PETERSON'S®
GRADUATE PROGRAMS IN THE HUMANITIES, ARTS & SOCIAL SCIENCES

2019

About Peterson's®

Peterson's® has been your trusted educational publisher for over 50 years. It's a milestone we're quite proud of, as we continue to offer the most accurate, dependable, high-quality educational content in the field, providing you with everything you need to succeed. No matter where you are on your academic or professional path, you can rely on Peterson's for its books, online information, expert test-prep tools, the most up-to-date education exploration data, and the highest quality career success resources—everything you need to achieve your education goals. For our complete line of products, visit **www.petersons.com**.

For more information about Peterson's range of educational products, contact Peterson's, 8740 Lucent Blvd., Suite 400 Highlands Ranch, CO 80129, or find us online at **www.petersons.com**.

CONTENTS

A Note from the Peterson's Editors

The six volumes of Peterson's *Graduate and Professional Programs*, the only annually updated reference work of its kind, provide wide-ranging information on the graduate and professional programs offered by accredited colleges and universities in the United States, U.S. territories, and Canada and by those institutions outside the United States that are accredited by U.S. accrediting bodies. More than 44,000 individual academic and professional programs at nearly 2,300 institutions are listed. Peterson's *Graduate and Professional Programs* have been used for more than fifty years by prospective graduate and professional students, placement counselors, faculty advisers, and all others interested in postbaccalaureate education.

Graduate & Professional Programs: An Overview contains information on institutions as a whole, while the other books in the series are devoted to specific academic and professional fields:

- *Graduate Programs in the Biological/Biomedical Sciences & Health-Related Medical Professions*

- *Graduate Programs in Business, Education, Information Studies, Law & Social Work*

- *Graduate Programs in Engineering & Applied Sciences*

- *Graduate Programs in the Humanities, Arts & Social Sciences*

- *Graduate Programs in the Physical Sciences, Mathematics, Agricultural Sciences, the Environment & Natural Resources*

The books may be used individually or as a set. For example, if you have chosen a field of study but do not know what institution you want to attend or if you have a college or university in mind but have not chosen an academic field of study, it is best to begin with the Overview guide.

Graduate & Professional Programs: An Overview presents several directories to help you identify programs of study that might interest you; you can then research those programs further in the other books in the series by using the Directory of Graduate and Professional Programs by Field, which lists 500 fields and gives the names of those institutions that offer graduate degree programs in each.

For geographical or financial reasons, you may be interested in attending a particular institution and will want to know what it has to offer. You should turn to the Directory of Institutions and Their Offerings, which lists the degree programs available at each institution. As in the Directory of Graduate and Professional Programs by Field, the level of degrees offered is also indicated.

All books in the series include advice on graduate education, including topics such as admissions tests, financial aid, and accreditation. **The Graduate Adviser** includes two essays and information about accreditation. The first essay, "The Admissions Process," discusses general admission requirements, admission tests, factors to consider when selecting a graduate school or program, when and how to apply, and how admission decisions are made. Special information for international students and tips for minority students are also included. The second essay, "Financial Support," is an overview of the broad range of support available at the graduate level. Fellowships, scholarships, and grants; assistantships and internships; federal and private loan programs, as well as Federal Work-Study; and the GI bill are detailed. This essay concludes with advice on applying for need-based financial aid. "Accreditation and Accrediting Agencies" gives information on accreditation and its purpose and lists institutional accrediting agencies first and then specialized accrediting agencies relevant to each volume's specific fields of study.

With information on more than 40,000 graduate programs in more than 500 disciplines, Peterson's *Graduate and Professional Programs* give you all the information you need about the programs that are of interest to you in three formats: **Profiles** (capsule summaries of basic information), **Displays** (information that an institution or program wants to emphasize), and **Close-Ups** (written by administrators, with more expansive information than the **Profiles**, emphasizing different aspects of the programs). By using these various formats of program information, coupled with **Appendixes** and **Indexes** covering directories and subject areas for all six books, you will find that these guides provide the most comprehensive, accurate, and up-to-date graduate study information available.

Peterson's publishes a full line of resources with information you need to guide you through the graduate admissions process. Peterson's publications can be found at college libraries and career centers and your local bookstore or library—or visit us on the Web at www.petersons.com.

Colleges and universities will be pleased to know that Peterson's helped you in your selection. Admissions staff members are more than happy to answer questions, address specific problems, and help in any way they can. The editors at Peterson's wish you great success in your graduate program search!

NOTICE: Certain portions of or information contained in this book have been submitted and paid for by the educational institution identified, and such institutions take full responsibility for the accuracy, timeliness, completeness and functionality of such contents. Such portions or information include (i) each display ad that comprises a half page of information covering a single educational institution or program and (ii) each two-page description or Close-Up of a graduate school or program that appear in the different sections of this guide. The "Close-Ups and Displays" are listed in various sections throughout the book.

THE GRADUATE ADVISER

The Admissions Process

Generalizations about graduate admissions practices are not always helpful because each institution has its own set of guidelines and procedures. Nevertheless, some broad statements can be made about the admissions process that may help you plan your strategy.

Factors Involved in Selecting a Graduate School or Program

Selecting a graduate school and a specific program of study is a complex matter. Quality of the faculty; program and course offerings; the nature, size, and location of the institution; admission requirements; cost; and the availability of financial assistance are among the many factors that affect one's choice of institution. Other considerations are job placement and achievements of the program's graduates and the institution's resources, such as libraries, laboratories, and computer facilities. If you are to make the best possible choice, you need to learn as much as you can about the schools and programs you are considering before you apply.

The following steps may help you narrow your choices.

- Talk to alumni of the programs or institutions you are considering to get their impressions of how well they were prepared for work in their fields of study.
- Remember that graduate school requirements change, so be sure to get the most up-to-date information possible.
- Talk to department faculty members and the graduate adviser at your undergraduate institution. They often have information about programs of study at other institutions.
- Visit the websites of the graduate schools in which you are interested to request a graduate catalog. Contact the department chair in your chosen field of study for additional information about the department and the field.
- Visit as many campuses as possible. Call ahead for an appointment with the graduate adviser in your field of interest and be sure to check out the facilities and talk to students.

General Requirements

Graduate schools and departments have requirements that applicants for admission must meet. Typically, these requirements include undergraduate transcripts (which provide information about undergraduate grade point average and course work applied toward a major), admission test scores, and letters of recommendation. Most graduate programs also ask for an essay or personal statement that describes your personal reasons for seeking graduate study. In some fields, such as art and music, portfolios or auditions may be required in addition to other evidence of talent. Some institutions require that the applicant have an undergraduate degree in the same subject as the intended graduate major.

Most institutions evaluate each applicant on the basis of the applicant's total record, and the weight accorded any given factor varies widely from institution to institution and from program to program.

The Application Process

You should begin the application process at least one year before you expect to begin your graduate study. Find out the application deadline for each institution (many are provided in the **Profile** section of this guide). Go to the institution's website and find out if you can apply online. If not, request a paper application form. Fill out this form thoroughly and neatly. Assume that the school needs all the information it is requesting and that the admissions officer will be sensitive to the neatness and overall quality of what you submit. Do not supply more information than the school requires.

The institution may ask at least one question that will require a three- or four-paragraph answer. Compose your response on the assumption that the admissions officer is interested in both what you think and how you express yourself. Keep your statement brief and to the point, but, at the same time, include all pertinent information about your past experiences and your educational goals. Individual statements vary greatly in style and content, which helps admissions officers differentiate among applicants. Many graduate departments give considerable weight to the statement in making their admissions decisions, so be sure to take the time to prepare a thoughtful and concise statement.

If recommendations are a part of the admissions requirements, carefully choose the individuals you ask to write them. It is generally best to ask current or former professors to write the recommendations, provided they are able to attest to your intellectual ability and motivation for doing the work required of a graduate student. It is advisable to provide stamped, preaddressed envelopes to people being asked to submit recommendations on your behalf.

Completed applications, including references, transcripts, and admission test scores, should be received at the institution by the specified date.

Be advised that institutions do not usually make admissions decisions until all materials have been received. Enclose a self-addressed postcard with your application, requesting confirmation of receipt. Allow at least ten days for the return of the postcard before making further inquiries.

If you plan to apply for financial support, it is imperative that you file your application early.

ADMISSION TESTS

The major testing program used in graduate admissions is the Graduate Record Examinations (GRE®) testing program, sponsored by the GRE Board and administered by Educational Testing Service, Princeton, New Jersey.

The Graduate Record Examinations testing program consists of a General Test and six Subject Tests. The General Test measures critical thinking, verbal reasoning, quantitative reasoning, and analytical writing skills. It is offered as an Internet-based test (iBT) in the United States, Canada, and many other countries.

The GRE® revised General Test's questions were designed to reflect the kind of thinking that students need to do in graduate or business school and demonstrate that students are indeed ready for graduate-level work.

- **Verbal Reasoning**—Measures ability to analyze and evaluate written material and synthesize information obtained from it, analyze relationships among component parts of sentences, and recognize relationships among words and concepts.
- **Quantitative Reasoning**—Measures problem-solving ability, focusing on basic concepts of arithmetic, algebra, geometry, and data analysis.
- **Analytical Writing**—Measures critical thinking and analytical writing skills, specifically the ability to articulate and support complex ideas clearly and effectively.

The computer-delivered GRE® revised General Test is offered year-round at Prometric™ test centers and on specific dates at testing locations outside of the Prometric test center network. Appointments are scheduled on a first-come, first-served basis. The GRE® revised General Test is also offered as a paper-based test three times a year in areas where computer-based testing is not available.

You can take the computer-delivered GRE® revised General Test once every twenty-one days, up to five times within any continuous rolling twelve-month period (365 days)—even if you canceled your

scores on a previously taken test. You may take the paper-based GRE® revised General Test as often as it is offered.

Three scores are reported on the revised General Test:

1. A **Verbal Reasoning score** is reported on a 130–170 score scale, in 1-point increments.

2. A **Quantitative Reasoning score** is reported on a 130–170 score scale, in 1-point increments.

3. An **Analytical Writing score** is reported on a 0–6 score level, in half-point increments.

The GRE® Subject Tests measure achievement and assume undergraduate majors or extensive background in the following six disciplines:

• Biology
• Chemistry
• Literature in English
• Mathematics
• Physics
• Psychology

The Subject Tests are available three times per year as paper-based administrations around the world. Testing time is approximately 2 hours and 50 minutes. You can obtain more information about the GRE® by visiting the ETS website at **www.ets.org** or consulting the *GRE® Information Bulletin*. The *Bulletin* can be obtained at many undergraduate colleges. You can also download it from the ETS website or obtain it by contacting Graduate Record Examinations, Educational Testing Service, P.O. Box 6000, Princeton, NJ 08541-6000; phone: 609-771-7670 or 866-473-4373.

If you expect to apply for admission to a program that requires any of the GRE® tests, you should select a test date well in advance of the application deadline. Scores on the computer-based General Test are reported within ten to fifteen days; scores on the paper-based Subject Tests are reported within six weeks.

Another testing program, the Miller Analogies Test® (MAT®), is administered at more than 500 Controlled Testing Centers in the United States, Canada, and other countries. The MAT® computer-based test is now available. Testing time is 60 minutes. The test consists of 120 partial analogies. You can obtain the *Candidate Information Booklet,* which contains a list of test centers and instructions for taking the test, from **www.milleranalogies.com** or by calling 800-328-5999 (toll-free).

Check the specific requirements of the programs to which you are applying.

How Admission Decisions Are Made

The program you apply to is directly involved in the admissions process. Although the final decision is usually made by the graduate dean (or an associate) or the faculty admissions committee, recommendations from faculty members in your intended field are important. At some institutions, an interview is incorporated into the decision process.

A Special Note for International Students

In addition to the steps already described, there are some special considerations for international students who intend to apply for graduate study in the United States. All graduate schools require an indication of competence in English. The purpose of the Test of English as a Foreign Language (TOEFL®) is to evaluate the English proficiency of people who are nonnative speakers of English and want to study at colleges and universities where English is the language of instruction. The TOEFL® is administered by Educational Testing Service (ETS) under the general direction of a policy board established by the College Board and the Graduate Record Examinations Board.

The TOEFL iBT® assesses four basic language skills: listening, reading, writing, and speaking. The Internet-based test is administered at secure, official test centers. The testing time is approximately 4 hours.

The TOEFL® is also offered in a paper-based format in areas of the world where internet-based testing is not available. In 2017, ETS launched a revised TOEFL® paper-based Test, that more closely aligned to the TOEFL iBT® test. This revised paper-based test consists of three sections—listening, reading, and writing. The testing time is approximately 3 hours.

You can obtain more information for both versions of the TOEFL® by visiting the ETS website at **www.ets.org/toefl**. Information can also be obtained by contacting TOEFL® Services, Educational Testing Service, P.O. Box 6151, Princeton, NJ 08541-6151. Phone: 609-771-7100 or 877-863-3546 (toll free).

International students should apply especially early because of the number of steps required to complete the admissions process. Furthermore, many United States graduate schools have a limited number of spaces for international students, and many more students apply than the schools can accommodate.

International students may find financial assistance from institutions very limited. The U.S. government requires international applicants to submit a certification of support, which is a statement attesting to the applicant's financial resources. In addition, international students *must* have health insurance coverage.

Tips for Minority Students

Indicators of a university's values in terms of diversity are found both in its recruitment programs and its resources directed to student success. Important questions: Does the institution vigorously recruit minorities for its graduate programs? Is there funding available to help with the costs associated with visiting the school? Are minorities represented in the institution's brochures or website or on their faculty rolls? What campus-based resources or services (including assistance in locating housing or career counseling and placement) are available? Is funding available to members of underrepresented groups?

At the program level, it is particularly important for minority students to investigate the "climate" of a program under consideration. How many minority students are enrolled and how many have graduated? What opportunities are there to work with diverse faculty and mentors whose research interests match yours? How are conflicts resolved or concerns addressed? How interested are faculty in building strong and supportive relations with students? "Climate" concerns should be addressed by posing questions to various individuals, including faculty members, current students, and alumni.

Information is also available through various organizations, such as the Hispanic Association of Colleges & Universities (HACU), and publications such as *Diverse Issues in Higher Education* and *Hispanic Outlook* magazine. There are also books devoted to this topic, such as *The Multicultural Student's Guide to Colleges* by Robert Mitchell.

Financial Support

The range of financial support at the graduate level is very broad. The following descriptions will give you a general idea of what you might expect and what will be expected of you as a financial support recipient.

Fellowships, Scholarships, and Grants

These are usually outright awards of a few hundred to many thousands of dollars with no service to the institution required in return. Fellowships and scholarships are usually awarded on the basis of merit and are highly competitive. Grants are made on the basis of financial need or special talent in a field of study. Many fellowships, scholarships, and grants not only cover tuition, fees, and supplies but also include stipends for living expenses with allowances for dependents. However, the terms of each should be examined because some do not permit recipients to supplement their income with outside work. Fellowships, scholarships, and grants may vary in the number of years for which they are awarded.

In addition to the availability of these funds at the university or program level, many excellent fellowship programs are available at the national level and may be applied for before and during enrollment in a graduate program. A listing of many of these programs can be found at the Council of Graduate Schools' website, **https://cgsnet.org/**. There is a wealth of information in the "Programs" and "Awards" sections.

Assistantships and Internships

Many graduate students receive financial support through assistantships, particularly involving teaching or research duties. It is important to recognize that such appointments should not be viewed simply as employment relationships but rather should constitute an integral and important part of a student's graduate education. As such, the appointments should be accompanied by strong faculty mentoring and increasingly responsible apprenticeship experiences. The specific nature of these appointments in a given program should be considered in selecting that graduate program.

TEACHING ASSISTANTSHIPS

These usually provide a salary and full or partial tuition remission and may also provide health benefits. Unlike fellowships, scholarships, and grants, which require no service to the institution, teaching assistantships require recipients to provide the institution with a specific amount of undergraduate teaching, ideally related to the student's field of study. Some teaching assistants are limited to grading papers, compiling bibliographies, taking notes, or monitoring laboratories. At some graduate schools, teaching assistants must carry lighter course loads than regular full-time students.

RESEARCH ASSISTANTSHIPS

These are very similar to teaching assistantships in the manner in which financial assistance is provided. The difference is that recipients are given basic research assignments in their disciplines rather than teaching responsibilities. The work required is normally related to the student's field of study; in most instances, the assistantship supports the student's thesis or dissertation research.

ADMINISTRATIVE INTERNSHIPS

These are similar to assistantships in application of financial assistance funds, but the student is given an assignment on a part-time basis, usually as a special assistant with one of the university's administrative offices. The assignment may not necessarily be directly related to the recipient's discipline.

RESIDENCE HALL AND COUNSELING ASSISTANTSHIPS

These assistantships are frequently assigned to graduate students in psychology, counseling, and social work, but they may be offered to students in other disciplines, especially if the student has worked in this capacity during his or her undergraduate years. Duties can vary from being available in a dean's office for a specific number of hours for consultation with undergraduates to living in campus residences and being responsible for both counseling and administrative tasks or advising student activity groups. Residence hall assistantships often include a room and board allowance and, in some cases, tuition assistance and stipends. Contact the Housing and Student Life Office for more information.

Health Insurance

The availability and affordability of health insurance is an important issue and one that should be considered in an applicant's choice of institution and program. While often included with assistantships and fellowships, this is not always the case and, even if provided, the benefits may be limited. It is important to note that the U.S. government requires international students to have health insurance.

The GI Bill

This provides financial assistance for students who are veterans of the United States armed forces. If you are a veteran, contact your local Veterans Administration office to determine your eligibility and to get full details about benefits. There are a number of programs that offer educational benefits to current military enlistees. Some states have tuition assistance programs for members of the National Guard. Contact the VA office at the college for more information.

Federal Work-Study Program (FWS)

Employment is another way some students finance their graduate studies. The federally funded Federal Work-Study Program provides eligible students with employment opportunities, usually in public and private nonprofit organizations. Federal funds pay up to 75 percent of the wages, with the remainder paid by the employing agency. FWS is available to graduate students who demonstrate financial need. Not all schools have these funds, and some only award them to undergraduates. Each school sets its application deadline and workstudy earnings limits. Wages vary and are related to the type of work done. You must file the Free Application for Federal Student Aid (FAFSA) to be eligible for this program.

Loans

Many graduate students borrow to finance their graduate programs when other sources of assistance (which do not have to be repaid) prove insufficient. You should always read and understand the terms of any loan program before submitting your application.

FEDERAL DIRECT LOANS

Federal Direct Loans. The Federal Direct Loan Program offers a variable-fixed interest rate loan to graduate students with the Department of Education acting as the lender. Students receive a new rate with each new loan, but that rate is fixed for the life of the loan. Beginning with loans made on or after July 1, 2013, the interest rate for loans made each July 1st to June 30th period are determined based on the last 10-year Treasury note auction prior to June 1st of that year, plus an added percentage. The interest rate can be no higher than 9.5%.

Beginning July 1, 2012, the Federal Direct Loan for graduate students is an unsubsidized loan. Under the *unsubsidized* program, the grad borrower pays the interest on the loan from the day proceeds are issued and is responsible for paying interest during all periods. If the borrower chooses not to pay the interest while in school, or during the grace periods, deferment, or forbearance, the interest accrues and will be capitalized.

Graduate students may borrow up to $20,500 per year through the Direct Loan Program, up to a cumulative maximum of $138,500, including undergraduate borrowing. No more than $65,500 of the $138,500 can be from subsidized loans, including loans the grad borrower may have received for periods of enrollment that began before July 1, 2012, or for prior undergraduate borrowing. You may borrow up to the cost of attendance at the school in which you are enrolled or will attend, minus estimated financial assistance from other federal, state, and private sources, up to a maximum of $20,500. Grad borrowers who reach the aggregate loan limit over the course of their education cannot receive additional loans; however, if they repay some of their loans to bring the outstanding balance below the aggregate limit, they could be eligible to borrow again, up to that limit.

Under the *subsidized* Federal Direct Loan Program, repayment begins six months after your last date of enrollment on at least a half-time basis. Under the *unsubsidized* program, repayment of interest begins within thirty days from disbursement of the loan proceeds, and repayment of the principal begins six months after your last enrollment on at least a half-time basis. Some borrowers may choose to defer interest payments while they are in school. The accrued interest is added to the loan balance when the borrower begins repayment. There are several repayment options.

Federal Perkins Loans. The Federal Perkins Loan is available to students demonstrating financial need and is administered directly by the school. Not all schools have these funds, and some may award them to undergraduates only. Eligibility is determined from the information you provide on the FAFSA. The school will notify you of your eligibility.

Eligible graduate students may borrow up to $8,000 per year, up to a maximum of $60,000, including undergraduate borrowing (even if your previous Perkins Loans have been repaid). The interest rate for Federal Perkins Loans is 5 percent, and no interest accrues while you remain in school at least half-time. Students who are attending less than half-time need to check with their school to determine the length of their grace period. There are no guarantee, loan, or disbursement fees. Repayment begins nine months after your last date of enrollment on at least a half-time basis and may extend over a maximum of ten years with no prepayment penalty.

Federal Direct Graduate PLUS Loans. Effective July 1, 2006, graduate and professional students are eligible for Graduate PLUS loans. This program allows students to borrow up to the cost of attendance, less any other aid received. These loans have a fixed interest rate (7.6% for loans first disbursed on or after July 1, 2018, and before July 1, 2019) and interest begins to accrue at the time of disbursement. Beginning with loans made on or after July 1, 2013, the interest rate for loans made each July 1st to June 30th period are determined based on the last 10-year Treasury note auction prior to June 1st of that year. The interest rate can be no higher than 10.5%. The PLUS loans do involve a credit check; a PLUS borrower may obtain a loan with a cosigner if his or her credit is not good enough. Grad PLUS loans may be deferred while a student is in school and for the six months following a drop below half-time enrollment. For more information, you should contact a representative in your college's financial aid office.

Deferring Your Federal Loan Repayments. If you borrowed under the Federal Direct Loan Program, Federal Direct PLUS Loan Program, or the Federal Perkins Loan Program for previous undergraduate or graduate study, your payments may be deferred when you return to graduate school, depending on when you borrowed and under which program.

There are other deferment options available if you are temporarily unable to repay your loan. Information about these deferments is provided at your entrance and exit interviews. If you believe you are eligible for a deferment of your loan payments, you must contact your lender or loan servicer to request a deferment. The deferment must be filed prior to the time your payment is due, and it must be re-filed when it expires if you remain eligible for deferment at that time.

SUPPLEMENTAL (PRIVATE) LOANS

Many lending institutions offer supplemental loan programs and other financing plans, such as the ones described here, to students seeking additional assistance in meeting their education expenses. Some loan programs target all types of graduate students; others are designed specifically for business, law, or medical students. In addition, you can use private loans not specifically designed for education to help finance your graduate degree.

If you are considering borrowing through a supplemental or private loan program, you should carefully consider the terms and be sure to read the fine print. Check with the program sponsor for the most current terms that will be applicable to the amounts you intend to borrow for graduate study. Most supplemental loan programs for graduate study offer unsubsidized, credit-based loans. In general, a credit-ready borrower is one who has a satisfactory credit history or no credit history at all. A creditworthy borrower generally must pass a credit test to be eligible to borrow or act as a cosigner for the loan funds.

Many supplemental loan programs have minimum and maximum annual loan limits. Some offer amounts equal to the cost of attendance minus any other aid you will receive for graduate study. If you are planning to borrow for several years of graduate study, consider whether there is a cumulative or aggregate limit on the amount you may borrow. Often this cumulative or aggregate limit will include any amounts you borrowed and have not repaid for undergraduate or previous graduate study.

The combination of the annual interest rate, loan fees, and the repayment terms you choose will determine how much you will repay over time. Compare these features in combination before you decide which loan program to use. Some loans offer interest rates that are adjusted monthly, quarterly, or annually. Some offer interest rates that are lower during the in-school, grace, and deferment periods and then increase when you begin repayment. Some programs include a loan origination fee, which is usually deducted from the principal amount you receive when the loan is disbursed and must be repaid along with the interest and other principal when you graduate, withdraw from school, or drop below half-time study. Sometimes the loan fees are reduced if you borrow with a qualified cosigner. Some programs allow you to defer interest and/or principal payments while you are enrolled in graduate school. Many programs allow you to capitalize your interest payments; the interest due on your loan is added to the outstanding balance of your loan, so you don't have to repay immediately, but this increases the amount you owe. Other programs allow you to pay the interest as you go, which reduces the amount you later have to repay. The private loan market is very competitive, and your financial aid office can help you evaluate these programs.

Applying for Need-Based Financial Aid

Schools that award federal and institutional financial assistance based on need will require you to complete the FAFSA and, in some cases, an institutional financial aid application.

If you are applying for federal student assistance, you **must** complete the FAFSA. A service of the U.S. Department of Education, the FAFSA is free to all applicants. Most applicants apply online at **www.fafsa.ed.gov**. Paper applications are available at the financial aid office of your local college.

After your FAFSA information has been processed, you will receive a Student Aid Report (SAR). If you provided an e-mail address on the FAFSA, this will be sent to you electronically; otherwise, it will be mailed to your home address.

Follow the instructions on the SAR if you need to correct information reported on your original application. If your situation changes after you file your FAFSA, contact your financial aid officer to discuss amending

your information. You can also appeal your financial aid award if you have extenuating circumstances.

If you would like more information on federal student financial aid, visit the FAFSA website or download the most recent version of *Do You Need Money for College* at www.studentaid.ed.gov/sa/sites/default/files/2018-19-do-you-need-money.pdf. This guide is also available in Spanish.

The U.S. Department of Education also has a toll-free number for questions concerning federal student aid programs. The number is 1-800-4-FED AID (1-800-433-3243). If you are hearing impaired, call toll-free, 1-800-730-8913.

Summary

Remember that these are generalized statements about financial assistance at the graduate level. Because each institution allots its aid differently, you should communicate directly with the school and the specific department of interest to you. It is not unusual, for example, to find that an endowment vested within a specific department supports one or more fellowships. You may fit its requirements and specifications precisely.

Accreditation and Accrediting Agencies

Colleges and universities in the United States, and their individual academic and professional programs, are accredited by nongovernmental agencies concerned with monitoring the quality of education in this country. Agencies with both regional and national jurisdictions grant accreditation to institutions as a whole, while specialized bodies acting on a nationwide basis—often national professional associations—grant accreditation to departments and programs in specific fields.

Institutional and specialized accrediting agencies share the same basic concerns: the purpose an academic unit—whether university or program—has set for itself and how well it fulfills that purpose, the adequacy of its financial and other resources, the quality of its academic offerings, and the level of services it provides. Agencies that grant institutional accreditation take a broader view, of course, and examine university-wide or college-wide services with which a specialized agency may not concern itself.

Both types of agencies follow the same general procedures when considering an application for accreditation. The academic unit prepares a self-evaluation, focusing on the concerns mentioned above and usually including an assessment of both its strengths and weaknesses; a team of representatives of the accrediting body reviews this evaluation, visits the campus, and makes its own report; and finally, the accrediting body makes a decision on the application. Often, even when accreditation is granted, the agency makes a recommendation regarding how the institution or program can improve. All institutions and programs are also reviewed every few years to determine whether they continue to meet established standards; if they do not, they may lose their accreditation.

Accrediting agencies themselves are reviewed and evaluated periodically by the U.S. Department of Education and the Council for Higher Education Accreditation (CHEA). Recognized agencies adhere to certain standards and practices, and their authority in matters of accreditation is widely accepted in the educational community.

This does not mean, however, that accreditation is a simple matter, either for schools wishing to become accredited or for students deciding where to apply. Indeed, in certain fields the very meaning and methods of accreditation are the subject of a good deal of debate. For their part, those applying to graduate school should be aware of the safeguards provided by regional accreditation, especially in terms of degree acceptance and institutional longevity. Beyond this, applicants should understand the role that specialized accreditation plays in their field, as this varies considerably from one discipline to another. In certain professional fields, it is necessary to have graduated from a program that is accredited in order to be eligible for a license to practice, and in some fields the federal government also makes this a hiring requirement. In other disciplines, however, accreditation is not as essential, and there can be excellent programs that are not accredited. In fact, some programs choose not to seek accreditation, although most do.

Institutions and programs that present themselves for accreditation are sometimes granted the status of candidate for accreditation, or what is known as "preaccreditation." This may happen, for example, when an academic unit is too new to have met all the requirements for accreditation. Such status signifies initial recognition and indicates that the school or program in question is working to fulfill all requirements; it does not, however, guarantee that accreditation will be granted.

Institutional Accrediting Agencies—Regional

MIDDLE STATES COMMISSION ON HIGHER EDUCATION

Accredits institutions in Delaware, District of Columbia, Maryland, New Jersey, New York, Pennsylvania, Puerto Rico, and the Virgin Islands.

Dr. Elizabeth Sibolski, President
Middle States Commission on Higher Education
3624 Market Street, Second Floor West
Philadelphia, Pennsylvania 19104
Phone: 267-284-5000
Fax: 215-662-5501
E-mail: info@msche.org
Website: www.msche.org

NEW ENGLAND ASSOCIATION OF SCHOOLS AND COLLEGES

Accredits institutions in Connecticut, Maine, Massachusetts, New Hampshire, Rhode Island, and Vermont.

Dr. Barbara E. Brittingham, President/Director
Commission on Institutions of Higher Education
3 Burlington Woods Drive, Suite 100
Burlington, Massachusetts 01803-4531
Phone: 855-886-3272 or 781-425-7714
Fax: 781-425-1001
E-mail: cihe@neasc.org
Website: https://cihe.neasc.org

THE HIGHER LEARNING COMMISSION

Accredits institutions in Arizona, Arkansas, Colorado, Illinois, Indiana, Iowa, Kansas, Michigan, Minnesota, Missouri, Nebraska, New Mexico, North Dakota, Ohio, Oklahoma, South Dakota, West Virginia, Wisconsin, and Wyoming.

Dr. Barbara Gellman-Danley, President
The Higher Learning Commission
230 South LaSalle Street, Suite 7-500
Chicago, Illinois 60604-1413
Phone: 800-621-7440 or 312-263-0456
Fax: 312-263-7462
E-mail: info@hlcommission.org
Website: www.hlcommission.org

NORTHWEST COMMISSION ON COLLEGES AND UNIVERSITIES

Accredits institutions in Alaska, Idaho, Montana, Nevada, Oregon, Utah, and Washington.

Dr. Sandra E. Elman, President
8060 165th Avenue, NE, Suite 100
Redmond, Washington 98052
Phone: 425-558-4224
Fax: 425-376-0596
E-mail: selman@nwccu.org
Website: www.nwccu.org

SOUTHERN ASSOCIATION OF COLLEGES AND SCHOOLS

Accredits institutions in Alabama, Florida, Georgia, Kentucky, Louisiana, Mississippi, North Carolina, South Carolina, Tennessee, Texas, and Virginia.

Dr. Belle S. Wheelan, President
Commission on Colleges
1866 Southern Lane
Decatur, Georgia 30033-4097
Phone: 404-679-4500 Ext. 4504
Fax: 404-679-4558
E-mail: questions@sacscoc.org
Website: www.sacscoc.org

WESTERN ASSOCIATION OF SCHOOLS AND COLLEGES

Accredits institutions in California, Guam, and Hawaii.

Jamienne S. Studley, President
WASC Senior College and University Commission
985 Atlantic Avenue, Suite 100
Alameda, California 94501
Phone: 510-748-9001
Fax: 510-748-9797
E-mail: wasc@wscuc.org
Website: https://www.wscuc.org/

Institutional Accrediting Agencies—Other

ACCREDITING COUNCIL FOR INDEPENDENT COLLEGES AND SCHOOLS
Michelle Edwards, President
750 First Street NE, Suite 980
Washington, DC 20002-4223
Phone: 202-336-6780
Fax: 202-842-2593
E-mail: info@acics.org
Website: www.acics.org

DISTANCE EDUCATION ACCREDITING COMMISSION (DEAC)
Leah Matthews, Executive Director
1101 17th Street NW, Suite 808
Washington, DC 20036-4704
Phone: 202-234-5100
Fax: 202-332-1386
E-mail: info@deac.org
Website: www.deac.org

Specialized Accrediting Agencies

ACUPUNCTURE AND ORIENTAL MEDICINE
Mark S. McKenzie, LAc MsOM DiplOM, Executive Director
Accreditation Commission for Acupuncture and Oriental Medicine
8941 Aztec Drive, Suite 2
Eden Prairie, Minnesota 55347
Phone: 952-212-2434
Fax: 301-313-0912
E-mail: info@acaom.org
Website: www.acaom.org

ALLIED HEALTH
Kathleen Megivern, Executive Director
Commission on Accreditation of Allied Health Education Programs (CAAHEP)
25400 US Hwy 19 North, Suite 158
Clearwater, Florida 33763
Phone: 727-210-2350
Fax: 727-210-2354
E-mail: mail@caahep.org
Website: www.caahep.org

ART AND DESIGN
Karen P. Moynahan, Executive Director
National Association of Schools of Art and Design (NASAD)
Commission on Accreditation
11250 Roger Bacon Drive, Suite 21
Reston, Virginia 20190-5248
Phone: 703-437-0700
Fax: 703-437-6312
E-mail: info@arts-accredit.org
Website: http://nasad.arts-accredit.org

ATHLETIC TRAINING EDUCATION
Pamela Hansen, CAATE Director of Accreditation
Commission on Accreditation of Athletic Training Education (CAATE)
6850 Austin Center Blvd., Suite 100
Austin, Texas 78731-3184
Phone: 512-733-9700
E-mail: pamela@caate.net
Website: www.caate.net

AUDIOLOGY EDUCATION
Meggan Olek, Director
Accreditation Commission for Audiology Education (ACAE)
11480 Commerce Park Drive, Suite 220
Reston, Virginia 20191
Phone: 202-986-9500
Fax: 202-986-9550
E-mail: info@acaeaccred.org
Website: https://acaeaccred.org/

AVIATION
Dr. Gary J. Northam, President
Aviation Accreditation Board International (AABI)
3410 Skyway Drive
Auburn, Alabama 36830
Phone: 334-844-2431
Fax: 334-844-2432
E-mail: gary.northam@auburn.edu
Website: www.aabi.aero

BUSINESS
Stephanie Bryant, Executive Vice President and Chief Accreditation Officer
AACSB International—The Association to Advance Collegiate Schools of Business
777 South Harbour Island Boulevard, Suite 750
Tampa, Florida 33602
Phone: 813-769-6500
Fax: 813-769-6559
E-mail: stephanie.bryant@aacsb.edu
Website: www.aacsb.edu

BUSINESS EDUCATION
Dr. Phyllis Okrepkie, President
International Assembly for Collegiate Business Education (IACBE)
11374 Strang Line Road
Lenexa, Kansas 66215
Phone: 913-631-3009
Fax: 913-631-9154
E-mail: iacbe@iacbe.org
Website: www.iacbe.org

CHIROPRACTIC
Dr. Craig S. Little, President
Council on Chiropractic Education (CCE)
Commission on Accreditation
8049 North 85th Way
Scottsdale, Arizona 85258-4321
Phone: 480-443-8877 or 888-443-3506
Fax: 480-483-7333
E-mail: cce@cce-usa.org
Website: www.cce-usa.org

CLINICAL LABORATORY SCIENCES
Dianne M. Cearlock, Ph.D., Chief Executive Officer
National Accrediting Agency for Clinical Laboratory Sciences
5600 North River Road, Suite 720
Rosemont, Illinois 60018-5119
Phone: 773-714-8880 or 847-939-3597
Fax: 773-714-8886
E-mail: info@naacls.org
Website: www.naacls.org

CLINICAL PASTORAL EDUCATION
Trace Haythorn, Ph.D., Executive Director/CEO
Association for Clinical Pastoral Education, Inc.
One West Court Square, Suite 325
Decatur, Georgia 30030-2576
Phone: 678-363-6226
Fax: 404-320-0849
E-mail: acpe@acpe.edu
Website: www.acpe.edu

DANCE
Karen P. Moynahan, Executive Director
National Association of Schools of Dance (NASD)
Commission on Accreditation
11250 Roger Bacon Drive, Suite 21
Reston, Virginia 20190-5248
Phone: 703-437-0700
Fax: 703-437-6312
E-mail: info@arts-accredit.org
Website: http://nasd.arts-accredit.org

DENTISTRY
Dr. Kathleen T. O'Loughlin, Executive Director
Commission on Dental Accreditation
American Dental Association
211 East Chicago Avenue
Chicago, Illinois 60611
Phone: 312-440-2500
E-mail: accreditation@ada.org
Website: www.ada.org

DIETETICS AND NUTRITION
Mary B. Gregoire, Ph.D., Executive Director; RD, FADA, FAND
Academy of Nutrition and Dietetics
Accreditation Council for Education in Nutrition and Dietetics (ACEND)
120 South Riverside Plaza
Chicago, Illinois 60606-6995
Phone: 800-877-1600 or 312-899-0040
E-mail: acend@eatright.org
Website: www.eatright.org/cade

EDUCATION PREPARATION
Christopher Koch, President
Council for the Accreditation of Educator Preparation (CAEP)
1140 19th Street NW, Suite 400
Washington, DC 20036
Phone: 202-223-0077
Fax: 202-296-6620
E-mail: caep@caepnet.org
Website: www.caepnet.org

ENGINEERING
Michael Milligan, Ph.D., PE, Executive Director
Accreditation Board for Engineering and Technology, Inc. (ABET)
415 North Charles Street
Baltimore, Maryland 21201
Phone: 410-347-7700
E-mail: accreditation@abet.org
Website: www.abet.org

FORENSIC SCIENCES
Nancy J. Jackson, Director of Development and Accreditation
American Academy of Forensic Sciences (AAFS)
Forensic Science Education Program Accreditation Commission (FEPAC)
410 North 21st Street
Colorado Springs, Colorado 80904
Phone: 719-636-1100
Fax: 719-636-1993
E-mail: njackson@aafs.org
Website: www.fepac-edu.org

FORESTRY
Carol L. Redelsheimer
Director of Science and Education
Society of American Foresters
10100 Laureate Way
Bethesda, Maryland 20814-2198
Phone: 301-897-8720 or 866-897-8720
Fax: 301-897-3690
E-mail: membership@safnet.org
Website: www.eforester.com

HEALTHCARE MANAGEMENT
Commission on Accreditation of Healthcare Management Education (CAHME)
Anthony Stanowski, President and CEO
6110 Executive Boulevard, Suite 614
Rockville, Maryland 20852
Phone: 301-298-1820
E-mail: info@cahme.org
Website: www.cahme.org

HEALTH INFORMATICS AND HEALTH MANAGEMENT
Angela Kennedy, EdD, MBA, RHIA, Chief Executive Officer
Commission on Accreditation for Health Informatics and Information Management Education (CAHIIM)
233 North Michigan Avenue, 21st Floor
Chicago, Illinois 60601-5800
Phone: 312-233-1134
Fax: 312-233-1948
E-mail: info@cahiim.org
Website: www.cahiim.org

HUMAN SERVICE EDUCATION
Dr. Elaine Green, President
Council for Standards in Human Service Education (CSHSE)
3337 Duke Street
Alexandria, Virginia 22314
Phone: 571-257-3959
E-mail: info@cshse.org
Website: www.cshse.org

INTERIOR DESIGN
Holly Mattson, Executive Director
Council for Interior Design Accreditation
206 Grandview Avenue, Suite 350
Grand Rapids, Michigan 49503-4014
Phone: 616-458-0400
Fax: 616-458-0460
E-mail: info@accredit-id.org
Website: www.accredit-id.org

JOURNALISM AND MASS COMMUNICATIONS
Patricia Thompson, Executive Director
Accrediting Council on Education in Journalism and Mass Communications (ACEJMC)
201 Bishop Hall
P.O. Box 1848
University, MS 38677-1848
Phone: 662-915-5504
E-mail: pthomps1@olemiss.edu
Website: www.acejmc.org

LANDSCAPE ARCHITECTURE
Nancy Somerville, Executive Vice President, CEO
American Society of Landscape Architects (ASLA)
636 Eye Street, NW
Washington, DC 20001-3736
Phone: 202-898-2444
Fax: 202-898-1185
E-mail: info@asla.org
Website: www.asla.org

LAW
Barry Currier, Managing Director of Accreditation & Legal Education
American Bar Association
321 North Clark Street, 21st Floor
Chicago, Illinois 60654
Phone: 312-988-6738
Fax: 312-988-5681
E-mail: legaled@americanbar.org
Website: https://www.americanbar.org/groups/legal_education/accreditation.html

LIBRARY
Karen O'Brien, Director
Office for Accreditation
American Library Association
50 East Huron Street
Chicago, Illinois 60611-2795
Phone: 800-545-2433, ext. 2432 or 312-280-2432
Fax: 312-280-2433
E-mail: accred@ala.org
Website: http://www.ala.org/aboutala/offices/accreditation/

MARRIAGE AND FAMILY THERAPY
Tanya A. Tamarkin, Director of Educational Affairs
Commission on Accreditation for Marriage and Family Therapy
    Education (COAMFTE)
American Association for Marriage and Family Therapy
112 South Alfred Street
Alexandria, Virginia 22314-3061
Phone: 703-838-9808
Fax: 703-838-9805
E-mail: coa@aamft.org
Website: www.aamft.org

MEDICAL ILLUSTRATION
Kathleen Megivern, Executive Director
Commission on Accreditation of Allied Health Education Programs
    (CAAHEP)
25400 US Highway 19 North, Suite 158
Clearwater, Florida 33756
Phone: 727-210-2350
Fax: 727-210-2354
E-mail: mail@caahep.org
Website: www.caahep.org

MEDICINE
Liaison Committee on Medical Education (LCME)
Robert B. Hash, M.D., LCME Secretary
American Medical Association
Council on Medical Education
330 North Wabash Avenue, Suite 39300
Chicago, Illinois 60611-5885
Phone: 312-464-4933
E-mail: lcme@aamc.org
Website: www.ama-assn.org

Liaison Committee on Medical Education (LCME)
Heather Lent, M.A., Director
Accreditation Services
Association of American Medical Colleges
655 K Street, NW
Washington, DC 20001-2399
Phone: 202-828-0596
E-mail: lcme@aamc.org
Website: www.lcme.org

MUSIC
Karen P. Moynahan, Executive Director
National Association of Schools of Music (NASM)
Commission on Accreditation
11250 Roger Bacon Drive, Suite 21
Reston, Virginia 20190-5248
Phone: 703-437-0700
Fax: 703-437-6312
E-mail: info@arts-accredit.org
Website: http://nasm.arts-accredit.org/

NATUROPATHIC MEDICINE
Daniel Seitz, J.D., Ed.D., Executive Director
Council on Naturopathic Medical Education
P.O. Box 178
Great Barrington, Massachusetts 01230
Phone: 413-528-8877
E-mail: https://cnme.org/contact-us/
Website: www.cnme.org

NURSE ANESTHESIA
Francis R.Gerbasi, Ph.D., CRNA, COA Executive Director
Council on Accreditation of Nurse Anesthesia Educational Programs
    (CoA-NAEP)
American Association of Nurse Anesthetists
222 South Prospect Avenue
Park Ridge, Illinois 60068-4001
Phone: 847-655-1160
Fax: 847-692-7137
E-mail: accreditation@coa.us.com
Website: http://www.coacrna.org

NURSE EDUCATION
Jennifer L. Butlin, Executive Director
Commission on Collegiate Nursing Education (CCNE)
One Dupont Circle, NW, Suite 530
Washington, DC 20036-1120
Phone: 202-887-6791
Fax: 202-887-8476
E-mail: jbutlin@aacn.nche.edu
Website: www.aacn.nche.edu/accreditation

Marsal P. Stoll, Chief Executive Officer
Accreditation Commission for Education in Nursing (ACEN)
3343 Peachtree Road, NE, Suite 850
Atlanta, Georgia 30326
Phone: 404-975-5000
Fax: 404-975-5020
E-mail: mstoll@acenursing.org
Website: www.acenursing.org

NURSE MIDWIFERY
Heather L. Maurer, M.A., Executive Director
Accreditation Commission for Midwifery Education (ACME)
American College of Nurse-Midwives
8403 Colesville Road, Suite 1550
Silver Spring, Maryland 20910
Phone: 240-485-1800
Fax: 240-485-1818
E-mail: info@acnm.org
Website: www.midwife.org/Program-Accreditation

NURSE PRACTITIONER
Gay Johnson, CEO
National Association of Nurse Practitioners in Women's Health
Council on Accreditation
505 C Street, NE
Washington, DC 20002
Phone: 202-543-9693 Ext. 1
Fax: 202-543-9858
E-mail: info@npwh.org
Website: www.npwh.org

NURSING
Marsal P. Stoll, Chief Executive Director
Accreditation Commission for Education in Nursing (ACEN)
3343 Peachtree Road, NE, Suite 850
Atlanta, Georgia 30326
Phone: 404-975-5000
Fax: 404-975-5020
E-mail: info@acenursing.org
Website: www.acenursing.org

OCCUPATIONAL THERAPY
Heather Stagliano, DHSc, OTR/L, Executive Director
The American Occupational Therapy Association, Inc.
4720 Montgomery Lane, Suite 200
Bethesda, Maryland 20814-3449
Phone: 301-652-6611 Ext. 2682
TDD: 800-377-8555
Fax: 240-762-5150
E-mail: accred@aota.org
Website: www.aoteonline.org

OPTOMETRY
Joyce L. Urbeck, Administrative Director
Accreditation Council on Optometric Education (ACOE)
American Optometric Association
243 North Lindbergh Boulevard
St. Louis, Missouri 63141-7881
Phone: 314-991-4100, Ext. 4246
Fax: 314-991-4101
E-mail: accredit@aoa.org
Website: www.theacoe.org

OSTEOPATHIC MEDICINE
Director, Department of Accreditation
Commission on Osteopathic College Accreditation (COCA)
American Osteopathic Association
142 East Ontario Street
Chicago, Illinois 60611
Phone: 312-202-8048
Fax: 312-202-8202
E-mail: predoc@osteopathic.org
Website: www.aoacoca.org

PHARMACY
Peter H. Vlasses, PharmD, Executive Director
Accreditation Council for Pharmacy Education
135 South LaSalle Street, Suite 4100
Chicago, Illinois 60603-4810
Phone: 312-664-3575
Fax: 312-664-4652
E-mail: csinfo@acpe-accredit.org
Website: www.acpe-accredit.org

PHYSICAL THERAPY
Sandra Wise, Senior Director
Commission on Accreditation in Physical Therapy Education (CAPTE)
American Physical Therapy Association (APTA)
1111 North Fairfax Street
Alexandria, Virginia 22314-1488
Phone: 703-706-3245
Fax: 703-706-3387
E-mail: accreditation@apta.org
Website: www.capteonline.org

PHYSICIAN ASSISTANT STUDIES
Sharon L. Luke, Executive Director
Accredittion Review Commission on Education for the Physician
    Assistant, Inc. (ARC-PA)
12000 Findley Road, Suite 275
Johns Creek, Georgia 30097
Phone: 770-476-1224
Fax: 770-476-1738
E-mail: arc-pa@arc-pa.org
Website: www.arc-pa.org

PLANNING
Jesmarie Soto Johnson, Executive Director
American Institute of Certified Planners/Association of Collegiate
    Schools of Planning/American Planning Association
Planning Accreditation Board (PAB)
2334 West Lawrence Avenue, Suite 209
Chicago, Illinois 60625
Phone: 773-334-7200
E-mail: smerits@planningaccreditationboard.org
Website: www.planningaccreditationboard.org

PODIATRIC MEDICINE
Heather Stagliano, OTR/L, DHSc, Executive Director
Council on Podiatric Medical Education (CPME)
American Podiatric Medical Association (APMA)
9312 Old Georgetown Road
Bethesda, Maryland 20814-1621
Phone: 301-581-9200
Fax: 301-571-4903
Website: www.cpme.org

PSYCHOLOGY AND COUNSELING
Jacqueline Remondet, Associate Executive Director, CEO of the
Accrediting Unit,
Office of Program Consultation and Accreditation
American Psychological Association
750 First Street, NE
Washington, DC 20002-4202
Phone: 202-336-5979 or 800-374-2721
TDD/TTY: 202-336-6123
Fax: 202-336-5978
E-mail: apaaccred@apa.org
Website: www.apa.org/ed/accreditation

Kelly Coker, Executive Director
Council for Accreditation of Counseling and Related Educational
    Programs (CACREP)
1001 North Fairfax Street, Suite 510
Alexandria, Virginia 22314
Phone: 703-535-5990
Fax: 703-739-6209
E-mail: cacrep@cacrep.org
Website: www.cacrep.org

Richard M. McFall, Executive Director
Psychological Clinical Science Accreditation System (PCSAS)
1101 East Tenth Street
IU Psychology Building
Bloomington, Indiana 47405-7007
Phone: 812-856-2570
Fax: 812-322-5545
E-mail: rmmcfall@pcsas.org
Website: www.pcsas.org

PUBLIC HEALTH
Laura Rasar King, M.P.H., MCHES, Executive Director
Council on Education for Public Health
1010 Wayne Avenue, Suite 220
Silver Spring, Maryland 20910
Phone: 202-789-1050
Fax: 202-789-1895
E-mail: Lking@ceph.org
Website: www.ceph.org

PUBLIC POLICY, AFFAIRS AND ADMINISTRATION
Crystal Calarusse, Chief Accreditation Officer
Commission on Peer Review and Accreditation
Network of Schools of Public Policy, Affairs, and Administration
(NASPAA-COPRA)
1029 Vermont Avenue, NW, Suite 1100
Washington, DC 20005
Phone: 202-628-8965
Fax: 202-626-4978
E-mail: copra@naspaa.org
Website: accreditation.naspaa.org

RADIOLOGIC TECHNOLOGY
Leslie Winter, Chief Executive Officer Joint Review Committee on
Education in Radiologic Technology (JRCERT)
20 North Wacker Drive, Suite 2850
Chicago, Illinois 60606-3182
Phone: 312-704-5300
Fax: 312-704-5304
E-mail: mail@jrcert.org
Website: www.jrcert.org

REHABILITATION EDUCATION
Frank Lane, Ph.D., Executive Director
Council for Accreditation of Counseling and Related Educational
    Programs (CACREP)
1001 North Fairfax Street, Suite 510
Alexandria, Virginia 22314
Phone: 703-535-5990
Fax: 703-739-6209
E-mail: cacrep@cacrep.org
Website: www.cacrep.org

RESPIRATORY CARE
Thomas Smalling, Executive Director
Commission on Accreditation for Respiratory Care (CoARC)
1248 Harwood Road
Bedford, Texas 76021-4244
Phone: 817-283-2835
Fax: 817-354-8519
E-mail: tom@coarc.com
Website: www.coarc.com

SOCIAL WORK
Dr. Stacey Borasky, Director of Accreditation
Office of Social Work Accreditation
Council on Social Work Education
1701 Duke Street, Suite 200
Alexandria, Virginia 22314
Phone: 703-683-8080
Fax: 703-519-2078
E-mail: info@cswe.org
Website: www.cswe.org

SPEECH-LANGUAGE PATHOLOGY AND AUDIOLOGY
Kimberlee Moore, Accreditation Executive Director
American Speech-Language-Hearing Association
Council on Academic Accreditation in Audiology and Speech-Language
  Pathology
2200 Research Boulevard #310
Rockville, Maryland 20850-3289
Phone: 301-296-5700
Fax: 301-296-8750
E-mail: accreditation@asha.org
Website: http://caa.asha.org

TEACHER EDUCATION
Christopher A. Koch, President
National Council for Accreditation of Teacher Education (NCATE)
Teacher Education Accreditation Council (TEAC)
1140 19th Street, Suite 400
Washington, DC 20036
Phone: 202-223-0077
Fax: 202-296-6620
E-mail: caep@caepnet.org
Website: www.ncate.org

TECHNOLOGY
Michale S. McComis, Ed.D., Executive Director
Accrediting Commission of Career Schools and Colleges
2101 Wilson Boulevard, Suite 302
Arlington, Virginia 22201
Phone: 703-247-4212
Fax: 703-247-4533
E-mail: mccomis@accsc.org
Website: www.accsc.org

TECHNOLOGY, MANAGEMENT, AND APPLIED ENGINEERING
Kelly Schild, Director of Accreditation
The Association of Technology, Management, and Applied Engineering
(ATMAE)
275 N. York Street, Suite 401
Elmhurst, Illinois 60126
Phone: 630-433-4514
Fax: 630-563-9181
E-mail: Kelly@atmae.org
Website: www.atmae.org

THEATER
Karen P. Moynahan, Executive Director
National Association of Schools of Theatre Commission on
  Accreditation
11250 Roger Bacon Drive, Suite 21
Reston, Virginia 20190
Phone: 703-437-0700
Fax: 703-437-6312
E-mail: info@arts-accredit.org
Website: http://nast.arts-accredit.org/

THEOLOGY
Dr. Bernard Fryshman, Executive VP
Emeritus and Interim Executive Director
Association of Advanced Rabbinical and Talmudic Schools (AARTS)
Accreditation Commission
11 Broadway, Suite 405
New York, New York 10004
Phone: 212-363-1991
Fax: 212-533-5335
E-mail: k.sharfman.aarts@gmail.com

Frank Yamada, Executive Director
Association of Theological Schools in the United States and Canada
  (ATS)
Commission on Accrediting
10 Summit Park Drive
Pittsburgh, Pennsylvania 15275
Phone: 412-788-6505
Fax: 412-788-6510
E-mail: ats@ats.edu
Website: www.ats.edu

Dr. Timothy Eaton, President
Transnational Association of Christian Colleges and Schools (TRACS)
Accreditation Commission
15935 Forest Road
Forest, Virginia 24551
Phone: 434-525-9539
Fax: 434-525-9538
E-mail: info@tracs.org
Website: www.tracs.org

VETERINARY MEDICINE
Dr. Karen Brandt, Director of Education and Research
American Veterinary Medical Association (AVMA)
Council on Education
1931 North Meacham Road, Suite 100
Schaumburg, Illinois 60173-4360
Phone: 847-925-8070 Ext. 6674
Fax: 847-285-5732
E-mail: info@avma.org
Website: www.avma.org

How to Use These Guides

As you identify the particular programs and institutions that interest you, you can use both the *Graduate & Professional Programs: An Overview* volume and the specialized volumes in the series to obtain detailed information.

- *Graduate Programs in the Biological/Biomedical Sciences & Health-Related Professions*
- *Graduate Programs in Business, Education, Information Studies, Law & Social Work*
- *Graduate Programs in Engineering & Applied Sciences*
- *Graduate Programs the Humanities, Arts & Social Sciences*
- *Graduate Programs in the Physical Sciences, Mathematics, Agricultural Sciences, the Environment & Natural Resources*

Each of the specialized volumes in the series is divided into sections that contain one or more directories devoted to programs in a particular field. If you do not find a directory devoted to your field of interest in a specific volume, consult "Directories and Subject Areas" (located at the end of each volume). After you have identified the correct volume, consult the "Directories and Subject Areas in This Book" index, which shows (as does the more general directory) what directories cover subjects not specifically named in a directory or section title.

Each of the specialized volumes in the series has a number of general directories. These directories have entries for the largest unit at an institution granting graduate degrees in that field. For example, the general Engineering and Applied Sciences directory in the *Graduate Programs in Engineering & Applied Sciences* volume consists of *Profiles* for colleges, schools, and departments of engineering and applied sciences.

General directories are followed by other directories, or sections, that give more detailed information about programs in particular areas of the general field that has been covered. The general Engineering and Applied Sciences directory, in the previous example, is followed by nineteen sections with directories in specific areas of engineering, such as Chemical Engineering, Industrial/Management Engineering, and Mechanical Engineering.

Because of the broad nature of many fields, any system of organization is bound to involve a certain amount of overlap. Environmental studies, for example, is a field whose various aspects are studied in several types of departments and schools. Readers interested in such studies will find information on relevant programs in the *Graduate Programs in the Biological/Biomedical Sciences & Health-Related Professions* volume under Ecology and Environmental Biology and Environmental and Occupational Health; in the *Graduate Programs in the Physical Sciences, Mathematics, Agricultural Sciences, the Environment & Natural Resources* volume under Environmental Management and Policy and Natural Resources; and in the *Graduate Programs in Engineering & Applied Sciences* volume under Energy Management and Policy and Environmental Engineering. To help you find all of the programs of interest to you, the introduction to each section within the specialized volumes includes, if applicable, a paragraph suggesting other sections and directories with information on related areas of study.

Directory of Institutions with Programs in the Physical Sciences, Mathematics, Agricultural Sciences, the Environment & Natural Resources

This directory lists institutions in alphabetical order and includes beneath each name the academic fields in which each institution offers graduate programs. The degree level in each field is also indicated, provided that the institution has supplied that information in response to Peterson's Annual Survey of Graduate and Professional Institutions.

An M indicates that a master's degree program is offered; a D indicates that a doctoral degree program is offered; an O signifies that other advanced degrees (e.g., certificates or specialist degrees) are offered; and an * (asterisk) indicates that a **Close-Up** and/or **Display** is located in this volume. See the index, "Close-Ups and Displays," for the specific page number.

Profiles of Academic and Professional Programs in the Specialized Volumes

Each section of **Profiles** has a table of contents that lists the Program Directories, **Displays**, and **Close-Ups**. Program Directories consist of the **Profiles** of programs in the relevant fields, with **Displays** following if programs have chosen to include them. **Close-Ups**, which are more individualized statements, are also listed for those graduate schools or programs that have chosen to submit them.

The **Profiles** found in the 500 directories in the specialized volumes provide basic data about the graduate units in capsule form for quick reference. To make these directories as useful as possible, **Profiles** are generally listed for an institution's smallest academic unit within a subject area. In other words, if an institution has a College of Liberal Arts that administers many related programs, the **Profile** for the individual program (e.g., Program in History), not the entire College, appears in the directory.

There are some programs that do not fit into any current directory and are not given individual **Profiles**. The directory structure is reviewed annually in order to keep this number to a minimum and to accommodate major trends in graduate education.

The following outline describes the **Profile** information found in the guides and explains how best to use that information. Any item that does not apply to or was not provided by a graduate unit is omitted from its listing. The format of the **Profiles** is constant, making it easy to compare one institution with another and one program with another.

A ★ graphic next to the school's name indicates the institution has additional detailed information in a "Premium Profile" on Petersons.com. After reading their information here, you can learn more about the school by visiting www.petersons.com and searching for that particular college or university's graduate program.

Identifying Information. The institution's name, in boldface type, is followed by a complete listing of the administrative structure for that field of study. (For example, University of Akron, Buchtel College of Arts and Sciences, Department of Theoretical and Applied Mathematics, Program in Mathematics.) The last unit listed is the one to which all information in the **Profile** pertains. The institution's city, state, and ZIP code follow.

Offerings. Each field of study offered by the unit is listed with all postbaccalaureate degrees awarded. Degrees that are not preceded by a specific concentration are awarded in the general field listed in the unit name. Frequently, fields of study are broken down into subspecializations, and those appear following the degrees awarded; for example, "Offerings in secondary education (M.Ed.), including English education, mathematics education, science education." Students enrolled in the M.Ed. program would be able to specialize in any of the three fields mentioned.

Professional Accreditation. Some **Profiles** indicate whether a program is professionally accredited. Because it is possible for a program to receive or lose professional accreditation at any time, students entering fields in which accreditation is important to a career should verify the status of programs by contacting either the chairperson or the appropriate accrediting association.

Jointly Offered Degrees. Explanatory statements concerning programs that are offered in cooperation with other institutions are

included in the list of degrees offered. This occurs most commonly on a regional basis (for example, two state universities offering a cooperative Ph.D. in special education) or where the specialized nature of the institutions encourages joint efforts (a J.D./M.B.A. offered by a law school at an institution with no formal business programs and an institution with a business school but lacking a law school). Only programs that are truly cooperative are listed; those involving only limited course work at another institution are not. Interested students should contact the heads of such units for further information.

Program Availability. This may include the following: part-time, evening/weekend, online only, 100% online, blended/hybrid learning, and/or minimal on-campus study. When information regarding the availability of part-time or evening/weekend study appears in the **Profile**, it means that students are able to earn a degree exclusively through such study. Blended/hybrid learning describes those courses in which some traditional in-class time has been replaced by online learning activities. Hybrid courses take advantage of the best features of both face-to-face and online learning.

Faculty. Figures on the number of faculty members actively involved with graduate students through teaching or research are separated into full- and part-time as well as men and women whenever the information has been supplied.

Students. Figures for the number of students enrolled in graduate and professional programs pertain to the semester of highest enrollment from the 2017–18 academic year. These figures are broken down into full- and part-time and men and women whenever the data have been supplied. Information on the number of matriculated students enrolled in the unit who are members of a minority group or are international students appears here. The average age of the matriculated students is followed by the number of applicants, the percentage accepted, and the number enrolled for fall 2017.

Degrees Awarded. The number of degrees awarded in the calendar year is listed. Many doctoral programs offer a terminal master's degree if students leave the program after completing only part of the requirements for a doctoral degree; that is indicated here. All degrees are classified into one of four types: master's, doctoral, first professional, and other advanced degrees. A unit may award one or several degrees at a given level; however, the data are only collected by type and may therefore represent several different degree programs.

Degree Requirements. The information in this section is also broken down by type of degree, and all information for a degree level pertains to all degrees of that type unless otherwise specified. Degree requirements are collected in a simplified form to provide some very basic information on the nature of the program and on foreign language, thesis or dissertation, comprehensive exam, and registration requirements. Many units also provide a short list of additional requirements, such as fieldwork or an internship. For complete information on graduation requirements, contact the graduate school or program directly.

Entrance Requirements. Entrance requirements are broken down into the four degree levels of master's, doctoral, first professional, and other advanced degrees. Within each level, information may be provided in two basic categories: entrance exams and other requirements. The entrance exams are identified by the standard acronyms used by the testing agencies, unless they are not well known. Other entrance requirements are quite varied, but they often contain an undergraduate or graduate grade point average (GPA). Unless otherwise stated, the GPA is calculated on a 4.0 scale and is listed as a minimum required for admission. Additional exam requirements/recommendations for international students may be listed here. Application deadlines for domestic and international students, the application fee, and whether electronic applications are accepted may be listed here. Note that the deadline should be used for reference only; these dates are subject to change, and students interested in applying should always contact the graduate unit directly about application procedures and deadlines.

Expenses. The typical cost of study for the 2018–2019 academic year (2017–18 if 2018–19 figures were not available) is given in two basic categories: tuition and fees. Cost of study may be quite complex at a graduate institution. There are often sliding scales for part-time study, a different cost for first-year students, and other variables that make it impossible to completely cover the cost of study for each graduate program. To provide the most usable information, figures are given for full-time study for a full year where available and for part-time study in terms of a per-unit rate (per credit, per semester hour, etc.). Occa-

sionally, variances may be noted in tuition and fees for reasons such as the type of program, whether courses are taken during the day or evening, whether courses are at the master's or doctoral level, or other institution-specific reasons. Respondents were also given the opportunity to provide more specific and detailed tuition and fees information at the unit level. When provided, this information will appear in place of any typical costs entered elsewhere on the university-level survey. Expenses are usually subject to change; for exact costs at any given time, contact your chosen schools and programs directly. Keep in mind that the tuition of Canadian institutions is usually given in Canadian dollars.

Financial Support. This section contains data on the number of awards administered by the institution and given to graduate students during the 2017–18 academic year. The first figure given represents the total number of students receiving financial support enrolled in that unit. If the unit has provided information on graduate appointments, these are broken down into three major categories: fellowships give money to graduate students to cover the cost of study and living expenses and are not based on a work obligation or research commitment, research assistantships provide stipends to graduate students for assistance in a formal research project with a faculty member, and teaching assistantships provide stipends to graduate students for teaching or for assisting faculty members in teaching undergraduate classes. Within each category, figures are given for the total number of awards, the average yearly amount per award, and whether full or partial tuition reimbursements are awarded. In addition to graduate appointments, the availability of several other financial aid sources is covered in this section. Tuition waivers are routinely part of a graduate appointment, but units sometimes waive part or all of a student's tuition even if a graduate appointment is not available. Federal Work Study is made available to students who demonstrate need and meet the federal guidelines; this form of aid normally includes 10 or more hours of work per week in an office of the institution. Institutionally sponsored loans are low-interest loans available to graduate students to cover both educational and living expenses. Career-related internships or fieldwork offer money to students who are participating in a formal off-campus research project or practicum. Grants, scholarships, traineeships, unspecified assistantships, and other awards may also be noted. The availability of financial support to part-time students is also indicated here.

Some programs list the financial aid application deadline and the forms that need to be completed for students to be eligible for financial awards. There are two forms: FAFSA, the Free Application for Federal Student Aid, which is required for federal aid, and the CSS PROFILE®.

Faculty Research. Each unit has the opportunity to list several keyword phrases describing the current research involving faculty members and graduate students. Space limitations prevent the unit from listing complete information on all research programs. The total expenditure for funded research from the previous academic year may also be included.

Unit Head and Application Contact. The head of the graduate program for each unit may be listed with academic title, phone and fax numbers, and e-mail address. In addition to the unit head's contact information, many graduate programs also list a separate contact for application and admission information, followed by the graduate school, program, or department's website. If no unit head or application contact is given, you should contact the overall institution for information on graduate admissions.

Displays and Close-Ups

The **Displays** and **Close-Ups** are supplementary insertions submitted by deans, chairs, and other administrators who wish to offer an additional, more individualized statement to readers. A number of graduate school and program administrators have attached a **Display** ad near the **Profile** listing. Here you will find information that an institution or program wants to emphasize. The **Close-Ups** are by their very nature more expansive and flexible than the **Profiles**, and the administrators who have written them may emphasize different aspects of their programs. All of the **Close-Ups** are organized in the same way (with the exception of a few that describe research and training opportunities instead of degree programs), and in each one

you will find information on the same basic topics, such as programs of study, research facilities, tuition and fees, financial aid, and application procedures. If an institution or program has submitted a **Close-Up**, a boldface cross-reference appears below its **Profile**. As with the **Displays**, all of the **Close-Ups** in the guides have been submitted by choice; the absence of a **Display** or **Close-Up** does not reflect any type of editorial judgment on the part of Peterson's, and their presence in the guides should not be taken as an indication of status, quality, or approval. Statements regarding a university's objectives and accomplishments are a reflection of its own beliefs and are not the opinions of the Peterson's editors.

Appendixes

This section contains two appendixes. The first, "Institutional Changes Since the 2018 Edition," lists institutions that have closed, merged, or changed their name or status since the last edition of the guides. The second, "Abbreviations Used in the Guides," gives abbreviations of degree names, along with what those abbreviations stand for. These appendixes are identical in all six volumes of *Peterson's Graduate and Professional Programs*.

Indexes

There are three indexes presented here. The first index, "Close-Ups and Displays," gives page references for all programs that have chosen to place **Close-Ups** and **Displays** in this volume. It is arranged alphabetically by institution; within institutions, the arrangement is alphabetical by subject area. It is not an index to all programs in the book's directories of **Profiles**; readers must refer to the directories themselves for **Profile** information on programs that have not submitted the additional, more individualized statements. The second index, "Directories and Subject Areas in Other Books in This Series", gives book references for the directories in the specialized volumes and also includes cross-references for subject area names not used in the directory structure, for example, "Computing Technology (see Computer Science)." The third index, "Directories and Subject Areas in This Book," gives page references for the directories in this volume and cross-references for subject area names not used in this volume's directory structure.

Data Collection Procedures

The information published in the directories and Profiles of all the books is collected through Peterson's Annual Survey of Graduate and Professional Institutions. The survey is sent each spring to nearly 2,300 institutions offering postbaccalaureate degree programs, including accredited institutions in the United States, U.S. territories, and Canada and those institutions outside the United States that are accredited by

U.S. accrediting bodies. Deans and other administrators complete these surveys, providing information on programs in the 500 academic and professional fields covered in the guides as well as overall institutional information. While every effort has been made to ensure the accuracy and completeness of the data, information is sometimes unavailable or changes occur after publication deadlines. All usable information received in time for publication has been included. The omission of any particular item from a directory or Profile signifies either that the item is not applicable to the institution or program or that information was not available. Profiles of programs scheduled to begin during the 2018–19 academic year cannot, obviously, include statistics on enrollment or, in many cases, the number of faculty members. If no usable data were submitted by an institution, its name, address, and program name appear in order to indicate the availability of graduate work.

Criteria for Inclusion in This Guide

To be included in this guide, an institution must have full accreditation or be a candidate for accreditation (preaccreditation) status by an institutional or specialized accrediting body recognized by the U.S. Department of Education or the Council for Higher Education Accreditation (CHEA). Institutional accrediting bodies, which review each institution as a whole, include the six regional associations of schools and colleges (Middle States, New England, North Central, Northwest, Southern, and Western), each of which is responsible for a specified portion of the United States and its territories. Other institutional accrediting bodies are national in scope and accredit specific kinds of institutions (e.g., Bible colleges, independent colleges, and rabbinical and Talmudic schools). Program registration by the New York State Board of Regents is considered to be the equivalent of institutional accreditation, since the board requires that all programs offered by an institution meet its standards before recognition is granted. A Canadian institution must be chartered and authorized to grant degrees by the provincial government, affiliated with a chartered institution, or accredited by a recognized U.S. accrediting body. This guide also includes institutions outside the United States that are accredited by these U.S. accrediting bodies. There are recognized specialized or professional accrediting bodies in more than fifty different fields, each of which is authorized to accredit institutions or specific programs in its particular field. For specialized institutions that offer programs in one field only, we designate this to be the equivalent of institutional accreditation. A full explanation of the accrediting process and complete information on recognized institutional (regional and national) and specialized accrediting bodies can be found online at **www.chea.org** or at **www.ed.gov/admins/finaid/accred/index.html**.

DIRECTORY OF INSTITUTIONS WITH PROGRAMS IN THE HUMANITIES, ARTS & SOCIAL SCIENCES

ABILENE CHRISTIAN UNIVERSITY
Clinical Psychology — M
Communication—General — M
Conflict Resolution and
  Mediation/Peace Studies — M,O
Counseling Psychology — M
English — M
Liberal Studies — M
Marriage and Family Therapy — M
Missions and Missiology — M
Pastoral Ministry and Counseling — M,D
Psychology—General — M
Religion — M
Rhetoric — M
School Psychology — O
Theology — M
Writing — M

ACADEMY FOR JEWISH RELIGION CALIFORNIA
Jewish Studies — M

ACADEMY OF ART UNIVERSITY
Applied Arts and Design—
  General — M
Architecture — M
Art History — M
Art/Fine Arts — M
Arts Journalism — M
Computer Art and Design — M
Film, Television, and Video
  Production — M
Graphic Design — M
Illustration — M
Industrial Design — M
Interior Design — M
Internet and Interactive
  Multimedia — M
Landscape Architecture — M
Music — M
Photography — M
Textile Design — M
Theater — M
Writing — M

ACADIA UNIVERSITY
Clinical Psychology — M
English — M
Geographic Information Systems — M
Missions and Missiology — M,D
Pastoral Ministry and Counseling — M,D
Philosophy — M
Political Science — M
Psychology—General — M
Sociology — M
Theology — M,D

ADAMS STATE UNIVERSITY
Clinical Psychology — M,D
History — M
Humanities — M
Public Administration — M
Sport Psychology — M

ADELPHI UNIVERSITY
Art/Fine Arts — M
Clinical Psychology — D
Counseling Psychology — M
Emergency Management — O
Gerontology — M,O
Psychology—General — M
School Psychology — M
Writing — M

ADLER GRADUATE SCHOOL
Addictions/Substance Abuse
  Counseling — M
Art Therapy — M
Clinical Psychology — M
Counseling Psychology — M
Marriage and Family Therapy — M
Psychoanalysis and Psychotherapy — M

ADLER UNIVERSITY
Addictions/Substance Abuse
  Counseling — O
Applied Psychology — M
Art Therapy — M,D
Clinical Psychology — M,D
Counseling Psychology — M
Criminal Justice and Criminology — M
Emergency Management — M
Forensic Psychology — M
Gender Studies — M
Health Psychology — M
Industrial and Organizational
  Psychology — M,D
Marriage and Family Therapy — M,D,O
Media Studies — M
Military and Defense Studies — M
Public Administration — M
Public Policy — M
Rehabilitation Counseling — M
School Psychology — M
Social Psychology — M
Sport Psychology — M

ADRIAN COLLEGE
Criminal Justice and Criminology — M

ALABAMA AGRICULTURAL AND MECHANICAL UNIVERSITY
Child and Family Studies — M
Clinical Psychology — M,O
Clothing and Textiles — M
Counseling Psychology — M,O
Family and Consumer
  Sciences-General — M
Human Development — M
Psychology—General — M,O
Rehabilitation Counseling — M,O
School Psychology — M,O
Urban and Regional Planning — M

ALABAMA STATE UNIVERSITY
Forensic Sciences — M
History — M

Rehabilitation Counseling — M

ALASKA PACIFIC UNIVERSITY
Counseling Psychology — M
Interdisciplinary Studies — M
Liberal Studies — M

ALBANY STATE UNIVERSITY
Criminal Justice and Criminology — M
Economic Development — M
Economics — M
Public Administration — M
Public Policy — M

ALBERTUS MAGNUS COLLEGE
Art Therapy — M
Criminal Justice and Criminology — M
Liberal Studies — M
Writing — M

ALCORN STATE UNIVERSITY
Agricultural Economics and
  Agribusiness — M

ALFRED UNIVERSITY
Applied Arts and Design—
  General — M
Art/Fine Arts — M,D
Computer Art and Design — M
Counseling Psychology — M,D,O
Internet and Interactive
  Multimedia — M
Public Administration — M
School Psychology — M,D,O

ALLIANT INTERNATIONAL UNIVERSITY–FRESNO
Clinical Psychology — D
Forensic Psychology — D
Industrial and Organizational
  Psychology — M,D
Psychology—General — M,D

ALLIANT INTERNATIONAL UNIVERSITY–IRVINE
Forensic Psychology — D
Forensic Sciences — D
Marriage and Family Therapy — M,D
School Psychology — M,D,O

ALLIANT INTERNATIONAL UNIVERSITY–LOS ANGELES
Addictions/Substance Abuse
  Counseling — M
Clinical Psychology — D
Forensic Psychology — D
Gerontology — M
Health Psychology — D
Industrial and Organizational
  Psychology — M,D
Marriage and Family Therapy — M,D
Psychology—General — M,D
School Psychology — M,D,O
Social Psychology — D

ALLIANT INTERNATIONAL UNIVERSITY–SACRAMENTO
Clinical Psychology — D
Forensic Psychology — D
Marriage and Family Therapy — M,D
Psychology—General — M,D

ALLIANT INTERNATIONAL UNIVERSITY–SAN DIEGO
Clinical Psychology — M,D
Forensic Psychology — D
Industrial and Organizational
  Psychology — M,D
Marriage and Family Therapy — M,D
Psychology—General — M,D
School Psychology — M,D,O

ALLIANT INTERNATIONAL UNIVERSITY–SAN FRANCISCO
Clinical Psychology — M,D,O
Criminal Justice and Criminology — M
Forensic Psychology — M,D
Industrial and Organizational
  Psychology — M,D
Psychology—General — M,D,O
School Psychology — M,D,O

ALVERNIA UNIVERSITY
Liberal Studies — M
Social Psychology — M

ALVERNO COLLEGE
Social Psychology — M

AMBERTON UNIVERSITY
Child and Family Studies — M
Counseling Psychology — M
Interdisciplinary Studies — M
Marriage and Family Therapy — M

AMBROSE UNIVERSITY
Pastoral Ministry and Counseling — M,O
Religion — M,O
Theology — M,O

AMERICAN BAPTIST SEMINARY OF THE WEST
Pastoral Ministry and Counseling — M
Theology — M

AMERICAN COLLEGE DUBLIN
Writing — M

AMERICAN CONSERVATORY THEATER
Theater — M,O

AMERICAN FILM INSTITUTE CONSERVATORY
Film, Television, and Video
  Production — M

AMERICAN GRADUATE SCHOOL IN PARIS
International Affairs — M,D

AMERICAN INTERCONTINENTAL UNIVERSITY ONLINE
Industrial and Organizational
  Psychology — M

AMERICAN INTERNATIONAL COLLEGE
Clinical Psychology — M,D,O
Counseling Psychology — M,D
Forensic Psychology — M,D,O
Psychology—General — M,D,O

AMERICAN JEWISH UNIVERSITY
Jewish Studies — M
Theology — M

AMERICAN MUSEUM OF NATURAL HISTORY–RICHARD GILDER GRADUATE SCHOOL
Museum Studies — D

AMERICAN PUBLIC UNIVERSITY SYSTEM
American Studies — M,D
Conflict Resolution and
  Mediation/Peace Studies — M,D
Criminal Justice and Criminology — M,D
History — M,D
International Affairs — M,D
Military and Defense Studies — M,D
National Security — M,D
Political Science — M,D
Public Policy — M,D

AMERICAN UNIVERSITY
American Studies — M,D,O
Anthropology — M,D,O
Applied Social Research — M,O
Art History — M
Arts Administration — M,O
Asian Studies — O
Clinical Psychology — M,D,O
Cognitive Sciences — M,D,O
Communication—General — M,D,O
Comparative Literature — M
Conflict Resolution and
  Mediation/Peace Studies — M,D,O
Corporate and Organizational
  Communication — M
Criminal Justice and Criminology — M,D
Cultural Studies — M,D,O
Economics — M,D,O
Ethics — M,D,O
Film, Television, and Video
  Production — M
French — M,O
Gender Studies — M,D,O
History — M,D
International Affairs — M,D,O
International Development — M,D,O
International Economics — M,D,O
Journalism — M
Latin American Studies — M,O
Mass Communication — M,D
Media Studies — M,D
Music — M,O
National Security — M,D,O
Philosophy — M
Political Science — M,D,O
Psychology—General — M,D,O
Public Administration — M,D,O
Public Policy — M,D,O
Russian — M,O
Sociology — M,O
Spanish — M,O
Sustainable Development — M,D,O
Western European Studies — M,D,O
Women's Studies — O
Writing — M

THE AMERICAN UNIVERSITY IN CAIRO
Broadcast Journalism — M,O
Communication—General — M,D,O
Comparative Literature — M,O
Economic Development — M,O
Economics — M,O
English — M,O
Gender Studies — M,O
Humanities — M,O
International Affairs — M,O
Journalism — M,O
Mass Communication — M,O
Near and Middle Eastern Languages — M,O
Near and Middle Eastern Studies — M,O
Philosophy — M,O
Psychology—General — M,O
Public Administration — M,O
Public Policy — M,O
Sustainable Development — M,D,O
Women's Studies — M,O

AMERICAN UNIVERSITY OF ARMENIA
Economics — M
International Affairs — M
Political Science — M

AMERICAN UNIVERSITY OF BEIRUT
Agricultural Economics and
  Agribusiness — M
Anthropology — M,D
Archaeology — M,D
Art History — M,D
Clinical Psychology — M,D
Economics — M,D
English — M,D
History — M,D
International Affairs — M,D
Media Studies — M,D
Near and Middle Eastern Languages — M,D
Near and Middle Eastern Studies — M,D
Philosophy — M,D
Political Science — M,D
Psychology—General — M,D
Public Administration — M,D
Public Policy — M,D
School Psychology — M,D
Sociology — M,D

Urban and Regional Planning — M,D
Urban Design — M,D

THE AMERICAN UNIVERSITY OF PARIS
Communication—General — M
Conflict Resolution and
  Mediation/Peace Studies — M
Cultural Studies — M
International Affairs — M
Near and Middle Eastern Studies — M
Public Policy — M

AMERICAN UNIVERSITY OF PUERTO RICO
Criminal Justice and Criminology — M

THE AMERICAN UNIVERSITY OF ROME
Historic Preservation — M
Religion — M

AMERICAN UNIVERSITY OF SHARJAH
Translation and Interpretation — M
Urban and Regional Planning — M,D

AMRIDGE UNIVERSITY
Counseling Psychology — M,D
Marriage and Family Therapy — M,D
Pastoral Ministry and Counseling — M,D
Religion — M,D
Theology — M,D

ANABAPTIST MENNONITE BIBLICAL SEMINARY
Conflict Resolution and
  Mediation/Peace Studies — M,O
Ethics — M,O
International Affairs — M,O
Pastoral Ministry and Counseling — M,O
Public Administration — M,O
Theology — M,O

ANDERSON UNIVERSITY (IN)
Missions and Missiology — M,D
Theology — M,D

ANDERSON UNIVERSITY (SC)
Criminal Justice and Criminology — M
Pastoral Ministry and Counseling — M,D

ANDREWS UNIVERSITY
Architecture — M
Clinical Psychology — M
Communication—General — M
Counseling Psychology — M,D
Developmental Psychology — M,D
Economics — M
English — M
International Development — M
Music — M
Pastoral Ministry and Counseling — M,D,O
Psychology—General — M,D,O
School Psychology — M,O
Social Psychology — M
Theology — M,D,O
Urban and Regional Planning — M

ANGELO STATE UNIVERSITY
Communication—General — M
Criminal Justice and Criminology — M
English — M
Homeland Security — M
Industrial and Organizational
  Psychology — M
Media Studies — M
National Security — M
Psychology—General — M
Sociology — M

ANNA MARIA COLLEGE
Art/Fine Arts — M,O
Counseling Psychology — M
Criminal Justice and Criminology — M
Emergency Management — M,O
Industrial and Organizational
  Psychology — M
Public Administration — M

ANTIOCH UNIVERSITY LOS ANGELES
Clinical Psychology — M
Psychology—General — M
Sustainable Development — M

ANTIOCH UNIVERSITY NEW ENGLAND
Addictions/Substance Abuse
  Counseling — M
Applied Behavior Analysis — M,O
Applied Psychology — M,D,O
Clinical Psychology — M,D
Counseling Psychology — M
Humanities — M
Interdisciplinary Studies — M
Marriage and Family Therapy — M,D,O
Sustainable Development — M,O
Therapies—Dance, Drama, and
  Music — M,O

ANTIOCH UNIVERSITY SANTA BARBARA
Clinical Psychology — M,D
Writing — M

ANTIOCH UNIVERSITY SEATTLE
Clinical Psychology — M,D
Marriage and Family Therapy — M,D
Therapies—Dance, Drama, and
  Music — M,D

APEX SCHOOL OF THEOLOGY
Theology — M,D

APPALACHIAN BIBLE COLLEGE
Pastoral Ministry and Counseling — M

APPALACHIAN STATE UNIVERSITY
American Studies — M
Clinical Psychology — M
Counseling Psychology — M
Cultural Studies — M
English — M
Geographic Information Systems — M

Geography M
Health Psychology M
History M
Marriage and Family Therapy M
Music M
Political Science M
Psychology—General M
Public Administration M
School Psychology M
Therapies—Dance, Drama, and Music M

AQUINAS INSTITUTE OF THEOLOGY
Music M,D,O
Pastoral Ministry and Counseling M,D,O
Theology M,D,O

ARCADIA UNIVERSITY
Applied Behavior Analysis M
Conflict Resolution and Mediation/Peace Studies M
Counseling Psychology M
English M
Forensic Sciences M
Genetic Counseling M
Humanities M
International Affairs M
Marriage and Family Therapy M
Psychology—General M,D,O
Theater M,D,O
Writing M

ARGOSY UNIVERSITY, ATLANTA
Clinical Psychology M,D,O
Forensic Psychology M,D,O
Health Psychology M,D,O
Industrial and Organizational Psychology M,D,O
Marriage and Family Therapy M,D,O
Psychology—General M,D,O
Social Psychology M,D,O
Sport Psychology M,D,O

ARGOSY UNIVERSITY, CHICAGO
Clinical Psychology M,D
Counseling Psychology D
Forensic Psychology D
Health Psychology D
Human Development D
Industrial and Organizational Psychology M,D
Marriage and Family Therapy D
Psychoanalysis and Psychotherapy D
Psychology—General M,D
Public Administration M,D
Social Psychology M,D

ARGOSY UNIVERSITY, HAWAII
Addictions/Substance Abuse Counseling O
Clinical Psychology M,D,O
Counseling Psychology D
Forensic Psychology M
Marriage and Family Therapy M
Psychology—General M,D,O
School Psychology M

ARGOSY UNIVERSITY, LOS ANGELES
Clinical Psychology M,D
Counseling Psychology M,D
Forensic Psychology M,D
Marriage and Family Therapy M,D
Psychology—General M,D
Public Administration M,D

ARGOSY UNIVERSITY, NORTHERN VIRGINIA
Clinical Psychology M,D
Counseling Psychology M,D
Forensic Psychology M,D
Health Psychology M,D
Marriage and Family Therapy M,D
Psychology—General M,D
Public Administration M,D,O
Social Psychology M,D

ARGOSY UNIVERSITY, ORANGE COUNTY
Clinical Psychology M,D
Counseling Psychology M,D
Forensic Psychology M
Marriage and Family Therapy M,D
Psychology—General M,D
Public Administration M,D,O
Sport Psychology M

ARGOSY UNIVERSITY, PHOENIX
Clinical Psychology M,D
Counseling Psychology M
Forensic Psychology M
Industrial and Organizational Psychology M
Psychology—General M,D
Public Administration M,D
School Psychology M,D
Sport Psychology M,D

ARGOSY UNIVERSITY, SEATTLE
Clinical Psychology M,D,O
Counseling Psychology M,D
Psychology—General M,D,O
Public Administration M,D

ARGOSY UNIVERSITY, TAMPA
Clinical Psychology M,D
Counseling Psychology M,D
Industrial and Organizational Psychology M,D
Marriage and Family Therapy M,D
Psychology—General M,D
Public Administration M,D

ARGOSY UNIVERSITY, TWIN CITIES
Clinical Psychology M,D,O
Forensic Psychology M,D,O
Health Psychology M,D,O
Industrial and Organizational Psychology M,D,O
Marriage and Family Therapy M,D,O
Psychology—General M,D,O
Public Administration M,D

ARIZONA STATE UNIVERSITY AT THE TEMPE CAMPUS
African Studies M,D,O
Agricultural Economics and Agribusiness D
Anthropology M,D,O
Applied Arts and Design—General M,D
Applied Behavior Analysis M,D
Applied Psychology M
Archaeology M,D,O
Architectural History D
Architecture M,D
Art History M,D
Art/Fine Arts M,D
Arts Administration M,D
Building Science M,D
Child and Family Studies M,D
Chinese M,D
Clinical Psychology M,D
Cognitive Sciences M,D
Communication—General M,D
Comparative Literature M,D,O
Counseling Psychology D
Criminal Justice and Criminology M,D,O
Cultural Studies M,D
Dance M
Developmental Psychology M,D
Economics D
Emergency Management M,D
English M,D,O
Environmental Design D
Ethics M,D
Film, Television, and Video Production M
French M
Gender Studies M,D,O
Geographic Information Systems M,D,O
Geography M,D,O
German M
Gerontology M,D,O
History of Science and Technology M,D
History M,D,O
Homeland Security M,D
Human Development M,D
Interdisciplinary Studies M
Japanese M
Journalism M,D
Landscape Architecture M,D
Liberal Studies M
Linguistics M,D,O
Marriage and Family Therapy M,D
Mass Communication M,D
Media Studies M,D
Medieval and Renaissance Studies M,D,O
Museum Studies M,D,O
Music M,D
Philosophy M,D,O
Political Science M,D
Psychology—General M,D
Public Administration M,D
Public Affairs M,D
Public History M,D,O
Public Policy M,D
Publishing M,D,O
Religion M,D,O
Rhetoric M,D,O
Social Psychology M,D
Sociology M,D
Spanish M,D
Sustainable Development M,D,O
Textile Design M,D
Theater M,D
Therapies—Dance, Drama, and Music M,D
Translation and Interpretation M,D,O
Urban and Regional Planning M,D,O
Urban Design M,D
Urban Studies M,D,O
Writing M,D

ARKANSAS STATE UNIVERSITY
Addictions/Substance Abuse Counseling M,O
Clinical Psychology M,O
Communication—General M,O
Criminal Justice and Criminology M,O
Emergency Management M,O
English M,O
Gerontology M,D,O
Health Communication M,O
Historic Preservation M,D
History M,O
Journalism M
Mass Communication M
Media Studies M
Music M,O
Political Science M,O
Public Administration M,O
Rehabilitation Counseling M,O
School Psychology M,O
Sociology M,O

ARKANSAS TECH UNIVERSITY
Emergency Management M
English M
History M
Journalism M
Liberal Studies M
Psychology—General M
Sociology M

ARLINGTON BAPTIST UNIVERSITY
Theology M

ARTCENTER COLLEGE OF DESIGN
Art/Fine Arts M
Computer Art and Design M
Environmental Design M
Film, Television, and Video Production M
Graphic Design M
Industrial Design M

THE ART INSTITUTE OF DALLAS, A BRANCH OF MIAMI INTERNATIONAL UNIVERSITY OF ART & DESIGN
Applied Arts and Design—General M

ASBURY THEOLOGICAL SEMINARY
Missions and Missiology M,D,O
Pastoral Ministry and Counseling M,D,O
Theology M,D,O

ASBURY UNIVERSITY
Child and Family Studies M
Classics M
English M
French M
Spanish M
Writing M

ASHLAND THEOLOGICAL SEMINARY
Clinical Psychology M,D
Pastoral Ministry and Counseling M,D
Theology M,D

ASHLAND UNIVERSITY
Communication—General M
Corporate and Organizational Communication M
History M
Political Science M
Writing M

ASHWORTH COLLEGE
Criminal Justice and Criminology M

ASSEMBLIES OF GOD THEOLOGICAL SEMINARY
Cultural Studies M,D
Missions and Missiology M,D
Pastoral Ministry and Counseling M,D
Theology M,D

ASSUMPTION COLLEGE
Addictions/Substance Abuse Counseling O
Applied Behavior Analysis M,O
Child and Family Studies M,O
Counseling Psychology M,O
Economics M,O
Rehabilitation Counseling M,O
School Psychology M,O
Social Sciences O

ATHABASCA UNIVERSITY
Applied Psychology M,O
Architecture M,O
Art Therapy M,O
Counseling Psychology M,O
Cultural Studies M,O
Interdisciplinary Studies M,O
International Development M,O

THE ATHENAEUM OF OHIO
Theology M,O

ATHENS STATE UNIVERSITY
Religion M

ATLANTIC SCHOOL OF THEOLOGY
Pastoral Ministry and Counseling M,O
Theology M,O

ATLANTIC UNIVERSITY
Pastoral Ministry and Counseling O
Psychoanalysis and Psychotherapy O
Transpersonal and Humanistic Psychology M

ATLANTIC UNIVERSITY COLLEGE
Graphic Design M

A.T. STILL UNIVERSITY
Sport Psychology M,D,O

AUBURN UNIVERSITY
Agricultural Economics and Agribusiness M
Applied Economics M,D
Architecture M
Child and Family Studies M,D
Clothing and Textiles M,D
Communication—General M,O
Economics M,D
English M,D,O*
Geography M
History M,D,O
Human Development M,D
Industrial Design M
Landscape Architecture M
Political Science M,D,O
Psychology—General M,D
Public Administration M,D,O
Sociology M
Spanish M
Technical Communication M,D,O
Urban and Regional Planning M

AUBURN UNIVERSITY AT MONTGOMERY
Applied Economics M
Clinical Psychology M,O
Criminal Justice and Criminology M
Economics M
Emergency Management M
Geographic Information Systems M
Homeland Security M
Liberal Studies M
Political Science M,D
Psychology—General M
Public Administration M,D
Public Policy M,D
School Psychology M,O
Writing M

AUGUSTANA UNIVERSITY
Genetic Counseling M

AUGUSTA UNIVERSITY
Clinical Psychology M,O
Medical Illustration M
Psychology—General M
School Psychology M,O
Social Sciences M

AURORA UNIVERSITY
Applied Behavior Analysis M,D
Homeland Security M
Public Policy M

AUSTIN GRADUATE SCHOOL OF THEOLOGY
Theology M

AUSTIN PEAY STATE UNIVERSITY
Clinical Psychology M
Communication—General M
Corporate and Organizational Communication M
Counseling Psychology M
English M
Industrial and Organizational Psychology M
Media Studies M
Military and Defense Studies M
Music M
Psychology—General M

AUSTIN PRESBYTERIAN THEOLOGICAL SEMINARY
Pastoral Ministry and Counseling M,D
Theology M,D

AVE MARIA UNIVERSITY
Pastoral Ministry and Counseling M,D
Theology M,D

AVILA UNIVERSITY
Counseling Psychology M
Psychology—General M

AZUSA PACIFIC UNIVERSITY
Art/Fine Arts M
Clinical Psychology D
Developmental Psychology M
English M
Ethics M
Experimental Psychology M
Film, Television, and Video Production M
Industrial and Organizational Psychology M
Marriage and Family Therapy D
Music M
Pastoral Ministry and Counseling M
Psychology—General M
School Psychology M,D
Theology M,D
Urban Studies M

BABEL UNIVERSITY PROFESSIONAL SCHOOL OF TRANSLATION
Translation and Interpretation M

BAKER UNIVERSITY
Liberal Studies M

BAKKE GRADUATE UNIVERSITY
Pastoral Ministry and Counseling M,D
Theology M,D

BALL STATE UNIVERSITY
Anthropology M,O
Applied Behavior Analysis M,O
Architecture M
Art/Fine Arts M
Clinical Psychology M,D
Cognitive Sciences M
Communication—General M,O
Counseling Psychology M,O
Criminal Justice and Criminology M,O
Economic Development M,O
Emergency Management M,O
English M,D
Family and Consumer Sciences-General M
Geographic Information Systems M,O
Geography M,O
Historic Preservation M
History M
Homeland Security M,O
Human Development M,D,O
Interior Design M
Internet and Interactive Multimedia M
Journalism M
Landscape Architecture M
Linguistics M
Music M,D,O
Photography M
Political Science M
Psychology—General M
Public Administration M,O
Rehabilitation Counseling M,O
Rhetoric M,D
School Psychology M,D,O
Social Psychology M
Sociology M
Speech and Interpersonal Communication M
Sport Psychology M
Urban and Regional Planning M,O
Urban Design M

*M—masters degree; D—doctorate; O—other advanced degree; *—Close-Up and/or Display*

Writing — M,D

BANK STREET COLLEGE OF EDUCATION
Child and Family Studies — M

BAPTIST BIBLE COLLEGE
Pastoral Ministry and Counseling — M
Theology — M

THE BAPTIST COLLEGE OF FLORIDA
Music — M
Pastoral Ministry and Counseling — M
Religion — M
Theology — M

BAPTIST MISSIONARY ASSOCIATION THEOLOGICAL SEMINARY
Theology — M

BAPTIST THEOLOGICAL SEMINARY AT RICHMOND
Pastoral Ministry and Counseling — M,D,O
Religion — M,D,O
Theology — M,D,O

BARCLAY COLLEGE
Theology — M

BARD COLLEGE
Art/Fine Arts — M
Economics — M
English — M
Film, Television, and Video Production — M
History — M
Museum Studies — M
Music — M,O
Photography — M
Spanish — M
Writing — M

BARD GRADUATE CENTER
Art History — M,D*
Decorative Arts — M,D

BARRY UNIVERSITY
Art/Fine Arts — M
Clinical Psychology — M,O
Communication—General — M,O
Corporate and Organizational Communication — M,O
Liberal Studies — M
Marriage and Family Therapy — M,O
Pastoral Ministry and Counseling — M,D
Photography — M
Psychology—General — M,O
Public Administration — M
Rehabilitation Counseling — M,O
School Psychology — M,O
Sport Psychology — M
Theology — M,D

BARUCH COLLEGE OF THE CITY UNIVERSITY OF NEW YORK
Arts Administration — M
Corporate and Organizational Communication — M
Counseling Psychology — M
Economics — M
Industrial and Labor Relations — M
Industrial and Organizational Psychology — M,D
International Affairs — M*
International Economics — M
International Trade Policy — M
Public Administration — M
Public Policy — M
Sustainable Development — M

BASTYR UNIVERSITY
Counseling Psychology — M,O
Health Psychology — M,O

BAYAMÓN CENTRAL UNIVERSITY
Industrial and Organizational Psychology — M
Marriage and Family Therapy — M,O
Rehabilitation Counseling — M,O

BAYLOR COLLEGE OF MEDICINE
Genetic Counseling — M

BAYLOR UNIVERSITY
American Studies — M
Applied Behavior Analysis — M,D,O
Clinical Psychology — D
Communication—General — M
Economics — M
English — M,D
History — M,D
Interdisciplinary Studies — D
International Affairs — M,D
Journalism — M
Museum Studies — M
Music — M,D
Philosophy — M,D
Political Science — M,D
Psychology—General — M,D
Public Administration — M,D
Public Policy — M,D
Religion — M,D
School Psychology — M,D,O
Sociology — M,D
Spanish — M
Theater — M
Theology — M,D

BAY PATH UNIVERSITY
Addictions/Substance Abuse Counseling — M
Applied Behavior Analysis — M
Clinical Psychology — M
Developmental Psychology — M
Forensic Sciences — M
Genetic Counseling — M
Writing — M

BECKER COLLEGE
Counseling Psychology — M
Social Psychology — M

BELHAVEN UNIVERSITY (MS)
Public Administration — M

BELLARMINE UNIVERSITY
Communication—General — M

BELLEVUE UNIVERSITY
Corporate and Organizational Communication — M
Criminal Justice and Criminology — M
Military and Defense Studies — M
National Security — M
Public Administration — M

BEMIDJI STATE UNIVERSITY
English — M

BENEDICTINE UNIVERSITY
Clinical Psychology — M
Emergency Management — M
Women's Studies — M

BENNINGTON COLLEGE
Dance — M
Music — M
Writing — M

BERKLEE COLLEGE OF MUSIC
Music — M,O
Theater — M,O

BETHANY GLOBAL UNIVERSITY
Pastoral Ministry and Counseling — M

BETHANY THEOLOGICAL SEMINARY
Conflict Resolution and Mediation/Peace Studies — M,O
Pastoral Ministry and Counseling — M,O
Religion — M,O
Theology — M,O

BETHEL COLLEGE
Pastoral Ministry and Counseling — M
Theology — M

BETHEL SEMINARY
Classics — M,D,O
Clinical Psychology — M,D,O
Marriage and Family Therapy — M,D,O
Missions and Missiology — M,D,O
Near and Middle Eastern Languages — M,D,O
Pastoral Ministry and Counseling — M,D,O
Religion — M,D,O
Theology — M,D,O

BETHEL UNIVERSITY (MN)
Counseling Psychology — M,D,O

BETHEL UNIVERSITY (TN)
Conflict Resolution and Mediation/Peace Studies — M

BETHESDA UNIVERSITY
Music — M
Religion — M
Theology — M

BETH HAMEDRASH SHAAREI YOSHER INSTITUTE
Theology — M

BETH HATALMUD RABBINICAL COLLEGE
Theology — M

BETHLEHEM COLLEGE & SEMINARY
Theology — M

BETH MEDRASH GOVOHA
Theology — M

BETHUNE-COOKMAN UNIVERSITY
Theology — M

BEULAH HEIGHTS UNIVERSITY
Religion — M

BEXLEY SEABURY SEMINARY
Theology — M,D,O

BIBLICAL THEOLOGICAL SEMINARY
Missions and Missiology — M,D,O
Pastoral Ministry and Counseling — M,D,O
Theology — M,D,O

BINGHAMTON UNIVERSITY, STATE UNIVERSITY OF NEW YORK
Anthropology — M,D
Art History — M,D
Asian Studies — M,O
Asian-American Studies — M,O
Clinical Psychology — D
Cognitive Sciences — D
Comparative Literature — M,D
Economics — M,D
English — M,D
French — M
Geography — M
History — M,D
Italian — M
Liberal Studies — M
Music — M
Philosophy — M,D
Political Science — M,D
Psychology—General — D
Public Administration — M
Public Affairs — D
Sociology — M,D
Spanish — M
Sustainable Development — M
Theater — M
Translation and Interpretation — D,O
Writing — M,D

BIOLA UNIVERSITY
Anthropology — M,D,O
Clinical Psychology — D
Cultural Studies — M,D,O

Jewish Studies — M,D,O
Linguistics — M,D,O
Missions and Missiology — M,D,O
Pastoral Ministry and Counseling — M,D,O
Psychology—General — D
Religion — M,D,O
Theology — M,D,O

BOB JONES UNIVERSITY
Art/Fine Arts — M,D,O
English — M,D,O
Film, Television, and Video Production — M,D,O
Graphic Design — M,D,O
History — M,D,O
Illustration — M,D,O
Journalism — M,D,O
Media Studies — M,D,O
Music — M,D,O
Pastoral Ministry and Counseling — M,D,O
Religion — M,D,O
Rhetoric — M,D,O
Speech and Interpersonal Communication — M,D,O
Theater — M,D,O
Theology — M,D,O

BOISE STATE UNIVERSITY
Anthropology — M
Art/Fine Arts — M
Communication—General — M
Criminal Justice and Criminology — M
Economics — M
History — M
Interdisciplinary Studies — M
Music — M
Political Science — M
Public Administration — M,D,O
Public Policy — M,D,O
Rhetoric — M
Technical Communication — M

BORICUA COLLEGE
Latin American Studies — M

BOSTON ARCHITECTURAL COLLEGE
Architecture — M
Historic Preservation — M
Interior Design — M
Landscape Architecture — M
Sustainable Development — M

BOSTON COLLEGE
Applied Psychology — M,D
Classics — M
Counseling Psychology — M,D
Developmental Psychology — M,D
East European and Russian Studies — M
Economics — D
English — M
French — M
History — M
Italian — M
Linguistics — M
Pastoral Ministry and Counseling — M,D,O
Philosophy — M,D
Political Science — M,D
Psychology—General — D
Russian — M
Sociology — M,D
Spanish — M
Theology — M,D,O
Western European Studies — M

BOSTON GRADUATE SCHOOL OF PSYCHOANALYSIS
Counseling Psychology — M
Developmental Psychology — O
Psychoanalysis and Psychotherapy — M,D,O
Psychology—General — M

BOSTON UNIVERSITY
African-American Studies — M
American Studies — D
Anthropology — M,D
Archaeology — M,D
Art History — M,D,O
Art/Fine Arts — M
Arts Administration — M,O
Classics — M,D
Communication—General — M
Corporate and Organizational Communication — M
Counseling Psychology — M
Criminal Justice and Criminology — M
Cultural Studies — M
Economic Development — M
Economics — M
Emergency Management — M
English — M,D
Ethics — M,D
Film, Television, and Video Production — M
Forensic Sciences — M
Genetic Counseling — M
Geographic Information Systems — M
Graphic Design — M
Health Communication — M
Hispanic and Latin American Languages — M,D
Historic Preservation — M
History — M,D
International Affairs — M*
Internet and Interactive Multimedia — M,O
Journalism — M
Latin American Studies — M
Linguistics — M
Mass Communication — M
Media Studies — M
Missions and Missiology — M
Museum Studies — M,D,O
Music — M,D
Pastoral Ministry and Counseling — M,D
Philosophy — M,D
Political Science — D

Psychology—General — M,D
Religion — M,D
Romance Languages — M,D
Sociology — M,D
Theater — M,O
Theology — M,D
Urban and Regional Planning — M
Urban Studies — M
Writing — M

BOWIE STATE UNIVERSITY
Corporate and Organizational Communication — M,O
Counseling Psychology — M
English — M
Public Administration — M

BOWLING GREEN STATE UNIVERSITY
American Studies — M,D
Applied Arts and Design—General — M
Art History — M
Art/Fine Arts — M
Clinical Psychology — M,D
Communication—General — M,D
Computer Art and Design — M
Criminal Justice and Criminology — M
Demography and Population Studies — M,D
Developmental Psychology — M,D
Economics — M
English — M,D
Experimental Psychology — M,D
Film, Television, and Video Production — M,D
French — M
German — M
Graphic Design — M
History — M,D
Industrial and Organizational Psychology — M,D
Interdisciplinary Studies — M,D
Media Studies — M,D
Music — M,D
Philosophy — M,D
Psychology—General — M,D
Public Administration — M
Rhetoric — M,D
Social Psychology — M,D
Sociology — M,D
Spanish — M
Technical Communication — M,D
Theater — M,D
Writing — M,D

BRADLEY UNIVERSITY
Art/Fine Arts — M
Clinical Psychology — M
Counseling Psychology — M
English — M
Graphic Design — M
Human Development — M
Photography — M

BRANDEIS UNIVERSITY
Anthropology — M,D
Applied Economics — M
Art/Fine Arts — O
Child and Family Studies — M,D
Chinese — M
Classics — M
Cognitive Sciences — M,D
Conflict Resolution and Mediation/Peace Studies — M,D
Cultural Anthropology — M,D
Developmental Psychology — M,D
Disability Studies — D
Economics — M,D
English — M,D
Gender Studies — M
Genetic Counseling — M
History — M,D
Humanities — M
International Affairs — M
Internet and Interactive Multimedia — M
Jewish Studies — M,D
Linguistics — M
Music — M,D
Near and Middle Eastern Languages — M,D
Near and Middle Eastern Studies — M,D
Philosophy — M
Political Science — M,D
Psychology—General — M,D
Public Policy — M
Social Psychology — M,D
Sociology — M,D
Sustainable Development — M
Theater — M
Women's Studies — M,D

BRANDMAN UNIVERSITY
Counseling Psychology — M
Marriage and Family Therapy — M
Psychology—General — M
Public Administration — M

BRANDON UNIVERSITY
Music — M
Rural Planning and Studies — M,O

BRENAU UNIVERSITY
Interior Design — M
Psychology—General — M

BRIDGEWATER STATE UNIVERSITY
Criminal Justice and Criminology — M
English — M
Psychology—General — M
Public Administration — M

BRIERCREST SEMINARY
Marriage and Family Therapy — M
Missions and Missiology — M
Pastoral Ministry and Counseling — M
Religion — M
Theology — M

BRIGHAM YOUNG UNIVERSITY

Anthropology	M
Art/Fine Arts	M
Child and Family Studies	M,D
Classics	M
Clinical Psychology	D
Cognitive Sciences	D
Communication—General	M
Comparative and Interdisciplinary Arts	M
Comparative Literature	M
Counseling Psychology	M,D,O
English	M
Film, Television, and Video Production	M
French	M
Hispanic and Latin American Languages	M
Human Development	M,D
Humanities	M
International Affairs	M
Linguistics	M
Marriage and Family Therapy	M,D
Mass Communication	M
Music	M
Political Science	M
Portuguese	M
Psychology—General	D
Public Administration	M
Rhetoric	M
School Psychology	M,D,O
Sociology	M
Spanish	M
Theater	M
Writing	M

BRITE DIVINITY SCHOOL

Pastoral Ministry and Counseling	M,D,O
Theology	M,D,O

BROCK UNIVERSITY

Child and Family Studies	M
Classics	M
Comparative Literature	M
Cultural Studies	M
Disability Studies	M,O
Economics	M
English	M
Geography	M
History	M
Human Development	M,D
International Affairs	M
Philosophy	M
Political Science	M
Psychology—General	M,D
Public Policy	M
Social Psychology	M,D
Sociology	M

BROOKLYN COLLEGE OF THE CITY UNIVERSITY OF NEW YORK

Art History	M
Art/Fine Arts	M
Arts Administration	M
Counseling Psychology	M,D,O
Economics	M
English	M
Experimental Psychology	M,D
Film, Television, and Video Production	M
Film, Television, and Video Theory and Criticism	M
French	M
History	M
Industrial and Organizational Psychology	M,D
International Affairs	M
Internet and Interactive Multimedia	M
Jewish Studies	M
Liberal Studies	M
Media Studies	M
Music	M
Photography	M
Political Science	M
Psychology—General	M,D
Public Policy	M
School Psychology	M,O
Social Psychology	M,D
Sociology	M,D
Spanish	M
Speech and Interpersonal Communication	M,D
Thanatology	M
Theater	M
Urban Studies	M
Writing	M

BROWN UNIVERSITY

American Studies	M,D
Anthropology	M,D
Archaeology	D
Art History	D
Asian Studies	D
Classics	M,D
Cognitive Sciences	M,D
Comparative Literature	D
East European and Russian Studies	M,D
Economics	D
English	M,D
French	D
German	D
Hispanic Studies	D
History of Science and Technology	D
History	M,D
Italian	D
Latin American Studies	M,D
Linguistics	M,D
Music	D
Near and Middle Eastern Studies	D
Philosophy	D
Political Science	D

Psychology—General	M,D
Public Policy	M
Publishing	M,D
Religion	D
Russian	M,D
Slavic Languages	M,D
Sociology	M,D
Theater	M,D
Western European Studies	M,D
Writing	M,D

BRYAN COLLEGE

Pastoral Ministry and Counseling	M

BRYANT UNIVERSITY

Applied Economics	M,O
Communication—General	M,O
Corporate and Organizational Communication	M,O
International Economics	M
Mass Communication	M,O

BRYN ATHYN COLLEGE OF THE NEW CHURCH

Religion	M
Theology	M

BRYN MAWR COLLEGE

Archaeology	M,D
Art History	M,D
Classics	M,D

BUCKNELL UNIVERSITY

English	M
Psychology—General	M

BUFFALO STATE COLLEGE, STATE UNIVERSITY OF NEW YORK

Applied Economics	M
Criminal Justice and Criminology	M
Economics	M
English	M
Historic Preservation	M,O
History	M
Interdisciplinary Studies	M

BUTLER UNIVERSITY

Art/Fine Arts	M
Clinical Psychology	M,O
English	M
History	M
Music	M
Writing	M

BYZANTINE CATHOLIC SEMINARY OF SAINTS CYRIL AND METHODIUS

Theology	M

CABRINI UNIVERSITY

Communication—General	M,D
Criminal Justice and Criminology	M,D
English	M,D
History	M,D

CAIRN UNIVERSITY

Applied Behavior Analysis	M,O
Pastoral Ministry and Counseling	M
Religion	M
Theology	M

CALDWELL UNIVERSITY

Applied Behavior Analysis	M,D,O
Art Therapy	M,O
Counseling Psychology	M,O
School Psychology	M,O

CALIFORNIA BAPTIST UNIVERSITY

Architecture	M
Communication—General	M
Counseling Psychology	M
Disability Studies	M
English	M
Forensic Psychology	M
Music	M
Pastoral Ministry and Counseling	M
Public Administration	M
School Psychology	M

CALIFORNIA COAST UNIVERSITY

Criminal Justice and Criminology	M
Psychology—General	M

CALIFORNIA COLLEGE OF THE ARTS

Applied Arts and Design— General	M
Architecture	M
Art/Fine Arts	M
Computer Art and Design	M
Film, Television, and Video Production	M
Film, Television, and Video Theory and Criticism	M
Graphic Design	M
Illustration	M
Industrial Design	M
Museum Studies	M
Writing	M

CALIFORNIA INSTITUTE OF INTEGRAL STUDIES

Art Therapy	M,D
Asian Studies	M,D,O
Clinical Psychology	M,D
Counseling Psychology	M,D
Cultural Anthropology	M,D,O
Health Psychology	M,D
Humanities	M,D,O
Interdisciplinary Studies	M,D,O
Philosophy	M,D,O
Psychology—General	M,D,O
Religion	M,D,O
Social Psychology	M,D
Theology	M,D,O
Therapies—Dance, Drama, and Music	M,D

Transpersonal and Humanistic Psychology	M,D,O
Women's Studies	M,D,O
Writing	M,D,O

CALIFORNIA INSTITUTE OF TECHNOLOGY

Social Sciences	M,D

CALIFORNIA INSTITUTE OF THE ARTS

Applied Arts and Design— General	M,O
Art/Fine Arts	M,O
Dance	M,O
Film, Television, and Video Production	M,O
Graphic Design	M,O
Music	M,O
Photography	M,O
Theater	M,O
Writing	M,O

CALIFORNIA LUTHERAN UNIVERSITY

Clinical Psychology	M,D
Marriage and Family Therapy	M,D
Psychology—General	M,D
Public Policy	M
Theology	M,D,O

CALIFORNIA POLYTECHNIC STATE UNIVERSITY, SAN LUIS OBISPO

Architecture	M
Economics	M
English	M
History	M
Political Science	M
Psychology—General	M
Urban and Regional Planning	M*

CALIFORNIA STATE POLYTECHNIC UNIVERSITY, POMONA

Architecture	M
Economics	M
English	M
History	M
Interior Design	M
Landscape Architecture	M
Psychology—General	M
Public Administration	M
Urban and Regional Planning	M

CALIFORNIA STATE UNIVERSITY, BAKERSFIELD

Anthropology	M
Counseling Psychology	M
English	M
History	M
Interdisciplinary Studies	M
Public Administration	M
Sociology	M
Spanish	M

CALIFORNIA STATE UNIVERSITY, CHICO

Anthropology	M
Applied Psychology	M
Art History	M
Art/Fine Arts	M
Communication—General	M
English	M
History	M
Marriage and Family Therapy	M
Museum Studies	M
Political Science	M
Psychology—General	M
Public Administration	M
School Psychology	M
Social Sciences	M

CALIFORNIA STATE UNIVERSITY, DOMINGUEZ HILLS

Applied Social Research	M
Clinical Psychology	M
Conflict Resolution and Mediation/Peace Studies	M
English	M,O
Health Psychology	M
Humanities	M
Marriage and Family Therapy	M
Psychology—General	M
Public Administration	M
Rhetoric	M,O
School Psychology	M
Sociology	M

CALIFORNIA STATE UNIVERSITY, EAST BAY

Anthropology	M
Child and Family Studies	M
Communication—General	M
Economics	M
English	M
Geography	M
History	M
Interdisciplinary Studies	M
Internet and Interactive Multimedia	M
Marriage and Family Therapy	M
Music	M
Public Administration	M
Public History	M
Public Policy	M
Social Psychology	M

CALIFORNIA STATE UNIVERSITY, FRESNO

Applied Arts and Design— General	M
Applied Behavior Analysis	M,O
Art/Fine Arts	M
Communication—General	M
Counseling Psychology	M
Criminal Justice and Criminology	M
English	M

Experimental Psychology	M,O
History	M
Human Development	M,D
Linguistics	M
Marriage and Family Therapy	M
Music	M
Psychology—General	M,O
Public Administration	M
Rehabilitation Counseling	M
Rhetoric	M
School Psychology	M,O
Spanish	M
Sport Psychology	M
Writing	M

CALIFORNIA STATE UNIVERSITY, FULLERTON

American Studies	M
Anthropology	M
Applied Arts and Design— General	M
Art History	M
Art/Fine Arts	M
Clinical Psychology	M
Communication—General	M
Economics	M
English	M
Film, Television, and Video Production	M
Geography	M
Gerontology	M
Graphic Design	M
History	M
Illustration	M
Linguistics	M
Mass Communication	M
Museum Studies	M
Music	M
Photography	M
Political Science	M
Psychology—General	M
Public Administration	M
Social Psychology	M
Sociology	M
Spanish	M
Speech and Interpersonal Communication	M
Theater	M

CALIFORNIA STATE UNIVERSITY, LONG BEACH

African Studies	M
Anthropology	M
Art/Fine Arts	M
Asian Studies	M
Asian-American Studies	M
Communication—General	M
Criminal Justice and Criminology	M
Dance	M
Economics	M
Emergency Management	M
English	M
French	M
Geography	M
German	M
Gerontology	M
History	M
Industrial and Organizational Psychology	M
Linguistics	M,O
Marriage and Family Therapy	M,D
Music	M
Near and Middle Eastern Studies	M
Philosophy	M
Political Science	M
Psychology—General	M
Public Administration	M,O
Public Policy	M,O
Religion	M
Spanish	M
Sport Psychology	M
Theater	M
Writing	M

CALIFORNIA STATE UNIVERSITY, LOS ANGELES

Anthropology	M
Applied Arts and Design— General	M
Art History	M
Art Therapy	M
Art/Fine Arts	M
Child and Family Studies	M
Child Development	M
Communication—General	M
Criminal Justice and Criminology	M
Economics	M
English	M,O
French	M
Geography	M
Graphic Design	M
Hispanic Studies	M
History	M
Latin American Studies	M
Music	M
Philosophy	M,O
Photography	M
Political Science	M
Psychology—General	M
Public Administration	M
Rehabilitation Counseling	M,D
School Psychology	M,D
Sociology	M
Spanish	M
Textile Design	M
Theater	M

CALIFORNIA STATE UNIVERSITY MARITIME ACADEMY

Emergency Management	M

CALIFORNIA STATE UNIVERSITY, NORTHRIDGE

Anthropology	M
Archaeology	M
Art History	M
Art/Fine Arts	M
Clinical Psychology	M
Communication—General	M
Comparative Literature	M
English	M
Experimental Psychology	M
Family and Consumer Sciences-General	M
Film, Television, and Video Production	M
Geography	M
Hispanic Studies	M
History	M
Journalism	M
Linguistics	M
Marriage and Family Therapy	M
Mass Communication	M
Music	M
Political Science	M
Psychology—General	M
Public Administration	M,O
Rhetoric	M
School Psychology	M
Sociology	M
Spanish	M
Speech and Interpersonal Communication	M
Theater	M
Writing	M

CALIFORNIA STATE UNIVERSITY, SACRAMENTO

Anthropology	M
Applied Behavior Analysis	M
Art/Fine Arts	M
Child Development	M,D,O
Communication—General	M
Criminal Justice and Criminology	M
English	M
Industrial and Organizational Psychology	M
Music	M
Political Science	M
Psychology—General	M
Public Administration	M
Public History	M,D
Public Policy	M
School Psychology	M,D,O
Sociology	M
Writing	M

CALIFORNIA STATE UNIVERSITY, SAN BERNARDINO

Archaeology	M
Art/Fine Arts	M
Child Development	M
Clinical Psychology	M
Communication—General	M
Corporate and Organizational Communication	M
Counseling Psychology	M
Criminal Justice and Criminology	M
English	M
Industrial and Organizational Psychology	M
Interdisciplinary Studies	M
National Security	M
Psychology—General	M
Public Administration	M
Rehabilitation Counseling	M
Social Sciences	M
Spanish	M
Writing	M

CALIFORNIA STATE UNIVERSITY, SAN MARCOS

Child and Family Studies	M
English	M
Hispanic and Latin American Languages	M
Hispanic Studies	M
History	M
Psychology—General	M
Sociology	M
Spanish	M
Writing	M

CALIFORNIA STATE UNIVERSITY, STANISLAUS

Applied Behavior Analysis	M
Counseling Psychology	M
Criminal Justice and Criminology	M
English	M,O
Genetic Counseling	M
History	M
Interdisciplinary Studies	M
Psychology—General	M
Public Administration	M
Rhetoric	M,O
Sustainable Development	M
Writing	M,O

CALIFORNIA UNIVERSITY OF MANAGEMENT AND SCIENCES

Economics	M,D

CALIFORNIA UNIVERSITY OF PENNSYLVANIA

Clinical Psychology	M
Conflict Resolution and Mediation/Peace Studies	M
Counseling Psychology	M
Criminal Justice and Criminology	M
School Psychology	M
Sport Psychology	M

CALUMET COLLEGE OF SAINT JOSEPH

Criminal Justice and Criminology	M

CALVARY UNIVERSITY

Pastoral Ministry and Counseling	M
Theology	M

CALVIN THEOLOGICAL SEMINARY

Missions and Missiology	M,D
Pastoral Ministry and Counseling	M,D
Religion	M,D
Theology	M,D

CAMBRIDGE COLLEGE

Addictions/Substance Abuse Counseling	M,O
Conflict Resolution and Mediation/Peace Studies	M
Counseling Psychology	M,O
Forensic Psychology	M,O
Interdisciplinary Studies	M,D,O
Marriage and Family Therapy	M,O
Psychology—General	M,O
School Psychology	M,D,O

CAMERON UNIVERSITY

Psychology—General	M

CAMPBELLSVILLE UNIVERSITY

Economics	M,D
Marriage and Family Therapy	M
Music	M
School Psychology	M
Social Sciences	M
Theology	M

CAMPBELL UNIVERSITY

Interdisciplinary Studies	M
Pastoral Ministry and Counseling	M,D
Theology	M,D

CANADIAN SOUTHERN BAPTIST SEMINARY

Pastoral Ministry and Counseling	M
Religion	M
Theology	M

CANISIUS COLLEGE

Anthropology	M
Corporate and Organizational Communication	M
School Psychology	M
Social Psychology	M

CAPELLA UNIVERSITY

Addictions/Substance Abuse Counseling	M,D
Applied Behavior Analysis	M
Child and Family Studies	M,D
Clinical Psychology	M,D
Counseling Psychology	M,D
Criminal Justice and Criminology	M,D
Developmental Psychology	M
Emergency Management	M,D
Gerontology	M
Homeland Security	M
Industrial and Organizational Psychology	M,D
Marriage and Family Therapy	M
Psychology—General	M,D
Public Administration	M,D
School Psychology	M,D
Sport Psychology	M

CAPITAL UNIVERSITY

Music	M

CARDINAL STRITCH UNIVERSITY

Clinical Psychology	M
Criminal Justice and Criminology	M
Liberal Studies	M
Pastoral Ministry and Counseling	M
Psychology—General	M
Religion	M

CAREY THEOLOGICAL COLLEGE

Theology	M,D

CARIBBEAN UNIVERSITY

Art History	M,D
Criminal Justice and Criminology	M,D
Museum Studies	M,D

CARLETON UNIVERSITY

Anthropology	M
Architecture	M
Art History	M
Canadian Studies	M,D
Cognitive Sciences	D
Communication—General	M,D
Comparative Literature	D
Conflict Resolution and Mediation/Peace Studies	M,O
East European and Russian Studies	M,O
Economics	M,D
English	M,D
Film, Television, and Video Production	M
French	M
Geography	M,D
History	M,D
Industrial Design	M
International Affairs	M,D
Journalism	M,D
Linguistics	M
Music	M
Philosophy	M
Political Science	M,D
Psychology—General	M,D
Public Administration	M,D
Public Policy	M,D
Sociology	M,D
Western European Studies	M,O

CARLOS ALBIZU UNIVERSITY

Clinical Psychology	M,D
Industrial and Organizational Psychology	M,D
Psychology—General	M,D

CARLOS ALBIZU UNIVERSITY, MIAMI CAMPUS

Clinical Psychology	M,D
Counseling Psychology	M,D
Industrial and Organizational Psychology	M,D
Marriage and Family Therapy	M,D
Psychology—General	M,D

CARLOW UNIVERSITY

Art/Fine Arts	M
Counseling Psychology	M,D,O
Forensic Sciences	M
Psychology—General	M
Writing	M

CARNEGIE MELLON UNIVERSITY

African Studies	D
African-American Studies	D
Applied Arts and Design—General	M,D
Architecture	M,D
Art/Fine Arts	M
Arts Administration	M
Building Science	M,D
Cognitive Sciences	D
Communication—General	M,D
Comparative Literature	M,D
Computer Art and Design	M
Corporate and Organizational Communication	M
Criminal Justice and Criminology	M,D
Cultural Studies	D
Developmental Psychology	D
Economics	D
English	M,D
Film, Television, and Video Production	M
Gender Studies	D
History of Science and Technology	D
History	D
Industrial and Labor Relations	D
Linguistics	M,D
Media Studies	M
Music	M
Philosophy	M,D
Psychology—General	D
Public Administration	M
Public Policy	M,D
Publishing	M
Rhetoric	M,D
Social Psychology	D
Social Sciences	D
Sustainable Development	M,D
Technical Writing	M
Theater	M
Urban Design	M,D
Women's Studies	D
Writing	M

CAROLINA CHRISTIAN COLLEGE

Pastoral Ministry and Counseling	M

CARSON-NEWMAN UNIVERSITY

Theology	M

CASE WESTERN RESERVE UNIVERSITY

Anthropology	M,D
Art History	M,D
Clinical Psychology	D
Cognitive Sciences	M
Comparative Literature	M
Dance	M
English	M,D
Experimental Psychology	D
French	M
Genetic Counseling	M,D
History	M,D
Linguistics	M
Museum Studies	M
Music	M,D
Political Science	M,D
Psychology—General	M,D
Sociology	M,D
Theater	M

CASTLETON UNIVERSITY

Forensic Psychology	M
Psychology—General	M

CATHOLIC DISTANCE UNIVERSITY

Theology	M

CATHOLIC THEOLOGICAL UNION

Missions and Missiology	M,D,O
Pastoral Ministry and Counseling	M,D,O
Theology	M,D,O

THE CATHOLIC UNIVERSITY OF AMERICA

American Studies	M,D
Anthropology	M
Applied Psychology	M,O
Architecture	M,O
Classics	M,D,O
Clinical Psychology	M,D
Criminal Justice and Criminology	M
Economic Development	M
English	M,D,O
Experimental Psychology	M,D
Hispanic Studies	M,D
History	M,D
International Affairs	M,D
Medieval and Renaissance Studies	M,D,O
Music	M,D,O
Near and Middle Eastern Languages	M,D
Near and Middle Eastern Studies	M,D,O
Pastoral Ministry and Counseling	M,D,O
Philosophy	M,D,O
Political Science	M,D
Psychology—General	M,D
Public Policy	M
Religion	M,D,O
Rhetoric	M,D,O
Sociology	M
Spanish	M,D
Sustainable Development	M,O
Theater	M,O
Theology	M,D,O
Urban and Regional Planning	M,O
Western European Studies	M,D

CEDAR CREST COLLEGE

Art Therapy	M
Forensic Sciences	M
Writing	M

CEDARVILLE UNIVERSITY

Missions and Missiology	M,D
Pastoral Ministry and Counseling	M,D

CENTENARY UNIVERSITY

Counseling Psychology	M

CENTRAL BAPTIST THEOLOGICAL SEMINARY

Missions and Missiology	M,O
Theology	M,O

CENTRAL CONNECTICUT STATE UNIVERSITY

Communication—General	M,O
Criminal Justice and Criminology	M
English	M,O
French	M,O
Geography	M
German	M,O
Graphic Design	M
History	M,O
International Affairs	M
Italian	M,O
Marriage and Family Therapy	M,O
Psychology—General	M
Rehabilitation Counseling	M,O
School Psychology	M,O
Spanish	M,O

CENTRAL EUROPEAN UNIVERSITY

Anthropology	M,D
Cognitive Sciences	D
Economics	M,D
Gender Studies	M,D
History	M,D
International Affairs	M,D
Medieval and Renaissance Studies	M,D
Philosophy	M,D
Political Science	M,D
Public Administration	M,D
Public Policy	M,D
Sociology	M,D

CENTRAL MICHIGAN UNIVERSITY

American Indian/Native American Studies	M
American Studies	M,O
Applied Psychology	M,D
Child and Family Studies	M,O
Clinical Psychology	D
Clothing and Textiles	M,O
Communication—General	M
Counseling Psychology	M,D,O
Cultural Studies	M
Economics	M
English	M
Experimental Psychology	M,D
Family and Consumer Sciences-General	M,O
Film, Television, and Video Production	M
Film, Television, and Video Theory and Criticism	M
Gender Studies	M
Geographic Information Systems	M
Gerontology	M,O
Health Psychology	M,D
History	M,O
Human Development	M,O
Humanities	M
Industrial and Organizational Psychology	M,D
International Affairs	M,O
Media Studies	M
Music	M
Political Science	M,O
Psychology—General	M,D,O
Public Administration	M,O
School Psychology	D,O
Spanish	M,O
Western European Studies	M,O
Writing	M

CENTRAL WASHINGTON UNIVERSITY

Anthropology	M
Art/Fine Arts	M
Child and Family Studies	M
Counseling Psychology	M
English	M
Experimental Psychology	M
Family and Consumer Sciences-General	M
Geography	M
Graphic Design	M
History	M
Interdisciplinary Studies	M
Music	M
Photography	M
Psychology—General	M,O
School Psychology	O
Theater	M
Writing	M

CENTRAL YESHIVA TOMCHEI TMIMIM-LUBAVITCH

Jewish Studies	M
Theology	M

CENTRO DE ESTUDIOS AVANZADOS DE PUERTO RICO Y EL CARIBE

History	M,D
Latin American Studies	M,D

CHAMINADE UNIVERSITY OF HONOLULU

Child Development	M
Counseling Psychology	M
Criminal Justice and Criminology	M
Marriage and Family Therapy	M
Pastoral Ministry and Counseling	M
School Psychology	M

Theology M

CHAMPLAIN COLLEGE
Conflict Resolution and
  Mediation/Peace Studies M
Forensic Sciences M
Internet and Interactive
  Multimedia M
Media Studies M

CHAPMAN UNIVERSITY
Communication—General M
Cultural Studies M,D,O
Disability Studies M,D,O
English M
Film, Television, and Video
  Production M
Holocaust and Genocide Studies M
International Affairs M
Marriage and Family Therapy M
School Psychology M,D,O
Writing M

CHARLESTON SOUTHERN UNIVERSITY
Criminal Justice and Criminology M

CHARLOTTE CHRISTIAN COLLEGE AND THEOLOGICAL SEMINARY
Cultural Studies M,D
Pastoral Ministry and Counseling M,D
Religion M,D
Theology M,D

CHATHAM UNIVERSITY
Communication—General M
Computer Art and Design M
Counseling Psychology M,D
Developmental Psychology M,D
Film, Television, and Video
  Production M
Health Communication M
Health Psychology M,D
Industrial and Organizational
  Psychology M,D
Interior Design M
Marriage and Family Therapy M,D
Sport Psychology M,D
Women's Studies M
Writing M

CHESTNUT HILL COLLEGE
Clinical Psychology M,D,O
Counseling Psychology M,O
Marriage and Family Therapy M,D,O
Psychology—General M,D,O

CHEYNEY UNIVERSITY OF PENNSYLVANIA
Public Administration M

THE CHICAGO SCHOOL OF PROFESSIONAL PSYCHOLOGY
Applied Behavior Analysis M,D
Clinical Psychology M,D
Forensic Psychology M,D
Industrial and Organizational
  Psychology M,D
Psychology—General M,D
School Psychology D,O

THE CHICAGO SCHOOL OF PROFESSIONAL PSYCHOLOGY AT DOWNTOWN LOS ANGELES
Applied Behavior Analysis M,D
Clinical Psychology M,D
Forensic Psychology D
Industrial and Organizational
  Psychology M
Marriage and Family Therapy M,D

THE CHICAGO SCHOOL OF PROFESSIONAL PSYCHOLOGY AT IRVINE
Clinical Psychology D
Forensic Psychology D
Marriage and Family Therapy M,D
Psychology—General D

THE CHICAGO SCHOOL OF PROFESSIONAL PSYCHOLOGY AT WASHINGTON DC
School Psychology O

THE CHICAGO SCHOOL OF PROFESSIONAL PSYCHOLOGY: ONLINE
Applied Psychology M,O
Clinical Psychology M
Forensic Psychology M,O
Industrial and Organizational
  Psychology M,D,O
Psychology—General M,D

CHICAGO STATE UNIVERSITY
Clinical Psychology M
Criminal Justice and Criminology M
English M
Geographic Information Systems M
History M
Writing M

CHICAGO THEOLOGICAL SEMINARY
Ethics M,D
Pastoral Ministry and Counseling M,D
Religion M,D
Theology M,D

CHRISTENDOM COLLEGE
Theology M

CHRISTIAN BROTHERS UNIVERSITY
Religion M

CHRISTIAN THEOLOGICAL SEMINARY
Marriage and Family Therapy M,D
Pastoral Ministry and Counseling M,D

Religion M,D
Theology M,D

CHRISTIE'S EDUCATION
Art History M
Art/Fine Arts O
Arts Administration M,O
Museum Studies M

CHRIST THE KING SEMINARY
Pastoral Ministry and Counseling M
Theology M

CHURCH DIVINITY SCHOOL OF THE PACIFIC
Theology M,D,O

CINCINNATI CHRISTIAN UNIVERSITY
Pastoral Ministry and Counseling M
Religion M
Theology M

THE CITADEL, THE MILITARY COLLEGE OF SOUTH CAROLINA
English M
Hispanic Studies O
History M,O
Homeland Security M,O
Interdisciplinary Studies M,O
Military and Defense Studies M,O
National Security M,O
Political Science M
Psychology—General M,O
School Psychology M,O
Social Sciences M

CITY COLLEGE OF THE CITY UNIVERSITY OF NEW YORK
Architecture M
Art History M
Art/Fine Arts M
Classics M
Clinical Psychology M,D
Computer Art and Design M
Corporate and Organizational
  Communication M
Economics M
English M
Graphic Design M
History M
International Affairs M
Landscape Architecture M
Media Studies M
Museum Studies M
Psychology—General M
Public Administration M,D
Sociology M
Spanish M
Sustainable Development M
Urban Design M
Writing M

CITY UNIVERSITY OF SEATTLE
Counseling Psychology M

CITY VISION UNIVERSITY
Pastoral Ministry and Counseling M

CLAREMONT GRADUATE UNIVERSITY
African Studies M,D,O
American Studies M,D,O
Art/Fine Arts M
Arts Administration M
Cognitive Sciences M,D,O
Comparative Literature M,D
Computer Art and Design M
Cultural Studies M,D,O
Developmental Psychology M,D,O
Economic Development M,D,O
Economics M,D,O
English M,D
Ethics M,D
Film, Television, and Video
  Theory and Criticism M
Geographic Information Systems M,D,O
Health Psychology M,D,O
History M,D,O
Human Development M,D,O
Humanities M,D,O
Industrial and Organizational
  Psychology M,D,O
International Affairs M,D
International Economics M,D,O
Media Studies M,D,O
Museum Studies M,D
Music M,D
Philosophy M,D
Photography M
Political Science M,D
Psychology—General M,D,O
Public Policy M,D,O
Religion M,D
Social Psychology M,D,O
Theology M,D
Western European Studies M,D,O
Women's Studies M,D
Writing M,D

CLAREMONT LINCOLN UNIVERSITY
Ethics M
Pastoral Ministry and Counseling M
Religion M

CLAREMONT SCHOOL OF THEOLOGY
Ethics M,D
Pastoral Ministry and Counseling M,D
Religion M,D
Theology M,D

CLARION UNIVERSITY OF PENNSYLVANIA
Communication—General M
Journalism M
Mass Communication M
Media Studies M

CLARK ATLANTA UNIVERSITY
African-American Studies M,D
Criminal Justice and Criminology M
Economics M
English M,D
Political Science M,D
Public Administration M
Sociology M

CLARKSON UNIVERSITY
Interdisciplinary Studies M,D
Sustainable Development M,D

CLARKS SUMMIT UNIVERSITY
Communication—General M
English M
Missions and Missiology M
Pastoral Ministry and Counseling M,D
Religion M,D
Theology M,D

CLARK UNIVERSITY
American Studies D
Clinical Psychology D
Communication—General M
Developmental Psychology D
Economics M
English M
Geographic Information Systems M
Geography D
History D
Holocaust and Genocide Studies D
International Development M,O
Public Administration M,O
Social Psychology D
Sustainable Development M
Urban and Regional Planning M

CLAYTON STATE UNIVERSITY
Applied Psychology M
Clinical Psychology M
Criminal Justice and Criminology M
Developmental Psychology M
History M
Liberal Studies M
Psychology—General M

CLEMSON UNIVERSITY
Anthropology M
Applied Economics M,D
Applied Psychology M,D
Architecture M,D,O
Art/Fine Arts M
Clinical Psychology M,D,O
Communication—General M
Criminal Justice and Criminology M
Economics M,D
Family and Consumer
  Sciences-General D,O
Historic Preservation M,O
History M
Industrial and Organizational
  Psychology M,D
Landscape Architecture M
Public Administration M,D,O
Public Policy D,O
Rhetoric M,D
Sociology M
Writing M,D

CLEVELAND INSTITUTE OF MUSIC
Music M,D,O

CLEVELAND STATE UNIVERSITY
Art History M
Communication—General M,D,O
Counseling Psychology M,D,O
Economic Development M,O
Economics M,O
English M
Geographic Information Systems M,O
Historic Preservation M
History M
Industrial and Labor Relations M
International Affairs M
International Economics M
Museum Studies M
Music M
Philosophy M,O
Psychology—General M,D,O
Public Administration M,D,O
Public Affairs D
Spanish M
Sustainable Development M
Urban and Regional Planning M,O
Urban Studies M,D,O
Writing M

COASTAL CAROLINA UNIVERSITY
Liberal Studies M
Writing M

COKER COLLEGE
Criminal Justice and Criminology M

THE COLBURN SCHOOL CONSERVATORY OF MUSIC
Music M,O

COLGATE ROCHESTER CROZER DIVINITY SCHOOL
Conflict Resolution and
  Mediation/Peace Studies M,D,O
Theology M,D,O

THE COLLEGE AT BROCKPORT, STATE UNIVERSITY OF NEW YORK
American Studies M
Art/Fine Arts M
Arts Administration M,O
Communication—General M
Counseling Psychology M,O
Dance M
English M,O
Gerontology M,O

History of Medicine M,O
History M
Liberal Studies M
Psychology—General M
Public Administration M,O
Public History M
Writing M,O

COLLÈGE DOMINICAIN DE PHILOSOPHIE ET DE THÉOLOGIE
Philosophy M
Theology M,D,O

COLLEGE FOR CREATIVE STUDIES
Applied Arts and Design—
  General M
Art/Fine Arts M

COLLEGE OF CHARLESTON
Arts Administration O
English M
Historic Preservation M
History M
Public Administration M
Urban and Regional Planning O
Writing M

COLLEGE OF EMMANUEL AND ST. CHAD
Theology M,D,O

THE COLLEGE OF NEW JERSEY
Addictions/Substance Abuse
  Counseling M,O
English O
Gender Studies O
Health Communication M
Marriage and Family Therapy O

THE COLLEGE OF NEW ROCHELLE
Art Therapy M
Communication—General M,O
Counseling Psychology M
Marriage and Family Therapy M
Public Administration M
School Psychology M
Thanatology M,O

COLLEGE OF SAINT ELIZABETH
Applied Behavior Analysis M,O
Counseling Psychology M,D
Criminal Justice and Criminology M,O
Holocaust and Genocide Studies M,O
Internet and Interactive
  Multimedia M
Pastoral Ministry and Counseling M,O
Psychology—General M,D
Public Administration M
School Psychology M,D
Theology M,O

COLLEGE OF ST. JOSEPH
Addictions/Substance Abuse
  Counseling M
Clinical Psychology M
Counseling Psychology M
Psychology—General M
School Psychology M
Social Psychology M

THE COLLEGE OF SAINT ROSE
Counseling Psychology M,O
School Psychology M,O

COLLEGE OF STATEN ISLAND OF THE CITY UNIVERSITY OF NEW YORK
African Studies M
American Studies M
Asian Studies M
Clinical Psychology M
Counseling Psychology M,O
English M
Film, Television, and Video
  Theory and Criticism M
History M
Latin American Studies M
Liberal Studies M
Media Studies M
Near and Middle Eastern Studies M
Public History O
Western European Studies M

THE COLLEGE OF WILLIAM AND MARY
Addictions/Substance Abuse
  Counseling M,D
American Studies M,D
Anthropology M,D
English M
Geographic Information Systems M,D
History M,D
International Development M
Marriage and Family Therapy M,D
Psychology—General M
Public Policy M
School Psychology M,O

COLORADO CHRISTIAN UNIVERSITY
Counseling Psychology M

THE COLORADO COLLEGE
American Studies M
Humanities M
Liberal Studies M

COLORADO SCHOOL OF MINES
Humanities O
Mineral Economics M,D
Social Sciences M

COLORADO STATE UNIVERSITY
Agricultural Economics and
  Agribusiness M,D
Anthropology M,D
Art History M
Art/Fine Arts M
Child and Family Studies M,D

---

*M—masters degree; D—doctorate; O—other advanced degree; *—Close-Up and/or Display*

Consumer Economics — M
Economics — M,D
English — M
Ethnic Studies — M
French — M
History — M
Human Development — M,D
Interdisciplinary Studies — M,D
Landscape Architecture — M,D
Liberal Studies — M
Marriage and Family Therapy — M,D
Media Studies — M,D
Music — M
Philosophy — M
Political Science — M,D
Psychology—General — M,D
Rhetoric — M,D
Sociology — M,D
Speech and Interpersonal Communication — M,D
Sustainable Development — M,O
Writing — M

COLORADO STATE UNIVERSITY–GLOBAL CAMPUS
Criminal Justice and Criminology — M

COLORADO TECHNICAL UNIVERSITY AURORA
Conflict Resolution and Mediation/Peace Studies — M
Criminal Justice and Criminology — M

COLORADO TECHNICAL UNIVERSITY COLORADO SPRINGS
Conflict Resolution and Mediation/Peace Studies — M,D
Criminal Justice and Criminology — M

COLUMBIA COLLEGE (MO)
Criminal Justice and Criminology — M

COLUMBIA COLLEGE (SC)
Criminal Justice and Criminology — M

COLUMBIA COLLEGE CHICAGO
Art History — M
Art/Fine Arts — M
Communication—General — M
English — M
Film, Television, and Video Production — M
Music — M
Photography — M
Writing — M

COLUMBIA INTERNATIONAL UNIVERSITY
Cultural Studies — M,D,O
Missions and Missiology — M,D,O
Pastoral Ministry and Counseling — M,D,O
Theology — M,D,O

COLUMBIA SOUTHERN UNIVERSITY
Criminal Justice and Criminology — M
Emergency Management — M

COLUMBIA THEOLOGICAL SEMINARY
Theology — M,D

COLUMBIA UNIVERSITY
African Studies — M,D
African-American Studies — M,D
American Studies — M,D
Anthropology — M,D
Archaeology — M,D
Architecture — M,D
Art History — M,D
Art/Fine Arts — M,D*
Asian Studies — M,D,O
Classics — M,D
Communication—General — M,D
Comparative Literature — M,D
Conflict Resolution and Mediation/Peace Studies — M
Corporate and Organizational Communication — M
East European and Russian Studies — M,D
Economics — M,D
English — M,D
Environmental Design — M
Ethics — M
Film, Television, and Video Production — M
Film, Television, and Video Theory and Criticism — M
French — M,D
German — M,D
Hispanic Studies — M,D
Historic Preservation — M,D,O
History — M,D
International Affairs — M,D
Italian — M,D
Japanese — M,D
Jewish Studies — M,D
Journalism — M,D
Landscape Architecture — M
Latin American Studies — M,D
Media Studies — M
Medieval and Renaissance Studies — M,D
Museum Studies — M,D
Music — M,D
Near and Middle Eastern Studies — M,D
Philosophy — M,D
Political Science — M,D
Psychology—General — M,D
Public Administration — M
Public Policy — M
Religion — M,D
Romance Languages — M,D
Russian — M,D
Slavic Languages — M,D
Social Sciences — M,D
Sociology — M,D
Spanish — M,D
Sustainable Development — M,D
Theater — M,D

Translation and Interpretation — M,D
Urban and Regional Planning — M,D
Western European Studies — M,D
Writing — M

COLUMBUS COLLEGE OF ART & DESIGN
Art/Fine Arts — M

COLUMBUS STATE UNIVERSITY
Clinical Psychology — M,D,O
Criminal Justice and Criminology — M
History — M,O
Homeland Security — M
Music — M,O
Political Science — M
Public Administration — M
Theater — M
Urban Studies — M

CONCORDIA LUTHERAN SEMINARY
Theology — M,O

CONCORDIA SEMINARY
Theology — M,D,O

CONCORDIA THEOLOGICAL SEMINARY
Theology — M,D

CONCORDIA UNIVERSITY (CANADA)
Anthropology — M,D
Applied Arts and Design—General — M,O
Art History — M,D
Art Therapy — M
Art/Fine Arts — M
Child and Family Studies — M
Clinical Psychology — D,O
Communication—General — M,D,O
Computer Art and Design — M,O
Cultural Anthropology — M,D
Economic Development — O
Economics — M,D,O
English — M,D
Film, Television, and Video Production — M,D
French — M,O
Geography — M,D,O
History — M,D
Humanities — D
Interdisciplinary Studies — M,D
Internet and Interactive Multimedia — M,D,O
Jewish Studies — M
Journalism — M,O
Linguistics — M,O
Media Studies — M,D,O
Music — O
Philosophy — M
Political Science — M,D
Psychology—General — M
Public Administration — M,D
Public Affairs — O
Public Policy — M,D
Religion — M,D
Sociology — M,D
Textile Design — M
Theology — M
Therapies—Dance, Drama, and Music — M
Translation and Interpretation — M,O
Urban and Regional Planning — O
Urban Studies — M,D,O
Writing — M

CONCORDIA UNIVERSITY CHICAGO
Counseling Psychology — M
Gerontology — M
Liberal Studies — M
Music — M
Psychology—General — M
Religion — M

CONCORDIA UNIVERSITY IRVINE
Applied Social Research — M
Cultural Studies — M
International Affairs — M*
Religion — M
Theology — M

CONCORDIA UNIVERSITY, NEBRASKA
Pastoral Ministry and Counseling — M

CONCORDIA UNIVERSITY OF EDMONTON
Religion — M
Theology — M

CONCORDIA UNIVERSITY, ST. PAUL
Corporate and Organizational Communication — M

CONCORDIA UNIVERSITY WISCONSIN
Child and Family Studies — M
Corporate and Organizational Communication — M
Music — M
Public Administration — M

CONSERVATORIO DE MUSICA DE PUERTO RICO
Music — O

CONVERSE COLLEGE
English — M
History — M
Liberal Studies — M
Marriage and Family Therapy — M
Music — M
Political Science — M
Writing — M

THE CONWAY SCHOOL
Landscape Architecture — M

COOPER UNION FOR THE ADVANCEMENT OF SCIENCE AND ART
Architecture — M

COPENHAGEN BUSINESS SCHOOL
Economics — M,D
Public Administration — M,D

COPPIN STATE UNIVERSITY
Addictions/Substance Abuse Counseling — M
Criminal Justice and Criminology — M
Rehabilitation Counseling — M

CORBAN UNIVERSITY
Pastoral Ministry and Counseling — M,D,O
Theology — M,D,O

CORNELL UNIVERSITY
African Studies — M,D
African-American Studies — M,D
Agricultural Economics and Agribusiness — M,D
American Studies — M,D
Anthropology — D
Applied Economics — M,D
Archaeology — M,D
Architectural History — M,D
Architecture — M,D
Art History — D
Art/Fine Arts — M
Asian Languages — M,D
Asian Studies — M,D
Child and Family Studies — M,D
Classics — D
Clothing and Textiles — M,D
Cognitive Sciences — D
Communication—General — M,D
Comparative Literature — D
Computer Art and Design — M,D
Conflict Resolution and Mediation/Peace Studies — M,D
Consumer Economics — M,D
Corporate and Organizational Communication — M,D
Cultural Anthropology — D
Cultural Studies — M,D
Demography and Population Studies — M,D
Developmental Psychology — M,D
East European and Russian Studies — M,D
Economic Development — M,D
Economics — M,D
English — M,D
Environmental Design — M
Ethnic Studies — M,D
Experimental Psychology — D
French — D
Gender Studies — M,D
German — M,D
Health Communication — M,D
Hispanic and Latin American Languages — D
Historic Preservation — M,D
History of Science and Technology — M,D
History — M,D
Human Development — M,D
Industrial and Labor Relations — M,D
Interior Design — M
International Affairs — D
Italian — D
Jewish Studies — M,D
Landscape Architecture — M
Latin American Studies — M,D
Linguistics — M,D
Media Studies — M,D
Medieval and Renaissance Studies — M,D
Music — M,D
Near and Middle Eastern Studies — M,D
Philosophy — D
Photography — M,D
Political Science — D
Psychology—General — D
Public Affairs — M
Public Policy — M,D
Religion — M,D
Romance Languages — M,D
Rural Sociology — M,D
Scandinavian Languages — M,D
Slavic Languages — M,D
Social Psychology — M,D
Sociology — M,D
Spanish — D
Sustainable Development — M,D
Textile Design — M,D
Theater — D
Urban and Regional Planning — M,D
Urban Design — M,D
Western European Studies — M,D
Women's Studies — M,D
Writing — M,D

COVENANT THEOLOGICAL SEMINARY
Pastoral Ministry and Counseling — M,D,O
Theology — M,D,O

CRANBROOK ACADEMY OF ART
Architecture — M
Art/Fine Arts — M
Photography — M
Textile Design — M

CREIGHTON UNIVERSITY
Anthropology — M
Conflict Resolution and Mediation/Peace Studies — M,D,O
English — M
School Psychology — M
Theology — M
Writing — M

CRISWELL COLLEGE
Jewish Studies — M
Pastoral Ministry and Counseling — M
Theology — M

CROWN COLLEGE
Theology — M

CUMBERLAND UNIVERSITY
Public Administration — M

CUNY GRADUATE SCHOOL OF JOURNALISM
Journalism — M

CURRY COLLEGE
Criminal Justice and Criminology — M

CURTIS INSTITUTE OF MUSIC
Music — M

DAEMEN COLLEGE
Arts Administration — M

DALHOUSIE UNIVERSITY
Anthropology — M,D
Architecture — M
Classics — M,D
Clinical Psychology — M,D
Economics — M,D
English — M,D
French — M,D
German — M
History — M,D
Interdisciplinary Studies — D
International Development — M
Music — M
Philosophy — M,D
Political Science — M,D
Psychology—General — M,D
Public Administration — M,O
Rural Planning and Studies — M
Sociology — M,D
Urban and Regional Planning — M

DALLAS BAPTIST UNIVERSITY
Asian Studies — M
Communication—General — M
Conflict Resolution and Mediation/Peace Studies — M
Corporate and Organizational Communication — M
Criminal Justice and Criminology — M
Interdisciplinary Studies — M
International Affairs — M
Liberal Studies — M
Missions and Missiology — M
Pastoral Ministry and Counseling — M,D
Religion — M
Theology — M
Western European Studies — M

DALLAS THEOLOGICAL SEMINARY
Child and Family Studies — M,D,O
Jewish Studies — M,D,O
Media Studies — M,D,O
Missions and Missiology — M,D,O
Pastoral Ministry and Counseling — M,D,O
Philosophy — M,D,O
Religion — M,D,O
Theology — M,D,O

DANIEL MORGAN GRADUATE SCHOOL OF NATIONAL SECURITY
National Security — M

DARTMOUTH COLLEGE
Cognitive Sciences — D
Comparative Literature — M
Liberal Studies — M*
Music — M
Psychology—General — D
Sustainable Development — D

DELAWARE STATE UNIVERSITY
Historic Preservation — M

DELAWARE VALLEY UNIVERSITY
Agricultural Economics and Agribusiness — M
Counseling Psychology — M
Developmental Psychology — M
Social Psychology — M

DELL'ARTE INTERNATIONAL SCHOOL OF PHYSICAL THEATRE
Theater — M

DELTA STATE UNIVERSITY
Criminal Justice and Criminology — M
Gender Studies — M
Liberal Studies — M
Philosophy — M
Religion — M
Urban and Regional Planning — M

DENVER SEMINARY
Marriage and Family Therapy — M,D,O
Pastoral Ministry and Counseling — M,D,O
Religion — M,D,O
Theology — M,D,O

DEPAUL UNIVERSITY
Applied Economics — M,D
Chinese — M
Clinical Psychology — M,D
Communication—General — M
Computer Art and Design — M,D
Corporate and Organizational Communication — M
Counseling Psychology — M,D
Economics — M,D
English — M
Ethnic Studies — M
Film, Television, and Video Production — M,D
Film, Television, and Video Theory and Criticism — M
French — M
Gender Studies — M
German — M
Health Communication — M
History — M
Interdisciplinary Studies — M
International Affairs — M
Internet and Interactive Multimedia — M,D

Italian M
Japanese M
Journalism M
Liberal Studies M
Media Studies M
Music M,O
Near and Middle Eastern Languages M
Psychology—General M,D
Public Administration M
Public Policy M
Publishing M
Rhetoric M
School Psychology M,D
Sociology M
Spanish M
Sustainable Development M
Theater M
Urban Design M
Women's Studies M
Writing M

DEREE - THE AMERICAN COLLEGE OF GREECE
Applied Psychology M
Communication—General M

DESALES UNIVERSITY
Criminal Justice and Criminology M,O
Forensic Sciences M,O
Gerontology M,D,O

DEVRY UNIVERSITY–FOLSOM CAMPUS
Public Administration M

DIGIPEN INSTITUTE OF TECHNOLOGY
Computer Art and Design M

DIVINE MERCY UNIVERSITY
Clinical Psychology M,D
Psychology—General M

DOANE UNIVERSITY
School Psychology M,D,O

DOMINICAN HOUSE OF STUDIES, PONTIFICAL FACULTY OF THE IMMACULATE CONCEPTION
Theology M,D,O

DOMINICAN SCHOOL OF PHILOSOPHY AND THEOLOGY
Philosophy M,O
Theology M,O

DOMINICAN UNIVERSITY OF CALIFORNIA
Art History M
Counseling Psychology M
Gender Studies M
History M
Humanities M
Liberal Studies M
Marriage and Family Therapy M
Music M
Philosophy M
Political Science M
Religion M
Writing M

DRAKE UNIVERSITY
Applied Behavior Analysis M,D,O
Communication—General M
Public Administration M
Public Affairs M

DREW UNIVERSITY
American Studies M,D,O
Art/Fine Arts M,D,O
Conflict Resolution and Mediation/Peace Studies M,D,O
Cultural Studies M,D,O
English M,D,O
French M,D,O
History M,D,O
Italian M,D,O
Liberal Studies M,D,O
Public History M,D,O
Religion M,D,O
Theology M,D,O
Western European Studies M,D,O
Writing M,D,O

DREXEL UNIVERSITY
Applied Arts and Design—General M,D
Applied Behavior Analysis M,D
Art Therapy M,O
Arts Administration M
Clinical Psychology D
Clothing and Textiles M
Communication—General M
Computer Art and Design M,D
Corporate and Organizational Communication M
Economics M,D,O
Emergency Management M
Film, Television, and Video Production M
Forensic Psychology D
Health Psychology D
History of Science and Technology M
Homeland Security M
Interior Design M
Marriage and Family Therapy M,D
Mass Communication M
Media Studies M
Psychology—General M,D
Technical Communication M
Technical Writing M
Textile Design M
Therapies—Dance, Drama, and Music M,O
Urban Design M

DRURY UNIVERSITY
Communication—General M

DUKE UNIVERSITY
Art History M,D
Art/Fine Arts M,D
Asian Studies M,O
Biological Anthropology D
Classics D
Clinical Psychology D
Cognitive Sciences D
Comparative Literature D
Cultural Anthropology D
Developmental Psychology D
Economics M,D
English D
Ethics M,O
Experimental Psychology D
French D
German D
Gerontology M,D,O
Health Psychology D
History M,D
Human Development D
Humanities M
International Development M
Italian D
Latin American Studies M,D
Liberal Studies M
Media Studies M
Music D
Philosophy D
Political Science M,D
Psychology—General D
Public Policy M,D
Religion M,D
Slavic Languages M,O
Sociology M,D
Spanish D
Theology M,D

DUQUESNE UNIVERSITY
Classics M
Clinical Psychology M,D,O
Communication—General M,D
Counseling Psychology M,D,O
English M,D
Forensic Sciences M
History M
Marriage and Family Therapy M,D,O
Music M,D
Philosophy M,D
Psychology—General D
Public History M
Rhetoric M,D
School Psychology M,D
Theology M,D

EARLHAM SCHOOL OF RELIGION
Pastoral Ministry and Counseling M
Religion M
Theology M

EAST CAROLINA UNIVERSITY
Addictions/Substance Abuse Counseling M,D,O
American Studies M
Anthropology M
Applied Economics M
Art/Fine Arts M
Child and Family Studies M,D
Child Development M,D
Clinical Psychology M,D,O
Comparative Literature M,D,O
Corporate and Organizational Communication M,D,O
Criminal Justice and Criminology M,O
Economic Development M,O
English M,D,O
Geographic Information Systems M,D,O
Geography M,O
Gerontology M,O
Graphic Design M
Health Communication M,O
Health Psychology M,D,O
History M
Illustration M
Industrial and Organizational Psychology M,D,O
International Affairs M,O
Linguistics M,D,O
Marriage and Family Therapy M,D
Military and Defense Studies M,O
Music M
Photography M
Political Science M,O
Public Administration M,O
Public History M
Rehabilitation Counseling M,D,O
Rhetoric M,D,O
Rural Planning and Studies M,O
Social Sciences M,D,O
Sociology M
Technical Communication M,D,O
Textile Design M
Therapies—Dance, Drama, and Music M,O
Urban and Regional Planning M,O
Western European Studies M
Writing M,D,O

EAST CENTRAL UNIVERSITY
Clinical Psychology M
Criminal Justice and Criminology M
Psychology—General M
Rehabilitation Counseling M

EASTERN ILLINOIS UNIVERSITY
Art/Fine Arts M
Clinical Psychology M,O
Communication—General M
Economics M
English M
Geographic Information Systems M
Gerontology M
History M
Human Development M
Music M
Political Science M
Psychology—General M,O
School Psychology M,O
Sustainable Development M

EASTERN KENTUCKY UNIVERSITY
Clinical Psychology M,O
Criminal Justice and Criminology M
English M
History M
Industrial and Organizational Psychology M,O
Music M
Political Science M
Psychology—General M,O
Public Administration M
School Psychology M,O
Urban and Regional Planning M
Writing M

EASTERN MENNONITE UNIVERSITY
Conflict Resolution and Mediation/Peace Studies M,O
Pastoral Ministry and Counseling M,O
Religion M,O
Theology M,O

EASTERN MICHIGAN UNIVERSITY
African-American Studies O
Art/Fine Arts M
Arts Administration M
Clinical Psychology M,D
Clothing and Textiles M
Communication—General M
Corporate and Organizational Communication M,O
Criminal Justice and Criminology M
Cultural Studies O
Dance M
Economics M,O
English M
Gender Studies M,O
Geographic Information Systems M,O
Gerontology O
Historic Preservation M,O
History M
Interior Design M
Linguistics M
Museum Studies M,O
Music M
Philosophy M
Psychology—General M,D
Public Administration M,O
Public Policy M,O
Social Sciences M
Sociology M
Sustainable Development M,O
Technical Communication M,O
Theater M
Urban and Regional Planning M,O
Women's Studies M,O
Writing M,O

EASTERN NAZARENE COLLEGE
Counseling Psychology M
Marriage and Family Therapy M

EASTERN NEW MEXICO UNIVERSITY
Anthropology M
Communication—General M
English M

EASTERN UNIVERSITY
Child and Family Studies D
Communication—General M,O
Counseling Psychology M,O
International Affairs M
International Development M
Marriage and Family Therapy D
Missions and Missiology M
Music M,O
Public Administration D,O
School Psychology M,O
Spanish M,O
Theology M
Urban and Regional Planning M

EASTERN VIRGINIA MEDICAL SCHOOL
Art Therapy M
Clinical Psychology D

EASTERN WASHINGTON UNIVERSITY
Applied Psychology M
Clinical Psychology M
Communication—General M
Counseling Psychology M
English M
Experimental Psychology M
History M
Interdisciplinary Studies M
Liberal Studies M
Music M
Psychology—General M,O
Public Administration M
Rhetoric M
School Psychology O
Technical Communication M

EAST STROUDSBURG UNIVERSITY OF PENNSYLVANIA
Geography M
History M
Political Science M
Public Administration M

EAST TENNESSEE STATE UNIVERSITY
Art/Fine Arts M
Clinical Psychology M,D
Communication—General M,O
Computer Art and Design M
Criminal Justice and Criminology M,O
Economic Development M,O
English M,O
Experimental Psychology D
Geographic Information Systems M,O
Gerontology M,D,O
History M,O
Liberal Studies M,O
Marriage and Family Therapy M
Psychology—General D
Public Administration M,O
School Psychology M
Sociology M
Translation and Interpretation M,O
Urban and Regional Planning M,O

EAST TEXAS BAPTIST UNIVERSITY
Counseling Psychology M
Religion M

ECCLESIA COLLEGE
Missions and Missiology M

ECUMENICAL THEOLOGICAL SEMINARY
Pastoral Ministry and Counseling D
Theology M

EDEN THEOLOGICAL SEMINARY
Theology M,D

EDINBORO UNIVERSITY OF PENNSYLVANIA
Anthropology M
Art Therapy M,O
Art/Fine Arts M
Clinical Psychology M,O
Communication—General M
Counseling Psychology M,O
History M
Political Science M
Rehabilitation Counseling M,O
School Psychology M,O

ELIZABETH CITY STATE UNIVERSITY
Geographic Information Systems M
Psychology—General M

ELMHURST COLLEGE
Geographic Information Systems M
Industrial and Organizational Psychology M

ELMS COLLEGE
Applied Behavior Analysis M,O
Religion M
Social Sciences M,O

ELON UNIVERSITY
Internet and Interactive Multimedia M

EMBRY-RIDDLE AERONAUTICAL UNIVERSITY–PRESCOTT
Military and Defense Studies M

EMBRY-RIDDLE AERONAUTICAL UNIVERSITY–WORLDWIDE
International Affairs M

EMERSON COLLEGE
Publishing M
Writing M

EMILY CARR UNIVERSITY OF ART + DESIGN
Applied Arts and Design—General M
Art/Fine Arts M
Computer Art and Design M

EMORY & HENRY COLLEGE
American Studies M,D
History M,D

EMORY UNIVERSITY
Anthropology D
Art History D
Clinical Psychology D
Cognitive Sciences D
Comparative Literature D,O
Developmental Psychology D
Economics D
English D,O
Ethics M,D
Film, Television, and Video Theory and Criticism M,D,O
French D
Genetic Counseling M
History D
Interdisciplinary Studies D
Music M
Pastoral Ministry and Counseling M,D
Philosophy D,O
Political Science D
Portuguese D,O
Psychology—General D
Religion D
Sociology D
Spanish D,O
Sustainable Development M
Theology M,D
Women's Studies D,O

EMPORIA STATE UNIVERSITY
Art Therapy M
Clinical Psychology M
Counseling Psychology M
English M
Forensic Sciences M,O
History M
Industrial and Organizational Psychology M
Music M
Psychology—General M

*M—masters degree; D—doctorate; O—other advanced degree; *—Close-Up and/or Display*

Rehabilitation Counseling — M
School Psychology — M,O

ENDICOTT COLLEGE
Applied Behavior Analysis — M,D,O
Emergency Management — M,O
Homeland Security — M,O
Interior Design — M

ERIKSON INSTITUTE
Child Development — M
Developmental Psychology — M,O
Human Development — M

ERSKINE THEOLOGICAL SEMINARY
Theology — M,D

EVANGELICAL SEMINARY
Marriage and Family Therapy — M
Missions and Missiology — M
Pastoral Ministry and Counseling — M
Theology — M

EVANGELICAL SEMINARY OF PUERTO RICO
Theology — M,D

EVANGEL UNIVERSITY
Clinical Psychology — M
Counseling Psychology — M
School Psychology — M
Social Sciences — M

THE EVERGREEN STATE COLLEGE
Public Administration — M

EXCELSIOR COLLEGE
Conflict Resolution and Mediation/Peace Studies — M,O
Criminal Justice and Criminology — M,O
Emergency Management — M
Homeland Security — M
Internet and Interactive Multimedia — M,O
Liberal Studies — M
Public Administration — M
Public Policy — M,O

FAIRFIELD UNIVERSITY
Addictions/Substance Abuse Counseling — M,O
American Studies — M
Applied Behavior Analysis — M,O
Applied Psychology — M,O
Child and Family Studies — M,O
Clinical Psychology — M,O
Communication—General — M
Counseling Psychology — M,O
Internet and Interactive Multimedia — M,O
Marriage and Family Therapy — M,O
Pastoral Ministry and Counseling — M,O
Public Administration — M
School Psychology — M,O
Writing — M

FAIRLEIGH DICKINSON UNIVERSITY, FLORHAM CAMPUS
Clinical Psychology — M
Corporate and Organizational Communication — M
Counseling Psychology — M
Industrial and Organizational Psychology — M
Psychology—General — M,O
Public Administration — M
Writing — M

FAIRLEIGH DICKINSON UNIVERSITY, METROPOLITAN CAMPUS
Art/Fine Arts — M
Clinical Psychology — M,D
Communication—General — M
Comparative Literature — M
Criminal Justice and Criminology — M
English — M
Experimental Psychology — M,O
Forensic Psychology — M
History — M
Homeland Security — M
International Affairs — M
Media Studies — M
Political Science — M
Psychology—General — M,D,O
Public Administration — M,O
School Psychology — M

FAIRMONT STATE UNIVERSITY
Criminal Justice and Criminology — M

FAITH BAPTIST BIBLE COLLEGE AND THEOLOGICAL SEMINARY
Pastoral Ministry and Counseling — M
Religion — M
Theology — M

FAITH INTERNATIONAL UNIVERSITY
Theology — M

FAITH THEOLOGICAL SEMINARY
Theology — M,D

FASHION INSTITUTE OF TECHNOLOGY
Applied Arts and Design—General — M
Art History — M
Arts Administration — M
Clothing and Textiles — M
Illustration — M
Museum Studies — M

FAULKNER UNIVERSITY
Criminal Justice and Criminology — M
Humanities — M,D
Pastoral Ministry and Counseling — M,D
Theology — M,D

FAYETTEVILLE STATE UNIVERSITY
Criminal Justice and Criminology — M
Psychology—General — M

Sociology — M

FELICIAN UNIVERSITY
Counseling Psychology — M,D

FERRIS STATE UNIVERSITY
Applied Arts and Design—General — M
Architecture — M
Art/Fine Arts — M
Criminal Justice and Criminology — M
Photography — M

FIELDING GRADUATE UNIVERSITY
Child Development — M,D,O
Clinical Psychology — M,D,O
Developmental Psychology — M,D,O
Human Development — M,D,O
Marriage and Family Therapy — M
Media Studies — M,D,O
Psychology—General — M,D,O

FISK UNIVERSITY
Clinical Psychology — M
Psychology—General — M

FITCHBURG STATE UNIVERSITY
Communication—General — M,O
Counseling Psychology — M
English — M,O
History — M
Interdisciplinary Studies — O
Psychology—General — O
Writing — M

FIVE TOWNS COLLEGE
Music — M,D

FLORIDA AGRICULTURAL AND MECHANICAL UNIVERSITY
Architecture — M
Criminal Justice and Criminology — M
History — M
Journalism — M
Landscape Architecture — M
Political Science — M
Psychology—General — M
Public Administration — M
Social Psychology — M
Social Sciences — M

FLORIDA ATLANTIC UNIVERSITY
Anthropology — M
Applied Arts and Design—General — M
Art/Fine Arts — M
Communication—General — M,O
Comparative and Interdisciplinary Arts — D
Comparative Literature — M
Criminal Justice and Criminology — M
Economics — M
English — M
Film, Television, and Video Production — M,O
French — M
German — M
Graphic Design — M
History — M
Linguistics — M
Media Studies — M,O
Music — M
Political Science — M
Psychology—General — M
Public Administration — M,D
Sociology — M
Spanish — M
Theater — M
Urban and Regional Planning — M
Women's Studies — M

FLORIDA GULF COAST UNIVERSITY
Clinical Psychology — M
Criminal Justice and Criminology — M
English — M
Forensic Sciences — M
History — M
Interdisciplinary Studies — M
Public Administration — M
School Psychology — M

FLORIDA INSTITUTE OF TECHNOLOGY
Applied Behavior Analysis — M,D
Clinical Psychology — D
Communication—General — M
Emergency Management — M,D
Industrial and Organizational Psychology — M,D
Interdisciplinary Studies — M
Psychology—General — M,D
Public Administration — M,D

FLORIDA INTERNATIONAL UNIVERSITY
African Studies — M
Applied Behavior Analysis — M,D
Architecture — M
Art/Fine Arts — M,O
Asian Studies — M
Clinical Psychology — M,D,O
Cognitive Sciences — M,D
Communication—General — M
Counseling Psychology — M,D,O
Criminal Justice and Criminology — M,D
Developmental Psychology — M,D
Economics — M,D
Emergency Management — M
English — M
Forensic Sciences — M
History — M,D
Industrial and Organizational Psychology — M,D
Interior Design — M
International Affairs — M,D
Journalism — M
Landscape Architecture — M
Latin American Studies — M
Liberal Studies — M
Linguistics — M

Mass Communication — M
Museum Studies — M,O
Music — M
Political Science — M,D
Psychology—General — M,D
Public Administration — M,D
Public Affairs — M,D
Rehabilitation Counseling — M,D,O
Religion — M
School Psychology — M,D,O
Sociology — M,D
Spanish — M
Writing — M

FLORIDA NATIONAL UNIVERSITY
Public Administration — M

FLORIDA STATE UNIVERSITY
American Studies — M,D
Applied Behavior Analysis — M
Applied Economics — M,D
Applied Social Research — M,D
Archaeology — M,D
Architecture — M
Art History — M,D
Art Therapy — M
Art/Fine Arts — M
Arts Administration — M,D
Asian Studies — M
Child and Family Studies — M,D
Classics — M,D
Clinical Psychology — D
Cognitive Sciences — D
Communication—General — M,D
Corporate and Organizational Communication — M,D
Criminal Justice and Criminology — M,D
Cultural Studies — M,D
Dance — M
Demography and Population Studies — M,D
Developmental Psychology — D
East European and Russian Studies — M
Economics — M,D
English — M,D
Family and Consumer Sciences-General — M,D
Film, Television, and Video Production — M
French — M,D
Geographic Information Systems — M,D
Geography — M,D
German — M
History — M,D
Human Development — M,D
Industrial Design — M
Interior Design — M
International Affairs — M
Italian — M
Marriage and Family Therapy — M,D
Media Studies — M,D
Museum Studies — M,D
Music — M,D
Philosophy — M,D
Political Science — M,D
Psychology—General — M,D
Public Administration — M,D,O
Public History — M,D
Public Policy — M,D,O
Religion — M,D
Rhetoric — M,D
School Psychology — M,D,O
Slavic Languages — M
Social Psychology — D
Sociology — M,D
Spanish — M,D
Sport Psychology — M,D,O
Theater — M,D
Therapies—Dance, Drama, and Music — M,D
Urban and Regional Planning — M,D
Writing — M,D

FONTBONNE UNIVERSITY
Art/Fine Arts — M
Family and Consumer Sciences-General — M
Health Communication — M
Theater — M

FORDHAM UNIVERSITY
Applied Psychology — M,D
Classics — M,D
Clinical Psychology — D
Communication—General — M,D
Counseling Psychology — M,D
Developmental Psychology — D
Economic Development — M,O
Economics — M,D,O
Emergency Management — M
English — M,D
Ethics — M,O
History — M,D
International Affairs — M,O
International Development — M,O
International Economics — M,D,O
Mass Communication — M
Media Studies — M
Medieval and Renaissance Studies — M,O
Pastoral Ministry and Counseling — M,O
Philosophy — M,D
Political Science — M,D
Psychology—General — M,D
Religion — M,D,O
School Psychology — M,D
Theater — M
Theology — M,D
Urban Studies — M

FORT HAYS STATE UNIVERSITY
Art/Fine Arts — M
Communication—General — M
English — M
Geography — M
History — M
Liberal Studies — M
Psychology—General — M,O

School Psychology — O

FORT VALLEY STATE UNIVERSITY
Counseling Psychology — M
Rehabilitation Counseling — M

FRAMINGHAM STATE UNIVERSITY
Counseling Psychology — M
English — M
Public Administration — M

FRANCISCAN SCHOOL OF THEOLOGY
Theology — M

FRANCISCAN UNIVERSITY OF STEUBENVILLE
Clinical Psychology — M
Counseling Psychology — M
Philosophy — M
Theology — M

FRANCIS MARION UNIVERSITY
Applied Psychology — M,O
Clinical Psychology — M,O
Counseling Psychology — M,O
Psychology—General — M,O
School Psychology — M,O

FRANKLIN UNIVERSITY
Corporate and Organizational Communication — M

FREDERICK S. PARDEE RAND GRADUATE SCHOOL
Public Policy — D

FREED-HARDEMAN UNIVERSITY
Ethics — M
Pastoral Ministry and Counseling — M
Theology — M

FRESNO PACIFIC UNIVERSITY
Conflict Resolution and Mediation/Peace Studies — M,O
Interdisciplinary Studies — M
Marriage and Family Therapy — M
Missions and Missiology — M
Pastoral Ministry and Counseling — M
School Psychology — M
Theology — M
Urban Studies — M

FRIENDS UNIVERSITY
Marriage and Family Therapy — M

FROSTBURG STATE UNIVERSITY
Counseling Psychology — M
Interdisciplinary Studies — M,D
Psychology—General — M

FULLER THEOLOGICAL SEMINARY
Clinical Psychology — M,D,O
Marriage and Family Therapy — M,D,O
Missions and Missiology — M,D,O
Music — M,D,O
Pastoral Ministry and Counseling — M,D,O
Theology — M,D,O

FULL SAIL UNIVERSITY
Art/Fine Arts — M
Computer Art and Design — M
Graphic Design — M
Internet and Interactive Multimedia — M
Journalism — M
Media Studies — M
Writing — M

FUTURE GENERATIONS UNIVERSITY
Social Psychology — M
Sustainable Development — M
Urban and Regional Planning — M

GALLAUDET UNIVERSITY
Clinical Psychology — M,D,O
Counseling Psychology — M,D,O
Linguistics — M,D,O
Public Administration — M,D,O
School Psychology — M,D,O
Translation and Interpretation — M,D,O

GANNON UNIVERSITY
Clinical Psychology — M
Counseling Psychology — M
Criminal Justice and Criminology — M
English — M
Health Communication — M
Pastoral Ministry and Counseling — M,O
Public Administration — M
Theology — M,O

GARDNER-WEBB UNIVERSITY
Counseling Psychology — M
Cultural Studies — M,D
English — M
Missions and Missiology — M,D
Pastoral Ministry and Counseling — M,D
Psychology—General — M
School Psychology — M
Theology — M,D

GARRETT-EVANGELICAL THEOLOGICAL SEMINARY
Music — M,D
Pastoral Ministry and Counseling — M,D
Theology — M,D

GATEWAY SEMINARY
Pastoral Ministry and Counseling — M,D,O
Theology — M,D,O

GENERAL THEOLOGICAL SEMINARY
Pastoral Ministry and Counseling — M,D,O
Religion — M,D,O
Theology — M,D,O

GENEVA COLLEGE
Clinical Psychology — M
Counseling Psychology — M
Marriage and Family Therapy — M
Pastoral Ministry and Counseling — M

Psychology—General M

GEORGE FOX UNIVERSITY
Clinical Psychology M,D,O
Counseling Psychology M,O
Cultural Studies M,O
Marriage and Family Therapy M
Pastoral Ministry and Counseling M,D,O
School Psychology M,O
Theology M,D,O

GEORGE MASON UNIVERSITY
Anthropology M,D
Art History M
Art/Fine Arts M
Arts Administration M
Clinical Psychology M,D,O
Cognitive Sciences M,D,O
Communication—General M,D,O
Conflict Resolution and
  Mediation/Peace Studies M,D,O
Criminal Justice and Criminology M,D
Cultural Studies D
Developmental Psychology M,D,O
Economics M,D
English M
Ethics M
Forensic Sciences M
French M
Gender Studies M
Geographic Information Systems M,D,O
Geography M,D,O
Graphic Design M
History M,D,O
Industrial and Organizational
  Psychology M,D,O
Interdisciplinary Studies M
International Affairs M
Linguistics M,D,O
Music M,D
National Security M,D,O
Near and Middle Eastern Studies M,O
Philosophy M
Political Science M,D
Psychology—General M
Public Administration M
Public Affairs M
Public Policy M,D
Religion M
Rhetoric M,D,O
Sociology M
Spanish M
Theater M
Women's Studies M
Writing M

GEORGETOWN UNIVERSITY
American Studies M,D
Asian Studies M
Communication—General M
Comparative Literature M,D
Conflict Resolution and
  Mediation/Peace Studies M
East European and Russian Studies M
Economic Development D
Economics D
Emergency Management M,D
English M
Ethics M,D
German M,D
History M,D
Human Development M,D
Humanities M,D
Industrial and Labor Relations D
Interdisciplinary Studies M,D
International Affairs M,D
International Development M
Internet and Interactive
  Multimedia M
Journalism M,D
Latin American Studies M,D
Liberal Studies M,D
Linguistics M,D
Media Studies M,D
Medieval and Renaissance Studies M,D
Near and Middle Eastern Languages M,O
Near and Middle Eastern Studies M,O
Philosophy M,D
Political Science M,D
Psychology—General D
Public Policy M,D
Religion M,D
Spanish M,D
Theology D
Urban and Regional Planning M
Western European Studies M

THE GEORGE WASHINGTON UNIVERSITY
Addictions/Substance Abuse
  Counseling M
American Studies M,D
Anthropology D
Applied Psychology D
Art History M
Art Therapy M,O
Art/Fine Arts M,O
Asian Studies M
Clinical Psychology M,D
Cognitive Sciences D
Communication—General M
Criminal Justice and Criminology M,O
Dance M,O
East European and Russian Studies M
Economics M,D
Emergency Management M,D,O
English M,D
Folklore M,D
Forensic Psychology O
Forensic Sciences M
Gender Studies O
Geography M,O

Health Communication M,D
Historic Preservation M,D
History M,D
Human Development M
Interior Design M
International Affairs M,D
International Development M,D
International Trade Policy M
Latin American Studies M
Mass Communication M,O
Military and Defense Studies M
Museum Studies M,D,O
National Security M
Near and Middle Eastern Studies M
Philosophy M
Photography M,O
Political Science M,D
Psychology—General M,D,O
Public Administration M,D
Public Affairs M,O
Public Policy M,D
Publishing M
Rehabilitation Counseling M
Religion M
Social Psychology D
Sociology M
Theater M,O
Western European Studies M
Women's Studies M,O

GEORGIA COLLEGE & STATE UNIVERSITY
Art Therapy M
Criminal Justice and Criminology M
English M
Public Administration M
Therapies—Dance, Drama, and
  Music M
Writing M

GEORGIA INSTITUTE OF TECHNOLOGY
Architecture M,D
Building Science M,D
Computer Art and Design M,D
Economic Development M,D
Economics M,D
Geographic Information Systems M,D
History of Science and Technology M,D
Industrial Design M
International Affairs M
Internet and Interactive
  Multimedia M,D
Music M,D
Psychology—General M,D
Public Policy M,D
Urban and Regional Planning M,D
Urban Design M,D

GEORGIAN COURT UNIVERSITY
Applied Behavior Analysis M,O
Clinical Psychology M,O
Computer Art and Design M,O
Counseling Psychology M,O
Criminal Justice and Criminology M,O
Health Psychology M,O
Homeland Security M,O
School Psychology M,O
Theology M,O

GEORGIA SOUTHERN UNIVERSITY
Applied Economics M,O
Art/Fine Arts M
Clinical Psychology M,D
Counseling Psychology M
English M
Graphic Design M
History M,O
Music M
Psychology—General M,D
Public Administration M
Public History M,O
School Psychology M,O
Sociology M
Spanish M

GEORGIA SOUTHERN UNIVERSITY–ARMSTRONG CAMPUS
American Studies M
Corporate and Organizational
  Communication M,O
Criminal Justice and Criminology M,O
History M
Public History M
Western European Studies M
Writing M,O

GEORGIA STATE UNIVERSITY
African-American Studies M
Anthropology M
Art History M
Art/Fine Arts M
Clinical Psychology D
Clothing and Textiles M
Cognitive Sciences D
Communication—General M,D
Counseling Psychology M,O
Criminal Justice and Criminology M,D,O
Cultural Studies M,O
Developmental Psychology D
Economic Development M,D,O
Economics M,D
Emergency Management M,D,O
English M,D
Film, Television, and Video
  Production M,D
Forensic Sciences M,O
French M,O
Gender Studies M,O
Geographic Information Systems O
Geography M,D
German O
Gerontology M,O
Graphic Design M

Historic Preservation M,D
History M,D
Human Development M,D,O
Industrial and Labor Relations M,D
Interior Design M
Latin American Studies M,O
Linguistics M,D
Mass Communication M,D
Media Studies M,D
Music M,D,O
Philosophy M
Photography M,D
Political Science M,D
Psychology—General D
Public Administration M,D,O
Public History M,D
Public Policy M,D,O
Rehabilitation Counseling M
Religion M
Rhetoric M
School Psychology M,D,O
Social Psychology D
Sociology M,D
Spanish M,O
Speech and Interpersonal
  Communication M,D
Translation and Interpretation O
Urban and Regional Planning M,D,O
Women's Studies M,O
Writing M,D

GLOBAL UNIVERSITY
Missions and Missiology M,D
Pastoral Ministry and Counseling M,D
Theology M,D

GODDARD COLLEGE
Art Therapy M
Clinical Psychology M
Comparative and Interdisciplinary
  Arts M
Interdisciplinary Studies M
Psychology—General M
Writing M

GOLDEN GATE UNIVERSITY
Forensic Sciences M,O
Psychology—General M,D,O
Public Administration M,D,O

GONZAGA UNIVERSITY
Marriage and Family Therapy M,D
Philosophy M
Theology M

GORDON-CONWELL THEOLOGICAL SEMINARY
Archaeology M,D
Missions and Missiology M,D
Pastoral Ministry and Counseling M,D
Religion M,D
Theology M,D

GOUCHER COLLEGE
Arts Administration M
Computer Art and Design M
Cultural Studies M
Historic Preservation M
Writing M

GOVERNORS STATE UNIVERSITY
Addictions/Substance Abuse
  Counseling M
Art/Fine Arts M
Communication—General M
Counseling Psychology M
Criminal Justice and Criminology M
English M
Film, Television, and Video
  Production M
Photography M
Political Science M
Psychology—General M
Public Administration M

GRACE COLLEGE
Clinical Psychology M

GRACE COLLEGE OF DIVINITY
Religion M

GRACELAND UNIVERSITY (IA)
Religion M
Theology M

GRACE MISSION UNIVERSITY
Missions and Missiology M,D

GRACE SCHOOL OF THEOLOGY
Theology M

GRACE THEOLOGICAL SEMINARY
Cultural Studies M,D,O
Missions and Missiology M,D,O
Pastoral Ministry and Counseling M,D,O
Theology M,D,O
Women's Studies M,D,O

THE GRADUATE CENTER, CITY UNIVERSITY OF NEW YORK
Anthropology D
Archaeology D
Architectural History D
Art History D
Classics M,D
Clinical Psychology D
Cognitive Sciences D
Comparative Literature M,D
Criminal Justice and Criminology D
Cultural Anthropology D
Developmental Psychology D
Economics D
English D
Experimental Psychology D
French D

Historic Preservation M,D
History M,D,O
Human Development M,D,O
Industrial and Labor Relations M,D
Interior Design M
Latin American Studies M,O
Linguistics M,D
Mass Communication M,D
Media Studies M,D
Music M,D,O
Philosophy M
Photography M,D
Political Science M,D
Psychology—General D
Public Administration M,D,O
Public History M,D
Public Policy M,D,O
Rehabilitation Counseling M
Religion M
Rhetoric M
School Psychology M,D,O
Social Psychology D
Sociology M,D
Spanish M,O
Speech and Interpersonal
  Communication M,D
Translation and Interpretation O
Urban and Regional Planning M,D,O
Women's Studies M,O
Writing M,D

Hispanic and Latin American
  Languages D
History D
Industrial and Organizational
  Psychology D
Italian M,D
Liberal Studies M
Linguistics M,D
Music D
Philosophy M,D
Political Science M,D
Psychology—General D
Social Psychology D
Sociology D
Theater D

GRADUATE INSTITUTE OF APPLIED LINGUISTICS
Linguistics M,O

GRADUATE THEOLOGICAL UNION
Art History M,D,O
Cultural Studies M,D,O
Ethics M,D,O
Jewish Studies M,D,O
Religion M,D,O
Social Sciences M,D,O
Theology M,D,O

GRAMBLING STATE UNIVERSITY
Criminal Justice and Criminology M
English M,D,O
Mass Communication M
Political Science M
Public Administration M

GRAND CANYON UNIVERSITY
Cognitive Sciences D
Emergency Management M
Industrial and Organizational
  Psychology D
Pastoral Ministry and Counseling D
Psychology—General D

GRAND RAPIDS THEOLOGICAL SEMINARY OF CORNERSTONE UNIVERSITY
Interdisciplinary Studies M
Pastoral Ministry and Counseling M
Religion M
Theology M

GRAND VALLEY STATE UNIVERSITY
Communication—General M
Criminal Justice and Criminology M
English M
Linguistics M
Public Administration M
School Psychology M,O

GRATZ COLLEGE
Holocaust and Genocide Studies M,D
Jewish Studies M,O

GREENVILLE UNIVERSITY
Pastoral Ministry and Counseling M

HAMLINE UNIVERSITY
Public Administration M,D
Writing M

HAMPTON UNIVERSITY
Liberal Studies M,D,O
Marriage and Family Therapy M
Pastoral Ministry and Counseling M,D,O
Psychology—General M

HARDING SCHOOL OF THEOLOGY
Pastoral Ministry and Counseling M,D
Theology M,D

HARDING UNIVERSITY
Pastoral Ministry and Counseling M

HARDIN-SIMMONS UNIVERSITY
Counseling Psychology M
English M
History M
Marriage and Family Therapy M
Music M
Pastoral Ministry and Counseling M
Psychology—General M
Religion M
Theology M,D

HARRISON MIDDLETON UNIVERSITY
Comparative Literature M,D
Humanities M,D
Interdisciplinary Studies M,D
Philosophy M,D
Religion M,D
Social Sciences M,D

HARTFORD SEMINARY
Pastoral Ministry and Counseling M,D,O
Religion M,D,O
Theology M,D,O

HARVARD UNIVERSITY
African Studies D
African-American Studies D
American Studies D
Anthropology M,D
Archaeology M,D
Architectural History D
Architecture M,D
Art History D
Asian Languages M,D
Asian Studies M,D
Celtic Languages D
Chinese D
Classics D
Cognitive Sciences M,D
Communication—General M,O
Comparative Literature D
Demography and Population Studies M,D

---

*M—masters degree; D—doctorate; O—other advanced degree; *—Close-Up and/or Display*

Developmental Psychology	D
East European and Russian Studies	M
Economics	D
English	M,D,O
Experimental Psychology	D
French	M,D
German	D
History of Science and Technology	M,D
History	D
Human Development	M
International Affairs	D
International Development	M
Italian	M,D
Japanese	D
Jewish Studies	M,D
Journalism	M,O
Landscape Architecture	M,D
Liberal Studies	M,O
Linguistics	D
Medieval and Renaissance Studies	D
Museum Studies	M,O
Music	M,D
Near and Middle Eastern Languages	M,D
Near and Middle Eastern Studies	M,D
Philosophy	M,D
Political Science	M,D
Portuguese	M,D
Psychology—General	D
Public Administration	M
Public Policy	M,D
Religion	D
Russian	D
Scandinavian Languages	D
Slavic Languages	D
Social Psychology	D
Sociology	D
Spanish	M,D
Technical Communication	M
Theology	M
Urban and Regional Planning	M,D
Urban Design	M

HAWAI'I PACIFIC UNIVERSITY

Clinical Psychology	M
Communication—General	M
Liberal Studies	M
Military and Defense Studies	M
Public Administration	M
Sustainable Development	M

HAZELDEN BETTY FORD GRADUATE SCHOOL OF ADDICTION STUDIES

Addictions/Substance Abuse Counseling	M,O

HEBREW COLLEGE

Jewish Studies	M,O
Music	M,O
Theology	M

HEBREW UNION COLLEGE–JEWISH INSTITUTE OF RELIGION (NY)

Jewish Studies	M
Music	M
Near and Middle Eastern Languages	D
Theology	M,D

HEC MONTREAL

Applied Economics	M,D
Arts Administration	O
Corporate and Organizational Communication	O
Sustainable Development	O

HEIDELBERG UNIVERSITY

Clinical Psychology	M
Counseling Psychology	M
School Psychology	M

HENDERSON STATE UNIVERSITY

Counseling Psychology	M,O
Liberal Studies	M

HENLEY-PUTNAM SCHOOL OF STRATEGIC SECURITY

Conflict Resolution and Mediation/Peace Studies	M
Homeland Security	M
Military and Defense Studies	M
National Security	D

HERITAGE CHRISTIAN UNIVERSITY

Classics	M
Pastoral Ministry and Counseling	M
Religion	M

HERITAGE COLLEGE AND SEMINARY

Theology	M,O

HERITAGE UNIVERSITY

English	M

HIGH POINT UNIVERSITY

Corporate and Organizational Communication	M,D

HILBERT COLLEGE

Criminal Justice and Criminology	M
Public Administration	M

HILLSDALE COLLEGE

Political Science	M,D

HIRAM COLLEGE

Interdisciplinary Studies	M

HODGES UNIVERSITY

Clinical Psychology	M
Counseling Psychology	M

HOFSTRA UNIVERSITY

Addictions/Substance Abuse Counseling	M,O
Applied Behavior Analysis	M,D,O
Art Therapy	M,O
Chinese	M,D,O
Clinical Psychology	M,D
Counseling Psychology	M,O
English	M
Family and Consumer Sciences-General	M,D,O
French	M,D,O
German	M,D,O
Human Development	M,D,O
Humanities	M,D,O
Industrial and Organizational Psychology	M,D
Italian	M,D,O
Journalism	M
Linguistics	M,D,O
Marriage and Family Therapy	M,O
Near and Middle Eastern Languages	M,D,O
Psychology—General	M,D
Rehabilitation Counseling	M,O
Russian	M,D,O
School Psychology	M,D
Social Psychology	M,D
Spanish	M,D,O
Sustainable Development	M
Urban Design	M
Writing	M

HOLLINS UNIVERSITY

Art/Fine Arts	M
Dance	M
English	M,O
Film, Television, and Video Production	M
Film, Television, and Video Theory and Criticism	M
Humanities	M
Illustration	M,O
Interdisciplinary Studies	M
Liberal Studies	M
Music	M
Social Sciences	M
Theater	M,O
Writing	M,O

HOLMES INSTITUTE

Pastoral Ministry and Counseling	M

HOLY APOSTLES COLLEGE AND SEMINARY

Theology	M,O

HOLY CROSS GREEK ORTHODOX SCHOOL OF THEOLOGY

Theology	M

HOLY FAMILY UNIVERSITY

Counseling Psychology	M
Criminal Justice and Criminology	M

HOLY NAMES UNIVERSITY

Counseling Psychology	M
Forensic Psychology	M
Music	M,O
Pastoral Ministry and Counseling	M
Writing	M

HOOD COLLEGE

Art/Fine Arts	M,O
Clinical Psychology	M
Geographic Information Systems	M,O
Human Development	M,O
Humanities	M
Interdisciplinary Studies	M,O
Psychology—General	M,O
Public Administration	M,O
School Psychology	M
Thanatology	M,O

HOOD THEOLOGICAL SEMINARY

Theology	M,D

HOPE INTERNATIONAL UNIVERSITY

International Development	M
Marriage and Family Therapy	M
Missions and Missiology	M
Music	M
Religion	M

HOUGHTON COLLEGE

Music	M

HOUSTON BAPTIST UNIVERSITY

Addictions/Substance Abuse Counseling	M
Art/Fine Arts	M
Counseling Psychology	M
English	M,D
Liberal Studies	M
Marriage and Family Therapy	M
Music	M,D
Near and Middle Eastern Languages	M
Pastoral Ministry and Counseling	M
Philosophy	M
Psychology—General	M
School Psychology	M
Spanish	M
Theology	M

HOUSTON GRADUATE SCHOOL OF THEOLOGY

Pastoral Ministry and Counseling	M,D
Theology	M,D

HOWARD PAYNE UNIVERSITY

Criminal Justice and Criminology	M
Pastoral Ministry and Counseling	M
Theology	M

HOWARD UNIVERSITY

African Studies	M,D
Applied Arts and Design—General	M
Art History	M
Art/Fine Arts	M
Clinical Psychology	M,D
Communication—General	M,D
Corporate and Organizational Communication	M,D
Counseling Psychology	D
Developmental Psychology	M,D
Economics	M,D
English	M,D
Experimental Psychology	M,D
Film, Television, and Video Production	M
French	M
History	M,D
Mass Communication	M,D
Media Studies	M,D
Music	M
Philosophy	M
Photography	M
Political Science	M,D
Psychology—General	M,D
Public Administration	M
School Psychology	M,D
Social Psychology	M,D
Sociology	M,D
Spanish	M
Theology	M,D

HUMBOLDT STATE UNIVERSITY

Anthropology	M
Counseling Psychology	M
Developmental Psychology	M
English	M
Psychology—General	M
School Psychology	M
Social Psychology	M
Social Sciences	M
Sociology	M

HUNTER COLLEGE OF THE CITY UNIVERSITY OF NEW YORK

Anthropology	M
Applied Social Research	M
Art History	M
Art/Fine Arts	M
Chinese	M
Classics	M
Comparative Literature	M
Economics	M
French	M
Geographic Information Systems	M,O
Geography	M,O
History	M
Italian	M
Media Studies	M
Music	M
Psychology—General	M,O
Rehabilitation Counseling	M
Romance Languages	M
Sociology	M
Spanish	M
Sustainable Development	M,O
Theater	M
Urban and Regional Planning	M
Urban Studies	M
Writing	M

HUNTINGTON UNIVERSITY

Pastoral Ministry and Counseling	M,D

HUNTSVILLE BIBLE COLLEGE

Pastoral Ministry and Counseling	M

HUSSON UNIVERSITY

Clinical Psychology	M
Counseling Psychology	M
Criminal Justice and Criminology	M
School Psychology	M
Social Psychology	M

ICAHN SCHOOL OF MEDICINE AT MOUNT SINAI

Genetic Counseling	M,D

IDAHO STATE UNIVERSITY

Anthropology	M
Art/Fine Arts	M
Clinical Psychology	D
Communication—General	M
Counseling Psychology	M,D,O
English	M,D,O
Experimental Psychology	D
Geographic Information Systems	M,O
History	M
Marriage and Family Therapy	M,D,O
Political Science	M,D
Psychology—General	D
Public Administration	M
School Psychology	M,D,O
Sociology	M
Theater	M

IGLOBAL UNIVERSITY

Public Administration	M

ILIFF SCHOOL OF THEOLOGY

Pastoral Ministry and Counseling	M,D
Religion	M,D
Theology	M,D

ILLINOIS INSTITUTE OF TECHNOLOGY

Applied Arts and Design—General	M,D
Architecture	M,D
Clinical Psychology	M,D
Communication—General	M,D
Corporate and Organizational Communication	M
Humanities	M,D
Industrial and Organizational Psychology	M,D
Landscape Architecture	M,D
Psychology—General	M,D
Public Administration	M
Rehabilitation Counseling	M,D
Technical Writing	M,D

ILLINOIS STATE UNIVERSITY

Agricultural Economics and Agribusiness	M
Archaeology	M
Art History	M
Art/Fine Arts	M
Clinical Psychology	M,D,O
Cognitive Sciences	M,D,O
Communication—General	M
Counseling Psychology	M,D,O
Criminal Justice and Criminology	M
Developmental Psychology	M,D,O
Economics	M
English	M,D,O
Family and Consumer Sciences-General	M
French	M
German	M
Graphic Design	M
History	M
Industrial and Organizational Psychology	M,D,O
Music	M
Photography	M
Political Science	M
Psychology—General	M,D,O
School Psychology	D,O
Sociology	M
Spanish	M
Textile Design	M
Theater	M
Writing	O

IMMACULATA UNIVERSITY

Clinical Psychology	M,D,O
Counseling Psychology	M,D,O
Forensic Psychology	M,D,O
Psychoanalysis and Psychotherapy	M,D,O
Psychology—General	M,D,O
School Psychology	M,D,O
Therapies—Dance, Drama, and Music	M

INDIANA STATE UNIVERSITY

Art/Fine Arts	M
Clinical Psychology	M,D,O
Communication—General	M
Criminal Justice and Criminology	M
English	M
Graphic Design	M
History	M
Linguistics	M,D,O
Media Studies	M
Music	M
Photography	M
Psychology—General	M,D
Public Administration	M
School Psychology	M,D,O
Spanish	M,D,O
Writing	M

INDIANA TECH

Psychology—General	M

INDIANA UNIVERSITY BLOOMINGTON

African Studies	M
African-American Studies	M,D
Anthropology	M,D
Applied Arts and Design—General	M
Archaeology	M,D
Art/Fine Arts	M
Arts Administration	M
Asian Languages	M,D
Asian Studies	M,D
Chinese	M,D
Classics	M,D
Cognitive Sciences	D
Comparative Literature	M,D
Criminal Justice and Criminology	M,D
Developmental Psychology	D
East European and Russian Studies	M,O
Economic Development	M,D,O
Economics	M,D
English	M,D
Folklore	M,D
French	M,D
Gender Studies	D
Geography	D
German	M,D
Hispanic and Latin American Languages	M,D
History of Science and Technology	M,D
History	M,D,O
International Affairs	M
International Development	M,D,O
Italian	M,D
Japanese	M,D
Jewish Studies	M
Latin American Studies	M
Linguistics	M,D
Media Studies	M,D
Medieval and Renaissance Studies	M,D
Music	M,D,O
Near and Middle Eastern Languages	M,D
Philosophy	M,D,O
Political Science	M,D
Portuguese	M,D
Psychology—General	D
Public Administration	M,D,O
Public Affairs	M,D,O
Public Policy	M,D,O
Religion	M,D
Rhetoric	M,D
School Psychology	M,D,O
Slavic Languages	M,D
Social Psychology	D
Social Sciences	M,D,O
Sociology	M,D
Spanish	M,D
Theater	M,D
Western European Studies	M
Writing	M,D

INDIANA UNIVERSITY KOKOMO

Public Administration	M,O
Public Policy	M,O

INDIANA UNIVERSITY NORTHWEST

Addictions/Substance Abuse Counseling	M,O
Counseling Psychology	M,O
Criminal Justice and Criminology	M,O
Gender Studies	M,O
Liberal Studies	M,O
Public Administration	M,O
Public Affairs	M,O

Urban Studies — M,O

INDIANA UNIVERSITY OF PENNSYLVANIA
Archaeology — M
Art/Fine Arts — M
Clinical Psychology — M,D
Communication—General — M
Criminal Justice and Criminology — M,D
English — M,D
Geographic Information Systems — M,O
Geography — M
Hispanic and Latin American Languages — M
History — M
Industrial and Labor Relations — M
Media Studies — D
Music — M
Psychology—General — M,D
Public Affairs — M
Public History — M
School Psychology — D,O
Social Psychology — M
Sociology — M
Urban and Regional Planning — M

INDIANA UNIVERSITY–PURDUE UNIVERSITY FORT WAYNE
Communication—General — M
English — M,O
Marriage and Family Therapy — M,O
Public Policy — M,O

INDIANA UNIVERSITY–PURDUE UNIVERSITY INDIANAPOLIS
American Studies — M,D
Art Therapy — M
Art/Fine Arts — M
Clinical Psychology — M,D
Communication—General — M,D
Computer Art and Design — M
Criminal Justice and Criminology — M,O
Economics — M
Emergency Management — M,O
English — M,O
Forensic Sciences — M
Geographic Information Systems — M
Graphic Design — M
Health Communication — M,D
History — M
Homeland Security — M,O
Industrial and Organizational Psychology — M,D
Liberal Studies — M,D,O
Museum Studies — M,O
Music — M,D
Philanthropic Studies — M,D
Philosophy — M,O
Photography — M
Political Science — M
Psychology—General — M,D
Public Administration — M,O
Public Affairs — M,O
Public History — M
Social Psychology — M,D
Social Sciences — M,D,O
Sociology — M
Technical Communication — M
Therapies—Dance, Drama, and Music — M,D
Western European Studies — M
Writing — M,O

INDIANA UNIVERSITY SOUTH BEND
Addictions/Substance Abuse Counseling — M,O
Clinical Psychology — M,O
Communication—General — M,D
Counseling Psychology — M,O
English — M,O
International Affairs — M,O
Liberal Studies — M,O
Marriage and Family Therapy — M,O
Music — M,D
Public Administration — M,O
Public Affairs — M,O
School Psychology — M,O
Writing — M,O

INDIANA UNIVERSITY SOUTHEAST
Interdisciplinary Studies — M

INDIANA WESLEYAN UNIVERSITY
Addictions/Substance Abuse Counseling — M
Counseling Psychology — M
Marriage and Family Therapy — M
Pastoral Ministry and Counseling — M
Social Psychology — M
Theology — M

INSTITUTE FOR CHRISTIAN STUDIES
Philosophy — M,D
Political Science — M,D
Theology — M,D

INSTITUTE FOR DOCTORAL STUDIES IN THE VISUAL ARTS
Art/Fine Arts — D
Philosophy — D

INSTITUTE OF AMERICAN INDIAN ARTS
Writing — M

INSTITUTE OF PUBLIC ADMINISTRATION
Public Administration — M,O

THE INSTITUTE OF WORLD POLITICS
Military and Defense Studies — M,O
National Security — M,O
Political Science — M
Public Affairs — M,O
Public Policy — M,O

INSTITUTO CENTROAMERICANO DE ADMINISTRACIÓN DE EMPRESAS
Agricultural Economics and Agribusiness — M
Sustainable Development — M

INSTITUTO TECNOLOGICO DE SANTO DOMINGO
Communication—General — M,O
Counseling Psychology — M,O
Economics — M,O
Gender Studies — M,O
Humanities — M,O
International Affairs — M,O
Linguistics — M,O
Marriage and Family Therapy — M,O
Sustainable Development — M,O

INSTITUTO TECNOLÓGICO Y DE ESTUDIOS SUPERIORES DE MONTERREY, CAMPUS CENTRAL DE VERACRUZ
Humanities — M

INSTITUTO TECNOLÓGICO Y DE ESTUDIOS SUPERIORES DE MONTERREY, CAMPUS CIUDAD DE MÉXICO
Economics — M,D
Humanities — M,D

INSTITUTO TECNOLÓGICO Y DE ESTUDIOS SUPERIORES DE MONTERREY, CAMPUS CIUDAD JUÁREZ
Humanities — M
Public Administration — M

INSTITUTO TECNOLÓGICO Y DE ESTUDIOS SUPERIORES DE MONTERREY, CAMPUS CIUDAD OBREGÓN
Communication—General — M
International Affairs — M

INSTITUTO TECNOLÓGICO Y DE ESTUDIOS SUPERIORES DE MONTERREY, CAMPUS ESTADO DE MÉXICO
Architecture — M,D
Humanities — M,D

INSTITUTO TECNOLÓGICO Y DE ESTUDIOS SUPERIORES DE MONTERREY, CAMPUS IRAPUATO
Architecture — M,D
Humanities — M,D

INSTITUTO TECNOLÓGICO Y DE ESTUDIOS SUPERIORES DE MONTERREY, CAMPUS MONTERREY
Communication—General — M,D

INTER AMERICAN UNIVERSITY OF PUERTO RICO, AGUADILLA CAMPUS
Counseling Psychology — M
Criminal Justice and Criminology — M

INTER AMERICAN UNIVERSITY OF PUERTO RICO, BARRANQUITAS CAMPUS
Criminal Justice and Criminology — M
History — M

INTER AMERICAN UNIVERSITY OF PUERTO RICO, METROPOLITAN CAMPUS
American Studies — M,D
Counseling Psychology — M
Criminal Justice and Criminology — M
English — M
History — M,D
Industrial and Labor Relations — M
Industrial and Organizational Psychology — M,D
Pastoral Ministry and Counseling — D
Psychology—General — M,D
School Psychology — M,D
Spanish — M
Theology — D
Women's Studies — M

INTER AMERICAN UNIVERSITY OF PUERTO RICO, PONCE CAMPUS
Criminal Justice and Criminology — M
Spanish — M

INTER AMERICAN UNIVERSITY OF PUERTO RICO, SAN GERMÁN CAMPUS
Art/Fine Arts — M
Counseling Psychology — M,D
Graphic Design — M
Music — M
Photography — M
Psychology—General — M,D
School Psychology — M,D

INTERDENOMINATIONAL THEOLOGICAL CENTER
Pastoral Ministry and Counseling — M,D
Theology — M,D

INTERIOR DESIGNERS INSTITUTE
Interior Design — M

INTERNATIONAL BAPTIST COLLEGE AND SEMINARY
Pastoral Ministry and Counseling — M,D
Theology — M

INTERNATIONAL TECHNOLOGICAL UNIVERSITY
Computer Art and Design — M

INTERNATIONAL UNIVERSITY IN GENEVA
Communication—General — M,D
International Affairs — M,D
Media Studies — M,D
Public Administration — M,D

IONA COLLEGE
Counseling Psychology — M,O
Criminal Justice and Criminology — M,O
English — M
Experimental Psychology — M,O
Forensic Sciences — M,O
History — M
Industrial and Organizational Psychology — M,O
Marriage and Family Therapy — M
Mass Communication — M,O
Psychology—General — M,O
School Psychology — M,O
Spanish — M

IOWA STATE UNIVERSITY OF SCIENCE AND TECHNOLOGY
Agricultural Economics and Agribusiness — M,D
Anthropology — M
Applied Arts and Design—General — M,D
Architecture — M
Art/Fine Arts — M
Child and Family Studies — M,D
Clothing and Textiles — M,D
Cognitive Sciences — M,D
Corporate and Organizational Communication — M,D
Counseling Psychology — M,D
Economics — M,D
English — M,D
Family and Consumer Sciences-General — M
Graphic Design — M
History — M,D
Human Development — M,D
Industrial Design — M
Interdisciplinary Studies — M
Interior Design — M
Journalism — M
Landscape Architecture — M
Linguistics — M,D
Mass Communication — M
Political Science — M
Psychology—General — M,D
Public Administration — M,D
Rhetoric — M,D
Rural Planning and Studies — D
Rural Sociology — M,D
Social Psychology — M,D
Sociology — M,D
Sustainable Development — M,D
Urban and Regional Planning — M
Writing — M,D

ITHACA COLLEGE
Art/Fine Arts — M
Internet and Interactive Multimedia — M
Music — M
Photography — M
Writing — M

JACKSON STATE UNIVERSITY
Clinical Psychology — M,D
Criminal Justice and Criminology — M
English — M
History — M
Political Science — M
Psychology—General — D
Public Administration — M,D
Public Affairs — M,D
Public Policy — M,D
School Psychology — M
Sociology — M
Urban and Regional Planning — M,D

JACKSONVILLE STATE UNIVERSITY
Criminal Justice and Criminology — M
Emergency Management — M,D
English — M
History — M
Liberal Studies — M
Music — M
Political Science — M
Psychology—General — M

JACKSONVILLE UNIVERSITY
Art/Fine Arts — M
Counseling Psychology — M
Dance — M
Marriage and Family Therapy — M
Public Policy — M

JAMES MADISON UNIVERSITY
American Studies — M
Applied Behavior Analysis — M
Art History — M
Art/Fine Arts — M
Clinical Psychology — D
Communication—General — M
Counseling Psychology — D
English — M
Experimental Psychology — M
Forensic Sciences — M
History — M
Music — M,D
Photography — M
Political Science — M
Psychology—General — M
Public Administration — M
Public History — M
Rhetoric — M
School Psychology — M,D,O
Technical Writing — M

INTERNATIONAL UNIVERSITY IN GENEVA (continued)
Writing — M

THE JEWISH THEOLOGICAL SEMINARY
Jewish Studies — M,D
Music — M
Religion — M,D
Theology — M,D,O
Women's Studies — M,D

JOHN BROWN UNIVERSITY
Clinical Psychology — M,O
Counseling Psychology — M,O
Ethics — M
Marriage and Family Therapy — M,O

JOHN CARROLL UNIVERSITY
Counseling Psychology — M
English — M
Humanities — M
Religion — M
Theology — M

JOHN F. KENNEDY UNIVERSITY
Art/Fine Arts — M
Comparative and Interdisciplinary Arts — M
Counseling Psychology — M
Health Psychology — M
Industrial and Organizational Psychology — M,O
Museum Studies — M,O
Psychology—General — M,D,O
Sport Psychology — M
Transpersonal and Humanistic Psychology — M

JOHN JAY COLLEGE OF CRIMINAL JUSTICE OF THE CITY UNIVERSITY OF NEW YORK
Criminal Justice and Criminology — M,D
Forensic Psychology — M,D
Forensic Sciences — M,D
Public Administration — M
Public Policy — M,D

JOHN PAUL THE GREAT CATHOLIC UNIVERSITY
Theology — M

JOHNS HOPKINS UNIVERSITY
Anthropology — D
Applied Behavior Analysis — O
Applied Economics — M
Archaeology — D
Art History — M,D
Asian Studies — M,D,O
Classics — D
Clinical Psychology — M,D
Cognitive Sciences — M,D
Communication—General — M,O
Comparative Literature — D
Counseling Psychology — M
Demography and Population Studies — M,D
Economics — D
English — M,D
Film, Television, and Video Production — M
French — M,D
Genetic Counseling — M
Geographic Information Systems — M,O
German — M,D
Health Communication — M,D
History of Science and Technology — M,D
History — M
Homeland Security — M,O
International Affairs — M,D,O
International Development — M,D,O
International Economics — M,D,O
Italian — M,D
Liberal Studies — M,O
Media Studies — M
Medical Illustration — M
Military and Defense Studies — M
Museum Studies — M,O
Music — M,D,O
Near and Middle Eastern Languages — D
Near and Middle Eastern Studies — D
Philosophy — M,D
Political Science — M,D,O
Psychology—General — D
Public Administration — M,O
Public Policy — M,D
Romance Languages — M
Sociology — D
Spanish — M,D
Technical Writing — M,O
Writing — M,O

JOHNSON & WALES UNIVERSITY
Addictions/Substance Abuse Counseling — M
Clinical Psychology — M
Criminal Justice and Criminology — M
Economic Development — M
Sustainable Development — M

JOHNSON UNIVERSITY
Clinical Psychology — M,D,O
Cultural Studies — M,D,O
Pastoral Ministry and Counseling — M,D,O
Theology — M,D,O

JOHNSON UNIVERSITY FLORIDA
Pastoral Ministry and Counseling — M

THE JUDGE ADVOCATE GENERAL'S SCHOOL, U.S. ARMY
Military and Defense Studies — M

JUDSON UNIVERSITY
Architecture — M
Clinical Psychology — M
Pastoral Ministry and Counseling — M
Sustainable Development — M
Urban Design — M

*M—masters degree; D—doctorate; O—other advanced degree; *—Close-Up and/or Display*

THE JUILLIARD SCHOOL
Music — M,D,O
Theater — M,D,O

KANSAS STATE UNIVERSITY
Agricultural Economics and Agribusiness — M,D
Architecture — M
Art/Fine Arts — M
Child and Family Studies — M,D,O
Child Development — M,D,O
Clothing and Textiles — M,D
Communication—General — M,D,O
Conflict Resolution and Mediation/Peace Studies — M,D,O
Consumer Economics — M,D,O
Economics — M,D
English — M,O
Environmental Design — D
Family and Consumer Sciences-General — M,D,O
French — M
Gender Studies — O
Geographic Information Systems — M,D,O
Geography — M,D,O
German — M
Gerontology — M,O
Health Communication — M
History — M,D
Human Development — M,D,O
Interdisciplinary Studies — M,O
Journalism — M
Landscape Architecture — M
Marriage and Family Therapy — M,D,O
Mass Communication — M
Music — M
National Security — M,D
Political Science — M
Psychology—General — M,D
Public Administration — M
Sociology — M,D
Spanish — M
Theater — M
Urban and Regional Planning — M
Women's Studies — O

KEAN UNIVERSITY
Addictions/Substance Abuse Counseling — M
Child and Family Studies — M
Clinical Psychology — M,D
Communication—General — M
Counseling Psychology — M
Criminal Justice and Criminology — M
Forensic Psychology — M
Holocaust and Genocide Studies — M
Industrial and Organizational Psychology — M
Liberal Studies — M
Marriage and Family Therapy — M
Psychology—General — M
Public Administration — M
School Psychology — D,O
Writing — M

KEENE STATE COLLEGE
School Psychology — M,O

KEHILATH YAKOV RABBINICAL SEMINARY
Theology — M

KEISER UNIVERSITY
Criminal Justice and Criminology — M
Homeland Security — M
Industrial and Organizational Psychology — M,D
Psychology—General — M,D

KENNESAW STATE UNIVERSITY
American Studies — M
Architecture — M
Communication—General — M
Conflict Resolution and Mediation/Peace Studies — M,D
Criminal Justice and Criminology — M
Ethics — O
International Affairs — M
Public Administration — M
Writing — M

KENRICK-GLENNON SEMINARY
Theology — M

KENT STATE UNIVERSITY
Anthropology — M
Architecture — M
Art History — M
Art/Fine Arts — M
Biological Anthropology — M,D
Child and Family Studies — M
Clinical Psychology — M,D
Communication—General — M
Conflict Resolution and Mediation/Peace Studies — M,D
Counseling Psychology — M
Criminal Justice and Criminology — M
Economics — M
English — M,D
Environmental Design — M
Experimental Psychology — M,D
French — M,D
Geographic Information Systems — M,D
Geography — M,D
German — M,D
Gerontology — M,D
Graphic Design — M
History — M,D
Human Development — M,D
Illustration — M
Japanese — M,D
Journalism — M
Landscape Architecture — M
Liberal Studies — M
Linguistics — M,D
Mass Communication — M
Media Studies — M

Music — M
Near and Middle Eastern Languages — M,D
Philosophy — M
Photography — M
Political Science — M
Psychology—General — M,D
Public Administration — M,D
Rehabilitation Counseling — M
Rhetoric — M,D
Russian — M
School Psychology — M,D,O
Sociology — M,D
Spanish — M,D
Textile Design — M
Theater — M
Translation and Interpretation — M,D
Urban Design — M
Writing — M

KENTUCKY CHRISTIAN UNIVERSITY
Religion — M
Theology — M

KENTUCKY STATE UNIVERSITY
Psychology—General — M
Public Administration — M,D

KEUKA COLLEGE
Criminal Justice and Criminology — M

THE KING'S UNIVERSITY
Pastoral Ministry and Counseling — M,D,O
Theology — M,D,O

KINGSWOOD UNIVERSITY
Pastoral Ministry and Counseling — M
Theology — M

KNOX COLLEGE
Theology — M,D

KNOX THEOLOGICAL SEMINARY
Classics — M
Pastoral Ministry and Counseling — D
Religion — M
Theology — M

KUTZTOWN UNIVERSITY OF PENNSYLVANIA
Arts Administration — M
Clinical Psychology — M
Counseling Psychology — M
English — M
Internet and Interactive Multimedia — M
Marriage and Family Therapy — M
Public Administration — M

LAGRANGE COLLEGE
Clinical Psychology — M

LAGUNA COLLEGE OF ART & DESIGN
Art/Fine Arts — M

LAKE FOREST COLLEGE
American Studies — M
Art/Fine Arts — M
Film, Television, and Video Production — M
French — M
History — M
Liberal Studies — M
Philosophy — M
Spanish — M
Writing — M

LAKEHEAD UNIVERSITY
Clinical Psychology — M,D
Economics — M
English — M
Experimental Psychology — M,D
Gerontology — M
History — M,D
Psychology—General — M,D
Sociology — M
Women's Studies — M,D

LAKELAND UNIVERSITY
Theology — M

LAMAR UNIVERSITY
Clinical Psychology — M
Counseling Psychology — M
Criminal Justice and Criminology — M
English — M
Family and Consumer Sciences-General — M
History — M
Industrial and Organizational Psychology — M
Music — M
Political Science — M
Psychology—General — M
Public Administration — M
Spanish — M

LANCASTER BIBLE COLLEGE
Counseling Psychology — M,D
Marriage and Family Therapy — M,D
Pastoral Ministry and Counseling — M,D,O
Theology — M

LANCASTER THEOLOGICAL SEMINARY
Art History — M,D,O
Ethics — M,D,O
Religion — M,D,O
Theology — M,D,O

LANDER UNIVERSITY
Emergency Management — M

LANGSTON UNIVERSITY
Rehabilitation Counseling — M

LA SALLE UNIVERSITY
American Studies — M,O
Clinical Psychology — M,D
Communication—General — M,O
Corporate and Organizational Communication — M,O
Counseling Psychology — M

Developmental Psychology — M,D
English — M,O
Forensic Sciences — M,O
Gerontology — M,D,O
Health Psychology — M,D
Hispanic Studies — M
History — M,O
Industrial and Organizational Psychology — M
Latin American Studies — M,O
Marriage and Family Therapy — M
Media Studies — M,O
Psychology—General — M,D
Public History — M,O
Translation and Interpretation — M,O
Western European Studies — M,O

LASELL COLLEGE
Communication—General — M,O
Corporate and Organizational Communication — M,O
Criminal Justice and Criminology — M,O
Emergency Management — M,O
Health Communication — M,O
Homeland Security — M,O

LA SIERRA UNIVERSITY
Communication—General — M
English — M
Pastoral Ministry and Counseling — M
Religion — M
School Psychology — M,O
Writing — M

LAURENTIAN UNIVERSITY
Applied Psychology — M
Applied Social Research — M
Experimental Psychology — M
History — M
Human Development — M
Humanities — M
Psychology—General — M
Sociology — M
Technical Writing — O

LAWRENCE TECHNOLOGICAL UNIVERSITY
Architecture — M,O
Communication—General — M,O
Interior Design — M,O
Technical Communication — M,O
Urban Design — M,O

LEBANESE AMERICAN UNIVERSITY
International Affairs — M

LEBANON VALLEY COLLEGE
Ethics — M

LEE UNIVERSITY
Art/Fine Arts — M,O
Child Development — M
Counseling Psychology — M
Economics — M,O
English — M,O
Ethics — M
History — M,O
Marriage and Family Therapy — M
Music — M
Pastoral Ministry and Counseling — M
Religion — M
Spanish — M
Theology — M

LEHIGH UNIVERSITY
African Studies — M,O
American Studies — M,D,O
Counseling Psychology — M,D,O
Economics — M,D
English — M,D
History — M,D
Interdisciplinary Studies — M,D
Political Science — M
Psychology—General — M,D
Public History — M,D
School Psychology — D,O
Sociology — M
Sustainable Development — M,O

LEHMAN COLLEGE OF THE CITY UNIVERSITY OF NEW YORK
Art/Fine Arts — M
English — M
History — M
Spanish — M

LE MOYNE COLLEGE
Arts Administration — M
Urban Studies — M,O

LENOIR-RHYNE UNIVERSITY
Addictions/Substance Abuse Counseling — M
Clinical Psychology — M
Counseling Psychology — M
Sustainable Development — M
Theology — M
Writing — M

LESLEY UNIVERSITY
Art Therapy — M,D,O
Art/Fine Arts — M,D,O
Clinical Psychology — M,D,O
Conflict Resolution and Mediation/Peace Studies — M,D,O
Counseling Psychology — M,D,O
Health Psychology — M,D,O
Interdisciplinary Studies — M,D,O
International Affairs — M,D,O
Photography — M
Psychology—General — M,D,O
School Psychology — M,D,O
Social Psychology — M,D,O
Sustainable Development — M,D,O
Therapies—Dance, Drama, and Music — M,D,O
Urban and Regional Planning — M,D,O
Women's Studies — M,D,O

Writing — M,D,O

LETOURNEAU UNIVERSITY
Counseling Psychology — M
Marriage and Family Therapy — M
Psychology—General — M
School Psychology — M

LEWIS & CLARK COLLEGE
Addictions/Substance Abuse Counseling — M
Counseling Psychology — M
Marriage and Family Therapy — M
School Psychology — M,O

LEWIS UNIVERSITY
Clinical Psychology — M
Counseling Psychology — M
Criminal Justice and Criminology — M

LEXINGTON THEOLOGICAL SEMINARY
Theology — M,D

LIBERTY UNIVERSITY
Addictions/Substance Abuse Counseling — M,D,O
Applied Psychology — M,D,O
Art/Fine Arts — M
Child and Family Studies — M,D,O
Clinical Psychology — M,D,O
Communication—General — M
Counseling Psychology — M,D,O
Criminal Justice and Criminology — M,D,O
Developmental Psychology — M,D,O
Emergency Management — M,D,O
English — M
Forensic Psychology — M
Graphic Design — M
History — M
Homeland Security — M
Industrial and Organizational Psychology — M,D,O
International Affairs — M,D
Internet and Interactive Multimedia — M
Marriage and Family Therapy — M,D,O
Military and Defense Studies — M,D
Missions and Missiology — M,D
Music — M,D
Pastoral Ministry and Counseling — M,D,O
Political Science — M
Psychology—General — M,D,O
Public Administration — M,D
Public Policy — M
Religion — M,D
School Psychology — M,D,O
Theology — M,D,O

LIM COLLEGE
Clothing and Textiles — M

LINCOLN CHRISTIAN SEMINARY
Pastoral Ministry and Counseling — M,D
Theology — M,D

LINCOLN CHRISTIAN UNIVERSITY
Cultural Studies — M
Pastoral Ministry and Counseling — M
Philosophy — M
Religion — M
Theology — M

LINCOLN UNIVERSITY (MO)
Criminal Justice and Criminology — M
History — M
Public Administration — M
Public Policy — M
Sociology — M

LINDENWOOD UNIVERSITY
Applied Behavior Analysis — M,D,O
Art History — M
Communication—General — M,O
Counseling Psychology — M,D,O
Criminal Justice and Criminology — M,O
Film, Television, and Video Production — M
Internet and Interactive Multimedia — M
Journalism — M
Mass Communication — M
Media Studies — M,O
Public Administration — M
School Psychology — M,D,O
Writing — M,O

LINDENWOOD UNIVERSITY–BELLEVILLE
Communication—General — M
Computer Art and Design — M
Criminal Justice and Criminology — M
Internet and Interactive Multimedia — M
Media Studies — M

LINDSEY WILSON COLLEGE
Counseling Psychology — M,D
Human Development — M,D
Internet and Interactive Multimedia — M

LIPSCOMB UNIVERSITY
Applied Behavior Analysis — M,D,O
Clinical Psychology — M,O
Conflict Resolution and Mediation/Peace Studies — M,O
Counseling Psychology — M,O
English — M,D,O
Film, Television, and Video Production — M
International Affairs — M,O
Marriage and Family Therapy — M,O
Pastoral Ministry and Counseling — M,D
Psychology—General — M,O
Public Administration — M
Public Policy — M
School Psychology — M,D,O
Sustainable Development — M,O
Theology — M,D

Writing | M

LOCK HAVEN UNIVERSITY OF PENNSYLVANIA
Clinical Psychology | M
Counseling Psychology | M
Sport Psychology | M

LOGOS EVANGELICAL SEMINARY
Theology | M,D,O

LOMA LINDA UNIVERSITY
Addictions/Substance Abuse Counseling | M,D,O
Applied Social Research | M,D
Child and Family Studies | M,D,O
Clinical Psychology | D
Criminal Justice and Criminology | M,D
Gerontology | M,D
Marriage and Family Therapy | M,D,O
Psychology—General | D
Religion | M

LONDON METROPOLITAN UNIVERSITY
Applied Psychology | M,D
Architecture | M,D
Arts Administration | M,D
Child and Family Studies | M,D
Clinical Psychology | M,D
Conflict Resolution and Mediation/Peace Studies | M,D
Counseling Psychology | M,D
Criminal Justice and Criminology | M,D
Emergency Management | M,D
Forensic Psychology | M,D
Homeland Security | M,D
Industrial and Organizational Psychology | M,D
International Affairs | M,D
Internet and Interactive Multimedia | M,D
Military and Defense Studies | M,D
Near and Middle Eastern Languages | M,D
Public Administration | M,D
Public Policy | M,D
Translation and Interpretation | M,D
Urban Design | M,D
Women's Studies | M,D
Writing | M,D

LONG ISLAND UNIVERSITY–BRENTWOOD CAMPUS
Clinical Psychology | M,O
Counseling Psychology | M,O
Criminal Justice and Criminology | M,O

LONG ISLAND UNIVERSITY–HUDSON
Addictions/Substance Abuse Counseling | M,O
Counseling Psychology | M,O
Marriage and Family Therapy | M,O
Public Administration | M,O
School Psychology | M,O

LONG ISLAND UNIVERSITY–LIU BROOKLYN
Applied Behavior Analysis | M,O
Clinical Psychology | M,D,O
Counseling Psychology | M,O
English | M,D,O
Forensic Sciences | M,D,O
Gerontology | M,O
Marriage and Family Therapy | M,O
Media Studies | M,D,O
Political Science | M,D,O
Psychology—General | M,D,O
Public Administration | M,O
Urban Studies | M,D,O
Writing | M,D,O

LONG ISLAND UNIVERSITY–LIU POST
Applied Behavior Analysis | M,O
Art Therapy | M
Art/Fine Arts | M
Clinical Psychology | M,D,O
Counseling Psychology | M,D,O
Criminal Justice and Criminology | M,O
English | M,O
Genetic Counseling | M,O
Gerontology | M,O
History | M,O
Interdisciplinary Studies | M,D,O
Internet and Interactive Multimedia | M
Museum Studies | M
Music | M
Political Science | M,O
Psychology—General | M,O
Public Administration | M,O
School Psychology | M,D,O
Sustainable Development | M,O
Theater | M

LONG ISLAND UNIVERSITY–RIVERHEAD
Applied Behavior Analysis | M,O
Homeland Security | M,O

LORAS COLLEGE
Applied Psychology | M
Pastoral Ministry and Counseling | M
Theology | M

LOUISIANA COLLEGE
Pastoral Ministry and Counseling | M
Theology | M

LOUISIANA STATE UNIVERSITY AND AGRICULTURAL & MECHANICAL COLLEGE
Agricultural Economics and Agribusiness | M,D
Anthropology | M,D

Applied Arts and Design—General | M
Architecture | M
Art History | M
Art/Fine Arts | M
Clinical Psychology | M,D
Cognitive Sciences | M,D
Communication—General | M,D
Comparative Literature | M,D
Developmental Psychology | M,D
Economics | M,D
English | M,D
Family and Consumer Sciences-General | M,D
French | M,D
Geography | M,D
Graphic Design | M
Hispanic Studies | M
History | M,D
Internet and Interactive Multimedia | M
Landscape Architecture | M
Liberal Studies | M
Mass Communication | M,D
Media Studies | M,D
Music | M
Philosophy | M
Photography | M
Political Science | M,D
Psychology—General | M,D
Public Administration | M,D
School Psychology | M,D
Sociology | M,D
Theater | M,D
Writing | M,D

LOUISIANA STATE UNIVERSITY HEALTH SCIENCES CENTER
Rehabilitation Counseling | M

LOUISIANA STATE UNIVERSITY IN SHREVEPORT
Liberal Studies | M
School Psychology | O

LOUISIANA TECH UNIVERSITY
Architecture | M,D,O
Art/Fine Arts | M,D,O
Clinical Psychology | M,D,O
Counseling Psychology | M,D,O
English | M,D,O
Graphic Design | M,D,O
History | M,D,O
Industrial and Organizational Psychology | M,D,O
Photography | M,D,O
Technical Writing | M,D,O

LOUISVILLE PRESBYTERIAN THEOLOGICAL SEMINARY
Religion | M,D
Theology | M,D

LOURDES UNIVERSITY
Theology | M

LOYOLA MARYMOUNT UNIVERSITY
Art/Fine Arts | M
Communication—General | M
Counseling Psychology | M
English | M
Film, Television, and Video Production | M
Marriage and Family Therapy | M
Pastoral Ministry and Counseling | M
Philosophy | M
School Psychology | M
Theology | M
Writing | M

LOYOLA UNIVERSITY CHICAGO
Clinical Psychology | M,D,O
Communication—General | M
Corporate and Organizational Communication | M
Counseling Psychology | M,D,O
Criminal Justice and Criminology | M
Developmental Psychology | M,D
Economics | M
English | M,D
Ethics | M
History | M,D
Humanities | M
Medieval and Renaissance Studies | M,D
Pastoral Ministry and Counseling | M,O
Philosophy | M,D
Political Science | M,D
Psychology—General | M,D
Public History | M,D
Public Policy | M
School Psychology | D,O
Social Psychology | M,O
Sociology | M,D
Spanish | M
Theology | M,D,O
Urban Studies | M

LOYOLA UNIVERSITY MARYLAND
Clinical Psychology | M,D,O
Counseling Psychology | M,D,O
Media Studies | M
Psychology—General | M,D,O
Theology | M

LOYOLA UNIVERSITY NEW ORLEANS
Clinical Psychology | M
Criminal Justice and Criminology | M
Marriage and Family Therapy | M
Music | M
Theology | M,O
Therapies—Dance, Drama, and Music | M

LUBBOCK CHRISTIAN UNIVERSITY
Theology | M

LUTHERAN SCHOOL OF THEOLOGY AT CHICAGO
Pastoral Ministry and Counseling | M,D
Theology | M,D

LUTHERAN THEOLOGICAL SEMINARY SASKATOON
Ethics | M,D
Pastoral Ministry and Counseling | M,D
Religion | M,D
Theology | M,D

LUTHER RICE COLLEGE & SEMINARY
Pastoral Ministry and Counseling | M,D
Religion | M,D
Theology | M,D

LUTHER SEMINARY
Missions and Missiology | M,D
Pastoral Ministry and Counseling | M,D
Theology | M,D

LYNN UNIVERSITY
Applied Psychology | M
Communication—General | M,O
Computer Art and Design | M,O
Counseling Psychology | M
Criminal Justice and Criminology | M
Graphic Design | M,O
Industrial and Organizational Psychology | M
Internet and Interactive Multimedia | M,O
Mass Communication | M,O
Media Studies | M,O
Music | M,O
Psychology—General | M

MACHZIKEI HADATH RABBINICAL COLLEGE
Theology | O

MADONNA UNIVERSITY
Clinical Psychology | M
Criminal Justice and Criminology | M
Liberal Studies | M
Pastoral Ministry and Counseling | M
Psychology—General | M
Theology | M

MAHARISHI UNIVERSITY OF MANAGEMENT
Asian Studies | M,D
Writing | M

MAINE COLLEGE OF ART
Art/Fine Arts | M

MALONE UNIVERSITY
Theology | M

MANHATTAN COLLEGE
Counseling Psychology | M,O
English | M,O
Marriage and Family Therapy | M

MANHATTAN SCHOOL OF MUSIC
Music | M,D,O

MANHATTANVILLE COLLEGE
Classics | M,O
Corporate and Organizational Communication | M,O
English | M,O
French | M,O
Italian | M,O
Spanish | M,O
Sustainable Development | M,O
Writing | M

MANSFIELD UNIVERSITY OF PENNSYLVANIA
Music | M
Psychology—General | M

MAPLE SPRINGS BAPTIST BIBLE COLLEGE AND SEMINARY
Pastoral Ministry and Counseling | M,D,O
Theology | M,D,O

MARANATHA BAPTIST UNIVERSITY
Cultural Studies | M
Pastoral Ministry and Counseling | M,D
Religion | M
Theology | M

MARIAN UNIVERSITY (IN)
Counseling Psychology | M

MARIAN UNIVERSITY (WI)
Thanatology | M

MARIETTA COLLEGE
Psychology—General | M

MARIST COLLEGE
Communication—General | M
Corporate and Organizational Communication | M
Counseling Psychology | M,O
Museum Studies | M
Psychology—General | M,O
Public Administration | M
School Psychology | M,O

MARQUETTE UNIVERSITY
Clinical Psychology | M,D
Communication—General | M,O
Counseling Psychology | M,O
Economics | M,D
English | M,D
Ethics | M,O
Health Communication | M,O
History | M,D
Interdisciplinary Studies | D

International Affairs | M,D
Journalism | M,O
Mass Communication | M,O
Philosophy | M,D
Political Science | M
Psychology—General | D
Social Psychology | M,D
Spanish | M
Speech and Interpersonal Communication | M,O
Theology | M,D

MARSHALL UNIVERSITY
Clinical Psychology | M,D,O
Communication—General | M
Criminal Justice and Criminology | M
English | M,O
Forensic Sciences | M,O
Geography | M,O
History | M,O
Humanities | M,O
Journalism | M,O
Music | M
Political Science | M
Psychology—General | M,D,O
Public Administration | M
School Psychology | O
Sociology | M

MARTIN UNIVERSITY
Pastoral Ministry and Counseling | M
Psychology—General | M
Social Psychology | M

MARY BALDWIN UNIVERSITY
English | M
Theater | M

MARYLAND INSTITUTE COLLEGE OF ART
Applied Arts and Design—General | M
Art/Fine Arts | M,O
Film, Television, and Video Production | M
Graphic Design | M
Illustration | M
Museum Studies | M
Photography | M

MARYMOUNT CALIFORNIA UNIVERSITY
International Development | M
Social Psychology | M

MARYMOUNT UNIVERSITY
Clinical Psychology | M
Counseling Psychology | M
English | M,O
Forensic Psychology | M
Interior Design | M
Pastoral Ministry and Counseling | M

MARYVILLE UNIVERSITY OF SAINT LOUIS
Addictions/Substance Abuse Counseling | M
Marriage and Family Therapy | M
Rehabilitation Counseling | M
Therapies—Dance, Drama, and Music | M

MARYWOOD UNIVERSITY
Architecture | M
Art Therapy | M,O
Art/Fine Arts | M
Clinical Psychology | M,D
Communication—General | M
Counseling Psychology | M
Criminal Justice and Criminology | M
Gerontology | M
Graphic Design | M
Human Development | D
Illustration | M
Interdisciplinary Studies | D
Interior Design | M
Photography | M
Psychology—General | M
Public Administration | M

MASSACHUSETTS COLLEGE OF ART AND DESIGN
Applied Arts and Design—General | M,O
Architecture | M
Art/Fine Arts | M,O
Film, Television, and Video Production | M,O
Interdisciplinary Studies | M,O
Media Studies | M,O
Photography | M,O
Textile Design | M,O

MASSACHUSETTS INSTITUTE OF TECHNOLOGY
Archaeology | M,D,O
Architectural History | M,D
Architecture | M,D
Art History | M,D
Cognitive Sciences | D
Economics | M,D
History of Science and Technology | D
Linguistics | D
Media Studies | M,D
Philosophy | D
Political Science | M,D
Social Sciences | D
Technical Writing | M
Urban and Regional Planning | M,D
Urban Studies | M,D
Writing | M

MASSACHUSETTS MARITIME ACADEMY
Emergency Management | M

*M—masters degree; D—doctorate; O—other advanced degree; *—Close-Up and/or Display*

THE MASTER'S UNIVERSITY
Pastoral Ministry and Counseling — M,D
Theology — M,D

MCCORMICK THEOLOGICAL SEMINARY
Pastoral Ministry and Counseling — M,D,O
Theology — M,D,O

MCDANIEL COLLEGE
Gerontology — M,O
Liberal Studies — M,O
Writing — M,O

MCGILL UNIVERSITY
Agricultural Economics and Agribusiness — M
Anthropology — M,D
Architecture — M,D,O
Art History — M,D
Asian Studies — M,D
Clinical Psychology — M,D
Communication—General — M,D
Counseling Psychology — M,D,O
Developmental Psychology — M,D,O
Economics — M,D
English — M,D
Experimental Psychology — M,D
Forensic Sciences — M,D,O
French — M,D
Genetic Counseling — M
Geography — M,D
German — M,D
Hispanic Studies — M,D
History of Medicine — M,D
History — M,D
International Development — M,D,O
Italian — M,D
Jewish Studies — M
Linguistics — M,D
Music — M,D
Near and Middle Eastern Studies — M,D,O
Philosophy — M,D
Political Science — M,D
Psychology—General — M,D
Religion — M,D
Russian — M,D
School Psychology — M,D,O
Sociology — M,D,O
Theology — M,D
Urban and Regional Planning — M,D

MCKENDREE UNIVERSITY
Clinical Psychology — M
Counseling Psychology — M

MCMASTER UNIVERSITY
Anthropology — M,D
Classics — M,D
Cultural Studies — M,D
Economics — M,D
English — M,D
French — M
Geography — M,D
History — M,D
Industrial and Labor Relations — M
International Affairs — M,D
Pastoral Ministry and Counseling — M,D,O
Philosophy — M,D
Political Science — M,D
Psychology—General — M,D
Public Administration — M,D
Public Affairs — M,D
Public Policy — M,D
Religion — M,D
Sociology — M,D
Theology — M,D,O

MCNEESE STATE UNIVERSITY
Applied Behavior Analysis — M,O
Counseling Psychology — M,O
Criminal Justice and Criminology — M
English — M
Experimental Psychology — M,O
Psychology—General — M,O
School Psychology — M,O
Writing — M

MEADVILLE LOMBARD THEOLOGICAL SCHOOL
Pastoral Ministry and Counseling — M,D
Theology — M,D

MEDAILLE COLLEGE
Clinical Psychology — M,D
Counseling Psychology — M,D
Marriage and Family Therapy — M,D
Psychology—General — M,D

MEMORIAL UNIVERSITY OF NEWFOUNDLAND
Anthropology — M,D
Archaeology — M,D
Classics — M
Clinical Psychology — M,D
Cultural Anthropology — M,D
Economics — M
English — M,D
Experimental Psychology — M,D
Folklore — M,D
French — M
Gender Studies — M,D
Geography — M,D
German — M
History — M,D
Humanities — M
Industrial and Labor Relations — M
Linguistics — M,D
Music — M,D
Philosophy — M,D
Political Science — M
Psychology—General — M
Religion — M
Sociology — M

MEMPHIS THEOLOGICAL SEMINARY
Theology — M,D

MERCER UNIVERSITY
Clinical Psychology — M,D
Criminal Justice and Criminology — M,D
Gerontology — M,D
Music — M
Pastoral Ministry and Counseling — M,D
Rehabilitation Counseling — M,D
School Psychology — M,D
Theology — M,D

MERCY COLLEGE
Counseling Psychology — M,O
English — M
Marriage and Family Therapy — M,O
Psychology—General — M
School Psychology — M

MERCYHURST UNIVERSITY
Anthropology — M
Applied Behavior Analysis — M
Archaeology — M
Biological Anthropology — M
Criminal Justice and Criminology — M
Forensic Sciences — M

MEREDITH COLLEGE
Industrial and Organizational Psychology — M
Psychology—General — M

MERRIMACK COLLEGE
Clinical Psychology — M,O
Criminal Justice and Criminology — M,O
Public Affairs — M,O
School Psychology — M,O
Theology — M,O

MESIVTA OF EASTERN PARKWAY–YESHIVA ZICHRON MEILECH
Theology

MESIVTA TORAH VODAATH RABBINICAL SEMINARY
Pastoral Ministry and Counseling — O
Theology — O

MESIVTHA TIFERETH JERUSALEM OF AMERICA
Theology

MESSIAH COLLEGE
Clinical Psychology — M,O
Counseling Psychology — M,O
Marriage and Family Therapy — M,O
Music — M

METHODIST THEOLOGICAL SCHOOL IN OHIO
Theology — M,D

METHODIST UNIVERSITY
Criminal Justice and Criminology — M

METROPOLITAN COLLEGE OF NEW YORK
Emergency Management — M
Media Studies — M
Public Administration — M
Public Affairs — M

METROPOLITAN STATE UNIVERSITY
Criminal Justice and Criminology — M
Liberal Studies — M
Technical Writing — M

MIAMI INTERNATIONAL UNIVERSITY OF ART & DESIGN
Applied Arts and Design—General — M
Film, Television, and Video Production — M

MIAMI UNIVERSITY
Architecture — M
Art/Fine Arts — M
Child and Family Studies — M
Demography and Population Studies — M,D
Economics — M
English — M,D
French — M
Geography — M
Gerontology — M,D
History — M
Interior Design — M
Music — M
Philosophy — M
Political Science — M
Psychology—General — M,D
Theater — M

MICHIGAN SCHOOL OF PROFESSIONAL PSYCHOLOGY
Clinical Psychology — M,D
Psychology—General — M,D
Transpersonal and Humanistic Psychology — M,D

MICHIGAN STATE UNIVERSITY
African Studies — M,D
African-American Studies — M,D
Agricultural Economics and Agribusiness — M,D
American Studies — M,D
Anthropology — M,D
Art/Fine Arts — M
Child and Family Studies — M,D
Child Development — M,D
Communication—General — M,D
Computer Art and Design — M
Criminal Justice and Criminology — M,D
Economics — M,D
English — M,D
Environmental Design — M,D
Forensic Sciences — M,D
French — M,D
Geography — M,D
German — M,D
Health Communication — M

Hispanic and Latin American Languages — M,D
Hispanic Studies — M,D
History — M,D
Industrial and Labor Relations — M,D
Interior Design — M,D
Journalism — M
Latin American Studies — D
Linguistics — M,D
Marriage and Family Therapy — M,D
Media Studies — M,D
Music — M,D
Philosophy — M,D
Political Science — M,D
Portuguese — M,D
Psychology—General — M,D
Rehabilitation Counseling — M,D,O
Rhetoric — M,D
Romance Languages — M,D
School Psychology — M,D,O
Sociology — M,D
Spanish — M,D
Theater — M
Therapies—Dance, Drama, and Music — M,D
Urban and Regional Planning — M,D
Writing — M,D

MICHIGAN TECHNOLOGICAL UNIVERSITY
Archaeology — M,D
Cognitive Sciences — M,D,O
Cultural Studies — M,D
Geographic Information Systems — M
Interdisciplinary Studies — M,D,O
Mineral Economics — M,D
Rhetoric — M,D

MID-AMERICA BAPTIST THEOLOGICAL SEMINARY
Missions and Missiology — M,D
Pastoral Ministry and Counseling — M,D
Theology — M,D

MID-AMERICA BAPTIST THEOLOGICAL SEMINARY NORTHEAST BRANCH
Theology — M

MID-AMERICA CHRISTIAN UNIVERSITY
Counseling Psychology — M
Marriage and Family Therapy — M
Pastoral Ministry and Counseling — M
Public Administration — M

MIDAMERICA NAZARENE UNIVERSITY
Clinical Psychology — M
Marriage and Family Therapy — M
School Psychology — M

MID-AMERICA REFORMED SEMINARY
Theology — M

MIDDLEBURY COLLEGE
Chinese — M
English — M,D
French — M,D
German — M,D
Italian — M,D
Near and Middle Eastern Languages — M
Russian — M,D
Spanish — M,D

MIDDLEBURY INSTITUTE OF INTERNATIONAL STUDIES AT MONTEREY
Conflict Resolution and Mediation/Peace Studies — M
International Affairs — M
International Development — M
International Trade Policy — M
Public Administration — M
Translation and Interpretation — M

MIDDLE GEORGIA STATE UNIVERSITY
Forensic Sciences — M

MIDDLE TENNESSEE STATE UNIVERSITY
Clinical Psychology — M,O
Counseling Psychology — M
Criminal Justice and Criminology — M
Economics — M,D
English — M,D
Experimental Psychology — M,O
French — M
Gender Studies — O
German — M
Gerontology — O
History — M
Industrial and Organizational Psychology — M,O
International Affairs — M
Mass Communication — M
Music — M
Political Science — M
Psychology—General — M,O
Public History — D
School Psychology — M,O
Sociology — M
Spanish — M
Women's Studies — O

MIDWESTERN BAPTIST THEOLOGICAL SEMINARY
Music — M,D,O
Pastoral Ministry and Counseling — M,D,O
Theology — M,D,O

MIDWESTERN STATE UNIVERSITY
Clinical Psychology — M
Counseling Psychology — M
Criminal Justice and Criminology — M,O
English — M
History — M
Philosophy — M,D
Political Science — M

MIDWESTERN UNIVERSITY, DOWNERS GROVE CAMPUS
Clinical Psychology — M,D

MIDWESTERN UNIVERSITY, GLENDALE CAMPUS
Clinical Psychology — D

MILLERSVILLE UNIVERSITY OF PENNSYLVANIA
Applied Arts and Design—General — M
Art/Fine Arts — M
Clinical Psychology — M
Emergency Management — M
English — M,O
French — M
Geographic Information Systems — M
German — M
History — M
Psychology—General — M
School Psychology — M
Spanish — M
Writing — M,O

MILLIGAN COLLEGE
Clinical Psychology — M,O
Missions and Missiology — M,D,O
Pastoral Ministry and Counseling — M,D,O
Religion — M,D,O
Theology — M,D,O

MILLS COLLEGE
Applied Economics — M
Art/Fine Arts — M
Dance — M
English — M,O
Illustration — M,O
Interdisciplinary Studies — M,O
Music — M
Photography — M
Public Policy — M
Translation and Interpretation — M,O
Writing — M,O

MINNEAPOLIS COLLEGE OF ART AND DESIGN
Applied Arts and Design—General — M
Art/Fine Arts — M,O
Computer Art and Design — O
Film, Television, and Video Production — M
Graphic Design — M,O
Illustration — M
Internet and Interactive Multimedia — M
Photography — M
Sustainable Development — M,O

MINNESOTA STATE UNIVERSITY MANKATO
Anthropology — M
Art/Fine Arts — M
Clinical Psychology — M,D
Communication—General — M,O
Corporate and Organizational Communication — M,O
Counseling Psychology — M,D
Criminal Justice and Criminology — M
English — M,O
Ethnic Studies — M
French — M
Gender Studies — M
Geography — M
Gerontology — M
History — M
Industrial and Organizational Psychology — M,D
Interdisciplinary Studies — M
Music — M
Psychology—General — M,D
Public Administration — M
Rehabilitation Counseling — M
School Psychology — M,D
Sociology — M
Spanish — M
Technical Communication — M,O
Theater — M
Urban and Regional Planning — M,O
Urban Studies — M,O
Women's Studies — M
Writing — M,O

MINNESOTA STATE UNIVERSITY MOORHEAD
School Psychology — M,O

MINOT STATE UNIVERSITY
School Psychology — O

MIRRER YESHIVA CENTRAL INSTITUTE
Theology

MISSISSIPPI COLLEGE
Art/Fine Arts — M
Communication—General — M
Corporate and Organizational Communication — M
Counseling Psychology — M,O
Criminal Justice and Criminology — M,O
English — M
History — M,O
Liberal Studies — M
Marriage and Family Therapy — M,O
Music — M
Political Science — M,O
Social Sciences — M,O

MISSISSIPPI STATE UNIVERSITY
Agricultural Economics and Agribusiness — M
Anthropology — M,D
Applied Psychology — M,D
Child and Family Studies — M,D
Clinical Psychology — M,D,O
Clothing and Textiles — M,D

Cognitive Sciences — M,D
Communication—General — M,D
Economics — M,D
English — M
Geography — M,D
History — M,D
Human Development — M,D
Landscape Architecture — M
Political Science — M,D
Psychology—General — M,D
Public Administration — M,D
Public Policy — M,D
Rehabilitation Counseling — M,D,O
School Psychology — M,D,O
Sociology — M,D
Sustainable Development — M,D

MISSISSIPPI VALLEY STATE UNIVERSITY
Criminal Justice and Criminology — M

MISSOURI BAPTIST UNIVERSITY
Pastoral Ministry and Counseling — M,O

MISSOURI SOUTHERN STATE UNIVERSITY
Criminal Justice and Criminology — M

MISSOURI STATE UNIVERSITY
Applied Behavior Analysis — M,O
Art/Fine Arts — M
Child and Family Studies — M
Clinical Psychology — M,O
Communication—General — M,O
Counseling Psychology — M
Criminal Justice and Criminology — M,O
English — M,O
Experimental Psychology — M,O
Film, Television, and Video
  Production — M,O
Geography — M,O
History — M,O
Homeland Security — M,O
Industrial and Organizational
  Psychology — M,O
International Affairs — M
Military and Defense Studies — M,O
Music — M
Political Science — M,O
Psychology—General — M,O
Public Administration — M,O
Religion — M,O
Theater — M
Urban and Regional Planning — M,O
Writing — M

MISSOURI UNIVERSITY OF SCIENCE AND TECHNOLOGY
Industrial and Organizational
  Psychology — M
Technical Communication — M

MISSOURI VALLEY COLLEGE
Social Psychology — M

MISSOURI WESTERN STATE UNIVERSITY
Forensic Sciences — M,O
Media Studies — M,O
Rhetoric — M,O
Technical Communication — M,O
Writing — M,O

MOLLOY COLLEGE
Clinical Psychology — M
Criminal Justice and Criminology — M
Therapies—Dance, Drama, and
  Music — M

MONMOUTH UNIVERSITY
Addictions/Substance Abuse
  Counseling — M,O
American Studies — M
Anthropology — M
Applied Behavior Analysis — M,D,O
Communication—General — M,O
Corporate and Organizational
  Communication — M,O
Counseling Psychology — M,O
Criminal Justice and Criminology — M,O
English — M
History — M
Homeland Security — M,O
Media Studies — M,O
Psychology—General — M,O
Rhetoric — M
School Psychology — M,D,O
Western European Studies — M
Writing — M

MONROE COLLEGE
Criminal Justice and Criminology — M

MONTANA STATE UNIVERSITY
American Indian/Native American
  Studies — M
Architecture — M
Art History — M
Art/Fine Arts — M
English — M
Film, Television, and Video
  Production — M
History — M,D
Human Development — M
Psychology—General — M
Public Administration — M
School Psychology — M,D,O

MONTANA STATE UNIVERSITY BILLINGS
Applied Behavior Analysis — M
Communication—General — M
Counseling Psychology — M
Interdisciplinary Studies — M
Psychology—General — M

Rehabilitation Counseling — M

MONTANA TECH OF THE UNIVERSITY OF MONTANA
Interdisciplinary Studies — M
Technical Communication — M

MONTCLAIR STATE UNIVERSITY
Addictions/Substance Abuse
  Counseling — O
Art/Fine Arts — M
Arts Administration — M
Child and Family Studies — M,D,O
Child Development — M,O
Clinical Psychology — M
Conflict Resolution and
  Mediation/Peace Studies — M,O
Corporate and Organizational
  Communication — M
Disability Studies — M,O
English — M
Forensic Psychology — O
French — M
Geographic Information Systems — O
Industrial and Organizational
  Psychology — M
Linguistics — M,O
Music — M,O
Political Science — M,O
Psychology—General — M
Social Sciences — M
Spanish — M
Sustainable Development — M
Theater — M
Therapies—Dance, Drama, and
  Music — M,O
Translation and Interpretation — O
Writing — O

MOODY BIBLE INSTITUTE
Pastoral Ministry and Counseling — M,O
Theology — M,O
Urban Studies — M,O

MOODY THEOLOGICAL SEMINARY–MICHIGAN
Counseling Psychology — M,O
Religion — M,O
Theology — M,O

MOORE COLLEGE OF ART & DESIGN
Art/Fine Arts — M
Arts Administration — M
Communication—General — M
Interior Design — M

MORAVIAN THEOLOGICAL SEMINARY
Theology — M,O

MOREHEAD STATE UNIVERSITY
Art/Fine Arts — M
Clinical Psychology — M
Communication—General — M
Counseling Psychology — M
Criminal Justice and Criminology — M
English — M
Experimental Psychology — M
Gerontology — M
Graphic Design — M
Music — M
Psychology—General — M
Public Administration — M
Public Policy — M
Sociology — M

MORGAN STATE UNIVERSITY
African-American Studies — M,D
Architecture — M
Economics — M
English — M,D
Historic Preservation — M,D
History — M,D
International Affairs — M
Landscape Architecture — M
Museum Studies — M,D
Music — M
Psychology—General — M,D
Sociology — M
Urban and Regional Planning — M

MOUNT ALOYSIUS COLLEGE
Social Psychology — M

MOUNT ANGEL SEMINARY
Theology — M

MOUNT MARTY COLLEGE
Pastoral Ministry and Counseling — M

MOUNT MARY UNIVERSITY
Art Therapy — M,D
Clinical Psychology — M,O
Counseling Psychology — M,O
English — M
Internet and Interactive
  Multimedia — M
Rehabilitation Counseling — M,O
Writing — M

MOUNT MERCY UNIVERSITY
Criminal Justice and Criminology — M
Marriage and Family Therapy — M

MOUNT ST. JOSEPH UNIVERSITY
Pastoral Ministry and Counseling — M,O
Religion — M,O
Theology — M,O

MOUNT SAINT MARY COLLEGE
Child Development — M,O

MOUNT SAINT MARY'S UNIVERSITY (CA)
Counseling Psychology — M,D,O
English — M,D,O

Film, Television, and Video
  Production — M,D,O
Humanities — M,D,O
Religion — M,D,O
Writing — M,D,O

MOUNT ST. MARY'S UNIVERSITY (MD)
Philosophy — M
Theology — M

MOUNT SAINT VINCENT UNIVERSITY
Child and Family Studies — M
Gerontology — M
School Psychology — M
Women's Studies — M

MOUNT VERNON NAZARENE UNIVERSITY
Theology — M

MULTNOMAH UNIVERSITY
Theology — M,D

MURRAY STATE UNIVERSITY
Clinical Psychology — M,O
Corporate and Organizational
  Communication — M
Economic Development — M
Economics — M
English — M,D,O
Experimental Psychology — M,O
Gender Studies — M,D,O
History — M,D,O
Human Development — M,D,O
Interdisciplinary Studies — M,O
Journalism — M
Mass Communication — M
Music — M
Political Science — M
Psychology—General — M,O
School Psychology — M,D,O
Sociology — M
Writing — M,D,O

NAROPA UNIVERSITY
Art Therapy — M
Counseling Psychology — M
Psychoanalysis and Psychotherapy — M
Psychology—General — M
Religion — M
Theater — M
Theology — M
Therapies—Dance, Drama, and
  Music — M
Writing — M

NASHOTAH HOUSE THEOLOGICAL SEMINARY
Pastoral Ministry and Counseling — M,D,O
Religion — M,D,O
Theology — M,D,O

NATIONAL AMERICAN UNIVERSITY (TX)
Criminal Justice and Criminology — M,D

NATIONAL DEFENSE UNIVERSITY
Homeland Security — M
Military and Defense Studies — M
National Security — M

THE NATIONAL GRADUATE SCHOOL OF QUALITY MANAGEMENT
Homeland Security — M,D

NATIONAL INTELLIGENCE UNIVERSITY
Military and Defense Studies — M

NATIONAL LOUIS UNIVERSITY
Human Development — M,D,O
Psychology—General — M,D,O
Public Policy — M,D,O
School Psychology — M,D,O
Writing — M,D,O

NATIONAL UNIVERSITY
Applied Behavior Analysis — M,O
Clinical Psychology — M,O
Counseling Psychology — M,O
Criminal Justice and Criminology — M
Emergency Management — M
English — M,O
Film, Television, and Video
  Production — M
Film, Television, and Video
  Theory and Criticism — M,O
Forensic Sciences — M,O
Homeland Security — M
Internet and Interactive
  Multimedia — M
Journalism — M
Marriage and Family Therapy — M,O
Public Administration — M
School Psychology — M,O
Writing — M

NAVAJO TECHNICAL UNIVERSITY
American Indian/Native American
  Studies — M

NAVAL POSTGRADUATE SCHOOL
Conflict Resolution and
  Mediation/Peace Studies — M,D
Geographic Information Systems — M,D,O
Homeland Security — M,D
Military and Defense Studies — M,D
National Security — M,D,O

NAVAL WAR COLLEGE
National Security — M

NAZARENE THEOLOGICAL SEMINARY
Cultural Studies — M,D,O
Theology — M,D,O

NAZARETH COLLEGE OF ROCHESTER
Art Therapy — M
Music — M

Therapies—Dance, Drama, and
  Music — M

NEBRASKA WESLEYAN UNIVERSITY
Forensic Sciences — M
History — M

NER ISRAEL RABBINICAL COLLEGE
Theology — M,D,O

NER ISRAEL YESHIVA COLLEGE OF TORONTO
Theology — M

NEUMANN UNIVERSITY
Clinical Psychology — M,D,O
Pastoral Ministry and Counseling — M,D,O

NEW BRUNSWICK THEOLOGICAL SEMINARY
Pastoral Ministry and Counseling — M,D
Theology — M,D

NEW CHARTER UNIVERSITY
Criminal Justice and Criminology — M
Public Administration — M

NEW ENGLAND COLLEGE
Counseling Psychology — M
International Affairs — M
Public Policy — M
Writing — M

NEW ENGLAND COLLEGE OF BUSINESS AND FINANCE
Ethics — M

NEW ENGLAND CONSERVATORY OF MUSIC
Music — M,D,O

NEW ENGLAND INSTITUTE OF TECHNOLOGY
Applied Arts and Design—
  General — M

NEW HAMPSHIRE INSTITUTE OF ART
Art/Fine Arts — M
Photography — M
Writing — M

NEW JERSEY CITY UNIVERSITY
Art/Fine Arts — M
Criminal Justice and Criminology — M,D,O
Music — M
National Security — M,D,O
Urban Studies — M

NEW JERSEY INSTITUTE OF TECHNOLOGY
Architecture — M,D
Emergency Management — M,D,O
History — M,D,O
Sustainable Development — M,D,O
Technical Communication — M,D,O
Urban Studies — M

NEWMAN THEOLOGICAL COLLEGE
Theology — M

NEWMAN UNIVERSITY
Theology — M

NEW MEXICO HIGHLANDS UNIVERSITY
American Studies — M
Anthropology — M
Clinical Psychology — M
Computer Art and Design — M
Counseling Psychology — M
English — M
History — M
Internet and Interactive
  Multimedia — M
Media Studies — M
Political Science — M
Psychology—General — M
Public Affairs — M
Rhetoric — M
Sociology — M
Writing — M

NEW MEXICO STATE UNIVERSITY
Agricultural Economics and
  Agribusiness — M,D
Anthropology — M,O
Art History — M
Art/Fine Arts — M
Clothing and Textiles — M
Communication—General — M
Corporate and Organizational
  Communication — M,D
Counseling Psychology — M,D,O
Criminal Justice and Criminology — M,D,O
Cultural Studies — M,D,O
Dance — M,D,O
Economic Development — M,D,O
Economics — M,D,O
English — M,D
Family and Consumer
  Sciences-General — M
Geography — M
History — M
Interdisciplinary Studies — M,D
Museum Studies — M,O
Music — M
Political Science — M
Psychology—General — M,D
Public Administration — M
Rhetoric — M,D
School Psychology — M,D,O
Sociology — M
Spanish — M,D,O
Writing — M,D

NEW ORLEANS BAPTIST THEOLOGICAL SEMINARY
Music — M,D

---

*M—masters degree; D—doctorate; O—other advanced degree; *—Close-Up and/or Display*

Pastoral Ministry and Counseling M,D
Theology M,D

NEW SAINT ANDREWS COLLEGE
Religion M,O
Theology M,O
Writing M,O

THE NEW SCHOOL
Anthropology M,D
Applied Arts and Design—
    General M
Applied Social Research M,D
Architecture M
Art/Fine Arts M
Clinical Psychology M,D
Clothing and Textiles M
Cognitive Sciences M
Computer Art and Design M
Economics M,D
History M
Industrial Design M
Interior Design M
International Affairs M
International Economics M,D
Internet and Interactive
    Multimedia M
Liberal Studies M
Lighting Design M
Media Studies M,O
Museum Studies M
Music M,O
Philosophy M,D
Photography M
Political Science M,D
Psychoanalysis and Psychotherapy M,D
Psychology—General M,D
Public Policy M,D
Social Psychology M,D
Social Sciences M,D
Sociology M,D
Textile Design M
Theater M
Urban Design M
Writing M

NEWSCHOOL OF ARCHITECTURE AND DESIGN
Architecture M

NEW YORK ACADEMY OF ART
Art/Fine Arts M

NEW YORK FILM ACADEMY
Film, Television, and Video
    Production M
Photography M

NEW YORK INSTITUTE OF TECHNOLOGY
Applied Arts and Design—
    General M
Architecture M
Art/Fine Arts M
Communication—General M
Computer Art and Design M
Graphic Design M
Industrial and Labor Relations M,O
Interdisciplinary Studies M,O
Urban Design M

NEW YORK MEDICAL COLLEGE
Emergency Management M,D,O
Psychology—General M,D,O

NEW YORK SCHOOL OF INTERIOR DESIGN
Interior Design M
Lighting Design M
Sustainable Development M

NEW YORK STUDIO SCHOOL OF DRAWING, PAINTING AND SCULPTURE
Art/Fine Arts M,O*

NEW YORK THEOLOGICAL SEMINARY
Theology M,D

NEW YORK UNIVERSITY
African Studies M,D,O
American Studies M,D
Anthropology M,D
Applied Arts and Design—
    General M
Applied Economics M,D,O
Applied Psychology M,D,O
Applied Social Research M
Archaeology M,D
Architectural History M
Art History M,D
Art Therapy M
Art/Fine Arts M,D,O
Arts Administration M
Asian Studies M,D
Chinese M,D,O
Classics M,D,O
Cognitive Sciences M,D,O
Communication—General M,D
Comparative Literature M,D
Conflict Resolution and
    Mediation/Peace Studies M
Corporate and Organizational
    Communication M
Counseling Psychology M,D,O
Cultural Studies M,D,O
Dance M,D,O
Demography and Population Studies M,D
Developmental Psychology M,D
Economics M,D,O
English M,D
Film, Television, and Video
    Production M
Film, Television, and Video
    Theory and Criticism M,D
French M,D,O
Gender Studies M
German M,D
Historic Preservation M

History M,D,O
Human Development M,D,O
Humanities M,O
Industrial and Organizational
    Psychology M,D,O
Interdisciplinary Studies M
International Affairs M,D
Internet and Interactive
    Multimedia M
Italian M,D,O
Japanese M,D,O
Jewish Studies M,D,O
Journalism M,D,O
Latin American Studies M,O
Linguistics M,D
Media Studies M,D
Museum Studies M,O
Music M,D,O
Near and Middle Eastern Studies M,D
Philosophy M,D
Political Science M,D
Portuguese M,D
Psychoanalysis and Psychotherapy M,D,O
Psychology—General M,D,O
Public Administration M,D,O
Public History M,D,O
Public Policy M
Publishing M
Religion M,O
Romance Languages M,D
Russian M
Slavic Languages M
Social Psychology M,D,O
Social Sciences M,D
Sociology M,D,O
Spanish M,D,O
Speech and Interpersonal
    Communication M,D
Sustainable Development M
Theater M,D,O
Therapies—Dance, Drama, and
    Music M
Translation and Interpretation M
Urban and Regional Planning M
Urban Studies M
Western European Studies M
Writing M

NIAGARA UNIVERSITY
Applied Behavior Analysis M,D,O
Counseling Psychology M,D,O
Criminal Justice and Criminology M
Forensic Sciences M
Interdisciplinary Studies M
School Psychology M

NICHOLLS STATE UNIVERSITY
Clinical Psychology M,O
School Psychology M,O

NICHOLS COLLEGE
Homeland Security M

NORFOLK STATE UNIVERSITY
Art/Fine Arts M
Clinical Psychology M
Communication—General M
Criminal Justice and Criminology M
Media Studies M
Music M
Psychology—General M,D
Social Psychology M
Urban Studies M

NORTH CAROLINA AGRICULTURAL AND TECHNICAL STATE UNIVERSITY
African-American Studies M
Agricultural Economics and
    Agribusiness M
Applied Economics M
Child and Family Studies M
Child Development M
Computer Art and Design M
Consumer Economics M
English M
Graphic Design M

NORTH CAROLINA CENTRAL UNIVERSITY
Clinical Psychology M
Criminal Justice and Criminology M
English M
Geographic Information Systems M
History M
Music M
Psychology—General M
Public Administration M

NORTH CAROLINA STATE UNIVERSITY
Agricultural Economics and
    Agribusiness M
Anthropology M
Applied Arts and Design—
    General M,D
Architecture M
Clothing and Textiles D
Communication—General M
Computer Art and Design D
Cultural Anthropology M
Developmental Psychology M,D
Economics M,D
English M
Experimental Psychology M
French M
Geographic Information Systems M,D
Graphic Design M
History M
Industrial and Organizational
    Psychology D
Industrial Design M
International Affairs M
Landscape Architecture M
Liberal Studies M
Psychology—General D
Public Administration M,D
Public History M

Rhetoric D
School Psychology D
Social Psychology M
Sociology M,D
Spanish M
Technical Communication M
Writing M

NORTH CENTRAL COLLEGE
Cultural Studies M
Liberal Studies M

NORTHCENTRAL UNIVERSITY
Marriage and Family Therapy M,D,O
Psychology—General M,D,O

NORTH DAKOTA STATE UNIVERSITY
Agricultural Economics and
    Agribusiness M
Anthropology M
Architecture M
Child and Family Studies M,D,O*
Child Development M
Clinical Psychology M,D
Clothing and Textiles M,O
Cognitive Sciences M,D
Communication—General M,D
Consumer Economics M,O
Counseling Psychology M,D
Criminal Justice and Criminology M,D
Developmental Psychology D
English M,D
Family and Consumer
    Sciences-General M
Gerontology M,O
Health Psychology M,D
History M,D
Marriage and Family Therapy D
Mass Communication M,D
Music M,D
Psychology—General M,D
Rhetoric M,D*
School Psychology M,D
Social Psychology M,D
Social Sciences M
Sociology M
Speech and Interpersonal
    Communication M,D
Urban and Regional Planning M
Urban Studies M,D
Writing M,D

NORTHEASTERN ILLINOIS UNIVERSITY
English M
Geographic Information Systems M,O
Geography M,O
Gerontology M
History M
Latin American Studies M
Linguistics M
Marriage and Family Therapy M
Music M
Political Science M
Rehabilitation Counseling M
Speech and Interpersonal
    Communication M

NORTHEASTERN SEMINARY AT ROBERTS WESLEYAN COLLEGE
Theology M,D

NORTHEASTERN STATE UNIVERSITY
American Indian/Native American
    Studies M
Communication—General M
Criminal Justice and Criminology M
English M
Psychology—General M

NORTHEASTERN UNIVERSITY
Applied Arts and Design—
    General M
Applied Behavior Analysis M,D,O
Architecture M
Art/Fine Arts M
Corporate and Organizational
    Communication M
Counseling Psychology M,D,O
Criminal Justice and Criminology M,D
Economic Development M
Economics M,D
English M,D
Geographic Information Systems M
History M,D
Homeland Security M,D
Interdisciplinary Studies M,D,O
International Affairs M,D
Internet and Interactive
    Multimedia M
Journalism M
Political Science M,D
Psychology—General M,D
Public Administration M,D
Public Policy M,D,O
School Psychology M,D,O
Sociology M,D
Technical Communication M
Urban Studies M,D

NORTHEAST OHIO MEDICAL UNIVERSITY
Humanities M,D,O

NORTHERN ARIZONA UNIVERSITY
American Indian/Native American
    Studies O
Anthropology M
Communication—General M,O
Counseling Psychology M,D,O
Criminal Justice and Criminology M,O
English M,D,O
Ethnic Studies O
Gender Studies O
Geographic Information Systems M,O
Geography M,O
History M
Human Development O

Liberal Studies M
Linguistics M,D,O
Music M,O
Political Science M,D,O
Psychology—General M
Public Administration M,D,O
Rhetoric M,D,O
School Psychology M,D,O
Sociology M
Spanish M
Sustainable Development M
Urban and Regional Planning M,O
Women's Studies O
Writing M,D,O

NORTHERN ILLINOIS UNIVERSITY
Anthropology M
Art/Fine Arts M
Child and Family Studies M
Communication—General M
Dance M
Economics M,D
English M,D
French M
Geography M,D
History M,D
Music M,O
Philosophy M
Political Science M,D
Psychology—General M,D
Public Administration M
Romance Languages M
Sociology M
Spanish M
Theater M

NORTHERN KENTUCKY UNIVERSITY
Clinical Psychology M
Communication—General M,O
Counseling Psychology M
Cultural Studies M,O
English M,O
Geographic Information Systems M
Health Psychology M,O
Industrial and Organizational
    Psychology M,O
Liberal Studies M
Marriage and Family Therapy M,O
Media Studies M
Public Administration M,O
Public History M
Rhetoric M,O
Writing M,O

NORTHERN MICHIGAN UNIVERSITY
Applied Behavior Analysis M
English M,O
Psychology—General M
Theater M,O
Writing M,O

NORTHERN SEMINARY
Missions and Missiology M,D
Pastoral Ministry and Counseling M,D
Religion M,D
Theology M,D

NORTHERN STATE UNIVERSITY
Clinical Psychology M
Counseling Psychology M

NORTHERN VERMONT UNIVERSITY–JOHNSON
Addictions/Substance Abuse
    Counseling M
Applied Behavior Analysis M
Art/Fine Arts M
Computer Art and Design M
Photography M
School Psychology M

NORTH GREENVILLE UNIVERSITY
Pastoral Ministry and Counseling M,D

NORTH PARK THEOLOGICAL SEMINARY
Pastoral Ministry and Counseling M,O
Theology M,D

NORTH PARK UNIVERSITY
Music M

NORTHWEST CHRISTIAN UNIVERSITY
Counseling Psychology M

NORTHWESTERN OKLAHOMA STATE UNIVERSITY
American Studies M
Counseling Psychology M

NORTHWESTERN STATE UNIVERSITY OF LOUISIANA
Art/Fine Arts M
Clinical Psychology M
English M
Homeland Security M
Music M
Psychology—General M

NORTHWESTERN UNIVERSITY
African Studies O
African-American Studies D
American Studies M
Anthropology D
Art History D
Art/Fine Arts M
Arts Administration M
Broadcast Journalism M
Clinical Psychology D
Cognitive Sciences M
Communication—General M,D
Comparative Literature M,D
Corporate and Organizational
    Communication M,D
Economics D
English M,D
Ethics M

Film, Television, and Video
  Production — M,D
French — D,O
Gender Studies — O
Genetic Counseling — M
German — D
History — M,D
Human Development — D
International Affairs — M,D,O
Internet and Interactive
  Multimedia — M
Italian — D,O
Journalism — M
Liberal Studies — M
Linguistics — D
Marriage and Family Therapy — M
Media Studies — M,D
Music — M,D
Philosophy — D
Political Science — D
Portuguese — D
Psychology—General — D
Public Administration — M
Public Policy — M,D
Publishing — M
Religion — M,D
Rhetoric — M,D
Slavic Languages — D
Social Psychology — D
Sociology — M,D
Spanish — D
Speech and Interpersonal
  Communication — M,D
Theater — M,D
Writing — M

NORTHWEST MISSOURI STATE UNIVERSITY
Agricultural Economics and
  Agribusiness — M
English — M,O
Geographic Information Systems — M,O

NORTHWEST NAZARENE UNIVERSITY
Addictions/Substance Abuse
  Counseling — M
Clinical Psychology — M
Marriage and Family Therapy — M
Missions and Missiology — M
Pastoral Ministry and Counseling — M
Religion — M
School Psychology — M
Theology — M

NORTHWEST UNIVERSITY
Counseling Psychology — M,D
Cultural Studies — M
Missions and Missiology — M
Pastoral Ministry and Counseling — M
Psychology—General — M,D
Theology — M
Urban and Regional Planning — M,D

NORWICH UNIVERSITY
Conflict Resolution and
  Mediation/Peace Studies — M
Criminal Justice and Criminology — M
Emergency Management — M
History — M
International Affairs — M
International Development — M
Military and Defense Studies — M
Public Administration — M
Public Policy — M

NOTRE DAME COLLEGE (OH)
Homeland Security — M,O

NOTRE DAME DE NAMUR UNIVERSITY
Art Therapy — M,D
Clinical Psychology — M
Marriage and Family Therapy — M
Public Administration — M
Public Affairs — M

NOTRE DAME OF MARYLAND UNIVERSITY
Communication—General — M
Liberal Studies — M

NOTRE DAME SEMINARY
Theology — M

NOVA SOUTHEASTERN UNIVERSITY
Addictions/Substance Abuse
  Counseling — M,D,O
Art/Fine Arts — M,D,O
Clinical Psychology — M,D,O
Conflict Resolution and
  Mediation/Peace Studies — M,D,O
Counseling Psychology — M,D,O
Criminal Justice and Criminology — M,D,O
Emergency Management — M,D,O
Experimental Psychology — M,D,O
Forensic Psychology — M,D,O
Humanities — M,D,O
Interdisciplinary Studies — M,D,O
Marriage and Family Therapy — M,D,O
Psychology—General — M,D,O
Public Administration — M
School Psychology — M,D,O
Social Sciences — M,D,O

NSCAD UNIVERSITY
Applied Arts and Design—
  General — M
Art/Fine Arts — M

NYACK COLLEGE
Counseling Psychology — M
Marriage and Family Therapy — M
Missions and Missiology — M,D
Pastoral Ministry and Counseling — M,D
Religion — M

Theology — M,D

OAKLAND CITY UNIVERSITY
Theology — M,D

OAKLAND UNIVERSITY
Applied Behavior Analysis — M,O
Counseling Psychology — M,D,O
Economics — M,O
English — M
History — M
Liberal Studies — M
Linguistics — M,O
Music — M
Public Administration — M,O

OAKWOOD UNIVERSITY
Pastoral Ministry and Counseling — M

OBERLIN COLLEGE
Music — M,O

OBLATE SCHOOL OF THEOLOGY
African-American Studies — M,D,O
Pastoral Ministry and Counseling — M,D,O
Religion — M,D,O
Theology — M,D,O

OHIO CHRISTIAN UNIVERSITY
Pastoral Ministry and Counseling — M
Theology — M

OHIO DOMINICAN UNIVERSITY
English — M
Theology — M

THE OHIO STATE UNIVERSITY
African Studies — M,D
African-American Studies — M,D
Agricultural Economics and
  Agribusiness — M,D
Anthropology — M,D
Architecture — M,D
Art History — M,D
Art/Fine Arts — M
Arts Administration — M
Asian Languages — M
Asian Studies — M
Child and Family Studies — M,D
Chinese — M,D
Classics — M,D
Clinical Psychology — D
Cognitive Sciences — D
Communication—General — M,D
Computer Art and Design — M
Dance — M,D
Developmental Psychology — D
East European and Russian Studies — M,D
Economics — M,D
English — M,D
Family and Consumer
  Sciences-General — M,D
French — M,D
Gender Studies — M,D
Geography — M,D
German — M,D
History — M,D
Human Development — M,D
Industrial and Labor Relations — M,D
Industrial Design — M
Interdisciplinary Studies — M,D
Interior Design — M
Internet and Interactive
  Multimedia — M
Italian — M,D
Japanese — M,D
Landscape Architecture — M,D
Latin American Studies — M
Linguistics — M,D
Music — M,D
Near and Middle Eastern Languages — M,D
Philosophy — M,D
Political Science — D
Portuguese — M,D
Psychology—General — D
Public Administration — M,D
Public Affairs — M,D
Public Policy — M,D
Rural Sociology — M,D
Slavic Languages — M,D
Social Psychology — D
Social Sciences — M,D
Sociology — D
Spanish — M,D
Theater — M,D
Urban and Regional Planning — M,D
Women's Studies — M,D

OHIO UNIVERSITY
African Studies — M
Applied Economics — M
Art History — M
Art/Fine Arts — M
Asian Studies — M
Child and Family Studies — M
Child Development — M
Clinical Psychology — M
Communication—General — M,D
Comparative and Interdisciplinary
  Arts — D
Consumer Economics — M
Corporate and Organizational
  Communication — M,D
Economics — M
English — M,D
Experimental Psychology — D
Film, Television, and Video
  Production — M
Film, Television, and Video
  Theory and Criticism — M
French — M
Geography — M
Graphic Design — M
Health Communication — M,D

History — M,D
Industrial and Organizational
  Psychology — D
International Affairs — M
International Development — M
Internet and Interactive
  Multimedia — M
Journalism — M,D
Latin American Studies — M
Linguistics — M
Media Studies — M,D
Music — M,O
Philosophy — M
Photography — M
Political Science — M
Psychology—General — D
Public Administration — M,O
Rehabilitation Counseling — M,D
Rhetoric — M,D
Social Sciences — M
Sociology — M
Spanish — M
Speech and Interpersonal
  Communication — M,D
Theater
Therapies—Dance, Drama, and
  Music — M,O

OHR HAMEIR THEOLOGICAL SEMINARY
Theology

OKLAHOMA BAPTIST UNIVERSITY
Marriage and Family Therapy — M

OKLAHOMA CHRISTIAN UNIVERSITY
Theology — M

OKLAHOMA CITY UNIVERSITY
Applied Behavior Analysis — M
Criminal Justice and Criminology — M
Music — M
Photography — M
Sociology — M
Writing — M

OKLAHOMA STATE UNIVERSITY
Agricultural Economics and
  Agribusiness — M,D
Applied Arts and Design—
  General — M
Applied Behavior Analysis — M,D,O
Applied Psychology — M,D,O
Art History — M
Child and Family Studies — M,D
Clinical Psychology — M,D
Clothing and Textiles — M,D
Consumer Economics — M,D
Economics — M,D
Emergency Management — M,D
English — M,D
Family and Consumer
  Sciences-General — M,D
Geography — M,D
Graphic Design — M
Health Psychology — M,D,O
History — M,D
International Affairs — M,D,O
Landscape Architecture — M,D
Mass Communication — M
Music — M
Philosophy — M
Political Science — M,D
Psychology—General — M,D
Sociology — M,D
Theater — M
Writing — M,D

OKLAHOMA STATE UNIVERSITY CENTER FOR HEALTH SCIENCES
Forensic Sciences — M

OKLAHOMA WESLEYAN UNIVERSITY
Theology — M

OLD DOMINION UNIVERSITY
Applied Psychology — D
Clinical Psychology — D
Communication—General — M,O
Computer Art and Design — M
Conflict Resolution and
  Mediation/Peace Studies — M,D
Counseling Psychology — M,D,O
Criminal Justice and Criminology — M,D
Cultural Studies — M,D,O
Economics — M
English — M,D
Gender Studies — M,O
History — M
Humanities — M,O
Industrial and Organizational
  Psychology — D
International Affairs — M,D
International Development — M,D
Linguistics — M
Media Studies — M,O
Music — M
Philosophy — M,O
Psychology—General — M,D
Public Administration — M
Rhetoric — M
School Psychology — M,D,O
Sociology — M
Speech and Interpersonal
  Communication — M
Women's Studies — M
Writing — M

OLIVET NAZARENE UNIVERSITY
Religion — M
Theology — M

OPEN UNIVERSITY
History — M
Music — M

Philosophy — M

ORAL ROBERTS UNIVERSITY
Addictions/Substance Abuse
  Counseling — M,D
Marriage and Family Therapy — M,D
Missions and Missiology — M,D
Near and Middle Eastern Languages — M,D
Pastoral Ministry and Counseling — M,D
Theology — M,D

OREGON COLLEGE OF ART AND CRAFT
Art/Fine Arts — M

OREGON HEALTH & SCIENCE UNIVERSITY
Gerontology — M,O

OREGON STATE UNIVERSITY
Anthropology — M
Applied Economics — M,D
Child and Family Studies — M,D
Clinical Psychology — M,D
Cognitive Sciences — M,D
English — M
Ethics — M
Gender Studies — M,D
Geographic Information Systems — M
Geography — M,D
Health Psychology — M,D
Hispanic Studies — M
History of Science and Technology — M,D
Human Development — M,D
Interdisciplinary Studies — M
Psychology—General — M,D
Public Policy — M,D
Rhetoric — M
School Psychology — M,D
Social Sciences — M,D
Women's Studies — M,D
Writing — M

OREGON STATE UNIVERSITY–CASCADES
School Psychology — M
Social Psychology — M

OTIS COLLEGE OF ART AND DESIGN
Art/Fine Arts — M
Graphic Design — M
Photography — M
Writing — M

OTTAWA UNIVERSITY
Art Therapy — M
Counseling Psychology — M
Marriage and Family Therapy — M
Pastoral Ministry and Counseling — M
School Psychology — M

OUR LADY OF THE LAKE UNIVERSITY
Counseling Psychology — D
English — M
Marriage and Family Therapy — M
Psychology—General — M
School Psychology — M
Sociology — M
Writing — M

OXFORD GRADUATE SCHOOL
Child and Family Studies — M,D
Religion — M,D
Sociology — M,D

PACE UNIVERSITY
Addictions/Substance Abuse
  Counseling — M,D
Clinical Psychology — M,D
Communication—General — M
Counseling Psychology — M,D
Developmental Psychology — M,D
Economics — O
Emergency Management — M
English — M,O
Forensic Sciences — M
Homeland Security — M
International Economics — O
Internet and Interactive
  Multimedia — M,D,O
Media Studies — M
Psychology—General — M
Public Administration — M
Publishing — M,O
School Psychology — M,D
Theater — M

PACIFICA GRADUATE INSTITUTE
Clinical Psychology — M,D
Counseling Psychology — M,D
Psychology—General — M,D

PACIFIC LUTHERAN UNIVERSITY
Marriage and Family Therapy — M
Writing — M

PACIFIC NORTHWEST COLLEGE OF ART
Applied Arts and Design—
  General — M
Art/Fine Arts — M
Cultural Studies — M

PACIFIC OAKS COLLEGE
Human Development — M
Marriage and Family Therapy — M

PACIFIC RIM CHRISTIAN UNIVERSITY
Pastoral Ministry and Counseling — M

PACIFIC SCHOOL OF RELIGION
Religion — M,D,O
Theology — M,D,O

PACIFIC UNIVERSITY
Clinical Psychology — M,D

---

*M—masters degree; D—doctorate; O—other advanced degree; *—Close-Up and/or Display*

Psychology—General M,D
Writing M

PALM BEACH ATLANTIC UNIVERSITY
Addictions/Substance Abuse
   Counseling M
Counseling Psychology M
Marriage and Family Therapy M
Theology M

PALO ALTO UNIVERSITY
Clinical Psychology M,D
Counseling Psychology M
Marriage and Family Therapy M
Psychology—General M,D

PARIS COLLEGE OF ART
Art/Fine Arts M
Interior Design M
Media Studies M
Photography M
Textile Design M

PARK UNIVERSITY
Emergency Management M,O
Music M,O
Public Administration M,O
Public Affairs M,O
Writing M

PAYNE THEOLOGICAL SEMINARY
Theology M

PENN STATE ERIE, THE BEHREND COLLEGE
Applied Psychology M
Clinical Psychology M

PENN STATE HARRISBURG
American Studies M,D,O
Applied Behavior Analysis M,D,O
Applied Psychology M,D,O
Clinical Psychology M,D,O
Communication—General M,D,O
Criminal Justice and Criminology M,D,O
Folklore M,D,O
Health Psychology M,D,O
Historic Preservation M,D,O
Homeland Security M,D,O
Humanities M,D,O
Museum Studies M,D,O
Psychology—General M,D,O
Public Administration M,D,O
Public Affairs M,D,O
Social Psychology M,D,O

PENN STATE UNIVERSITY PARK
Agricultural Economics and
   Agribusiness M,D,O
Anthropology M,D
Architecture M,D
Art History M,D
Art/Fine Arts M,D,O
Child and Family Studies M,D
Communication—General M,D
Comparative Literature M,D
Criminal Justice and Criminology M,D
Economics M,D
English M,D
Forensic Sciences M
French M,D
Geography M,D
German M,D
History M,D
Human Development M,D
Industrial and Labor Relations M
International Affairs M
Landscape Architecture M,D
Linguistics M,D
Mass Communication M,D
Media Studies M,D
Music M,D,O
Philosophy M,D
Political Science M,D
Psychology—General M,D
Rural Sociology M,D
Russian M,D
School Psychology M,D,O
Sociology M,D
Spanish M,D
Sustainable Development M
Theater M

PENNSYLVANIA ACADEMY OF THE FINE ARTS
Art/Fine Arts M,O

PENSACOLA CHRISTIAN COLLEGE
Art/Fine Arts M,D,O
Graphic Design M,D,O
Music M,D,O
Theater M,D,O

PENTECOSTAL THEOLOGICAL SEMINARY
Pastoral Ministry and Counseling M,D
Theology M,D

PEPPERDINE UNIVERSITY
American Studies M
Clinical Psychology M,D
Communication—General M
Conflict Resolution and
   Mediation/Peace Studies M
Economics M
Humanities M
International Affairs M,D
Marriage and Family Therapy M,D
Media Studies M
Pastoral Ministry and Counseling M
Political Science M
Psychology—General M,D
Public Policy M
Religion M
Writing M

PERU STATE COLLEGE
Economics M

PFEIFFER UNIVERSITY
Theology M

PHILADELPHIA COLLEGE OF OSTEOPATHIC MEDICINE
Applied Behavior Analysis M,D,O
Clinical Psychology M,D,O
Counseling Psychology M,D,O
Forensic Sciences M
Industrial and Organizational
   Psychology M,D,O
Psychology—General M,D,O*
School Psychology M,D,O

PHILLIPS GRADUATE UNIVERSITY
Art Therapy M
Marriage and Family Therapy M
Psychology—General M
School Psychology M

PHILLIPS THEOLOGICAL SEMINARY
Ethics M,D
Missions and Missiology M,D
Music M,D
Pastoral Ministry and Counseling D
Theology M,D

PHOENIX SEMINARY
Counseling Psychology M,D,O
Pastoral Ministry and Counseling M,D,O
Theology M,D,O

PIEDMONT INTERNATIONAL UNIVERSITY
Pastoral Ministry and Counseling M,D
Theology M,D

PILLAR COLLEGE
Clinical Psychology M
Marriage and Family Therapy M

PITTSBURGH THEOLOGICAL SEMINARY
Pastoral Ministry and Counseling M,D
Theology M,D

PITTSBURG STATE UNIVERSITY
Clinical Psychology M
Communication—General M
English M
Graphic Design M
History M
Music M
Psychology—General M
School Psychology O
Writing M

PLYMOUTH STATE UNIVERSITY
Clinical Psychology M,O
Cultural Studies M
Historic Preservation M
School Psychology M,O

POINT LOMA NAZARENE UNIVERSITY
Clinical Psychology M
Marriage and Family Therapy M
Pastoral Ministry and Counseling M
Theology M

POINT PARK UNIVERSITY
Clinical Psychology M,D
Communication—General M
Criminal Justice and Criminology M
Journalism M
Mass Communication M
Media Studies M
Music M
Theater M

POINT UNIVERSITY
Pastoral Ministry and Counseling M

POLYTECHNIC UNIVERSITY OF PUERTO RICO
Landscape Architecture M

PONCE HEALTH SCIENCES UNIVERSITY
Clinical Psychology D

PONTIFICAL CATHOLIC UNIVERSITY OF PUERTO RICO
Art/Fine Arts M
Clinical Psychology D
Criminal Justice and Criminology M
Hispanic Studies M,O
History M
Industrial and Organizational
   Psychology D
Psychology—General M,D
Public Administration M
Rehabilitation Counseling M
Spanish M,O
Theology M

PONTIFICAL COLLEGE JOSEPHINUM
Theology M

PONTIFICAL JOHN PAUL II INSTITUTE FOR STUDIES ON MARRIAGE AND FAMILY
Ethics M,D,O
Marriage and Family Therapy M,D,O
Theology M,D,O

PONTIFICIA UNIVERSIDAD CATOLICA MADRE Y MAESTRA
Architecture M
Building Science M
Clinical Psychology M
Criminal Justice and Criminology M
Developmental Psychology M
Forensic Psychology M
Interior Design M
International Affairs M
Landscape Architecture M
Psychology—General M

POPE ST. JOHN XXIII NATIONAL SEMINARY
Theology M

PORTLAND STATE UNIVERSITY
American Studies M
Anthropology M,D,O
Applied Social Research M,D
Architecture M
Art/Fine Arts M
Conflict Resolution and
   Mediation/Peace Studies M
Criminal Justice and Criminology M
Economics M,D,O
English M
French M
Geography M,D
German M
History M
International Affairs M
Japanese M
Music M
Political Science M
Psychology—General M,D,O
Public Administration M,D,O
Public Affairs M,D,O
Public Policy M,D,O
Sociology M,D,O
Spanish M
Speech and Interpersonal
   Communication M,O
Theater M
Writing M

POST UNIVERSITY
Addictions/Substance Abuse
   Counseling M
Clinical Psychology M
Emergency Management M
Forensic Psychology M
Homeland Security M
Public Administration M

PRAIRIE VIEW A&M UNIVERSITY
Architecture M
Clinical Psychology M,D
Forensic Psychology M,D
Sociology M

PRATT INSTITUTE
Applied Arts and Design—
   General M,O*
Architecture M*
Art History M
Art Therapy M
Art/Fine Arts M*
Arts Administration M
Graphic Design M
Historic Preservation M
Industrial Design M
Interior Design M
Internet and Interactive
   Multimedia M
Media Studies M*
Music M
Sustainable Development M
Therapies—Dance, Drama, and
   Music M
Urban and Regional Planning M
Urban Design M
Writing M

PRESCOTT COLLEGE
Art Therapy M
Art/Fine Arts M
Counseling Psychology M
Health Psychology M
Humanities M
Psychoanalysis and Psychotherapy M

PRINCETON THEOLOGICAL SEMINARY
Religion M,D
Theology M,D

PRINCETON UNIVERSITY
Anthropology D
Archaeology D
Architecture M,D
Asian Studies D
Classics D
Comparative Literature D
Demography and Population Studies D,O
Economics D,O
English D
French D
German D
History of Science and Technology D
History D
International Affairs M,D
Music D
Near and Middle Eastern Studies M,D
Philosophy D
Political Science D
Portuguese D
Psychology—General D
Public Affairs M,D,O
Public Policy M,D
Religion D
Russian D
Slavic Languages D
Sociology D,O
Spanish D

PROVIDENCE COLLEGE
American Studies M
History M
Theology M

PROVIDENCE UNIVERSITY COLLEGE & THEOLOGICAL SEMINARY
Counseling Psychology M,D,O
Missions and Missiology M,D,O
Pastoral Ministry and Counseling M,D,O
Theology M,D,O

PURCHASE COLLEGE, STATE UNIVERSITY OF NEW YORK
Art History M
Art/Fine Arts M
Arts Administration M
Computer Art and Design M
Media Studies M
Music M

PURDUE UNIVERSITY
Agricultural Economics and
   Agribusiness M,D
American Studies M,D
Anthropology M,D
Applied Arts and Design—
   General M,D
Art/Fine Arts M,D
Child and Family Studies M,D
Child Development M,D
Clinical Psychology D
Cognitive Sciences D
Communication—General M,D
Comparative Literature M,D
Computer Art and Design M,D
Consumer Economics M,D
Economics D
English M,D
French M,D
German M,D
History M,D
Human Development M,D
Industrial and Organizational
   Psychology D
Industrial Design M,D
Interior Design M,D
Japanese M,D
Linguistics M,D
Marriage and Family Therapy M,D
Philosophy M,D
Photography M,D
Political Science M,D
Psychology—General D
Sociology M,D
Spanish M,D
Sport Psychology M,D
Theater M
Writing M,D

PURDUE UNIVERSITY GLOBAL
Criminal Justice and Criminology M
Political Science M

PURDUE UNIVERSITY NORTHWEST
Child and Family Studies M
Child Development M
Communication—General M
Counseling Psychology M
English M
History M
Marriage and Family Therapy M
School Psychology M

QUEENS COLLEGE OF THE CITY UNIVERSITY OF NEW YORK
Applied Behavior Analysis M
Applied Social Research M
Art History M
Art/Fine Arts M
Child and Family Studies M,O
Counseling Psychology M,O
English M
Family and Consumer
   Sciences-General M,O
French M
Hispanic and Latin American
   Languages M
History M
Italian M
Liberal Studies M
Linguistics M,O
Media Studies M
Music M,O
Psychology—General M
Romance Languages M
School Psychology M,O
Sociology M
Spanish M
Urban Studies M
Writing M

QUEEN'S UNIVERSITY AT KINGSTON
Canadian Studies M,D
Classics M
Clinical Psychology M,D
Cognitive Sciences M,D
Communication—General M,D
Developmental Psychology M,D
English M,D
French M,D
Gender Studies M,D
Geography M,D
German M,D
Hispanic Studies M
Industrial and Labor Relations M
International Affairs M,D
Philosophy M,D
Political Science M,D
Psychology—General M,D
Public Policy M
Religion M
Social Psychology M,D
Sociology M,D
Spanish M
Sport Psychology M,D
Theology M,O
Urban and Regional Planning M
Women's Studies M,D

QUEENS UNIVERSITY OF CHARLOTTE
Communication—General M
Interior Design M
Writing M

QUINCY UNIVERSITY
Clinical Psychology M
School Psychology M

QUINNIPIAC UNIVERSITY
Broadcast Journalism M
Communication—General M
Film, Television, and Video
   Production M

Internet and Interactive
    Multimedia — M
Journalism — M

RABBINICAL ACADEMY MESIVTA RABBI CHAIM BERLIN
Theology — O

RABBINICAL COLLEGE BETH SHRAGA
Theology — M

RABBINICAL COLLEGE BOBOVER YESHIVA B'NEI ZION
Theology — O

RABBINICAL COLLEGE OF LONG ISLAND
Theology — M

RABBINICAL SEMINARY OF AMERICA
Theology — M

RADFORD UNIVERSITY
Art/Fine Arts — M
Clinical Psychology — M
Corporate and Organizational
    Communication — M
Counseling Psychology — D
Criminal Justice and Criminology — M,O
English — M
Experimental Psychology — M
Industrial and Organizational
    Psychology — M
Music — M
Psychology—General — M
School Psychology — O

RANDALL UNIVERSITY
Pastoral Ministry and Counseling — M

RANDOLPH COLLEGE
Writing — M

RECONSTRUCTIONIST RABBINICAL COLLEGE
Jewish Studies — M,D,O
Theology — M,D,O
Women's Studies — M,D,O

REED COLLEGE
Liberal Studies — M

REFORMED EPISCOPAL SEMINARY
Theology — M

REFORMED PRESBYTERIAN THEOLOGICAL SEMINARY
Theology — M,D

REFORMED THEOLOGICAL SEMINARY–ATLANTA CAMPUS
Theology — M,D,O

REFORMED THEOLOGICAL SEMINARY–CHARLOTTE CAMPUS
Pastoral Ministry and Counseling — M,D
Religion — M,D
Theology — M,D

REFORMED THEOLOGICAL SEMINARY–DALLAS CAMPUS
Theology — M

REFORMED THEOLOGICAL SEMINARY–HOUSTON CAMPUS
Religion — M

REFORMED THEOLOGICAL SEMINARY–JACKSON CAMPUS
Marriage and Family Therapy — M,D,O
Missions and Missiology — M,D,O
Pastoral Ministry and Counseling — M,D,O
Religion — M,D,O
Theology — M,D,O

REFORMED THEOLOGICAL SEMINARY–ORLANDO CAMPUS
Pastoral Ministry and Counseling — M,D,O
Theology — M,D,O

REFORMED THEOLOGICAL SEMINARY–WASHINGTON D.C.
Religion — M
Theology — M

REGENT COLLEGE
Theology — M,O

REGENT'S UNIVERSITY LONDON
International Affairs — M

REGENT UNIVERSITY
Addictions/Substance Abuse
    Counseling — M,D,O
American Studies — M
Clinical Psychology — M,D,O
Communication—General — M,D
Conflict Resolution and
    Mediation/Peace Studies — M,D
Corporate and Organizational
    Communication — M,D
Counseling Psychology — M,D,O
Criminal Justice and Criminology — M,D,O
Cultural Studies — M,D
Economics — M,D,O
Emergency Management — M
Film, Television, and Video
    Production — M,D
Homeland Security — M
Interdisciplinary Studies — M,D,O
International Affairs — M
Journalism — M,D
Marriage and Family Therapy — M,D,O
Missions and Missiology — M,D
National Security — M,D
Pastoral Ministry and Counseling — M,D,O
Political Science — M
Public Administration — M

Public Policy — M
Religion — M,D
Theater — M,D
Theology — M,D
Writing — M

REGIS COLLEGE (CANADA)
Pastoral Ministry and Counseling — M,D,O
Philosophy — M,D,O
Theology — M,D,O

REGIS COLLEGE (MA)
Applied Behavior Analysis — M
Corporate and Organizational
    Communication — M
Counseling Psychology — M,D,O

REGIS UNIVERSITY
Criminal Justice and Criminology — M,O
Developmental Psychology — M,D,O
Economics — M,O
Marriage and Family Therapy — M,D,O
Writing — M,O

REINHARDT UNIVERSITY
Public Administration — M
Writing — M

RENSSELAER POLYTECHNIC INSTITUTE
Architecture — M
Art/Fine Arts — D
Cognitive Sciences — D
Computer Art and Design — M
History of Science and Technology — M,D
Interdisciplinary Studies — M,D
Lighting Design — M,D
Rhetoric — M,D
Speech and Interpersonal
    Communication — M,D

RHODE ISLAND COLLEGE
Art/Fine Arts — M
Arts Administration — M
Counseling Psychology — M,O
English — M,O
Health Psychology — M,O
History — M
Psychology—General — M,O
Public Administration — M
School Psychology — M,O
Writing — M

RHODE ISLAND SCHOOL OF DESIGN
Applied Arts and Design—
    General — M
Architecture — M
Art/Fine Arts — M
Computer Art and Design — M
Graphic Design — M
Industrial Design — M
Interior Design — M
Landscape Architecture — M
Media Studies — M
Photography — M
Textile Design — M

RICE UNIVERSITY
African Studies — D
American Studies — D
Anthropology — M,D
Archaeology — M,D
Architecture — M,D
Art History — D
Cognitive Sciences — M,D
Cultural Anthropology — M,D
Economics — M,D
English — M,D
History — M,D
Industrial and Organizational
    Psychology — M,D
Jewish Studies — D
Liberal Studies — M
Linguistics — M,D
Music — M,D
Near and Middle Eastern Studies — D
Philosophy — M,D
Political Science — D
Psychology—General — M,D
Religion — D
Sociology — D
Urban Design — M,D

RICHMOND, THE AMERICAN INTERNATIONAL UNIVERSITY IN LONDON
Art History — M
International Affairs — M

RICHMONT GRADUATE UNIVERSITY
Clinical Psychology — M
Marriage and Family Therapy — M
Pastoral Ministry and Counseling — M,O

RIDER UNIVERSITY
Addictions/Substance Abuse
    Counseling — M,O
Clinical Psychology — M,O
Corporate and Organizational
    Communication — M
French — O
German — O
Health Communication — M
Homeland Security — M
Music — M
School Psychology — O
Spanish — O

RIVIER UNIVERSITY
Clinical Psychology — M
Counseling Psychology — M,D,O
English — M
Experimental Psychology — M
Psychology—General — M
Writing — M

THE ROBERT E. WEBBER INSTITUTE FOR WORSHIP STUDIES
Religion — M,D

ROBERT MORRIS UNIVERSITY
Counseling Psychology — M,D,O
Internet and Interactive
    Multimedia — M,D

ROBERT MORRIS UNIVERSITY ILLINOIS
Criminal Justice and Criminology — M

ROBERTS WESLEYAN COLLEGE
Child and Family Studies — M
Clinical Psychology — M,D
Psychology—General — M,D
School Psychology — M,D

ROCHESTER COLLEGE
Missions and Missiology — M

ROCHESTER INSTITUTE OF TECHNOLOGY
Architecture — M
Art/Fine Arts — M
Cognitive Sciences — O
Communication—General — M
Computer Art and Design — M
Criminal Justice and Criminology — M
Experimental Psychology — M
Film, Television, and Video
    Production — M
Graphic Design — M
Industrial Design — M
Interdisciplinary Studies — M
Internet and Interactive
    Multimedia — O
Media Studies — M
Medical Illustration — M
Photography — M
Psychology—General — M,O
Public Policy — M
School Psychology — M,O
Sustainable Development — M,D
Translation and Interpretation — M

ROCKY MOUNTAIN COLLEGE OF ART + DESIGN
Arts Administration — M
Internet and Interactive
    Multimedia — M

ROGER WILLIAMS UNIVERSITY
Architectural History — M,O
Architecture — M,O
Art History — M,O
Clinical Psychology — M
Criminal Justice and Criminology — M
Forensic Psychology — M
Historic Preservation — M,O
Public Administration — M
Urban and Regional Planning — M,O

ROLLINS COLLEGE
Applied Behavior Analysis — M
Liberal Studies — M

ROOSEVELT UNIVERSITY
Arts Administration — M,O
Clinical Psychology — M
Communication—General — M
Corporate and Organizational
    Communication — M
Economics — M
History — M
Humanities — M
Industrial and Organizational
    Psychology — M,D
Music — M,O
Philosophy — M
Psychology—General — M,D
School Psychology — M
Sociology — M
Theater — M
Writing — M

ROSALIND FRANKLIN UNIVERSITY OF MEDICINE AND SCIENCE
Clinical Psychology — M,D
Interdisciplinary Studies — D
Psychology—General — M,D

ROSEMONT COLLEGE
Counseling Psychology — M
Publishing — M
Writing — M

ROWAN UNIVERSITY
Applied Behavior Analysis — M,O
Arts Administration — M
Clinical Psychology — M,O
Corporate and Organizational
    Communication — O
Criminal Justice and Criminology — M,O
History — M,O
Media Studies — O
Music — M
Psychology—General — M,O
Publishing — O
Rhetoric — O
School Psychology — M,O
Theater — M
Writing — M,O

ROYAL MILITARY COLLEGE OF CANADA
Military and Defense Studies — M,D

ROYAL ROADS UNIVERSITY
Conflict Resolution and
    Mediation/Peace Studies — M,O
Emergency Management — M,O

RUTGERS UNIVERSITY–CAMDEN
Child Development — M,D
Criminal Justice and Criminology — M

English — M
History — M
International Affairs — M
International Development — M
Liberal Studies — M
Psychology—General — M
Public Administration — M
Public History — M
Public Policy — M
Writing — M

RUTGERS UNIVERSITY–NEWARK
American Studies — M,D
Clothing and Textiles — M
Cognitive Sciences — D
Criminal Justice and Criminology — M,D
Economics — M,D
English — M
History — M
International Affairs — M,D
Music — M
Political Science — M
Psychology—General — D
Public Administration — M
Public Policy — M,D,O
Rehabilitation Counseling — M
Social Psychology — D
Urban Studies — M,D
Writing — M

RUTGERS UNIVERSITY–NEW BRUNSWICK
African Studies — D
African-American Studies — D
Agricultural Economics and
    Agribusiness — M
Anthropology — M,D
Applied Arts and Design—
    General — M
Applied Psychology — M,D
Art History — M,D,O
Art/Fine Arts — M
Asian Studies — M,D
Classics — M,D
Clinical Psychology — D
Cognitive Sciences — D
Communication—General — D
Comparative Literature — M,D
Counseling Psychology — M
Economics — M,D
Emergency Management — M,D,O
English — M
French — M,D
Gender Studies — M,D
Geography — M,D
German — M,D
Health Psychology — D
Historic Preservation — M,D,O
History of Medicine — D
History of Science and Technology — D
History — D
Industrial and Labor Relations — M,D
Interdisciplinary Studies — D
International Affairs — M,D
Italian — M,D
Jewish Studies — M,O
Linguistics — D
Medieval and Renaissance Studies — D
Music — M,D,O
Philosophy — D
Political Science — M,D
Psychology—General — D
Public Policy — M,D
Religion — M,O
School Psychology — M,D
Social Psychology — D
Sociology — M,D
Spanish — M,D
Theater — M
Translation and Interpretation — M,D
Urban and Regional Planning — M,D
Women's Studies — M,D
Writing — M

RYERSON UNIVERSITY
Arts Administration — M

SACRED HEART MAJOR SEMINARY
Pastoral Ministry and Counseling — M
Theology — M

SACRED HEART SEMINARY AND SCHOOL OF THEOLOGY
Theology — M,O

SACRED HEART UNIVERSITY
Applied Psychology — M
Communication—General — M
Criminal Justice and Criminology — M
Film, Television, and Video
    Production — M
Industrial and Organizational
    Psychology — M
Journalism — M
Public Administration — M
Social Psychology — M

SAGE GRADUATE SCHOOL
Applied Behavior Analysis — M,O
Counseling Psychology — M
Forensic Psychology — M,O
Gerontology — M
Psychology—General — M,O
Social Psychology — M

SAGINAW VALLEY STATE UNIVERSITY
Chinese — M
Communication—General — M
Media Studies — M
Public Administration — M

ST. AMBROSE UNIVERSITY
Criminal Justice and Criminology — M
Pastoral Ministry and Counseling — M

---

*M—masters degree; D—doctorate; O—other advanced degree; *—Close-Up and/or Display*

ST. ANDREW'S COLLEGE
Theology — M,D,O

ST. ANDREW'S COLLEGE IN WINNIPEG
Theology — M

ST. AUGUSTINE'S SEMINARY OF TORONTO
Pastoral Ministry and Counseling — M,O
Theology — M,O

ST. BERNARD'S SCHOOL OF THEOLOGY AND MINISTRY
Pastoral Ministry and Counseling — M,O
Theology — M,O

ST. BONAVENTURE UNIVERSITY
Corporate and Organizational
 Communication — M
Counseling Psychology — M,O
Rehabilitation Counseling — M,O
Social Psychology — M,O

ST. CATHERINE UNIVERSITY
Pastoral Ministry and Counseling — M,O
Theology — M,O

SAINT CHARLES BORROMEO SEMINARY, OVERBROOK
Religion — M
Theology — M

ST. CLOUD STATE UNIVERSITY
Applied Behavior Analysis — M
Applied Economics — M
Archaeology — M
Child and Family Studies — M
Criminal Justice and Criminology — M
Economics — M
English — M
Geography — M
Gerontology — M
Historic Preservation — M
History — M
Industrial and Organizational
 Psychology — M
Marriage and Family Therapy — M
Mass Communication — M
Music — M
Psychology—General — M,D
Rehabilitation Counseling — M
Social Psychology — M

ST. EDWARD'S UNIVERSITY
Counseling Psychology — M
Humanities — M,O
Liberal Studies — M,O
Sustainable Development — M

ST. FRANCIS XAVIER UNIVERSITY
Cultural Studies — M
Urban and Regional Planning — M

ST. JOHN FISHER COLLEGE
Counseling Psychology — M
French — M

ST. JOHN'S COLLEGE (MD)
Liberal Studies — M

ST. JOHN'S COLLEGE (NM)
Asian Languages — M
Asian Studies — M
Liberal Studies — M

ST. JOHN'S SEMINARY (CA)
Pastoral Ministry and Counseling — M
Theology — M

SAINT JOHN'S SEMINARY (MA)
Religion — M
Theology — M

SAINT JOHN'S UNIVERSITY (MN)
Music — M
Pastoral Ministry and Counseling — M
Theology — M

ST. JOHN'S UNIVERSITY (NY)
Asian Studies — M
Clinical Psychology — M,D,O
Counseling Psychology — M,O
Criminal Justice and Criminology — M
English — M,D
History — M,D
Homeland Security — M
Liberal Studies — M
Mass Communication — M
Museum Studies — M
Political Science — M,O
Psychology—General — M
Public Administration — M,O
Public History — M,D
School Psychology — M,D
Sociology — M
Spanish — M
Theology — M

ST. JOSEPH'S COLLEGE, LONG ISLAND CAMPUS
Forensic Sciences — M

ST. JOSEPH'S COLLEGE, NEW YORK
Forensic Sciences — M
Writing — M

SAINT JOSEPH'S COLLEGE OF MAINE
Pastoral Ministry and Counseling — M

ST. JOSEPH'S SEMINARY
Pastoral Ministry and Counseling — M
Religion — M
Theology — M

SAINT JOSEPH'S UNIVERSITY
Criminal Justice and Criminology — M,O
Psychology—General — M,O
Writing — M

ST. LAWRENCE UNIVERSITY
Human Development — M,O

SAINT LEO UNIVERSITY
Criminal Justice and Criminology — M
Emergency Management — M
Forensic Sciences — M
Theology — M,O
Writing — M

SAINT LOUIS UNIVERSITY
American Studies — M,D
Applied Behavior Analysis — M,D
Clinical Psychology — M,D
Communication—General — M
Criminal Justice and Criminology — M
Emergency Management — M
English — M,D
Experimental Psychology — M,D
French — M
History — M,D
Industrial and Organizational
 Psychology — M,D
Philosophy — M,D
Political Science — M
Psychology—General — M
Spanish — M
Theology — M,D
Urban and Regional Planning — M

SAINT LOUIS UNIVERSITY–MADRID CAMPUS
English — M
Spanish — M

SAINT MARTIN'S UNIVERSITY
Counseling Psychology — M
Social Psychology — M

SAINT MARY-OF-THE-WOODS COLLEGE
Art Therapy — M,O
Therapies—Dance, Drama, and
 Music — M

SAINT MARY'S COLLEGE OF CALIFORNIA
Conflict Resolution and
 Mediation/Peace Studies — M
Dance — M
Marriage and Family Therapy — M,O
School Psychology — M,O
Writing — M

SAINT MARY SEMINARY AND GRADUATE SCHOOL OF THEOLOGY
Theology — M,D

ST. MARY'S SEMINARY AND UNIVERSITY
Theology — M,D,O

SAINT MARY'S UNIVERSITY (CANADA)
Applied Psychology — M,D
Canadian Studies — M,O
Criminal Justice and Criminology — M
Gender Studies — M
History — M
Industrial and Organizational
 Psychology — M,D
International Development — M,O
Philosophy — M
Psychology—General — M,D
Religion — M
Theology — M
Women's Studies — M

ST. MARY'S UNIVERSITY (UNITED STATES)
Communication—General — M
Conflict Resolution and
 Mediation/Peace Studies — M,O
Counseling Psychology — M
Criminal Justice and Criminology — M
English — M
Homeland Security — M,O
Industrial and Organizational
 Psychology — M
International Affairs — M,O
International Development — M,O
Public Administration — M,O
Theology — M

SAINT MARY'S UNIVERSITY OF MINNESOTA
Addictions/Substance Abuse
 Counseling — M,O
Counseling Psychology — M,D,O
Geographic Information Systems — M,O
Human Development — M
International Development — M
Marriage and Family Therapy — M
Philanthropic Studies — M
Public Administration — M

SAINT MEINRAD SCHOOL OF THEOLOGY
Theology — M

SAINT MICHAEL'S COLLEGE
Clinical Psychology — M

ST. NORBERT COLLEGE
Liberal Studies — M
Theology — M

ST. PATRICK'S SEMINARY & UNIVERSITY
Theology — M,O

SAINT PAUL SCHOOL OF THEOLOGY
Theology — M,D

SAINT PAUL UNIVERSITY
Conflict Resolution and
 Mediation/Peace Studies — M
Counseling Psychology — M
Marriage and Family Therapy — M
Missions and Missiology — M
Pastoral Ministry and Counseling — M,D,O
Theology — M,D,O

ST. PETER'S SEMINARY
Theology — M

SAINT PETER'S UNIVERSITY
Applied Behavior Analysis — M,D,O
Criminal Justice and Criminology — M
Public Administration — M

SAINTS CYRIL AND METHODIUS SEMINARY
Pastoral Ministry and Counseling — M
Theology — M

ST. STEPHEN'S COLLEGE
Pastoral Ministry and Counseling — M,D
Theology — M,D

ST. THOMAS UNIVERSITY
Arts Administration — M
Communication—General — M,D,O
Counseling Psychology — M
Criminal Justice and Criminology — M,O
Film, Television, and Video
 Production — M
Hispanic Studies — M,O
Marriage and Family Therapy — M,O
Pastoral Ministry and Counseling — M,O
Public Administration — M,O
Theology — M,D,O

ST. TIKHON'S ORTHODOX THEOLOGICAL SEMINARY
Theology — M

ST. VINCENT DE PAUL REGIONAL SEMINARY
Theology — M

SAINT VINCENT SEMINARY
Pastoral Ministry and Counseling — M
Theology — M

ST. VLADIMIR'S ORTHODOX THEOLOGICAL SEMINARY
Theology — M,D

SAINT XAVIER UNIVERSITY
Spanish — M

SALEM COLLEGE
Music — M

SALEM STATE UNIVERSITY
Counseling Psychology — M,O
Criminal Justice and Criminology — M
English — M
Geography — M
History — M
Psychology—General — M,O
Spanish — M

SALISBURY UNIVERSITY
American Studies — M
Conflict Resolution and
 Mediation/Peace Studies — M
English — M
Geographic Information Systems — M
History — M

SALVE REGINA UNIVERSITY
Addictions/Substance Abuse
 Counseling — M,O
Applied Behavior Analysis — M,O
Conflict Resolution and
 Mediation/Peace Studies — M,D
Counseling Psychology — M,O
Criminal Justice and Criminology — M,O
Forensic Sciences — M,O
Homeland Security — M,O
Humanities — M,D
International Affairs — M,O
Rehabilitation Counseling — M,D
Religion — M,D
Writing — M

SAMFORD UNIVERSITY
Music — M
Theology — M,D

SAM HOUSTON STATE UNIVERSITY
Clinical Psychology — M,D,O
Communication—General — M
Criminal Justice and Criminology — M,D
Dance — M
English — M
Family and Consumer
 Sciences-General — M
Forensic Sciences — M,D
Geographic Information Systems — M,O
History — M
Homeland Security — M
Humanities — M,D,O
Internet and Interactive
 Multimedia — M
Music — M
Political Science — M
Psychology—General — M,D,O
Public Administration — M
Publishing — M
School Psychology — M,D,O
Sociology — M
Spanish — M
Writing — M

SAN DIEGO STATE UNIVERSITY
Anthropology — M
Applied Arts and Design—
 General — M
Art History — M
Art/Fine Arts — M
Asian Studies — M
Child and Family Studies — M
Child Development — M
Clinical Psychology — M,D
Communication—General — M
Criminal Justice and Criminology — M
Economics — M
Emergency Management — M,D
English — M

Environmental Design — M
Film, Television, and Video
 Production — M,O
Gender Studies — O
Geography — M,D
Gerontology — M
Graphic Design — M
Health Psychology — M,D
History — M
Industrial and Organizational
 Psychology — M,D
Interdisciplinary Studies — M
Interior Design — M
Internet and Interactive
 Multimedia — M
Latin American Studies — M
Liberal Studies — M
Linguistics — M,O
Media Studies — M
Music — M
Philosophy — M
Political Science — M
Psychology—General — M,D
Public Administration — M
Rehabilitation Counseling — M
Rhetoric — M
Romance Languages — M
School Psychology — M
Sociology — M
Spanish — M
Theater — M
Urban and Regional Planning — M
Western European Studies — M
Women's Studies — M
Writing — M

SAN FRANCISCO ART INSTITUTE
Art History — M
Art/Fine Arts — M,O
Museum Studies — M

SAN FRANCISCO CONSERVATORY OF MUSIC
Music — M,O

SAN FRANCISCO STATE UNIVERSITY
Anthropology — M
Applied Arts and Design—
 General — M
Archaeology — M
Art/Fine Arts — M
Asian-American Studies — M
Chinese — M
Classics — M
Clinical Psychology — M,O
Comparative Literature — M
Criminal Justice and Criminology — M
Cultural Anthropology — M
Cultural Studies — M
Developmental Psychology — M,O
Economics — M
English — M,O
Ethnic Studies — M
Family and Consumer
 Sciences-General — M
Film, Television, and Video
 Production — M
Film, Television, and Video
 Theory and Criticism — M
French — M
Geographic Information Systems — M
Geography — M
German — M
Gerontology — M
History — M
Humanities — M
Industrial and Organizational
 Psychology — M,O
International Affairs — M
Italian — M
Japanese — M
Liberal Studies — M
Linguistics — M
Marriage and Family Therapy — M
Media Studies — M
Museum Studies — M
Music — M
Philosophy — M
Political Science — M
Psychology—General — M,O
Public Administration — M
Public Policy — M
School Psychology — M,O
Social Psychology — M,O
Spanish — M
Speech and Interpersonal
 Communication — M
Theater — M
Women's Studies — M
Writing — M

SAN FRANCISCO THEOLOGICAL SEMINARY
Theology — M,D

SAN JOSE STATE UNIVERSITY
Anthropology — M
Art History — M
Child Development — M,D
Clinical Psychology — M
Communication—General — M
Criminal Justice and Criminology — M
Economics — M
English — M
Experimental Psychology — M
Geography — M
Hispanic Studies — M
History — M
Industrial and Organizational
 Psychology — M
Linguistics — M
Mass Communication — M
Media Studies — M
Music — M
Philosophy — M
Photography — M

Psychology—General M
Public Administration M
Sociology M
Spanish M
Writing M

SANTA CLARA UNIVERSITY
Counseling Psychology M,O
Ethics M,D,O
Pastoral Ministry and Counseling M
Religion M,D,O
Theology M,D,O

SARAH LAWRENCE COLLEGE
Child Development M
Dance M
Genetic Counseling M
History M
Theater M
Women's Studies M
Writing M

SAVANNAH COLLEGE OF ART AND DESIGN
Applied Arts and Design—
General M
Architectural History M
Architecture M
Art History M
Art/Fine Arts M
Arts Administration M
Clothing and Textiles M
Computer Art and Design M
Film, Television, and Video
Production M
Film, Television, and Video
Theory and Criticism M
Graphic Design M
Historic Preservation M
Illustration M
Industrial Design M
Interior Design M
Internet and Interactive
Multimedia M
Media Studies M
Music M
Photography M
Sustainable Development M
Textile Design M
Theater M
Urban Design M
Writing M

SAVANNAH STATE UNIVERSITY
Public Administration M
Urban and Regional Planning M
Urban Studies M

SAYBROOK UNIVERSITY
Clinical Psychology M
Counseling Psychology M
Health Psychology M,D
Marriage and Family Therapy M,D
Psychology—General M,D
Sustainable Development M,D
Transpersonal and Humanistic
Psychology M,D

SCHILLER INTERNATIONAL UNIVERSITY
International Affairs M

SCHOOL OF ADVANCED AIR AND SPACE STUDIES
Military and Defense Studies M

SCHOOL OF ARCHITECTURE AT TALIESIN
Architecture M

SCHOOL OF THE ART INSTITUTE OF CHICAGO
Applied Arts and Design—
General M
Architecture M
Art History M
Art Therapy M
Art/Fine Arts M
Arts Administration M
Arts Journalism M
Film, Television, and Video
Production M
Graphic Design M
Historic Preservation M
Interior Design M
Journalism M
Music M
Photography M
Textile Design M,O
Writing M,O

SCHOOL OF VISUAL ARTS (NY)
Applied Arts and Design—
General M
Art History M
Art Therapy M
Art/Fine Arts M
Computer Art and Design M
Cultural Studies M
Film, Television, and Video
Production M
Graphic Design M
Illustration M
Internet and Interactive
Multimedia M
Photography M
Writing M

SCHREINER UNIVERSITY
Ethics M

SEATTLE PACIFIC UNIVERSITY
Clinical Psychology D
Industrial and Organizational
Psychology M,D

Marriage and Family Therapy M,O
Religion M,O
Theology M,O
Writing M

THE SEATTLE SCHOOL OF THEOLOGY AND PSYCHOLOGY
Counseling Psychology M
Psychology—General M
Religion M
Theology M

SEATTLE UNIVERSITY
Arts Administration M
Criminal Justice and Criminology M,O
Forensic Sciences M,O
Marriage and Family Therapy M
Pastoral Ministry and Counseling M
Psychology—General M
Public Administration M
School Psychology M,O
Theology M,D,O
Transpersonal and Humanistic
Psychology M

SELMA UNIVERSITY
Pastoral Ministry and Counseling M
Religion M

SEMINARY OF THE SOUTHWEST
Clinical Psychology M,O
Pastoral Ministry and Counseling M,O
Religion M,O
Theology M,O

SETON HALL UNIVERSITY
Asian Studies M
Communication—General M
Corporate and Organizational
Communication M
Counseling Psychology M,D
English M
Experimental Psychology M
History M
International Affairs M,O
Jewish Studies M,O
Marriage and Family Therapy M
Museum Studies M
Pastoral Ministry and Counseling M,O
Psychology—General M,D
Public Administration M,O
Public Policy M,O
Religion M,O
School Psychology M
Speech and Interpersonal
Communication M
Sport Psychology M
Theology M,O

SETON HILL UNIVERSITY
Art Therapy M
Marriage and Family Therapy M
Writing M

SHASTA BIBLE COLLEGE
Pastoral Ministry and Counseling M

SHAW UNIVERSITY
Theology M

SHENANDOAH UNIVERSITY
Applied Behavior Analysis M
Music M,D,O
Therapies—Dance, Drama, and
Music M,D,O
Writing M

SHEPHERDS THEOLOGICAL SEMINARY
Pastoral Ministry and Counseling M
Theology M

SHILOH UNIVERSITY
Pastoral Ministry and Counseling M,D
Theology M,D

SHIPPENSBURG UNIVERSITY OF PENNSYLVANIA
Clinical Psychology M,D
Communication—General M
Criminal Justice and Criminology M
Geography M
History M
Psychology—General M
Public Administration M
Public History M
Sociology M

SH'OR YOSHUV RABBINICAL COLLEGE
Theology M

SIENA HEIGHTS UNIVERSITY
Clinical Psychology M,O
Counseling Psychology M,O

SILVER LAKE COLLEGE OF THE HOLY FAMILY
Music M

SIMMONS COLLEGE
Applied Behavior Analysis M,D,O
Communication—General M
Cultural Studies M
English M
Gender Studies M
History M
Public Policy M
Writing M,D,O

SIMON FRASER UNIVERSITY
Anthropology M,D
Archaeology M,D
Communication—General M,D
Comparative and Interdisciplinary
Arts M
Criminal Justice and Criminology M,D
Cultural Studies D
Economics M,D

English M,D
French M
Gender Studies M,D
Geography M,D
Gerontology M,D
History M,D
Humanities M
International Affairs M
Latin American Studies M,O
Liberal Studies M
Linguistics M,D
Philosophy M
Political Science M,D
Psychology—General M,D
Public Policy M
Publishing M
Sociology M,D
Urban Studies M,O
Women's Studies M,D

SIMPSON COLLEGE
Criminal Justice and Criminology M

SIMPSON UNIVERSITY
Counseling Psychology M
Missions and Missiology M
Pastoral Ministry and Counseling M

SIOUX FALLS SEMINARY
Marriage and Family Therapy M
Pastoral Ministry and Counseling M
Religion M
Theology M,D,O

SIT GRADUATE INSTITUTE
Conflict Resolution and
Mediation/Peace Studies M
International Affairs M
Sustainable Development M

SLIPPERY ROCK UNIVERSITY OF PENNSYLVANIA
Clinical Psychology M
Counseling Psychology M
Criminal Justice and Criminology M
English M
History M
School Psychology M
Therapies—Dance, Drama, and
Music M

SMITH COLLEGE
Dance M
History M
Theater M
Women's Studies O

SOFIA UNIVERSITY
Clinical Psychology M,D
Counseling Psychology M,D
Psychology—General M,D
Transpersonal and Humanistic
Psychology M,D

SONOMA STATE UNIVERSITY
Anthropology M
Clinical Psychology M
Counseling Psychology M
English M
History M
Interdisciplinary Studies M
Political Science M
Public Administration M
Public History M
School Psychology M
Writing M

SOTHEBY'S INSTITUTE OF ART–LONDON
Art/Fine Arts M
Arts Administration M
Decorative Arts M

SOTHEBY'S INSTITUTE OF ART–NEW YORK
Art/Fine Arts M
Arts Administration M
Decorative Arts M

SOUTH CAROLINA STATE UNIVERSITY
Agricultural Economics and
Agribusiness M
Child and Family Studies M
English M
Family and Consumer
Sciences-General M
Rehabilitation Counseling M

SOUTH DAKOTA STATE UNIVERSITY
Communication—General M
Consumer Economics M
Economics M
English M
Family and Consumer
Sciences-General M
Geography M
Industrial and Organizational
Psychology M
Journalism M
Sociology M,D

SOUTHEASTERN BAPTIST THEOLOGICAL SEMINARY
Ethics M,D
Missions and Missiology M,D
Music M,D
Philosophy M,D
Psychology—General M,D
Theology M,D
Women's Studies M,D

SOUTHEASTERN LOUISIANA UNIVERSITY
Communication—General M
English M

Health Communication M
History M
Industrial and Organizational
Psychology M
Journalism M
Music M
Psychology—General M
Sociology M
Writing M

SOUTHEASTERN OKLAHOMA STATE UNIVERSITY
Clinical Psychology M
Counseling Psychology M

SOUTHEASTERN UNIVERSITY (FL)
Counseling Psychology M
Marriage and Family Therapy M
Pastoral Ministry and Counseling M,D
Theology M,D
Urban and Regional Planning M

SOUTHEAST MISSOURI STATE UNIVERSITY
Counseling Psychology M,O
Criminal Justice and Criminology M
English M
Historic Preservation M,O
History M,O
Public Administration M
Public History M,O

SOUTHERN ADVENTIST UNIVERSITY
Counseling Psychology M
Missions and Missiology M
Psychology—General M
Religion M
Theology M

SOUTHERN ARKANSAS UNIVERSITY–MAGNOLIA
Public Administration M

THE SOUTHERN BAPTIST THEOLOGICAL SEMINARY
Missions and Missiology M,D
Pastoral Ministry and Counseling M,D
Philosophy M,D
Religion M,D
Theology M,D

SOUTHERN CALIFORNIA INSTITUTE OF ARCHITECTURE
Architecture M*

SOUTHERN CALIFORNIA SEMINARY
Counseling Psychology M,D
Marriage and Family Therapy M,D
Psychology—General M,D
Religion M,D
Theology M,D

SOUTHERN CONNECTICUT STATE UNIVERSITY
English M
History M
Political Science M
Psychology—General M
School Psychology M,O
Sociology M
Women's Studies M

SOUTHERN EVANGELICAL SEMINARY
Jewish Studies M,D,O
Missions and Missiology M,D,O
Near and Middle Eastern Studies M,D,O
Pastoral Ministry and Counseling M,D,O
Philosophy M,D,O
Religion M,D,O
Theology M,D,O

SOUTHERN ILLINOIS UNIVERSITY CARBONDALE
Agricultural Economics and
Agribusiness M
Anthropology M,D
Applied Arts and Design—
General M
Architecture M
Art/Fine Arts M
Clinical Psychology M,D
Communication—General M,D
Counseling Psychology M,D
Criminal Justice and Criminology M,D
Cultural Studies M
Economics M,D
English M,D
Experimental Psychology M,D
Geography M,D
History M,D
Homeland Security M
Linguistics M
Mass Communication M,D
Media Studies M,D
Music M
Philosophy M,D
Political Science M,D
Psychology—General M,D
Public Administration M
Rhetoric M
Sociology M,D
Speech and Interpersonal
Communication M,D
Theater M,D
Writing M,D

SOUTHERN ILLINOIS UNIVERSITY EDWARDSVILLE
Art Therapy M
Art/Fine Arts M
Clinical Psychology M
Corporate and Organizational
Communication M
Cultural Anthropology M

Economics — M
English — M,O
Geography — M
Health Communication — M
History — M
Industrial and Organizational Psychology — M
Interdisciplinary Studies — M
Mass Communication — M
Media Studies — O
Museum Studies — O
Music — M
Psychology—General — M,O
Public Administration — M
School Psychology — O
Sociology — M
Speech and Interpersonal Communication — M
Sport Psychology — M
Sustainable Development — M
Writing — M

SOUTHERN METHODIST UNIVERSITY
Anthropology — M,D
Applied Economics — M,D
Art History — M,D
Art/Fine Arts — M
Arts Administration — M
Clinical Psychology — D
Conflict Resolution and Mediation/Peace Studies — M
Economics — M,D
English — M,D
Ethics — M,D
Experimental Psychology — M,D
History — M,D
Liberal Studies — M
Medieval and Renaissance Studies — M
Music — M
Photography — M
Psychology—General — D
Religion — M,D
Sustainable Development — M,D
Theater — M
Theology — M,D

SOUTHERN NAZARENE UNIVERSITY
Counseling Psychology — M
Marriage and Family Therapy — M
Psychology—General — M

SOUTHERN NEW HAMPSHIRE UNIVERSITY
Applied Economics — M,D,O
Clinical Psychology — M
Criminal Justice and Criminology — M
Economic Development — M,D,O
Economics — M,D,O
English — M
History — M
Internet and Interactive Multimedia — M,D,O
Political Science — M
Psychology—General — M
Public Administration — M,D,O
Writing — M

SOUTHERN OREGON UNIVERSITY
Counseling Psychology — M
French — M
Interdisciplinary Studies — M
Music — M
Psychology—General — M
Spanish — M
Theater — M

SOUTHERN UNIVERSITY AND AGRICULTURAL AND MECHANICAL COLLEGE
Criminal Justice and Criminology — M
History — M
Mass Communication — M
Political Science — M
Psychology—General — M
Public Administration — M
Public Policy — D
Rehabilitation Counseling — M
Social Sciences — M

SOUTHERN UNIVERSITY AT NEW ORLEANS
Criminal Justice and Criminology — M
Museum Studies — M

SOUTHERN UTAH UNIVERSITY
Arts Administration — M
Communication—General — M
Interdisciplinary Studies — M
Music — M
Public Administration — M

SOUTHERN WESLEYAN UNIVERSITY
Pastoral Ministry and Counseling — M

SOUTH FLORIDA BIBLE COLLEGE AND THEOLOGICAL SEMINARY
Theology — M

SOUTH UNIVERSITY (AL)
Counseling Psychology — M
Criminal Justice and Criminology — M
Public Administration — M

SOUTH UNIVERSITY
Counseling Psychology — M
Criminal Justice and Criminology — M
Public Administration — M

SOUTH UNIVERSITY
Criminal Justice and Criminology — M

SOUTH UNIVERSITY (GA)
Counseling Psychology — M
Criminal Justice and Criminology — M
Pastoral Ministry and Counseling — D
Public Administration — M

SOUTH UNIVERSITY (SC)
Counseling Psychology — M

Criminal Justice and Criminology — M

SOUTH UNIVERSITY (TX)
Counseling Psychology — M

SOUTH UNIVERSITY
Counseling Psychology — M

SOUTH UNIVERSITY
Counseling Psychology — M

SOUTHWESTERN ASSEMBLIES OF GOD UNIVERSITY
Counseling Psychology — M
History — M
Missions and Missiology — M
Pastoral Ministry and Counseling — M
Religion — M
Theology — M

SOUTHWESTERN BAPTIST THEOLOGICAL SEMINARY
Missions and Missiology — M,D
Music — M
Near and Middle Eastern Studies — M,D
Pastoral Ministry and Counseling — M,D
Theology — M,D

SOUTHWESTERN CHRISTIAN UNIVERSITY
Missions and Missiology — M
Pastoral Ministry and Counseling — M

SOUTHWESTERN COLLEGE (KS)
Criminal Justice and Criminology — M

SOUTHWESTERN COLLEGE (NM)
Art Therapy — M
Counseling Psychology — M,O
Health Psychology — O
Psychology—General — O
Social Psychology — O
Thanatology — M,O

SOUTHWESTERN OKLAHOMA STATE UNIVERSITY
Music — M
School Psychology — M

SOUTHWEST UNIVERSITY
Criminal Justice and Criminology — M

SOUTHWEST UNIVERSITY OF VISUAL ARTS
Art/Fine Arts — M
Photography — M

SPALDING UNIVERSITY
Clinical Psychology — M,D
Corporate and Organizational Communication — M
Psychology—General — M,D
Writing — M

SPERTUS INSTITUTE FOR JEWISH LEARNING AND LEADERSHIP
Jewish Studies — M,D

SPRING ARBOR UNIVERSITY
Child and Family Studies — M
Communication—General — M
Counseling Psychology — M
Pastoral Ministry and Counseling — M
Theology — M

SPRINGFIELD COLLEGE
Art Therapy — M,O
Clinical Psychology — M,D,O
Counseling Psychology — M,D,O
Industrial and Organizational Psychology — M,D,O
Rehabilitation Counseling — M
Sport Psychology — M,D,O

SPRING HILL COLLEGE
Art/Fine Arts — M,O
English — M,O
Ethics — M,O
Liberal Studies — M,O
Pastoral Ministry and Counseling — M,O
Theology — M,O

STANFORD UNIVERSITY
Anthropology — M,D
Applied Arts and Design—General — M,D,O
Archaeology — M,D
Art/Fine Arts — M,D
Asian Languages — M,D
Asian Studies — M
Chinese — M,D
Classics — M,D
Communication—General — M,D
Comparative Literature — D
Cultural Studies — M
East European and Russian Studies — M
Economics — D
English — M,D
Film, Television, and Video Production — M,D
French — M,D
German — M,D
History — M,D
Italian — M,D
Japanese — M,D
Linguistics — M,D
Music — M,D
Philosophy — M,D
Political Science — M,D
Psychology—General — D
Religion — D
Slavic Languages — D
Sociology — D
Spanish — M,D
Sustainable Development — M,D,O
Theater — M,D

STARR KING SCHOOL FOR THE MINISTRY
Theology — M

STATE UNIVERSITY OF NEW YORK AT FREDONIA
English — M,O
Interdisciplinary Studies — M,O
Music — M,O
Writing — M,O

STATE UNIVERSITY OF NEW YORK AT NEW PALTZ
Art/Fine Arts — M
Clinical Psychology — M,O
Counseling Psychology — M,O
English — M,O
French — M,O
Music — M
Psychology—General — M,O
Spanish — M,O
Therapies—Dance, Drama, and Music — M

STATE UNIVERSITY OF NEW YORK AT OSWEGO
Art/Fine Arts — M
Child and Family Studies — M
Communication—General — M
Consumer Economics — M
Corporate and Organizational Communication — M
Counseling Psychology — M
English — M
Graphic Design — M
Health Communication — M
History — M
Internet and Interactive Multimedia — M

STATE UNIVERSITY OF NEW YORK AT PLATTSBURGH
Clinical Psychology — M,O
Counseling Psychology — M,O
Psychology—General — M,O
School Psychology — M,O

STATE UNIVERSITY OF NEW YORK COLLEGE AT CORTLAND
English — M
History — M

STATE UNIVERSITY OF NEW YORK COLLEGE AT GENESEO
French — M
Spanish — M

STATE UNIVERSITY OF NEW YORK COLLEGE AT OLD WESTBURY
Counseling Psychology — M
Liberal Studies — M

STATE UNIVERSITY OF NEW YORK COLLEGE AT ONEONTA
Museum Studies — M

STATE UNIVERSITY OF NEW YORK COLLEGE AT POTSDAM
Communication—General — M
English — M
Music — M

STATE UNIVERSITY OF NEW YORK COLLEGE OF ENVIRONMENTAL SCIENCE AND FORESTRY
Economics — M,D
Geographic Information Systems — M,D
Landscape Architecture — M
Sustainable Development — M,D,O
Urban and Regional Planning — M,D
Urban Design — M

STATE UNIVERSITY OF NEW YORK EMPIRE STATE COLLEGE
Economic Development — M
Industrial and Labor Relations — M
Liberal Studies — M
Public Policy — M

STEPHEN F. AUSTIN STATE UNIVERSITY
Applied Arts and Design—General — M
Art/Fine Arts — M
Communication—General — M
English — M
Family and Consumer Sciences-General — M
History — M
Interdisciplinary Studies — M
Mass Communication — M
Music — M
Psychology—General — M
Public Administration — M
School Psychology — M

STEPHENS COLLEGE
Addictions/Substance Abuse Counseling — M,O
Clinical Psychology — M,O
Writing — M,O

STETSON UNIVERSITY
Counseling Psychology — M
Marriage and Family Therapy — M
Writing — M

STEVENS INSTITUTE OF TECHNOLOGY
Communication—General — M,D,O
Computer Art and Design — M,D,O
Corporate and Organizational Communication — O
Ethics — M,O
Film, Television, and Video Production — M
Internet and Interactive Multimedia — M,D,O
Media Studies — M

STEVENSON UNIVERSITY
Communication—General — M
Forensic Sciences — M

STOCKTON UNIVERSITY
American Studies — M,O
Criminal Justice and Criminology — M
Holocaust and Genocide Studies — M

STONY BROOK UNIVERSITY, STATE UNIVERSITY OF NEW YORK
Addictions/Substance Abuse Counseling — M,O
African Studies — M,O
Anthropology — M,D
Art History — M,D
Art/Fine Arts — M
Asian Studies — M
Asian-American Studies — M
Clinical Psychology — D
Cognitive Sciences — D
Comparative Literature — M,D,O
Cultural Studies — M,D,O
Economics — M,D
English — M,D,O
Film, Television, and Video Production — M
French — M
Gender Studies — O
Geographic Information Systems — O
Health Communication — M,O
Health Psychology — D
Hispanic and Latin American Languages — M,D
History — M,D
Italian — M
Journalism — M,O
Liberal Studies — M,O
Linguistics — M,D
Music — M,D
Philosophy — M,D,O
Political Science — M,D
Psychology—General — M,D
Public Policy — M
Romance Languages — M
Social Psychology — D
Sociology — M,D
Theater — M
Women's Studies — O
Writing — M,O

STRATFORD UNIVERSITY (VA)
Forensic Sciences — M,D

STRAYER UNIVERSITY
Public Administration — M

SUFFOLK UNIVERSITY
Applied Arts and Design—General — M
Clinical Psychology — M,D,O
Corporate and Organizational Communication — M
Counseling Psychology — M,D,O
Criminal Justice and Criminology — M,O
Ethics — M,O
Graphic Design — M
Interior Design — M
Political Science — M,O
Psychology—General — M,D,O
Public Administration — M
Public Policy — M,O

SUL ROSS STATE UNIVERSITY
Art History — M
Art/Fine Arts — M
Criminal Justice and Criminology — M
Emergency Management — M
English — M
History — M
Political Science — M
Psychology—General — M

SUM BIBLE COLLEGE & THEOLOGICAL SEMINARY
Pastoral Ministry and Counseling — M
Religion — M
Theology — M

SYRACUSE UNIVERSITY
Addictions/Substance Abuse Counseling — M,O
African Studies — M
African-American Studies — M
Anthropology — M,D
Applied Arts and Design—General — M
Architecture — M
Art History — M
Art/Fine Arts — M
Arts Journalism — M
Broadcast Journalism — M
Child and Family Studies — M,D
Clinical Psychology — M,D
Cognitive Sciences — D
Communication—General — M,D
Computer Art and Design — M
Conflict Resolution and Mediation/Peace Studies — O
Disability Studies — O
Economics — M,D
Emergency Management — O
English — M,D
Film, Television, and Video Production — M
Forensic Sciences — M,O
French — M
Geography — M,D
History — M,D
Human Development — M,D
Illustration — M
International Affairs — M
Journalism — M
Linguistics — M
Marriage and Family Therapy — M,D
Mass Communication — M,D
Media Studies — M
Museum Studies — M
Music — M
Philosophy — M,D

Photography | M
Political Science | M,D,O
Psychology—General | D
Public Administration | M,D
Public Affairs | M
Religion | M,D
Rhetoric | M,D
School Psychology | M,D,O
Social Psychology | D
Social Sciences | M,D
Sociology | M
Spanish | M
Urban and Regional Planning | O
Writing | M,D

TALMUDIC UNIVERSITY
Theology | M

TARLETON STATE UNIVERSITY
Applied Psychology | M
Clinical Psychology | M,O
Communication—General | M
Counseling Psychology | M
Criminal Justice and Criminology | M
English | M
History | M
Political Science | M
Public Administration | M

TAYLOR COLLEGE AND SEMINARY
Cultural Studies | M,O
Missions and Missiology | M,O
Theology | M,O

TEACHERS COLLEGE, COLUMBIA UNIVERSITY
Anthropology | M,D
Applied Behavior Analysis | M,D,O
Applied Psychology | M
Arts Administration | M,D,O
Clinical Psychology | M,D
Communication—General | M,D
Counseling Psychology | M,D
Developmental Psychology | M,D
Economics | M,D
Industrial and Organizational Psychology | M,D
Interdisciplinary Studies | M,D
International Affairs | M,D,O
Linguistics | M,D,O
Philosophy | M,D,O
Political Science | M,D
Psychology—General | M,D
School Psychology | M,D,O
Social Psychology | M,D
Sociology | M,D

TELSHE YESHIVA–CHICAGO
Jewish Studies | O

TEMPLE UNIVERSITY
African-American Studies | M,D
Anthropology | D
Applied Behavior Analysis | M,D,O
Architecture | M
Art History | M,D
Art/Fine Arts | M
Arts Administration | M,D
Communication—General | M,D
Corporate and Organizational Communication | M,D
Counseling Psychology | M,D,O
Criminal Justice and Criminology | M,D
Dance | M,D
Economics | M,D
English | M,D
Film, Television, and Video Production | M
Geographic Information Systems | M,D,O
Geography | M,D,O
Gerontology | D
Graphic Design | M
History | M,D
Industrial and Labor Relations | M,O
Journalism | M
Landscape Architecture | M
Media Studies | M
Music | M,D
Philosophy | M,D
Photography | M
Political Science | M,D
Psychology—General | M,D
Religion | M,D
School Psychology | M,D,O
Social Psychology | M,D,O
Sociology | M,D
Spanish | M,D
Sustainable Development | M,O
Textile Design | M
Theater | M
Therapies—Dance, Drama, and Music | M,D
Urban and Regional Planning | M,O
Urban Studies | M,D,O
Writing | M

TENNESSEE STATE UNIVERSITY
Counseling Psychology | M
Criminal Justice and Criminology | M
Family and Consumer Sciences-General | M,D
Psychology—General | M,D
Public Administration | M,D

TENNESSEE TECHNOLOGICAL UNIVERSITY
Applied Behavior Analysis | D
English | M
Internet and Interactive Multimedia | M

TEXAS A&M INTERNATIONAL UNIVERSITY
Counseling Psychology | M

Criminal Justice and Criminology | M
English | M
Hispanic Studies | M,D
History | M,D
Political Science | M,D
Psychology—General | M
Public Administration | M
Social Sciences | M
Translation and Interpretation | M,D

TEXAS A&M UNIVERSITY
Agricultural Economics and Agribusiness | M,D
Anthropology | M,D
Architecture | M,D
Art/Fine Arts | M
Clinical Psychology | M,D
Communication—General | M,D
Counseling Psychology | M,D
Cultural Studies | M
Economics | M,D
English | M,D
Geography | M,D
History | M,D
Homeland Security | M,O
Industrial and Organizational Psychology | M,D
International Affairs | M,O
Landscape Architecture | M
Music | M
National Security | M,D
Philosophy | M,D
Political Science | M,D
Psychology—General | M,D
Public Administration | M,O
Public Affairs | M,O
School Psychology | M,D
Sociology | M,D
Spanish | M,D
Urban and Regional Planning | M,D

TEXAS A&M UNIVERSITY–CENTRAL TEXAS
Clinical Psychology | M,O
Criminal Justice and Criminology | M,O
Experimental Psychology | M,O
History | M,O
Liberal Studies | M
Marriage and Family Therapy | M,O
Political Science | M,O
School Psychology | M,O

TEXAS A&M UNIVERSITY–COMMERCE
Art/Fine Arts | M,D,O
Criminal Justice and Criminology | M,D,O
English | M,D,O
Film, Television, and Video Theory and Criticism | M,D,O
History | M,D,O
Holocaust and Genocide Studies | M,D,O
Homeland Security | M,D,O
Linguistics | M,D,O
Music | M,D,O
Political Science | M,D,O
Psychology—General | M,D,O
Public History | M,D,O
Sociology | M,D,O
Spanish | M,D,O
Theater | M,D,O
Writing | M,D,O

TEXAS A&M UNIVERSITY–CORPUS CHRISTI
Art/Fine Arts | M
Clinical Psychology | M
Communication—General | M
English | M
Geographic Information Systems | M,D
History | M
Human Development | M,D
Psychology—General | M
Public Administration | M

TEXAS A&M UNIVERSITY–KINGSVILLE
Agricultural Economics and Agribusiness | M,D
Criminal Justice and Criminology | M
Cultural Studies | M
English | M
Family and Consumer Sciences-General | M
Hispanic Studies | D
Music | M
Psychology—General | M
Sociology | M
Spanish | M
Sustainable Development | D

TEXAS A&M UNIVERSITY–SAN ANTONIO
Clinical Psychology | M
English | M
Marriage and Family Therapy | M

TEXAS A&M UNIVERSITY–TEXARKANA
Counseling Psychology | M
English | M
Interdisciplinary Studies | M
Psychology—General | M

TEXAS CHRISTIAN UNIVERSITY
American Studies | M,D
Art History | M
Art/Fine Arts | M
Cognitive Sciences | M,D
Communication—General | M
Corporate and Organizational Communication | M
Criminal Justice and Criminology | M
Developmental Psychology | M,D
English | M,D
Experimental Psychology | M,D
Gerontology | D

History | M,D
Latin American Studies | M,D
Liberal Studies | M
Mass Communication | M
Music | M,D
Psychology—General | M,D
Rhetoric | M,D
Social Psychology | M,D
Speech and Interpersonal Communication | M

TEXAS SOUTHERN UNIVERSITY
Art/Fine Arts | M
Communication—General | M
Criminal Justice and Criminology | M,D
English | M
Family and Consumer Sciences-General | M
History | M
Music | M
Psychology—General | M
Public Administration | M
Sociology | M
Urban and Regional Planning | M,D

TEXAS STATE UNIVERSITY
Anthropology | M
Applied Arts and Design—General | M
Child and Family Studies | M
Clinical Psychology | M
Communication—General | M
Computer Art and Design | M
Criminal Justice and Criminology | M,D
English | M
Ethics | M
Family and Consumer Sciences-General | M
Geographic Information Systems | M,D
Geography | M
Gerontology | M
Graphic Design | M
History | M
Interdisciplinary Studies | M
International Affairs | M
Marriage and Family Therapy | M
Mass Communication | M
Music | M
Philosophy | M
Political Science | M
Psychology—General | M
Public Administration | M
Rhetoric | M
School Psychology | O
Sociology | M
Spanish | M
Sustainable Development | M
Technical Communication | M
Theater | M
Writing | M

TEXAS TECH UNIVERSITY
Agricultural Economics and Agribusiness | M,D
Anthropology | M,D
Applied Economics | M,D
Architecture | M,D
Art History | M
Art/Fine Arts | M,D
Child and Family Studies | M,D
Clinical Psychology | M,D
Communication—General | M
Consumer Economics | M,D
Counseling Psychology | M,D
Cultural Studies | M,D
Economics | M,D
English | M,D
Environmental Design | M,D
Experimental Psychology | M,D
Forensic Sciences | M
Geography | M,D
Gerontology | M,D
History | M,D
Human Development | M,D
Interdisciplinary Studies | M,D
Interior Design | M,D
Landscape Architecture | M
Marriage and Family Therapy | M,D
Mass Communication | M,D
Media Studies | M,D
Museum Studies | M,D
Music | M,D
Philosophy | M
Political Science | M,D
Psychology—General | M,D
Public Administration | M,D
Rhetoric | M,D
Romance Languages | M,D
Sociology | M
Spanish | M,D
Sustainable Development | M
Technical Writing | M,D
Theater | M

TEXAS TECH UNIVERSITY HEALTH SCIENCES CENTER
Addictions/Substance Abuse Counseling | M
Clinical Psychology | M
Rehabilitation Counseling | M

TEXAS WOMAN'S UNIVERSITY
Art History | M
Art/Fine Arts | M
Child and Family Studies | M,D
Child Development | M,D
Counseling Psychology | M,D,O
Dance | M
English | M,D
Gender Studies | M,D
Graphic Design | M
History | M

Internet and Interactive Multimedia | M
Marriage and Family Therapy | M,D
Music | M
Photography | M
Political Science | M
Psychology—General | M,D,O
Rhetoric | M,D
School Psychology | M,D,O
Sociology | M,D
Theater | M
Therapies—Dance, Drama, and Music | M,D
Women's Studies | M,D

THEOLOGICAL UNIVERSITY OF THE CARIBBEAN
Missions and Missiology | M,D
Pastoral Ministry and Counseling | M,D

THOMAS EDISON STATE UNIVERSITY
Economic Development | M
Homeland Security | M
Industrial and Organizational Psychology | M,O
Liberal Studies | M,O
Public Administration | M
Urban and Regional Planning | M

THOMAS JEFFERSON UNIVERSITY
Applied Economics | M,D,O
Architecture | M
Art/Fine Arts | M
Clothing and Textiles | M
Emergency Management | M
Genetic Counseling | M
Geography | M
Industrial Design | M
Interior Design | M
Internet and Interactive Multimedia | M
Marriage and Family Therapy | M
Social Psychology | M
Sustainable Development | M
Textile Design | M
Urban and Regional Planning | M

THOMAS UNIVERSITY
Rehabilitation Counseling | M
Social Psychology | M

TIFFIN UNIVERSITY
Art/Fine Arts | M
Communication—General | M
Criminal Justice and Criminology | M
English | M
Film, Television, and Video Theory and Criticism | M
Forensic Psychology | M
Homeland Security | M
Humanities | M
Psychology—General | M
Writing | M

TORONTO SCHOOL OF THEOLOGY
Theology | M,D

TOURO COLLEGE
Counseling Psychology | M,D
Industrial and Organizational Psychology | M,D
Internet and Interactive Multimedia | M
Jewish Studies | M

TOWSON UNIVERSITY
Art History | M
Art/Fine Arts | M
Child and Family Studies | M,O
Communication—General | M
Corporate and Organizational Communication | M
Counseling Psychology | M
Experimental Psychology | M
Forensic Sciences | M
Geography | M
Homeland Security | M,O
Humanities | M
Internet and Interactive Multimedia | M,O
Jewish Studies | M,O
Liberal Studies | M
Music | M
Psychology—General | M
School Psychology | M
Social Sciences | M
Theater | M
Women's Studies | M,O
Writing | M

TRENT UNIVERSITY
American Indian/Native American Studies | M,D
Anthropology | M
Canadian Studies | M,D
Cultural Studies | D
Geography | M,D

TREVECCA NAZARENE UNIVERSITY
Marriage and Family Therapy | M,D
Pastoral Ministry and Counseling | M,D
Religion | M

TRIDENT UNIVERSITY INTERNATIONAL
Conflict Resolution and Mediation/Peace Studies | M,D
Criminal Justice and Criminology | M,D
Emergency Management | M,D,O
Public Administration | M,D

TRINE UNIVERSITY
Criminal Justice and Criminology | M
Emergency Management | M

TRINITY BAPTIST COLLEGE
Religion — M

TRINITY BIBLE COLLEGE AND GRADUATE SCHOOL
Missions and Missiology — M
Pastoral Ministry and Counseling — M
Theology — M

TRINITY CHRISTIAN COLLEGE
Counseling Psychology — M

TRINITY COLLEGE (CANADA)
Music — M,D,O
Pastoral Ministry and Counseling — M,D,O
Theology — M,D,O

TRINITY COLLEGE (UNITED STATES)
American Studies — M
Cultural Studies — M
English — M
Media Studies — M
Museum Studies — M
Public Policy — M
Writing — M

TRINITY INTERNATIONAL UNIVERSITY
Archaeology — M,D,O
Counseling Psychology — M,D,O
Missions and Missiology — M,D,O
Pastoral Ministry and Counseling — M,D,O
Theology — M,D,O

TRINITY INTERNATIONAL UNIVERSITY FLORIDA
Counseling Psychology — M
Religion — M,O

TRINITY LUTHERAN SEMINARY
African-American Studies — M
Missions and Missiology — M
Music — M
Pastoral Ministry and Counseling — M
Theology — M

TRINITY SCHOOL FOR MINISTRY
Missions and Missiology — M,D,O
Pastoral Ministry and Counseling — M,D,O
Religion — M,D,O
Theology — M,D,O

TRINITY UNIVERSITY
School Psychology — M

TRINITY WASHINGTON UNIVERSITY
Clinical Psychology — M
Communication—General — M
Counseling Psychology — M
National Security — M

TRINITY WESTERN UNIVERSITY
Counseling Psychology — M
English — M
History — M
Humanities — M
Interdisciplinary Studies — M
Linguistics — M
Pastoral Ministry and Counseling — M,D
Philosophy — M
Theology — M,D

TRI-STATE BIBLE COLLEGE
Theology — M

TROPICAL AGRICULTURE RESEARCH AND HIGHER EDUCATION CENTER
Agricultural Economics and Agribusiness — M,D

TROY UNIVERSITY
Communication—General — M
Corporate and Organizational Communication — M
Criminal Justice and Criminology — M
Economic Development — M
Economics — M
History — M
International Affairs — M
Public Administration — M
Social Sciences — M

TRUETT MCCONNELL UNIVERSITY
Counseling Psychology — M
Theology — M

TRUMAN STATE UNIVERSITY
English — M
Music — M

TUFTS UNIVERSITY
Art History — M
Art/Fine Arts — M,O
Child and Family Studies — M,D
Child Development — M
Classics — M
Cognitive Sciences — M,D
Economics — M,D
English — M
Family and Consumer Sciences-General — M,D
French — M
German — M
Health Communication — M,D,O
History — M,D
Human Development — M
Interdisciplinary Studies — D
International Affairs — M
International Development — M
Museum Studies — M,D,O
Music — M
Philosophy — M
Psychology—General — M,D
Public Administration — O
Public Policy — M,D
School Psychology — M,O
Theater — M
Urban and Regional Planning — M
Urban Studies — M

TULANE UNIVERSITY
Anthropology — D
Architecture — M
Art History — M
Art/Fine Arts — M
Classics — M
Dance — M
Economics — M,D
Emergency Management — M
English — M
French — M,D
History — M,D
Homeland Security — M
Interdisciplinary Studies — D
International Development — M,D
Latin American Studies — M
Liberal Studies — M
Music — M
Philosophy — M,D
Political Science — D
Portuguese — M,D
Psychology—General — M,D
Sociology — M
Spanish — M,D
Theater — M

TUSKEGEE UNIVERSITY
Agricultural Economics and Agribusiness — M

TYNDALE UNIVERSITY COLLEGE & SEMINARY
Missions and Missiology — M,O
Pastoral Ministry and Counseling — M,O
Theology — M,O

UNIFICATION THEOLOGICAL SEMINARY
Theology — M,D

UNIFORMED SERVICES UNIVERSITY OF THE HEALTH SCIENCES
Clinical Psychology — D
Psychology—General — D

UNION COLLEGE (KY)
Clinical Psychology — M
Counseling Psychology — M
Psychology—General — M
School Psychology — M

UNION INSTITUTE & UNIVERSITY
Clinical Psychology — M
Cultural Studies — M,D
History — M
Humanities — D
Interdisciplinary Studies — D
Public Policy — M,D
Writing — M

UNION THEOLOGICAL SEMINARY IN THE CITY OF NEW YORK
Theology — M,D

UNION UNIVERSITY
Cultural Studies — M
Pastoral Ministry and Counseling — M,D
Religion — M,D

UNITED LUTHERAN SEMINARY
Pastoral Ministry and Counseling — M
Religion — M,D
Theology — M,D

UNITED LUTHERAN SEMINARY
Pastoral Ministry and Counseling — M,D,O
Religion — M,D,O
Theology — M,D,O

UNITED STATES ARMY COMMAND AND GENERAL STAFF COLLEGE
Military and Defense Studies — M

UNITED STATES INTERNATIONAL UNIVERSITY–AFRICA
Addictions/Substance Abuse Counseling — M
Conflict Resolution and Mediation/Peace Studies — M
Counseling Psychology — M
Health Psychology — M
International Affairs — M

UNITED TALMUDICAL SEMINARY
Theology — M

UNITED THEOLOGICAL SEMINARY
Pastoral Ministry and Counseling — M,D
Theology — M,D

UNITED THEOLOGICAL SEMINARY OF THE TWIN CITIES
Art/Fine Arts — M,D,O
Asian Studies — M,D,O
Conflict Resolution and Mediation/Peace Studies — M,D,O
Ethnic Studies — M,D,O
Humanities — M,D,O
Pastoral Ministry and Counseling — M,D,O
Religion — M,D,O
Theology — M,D,O
Women's Studies — M,D,O

UNITY COLLEGE
Sustainable Development — M

UNIVERSIDAD AUTONOMA DE GUADALAJARA
Architecture — M,D
Computer Art and Design — M,D
Corporate and Organizational Communication — M,D
Film, Television, and Video Production — M,D
Internet and Interactive Multimedia — M,D
Philosophy — M,D
Public Policy — M,D
Spanish — M,D

Translation and Interpretation — M,D

UNIVERSIDAD CENTRAL DEL CARIBE
Addictions/Substance Abuse Counseling — M

UNIVERSIDAD DE IBEROAMERICA
Clinical Psychology — M,D
Forensic Psychology — M,D

UNIVERSIDAD DE LAS AMERICAS, A.C.
International Affairs — M
Marriage and Family Therapy — M
Psychology—General — M

UNIVERSIDAD DE LAS AMÉRICAS PUEBLA
American Studies — M
Anthropology — M
Archaeology — M
Computer Art and Design — M
Economics — M
English — M
Linguistics — M
Psychology—General — M

UNIVERSIDAD DEL ESTE
Agricultural Economics and Agribusiness — M
Criminal Justice and Criminology — M
Public Policy — M

UNIVERSIDAD DEL TURABO
Art/Fine Arts — M
Arts Administration — M
Conflict Resolution and Mediation/Peace Studies — M
Counseling Psychology — M,D
Criminal Justice and Criminology — M
Forensic Psychology — M,D,O
Forensic Sciences — M

UNIVERSIDAD IBEROAMERICANA
Corporate and Organizational Communication — M,D

UNIVERSIDAD METROPOLITANA
Counseling Psychology — M

UNIVERSIDAD NACIONAL PEDRO HENRIQUEZ URENA
Architecture — M
Historic Preservation — M
International Affairs — M
Political Science — M

UNIVERSITÉ DE MONCTON
Economics — M
French — M,D
History — M
Public Administration — M

UNIVERSITÉ DE MONTRÉAL
Anthropology — M,D
Art History — M,D
Classics — M
Communication—General — M,D
Comparative Literature — M,D
Criminal Justice and Criminology — M,D
Demography and Population Studies — M,D
Developmental Psychology — M
Economics — M,D,O
Emergency Management — O
English — M,D
Environmental Design — M,D,O
Film, Television, and Video Theory and Criticism — M,D
French — M,D
Genetic Counseling — O
Geography — M,D,O
German — M
Hispanic and Latin American Languages — M,D
History — M,D
Industrial and Labor Relations — M,D,O
International Affairs — M,O
Linguistics — M,D,O
Museum Studies — M
Music — M,D,O
Philosophy — M,D
Political Science — M,D
Psychology—General — M,D
Public Policy — O
Religion — M,D
Sociology — M,D
Spanish — M
Theology — M,D,O
Translation and Interpretation — M,D
Urban and Regional Planning — M,D,O

UNIVERSITÉ DE SAINT-BONIFACE
Canadian Studies — M

UNIVERSITÉ DE SHERBROOKE
Canadian Studies — M,D
Comparative Literature — M,D
Conflict Resolution and Mediation/Peace Studies — M,D
Corporate and Organizational Communication — M
Economic Development — D
Economics — M
Ethics — M,D,O
French — M,D
Geography — M,D
Gerontology — M
History — M
Linguistics — M,D
Philosophy — M,D,O
Psychology—General — M
Public Administration — M
Religion — M,D,O
Theater — M
Theology — M,D,O

UNIVERSITÉ DU QUÉBEC À CHICOUTIMI
Art/Fine Arts — M
Canadian Studies — M
Comparative Literature — M

Ethics — O
French — O
Linguistics — M
Theology — M

UNIVERSITÉ DU QUÉBEC À MONTRÉAL
Art History — M,D
Art/Fine Arts — M
Communication—General — M,D
Comparative Literature — M,D
Dance — M
Economics — M,D
Geographic Information Systems — O
Geography — M
History — M,D
Linguistics — M,D
Museum Studies — M
Philosophy — M,D
Political Science — M,D
Psychology—General — D
Public Administration — M
Religion — M,D
Sociology — M,D
Urban Studies — M,D

UNIVERSITÉ DU QUÉBEC À RIMOUSKI
Comparative Literature — M
Ethics — M,O
Social Psychology — M
Urban and Regional Planning — M,D,O

UNIVERSITÉ DU QUÉBEC À TROIS-RIVIÈRES
Communication—General — M,O
Comparative Literature — M
Industrial and Labor Relations — O
Philosophy — M,D
Psychology—General — D,O

UNIVERSITÉ DU QUÉBEC, ÉCOLE NATIONALE D'ADMINISTRATION PUBLIQUE
Public Administration — D,O
Urban Studies — M

UNIVERSITÉ DU QUÉBEC EN OUTAOUAIS
Industrial and Labor Relations — M,D,O
Urban and Regional Planning — M

UNIVERSITÉ DU QUÉBEC, INSTITUT NATIONAL DE LA RECHERCHE SCIENTIFIQUE
Demography and Population Studies — M,D,O
Urban Studies — M,D,O

UNIVERSITÉ LAVAL
Agricultural Economics and Agribusiness — M
Anthropology — M,D
Archaeology — M,D
Architecture — M
Art History — M,D
Art/Fine Arts — M
Clinical Psychology — D
Comparative Literature — M,D
Consumer Economics — O
Economics — M,D
English — M,D
Ethics — O
Ethnic Studies — M,D
Film, Television, and Video Theory and Criticism — M,D
Geographic Information Systems — M,O
Geography — M,D
Gerontology — O
Graphic Design — M
History — M,D
Industrial and Labor Relations — M,D
International Affairs — M,D
Journalism — O
Linguistics — M,D
Mass Communication — M,D
Museum Studies — O
Music — M,D
Philosophy — M,D
Political Science — M,D
Psychology—General — D
Religion — M,D
Rural Planning and Studies — O
Social Psychology — M,D
Sociology — M,D
Spanish — M,D
Theater — M,D
Theology — M,D
Translation and Interpretation — M,O
Urban and Regional Planning — M,D
Women's Studies — O

UNIVERSITY AT ALBANY, STATE UNIVERSITY OF NEW YORK
African Studies — M
African-American Studies — M
Anthropology — M,D
Art/Fine Arts — M
Clinical Psychology — M,D
Cognitive Sciences — M,D
Communication—General — M,D
Counseling Psychology — M,D,O
Criminal Justice and Criminology — M,D
Demography and Population Studies — M,D,O
Economics — M,D,O
Emergency Management — M,D,O
English — M,D
Forensic Sciences — M
Gender Studies — M
Geographic Information Systems — M,O
Geography — M,O
History — M,D,O
Homeland Security — M,D,O
Industrial and Organizational Psychology — M,D
Latin American Studies — M,D,O
Liberal Studies — M
Philosophy — M,D
Political Science — M,D

Psychology—General	M,D
Public Administration	M,D,O
Public History	M,D,O
Public Policy	M,D,O
Social Psychology	M,D
Sociology	M,D,O
Spanish	M,D
Urban and Regional Planning	M,O
Urban Studies	M,D,O
Women's Studies	M

UNIVERSITY AT BUFFALO, THE STATE UNIVERSITY OF NEW YORK

American Studies	M,D
Anthropology	M,D
Architecture	M
Art History	M,D
Art/Fine Arts	M
Arts Administration	M
Canadian Studies	M,D
Classics	M,D,O
Communication—General	M,D
Comparative Literature	M,D
Counseling Psychology	M,D,O
Dance	M,D
Economic Development	M,D,O
Economics	M,D,O
English	M,D,O
Film, Television, and Video Theory and Criticism	M,D,O
French	M,D,O
Gender Studies	M,D
Geographic Information Systems	M,D
Geography	M,D
German	M,D,O
Historic Preservation	M,D,O
History	M,D,O
Humanities	M
Interdisciplinary Studies	M,D
Linguistics	M,D
Media Studies	M,D,O
Museum Studies	M,D
Music	M,D,O
Philosophy	M,D
Political Science	M,D
Psychology—General	M,D
Public History	M,D,O
Rehabilitation Counseling	M,D,O
Romance Languages	M,D
Social Sciences	M
Sociology	M,D
Spanish	M,D,O
Sustainable Development	M,D
Theater	M,D
Urban and Regional Planning	M,D,O
Urban Design	M,D,O

UNIVERSITY OF ADVANCING TECHNOLOGY

Internet and Interactive Multimedia	M

THE UNIVERSITY OF AKRON

Arts Administration	M
Child and Family Studies	M
Child Development	M
Clinical Psychology	M
Clothing and Textiles	M
Communication—General	M
Counseling Psychology	M,D
Economics	M
English	M
Gerontology	D
History	M,D
Industrial and Organizational Psychology	M,D
Marriage and Family Therapy	M
Music	M
Political Science	M
Psychology—General	M,D
Public Administration	M
School Psychology	M
Sociology	M,D
Spanish	M
Theater	M
Writing	M

THE UNIVERSITY OF ALABAMA

American Studies	M
Anthropology	M,D
Art History	M
Art/Fine Arts	M
Child and Family Studies	M
Clinical Psychology	D
Clothing and Textiles	M
Communication—General	M,D
Consumer Economics	M
Criminal Justice and Criminology	M
Economics	M,D
English	M,D
Experimental Psychology	D
Family and Consumer Sciences-General	M,D
French	M,D
Geographic Information Systems	M,D
Geography	M,D
German	M,D
History	M,D
Human Development	M
Interdisciplinary Studies	D
Journalism	M
Marriage and Family Therapy	M
Mass Communication	D
Music	M,D
Photography	M
Political Science	M,D
Psychology—General	D
Public Administration	M,D
Rhetoric	M,D
Romance Languages	M,D
Spanish	M,D
Speech and Interpersonal Communication	M
Theater	M
Women's Studies	M
Writing	M,D

THE UNIVERSITY OF ALABAMA AT BIRMINGHAM

Anthropology	M
Art History	M
Clinical Psychology	M,D
Communication—General	M
Criminal Justice and Criminology	M
Developmental Psychology	M,D
English	M
Forensic Sciences	M
Genetic Counseling	M
Health Psychology	M,D
History	M
Psychology—General	M,D
Public Administration	M
Rhetoric	M
Sociology	D
Sustainable Development	M
Writing	M

THE UNIVERSITY OF ALABAMA IN HUNTSVILLE

English	M,O
History	M
Industrial and Organizational Psychology	M
Psychology—General	M
Public Affairs	M
Technical Writing	M,O

UNIVERSITY OF ALASKA ANCHORAGE

Anthropology	M
Clinical Psychology	M,D
English	M
Interdisciplinary Studies	M
Psychology—General	M,D
Public Administration	M
Social Psychology	M,D
Writing	M

UNIVERSITY OF ALASKA FAIRBANKS

Anthropology	M,D
Art/Fine Arts	M
Clinical Psychology	D
Communication—General	M
Computer Art and Design	M
Corporate and Organizational Communication	M
Criminal Justice and Criminology	M
Cultural Studies	M
Economics	M
Emergency Management	M
English	M
Geographic Information Systems	M
History	M
Homeland Security	M
Interdisciplinary Studies	M,D
Linguistics	M
Music	M
Northern Studies	M
Photography	M
Psychology—General	D
Rural Planning and Studies	M
Social Psychology	M,D,O
Sustainable Development	M,D
Writing	M

UNIVERSITY OF ALASKA SOUTHEAST

Public Administration	M

UNIVERSITY OF ALBERTA

Agricultural Economics and Agribusiness	M,D
Anthropology	M,D
Applied Arts and Design—General	M
Archaeology	M,D
Art History	M
Art/Fine Arts	M
Asian Studies	M
Chinese	M
Classics	M,D
Clothing and Textiles	M,D
Communication—General	M
Counseling Psychology	M,D
Criminal Justice and Criminology	M,D
Demography and Population Studies	M,D
East European and Russian Studies	M,D
Economics	M,D
English	M,D
Family and Consumer Sciences-General	M,D
Folklore	M,D
French	M,D
German	M,D
Hispanic Studies	M,D
History	M,D
Industrial and Labor Relations	D
Italian	M,D
Japanese	M
Linguistics	M,D
Music	M,D
Philosophy	M,D
Political Science	M,D
Psychology—General	M,D
Rural Sociology	M,D
School Psychology	M,D
Slavic Languages	M,D
Sociology	M,D
Theater	M

UNIVERSITY OF ANTELOPE VALLEY

Criminal Justice and Criminology	M

THE UNIVERSITY OF ARIZONA

African Studies	M,D,O
Agricultural Economics and Agribusiness	M
American Indian/Native American Studies	M,D
Anthropology	M,D,O
Applied Economics	M
Architecture	M
Art History	M,D
Art/Fine Arts	M
Asian Studies	M,D
Child and Family Studies	M,D,O
Classics	M
Communication—General	M,D
Counseling Psychology	M
Dance	M
Economics	M,D
English	M,D
Family and Consumer Sciences-General	D
Film, Television, and Video Theory and Criticism	M
French	M
Gender Studies	M,D,O
Geographic Information Systems	M,D,O
Geography	M,D,O
German	M,D
History	M,D,O
Human Development	M,D,O
Interdisciplinary Studies	M,D
Journalism	M
Landscape Architecture	M
Latin American Studies	M
Linguistics	M,D
Music	M,D
Near and Middle Eastern Studies	M,D,O
Philosophy	M,D
Political Science	M,D
Psychology—General	M,D
Public Administration	M,D,O
Public Policy	M,D,O
Rehabilitation Counseling	M,D
Rhetoric	M,D
Russian	M
School Psychology	D,O
Sociology	M,D
Spanish	M,D
Theater	M
Urban and Regional Planning	M
Women's Studies	M,D,O
Writing	M

UNIVERSITY OF ARKANSAS

Agricultural Economics and Agribusiness	M
Anthropology	M,D
Art/Fine Arts	M
Communication—General	M
Comparative Literature	M,D
Cultural Studies	M,D
Economics	M,D
English	M,D
Family and Consumer Sciences-General	M
French	M
Geography	M
German	M
History	M,D
Journalism	M
Music	M
Philosophy	M,D
Political Science	M
Psychology—General	M,D
Public Administration	M
Public Policy	D
Rehabilitation Counseling	M,D
Sociology	M
Spanish	M
Theater	M
Writing	M

UNIVERSITY OF ARKANSAS AT LITTLE ROCK

Applied Psychology	M
Art History	M
Art/Fine Arts	M
Conflict Resolution and Mediation/Peace Studies	O
Criminal Justice and Criminology	M,D
Gerontology	O
Interdisciplinary Studies	M
Mass Communication	M
Psychology—General	M
Public Administration	M
Public Affairs	M,O
Public History	M
Rehabilitation Counseling	M,O
Rhetoric	M
Speech and Interpersonal Communication	M
Technical Writing	M
Writing	M

UNIVERSITY OF ARKANSAS FOR MEDICAL SCIENCES

Genetic Counseling	M,D

UNIVERSITY OF BALTIMORE

Applied Arts and Design—General	M
Applied Psychology	M
Conflict Resolution and Mediation/Peace Studies	M
Counseling Psychology	M
Criminal Justice and Criminology	M
Ethics	M
Graphic Design	M,D
Public Administration	M,D
Public Affairs	M,D
Publishing	M
Writing	M

UNIVERSITY OF BRIDGEPORT

Applied Arts and Design—General	M
Asian Studies	M
Clinical Psychology	M
Communication—General	M
Conflict Resolution and Mediation/Peace Studies	M
Counseling Psychology	M
International Affairs	M
Media Studies	M
Social Psychology	M

THE UNIVERSITY OF BRITISH COLUMBIA

Agricultural Economics and Agribusiness	M
Anthropology	M,D
Archaeology	M
Architecture	M
Art History	M,D
Art/Fine Arts	M,D
Asian Studies	M,D
Classics	M,D
Clinical Psychology	M,D
Cognitive Sciences	M,D
Counseling Psychology	M,D,O
Developmental Psychology	M,D
East European and Russian Studies	M,D
Economics	M,D
English	M,D
Ethnic Studies	M
Film, Television, and Video Production	M
Film, Television, and Video Theory and Criticism	M
French	M,D
Gender Studies	M,D
Genetic Counseling	M
Geography	M,D
German	M,D
Health Psychology	M,D
Hispanic Studies	M,D
History	M,D
Human Development	M,D,O
International Affairs	M
Internet and Interactive Multimedia	M
Journalism	M
Landscape Architecture	M
Linguistics	M,D
Museum Studies	M,D
Music	M,D
Pacific Area/Pacific Rim Studies	M
Philosophy	M,D
Political Science	M,D
Psychology—General	M,D
Public Policy	M
Religion	M,D
School Psychology	M,D,O
Social Psychology	M,D
Sociology	M,D
Sustainable Development	M
Theater	M,D
Urban and Regional Planning	M,D
Urban Design	M
Writing	M,D

UNIVERSITY OF CALGARY

Anthropology	M,D
Applied Psychology	M,D
Archaeology	M
Architecture	M,D
Art/Fine Arts	M
Classics	M,D
Clinical Psychology	M,D
Communication—General	M,D
Counseling Psychology	M,D
Economics	M,D
English	M,D
Environmental Design	M,D
French	M,D
Geography	M,D
German	M,D
History	M,D
Landscape Architecture	M,D
Linguistics	M,D
Military and Defense Studies	M,D
Music	M,D
Philosophy	M,D
Political Science	M,D
Psychology—General	M,D
Public Policy	M
Religion	M,D
School Psychology	M,D
Sociology	M,D
Spanish	M,D
Sustainable Development	M,D
Theater	M

UNIVERSITY OF CALIFORNIA, BERKELEY

Addictions/Substance Abuse Counseling	O
African-American Studies	D
Agricultural Economics and Agribusiness	D
Anthropology	D
Applied Arts and Design—General	O
Archaeology	M,D
Architectural History	M,D
Architecture	M,D
Art History	D
Art/Fine Arts	M,O
Asian Languages	M,D
Asian Studies	M,D
Building Science	M,D
Chinese	D
Classics	M,D
Comparative Literature	D

*M—masters degree; D—doctorate; O—other advanced degree; *—Close-Up and/or Display*

Counseling Psychology	O
Demography and Population Studies	M,D
Economics	D
English	D
Environmental Design	M,D
Ethnic Studies	D
Film, Television, and Video Theory and Criticism	D
Folklore	M
French	D
Geography	D
German	D
Hispanic and Latin American Languages	D
History of Science and Technology	D
History	M,D
Human Development	M,D
Industrial and Labor Relations	D
Interior Design	O
International Affairs	M
Italian	D
Japanese	D
Journalism	M
Landscape Architecture	M,D,O
Linguistics	D
Music	D
Near and Middle Eastern Studies	M,D
Philosophy	D
Political Science	D
Psychology—General	D
Public Affairs	M
Public Policy	M,D
Religion	D
Rhetoric	D
Romance Languages	D
Russian	D
Scandinavian Languages	D
Slavic Languages	D
Sociology	D
Spanish	D
Sustainable Development	M,O
Theater	D
Urban and Regional Planning	M,D
Urban Design	M,D
Writing	O

UNIVERSITY OF CALIFORNIA, DAVIS

Agricultural Economics and Agribusiness	M,D
American Indian/Native American Studies	M,D
Anthropology	M,D
Art History	M
Art/Fine Arts	M
Child Development	M
Clothing and Textiles	M
Communication—General	M
Comparative Literature	D
Cultural Studies	M,D
Economics	M,D
English	M,D
Forensic Sciences	M
French	D
Geography	M,D
German	M,D
History	M,D
Human Development	D
Linguistics	M,D
Music	M,D
Philosophy	M,D
Political Science	M,D
Psychology—General	D
Sociology	M,D
Spanish	M,D
Textile Design	M
Theater	M
Urban and Regional Planning	M
Writing	M,D

UNIVERSITY OF CALIFORNIA, IRVINE

Anthropology	M,D
Art/Fine Arts	M,D
Asian Languages	M,D
Chinese	M,D
Classics	M,D
Comparative Literature	M,D
Criminal Justice and Criminology	M,D
Cultural Studies	D
Dance	M
Demography and Population Studies	M
Economics	M,D
English	M,D
Environmental Design	D
French	M,D
Genetic Counseling	M
German	M,D
History	M,D
Japanese	M,D
Music	M
Philosophy	M,D
Political Science	D
Psychology—General	D
Sociology	D
Spanish	M,D
Theater	M,D
Urban and Regional Planning	M,D
Urban Studies	M,D
Writing	M

UNIVERSITY OF CALIFORNIA, LOS ANGELES

African Studies	M
African-American Studies	M
American Indian/Native American Studies	M
Anthropology	M,D
Applied Arts and Design—General	M
Applied Economics	M
Archaeology	M,D
Architecture	M,D
Art History	M,D
Art/Fine Arts	M
Asian Languages	M,D
Asian Studies	M,D
Asian-American Studies	M
Classics	M,D
Comparative Literature	M,D
Dance	M,D
Economics	D*
English	M,D
Film, Television, and Video Production	M,D
French	M,D
Gender Studies	M,D
Geography	M,D
German	M,D
Hispanic and Latin American Languages	D
Historic Preservation	M
History	M,D
Italian	M,D
Latin American Studies	M
Linguistics	M,D
Media Studies	M,D
Music	M,D
Near and Middle Eastern Languages	M,D
Near and Middle Eastern Studies	M,D
Philosophy	M,D
Political Science	M,D
Portuguese	M
Psychology—General	M,D
Public Affairs	M,D
Public Policy	M
Scandinavian Languages	M
Slavic Languages	M,D
Sociology	M,D
Spanish	M
Theater	M,D
Urban and Regional Planning	M,D
Urban Design	M,D

UNIVERSITY OF CALIFORNIA, MERCED

Cognitive Sciences	M,D
Humanities	M,D
Psychology—General	M,D
Social Sciences	M,D
Sociology	M,D

UNIVERSITY OF CALIFORNIA, RIVERSIDE

Anthropology	M,D
Applied Behavior Analysis	M,D,O
Art History	M,D
Art/Fine Arts	M
Asian Studies	M
Classics	D
Comparative Literature	M,D
Cultural Studies	D
Dance	M
Economics	M,D
English	M,D
Ethnic Studies	D
Hispanic Studies	M,D
History	M,D
Music	M,D
Philosophy	M,D
Political Science	M,D
Psychology—General	D
Public Policy	M,D
Religion	M,D
School Psychology	M,D,O
Sociology	M,D
Spanish	M,D
Writing	M

UNIVERSITY OF CALIFORNIA, SAN DIEGO

Anthropology	D
Art History	M,D
Art/Fine Arts	M,D
Clinical Psychology	D
Cognitive Sciences	D
Communication—General	D
Dance	M,D
Economics	D
English	M,D
Ethnic Studies	D
History of Science and Technology	D
History	M,D
International Affairs	M,D
International Development	M
International Economics	M
Jewish Studies	M,D
Latin American Studies	M
Linguistics	D
Music	M,D
Philosophy	D
Political Science	M,D
Psychology—General	D
Public Policy	M
Sociology	D
Theater	M,D
Writing	M,D

UNIVERSITY OF CALIFORNIA, SAN FRANCISCO

Anthropology	D
History of Science and Technology	M,D
Sociology	D

UNIVERSITY OF CALIFORNIA, SANTA BARBARA

African-American Studies	D
Agricultural Economics and Agribusiness	M,D
Anthropology	M,D
Art History	D
Art/Fine Arts	M
Asian Languages	M,D
Asian Studies	M,D
Classics	M,D
Clinical Psychology	M,D,O
Cognitive Sciences	M,D
Communication—General	D
Comparative Literature	D
Counseling Psychology	M,D,O
Cultural Anthropology	M,D
Cultural Studies	M,D
Economics	M,D
English	D
Film, Television, and Video Production	D
French	D
Geography	M,D
Hispanic and Latin American Languages	M,D
Hispanic Studies	M,D
History	D
Interdisciplinary Studies	D
International Affairs	M,D
Latin American Studies	M
Linguistics	M,D
Media Studies	M,D
Medieval and Renaissance Studies	M,D
Music	M,D
Philosophy	D
Political Science	M,D
Portuguese	M,D
Psychology—General	D
Public History	D
Religion	M,D
School Psychology	M,D,O
Social Sciences	D
Sociology	D
Spanish	M,D
Speech and Interpersonal Communication	D
Sustainable Development	M,D
Theater	M,D
Translation and Interpretation	M,D
Women's Studies	M,D
Writing	D

UNIVERSITY OF CALIFORNIA, SANTA CRUZ

Anthropology	D
Applied Economics	M
Art/Fine Arts	M,D
Communication—General	O
Comparative Literature	M,D
Computer Art and Design	M,D
Cultural Anthropology	D
Economics	D
English	M,D
Film, Television, and Video Theory and Criticism	D
History	M,D
Humanities	D
Interdisciplinary Studies	M,D
International Affairs	D
Internet and Interactive Multimedia	M,D
Linguistics	M,D
Music	M,D
Philosophy	M,D
Political Science	D
Psychology—General	D
Social Sciences	D
Sociology	D
Theater	O
Writing	M

UNIVERSITY OF CENTRAL ARKANSAS

Computer Art and Design	M
Counseling Psychology	M,O
Economic Development	M,O
Economics	M,O
English	M
Family and Consumer Sciences-General	M
Film, Television, and Video Production	M
Geographic Information Systems	M,O
Geography	M,O
History	M
Music	M,O
Psychology—General	M,D,O
School Psychology	M,D,O
Social Psychology	M
Urban and Regional Planning	M,O
Writing	M

UNIVERSITY OF CENTRAL FLORIDA

Anthropology	M
Art/Fine Arts	M
Clinical Psychology	M,D
Cognitive Sciences	D
Communication—General	M,O
Computer Art and Design	M
Corporate and Organizational Communication	M,O
Criminal Justice and Criminology	M,D,O
Emergency Management	M,O
English	M,D,O
Film, Television, and Video Production	M
Forensic Sciences	M,D
Geographic Information Systems	M,O
History	M
Homeland Security	M,O
Industrial and Organizational Psychology	M,D
Interdisciplinary Studies	M,O
Marriage and Family Therapy	M,O
Music	M
National Security	M,D,O
Political Science	M,D,O
Psychology—General	M,D
Public Administration	M,O
Public Affairs	D
School Psychology	O
Sociology	M,D
Spanish	M
Theater	M
Urban and Regional Planning	M,O
Writing	M,D,O

UNIVERSITY OF CENTRAL MISSOURI

Communication—General	M,D,O
Counseling Psychology	M,D,O
Criminal Justice and Criminology	M,D,O
English	M,D,O
Gerontology	M,D,O
History	M,D,O
Music	M,D,O
Psychology—General	M,D,O
Sociology	M,D,O
Theater	M,D,O

UNIVERSITY OF CENTRAL OKLAHOMA

Addictions/Substance Abuse Counseling	M
Applied Arts and Design—General	M
Child and Family Studies	M
Counseling Psychology	M
Criminal Justice and Criminology	M
English	M
Experimental Psychology	M
Family and Consumer Sciences-General	M
Forensic Psychology	M
Forensic Sciences	M
Gerontology	M
History	M
Human Development	M
Interdisciplinary Studies	M
Liberal Studies	M
Marriage and Family Therapy	M
Museum Studies	M
Music	M
Political Science	M
Psychology—General	M
Public Administration	M
Rhetoric	M
School Psychology	M
Sociology	M
Urban and Regional Planning	M
Writing	M

UNIVERSITY OF CHARLESTON

Forensic Sciences	M

UNIVERSITY OF CHICAGO

Anthropology	D
Archaeology	D
Art History	M,D
Art/Fine Arts	M
Asian Languages	D
Asian Studies	M,D
Classics	M,D
Comparative Literature	M,D
Economics	M,D,O
Emergency Management	M
English	M,D
Ethics	D
Film, Television, and Video Theory and Criticism	D
French	D
Gender Studies	D
German	M,D
History	D
Human Development	D
Humanities	M
International Affairs	M
Internet and Interactive Multimedia	M
Italian	D
Latin American Studies	M
Liberal Studies	M
Linguistics	M,D
Media Studies	M,D
Medieval and Renaissance Studies	D
Music	M,D
Near and Middle Eastern Languages	D
Near and Middle Eastern Studies	M,D
Pastoral Ministry and Counseling	M
Philosophy	M,D
Political Science	D
Psychology—General	D
Public Policy	M,D
Religion	M,D
Romance Languages	M,D
Slavic Languages	M
Social Sciences	M,D
Sociology	D
Spanish	D
Theater	M
Theology	D
Writing	M

UNIVERSITY OF CINCINNATI

Addictions/Substance Abuse Counseling	M,D,O
Anthropology	M
Applied Arts and Design—General	M
Applied Economics	M
Architecture	M
Art History	M
Art/Fine Arts	M
Arts Administration	M,D
Classics	M,D
Clinical Psychology	D
Communication—General	M
Criminal Justice and Criminology	M,D
Economics	D
English	M,D
Experimental Psychology	D
French	M,D
Genetic Counseling	M
Geography	M,D
German	M,D
Graphic Design	M
History	M,D
Industrial and Labor Relations	M
Industrial Design	M
Interdisciplinary Studies	D
Interior Design	M
Music	M,D,O
Philosophy	M,D
Political Science	M,D
Psychology—General	D
Romance Languages	M,D
School Psychology	D,O
Sociology	M,D
Spanish	M,D
Textile Design	M
Theater	M,D

Urban and Regional Planning M,O
Women's Studies M

UNIVERSITY OF COLORADO BOULDER
Anthropology M,D
Art History M
Art/Fine Arts M
Asian Studies M,D
Chinese M,D
Classics M,D
Communication—General M,D
Dance M
East European and Russian Studies M
Economics M,D
English M,D
Ethnic Studies D
Film, Television, and Video
　Production M
French M,D
Geography M,D
German M
Hispanic and Latin American
　Languages M,D
History M,D
Internet and Interactive
　Multimedia D
Japanese M,D
Journalism M,D
Linguistics M,D
Mass Communication M,D
Media Studies M,D
Museum Studies M
Music M,D
Philosophy M,D
Photography M
Political Science M,D
Psychology—General M,D
Religion M
Sociology D
Spanish M,D
Theater M,D
Writing M

UNIVERSITY OF COLORADO COLORADO SPRINGS
Communication—General M
Criminal Justice and Criminology M
Geography M
History M
Interdisciplinary Studies M
Psychology—General M,D
Public Administration M
Public Affairs M
Sociology M

UNIVERSITY OF COLORADO DENVER
American Studies M
Anthropology M
Archaeology M
Architectural History D
Architecture M
Art/Fine Arts M
Clinical Psychology M,D
Communication—General M
Corporate and Organizational
　Communication M
Counseling Psychology M
Criminal Justice and Criminology M,D
Economic Development M
Economics M
Emergency Management M,D
English M
Forensic Sciences M
Gender Studies M
Genetic Counseling M
Geographic Information Systems M,D
Health Psychology M,D
Historic Preservation M
History M
Homeland Security M,D
Human Development M,D,O
Humanities M
International Affairs M
Landscape Architecture M
Linguistics M
Marriage and Family Therapy M
Military and Defense Studies M,D
Music M
Political Science M,D
Public Administration M
Public Affairs M,D
Public History M
Rhetoric M
School Psychology M,D,O
Sociology M
Spanish M
Sustainable Development M,D
Urban and Regional Planning M,D
Urban Design M
Western European Studies M
Women's Studies M
Writing M

UNIVERSITY OF CONNECTICUT
Agricultural Economics and
　Agribusiness M,D
Anthropology M,D
Applied Arts and Design—
　General M
Child and Family Studies M,D
Clinical Psychology M,D
Cognitive Sciences M,D
Communication—General M,D
Counseling Psychology M,D
Developmental Psychology M,D
Economics M,D
English M,D
Experimental Psychology M,D
Geography M,D
History M,D
Human Development M,D

Industrial and Organizational
　Psychology M,D
International Affairs M
Jewish Studies M
Latin American Studies M
Linguistics M,D
Medieval and Renaissance Studies M
Music M,D
Philosophy M,D
Political Science M,D
Psychology—General M,D
Public Administration M
Social Psychology M,D
Sociology M,D
Theater M
Western European Studies M

UNIVERSITY OF DALLAS
American Studies M
Art/Fine Arts M
Classics M
Clinical Psychology M
Comparative Literature D
English M
Humanities M
Pastoral Ministry and Counseling M
Philosophy M,D
Political Science M,D
Psychology—General M
Theology M

UNIVERSITY OF DAYTON
Art/Fine Arts M
Clinical Psychology M,O
Communication—General M
Counseling Psychology M,O
Cultural Studies M
English M
Human Development M,O
Interdisciplinary Studies M
Pastoral Ministry and Counseling M,D
Psychology—General M
Public Administration M
Rhetoric M
School Psychology M,O
Theology M,D
Writing M

UNIVERSITY OF DELAWARE
Agricultural Economics and
　Agribusiness M
American Studies M
Applied Arts and Design—
　General M
Art History M,D
Art/Fine Arts M
Child and Family Studies M,D
Chinese M
Clinical Psychology D
Clothing and Textiles M
Cognitive Sciences M,D
Communication—General M
Criminal Justice and Criminology M,D
Economics M,D
Emergency Management M,D
English M,D
French M
Geography M,D
German M
Historic Preservation M
History of Science and Technology M,D
History M,D
Human Development M,D
International Affairs M,D
Liberal Studies M
Linguistics M,D
Music M
Political Science M,D
Psychology—General D
Public Administration M*
Public Policy M,D
School Psychology M,D,O
Social Psychology D
Sociology M,D
Spanish M
Theater M
Translation and Interpretation M
Urban Studies M,D

UNIVERSITY OF DENVER
Anthropology M
Archaeology M
Art History M
Art/Fine Arts M
Child and Family Studies M,D,O
Clinical Psychology M,D,O
Communication—General M,D,O
Computer Art and Design M
Conflict Resolution and
　Mediation/Peace Studies M
Counseling Psychology M,D,O
Criminal Justice and Criminology M,O
Cultural Anthropology M
Cultural Studies M,O
Developmental Psychology D
Economics M
Emergency Management M,O
English M,D
Forensic Psychology M,D,O
Geographic Information Systems M,D,O
Geography M,D
History M,O
Homeland Security M,D,O
International Affairs M,D,O
International Development M,D,O
Marriage and Family Therapy M,D,O
Mass Communication M
Media Studies M
Museum Studies M
Music M,O
Psychology—General M,D,O
Public Policy M

Religion M,D,O
Rhetoric M,D
School Psychology M,D,O
Social Psychology D
Speech and Interpersonal
　Communication M,D
Sport Psychology M,D,O
Theology D,O
Translation and Interpretation M
Writing M

UNIVERSITY OF DETROIT MERCY
Addictions/Substance Abuse
　Counseling M,D,O
Clinical Psychology M,D,O
Criminal Justice and Criminology M,D,O
Economics M,D,O
Ethics M,O
Forensic Sciences M,O
Industrial and Organizational
　Psychology M,D,O
Industrial Design M,D
Liberal Studies M,D,O
School Psychology M,D,O
Urban and Regional Planning M

UNIVERSITY OF DUBUQUE
Communication—General M
Theology M,D

UNIVERSITY OF EVANSVILLE
Public Administration M

THE UNIVERSITY OF FINDLAY
Linguistics M,D
Public Administration M,D
Rhetoric M,D
Writing M,D

UNIVERSITY OF FLORIDA
Agricultural Economics and
　Agribusiness M,D
Anthropology M,D
Architecture M,D
Art History M,D
Art/Fine Arts M,D
Child Development M
Classics M,D
Clinical Psychology M,D
Communication—General M,D
Computer Art and Design M,D
Counseling Psychology M,D
Criminal Justice and Criminology M,D
Economics M,D
Emergency Management M
English M,D
Family and Consumer
　Sciences-General M
Forensic Sciences M,O
French M,D
Gender Studies M,O
Geographic Information Systems M,O
Geography M,D
German M,D
Health Communication M,D,O
Health Psychology M,D
Historic Preservation M,D
History M,D
Interdisciplinary Studies M,D
Interior Design M,D
International Affairs M
International Development M,D,O
Jewish Studies M,D
Journalism M,D
Landscape Architecture M,D
Latin American Studies M,O
Linguistics M,D
Marriage and Family Therapy M,D,O
Mass Communication M,D
Museum Studies M,D
Music M,D
Philosophy M,D
Political Science M,D,O
Psychology—General M,D
Public Affairs M,D,O
Religion M,D
School Psychology M,D,O
Social Sciences M,D,O
Sociology M,D
Spanish M,D
Sustainable Development M,D
Theater M
Urban and Regional Planning M,D
Women's Studies M,O
Writing M,D

UNIVERSITY OF FORT LAUDERDALE
Pastoral Ministry and Counseling M

UNIVERSITY OF GEORGIA
Agricultural Economics and
　Agribusiness M,D
Anthropology M,D
Applied Economics M,D
Art History M,D
Art/Fine Arts M,D
Child and Family Studies M
Classics M
Clothing and Textiles M,D
Communication—General M,D
Comparative Literature M,D
Economics M,D
English M,D
Environmental Design M
Family and Consumer
　Sciences-General M,D
French M,D
Geography M,D
German M,D
Gerontology O
Historic Preservation M
History M,D
Interior Design M,D

International Affairs M,D
Italian M,D
Journalism M,D
Landscape Architecture M
Linguistics M,D
Mass Communication M,D
Music M,D
Philosophy M,D
Political Science M,D
Portuguese M,D
Psychology—General D
Public Administration M,D
Public Policy M,D
Religion M
Sociology M,D
Spanish M,D
Sustainable Development M,D
Theater M,D
Women's Studies O

UNIVERSITY OF GUAM
Art/Fine Arts M
English M
Graphic Design M
Pacific Area/Pacific Rim Studies M
Public Administration M

UNIVERSITY OF GUELPH
Agricultural Economics and
　Agribusiness M,D
Anthropology M,D
Applied Psychology M,D
Art/Fine Arts M
Child and Family Studies M,D
Clinical Psychology M,D
Cognitive Sciences M,D
Comparative Literature D
Consumer Economics M,D
Criminal Justice and Criminology M,D
Demography and Population Studies M,D
Economics M,D
English M,D
French M
Geography M,D
History M,D
Human Development M,D
Industrial and Organizational
　Psychology M,D
International Development M,D
Landscape Architecture M,D
Marriage and Family Therapy M,D
Medieval and Renaissance Studies D
Philosophy M,D
Political Science M
Psychology—General M,D
Public Administration M
Public Policy M
Rural Planning and Studies M,D
Social Psychology M,D
Sociology M,D
Theater M
Western European Studies M

UNIVERSITY OF HARTFORD
Architecture M
Art/Fine Arts M
Clinical Psychology M,D
Communication—General M
Experimental Psychology M
Music M,D,O
Psychology—General M,D
School Psychology M

UNIVERSITY OF HAWAII AT HILO
Counseling Psychology M
Cultural Studies M,D

UNIVERSITY OF HAWAII AT MANOA
American Studies M,D
Anthropology M,D
Architecture D
Art History M
Art/Fine Arts M
Asian Languages M,D
Asian Studies O
Chinese M,D
Clinical Psychology M,D,O
Communication—General M,O
Conflict Resolution and
　Mediation/Peace Studies M,O
Cultural Studies O
Dance M,D
Demography and Population Studies O
Disability Studies O
Economics M,D
Emergency Management O
English M
French M
Geography M,D,O
Historic Preservation O
History M,D
International Affairs O
International Development M,D,O
Japanese M,D
Linguistics M,D
Museum Studies O
Music M,D
Pacific Area/Pacific Rim Studies M,O
Philosophy M,D
Political Science M,D
Psychology—General M,D,O
Public Administration M,D
Public Policy O
Religion M
Social Psychology M,D,O
Sociology M,D
Spanish M
Speech and Interpersonal
　Communication M
Sustainable Development M,D,O
Theater M,D
Urban and Regional Planning M,D,O

*M—masters degree; D—doctorate; O—other advanced degree; *—Close-Up and/or Display*

Women's Studies O

UNIVERSITY OF HOLY CROSS
Marriage and Family Therapy M,D
Theology M,D

UNIVERSITY OF HOUSTON
Anthropology M
Applied Economics M,D
Architecture M
Art History M
Art/Fine Arts M
Clinical Psychology M,D
Communication—General M
Comparative Literature M
Counseling Psychology M,D
Cultural Studies M
Developmental Psychology M,D
Economics M,D
Family and Consumer Sciences-General M
Health Communication M
Hispanic Studies M,D
History M,D
Industrial and Organizational Psychology M,D
Linguistics M,D
Mass Communication M
Music M,D
Philosophy M
Political Science M,D
Psychology—General M,D
Public Administration M,D
Public Policy M
Social Psychology M,D
Sociology M
Spanish M,D
Speech and Interpersonal Communication M
Sustainable Development M
Theater M
Urban Design M
Writing M,D

UNIVERSITY OF HOUSTON–CLEAR LAKE
Clinical Psychology M
Criminal Justice and Criminology M
Cultural Studies M
English M
History M
Humanities M
Marriage and Family Therapy M
Psychology—General M
School Psychology M
Sociology M

UNIVERSITY OF HOUSTON–DOWNTOWN
Criminal Justice and Criminology M
English M
Rhetoric M
Technical Communication M

UNIVERSITY OF HOUSTON–VICTORIA
Counseling Psychology M
Economic Development M
Forensic Psychology M
Forensic Sciences M
Interdisciplinary Studies M
Psychology—General M
Publishing M
School Psychology M
Writing M

UNIVERSITY OF IDAHO
Agricultural Economics and Agribusiness M
Anthropology M
Architecture M
Art/Fine Arts M
Consumer Economics M
Experimental Psychology M,D
Geography M,D
History M,D
Interdisciplinary Studies M
Music M
Philosophy M,D
Political Science M,D
Psychology—General M,D
Public Administration M,D
Rehabilitation Counseling M,O
Theater M
Urban and Regional Planning M
Writing M

UNIVERSITY OF ILLINOIS AT CHICAGO
Anthropology M,D
Applied Arts and Design—General M
Architecture M
Art History M,D
Art/Fine Arts M,D
Communication—General M,D
Criminal Justice and Criminology M,D
Developmental Psychology M,D
Disability Studies M,D
East European and Russian Studies M,D
Economics M,D
English M,D
Forensic Sciences M
French M
Geography M
German M
Graphic Design M
Hispanic and Latin American Languages M,D
Hispanic Studies M,D
History M,D
Human Development M
Interdisciplinary Studies D
Latin American Studies M
Linguistics M
Medical Illustration M
Museum Studies M
Philosophy M,D

Political Science M
Psychology—General M,D
Public Administration M,D
Slavic Languages M,D
Sociology M,D
Spanish M,D
Urban and Regional Planning M,D

UNIVERSITY OF ILLINOIS AT SPRINGFIELD
Addictions/Substance Abuse Counseling M,O
Child and Family Studies M
Communication—General M
Emergency Management M,O
English M,O
Gerontology M,O
History M
Homeland Security M,O
Human Development M
Interdisciplinary Studies M
Journalism M
Political Science M
Public Administration M,D,O
Public History M
Social Sciences M,O

UNIVERSITY OF ILLINOIS AT URBANA–CHAMPAIGN
African Studies M
Agricultural Economics and Agribusiness M,D
Anthropology M,D
Applied Arts and Design—General M,D
Applied Economics M,D
Architecture M,D
Art History M
Art/Fine Arts M
Asian Languages M,D
Asian Studies M,D
Classics M,D
Communication—General M,D
Comparative Literature M,D
Consumer Economics M,D
Corporate and Organizational Communication M
Dance M
East European and Russian Studies M
Economics M,D
English M,D
French M,D
Geography M,D
German M,D
Graphic Design M
History M,D
Human Development M,D
Industrial and Labor Relations M,D
Industrial Design M
Interdisciplinary Studies D
Italian M,D
Journalism M
Landscape Architecture M,D
Latin American Studies M
Linguistics M,D
Media Studies M,D
Music M
Near and Middle Eastern Studies M
Philosophy M,D
Photography M
Political Science M,D
Portuguese M,D
Psychology—General M,D
Religion M
Romance Languages D
Slavic Languages M,D
Sociology M,D
Spanish M,D
Theater M,D
Translation and Interpretation M
Urban and Regional Planning M,D
Western European Studies M
Writing M,D

UNIVERSITY OF INDIANAPOLIS
Anthropology M
Art/Fine Arts M
Clinical Psychology M,D
Counseling Psychology M
English M
Gerontology M,D,O
History M
International Affairs M
Psychology—General M,D
Sociology M

THE UNIVERSITY OF IOWA
American Studies M,D
Anthropology M,D
Art History M,D
Art/Fine Arts M
Asian Languages M
Asian Studies M
Chinese M
Classics M,D
Communication—General M,D
Counseling Psychology M,D,O
Dance M
Economics D
English M,D
Film, Television, and Video Production M
Film, Television, and Video Theory and Criticism M,D
French M,D
Geographic Information Systems M,D,O
Geography M,D,O
History M,D
Journalism M,D
Linguistics M,D
Marriage and Family Therapy M,D
Mass Communication M,D
Media Studies M,D
Music M,D
Philosophy D

Political Science D
Psychology—General M,D,O
Rehabilitation Counseling M,D
Religion M,D
Rhetoric M,D
School Psychology M,D,O
Sociology M,D
Spanish M,D
Speech and Interpersonal Communication M,D
Sustainable Development M,D
Theater M
Urban and Regional Planning M
Women's Studies O
Writing M

THE UNIVERSITY OF KANSAS
African Studies M,O
African-American Studies M,O
American Indian/Native American Studies M,O
American Studies M,D
Anthropology M,D
Applied Arts and Design—General M
Applied Behavior Analysis M,D,O
Architecture M,D,O
Art History M,D
Art/Fine Arts M,D
Asian Languages M,O
Asian Studies M,O
Classics M
Clinical Psychology M,D
Cognitive Sciences M,D
Communication—General M,D,O
Counseling Psychology M,D
Cultural Studies M,D
Developmental Psychology M,D
East European and Russian Studies M,O
Economics M,D
English M,D
Film, Television, and Video Theory and Criticism M,D
French M,D
Geographic Information Systems M,D,O
Geography M,D,O
Gerontology D
Historic Preservation M,D,O
History M,D
Interdisciplinary Studies D
International Affairs M
Journalism M,D
Latin American Studies M,D
Linguistics M,D
Media Studies M,D
Museum Studies M,O
Music M,D
Near and Middle Eastern Studies M,O
Philosophy M,D
Political Science M,D
Psychology—General M,D,O
Public Administration M,D,O
Religion M,O
School Psychology D,O
Slavic Languages M,D
Social Psychology M,D
Sociology D
Spanish M,D
Textile Design M
Theater M,D
Therapies—Dance, Drama, and Music M,D
Urban and Regional Planning M
Urban Design M,D,O
Writing M,D

UNIVERSITY OF KENTUCKY
Agricultural Economics and Agribusiness M,D
Anthropology M,D
Applied Arts and Design—General M
Architecture M
Art History M
Art/Fine Arts M
Arts Administration M
Child and Family Studies M,D
Classics M
Communication—General M,D
Counseling Psychology M,D,O
Economics M,D
English M,D
Geography M,D
German M
Gerontology D,O
Hispanic Studies M,D
Historic Preservation M
History M,D
Interior Design M
International Affairs M
Music M,D
Philosophy M,D
Political Science M,D
Psychology—General M,D
Public Administration M,D,O
Public Policy M,D,O
Rehabilitation Counseling M,D
School Psychology M,D,O
Sociology M,D
Therapies—Dance, Drama, and Music M,D

UNIVERSITY OF KING'S COLLEGE
Journalism M
Writing M

UNIVERSITY OF LA VERNE
Child and Family Studies M
Child Development M
Clinical Psychology D
English M,O
Gerontology M,O
Marriage and Family Therapy M
Psychology—General M,D
Public Administration M,D

School Psychology M,O

UNIVERSITY OF LETHBRIDGE
Addictions/Substance Abuse Counseling M,D
American Indian/Native American Studies M,D
Anthropology M,D
Archaeology M,D
Art/Fine Arts M,D
Canadian Studies M,D
Counseling Psychology M,D
Economics M,D
English M,D
French M,D
Gender Studies M,D
Geographic Information Systems M,D
Geography M,D
German M,D
Media Studies M,D
Music M,D
Philosophy M,D
Political Science M,D
Psychology—General M,D
Religion M,D
Sociology M,D
Spanish M,D
Theater M,D
Urban Studies M,D
Women's Studies M,D

UNIVERSITY OF LOUISIANA AT LAFAYETTE
American Studies D
Cognitive Sciences D
Communication—General M
English M,D
Folklore M,D
French M,D
History M
Mass Communication M
Music M
Psychology—General M
Rehabilitation Counseling M
Rhetoric M,D
Writing M,D

UNIVERSITY OF LOUISIANA AT MONROE
Clinical Psychology M
Communication—General M
Counseling Psychology M
Criminal Justice and Criminology M
English M
Forensic Psychology M
Gerontology M,O
History M
Marriage and Family Therapy M,D
Psychology—General M
Public Administration M

UNIVERSITY OF LOUISVILLE
Addictions/Substance Abuse Counseling M,D,O
African Studies M
African-American Studies M
Anthropology M
Applied Arts and Design—General M,D
Applied Behavior Analysis M,D,O
Art History M,D
Art Therapy M,D
Clinical Psychology D
Cognitive Sciences M
Communication—General M
Counseling Psychology M,D
Criminal Justice and Criminology M,D
Cultural Studies M,D
Developmental Psychology D
English M,D
Experimental Psychology D
French M,O
Geography M
Gerontology M,D,O
History M,O
Humanities M,D
Interdisciplinary Studies M,D
Linguistics M,D
Marriage and Family Therapy M,D,O
Museum Studies M,D
Music M
Philosophy M,D
Political Science M
Psychology—General D
Public Administration M,D
Public Affairs M,D
Public History M,O
Public Policy M,D
Rhetoric M,D
School Psychology M,D
Sociology M,D
Spanish M,O
Theater M
Urban and Regional Planning M,D
Urban Studies M,D
Women's Studies M,O
Writing M,D

UNIVERSITY OF LYNCHBURG
Clinical Psychology M
Counseling Psychology M
Criminal Justice and Criminology M
School Psychology M

UNIVERSITY OF MAINE
Agricultural Economics and Agribusiness M
Anthropology D
Art/Fine Arts M
Communication—General M,D
Economics M
English M
French M
History M,D
Human Development M,D,O
Interdisciplinary Studies M,D

International Affairs — M
Music
Psychology—General — M,D

UNIVERSITY OF MANAGEMENT AND TECHNOLOGY
Criminal Justice and Criminology — M,O
Homeland Security — M
Public Administration — M,O

THE UNIVERSITY OF MANCHESTER
Anthropology — M,D
Archaeology — M,D
Architecture — M,D
Art History — D
Art/Fine Arts — M,D
Arts Administration — D
Asian Studies — M,D
Chinese — M,D
Classics — D
Clinical Psychology — M,D
Clothing and Textiles — M,D
Conflict Resolution and
   Mediation/Peace Studies — D
Counseling Psychology — M,D
Criminal Justice and Criminology — M,D
Cultural Studies — M,D
Developmental Psychology — M,D
Economics — D
English — D
Environmental Design — M,D
French — M,D
Geography — M,D
German — M,D
Hispanic Studies — M,D
History of Medicine — M,D
History of Science and Technology — M,D
History — D
Industrial and Labor Relations — M
Industrial and Organizational
   Psychology — M
International Affairs
International Development — M,D
Italian — M,D
Japanese — M,D
Landscape Architecture — M,D
Latin American Studies — M,D
Linguistics — D
Museum Studies — D
Music
Near and Middle Eastern Languages — M,D
Near and Middle Eastern Studies — M,D
Philosophy — M,D
Political Science — M,D
Psychology—General — M,D
Religion — D
Russian — M,D
Slavic Languages — M,D
Social Sciences — M,D
Sociology — M,D
Spanish — M,D
Textile Design — M,D
Theater — D
Theology — D
Translation and Interpretation — M,D
Writing — D

UNIVERSITY OF MANITOBA
Agricultural Economics and
   Agribusiness — M,D
American Indian/Native American
   Studies — M
Anthropology — M,D
Architecture — M
Canadian Studies — M
Classics — M
Clinical Psychology — M,D
Disability Studies — M
Economics — M,D
English — M,D
French — M,D
Genetic Counseling — M,D
Geography — M,D
German — M,D
History — M,D
Interdisciplinary Studies — M,D
Interior Design — M
Landscape Architecture — M
Linguistics — M,D
Music — M
Northern Studies — M
Philosophy — M
Political Science — M
Psychoanalysis and Psychotherapy — M
Psychology—General — M,D
Public Administration — M
Religion — M,D
School Psychology — M,D
Slavic Languages — M
Sociology — M,D
Urban and Regional Planning — M

UNIVERSITY OF MARY HARDIN-BAYLOR
Clinical Psychology — M
Counseling Psychology — M
Marriage and Family Therapy — M

UNIVERSITY OF MARYLAND, BALTIMORE
Ethics — O
Forensic Sciences — M
Genetic Counseling — M
Gerontology — M,D
Thanatology — O

UNIVERSITY OF MARYLAND, BALTIMORE COUNTY
Applied Psychology — D
Clinical Psychology — M,D
Cognitive Sciences — D
Communication—General — M
Computer Art and Design — M
Dance — M

Developmental Psychology — D
Economics — M,D
Emergency Management — M,D,O
English — M
Geographic Information Systems — M,O
Geography — M,D
Gerontology — M,D
History — M
Industrial and Organizational
   Psychology — M
Linguistics — M
Music — O
Psychology—General — M,D
Public History — M,D
Public Policy — M,D,O
Social Psychology — M,D
Social Sciences — D
Sociology — M
Theater — M
Urban Studies — M,D

UNIVERSITY OF MARYLAND, COLLEGE PARK
Agricultural Economics and
   Agribusiness — M,D
American Studies — M,D
Anthropology — M
Architecture — M
Art History — M,D
Art Therapy — M,D,O
Art/Fine Arts — M
Broadcast Journalism — M,D
Child and Family Studies — M,D
Classics — M
Clinical Psychology — M,D
Cognitive Sciences — D
Communication—General — M,D
Comparative Literature — M,D
Counseling Psychology — M,D,O
Criminal Justice and Criminology — M,D
Dance — M
Developmental Psychology — M,D
Economics — M,D
English — M,D
Experimental Psychology — M,D
Family and Consumer
   Sciences-General — M,D
French — M,D
Geography — M,D
German — M,D
Historic Preservation — M,O
History — M,D
Human Development — M,D
Industrial and Organizational
   Psychology — M,D
Jewish Studies — M
Journalism — M,D
Landscape Architecture — M
Linguistics — M,D
Marriage and Family Therapy — M
Media Studies — M,D
Music — M,D
Philosophy — M,D
Political Science — D
Portuguese — M,D
Psychology—General — M,D
Public Administration — M
Public Policy — M,D
Rehabilitation Counseling — M,D,O
School Psychology — M,D,O
Social Psychology — M,D
Sociology — M,D
Spanish — M,D
Speech and Interpersonal
   Communication — M,D
Survey Methodology — M,D
Sustainable Development — M
Theater — M,D
Urban and Regional Planning — M,D
Women's Studies — M,D
Writing — M,D

UNIVERSITY OF MARYLAND EASTERN SHORE
Criminal Justice and Criminology — M
Rehabilitation Counseling — M

UNIVERSITY OF MASSACHUSETTS AMHERST
African-American Studies — M,D
Agricultural Economics and
   Agribusiness — M,D
American Studies — M,D
Anthropology — M,D
Architecture — M
Art History — M
Art/Fine Arts — M
Child and Family Studies — M,D,O
Chinese — M
Classics — M
Clinical Psychology — M,D
Cognitive Sciences — M,D
Communication—General — M,D
Comparative Literature — M,D
Conflict Resolution and
   Mediation/Peace Studies — M,D
Developmental Psychology — M,D
Economics — M,D
English — M,D
French — M
Geography — M
German — M,D
Hispanic and Latin American
   Languages — M,D
Historic Preservation — M
History — M,D
Industrial and Labor Relations — M
Interior Design — M
Italian — M
Japanese — M
Landscape Architecture — M

Linguistics — M,D
Music — M,D
Philosophy — M,D
Political Science — M,D
Portuguese — M,D
Psychology—General — M,D
Public Administration — M
Public Policy — M
Rhetoric — M
Scandinavian Languages — M,D
School Psychology — M,D,O
Social Psychology — M,D
Sociology — M,D
Spanish — M,D
Sustainable Development — M
Theater — M
Urban and Regional Planning — M,D
Writing — M,D

UNIVERSITY OF MASSACHUSETTS BOSTON
American Studies — M
Applied Economics — M
Archaeology — M
Classics — M
Clinical Psychology — D
Cognitive Sciences — M
Conflict Resolution and
   Mediation/Peace Studies — M,O
Counseling Psychology — M
Cultural Studies — M
English — M
Gerontology — M,D,O
History — M
International Affairs — M
International Development — M
Linguistics — M,D
Marriage and Family Therapy — M
Public Administration — M
Public Policy — M,D
Rehabilitation Counseling — M
School Psychology — M,D
Sociology — M,D
Urban and Regional Planning — M
Writing — M

UNIVERSITY OF MASSACHUSETTS DARTMOUTH
Applied Behavior Analysis — M,O
Art History — M
Art/Fine Arts — M,O
Clinical Psychology — M,O
Experimental Psychology — M,O
Latin American Studies — M,D
Media Studies — M
Portuguese — M,D
Psychology—General — M,D
Public Administration — M,O
Public Policy — M,O
Writing — M,O

UNIVERSITY OF MASSACHUSETTS LOWELL
Conflict Resolution and
   Mediation/Peace Studies — M
Criminal Justice and Criminology — M
Economic Development — M,O
Economics — M,O
Music — M
Psychology—General — M
Social Psychology — M
Sociology — M,O
Urban and Regional Planning — M,O

UNIVERSITY OF MASSACHUSETTS MEDICAL SCHOOL
Interdisciplinary Studies — M,D

UNIVERSITY OF MEMPHIS
African-American Studies — M,D,O
Anthropology — M
Applied Behavior Analysis — M,D,O
Archaeology — M,D,O
Architecture — M
Art History — M,O
Art/Fine Arts — M,O
Clinical Psychology — M,D,O
Communication—General — M,D
Comparative Literature — M,D,O
Counseling Psychology — M,D
Criminal Justice and Criminology — M
Economics — M,D,O
English — M,D,O
Experimental Psychology — M,D,O
Film, Television, and Video
   Production — M,D
French — M
Gender Studies — O
Geographic Information Systems — M,D,O
Geography — M,D,O
Graphic Design — M,O
History — M,D
Interdisciplinary Studies — M,D,O
Journalism — M,O
Liberal Studies — M,O
Linguistics — M,O
Museum Studies — M,O
Music — M,D
Near and Middle Eastern Studies — M,D
Philosophy — M,D
Photography — M
Political Science — M
Psychology—General — M,D,O
Public Administration — M,O
Public Policy — M,O
Rehabilitation Counseling — M,D
School Psychology — M,D,O
Social Sciences — M
Sociology — M
Spanish — M
Theater — M
Urban and Regional Planning — M

Linguistics — M,D
Music — M,D
Philosophy — M,D
Political Science — M,D
Portuguese — M,D
Psychology—General — M,D
Public Administration — M
Public Policy — M
Rhetoric — M
Scandinavian Languages — M,D
School Psychology — M,D,O
Social Psychology — M,D
Sociology — M,D
Spanish — M,D
Sustainable Development — M
Theater — M
Urban and Regional Planning — M
Writing — M,D

Writing — M,D,O

UNIVERSITY OF MIAMI
Architecture — M
Art History — M
Art/Fine Arts — M
Broadcast Journalism — M,D
Clinical Psychology — M,D
Communication—General — M,D
Counseling Psychology — D
Developmental Psychology — M,D
English — M,D
Film, Television, and Video
   Production — M,D
Film, Television, and Video
   Theory and Criticism — M,D
French — D
Geography — M
Graphic Design — M
History — M,D
International Affairs — M,D
Internet and Interactive
   Multimedia — M
Journalism — M,D
Latin American Studies — M
Liberal Studies — M
Marriage and Family Therapy — M,O
Music — M,D,O
Philosophy — M,D
Photography — M
Political Science — M
Psychology—General — M,D
Romance Languages — D
Sociology — M,D
Spanish — M,D
Therapies—Dance, Drama, and
   Music — M,D,O
Urban Design — M
Writing — M,D

UNIVERSITY OF MICHIGAN
African Studies — M
American Studies — M,D
Anthropology — D
Applied Arts and Design—
   General — M,D
Applied Economics — M
Archaeology — M,D
Architecture — M
Art History — M,D
Art/Fine Arts — M
Asian Languages — D
Asian Studies — M,D,O
Classics — M,D,O
Clinical Psychology — D
Cognitive Sciences — D
Communication—General — D
Comparative Literature — D
Cultural Anthropology — D
Dance — M
Developmental Psychology — D
East European and Russian Studies — M,O
Economics — M,D
English — M,D,O
Film, Television, and Video
   Theory and Criticism — D,O
French — D
Genetic Counseling — M,D
German — M,D,O
History — D,O
Italian — D
Jewish Studies — M,D,O
Landscape Architecture — M
Linguistics — D
Media Studies — M
Music — M,D,O
Near and Middle Eastern Languages — M,D
Near and Middle Eastern Studies — M,D
Philosophy — M,D
Political Science — D
Psychology—General — D,O
Public Policy — M,D
Religion — M,D
Slavic Languages — M,D
Social Psychology — D
Social Sciences — D
Sociology — D
Spanish — D
Survey Methodology — M,D,O
Sustainable Development — M,D
Urban and Regional Planning — M,D
Urban Design — M
Women's Studies — D,O
Writing

UNIVERSITY OF MICHIGAN–DEARBORN
Applied Behavior Analysis — M
Clinical Psychology — M
Criminal Justice and Criminology — M
Health Psychology — M
Public Administration — M

UNIVERSITY OF MICHIGAN–FLINT
American Studies — M
Art/Fine Arts — M
Arts Administration — M
Communication—General — M
Criminal Justice and Criminology — M
English — M
Gender Studies — M
Gerontology — M,D,O
International Affairs — M
Museum Studies — M
Music — M
Political Science — M
Public Administration — M
Rhetoric — M
Social Sciences — M
Writing — M

UNIVERSITY OF MINNESOTA, DULUTH
Anthropology — M

*M—masters degree; D—doctorate; O—other advanced degree; *—Close-Up and/or Display*

Art/Fine Arts	M
Criminal Justice and Criminology	M
English	M
Graphic Design	M
Liberal Studies	M
Music	M
Sociology	M

UNIVERSITY OF MINNESOTA, TWIN CITIES CAMPUS

American Studies	D
Anthropology	M,D
Applied Arts and Design—General	M,D,O
Applied Economics	M,D
Archaeology	M,D
Architecture	M
Art History	M,D
Art/Fine Arts	M
Asian Languages	D
Asian Studies	D
Child and Family Studies	M,D
Child Development	M,D
Classics	M,D
Clinical Psychology	D
Clothing and Textiles	M,D,O
Cognitive Sciences	D
Communication—General	M,D,O
Comparative Literature	D
Counseling Psychology	D
Cultural Studies	D
Economics	M,D
English	M,D
French	M,D
Genetic Counseling	M,D
Geographic Information Systems	M,D
Geography	M,D
German	M,D
Hispanic and Latin American Languages	M,D
History of Medicine	M,D
History of Science and Technology	M,D
History	M,D
Industrial and Labor Relations	M
Industrial and Organizational Psychology	D
Interdisciplinary Studies	D
Interior Design	M,D,O
International Development	M
Landscape Architecture	M
Linguistics	M,D
Marriage and Family Therapy	M,D
Mass Communication	M,D
Medieval and Renaissance Studies	M,D
Music	M,D
Philosophy	M,D
Political Science	D
Portuguese	M,D
Psychology—General	D
Public Affairs	M,D
Public Policy	M,D
Religion	M,D
Scandinavian Languages	M,D
School Psychology	M,D,O
Social Psychology	D
Sociology	M,D
Spanish	M,D
Textile Design	M,D,O
Theater	M,D
Urban and Regional Planning	M,D
Women's Studies	D

UNIVERSITY OF MISSISSIPPI

Anthropology	M,D
Art/Fine Arts	M,D
Criminal Justice and Criminology	M,D
Economics	M,D
English	M,D
Experimental Psychology	M,D
Film, Television, and Video Production	M,D
History	M,D
Journalism	M
Music	M,D
Philosophy	M,D
Political Science	M,D
Writing	M,D

UNIVERSITY OF MISSOURI

Agricultural Economics and Agribusiness	M,D,O
Anthropology	M,D
Archaeology	M,D
Architecture	M,D
Art History	M,D
Art/Fine Arts	M
Child and Family Studies	M,D
Classics	M,D
Clothing and Textiles	M,D
Communication—General	M,D
Comparative Literature	M,D
Conflict Resolution and Mediation/Peace Studies	M,D,O
Consumer Economics	M,D,O
Counseling Psychology	M,D,O
Economics	M,D
English	M,D
Family and Consumer Sciences-General	M,D,O
French	M,D
Geographic Information Systems	M,D,O
Geography	M,O
German	M
Gerontology	M,D,O
Health Communication	M,D
History	M,D
Human Development	M,D
Journalism	M,D
Music	M
Philosophy	D
Political Science	M,D
Psychology—General	M,D
Public Administration	M,D,O
Public Affairs	M,D,O
Public Policy	M,D,O
Religion	M
Romance Languages	M,D
Rural Sociology	M,D
Russian	M
School Psychology	M,D,O
Sociology	D
Spanish	M,D
Theater	M,D

UNIVERSITY OF MISSOURI–KANSAS CITY

Art/Fine Arts	M,D
Counseling Psychology	M,D,O
Criminal Justice and Criminology	M
Economics	M,D
English	M,D
French	M
History	M,D
Interdisciplinary Studies	D
Music	M,D
Political Science	M
Psychology—General	M,D
Public Administration	M,D
Public Affairs	M,D
Romance Languages	M
Social Psychology	M,D
Sociology	M
Spanish	M
Theater	M
Therapies—Dance, Drama, and Music	M,D

UNIVERSITY OF MISSOURI–ST. LOUIS

American Studies	M,D
Clinical Psychology	M,D,O
Communication—General	M
Criminal Justice and Criminology	M,D
Economics	M
English	M
History	M,O
Museum Studies	M,O
Philosophy	M
Political Science	M,D
Psychology—General	M,D,O
Public Administration	M,D,O
Public Policy	M,D,O
School Psychology	M,O
Writing	M

UNIVERSITY OF MOBILE

Marriage and Family Therapy	M

UNIVERSITY OF MONTANA

Anthropology	M,D
Art History	M
Art/Fine Arts	M
Child and Family Studies	M,D,O
Clinical Psychology	M,D,O
Communication—General	M
Computer Art and Design	M
Counseling Psychology	M,D,O
Criminal Justice and Criminology	M
Cultural Studies	M,D,O
Developmental Psychology	M,D,O
Economics	M
English	M
Experimental Psychology	M,D,O
Film, Television, and Video Production	M
French	M
Geography	M
German	M
History	M,D
Interdisciplinary Studies	M,D
Internet and Interactive Multimedia	M
Journalism	M
Linguistics	M,D
Music	M
Philosophy	M
Photography	M
Political Science	M
Psychology—General	M,D,O
Public Administration	M
Rural Planning and Studies	M
Rural Sociology	M
School Psychology	M,D,O
Sociology	M
Spanish	M
Theater	M
Writing	M

UNIVERSITY OF MONTEVALLO

English	M

UNIVERSITY OF NEBRASKA AT KEARNEY

Counseling Psychology	M,O
English	M
History	M
School Psychology	M,O
Writing	M

UNIVERSITY OF NEBRASKA AT OMAHA

Applied Behavior Analysis	M,D,O
Art/Fine Arts	M
Communication—General	M,O
Criminal Justice and Criminology	M,D,O
Economics	M,O
English	M,O
Geographic Information Systems	M,O
Geography	M,O
Gerontology	M,D,O
History	M
Industrial and Organizational Psychology	M,D,O
Music	M
National Security	M,O
Political Science	M,O
Psychology—General	M,D,O
Public Administration	M,D,O
School Psychology	M,D,O
Sociology	M
Technical Communication	M,O
Writing	M,O

UNIVERSITY OF NEBRASKA–LINCOLN

Agricultural Economics and Agribusiness	M,D
Anthropology	M
Archaeology	M,D
Architecture	M,D
Art History	M
Art/Fine Arts	M
Child and Family Studies	M,D
Child Development	M,D
Classics	M
Clinical Psychology	M,D
Clothing and Textiles	M,D
Cognitive Sciences	M,D,O
Communication—General	M,D
Comparative Literature	M,D
Consumer Economics	M,D
Corporate and Organizational Communication	M,D
Counseling Psychology	M,D,O
Developmental Psychology	M,D,O
Economics	M,D
English	M,D
Family and Consumer Sciences-General	M,D
French	M,D
Geography	M,D
German	M,D
Gerontology	M,D
History	M,D
Human Development	M,D,O
Interior Design	M,D
Journalism	M
Marriage and Family Therapy	M,D
Mass Communication	M,D
Music	M,D
Philosophy	M,D
Political Science	M,D,O
Psychology—General	M,D,O
Public Policy	M,D,O
Rhetoric	M,D
School Psychology	M,D,O
Social Psychology	M,D
Sociology	M,D
Spanish	M,D
Speech and Interpersonal Communication	M,D
Survey Methodology	M,D
Theater	M
Urban and Regional Planning	M,D
Writing	M,D

UNIVERSITY OF NEBRASKA MEDICAL CENTER

Applied Behavior Analysis	M,D
Emergency Management	M

UNIVERSITY OF NEVADA, LAS VEGAS

Addictions/Substance Abuse Counseling	M,D,O
Anthropology	M,D
Applied Economics	M,O
Architecture	M,O
Art/Fine Arts	M
Clinical Psychology	M,D,O
Communication—General	M
Counseling Psychology	M,D,O
Criminal Justice and Criminology	M,D
Economics	M
Emergency Management	M,D,O
English	M,D
Film, Television, and Video Production	M,O
Hispanic Studies	M,O
History	M,D
Journalism	M
Marriage and Family Therapy	M
Media Studies	M
Music	M,D,O
Political Science	M,D
Psychology—General	M,D,O
Public Administration	M,D,O
Public Affairs	M,D,O
Public Policy	M,D,O
Sociology	M,D
Theater	M
Translation and Interpretation	M,O
Writing	M,D,O

UNIVERSITY OF NEVADA, RENO

Agricultural Economics and Agribusiness	M,D
Anthropology	M,D
Applied Economics	M,D
Art/Fine Arts	M
Child and Family Studies	M
Clinical Psychology	D
Cognitive Sciences	M,D
Criminal Justice and Criminology	M
Economics	M
English	M,D
French	M
Geography	M,D
German	M
History	M,D
Human Development	M
Journalism	M
Music	M
Philosophy	M
Political Science	M,D
Psychology—General	M,D
Public Administration	M
Social Psychology	D
Sociology	M
Spanish	M
Speech and Interpersonal Communication	M
Western European Studies	D

UNIVERSITY OF NEW BRUNSWICK FREDERICTON

Anthropology	M
Applied Economics	M
Classics	M
Conflict Resolution and Mediation/Peace Studies	M
Economics	M
English	M,D
History	M,D
Interdisciplinary Studies	M,D
International Development	M
Political Science	M
Psychology—General	M,D
Public Administration	M
Public Policy	M
Sociology	M,D
Sustainable Development	M
Urban and Regional Planning	M

UNIVERSITY OF NEW BRUNSWICK SAINT JOHN

Clinical Psychology	M,D
Experimental Psychology	M,D
Psychology—General	M,D

UNIVERSITY OF NEW HAMPSHIRE

Addictions/Substance Abuse Counseling	M,O
Child and Family Studies	M,O
Economic Development	M
Economics	M,D
English	M,D
Geographic Information Systems	O
History	M,D
Liberal Studies	M
Linguistics	M,D
Marriage and Family Therapy	M,O
Museum Studies	M,D
Music	M
Political Science	M,O
Psychology—General	D
Public Administration	M,O
Public Policy	M
Sociology	M,D
Spanish	M,O
Women's Studies	O
Writing	M,D

UNIVERSITY OF NEW HAVEN

Conflict Resolution and Mediation/Peace Studies	M,O
Criminal Justice and Criminology	M,D,O*
Emergency Management	M,O
Forensic Psychology	M,O
Forensic Sciences	M,O
Geographic Information Systems	M
Industrial and Organizational Psychology	M,O*
National Security	M,O
Public Administration	M,O
Social Psychology	M,O*

UNIVERSITY OF NEW MEXICO

American Indian/Native American Studies	M,D
American Studies	M,D
Anthropology	M,D
Archaeology	M,D
Architecture	M,D
Art History	M,D
Art/Fine Arts	M
Child and Family Studies	M,D
Clinical Psychology	D
Cognitive Sciences	D
Communication—General	M,D
Comparative Literature	M,D
Cultural Studies	M,D
Dance	M
Developmental Psychology	D
Economics	M,D
English	M,D
Ethnic Studies	M,D
French	M,D
Geography	M
German	M,D
Health Psychology	D
Historic Preservation	O
History	M,D
Human Development	M,D
International Development	M,D
International Economics	M,D
Landscape Architecture	M
Latin American Studies	M,D
Linguistics	M,D
Music	M
Philosophy	M,D
Photography	M,D
Political Science	M,D
Portuguese	M,D
Psychology—General	D
Public Administration	M,D
Sociology	M,D
Spanish	M,D
Theater	M
Urban and Regional Planning	M
Writing	M

UNIVERSITY OF NEW ORLEANS

Art/Fine Arts	M
Arts Administration	M
Economics	D
English	M
Film, Television, and Video Production	M
Geography	M
History	M
Music	M
Political Science	M,D
Psychology—General	M,D
Public Administration	M
Romance Languages	M
Sociology	M
Theater	M
Urban and Regional Planning	M
Urban Studies	M,D

UNIVERSITY OF NORTH ALABAMA

Child and Family Studies	M
Clinical Psychology	M
Criminal Justice and Criminology	M

Economic Development M
English M
Geographic Information Systems M
Historic Preservation M
History M
Interdisciplinary Studies M
Political Science M
Public History M
Rhetoric M
Technical Writing M
Writing M

UNIVERSITY OF NORTH CAROLINA AT ASHEVILLE
Cultural Studies M,O
Liberal Studies M,O
Sustainable Development M,O

THE UNIVERSITY OF NORTH CAROLINA AT CHAPEL HILL
Anthropology M,D
Archaeology M,D
Art History M,D
Art/Fine Arts M
Classics M,D
Clinical Psychology D
Cognitive Sciences D
Communication—General M,D,O
Developmental Psychology D
East European and Russian Studies M
Economics M,D
English M,D
Folklore M
French M,D
Geography M,D
German D
Health Communication M,D,O
Health Psychology M,D
History M,D
International Affairs M
Italian M,D
Journalism M,D,O
Latin American Studies M
Linguistics M
Media Studies M,D,O
Music M,D
Philosophy M,D
Political Science M,D,O
Portuguese M,D
Psychology—General D
Public Administration M
Public Policy D
Rehabilitation Counseling M
Religion M,D
Romance Languages M,D
School Psychology M,D
Slavic Languages D
Social Psychology D
Sociology M,D
Spanish M,D
Theater M
Urban and Regional Planning M,D

THE UNIVERSITY OF NORTH CAROLINA AT CHARLOTTE
Addictions/Substance Abuse Counseling M,D,O
African Studies O
Anthropology M
Applied Economics M,O
Architecture M
Arts Administration M,O
Child and Family Studies M,D,O
Child Development M,D,O
Cognitive Sciences M,D,O
Communication—General M
Criminal Justice and Criminology M
Cultural Studies M,O
Economics M,O
Emergency Management M,O
English M,O
Ethics M,O
Gender Studies M,D,O
Geographic Information Systems M,D
Geography M,D
Gerontology M,D,O
Health Psychology M,D,O
History M
Industrial and Organizational Psychology M,D,O
Interdisciplinary Studies M,D,O
Latin American Studies M,D,O
Liberal Studies M,D,O
Linguistics M,O
Music O
Philosophy M,O
Psychology—General M,D,O
Public Administration M,O
Public Policy M,D,O
Religion M
Sociology M
Spanish M,O
Technical Writing M,O
Theater M,D,O
Urban and Regional Planning M,O
Urban Design M
Women's Studies M,D,O
Writing M

THE UNIVERSITY OF NORTH CAROLINA AT GREENSBORO
Applied Economics M
Architecture M,O
Art/Fine Arts M
Child and Family Studies M,D
Classics M
Clinical Psychology M,D
Cognitive Sciences M,D
Communication—General M
Conflict Resolution and Mediation/Peace Studies M,O
Counseling Psychology M,D,O

Criminal Justice and Criminology M
Dance M
Developmental Psychology M,D
Economic Development M,D,O
Economics D
English M,D
Film, Television, and Video Production M
French M
Gender Studies M,O
Genetic Counseling M
Geographic Information Systems M,D,O
Geography M,D,O
Gerontology M,O
Hispanic and Latin American Languages M,O
Hispanic Studies M,O
Historic Preservation M,D
History M,D
Human Development M,D
Interior Design M
Liberal Studies M
Marriage and Family Therapy M,D,O
Media Studies M
Museum Studies M,D,O
Music M,D
Political Science M,O
Psychology—General M,D
Public Affairs M,O
Rhetoric M
School Psychology M,D,O
Social Psychology M,D
Sociology M
Spanish M,O
Technical Writing M,D,O
Textile Design M,D
Theater M
Women's Studies M,D,O
Writing M

THE UNIVERSITY OF NORTH CAROLINA AT PEMBROKE
Counseling Psychology M
Criminal Justice and Criminology M
Emergency Management M
Public Administration M

UNIVERSITY OF NORTH CAROLINA SCHOOL OF THE ARTS
Film, Television, and Video Production M
Music M,O
Theater M

THE UNIVERSITY OF NORTH CAROLINA WILMINGTON
Applied Behavior Analysis M,D
Clinical Psychology M,D
Conflict Resolution and Mediation/Peace Studies M
Criminal Justice and Criminology M
English M
Geographic Information Systems M,O
Gerontology M
Hispanic Studies M,O
History M
Liberal Studies M
Psychology—General M,D
Public Administration M
Sociology M
Spanish M,O
Writing M

UNIVERSITY OF NORTH DAKOTA
Applied Economics M
Art/Fine Arts M
Clinical Psychology M,D
Communication—General D
Counseling Psychology M,D
Criminal Justice and Criminology D
English M,D
Forensic Psychology M
Geographic Information Systems M
Geography M
History M,D
Linguistics M
Music M,D
Psychology—General M,D
Public Administration M
Sociology M

UNIVERSITY OF NORTHERN BRITISH COLUMBIA
Disability Studies M,D,O
Gender Studies M,D,O
History M,D,O
Interdisciplinary Studies M,D,O
International Affairs M,D,O
Political Science M,D,O
Psychology—General M,D,O

UNIVERSITY OF NORTHERN COLORADO
Art History M
Art/Fine Arts M
Clinical Psychology M
Communication—General M
Counseling Psychology D
Criminal Justice and Criminology M
English M
Gerontology M,D
History M
Music M,D
Rehabilitation Counseling M,D
School Psychology O
Sociology M
Translation and Interpretation M

UNIVERSITY OF NORTHERN IOWA
Art/Fine Arts M
Communication—General M
Counseling Psychology M
English M

Gender Studies M
Geography M
History M
Music M
Psychology—General M
Public History M
Public Policy M
School Psychology M,O
Social Sciences M
Spanish M
Women's Studies M
Writing M

UNIVERSITY OF NORTH FLORIDA
Applied Behavior Analysis M
Counseling Psychology M
Criminal Justice and Criminology M
Economics M
English M
Ethics M,O
History M
Philosophy M,O
Psychology—General M
Public Administration M
Translation and Interpretation M
Writing M

UNIVERSITY OF NORTH GEORGIA
Anthropology M
Counseling Psychology M
Criminal Justice and Criminology M
History M
International Affairs M
Philosophy M
Public Administration M

UNIVERSITY OF NORTH TEXAS
Anthropology M,D,O
Applied Arts and Design— General M,D,O
Applied Behavior Analysis M,D,O
Art History M,D,O
Art/Fine Arts M,D,O
Child and Family Studies M,D,O
Clinical Psychology M,D,O
Communication—General M,D,O
Counseling Psychology M,D,O
Criminal Justice and Criminology M,D,O
Economics M,D,O
Emergency Management M,D,O
English M,D,O
Film, Television, and Video Production M,D,O
French M,D,O
Geography M,D,O
Gerontology M,D,O
History M,D,O
Human Development M,D,O
Interdisciplinary Studies M,D,O
Interior Design M,D,O
International Affairs M,D,O
Internet and Interactive Multimedia M,D,O
Journalism M,D,O
Linguistics M,D,O
Museum Studies M,D,O
Music M,D,O
Philosophy M,D,O
Political Science M,D,O
Psychology—General M,D,O
Public Administration M,D,O
Rehabilitation Counseling M,D,O
Sociology M,D,O
Spanish M,D,O
Textile Design M,D,O
Writing M,D,O

UNIVERSITY OF NORTH TEXAS AT DALLAS
Clinical Psychology M
Criminal Justice and Criminology M
Public Administration M

UNIVERSITY OF NORTH TEXAS HEALTH SCIENCE CENTER AT FORT WORTH
Forensic Sciences M,D
Geographic Information Systems M,D,O

UNIVERSITY OF NORTHWESTERN–ST. PAUL
Pastoral Ministry and Counseling M
Theology M

UNIVERSITY OF NOTRE DAME
Applied Arts and Design— General M
Architecture M
Art History M
Art/Fine Arts M
Cognitive Sciences D
Comparative Literature D
Conflict Resolution and Mediation/Peace Studies M,D
Counseling Psychology D
Developmental Psychology D
Economics M,D
English M,D
French M
Graphic Design M
History of Science and Technology M,D
History M,D
Industrial Design M
International Affairs M
Italian M
Latin American Studies M
Medieval and Renaissance Studies M,D
Philosophy D
Photography M
Political Science D
Psychology—General D
Religion M
Romance Languages M
Sociology D

Spanish M
Sustainable Development M
Theology M,D
Writing M

UNIVERSITY OF OKLAHOMA
Addictions/Substance Abuse Counseling M
American Indian/Native American Studies M,D
Anthropology M,D
Applied Arts and Design— General M,D
Applied Behavior Analysis M,D
Applied Economics M,D
Archaeology M,D
Architecture M,D
Art History M
Art/Fine Arts M
Clinical Psychology M,D
Communication—General M,D,O
Corporate and Organizational Communication M,D
Counseling Psychology M
Criminal Justice and Criminology M,O
Cultural Studies M,D
Dance M
Economic Development M,D
Economics M
English M,D
Film, Television, and Video Theory and Criticism M,D
French M
Gender Studies O
Geography M
German M
Health Communication M,D
History of Science and Technology M,D
History M,D
Industrial and Organizational Psychology M,D
Interdisciplinary Studies M,D
Interior Design M,O
International Affairs M
Journalism M,D
Landscape Architecture M
Mass Communication M,D
Media Studies M,D
Museum Studies M,O
Music M,D,O
Philosophy M,D
Photography M,D
Political Science M,D
Psychology—General M,D,O
Public Administration M
Public Policy M
Rhetoric M
School Psychology M
Sociology M,D
Spanish M,D
Sustainable Development M
Urban and Regional Planning M,D
Women's Studies O
Writing M,D

UNIVERSITY OF OKLAHOMA HEALTH SCIENCES CENTER
Genetic Counseling M
Homeland Security M

UNIVERSITY OF OREGON
Anthropology M,D
Applied Arts and Design— General M
Architecture M
Art History M,D
Art/Fine Arts M
Asian Languages M,D
Asian Studies M
Chinese M,D
Classics M
Clinical Psychology D
Cognitive Sciences M,D
Communication—General M,D
Comparative Literature M,D
Counseling Psychology M,D
Dance M
Developmental Psychology M,D
Economics M,D
English M,D
Folklore M
French M
Geography M,D
German M,D
Historic Preservation M
History M,D
Interdisciplinary Studies M
Interior Design M
International Affairs M
Italian M
Japanese M,D
Journalism M,D
Landscape Architecture M,D
Linguistics M,D
Marriage and Family Therapy M,D
Media Studies M,D
Music M,D
Philosophy M,D
Political Science M,D
Psychology—General M,D
Public Administration M
Romance Languages M
Russian M
School Psychology M,D
Social Psychology M,D
Sociology M
Spanish M
Theater M,D
Urban and Regional Planning M
Writing M

*M—masters degree; D—doctorate; O—other advanced degree; *—Close-Up and/or Display*

UNIVERSITY OF OTTAWA
Anthropology M
Canadian Studies D
Classics M,D
Communication—General M
Criminal Justice and Criminology M,D
Economics M,D
English M,D
French M,D
Geography M,D
History M,D
Interdisciplinary Studies D,O
International Development M
Linguistics M,D
Music M,O
Philosophy M,D
Political Science M,D
Psychology—General D
Public Administration D,O
Religion M,D
Sociology M
Spanish M,D
Theater M
Translation and Interpretation M,D
Women's Studies M

UNIVERSITY OF PENNSYLVANIA
African Studies M,D
Anthropology M,D
Applied Economics D
Applied Psychology M
Archaeology M,D
Architecture M,D,O
Art History M,D
Art/Fine Arts M,O
Asian Studies M,D
Classics M,D
Communication—General D
Comparative Literature M,D
Computer Art and Design M,D
Counseling Psychology M
Criminal Justice and Criminology M,D
Demography and Population Studies M,D
Economic Development M,O
Economics M,D
English M,D
Ethics M,D
French M,D
Geographic Information Systems M,D,O
German M,D
Graphic Design M,O
Historic Preservation M,O
History of Science and Technology M,D
History M,D
Human Development M,D
International Affairs M
Internet and Interactive Multimedia M,O
Italian M,D
Landscape Architecture M,O
Liberal Studies M
Linguistics M,D
Music M,D
Near and Middle Eastern Studies M,D
Philosophy M,D
Political Science M,D,O
Psychology—General D
Public Administration M,O
Public Policy M,D
Religion D
Romance Languages M,D
Sociology M,D
Spanish M,D
Urban and Regional Planning M,D,O
Urban Design M,D,O

UNIVERSITY OF PHILOSOPHICAL RESEARCH
Psychology—General M
Theology M

UNIVERSITY OF PHOENIX–BAY AREA CAMPUS
Criminal Justice and Criminology M
Marriage and Family Therapy M
Public Administration M,D

UNIVERSITY OF PHOENIX–CENTRAL VALLEY CAMPUS
Gerontology M
Marriage and Family Therapy M
Public Administration M

UNIVERSITY OF PHOENIX–DALLAS CAMPUS
Criminal Justice and Criminology M
Public Administration M

UNIVERSITY OF PHOENIX–HAWAII CAMPUS
Gerontology M
Public Administration M

UNIVERSITY OF PHOENIX–HOUSTON CAMPUS
Public Administration M

UNIVERSITY OF PHOENIX–LAS VEGAS CAMPUS
Counseling Psychology M
Marriage and Family Therapy M
Public Administration M
School Psychology M

UNIVERSITY OF PHOENIX–ONLINE CAMPUS
Conflict Resolution and Mediation/Peace Studies M,O
Criminal Justice and Criminology M,O
Homeland Security M
Industrial and Organizational Psychology M,D,O
Psychology—General M,O
Public Administration M,O

UNIVERSITY OF PHOENIX–PHOENIX CAMPUS
Clinical Psychology M
Counseling Psychology M
Criminal Justice and Criminology M
Homeland Security M
Marriage and Family Therapy M
Psychology—General M
Public Administration M
Social Psychology M

UNIVERSITY OF PHOENIX–SACRAMENTO VALLEY CAMPUS
Public Administration M

UNIVERSITY OF PHOENIX–SAN ANTONIO CAMPUS
Criminal Justice and Criminology M
Public Administration M

UNIVERSITY OF PHOENIX–SAN DIEGO CAMPUS
Public Administration M

UNIVERSITY OF PITTSBURGH
African Studies O
Anthropology M,D
Applied Behavior Analysis M,D
Applied Psychology M,D
Architectural History M,D
Art History M,D
Asian Studies M,O
Chinese M
Clinical Psychology M,D
Communication—General M,D
Criminal Justice and Criminology M
Cultural Studies O
Developmental Psychology M,D
Disability Studies O
East European and Russian Studies O
Economics M,D
English M,D
Film, Television, and Video Theory and Criticism M,D,O
French M,D
Genetic Counseling M,D,O
Geographic Information Systems M,D
Health Psychology D
History of Science and Technology D
History M,D
Interdisciplinary Studies D
International Affairs M,D,O
International Development M,D
Italian M,D
Japanese M
Latin American Studies O
Linguistics M,D
Medieval and Renaissance Studies O
Military and Defense Studies M
Music M,D
Philosophy D
Political Science M,D
Psychology—General D
Public Administration M,D
Public Policy M,D
Rehabilitation Counseling M,D
Slavic Languages M,D
Social Psychology D
Sociology M,D
Spanish D
Theater M,D
Urban and Regional Planning M
Western European Studies O
Women's Studies O
Writing M,D

UNIVERSITY OF PORTLAND
Communication—General M
Corporate and Organizational Communication M
Pastoral Ministry and Counseling M
Theater M

UNIVERSITY OF PRINCE EDWARD ISLAND
Geography M

UNIVERSITY OF PROVIDENCE
Counseling Psychology M
Criminal Justice and Criminology M

UNIVERSITY OF PUERTO RICO–MAYAGÜEZ
Agricultural Economics and Agribusiness M
English M
Hispanic Studies M
Rural Sociology M

UNIVERSITY OF PUERTO RICO–MEDICAL SCIENCES CAMPUS
Demography and Population Studies M
Gerontology M,O

UNIVERSITY OF PUERTO RICO–RÍO PIEDRAS
Architecture M
Clinical Psychology M,D
Communication—General M
Comparative Literature M
Economic Development M
Economics M
English M,D
Family and Consumer Sciences-General M
Hispanic Studies M,D
History M,D
Industrial and Organizational Psychology M,D
Journalism M
Linguistics M,D
Mass Communication M
Philosophy M
Psychology—General M,D
Public Administration M
Public Policy M
Rehabilitation Counseling M
Social Psychology M,D
Sociology M
Translation and Interpretation M,O
Urban and Regional Planning M

UNIVERSITY OF PUGET SOUND
Counseling Psychology M

UNIVERSITY OF REDLANDS
Geographic Information Systems M
Music M

UNIVERSITY OF REGINA
Anthropology M
Applied Economics M
Applied Psychology M,D
Art/Fine Arts M
Canadian Studies M,D
Clinical Psychology M,D
Criminal Justice and Criminology M
Economics M,D,O
English M,D
Experimental Psychology M,D
Film, Television, and Video Production M
French M
Geography M,D
Gerontology M
History M
Interdisciplinary Studies M
Journalism M
Linguistics M
Music M
Philosophy M
Political Science M
Psychology—General M,D
Public Administration M,D,O
Public Policy M,D,O
Religion M
Social Sciences M
Sociology M
Women's Studies M
Writing M,D

UNIVERSITY OF RHODE ISLAND
Anthropology M
Archaeology M
Child and Family Studies M
Clinical Psychology M,D
Clothing and Textiles M,O
Communication—General M
Computer Art and Design M
Counseling Psychology M
Economics M,D
English M,D
Film, Television, and Video Production M,D
Forensic Sciences M,D,O
Gender Studies M,D,O
History M
Human Development M
Industrial and Labor Relations M,O
Marriage and Family Therapy M
Music M
Political Science M
Psychology—General M,D
Public Administration M
Public Policy M
School Psychology M,D
Spanish M
Sport Psychology M
Women's Studies O
Writing M,D

UNIVERSITY OF ROCHESTER
Art History D
Art/Fine Arts D
Clinical Psychology D
Cognitive Sciences D
Comparative Literature M
Developmental Psychology D
Economics D
English M,D
Historic Preservation M
History M,D
Human Development M,D
Linguistics M
Marriage and Family Therapy M
Music M,D
Philosophy D
Photography M
Political Science D
Psychology—General D
Social Psychology M,D
Translation and Interpretation M,O

UNIVERSITY OF ST. FRANCIS (IL)
Forensic Sciences M,O

UNIVERSITY OF SAINT FRANCIS (IN)
Art/Fine Arts M
Clinical Psychology M,O
Counseling Psychology M,O

UNIVERSITY OF SAINT JOSEPH
Clinical Psychology M
Counseling Psychology M
Marriage and Family Therapy M

UNIVERSITY OF SAINT MARY
Counseling Psychology M
Psychology—General M

UNIVERSITY OF SAINT MARY OF THE LAKE–MUNDELEIN SEMINARY
Pastoral Ministry and Counseling M,D
Theology M,D

UNIVERSITY OF ST. MICHAEL'S COLLEGE
Jewish Studies M,D,O
Pastoral Ministry and Counseling M,D,O
Theology M,D,O

UNIVERSITY OF ST. THOMAS (MN)
Art History M,O
Counseling Psychology M,D
English M,O
Ethics M,D
Health Communication M
Human Development D
Museum Studies M,O
Music M,D
Pastoral Ministry and Counseling M
Publishing M,O
Religion M
Theology M
Writing M,O

UNIVERSITY OF ST. THOMAS (TX)
Liberal Studies M
Music M
Pastoral Ministry and Counseling M
Philosophy M,D
Public Administration M
Public Policy M
Religion M
Theology M

UNIVERSITY OF SAN DIEGO
Conflict Resolution and Mediation/Peace Studies M
Counseling Psychology M
Criminal Justice and Criminology M
International Affairs M
Marriage and Family Therapy M
School Psychology M
Theater M

UNIVERSITY OF SAN FRANCISCO
Applied Behavior Analysis M
Asian Studies M
Clinical Psychology D
Communication—General M
Counseling Psychology M
Economics M
International Affairs M
International Development M
Marriage and Family Therapy M
Museum Studies M
Pacific Area/Pacific Rim Studies M
Public Administration M
Public Affairs M
Urban Studies M
Writing M

UNIVERSITY OF SASKATCHEWAN
Agricultural Economics and Agribusiness M,D,O
Anthropology M
Archaeology M,D
Art/Fine Arts M
Canadian Studies M,D
East European and Russian Studies M
Economics M,O
English M,D
French M
Gender Studies M,D
Geography M,D
German M
History M,D
Music M
Philosophy M
Political Science M
Psychology—General M,D
Public Affairs M,D
Public Policy M,D
Religion M
Sociology M,D
Theater M
Women's Studies M,D

THE UNIVERSITY OF SCRANTON
Art/Fine Arts M
Clinical Psychology M
Counseling Psychology M
Rehabilitation Counseling M
Theology M

UNIVERSITY OF SOUTH AFRICA
Anthropology M,D
Archaeology M,D
Art History M,D
Classics M,D
Clinical Psychology M,D
Communication—General M,D
Counseling Psychology M,D
Criminal Justice and Criminology M,D
Economics M,D
English M,D
Ethics M,D
Family and Consumer Sciences-General M,D
French M,D
Geography M,D
German M,D
History M,D
Human Development M,D
Industrial and Organizational Psychology M,D
Italian M,D
Linguistics M,D
Missions and Missiology M,D
Music M,D
Near and Middle Eastern Languages M,D
Near and Middle Eastern Studies M,D
Pastoral Ministry and Counseling M,D
Philosophy M,D
Political Science M,D
Portuguese M,D
Psychology—General M,D
Public Administration M,D
Religion M,D
Romance Languages M,D
Russian M,D
Sociology M,D
Spanish M,D
Theology M,D

UNIVERSITY OF SOUTH ALABAMA
Art/Fine Arts M
Clinical Psychology M,D,O
Communication—General M

Counseling Psychology	M,D,O
English	M
History	M
Music	M
Psychology—General	M
Public Administration	M
Sociology	M
Writing	M

UNIVERSITY OF SOUTH CAROLINA

Anthropology	M,D
Art History	M
Art/Fine Arts	M
Clinical Psychology	M,D
Comparative Literature	M,D
Consumer Economics	M
Criminal Justice and Criminology	M,D
Economics	M,D
English	M,D
Experimental Psychology	M,D
French	M,D
Genetic Counseling	M
Geography	M,D
German	M,D
Gerontology	O
Historic Preservation	M,O
History	M,D,O
International Affairs	M,D
Journalism	M,D
Linguistics	M,D,O
Media Studies	M
Museum Studies	M,O
Music	M,D,O
Philosophy	M,D
Political Science	M,D
Psychology—General	M,D
Public Administration	M
Public History	M,O
Rehabilitation Counseling	M,O
Religion	M
School Psychology	D
Social Psychology	M,D
Sociology	M,D
Spanish	M,D
Speech and Interpersonal Communication	M,D
Theater	M,D
Women's Studies	O
Writing	M,D

UNIVERSITY OF SOUTH CAROLINA AIKEN

Applied Psychology	M
Clinical Psychology	M

UNIVERSITY OF SOUTH DAKOTA

Addictions/Substance Abuse Counseling	M
American Indian/Native American Studies	M,D,O
Art/Fine Arts	M
Clinical Psychology	M,D
Communication—General	M
Counseling Psychology	M,D,O
Criminal Justice and Criminology	M
English	M,D
Graphic Design	M
History	M
Human Development	M,D,O
Interdisciplinary Studies	M
Music	M
Photography	M
Psychology—General	M,D
School Psychology	M,D,O
Sustainable Development	M,D
Theater	M

UNIVERSITY OF SOUTHERN CALIFORNIA

American Studies	D
Architecture	M,D
Art History	M,D,O
Art/Fine Arts	M,D,O
Arts Administration	M
Asian Languages	M,D
Asian Studies	M,D
Child and Family Studies	M,D
Classics	M,D
Clinical Psychology	M,D
Cognitive Sciences	M,D
Communication—General	M,D
Comparative Literature	D
Computer Art and Design	M
Corporate and Organizational Communication	M
Cultural Studies	D
Developmental Psychology	M,D
Economic Development	M,D
Economics	M,D
English	M,D
Film, Television, and Video Production	M
Film, Television, and Video Theory and Criticism	M,D
Geographic Information Systems	M,O
Geography	M,O
Gerontology	M,D,O*
Health Communication	M,D
History	D
Homeland Security	M,O
International Affairs	M,D
Internet and Interactive Multimedia	M,D,O
Journalism	M
Latin American Studies	D
Linguistics	M,D
Marriage and Family Therapy	M
Media Studies	M,D
Music	M,D,O
Philosophy	M,D
Photography	M
Political Science	M,D

Psychology—General	M,D
Public Administration	M,O
Public Policy	M,D,O
Rhetoric	D
Slavic Languages	M,D
Social Psychology	M,D
Sociology	D
Spanish	D
Sustainable Development	M,D,O
Theater	M
Urban and Regional Planning	M,D,O
Writing	M,D

UNIVERSITY OF SOUTHERN INDIANA

Communication—General	M
Cultural Studies	M
English	M
Gerontology	M,D,O
Liberal Studies	M
Public Administration	M

UNIVERSITY OF SOUTHERN MAINE

Addictions/Substance Abuse Counseling	M,O
American Studies	M,O
Applied Behavior Analysis	M,O
Counseling Psychology	M,O
Cultural Studies	M,O
Music	M
Public Policy	M
Rehabilitation Counseling	M,O
School Psychology	M,D
Urban and Regional Planning	M,O
Writing	M

UNIVERSITY OF SOUTHERN MISSISSIPPI

Anthropology	M
Child and Family Studies	M
Criminal Justice and Criminology	M,D
Economic Development	M
Economics	M
English	M,D
Forensic Sciences	M
Geography	M,D
History	M,D
International Development	M,D
Music	M,D
Political Science	M,D
Psychology—General	M,D
Spanish	M
Speech and Interpersonal Communication	M,D
Theater	M
Writing	M,D

UNIVERSITY OF SOUTH FLORIDA

Addictions/Substance Abuse Counseling	M,D
African Studies	M,D,O
American Studies	M,D
Anthropology	M,D,O
Applied Behavior Analysis	M,D
Archaeology	M,D,O
Architecture	M
Art History	M
Art/Fine Arts	M
Child and Family Studies	M,D,O
Clinical Psychology	D
Cognitive Sciences	D
Communication—General	M,D
Comparative Literature	O
Corporate and Organizational Communication	M,O
Counseling Psychology	M,D,O
Criminal Justice and Criminology	M,D,O
Economics	M,D
Emergency Management	O
English	M,D,O
Film, Television, and Video Theory and Criticism	M
Forensic Sciences	M,D,O
French	M,D
Gender Studies	M,O
Geographic Information Systems	M,D,O
Geography	O
Gerontology	M,D,O
History	M,D
Humanities	M
Industrial and Organizational Psychology	D
Interdisciplinary Studies	M,D
International Affairs	O
Internet and Interactive Multimedia	M,O
Journalism	M,O
Latin American Studies	M,D,O
Liberal Studies	M,D
Linguistics	M,D
Marriage and Family Therapy	M,D,O
Mass Communication	M,O
Media Studies	M
Museum Studies	O
Music	M,D
Philosophy	M,D
Political Science	M,D,O
Psychology—General	D
Public Administration	O
Public Affairs	O
Rehabilitation Counseling	M,D,O
Religion	M,D
Rhetoric	M,D
School Psychology	M,D,O
Sociology	M,D
Spanish	M,D
Sustainable Development	M,O
Technical Communication	O
Urban and Regional Planning	O
Urban Design	M
Western European Studies	M,D
Women's Studies	M
Writing	M,D,O

UNIVERSITY OF SOUTH FLORIDA, ST. PETERSBURG

Computer Art and Design	M
Journalism	M
Liberal Studies	M
Media Studies	M
Psychology—General	M

UNIVERSITY OF SOUTH FLORIDA SARASOTA-MANATEE

Criminal Justice and Criminology	M
Liberal Studies	M
Social Sciences	M

THE UNIVERSITY OF TAMPA

Criminal Justice and Criminology	M
Writing	M

THE UNIVERSITY OF TENNESSEE

Anthropology	M,D
Applied Psychology	M,D
Archaeology	M,D
Architecture	M
Art/Fine Arts	M
Child and Family Studies	M,D
Clinical Psychology	M,D
Clothing and Textiles	M,D
Communication—General	M,D
Consumer Economics	M,D
Counseling Psychology	M,D
Criminal Justice and Criminology	M,D
Cultural Anthropology	M,D
Economics	M,D
English	M,D
Experimental Psychology	M,D
Family and Consumer Sciences-General	D
French	M,D
Geography	M,D
German	M,D
Gerontology	M
Graphic Design	M
History	M,D
Industrial and Organizational Psychology	D
Italian	D
Journalism	M,D
Landscape Architecture	M
Linguistics	D
Media Studies	M,D
Music	M
Philosophy	M,D
Photography	M
Political Science	M,D
Portuguese	D
Psychology—General	M,D
Public Administration	M
Rehabilitation Counseling	M,D
Religion	M,D
Russian	D
School Psychology	M,D,O
Sociology	M,D
Spanish	M,D
Speech and Interpersonal Communication	M,D
Theater	M

THE UNIVERSITY OF TENNESSEE AT CHATTANOOGA

Criminal Justice and Criminology	M
English	M
Ethics	M,O
Experimental Psychology	M
Industrial and Organizational Psychology	M
Interior Design	M
Music	M
Psychology—General	M
Public Administration	M,O
Rhetoric	M
School Psychology	M,D,O
Social Psychology	M,D,O
Writing	M

THE UNIVERSITY OF TENNESSEE AT MARTIN

Addictions/Substance Abuse Counseling	M
Agricultural Economics and Agribusiness	M
Child and Family Studies	M
Child Development	M
Communication—General	M
Family and Consumer Sciences-General	M
Interdisciplinary Studies	M
Social Psychology	M

THE UNIVERSITY OF TEXAS AT ARLINGTON

Anthropology	M
Architecture	M
Art/Fine Arts	M
Communication—General	M
Criminal Justice and Criminology	M
Economics	M
English	M,D
Experimental Psychology	M,D
Film, Television, and Video Production	M
French	M
Health Psychology	M,D
History	M,D
Industrial and Organizational Psychology	M,D
Landscape Architecture	M
Linguistics	M,D
Music	M
Political Science	M
Psychology—General	M,D
Public Administration	M
Public Policy	M,D

Sociology	M
Spanish	M
Urban and Regional Planning	D

THE UNIVERSITY OF TEXAS AT AUSTIN

African Studies	M,D
American Studies	M,D
Anthropology	M,D
Applied Arts and Design—General	M
Archaeology	M,D
Architectural History	M,D
Architecture	M
Art History	M,D
Art/Fine Arts	M
Asian Languages	M,D
Asian Studies	M,D
Child and Family Studies	M,D
Child Development	M,D
Classics	M,D
Clinical Psychology	D
Communication—General	M,D
Comparative Literature	M,D
Counseling Psychology	M,D
Cultural Studies	M,D
Dance	M,D
Developmental Psychology	D
East European and Russian Studies	M
Economics	M,D
English	M,D
Family and Consumer Sciences-General	M,D
Film, Television, and Video Production	M,D
Folklore	M,D
French	M,D
Geography	M,D
German	M,D
Hispanic and Latin American Languages	M,D
Hispanic Studies	M
Historic Preservation	M
History	M,D
Human Development	M,D
Interior Design	M
Italian	M,D
Journalism	M,D
Landscape Architecture	M
Latin American Studies	M,D
Linguistics	M,D
Media Studies	M,D
Mineral Economics	M
Music	M,D
Near and Middle Eastern Languages	M,D
Near and Middle Eastern Studies	M,D
Philosophy	D
Political Science	M,D
Portuguese	M,D
Psychology—General	D
Public Administration	M,D
Public Affairs	M,D
Public History	M,D
Public Policy	M,D
Rehabilitation Counseling	M,D
Romance Languages	M,D
School Psychology	M,D
Slavic Languages	M,D
Sociology	M,D
Spanish	M,D
Sport Psychology	M,D
Sustainable Development	M
Theater	M,D
Urban and Regional Planning	M,D
Urban Design	M
Writing	M,D

THE UNIVERSITY OF TEXAS AT DALLAS

Art History	M,D
Child and Family Studies	M,D
Cognitive Sciences	M,D
Communication—General	M,D
Comparative Literature	M,D
Criminal Justice and Criminology	M,D
Economics	M,D
Geographic Information Systems	M,D
Geography	M,D
History	M,D
Humanities	M,D
Interdisciplinary Studies	M
Internet and Interactive Multimedia	M,D
Latin American Studies	M,D
Political Science	M,D
Psychology—General	M,D
Public Administration	M,D
Public Policy	M,D

THE UNIVERSITY OF TEXAS AT EL PASO

Anthropology	M,O
Applied Psychology	M,D
Art/Fine Arts	M
Clinical Psychology	M,D
Communication—General	M
Economics	M
English	M,D,O
Experimental Psychology	M,D
History	M,D
Interdisciplinary Studies	M,D
Liberal Studies	M
Linguistics	M,O
Music	M
Philosophy	M
Political Science	M
Psychology—General	M,D
Rehabilitation Counseling	M
Rhetoric	M,D,O
Sociology	M,O
Spanish	M,O
Writing	M,D,O

*M—masters degree; D—doctorate; O—other advanced degree; *—Close-Up and/or Display*

THE UNIVERSITY OF TEXAS AT SAN ANTONIO
Anthropology — M,D
Applied Behavior Analysis — M,O
Architecture — M
Art History — M
Art/Fine Arts — M
Communication—General — M
Criminal Justice and Criminology — M
Cultural Studies — M,D
Demography and Population Studies — D
Economics — M
English — M,D
History — M
Interdisciplinary Studies — M,D
Music — M
Philosophy — M
Political Science — M
Psychology—General — M,D
Public Administration — M
School Psychology — M,O
Sociology — M
Spanish — M
Urban and Regional Planning — M

THE UNIVERSITY OF TEXAS AT TYLER
Art History — M
Art/Fine Arts — M
Clinical Psychology — M
Communication—General — M
Counseling Psychology — M
Criminal Justice and Criminology — M
English — M
History — M
Interdisciplinary Studies — M
Marriage and Family Therapy — M
Political Science — M
Psychology—General — M
Public Administration — M
School Psychology — M
Social Sciences — M
Sociology — M

THE UNIVERSITY OF TEXAS HEALTH SCIENCE CENTER AT HOUSTON
Genetic Counseling — M,D

THE UNIVERSITY OF TEXAS HEALTH SCIENCE CENTER AT SAN ANTONIO
Interdisciplinary Studies — D

THE UNIVERSITY OF TEXAS MEDICAL BRANCH
Demography and Population Studies — D
Humanities — M,D

THE UNIVERSITY OF TEXAS OF THE PERMIAN BASIN
Applied Psychology — M
Clinical Psychology — M
Criminal Justice and Criminology — M
English — M
Experimental Psychology — M
History — M
Political Science — M
Psychology—General — M
Spanish — M

THE UNIVERSITY OF TEXAS RIO GRANDE VALLEY
Art/Fine Arts — M
Clinical Psychology — M
Communication—General — M
Criminal Justice and Criminology — M
Emergency Management — M
English — M
Experimental Psychology — M
History — M
Interdisciplinary Studies — M
Music — M
Psychology—General — M
Public Administration — M
Public Affairs — M
Public Policy — M
Rehabilitation Counseling — M,D
School Psychology — M
Sociology — M
Spanish — M
Sustainable Development — M
Translation and Interpretation — M
Writing — M

THE UNIVERSITY OF TEXAS SOUTHWESTERN MEDICAL CENTER
Clinical Psychology — D
Rehabilitation Counseling — M

THE UNIVERSITY OF THE ARTS
Art/Fine Arts — M
Industrial Design — M
Museum Studies — M
Music — M

UNIVERSITY OF THE CUMBERLANDS
Clinical Psychology — D
Counseling Psychology — M
Religion — M
Theater — M,D,O

UNIVERSITY OF THE DISTRICT OF COLUMBIA
Architecture — M
Counseling Psychology — M
Homeland Security — M
Public Administration — M
Rehabilitation Counseling — M

UNIVERSITY OF THE FRASER VALLEY
Criminal Justice and Criminology — M

UNIVERSITY OF THE INCARNATE WORD
Clothing and Textiles — M
Communication—General — M,D
Industrial and Organizational Psychology — M,D
Pastoral Ministry and Counseling — M

UNIVERSITY OF THE PACIFIC
Communication—General — M
International Affairs — M,D
Music — M
Psychology—General — M
Public Policy — M,D
School Psychology — M,D,O
Therapies—Dance, Drama, and Music — M

UNIVERSITY OF THE ROCKIES
Psychology—General — M,D

UNIVERSITY OF THE SACRED HEART
Broadcast Journalism — M,O
Communication—General — M,O
Conflict Resolution and Mediation/Peace Studies — M
Cultural Studies — M
Film, Television, and Video Production — M,O
Internet and Interactive Multimedia — M,O
Writing — M,O

UNIVERSITY OF THE SCIENCES
Health Psychology — M
Technical Writing — M

THE UNIVERSITY OF THE SOUTH
English — M
Theology — M,D
Writing — M

UNIVERSITY OF THE SOUTHWEST
Counseling Psychology — M

UNIVERSITY OF THE VIRGIN ISLANDS
Liberal Studies — M
School Psychology — M,D,O
Social Sciences — M

UNIVERSITY OF THE WEST
Psychology—General — M
Religion — M,D
Theology — M

THE UNIVERSITY OF TOLEDO
Clinical Psychology — M,D
Communication—General — O
Criminal Justice and Criminology — M,O
Economics — M,D,O
Emergency Management — M,O
English — M,O
Experimental Psychology — M,D
French — M
Gender Studies — O
Geographic Information Systems — M,D,O
Geography — M,D,O
German — M
Gerontology — M,O
History — M,D
Liberal Studies — M
Music — M,O
Philosophy — M
Political Science — M,O
Psychology—General — M,D
Public Administration — M
School Psychology — M,D,O
Sociology — M
Spanish — M
Urban and Regional Planning — M,D,O
Women's Studies — O
Writing — M,O

UNIVERSITY OF TORONTO
Anthropology — M,D
Architecture — M
Art History — M,D
Asian Studies — M,D
Classics — M,D
Comparative Literature — M,D
Criminal Justice and Criminology — M,D
East European and Russian Studies — M
Economics — M,D
English — M,D
Film, Television, and Video Theory and Criticism — M,D
French — M,D
Gender Studies — M,D
Genetic Counseling — M,D
Geography — M,D
German — M,D
History of Science and Technology — M,D
History — M,D
Industrial and Labor Relations — M,D
International Affairs — M
Italian — M,D
Landscape Architecture — M
Linguistics — M,D
Medieval and Renaissance Studies — M,D
Museum Studies — M
Music — M,D
Near and Middle Eastern Studies — M,D
Philosophy — M,D
Political Science — M,D
Portuguese — M,D
Psychology—General — M,D
Religion — M,D
Slavic Languages — M,D
Social Sciences — M,D
Sociology — M,D
Spanish — M,D
Theater — M,D
Urban and Regional Planning — M,D
Urban Design — M,D
Women's Studies — M,D
Writing — M,D

THE UNIVERSITY OF TULSA
American Indian/Native American Studies — M,D,O
Anthropology — M,D
Applied Arts and Design— General — M
Art History — M
Art/Fine Arts — M

Clinical Psychology — M,D
English — M,D
History — M
Industrial and Organizational Psychology — M,D
Museum Studies — M
Psychology—General — M,D

UNIVERSITY OF UTAH
American Studies — M,D
Anthropology — M,D
Applied Behavior Analysis — M
Architecture — M
Art History — M
Art/Fine Arts — M
Asian Studies — M
Child and Family Studies — M
Clinical Psychology — M,D,O
Communication—General — M,D
Comparative Literature — M,D
Counseling Psychology — M,D,O
Cultural Studies — M,D
Dance — M,O
Developmental Psychology — D
Economics — M,D
English — M,D
Film, Television, and Video Production — M
French — M,D
Geographic Information Systems — M,D
Geography — M,D
Gerontology — M,O
Graphic Design — M
History — M,D
Human Development — M
Humanities — M
International Affairs — M,D
Internet and Interactive Multimedia — M,D
Latin American Studies — M
Linguistics — M,D
Music — M,D
Near and Middle Eastern Languages — M,D
Near and Middle Eastern Studies — M,D
Philosophy — M,D
Photography — M
Political Science — M,D
Psychology—General — D
Public Administration — M,D
Public Policy — M
Rhetoric — M,D
School Psychology — M,D,O
Social Psychology — D
Sociology — M,D
Spanish — M,D
Urban and Regional Planning — M,D
Urban Design — M,D
Writing — M,D

UNIVERSITY OF VALLEY FORGE
Music — M
Religion — M
Theology — M

UNIVERSITY OF VERMONT
Agricultural Economics and Agribusiness — M
Applied Economics — M
Classics — M,O
Clinical Psychology — M
Counseling Psychology — M
Developmental Psychology — D
Economics — M,D,O
English — M
Experimental Psychology — D
German — M
Historic Preservation — M
History — M
Interdisciplinary Studies — M
Psychology—General — D
Public Administration — M
School Psychology — M
Social Psychology — D
Sustainable Development — M

UNIVERSITY OF VICTORIA
Anthropology — M
Art History — M
Art/Fine Arts — M
Asian Studies — M
Child and Family Studies — M,D
Classics — M,D
Clinical Psychology — M,D
Computer Art and Design — M
Conflict Resolution and Mediation/Peace Studies — M,D
Counseling Psychology — M,D
Developmental Psychology — M,D
Economics — M,D
English — M,D
Experimental Psychology — M,D
Film, Television, and Video Production — M
French — M
Geography — M
German — M
Hispanic Studies — M
History — M,D
Human Development — M,D
Italian — M
Linguistics — M,D
Music — M
Pacific Area/Pacific Rim Studies — M
Philosophy — M
Photography — M
Political Science — M,D
Psychology—General — M,D
Public Administration — M,D
Social Psychology — M,D
Sociology — M,D
Theater — M
Writing — M

UNIVERSITY OF VIRGINIA
Anthropology — M,D
Architectural History — M,D

Architecture — M
Art History — M,D
Asian Studies — M
Classics — M,D
Clinical Psychology — D
Economics — M,D
English — M,D
French — M,D
German — M
History — M,D
Interdisciplinary Studies — M,D
International Affairs — M,D
Landscape Architecture — M
Linguistics — M
Music — M
Near and Middle Eastern Studies — M,D
Philosophy — M,D
Political Science — M,D
Psychology—General — M,D
Public Policy — M
Religion — M,D
School Psychology — M,D
Slavic Studies — M,D
Sociology — M,D
Spanish — M,D
Theater — M
Urban and Regional Planning — M
Western European Studies — M,D
Writing — M

UNIVERSITY OF WASHINGTON
Anthropology — M,D
Applied Arts and Design— General — M
Architecture — M,D,O
Art History — M,D
Art/Fine Arts — M
Asian Languages — M,D
Asian Studies — M,D
Chinese — M,D
Classics — M,D
Clinical Psychology — M,D
Cognitive Sciences — M,D
Communication—General — M,D
Comparative Literature — M,D
Dance — M
Developmental Psychology — M,D
East European and Russian Studies — M
Economics — D
English — M,D
French — M,D
Geography — M,D
German — M,D
Hispanic and Latin American Languages — M
Historic Preservation — O
History — M,D
Human Development — M,D
Industrial Design — M
International Affairs — M,D
Italian — M,D
Japanese — M,D
Landscape Architecture — M
Lighting Design — M,D,O
Linguistics — M,D
Museum Studies — M
Music — M,D
Near and Middle Eastern Studies — M,D
Philosophy — M,D
Photography — M
Political Science — M,D
Portuguese — M
Psychology—General — M,D
Public Administration — M,D
Public Affairs — M,D
Public Policy — M,D
Religion — M,D
Russian — M,D
Scandinavian Languages — M,D
School Psychology — M,D
Slavic Languages — M,D
Social Psychology — M,D
Social Sciences — M,D
Sociology — M,D
Spanish — M
Sustainable Development — M,D
Theater — M,D
Urban and Regional Planning — M,D
Urban Design — M,D,O
Women's Studies — M,D
Writing — M

UNIVERSITY OF WASHINGTON, BOTHELL
Cultural Studies — M
Public Policy — M
Writing — M

UNIVERSITY OF WASHINGTON, TACOMA
Interdisciplinary Studies — M

UNIVERSITY OF WATERLOO
Anthropology — M
Architecture — M
Art/Fine Arts — M
Economic Development — M
Economics — M,D
English — M,D
French — M,D
Geography — M,D
German — M,D
History — M,D
International Affairs — M
Near and Middle Eastern Studies — M
Philosophy — M,D
Political Science — M,D
Psychology—General — M,D
Public Affairs — M
Religion — D
Russian — M,D
Sociology — M,D
Technical Writing — M,D
Urban and Regional Planning — M,D

THE UNIVERSITY OF WEST ALABAMA

Child Development	M,O
Clinical Psychology	M
Experimental Psychology	M
History	M
Marriage and Family Therapy	M

THE UNIVERSITY OF WESTERN ONTARIO

Anthropology	M,D
Classics	M
Comparative Literature	M,D
Counseling Psychology	M
Economics	M,D
English	M,D
French	M,D
Geography	M,D
History	M,D
Interdisciplinary Studies	M,D
Journalism	M
Media Studies	M,D
Music	M,D
Philosophy	M,D
Political Science	M,D
Psychology—General	M,D
Sociology	M,D
Spanish	M,D
Sustainable Development	M,D

UNIVERSITY OF WEST FLORIDA

American Studies	M
Anthropology	M
Applied Behavior Analysis	M
Applied Psychology	M
Archaeology	M
Communication—General	M
Counseling Psychology	M
Criminal Justice and Criminology	M
English	M
Experimental Psychology	M
Geographic Information Systems	M
History	M
Industrial and Organizational Psychology	M
Political Science	M
Psychology—General	M
Public Administration	M
Public History	M
Writing	M

UNIVERSITY OF WEST GEORGIA

Criminal Justice and Criminology	M,D,O
English	M,O
Geographic Information Systems	M,O
History	M,O
Museum Studies	M,O
Music	M,O
Psychology—General	M,D,O
Public Administration	M,D,O
Public History	M,O
Sociology	M,D,O
Urban and Regional Planning	M,D,O

UNIVERSITY OF WINDSOR

Applied Psychology	M,D
Art/Fine Arts	M
Clinical Psychology	M,D
Communication—General	M
Criminal Justice and Criminology	M,D
Economics	M
English	M
History	M
Philosophy	M
Political Science	M
Psychology—General	M,D
Social Psychology	M,D
Sociology	M,D
Writing	M

THE UNIVERSITY OF WINNIPEG

History	M
Marriage and Family Therapy	M,O
Public Administration	M
Religion	M
Theology	M,O

UNIVERSITY OF WISCONSIN–EAU CLAIRE

English	M
History	M
Psychology—General	M,O
School Psychology	M,O
Writing	M

UNIVERSITY OF WISCONSIN–LA CROSSE

Psychology—General	M,O
School Psychology	M,O

UNIVERSITY OF WISCONSIN–MADISON

African Studies	M,D
African-American Studies	M
Agricultural Economics and Agribusiness	M,D
American Studies	M,D
Anthropology	D
Applied Arts and Design—General	M,D
Applied Economics	M,D
Archaeology	D
Art History	M,D
Art/Fine Arts	M
Arts Administration	M
Asian Languages	M,D
Asian Studies	M,D
Child and Family Studies	M,D
Chinese	M,D
Classics	M,D
Clinical Psychology	D
Cognitive Sciences	D
Communication—General	M,D
Comparative Literature	M,D
Consumer Economics	M,D
Counseling Psychology	D
Cultural Anthropology	D
Demography and Population Studies	M,D
Developmental Psychology	D
Economics	D
English	M,D
Family and Consumer Sciences-General	M,D
Film, Television, and Video Theory and Criticism	M,D
Folklore	M,D
French	M,D,O
Genetic Counseling	M,D
Geographic Information Systems	M,D,O
Geography	M,D,O
German	M,D
History of Science and Technology	M,D
History	M,D
Human Development	M,D
Italian	M,D
Japanese	M,D
Jewish Studies	M,D
Journalism	M,D
Landscape Architecture	M,D
Latin American Studies	M,D
Linguistics	M,D
Mass Communication	M,D
Media Studies	M,D
Music	M,D
Near and Middle Eastern Languages	M,D
Near and Middle Eastern Studies	M,D
Philosophy	M,D
Political Science	D
Portuguese	M,D
Psychology—General	D
Public Affairs	M
Rehabilitation Counseling	M,D
Rhetoric	M,D
Rural Sociology	M,D
Scandinavian Languages	M,D
Slavic Languages	M,D
Social Psychology	D
Sociology	M,D
Spanish	M,D
Speech and Interpersonal Communication	M,D
Sustainable Development	M
Theater	M,D
Urban and Regional Planning	M,D
Women's Studies	M,D
Writing	M,D

UNIVERSITY OF WISCONSIN–MILWAUKEE

African Studies	D
Anthropology	M,D,O
Applied Arts and Design—General	M
Architecture	M,D,O
Art History	M
Classics	M,O
Communication—General	M,D,O
Comparative Literature	M,O
Conflict Resolution and Mediation/Peace Studies	M,D,O
Counseling Psychology	M,D,O
Criminal Justice and Criminology	M,O
Developmental Psychology	M,D,O
Economics	M,D
English	M,D
Film, Television, and Video Theory and Criticism	M,D
French	M,O
Gender Studies	M,O
Geographic Information Systems	M,D,O
Geography	M,D
German	M,O
Gerontology	M,D,O
History	M,D
Industrial and Labor Relations	M,O
Latin American Studies	M,O
Liberal Studies	M
Linguistics	M,D,O
Media Studies	M,D
Museum Studies	M,D,O
Philosophy	M
Political Science	M,D
Portuguese	M
Psychology—General	M,D
Public Administration	M
Rhetoric	M,D,O
School Psychology	M,D,O
Sociology	M,O
Spanish	M,O
Translation and Interpretation	M,O
Urban and Regional Planning	M
Urban Studies	M,D
Women's Studies	M,O
Writing	M,D

UNIVERSITY OF WISCONSIN–OSHKOSH

English	M
Experimental Psychology	M
Industrial and Organizational Psychology	M
Psychology—General	M
Public Administration	M

UNIVERSITY OF WISCONSIN–PARKSIDE

Clinical Psychology	M

UNIVERSITY OF WISCONSIN–PLATTEVILLE

Criminal Justice and Criminology	M

UNIVERSITY OF WISCONSIN–RIVER FALLS

Art/Fine Arts	M
School Psychology	M,O

UNIVERSITY OF WISCONSIN–STEVENS POINT

Communication—General	M
Corporate and Organizational Communication	M
English	M
Family and Consumer Sciences-General	M
History	M
Human Development	M
Media Studies	M
Speech and Interpersonal Communication	M
Sustainable Development	D

UNIVERSITY OF WISCONSIN–STOUT

Applied Psychology	M
Art/Fine Arts	M
Clinical Psychology	M
Counseling Psychology	M
Marriage and Family Therapy	M
Rehabilitation Counseling	M
School Psychology	M,O
Technical Communication	M

UNIVERSITY OF WISCONSIN–SUPERIOR

Art History	M
Art Therapy	M
Art/Fine Arts	M
Communication—General	M
Mass Communication	M
School Psychology	M
Social Psychology	M
Speech and Interpersonal Communication	M
Theater	M

UNIVERSITY OF WISCONSIN–WHITEWATER

Communication—General	M
Corporate and Organizational Communication	M
Mass Communication	M
Psychology—General	M,O
School Psychology	M,O

UNIVERSITY OF WYOMING

Agricultural Economics and Agribusiness	M
American Studies	M
Anthropology	M,D
Applied Economics	M
Child Development	M
Communication—General	M
Consumer Economics	M
Economics	M,D
English	M
French	M
Geography	M
German	M
History	M
International Affairs	M
Music	M
Philosophy	M
Political Science	M
Psychology—General	M,D
Public Administration	M
Rural Planning and Studies	M
Sociology	M
Spanish	M
Writing	M

UPPER IOWA UNIVERSITY

Emergency Management	M
Homeland Security	M
Public Administration	M

URBANA UNIVERSITY–A BRANCH CAMPUS OF FRANKLIN UNIVERSITY

Criminal Justice and Criminology	M

URSHAN GRADUATE SCHOOL OF THEOLOGY

Theology	M

URSULINE COLLEGE

Art Therapy	M
Historic Preservation	M
Liberal Studies	M
Pastoral Ministry and Counseling	M
Theology	M

UTAH STATE UNIVERSITY

Agricultural Economics and Agribusiness	M,D
American Studies	M
Anthropology	M,D
Applied Economics	M,D
Art/Fine Arts	M
Child and Family Studies	M,D
Clinical Psychology	M,D
Communication—General	M
Consumer Economics	M
Counseling Psychology	M,D
Disability Studies	M,D,O
Economics	M
English	M
Family and Consumer Sciences-General	M,D
Folklore	M
Geography	M,D
History	M
Human Development	M,D
Landscape Architecture	M
Marriage and Family Therapy	M,D
Music	M
Political Science	M
Psychology—General	M,D
Rehabilitation Counseling	M
School Psychology	M,D
Sociology	M,D
Theater	M
Urban and Regional Planning	M,D
Writing	M

UTICA COLLEGE

Criminal Justice and Criminology	M

VALDOSTA STATE UNIVERSITY

English	M
Industrial and Organizational Psychology	M,O
Marriage and Family Therapy	M,O
Psychology—General	M,O
Public Administration	M,D

VALPARAISO UNIVERSITY

Arts Administration	M
Clinical Psychology	M
Communication—General	M,O
English	M
Ethics	M,O
International Economics	M
International Trade Policy	M
Media Studies	M,O
School Psychology	M,O

VANCOUVER SCHOOL OF THEOLOGY

Religion	M,O
Theology	M,O

VANDERBILT UNIVERSITY

Anthropology	M,D
Child and Family Studies	M
Classics	M
Economic Development	M,D
Economics	M,D
English	M,D
French	M,D
German	M,D
History	M,D
Human Development	M
Latin American Studies	M
Liberal Studies	M
Philosophy	M,D
Political Science	M,D
Portuguese	M,D
Psychology—General	D
Public Policy	D
Religion	M,D
Sociology	M,D
Spanish	M,D
Theology	M
Urban and Regional Planning	M
Writing	M

VANGUARD UNIVERSITY OF SOUTHERN CALIFORNIA

Clinical Psychology	M
Religion	M
Theology	M

VERMONT COLLEGE OF FINE ARTS

Art/Fine Arts	M
Film, Television, and Video Production	M
Graphic Design	M
Music	M
Publishing	M
Writing	M

VICTORIA UNIVERSITY

Theology	M,D,O

VILLANOVA UNIVERSITY

Classics	M
Communication—General	M
English	M
Hispanic Studies	M
History	M
Liberal Studies	M
Missions and Missiology	M
Philosophy	D
Political Science	M
Psychology—General	M
Public Administration	M,O
Theater	M
Theology	M,D

VIRGINIA BAPTIST COLLEGE

Theology	M

VIRGINIA BEACH THEOLOGICAL SEMINARY

Pastoral Ministry and Counseling	M
Theology	M

VIRGINIA COMMONWEALTH UNIVERSITY

Art History	M,D
Art/Fine Arts	M,D
Clinical Psychology	D
Communication—General	D
Counseling Psychology	M,D
Criminal Justice and Criminology	M,O
Economics	M
Emergency Management	M,O
English	M
Film, Television, and Video Production	M,D
Forensic Sciences	M
Geographic Information Systems	O
Gerontology	M,D
Health Psychology	D
History	M
Homeland Security	M,O
Interdisciplinary Studies	M
Interior Design	M,D
Journalism	M
Mass Communication	M
Media Studies	M,D
Museum Studies	M,D
Music	M
Photography	M,D
Political Science	M,D,O
Public Administration	M,D
Public Affairs	M,D,O
Public Policy	D

*M—masters degree; D—doctorate; O—other advanced degree; *—Close-Up and/or Display*

Rehabilitation Counseling — M
Sociology — M
Theater — M
Urban and Regional Planning — M
Writing — M

VIRGINIA INTERNATIONAL UNIVERSITY
Computer Art and Design — M,O
International Affairs — M
Linguistics — M
Public Administration — M

VIRGINIA POLYTECHNIC INSTITUTE AND STATE UNIVERSITY
Agricultural Economics and Agribusiness — M,D
Applied Economics — M,D
Communication—General — M,D,O
Economics — M,D
English — M,D,O
Environmental Design — M,D
Geography — M,D
Humanities — M,D,O
Interdisciplinary Studies — M,D
International Affairs — M,D
Internet and Interactive Multimedia — M,D
Landscape Architecture — M,D
Liberal Studies — M,O
National Security — M,O
Political Science — M,O
Psychology—General — M,D
Public Administration — M,D
Public Affairs — M,D
Public Policy — M,D
Urban and Regional Planning — M,D
Urban Studies — M,D
Writing — M,D,O

VIRGINIA STATE UNIVERSITY
Clinical Psychology — M,D
Criminal Justice and Criminology — M
Economics — M
Health Psychology — M
Interdisciplinary Studies — M
Media Studies — M
Psychology—General — M,D

VIRGINIA THEOLOGICAL SEMINARY
Theology — M,D

VIRGINIA UNION UNIVERSITY
Theology — M,D

VIRGINIA UNIVERSITY OF LYNCHBURG
Pastoral Ministry and Counseling — M,D
Religion — M,D

VITERBO UNIVERSITY
Addictions/Substance Abuse Counseling — M
Counseling Psychology — M
Developmental Psychology — M
Ethics — M,O
Health Psychology — M
Pastoral Ministry and Counseling — M

WAGNER COLLEGE
Media Studies — M

WAKE FOREST UNIVERSITY
Communication—General — M
English — M
Liberal Studies — M
Psychology—General — M
Religion — M
Speech and Interpersonal Communication — M

WALDEN UNIVERSITY
Addictions/Substance Abuse Counseling — M,D
Applied Psychology — M,D,O
Child and Family Studies — M,D
Clinical Psychology — M,D,O
Communication—General — M
Conflict Resolution and Mediation/Peace Studies — M,D,O
Counseling Psychology — M,D,O
Criminal Justice and Criminology — M,D,O
Emergency Management — M,D,O
Forensic Psychology — M,D
Gerontology — M,D
Health Psychology — M,D
Homeland Security — M,D,O
Industrial and Organizational Psychology — M,D,O
Interdisciplinary Studies — M,D,O
International Affairs — M,D,O
International Development — M,D,O
Marriage and Family Therapy — M,D
Political Science — M,D,O
Psychology—General — M,D,O
Public Administration — M,D,O
Public Policy — M,D,O
Social Psychology — M,D,O
Sustainable Development — M,D,O

WALDORF UNIVERSITY
Criminal Justice and Criminology — M
Emergency Management — M
Public Administration — M

WALLA WALLA UNIVERSITY
Communication—General — M
Film, Television, and Video Theory and Criticism — M
Internet and Interactive Multimedia — M
Pastoral Ministry and Counseling — M
Religion — M

WALSH UNIVERSITY
Counseling Psychology — M
Pastoral Ministry and Counseling — M
Theology — M

WARREN WILSON COLLEGE
Art/Fine Arts — M

Writing — M

WARTBURG THEOLOGICAL SEMINARY
Theology — M

WASHBURN UNIVERSITY
Addictions/Substance Abuse Counseling — M
Clinical Psychology — M
Criminal Justice and Criminology — M
Liberal Studies — M
Psychology—General — M

WASHINGTON ADVENTIST UNIVERSITY
Counseling Psychology — M
Public Administration — M
Religion — M

WASHINGTON & JEFFERSON COLLEGE
Applied Economics — M,O
Thanatology — M,O
Writing — M,O

WASHINGTON STATE UNIVERSITY
Agricultural Economics and Agribusiness — M,D,O
American Studies — M,D
Anthropology — M,D
Archaeology — M,D
Architecture — M
Art/Fine Arts — M
Clinical Psychology — M,D
Clothing and Textiles — M,D
Communication—General — M,D
Corporate and Organizational Communication — M,D
Counseling Psychology — M,D
Criminal Justice and Criminology — M,D
Cultural Anthropology — M,D
Cultural Studies — M,D
Economics — M,D,O
English — M,D
Experimental Psychology — M,D
History — M,D
Human Development — D
Interdisciplinary Studies — D
Interior Design — M
Landscape Architecture — M
Music — M
Political Science — M,D,O
Psychology—General — M,D
Public Affairs — M,D,O
Sociology — M,D

WASHINGTON UNIVERSITY IN ST. LOUIS
Anthropology — D
Archaeology — M,D
Architecture — M
Art History — M,D
Art/Fine Arts — M
Asian Languages — M,D
Asian Studies — M,D
Child and Family Studies — M,D
Chinese — M,D
Classics — M,D
Comparative Literature — M,D
Dance — M
Developmental Psychology — D
Economics — D
English — M,D
French — D
German — D
Gerontology — M,D
History — D
Japanese — M,D
Jewish Studies — M
Music — M,D
Near and Middle Eastern Studies — M
Philosophy — D
Political Science — D
Psychology—General — D
Religion — M
Romance Languages — D
Spanish — D
Speech and Interpersonal Communication — M,D
Theater — M
Urban Design — M
Writing — M

WATKINS COLLEGE OF ART, DESIGN, & FILM
Film, Television, and Video Production — M

WAYLAND BAPTIST UNIVERSITY
Counseling Psychology — M
Criminal Justice and Criminology — M
History — M
Homeland Security — M
Humanities — M
Pastoral Ministry and Counseling — M
Religion — M
Theology — M

WAYNESBURG UNIVERSITY
Addictions/Substance Abuse Counseling — M,D
Clinical Psychology — M,D
Counseling Psychology — M,D
Criminal Justice and Criminology — M,D

WAYNE STATE COLLEGE
Communication—General — M

WAYNE STATE UNIVERSITY
African-American Studies — M,D,O
Anthropology — M,D
Applied Behavior Analysis — M,D,O
Art History — M
Art/Fine Arts — M
Clinical Psychology — M,D
Clothing and Textiles — M
Cognitive Sciences — M,D
Communication—General — M,D,O
Conflict Resolution and Mediation/Peace Studies — M,D,O

Counseling Psychology — M,D,O
Criminal Justice and Criminology — M
Cultural Studies — M,D
Dance — M,D,O
Economic Development — M,D,O
Economics — M,D
English — M,D
Film, Television, and Video Theory and Criticism — M,D
French — M,D
Gender Studies — M,D,O
Genetic Counseling — M,D,O
German — M,D
Gerontology — M,D
Graphic Design — M
Health Communication — M,D,O
History — M,D,O
Industrial and Labor Relations — M,D
Industrial and Organizational Psychology — M,D
Industrial Design — M
Interior Design — M
International Economics — M,D
Italian — M,D
Journalism — M,D,O
Linguistics — M
Media Studies — M,D,O
Museum Studies — M,D,O
Music — M
Near and Middle Eastern Languages — M,D
Near and Middle Eastern Studies — M,D
Philosophy — M,D
Photography — M
Political Science — M,D
Psychology—General — M,D
Public Administration — M,D
Public History — M,D,O
Public Policy — M,D,O
Rehabilitation Counseling — M,D,O
Rhetoric — M,D
Romance Languages — M,D
School Psychology — M,D,O
Social Psychology — M,D,O
Sociology — M,D
Spanish — M,D
Textile Design — M
Theater — M
Urban and Regional Planning — M,O
Urban Studies — M,D,O
Women's Studies — M,D,O
Writing — M,D

WEBBER INTERNATIONAL UNIVERSITY
Criminal Justice and Criminology — M

WEBER STATE UNIVERSITY
Communication—General — M
English — M

WEBSTER UNIVERSITY
Art History — M
Art/Fine Arts — M
Communication—General — M,O
Corporate and Organizational Communication — M
Counseling Psychology — M
Criminal Justice and Criminology — M,D,O
Forensic Sciences — M
Gerontology — M
International Affairs — M
Internet and Interactive Multimedia — M
Media Studies — M
Music — M
Psychology—General — M
Public Administration — M,D,O

WELCH COLLEGE
Pastoral Ministry and Counseling — M
Theology — M

WENTWORTH INSTITUTE OF TECHNOLOGY
Architecture — M

WESLEYAN UNIVERSITY
Liberal Studies — M,O
Music — M,D
Writing — M,O

WESLEY BIBLICAL SEMINARY
Linguistics — M
Missions and Missiology — M
Pastoral Ministry and Counseling — M
Religion — M
Theology — M
Translation and Interpretation — M

WESLEY THEOLOGICAL SEMINARY
Theology — M

WEST CHESTER UNIVERSITY OF PENNSYLVANIA
Clinical Psychology — M,D,O
Communication—General — M
Criminal Justice and Criminology — M
Cultural Studies — M,O
English — M,O
Ethics — M,O
French — M,O
Geographic Information Systems — M,O
Geography — M,O
German — M,O
Gerontology — M,O
History — M
Holocaust and Genocide Studies — M,O
Industrial and Organizational Psychology — M,D,O
Music — M,O
Philosophy — M,O
Psychology—General — M,D,O
Public Administration — M,O
Public Affairs — M,O
Spanish — M,O
Sustainable Development — M,O
Urban and Regional Planning — M,O
Writing — M,O

WESTERN CAROLINA UNIVERSITY
Applied Arts and Design— General — M
Art/Fine Arts — M
English — M,O
History — M
Psychology—General — M
Public Affairs — M
Rhetoric — M,O
Technical Writing — M,O
Writing — M,O

WESTERN CONNECTICUT STATE UNIVERSITY
Art/Fine Arts — M
Clinical Psychology — M
English — M
History — M
Illustration — M
Writing — M

WESTERN ILLINOIS UNIVERSITY
Clinical Psychology — M,O
Communication—General — M
Criminal Justice and Criminology — M
Economic Development — M
Economics — M
English — M,O
Experimental Psychology — M,O
Geographic Information Systems — M,O
Geography — M,O
History — M,O
Liberal Studies — M
Museum Studies — M,O
Music — M
Political Science — M
Psychology—General — M,O
School Psychology — M,O
Social Psychology — M,O
Sociology — M
Theater — M

WESTERN KENTUCKY UNIVERSITY
Anthropology — M
Applied Economics — M
Clinical Psychology — M,O
Communication—General — M,O
Comparative Literature — M
Corporate and Organizational Communication — M,O
Counseling Psychology — M
Criminal Justice and Criminology — M
English — M
Experimental Psychology — M
French — M
German — M
History — M
Homeland Security — M
Industrial and Organizational Psychology — M,O
Interdisciplinary Studies — M,O
Marriage and Family Therapy — M
Political Science — M
Psychology—General — M,O
Public Administration — M
School Psychology — M,O
Sociology — M
Spanish — M
Writing — M

WESTERN MICHIGAN UNIVERSITY
Anthropology — M
Applied Arts and Design— General — M
Applied Economics — M,D
Clinical Psychology — M,D
Communication—General — M
Counseling Psychology — M,D
Economics — M,D
English — M,D
Family and Consumer Sciences-General — M
Geographic Information Systems — M,O
Geography — M,O
History — M,D
Industrial and Organizational Psychology — M,D
International Affairs — M,O
Music — M,O
Philosophy — M
Political Science — M,D
Psychology—General — M,D
Public Administration — M,D,O
Public Affairs — M,D,O
Rehabilitation Counseling — M,O
Religion — M,O
Sociology — M,D
Spanish — M,D
Therapies—Dance, Drama, and Music — M,O
Writing — M

WESTERN MICHIGAN UNIVERSITY THOMAS M. COOLEY LAW SCHOOL
Homeland Security — M,D
National Security — M,D

WESTERN NEW ENGLAND UNIVERSITY
Applied Behavior Analysis — M,D
Communication—General — M
Writing — M

WESTERN NEW MEXICO UNIVERSITY
Interdisciplinary Studies — M

WESTERN OREGON UNIVERSITY
Criminal Justice and Criminology — M
Music — M
Rehabilitation Counseling — M

WESTERN SEMINARY
Pastoral Ministry and Counseling — M,D,O
Religion — M,O
Theology — M,O
Women's Studies — M

WESTERN SEMINARY–SACRAMENTO CAMPUS

Marriage and Family Therapy	M
Pastoral Ministry and Counseling	M,O
Theology	M,O
Women's Studies	O

WESTERN SEMINARY–SAN JOSE CAMPUS

Marriage and Family Therapy	M,O
Pastoral Ministry and Counseling	M,O
Theology	M,O
Women's Studies	M,O

WESTERN STATE COLORADO UNIVERSITY

Film, Television, and Video Production	M
Writing	M

WESTERN THEOLOGICAL SEMINARY

Pastoral Ministry and Counseling	M,D,O
Theology	M,D,O

WESTERN WASHINGTON UNIVERSITY

Anthropology	M
Counseling Psychology	M
English	M
Experimental Psychology	M
Geography	M
History	M
Music	M
Political Science	M
Psychology—General	M
Rehabilitation Counseling	M

WESTFIELD STATE UNIVERSITY

Applied Behavior Analysis	M
Counseling Psychology	M
Criminal Justice and Criminology	M
English	M
Forensic Psychology	M
Psychology—General	M
Public Administration	M

WESTMINSTER COLLEGE (PA)

Clinical Psychology	M

WESTMINSTER COLLEGE (UT)

Communication—General	M
Counseling Psychology	M
Writing	M

WESTMINSTER SEMINARY CALIFORNIA

Religion	M
Theology	M

WESTMINSTER THEOLOGICAL SEMINARY

Missions and Missiology	M,D,O
Pastoral Ministry and Counseling	M,D,O
Religion	M,D,O
Theology	M,D,O

WEST TEXAS A&M UNIVERSITY

Agricultural Economics and Agribusiness	M
Art/Fine Arts	M
Communication—General	M
Criminal Justice and Criminology	M
Economics	M
English	M
History	M
Interdisciplinary Studies	M
Music	M
Psychology—General	M

WEST VIRGINIA STATE UNIVERSITY

Criminal Justice and Criminology	M
Media Studies	M

WEST VIRGINIA UNIVERSITY

Art History	M,D
Art/Fine Arts	M,D
Clinical Psychology	M,D
Communication—General	M
Corporate and Organizational Communication	M,O
Counseling Psychology	M,D
Economics	M,D,O
English	M,D
Forensic Sciences	M,D
Geography	M,D
Graphic Design	M,D
History	M
Industrial and Labor Relations	M,D,O
Journalism	M,O
Landscape Architecture	M,D
Media Studies	M,O
Music	M
Photography	M,D
Political Science	M,D
Psychology—General	M,D
Public Administration	M,D
Rehabilitation Counseling	M,D
Sociology	M,D
Sport Psychology	M,D
Theater	M,D
Writing	M,D

WEST VIRGINIA WESLEYAN COLLEGE

Writing	M

WHEATON COLLEGE

Archaeology	M,D
Clinical Psychology	M,D
Counseling Psychology	M,D
Cultural Studies	M,O
Emergency Management	M

WHITTIER COLLEGE

Child Development	M

WHITWORTH UNIVERSITY

Missions and Missiology	M
Pastoral Ministry and Counseling	M
Theology	M

WICHITA STATE UNIVERSITY

Anthropology	M
Art/Fine Arts	M
Clinical Psychology	D
Communication—General	M
Criminal Justice and Criminology	M
Economics	M
English	M
Gerontology	M
History	M
International Economics	M
Liberal Studies	M
Music	M
Photography	M
Psychology—General	D
Public Administration	M
School Psychology	M,D,O
Social Psychology	D
Sociology	M
Spanish	M
Writing	M

WIDENER UNIVERSITY

Clinical Psychology	D
Criminal Justice and Criminology	M
Psychology—General	
Public Administration	M

WILBERFORCE UNIVERSITY

Rehabilitation Counseling	M

WILFRID LAURIER UNIVERSITY

American Studies	M,D
Canadian Studies	M,D
Cognitive Sciences	M,D
Communication—General	M
Conflict Resolution and Mediation/Peace Studies	D
Criminal Justice and Criminology	M
Cultural Studies	M
Developmental Psychology	M,D
Economics	M,D
English	M,D
Film, Television, and Video Theory and Criticism	M,D
Gender Studies	M
Geography	M,D
History	M,D
International Affairs	M,D
International Economics	M
Media Studies	M
Pastoral Ministry and Counseling	M,D,O
Philosophy	M
Political Science	M,D
Psychology—General	M,D
Public Policy	M
Religion	M,D
Social Psychology	M,D
Social Sciences	M
Sociology	M
Theology	M,D,O
Therapies—Dance, Drama, and Music	M

WILKES UNIVERSITY

Writing	M

WILLAMETTE UNIVERSITY

Conflict Resolution and Mediation/Peace Studies	M,D

WILLIAM CAREY UNIVERSITY

Counseling Psychology	M
Psychology—General	M

WILLIAM JAMES COLLEGE

Applied Psychology	M,D,O
Clinical Psychology	M,D,O
Counseling Psychology	M,D,O
Forensic Psychology	M,D,O
Industrial and Organizational Psychology	M,D,O
Psychology—General	M,D,O
School Psychology	M,D,O

WILLIAM PATERSON UNIVERSITY OF NEW JERSEY

Clinical Psychology	M,D,O
Counseling Psychology	M,D,O
English	M,D,O
History	M
Music	M
Public Policy	M,D,O
Sociology	M,D,O
Writing	M,D,O

WILLIAMS COLLEGE

Art History	M
Economic Development	M

WILMINGTON UNIVERSITY

Clinical Psychology	M
Counseling Psychology	M
Criminal Justice and Criminology	M
Homeland Security	M,D

WILSON COLLEGE

Internet and Interactive Multimedia	M
Public Administration	M,D

WILSON COLLEGE

Art/Fine Arts	M
Cultural Studies	M
Dance	M
English	M
Humanities	M
Women's Studies	M

WINEBRENNER THEOLOGICAL SEMINARY

Counseling Psychology	M,D
Theology	M,D

WINONA STATE UNIVERSITY

Addictions/Substance Abuse Counseling	M,O
Clinical Psychology	M,O
English	M

WINSTON-SALEM STATE UNIVERSITY

Rehabilitation Counseling	M

WINTHROP UNIVERSITY

Art/Fine Arts	M
Arts Administration	M
English	M
History	M
Liberal Studies	M
Music	M
Psychology—General	M,O

WISCONSIN SCHOOL OF PROFESSIONAL PSYCHOLOGY

Clinical Psychology	M,D
Psychology—General	M,D

WON INSTITUTE OF GRADUATE STUDIES

Religion	M

WOODBURY UNIVERSITY

Architecture	M

WORCESTER POLYTECHNIC INSTITUTE

Interdisciplinary Studies	M,D,O
Internet and Interactive Multimedia	M
Social Sciences	M,D,O

WORCESTER STATE UNIVERSITY

History	M
School Psychology	M,O
Spanish	M

WORLD MISSION UNIVERSITY

Music	M,D
Pastoral Ministry and Counseling	M,D
Theology	M,D

THE WRIGHT INSTITUTE

Clinical Psychology	D
Counseling Psychology	M
Psychology—General	D

WRIGHT STATE UNIVERSITY

Applied Behavior Analysis	M
Applied Economics	M
Clinical Psychology	D
Criminal Justice and Criminology	M
Economics	M
English	M
History	M
Humanities	M
Industrial and Organizational Psychology	M,D
Psychology—General	M,D
Public Administration	M
Rehabilitation Counseling	M

WYCLIFFE COLLEGE

Religion	M,D,O
Theology	M,D,O

XAVIER UNIVERSITY

Clinical Psychology	M,D
Counseling Psychology	M
Criminal Justice and Criminology	M
English	M
Ethics	M
Industrial and Organizational Psychology	M,D
Pastoral Ministry and Counseling	M
Psychology—General	M,D
Sustainable Development	M
Theology	M

XAVIER UNIVERSITY OF LOUISIANA

Pastoral Ministry and Counseling	M
Theology	M

YALE UNIVERSITY

African Studies	M
African-American Studies	D
American Studies	D
Anthropology	M,D
Applied Arts and Design—General	M
Archaeology	M,D
Architecture	M,D
Art History	D
Art/Fine Arts	M
Asian Languages	D
Asian Studies	M
Classics	M,D
Clinical Psychology	D
Cognitive Sciences	D
Comparative Literature	D
Developmental Psychology	D
East European and Russian Studies	M,D
Economic Development	M
Economics	M,D
English	M,D
Environmental Design	M,D
Film, Television, and Video Theory and Criticism	D
French	M,D
German	D
Graphic Design	M
History of Medicine	M,D
History of Science and Technology	M,D
History	M
International Affairs	M
International Economics	M
Italian	D
Latin American Studies	M
Linguistics	D
Medieval and Renaissance Studies	M,D
Music	M,D,O
Near and Middle Eastern Languages	M,D
Near and Middle Eastern Studies	M,D
Philosophy	D
Photography	M
Political Science	D
Portuguese	D
Psychology—General	D
Religion	D
Russian	D
Slavic Languages	D
Social Psychology	D
Social Sciences	M,D
Sociology	D
Spanish	D
Theater	M,D,O
Theology	M
Writing	M,D,O

YESHIVA BETH MOSHE

Theology	O

YESHIVA DERECH CHAIM

Religion	D

YESHIVA KARLIN STOLIN

Theology	O

YESHIVA OF NITRA RABBINICAL COLLEGE

Theology	O

YESHIVA SHAAR HATORAH TALMUDIC RESEARCH INSTITUTE

Theology	

YESHIVATH ZICHRON MOSHE

Theology	O

YESHIVA UNIVERSITY

Clinical Psychology	D
Conflict Resolution and Mediation/Peace Studies	M,D
Counseling Psychology	M
Economics	M
Health Psychology	D
Jewish Studies	M,D
Psychology—General	M,D
School Psychology	D

YORK UNIVERSITY

Anthropology	M,D
Applied Arts and Design—General	M
Art History	M,D
Art/Fine Arts	M,D
Communication—General	M,D
Dance	M,D
Disability Studies	M,D
Economics	M,D
Emergency Management	M
English	M,D
Film, Television, and Video Production	M,D
French	M,D
Gender Studies	M,D
Geography	M,D
History	M,D
Humanities	M,D
Interdisciplinary Studies	M
International Affairs	M
Linguistics	M,D
Music	M,D
Philosophy	M,D
Political Science	M,D
Psychology—General	M,D
Public Administration	M
Public Affairs	M
Public Policy	M
Sociology	M,D
Theater	M,D
Translation and Interpretation	M
Women's Studies	M,D

YOUNGSTOWN STATE UNIVERSITY

Applied Behavior Analysis	M
Counseling Psychology	M
Criminal Justice and Criminology	M
Economics	M
English	M
Gerontology	M
History	M
Music	M
Psychology—General	M
School Psychology	M

M—masters degree; D—doctorate; O—other advanced degree; *—Close-Up and/or Display

ACADEMIC AND PROFESSIONAL PROGRAMS IN THE ARTS AND ARCHITECTURE

Section 1
Applied Arts and Design

This section contains a directory of institutions offering graduate work in applied arts and design, followed by in-depth entries submitted by institutions that chose to prepare detailed program descriptions. Additional information about programs listed in the directory but not augmented by an in-depth entry may be obtained by writing directly to the dean of a graduate school or chair of a department at the address given in the directory.

For programs offering related work, see also in this book *Architecture* and *Art and Art History.* In another guide in this series:

Graduate Programs in Business, Education, Information Studies, Law & Social Work

See *Advertising and Public Relations*

CONTENTS

Program Directories

Featured Schools: Displays and Close-Ups

See also:

Applied Arts and Design—General

Academy of Art University, Graduate Programs, School of Advertising, San Francisco, CA 94105-3410. Offers advertising (MFA); advertising and branded media technology (MA). *Program availability:* Part-time, 100% online. *Faculty:* 5 full-time (2 women), 13 part-time/adjunct (6 women). *Students:* 59 full-time (41 women), 34 part-time (24 women); includes 16 minority (5 Black or African American, non-Hispanic/Latino; 6 Asian, non-Hispanic/Latino; 5 Hispanic/Latino), 57 international. Average age 28. 29 applicants, 100% accepted, 23 enrolled. In 2017, 61 master's awarded. *Degree requirements:* For master's, final review. *Entrance requirements:* For master's, statement of intent; resume; portfolio/reel; official college transcripts. *Application deadline:* Applications are processed on a rolling basis. Application fee: $50. Electronic applications accepted. *Expenses: Tuition:* Part-time $982 per unit. *Financial support:* Career-related internships or fieldwork, Federal Work-Study, and scholarships/grants available. Financial award application deadline: 8/10; financial award applicants required to submit FAFSA. *Unit head:* 800-544-ARTS, E-mail: info@academyart.edu. *Application contact:* 800-544-ARTS, E-mail: info@academyart.edu.
Website: https://www.academyart.edu/academics/advertising

Alfred University, Graduate School, College of Ceramics, School of Art and Design, Alfred, NY 14802. Offers ceramic art (MFA); electronic integrated arts (MFA); painting (MFA); sculpture/dimensional studies (MFA). *Accreditation:* NASAD. *Degree requirements:* For master's, thesis, exhibit. *Entrance requirements:* For master's, portfolio. Additional exam requirements/recommendations for international students: Required—TOEFL (minimum score 550 paper-based; 80 iBT), IELTS (minimum score 6). Electronic applications accepted. *Expenses:* Contact institution. *Faculty research:* Ceramic art, sculpture, glass art, new media, time-based media.

Arizona State University at the Tempe campus, Herberger Institute for Design and the Arts, The Design School, Tempe, AZ 85287-1605. Offers architecture (M Arch); building design/built environment (MS); design (MSD), including arts, media, and engineering, healthcare and healing environments (MSD, PhD), industrial design, interaction design, interior design, new product innovation, visual communication design; design, environment and the arts (PhD), including design, digital culture, healthcare and healing environments (MSD, PhD), history, theory, and criticism; landscape architecture (MLA); urban design (MUD); MA/MBA. *Accreditation:* NASAD. Terminal master's awarded for partial completion of doctoral program. *Degree requirements:* For master's, thesis optional, interactive Program of Study (iPOS) submitted before completing 50 percent of required credit hours; for doctorate, comprehensive exam, thesis/dissertation, interactive Program of Study (iPOS) submitted before completing 50 percent of required credit hours. *Entrance requirements:* For master's, GRE General Test, minimum GPA of 3.0 or equivalent in last 2 years of work leading to bachelor's degree, design/creative works portfolio, 3 references, statement of intent; for doctorate, GRE, master's degree in architecture, graphic design, industrial design, interior design, landscape architecture, or art history or equivalent standing; statement of purpose; 3 letters of recommendation; indication of potential faculty mentor; sample of written work. Additional exam requirements/recommendations for international students: Required—TOEFL (minimum score 600 paper-based; 100 iBT). Electronic applications accepted.

The Art Institute of Dallas, a branch of Miami International University of Art & Design, Program in Design and Media Management, Dallas, TX 75231-5993. Offers MA.

Bowling Green State University, Graduate College, College of Arts and Sciences, School of Art, Bowling Green, OH 43403. Offers 2-D studio art (MA, MFA); 3-D studio art (MA, MFA); art education (MA); art history (MA); computer art (MA); design (MFA); digital arts (MFA); graphics (MFA). *Accreditation:* NASAD. *Program availability:* Part-time. *Degree requirements:* For master's, thesis or alternative, final exhibit (MFA). *Entrance requirements:* For master's, GRE General Test (for MA), slide portfolio (15-20 slides). Additional exam requirements/recommendations for international students: Required—TOEFL. Electronic applications accepted. *Faculty research:* Computer animation and virtual reality, Spanish still-life painting from 1600 to 1800, art and psychotherapy, Japanese wood-firing techniques in ceramics, non-toxic printmaking technologies.

California College of the Arts, Graduate Programs, Design Program, San Francisco, CA 94107. Offers graphic design (MFA); industrial design (MFA); interaction design (MFA). *Accreditation:* NASAD. *Faculty:* 14 full-time (4 women), 40 part-time/adjunct (14 women). *Students:* 109 full-time (64 women); includes 18 minority (1 Black or African American, non-Hispanic/Latino; 12 Asian, non-Hispanic/Latino; 5 Hispanic/Latino), 64 international. Average age 26. 618 applicants, 35% accepted, 76 enrolled. In 2017, 54 master's awarded. *Degree requirements:* For master's, thesis, exhibit. *Entrance requirements:* For master's, appropriate bachelor's degree, portfolio, resume, letters of recommendation, transcripts. Additional exam requirements/recommendations for international students: Required—TOEFL, IELTS, or PTE. *Application deadline:* For fall admission, 1/31 priority date for domestic and international students. Applications are processed on a rolling basis. Application fee: $70. Electronic applications accepted. *Expenses:* Contact institution. *Financial support:* In 2017–18, fellowships (averaging $22,000 per year), teaching assistantships (averaging $2,000 per year) were awarded; career-related internships or fieldwork, Federal Work-Study, scholarships/grants, health care benefits, and unspecified assistantships also available. Financial award application deadline: 7/31; financial award applicants required to submit FAFSA. *Unit head:* Kristian Simsarian, Graduate Chair, 415-551-9283, Fax: 415-703-9539, E-mail: ksimsarian@cca.edu. *Application contact:* Wes Fanelli, Assistant Director of Graduate Admissions, 415-703-9533, Fax: 415-703-9539, E-mail: wfanelli@cca.edu.

California College of the Arts, Graduate Programs, MBA in Design Strategy Program, San Francisco, CA 94107. Offers MBA. *Accreditation:* NASAD. *Faculty:* 1 (woman) full-time, 16 part-time/adjunct (5 women). *Students:* 88 full-time (62 women); includes 24 minority (3 Black or African American, non-Hispanic/Latino; 14 Asian, non-Hispanic/Latino; 6 Hispanic/Latino; 1 Native Hawaiian or other Pacific Islander, non-Hispanic/Latino), 26 international. Average age 30. 187 applicants, 68% accepted, 49 enrolled. In 2017, 53 master's awarded. *Degree requirements:* For master's, thesis. *Entrance requirements:* Additional exam requirements/recommendations for international students: Required—TOEFL, IELTS, or PTE. *Application deadline:* For fall admission, 1/31 priority date for domestic and international students. Applications are processed on a rolling basis. Application fee: $70. Electronic applications accepted. *Expenses:* $49,230 per year full-time tuition, $490 per year fees; $1,641 per unit part-time tuition. *Financial support:* Federal Work-Study and scholarships/grants available. Financial award application deadline: 7/31; financial award applicants required to submit FAFSA. *Unit head:* Andy Dong, Program Chair, 800-447-1ART, E-mail: andy@cca.edu. *Application contact:* Wes Fanelli, Assistant Director of Graduate Admissions, 415-703-9533, Fax: 415-703-9539, E-mail: wfanelli@cca.edu.

California Institute of the Arts, School of Art, Valencia, CA 91355-2340. Offers art (MFA, Adv C); graphic design (MFA, Adv C); photography (MFA, Adv C). *Accreditation:* NASAD (one or more programs are accredited). *Degree requirements:* For master's, final project. *Entrance requirements:* For master's, portfolio. Additional exam requirements/recommendations for international students: Required—TOEFL. Electronic applications accepted.

California State University, Fresno, Division of Research and Graduate Studies, College of Arts and Humanities, Department of Art and Design, Fresno, CA 93740-8027. Offers art (MA). *Program availability:* Part-time, evening/weekend. *Degree requirements:* For master's, thesis or alternative. *Entrance requirements:* For master's, GRE General Test, minimum GPA of 3.0, portfolio. Additional exam requirements/recommendations for international students: Required—TOEFL. Electronic applications accepted. *Faculty research:* Art history, graphic design, studio art.

California State University, Fullerton, Graduate Studies, College of the Arts, Department of Visual Arts, Fullerton, CA 92831-3599. Offers art (MA, MFA), including art history (MA), ceramics (MFA), crafts, creative photography, exhibition design, glass, graphic design, illustration, sculpture. *Accreditation:* NASAD (one or more programs are accredited). *Program availability:* Part-time. *Faculty:* 17 full-time (7 women), 4 part-time/adjunct (3 women). *Students:* 35 full-time (22 women), 24 part-time (14 women); includes 26 minority (3 Black or African American, non-Hispanic/Latino; 7 Asian, non-Hispanic/Latino; 14 Hispanic/Latino; 2 Two or more races, non-Hispanic/Latino), 6 international. Average age 33. 81 applicants, 31% accepted, 21 enrolled. In 2017, 17 master's awarded. *Entrance requirements:* For master's, minimum GPA of 2.5 in last 60 units of course work, portfolio. Application fee: $55. *Financial support:* Career-related internships or fieldwork, Federal Work-Study, institutionally sponsored loans, and scholarships/grants available. Support available to part-time students. Financial award application deadline: 3/1; financial award applicants required to submit FAFSA. *Unit head:* Dana Lamb, Chair, 657-278-2076.
Website: http://www.fullerton.edu/arts/art/

California State University, Los Angeles, Graduate Studies, College of Arts and Letters, Department of Art, Los Angeles, CA 90032-8530. Offers art (MA), including art education, art history, art therapy, ceramics, metals, and textiles, design (MA, MFA), painting, sculpture, and graphic arts, photography; fine arts (MFA), including crafts, design (MA, MFA), studio arts. *Accreditation:* NASAD (one or more programs are accredited). *Program availability:* Part-time, evening/weekend. *Degree requirements:* For master's, comprehensive exam, project or thesis. *Entrance requirements:* For master's, portfolio. Additional exam requirements/recommendations for international students: Required—TOEFL (minimum score 500 paper-based). Electronic applications accepted. *Faculty research:* The artist and the book, conceptual art, ceramic processes, computer graphics, architectural graphics.

Carnegie Mellon University, College of Fine Arts, School of Design, Program in Design, Pittsburgh, PA 15213-3891. Offers MA, D Des, PhD. *Degree requirements:* For doctorate, one foreign language, comprehensive exam, thesis/dissertation. *Entrance requirements:* For doctorate, GRE, portfolio of relevant work. Additional exam requirements/recommendations for international students: Required—TOEFL (minimum score 600 paper-based). *Faculty research:* Design theory, typography and information design, new product development, organizational behavior, interaction design.

College for Creative Studies, Graduate Programs, Detroit, MI 48202-4034. Offers color and materials design (MFA); integrated design (MFA); interaction design (MFA); transportation design (MFA). *Accreditation:* NASAD.

Concordia University, School of Graduate Studies, Faculty of Fine Arts, Department of Design and Computation Arts, Montréal, QC H3G 1M8, Canada. Offers design (M Des); digital technologies in design art practice (Certificate).

Drexel University, Westphal College of Media Arts and Design, Philadelphia, PA 19104-2875. Offers arts administration (MS); design research (MS); digital media (MS, PhD); fashion design (MS); interior architecture and design (MS); museum leadership (MS); retail and merchandising (MS); television management (MS); urban strategy (MS); MS/MBA. *Accreditation:* NASAD. *Program availability:* Part-time, evening/weekend. *Entrance requirements:* For master's, interview. Additional exam requirements/recommendations for international students: Required—TOEFL. Electronic applications accepted. *Expenses:* Contact institution.

Emily Carr University of Art + Design, Program in Applied Arts, Vancouver, BC V6H 3R9, Canada. Offers design (M Des); media arts (MAA); visual arts (MAA). *Degree requirements:* For master's, internship, thesis project. *Entrance requirements:* For master's, minimum overall GPA of 3.0, visual portfolio, 3 letters of recommendation, resume/curriculum vitae. Additional exam requirements/recommendations for international students: Required—TOEFL (minimum score 570 paper-based; 84 iBT), IELTS (minimum score 6.5), Michigan English Language Assessment Battery (minimum score 81). Electronic applications accepted.

Fashion Institute of Technology, School of Graduate Studies, New York, NY 10001-5992. Offers MA, MFA, MPS. *Accreditation:* NASAD. *Program availability:* Part-time, evening/weekend. *Degree requirements:* For master's, thesis. *Entrance requirements:* For master's, portfolio, letters of recommendation, resume, interview. Additional exam requirements/recommendations for international students: Required—TOEFL (minimum score 550 paper-based; 80 iBT). Electronic applications accepted. *Faculty research:* Fashion history, material conservation, international marketing and global sourcing, sustainable economic development, luxury braiding in China.

Ferris State University, Kendall College of Art and Design, Grand Rapids, MI 49503. Offers architecture (M Arch); art education (MAE); design (MA); drawing (MFA); painting (MFA); photography (MFA); printmaking (MFA); visual and critical studies (MA). *Program availability:* Part-time. *Faculty:* 21 full-time (15 women), 6 part-time/adjunct (2 women). *Students:* 39 full-time (29 women), 15 part-time (9 women); includes 12 minority (4 Black or African American, non-Hispanic/Latino; 1 American Indian or Alaska Native, non-Hispanic/Latino; 3 Asian, non-Hispanic/Latino; 4 Hispanic/Latino), 6 international. Average age 31. 48 applicants, 60% accepted, 17 enrolled. In 2017, 12 master's awarded. *Degree requirements:* For master's, thesis, seminars. *Entrance requirements:* For master's, portfolio, 3 letters of recommendation, curriculum vitae, artist statement, letter of intent. Additional exam requirements/recommendations for international students: Required—TOEFL (minimum score 79 iBT). *Application deadline:* For fall admission, 2/1 priority date for domestic and international students; for spring admission, 11/1 priority date for domestic and international students. Applications are processed on a rolling basis. Application fee: $0. Electronic applications accepted. *Expenses:* Contact institution. *Financial support:* In 2017–18, 32 students received support, including 8 fellowships (averaging $16,781 per year); scholarships/grants and unspecified assistantships also available. Financial award application deadline: 2/1;

financial award applicants required to submit FAFSA. *Unit head:* Leslie Bellavance, President, 616-451-2787. *Application contact:* Thomas Post, Graduate Recruitment Specialist, 616-451-2787, Fax: 616-831-9689, E-mail: thomaspost@ferris.edu. Website: http://www.kcad.edu/

Florida Atlantic University, Dorothy F. Schmidt College of Arts and Letters, Department of Visual Arts and Art History, Boca Raton, FL 33431-0991. Offers visual art (MFA), including ceramics, graphic design, visual art. *Faculty:* 14 full-time (10 women). *Students:* 13 full-time (10 women), 3 part-time (2 women); includes 5 minority (2 Black or African American, non-Hispanic/Latino; 1 Asian, non-Hispanic/Latino; 2 Hispanic/Latino). Average age 37. 31 applicants, 23% accepted, 5 enrolled. In 2017, 4 master's awarded. *Degree requirements:* For master's, one foreign language, project. *Entrance requirements:* For master's, GRE General Test, minimum GPA of 3.0 during last 60 hours of course work, slide portfolio. *Application deadline:* For fall admission, 2/21 for domestic and international students; for spring admission, 10/1 for domestic and international students. Application fee: $30. Electronic applications accepted. *Expenses:* Tuition, state resident: full-time $7400; part-time $369.82 per credit. Tuition, nonresident: full-time $20,496; part-time $1042.81 per credit. *Financial support:* Research assistantships with full tuition reimbursements, teaching assistantships with full tuition reimbursements, career-related internships or fieldwork, Federal Work-Study, and institutionally sponsored loans available. Financial award applicants required to submit FAFSA. *Faculty research:* Painting, ceramics (traditional and non-traditional), installation, video and interactive sculpture. *Unit head:* Dr. Eric Landes, Chair, 954-236-1106, E-mail: elandes1@fau.edu. Website: http://www.fau.edu/VAAH/

Howard University, Graduate School, Division of Fine Arts, Department of Art, Program in Fine Arts, Washington, DC 20059-0002. Offers 3D reality (sculpture and ceramics) (MFA); design (MFA); electronic studio (MFA); painting (MFA); photography (MFA). *Accreditation:* NASAD. *Degree requirements:* For master's, comprehensive exam, thesis, exhibit. *Entrance requirements:* For master's, minimum GPA of 3.0, portfolio.

Illinois Institute of Technology, Graduate College, Institute of Design, Chicago, IL 60654. Offers M Des, MDM, PhD, M Des/MBA. *Program availability:* Part-time. Terminal master's awarded for partial completion of doctoral program. *Degree requirements:* For master's, comprehensive exam (for some programs), thesis (for some programs); for doctorate, one foreign language, comprehensive exam, thesis/dissertation. *Entrance requirements:* For master's, GRE (minimum score 310); GMAT (minimum score 600), bachelor's degree, minimum GPA of 3.0, official transcripts, portfolio (for applicants with design degrees), minimum of two years of professional experience; for doctorate, GRE General Test (minimum score 1000 Quantitative and Verbal, 3.5 Analytical Writing), master's degree in design from accredited institution, official transcripts, portfolio. Additional exam requirements/recommendations for international students: Required—TOEFL (minimum score 100 iBT); Recommended—IELTS (minimum score 7). Electronic applications accepted. *Expenses:* Contact institution. *Faculty research:* Data visualization, urbanism, big data, digital tools, future of work.

Indiana University Bloomington, University Graduate School, College of Arts and Sciences, School of Art and Design, Bloomington, IN 47405-7000. Offers apparel merchandising (MS); studio art (MFA). *Accreditation:* NASAD (one or more programs are accredited). *Entrance requirements:* For master's, portfolio (MFA). Additional exam requirements/recommendations for international students: Required—TOEFL. Electronic applications accepted.

Iowa State University of Science and Technology, Department of Apparel, Events, and Hospitality Management, Ames, IA 50011-1078. Offers apparel, merchandising, and design (MS, PhD); hospitality management (MS, PhD). *Program availability:* Online learning. *Degree requirements:* For doctorate, thesis/dissertation. *Entrance requirements:* For master's and doctorate, GRE General Test. Additional exam requirements/recommendations for international students: Required—TOEFL (minimum score 550 paper-based; 79 iBT), IELTS (minimum score 6.5). Electronic applications accepted.

Louisiana State University and Agricultural & Mechanical College, Graduate School, College of Art and Design, Baton Rouge, LA 70803. Offers M Arch, MA, MFA, MLA. *Accreditation:* ASLA (one or more programs are accredited); NASAD (one or more programs are accredited). *Faculty:* 51 full-time (18 women). *Students:* 100 full-time (60 women), 11 part-time (7 women); includes 19 minority (6 Black or African American, non-Hispanic/Latino; 7 Asian, non-Hispanic/Latino; 6 Hispanic/Latino), 36 international. Average age 29. 163 applicants, 34% accepted, 29 enrolled. In 2017, 36 master's awarded. *Financial support:* In 2017–18, 10 research assistantships (averaging $10,907 per year), 68 teaching assistantships (averaging $10,996 per year) were awarded. *Total annual research expenditures:* $28,201.

Maryland Institute College of Art, Graduate Studies, Design Leadership MBA/MA Program, Baltimore, MD 21201. Offers MBA/MA. Program offered in collaboration with The Johns Hopkins University. *Entrance requirements:* Additional exam requirements/recommendations for international students: Required—TOEFL (minimum score 100 iBT) or IELTS (minimum score 7). Electronic applications accepted. *Expenses:* Contact institution.

Maryland Institute College of Art, Graduate Studies, MPS Program in Business of Art and Design, Baltimore, MD 21201. Offers MPS. *Program availability:* Part-time. *Degree requirements:* For master's, business plan presentation. *Entrance requirements:* For master's, essay, resume. Additional exam requirements/recommendations for international students: Required—TOEFL (minimum score 550 paper-based; 80 iBT), IELTS (minimum score 6.5). Electronic applications accepted. *Expenses:* Contact institution.

Maryland Institute College of Art, Graduate Studies, MPS Program in Information Visualization, Baltimore, MD 21201. Offers MPS. *Program availability:* Part-time, online learning. *Entrance requirements:* For master's, curriculum vitae/resume, visualization portfolio, bachelor's degree in any field. Additional exam requirements/recommendations for international students: Required—TOEFL (minimum score 550 paper-based; 80 iBT). Electronic applications accepted. *Expenses:* Contact institution.

Maryland Institute College of Art, Graduate Studies, Program in Social Design, Baltimore, MD 21201. Offers MA. *Degree requirements:* For master's, thesis, thesis project, exhibition, project presentation. *Entrance requirements:* For master's, portfolio, bachelor's degree in any field. Additional exam requirements/recommendations for international students: Required—TOEFL (minimum score 550 paper-based; 80 iBT), IELTS (minimum score 6.5). Electronic applications accepted. *Expenses:* Contact institution.

Massachusetts College of Art and Design, Graduate Programs, MFA Program, Boston, MA 02115-5882. Offers 2D fine arts (MFA), including painting, printmaking; 3D fine arts (MFA), including ceramics, fibers, glass, jewelry and metalsmithing, sculpture; design (MFA, Postbaccalaureate Certificate), including dynamic media; fine arts (MFA), including interdisciplinary; media arts (MFA, Postbaccalaureate Certificate), including film/video (MFA), photography. *Accreditation:* NASAD. *Faculty:* 28 full-time (8 women), 28 part-time/adjunct (17 women). *Students:* 44 full-time (26 women), 28 part-time (17 women); includes 8 minority (5 Asian, non-Hispanic/Latino; 3 Hispanic/Latino), 18 international. 247 applicants, 52% accepted, 47 enrolled. In 2017, 42 master's, 5 other advanced degrees awarded. *Degree requirements:* For master's, thesis, thesis exhibition (for fine arts programs); thesis project and document (for design/dynamic media program). *Entrance requirements:* For master's, portfolio, college transcripts, resume, statement of purpose, letters of reference, interview, 6 credits of art history taken prior to or during MFA program; for Postbaccalaureate Certificate, portfolio, college transcripts, resume, statement of purpose, letters of reference, interview. Additional exam requirements/recommendations for international students: Required—TOEFL (minimum score 550 paper-based, 85 iBT) or IELTS (6). *Application deadline:* For fall admission, 1/4 priority date for domestic and international students; for summer admission, 1/4 priority date for domestic and international students. Applications are processed on a rolling basis. Application fee: $90. Electronic applications accepted. *Expenses:* $780 per credit. *Financial support:* In 2017–18, 51 students received support, including 1 research assistantship (averaging $2,160 per year), 33 teaching assistantships (averaging $2,160 per year); fellowships, career-related internships or fieldwork, scholarships/grants, tuition waivers (partial), unspecified assistantships, and adjunct co-teaching positions also available. Support available to part-time students. Financial award application deadline: 1/4; financial award applicants required to submit FAFSA. *Faculty research:* Painting and printmaking, sculpture, photography, film and video, dynamic media design. *Unit head:* Paul Paturzo, Dean of Graduate Studies, 617-879-7166, E-mail: pjpaturzo@massart.edu. *Application contact:* Lauren O'Neill, Assistant Director of Graduate Admissions, 617-879-7222, E-mail: gradadmissions@massart.edu. Website: http://www.massart.edu/Admissions/Graduate_Programs.html

Massachusetts College of Art and Design, Graduate Programs, Program in Design Innovation, Boston, MA 02115-5882. Offers M Des. *Faculty:* 5 full-time (1 woman), 9 part-time/adjunct (2 women). *Students:* 14 full-time (8 women); includes 4 minority (all Asian, non-Hispanic/Latino), 3 international. 42 applicants, 48% accepted, 9 enrolled. *Degree requirements:* For master's, thesis, thesis project. *Entrance requirements:* For master's, portfolio, college transcripts, resume, statement of purpose, letters of reference, interview. Additional exam requirements/recommendations for international students: Required—TOEFL (minimum score 550 paper-based; 85 iBT); Recommended—IELTS (minimum score 6.5). *Application deadline:* For fall admission, 1/4 priority date for domestic and international students. Application fee: $90. Electronic applications accepted. *Expenses:* $780 per credit. *Financial support:* In 2017–18, 11 students received support, including 8 teaching assistantships (averaging $2,160 per year); research assistantships, career-related internships or fieldwork, Federal Work-Study, scholarships/grants, tuition waivers (partial), and unspecified assistantships also available. Support available to part-time students. Financial award application deadline: 1/4; financial award applicants required to submit FAFSA. *Unit head:* Paul Paturzo, Dean of Graduate Studies, 617-879-7166, E-mail: pjpaturzo@massart.edu. *Application contact:* Lauren O'Neill, Assistant Director of Graduate Admissions, 617-879-7222, E-mail: gradadmissions@massart.edu. Website: http://www.massart.edu/Admissions/Graduate_Programs.html

Miami International University of Art & Design, Program in Design and Media Management, Miami, FL 33132-1418. Offers MA.

Millersville University of Pennsylvania, College of Graduate Studies and Adult Learning, College of Arts, Humanities and Social Sciences, Department of Art and Design, Millersville, PA 17551-0302. Offers art education (M Ed). *Accreditation:* NASAD; NCATE. *Program availability:* Part-time. *Faculty:* 3 full-time (all women), 3 part-time/adjunct (2 women). *Students:* 3 full-time (2 women), 11 part-time (9 women); includes 3 minority (2 Asian, non-Hispanic/Latino; 1 Hispanic/Latino). Average age 34. 5 applicants, 100% accepted, 1 enrolled. In 2017, 8 master's awarded. *Degree requirements:* For master's, comprehensive exam, thesis optional. *Entrance requirements:* For master's, teaching certificate (unless enrolled in post baccalaureate certificate at same time); portfolio (if not MU graduate); minimum undergraduate and post baccalaureate GPA of 3.0 cumulative, 3.25 in art and art education courses; three letters of recommendation; professional goals as stated by the applicant. Additional exam requirements/recommendations for international students: Required—TOEFL (minimum score 80 iBT), IELTS (minimum score 6.5), PTE (minimum score 60). *Application deadline:* Applications are processed on a rolling basis. Application fee: $40. Electronic applications accepted. *Expenses:* $500 per credit resident tuition and fees; $750 per credit non-resident tuition and fees; $114.75 per credit general fee (maximum of 12 credits); technology fee $27 per credit (resident), $39 per credit (non-resident). *Financial support:* Unspecified assistantships available. Financial award application deadline: 3/15; financial award applicants required to submit FAFSA. *Faculty research:* Ceramics; representational painting; material investigations involving bronze casting, steel forming and fabrication, mold-making, wood working; art educator's professional learning, assessment in the arts, and postmodern; interactive design fundamentals, interdisciplinary design, interaction, visual storytelling and digital narrative forms and choice-based approaches to teaching art. *Unit head:* Deborah S. Sigel, Chairperson, 717-871-7248, Fax: 717-871-2004, E-mail: deborah.sigel@millersville.edu. *Application contact:* Dr. Victor S. DeSantis, Dean of College of Graduate Studies and Adult Learning/Associate Provost for Civic and Community Engagement, 717-871-7619, Fax: 717-871-7954, E-mail: victor.desantis@millersville.edu. Website: http://www.millersville.edu/art/

Minneapolis College of Art and Design, Program in Visual Studies, Minneapolis, MN 55404-4347. Offers animation (MFA); comic art (MFA); drawing (MFA); filmmaking (MFA); fine arts (MFA); furniture design (MFA); graphic design (MFA); illustration (MFA); interactive media (MFA); painting (MFA); photography (MFA); printmaking (MFA); sculpture (MFA). *Accreditation:* NASAD. *Program availability:* Part-time. *Faculty:* 42 full-time (13 women). *Students:* 30 full-time (23 women); includes 3 minority (2 Asian, non-Hispanic/Latino; 1 Hispanic/Latino), 13 international. 166 applicants, 28% accepted, 12 enrolled. In 2017, 10 master's awarded. *Degree requirements:* For master's, thesis, thesis exhibit. *Entrance requirements:* For master's, portfolio of visual artwork, resume, 3 letters of recommendation. Additional exam requirements/recommendations for international students: Required—TOEFL (minimum score 550 paper-based; 79 iBT). *Application deadline:* For fall admission, 1/15 for domestic and international students. Application fee: $50. Electronic applications accepted. *Expenses:* Tuition: Full-time $38,670. *Required fees:* $450. One-time fee: $300 full-time. *Financial support:* In 2017–18, 23 students received support, including 15 teaching assistantships (averaging $6,000 per year); career-related internships or fieldwork, Federal Work-Study, scholarships/grants, and unspecified assistantships also available. Support available to part-time students. Financial award application deadline: 3/15; financial award applicants required to submit FAFSA. *Faculty research:* Visual arts: animation, comic art, drawing, filmmaking, furniture design, graphic design, illustration, interactive media, painting, photography, printmaking, sculpture. *Unit head:* Graduate Director, 612-209-1471, E-mail: admissions@mcad.edu. *Application contact:* Mary Kazura, Associate Director of Admissions, 612-874-3760, Fax: 612-874-3701, E-mail: mary_kazura@mcad.edu. Website: http://mcad.edu/mfa

Applied Arts and Design—General

New England Institute of Technology, Program in Applied Design, East Greenwich, RI 02818. Offers MAD. *Program availability:* Part-time-only, evening/weekend, 100% online, blended/hybrid learning, low-residency. *Entrance requirements:* For master's, minimum GPA of 2.5; bachelor's degree in any field from accredited institution. Additional exam requirements/recommendations for international students: Required—TOEFL. *Application deadline:* Applications are processed on a rolling basis. Application fee: $25. Electronic applications accepted. *Expenses:* $550 per credit. *Unit head:* Douglas H. Sherman, Senior Vice President and Provost, 401-739-5000 Ext. 3481, Fax: 401-886-0859, E-mail: dsherman@neit.edu. *Application contact:* Michael Caruso, Director of Admissions, 800-736-7744 Ext. 3411, Fax: 401-886-0868, E-mail: mcaruso@neit.edu.
Website: https://www.neit.edu/Programs/Online-and-Hybrid-Degree-Programs/Master-of-Applied-Design

The New School, Parsons Paris, Paris, NY 10011, France. Offers MA. *Program availability:* Part-time. *Faculty:* 5 full-time (2 women), 46 part-time/adjunct (31 women). *Students:* 35 full-time (32 women), 3 part-time (2 women); includes 9 minority (2 Black or African American, non-Hispanic/Latino; 3 Asian, non-Hispanic/Latino; 3 Hispanic/Latino; 1 Two or more races, non-Hispanic/Latino), 20 international. Average age 26. 42 applicants, 93% accepted, 24 enrolled. In 2017, 15 master's awarded. *Degree requirements:* For master's, one foreign language, thesis (for some programs). *Entrance requirements:* For master's, transcripts, resume, statement of purpose, recommendation letters, interviews. Additional exam requirements/recommendations for international students: Required—TOEFL (minimum score 100 iBT), IELTS (minimum score 7), PTE (minimum score 68). *Application deadline:* For fall admission, 1/1 priority date for domestic and international students. Applications are processed on a rolling basis. Application fee: $50. Electronic applications accepted. *Expenses:* $19,203 per term full-time, $1,339 per credit part-time; $100 fee per term for maintenance of status. *Financial support:* In 2017–18, 29 students received support. Career-related internships or fieldwork and scholarships/grants available. Financial award application deadline: 2/1; financial award applicants required to submit FAFSA. *Unit head:* Florence Leclerc-Dickler, Dean, 33-176217661, E-mail: leclercf@newschool.edu. *Application contact:* Mike Fakih, Director of Admissions, Parsons Paris, 33 176 21 76 67, E-mail: thinkparsonsparis@newschool.edu.
Website: https://www.newschool.edu/parsons-paris/

The New School, Parsons School of Design, Program in Design Studies, New York, NY 10011. Offers MA. *Program availability:* Part-time. *Faculty:* 2 full-time (both women), 3 part-time/adjunct (1 woman). *Students:* 12 full-time (10 women), 3 part-time (2 women); includes 3 minority (1 Asian, non-Hispanic/Latino; 2 Hispanic/Latino), 8 international. Average age 31. 30 applicants, 80% accepted, 4 enrolled. In 2017, 6 master's awarded. *Degree requirements:* For master's, thesis/capstone paper, project/oral examination. *Entrance requirements:* For master's, transcripts, resume, statement of purpose, recommendation letters, interview. Additional exam requirements/recommendations for international students: Required—TOEFL (minimum score 92 iBT), IELTS (minimum score 7), PTE (minimum score 63). *Application deadline:* Applications are processed on a rolling basis. Application fee: $50. Electronic applications accepted. *Expenses:* $24,922 per semester full-time, $1,744 per credit part-time, $100 maintenance of status fee. *Financial support:* In 2017–18, 12 students received support, including 7 teaching assistantships (averaging $10,122 per year); career-related internships or fieldwork, scholarships/grants, and unspecified assistantships also available. Support available to part-time students. Financial award application deadline: 2/1; financial award applicants required to submit FAFSA. *Total annual research expenditures:* $106,000. *Unit head:* Susan Yelavich, Director, 212-229-8916 Ext. 3767, E-mail: yelavics@newschool.edu. *Application contact:* Courtney Malenius, Director of Graduate Admission, 212-229-5150 Ext. 4011, E-mail: thinkparsonsgrad@newschool.edu.
Website: https://www.newschool.edu/parsons/ma-design-studies-research/

The New School, Parsons School of Design, Program in Transdisciplinary Design, New York, NY 10011. Offers MFA. *Program availability:* Part-time. *Faculty:* 8 full-time (3 women), 2 part-time/adjunct (both women). *Students:* 33 full-time (24 women), 1 (woman) part-time; includes 7 minority (1 American Indian or Alaska Native, non-Hispanic/Latino; 4 Asian, non-Hispanic/Latino; 2 Hispanic/Latino), 21 international. Average age 28. 79 applicants, 72% accepted, 19 enrolled. In 2017, 19 master's awarded. *Degree requirements:* For master's, thesis. *Entrance requirements:* For master's, transcripts, resume, statement of purpose, recommendation letters, portfolio, interview. Additional exam requirements/recommendations for international students: Required—TOEFL (minimum score 91 iBT), IELTS (minimum score 7), PTE (minimum score 63). *Application deadline:* For fall admission, 1/1 priority date for domestic and international students. Applications are processed on a rolling basis. Application fee: $50. Electronic applications accepted. *Expenses:* $24,922 per semester full-time, $1,744 per credit part-time, $198 fee per term. *Financial support:* In 2017–18, 28 students received support, including 6 fellowships (averaging $6,202 per year); career-related internships or fieldwork, scholarships/grants, and unspecified assistantships also available. Support available to part-time students. Financial award application deadline: 2/1; financial award applicants required to submit FAFSA. *Unit head:* Lara Penin, Program Director, 212-229-8908 Ext. 4329, E-mail: peninl@newschool.edu. *Application contact:* Courtney Malenius, Director of Graduate Admissions, 212-229-5150 Ext. 4011, E-mail: maleniuc@newschool.edu.
Website: https://www.newschool.edu/parsons/mfa-transdisciplinary-design/

New York Institute of Technology, College of Arts and Sciences, Department of Digital Art and Design, Old Westbury, NY 11568-8000. Offers computer graphics (MFA), including animation, fine arts and technology, graphic design. *Program availability:* Part-time, evening/weekend. *Faculty:* 7 full-time (4 women), 6 part-time/adjunct (2 women). *Students:* 35 full-time (24 women), 12 part-time (7 women); includes 7 minority (4 Black or African American, non-Hispanic/Latino; 1 Asian, non-Hispanic/Latino; 2 Hispanic/Latino), 35 international. Average age 26. 37 applicants, 73% accepted, 9 enrolled. In 2017, 27 master's awarded. *Degree requirements:* For master's, thesis. *Entrance requirements:* For master's, BFA or equivalent; minimum undergraduate GPA of 3.0; digital portfolio. Additional exam requirements/recommendations for international students: Required—TOEFL (minimum score 79 iBT), IELTS (minimum score 6). *Application deadline:* For fall admission, 6/1 for domestic and international students. Applications are processed on a rolling basis. Application fee: $50. Electronic applications accepted. *Expenses:* $1,285 per credit plus fees. *Financial support:* Career-related internships or fieldwork, Federal Work-Study, scholarships/grants, tuition waivers (full and partial), and unspecified assistantships available. Support available to part-time students. Financial award application deadline: 2/15; financial award applicants required to submit FAFSA. *Faculty research:* Graphic design, animation, art and technology, virtual reality, sculpture. *Unit head:* Terry Nauheim, Department Chair, 516-686-7881, Fax: 212-261-1742, E-mail: tnauheim@nyit.edu. *Application contact:* Alice Dolitsky, Director, Graduate Admissions, 516-686-7520, Fax: 516-686-1116, E-mail: nyitgrad@nyit.edu.
Website: http://www.nyit.edu/departments/digital_art_and_design

New York University, Tisch School of the Arts, Department of Design for Stage and Film, New York, NY 10012-1019. Offers MFA. *Faculty:* 10 full-time, 11 part-time/adjunct. *Students:* 50 full-time (32 women); includes 5 minority (2 Black or African American, non-Hispanic/Latino; 1 Asian, non-Hispanic/Latino; 1 Hispanic/Latino; 1 Two or more races, non-Hispanic/Latino), 17 international. 94 applicants, 23% accepted, 18 enrolled. In 2017, 18 master's awarded. *Degree requirements:* For master's, thesis. *Entrance requirements:* For master's, interview, portfolio. Additional exam requirements/recommendations for international students: Required—TOEFL (minimum score 620 paper-based; 105 iBT), IELTS. *Application deadline:* For fall admission, 1/1 priority date for domestic and international students. Application fee: $60. Electronic applications accepted. *Expenses: Tuition:* Full-time $41,352; part-time $19,968 per year. *Required fees:* $2496; $1628 per unit. $814 per term. Tuition and fees vary according to course load and program. *Financial support:* In 2017–18, 28 students received support, including 12 fellowships with full and partial tuition reimbursements available; Federal Work-Study, institutionally sponsored loans, tuition waivers (partial), and unspecified assistantships also available. Financial award application deadline: 2/15; financial award applicants required to submit FAFSA. *Unit head:* Susan Hilferty, Chair, 212-998-1950, Fax: 212-998-1953, E-mail: tisch.design@nyu.edu. *Application contact:* Dan Sandford, Director of Graduate Admissions, 212-998-1918, Fax: 212-995-4060, E-mail: tisch.gradadmissions@nyu.edu.
Website: http://www.design.tisch.nyu.edu/

North Carolina State University, Graduate School, College of Design, Program in Art and Design, Raleigh, NC 27695. Offers MAD. *Degree requirements:* For master's, thesis optional. Electronic applications accepted.

North Carolina State University, Graduate School, College of Design, Program in Design, Raleigh, NC 27695. Offers PhD. *Degree requirements:* For doctorate, thesis/dissertation. *Entrance requirements:* For doctorate, GRE. Electronic applications accepted. *Faculty research:* Design and cognition, children's environments, community design, ecological design, sustainable communities and urban spatial development.

Northeastern University, College of Arts, Media and Design, Boston, MA 02115-5096. Offers architecture (M Arch); game science and design (MS); information design and visualization (MFA); interdisciplinary arts (MFA); journalism (MA); music industry leadership (MS); studio art (MFA); sustainable building systems (MS); sustainable urban environments (M Des). *Faculty:* 145. *Students:* 259. In 2017, 83 master's awarded. Application fee: $75. Electronic applications accepted. *Expenses:* Contact institution. *Financial support:* Applicants required to submit FAFSA. *Unit head:* Dr. Elizabeth Hudson, Dean, 617-373-5088, E-mail: n.elysse@northeastern.edu. *Application contact:* Jane Amidon, Associate Dean for Graduate Programs and Research, 617-373-4614, E-mail: gscamd@northeastern.edu.
Website: http://www.northeastern.edu/camd/

NSCAD University, Program in Fine Arts, Halifax, NS B3J 3J6, Canada. Offers craft (MFA); design (M Des); fine and media arts (MFA). *Degree requirements:* For master's, thesis, exhibit. *Entrance requirements:* For master's, portfolio, at least 5 art history classes. Additional exam requirements/recommendations for international students: Required—Michigan English Language Assessment Battery (minimum score: 80), CanTEST (minimum score: 4.5), CAEL (minimum score: 70); Recommended—TOEFL (minimum score 575 paper-based; 90 iBT), IELTS (minimum score 6.5).

Oklahoma State University, College of Human Sciences, Department of Design, Housing and Merchandising, Stillwater, OK 74078. Offers MS, PhD. *Faculty:* 16 full-time (12 women). *Students:* 10 part-time (7 women); includes 3 minority (1 Black or African American, non-Hispanic/Latino; 1 Hispanic/Latino; 1 Two or more races, non-Hispanic/Latino), 5 international. Average age 28. 11 applicants, 27% accepted, 3 enrolled. In 2017, 1 master's, 1 doctorate awarded. *Entrance requirements:* For master's and doctorate, GRE or GMAT. Additional exam requirements/recommendations for international students: Required—TOEFL (minimum score 550 paper-based; 79 iBT). *Application deadline:* For fall admission, 3/1 priority date for international students; for spring admission, 8/1 priority date for international students. Applications are processed on a rolling basis. Application fee: $40 ($75 for international students). Electronic applications accepted. *Expenses:* Tuition, state resident: full-time $4019; part-time $2679.60 per year. Tuition, nonresident: full-time $15,286; part-time $10,190.40 per year. *Required fees:* $2129; $1419 per unit. Tuition and fees vary according to program. *Financial support:* Research assistantships, teaching assistantships, career-related internships or fieldwork, Federal Work-Study, scholarships/grants, health care benefits, tuition waivers (partial), and unspecified assistantships available. Support available to part-time students. Financial award application deadline: 3/1; financial award applicants required to submit FAFSA. *Faculty research:* Environmental sciences design, housing and merchandising; creativity and physical environment; product development, production and evaluation; experimental learning and critical thinking; technology strategies and assessment; customer expectation and satisfaction. *Unit head:* Dr. Jane Swinney, Interim Department Head, 405-744-6552, Fax: 405-744-6910, E-mail: jane.swinney@okstate.edu. *Application contact:* Dr. Christine Johnson, Associate Dean for Research and Graduate Studies, 405-744-1744, E-mail: christine.johnson@okstate.edu.
Website: https://humansciences.okstate.edu/dhm/

Pacific Northwest College of Art, Program in Applied Craft and Design, Portland, OR 97209. Offers MFA. Program offered in collaboration with Oregon College of Art & Craft. *Accreditation:* NASAD. *Entrance requirements:* For master's, resume, 2 letters of recommendation, portfolio.

Pacific Northwest College of Art, Program in Collaborative Design, Portland, OR 97209. Offers MFA.

Pratt Institute, School of Art, Brooklyn, NY 11205-3899. Offers MA, MFA, MPS, MS, Adv C, MS/MFA. *Accreditation:* NASAD (one or more programs are accredited). *Program availability:* Part-time. *Students:* 251 full-time (187 women), 95 part-time (92 women); includes 89 minority (33 Black or African American, non-Hispanic/Latino; 1 American Indian or Alaska Native, non-Hispanic/Latino; 14 Asian, non-Hispanic/Latino; 32 Hispanic/Latino; 9 Two or more races, non-Hispanic/Latino), 135 international. Average age 28. 906 applicants, 50% accepted, 147 enrolled. In 2017, 211 master's awarded. *Degree requirements:* For master's, thesis. *Entrance requirements:* For master's, portfolio. Additional exam requirements/recommendations for international students: Required—TOEFL (minimum score 550 paper-based; 79 iBT). *Application deadline:* For fall admission, 1/5 for domestic and international students; for spring admission, 10/1 for domestic and international students. Application fee: $50 ($90 for international students). Electronic applications accepted. *Expenses: Tuition:* Full-time $30,834. *Required fees:* $1974. *Financial support:* Career-related internships or fieldwork, Federal Work-Study, institutionally sponsored loans, scholarships/grants, health care benefits, and unspecified assistantships available. Support available to part-time students. Financial award application deadline: 2/1; financial award applicants required to submit FAFSA. *Faculty research:* Painting, drawing, photography, sculpture, integrated practices and printmaking; art therapy; four-dimensional design; digital arts; art and design education. *Unit head:* Gerry Snyder, Dean, 718-636-3619, E-mail: gsnyder@pratt.edu. *Application contact:* Natalie Capannelli, Director of Graduate Admissions, 718-636-3551, Fax: 718-399-4242, E-mail: ncapanne@pratt.edu.
Website: https://www.pratt.edu/academics/school-of-art/graduate-school-of-art/

See Display on page 141 and Close-Up on page 189.

Pratt Institute, School of Design, Brooklyn, NY 11205-3899. Offers MFA, MID, MS. *Program availability:* Part-time. *Students:* 376 full-time (288 women), 14 part-time (10 women); includes 50 minority (8 Black or African American, non-Hispanic/Latino; 23 Asian, non-Hispanic/Latino; 17 Hispanic/Latino; 2 Two or more races, non-Hispanic/Latino), 267 international. Average age 26. 905 applicants, 56% accepted, 183 enrolled. In 2017, 121 master's awarded. *Degree requirements:* For master's, thesis. *Entrance requirements:* For master's, letters of recommendation, portfolio. Additional exam requirements/recommendations for international students: Required—TOEFL (minimum score 575 paper-based; 90 iBT). *Application deadline:* For fall admission, 1/5 for domestic and international students; for spring admission, 10/1 for domestic and international students. Application fee: $50 ($90 for international students). Electronic applications accepted. *Expenses: Tuition:* Full-time $30,834. *Required fees:* $1974. *Financial support:* Career-related internships or fieldwork, Federal Work-Study, institutionally sponsored loans, scholarships/grants, health care benefits, and unspecified assistantships available. Support available to part-time students. Financial award application deadline: 2/1; financial award applicants required to submit FAFSA. *Unit head:* Anita Cooney, Dean, School of Design, 718-687-5744, Fax: 718-636-3410, E-mail: acooney@pratt.edu. *Application contact:* Natalie Capannelli, Director of Graduate Admissions, 718-636-3551, Fax: 718-636-3670, E-mail: ncapanne@pratt.edu. Website: https://www.pratt.edu/academics/school-of-design/graduate-school-of-design/

See Display on this page and Close-Up on page 97.

Pratt Institute, School of Liberal Arts and Sciences, History of Art and Design Program, Brooklyn, NY 11205-3899. Offers MA, MA/MFA, MA/MSLIS. *Accreditation:* NASAD. *Program availability:* Part-time. *Students:* 18 full-time (17 women), 8 part-time (7 women); includes 6 minority (1 American Indian or Alaska Native, non-Hispanic/Latino; 3 Hispanic/Latino; 2 Two or more races, non-Hispanic/Latino), 2 international. Average age 27. 38 applicants, 87% accepted, 7 enrolled. In 2017, 10 master's awarded. *Degree requirements:* For master's, one foreign language, thesis. *Entrance requirements:* For master's, GRE General Test, letters of recommendation, writing sample, portfolio. Additional exam requirements/recommendations for international students: Required—TOEFL (minimum score 600 paper-based; 100 iBT). *Application deadline:* For fall admission, 1/5 for domestic and international students; for spring admission, 10/1 for domestic and international students. Application fee: $50 ($90 for international students). Electronic applications accepted. *Expenses: Tuition:* Full-time $30,834. *Required fees:* $1974. *Financial support:* Career-related internships or fieldwork, Federal Work-Study, institutionally sponsored loans, scholarships/grants, health care benefits, and unspecified assistantships available. Support available to part-time students. Financial award application deadline: 2/1; financial award applicants required to submit FAFSA. *Faculty research:* Conservation techniques, women artists from previous centuries, art of sixteenth-century Veneto, design history, nineteenth-century Germany. *Unit head:* John Decker, Chairperson, 718-636-3598, E-mail: jdecker@pratt.edu. *Application contact:* Natalie Capannelli, Director of Graduate Admissions, 718-636-3551, Fax: 718-399-4242, E-mail: ncapanne@pratt.edu. Website: https://www.pratt.edu/academics/liberal-arts-and-sciences/history-of-art-design-grad/

See Display on page 725 and Close-Up on page 749.

Purdue University, Graduate School, College of Liberal Arts, Department of Art and Design, West Lafayette, IN 47907. Offers art education (MA, PhD); industrial design (MFA); integrated studio arts (MFA); interior design (MFA); photography (MFA); visual communications design (MFA). *Accreditation:* NASAD; NAST. *Program availability:* Part-time. *Students:* 20 full-time (14 women), 1 part-time (0 women); includes 1 minority (Two or more races, non-Hispanic/Latino), 16 international. Average age 26. 97 applicants, 26% accepted, 10 enrolled. In 2017, 6 master's awarded. *Degree requirements:* For master's, terminal exhibit, project, or thesis. *Entrance requirements:* For master's, GRE General Test (for art education), minimum undergraduate GPA of 3.0 or equivalent; 9 undergraduate hours in an art or design history; BA in art (for MA in art education); for doctorate, GRE General Test (minimum scores 600 in verbal and 1000 total), master's degree in art education or art with teaching certification; 3 years of teaching experience at the K-12 level. Additional exam requirements/recommendations for international students: Required—TOEFL (minimum score 550 paper-based; 77 iBT). *Application deadline:* For fall admission, 2/1 for domestic students, 2/1 priority date for international students. Applications are processed on a rolling basis. Application fee: $60 ($75 for international students). Electronic applications accepted. *Financial support:* Teaching assistantships with tuition reimbursements and career-related internships or fieldwork available. Support available to part-time students. Financial award applicants required to submit FAFSA. *Faculty research:* Design, fine arts, photography, acting, directing, theatre technology. *Unit head:* Harry T. Bulow, Head of the Graduate Program, 765-494-3056, E-mail: hbulow@purdue.edu. *Application contact:* Sara J. Unser, Graduate Contact, 765-494-8662, E-mail: sunser@purdue.edu. Website: https://www.cla.purdue.edu/vpa/ad/

Rhode Island School of Design, Department of Furniture Design, Providence, RI 02903-2784. Offers MFA. *Faculty:* 4 full-time (2 women), 11 part-time/adjunct (5 women). *Students:* 21 full-time (10 women); includes 7 minority (4 Asian, non-Hispanic/Latino; 1 Hispanic/Latino; 2 Two or more races, non-Hispanic/Latino), 8 international. Average age 28. 35 applicants, 46% accepted, 11 enrolled. In 2017, 8 master's awarded. *Degree requirements:* For master's, thesis, exhibition. *Entrance requirements:* For master's, portfolio, statement of purpose, 3 letters of recommendation. Additional exam requirements/recommendations for international students: Required—TOEFL (minimum score 580 paper-based; 93 iBT). *Application deadline:* For fall admission, 1/10 for domestic and international students. Application fee: $60. Electronic applications accepted. *Expenses: Tuition:* Full-time $48,210. *Required fees:* $260. *Financial support:* Fellowships, research assistantships, teaching assistantships, Federal Work-Study, scholarships/grants, and unspecified assistantships available. Financial award application deadline: 2/15; financial award applicants required to submit FAFSA. *Unit head:* Lothar Windels, Department Head, 401-454-6102, E-mail: furniture@risd.edu. *Application contact:* Molly Pettengill, Assistant Director for Graduate Recruitment, 401-454-6312, Fax: 401-454-6309, E-mail: mpetteng@risd.edu. Website: http://www.risd.edu/academics/furniture-design/

Rutgers University–New Brunswick, Mason Gross School of the Arts, Theater Department, New Brunswick, NJ 08901. Offers acting (MFA); design (MFA); playwriting (MFA); stage management (MFA); technical direction (MFA). *Degree requirements:* For master's, thesis (for some programs), performance project. *Entrance requirements:* For master's, audition, interview, portfolio. Additional exam requirements/recommendations for international students: Required—TOEFL (minimum score 550 paper-based), IELTS (minimum score 7). Electronic applications accepted. *Faculty research:* Faculty of working professional.

San Diego State University, Graduate and Research Affairs, College of Professional Studies and Fine Arts, School of Art, Design and Art History, San Diego, CA 92182. Offers art history (MA); studio arts (MA, MFA), including applied design, environmental design, graphic design, interior design, painting and printmaking, sculpture. *Accreditation:* NASAD (one or more programs are accredited). *Degree*

requirements: For master's, variable foreign language requirement, thesis. *Entrance requirements:* For master's, GRE General Test, bachelor's degree in related field, slide portfolio, typed slide information sheet, 2 letters of recommendation. Additional exam requirements/recommendations for international students: Required—TOEFL. Electronic applications accepted.

San Francisco State University, Division of Graduate Studies, College of Liberal and Creative Arts, School of Design, San Francisco, CA 94132-1722. Offers industrial arts (MA). *Unit head:* Mari Hulick, Director, 415-338-2211, Fax: 415-338-7770, E-mail: design@sfsu.edu. *Application contact:* Prof. Hsiao-Yun Chu, Graduate Coordinator, 415-338-2430, Fax: 415-338-7770, E-mail: hychu@sfsu.edu.
Website: http://design.sfsu.edu/

Savannah College of Art and Design, Program in Service Design, Savannah, GA 31402-3146. Offers MFA. *Program availability:* Part-time. *Faculty:* 2 full-time (1 woman). *Students:* 12 full-time (6 women), 6 part-time (5 women); includes 2 minority (1 Black or African American, non-Hispanic/Latino; 1 Asian, non-Hispanic/Latino), 10 international. Average age 28. 50 applicants, 56% accepted, 3 enrolled. In 2017, 2 master's awarded. *Degree requirements:* For master's, thesis. *Entrance requirements:* For master's, GRE (recommended), portfolio (submitted in digital format), audition or writing submission, resume, statement of purpose, two letters of recommendation. Additional exam requirements/recommendations for international students: Recommended—TOEFL (minimum score 550 paper-based; 85 iBT), IELTS (minimum score 6.5). *Application deadline:* For fall admission, 4/1 for domestic and international students. Applications are processed on a rolling basis. Application fee: $40. Electronic applications accepted. *Expenses: Tuition:* Full-time $36,765; part-time $817 per credit hour. One-time fee: $500. *Financial support:* Career-related internships or fieldwork, Federal Work-Study, and scholarships/grants available. Financial award application deadline: 4/1; financial award applicants required to submit FAFSA. *Unit head:* Xenia Viladas, Academic Program Coordinator. *Application contact:* Jenny Jaquillard, Executive Director of Admissions, Recruitment and Events, 912-525-5100, Fax: 912-525-5985, E-mail: admission@scad.edu.
Website: http://www.scad.edu/academics/programs/service-design

School of the Art Institute of Chicago, Graduate Division, Department of Architecture, Interior Architecture, and Designed Objects, Program in Designed Objects, Chicago, IL 60603-3103. Offers M Des. *Entrance requirements:* Additional exam requirements/recommendations for international students: Required—TOEFL, IELTS.

School of the Art Institute of Chicago, Graduate Division, Department of Architecture, Interior Architecture, and Designed Objects, Program in Design for Emerging Technologies, Chicago, IL 60603-3103. Offers MFA. *Entrance requirements:* Additional exam requirements/recommendations for international students: Required—TOEFL, IELTS.

School of the Art Institute of Chicago, Graduate Division, Department of Architecture, Interior Architecture, and Designed Objects, Program in Interior Architecture, Chicago, IL 60603-3103. Offers M Arc. *Entrance requirements:* Additional exam requirements/recommendations for international students: Required—TOEFL, IELTS.

School of Visual Arts, Graduate Programs, Design Department, New York, NY 10010-3994. Offers MFA. *Accreditation:* NASAD. *Degree requirements:* For master's, thesis, 60 credits, including all required courses; minimum cumulative GPA of 3.0; residency of two academic years. *Entrance requirements:* For master's, portfolio that reflects wide range of design work and fluency in type and typography. Additional exam requirements/recommendations for international students: Required—TOEFL (minimum score 550 paper-based; 79 iBT). *Expenses:* Contact institution. *Faculty research:* Design, graphic design, multimedia.

School of Visual Arts, Graduate Programs, Design for Social Innovation Department, New York, NY 10010-3994. Offers MFA. *Degree requirements:* For master's, thesis, 60 credits, including all required courses, with minimum cumulative GPA of 3.0; residency of two academic years. *Entrance requirements:* For master's, resume/curriculum vitae; statement of purpose; portfolio; personal interview. Additional exam requirements/recommendations for international students: Required—TOEFL (minimum score 550 paper-based; 79 iBT). Electronic applications accepted. *Expenses:* Contact institution.

School of Visual Arts, Graduate Programs, Products of Design Department, New York, NY 10010-3994. Offers MFA. *Degree requirements:* For master's, thesis, 60 credits, including all required courses; minimum cumulative GPA 3.0; residency of two academic years. *Entrance requirements:* For master's, portfolio. Additional exam requirements/recommendations for international students: Required—TOEFL (minimum score 550 paper-based; 79 iBT). Electronic applications accepted.

School of Visual Arts, Graduate Programs, Program in Branding, New York, NY 10010-3994. Offers MPS. *Degree requirements:* For master's, thesis, 36 credits, including all required courses; minimum cumulative GPA of 3.0; residency of one academic year. *Entrance requirements:* For master's, writing sample, statement of purpose. Additional exam requirements/recommendations for international students: Required—TOEFL (minimum score 550 paper-based; 79 iBT). *Expenses:* Contact institution.

School of Visual Arts, Graduate Programs, Program in Design Research, Writing and Criticism, New York, NY 10010-3994. Offers MA. *Degree requirements:* For master's, thesis, 64 credits, including all required courses, with minimum cumulative GPA of 3.0; residency of two academic years. *Entrance requirements:* For master's, short essay critiquing design object, event or concept; writing sample of published or unpublished writing between 1,000 and 2,000 words; personal interview. Additional exam requirements/recommendations for international students: Required—TOEFL (minimum score 550 paper-based; 79 iBT). Electronic applications accepted.

Southern Illinois University Carbondale, Graduate School, College of Liberal Arts, School of Art and Design, Carbondale, IL 62901-4701. Offers drawing (MFA); fiber/weaving (MFA); glass (MFA); metalsmithing/blacksmithing (MFA); painting (MFA). *Accreditation:* NASAD. *Degree requirements:* For master's, thesis or alternative. *Entrance requirements:* For master's, minimum GPA of 2.7, portfolio, slides. Additional exam requirements/recommendations for international students: Required—TOEFL. *Faculty research:* Prints/woodcuts, foundry, watercolor.

Stanford University, School of Engineering, Department of Civil and Environmental Engineering, Stanford, CA 94305-2004. Offers atmosphere and energy (MS, PhD); construction (MS), including construction engineering and management, design-construction integration, sustainable design and construction; environmental engineering and science (MS, PhD, Eng); environmental fluid mechanics and hydrology (PhD); geomechanics (MS); structural engineering (MS). Terminal master's awarded for partial completion of doctoral program. *Degree requirements:* For doctorate, thesis/dissertation, qualifying exam; for Eng, thesis. *Entrance requirements:* For master's, doctorate, and Eng, GRE General Test. Additional exam requirements/recommendations for international students: Required—TOEFL. Electronic applications accepted. *Expenses: Tuition:* Full-time $48,987; part-time $10,620 per quarter. One-time fee: $400. Tuition and fees vary according to program.

Stanford University, School of Humanities and Sciences, Department of Art and Art History, Stanford, CA 94305-2004. Offers art history (PhD); art practice (MFA); design (MFA); documentary film and video (MFA); MS/MFA. *Degree requirements:* For master's, thesis (for some programs), faculty reviews; for doctorate, 2 foreign languages, thesis/dissertation. *Entrance requirements:* For master's and doctorate, GRE General Test. Additional exam requirements/recommendations for international students: Required—TOEFL. Electronic applications accepted. *Expenses: Tuition:* Full-time $48,987; part-time $10,620 per quarter. One-time fee: $400. Tuition and fees vary according to program.

Stephen F. Austin State University, Graduate School, College of Fine Arts, School of Art, Nacogdoches, TX 75962. Offers art (MA); design (MFA); drawing (MFA); painting (MFA); sculpture (MFA). *Accreditation:* NASAD. *Program availability:* Part-time. *Degree requirements:* For master's, comprehensive exam, thesis, exhibit. *Entrance requirements:* For master's, GRE General Test, portfolio. Additional exam requirements/recommendations for international students: Required—TOEFL. *Faculty research:* Printmaking, jewelry, photography, ceramics, art history.

Suffolk University, New England School of Art and Design, Boston, MA 02108-2770. Offers graphic design (MA); interior architecture (MA). *Program availability:* Part-time, evening/weekend. *Faculty:* 13 full-time (8 women), 10 part-time/adjunct (5 women). *Students:* 33 full-time (28 women), 25 part-time (23 women); includes 12 minority (1 Black or African American, non-Hispanic/Latino; 7 Asian, non-Hispanic/Latino; 4 Hispanic/Latino), 16 international. Average age 28. 58 applicants, 57% accepted, 10 enrolled. In 2017, 37 master's awarded. *Entrance requirements:* For master's, GRE (for MFA), art portfolio, interview, 2 letters of recommendation, resume; letter of intent (for MFA). Additional exam requirements/recommendations for international students: Required—TOEFL (minimum score 550 paper-based; 80 iBT). *Application deadline:* For fall admission, 3/15 priority date for domestic and international students; for spring admission, 10/15 priority date for domestic and international students. Applications are processed on a rolling basis. Application fee: $50. Electronic applications accepted. *Expenses:* $29,520 per year full-time tuition; $1,230 per credit part-time. *Financial support:* In 2017–18, 46 students received support, including 4 fellowships (averaging $6,062 per year); career-related internships or fieldwork, Federal Work-Study, institutionally sponsored loans, scholarships/grants, and unspecified assistantships also available. Financial award application deadline: 4/1; financial award applicants required to submit FAFSA. *Faculty research:* Sustainable design, lighting and technology, design education, environmental graphic design, designing for the non-profit sector. *Unit head:* Audrey Goldstein, Department Chair, 617-997-4290, E-mail: agoldstein@suffolk.edu. *Application contact:* Mara Marzocchi, Associate Director of Graduate Admissions, 617-573-8302, Fax: 617-305-1733, E-mail: grad.admission@suffolk.edu.
Website: http://www.suffolk.edu/nesad/

Syracuse University, College of Visual and Performing Arts, MFA Program in Art Video, Syracuse, NY 13244. Offers MFA. *Accreditation:* NASAD. *Program availability:* Part-time, online learning. *Degree requirements:* For master's, thesis or alternative. *Entrance requirements:* For master's, portfolio, artist statement, three letters of recommendation, transcripts, personal statement/essay, resume. Additional exam requirements/recommendations for international students: Required—TOEFL (minimum score 100 iBT), IELTS. *Application deadline:* For fall admission, 2/1 priority date for domestic and international students. Application fee: $75. Electronic applications accepted. *Financial support:* Fellowships with full tuition reimbursements, teaching assistantships with tuition reimbursements, and tuition waivers available. Financial award application deadline: 1/1; financial award applicants required to submit FAFSA. *Faculty research:* Aesthetic possibilities of subject, genre, and media technologies from personal points of view. *Unit head:* Prof. Tom Sherman, Department of Transmedia, 315-443-1202, E-mail: twsherma@syr.edu. *Application contact:* Caitlin Jarvis, Graduate Recruitment Specialist, 315-443-2769, E-mail: admissg@syr.edu.
Website: http://vpa.syr.edu/academics/transmedia/graduate/art-video/

Texas State University, The Graduate College, College of Fine Arts and Communication, Program in Theatre Arts, San Marcos, TX 78666. Offers design (MFA); directing (MFA); dramatic writing (MFA); theatre history, dramatic criticism and dramaturgy (MA). *Program availability:* Part-time, evening/weekend. *Faculty:* 20 full-time (10 women), 5 part-time/adjunct (3 women). *Students:* 27 full-time (12 women), 1 (woman) part-time; includes 5 minority (2 Black or African American, non-Hispanic/Latino; 2 Hispanic/Latino; 1 Two or more races, non-Hispanic/Latino). Average age 31. 35 applicants, 40% accepted, 12 enrolled. In 2017, 3 master's awarded. *Degree requirements:* For master's, comprehensive exam, thesis (for some programs). *Entrance requirements:* For master's, GRE General Test with minimum preferred score of 300 verbal and quantitative combined (for MA), baccalaureate degree from regionally-accredited institution with minimum GPA of 2.75 in last 60 hours of undergraduate course work, 2 letters of recommendation, statement of purpose, curriculum vitae/resume; writing sample (for playwriting applicants only); interview (for directing applicants only). Additional exam requirements/recommendations for international students: Required—TOEFL (minimum score 550 paper-based; 78 iBT), IELTS (minimum score 6). *Application deadline:* For fall admission, 3/15 for domestic and international students. Applications are processed on a rolling basis. Application fee: $40 ($90 for international students). Electronic applications accepted. *Expenses:* Tuition, state resident: full-time $7868; part-time $3934 per semester. Tuition, nonresident: full-time $17,828; part-time $8914 per semester. *Required fees:* $2092; $1435 per semester. Tuition and fees vary according to course load. *Financial support:* In 2017–18, 25 teaching assistantships (averaging $12,453 per year) were awarded; research assistantships, Federal Work-Study, institutionally sponsored loans, scholarships/grants, and unspecified assistantships also available. Support available to part-time students. Financial award application deadline: 3/1; financial award applicants required to submit FAFSA. *Faculty research:* Black and Latino playwright conference, creation in motion. *Total annual research expenditures:* $2,900. *Unit head:* Dr. Sandra Mayo, Graduate Advisor, 512-245-7889, Fax: 512-245-8440, E-mail: th_gradadvisor@txstate.edu. *Application contact:* Dr. Andrea Golato, Dean of Graduate School, 512-245-2581, Fax: 512-245-8365, E-mail: gradcollege@txstate.edu.
Website: http://www.theatreanddance.txstate.edu/

University of Alberta, Faculty of Graduate Studies and Research, Department of Art and Design, Edmonton, AB T6G 2E1, Canada. Offers drawing (MFA); history of art, design, and visual culture (MA); industrial design (M Des); painting (MFA); printmaking (MFA); sculpture (MFA); visual communication design (M Des). *Degree requirements:* For master's, thesis. *Entrance requirements:* For master's, portfolio (MFA and MDES). Additional exam requirements/recommendations for international students: Required—TOEFL (minimum score 550 paper-based).

University of Baltimore, Graduate School, Yale Gordon College of Arts and Sciences, Program in Integrated Design, Baltimore, MD 21201-5779. Offers MFA. *Program availability:* Part-time, evening/weekend. *Entrance requirements:* Additional exam requirements/recommendations for international students: Required—TOEFL (minimum score 550 paper-based). Electronic applications accepted. *Expenses:* Contact institution. *Faculty research:* Information and graphics design, economics, hypermedia communications.

University of Bridgeport, Shintaro Akatsu School of Design, Bridgeport, CT 06604. Offers design management (MPS). *Program availability:* Part-time, evening/weekend. *Entrance requirements:* Additional exam requirements/recommendations for international students: Recommended—TOEFL (minimum score 550 paper-based; 80 iBT), IELTS (minimum score 6.5). Electronic applications accepted.

University of California, Berkeley, UC Berkeley Extension, Certificate Programs in Art and Design, Berkeley, CA 94720-1500. Offers interior design and interior architecture (Certificate); landscape architecture (Certificate); visual arts (Postbaccalaureate Certificate).

University of California, Los Angeles, Graduate Division, School of the Arts and Architecture, Department of Design Media Arts, Los Angeles, CA 90095. Offers MFA. *Degree requirements:* For master's, comprehensive exam. *Entrance requirements:* For master's, bachelor's degree; minimum undergraduate GPA of 3.0 (or its equivalent if letter grade system not used); portfolio. Additional exam requirements/recommendations for international students: Required—TOEFL. Electronic applications accepted. *Expenses:* Contact institution.

University of Central Oklahoma, The Jackson College of Graduate Studies, College of Fine Arts and Design, Department of Design, Edmond, OK 73034-5209. Offers design (MFA). *Accreditation:* NASAD. *Program availability:* Part-time. *Faculty:* 4 full-time (3 women). *Students:* 11 full-time (5 women), 2 part-time (1 woman); includes 1 minority (American Indian or Alaska Native, non-Hispanic/Latino), 6 international. Average age 30. 8 applicants, 100% accepted, 4 enrolled. In 2017, 2 master's awarded. *Degree requirements:* For master's, thesis. *Entrance requirements:* For master's, essay, portfolio. Additional exam requirements/recommendations for international students: Required—TOEFL (minimum score 550 paper-based; 79 iBT), IELTS (minimum score 6.5). *Application deadline:* For fall admission, 4/1 for domestic and international students; for spring admission, 10/1 for domestic and international students. Applications are processed on a rolling basis. Application fee: $60. Electronic applications accepted. *Expenses:* Tuition, state resident: full-time $5375; part-time $268.75 per credit hour. Tuition, nonresident: full-time $13,295; part-time $664.75 per credit hour. *Required fees:* $626; $31.30 per credit hour. One-time fee: $50. Tuition and fees vary according to program. *Financial support:* In 2017–18, 5 students received support, including 1 research assistantship with partial tuition reimbursement available (averaging $11,830 per year), 2 teaching assistantships with partial tuition reimbursements available (averaging $5,915 per year); career-related internships or fieldwork, scholarships/grants, tuition waivers (partial), and unspecified assistantships also available. Financial award application deadline: 3/31; financial award applicants required to submit FAFSA. *Unit head:* Amy Johnson, Chair, 405-974-5200, Fax: 405-974-3775, E-mail: gradcoll@uco.edu.
Website: http://sites.uco.edu/cfad/academics/design/index.asp

University of Cincinnati, Graduate School, College of Design, Architecture, Art, and Planning, School of Design, Cincinnati, OH 45221. Offers fashion design (M Des); graphic design (M Des); industrial design (M Des); interaction design (M Des); product development (M Des). *Accreditation:* NASAD. *Degree requirements:* For master's, thesis. *Entrance requirements:* For master's, undergraduate degree in design or related field, 2 years of work experience in design or related field. Additional exam requirements/recommendations for international students: Required—TOEFL. Electronic applications accepted. *Expenses: Tuition, area resident:* Full-time $14,468. Tuition, state resident: full-time $14,968; part-time $754 per credit hour. Tuition, nonresident: full-time $24,210; part-time $1311 per credit hour. *International tuition:* $26,460 full-time. *Required fees:* $3958; $84 per credit hour. One-time fee: $85 full-time. Tuition and fees vary according to course load, degree level and program. *Faculty research:* Design theory, interdisciplinary design topics.

University of Connecticut, Graduate School, School of Fine Arts, Department of Dramatic Arts, Storrs, CT 06269. Offers acting (MA, MFA); design (MA, MFA); puppetry (MA, MFA); technical direction (MA, MFA). *Degree requirements:* For master's, comprehensive exam. *Entrance requirements:* Additional exam requirements/recommendations for international students: Required—TOEFL (minimum score 550 paper-based). Electronic applications accepted.

University of Delaware, College of Arts and Sciences, Department of Art, Newark, DE 19716. Offers MA, MFA. *Degree requirements:* For master's, exposition paper final exhibition. *Entrance requirements:* For master's, portfolio of creative work. Electronic applications accepted. *Faculty research:* Painting, printmaking, ceramics, photography, sculpture.

University of Illinois at Chicago, College of Architecture, Design and the Arts, School of Design, Chicago, IL 60607-7128. Offers graphic design (M Des); industrial design (M Des). *Degree requirements:* For master's, thesis, exhibit. *Entrance requirements:* For master's, MAT, portfolio. Additional exam requirements/recommendations for international students: Required—TOEFL. Electronic applications accepted. *Expenses:* Contact institution.

University of Illinois at Urbana–Champaign, Graduate College, College of Fine and Applied Arts, School of Art and Design, Champaign, IL 61820. Offers Ed M, MA, MFA, PhD. *Accreditation:* NASAD. *Entrance requirements:* For master's, minimum GPA of 3.0.

The University of Kansas, Graduate Studies, School of Architecture and Design, Department of Design, Lawrence, KS 66045. Offers design management (MA); interaction design (MA). *Accreditation:* NASAD. *Program availability:* Part-time. *Students:* 2 full-time (1 woman), 18 part-time (10 women); includes 4 minority (1 Black or African American, non-Hispanic/Latino; 1 Asian, non-Hispanic/Latino; 2 Two or more races, non-Hispanic/Latino), 3 international. Average age 35. 14 applicants, 64% accepted, 3 enrolled. In 2017, 8 master's awarded. *Entrance requirements:* For master's, GRE (preferred), curriculum vitae or resume; statement of design philosophy and approach; official transcripts; three recommendations; portfolio of design work or, if previous degree was not in design-related discipline, samples of written work or other creative artifacts produced. Additional exam requirements/recommendations for international students: Required—TOEFL, IELTS. *Application deadline:* For fall admission, 4/15 priority date for domestic and international students; for spring admission, 11/15 priority date for domestic and international students. Application fee: $65 ($85 for international students). Electronic applications accepted. *Financial support:* Fellowships, teaching assistantships, Federal Work-Study, scholarships/grants, and unspecified assistantships available. Financial award application deadline: 2/1; financial award applicants required to submit FAFSA. *Faculty research:* Interaction design, design management, photography, graphic design, industrial design. *Unit head:* Andrea Herstowski, Chair, 785-864-2956, E-mail: hestow@ku.edu. *Application contact:* Gera Elliott, Graduate Admission Coordinator, 785-864-3167, E-mail: archku@ku.edu. Website: http://design.ku.edu/

University of Kentucky, Graduate School, College of Design, Lexington, KY 40506-0032. Offers M Arch, MAIDM, MHP, MSIDM. *Accreditation:* NASAD. *Entrance requirements:* For master's, GRE, minimum GPA of 2.75. Additional exam requirements/recommendations for international students: Required—TOEFL (minimum score 550 paper-based). Electronic applications accepted.

University of Louisville, Graduate School, College of Arts and Sciences, Department of Fine Arts, Louisville, KY 40292. Offers art history (MA, PhD); curatorial studies (MA); studio art (MFA), including design. *Program availability:* Online learning. *Faculty:* 23 full-time (9 women), 6 part-time/adjunct (3 women). *Students:* 24 full-time (17 women), 1 (woman) part-time; includes 3 minority (1 Asian, non-Hispanic/Latino; 1 Hispanic/Latino; 1 Two or more races, non-Hispanic/Latino). Average age 35. 16 applicants, 63% accepted, 7 enrolled. In 2017, 5 master's awarded. *Degree requirements:* For master's, one foreign language, thesis. *Entrance requirements:* For doctorate, MA. Additional exam requirements/recommendations for international students: Required—TOEFL (minimum score 550 paper-based; 80 iBT), IELTS (minimum score 6.5). *Application deadline:* For fall admission, 3/1 priority date for domestic and international students. Application fee: $65. *Expenses:* $12,500. *Financial support:* In 2017–18, 7 teaching assistantships with full tuition reimbursements (averaging $14,000 per year) were awarded; research assistantships, scholarships/grants, health care benefits, and unspecified assistantships also available. Financial award application deadline: 3/1. *Faculty research:* Sustainability and environmental design, media theory, cross cultural and critical theories, Installation, urban and public art. *Total annual research expenditures:* $75,000. *Unit head:* Dr. Scott L. Massey, Associate Professor and Chair, 502-852-6794, Fax: 502-852-6791, E-mail: s.massey@louisville.edu. *Application contact:* Theresa Berbet, Senior Advisor, 502-852-6147, Fax: 502-852-6791, E-mail: tberbet@louisville.edu.
Website: http://art.louisville.edu

University of Louisville, Graduate School, College of Arts and Sciences, Department of Theatre Arts, Louisville, KY 40292-0001. Offers design (MFA); performance (MFA). *Accreditation:* NAST. *Program availability:* Part-time. *Faculty:* 11 full-time (5 women), 4 part-time/adjunct (3 women). *Students:* 11 full-time (7 women); includes 6 minority (5 Black or African American, non-Hispanic/Latino; 1 Hispanic/Latino), 1 international. Average age 30. 6 applicants, 100% accepted, 4 enrolled. In 2017, 3 master's awarded. *Degree requirements:* For master's, variable foreign language requirement, performance project and monograph. *Entrance requirements:* For master's, audition. Additional exam requirements/recommendations for international students: Required—TOEFL. *Application deadline:* For spring admission, 4/15 for domestic and international students. Application fee: $65. Electronic applications accepted. *Expenses:* Contact institution. *Financial support:* In 2017–18, 3 teaching assistantships (averaging $12,000 per year) were awarded; health care benefits also available. Financial award application deadline: 2/15; financial award applicants required to submit FAFSA. *Faculty research:* Social justice, African American theatre, African diaspora theatre, costume history and design, lighting design, scenic design. *Unit head:* Dr. Kevin Gawley, Chair, 502-852-8683, Fax: 502-852-7235, E-mail: kevin.gawley@louisville.edu. *Application contact:* Latonia Craig, Director of Graduate Recruitment and Diversity Retention, 502-852-5207, Fax: 502-852-6536, E-mail: gradadm@louisville.edu.
Website: http://louisville.edu/theatrearts/

University of Michigan, College of Engineering, Department of Integrative Systems and Design, Ann Arbor, MI 48109. Offers automotive engineering (M Eng); design science (MS, PhD); energy systems engineering (M Eng, MS); global automotive and manufacturing engineering (M Eng); manufacturing engineering (M Eng, D Eng); pharmaceutical engineering (M Eng); robotics and autonomous vehicles (M Eng); systems engineering and design (M Eng); MBA/M Eng; MSE/MS. *Program availability:* Part-time, online learning. *Students:* 165 full-time (37 women), 281 part-time (47 women). 406 applicants, 10% accepted, 20 enrolled. In 2017, 113 master's, 1 doctorate awarded. Terminal master's awarded for partial completion of doctoral program. *Degree requirements:* For master's, capstone project; for doctorate, thesis/dissertation. *Entrance requirements:* For master's, GRE; for doctorate, GRE, 2 years of work experience. Additional exam requirements/recommendations for international students: Required—TOEFL (minimum score 560 paper-based). *Application deadline:* Applications are processed on a rolling basis. Electronic applications accepted. *Expenses:* Tuition, state resident: full-time $22,368; part-time $1201 per credit hour. Tuition, nonresident: full-time $45,156; part-time $2467 per credit hour. *Required fees:* $376 per term. Tuition and fees vary according to course load, degree level and program. *Financial support:* Fellowships, research assistantships with full tuition reimbursements, teaching assistantships with full tuition reimbursements, career-related internships or fieldwork, scholarships/grants, and unspecified assistantships available. Financial award applicants required to submit FAFSA. *Faculty research:* Automotive engineering, design science, energy systems engineering, engineering sustainable systems, financial engineering, global automotive and manufacturing engineering, integrated microsystems, manufacturing engineering, pharmaceutical engineering, robotics and autonomous vehicles. *Total annual research expenditures:* $586,040. *Unit head:* Prof. Panos Papalambros, Department Chair, 734-647-8401, E-mail: pyp@umich.edu. *Application contact:* Kathy Bishar, Senior Graduate Coordinator, 734-764-3312, E-mail: kbishar@umich.edu.
Website: http://www.isd.engin.umich.edu

University of Michigan, Rackham Graduate School, Penny W. Stamps School of Art and Design, Ann Arbor, MI 48109-2069. Offers art and design (MFA); integrative design (M Des). *Accreditation:* NASAD. *Faculty:* 37. *Students:* 18 (12 women). 179 applicants, 6% accepted, 10 enrolled. In 2017, 9 master's awarded. *Degree requirements:* For master's, thesis, exhibit (MFA), slide lecture. *Entrance requirements:* For master's, portfolio. Additional exam requirements/recommendations for international students: Required—TOEFL (minimum score 560 paper-based; 84 iBT), IELTS (minimum score 6.5). *Application deadline:* For fall admission, 1/1 for domestic and international students. Application fee: $75 ($90 for international students). Electronic applications accepted. *Expenses:* Tuition, state resident: full-time $22,368; part-time $1201 per credit hour. Tuition, nonresident: full-time $45,156; part-time $2467 per credit hour. *Required fees:* $376 per term. Tuition and fees vary according to course load, degree level and program. *Financial support:* In 2017–18, 19 students received support. Fellowships with full tuition reimbursements available, research assistantships with full tuition reimbursements available, teaching assistantships with full tuition reimbursements available, career-related internships or fieldwork, Federal Work-Study, institutionally sponsored loans, scholarships/grants, health care benefits, tuition waivers (full and partial), and unspecified assistantships available. Support available to part-time students. Financial award application deadline: 1/1. *Faculty research:* Creative expression, social engagement, commercial design, collaborative research, preparation for teaching. *Unit head:* Gunalan Nadarajan, Dean, 734-764-0397, E-mail: artdes-dean@umich.edu. *Application contact:* Meghan Jellema, Graduate Programs Coordinator, 734-763-5247, E-mail: stamps-graduate-info@umich.edu.
Website: http://stamps.umich.edu/

University of Minnesota, Twin Cities Campus, Graduate School, College of Design, Department of Design, Housing, and Apparel, Minneapolis, MN 55455-0213. Offers apparel (MA, MS, PhD); design communication (MA, MS, PhD); housing studies (MA, MS, PhD, Postbaccalaureate Certificate); interactive design (MFA); interior design (MA, MS, PhD). *Program availability:* Part-time. *Degree requirements:* For master's and Postbaccalaureate Certificate, comprehensive exam, thesis (for some programs); for doctorate, comprehensive exam, thesis/dissertation. *Entrance requirements:* For master's, GRE General Test, minimum GPA of 3.0 (preferred), portfolio, 3 letters of

recommendation; for doctorate, GRE General Test, minimum GPA of 3.0 (preferred), portfolio, 3 letters of recommendation, writing sample; for Postbaccalaureate Certificate, GRE General Test, minimum GPA of 3.0 (preferred). Additional exam requirements/ recommendations for international students: Required—TOEFL (minimum score 550 paper-based; 79 iBT). Electronic applications accepted. *Faculty research:* Housing policy and community development; consumer behavior; interactive design; design history; social, cultural, and behavioral issues related to designed environments.

University of North Texas, Robert B. Toulouse School of Graduate Studies, Denton, TX 76203-5459. Offers accounting (MS); applied anthropology (MA, MS); applied behavior analysis (Certificate); applied geography (MA); applied technology and performance improvement (M Ed, MS); art education (MA); art history (MA); art museum education (Certificate); arts leadership (Certificate); audiology (Au D); behavior analysis (MS); behavioral science (PhD); biochemistry and molecular biology (MS); biology (MA, MS); biomedical engineering (MS); business analysis (MS); chemistry (MS); clinical health psychology (PhD); communication studies (MA, MS); computer engineering (MS); computer science (MS); counseling (M Ed, MS), including clinical mental health counseling (MS), college and university counseling, elementary school counseling, secondary school counseling; creative writing (MA); criminal justice (MS); curriculum and instruction (M Ed); decision sciences (MBA); design (MA, MFA), including fashion design (MFA), innovation studies, interior design (MFA); early childhood studies (MS); economics (MS); educational leadership (M Ed, Ed D); educational psychology (MS, PhD), including family studies (MS), gifted and talented (MS), human development (MS), learning and cognition (MS), research, measurement and evaluation (MS); electrical engineering (MS); emergency management (MPA); engineering technology (MS); English (MA); English as a second language (MA); environmental science (MS); finance (MBA, MS); financial management (MPA); French (MA); health services management (MBA); higher education (M Ed, Ed D); history (MA, MS); hospitality management (MS); human resources management (MPA); information science (MS); information systems (PhD); information technologies (MBA); interdisciplinary studies (MA, MS); international studies (MA); international sustainable tourism (MS); jazz studies (MM); journalism (MA, MJ, Graduate Certificate), including interactive and virtual digital communication (Graduate Certificate), narrative journalism (Graduate Certificate), public relations (Graduate Certificate); kinesiology (MS); linguistics (MA); local government management (MPA); logistics (PhD); logistics and supply chain management (MBA); long-term care, senior housing, and aging services (MA); management (PhD); marketing (MBA); mathematics (MA, MS); mechanical and energy engineering (MS, PhD); music (MA), including ethnomusicology, music theory, musicology, performance; music composition (PhD); music education (MM Ed, PhD); nonprofit management (MPA); operations and supply chain management (MBA); performance (MM, DMA); philosophy (MA); political science (MA); professional and technical communication (MA); radio, television and film (MA, MFA); rehabilitation counseling (Certificate); sociology (MA); Spanish (MA); special education (M Ed); speech-language pathology (MA); strategic management (MBA); studio art (MFA); teaching (M Ed); MBA/MS. *Program availability:* Part-time, evening/weekend, online learning. Terminal master's awarded for partial completion of doctoral program. *Degree requirements:* For master's, variable foreign language requirement, comprehensive exam (for some programs), thesis (for some programs); for doctorate, variable foreign language requirement, comprehensive exam (for some programs), thesis/dissertation; for other advanced degree, variable foreign language requirement, comprehensive exam (for some programs). *Entrance requirements:* For master's and doctorate, GRE, GMAT. Additional exam requirements/ recommendations for international students: Required—TOEFL (minimum score 550 paper-based; 79 iBT). Electronic applications accepted.

University of Notre Dame, Graduate School, College of Arts and Letters, Division of Humanities, Department of Art, Art History, and Design, Notre Dame, IN 46556. Offers art history (MA); design (MFA), including graphic design, industrial design; studio art (MFA), including ceramics, painting, photography, printmaking, sculpture. *Accreditation:* NASAD. *Degree requirements:* For master's, comprehensive exam (for some programs), thesis. *Entrance requirements:* For master's, GRE General Test, minimum GPA of 3.0. Additional exam requirements/recommendations for international students: Required—TOEFL (minimum score 600 paper-based; 80 iBT). Electronic applications accepted. *Faculty research:* Studio art practice in ceramics, printing, photography, printmaking and sculpture, graphic design and industrial design, digital imaging in design and photography, Renaissance and American art history, contemporary art theory and criticism.

University of Oklahoma, Weitzenhoffer Family College of Fine Arts, School of Visual Arts, Norman, OK 73019. Offers art (MFA), including art and technology, ceramics, film, painting, photography, printmaking, sculpture, video, visual communication; art history (MA, PhD), including art history (MA), art of the American West (PhD), Native American art history (PhD); design (MFA). *Faculty:* 24 full-time (8 women). *Students:* 22 full-time (17 women), 9 part-time (all women); includes 9 minority (1 American Indian or Alaska Native, non-Hispanic/Latino; 1 Asian, non-Hispanic/Latino; 4 Hispanic/Latino; 3 Two or more races, non-Hispanic/Latino). Average age 33. 28 applicants, 25% accepted, 6 enrolled. In 2017, 6 master's, 3 doctorates awarded. *Degree requirements:* For master's, 2 foreign languages, comprehensive exam (for some programs), thesis (for some programs); for doctorate, 2 foreign languages, comprehensive exam, thesis/dissertation. *Entrance requirements:* For master's and doctorate, GRE. Additional exam requirements/recommendations for international students: Required—TOEFL (minimum score 79 iBT) or IELTS (minimum score 6.5). *Application deadline:* For fall admission, 2/1 for domestic and international students. Application fee: $50 ($100 for international students). Electronic applications accepted. *Expenses:* Tuition, state resident: full-time $5119; part-time $213.30 per credit hour. Tuition, nonresident: full-time $19,778; part-time $824.10 per credit hour. *Required fees:* $3458; $133.55 per credit hour. $126.50 per semester. *Financial support:* In 2017–18, 30 students received support, including 1 research assistantship with full tuition reimbursement available (averaging $10,373 per year), 16 teaching assistantships with full tuition reimbursements available (averaging $10,377 per year); fellowships with full tuition reimbursements available, career-related internships or fieldwork, Federal Work-Study, institutionally sponsored loans, scholarships/grants, health care benefits, tuition waivers (full and partial), and unspecified assistantships also available. Support available to part-time students. Financial award application deadline: 6/1; financial award applicants required to submit FAFSA. *Faculty research:* Art history, studio arts, 3D printing, installation art, photography. *Unit head:* Dr. Bette Talvacchia, Director, 405-325-2691, Fax: 405-325-1668, E-mail: bette.talvacchia-1@ou.edu. *Application contact:* Peter Froslie, MFA Coordinator, E-mail: froslie@ou.edu.
Website: http://art.ou.edu

University of Oregon, Graduate School, College of Design, Department of Product Design, Eugene, OR 97403. Offers sports product design (MS).

The University of Texas at Austin, Graduate School, College of Fine Arts, Department of Art and Art History, Program in Design, Austin, TX 78712-1111. Offers MFA. *Accreditation:* NASAD. *Degree requirements:* For master's, thesis, oral exam, exhibition. *Entrance requirements:* For master's, minimum GPA of 3.0, portfolio. Electronic applications accepted.

The University of Tulsa, Graduate School, Kendall College of Arts and Sciences, School of Art, Design, and Art History, Tulsa, OK 74104-3189. Offers MA, MFA, MTA. *Program availability:* Part-time. *Faculty:* 7 full-time (4 women), 6 part-time/adjunct (3 women). *Students:* 6 full-time (5 women), 1 part-time (0 women); includes 1 minority (Asian, non-Hispanic/Latino). Average age 35. 15 applicants, 13% accepted, 2 enrolled. In 2017, 3 master's awarded. *Degree requirements:* For master's, comprehensive exam (for some programs), thesis (for some programs). *Entrance requirements:* For master's, portfolio. Additional exam requirements/recommendations for international students: Required—TOEFL (minimum score 577 paper-based; 91 iBT), IELTS (minimum score 6.5). *Application deadline:* For fall admission, 2/1 for domestic and international students. Application fee: $55. Electronic applications accepted. *Expenses: Tuition:* Full-time $22,230. *Required fees:* $2000. Tuition and fees vary according to course load and program. *Financial support:* In 2017–18, 6 students received support, including 5 fellowships with full tuition reimbursements available (averaging $5,200 per year), 5 teaching assistantships with full tuition reimbursements available (averaging $13,410 per year); career-related internships or fieldwork, Federal Work-Study, scholarships/ grants, traineeships, health care benefits, tuition waivers (full and partial), and unspecified assistantships also available. Support available to part-time students. Financial award application deadline: 2/1; financial award applicants required to submit FAFSA. *Faculty research:* Drawing, painting, printmaking, graphic design, photography. *Unit head:* Prof. Teresa Valero, Director, 918-631-3513, Fax: 918-631-3423, E-mail: maria-valero@utulsa.edu. *Application contact:* Prof. Michelle Martin, Program Advisor, 918-631-2736, Fax: 918-631-3423, E-mail: michelle-martin@utulsa.edu.
Website: http://artsandsciences.utulsa.edu/academics/departments-schools/art/

University of Washington, Graduate School, College of Arts and Sciences, School of Art, Division of Design, Seattle, WA 98195. Offers industrial design (MFA); visual communication design (MFA).

University of Wisconsin–Madison, Graduate School, School of Human Ecology, Program in Design Studies, Madison, WI 53706. Offers MFA, MS, PhD. *Degree requirements:* For master's, thesis (for some programs); for doctorate, comprehensive exam, thesis/dissertation. *Entrance requirements:* For master's, portfolio, scholarly paper, 3 letters of recommendation from faculty; for doctorate, letters of recommendation, scholarly paper. Additional exam requirements/recommendations for international students: Required—TOEFL (minimum score 580 paper-based; 92 iBT). *Faculty research:* Feng shui, material culture, behavior and environment, use of pattern to enhance environment, design visualization.

University of Wisconsin–Milwaukee, Graduate School, College of Health Sciences, Department of Occupational Science and Technology, Milwaukee, WI 53201-0413. Offers assistive technology and design (MS); disability and occupation (MS); ergonomics (MS); therapeutic recreation (MS). *Accreditation:* AOTA. *Students:* 86 full-time (74 women), 1 (woman) part-time; includes 6 minority (3 Asian, non-Hispanic/ Latino; 1 Hispanic/Latino; 2 Two or more races, non-Hispanic/Latino), 1 international. Average age 27. 115 applicants, 30% accepted, 32 enrolled. In 2017, 22 master's awarded. *Degree requirements:* For master's, thesis or alternative. *Entrance requirements:* Additional exam requirements/recommendations for international students: Required—TOEFL (minimum score 550 paper-based; 79 iBT), IELTS (minimum score 6.5). *Application deadline:* For fall admission, 1/1 priority date for domestic students; for spring admission, 9/1 for domestic students. Applications are processed on a rolling basis. Application fee: $56 ($75 for international students). *Financial support:* Fellowships, research assistantships, teaching assistantships, and unspecified assistantships available. Support available to part-time students. Financial award application deadline: 4/15. *Unit head:* Jay Kapellusch, PhD, Department Chair, 414-229-5292, Fax: 414-229-2619, E-mail: kap@uwm.edu. *Application contact:* Bhagwant S. Sindhu, PhD, Graduate Program Coordinator, 414-229-1180, Fax: 414-229-5100, E-mail: sindhu@uwm.edu.
Website: http://uwm.edu/healthsciences/academics/occupational-science-technology/

Western Carolina University, Graduate School, College of Fine and Performing Arts, School of Art and Design, Cullowhee, NC 28723. Offers MFA. *Accreditation:* NASAD. *Program availability:* Part-time. *Degree requirements:* For master's, thesis. *Entrance requirements:* For master's, GRE, appropriate undergraduate degree, portfolio, letters of recommendation. Additional exam requirements/recommendations for international students: Required—TOEFL (minimum score 550 paper-based; 79 iBT). *Expenses:* Tuition, state resident: full-time $4436. Tuition, nonresident: full-time $14,842. *Required fees:* $2926. *Faculty research:* Art and society, visual literacy, vernacular cultural studies and oral history, environments for aging, health and leisure.

Western Michigan University, Graduate College, College of Fine Arts, Gwen Frostic School of Art, Kalamazoo, MI 49008. Offers art education (MA). *Accreditation:* NASAD. *Degree requirements:* For master's, thesis or alternative.

Yale University, School of Art, New Haven, CT 06520-8339. Offers graphic design (MFA); painting/printmaking (MFA); photography (MFA); sculpture (MFA). *Degree requirements:* For master's, thesis (for some programs). *Entrance requirements:* Additional exam requirements/recommendations for international students: Required—TOEFL (minimum score 550 paper-based; 100 iBT). Electronic applications accepted. *Expenses:* Contact institution.

York University, Faculty of Graduate Studies, Faculty of Fine Arts, Program in Design, Toronto, ON M3J 1P3, Canada. Offers M Des. Electronic applications accepted.

Computer Art and Design

Academy of Art University, Graduate Programs, School of Graphic Design, San Francisco, CA 94105-3410. Offers graphic design (MFA); graphic design and digital media (MA). *Accreditation:* NASAD. *Program availability:* Part-time, 100% online. *Faculty:* 6 full-time (2 women), 27 part-time/adjunct (13 women). *Students:* 187 full-time (134 women), 188 part-time (142 women); includes 51 minority (12 Black or African American, non-Hispanic/Latino; 1 American Indian or Alaska Native, non-Hispanic/Latino; 14 Asian, non-Hispanic/Latino; 20 Hispanic/Latino; 2 Native Hawaiian or other Pacific Islander, non-Hispanic/Latino; 2 Two or more races, non-Hispanic/Latino), 239 international. Average age 29. 146 applicants, 100% accepted, 97 enrolled. In 2017, 82 master's awarded. *Degree requirements:* For master's, final review. *Entrance requirements:* For master's, statement of intent; resume; portfolio/reel; official college transcripts. *Application deadline:* Applications are processed on a rolling basis. Application fee: $50. Electronic applications accepted. *Expenses: Tuition:* Part-time $982 per unit. *Financial support:* Career-related internships or fieldwork, Federal Work-Study, and scholarships/grants available. Financial award application deadline: 8/10; financial award applicants required to submit FAFSA. *Unit head:* 800-544-ARTS, E-mail: info@academyart.edu. *Application contact:* 800-544-ARTS, E-mail: info@academyart.edu.
Website: https://www.academyart.edu/academics/graphic-design

Academy of Art University, Graduate Programs, School of Visual Development, San Francisco, CA 94105-3410. Offers MA, MFA. *Program availability:* Part-time, 100% online. *Faculty:* 5 full-time (0 women), 13 part-time/adjunct (1 woman). *Students:* 105 full-time (67 women), 79 part-time (40 women); includes 38 minority (8 Black or African American, non-Hispanic/Latino; 1 American Indian or Alaska Native, non-Hispanic/Latino; 14 Asian, non-Hispanic/Latino; 12 Hispanic/Latino; 3 Two or more races, non-Hispanic/Latino), 88 international. Average age 29. 37 applicants, 100% accepted, 33 enrolled. In 2017, 48 master's awarded. *Degree requirements:* For master's, final review. *Entrance requirements:* For master's, statement of intent; resume; portfolio/reel; official college transcripts. *Application deadline:* Applications are processed on a rolling basis. Application fee: $50. Electronic applications accepted. *Expenses: Tuition:* Part-time $982 per unit. *Financial support:* Career-related internships or fieldwork, Federal Work-Study, and scholarships/grants available. Financial award application deadline: 8/10; financial award applicants required to submit FAFSA. *Unit head:* 800-544-ARTS, E-mail: info@academyart.edu. *Application contact:* 800-544-ARTS, E-mail: info@academyart.edu.
Website: https://www.academyart.edu/academics/visual-development

Academy of Art University, Graduate Programs, School of Web Design and New Media, San Francisco, CA 94105-3410. Offers MA, MFA. *Program availability:* Part-time, 100% online. *Faculty:* 8 full-time (3 women), 29 part-time/adjunct (9 women). *Students:* 272 full-time (183 women), 149 part-time (100 women); includes 60 minority (8 Black or African American, non-Hispanic/Latino; 36 Asian, non-Hispanic/Latino; 11 Hispanic/Latino; 1 Native Hawaiian or other Pacific Islander, non-Hispanic/Latino; 4 Two or more races, non-Hispanic/Latino), 298 international. Average age 29. 107 applicants, 100% accepted, 102 enrolled. In 2017, 138 master's awarded. *Degree requirements:* For master's, final review. *Entrance requirements:* For master's, statement of intent; resume; portfolio/reel; official college transcripts. *Application deadline:* Applications are processed on a rolling basis. Application fee: $50. Electronic applications accepted. *Expenses: Tuition:* Part-time $982 per unit. *Financial support:* Career-related internships or fieldwork, Federal Work-Study, and scholarships/grants available. Financial award application deadline: 8/10; financial award applicants required to submit FAFSA. *Unit head:* 800-544-ARTS, E-mail: info@academyart.edu. *Application contact:* 800-544-ARTS, E-mail: info@academyart.edu.
Website: http://www.academyart.edu/computer-arts-school/index.html

Alfred University, Graduate School, College of Ceramics, School of Art and Design, Alfred, NY 14802. Offers ceramic art (MFA); electronic integrated arts (MFA); painting (MFA); sculpture/dimensional studies (MFA). *Accreditation:* NASAD. *Degree requirements:* For master's, thesis, exhibit. *Entrance requirements:* For master's, portfolio. Additional exam requirements/recommendations for international students: Required—TOEFL (minimum score 550 paper-based; 80 iBT), IELTS (minimum score 6). Electronic applications accepted. *Expenses:* Contact institution. *Faculty research:* Ceramic art, sculpture, glass art, new media, time-based media.

ArtCenter College of Design, Graduate Media Design Practices Program, Pasadena, CA 91103. Offers MFA. *Accreditation:* NASAD.

Bowling Green State University, Graduate College, College of Arts and Sciences, School of Art, Bowling Green, OH 43403. Offers 2-D studio art (MA, MFA); 3-D studio art (MA, MFA); art education (MA); art history (MA); computer art (MA); design (MFA); digital arts (MFA); graphics (MFA). *Accreditation:* NASAD. *Program availability:* Part-time. *Degree requirements:* For master's, thesis or alternative, final exhibit (MFA). *Entrance requirements:* For master's, GRE General Test (for MA), slide portfolio (15-20 slides). Additional exam requirements/recommendations for international students: Required—TOEFL. Electronic applications accepted. *Faculty research:* Computer animation and virtual reality, Spanish still-life painting from 1600 to 1800, art and psychotherapy, Japanese wood-firing techniques in ceramics, non-toxic printmaking technologies.

California College of the Arts, Graduate Programs, Design Program, San Francisco, CA 94107. Offers graphic design (MFA); industrial design (MFA); interaction design (MFA). *Accreditation:* NASAD. *Faculty:* 14 full-time (4 women), 40 part-time/adjunct (14 women). *Students:* 109 full-time (64 women); includes 18 minority (1 Black or African American, non-Hispanic/Latino; 12 Asian, non-Hispanic/Latino; 5 Hispanic/Latino), 64 international. Average age 26. 618 applicants, 35% accepted, 76 enrolled. In 2017, 54 master's awarded. *Degree requirements:* For master's, thesis, exhibit. *Entrance requirements:* For master's, appropriate bachelor's degree, portfolio, resume, letters of recommendation, transcripts. Additional exam requirements/recommendations for international students: Required—TOEFL, IELTS, or PTE. *Application deadline:* For fall admission, 1/31 priority date for domestic and international students. Applications are processed on a rolling basis. Application fee: $70. Electronic applications accepted. *Expenses:* Contact institution. *Financial support:* In 2017–18, fellowships (averaging $22,000 per year), teaching assistantships (averaging $2,000 per year) were awarded; career-related internships or fieldwork, Federal Work-Study, scholarships/grants, health care benefits, and unspecified assistantships also available. Financial award application deadline: 7/31; financial award applicants required to submit FAFSA. *Unit head:* Kristian Simsarian, Graduate Chair, 415-551-9283, Fax: 415-703-9539, E-mail: ksimsarian@cca.edu. *Application contact:* Wes Fanelli, Assistant Director of Graduate Admissions, 415-703-9533, Fax: 415-703-9539, E-mail: wfanelli@cca.edu.

Carnegie Mellon University, College of Fine Arts, School of Design, Program in Design for Interactions, Pittsburgh, PA 15213-3891. Offers M Des. *Program availability:*

Part-time. *Degree requirements:* For master's, thesis. *Entrance requirements:* For master's, GRE, portfolio of relevant work. Additional exam requirements/recommendations for international students: Required—TOEFL (minimum score 600 paper-based). *Faculty research:* Interaction and emotion, visual interface design, robotics, visualization and diagramming, design theory.

Chatham University, Program in Film and Digital Technology, Pittsburgh, PA 15232-2826. Offers MFA. *Program availability:* Part-time, evening/weekend. *Faculty:* 3 full-time (2 women), 2 part-time/adjunct (1 woman). *Students:* 7 full-time (3 women), 1 (woman) part-time; includes 3 minority (all Black or African American, non-Hispanic/Latino), 2 international. Average age 28. 10 applicants, 60% accepted, 5 enrolled. In 2017, 4 master's awarded. *Degree requirements:* For master's, thesis, capstone project. *Entrance requirements:* Additional exam requirements/recommendations for international students: Required—TOEFL (minimum score 600 paper-based; 100 iBT), IELTS (minimum score 7), TWE. *Application deadline:* For fall admission, 4/1 priority date for domestic and international students; for spring admission, 11/1 priority date for domestic students, 10/1 priority date for international students. Applications are processed on a rolling basis. Application fee: $45. Electronic applications accepted. Application fee is waived when completed online. *Expenses: Tuition:* Full-time $16,740; part-time $930 per credit. *Required fees:* $486; $27 per credit. $243 per semester. *Financial support:* Applicants required to submit FAFSA. *Unit head:* Dr. Prajna Parasher, Director, 412-365-1182, E-mail: parasher@chatham.edu. *Application contact:* Katie Noel, Assistant Director of Graduate Admission, 412-365-2758, Fax: 412-365-1609, E-mail: gradadmissions@chatham.edu.
Website: http://www.chatham.edu/mfafilm

City College of the City University of New York, Graduate School, Division of Humanities and the Arts, Department of Art, Program in Fine Arts, New York, NY 10031-9198. Offers advertising design (MFA); ceramic design (MFA); digital and interdisciplinary art practice (MFA); painting (MFA); printmaking (MFA); sculpture (MFA); wood and metal design (MFA). *Degree requirements:* For master's, thesis exhibit. *Entrance requirements:* For master's, 20-slide portfolio. Additional exam requirements/recommendations for international students: Required—TOEFL (minimum score 577 paper-based; 90 iBT). Electronic applications accepted.

Claremont Graduate University, Graduate Programs, School of Arts and Humanities, Department of Art, Claremont, CA 91711. Offers digital media (MFA); drawing (MFA); installation (MFA); painting (MFA); performance (MFA); photography (MFA); sculpture (MFA); studio (MFA). *Program availability:* Part-time. *Degree requirements:* For master's, final project show. *Entrance requirements:* For master's, BA in art or BFA, slide review. Additional exam requirements/recommendations for international students: Required—TOEFL (minimum score 75 iBT). Electronic applications accepted. *Expenses:* Contact institution. *Faculty research:* Acoustic sculpture, feminization of abstraction, installation sculpture.

Concordia University, School of Graduate Studies, Faculty of Fine Arts, Department of Design and Computation Arts, Montréal, QC H3G 1M8, Canada. Offers design (M Des); digital technologies in design art practice (Certificate).

Cornell University, Graduate School, Graduate Fields of Architecture, Art and Planning, Field of Architecture, Ithaca, NY 14853. Offers architectural design (M Arch); architectural science (MS); computer graphics (MS); history of architecture (MA, PhD); history of urban development (MA, PhD); theory and criticism of architecture (M Arch); urban design (M Arch). *Degree requirements:* For master's, one foreign language, thesis (MA, MS); for doctorate, 2 foreign languages, comprehensive exam, thesis/dissertation. *Entrance requirements:* For master's, GRE General Test, 5-year bachelor's degree in architecture, portfolio (M Arch), 3 letters of recommendation; for doctorate, GRE General Test, 3 letters of recommendation. Additional exam requirements/recommendations for international students: Required—TOEFL (minimum score 600 paper-based; 77 iBT). Electronic applications accepted. *Faculty research:* Architectural design and urban design, theory and criticism of architecture, computer graphics, building technology and environmental science, history of architecture and history of urban-development.

DePaul University, College of Computing and Digital Media, Chicago, IL 60604. Offers animation (MA, MFA); applied technology (MS); business information technology (MS); computational finance (MS); computer and information sciences (PhD); computer science (MS); creative producing (MFA); cybersecurity (MS); data science (MS); digital communication and media arts (MA); documentary (MFA); e-commerce technology (MS); experience design (MA); film and television (MS); film and television directing (MFA); game design (MFA); game programming (MS); health informatics (MS); human centered design (PhD); human-computer interaction (MS); information systems (MS); network engineering and security (MS); product innovation and computing (MS); screenwriting (MFA); software engineering (MS); JD/MS. *Program availability:* Part-time, evening/weekend, online learning. *Degree requirements:* For master's, thesis (for some programs); for doctorate, comprehensive exam, thesis/dissertation. *Entrance requirements:* For master's, GRE or GMAT (for MS in computational finance only), bachelor's degree, resume (MS in predictive analytics only), IT experience (MS in information technology project management only), portfolio review (all MFA programs and MA in animation); for doctorate, GRE, master's degree in computer science. Additional exam requirements/recommendations for international students: Required—TOEFL (minimum score 590 paper-based; 80 iBT), IELTS (minimum score 6.5), PTE (minimum score 53). *Application deadline:* For fall admission, 8/1 priority date for domestic students, 6/15 priority date for international students; for winter admission, 12/1 priority date for domestic students, 10/15 priority date for international students; for spring admission, 3/1 priority date for domestic students, 1/15 priority date for international students; for summer admission, 5/1 for domestic students, 4/15 for international students. Applications are processed on a rolling basis. Application fee: $25. Electronic applications accepted. *Expenses:* Contact institution. *Financial support:* Fellowships with full tuition reimbursements, research assistantships with full and partial tuition reimbursements, teaching assistantships with full and partial tuition reimbursements, Federal Work-Study, scholarships/grants, tuition waivers (full and partial), and unspecified assistantships available. Support available to part-time students. Financial award application deadline: 4/20; financial award applicants required to submit FAFSA. *Faculty research:* Data mining, computer science, human-computer interaction, security, animation and film. *Unit head:* Elly Kafritsas-Wessels, Communications Manager, 312-362-5816, Fax: 312-362-5185, E-mail: ekafrits@cdm.depaul.edu. *Application contact:* Office of Admission, 312-362-8714, E-mail: admission@cdm.depaul.edu.
Website: http://cdm.depaul.edu

DigiPen Institute of Technology, Graduate Programs, Redmond, WA 98052. Offers computer science (MS); digital art and animation (MFA). *Program availability:* Part-time. *Faculty:* 36 full-time (8 women), 16 part-time/adjunct (1 woman). *Students:* 44

full-time (7 women), 30 part-time (6 women); includes 31 minority (1 Black or African American, non-Hispanic/Latino; 23 Asian, non-Hispanic/Latino; 5 Hispanic/Latino; 2 Two or more races, non-Hispanic/Latino), 15 international. Average age 28. 122 applicants, 37% accepted, 30 enrolled. In 2017, 17 master's awarded. *Degree requirements:* For master's, comprehensive exam (for some programs), thesis (for some programs). *Entrance requirements:* For master's, GRE General Test (for MSCS), art portfolio (for MFA); official transcripts from all post-secondary education including final transcript indicating degree earned, statement of purpose, and 2 letters of recommendation. Additional exam requirements/recommendations for international students: Required—TOEFL (minimum score 550 paper-based; 80 iBT). *Application deadline:* For fall admission, 2/1 priority date for domestic and international students; for spring admission, 7/1 for domestic and international students. Applications are processed on a rolling basis. Application fee: $60. Electronic applications accepted. *Expenses:* Contact institution. *Financial support:* Fellowships, career-related internships or fieldwork, and scholarships/grants available. Financial award application deadline: 5/1; financial award applicants required to submit FAFSA. *Faculty research:* Procedural modeling, computer graphics and visualization, human-computer interaction, fuzzy numbers and fuzzy analysis, modeling under spistemic uncertainty, nonlinear image processing, mathematical representation of surfaces, advanced computer graphic rendering techniques, mathematical physics, computer music and sound synthesis. *Unit head:* Angela Kugler, Senior Vice President, 425-895-4438, Fax: 425-558-0378, E-mail: akugler@digipen.edu. *Application contact:* Danial Powers, Director of Admissions, 425-629-5071, Fax: 425-558-0378, E-mail: dpowers@digipen.edu.

Drexel University, Westphal College of Media Arts and Design, Program in Digital Media, Philadelphia, PA 19104-2875. Offers MS, PhD. *Degree requirements:* For master's, thesis (including oral presentation, written statement, and copy of completed media work). *Entrance requirements:* For master's, interview. Additional exam requirements/recommendations for international students: Required—TOEFL. Electronic applications accepted.

East Tennessee State University, School of Graduate Studies, College of Business and Technology, Department of Engineering, Engineering Technology, and Surveying, Johnson City, TN 37614. Offers technology (MS). *Program availability:* Part-time. *Degree requirements:* For master's, comprehensive exam, thesis optional, capstone. *Entrance requirements:* For master's, bachelor's degree in technical or related area, minimum GPA of 3.0, undergraduate course in probability and statistics. Additional exam requirements/recommendations for international students: Required—TOEFL (minimum score 550 paper-based; 79 iBT). *Application deadline:* For fall admission, 6/1 for domestic students, 4/29 for international students; for spring admission, 11/1 for domestic students, 9/29 for international students. Application fee: $55 ($65 for international students). Electronic applications accepted. *Financial support:* Research assistantships with full tuition reimbursements, career-related internships or fieldwork, institutionally sponsored loans, scholarships/grants, and unspecified assistantships available. Financial award application deadline: 7/1; financial award applicants required to submit FAFSA. *Faculty research:* Computer-integrated manufacturing, alternative energy, sustainability, CAD/CAM, organizational change. *Unit head:* Dr. Keith V. Johnson, Chair, 423-439-7813, Fax: 423-439-7750, E-mail: johnsonk@etsu.edu. *Application contact:* Moin Uddin, Graduate Coordinator, 423-439-4164, E-mail: uddinm@etsu.edu.
Website: http://www.etsu.edu/cbat/applieddesign/

Emily Carr University of Art + Design, Program in Digital Media, Vancouver, BC V5T 0C6, Canada. Offers MDM. *Degree requirements:* For master's, internship. *Entrance requirements:* For master's, portfolio, minimum undergraduate B+ average, 3 reference letters. Additional exam requirements/recommendations for international students: Required—TOEFL (minimum score 93 iBT), IELTS (minimum score 6.5), PTE (minimum score 62). Electronic applications accepted.

Full Sail University, Game Design Master of Science Program - Campus, Winter Park, FL 32792-7437. Offers MS.

Georgia Institute of Technology, Graduate Studies, Ivan Allen College of Liberal Arts, School of Literature, Media, and Communication, Atlanta, GA 30332-0001. Offers digital media (MS, PhD). *Program availability:* Part-time. Terminal master's awarded for partial completion of doctoral program. *Degree requirements:* For master's, thesis optional, project studio, paid internship, responsible conduct of research training; for doctorate, comprehensive exam, thesis/dissertation, portfolio review, responsible conduct of research training. *Entrance requirements:* For master's and doctorate, GRE, three letters of recommendation, transcripts from each college/university attended, design portfolio, statement of purpose. Additional exam requirements/recommendations for international students: Required—TOEFL (minimum score 650 paper-based; 114 iBT). Electronic applications accepted. *Faculty research:* New media studies.

Georgian Court University, School of Business and Digital Media, Lakewood, NJ 08701-2697. Offers business (MBA); business essentials (Certificate); nonprofit management (Certificate). *Program availability:* Part-time, evening/weekend. *Faculty:* 6 full-time (3 women), 11 part-time/adjunct (3 women). *Students:* 29 full-time (19 women), 31 part-time (24 women); includes 17 minority (7 Black or African American, non-Hispanic/Latino; 3 Asian, non-Hispanic/Latino; 4 Hispanic/Latino; 3 Two or more races, non-Hispanic/Latino), 2 international. Average age 31. 54 applicants, 65% accepted, 21 enrolled. In 2017, 33 master's, 7 other advanced degrees awarded. *Entrance requirements:* For master's, GMAT or CPA exam, 3 letters of recommendation. Additional exam requirements/recommendations for international students: Required—TOEFL (minimum score 550 paper-based). *Application deadline:* For fall admission, 8/15 priority date for domestic students, 5/1 for international students; for spring admission, 1/15 priority date for domestic students, 10/1 for international students. Applications are processed on a rolling basis. Application fee: $40. Electronic applications accepted. *Expenses: Tuition:* Part-time $839 per credit. *Required fees:* $248 per semester. Tuition and fees vary according to campus/location and program. *Financial support:* Scholarships/grants, health care benefits, and unspecified assistantships available. Financial award application deadline: 4/15; financial award applicants required to submit FAFSA. *Unit head:* Dr. Cathleen McQuillen, Dean, 732-987-2623, Fax: 732-987-2024, E-mail: cmcquillen@georgian.edu. *Application contact:* Patrick Givens, Director of Graduate and Professional Studies Admissions, 732-987-2736, Fax: 732-987-2000, E-mail: gps@georgian.edu.
Website: http://georgian.edu/academics/school-of-business/

Goucher College, MA and MFA Programs, Baltimore, MD 21204-2794. Offers art and technology (MFA); arts administration (MA); cultural sustainability (MA); digital arts (MA); historic preservation (MA); nonfiction (MFA). *Program availability:* Part-time, evening/weekend, blended/hybrid learning. *Degree requirements:* For master's, thesis, e-portfolio. *Entrance requirements:* For master's, digital portfolio (for MA, MFA in digital arts); writing sample (for MFA in creative nonfiction). Additional exam requirements/recommendations for international students: Required—TOEFL (minimum score 550 paper-based; 80 iBT). *Application deadline:* Applications are processed on a rolling basis. Application fee: $75. Electronic applications accepted. *Expenses:* Contact institution. *Financial support:* Scholarships/grants and unspecified assistantships available. Financial award application deadline: 4/15; financial award applicants required to submit FAFSA. *Unit head:* Leslie Rubinkowski, Acting Assistant Provost for Limited Residency Graduate Programs, 410-337-6200, E-mail: leslie.rubinkowski@goucher.edu. *Application contact:* Carlton E. Surbeck, III, Director of Admissions, 410-337-6100, Fax: 410-337-6200, E-mail: admissions@goucher.edu.
Website: http://www.goucher.edu/grad

Indiana University–Purdue University Indianapolis, Herron School of Art and Design, Indianapolis, IN 46202. Offers art therapy (MA); visual art (MFA), including ceramics, furniture design, painting and drawing, photography and intermedia, printmaking, sculpture; visual communication design (MFA). *Degree requirements:* For master's, thesis. *Entrance requirements:* For master's, personal statement, resume, recommendations, portfolio, transcripts (18 credit hours of studio art and 12 credit hours of psychology, including 3 credit hours of developmental psychology and 3 credit hours of abnormal psychology for MA). Additional exam requirements/recommendations for international students: Recommended—TOEFL (minimum score 550 paper-based; 79 iBT), IELTS (minimum score 6.5). Electronic applications accepted. *Expenses:* Contact institution. *Faculty research:* Contemporary digital narratives for the homoerotic trope; sound articulated 3D print; neuroscience, art and related therapeutics; automotive and aeronautical design and fabrication; technological detritus.

International Technological University, Program in Digital Arts, San Jose, CA 95134. Offers MA. *Program availability:* Part-time. *Degree requirements:* For master's, capstone project. *Entrance requirements:* Additional exam requirements/recommendations for international students: Required—TOEFL, IELTS. Electronic applications accepted.

Lindenwood University–Belleville, Graduate Programs, Belleville, IL 62226. Offers business administration (MBA); communications (MA), including digital and multimedia, media management, promotions, training and development; counseling (MA); criminal justice administration (MS); education (MA); healthcare administration (MS); human resource management (MS); school administration (MA); teaching (MAT).

Lynn University, Eugene M. and Christine E. Lynn College of Communication and Design, Boca Raton, FL 33431-5598. Offers communication and media (MS), including design strategies for Web development, digital media, media studies and practice; digital media (Certificate); graphic and Web design (MFA); visual effects animation (MFA); Web design and technology (MS). *Program availability:* Part-time, evening/weekend. *Faculty:* 14 full-time (9 women), 7 part-time/adjunct (1 woman). *Students:* 35 full-time (21 women), 33 part-time (13 women); includes 31 minority (12 Black or African American, non-Hispanic/Latino; 2 American Indian or Alaska Native, non-Hispanic/Latino; 2 Asian, non-Hispanic/Latino; 14 Hispanic/Latino; 1 Two or more races, non-Hispanic/Latino), 12 international. Average age 27. 59 applicants, 92% accepted, 44 enrolled. In 2017, 17 master's awarded. *Degree requirements:* For master's, thesis (for some programs), completion of degree in four calendar years; minimum cumulative GPA of 3.0 and C grade or higher in each course; orientation seminar (one credit); 36 credits of foundation and specialization or a thesis. *Entrance requirements:* For master's, bachelor's degree from accredited institution, minimum undergraduate GPA of 3.0, official undergraduate transcripts, letter of recommendation from academic or professional source, writing sample demonstrating capacity to perform at graduate level. Additional exam requirements/recommendations for international students: Required—TOEFL (minimum score 550 paper-based; 80 iBT), IELTS (minimum score 6.5). *Application deadline:* For fall admission, 8/18 for domestic students, 8/4 for international students; for spring admission, 12/15 for domestic students, 12/1 for international students; for summer admission, 4/17 for domestic students, 4/3 for international students. Applications are processed on a rolling basis. Application fee: $45. Electronic applications accepted. *Expenses:* $740 per credit. *Financial support:* Career-related internships or fieldwork, Federal Work-Study, institutionally sponsored loans, scholarships/grants, tuition waivers (partial), and unspecified assistantships available. Support available to part-time students. Financial award application deadline: 8/1; financial award applicants required to submit FAFSA. *Unit head:* Dr. David L. Jaffe, Dean, 561-237-7099, Fax: 561-237-7097, E-mail: djaffe@lynn.edu. *Application contact:* Steven Pruitt, Director of Graduate Admission, 561-237-7834, Fax: 561-237-7100, E-mail: admission@lynn.edu.
Website: https://www.lynn.edu/academics/colleges-schools/communication-and-design

Michigan State University, The Graduate School, College of Communication Arts and Sciences, Department of Telecommunication, Information Studies, and Media, East Lansing, MI 48824. Offers digital media arts and technology (MA); information and telecommunication management (MA); information, policy and society (MA); serious game design (MA). *Entrance requirements:* Additional exam requirements/recommendations for international students: Required—TOEFL. Electronic applications accepted.

Minneapolis College of Art and Design, Certificate Programs, Minneapolis, MN 55404-4347. Offers graphic design (Certificate); media (Certificate); sustainable design (Certificate). *Program availability:* Part-time, 100% online, blended/hybrid learning. *Faculty:* 42 full-time (29 women). *Students:* 29 full-time (21 women), 5 part-time (all women); includes 6 minority (2 Black or African American, non-Hispanic/Latino; 1 Asian, non-Hispanic/Latino; 3 Hispanic/Latino), 1 international. In 2017, 15 Certificates awarded. *Degree requirements:* For Certificate, final project. *Entrance requirements:* For degree, resume, portfolio, letter of recommendation. Additional exam requirements/recommendations for international students: Required—TOEFL (minimum score 550 paper-based; 79 iBT). *Application deadline:* For fall admission, 1/15 for domestic and international students; for spring admission, 10/15 for domestic and international students. Application fee: $50. Electronic applications accepted. *Expenses: Tuition:* Full-time $38,670. *Required fees:* $450. One-time fee: $300 full-time. *Financial support:* Career-related internships or fieldwork and scholarships/grants available. Financial award application deadline: 3/15; financial award applicants required to submit FAFSA. *Faculty research:* Visual arts. *Unit head:* Lara Roy, Senior Director of Continuing Education, 612-874-3778, E-mail: continuing_education@mcad.edu.
Website: http://www.mcad.edu/showPage.php?pageID-1216

New Mexico Highlands University, Graduate Studies, School of Business, Media and Technology, Department of Media Arts and Technology, Las Vegas, NM 87701. Offers media arts and computer science (MA), including media arts.

The New School, Parsons School of Design, Program in Design and Technology, New York, NY 10011. Offers MFA. Program also offered at Paris, France campus. *Program availability:* Part-time. *Faculty:* 10 full-time (5 women), 43 part-time/adjunct (18 women). *Students:* 177 full-time (125 women), 2 part-time (1 woman); includes 28 minority (9 Black or African American, non-Hispanic/Latino; 1 American Indian or Alaska Native, non-Hispanic/Latino; 10 Asian, non-Hispanic/Latino; 7 Hispanic/Latino; 1 Two or more races, non-Hispanic/Latino), 131 international. Average age 26. 394 applicants, 69% accepted, 97 enrolled. In 2017, 75 master's awarded. *Degree requirements:* For master's, thesis or alternative. *Entrance requirements:* For master's, transcripts, resume, statement of purpose, recommendation letters, portfolio, interview. Additional exam requirements/recommendations for international students: Required—TOEFL (minimum score 92 iBT), IELTS (minimum score 7), PTE (minimum score 63). *Application deadline:* For fall admission, 1/1 for domestic students, 1/1 priority date for international students; for summer admission, 1/1 priority date for domestic and international students. Applications are processed on a rolling basis. Application fee:

$50. Electronic applications accepted. *Expenses:* $24,922 per semester full-time, $1,744 per credit part-time. *Financial support:* In 2017–18, 97 students received support, including 16 teaching assistantships (averaging $6,140 per year); career-related internships or fieldwork, Federal Work-Study, scholarships/grants, and travel funding; tuition waivers for students who are also New School employees also available. Support available to part-time students. Financial award application deadline: 2/1; financial award applicants required to submit FAFSA. *Unit head:* John Sharp, Program Director, E-mail: sharp@newschool.edu. *Application contact:* Courtney Malenius, Director of Graduate Admission, 212-229-5150 Ext. 4011, E-mail: thinkparsonsgrad@newschool.edu.
Website: https://www.newschool.edu/parsons/mfa-design-technology/

New York Institute of Technology, College of Arts and Sciences, Department of Digital Art and Design, Old Westbury, NY 11568-8000. Offers computer graphics (MFA), including animation, fine arts and technology, graphic design. *Program availability:* Part-time, evening/weekend. *Faculty:* 7 full-time (4 women), 6 part-time/adjunct (2 women). *Students:* 35 full-time (24 women), 12 part-time (7 women); includes 7 minority (4 Black or African American, non-Hispanic/Latino; 1 Asian, non-Hispanic/Latino; 2 Hispanic/Latino), 35 international. Average age 26. 37 applicants, 73% accepted, 9 enrolled. In 2017, 27 master's awarded. *Degree requirements:* For master's, thesis. *Entrance requirements:* For master's, BFA or equivalent; minimum undergraduate GPA of 3.0; digital portfolio. Additional exam requirements/recommendations for international students: Required—TOEFL (minimum score 79 iBT), IELTS (minimum score 6). *Application deadline:* For fall admission, 6/1 for domestic and international students. Applications are processed on a rolling basis. Application fee: $50. Electronic applications accepted. *Expenses:* $1,285 per credit plus fees. *Financial support:* Career-related internships or fieldwork, Federal Work-Study, scholarships/grants, tuition waivers (full and partial), and unspecified assistantships available. Support available to part-time students. Financial award application deadline: 2/15; financial award applicants required to submit FAFSA. *Faculty research:* Graphic design, animation, art and technology, virtual reality, sculpture. *Unit head:* Terry Nauheim, Department Chair, 516-686-7881, Fax: 212-261-1742, E-mail: tnauheim@nyit.edu. *Application contact:* Alice Dolitsky, Director, Graduate Admissions, 516-686-7520, Fax: 516-686-1116, E-mail: nyitgrad@nyit.edu.
Website: http://www.nyit.edu/departments/digital_art_and_design

North Carolina Agricultural and Technical State University, School of Graduate Studies, School of Technology, Department of Graphic Communication Systems and Technological Studies, Greensboro, NC 27411. Offers graphic communication systems (MSTM); technology education (MAT). *Accreditation:* NCATE (one or more programs are accredited). *Program availability:* Part-time, evening/weekend. *Degree requirements:* For master's, comprehensive exam, thesis or alternative, qualifying exam. *Entrance requirements:* For master's, GRE General Test, minimum GPA of 3.0.

North Carolina State University, Graduate School, College of Humanities and Social Sciences, Program in Communication, Rhetoric, and Digital Media, Raleigh, NC 27695. Offers PhD.

Northern Vermont University–Johnson, Program in Studio Arts, Johnson, VT 05656. Offers ceramics (MFA); digital media (MFA); drawing (MFA); painting (MFA); photography (MFA); printmaking (MFA); sculpture (MFA). *Program availability:* Part-time, online learning. *Faculty:* 3 full-time (1 woman). *Students:* 5 full-time (3 women), 2 part-time (1 woman). In 2017, 2 master's awarded. *Degree requirements:* For master's, thesis. *Entrance requirements:* For master's, portfolio. Additional exam requirements/recommendations for international students: Required—TOEFL. *Application deadline:* For fall admission, 3/1 for domestic students, 2/1 for international students. Applications are processed on a rolling basis. Electronic applications accepted. *Expenses:* Contact institution. *Financial support:* Teaching assistantships and unspecified assistantships available. Support available to part-time students. Financial award application deadline: 3/1; financial award applicants required to submit FAFSA. *Application contact:* Catherine H. Higley, Administrative Assistant, 800-635-2356 Ext. 1244, Fax: 802-635-1248, E-mail: catherine.higley@jsc.edu.
Website: http://www.jsc.edu/academics/fine-arts-department/majors-and-minors/mfa-in-studio-arts/

The Ohio State University, Graduate School, College of Arts and Sciences, Division of Arts and Humanities, Department of Design, Columbus, OH 43210. Offers design (MA); design research and development (MFA); digital animation and interactive media (MFA). *Accreditation:* NASAD. *Program availability:* Part-time. *Faculty:* 16. *Students:* 25 (15 women), 8 international. Average age 28. In 2017, 10 master's awarded. *Entrance requirements:* For master's, GRE General Test (for all applicants with cumulative GPA below 3.0), portfolio. Additional exam requirements/recommendations for international students: Recommended—TOEFL (minimum score 550 paper-based; 79 iBT). *Application deadline:* For fall admission, 12/13 priority date for domestic students, 11/30 priority date for international students; for spring admission, 3/1 for domestic students, 2/1 for international students. Applications are processed on a rolling basis. Application fee: $60 ($70 for international students). Electronic applications accepted. *Financial support:* Fellowships, research assistantships, teaching assistantships, career-related internships or fieldwork, Federal Work-Study, institutionally sponsored loans, and unspecified assistantships available. Support available to part-time students. Financial award application deadline: 5/1. *Unit head:* Dr. Mary Anne Beecher, Chair, 614-688-6746, E-mail: beecher.17@osu.edu. *Application contact:* Graduate and Professional Admissions, 614-292-9444, Fax: 614-292-3895, E-mail: gpadmissions@osu.edu.
Website: http://design.osu.edu/

Old Dominion University, College of Arts and Letters, Program in Lifespan and Digital Communication, Norfolk, VA 23529. Offers MA. *Accreditation:* NASAD. *Program availability:* Part-time, evening/weekend. *Faculty:* 11 full-time (3 women). *Students:* 9 full-time (5 women), 16 part-time (12 women); includes 14 minority (7 Black or African American, non-Hispanic/Latino; 1 Asian, non-Hispanic/Latino; 3 Hispanic/Latino; 3 Two or more races, non-Hispanic/Latino), 1 international. Average age 34. 14 applicants, 86% accepted, 12 enrolled. In 2017, 5 master's awarded. *Degree requirements:* For master's, thesis or capstone project. *Entrance requirements:* For master's, GRE. Additional exam requirements/recommendations for international students: Required—TOEFL (minimum score 550 paper-based; 79 iBT). *Application deadline:* For fall admission, 6/15 for domestic students, 4/15 for international students. Applications are processed on a rolling basis. Application fee: $50. Electronic applications accepted. *Expenses:* $8,928 in-state tuition, $300 in-state fees. *Financial support:* In 2017–18, 10 students received support, including 10 research assistantships (averaging $10,000 per year), 10 teaching assistantships (averaging $10,000 per year); 10 assistantships (averaging $5000) also available. Financial award application deadline: 6/15. *Faculty research:* Lifespan digital media studies, lifespan relational communication, social media, screenwriting, media industries. *Unit head:* Dr. Thomas J. Socha, Graduate Program Director, 757-683-3833, E-mail: tsocha@odu.edu. *Application contact:* Dr. Dale Miller, Associate Dean for Research and Graduate Studies, 757-683-3866, E-mail: demiller@odu.edu.
Website: http://www.odu.edu/commtheatre/graduate#.WtdfPme-YSk

Purchase College, State University of New York, School of Art and Design, Purchase, NY 10577-1400. Offers art history/visual arts (MA); visual arts (MFA). *Accreditation:* NASAD. *Degree requirements:* For master's, thesis, exhibit. *Entrance requirements:* For master's, portfolio. *Application deadline:* For fall admission, 2/15 for domestic students. Applications are processed on a rolling basis. Application fee: $85. Electronic applications accepted. *Financial support:* Fellowships, teaching assistantships, Federal Work-Study, scholarships/grants, and tuition waivers (partial) available. Support available to part-time students. Financial award application deadline: 3/15; financial award applicants required to submit FAFSA. *Unit head:* Steven Lam, Director, 914-251-6750, Fax: 914-251-6793, E-mail: steven.lam@purchase.edu. *Application contact:* Garrett Marino, Associate Director of Admissions, 914-251-6316, Fax: 914-251-6314, E-mail: admissn@purchase.edu.
Website: https://www.purchase.edu/academics/art-and-design/

Purdue University, Graduate School, College of Technology, Department of Computer Graphics Technology, West Lafayette, IN 47907. Offers MS, PhD. *Faculty:* 20 full-time (5 women). *Students:* 33 full-time (13 women), 17 part-time (8 women); includes 6 minority (1 Black or African American, non-Hispanic/Latino; 2 American Indian or Alaska Native, non-Hispanic/Latino; 2 Asian, non-Hispanic/Latino; 1 Hispanic/Latino), 25 international. Average age 25. 40 applicants, 75% accepted, 20 enrolled. In 2017, 10 master's awarded. *Degree requirements:* For master's, thesis; for doctorate, thesis/dissertation. *Entrance requirements:* For master's, GRE (minimum scores: 50th percentile, 150 on verbal, 150 on quantitative, 4.0 analytical). Additional exam requirements/recommendations for international students: Required—TOEFL (minimum score 550 paper-based; 77 iBT); Recommended—TWE. *Application deadline:* For fall admission, 4/1 for domestic and international students; for spring admission, 10/1 for domestic students, 9/1 for international students; for summer admission, 4/1 for domestic students, 2/15 for international students. Applications are processed on a rolling basis. Application fee: $60 ($75 for international students). Electronic applications accepted. *Financial support:* Research assistantships and teaching assistantships available. *Unit head:* Nathan W. Hartman, Interim Head of the Graduate Program, 765-496-6104, E-mail: nhartman@purdue.edu. *Application contact:* Cathy Noerenberg, Graduate Contact, 765-496-6368, E-mail: cnoerenb@purdue.edu.
Website: http://www.tech.purdue.edu/cgt/

Rensselaer Polytechnic Institute, Graduate School, School of Humanities, Arts, and Social Sciences, Program in Electronic Arts, Troy, NY 12180-3590. Offers PhD. *Faculty:* 25 full-time (10 women), 9 part-time/adjunct (5 women). *Students:* 20 full-time (12 women), 3 part-time (2 women); includes 4 minority (1 Asian, non-Hispanic/Latino; 2 Hispanic/Latino; 1 Two or more races, non-Hispanic/Latino), 4 international. Average age 35. 29 applicants, 24% accepted, 5 enrolled. In 2017, 1 doctorate awarded. *Degree requirements:* For doctorate, comprehensive exam. *Entrance requirements:* For doctorate, portfolio, research proposal, writing sample. Additional exam requirements/recommendations for international students: Required—TOEFL (minimum score 570 paper-based; 88 iBT), IELTS (minimum score 6.5), PTE (minimum score 60). *Application deadline:* For fall admission, 1/1 priority date for domestic and international students. Applications are processed on a rolling basis. Application fee: $75. Electronic applications accepted. *Expenses: Tuition:* Full-time $52,550; part-time $2125 per credit hour. *Required fees:* $2890. *Financial support:* In 2017–18, research assistantships (averaging $23,000 per year), teaching assistantships with full tuition reimbursements (averaging $23,000 per year) were awarded; scholarships/grants also available. Financial award application deadline: 1/1. *Unit head:* Dr. Tomie Hahn, Graduate Program Director, 518-276-2379, E-mail: hahnt@rpi.edu.
Website: http://www.arts.rpi.edu/pl/graduate-programs

Rhode Island School of Design, Department of Digital and Media, Providence, RI 02903-2784. Offers MFA. *Faculty:* 2 full-time (0 women), 11 part-time/adjunct (5 women). *Students:* 19 full-time (9 women); includes 2 minority (1 Asian, non-Hispanic/Latino; 1 Two or more races, non-Hispanic/Latino), 10 international. Average age 26. 143 applicants, 18% accepted, 11 enrolled. In 2017, 15 master's awarded. *Degree requirements:* For master's, thesis, exhibition. *Entrance requirements:* For master's, portfolio, statement of purpose, 3 letters of recommendation. Additional exam requirements/recommendations for international students: Required—TOEFL (minimum score 580 paper-based; 93 iBT). *Application deadline:* For fall admission, 1/10 for domestic and international students. Application fee: $60. Electronic applications accepted. *Expenses: Tuition:* Full-time $48,210. *Required fees:* $260. *Financial support:* Fellowships, research assistantships, teaching assistantships, Federal Work-Study, scholarships/grants, and unspecified assistantships available. Financial award application deadline: 2/15; financial award applicants required to submit FAFSA. *Unit head:* Shona Kitchen, Department Head and Graduate Program Director, 401-454-6139, Fax: 401-277-4966, E-mail: digital@risd.edu. *Application contact:* Molly Pettengill, Assistant Director for Graduate Recruitment, 401-454-6312, Fax: 401-454-6309, E-mail: mpetteng@risd.edu.
Website: http://www.risd.edu/academics/digital-media/

Rochester Institute of Technology, Graduate Enrollment Services, College of Imaging Arts and Sciences, School of Design, MFA Program in Visual Communication Design, Rochester, NY 14623-5603. Offers MFA. *Accreditation:* NASAD. *Program availability:* Part-time. *Students:* 66 full-time (52 women), 39 part-time (29 women); includes 7 minority (2 Asian, non-Hispanic/Latino; 2 Hispanic/Latino; 3 Two or more races, non-Hispanic/Latino), 80 international. Average age 29. 186 applicants, 58% accepted, 29 enrolled. In 2017, 13 master's awarded. *Degree requirements:* For master's, thesis, thesis exhibition. *Entrance requirements:* For master's, GRE, portfolio, minimum GPA of 3.0 (recommended). Additional exam requirements/recommendations for international students: Required—TOEFL (minimum score 550 paper-based; 90 iBT), IELTS (minimum score 7), PTE (minimum score 58). *Application deadline:* For fall admission, 2/15 priority date for domestic and international students. Applications are processed on a rolling basis. Application fee: $65. Electronic applications accepted. *Expenses:* $1,815 per credit hour. *Financial support:* In 2017–18, 52 students received support. Teaching assistantships with partial tuition reimbursements available, career-related internships or fieldwork, scholarships/grants, and unspecified assistantships available. Support available to part-time students. Financial award applicants required to submit FAFSA. *Faculty research:* Motion graphics for design and interaction; experiential design for physical and digital environments; augmented and virtual reality applications within education, advertising and consumer products; visual design for user experience and interactive solutions. *Unit head:* Adam Smith, Graduate Program Director, 585-475-4552, Fax: 585-475-7533, E-mail: aesfaa@rit.edu. *Application contact:* Diane Ellison, Senior Associate Vice President, Graduate Enrollment Services, 585-475-2229, Fax: 585-475-7164, E-mail: gradinfo@rit.edu.
Website: http://cias.rit.edu/schools/design/graduate-visual-communication-design

Rochester Institute of Technology, Graduate Enrollment Services, College of Imaging Arts and Sciences, School of Film and Animation, MFA Program in Film and Animation, Rochester, NY 14623. Offers MFA. *Program availability:* Part-time. *Students:* 41 full-time (19 women), 12 part-time (6 women); includes 3 minority (1 Asian, non-Hispanic/Latino; 2 Hispanic/Latino), 33 international. Average age 26. 116 applicants, 14% accepted, 11 enrolled. In 2017, 4 master's awarded. *Degree requirements:* For master's, thesis. *Entrance requirements:* For master's, GRE, portfolio, minimum GPA of

3.0 (recommended). Additional exam requirements/recommendations for international students: Required—TOEFL (minimum score 550 paper-based; 82 iBT), IELTS (minimum score 6.5), PTE (minimum score 58). *Application deadline:* For fall admission, 2/15 priority date for domestic and international students. Applications are processed on a rolling basis. Application fee: $65. Electronic applications accepted. *Expenses:* $1,815 per credit hour. *Financial support:* In 2017–18, 31 students received support. Teaching assistantships with partial tuition reimbursements available, career-related internships or fieldwork, scholarships/grants, and unspecified assistantships available. Support available to part-time students. Financial award applicants required to submit FAFSA. *Faculty research:* 3-D printing, super 8 cameras, color and projection, gaming and storytelling, special effects including virtual reality. *Unit head:* Thomas Gasek, Graduate Program Director, 585-475-7403, E-mail: tdgpph@rit.edu. *Application contact:* Diane Ellison, Senior Associate Vice President, Graduate Enrollment Services, 585-475-2229, Fax: 585-475-7164, E-mail: gradinfo@rit.edu.
Website: http://cias.rit.edu/schools/film-animation/graduate-film-and-animation

Savannah College of Art and Design, Program in Animation, Savannah, GA 31402-3146. Offers MA, MFA. *Program availability:* Part-time, 100% online. *Faculty:* 32 full-time (6 women), 6 part-time/adjunct (3 women). *Students:* 207 full-time (111 women), 72 part-time (38 women); includes 49 minority (29 Black or African American, non-Hispanic/Latino; 8 Asian, non-Hispanic/Latino; 12 Hispanic/Latino), 123 international. Average age 26. 220 applicants, 53% accepted, 64 enrolled. In 2017, 51 master's awarded. *Degree requirements:* For master's, final project (for MA); thesis (for MFA). *Entrance requirements:* For master's, GRE (recommended), portfolio (submitted in digital format), audition or writing submission, resume, statement of purpose, two letters of recommendation. Additional exam requirements/recommendations for international students: Recommended—TOEFL (minimum score 550 paper-based; 85 iBT), IELTS (minimum score 6.5). *Application deadline:* For fall admission, 4/1 for domestic and international students. Applications are processed on a rolling basis. Application fee: $40. Electronic applications accepted. *Expenses: Tuition:* Full-time $36,765; part-time $817 per credit hour. One-time fee: $500. *Financial support:* Career-related internships or fieldwork, Federal Work-Study, and scholarships/grants available. Financial award application deadline: 4/1; financial award applicants required to submit FAFSA. *Unit head:* Greg Araya, Chair, Animation. *Application contact:* Jenny Jaquillard, Executive Director of Admissions, Recruitment and Events, 912-525-5100, Fax: 912-525-5985, E-mail: admission@scad.edu.
Website: http://www.scad.edu/academics/programs/animation

Savannah College of Art and Design, Program in Interactive Design and Game Development, Savannah, GA 31402-3146. Offers MA, MFA. *Program availability:* Part-time, 100% online. *Faculty:* 16 full-time (4 women), 4 part-time/adjunct (1 woman). *Students:* 74 full-time (28 women), 27 part-time (9 women); includes 11 minority (3 Black or African American, non-Hispanic/Latino; 6 Asian, non-Hispanic/Latino; 2 Hispanic/Latino), 58 international. Average age 27. 145 applicants, 41% accepted, 26 enrolled. In 2017, 34 master's awarded. *Degree requirements:* For master's, final project (for MA); thesis (for MFA). *Entrance requirements:* For master's, GRE (recommended), portfolio (submitted in digital format), audition or writing submission, resume, statement of purpose, two letters of recommendation. Additional exam requirements/recommendations for international students: Recommended—TOEFL (minimum score 550 paper-based; 85 iBT), IELTS (minimum score 6.5). *Application deadline:* For fall admission, 4/1 for domestic and international students. Applications are processed on a rolling basis. Application fee: $40. Electronic applications accepted. *Expenses: Tuition:* Full-time $36,765; part-time $817 per credit hour. One-time fee: $500. *Financial support:* Career-related internships or fieldwork, Federal Work-Study, and scholarships/grants available. Financial award application deadline: 4/1; financial award applicants required to submit FAFSA. *Unit head:* SuAnne Fu, Chair, Interactive Design and Game Development. *Application contact:* Jenny Jaquillard, Executive Director of Admissions, Recruitment and Events, 912-525-5100, Fax: 912-525-5985, E-mail: admission@scad.edu.
Website: http://www.scad.edu/academics/programs/interactive-design-and-game-development

Savannah College of Art and Design, Program in Motion Media Design, Savannah, GA 31402-3146. Offers MA, MFA. *Program availability:* Part-time, 100% online. *Faculty:* 16 full-time (3 women), 7 part-time/adjunct (5 women). *Students:* 49 full-time (29 women), 28 part-time (12 women); includes 12 minority (7 Black or African American, non-Hispanic/Latino; 1 Asian, non-Hispanic/Latino; 4 Hispanic/Latino), 38 international. Average age 30. 34 applicants, 53% accepted, 13 enrolled. In 2017, 23 master's awarded. *Degree requirements:* For master's, final project (for MA); thesis (for MFA). *Entrance requirements:* For master's, GRE (recommended), portfolio (submitted in digital format), audition or writing submission, resume, statement of purpose, two letters of recommendation. Additional exam requirements/recommendations for international students: Recommended—TOEFL (minimum score 550 paper-based; 85 iBT), IELTS (minimum score 6.5). *Application deadline:* For fall admission, 4/1 for domestic and international students. Applications are processed on a rolling basis. Application fee: $40. Electronic applications accepted. *Expenses: Tuition:* Full-time $36,765; part-time $817 per credit hour. One-time fee: $500. *Financial support:* Career-related internships or fieldwork, Federal Work-Study, and scholarships/grants available. Financial award application deadline: 4/1; financial award applicants required to submit FAFSA. *Unit head:* Kelly Carlton, Chair, Motion Media Design. *Application contact:* Jenny Jaquillard, Executive Director of Admissions, Recruitment and Events, 912-525-5100, Fax: 912-525-5985, E-mail: admission@scad.edu.
Website: http://www.scad.edu/academics/programs/motion-media-design

School of Visual Arts, Graduate Programs, Computer Art Department, New York, NY 10010-3994. Offers MFA. *Accreditation:* NASAD. *Degree requirements:* For master's, thesis, 60 credits, including all required courses; minimum GPA of 3.0; matriculation of two academic years. *Entrance requirements:* For master's, portfolio; 3-5 minute sample reel showing best work; statement of purpose; official transcript; 3 letters of recommendation; resume/curriculum vitae. Additional exam requirements/recommendations for international students: Required—TOEFL (minimum score 550 paper-based; 79 iBT). Electronic applications accepted. *Expenses:* Contact institution.

Stevens Institute of Technology, Graduate School, Charles V. Schaefer Jr. School of Engineering and Science, Department of Computer Science, Hoboken, NJ 07030. Offers computer graphics (Certificate), including computer graphics; computer science (MS, PhD); computer systems (Certificate), including computer systems; cybersecurity (MS); database management systems (Certificate), including databases; distributed systems (Certificate), including distributed systems; elements of computer science (Certificate), including cybersecurity; enterprise and cloud computing (MS); enterprise computing (Certificate), including enterprise and cloud computing; enterprise security and information assurance (Certificate), including enterprise security and information assurance; health informatics (Certificate), including health informatics; multimedia experience and management (Certificate), including multimedia experience and management; networks and systems administration (Certificate), including cloud computing; service oriented computing (Certificate), including service oriented computing. *Program availability:* Part-time, evening/weekend. *Faculty:* 20 full-time (4 women), 13 part-time/adjunct (3 women). *Students:* 462 full-time (100 women), 65 part-time (13 women); includes 27 minority (4 Black or African American, non-Hispanic/Latino; 22 Asian, non-Hispanic/Latino; 1 Hispanic/Latino), 427 international. Average age 25. 1,354 applicants, 57% accepted, 181 enrolled. In 2017, 269 master's, 7 doctorates, 8 other advanced degrees awarded. Terminal master's awarded for partial completion of doctoral program. *Degree requirements:* For master's, thesis optional, minimum B average in major field and overall; for doctorate, comprehensive exam (for some programs), thesis/dissertation; for Certificate, minimum B average. *Entrance requirements:* Additional exam requirements/recommendations for international students: Required—TOEFL (minimum score 74 iBT), IELTS (minimum score 6). *Application deadline:* For fall admission, 7/1 for domestic students, 4/15 for international students; for spring admission, 12/1 for domestic and international students. Applications are processed on a rolling basis. Application fee: $60. Electronic applications accepted. *Expenses: Tuition:* Full-time $34,494; part-time $1554 per credit. *Required fees:* $291 per semester. *Financial support:* Fellowships, research assistantships, teaching assistantships, career-related internships or fieldwork, Federal Work-Study, scholarships/grants, and unspecified assistantships available. Financial award application deadline: 2/15; financial award applicants required to submit FAFSA. *Faculty research:* Computer security, computer vision, dynamic scene analysis, privacy-preserving data mining, visualization. *Unit head:* Giuseppe Ateniese, Director, 201-216-3741, E-mail: gatenies@stevens.edu. *Application contact:* Graduate Admissions, 888-783-8367, Fax: 888-511-1306, E-mail: graduate@stevens.edu.
Website: https://www.stevens.edu/schaefer-school-engineering-science/departments/computer-science

Syracuse University, College of Visual and Performing Arts, MFA Program in Computer Art, Syracuse, NY 13244. Offers MFA. *Degree requirements:* For master's, thesis or alternative. *Entrance requirements:* For master's, portfolio, artist statement, three letters of recommendation, transcripts, personal statement/essay, resume. Additional exam requirements/recommendations for international students: Required—TOEFL (minimum score 100 iBT), IELTS. *Application deadline:* For fall admission, 2/1 priority date for domestic and international students. Application fee: $75. Electronic applications accepted. *Financial support:* Fellowships with full tuition reimbursements and teaching assistantships with tuition reimbursements available. Financial award application deadline: 1/1; financial award applicants required to submit FAFSA. *Faculty research:* Aesthetic possibilities of subject, genre, media technologies from personal points of view, strategies for making art in the video medium, including performance, narrative, documentary, site-specific, and multi-channel installation. *Unit head:* Prof. Heath Hanlin, Associate Professor, Computer Art and Animation/Program Coordinator, 315-443-1210, E-mail: hahanlin@syr.edu. *Application contact:* Caitlin Jarvis, Graduate Recruitment Specialist, 315-443-2769, E-mail: admissg@syr.edu.
Website: http://vpa.syr.edu/academics/transmedia/graduate/computer-art/

Texas State University, The Graduate College, College of Fine Arts and Communication, Program in Communication Design, San Marcos, TX 78666. Offers MFA. *Program availability:* Part-time. *Faculty:* 26 full-time (14 women), 4 part-time/adjunct (2 women). *Students:* 15 full-time (10 women), 20 part-time (14 women); includes 13 minority (1 Black or African American, non-Hispanic/Latino; 1 Asian, non-Hispanic/Latino; 9 Hispanic/Latino; 2 Two or more races, non-Hispanic/Latino), 4 international. Average age 33. 25 applicants, 28% accepted, 2 enrolled. In 2017, 7 master's awarded. *Degree requirements:* For master's, comprehensive exam, thesis. *Entrance requirements:* For master's, related baccalaureate degree from regionally-accredited institution with minimum GPA of 2.75 in last 60 hours of undergraduate course work, 3 letters of recommendation, academic and professional statement of purpose, online portfolio showcasing at least 20 works in communication design. Additional exam requirements/recommendations for international students: Required—TOEFL (minimum score 550 paper-based; 78 iBT), IELTS (minimum score 6), TOEFL (minimum iBT scores: 19 listening, 19 reading, 19 speaking, 18 writing). *Application deadline:* For fall admission, 3/31 for domestic and international students; for spring admission, 10/31 for domestic students, 10/1 for international students. Applications are processed on a rolling basis. Application fee: $40 ($90 for international students). Electronic applications accepted. *Expenses:* Tuition, state resident: full-time $7868; part-time $3934 per semester. Tuition, nonresident: full-time $17,828; part-time $8914 per semester. *Required fees:* $2092; $1435 per semester. Tuition and fees vary according to course load. *Financial support:* In 2017–18, 23 students received support, including 10 teaching assistantships (averaging $12,926 per year); research assistantships, Federal Work-Study, institutionally sponsored loans, scholarships/grants, and unspecified assistantships also available. Support available to part-time students. Financial award application deadline: 3/1; financial award applicants required to submit FAFSA. *Unit head:* Claudia Roeschmann, Graduate Advisor, 512-245-7450, E-mail: cr29@txstate.edu. *Application contact:* Dr. Andrea Golato, Dean of Graduate School, 512-245-2581, Fax: 512-245-8365, E-mail: gradcollege@txstate.edu.
Website: http://www.finearts.txstate.edu/Art/mfacomdes/

Universidad Autonoma de Guadalajara, Graduate Programs, Guadalajara, Mexico. Offers administrative law and justice (LL M); advertising and corporate communications (MA); architecture (M Arch); business (MBA); computational science (MCC); education (Ed M, Ed D); English-Spanish translation (MA); entrepreneurship and management (MBA); integrated management of digital animation (MA); international business (MIB); international corporate law (LL M); internet technologies (MS); manufacturing systems (MMS); occupational health (MS); philosophy (MA, PhD); power electronics (MS); quality systems (MQS); renewable energy (MS); social evaluation of projects (MBA); strategic market research (MBA); tax law (MA); teaching mathematics (MA).

Universidad de las Américas Puebla, Division of Graduate Studies, School of Humanities, Program in Information Design, Puebla, Mexico. Offers MA. *Program availability:* Part-time, evening/weekend. *Degree requirements:* For master's, one foreign language, thesis. *Entrance requirements:* Additional exam requirements/recommendations for international students: Required—TOEFL. *Faculty research:* Typography, project development, organizational image.

University of Alaska Fairbanks, College of Liberal Arts, Department of Art, Fairbanks, AK 99775-5640. Offers art (MFA); ceramics (MFA); computer art (MFA); drawing (MFA); painting (MFA); photography (MFA); printmaking (MFA); sculpture (MFA). *Program availability:* Part-time. *Degree requirements:* For master's, comprehensive exam, oral defense of project or thesis. *Entrance requirements:* For master's, portfolio of work including about 20 slides or appropriate equivalent depending on field of study. Additional exam requirements/recommendations for international students: Required—TOEFL (minimum score 550 paper-based; 79 iBT), IELTS (minimum score 6.5). Electronic applications accepted. *Faculty research:* Computer art, survey of arts in Alaska, found object art, visualization and animation, painting from the wilderness.

University of California, Santa Cruz, Division of Graduate Studies, Division of the Arts, Department of Film and Digital Media, Santa Cruz, CA 95064. Offers PhD. *Degree requirements:* For doctorate, one foreign language, thesis/dissertation, qualifying exams. *Entrance requirements:* For doctorate, GRE. Additional exam requirements/recommendations for international students: Required—TOEFL (minimum score 550 paper-based; 83 iBT); Recommended—IELTS (minimum score 8). Electronic

applications accepted. *Faculty research:* Integrating critical and creative practice, working across media, pursuing new modes of social and political engagement, fostering global cultural citizenship.

University of California, Santa Cruz, Division of Graduate Studies, Division of the Arts, Program in Digital Arts and New Media, Santa Cruz, CA 95064. Offers MFA. *Degree requirements:* For master's, thesis, written paper. *Entrance requirements:* Additional exam requirements/recommendations for international students: Required— TOEFL (minimum score 550 paper-based; 83 iBT); Recommended—IELTS (minimum score 8). Electronic applications accepted. *Faculty research:* Mechatronics, participatory culture, performative technologies, playable media.

University of Central Arkansas, Graduate School, College of Fine Arts and Communication, Program in Digital Filmmaking, Conway, AR 72035-0001. Offers MFA. *Accreditation:* NASAD. *Degree requirements:* For master's, thesis. *Entrance requirements:* For master's, GRE General Test, minimum GPA of 2.7. Additional exam requirements/recommendations for international students: Required—TOEFL (minimum score 550 paper-based). Electronic applications accepted.

University of Central Florida, College of Arts and Humanities, School of Visual Arts and Design, Orlando, FL 32816. Offers digital media (MA); emerging media (MFA), including animation and visual effects, digital media, entrepreneurial digital cinema, studio art and the computer. *Program availability:* Part-time. *Students:* 38 full-time (13 women), 9 part-time (3 women); includes 16 minority (6 Black or African American, non-Hispanic/Latino; 2 Asian, non-Hispanic/Latino; 8 Hispanic/Latino), 3 international. Average age 30. 61 applicants, 54% accepted, 20 enrolled. In 2017, 8 master's awarded. *Degree requirements:* For master's, comprehensive exam, thesis or alternative. *Entrance requirements:* For master's, GRE, letter of recommendation. Additional exam requirements/recommendations for international students: Required— TOEFL. *Application deadline:* For fall admission, 7/1 for domestic students. Application fee: $30. Electronic applications accepted. *Expenses:* Tuition, state resident: part-time $288.16 per credit hour. Tuition, nonresident: part-time $1073.31 per credit hour. Tuition and fees vary according to program. *Financial support:* In 2017–18, 17 students received support, including 7 fellowships with partial tuition reimbursements available (averaging $10,000 per year), 3 research assistantships with partial tuition reimbursements available (averaging $6,355 per year), 15 teaching assistantships with partial tuition reimbursements available (averaging $8,208 per year); scholarships/ grants, health care benefits, and unspecified assistantships also available. Financial award application deadline: 3/1; financial award applicants required to submit FAFSA. *Unit head:* Dr. Rudy McDaniel, Director, 407-823-3145, E-mail: rudy@ucf.edu. *Application contact:* Associate Director, Graduate Admissions, 407-823-2766, Fax: 407-823-6442, E-mail: gradadmissions@ucf.edu.
Website: http://svad.cah.ucf.edu/

University of Denver, Division of Arts, Humanities and Social Sciences, Program in Emergent Digital Practices, Denver, CO 80208. Offers MA, MFA. *Program availability:* Part-time. *Students:* Average age 33. 121 applicants, 86% accepted, 70 enrolled. In 2017, 87 master's awarded. *Degree requirements:* For master's, thesis (for some programs), project or thesis. *Entrance requirements:* For master's, GRE General Test, bachelor's degree, transcripts, personal statement, resume or curriculum vitae, three letters of recommendation. Additional exam requirements/recommendations for international students: Required—TOEFL (minimum score 620 paper-based; 105 iBT). *Application deadline:* For fall admission, 1/20 priority date for domestic and international students. Applications are processed on a rolling basis. Application fee: $65. Electronic applications accepted. *Expenses:* Contact institution. *Financial support:* In 2017–18, 10 students received support, including 4 teaching assistantships with tuition reimbursements available (averaging $7,500 per year); Federal Work-Study, scholarships/grants, and unspecified assistantships also available. Financial award application deadline: 2/15; financial award applicants required to submit FAFSA. *Faculty research:* Bio-art, humane games, creative coding, audio/video art and animation, online activism. *Unit head:* Dr. Rafael Fajardo, Associate Professor and Director, 303-871-7716, E-mail: rfajardo@du.edu. *Application contact:* Dr. Laleh Mehran, Assistant Professor and Graduate Director, 303-871-3264, E-mail: laleh.mehran@du.edu.
Website: http://www.du.edu/ahss/edp

University of Florida, Graduate School, College of The Arts, School of Art and Art History, Gainesville, FL 32611. Offers art (MA), including digital arts and sciences; art education (MA); art history (MA, PhD); museology (MA), including historic preservation. *Accreditation:* NASAD. *Program availability:* Online learning. *Degree requirements:* For master's, project or thesis (MFA); 1 foreign language (MA in art history); for doctorate, 2 foreign languages, comprehensive exam, thesis/dissertation. *Entrance requirements:* For master's, GRE General Test, portfolio (MFA), writing sample (MA), minimum GPA 3.0; for doctorate, GRE General Test, minimum GPA of 3.0. Additional exam requirements/recommendations for international students: Required—TOEFL (minimum score 550 paper-based; 80 iBT), IELTS (minimum score 6). Electronic applications accepted. *Faculty research:* Studio production, art historical studies of style context.

University of Florida, Graduate School, Herbert Wertheim College of Engineering and College of Liberal Arts and Sciences, Department of Computer and Information Science and Engineering, Gainesville, FL 32611. Offers computer engineering (ME, MS, PhD); computer science (MS); digital arts and sciences (MS). *Program availability:* Part-time, online learning. Terminal master's awarded for partial completion of doctoral program. *Degree requirements:* For master's, comprehensive exam, thesis optional; for doctorate, comprehensive exam, thesis/dissertation. *Entrance requirements:* For master's and doctorate, minimum GPA of 3.0. Additional exam requirements/ recommendations for international students: Required—TOEFL (minimum score 550 paper-based; 80 iBT), IELTS (minimum score 6). Electronic applications accepted. *Faculty research:* Computer systems and computer networking; high-performance computing and algorithm; database and machine learning; computer graphics, vision, and intelligent systems; human center computing and digital art.

University of Maryland, Baltimore County, The Graduate School, College of Arts, Humanities and Social Sciences, Department of Visual Arts, MFA in Intermedia and Digital Arts Program, Baltimore, MD 21250. Offers MFA. *Faculty:* 24 full-time (13 women), 15 part-time/adjunct (7 women). *Students:* 15 full-time (8 women); includes 4 minority (1 Black or African American, non-Hispanic/Latino; 1 Asian, non-Hispanic/ Latino; 2 Two or more races, non-Hispanic/Latino). Average age 30. 22 applicants, 27% accepted, 4 enrolled. In 2017, 3 master's awarded. *Degree requirements:* For master's, oral defense, exhibition, written thesis. *Entrance requirements:* For master's, minimum GPA of 3.0, portfolio. Additional exam requirements/recommendations for international students: Required—TOEFL. *Application deadline:* For fall admission, 2/1 for domestic and international students. Applications are processed on a rolling basis. Application fee: $50. Electronic applications accepted. *Expenses:* Contact institution. *Financial*

support: In 2017–18, 16 students received support, including 16 research assistantships with partial tuition reimbursements available (averaging $22,325 per year); institutionally sponsored loans, scholarships/grants, health care benefits, and unspecified assistantships also available. Financial award application deadline: 2/1. *Faculty research:* Interactive art, video, electronic media, photography, animation, print media, sound, performance, installation, cinematic arts. *Unit head:* Prof. Lisa Moren, Graduate Program Director, 410-455-2490, Fax: 410-455-1053, E-mail: lmoren@umbc.edu.
Website: http://imda.umbc.edu

University of Montana, Graduate School, College of Visual and Performing Arts, School of Media Arts, Missoula, MT 59812. Offers digital filmmaking (MFA); integrated digital media (MFA).

University of Pennsylvania, School of Engineering and Applied Science, Department of Computer and Information Science, Philadelphia, PA 19104. Offers computer and information science (MSE, PhD); computer and information technology (MCIT); computer graphics and game technology (MSE). *Program availability:* Part-time. *Faculty:* 52 full-time (8 women), 8 part-time/adjunct (0 women). *Students:* 272 full-time (78 women), 116 part-time (36 women); includes 45 minority (4 Black or African American, non-Hispanic/Latino; 32 Asian, non-Hispanic/Latino; 5 Hispanic/Latino; 4 Two or more races, non-Hispanic/Latino), 245 international. Average age 26. 2,559 applicants, 14% accepted, 216 enrolled. In 2017, 130 master's, 15 doctorates awarded. Terminal master's awarded for partial completion of doctoral program. *Degree requirements:* For master's, comprehensive exam, thesis optional; for doctorate, comprehensive exam, thesis/dissertation. *Entrance requirements:* For master's and doctorate, GRE, bachelor's degree, letters of recommendation, resume, personal statement. Additional exam requirements/recommendations for international students: Required—TOEFL (minimum score 100 iBT), IELTS (minimum score 7). *Application deadline:* For fall admission, 12/15 priority date for domestic and international students. Application fee: $80. Electronic applications accepted. *Expenses:* $7,022 per course. *Faculty research:* Artificial intelligence, bioinformatics and computational biology, embedded and real-time systems, machine learning, security and information assurance. *Application contact:* William Fenton, Assistant Director of Graduate Admissions, 215-898-4542, Fax: 215-573-5577, E-mail: gradstudies@seas.upenn.edu.
Website: http://www.cis.upenn.edu/prospective-students/graduate/

University of Rhode Island, Graduate School, College of Arts and Sciences, Graduate School of Library and Information Studies, Kingston, RI 02881. Offers libraries, leadership and transforming communities (MLIS); organization of digital media (MLIS); school library media (MLIS); MLIS/MA; MLIS/MPA. *Accreditation:* ALA (one or more programs are accredited). *Program availability:* Part-time. *Faculty:* 4 full-time (all women). *Students:* 17 full-time (12 women), 85 part-time (74 women); includes 13 minority (2 Black or African American, non-Hispanic/Latino; 3 Asian, non-Hispanic/ Latino; 3 Hispanic/Latino; 1 Native Hawaiian or other Pacific Islander, non-Hispanic/ Latino; 4 Two or more races, non-Hispanic/Latino). 47 applicants, 89% accepted, 26 enrolled. In 2017, 41 master's awarded. *Entrance requirements:* For master's, GRE or MAT if undergraduate GPA below 3.3, 2 letters of recommendation. Additional exam requirements/recommendations for international students: Required—TOEFL. *Application deadline:* For fall admission, 6/15 for domestic students, 2/1 for international students; for spring admission, 10/15 for domestic students, 7/15 for international students; for summer admission, 3/15 for domestic students. Application fee: $65. Electronic applications accepted. *Expenses:* Tuition, state resident: full-time $12,706; part-time $786 per credit. Tuition, nonresident: full-time $25,216; part-time $1401 per credit. *Required fees:* $1598; $45 per credit. One-time fee: $30 part-time. *Financial support:* Research assistantships and teaching assistantships available. Financial award application deadline: 1/15; financial award applicants required to submit FAFSA. *Unit head:* Dr. Valerie Karno, Director, Graduate School of Library and Information Studies, 401-874-4682, Fax: 401-874-4127, E-mail: karno@uri.edu.
Website: http://www.uri.edu/artsci/lsc/

University of Southern California, Graduate School, School of Cinematic Arts, Division of Animation and Digital Arts, Los Angeles, CA 90089. Offers MFA. *Degree requirements:* For master's, thesis, digital media and research documentation. *Entrance requirements:* Additional exam requirements/recommendations for international students: Recommended—TOEFL. Electronic applications accepted. *Expenses:* Contact institution. *Faculty research:* Character animation, visual effects, motion graphics, documentary animation, experimental animation.

University of South Florida, St. Petersburg, College of Arts and Sciences, St. Petersburg, FL 33701. Offers digital journalism and design (MA); environmental science and policy (MA, MS); Florida studies (MLA); journalism and media studies (MA); liberal studies (MLA); psychology (MA). *Program availability:* Part-time, online learning. *Degree requirements:* For master's, comprehensive exam, thesis or project. *Entrance requirements:* For master's, GRE, LSAT, MCAT (varies by program), letter of intent, 3 letters of recommendation, writing samples, bachelor's degree from regionally-accredited institution with minimum GPA of 3.0 overall or in upper two years. Additional exam requirements/recommendations for international students: Required—TOEFL (minimum score 550 paper-based; 79 iBT); Recommended—IELTS. Electronic applications accepted.

University of Victoria, Faculty of Graduate Studies, Faculty of Fine Arts, Department of Visual Arts, Victoria, BC V8W 2Y2, Canada. Offers digital multimedia (MFA); drawing (MFA); painting (MFA); photography (MFA); sculpture (MFA); video (MFA). *Degree requirements:* For master's, exhibit, oral exam. *Entrance requirements:* For master's, portfolio, BFA. Additional exam requirements/recommendations for international students: Required—TOEFL (minimum score 575 paper-based), IELTS (minimum score 7). Electronic applications accepted.

Virginia International University, School of Computer Information Systems, Fairfax, VA 22030. Offers business intelligence (Graduate Certificate); business intelligence and data analytics (MIS); computer science (MS), including computer animation and gaming, cybersecurity, data management networking, intelligent systems, software applications development, software engineering; cybersecurity (MIS); data management (MIS); enterprise project management (MIS); health informatics (MIS); information assurance (MIS); information systems (Graduate Certificate); information systems management (MS, Graduate Certificate); information technology (MS); information technology audit and compliance (Graduate Certificate); knowledge management (MIS); software engineering (MS). *Program availability:* Part-time, online learning. *Entrance requirements:* For master's, bachelor's degree. Additional exam requirements/recommendations for international students: Required—TOEFL (minimum score 550 paper-based; 80 iBT), IELTS. Electronic applications accepted.

Graphic Design

Academy of Art University, Graduate Programs, School of Graphic Design, San Francisco, CA 94105-3410. Offers graphic design (MFA); graphic design and digital media (MA). *Accreditation:* NASAD. *Program availability:* Part-time, 100% online. *Faculty:* 6 full-time (2 women), 27 part-time/adjunct (13 women). *Students:* 187 full-time (134 women), 188 part-time (142 women); includes 51 minority (12 Black or African American, non-Hispanic/Latino; 1 American Indian or Alaska Native, non-Hispanic/Latino; 14 Asian, non-Hispanic/Latino; 20 Hispanic/Latino; 2 Native Hawaiian or other Pacific Islander, non-Hispanic/Latino; 2 Two or more races, non-Hispanic/Latino), 239 international. Average age 29. 146 applicants, 100% accepted, 97 enrolled. In 2017, 82 master's awarded. *Degree requirements:* For master's, final review. *Entrance requirements:* For master's, statement of intent; resume; portfolio/reel; official college transcripts. *Application deadline:* Applications are processed on a rolling basis. Application fee: $50. Electronic applications accepted. *Expenses: Tuition:* Part-time $982 per unit. *Financial support:* Career-related internships or fieldwork, Federal Work-Study, and scholarships/grants available. Financial award application deadline: 8/10; financial award applicants required to submit FAFSA. *Unit head:* 800-544-ARTS, E-mail: info@academyart.edu. *Application contact:* 800-544-ARTS, E-mail: info@academyart.edu.
Website: https://www.academyart.edu/academics/graphic-design

ArtCenter College of Design, Graduate Graphic Design Program, Pasadena, CA 91103. Offers MFA.

Atlantic University College, Program in Graphic Arts, Guaynabo, PR 00970. Offers digital graphic design (MGD). *Program availability:* Part-time. *Degree requirements:* For master's, thesis. *Entrance requirements:* For master's, minimum GPA of 3.0, 2 letters of recommendation, portfolio, interview. *Faculty research:* Digital design, technology.

Bob Jones University, Graduate Programs, Greenville, SC 29614. Offers accountancy (MS); Bible (MA); Bible translation (MA); Biblical studies (Certificate); broadcast management (MS); business administration (MBA); church history (MA, PhD); church ministries (MA); church music (MM); cinema and video production (MA); counseling (MS); curriculum and instruction (Ed D); divinity (M Div); dramatic production (MA); educational leadership (MS, Ed D, Ed S); elementary education (M Ed, MAT); English (M Ed, MA, MAT); fine arts (MA); graphic design (MA); history (M Ed, MA); illustration (MA); interpretative speech (MA); mathematics (M Ed, MAT); medical missions (Certificate); ministry (MM, D Min); multi-categorical special education (M Ed, MAT); music (M Ed); New Testament interpretation (PhD); Old Testament interpretation (PhD); orchestral instrument performance (MM); organ performance (MM); pastoral studies (MA); personnel services (MS, Ed S); piano pedagogy (MM); piano performance (MM); platform arts (MA); radio and television broadcasting (MS); rhetoric and public address (MA); secondary education (M Ed); studio art (MA); teaching Bible (MA); theology (MA, PhD); voice performance (MM); youth ministries (MA); M Div/MM.

Boston University, College of Fine Arts, School of Visual Arts, Boston, MA 02215. Offers art education (MA); graphic design (MFA); painting (MFA); sculpture (MFA); studio teaching (MA). *Faculty:* 17 full-time, 4 part-time/adjunct. *Students:* 161 full-time (139 women), 3 part-time (all women); includes 19 minority (2 Black or African American, non-Hispanic/Latino; 6 Asian, non-Hispanic/Latino; 9 Hispanic/Latino; 2 Two or more races, non-Hispanic/Latino), 37 international. Average age 30. 365 applicants, 27% accepted, 21 enrolled. In 2017, 85 master's awarded. *Entrance requirements:* For master's, portfolio. Additional exam requirements/recommendations for international students: Required—TOEFL (minimum score 90 iBT), IELTS (minimum score 7). *Application deadline:* For fall admission, 2/1 for domestic and international students. Applications are processed on a rolling basis. Application fee: $95. *Expenses:* Contact institution. *Financial support:* In 2017–18, 36 students received support. Fellowships, teaching assistantships, scholarships/grants, and unspecified assistantships available. Financial award application deadline: 2/1. *Unit head:* Lynne Allen, Director, 617-353-3371. *Application contact:* Jessica Caccamo, Assistant Director of Admissions, 617-353-3371, E-mail: visuarts@bu.edu.

Bowling Green State University, Graduate College, College of Arts and Sciences, School of Art, Bowling Green, OH 43403. Offers 2-D studio art (MA, MFA); 3-D studio art (MA, MFA); art education (MA); art history (MA); computer art (MA); design (MFA); digital arts (MFA); graphics (MFA). *Accreditation:* NASAD. *Program availability:* Part-time. *Degree requirements:* For master's, thesis or alternative, final exhibit (MFA). *Entrance requirements:* For master's, GRE General Test (for MA), slide portfolio (15-20 slides). Additional exam requirements/recommendations for international students: Required—TOEFL. Electronic applications accepted. *Faculty research:* Computer animation and virtual reality, Spanish still-life painting from 1600 to 1800, art and psychotherapy, Japanese wood-firing techniques in ceramics, non-toxic printmaking technologies.

Bradley University, The Graduate School, Slane College of Communications and Fine Arts, Department of Art, Peoria, IL 61625-0002. Offers ceramics (MA, MFA); drawing (MA, MFA); graphic design (MA, MFA); painting (MA, MFA); photography (MA, MFA); printmaking (MA, MFA); sculpture (MA, MFA). *Accreditation:* NASAD. *Program availability:* Part-time. *Degree requirements:* For master's, comprehensive exam, thesis, final exhibit. *Entrance requirements:* For master's, portfolio, 2 letters of recommendation. Additional exam requirements/recommendations for international students: Required—TOEFL (minimum score 550 paper-based; 79 iBT). Electronic applications accepted.

California College of the Arts, Graduate Programs, Design Program, San Francisco, CA 94107. Offers graphic design (MFA); industrial design (MFA); interaction design (MFA). *Accreditation:* NASAD. *Faculty:* 14 full-time (4 women), 40 part-time/adjunct (14 women). *Students:* 109 full-time (64 women); includes 18 minority (1 Black or African American, non-Hispanic/Latino; 12 Asian, non-Hispanic/Latino; 5 Hispanic/Latino), 64 international. Average age 26. 618 applicants, 35% accepted, 76 enrolled. In 2017, 54 master's awarded. *Degree requirements:* For master's, thesis, exhibit. *Entrance requirements:* For master's, appropriate bachelor's degree, portfolio, resume, letters of recommendation, transcripts. Additional exam requirements/recommendations for international students: Required—TOEFL, IELTS, or PTE. *Application deadline:* For fall admission, 1/31 priority date for domestic and international students. Applications are processed on a rolling basis. Application fee: $70. Electronic applications accepted. *Expenses:* Contact institution. *Financial support:* In 2017–18, fellowships (averaging $22,000 per year), teaching assistantships (averaging $2,000 per year) were awarded; career-related internships or fieldwork, Federal Work-Study, scholarships/grants, health care benefits, and unspecified assistantships also available. Financial award application deadline: 7/31; financial award applicants required to submit FAFSA. *Unit head:* Kristian Simsarian, Graduate Chair, 415-551-9283, Fax: 415-703-9539, E-mail:

ksimsarian@cca.edu. *Application contact:* Wes Fanelli, Assistant Director of Graduate Admissions, 415-703-9533, Fax: 415-703-9539, E-mail: wfanelli@cca.edu.

California Institute of the Arts, School of Art, Valencia, CA 91355-2340. Offers art (MFA, Adv C); graphic design (MFA, Adv C); photography (MFA, Adv C). *Accreditation:* NASAD (one or more programs are accredited). *Degree requirements:* For master's, final project. *Entrance requirements:* For master's, portfolio. Additional exam requirements/recommendations for international students: Required—TOEFL. Electronic applications accepted.

California State University, Fullerton, Graduate Studies, College of the Arts, Department of Visual Arts, Fullerton, CA 92831-3599. Offers art (MA, MFA), including art history (MA), ceramics (MFA), crafts, creative photography, exhibition design, glass, graphic design, illustration, sculpture. *Accreditation:* NASAD (one or more programs are accredited). *Program availability:* Part-time. *Faculty:* 17 full-time (7 women), 4 part-time/adjunct (3 women). *Students:* 35 full-time (22 women), 24 part-time (14 women); includes 26 minority (3 Black or African American, non-Hispanic/Latino; 7 Asian, non-Hispanic/Latino; 14 Hispanic/Latino; 2 Two or more races, non-Hispanic/Latino), 6 international. Average age 33. 81 applicants, 31% accepted, 21 enrolled. In 2017, 17 master's awarded. *Entrance requirements:* For master's, minimum GPA of 2.5 in last 60 units of course work, portfolio. Application fee: $55. *Financial support:* Career-related internships or fieldwork, Federal Work-Study, institutionally sponsored loans, and scholarships/grants available. Support available to part-time students. Financial award application deadline: 3/1; financial award applicants required to submit FAFSA. *Unit head:* Dana Lamb, Chair, 657-278-2076.
Website: http://www.fullerton.edu/arts/art/

California State University, Los Angeles, Graduate Studies, College of Arts and Letters, Department of Art, Los Angeles, CA 90032-8530. Offers art (MA), including art education, art history, art therapy, ceramics, metals, and textiles, design (MA, MFA), painting, sculpture, and graphic arts, photography; fine arts (MFA), including crafts, design (MA, MFA), studio arts. *Accreditation:* NASAD (one or more programs are accredited). *Program availability:* Part-time, evening/weekend. *Degree requirements:* For master's, comprehensive exam, project or thesis. *Entrance requirements:* For master's, portfolio. Additional exam requirements/recommendations for international students: Required—TOEFL (minimum score 500 paper-based). Electronic applications accepted. *Faculty research:* The artist and the book, conceptual art, ceramic processes, computer graphics, architectural graphics.

Central Connecticut State University, School of Graduate Studies, College of Liberal Arts and Social Sciences, Department of Design, New Britain, CT 06050-4010. Offers information design (MA). *Program availability:* Part-time, evening/weekend. *Faculty:* 1 full-time (0 women), 1 (woman) part-time/adjunct. *Students:* 10 full-time (5 women), 6 part-time (5 women); includes 2 minority (1 Black or African American, non-Hispanic/Latino; 1 Two or more races, non-Hispanic/Latino). Average age 28. 15 applicants, 87% accepted, 11 enrolled. In 2017, 6 master's awarded. *Degree requirements:* For master's, thesis or alternative, research project. *Entrance requirements:* For master's, portfolio, minimum undergraduate GPA of 3.0, essay. Additional exam requirements/recommendations for international students: Required—TOEFL (minimum score 550 paper-based; 79 iBT); Recommended—IELTS (minimum score 6.5). *Application deadline:* For fall admission, 8/1 for domestic students, 5/1 for international students; for spring admission, 11/1 for domestic and international students. Applications are processed on a rolling basis. Application fee: $50. Electronic applications accepted. *Expenses: Tuition, area resident:* Full-time $6757. Tuition, state resident: full-time $9750; part-time $374 per credit. Tuition, nonresident: full-time $18,102; part-time $374 per credit. *Required fees:* $4635; $255 per credit. *Financial support:* In 2017–18, 7 students received support. Career-related internships or fieldwork, Federal Work-Study, scholarships/grants, and unspecified assistantships available. Support available to part-time students. Financial award application deadline: 3/1; financial award applicants required to submit FAFSA. *Unit head:* Dr. Eleanor Thornton, Chair, 860-832-2564, E-mail: thorntone@ccsu.edu. *Application contact:* Patricia Gardner, Associate Director of Graduate Studies, 860-832-2350, Fax: 860-832-2362.
Website: http://www.design.ccsu.edu/

Central Washington University, School of Graduate Studies and Research, College of Arts and Humanities, Department of Art and Design, Ellensburg, WA 98926. Offers ceramics (MFA); computer arts (MFA); jewelry and metalsmithing (MFA); painting and drawing (MFA); photography (MFA); sculpture (MFA). *Entrance requirements:* For master's, minimum GPA of 3.0, portfolio. Additional exam requirements/recommendations for international students: Required—TOEFL (minimum score 550 paper-based; 79 iBT) or IELTS (minimum score 6.5). *Application deadline:* For fall admission, 2/1 for domestic students; for winter admission, 10/1 for domestic students; for spring admission, 1/1 for domestic students. Applications are processed on a rolling basis. Application fee: $50. Electronic applications accepted. *Financial support:* Application deadline: 3/1; applicants required to submit FAFSA. *Unit head:* Prof. Rachel Kirk, Chair, 509-963-2665, E-mail: rachel.kirk@cwu.edu. *Application contact:* Justine Eason, Admissions Program Coordinator, 509-963-3103, Fax: 509-963-1799, E-mail: masters@cwu.edu.
Website: http://www.cwu.edu/~art/

City College of the City University of New York, Graduate School, Division of Humanities and the Arts, Department of Art, Program in Fine Arts, New York, NY 10031-9198. Offers advertising design (MFA); ceramic design (MFA); digital and interdisciplinary art practice (MFA); painting (MFA); printmaking (MFA); sculpture (MFA); wood and metal design (MFA). *Degree requirements:* For master's, thesis exhibit. *Entrance requirements:* For master's, 20-slide portfolio. Additional exam requirements/recommendations for international students: Required—TOEFL (minimum score 577 paper-based; 90 iBT). Electronic applications accepted.

East Carolina University, Graduate School, College of Fine Arts and Communication, School of Art and Design, Greenville, NC 27858-4353. Offers art education (MA Ed); ceramics (MFA); graphic design (MFA); illustration (MFA); metal design (MFA); painting and drawing (MFA); photography (MFA); printmaking (MFA); sculpture (MFA); textile design (MFA); wood design (MFA). *Accreditation:* NASAD (one or more programs are accredited). *Program availability:* Part-time, evening/weekend. *Students:* 24 full-time (14 women), 12 part-time (10 women); includes 6 minority (3 Asian, non-Hispanic/Latino; 2 Hispanic/Latino; 1 Two or more races, non-Hispanic/Latino). Average age 33. 27 applicants, 70% accepted, 12 enrolled. In 2017, 16 master's awarded. *Degree requirements:* For master's, comprehensive exam (for some programs), thesis (for some programs). *Entrance requirements:* For master's, portfolio. *Application deadline:* For fall admission, 2/1 for domestic students; for spring admission, 10/1 for domestic students. Applications are processed on a rolling basis. Application

fee: $75. Electronic applications accepted. *Expenses:* Tuition, state resident: full-time $4749; part-time $297 per credit hour. Tuition, nonresident: full-time $17,898; part-time $1119 per credit hour. *Required fees:* $2691; $224 per credit hour. Part-time tuition and fees vary according to course load and program. *Financial support:* Research assistantships with partial tuition reimbursements, teaching assistantships with partial tuition reimbursements, and Federal Work-Study available. Support available to part-time students. Financial award application deadline: 6/1. *Unit head:* Michael H. Drought, Director, 252-328-6665, E-mail: droughtm@ecu.edu. *Application contact:* Dr. Linda H. Nelson, Information Contact, 252-328-1286, E-mail: nelsonlh@ecu.edu.
Website: http://www.ecu.edu/soad/

Florida Atlantic University, Dorothy F. Schmidt College of Arts and Letters, Department of Visual Arts and Art History, Boca Raton, FL 33431-0991. Offers visual art (MFA), including ceramics, graphic design, visual art. *Faculty:* 14 full-time (10 women). *Students:* 13 full-time (10 women), 3 part-time (2 women); includes 5 minority (2 Black or African American, non-Hispanic/Latino; 1 Asian, non-Hispanic/Latino; 2 Hispanic/Latino). Average age 37. 31 applicants, 23% accepted, 5 enrolled. In 2017, 4 master's awarded. *Degree requirements:* For master's, one foreign language, project. *Entrance requirements:* For master's, GRE General Test, minimum GPA of 3.0 during last 60 hours of course work, slide portfolio. *Application deadline:* For fall admission, 2/21 for domestic and international students; for spring admission, 10/1 for domestic and international students. Application fee: $30. Electronic applications accepted. *Expenses:* Tuition, state resident: full-time $7400; part-time $369.82 per credit. Tuition, nonresident: full-time $20,496; part-time $1042.81 per credit. *Financial support:* Research assistantships with full tuition reimbursements, teaching assistantships with full tuition reimbursements, career-related internships or fieldwork, Federal Work-Study, and institutionally sponsored loans available. Financial award applicants required to submit FAFSA. *Faculty research:* Painting, ceramics (traditional and non-traditional), installation, video and interactive sculpture. *Unit head:* Dr. Eric Landes, Chair, 954-236-1106, E-mail: elandes1@fau.edu.
Website: http://www.fau.edu/VAAH/

Full Sail University, Game Design Master of Science Program - Campus, Winter Park, FL 32792-7437. Offers MS.

George Mason University, College of Visual and Performing Arts, Program in Graphic Design, Fairfax, VA 22030. Offers MA. *Faculty:* 21 full-time (10 women), 26 part-time/adjunct (12 women). *Students:* 2 full-time (both women), 7 part-time (5 women); includes 5 minority (3 Black or African American, non-Hispanic/Latino; 2 Hispanic/Latino), 3 international. Average age 28. 7 applicants, 29% accepted, 1 enrolled. In 2017, 4 master's awarded. *Degree requirements:* For master's, thesis, exhibition, publication, or portfolio. *Entrance requirements:* For master's, portfolio presentation; artist statement; recommendations; transcript. Additional exam requirements/recommendations for international students: Required—TOEFL (minimum score 575 paper-based; 88 iBT), IELTS (minimum score 6.5), PTE (minimum score 59). *Application deadline:* For fall admission, 2/1 for domestic and international students. Application fee: $75 ($80 for international students). Electronic applications accepted. *Expenses:* Tuition, state resident: full-time $11,228; part-time $459.50 per credit. Tuition, nonresident: full-time $30,932; part-time $1280.50 per credit. *Required fees:* $3252; $135.50 per credit. Part-time tuition and fees vary according to course load and program. *Financial support:* Career-related internships or fieldwork, Federal Work-Study, and scholarships/grants available. Support available to part-time students. Financial award application deadline: 3/1; financial award applicants required to submit FAFSA. *Faculty research:* Web design; publication design; motion graphics; information design; branding. *Unit head:* Don Starr, Director, 703-993-8642, Fax: 703-993-8798, E-mail: dstarr@gmu.edu. *Application contact:* Nikki Brugnoli-Whipkey, Administrative Assistant for Graduate Study, 703-993-5792, Fax: 703-993-8798, E-mail: nbrugnol@gmu.edu.
Website: http://soa.gmu.edu/areasofconcentration/graphicdesign/

George Mason University, College of Visual and Performing Arts, Program in Visual and Performing Arts, Fairfax, VA 22030. Offers dance (MFA); graphic design (MFA); theater (MFA); visual art (MFA). *Accreditation:* NASAD. *Faculty:* 18 full-time (9 women), 39 part-time/adjunct (20 women). *Students:* 4 full-time (3 women), 7 part-time (3 women); includes 3 minority (1 Hispanic/Latino; 2 Two or more races, non-Hispanic/Latino). Average age 33. 22 applicants, 45% accepted, 5 enrolled. In 2017, 3 master's awarded. *Degree requirements:* For master's, comprehensive experience, studio project or thesis. *Entrance requirements:* For master's, official transcripts; 3 letters of recommendation; letter of intent; resume; professional goals statement. Additional exam requirements/recommendations for international students: Required—TOEFL (minimum score 575 paper-based; 88 iBT), IELTS (minimum score 6.5), PTE (minimum score 59). Application fee: $75 ($80 for international students). Electronic applications accepted. *Expenses:* Tuition, state resident: full-time $11,228; part-time $459.50 per credit. Tuition, nonresident: full-time $30,932; part-time $1280.50 per credit. *Required fees:* $3252; $135.50 per credit. Part-time tuition and fees vary according to course load and program. *Financial support:* In 2017–18, 2 students received support, including 3 teaching assistantships (averaging $4,123 per year); career-related internships or fieldwork, Federal Work-Study, scholarships/grants, unspecified assistantships, and health care benefits (for full-time research or teaching assistantship recipients) also available. Support available to part-time students. Financial award application deadline: 3/1; financial award applicants required to submit FAFSA. *Faculty research:* Digital arts, painting, photography, print-making, sculpture; combined art forms in in-disciplinary projects including installation, performance, publishing, time or writing-based; combined creative and critical approaches. *Unit head:* Lisa Kahn, Associate Dean, 703-993-4541, E-mail: lkahn2@gmu.edu. *Application contact:* Nikki Brugnoli-Whipkey, Graduate Studies Administrative Assistant, 703-993-5792, Fax: 703-993-8798, E-mail: rbrugnol@gmu.edu.
Website: http://soa.gmu.edu

Georgia Southern University, Jack N. Averitt College of Graduate Studies, College of Liberal Arts and Social Sciences, Program in Art, Statesboro, GA 30460. Offers fine arts (MFA), including 2D graphic design, 2D studio art, 3D studio art. *Accreditation:* NASAD. *Program availability:* Part-time. *Faculty:* 19 full-time (9 women). *Students:* 18 full-time (14 women), 2 part-time (0 women); includes 3 minority (2 Black or African American, non-Hispanic/Latino; 1 Hispanic/Latino), 3 international. Average age 33. 4 applicants, 100% accepted, 4 enrolled. *Degree requirements:* For master's, thesis, exhibition. *Entrance requirements:* For master's, minimum GPA of 3.0; 18 semester hours of course work in studio art, 9 in art history; portfolio; letters of reference. Additional exam requirements/recommendations for international students: Required—TOEFL (minimum score 550 paper-based; 80 iBT), IELTS (minimum score 6). *Application deadline:* For fall admission, 3/1 priority date for domestic and international students; for spring admission, 10/1 priority date for domestic students, 10/1 for international students. Applications are processed on a rolling basis. Application fee: $50. Electronic applications accepted. *Expenses:* Tuition, state resident: full-time $4986; part-time $3324 per year. Tuition, nonresident: full-time $21,982; part-time $15,352 per year. *Required fees:* $2092; $1802 per credit hour. $901 per semester. Tuition and fees vary according to course load, campus/location and program. *Financial support:* In 2017–18, 11 students received support, including 4 fellowships with full tuition reimbursements available (averaging $7,750 per year); career-related internships or fieldwork, Federal Work-Study, scholarships/grants, tuition waivers (full), and unspecified assistantships also available. Support available to part-time students. Financial award application deadline: 4/15; financial award applicants required to submit FAFSA. *Faculty research:* International design trends; graphic design social awareness campaigns; functional design; public sculpture; fine art painting, drawing, printmaking, paper and book arts; folk art; Georgia artists archive, technology, design, contemporary, traditional studio. *Unit head:* Dr. Robert Farber, Department Chair, 912-478-5358, Fax: 912-478-5104, E-mail: rfarber@georgiasouthern.edu.
Website: http://class.georgiasouthern.edu/art

Georgia State University, Ernest G. Welch School of Art and Design, Program in Studio Art, Atlanta, GA 30302-3083. Offers ceramics (MFA); drawing and painting (MFA); graphic design (MFA); interior design (MFA); photography (MFA); printmaking (MFA); sculpture (MFA); textiles (MFA). *Accreditation:* NASAD. Application fee: $50. Electronic applications accepted. *Expenses:* Tuition, state resident: full-time $7020. Tuition, nonresident: full-time $22,518. *Required fees:* $2128. Tuition and fees vary according to degree level and program. *Financial support:* Fellowships, research assistantships, teaching assistantships, scholarships/grants, and unspecified assistantships available. Financial award application deadline: 4/15; financial award applicants required to submit FAFSA. *Faculty research:* Advertising and typography, new media, traditional media, three-dimensional art, architectural and environmental design. *Unit head:* Michael White, Director, Welch School of Art and Design, 404-413-5221, Fax: 404-413-5261, E-mail: mwhite@gsu.edu. *Application contact:* Hubert Stanley Anderson, Director of Graduate Studies, 404-413-5229, Fax: 404-413-5261, E-mail: artgrad@gsu.edu.
Website: http://artdesign.gsu.edu/graduate/admissions/masters-of-fine-arts-in-studio/

Illinois State University, Graduate School, College of Fine Arts, School of Art, Normal, IL 61790. Offers art history (MA, MS); ceramics (MFA, MS); drawing (MFA, MS); fibers (MFA, MS); glass (MFA, MS); graphic design (MFA, MS); metals (MFA, MS); painting (MFA, MS); photography (MFA, MS); printmaking (MFA, MS); sculpture (MFA, MS). *Accreditation:* NASAD (one or more programs are accredited). *Degree requirements:* For master's, thesis or alternative, internship. *Entrance requirements:* For master's, portfolio, sample of scholarly writing.

Indiana State University, College of Graduate and Professional Studies, College of Arts and Sciences, Department of Art and Design, Terre Haute, IN 47809. Offers ceramics (MA, MFA); drawing (MA, MFA); graphic design (MA, MFA); painting (MA, MFA); photography (MA, MFA); printmaking (MA, MFA); sculpture (MA, MFA). *Accreditation:* NASAD (one or more programs are accredited). *Program availability:* Part-time. *Degree requirements:* For master's, thesis or alternative, departmental qualifying exam. *Entrance requirements:* For master's, portfolio. Additional exam requirements/recommendations for international students: Required—TOEFL (minimum score 550 paper-based).

Indiana University–Purdue University Indianapolis, Herron School of Art and Design, Indianapolis, IN 46202. Offers art therapy (MA); visual art (MFA), including ceramics, furniture design, painting and drawing, photography and intermedia, printmaking, sculpture; visual communication design (MFA). *Degree requirements:* For master's, thesis. *Entrance requirements:* For master's, personal statement, resume, recommendations, portfolio, transcripts (18 credit hours of studio art and 12 credit hours of psychology, including 3 credit hours of developmental psychology and 3 credit hours of abnormal psychology for MA). Additional exam requirements/recommendations for international students: Recommended—TOEFL (minimum score 550 paper-based; 79 iBT), IELTS (minimum score 6.5). Electronic applications accepted. *Expenses:* Contact institution. *Faculty research:* Contemporary digital narratives for the homoerotic trope; sound articulated 3D print; neuroscience, art and related therapeutics; automotive and aeronautical design and fabrication; technological detritus.

Inter American University of Puerto Rico, San Germán Campus, Graduate Studies Center, Program in Fine Arts, San Germán, PR 00683-5008. Offers drawing (MFA); graphic design (MFA); painting (MFA); photography (MFA); printmaking (MFA); sculpture (MFA). *Program availability:* Part-time, evening/weekend. *Degree requirements:* For master's, comprehensive exam, thesis. *Entrance requirements:* For master's, GRE General Test or EXADEP, minimum GPA of 3.0.

Iowa State University of Science and Technology, Program in Graphic Design, Ames, IA 50011. Offers MA, MFA. *Accreditation:* NASAD. *Entrance requirements:* Additional exam requirements/recommendations for international students: Required—TOEFL (minimum score 550 paper-based; 79 iBT), IELTS (minimum score 6). Electronic applications accepted.

Kent State University, College of Communication and Information, School of Visual Communication Design, Kent, OH 44242-0001. Offers MA, MFA. *Accreditation:* NASAD. *Program availability:* Part-time. *Faculty:* 10 full-time (5 women), 6 part-time/adjunct (1 woman). *Students:* 18 full-time (13 women), 9 part-time (6 women); includes 4 minority (3 Black or African American, non-Hispanic/Latino; 1 Two or more races, non-Hispanic/Latino), 9 international. Average age 29. 16 applicants, 81% accepted, 7 enrolled. In 2017, 17 master's awarded. *Degree requirements:* For master's, project (MA); thesis (MFA). *Entrance requirements:* For master's, undergraduate degree in design or closely-related program, minimum major GPA of 3.0, goal statement, autobiographical statement, 3 letters of recommendation, resume, transcripts, link to personal online portfolio. Additional exam requirements/recommendations for international students: Required—TOEFL (minimum score 587 paper-based, 94 iBT), Michigan English Language Assessment Battery (minimum score 82), IELTS (minimum score 7.0) or PTE (minimum score 65). *Application deadline:* For fall admission, 3/1 for domestic and international students; for spring admission, 10/1 for domestic and international students. Applications are processed on a rolling basis. Application fee: $45 ($70 for international students). Electronic applications accepted. *Expenses:* Tuition, state resident: full-time $11,310; part-time $515 per credit hour. Tuition, nonresident: full-time $20,396; part-time $928 per credit hour. *International tuition:* $18,544 full-time. *Financial support:* Scholarships/grants and unspecified assistantships available. Financial award application deadline: 4/9. *Unit head:* Dr. David Robins, Interim Director, 330-672-2782, E-mail: drobins@kent.edu. *Application contact:* Ken Visocky O'Grady, Graduate Coordinator and Associate Professor, 330-672-1353, E-mail: kogrady@kent.edu.
Website: http://www.kent.edu/vcd/

Liberty University, School of Visual and Performing Arts, Lynchburg, VA 24515. Offers graphic design (MFA); studio art (MFA); visual communication design (MA). *Students:* 37 full-time (19 women), 24 part-time (17 women); includes 9 minority (3 Black or African American, non-Hispanic/Latino; 1 Asian, non-Hispanic/Latino; 1 Hispanic/Latino; 4 Two or more races, non-Hispanic/Latino), 2 international. Average age 31. 109 applicants, 23% accepted, 12 enrolled. In 2017, 12 master's awarded. Application fee: $50. Electronic applications accepted. *Unit head:* Scott Hayes, Dean, E-mail: smhayes@liberty.edu. *Application contact:* Jay Bridge, Director of Admissions, 800-424-9595, Fax: 800-628-7977, E-mail: gradadmissions@liberty.edu.

Louisiana State University and Agricultural & Mechanical College, Graduate School, College of Art and Design, School of Art, Program in Studio Art, Baton Rouge, LA 70803. Offers ceramics (MFA); graphic design (MFA); painting and drawing

Graphic Design

(MFA); photography (MFA); printmaking (MFA); sculpture (MFA). *Accreditation:* NASAD. *Students:* 36 full-time (20 women), 1 (woman) part-time; includes 1 minority (Hispanic/Latino), 5 international. Average age 29. 58 applicants, 24% accepted, 13 enrolled. In 2017, 13 master's awarded.

Louisiana Tech University, Graduate School, College of Liberal Arts, Ruston, LA 71272. Offers architecture (M Arch); art (MFA), including graphic design, photography, studio; audiology (Au D); communication (MA), including speech communication, theatre; English (MA), including literature, technical writing; history (MA); speech pathology (MA); technical writing and communication (Graduate Certificate). *Program availability:* Part-time. *Faculty:* 63 full-time (25 women), 5 part-time/adjunct (3 women). *Students:* 114 full-time (29 women), 31 part-time (19 women); includes 12 minority (4 Black or African American, non-Hispanic/Latino; 1 Asian, non-Hispanic/Latino; 3 Hispanic/Latino; 4 Two or more races, non-Hispanic/Latino), 5 international. Average age 30. 146 applicants, 59% accepted, 37 enrolled. In 2017, 49 master's, 3 doctorates awarded. *Degree requirements:* For master's, thesis (for some programs); for doctorate, thesis/dissertation. *Entrance requirements:* For master's, GRE General Test; for doctorate, GRE General Test, bachelor's degree, minimum GPA of 3.0 or 3.2 on last 60 hours attempted. Additional exam requirements/recommendations for international students: Required—TOEFL (minimum score 550 paper-based; 80 iBT), IELTS (minimum score 6.5). *Application deadline:* For fall admission, 8/1 priority date for domestic students, 6/1 for international students; for winter admission, 11/1 priority date for domestic students, 9/1 for international students; for spring admission, 2/1 priority date for domestic students, 12/1 for international students; for summer admission, 5/1 priority date for domestic students, 3/1 for international students. Application fee: $40 ($50 for international students). Electronic applications accepted. *Expenses:* Tuition, state resident: full-time $5146. Tuition, nonresident: full-time $10,147. International tuition: $10,267 full-time. *Required fees:* $2273. *Financial support:* In 2017–18, 63 students received support, including 46 research assistantships (averaging $5,229 per year), 7 teaching assistantships (averaging $5,543 per year); fellowships, career-related internships or fieldwork, Federal Work-Study, institutionally sponsored loans, tuition waivers (partial), and unspecified assistantships also available. Financial award application deadline: 2/1. *Faculty research:* Contributing to the expansion of historical and social scientific knowledge and understanding through original research and publication; diverse language, ethnic, cultural, and socioeconomic backgrounds with disorders of speech, language, swallowing, hearing, and cognitive aspects of communication; prevention of communication, swallowing, and hearing disorders. *Unit head:* Dr. Donald P. Kaczvinsky, Dean, 318-257-4805, Fax: 318-257-3935, E-mail: dkaczv@latech.edu. *Application contact:* Mary Green, Administrative Assistant, 318-257-2924, Fax: 318-257-4487, E-mail: meg@latech.edu.
Website: http://liberalarts.latech.edu/

Lynn University, Eugene M. and Christine E. Lynn College of Communication and Design, Boca Raton, FL 33431-5598. Offers communication and media (MS), including design strategies for Web development, digital media, media studies and practice; digital media (Certificate); graphic and Web design (MFA); visual effects animation (MFA); Web design and technology (MS). *Program availability:* Part-time, evening/weekend. *Faculty:* 14 full-time (9 women), 7 part-time/adjunct (1 woman). *Students:* 35 full-time (21 women), 33 part-time (13 women); includes 31 minority (12 Black or African American, non-Hispanic/Latino; 2 American Indian or Alaska Native, non-Hispanic/Latino; 2 Asian, non-Hispanic/Latino; 14 Hispanic/Latino; 1 Two or more races, non-Hispanic/Latino), 12 international. Average age 27. 59 applicants, 92% accepted, 44 enrolled. In 2017, 17 master's awarded. *Degree requirements:* For master's, thesis (for some programs), completion of degree in four calendar years; minimum cumulative GPA of 3.0 and C grade or higher in each course; orientation seminar (one credit); 36 credits of foundation and specialization or a thesis. *Entrance requirements:* For master's, bachelor's degree from accredited institution, minimum undergraduate GPA of 3.0, official undergraduate transcripts, letter of recommendation from academic or professional source, writing sample demonstrating capacity to perform at graduate level. Additional exam requirements/recommendations for international students: Required—TOEFL (minimum score 550 paper-based; 80 iBT), IELTS (minimum score 6.5). *Application deadline:* For fall admission, 8/18 for domestic students, 8/4 for international students; for spring admission, 12/15 for domestic students, 12/1 for international students; for summer admission, 4/17 for domestic students, 4/3 for international students. Applications are processed on a rolling basis. Application fee: $45. Electronic applications accepted. *Expenses:* $740 per credit. *Financial support:* Career-related internships or fieldwork, Federal Work-Study, institutionally sponsored loans, scholarships/grants, tuition waivers (partial), and unspecified assistantships available. Support available to part-time students. Financial award application deadline: 8/1; financial award applicants required to submit FAFSA. *Unit head:* Dr. David L. Jaffe, Dean, 561-237-7099, Fax: 561-237-7097, E-mail: djaffe@lynn.edu. *Application contact:* Steven Pruitt, Director of Graduate Admission, 561-237-7834, Fax: 561-237-7100, E-mail: admission@lynn.edu.
Website: https://www.lynn.edu/academics/colleges-schools/communication-and-design

Maryland Institute College of Art, Graduate Studies, MA Program in Graphic Design, Baltimore, MD 21201. Offers MA. *Entrance requirements:* Additional exam requirements/recommendations for international students: Required—TOEFL (minimum score 550 paper-based; 80 iBT), IELTS (minimum score 6.5). Electronic applications accepted.

Maryland Institute College of Art, Graduate Studies, MFA Program in Graphic Design, Baltimore, MD 21201. Offers MFA. *Degree requirements:* For master's, thesis, exhibit and thesis documentation. *Entrance requirements:* For master's, portfolio, bachelor's degree in any field. Additional exam requirements/recommendations for international students: Required—TOEFL (minimum score 550 paper-based; 80 iBT), IELTS (minimum score 6.5). Electronic applications accepted. *Expenses:* Contact institution.

Marywood University, Academic Affairs, Insalaco College of Creative and Performing Arts, Art Department, Program in Visual Arts, Scranton, PA 18509-1598. Offers clay (MFA); graphic design (MFA); illustration (MFA); painting (MFA); photography (MFA); printmaking (MFA); sculpture (MFA). *Accreditation:* NASAD. *Program availability:* Part-time. Electronic applications accepted. *Expenses:* Contact institution.

Minneapolis College of Art and Design, Certificate Programs, Minneapolis, MN 55404-4347. Offers graphic design (Certificate); media (Certificate); sustainable design (Certificate). *Program availability:* Part-time, 100% online, blended/hybrid learning. *Faculty:* 42 full-time (29 women). *Students:* 29 full-time (21 women), 5 part-time (all women); includes 6 minority (2 Black or African American, non-Hispanic/Latino; 1 Asian, non-Hispanic/Latino; 3 Hispanic/Latino), 1 international. In 2017, 15 Certificates awarded. *Degree requirements:* For Certificate, final project. *Entrance requirements:* For degree, resume, portfolio, letter of recommendation. Additional exam requirements/recommendations for international students: Required—TOEFL (minimum score 550 paper-based; 79 iBT). *Application deadline:* For fall admission, 1/15 for domestic and international students; for spring admission, 10/15 for domestic and international students. Application fee: $50. Electronic applications accepted. *Expenses: Tuition:* Full-time $38,670. *Required fees:* $450. One-time fee: $300 full-time. *Financial support:*

Career-related internships or fieldwork and scholarships/grants available. Financial award application deadline: 3/15; financial award applicants required to submit FAFSA. *Faculty research:* Visual arts. *Unit head:* Lara Roy, Senior Director of Continuing Education, 612-874-3778, E-mail: continuing_education@mcad.edu.
Website: http://www.mcad.edu/showPage.php?pageID=1216

Minneapolis College of Art and Design, Program in Graphic and Web Design, Minneapolis, MN 55404-4347. Offers MA. *Expenses: Tuition:* Full-time $38,670. *Required fees:* $450. One-time fee: $300 full-time.

Minneapolis College of Art and Design, Program in Visual Studies, Minneapolis, MN 55404-4347. Offers animation (MFA); comic art (MFA); drawing (MFA); filmmaking (MFA); fine arts (MFA); furniture design (MFA); graphic design (MFA); illustration (MFA); interactive media (MFA); painting (MFA); photography (MFA); printmaking (MFA); sculpture (MFA). *Accreditation:* NASAD. *Program availability:* Part-time. *Faculty:* 42 full-time (13 women). *Students:* 30 full-time (23 women); includes 3 minority (2 Asian, non-Hispanic/Latino; 1 Hispanic/Latino), 13 international. 166 applicants, 28% accepted, 12 enrolled. In 2017, 10 master's awarded. *Degree requirements:* For master's, thesis, thesis exhibit. *Entrance requirements:* For master's, portfolio of visual artwork, resume, 3 letters of recommendation. Additional exam requirements/recommendations for international students: Required—TOEFL (minimum score 550 paper-based; 79 iBT). *Application deadline:* For fall admission, 1/15 for domestic and international students. Application fee: $50. Electronic applications accepted. *Expenses: Tuition:* Full-time $38,670. *Required fees:* $450. One-time fee: $300 full-time. *Financial support:* In 2017–18, 23 students received support, including 15 teaching assistantships (averaging $6,000 per year); career-related internships or fieldwork, Federal Work-Study, scholarships/grants, and unspecified assistantships also available. Support available to part-time students. Financial award application deadline: 3/15; financial award applicants required to submit FAFSA. *Faculty research:* Visual arts: animation, comic art, drawing, filmmaking, furniture design, graphic design, illustration, interactive media, painting, photography, printmaking, sculpture. *Unit head:* Graduate Director, 612-209-1471, E-mail: admissions@mcad.edu. *Application contact:* Mary Kazura, Associate Director of Admissions, 612-874-3760, Fax: 612-874-3701, E-mail: mary_kazura@mcad.edu.
Website: http://mcad.edu/mfa

Morehead State University, Graduate Programs, Caudill College of Arts, Humanities and Social Sciences, Department of Art and Design, Morehead, KY 40351. Offers art education (MA); graphic design (MA); studio art (MA). *Accreditation:* NASAD. *Program availability:* Part-time, evening/weekend. *Degree requirements:* For master's, comprehensive exam, thesis (for some programs), oral exam during exhibition. *Entrance requirements:* For master's, GRE General Test, minimum undergraduate GPA of 3.0 in major, 2.5 overall; portfolio; bachelor's degree in art. Additional exam requirements/recommendations for international students: Required—TOEFL (minimum score 500 paper-based). Electronic applications accepted. *Faculty research:* Computer art, painting, drawing, ceramics, photography.

New York Institute of Technology, College of Arts and Sciences, Department of Digital Art and Design, Old Westbury, NY 11568-8000. Offers computer graphics (MFA), including animation, fine arts and technology, graphic design. *Program availability:* Part-time, evening/weekend. *Faculty:* 7 full-time (4 women), 6 part-time/adjunct (2 women). *Students:* 35 full-time (24 women), 12 part-time (7 women); includes 7 minority (4 Black or African American, non-Hispanic/Latino; 1 Asian, non-Hispanic/Latino; 2 Hispanic/Latino), 35 international. Average age 26. 37 applicants, 73% accepted, 9 enrolled. In 2017, 27 master's awarded. *Degree requirements:* For master's, thesis. *Entrance requirements:* For master's, BFA or equivalent; minimum undergraduate GPA of 3.0; digital portfolio. Additional exam requirements/recommendations for international students: Required—TOEFL (minimum score 79 iBT), IELTS (minimum score 6). *Application deadline:* For fall admission, 6/1 for domestic and international students. Applications are processed on a rolling basis. Application fee: $50. Electronic applications accepted. *Expenses:* $1,285 per credit plus fees. *Financial support:* Career-related internships or fieldwork, Federal Work-Study, scholarships/grants, tuition waivers (full and partial), and unspecified assistantships available. Support available to part-time students. Financial award application deadline: 2/15; financial award applicants required to submit FAFSA. *Faculty research:* Graphic design, animation, art and technology, virtual reality, sculpture. *Unit head:* Terry Nauheim, Department Chair, 516-686-7881, Fax: 212-261-1742, E-mail: tnauheim@nyit.edu. *Application contact:* Alice Dolitsky, Director, Graduate Admissions, 516-686-7520, Fax: 516-686-1116, E-mail: nyitgrad@nyit.edu.
Website: http://www.nyit.edu/departments/digital_art_and_design

North Carolina Agricultural and Technical State University, School of Graduate Studies, School of Technology, Department of Graphic Communication Systems and Technological Studies, Greensboro, NC 27411. Offers graphic communication systems (MSTM); technology education (MAT). *Accreditation:* NCATE (one or more programs are accredited). *Program availability:* Part-time, evening/weekend. *Degree requirements:* For master's, comprehensive exam, thesis or alternative, qualifying exam. *Entrance requirements:* For master's, GRE General Test, minimum GPA of 3.0.

North Carolina State University, Graduate School, College of Design, Department of Graphic Design, Raleigh, NC 27695. Offers MGD. *Accreditation:* NASAD. *Degree requirements:* For master's, thesis optional, oral exam. *Entrance requirements:* For master's, GRE General Test, portfolio. Electronic applications accepted. *Faculty research:* Typography, graphic design, interaction design, design and cognition, design and culture.

Ohio University, Graduate College, College of Fine Arts, School of Art, Athens, OH 45701-2979. Offers art history (MA); ceramics (MFA); graphic design (MFA); painting (MFA); photography (MFA); printmaking (MFA); sculpture (MFA). *Program availability:* Part-time. *Degree requirements:* For master's, thesis. *Entrance requirements:* For master's, portfolio. Additional exam requirements/recommendations for international students: Required—TOEFL (minimum score 550 paper-based; 80 iBT) or IELTS (minimum score 6.5). Electronic applications accepted. *Faculty research:* Vapor-fired ceramics, video installation, art theory, digital photography, mixed and interdisciplinary media work.

Oklahoma State University, College of Arts and Sciences, Department of Art, Graphic Design and Art History, Stillwater, OK 74078. Offers art history (MA); graphic design (MA). *Faculty:* 22 full-time (12 women), 2 part-time/adjunct (1 woman). *Students:* 6 full-time (3 women), 4 part-time (all women); includes 1 minority (Black or African American, non-Hispanic/Latino), 3 international. Average age 29. 16 applicants, 44% accepted, 7 enrolled. In 2017, 5 master's awarded. *Entrance requirements:* Additional exam requirements/recommendations for international students: Required—TOEFL. *Application deadline:* For fall admission, 3/1 for domestic students; for spring admission, 8/1 for domestic students. Application fee: $40 ($75 for international students). Electronic applications accepted. *Expenses:* Tuition, state resident: full-time $4019; part-time $2679.60 per year. Tuition, nonresident: full-time $15,286; part-time $10,190.40 per year. *Required fees:* $2129; $1419 per unit. Tuition and fees vary according to program. *Financial support:* Research assistantships and teaching

assistantships available. Financial award applicants required to submit FAFSA. *Unit head:* Dr. Rebecca Brienen, Head, E-mail: rebecca.brienen@okstate.edu.
Website: http://art.okstate.edu/

Otis College of Art and Design, Program in Graphic Design, Los Angeles, CA 90045-9785. Offers MFA. *Entrance requirements:* Additional exam requirements/recommendations for international students: Required—TOEFL (minimum score 600 paper-based). Electronic applications accepted.

Pensacola Christian College, Graduate Studies, Pensacola, FL 32503-2267. Offers business administration (MBA); curriculum and instruction (MS, Ed D, Ed S); dramatics (MFA); educational leadership (MS, Ed D, Ed S); graphic design (MA, MFA); music (MA); nursing (MSN); performance studies (MA); studio art (MA, MFA).

Pittsburg State University, Graduate School, College of Technology, Department of Technology and Workforce Learning, Pittsburg, KS 66762. Offers career and technical education (MS); human resource development (MS); technology (MS), including automotive technology, construction management, graphic design, graphics management, information technology, innovation in technology, personnel development, technology management, workforce learning; workforce development and education (Ed S). *Program availability:* Part-time, evening/weekend, 100% online, blended/hybrid learning. *Students:* 129 (66 women); includes 18 minority (7 Black or African American, non-Hispanic/Latino; 3 American Indian or Alaska Native, non-Hispanic/Latino; 1 Asian, non-Hispanic/Latino; 3 Hispanic/Latino; 4 Two or more races, non-Hispanic/Latino), 29 international. In 2017, 62 master's, 2 other advanced degrees awarded. *Degree requirements:* For master's, thesis or alternative; for Ed S, thesis optional. *Entrance requirements:* Additional exam requirements/recommendations for international students: Required—TOEFL (minimum score 520 paper-based; 68 iBT), IELTS (minimum score 6), PTE (minimum score 47). *Application deadline:* For fall admission, 7/15 for domestic students, 6/1 for international students; for spring admission, 12/15 for domestic students, 10/15 for international students; for summer admission, 5/15 for domestic students, 4/1 for international students. Applications are processed on a rolling basis. Application fee: $35 ($60 for international students). Electronic applications accepted. *Expenses:* Contact institution. *Financial support:* In 2017–18, 8 teaching assistantships with full tuition reimbursements (averaging $5,500 per year) were awarded; career-related internships or fieldwork also available. Financial award application deadline: 2/1; financial award applicants required to submit FAFSA. *Unit head:* Dr. John Iley, Chairperson, 620-235-4373, E-mail: jiley@pittstate.edu. *Application contact:* Lisa Allen, Assistant Director of Graduate and Continuing Studies, 620-235-4218, Fax: 620-235-4219, E-mail: lallen@pittstate.edu.

Pratt Institute, School of Art, Program in Digital Arts, Brooklyn, NY 11205-3899. Offers MFA, MS/MFA. *Accreditation:* NASAD. *Students:* 47 full-time (34 women), 5 part-time (3 women); includes 2 minority (1 Asian, non-Hispanic/Latino; 1 Hispanic/Latino), 42 international. Average age 26. 218 applicants, 34% accepted, 18 enrolled. In 2017, 26 master's awarded. *Degree requirements:* For master's, thesis, exhibit. *Entrance requirements:* For master's, portfolio or video, letters of recommendation. Additional exam requirements/recommendations for international students: Required—TOEFL (minimum score 550 paper-based; 79 iBT). *Application deadline:* For fall admission, 1/5 for domestic and international students; for spring admission, 10/1 for domestic and international students. Application fee: $50 ($90 for international students). Electronic applications accepted. *Expenses: Tuition:* Full-time $30,834. *Required fees:* $1974. *Financial support:* Career-related internships or fieldwork, Federal Work-Study, institutionally sponsored loans, scholarships/grants, health care benefits, and unspecified assistantships available. Support available to part-time students. Financial award application deadline: 2/1; financial award applicants required to submit FAFSA. *Unit head:* Peter Patchen, Chair, 718-636-3693, Fax: 718-399-4494, E-mail: ppatchen@pratt.edu. *Application contact:* Natalie Capannelli, Director of Graduate Admissions, 718-636-3551, Fax: 718-399-4242, E-mail: ncapanne@pratt.edu.
Website: https://www.pratt.edu/academics/school-of-art/graduate-school-of-art/digital-arts-grad/

See Display on page 141 and Close-Up on page 189.

Pratt Institute, School of Design, Program in Communications Design, Brooklyn, NY 10011. Offers MFA. *Accreditation:* NASAD. *Program availability:* Part-time. *Students:* 125 full-time (95 women), 5 part-time (4 women); includes 13 minority (3 Black or African American, non-Hispanic/Latino; 4 Asian, non-Hispanic/Latino; 6 Hispanic/Latino), 98 international. Average age 25. 350 applicants, 62% accepted, 73 enrolled. In 2017, 52 master's awarded. *Degree requirements:* For master's, thesis. *Entrance requirements:* For master's, portfolio, letters of recommendation. Additional exam requirements/recommendations for international students: Required—TOEFL (minimum score 575 paper-based; 90 iBT). *Application deadline:* For fall admission, 1/5 for domestic and international students; for spring admission, 10/1 for domestic and international students. Application fee: $50 ($90 for international students). Electronic applications accepted. *Expenses: Tuition:* Full-time $30,834. *Required fees:* $1974. *Financial support:* Career-related internships or fieldwork, Federal Work-Study, institutionally sponsored loans, scholarships/grants, health care benefits, and unspecified assistantships available. Support available to part-time students. Financial award application deadline: 2/1; financial award applicants required to submit FAFSA. *Faculty research:* Graphics, film, photography, media presentations, computer graphics for community service organizations. *Unit head:* Santiago Piedrafita Iglesias, Chairperson, 212-687-5313, Fax: 718-399-4495, E-mail: spiedraf@pratt.edu. *Application contact:* Natalie Capannelli, Director of Graduate Admissions, 718-636-3551, Fax: 718-399-4242, E-mail: ncapanne@pratt.edu.
Website: https://www.pratt.edu/academics/school-of-design/graduate-school-of-design/grad-communications-design/

See Display on page 65 and Close-Up on page 97.

Rhode Island School of Design, Department of Graphic Design, Providence, RI 02903-2784. Offers MFA. *Accreditation:* NASAD. *Faculty:* 11 full-time (5 women), 14 part-time/adjunct (6 women). *Students:* 37 full-time (25 women); includes 7 minority (5 Asian, non-Hispanic/Latino; 1 Hispanic/Latino; 1 Two or more races, non-Hispanic/Latino), 8 international. Average age 29. 289 applicants, 8% accepted, 15 enrolled. In 2017, 14 master's awarded. *Degree requirements:* For master's, thesis, exhibition. *Entrance requirements:* For master's, portfolio, statement of purpose, 3 letters of recommendation. Additional exam requirements/recommendations for international students: Required—TOEFL (minimum score 580 paper-based; 93 iBT). *Application deadline:* For fall admission, 1/10 for domestic and international students. Application fee: $60. Electronic applications accepted. *Expenses: Tuition:* Full-time $48,210. *Required fees:* $260. *Financial support:* Fellowships, research assistantships, teaching assistantships, Federal Work-Study, scholarships/grants, and unspecified assistantships available. Financial award application deadline: 2/15; financial award applicants required to submit FAFSA. *Unit head:* John Caserta, Department Head, 401-454-6171, Fax: 401-454-6117, E-mail: gd@risd.edu. *Application contact:* Molly Pettengill, Assistant Director for Graduate Recruitment, 401-454-6312, Fax: 401-454-6309, E-mail: mpetteng@risd.edu.
Website: http://www.risd.edu/academics/graphic-design/

Rochester Institute of Technology, Graduate Enrollment Services, College of Imaging Arts and Sciences, School of Design, MFA Program in Visual Communication Design, Rochester, NY 14623-5603. Offers MFA. *Accreditation:* NASAD. *Program availability:* Part-time. *Students:* 66 full-time (52 women), 39 part-time (29 women); includes 7 minority (2 Asian, non-Hispanic/Latino; 2 Hispanic/Latino; 3 Two or more races, non-Hispanic/Latino), 80 international. Average age 29. 186 applicants, 58% accepted, 29 enrolled. In 2017, 13 master's awarded. *Degree requirements:* For master's, thesis, thesis exhibition. *Entrance requirements:* For master's, GRE, portfolio, minimum GPA of 3.0 (recommended). Additional exam requirements/recommendations for international students: Required—TOEFL (minimum score 550 paper-based; 90 iBT), IELTS (minimum score 7), PTE (minimum score 58). *Application deadline:* For fall admission, 2/15 priority date for domestic and international students. Applications are processed on a rolling basis. Application fee: $65. Electronic applications accepted. *Expenses:* $1,815 per credit hour. *Financial support:* In 2017–18, 52 students received support. Teaching assistantships with partial tuition reimbursements available, career-related internships or fieldwork, scholarships/grants, and unspecified assistantships available. Support available to part-time students. Financial award applicants required to submit FAFSA. *Faculty research:* Motion graphics for design and interaction; experiential design for physical and digital environments; augmented and virtual reality applications within education, advertising and consumer products; visual design for user experience and interactive solutions. *Unit head:* Adam Smith, Graduate Program Director, 585-475-4552, Fax: 585-475-7533, E-mail: aesfaa@rit.edu. *Application contact:* Diane Ellison, Senior Associate Vice President, Graduate Enrollment Services, 585-475-2229, Fax: 585-475-7164, E-mail: gradinfo@rit.edu.
Website: http://cias.rit.edu/schools/design/graduate-visual-communication-design

Rochester Institute of Technology, Graduate Enrollment Services, College of Imaging Arts and Sciences, School of Media Sciences, MS Program in Print Media, Rochester, NY 14623-5603. Offers MS. *Program availability:* Part-time. *Students:* 25 full-time (12 women), 6 part-time (3 women); includes 3 minority (1 Black or African American, non-Hispanic/Latino; 2 Asian, non-Hispanic/Latino), 21 international. Average age 26. 6 applicants, 50% accepted, 3 enrolled. In 2017, 1 master's awarded. *Degree requirements:* For master's, thesis. *Entrance requirements:* For master's, GRE, minimum GPA of 3.0 (recommended). Additional exam requirements/recommendations for international students: Required—TOEFL (minimum score 550 paper-based; 80 iBT), IELTS (minimum score 6.5), PTE (minimum score 58). *Application deadline:* For fall admission, 2/15 priority date for domestic and international students. Applications are processed on a rolling basis. Application fee: $65. Electronic applications accepted. *Expenses:* $1,815 per credit hour. *Financial support:* In 2017–18, 7 students received support. Research assistantships with partial tuition reimbursements available, teaching assistantships with partial tuition reimbursements available, career-related internships or fieldwork, scholarships/grants, and unspecified assistantships available. Support available to part-time students. Financial award applicants required to submit FAFSA. *Faculty research:* 3D, functional, and packaging print processes; color management; cross-media publishing; operations management; digital printing. *Unit head:* Christine Heusner, Graduate Program Director, 585-475-4627, E-mail: cxhppr@rit.edu. *Application contact:* Diane Ellison, Senior Associate Vice President, Graduate Enrollment Services, 585-475-2229, Fax: 585-475-7164, E-mail: gradinfo@rit.edu.
Website: http://cias.rit.edu/schools/media-sciences/graduate-graduate-print-media

San Diego State University, Graduate and Research Affairs, College of Professional Studies and Fine Arts, School of Art, Design and Art History, San Diego, CA 92182. Offers art history (MA); studio arts (MA, MFA), including applied design, environmental design, graphic design, interior design, painting and printmaking, sculpture. *Accreditation:* NASAD (one or more programs are accredited). *Degree requirements:* For master's, variable foreign language requirement, thesis. *Entrance requirements:* For master's, GRE General Test, bachelor's degree in related field, slide portfolio, typed slide information sheet, 2 letters of recommendation. Additional exam requirements/recommendations for international students: Required—TOEFL. Electronic applications accepted.

Savannah College of Art and Design, Program in Advertising, Savannah, GA 31402-3146. Offers MA, MFA. *Program availability:* Part-time. *Faculty:* 10 full-time (3 women), 5 part-time/adjunct (2 women). *Students:* 21 full-time (11 women), 9 part-time (4 women); includes 14 minority (9 Black or African American, non-Hispanic/Latino; 2 Asian, non-Hispanic/Latino; 3 Hispanic/Latino), 11 international. Average age 27. 59 applicants, 22% accepted, 9 enrolled. In 2017, 23 master's awarded. *Degree requirements:* For master's, final project (for MA); thesis (for MFA). *Entrance requirements:* For master's, GRE (recommended), portfolio (submitted in digital format), audition or writing submission, resume, statement of purpose, two letters of recommendation. Additional exam requirements/recommendations for international students: Recommended—TOEFL (minimum score 550 paper-based; 85 iBT), IELTS (minimum score 6.5). *Application deadline:* For fall admission, 4/1 for domestic and international students. Applications are processed on a rolling basis. Application fee: $40. Electronic applications accepted. *Expenses: Tuition:* Full-time $36,765; part-time $817 per credit hour. One-time fee: $500. *Financial support:* Career-related internships or fieldwork, Federal Work-Study, and scholarships/grants available. Financial award application deadline: 4/1; financial award applicants required to submit FAFSA. *Unit head:* Emily Sander, Chair of Advertising Design. *Application contact:* Jenny Jaquillard, Executive Director of Admissions, Recruitment and Events, 912-525-5100, Fax: 912-525-5985, E-mail: admission@scad.edu.
Website: http://www.scad.edu/academics/programs/advertising

Savannah College of Art and Design, Program in Graphic Design and Visual Experience, Savannah, GA 31402-3146. Offers MA, MFA. *Program availability:* Part-time, 100% online. *Faculty:* 20 full-time (9 women), 8 part-time/adjunct (3 women). *Students:* 96 full-time (63 women), 47 part-time (28 women); includes 16 minority (6 Black or African American, non-Hispanic/Latino; 4 Asian, non-Hispanic/Latino; 6 Hispanic/Latino), 85 international. Average age 28. 333 applicants, 35% accepted, 49 enrolled. In 2017, 36 master's awarded. *Degree requirements:* For master's, capstone course (for MA); thesis (for MFA). *Entrance requirements:* For master's, GRE (recommended), portfolio (submitted in digital format), audition or writing submission, resume, statement of purpose, two letters of recommendation. Additional exam requirements/recommendations for international students: Recommended—TOEFL (minimum score 550 paper-based; 85 iBT), IELTS (minimum score 6.5). *Application deadline:* For fall admission, 4/1 for domestic and international students. Applications are processed on a rolling basis. Application fee: $40. Electronic applications accepted. *Expenses: Tuition:* Full-time $36,765; part-time $817 per credit hour. One-time fee: $500. *Financial support:* Career-related internships or fieldwork, Federal Work-Study, and scholarships/grants available. Financial award application deadline: 4/1; financial award applicants required to submit FAFSA. *Unit head:* Jason Fox, Chair, Graphic Design and Visual Experience. *Application contact:* Jenny Jaquillard, Executive Director of Admissions, Recruitment and Events, 912-525-5100, Fax: 912-525-5985, E-mail: admission@scad.edu.
Website: http://www.scad.edu/academics/programs/graphic-design

School of the Art Institute of Chicago, Graduate Division, Department of Visual Communication, Chicago, IL 60603-3103. Offers MFA. *Entrance requirements:* Additional exam requirements/recommendations for international students: Required—TOEFL, IELTS.

Graphic Design

School of Visual Arts, Graduate Programs, Program in Visual Narrative, New York, NY 10010-3994. Offers MFA. Summer admission only. *Degree requirements:* For master's, thesis, 60 credits, including all required courses. *Entrance requirements:* For master's, portfolio, statement of purpose; unique and complete short story/visual narrative (minimum 2-5 pages/images, or 2-5 minutes for video or animation submissions). Additional exam requirements/recommendations for international students: Required—TOEFL (minimum score 550 paper-based; 79 iBT). Electronic applications accepted. *Faculty research:* Storytelling, animation, design, illustration, art history, painting, printmaking, writing, graphic novels.

State University of New York at Oswego, Graduate Studies, Department of Art, Oswego, NY 13126. Offers art (MA); graphic design and digital media (MA). *Accreditation:* NASAD. *Program availability:* Part-time. *Degree requirements:* For master's, exhibit, final presentation. *Entrance requirements:* For master's, slides of previous work. Additional exam requirements/recommendations for international students: Required—TOEFL (minimum score 560 paper-based). *Faculty research:* Ancient and primitive art, nineteenth century art, medieval art, Renaissance art.

Suffolk University, New England School of Art and Design, Boston, MA 02108-2770. Offers graphic design (MA); interior architecture (MA). *Program availability:* Part-time, evening/weekend. *Faculty:* 13 full-time (8 women), 10 part-time/adjunct (5 women). *Students:* 33 full-time (28 women), 25 part-time (23 women); includes 12 minority (1 Black or African American, non-Hispanic/Latino; 7 Asian, non-Hispanic/Latino; 4 Hispanic/Latino), 16 international. Average age 28. 58 applicants, 57% accepted, 10 enrolled. In 2017, 37 master's awarded. *Entrance requirements:* For master's, GRE (for MFA), art portfolio, interview, 2 letters of recommendation, resume; letter of intent (for MFA). Additional exam requirements/recommendations for international students: Required—TOEFL (minimum score 550 paper-based; 80 iBT). *Application deadline:* For fall admission, 3/15 priority date for domestic and international students; for spring admission, 10/15 priority date for domestic and international students. Applications are processed on a rolling basis. Application fee: $50. Electronic applications accepted. *Expenses:* $29,520 per year full-time tuition; $1,230 per credit part-time. *Financial support:* In 2017–18, 46 students received support, including 4 fellowships (averaging $6,062 per year); career-related internships or fieldwork, Federal Work-Study, institutionally sponsored loans, scholarships/grants, and unspecified assistantships also available. Financial award application deadline: 4/1; financial award applicants required to submit FAFSA. *Faculty research:* Sustainable design, lighting and technology, design education, environmental graphic design, designing for the non-profit sector. *Unit head:* Audrey Goldstein, Department Chair, 617-997-4290, E-mail: agoldstein@suffolk.edu. *Application contact:* Mara Marzocchi, Associate Director of Graduate Admissions, 617-573-8302, Fax: 617-305-1733, E-mail: grad.admission@suffolk.edu.
Website: http://www.suffolk.edu/nesad/

Temple University, Tyler School of Art, Department of Graphic Arts and Design, Philadelphia, PA 19122-6096. Offers graphic and interactive design (MFA); photography (MFA); printmaking (MFA). *Faculty:* 12 full-time (5 women), 31 part-time/adjunct (12 women). *Students:* 19 full-time (12 women); includes 3 minority (2 Asian, non-Hispanic/Latino; 1 Two or more races, non-Hispanic/Latino), 5 international. 117 applicants, 18% accepted, 10 enrolled. In 2017, 8 master's awarded. *Entrance requirements:* For master's, minimum GPA of 3.0, slide portfolio, 40 credits in studio art, 12 credits in art history, letters of recommendation, resume/curriculum vitae. Additional exam requirements/recommendations for international students: Required—TOEFL (minimum score 550 paper-based; 79 iBT), IELTS (minimum score 6.5). *Application deadline:* For fall admission, 1/15 for domestic students, 12/15 for international students. Application fee: $60. Electronic applications accepted. *Expenses:* Contact institution. *Financial support:* Fellowships, research assistantships, teaching assistantships, and Federal Work-Study available. Support available to part-time students. Financial award application deadline: 1/15; financial award applicants required to submit FAFSA. *Unit head:* Dermot Mac Cormack, Chair, 215-777-9179, Fax: 215-782-2799, E-mail: dermot@temple.edu. *Application contact:* Tamryn McDermott, Director of Admissions, 215-777-9090, E-mail: tylerart@temple.edu.
Website: http://tyler.temple.edu/graduate

Texas State University, The Graduate College, College of Fine Arts and Communication, Program in Communication Design, San Marcos, TX 78666. Offers MFA. *Program availability:* Part-time. *Faculty:* 26 full-time (14 women), 4 part-time/adjunct (2 women). *Students:* 15 full-time (10 women), 20 part-time (14 women); includes 13 minority (1 Black or African American, non-Hispanic/Latino; 1 Asian, non-Hispanic/Latino; 9 Hispanic/Latino; 2 Two or more races, non-Hispanic/Latino), 4 international. Average age 33. 25 applicants, 28% accepted, 2 enrolled. In 2017, 7 master's awarded. *Degree requirements:* For master's, comprehensive exam, thesis. *Entrance requirements:* For master's, related baccalaureate degree from regionally-accredited institution with minimum GPA of 2.75 in last 60 hours of undergraduate course work, 3 letters of recommendation, academic and professional statement of purpose, online portfolio showcasing at least 20 works in communication design. Additional exam requirements/recommendations for international students: Required—TOEFL (minimum score 550 paper-based; 78 iBT), IELTS (minimum score 6), TOEFL (minimum iBT scores: 19 listening, 19 reading, 19 speaking, 18 writing). *Application deadline:* For fall admission, 3/31 for domestic and international students; for spring admission, 10/31 for domestic students, 10/1 for international students. Applications are processed on a rolling basis. Application fee: $40 ($90 for international students). Electronic applications accepted. *Expenses:* Tuition, state resident: full-time $7868; part-time $3934 per semester. Tuition, nonresident: full-time $17,828; part-time $8914 per semester. *Required fees:* $2092; $1435 per semester. Tuition and fees vary according to course load. *Financial support:* In 2017–18, 23 students received support, including 10 teaching assistantships (averaging $12,926 per year); research assistantships, Federal Work-Study, institutionally sponsored loans, scholarships/grants, and unspecified assistantships also available. Support available to part-time students. Financial award application deadline: 3/1; financial award applicants required to submit FAFSA. *Unit head:* Claudia Roeschmann, Graduate Advisor, 512-245-7450, E-mail: cr29@txstate.edu. *Application contact:* Dr. Andrea Golato, Dean of Graduate School, 512-245-2581, Fax: 512-245-8365, E-mail: gradcollege@txstate.edu.
Website: http://www.finearts.txstate.edu/Art/mfacomdes/

Texas Woman's University, Graduate School, College of Arts and Sciences, School of the Arts, Department of Visual Arts, Denton, TX 76204. Offers art (MA, MAT, MFA), including art education (MA, MAT), art history (MA), ceramics (MFA), graphic design (MA), intermedia (MFA), painting (MFA), photography (MFA), sculpture (MFA). MFA degrees are granted through the Federation of North Texas Area Universities (The University of North Texas, Texas A&M Commerce, and Texas Woman's University). *Faculty:* 6 full-time (3 women). *Students:* 8 full-time (6 women), 9 part-time (8 women); includes 7 minority (1 Black or African American, non-Hispanic/Latino; 1 American Indian or Alaska Native, non-Hispanic/Latino; 4 Hispanic/Latino; 1 Two or more races, non-Hispanic/Latino). Average age 33. 10 applicants, 50% accepted, 2 enrolled. In 2017, 10 master's awarded. *Degree requirements:* For master's, comprehensive exam, thesis (for some programs), exhibit (MFA), oral exam, thesis or professional paper (MA). *Entrance requirements:* For master's, portfolio, interview, current curriculum vitae, letter of intent, 3 letters of recommendation, artist statement, 2 research papers (for art history or art education). Additional exam requirements/recommendations for international students: Required—TOEFL (minimum score 550 paper-based; 79 iBT); Recommended—IELTS (minimum score 6.5), TSE (minimum score 53). *Application deadline:* For fall admission, 1/31 priority date for domestic and international students; for spring admission, 10/15 priority date for domestic students, 7/1 priority date for international students. Applications are processed on a rolling basis. Application fee: $50 ($75 for international students). Electronic applications accepted. *Expenses:* $7,520 per year full-time in-state; $16,820 per year full-time out-of-state. *Financial support:* In 2017–18, 9 students received support, including 5 teaching assistantships (averaging $9,780 per year); career-related internships or fieldwork, Federal Work-Study, institutionally sponsored loans, scholarships/grants, traineeships, health care benefits, and unspecified assistantships also available. Support available to part-time students. Financial award application deadline: 3/1; financial award applicants required to submit FAFSA. *Faculty research:* Art education and electronic technology, film noir, one-of-a-kind art books, new media, early video art from 1960-1980. *Unit head:* Dr. Vagner Whitehead, Chair, 940-898-2530, Fax: 940-898-2496, E-mail: visualarts@twu.edu. *Application contact:* Korie Hawkins, Associate Director of Admissions, Graduate Recruitment, 940-898-3188, Fax: 940-898-3081, E-mail: admissions@twu.edu.
Website: http://www.twu.edu/visual-arts/

Université Laval, Faculty of Architecture, Planning and Visual Arts, School of Visual Arts, Programs in Visual Arts, Québec, QC G1K 7P4, Canada. Offers graphic design and multimedia (MA); visual arts (MA). *Degree requirements:* For master's, thesis (for some programs). *Entrance requirements:* For master's, technical exam, interview, mastery of pertinent software, knowledge of French. Electronic applications accepted.

University of Baltimore, Graduate School, Yale Gordon College of Arts and Sciences, Doctoral Program in Information and Interaction Design, Baltimore, MD 21201-5779. Offers DS. *Program availability:* Part-time, evening/weekend. *Entrance requirements:* For doctorate, minimum GPA of 3.2, previous graduate study in related discipline, portfolio, resume. Electronic applications accepted.

University of Baltimore, Graduate School, Yale Gordon College of Arts and Sciences, Program in Publications Design, Baltimore, MD 21201-5779. Offers MA. *Program availability:* Part-time, evening/weekend. *Degree requirements:* For master's, seminar project. *Entrance requirements:* For master's, minimum GPA of 3.0, portfolio, interview. Additional exam requirements/recommendations for international students: Required—TOEFL (minimum score 550 paper-based). Electronic applications accepted. *Faculty research:* Communication theory, graphic design, media technology.

University of Cincinnati, Graduate School, College of Design, Architecture, Art, and Planning, School of Design, Cincinnati, OH 45221. Offers fashion design (M Des); graphic design (M Des); industrial design (M Des); interaction design (M Des); product development (M Des). *Accreditation:* NASAD. *Degree requirements:* For master's, thesis. *Entrance requirements:* For master's, undergraduate degree in design or related field, 2 years of work experience in design or related field. Additional exam requirements/recommendations for international students: Required—TOEFL. Electronic applications accepted. *Expenses:* Tuition, area resident: Full-time $14,468. Tuition, state resident: full-time $14,968; part-time $754 per credit hour. Tuition, nonresident: full-time $24,210; part-time $1311 per credit hour. *International tuition:* $26,460 full-time. *Required fees:* $3958; $84 per credit hour. One-time fee: $85 full-time. Tuition and fees vary according to course load, degree level and program. *Faculty research:* Design theory, interdisciplinary design topics.

University of Guam, Office of Graduate Studies, College of Liberal Arts and Social Sciences, Division of Fine Arts, Mangilao, GU 96923. Offers ceramics (MA); graphics (MA); painting (MA). *Degree requirements:* For master's, thesis or alternative, exhibit, final oral exam. *Entrance requirements:* For master's, GRE General Test, portfolio. Additional exam requirements/recommendations for international students: Required—TOEFL.

University of Illinois at Chicago, College of Architecture, Design and the Arts, School of Design, Chicago, IL 60607-7128. Offers graphic design (M Des); industrial design (M Des). *Degree requirements:* For master's, thesis, exhibit. *Entrance requirements:* For master's, MAT, portfolio. Additional exam requirements/recommendations for international students: Required—TOEFL. Electronic applications accepted. *Expenses:* Contact institution.

University of Illinois at Urbana–Champaign, Graduate College, College of Fine and Applied Arts, School of Art and Design, Program in Design and Media, Champaign, IL 61820. Offers art and design (MFA), including new media; graphic design (MFA); industrial design (MFA). *Accreditation:* NASAD.

University of Memphis, Graduate School, College of Communication and Fine Arts, Department of Art, Memphis, TN 38152. Offers art history (MA), including Egyptian art and archaeology, general art history; ceramics (MFA); graphic design (MFA); museum studies (Graduate Certificate); painting (MFA); printmaking/photography (MFA); sculpture (MFA). *Accreditation:* NASAD (one or more programs are accredited). *Program availability:* Part-time. *Faculty:* 18 full-time (7 women), 2 part-time/adjunct (1 woman). *Students:* 21 full-time (17 women), 5 part-time (all women); includes 8 minority (2 Black or African American, non-Hispanic/Latino; 1 Asian, non-Hispanic/Latino; 4 Hispanic/Latino; 1 Two or more races, non-Hispanic/Latino). Average age 29. 11 applicants, 73% accepted, 5 enrolled. In 2017, 5 master's, 5 other advanced degrees awarded. *Degree requirements:* For master's, 2 foreign languages, comprehensive exam, thesis, image identification exam, qualifying exam; for Graduate Certificate, internship. *Entrance requirements:* For master's, GRE General Test or MAT, portfolio (MFA), letter of intent, sample of undergraduate writing, two letters of recommendation; for Graduate Certificate, three letters of recommendation, letter of intent. *Application deadline:* For fall admission, 2/15 for domestic students; for spring admission, 11/1 for domestic students. Applications are processed on a rolling basis. Application fee: $35 ($60 for international students). *Expenses:* Contact institution. *Financial support:* In 2017–18, 36 students received support, including 15 research assistantships with full tuition reimbursements available (averaging $11,600 per year); teaching assistantships with full tuition reimbursements available, Federal Work-Study, scholarships/grants, and unspecified assistantships also available. Financial award application deadline: 2/1; financial award applicants required to submit FAFSA. *Faculty research:* Online collaborative learning, advanced art history studies, electronic publishing/design, studio arts, architectural studies. *Unit head:* Prof. Richard Lou, Chair, 901-678-2217, Fax: 901-678-2735, E-mail: ralou@memphis.edu. *Application contact:* Niles Wallice, Coordinator of Graduate Studies, 901-678-4899.
Website: http://memphis.edu/art/

University of Miami, Graduate School, College of Arts and Sciences, Department of Art and Art History, Coral Gables, FL 33124. Offers art history (MA); ceramics/glass (MFA); graphic design/multimedia (MFA); painting (MFA); photography/digital imaging (MFA); printmaking (MFA); sculpture (MFA). *Program availability:* Part-time. *Degree requirements:* For master's, variable foreign language requirement, thesis, exhibit (MFA), comprehensive exam (MA). *Entrance requirements:* For master's, GRE General Test (MA), research paper (MA), slide portfolio (MFA). Additional exam requirements/

recommendations for international students: Required—TOEFL. Electronic applications accepted. *Faculty research:* Installation art, public art.

University of Minnesota, Duluth, Graduate School, School of Fine Arts, Department of Art and Design, Duluth, MN 55812-2496. Offers graphic design (MFA). *Accreditation:* NASAD. *Program availability:* Part-time. *Degree requirements:* For master's, final exhibit, project, supporting paper. *Entrance requirements:* For master's, minimum GPA of 3.0, writing sample, slide portfolio. Additional exam requirements/recommendations for international students: Required—TOEFL (minimum score 550 paper-based). *Faculty research:* Motion graphics, graphic design history, interactive design, typography, education.

University of Notre Dame, Graduate School, College of Arts and Letters, Division of Humanities, Department of Art, Art History, and Design, Notre Dame, IN 46556. Offers art history (MA); design (MFA), including graphic design, industrial design; studio art (MFA), including ceramics, painting, photography, printmaking, sculpture. *Accreditation:* NASAD. *Degree requirements:* For master's, comprehensive exam (for some programs), thesis. *Entrance requirements:* For master's, GRE General Test, minimum GPA of 3.0. Additional exam requirements/recommendations for international students: Required—TOEFL (minimum score 600 paper-based; 80 iBT). Electronic applications accepted. *Faculty research:* Studio art practice in ceramics, printing, photography, printmaking and sculpture, graphic design and industrial design, digital imaging in design and photography, Renaissance and American art history, contemporary art theory and criticism.

University of Pennsylvania, School of Design, Department of Fine Arts, Philadelphia, PA 19104. Offers emerging design and research (Certificate); fine arts (MFA); time-based and interactive media (Certificate). *Faculty:* 8 full-time (4 women), 1 part-time/adjunct (0 women). *Students:* 25 full-time (11 women); includes 8 minority (3 Black or African American, non-Hispanic/Latino; 1 Asian, non-Hispanic/Latino; 3 Hispanic/Latino; 1 Two or more races, non-Hispanic/Latino), 10 international. Average age 30. 123 applicants, 41% accepted, 15 enrolled. In 2017, 16 master's, 1 other advanced degree awarded. *Degree requirements:* For master's, thesis. *Application deadline:* Applications are processed on a rolling basis. Electronic applications accepted. *Financial support:* In 2017–18, 30 students received support, including teaching assistantships (averaging $6,000 per year); fellowships with full tuition reimbursements available, research assistantships, Federal Work-Study, scholarships/grants, health care benefits, and unspecified assistantships also available. Financial award applicants required to submit FAFSA. *Faculty research:* Performance art, photography and video, drawing and painting, sculpture, animation and creative research. *Unit head:* Joshua Mosley, Professor/Chair/Director of Graduate Program, 215-898-8374, E-mail: jmosley@design.upenn.edu. *Application contact:* Leighann Bogner, Administrative Assistant, 215-898-8374, Fax: 215-573-2459, E-mail: mfa@pobox.upenn.edu.
Website: http://www.design.upenn.edu/mfa

University of South Dakota, Graduate School, College of Fine Arts, Department of Art, Vermillion, SD 57069. Offers art education (MFA); ceramics (MFA); graphic design (MFA); painting (MFA); photography (MFA); printmaking (MFA); sculpture (MFA). *Accreditation:* NASAD. *Degree requirements:* For master's, thesis or alternative. *Entrance requirements:* For master's, portfolio, minimum GPA of 2.7. Additional exam requirements/recommendations for international students: Required—TOEFL (minimum score 550 paper-based; 79 iBT). *Application deadline:* Applications are processed on a rolling basis. Application fee: $35. Electronic applications accepted. *Financial support:* Research assistantships with partial tuition reimbursements, teaching assistantships with partial tuition reimbursements, Federal Work-Study, and unspecified assistantships available. Support available to part-time students. Financial award applicants required to submit FAFSA. *Application contact:* Graduate School, 605-658-6140, Fax: 605-677-6118, E-mail: grad@usd.edu.
Website: http://www.usd.edu/fine-arts/art

The University of Tennessee, Graduate School, College of Arts and Sciences, School of Art, Knoxville, TN 37996. Offers ceramics (MFA); drawing (MFA); graphic design (MFA); inter-area studies (MFA); media arts (MFA); painting (MFA); printmaking (MFA); sculpture (MFA); watercolor (MFA). *Accreditation:* NASAD. *Degree requirements:* For master's, thesis or alternative, exhibit. *Entrance requirements:* For master's, portfolio, minimum GPA of 2.7. Additional exam requirements/recommendations for international students: Required—TOEFL. Electronic applications accepted.

University of Utah, Graduate School, College of Fine Arts, Department of Art and Art History, Salt Lake City, UT 84112-0380. Offers art history (MA); ceramics (MFA); community-based art education (MFA); drawing (MFA); graphic design (MFA); painting (MFA); photography/digital imaging (MFA); printmaking (MFA); sculpture/intermedia (MFA). *Faculty:* 19 full-time (9 women), 23 part-time/adjunct (11 women). *Students:* 6 full-time (3 women); includes 1 minority (Asian, non-Hispanic/Latino). Average age 24. 48 applicants, 31% accepted, 3 enrolled. In 2017, 6 master's awarded. *Degree requirements:* For master's, variable foreign language requirement, comprehensive exam (for some programs), thesis or alternative, exhibit and final project paper (for MFA). *Entrance requirements:* For master's, CD portfolio (MFA), writing sample (MA), curriculum vitae, letters of recommendation, letter of intent. Additional exam requirements/recommendations for international students: Required—TOEFL (minimum score 575 paper-based; 75 iBT). *Application deadline:* For fall admission, 1/15 priority date for domestic and international students. Application fee: $55 ($65 for international students). Electronic applications accepted. *Expenses:* Contact institution. *Financial support:* In 2017–18, 6 students received support, including 2 fellowships, 6 research assistantships with partial tuition reimbursements available, 34 teaching assistantships with partial tuition reimbursements available; Federal Work-Study, institutionally sponsored loans, scholarships/grants, tuition waivers (partial), unspecified assistantships, and stipends also available. Financial award application deadline: 1/15; financial award applicants required to submit FAFSA. *Faculty research:* Studio art, European art history, Asian art history, Latin American art history, twentieth-century/contemporary art history. Total annual research expenditures: $54,906. *Unit head:* Prof. Brian Snapp, Chair, 801-581-8677, Fax: 801-585-6171, E-mail: b.snapp@utah.edu. *Application contact:* Prof. Kim Martinez, Director of Graduate Studies, 801-581-8677, Fax: 801-585-6171, E-mail: kim.martinez@art.utah.edu.
Website: http://www.art.utah.edu/

Vermont College of Fine Arts, MFA in Graphic Design Program, Montpelier, VT 05602. Offers MFA. *Accreditation:* NASAD. *Faculty:* 10 part-time/adjunct (5 women). *Students:* 32 full-time (15 women); includes 5 minority (1 Asian, non-Hispanic/Latino; 3 Hispanic/Latino; 1 Two or more races, non-Hispanic/Latino), 1 international. Average age 35. 31 applicants, 74% accepted, 14 enrolled. In 2017, 12 master's awarded. *Application deadline:* Applications are processed on a rolling basis. Application fee: $75. Electronic applications accepted. *Expenses:* Contact institution. *Financial support:* In 2017–18, 28 students received support. Scholarships/grants available. Financial award applicants required to submit FAFSA. *Unit head:* Jennifer Renko, Program Director, 866-934-8232 Ext. 8896, E-mail: jennifer.renko@vcfa.edu.
Website: http://www.vcfa.edu/graphic-design

Wayne State University, College of Fine, Performing and Communication Arts, James Pearson Duffy Department of Art and Art History, Detroit, MI 48202. Offers art (MA, MFA), including ceramics, drawing, fashion design and merchandising (MA), fibers, graphic design, industrial design (MA), interior design (MA), metalsmithing, painting, photography, printmaking, sculpture; art history (MA). *Students:* 13 full-time (8 women), 12 part-time (9 women); includes 5 minority (3 Black or African American, non-Hispanic/Latino; 1 Asian, non-Hispanic/Latino; 1 Hispanic/Latino), 2 international. Average age 34. 46 applicants, 24% accepted, 6 enrolled. In 2017, 5 master's awarded. *Degree requirements:* For master's, thesis (for some programs), essay or thesis. *Entrance requirements:* For master's, BFA or another degree and equivalent course work, portfolio, personal interview, reference letters, statement of intent (except for art history program). Additional exam requirements/recommendations for international students: Required—TOEFL (minimum score 550 paper-based; 79 iBT), TWE (minimum score 5.5), Michigan English Language Assessment Battery (minimum score 85); Recommended—IELTS (minimum score 6.5). *Application deadline:* For fall admission, 2/1 for domestic and international students; for winter admission, 10/1 for domestic and international students. Application fee: $50. Electronic applications accepted. *Expenses:* Contact institution. *Financial support:* In 2017–18, 18 students received support, including 1 research assistantship (averaging $22,241 per year), 6 teaching assistantships with tuition reimbursements available (averaging $18,534 per year); fellowships with tuition reimbursements available, scholarships/grants, and unspecified assistantships also available. Support available to part-time students. Financial award applicants required to submit FAFSA. *Unit head:* Dr. John Richardson, Chair, 313-577-2980, Fax: 313-577-3491, E-mail: af5343@wayne.edu. *Application contact:* 313-577-2980, E-mail: art@wayne.edu.
Website: http://art.wayne.edu/

West Virginia University, College of Creative Arts, Morgantown, WV 26506. Offers acting (MFA); art education (MA); art history (MA); ceramics (MFA); collaborative piano (MM, DMA); composition (MM, DMA); conducting (MM, DMA); costume design and technology (MFA); graphic design (MFA); jazz pedagogy (MM); lighting design and technology (MFA); music (PhD); music education (MM, PhD); music industry (MA); music theory (MM); musicology (MA); painting and printmaking (MFA); performance (MM, DMA); photography (MFA); piano pedagogy (MM); scenic design and technology (MFA); sculpture (MFA); studio art (MA); technical direction (MFA); vocal pedagogy and performance (DMA). *Program availability:* Part-time. *Students:* 114 full-time (64 women), 39 part-time (21 women); includes 19 minority (11 Black or African American, non-Hispanic/Latino; 1 Asian, non-Hispanic/Latino; 6 Hispanic/Latino; 1 Two or more races, non-Hispanic/Latino), 33 international. *Degree requirements:* For master's, thesis, recitals; for doctorate, comprehensive exam, thesis/dissertation, recitals (DMA). *Entrance requirements:* For doctorate, minimum GPA of 3.0, audition. Additional exam requirements/recommendations for international students: Required—TOEFL. *Application deadline:* For fall admission, 3/1 priority date for domestic students, 2/15 for international students; for spring admission, 11/1 for domestic students, 9/15 for international students. Applications are processed on a rolling basis. Application fee: $60. Electronic applications accepted. *Expenses:* Tuition, state resident: full-time $9450. Tuition, nonresident: full-time $24,390. *Financial support:* Research assistantships, teaching assistantships, career-related internships or fieldwork, Federal Work-Study, institutionally sponsored loans, scholarships/grants, health care benefits, tuition waivers (partial), and administrative assistantships available. Financial award applicants required to submit FAFSA. *Faculty research:* Professional directing, consulting, acting design, music education, jazz history. *Unit head:* Dr. Paul Kreider, Dean, 304-293-4841 Ext. 3109, Fax: 304-293-6896, E-mail: paul.kreider@mail.wvu.edu. *Application contact:* Records Officer, 304-293-4841, Fax: 304-293-2533, E-mail: rachel.hanks@mail.wvu.edu.
Website: http://www.ccarts.wvu.edu

Yale University, School of Art, New Haven, CT 06520-8339. Offers graphic design (MFA); painting/printmaking (MFA); photography (MFA); sculpture (MFA). *Degree requirements:* For master's, thesis (for some programs). *Entrance requirements:* Additional exam requirements/recommendations for international students: Required—TOEFL (minimum score 550 paper-based; 100 iBT). Electronic applications accepted. *Expenses:* Contact institution.

Illustration

Academy of Art University, Graduate Programs, School of Illustration, San Francisco, CA 94105-3410. Offers MA, MFA. *Accreditation:* NASAD. *Program availability:* Part-time, 100% online. *Faculty:* 10 full-time (2 women), 39 part-time/adjunct (16 women). *Students:* 123 full-time (82 women), 95 part-time (67 women); includes 39 minority (15 Black or African American, non-Hispanic/Latino; 7 Asian, non-Hispanic/Latino; 12 Hispanic/Latino; 5 Two or more races, non-Hispanic/Latino), 104 international. Average age 31. 67 applicants, 100% accepted, 46 enrolled. In 2017, 68 master's awarded. *Degree requirements:* For master's, final review. *Entrance requirements:* For master's, statement of intent; resume; portfolio/reel; official college transcripts. *Application deadline:* Applications are processed on a rolling basis. Application fee: $50. Electronic applications accepted. *Expenses: Tuition:* Part-time $982 per unit. *Financial support:* Career-related internships or fieldwork, Federal Work-Study, and scholarships/grants available. Financial award application deadline: 8/10; financial award applicants required to submit FAFSA. *Unit head:* 800-544-ARTS, E-mail: info@academyart.edu. *Application contact:* 800-544-ARTS, E-mail: info@academyart.edu.
Website: http://www.academyart.edu/illustration-school/index.html

Bob Jones University, Graduate Programs, Greenville, SC 29614. Offers accountancy (MS); Bible (MA); Bible translation (MA); Biblical studies (Certificate); broadcast management (MS); business administration (MBA); church history (MA, PhD); church ministries (MA); church music (MM); cinema and video production (MA);

counseling (MS); curriculum and instruction (Ed D); divinity (M Div); dramatic production (MA); educational leadership (MS, Ed D, Ed S); elementary education (M Ed, MAT); English (M Ed, MA, MAT); fine arts (MA); graphic design (MA); history (M Ed, MA); illustration (MA); interpretative speech (MA); mathematics (M Ed, MAT); medical missions (Certificate); ministry (MM, D Min); multi-categorical special education (M Ed, MAT); music (M Ed); New Testament interpretation (PhD); Old Testament interpretation (PhD); orchestral instrument performance (MM); organ performance (MM); pastoral studies (MA); personnel services (MS, Ed S); piano pedagogy (MM); piano performance (MM); platform arts (MA); radio and television broadcasting (MS); rhetoric and public address (MA); secondary education (M Ed); studio art (MA); teaching Bible (MA); theology (MA, PhD); voice performance (MM); youth ministries (MA); M Div/MM.

California College of the Arts, Graduate Programs, MFA in Comics Program, San Francisco, CA 94107. Offers MFA. *Program availability:* Part-time-only. *Faculty:* 5 full-time (0 women), 12 part-time/adjunct (3 women). *Students:* 19 full-time (10 women); includes 10 minority (2 Black or African American, non-Hispanic/Latino; 2 Asian, non-Hispanic/Latino; 6 Hispanic/Latino), 2 international. Average age 28. 31 applicants, 68% accepted, 11 enrolled. In 2017, 13 master's awarded. *Degree requirements:* For master's, thesis. *Entrance requirements:* For master's, portfolio, personal essay, resume, two letters of recommendation, college transcripts, interview. Additional exam requirements/recommendations for international students: Required—TOEFL, IELTS, or PTE. *Application deadline:* For fall admission, 1/31 priority date for domestic and international students. Applications are processed on a rolling basis. Application fee: $70. Electronic applications accepted. *Expenses:* $31,536 per year full-time tuition, $1,314 per credit part-time; $390 fees per year. *Financial support:* Applicants required to submit FAFSA. *Unit head:* Matt Silady, Chair, E-mail: msilady@cca.edu. *Application contact:* Wes Fanelli, Assistant Director of Graduate Admissions, 415-703-9533, Fax: 415-703-9539, E-mail: wfanelli@cca.edu.
Website: https://www.cca.edu/academics/graduate/comics

California State University, Fullerton, Graduate Studies, College of the Arts, Department of Visual Arts, Fullerton, CA 92831-3599. Offers art (MA, MFA), including art history (MA); ceramics (MFA); crafts, creative photography, exhibition design, glass, graphic design, illustration, sculpture. *Accreditation:* NASAD (one or more programs are accredited). *Program availability:* Part-time. *Faculty:* 17 full-time (7 women), 4 part-time/adjunct (3 women). *Students:* 35 full-time (22 women), 24 part-time (14 women); includes 26 minority (3 Black or African American, non-Hispanic/Latino; 7 Asian, non-Hispanic/Latino; 14 Hispanic/Latino; 2 Two or more races, non-Hispanic/Latino), 6 international. Average age 33. 81 applicants, 31% accepted, 21 enrolled. In 2017, 17 master's awarded. *Entrance requirements:* For master's, minimum GPA of 2.5 in last 60 units of course work, portfolio. Application fee: $55. *Financial support:* Career-related internships or fieldwork, Federal Work-Study, institutionally sponsored loans, and scholarships/grants available. Support available to part-time students. Financial award application deadline: 3/1; financial award applicants required to submit FAFSA. *Unit head:* Dana Lamb, Chair, 657-278-2076.
Website: http://www.fullerton.edu/arts/art/

East Carolina University, Graduate School, College of Fine Arts and Communication, School of Art and Design, Greenville, NC 27858-4353. Offers art education (MA Ed); ceramics (MFA); graphic design (MFA); illustration (MFA); metal design (MFA); painting and drawing (MFA); photography (MFA); printmaking (MFA); sculpture (MFA); textile design (MFA); wood design (MFA). *Accreditation:* NASAD (one or more programs are accredited). *Program availability:* Part-time, evening/weekend. *Students:* 24 full-time (14 women), 12 part-time (10 women); includes 6 minority (3 Asian, non-Hispanic/Latino; 2 Hispanic/Latino; 1 Two or more races, non-Hispanic/Latino). Average age 33. 27 applicants, 70% accepted, 12 enrolled. In 2017, 16 master's awarded. *Degree requirements:* For master's, comprehensive exam (for some programs), thesis (for some programs). *Entrance requirements:* For master's, portfolio. *Application deadline:* For fall admission, 2/1 for domestic students; for spring admission, 10/1 for domestic students. Applications are processed on a rolling basis. Application fee: $75. Electronic applications accepted. *Expenses:* Tuition, state resident: full-time $4749; part-time $297 per credit hour. Tuition, nonresident: full-time $17,898; part-time $1119 per credit hour. *Required fees:* $2691; $224 per credit hour. Part-time tuition and fees vary according to course load and program. *Financial support:* Research assistantships with partial tuition reimbursements, teaching assistantships with partial tuition reimbursements, and Federal Work-Study available. Support available to part-time students. Financial award application deadline: 6/1. *Unit head:* Michael H. Drought, Director, 252-328-6665, E-mail: droughtm@ecu.edu. *Application contact:* Dr. Linda H. Nelson, Information Contact, 252-328-1286, E-mail: nelsonlh@ecu.edu.
Website: http://www.ecu.edu/soad/

Fashion Institute of Technology, School of Graduate Studies, Program in Illustration, New York, NY 10001-5992. Offers MFA. *Degree requirements:* For master's, thesis. *Entrance requirements:* Additional exam requirements/recommendations for international students: Required—TOEFL (minimum score 550 paper-based). Electronic applications accepted.

Hollins University, Graduate Programs, Program in Children's Literature, Roanoke, VA 24020. Offers children's book illustration (Certificate); children's book writing and illustrating (MFA); children's literature (MA, MFA). Program offered during summer only. *Program availability:* Part-time. *Faculty:* 2 full-time (both women), 8 part-time/adjunct (7 women). *Students:* 40 full-time (38 women), 6 part-time (5 women); includes 6 minority (1 Black or African American, non-Hispanic/Latino; 1 Asian, non-Hispanic/Latino; 3 Hispanic/Latino; 1 Two or more races, non-Hispanic/Latino). Average age 35. 24 applicants, 96% accepted, 10 enrolled. In 2017, 11 master's awarded. *Degree requirements:* For master's, one foreign language, comprehensive exam, thesis. *Entrance requirements:* For master's, transcripts, letters of recommendation, portfolio, personal statement of educational objectives. Additional exam requirements/recommendations for international students: Required—TOEFL (minimum score 550 paper-based; 79 iBT), IELTS (minimum score 6.5). *Application deadline:* For summer admission, 2/15 priority date for domestic and international students. Application fee: $40. Electronic applications accepted. *Expenses:* Contact institution. *Financial support:* Federal Work-Study and scholarships/grants available. Support available to part-time students. Financial award application deadline: 2/15; financial award applicants required to submit FAFSA. *Faculty research:* Fantasy, children's film, young adult fiction, picture books, mythology and folk tales. *Unit head:* Amanda Cockrell, Director, 540-362-6024, Fax: 540-362-6642, E-mail: acockrell@hollins.edu. *Application contact:* Cathy S. Koon, Manager of Graduate Services, 540-362-6326, Fax: 540-362-6288, E-mail: ckoon@hollins.edu.

Kent State University, College of Communication and Information, School of Visual Communication Design, Kent, OH 44242-0001. Offers MA, MFA. *Accreditation:* NASAD. *Program availability:* Part-time. *Faculty:* 10 full-time (5 women), 6 part-time/adjunct (1 woman). *Students:* 18 full-time (13 women), 9 part-time (6 women); includes 4 minority (3 Black or African American, non-Hispanic/Latino; 1 Two or more races, non-Hispanic/Latino), 9 international. Average age 29. 16 applicants, 81% accepted, 7 enrolled. In 2017, 17 master's awarded. *Degree requirements:* For master's, project (MA); thesis (MFA). *Entrance requirements:* For master's, undergraduate degree in design or closely-related program, minimum major GPA of 3.0, goal statement, autobiographical

statement, 3 letters of recommendation, resume, transcripts, link to personal online portfolio. Additional exam requirements/recommendations for international students: Required—TOEFL (minimum score 587 paper-based, 94 iBT), Michigan English Language Assessment Battery (minimum score 82), IELTS (minimum score 7.0) or PTE (minimum score 65). *Application deadline:* For fall admission, 3/1 for domestic and international students; for spring admission, 10/1 for domestic and international students. Applications are processed on a rolling basis. Application fee: $45 ($70 for international students). Electronic applications accepted. *Expenses:* Tuition, state resident: full-time $11,310; part-time $515 per credit hour. Tuition, nonresident: full-time $20,396; part-time $928 per credit hour. *International tuition:* $18,544 full-time. *Financial support:* Scholarships/grants and unspecified assistantships available. Financial award application deadline: 4/9. *Unit head:* Dr. David Robins, Interim Director, 330-672-2782, E-mail: drobins@kent.edu. *Application contact:* Ken Visocky O'Grady, Graduate Coordinator and Associate Professor, 330-672-1353, E-mail: kogrady@kent.edu.
Website: http://www.kent.edu/vcd/

Maryland Institute College of Art, Graduate Studies, Program in Illustration Practice, Baltimore, MD 21201. Offers MFA. *Degree requirements:* For master's, thesis, exhibition. *Entrance requirements:* For master's, portfolio, writing sample, bachelor's degree in any field. Additional exam requirements/recommendations for international students: Required—TOEFL (minimum score 550 paper-based; 80 iBT), IELTS (minimum score 6.5). Electronic applications accepted. *Expenses:* Contact institution.

Marywood University, Academic Affairs, Insalaco College of Creative and Performing Arts, Art Department, Program in Visual Arts, Scranton, PA 18509-1598. Offers clay (MFA); graphic design (MFA); illustration (MFA); painting (MFA); photography (MFA); printmaking (MFA); sculpture (MFA). *Accreditation:* NASAD. *Program availability:* Part-time. Electronic applications accepted. *Expenses:* Contact institution.

Mills College, Graduate Studies, Department of English, Oakland, CA 94613-1000. Offers book art and creative writing (MFA); literature (MA); poetry (MFA); prose (MFA); Spanish creative writing (Certificate); translation (MFA). *Program availability:* Part-time. *Faculty:* 6 full-time (5 women), 4 part-time/adjunct (all women). *Students:* 36 full-time (29 women), 21 part-time (14 women); includes 26 minority (9 Black or African American, non-Hispanic/Latino; 3 Asian, non-Hispanic/Latino; 9 Hispanic/Latino; 5 Two or more races, non-Hispanic/Latino). Average age 32. 100 applicants, 95% accepted, 27 enrolled. In 2017, 18 master's awarded. *Degree requirements:* For master's, comprehensive exam, thesis. *Entrance requirements:* For master's, 15-20 page writing sample. Additional exam requirements/recommendations for international students: Required—TOEFL (minimum score 600 paper-based; 100 iBT), IELTS (minimum score 7). *Application deadline:* For fall admission, 12/15 priority date for domestic students, 12/15 for international students. Applications are processed on a rolling basis. Application fee: $50. Electronic applications accepted. *Expenses:* Contact institution. *Financial support:* In 2017–18, 23 students received support, including 23 fellowships with partial tuition reimbursements available (averaging $6,327 per year), 21 teaching assistantships with tuition reimbursements available; research assistantships and scholarships/grants also available. Support available to part-time students. Financial award application deadline: 2/1; financial award applicants required to submit FAFSA. *Faculty research:* Creative writing, African-American literature, Victorian women writers, theories of sexuality, Shakespeare. *Unit head:* Dr. Thomas Strychacz, Chair of the English Department, 510-430-2208, E-mail: toms@mills.edu. *Application contact:* Robynne Lofton, Director of Admissions, 510-430-3295, Fax: 510-430-2159, E-mail: grad-admission@mills.edu.
Website: http://www.mills.edu/english/

Mills College, Graduate Studies, Program in Book Art and Creative Writing, Oakland, CA 94613-1000. Offers MFA. *Program availability:* Part-time. *Faculty:* 3 full-time (all women), 6 part-time/adjunct (5 women). *Students:* 2 full-time (both women), 2 part-time (both women). Average age 31. 16 applicants, 81% accepted, 1 enrolled. In 2017, 3 master's awarded. *Degree requirements:* For master's, thesis project. *Entrance requirements:* For master's, visual portfolio of 15-25 images, written portfolio sample (for creative writing program). Additional exam requirements/recommendations for international students: Required—TOEFL (minimum score 600 paper-based; 100 iBT), IELTS (minimum score 7). *Application deadline:* For fall admission, 12/15 priority date for domestic students, 12/15 for international students. Application fee: $50. Electronic applications accepted. *Expenses:* Tuition: Full-time $33,480; part-time $1000 per credit. *Required fees:* $1479. Tuition and fees vary according to program. *Financial support:* In 2017–18, 4 students received support, including 4 fellowships with tuition reimbursements available (averaging $5,323 per year), 3 teaching assistantships with tuition reimbursements available. Financial award application deadline: 2/1; financial award applicants required to submit FAFSA. *Unit head:* Kathleen Walkup, Professor of Book Arts, 510-430-2001, Fax: 510-430-2159, E-mail: kwalk@mills.edu. *Application contact:* Robynne Lofton, Director of Admissions, 510-430-3295, Fax: 510-430-2159, E-mail: grad-admission@mills.edu.
Website: http://www.mills.edu/academics/graduate/eng/programs/MFA_in_bookart.php

Minneapolis College of Art and Design, Program in Visual Studies, Minneapolis, MN 55404-4347. Offers animation (MFA); comic art (MFA); drawing (MFA); filmmaking (MFA); fine arts (MFA); furniture design (MFA); graphic design (MFA); illustration (MFA); interactive media (MFA); painting (MFA); photography (MFA); printmaking (MFA); sculpture (MFA). *Accreditation:* NASAD. *Program availability:* Part-time. *Faculty:* 42 full-time (13 women). *Students:* 30 full-time (23 women); includes 3 minority (2 Asian, non-Hispanic/Latino; 1 Hispanic/Latino), 13 international. 166 applicants, 28% accepted, 12 enrolled. In 2017, 10 master's awarded. *Degree requirements:* For master's, thesis, thesis exhibit. *Entrance requirements:* For master's, portfolio of visual artwork, resume, 3 letters of recommendation. Additional exam requirements/recommendations for international students: Required—TOEFL (minimum score 550 paper-based; 79 iBT). *Application deadline:* For fall admission, 1/15 for domestic and international students. Application fee: $50. Electronic applications accepted. *Expenses:* Tuition: Full-time $38,670. *Required fees:* $450. One-time fee: $300 full-time. *Financial support:* In 2017–18, 23 students received support, including 15 teaching assistantships (averaging $6,000 per year); career-related internships or fieldwork, Federal Work-Study, scholarships/grants, and unspecified assistantships also available. Support available to part-time students. Financial award application deadline: 3/15; financial award applicants required to submit FAFSA. *Faculty research:* Visual arts: animation, comic art, drawing, filmmaking, furniture design, graphic design, illustration, interactive media, painting, photography, printmaking, sculpture. *Unit head:* Graduate Director, 612-209-1471, E-mail: admissions@mcad.edu. *Application contact:* Mary Kazura, Associate Director of Admissions, 612-874-3760, Fax: 612-874-3701, E-mail: mary_kazura@mcad.edu.
Website: http://mcad.edu/mfa

Savannah College of Art and Design, Program in Illustration, Savannah, GA 31402-3146. Offers MA, MFA. *Program availability:* Part-time, 100% online. *Faculty:* 17 full-time (3 women), 4 part-time/adjunct (2 women). *Students:* 113 full-time (85 women), 48 part-time (31 women); includes 18 minority (6 Black or African American, non-Hispanic/Latino; 1 American Indian or Alaska Native, non-Hispanic/Latino; 6 Asian, non-Hispanic/Latino; 5 Hispanic/Latino), 82 international. Average age 28. 171 applicants,

45% accepted, 41 enrolled. In 2017, 43 master's awarded. *Degree requirements:* For master's, final project (for MA); thesis (for MFA). *Entrance requirements:* For master's, GRE (recommended), portfolio (submitted in digital format), audition or writing submission, resume, statement of purpose, two letters of recommendation. Additional exam requirements/recommendations for international students: Recommended—TOEFL (minimum score 550 paper-based; 85 iBT), IELTS (minimum score 6.5). *Application deadline:* For fall admission, 4/1 for domestic and international students. Applications are processed on a rolling basis. Application fee: $40. Electronic applications accepted. *Expenses: Tuition:* Full-time $36,765; part-time $817 per credit hour. One-time fee: $500. *Financial support:* Career-related internships or fieldwork, Federal Work-Study, and scholarships/grants available. Financial award application deadline: 4/1; financial award applicants required to submit FAFSA. *Unit head:* George Spears, Chair, Illustration and Sequential Art. *Application contact:* Jenny Jaquillard, Executive Director of Admissions, Recruitment and Events, 912-525-5100, Fax: 912-525-5985, E-mail: admission@scad.edu.
Website: http://www.scad.edu/academics/programs/illustration

Savannah College of Art and Design, Program in Sequential Art, Savannah, GA 31402-3146. Offers MA, MFA. *Program availability:* Part-time. *Faculty:* 11 full-time (0 women), 6 part-time/adjunct (3 women). *Students:* 42 full-time (32 women), 4 part-time (3 women); includes 11 minority (3 Black or African American, non-Hispanic/Latino; 2 Asian, non-Hispanic/Latino; 6 Hispanic/Latino), 16 international. Average age 27. 40 applicants, 50% accepted, 12 enrolled. In 2017, 11 master's awarded. *Degree requirements:* For master's, final project (for MA); thesis (for MFA). *Entrance requirements:* For master's, GRE (recommended), portfolio (submitted in digital format), audition or writing submission, resume, statement of purpose, two letters of recommendation. Additional exam requirements/recommendations for international students: Recommended—TOEFL (minimum score 550 paper-based; 85 iBT), IELTS (minimum score 6.5). *Application deadline:* For fall admission, 4/1 for domestic and international students. Applications are processed on a rolling basis. Application fee: $40. Electronic applications accepted. *Expenses: Tuition:* Full-time $36,765; part-time $817 per credit hour. One-time fee: $500. *Financial support:* Career-related internships or fieldwork, Federal Work-Study, and scholarships/grants available. Financial award application deadline: 4/1; financial award applicants required to submit FAFSA. *Unit head:* George Spears, Chair, Illustration and Sequential Art. *Application contact:* Jenny Jaquillard, Executive Director of Admissions, Recruitment and Events, 912-525-5100, Fax: 912-525-5985, E-mail: admission@scad.edu.
Website: http://www.scad.edu/academics/programs/sequential-art

School of Visual Arts, Graduate Programs, Illustration as Visual Essay Department, New York, NY 10010-3994. Offers MFA. *Accreditation:* NASAD. *Degree requirements:* For master's, thesis, 60 credits, including all required courses; residency of two academic years. *Entrance requirements:* For master's, portfolio of work (still images) submitted through SlideRoom. Additional exam requirements/recommendations for international students: Required—TOEFL (minimum score 100 iBT). Electronic applications accepted. *Faculty research:* Illustration, fine arts, computer art, writing, art history, art direction.

Syracuse University, College of Visual and Performing Arts, MFA Program in Illustration, Syracuse, NY 13244. Offers MFA. In 2017, 1 master's awarded. *Degree requirements:* For master's, thesis or alternative. *Entrance requirements:* For master's, portfolio, artist statement, three letters of recommendation, academic transcripts, personal statement/essay, resume. Additional exam requirements/recommendations for international students: Required—TOEFL (minimum score 100 iBT), IELTS. *Application deadline:* For fall admission, 2/1 priority date for domestic and international students. Application fee: $75. Electronic applications accepted. *Financial support:* Fellowships with full tuition reimbursements and teaching assistantships with tuition reimbursements available. Financial award application deadline: 1/1. *Faculty research:* Illustration skills and concepts. *Unit head:* Prof. James Ransome, Associate Professor/Graduate Program Coordinator, 315-443-1138, E-mail: jransome@syr.edu. *Application contact:* Caitlin Jarvis, Graduate Recruitment Specialist, 315-443-2769, E-mail: admissg@syr.edu.
Website: http://vpa.syr.edu/academics/art/graduate/illustration/

Western Connecticut State University, Division of Graduate Studies, School of Visual and Performing Arts, Department of Art, Danbury, CT 06810-6885. Offers illustration (MFA); painting (MFA). *Program availability:* Part-time. *Degree requirements:* For master's, individual exhibition of artwork, review of student's progress prior to admission to final semester, completion of program in 6 years. *Entrance requirements:* For master's, portfolio review, minimum GPA of 2.5. Additional exam requirements/recommendations for international students: Recommended—TOEFL (minimum score 550 paper-based; 79 iBT), IELTS (minimum score 6). *Expenses:* Contact institution. *Faculty research:* Proficiency in both traditional and digital processes.

Industrial Design

Academy of Art University, Graduate Programs, School of Industrial Design, San Francisco, CA 94105-3410. Offers MA, MFA. *Program availability:* Part-time, 100% online. *Faculty:* 5 full-time (0 women), 27 part-time/adjunct (5 women). *Students:* 73 full-time (25 women), 56 part-time (21 women); includes 15 minority (2 Black or African American, non-Hispanic/Latino; 6 Asian, non-Hispanic/Latino; 6 Hispanic/Latino; 1 Native Hawaiian or other Pacific Islander, non-Hispanic/Latino), 96 international. Average age 28. 75 applicants, 100% accepted, 37 enrolled. In 2017, 52 master's awarded. *Degree requirements:* For master's, final review. *Entrance requirements:* For master's, statement of intent; resume; portfolio/reel; official college transcripts. *Application deadline:* Applications are processed on a rolling basis. Application fee: $50. Electronic applications accepted. *Expenses: Tuition:* Part-time $982 per unit. *Financial support:* Career-related internships or fieldwork, Federal Work-Study, and scholarships/grants available. Financial award application deadline: 8/10; financial award applicants required to submit FAFSA. *Unit head:* 800-544-ARTS, E-mail: info@academyart.edu. *Application contact:* 800-544-ARTS, E-mail: info@academyart.edu.
Website: http://www.academyart.edu/industrial-design-school/index.html

ArtCenter College of Design, Graduate Industrial Design Program, Pasadena, CA 91103. Offers MS. *Accreditation:* NASAD.

Auburn University, Graduate School, College of Architecture, Design, and Construction, Department of Industrial Design, Auburn University, AL 36849. Offers MID. *Accreditation:* NASAD. *Program availability:* Part-time. *Faculty:* 19 full-time (4 women), 2 part-time/adjunct (1 woman). *Students:* 31 full-time (19 women), 10 part-time (2 women); includes 1 minority (Black or African American, non-Hispanic/Latino), 33 international. Average age 24. 50 applicants, 48% accepted, 16 enrolled. In 2017, 5 master's awarded. *Entrance requirements:* For master's, GRE General Test. *Application deadline:* Applications are processed on a rolling basis. Application fee: $50 ($60 for international students). Electronic applications accepted. *Expenses:* Tuition, state resident: full-time $10,974; part-time $519 per credit hour. Tuition, nonresident: full-time $29,658; part-time $1557 per credit hour. *Required fees:* $816 per semester. Tuition and fees vary according to degree level and program. *Financial support:* Federal Work-Study available. Support available to part-time students. Financial award application deadline: 3/15; financial award applicants required to submit FAFSA. *Faculty research:* Design of space living facilities, color use in business communications. *Unit head:* Clark E. Lundell, Head, 334-844-2364. *Application contact:* Dr. George Flowers, Dean of the Graduate School, 334-844-2125.
Website: http://www.auburn.edu/academic/architecture/ind/menu.html

California College of the Arts, Graduate Programs, Design Program, San Francisco, CA 94107. Offers graphic design (MFA); industrial design (MFA); interaction design (MFA). *Accreditation:* NASAD. *Faculty:* 14 full-time (4 women), 40 part-time/adjunct (14 women). *Students:* 109 full-time (64 women); includes 18 minority (1 Black or African American, non-Hispanic/Latino; 12 Asian, non-Hispanic/Latino; 5 Hispanic/Latino), 64 international. Average age 26. 618 applicants, 35% accepted, 76 enrolled. In 2017, 54 master's awarded. *Degree requirements:* For master's, thesis, exhibit. *Entrance requirements:* For master's, appropriate bachelor's degree, portfolio, resume, letters of recommendation, transcripts. Additional exam requirements/recommendations for international students: Required—TOEFL, IELTS, or PTE. *Application deadline:* For fall admission, 1/31 priority date for domestic and international students. Applications are processed on a rolling basis. Application fee: $70. Electronic applications accepted. *Expenses:* Contact institution. *Financial support:* In 2017–18, fellowships (averaging $22,000 per year), teaching assistantships (averaging $2,000 per year) were awarded; career-related internships or fieldwork, Federal Work-Study, scholarships/grants, health care benefits, and unspecified assistantships also available. Financial award application deadline: 7/31; financial award applicants required to submit FAFSA. *Unit head:* Kristian Simsarian, Graduate Chair, 415-551-9283, Fax: 415-703-9539, E-mail: ksimsarian@cca.edu. *Application contact:* Wes Fanelli, Assistant Director of Graduate Admissions, 415-703-9533, Fax: 415-703-9539, E-mail: wfanelli@cca.edu.

Carleton University, Faculty of Graduate Studies, Faculty of Engineering and Design, School of Industrial Design, Ottawa, ON K1S 5B6, Canada. Offers M Des. *Degree requirements:* For master's, thesis optional. *Entrance requirements:* For master's, honors degree. Additional exam requirements/recommendations for international students: Required—TOEFL.

Florida State University, The Graduate School, College of Human Sciences, Department of Retail, Merchandising and Product Development, Tallahassee, FL 32306-1492. Offers MS. *Program availability:* Part-time. *Faculty:* 5 full-time (4 women). *Students:* 3 full-time (all women); all minorities (1 Black or African American, non-Hispanic/Latino; 2 Two or more races, non-Hispanic/Latino). Average age 29. In 2017, 4 master's awarded. *Degree requirements:* For master's, thesis optional. *Entrance requirements:* For master's, GRE General Test, minimum upper-division GPA of 3.0. Additional exam requirements/recommendations for international students: Required—TOEFL (minimum score 550 paper-based; 80 iBT). *Application deadline:* For fall admission, 4/1 for domestic and international students; for spring admission, 10/1 for domestic and international students. Applications are processed on a rolling basis. Application fee: $30. Electronic applications accepted. *Expenses:* $480 per credit hour in-state; $1,111 per credit hour out-of-state. *Financial support:* In 2017–18, 3 students received support, including 2 research assistantships (averaging $9,332 per year), 1 teaching assistantship with full tuition reimbursement available (averaging $5,365 per year); career-related internships or fieldwork, institutionally sponsored loans, scholarships/grants, and unspecified assistantships also available. Financial award application deadline: 1/15; financial award applicants required to submit FAFSA. *Faculty research:* Global merchandising and product development. *Total annual research expenditures:* $19,383. *Unit head:* Dr. Robert C. Hickner, Interim Department Chair, 850-644-2498, Fax: 850-645-4673, E-mail: rhickner@fsu.edu.

Georgia Institute of Technology, Graduate Studies, College of Design, School of Industrial Design, Atlanta, GA 30332-0001. Offers MID. *Accreditation:* NASAD. *Degree requirements:* For master's, thesis optional.

Iowa State University of Science and Technology, Program in Industrial Design, Ames, IA 50011. Offers MID. *Accreditation:* NASAD. *Entrance requirements:* For master's, GRE, curriculum vitae, portfolio, letters of recommendation, interview. Additional exam requirements/recommendations for international students: Required—TOEFL (minimum score 587 paper-based; 95 iBT), IELTS (minimum score 7). Electronic applications accepted.

The New School, Parsons School of Design, Program in Industrial Design, New York, NY 10011. Offers MFA. *Program availability:* Part-time. *Faculty:* 8 full-time (2 women), 11 part-time/adjunct (5 women). *Students:* 40 full-time (25 women); includes 3 minority (1 Black or African American, non-Hispanic/Latino; 2 Hispanic/Latino), 29 international. Average age 27. 150 applicants, 39% accepted, 24 enrolled. In 2017, 14 master's awarded. *Degree requirements:* For master's, thesis. *Entrance requirements:* For master's, transcripts, resume, statement of purpose, recommendation letters, portfolio, interview. Additional exam requirements/recommendations for international students: Required—TOEFL (minimum score 92 iBT), IELTS (minimum score 7), PTE (minimum score 63). *Application deadline:* For fall admission, 1/1 priority date for domestic and international students; for summer admission, 1/1 priority date for domestic and international students. Applications are processed on a rolling basis. Application fee: $50. Electronic applications accepted. *Expenses:* $24,922 per semester full-time, $1,744 per credit part-time, $100 maintenance of status fee. *Financial support:* In 2017–18, 26 students received support, including 4 teaching assistantships (averaging $3,349 per year); career-related internships or fieldwork, scholarships/grants, unspecified assistantships, and travel funding; tuition waivers for students who are also New School employees also available. Support available to part-time students. Financial award application deadline: 2/1; financial award applicants required to submit FAFSA. *Total annual research expenditures:* $106,000. *Unit head:* Rama Chorpash, Program Director, 212-229-5600, E-mail: chorpasr@newschool.edu. *Application contact:* Courtney Malenius, Director of Graduate Admissions, 212-229-5150 Ext. 4011, E-mail: maleniuc@newschool.edu.
Website: https://www.newschool.edu/parsons/mfa-industrial-design/

Industrial Design

North Carolina State University, Graduate School, College of Design, Department of Industrial Design, Raleigh, NC 27695. Offers MID. *Accreditation:* NASAD. *Program availability:* Part-time. *Degree requirements:* For master's, thesis optional, oral exam, project. *Entrance requirements:* For master's, GRE General Test (recommended), portfolio. Electronic applications accepted. *Faculty research:* Computer graphics, ergonomics, product design.

The Ohio State University, Graduate School, College of Arts and Sciences, Division of Arts and Humanities, Department of Design, Columbus, OH 43210. Offers design (MA); design research and development (MFA); digital animation and interactive media (MFA). *Accreditation:* NASAD. *Program availability:* Part-time. *Faculty:* 16. *Students:* 25 (15 women), 8 international. Average age 28. In 2017, 10 master's awarded. *Entrance requirements:* For master's, GRE General Test (for all applicants with cumulative GPA below 3.0), portfolio. Additional exam requirements/recommendations for international students: Recommended—TOEFL (minimum score 550 paper-based; 79 iBT). *Application deadline:* For fall admission, 12/13 priority date for domestic students, 11/30 priority date for international students; for spring admission, 3/1 for domestic students, 2/1 for international students. Applications are processed on a rolling basis. Application fee: $60 ($70 for international students). Electronic applications accepted. *Financial support:* Fellowships, research assistantships, teaching assistantships, career-related internships or fieldwork, Federal Work-Study, institutionally sponsored loans, and unspecified assistantships available. Support available to part-time students. Financial award application deadline: 5/1. *Unit head:* Dr. Mary Anne Beecher, Chair, 614-688-6746, E-mail: beecher.17@osu.edu. *Application contact:* Graduate and Professional Admissions, 614-292-9444, Fax: 614-292-3895, E-mail: gpadmissions@osu.edu.
Website: http://design.osu.edu/

Pratt Institute, School of Design, Program in Industrial Design, Brooklyn, NY 11205-3899. Offers MID. *Accreditation:* NASAD. *Program availability:* Part-time. *Students:* 73 full-time (42 women), 2 part-time (0 women); includes 10 minority (5 Asian, non-Hispanic/Latino; 3 Hispanic/Latino; 2 Two or more races, non-Hispanic/Latino), 46 international. Average age 26. 258 applicants, 33% accepted, 27 enrolled. In 2017, 21 master's awarded. *Degree requirements:* For master's, thesis. *Entrance requirements:* For master's, portfolio, letters of recommendation. Additional exam requirements/recommendations for international students: Required—TOEFL (minimum score 575 paper-based; 90 iBT). *Application deadline:* For fall admission, 1/5 for domestic and international students; for spring admission, 10/1 for domestic and international students. Application fee: $50 ($90 for international students). Electronic applications accepted. *Expenses: Tuition:* Full-time $30,834. *Required fees:* $1974. *Financial support:* Career-related internships or fieldwork, Federal Work-Study, institutionally sponsored loans, scholarships/grants, health care benefits, and unspecified assistantships available. Support available to part-time students. Financial award application deadline: 2/1; financial award applicants required to submit FAFSA. *Faculty research:* Universal design, design ethics, sustainability in design. *Unit head:* Constantin Boym, Chairperson, 718-636-3520, Fax: 718-636-3553, E-mail: cboym@pratt.edu. *Application contact:* Natalie Capannelli, Director of Graduate Admissions, 718-636-3551, Fax: 718-399-4242, E-mail: ncapanne@pratt.edu.
Website: https://www.pratt.edu/academics/school-of-design/graduate-school-of-design/industrial-design-grad/

See Display on page 65 and Close-Up on page 97.

Pratt Institute, School of Design, Program in Package Design, Brooklyn, NY 10011. Offers MS. *Accreditation:* NASAD. *Program availability:* Part-time. *Students:* 36 full-time (28 women), 1 (woman) part-time; includes 8 minority (1 Black or African American, non-Hispanic/Latino; 4 Asian, non-Hispanic/Latino; 3 Hispanic/Latino), 24 international. Average age 26. 31 applicants, 90% accepted, 14 enrolled. In 2017, 14 master's awarded. *Degree requirements:* For master's, thesis. *Entrance requirements:* For master's, portfolio, letters of recommendation. Additional exam requirements/recommendations for international students: Required—TOEFL (minimum score 575 paper-based; 90 iBT). *Application deadline:* For fall admission, 1/5 for domestic and international students; for spring admission, 10/1 for domestic and international students. Application fee: $50 ($90 for international students). Electronic applications accepted. *Expenses: Tuition:* Full-time $30,834. *Required fees:* $1974. *Financial support:* Career-related internships or fieldwork, Federal Work-Study, institutionally sponsored loans, scholarships/grants, health care benefits, and unspecified assistantships available. Support available to part-time students. Financial award application deadline: 2/1; financial award applicants required to submit FAFSA. *Unit head:* Santiago Piedrafita Iglesias, Chairperson, 718-648-5313, Fax: 718-399-4495, E-mail: spiedraf@pratt.edu. *Application contact:* Natalie Capannelli, Director of Graduate Admissions, 718-636-3551, Fax: 718-399-4242, E-mail: ncapanne@pratt.edu.
Website: https://www.pratt.edu/academics/school-of-design/graduate-school-of-design/grad-communications-design/package-design-ms/

See Display on page 65 and Close-Up on page 97.

Purdue University, Graduate School, College of Liberal Arts, Department of Art and Design, West Lafayette, IN 47907. Offers art education (MA, PhD); industrial design (MFA); integrated studio arts (MFA); interior design (MFA); photography (MFA); visual communications design (MFA). *Accreditation:* NASAD; NAST. *Program availability:* Part-time. *Students:* 20 full-time (14 women), 1 part-time (0 women); includes 1 minority (Two or more races, non-Hispanic/Latino), 16 international. Average age 26. 97 applicants, 26% accepted, 10 enrolled. In 2017, 6 master's awarded. *Degree requirements:* For master's, terminal exhibit, project, or thesis. *Entrance requirements:* For master's, GRE General Test (for art education), minimum undergraduate GPA of 3.0 or equivalent; 9 undergraduate hours in an art or design history; BA in art (for MA in art education); for doctorate, GRE General Test (minimum scores 600 in verbal and 1000 total), master's degree in art education or art with teaching certification; 3 years of teaching experience at the K-12 level. Additional exam requirements/recommendations for international students: Required—TOEFL (minimum score 550 paper-based; 77 iBT). *Application deadline:* For fall admission, 2/1 for domestic students, 2/1 priority date for international students. Applications are processed on a rolling basis. Application fee: $60 ($75 for international students). Electronic applications accepted. *Financial support:* Teaching assistantships with tuition reimbursements and career-related internships or fieldwork available. Support available to part-time students. Financial award applicants required to submit FAFSA. *Faculty research:* Design, fine arts, photography, acting, directing, theatre technology. *Unit head:* Harry T. Bulow, Head of the Graduate Program, 765-494-3056, E-mail: hbulow@purdue.edu. *Application contact:* Sara J. Unser, Graduate Contact, 765-494-8662, E-mail: sunser@purdue.edu.
Website: https://www.cla.purdue.edu/vpa/ad/

Rhode Island School of Design, Department of Industrial Design, Providence, RI 02903-2784. Offers MID. *Accreditation:* NASAD. *Faculty:* 5 full-time (2 women), 18 part-time/adjunct (8 women). *Students:* 37 full-time (16 women); includes 6 minority (4 Asian, non-Hispanic/Latino; 1 Hispanic/Latino; 1 Two or more races, non-Hispanic/Latino), 14 international. Average age 27. 218 applicants, 24% accepted, 12 enrolled. In 2017, 19 master's awarded. *Degree requirements:* For master's, thesis, exhibition. *Entrance requirements:* For master's, portfolio, statement of purpose, 3 letters of recommendation. Additional exam requirements/recommendations for international students: Required—TOEFL (minimum score 580 paper-based; 93 iBT). *Application deadline:* For fall admission, 1/10 for domestic and international students. Application fee: $60. Electronic applications accepted. *Expenses: Tuition:* Full-time $48,210. *Required fees:* $260. *Financial support:* Fellowships, research assistantships, teaching assistantships, Federal Work-Study, scholarships/grants, and unspecified assistantships available. Financial award application deadline: 2/15; financial award applicants required to submit FAFSA. *Unit head:* Charlie Cannon, Department Head, 401-454-6160, Fax: 401-454-6157, E-mail: idgradprogram@risd.edu. *Application contact:* Molly Pettengill, Assistant Director for Graduate Recruitment, 401-454-6312, Fax: 401-454-6309, E-mail: mpetteng@risd.edu.
Website: http://www.risd.edu/academics/industrial-design/

Rochester Institute of Technology, Graduate Enrollment Services, College of Imaging Arts and Sciences, School of Design, MFA Program in Industrial Design, Rochester, NY 14623-5603. Offers MFA. *Accreditation:* NASAD. *Program availability:* Part-time. *Students:* Average age 26. 189 applicants, 32% accepted, 20 enrolled. In 2017, 10 master's awarded. *Degree requirements:* For master's, thesis, thesis exhibition. *Entrance requirements:* For master's, GRE, portfolio, minimum GPA of 3.0 (recommended). Additional exam requirements/recommendations for international students: Required—TOEFL (minimum score 550 paper-based; 90 iBT), IELTS (minimum score 7), PTE (minimum score 58). *Application deadline:* For fall admission, 2/15 priority date for domestic and international students. Applications are processed on a rolling basis. Application fee: $65. Electronic applications accepted. *Expenses:* $1,815 per credit hour. *Financial support:* In 2017–18, 31 students received support. Teaching assistantships with partial tuition reimbursements available, career-related internships or fieldwork, scholarships/grants, and unspecified assistantships available. Support available to part-time students. Financial award applicants required to submit FAFSA. *Faculty research:* User-centered design, accessible technology, interdisciplinary collaboration, digital fabrication, sustainability. *Unit head:* Alex Lobos, Graduate Program Director, 585-475-7417, E-mail: alex.lobos@rit.edu. *Application contact:* Diane Ellison, Senior Associate Vice President, Graduate Enrollment Services, 585-475-2229, Fax: 585-475-7164, E-mail: gradinfo@rit.edu.
Website: http://cias.rit.edu/schools/design/graduate-industrial-design

Savannah College of Art and Design, Program in Industrial Design, Savannah, GA 31402-3146. Offers MA, MFA. *Program availability:* Part-time. *Faculty:* 14 full-time (1 woman), 3 part-time/adjunct (1 woman). *Students:* 118 full-time (52 women), 25 part-time (10 women); includes 8 minority (3 Black or African American, non-Hispanic/Latino; 3 Asian, non-Hispanic/Latino; 2 Hispanic/Latino), 123 international. Average age 26. 152 applicants, 74% accepted, 36 enrolled. In 2017, 36 master's awarded. *Degree requirements:* For master's, final project (for MA); thesis (for MFA). *Entrance requirements:* For master's, GRE (recommended), portfolio (submitted in digital format), audition or writing submission, resume, statement of purpose, two letters of recommendation. Additional exam requirements/recommendations for international students: Recommended—TOEFL (minimum score 550 paper-based; 85 iBT), IELTS (minimum score 6.5). *Application deadline:* For fall admission, 4/1 for domestic and international students. Applications are processed on a rolling basis. Application fee: $40. Electronic applications accepted. *Expenses: Tuition:* Full-time $36,765; part-time $817 per credit hour. One-time fee: $500. *Financial support:* Career-related internships or fieldwork, Federal Work-Study, and scholarships/grants available. Financial award application deadline: 4/1; financial award applicants required to submit FAFSA. *Unit head:* Victor Ermoli, Dean, School of Design. *Application contact:* Jenny Jaquillard, Executive Director of Admissions, Recruitment and Events, 912-525-5100, Fax: 912-525-5985, E-mail: admission@scad.edu.
Website: http://www.scad.edu/academics/programs/industrial-design

Thomas Jefferson University, Kanbar College of Design, Engineering and Commerce, Program in Industrial Design, Philadelphia, PA 19107. Offers MS. *Accreditation:* NASAD. *Program availability:* Part-time, evening/weekend. *Degree requirements:* For master's, project. *Entrance requirements:* For master's, essay; portfolio (recommended). Additional exam requirements/recommendations for international students: Required—TOEFL (minimum score 79 iBT), IELTS (minimum score 6.5).

University of Cincinnati, Graduate School, College of Design, Architecture, Art, and Planning, School of Design, Cincinnati, OH 45221. Offers fashion design (M Des); graphic design (M Des); industrial design (M Des); interaction design (M Des); product development (M Des). *Accreditation:* NASAD. *Degree requirements:* For master's, thesis. *Entrance requirements:* For master's, undergraduate degree in design or related field, 2 years of work experience in design or related field. Additional exam requirements/recommendations for international students: Required—TOEFL. Electronic applications accepted. *Expenses: Tuition, area resident:* Full-time $14,468. Tuition, state resident: full-time $14,968; part-time $754 per credit hour. Tuition, nonresident: full-time $24,210; part-time $1311 per credit hour. *International tuition:* $26,460 full-time. *Required fees:* $3958; $84 per credit hour. One-time fee: $85 full-time. Tuition and fees vary according to course load, degree level and program. *Faculty research:* Design theory, interdisciplinary design topics.

University of Detroit Mercy, College of Engineering and Science, Detroit, MI 48221. Offers chemistry (MS); civil and environmental engineering (DE); electrical and computer engineering (ME); electrical engineering (DE); engineering management (M Eng Mgt); environmental engineering (MEE); mechanical engineering (MME, DE); product development (MS); software engineering (MSSE); teaching of mathematics (MATM). *Program availability:* Part-time, evening/weekend. *Degree requirements:* For doctorate, thesis/dissertation. Electronic applications accepted. Application fee is waived when completed online. *Expenses:* Contact institution.

University of Illinois at Urbana–Champaign, Graduate College, College of Fine and Applied Arts, School of Art and Design, Program in Design and Media, Champaign, IL 61820. Offers art and design (MFA), including new media; graphic design (MFA); industrial design (MFA). *Accreditation:* NASAD.

University of Notre Dame, Graduate School, College of Arts and Letters, Division of Humanities, Department of Art, Art History, and Design, Notre Dame, IN 46556. Offers art history (MA); design (MFA), including graphic design, industrial design; studio art (MFA), including ceramics, painting, photography, printmaking, sculpture. *Accreditation:* NASAD. *Degree requirements:* For master's, comprehensive exam (for some programs), thesis. *Entrance requirements:* For master's, GRE General Test, minimum GPA of 3.0. Additional exam requirements/recommendations for international students: Required—TOEFL (minimum score 600 paper-based; 80 iBT). Electronic applications accepted. *Faculty research:* Studio art practice in ceramics, printing, photography, printmaking and sculpture, graphic design and industrial design, digital imaging in design and photography, Renaissance and American art history, contemporary art theory and criticism.

The University of the Arts, College of Art, Media and Design, Department of Industrial Design, Philadelphia, PA 19102-4944. Offers MID. *Accreditation:* NASAD. *Degree requirements:* For master's, thesis. *Entrance requirements:* For master's, portfolio of 20 pieces that showcases self-generated projects, professional assignments

or projects developed in a previous program; official transcripts; three letters of recommendation; one- to two-page statement of professional plans and goals; personal interview; resume or curriculum vitae; statement of intent. Additional exam requirements/recommendations for international students: Required—TOEFL (minimum score 580 paper-based, 92 iBT) or IELTS (minimum score 6.5).

University of Washington, Graduate School, College of Arts and Sciences, School of Art, Division of Design, Seattle, WA 98195. Offers industrial design (MFA); visual communication design (MFA).

Wayne State University, College of Fine, Performing and Communication Arts, James Pearson Duffy Department of Art and Art History, Detroit, MI 48202. Offers art (MA, MFA), including ceramics, drawing, fashion design and merchandising (MA), fibers, graphic design, industrial design (MA), interior design (MA), metalsmithing, painting, photography, printmaking, sculpture; art history (MA). *Students:* 13 full-time (8 women), 12 part-time (9 women); includes 5 minority (3 Black or African American, non-Hispanic/Latino; 1 Asian, non-Hispanic/Latino; 1 Hispanic/Latino), 2 international. Average age 34. 46 applicants, 24% accepted, 6 enrolled. In 2017, 5 master's awarded. *Degree requirements:* For master's, thesis (for some programs), essay or thesis.

Entrance requirements: For master's, BFA or another degree and equivalent course work, portfolio, personal interview, reference letters, statement of intent (except for art history program). Additional exam requirements/recommendations for international students: Required—TOEFL (minimum score 550 paper-based; 79 iBT), TWE (minimum score 5.5), Michigan English Language Assessment Battery (minimum score 85); Recommended—IELTS (minimum score 6.5). *Application deadline:* For fall admission, 2/1 for domestic and international students; for winter admission, 10/1 for domestic and international students. Application fee: $50. Electronic applications accepted. *Expenses:* Contact institution. *Financial support:* In 2017–18, 18 students received support, including 1 research assistantship (averaging $22,241 per year), 6 teaching assistantships with tuition reimbursements available (averaging $18,534 per year); fellowships with tuition reimbursements available, scholarships/grants, and unspecified assistantships also available. Support available to part-time students. Financial award applicants required to submit FAFSA. *Unit head:* Dr. John Richardson, Chair, 313-577-2980, Fax: 313-577-3491, E-mail: af5343@wayne.edu. *Application contact:* 313-577-2980, E-mail: art@wayne.edu. Website: http://art.wayne.edu/

Interior Design

Academy of Art University, Graduate Programs, School of Interior Architecture and Design, San Francisco, CA 94105-3410. Offers MA, MFA. *Accreditation:* CIDA. *Program availability:* Part-time, 100% online. *Faculty:* 3 full-time (2 women), 26 part-time/adjunct (10 women). *Students:* 150 full-time (109 women), 136 part-time (121 women); includes 46 minority (20 Black or African American, non-Hispanic/Latino; 9 Asian, non-Hispanic/Latino; 13 Hispanic/Latino; 4 Two or more races, non-Hispanic/Latino), 127 international. Average age 32. 119 applicants, 100% accepted, 78 enrolled. In 2017, 53 master's awarded. *Degree requirements:* For master's, final review. *Entrance requirements:* For master's, statement of intent; resume; portfolio/reel; official college transcripts. *Application deadline:* Applications are processed on a rolling basis. Application fee: $50. Electronic applications accepted. *Expenses: Tuition:* Part-time $982 per unit. *Financial support:* Career-related internships or fieldwork, Federal Work-Study, and scholarships/grants available. Financial award application deadline: 8/10; financial award applicants required to submit FAFSA. *Unit head:* 800-544-ARTS, E-mail: info@academyart.edu. *Application contact:* 800-544-ARTS, E-mail: info@academyart.edu.
Website: http://www.academyart.edu/interior-design-school/index.html

Ball State University, Graduate School, Teachers College, Department of Family, Consumer, and Technology Education, Muncie, IN 47306. Offers family and consumer science (MS), including apparel design (MA, MS), fashion merchandising (MA, MS), interior design (MA, MS), residential property management (MA, MS); family and consumer sciences (MA), including apparel design (MA, MS), fashion merchandising (MA, MS), interior design (MA, MS), residential property management (MA, MS); nutrition and dietetics (MA, MS). *Program availability:* Part-time, evening/weekend, 100% online. *Students:* 9 full-time (5 women), 54 part-time (20 women); includes 9 minority (5 Black or African American, non-Hispanic/Latino; 1 Asian, non-Hispanic/Latino; 3 Hispanic/Latino), 6 international. Average age 36. 63 applicants, 48% accepted, 26 enrolled. In 2017, 19 master's awarded. *Entrance requirements:* For master's, letter of intent, resume, two letters of recommendation, portfolio (for interior design option). Additional exam requirements/recommendations for international students: Required—TOEFL (minimum score 550 paper-based; 79 iBT), IELTS (minimum score 6.5). *Application deadline:* For fall admission, 2/15 for domestic students; for spring admission, 9/25 for domestic students. Applications are processed on a rolling basis. Application fee: $60. Electronic applications accepted. *Financial support:* Research assistantships with partial tuition reimbursements and unspecified assistantships available. Financial award application deadline: 3/1; financial award applicants required to submit FAFSA. *Unit head:* Dr. Scott Hall, Chairperson, 765-285-5943, Fax: 765-285-2314, E-mail: sshall@bsu.edu. *Application contact:* Dr. Scott Hall, Chairperson, 765-285-5943, Fax: 765-285-2314, E-mail: sshall@bsu.edu.
Website: http://www.bsu.edu/fcs/

Boston Architectural College, Graduate Programs, Boston, MA 02115-2795. Offers architecture (M Arch); historic preservation (MDS); interior design (MID); landscape architecture (MLA); sustainable design (MDS). *Accreditation:* CIDA. *Degree requirements:* For master's, thesis. *Entrance requirements:* For master's, portfolio (recommended). Electronic applications accepted.

Brenau University, Sydney O. Smith Graduate School, College of Fine Arts and Humanities, Gainesville, GA 30501. Offers interior design (MID). *Accreditation:* CIDA. *Program availability:* Part-time. *Degree requirements:* For master's, internship; portfolio. *Entrance requirements:* For master's, portfolio review, minimum GPA of 3.0, resume. Additional exam requirements/recommendations for international students: Required—TOEFL (minimum score 500 paper-based; 61 iBT); Recommended—IELTS (minimum score 5). Electronic applications accepted.

California State Polytechnic University, Pomona, Program in Interior Architecture, Pomona, CA 91768-2557. Offers MIA. Program offered in partnership with UCLA Extension. *Accreditation:* CIDA. *Program availability:* Part-time, evening/weekend. *Students:* 17 full-time (15 women), 32 part-time (29 women); includes 12 minority (2 Black or African American, non-Hispanic/Latino; 9 Asian, non-Hispanic/Latino; 1 Two or more races, non-Hispanic/Latino), 22 international. Average age 30. 41 applicants, 54% accepted, 18 enrolled. In 2017, 39 master's awarded. *Entrance requirements:* Additional exam requirements/recommendations for international students: Required—TOEFL (minimum score 550 paper-based). *Application deadline:* Applications are processed on a rolling basis. Application fee: $55. Electronic applications accepted. *Expenses:* Contact institution. *Financial support:* Application deadline: 3/2; applicants required to submit FAFSA. *Unit head:* Prof. Irma Ramirez, Professor/Coordinator, 909-869-5355, Fax: 909-869-4331, E-mail: ieramirez@cpp.edu. *Application contact:* Deborah L. Brandon, Executive Director of Admissions and Enrollment Planning, 909-869-3427, Fax: 909-869-5315, E-mail: dlbrandon@cpp.edu. Website: http://www.cpp.edu/~ceu/degree-programs/interior-architecture/index.shtml

Chatham University, Program in Interior Architecture, Pittsburgh, PA 15232-2826. Offers MIA. *Program availability:* Part-time, evening/weekend, online learning. *Faculty:* 1 (woman) full-time, 5 part-time/adjunct (2 women). *Students:* 19 full-time (18 women), 5 part-time (all women); includes 2 minority (1 Black or African American, non-Hispanic/Latino; 1 Asian, non-Hispanic/Latino), 5 international. Average age 31. 32 applicants, 53% accepted, 11 enrolled. In 2017, 14 master's awarded. *Entrance requirements:* Additional exam requirements/recommendations for international students: Required—

TOEFL (minimum score 600 paper-based; 100 iBT), IELTS (minimum score 7), TWE. *Application deadline:* For fall admission, 4/1 priority date for domestic and international students; for spring admission, 11/1 priority date for domestic students, 10/1 priority date for international students. Applications are processed on a rolling basis. Application fee: $45. Electronic applications accepted. Application fee is waived when completed online. *Expenses: Tuition:* Full-time $16,740; part-time $930 per credit. *Required fees:* $486; $27 per credit. $243 per semester. *Financial support:* Applicants required to submit FAFSA. *Faculty research:* Sustainability. *Unit head:* Dr. Thelma Lazo-Flores, Director, 412-365-2977, E-mail: tlazoflores@chatham.edu.
Website: http://www.chatham.edu/departments/artdesign/graduate/MIA/index.cfm

Cornell University, Graduate School, Graduate Fields of Human Ecology, Field of Design and Environmental Analysis, Ithaca, NY 14853. Offers applied research in human-environment relations (MS); facilities planning and management (MS); housing and design (MS); human factors and ergonomics (MS); human-environment relations (MS); interior design (MA, MPS). *Degree requirements:* For master's, thesis. *Entrance requirements:* For master's, GRE General Test, portfolio or slides of recent work; bachelor's degree in interior design, architecture or related design discipline; 2 letters of recommendation. Additional exam requirements/recommendations for international students: Required—TOEFL (minimum score 600 paper-based; 105 iBT). Electronic applications accepted. *Faculty research:* Facility planning and management, environmental psychology, housing, interior design, ergonomics and human factors.

Drexel University, Westphal College of Media Arts and Design, Program in Interior Architecture and Design, Philadelphia, PA 19104-2875. Offers MS. *Accreditation:* CIDA; NASAD. *Degree requirements:* For master's, comprehensive exam, thesis. *Entrance requirements:* For master's, interview. Additional exam requirements/recommendations for international students: Required—TOEFL. Electronic applications accepted. *Faculty research:* History of commercial interiors, hospice spaces, environmental sculpture, painting.

Eastern Michigan University, Graduate School, College of Technology, School of Visual and Built Environments, Program in Interior Design, Ypsilanti, MI 48197. Offers MS. *Program availability:* Part-time, evening/weekend, online learning. *Students:* 4 full-time (all women), 4 part-time (all women), 4 international. Average age 27. 9 applicants, 67% accepted, 1 enrolled. In 2017, 9 master's awarded. *Entrance requirements:* Additional exam requirements/recommendations for international students: Required—TOEFL. *Application deadline:* Applications are processed on a rolling basis. Application fee: $45. *Financial support:* Fellowships, research assistantships with full tuition reimbursements, teaching assistantships with full tuition reimbursements, career-related internships or fieldwork, Federal Work-Study, institutionally sponsored loans, scholarships/grants, tuition waivers (partial), and unspecified assistantships available. Support available to part-time students. Financial award applicants required to submit FAFSA. *Application contact:* Dr. Shinming Shyu, Graduate Program Coordinator, 734-487-6419, Fax: 734-487-8755, E-mail: sshyu@emich.edu.

Endicott College, Van Loan School of Graduate and Professional Studies, Program in Interior Architecture, Beverly, MA 01915-2096. Offers MA, MFA. *Accreditation:* NASAD. *Faculty:* 2 full-time (1 woman), 9 part-time/adjunct (5 women). *Students:* 12 full-time (11 women), 7 part-time (5 women); includes 3 minority (2 Asian, non-Hispanic/Latino; 1 Hispanic/Latino), 2 international. Average age 29. 6 applicants, 100% accepted, 2 enrolled. In 2017, 5 master's awarded. *Degree requirements:* For master's, thesis. *Entrance requirements:* For master's, statement of professional goals, two letters of recommendation, interview, undergraduate transcript. Additional exam requirements/recommendations for international students: Required—TOEFL (minimum score 550 paper-based; 79 iBT). *Application deadline:* Applications are processed on a rolling basis. Application fee: $50. Electronic applications accepted. *Expenses:* Contact institution. *Financial support:* Applicants required to submit FAFSA. *Faculty research:* Community outreach design studio, interior design practice. *Unit head:* Myoung Joo Chun, Director of Graduate Interior Design Programs, 978-232-2545, Fax: 978-232-3000, E-mail: mchun@endicott.edu. *Application contact:* Ian Menchini, Director, Graduate Enrollment and Advising, 978-232-5292, Fax: 978-232-3000, E-mail: imenchin@endicott.edu.
Website: https://vanloan.endicott.edu/programs-of-study/masters-programs/interior-architecture-program

Florida International University, College of Communication, Architecture and The Arts, Department of Interior Architecture, Miami, FL 33199. Offers MA, MIA, Certificate. *Accreditation:* CIDA. *Faculty:* 3 full-time (1 woman), 5 part-time/adjunct (4 women). *Students:* 42 full-time (34 women), 2 part-time (both women); includes 23 minority (1 Black or African American, non-Hispanic/Latino; 1 Asian, non-Hispanic/Latino; 21 Hispanic/Latino), 11 international. Average age 27. 12 applicants, 67% accepted, 6 enrolled. In 2017, 19 master's awarded. *Entrance requirements:* For master's, GRE or minimum GPA of 3.0 in upper-level undergraduate work, portfolio. Additional exam requirements/recommendations for international students: Required—TOEFL (minimum score 550 paper-based; 80 iBT). *Application deadline:* For fall admission, 2/1 for domestic and international students. Application fee: $30. Electronic applications accepted. *Expenses:* Tuition, state resident: full-time $8912; part-time $446 per credit hour. Tuition, nonresident: full-time $21,393; part-time $992 per credit hour. *Required fees:* $390; $195 per semester. *Financial support:* Institutionally sponsored

loans and scholarships/grants available. Financial award application deadline: 3/1; financial award applicants required to submit FAFSA. *Total annual research expenditures:* $27. *Unit head:* Janine King, Chair, 305-348-6630, Fax: 305-348-2650, E-mail: janine.king@fiu.edu. *Application contact:* Nanett Rojas, Assistant Director, Graduate Admissions, 305-348-7464, Fax: 305-348-7441, E-mail: gradadm@fiu.edu. Website: http://carta.fiu.edu

Florida State University, The Graduate School, College of Fine Arts, Department of Interior Architecture and Design, Tallahassee, FL 32306. Offers MFA, MS. *Accreditation:* NASAD (one or more programs are accredited). *Program availability:* Part-time. *Faculty:* 9 full-time (7 women), 4 part-time/adjunct (1 woman). *Students:* 18 full-time (15 women), 1 (woman) part-time; includes 2 minority (1 Black or African American, non-Hispanic/Latino; 1 Hispanic/Latino), 7 international. Average age 25. 37 applicants, 54% accepted, 9 enrolled. In 2017, 17 master's awarded. *Degree requirements:* For master's, thesis or alternative. *Entrance requirements:* For master's, GRE General Test, minimum GPA of 3.0 during previous 2 years. Additional exam requirements/recommendations for international students: Required—TOEFL (minimum score 550 paper-based; 80 iBT). *Application deadline:* For fall admission, 7/1 for domestic students, 5/1 for international students; for summer admission, 3/1 for domestic and international students. Applications are processed on a rolling basis. Application fee: $30. Electronic applications accepted. *Financial support:* In 2017–18, 13 teaching assistantships with tuition reimbursements (averaging $5,000 per year) were awarded; career-related internships or fieldwork and unspecified assistantships also available. Financial award applicants required to submit FAFSA. *Faculty research:* Social responsibility issues, graphics techniques, history of interiors, computer-aided design and drafting, pedagogy. *Unit head:* Dr. Lisa K. Waxman, Chairman, 850-644-8326, Fax: 850-644-3112, E-mail: lwaxman@fsu.edu. *Application contact:* Dr. Marlo Ransdell, Director of Graduate Studies, 850-645-6831, Fax: 850-644-3112, E-mail: mransdell@fsu.edu. Website: http://interiordesign.fsu.edu/

The George Washington University, Columbian College of Arts and Sciences, Corcoran School of the Arts and Design, Washington, DC 20007. Offers art and the book (MA); art education (MA, MAT); decorative arts and design history (MA); exhibition design (MA); interior design (MA); new media photojournalism (MA). MA in decorative arts and design history offered in partnership with Smithsonian Associates. *Accreditation:* NASAD. *Program availability:* Part-time. *Entrance requirements:* Additional exam requirements/recommendations for international students: Required—TOEFL (minimum score 95 iBT). *Expenses: Tuition:* Full-time $28,800; part-time $1655 per credit hour. *Required fees:* $45; $2.75 per credit hour.

The George Washington University, Columbian College of Arts and Sciences, Department of Fine Arts and Art History, Program in Interior Design, Washington, DC 20052. Offers MA, MFA. *Accreditation:* CIDA. *Faculty:* 2 full-time (0 women), 2 part-time/adjunct (both women). *Students:* 29 full-time (26 women); includes 14 minority (7 Black or African American, non-Hispanic/Latino; 2 Asian, non-Hispanic/Latino; 4 Hispanic/Latino; 1 Two or more races, non-Hispanic/Latino), 3 international. Average age 30. 45 applicants, 58% accepted, 13 enrolled. In 2017, 21 master's awarded. *Entrance requirements:* Additional exam requirements/recommendations for international students: Required—TOEFL (minimum score 550 paper-based; 80 iBT). *Application deadline:* For fall admission, 3/1 for domestic students, 1/15 for international students; for spring admission, 10/1 for domestic students, 9/1 for international students. *Expenses: Tuition:* Full-time $28,800; part-time $1655 per credit hour. *Required fees:* $45; $2.75 per credit hour. *Financial support:* Application deadline: 1/15. *Unit head:* Stephanie Travis, Chair, E-mail: stravis@gwu.edu. *Application contact:* Information Contact, 202-994-6085, Fax: 202-994-8657, E-mail: art@gwu.edu.

Georgia State University, Ernest G. Welch School of Art and Design, Program in Studio Art, Atlanta, GA 30302-3083. Offers ceramics (MFA); drawing and painting (MFA); graphic design (MFA); interior design (MFA); photography (MFA); printmaking (MFA); sculpture (MFA); textiles (MFA). *Accreditation:* NASAD. Application fee: $50. Electronic applications accepted. *Expenses:* Tuition, state resident: full-time $7020. Tuition, nonresident: full-time $22,518. *Required fees:* $2128. Tuition and fees vary according to degree level and program. *Financial support:* Fellowships, research assistantships, teaching assistantships, scholarships/grants, and unspecified assistantships available. Financial award application deadline: 4/15; financial award applicants required to submit FAFSA. *Faculty research:* Advertising and typography, new media, traditional media, three-dimensional art, architectural and environmental design. *Unit head:* Michael White, Director, Welch School of Art and Design, 404-413-5221, Fax: 404-413-5261, E-mail: mwhite@gsu.edu. *Application contact:* Hubert Stanley Anderson, Director of Graduate Studies, 404-413-5229, Fax: 404-413-5261, E-mail: artgrad@gsu.edu. Website: http://artdesign.gsu.edu/graduate/admissions/masters-of-fine-arts-in-studio/

Interior Designers Institute, Graduate Program, Newport Beach, CA 92660. Offers MA.

Iowa State University of Science and Technology, Program in Interior Design, Ames, IA 50011. Offers MA, MFA. *Accreditation:* NASAD. *Entrance requirements:* For master's, GRE. Additional exam requirements/recommendations for international students: Required—TOEFL (minimum score 550 paper-based; 79 iBT), IELTS (minimum score 6.5). Electronic applications accepted.

Lawrence Technological University, College of Architecture and Design, Southfield, MI 48075-1058. Offers architecture (M Arch, MA), including interior architecture (M Arch); build information modeling (Graduate Certificate); interior design (MID); social practice (MFA); transportation design (Graduate Certificate); urban design (MUD). *Accreditation:* NASAD. *Program availability:* Part-time, evening/weekend. *Faculty:* 14 full-time (1 woman), 3 part-time/adjunct (1 woman). *Students:* 6 full-time (2 women), 115 part-time (50 women); includes 11 minority (3 Black or African American, non-Hispanic/Latino; 1 Asian, non-Hispanic/Latino; 6 Hispanic/Latino; 1 Two or more races, non-Hispanic/Latino), 32 international. Average age 30. 150 applicants, 55% accepted, 50 enrolled. In 2017, 82 master's, 3 other advanced degrees awarded. *Degree requirements:* For master's, thesis optional. *Entrance requirements:* Additional exam requirements/recommendations for international students: Required—TOEFL (minimum score 550 paper-based; 79 iBT). *Application deadline:* For fall admission, 5/27 for international students; for spring admission, 10/8 for international students; for summer admission, 2/14 for international students. Applications are processed on a rolling basis. Application fee: $50. Electronic applications accepted. *Expenses: Tuition:* Full-time $15,274; part-time $1091 per credit. One-time fee: $150. *Financial support:* In 2017–18, 45 students received support, including 8 research assistantships with partial tuition reimbursements available (averaging $6,000 per year); career-related internships or fieldwork, scholarships/grants, and unspecified assistantships also available. Financial award application deadline: 4/1; financial award applicants required to submit FAFSA. *Faculty research:* Symmetry within the design process, public interest design, transdisciplinary design, adaptive reuse, digital craft, and integration of the use of daylight in architecture and urban design. *Total annual research expenditures:* $209,672. *Unit head:* Prof. Karl Daubmann, Dean/Professor, 248-204-2805, E-mail: archdean@ltu.edu. *Application contact:* Jane Rohrback, Director of Admissions, 248-

204-3160, Fax: 248-204-2228, E-mail: admissions@ltu.edu. Website: http://www.ltu.edu/architecture_and_design/index.asp

Marymount University, School of Arts and Sciences, Program in Interior Design, Arlington, VA 22207-4299. Offers MA. *Accreditation:* CIDA. *Program availability:* Part-time, evening/weekend. *Faculty:* 7 full-time (4 women), 4 part-time/adjunct (3 women). *Students:* 46 full-time (45 women), 28 part-time (25 women); includes 24 minority (13 Black or African American, non-Hispanic/Latino; 3 Asian, non-Hispanic/Latino; 6 Hispanic/Latino; 1 Native Hawaiian or other Pacific Islander, non-Hispanic/Latino; 1 Two or more races, non-Hispanic/Latino), 10 international. Average age 34. 32 applicants, 97% accepted, 20 enrolled. In 2017, 10 master's awarded. *Degree requirements:* For master's, thesis, 3-6 semesters of applied design studio work. *Entrance requirements:* For master's, 2 letters of recommendation, resume, personal statement, portfolio, transcript showing minimum of 30 credits in liberal arts and sciences coursework. Additional exam requirements/recommendations for international students: Required—TOEFL (minimum score 600 paper-based; 96 iBT), IELTS (minimum score 6.5). *Application deadline:* For fall admission, 7/15 priority date for domestic and international students; for spring admission, 11/1 priority date for domestic and international students; for summer admission, 4/15 priority date for domestic and international students. Applications are processed on a rolling basis. Application fee: $40. Electronic applications accepted. *Expenses: Tuition:* Full-time $17,550; part-time $975 per credit hour. *Required fees:* $198; $11 per credit hour. One-time fee: $250. Tuition and fees vary according to program. *Financial support:* In 2017–18, 7 students received support, including 1 research assistantship with full and partial tuition reimbursement available (averaging $5,850 per year), 2 teaching assistantships with full and partial tuition reimbursements available (averaging $5,850 per year); career-related internships or fieldwork, Federal Work-Study, scholarships/grants, and unspecified assistantships also available. Support available to part-time students. Financial award application deadline: 3/1; financial award applicants required to submit FAFSA. *Unit head:* Douglas R. Seidler, Chair, Interior Design, 703-284-1671, Fax: 703-284-3859, E-mail: douglas.seidler@marymount.edu. *Application contact:* Francesca Reed, Director, Graduate Admissions, 703-284-5901, Fax: 703-527-3815, E-mail: grad.admissions@marymount.edu. Website: http://www.marymount.edu/Academics/School-of-Arts-Sciences/Graduate-Programs/Interior-Design-MA

Marywood University, Academic Affairs, School of Architecture, Program in Interior Architecture/Design, Scranton, PA 18509-1598. Offers MA. *Degree requirements:* For master's, thesis. *Entrance requirements:* For master's, resume, personal essay, portfolio.

Miami University, College of Creative Arts, Department of Architecture and Interior Design, Oxford, OH 45056. Offers M Arch. *Accreditation:* NASAD. *Students:* 26 full-time (9 women); includes 3 minority (1 Black or African American, non-Hispanic/Latino; 1 Hispanic/Latino; 1 Two or more races, non-Hispanic/Latino), 10 international. Average age 26. In 2017, 10 master's awarded. *Expenses:* Tuition, state resident: full-time $13,812; part-time $575 per credit hour. Tuition, nonresident: full-time $30,860; part-time $1286 per credit hour. *Unit head:* Graham Cairns, Chair and Professor, 513-529-6431, E-mail: cairnsgj@miamioh.edu. *Application contact:* Craig Hinrichs, Professor/Director of Graduate Studies, 513-529-7036, E-mail: hinriccl@miamioh.edu. Website: http://www.MiamiOH.edu/architecture

Michigan State University, The Graduate School, College of Agriculture and Natural Resources and College of Social Science, School of Planning, Design and Construction, East Lansing, MI 48824. Offers construction management (MS, PhD); environmental design (MA); interior design and facilities management (MA); international planning studies (MIPS); urban and regional planning (MURP). *Degree requirements:* For master's, thesis or alternative. *Entrance requirements:* Additional exam requirements/recommendations for international students: Required—TOEFL. Electronic applications accepted.

Moore College of Art & Design, Program in Interior Design, Philadelphia, PA 19103. Offers MFA. *Accreditation:* NASAD. *Program availability:* Evening/weekend. *Degree requirements:* For master's, thesis, internship, thesis exhibition. *Entrance requirements:* For master's, minimum GPA of 3.0, on-site interview, portfolio, 3 letters of recommendation, resume.

The New School, Parsons School of Design, Program in Interior Design, New York, NY 10011. Offers interior design (MFA); interior/lighting design (MFA). *Program availability:* Part-time. *Faculty:* 13 full-time (4 women), 3 part-time/adjunct (1 woman). *Students:* 53 full-time (43 women); includes 5 minority (3 Black or African American, non-Hispanic/Latino; 1 Hispanic/Latino; 1 Native Hawaiian or other Pacific Islander, non-Hispanic/Latino), 31 international. Average age 27. 213 applicants, 44% accepted, 26 enrolled. In 2017, 27 master's awarded. *Degree requirements:* For master's, thesis. *Entrance requirements:* For master's, transcripts, resume, statement of purpose, recommendation letters, portfolio, interviews. Additional exam requirements/recommendations for international students: Required—TOEFL (minimum score 92 iBT), IELTS (minimum score 7), PTE (minimum score 63). *Application deadline:* For fall admission, 1/1 priority date for domestic and international students; for summer admission, 1/1 for domestic students, 1/1 priority date for international students. Applications are processed on a rolling basis. Application fee: $50. Electronic applications accepted. *Expenses:* $24,922 per semester full-time, $1,744 per credit part-time, $100 maintenance of status fee. *Financial support:* In 2017–18, 33 students received support, including 4 teaching assistantships (averaging $2,679 per year); career-related internships or fieldwork, scholarships/grants, and unspecified assistantships also available. Support available to part-time students. Financial award application deadline: 2/1; financial award applicants required to submit FAFSA. *Unit head:* Alfred Zollinger, Director, 212-229-8955 Ext. 2779, E-mail: zollinga@newschool.edu. *Application contact:* Courtney Malenius, Director of Graduate Admissions, 212-229-5150 Ext. 4011, E-mail: maleniuc@newschool.edu. Website: https://www.newschool.edu/parsons/mfa-interior-design/

The New School, Parsons School of Design, Program in Lighting Design, New York, NY 10011. Offers interior design/lighting design (MFA); lighting design (MFA); M Arch/MFA. *Faculty:* 6 full-time (2 women), 13 part-time/adjunct (4 women). *Students:* 26 full-time (20 women); includes 2 minority (1 Asian, non-Hispanic/Latino; 1 Hispanic/Latino), 21 international. Average age 27. 44 applicants, 75% accepted, 8 enrolled. In 2017, 21 master's awarded. *Degree requirements:* For master's, thesis. *Entrance requirements:* For master's, transcripts, resume, statement of purpose, recommendation letters, portfolio, interviews. Additional exam requirements/recommendations for international students: Required—TOEFL (minimum score 92 iBT), IELTS (minimum score 7), PTE (minimum score 63). *Application deadline:* For fall admission, 1/1 priority date for domestic and international students; for summer admission, 1/1 priority date for domestic and international students. Applications are processed on a rolling basis. Application fee: $50. Electronic applications accepted. *Expenses:* $24,922 per semester full-time, $1,744 per credit part-time, $100 maintenance of status fee. *Financial support:* In 2017–18, 17 students received support, including 4 teaching assistantships (averaging $2,344 per year); career-related internships or fieldwork, scholarships/grants, and unspecified assistantships also available. Support available to part-time students. Financial award application deadline: 2/1; financial award applicants required

to submit FAFSA. *Unit head:* Glenn Shrum, Director, 212-229-8900 Ext. 4853, E-mail: shrumg@newschool.edu. *Application contact:* Courtney Malenius, Director of Graduate Admissions, 212-229-5150 Ext. 4011, E-mail: maleniuc@newschool.edu.
Website: https://www.newschool.edu/parsons/lighting-design/

New York School of Interior Design, Program in Healthcare Interior Design, New York, NY 10021-5110. Offers MPS. *Entrance requirements:* For master's, portfolio, resume, undergraduate degree in interior design or closely-related field. Additional exam requirements/recommendations for international students: Required—TOEFL (minimum score 550 paper-based; 79 iBT). Electronic applications accepted.

New York School of Interior Design, Program in Interior Design (Post-Professional Level), New York, NY 10021-5110. Offers MFA. *Degree requirements:* For master's, thesis. *Entrance requirements:* For master's, portfolio, resume, undergraduate degree in interior design or closely-related field. Additional exam requirements/recommendations for international students: Required—TOEFL (minimum score 550 paper-based; 79 iBT). Electronic applications accepted.

New York School of Interior Design, Program in Interior Design (Professional-Level), New York, NY 10021-5110. Offers MFA. *Accreditation:* NASAD. *Degree requirements:* For master's, thesis. *Entrance requirements:* For master's, portfolio, resume, undergraduate degree in interior design or closely-related field. Additional exam requirements/recommendations for international students: Required—TOEFL (minimum score 550 paper-based; 79 iBT). Electronic applications accepted. *Faculty research:* History, theory, aesthetics, sociology, and green design; landscape, lighting, furniture, product, and set design.

The Ohio State University, Graduate School, College of Arts and Sciences, Division of Arts and Humanities, Department of Design, Columbus, OH 43210. Offers design (MA); design research and development (MFA); digital animation and interactive media (MFA). *Accreditation:* NASAD. *Program availability:* Part-time. *Faculty:* 16. *Students:* 25 (15 women), 8 international. Average age 28. In 2017, 10 master's awarded. *Entrance requirements:* For master's, GRE General Test (for all applicants with cumulative GPA below 3.0), portfolio. Additional exam requirements/recommendations for international students: Recommended—TOEFL (minimum score 550 paper-based; 79 iBT). *Application deadline:* For fall admission, 12/13 priority date for domestic students, 11/30 priority date for international students; for spring admission, 3/1 for domestic students, 2/1 for international students. Applications are processed on a rolling basis. Application fee: $60 ($70 for international students). Electronic applications accepted. *Financial support:* Fellowships, research assistantships, teaching assistantships, career-related internships or fieldwork, Federal Work-Study, institutionally sponsored loans, and unspecified assistantships available. Support available to part-time students. Financial award application deadline: 5/1. *Unit head:* Dr. Mary Anne Beecher, Chair, 614-688-6746, E-mail: beecher.17@osu.edu. *Application contact:* Graduate and Professional Admissions, 614-292-9444, Fax: 614-292-3895, E-mail: gpadmissions@osu.edu.
Website: http://design.osu.edu/

Paris College of Art, Graduate Programs, Paris, France. Offers accessories design (MA); fashion design: new materials and technologies (MA); fashion film and photography (MA); interior design (MA); transdisciplinary new media (MA, MFA). *Entrance requirements:* Additional exam requirements/recommendations for international students: Required—TOEFL or IELTS.

Pontificia Universidad Catolica Madre y Maestra, Graduate School, Faculty of Sciences and Humanities, Santiago, Dominican Republic. Offers architecture (M Arch), including architecture of interiors, architecture of tourist lodgings, landscaping; early childhood education (M Ed).

Pratt Institute, School of Design, Program in Interior Design, Brooklyn, NY 11205-3899. Offers MFA. *Accreditation:* NASAD. *Program availability:* Part-time. *Students:* 142 full-time (123 women), 6 part-time (5 women); includes 19 minority (4 Black or African American, non-Hispanic/Latino; 10 Asian, non-Hispanic/Latino; 5 Hispanic/Latino), 99 international. Average age 26. 266 applicants, 65% accepted, 69 enrolled. In 2017, 34 master's awarded. *Degree requirements:* For master's, thesis. *Entrance requirements:* For master's, portfolio, letters of recommendation. Additional exam requirements/recommendations for international students: Required—TOEFL (minimum score 575 paper-based; 90 iBT). *Application deadline:* For fall admission, 1/5 for domestic and international students; for spring admission, 10/1 for domestic and international students. Application fee: $50 ($90 for international students). Electronic applications accepted. *Expenses: Tuition:* Full-time $30,834. *Required fees:* $1974. *Financial support:* Career-related internships or fieldwork, Federal Work-Study, institutionally sponsored loans, scholarships/grants, health care benefits, and unspecified assistantships available. Support available to part-time students. Financial award application deadline: 2/1; financial award applicants required to submit FAFSA. *Unit head:* Alison Snyder, Chairperson, 718-636-3630, E-mail: asnyder@pratt.edu. *Application contact:* Natalie Capannelli, Director of Graduate Admissions, 718-636-3551, Fax: 718-636-3670, E-mail: ncapanne@pratt.edu.
Website: https://www.pratt.edu/academics/school-of-design/graduate-school-of-design/interior-design-grad/

See Display on page 65 and Close-Up on page 97.

Purdue University, Graduate School, College of Liberal Arts, Department of Art and Design, West Lafayette, IN 47907. Offers art education (MA, PhD); industrial design (MFA); integrated studio arts (MFA); interior design (MFA); photography (MFA); visual communications design (MFA). *Accreditation:* NASAD; NAST. *Program availability:* Part-time. *Students:* 20 full-time (14 women), 1 part-time (0 women); includes 1 minority (Two or more races, non-Hispanic/Latino), 16 international. Average age 26. 97 applicants, 26% accepted, 10 enrolled. In 2017, 6 master's awarded. *Degree requirements:* For master's, terminal exhibit, project, or thesis. *Entrance requirements:* For master's, GRE General Test (for art education), minimum undergraduate GPA of 3.0 or equivalent; 9 undergraduate hours in an art or design history; BA in art (for MA in art education); for doctorate, GRE General Test (minimum scores 600 in verbal and 1000 total), master's degree in art education or art with teaching certification; 3 years of teaching experience at the K-12 level. Additional exam requirements/recommendations for international students: Required—TOEFL (minimum score 550 paper-based; 77 iBT). *Application deadline:* For fall admission, 2/1 for domestic students, 2/1 priority date for international students. Applications are processed on a rolling basis. Application fee: $60 ($75 for international students). Electronic applications accepted. *Financial support:* Teaching assistantships with tuition reimbursements and career-related internships or fieldwork available. Support available to part-time students. Financial award applicants required to submit FAFSA. *Faculty research:* Design, fine arts, photography, acting, directing, theatre technology. *Unit head:* Harry T. Bulow, Head of the Graduate Program, 765-494-3056, E-mail: hbulow@purdue.edu. *Application contact:* Sara J. Unser, Graduate Contact, 765-494-8662, E-mail: sunser@purdue.edu.
Website: https://www.cla.purdue.edu/vpa/ad/

Queens University of Charlotte, College of Arts and Sciences, Charlotte, NC 28274-0002. Offers creative writing (MFA); interior design (MA). *Program availability:* Part-time, online learning. Electronic applications accepted.

Rhode Island School of Design, Department of Interior Architecture, Providence, RI 02903-2784. Offers exhibition and narrative environments (M Des); interior studies/adaptive reuse (M Des, MA). *Faculty:* 9 full-time (2 women), 21 part-time/adjunct (5 women). *Students:* 74 full-time (55 women); includes 6 minority (2 Black or African American, non-Hispanic/Latino; 2 Asian, non-Hispanic/Latino; 1 Hispanic/Latino; 1 Two or more races, non-Hispanic/Latino), 55 international. Average age 26. 174 applicants, 46% accepted, 46 enrolled. In 2017, 37 master's awarded. *Degree requirements:* For master's, thesis, exhibition. *Entrance requirements:* For master's, portfolio, statement of purpose, 3 letters of recommendation. Additional exam requirements/recommendations for international students: Required—TOEFL (minimum score 580 paper-based; 93 iBT). *Application deadline:* For fall admission, 1/10 for domestic and international students. Application fee: $60. Electronic applications accepted. *Expenses: Tuition:* Full-time $48,210. *Required fees:* $260. *Financial support:* Fellowships, research assistantships, teaching assistantships, Federal Work-Study, scholarships/grants, and unspecified assistantships available. Financial award application deadline: 2/15; financial award applicants required to submit FAFSA. *Unit head:* Liliane Wong, Department Head, 401-454-6272, Fax: 401-277-4962, E-mail: lwong@risd.edu. *Application contact:* Molly Pettengill, Assistant Director for Graduate Recruitment, 401-454-6312, Fax: 401-454-6309, E-mail: mpetteng@risd.edu.
Website: http://www.risd.edu/academics/interior-architecture/

San Diego State University, Graduate and Research Affairs, College of Professional Studies and Fine Arts, School of Art, Design and Art History, San Diego, CA 92182. Offers art history (MA); studio arts (MA, MFA), including applied design, environmental design, graphic design, interior design, painting and printmaking, sculpture. *Accreditation:* NASAD (one or more programs are accredited). *Degree requirements:* For master's, variable foreign language requirement, thesis. *Entrance requirements:* For master's, GRE General Test, bachelor's degree in related field, slide portfolio, typed slide information sheet, 2 letters of recommendation. Additional exam requirements/recommendations for international students: Required—TOEFL. Electronic applications accepted.

Savannah College of Art and Design, Program in Interior Design, Savannah, GA 31402-3146. Offers MA, MFA. *Program availability:* Part-time, 100% online. *Faculty:* 16 full-time (8 women), 6 part-time/adjunct (4 women). *Students:* 96 full-time (74 women), 24 part-time (20 women); includes 6 minority (1 Black or African American, non-Hispanic/Latino; 2 Asian, non-Hispanic/Latino; 3 Hispanic/Latino), 97 international. Average age 26. 237 applicants, 39% accepted, 40 enrolled. In 2017, 33 master's awarded. *Degree requirements:* For master's, final project (for MA); thesis (for MFA). *Entrance requirements:* For master's, GRE (recommended), portfolio (submitted in digital format), audition or writing submission, resume, statement of purpose, two letters of recommendation. Additional exam requirements/recommendations for international students: Recommended—TOEFL (minimum score 550 paper-based; 85 iBT), IELTS (minimum score 6.5). *Application deadline:* For fall admission, 4/1 for domestic and international students. Applications are processed on a rolling basis. Application fee: $40. Electronic applications accepted. *Expenses: Tuition:* Full-time $36,765; part-time $817 per credit hour. One-time fee: $500. *Financial support:* Career-related internships or fieldwork, Federal Work-Study, and scholarships/grants available. Financial award application deadline: 4/1; financial award applicants required to submit FAFSA. *Unit head:* Khoi Vo, Chair, Interior Design. *Application contact:* Jenny Jaquillard, Executive Director of Admissions, Recruitment and Events, 912-525-5100, Fax: 912-525-5985, E-mail: admission@scad.edu.
Website: http://www.scad.edu/academics/programs/interior-design

School of the Art Institute of Chicago, Graduate Division, Department of Architecture, Interior Architecture, and Designed Objects, Chicago, IL 60603-3103. Offers architecture (M Arch); design for emerging technologies (MFA); designed objects (M Des); interior architecture (M Arc). *Entrance requirements:* Additional exam requirements/recommendations for international students: Required—TOEFL, IELTS.

Suffolk University, New England School of Art and Design, Boston, MA 02108-2770. Offers graphic design (MA); interior architecture (MA). *Program availability:* Part-time, evening/weekend. *Faculty:* 13 full-time (8 women), 10 part-time/adjunct (5 women). *Students:* 33 full-time (28 women), 25 part-time (23 women); includes 12 minority (1 Black or African American, non-Hispanic/Latino; 7 Asian, non-Hispanic/Latino; 4 Hispanic/Latino), 16 international. Average age 28. 58 applicants, 57% accepted, 10 enrolled. In 2017, 37 master's awarded. *Entrance requirements:* For master's, GRE (for MFA), art portfolio, interview, 2 letters of recommendation, resume; letter of intent (for MFA). Additional exam requirements/recommendations for international students: Required—TOEFL (minimum score 550 paper-based; 80 iBT). *Application deadline:* For fall admission, 3/15 priority date for domestic and international students; for spring admission, 10/15 priority date for domestic and international students. Applications are processed on a rolling basis. Application fee: $50. Electronic applications accepted. *Expenses:* $29,520 per year full-time tuition; $1,230 per credit part-time. *Financial support:* In 2017–18, 46 students received support, including 4 fellowships (averaging $6,062 per year); career-related internships or fieldwork, Federal Work-Study, institutionally sponsored loans, scholarships/grants, and unspecified assistantships also available. Financial award application deadline: 4/1; financial award applicants required to submit FAFSA. *Faculty research:* Sustainable design, lighting and technology, design education, environmental graphic design, designing for the non-profit sector. *Unit head:* Audrey Goldstein, Department Chair, 617-997-4290, E-mail: agoldstein@suffolk.edu. *Application contact:* Mara Marzocchi, Associate Director of Graduate Admissions, 617-573-8302, Fax: 617-305-1733, E-mail: grad.admission@suffolk.edu.
Website: http://www.suffolk.edu/nesad/

Texas Tech University, Graduate School, College of Human Sciences, Department of Design, Lubbock, TX 79409-1220. Offers environmental design (MS); interior and environmental design (PhD). *Program availability:* Part-time. *Faculty:* 11 full-time (9 women), 1 (woman) part-time/adjunct. *Students:* 16 full-time (12 women), 4 part-time (2 women); includes 3 minority (all Hispanic/Latino), 13 international. Average age 33. 16 applicants, 63% accepted, 5 enrolled. In 2017, 5 master's, 3 doctorates awarded. *Degree requirements:* For master's, comprehensive exam, thesis or alternative; for doctorate, comprehensive exam, thesis/dissertation. *Entrance requirements:* For master's, 3 recommendation letters, design portfolio, 500-word written statement (reason for pursuing degree), resume; for doctorate, GRE, 3 recommendation letters, design portfolio, 500-word written statement (reason for pursuing degree), resume. Additional exam requirements/recommendations for international students: Required—TOEFL (minimum score 550 paper-based, 79 iBT) or IELTS (6.5). *Application deadline:* For fall admission, 6/1 priority date for domestic students, 1/15 priority date for international students; for spring admission, 9/1 priority date for domestic students, 6/15 priority date for international students. Applications are processed on a rolling basis. Application fee: $60. Electronic applications accepted. *Expenses:* Contact institution. *Financial support:* In 2017–18, 15 students received support, including 13 fellowships (averaging $6,394 per year), 10 research assistantships (averaging $8,383 per year); teaching assistantships, scholarships/grants, and unspecified assistantships also available. Financial award application deadline: 4/15; financial award applicants required to submit FAFSA. *Faculty research:* Healthcare and the built environment, sustainability,

vulnerable populations, historic preservation, evidence-based design, environmental design, interior design, clothing design, creative scholarship (juried exhibitions). *Total annual research expenditures:* $137,557. *Unit head:* Dr. Sharran F. Parkinson, Department Chairperson/Professor, 806-742-3031, Fax: 806-742-1639, E-mail: sharran.parkinson@ttu.edu. *Application contact:* Erin Rebecca Sopronyi, Senior Office Manager, 806-742-3050, Fax: 806-742-1639, E-mail: erin.r.sopronyi@ttu.edu.
Website: http://www.depts.ttu.edu/hs/dod/

Thomas Jefferson University, College of Architecture and the Built Environment, Program in Interior Architecture, Philadelphia, PA 19107. Offers MS.

University of California, Berkeley, UC Berkeley Extension, Certificate Programs in Art and Design, Berkeley, CA 94720-1500. Offers interior design and interior architecture (Certificate); landscape architecture (Certificate); visual arts (Postbaccalaureate Certificate).

University of Cincinnati, Graduate School, College of Design, Architecture, Art, and Planning, School of Architecture and Interior Design, Cincinnati, OH 45221. Offers architecture (M Arch). *Accreditation:* NASAD. *Degree requirements:* For master's, one foreign language, thesis. *Entrance requirements:* Additional exam requirements/recommendations for international students: Required—TOEFL. *Expenses: Tuition, area resident:* Full-time $14,468. Tuition, state resident: full-time $14,968; part-time $754 per credit hour. Tuition, nonresident: full-time $24,210; part-time $1311 per credit hour. *International tuition:* $26,460 full-time. *Required fees:* $3958; $84 per credit hour. One-time fee: $85 full-time. Tuition and fees vary according to course load, degree level and program. *Faculty research:* Theory and history of architecture.

University of Florida, Graduate School, College of Design, Construction and Planning, Department of Interior Design, Gainesville, FL 32611. Offers historic preservation (MID); interior design (MID); sustainable design (MID). *Degree requirements:* For master's, thesis. *Entrance requirements:* For master's, GRE General Test, minimum GPA of 3.0. Additional exam requirements/recommendations for international students: Required—TOEFL (minimum score 550 paper-based; 80 iBT), IELTS (minimum score 6). *Faculty research:* Sustainable design and environmentally significant behaviors; design innovation, creativity, methods and pedagogy; lighting and color design and perception; historic preservation; design for special populations.

University of Florida, Graduate School, College of Design, Construction and Planning, Doctoral Program in Design, Construction and Planning, Gainesville, FL 32611. Offers construction management (PhD); design, construction and planning (PhD); geographic information systems (PhD); historic preservation (PhD); interior design (PhD); landscape architecture (PhD); urban and regional planning (PhD). *Degree requirements:* For doctorate, thesis/dissertation. *Entrance requirements:* For doctorate, GRE General Test, minimum GPA of 3.0. Additional exam requirements/recommendations for international students: Required—TOEFL (minimum score 550 paper-based; 80 iBT), IELTS (minimum score 6). Electronic applications accepted. *Faculty research:* Architecture, building construction, urban and regional planning.

University of Georgia, College of Family and Consumer Sciences, Department of Textiles, Merchandising, and Interiors, Athens, GA 30602. Offers historical and cultural aspects of dress and textiles (MS); interior environments (MS); international merchandising (PhD); merchandising and international trade (MS); polymer, fiber and textile science (MS); polymer, fiber, and textile sciences (PhD). *Accreditation:* NASAD. *Degree requirements:* For master's, thesis; for doctorate, thesis/dissertation. *Entrance requirements:* For master's and doctorate, GRE General Test. Electronic applications accepted.

University of Kentucky, Graduate School, College of Design, Program in Interior Design, Merchandising, and Textiles, Lexington, KY 40506-0032. Offers interior design (MA). *Degree requirements:* For master's, comprehensive exam, thesis optional. *Entrance requirements:* For master's, GRE General Test, minimum undergraduate GPA of 2.75. Additional exam requirements/recommendations for international students: Required—TOEFL (minimum score 550 paper-based). Electronic applications accepted. *Faculty research:* Interior design, apparel merchandising, textile evaluation, creativity in design, social-psychological aspects of dress and interiors.

University of Manitoba, Faculty of Graduate Studies, Faculty of Architecture, Department of Interior Design, Winnipeg, MB R3T 2N2, Canada. Offers MID. *Accreditation:* CIDA.

University of Massachusetts Amherst, Graduate School, College of Humanities and Fine Arts, Department of Architecture, Amherst, MA 01003. Offers architecture (M Arch); design (MS); design in historic preservation (MS). *Program availability:* Part-time. *Degree requirements:* For master's, thesis or alternative, project. *Entrance requirements:* For master's, GRE General Test (for M Arch only), 3 letters of recommendation (M Arch only); portfolio. Additional exam requirements/recommendations for international students: Required—TOEFL (minimum score 550 paper-based; 80 iBT), IELTS (minimum score 6.5). Electronic applications accepted.

University of Minnesota, Twin Cities Campus, Graduate School, College of Design, Department of Design, Housing, and Apparel, Minneapolis, MN 55455-0213. Offers apparel (MA, MS, PhD); design communication (MA, MS, PhD); housing studies (MA, MS, PhD, Postbaccalaureate Certificate); interactive design (MFA); interior design (MA, MS, PhD). *Program availability:* Part-time. *Degree requirements:* For master's and Postbaccalaureate Certificate, comprehensive exam, thesis (for some programs); for doctorate, comprehensive exam, thesis/dissertation. *Entrance requirements:* For master's, GRE General Test, minimum GPA of 3.0 (preferred), portfolio, 3 letters of recommendation; for doctorate, GRE General Test, minimum GPA of 3.0 (preferred), portfolio, 3 letters of recommendation, writing sample; for Postbaccalaureate Certificate, GRE General Test, minimum GPA of 3.0 (preferred). Additional exam requirements/recommendations for international students: Required—TOEFL (minimum score 550 paper-based; 79 iBT). Electronic applications accepted. *Faculty research:* Housing policy and community development; consumer behavior; interactive design; design history; social, cultural, and behavioral issues related to designed environments.

University of Nebraska–Lincoln, Graduate College, College of Architecture, Department of Architecture, Lincoln, NE 68588. Offers architecture (M Arch, MS, PhD); interior design (MS); M Arch/MBA; M Arch/MCRP. *Entrance requirements:* Additional exam requirements/recommendations for international students: Required—TOEFL. Electronic applications accepted.

The University of North Carolina at Greensboro, Graduate School, College of Arts and Sciences, Department of Interior Architecture, Greensboro, NC 27412-5001. Offers historic preservation (Certificate); interior architecture (MS); museum studies (Certificate). *Degree requirements:* For master's, thesis. *Entrance requirements:* For master's, GRE General Test or MAT, bachelor's degree in interior design, interview, portfolio. Additional exam requirements/recommendations for international students: Required—TOEFL. Electronic applications accepted.

University of North Texas, Robert B. Toulouse School of Graduate Studies, Denton, TX 76203-5459. Offers accounting (MS); applied anthropology (MA, MS); applied behavior analysis (Certificate); applied geography (MA); applied technology and performance improvement (M Ed, MS); art education (MA); art history (MA); art museum education (Certificate); arts leadership (Certificate); audiology (Au D); behavior analysis (MS); behavioral science (PhD); biochemistry and molecular biology (MS); biology (MA, MS); biomedical engineering (MS); business analysis (MS); chemistry (MS); clinical health psychology (PhD); communication studies (MA, MS); computer engineering (MS); computer science (MS); counseling (M Ed, MS), including clinical mental health counseling (MS), college and university counseling, elementary school counseling, secondary school counseling; creative writing (MA); criminal justice (MS); curriculum and instruction (M Ed); decision sciences (MBA); design (MA, MFA), including fashion design (MFA), innovation studies, interior design (MFA); early childhood studies (MS); economics (MS); educational leadership (M Ed, Ed D); educational psychology (MS, PhD), including family studies (MS), gifted and talented (MS), human development (MS), learning and cognition (MS), research, measurement and evaluation (MS); electrical engineering (MS); emergency management (MPA); engineering technology (MS); English (MA); English as a second language (MA); environmental science (MS); finance (MBA, MS); financial management (MPA); French (MA); health services management (MBA); higher education (M Ed, Ed D); history (MA, MS); hospitality management (MS); human resources management (MPA); information science (MS); information systems (PhD); information technologies (MBA); interdisciplinary studies (MA, MS); international studies (MA); international sustainable tourism (MS); jazz studies (MM); journalism (MA, MJ, Graduate Certificate), including interactive and virtual digital communication (Graduate Certificate), narrative journalism (Graduate Certificate), public relations (Graduate Certificate); kinesiology (MS); linguistics (MA); local government management (MPA); logistics (PhD); logistics and supply chain management (MBA); long-term care, senior housing, and aging services (MA); management (PhD); marketing (MBA); mathematics (MA, MS); mechanical and energy engineering (MS, PhD); music (MA), including ethnomusicology, music theory, musicology, performance; music composition (PhD); music education (MM Ed, PhD); nonprofit management (MPA); operations and supply chain management (MBA); performance (MM, DMA); philosophy (MA); political science (MA); professional and technical communication (MA); radio, television and film (MA, MFA); rehabilitation counseling (Certificate); sociology (MA); Spanish (MA); special education (M Ed); speech-language pathology (MA); strategic management (MBA); studio art (MFA); teaching (M Ed); MBA/MS. *Program availability:* Part-time, evening/weekend, online learning. Terminal master's awarded for partial completion of doctoral program. *Degree requirements:* For master's, variable foreign language requirement, comprehensive exam (for some programs), thesis (for some programs); for doctorate, variable foreign language requirement, comprehensive exam (for some programs), thesis/dissertation; for other advanced degree, variable foreign language requirement, comprehensive exam (for some programs). *Entrance requirements:* For master's and doctorate, GRE, GMAT. Additional exam requirements/recommendations for international students: Required—TOEFL (minimum score 550 paper-based; 79 iBT). Electronic applications accepted.

University of Oklahoma, Christopher C. Gibbs College of Architecture, Division of Interior Design, Norman, OK 73019. Offers interior design (MS); professional applications of interior design (Graduate Certificate). *Program availability:* Part-time. *Students:* 5 full-time (4 women), 2 part-time (both women); includes 2 minority (1 American Indian or Alaska Native, non-Hispanic/Latino; 1 Hispanic/Latino), 2 international. Average age 30. 5 applicants, 60% accepted, 1 enrolled. In 2017, 1 master's awarded. *Degree requirements:* For master's, comprehensive exam, project or thesis. *Entrance requirements:* For master's, graduate degree in interior design or related field, portfolio of design work, letter of intent limited to 500 words, three letters of recommendation; for Graduate Certificate, undergraduate degree in interior design or related field, portfolio of design work, letter of intent limited to 500 words, three letters of recommendation. Additional exam requirements/recommendations for international students: Required—TOEFL (minimum score 79 iBT) or IELTS (minimum score 6.5). *Application deadline:* Applications are processed on a rolling basis. Application fee: $50 ($100 for international students). Electronic applications accepted. *Expenses:* Tuition, state resident: full-time $5119; part-time $213.30 per credit hour. Tuition, nonresident: full-time $19,778; part-time $824.10 per credit hour. *Required fees:* $3458; $133.55 per credit hour. $126.50 per semester. *Financial support:* In 2017–18, 5 students received support, including 1 research assistantship with partial tuition reimbursement available (averaging $10,372 per year), 3 teaching assistantships with full and partial tuition reimbursements available (averaging $10,372 per year); career-related internships or fieldwork, scholarships/grants, and unspecified assistantships also available. Financial award application deadline: 6/1; financial award applicants required to submit FAFSA. *Faculty research:* Environment and human behavior; indoor environmental quality; pedagogical exploration; building information modeling (BIM) for cognitive spatial problem solving; community health and environmental design. *Unit head:* Elizabeth Pober, Academic Director and Associate Professor, 405-325-6764, Fax: 405-325-7558, E-mail: epober@ou.edu. *Application contact:* Dr. Suchismita Bhattacharjee, Assistant Professor and Graduate Liaison, 405-325-2548, Fax: 405-325-7558, E-mail: suchi@ou.edu.
Website: http://www.ou.edu/architecture/interior_design.html

University of Oregon, Graduate School, College of Design, Department of Architecture, Eugene, OR 97403. Offers architecture (M Arch); interior architecture (MI Arch). *Accreditation:* CIDA. *Degree requirements:* For master's, thesis (for some programs). *Entrance requirements:* For master's, GRE General Test. Additional exam requirements/recommendations for international students: Required—TOEFL. *Faculty research:* Innovation in housing design and design production, climate responsive design, passive heating and cooling, computer software development for design applications, vernacular architecture.

The University of Tennessee at Chattanooga, Program in Interior Design, Chattanooga, TN 37403. Offers MID, MS. *Students:* 5 full-time (4 women), 2 part-time (both women); includes 1 minority (Two or more races, non-Hispanic/Latino). Average age 37. 3 applicants, 100% accepted, 2 enrolled. *Degree requirements:* For master's, professional project or thesis. *Entrance requirements:* For master's, GRE, 3 letters of reference, minimum undergraduate GPA of 3.0, interview. Additional exam requirements/recommendations for international students: Required—TOEFL (minimum score 550 paper-based; 79 iBT), IELTS (minimum score 6). *Application deadline:* For fall admission, 6/15 priority date for domestic students, 7/1 for international students; for spring admission, 11/1 priority date for domestic students, 11/1 for international students. Applications are processed on a rolling basis. Application fee: $35 ($40 for international students). Electronic applications accepted. *Expenses:* Tuition, state resident: full-time $8244; part-time $458 per credit hour. Tuition, nonresident: full-time $24,362; part-time $1353 per credit hour. *Required fees:* $1776; $487 per semester. Tuition and fees vary according to course load. *Financial support:* Career-related internships or fieldwork, scholarships/grants, and unspecified assistantships available. Support available to part-time students. Financial award application deadline: 7/1; financial award applicants required to submit FAFSA. *Faculty research:* Impact of space planning on education, historic preservation, impact of space planning on health and safety. *Total annual research expenditures:* $3,000. *Unit head:* Dr. Dana Moody, Graduate Program Director, 423-425-4459, Fax: 423-425-4479, E-mail: dana-moody@utc.edu. *Application contact:* Dr. Joanne Romagni, Dean of the Graduate School, 423-425-4478, Fax: 423-425-5223, E-mail: joanne-romagni@utc.edu.
Website: https://www.utc.edu/interior-design/

The University of Texas at Austin, Graduate School, School of Architecture, Program in Interior Design, Austin, TX 78712-1111. Offers MID.

Virginia Commonwealth University, Graduate School, School of the Arts, Richmond, VA 23284-9005. Offers art education (MAE, PhD); art history (MA, PhD), including curatorial (PhD), historical studies, museum studies (MA); ceramics (MFA); design (MFA), including interior environments, visual communications; fibers (MFA); furniture design (MFA); glassworking (MFA); jewelry/metalworking (MFA); kinetic imaging (MFA); music (MM), including music education; painting (MFA); photography and film (MFA); printmaking (MFA); sculpture (MFA); theatre (MFA), including costume design, pedagogy/literature, pedagogy/performance, scene design/technical theatre. *Program availability:* Part-time. *Entrance requirements:* For doctorate, GRE General Test, writing sample. Additional exam requirements/recommendations for international students: Required—TOEFL (minimum score 600 paper-based; 100 iBT). Electronic applications accepted.

Washington State University, College of Agricultural, Human, and Natural Resource Sciences, Program in Interior Design and Landscape Architecture, Pullman, WA 99164-2220. Offers MA, MS. Programs offered at the Pullman campus. *Program availability:* Part-time. *Degree requirements:* For master's, comprehensive exam, thesis (for some programs), oral exam. *Entrance requirements:* For master's, portfolio. Additional exam requirements/recommendations for international students: Required—TOEFL or IELTS. Electronic applications accepted. *Faculty research:* Digital fabrication, design pedagogy, proportional systems, American architecture and urbanism, design leadership.

Wayne State University, College of Fine, Performing and Communication Arts, James Pearson Duffy Department of Art and Art History, Detroit, MI 48202. Offers art (MA, MFA), including ceramics, drawing, fashion design and merchandising (MA), fibers, graphic design, industrial design (MA), interior design (MA), metalsmithing, painting, photography, printmaking, sculpture; art history (MA). *Students:* 13 full-time (8 women), 12 part-time (9 women); includes 5 minority (3 Black or African American, non-Hispanic/Latino; 1 Asian, non-Hispanic/Latino; 1 Hispanic/Latino), 2 international. Average age 34. 46 applicants, 24% accepted, 6 enrolled. In 2017, 5 master's awarded. *Degree requirements:* For master's, thesis (for some programs), essay or thesis. *Entrance requirements:* For master's, BFA or another degree and equivalent course work, portfolio, personal interview, reference letters, statement of intent (except for art history program). Additional exam requirements/recommendations for international students: Required—TOEFL (minimum score 550 paper-based; 79 iBT), TWE (minimum score 5.5), Michigan English Language Assessment Battery (minimum score 85); Recommended—IELTS (minimum score 6.5). *Application deadline:* For fall admission, 2/1 for domestic and international students; for winter admission, 10/1 for domestic and international students. Application fee: $50. Electronic applications accepted. *Expenses:* Contact institution. *Financial support:* In 2017–18, 18 students received support, including 1 research assistantship (averaging $22,241 per year), 6 teaching assistantships with tuition reimbursements available (averaging $18,534 per year); fellowships with tuition reimbursements available, scholarships/grants, and unspecified assistantships also available. Support available to part-time students. Financial award applicants required to submit FAFSA. *Unit head:* Dr. John Richardson, Chair, 313-577-2980, Fax: 313-577-3491, E-mail: af5343@wayne.edu. *Application contact:* 313-577-2980, E-mail: art@wayne.edu.
Website: http://art.wayne.edu/

Medical Illustration

Augusta University, College of Allied Health Sciences, Program in Medical Illustration, Augusta, GA 30912. Offers MS. *Accreditation:* ARCMI. *Degree requirements:* For master's, thesis or alternative, project. *Entrance requirements:* For master's, GRE General Test, portfolio. Additional exam requirements/recommendations for international students: Required—TOEFL (minimum score 550 paper-based; 79 iBT). Electronic applications accepted. *Faculty research:* Digital visual communication modalities, information science education, Southwestern Native American art pedagogy, medical illustration pedagogy, public health/visual education.

Johns Hopkins University, School of Medicine, Graduate Programs in Medicine, Department of Art as Applied to Medicine, Baltimore, MD 21287. Offers medical and biological illustration (MA). *Faculty:* 10 full-time (4 women), 11 part-time/adjunct (3 women). *Students:* 12 full-time (11 women); includes 4 minority (2 Black or African American, non-Hispanic/Latino; 2 Asian, non-Hispanic/Latino), 2 international. Average age 26. 69 applicants, 10% accepted, 7 enrolled. In 2017, 7 master's awarded. *Degree requirements:* For master's, thesis. *Entrance requirements:* For master's, GRE General Test (encouraged). Additional exam requirements/recommendations for international students: Recommended—TOEFL, IELTS. *Application deadline:* For fall admission, 1/15 for domestic and international students. Application fee: $110. Electronic applications accepted. *Financial support:* In 2017–18, 12 students received support. Scholarships/grants available. Financial award application deadline: 5/31; financial award applicants required to submit FAFSA. *Faculty research:* Visualization, animation and 3D modeling, 3D printing, instructional design, anaplastology. *Unit head:* Corinne Sandone, Director, 410-955-3213, Fax: 410-955-1085, E-mail: medart-info@jhmi.edu. *Application contact:* Dacia M. Balch, Administrative Coordinator, 410-955-3213, Fax: 410-955-1085, E-mail: medart-info@jhmi.edu.
Website: http://medicalart.johnshopkins.edu/

Rochester Institute of Technology, Graduate Enrollment Services, College of Health Sciences and Technology, Health Sciences Department, MFA Program in Medical Illustration, Rochester, NY 14623-5603. Offers MFA. *Program availability:* Part-time. *Students:* 12 full-time (9 women), 2 part-time (1 woman); includes 5 minority (2 Black or African American, non-Hispanic/Latino; 2 Asian, non-Hispanic/Latino; 1 Hispanic/Latino), 4 international. Average age 26. 28 applicants, 50% accepted, 8 enrolled. In 2017, 3 master's awarded. *Degree requirements:* For master's, thesis. *Entrance requirements:* For master's, portfolio, minimum GPA of 3.0 (recommended). Additional exam requirements/recommendations for international students: Required—TOEFL (minimum score 550 paper-based; 79 iBT), IELTS (minimum score 6.5), PTE (minimum score 58). *Application deadline:* Applications are processed on a rolling basis. Application fee: $65. Electronic applications accepted. *Expenses:* $1,815 per credit hour. *Financial support:* In 2017–18, 11 students received support. Teaching assistantships with partial tuition reimbursements available, career-related internships or fieldwork, scholarships/grants, and unspecified assistantships available. Support available to part-time students. Financial award applicants required to submit FAFSA. *Faculty research:* Medical and scientific visualization, medical game design and interactive media, three-dimensional modeling and animation, medical information design and graphics, molecular graphics. *Unit head:* James Perkins, Graduate Program Director, 585-475-5697, Fax: 585-475-6447, E-mail: japfaa@rit.edu. *Application contact:* Diane Ellison, Senior Associate Vice President, Graduate Enrollment Services, 585-475-2229, Fax: 585-475-7164, E-mail: gradinfo@rit.edu.
Website: http://www.rit.edu/healthsciences/graduate-programs/medical-illustration

University of Illinois at Chicago, College of Applied Health Sciences, Program in Biomedical Visualization, Chicago, IL 60607-7128. Offers MS. *Accreditation:* ARCMI. *Degree requirements:* For master's, thesis. *Entrance requirements:* For master's, GRE General Test, minimum GPA of 2.75. Additional exam requirements/recommendations for international students: Required—TOEFL. Electronic applications accepted. *Expenses:* Contact institution. *Faculty research:* Medical illustration, graphics, reconstruction, anatomical modeling.

Photography

Academy of Art University, Graduate Programs, School of Photography, San Francisco, CA 94105-3410. Offers MA, MFA. *Accreditation:* NASAD. *Program availability:* Part-time, 100% online. *Faculty:* 9 full-time (5 women), 23 part-time/adjunct (8 women). *Students:* 128 full-time (62 women), 107 part-time (69 women); includes 43 minority (9 Black or African American, non-Hispanic/Latino; 5 American Indian or Alaska Native, non-Hispanic/Latino; 8 Asian, non-Hispanic/Latino; 13 Hispanic/Latino; 3 Native Hawaiian or other Pacific Islander, non-Hispanic/Latino; 5 Two or more races, non-Hispanic/Latino), 88 international. Average age 36. 65 applicants, 100% accepted, 48 enrolled. In 2017, 77 master's awarded. *Degree requirements:* For master's, final review. *Entrance requirements:* For master's, statement of intent; resume; portfolio/reel; official college transcripts. *Application deadline:* Applications are processed on a rolling basis. Application fee: $50. Electronic applications accepted. *Expenses:* Tuition: Part-time $982 per unit. *Financial support:* Career-related internships or fieldwork, Federal Work-Study, and scholarships/grants available. Financial award application deadline: 8/10; financial award applicants required to submit FAFSA. *Unit head:* 800-544-ARTS, E-mail: info@academyart.edu. *Application contact:* 800-544-ARTS, E-mail: info@academyart.edu.
Website: http://www.academyart.edu/photography-school/index.html

Ball State University, Graduate School, College of Fine Arts, School of Art, Muncie, IN 47306. Offers fine arts (MFA), including animation, glass; visual arts studio (MA), including ceramics, drawing, metals, painting, photography and intermedia arts, printmaking, sculpture. *Accreditation:* NASAD. *Program availability:* Part-time. *Faculty:* 17 full-time (7 women). *Students:* 16 full-time (11 women), 5 part-time (1 woman); includes 5 minority (2 Black or African American, non-Hispanic/Latino; 2 Asian, non-Hispanic/Latino; 1 Hispanic/Latino). Average age 28. 27 applicants, 59% accepted, 15 enrolled. In 2017, 4 master's awarded. *Entrance requirements:* For master's, minimum baccalaureate GPA of 2.75 or 3.0 in latter half of baccalaureate, goals statement, digital portfolio of artwork, resume, transcripts of all college-level course work, three letters of recommendation. Additional exam requirements/recommendations for international students: Required—TOEFL (minimum score 550 paper-based; 79 iBT), IELTS (minimum score 6.5). *Application deadline:* For fall admission, 3/31 for domestic students. Applications are processed on a rolling basis. Application fee: $60. Electronic applications accepted. *Financial support:* In 2017–18, 15 students received support, including 1 research assistantship with partial tuition reimbursement available (averaging $10,667 per year), 14 teaching assistantships with partial tuition reimbursements available (averaging $10,786 per year); unspecified assistantships also available. Financial award application deadline: 3/1; financial award applicants required to submit FAFSA. *Unit head:* Dr. Arne Flaten, Director, 765-285-5840, Fax: 765-285-5275, E-mail: arflaten@bsu.edu. *Application contact:* Zachary Craw, Graduate Advisor, 765-285-5838, Fax: 765-285-5275, E-mail: zacraw@bsu.edu.
Website: http://www.bsu.edu/art

Bard College, International Center of Photography, Annandale-on-Hudson, NY 12504. Offers advanced photographic studies (MFA).

Bard College, Milton Avery Graduate School of the Arts, Annandale-on-Hudson, NY 12504. Offers film/video (MFA); music/sound (MFA); painting (MFA); photography (MFA); sculpture (MFA); writing (MFA). *Degree requirements:* For master's, thesis, project, 8-week summer residency, independent study. *Entrance requirements:* For master's, interview, portfolio, 2 letters of recommendation, history of work in the arts. Additional exam requirements/recommendations for international students: Required—TOEFL (minimum score 550 paper-based). Electronic applications accepted. *Expenses:* Contact institution. *Faculty research:* Original work in painting, writing, sculpture, photography, video/film, sound/music.

Barry University, College of Arts and Sciences, Department of Fine Arts, Miami Shores, FL 33161-6695. Offers photography (MA, MFA). *Degree requirements:* For master's, thesis (for some programs). *Entrance requirements:* For master's, GRE General Test, minimum GPA of 3.0. Electronic applications accepted. *Faculty research:* Inclusion education, exceptional education, art-based assessments.

Photography

Bradley University, The Graduate School, Slane College of Communications and Fine Arts, Department of Art, Peoria, IL 61625-0002. Offers ceramics (MA, MFA); drawing (MA, MFA); graphic design (MA, MFA); painting (MA, MFA); photography (MA, MFA); printmaking (MA, MFA); sculpture (MA, MFA). *Accreditation:* NASAD. *Program availability:* Part-time. *Degree requirements:* For master's, comprehensive exam, thesis, final exhibit. *Entrance requirements:* For master's, portfolio, 2 letters of recommendation. Additional exam requirements/recommendations for international students: Required—TOEFL (minimum score 550 paper-based; 79 iBT). Electronic applications accepted.

Brooklyn College of the City University of New York, School of Visual, Media and Performing Arts, Department of Art, Brooklyn, NY 11210-2889. Offers art history (MA); digital art (MFA); drawing and painting (MFA); photography (MFA); printmaking (MFA); sculpture (MFA). *Program availability:* Part-time. *Degree requirements:* For master's, thesis. *Entrance requirements:* For master's, bachelor's degree in art, portfolio, 2 letters of recommendation. Additional exam requirements/recommendations for international students: Required—TOEFL (minimum score 500 paper-based; 61 iBT). Electronic applications accepted.

California Institute of the Arts, School of Art, Valencia, CA 91355-2340. Offers art (MFA, Adv C); graphic design (MFA, Adv C); photography (MFA, Adv C). *Accreditation:* NASAD (one or more programs are accredited). *Degree requirements:* For master's, final project. *Entrance requirements:* For master's, portfolio. Additional exam requirements/recommendations for international students: Required—TOEFL. Electronic applications accepted.

California State University, Fullerton, Graduate Studies, College of the Arts, Department of Visual Arts, Fullerton, CA 92831-3599. Offers art (MA, MFA), including art history (MA), ceramics (MFA), crafts, creative photography, exhibition design, glass, graphic design, illustration, sculpture. *Accreditation:* NASAD (one or more programs are accredited). *Program availability:* Part-time. *Faculty:* 17 full-time (7 women), 4 part-time/adjunct (3 women). *Students:* 35 full-time (22 women), 24 part-time (14 women); includes 26 minority (3 Black or African American, non-Hispanic/Latino; 7 Asian, non-Hispanic/Latino; 14 Hispanic/Latino; 2 Two or more races, non-Hispanic/Latino), 6 international. Average age 33. 81 applicants, 31% accepted, 21 enrolled. In 2017, 17 master's awarded. *Entrance requirements:* For master's, minimum GPA of 2.5 in last 60 units of course work, portfolio. Application fee: $55. *Financial support:* Career-related internships or fieldwork, Federal Work-Study, institutionally sponsored loans, and scholarships/grants available. Support available to part-time students. Financial award application deadline: 3/1; financial award applicants required to submit FAFSA. *Unit head:* Dana Lamb, Chair, 657-278-2076. Website: http://www.fullerton.edu/arts/art/

California State University, Los Angeles, Graduate Studies, College of Arts and Letters, Department of Art, Los Angeles, CA 90032-8530. Offers art (MA), including art education, art history, art therapy, ceramics, metals, and textiles, design (MA, MFA), painting, sculpture, and graphic arts, photography; fine arts (MFA), including crafts, design (MA, MFA), studio arts. *Accreditation:* NASAD (one or more programs are accredited). *Program availability:* Part-time, evening/weekend. *Degree requirements:* For master's, comprehensive exam, project or thesis. *Entrance requirements:* For master's, portfolio. Additional exam requirements/recommendations for international students: Required—TOEFL (minimum score 500 paper-based). Electronic applications accepted. *Faculty research:* The artist and the book, conceptual art, ceramic processes, computer graphics, architectural graphics.

Central Washington University, School of Graduate Studies and Research, College of Arts and Humanities, Department of Art and Design, Ellensburg, WA 98926. Offers ceramics (MFA); computer arts (MFA); jewelry and metalsmithing (MFA); painting and drawing (MFA); photography (MFA); sculpture (MFA). *Entrance requirements:* For master's, minimum GPA of 3.0, portfolio. Additional exam requirements/recommendations for international students: Required—TOEFL (minimum score 550 paper-based; 79 iBT) or IELTS (minimum score 6.5). *Application deadline:* For fall admission, 2/1 for domestic students; for winter admission, 10/1 for domestic students; for spring admission, 1/1 for domestic students. Applications are processed on a rolling basis. Application fee: $50. Electronic applications accepted. *Financial support:* Application deadline: 3/1; applicants required to submit FAFSA. *Unit head:* Prof. Rachel Kirk, Chair, 509-963-2665, E-mail: rachel.kirk@cwu.edu. *Application contact:* Justine Eason, Admissions Program Coordinator, 509-963-3103, Fax: 509-963-1799, E-mail: masters@cwu.edu. Website: http://www.cwu.edu/~art/

Claremont Graduate University, Graduate Programs, School of Arts and Humanities, Department of Art, Claremont, CA 91711. Offers digital media (MFA); drawing (MFA); installation (MFA); painting (MFA); performance (MFA); photography (MFA); sculpture (MFA); studio (MFA). *Program availability:* Part-time. *Degree requirements:* For master's, final project show. *Entrance requirements:* For master's, BA in art or BFA, slide review. Additional exam requirements/recommendations for international students: Required—TOEFL (minimum score 75 iBT). Electronic applications accepted. *Expenses:* Contact institution. *Faculty research:* Acoustic sculpture, feminization of abstraction, installation sculpture.

Columbia College Chicago, School of Graduate Studies, Photography Department, Chicago, IL 60605-1996. Offers MFA. *Program availability:* Part-time. *Students:* 15 full-time (9 women), 1 part-time (0 women); includes 2 minority (1 Asian, non-Hispanic/Latino; 1 Hispanic/Latino), 5 international. 39 applicants, 44% accepted, 7 enrolled. *Degree requirements:* For master's, thesis. *Entrance requirements:* For master's, self-assessment essay, portfolio, resume, letters of recommendation, transcripts. Additional exam requirements/recommendations for international students: Required—TOEFL, IELTS. *Application deadline:* For fall admission, 1/15 priority date for domestic and international students. Applications are processed on a rolling basis. Application fee: $55 ($100 for international students). Electronic applications accepted. *Expenses:* Contact institution. *Financial support:* In 2017–18, 6 students received support. Career-related internships or fieldwork, Federal Work-Study, scholarships/grants, and unspecified assistantships available. Financial award application deadline: 1/15. *Unit head:* Peter Fitzpatrick, Chair, 312-369-7286, E-mail: pfitzpatrick@colum.edu. *Application contact:* David Marts, Graduate Admissions, 312-369-7942, E-mail: dmarts@colum.edu. Website: https://www.colum.edu/academics/fine-and-performing-arts/photography/index.html

Cornell University, Graduate School, Graduate Fields of Architecture, Art and Planning, Field of Art, Ithaca, NY 14853. Offers creative visual arts (MFA), including painting, photography, printmaking, sculpture. *Degree requirements:* For master's, thesis, exhibit. *Entrance requirements:* For master's, slide portfolio of 10-20 slides, 3 letters of recommendation, resume. Additional exam requirements/recommendations for international students: Required—TOEFL (minimum score 550 paper-based; 77 iBT). Electronic applications accepted. *Faculty research:* Painting, sculpture, photography, printmaking.

Cornell University, Graduate School, Graduate Fields of Arts and Sciences, Field of History of Art, Archaeology and Visual Studies, Ithaca, NY 14853. Offers 19th century

art (PhD); African, African American and African diaspora (PhD); American art (PhD); ancient art and archaeology (PhD); Asian American art (PhD); Baroque art (PhD); comparative modernities (PhD); digital art (PhD); East Asian art (PhD); history of photography (PhD); Islamic art (PhD); Latin American art (PhD); medieval art (PhD); modern art (PhD); Renaissance art (PhD); Southeast Asian art (PhD); theory and criticism (PhD); visual studies (PhD). *Degree requirements:* For doctorate, one foreign language, comprehensive exam, thesis/dissertation, general exams in 3 areas. *Entrance requirements:* For doctorate, GRE General Test, sample of written work, 3 letters of recommendation. Additional exam requirements/recommendations for international students: Required—TOEFL (minimum score 550 paper-based; 77 iBT). Electronic applications accepted.

Cranbrook Academy of Art, Program in Fine Arts, Bloomfield Hills, MI 48303-0801. Offers 2d design (MFA); 3d design (MFA); ceramics (MFA); fiber (MFA); metalsmithing (MFA); painting (MFA); photography (MFA); print media (MFA); sculpture (MFA). *Accreditation:* NASAD. *Degree requirements:* For master's, thesis, exhibit. *Entrance requirements:* Additional exam requirements/recommendations for international students: Required—TOEFL (minimum score 85 iBT). Electronic applications accepted.

East Carolina University, Graduate School, College of Fine Arts and Communication, School of Art and Design, Greenville, NC 27858-4353. Offers art education (MA Ed); ceramics (MFA); graphic design (MFA); illustration (MFA); metal design (MFA); painting and drawing (MFA); photography (MFA); printmaking (MFA); sculpture (MFA); textile design (MFA); wood design (MFA). *Accreditation:* NASAD (one or more programs are accredited). *Program availability:* Part-time, evening/weekend. *Students:* 24 full-time (14 women), 12 part-time (10 women); includes 6 minority (3 Asian, non-Hispanic/Latino; 2 Hispanic/Latino; 1 Two or more races, non-Hispanic/Latino). Average age 33. 27 applicants, 70% accepted, 12 enrolled. In 2017, 16 master's awarded. *Degree requirements:* For master's, comprehensive exam (for some programs), thesis (for some programs). *Entrance requirements:* For master's, portfolio. *Application deadline:* For fall admission, 2/1 for domestic students; for spring admission, 10/1 for domestic students. Applications are processed on a rolling basis. Application fee: $75. Electronic applications accepted. *Expenses:* Tuition, state resident: full-time $4749; part-time $297 per credit hour. Tuition, nonresident: full-time $17,898; part-time $1119 per credit hour. *Required fees:* $2691; $224 per credit hour. Part-time tuition and fees vary according to course load and program. *Financial support:* Research assistantships with partial tuition reimbursements, teaching assistantships with partial tuition reimbursements, and Federal Work-Study available. Support available to part-time students. Financial award application deadline: 6/1. *Unit head:* Michael H. Drought, Director, 252-328-6665, E-mail: droughtm@ecu.edu. *Application contact:* Dr. Linda H. Nelson, Information Contact, 252-328-1286, E-mail: nelsonlh@ecu.edu. Website: http://www.ecu.edu/soad/

Ferris State University, Kendall College of Art and Design, Grand Rapids, MI 49503. Offers architecture (M Arch); art education (MAE); design (MA); drawing (MFA); painting (MFA); photography (MFA); printmaking (MFA); visual and critical studies (MA). *Program availability:* Part-time. *Faculty:* 21 full-time (15 women), 6 part-time/adjunct (2 women). *Students:* 39 full-time (29 women), 15 part-time (9 women); includes 12 minority (4 Black or African American, non-Hispanic/Latino; 1 American Indian or Alaska Native, non-Hispanic/Latino; 3 Asian, non-Hispanic/Latino; 4 Hispanic/Latino), 6 international. Average age 31. 48 applicants, 60% accepted, 17 enrolled. In 2017, 12 master's awarded. *Degree requirements:* For master's, thesis, seminars. *Entrance requirements:* For master's, portfolio, 3 letters of recommendation, curriculum vitae, artist statement, letter of intent. Additional exam requirements/recommendations for international students: Required—TOEFL (minimum score 79 iBT). *Application deadline:* For fall admission, 2/1 priority date for domestic and international students; for spring admission, 11/1 priority date for domestic and international students. Applications are processed on a rolling basis. Application fee: $0. Electronic applications accepted. *Expenses:* Contact institution. *Financial support:* In 2017–18, 32 students received support, including 8 fellowships (averaging $16,781 per year); scholarships/grants and unspecified assistantships also available. Financial award application deadline: 2/1; financial award applicants required to submit FAFSA. *Unit head:* Leslie Bellavance, President, 616-451-2787. *Application contact:* Thomas Post, Graduate Recruitment Specialist, 616-451-2787, Fax: 616-831-9689, E-mail: thomaspost@ferris.edu. Website: http://www.kcad.edu/

The George Washington University, Columbian College of Arts and Sciences, Corcoran School of the Arts and Design, Washington, DC 20007. Offers art and the book (MA); art education (MA, MAT); decorative arts and design history (MA); exhibition design (MA); interior design (MA); new media photojournalism (MA). MA in decorative arts and design history offered in partnership with Smithsonian Associates. *Accreditation:* NASAD. *Program availability:* Part-time. *Entrance requirements:* Additional exam requirements/recommendations for international students: Required—TOEFL (minimum score 95 iBT). *Expenses:* Tuition: Full-time $28,800; part-time $1655 per credit hour. *Required fees:* $45; $2.75 per credit hour.

The George Washington University, Columbian College of Arts and Sciences, Department of Fine Arts and Art History, Washington, DC 20052. Offers art history (MA), including art history, museum training; ceramics (MFA); drawing/painting (MFA); interior design (MFA), including interior architecture and design; new media (MFA); photography (MFA); sculpture (MFA). *Accreditation:* CIDA. *Program availability:* Part-time, evening/weekend. *Faculty:* 14 full-time (6 women), 16 part-time/adjunct (10 women). *Students:* 60 full-time (50 women), 13 part-time (11 women); includes 15 minority (5 Black or African American, non-Hispanic/Latino; 3 Asian, non-Hispanic/Latino; 4 Hispanic/Latino; 3 Two or more races, non-Hispanic/Latino), 21 international. Average age 27. 138 applicants, 65% accepted, 31 enrolled. In 2017, 43 master's awarded. *Entrance requirements:* For master's, GRE General Test, bachelor's degree in field, minimum GPA of 3.0. Additional exam requirements/recommendations for international students: Required—TOEFL (minimum score 550 paper-based; 80 iBT). *Application deadline:* For fall admission, 3/1 priority date for domestic students, 1/15 priority date for international students; for spring admission, 10/1 priority date for domestic students, 9/1 priority date for international students. Applications are processed on a rolling basis. Application fee: $75. Electronic applications accepted. *Expenses:* Tuition: Full-time $28,800; part-time $1655 per credit hour. *Required fees:* $45; $2.75 per credit hour. *Financial support:* In 2017–18, 12 students received support. Fellowships, teaching assistantships, career-related internships or fieldwork, Federal Work-Study, and tuition waivers available. Financial award application deadline: 1/15. *Unit head:* Phil Jacks, Chair, 202-994-6085, E-mail: pjacks@gwu.edu. *Application contact:* Information Contact, 202-994-6085, Fax: 202-994-8657, E-mail: art@gwu.edu. Website: http://art.columbian.gwu.edu/

Georgia State University, College of Arts and Sciences, Department of Communication, Atlanta, GA 30302-3083. Offers film, video, and digital imaging (MA), including critical studies, production, screenwriting; human communication and social influence (MA); mass communication (MA); media and society (PhD); moving image studies (PhD); public communication (PhD); rhetoric and politics (PhD). *Program availability:* Part-time. *Faculty:* 57 full-time (34 women). *Students:* 71 full-time (51 women), 17 part-time (9 women); includes 36 minority (28 Black or African American,

non-Hispanic/Latino; 1 Asian, non-Hispanic/Latino; 4 Hispanic/Latino; 1 Native Hawaiian or other Pacific Islander, non-Hispanic/Latino; 2 Two or more races, non-Hispanic/Latino), 15 international. Average age 33. 63 applicants, 54% accepted, 17 enrolled. In 2017, 20 master's, 10 doctorates awarded. *Degree requirements:* For master's, variable foreign language requirement, thesis (for some programs); for doctorate, comprehensive exam, thesis/dissertation. *Entrance requirements:* For master's and doctorate, GRE. Additional exam requirements/recommendations for international students: Required—TOEFL (minimum score 550 paper-based; 80 iBT), IELTS (minimum score 6.5). *Application deadline:* For fall admission, 2/10 for domestic and international students; for spring admission, 10/15 for domestic and international students. Application fee: $50. Electronic applications accepted. *Expenses:* Tuition, state resident: full-time $7020. Tuition, nonresident: full-time $22,518. *Required fees:* $2128. Tuition and fees vary according to degree level and program. *Financial support:* In 2017–18, fellowships with tuition reimbursements (averaging $15,000 per year), teaching assistantships with tuition reimbursements (averaging $15,000 per year) were awarded; career-related internships or fieldwork and unspecified assistantships also available. Financial award applicants required to submit FAFSA. *Faculty research:* New media, mass media and journalism, rhetoric, film and media studies, film production. *Unit head:* Dr. Greg Lisby, Chair, 404-413-5639, Fax: 404-413-5634, E-mail: glisby@gsu.edu.
Website: http://communication.gsu.edu

Georgia State University, Ernest G. Welch School of Art and Design, Program in Studio Art, Atlanta, GA 30302-3083. Offers ceramics (MFA); drawing and painting (MFA); graphic design (MFA); interior design (MFA); photography (MFA); printmaking (MFA); sculpture (MFA); textiles (MFA). *Accreditation:* NASAD. Application fee: $50. Electronic applications accepted. *Expenses:* Tuition, state resident: full-time $7020. Tuition, nonresident: full-time $22,518. *Required fees:* $2128. Tuition and fees vary according to degree level and program. *Financial support:* Fellowships, research assistantships, teaching assistantships, scholarships/grants, and unspecified assistantships available. Financial award application deadline: 4/15; financial award applicants required to submit FAFSA. *Faculty research:* Advertising and typography, new media, traditional media, three-dimensional art, architectural and environmental design. *Unit head:* Michael White, Director, Welch School of Art and Design, 404-413-5221, Fax: 404-413-5261, E-mail: mwhite@gsu.edu. *Application contact:* Hubert Stanley Anderson, Director of Graduate Studies, 404-413-5229, Fax: 404-413-5261, E-mail: artgrad@gsu.edu.
Website: http://artdesign.gsu.edu/graduate/admissions/masters-of-fine-arts-in-studio/

Governors State University, College of Arts and Sciences, Program in Independent Film and Digital Imaging, University Park, IL 60484. Offers MFA. *Program availability:* Part-time. *Faculty:* 60 full-time (34 women), 115 part-time/adjunct (58 women). *Students:* 11 full-time (7 women), 8 part-time (6 women); includes 11 minority (10 Black or African American, non-Hispanic/Latino; 1 Two or more races, non-Hispanic/Latino), 1 international. Average age 40. 6 applicants, 50% accepted, 3 enrolled. In 2017, 8 master's awarded. *Application deadline:* For fall admission, 4/1 for domestic students. Applications are processed on a rolling basis. Application fee: $50. Electronic applications accepted. *Expenses:* Tuition, state resident: full-time $8472; part-time $353 per credit hour. Tuition, nonresident: full-time $16,944; part-time $706 per credit hour. *Required fees:* $1824; $76 per credit hour. $38 per term. Tuition and fees vary according to course load, degree level and program. *Financial support:* Application deadline: 5/1; applicants required to submit FAFSA. *Unit head:* Lori Montalbano, Chair, Division of Arts and Letters, 708-534-5000 Ext. 2802, E-mail: lmontalbano@govst.edu.

Howard University, Graduate School, Division of Fine Arts, Department of Art, Program in Fine Arts, Washington, DC 20059-0002. Offers 3D reality (sculpture and ceramics) (MFA); design (MFA); electronic studio (MFA); painting (MFA); photography (MFA). *Accreditation:* NASAD. *Degree requirements:* For master's, comprehensive exam, thesis, exhibit. *Entrance requirements:* For master's, minimum GPA of 3.0, portfolio.

Illinois State University, Graduate School, College of Fine Arts, School of Art, Normal, IL 61790. Offers art history (MA, MS); ceramics (MFA, MS); drawing (MFA, MS); fibers (MFA, MS); glass (MFA, MS); graphic design (MFA, MS); metals (MFA, MS); painting (MFA, MS); photography (MFA, MS); printmaking (MFA, MS); sculpture (MFA, MS). *Accreditation:* NASAD (one or more programs are accredited). *Degree requirements:* For master's, thesis or alternative, internship. *Entrance requirements:* For master's, portfolio, sample of scholarly writing.

Indiana State University, College of Graduate and Professional Studies, College of Arts and Sciences, Department of Art and Design, Terre Haute, IN 47809. Offers ceramics (MA, MFA); drawing (MA, MFA); graphic design (MA, MFA); painting (MA, MFA); photography (MA, MFA); printmaking (MA, MFA); sculpture (MA, MFA). *Accreditation:* NASAD (one or more programs are accredited). *Program availability:* Part-time. *Degree requirements:* For master's, thesis or alternative, departmental qualifying exam. *Entrance requirements:* For master's, portfolio. Additional exam requirements/recommendations for international students: Required—TOEFL (minimum score 550 paper-based).

Indiana University–Purdue University Indianapolis, Herron School of Art and Design, Indianapolis, IN 46202. Offers art therapy (MA); visual art (MFA), including ceramics, furniture design, painting and drawing, photography and intermedia, printmaking, sculpture; visual communication design (MFA). *Degree requirements:* For master's, thesis. *Entrance requirements:* For master's, personal statement, resume, recommendations, portfolio, transcripts (18 credit hours of studio art and 12 credit hours of psychology, including 3 credit hours of developmental psychology and 3 credit hours of abnormal psychology for MA). Additional exam requirements/recommendations for international students: Recommended—TOEFL (minimum score 550 paper-based; 79 iBT), IELTS (minimum score 6.5). Electronic applications accepted. *Expenses:* Contact institution. *Faculty research:* Contemporary digital narratives for the homoerotic trope; sound articulated 3D print; neuroscience, art and related therapeutics; automotive and aeronautical design and fabrication; technological detritus.

Inter American University of Puerto Rico, San Germán Campus, Graduate Studies Center, Program in Fine Arts, San Germán, PR 00683-5008. Offers drawing (MFA); graphic design (MFA); painting (MFA); photography (MFA); printmaking (MFA); sculpture (MFA). *Program availability:* Part-time, evening/weekend. *Degree requirements:* For master's, comprehensive exam, thesis. *Entrance requirements:* For master's, GRE General Test or EXADEP, minimum GPA of 3.0.

Ithaca College, Roy H. Park School of Communications, Program in Image Text, Ithaca, NY 14850. Offers MFA. *Program availability:* Part-time-only. *Faculty:* 9 full-time (2 women). *Students:* 18 part-time (9 women); includes 5 minority (3 Hispanic/Latino; 2 Two or more races, non-Hispanic/Latino). Average age 28. 20 applicants, 70% accepted, 10 enrolled. *Degree requirements:* For master's, thesis, field practicum. *Entrance requirements:* Additional exam requirements/recommendations for international students: Required—TOEFL (minimum score 550 paper-based; 80 iBT). *Application deadline:* For fall admission, 3/15 for domestic and international students; for spring admission, 12/1 for domestic and international students. Applications are processed on a rolling basis. Application fee: $40. Electronic applications accepted. *Expenses:* Contact institution. *Financial support:* In 2017–18, 18 students received support, including 18 fellowships (averaging $4,868 per year); career-related internships or fieldwork, Federal Work-Study, and scholarships/grants also available. Support available to part-time students. Financial award application deadline: 3/1; financial award applicants required to submit FAFSA. *Unit head:* Nicholas Muellner, Co-Director, 607-274-1984, E-mail: nmuellner@ithaca.edu. *Application contact:* Nicole Eversley Bradwell, Director, Office of Admission, 607-274-3124, Fax: 607-274-1263, E-mail: admission@ithaca.edu.
Website: http://www.ithaca.edu/gradprograms/image-text

James Madison University, The Graduate School, College of Visual and Performing Arts, School of Art, Design and Art History, Harrisonburg, VA 22801. Offers art education (MA); studio art (MA, MFA), including ceramics (MFA), drawing/painting (MFA), intermedia (MFA), metal/jewelry (MFA), photography (MFA), sculpture (MFA). *Accreditation:* NASAD. *Program availability:* Part-time. *Students:* 7 full-time (5 women), 1 (woman) part-time. Average age 30. In 2017, 5 master's awarded. Application fee: $55. Electronic applications accepted. *Expenses:* Tuition, state resident: full-time $10,512; part-time $438 per credit hour. Tuition, nonresident: full-time $28,358; part-time $1162 per credit hour. *Required fees:* $1128. *Financial support:* In 2017–18, 7 students received support, including 4 teaching assistantships with full tuition reimbursements available (averaging $9,284 per year); Federal Work-Study and 3 assistantships (averaging $7911) also available. Financial award application deadline: 3/1; financial award applicants required to submit FAFSA. *Unit head:* Dr. Kathy A. Schwartz, Director of School of Art, Design and Art History, 540-568-6216, E-mail: schwarka@jmu.edu. *Application contact:* Lynette D. Michael, Director of Graduate Student Admissions, 540-568-6131 Ext. 6395, Fax: 540-568-7860, E-mail: michaeld@jmu.edu.
Website: http://www.jmu.edu/artandarthistory

Kent State University, College of the Arts, School of Art, Kent, OH 44242-0001. Offers art education (MA); art history (MA); crafts (MA), including glass (MA, MFA); fine arts (MA), including fashion; studio art (MFA), including ceramics, drawing, glass (MA, MFA), jewelry, metals and enameling, painting, print media and photography, sculpture, textiles. *Accreditation:* NASAD (one or more programs are accredited). *Program availability:* Part-time, online learning. *Faculty:* 24 full-time (13 women), 3 part-time/adjunct (all women). *Students:* 40 full-time (27 women), 22 part-time (19 women); includes 3 minority (2 Black or African American, non-Hispanic/Latino; 1 Two or more races, non-Hispanic/Latino). Average age 31. 40 applicants, 75% accepted, 23 enrolled. In 2017, 22 master's awarded. *Degree requirements:* For master's, comprehensive exam, thesis (for some programs), 1 foreign language (for art history); final project (for crafts and fine arts). *Entrance requirements:* For master's, transcripts, goal statement, 3 letters of recommendation, curriculum vitae, portfolio. Additional exam requirements/recommendations for international students: Required—TOEFL (minimum score 550 paper-based, 79 iBT), Michigan English Language Assessment Battery (minimum score 77), IELTS (minimum score 6.5) or PTE (minimum score 58). *Application deadline:* For fall admission, 2/2 for domestic and international students; for spring admission, 10/15 for domestic and international students. Applications are processed on a rolling basis. Application fee: $45 ($70 for international students). Electronic applications accepted. *Expenses:* Tuition, state resident: full-time $11,310; part-time $515 per credit hour. Tuition, nonresident: full-time $20,396; part-time $928 per credit hour. *International tuition:* $18,544 full-time. *Financial support:* Career-related internships or fieldwork, scholarships/grants, and unspecified assistantships available. Financial award application deadline: 3/16. *Unit head:* Marie Bukowski, Director, 330-672-2192, E-mail: mbukows1@kent.edu. *Application contact:* Linda Hoeptner Poling, Graduate Coordinator and Associate Professor of Art Education, 330-672-7895, E-mail: lhoeptne@kent.edu.
Website: http://www.kent.edu/art

Lesley University, College of Art and Design, Cambridge, MA 02138-2790. Offers photography (MFA); visual arts (MFA). *Program availability:* Part-time. *Degree requirements:* For master's, thesis, final exhibition of thesis work. *Entrance requirements:* For master's, portfolio, resume, personal statement. Additional exam requirements/recommendations for international students: Required—TOEFL (minimum score 550 paper-based; 80 iBT). Electronic applications accepted. *Faculty research:* Graphic design; Web and multimedia design; book, advertising and editorial illustration; animation; documentary photography; photojournalism; fine arts photography; fine arts; art education.

Louisiana State University and Agricultural & Mechanical College, Graduate School, College of Art and Design, School of Art, Program in Studio Art, Baton Rouge, LA 70803. Offers ceramics (MFA); graphic design (MFA); painting and drawing (MFA); photography (MFA); printmaking (MFA); sculpture (MFA). *Accreditation:* NASAD. *Students:* 36 full-time (20 women), 1 (woman) part-time; includes 1 minority (Hispanic/Latino), 5 international. Average age 29. 58 applicants, 24% accepted, 13 enrolled. In 2017, 13 master's awarded.

Louisiana Tech University, Graduate School, College of Liberal Arts, Ruston, LA 71272. Offers architecture (M Arch); art (MFA), including graphic design, photography, studio; audiology (Au D); communication (MA), including speech communication, theatre; English (MA), including literature, technical writing; history (MA); speech pathology (MA); technical writing and communication (Graduate Certificate). *Program availability:* Part-time. *Faculty:* 63 full-time (25 women), 5 part-time/adjunct (3 women). *Students:* 114 full-time (29 women), 31 part-time (19 women); includes 12 minority (4 Black or African American, non-Hispanic/Latino; 1 Asian, non-Hispanic/Latino; 3 Hispanic/Latino; 4 Two or more races, non-Hispanic/Latino), 5 international. Average age 30. 146 applicants, 59% accepted, 37 enrolled. In 2017, 49 master's, 3 doctorates awarded. *Degree requirements:* For master's, thesis (for some programs); for doctorate, thesis/dissertation. *Entrance requirements:* For master's, GRE General Test; for doctorate, GRE General Test, bachelor's degree, minimum GPA of 3.0 or 3.2 on last 60 hours attempted. Additional exam requirements/recommendations for international students: Required—TOEFL (minimum score 550 paper-based; 80 iBT), IELTS (minimum score 6.5). *Application deadline:* For fall admission, 8/1 priority date for domestic students, 6/1 for international students; for winter admission, 11/1 priority date for domestic students, 9/1 for international students; for spring admission, 2/1 priority date for domestic students, 12/1 for international students; for summer admission, 5/1 priority date for domestic students, 3/1 for international students. Application fee: $40 ($50 for international students). Electronic applications accepted. *Expenses:* Tuition, state resident: full-time $5146. Tuition, nonresident: full-time $10,147. *International tuition:* $10,267 full-time. *Required fees:* $2273. *Financial support:* In 2017–18, 63 students received support, including 46 research assistantships (averaging $5,229 per year), 7 teaching assistantships (averaging $5,543 per year); fellowships, career-related internships or fieldwork, Federal Work-Study, institutionally sponsored loans, tuition waivers (partial), and unspecified assistantships also available. Financial award application deadline: 2/1. *Faculty research:* Contributing to the expansion of historical and social scientific knowledge and understanding through original research and publication; diverse language, ethnic, cultural, and socioeconomic backgrounds with disorders of speech, language, swallowing, hearing, and cognitive aspects of communication; prevention of communication, swallowing, and hearing disorders. *Unit head:* Dr. Donald P. Kaczvinsky, Dean, 318-257-4805, Fax: 318-257-3935, E-mail: dkaczv@latech.edu. *Application contact:* Mary Green, Administrative Assistant, 318-257-2924, Fax: 318-257-4487, E-mail: meg@latech.edu.
Website: http://liberalarts.latech.edu/

Photography

Maryland Institute College of Art, Graduate Studies, MFA Program in Photographic and Electronic Media, Baltimore, MD 21201. Offers MFA. *Accreditation:* NASAD. *Degree requirements:* For master's, thesis, exhibit and thesis documentation. *Entrance requirements:* For master's, portfolio, bachelor's degree in any field. Additional exam requirements/recommendations for international students: Required—TOEFL (minimum score 550 paper-based; 80 iBT), IELTS (minimum score 6.5). Electronic applications accepted. *Expenses:* Contact institution.

Marywood University, Academic Affairs, Insalaco College of Creative and Performing Arts, Art Department, Program in Studio Art, Scranton, PA 18509-1598. Offers clay (MA); painting (MA); photography (MA); printmaking (MA); sculpture (MA). *Accreditation:* NASAD. Electronic applications accepted. *Faculty research:* Texture and line in clay, cast bronze sculpture, color theories, book art and illustration, sculptural form.

Marywood University, Academic Affairs, Insalaco College of Creative and Performing Arts, Art Department, Program in Visual Arts, Scranton, PA 18509-1598. Offers clay (MFA); graphic design (MFA); illustration (MFA); painting (MFA); photography (MFA); printmaking (MFA); sculpture (MFA). *Accreditation:* NASAD. *Program availability:* Part-time. Electronic applications accepted. *Expenses:* Contact institution.

Massachusetts College of Art and Design, Graduate Programs, MFA Program, Boston, MA 02115-5882. Offers 2D fine arts (MFA), including painting, printmaking; 3D fine arts (MFA), including ceramics, fibers, glass, jewelry and metalsmithing, sculpture; design (MFA, Postbaccalaureate Certificate), including dynamic media; fine arts (MFA), including interdisciplinary; media arts (MFA, Postbaccalaureate Certificate), including film/video (MFA), photography. *Accreditation:* NASAD. *Faculty:* 28 full-time (8 women), 28 part-time/adjunct (17 women). *Students:* 44 full-time (26 women), 28 part-time (17 women); includes 8 minority (5 Asian, non-Hispanic/Latino; 3 Hispanic/Latino), 18 international. 247 applicants, 52% accepted, 47 enrolled. In 2017, 42 master's, 5 other advanced degrees awarded. *Degree requirements:* For master's, thesis, thesis exhibition (for fine arts programs); thesis project and document (for design/dynamic media program). *Entrance requirements:* For master's, portfolio, college transcripts, resume, statement of purpose, letters of reference, interview, 6 credits of art history taken prior to or during MFA program; for Postbaccalaureate Certificate, portfolio, college transcripts, resume, statement of purpose, letters of reference, interview. Additional exam requirements/recommendations for international students: Required—TOEFL (minimum score 550 paper-based, 85 iBT) or IELTS (6). *Application deadline:* For fall admission, 1/4 priority date for domestic and international students; for summer admission, 1/4 priority date for domestic and international students. Applications are processed on a rolling basis. Application fee: $90. Electronic applications accepted. *Expenses:* $780 per credit. *Financial support:* In 2017–18, 51 students received support, including 1 research assistantship (averaging $2,160 per year), 33 teaching assistantships (averaging $2,160 per year); fellowships, career-related internships or fieldwork, scholarships/grants, tuition waivers (partial), unspecified assistantships, and adjunct co-teaching positions also available. Support available to part-time students. Financial award application deadline: 1/4; financial award applicants required to submit FAFSA. *Faculty research:* Painting and printmaking, sculpture, photography, film and video, dynamic media design. *Unit head:* Paul Paturzo, Dean of Graduate Studies, 617-879-7166, E-mail: pjpaturzo@massart.edu. *Application contact:* Lauren O'Neill, Assistant Director of Graduate Admissions, 617-879-7222, E-mail: gradadmissions@massart.edu.
Website: http://www.massart.edu/Admissions/Graduate_Programs.html

Mills College, Graduate Studies, Department of Art, Oakland, CA 94613-1000. Offers art (MFA); ceramics (MFA); intermedia (MFA); painting (MFA); photography (MFA); sculpture (MFA). *Faculty:* 3 full-time (2 women), 5 part-time/adjunct (3 women). *Students:* 20 full-time (11 women); includes 4 minority (1 Asian, non-Hispanic/Latino; 2 Hispanic/Latino; 1 Two or more races, non-Hispanic/Latino). Average age 30. 31 applicants, 74% accepted, 9 enrolled. In 2017, 9 master's awarded. *Degree requirements:* For master's, thesis or alternative, exhibit. *Entrance requirements:* For master's, portfolio, artist statement. Additional exam requirements/recommendations for international students: Required—TOEFL (minimum score 550 paper-based; 80 iBT) or IELTS (minimum score 6). *Application deadline:* For fall admission, 2/1 for domestic students, 12/15 for international students. Application fee: $50. Electronic applications accepted. *Expenses:* Contact institution. *Financial support:* In 2017–18, 21 students received support, including 21 fellowships with partial tuition reimbursements available (averaging $11,386 per year), 8 teaching assistantships with partial tuition reimbursements available; scholarships/grants and unspecified assistantships also available. Financial award application deadline: 2/1; financial award applicants required to submit FAFSA. *Faculty research:* Experimental film and video, public art projects, ecological design, contemporary art philosophy, sound installations. *Unit head:* Catherine Wagner, Professor of Studio Art, 510-430-3288. *Application contact:* Robynne Lofton, Director of Admissions, 510-430-3295, Fax: 510-430-2159, E-mail: grad-admission@mills.edu.
Website: http://www.mills.edu/art

Minneapolis College of Art and Design, Program in Visual Studies, Minneapolis, MN 55404-4347. Offers animation (MFA); comic art (MFA); drawing (MFA); filmmaking (MFA); fine arts (MFA); furniture design (MFA); graphic design (MFA); illustration (MFA); interactive media (MFA); painting (MFA); photography (MFA); printmaking (MFA); sculpture (MFA). *Accreditation:* NASAD. *Program availability:* Part-time. *Faculty:* 42 full-time (13 women). *Students:* 30 full-time (23 women); includes 3 minority (2 Asian, non-Hispanic/Latino; 1 Hispanic/Latino), 13 international. 166 applicants, 28% accepted, 12 enrolled. In 2017, 10 master's awarded. *Degree requirements:* For master's, thesis, thesis exhibit. *Entrance requirements:* For master's, portfolio of visual artwork, resume, 3 letters of recommendation. Additional exam requirements/recommendations for international students: Required—TOEFL (minimum score 550 paper-based; 79 iBT). *Application deadline:* For fall admission, 1/15 for domestic and international students. Application fee: $50. Electronic applications accepted. *Expenses: Tuition:* Full-time $38,670. *Required fees:* $450. One-time fee: $300 full-time. *Financial support:* In 2017–18, 23 students received support, including 15 teaching assistantships (averaging $6,000 per year); career-related internships or fieldwork, Federal Work-Study, scholarships/grants, and unspecified assistantships also available. Support available to part-time students. Financial award application deadline: 3/15; financial award applicants required to submit FAFSA. *Faculty research:* Visual arts: animation, comic art, drawing, filmmaking, furniture design, graphic design, illustration, interactive media, painting, photography, printmaking, sculpture. *Unit head:* Graduate Director, 612-209-1471, E-mail: admissions@mcad.edu. *Application contact:* Mary Kazura, Associate Director of Admissions, 612-874-3760, Fax: 612-874-3701, E-mail: mary_kazura@mcad.edu.
Website: http://mcad.edu/mfa

New Hampshire Institute of Art, Graduate Studies, Manchester, NH 03104. Offers art education (MA); creative writing (MFA); photography (MFA); teaching visual arts (MAT); visual arts (MFA). *Accreditation:* NASAD. *Faculty:* 31 part-time/adjunct (14 women). *Students:* 59 full-time (42 women), 6 part-time (3 women); includes 2 minority (1 Asian, non-Hispanic/Latino; 1 Hispanic/Latino). Average age 43. 33 applicants, 36% accepted, 5 enrolled. In 2017, 2 master's awarded. *Degree requirements:* For master's, thesis, corresponding exhibition and artist talk. *Entrance requirements:* For master's, writing sample or visual art portfolio; curriculum vitae; transcripts; letters of recommendation. Additional exam requirements/recommendations for international students: Required—TOEFL (minimum score 550 paper-based; 80 iBT), IELTS (minimum score 6.5). *Application deadline:* For fall admission, 5/1 priority date for domestic students; for spring admission, 11/1 priority date for domestic students. Applications are processed on a rolling basis. Application fee: $75. Electronic applications accepted. *Expenses:* Contact institution. *Financial support:* In 2017–18, 2 teaching assistantships (averaging $1,200 per year) were awarded; scholarships/grants and unspecified assistantships also available. Support available to part-time students. Financial award application deadline: 6/1; financial award applicants required to submit FAFSA. *Faculty research:* Fine arts - visual arts, photography, creative writing; art education. *Unit head:* Lucinda Bliss, Dean of Graduate Studies, 603-836-2522, E-mail: lucindabliss@nhia.edu. *Application contact:* Moriah Billups, Graduate Admissions Coordinator, 603-836 2588, E-mail: gradadmissions@nhia.edu.
Website: http://www.nhia.edu/graduate-studies

The New School, Parsons School of Design, Program in Photography, New York, NY 10011. Offers MFA. *Program availability:* Part-time. *Faculty:* 4 full-time (1 woman), 10 part-time/adjunct (8 women). *Students:* 14 full-time (10 women), 24 part-time (15 women); includes 12 minority (2 Black or African American, non-Hispanic/Latino; 6 Asian, non-Hispanic/Latino; 3 Hispanic/Latino; 1 Two or more races, non-Hispanic/Latino), 17 international. Average age 28. 86 applicants, 42% accepted, 15 enrolled. In 2017, 8 master's awarded. *Degree requirements:* For master's, thesis. *Entrance requirements:* For master's, transcripts, resume, statement of purpose, recommendation letters, portfolio, interview. Additional exam requirements/recommendations for international students: Required—TOEFL (minimum score 92 iBT), IELTS (minimum score 7), PTE (minimum score 63). *Application deadline:* For fall admission, 1/1 priority date for domestic and international students; for summer admission, 1/1 priority date for domestic and international students. Applications are processed on a rolling basis. Application fee: $50. Electronic applications accepted. *Expenses:* $24,922 per semester full-time, $1,744 per credit part-time, $100 maintenance of status fee. *Financial support:* In 2017–18, 25 students received support, including 10 teaching assistantships (averaging $3,572 per year); career-related internships or fieldwork, scholarships/grants, unspecified assistantships, and travel funding; tuition waivers for students who are also New School employees also available. Support available to part-time students. Financial award application deadline: 2/1; financial award applicants required to submit FAFSA. *Unit head:* Jeanine Oleson, Associate Director, 212-229-5100 Ext. 3919, E-mail: olesonj@newschool.edu. *Application contact:* Courtney Malenius, Director of Graduate Admissions, 212-229-5150 Ext. 4011, E-mail: maleniuc@newschool.edu.
Website: https://www.newschool.edu/parsons/mfa-photography/

New York Film Academy, Program in Filmmaking–Los Angeles, Burbank, CA 91505. Offers acting for film (MFA); cinematography (MFA); documentary film (MFA); film and media production (MA); filmmaking (MFA); game design (MFA); photography (MFA); producing (MA, MFA); screenwriting (MA, MFA). *Accreditation:* NASAD.

New York Film Academy, Program in Filmmaking–South Beach, Florida, Miami Beach, FL 33139. Offers acting for film (MFA); cinematography (MFA); documentary film (MFA); film and media production (MA); filmmaking (MFA); game design (MFA); photography (MFA); producing (MA, MFA); screenwriting (MA, MFA).

Northern Vermont University–Johnson, Program in Studio Arts, Johnson, VT 05656. Offers ceramics (MFA); digital media (MFA); drawing (MFA); painting (MFA); photography (MFA); printmaking (MFA); sculpture (MFA). *Program availability:* Part-time, online learning. *Faculty:* 3 full-time (1 woman). *Students:* 5 full-time (3 women), 2 part-time (1 woman). In 2017, 2 master's awarded. *Degree requirements:* For master's, thesis. *Entrance requirements:* For master's, portfolio. Additional exam requirements/recommendations for international students: Required—TOEFL. *Application deadline:* For fall admission, 3/1 for domestic students, 2/1 for international students. Applications are processed on a rolling basis. Electronic applications accepted. *Expenses:* Contact institution. *Financial support:* Teaching assistantships and unspecified assistantships available. Support available to part-time students. Financial award application deadline: 3/1; financial award applicants required to submit FAFSA. *Application contact:* Catherine H. Higley, Administrative Assistant, 800-635-2356 Ext. 1244, Fax: 802-635-1248, E-mail: catherine.higley@jsc.edu.
Website: http://www.jsc.edu/academics/fine-arts-department/majors-and-minors/mfa-in-studio-arts/

Ohio University, Graduate College, College of Fine Arts, School of Art, Athens, OH 45701-2979. Offers art history (MA); ceramics (MFA); graphic design (MFA); painting (MFA); photography (MFA); printmaking (MFA); sculpture (MFA). *Program availability:* Part-time. *Degree requirements:* For master's, thesis. *Entrance requirements:* For master's, portfolio. Additional exam requirements/recommendations for international students: Required—TOEFL (minimum score 550 paper-based; 80 iBT) or IELTS (minimum score 6.5). Electronic applications accepted. *Faculty research:* Vapor-fired ceramics, video installation, art theory, digital photography, mixed and interdisciplinary media work.

Ohio University, Graduate College, Scripps College of Communication, School of Visual Communication, Athens, OH 45701-2979. Offers MA. *Entrance requirements:* For master's, minimum GPA of 2.5, portfolio. Additional exam requirements/recommendations for international students: Required—TOEFL (minimum score 600 paper-based; 100 iBT) or IELTS (minimum score 7). Electronic applications accepted. *Faculty research:* Photojournalism (including documentary photography), commercial photography (including illustrative photography), picture editing, informational graphics/publication design, interactive multimedia, visual media management.

Oklahoma City University, Petree College of Arts and Sciences, Oklahoma City, OK 73106-1402. Offers applied behavioral studies (M Ed); applied sociology: nonprofit leadership (MA); creative writing (MFA); criminology (MS); early childhood education (M Ed); elementary education (M Ed); general studies (MLA); leadership/management (MLA); moving image arts (MFA); professional counseling (M Ed); teaching (MA); teaching English to speakers of other languages (MA). *Program availability:* Part-time, evening/weekend. *Faculty:* 6 full-time (2 women), 16 part-time/adjunct (10 women). *Students:* 84 full-time (61 women), 32 part-time (23 women); includes 31 minority (13 Black or African American, non-Hispanic/Latino; 3 American Indian or Alaska Native, non-Hispanic/Latino; 1 Asian, non-Hispanic/Latino; 9 Hispanic/Latino; 5 Two or more races, non-Hispanic/Latino), 30 international. Average age 34. 192 applicants, 67% accepted, 57 enrolled. In 2017, 65 master's awarded. *Degree requirements:* For master's, capstone/practicum. *Entrance requirements:* For master's, bachelor's degree from accredited institution with minimum GPA of 3.0, essay, recommendation letters. Additional exam requirements/recommendations for international students: Required—TOEFL (minimum score 550 paper-based; 80 iBT). *Application deadline:* Applications are processed on a rolling basis. Application fee: $50. Electronic applications accepted. *Expenses:* $8,580. *Financial support:* In 2017–18, 19 students received support. Federal Work-Study, institutionally sponsored loans, scholarships/grants, and tuition waivers (full and partial) available. Support available to part-time students. Financial award application deadline: 6/1; financial award applicants required to submit FAFSA.

Unit head: Dr. Amy Cataldi, Dean, 405-208-5446, Fax: 405-208-5447, E-mail: acataldi@okcu.edu. *Application contact:* Michael Harrington, Director of Graduate Admissions, 800-633-7242, Fax: 405-208-5356, E-mail: gadmissions@okcu.edu. Website: https://www.okcu.edu/artsci/home

Otis College of Art and Design, Program in Fine Arts, Los Angeles, CA 90045-9785. Offers new genres (MFA); painting (MFA); photography (MFA); sculpture (MFA). *Accreditation:* NASAD. *Degree requirements:* For master's, thesis. *Entrance requirements:* For master's, portfolio. Additional exam requirements/recommendations for international students: Required—TOEFL (minimum score 600 paper-based). Electronic applications accepted.

Paris College of Art, Graduate Programs, Paris, France. Offers accessories design (MA); fashion design: new materials and technologies (MA); fashion film and photography (MA); interior design (MA); transdisciplinary new media (MA, MFA). *Entrance requirements:* Additional exam requirements/recommendations for international students: Required—TOEFL or IELTS.

Purdue University, Graduate School, College of Liberal Arts, Department of Art and Design, West Lafayette, IN 47907. Offers art education (MA, PhD); industrial design (MFA); integrated studio arts (MFA); interior design (MFA); photography (MFA); visual communications design (MFA). *Accreditation:* NASAD; NAST. *Program availability:* Part-time. *Students:* 20 full-time (14 women), 1 part-time (0 women); includes 1 minority (Two or more races, non-Hispanic/Latino), 16 international. Average age 26. 97 applicants, 26% accepted, 10 enrolled. In 2017, 6 master's awarded. *Degree requirements:* For master's, terminal exhibit, project, or thesis. *Entrance requirements:* For master's, GRE General Test (for art education), minimum undergraduate GPA of 3.0 or equivalent; 9 undergraduate hours in an art or design history; BA in art (for MA in art education); for doctorate, GRE General Test (minimum scores 600 in verbal and 1000 total), master's degree in art education or art with teaching certification; 3 years of teaching experience at the K-12 level. Additional exam requirements/recommendations for international students: Required—TOEFL (minimum score 550 paper-based; 77 iBT). *Application deadline:* For fall admission, 2/1 for domestic students, 2/1 priority date for international students. Applications are processed on a rolling basis. Application fee: $60 ($75 for international students). Electronic applications accepted. *Financial support:* Teaching assistantships with tuition reimbursements and career-related internships or fieldwork available. Support available to part-time students. Financial award applicants required to submit FAFSA. *Faculty research:* Design, fine arts, photography, acting, directing, theatre technology. *Unit head:* Harry T. Bulow, Head of the Graduate Program, 765-494-3056, E-mail: hbulow@purdue.edu. *Application contact:* Sara J. Unser, Graduate Contact, 765-494-8662, E-mail: sunser@purdue.edu. Website: https://www.cla.purdue.edu/vpa/ad/

Rhode Island School of Design, Department of Photography, Providence, RI 02903-2784. Offers MFA. *Accreditation:* NASAD. *Faculty:* 5 full-time (3 women), 8 part-time/adjunct (7 women). *Students:* 16 full-time (5 women); includes 5 minority (2 Black or African American, non-Hispanic/Latino; 3 Hispanic/Latino), 5 international. Average age 26. 105 applicants, 13% accepted, 9 enrolled. In 2017, 7 master's awarded. *Degree requirements:* For master's, thesis, exhibition. *Entrance requirements:* For master's, portfolio, statement of purpose, 3 letters of recommendation. Additional exam requirements/recommendations for international students: Required—TOEFL (minimum score 580 paper-based; 93 iBT). *Application deadline:* For fall admission, 1/10 for domestic and international students. Application fee: $60. Electronic applications accepted. *Expenses: Tuition:* Full-time $48,210. *Required fees:* $260. *Financial support:* Fellowships, research assistantships, teaching assistantships, Federal Work-Study, scholarships/grants, and unspecified assistantships available. Financial award application deadline: 2/15; financial award applicants required to submit FAFSA. *Unit head:* Brian Ulrich, Department Head, 401-454-6122, Fax: 401-454-6385, E-mail: photo@risd.edu. *Application contact:* Molly Pettengill, Assistant Director for Graduate Recruitment, 401-454-6312, Fax: 401-454-6309, E-mail: mpetteng@risd.edu. Website: http://www.risd.edu/academics/photography/

Rochester Institute of Technology, Graduate Enrollment Services, College of Imaging Arts and Sciences, School of Photographic Arts and Sciences, MFA Program in Photography and Related Media, Rochester, NY 14623-5603. Offers MFA. *Accreditation:* NASAD. *Program availability:* Part-time. *Students:* 15 full-time (8 women), 1 (woman) part-time; includes 5 minority (1 Asian, non-Hispanic/Latino; 3 Hispanic/Latino; 1 Two or more races, non-Hispanic/Latino), 6 international. Average age 28. 63 applicants, 40% accepted, 9 enrolled. In 2017, 5 master's awarded. *Degree requirements:* For master's, thesis, exhibit. *Entrance requirements:* For master's, GRE, portfolio, minimum GPA of 3.0 (recommended). Additional exam requirements/recommendations for international students: Required—TOEFL (minimum score 550 paper-based; 90 iBT), IELTS (minimum score 6.5), PTE (minimum score 58). *Application deadline:* For fall admission, 2/15 priority date for domestic and international students. Applications are processed on a rolling basis. Application fee: $65. Electronic applications accepted. *Expenses:* $1,815 per credit hour. *Financial support:* In 2017-18, 14 students received support. Teaching assistantships with partial tuition reimbursements available, career-related internships or fieldwork, scholarships/grants, and unspecified assistantships available. Support available to part-time students. Financial award applicants required to submit FAFSA. *Faculty research:* Histories and theories of photography, contemporary art, American art and visual culture, and critical theory; photo books, visual narrative and expanded/experimental forms of documentary; contemporary fine art photography practice as personal document; public space, social practice, sensory observation, walking and mapping; relationship between the constructed image, photography as object, and fiction in contemporary practice. *Unit head:* Christine Shank, Graduate Program Director, 585-475-2616, Fax: 585-475-5804, E-mail: crspph@rit.edu. *Application contact:* Diane Ellison, Senior Associate Vice President, Graduate Enrollment Services, 585-475-2229, Fax: 585-475-7164, E-mail: gradinfo@rit.edu. Website: http://cias.rit.edu/schools/photographic-arts-sciences/graduate-imaging-arts

San Jose State University, Graduate Studies and Research, College of Humanities and the Arts, San Jose, CA 95192-0088. Offers art (MA, MFA), including digital media art (MFA), history and visual culture (MA), photography (MFA), pictorial art (MFA), spatial art (MFA); English (MA, MFA), including creative writing (MFA); linguistics (MA); music (MM); music education (MA); philosophy (MA); Spanish (MA); teaching English to speakers of other languages (MA). *Program availability:* Part-time. *Faculty:* 35 full-time (17 women), 19 part-time/adjunct (11 women). *Students:* 129 full-time (79 women), 106 part-time (71 women); includes 117 minority (5 Black or African American, non-Hispanic/Latino; 29 Asian, non-Hispanic/Latino; 44 Hispanic/Latino; 39 Two or more races, non-Hispanic/Latino), 28 international. Average age 35. 204 applicants, 65% accepted, 79 enrolled. In 2017, 85 master's awarded. *Degree requirements:* For master's, one foreign language, comprehensive exam (for some programs), thesis (for some programs), graduate writing assessment, special study/project, recital. *Entrance requirements:* Additional exam requirements/recommendations for international students: Required—TOEFL (minimum score 550 paper-based; 80 iBT), IELTS (minimum score 6.5), PTE (minimum score 53). *Application deadline:* For fall admission, 2/1 for domestic and international students. Applications are processed on a rolling basis. Application fee: $55. Electronic applications accepted. *Expenses:* Tuition, state

resident: full-time $7176. Tuition, nonresident: full-time $16,680. Tuition and fees vary according to course load and program. *Financial support:* Fellowships, research assistantships, Federal Work-Study, scholarships/grants, traineeships, tuition waivers (full and partial), and unspecified assistantships available. Support available to part-time students. Financial award application deadline: 4/28; financial award applicants required to submit FAFSA. *Unit head:* Dr. Shannon Miller, Dean, 408-924-4300, Fax: 408-924-4365, E-mail: shannon.miller@sjsu.edu. Website: http://www.sjsu.edu/humanitiesandarts/

Savannah College of Art and Design, Program in Photography, Savannah, GA 31402-3146. Offers MA, MFA. *Program availability:* Part-time, 100% online. *Faculty:* 21 full-time (8 women), 6 part-time/adjunct (1 woman). *Students:* 59 full-time (28 women), 26 part-time (16 women); includes 19 minority (8 Black or African American, non-Hispanic/Latino; 1 American Indian or Alaska Native, non-Hispanic/Latino; 3 Asian, non-Hispanic/Latino; 6 Hispanic/Latino; 1 Native Hawaiian or other Pacific Islander, non-Hispanic/Latino), 26 international. Average age 33. 116 applicants, 28% accepted, 15 enrolled. In 2017, 29 master's awarded. *Degree requirements:* For master's, final portfolio (for MA); thesis (for MFA). *Entrance requirements:* For master's, GRE (recommended), portfolio (submitted in digital format), audition or writing submission, resume, statement of purpose, two letters of recommendation. *Application deadline:* For fall admission, 4/1 for domestic and international students. Applications are processed on a rolling basis. Application fee: $40. Electronic applications accepted. *Expenses: Tuition:* Full-time $36,765; part-time $817 per credit hour. One-time fee: $500. *Financial support:* Career-related internships or fieldwork, Federal Work-Study, and scholarships/grants available. Financial award application deadline: 4/1; financial award applicants required to submit FAFSA. *Unit head:* Rick English, Chair, Photography. *Application contact:* Jenny Jaquillard, Executive Director of Admissions, Recruitment and Events, 912-525-5100, Fax: 912-525-5985, E-mail: admission@scad.edu. Website: http://www.scad.edu/academics/programs/photography

School of the Art Institute of Chicago, Graduate Division, Department of Photography, Chicago, IL 60603-3103. Offers MFA. *Accreditation:* NASAD. *Entrance requirements:* Additional exam requirements/recommendations for international students: Required—TOEFL.

School of Visual Arts, Graduate Programs, Digital Photography Department, New York, NY 10010-3994. Offers MPS. *Program availability:* Part-time, online learning. *Degree requirements:* For master's, thesis, 33 credits, including all required courses; minimum GPA of 3.0; thesis project culminating in online project, printed book and exhibition. *Entrance requirements:* For master's, image portfolio which represents 1-3 photographically cohesive bodies of work based on style, concept and execution. Additional exam requirements/recommendations for international students: Required—TOEFL (minimum score 550 paper-based; 79 iBT). Electronic applications accepted. *Faculty research:* Professional photography, digital-imaging technologies.

School of Visual Arts, Graduate Programs, Fashion Photography Department, New York, NY 10010-3994. Offers MPS. *Degree requirements:* For master's, 30 credits, including all required courses; minimum cumulative GPA of 3.0; original, challenging and provocative portfolio of images. *Entrance requirements:* For master's, portfolio, writing sample. Additional exam requirements/recommendations for international students: Required—TOEFL (minimum score 550 paper-based; 79 iBT). Electronic applications accepted. *Expenses:* Contact institution.

School of Visual Arts, Graduate Programs, Program in Photography, Video and Related Media, New York, NY 10010-3994. Offers MFA. *Accreditation:* NASAD. *Degree requirements:* For master's, thesis, 60 credits and all course requirements; minimum GPA of 3.3; thesis project. *Entrance requirements:* For master's, portfolio (still images and/or videos) through SlideRoom. Additional exam requirements/recommendations for international students: Required—TOEFL (minimum score 550 paper-based; 79 iBT). Electronic applications accepted. *Faculty research:* Contemporary and responsible creative initiatives, including experimental, narrative or documentary video, installation and conceptual art, tableau and real-world-witness photography.

Southern Methodist University, Meadows School of the Arts, Division of Art, Dallas, TX 75275. Offers studio art (MFA), including ceramics, drawing, painting, photography, printmaking, sculpture. *Accreditation:* NASAD. *Degree requirements:* For master's, thesis or alternative, exhibit. *Entrance requirements:* For master's, BFA or equivalent, letters of recommendation, portfolio. Additional exam requirements/recommendations for international students: Required—TOEFL (minimum score 550 paper-based; 80 iBT). *Faculty research:* American stoneware, Southwestern furniture traditions, photographic apparatus and techniques, American ceramists, architecture.

Southwest University of Visual Arts, MFA Programs, Tucson, AZ 85716-2505. Offers motion arts (MFA); painting and drawing (MFA); photography (MFA).

Syracuse University, College of Visual and Performing Arts, MFA Program in Art Photography, Syracuse, NY 13244. Offers MFA. *Accreditation:* NASAD. *Degree requirements:* For master's, thesis or alternative. *Entrance requirements:* For master's, personal statement, portfolio, three letters of recommendation, transcripts. Additional exam requirements/recommendations for international students: Required—TOEFL (minimum score 100 iBT). *Application deadline:* For fall admission, 2/1 priority date for domestic and international students. Application fee: $75. Electronic applications accepted. *Financial support:* Fellowships with full tuition reimbursements, teaching assistantships with tuition reimbursements, and tuition waivers available. Financial award application deadline: 1/1. *Faculty research:* Light work, art photography, art theory, art criticism. *Unit head:* Prof. Laura Heyman, Associate Professor/Program Coordinator, 315-443-1198, E-mail: lheyman@syr.edu. *Application contact:* Caitlin Jarvis, Graduate Recruitment Specialist, 315-443-2769, E-mail: admissg@syr.edu. Website: http://vpa.syr.edu/academics/transmedia/graduate/art-photography/

Syracuse University, S. I. Newhouse School of Public Communications, MS in Photography Program, Syracuse, NY 13244. Offers MS. *Students:* Average age 29. *Degree requirements:* For master's, thesis optional, special project. *Entrance requirements:* For master's, portfolio, resume, official transcripts, personal statement, three letters of recommendation. Additional exam requirements/recommendations for international students: Required—TOEFL (minimum score 600 paper-based; 100 iBT). *Application deadline:* For summer admission, 1/15 priority date for domestic and international students. Application fee: $45. Electronic applications accepted. *Financial support:* Fellowships with full tuition reimbursements, research assistantships with partial tuition reimbursements, teaching assistantships with partial tuition reimbursements, and Federal Work-Study available. Financial award application deadline: 2/1. *Faculty research:* Visual communications theory and practice, advertising and illustration photography, picture and multimedia editing, media law. *Unit head:* Prof. Bruce Strong, Chair, Multimedia Photography and Design, 315-443-2304, Fax: 315-443-3946, E-mail: pcgrad@syr.edu. *Application contact:* Martha Coria, Graduate Records, 315-443-4039, Fax: 315-443-1834, E-mail: pcgrad@syr.edu. Website: http://newhouse.syr.edu/academics/degrees/masters/photography

Temple University, Tyler School of Art, Department of Graphic Arts and Design, Philadelphia, PA 19122-6096. Offers graphic and interactive design (MFA); photography (MFA); printmaking (MFA). *Faculty:* 12 full-time (5 women), 31 part-time/adjunct (12 women). *Students:* 19 full-time (12 women); includes 3 minority (2 Asian, non-Hispanic/

Latino; 1 Two or more races, non-Hispanic/Latino), 5 international. 117 applicants, 18% accepted, 10 enrolled. In 2017, 8 master's awarded. *Entrance requirements:* For master's, minimum GPA of 3.0, slide portfolio, 40 credits in studio art, 12 credits in art history, letters of recommendation, resume/curriculum vitae. Additional exam requirements/recommendations for international students: Required—TOEFL (minimum score 550 paper-based; 79 iBT), IELTS (minimum score 6.5). *Application deadline:* For fall admission, 1/15 for domestic students, 12/15 for international students. Application fee: $60. Electronic applications accepted. *Expenses:* Contact institution. *Financial support:* Fellowships, research assistantships, teaching assistantships, and Federal Work-Study available. Support available to part-time students. Financial award application deadline: 1/15; financial award applicants required to submit FAFSA. *Unit head:* Dermot Mac Cormack, Chair, 215-777-9179, Fax: 215-782-2799, E-mail: dermot@temple.edu. *Application contact:* Tamryn McDermott, Director of Admissions, 215-777-9090, E-mail: tylerart@temple.edu.
Website: http://tyler.temple.edu/graduate

Texas Woman's University, Graduate School, College of Arts and Sciences, School of the Arts, Department of Visual Arts, Denton, TX 76204. Offers art (MA, MAT, MFA), including art education (MA, MAT), art history (MA), ceramics (MFA), graphic design (MA), intermedia (MFA), painting (MFA), photography (MFA), sculpture (MFA). MFA degrees are granted through the Federation of North Texas Area Universities (The University of North Texas, Texas A&M Commerce, and Texas Woman's University). *Faculty:* 6 full-time (3 women). *Students:* 8 full-time (6 women), 9 part-time (8 women); includes 7 minority (1 Black or African American, non-Hispanic/Latino; 1 American Indian or Alaska Native, non-Hispanic/Latino; 4 Hispanic/Latino; 1 Two or more races, non-Hispanic/Latino). Average age 33. 10 applicants, 50% accepted, 2 enrolled. In 2017, 10 master's awarded. *Degree requirements:* For master's, comprehensive exam, thesis (for some programs), exhibit (MFA), oral exam, thesis or professional paper (MA). *Entrance requirements:* For master's, portfolio, interview, current curriculum vitae, letter of intent, 3 letters of recommendation, artist statement, 2 research papers (for art history or art education). Additional exam requirements/recommendations for international students: Required—TOEFL (minimum score 550 paper-based; 79 iBT); Recommended—IELTS (minimum score 6.5), TSE (minimum score 53). *Application deadline:* For fall admission, 1/31 priority date for domestic and international students; for spring admission, 10/15 priority date for domestic students, 7/1 priority date for international students. Applications are processed on a rolling basis. Application fee: $50 ($75 for international students). Electronic applications accepted. *Expenses:* $7,520 per year full-time in-state; $16,820 per year full-time out-of-state. *Financial support:* In 2017–18, 9 students received support, including 5 teaching assistantships (averaging $9,780 per year); career-related internships or fieldwork, Federal Work-Study, institutionally sponsored loans, scholarships/grants, traineeships, health care benefits, and unspecified assistantships also available. Support available to part-time students. Financial award application deadline: 3/1; financial award applicants required to submit FAFSA. *Faculty research:* Art education and electronic technology, film noir, one-of-a kind art books, new media, early video art from 1960-1980. *Unit head:* Dr. Vagner Whitehead, Chair, 940-898-2530, Fax: 940-898-2496, E-mail: visualarts@twu.edu. *Application contact:* Korie Hawkins, Associate Director of Admissions, Graduate Recruitment, 940-898-3188, Fax: 940-898-3081, E-mail: admissions@twu.edu.
Website: http://www.twu.edu/visual-arts/

The University of Alabama, Graduate School, College of Arts and Sciences, Department of Art and Art History, Tuscaloosa, AL 35487. Offers art history (MA); studio art (MA, MFA), including ceramics, painting, photography, printmaking, sculpture. *Accreditation:* NASAD. *Program availability:* Part-time. *Faculty:* 18 full-time (11 women), 1 part-time/adjunct (0 women). *Students:* 16 full-time (11 women), 1 part-time (0 women); includes 2 minority (1 Black or African American, non-Hispanic/Latino; 1 Hispanic/Latino), 2 international. Average age 31. 22 applicants, 73% accepted, 9 enrolled. In 2017, 10 master's awarded. *Degree requirements:* For master's, one foreign language, comprehensive exam (for some programs), oral exam, thesis statement, exhibit (studio art), thesis (art history). *Entrance requirements:* For master's, GRE General Test or MAT (art history), minimum GPA of 3.0, BFA or equivalent (studio art). Additional exam requirements/recommendations for international students: Required—TOEFL (minimum score 550 paper-based). *Application deadline:* For fall admission, 3/15 for domestic and international students; for spring admission, 10/15 for domestic and international students. Applications are processed on a rolling basis. Application fee: $50 ($60 for international students). Electronic applications accepted. *Financial support:* In 2017–18, 8 students received support, including 2 fellowships with full tuition reimbursements available, 14 teaching assistantships with tuition reimbursements available (averaging $15,427 per year); career-related internships or fieldwork, institutionally sponsored loans, scholarships/grants, and unspecified assistantships also available. Financial award application deadline: 7/14. *Faculty research:* Nineteenth-century American, Medieval Europe, Baroque, twentieth-century, and African American art history. *Unit head:* Jason Guynes, Chair, 205-348-9944, Fax: 205-348-0287, E-mail: jguynes@ua.edu. *Application contact:* Sarah Marshall, Graduate Coordinator, 205-348-1890, Fax: 205-348-5967, E-mail: smarsh@ua.edu.
Website: http://www.art.ua.edu/

University of Alaska Fairbanks, College of Liberal Arts, Department of Art, Fairbanks, AK 99775-5640. Offers art (MFA); ceramics (MFA); computer art (MFA); drawing (MFA); painting (MFA); photography (MFA); printmaking (MFA); sculpture (MFA). *Program availability:* Part-time. *Degree requirements:* For master's, comprehensive exam, oral defense of project or thesis. *Entrance requirements:* For master's, portfolio of work including about 20 slides or appropriate equivalent depending on field of study. Additional exam requirements/recommendations for international students: Required—TOEFL (minimum score 550 paper-based; 79 iBT), IELTS (minimum score 6.5). Electronic applications accepted. *Faculty research:* Computer art, survey of arts in Alaska, found object art, visualization and animation, painting from the wilderness.

University of Colorado Boulder, Graduate School, College of Arts and Sciences, Department of Art and Art History, Boulder, CO 80309. Offers art history (MA), including contemporary art criticism, early twentieth-century art, nineteenth-century art, Russian and Soviet art; ceramics (MFA); photography and media arts (MFA); printmaking (MFA); sculpture (MFA). *Faculty:* 23 full-time (10 women). *Students:* 42 full-time (30 women), 3 part-time (2 women); includes 7 minority (4 Hispanic/Latino; 3 Two or more races, non-Hispanic/Latino). Average age 29. 152 applicants, 18% accepted, 15 enrolled. In 2017, 16 master's awarded. Terminal master's awarded for partial completion of doctoral program. *Degree requirements:* For master's, variable foreign language requirement, comprehensive exam, thesis (for some programs). *Entrance requirements:* For master's, GRE General Test, minimum undergraduate GPA of 3.0, portfolio. *Application deadline:* For fall admission, 1/10 for domestic students; for spring admission, 12/1 for domestic students. Application fee: $60 ($80 for international students). Electronic applications accepted. Application fee is waived when completed online. *Financial support:* In 2017–18, 140 students received support, including 43 fellowships (averaging $2,068 per year), 41 teaching assistantships with full and partial tuition reimbursements available (averaging $26,884 per year); institutionally sponsored loans, scholarships/grants, health care benefits, and unspecified assistantships also available. Financial award application deadline: 2/15; financial award applicants required to submit FAFSA. *Faculty research:* Visual arts; sculpture; fine arts; installation art; mixed-media art. *Total annual research expenditures:* $17,000. *Application contact:* E-mail: finearts@colorado.edu.
Website: http://www.colorado.edu/arts

University of Illinois at Urbana–Champaign, Graduate College, College of Fine and Applied Arts, School of Art and Design, Program in Studio Arts, Champaign, IL 61820. Offers art and design (MFA); crafts (MFA); metals (MFA); painting (MFA); photography (MFA); sculpture (MFA). *Accreditation:* NASAD. *Entrance requirements:* For master's, minimum GPA of 3.0.

University of Memphis, Graduate School, College of Communication and Fine Arts, Department of Art, Memphis, TN 38152. Offers art history (MA), including Egyptian art and archaeology, general art history; ceramics (MFA); graphic design (MFA); museum studies (Graduate Certificate); painting (MFA); printmaking/photography (MFA); sculpture (MFA). *Accreditation:* NASAD (one or more programs are accredited). *Program availability:* Part-time. *Faculty:* 18 full-time (7 women), 2 part-time/adjunct (1 woman). *Students:* 21 full-time (17 women), 5 part-time (all women); includes 8 minority (2 Black or African American, non-Hispanic/Latino; 1 Asian, non-Hispanic/Latino; 4 Hispanic/Latino; 1 Two or more races, non-Hispanic/Latino). Average age 29. 11 applicants, 73% accepted, 5 enrolled. In 2017, 5 master's, 5 other advanced degrees awarded. *Degree requirements:* For master's, 2 foreign languages, comprehensive exam, thesis, image identification exam, qualifying exam; for Graduate Certificate, internship. *Entrance requirements:* For master's, GRE General Test or MAT, portfolio (MFA), letter of intent, sample of undergraduate writing, two letters of recommendation; for Graduate Certificate, three letters of recommendation, letter of intent. *Application deadline:* For fall admission, 2/15 for domestic students; for spring admission, 11/1 for domestic students. Applications are processed on a rolling basis. Application fee: $35 ($60 for international students). *Expenses:* Contact institution. *Financial support:* In 2017–18, 36 students received support, including 15 research assistantships with full tuition reimbursements available (averaging $11,600 per year); teaching assistantships with full tuition reimbursements available, Federal Work-Study, scholarships/grants, and unspecified assistantships also available. Financial award application deadline: 2/1; financial award applicants required to submit FAFSA. *Faculty research:* Online collaborative learning, advanced art history studies, electronic publishing/design, studio arts, architectural studies. *Unit head:* Prof. Richard Lou, Chair, 901-678-2217, Fax: 901-678-2735, E-mail: ralou@memphis.edu. *Application contact:* Niles Wallice, Coordinator of Graduate Studies, 901-678-4899.
Website: http://memphis.edu/art/

University of Miami, Graduate School, College of Arts and Sciences, Department of Art and Art History, Coral Gables, FL 33124. Offers art history (MA); ceramics/glass (MFA); graphic design/multimedia (MFA); painting (MFA); photography/digital imaging (MFA); printmaking (MFA); sculpture (MFA). *Program availability:* Part-time. *Degree requirements:* For master's, variable foreign language requirement, thesis, exhibit (MFA), comprehensive exam (MA). *Entrance requirements:* For master's, GRE General Test (MA), research paper (MA), slide portfolio (MFA). Additional exam requirements/recommendations for international students: Required—TOEFL. Electronic applications accepted. *Faculty research:* Installation art, public art.

University of Montana, Graduate School, College of Visual and Performing Arts, School of Art, Missoula, MT 59812. Offers fine arts (MA), including art, art history; photography (MFA). *Accreditation:* NASAD (one or more programs are accredited). *Degree requirements:* For master's, thesis exhibit. *Entrance requirements:* For master's, GRE General Test, portfolio.

University of New Mexico, Graduate Studies, College of Fine Arts, Program in Art History, Albuquerque, NM 87131. Offers art history (MA); art of the Americas (MA); history of architecture (PhD); history of graphic arts (PhD); history of photography (PhD); modern Latin American art (PhD); Native American art (PhD); Pre-Columbian art and architecture (PhD); Spanish colonial art (PhD). *Program availability:* Part-time. *Faculty:* 7 full-time (5 women). *Students:* 7 full-time (all women), 18 part-time (15 women); includes 8 minority (2 American Indian or Alaska Native, non-Hispanic/Latino; 5 Hispanic/Latino; 1 Two or more races, non-Hispanic/Latino), 2 international. Average age 41. 21 applicants, 33% accepted, 5 enrolled. In 2017, 5 master's, 1 doctorate awarded. *Degree requirements:* For master's, one foreign language, comprehensive exam (for some programs), thesis, symposium; for doctorate, 2 foreign languages, comprehensive exam, thesis/dissertation, symposium. *Entrance requirements:* Additional exam requirements/recommendations for international students: Required—TOEFL (minimum score 550 paper-based), IELTS (minimum score 6). *Application deadline:* For fall admission, 1/15 for domestic students; for spring admission, 1/15 for domestic students. Application fee: $50. Electronic applications accepted. *Financial support:* Fellowships, research assistantships, teaching assistantships with partial tuition reimbursements, Federal Work-Study, institutionally sponsored loans, scholarships/grants, health care benefits, and unspecified assistantships available. Support available to part-time students. Financial award application deadline: 3/1; financial award applicants required to submit FAFSA. *Faculty research:* Native American, modern Latin American, pre-Columbian, architectural, American, medieval, Spanish Colonial, and Latin American art; history of photography. *Unit head:* Prof. Mary Tsiongas, Chair, 505-277-5861, Fax: 505-277-5955, E-mail: tsiongas@unm.edu. *Application contact:* Kat Heatherington, Graduate Advisor, 505-277-6672, Fax: 505-277-5955, E-mail: art255@unm.edu.
Website: http://art.unm.edu/

University of Notre Dame, Graduate School, College of Arts and Letters, Division of Humanities, Department of Art, Art History, and Design, Notre Dame, IN 46556. Offers art history (MA); design (MFA), including graphic design, industrial design; studio art (MFA), including ceramics, painting, photography, printmaking, sculpture. *Accreditation:* NASAD. *Degree requirements:* For master's, comprehensive exam (for some programs), thesis. *Entrance requirements:* For master's, GRE General Test, minimum GPA of 3.0. Additional exam requirements/recommendations for international students: Required—TOEFL (minimum score 600 paper-based; 80 iBT). Electronic applications accepted. *Faculty research:* Studio art practice in ceramics, printing, photography, printmaking and sculpture, graphic design and industrial design, digital imaging in design and photography, Renaissance and American art history, contemporary art theory and criticism.

University of Oklahoma, Weitzenhoffer Family College of Fine Arts, School of Visual Arts, Norman, OK 73019. Offers art (MFA), including art and technology, ceramics, film, painting, photography, printmaking, sculpture, video, visual communication; art history (MA, PhD), including art history (MA), art of the American West (PhD), Native American art history (PhD); design (MFA). *Faculty:* 24 full-time (8 women). *Students:* 22 full-time (17 women), 9 part-time (all women); includes 9 minority (1 American Indian or Alaska Native, non-Hispanic/Latino; 1 Asian, non-Hispanic/Latino; 4 Hispanic/Latino; 3 Two or more races, non-Hispanic/Latino). Average age 33. 28 applicants, 25% accepted, 6 enrolled. In 2017, 6 master's, 3 doctorates awarded. *Degree requirements:* For master's, 2 foreign languages, comprehensive exam (for some programs), thesis (for some programs); for doctorate, 2 foreign languages, comprehensive exam, thesis/dissertation. *Entrance requirements:* For master's and doctorate, GRE. Additional exam requirements/recommendations for international students: Required—TOEFL (minimum score 79 iBT) or IELTS (minimum score 6.5). *Application deadline:* For fall admission, 2/1 for domestic and international students.

Application fee: $50 ($100 for international students). Electronic applications accepted. *Expenses:* Tuition, state resident: full-time $5119; part-time $213.30 per credit hour. Tuition, nonresident: full-time $19,778; part-time $824.10 per credit hour. *Required fees:* $3458; $133.55 per credit hour. $126.50 per semester. *Financial support:* In 2017–18, 30 students received support, including 1 research assistantship with full tuition reimbursement available (averaging $10,373 per year), 16 teaching assistantships with full tuition reimbursements available (averaging $10,377 per year); fellowships with full tuition reimbursements available, career-related internships or fieldwork, Federal Work-Study, institutionally sponsored loans, scholarships/grants, health care benefits, tuition waivers (full and partial), and unspecified assistantships also available. Support available to part-time students. Financial award application deadline: 6/1; financial award applicants required to submit FAFSA. *Faculty research:* Art history, studio arts, 3D printing, installation art, photography. *Unit head:* Dr. Bette Talvacchia, Director, 405-325-2691, Fax: 405-325-1668, E-mail: bette.talvacchia-1@ou.edu. *Application contact:* Peter Froslie, MFA Coordinator, E-mail: froslie@ou.edu.
Website: http://art.ou.edu

University of Rochester, School of Arts and Sciences, Program in Photographic Preservation and Collections Management, Rochester, NY 14627. Offers MA. Program offered jointly with George Eastman Museum. *Students:* 9 full-time (6 women), 1 (woman) part-time; includes 1 minority (Black or African American, non-Hispanic/Latino). Average age 28. 14 applicants, 86% accepted, 4 enrolled. In 2017, 9 master's awarded. *Degree requirements:* For master's, essay (counts as qualifying exam). *Entrance requirements:* For master's, writing sample, transcripts, three letters of recommendation, one- to two-page statement of purpose. Additional exam requirements/recommendations for international students: Required—TOEFL. *Application deadline:* For fall admission, 1/15 for domestic and international students. Application fee: $60. Electronic applications accepted. *Expenses:* $1,596 per credit hour. *Financial support:* In 2017–18, 4 students received support. Tuition waivers (partial) available. Financial award application deadline: 1/15. *Unit head:* Jacob Lewis, Associate Academic Director, 585-275-4287, E-mail: joan.saab@rochester.edu. *Application contact:* Martin Collier, Administrator, 585-275-7451, E-mail: marty.collier@rochester.edu.
Website: https://www.sas.rochester.edu/ppc/

University of South Dakota, Graduate School, College of Fine Arts, Department of Art, Vermillion, SD 57069. Offers art education (MFA); ceramics (MFA); graphic design (MFA); painting (MFA); photography (MFA); printmaking (MFA); sculpture (MFA). *Accreditation:* NASAD. *Degree requirements:* For master's, thesis or alternative. *Entrance requirements:* For master's, portfolio, minimum GPA of 2.7. Additional exam requirements/recommendations for international students: Required—TOEFL (minimum score 550 paper-based; 79 iBT). *Application deadline:* Applications are processed on a rolling basis. Application fee: $35. Electronic applications accepted. *Financial support:* Research assistantships with partial tuition reimbursements, teaching assistantships with partial tuition reimbursements, Federal Work-Study, and unspecified assistantships available. Support available to part-time students. Financial award applicants required to submit FAFSA. *Application contact:* Graduate School, 605-658-6140, Fax: 605-677-6118, E-mail: grad@usd.edu.
Website: http://www.usd.edu/fine-arts/art

University of Southern California, Graduate School, Roski School of Fine Arts, Graduate Programs in Fine Arts, Los Angeles, CA 90089. Offers new genres (MFA); painting/drawing (MFA); photography (MFA); sculpture (MFA). *Degree requirements:* For master's, thesis. *Entrance requirements:* For master's, portfolio, artist statement, 3 letters of recommendation. Additional exam requirements/recommendations for international students: Required—TOEFL (minimum score 600 paper-based; 100 iBT). Electronic applications accepted. *Faculty research:* Fine art production in the areas of photography, video, sculpture, drawing, and performance.

The University of Tennessee, Graduate School, College of Arts and Sciences, School of Art, Knoxville, TN 37996. Offers ceramics (MFA); drawing (MFA); graphic design (MFA); inter-area studies (MFA); media arts (MFA); painting (MFA); printmaking (MFA); sculpture (MFA); watercolor (MFA). *Accreditation:* NASAD. *Degree requirements:* For master's, thesis or alternative, exhibit. *Entrance requirements:* For master's, portfolio, minimum GPA of 2.7. Additional exam requirements/recommendations for international students: Required—TOEFL. Electronic applications accepted.

University of Utah, Graduate School, College of Fine Arts, Department of Art and Art History, Salt Lake City, UT 84112-0380. Offers art history (MA); ceramics (MFA); community-based art education (MFA); drawing (MFA); graphic design (MFA); painting (MFA); photography/digital imaging (MFA); printmaking (MFA); sculpture/intermedia (MFA). *Faculty:* 19 full-time (9 women), 23 part-time/adjunct (11 women). *Students:* 6 full-time (3 women); includes 1 minority (Asian, non-Hispanic/Latino). Average age 24. 48 applicants, 31% accepted, 3 enrolled. In 2017, 6 master's awarded. *Degree requirements:* For master's, variable foreign language requirement, comprehensive exam (for some programs), thesis or alternative, exhibit and final project paper (for MFA). *Entrance requirements:* For master's, CD portfolio (MFA), writing sample (MA), curriculum vitae, letters of recommendation, letter of intent. Additional exam requirements/recommendations for international students: Required—TOEFL (minimum score 575 paper-based; 75 iBT). *Application deadline:* For fall admission, 1/15 priority date for domestic and international students. Application fee: $55 ($65 for international students). Electronic applications accepted. *Expenses:* Contact institution. *Financial support:* In 2017–18, 6 students received support, including 2 fellowships, 6 research assistantships with partial tuition reimbursements available, 34 teaching assistantships with partial tuition reimbursements available; Federal Work-Study, institutionally sponsored loans, scholarships/grants, tuition waivers (partial), unspecified assistantships, and stipends also available. Financial award application deadline: 1/15; financial award applicants required to submit FAFSA. *Faculty research:* Studio art, European art history, Asian art history, Latin American art history, twentieth-century/contemporary art history. *Total annual research expenditures:* $54,906. *Unit head:* Prof. Brian Snapp, Chair, 801-581-8677, Fax: 801-585-6171, E-mail: b.snapp@utah.edu. *Application contact:* Prof. Kim Martinez, Director of Graduate Studies, 801-581-8677, Fax: 801-585-6171, E-mail: kim.martinez@art.utah.edu.
Website: http://www.art.utah.edu/

University of Victoria, Faculty of Graduate Studies, Faculty of Fine Arts, Department of Visual Arts, Victoria, BC V8W 2Y2, Canada. Offers digital multimedia (MFA); drawing (MFA); painting (MFA); photography (MFA); sculpture (MFA); video (MFA). *Degree requirements:* For master's, exhibit, oral exam. *Entrance requirements:* For master's, portfolio, BFA. Additional exam requirements/recommendations for international students: Required—TOEFL (minimum score 575 paper-based), IELTS (minimum score 7). Electronic applications accepted.

University of Washington, Graduate School, College of Arts and Sciences, School of Art, Division of Art, Seattle, WA 98195. Offers painting and drawing (MFA); photography (MFA). *Degree requirements:* For master's, thesis, exhibit. *Entrance requirements:* For master's, BFA or equivalent academic work in art, 20 slide portfolio. Additional exam requirements/recommendations for international students: Required—TOEFL. Electronic applications accepted.

Virginia Commonwealth University, Graduate School, School of the Arts, Richmond, VA 23284-9005. Offers art education (MAE, PhD); art history (MA, PhD), including curatorial (PhD), historical studies, museum studies (MA); ceramics (MFA); design (MFA), including interior environments, visual communications; fibers (MFA); furniture design (MFA); glassworking (MFA); jewelry/metalworking (MFA); kinetic imaging (MFA); music (MM), including music education; painting (MFA); photography and film (MFA); printmaking (MFA); sculpture (MFA); theatre (MFA), including costume design, pedagogy/literature, pedagogy/performance, scene design/technical theatre. *Program availability:* Part-time. *Entrance requirements:* For doctorate, GRE General Test, writing sample. Additional exam requirements/recommendations for international students: Required—TOEFL (minimum score 600 paper-based; 100 iBT). Electronic applications accepted.

Wayne State University, College of Fine, Performing and Communication Arts, James Pearson Duffy Department of Art and Art History, Detroit, MI 48202. Offers art (MA, MFA), including ceramics, drawing, fashion design and merchandising (MA), fibers, graphic design, industrial design (MA), interior design (MA), metalsmithing, painting, photography, printmaking, sculpture; art history (MA). *Students:* 13 full-time (8 women), 12 part-time (9 women); includes 5 minority (3 Black or African American, non-Hispanic/Latino; 1 Asian, non-Hispanic/Latino; 1 Hispanic/Latino), 2 international. Average age 34. 46 applicants, 24% accepted, 6 enrolled. In 2017, 5 master's awarded. *Degree requirements:* For master's, thesis (for some programs), essay or thesis. *Entrance requirements:* For master's, BFA or another degree and equivalent course work, portfolio, personal interview, reference letters, statement of intent (except for art history program). Additional exam requirements/recommendations for international students: Required—TOEFL (minimum score 550 paper-based; 79 iBT), TWE (minimum score 5.5), Michigan English Language Assessment Battery (minimum score 85); Recommended—IELTS (minimum score 6.5). *Application deadline:* For fall admission, 2/1 for domestic and international students; for winter admission, 10/1 for domestic and international students. Application fee: $50. Electronic applications accepted. *Expenses:* Contact institution. *Financial support:* In 2017–18, 18 students received support, including 1 research assistantship (averaging $22,241 per year), 6 teaching assistantships with tuition reimbursements available (averaging $18,534 per year); fellowships with tuition reimbursements available, scholarships/grants, and unspecified assistantships also available. Support available to part-time students. Financial award applicants required to submit FAFSA. *Unit head:* Dr. John Richardson, Chair, 313-577-2980, Fax: 313-577-3491, E-mail: af5343@wayne.edu. *Application contact:* 313-577-2980, E-mail: art@wayne.edu.
Website: http://art.wayne.edu/

West Virginia University, College of Creative Arts, Morgantown, WV 26506. Offers acting (MFA); art education (MA); art history (MA); ceramics (MFA); collaborative piano (MM, DMA); composition (MM, DMA); conducting (MM, DMA); costume design and technology (MFA); graphic design (MFA); jazz pedagogy (MM); lighting design and technology (MFA); music (PhD); music education (MM, PhD); music industry (MA); music theory (MM); musicology (MA); painting and printmaking (MFA); performance (MM, DMA); photography (MFA); piano pedagogy (MM); scenic design and technology (MFA); sculpture (MFA); studio art (MA); technical direction (MFA); vocal pedagogy and performance (DMA). *Program availability:* Part-time. *Students:* 114 full-time (64 women), 39 part-time (21 women); includes 19 minority (11 Black or African American, non-Hispanic/Latino; 1 Asian, non-Hispanic/Latino; 6 Hispanic/Latino; 1 Two or more races, non-Hispanic/Latino), 33 international. *Degree requirements:* For master's, thesis, recitals; for doctorate, comprehensive exam, thesis/dissertation, recitals (DMA). *Entrance requirements:* For doctorate, minimum GPA of 3.0, audition. Additional exam requirements/recommendations for international students: Required—TOEFL. *Application deadline:* For fall admission, 3/1 priority date for domestic students, 2/15 for international students; for spring admission, 11/1 for domestic students, 9/15 for international students. Applications are processed on a rolling basis. Application fee: $60. Electronic applications accepted. *Expenses:* Tuition, state resident: full-time $9450. Tuition, nonresident: full-time $24,390. *Financial support:* Research assistantships, teaching assistantships, career-related internships or fieldwork, Federal Work-Study, institutionally sponsored loans, scholarships/grants, health care benefits, tuition waivers (partial), and administrative assistantships available. Financial award applicants required to submit FAFSA. *Faculty research:* Professional directing, consulting, acting design, music education, jazz history. *Unit head:* Dr. Paul Kreider, Dean, 304-293-4841 Ext. 3109, Fax: 304-293-6896, E-mail: paul.kreider@mail.wvu.edu. *Application contact:* Records Officer, 304-293-4841, Fax: 304-293-2533, E-mail: rachel.hanks@mail.wvu.edu.
Website: http://www.ccarts.wvu.edu

Wichita State University, Graduate School, College of Fine Arts, School of Art, Design and Creative Industries, Wichita, KS 67260. Offers studio arts (MFA), including ceramics, painting, photo media, printmaking, sculpture. *Accreditation:* NASAD. *Unit head:* Prof. Jeff Pulaski, Director, 316-978-3555, Fax: 316-978-5418, E-mail: jeff.pulaski1@wichita.edu. *Application contact:* Jordan Oleson, Admissions Coordinator, 316-978-3095, Fax: 316-978-3253, E-mail: jordan.oleson@wichita.edu.
Website: http://www.wichita.edu/artdesign

Yale University, School of Art, New Haven, CT 06520-8339. Offers graphic design (MFA); painting/printmaking (MFA); photography (MFA); sculpture (MFA). *Degree requirements:* For master's, thesis (for some programs). *Entrance requirements:* Additional exam requirements/recommendations for international students: Required—TOEFL (minimum score 550 paper-based; 100 iBT). Electronic applications accepted. *Expenses:* Contact institution.

Textile Design

Academy of Art University, Graduate Programs, Program in Costume Design, San Francisco, CA 94105-3410. Offers MA, MFA. *Program availability:* Part-time, evening/weekend, 100% online. *Faculty:* 26 full-time (17 women), 54 part-time/adjunct (44 women). *Students:* 14 full-time (all women), 7 part-time (all women); includes 3 minority (2 Asian, non-Hispanic/Latino; 1 Hispanic/Latino), 6 international. Average age 33. 5 applicants, 100% accepted, 3 enrolled. In 2017, 1 master's awarded. *Degree requirements:* For master's, final review. *Entrance requirements:* For master's, statement of intent; resume; portfolio/reel; official college transcripts. *Application deadline:* Applications are processed on a rolling basis. Application fee: $50. Electronic applications accepted. *Expenses: Tuition:* Part-time $982 per unit. *Financial support:* Career-related internships or fieldwork, Federal Work-Study, and scholarships/grants available. Financial award application deadline: 8/10; financial award applicants required to submit FAFSA. *Unit head:* 800-544-ARTS, E-mail: info@academyart.edu. *Application contact:* 800-544-ARTS, E-mail: info@academyart.edu.
Website: http://www.academyart.edu/academics/fashion/graduate-degrees

Academy of Art University, Graduate Programs, School of Fashion, San Francisco, CA 94105-3410. Offers fashion (MA, MFA); fashion merchandising (MA); fashion merchandising and management (MFA); fashion product development (MFA); knitwear design (MFA); textile design (MFA). *Program availability:* Part-time, 100% online. *Faculty:* 26 full-time (17 women), 54 part-time/adjunct (44 women). *Students:* 325 full-time (297 women), 186 part-time (167 women); includes 115 minority (61 Black or African American, non-Hispanic/Latino; 2 American Indian or Alaska Native, non-Hispanic/Latino; 27 Asian, non-Hispanic/Latino; 17 Hispanic/Latino; 1 Native Hawaiian or other Pacific Islander, non-Hispanic/Latino; 7 Two or more races, non-Hispanic/Latino), 291 international. Average age 29. 157 applicants, 100% accepted, 110 enrolled. In 2017, 205 master's awarded. *Degree requirements:* For master's, final review. *Entrance requirements:* For master's, statement of intent; resume; portfolio/reel; official college transcripts. *Application deadline:* Applications are processed on a rolling basis. Application fee: $50. Electronic applications accepted. *Expenses: Tuition:* Part-time $982 per unit. *Financial support:* Career-related internships or fieldwork, Federal Work-Study, and scholarships/grants available. Financial award application deadline: 8/10; financial award applicants required to submit FAFSA. *Unit head:* 800-544-ARTS, E-mail: info@academyart.edu. *Application contact:* 800-544-ARTS, E-mail: info@academyart.edu.
Website: http://www.academyart.edu/fashion-school/index.html

Arizona State University at the Tempe campus, Herberger Institute for Design and the Arts, School of Art, Tempe, AZ 85287-1505. Offers art education (MA); art history (MA); ceramics (MFA); design, environment and the arts (PhD), including history, theory and criticism; drawing (MFA); fibers (MFA); intermedia (MFA); metals (MFA); museum studies (MFA); painting (MFA); printmaking (MFA); sculpture (MFA); wood (MFA); MFA/MA. Terminal master's awarded for partial completion of doctoral program. *Degree requirements:* For master's, thesis/exhibition (MFA, MA in art education); interactive Program of Study (iPOS) submitted before completing 50 percent of required credit hours; for doctorate, comprehensive exam, thesis/dissertation, interactive Program of Study (iPOS) submitted before completing 50 percent of required credit hours. *Entrance requirements:* For master's, GRE or MAT, minimum GPA of 3.0 or equivalent in last 2 years of work leading to bachelor's degree; for doctorate, GRE, master's degree in architecture, graphic design, industrial design, interior design, landscape architecture, or art history or equivalent standing; statement of purpose; 3 letters of recommendation; indication of potential faculty mentor; sample of written work. Additional exam requirements/recommendations for international students: Required—TOEFL, IELTS, or PTE. Electronic applications accepted.

California State University, Los Angeles, Graduate Studies, College of Arts and Letters, Department of Art, Los Angeles, CA 90032-8530. Offers art (MA), including art education, art history, art therapy, ceramics, metals, and textiles, design (MA, MFA), painting, sculpture, and graphic arts, photography; fine arts (MFA), including crafts, design (MA, MFA), studio arts. *Accreditation:* NASAD (one or more programs are accredited). *Program availability:* Part-time, evening/weekend. *Degree requirements:* For master's, comprehensive exam, project or thesis. *Entrance requirements:* For master's, portfolio. Additional exam requirements/recommendations for international students: Required—TOEFL (minimum score 500 paper-based). Electronic applications accepted. *Faculty research:* The artist and the book, conceptual art, ceramic processes, computer graphics, architectural graphics.

Concordia University, School of Graduate Studies, Faculty of Fine Arts, Department of Studio Arts, Montréal, QC H3G 1M8, Canada. Offers studio arts (MFA), including fibers and material practices, film production, intermedia, painting and drawing, photography, print media, sculpture. *Degree requirements:* For master's, thesis or alternative. *Entrance requirements:* For master's, portfolio.

Cornell University, Graduate School, Graduate Fields of Human Ecology, Field of Fiber Science and Apparel Design, Ithaca, NY 14853. Offers apparel design (MA, MPS); fiber science (MS, PhD); polymer science (MS, PhD); textile science (MS, PhD). *Degree requirements:* For master's, thesis (MA, MS), project paper (MPS); for doctorate, comprehensive exam, thesis/dissertation. *Entrance requirements:* For master's, GRE General Test, 2 letters of recommendation, portfolio (for functional apparel design); for doctorate, GRE General Test, 2 letters of recommendation. Additional exam requirements/recommendations for international students: Required—TOEFL (minimum score 600 paper-based; 77 iBT). Electronic applications accepted. *Faculty research:* Apparel design, consumption, mass customization, 3-D body scanning.

Cranbrook Academy of Art, Program in Fine Arts, Bloomfield Hills, MI 48303-0801. Offers 2d design (MFA); 3d design (MFA); ceramics (MFA); fiber (MFA); metalsmithing (MFA); painting (MFA); photography (MFA); print media (MFA); sculpture (MFA). *Accreditation:* NASAD. *Degree requirements:* For master's, thesis, exhibit. *Entrance requirements:* Additional exam requirements/recommendations for international students: Required—TOEFL (minimum score 85 iBT). Electronic applications accepted.

Drexel University, Westphal College of Media Arts and Design, Program in Fashion Design, Philadelphia, PA 19104-2875. Offers MS. *Accreditation:* NASAD. *Degree requirements:* For master's, thesis, portfolio review. *Entrance requirements:* For master's, interview. Additional exam requirements/recommendations for international students: Required—TOEFL. Electronic applications accepted.

East Carolina University, Graduate School, College of Fine Arts and Communication, School of Art and Design, Greenville, NC 27858-4353. Offers art education (MA Ed); ceramics (MFA); graphic design (MFA); illustration (MFA); metal design (MFA); painting and drawing (MFA); photography (MFA); printmaking (MFA); sculpture (MFA); textile design (MFA); wood design (MFA). *Accreditation:* NASAD (one or more programs are accredited). *Program availability:* Part-time, evening/weekend. *Students:* 24 full-time (14 women), 12 part-time (10 women); includes 6 minority (3 Asian, non-Hispanic/Latino; 2 Hispanic/Latino; 1 Two or more races, non-Hispanic/Latino). Average age 33. 27 applicants, 70% accepted, 12 enrolled. In 2017, 16 master's awarded. *Degree requirements:* For master's, comprehensive exam (for some programs), thesis (for some programs). *Entrance requirements:* For master's, portfolio. *Application deadline:* For fall admission, 2/1 for domestic students; for spring admission, 10/1 for domestic students. Applications are processed on a rolling basis. Application fee: $75. Electronic applications accepted. *Expenses:* Tuition, state resident: full-time $4749; part-time $297 per credit hour. Tuition, nonresident: full-time $17,898; part-time $1119 per credit hour. *Required fees:* $2691; $224 per credit hour. Part-time tuition and fees vary according to course load and program. *Financial support:* Research assistantships with partial tuition reimbursements, teaching assistantships with partial tuition reimbursements, and Federal Work-Study available. Support available to part-time students. Financial award application deadline: 6/1. *Unit head:* Michael H. Drought, Director, 252-328-6665, E-mail: droughtm@ecu.edu. *Application contact:* Dr. Linda H. Nelson, Information Contact, 252-328-1286, E-mail: nelsonlh@ecu.edu.
Website: http://www.ecu.edu/soad/

Illinois State University, Graduate School, College of Fine Arts, School of Art, Normal, IL 61790. Offers art history (MA, MS); ceramics (MFA, MS); drawing (MFA, MS); fibers (MFA, MS); glass (MFA, MS); graphic design (MFA, MS); metals (MFA, MS); painting (MFA, MS); photography (MFA, MS); printmaking (MFA, MS); sculpture (MFA, MS). *Accreditation:* NASAD (one or more programs are accredited). *Degree requirements:* For master's, thesis or alternative, internship. *Entrance requirements:* For master's, portfolio, sample of scholarly writing.

Kent State University, College of the Arts, School of Art, Kent, OH 44242-0001. Offers art education (MA); art history (MA); crafts (MA), including glass (MA, MFA); fine arts (MA), including fashion; studio art (MFA), including ceramics, drawing, glass (MA, MFA), jewelry, metals and enameling, painting, print media and photography, sculpture, textiles. *Accreditation:* NASAD (one or more programs are accredited). *Program availability:* Part-time, online learning. *Faculty:* 24 full-time (13 women), 3 part-time/adjunct (all women). *Students:* 40 full-time (27 women), 22 part-time (19 women); includes 3 minority (2 Black or African American, non-Hispanic/Latino; 1 Two or more races, non-Hispanic/Latino). Average age 31. 40 applicants, 75% accepted, 23 enrolled. In 2017, 22 master's awarded. *Degree requirements:* For master's, comprehensive exam, thesis (for some programs), 1 foreign language (for art history); final project (for crafts and fine arts). *Entrance requirements:* For master's, transcripts, goal statement, 3 letters of recommendation, curriculum vitae, portfolio. Additional exam requirements/recommendations for international students: Required—TOEFL (minimum score 550 paper-based, 79 iBT), Michigan English Language Assessment Battery (minimum score 77), IELTS (minimum score 6.5) or PTE (minimum score 58). *Application deadline:* For fall admission, 2/2 for domestic and international students; for spring admission, 10/15 for domestic and international students. Applications are processed on a rolling basis. Application fee: $45 ($70 for international students). Electronic applications accepted. *Expenses:* Tuition, state resident: full-time $11,310; part-time $515 per credit hour. Tuition, nonresident: full-time $20,396; part-time $928 per credit hour. *International tuition:* $18,544 full-time. *Financial support:* Career-related internships or fieldwork, scholarships/grants, and unspecified assistantships available. Financial award application deadline: 3/16. *Unit head:* Marie Bukowski, Director, 330-672-2192, E-mail: mbukows1@kent.edu. *Application contact:* Linda Hoeptner Poling, Graduate Coordinator and Associate Professor of Art Education, 330-672-7895, E-mail: lhoeptne@kent.edu.
Website: http://www.kent.edu/art

Massachusetts College of Art and Design, Graduate Programs, MFA Program, Boston, MA 02115-5882. Offers 2D fine arts (MFA), including painting, printmaking; 3D fine arts (MFA), including ceramics, fibers, glass, jewelry and metalsmithing, sculpture; design (MFA, Postbaccalaureate Certificate), including dynamic media; fine arts (MFA), including interdisciplinary; media arts (MFA, Postbaccalaureate Certificate), including film/video (MFA), photography. *Accreditation:* NASAD. *Faculty:* 28 full-time (8 women), 28 part-time/adjunct (17 women). *Students:* 44 full-time (26 women), 28 part-time (17 women); includes 8 minority (5 Asian, non-Hispanic/Latino; 3 Hispanic/Latino), 18 international. 247 applicants, 52% accepted, 47 enrolled. In 2017, 42 master's, 5 other advanced degrees awarded. *Degree requirements:* For master's, thesis, thesis exhibition (for fine arts programs); thesis project and document (for design/dynamic media program). *Entrance requirements:* For master's, portfolio, college transcripts, resume, statement of purpose, letters of reference, interview, 6 credits of art history taken prior to or during MFA program; for Postbaccalaureate Certificate, portfolio, college transcripts, resume, statement of purpose, letters of reference, interview. Additional exam requirements/recommendations for international students: Required—TOEFL (minimum score 550 paper-based, 85 iBT) or IELTS (6). *Application deadline:* For fall admission, 1/4 priority date for domestic and international students; for summer admission, 1/4 priority date for domestic and international students. Applications are processed on a rolling basis. Application fee: $90. Electronic applications accepted. *Expenses:* $780 per credit. *Financial support:* In 2017–18, 51 students received support, including 1 research assistantship (averaging $2,160 per year), 33 teaching assistantships (averaging $2,160 per year); fellowships, career-related internships or fieldwork, scholarships/grants, tuition waivers (partial), unspecified assistantships, and adjunct co-teaching positions also available. Support available to part-time students. Financial award application deadline: 1/4; financial award applicants required to submit FAFSA. *Faculty research:* Painting and printmaking, sculpture, photography, film and video, dynamic media design. *Unit head:* Paul Paturzo, Dean of Graduate Studies, 617-879-7166, E-mail: pjpaturzo@massart.edu. *Application contact:* Lauren O'Neill, Assistant Director of Graduate Admissions, 617-879-7222, E-mail: gradadmissions@massart.edu.
Website: http://www.massart.edu/Admissions/Graduate_Programs.html

The New School, Parsons School of Design, Program in Fashion Design and Society, New York, NY 10011. Offers MFA. *Program availability:* Part-time. *Faculty:* 2 full-time (1 woman), 5 part-time/adjunct (2 women). *Students:* 33 full-time (27 women); includes 1 minority (Asian, non-Hispanic/Latino), 30 international. Average age 25. 211 applicants, 13% accepted, 18 enrolled. In 2017, 10 master's awarded. *Degree requirements:* For master's, thesis. *Entrance requirements:* For master's, transcripts, resume, statement of purpose, recommendation letters, portfolio. Additional exam requirements/recommendations for international students: Required—TOEFL (minimum score 92 iBT), IELTS (minimum score 7), PTE (minimum score 63). *Application deadline:* For fall admission, 1/1 priority date for domestic and international students; for summer admission, 1/1 for domestic students, 1/1 priority date for international students. Applications are processed on a rolling basis. Application fee: $50. Electronic applications accepted. *Expenses:* $24,922 per semester full-time, $1,744 per credit part-

time, $100 maintenance of status fee. *Financial support:* In 2017–18, 26 students received support. Career-related internships or fieldwork, scholarships/grants, and unspecified assistantships available. Support available to part-time students. Financial award application deadline: 2/1; financial award applicants required to submit FAFSA. *Unit head:* Shelley Fox, Program Director, 212-229-8966 Ext. 2746, E-mail: foxs@newschool.edu. *Application contact:* Courtney Malenius, Director of Graduate Admissions, 212-229-5150 Ext. 4011, E-mail: maleniuc@newschool.edu.
Website: https://www.newschool.edu/parsons/mfa-fashion-design-society/

The New School, Parsons School of Design, Program in Fashion Studies, New York, NY 10011. Offers MA. Program also offered at Paris, France campus. *Program availability:* Part-time. *Faculty:* 13 full-time (11 women), 1 part-time/adjunct (0 women). *Students:* 50 full-time (38 women), 5 part-time (all women); includes 16 minority (9 Black or African American, non-Hispanic/Latino; 4 Asian, non-Hispanic/Latino; 2 Hispanic/Latino; 1 Two or more races, non-Hispanic/Latino), 27 international. Average age 25. 123 applicants, 44% accepted, 29 enrolled. In 2017, 23 master's awarded. *Degree requirements:* For master's, thesis. *Entrance requirements:* For master's, transcripts, resume, statement of purpose, recommendation letters, interview. Additional exam requirements/recommendations for international students: Required—TOEFL (minimum score 92 iBT), IELTS (minimum score 7), PTE (minimum score 63). *Application deadline:* For fall admission, 1/1 priority date for domestic and international students; for summer admission, 1/1 priority date for domestic and international students. Applications are processed on a rolling basis. Application fee: $50. Electronic applications accepted. *Expenses:* $24,922 per semester full-time, $1,744 per credit part-time, $100 maintenance of status fee. *Financial support:* In 2017–18, 28 students received support. Career-related internships or fieldwork, scholarships/grants, unspecified assistantships, and travel funding; tuition waivers for students who are also New School employees available. Support available to part-time students. Financial award application deadline: 2/1; financial award applicants required to submit FAFSA. *Unit head:* Hazel Clark, Program Director, 212-229-8916 Ext. 4083, E-mail: clarkh@newschool.edu. *Application contact:* Courtney Malenius, Director of Graduate Admissions, 212-229-5150 Ext. 4011, E-mail: maleniuc@newschool.edu.
Website: https://www.newschool.edu/parsons/ma-fashion-studies/

Paris College of Art, Graduate Programs, Paris, France. Offers accessories design (MA); fashion design: new materials and technologies (MA); fashion film and photography (MA); interior design (MA); transdisciplinary new media (MA, MFA). *Entrance requirements:* Additional exam requirements/recommendations for international students: Required—TOEFL or IELTS.

Rhode Island School of Design, Department of Textiles, Providence, RI 02903-2784. Offers MFA. *Accreditation:* NASAD. *Faculty:* 4 full-time (3 women), 5 part-time/adjunct (4 women). *Students:* 12 full-time (9 women); includes 4 minority (1 Black or African American, non-Hispanic/Latino; 1 Asian, non-Hispanic/Latino; 1 Hispanic/Latino; 1 Two or more races, non-Hispanic/Latino), 3 international. Average age 28. 55 applicants, 18% accepted, 6 enrolled. In 2017, 5 master's awarded. *Degree requirements:* For master's, thesis, exhibition. *Entrance requirements:* For master's, portfolio, statement of purpose, 3 letters of recommendation. Additional exam requirements/recommendations for international students: Required—TOEFL (minimum score 580 paper-based; 93 iBT). *Application deadline:* For fall admission, 1/10 for domestic and international students. Application fee: $60. Electronic applications accepted. *Expenses: Tuition:* Full-time $48,210. *Required fees:* $260. *Financial support:* Fellowships, research assistantships, teaching assistantships, Federal Work-Study, scholarships/grants, and unspecified assistantships available. Financial award application deadline: 2/15; financial award applicants required to submit FAFSA. *Unit head:* MaryAnne Friel, Department Head, 401-427-6967, Fax: 401-277-4883, E-mail: textiles@risd.edu. *Application contact:* Molly Pettengill, Assistant Director for Graduate Recruitment, 401-454-6312, Fax: 401-454-6309, E-mail: mpetteng@risd.edu.
Website: http://www.risd.edu/academics/textiles/

Savannah College of Art and Design, Program in Fashion, Savannah, GA 31402-3146. Offers MA, MFA. *Program availability:* Part-time, 100% online. *Faculty:* 23 full-time (13 women), 4 part-time/adjunct (all women). *Students:* 64 full-time (56 women), 25 part-time (22 women); includes 18 minority (15 Black or African American, non-Hispanic/Latino; 3 Asian, non-Hispanic/Latino), 60 international. Average age 28. 114 applicants, 41% accepted, 23 enrolled. In 2017, 11 master's awarded. *Degree requirements:* For master's, final project (for MA); thesis (for MFA). *Entrance requirements:* For master's, GRE (recommended), portfolio (submitted in digital format), audition or writing submission, resume, statement of purpose, two letters of recommendation. Additional exam requirements/recommendations for international students: Recommended—TOEFL (minimum score 550 paper-based; 85 iBT), IELTS (minimum score 6.5). *Application deadline:* For fall admission, 4/1 for domestic and international students. Applications are processed on a rolling basis. Application fee: $40. Electronic applications accepted. *Expenses: Tuition:* Full-time $36,765; part-time $817 per credit hour. One-time fee: $500. *Financial support:* Career-related internships or fieldwork, Federal Work-Study, and scholarships/grants available. Financial award application deadline: 4/1; financial award applicants required to submit FAFSA. *Application contact:* Jenny Jaquillard, Executive Director of Admissions, Recruitment and Events, 912-525-5100, Fax: 912-525-5985, E-mail: admission@scad.edu.
Website: http://www.scad.edu/academics/programs/fashion

Savannah College of Art and Design, Program in Fibers, Savannah, GA 31402-3146. Offers MA, MFA. *Program availability:* Part-time. *Faculty:* 8 full-time (7 women), 3 part-time/adjunct (all women). *Students:* 18 full-time (17 women), 9 part-time (8 women); includes 3 minority (1 Black or African American, non-Hispanic/Latino; 1 Asian, non-Hispanic/Latino; 1 Hispanic/Latino), 12 international. Average age 26. 30 applicants, 47% accepted, 9 enrolled. In 2017, 8 master's awarded. *Degree requirements:* For master's, final project (for MA); thesis (for MFA). *Entrance requirements:* For master's, GRE (recommended), portfolio (submitted in digital format), audition or writing submission, resume, statement of purpose, two letters of recommendation. Additional exam requirements/recommendations for international students: Recommended—TOEFL (minimum score 550 paper-based; 85 iBT), IELTS (minimum score 6.5). *Application deadline:* For fall admission, 4/1 for domestic and international students. Applications are processed on a rolling basis. Application fee: $40. Electronic applications accepted. *Expenses: Tuition:* Full-time $36,765; part-time $817 per credit hour. One-time fee: $500. *Financial support:* Career-related internships or fieldwork, Federal Work-Study, and scholarships/grants available. Financial award application deadline: 4/1; financial award applicants required to submit FAFSA. *Unit head:* Cayewah Easley, Chair, Fibers. *Application contact:* Jenny Jaquillard, Executive Director of Admissions, Recruitment and Events, 912-525-5100, Fax: 912-525-5985, E-mail: admission@scad.edu.
Website: http://www.scad.edu/academics/programs/fibers

Savannah College of Art and Design, Program in Luxury and Fashion Management, Savannah, GA 31402-3146. Offers MA, MFA. *Program availability:* Part-time, 100% online. *Faculty:* 12 full-time (5 women). *Students:* 125 full-time (110 women), 46 part-time (41 women); includes 47 minority (35 Black or African American, non-Hispanic/Latino; 5 Asian, non-Hispanic/Latino; 7 Hispanic/Latino), 88 international. Average age 26. 192 applicants, 40% accepted, 51 enrolled. In 2017, 46 master's awarded. *Degree requirements:* For master's, final project (for MA); thesis (for MFA). *Entrance requirements:* For master's, GRE (recommended), portfolio (submitted in digital format), audition or writing submission, resume, statement of purpose, two letters of recommendation. Additional exam requirements/recommendations for international students: Recommended—TOEFL (minimum score 550 paper-based; 85 iBT), IELTS (minimum score 6.5). *Application deadline:* For fall admission, 4/1 for domestic and international students. Applications are processed on a rolling basis. Application fee: $40. Electronic applications accepted. *Expenses: Tuition:* Full-time $36,765; part-time $817 per credit hour. One-time fee: $500. *Financial support:* Career-related internships or fieldwork, Federal Work-Study, and scholarships/grants available. Financial award application deadline: 4/1; financial award applicants required to submit FAFSA. *Unit head:* Alessandro Cannata, Academic Program Coordinator. *Application contact:* Jenny Jaquillard, Executive Director of Admissions, Recruitment and Events, 912-525-5100, Fax: 912-525-5985, E-mail: admission@scad.edu.
Website: http://www.scad.edu/academics/programs/luxury-and-fashion-management

School of the Art Institute of Chicago, Graduate Division, Program in Fashion, Body, and Garment, Chicago, IL 60603-3103. Offers M Des, Certificate.

Temple University, Tyler School of Art, Department of Crafts, Philadelphia, PA 19122-6096. Offers ceramics (MFA); fibers and material studies (MFA); glass (MFA); metals/jewelry/CAD-CAM (MFA). *Faculty:* 8 full-time (5 women), 21 part-time/adjunct (18 women). *Students:* 15 full-time (11 women); includes 2 minority (both Hispanic/Latino). 67 applicants, 25% accepted, 8 enrolled. In 2017, 11 master's awarded. *Entrance requirements:* For master's, minimum GPA of 3.0, slide portfolio, 40 credits in studio art, 12 credits in art history, letters of recommendation, resume/curriculum vitae. Additional exam requirements/recommendations for international students: Required—TOEFL (minimum score 550 paper-based; 79 iBT), IELTS (minimum score 6.5). *Application deadline:* For fall admission, 1/15 for domestic students, 12/15 for international students. Application fee: $60. Electronic applications accepted. *Expenses:* Contact institution. *Financial support:* Fellowships, research assistantships, teaching assistantships, and Federal Work-Study available. Support available to part-time students. Financial award application deadline: 1/15; financial award applicants required to submit FAFSA. *Unit head:* Nicholas Kripal, Chair, 215-782-2790, Fax: 215-782-2799, E-mail: nkripal@temple.edu. *Application contact:* Tamryn McDermott, Director of Admissions, 215-777-9090, E-mail: tylerart@temple.edu.

Thomas Jefferson University, Kanbar College of Design, Engineering and Commerce, Program in Textile Design, Philadelphia, PA 19107. Offers MS. *Program availability:* Part-time. *Entrance requirements:* For master's, GRE or MAT, minimum GPA of 2.8. Additional exam requirements/recommendations for international students: Required—TOEFL (minimum score 550 paper-based; 79 iBT). Electronic applications accepted.

University of California, Davis, Graduate Studies, Program in Textile Arts and Costume Design, Davis, CA 95616. Offers MFA. *Degree requirements:* For master's, presentation of an individual project/body of work. *Entrance requirements:* For master's, minimum GPA of 3.0, portfolio. Additional exam requirements/recommendations for international students: Required—TOEFL (minimum score 550 paper-based). Electronic applications accepted. *Faculty research:* Historic ethnographic and contemporary costume and textile design, computer-aided design.

University of Cincinnati, Graduate School, College of Design, Architecture, Art, and Planning, School of Design, Cincinnati, OH 45221. Offers fashion design (M Des); graphic design (M Des); industrial design (M Des); interaction design (M Des); product development (M Des). *Accreditation:* NASAD. *Degree requirements:* For master's, thesis. *Entrance requirements:* For master's, undergraduate degree in design or related field, 2 years of work experience in design or related field. Additional exam requirements/recommendations for international students: Required—TOEFL. Electronic applications accepted. *Expenses: Tuition, area resident:* Full-time $14,468. Tuition, state resident: full-time $14,968; part-time $754 per credit hour. Tuition, nonresident: full-time $24,210; part-time $1311 per credit hour. *International tuition:* $26,460 full-time. *Required fees:* $3958; $84 per credit hour. One-time fee: $85 full-time. Tuition and fees vary according to course load, degree level and program. *Faculty research:* Design theory, interdisciplinary design topics.

The University of Kansas, Graduate Studies, College of Liberal Arts and Sciences, Department of Visual Art, Lawrence, KS 66045. Offers ceramics (MFA); drawing and painting (MFA); expanded media (MFA); metalsmithing/jewelry (MFA); sculpture (MFA); textiles/fibers (MFA); visual art education (MA). *Accreditation:* NASAD. *Program availability:* Part-time. *Students:* 26 full-time (13 women), 2 part-time (both women); includes 3 minority (1 American Indian or Alaska Native, non-Hispanic/Latino; 1 Hispanic/Latino; 1 Two or more races, non-Hispanic/Latino), 4 international. Average age 30. 58 applicants, 16% accepted, 6 enrolled. In 2017, 6 master's awarded. *Entrance requirements:* For master's, portfolio, official transcript, minimum GPA of 3.0, 3 letters of recommendation. Additional exam requirements/recommendations for international students: Required—TOEFL. *Application deadline:* For fall admission, 5/1 for domestic and international students; for spring admission, 12/1 for domestic and international students. Application fee: $65 ($85 for international students). Electronic applications accepted. *Financial support:* Fellowships, teaching assistantships, Federal Work-Study, scholarships/grants, and unspecified assistantships available. Financial award application deadline: 1/15; financial award applicants required to submit FAFSA. *Faculty research:* Metal and glass casting; mapping, indigenous lands and history; wood fire kilns; Japanese block printing techniques. *Unit head:* Mary Anne Jordan, Chair, 785-864-2952, E-mail: majordan@ku.edu. *Application contact:* Lauren Chaney, Graduate Admissions Contact, 785-864-2306, E-mail: lkchaney@ku.edu.
Website: http://art.ku.edu/

The University of Manchester, School of Materials, Manchester, United Kingdom. Offers advanced aerospace materials engineering (M Sc); advanced metallic systems (PhD); biomedical materials (M Phil, M Sc, PhD); ceramics and glass (M Phil, M Sc, PhD); composite materials (M Sc, PhD); corrosion and protection (M Phil, M Sc, PhD); materials (M Phil, PhD); metallic materials (M Phil, M Sc, PhD); nanostructural materials (M Phil, M Sc, PhD); paper science (M Phil, M Sc, PhD); polymer science and engineering (M Phil, M Sc, PhD); technical textiles (M Sc); textile design, fashion and management (M Phil, M Sc, PhD); textile science and technology (M Phil, M Sc, PhD); textiles (M Phil, PhD); textiles and fashion (M Ent).

University of Minnesota, Twin Cities Campus, Graduate School, College of Design, Department of Design, Housing, and Apparel, Minneapolis, MN 55455-0213. Offers apparel (MA, MS, PhD); design communication (MA, MS, PhD); housing studies (MA, MS, PhD, Postbaccalaureate Certificate); interactive design (MFA); interior design (MA, MS, PhD). *Program availability:* Part-time. *Degree requirements:* For master's and Postbaccalaureate Certificate, comprehensive exam, thesis (for some programs); for doctorate, comprehensive exam, thesis/dissertation. *Entrance requirements:* For master's, GRE General Test, minimum GPA of 3.0 (preferred), portfolio, 3 letters of recommendation; for doctorate, GRE General Test, minimum GPA of 3.0 (preferred), portfolio, 3 letters of recommendation, writing sample; for Postbaccalaureate Certificate, GRE General Test, minimum GPA of 3.0 (preferred). Additional exam requirements/recommendations for international students: Required—TOEFL (minimum score 550

paper-based; 79 iBT). Electronic applications accepted. *Faculty research:* Housing policy and community development; consumer behavior; interactive design; design history; social, cultural, and behavioral issues related to designed environments.

The University of North Carolina at Greensboro, Graduate School, Bryan School of Business and Economics, Department of Consumer, Apparel, and Retail Studies, Greensboro, NC 27412-5001. Offers MS, PhD. *Degree requirements:* For master's, one foreign language; for doctorate, one foreign language, thesis/dissertation. *Entrance requirements:* For master's and doctorate, GRE General Test. Additional exam requirements/recommendations for international students: Required—TOEFL. Electronic applications accepted. *Faculty research:* Impact of phosphate removal, protective clothing for pesticide workers, fabric hand: subjective and objective measurements.

University of North Texas, Robert B. Toulouse School of Graduate Studies, Denton, TX 76203-5459. Offers accounting (MS); applied anthropology (MA, MS); applied behavior analysis (Certificate); applied geography (MA); applied technology and performance improvement (M Ed, MS); art education (MA); art history (MA); art museum education (Certificate); arts leadership (Certificate); audiology (Au D); behavior analysis (MS); behavioral science (PhD); biochemistry and molecular biology (MS); biology (MA, MS); biomedical engineering (MS); business analysis (MS); chemistry (MS); clinical health psychology (PhD); communication studies (MA, MS); computer engineering (MS); computer science (MS); counseling (M Ed, MS), including clinical mental health counseling (MS), college and university counseling, elementary school counseling, secondary school counseling; creative writing (MA); criminal justice (MS); curriculum and instruction (M Ed); decision sciences (MBA); design (MA, MFA), including fashion design (MFA), innovation studies, interior design (MFA); early childhood studies (MS); economics (MS); educational leadership (M Ed, Ed D); educational psychology (MS, PhD), including family studies (MS), gifted and talented (MS), human development (MS), learning and cognition (MS), research, measurement and evaluation (MS); electrical engineering (MS); emergency management (MPA); engineering technology (MS); English (MA); English as a second language (MA); environmental science (MS); finance (MBA, MS); financial management (MPA); French (MA); health services management (MBA); higher education (M Ed, Ed D); history (MA, MS); hospitality management (MS); human resources management (MPA); information science (MS); information systems (PhD); information technologies (MBA); interdisciplinary studies (MA, MS); international studies (MA); international sustainable tourism (MS); jazz studies (MM); journalism (MA, MJ, Graduate Certificate), including interactive and virtual digital communication (Graduate Certificate), narrative journalism (Graduate Certificate), public relations (Graduate Certificate); kinesiology (MS); linguistics (MA); local government management (MPA); logistics (PhD); logistics and supply chain management (MBA); long-term care, senior housing, and aging services (MA); management (PhD); marketing (MBA); mathematics (MA, MS); mechanical and energy engineering (MS, PhD); music (MA), including ethnomusicology, music theory, musicology, performance; music composition (PhD); music education (MM Ed, PhD); nonprofit management (MPA); operations and supply chain management (MBA); performance (MM, DMA); philosophy (MA); political science (MA); professional and technical communication (MA); radio, television and film (MA, MFA); rehabilitation counseling (Certificate); sociology (MA); Spanish (MA); special education (M Ed); speech-language pathology (MA); strategic management (MBA); studio art (MFA); teaching (M Ed); MBA/MS. *Program availability:* Part-time, evening/weekend, online learning. Terminal master's awarded for partial completion of doctoral program. *Degree requirements:* For master's, variable foreign language requirement, comprehensive exam (for some programs), thesis (for some programs); for doctorate, variable foreign language requirement, comprehensive exam (for some programs), thesis/dissertation; for other advanced degree, variable foreign language requirement, comprehensive exam (for some programs). *Entrance requirements:* For master's and doctorate, GRE, GMAT. Additional exam requirements/recommendations for international students: Required—TOEFL (minimum score 550 paper-based; 79 iBT). Electronic applications accepted.

Wayne State University, College of Fine, Performing and Communication Arts, James Pearson Duffy Department of Art and Art History, Detroit, MI 48202. Offers art (MA, MFA), including ceramics, drawing, fashion design and merchandising (MA), fibers, graphic design, industrial design (MA), interior design (MA), metalsmithing, painting, photography, printmaking, sculpture; art history (MA). *Students:* 13 full-time (8 women), 12 part-time (9 women); includes 5 minority (3 Black or African American, non-Hispanic/Latino; 1 Asian, non-Hispanic/Latino; 1 Hispanic/Latino), 2 international. Average age 34. 46 applicants, 24% accepted, 6 enrolled. In 2017, 5 master's awarded. *Degree requirements:* For master's, thesis (for some programs), essay or thesis. *Entrance requirements:* For master's, BFA or another degree and equivalent course work, portfolio, personal interview, reference letters, statement of intent (except for art history program). Additional exam requirements/recommendations for international students: Required—TOEFL (minimum score 550 paper-based; 79 iBT), TWE (minimum score 5.5), Michigan English Language Assessment Battery (minimum score 85); Recommended—IELTS (minimum score 6.5). *Application deadline:* For fall admission, 2/1 for domestic and international students; for winter admission, 10/1 for domestic and international students. Application fee: $50. Electronic applications accepted. *Expenses:* Contact institution. *Financial support:* In 2017–18, 18 students received support, including 1 research assistantship (averaging $22,241 per year), 6 teaching assistantships with tuition reimbursements available (averaging $18,534 per year); fellowships with tuition reimbursements available, scholarships/grants, and unspecified assistantships also available. Support available to part-time students. Financial award applicants required to submit FAFSA. *Unit head:* Dr. John Richardson, Chair, 313-577-2980, Fax: 313-577-3491, E-mail: af5343@wayne.edu. *Application contact:* 313-577-2980, E-mail: art@wayne.edu.
Website: http://art.wayne.edu/

PRATT INSTITUTE
School of Design

Programs of Study

Pratt has been educating professionals for productive careers in the field of design since its founding in 1887. Pratt's School of Design, one of the largest of its kind, offers an outstanding professional art and design education taught by a faculty of working professionals who bring high standards and current practices to the classroom. Faculty members have received more than eighteen Tiffany, Fulbright, and Guggenheim awards as well as other prestigious professional awards. Pratt's graduate interior design program was ranked first nationally by *DesignIntelligence* (2017). *U.S. News & World Report* ranked Pratt's interior design program among the best in the country, communications design was ranked twelfth, and industrial design was ranked fifth.

Pratt offers master's degrees in a variety of programs, including Master of Fine Arts in Communications Design and Interior Design, Master of Science in Package Design, and Master of Industrial Design. All are located on the main Brooklyn campus.

Graduates of Pratt's design programs have the competitive edge needed to obtain top administrative and creative positions in design studios, businesses, various industries, and arts organizations.

All graduate design curricula include supportive course work in the humanities. Students can choose from a wide array of course offerings, including art and design history, comparative literature, philosophy, foreign languages, and social sciences. The graduate programs require the completion of 30 to 68 credits and last from 1½ to 3 years, depending on the curriculum and the number of prerequisites that have not been met at the time of admission. For the granting of degrees, all of the graduate programs require the submission of a thesis or a comparable effort. For the M.F.A., an exhibition and supporting corollary statement are required. Candidates for the M.S. and the M.I.D. degrees must present a thesis project that demonstrates a meaningful contribution to design and documents the supportive research that informs all phases of design and construction.

Research Facilities

The Pratt Library contains 186,589 bound volumes, serial backfiles, and other material (including government documents); 251,603 audiovisual materials; and 3,996 microforms and subscribes to 925 periodicals.

Pratt maintains numerous studios, shops, and technical facilities for work in all media as well as state-of-the-art computer facilities. Digital arts labs include state-of-the-art Macintosh, PC/NT, and UNIX operating systems as well as digital video and audio systems. Pratt also has extensive gallery space for exhibitions.

Financial Aid

Financial aid awards are offered through a variety of institutional, state, and federally funded programs. These include Graduate Scholarships awarded by departments to incoming students on the basis of merit, endowed and restricted scholarships for continuing students, and student employment. Assistantships are awarded on a competitive basis to continuing students in all departments. Special alumni-sponsored fellowships are also available.

Cost of Study

Graduate tuition for 2018–19 is $32,004 per year (full-time 18 credits, $1,778 per credit) and student fees are $1,980 per year. The cost of books and supplies varies widely, depending on the program in which the student is enrolled.

Living and Housing Costs

Limited campus housing is available on a first-come, first-served basis. Housing costs average $19,550 per academic year. There is a plentiful supply of moderately priced rentals in the immediate area and in adjacent neighborhoods for married students seeking housing and for those students choosing to reside off campus.

Student Group

In educating more than four generations of students to be creative, technically skilled, and adaptable professionals, Pratt has gained an international reputation that attracts more than 4,800 undergraduate and graduate students annually from forty-eight states and eighty-four countries.

Location

Pratt Institute's 25-acre, parklike main campus is situated among the turn-of-the-century mansions, Victorian brownstones, and wide, tree-lined boulevards of Clinton Hill, one of Brooklyn's historic neighborhoods. Midtown Manhattan, the heart of New York City, is only 25 minutes away by subway and offers students a vast array of professional, cultural, and recreational opportunities. Pratt's Manhattan campus is located in the Chelsea district.

The Institute

A private, nonsectarian institute of higher education, Pratt Institute was founded by the industrialist and philanthropist Charles Pratt. Changing with the needs and requirements of the professional world for which it prepares its graduates, Pratt today educates 3,439 undergraduate and 1,390 graduate students for careers in art and design, architecture, and library and information science.

Applying

The deadline for applications and all supporting materials, including portfolio, is January 5. Applicants should complete the application process online. Early submission of applications with all necessary credentials is highly desirable. Applications received after these dates are considered if openings exist in a particular program. For applicants who intend to file for financial aid, the FAFSA should be filed by March 1 for fall entrance and by October 1 for spring entrance.

Correspondence and Information

Graduate Admissions Office
Pratt Institute
200 Willoughby Avenue
Brooklyn, New York 11205
United States
Phone: 718-636-3514
   800-331-0834 (toll-free)
Fax: 718-399-4242
E-mail: admissions@pratt.edu
Website: http://www.pratt.edu
   http://www.pratt.edu/admissions/request-information (to request information)

THE FACULTY

Anita Cooney, Dean

T. Camille Martin, Assistant Dean

Communications/Package Design
Santiago Piedrafita, Chair, Associate Professor; M.S. Pratt.
Barry Berger, Associate Professor; B.I.D., Pratt.
Jean Brennan, Adjunct Professor; M.S., Pratt, CCE.
Thomas Delaney, Visiting Instructor; A.A.S., F.I.T.
Antonio DiSpigna, Professor; B.F.A., Pratt.
David Frisco, Adjunct Professor; M.F.A., Yale, CCE.
Kevin Gatta, Professor; M.S., Pratt.
J. Roger Guilfoyle, Adjunct Professor; B.A., Creighton; CCE.
William Hilson, Adjunct Professor; M.S., NYIT; CCE.
Michelle Hinebrook, Adjunct Associate Professor; M.F.A., Cranbrook.
Thomas Klinkowstein, Adjunct Professor; M.S., Syracuse; CCE.
Gusty Lange, Adjunct Professor; M.P.S., Pratt, CCE.
Christina Latina, Visiting Assistant Professor; M.F.A. Pratt.
Alex Liebergesell, Associate Professor; M.F.A., Yale.
Katya Moorman, Associate Professor; M.F.A., Cranbrook.
Ann Morris, Adjunct Assistant Professor; M.A., CUNY, Hunter.
Eric O'Toole, Associate Professor; M.F.A., Pratt.
Marc Rosen, Visiting Associate Professor; M.S., Pratt.
Dr. Gaia Scagnetti, Assistant Professor; Ph.D., Politecnico di Milano.
Ryan Waller, Adjunct Assistant Professor; M.F.A., Yale.
Pirco Wolfframm, Adjunct Associate Professor; M.F.A., California Institute of the Arts; CCE.
Alisa Zamir, Professor; M.S., Pratt.

Industrial Design
Constantin Boym, Chair, Professor; M.Design, Domus Academy (Milan).
Hlynur Atlason, Visiting Assistant Professor; B.A., Parsons.
Lawrence Au, Visiting Instructor; B.I.D., Pratt.
Peter Barna, Associate Professor; M.I.D., Pratt.
Mark Belkin, Visiting Assistant Professor; J.D., Albany Law School.
Harvey Bernstein, Adjunct Professor; M.S., Pratt; CCE.
Meri Bourgard-Rohrs, Visiting Professor; M.F.A., Pratt; CCE.
Gina Caspi, Visiting Professor; M.I.D., Pratt.
Esther Beke Cohen, Visiting Instructor; M.I.D. Pratt.
Justin Crocker, Visiting Instructor, M.I.D. Pratt.
Lucia DeRespinis, Adjunct Professor; B.I.D., Pratt; CCE.
Kathryn Filla, Adjunct Professor; M.I.D. Pratt, CCE.
Kate Hixon, Adjunct Associate Professor; B.I.D., Pratt, CCE.
Matthew Hoey, Visiting Assistant Professor; B.Arch, Temple University.
Jeffrey Kapec, Visiting Associate Professor; B.I.D., Pratt.
Robert Langhorn, Adjunct Associate Professor; Royal College of Art, London.
Kate Lewis, Visiting Assistant Professor; M.A., Central Saint Martins.

Pratt Institute

Jong. S. (Mark) Lim, Adjunct Professor; M.F.A., Pratt, CCE.
Scott Lundberg, Adjunct Associate Professor; M.I.D., Pratt; CCE.
Frederick McSwain, Visiting Assistant Professor; B.A., University of North Carolina at Wilmington.
Frank Millero, Visiting Assistant Professor; M.I.D., Pratt.
Katrin Mueller-Russo, Professor; Dipl Des., Hochschule fur Dildende Kunste (Germany).
Karol Murlak, Associate Professor; Ph.D., Academy of Fine Arts in Warsaw, Poland.
William Niemeier, Visiting Assistant Professor; A.A.S., F.I.T.
Matte Nyberg, Visiting Instructor; M.I.D., Pratt.
Judith Nylen, Visiting Assistant Professor; M.F.A., Pratt.
Rebeccah Pailes-Friedman, Adjunct Associate Professor; M.I.D., Pratt.
Peter Ragonetti, Visiting Instructor; B.I.D., Pratt.
Andrew Raible, Visiting Assistant Professor; M.I.D., Pratt.
Alex Schweder, Visiting Associate Professor; Ph.D., University of Cambridge.
Irvin Tepper, Adjunct Professor; M.F.A., Washington (Seattle), CCE.
Jonathan Thayer, Associate Professor; B.I.D., Pratt.
Marc Thorpe, Visiting Assistant Professor; M.I.D., Parsons.
William Jeffrey Tolbert, Adjunct Associate Professor; M.F.A., Yale.
Danielle Trofe, Visiting Instructor; M.I.D., Florence Design Academy.
Ignacio Urbina Polo, Associate Professor; M.S., Universidad Federal de Santa Catarina (Brazil).
Rebecca Welz, Adjunct Professor; B.A., SUNY Empire State College; CCE.
Allen Wilpon, Visiting Associate Professor; M.I.D., Pratt; M.D., Domus Academy, Milan.
Laura Wing, Visiting Assistant Professor; M.F.A. Parsons.
Henry Yoo, Adjunct Professor; M.I.D., Pratt, CCE.

Interior Design

Alison B. Snyder, Chair, Professor; M.Arch., GSAPP, Columbia University.
Tania Sofia Branquinho, Assistant Chair, Adjunct Professor; M.Arch., Pratt.
Virna Abraham, Visiting Assistant Professor; M.F.A., Parsons.
Severino Alfonso, Visiting Assistant Professor; M.S., Columbia.
Eric Ansel, Visiting Assistant Professor; M.Arch., Pratt.
Tarek Ashkar, Visiting Assistant Professor; M.Arch., Harvard.
Peter Lind Barna, Professor; M.I.D., Pratt.
Francesca Bastianini, Visiting Instructor; M.F.A., Parsons.
Jacob Bek, Visiting Assistant Professor; M.Sc., Architectural Association School of Architecture.
David Black, Visiting Assistant Professor; M.Arch, Illinois at Chicago.
Nick Brinen, Visiting Assistant Professor; M.Arch, University of Texas at Austin.
Greg Bugel, Visiting Assistant Professor; M.Arch, Columbia.
Mary Burke, Adjunct Associate Professor; M.S., Columbia.
Tania Chau, Visiting Assistant Professor; M.S., Pratt.
Ike Cheung, Visiting Instructor, Lecturer; B.Arch., Pratt.
Der Sean Chou, Visiting Assistant Professor; M.S., NYU.
Annie Coggan, Visiting Assistant Professor; M.Arch., Southern California Institute of Architecture.
James Conti, Adjunct Associate Professor; M.F.A., Ohio State.
James Counts, Visiting Assistant Professor; M.S., Columbia.
Wendy Cronk, Visiting Assistant Professor; M.Arch., Harvard.
Asli Erdem, Visiting Assistant Professor; M.Arch, Rensselaer.
Kim Farrah, Visiting Assistant Professor; M.S. Pratt.
Philip Farrell, Adjunct Professor; M.S., Pratt.
David C. Foley, Visiting Professor; M.Arch., Notre Dame.
Nancy Gesimondo, Visiting Instructor; M.F.A., Parsons.
Randi Halpern, Visiting Assistant Professor; B.F.A. NYIT.
Dalia Hamati, Visiting Assistant Professor; M.S., Columbia.
Adam Hayes, Visiting Instructor; B.Arch., Rice.
John Heida, Visiting Assistant Professor; B.Arch., Rice.
Claudia Hernandez, Visiting Assistant Professor; M.S., Columbia.
Sarah Hill, Visiting Assistant Professor; M.S., Pratt.
Lindsay Homer, Visiting Associate Professor; M.S., Pratt.
Benjamin Howes, Visiting Assistant Professor; M.S., Stevens.
Sheryl Kasak, Adjunct Associate Professor; M.S., Columbia.
Ted Kilcommons, Visiting Instructor; B.A., Texas.
Olivia Knott, Visiting Assistant Professor; M.Arch Parsons.
Eugene Kwak, Visiting Associate Professor; M.S., Columbia.
Chelsea Limbird, Visiting Assistant Professor; M.Arch., Rhode Island School of Design.
Jason Livingston, Visiting Assistant Professor; M.F.A., NYU.
Cam Lorendo, Adjunct Associate Professor; B.A., Parsons.
Addy Madorsky, Visiting Assistant Professor; M.S., Pratt.
Michael Maggio, Visiting Assistant Professor; M.A., Buffalo, SUNY.
William Mangold, Adjunct Assistant Professor; Ph.D., CUNY Graduate Center.
William McLoughlin, Visiting Instructor; B.Arch, Rhode Island School of Design/Brown.
Anthony Mekel, Adjunct Professor; B.Arch., Pratt.
Francine Monaco, Adjunct Associate Professor; B.Arch., Cincinnati.
John Nafziger, Visiting Assistant Professor; M.Arch. II, Yale.
Robert Nassar, Visiting Associate Professor; B.F.A., Syracuse.
Latoya Nelson, Visiting Assistant Professor; M.Arch., Pennsylvania.
Tetsu Ohara, Visiting Assistant Professor; certificate of architecture, Harvard.
Jon Otis, Professor; M.S., Massachusetts.

Danny Pang, Visiting Assistant Professor; M.S., Pratt.
Leticia Pardo Rojo, Visiting Assistant Professor; M.S., Pratt.
Rachel Paupek, Visiting Assistant Professor; M.Arch, RISD.
Regis Pean, Visiting Assistant Professor; M.Arch, Technical University (Austria).
Sal Raffone, Visiting Assistant Professor; M.Arch., Harvard; M.B.A., Columbia.
J. Woodson Rainey Jr., Visiting Assistant Professor; B.Arch., Utah.
Christian Rietzke, Visiting Assistant Professor; M.Arch., Pratt.
Ben Rosenblum, Visiting Assistant Professor; M.Arch, Yale.
Rachely Rotem, Visiting Assistant Professor; M.S., Columbia.
Mary-Jo Schlachter, Visiting Assistant Professor; M.Arch., Pennsylvania.
Irina Schneid, Visiting Assistant Professor; M.Arch., Cornell.
Deborah Schneiderman, Professor; M.Arch., Southern California Institute of Architecture.
Alex Schweder, Visiting Associate Professor; Ph.D., University of Cambridge, U.K.
Coren Sharples, Visiting Assistant Professor; M.Arch., Columbia.
Hazel Siegel, Visiting Assistant Professor; M.F.A., CUNY, Hunter.
Andrew Simons, Visiting Assistant Professor; B.F.A., Carnegie Mellon.
Darius Somers, Visiting Assistant Professor; M.S., Columbia.
Suzanne Song, Visiting Assistant Professor; M.S.A.A.D., GSAPP, Columbia.
Scott Sorenson, Visiting Assistant Professor; B.Arch, Pratt.
Sarah Strauss, Visiting Associate Professor; M.Arch., Yale.
Keena Suh, Associate Professor; M.Arch., Columbia.
Myonggi Sul, Professor; M.S., Pratt.
Karin Tehve, Associate Professor; M.Arch., Harvard.
Jack Travis, Adjunct Professor; M.Arch., Illinois at Urbana–Champaign.
Loukia Tsafoulia, Visiting Assistant Professor; M.S.A.A.D., Columbia.
Kathryn van Voorhees, Visiting Assistant Professor; M.ARch, Columbia.
Kevin Walz, Visiting Associate Professor; Pratt.
William Watson, Visiting Assistant Professor; M.Arch., Texas at Austin.
Henry Weintraub, Visiting Assistant Professor; M.Arch, Harvard.
Alexandra Winton, Visiting Associate Professor; M.A., Bard.
Piotr Woronkowicz, Visiting Instructor; B.S., Art Center College of Design.
Edwin Zawadzki, Visiting Assistant Professor; M.Arch., Yale.
Michael Zuckerman, Adjunct Professor; B.Arch., CUNY, City College.

© 2017 Bob Handelman

© 2017 Bob Handelman

Section 2
Architecture

This section contains a directory of institutions offering graduate work in architecture, followed by in-depth entries submitted by institutions that chose to prepare detailed program descriptions. Additional information about programs listed in the directory but not augmented by an in-depth entry may be obtained by writing directly to the dean of a graduate school or chair of a department at the address given in the directory.

For programs offering related work, see also in this book *Applied Arts and Design, Art and Art History,* and *Public, Regional, and Industrial Affairs.* In another guide in this series:

Graduate Programs in Engineering & Applied Sciences
See *Civil and Environmental Engineering*

CONTENTS

Program Directories

Featured Schools: Displays and Close-Ups

Architectural History

Arizona State University at the Tempe campus, Herberger Institute for Design and the Arts, The Design School, PhD Program in Design, Environment and the Arts, Tempe, AZ 85287-2105. Offers design (PhD); digital culture (PhD); healthcare and healing environments (PhD); history, theory, and criticism (PhD). *Degree requirements:* For doctorate, comprehensive exam, thesis/dissertation, interactive Program of Study (iPOS) submitted before completing 50 percent of required credit hours. *Entrance requirements:* For doctorate, GRE, master's degree in architecture, graphic design, industrial design, interior design, landscape architecture, or art history or equivalent standing; statement of purpose; 3 letters of recommendation; indication of potential faculty mentor; sample of written work. Additional exam requirements/recommendations for international students: Required—TOEFL, IELTS, or PTE. Electronic applications accepted. *Expenses:* Contact institution.

Cornell University, Graduate School, Graduate Fields of Architecture, Art and Planning, Field of Architecture, Ithaca, NY 14853. Offers architectural design (M Arch); architectural science (MS); computer graphics (MS); history of architecture (MA, PhD); history of urban development (MA, PhD); theory and criticism of architecture (M Arch); urban design (M Arch). *Degree requirements:* For master's, one foreign language, thesis (MA, MS); for doctorate, 2 foreign languages, comprehensive exam, thesis/dissertation. *Entrance requirements:* For master's, GRE General Test, 5-year bachelor's degree in architecture, portfolio (M Arch), 3 letters of recommendation; for doctorate, GRE General Test, 3 letters of recommendation. Additional exam requirements/recommendations for international students: Required—TOEFL (minimum score 600 paper-based; 77 iBT). Electronic applications accepted. *Faculty research:* Architectural design and urban design, theory and criticism of architecture, computer graphics, building technology and environmental science, history of architecture and history of urban-development.

The Graduate Center, City University of New York, Graduate Studies, Program in Art History, New York, NY 10016-4039. Offers architecture (PhD); graphic arts (PhD); painting (PhD); photography (PhD); sculpture (PhD). *Faculty:* 16 full-time (11 women). *Students:* 112 full-time (100 women); includes 11 minority (1 Black or African American, non-Hispanic/Latino; 3 Asian, non-Hispanic/Latino; 5 Hispanic/Latino; 1 Native Hawaiian or other Pacific Islander, non-Hispanic/Latino; 1 Two or more races, non-Hispanic/Latino), 16 international. Average age 34. 104 applicants, 15% accepted, 9 enrolled. In 2017, 13 doctorates awarded. *Degree requirements:* For doctorate, 2 foreign languages, thesis/dissertation. *Entrance requirements:* For doctorate, GRE General Test. Additional exam requirements/recommendations for international students: Required—TOEFL. *Application deadline:* For fall admission, 4/15 for domestic students; for spring admission, 11/15 for domestic students. Application fee: $125. Electronic applications accepted. *Financial support:* In 2017–18, 91 students received support, including 70 fellowships, 4 research assistantships, 12 teaching assistantships; career-related internships or fieldwork, Federal Work-Study, institutionally sponsored loans, and tuition waivers (full and partial) also available. Financial award application deadline: 2/1; financial award applicants required to submit FAFSA. *Unit head:* Dr. Rachel Kousser, Executive Officer, 212-817-8035, Fax: 212-817-1502, E-mail: rkousser@gc.cuny.edu. *Application contact:* Les Gribben, Director of Admissions, 212-817-7470, Fax: 212-817-1624, E-mail: lgribben@gc.cuny.edu.

Harvard University, Graduate School of Arts and Sciences, Department of History of Art and Architecture, Cambridge, MA 02138. Offers ancient art (PhD); ancient Near Eastern art (PhD); Baroque art (PhD); Byzantine art (PhD); classical art (PhD); Indian art (PhD); Islamic art (PhD); Japanese and Chinese art (PhD); medieval art (PhD); modern art (PhD); Renaissance and modern architecture (PhD); Renaissance art (PhD). *Degree requirements:* For doctorate, variable foreign language requirement, thesis/dissertation, general exams; reading exams in French, German, and Italian. *Entrance requirements:* For doctorate, GRE General Test. Additional exam requirements/recommendations for international students: Required—TOEFL.

Massachusetts Institute of Technology, School of Architecture and Planning, Department of Architecture, Cambridge, MA 02139. Offers architecture (M Arch, PhD), including building technology (PhD), design and computation (PhD), history and theory of architecture (PhD), history and theory of art (PhD); architecture studies (SM Arch S); art, culture and technology (SMACT); building technology (SMBT). *Degree requirements:* For master's, thesis; for doctorate, comprehensive exam, thesis/dissertation. *Entrance requirements:* For master's and doctorate, GRE General Test. Additional exam requirements/recommendations for international students: Required—TOEFL, IELTS. Electronic applications accepted. *Faculty research:* Architecture; urbanism; building technology and sustainability; computation and design; history, theory, and criticism; art, culture, and technology.

New York University, Graduate School of Arts and Science, Program in Historical and Sustainable Architecture, New York, NY 10012-1019. Offers MA. *Students:* Average age 25. 17 applicants, 100% accepted, 12 enrolled. In 2017, 14 master's awarded. *Entrance requirements:* For master's, GRE, writing sample. *Application deadline:* For fall admission, 3/1 for domestic and international students. Application fee: $100. *Expenses: Tuition:* Full-time $41,352; part-time $19,968 per year. *Required fees:* $2496; $1628 per unit. $814 per term. Tuition and fees vary according to course load and program. *Financial support:* Application deadline: 3/1. *Unit head:* Mosette Broderick, Director of Graduate Studies, 212-998-8180, Fax: 212-995-4152, E-mail: histsust@nyu.edu. *Application contact:* Jon Ritter, Assistant Director, 212-998-8180, Fax: 212-995-4152, E-mail: histsust@nyu.edu.
Website: http://arthistory.as.nyu.edu/

Roger Williams University, School of Architecture, Art and Historic Preservation, Bristol, RI 02809. Offers architecture (M Arch); art and architectural history (MA); historical preservation (MS, Certificate); urban and regional planning (Certificate). *Faculty:* 18 full-time (5 women), 9 part-time/adjunct (1 woman). *Students:* 107 full-time (52 women), 9 part-time (5 women); includes 10 minority (1 Asian, non-Hispanic/Latino; 7 Hispanic/Latino; 2 Two or more races, non-Hispanic/Latino), 5 international. Average age 26. 92 applicants, 93% accepted, 58 enrolled. In 2017, 46 master's, 1 other advanced degree awarded. *Degree requirements:* For master's, thesis. *Entrance requirements:* For master's, portfolio, 2 letters of recommendation, college transcript, letter of intent. Additional exam requirements/recommendations for international students: Required—TOEFL (minimum score 85 iBT), IELTS (minimum score 6.5). *Application deadline:* For fall admission, 4/1 for domestic students; for spring admission, 11/15 for domestic students. Application fee: $50. Electronic applications accepted. *Expenses:* $1,463 per credit hour (for M Arch); $876 per credit hour (for MS and MA); $258 graduation fee. *Financial support:* In 2017–18, 116 students received support, including 116 research assistantships (averaging $2,776 per year); career-related internships or fieldwork, scholarships/grants, and unspecified assistantships also available. Financial award application deadline: 4/1; financial award applicants required to submit FAFSA. *Unit head:* Stephen White, Dean, 401-254-3607, E-mail: swhite@rwu.edu. *Application contact:* Marcus Hanscom, Director of Graduate Admissions, 401-254-3345, Fax: 401-254-3557, E-mail: gradadmit@rwu.edu.
Website: http://www.rwu.edu/graduate/programs/graduate-programs/architecture

Savannah College of Art and Design, Program in Architectural History, Savannah, GA 31402-3146. Offers MFA. *Program availability:* Part-time. *Faculty:* 9 full-time (1 woman). *Students:* 2 full-time (both women), 1 (woman) part-time. Average age 25. 7 applicants, 43% accepted, 2 enrolled. In 2017, 1 master's awarded. *Degree requirements:* For master's, thesis. *Entrance requirements:* For master's, GRE (recommended), portfolio (submitted in digital format), audition or writing submission, resume, statement of purpose, two letters of recommendation. Additional exam requirements/recommendations for international students: Recommended—TOEFL (minimum score 550 paper-based; 85 iBT), IELTS (minimum score 6.5). *Application deadline:* For fall admission, 4/1 for domestic and international students. Applications are processed on a rolling basis. Application fee: $40. Electronic applications accepted. *Expenses: Tuition:* Full-time $36,765; part-time $817 per credit hour. One-time fee: $500. *Financial support:* Career-related internships or fieldwork, Federal Work-Study, and scholarships/grants available. Financial award application deadline: 4/1; financial award applicants required to submit FAFSA. *Unit head:* Dr. Robin Williams, Chair, Architectural History. *Application contact:* Jenny Jaquillard, Executive Director of Admissions, Recruitment and Events, 912-525-5100, Fax: 912-525-5985, E-mail: admission@scad.edu.
Website: http://www.scad.edu/academics/programs/architectural-history

University of California, Berkeley, Graduate Division, College of Environmental Design, Department of Architecture, Berkeley, CA 94720-1500. Offers architecture (M Arch); building science (MS, PhD); building structures, construction and materials (MS, PhD); design theories, methods, and practices (MS, PhD); environmental design in developing countries (MS, PhD); history of architecture and urbanism (MS, PhD); social and cultural processes in architecture and urbanism (MS, PhD); M Arch/MCP; M Arch/MS; MLA/M Arch. *Degree requirements:* For master's, thesis; for doctorate, thesis/dissertation, qualifying exam. *Entrance requirements:* For master's and doctorate, GRE General Test, minimum GPA of 3.0, 3 letters of recommendation. Additional exam requirements/recommendations for international students: Required—TOEFL (minimum score 570 paper-based; 90 iBT). Electronic applications accepted. Application fee is waived when completed online.

University of Colorado Denver, College of Architecture and Planning, Program in Design and Planning, Denver, CO 80217. Offers history of architecture, landscape and urbanism (PhD); sustainable and healthy environments (PhD). *Program availability:* Part-time. *Degree requirements:* For doctorate, comprehensive exam, thesis/dissertation. *Entrance requirements:* For doctorate, GRE (minimum score of 158 for both verbal and quantitative; writing 4.0), minimum undergraduate GPA of 3.0, graduate 3.5; writing sample; three letters of recommendation; statement of personal and professional goals. Additional exam requirements/recommendations for international students: Required—TOEFL (minimum score 80 iBT); Recommended—IELTS (minimum score 6.8). Electronic applications accepted. *Expenses:* Contact institution. *Faculty research:* Land use and environmental planning and design; design and planning processes and practices; history, theory, and criticism of the built environment.

University of Pittsburgh, Kenneth P. Dietrich School of Arts and Sciences, Department of History of Art and Architecture, Pittsburgh, PA 15260. Offers MA, PhD. *Faculty:* 13 full-time (6 women). *Students:* 36 full-time (31 women); includes 7 minority (2 Hispanic/Latino; 1 Native Hawaiian or other Pacific Islander, non-Hispanic/Latino; 4 Two or more races, non-Hispanic/Latino), 7 international. Average age 32. 44 applicants, 20% accepted, 5 enrolled. In 2017, 3 master's, 5 doctorates awarded. *Degree requirements:* For master's, one foreign language, thesis or alternative, paper; for doctorate, 2 foreign languages, comprehensive exam, thesis/dissertation, teaching portfolio. *Entrance requirements:* For master's and doctorate, GRE General Test, 3 letters of recommendation, writing sample, personal statement, transcripts, foreign language questionnaire. Additional exam requirements/recommendations for international students: Required—TOEFL (minimum score 550 paper-based; 90 iBT). *Application deadline:* For fall admission, 12/15 for domestic and international students. Application fee: $50. Electronic applications accepted. *Expenses:* $22,290 full-time resident per year, $36,980 full-time nonresident. *Financial support:* In 2017–18, 24 students received support, including 9 fellowships with full tuition reimbursements available (averaging $22,042 per year), 5 research assistantships with full tuition reimbursements available (averaging $18,620 per year), 6 teaching assistantships with full tuition reimbursements available (averaging $18,620 per year); career-related internships or fieldwork, scholarships/grants, health care benefits, tuition waivers (partial), and unspecified assistantships also available. Financial award application deadline: 12/15. *Faculty research:* Medieval European art and architecture, modern architecture, modern and contemporary art, history of photography, Japanese art, 20th century German art, contemporary Chinese art, art of the United States, ancient Roman art. *Unit head:* Dr. Barbara McCloskey, Chair, 412-648-2417, Fax: 412-648-2792, E-mail: barbara.mccloskey@pitt.edu. *Application contact:* Karoline Swinotek, Graduate Administrator, 412-648-2400, Fax: 412-648-2792, E-mail: karoline@pitt.edu.
Website: http://www.haa.pitt.edu

The University of Texas at Austin, Graduate School, School of Architecture, Program in Architectural History, Austin, TX 78712-1111. Offers MA, PhD. *Degree requirements:* For doctorate, thesis/dissertation.

University of Virginia, School of Architecture, Department of Architectural History, Charlottesville, VA 22903. Offers M Arch H, PhD. *Faculty:* 4 full-time (1 woman). *Students:* 11 full-time (8 women), 3 part-time (all women); includes 2 minority (1 Asian, non-Hispanic/Latino; 1 Two or more races, non-Hispanic/Latino), 1 international. Average age 29. 16 applicants, 94% accepted, 7 enrolled. In 2017, 6 master's awarded. *Degree requirements:* For master's, one foreign language, thesis. *Entrance requirements:* For master's, GRE General Test, 3 letters of recommendation. Additional exam requirements/recommendations for international students: Required—TOEFL (minimum score 600 paper-based; 90 iBT). *Application deadline:* For fall admission, 1/5 for domestic and international students. Applications are processed on a rolling basis. Application fee: $60. Electronic applications accepted. *Financial support:* Career-related internships or fieldwork, Federal Work-Study, and institutionally sponsored loans available. Financial award applicants required to submit FAFSA. *Faculty research:* Urban form, nineteenth- and Twentieth-Century American architecture. *Unit head:* Sheila Crane, Chair, 434-243-2342, Fax: 434-982-2678, E-mail: scrane@virginia.edu. *Application contact:* Director of Admissions and Financial Aid, 434-924-6442, Fax: 434-982-2678, E-mail: a-school-admissions@virginia.edu.
Website: http://www.arch.virginia.edu/academics/disciplines/history

Architecture

Academy of Art University, Graduate Programs, School of Architecture, San Francisco, CA 94105-3410. Offers advanced architectural design (MA); architecture (M Arch). *Program availability:* Part-time, 100% online. *Faculty:* 8 full-time (2 women), 32 part-time/adjunct (10 women). *Students:* 98 full-time (43 women), 83 part-time (35 women); includes 39 minority (10 Black or African American, non-Hispanic/Latino; 8 Asian, non-Hispanic/Latino; 19 Hispanic/Latino; 2 Two or more races, non-Hispanic/Latino), 53 international. Average age 33. 87 applicants, 100% accepted, 34 enrolled. In 2017, 34 master's awarded. *Degree requirements:* For master's, final review. *Entrance requirements:* For master's, statement of intent; resume; portfolio/reel; official college transcripts. *Application deadline:* Applications are processed on a rolling basis. Application fee: $50. Electronic applications accepted. *Expenses: Tuition:* Part-time $982 per unit. *Financial support:* Career-related internships or fieldwork, Federal Work-Study, and scholarships/grants available. Financial award application deadline: 8/10; financial award applicants required to submit FAFSA. *Unit head:* 800-544-ARTS, E-mail: info@academyart.edu. *Application contact:* 800-544-ARTS, E-mail: info@academyart.edu.
Website: http://www.academyart.edu/architecture-school/index.html

Andrews University, School of Graduate Studies, School of Architecture, Art and Design, Berrien Springs, MI 49104. Offers M Arch. *Faculty:* 9 full-time (3 women), 1 (woman) part-time/adjunct. *Students:* 17 full-time (7 women), 1 part-time (0 women); includes 6 minority (3 Black or African American, non-Hispanic/Latino; 3 Hispanic/Latino), 5 international. Average age 26. 15 applicants, 100% accepted, 7 enrolled. In 2017, 9 master's awarded. *Entrance requirements:* For master's, GRE. Additional exam requirements/recommendations for international students: Required—TOEFL (minimum score 550 paper-based). *Application deadline:* Applications are processed on a rolling basis. Application fee: $40. Electronic applications accepted. *Faculty research:* Irish archaeology, place making, town planning, Waldensian architecture, international community development. *Unit head:* Carey Carscallen, Dean, 269-471-6003. *Application contact:* Justina Clayburn, Supervisor of Graduate Admission, 800-253-2874, Fax: 269-471-6321, E-mail: graduate@andrews.edu.

Arizona State University at the Tempe campus, Herberger Institute for Design and the Arts, The Design School, Tempe, AZ 85287-1605. Offers architecture (M Arch); building design/built environment (MS); design (MSD), including arts, media, and engineering, healthcare and healing environments (MSD, PhD), industrial design, interaction design, interior design, new product innovation, visual communication design; design, environment and the arts (PhD), including design, digital culture, healthcare and healing environments (MSD, PhD), history, theory, and criticism; landscape architecture (MLA); urban design (MUD); MA/MBA. *Accreditation:* NASAD. Terminal master's awarded for partial completion of doctoral program. *Degree requirements:* For master's, thesis optional, interactive Program of Study (iPOS) submitted before completing 50 percent of required credit hours; for doctorate, comprehensive exam, thesis/dissertation, interactive Program of Study (iPOS) submitted before completing 50 percent of required credit hours. *Entrance requirements:* For master's, GRE General Test, minimum GPA of 3.0 or equivalent in last 2 years of work leading to bachelor's degree, design/creative works portfolio, 3 references, statement of intent; for doctorate, GRE, master's degree in architecture, graphic design, industrial design, interior design, landscape architecture, or art history or equivalent standing; statement of purpose; 3 letters of recommendation; indication of potential faculty mentor; sample of written work. Additional exam requirements/recommendations for international students: Required—TOEFL (minimum score 600 paper-based; 100 iBT). Electronic applications accepted.

Athabasca University, Faculty of Science and Technology, Athabasca, AB T9S 3A3, Canada. Offers architecture (Postgraduate Diploma); information systems (M Sc). *Program availability:* Part-time, online learning. *Degree requirements:* For master's, thesis optional. *Entrance requirements:* For master's, B Sc in computing or other bachelor's degree and IT experience. Electronic applications accepted. *Expenses:* Contact institution. *Faculty research:* Distributed systems multimedia, computer science education, e-services.

Auburn University, Graduate School, College of Architecture, Design, and Construction, Auburn University, AL 36849. Offers MBC, MCP, MID, ML Arch, MPA/MCP. *Program availability:* Part-time. *Faculty:* 61 full-time (15 women), 15 part-time/adjunct (3 women). *Students:* 66 full-time (34 women), 71 part-time (20 women); includes 23 minority (8 Black or African American, non-Hispanic/Latino; 5 Asian, non-Hispanic/Latino; 8 Hispanic/Latino; 1 Native Hawaiian or other Pacific Islander, non-Hispanic/Latino; 1 Two or more races, non-Hispanic/Latino), 51 international. Average age 32. 144 applicants, 69% accepted, 60 enrolled. In 2017, 63 master's awarded. *Entrance requirements:* For master's, GRE General Test. *Application deadline:* Applications are processed on a rolling basis. Application fee: $50 ($60 for international students). Electronic applications accepted. *Expenses:* Contact institution. *Financial support:* Fellowships and Federal Work-Study available. Support available to part-time students. Financial award application deadline: 3/15; financial award applicants required to submit FAFSA. *Unit head:* Dr. Vini Nathan, Dean/Chair, 334-844-4285. *Application contact:* Dr. George Flowers, Dean of the Graduate School, 334-844-2125.
Website: http://www.cadc.auburn.edu/

Ball State University, Graduate School, College of Architecture and Planning, Department of Architecture, Program in Architecture, Muncie, IN 47306. Offers architecture (M Arch, M Arch II). *Program availability:* Part-time. *Students:* 52 full-time (22 women), 15 part-time (9 women); includes 5 minority (2 Black or African American, non-Hispanic/Latino; 2 Hispanic/Latino; 1 Two or more races, non-Hispanic/Latino), 6 international. Average age 24. 53 applicants, 75% accepted, 26 enrolled. In 2017, 31 master's awarded. *Degree requirements:* For master's, thesis. *Entrance requirements:* For master's, GRE (if cumulative baccalaureate GPA is below 3.0), minimum baccalaureate GPA of 2.75 or 3.0 in latter half of baccalaureate, resume, statement of purpose, portfolio, three letters of reference. Additional exam requirements/recommendations for international students: Required—TOEFL (minimum score 550 paper-based; 79 iBT), IELTS (minimum score 6.5). *Application deadline:* For fall admission, 1/15 priority date for domestic students. Applications are processed on a rolling basis. Application fee: $60. Electronic applications accepted. *Expenses:* Contact institution. *Financial support:* Research assistantships with partial tuition reimbursements, teaching assistantships with partial tuition reimbursements, and unspecified assistantships available. Financial award application deadline: 3/1; financial award applicants required to submit FAFSA. *Unit head:* Andrea Swartz, Chairperson, 765-285-1904, E-mail: aswartz@bsu.edu. *Application contact:* Janice Shimizu, Graduate Program Director, 765-285-7162, Fax: 765-285-1765, E-mail: jhshimizu@bsu.edu.
Website: http://www.bsu.edu/architecture

Boston Architectural College, Graduate Programs, Boston, MA 02115-2795. Offers architecture (M Arch); historic preservation (MDS); interior design (MID); landscape architecture (MLA); sustainable design (MDS). *Accreditation:* CIDA. *Degree requirements:* For master's, thesis. *Entrance requirements:* For master's, portfolio (recommended). Electronic applications accepted.

California Baptist University, Program in Architecture, Riverside, CA 92504-3206. Offers M Arch. *Faculty:* 5 full-time (1 woman). *Students:* 9 full-time (5 women), 1 (woman) part-time; includes 7 minority (2 Black or African American,. non-Hispanic/Latino; 5 Hispanic/Latino). Average age 25. 12 applicants, 100% accepted, 10 enrolled. *Degree requirements:* For master's, thesis, internship, professional practice, minimum cumulative GPA of 2.75 by the end of the first semester of the third year, progress review after the fifth full-time semester in the program. *Entrance requirements:* Additional exam requirements/recommendations for international students: Required—TOEFL (minimum score 80 iBT). *Application deadline:* For fall admission, 8/1 priority date for domestic students, 7/1 for international students; for spring admission, 12/1 priority date for domestic students, 11/1 for international students. Applications are processed on a rolling basis. Application fee: $45. Electronic applications accepted. *Expenses:* Contact institution. *Financial support:* Federal Work-Study and scholarships/grants available. Financial award applicants required to submit CSS PROFILE or FAFSA. *Faculty research:* Architectural design, urbanism, interdisciplinary design thought, psychology of human interaction to the built environment, aesthetic perception. *Unit head:* Mark Roberson, Dean, College of Architecture, Visual Arts and Design, 951-552-8652, E-mail: maroberson@calbaptist.edu.
Website: http://cbucavad.com/architecture/

California College of the Arts, Graduate Programs, Master of Architecture Program, San Francisco, CA 94107. Offers advanced architecture design (MAAD); architecture (M Arch). *Faculty:* 6 full-time (2 women), 9 part-time/adjunct (2 women). *Students:* 66 full-time (33 women), 9 part-time (5 women); includes 25 minority (3 Black or African American, non-Hispanic/Latino; 1 American Indian or Alaska Native, non-Hispanic/Latino; 9 Asian, non-Hispanic/Latino; 12 Hispanic/Latino), 32 international. Average age 29. In 2017, 13 master's awarded. *Degree requirements:* For master's, thesis. *Entrance requirements:* For master's, appropriate bachelor's degree, portfolio, resume, minimum 2 letters of recommendation, essay, transcripts. Additional exam requirements/recommendations for international students: Required—TOEFL, IELTS, or PTE. *Application deadline:* For fall admission, 1/31 priority date for domestic and international students. Applications are processed on a rolling basis. Application fee: $70. Electronic applications accepted. *Expenses:* $49,230 per year full-time tuition, $490 per year fees; $1,641 per unit part-time tuition. *Financial support:* In 2017–18, fellowships (averaging $22,000 per year), teaching assistantships (averaging $2,000 per year) were awarded; career-related internships or fieldwork, Federal Work-Study, scholarships/grants, and health care benefits also available. Financial award application deadline: 7/31; financial award applicants required to submit FAFSA. *Unit head:* Antje Steinmuller, Chair, E-mail: asteinmuller@cca.edu. *Application contact:* Wes Fanelli, Assistant Director of Graduate Admissions, 415-703-9533, Fax: 415-703-9539, E-mail: wfanelli@cca.edu.

California Polytechnic State University, San Luis Obispo, College of Architecture and Environmental Design, Department of Architecture, San Luis Obispo, CA 93407. Offers MS. *Program availability:* Part-time. *Faculty:* 3 full-time (1 woman). *Students:* 3 full-time (1 woman), 2 part-time (1 woman), 2 international. Average age 26. 19 applicants, 42% accepted, 1 enrolled. In 2017, 10 master's awarded. *Degree requirements:* For master's, thesis. *Application deadline:* For fall admission, 4/1 for domestic and international students; for winter admission, 11/1 for domestic students, 6/30 for international students. Applications are processed on a rolling basis. Application fee: $55. Electronic applications accepted. *Expenses:* Tuition, state resident: full-time $7176; part-time $4164 per year. *Required fees:* $3690; $3219 per year. $1073 per trimester. *Financial support:* Fellowships, research assistantships, teaching assistantships, and institutionally sponsored loans available. Financial award application deadline: 3/2; financial award applicants required to submit FAFSA. *Faculty research:* Computer-assisted design, decision support systems, building science, facilities management. *Unit head:* Thomas Fowler, Graduate Coordinator, 805-756-2981, E-mail: tfowler@calpoly.edu.
Website: http://www.architecture.calpoly.edu/

California State Polytechnic University, Pomona, Program in Architecture, Pomona, CA 91768-2557. Offers M Arch. *Program availability:* Part-time, evening/weekend. *Students:* 37 full-time (19 women), 7 part-time (5 women); includes 23 minority (9 Asian, non-Hispanic/Latino; 14 Hispanic/Latino), 3 international. Average age 30. 88 applicants, 51% accepted, 14 enrolled. In 2017, 12 master's awarded. *Entrance requirements:* Additional exam requirements/recommendations for international students: Required—TOEFL (minimum score 550 paper-based). *Application deadline:* Applications are processed on a rolling basis. Application fee: $55. Electronic applications accepted. *Expenses:* Contact institution. *Financial support:* Application deadline: 3/2; applicants required to submit FAFSA. *Unit head:* Prof. Kip A. Dickson, Professor/Graduate Coordinator, 909-869-2682, Fax: 909-869-4331, E-mail: kadickson@cpp.edu. *Application contact:* Deborah L. Brandon, Executive Director of Admissions and Enrollment Planning, 909-869-3427, Fax: 909-869-5315, E-mail: dlbrandon@cpp.edu.
Website: https://env.cpp.edu/arc/degree/master-architecture

Carleton University, Faculty of Graduate Studies, Faculty of Engineering and Design, School of Architecture, Ottawa, ON K1S 5B6, Canada. Offers design studies (M Arch). *Degree requirements:* For master's, thesis. *Entrance requirements:* For master's, honors degree. Additional exam requirements/recommendations for international students: Required—TOEFL. *Faculty research:* Theoretical issues in architecture and culture, cultural diversity, architecture and technoscientific culture.

Carnegie Mellon University, College of Fine Arts, School of Architecture, Pittsburgh, PA 15213-3891. Offers architecture (MSA); architecture, engineering, and construction management (PhD); building performance and diagnostics (MS, PhD); computational design (MS, PhD); engineering construction management (MSA); tangible interaction design (MTID); urban design (MUD). Terminal master's awarded for partial completion of doctoral program. *Degree requirements:* For doctorate, thesis/dissertation. *Entrance requirements:* For master's and doctorate, GRE General Test. Additional exam requirements/recommendations for international students: Required—TOEFL.

The Catholic University of America, School of Architecture and Planning, Washington, DC 20064. Offers architecture and planning (M Arch, MS Arch St); city and regional planning (M Arch); facilities management (MS Arch); regional development (Certificate); sustainable design (M Arch, Certificate). *Program availability:* Part-time.

Faculty: 19 full-time (7 women), 9 part-time/adjunct (1 woman). *Students:* 61 full-time (24 women), 13 part-time (7 women); includes 31 minority (12 Black or African American, non-Hispanic/Latino; 1 American Indian or Alaska Native, non-Hispanic/Latino; 3 Asian, non-Hispanic/Latino; 8 Hispanic/Latino; 7 Two or more races, non-Hispanic/Latino), 11 international. Average age 28. 61 applicants, 90% accepted, 28 enrolled. In 2017, 46 master's awarded. *Degree requirements:* For master's, thesis. *Entrance requirements:* For master's, GRE (minimum score: 1000), minimum GPA of 2.8, portfolio, statement of purpose, official copies of academic transcripts, three letters of recommendation. Additional exam requirements/recommendations for international students: Required—TOEFL (minimum score 550 paper-based; 80 iBT). *Application deadline:* For fall admission, 1/15 priority date for domestic students, 7/1 for international students; for spring admission, 10/15 priority date for domestic students, 11/1 for international students. Applications are processed on a rolling basis. Application fee: $55. Electronic applications accepted. *Expenses:* Contact institution. *Financial support:* Fellowships, research assistantships, teaching assistantships, Federal Work-Study, scholarships/grants, tuition waivers (full and partial), and unspecified assistantships available. Financial award application deadline: 2/1; financial award applicants required to submit FAFSA. *Faculty research:* Architectural history, cultural studies/sacred space, design technologies, digital media, real estate development, urban design. *Total annual research expenditures:* $106,977. *Unit head:* Randall Ott, Dean, 202-319-5784, Fax: 202-319-2023, E-mail: ott@cua.edu. *Application contact:* Dr. Steven Brown, Director of Graduate Admissions, 202-319-5057, Fax: 202-319-6533, E-mail: cua-admissions@cua.edu.
Website: https://architecture.catholic.edu/

City College of the City University of New York, Graduate School, The Bernard and Anne Spitzer School of Architecture, Program in Architecture, New York, NY 10031-9198. Offers M Arch. *Entrance requirements:* For master's, GRE. Additional exam requirements/recommendations for international students: Required—TOEFL (minimum score 550 paper-based).

Clemson University, Graduate School, College of Architecture, Arts, and Humanities, School of Architecture, Clemson, SC 29634. Offers architecture (M Arch, MS, Certificate), including community build (Certificate); architecture and health (M Arch); digital ecologies (Certificate); historic preservation (MS, Certificate); integrated project delivery (Certificate); landscape architecture (MLA); planning, design and the built environment (PhD); resilient urban design (MRUD). *Faculty:* 38 full-time (13 women), 13 part-time/adjunct (6 women). *Students:* 149 full-time (98 women); includes 17 minority (2 Black or African American, non-Hispanic/Latino; 6 Asian, non-Hispanic/Latino; 9 Hispanic/Latino), 53 international. Average age 25. 317 applicants, 63% accepted, 54 enrolled. In 2017, 92 master's, 4 doctorates, 12 other advanced degrees awarded. *Degree requirements:* For master's, thesis (for some programs); for doctorate, comprehensive exam, thesis/dissertation. *Entrance requirements:* For master's, GRE General Test, design portfolio, unofficial transcripts, letters of recommendation, personal statement. Additional exam requirements/recommendations for international students: Required—TOEFL (minimum score 80 iBT); Recommended—IELTS (minimum score 6.5), TSE (minimum score 54). *Application deadline:* For fall admission, 1/15 for domestic and international students. Applications are processed on a rolling basis. Application fee: $80 ($90 for international students). Electronic applications accepted. *Expenses:* $6,564 per semester full-time resident, $12,538 per semester full-time non-resident, $743 per credit hour part-time resident, $1,486 per credit hour part-time non-resident, $1,203 per credit hour online, other fees may apply per session. *Financial support:* In 2017–18, 131 students received support, including 63 fellowships with partial tuition reimbursements available (averaging $2,206 per year), 24 research assistantships with partial tuition reimbursements available (averaging $16,900 per year), 7 teaching assistantships with partial tuition reimbursements available (averaging $16,629 per year); career-related internships or fieldwork and unspecified assistantships also available. Financial award application deadline: 1/15. *Faculty research:* Architecture and health, sustainable design, community design-build, architectural robotics, digital fabrication. *Total annual research expenditures:* $110,347. *Unit head:* Kate Schwennsen, Program Director, 864-656-3895, E-mail: kschwen@clemson.edu. *Application contact:* Dr. Dan Harding, Graduate Director, 864-606-6645, E-mail: hardin4@clemson.edu.
Website: https://www.clemson.edu/caah/departments/architecture/index.html

Columbia University, Graduate School of Architecture, Planning, and Preservation, Program in Advanced Architectural Design, New York, NY 10027. Offers MS. *Entrance requirements:* For master's, GRE General Test. *Expenses: Tuition:* Full-time $44,864; part-time $1704 per credit. *Required fees:* $2370 per semester. One-time fee: $105.

Columbia University, Graduate School of Architecture, Planning, and Preservation, Program in Architecture, New York, NY 10027. Offers M Arch, PhD, M Arch/MS. PhD offered through the Graduate School of Arts and Science. *Degree requirements:* For master's, thesis optional. *Entrance requirements:* For master's, GRE General Test. *Expenses: Tuition:* Full-time $44,864; part-time $1704 per credit. *Required fees:* $2370 per semester. One-time fee: $105.

Cooper Union for the Advancement of Science and Art, Irwin S. Chanin School of Architecture, New York, NY 10003-7120. Offers M Arch II. *Faculty:* 3 full-time (2 women), 14 part-time/adjunct (6 women). *Students:* 9 full-time (3 women); includes 1 minority (Asian, non-Hispanic/Latino), 7 international. Average age 27. 75 applicants, 31% accepted, 10 enrolled. In 2017, 11 master's awarded. *Degree requirements:* For master's, thesis. *Entrance requirements:* For master's, GRE, official transcripts from all colleges and universities from which applicant received credit; three recommendation letters; resumé/curriculum vitae; written essay, portfolio, examples of written work. Additional exam requirements/recommendations for international students: Required—TOEFL (minimum score 600 paper-based; 100 iBT). *Application deadline:* For fall admission, 1/31 for domestic and international students. Application fee: $75. Electronic applications accepted. *Expenses:* $21,625 per term. *Financial support:* In 2017–18, 9 students received support. Tuition waivers (partial) and tuition scholarships offered to exceptional students available. Financial award application deadline: 5/1; financial award applicants required to submit FAFSA. *Unit head:* Nader Tehrani, Dean, 212-353-4220, E-mail: ntehrani@cooper.edu. *Application contact:* Chabeli Lajara, Administrative Assistant, 212-353-4120, E-mail: admissions@cooper.edu.
Website: http://cooper.edu/architecture

Cornell University, Graduate School, Graduate Fields of Architecture, Art and Planning, Field of Architecture, Ithaca, NY 14853. Offers architectural design (M Arch); architectural science (MS); computer graphics (MS); history of architecture (MA, PhD); history of urban development (MA, PhD); theory and criticism of architecture (M Arch); urban design (M Arch). *Degree requirements:* For master's, one foreign language, thesis (MA, MS); for doctorate, 2 foreign languages, comprehensive exam, thesis/dissertation. *Entrance requirements:* For master's, GRE General Test, 5-year bachelor's degree in architecture, portfolio (M Arch), 3 letters of recommendation; for doctorate, GRE General Test, 3 letters of recommendation. Additional exam requirements/recommendations for international students: Required—TOEFL (minimum score 600 paper-based; 77 iBT). Electronic applications accepted. *Faculty research:* Architectural design and urban design, theory and criticism of architecture, computer graphics, building technology and environmental science, history of architecture and history of urban-development.

Cranbrook Academy of Art, Program in Architecture, Bloomfield Hills, MI 48303-0801. Offers M Arch. *Degree requirements:* For master's, thesis, exhibit. *Entrance requirements:* Additional exam requirements/recommendations for international students: Required—TOEFL (minimum score 85 iBT). Electronic applications accepted.

Dalhousie University, Faculty of Architecture and Planning, Halifax, NS B3J 2X4, Canada. Offers M Arch, M Eng, M Plan, MEDS, MPS. *Degree requirements:* For master's, thesis. *Entrance requirements:* Additional exam requirements/recommendations for international students: Required—1 of 5 approved tests: TOEFL, IELTS, CANTEST, CAEL, Michigan English Language Assessment Battery. Electronic applications accepted.

Ferris State University, Kendall College of Art and Design, Grand Rapids, MI 49503. Offers architecture (M Arch); art education (MAE); design (MA); drawing (MFA); painting (MFA); photography (MFA); printmaking (MFA); visual and critical studies (MA). *Program availability:* Part-time. *Faculty:* 21 full-time (15 women), 6 part-time/adjunct (2 women). *Students:* 39 full-time (29 women), 15 part-time (9 women); includes 12 minority (4 Black or African American, non-Hispanic/Latino; 1 American Indian or Alaska Native, non-Hispanic/Latino; 3 Asian, non-Hispanic/Latino; 4 Hispanic/Latino), 6 international. Average age 31. 48 applicants, 60% accepted, 17 enrolled. In 2017, 12 master's awarded. *Degree requirements:* For master's, thesis, seminars. *Entrance requirements:* For master's, portfolio, 3 letters of recommendation, curriculum vitae, artist statement, letter of intent. Additional exam requirements/recommendations for international students: Required—TOEFL (minimum score 79 iBT). *Application deadline:* For fall admission, 2/1 priority date for domestic and international students; for spring admission, 11/1 priority date for domestic and international students. Applications are processed on a rolling basis. Application fee: $0. Electronic applications accepted. *Expenses:* Contact institution. *Financial support:* In 2017–18, 32 students received support, including 8 fellowships (averaging $16,781 per year); scholarships/grants and unspecified assistantships also available. Financial award application deadline: 2/1; financial award applicants required to submit FAFSA. *Unit head:* Leslie Bellavance, President, 616-451-2787. *Application contact:* Thomas Post, Graduate Recruitment Specialist, 616-451-2787, Fax: 616-831-9689, E-mail: thomaspost@ferris.edu.
Website: http://www.kcad.edu/

Florida Agricultural and Mechanical University, Division of Graduate Studies, Research, and Continuing Education, School of Architecture, Tallahassee, FL 32307-3200. Offers architectural studies (MS Arch); architecture (professional) (M Arch); landscape architecture (MLA). *Program availability:* Part-time. *Degree requirements:* For master's, thesis. *Entrance requirements:* For master's, GRE General Test, minimum GPA of 3.0, portfolio. Additional exam requirements/recommendations for international students: Required—TOEFL (minimum score 550 paper-based). *Faculty research:* Environmental technology, post-occupancy evaluation, building economics, design methods, computer-aided design.

Florida International University, College of Communication, Architecture and The Arts, Department of Architecture, Miami, FL 33199. Offers M Arch, MA. *Program availability:* Part-time, evening/weekend. *Faculty:* 12 full-time (1 woman), 16 part-time/adjunct (7 women). *Students:* 129 full-time (71 women), 18 part-time (11 women); includes 100 minority (7 Black or African American, non-Hispanic/Latino; 1 Asian, non-Hispanic/Latino; 91 Hispanic/Latino; 1 Two or more races, non-Hispanic/Latino), 27 international. Average age 26. 122 applicants, 34% accepted, 19 enrolled. In 2017, 96 master's awarded. *Entrance requirements:* For master's, GRE or minimum GPA of 3.0 in upper-level undergraduate work, portfolio. Additional exam requirements/recommendations for international students: Required—TOEFL (minimum score 550 paper-based; 80 iBT). *Application deadline:* For fall admission, 2/1 for domestic and international students. Application fee: $30. Electronic applications accepted. *Expenses:* Tuition, state resident: full-time $8912; part-time $446 per credit hour. Tuition, nonresident: full-time $21,393; part-time $992 per credit hour. *Required fees:* $390; $195 per semester. *Financial support:* Institutionally sponsored loans and scholarships/grants available. Financial award application deadline: 3/1; financial award applicants required to submit FAFSA. *Unit head:* Jason Chandler, Chair, 305-348-6913, E-mail: jason.chandler@fiu.edu. *Application contact:* Nanett Rojas, Assistant Director, Graduate Admissions, 305-348-7464, Fax: 305-348-7441, E-mail: gradadm@fiu.edu.
Website: http://carta.fiu.edu/

Florida State University, The Graduate School, College of Fine Arts, Department of Interior Architecture and Design, Tallahassee, FL 32306. Offers MFA, MS. *Accreditation:* NASAD (one or more programs are accredited). *Program availability:* Part-time. *Faculty:* 9 full-time (7 women), 4 part-time/adjunct (1 woman). *Students:* 18 full-time (15 women), 1 (woman) part-time; includes 2 minority (1 Black or African American, non-Hispanic/Latino; 1 Hispanic/Latino), 7 international. Average age 25. 37 applicants, 54% accepted, 9 enrolled. In 2017, 17 master's awarded. *Degree requirements:* For master's, thesis or alternative. *Entrance requirements:* For master's, GRE General Test, minimum GPA of 3.0 during previous 2 years. Additional exam requirements/recommendations for international students: Required—TOEFL (minimum score 550 paper-based; 80 iBT). *Application deadline:* For fall admission, 7/1 for domestic students, 5/1 for international students; for summer admission, 3/1 for domestic and international students. Applications are processed on a rolling basis. Application fee: $30. Electronic applications accepted. *Financial support:* In 2017–18, 13 teaching assistantships with tuition reimbursements (averaging $5,000 per year) were awarded; career-related internships or fieldwork and unspecified assistantships also available. Financial award applicants required to submit FAFSA. *Faculty research:* Social responsibility issues, graphics techniques, history of interiors, computer-aided design and drafting, pedagogy. *Unit head:* Dr. Lisa K. Waxman, Chairman, 850-644-8326, Fax: 850-644-3112, E-mail: lwaxman@fsu.edu. *Application contact:* Dr. Marlo Ransdell, Director of Graduate Studies, 850-645-6831, Fax: 850-644-3112, E-mail: mransdell@fsu.edu.
Website: http://interiordesign.fsu.edu/

Georgia Institute of Technology, Graduate Studies, College of Design, Doctoral Program in Architecture, Atlanta, GA 30332-0001. Offers PhD. *Program availability:* Part-time, online learning. *Degree requirements:* For doctorate, comprehensive exam, thesis/dissertation. *Entrance requirements:* For doctorate, GRE General Test. Additional exam requirements/recommendations for international students: Required—TOEFL (minimum score 600 paper-based). Electronic applications accepted.

Georgia Institute of Technology, Graduate Studies, College of Design, Master's Program in Architecture, Atlanta, GA 30332-0001. Offers M Arch, MS, M Arch/MCRP. *Program availability:* Part-time. *Degree requirements:* For master's, thesis or alternative. *Entrance requirements:* For master's, GRE General Test. Additional exam requirements/recommendations for international students: Required—TOEFL (minimum score 600 paper-based). Electronic applications accepted.

Georgia Institute of Technology, Graduate Studies, College of Design, School of City and Regional Planning, Atlanta, GA 30332-0001. Offers city and regional planning (PhD); economic development (MCRP); environmental planning and management (MCRP); geographic information systems (MCRP); land and community development (MCRP); land use planning (MCRP); transportation (MCRP); urban design (MCRP); MCP/MSCE. *Accreditation:* ACSP. *Degree requirements:* For master's, thesis,

internship. *Entrance requirements:* For master's, GRE General Test, minimum GPA of 2.7. Additional exam requirements/recommendations for international students: Required—TOEFL. Electronic applications accepted.

Harvard University, Graduate School of Arts and Sciences, Committee on Architecture, Landscape Architecture, and Urban Planning, Cambridge, MA 02138. Offers architecture (PhD); landscape architecture (PhD); urban planning (PhD). *Accreditation:* ACSP. *Degree requirements:* For doctorate, one foreign language, thesis/ dissertation, oral exam. *Entrance requirements:* For doctorate, GRE General Test. Additional exam requirements/recommendations for international students: Required— TOEFL.

Harvard University, Graduate School of Design, Department of Architecture, Cambridge, MA 02138. Offers M Arch. *Degree requirements:* For master's, thesis (for some programs). *Entrance requirements:* For master's, GRE General Test. Additional exam requirements/recommendations for international students: Required—TOEFL (minimum score 600 paper-based; 104 iBT). Electronic applications accepted.

Harvard University, Graduate School of Design, Program in Design, Cambridge, MA 02138. Offers Dr DES. *Entrance requirements:* For doctorate, GRE General Test. Additional exam requirements/recommendations for international students: Required— TOEFL (minimum score 600 paper-based; 104 iBT). Electronic applications accepted.

Harvard University, Graduate School of Design, Program in Design Studies, Cambridge, MA 02138. Offers M Des S. *Entrance requirements:* For master's, GRE General Test. Additional exam requirements/recommendations for international students: Required—TOEFL (minimum score 600 paper-based; 104 iBT). Electronic applications accepted.

Illinois Institute of Technology, Graduate College, College of Architecture, Chicago, IL 60616. Offers M Arch, MLA, MS Arch, PhD, MLA/M Arch. *Accreditation:* ASLA. *Program availability:* Part-time. Terminal master's awarded for partial completion of doctoral program. *Degree requirements:* For master's, comprehensive exam (for some programs), thesis (for some programs); for doctorate, comprehensive exam, thesis/dissertation. *Entrance requirements:* For master's, GRE General Test (minimum score 292 Quantitative and Verbal, 2.5 Analytical Writing), minimum college GPA of 3.0, official transcripts, portfolio, 3 letters of recommendation, professional statement; for doctorate, GRE General Test (minimum score 900 Quantitative and Verbal, 2.5 Analytical Writing), minimum GPA of 3.5, official transcripts, portfolio, 3 letters of recommendation, professional statement. Additional exam requirements/ recommendations for international students: Required—TOEFL (minimum score 550 paper-based; 80 iBT). Electronic applications accepted. *Faculty research:* Sustainable design and efficiency; the influence of climate and environment on building form; emerging urbanisms; computer applications (such as 3-D modeling); the design, planning and structure of high-rise buildings.

Instituto Tecnológico y de Estudios Superiores de Monterrey, Campus Estado de México, Professional and Graduate Division, Estado de Mexico, Mexico. Offers administration of information technologies (MITA); architecture (M Arch); business administration (GMBA, MBA); computer sciences (MCS, PhD); education (M Ed); educational institution administration (MAD); educational technology and innovation (PhD); electronic commerce (MEC); environmental systems (MS); finance (MAF); humanistic studies (MHS); information sciences and knowledge management (MISKM); information systems (MS); manufacturing systems (MS); marketing (MEM); quality systems and productivity (MS); science and materials engineering (PhD); telecommunications management (MTM). *Program availability:* Part-time, online learning. *Degree requirements:* For master's, one foreign language, thesis (for some programs); for doctorate, one foreign language, thesis/dissertation. *Entrance requirements:* For master's, E-PAEP 500, interview; for doctorate, E-PAEP 500, research proposal. Additional exam requirements/recommendations for international students: Required—TOEFL (minimum score 550 paper-based). *Faculty research:* Surface treatments by plasmas, mechanical properties, robotics, graphical computing, mechatronics security protocols.

Instituto Tecnológico y de Estudios Superiores de Monterrey, Campus Irapuato, Graduate Programs, Irapuato, Mexico. Offers administration (MBA); administration of information technology (MAIT); administration of telecommunications (MAT); architecture (M Arch); computer science (MCS); education (M Ed); educational administration (MEA); educational innovation and technology (DEIT); educational technology (MET); electronic commerce (MBA); environmental administration and planning (MEAP); environmental systems (MES); finances (MBA); humanistic studies (MHS); international management for Latin American executives (MIMLAE); library and information science (MLIS); manufacturing quality management (MMQM); marketing research (MBA).

Iowa State University of Science and Technology, Department of Architecture, Ames, IA 50011. Offers architectural studies (MSAS); architecture (M Arch, MS); M Arch/MBA; M Arch/MCRP; M Arch/MS. *Degree requirements:* For master's, thesis (for some programs). *Entrance requirements:* For master's, GRE General Test, portfolio, letters of reference. Additional exam requirements/recommendations for international students: Required—TOEFL (minimum score 600 paper-based; 79 iBT), IELTS (minimum score 7). Electronic applications accepted. *Faculty research:* Computer-aided architectural design, social dimensions of urban architecture, designing for the elderly, energy utilization in buildings, architectural theory.

Judson University, Master of Architecture Program, Elgin, IL 60123-1498. Offers architecture (M Arch); sustainable design (M Arch); traditional architecture and urbanism (M Arch). *Program availability:* Part-time. *Faculty:* 9 full-time (3 women), 3 part-time/ adjunct (1 woman). *Students:* 11 full-time (4 women). Average age 23. 24 applicants, 83% accepted, 11 enrolled. In 2017, 6 master's awarded. *Degree requirements:* For master's, thesis optional, 1600-hour practicum/preceptorship completed prior to enrollment. *Entrance requirements:* For master's, GRE, Judson BA in architecture or equivalent; minimum cumulative undergraduate GPA of 2.75, 3.0 in architecture; comprehensive portfolio; letter of intent. Additional exam requirements/ recommendations for international students: Required—TOEFL (minimum score 550 paper-based), IELTS (minimum score 6.5). *Application deadline:* For fall admission, 2/15 priority date for domestic and international students; for winter admission, 11/15 for domestic students; for spring admission, 11/15 for domestic and international students. Applications are processed on a rolling basis. Application fee: $100. Electronic applications accepted. *Expenses:* Contact institution. *Financial support:* In 2017–18, 9 students received support. Fellowships, research assistantships, teaching assistantships, scholarships/grants, and 8 assistantships available. Financial award application deadline: 5/1; financial award applicants required to submit FAFSA. *Faculty research:* Sustainable design, urbanism, daylighting, acoustics, digital media and fabrication. *Unit head:* Dr. David M. Ogoli, Chair, 847-628-1018, E-mail: dogoli@judsonu.edu. *Application contact:* Molly Smith, Director of Admissions, 847-628-2521, E-mail: molly.smith@judsonu.edu.
Website: http://www.judsonu.edu/ArchMaster/

Kansas State University, Graduate School, College of Architecture, Planning and Design, Department of Architecture, Manhattan, KS 66506. Offers M Arch, MS Arch. *Program availability:* Part-time. *Degree requirements:* For master's, thesis optional,

residency. *Entrance requirements:* For master's, portfolio, minimum GPA of 3.0. Additional exam requirements/recommendations for international students: Required— TOEFL (minimum score 95 iBT), IELTS (minimum score 7). Electronic applications accepted. *Faculty research:* Design theory, environment behavior and place studies, ecological and sustainable design, computer-assisted design and fabrication.

Kennesaw State University, College of Architecture and Construction Management, Department of Architecture, Kennesaw, GA 30144. Offers MS Arch.

Kent State University, College of Architecture and Environmental Design, Kent, OH 44242-0001. Offers architecture (M Arch); architecture and environmental design (MS); health care design (MHCD); landscape architecture (MLA); urban design (MUD); M Arch/MBA; M Arch/MUD. *Program availability:* Part-time. *Faculty:* 19 full-time (2 women), 15 part-time/adjunct (6 women). *Students:* 70 full-time (27 women), 13 part-time (7 women); includes 8 minority (1 Black or African American, non-Hispanic/Latino; 1 Asian, non-Hispanic/Latino; 4 Hispanic/Latino; 2 Two or more races, non-Hispanic/ Latino), 13 international. Average age 26. 100 applicants, 82% accepted, 57 enrolled. In 2017, 59 master's awarded. *Degree requirements:* For master's, thesis (for some programs), capstone project (for some programs). *Entrance requirements:* For master's, GRE with minimum scores 151 (460) verbal reasoning, 150 (620) quantitative reasoning, and 4.25 analytical writing (except for MHCD), letters of recommendation, portfolio. Additional exam requirements/recommendations for international students: Required—TOEFL (minimum score 550 paper-based; 80 iBT), IELTS (minimum score 6.5), PTE (minimum score 54), Michigan English Language Assessment Battery (minimum score 77). *Application deadline:* Applications are processed on a rolling basis. Application fee: $45 ($70 for international students). Electronic applications accepted. *Expenses:* Tuition, state resident: full-time $11,310; part-time $515 per credit hour. Tuition, nonresident: full-time $20,396; part-time $928 per credit hour. International tuition: $18,544 full-time. *Financial support:* Research assistantships with full tuition reimbursements, teaching assistantships with full tuition reimbursements, Federal Work-Study, scholarships/grants, and unspecified assistantships available. Financial award application deadline: 2/1; financial award applicants required to submit FAFSA. *Unit head:* Mark Mistur, Dean, E-mail: mmistur1@kent.edu. *Application contact:* Johnathan Fleming, Assistant Professor and Director, Master of Architecture, 330-672-0934, E-mail: jpflemi1@kent.edu.
Website: http://www.kent.edu/caed

Lawrence Technological University, College of Architecture and Design, Southfield, MI 48075-1058. Offers architecture (M Arch, MA), including interior architecture (M Arch); build information modeling (Graduate Certificate); interior design (MID); social practice (MFA); transportation design (Graduate Certificate); urban design (MUD). *Accreditation:* NASAD. *Program availability:* Part-time, evening/weekend. *Faculty:* 14 full-time (1 woman), 3 part-time/adjunct (1 woman). *Students:* 6 full-time (2 women), 115 part-time (50 women); includes 11 minority (3 Black or African American, non-Hispanic/Latino; 1 Asian, non-Hispanic/Latino; 6 Hispanic/Latino; 1 Two or more races, non-Hispanic/Latino), 32 international. Average age 30. 150 applicants, 55% accepted, 50 enrolled. In 2017, 82 master's, 3 other advanced degrees awarded. *Degree requirements:* For master's, thesis optional. *Entrance requirements:* Additional exam requirements/recommendations for international students: Required—TOEFL (minimum score 550 paper-based; 79 iBT). *Application deadline:* For fall admission, 5/27 for international students; for spring admission, 10/8 for international students; for summer admission, 2/14 for international students. Applications are processed on a rolling basis. Application fee: $50. Electronic applications accepted. *Expenses:* Tuition: Full-time $15,274; part-time $1091 per credit. One-time fee: $150. *Financial support:* In 2017–18, 45 students received support, including 8 research assistantships with partial tuition reimbursements available (averaging $6,000 per year); career-related internships or fieldwork, scholarships/grants, and unspecified assistantships also available. Financial award application deadline: 4/1; financial award applicants required to submit FAFSA. *Faculty research:* Symmetry within the design process, public interest design, transdisciplinary design, adaptive reuse, digital craft, and integration of the use of daylight in architecture and urban design. *Total annual research expenditures:* $209,672. *Unit head:* Prof. Karl Daubmann, Dean/Professor, 248-204-2805, E-mail: archdean@ltu.edu. *Application contact:* Jane Rohrback, Director of Admissions, 248-204-3160, Fax: 248-204-2228, E-mail: admissions@ltu.edu.
Website: http://www.ltu.edu/architecture_and_design/index.asp

London Metropolitan University, Graduate Programs, London, United Kingdom. Offers applied psychology (M Sc); architecture (MA); biomedical science (M Sc); blood science (M Sc); cancer pharmacology (M Sc); computer networking and cyber security (M Sc); computing and information systems (M Sc); conference interpreting (MA); counter-terrorism studies (M Sc); creative, digital and professional writing (MA); crime, violence and prevention (M Sc); criminology (M Sc); curating contemporary art (MA); data analytics (M Sc); digital media (MA); early childhood studies (MA); education (MA, Ed D); financial services law, regulation and compliance (LL M); food science (M Sc); forensic psychology (M Sc); health and social care management and policy (M Sc); human nutrition (M Sc); human resource management (MA); human rights and international conflict (MA); information technology (M Sc); intelligence and security studies (M Sc); international oil, gas and energy law (LL M); international relations (MA); interpreting (MA); learning and teaching in higher education (MA); legal practice (LL M); media and entertainment law (LL M); organizational and consumer psychology (M Sc); psychological therapy (M Sc); psychology of mental health (M Sc); public health (M Sc); public policy and management (MPA); security studies (M Sc); social work (M Sc); spatial planning and urban design (MA); sports therapy (M Sc); supporting older children and young people with dyslexia (MA); teaching languages (MA), including Arabic, English; translation (MA); woman and child abuse (MA).

Louisiana State University and Agricultural & Mechanical College, Graduate School, College of Art and Design, School of Architecture, Baton Rouge, LA 70803. Offers M Arch. *Faculty:* 12 full-time (3 women). *Students:* 22 full-time (11 women), 1 part-time (0 women); includes 7 minority (3 Black or African American, non-Hispanic/Latino; 2 Asian, non-Hispanic/Latino; 2 Hispanic/Latino), 3 international. Average age 28. 4 applicants, 25% accepted, 1 enrolled. In 2017, 7 master's awarded. *Financial support:* In 2017–18, 2 research assistantships (averaging $14,667 per year), 13 teaching assistantships (averaging $11,326 per year) were awarded.

Louisiana Tech University, Graduate School, College of Liberal Arts, Ruston, LA 71272. Offers architecture (M Arch); art (MFA), including graphic design, photography, studio; audiology (Au D); communication (MA), including speech communication, theatre; English (MA), including literature, technical writing; history (MA); speech pathology (MA); technical writing and communication (Graduate Certificate). *Program availability:* Part-time. *Faculty:* 63 full-time (25 women), 5 part-time/adjunct (3 women). *Students:* 114 full-time (29 women), 31 part-time (19 women); includes 12 minority (4 Black or African American, non-Hispanic/Latino; 1 Asian, non-Hispanic/Latino; 3 Hispanic/Latino; 4 Two or more races, non-Hispanic/Latino), 5 international. Average age 30. 146 applicants, 59% accepted, 37 enrolled. In 2017, 49 master's, 3 doctorates awarded. *Degree requirements:* For master's, thesis (for some programs); for doctorate, thesis/dissertation. *Entrance requirements:* For master's, GRE General Test; for doctorate, GRE General Test, bachelor's degree, minimum GPA of 3.0 or 3.2 on last 60 hours attempted. Additional exam requirements/recommendations for international

students: Required—TOEFL (minimum score 550 paper-based; 80 iBT), IELTS (minimum score 6.5). *Application deadline:* For fall admission, 8/1 priority date for domestic students, 6/1 for international students; for winter admission, 11/1 priority date for domestic students, 9/1 for international students; for spring admission, 2/1 priority date for domestic students, 12/1 for international students; for summer admission, 5/1 priority date for domestic students, 3/1 for international students. Application fee: $40 ($50 for international students). Electronic applications accepted. *Expenses:* Tuition, state resident: full-time $5146. Tuition, nonresident: full-time $10,147. *International tuition:* $10,267 full-time. *Required fees:* $2273. *Financial support:* In 2017–18, 63 students received support, including 46 research assistantships (averaging $5,229 per year), 7 teaching assistantships (averaging $5,543 per year); fellowships, career-related internships or fieldwork, Federal Work-Study, institutionally sponsored loans, tuition waivers (partial), and unspecified assistantships also available. Financial award application deadline: 2/1. *Faculty research:* Contributing to the expansion of historical and social scientific knowledge and understanding through original research and publication; diverse language, ethnic, cultural, and socioeconomic backgrounds with disorders of speech, language, swallowing, hearing, and cognitive aspects of communication; prevention of communication, swallowing, and hearing disorders. *Unit head:* Dr. Donald P. Kaczvinsky, Dean, 318-257-4805, Fax: 318-257-3935, E-mail: dkaczv@latech.edu. *Application contact:* Mary Green, Administrative Assistant, 318-257-2924, Fax: 318-257-4487, E-mail: meg@latech.edu.
Website: http://liberalarts.latech.edu/

Marywood University, Academic Affairs, School of Architecture, Program in Architecture, Scranton, PA 18509-1598. Offers M Arch. *Program availability:* Part-time. *Degree requirements:* For master's, thesis project.

Massachusetts College of Art and Design, Graduate Programs, Program in Architecture, Boston, MA 02115-5882. Offers M Arch. *Faculty:* 5 full-time (4 women), 14 part-time/adjunct (1 woman). *Students:* 24 full-time (10 women), 5 part-time (4 women); includes 8 minority (3 Black or African American, non-Hispanic/Latino; 2 Asian, non-Hispanic/Latino; 3 Hispanic/Latino), 7 international. 43 applicants, 79% accepted, 12 enrolled. In 2017, 6 master's awarded. *Entrance requirements:* For master's, portfolio, college transcripts, resume, statement of purpose, letters of reference, interview. Additional exam requirements/recommendations for international students: Required—TOEFL (minimum score 550 paper-based; 85 iBT); Recommended—IELTS (minimum score 6). *Application deadline:* For summer admission, 1/4 priority date for domestic and international students. Application fee: $90. Electronic applications accepted. *Expenses:* $780 per credit. *Financial support:* In 2017–18, 16 students received support, including 8 teaching assistantships (averaging $2,160 per year); research assistantships, career-related internships or fieldwork, scholarships/grants, tuition waivers (partial), and unspecified assistantships also available. Support available to part-time students. Financial award application deadline: 1/4; financial award applicants required to submit FAFSA. *Faculty research:* Sustainability, civic engagement, community development, digital teaching tools. *Unit head:* Paul Paturzo, Dean of Graduate Studies, 617-879-7166, E-mail: pjpaturzo@massart.edu. *Application contact:* Lauren O'Neill, Assistant Director of Graduate Admissions, 617-879-7222, E-mail: gradadmissions@massart.edu.
Website: http://www.massart.edu/Admissions/Graduate_Programs.html

Massachusetts Institute of Technology, School of Architecture and Planning, Department of Architecture, Cambridge, MA 02139. Offers architecture (M Arch, PhD), including building technology (PhD), design and computation (PhD), history and theory of architecture (PhD), history and theory of art (PhD); architecture studies (SM Arch S); art, culture and technology (SMACT); building technology (SMBT). *Degree requirements:* For master's, thesis; for doctorate, comprehensive exam, thesis/dissertation. *Entrance requirements:* For master's and doctorate, GRE General Test. Additional exam requirements/recommendations for international students: Required—TOEFL, IELTS. Electronic applications accepted. *Faculty research:* Architecture; urbanism; building technology and sustainability; computation and design; history, theory, and criticism; art, culture, and technology.

McGill University, Faculty of Graduate and Postdoctoral Studies, Faculty of Engineering, School of Architecture, Montréal, QC H3A 2T5, Canada. Offers affordable homes (M Arch II, Diploma); architectural history and theory (M Arch II); architecture (PhD); domestic environment (M Arch II); domestic environments (Diploma); minimum cost housing in developing countries (M Arch II, Diploma); professional architecture (M Arch I).

Miami University, College of Creative Arts, Department of Architecture and Interior Design, Oxford, OH 45056. Offers M Arch. *Accreditation:* NASAD. *Students:* 26 full-time (9 women); includes 3 minority (1 Black or African American, non-Hispanic/Latino; 1 Hispanic/Latino; 1 Two or more races, non-Hispanic/Latino), 10 international. Average age 26. In 2017, 10 master's awarded. *Expenses:* Tuition, state resident: full-time $13,812; part-time $575 per credit hour. Tuition, nonresident: full-time $30,860; part-time $1286 per credit hour. *Unit head:* Graham Cairns, Chair and Professor, 513-529-6431, E-mail: cairnsgj@miamioh.edu. *Application contact:* Craig Hinrichs, Professor/Director of Graduate Studies, 513-529-7036, E-mail: hinriccl@miamioh.edu.
Website: http://www.MiamiOH.edu/architecture

Montana State University, The Graduate School, College of Arts and Architecture, School of Architecture, Bozeman, MT 59717. Offers M Arch. *Program availability:* Part-time. *Degree requirements:* For master's, comprehensive exam. *Entrance requirements:* For master's, GRE General Test, minimum cumulative GPA of 3.0, portfolio, 3 letters of recommendation. Additional exam requirements/recommendations for international students: Required—TOEFL (minimum score 550 paper-based). Electronic applications accepted. *Faculty research:* Sustainability, architecture as craft, visualization, stewardship, community design, design build.

Morgan State University, School of Graduate Studies, School of Architecture and Planning, Program in Architecture, Baltimore, MD 21251. Offers M Arch. *Entrance requirements:* Additional exam requirements/recommendations for international students: Required—TOEFL (minimum score 550 paper-based). *Application deadline:* For fall admission, 2/1 priority date for domestic students; for spring admission, 10/1 priority date for domestic students. Applications are processed on a rolling basis. Application fee: $0. *Expenses:* Tuition, state resident: part-time $433 per credit. Tuition, nonresident: part-time $851 per credit. *Required fees:* $81.50 per credit. *Financial support:* Application deadline: 2/1. *Unit head:* Jeremy Kargon, Graduate Program Director, 443-885-3511, E-mail: jeremy.kargon@morgan.edu. *Application contact:* Dr. Dean Campbell, Graduate Recruitment Specialist, 443-885-3185, Fax: 443-885-8226, E-mail: dean.campbell@morgan.edu.

New Jersey Institute of Technology, College of Architecture and Design, Newark, NJ 07102. Offers architecture (M Arch, MS Arch); infrastructure planning (MIP); urban systems (PhD). *Program availability:* Part-time, evening/weekend. *Faculty:* 31 full-time (8 women), 37 part-time/adjunct (14 women). *Students:* 40 full-time (23 women), 6 part-time (0 women); includes 10 minority (1 Black or African American, non-Hispanic/Latino; 3 Asian, non-Hispanic/Latino; 5 Hispanic/Latino; 1 Two or more races, non-Hispanic/Latino), 19 international. Average age 30. 129 applicants, 37% accepted, 10 enrolled. In 2017, 16 master's, 4 doctorates awarded. Terminal master's awarded for partial completion of doctoral program. *Degree requirements:* For master's, thesis (for some programs). *Entrance requirements:* For master's, GRE General Test, minimum GPA of 3.0. Additional exam requirements/recommendations for international students: Required—TOEFL (minimum score 550 paper-based; 79 iBT). *Application deadline:* For fall admission, 6/1 priority date for domestic students, 5/1 priority date for international students; for spring admission, 11/15 priority date for domestic and international students. Applications are processed on a rolling basis. Application fee: $75. Electronic applications accepted. *Expenses:* Contact institution. *Financial support:* In 2017–18, 31 students received support, including 6 fellowships (averaging $6,825 per year), 8 teaching assistantships (averaging $24,834 per year); career-related internships or fieldwork, Federal Work-Study, institutionally sponsored loans, scholarships/grants, traineeships, unspecified assistantships, and studio assistantships (1 averaging $10,000) also available. Financial award application deadline: 1/15. *Faculty research:* Building sciences, community and urban design history and theory, computer-aided architecture, material dynamics. *Unit head:* Anthony W. Schuman, Interim Dean, 973-596-6370, E-mail: anthony.w.schuman@njit.edu. *Application contact:* Stephen Eck, Director of Admissions, 973-596-3300, Fax: 973-596-3461, E-mail: admissions@njit.edu.
Website: http://architecture.njit.edu/

The New School, Parsons School of Design, Program in Architecture, New York, NY 10011. Offers M Arch, M Arch/MFA. *Faculty:* 15 full-time (5 women), 17 part-time/adjunct (9 women). *Students:* 66 full-time (39 women), 1 part-time (0 women); includes 21 minority (4 Black or African American, non-Hispanic/Latino; 7 Asian, non-Hispanic/Latino; 9 Hispanic/Latino; 1 Two or more races, non-Hispanic/Latino), 20 international. Average age 26. 170 applicants, 82% accepted, 27 enrolled. In 2017, 54 master's awarded. *Degree requirements:* For master's, thesis. *Entrance requirements:* For master's, GRE, transcripts, resume, statement of purpose, recommendation letters, portfolio, interview. Additional exam requirements/recommendations for international students: Required—TOEFL (minimum score 92 iBT), IELTS (minimum score 7), PTE (minimum score 63). *Application deadline:* For fall admission, 1/1 for domestic and international students. Applications are processed on a rolling basis. Application fee: $50. Electronic applications accepted. *Expenses:* $24,922 per semester full-time, $1,744 per credit part-time. *Financial support:* In 2017–18, 54 students received support, including 7 teaching assistantships (averaging $3,572 per year); career-related internships or fieldwork, Federal Work-Study, scholarships/grants, unspecified assistantships, and travel funding; tuition waivers for students who are also New School employees also available. Support available to part-time students. Financial award application deadline: 2/1; financial award applicants required to submit FAFSA. *Unit head:* Joel Towers, Executive Dean, Parsons School of Design, 212-229-8950 Ext. 4393, E-mail: towersj@newschool.edu. *Application contact:* Courtney Malenius, Director of Graduate Admission, 212-229-5150 Ext. 4011, E-mail: thinkparsonsgrad@newschool.edu.
Website: https://www.newschool.edu/parsons/masters-architecture/

NewSchool of Architecture and Design, Program in Architecture, San Diego, CA 92101-6634. Offers M Arch, MS. *Program availability:* Part-time, online learning. *Degree requirements:* For master's, thesis. *Entrance requirements:* For master's, portfolio, interview. Additional exam requirements/recommendations for international students: Required—TOEFL, IELTS. *Faculty research:* Urban studies, regional studies, environmental design, structures, cross-cultural studies.

New York Institute of Technology, School of Architecture and Design, Old Westbury, NY 11568-8000. Offers architecture (M Arch); architecture, urban and regional design (MS). *Program availability:* Part-time. *Faculty:* 3 full-time (1 woman), 3 part-time/adjunct (0 women). *Students:* 14 full-time (11 women), all international. Average age 26. 45 applicants, 44% accepted, 8 enrolled. In 2017, 14 master's awarded. *Entrance requirements:* For master's, professional architecture or landscape architecture degree from accredited college or university approved by the NAAB or equivalent; minimum undergraduate GPA of 3.0; digital portfolio; curriculum vitae; personal essay; two letters of recommendation. Additional exam requirements/recommendations for international students: Required—TOEFL (minimum score 79 iBT), IELTS (minimum score 6). *Application deadline:* For fall admission, 3/1 for domestic and international students. Applications are processed on a rolling basis. Application fee: $50. Electronic applications accepted. *Expenses:* $1,285 per credit plus fees. *Financial support:* Career-related internships or fieldwork, Federal Work-Study, institutionally sponsored loans, scholarships/grants, tuition waivers (full and partial), and unspecified assistantships available. Support available to part-time students. Financial award application deadline: 2/15; financial award applicants required to submit FAFSA. *Faculty research:* Resilient cities, compact morphology, new town development, pedestrian-friendly public realm. *Unit head:* Jeffrey Raven, Graduate Director, 212-261-1547, E-mail: jraven@nyit.edu. *Application contact:* Alice Dolitsky, Director, Graduate Admissions, 516-686-7520, Fax: 516-686-1116, E-mail: nyitgrad@nyit.edu.
Website: http://www.nyit.edu/architecture

North Carolina State University, Graduate School, College of Design, School of Architecture, Raleigh, NC 27695. Offers M Arch. *Degree requirements:* For master's, thesis optional, oral exam, project. *Entrance requirements:* For master's, GRE General Test, portfolio. Electronic applications accepted. *Faculty research:* Architectural design, architectural history and theory, construction materials, sustainable design.

North Dakota State University, College of Graduate and Interdisciplinary Studies, College of Arts, Humanities and Social Sciences, Department of Architecture and Landscape Architecture, Fargo, ND 58102. Offers architecture (M Arch). Electronic applications accepted.

Northeastern University, College of Arts, Media and Design, Boston, MA 02115-5096. Offers architecture (M Arch); game science and design (MS); information design and visualization (MFA); interdisciplinary arts (MFA); journalism (MA); music industry leadership (MS); studio art (MFA); sustainable building systems (MS); sustainable urban environments (M Des). *Faculty:* 145. *Students:* 259. In 2017, 83 master's awarded. Application fee: $75. Electronic applications accepted. *Expenses:* Contact institution. *Financial support:* Applicants required to submit FAFSA. *Unit head:* Dr. Elizabeth Hudson, Dean, 617-373-5088, E-mail: n.elysse@northeastern.edu. *Application contact:* Jane Amidon, Associate Dean for Graduate Programs and Research, 617-373-4614, E-mail: gscamd@northeastern.edu.
Website: http://www.northeastern.edu/camd/

The Ohio State University, Graduate School, College of Engineering, Austin E. Knowlton School of Architecture, Columbus, OH 43210. Offers architecture (M Arch); city and regional planning (MCRP, PhD); landscape architecture (M Land Arch). *Accreditation:* ACSP; ASLA. *Faculty:* 41. *Students:* 197 full-time (84 women), 6 part-time (2 women); includes 34 minority (9 Black or African American, non-Hispanic/Latino; 5 Asian, non-Hispanic/Latino; 15 Hispanic/Latino; 5 Two or more races, non-Hispanic/Latino), 35 international. Average age 26. In 2017, 66 master's, 8 doctorates awarded. *Entrance requirements:* For master's, GRE or GMAT (city and regional planning), portfolio (for architecture and landscape architecture); for doctorate, GRE or GMAT (city and regional planning), example of research or written work. Additional exam requirements/recommendations for international students: Required—TOEFL (minimum score 600 paper-based; 100 iBT), Michigan English Language Assessment Battery (minimum score 86); Recommended—IELTS (minimum score 8). *Application deadline:*

For fall admission, 1/1 priority date for domestic students, 11/30 priority date for international students. Applications are processed on a rolling basis. Application fee: $60 ($70 for international students). Electronic applications accepted. *Financial support:* Fellowships, research assistantships, Federal Work-Study, institutionally sponsored loans, and unspecified assistantships available. Support available to part-time students. *Unit head:* Michael B. Cadwell, Professor/Director, 614-292-3174, E-mail: cadwell.1@osu.edu. *Application contact:* Graduate and Professional Admissions, 614-292-9444, Fax: 614-292-3895, E-mail: gpadmissions@osu.edu. Website: http://knowlton.osu.edu/

Penn State University Park, Graduate School, College of Arts and Architecture, Stuckeman School of Architecture and Landscape Architecture, University Park, PA 16802. Offers architecture (M Arch, MS, PhD); landscape architecture (MLA, MS). *Accreditation:* ASLA. *Unit head:* Dr. Barbara O. Korner, Dean, 814-865-2592, Fax: 814-865-2018. *Application contact:* Lori Hawn, Director, Graduate Student Services, 814-865-1795, Fax: 814-863-4627, E-mail: l-gswww@lists.psu.edu. Website: https://stuckeman.psu.edu/

Pontificia Universidad Catolica Madre y Maestra, Graduate School, Faculty of Sciences and Humanities, Santiago, Dominican Republic. Offers architecture (M Arch), including architecture of interiors, architecture of tourist lodgings, landscaping; early childhood education (M Ed).

Portland State University, Graduate Studies, College of the Arts, School of Architecture, Portland, OR 97207-0751. Offers M Arch. *Faculty:* 11 full-time (3 women), 15 part-time/adjunct (5 women). *Students:* 46 full-time (28 women), 3 part-time (2 women); includes 9 minority (3 Asian, non-Hispanic/Latino; 5 Hispanic/Latino; 1 Two or more races, non-Hispanic/Latino), 5 international. Average age 32. 28 applicants, 68% accepted, 6 enrolled. In 2017, 21 master's awarded. *Degree requirements:* For master's, thesis optional. *Entrance requirements:* For master's, GRE General Test, statement of intent, resume, 3 letters of recommendation, writing sample, portfolio. Additional exam requirements/recommendations for international students: Required—TOEFL (minimum score 550 paper-based; 80 iBT), IELTS (minimum score 6.5). *Application deadline:* For fall admission, 6/22 for domestic students; for summer admission, 5/23 for domestic students. Applications are processed on a rolling basis. Application fee: $65. Electronic applications accepted. *Expenses:* Contact institution. *Financial support:* In 2017–18, 22 students received support, including 5 research assistantships with tuition reimbursements available (averaging $6,284 per year), 7 teaching assistantships with tuition reimbursements available (averaging $5,325 per year); Federal Work-Study, institutionally sponsored loans, scholarships/grants, and unspecified assistantships also available. Support available to part-time students. *Total annual research expenditures:* $399,278. *Unit head:* Prof. Clive Knights, Director, 503-725-3349, E-mail: knightsc@pdx.edu. *Application contact:* 503-725-8405, Fax: 503-725-8318, E-mail: architec@pdx.edu. Website: https://www.pdx.edu/architecture/

Prairie View A&M University, School of Architecture, Prairie View, TX 77446. Offers M Arch, MCD. *Program availability:* Part-time, evening/weekend. *Faculty:* 3 full-time (0 women), 3 part-time/adjunct (2 women). *Students:* 42 full-time (22 women), 16 part-time (7 women); includes 50 minority (42 Black or African American, non-Hispanic/Latino; 7 Hispanic/Latino; 1 Native Hawaiian or other Pacific Islander, non-Hispanic/Latino), 7 international. Average age 29. 51 applicants, 88% accepted, 34 enrolled. In 2017, 39 master's awarded. *Degree requirements:* For master's, comprehensive exam, thesis. *Entrance requirements:* For master's, GRE General Test, portfolio (M Arch), minimum GPA of 2.75. Additional exam requirements/recommendations for international students: Required—TOEFL (minimum score 550 paper-based; 79 iBT). *Application deadline:* For fall admission, 5/1 priority date for domestic and international students; for spring admission, 10/1 priority date for domestic students, 9/1 priority date for international students; for summer admission, 3/1 priority date for domestic students, 2/1 priority date for international students. Applications are processed on a rolling basis. Application fee: $50. Electronic applications accepted. *Expenses:* Tuition, state resident: part-time $242 per credit. Tuition, nonresident: part-time $695 per credit. *Required fees:* $149 per credit. *Financial support:* Career-related internships or fieldwork, Federal Work-Study, institutionally sponsored loans, scholarships/grants, tuition waivers (full and partial), and unspecified assistantships available. Support available to part-time students. Financial award application deadline: 4/1; financial award applicants required to submit FAFSA. *Faculty research:* Community management, sustainable design. *Unit head:* Dr. Ikhlas Sabouni, Dean, 936-261-9800, Fax: 936-261-2350, E-mail: isabouni@pvamu.edu. *Application contact:* Pauline Walker, Administrative Assistant II, Research and Graduate Studies, 936-261-3521, Fax: 936-261-3529, E-mail: pmwalker@pvamu.edu.

Pratt Institute, School of Architecture, Program in Architecture, Brooklyn, NY 11205-3899. Offers architecture (first-professional) (M Arch); architecture (post-professional) (MS Arch). *Students:* 173 full-time (93 women), 4 part-time (1 woman); includes 24 minority (2 Black or African American, non-Hispanic/Latino; 8 Asian, non-Hispanic/Latino; 13 Hispanic/Latino; 1 Two or more races, non-Hispanic/Latino), 104 international. Average age 26. 442 applicants, 83% accepted, 56 enrolled. In 2017, 79 master's awarded. *Degree requirements:* For master's, thesis. *Entrance requirements:* For master's, GRE (for M Arch only), B Arch (for MS Arch only), portfolio, letters of recommendation. Additional exam requirements/recommendations for international students: Required—TOEFL (minimum score 550 paper-based; 79 iBT). *Application deadline:* For fall admission, 1/5 for domestic and international students; for spring admission, 10/1 for domestic and international students. Application fee: $50 ($90 for international students). Electronic applications accepted. *Expenses: Tuition:* Full-time $30,834. *Required fees:* $1974. *Financial support:* Career-related internships or fieldwork, Federal Work-Study, institutionally sponsored loans, scholarships/grants, health care benefits, and unspecified assistantships available. Support available to part-time students. Financial award application deadline: 2/1; financial award applicants required to submit FAFSA. *Faculty research:* Design theory, advanced structural systems, urban investigations. *Unit head:* David Erdman, Chairperson, 718-399-4327, E-mail: derdman@pratt.edu. *Application contact:* Natalie Capannelli, Director of Graduate Admissions, 718-636-3551, Fax: 718-399-4242, E-mail: ncapanne@pratt.edu. Website: https://www.pratt.edu/academics/architecture/grad-arch-urban-design/grad-dept-architecture/

See Display on this page and Close-Up on page 125.

Princeton University, Graduate School, School of Architecture, Princeton, NJ 08544-1019. Offers M Arch, PhD. Terminal master's awarded for partial completion of doctoral program. *Degree requirements:* For master's, thesis; for doctorate, 2 foreign languages, comprehensive exam, thesis/dissertation. *Entrance requirements:* For master's, GRE General Test, design portfolio, math, 2 semesters of physics, and art/architecture survey; for doctorate, GRE General Test, samples of written work. Additional exam requirements/recommendations for international students: Required—TOEFL (minimum score 600 paper-based). Electronic applications accepted. *Faculty research:* Design, urban studies, landscape architecture, media and information technologies in architecture.

Rensselaer Polytechnic Institute, Graduate School, School of Architecture, Program in Architecture, Troy, NY 12180-3590. Offers M Arch. *Faculty:* 33 full-time (8 women), 13 part-time/adjunct (1 woman). *Students:* 22 full-time (13 women); includes 5 minority (1 Black or African American, non-Hispanic/Latino; 2 Asian, non-Hispanic/Latino; 2 Hispanic/Latino), 7 international. Average age 26. 83 applicants, 77% accepted, 9 enrolled. *Degree requirements:* For master's, thesis. *Entrance requirements:* For master's, GRE, portfolio. Additional exam requirements/recommendations for international students: Required—TOEFL (minimum score 570 paper-based; 88 iBT), IELTS (minimum score 6.5), PTE (minimum score 60). *Application deadline:* For fall admission, 1/1 priority date for domestic and international students; for summer admission, 1/1 priority date for domestic and international students. Applications are processed on a rolling basis. Application fee: $75. Electronic applications accepted. *Expenses: Tuition:* Full-time $52,550; part-time $2125 per credit hour. *Required fees:* $2890. *Financial support:* Scholarships/grants available. Financial award application deadline: 1/1. *Faculty research:* Environmental parametrics, geofutures. *Total annual research expenditures:* $652,863. *Unit head:* Lonn Combs, Graduate Program Director, 518-276-8718, E-mail: combsl@rpi.edu.
Website: http://march1.arch.rpi.edu/

Rensselaer Polytechnic Institute, Graduate School, School of Architecture, Program in Lighting, Troy, NY 12180-3590. Offers MS. *Faculty:* 33 full-time (8 women), 13 part-time/adjunct (1 woman). *Students:* 4 full-time (3 women); includes 1 minority (Black or African American, non-Hispanic/Latino). Average age 25. 10 applicants, 60% accepted, 4 enrolled. *Degree requirements:* For master's, comprehensive exam, thesis. *Entrance requirements:* For master's, GRE. Additional exam requirements/recommendations for international students: Required—TOEFL (minimum score 570 paper-based; 88 iBT), IELTS (minimum score 6.5), PTE (minimum score 60). *Application deadline:* For fall admission, 1/1 priority date for domestic and international students. Applications are processed on a rolling basis. Application fee: $75. Electronic applications accepted. *Expenses: Tuition:* Full-time $52,550; part-time $2125 per credit hour. *Required fees:* $2890. *Financial support:* In 2017–18, research assistantships (averaging $23,000 per year), teaching assistantships with full tuition reimbursements (averaging $23,000 per year) were awarded; fellowships also available. Financial award application deadline: 1/1. *Faculty research:* Applications and design, automotive and street lighting, aviation lighting, controls, daylighting, energy and environment, health and vision, LEDs, outdoor lighting, residential lighting, security lighting. *Unit head:* Nadarajah Narendran, Graduate Program Director, 518-687-7100, E-mail: narenn2@rpi.edu.
Website: http://www.arch.rpi.edu/academic/graduate/lighting/

Rhode Island School of Design, Department of Architecture, Providence, RI 02903-2784. Offers M Arch. *Faculty:* 16 full-time (8 women), 31 part-time/adjunct (14 women). *Students:* 85 full-time (50 women); includes 16 minority (3 Black or African American, non-Hispanic/Latino; 5 Asian, non-Hispanic/Latino; 8 Hispanic/Latino), 48 international. Average age 26. 314 applicants, 47% accepted, 37 enrolled. In 2017, 32 master's awarded. *Degree requirements:* For master's, thesis, exhibition. *Entrance requirements:* For master's, portfolio, statement of purpose, 3 letters of recommendation. Additional exam requirements/recommendations for international students: Required—TOEFL (minimum score 580 paper-based; 93 iBT). *Application deadline:* For fall admission, 1/10 for domestic and international students. Application fee: $60. Electronic applications accepted. *Expenses: Tuition:* Full-time $48,210. *Required fees:* $260. *Financial support:* Fellowships, research assistantships, teaching assistantships, Federal Work-Study, scholarships/grants, and unspecified assistantships available. Financial award application deadline: 2/15; financial award applicants required to submit FAFSA. *Unit head:* Amy Kulper, Department Head, 401-454-6281, Fax: 401-454-6299, E-mail: archgrad@risd.edu. *Application contact:* Molly Pettengill, Assistant Director for Graduate Recruitment, 401-454-6312, Fax: 401-454-6309, E-mail: mpetteng@risd.edu.
Website: http://www.risd.edu/academics/architecture/

Rice University, Graduate Programs, School of Architecture, Houston, TX 77251-1892. Offers architecture (M Arch, D Arch); urban design (M Arch). *Degree requirements:* For master's, thesis optional; for doctorate, thesis/dissertation. *Entrance requirements:* For master's and doctorate, GRE. Additional exam requirements/recommendations for international students: Required—TOEFL (minimum score 600 paper-based; 100 iBT). Electronic applications accepted.

Rochester Institute of Technology, Graduate Enrollment Services, Golisano Institute for Sustainability, Architecture and Sustainability Department, M Arch Program in Architecture, Rochester, NY 14623. Offers M Arch. *Students:* 34 full-time (17 women), 13 part-time (6 women), 28 international. Average age 29. 68 applicants, 75% accepted, 6 enrolled. In 2017, 2 master's awarded. *Entrance requirements:* For master's, GRE, minimum GPA of 3.0 (recommended), portfolio. Additional exam requirements/recommendations for international students: Required—TOEFL (minimum score 550 paper-based; 79 iBT), IELTS (minimum score 6.5), PTE (minimum score 58). *Application deadline:* For fall admission, 2/15 priority date for domestic and international students. Applications are processed on a rolling basis. Application fee: $65. Electronic applications accepted. *Expenses:* $1,815 per credit hour. *Financial support:* In 2017–18, 35 students received support. Teaching assistantships with partial tuition reimbursements available, career-related internships or fieldwork, scholarships/grants, and unspecified assistantships available. Financial award applicants required to submit FAFSA. *Faculty research:* Architecture and sustainability, design resiliency, and net zero energy/high performance buildings; renewable energy, environmentally responsive architecture and passive/natural building design and systems; sustainable urban design; socially responsible design and livable communities; traditional and classical architecture; theory and history of architecture and urban form. *Unit head:* Dennis Andrejko, Program Chairman, 585-475-7363, E-mail: info@sustainability.rit.edu. *Application contact:* Diane Ellison, Senior Associate Vice President, Graduate Enrollment Services, 585-475-2229, Fax: 585-475-7164, E-mail: gradinfo@rit.edu.
Website: http://www.rit.edu/gis/academics/master-architecture/overview

Roger Williams University, School of Architecture, Art and Historic Preservation, Bristol, RI 02809. Offers architecture (M Arch); art and architectural history (MA); historical preservation (MS, Certificate); urban and regional planning (Certificate). *Faculty:* 18 full-time (5 women), 9 part-time/adjunct (1 woman). *Students:* 107 full-time (52 women), 9 part-time (5 women); includes 10 minority (1 Asian, non-Hispanic/Latino; 7 Hispanic/Latino; 2 Two or more races, non-Hispanic/Latino), 5 international. Average age 26. 92 applicants, 93% accepted, 58 enrolled. In 2017, 46 master's, 1 other advanced degree awarded. *Degree requirements:* For master's, thesis. *Entrance requirements:* For master's, portfolio, 2 letters of recommendation, college transcript, letter of intent. Additional exam requirements/recommendations for international students: Required—TOEFL (minimum score 85 iBT), IELTS (minimum score 6.5). *Application deadline:* For fall admission, 4/1 for domestic students; for spring admission, 11/15 for domestic students. Application fee: $50. Electronic applications accepted. *Expenses:* $1,463 per credit hour (for M Arch); $876 per credit hour (for MS and MA); $258 graduation fee. *Financial support:* In 2017–18, 116 students received support, including 116 research assistantships (averaging $2,776 per year); career-related internships or fieldwork, scholarships/grants, and unspecified assistantships also available. Financial award application deadline: 4/1; financial award applicants required to submit FAFSA. *Unit head:* Stephen White, Dean, 401-254-3607, E-mail: swhite@rwu.edu. *Application contact:* Marcus Hanscom, Director of Graduate Admissions, 401-254-3345, Fax: 401-254-3557, E-mail: gradadmit@rwu.edu.
Website: http://www.rwu.edu/graduate/programs/graduate-programs/architecture

Savannah College of Art and Design, Program in Architecture, Savannah, GA 31402-3146. Offers M Arch. *Program availability:* Part-time. *Faculty:* 19 full-time (7 women), 5 part-time/adjunct (0 women). *Students:* 72 full-time (32 women), 19 part-time (7 women); includes 15 minority (4 Black or African American, non-Hispanic/Latino; 1 Asian, non-Hispanic/Latino; 10 Hispanic/Latino), 44 international. Average age 26. 142 applicants, 58% accepted, 28 enrolled. In 2017, 46 master's awarded. *Degree requirements:* For master's, thesis. *Entrance requirements:* For master's, GRE (recommended), portfolio (submitted in digital format), audition or writing submission, resume, statement of purpose, two letters of recommendation. Additional exam requirements/recommendations for international students: Recommended—TOEFL (minimum score 550 paper-based; 85 iBT), IELTS (minimum score 6.5). *Application deadline:* For fall admission, 4/1 for domestic and international students. Applications are processed on a rolling basis. Application fee: $40. Electronic applications accepted. *Expenses: Tuition:* Full-time $36,765; part-time $817 per credit hour. One-time fee: $500. *Financial support:* Career-related internships or fieldwork, Federal Work-Study, and scholarships/grants available. Financial award application deadline: 4/1; financial award applicants required to submit FAFSA. *Unit head:* Ivan Chow, Dean, School of Building Arts. *Application contact:* Jenny Jaquillard, Executive Director of Admissions, Recruitment and Events, 912-525-5100, Fax: 912-525-5985, E-mail: admission@scad.edu.
Website: http://www.scad.edu/academics/programs/architecture

School of Architecture at Taliesin, Graduate Program, Scottsdale, AZ 85259. Offers M Arch. Summer session held in Spring Green, WI. *Degree requirements:* For master's, thesis or alternative. *Entrance requirements:* For master's, interviews, portfolio, statement of purpose, resume, 3 letters of recommendation, transcripts. Additional exam requirements/recommendations for international students: Required—TOEFL, IELTS. Electronic applications accepted. Application fee is waived when completed online. *Expenses:* Contact institution. *Faculty research:* Architecture, landscape architecture, materials design, design.

School of the Art Institute of Chicago, Graduate Division, Department of Architecture, Interior Architecture, and Designed Objects, Chicago, IL 60603-3103. Offers architecture (M Arc); design for emerging technologies (MFA); designed objects (M Des); interior architecture (M Arc). *Entrance requirements:* Additional exam requirements/recommendations for international students: Required—TOEFL, IELTS.

Southern California Institute of Architecture, Graduate Program in Architecture, Los Angeles, CA 90013. Offers M Arch. *Degree requirements:* For master's, thesis, final thesis project. *Entrance requirements:* For master's, GRE General Test, portfolio, 3 letters of recommendation, transcripts, statement of purpose, resume. Additional exam requirements/recommendations for international students: Required—TOEFL (minimum score 583 paper-based, 90 iBT) or IELTS (minimum score 6.5). Electronic applications accepted.
See Display on the next page and Close-Up on page 127.

Southern Illinois University Carbondale, Graduate School, College of Applied Science, School of Architecture, Carbondale, IL 62901-4701. Offers M Arch. *Entrance requirements:* Additional exam requirements/recommendations for international students: Required—TOEFL (minimum score 550 paper-based; 80 iBT). Electronic applications accepted.

Syracuse University, School of Architecture, Master of Architecture Program, Syracuse, NY 13244. Offers M Arch. *Entrance requirements:* For master's, GRE, online portfolio of creative and/or professional work in architecture, the visual arts, design, and/or affiliated fields; personal statement of purpose; official transcripts; three letters of recommendation. Additional exam requirements/recommendations for international students: Required—TOEFL, IELTS. *Application deadline:* For fall admission, 1/15 priority date for domestic students, 1/1 priority date for international students. *Financial support:* Fellowships, research assistantships, teaching assistantships, and scholarships/grants available. *Unit head:* Brian Lonsway, Chair, 315-443-2316, E-mail: blonsway@syr.edu. *Application contact:* Vittoria Buccina, Director, Graduate and Undergraduate Recruitment, 315-443-5074, E-mail: vabuccin@syr.edu.
Website: http://soa.syr.edu/programs/graduate/march/

Syracuse University, School of Architecture, MS in Architecture Program, Syracuse, NY 13244. Offers MS. *Entrance requirements:* For master's, GRE (recommended), online portfolio of creative and/or professional work in architecture, the visual arts, design, and/or affiliated fields; personal statement of purpose; research proposal; official transcripts; three letters of recommendation. Additional exam requirements/recommendations for international students: Required—TOEFL, IELTS. *Application deadline:* For fall admission, 1/15 for domestic and international students. *Financial support:* Fellowships, research assistantships, teaching assistantships, and scholarships/grants available. *Unit head:* Brian Lonsway, Associate Professor/Graduate Chair, 315-443-2316, E-mail: blonsway@syr.edu. *Application contact:* Vittoria Buccina, Director, Graduate and Undergraduate Recruitment, 315-443-5074, E-mail: vabuccin@syr.edu.
Website: http://soa.syr.edu/programs/graduate/ms-in-architecture/

Temple University, Tyler School of Art, Department of Architecture, Philadelphia, PA 19122-6096. Offers M Arch. *Program availability:* Part-time. *Faculty:* 10 full-time (3 women), 4 part-time/adjunct (0 women). *Students:* 36 full-time (17 women), 1 part-time (0 women); includes 10 minority (2 Black or African American, non-Hispanic/Latino; 2 Asian, non-Hispanic/Latino; 2 Hispanic/Latino; 4 Two or more races, non-Hispanic/Latino), 3 international. 44 applicants, 64% accepted, 8 enrolled. In 2017, 12 master's awarded. *Entrance requirements:* For master's, GRE, portfolio, letters of recommendation, resume/curriculum vitae, minimum GPA of 3.0. Additional exam requirements/recommendations for international students: Required—TOEFL (minimum score 550 paper-based; 79 iBT), IELTS (minimum score 6.5). *Application deadline:* For fall admission, 1/15 for domestic students, 1/15 priority date for international students. Applications are processed on a rolling basis. Application fee: $60. Electronic applications accepted. *Expenses:* Contact institution. *Financial support:* Career-related internships or fieldwork, Federal Work-Study, and institutionally sponsored loans available. Support available to part-time students. Financial award application deadline: 1/15; financial award applicants required to submit FAFSA. *Unit head:* Rashida Ng, Chair, 215-204-8813, Fax: 215-204-5481, E-mail: architecture@temple.edu. *Application contact:* Tamryn McDermott, Director of Admissions, 215-777-9090, E-mail: tylerart@temple.edu.
Website: https://tyler.temple.edu/programs/architecture

Texas A&M University, College of Architecture, Department of Architecture, College Station, TX 77843. Offers architecture (M Arch, MS, PhD). *Faculty:* 41. *Students:* 166 full-time (95 women), 13 part-time (4 women); includes 27 minority (2 Black or African American, non-Hispanic/Latino; 5 Asian, non-Hispanic/Latino; 19

SCI-ARc

Los Angeles

Master of Architecture — M.Arch

MS in Architectural Technologies

MS in Design Theory and Pedagogy

MS in Design of Cities

MA in Fiction and Entertainment

sciarc.edu

Hispanic/Latino; 1 Two or more races, non-Hispanic/Latino), 92 international. Average age 29. 200 applicants, 69% accepted, 56 enrolled. In 2017, 38 master's, 10 doctorates awarded. *Degree requirements:* For master's, comprehensive exam, thesis; for doctorate, comprehensive exam, thesis/dissertation. *Entrance requirements:* For master's, GRE General Test, portfolio, letters of recommendation; for doctorate, GRE General Test. Additional exam requirements/recommendations for international students: Required—TOEFL (minimum score 550 paper-based; 80 iBT), IELTS (minimum score 6), PTE (minimum score 53). *Application deadline:* For fall admission, 12/15 priority date for domestic and international students. Applications are processed on a rolling basis. Application fee: $50 ($90 for international students). Electronic applications accepted. *Expenses:* Contact institution. *Financial support:* In 2017–18, 119 students received support, including 3 fellowships with tuition reimbursements available (averaging $17,837 per year), 36 research assistantships with tuition reimbursements available (averaging $6,240 per year), 59 teaching assistantships with tuition reimbursements available (averaging $6,503 per year); career-related internships or fieldwork, institutionally sponsored loans, scholarships/grants, traineeships, health care benefits, tuition waivers (full and partial), and unspecified assistantships also available. Support available to part-time students. Financial award application deadline: 3/15; financial award applicants required to submit FAFSA. *Faculty research:* Energy optimization, architecture pedagogy, environment and behavior. *Unit head:* Dr. Ward Wells, Head, 979-845-1015, Fax: 979-862-1571, E-mail: ward-wells@tamu.edu. *Application contact:* Graduate Admissions, 979-845-1060, E-mail: graduate-admissions@tamu.edu.
Website: http://dept.arch.tamu.edu/

Texas Tech University, Graduate School, College of Architecture, Lubbock, TX 79409. Offers architecture (M Arch, MS); land-use planning, management, and design (PhD); MBA/M Arch. *Program availability:* Part-time. *Faculty:* 32 full-time (8 women), 15 part-time/adjunct (3 women). *Students:* 62 full-time (19 women), 26 part-time (10 women); includes 33 minority (4 Black or African American, non-Hispanic/Latino; 29 Hispanic/Latino), 19 international. Average age 27. 55 applicants, 56% accepted, 15 enrolled. In 2017, 56 master's awarded. *Degree requirements:* For master's, comprehensive exam (for some programs), thesis (for some programs); for doctorate, comprehensive exam, thesis/dissertation. *Entrance requirements:* For master's, GRE General Test, portfolio; for doctorate, GRE General Test. Additional exam requirements/recommendations for international students: Required—TOEFL (minimum score 550 paper-based; 79 iBT). *Application deadline:* For fall admission, 6/1 priority date for domestic students, 1/15 priority date for international students; for spring admission, 9/1 priority date for domestic students, 6/15 priority date for international students. Applications are processed on a rolling basis. Application fee: $60. Electronic applications accepted. *Expenses:* Contact institution. *Financial support:* In 2017–18, 69 students received support, including 69 fellowships (averaging $4,740 per year); research assistantships, teaching assistantships, career-related internships or fieldwork, Federal Work-Study, institutionally sponsored loans, scholarships/grants, traineeships, health care benefits, and unspecified assistantships also available. Support available to part-time students. Financial award application deadline: 2/1; financial award applicants required to submit FAFSA. *Faculty research:* Architectural design, digital design and fabrication, community development and urban design, health care and design, historic preservation. *Total annual research expenditures:* $43,633. *Unit head:* Prof. James Williamson, Dean, 806-742-3136, Fax: 806-742-1400, E-mail: james.p.williamson@ttu.edu. *Application contact:* Jeff Rammage, Graduate Advisor, 806-742-3169, Fax: 806-742-1400, E-mail: jeffrey.rammage@ttu.edu.
Website: http://www.arch.ttu.edu/architecture/

Thomas Jefferson University, College of Architecture and the Built Environment, Program in Architecture, Philadelphia, PA 19107. Offers M Arch, MS. *Entrance requirements:* For master's, bachelor's degree, official undergraduate transcripts, current resume, two letters of recommendation, portfolio of relevant work, personal essay describing intended research.

Tulane University, School of Architecture, New Orleans, LA 70118-5669. Offers M Arch, M Arch II, MPS, MSRED. *Program availability:* Part-time. *Degree requirements:* For master's, thesis. *Entrance requirements:* For master's, GRE, portfolio. Additional exam requirements/recommendations for international students: Required—TOEFL. *Expenses:* Contact institution. *Faculty research:* Design topics, preservation and environmental conservation, architecture and human health, computing.

Universidad Autonoma de Guadalajara, Graduate Programs, Guadalajara, Mexico. Offers administrative law and justice (LL M); advertising and corporate communications (MA); architecture (M Arch); business (MBA); computational science (MCC); education (Ed M, Ed D); English-Spanish translation (MA); entrepreneurship and management (MBA); integrated management of digital animation (MA); international business (MIB); international corporate law (LL M); internet technologies (MS); manufacturing systems (MMS); occupational health (MS); philosophy (MA, PhD); power electronics (MS); quality systems (MQS); renewable energy (MS); social evaluation of projects (MBA); strategic market research (MBA); tax law (MA); teaching mathematics (MA).

Universidad Nacional Pedro Henriquez Urena, Graduate School, Santo Domingo, Dominican Republic. Offers agricultural diversity (MS), including horticultural/fruit production, tropical animal production; conservation of monuments and cultural assets (M Arch); ecology and environment (MS); environmental engineering (MEE); international relations (MA); natural resource management (MS); political science (MA); project optimization (MPM); project feasibility (MPM); project management (MPM); sanitation engineering (ME); science for teachers (MS); tropical Caribbean architecture (M Arch).

Université Laval, Faculty of Architecture, Planning and Visual Arts, School of Architecture, Program in Architecture, Québec, QC G1K 7P4, Canada. Offers M Arch, M Sc. *Program availability:* Part-time. *Degree requirements:* For master's, thesis (for some programs). *Entrance requirements:* For master's, mastery of software (CAO), knowledge of French and English. Electronic applications accepted.

University at Buffalo, the State University of New York, Graduate School, School of Architecture and Planning, Department of Architecture, Buffalo, NY 14260. Offers architecture (M Arch); ecological practices (MS Arch); M Arch/MBA; M Arch/MFA; M Arch/MUP. *Program availability:* Part-time. *Faculty:* 34 full-time (11 women), 11 part-time/adjunct (5 women). *Students:* 104 full-time (46 women), 10 part-time (4 women); includes 26 minority (12 Black or African American, non-Hispanic/Latino; 3 Asian, non-Hispanic/Latino; 8 Hispanic/Latino; 3 Two or more races, non-Hispanic/Latino), 21 international. Average age 25. 215 applicants, 27% accepted, 32 enrolled. In 2017, 61 master's awarded. *Degree requirements:* For master's, thesis or alternative, project, portfolio. *Entrance requirements:* For master's, GRE, portfolio, three letters of recommendation, transcripts, personal statement. Additional exam requirements/recommendations for international students: Required—TOEFL (minimum score 79 iBT), IELTS (minimum score 6.5). *Application deadline:* For fall admission, 1/1 priority date for domestic and international students. Application fee: $75. Electronic applications accepted. *Expenses:* $16,292 (for M Arch); $13,382 (for MS). *Financial support:* In 2017–18, 75 students received support, including 6 fellowships with full tuition reimbursements available (averaging $15,000 per year), 2 research

assistantships with partial tuition reimbursements available (averaging $14,967 per year), 43 teaching assistantships with partial tuition reimbursements available (averaging $4,900 per year); career-related internships or fieldwork, Federal Work-Study, scholarships/grants, health care benefits, and unspecified assistantships also available. Financial award application deadline: 3/1; financial award applicants required to submit FAFSA. *Faculty research:* Ecological practices, inclusive design, material culture, situated technologies, urban design. *Total annual research expenditures:* $2.5 million. *Unit head:* Prof. Omar Khan, Chair, 716-829-3486, Fax: 716-829-3256, E-mail: omar.khan@buffalo.edu. *Application contact:* Debra Eggebrecht, Assistant to the Chair, 716-829-3486, Fax: 716-829-3256, E-mail: dle2@buffalo.edu.
Website: http://www.ap.buffalo.edu/architecture/

The University of Arizona, College of Architecture, Planning, and Landscape Architecture, School of Architecture, Tucson, AZ 85721. Offers M Arch, MS. *Entrance requirements:* For master's, GRE, 3 letters of recommendation, statement of purpose, portfolio, resume. Additional exam requirements/recommendations for international students: Required—TOEFL (minimum score 550 paper-based; 79 iBT). Electronic applications accepted.

The University of British Columbia, Faculty of Applied Science, School of Architecture and Landscape Architecture, Vancouver, BC V6T 1Z2, Canada. Offers architecture (M Arch, MASA); landscape architecture (MASLA, MLA, MUD), including advanced studies in landscape architecture (MASLA), landscape architecture (MLA), urban design (MUD); M Arch/MLA. *Degree requirements:* For master's, thesis. *Entrance requirements:* For master's, portfolio, resume, statement of interest, 3 reference letters. Additional exam requirements/recommendations for international students: Required—TOEFL, IELTS. Electronic applications accepted. *Expenses:* Contact institution. *Faculty research:* Energy and resource use of buildings, advanced design research, urban design and community activism, advanced research in computer applications, cultural studies.

University of Calgary, Faculty of Graduate Studies, Faculty of Environmental Design, Calgary, AB T2N 1N4, Canada. Offers architecture (M Arch); environmental design (M Env Des, PhD); landscape architecture (MLA); planning (M Plan). *Degree requirements:* For master's, thesis; for doctorate, thesis/dissertation. *Entrance requirements:* For master's, minimum GPA of 3.0; for doctorate, minimum GPA of 3.5. Additional exam requirements/recommendations for international students: Required—TOEFL (minimum score 550 paper-based). *Faculty research:* Sustainable development in architecture, planning and product design, energy and environment, impact assessment, ecotourism.

University of California, Berkeley, Graduate Division, College of Environmental Design, Department of Architecture, Berkeley, CA 94720-1500. Offers architecture (M Arch); building science (MS, PhD); building structures, construction and materials (MS, PhD); design theories, methods, and practices (MS, PhD); environmental design in developing countries (MS, PhD); history of architecture and urbanism (MS, PhD); social and cultural processes in architecture and urbanism (MS, PhD); M Arch/MCP; M Arch/MS; MLA/M Arch. *Degree requirements:* For master's, thesis; for doctorate, thesis/dissertation, qualifying exam. *Entrance requirements:* For master's and doctorate, GRE General Test, minimum GPA of 3.0, 3 letters of recommendation. Additional exam requirements/recommendations for international students: Required—TOEFL (minimum score 570 paper-based; 90 iBT). Electronic applications accepted. Application fee is waived when completed online.

University of California, Los Angeles, Graduate Division, School of the Arts and Architecture, Department of Architecture and Urban Design, Los Angeles, CA 90095. Offers M Arch, MA, PhD. *Degree requirements:* For master's, comprehensive exam (M Arch I, II); thesis (MA); for doctorate, 2 foreign languages, thesis/dissertation, oral and written qualifying exams. *Entrance requirements:* For master's, GRE General Test, bachelor's degree; minimum undergraduate GPA of 3.0 (or its equivalent if letter grade system not used); writing sample (MA only); portfolio (M Arch only); for doctorate, GRE General Test, bachelor's degree; minimum undergraduate GPA of 3.5 (or its equivalent if letter grade system not used); writing sample. Additional exam requirements/recommendations for international students: Required—TOEFL. Electronic applications accepted. *Expenses:* Contact institution.

University of Cincinnati, Graduate School, College of Design, Architecture, Art, and Planning, School of Architecture and Interior Design, Cincinnati, OH 45221. Offers architecture (M Arch). *Accreditation:* NASAD. *Degree requirements:* For master's, one foreign language, thesis. *Entrance requirements:* Additional exam requirements/recommendations for international students: Required—TOEFL. *Expenses: Tuition, area resident:* Full-time $14,468. Tuition, state resident: full-time $14,968; part-time $754 per credit hour. Tuition, nonresident: full-time $24,210; part-time $1311 per credit hour. *International tuition:* $26,460 full-time. *Required fees:* $3958; $84 per credit hour. One-time fee: $85 full-time. Tuition and fees vary according to course load, degree level and program. *Faculty research:* Theory and history of architecture.

University of Colorado Denver, College of Architecture and Planning, Program in Architecture, Denver, CO 80217. Offers M Arch. *Program availability:* Part-time. *Degree requirements:* For master's, thesis optional. *Entrance requirements:* For master's, GRE, portfolio; sample of writing or work project; three letters of recommendation; statement of purpose. Additional exam requirements/recommendations for international students: Required—TOEFL (minimum score 75 iBT). Electronic applications accepted. *Expenses:* Contact institution. *Faculty research:* Architectural design; history, theory, and criticism of architecture; regional and environmental issues; sustainability; intervention and transformation in the urban and rural landscape.

University of Florida, Graduate School, College of Design, Construction and Planning, Doctoral Program in Design, Construction and Planning, Gainesville, FL 32611. Offers construction management (PhD); design, construction and planning (PhD); geographic information systems (PhD); historic preservation (PhD); interior design (PhD); landscape architecture (PhD); urban and regional planning (PhD). *Degree requirements:* For doctorate, thesis/dissertation. *Entrance requirements:* For doctorate, GRE General Test, minimum GPA of 3.0. Additional exam requirements/recommendations for international students: Required—TOEFL (minimum score 550 paper-based; 80 iBT), IELTS (minimum score 6). Electronic applications accepted. *Faculty research:* Architecture, building construction, urban and regional planning.

University of Florida, Graduate School, College of Design, Construction and Planning, School of Architecture, Gainesville, FL 32611. Offers architecture (M Arch, MSAS); historic preservation (M Arch, MSAS); sustainable architecture (M Arch, MSAS); sustainable design (M Arch, MSAS). *Program availability:* Online learning. *Entrance requirements:* For master's, GRE General Test, minimum GPA of 3.0. Additional exam requirements/recommendations for international students: Required—TOEFL (minimum score 550 paper-based; 80 iBT), IELTS (minimum score 6).

University of Hartford, College of Engineering, Technology and Architecture, Program in Architecture, West Hartford, CT 06117-1599. Offers M Arch. *Entrance requirements:* For master's, 3 letters of recommendation, portfolio. Additional exam requirements/recommendations for international students: Required—TOEFL (minimum score 550 paper-based).

University of Hawaii at Manoa, School of Architecture, Honolulu, HI 96822. Offers D Arch. *Program availability:* Part-time. *Entrance requirements:* Additional exam requirements/recommendations for international students: Required—TOEFL, IELTS. *Faculty research:* Housing, future cities, environmental studies, preservation, professional practice.

University of Houston, Gerald D. Hines College of Architecture and Design, Houston, TX 77204-4000. Offers architectural studies (MA); architecture (M Arch, MS), including media and fabrication (MS), sustainable design (MS), sustainable urban systems (MS), urban design (MS); industrial design (MS). *Faculty:* 15 full-time (4 women), 13 part-time/adjunct (3 women). *Students:* 92 full-time (40 women), 6 part-time (2 women); includes 23 minority (1 Black or African American, non-Hispanic/Latino; 1 American Indian or Alaska Native, non-Hispanic/Latino; 9 Asian, non-Hispanic/Latino; 9 Hispanic/Latino; 3 Two or more races, non-Hispanic/Latino), 20 international. Average age 28. 192 applicants, 45% accepted, 47 enrolled. In 2017, 21 master's awarded. *Degree requirements:* For master's, thesis (for some programs). *Entrance requirements:* For master's, GRE General Test, digital portfolio. Additional exam requirements/recommendations for international students: Required—TOEFL (minimum score 550 paper-based; 79 iBT), IELTS (minimum score 6.5). *Application deadline:* For fall admission, 2/1 priority date for domestic students, 2/1 for international students. Applications are processed on a rolling basis. Application fee: $50. Electronic applications accepted. *Expenses:* Contact institution. *Financial support:* In 2017–18, 15 students received support, including 2 research assistantships with partial tuition reimbursements available (averaging $7,720 per year), 11 teaching assistantships with partial tuition reimbursements available (averaging $5,264 per year); career-related internships or fieldwork, Federal Work-Study, institutionally sponsored loans, scholarships/grants, health care benefits, and unspecified assistantships also available. Support available to part-time students. Financial award application deadline: 2/1. *Faculty research:* Community-based design; twentieth-century architecture, urbanism, and design; extreme environments; design build; green building components; digital technology; preservation; industrial design; interior architecture. *Total annual research expenditures:* $150,000. *Unit head:* Patricia Belton Oliver, Dean, 713-743-2400, Fax: 713-743-2358, E-mail: poliver@central.uh.edu. *Application contact:* Trang Phan, Assistant Dean, 713-743-2400, Fax: 713-743-2358, E-mail: tphan@uh.edu.
Website: http://www.uh.edu/architecture/

University of Idaho, College of Graduate Studies, College of Art and Architecture, Moscow, ID 83844. Offers M Arch, MFA, MLA, MS. *Accreditation:* NASAD. *Faculty:* 20 full-time (7 women). *Students:* 67 full-time, 7 part-time. Average age 28. In 2017, 43 master's awarded. *Entrance requirements:* For master's, minimum GPA of 3.0. Additional exam requirements/recommendations for international students: Required—TOEFL (minimum score 79 iBT). *Application deadline:* For fall admission, 8/1 for domestic students; for spring admission, 12/15 for domestic students. Applications are processed on a rolling basis. Application fee: $60. Electronic applications accepted. *Expenses:* Tuition, state resident: full-time $6722; part-time $430 per credit hour. Tuition, nonresident: full-time $23,046; part-time $1337 per credit hour. *Required fees:* $2142; $63 per credit hour. *Financial support:* Applicants required to submit FAFSA. *Faculty research:* Sustainability in communities, urban research, virtual technology, bioregional planning, environment and behavior interaction. *Unit head:* Dr. Shauna Corry, Interim Dean, 208-885-4409, E-mail: caa@uidaho.edu. *Application contact:* Sean Scoggin, Graduate Recruitment Coordinator, 208-885-4001, Fax: 208-885-4406, E-mail: graduateadmissions@uidaho.edu.
Website: http://www.uidaho.edu/caa

University of Illinois at Chicago, College of Architecture, Design and the Arts, School of Architecture, Chicago, IL 60607-7128. Offers M Arch, MA, MS, MS Arch. *Entrance requirements:* For master's, GRE General Test, portfolio, minimum GPA of 3.0 in the last 60 hours of coursework, 3 letters of recommendation, statement of intent. Additional exam requirements/recommendations for international students: Required—TOEFL or IELTS. Electronic applications accepted. *Expenses:* Contact institution. *Faculty research:* Contemporary design, history and theory, technology, urbanism.

University of Illinois at Urbana–Champaign, Graduate College, College of Fine and Applied Arts, School of Architecture, Champaign, IL 61820. Offers architectural studies (MS); architecture (M Arch, PhD); M Arch/MBA; M Arch/MS; M Arch/MUP; MCS/M Arch.

The University of Kansas, Graduate Studies, School of Architecture and Design, Department of Architecture, Lawrence, KS 66045. Offers architectural acoustics (Certificate); architecture (M Arch, PhD); health and wellness (Certificate); historic preservation (Certificate); urban design (Certificate). *Students:* 91 full-time (43 women), 14 part-time (6 women); includes 14 minority (3 Black or African American, non-Hispanic/Latino; 4 Asian, non-Hispanic/Latino; 4 Hispanic/Latino; 3 Two or more races, non-Hispanic/Latino), 21 international. Average age 25. 100 applicants, 52% accepted, 20 enrolled. In 2017, 77 master's, 7 doctorates, 5 other advanced degrees awarded. Terminal master's awarded for partial completion of doctoral program. *Entrance requirements:* For master's, GRE, transcript; resume; minimum GPA of 3.0; statement of purpose; letters of recommendation; portfolio of design work, or samples of written work or other creative artifacts produced if previous degree was not in a design-related discipline; for doctorate, GRE, transcript, resume, minimum GPA of 3.0, statement of purpose, letters of recommendation, research-informed writing sample, exhibit of work illustrating applicant's interests and abilities in areas related to the design disciplines. Additional exam requirements/recommendations for international students: Required—TOEFL, IELTS. *Application deadline:* For fall admission, 1/15 priority date for domestic and international students; for summer admission, 1/15 priority date for domestic and international students. Application fee: $65 ($85 for international students). Electronic applications accepted. *Financial support:* Fellowships, research assistantships, teaching assistantships, scholarships/grants, health care benefits, and unspecified assistantships available. Financial award application deadline: 1/15; financial award applicants required to submit FAFSA. *Faculty research:* Design build, sustainability, emergent technology, healthy places, urban design. *Unit head:* Prof. Jae Chang, Chair, 785-864-1446, E-mail: jdchang@ku.edu. *Application contact:* Gera Elliott, Admissions Coordinator, 785-864-3167, Fax: 785-864-5185, E-mail: archku@ku.edu.
Website: http://architecture.ku.edu/

University of Kentucky, Graduate School, College of Design, School of Architecture, Lexington, KY 40506-0032. Offers M Arch. *Degree requirements:* For master's, comprehensive exam. *Entrance requirements:* For master's, GRE General Test, minimum undergraduate GPA of 2.75. Additional exam requirements/recommendations for international students: Required—TOEFL (minimum score 550 paper-based). Electronic applications accepted.

The University of Manchester, School of Environment and Development, Manchester, United Kingdom. Offers architecture (M Phil, PhD); development policy and management (M Phil, PhD); human geography (M Phil, PhD); physical geography (M Phil, PhD); planning and landscape (M Phil, PhD).

University of Manitoba, Faculty of Graduate Studies, Faculty of Architecture, Department of Architecture, Winnipeg, MB R3T 2N2, Canada. Offers M Arch. *Degree requirements:* For master's, thesis or alternative.

University of Maryland, College Park, Academic Affairs, School of Architecture, Planning and Preservation, Program in Architecture, College Park, MD 20742. Offers M Arch, M Arch/MCP. *Program availability:* Part-time, evening/weekend. *Entrance requirements:* For master's, GRE General Test, portfolio, minimum GPA of 3.0, letters of recommendation. Additional exam requirements/recommendations for international students: Required—TOEFL. Electronic applications accepted. *Faculty research:* Design, history, theory.

University of Massachusetts Amherst, Graduate School, College of Humanities and Fine Arts, Department of Architecture, Amherst, MA 01003. Offers architecture (M Arch); design (MS); design in historic preservation (MS). *Program availability:* Part-time. *Degree requirements:* For master's, thesis or alternative, project. *Entrance requirements:* For master's, GRE General Test (for M Arch only), 3 letters of recommendation (M Arch only); portfolio. Additional exam requirements/ recommendations for international students: Required—TOEFL (minimum score 550 paper-based; 80 iBT), IELTS (minimum score 6.5). Electronic applications accepted.

University of Memphis, Graduate School, College of Communication and Fine Arts, Department of Architecture, Memphis, TN 38152. Offers M Arch. *Program availability:* Part-time. *Faculty:* 5 full-time (3 women), 2 part-time/adjunct (both women). *Students:* 12 full-time (6 women); includes 4 minority (1 Black or African American, non-Hispanic/Latino; 1 Asian, non-Hispanic/Latino; 2 Hispanic/Latino), 2 international. Average age 29. 6 applicants, 100% accepted, 4 enrolled. In 2017, 5 master's awarded. *Degree requirements:* For master's, thesis or alternative. *Entrance requirements:* For master's, portfolio; letters of recommendation; statement of intent; pre-professional undergraduate degree in architecture, environmental design, or equivalent. Additional exam requirements/recommendations for international students: Required—TOEFL (minimum score 550 paper-based; 79 iBT). *Application deadline:* For fall admission, 3/15 for domestic students. Application fee: $35 ($60 for international students). Electronic applications accepted. *Expenses:* Contact institution. *Financial support:* In 2017–18, 7 students received support, including 7 research assistantships with full tuition reimbursements available (averaging $10,142 per year); teaching assistantships with full tuition reimbursements available, Federal Work-Study, scholarships/grants, and unspecified assistantships also available. Financial award application deadline: 2/1; financial award applicants required to submit FAFSA. *Unit head:* Michael D. Hagge, Chair, 901-678-2724, Fax: 901-678-1755, E-mail: mdhagge@memphis.edu. *Application contact:* Sherry Brian, Director of Graduate Studies, 901-678-3302, Fax: 901-678-1755. Website: http://architecture.memphis.edu

University of Miami, Graduate School, School of Architecture, Professional Program in Architecture, Coral Gables, FL 33124. Offers M Arch. *Entrance requirements:* For master's, GRE General Test, minimum GPA of 3.0, portfolio. Additional exam requirements/recommendations for international students: Required— TOEFL. Electronic applications accepted. *Faculty research:* Urbanism, landscape architecture.

University of Michigan, Taubman College of Architecture and Urban Planning, Master of Architecture Program, Ann Arbor, MI 48109. Offers M Arch, M Arch/M Eng, M Arch/MSE, M Arch/MUD, MBA/M Arch. *Degree requirements:* For master's, thesis or alternative, thesis studio. *Entrance requirements:* Additional exam requirements/ recommendations for international students: Required—TOEFL (minimum score 100 iBT), GRE. Electronic applications accepted. *Expenses:* Contact institution.

University of Michigan, Taubman College of Architecture and Urban Planning, Master of Science in Architecture Design and Research Program, Ann Arbor, MI 48109. Offers design and health (MS); digital technologies (MS); material systems (MS). *Degree requirements:* For master's, thesis or alternative, capstone studio. *Entrance requirements:* Additional exam requirements/recommendations for international students: Required—TOEFL (minimum score 83 iBT), GRE. Electronic applications accepted. *Expenses:* Contact institution.

University of Minnesota, Twin Cities Campus, Graduate School, College of Design, School of Architecture, Minneapolis, MN 55455-0213. Offers architecture (M Arch); sustainable design (MS). First professional and post-professional tracks available in M Arch program. *Degree requirements:* For master's, thesis (for some programs). *Entrance requirements:* For master's, GRE General Test, suggested GPA of 3.0, portfolio. Additional exam requirements/recommendations for international students: Required—TOEFL (minimum score 550 paper-based; 79 iBT). *Expenses:* Contact institution. *Faculty research:* History, daylighting, computer-aided design, sustainable design, structures.

University of Missouri, Office of Research and Graduate Studies, College of Human Environmental Sciences, Department of Architectural Studies, Columbia, MO 65211. Offers M Arch, PhD. *Entrance requirements:* For master's, GRE General Test, minimum GPA of 3.0. Additional exam requirements/recommendations for international students: Required—TOEFL (minimum score 500 paper-based; 61 iBT). Electronic applications accepted.

University of Nebraska–Lincoln, Graduate College, College of Architecture, Department of Architecture, Graduate Program in Architecture, Lincoln, NE 68588. Offers MS, PhD. *Degree requirements:* For master's, comprehensive exam, thesis. *Entrance requirements:* For master's, GRE General Test. Additional exam requirements/ recommendations for international students: Required—TOEFL (minimum score 550 paper-based). Electronic applications accepted. *Faculty research:* Housing, environmental design, architectural history, sustainable design, rural architecture.

University of Nebraska–Lincoln, Graduate College, College of Architecture, Department of Architecture, Professional Program in Architecture, Lincoln, NE 68588. Offers M Arch, M Arch/MBA, M Arch/MCRP. *Entrance requirements:* For master's, GRE General Test. Additional exam requirements/recommendations for international students: Required—TOEFL. *Faculty research:* Housing, environmental design, architectural history, sustainable design, rural architecture.

University of Nevada, Las Vegas, Graduate College, College of Fine Arts, School of Architecture, Las Vegas, NV 89154. Offers architecture (M Arch); healthcare interior design (MHID); hospitality design (Certificate). *Program availability:* Part-time. *Faculty:* 9 full-time (3 women), 7 part-time/adjunct (0 women). *Students:* 34 full-time (19 women), 9 part-time (4 women); includes 26 minority (9 Asian, non-Hispanic/Latino; 14 Hispanic/Latino; 1 Native Hawaiian or other Pacific Islander, non-Hispanic/Latino; 2 Two or more races, non-Hispanic/Latino), 5 international. Average age 30. 31 applicants, 81% accepted, 15 enrolled. In 2017, 19 master's, 4 Certificates awarded. *Degree requirements:* For master's, thesis (for some programs), professional project; for Certificate, defense of design/research presentation. *Entrance requirements:* For master's, GRE General Test, design portfolio; writing sample; bachelor's degree with minimum GPA of 3.0; for Certificate, portfolio of original work. Additional exam requirements/recommendations for international students: Required—TOEFL (minimum score 550 paper-based; 80 iBT), IELTS (minimum score 7). *Application deadline:* For fall admission, 1/15 for domestic students. Application fee: $60 ($95 for international students). Electronic applications accepted. *Expenses:* $275 per credit, $850 per course, $7,969 per year resident, $22,157 per year non-resident, $7,094 non-resident fee (7 credits or more), $1,307 annual health insurance fee. *Financial support:* In 2017–18, 14 students received support, including 1 research assistantship with full tuition

reimbursement available (averaging $14,333 per year), 13 teaching assistantships with full tuition reimbursements available (averaging $15,000 per year); institutionally sponsored loans, scholarships/grants, health care benefits, and unspecified assistantships also available. Financial award application deadline: 3/15; financial award applicants required to submit FAFSA. *Faculty research:* Hospitality design, urban studies/design, building science and sustainability, healthcare design, design for aging populations, educational design. *Total annual research expenditures:* $101,994. *Unit head:* Dr. Alfredo Fernandez-Gonzalez, Director/Professor, 702-895-1141, Fax: 702-895-1119, E-mail: alfredo.fernandez@unlv.edu. *Application contact:* Dr. Glenn Nowak, Graduate Coordinator, 702-895-1076, Fax: 702-895-1119, E-mail: glenn.nowak@unlv.edu.
Website: http://architecture.unlv.edu/

University of New Mexico, Graduate Studies, College of Fine Arts, Program in Art History, Albuquerque, NM 87131. Offers art history (MA); art of the Americas (MA); history of architecture (PhD); history of graphic arts (PhD); history of photography (PhD); modern Latin American art (PhD); Native American art (PhD); Pre-Columbian art and architecture (PhD); Spanish colonial art (PhD). *Program availability:* Part-time. *Faculty:* 7 full-time (5 women). *Students:* 7 full-time (all women), 18 part-time (15 women); includes 8 minority (2 American Indian or Alaska Native, non-Hispanic/Latino; 5 Hispanic/Latino; 1 Two or more races, non-Hispanic/Latino), 2 international. Average age 41. 21 applicants, 33% accepted, 5 enrolled. In 2017, 5 master's, 1 doctorate awarded. *Degree requirements:* For master's, one foreign language, comprehensive exam (for some programs), thesis, symposium; for doctorate, 2 foreign languages, comprehensive exam, thesis/dissertation, symposium. *Entrance requirements:* Additional exam requirements/recommendations for international students: Required—TOEFL (minimum score 550 paper-based), IELTS (minimum score 6). *Application deadline:* For fall admission, 1/15 for domestic students; for spring admission, 1/15 for domestic students. Application fee: $50. Electronic applications accepted. *Financial support:* Fellowships, research assistantships, teaching assistantships with partial tuition reimbursements, Federal Work-Study, institutionally sponsored loans, scholarships/grants, health care benefits, and unspecified assistantships available. Support available to part-time students. Financial award application deadline: 3/1; financial award applicants required to submit FAFSA. *Faculty research:* Native American, modern Latin American, pre-Columbian, architectural, American, medieval, Spanish Colonial, and Latin American art; history of photography. *Unit head:* Prof. Mary Tsiongas, Chair, 505-277-5861, Fax: 505-277-5955, E-mail: tsiongas@unm.edu. *Application contact:* Kat Heatherington, Graduate Advisor, 505-277-6672, Fax: 505-277-5955, E-mail: art255@unm.edu.
Website: http://art.unm.edu/

University of New Mexico, Graduate Studies, School of Architecture and Planning, Program in Architecture, Albuquerque, NM 87131-2039. Offers M Arch. *Faculty:* 22 full-time (9 women), 9 part-time/adjunct (3 women). *Students:* 109 full-time (48 women), 8 part-time (5 women); includes 41 minority (1 Black or African American, non-Hispanic/ Latino; 2 American Indian or Alaska Native, non-Hispanic/Latino; 3 Asian, non-Hispanic/ Latino; 31 Hispanic/Latino; 4 Two or more races, non-Hispanic/Latino), 32 international. Average age 30. 111 applicants, 46% accepted, 51 enrolled. In 2017, 30 master's awarded. *Degree requirements:* For master's, thesis (for some programs). *Entrance requirements:* For master's, experience in field. Additional exam requirements/ recommendations for international students: Required—TOEFL (minimum score 550 paper-based; 79 iBT). *Application deadline:* For fall admission, 2/1 priority date for domestic students. Application fee: $50. Electronic applications accepted. *Financial support:* Fellowships, research assistantships with partial tuition reimbursements, scholarships/grants, health care benefits, and unspecified assistantships available. Financial award application deadline: 3/1; financial award applicants required to submit FAFSA. *Faculty research:* Professional practice, design theory, sustainable environments, architecture and children, environment and behavior. *Unit head:* Geraldine Forbes Isais, Director, 505-277-3303, Fax: 505-277-0076, E-mail: gforbes@unm.edu. *Application contact:* Elizabeth M. Rowe, Senior Academic Advisor, 505-277-1303, Fax: 505-277-0076, E-mail: mitziv@unm.edu.
Website: http://saap.unm.edu/

The University of North Carolina at Charlotte, College of Arts and Architecture, School of Architecture, Charlotte, NC 28223-0001. Offers architecture (M Arch I, M Arch II, MS); urban design (MUD). *Faculty:* 26 full-time (9 women). *Students:* 81 full-time (45 women), 2 part-time (both women); includes 16 minority (10 Black or African American, non-Hispanic/Latino; 5 Hispanic/Latino; 1 Two or more races, non-Hispanic/Latino), 27 international. Average age 25. 120 applicants, 86% accepted, 33 enrolled. In 2017, 55 master's awarded. *Degree requirements:* For master's, design studio or thesis. *Entrance requirements:* For master's, GRE, official transcripts from all previous college-level institution(s); statement of purpose explaining reasons for wanting to study in the School of Architecture; three recommendations from persons familiar with the applicant's personal and professional qualifications; resume or curriculum vitae; portfolio. Additional exam requirements/recommendations for international students: Required—TOEFL (minimum score 523 paper-based, 70 iBT) or IELTS (6.5). *Application deadline:* For fall admission, 1/15 priority date for domestic and international students. Applications are processed on a rolling basis. Application fee: $75. Electronic applications accepted. *Expenses:* Contact institution. *Financial support:* In 2017–18, 33 students received support, including 30 research assistantships (averaging $6,644 per year), 2 teaching assistantships (averaging $5,000 per year); institutionally sponsored loans, scholarships/grants, unspecified assistantships, and administrative assistantship also available. Financial award application deadline: 3/1; financial award applicants required to submit FAFSA. *Faculty research:* Urban design studies for local and regional municipalities and community groups, high performance building and optimization protocols, daylighting and energy analysis, digital design and fabrication components, and interactive visualization; refinement of regionally specific computer-aided analysis tools used to evaluate total building energy performance, and the economic valuation of architectural systems and their design attributes. *Total annual research expenditures:* $35,526. *Unit head:* Kenneth A. Lambla, Dean, 704-687-0090, E-mail: kalambla@uncc.edu. *Application contact:* Kathy B. Giddings, Director of Graduate Admissions, 704-687-5503, Fax: 704-687-1668, E-mail: gradadm@uncc.edu.
Website: http://coaa.uncc.edu/academics/school-of-architecture

The University of North Carolina at Greensboro, Graduate School, College of Arts and Sciences, Department of Interior Architecture, Greensboro, NC 27412-5001. Offers historic preservation (Certificate); interior architecture (MS); museum studies (Certificate). *Degree requirements:* For master's, thesis. *Entrance requirements:* For master's, GRE General Test or MAT, bachelor's degree in interior design, interview, portfolio. Additional exam requirements/recommendations for international students: Required—TOEFL. Electronic applications accepted.

University of Notre Dame, Graduate School, School of Architecture, Notre Dame, IN 46556. Offers architectural design and urbanism (M ADU); architecture (M Arch). *Degree requirements:* For master's, thesis or alternative. *Entrance requirements:* For master's, GRE General Test, portfolio. Additional exam requirements/recommendations for international students: Required—TOEFL (minimum score 600 paper-based; 80 iBT). Electronic applications accepted. *Faculty research:* Architectural theory, urban design, classical and traditional architecture and urbanism.

University of Oklahoma, Christopher C. Gibbs College of Architecture, Division of Architecture, Norman, OK 73019. Offers architecture (MS); data and digital representation (M Arch); design entrepreneurship and real estate (M Arch); planning, design and construction (PhD); resilient planning, design, and construction (M Arch). *Program availability:* Part-time. *Faculty:* 32 full-time (12 women), 2 part-time/adjunct (0 women). *Students:* 33 full-time (22 women), 9 part-time (2 women); includes 6 minority (2 Black or African American, non-Hispanic/Latino; 1 American Indian or Alaska Native, non-Hispanic/Latino; 1 Hispanic/Latino; 2 Two or more races, non-Hispanic/Latino), 13 international. Average age 29. 25 applicants, 72% accepted, 11 enrolled. In 2017, 7 master's awarded. Terminal master's awarded for partial completion of doctoral program. *Degree requirements:* For master's, variable foreign language requirement; for doctorate, variable foreign language requirement, comprehensive exam, thesis/dissertation. *Entrance requirements:* Additional exam requirements/recommendations for international students: Required—TOEFL (minimum score 79 iBT) or IELTS (minimum score 6.5). *Application deadline:* For spring admission, 5/1 for domestic students, 3/1 for international students. Applications are processed on a rolling basis. Application fee: $50 ($100 for international students). Electronic applications accepted. *Expenses:* Tuition, state resident: full-time $5119; part-time $213.30 per credit hour. Tuition, nonresident: full-time $19,778; part-time $824.10 per credit hour. *Required fees:* $3458; $133.55 per credit hour. $126.50 per semester. *Financial support:* In 2017–18, 34 students received support, including 17 research assistantships with partial tuition reimbursements available (averaging $12,585 per year), 1 teaching assistantship with partial tuition reimbursement available (averaging $10,372 per year); career-related internships or fieldwork, scholarships/grants, health care benefits, tuition waivers, and unspecified assistantships also available. Financial award application deadline: 6/1; financial award applicants required to submit FAFSA. *Faculty research:* Resiliency and sustainability; data and digital representation; design entrepreneurship and real estate. *Unit head:* Dr. Stephanie Pilat, Director, 405-325-9352, Fax: 405-325-7588, E-mail: architecture.director@ou.edu. *Application contact:* Marjorie Callahan, Graduate Liaison, Fax: 405-325-7588, E-mail: mcallahan@ou.edu.
Website: http://arch.coa.ou.edu

University of Oregon, Graduate School, College of Design, Department of Architecture, Eugene, OR 97403. Offers architecture (M Arch); interior architecture (MI Arch). *Accreditation:* CIDA. *Degree requirements:* For master's, thesis (for some programs). *Entrance requirements:* For master's, GRE General Test. Additional exam requirements/recommendations for international students: Required—TOEFL. *Faculty research:* Innovation in housing design and design production, climate responsive design, passive heating and cooling, computer software development for design applications, vernacular architecture.

University of Pennsylvania, School of Design, Department of Architecture, Philadelphia, PA 19104. Offers architecture (M Arch, PhD); ecological architecture (Certificate); environmental building design (MEBD). *Program availability:* Part-time. *Faculty:* 13 full-time (4 women), 12 part-time/adjunct (3 women). *Students:* 375 full-time (208 women), 3 part-time (1 woman); includes 48 minority (6 Black or African American, non-Hispanic/Latino; 25 Asian, non-Hispanic/Latino; 13 Hispanic/Latino; 4 Two or more races, non-Hispanic/Latino), 249 international. Average age 26. 876 applicants, 49% accepted, 184 enrolled. In 2017, 132 master's, 4 doctorates, 31 other advanced degrees awarded.

University of Puerto Rico–Río Piedras, School of Architecture, San Juan, PR 00931-3300. Offers M Arch. *Program availability:* Part-time. *Degree requirements:* For master's, comprehensive exam, thesis, design project. *Entrance requirements:* For master's, PAEG or GRE, bachelor's degree in architecture, interview, minimum GPA of 3.0, portfolio, 2 letters of recommendation.

University of Southern California, Graduate School, School of Architecture, Los Angeles, CA 90089. Offers M Arch, MBS, MHP, MLA, PhD, M Arch/M Pl, MLA/M Pl. Terminal master's awarded for partial completion of doctoral program. *Degree requirements:* For master's, thesis (for some programs); for doctorate, thesis/dissertation. *Entrance requirements:* For master's and doctorate, GRE. Additional exam requirements/recommendations for international students: Required—TOEFL (minimum score 100 iBT). Electronic applications accepted. *Faculty research:* Urban housing; advanced digital simulation, computation, and representation; building skins; parametric design; advanced seismic research.

University of South Florida, College of The Arts, School of Architecture and Community Design, Tampa, FL 33620-9951. Offers architecture (M Arch); urban and community design (MUCD). *Faculty:* 10 full-time (1 woman). *Students:* 92 full-time (40 women), 18 part-time (5 women); includes 38 minority (6 Black or African American, non-Hispanic/Latino; 7 Asian, non-Hispanic/Latino; 22 Hispanic/Latino; 3 Two or more races, non-Hispanic/Latino), 23 international. Average age 26. 61 applicants, 44% accepted, 22 enrolled. In 2017, 48 master's awarded. *Degree requirements:* For master's, comprehensive exam, thesis. *Entrance requirements:* For master's, GRE General Test, minimum undergraduate GPA of 3.0 in last 60 hours of coursework; three letters of recommendation; portfolio or creative work; written statement of intent; prerequisite courses in physics, calculus, and AutoCAD. Additional exam requirements/recommendations for international students: Required—TOEFL (minimum score 550 paper-based; 79 iBT) or IELTS (minimum score 6.5). *Application deadline:* For fall admission, 2/1 priority date for domestic students, 2/1 for international students. Applications are processed on a rolling basis. Application fee: $30. Electronic applications accepted. *Financial support:* In 2017–18, 34 students received support, including 3 teaching assistantships with tuition reimbursements available (averaging $9,360 per year); Federal Work-Study, scholarships/grants, and unspecified assistantships also available. *Faculty research:* Urban community design and planning; public space infrastructure; conditions of suburban sprawl; redevelopment strategies for abandoned commercial centers and edges; sustainability; influences of technology, cultural identity and interpretation and social values on architectural design; epistemology of design thinking; tropical architecture; high-density urbanism; design benevolence; economic development/community revitalization; housing/residential development; development regulations. *Total annual research expenditures:* $187,157. *Unit head:* Dr. Robert MacLeod, Director and Professor, School of Architecture and Community Design, 813-974-6015, Fax: 813-974-2557, E-mail: rmacleod@arch.usf.edu. *Application contact:* Mildred Abreu, Academic Advisor, 813-974-1216, Fax: 813-974-2557, E-mail: abreu@arch.usf.edu.
Website: http://www.arch.usf.edu/

The University of Tennessee, Graduate School, College of Architecture and Design, Program in Architecture, Knoxville, TN 37996. Offers architecture (professional) (M Arch); architecture (research) (M Arch). *Degree requirements:* For master's, thesis. *Entrance requirements:* For master's, GRE General Test, minimum GPA of 3.0, 3 letters of recommendation, samples of portfolio work (highly recommended for professional track). Additional exam requirements/recommendations for international students: Required—TOEFL (minimum score 550 paper-based).

The University of Texas at Arlington, Graduate School, College of Architecture, Planning and Public Affairs, Program in Architecture, Arlington, TX 76019. Offers M Arch. *Degree requirements:* For master's, thesis. *Entrance requirements:* For master's, GRE General Test, minimum GPA of 3.0, portfolio (for those with previous design degrees). Additional exam requirements/recommendations for international students: Required—TOEFL (minimum score 575 paper-based; 91 iBT). *Faculty research:* Regional landscapes/native materials, urban densification, urban design, sustainable design principles.

The University of Texas at Austin, Graduate School, School of Architecture, Program in Architecture, Austin, TX 78712-1111. Offers M Arch, MSAS. *Entrance requirements:* For master's, GRE, transcripts, portfolio, statement of interest, references.

The University of Texas at San Antonio, College of Architecture, Construction and Planning, Department of Architecture, San Antonio, TX 78249-0617. Offers M Arch, MS Arch. *Program availability:* Part-time. *Faculty:* 17 full-time (5 women), 4 part-time/adjunct (0 women). *Students:* 82 full-time (39 women), 15 part-time (6 women); includes 63 minority (2 Black or African American, non-Hispanic/Latino; 4 Asian, non-Hispanic/Latino; 57 Hispanic/Latino), 13 international. Average age 28. 54 applicants, 85% accepted, 30 enrolled. In 2017, 25 master's awarded. *Degree requirements:* For master's, comprehensive exam (for some programs), thesis optional. *Entrance requirements:* For master's, GRE General Test, bachelor's degree with 18 credit hours in field of study or in another appropriate field of study, 2 letters of recommendation, statement of purpose. Additional exam requirements/recommendations for international students: Required—TOEFL (minimum score 550 paper-based; 79 iBT), IELTS (minimum score 6.5). *Application deadline:* For fall admission, 6/15 for domestic students, 3/1 for international students. Application fee: $50 ($90 for international students). Electronic applications accepted. *Expenses:* Tuition, state resident: full-time $5495. Tuition, nonresident: full-time $21,938. *Required fees:* $1915. Tuition and fees vary according to program. *Financial support:* In 2017–18, research assistantships (averaging $3,500 per year) were awarded; teaching assistantships and tuition waivers (partial) also available. Financial award applicants required to submit FAFSA. *Faculty research:* Building energy performance and sustainability, architectural and heritage tourism, regionalism and architectural theory, Mexican and Latin American architecture, Medieval and Renaissance architecture, historic preservation and conservation, urban and regional planning, materials. *Total annual research expenditures:* $130,876. *Unit head:* Dr. Sedef Doganer, Chair, 210-458-3037, E-mail: sedef.doganer@utsa.edu.
Website: http://architecture.utsa.edu/academic-programs/department-of-architecture/

University of the District of Columbia, College of Agriculture, Urban Sustainability and Environmental Sciences, Program in Architecture, Washington, DC 20008-1175. Offers M Arch, M Arch II.

University of Toronto, School of Graduate Studies, John H. Daniels Faculty of Architecture, Landscape, and Design, Toronto, ON M5S 1A1, Canada. Offers M Arch, MLA, MUD, MVS. *Entrance requirements:* For master's, minimum B average; 3 letters of reference; resume; 3 writing samples; 5 samples of design work, drawing, or work in a related field, statement of interest. Additional exam requirements/recommendations for international students: Required—TOEFL (minimum score 580 paper-based; 93 iBT), IELTS (minimum score 7), TWE (minimum score 5), Michigan English Language Assessment Battery (minimum score 85), COPE (minimum score 76). Electronic applications accepted. *Expenses:* Contact institution.

University of Utah, Graduate School, College of Architecture and Planning, School of Architecture, Salt Lake City, UT 84112. Offers architectural studies (MS); architecture (M Arch). *Program availability:* Part-time. *Faculty:* 12 full-time (7 women), 11 part-time/adjunct (3 women). *Students:* 59 full-time (17 women), 2 part-time (1 woman); includes 10 minority (2 Asian, non-Hispanic/Latino; 5 Hispanic/Latino; 3 Two or more races, non-Hispanic/Latino), 6 international. Average age 23. 67 applicants, 87% accepted, 34 enrolled. In 2017, 37 master's awarded. *Entrance requirements:* For master's, minimum undergraduate GPA of 3.0; portfolio; statement of purpose; letters of recommendation. Additional exam requirements/recommendations for international students: Required—TOEFL (minimum score 575 paper-based). *Application deadline:* For fall admission, 1/1 for domestic students, 12/1 for international students. Application fee: $55 ($65 for international students). Electronic applications accepted. *Expenses:* Contact institution. *Financial support:* In 2017–18, 36 students received support, including 15 fellowships (averaging $3,375 per year), 29 teaching assistantships (averaging $3,375 per year); research assistantships, career-related internships or fieldwork, scholarships/grants, and unspecified assistantships also available. Financial award application deadline: 3/1; financial award applicants required to submit FAFSA. *Faculty research:* History, design, acoustics, photography, structures, architecture of the American West, architectural communication and representation, impact of technology, design-build. *Total annual research expenditures:* $62,017. *Unit head:* Mira Locher, Chair, 801-585-8946, E-mail: locher@arch.utah.edu. *Application contact:* Mayra Godin Focht, Administrative Officer/Advisor, 801-585-5354, Fax: 801-585-1565, E-mail: mayra@arch.utah.edu.
Website: http://www.arch.utah.edu/?school_of_architecture

University of Virginia, School of Architecture, Department of Architecture, Charlottesville, VA 22903. Offers M Arch. *Faculty:* 25 full-time (9 women), 2 part-time/adjunct (1 woman). *Students:* 90 full-time (39 women); includes 10 minority (4 Asian, non-Hispanic/Latino; 3 Hispanic/Latino; 3 Two or more races, non-Hispanic/Latino), 50 international. Average age 25. 395 applicants, 45% accepted, 34 enrolled. In 2017, 30 master's awarded. *Entrance requirements:* For master's, GRE General Test, 3 letters of recommendation; portfolio. Additional exam requirements/recommendations for international students: Required—TOEFL (minimum score 600 paper-based; 90 iBT). *Application deadline:* For fall admission, 1/5 for domestic and international students. Applications are processed on a rolling basis. Application fee: $60. Electronic applications accepted. *Financial support:* Career-related internships or fieldwork, Federal Work-Study, and institutionally sponsored loans available. Financial award applicants required to submit FAFSA. *Unit head:* Bill Sherman, Chair, 434-924-7592, Fax: 434-982-2678, E-mail: whs2b@virginia.edu. *Application contact:* Jeana Ripple, Director, Architecture Graduate Program, 434-924-6365, Fax: 434-982-2678, E-mail: ripple@virginia.edu.

University of Washington, Graduate School, College of Built Environments, Department of Architecture, Seattle, WA 98195. Offers architecture (M Arch, MS); built environment (PhD); design computing (Certificate); design firm leadership and management (Certificate); historic preservation (Certificate); lighting (Certificate); urban design (Certificate). *Degree requirements:* For master's, thesis. *Entrance requirements:* For master's, GRE General Test, minimum GPA of 3.0, portfolio, 3 letters of recommendation. Additional exam requirements/recommendations for international students: Required—TOEFL. *Faculty research:* Lighting, materials, computing theory, media, culture, environment.

University of Waterloo, Graduate Studies, Faculty of Engineering, School of Architecture, Waterloo, ON N2L 3G1, Canada. Offers M Arch. *Program availability:* Part-time. *Degree requirements:* For master's, thesis. *Entrance requirements:* For master's, bachelor's degree in pre-professional architecture. Additional exam requirements/recommendations for international students: Required—TOEFL, IELTS, PTE. Electronic applications accepted.

University of Wisconsin–Milwaukee, Graduate School, School of Architecture and Urban Planning, Department of Architecture, Milwaukee, WI 53201-0413. Offers architecture (M Arch, MS Arch, PhD); geographic information systems (Graduate Certificate). *Students:* 97 full-time (47 women), 13 part-time (4 women); includes 15

minority (2 Black or African American, non-Hispanic/Latino; 1 American Indian or Alaska Native, non-Hispanic/Latino; 4 Asian, non-Hispanic/Latino; 1 Hispanic/Latino; 7 Two or more races, non-Hispanic/Latino), 16 international. Average age 29. 145 applicants, 55% accepted, 35 enrolled. In 2017, 39 master's, 5 doctorates, 9 other advanced degrees awarded. *Degree requirements:* For master's, comprehensive exam, thesis; for doctorate, comprehensive exam, thesis/dissertation. *Entrance requirements:* For master's, GRE General Test, portfolio. Additional exam requirements/recommendations for international students: Required—TOEFL (minimum score 600 paper-based; 100 iBT), IELTS (minimum score 7). *Application deadline:* For fall admission, 1/1 priority date for domestic students; for spring admission, 9/1 for domestic students. Application fee: $56 ($96 for international students). Electronic applications accepted. *Financial support:* Fellowships, teaching assistantships, career-related internships or fieldwork, health care benefits, unspecified assistantships, and project assistantships available. Support available to part-time students. Financial award application deadline: 4/15; financial award applicants required to submit FAFSA. *Unit head:* Robert Greenstreet, Dean, 414-229-4016. *Application contact:* Student Advising Office, 414-229-4015, E-mail: sarup-grad@uwm.edu. Website: https://uwm.edu/sarup/architecture/

Washington State University, Voiland College of Engineering and Architecture, Program in Architecture, Pullman, WA 99164-2220. Offers architecture (M Arch). *Degree requirements:* For master's, comprehensive exam, thesis, oral exam. *Entrance requirements:* For master's, minimum GPA of 3.0, 3 letters of recommendation, personal statement, portfolio. Additional exam requirements/recommendations for international students: Required—TOEFL (minimum score 80 iBT), IELTS. *Faculty research:* Cultural, technological, and environmental design; integrated project delivery; American architecture and urbanism; land use and planning; design for rural communities and aging populations.

Washington University in St. Louis, Sam Fox School of Design and Visual Arts, Program in Architecture, St. Louis, MO 63130-4899. Offers M Arch, MLA, M Arch/MBA, M Arch/MCM, M Arch/MSW, M Arch/MUD, MLA/M Arch. *Degree requirements:* For master's, final project. *Entrance requirements:* For master's, GRE General Test, portfolio. Additional exam requirements/recommendations for international students:

Required—TOEFL (minimum score 550 paper-based; 80 iBT), TWE. Electronic applications accepted. *Faculty research:* Urban design development issues.

Wentworth Institute of Technology, Department of Architecture, Boston, MA 02115-5998. Offers M Arch. *Faculty:* 19 full-time (8 women), 20 part-time/adjunct (7 women). *Students:* 84 full-time (27 women), 3 part-time (1 woman); includes 11 minority (4 Asian, non-Hispanic/Latino; 3 Hispanic/Latino; 4 Two or more races, non-Hispanic/ Latino), 3 international. Average age 23. 131 applicants, 87% accepted, 83 enrolled. In 2017, 74 master's awarded. *Degree requirements:* For master's, thesis project. *Entrance requirements:* For master's, GRE, statement of objectives, resume or curriculum vitae, recommendation letters, official transcripts, portfolio. Additional exam requirements/recommendations for international students: Required—TOEFL (minimum score 525 paper-based). *Application deadline:* For fall admission, 1/15 priority date for domestic and international students. Applications are processed on a rolling basis. Application fee: $50. Electronic applications accepted. *Expenses:* $20,123 per year. *Financial support:* In 2017–18, 83 students received support, including 80 fellowships (averaging $7,256 per year), 37 teaching assistantships (averaging $2,500 per year). Financial award application deadline: 5/1; financial award applicants required to submit FAFSA. *Unit head:* Sharon Matthews, Interim Department Chair, 617-989-4622, E-mail: matthewss3@wit.edu. *Application contact:* Kelly Hutzell, Director of Graduate Programs, 617-989-4494, E-mail: hutzelk@wit.edu. Website: https://wit.edu/architecture

Woodbury University, School of Architecture, Burbank, CA 91504. Offers M Arch, MIA, MS Arch. *Degree requirements:* For master's, thesis. *Entrance requirements:* For master's, GRE (if undergraduate GPA is below 3.0), 3 letters of recommendation, portfolio, essay, interview, resume, academic transcripts. Additional exam requirements/ recommendations for international students: Required—TOEFL (minimum score 550 paper-based; 83 iBT), IELTS (minimum score 6.5). *Expenses:* Contact institution.

Yale University, School of Architecture, New Haven, CT 06520. Offers M Arch, M Env Des, MEM, PhD, M Arch/M Env Des, M Arch/MBA. *Entrance requirements:* For master's, GRE General Test, design portfolio. Additional exam requirements/ recommendations for international students: Required—TOEFL. Electronic applications accepted. *Expenses:* Contact institution.

Building Science

Arizona State University at the Tempe campus, Herberger Institute for Design and the Arts, The Design School, Tempe, AZ 85287-1605. Offers architecture (M Arch); building design/built environment (MS); design (MSD), including arts, media, and engineering, healthcare and healing environments (MSD, PhD), industrial design; interaction design, interior design, new product innovation, visual communication design; design, environment and the arts (PhD), including design, digital culture, healthcare and healing environments (MSD, PhD), history, theory, and criticism; landscape architecture (MLA); urban design (MUD); MA/MBA. *Accreditation:* NASAD. Terminal master's awarded for partial completion of doctoral program. *Degree requirements:* For master's, thesis optional, interactive Program of Study (iPOS) submitted before completing 50 percent of required credit hours; for doctorate, comprehensive exam, thesis/dissertation, interactive Program of Study (iPOS) submitted before completing 50 percent of required credit hours. *Entrance requirements:* For master's, GRE General Test, minimum GPA of 3.0 or equivalent in last 2 years of work leading to bachelor's degree, design/creative works portfolio, 3 references, statement of intent; for doctorate, GRE, master's degree in architecture, graphic design, industrial design, interior design, landscape architecture, or art history or equivalent standing; statement of purpose; 3 letters of recommendation; indication of potential faculty mentor; sample of written work. Additional exam requirements/recommendations for international students: Required—TOEFL (minimum score 600 paper-based; 100 iBT). Electronic applications accepted.

Carnegie Mellon University, College of Fine Arts, School of Architecture, Pittsburgh, PA 15213-3891. Offers architecture (MSA); architecture, engineering, and construction management (PhD); building performance and diagnostics (MS, PhD); computational design (MS, PhD); engineering construction management (MSA); tangible interaction design (MTID); urban design (MUD). Terminal master's awarded for partial completion of doctoral program. *Degree requirements:* For doctorate, thesis/ dissertation. *Entrance requirements:* For master's and doctorate, GRE General Test.

Additional exam requirements/recommendations for international students: Required— TOEFL.

Georgia Institute of Technology, Graduate Studies, College of Design, School of Building Construction, Atlanta, GA 30332-0001. Offers building construction (PhD); integrated facility and property management (MS); integrated project delivery systems (MS); program management (MS); residential construction development (MS). *Program availability:* Part-time, evening/weekend. *Entrance requirements:* For master's and doctorate, GRE or GMAT. Additional exam requirements/recommendations for international students: Required—TOEFL (minimum score 550 paper-based). Electronic applications accepted. *Faculty research:* Design-build, mold, indoor air quality, real estate.

Pontificia Universidad Catolica Madre y Maestra, Graduate School, Faculty of Engineering Sciences, Santiago, Dominican Republic. Offers earthquake engineering (ME); logistics management (ME).

University of California, Berkeley, Graduate Division, College of Environmental Design, Department of Architecture, Berkeley, CA 94720-1500. Offers architecture (M Arch); building science (MS, PhD); building structures, construction and materials (MS, PhD); design theories, methods, and practices (MS, PhD); environmental design in developing countries (MS, PhD); history of architecture and urbanism (MS, PhD); social and cultural processes in architecture and urbanism (MS, PhD); M Arch/MCP; M Arch/ MS; MLA/M Arch. *Degree requirements:* For master's, thesis; for doctorate, thesis/ dissertation, qualifying exam. *Entrance requirements:* For master's and doctorate, GRE General Test, minimum GPA of 3.0, 3 letters of recommendation. Additional exam requirements/recommendations for international students: Required—TOEFL (minimum score 570 paper-based; 90 iBT). Electronic applications accepted. Application fee is waived when completed online.

Environmental Design

Arizona State University at the Tempe campus, Herberger Institute for Design and the Arts, The Design School, PhD Program in Design, Environment and the Arts, Tempe, AZ 85287-2105. Offers design (PhD); digital culture (PhD); healthcare and healing environments (PhD); history, theory, and criticism (PhD). *Degree requirements:* For doctorate, comprehensive exam, thesis/dissertation, interactive Program of Study (iPOS) submitted before completing 50 percent of required credit hours. *Entrance requirements:* For doctorate, GRE, master's degree in architecture, graphic design, industrial design, interior design, landscape architecture, or art history or equivalent standing; statement of purpose; 3 letters of recommendation; indication of potential faculty mentor; sample of written work. Additional exam requirements/recommendations for international students: Required—TOEFL, IELTS, or PTE. Electronic applications accepted. *Expenses:* Contact institution.

ArtCenter College of Design, Graduate Environmental Design Program, Pasadena, CA 91103. Offers furniture and fixtures (MS); spatial experience (MS).

Columbia University, School of Professional Studies, Program in Landscape Design, New York, NY 10027. Offers MS. *Program availability:* Part-time. *Entrance requirements:* For master's, minimum undergraduate GPA of 3.0. Additional exam requirements/recommendations for international students: Required—American Language Program placement test. *Expenses:* Tuition: Full-time $44,864; part-time $1704 per credit. *Required fees:* $2370 per semester. One-time fee: $105.

Cornell University, Graduate School, Graduate Fields of Human Ecology, Field of Design and Environmental Analysis, Ithaca, NY 14853. Offers applied research in human-environment relations (MS); facilities planning and management (MS); housing

and design (MS); human factors and ergonomics (MS); human-environment relations (MS); interior design (MA, MPS). *Degree requirements:* For master's, thesis. *Entrance requirements:* For master's, GRE General Test, portfolio or slides of recent work; bachelor's degree in interior design, architecture or related design discipline; 2 letters of recommendation. Additional exam requirements/recommendations for international students: Required—TOEFL (minimum score 600 paper-based; 105 iBT). Electronic applications accepted. *Faculty research:* Facility planning and management, environmental psychology, housing, interior design, ergonomics and human factors.

Kansas State University, Graduate School, College of Architecture, Planning and Design, Interdisciplinary Doctoral Program in Environmental Design and Planning, Manhattan, KS 66506. Offers PhD. *Degree requirements:* For doctorate, comprehensive exam, thesis/dissertation, preliminary exam, oral exam. *Entrance requirements:* For doctorate, GRE, transcript(s), statement of intent, three letters of recommendation, portfolio. Additional exam requirements/recommendations for international students: Required—TOEFL (minimum score 600 paper-based; 100 iBT), IELTS (minimum score 7), PTE (minimum score 70). Electronic applications accepted. *Faculty research:* Sustainability, place-making, design, planning.

Kent State University, College of Architecture and Environmental Design, Kent, OH 44242-0001. Offers architecture (M Arch); architecture and environmental design (MS); health care design (MHCD); landscape architecture (MLA); urban design (MUD); M Arch/MBA; M Arch/MUD. *Program availability:* Part-time. *Faculty:* 19 full-time (2 women), 15 part-time/adjunct (6 women). *Students:* 70 full-time (27 women), 13 part-time (7 women); includes 8 minority (1 Black or African American, non-Hispanic/Latino;

1 Asian, non-Hispanic/Latino; 4 Hispanic/Latino; 2 Two or more races, non-Hispanic/Latino), 13 international. Average age 26. 100 applicants, 82% accepted, 57 enrolled. In 2017, 59 master's awarded. *Degree requirements:* For master's, thesis (for some programs), capstone project (for some programs). *Entrance requirements:* For master's, GRE with minimum scores 151 (460) verbal reasoning, 150 (620) quantitative reasoning, and 4.25 analytical writing (except for MHCD), letters of recommendation, portfolio. Additional exam requirements/recommendations for international students: Required—TOEFL (minimum score 550 paper-based; 80 iBT), IELTS (minimum score 6.5), PTE (minimum score 54), Michigan English Language Assessment Battery (minimum score 77). *Application deadline:* Applications are processed on a rolling basis. Application fee: $45 ($70 for international students). Electronic applications accepted. *Expenses:* Tuition, state resident: full-time $11,310; part-time $515 per credit hour. Tuition, nonresident: full-time $20,396; part-time $928 per credit hour. *International tuition:* $18,544 full-time. *Financial support:* Research assistantships with full tuition reimbursements, teaching assistantships with full tuition reimbursements, Federal Work-Study, scholarships/grants, and unspecified assistantships available. Financial award application deadline: 2/1; financial award applicants required to submit FAFSA. *Unit head:* Mark Mistur, Dean, E-mail: mmistur1@kent.edu. *Application contact:* Johnathan Fleming, Assistant Professor and Director, Master of Architecture, 330-672-0934, E-mail: jpflemi1@kent.edu.
Website: http://www.kent.edu/caed

Michigan State University, The Graduate School, College of Agriculture and Natural Resources and College of Social Science, School of Planning, Design and Construction, East Lansing, MI 48824. Offers construction management (MS, PhD); environmental design (MA); interior design and facilities management (MA); international planning studies (MIPS); urban and regional planning (MURP). *Degree requirements:* For master's, thesis or alternative. *Entrance requirements:* Additional exam requirements/recommendations for international students: Required—TOEFL. Electronic applications accepted.

San Diego State University, Graduate and Research Affairs, College of Professional Studies and Fine Arts, School of Art, Design and Art History, San Diego, CA 92182. Offers art history (MA); studio arts (MA, MFA), including applied design, environmental design, graphic design, interior design, painting and printmaking, sculpture. *Accreditation:* NASAD (one or more programs are accredited). *Degree requirements:* For master's, variable foreign language requirement, thesis. *Entrance requirements:* For master's, GRE General Test, bachelor's degree in related field, slide portfolio, typed slide information sheet, 2 letters of recommendation. Additional exam requirements/recommendations for international students: Required—TOEFL. Electronic applications accepted.

Texas Tech University, Graduate School, College of Human Sciences, Department of Design, Lubbock, TX 79409-1220. Offers environmental design (MS); interior and environmental design (PhD). *Program availability:* Part-time. *Faculty:* 11 full-time (9 women), 1 (woman) part-time/adjunct. *Students:* 16 full-time (12 women), 4 part-time (2 women); includes 3 minority (all Hispanic/Latino), 13 international. Average age 33. 16 applicants, 63% accepted, 5 enrolled. In 2017, 5 master's, 3 doctorates awarded. *Degree requirements:* For master's, comprehensive exam, thesis or alternative; for doctorate, comprehensive exam, thesis/dissertation. *Entrance requirements:* For master's, 3 recommendation letters, design portfolio, 500-word written statement (reason for pursuing degree), resume; for doctorate, GRE, 3 recommendation letters, design portfolio, 500-word written statement (reason for pursuing degree), resume. Additional exam requirements/recommendations for international students: Required—TOEFL (minimum score 550 paper-based, 79 iBT) or IELTS (6.5). *Application deadline:* For fall admission, 6/1 priority date for domestic students, 1/15 priority date for international students; for spring admission, 9/1 priority date for domestic students, 6/15 priority date for international students. Applications are processed on a rolling basis. Application fee: $60. Electronic applications accepted. *Expenses:* Contact institution. *Financial support:* In 2017–18, 15 students received support, including 13 fellowships (averaging $6,394 per year), 10 research assistantships (averaging $8,383 per year); teaching assistantships, scholarships/grants, and unspecified assistantships also available. Financial award application deadline: 4/15; financial award applicants required to submit FAFSA. *Faculty research:* Healthcare and the built environment, sustainability, vulnerable populations, historic preservation, evidence-based design, environmental design, interior design, clothing design, creative scholarship (juried exhibitions). *Total annual research expenditures:* $137,557. *Unit head:* Dr. Sharran F. Parkinson, Department Chairperson/Professor, 806-742-3031, Fax: 806-742-1639, E-mail: sharran.parkinson@ttu.edu. *Application contact:* Erin Rebecca Sopronyi, Senior Office Manager, 806-742-3050, Fax: 806-742-1639, E-mail: erin.r.sopronyi@ttu.edu.
Website: http://www.depts.ttu.edu/hs/dod/

Université de Montréal, Faculty of Environmental Design and Planning, Montréal, QC H3C 3J7, Canada. Offers environmental design and planning (M Sc A, PhD); environmental planning and design projects (DESS); game design (DESS); urban management for developing countries (DESS); urban planning (M Urb). DESS programs offered jointly with HEC Montreal and École Polytechnique de Montréal. *Accreditation:* ACSP. *Degree requirements:* For doctorate, thesis/dissertation, general exam. Electronic applications accepted. *Expenses:* Contact institution. *Faculty research:* Wayfinding, environmental evaluation, housing studies, urban design, urban and regional planning.

University of Calgary, Faculty of Graduate Studies, Faculty of Environmental Design, Calgary, AB T2N 1N4, Canada. Offers architecture (M Arch); environmental design (M Env Des, PhD); landscape architecture (MLA); planning (M Plan). *Degree requirements:* For master's, thesis; for doctorate, thesis/dissertation. *Entrance requirements:* For master's, minimum GPA of 3.0; for doctorate, minimum GPA of 3.5. Additional exam requirements/recommendations for international students: Required—TOEFL (minimum score 550 paper-based). *Faculty research:* Sustainable development in architecture, planning and product design, energy and environment, impact assessment, ecotourism.

University of California, Berkeley, Graduate Division, College of Environmental Design, Department of Landscape Architecture and Environmental Planning, Berkeley, CA 94720-1500. Offers landscape architecture (MLA), including environmental planning, landscape design and site planning, urban and community design; landscape architecture and environmental planning (PhD); MLA/M Arch; MLA/MCP. *Accreditation:* ASLA (one or more programs are accredited). *Degree requirements:* For master's, comprehensive exam (for some programs), thesis (for some programs), professional project or thesis; for doctorate, one foreign language, thesis/dissertation, qualifying exam. *Entrance requirements:* For master's, GRE General Test, minimum GPA of 3.0, portfolio; for doctorate, GRE General Test, master's degree (strongly recommended), minimum GPA of 3.0, sample of written work, 3 letters of recommendation. Additional exam requirements/recommendations for international students: Required—TOEFL (minimum score 570 paper-based; 90 iBT). Electronic applications accepted.

University of California, Irvine, School of Social Ecology, Programs in Social Ecology, Irvine, CA 92697. Offers environmental analysis and design (PhD); epidemiology and public health (PhD); social ecology (PhD). *Students:* 9 full-time (8 women), 1 (woman) part-time; includes 1 minority (Hispanic/Latino), 1 international. Average age 30. 14 applicants, 43% accepted, 3 enrolled. In 2017, 2 doctorates awarded. Application fee: $105 ($125 for international students). *Unit head:* Tim-Allen Bruckner, Professor, 949-824-5797, Fax: 949-824-1845, E-mail: tim.bruckner@uci.edu. *Application contact:* Jennifer Craig, Director of Graduate Student Services, 949-824-5918, Fax: 949-824-1845, E-mail: craigj@uci.edu.
Website: http://socialecology.uci.edu/core/graduate-se-core-programs

University of Georgia, College of Environment and Design, Athens, GA 30602. Offers environmental planning and design (MEPD); historic preservation (MHP); landscape architecture (MLA). *Accreditation:* ACSP.

The University of Manchester, School of Environment and Development, Manchester, United Kingdom. Offers architecture (M Phil, PhD); development policy and management (M Phil, PhD); human geography (M Phil, PhD); physical geography (M Phil, PhD); planning and landscape (M Phil, PhD).

Virginia Polytechnic Institute and State University, Graduate School, College of Architecture and Urban Studies, Blacksburg, VA 24061. Offers architecture (M Arch, MS); architecture and design research (PhD); building construction science management (MS); creative technologies (MFA); environmental design and planning (PhD); government and international affairs (MPIA); landscape architecture (MLA, PhD); planning, governance, and globalization (PhD); public administration and public affairs (MPA, PhD); urban and regional planning (MURPL). *Accreditation:* ASLA (one or more programs are accredited). *Faculty:* 139 full-time (58 women), 1 (woman) part-time/adjunct. *Students:* 339 full-time (165 women), 210 part-time (97 women); includes 115 minority (49 Black or African American, non-Hispanic/Latino; 1 American Indian or Alaska Native, non-Hispanic/Latino; 30 Asian, non-Hispanic/Latino; 29 Hispanic/Latino; 6 Two or more races, non-Hispanic/Latino), 136 international. Average age 32. 649 applicants, 49% accepted, 105 enrolled. In 2017, 142 master's, 18 doctorates awarded. *Degree requirements:* For master's, comprehensive exam (for some programs), thesis (for some programs); for doctorate, comprehensive exam (for some programs), thesis/dissertation (for some programs). *Entrance requirements:* For master's and doctorate, GRE/GMAT. Additional exam requirements/recommendations for international students: Required—TOEFL (minimum score 80 iBT). *Application deadline:* For fall admission, 8/1 for domestic students, 4/1 for international students; for spring admission, 1/1 for domestic students, 9/1 for international students. Applications are processed on a rolling basis. Application fee: $75. Electronic applications accepted. *Expenses:* Tuition, state resident: full-time $15,072; part-time $718.50 per credit hour. Tuition, nonresident: full-time $28,810; part-time $1448.25 per credit hour. *Required fees:* $2741; $502 per semester. Tuition and fees vary according to course load, campus/location and program. *Financial support:* In 2017–18, 17 research assistantships with full tuition reimbursements (averaging $18,561 per year), 41 teaching assistantships with full tuition reimbursements (averaging $17,340 per year) were awarded. Financial award application deadline: 3/1; financial award applicants required to submit FAFSA. *Total annual research expenditures:* $3.1 million. *Unit head:* Dr. Richard Blythe, Dean, 540-231-6416, Fax: 540-231-6332, E-mail: richbl1@vt.edu. *Application contact:* Christine Mattsson-Coon, Executive Assistant, 540-231-6416, Fax: 540-231-6332, E-mail: cmattsso@vt.edu.
Website: http://www.caus.vt.edu/

Yale University, School of Architecture, New Haven, CT 06520. Offers M Arch, M Env Des, MEM, PhD, M Arch/M Env Des, M Arch/MBA. *Entrance requirements:* For master's, GRE General Test, design portfolio. Additional exam requirements/recommendations for international students: Required—TOEFL. Electronic applications accepted. *Expenses:* Contact institution.

Historic Preservation

The American University of Rome, Graduate School, Rome, Italy. Offers religious studies (MA); sustainable cultural heritage (MA). *Degree requirements:* For master's, thesis, internship. *Entrance requirements:* For master's, bachelor's degree in the liberal arts, humanities or social sciences; minimum GPA of 2.75. Additional exam requirements/recommendations for international students: Required—TOEFL (minimum score 550 paper-based; 80 iBT), IELTS (minimum score 6.5). Electronic applications accepted. *Faculty research:* Sustainable cultural heritage, archaeology in Europe and Italy.

Arkansas State University, Graduate School, College of Humanities and Social Sciences, Heritage Studies Program, State University, AR 72467. Offers heritage studies (MA, PhD). *Program availability:* Part-time. *Degree requirements:* For master's, comprehensive exam, thesis or alternative, portfolio; for doctorate, comprehensive exam, thesis/dissertation, portfolio. *Entrance requirements:* For master's, GRE, MAT or GMAT, appropriate bachelor's degree, letters of reference, official transcript, interview, letter of interest, writing sample, immunization records; for doctorate, GRE, MAT, or GMAT, appropriate bachelor's or master's degree, interview, letters of reference, official transcript, letter of interest, writing sample, immunization records. Additional exam requirements/recommendations for international students: Required—TOEFL (minimum score 550 paper-based; 79 iBT), IELTS (minimum score 6), PTE (minimum score 56). Electronic applications accepted.

Ball State University, Graduate School, College of Architecture and Planning, Department of Architecture, Program in Historic Preservation, Muncie, IN 47306. Offers MS. *Program availability:* Part-time. *Students:* 11 full-time (8 women), 1 (woman) part-time. Average age 29. 15 applicants, 87% accepted, 6 enrolled. In 2017, 8 master's awarded. *Entrance requirements:* For master's, minimum baccalaureate GPA of 2.75 or 3.0 in latter half of baccalaureate, resume, statement of purpose, academic writing sample, three letters of recommendation. Additional exam requirements/recommendations for international students: Required—TOEFL (minimum score 550 paper-based; 79 iBT), IELTS (minimum score 6.5). *Application deadline:* Applications are processed on a rolling basis. Application fee: $60. Electronic applications accepted.

Expenses: Contact institution. *Financial support:* Research assistantships with partial tuition reimbursements and teaching assistantships with partial tuition reimbursements available. Financial award application deadline: 3/1; financial award applicants required to submit FAFSA. *Unit head:* Andrea Swartz, Chairperson, 765-285-1904, Fax: 765-285-1765, E-mail: aswartz@bsu.edu.
Website: http://cms.bsu.edu/Academics/CollegesandDepartments/CAP/Programs/Architecture/AboutUs/Centers/CenterHistoric.aspx

Boston Architectural College, Graduate Programs, Boston, MA 02115-2795. Offers architecture (M Arch); historic preservation (MDS); interior design (MID); landscape architecture (MLA); sustainable design (MDS). *Accreditation:* CIDA. *Degree requirements:* For master's, thesis. *Entrance requirements:* For master's, portfolio (recommended). Electronic applications accepted.

Boston University, Graduate School of Arts and Sciences, Program in Preservation Studies, Boston, MA 02215. Offers MA, JD/MA. *Students:* 4 full-time (all women), 2 part-time (1 woman); includes 1 minority (Hispanic/Latino), 2 international. Average age 26. 13 applicants, 100% accepted. In 2017, 3 master's awarded. *Degree requirements:* For master's, thesis or alternative, internship, major project. *Entrance requirements:* For master's, GRE General Test, scholarly writing sample, 3 letters of recommendation, transcripts, curriculum vitae, personal statement. Additional exam requirements/recommendations for international students: Required—TOEFL (minimum score 550 paper-based; 84 iBT). *Application deadline:* For fall admission, 4/1 for domestic and international students; for spring admission, 11/15 for domestic and international students. Application fee: $95. Electronic applications accepted. *Financial support:* In 2017–18, 5 students received support. Career-related internships or fieldwork, Federal Work-Study, scholarships/grants, and unspecified assistantships available. Support available to part-time students. Financial award application deadline: 1/15. *Unit head:* Daniel Bluestone, Director, 617-358-7332, Fax: 617-353-2556, E-mail: dblues@bu.edu. *Application contact:* Julia Kline, Senior Program Coordinator, 617-353-2948, Fax: 617-353-2556, E-mail: jgawle@bu.edu.
Website: http://www.bu.edu/amnesp/ma/

Buffalo State College, State University of New York, The Graduate School, Faculty of Arts and Humanities, Department of Art Conservation, Buffalo, NY 14222-1095. Offers art conservation (CAS); conservation of historic works and art works (MA). *Degree requirements:* For master's, final oral exam; for CAS, internship. *Entrance requirements:* For master's, GRE General Test, minimum GPA of 2.8. Additional exam requirements/recommendations for international students: Required—TOEFL (minimum score 550 paper-based). *Faculty research:* Mechanics of deterioration of art, conservation of materials.

Clemson University, Graduate School, College of Architecture, Arts, and Humanities, School of Architecture, Master of Science Program in Historic Preservation, Charleston, SC 29403. Offers MS, Certificate. *Faculty:* 2 full-time (1 woman), 10 part-time/adjunct (5 women). *Students:* 26 full-time (22 women); includes 6 minority (2 Asian, non-Hispanic/Latino; 4 Hispanic/Latino), 2 international. Average age 27. 38 applicants, 92% accepted, 13 enrolled. In 2017, 24 master's, 2 other advanced degrees awarded. *Degree requirements:* For master's, thesis. *Entrance requirements:* For master's, GRE General Test, official transcripts, letters of recommendation. Additional exam requirements/recommendations for international students: Required—TOEFL (minimum score 80 iBT), IELTS (minimum score 6.5), PTE (minimum score 54). *Application deadline:* For fall admission, 2/15 for domestic and international students. Application fee: $80 ($90 for international students). Electronic applications accepted. *Expenses:* Contact institution. *Financial support:* In 2017–18, 10 students received support, including 10 fellowships with partial tuition reimbursements available (averaging $5,700 per year). Financial award application deadline: 2/15. *Faculty research:* Historic preservation, architectural history, architectural forensics, materials science, cultural landscapes. *Unit head:* Kate Schwennsen, Director, School of Architecture, 864-656-3895, E-mail: kschwen@clemson.edu. *Application contact:* Dr. Carter Hudgins, Director of the Graduate Program in Historic Preservation, 843-937-9596, E-mail: chudgin@clemson.edu.
Website: http://www.clemson.edu/caah/departments/historic-preservation/

Cleveland State University, College of Graduate Studies, Maxine Goodman Levin College of Urban Affairs, Program in Urban Planning and Development, Cleveland, OH 44115. Offers economic development (MUPD); environmental sustainability (MUPD); historic preservation (MUPD); housing and neighborhood development (MUPD); real estate development and finance (MUPD); urban economic development (Certificate); urban geographic information systems (MUPD); JD/MUPDD. *Accreditation:* ACSP. *Program availability:* Part-time, evening/weekend. *Faculty:* 16 full-time (8 women), 13 part-time/adjunct (5 women). *Students:* 20 full-time (7 women), 15 part-time (5 women); includes 1 minority (Black or African American, non-Hispanic/Latino), 2 international. Average age 28. 48 applicants, 56% accepted, 14 enrolled. In 2017, 24 master's awarded. *Degree requirements:* For master's, thesis or alternative, exit project. *Entrance requirements:* For master's, GRE General Test (minimum score: 50th percentile combined verbal and quantitative, 4.0 analytical writing), minimum GPA of 3.0. Additional exam requirements/recommendations for international students: Required—TOEFL (minimum score 550 paper-based; 78 iBT), IELTS (6.0), or International Test of English Proficiency (iTEP). *Application deadline:* For fall admission, 7/1 priority date for domestic students, 5/15 for international students; for spring admission, 11/15 for domestic students, 11/1 for international students; for summer admission, 4/1 for domestic students, 3/15 for international students. Applications are processed on a rolling basis. Application fee: $40. Electronic applications accepted. *Expenses:* Contact institution. *Financial support:* In 2017–18, 10 students received support, including 5 research assistantships with full tuition reimbursements available (averaging $7,200 per year), 3 teaching assistantships with partial tuition reimbursements available (averaging $2,400 per year); scholarships/grants, tuition waivers (full and partial), and unspecified assistantships also available. Support available to part-time students. Financial award application deadline: 3/1; financial award applicants required to submit FAFSA. *Faculty research:* Housing and neighborhood development, urban housing policy, environmental sustainability, economic development, GIS and planning decision support. *Unit head:* Dr. Stephanie Ryberg-Webster, Assistant Professor/Program Director, 216-802-3386, Fax: 216-687-2013, E-mail: s.ryberg@csuohio.edu. *Application contact:* David Arrighi, Graduate Academic Advisor, 216-523-7522, Fax: 216-687-5398, E-mail: d.arrighi@csuohio.edu.
Website: http://www.csuohio.edu/urban/mupd/mupd

College of Charleston, Graduate School, School of the Arts, Program in Historic Preservation, Charleston, SC 29424-0001. Offers MS. Program offered in collaboration with Clemson University. *Degree requirements:* For master's, thesis optional. *Entrance requirements:* For master's, GRE. Additional exam requirements/recommendations for international students: Required—TOEFL (minimum score 81 iBT). Electronic applications accepted.

Columbia University, Graduate School of Architecture, Planning, and Preservation, Program in Historic Preservation, New York, NY 10027. Offers MS, PhD, Certificate, M Arch/MS, MS/MS. *Degree requirements:* For master's, thesis. *Entrance requirements:* For master's, GRE General Test. *Expenses: Tuition:* Full-time $44,864; part-time $1704 per credit. *Required fees:* $2370 per semester. One-time fee: $105.

Cornell University, Graduate School, Graduate Fields of Architecture, Art and Planning, Field of City and Regional Planning, Ithaca, NY 14853. Offers city and regional planning (MRP, PhD); environmental planning and design (MRP, PhD); historic preservation planning (MA); international development planning (MRP, PhD); planning theory and systems analysis (MRP, PhD); regional economics and development planning (MRP, PhD); regional science (MRP, PhD); social and health systems planning (MRP, PhD); urban and regional theory (MRP, PhD); urban planning history (MRP, PhD). *Accreditation:* ACSP (one or more programs are accredited). *Degree requirements:* For master's, thesis (MA); for doctorate, comprehensive exam, thesis/dissertation. *Entrance requirements:* For master's and doctorate, GRE General Test, 2 letters of recommendation. Additional exam requirements/recommendations for international students: Required—TOEFL (minimum score 600 paper-based; 77 iBT). Electronic applications accepted. *Faculty research:* Land use planning, economic development, international development, historic preservation, community development.

Delaware State University, Graduate Programs, Department of History, Philosophy and Political Sciences, Dover, DE 19901-2277. Offers historic preservation (MA). *Entrance requirements:* Additional exam requirements/recommendations for international students: Required—TOEFL (minimum score 550 paper-based). Electronic applications accepted.

Eastern Michigan University, Graduate School, College of Arts and Sciences, Department of Geography and Geology, Programs in Historic Preservation, Ypsilanti, MI 48197. Offers heritage interpretation and museum practice (MS); historic preservation (Graduate Certificate); preservation planning and administration (MS); recording, documentation and digital cultural heritage (MS). *Program availability:* Part-time, evening/weekend, online learning. *Students:* 7 full-time (5 women), 39 part-time (28 women); includes 6 minority (1 Black or African American, non-Hispanic/Latino; 3 Hispanic/Latino; 2 Two or more races, non-Hispanic/Latino), 1 international. Average age 37. 19 applicants, 89% accepted, 9 enrolled. In 2017, 18 master's, 2 other advanced degrees awarded. *Entrance requirements:* Additional exam requirements/recommendations for international students: Required—TOEFL. *Application deadline:* Applications are processed on a rolling basis. Application fee: $45. *Financial support:* Fellowships, research assistantships with full tuition reimbursements, teaching assistantships with full tuition reimbursements, career-related internships or fieldwork, Federal Work-Study, institutionally sponsored loans, scholarships/grants, tuition waivers (partial), and unspecified assistantships available. Support available to part-time students. Financial award applicants required to submit FAFSA. *Application contact:* Dr. Ted Ligibel, Program Director, 734-487-0232, Fax: 734-487-6979, E-mail: tligibel@emich.edu.

The George Washington University, Columbian College of Arts and Sciences, Department of American Studies, Washington, DC 20052. Offers American studies (PhD); folk life (MA); historic preservation (MA); material culture (MA). *Program availability:* Part-time, evening/weekend. *Faculty:* 10 full-time (5 women), 1 part-time/adjunct (0 women). *Students:* 18 full-time (14 women), 17 part-time (13 women); includes 13 minority (6 Black or African American, non-Hispanic/Latino; 3 Asian, non-Hispanic/Latino; 2 Hispanic/Latino; 2 Two or more races, non-Hispanic/Latino). Average age 28. 103 applicants, 31% accepted, 12 enrolled. In 2017, 9 master's, 2 doctorates awarded. Terminal master's awarded for partial completion of doctoral program. *Degree requirements:* For master's, comprehensive exam; for doctorate, one foreign language, thesis/dissertation, general exam. *Entrance requirements:* For master's and doctorate, GRE General Test, minimum GPA of 3.0. Additional exam requirements/recommendations for international students: Required—TOEFL (minimum score 550 paper-based; 80 iBT). *Application deadline:* For fall admission, 1/15 priority date for domestic and international students; for spring admission, 10/1 for domestic students. Application fee: $75. *Expenses: Tuition:* Full-time $28,800; part-time $1655 per credit hour. *Required fees:* $45; $2.75 per credit hour. *Financial support:* In 2017–18, 22 students received support. Fellowships, research assistantships, teaching assistantships, career-related internships or fieldwork, Federal Work-Study, institutionally sponsored loans, and tuition waivers available. Financial award application deadline: 1/15. *Unit head:* Melanie McAlister, Chair, 202-994-7244, E-mail: jam@gwu.edu. *Application contact:* Information Contact, 202-994-6070, Fax: 202-994-8651, E-mail: amst@gwu.edu.
Website: http://departments.columbian.gwu.edu/americanstudies/

Georgia State University, College of Arts and Sciences, Department of History, Program in Heritage Preservation, Atlanta, GA 30302-3083. Offers MHP. *Program availability:* Part-time. *Entrance requirements:* For master's, GRE General Test, statement of purpose, three letters of recommendation, official transcripts. Additional exam requirements/recommendations for international students: Required—TOEFL (minimum score 550 paper-based; 80 iBT). *Application deadline:* Applications are processed on a rolling basis. Application fee: $50. Electronic applications accepted. *Expenses:* Tuition, state resident: full-time $7020. Tuition, nonresident: full-time $22,518. *Required fees:* $2128. Tuition and fees vary according to degree level and program. *Financial support:* Fellowships, research assistantships, career-related internships or fieldwork, Federal Work-Study, scholarships/grants, and unspecified assistantships available. Support available to part-time students. Financial award application deadline: 7/15. *Faculty research:* Materials conservation, preservation planning, cultural preservation, public history, oral history, twentieth-century American history. *Unit head:* Dr. Michelle Brattain, Chair, 404-413-6352, E-mail: mbrattain@gsu.edu. *Application contact:* Richard Laub, Director of Heritage Preservation Program, 404-413-6365, E-mail: rlaub@gsu.edu.
Website: http://www.gsu.edu/~wwwhis/

Georgia State University, College of Arts and Sciences, Department of History, Program in History, Atlanta, GA 30302-3083. Offers historic preservation (MA); history (PhD); public history (MA); world history (MA). *Program availability:* Part-time, evening/weekend. Terminal master's awarded for partial completion of doctoral program. *Entrance requirements:* For master's, GRE, BA in history; statement of purpose; writing sample; three letters of recommendation; official transcripts; for doctorate, GRE, MA in history; master's thesis; statement of purpose; writing sample; three letters of recommendation; official transcripts; appropriate language skills. Additional exam requirements/recommendations for international students: Required—TOEFL (minimum score 550 paper-based; 80 iBT). *Application deadline:* Applications are processed on a rolling basis. Application fee: $50. Electronic applications accepted. *Expenses:* Tuition, state resident: full-time $7020. Tuition, nonresident: full-time $22,518. *Required fees:* $2128. Tuition and fees vary according to degree level and program. *Financial support:* Research assistantships, teaching assistantships, and scholarships/grants available. Financial award application deadline: 2/15; financial award applicants required to submit FAFSA. *Faculty research:* Nineteenth- and twentieth-century U.S. history, early modern European history, modern European history, world history, public history. *Unit head:* Dr. Michelle Brattain, Chair, 404-413-6352, Fax: 404-413-6384, E-mail: mbrattain@gsu.edu. *Application contact:* Dr. Joe Perry, Director of Graduate Studies, 404-413-6374, Fax: 404-413-6384, E-mail: jbperry@gsu.edu.
Website: http://www.gsu.edu/~wwwhis/

Goucher College, MA and MFA Programs, Baltimore, MD 21204-2794. Offers art and technology (MFA); arts administration (MA); cultural sustainability (MA); digital arts

(MA); historic preservation (MA); nonfiction (MFA). *Program availability:* Part-time, evening/weekend, blended/hybrid learning. *Degree requirements:* For master's, thesis, e-portfolio. *Entrance requirements:* For master's, digital portfolio (for MA, MFA in digital arts); writing sample (for MFA in creative nonfiction). Additional exam requirements/recommendations for international students: Required—TOEFL (minimum score 550 paper-based; 80 iBT). *Application deadline:* Applications are processed on a rolling basis. Application fee: $75. Electronic applications accepted. *Expenses:* Contact institution. *Financial support:* Scholarships/grants and unspecified assistantships available. Financial award application deadline: 4/15; financial award applicants required to submit FAFSA. *Unit head:* Leslie Rubinkowski, Acting Assistant Provost for Limited Residency Graduate Programs, 410-337-6200, E-mail: leslie.rubinkowski@goucher.edu. *Application contact:* Carlton E. Surbeck, III, Director of Admissions, 410-337-6100, Fax: 410-337-6200, E-mail: admissions@goucher.edu.
Website: http://www.goucher.edu/grad

Morgan State University, School of Graduate Studies, College of Liberal Arts, Department of History and Geography, Baltimore, MD 21251. Offers African-American studies (MA); history (MA, PhD); museum studies and historic preservation (MA). *Program availability:* Part-time, evening/weekend. *Degree requirements:* For master's, comprehensive exam, thesis; for doctorate, comprehensive exam, thesis/dissertation. *Entrance requirements:* For master's, minimum GPA of 2.5; for doctorate, GRE or MAT. Additional exam requirements/recommendations for international students: Required—TOEFL (minimum score 550 paper-based). *Application deadline:* For fall admission, 2/1 priority date for domestic students; for spring admission, 10/1 priority date for domestic students. Applications are processed on a rolling basis. Application fee: $0. *Expenses:* Tuition, state resident: part-time $433 per credit. Tuition, nonresident: part-time $851 per credit. *Required fees:* $81.50 per credit. *Financial support:* Application deadline: 2/1. *Faculty research:* Women's history, African diaspora history, urban history. *Unit head:* Dr. Jeremiah I. Dibua, Graduate Coordinator, 443-885-3400, Fax: 443-885-8227, E-mail: jeremiah.dibua@morgan.edu. *Application contact:* Dr. Dean Campbell, Graduate Recruitment Specialist, 443-885-3185, Fax: 443-885-8226, E-mail: dean.campbell@morgan.edu.

New York University, Graduate School of Arts and Science, Institute of Fine Arts, Program in Conservation Training, New York, NY 10012-1019. Offers MA/Diploma. *Students:* 35 applicants, 31% accepted, 4 enrolled. *Application deadline:* For fall admission, 12/18 for domestic and international students. Application fee: $95. *Expenses: Tuition:* Full-time $41,352; part-time $19,968 per year. *Required fees:* $2496; $1628 per unit. $814 per term. Tuition and fees vary according to course load and program. *Financial support:* Career-related internships or fieldwork, Federal Work-Study, and institutionally sponsored loans available. Financial award application deadline: 12/18; financial award applicants required to submit FAFSA. *Unit head:* Michele Marincola, Chair, Conservation Center, 212-992-5800, Fax: 212-992-5807, E-mail: ifa.program@nyu.edu. *Application contact:* Kevin Martin, Graduate Advisor, 212-992-5800, Fax: 212-992-5807, E-mail: ifa.program@nyu.edu.
Website: http://www.nyu.edu/gsas/dept/fineart/

Penn State Harrisburg, Graduate School, School of Humanities, Middletown, PA 17057. Offers American studies (MA, PhD); communications (MA); folklore and ethnography (Certificate); heritage and museum practice (Certificate); humanities (MA). *Program availability:* Evening/weekend. *Unit head:* Dr. Mukund S. Kulkarni, Chancellor, 717-948-6105, Fax: 717-948-6452. *Application contact:* Robert W. Coffman, Jr., Director of Enrollment Management, Recruitment and Admissions, 717-948-6250, Fax: 717-948-6325, E-mail: hbgadmit@psu.edu.
Website: https://harrisburg.psu.edu/humanities

Plymouth State University, Program in Historic Preservation, Plymouth, NH 03264-1595. Offers MA. *Degree requirements:* For master's, thesis or practicum.

Pratt Institute, School of Architecture, Program in Historic Preservation, New York, NY 10011. Offers MS. *Program availability:* Part-time. *Students:* 26 full-time (18 women), 2 part-time (1 woman); includes 5 minority (4 Hispanic/Latino; 1 Two or more races, non-Hispanic/Latino), 12 international. Average age 28. 24 applicants, 96% accepted, 10 enrolled. In 2017, 9 master's awarded. *Degree requirements:* For master's, thesis. *Entrance requirements:* For master's, writing sample, bachelor's degree, transcripts, letters of recommendation, portfolio. Additional exam requirements/recommendations for international students: Required—TOEFL (minimum score 575 paper-based; 90 iBT). *Application deadline:* For fall admission, 1/5 for domestic and international students; for spring admission, 10/1 for domestic and international students. Application fee: $50 ($90 for international students). Electronic applications accepted. *Expenses: Tuition:* Full-time $30,834. *Required fees:* $1974. *Financial support:* Career-related internships or fieldwork, Federal Work-Study, institutionally sponsored loans, scholarships/grants, health care benefits, and unspecified assistantships available. Support available to part-time students. Financial award application deadline: 2/1; financial award applicants required to submit FAFSA. *Unit head:* Eve Baron, Chairperson, 718-687-5641, Fax: 718-636-3709, E-mail: ebaron@pratt.edu. *Application contact:* Natalie Capannelli, Director of Graduate Admissions, 718-636-3551, Fax: 718-399-4242, E-mail: ncapanne@pratt.edu.
Website: https://www.pratt.edu/academics/architecture/historic-preservation/

See Display on page 105 and Close-Up on page 125.

Roger Williams University, School of Architecture, Art and Historic Preservation, Bristol, RI 02809. Offers architecture (M Arch); art and architectural history (MA); historical preservation (MS, Certificate); urban and regional planning (Certificate). *Faculty:* 18 full-time (5 women), 9 part-time/adjunct (1 woman). *Students:* 107 full-time (52 women), 9 part-time (5 women); includes 10 minority (1 Asian, non-Hispanic/Latino; 7 Hispanic/Latino; 2 Two or more races, non-Hispanic/Latino), 5 international. Average age 26. 92 applicants, 93% accepted, 58 enrolled. In 2017, 46 master's, 1 other advanced degree awarded. *Degree requirements:* For master's, thesis. *Entrance requirements:* For master's, portfolio, 2 letters of recommendation, college transcript, letter of intent. Additional exam requirements/recommendations for international students: Required—TOEFL (minimum score 85 iBT), IELTS (minimum score 6.5). *Application deadline:* For fall admission, 4/1 for domestic students; for spring admission, 11/15 for domestic students. Application fee: $50. Electronic applications accepted. *Expenses:* $1,463 per credit hour (for M Arch); $876 per credit hour (for MS and MA); $258 graduation fee. *Financial support:* In 2017–18, 116 students received support, including 116 research assistantships (averaging $2,776 per year); career-related internships or fieldwork, scholarships/grants, and unspecified assistantships also available. Financial award application deadline: 4/1; financial award applicants required to submit FAFSA. *Unit head:* Stephen White, Dean, 401-254-3607, E-mail: swhite@rwu.edu. *Application contact:* Marcus Hanscom, Director of Graduate Admissions, 401-254-3345, Fax: 401-254-3557, E-mail: gradadmit@rwu.edu.
Website: http://www.rwu.edu/graduate/programs/graduate-programs/architecture

Rutgers University–New Brunswick, Graduate School-New Brunswick, Program in Art History, Piscataway, NJ 08854-8097. Offers art history (MA, PhD); curatorial studies (Certificate); historic preservation (Certificate). *Program availability:* Part-time. Terminal master's awarded for partial completion of doctoral program. *Degree requirements:* For master's, one foreign language, comprehensive exam; for doctorate, 2 foreign languages, comprehensive exam, thesis/dissertation. *Entrance requirements:* For master's and doctorate, GRE General Test, writing sample. Additional exam requirements/recommendations for international students: Required—TOEFL (minimum score 550 paper-based). Electronic applications accepted. *Faculty research:* Ancient and medieval art and architecture; Renaissance and Baroque art and architecture; modern and contemporary art and architecture; Italian studies; the arts of Asia, Africa, and the Americas.

Rutgers University–New Brunswick, Graduate School-New Brunswick, Program in Cultural Heritage and Preservation Studies, Piscataway, NJ 08854-8097. Offers cultural heritage and preservation studies (MA); historic preservation (Certificate).

St. Cloud State University, School of Graduate Studies, College of Social Sciences, Program in Cultural Resource Management Archeology, St. Cloud, MN 56301-4498. Offers MS. *Entrance requirements:* For master's, GRE General Test, minimum GPA of 2.75. Additional exam requirements/recommendations for international students: Required—Michigan English Language Assessment Battery; Recommended—TOEFL (minimum score 550 paper-based).

Savannah College of Art and Design, Program in Preservation Design, Savannah, GA 31402-3146. Offers MA, MFA. *Program availability:* Part-time, 100% online. *Faculty:* 4 full-time (1 woman). *Students:* 19 full-time (13 women), 26 part-time (24 women); includes 1 minority (Hispanic/Latino). Average age 33. 52 applicants, 37% accepted, 9 enrolled. In 2017, 13 master's awarded. *Degree requirements:* For master's, thesis (for some programs), preservation practicum (for MA); thesis (for MFA). *Entrance requirements:* For master's, GRE (recommended), portfolio (submitted in digital format), audition or writing submission, resume, statement of purpose, two letters of recommendation. Additional exam requirements/recommendations for international students: Recommended—TOEFL (minimum score 550 paper-based; 85 iBT), IELTS (minimum score 6.5). *Application deadline:* For fall admission, 4/1 for domestic and international students. Applications are processed on a rolling basis. Application fee: $40. Electronic applications accepted. *Expenses: Tuition:* Full-time $36,765; part-time $817 per credit hour. One-time fee: $500. *Financial support:* Career-related internships or fieldwork, Federal Work-Study, and scholarships/grants available. Financial award application deadline: 4/1; financial award applicants required to submit FAFSA. *Unit head:* Ivan Chow, Dean, School of Building Arts. *Application contact:* Jenny Jaquillard, Executive Director of Admissions, Recruitment and Events, 912-525-5100, Fax: 912-525-5985, E-mail: admission@scad.edu.
Website: http://www.scad.edu/academics/programs/preservation-design

School of the Art Institute of Chicago, Graduate Division, Program in Historic Preservation, Chicago, IL 60603-3103. Offers MSHP. *Entrance requirements:* Additional exam requirements/recommendations for international students: Required—TOEFL, IELTS.

Southeast Missouri State University, School of Graduate Studies, Department of History, Cape Girardeau, MO 63701-4799. Offers heritage interpretation (Certificate); historic preservation (Certificate); history (MA); public history (MA), including heritage education, historic preservation. *Program availability:* Part-time, evening/weekend. *Faculty:* 10 full-time (4 women). *Students:* 12 full-time (7 women), 14 part-time (5 women); includes 3 minority (2 Black or African American, non-Hispanic/Latino; 1 Hispanic/Latino). Average age 32. 12 applicants, 100% accepted, 10 enrolled. In 2017, 8 master's awarded. *Degree requirements:* For master's, comprehensive exam (for some programs), thesis or comprehensive exams plus a capstone project/paper (for history); thesis or internship plus advanced project in applied history and comprehensive exams (for public history). *Entrance requirements:* For master's, minimum GPA of 2.75; 24 semester hours of undergraduate credit in history; letter of intent indicating how past experiences have prepared the candidate for graduate study and what the candidate expects to achieve through graduate study; two letters of recommendation; academic or professional writing sample; for Certificate, minimum GPA of 2.75; letter of intent indicating how past experiences have prepared the candidate for graduate study and what the candidate expects to achieve through graduate study; two letters of recommendation; academic or professional writing sample. Additional exam requirements/recommendations for international students: Required—TOEFL (minimum score 550 paper-based; 79 iBT), IELTS (minimum score 6), PTE (minimum score 53). *Application deadline:* For fall admission, 8/1 for domestic students, 6/1 for international students; for spring admission, 11/21 for domestic students, 10/1 for international students; for summer admission, 5/15 for domestic students. Applications are processed on a rolling basis. Application fee: $30 ($40 for international students). Electronic applications accepted. *Expenses:* $270.35 per credit hour in-state tuition, $33.40 per credit hour fees. *Financial support:* In 2017–18, 4 students received support, including 4 teaching assistantships with full tuition reimbursements available; career-related internships or fieldwork, Federal Work-Study, scholarships/grants, traineeships, tuition waivers (full), and unspecified assistantships also available. Financial award application deadline: 6/30; financial award applicants required to submit FAFSA. *Faculty research:* Medieval Europe; modern Europe including Britain, Germany, France, Russia, and Spain; colonial and nineteenth-century America; twentieth-century America and American West; public history and medieval Europe; modern Europe including Britain, Germany, France, Russia, and Spain; colonial and nineteenth-century America; twentieth-century America and American West; public history and historic preservation; Latin America. *Unit head:* Dr. Toni Alexander, Chairperson/Professor of History, 573-651-2179, Fax: 573-651-5114, E-mail: talexander@semo.edu. *Application contact:* Dr. Vicky McAlister, Graduate Coordinator/Assistant Professor of History, 573-651-2763, Fax: 573-651-5114, E-mail: vmcalister@semo.edu.

Universidad Nacional Pedro Henriquez Urena, Graduate School, Santo Domingo, Dominican Republic. Offers agricultural diversity (MS), including horticultural/fruit production, tropical animal production; conservation of monuments and cultural assets (M Arch); ecology and environment (MS); environmental engineering (MEE); international relations (MA); natural resource management (MS); political science (MA); project optimization (MPM); project feasibility (MPM); project management (MPM); sanitation engineering (ME); science for teachers (MS); tropical Caribbean architecture (M Arch).

University at Buffalo, the State University of New York, Graduate School, School of Architecture and Planning, Department of Urban and Regional Planning, Buffalo, NY 12414. Offers community health and food systems (MUP); economic development (MUP); environment/land use (MUP); historic preservation (MUP, Certificate); neighborhood/community development (MUP); real estate development (MSRED); urban and regional planning (PhD); urban design (MUP); JD/MUP; M Arch/MUP. *Accreditation:* ACSP. *Program availability:* Part-time. *Faculty:* 13 full-time (6 women), 12 part-time/adjunct (3 women). *Students:* 76 full-time (27 women), 20 part-time (9 women); includes 17 minority (9 Black or African American, non-Hispanic/Latino; 5 Hispanic/Latino; 3 Two or more races, non-Hispanic/Latino), 20 international. Average age 27. 196 applicants, 20% accepted, 32 enrolled. In 2017, 35 master's, 1 doctorate, 5 other advanced degrees awarded. *Degree requirements:* For master's, thesis or alternative, project; for doctorate, comprehensive exam, thesis/dissertation. *Entrance requirements:* For master's, resume, three letters of recommendation, personal statement, transcripts; for doctorate, GRE, transcripts, three letters of recommendation, resume, research statement, writing sample. Additional exam requirements/

recommendations for international students: Required—TOEFL (minimum score 79 iBT), IELTS (minimum score 6.5). *Application deadline:* For fall admission, 3/1 priority date for domestic and international students; for spring admission, 10/31 priority date for domestic students, 10/1 priority date for international students. Applications are processed on a rolling basis. Application fee: $75. Electronic applications accepted. *Expenses:* $13,382. *Financial support:* In 2017–18, 45 students received support, including 3 fellowships with full tuition reimbursements available (averaging $15,600 per year), 2 research assistantships with partial tuition reimbursements available (averaging $13,390 per year), 15 teaching assistantships with partial tuition reimbursements available (averaging $4,800 per year); career-related internships or fieldwork, Federal Work-Study, institutionally sponsored loans, scholarships/grants, health care benefits, and unspecified assistantships also available. Financial award application deadline: 3/1; financial award applicants required to submit FAFSA. *Faculty research:* Economic and international development, environmental and land use planning, GIS and spatial analysis, urban design and physical planning, neighborhood planning and community development, historic preservation. *Total annual research expenditures:* $1.3 million. *Unit head:* Dr. Daniel B. Hess, Professor and Chair, 716-829-3671 Ext. 109, Fax: 716-829-3256, E-mail: dbhess@buffalo.edu. *Application contact:* Donna Rogalski, Department Secretary, 716-829-3671, Fax: 716-829-3256, E-mail: dmr1@buffalo.edu.
Website: http://www.ap.buffalo.edu/planning/

University of California, Los Angeles, Graduate Division, College of Letters and Science, Interdepartmental Program in Conservation of Archaeological and Ethnographic Materials, Los Angeles, CA 90095. Offers MA. *Degree requirements:* For master's, one foreign language, thesis, eleven-month internship. *Entrance requirements:* For master's, GRE General Test, bachelor's degree; minimum undergraduate GPA of 3.0 (or its equivalent if letter grade system not used); proficiency in one foreign language; portfolio; writing sample; documented practical experience; interview. Additional exam requirements/recommendations for international students: Required—TOEFL.

University of Colorado Denver, College of Architecture and Planning, Program in Historic Preservation, Denver, CO 80217. Offers MS. *Degree requirements:* For master's, thesis, 45 credit hours. *Entrance requirements:* For master's, GRE (recommended, especially for students with an undergraduate GPA of less than 3.0), portfolio of creative work; sample of writing or work project. Additional exam requirements/recommendations for international students: Required—TOEFL (minimum score 75 iBT). Electronic applications accepted. *Expenses:* Contact institution. *Faculty research:* Rural cultural landscapes; vernacular architecture; cultural preservation; architectural conservation, heritage, and policy.

University of Delaware, College of Arts and Sciences, Department of Art Conservation, Newark, DE 19716. Offers art conservation (MS); preservation studies (PhD). *Degree requirements:* For master's, internship, portfolio, oral exam, oral presentation. *Entrance requirements:* For master's, GRE General Test, course work in chemistry, art history/anthropology and studio art; minimum of 400 hours of conservation experience. Additional exam requirements/recommendations for international students: Recommended—TOEFL. Electronic applications accepted. *Faculty research:* Emergency response cleaning techniques, degradation process, art history, artists, materials, techniques of preservation and treatment.

University of Delaware, College of Arts and Sciences, School of Public Policy and Administration, Program in Urban Affairs and Public Policy, Newark, DE 19716. Offers governance planning and management (PhD); historic preservation (MA); social and urban policy (PhD); technology, environment and society (PhD); urban affairs and public policy (MA). *Program availability:* Part-time. Terminal master's awarded for partial completion of doctoral program. *Degree requirements:* For master's, analytical paper or thesis; for doctorate, thesis/dissertation. *Entrance requirements:* For master's, GRE General Test, minimum GPA of 3.0; for doctorate, GRE General Test, minimum GPA of 3.5. Additional exam requirements/recommendations for international students: Required—TOEFL. Electronic applications accepted. *Faculty research:* Political economy; social policy analysis; technology and society; historic preservation; urban policy.

University of Florida, Graduate School, College of Liberal Arts and Sciences, Department of History, Gainesville, FL 32611. Offers historic preservation (MA, PhD); history (MA, PhD); Jewish studies (MA); women's and gender studies (PhD); JD/MA; JD/PhD. *Program availability:* Part-time. Terminal master's awarded for partial completion of doctoral program. *Degree requirements:* For master's, variable foreign language requirement, thesis optional, 30 credit hours; for doctorate, variable foreign language requirement, comprehensive exam, thesis/dissertation, 90 credit hours. *Entrance requirements:* For master's and doctorate, GRE General Test, minimum GPA of 3.0. Additional exam requirements/recommendations for international students: Required—TOEFL (minimum score 550 paper-based; 80 iBT), IELTS (minimum score 6). Electronic applications accepted. *Faculty research:* Latin American and Caribbean history, nineteenth century U.S. history, medieval European history, African history and Atlantic world history.

University of Georgia, College of Environment and Design, Athens, GA 30602. Offers environmental planning and design (MEPD); historic preservation (MHP); landscape architecture (MLA). *Accreditation:* ACSP.

University of Hawaii at Manoa, Office of Graduate Education, College of Arts and Humanities, Department of American Studies, Program in Historic Preservation, Honolulu, HI 96822. Offers Graduate Certificate. *Program availability:* Part-time. *Entrance requirements:* Additional exam requirements/recommendations for international students: Required—TOEFL (minimum score 600 paper-based; 100 iBT), IELTS (minimum score 7).

The University of Kansas, Graduate Studies, School of Architecture and Design, Department of Architecture, Lawrence, KS 66045. Offers architectural acoustics (Certificate); architecture (M Arch, PhD); health and wellness (Certificate); historic preservation (Certificate); urban design (Certificate). *Students:* 91 full-time (43 women), 14 part-time (6 women); includes 14 minority (3 Black or African American, non-Hispanic/Latino; 4 Asian, non-Hispanic/Latino; 4 Hispanic/Latino; 3 Two or more races, non-Hispanic/Latino), 21 international. Average age 25. 100 applicants, 52% accepted, 20 enrolled. In 2017, 77 master's, 7 doctorates, 5 other advanced degrees awarded. Terminal master's awarded for partial completion of doctoral program. *Entrance requirements:* For master's, GRE, transcript; resume; minimum GPA of 3.0; statement of purpose; letters of recommendation; portfolio of design work, or samples of written work or other creative artifacts produced if previous degree was not in a design-related discipline; for doctorate, GRE, transcript, resume, minimum GPA of 3.0, statement of purpose, letters of recommendation, research-informed writing sample, exhibit of work illustrating applicant's interests and abilities in areas related to the design disciplines. Additional exam requirements/recommendations for international students: Required—TOEFL, IELTS. *Application deadline:* For fall admission, 1/15 priority date for domestic and international students; for summer admission, 1/15 priority date for domestic and international students. Application fee: $65 ($85 for international students). Electronic applications accepted. *Financial support:* Fellowships, research assistantships, teaching assistantships, scholarships/grants, health care benefits, and unspecified assistantships available. Financial award application deadline: 1/15; financial award applicants required to submit FAFSA. *Faculty research:* Design build, sustainability, emergent technology, healthy places, urban design. *Unit head:* Prof. Jae Chang, Chair, 785-864-1446, E-mail: jdchang@ku.edu. *Application contact:* Gera Elliott, Admissions Coordinator, 785-864-3167, Fax: 785-864-5185, E-mail: archku@ku.edu.
Website: http://architecture.ku.edu/

University of Kentucky, Graduate School, College of Design, Department of Historic Preservation, Lexington, KY 40506-0032. Offers MHP. *Degree requirements:* For master's, comprehensive exam. *Entrance requirements:* For master's, GRE General Test, minimum undergraduate GPA of 2.75. Additional exam requirements/recommendations for international students: Required—TOEFL (minimum score 550 paper-based). Electronic applications accepted.

University of Maryland, College Park, Academic Affairs, School of Architecture, Planning and Preservation, Program in Historic Preservation, College Park, MD 20742. Offers MHP, Certificate. *Degree requirements:* For Certificate, thesis. *Entrance requirements:* For master's, GRE, minimum GPA of 3.0, 3 letters of recommendation, writing sample. Additional exam requirements/recommendations for international students: Required—TOEFL. Electronic applications accepted.

University of Massachusetts Amherst, Graduate School, College of Humanities and Fine Arts, Department of Architecture, Amherst, MA 01003. Offers architecture (M Arch); design (MS); design in historic preservation (MS). *Program availability:* Part-time. *Degree requirements:* For master's, thesis or alternative, project. *Entrance requirements:* For master's, GRE General Test (for M Arch only), 3 letters of recommendation (M Arch only); portfolio. Additional exam requirements/recommendations for international students: Required—TOEFL (minimum score 550 paper-based; 80 iBT), IELTS (minimum score 6.5). Electronic applications accepted.

University of New Mexico, Graduate Studies, School of Architecture and Planning, Program in Historic Preservation and Regionalism, Albuquerque, NM 87131-2039. Offers Graduate Certificate. *Program availability:* Part-time, evening/weekend. *Faculty:* 2 full-time (both women). *Students:* 1 (woman) full-time, 5 part-time (3 women). Average age 44. 4 applicants, 100% accepted, 3 enrolled. In 2017, 9 Graduate Certificates awarded. *Application deadline:* For fall admission, 11/1 priority date for domestic students; for spring admission, 3/1 priority date for domestic students. Application fee: $50. Electronic applications accepted. *Financial support:* Research assistantships, career-related internships or fieldwork, and scholarships/grants available. Support available to part-time students. *Unit head:* Chris Wilson, Director, 505-277-3303, Fax: 505-277-0897, E-mail: chwilson@unm.edu. *Application contact:* Elizabeth M. Rowe, Senior Academic Adviser, 505-277-1303, Fax: 505-277-0076, E-mail: erowe@unm.edu.
Website: http://saap.unm.edu/

University of North Alabama, College of Arts and Sciences, Department of History, Program in Public History, Florence, AL 35632-0001. Offers historic preservation (MA); historical administration (MA). *Program availability:* Part-time. *Faculty:* 9 full-time (3 women), 3 part-time/adjunct (2 women). *Students:* 5 full-time (3 women), 3 part-time (2 women). Average age 35. 4 applicants, 100% accepted, 4 enrolled. In 2017, 3 master's awarded. *Degree requirements:* For master's, comprehensive exam (for some programs), thesis optional. *Entrance requirements:* For master's, GRE, three letters of recommendation; essay; writing sample. Additional exam requirements/recommendations for international students: Required—TOEFL (minimum score 79 iBT), IELTS (minimum score 6), TWE, PTE (minimum score 54). *Application deadline:* Applications are processed on a rolling basis. Application fee: $50 ($100 for international students). Electronic applications accepted. *Expenses:* Tuition, state resident: full-time $7824; part-time $5943 per year. Tuition, nonresident: full-time $15,648; part-time $11,736 per year. *Required fees:* $3064; $2298 per unit. Tuition and fees vary according to course load and reciprocity agreements. *Financial support:* In 2017–18, 5 students received support. Federal Work-Study, scholarships/grants, and unspecified assistantships available. Financial award application deadline: 2/1; financial award applicants required to submit FAFSA. *Unit head:* Dr. Jeffrey Bibbee, Chair, 256-765-4306, E-mail: jrbibbee@una.edu. *Application contact:* Hillary N. Coats, Graduate Admissions Coordinator, 256-765-4447, E-mail: graduate@una.edu.
Website: https://www.una.edu/history/graduate-students/master-of-arts-in-public-history.html

The University of North Carolina at Greensboro, Graduate School, College of Arts and Sciences, Department of Interior Architecture, Greensboro, NC 27412-5001. Offers historic preservation (Certificate); interior architecture (MS); museum studies (Certificate). *Degree requirements:* For master's, thesis. *Entrance requirements:* For master's, GRE General Test or MAT, bachelor's degree in interior design, interview, portfolio. Additional exam requirements/recommendations for international students: Required—TOEFL. Electronic applications accepted.

University of Oregon, Graduate School, College of Design, Program in Historic Preservation, Eugene, OR 97403. Offers MS. *Degree requirements:* For master's, thesis, internship. *Entrance requirements:* For master's, participation in Pacific Northwest Field School. Additional exam requirements/recommendations for international students: Required—TOEFL. *Faculty research:* Vernacular architecture, Native American architecture, masonry structure and details, wood construction systems, cultural landscapes.

University of Pennsylvania, School of Design, Program in Historic Preservation, Philadelphia, PA 19104. Offers MS, Certificate. *Faculty:* 3 full-time (0 women), 3 part-time/adjunct (1 woman). *Students:* 44 full-time (34 women), 1 (woman) part-time; includes 9 minority (1 Black or African American, non-Hispanic/Latino; 1 Asian, non-Hispanic/Latino; 6 Hispanic/Latino; 1 Two or more races, non-Hispanic/Latino), 10 international. Average age 27. 50 applicants, 94% accepted, 19 enrolled. In 2017, 20 master's, 6 other advanced degrees awarded. *Degree requirements:* For master's, thesis. *Entrance requirements:* For master's, GRE, official academic transcripts, 3 letters of recommendation, course in computer-aided drafting (preferably AutoCad). Additional exam requirements/recommendations for international students: Required—TOEFL (minimum score 600 paper-based; 100 iBT). *Application deadline:* For fall admission, 1/12 for domestic students. Application fee: $80. *Financial support:* Research assistantships, teaching assistantships, career-related internships or fieldwork, Federal Work-Study, institutionally sponsored loans, scholarships/grants, and unspecified assistantships available. Financial award application deadline: 4/15; financial award applicants required to submit FAFSA. *Faculty research:* Theories and methods of preservation planning, historic building technology and conservation of building materials, ways in which visual culture inform planning and design, cultural policy and the economics of preservation. *Unit head:* Dr. Randall F. Mason, Chair/Associate Professor, 215-898-3169, Fax: 215-573-6326, E-mail: rfmason@upenn.edu. *Application contact:* Nadine Beauharnois, Administrative Assistant, 215-898-3169, Fax: 215-573-6326, E-mail: pennhsvp@upenn.edu.
Website: http://www.design.upenn.edu/historic-preservation

University of Rochester, School of Arts and Sciences, Program in Photographic Preservation and Collections Management, Rochester, NY 14627. Offers MA. Program offered jointly with George Eastman Museum. *Students:* 9 full-time (6 women), 1 (woman) part-time; includes 1 minority (Black or African American, non-Hispanic/Latino).

Average age 28. 14 applicants, 86% accepted, 4 enrolled. In 2017, 9 master's awarded. *Degree requirements:* For master's, essay (counts as qualifying exam). *Entrance requirements:* For master's, writing sample, transcripts, three letters of recommendation, one- to two-page statement of purpose. Additional exam requirements/recommendations for international students: Required—TOEFL. *Application deadline:* For fall admission, 1/15 for domestic and international students. Application fee: $60. Electronic applications accepted. *Expenses:* $1,596 per credit hour. *Financial support:* In 2017–18, 4 students received support. Tuition waivers (partial) available. Financial award application deadline: 1/15. *Unit head:* Jacob Lewis, Associate Academic Director, 585-275-4287, E-mail: joan.saab@rochester.edu. *Application contact:* Martin Collier, Administrator, 585-275-7451, E-mail: marty.collier@rochester.edu.
Website: https://www.sas.rochester.edu/ppc/

University of South Carolina, The Graduate School, College of Arts and Sciences, Department of History, Program in Public History, Columbia, SC 29208. Offers archive management (MA); historic preservation (MA); museum administration (MA); museum management (Certificate); MLIS/MA. *Degree requirements:* For master's, one foreign language, thesis, internship. *Entrance requirements:* For master's, GRE General Test, writing sample. Additional exam requirements/recommendations for international students: Required—TOEFL. Electronic applications accepted. *Faculty research:* Museum studies, historic preservation, archives administration.

The University of Texas at Austin, Graduate School, School of Architecture, Program in Historic Preservation, Austin, TX 78712-1111. Offers M Arch, MS, MSCRP.

University of Vermont, Graduate College, College of Arts and Sciences, Program in Historic Preservation, Burlington, VT 05405. Offers MS. *Students:* 11 (6 women). 12 applicants, 100% accepted, 5 enrolled. In 2017, 6 master's awarded. *Entrance requirements:* For master's, GRE General Test, writing sample or sample project. Additional exam requirements/recommendations for international students: Required—TOEFL (minimum score 550 paper-based, 90 iBT) or IELTS (6.5). *Application deadline:* For fall admission, 3/1 priority date for domestic and international students. Applications are processed on a rolling basis. Application fee: $65. Electronic applications accepted. *Expenses:* $646 per credit in-state, $1,130 per credit out-of-state. *Financial support:* In 2017–18, 5 students received support, including 5 teaching assistantships with partial tuition reimbursements available (averaging $8,000 per year); fellowships, Federal Work-Study, scholarships/grants, and health care benefits also available. Financial award application deadline: 3/1. *Faculty research:* Architectural environment. *Unit head:* Thomas Visser, Director, 802-656-3180, E-mail: histpres@uvm.edu.
Website: http://www.uvm.edu/~histpres/

University of Washington, Graduate School, College of Built Environments, Interdisciplinary Program in Historic Preservation, Seattle, WA 98195. Offers Certificate. Offered in cooperation with the Departments of Architecture, Landscape Architecture, and Urban Design and Planning. *Program availability:* Part-time. Electronic applications accepted. *Faculty research:* History of the built environment, historic preservation planning, vernacular architecture, ethnic and gender issues in preservation, restoration.

Ursuline College, School of Graduate and Professional Studies, Program in Historic Preservation, Pepper Pike, OH 44124-4398. Offers MA. *Program availability:* Part-time. *Faculty:* 1 (woman) full-time. *Students:* 4 full-time (all women), 2 part-time (both women). Average age 41. 2 applicants, 100% accepted, 2 enrolled. In 2017, 3 master's awarded. *Degree requirements:* For master's, thesis. *Entrance requirements:* For master's, minimum undergraduate GPA of 3.0. Additional exam requirements/recommendations for international students: Required—TOEFL (minimum score 500 paper-based; 80 iBT). *Application deadline:* For fall admission, 8/1 priority date for domestic students. Applications are processed on a rolling basis. Application fee: $25. Electronic applications accepted. *Expenses:* $1,094 per credit hour. *Financial support:* In 2017–18, 2 students received support. Scholarships/grants available. Financial award application deadline: 3/1; financial award applicants required to submit FAFSA. *Faculty research:* Women representation in historic landmarks, geographic history, digital humanities. *Unit head:* Dr. Bari Stith, Director, 440-646-8135, Fax: 440-684-6088, E-mail: bstith@ursuline.edu. *Application contact:* Melanie Steele, Director, Graduate Admission, 440-646-8146, Fax: 440-684-6138, E-mail: graduateadmissions@ursuline.edu.

Landscape Architecture

Academy of Art University, Graduate Programs, School of Landscape Architecture, San Francisco, CA 94105-3410. Offers MA, MFA. *Program availability:* Part-time, 100% online. *Faculty:* 2 full-time (1 woman), 11 part-time/adjunct (5 women). *Students:* 25 full-time (15 women), 8 part-time (0 women); includes 1 minority (Hispanic/Latino), 30 international. Average age 28. 11 applicants, 100% accepted, 5 enrolled. In 2017, 17 master's awarded. *Degree requirements:* For master's, final review. *Entrance requirements:* For master's, statement of intent; resume; portfolio/reel; official college transcripts. *Application deadline:* Applications are processed on a rolling basis. Application fee: $50. Electronic applications accepted. *Expenses: Tuition:* Part-time $982 per unit. *Financial support:* Career-related internships or fieldwork, Federal Work-Study, and scholarships/grants available. Financial award application deadline: 8/10; financial award applicants required to submit FAFSA. *Unit head:* 800-544-ARTS, E-mail: info@academyart.edu. *Application contact:* 800-544-ARTS, E-mail: info@academyart.edu.
Website: http://www.academyart.edu/landscape-architecture-school/index.html

Arizona State University at the Tempe campus, Herberger Institute for Design and the Arts, The Design School, Tempe, AZ 85287-1605. Offers architecture (M Arch); building design/built environment (MS); design (MSD), including arts, media, and engineering, healthcare and healing environments (MSD, PhD), industrial design, interaction design, interior design, new product innovation, visual communication design; design, environment and the arts (PhD), including design, digital culture, healthcare and healing environments (MSD, PhD), history, theory, and criticism; landscape architecture (MLA); urban design (MUD); MA/MBA. *Accreditation:* NASAD. Terminal master's awarded for partial completion of doctoral program. *Degree requirements:* For master's, thesis optional, interactive Program of Study (iPOS) submitted before completing 50 percent of required credit hours; for doctorate, comprehensive exam, thesis/dissertation, interactive Program of Study (iPOS) submitted before completing 50 percent of required credit hours. *Entrance requirements:* For master's, GRE General Test, minimum GPA of 3.0 or equivalent in last 2 years of work leading to bachelor's degree, design/creative works portfolio, 3 references, statement of intent; for doctorate, GRE, master's degree in architecture, graphic design, industrial design, interior design, landscape architecture, or art history or equivalent standing; statement of purpose; 3 letters of recommendation; indication of potential faculty mentor; sample of written work. Additional exam requirements/recommendations for international students: Required—TOEFL (minimum score 600 paper-based; 100 iBT). Electronic applications accepted.

Auburn University, Graduate School, College of Architecture, Design, and Construction, Program in Landscape Architecture, Auburn University, AL 36849. Offers ML Arch. *Accreditation:* ASLA. *Faculty:* 23 full-time (8 women), 8 part-time/adjunct (0 women). *Students:* 20 full-time (12 women); includes 1 minority (Asian, non-Hispanic/Latino), 13 international. Average age 25. 34 applicants, 71% accepted, 12 enrolled. In 2017, 16 master's awarded. *Entrance requirements:* For master's, 3 letters of recommendation. Application fee: $50 ($60 for international students). *Expenses:* Tuition, state resident: full-time $10,974; part-time $519 per credit hour. Tuition, nonresident: full-time $29,658; part-time $1557 per credit hour. *Required fees:* $816 per semester. Tuition and fees vary according to degree level and program. *Financial support:* Applicants required to submit FAFSA. *Unit head:* David Hill, Chair, 334-844-5449. *Application contact:* Dr. George Flowers, Dean of the Graduate School, 334-844-2125.

Ball State University, Graduate School, College of Architecture and Planning, Department of Landscape Architecture, Muncie, IN 47306. Offers MLA. *Accreditation:* ASLA. *Program availability:* Part-time. *Faculty:* 13 full-time (6 women). *Students:* 24 full-time (14 women), 6 part-time (4 women), 15 international. Average age 30. 23 applicants, 78% accepted, 7 enrolled. In 2017, 18 master's awarded. *Entrance requirements:* For master's, minimum baccalaureate GPA of 2.75 or 3.0 in latter half of baccalaureate, resume, three letters of reference, copies of all transcripts, portfolio, writing sample. Additional exam requirements/recommendations for international students: Required—TOEFL (minimum score 550 paper-based; 79 iBT), IELTS (minimum score 6.5). *Application deadline:* Applications are processed on a rolling basis. Application fee: $60. Electronic applications accepted. *Expenses:* Contact institution. *Financial support:* In 2017–18, 11 students received support, including 1 research assistantship with partial tuition reimbursement available (averaging $3,425 per year), 9 teaching assistantships with partial tuition reimbursements available (averaging $4,306 per year); unspecified assistantships also available. Financial award application deadline: 3/1; financial award applicants required to submit FAFSA. *Unit head:* Joseph Blalock, Chairperson, 765-285-4258, Fax: 765-285-1983, E-mail: jblalock@bsu.edu.
Website: http://www.bsu.edu/landscape

Boston Architectural College, Graduate Programs, Boston, MA 02115-2795. Offers architecture (M Arch); historic preservation (MDS); interior design (MID); landscape architecture (MLA); sustainable design (MDS). *Accreditation:* CIDA. *Degree requirements:* For master's, thesis. *Entrance requirements:* For master's, portfolio (recommended). Electronic applications accepted.

California State Polytechnic University, Pomona, Program in Landscape Architecture, Pomona, CA 91768-2557. Offers M Land Arch. *Accreditation:* ASLA. *Program availability:* Part-time, evening/weekend. *Students:* 31 full-time (19 women); includes 14 minority (6 Asian, non-Hispanic/Latino; 8 Hispanic/Latino), 5 international. Average age 30. 45 applicants, 67% accepted, 18 enrolled. In 2017, 11 master's awarded. *Entrance requirements:* Additional exam requirements/recommendations for international students: Required—TOEFL (minimum score 550 paper-based). *Application deadline:* Applications are processed on a rolling basis. Application fee: $55. Electronic applications accepted. *Expenses:* Contact institution. *Financial support:* Application deadline: 3/2; applicants required to submit FAFSA. *Unit head:* Prof. Gerald O. Taylor, Graduate Coordinator, 909-869-6891, Fax: 909-869-2580, E-mail: jotaylor@cpp.edu. *Application contact:* Deborah L. Brandon, Executive Director of Admissions and Enrollment Planning, 909-869-3427, Fax: 909-869-5315, E-mail: dlbrandon@cpp.edu.
Website: https://env.cpp.edu/la/degree/master-landscape-architecture

City College of the City University of New York, Graduate School, The Bernard and Anne Spitzer School of Architecture, Program in Landscape Architecture, New York, NY 10031-9198. Offers MLA. *Accreditation:* ASLA.

Clemson University, Graduate School, College of Architecture, Arts, and Humanities, School of Architecture, Clemson, SC 29634. Offers architecture (M Arch, MS, Certificate), including community build (Certificate); architecture and health (M Arch); digital ecologies (Certificate); historic preservation (MS, Certificate); integrated project delivery (Certificate); landscape architecture (MLA); planning, design and the built environment (PhD); resilient urban design (MRUD). *Faculty:* 38 full-time (13 women), 13 part-time/adjunct (6 women). *Students:* 149 full-time (98 women); includes 17 minority (2 Black or African American, non-Hispanic/Latino; 6 Asian, non-Hispanic/Latino; 9 Hispanic/Latino), 53 international. Average age 25. 317 applicants, 63% accepted, 54 enrolled. In 2017, 92 master's, 4 doctorates, 12 other advanced degrees awarded. *Degree requirements:* For master's, thesis (for some programs); for doctorate, comprehensive exam, thesis/dissertation. *Entrance requirements:* For master's, GRE General Test, design portfolio, unofficial transcripts, letters of recommendation, personal statement. Additional exam requirements/recommendations for international students: Required—TOEFL (minimum score 80 iBT); Recommended—IELTS (minimum score 6.5), TSE (minimum score 54). *Application deadline:* For fall admission, 1/15 for domestic and international students. Applications are processed on a rolling basis. Application fee: $80 ($90 for international students). Electronic applications accepted. *Expenses:* $6,564 per semester full-time resident, $12,538 per semester full-time non-resident, $743 per credit hour part-time resident, $1,486 per credit hour part-time non-resident, $1,203 per credit hour online, other fees may apply per session. *Financial support:* In 2017–18, 131 students received support, including 63 fellowships with partial tuition reimbursements available (averaging $2,206 per year), 24 research assistantships with partial tuition reimbursements available (averaging $16,900 per year), 7 teaching assistantships with partial tuition reimbursements available (averaging $16,629 per year); career-related internships or fieldwork and unspecified assistantships also available. Financial award application deadline: 1/15. *Faculty research:* Architecture and health, sustainable design, community design-build, architectural robotics, digital fabrication. *Total annual research expenditures:* $110,347. *Unit head:* Kate Schwennsen, Program Director, 864-656-3895, E-mail: kschwen@clemson.edu. *Application contact:* Dr. Dan Harding, Graduate Director, 864-606-6645, E-mail: hardin4@clemson.edu.
Website: https://www.clemson.edu/caah/departments/architecture/index.html

Colorado State University, College of Agricultural Sciences, Department of Horticulture and Landscape Architecture, Fort Collins, CO 80523-1173. Offers MLA, MS, PhD. *Faculty:* 15 full-time (4 women), 2 part-time/adjunct (1 woman). *Students:* 17 full-time (7 women), 19 part-time (9 women); includes 2 minority (both Hispanic/Latino), 15 international. Average age 34. 50 applicants, 52% accepted, 4 enrolled. In 2017, 11 master's awarded. Terminal master's awarded for partial completion of doctoral program. *Degree requirements:* For master's, thesis (for some programs), research paper; for doctorate, thesis/dissertation. *Entrance requirements:* For master's, GRE General Test (minimum score of 300 combined Verbal and Quantitative sections), minimum GPA of 3.0, letters of reference, transcripts, resume/curriculum vitae, statement of purpose; for doctorate, GRE General Test (minimum score of 300 combined Verbal and Quantitative sections), minimum GPA of 3.0, letters of reference, statement of purpose, resume/curriculum vitae, transcripts. Additional exam requirements/recommendations for international students: Required—TOEFL (minimum score 550 paper-based), IELTS. *Application deadline:* For fall admission, 4/1 for domestic and international students; for spring admission, 9/1 for domestic and international students; for summer admission, 1/1 for domestic and international students. Application fee: $60 ($70 for international students). Electronic applications accepted. *Expenses:* Tuition, state resident: full-time $9917. Tuition, nonresident: full-time $24,312. *Required fees:* $2284. Tuition and fees vary according to course load and program. *Financial support:* In 2017–18, 9 research assistantships with partial tuition reimbursements (averaging $19,924 per year), 6 teaching assistantships with partial tuition reimbursements (averaging $13,068 per year) were awarded; scholarships/grants and unspecified assistantships also available. Financial award application deadline: 2/15. *Faculty research:* Specialty crops, environmental physiology, water requirements for plant life, biochemical diversity, land reclamation within post-mined landscapes. *Total annual research expenditures:* $1.2 million. *Unit head:* Dr. Jessica G. Davis, Department Head/Professor, 970-491-7018, Fax: 970-491-7745, E-mail: jessica.davis@colostate.edu. *Application contact:* Kathi Nietfeld, Graduate Coordinator, 970-491-7018, Fax: 970-491-7745, E-mail: kathi.nietfeld@colostate.edu. Website: http://hortla.agsci.colostate.edu

Columbia University, School of Professional Studies, Program in Landscape Design, New York, NY 10027. Offers MS. *Program availability:* Part-time. *Entrance requirements:* For master's, minimum undergraduate GPA of 3.0. Additional exam requirements/recommendations for international students: Required—American Language Program placement test. *Expenses: Tuition:* Full-time $44,864; part-time $1704 per credit. *Required fees:* $2370 per semester. One-time fee: $105.

The Conway School, Program in Ecological Design, Conway, MA 01341-0179. Offers MS. *Faculty:* 2 full-time (1 woman), 10 part-time/adjunct (6 women). *Students:* 18 full-time (9 women). Average age 41. *Degree requirements:* For master's, projects. *Application deadline:* For fall admission, 2/1 priority date for domestic students. Applications are processed on a rolling basis. Application fee: $50. *Expenses:* $35,998 tuition. *Financial support:* Career-related internships or fieldwork, institutionally sponsored loans, and scholarships/grants available. Financial award application deadline: 11/9; financial award applicants required to submit FAFSA. *Faculty research:* Restoration of native plant communities; integration of humanities, environment, and design. *Unit head:* Ken Byrne, Academic Coordinator, 413-369-4044. *Application contact:* Kate Cholakis, Director of Admissions, 413-369-4044, E-mail: admissions@csld.edu. Website: http://www.csld.edu/

Cornell University, Graduate School, Graduate Fields of Agriculture and Life Sciences and Graduate Fields of Architecture, Art and Planning, Field of Landscape Architecture, Ithaca, NY 14853. Offers MLA, MPS. *Accreditation:* ASLA. *Degree requirements:* For master's, project or thesis. *Entrance requirements:* For master's, GRE General Test (recommended), portfolio, 2 letters of recommendation. Additional exam requirements/recommendations for international students: Required—TOEFL (minimum score 550 paper-based; 77 iBT). Electronic applications accepted. *Faculty research:* Urban horticulture and landscape design, urban design research, cultural landscape history, women in landscape architecture, landscape design language, Japanese landscape architecture.

Florida Agricultural and Mechanical University, Division of Graduate Studies, Research, and Continuing Education, School of Architecture, Tallahassee, FL 32307-3200. Offers architectural studies (MS Arch); architecture (professional) (M Arch); landscape architecture (MLA). *Program availability:* Part-time. *Degree requirements:* For master's, thesis. *Entrance requirements:* For master's, GRE General Test, minimum GPA of 3.0, portfolio. Additional exam requirements/recommendations for international students: Required—TOEFL (minimum score 550 paper-based). *Faculty research:* Environmental technology, post-occupancy evaluation, building economics, design methods, computer-aided design.

Florida International University, College of Communication, Architecture and The Arts, Department of Landscape Architecture, Miami, FL 33199. Offers MLA. *Accreditation:* ASLA. *Program availability:* Part-time. *Faculty:* 4 full-time (2 women), 3 part-time/adjunct (2 women). *Students:* 34 full-time (17 women), 5 part-time (2 women); includes 23 minority (4 Black or African American, non-Hispanic/Latino; 1 Asian, non-Hispanic/Latino; 17 Hispanic/Latino; 1 Two or more races, non-Hispanic/Latino), 6 international. Average age 28. 27 applicants, 33% accepted, 6 enrolled. In 2017, 13 master's awarded. *Entrance requirements:* For master's, GRE or minimum GPA of 3.0 in upper-level undergraduate work, portfolio. Additional exam requirements/recommendations for international students: Required—TOEFL (minimum score 550 paper-based; 80 iBT). *Application deadline:* For fall admission, 2/1 for domestic and international students. Application fee: $30. Electronic applications accepted. *Expenses:* Tuition, state resident: full-time $8912; part-time $446 per credit hour. Tuition, nonresident: full-time $21,393; part-time $992 per credit hour. *Required fees:* $390; $195 per semester. *Financial support:* Institutionally sponsored loans and scholarships/grants available. Financial award application deadline: 3/1; financial award applicants required to submit FAFSA. *Unit head:* Jason Chandler, Chair, 305-348-6913, E-mail: jason.chandler@fiu.edu. *Application contact:* Nanett Rojas, Assistant Director, Graduate Admissions, 305-348-7464, Fax: 305-348-7441, E-mail: gradadm@fiu.edu. Website: http://carta.fiu.edu/landscape/

Harvard University, Graduate School of Arts and Sciences, Committee on Architecture, Landscape Architecture, and Urban Planning, Cambridge, MA 02138. Offers architecture (PhD); landscape architecture (PhD); urban planning (PhD). *Accreditation:* ACSP. *Degree requirements:* For doctorate, one foreign language, thesis/dissertation, oral exam. *Entrance requirements:* For doctorate, GRE General Test. Additional exam requirements/recommendations for international students: Required—TOEFL.

Harvard University, Graduate School of Design, Department of Landscape Architecture, Cambridge, MA 02138. Offers MLA. *Accreditation:* ASLA. *Entrance requirements:* For master's, GRE General Test. Additional exam requirements/recommendations for international students: Required—TOEFL (minimum score 600 paper-based; 104 iBT). Electronic applications accepted.

Illinois Institute of Technology, Graduate College, College of Architecture, Chicago, IL 60616. Offers M Arch, MLA, MS Arch, PhD, MLA/M Arch. *Accreditation:* ASLA. *Program availability:* Part-time. Terminal master's awarded for partial completion of doctoral program. *Degree requirements:* For master's, comprehensive exam (for some programs), thesis (for some programs); for doctorate, comprehensive exam, thesis/dissertation. *Entrance requirements:* For master's, GRE General Test (minimum score 292 Quantitative and Verbal, 2.5 Analytical Writing), minimum college GPA of 3.0, official transcripts, portfolio, 3 letters of recommendation, professional statement; for doctorate, GRE General Test (minimum score 900 Quantitative and Verbal, 2.5 Analytical Writing), minimum GPA of 3.5, official transcripts, portfolio, 3 letters of recommendation, professional statement. Additional exam requirements/recommendations for international students: Required—TOEFL (minimum score 550 paper-based; 80 iBT). Electronic applications accepted. *Faculty research:* Sustainable design and efficiency; the influence of climate and environment on building form; emerging urbanisms; computer applications (such as 3-D modeling); the design, planning and structure of high-rise buildings.

Iowa State University of Science and Technology, Department of Landscape Architecture, Ames, IA 50011. Offers MLA, MS, MCRP/MLA. *Accreditation:* ASLA. *Program availability:* Part-time. *Degree requirements:* For master's, thesis. *Entrance requirements:* For master's, GRE (highly recommended), portfolio. Additional exam requirements/recommendations for international students: Required—TOEFL (minimum score 600 paper-based; 79 iBT), IELTS (minimum score 7). Electronic applications accepted. *Faculty research:* Landscape ecology, geographic information systems, landscape perception, historic preservation, resource management, design.

Kansas State University, Graduate School, College of Architecture, Planning and Design, Department of Landscape Architecture and Regional and Community Planning, Manhattan, KS 66506. Offers community development (MS); landscape architecture (MLA); regional and community planning (MRCP). MS offered online through the Great Plains Interactive Distance Education Alliance: Iowa State University, University of Nebraska, North Dakota State University, South Dakota State University. *Accreditation:* ACSP; ASLA. *Program availability:* Part-time, 100% online. Terminal master's awarded for partial completion of doctoral program. *Degree requirements:* For master's, thesis, oral exam. *Entrance requirements:* Additional exam requirements/recommendations for international students: Required—TOEFL (minimum score 600 paper-based), IELTS (minimum score 6.5). Electronic applications accepted. *Faculty research:* Community planning and design, design and implementation, geospatial modeling, fluvial and green systems, transportation systems.

Kent State University, College of Architecture and Environmental Design, Kent, OH 44242-0001. Offers architecture (M Arch); architecture and environmental design (MS); health care design (MHCD); landscape architecture (MLA); urban design (MUD); M Arch/MBA; M Arch/MUD. *Program availability:* Part-time. *Faculty:* 19 full-time (2 women), 15 part-time/adjunct (6 women). *Students:* 70 full-time (27 women), 13 part-time (7 women); includes 8 minority (1 Black or African American, non-Hispanic/Latino; 1 Asian, non-Hispanic/Latino; 4 Hispanic/Latino; 2 Two or more races, non-Hispanic/Latino), 13 international. Average age 26. 100 applicants, 82% accepted, 57 enrolled. In 2017, 59 master's awarded. *Degree requirements:* For master's, thesis (for some programs), capstone project (for some programs). *Entrance requirements:* For master's, GRE with minimum scores 151 (460) verbal reasoning, 150 (620) quantitative reasoning, and 4.25 analytical writing (except for MHCD), letters of recommendation, portfolio. Additional exam requirements/recommendations for international students: Required—TOEFL (minimum score 550 paper-based; 80 iBT), IELTS (minimum score 6.5), PTE (minimum score 54), Michigan English Language Assessment Battery (minimum score 77). *Application deadline:* Applications are processed on a rolling basis. Application fee: $45 ($70 for international students). Electronic applications accepted. *Expenses:* Tuition, state resident: full-time $11,310; part-time $515 per credit hour. Tuition, nonresident: full-time $20,396; part-time $928 per credit hour. *International tuition:* $18,544 full-time. *Financial support:* Research assistantships with full tuition reimbursements, teaching assistantships with full tuition reimbursements, Federal Work-Study, scholarships/grants, and unspecified assistantships available. Financial award application deadline: 2/1; financial award applicants required to submit FAFSA. *Unit head:* Mark Mistur, Dean, E-mail: mmistur1@kent.edu. *Application contact:* Johnathan Fleming, Assistant Professor and Director, Master of Architecture, 330-672-0934, E-mail: jpflemi1@kent.edu. Website: http://www.kent.edu/caed

Louisiana State University and Agricultural & Mechanical College, Graduate School, College of Art and Design, Robert Reich School of Landscape Architecture, Baton Rouge, LA 70803. Offers MLA. *Accreditation:* ASLA. *Faculty:* 9 full-time (1 woman). *Students:* 39 full-time (26 women), 2 part-time (0 women); includes 5 minority (3 Asian, non-Hispanic/Latino; 2 Hispanic/Latino), 27 international. Average age 28. 89 applicants, 36% accepted, 11 enrolled. In 2017, 13 master's awarded. *Financial support:* In 2017–18, 8 research assistantships (averaging $9,967 per year), 18 teaching assistantships (averaging $9,558 per year) were awarded. *Total annual research expenditures:* $17,665.

Mississippi State University, College of Agriculture and Life Sciences, Department of Landscape Architecture, Mississippi State, MS 39762. Offers MLA. *Accreditation:* ASLA. *Program availability:* Part-time. *Faculty:* 10 full-time (2 women). *Students:* 9 full-time (4 women), 2 part-time (1 woman); includes 3 minority (2 Black or African American, non-Hispanic/Latino; 1 Hispanic/Latino), 1 international. Average age 37. 12 applicants, 92% accepted, 3 enrolled. In 2017, 6 master's awarded. *Degree requirements:* For master's, thesis. *Entrance requirements:* For master's, GRE or minimum GPA of 3.0 in upper-division major emphasis courses from accredited university, minimum GPA of 2.8 on bachelor's degree. Additional exam requirements/recommendations for international students: Required—TOEFL (minimum score 600 paper-based; 100 iBT); Recommended—IELTS (minimum score 7.5). *Application deadline:* For fall admission, 7/1 for domestic students, 5/1 for international students; for spring admission, 10/1 for domestic students, 9/1 for international students. Applications are processed on a rolling basis. Application fee: $60 ($80 for international students). Electronic applications accepted. *Expenses:* Tuition, state resident: full-time $8318; part-time $462.12 per credit hour. Tuition, nonresident: full-time $22,358; part-time $1242.12 per credit hour. *Required fees:* $110; $12.24 per credit hour. $6.12 per semester. *Financial support:* In 2017–18, 2 research assistantships with full tuition reimbursements (averaging $16,360 per year), 4 teaching assistantships with partial tuition reimbursements (averaging $7,120 per year) were awarded; Federal Work-Study, institutionally sponsored loans, tuition waivers (partial), and unspecified assistantships also available. Financial award application deadline: 4/1; financial award applicants required to submit FAFSA. *Faculty research:* Design pedagogy, low impact development, conservation planning, wildlife/urban interfacing planning, sustainable communities, watershed planning, historical landscapes, decision support system development. *Unit head:* Dr. Sadik C. Artunc, Professor and Department Head, 662-325-7894, Fax: 662-325-7893, E-mail: sa305@msstate.edu. *Application contact:* Marina Hunt, Admissions and Enrollment Assistant, 662-325-5188, Fax: 662-325-7893, E-mail: mhunt@grad.msstate.edu. Website: http://www.lalc.msstate.edu

Landscape Architecture

Morgan State University, School of Graduate Studies, School of Architecture and Planning, Program in Landscape Architecture, Baltimore, MD 21251. Offers MLA. *Accreditation:* ASLA. *Entrance requirements:* Additional exam requirements/recommendations for international students: Required—TOEFL (minimum score 550 paper-based). *Application deadline:* For fall admission, 2/1 priority date for domestic students; for spring admission, 10/1 priority date for domestic students. Applications are processed on a rolling basis. Application fee: $0. *Expenses:* Tuition, state resident: part-time $433 per credit. Tuition, nonresident: part-time $851 per credit. *Required fees:* $81.50 per credit. *Financial support:* Application deadline: 2/1. *Faculty research:* Philosophy and design, urban design, design history and theory, computer-aided design and community design. *Unit head:* Paul Voos, Program Director, 443-885-1861, E-mail: paul.voos@morgan.edu. *Application contact:* Dr. Dean Campbell, Graduate Recruitment Specialist, 443-885-3185, Fax: 443-885-8226, E-mail: dean.campbell@morgan.edu.

North Carolina State University, Graduate School, College of Design, Department of Landscape Architecture, Raleigh, NC 27695. Offers MLA. *Accreditation:* ASLA. *Degree requirements:* For master's, thesis optional, oral exam, project. *Entrance requirements:* For master's, GRE General Test (recommended), portfolio. Electronic applications accepted. *Faculty research:* Community development and co-operative engagement, landscape planning and design.

The Ohio State University, Graduate School, College of Engineering, Austin E. Knowlton School of Architecture, Columbus, OH 43210. Offers architecture (M Arch); city and regional planning (MCRP, PhD); landscape architecture (M Land Arch). *Accreditation:* ACSP; ASLA. *Faculty:* 41. *Students:* 197 full-time (84 women), 6 part-time (2 women); includes 34 minority (9 Black or African American, non-Hispanic/Latino; 5 Asian, non-Hispanic/Latino; 15 Hispanic/Latino; 5 Two or more races, non-Hispanic/Latino), 35 international. Average age 26. In 2017, 66 master's, 8 doctorates awarded. *Entrance requirements:* For master's, GRE or GMAT (city and regional planning), portfolio (for architecture and landscape architecture); for doctorate, GRE or GMAT (city and regional planning), example of research or written work. Additional exam requirements/recommendations for international students: Required—TOEFL (minimum score 600 paper-based; 100 iBT), Michigan English Language Assessment Battery (minimum score 86); Recommended—IELTS (minimum score 8). *Application deadline:* For fall admission, 1/1 priority date for domestic students, 11/30 priority date for international students. Applications are processed on a rolling basis. Application fee: $60 ($70 for international students). Electronic applications accepted. *Financial support:* Fellowships, research assistantships, Federal Work-Study, institutionally sponsored loans, and unspecified assistantships available. Support available to part-time students. *Unit head:* Michael B. Cadwell, Professor/Director, 614-292-3174, E-mail: cadwell.1@osu.edu. *Application contact:* Graduate and Professional Admissions, 614-292-9444, Fax: 614-292-3895, E-mail: gpadmissions@osu.edu.
Website: http://knowlton.osu.edu/

Oklahoma State University, College of Agricultural Science and Natural Resources, Department of Horticulture and Landscape Architecture, Stillwater, OK 74078. Offers crop science (PhD); horticulture (M Ag, MS). *Faculty:* 17 full-time (5 women), 1 (woman) part-time/adjunct. *Students:* 15 part-time (5 women); includes 4 minority (1 Black or African American, non-Hispanic/Latino; 1 American Indian or Alaska Native, non-Hispanic/Latino; 1 Hispanic/Latino; 1 Two or more races, non-Hispanic/Latino), 7 international. Average age 28. 5 applicants, 60% accepted, 3 enrolled. In 2017, 2 master's awarded. *Entrance requirements:* For master's and doctorate, GRE or GMAT. Additional exam requirements/recommendations for international students: Required—TOEFL (minimum score 550 paper-based; 79 iBT). *Application deadline:* For fall admission, 3/1 priority date for international students; for spring admission, 8/1 priority date for international students. Applications are processed on a rolling basis. Application fee: $40 ($75 for international students). Electronic applications accepted. *Expenses:* Tuition, state resident: full-time $4019; part-time $2679.60 per year. Tuition, nonresident: full-time $15,286; part-time $10,190.40 per year. *Required fees:* $2129; $1419 per unit. Tuition and fees vary according to program. *Financial support:* Research assistantships, teaching assistantships, career-related internships or fieldwork, Federal Work-Study, scholarships/grants, health care benefits, tuition waivers (partial), and unspecified assistantships available. Support available to part-time students. Financial award application deadline: 3/1; financial award applicants required to submit FAFSA. *Faculty research:* Stress and postharvest physiology; water utilization and runoff; integrated pest management (IPM) systems and nursery, turf, floriculture, vegetable, net and fruit produces and natural resources, food extraction, and processing; public garden management. *Unit head:* Dr. Janet Cole, Department Head, 405-744-5414, Fax: 405-744-9709. *Application contact:* Dr. Sheryl Tucker, Dean, 405-744-7099, Fax: 405-744-0355, E-mail: gradi@okstate.edu.
Website: http://www.hortla.okstate.edu/

Penn State University Park, Graduate School, College of Arts and Architecture, Stuckeman School of Architecture and Landscape Architecture, University Park, PA 16802. Offers architecture (M Arch, MS, PhD); landscape architecture (MLA, MS). *Accreditation:* ASLA. *Unit head:* Dr. Barbara O. Korner, Dean, 814-865-2592, Fax: 814-865-2018. *Application contact:* Lori Hawn, Director, Graduate Student Services, 814-865-1795, Fax: 814-863-4627, E-mail: l-gswww@lists.psu.edu.
Website: https://stuckeman.psu.edu/

Polytechnic University of Puerto Rico, Graduate School, Hato Rey, PR 00918. Offers business administration (MBA), including computer information systems, general management, management of information systems, management of international enterprises; civil engineering (ME, MS); computer engineering (ME, MS); computer science (MCS, MS); electrical engineering (ME, MS); engineering management (MEM); environmental management (MEM); landscape architecture (M Land Arch); manufacturing competitiveness (MMC, MS); manufacturing engineering (ME, MS); mechanical engineering (M Mech E). *Program availability:* Part-time, evening/weekend. *Entrance requirements:* For master's, 3 letters of recommendation.

Pontificia Universidad Catolica Madre y Maestra, Graduate School, Faculty of Sciences and Humanities, Santiago, Dominican Republic. Offers architecture (M Arch), including architecture of interiors, architecture of tourist lodgings, landscaping; early childhood education (M Ed).

Rhode Island School of Design, Department of Landscape Architecture, Providence, RI 02903-2784. Offers MLA. *Accreditation:* ASLA. *Faculty:* 4 full-time (3 women), 23 part-time/adjunct (12 women). *Students:* 68 full-time (47 women); includes 2 minority (both Asian, non-Hispanic/Latino), 56 international. Average age 24. 116 applicants, 80% accepted, 22 enrolled. In 2017, 23 master's awarded. *Degree requirements:* For master's, thesis, exhibition. *Entrance requirements:* For master's, portfolio, statement of purpose, 3 letters of recommendation. Additional exam requirements/recommendations for international students: Required—TOEFL (minimum score 580 paper-based; 93 iBT). *Application deadline:* For fall admission, 1/10 for domestic and international students. Application fee: $60. Electronic applications accepted. *Expenses:* Tuition: Full-time $48,210. *Required fees:* $260. *Financial support:* Fellowships, research assistantships, teaching assistantships, Federal Work-Study, scholarships/grants, and unspecified assistantships available. Financial award application deadline: 2/15; financial award applicants required to submit FAFSA. *Unit head:* Emily Vogler, Department Head, 401-454-6282, Fax: 401-454-6299, E-mail:

ldardept@risd.edu. *Application contact:* Molly Pettengill, Assistant Director for Graduate Recruitment, 401-454-6312, Fax: 401-454-6309, E-mail: mpetteng@risd.edu.
Website: http://www.risd.edu/academics/landscape-architecture/

State University of New York College of Environmental Science and Forestry, Department of Landscape Architecture, Syracuse, NY 13210-2779. Offers community design and planning (MLA, MS); cultural landscape studies and conservation (MLA, MS); landscape and urban ecology (MLA, MS). *Accreditation:* ASLA (one or more programs are accredited). *Program availability:* Part-time. *Faculty:* 10 full-time (4 women), 7 part-time/adjunct (5 women). *Students:* 27 full-time (16 women), 5 part-time (3 women); includes 5 minority (3 Black or African American, non-Hispanic/Latino; 1 Asian, non-Hispanic/Latino; 1 Hispanic/Latino), 5 international. Average age 25. 31 applicants, 65% accepted, 10 enrolled. In 2017, 9 master's awarded. *Degree requirements:* For master's, comprehensive exam (for some programs), thesis (for some programs). *Entrance requirements:* For master's, GRE General Test, minimum GPA of 3.0. Additional exam requirements/recommendations for international students: Required—TOEFL (minimum score 550 paper-based; 80 iBT), IELTS (minimum score 6), or STEP Eiken (grade 1). *Application deadline:* For fall admission, 2/1 priority date for domestic and international students; for spring admission, 11/1 priority date for domestic and international students. Applications are processed on a rolling basis. Application fee: $60. Electronic applications accepted. *Expenses:* Tuition, state resident: full-time $10,870; part-time $453 per credit. Tuition, nonresident: full-time $22,210; part-time $925 per credit. *Required fees:* $1435; $70.85 per credit. One-time fee: $25 full-time. Part-time tuition and fees vary according to course load. *Financial support:* In 2017–18, 9 students received support. Unspecified assistantships available. Financial award application deadline: 6/30; financial award applicants required to submit FAFSA. *Faculty research:* Site analysis and design, city and regional planning, community environments. *Total annual research expenditures:* $216,783. *Unit head:* Dr. Douglas Johnston, Chair, 315-470-6544, Fax: 315-470-6540, E-mail: dmjohnst@esf.edu. *Application contact:* Scott Shannon, Associate Provost for Instruction/Dean of the Graduate School, 315-470-6599, Fax: 315-470-6978, E-mail: esfgrad@esf.edu.
Website: http://www.esf.edu/la/

Temple University, Tyler School of Art, Department of Landscape Architecture and Horticulture, Ambler, PA 19335. Offers landscape architecture (ML Arch), including ecological landscape restoration. *Accreditation:* ASLA. *Program availability:* Part-time. *Faculty:* 7 full-time (4 women), 7 part-time/adjunct (4 women). *Students:* 9 full-time (4 women), 4 part-time (3 women). 18 applicants, 72% accepted, 5 enrolled. In 2017, 8 master's awarded. *Entrance requirements:* For master's, GRE or GMAT, 2 letters of recommendation, minimum undergraduate GPA of 3.0, statement of goals. Additional exam requirements/recommendations for international students: Required—TOEFL (minimum score 550 paper-based; 79 iBT). *Application deadline:* For fall admission, 7/1 for domestic students, 12/15 for international students; for spring admission, 11/1 for domestic students, 8/1 for international students. Applications are processed on a rolling basis. Application fee: $60. *Expenses:* Tuition, state resident: full-time $16,164; part-time $898 per credit hour. Tuition, nonresident: full-time $22,158; part-time $1231 per credit hour. *Required fees:* $890; $445 per semester. Full-time tuition and fees vary according to course load, degree level, campus/location and program. *Financial support:* In 2017–18, 8 students received support. Application deadline: 1/15; applicants required to submit FAFSA. *Faculty research:* Seasonal landscape performance, landscape performance, green urban schoolyards, intersection of landscape arch practice and research, community engagement and service. *Unit head:* Baldev Lamba, Chair, 267-468-8181, Fax: 267-468-8188, E-mail: blamba@temple.edu.
Website: https://tyler.temple.edu/programs/landscape-architecture-horticulture

Texas A&M University, College of Architecture, Department of Landscape Architecture and Urban Planning, College Station, TX 77843. Offers land and property development (MLPD); landscape architecture (MLA); urban and regional planning (MUP); urban and regional science (PhD). *Accreditation:* ACSP (one or more programs are accredited); ASLA (one or more programs are accredited). *Faculty:* 30. *Students:* 163 full-time (84 women), 10 part-time (5 women); includes 22 minority (4 Black or African American, non-Hispanic/Latino; 4 Asian, non-Hispanic/Latino; 13 Hispanic/Latino; 1 Two or more races, non-Hispanic/Latino), 94 international. Average age 27. 186 applicants, 68% accepted, 62 enrolled. In 2017, 66 master's, 8 doctorates awarded. Terminal master's awarded for partial completion of doctoral program. *Degree requirements:* For master's, thesis optional, professional internship; for doctorate, comprehensive exam, thesis/dissertation, seminar. *Entrance requirements:* For master's, GMAT or GRE General Test, portfolio (MLA), minimum GPA of 3.0; for doctorate, GMAT or GRE General Test. Additional exam requirements/recommendations for international students: Required—TOEFL (minimum score 550 paper-based; 80 iBT), IELTS (minimum score 6), PTE (minimum score 53). *Application deadline:* For fall admission, 12/1 priority date for domestic and international students; for spring admission, 8/1 for domestic students. Applications are processed on a rolling basis. Application fee: $50 ($90 for international students). Electronic applications accepted. *Expenses:* Contact institution. *Financial support:* In 2017–18, 117 students received support, including 4 fellowships with tuition reimbursements available (averaging $25,450 per year), 45 research assistantships with tuition reimbursements available (averaging $6,952 per year), 18 teaching assistantships with tuition reimbursements available (averaging $8,427 per year); career-related internships or fieldwork, institutionally sponsored loans, scholarships/grants, traineeships, health care benefits, tuition waivers (full and partial), and unspecified assistantships also available. Support available to part-time students. Financial award application deadline: 3/15; financial award applicants required to submit FAFSA. *Faculty research:* Erosion control/water quality, geographic information systems/spatial information technology, transport hazards, international sustainable development. *Unit head:* Dr. Forster Ndubisi, Head, 979-845-1019, Fax: 979-862-1784. *Application contact:* Thena Morris, Administrative Assistant, 979-458-4306, E-mail: t-morris@tamu.edu.
Website: http://laup.arch.tamu.edu/

Texas Tech University, Graduate School, College of Agricultural Sciences and Natural Resources, Department of Landscape Architecture, Lubbock, TX 79409. Offers MLA. *Accreditation:* ASLA. *Program availability:* Part-time. *Faculty:* 7 full-time (4 women), 1 part-time/adjunct (0 women). *Students:* 3 full-time (1 woman), 2 part-time (1 woman). Average age 27. 9 applicants, 56% accepted, 1 enrolled. In 2017, 8 master's awarded. Terminal master's awarded for partial completion of doctoral program. *Degree requirements:* For master's, thesis or alternative. *Entrance requirements:* For master's, formal approval from departmental committee. Additional exam requirements/recommendations for international students: Required—TOEFL (minimum score 550 paper-based; 79 iBT). *Application deadline:* For fall admission, 6/1 priority date for domestic students, 1/15 priority date for international students; for spring admission, 9/1 priority date for domestic students, 6/15 priority date for international students. Applications are processed on a rolling basis. Application fee: $60. Electronic applications accepted. *Expenses:* Contact institution. *Financial support:* In 2017–18, 6 students received support. Fellowships, research assistantships, teaching assistantships, career-related internships or fieldwork, scholarships/grants, and unspecified assistantships available. Financial award application deadline: 4/15; financial award applicants required to submit FAFSA. *Faculty research:* Landscape performance, landscape modeling, environmental planning and design, therapeutic

landscapes, GIS and CAD fused workflows in landscape architecture. *Total annual research expenditures:* $78,879. *Unit head:* Prof. Eric A. Bernard, Professor and Chairperson, 806-742-2858, Fax: 806-742-0770, E-mail: eric.bernard@ttu.edu.
Website: http://www.larc.ttu.edu/

The University of Arizona, College of Architecture, Planning, and Landscape Architecture, Landscape Architecture Program, Tucson, AZ 85721. Offers ML Arch. *Accreditation:* ASLA. *Degree requirements:* For master's, thesis. *Entrance requirements:* For master's, minimum GPA of 3.2, 3 letters of reference, statement of intent, portfolio, transcripts. Additional exam requirements/recommendations for international students: Required—TOEFL (minimum score 600 paper-based). Electronic applications accepted. *Faculty research:* Children's environments, cultural landscapes, arid lands plant communities, geographic information systems and science, computer-aided drafting and design (CAD).

The University of British Columbia, Faculty of Applied Science, School of Architecture and Landscape Architecture, Program in Landscape Architecture, Vancouver, BC V6T 1Z2, Canada. Offers advanced studies in landscape architecture (MASLA); landscape architecture (MLA); urban design (MUD); M Arch/MLA. *Degree requirements:* For master's, comprehensive exam or thesis. *Entrance requirements:* For master's, portfolio. Additional exam requirements/recommendations for international students: Required—TOEFL. Electronic applications accepted. *Expenses:* Contact institution. *Faculty research:* Landscape design, urban-rural interface, urban ecology, sustainable development, collaborative planning and community forestry.

University of Calgary, Faculty of Graduate Studies, Faculty of Environmental Design, Calgary, AB T2N 1N4, Canada. Offers architecture (M Arch); environmental design (M Env Des, PhD); landscape architecture (MLA); planning (M Plan). *Degree requirements:* For master's, thesis; for doctorate, thesis/dissertation. *Entrance requirements:* For master's, minimum GPA of 3.0; for doctorate, minimum GPA of 3.5. Additional exam requirements/recommendations for international students: Required—TOEFL (minimum score 550 paper-based). *Faculty research:* Sustainable development in architecture, planning and product design, energy and environment, impact assessment, ecotourism.

University of California, Berkeley, Graduate Division, College of Environmental Design, Department of Landscape Architecture and Environmental Planning, Berkeley, CA 94720-1500. Offers landscape architecture (MLA), including environmental planning, landscape design and site planning, urban and community design; landscape architecture and environmental planning (PhD); MLA/M Arch; MLA/MCP. *Accreditation:* ASLA (one or more programs are accredited). *Degree requirements:* For master's, comprehensive exam (for some programs), thesis (for some programs), professional project or thesis; for doctorate, one foreign language, thesis/dissertation, qualifying exam. *Entrance requirements:* For master's, GRE General Test, minimum GPA of 3.0, portfolio; for doctorate, GRE General Test, master's degree (strongly recommended), minimum GPA of 3.0, sample of written work, 3 letters of recommendation. Additional exam requirements/recommendations for international students: Required—TOEFL (minimum score 570 paper-based; 90 iBT). Electronic applications accepted.

University of California, Berkeley, UC Berkeley Extension, Certificate Programs in Art and Design, Berkeley, CA 94720-1500. Offers interior design and interior architecture (Certificate); landscape architecture (Certificate); visual arts (Postbaccalaureate Certificate).

University of Colorado Denver, College of Architecture and Planning, Program in Landscape Architecture, Denver, CO 80217. Offers MLA. *Accreditation:* ASLA. *Program availability:* Part-time. *Degree requirements:* For master's, thesis optional, six-semester sequence of course work totaling 90 semester hours. *Entrance requirements:* For master's, GRE (recommended for students with an undergraduate GPA of 3.0 or lower), portfolio of creative work; statement of purpose; three letters of recommendation. Additional exam requirements/recommendations for international students: Required—TOEFL (minimum score 75 iBT). Electronic applications accepted. *Expenses:* Contact institution. *Faculty research:* Landscape architectural design theory and process, urban design, advanced landscape technologies, landscape planning.

University of Florida, Graduate School, College of Design, Construction and Planning, Department of Landscape Architecture, Gainesville, FL 32611. Offers geographic information systems (MLA); historic preservation (MLA); landscape architecture (MLA); sustainable design (MLA); wetland sciences (MLA). *Accreditation:* ASLA. *Program availability:* Part-time. *Degree requirements:* For master's, thesis, internship. *Entrance requirements:* For master's, GRE General Test, minimum GPA of 3.0. Additional exam requirements/recommendations for international students: Required—TOEFL (minimum score 550 paper-based; 80 iBT), IELTS (minimum score 6). Electronic applications accepted. *Faculty research:* Landscape reclamation, community development, landscape ethics, land-use planning, international conservation.

University of Florida, Graduate School, College of Design, Construction and Planning, Doctoral Program in Design, Construction and Planning, Gainesville, FL 32611. Offers construction management (PhD); design, construction and planning (PhD); geographic information systems (PhD); historic preservation (PhD); interior design (PhD); landscape architecture (PhD); urban and regional planning (PhD). *Degree requirements:* For doctorate, thesis/dissertation. *Entrance requirements:* For doctorate, GRE General Test, minimum GPA of 3.0. Additional exam requirements/recommendations for international students: Required—TOEFL (minimum score 550 paper-based; 80 iBT), IELTS (minimum score 6). Electronic applications accepted. *Faculty research:* Architecture, building construction, urban and regional planning.

University of Georgia, College of Environment and Design, Athens, GA 30602. Offers environmental planning and design (MEPD); historic preservation (MHP); landscape architecture (MLA). *Accreditation:* ACSP.

University of Guelph, Graduate Studies, Ontario Agricultural College, School of Environmental Design and Rural Development, Landscape Architecture Program, Guelph, ON N1G 2W1, Canada. Offers MLA. *Degree requirements:* For master's, thesis. *Entrance requirements:* For master's, minimum B- average during previous 2 years of honors degree, portfolio and questionnaire. Additional exam requirements/recommendations for international students: Required—TOEFL (minimum score 600 paper-based; 89 iBT), IELTS (minimum score 7), Canadian Academic Language Assessment, Michigan English Language Assessment Battery. Electronic applications accepted. *Faculty research:* Land planning, human factors in design, landscape assessment (biophysical and cultural), landscape ecology and restoration, community design.

University of Illinois at Urbana–Champaign, Graduate College, College of Fine and Applied Arts, Department of Landscape Architecture, Champaign, IL 61820. Offers MLA, PhD, MLA/MUP. *Accreditation:* ASLA.

The University of Manchester, School of Environment and Development, Manchester, United Kingdom. Offers architecture (M Phil, PhD); development policy and management (M Phil, PhD); human geography (M Phil, PhD); physical geography (M Phil, PhD); planning and landscape (M Phil, PhD).

University of Manitoba, Faculty of Graduate Studies, Faculty of Architecture, Department of Landscape Architecture, Winnipeg, MB R3T 2N2, Canada. Offers M Land Arch. *Accreditation:* ASLA. *Degree requirements:* For master's, thesis or alternative.

University of Maryland, College Park, Academic Affairs, College of Agriculture and Natural Resources, Department of Plant Science and Landscape Architecture, Landscape Architecture Program, College Park, MD 20742. Offers MLA. *Accreditation:* ASLA. *Entrance requirements:* Additional exam requirements/recommendations for international students: Required—TOEFL. Electronic applications accepted. *Faculty research:* Cereal crop production, soil and water conservation, turf management, x-ray diffraction.

University of Massachusetts Amherst, Graduate School, College of Social and Behavioral Sciences, Department of Landscape Architecture and Regional Planning, Dual Degree Program in Landscape Architecture and Regional Planning, Amherst, MA 01003. Offers MLA/MRP. *Accreditation:* ACSP; ASLA. *Program availability:* Part-time. *Entrance requirements:* Additional exam requirements/recommendations for international students: Required—TOEFL (minimum score 550 paper-based; 80 iBT), IELTS (minimum score 6.5). Electronic applications accepted.

University of Massachusetts Amherst, Graduate School, College of Social and Behavioral Sciences, Department of Landscape Architecture and Regional Planning, Program in Landscape Architecture, Amherst, MA 01003. Offers MLA, MLA/M Arch. *Accreditation:* ASLA. *Program availability:* Part-time. *Degree requirements:* For master's, thesis or alternative. *Entrance requirements:* For master's, GRE General Test, portfolio. Additional exam requirements/recommendations for international students: Required—TOEFL (minimum score 550 paper-based; 80 iBT), IELTS (minimum score 6.5). Electronic applications accepted.

University of Michigan, School for Environment and Sustainability, Program in Landscape Architecture, Ann Arbor, MI 48109. Offers MLA, MLA/M Arch, MLA/MBA, MURP/MLA. Offered through the Rackham Graduate School. *Accreditation:* ASLA (one or more programs are accredited). *Degree requirements:* For master's, thesis, practicum or group project. *Entrance requirements:* For master's, GRE General Test. Additional exam requirements/recommendations for international students: Required—TOEFL (minimum score 560 paper-based; 84 iBT) or IELTS (minimum score 6.5). Electronic applications accepted. *Expenses:* Tuition, state resident: full-time $22,368; part-time $1201 per credit hour. Tuition, nonresident: full-time $45,156; part-time $2467 per credit hour. *Required fees:* $376 per term. Tuition and fees vary according to course load, degree level and program. *Faculty research:* Environmentally responsible design, ecological processes, human behavior, and ecological function.

University of Minnesota, Twin Cities Campus, Graduate School, College of Design, Department of Landscape Architecture, Minneapolis, MN 55455-0213. Offers MLA, MS. *Accreditation:* ASLA (one or more programs are accredited). *Degree requirements:* For master's, thesis (MS). *Entrance requirements:* For master's, GRE General Test (MS), suggested GPA of 3.0. Additional exam requirements/recommendations for international students: Required—TOEFL (minimum score 550 paper-based; 79 iBT). Electronic applications accepted. *Expenses:* Contact institution. *Faculty research:* Landscape history, landscape ecology, urban design, sustainable design, public art/space.

University of New Mexico, Graduate Studies, School of Architecture and Planning, Department of Landscape Architecture, Albuquerque, NM 87131. Offers MLA. *Accreditation:* ASLA. *Program availability:* Part-time. *Faculty:* 1 (woman) full-time, 4 part-time/adjunct (1 woman). *Students:* 24 full-time (10 women), 2 part-time (1 woman); includes 3 minority (2 Black or African American, non-Hispanic/Latino; 1 Hispanic/Latino), 7 international. Average age 30. 21 applicants, 43% accepted, 5 enrolled. In 2017, 22 master's awarded. *Degree requirements:* For master's, comprehensive exam, thesis optional, portfolio review, thesis studio. *Entrance requirements:* For master's, minimum GPA of 3.0. Additional exam requirements/recommendations for international students: Required—TOEFL. *Application deadline:* For fall admission, 2/15 priority date for domestic students, 2/15 for international students; for spring admission, 11/1 for domestic and international students. Applications are processed on a rolling basis. Application fee: $50. Electronic applications accepted. *Expenses:* $8,500 per year. *Financial support:* Research assistantships with partial tuition reimbursements, teaching assistantships with partial tuition reimbursements, scholarships/grants, health care benefits, tuition waivers (partial), and unspecified assistantships available. Financial award application deadline: 3/1; financial award applicants required to submit FAFSA. *Faculty research:* Cultural landscape studies, urban design and sustainability, landscape and infrastructure. *Unit head:* Dr. Alfred Simon, Professor and Chair, 505-277-4120, Fax: 505-277-0897, E-mail: asimon@unm.edu. *Application contact:* Miquela Ortiz Upston, Senior Academic Advisor, 505-277-1303, Fax: 505-277-0076, E-mail: miquela@unm.edu.
Website: http://saap.unm.edu/

University of Oklahoma, Christopher C. Gibbs College of Architecture, Division of Landscape Architecture, Norman, OK 73019. Offers landscape architectural studies (MLA); landscape architecture (MLA); MRCP/MLA. *Accreditation:* ASLA. *Students:* 16 full-time (10 women), 7 part-time (3 women); includes 5 minority (1 American Indian or Alaska Native, non-Hispanic/Latino; 2 Asian, non-Hispanic/Latino; 2 Two or more races, non-Hispanic/Latino), 10 international. Average age 27. 14 applicants, 71% accepted, 5 enrolled. In 2017, 4 master's awarded. Terminal master's awarded for partial completion of doctoral program. *Degree requirements:* For master's, comprehensive exam. *Entrance requirements:* Additional exam requirements/recommendations for international students: Required—TOEFL (minimum score 79 iBT) or IELTS (minimum score 6.5). *Application deadline:* For fall admission, 2/15 priority date for domestic and international students. Applications are processed on a rolling basis. Application fee: $50 ($100 for international students). Electronic applications accepted. *Expenses:* Tuition, state resident: full-time $5119; part-time $213.30 per credit hour. Tuition, nonresident: full-time $19,778; part-time $824.10 per credit hour. *Required fees:* $3458; $133.55 per credit hour. $126.50 per semester. *Financial support:* In 2017–18, 21 students received support, including 7 research assistantships with full and partial tuition reimbursements available (averaging $13,334 per year); scholarships/grants and unspecified assistantships also available. Financial award application deadline: 6/1; financial award applicants required to submit FAFSA. *Faculty research:* Human behavior in environment, green roofs, geodesign. *Unit head:* Leehu Loon, Associate Dean and Director, 405-325-1519, Fax: 405-325-7558, E-mail: lloon@ou.edu.
Website: http://la.ou.edu

University of Oregon, Graduate School, College of Design, Department of Landscape Architecture, Eugene, OR 97403. Offers MLA, PhD. *Accreditation:* ASLA. *Degree requirements:* For master's, thesis or alternative, project. *Entrance requirements:* For master's, portfolio. Additional exam requirements/recommendations for international students: Required—TOEFL. *Faculty research:* Design, landscape planning analysis, history and theory, computer applications.

University of Pennsylvania, School of Design, Department of Landscape Architecture, Philadelphia, PA 19104. Offers landscape architecture (MLA); landscape studies (Certificate). *Accreditation:* ASLA (one or more programs are accredited).

Landscape Architecture

Program availability: Part-time. *Faculty:* 6 full-time (3 women), 4 part-time/adjunct (2 women). *Students:* 108 full-time (73 women), 3 part-time (1 woman); includes 9 minority (1 Black or African American, non-Hispanic/Latino; 2 Asian, non-Hispanic/Latino; 4 Hispanic/Latino; 2 Two or more races, non-Hispanic/Latino), 70 international. Average age 26. 344 applicants, 36% accepted, 45 enrolled. In 2017, 42 master's, 13 Certificates awarded. *Financial support:* Teaching assistantships available. Financial award application deadline: 2/1.

The University of Tennessee, Graduate School, College of Architecture and Design, Program in Landscape Architecture, Knoxville, TN 37996. Offers landscape architecture (MLA); landscape architecture (research) (MA, MS). *Accreditation:* ASLA. *Degree requirements:* For master's, oral exam, project and thesis optional (MLA), oral exam and thesis (MA, MS). *Entrance requirements:* For master's, GRE General Test, minimum GPA of 3.0, 3 letters of recommendation, samples of portfolio work. Additional exam requirements/recommendations for international students: Required—TOEFL (minimum score 550 paper-based).

The University of Texas at Arlington, Graduate School, College of Architecture, Planning and Public Affairs, Program in Landscape Architecture, Arlington, TX 76019. Offers MLA. *Accreditation:* ASLA. *Program availability:* Part-time, evening/weekend. *Degree requirements:* For master's, thesis. *Entrance requirements:* For master's, GRE General Test, minimum GPA of 3.0, portfolio. Additional exam requirements/recommendations for international students: Required—TOEFL (minimum score 575 paper-based; 80 iBT).

The University of Texas at Austin, Graduate School, School of Architecture, Program in Landscape Architecture, Austin, TX 78712-1111. Offers MLA. *Accreditation:* ASLA.

University of Toronto, School of Graduate Studies, John H. Daniels Faculty of Architecture, Landscape, and Design, Toronto, ON M5S 1A1, Canada. Offers M Arch, MLA, MUD, MVS. *Entrance requirements:* For master's, minimum B average; 3 letters of reference; resume; 3 writing samples; 5 samples of design work, drawing, or work in a related field, statement of interest. Additional exam requirements/recommendations for international students: Required—TOEFL (minimum score 580 paper-based; 93 iBT), IELTS (minimum score 7), TWE (minimum score 5), Michigan English Language Assessment Battery (minimum score 85), COPE (minimum score 76). Electronic applications accepted. *Expenses:* Contact institution.

University of Virginia, School of Architecture, Department of Landscape Architecture, Charlottesville, VA 22903. Offers M Land Arch. *Accreditation:* ASLA. *Faculty:* 7 full-time (4 women), 2 part-time/adjunct (both women). *Students:* 64 full-time (44 women); includes 3 minority (1 Asian, non-Hispanic/Latino; 1 Hispanic/Latino; 1 Two or more races, non-Hispanic/Latino), 35 international. Average age 25. 177 applicants, 56% accepted, 30 enrolled. In 2017, 19 master's awarded. *Entrance requirements:* For master's, GRE General Test, 3 letters of recommendation; portfolio. Additional exam requirements/recommendations for international students: Required—TOEFL (minimum score 600 paper-based; 90 iBT). *Application deadline:* For fall admission, 1/15 for domestic students, 1/16 for international students. Applications are processed on a rolling basis. Application fee: $60. Electronic applications accepted. *Financial support:* Applicants required to submit FAFSA. *Faculty research:* History of landscape architecture. *Unit head:* Brad Cantrell, Chair, 434-982-3287, Fax: 434-982-2678, E-mail: bec9n@virginia.edu. *Application contact:* Director of Graduate Admissions and Financial Aid, 434-924-6442, Fax: 434-982-2678, E-mail: a-school-admissions@virginia.edu. Website: http://www.arch.virginia.edu/academics/disciplines/landscape

University of Washington, Graduate School, College of Built Environments, Department of Landscape Architecture, Seattle, WA 98195. Offers MLA. *Accreditation:* ASLA. *Degree requirements:* For master's, thesis. *Entrance requirements:* For master's, GRE, minimum GPA of 3.0. Additional exam requirements/recommendations for international students: Required—TOEFL. *Faculty research:* Cultural landscape, history of gardens, urban stream restoration, campus master planning, urban ecology.

University of Wisconsin–Madison, Graduate School, College of Letters and Science, Department of Planning and Landscape Architecture, Madison, WI 53706-1380. Offers landscape architecture (MS); urban and regional planning (MS, PhD). *Accreditation:* ACSP (one or more programs are accredited). *Program availability:* Part-time. *Degree requirements:* For master's, thesis optional, internship; for doctorate, thesis/dissertation, 3 preliminary exams. *Entrance requirements:* For master's, GRE, minimum GPA of 3.0, previous course work in statistics; for doctorate, 1 year of experience, master's degree in related field. Electronic applications accepted. *Faculty research:* Land use, environmental planning, community development, economic development planning.

Utah State University, School of Graduate Studies, College of Agriculture and Applied Sciences, Department of Landscape Architecture and Environmental Planning, Logan, UT 84322. Offers bioregional planning (MS); landscape architecture (MLA). *Accreditation:* ASLA (one or more programs are accredited). *Degree requirements:* For master's, thesis. *Entrance requirements:* For master's, GRE General Test, minimum GPA of 3.0. Additional exam requirements/recommendations for international students: Required—TOEFL. *Faculty research:* Visual resource management, planning for wildlife, agricultural land preservation, watershed planning, community planning and design.

Virginia Polytechnic Institute and State University, Graduate School, College of Architecture and Urban Studies, Blacksburg, VA 24061. Offers architecture (M Arch, MS); architecture and design research (PhD); building construction science management (MS); creative technologies (MFA); environmental design and planning (PhD); government and international affairs (MPIA); landscape architecture (MLA, PhD); planning, governance, and globalization (PhD); public administration and public affairs (MPA, PhD); urban and regional planning (MURPL). *Accreditation:* ASLA (one or more programs are accredited). *Faculty:* 139 full-time (58 women), 1 (woman) part-time/adjunct. *Students:* 339 full-time (165 women), 210 part-time (97 women); includes 115 minority (49 Black or African American, non-Hispanic/Latino; 1 American Indian or Alaska Native, non-Hispanic/Latino; 30 Asian, non-Hispanic/Latino; 29 Hispanic/Latino; 6 Two or more races, non-Hispanic/Latino), 136 international. Average age 32. 649 applicants, 49% accepted, 105 enrolled. In 2017, 142 master's, 18 doctorates awarded. *Degree requirements:* For master's, comprehensive exam (for some programs), thesis (for some programs); for doctorate, comprehensive exam (for some programs), thesis/dissertation (for some programs). *Entrance requirements:* For master's and doctorate, GRE/GMAT. Additional exam requirements/recommendations for international students: Required—TOEFL (minimum score 80 iBT). *Application deadline:* For fall admission, 8/1 for domestic students, 4/1 for international students; for spring admission, 1/1 for domestic students, 9/1 for international students. Applications are processed on a rolling basis. Application fee: $75. Electronic applications accepted. *Expenses:* Tuition, state resident: full-time $15,072; part-time $718.50 per credit hour. Tuition, nonresident: full-time $28,810; part-time $1448.25 per credit hour. *Required fees:* $2741; $502 per semester. Tuition and fees vary according to course load, campus/location and program. *Financial support:* In 2017–18, 17 research assistantships with full tuition reimbursements (averaging $18,561 per year), 41 teaching assistantships with full tuition reimbursements (averaging $17,340 per year) were awarded. Financial award application deadline: 3/1; financial award applicants required to submit FAFSA. *Total annual research expenditures:* $3.1 million. *Unit head:* Dr. Richard Blythe, Dean, 540-231-6416, Fax: 540-231-6332, E-mail: richbl1@vt.edu. *Application contact:* Christine Mattsson-Coon, Executive Assistant, 540-231-6416, Fax: 540-231-6332, E-mail: cmattsso@vt.edu.
Website: http://www.caus.vt.edu/

Washington State University, College of Agricultural, Human, and Natural Resource Sciences, Program in Interior Design and Landscape Architecture, Pullman, WA 99164-2220. Offers MA, MS. Programs offered at the Pullman campus. *Program availability:* Part-time. *Degree requirements:* For master's, comprehensive exam, thesis (for some programs), oral exam. *Entrance requirements:* For master's, portfolio. Additional exam requirements/recommendations for international students: Required—TOEFL or IELTS. Electronic applications accepted. *Faculty research:* Digital fabrication, design pedagogy, proportional systems, American architecture and urbanism, design leadership.

West Virginia University, Davis College of Agriculture, Forestry and Consumer Sciences, Morgantown, WV 26506. Offers agricultural and extension education (MS, PhD); agriculture and resource management (MS); agriculture, natural resources and design (M Agr); agronomy (MS); animal and food science (PhD); animal physiology (MS); applied and environmental microbiology (MS); design and merchandising (MS); entomology (MS); forest resource science (PhD); forestry (MSF); genetics and developmental biology (MS, PhD); horticulture (MS); human and community development (PhD); landscape architecture (MLA); natural resource economics (PhD); nutritional and food science (MS); plant and soil science (PhD); plant pathology (MS); recreation, parks and tourism resources (MS); reproductive physiology (MS, PhD); wildlife and fisheries resources (PhD). *Program availability:* Part-time. *Students:* 200 full-time (97 women), 53 part-time (32 women); includes 27 minority (6 Black or African American, non-Hispanic/Latino; 1 American Indian or Alaska Native, non-Hispanic/Latino; 4 Asian, non-Hispanic/Latino; 11 Hispanic/Latino; 5 Two or more races, non-Hispanic/Latino), 67 international. *Degree requirements:* For master's, thesis; for doctorate, thesis/dissertation. *Entrance requirements:* Additional exam requirements/recommendations for international students: Required—TOEFL (minimum score 550 paper-based). *Application deadline:* For fall admission, 6/1 priority date for domestic students, 6/1 for international students; for spring admission, 1/5 for domestic and international students. Applications are processed on a rolling basis. Application fee: $60. Electronic applications accepted. *Expenses:* Tuition, state resident: full-time $9450. Tuition, nonresident: full-time $24,390. *Financial support:* Fellowships, research assistantships, teaching assistantships, career-related internships or fieldwork, Federal Work-Study, institutionally sponsored loans, tuition waivers (full and partial), and unspecified assistantships available. Financial award application deadline: 2/1; financial award applicants required to submit FAFSA. *Faculty research:* Reproductive physiology, soil and water quality, human nutrition, aquaculture, wildlife management. *Unit head:* Dr. Dan J. Robison, Dean, 304-293-2395, Fax: 304-293-3740, E-mail: dan.robison@mail.wvu.edu. *Application contact:* Dr. Dennis K. Smith, Associate Dean, 304-293-2275, Fax: 304-293-3740, E-mail: denny.smith@mail.wvu.edu.
Website: https://www.davis.wvu.edu

Lighting Design

The New School, Parsons School of Design, Program in Lighting Design, New York, NY 10011. Offers interior design/lighting design (MFA); lighting design (MFA); M Arch/MFA. *Faculty:* 6 full-time (2 women), 13 part-time/adjunct (4 women). *Students:* 26 full-time (20 women); includes 2 minority (1 Asian, non-Hispanic/Latino; 1 Hispanic/Latino), 21 international. Average age 27. 44 applicants, 75% accepted, 8 enrolled. In 2017, 21 master's awarded. *Degree requirements:* For master's, thesis. *Entrance requirements:* For master's, transcripts, resume, statement of purpose, recommendation letters, portfolio, interviews. Additional exam requirements/recommendations for international students: Required—TOEFL (minimum score 92 iBT), IELTS (minimum score 7), PTE (minimum score 63). *Application deadline:* For fall admission, 1/1 priority date for domestic and international students; for summer admission, 1/1 priority date for domestic and international students. Applications are processed on a rolling basis. Application fee: $50. Electronic applications accepted. *Expenses:* $24,922 per semester full-time, $1,744 per credit part-time, $100 maintenance of status fee. *Financial support:* In 2017–18, 17 students received support, including 4 teaching assistantships (averaging $2,344 per year); career-related internships or fieldwork, scholarships/grants, and unspecified assistantships also available. Support available to part-time students. Financial award application deadline: 2/1; financial award applicants required to submit FAFSA. *Unit head:* Glenn Shrum, Director, 212-229-8900 Ext. 4853, E-mail: shrumg@newschool.edu. *Application contact:* Courtney Malenius, Director of Graduate Admissions, 212-229-5150 Ext. 4011, E-mail: maleniuc@newschool.edu.
Website: https://www.newschool.edu/parsons/lighting-design/

New York School of Interior Design, Program in Interior Lighting Design, New York, NY 10021-5110. Offers MPS. *Entrance requirements:* For master's, portfolio, resume, undergraduate degree in interior design or closely-related field. Additional exam requirements/recommendations for international students: Required—TOEFL (minimum score 79 iBT). Electronic applications accepted.

Rensselaer Polytechnic Institute, Graduate School, School of Architecture, Program in Architectural Sciences, Troy, NY 12180-3590. Offers architectural acoustics (PhD); built ecologies (PhD); lighting (PhD). *Faculty:* 33 full-time (8 women), 13 part-time/adjunct (1 woman). *Students:* 21 full-time (4 women), 3 part-time (1 woman); includes 3 minority (all Asian, non-Hispanic/Latino), 9 international. Average age 29. 35 applicants, 43% accepted, 8 enrolled. *Degree requirements:* For doctorate, comprehensive exam (for some programs), thesis/dissertation. *Entrance requirements:* For doctorate, GRE, portfolio/personal statement. Additional exam requirements/recommendations for international students: Required—TOEFL (minimum score 570 paper-based; 88 iBT), IELTS (minimum score 6.5), PTE (minimum score 60).

Application deadline: For fall admission, 1/1 priority date for domestic and international students. Applications are processed on a rolling basis. Application fee: $75. Electronic applications accepted. *Expenses: Tuition:* Full-time $52,550; part-time $2125 per credit hour. *Required fees:* $2890. *Financial support:* In 2017–18, research assistantships (averaging $23,000 per year), teaching assistantships with full tuition reimbursements (averaging $23,000 per year) were awarded; fellowships also available. Financial award application deadline: 1/1. *Unit head:* Evan Douglis, Dean, School of Architecture, 518-276-3034, E-mail: douglis@rpi.edu.
Website: http://www.arch.rpi.edu/academic/graduate/phd-program/

Rensselaer Polytechnic Institute, Graduate School, School of Architecture, Program in Lighting, Troy, NY 12180-3590. Offers MS. *Faculty:* 33 full-time (8 women), 13 part-time/adjunct (1 woman). *Students:* 4 full-time (3 women); includes 1 minority (Black or African American, non-Hispanic/Latino). Average age 25. 10 applicants, 60% accepted, 4 enrolled. *Degree requirements:* For master's, comprehensive exam, thesis. *Entrance requirements:* For master's, GRE. Additional exam requirements/recommendations for international students: Required—TOEFL (minimum score 570 paper-based; 88 iBT), IELTS (minimum score 6.5), PTE (minimum score 60). *Application deadline:* For fall admission, 1/1 priority date for domestic and international students. Applications are processed on a rolling basis. Application fee: $75. Electronic

applications accepted. *Expenses: Tuition:* Full-time $52,550; part-time $2125 per credit hour. *Required fees:* $2890. *Financial support:* In 2017–18, research assistantships (averaging $23,000 per year), teaching assistantships with full tuition reimbursements (averaging $23,000 per year) were awarded; fellowships also available. Financial award application deadline: 1/1. *Faculty research:* Applications and design, automotive and street lighting, aviation lighting, controls, daylighting, energy and environment, health and vision, LEDs, outdoor lighting, residential lighting, security lighting. *Unit head:* Nadarajah Narendran, Graduate Program Director, 518-687-7100, E-mail: narenn2@rpi.edu.
Website: http://www.arch.rpi.edu/academic/graduate/lighting/

University of Washington, Graduate School, College of Built Environments, Department of Architecture, Seattle, WA 98195. Offers architecture (M Arch, MS); built environment (PhD); design computing (Certificate); design firm leadership and management (Certificate); historic preservation (Certificate); lighting (Certificate); urban design (Certificate). *Degree requirements:* For master's, thesis. *Entrance requirements:* For master's, GRE General Test, minimum GPA of 3.0, portfolio, 3 letters of recommendation. Additional exam requirements/recommendations for international students: Required—TOEFL. *Faculty research:* Lighting, materials, computing theory, media, culture, environment.

Urban Design

American University of Beirut, Graduate Programs, Maroun Semaan Faculty of Engineering and Architecture, 1107 2020, Lebanon. Offers applied energy (ME); civil engineering (PhD); electrical and computer engineering (PhD); energy studies (MS); engineering management (MEM); environmental and water resources (ME); environmental technology (MSES); mechanical engineering (ME, PhD); urban design (MUD); urban planning and policy (MUPP). *Program availability:* Part-time, 100% online. *Faculty:* 98 full-time (21 women), 88 part-time/adjunct (27 women). *Students:* 337 full-time (176 women), 114 part-time (42 women). Average age 26. 502 applicants, 65% accepted, 118 enrolled. In 2017, 71 master's, 16 doctorates awarded. Terminal master's awarded for partial completion of doctoral program. *Degree requirements:* For master's, one foreign language, comprehensive exam, thesis optional; for doctorate, one foreign language, comprehensive exam, thesis/dissertation. *Entrance requirements:* For doctorate, GRE. Additional exam requirements/recommendations for international students: Required—TOEFL (minimum score 573 paper-based; 88 iBT); Recommended—IELTS (minimum score 7). *Application deadline:* For fall admission, 4/4 for domestic and international students; for spring admission, 11/3 for domestic and international students; for summer admission, 4/4 for domestic and international students. Applications are processed on a rolling basis. Application fee: $50. Electronic applications accepted. *Expenses:* $34,056 (for non-thesis ME/MS); $31,993 (for thesis ME/MS); $49,536 (for PhD). *Financial support:* In 2017–18, 26 students received support, including 92 fellowships with full tuition reimbursements available (averaging $14,400 per year), 65 research assistantships with full and partial tuition reimbursements available (averaging $5,000 per year), 129 teaching assistantships with full and partial tuition reimbursements available (averaging $1,326 per year); scholarships/grants, tuition waivers (full and partial), and unspecified assistantships also available. Financial award application deadline: 4/2. *Faculty research:* All areas in engineering, architecture and design. *Total annual research expenditures:* $1.7 million. *Unit head:* Prof. Alan Shihade, Dean, 961-1-374374 Ext. 3400, Fax: 961-1-744462, E-mail: as20@aub.edu.lb. *Application contact:* Dr. Salim Kanaan, Director, Admissions Office, 961-1-374374 Ext. 2590, Fax: 961-1-750775, E-mail: sk00@aub.edu.lb.
Website: http://www.aub.edu.lb/msfea/pages/default.aspx

Arizona State University at the Tempe campus, Herberger Institute for Design and the Arts, The Design School, Tempe, AZ 85287-1605. Offers architecture (M Arch); building design/built environment (MS); design (MSD), including arts, media, and engineering, healthcare and healing environments (MSD, PhD), industrial design, interaction design, interior design, new product innovation, visual communication design; design, environment and the arts (PhD), including design, digital culture, healthcare and healing environments (MSD, PhD), history, theory, and criticism; landscape architecture (MLA); urban design (MUD); MA/MBA. *Accreditation:* NASAD. Terminal master's awarded for partial completion of doctoral program. *Degree requirements:* For master's, thesis optional, interactive Program of Study (iPOS) submitted before completing 50 percent of required credit hours; for doctorate, comprehensive exam, thesis/dissertation, interactive Program of Study (iPOS) submitted before completing 50 percent of required credit hours. *Entrance requirements:* For master's, GRE General Test, minimum GPA of 3.0 or equivalent in last 2 years of work leading to bachelor's degree, design/creative works portfolio, 3 references, statement of intent; for doctorate, GRE, master's degree in architecture, graphic design, industrial design, interior design, landscape architecture, or art history or equivalent standing; statement of purpose; 3 letters of recommendation; indication of potential faculty mentor; sample of written work. Additional exam requirements/recommendations for international students: Required—TOEFL (minimum score 600 paper-based; 100 iBT). Electronic applications accepted.

Ball State University, Graduate School, College of Architecture and Planning, Interdepartmental Program in Urban Design, Muncie, IN 47306. Offers MUD. *Students:* 8 full-time (1 woman); includes 3 minority (1 Black or African American, non-Hispanic/Latino; 1 Asian, non-Hispanic/Latino; 1 Hispanic/Latino). Average age 24. 13 applicants, 62% accepted, 7 enrolled. In 2017, 4 master's awarded. *Entrance requirements:* For master's, minimum cumulative baccalaureate GPA of 2.75 or 3.0 for latter half of baccalaureate, curriculum vitae or resume, statement of professional intent, portfolio of professional/academic work, writing sample. Additional exam requirements/recommendations for international students: Required—TOEFL (minimum score 550 paper-based; 79 iBT), IELTS (minimum score 6.5). *Application deadline:* Applications are processed on a rolling basis. Application fee: $60. Electronic applications accepted. *Expenses:* Contact institution. *Financial support:* Research assistantships with partial tuition reimbursements, teaching assistantships, and unspecified assistantships available. Financial award application deadline: 3/1; financial award applicants required to submit FAFSA. *Unit head:* Justin Ferguson, Director, 317-829-1025, E-mail: jferguson@bsu.edu.
Website: http://www.bsu.edu/urbandesign

Carnegie Mellon University, College of Fine Arts, School of Architecture, Pittsburgh, PA 15213-3891. Offers architecture (MSA); architecture, engineering, and construction management (PhD); building performance and diagnostics (MS, PhD); computational design (MS, PhD); engineering construction management (MSA); tangible interaction design (MTID); urban design (MUD). Terminal master's awarded for

partial completion of doctoral program. *Degree requirements:* For doctorate, thesis/dissertation. *Entrance requirements:* For master's and doctorate, GRE General Test. Additional exam requirements/recommendations for international students: Required—TOEFL.

City College of the City University of New York, Graduate School, The Bernard and Anne Spitzer School of Architecture, Program in Urban Design, New York, NY 10031-9198. Offers MUP. *Program availability:* Part-time. *Degree requirements:* For master's, thesis. *Entrance requirements:* For master's, portfolio, professional degree in architecture or equivalent. Additional exam requirements/recommendations for international students: Required—TOEFL (minimum score 550 paper-based). *Faculty research:* Real estate, planning, law.

Cornell University, Graduate School, Graduate Fields of Architecture, Art and Planning, Field of Architecture, Ithaca, NY 14853. Offers architectural design (M Arch); architectural science (MS); computer graphics (MS); history of architecture (MA, PhD); history of urban development (MA, PhD); theory and criticism of architecture (M Arch); urban design (M Arch). *Degree requirements:* For master's, one foreign language, thesis (MA, MS); for doctorate, 2 foreign languages, comprehensive exam, thesis/dissertation. *Entrance requirements:* For master's, GRE General Test, 5-year bachelor's degree in architecture, portfolio (M Arch), 3 letters of recommendation; for doctorate, GRE General Test, 3 letters of recommendation. Additional exam requirements/recommendations for international students: Required—TOEFL (minimum score 600 paper-based; 77 iBT). Electronic applications accepted. *Faculty research:* Architectural design and urban design, theory and criticism of architecture, computer graphics, building technology and environmental science, history of architecture and history of urban-development.

DePaul University, College of Liberal Arts and Social Sciences, Chicago, IL 60614. Offers Arabic (MA); Chinese (MA); critical ethnic studies (MA); English (MA); French (MA); German (MA); history (MA); interdisciplinary studies (MA, MS); international public service (MS); international studies (MA); Italian (MA); Japanese (MA); liberal studies (MA); nonprofit management (MNM); public administration (MPA); public health (MPH); public policy (MPP); public service management (MS); refugee and forced migration studies (MS); social work (MSW); sociology (MA); Spanish (MA); sustainable urban development (MA); women's and gender studies (MA); writing and publishing (MA); writing, rhetoric and discourse (MA); MA/PhD. *Program availability:* Part-time, evening/weekend, online learning. Terminal master's awarded for partial completion of doctoral program. *Degree requirements:* For master's, variable foreign language requirement, comprehensive exam (for some programs), thesis (for some programs). *Application deadline:* Applications are processed on a rolling basis. Application fee: $40. Electronic applications accepted. *Financial support:* Applicants required to submit FAFSA. *Unit head:* Dr. Guillermo Vasquez de Velasco, Dean, 773-325-7305. *Application contact:* Ann Spittle, Director of Graduate Admission, 773-325-8369, Fax: 312-476-3244, E-mail: graddepaul@depaul.edu.
Website: http://las.depaul.edu/

Drexel University, Westphal College of Media Arts and Design, Program in Urban Strategy, Philadelphia, PA 19104-2875. Offers MS.

Georgia Institute of Technology, Graduate Studies, College of Design, School of City and Regional Planning, Atlanta, GA 30332-0001. Offers city and regional planning (PhD); economic development (MCRP); environmental planning and management (MCRP); geographic information systems (MCRP); land and community development (MCRP); land use planning (MCRP); transportation (MCRP); urban design (MCRP); MCP/MSCE. *Accreditation:* ACSP. *Degree requirements:* For master's, thesis, internship. *Entrance requirements:* For master's, GRE General Test, minimum GPA of 2.7. Additional exam requirements/recommendations for international students: Required—TOEFL. Electronic applications accepted.

Harvard University, Graduate School of Design, Department of Urban Planning and Design, Cambridge, MA 02138. Offers urban planning (MUP); urban planning and design (MAUD, MLAUD). *Accreditation:* ACSP (one or more programs are accredited). *Entrance requirements:* For master's, GRE General Test. Additional exam requirements/recommendations for international students: Required—TOEFL (minimum score 600 paper-based; 104 iBT). Electronic applications accepted.

Hofstra University, College of Liberal Arts and Sciences, Programs in Biology, Hempstead, NY 11549. Offers biology (MA, MS); urban ecology (MA, MS). *Program availability:* Part-time, evening/weekend. *Students:* 17 full-time (10 women), 7 part-time (3 women); includes 18 minority (7 Black or African American, non-Hispanic/Latino; 1 American Indian or Alaska Native, non-Hispanic/Latino; 2 Asian, non-Hispanic/Latino; 6 Hispanic/Latino; 2 Two or more races, non-Hispanic/Latino). Average age 25. 18 applicants, 78% accepted, 8 enrolled. In 2017, 11 master's awarded. *Degree requirements:* For master's, thesis, minimum GPA of 3.0. *Entrance requirements:* For master's, GRE, bachelor's degree in biology or equivalent, 2 letters of recommendation, essay. Additional exam requirements/recommendations for international students: Required—TOEFL (minimum score 550 paper-based; 80 iBT). *Application deadline:* Applications are processed on a rolling basis. Application fee: $75. Electronic applications accepted. *Expenses: Tuition:* Full-time $1292. *Required fees:* $970. Tuition and fees vary according to program. *Financial support:* In 2017–18, 23 students

received support, including 18 fellowships with full and partial tuition reimbursements available (averaging $4,355 per year); research assistantships with full and partial tuition reimbursements available, career-related internships or fieldwork, Federal Work-Study, institutionally sponsored loans, scholarships/grants, tuition waivers (full and partial), and unspecified assistantships also available. Support available to part-time students. Financial award applicants required to submit FAFSA. *Faculty research:* Cellular communication through extracellular vesicle release; endocytic trafficking of g protein-coupled receptors in human diseases like vascular inflammation and cancer; ecological factors that promote the evolution of parental care behaviors; neurobiological, genetic, and hormonal regulation of mate choice and maternal behaviors in female songbirds and amphibians; applied and environmental microbiology; the scholarship of teaching and learning; biology education; metacognition. *Unit head:* Dr. Peter Daniel, Chairperson, 516-463-6718, Fax: 516-463-5112, E-mail: peter.c.daniel@hofstra.edu. *Application contact:* Sunil Samuel, Assistant Vice President of Admissions, 516-463-4723, Fax: 516-463-4664, E-mail: graduateadmission@hofstra.edu.
Website: http://www.hofstra.edu/hclas

Judson University, Master of Architecture Program, Elgin, IL 60123-1498. Offers architecture (M Arch); sustainable design (M Arch); traditional architecture and urbanism (M Arch). *Program availability:* Part-time. *Faculty:* 9 full-time (3 women), 3 part-time/adjunct (1 woman). *Students:* 11 full-time (4 women). Average age 23. 24 applicants, 83% accepted, 11 enrolled. In 2017, 6 master's awarded. *Degree requirements:* For master's, thesis optional, 1600-hour practicum/preceptorship completed prior to enrollment. *Entrance requirements:* For master's, GRE, Judson BA in architecture or equivalent; minimum cumulative undergraduate GPA of 2.75, 3.0 in architecture; comprehensive portfolio; letter of intent. Additional exam requirements/recommendations for international students: Required—TOEFL (minimum score 550 paper-based), IELTS (minimum score 6.5). *Application deadline:* For fall admission, 2/15 priority date for domestic and international students; for winter admission, 11/15 for domestic students; for spring admission, 11/15 for domestic and international students. Applications are processed on a rolling basis. Application fee: $100. Electronic applications accepted. *Expenses:* Contact institution. *Financial support:* In 2017–18, 9 students received support. Fellowships, research assistantships, teaching assistantships, scholarships/grants, and 8 assistantships available. Financial award application deadline: 5/1; financial award applicants required to submit FAFSA. *Faculty research:* Sustainable design, urbanism, daylighting, acoustics, digital media and fabrication. *Unit head:* Dr. David M. Ogoli, Chair, 847-628-1018, E-mail: dogoli@judsonu.edu. *Application contact:* Molly Smith, Director of Admissions, 847-628-2521, E-mail: molly.smith@judsonu.edu.
Website: http://www.judsonu.edu/ArchMaster/

Kent State University, College of Architecture and Environmental Design, Kent, OH 44242-0001. Offers architecture (M Arch); architecture and environmental design (MS); health care design (MHCD); landscape architecture (MLA); urban design (MUD); M Arch/MBA; M Arch/MUD. *Program availability:* Part-time. *Faculty:* 19 full-time (2 women), 15 part-time/adjunct (6 women). *Students:* 70 full-time (27 women), 13 part-time (7 women); includes 8 minority (1 Black or African American, non-Hispanic/Latino; 1 Asian, non-Hispanic/Latino; 4 Hispanic/Latino; 2 Two or more races, non-Hispanic/Latino), 13 international. Average age 26. 100 applicants, 82% accepted, 57 enrolled. In 2017, 59 master's awarded. *Degree requirements:* For master's, thesis (for some programs), capstone project (for some programs). *Entrance requirements:* For master's, GRE with minimum scores 151 (460) verbal reasoning, 150 (620) quantitative reasoning, and 4.25 analytical writing (except for MHCD), letters of recommendation, portfolio. Additional exam requirements/recommendations for international students: Required—TOEFL (minimum score 550 paper-based; 80 iBT), IELTS (minimum score 6.5), PTE (minimum score 54), Michigan English Language Assessment Battery (minimum score 77). *Application deadline:* Applications are processed on a rolling basis. Application fee: $45 ($70 for international students). Electronic applications accepted. *Expenses:* Tuition, state resident: full-time $11,310; part-time $515 per credit hour. Tuition, nonresident: full-time $20,396; part-time $928 per credit hour. *International tuition:* $18,544 full-time. *Financial support:* Research assistantships with full tuition reimbursements, teaching assistantships with full tuition reimbursements, Federal Work-Study, scholarships/grants, and unspecified assistantships available. Financial award application deadline: 2/1; financial award applicants required to submit FAFSA. *Unit head:* Mark Mistur, Dean, E-mail: mmistur1@kent.edu. *Application contact:* Johnathan Fleming, Assistant Professor and Director, Master of Architecture, 330-672-0934, E-mail: jpflemi1@kent.edu.
Website: http://www.kent.edu/caed

Lawrence Technological University, College of Architecture and Design, Southfield, MI 48075-1058. Offers architecture (M Arch, MA), including interior architecture (M Arch); build information modeling (Graduate Certificate); interior design (MID); social practice (MFA); transportation design (Graduate Certificate); urban design (MUD). *Accreditation:* NASAD. *Program availability:* Part-time, evening/weekend. *Faculty:* 14 full-time (1 woman), 3 part-time/adjunct (1 woman). *Students:* 6 full-time (2 women), 115 part-time (50 women); includes 11 minority (3 Black or African American, non-Hispanic/Latino; 1 Asian, non-Hispanic/Latino; 6 Hispanic/Latino; 1 Two or more races, non-Hispanic/Latino), 32 international. Average age 30. 150 applicants, 55% accepted, 50 enrolled. In 2017, 82 master's, 3 other advanced degrees awarded. *Degree requirements:* For master's, thesis optional. *Entrance requirements:* Additional exam requirements/recommendations for international students: Required—TOEFL (minimum score 550 paper-based; 79 iBT). *Application deadline:* For fall admission, 5/27 for international students; for spring admission, 10/8 for international students; for summer admission, 2/14 for international students. Applications are processed on a rolling basis. Application fee: $50. Electronic applications accepted. *Expenses: Tuition:* Full-time $15,274; part-time $1091 per credit. One-time fee: $150. *Financial support:* In 2017–18, 45 students received support, including 8 research assistantships with partial tuition reimbursements available (averaging $6,000 per year); career-related internships or fieldwork, scholarships/grants, and unspecified assistantships also available. Financial award application deadline: 4/1; financial award applicants required to submit FAFSA. *Faculty research:* Symmetry within the design process, public interest design, transdisciplinary design, adaptive reuse, digital craft, and integration of the use of daylight in architecture and urban design. *Total annual research expenditures:* $209,672. *Unit head:* Prof. Karl Daubmann, Dean/Professor, 248-204-2805, E-mail: archdean@ltu.edu. *Application contact:* Jane Rohrback, Director of Admissions, 248-204-3160, Fax: 248-204-2228, E-mail: admissions@ltu.edu.
Website: http://www.ltu.edu/architecture_and_design/index.asp

London Metropolitan University, Graduate Programs, London, United Kingdom. Offers applied psychology (M Sc); architecture (MA); biomedical science (M Sc); blood science (M Sc); cancer pharmacology (M Sc); computer networking and cyber security (M Sc); computing and information systems (M Sc); conference interpreting (MA); counter-terrorism studies (M Sc); creative, digital and professional writing (MA); crime, violence and prevention (M Sc); criminology (M Sc); curating contemporary art (MA); data analytics (M Sc); digital media (MA); early childhood studies (MA); education (MA, Ed D); financial services law, regulation and compliance (LL M); food science (M Sc); forensic psychology (M Sc); health and social care management and policy (M Sc); human nutrition (M Sc); human resource management (MA); human rights and international conflict (MA); information technology (M Sc); intelligence and security studies (M Sc); international oil, gas and energy law (LL M); international relations (MA); interpreting (MA); learning and teaching in higher education (MA); legal practice (LL M); media and entertainment law (LL M); organizational and consumer psychology (M Sc); psychological therapy (M Sc); psychology of mental health (M Sc); public health (M Sc); public policy and management (MPA); security studies (M Sc); social work (M Sc); spatial planning and urban design (MA); sports therapy (M Sc); supporting older children and young people with dyslexia (MA); teaching languages (MA), including Arabic, English; translation (MA); woman and child abuse (MA).

The New School, Parsons School of Design, Program in Design and Urban Ecologies, New York, NY 10011. Offers MS. *Program availability:* Part-time. *Faculty:* 7 full-time (3 women), 4 part-time/adjunct (2 women). *Students:* 30 full-time (22 women); includes 4 minority (2 Black or African American, non-Hispanic/Latino; 1 Asian, non-Hispanic/Latino; 1 Two or more races, non-Hispanic/Latino), 16 international. Average age 26. 42 applicants, 95% accepted, 16 enrolled. In 2017, 8 master's awarded. *Degree requirements:* For master's, thesis. *Entrance requirements:* For master's, transcripts, resume, statement of purpose, recommendation letters, portfolio, interview. Additional exam requirements/recommendations for international students: Required—TOEFL (minimum score 92 iBT), IELTS (minimum score 7), PTE (minimum score 63). *Application deadline:* For fall admission, 1/1 priority date for domestic and international students; for summer admission, 1/1 priority date for domestic and international students. Applications are processed on a rolling basis. Application fee: $50. Electronic applications accepted. *Expenses:* $24,922 per semester full-time, $1,744 per credit part-time, $100 maintenance of status fee. *Financial support:* In 2017–18, 29 students received support, including 16 teaching assistantships (averaging $6,140 per year); career-related internships or fieldwork, Federal Work-Study, scholarships/grants, unspecified assistantships, and travel funding; tuition waivers for students who are also New School employees also available. Support available to part-time students. Financial award application deadline: 2/1; financial award applicants required to submit FAFSA. *Unit head:* Miodrag Mitrasinovic, Chair, Urban Council, E-mail: mitrasim@newschool.edu. *Application contact:* Courtney Malenius, Director of Graduate Admission, 212-229-5150 Ext. 4011, E-mail: thinkparsonsgrad@newschool.edu.
Website: https://www.newschool.edu/parsons/ms-design-urban-ecology/

The New School, Parsons School of Design, Program in Theories of Urban Practice, New York, NY 10011. Offers MA. *Program availability:* Part-time. *Faculty:* 7 full-time (3 women), 3 part-time/adjunct (2 women). *Students:* 15 full-time (8 women), 2 part-time (both women); includes 6 minority (2 Black or African American, non-Hispanic/Latino; 2 Asian, non-Hispanic/Latino; 1 Hispanic/Latino; 1 Two or more races, non-Hispanic/Latino), 3 international. Average age 27. 15 applicants, 87% accepted, 7 enrolled. In 2017, 11 master's awarded. *Degree requirements:* For master's, thesis. *Entrance requirements:* For master's, transcripts, resume, statement of purpose, recommendation letters, portfolio or writing sample, interview. Additional exam requirements/recommendations for international students: Required—TOEFL (minimum score 92 iBT), IELTS (minimum score 7), PTE (minimum score 63). *Application deadline:* For fall admission, 1/1 priority date for domestic and international students. Applications are processed on a rolling basis. Application fee: $50. Electronic applications accepted. *Expenses:* $1,744 per credit. *Financial support:* In 2017–18, 13 students received support, including 1 teaching assistantship (averaging $4,467 per year); career-related internships or fieldwork, scholarships/grants, and unspecified assistantships also available. Support available to part-time students. Financial award application deadline: 2/1; financial award applicants required to submit FAFSA. *Unit head:* Gabriela Perez Rendon, Co-Chair, Urban Council, 212-229-8970 Ext. 1335, E-mail: perezreg@newschool.edu. *Application contact:* Courtney Malenius, Director of Graduate Admissions, 212-229-5150 Ext. 4011, E-mail: maleniuc@newschool.edu.
Website: https://www.newschool.edu/parsons/ma-theories-urban-research/

New York Institute of Technology, School of Architecture and Design, Old Westbury, NY 11568-8000. Offers architecture (M Arch); architecture, urban and regional design (MS). *Program availability:* Part-time. *Faculty:* 3 full-time (1 woman), 3 part-time/adjunct (0 women). *Students:* 14 full-time (11 women), all international. Average age 26. 45 applicants, 44% accepted, 8 enrolled. In 2017, 14 master's awarded. *Entrance requirements:* For master's, professional architecture or landscape architecture degree from accredited college or university approved by the NAAB or equivalent; minimum undergraduate GPA of 3.0; digital portfolio; curriculum vitae; personal essay; two letters of recommendation. Additional exam requirements/recommendations for international students: Required—TOEFL (minimum score 79 iBT), IELTS (minimum score 6). *Application deadline:* For fall admission, 3/1 for domestic and international students. Applications are processed on a rolling basis. Application fee: $50. Electronic applications accepted. *Expenses:* $1,285 per credit plus fees. *Financial support:* Career-related internships or fieldwork, Federal Work-Study, institutionally sponsored loans, scholarships/grants, tuition waivers (full and partial), and unspecified assistantships available. Support available to part-time students. Financial award application deadline: 2/15; financial award applicants required to submit FAFSA. *Faculty research:* Resilient cities, compact morphology, new town development, pedestrian-friendly public realm. *Unit head:* Jeffrey Raven, Graduate Director, 212-261-1547, E-mail: jraven@nyit.edu. *Application contact:* Alice Dolitsky, Director, Graduate Admissions, 516-686-7520, Fax: 516-686-1116, E-mail: nyitgrad@nyit.edu.
Website: http://www.nyit.edu/architecture

Pratt Institute, School of Architecture, Program in Architecture and Urban Design, Brooklyn, NY 11205-3899. Offers MS. *Students:* 7 full-time (3 women); includes 1 minority (Hispanic/Latino), 5 international. Average age 27. 57 applicants, 65% accepted, 7 enrolled. In 2017, 10 master's awarded. *Degree requirements:* For master's, thesis. *Entrance requirements:* For master's, portfolio, letters of recommendation. Additional exam requirements/recommendations for international students: Required—TOEFL (minimum score 550 paper-based; 79 iBT). *Application deadline:* For fall admission, 1/5 for domestic and international students; for spring admission, 10/1 for domestic and international students. Application fee: $50 ($90 for international students). Electronic applications accepted. *Expenses: Tuition:* Full-time $30,834. *Required fees:* $1974. *Financial support:* Career-related internships or fieldwork, Federal Work-Study, institutionally sponsored loans, scholarships/grants, health care benefits, and unspecified assistantships available. Support available to part-time students. Financial award application deadline: 2/1; financial award applicants required to submit FAFSA. *Faculty research:* Urban development process; historical, social, and economic implications of planning. *Unit head:* David Erdman, Chairperson, 718-399-4327, E-mail: derdman@pratt.edu. *Application contact:* Natalie Capannelli, Director of Graduate Admissions, 718-636-3551, Fax: 718-399-4242, E-mail: ncapanne@pratt.edu.
Website: https://www.pratt.edu/academics/architecture/grad-arch-urban-design/

See Display on page 105 and Close-Up on page 125.

Rice University, Graduate Programs, School of Architecture, Houston, TX 77251-1892. Offers architecture (M Arch, D Arch); urban design (M Arch). *Degree requirements:* For master's, thesis optional; for doctorate, thesis/dissertation. *Entrance requirements:* For master's and doctorate, GRE. Additional exam requirements/recommendations for international students: Required—TOEFL (minimum score 600 paper-based; 100 iBT). Electronic applications accepted.

Savannah College of Art and Design, Program in Urban Design, Savannah, GA 31402-3146. Offers MUD. *Program availability:* Part-time. *Faculty:* 1 full-time (0 women). *Students:* 7 full-time (5 women), 4 part-time (3 women), 9 international. Average age 27. 42 applicants, 57% accepted, 5 enrolled. In 2017, 4 master's awarded. *Degree requirements:* For master's, thesis. *Entrance requirements:* For master's, GRE (recommended), portfolio (submitted in digital format), audition or writing submission, resume, statement of purpose, two letters of recommendation. Additional exam requirements/recommendations for international students: Recommended—TOEFL (minimum score 550 paper-based; 85 iBT), IELTS (minimum score 6.5). *Application deadline:* For fall admission, 4/1 for domestic and international students. Applications are processed on a rolling basis. Application fee: $40. Electronic applications accepted. *Expenses: Tuition:* Full-time $36,765; part-time $817 per credit hour. One-time fee: $500. *Financial support:* Career-related internships or fieldwork, Federal Work-Study, and scholarships/grants available. Financial award application deadline: 4/1; financial award applicants required to submit FAFSA. *Unit head:* Ivan Chow, Dean, School of Building Arts. *Application contact:* Jenny Jaquillard, Executive Director of Admissions, Recruitment and Events, 912-525-5100, Fax: 912-525-5985, E-mail: admission@scad.edu.
Website: http://www.scad.edu/academics/programs/urban-design

State University of New York College of Environmental Science and Forestry, Department of Landscape Architecture, Syracuse, NY 13210-2779. Offers community design and planning (MLA, MS); cultural landscape studies and conservation (MLA, MS); landscape and urban ecology (MLA, MS). *Accreditation:* ASLA (one or more programs are accredited). *Program availability:* Part-time. *Faculty:* 10 full-time (4 women), 7 part-time/adjunct (5 women). *Students:* 27 full-time (16 women), 5 part-time (3 women); includes 5 minority (3 Black or African American, non-Hispanic/Latino; 1 Asian, non-Hispanic/Latino; 1 Hispanic/Latino), 5 international. Average age 25. 31 applicants, 65% accepted, 10 enrolled. In 2017, 9 master's awarded. *Degree requirements:* For master's, comprehensive exam (for some programs), thesis (for some programs). *Entrance requirements:* For master's, GRE General Test, minimum GPA of 3.0. Additional exam requirements/recommendations for international students: Required—TOEFL (minimum score 550 paper-based; 80 iBT), IELTS (minimum score 6), or STEP Eiken (grade 1). *Application deadline:* For fall admission, 2/1 priority date for domestic and international students; for spring admission, 11/1 priority date for domestic and international students. Applications are processed on a rolling basis. Application fee: $60. Electronic applications accepted. *Expenses:* Tuition, state resident: full-time $10,870; part-time $453 per credit. Tuition, nonresident: full-time $22,210; part-time $925 per credit. *Required fees:* $1435; $70.85 per credit. One-time fee: $25 full-time. Part-time tuition and fees vary according to course load. *Financial support:* In 2017–18, 9 students received support. Unspecified assistantships available. Financial award application deadline: 6/30; financial award applicants required to submit FAFSA. *Faculty research:* Site analysis and design, city and regional planning, community environments. *Total annual research expenditures:* $216,783. *Unit head:* Dr. Douglas Johnston, Chair, 315-470-6544, Fax: 315-470-6540, E-mail: dmjohnst@esf.edu. *Application contact:* Scott Shannon, Associate Provost for Instruction/Dean of the Graduate School, 315-470-6599, Fax: 315-470-6978, E-mail: esfgrad@esf.edu.
Website: http://www.esf.edu/la/

University at Buffalo, the State University of New York, Graduate School, School of Architecture and Planning, Department of Urban and Regional Planning, Buffalo, NY 12414. Offers community health and food systems (MUP); economic development (MUP); environment/land use (MUP); historic preservation (MUP, Certificate); neighborhood/community development (MUP); real estate development (MSRED); urban and regional planning (PhD); urban design (MUP); JD/MUP; M Arch/MUP. *Accreditation:* ACSP. *Program availability:* Part-time. *Faculty:* 13 full-time (6 women), 12 part-time/adjunct (3 women). *Students:* 76 full-time (27 women), 20 part-time (9 women); includes 17 minority (9 Black or African American, non-Hispanic/Latino; 5 Hispanic/Latino; 3 Two or more races, non-Hispanic/Latino), 20 international. Average age 27. 196 applicants, 20% accepted, 32 enrolled. In 2017, 35 master's, 1 doctorate, 5 other advanced degrees awarded. *Degree requirements:* For master's, thesis or alternative, project; for doctorate, comprehensive exam, thesis/dissertation. *Entrance requirements:* For master's, resume, three letters of recommendation, personal statement, transcripts; for doctorate, GRE, transcripts, three letters of recommendation, resume, research statement, writing sample. Additional exam requirements/recommendations for international students: Required—TOEFL (minimum score 79 iBT), IELTS (minimum score 6.5). *Application deadline:* For fall admission, 3/1 priority date for domestic and international students; for spring admission, 10/31 priority date for domestic students, 10/1 priority date for international students. Applications are processed on a rolling basis. Application fee: $75. Electronic applications accepted. *Expenses:* $13,382. *Financial support:* In 2017–18, 45 students received support, including 3 fellowships with full tuition reimbursements available (averaging $15,600 per year), 2 research assistantships with partial tuition reimbursements available (averaging $13,390 per year), 15 teaching assistantships with partial tuition reimbursements available (averaging $4,800 per year); career-related internships or fieldwork, Federal Work-Study, institutionally sponsored loans, scholarships/grants, health care benefits, and unspecified assistantships also available. Financial award application deadline: 3/1; financial award applicants required to submit FAFSA. *Faculty research:* Economic and international development, environmental and land use planning, GIS and spatial analysis, urban design and physical planning, neighborhood planning and community development, historic preservation. *Total annual research expenditures:* $1.3 million. *Unit head:* Dr. Daniel B. Hess, Professor and Chair, 716-829-3671 Ext. 109, Fax: 716-829-3256, E-mail: dbhess@buffalo.edu. *Application contact:* Donna Rogalski, Department Secretary, 716-829-3671, Fax: 716-829-3256, E-mail: dmr1@buffalo.edu.
Website: http://www.ap.buffalo.edu/planning/

The University of British Columbia, Faculty of Applied Science, School of Architecture and Landscape Architecture, Program in Landscape Architecture, Vancouver, BC V6T 1Z2, Canada. Offers advanced studies in landscape architecture (MASLA); landscape architecture (MLA); urban design (MUD); M Arch/MLA. *Degree requirements:* For master's, comprehensive exam or thesis. *Entrance requirements:* For master's, portfolio. Additional exam requirements/recommendations for international students: Required—TOEFL. Electronic applications accepted. *Expenses:* Contact institution. *Faculty research:* Landscape design, urban-rural interface, urban ecology, sustainable development, collaborative planning and community forestry.

University of California, Berkeley, Graduate Division, College of Environmental Design, Department of Architecture, Berkeley, CA 94720-1500. Offers architecture (M Arch); building science (MS, PhD); building structures, construction and materials (MS, PhD); design theories, methods, and practices (MS, PhD); environmental design in developing countries (MS, PhD); history of architecture and urbanism (MS, PhD); social and cultural processes in architecture and urbanism (MS, PhD); M Arch/MCP; M Arch/MS; MLA/M Arch. *Degree requirements:* For master's, thesis; for doctorate, thesis/dissertation, qualifying exam. *Entrance requirements:* For master's and doctorate, GRE General Test, minimum GPA of 3.0, 3 letters of recommendation. Additional exam requirements/recommendations for international students: Required—TOEFL (minimum score 570 paper-based; 90 iBT). Electronic applications accepted. Application fee is waived when completed online.

University of California, Berkeley, Graduate Division, College of Environmental Design, Department of Landscape Architecture and Environmental Planning, Berkeley, CA 94720-1500. Offers landscape architecture (MLA), including environmental planning, landscape design and site planning, urban and community design; landscape architecture and environmental planning (PhD); MLA/M Arch; MLA/MCP. *Accreditation:* ASLA (one or more programs are accredited). *Degree requirements:* For master's, comprehensive exam (for some programs), thesis (for some programs), professional project or thesis; for doctorate, one foreign language, thesis/dissertation, qualifying exam. *Entrance requirements:* For master's, GRE General Test, minimum GPA of 3.0, portfolio; for doctorate, GRE General Test, master's degree (strongly recommended), minimum GPA of 3.0, sample of written work, 3 letters of recommendation. Additional exam requirements/recommendations for international students: Required—TOEFL (minimum score 570 paper-based; 90 iBT). Electronic applications accepted.

University of California, Berkeley, Graduate Division, College of Environmental Design, Group in Urban Design, Berkeley, CA 94720-1500. Offers MUD. *Degree requirements:* For master's, thesis (for some programs), professional project or thesis. *Entrance requirements:* For master's, GRE General Test, minimum GPA of 3.0, portfolio, 3 letters of recommendation. Additional exam requirements/recommendations for international students: Required—TOEFL (minimum score 570 paper-based; 90 iBT). Electronic applications accepted.

University of California, Los Angeles, Graduate Division, School of the Arts and Architecture, Department of Architecture and Urban Design, Los Angeles, CA 90095. Offers M Arch, MA, PhD. *Degree requirements:* For master's, comprehensive exam (M Arch I, II); thesis (MA); for doctorate, 2 foreign languages, thesis/dissertation, oral and written qualifying exams. *Entrance requirements:* For master's, GRE General Test, bachelor's degree; minimum undergraduate GPA of 3.0 (or its equivalent if letter grade system not used); writing sample (MA only); portfolio (M Arch only); for doctorate, GRE General Test, bachelor's degree; minimum undergraduate GPA of 3.5 (or its equivalent if letter grade system not used); writing sample. Additional exam requirements/recommendations for international students: Required—TOEFL. Electronic applications accepted. *Expenses:* Contact institution.

University of Colorado Denver, College of Architecture and Planning, Program in Design and Planning, Denver, CO 80217. Offers history of architecture, landscape and urbanism (PhD); sustainable and healthy environments (PhD). *Program availability:* Part-time. *Degree requirements:* For doctorate, comprehensive exam, thesis/dissertation. *Entrance requirements:* For doctorate, GRE (minimum score of 158 for both verbal and quantitative; writing 4.0), minimum undergraduate GPA of 3.0, graduate 3.5; writing sample; three letters of recommendation; statement of personal and professional goals. Additional exam requirements/recommendations for international students: Required—TOEFL (minimum score 80 iBT); Recommended—IELTS (minimum score 6.8). Electronic applications accepted. *Expenses:* Contact institution. *Faculty research:* Land use and environmental planning and design; design and planning processes and practices; history, theory, and criticism of the built environment.

University of Colorado Denver, College of Architecture and Planning, Program in Urban Design, Denver, CO 80217. Offers MUD. *Program availability:* Part-time. *Degree requirements:* For master's, thesis optional, 36 credits, including an independent study, internship, or additional elective. *Entrance requirements:* For master's, GRE (for students with an undergraduate GPA below 3.0), BA in related field; prior professional degree; portfolio of creative work; statement of purpose; resume. Additional exam requirements/recommendations for international students: Required—TOEFL (minimum score 75 iBT). Electronic applications accepted. *Expenses:* Contact institution. *Faculty research:* Architecture of the city, architectural experimentation and exploration, composition and decomposition, intervention and transformation in the urban and rural landscape.

University of Colorado Denver, School of Education and Human Development, Program in Educational Leadership and Innovation, Denver, CO 80217. Offers educational studies and research (PhD), including administrative leadership and policy, early childhood special education, math education, research, assessment and evaluation, science education, urban ecologies. *Program availability:* Part-time, evening/weekend. *Degree requirements:* For doctorate, comprehensive exam, thesis/dissertation, 75 credit hours (for PhD). *Entrance requirements:* For doctorate, GRE or equivalent, resume or curriculum vitae, letters of recommendation, master's degree or equivalent, completion of basic or advanced statistics course with minimum B grade. Additional exam requirements/recommendations for international students: Required—TOEFL (minimum score 537 paper-based; 75 iBT); Recommended—IELTS (minimum score 6.5). Electronic applications accepted. *Expenses:* Contact institution. *Faculty research:* Administrative leadership and policy studies, early childhood education, research in diversity, paraprofessionals in education, urban schools lab.

University of Houston, Gerald D. Hines College of Architecture and Design, Houston, TX 77204-4000. Offers architectural studies (MA); architecture (M Arch, MS), including media and fabrication (MS), sustainable design (MS), sustainable urban systems (MS), urban design (MS); industrial design (MS). *Faculty:* 15 full-time (4 women), 13 part-time/adjunct (3 women). *Students:* 92 full-time (40 women), 6 part-time (2 women); includes 23 minority (1 Black or African American, non-Hispanic/Latino; 1 American Indian or Alaska Native, non-Hispanic/Latino; 9 Asian, non-Hispanic/Latino; 9 Hispanic/Latino; 3 Two or more races, non-Hispanic/Latino), 20 international. Average age 28. 192 applicants, 45% accepted, 47 enrolled. In 2017, 21 master's awarded. *Degree requirements:* For master's, thesis (for some programs). *Entrance requirements:* For master's, GRE General Test, digital portfolio. Additional exam requirements/recommendations for international students: Required—TOEFL (minimum score 550 paper-based; 79 iBT), IELTS (minimum score 6.5). *Application deadline:* For fall admission, 2/1 priority date for domestic students, 2/1 for international students. Applications are processed on a rolling basis. Application fee: $50. Electronic applications accepted. *Expenses:* Contact institution. *Financial support:* In 2017–18, 15 students received support, including 2 research assistantships with partial tuition reimbursements available (averaging $7,720 per year), 11 teaching assistantships with partial tuition reimbursements available (averaging $5,264 per year); career-related internships or fieldwork, Federal Work-Study, institutionally sponsored loans, scholarships/grants, health care benefits, and unspecified assistantships also available. Support available to part-time students. Financial award application deadline: 2/1. *Faculty research:* Community-based design; twentieth-century architecture, urbanism, and design; extreme environments; design build; green building components; digital technology; preservation; industrial design; interior architecture. *Total annual research expenditures:* $150,000. *Unit head:* Patricia Belton Oliver, Dean, 713-743-2400, Fax: 713-743-2358, E-mail: poliver@central.uh.edu. *Application contact:* Trang Phan, Assistant Dean, 713-743-2400, Fax: 713-743-2358, E-mail: tphan@uh.edu.
Website: http://www.uh.edu/architecture/

The University of Kansas, Graduate Studies, School of Architecture and Design, Department of Architecture, Lawrence, KS 66045. Offers architectural acoustics (Certificate); architecture (M Arch, PhD); health and wellness (Certificate); historic preservation (Certificate); urban design (Certificate). *Students:* 91 full-time (43 women), 14 part-time (6 women); includes 14 minority (3 Black or African American, non-Hispanic/Latino; 4 Asian, non-Hispanic/Latino; 4 Hispanic/Latino; 3 Two or more races,

non-Hispanic/Latino), 21 international. Average age 25. 100 applicants, 52% accepted, 20 enrolled. In 2017, 77 master's, 7 doctorates, 5 other advanced degrees awarded. Terminal master's awarded for partial completion of doctoral program. *Entrance requirements:* For master's, GRE, transcript; resume; minimum GPA of 3.0; statement of purpose; letters of recommendation; portfolio of design work, or samples of written work or other creative artifacts produced if previous degree was not in a design-related discipline; for doctorate, GRE, transcript, resume, minimum GPA of 3.0, statement of purpose, letters of recommendation, research-informed writing sample, exhibit of work illustrating applicant's interests and abilities in areas related to the design disciplines. Additional exam requirements/recommendations for international students: Required—TOEFL, IELTS. *Application deadline:* For fall admission, 1/15 priority date for domestic and international students; for summer admission, 1/15 priority date for domestic and international students. Application fee: $65 ($85 for international students). Electronic applications accepted. *Financial support:* Fellowships, research assistantships, teaching assistantships, scholarships/grants, health care benefits, and unspecified assistantships available. Financial award application deadline: 1/15; financial award applicants required to submit FAFSA. *Faculty research:* Design build, sustainability, emergent technology, healthy places, urban design. *Unit head:* Prof. Jae Chang, Chair, 785-864-1446, E-mail: jdchang@ku.edu. *Application contact:* Gera Elliott, Admissions Coordinator, 785-864-3167, Fax: 785-864-5185, E-mail: archku@ku.edu. Website: http://architecture.ku.edu/

University of Miami, Graduate School, School of Architecture, Program in Suburb and Town Design, Coral Gables, FL 33124. Offers M Arch. *Entrance requirements:* For master's, GRE General Test, minimum GPA of 3.0, portfolio. Additional exam requirements/recommendations for international students: Required—TOEFL. Electronic applications accepted.

University of Michigan, Taubman College of Architecture and Urban Planning, Master of Urban Design Program, Ann Arbor, MI 48109. Offers MUD, MUD/M Arch. *Degree requirements:* For master's, thesis or alternative. *Entrance requirements:* Additional exam requirements/recommendations for international students: Required—TOEFL (minimum score 100 iBT), GRE. Electronic applications accepted. *Expenses:* Contact institution.

The University of North Carolina at Charlotte, College of Arts and Architecture, School of Architecture, Charlotte, NC 28223-0001. Offers architecture (M Arch I, M Arch II, MS); urban design (MUD). *Faculty:* 26 full-time (9 women). *Students:* 81 full-time (45 women), 2 part-time (both women); includes 16 minority (10 Black or African American, non-Hispanic/Latino; 5 Hispanic/Latino; 1 Two or more races, non-Hispanic/Latino), 27 international. Average age 25. 120 applicants, 86% accepted, 33 enrolled. In 2017, 55 master's awarded. *Degree requirements:* For master's, design studio or thesis. *Entrance requirements:* For master's, GRE, official transcripts from all previous college-level institution(s); statement of purpose explaining reasons for wanting to study in the School of Architecture; three recommendations from persons familiar with the applicant's personal and professional qualifications; resume or curriculum vitae; portfolio. Additional exam requirements/recommendations for international students: Required—TOEFL (minimum score 523 paper-based, 70 iBT) or IELTS (6.5). *Application deadline:* For fall admission, 1/15 priority date for domestic and international students. Applications are processed on a rolling basis. Application fee: $75. Electronic applications accepted. *Expenses:* Contact institution. *Financial support:* In 2017–18, 33 students received support, including 30 research assistantships (averaging $6,644 per year), 2 teaching assistantships (averaging $5,000 per year); institutionally sponsored loans, scholarships/grants, unspecified assistantships, and administrative assistantship also available. Financial award application deadline: 3/1; financial award applicants required to submit FAFSA. *Faculty research:* Urban design studies for local and regional municipalities and community groups, high performance building and optimization protocols, daylighting and energy analysis, digital design and fabrication components, and interactive visualization; refinement of regionally specific computer-aided analysis tools used to evaluate total building energy performance, and the economic valuation of architectural systems and their design attributes. *Total annual research expenditures:* $35,526. *Unit head:* Kenneth A. Lambla, Dean, 704-687-0090, E-mail: kalambla@uncc.edu. *Application contact:* Kathy B. Giddings, Director of Graduate Admissions, 704-687-5503, Fax: 704-687-1668, E-mail: gradadm@uncc.edu. Website: http://coaa.uncc.edu/academics/school-of-architecture

University of Pennsylvania, School of Design, Department of City and Regional Planning, Philadelphia, PA 19104. Offers city and regional planning (PhD); city planning (MCP); GIS and spatial analysis (Certificate); land preservation (Certificate); urban design (Certificate); urban redevelopment (Certificate); urban spatial analytics (MUSA). *Accreditation:* ACSP (one or more programs are accredited). *Program availability:* Part-time. *Faculty:* 16 full-time (8 women), 3 part-time/adjunct (0 women). *Students:* 148 full-time (83 women), 5 part-time (2 women); includes 22 minority (5 Black or African American, non-Hispanic/Latino; 8 Asian, non-Hispanic/Latino; 6 Hispanic/Latino; 1 Native Hawaiian or other Pacific Islander, non-Hispanic/Latino; 2 Two or more races, non-Hispanic/Latino), 56 international. Average age 27. 395 applicants, 62% accepted, 101 enrolled. In 2017, 65 master's, 5 doctorates, 7 other advanced degrees awarded. *Degree requirements:* For doctorate, thesis/dissertation. *Entrance requirements:* Additional exam requirements/recommendations for international students: Required—TOEFL (minimum score 100 iBT); Recommended—IELTS (minimum score 7), TSE (minimum score 68). *Application deadline:* For spring admission, 1/12 for domestic students. Application fee: $80. Electronic applications accepted. *Financial support:* In 2017–18, 39 teaching assistantships (averaging $2,000 per year) were awarded; fellowships, research assistantships, and Federal Work-Study also available. Financial award application deadline: 2/15; financial award applicants required to submit FAFSA. *Faculty research:* Transportation planning, community and economic development, public private development, land use and environmental planning, urban design. *Unit head:* Dr. John Landis, Department Chair, 215-746-2340, E-mail: jlan@design.upenn.edu. *Application contact:* Roslynne Carter, Administrative Assistant, 215-898-8330, Fax: 215-898-5730, E-mail: admissions@design.upenn.edu. Website: https://www.design.upenn.edu/city-regional-planning

University of South Florida, College of The Arts, School of Architecture and Community Design, Tampa, FL 33620-9951. Offers architecture (M Arch); urban and community design (MUCD). *Faculty:* 10 full-time (1 woman). *Students:* 92 full-time (40 women), 18 part-time (5 women); includes 38 minority (6 Black or African American, non-Hispanic/Latino; 7 Asian, non-Hispanic/Latino; 22 Hispanic/Latino; 3 Two or more races, non-Hispanic/Latino), 23 international. Average age 26. 61 applicants, 44% accepted, 22 enrolled. In 2017, 48 master's awarded. *Degree requirements:* For master's, comprehensive exam, thesis. *Entrance requirements:* For master's, GRE General Test, minimum undergraduate GPA of 3.0 in last 60 hours of coursework; three letters of recommendation; portfolio or creative work; written statement of intent; prerequisite courses in physics, calculus, and AutoCAD. Additional exam requirements/

recommendations for international students: Required—TOEFL (minimum score 550 paper-based; 79 iBT) or IELTS (minimum score 6.5). *Application deadline:* For fall admission, 2/1 priority date for domestic students, 2/1 for international students. Applications are processed on a rolling basis. Application fee: $30. Electronic applications accepted. *Financial support:* In 2017–18, 34 students received support, including 3 teaching assistantships with tuition reimbursements available (averaging $9,360 per year); Federal Work-Study, scholarships/grants, and unspecified assistantships also available. *Faculty research:* Urban community design and planning; public space infrastructure; conditions of suburban sprawl; redevelopment strategies for abandoned commercial centers and edges; sustainability; influences of technology, cultural identity and interpretation and social values on architectural design; epistemology of design thinking; tropical architecture; high-density urbanism; design benevolence; economic development/community revitalization; housing/residential development; development regulations. *Total annual research expenditures:* $187,157. *Unit head:* Dr. Robert MacLeod, Director and Professor, School of Architecture and Community Design, 813-974-6015, Fax: 813-974-2557, E-mail: rmacleod@arch.usf.edu. *Application contact:* Mildred Abreu, Academic Advisor, 813-974-1216, Fax: 813-974-2557, E-mail: abreu@arch.usf.edu. Website: http://www.arch.usf.edu/

The University of Texas at Austin, Graduate School, School of Architecture, Program in Urban Design, Austin, TX 78712-1111. Offers M Arch, MSUD.

University of Toronto, School of Graduate Studies, Faculty of Arts and Science, Department of Geography, Program in Planning, Toronto, ON M5S 1A1, Canada. Offers M Sc Pl, MUDS, PhD. *Program availability:* Part-time. *Degree requirements:* For master's, summer internship. *Entrance requirements:* For master's, bachelor's degree in planning, geography, social science or a closely related professional field, minimum B+ average in final year, 3 letters of reference; for doctorate, minimum A- or equivalent standing in previous master's program. Additional exam requirements/recommendations for international students: Required—TOEFL (minimum score 580 paper-based; 93 iBT), TWE (minimum score 5). Electronic applications accepted. *Expenses:* Contact institution.

University of Toronto, School of Graduate Studies, John H. Daniels Faculty of Architecture, Landscape, and Design, Toronto, ON M5S 1A1, Canada. Offers M Arch, MLA, MUD, MVS. *Entrance requirements:* For master's, minimum B average; 3 letters of reference; resume; 3 writing samples; 5 samples of design work, drawing, or work in a related field, statement of interest. Additional exam requirements/recommendations for international students: Required—TOEFL (minimum score 580 paper-based; 93 iBT), IELTS (minimum score 7), TWE (minimum score 5), Michigan English Language Assessment Battery (minimum score 85), COPE (minimum score 76). Electronic applications accepted. *Expenses:* Contact institution.

University of Utah, Graduate School, College of Architecture and Planning, Department of City and Metropolitan Planning, Salt Lake City, UT 84112. Offers city and metropolitan planning (MCMP), including ecological planning, small town and resort planning, smart growth and transportation, urban design; metropolitan planning, policy and design (PhD). *Accreditation:* ACSP. *Program availability:* Part-time. *Faculty:* 4 full-time (2 women), 9 part-time/adjunct (2 women). *Students:* 41 full-time (17 women), 17 part-time (5 women); includes 10 minority (1 Black or African American, non-Hispanic/Latino; 1 Asian, non-Hispanic/Latino; 5 Hispanic/Latino; 3 Two or more races, non-Hispanic/Latino), 12 international. Average age 27. 33 applicants, 100% accepted, 16 enrolled. In 2017, 19 master's, 1 doctorate awarded. *Degree requirements:* For master's, thesis or alternative, comprehensive project; for doctorate, thesis/dissertation. *Entrance requirements:* For master's, GRE, minimum undergraduate GPA of 3.0; for doctorate, GRE, minimum GPA of 3.5. Additional exam requirements/recommendations for international students: Required—TOEFL (minimum score 500 paper-based; 61 iBT); Recommended—IELTS (minimum score 6). *Application deadline:* For fall admission, 1/15 priority date for domestic and international students; for spring admission, 11/1 for domestic and international students. Applications are processed on a rolling basis. Application fee: $55 ($65 for international students). Electronic applications accepted. *Expenses:* Contact institution. *Financial support:* In 2017–18, 25 students received support, including 1 fellowship with full tuition reimbursement available (averaging $25,000 per year), 3 research assistantships with tuition reimbursements available (averaging $16,000 per year), 21 teaching assistantships with tuition reimbursements available (averaging $10,000 per year); career-related internships or fieldwork, Federal Work-Study, scholarships/grants, health care benefits, and unspecified assistantships also available. Financial award application deadline: 1/15; financial award applicants required to submit FAFSA. *Faculty research:* Transportation, land-use, smart growth, public health, climate change, urban design, sustainable communities, community-based decision-making process, urban morphology, theory and practice in scenario-planning techniques, community-engaged teaching methodologies, interactions between federal environmental policies and state/local community development patterns, values in architecture and planning practices. *Total annual research expenditures:* $689,627. *Unit head:* Reid Ewing, Chair, 801-585-3745, Fax: 801-581-8217, E-mail: ewing@arch.utah.edu. *Application contact:* Saolo Utu, Recruitment and Admissions Advisor, 801-581-2361, Fax: 801-581-8217, E-mail: recruitment@arch.utah.edu. Website: http://www.plan.utah.edu/

University of Washington, Graduate School, College of Built Environments, Department of Urban Design and Planning, Seattle, WA 98195. Offers urban design and planning (PhD); urban planning (MUP). *Accreditation:* ACSP (one or more programs are accredited). *Degree requirements:* For master's, thesis or alternative; for doctorate, thesis/dissertation. *Entrance requirements:* For master's and doctorate, GRE General Test, minimum GPA of 3.0. Additional exam requirements/recommendations for international students: Required—TOEFL. *Faculty research:* Land-use and growth management, urban form and travel behavior, geographic information systems/remote sensing, historic preservation, urban ecology and environmental planning.

University of Washington, Graduate School, College of Built Environments, Interdisciplinary Program in Urban Design, Seattle, WA 98195. Offers Certificate. Electronic applications accepted. *Faculty research:* Urban design process; urban form; place theory; place analysis; race, class, and gender in community design.

Washington University in St. Louis, Sam Fox School of Design and Visual Arts, Program in Urban Design, St. Louis, MO 63130-4899. Offers MUD, M Arch/MUD, MUD/MSW. *Entrance requirements:* For master's, GRE General Test, portfolio. Additional exam requirements/recommendations for international students: Required—TOEFL (minimum score 600 paper-based; 100 iBT), TWE. *Faculty research:* Urban design development issues: city revitalization, sustainability and suburbanization; urban history and visualization of urban form.

PRATT INSTITUTE

School of Architecture

Pratt

★ For more information, visit http://petersons.to/prattarchitecture

Programs of Study

The School of Architecture is dedicated to maintaining the connection between design theory and practice and to extending the range of knowledge necessary to an understanding of the built environment. The diversity of programs within the School and the accessibility of other programs within the Institute enable students to pursue a wide range of interests. Students can take electives in fine arts, film, digital arts, industrial design, furniture design, interior design, and photography as well as electives in advanced architectural theory, design, technology, and management. The School has many internationally recognized faculty members who bring to the graduate programs a strong theoretical base and the high standards of their professional work. The programs are distinguished by strong studio cultures and creative approaches to architectural design. Many special courses are offered in contemporary theoretical and critical issues, advanced computing and media, building technology, architectural history, and experimental structures. Students are exposed to the professional world through optional internship programs that place them in outstanding New York architectural offices, public agencies, and nonprofit design institutions, giving them firsthand work experience and credit towards their degree.

The School of Architecture offers a total of nine graduate programs. There are two graduate architecture programs: the first-professional accredited Master of Architecture (M.Arch.) and the post-professional Master of Architecture (M.S.Arch.). There are also seven Master of Science programs: Architecture and Urban Design, City and Regional Planning, Sustainable Environmental Systems, Facilities Management, Historic Preservation, Urban Placemaking and Management, and Real Estate Practice.

The three-year M.Arch. first-professional program is designed for students holding a four-year undergraduate program in any field, including architecture. Graduate courses and seminars are designed to familiarize students with all aspects of the discipline and practice of architecture. Design studios at Pratt find many of their coordinates within the rich territory of New York City. However, the program also reaches into areas worldwide and into other frames, such as global marketplaces, digital worlds, and historical, theoretical, and political networks. This program is fully accredited by NAAB. Students with a B.S. in Architecture or other non-professional degree should apply for this M.Arch. program. Applicants with four-year, B.Sc. in Architecture or B.Sc.Eng. in Architecture may qualify for advanced standing (shortening the time to two years). The post-professional M.S.Arch., a summer/fall/spring program, is for those who hold an accredited architecture degree or the equivalent. The program takes three semesters to complete. Students with significant professional experience can also apply for work credit, which reduces total credit-hour requirements. The post-professional M.S.Arch. allows intensive theoretical and technical engagement of architecture and the city and stresses research and experimentation concentrating on the relations between architecture and other urban forms, scales, and forces. Research is conducted primarily within the analytic and synthetic content of the design studio and culminates in a required thesis.

The Master of Science in Architecture and Urban Design program is intended for students who are interested in careers that enhance the growth and development of the built urban environments, the context for an urban laboratory. The 33-credit program requires 17 hours of design studio and research, with the balance of the credits in required courses in urban history, theory, infrastructure, and implementation and electives in law, transportation, housing, and preservation. The program is open to those with professional undergraduate degrees in architecture and is a summer/fall/spring program.

The six programs offered by Pratt's Programs for Sustainable Planning and Development (PSPD)—the M.S. in City and Regional Planning (CRP), the M.S. in Sustainable Environmental Systems (SES), the M.S. in Historic Preservation, the M.S. in Urban Placemaking and Management, the M.S. in Facilities Management (FM), and the M.S. in Real Estate Practice (REP)—emphasize planning and preservation practice rooted in the principles of sustainability, equity, and public participation.

The curricula are designed to build the professional skills and knowledge of students who desire to affect the built, natural, and social environments of the nation's cities and communities in positive ways. CRP and SES courses are offered in the evenings, enabling students to work full-time. The City and Regional planning program offers specializations in community development, environmental planning, physical planning, and preservation planning. The CRP program requires the completion of 60 credits, including the thesis or the Demonstration of Professional Competence course. The Urban Placemaking and Management program requires the completion of 40 credits. The curriculum of study includes Design and Infrastructure, Economics, Planning and Policy and Management. The SES program requires 40 credits of course work and includes a focus on sustainability. The REP program is 36 credits designed to be completed in three full-time terms of study in the afternoon and evenings.

Students with undergraduate degrees in architecture and engineering may have up to 9 credits waived in either the CRP or SES program.

PSPD's Historic Preservation program is a two-year graduate program leading to the M.S. in Historic Preservation. The program, designed primarily for full-time students and based at the Brooklyn campus, is a 44-credit sequence of courses that provides studies in community planning, history, interpretation, design, policy, and regulatory practice.

Recognizing that today's field of preservation requires more than curatorial management, the program fosters the knowledge preservationists must have in order to participate in policy-making to revitalize urban areas, suburban communities, and rural landscapes. With its urban focus, the program emphasizes hands-on work and makes extensive use of New York City's rich resources.

All five graduate programs in the PSPD maintain strong ties with Pratt's architecture and design programs and with the Pratt Center for Community Development, an innovative center for the practice of planning, design, and policy work that focuses on increasing quality of life and affecting social change in New York City's diverse communities.

The M.S. in Facilities Management program prepares individuals to assume leadership roles in corporations, institutions, and government. The degree requires the completion of 45 credits of course work and the 5-credit Demonstration of Professional Competence course, for a total of 50 credits. Students entering the program with prior professional experience or graduate work in related fields may be eligible for advanced standing; up to 12 credits may be waived. The facilities management program, accredited by IFMA, is offered at the Pratt Manhattan Center on an evening schedule, allowing maximum flexibility to combine full-time work with study and research. Students may take courses in any of the programs in PSPD.

Research Facilities

The Pratt Library has grown with the Institute to house one of the finest collections of reference material on art, design, and architecture.

Pratt maintains numerous studios, shops, and technical facilities for work in all media, as well as state-of-the-art computer facilities. Pratt also has extensive gallery space for the exhibition of works by the student body, alumni, faculty members, and well-known architects and designers.

Financial Aid

Financial aid awards are offered through a variety of institutional, state, and federally funded programs. These include Graduate Scholarships awarded by departments to incoming students on the basis of merit, as well as endowed and restricted scholarships for continuing students, and student employment. Assistantships are awarded on a competitive basis to continuing students in all departments. Special alumni-sponsored fellowships are also available.

Cost of Study

Graduate tuition for 2018–19 is $ $32,004 per year (full-time 18 credits, $1,778 per credit). Student fees are $1,980 per semester. The cost of books and supplies varies widely, depending on the program in which the student is enrolled.

Living and Housing Costs

Campus housing continues to be expanded to meet student needs and is available for single students on a first-come, first-served basis. Housing costs average $18,880 per academic year. There is a plentiful supply of moderately priced rentals in the immediate area and in adjacent neighborhoods for married students seeking housing as well as for those students choosing to reside off campus.

Student Group

There are 370 students enrolled in Pratt's School of Architecture graduate programs; 58 percent are women. They come from all parts of the United States and the world. The graduate programs are noted for an exceptional placement ratio, with more than 85 percent of the graduating students finding employment before graduation.

Location

Pratt Institute is located in the Clinton Hill section of Brooklyn, on a 25-acre park-like campus. Pratt's Manhattan campus houses the Institute's graduate arts and cultural management, communications design, design management, facilities management, and library and information science programs as well as offering courses in architecture, city and regional planning, creative arts therapy, and urban design.

The Institute

A private, nonsectarian institute of higher education, Pratt Institute was founded in 1887 by the industrialist and philanthropist Charles Pratt. Today, Pratt educates 3,439 undergraduates and 1,390 graduate students for careers in art and design, architecture, and library and information science.

Applying

The deadline for applications and all supporting materials, including portfolio, is January 5. Applicants should complete the application process online. Early submission of applications with all necessary credentials is highly desirable. Applications received after these dates are considered if openings exist in a particular program. For applicants who intend to file for financial aid, the FAFSA should be filed by March 1 for fall entrance and by October 1 for spring entrance.

Correspondence and Information

Graduate Admissions Office
Pratt Institute
200 Willoughby Avenue
Brooklyn, New York 11205
Phone: 718-636-3514
800-331-0834 (toll-free outside New York State)
Fax: 718-399-4242
E-mail: admissions@pratt.edu
Website: http://www.pratt.edu

THE FACULTY

Thomas Hanrahan, Dean; M.Arch., Harvard; AIA, NCARB.

Architecture

David Erdman, Chair, Adjunct Associate Professor, M.Arch., Columbia.
Alexandra Barker, Assistant Chair, Adjunct Associate Professor; M.Arch., Harvard.

Nick Agneta, Adjunct Associate Professor; B.Arch., Cooper Union; AIA.
Jeffrey Anderson, Visiting Assistant Professor, M.Arch. II, Princeton
Carlos Arnaiz, Adjunct Assistant Professor; M.Arch., Harvard.
Kutan Ayata, Adjunct Assistant Professor; M.Arch., Princeton.
Dylan Baker-Rice, Visiting Professor, M.Arch., Columbia.
Gisela Baurmann, Visiting Assistant Professor, M.S.Columbia, Dip.Arch, Technical University of Berlin
Stephanie Bayard, Adjunct Assistant Professor; M.S., Columbia, Dip.Arch, Paris La Villette.
Joshua Bolchover, Visiting Professor, M.A., Cambridge, Dip.Arch, University College London.
Stuart Christopher Bridgett, Visiting Professor, B.Sc., University of Warwick.
Meta Brunzema, Adjunct Associate Professor; M.Arch., Columbia.
Robert Cervellione, Assistant Adjunct Instructor, M.Arch., Pratt.
Steven J. Chang, Adjunct Assistant Professor; B.Arch., Berkeley; AIA.
Jonas Coersmeier, Adjunct Assistant Professor, M.S., Columbia.
Cristobal Correa, Assistant Professor; M.S.C.E., MIT.
Theo David, Professor; M.Arch., Yale.
Manuel DeLanda, Adjunct Professor; B.F.A., School of Visual Arts.
Koray Duman, Visiting Assistant Professor, M.Arch., Columbia.
Deborah Gans, Professor; M.Arch., Princeton.
James Garrison, Adjunct Associate Professor; B.Arch., Syracuse.
Erik Ghenoiu, Adjunct Associate Professor; Ph.D., Harvard.
Jose Gonzalez, Visiting Assistant Professor; M.S., Columbia.
Nathan Hume, Visiting Assistant Professor, M.Arch., Yale.
Catherine Ingraham, Professor; Ph.D., Johns Hopkins.
Hina Jamelle, Visiting Assistant Professor; M.Arch., Michigan.
Robert Kearns, Visiting Assistant Professor; M.A.E., Penn State.
Karel Klein, Adjunct Associate Professor; M.Arch., Columbia.
Carisima Koenig, Visiting Instructor; M.Arch., Iowa State.
Mehmet Ferda Kolatan, Visiting Assistant Professor; M.S.A.A.D., Columbia, Arch.Dip., RWTH, Aachen..
Sulan Kolatan, Adjunct Professor; M.S.Arch., Columbia, Arch.Dip., RWTH, Aachen.
Craig Konyk, Adjunct Associate Professor; M.Arch., Virginia.
Christopher Kroner, Adjunct Assistant Professor; M.Arch., Columbia.
Sameer Kumar, Adjunct Assistant Professor; M.Arch., Pennsylvania.
Sanford Kwinter, Professor, Ph.D., Columbia.
Paul Laroque, Visiting Assistant Professor, M.Eng., MIT.
Thomas Leeser, Associate Professor, M.Arch., THD, Darmstadt, Germany.
Carla Leitao, Associate Professor; M.S.AAD., Columbia.
John Chun Han Lin, Visiting Professor, B.Arch., Cooper Union.
John Lobell, Professor; M.Arch., Pennsylvania.
Ariane Lourie-Harrison, Adjunct Associate Professor, Ph.D., NYU.
Peter Macapia, Adjunct Associate Professor; Ph.D., Columbia.
William MacDonald, Professor; M.S.Arch, Columbia.
Radhi Majmuder, Adjunct Assistant Professor; M.S., Columbia.
Rosalinda Malibiran, Visiting Assistant Professor; M.Arch., Columbia.
Elliott Maltby, Adjunct Associate Professor; M.L.A., Berkeley.
Hart Marlow, Adjunct Assistant Professor, M.Arch., Pratt.
Deborah McGuinness, Visiting Associate Professor, B.S., Villanova.
Benjamin Martinson, Adjunct Assistant Professor, M.Arch., Pratt.
Bruce Mau, Visiting Professor, studied at Ontario College of Art and Design.
Debora Mesa Molina, Visiting Associate Professor, Polytechnic Institute of Madrid.

SECTION 2: ARCHITECTURE

Pratt Institute

Danil Nagy, Visiting Assistant Professor, M.Arch., Columbia.
Hannibal Newsom, Visiting Assistant Professor.
Bruce Nichol, Visiting Professor, Graduate Diploma, Architecture,
   Oxford Brookes University; ARB, RIBA.
Signe Nielsen, Adjunct Professor; B.S., Pratt.
Christina Ostermier, Visiting Assistant Professor, M.Arch., Pratt.
Phillip Parker, Adjunct Associate Professor, M.Arch., Yale.
Shinjinee Pathak, Visiting Assistant Professor, M.A., UC Berkeley.
Florencia Pita, Visiting Professor, M.S. Columbia.
Keyan Rahimzadeh, Visiting Assistant Professor, M.Arch., Georgia Institute of Technology.
Brian Ringley, Visiting Assistant Professor; M.Arch., Cincinnati.
Linda Roy, Visiting Associate Professor, M.Arch., Columbia.
David Ruy, Professor; M.Arch., Columbia.
Richard Scherr, Director, Facilities Planning, Adjunct Professor; M.S.Arch., Columbia.
Erich Schoenenberger, Adjunct Associate Professor; M.S.AAD., Columbia.
Paul Segal, Adjunct Professor; M.F.A., Princeton; FAIA.
Benjamin Shepherd, Adjunct Associate Professor; M.A., Yale.
Maria Sieira, Associate Professor; M.Arch., Pennsylvania.
Henry Smith-Miller, Adjunct Professor; M.Arch., Pennsylvania.
Roland Snooks, Adjunct Assistant Professor; M.S.AAD., Columbia.
Michael Szivos, Visiting Assistant Professor; M.S.AAD., Columbia.
Jeffrey Taras, Visiting Instructor; M.Arch., Columbia.
Jeffrey Thompson, Visiting Assistant Professor, M.Eng., Washington University, St. Louis.
Maria Ludovica Tramontin, Adjunct Assistant Professor; Ph.D., Cagliari (Italy).
Nanako Umemoto-Reiser, Adjunct Professor; B.Arch., Cooper Union.
Joseph Vidich, Visiting Assistant Professor, M.Arch., Columbia.
Olivia Vien, Visiting Assistant Professor, M.Arch., Pratt.
Jason Vigneri-Beane, Adjunct Associate Professor; M.Arch., Iowa State.
John Christopher Whitelaw, Visiting Instructor; M.Arch., Columbia.
Corey Wowk, Visiting Assistant Professor, MDesS, Harvard.

Urban Design

David Erdman, Chair, Adjunct Associate Professor, M.Arch., Columbia.
Jose Coersmeier, Program Coordinator, Adjunct Associate Professor, M.S., Columbia.

Carlos Arnaiz, Adjunct Assistant Professor; M.Arch., Harvard.
Stephanie Bayard, Adjunct Assistant Professor; M.S.AAD, Columbia.
Meta Brunzema, Adjunct Associate Professor; M.Arch., Columbia.
Jose Gonzales, Visiting Assistant Professor; M.S.AAD., Columbia.
Mehmet Ferda Kolatan, Visiting Assistant Professor; M.S.AAD., Columbia.
Sulan Kolatan, Adjunct Professor; M.S.Arch., Columbia.
Carla Leitao, Adjunct Associate Professor; M.S.AAD., Columbia.
William MacDonald, Professor, M.S. Arch, Columbia.
Elliot Maltby, Adjunct Associate Professor; M.L.A., Berkeley.
Signe Nielsen, Adjunct Professor; B.S., Pratt.
Philip Parker, Adjunct Associate Professor, M.Arch., Yale.
David Ruy, Professor; M.Arch., Columbia.
Erich Schoenenberger, Adjunct Associate Professor; M.S.AAD., Columbia.
Nanako Umemoto-Reiser, Adjunct Professor; B.Arch., Cooper Union.
Jason Vigneri Beane, Adjunct Associate Professor, M.Arch., Iowa State University.

Planning and the Environment (City and Regional Planning, Sustainable Environmental Systems, Urban Placemaking and Management)

Eve Baron, Chair, Ph.D. Rutgers.
David Burney, Academic Coordinator of Urban Placemaking and Management,
   Associate Professor; M.S., London.
Jaime Stein, Academic Coordinator, Sustainable Environmental Systems; M.S., Pratt.

Bridget Anderson, Visiting Assistant Professor; M.P.A., Columbia.
Caron Atlas, Visiting Assistant Professor; M.A., Chicago.
Eddie Bautista, Visiting Assistant Professor; M.S.C.R.P., Pratt.
Jenifer Becker, Visiting Assistant Professor; M.S.C.R.P., Pratt.
Bethany Bingham, Visiting Assistant Professor, M.S., Pratt.
Michael Bobker, Visiting Assistant Professor; M.S., NYIT.
Jessie Braden, Visiting Assistant Professor, M.A., University of Toledo.
Ester Brunner, Visiting Assistant Professor, M.L.A., Columbia.
Joan Byron, Visiting Assistant Professor; M.P.A., Harvard.
Damon Chaky, Assistant Professor; Ph.D., Rensselaer Polytechnic Institute.
Carter Craft, Visiting Assistant Professor; M.U.P., NYU.
Steve Davies, Professor, M.Arch, California–Berkeley.
Raymond Figueroa, Visiting Instructor, Cornell University College of Human Ecology.
Mike Flynn, Visiting Assistant Professor; M.S.C.R.P., Pratt.
Michael Freedman-Schnapp, Visiting Assistant Professor; M.S.U.P., NYU.
Adam Friedman, Visiting Assistant Professor; J.D., Benjamin Cardozo School of Law.
Mindy Fullilove, Visiting Assistant Professor; M.D., Columbia.
Moses Gates, Visiting Assistant Professor; M.U.P., Hunter College.
Ben Gibberd, Visiting Assistant Professor; M.A., Edinburgh.
Ingrid Haftel, Visiting Assistant Professor; M.A., Chicago.
Eva Hanhardt, Visiting Assistant Professor; M.U.P., NYU.
Will Hart, Visiting Assistant Professor; M.L.A., Georgia.
Daniel Hernandez, Visiting Assistant Professor; M.Arch., UCLA.
George Jacquemart, Visiting Assistant Professor; M.S.U.P., Stanford; PE.
Laura Jay, Visiting Assistant Professor, M.S., Columbia.
Tom Jost, Visiting Assistant Professor; M.S Arch and U.D., Pratt.
David Kallick, Visiting Assistant Professor; B.A., Yale.
Gillian Kaye, Visiting Assistant Professor; B.A., Columbia.
Raj Kottamasu, Visiting Assistant Professor; M.C.P. with Urban Design Certificate, MIT.
Tanu Kumar, Visiting Assistant Professor; M.S., Cornell.
Frank Lang, Visiting Assistant Professor; M.Arch., Pennsylvania; RA.
Matthew Lister, Visiting Assistant Professor; M.S., MIT.
Setha Low, Visiting Assistant Professor; Ph.D., Berkeley.
Alan Mallach, Visiting Assistant Professor; B.A., Yale.
Elliott Maltby, Adjunct Associate Professor; M.L.A., Berkeley.
Paul Mankiewicz, Visiting Associate Professor; Ph.D., CUNY.
Michael Marella, Visiting Assistant Professor; M.C.P with Urban Design Certificate, MIT.
Jonathan Martin, Associate Professor; Ph.D., Cornell.
Jonathan Marvel, Visiting Assistant Professor; M.Arch., Harvard, FAIA.
Claudia Mausner, Visiting Assistant Professor, Ph.D., The Graduate Center, CUNY.
William Menking, Professor; M.S.C.R.P., Pratt.
Jon Meyers, Visiting Assistant Professor; M.B.A., Columbia.
Norman Mintz, Visiting Associate Professor; M.S., Columbia.
Mariana Mogilevich, Visiting Assistant Professor; Ph.D., Harvard.
Eliza Montgomery, Visiting Assistant Professor; AIA, M.Arch., Columbia.
Gita Nandan, Visiting Assistant Professor; M.Arch., Berkeley.
Mercedes Narciso, Adjunct Associate Professor; M.S.C.R.P., Pratt.
Marcel Negret, Visiting Assistant Professor, M.S., Pratt.
Signe Nielsen, Adjunct Professor; B.L.Arch., CUNY, City College.
Suzanne Nienaber, Visiting Assistant Professor.
Cynthia Nikitin, Visiting Assistant Professor; M.A., NYU.
Larisa Ortiz Pu-Folkes, Visiting Assistant Professor; M.S., MIT.
Juan Camilo Osorio, Visiting Assistant Professor; M.S., University of Massachusetts.
Leonel Ponce, Visiting Assistant Professor, M.S., Pratt.
Steven Romalewski, Visiting Assistant Professor; M.S., Columbia.
Carolyn Schaeberle, Visiting Assistant Professor; M.S.I.D., Pratt.
John Shapiro, Associate Professor; M.S.C.R.P., Pratt; AICP.

Ronald Shiffman, Professor; M.S.C.R.P., Pratt; FAICP, FAIA.
Mitchell Siver, Professor, M.S. Hunter College.
Toby Snyder, Visiting Assistant Professor; M.Arch., Rhode Island School of Design.
Christopher Starkey, Visiting Assistant Professor, M.Arch., M.F.M., Yale.
Ira Stern, Visiting Assistant Professor; M.S.C.R.P., Pratt.
Gelvin Stevenson, Visiting Associate Professor; Ph.D., Washington (St. Louis).
Samara Swanston, Visiting Assistant Professor; J.D., St. John's (New York).
Lacey Tauber, Visiting Assistant Professor; M.S., Pratt.
Meg Walker, Visiting Assistant Professor; M.Arch., Columbia.
Don Weinreich, Visiting Assistant Professor, M.Arch., Columbia.
Ben Wellington, Visiting Assistant Professor; Ph.D., NYU.
Barika Williams, Visiting Assistant Professor; M.C.P., MIT.
Ayse Yonder, Professor; Ph.D., Berkeley.

Historic Preservation

Nadya Nenadich, Adjunct Associate Professor, Academic Coordinator, Graduate Center for Planning;
   Ph.D., Polytechnic University of Cataluna.

Lisa Ackerman, Visiting Assistant Professor; M.S., Pratt.
Kate Allen, M.S., Columbia.
Beth Bingham, Visiting Assistant Professor; M.S., Pratt.
Glenn Boornazian, M.S., Columbia.
Patrick Ciccone, Visiting Assistant Professor; M.S., Columbia.
Carol Clark, Visiting Associate Professor; M.S., Columbia.
Pat Fisher-Olsen, Visiting Assistant Professor; M.S., Pratt.
Laura Klar Phillips, Visiting Assistant Professor, Ph.D., NYU.
Norman Mintz, Visiting Associate Professor, M.S. Columbia.
Christopher Neville, Visiting Assistant Professor; M.S., Columbia.
Kate Ottavino, M.S., Columbia.
Theodore Prudon, Adjunct Professor, Ph.D., Columbia.
Lacey Tauber Visiting Assistant Professor; M.S., Pratt.
Vicki Weiner, Adjunct Associate Professor; M.S., Columbia.
Aaron B. White, Adjunct Associate Professor, M.Arch., Pratt.
Kevin Wolfe, Visiting Assistant Professor; M.Arch., Columbia.

Facilities Management

Regina Ford Cahill, Chair, Associate Professor; M.S., Pratt.

Lennart Andersson, Visiting Assistant Professor; M.Arch., Savannah College of Art and Design.
Daniel Crow, Visiting Assistant Professor, J.D., New York Law School.
Matthias Ebinger, Visiting Assistant Professor; M.S., NYU.
William Henry, Visiting Assistant Professor; B.Arch., NYU.
Stephen LoGrasso, Visiting Assistant Professor; B.S., NYIT.
Gerald F. McGowan, Visiting Associate Professor; M.B.A., NYU.
Wilfredo Moran, Visiting Assistant Professor, M.B.A., Southern New Hampshire University.
Russell Olson, Visiting Assistant Professor; M.S., Pratt.
John Osborn, Visiting Associate Professor; J.D., South Carolina.
Edward Re, Adjunct Associate Professor; M.S., Pratt.
Audrey L. Schultz, Associate Professor; Ph.D., Salford; FMP, ASC, CIB.
Marjorie St. Elin, Visiting Assistant Professor; B.S., Pratt.
Mira Tsymuk, Visiting Assistant Professor; M.A., CUNY, Hunter.

Real Estate Practice

Howard Albert, Coordinator, Assistant Adjunct Professor, M.S., Columbia.
Desiree Aponte, Visiting Assistant Professor, M.B.A., NYU.
Christopher Cirillo, Visiting Assistant Professor, M.S., Pratt.
D. Nicole Ferreira, Visiting Assistant Professor, M.S., Pratt.
Frederick Harris, Visiting Assistant Professor, J.D., NYU.
Brian Schwagerl, Visiting Assistant Professor, J.D., St. John's University.

© 2017 Bob Handelman

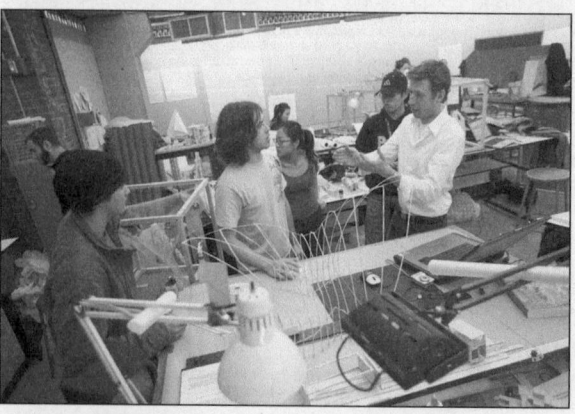

© 2017 Bob Handelman

SOUTHERN CALIFORNIA INSTITUTE OF ARCHITECTURE

Master of Architecture Programs

 For more information, visit http://petersons.to/scia

SCI⁻Arc

Programs of Study

The Master of Architecture (M.Arch.) programs at Southern California Institute of Architecture (SCI-Arc) seek to advance the next generation of the architectural discipline and practice. They emphasize formal exploration, innovation in architectural practice, contemporary experimentation, speculation, and creative freedom. The programs also give students the opportunity to work closely with expert faculty mentors and top consultants in the field.

The Southern California Institute of Architecture has received national recognition for excellence in architectural education. The M.Arch. programs have professional accreditation from the National Architectural Accrediting Board (NAAB). DesignIntelligence ranked the Institute in more categories on its list of America's Top Architectural Schools 2017 than any other school in the nation: #3 for Computer Applications, #3 for Top Regional Graduate Program in the West, #4 for Design Skills, and #4 for Graduate Programs Most Admired by Deans and Chairs.

M.Arch. 1 Program: This three-year (seven terms) program of rigorous course work is designed for individuals with bachelor's degrees in any field. Its curriculum consists of a core sequence, advanced studios, seminars, and a thesis.

The four semesters of core courses provide a framework for the field as well as a strong foundation for experimentation and critical inquiry. Each semester includes a design studio that links with courses in applied studies, visual studies, and history and theory. This provides students with an in-depth understanding of the relationship between architecture, representation, social change, and technology. With each semester, students strengthen their ability to address multifaceted architectural issues while testing their design and intellectual principles.

After completing the core sequence, students choose from an assortment of advanced studios and seminars. They explore the latest technological innovations, develop new approaches to design analysis, and use applied research to create new ideas and methods. Their studies culminate with an extensively researched architectural thesis that's presented at a public exhibition.

M.Arch. 2 Program: This two-year (five terms) program was created for individuals with four-year degrees in architecture (or the equivalent). It enables students to review and build upon knowledge acquired during their undergraduate studies. M.Arch. 2 provides a new environment for architects seeking to complement what may be a classical education with a more contemporary, cutting-edge one that incorporates new technology and fabrication, new theories, and new ways of thinking.

The program consists of a two-term core sequence, vertical studios, elective seminars, and a thesis. It provides extensive knowledge of design methodologies and their contemporary and historical contexts and also emphasizes the most current developments in design fabrication. It concludes with a thoroughly researched thesis that's presented at a public exhibition.

The program begins the Compositional Morphologies studio, which leads the conversation about the next in terms of aesthetic agendas, architecture's contemporary and future societal role, and the impact of theoretical and technological innovation on architecture's design and communicative repertoire.

The second M.Arch 2 studio focuses on computational design and places an emphasis on advancing formal strategies beyond the current state-of-the-art. Students integrate extra-disciplinary techniques and technologies into the design workflow in order to develop innovative architectures that respond to changing societal, ecological, and technological contexts. Students' design work engages issues that range from fundamental morphological transformations through rigorous 3D modeling, to the role of the image and digital sampling in the production of architectural form. These issues are explored through a highly resolved building design.

This second studio in the program combines the tools acquired during the first semester with the architectural background that students bring from their undergraduate degrees to create a contemporary architectural proposal.

Master of Science Degree: SCI-Arc EDGE is a new platform for advanced studies in architecture. Its innovative postgraduate degree programs are designed to test the theoretical and practical limits of architectural innovation in order to launch new architectural careers for the twenty-first century.

The MS in Architectural Technologies brings students together with some of the most progressive architects, designers and theorists in the field, to inventively speculate about the near future of architecture in the form of specific projects, sophisticated prototypes, complex tectonic and material systems and strange aesthetic objects.

The MS in Fiction and Entertainment is organized as a year-long thesis project. The three-semester sequence begins with a focus on world building, moves into storytelling in the second semester, and ends in the final semester with a focus on production. Within this framework, students are encouraged to develop their own unique body of work that may take the form of short films, animations, music videos, documentaries, video games, VR environments, theatre experiences, or performances.

The MS in Design of Cities is an urban design program that allows architects to reengage the ambition to design cities.

The MS in Design Theory and Pedagogy utilizes SCI-Arc itself as a hands-on teaching laboratory where the long-term project is to develop new design pedagogies and a new apparatus for the production of design theory.

Facilities

Within its quarter-mile-long campus, SCI-Arc offers students an integrated suite of resources that support academic progress and experimentation.

The Magic Box, SCI-Arc's technologically transformative digital fabrication lab, expands the school's experimental approach to design. The SCI-Arc Robot House is a platform for experimentation and speculation on the future of architecture, situated conceptually and physically between studio and shop, academy and industry.

SCI-Arc's 6,000-square-foot fabrication shop is equipped with a wide array of metal and woodworking machinery and tools, supporting hands-on experimentation with materials and construction. The SCI-Arc Art and Architecture Supply Store serves both the student body and the downtown community, offering competitive prices for architecture and art supplies. The Print Center at SCI-Arc provides students and faculty with access to a variety of regular and large-format high-resolution color plotters and printers at a fraction of typical service center prices.

SCI-Arc also has several galleries, making it the only cultural institution in Los Angeles committed to exhibiting experimental projects by contemporary architects. The Kappe Library is the largest academic library in Southern California focused on architecture, and welcomes both students and outside architectural researchers.

Financial Aid

SCI-Arc works with students to find the right means to fund their education. Available financial aid options include Federal Pell Grants, Federal Supplemental Educational Opportunity Grants (FSEOG), and Federal Education Loans. A limited number of merit- and need-based scholarships are also available for both U.S. and international students.

Cost of Study

For the 2018–19 academic year, tuition and fees for Master of Architecture programs total $21,900 per semester. The cost of course supplies and books is estimated at $3,050 per semester.

Southern California Institute of Architecture

Living and Housing Costs

SCI-Arc does not provide on-campus housing. Most students live in apartments or lofts close to the campus in the Arts District of downtown Los Angeles, or in surrounding communities, many accessible by bike or public transportation. Students live in the Arts District itself or the nearby communities of Little Tokyo, Echo Park, Chinatown, Silver Lake, and Koreatown. Each community has a distinctive flavor that can best be understood by visiting. Some have easily accessible public transportation, others may require a vehicle. While finding housing in any new city can be challenging, most SCI-Arc students are able to find suitable accommodations within a week or two. Room and board for an academic year is estimated at $5,500 per semester.

Student Outcomes

M.Arch. students graduate prepared to create structures and spaces that improve quality of life and change how humans interact with one other and their environments. Upon graduation, they enter a promising job market. According to the US Bureau of Labor Statistics, employment of architects is expected to grow 7 percent from 2014 to 2024. This is as fast as the average for all occupations.

Location

The Institute is located in the historic Santa Fe Freight Depot in the Arts District of Los Angeles (LA), California in the western region of the United States. Its campus includes vibrant design studios and galleries, supply store, library, print center and features one of the largest fabrication labs in a US architecture school. Located in downtown LA, the Arts District offers a variety of galleries, shops, restaurants, coffee shops, and nightlife venues. Attractions include ICA Museum, A+D Museum, Alchemy Works, Hauser & Wirth, and Hennessey + Ingalls.

The Institute

Founded in 1972, Southern California Institute of Architecture is one the few independent architecture schools in the nation. It offers undergraduate, graduate, and postgraduate programs in architecture.

SCI-Arc's mission is to reimagine the very edges of architecture, educating architects to engage, speculate, and innovate; to examine everything about the built environment, from design and materials to culture and experience; to ask provocative questions that provoke new thinking and prompt new theoretical constructs; to be international leaders in creating the future of architecture; and to create designs that change how people interact with each other and their environment.

For more than forty-five years, SCI-Arc has maintained a reputation of risk and excellence.

Faculty

Founded on the idea that architects should teach what they practice, SCI-Arc still believes that practicing architects can best communicate to students the complex realities of thinking about and making architecture. Today, SCI-Arc faculty is comprised of some of the most innovative thinkers in architecture, culture, history, and technology. Design Studio faculty are active practitioners working in many of LA's most cutting-edge architecture firms. The symbiotic relationship between practice and teaching produces a close dialogue between conceptual and professional practice.

Graduate Programs Chair, Elena Manferdini contributes more than fifteen years of professional experience to her role as Programs Chair. In 2004 Manferdini founded Atelier Manferdini in Venice, CA where she is principal. In 2011, she was one of the recipients of the prestigious annual grants from the United States Artists (USA) in the category of architecture and design. Manferdini was awarded the 2013 COLA Fellowship given by City of Los Angeles Department of Cultural Affairs to support the production of original artwork. That same year, she received a Graham Award for architecture, the 2013 ACADIA Innovative Research Award of Excellence, and was selected as recipient for the Educator of the Year presidential award given by the AIA Los Angeles.

David Ruy, Postgraduate Programs is an architect, theorist, and director of Ruy Klein. Ruy Klein examines contemporary design problems at the intersection of architecture, nature, and technology. Encompassing a wide array of experimentation, Ruy Klein's projects study the mutual imbrications of artificial and natural regimes that are shaping an ever more synthetic world. The work of Ruy Klein has been widely published and exhibited and has been the recipient of numerous awards recognizing the firm as one of the leading experimental practices in architecture today. Their work is part of the permanent collection of The Museum of Modern Art in New York City and The Frac Centre in Orléans, France.

Information about other faculty members can be found at https://sciarc.edu/institution/people/faculty.

SCI-Arc also provides lectures and symposia that enhance classroom and hands-on learning. Guest lecturers include prominent architects, artists, curators, historians, professors, writers, and other experts. Recent and upcoming symposia include Drawing Conclusions Symposium, Architecture in the Age of Digital Media, and SCI-Arc Tokyo Symposium.

Applying

SCI-Arc receives applications from throughout the United States and all around the world. SCI-Arc is committed to shaping student experiences as they pursue undergraduate, graduate, and postgraduate degrees. Applications for all graduate and postgraduate programs are accepted for the fall semester only. Successful applicants generally demonstrate a strong academic record, compelling letters of recommendation, and a portfolio of distinct work.

Applicants need to complete the online application form and submit all additional required application materials through SlideRoom. Required application materials include: online application form, $85 nonrefundable application fee, portfolio of creative work, personal statement, resume, academic transcripts, three letters of recommendation, GRE test scores (M.Arch programs only), and TOEFL/IELTS test scores (for students who completed their undergraduate degrees internationally).

Graduate applicants will be notified of their admission status between the months of March and April. Students who accept SCI-Arc's offer of admission are required to submit a nonrefundable deposit, which reserves their place in the entering class.

Applicants placed on the waiting list will be notified on a rolling basis as positions become available in the entering class.

Correspondence and Information

Southern California Institute of Architecture
960 East 3rd Street
Los Angeles, California 90013
United States
Phone: 213-356-5620
E-mail: admissions@sciarc.edu
Website: https://sciarc.edu

Section 3
Art and Art History

This section contains a directory of institutions offering graduate work in art and art history, followed by in-depth entries submitted by institutions that chose to prepare detailed program descriptions. Additional information about programs listed in the directory but not augmented by an in-depth entry may be obtained by writing directly to the dean of a graduate school or chair of a department at the address given in the directory.

For programs offering related work, see also in this book *Applied Arts and Design; Architecture; Area and Cultural Studies; Film, Television, and Video; Performing Arts;* and *Sociology, Anthropology, and Archaeology.* In another guide in this series:

Graduate Programs in Business, Education, Information Studies, Law & Social Work

See *Subject Areas (Art Education)*

CONTENTS

Art/Fine Arts

Academy of Art University, Graduate Programs, School of Fine Art, San Francisco, CA 94105-3410. Offers figurative painting (MFA). *Accreditation:* NASAD. *Program availability:* Part-time, 100% online. *Faculty:* 19 full-time (9 women), 29 part-time/adjunct (16 women). *Students:* 75 full-time (48 women), 143 part-time (112 women); includes 35 minority (7 Black or African American, non-Hispanic/Latino; 1 American Indian or Alaska Native, non-Hispanic/Latino; 7 Asian, non-Hispanic/Latino; 17 Hispanic/Latino; 2 Native Hawaiian or other Pacific Islander, non-Hispanic/Latino; 1 Two or more races, non-Hispanic/Latino), 54 international. Average age 41. 53 applicants, 100% accepted, 37 enrolled. In 2017, 55 master's awarded. *Degree requirements:* For master's, final review. *Entrance requirements:* For master's, statement of intent; resume; portfolio/reel; official college transcripts. *Application deadline:* Applications are processed on a rolling basis. Application fee: $50. Electronic applications accepted. *Expenses: Tuition:* Part-time $982 per unit. *Financial support:* Career-related internships or fieldwork, Federal Work-Study, and scholarships/grants available. Financial award application deadline: 8/10; financial award applicants required to submit FAFSA. *Unit head:* 800-544-ARTS, E-mail: info@academyart.edu. *Application contact:* 800-544-ARTS, E-mail: info@academyart.edu.
Website: http://www.academyart.edu/fine-art-school/index.html

Academy of Art University, Graduate Programs, School of Jewelry and Metal Arts, San Francisco, CA 94105-3410. Offers MA, MFA. *Program availability:* Part-time, 100% online. *Faculty:* 2 full-time (both women), 9 part-time/adjunct (5 women). *Students:* 22 full-time (21 women), 11 part-time (9 women); includes 3 minority (all Asian, non-Hispanic/Latino), 25 international. Average age 30. 12 applicants, 100% accepted, 4 enrolled. In 2017, 12 master's awarded. *Degree requirements:* For master's, final review. *Entrance requirements:* For master's, statement of intent; resume; portfolio/reel; official college transcripts. *Application deadline:* Applications are processed on a rolling basis. Application fee: $50. Electronic applications accepted. *Expenses: Tuition:* Part-time $982 per unit. *Financial support:* Career-related internships or fieldwork, Federal Work-Study, and scholarships/grants available. Financial award application deadline: 8/10; financial award applicants required to submit FAFSA. *Unit head:* 800-544-ARTS, E-mail: info@academyart.edu. *Application contact:* 800-544-ARTS, E-mail: info@academyart.edu.
Website: http://www.academyart.edu/jewelry-and-metal-arts-school/

Adelphi University, College of Arts and Sciences, Department of Art and Art History, Garden City, NY 11530-0701. Offers studio art (MA). *Program availability:* Part-time. *Faculty:* 8 full-time (5 women), 17 part-time/adjunct (12 women). In 2017, 2 master's awarded. *Entrance requirements:* For master's, essay, portfolio, 2 letters of recommendation. Additional exam requirements/recommendations for international students: Required—TOEFL (minimum score 550 paper-based; 80 iBT), IELTS (minimum score 6.5). *Application deadline:* For fall admission, 5/1 for international students; for spring admission, 12/1 for international students. Applications are processed on a rolling basis. Application fee: $50. Electronic applications accepted. *Expenses:* Contact institution. *Financial support:* Research assistantships with full and partial tuition reimbursements, teaching assistantships, career-related internships or fieldwork, institutionally sponsored loans, scholarships/grants, traineeships, and unspecified assistantships available. Support available to part-time students. Financial award application deadline: 2/15. *Unit head:* David Hornung, Chairperson, 516-877-4458, E-mail: hornung@adelphi.edu. *Application contact:* E-mail: graduateadmissions@adelphi.edu.
Website: http://academics.adelphi.edu/artsci/art/

Alfred University, Graduate School, College of Ceramics, Inamori School of Engineering, Alfred, NY 14802. Offers biomaterials engineering (MS); ceramic engineering (MS, PhD); electrical engineering (MS); glass science (MS, PhD); materials science and engineering (MS, PhD); mechanical engineering (MS). *Program availability:* Part-time. *Degree requirements:* For master's, thesis; for doctorate, thesis/dissertation. *Entrance requirements:* Additional exam requirements/recommendations for international students: Required—TOEFL (minimum score 590 paper-based; 90 iBT), IELTS (minimum score 6.5). Electronic applications accepted. *Expenses:* Contact institution. *Faculty research:* X-ray diffraction, biomaterials and polymers, thin-film processing, electronic and optical ceramics, solid-state chemistry.

Alfred University, Graduate School, College of Ceramics, School of Art and Design, Alfred, NY 14802. Offers ceramic art (MFA); electronic integrated arts (MFA); painting (MFA); sculpture/dimensional studies (MFA). *Accreditation:* NASAD. *Degree requirements:* For master's, thesis, exhibit. *Entrance requirements:* For master's, portfolio. Additional exam requirements/recommendations for international students: Required—TOEFL (minimum score 550 paper-based; 80 iBT), IELTS (minimum score 6). Electronic applications accepted. *Expenses:* Contact institution. *Faculty research:* Ceramic art, sculpture, glass art, new media, time-based media.

Anna Maria College, Graduate Division, Program in Education, Paxton, MA 01612. Offers early childhood education (M Ed); education (CAGS); elementary education (M Ed); English language arts (M Ed); visual arts (M Ed). *Program availability:* Part-time, evening/weekend. *Entrance requirements:* For master's, bachelor's degree in liberal arts or sciences, minimum GPA of 3.0. Additional exam requirements/recommendations for international students: Required—TOEFL (minimum score 500 paper-based). Electronic applications accepted.

Arizona State University at the Tempe campus, Herberger Institute for Design and the Arts, School of Art, Tempe, AZ 85287-1505. Offers art education (MA); art history (MA); ceramics (MFA); design, environment and the arts (PhD), including history, theory and criticism; drawing (MFA); fibers (MFA); intermedia (MFA); metals (MFA); museum studies (MFA); painting (MFA); printmaking (MFA); sculpture (MFA); wood (MFA); MFA/MA. Terminal master's awarded for partial completion of doctoral program. *Degree requirements:* For master's, thesis/exhibition (MFA, MA in art education); interactive Program of Study (iPOS) submitted before completing 50 percent of required credit hours; for doctorate, comprehensive exam, thesis/dissertation, interactive Program of Study (iPOS) submitted before completing 50 percent of required credit hours. *Entrance requirements:* For master's, GRE or MAT, minimum GPA of 3.0 or equivalent in last 2 years of work leading to bachelor's degree; for doctorate, GRE, master's degree in architecture, graphic design, industrial design, interior design, landscape architecture, or art history or equivalent standing; statement of purpose; 3 letters of recommendation; indication of potential faculty mentor; sample of written work. Additional exam requirements/recommendations for international students: Required—TOEFL, IELTS, or PTE. Electronic applications accepted.

ArtCenter College of Design, Graduate Art Program, Pasadena, CA 91103. Offers MFA. *Accreditation:* NASAD.

Azusa Pacific University, College of Music and the Arts, Azusa, CA 91702-7000. Offers composition (M Mus); conducting (M Mus); education (M Mus); modern art history, theory, and criticism (MA); music entrepreneurial studies (MA); performance (M Mus); screenwriting (MA); visual art (MFA). *Accreditation:* NASAD; NASM. *Program availability:* Part-time, evening/weekend. *Degree requirements:* For master's, recital. *Entrance requirements:* For master's, interview, audition. Additional exam requirements/recommendations for international students: Required—TOEFL (minimum score 550 paper-based).

Ball State University, Graduate School, College of Fine Arts, School of Art, Muncie, IN 47306. Offers fine arts (MFA), including animation, glass; visual arts studio (MA), including ceramics, drawing, metals, painting, photography and intermedia arts, printmaking, sculpture. *Accreditation:* NASAD. *Program availability:* Part-time. *Faculty:* 17 full-time (7 women). *Students:* 16 full-time (11 women), 5 part-time (1 woman); includes 5 minority (2 Black or African American, non-Hispanic/Latino; 2 Asian, non-Hispanic/Latino; 1 Hispanic/Latino). Average age 28. 27 applicants, 59% accepted, 15 enrolled. In 2017, 4 master's awarded. *Entrance requirements:* For master's, minimum baccalaureate GPA of 2.75 or 3.0 in latter half of baccalaureate, goals statement, digital portfolio of artwork, resume, transcripts of all college-level course work, three letters of recommendation. Additional exam requirements/recommendations for international students: Required—TOEFL (minimum score 550 paper-based; 79 iBT), IELTS (minimum score 6.5). *Application deadline:* For fall admission, 3/31 for domestic students. Applications are processed on a rolling basis. Application fee: $60. Electronic applications accepted. *Financial support:* In 2017–18, 15 students received support, including 1 research assistantship with partial tuition reimbursement available (averaging $10,667 per year), 14 teaching assistantships with partial tuition reimbursements available (averaging $10,786 per year); unspecified assistantships also available. Financial award application deadline: 3/1; financial award applicants required to submit FAFSA. *Unit head:* Dr. Arne Flaten, Director, 765-285-5840, Fax: 765-285-5275, E-mail: arflaten@bsu.edu. *Application contact:* Zachary Craw, Graduate Advisor, 765-285-5838, Fax: 765-285-5275, E-mail: zacraw@bsu.edu.
Website: http://www.bsu.edu/art

Bard College, Milton Avery Graduate School of the Arts, Annandale-on-Hudson, NY 12504. Offers film/video (MFA); music/sound (MFA); painting (MFA); photography (MFA); sculpture (MFA); writing (MFA). *Degree requirements:* For master's, thesis, project, 8-week summer residency, independent study. *Entrance requirements:* For master's, interview, portfolio, 2 letters of recommendation, history of work in the arts. Additional exam requirements/recommendations for international students: Required—TOEFL (minimum score 550 paper-based). Electronic applications accepted. *Expenses:* Contact institution. *Faculty research:* Original work in painting, writing, sculpture, photography, video/film, sound/music.

Barry University, College of Arts and Sciences, Department of Fine Arts, Miami Shores, FL 33161-6695. Offers photography (MA, MFA). *Degree requirements:* For master's, thesis (for some programs). *Entrance requirements:* For master's, GRE General Test, minimum GPA of 3.0. Electronic applications accepted. *Faculty research:* Inclusion education, exceptional education, art-based assessments.

Bob Jones University, Graduate Programs, Greenville, SC 29614. Offers accountancy (MS); Bible (MA); Bible translation (MA); Biblical studies (Certificate); broadcast management (MS); business administration (MBA); church history (MA, PhD); church ministries (MA); church music (MM); cinema and video production (MA); counseling (MS); curriculum and instruction (Ed D); divinity (M Div); dramatic production (MA); educational leadership (MS, Ed D, Ed S); elementary education (M Ed, MAT); English (M Ed, MA, MAT); fine arts (MA); graphic design (MA); history (M Ed, MA); illustration (MA); interpretative speech (MA); mathematics (M Ed, MAT); medical missions (Certificate); ministry (MM, D Min); multi-categorical special education (M Ed, MAT); music (M Ed); New Testament interpretation (PhD); Old Testament interpretation (PhD); orchestral instrument performance (MM); organ performance (MM); pastoral studies (MA); personnel services (MS, Ed S); piano pedagogy (MM); piano performance (MM); platform arts (MA); radio and television broadcasting (MS); rhetoric and public address (MA); secondary education (M Ed); studio art (MA); teaching Bible (MA); theology (MA, PhD); voice performance (MM); youth ministries (MA); M Div/MM.

Boise State University, College of Arts and Sciences, Department of Art, Boise, ID 83725-0399. Offers visual arts (MFA). *Program availability:* Part-time. *Students:* 8 full-time (5 women), 4 part-time (2 women); includes 1 minority (Hispanic/Latino). Average age 38. 22 applicants, 23% accepted, 4 enrolled. In 2017, 5 master's awarded. *Degree requirements:* For master's, thesis optional. *Entrance requirements:* For master's, minimum GPA of 3.0, portfolio. Additional exam requirements/recommendations for international students: Required—TOEFL (minimum score 550 paper-based; 80 iBT), IELTS (minimum score 6). *Application deadline:* For fall admission, 1/15 priority date for domestic and international students. Application fee: $80 ($110 for international students). Electronic applications accepted. *Expenses:* Tuition, state resident: full-time $6471; part-time $390 per credit. Tuition, nonresident: full-time $21,787; part-time $685 per credit. *Required fees:* $2283; $100 per term. Part-time tuition and fees vary according to course load and program. *Financial support:* Teaching assistantships, scholarships/grants, and unspecified assistantships available. Financial award application deadline: 1/15; financial award applicants required to submit FAFSA. *Unit head:* Dr. Kathleen Keys, Department Chair, 208-426-1230, E-mail: kathleenkeys@boisestate.edu. *Application contact:* Chad Erpelding, Graduate Program Coordinator, 208-426-4081, E-mail: chaderpelding@boisestate.edu.
Website: http://art.boisestate.edu/gradprogram/

Boston University, College of Fine Arts, School of Visual Arts, Boston, MA 02215. Offers art education (MA); graphic design (MFA); painting (MFA); sculpture (MFA); studio teaching (MA). *Faculty:* 17 full-time, 4 part-time/adjunct. *Students:* 161 full-time (139 women), 3 part-time (all women); includes 19 minority (2 Black or African American, non-Hispanic/Latino; 6 Asian, non-Hispanic/Latino; 9 Hispanic/Latino; 2 Two or more races, non-Hispanic/Latino), 37 international. Average age 30. 365 applicants, 27% accepted, 21 enrolled. In 2017, 85 master's awarded. *Entrance requirements:* For master's, portfolio. Additional exam requirements/recommendations for international students: Required—TOEFL (minimum score 90 iBT), IELTS (minimum score 7). *Application deadline:* For fall admission, 2/1 for domestic and international students. Applications are processed on a rolling basis. Application fee: $95. *Expenses:* Contact institution. *Financial support:* In 2017–18, 36 students received support. Fellowships, teaching assistantships, scholarships/grants, and unspecified assistantships available. Financial award application deadline: 2/1. *Unit head:* Lynne Allen, Director, 617-353-3371. *Application contact:* Jessica Caccamo, Assistant Director of Admissions, 617-353-3371, E-mail: visuarts@bu.edu.

Bowling Green State University, Graduate College, College of Arts and Sciences, School of Art, Bowling Green, OH 43403. Offers 2-D studio art (MA, MFA); 3-D studio art (MA, MFA); art education (MA); art history (MA); computer art (MA); design (MFA); digital arts (MFA); graphics (MFA). *Accreditation:* NASAD. *Program availability:* Part-time. *Degree requirements:* For master's, thesis or alternative, final exhibit (MFA). *Entrance requirements:* For master's, GRE General Test (for MA), slide portfolio (15-20 slides). Additional exam requirements/recommendations for international students: Required—

TOEFL. Electronic applications accepted. *Faculty research:* Computer animation and virtual reality, Spanish still-life painting from 1600 to 1800, art and psychotherapy, Japanese wood-firing techniques in ceramics, non-toxic printmaking technologies.

Bradley University, The Graduate School, Slane College of Communications and Fine Arts, Department of Art, Peoria, IL 61625-0002. Offers ceramics (MA, MFA); drawing (MA, MFA); graphic design (MA, MFA); painting (MA, MFA); photography (MA, MFA); printmaking (MA, MFA); sculpture (MA, MFA). *Accreditation:* NASAD. *Program availability:* Part-time. *Degree requirements:* For master's, comprehensive exam, thesis, final exhibit. *Entrance requirements:* For master's, portfolio, 2 letters of recommendation. Additional exam requirements/recommendations for international students: Required—TOEFL (minimum score 550 paper-based; 79 iBT). Electronic applications accepted.

Brandeis University, Graduate School of Arts and Sciences, Postbaccalaureate Program in Studio Art, Waltham, MA 02454-9110. Offers Postbaccalaureate Certificate. *Faculty:* 15 full-time (8 women), 2 part-time/adjunct (0 women). *Students:* 3 full-time (all women); includes 2 minority (both Hispanic/Latino). Average age 25. 6 applicants, 83% accepted, 1 enrolled. In 2017, 3 Postbaccalaureate Certificates awarded. *Degree requirements:* For Postbaccalaureate Certificate, exhibit of work. *Entrance requirements:* For degree, resume, statement of purpose, 12 images of recent work, letter of recommendation, transcripts. Additional exam requirements/recommendations for international students: Required—PTE (minimum score 68), TOEFL (minimum score 600 paper-based, 100 iBT) or IELTS (7). *Application deadline:* For fall admission, 6/15 for domestic students; for spring admission, 12/15 for domestic students. Applications are processed on a rolling basis. Application fee: $75. Electronic applications accepted. *Expenses:* $19,982 tuition, $88 fees. *Financial support:* In 2017–18, 5 students received support, including 12 teaching assistantships (averaging $2,000 per year); scholarships/grants and unspecified assistantships also available. Financial award application deadline: 6/15; financial award applicants required to submit FAFSA. *Faculty research:* Painting, sculpture. *Unit head:* Prof. Sean Downey, Faculty Coordinator, 781-736-2660, E-mail: sdowney@brandeis.edu. *Application contact:* Christine Dunant, Department Administrator, 781-736-2655, E-mail: cdunant@brandeis.edu.
Website: http://www.brandeis.edu/gsas/programs/studio_art.html

Brigham Young University, Graduate Studies, College of Fine Arts and Communications, Department of Art, Provo, UT 84602-6414. Offers art education (MA); studio arts (MFA). Art education applications accepted biennially. *Accreditation:* NASAD. *Faculty:* 13 full-time (2 women). *Students:* 26 full-time (18 women); includes 4 minority (3 Asian, non-Hispanic/Latino; 1 Hispanic/Latino). Average age 36. 22 applicants, 55% accepted, 10 enrolled. In 2017, 6 master's awarded. *Degree requirements:* For master's, one foreign language, comprehensive exam, thesis, selected project (for MFA); curriculum project (for art education). *Entrance requirements:* For master's, minimum GPA of 3.0 (for MFA, MA in art education), portfolio submitted on a flash drive (for MFA); writing samples (for MA). Additional exam requirements/recommendations for international students: Required—TOEFL (minimum score 580 paper-based, 85 iBT) or IELTS (7). *Application deadline:* For fall admission, 2/1 for domestic and international students. Application fee: $50. Electronic applications accepted. *Expenses:* $10,320 per academic year, $405 per credit hour for members of the Church of Jesus Christ of Latter-day Saints; $20,640 for the year, $810 per credit hour for those who are not members of the Church; lab fees: $25 per credit hour for printmaking, $25 for ceramics, and $15 for sculpture. *Financial support:* In 2017–18, 19 students received support, including 11 teaching assistantships with partial tuition reimbursements available; scholarships/grants also available. Financial award application deadline: 2/1. *Faculty research:* Methodology-standards-assessment, exploration of art making processes, new genre, installation, photography, theory and critical studies, art history. *Unit head:* Prof. Gary C. Barton, Chair, 801-422-4429, Fax: 801-422-0695, E-mail: garold_barton@byu.edu. *Application contact:* Sharon Lyn Heelis, Secretary, 801-422-4429, Fax: 801-422-0695, E-mail: sharon_heelis@byu.edu.
Website: http://art.byu.edu

Brooklyn College of the City University of New York, School of Visual, Media and Performing Arts, Department of Art, Brooklyn, NY 11210-2889. Offers art history (MA); digital art (MFA); drawing and painting (MFA); photography (MFA); printmaking (MFA); sculpture (MFA). *Program availability:* Part-time. *Degree requirements:* For master's, thesis. *Entrance requirements:* For master's, bachelor's degree in art, portfolio, 2 letters of recommendation. Additional exam requirements/recommendations for international students: Required—TOEFL (minimum score 500 paper-based; 61 iBT). Electronic applications accepted.

Butler University, Jordan College of the Arts, Indianapolis, IN 46208-3485. Offers composition (MM); conducting (MM), including choral, instrumental; music education (MM); musicology (MA); performance (MM); piano pedagogy (MM). *Accreditation:* NASM. *Program availability:* Part-time. *Faculty:* 25 full-time (7 women), 35 part-time/adjunct (18 women). *Students:* 12 full-time (3 women), 25 part-time (9 women); includes 8 minority (3 Black or African American, non-Hispanic/Latino; 2 Asian, non-Hispanic/Latino; 1 Hispanic/Latino; 2 Two or more races, non-Hispanic/Latino), 1 international. Average age 27. 36 applicants, 67% accepted, 14 enrolled. In 2017, 10 master's awarded. *Degree requirements:* For master's, variable foreign language requirement, comprehensive exam, thesis (for some programs). *Entrance requirements:* For master's, GRE General Test (for MA in musicology), audition, interview, three letters of recommendation, transcripts, sample works. Additional exam requirements/recommendations for international students: Required—TOEFL (minimum score 550 paper-based; 79 iBT), IELTS (minimum score 6). *Application deadline:* For fall admission, 2/1 for domestic and international students; for spring admission, 12/15 for domestic and international students; for summer admission, 4/15 for domestic and international students. Applications are processed on a rolling basis. Application fee: $0. Electronic applications accepted. *Expenses:* $560 per credit. *Financial support:* In 2017–18, 19 students received support. Scholarships/grants, tuition waivers (full and partial), and unspecified assistantships available. Financial award application deadline: 7/15; financial award applicants required to submit FAFSA. *Faculty research:* Music neuroscience; woodwind pedagogy and repertoire; Johannes Kepler and Carolus Luython; music criticism in early 20th-century Germany and Austria; Arabic choral music; pedagogy of music theory. *Unit head:* Wendy Meaden, Dean, 317-940-9229, E-mail: wmeaden@butler.edu. *Application contact:* Diane Dubord, Graduate Student Services Specialist, 317-940-8107, E-mail: ddubord@butler.edu.
Website: http://www.butler.edu/jca/

California College of the Arts, Graduate Programs, Fine Arts Programs, San Francisco, CA 94107. Offers film (MFA); fine arts (MFA). *Accreditation:* NASAD. *Faculty:* 62 full-time (34 women), 56 part-time/adjunct (34 women). *Students:* 80 full-time (55 women); includes 15 minority (4 Black or African American, non-Hispanic/Latino; 1 American Indian or Alaska Native, non-Hispanic/Latino; 3 Asian, non-Hispanic/Latino; 7 Hispanic/Latino), 33 international. Average age 29. 288 applicants, 57% accepted, 39 enrolled. In 2017, 45 master's awarded. *Degree requirements:* For master's, thesis, exhibit. *Entrance requirements:* For master's, appropriate bachelor's degree, portfolio, resume, 2 letters of recommendation, transcript. Additional exam requirements/recommendations for international students: Required—TOEFL, IELTS, or PTE. *Application deadline:* For fall admission, 1/31 priority date for domestic and international students. Applications are processed on a rolling basis. Application fee: $70. Electronic applications accepted. *Expenses:* $49,230 per year full-time tuition, $490 per year fees; $1,641 per unit part-time tuition. *Financial support:* In 2017–18, fellowships (averaging $42,000 per year), teaching assistantships (averaging $2,000 per year) were awarded; career-related internships or fieldwork, Federal Work-Study, scholarships/grants, health care benefits, and unspecified assistantships also available. Financial award application deadline: 7/31; financial award applicants required to submit FAFSA. *Unit head:* James Gobel, Chair, 415-551-9214, Fax: 415-703-9539, E-mail: jgobel@cca.edu. *Application contact:* Wes Fanelli, Assistant Director of Graduate Admissions, 415-703-9533, Fax: 415-703-9539, E-mail: wfanelli@cca.edu.

California College of the Arts, Graduate Programs, Visual and Critical Studies Program, San Francisco, CA 94107. Offers MA. *Faculty:* 2 full-time (both women), 3 part-time/adjunct (2 women). *Students:* 3 full-time (2 women); includes 2 minority (both Hispanic/Latino). Average age 40. 9 applicants, 100% accepted, 1 enrolled. In 2017, 1 master's awarded. *Degree requirements:* For master's, thesis. *Entrance requirements:* For master's, portfolio, resume, 2 letters of recommendation, transcripts, essay, interview. Additional exam requirements/recommendations for international students: Required—TOEFL, IELTS, or PTE. *Application deadline:* For fall admission, 1/31 priority date for domestic and international students. Applications are processed on a rolling basis. Application fee: $70. Electronic applications accepted. *Expenses:* $34,461 per year full-time tuition, $490 per year fees; $1,641 per unit part-time tuition. *Financial support:* Fellowships, teaching assistantships, career-related internships or fieldwork, Federal Work-Study, scholarships/grants, and health care benefits available. Financial award application deadline: 7/31; financial award applicants required to submit FAFSA. *Unit head:* Dr. Jacqueline Francis, Chair, E-mail: jfrancis@cca.edu. *Application contact:* Wes Fanelli, Assistant Director of Graduate Admissions, 415-703-9533, Fax: 415-703-9539, E-mail: wfanelli@cca.edu.
Website: https://www.cca.edu/academics/graduate/visual-critical-studies

California Institute of the Arts, School of Art, Valencia, CA 91355-2340. Offers art (MFA, Adv C); graphic design (MFA, Adv C); photography (MFA, Adv C). *Accreditation:* NASAD (one or more programs are accredited). *Degree requirements:* For master's, final project. *Entrance requirements:* For master's, portfolio. Additional exam requirements/recommendations for international students: Required—TOEFL. Electronic applications accepted.

California State University, Chico, Office of Graduate Studies, College of Humanities and Fine Arts, Department of Art and Art History, Program in Fine Arts, Chico, CA 95929-0722. Offers art studio (MFA). *Accreditation:* NASAD. *Degree requirements:* For master's, thesis or alternative, exhibition with written evaluation of work. *Entrance requirements:* For master's, three letters of recommendation, statement of purpose, media portfolio. Additional exam requirements/recommendations for international students: Required—TOEFL (minimum score 550 paper-based; 80 iBT), IELTS (minimum score 6.5), PTE (minimum score 59). Electronic applications accepted.

California State University, Fresno, Division of Research and Graduate Studies, College of Arts and Humanities, Department of Art and Design, Fresno, CA 93740-8027. Offers art (MA). *Program availability:* Part-time, evening/weekend. *Degree requirements:* For master's, thesis or alternative. *Entrance requirements:* For master's, GRE General Test, minimum GPA of 3.0, portfolio. Additional exam requirements/recommendations for international students: Required—TOEFL. Electronic applications accepted. *Faculty research:* Art history, graphic design, studio art.

California State University, Fullerton, Graduate Studies, College of the Arts, Department of Visual Arts, Fullerton, CA 92831-3599. Offers art (MA, MFA), including art history (MA), ceramics (MFA), crafts, creative photography, exhibition design, glass, graphic design, illustration, sculpture. *Accreditation:* NASAD (one or more programs are accredited). *Program availability:* Part-time. *Faculty:* 17 full-time (7 women), 4 part-time/adjunct (3 women). *Students:* 35 full-time (22 women), 24 part-time (14 women); includes 26 minority (3 Black or African American, non-Hispanic/Latino; 7 Asian, non-Hispanic/Latino; 14 Hispanic/Latino; 2 Two or more races, non-Hispanic/Latino), 6 international. Average age 33. 81 applicants, 31% accepted, 21 enrolled. In 2017, 17 master's awarded. *Entrance requirements:* For master's, minimum GPA of 2.5 in last 60 units of course work, portfolio. Application fee: $55. *Financial support:* Career-related internships or fieldwork, Federal Work-Study, institutionally sponsored loans, and scholarships/grants available. Support available to part-time students. Financial award application deadline: 3/1; financial award applicants required to submit FAFSA. *Unit head:* Dana Lamb, Chair, 657-278-2076.
Website: http://www.fullerton.edu/arts/art/

California State University, Long Beach, Graduate Studies, College of the Arts, Department of Art, Long Beach, CA 90840. Offers art education (MA); studio art (MFA). *Accreditation:* NASAD. *Program availability:* Part-time. *Degree requirements:* For master's, thesis (for some programs). *Entrance requirements:* For master's, minimum GPA of 3.0 in last 60 hours. Electronic applications accepted.

California State University, Los Angeles, Graduate Studies, College of Arts and Letters, Department of Art, Los Angeles, CA 90032-8530. Offers art (MA), including art education, art history, art therapy, ceramics, metals, and textiles, design (MA, MFA), painting, sculpture, and graphic arts, photography; fine arts (MFA), including crafts, design (MA, MFA), studio arts. *Accreditation:* NASAD (one or more programs are accredited). *Program availability:* Part-time, evening/weekend. *Degree requirements:* For master's, comprehensive exam, project or thesis. *Entrance requirements:* For master's, portfolio. Additional exam requirements/recommendations for international students: Required—TOEFL (minimum score 500 paper-based). Electronic applications accepted. *Faculty research:* The artist and the book, conceptual art, ceramic processes, computer graphics, architectural graphics.

California State University, Northridge, Graduate Studies, Mike Curb College of Arts, Media, and Communication, Department of Art, Northridge, CA 91330. Offers art education (MA); art history (MA); studio art (MA, MFA); visual communications (MA, MFA). *Accreditation:* NASAD. *Students:* 27 full-time (16 women), 9 part-time (6 women); includes 17 minority (1 Black or African American, non-Hispanic/Latino; 2 Asian, non-Hispanic/Latino; 11 Hispanic/Latino; 3 Two or more races, non-Hispanic/Latino). Average age 31. 58 applicants, 34% accepted, 20 enrolled. In 2017, 11 master's awarded. *Application deadline:* For fall admission, 11/30 for domestic students. Application fee: $55. *Financial support:* Application deadline: 3/1. *Unit head:* Prof. Edward Alfano, Chair, 818-677-2242, E-mail: art.dept@csun.edu.
Website: http://www.csun.edu/art/

California State University, Sacramento, College of Arts and Letters, Department of Art, Sacramento, CA 95819. Offers studio art (MA). *Accreditation:* NASAD. *Program availability:* Part-time. *Students:* 7 full-time (4 women), 3 part-time (2 women); includes 5 minority (1 American Indian or Alaska Native, non-Hispanic/Latino; 1 Asian, non-Hispanic/Latino; 3 Hispanic/Latino). Average age 31. 18 applicants, 44% accepted, 6 enrolled. In 2017, 4 master's awarded. *Degree requirements:* For master's, culminating exhibition of student's work; passage of writing proficiency examination or approved waiver. *Entrance requirements:* For master's, BA in art or its equivalent, including 12 units in art history; minimum GPA of 2.5 in last 60 units attempted; approval by studio faculty review of other submitted materials. Additional exam requirements/recommendations for international students: Required—TOEFL (minimum score 550 paper-based; 80 iBT). *Application deadline:* For fall admission, 2/15 for domestic students, 1/15 for international students; for spring admission, 9/15 for domestic students, 8/15 for international students. Applications

are processed on a rolling basis. Application fee: $55. Electronic applications accepted. *Expenses:* Contact institution. *Financial support:* Career-related internships or fieldwork and Federal Work-Study available. Support available to part-time students. Financial award application deadline: 3/1; financial award applicants required to submit FAFSA. *Unit head:* Carolyn Gibbs, Chair, 916-278-7515, Fax: 916-278-7287, E-mail: carolyng@csus.edu. *Application contact:* Jose Martinez, Graduate Admissions Supervisor, 916-278-7871, E-mail: martinj@skymail.csus.edu.
Website: http://www.al.csus.edu/art

California State University, San Bernardino, Graduate Studies, College of Arts and Letters, Program in Studio Art, San Bernardino, CA 92407. Offers MA. *Accreditation:* NASAD; NCATE. *Faculty:* 3 full-time (0 women). *Students:* 12 full-time (6 women), 1 (woman) part-time; includes 5 minority (1 Black or African American, non-Hispanic/Latino; 2 Hispanic/Latino; 2 Two or more races, non-Hispanic/Latino). Average age 36. 16 applicants, 38% accepted, 5 enrolled. In 2017, 4 master's awarded. *Entrance requirements:* Additional exam requirements/recommendations for international students: Required—TOEFL. Application fee: $55. *Unit head:* Dr. Matthew Poole, Dean, 909-537-5808, E-mail: matthew.poole@csusb.edu. *Application contact:* Dr. Dorota Huizinga, Dean of Graduate Studies, 909-537-5058, E-mail: dodrota.huizinga@csusb.edu.

Carlow University, College of Learning and Innovation, Program in Art, Pittsburgh, PA 15213-3165. Offers MA. *Program availability:* Part-time, evening/weekend. *Entrance requirements:* For master's, personal essay; resume or curriculum vitae; two recommendations; official transcripts; interview; minimum undergraduate GPA of 3.0. Additional exam requirements/recommendations for international students: Required—TOEFL (minimum score 550 paper-based). *Application deadline:* Applications are processed on a rolling basis. Electronic applications accepted. *Expenses: Tuition:* Full-time $12,103; part-time $825 per credit hour. Tuition and fees vary according to program. *Financial support:* Application deadline: 4/1; applicants required to submit FAFSA. *Unit head:* Dale Huffman, Chair, 412-578-6033, E-mail: dhuffman@carlow.edu. *Application contact:* E-mail: gradstudies@carlow.edu.
Website: http://www.carlow.edu/MA_art.aspx

Carnegie Mellon University, College of Fine Arts, School of Art, Pittsburgh, PA 15213-3891. Offers MFA. *Degree requirements:* For master's, thesis, exhibit. *Entrance requirements:* For master's, portfolio. Additional exam requirements/recommendations for international students: Required—TOEFL.

Central Washington University, School of Graduate Studies and Research, College of Arts and Humanities, Department of Art and Design, Ellensburg, WA 98926. Offers ceramics (MFA); computer arts (MFA); jewelry and metalsmithing (MFA); painting and drawing (MFA); photography (MFA); sculpture (MFA). *Entrance requirements:* For master's, minimum GPA of 3.0, portfolio. Additional exam requirements/recommendations for international students: Required—TOEFL (minimum score 550 paper-based; 79 iBT) or IELTS (minimum score 6.5). *Application deadline:* For fall admission, 2/1 for domestic students; for winter admission, 10/1 for domestic students; for spring admission, 1/1 for domestic students. Applications are processed on a rolling basis. Application fee: $50. Electronic applications accepted. *Financial support:* Application deadline: 3/1; applicants required to submit FAFSA. *Unit head:* Prof. Rachel Kirk, Chair, 509-963-2665, E-mail: rachel.kirk@cwu.edu. *Application contact:* Justine Eason, Admissions Program Coordinator, 509-963-3103, Fax: 509-963-1799, E-mail: masters@cwu.edu.
Website: http://www.cwu.edu/~art/

Christie's Education, Certificate Program in Modern and Contemporary Art in New York, New York, NY 10020. Offers Certificate. *Program availability:* Part-time. *Faculty:* 4 full-time (3 women). *Students:* 9. *Application deadline:* Applications are processed on a rolling basis. Application fee: $95. *Expenses:* Contact institution. *Unit head:* Dr. Julie Reiss, Program Director, 212-355-1501 Ext. 3307, E-mail: jreiss@christies.edu. *Application contact:* Hilary Smith, Recruitment and Admissions Officer, 212-355-1501 Ext. 3309, Fax: 212-355-7370, E-mail: hsmith@christies.edu.
Website: https://www.christies.edu/new-york/courses/certificate-modern-contemporary-art.aspx

City College of the City University of New York, Graduate School, Division of Humanities and the Arts, Department of Art, Program in Fine Arts, New York, NY 10031-9198. Offers advertising design (MFA); ceramic design (MFA); digital and interdisciplinary art practice (MFA); painting (MFA); printmaking (MFA); sculpture (MFA); wood and metal design (MFA). *Degree requirements:* For master's, thesis exhibit. *Entrance requirements:* For master's, 20-slide portfolio. Additional exam requirements/recommendations for international students: Required—TOEFL (minimum score 577 paper-based; 90 iBT). Electronic applications accepted.

Claremont Graduate University, Graduate Programs, School of Arts and Humanities, Department of Art, Claremont, CA 91711. Offers digital media (MFA); drawing (MFA); installation (MFA); painting (MFA); performance (MFA); photography (MFA); sculpture (MFA); studio (MFA). *Program availability:* Part-time. *Degree requirements:* For master's, final project show. *Entrance requirements:* For master's, BA in art or BFA, slide review. Additional exam requirements/recommendations for international students: Required—TOEFL (minimum score 75 iBT). Electronic applications accepted. *Expenses:* Contact institution. *Faculty research:* Acoustic sculpture, feminization of abstraction, installation sculpture.

Clemson University, Graduate School, College of Architecture, Arts, and Humanities, Department of Art, Clemson, SC 29634. Offers visual arts (MFA). *Accreditation:* NASAD. *Faculty:* 14 full-time (7 women), 1 (woman) part-time/adjunct. *Students:* 36 full-time (28 women); includes 4 minority (2 Black or African American, non-Hispanic/Latino; 2 Hispanic/Latino). Average age 29. 29 applicants, 24% accepted, 5 enrolled. In 2017, 4 master's awarded. *Degree requirements:* For master's, thesis. *Entrance requirements:* For master's, portfolio, unofficial transcripts, letters of recommendation, resume, letter of intent, artist statement. Additional exam requirements/recommendations for international students: Required—TOEFL (minimum score 80 iBT), IELTS (minimum score 6.5), PTE (minimum score 54). *Application deadline:* For fall admission, 3/15 priority date for domestic and international students. Application fee: $80 ($90 for international students). Electronic applications accepted. *Expenses:* $5,767 per semester full-time resident, $10,918 per semester full-time non-resident, $656 per credit hour part-time resident, $1,310 per credit hour part-time non-resident, $915 per credit hour online; other fees may apply per session. *Financial support:* In 2017–18, 16 students received support, including 1 fellowship with partial tuition reimbursement available (averaging $2,500 per year), 4 teaching assistantships with partial tuition reimbursements available (averaging $3,485 per year); unspecified assistantships also available. Financial award application deadline: 3/15. *Total annual research expenditures:* $7,474. *Unit head:* Valarie Zimany, Interim Department Chair, 864-656-3880. *Application contact:* David Detrich, Graduate Program Coordinator, 864-656-3890, E-mail: ddavid@clemson.edu.
Website: http://www.clemson.edu/caah/departments/art/index.html

The College at Brockport, State University of New York, School of Arts and Sciences, Visual Studies Workshop, Brockport, NY 14420-2997. Offers MFA. *Faculty:* 2 full-time (1 woman). *Students:* 11 full-time (7 women), 3 part-time (1 woman); includes 2 minority (1 Asian, non-Hispanic/Latino; 1 Two or more races, non-Hispanic/Latino), 1 international. 7 applicants, 71% accepted, 2 enrolled. In 2017, 4 master's awarded. *Degree requirements:* For master's, thesis or alternative, internship, final project. *Entrance requirements:* For master's, slides, portfolio, video or CD/DVD, including work description; letters of recommendation; minimum GPA of 3.0; statement of objectives. Additional exam requirements/recommendations for international students: Required—TOEFL (minimum score 550 paper-based; 79 iBT), IELTS (minimum score 6.5). *Application deadline:* For fall admission, 2/15 priority date for domestic and international students. Application fee: $50. Electronic applications accepted. *Expenses:* Tuition, state resident: full-time $10,870; part-time $453 per credit hour. Tuition, nonresident: full-time $22,210. *Required fees:* $988; $246 per semester. *Financial support:* Federal Work-Study and scholarships/grants available. Support available to part-time students. Financial award application deadline: 3/15; financial award applicants required to submit FAFSA. *Faculty research:* Photography, film, video, digital media, artists' books. *Unit head:* Tate Shaw, Executive Director, 585-442-8676, Fax: 585-442-1992, E-mail: tshaw@brockport.edu. *Application contact:* Danielle A. Welch, Graduate Admissions Counselor, 585-395-5465, Fax: 585-395-2515.
Website: https://www.brockport.edu/academics/visual/graduate/masters.html

College for Creative Studies, Graduate Programs, Detroit, MI 48202-4034. Offers color and materials design (MFA); integrated design (MFA); interaction design (MFA); transportation design (MFA). *Accreditation:* NASAD.

Colorado State University, College of Liberal Arts, Department of Art and Art History, Fort Collins, CO 80523-1779. Offers studio art (MFA). *Faculty:* 15 full-time (8 women), 2 part-time/adjunct (1 woman). *Students:* 18 full-time (10 women), 2 part-time (both women); includes 6 minority (1 Black or African American, non-Hispanic/Latino; 1 American Indian or Alaska Native, non-Hispanic/Latino; 3 Hispanic/Latino; 1 Two or more races, non-Hispanic/Latino). Average age 32. 46 applicants, 17% accepted, 6 enrolled. In 2017, 2 master's awarded. *Degree requirements:* For master's, comprehensive exam (for some programs), thesis, exhibition. *Entrance requirements:* For master's, portfolio, three letters of recommendation, transcripts, statement of purpose, resume, artist statement; 20 images of work (including video, if applicable). Additional exam requirements/recommendations for international students: Required—TOEFL (minimum score 550 paper-based; 80 iBT). *Application deadline:* For fall admission, 2/1 priority date for domestic and international students. Applications are processed on a rolling basis. Application fee: $60 ($70 for international students). Electronic applications accepted. *Expenses:* Tuition, state resident: full-time $9917. Tuition, nonresident: full-time $24,312. *Required fees:* $2284. Tuition and fees vary according to course load and program. *Financial support:* In 2017–18, 8 teaching assistantships with full tuition reimbursements (averaging $12,474 per year) were awarded; fellowships with partial tuition reimbursements, scholarships/grants, and unspecified assistantships also available. *Faculty research:* African art history, bronze castings, etching/lithography, pre-Columbian art history, contemporary crafts. *Total annual research expenditures:* $15,357. *Unit head:* Suzanne Faris, Department Chair/Associate Professor, 970-491-6774, Fax: 970-491-0505, E-mail: suzanne.faris@colostate.edu. *Application contact:* Kathleen Chynoweth, Graduate Contact, 970-491-6775, E-mail: kathleen.chynoweth@colostate.edu.
Website: http://art.colostate.edu/

Columbia College Chicago, School of Graduate Studies, Art and Art History Department, Chicago, IL 60605-1996. Offers fine arts (MFA). *Program availability:* Part-time, evening/weekend. *Students:* 17 full-time (13 women), 3 part-time (2 women); includes 4 minority (1 Black or African American, non-Hispanic/Latino; 2 Hispanic/Latino; 1 Two or more races, non-Hispanic/Latino), 4 international. 29 applicants, 69% accepted, 8 enrolled. *Degree requirements:* For master's, thesis. *Entrance requirements:* For master's, self-assessment essay, work sample, interview, letters of recommendation, transcripts. Additional exam requirements/recommendations for international students: Required—TOEFL, IELTS. *Application deadline:* For fall admission, 1/15 priority date for domestic and international students. Applications are processed on a rolling basis. Application fee: $55 ($100 for international students). Electronic applications accepted. *Expenses: Tuition:* Full-time $26,808; part-time $1117 per credit. *Required fees:* $572; $155 per credit. *Financial support:* In 2017–18, 10 students received support. Career-related internships or fieldwork, Federal Work-Study, scholarships/grants, and unspecified assistantships available. Financial award application deadline: 1/15. *Unit head:* Duncan Mackenzie, Chair, 312-369-8663, E-mail: dmackenzie@colum.edu. *Application contact:* David Marts, Graduate Admissions, 312-369-7942, E-mail: dmarts@colum.edu.

Columbia University, Graduate School of Arts and Sciences, New York, NY 10027. Offers African-American studies (MA); American studies (MA); anthropology (MA, PhD); art history and archaeology (MA, PhD); astronomy (PhD); biological sciences (PhD); biotechnology (MA); chemical physics (PhD); chemistry (PhD); classical studies (MA, PhD); classics (MA, PhD); climate and society (MA); conservation biology (MA); earth and environmental sciences (PhD); East Asia: regional studies (MA); East Asian languages and cultures (MA, PhD); ecology, evolution and environmental biology (MA), including conservation biology; ecology, evolution, and environmental biology (PhD), including ecology and evolutionary biology, evolutionary primatology; economics (MA, PhD); English and comparative literature (MA, PhD); French and Romance philology (MA, PhD); Germanic languages (MA, PhD); global French studies (MA); global thought (MA); Hispanic cultural studies (MA); history (PhD); history and literature (MA); human rights studies (MA); Islamic studies (MA); Italian (MA, PhD); Japanese pedagogy (MA); Jewish studies (MA); Latin America and the Caribbean: regional studies (MA); Latin American and Iberian cultures (PhD); mathematics (MA, PhD), including finance (MA); medieval and Renaissance studies (MA); Middle Eastern, South Asian, and African studies (MA, PhD); modern art: critical and curatorial studies (MA); modern European studies (MA); museum anthropology (MA); music (DMA, PhD); oral history (MA); philosophical foundations of physics (MA); philosophy (MA, PhD); physics (PhD); political science (MA, PhD); psychology (PhD); quantitative methods in the social sciences (MA); religion (MA, PhD); Russia, Eurasia and East Europe: regional studies (MA); Russian translation (MA); Slavic cultures (MA); Slavic languages (MA, PhD); sociology (MA, PhD); South Asian studies (MA); statistics (MA, PhD); theatre (PhD). Dual-degree programs require admission to both Graduate School of Arts and Sciences and another Columbia school. *Program availability:* Part-time. Terminal master's awarded for partial completion of doctoral program. *Degree requirements:* For master's, variable foreign language requirement, comprehensive exam (for some programs), thesis (for some programs); for doctorate, variable foreign language requirement, comprehensive exam (for some programs), thesis/dissertation. *Entrance requirements:* For master's and doctorate, GRE General Test, GRE Subject Test (for some programs). Additional exam requirements/recommendations for international students: Required—TOEFL, IELTS. Electronic applications accepted. *Expenses: Tuition:* Full-time $44,864; part-time $1704 per credit. *Required fees:* $2370 per semester. One-time fee: $105.

Columbia University, School of the Arts, Sound Art Program, New York, NY 10027. Offers MFA. *Expenses: Tuition:* Full-time $44,864; part-time $1704 per credit. *Required fees:* $2370 per semester. One-time fee: $105. *Unit head:* Miya Masaoka, Director, E-mail: soundart@columbia.edu. *Application contact:* Kenny Wong, Director of Admissions and Financial Aid, 212-854-2134, E-mail: admissions-arts@columbia.edu.
Website: https://arts.columbia.edu/sound-art

Columbia University, School of the Arts, Visual Arts Program, New York, NY 10027. Offers new genres (MFA). Program is interdisciplinary across all genres. *Faculty:* 11 full-time (5 women), 47 part-time/adjunct (29 women). *Students:* 54 full-time (34 women); includes 20 minority (4 Black or African American, non-Hispanic/Latino; 7 Asian, non-

Hispanic/Latino; 6 Hispanic/Latino; 3 Two or more races, non-Hispanic/Latino), 11 international. Average age 28. 626 applicants, 6% accepted, 27 enrolled. In 2017, 29 master's awarded. *Degree requirements:* For master's, thesis. *Entrance requirements:* For master's, 3 letters of recommendation, portfolio, resume. Additional exam requirements/recommendations for international students: Required—TOEFL (minimum score 600 paper-based; 100 iBT). *Application deadline:* For fall admission, 1/15 for domestic and international students. Application fee: $110. Electronic applications accepted. *Expenses:* Contact institution. *Financial support:* In 2017–18, 45 students received support, including 53 teaching assistantships with full and partial tuition reimbursements available; fellowships, research assistantships, career-related internships or fieldwork, Federal Work-Study, scholarships/grants, and unspecified assistantships also available. Financial award application deadline: 2/1; financial award applicants required to submit FAFSA. *Unit head:* Matthew Buckingham, Chair, 212-854-4065, E-mail: visualarts@columbia.edu. *Application contact:* Kenny Wong, Director of Admissions and Financial Aid, 212-854-2134, E-mail: admissions-arts@columbia.edu. Website: http://arts.columbia.edu/visual-arts

See Display below and Close-Up on page 185.

Columbus College of Art & Design, Graduate Programs, Columbus, OH 43215. Offers integrative design (M Des); visual arts (MFA). *Accreditation:* NASAD. *Program availability:* Part-time. *Faculty:* 64 full-time (28 women), 111 part-time/adjunct (52 women). *Students:* 50 full-time (35 women), 1 part-time (0 women); includes 21 minority (4 Black or African American, non-Hispanic/Latino; 14 Asian, non-Hispanic/Latino; 2 Hispanic/Latino; 1 Two or more races, non-Hispanic/Latino). Average age 32. 61 applicants, 77% accepted, 31 enrolled. In 2017, 20 master's awarded. *Degree requirements:* For master's, thesis, thesis exhibition. *Entrance requirements:* For master's, portfolio, resume/curriculum vitae, three letters of recommendation, minimum GPA of 3.0. Additional exam requirements/recommendations for international students: Required—TOEFL (minimum score 80 iBT), IELTS (minimum score 6.5). *Application deadline:* For fall admission, 2/1 priority date for domestic and international students. Applications are processed on a rolling basis. Application fee: $65. Electronic applications accepted. *Expenses: Tuition:* Full-time $34,920. *Financial support:* In 2017–18, 30 students received support. Teaching assistantships, scholarships/grants, and unspecified assistantships available. Support available to part-time students. Financial award application deadline: 2/1; financial award applicants required to submit FAFSA. *Faculty research:* Sculpture, design, strategy, business, art. *Unit head:* Ric Petry, Director of Graduate Studies/MFA Professor, 614-222-3227, E-mail: rpetry@ccad.edu. *Application contact:* John Cairns, Senior Admissions Counselor, Graduate Studies, 614-222-3249, E-mail: jcairns.1@ccad.edu. Website: https://www.ccad.edu/

Concordia University, School of Graduate Studies, Faculty of Fine Arts, Department of Studio Arts, Montréal, QC H3G 1M8, Canada. Offers studio arts (MFA), including fibers and material practices, film production, intermedia, painting and drawing, photography, print media, sculpture. *Degree requirements:* For master's, thesis or alternative. *Entrance requirements:* For master's, portfolio.

Cornell University, Graduate School, Graduate Fields of Architecture, Art and Planning, Field of Art, Ithaca, NY 14853. Offers creative visual arts (MFA), including painting, photography, printmaking, sculpture. *Degree requirements:* For master's, thesis, exhibit. *Entrance requirements:* For master's, slide portfolio of 10-20 slides, 3 letters of recommendation, resume. Additional exam requirements/recommendations for international students: Required—TOEFL (minimum score 550 paper-based; 77 iBT). Electronic applications accepted. *Faculty research:* Painting, sculpture, photography, printmaking.

Cranbrook Academy of Art, Program in Fine Arts, Bloomfield Hills, MI 48303-0801. Offers 2d design (MFA); 3d design (MFA); ceramics (MFA); fiber (MFA); metalsmithing

(MFA); painting (MFA); photography (MFA); print media (MFA); sculpture (MFA). *Accreditation:* NASAD. *Degree requirements:* For master's, thesis, exhibit. *Entrance requirements:* Additional exam requirements/recommendations for international students: Required—TOEFL (minimum score 85 iBT). Electronic applications accepted.

Drew University, Caspersen School of Graduate Studies, Madison, NJ 07940-1493. Offers conflict resolution and leadership (Certificate), including community leadership, moderation, peace building; education (M Ed); finance (MA); history and culture (MA, PhD), including American history, book history, British history, European history, Holocaust and genocide (M Litt, MA, D Litt, PhD), intellectual history, Irish history, print culture, public history; K-12 education (MAT), including art, biology, chemistry, elementary education, English, French, Italian, math, secondary education, special education, teacher of students with disabilities; liberal studies (M Litt, D Litt), including history, Holocaust and genocide (M Litt, MA, D Litt, PhD), Irish/Irish-American studies, literature (M Litt, MMH, D Litt, DMH, CMH), religion, spirituality, teaching in the two-year college, writing; medical humanities (MMH, DMH, CMH), including arts, health, healthcare, literature (M Litt, MMH, D Litt, DMH, CMH), scientific research; poetry (MFA). *Program availability:* Part-time, evening/weekend. *Faculty:* 4 full-time (2 women), 29 part-time/adjunct (15 women). *Students:* 77 full-time (42 women), 175 part-time (114 women); includes 39 minority (12 Black or African American, non-Hispanic/Latino; 6 Asian, non-Hispanic/Latino; 16 Hispanic/Latino; 5 Two or more races, non-Hispanic/Latino), 11 international. Average age 41. 126 applicants, 75% accepted, 52 enrolled. In 2017, 38 master's, 23 doctorates, 35 other advanced degrees awarded. Terminal master's awarded for partial completion of doctoral program. *Degree requirements:* For master's and other advanced degree, thesis (for some programs); for doctorate, one foreign language, comprehensive exam (for some programs), thesis/dissertation. *Entrance requirements:* For master's, PRAXIS Core and Subject Area tests (for MAT), GRE/GMAT (for M Fin), resume, transcripts, writing sample, personal statement, letters of recommendation; for doctorate, GRE (PhD in history and culture), resume, transcripts, writing sample, personal statement, letters of recommendation; for other advanced degree, resume, transcripts, personal statement. Additional exam requirements/recommendations for international students: Required—TOEFL (minimum score 587 paper-based; 80 iBT), IELTS (minimum score 6), TWE (minimum score 4). *Application deadline:* For fall admission, 8/1 for domestic students, 6/1 for international students; for spring admission, 12/1 for domestic students, 10/1 for international students. Applications are processed on a rolling basis. Application fee: $35. Electronic applications accepted. *Financial support:* Fellowships, research assistantships, teaching assistantships, career-related internships or fieldwork, Federal Work-Study, scholarships/grants, and unspecified assistantships available. Support available to part-time students. Financial award applicants required to submit FAFSA. *Faculty research:* Irish history and culture, conflict resolution and leadership. *Application contact:* Leanne Horinko, Director of Caspersen Admissions, 973-408-3280, E-mail: gradm@drew.edu. Website: http://www.drew.edu/caspersen

Duke University, Graduate School, Department of Art, Art History and Visual Studies, Durham, NC 27708-0764. Offers historical and cultural visualization (MA); history of art (PhD). *Degree requirements:* For doctorate, thesis/dissertation. *Entrance requirements:* For doctorate, GRE General Test. Additional exam requirements/recommendations for international students: Required—TOEFL (minimum score 577 paper-based; 90 iBT) or IELTS (minimum score 7). Electronic applications accepted.

East Carolina University, Graduate School, College of Fine Arts and Communication, School of Art and Design, Greenville, NC 27858-4353. Offers art education (MA Ed); ceramics (MFA); graphic design (MFA); illustration (MFA); metal design (MFA); painting and drawing (MFA); photography (MFA); printmaking (MFA); sculpture (MFA); textile design (MFA); wood design (MFA). *Accreditation:* NASAD (one or more programs are accredited). *Program availability:* Part-time, evening/weekend. *Students:* 24 full-time (14 women), 12 part-time (10 women); includes 6 minority (3 Asian, non-Hispanic/Latino; 2

Hispanic/Latino; 1 Two or more races, non-Hispanic/Latino). Average age 33. 27 applicants, 70% accepted, 12 enrolled. In 2017, 16 master's awarded. *Degree requirements:* For master's, comprehensive exam (for some programs), thesis (for some programs). *Entrance requirements:* For master's, portfolio. *Application deadline:* For fall admission, 2/1 for domestic students; for spring admission, 10/1 for domestic students. Applications are processed on a rolling basis. Application fee: $75. Electronic applications accepted. *Expenses:* Tuition, state resident: full-time $4749; part-time $297 per credit hour. Tuition, nonresident: full-time $17,898; part-time $1119 per credit hour. *Required fees:* $2691; $224 per credit hour. Part-time tuition and fees vary according to course load and program. *Financial support:* Research assistantships with partial tuition reimbursements, teaching assistantships with partial tuition reimbursements, and Federal Work-Study available. Support available to part-time students. Financial award application deadline: 6/1. *Unit head:* Michael H. Drought, Director, 252-328-6665, E-mail: droughtm@ecu.edu. *Application contact:* Dr. Linda H. Nelson, Information Contact, 252-328-1286, E-mail: nelsonlh@ecu.edu.
Website: http://www.ecu.edu/soad/

Eastern Illinois University, Graduate School, College of Liberal Arts and Sciences, Department of Art, Charleston, IL 61920. Offers art (MA); art education (MA); community arts (MA). *Accreditation:* NASAD. *Program availability:* Part-time, evening/weekend, online learning. *Degree requirements:* For master's, comprehensive exam (for some programs), thesis (for some programs). *Entrance requirements:* For master's, GMAT or GRE. Additional exam requirements/recommendations for international students: Required—TOEFL (minimum score 500 paper-based; 61 iBT), IELTS (minimum score 6). *Application deadline:* For fall admission, 5/15 for domestic and international students; for spring admission, 10/15 for domestic and international students. Applications are processed on a rolling basis. Application fee: $30. Electronic applications accepted. *Financial support:* Teaching assistantships with tuition reimbursements, career-related internships or fieldwork, Federal Work-Study, and unspecified assistantships available. Support available to part-time students. Financial award application deadline: 3/1; financial award applicants required to submit FAFSA. *Unit head:* Chris Kahler, Chair, 217-581-3410, Fax: 217-581-6199, E-mail: cbkahler@eiu.edu. *Application contact:* Patricia K. Belleville, Program Director, 217-581-7009, Fax: 217-581-6199, E-mail: pkbelleville@eiu.edu.
Website: http://www.eiu.edu/artgrad/index.php

Eastern Michigan University, Graduate School, College of Arts and Sciences, School of Art and Design, Program in Studio Art, Ypsilanti, MI 48197. Offers MA, MFA. *Accreditation:* NASAD. *Program availability:* Part-time, evening/weekend, online learning. *Students:* 15 full-time (14 women), 5 part-time (3 women); includes 2 minority (1 Asian, non-Hispanic/Latino; 1 Two or more races, non-Hispanic/Latino). Average age 38. 23 applicants, 52% accepted, 4 enrolled. In 2017, 10 master's awarded. *Application deadline:* Applications are processed on a rolling basis. Application fee: $45. *Financial support:* Fellowships, research assistantships with full tuition reimbursements, teaching assistantships with full tuition reimbursements, career-related internships or fieldwork, Federal Work-Study, institutionally sponsored loans, scholarships/grants, and unspecified assistantships available. Support available to part-time students. *Application contact:* Michael Reedy, Graduate Coordinator, 734-487-1268, Fax: 734-487-2324, E-mail: mreedy@emich.edu.

East Tennessee State University, School of Graduate Studies, College of Arts and Sciences, Department of Art and Design, Johnson City, TN 37614. Offers studio art (MFA). *Accreditation:* NASAD. *Students:* 13 (7 women). *Degree requirements:* For master's, thesis, exhibit, oral exam. *Entrance requirements:* For master's, GRE General Test, portfolio, bachelor's degree in art, minimum GPA of 3.0, three letters of recommendation. Additional exam requirements/recommendations for international students: Required—TOEFL (minimum score 550 paper-based; 79 iBT). *Application deadline:* For fall admission, 2/1 for domestic and international students. Applications are processed on a rolling basis. Application fee: $55 ($65 for international students). Electronic applications accepted. *Financial support:* Research assistantships with full tuition reimbursements, teaching assistantships with full tuition reimbursements, career-related internships or fieldwork, institutionally sponsored loans, scholarships/grants, and unspecified assistantships available. Financial award application deadline: 7/1; financial award applicants required to submit FAFSA. *Faculty research:* Art history, ceramics, drawing, fibers, graphic design, installation, jewelry/metalsmithing, mixed media, new media, painting, photography, printmaking, sculpture, video. *Unit head:* Prof. Mira Gerard, Chair, 423-439-4247, Fax: 423-439-4393, E-mail: gerard@etsu.edu. *Application contact:* Travis Graves, Graduate Coordinator, 423-439-8303, E-mail: gravest@etsu.edu.
Website: http://www.etsu.edu/cas/art/

Edinboro University of Pennsylvania, Department of Art, Edinboro, PA 16444. Offers art education (MA); fine arts (MFA), including ceramics (MA, MFA), metals/jewelry, painting (MA, MFA), printmaking (MA, MFA), sculpture (MA, MFA); studio art (MA), including ceramics (MA, MFA), jewelry/metals, painting (MA, MFA), printmaking (MA, MFA), sculpture (MA, MFA). *Accreditation:* NASAD. *Program availability:* Evening/weekend. *Degree requirements:* For master's, comprehensive exam, thesis or alternative, competency exam, exhibit, portfolio. *Entrance requirements:* For master's, GRE or MAT, interview, minimum QPA of 2.5, portfolio. Electronic applications accepted.

Emily Carr University of Art + Design, Program in Applied Arts, Vancouver, BC V6H 3R9, Canada. Offers design (M Des); media arts (MAA); visual arts (MAA). *Degree requirements:* For master's, internship, thesis project. *Entrance requirements:* For master's, minimum overall GPA of 3.0, visual portfolio, 3 letters of recommendation, resume/curriculum vitae. Additional exam requirements/recommendations for international students: Required—TOEFL (minimum score 570 paper-based; 84 iBT), IELTS (minimum score 6.5), Michigan English Language Assessment Battery (minimum score 81). Electronic applications accepted.

Fairleigh Dickinson University, Metropolitan Campus, University College: Arts, Sciences, and Professional Studies, School of Art and Media Studies, Teaneck, NJ 07666-1914. Offers MA.

Ferris State University, Kendall College of Art and Design, Grand Rapids, MI 49503. Offers architecture (M Arch); art education (MAE); design (MA); drawing (MFA); painting (MFA); photography (MFA); printmaking (MFA); visual and critical studies (MA). *Program availability:* Part-time. *Faculty:* 21 full-time (15 women), 6 part-time/adjunct (2 women). *Students:* 39 full-time (29 women), 15 part-time (9 women); includes 12 minority (4 Black or African American, non-Hispanic/Latino; 1 American Indian or Alaska Native, non-Hispanic/Latino; 3 Asian, non-Hispanic/Latino; 4 Hispanic/Latino), 6 international. Average age 31. 48 applicants, 60% accepted, 17 enrolled. In 2017, 12 master's awarded. *Degree requirements:* For master's, thesis, seminars. *Entrance requirements:* For master's, portfolio, 3 letters of recommendation, curriculum vitae, artist statement, letter of intent. Additional exam requirements/recommendations for international students: Required—TOEFL (minimum score 79 iBT). *Application deadline:* For fall admission, 2/1 priority date for domestic and international students; for spring admission, 11/1 priority date for domestic and international students. Applications are processed on a rolling basis. Application fee: $0. Electronic applications accepted. *Expenses:* Contact institution. *Financial support:* In 2017–18, 32 students received support, including 8 fellowships (averaging $16,781 per year); scholarships/grants and unspecified assistantships also available. Financial award application deadline: 2/1; financial award applicants required to submit FAFSA. *Unit head:* Leslie Bellavance, President, 616-451-2787. *Application contact:* Thomas Post, Graduate Recruitment Specialist, 616-451-2787, Fax: 616-831-9689, E-mail: thomaspost@ferris.edu.
Website: http://www.kcad.edu/

Florida Atlantic University, Dorothy F. Schmidt College of Arts and Letters, Department of Visual Arts and Art History, Boca Raton, FL 33431-0991. Offers visual art (MFA), including ceramics, graphic design, visual art. *Faculty:* 14 full-time (10 women). *Students:* 13 full-time (10 women), 3 part-time (2 women); includes 5 minority (2 Black or African American, non-Hispanic/Latino; 1 Asian, non-Hispanic/Latino; 2 Hispanic/Latino). Average age 37. 31 applicants, 23% accepted, 5 enrolled. In 2017, 4 master's awarded. *Degree requirements:* For master's, one foreign language, project. *Entrance requirements:* For master's, GRE General Test, minimum GPA of 3.0 during last 60 hours of course work, slide portfolio. *Application deadline:* For fall admission, 2/21 for domestic and international students; for spring admission, 10/1 for domestic and international students. Application fee: $30. Electronic applications accepted. *Expenses:* Tuition, state resident: full-time $7400; part-time $369.82 per credit. Tuition, nonresident: full-time $20,496; part-time $1042.81 per credit. *Financial support:* Research assistantships with full tuition reimbursements, teaching assistantships with full tuition reimbursements, career-related internships or fieldwork, Federal Work-Study, and institutionally sponsored loans available. Financial award applicants required to submit FAFSA. *Faculty research:* Painting, ceramics (traditional and non-traditional), installation, video and interactive sculpture. *Unit head:* Dr. Eric Landes, Chair, 954-236-1106, E-mail: elandes1@fau.edu.
Website: http://www.fau.edu/VAAH/

Florida International University, College of Communication, Architecture and The Arts, Department of Art and Art History, Miami, FL 33199. Offers museum studies (Graduate Certificate); studio art (MFA). *Accreditation:* NASAD. *Program availability:* Part-time, evening/weekend. *Faculty:* 13 full-time (6 women), 20 part-time/adjunct (13 women). *Students:* 28 full-time (21 women), 19 part-time (15 women); includes 36 minority (5 Black or African American, non-Hispanic/Latino; 30 Hispanic/Latino; 1 Two or more races, non-Hispanic/Latino), 3 international. Average age 31. 25 applicants, 72% accepted, 15 enrolled. In 2017, 15 master's awarded. *Entrance requirements:* For master's, minimum GPA of 3.0 in upper-level coursework, 3 letters of recommendation, 20 slides of creative work. Additional exam requirements/recommendations for international students: Required—TOEFL (minimum score 550 paper-based; 80 iBT). *Application deadline:* For fall admission, 2/1 for domestic and international students. Application fee: $30. Electronic applications accepted. *Expenses:* Tuition, state resident: full-time $8912; part-time $446 per credit hour. Tuition, nonresident: full-time $21,393; part-time $992 per credit hour. *Required fees:* $390; $195 per semester. *Financial support:* Institutionally sponsored loans and scholarships/grants available. Financial award application deadline: 3/1; financial award applicants required to submit FAFSA. *Unit head:* Dr. Jacek Kolasinski, Chair, 305-348-3362, Fax: 305-348-0513, E-mail: jacek.kolasinski@fiu.edu. *Application contact:* Nanett Rojas, Assistant Director, Graduate Admissions, 305-348-7464, Fax: 305-348-7441, E-mail: gradadm@fiu.edu.
Website: http://carta.fiu.edu/arts/

Florida State University, The Graduate School, College of Fine Arts, Department of Art, Tallahassee, FL 32306. Offers MFA. *Accreditation:* NASAD. *Faculty:* 20 full-time (12 women), 33 part-time/adjunct (22 women). *Students:* 30 full-time (20 women); includes 8 minority (4 Black or African American, non-Hispanic/Latino; 4 Hispanic/Latino). Average age 26. 59 applicants, 25% accepted, 9 enrolled. In 2017, 8 master's awarded. *Degree requirements:* For master's, thesis, creative thesis project, short thesis paper. *Entrance requirements:* Additional exam requirements/recommendations for international students: Required—TOEFL (minimum score 550 paper-based). *Application deadline:* For fall admission, 2/1 priority date for domestic and international students. Application fee: $30. Electronic applications accepted. *Financial support:* In 2017–18, 30 students received support, including 30 teaching assistantships (averaging $5,900 per year); fellowships, Federal Work-Study, scholarships/grants, tuition waivers (full), and unspecified assistantships also available. *Faculty research:* Photography, painting, sculpture, printmaking, ceramics. *Unit head:* David Gussak, Department Chair, 850-644-7254, E-mail: dgussak@fsu.edu. *Application contact:* Haley Lauw, Graduate Coordinator, 850-644-7254, E-mail: hlauw@fsu.edu.
Website: http://art.fsu.edu/

Fontbonne University, Graduate Programs, St. Louis, MO 63105-3098. Offers accounting (MBA, MS); art (MA); art (K-12) (MAT); business (MBA); computer science (MS); deaf education (MA); early intervention in deaf education (MA); education (MA), including autism spectrum disorders, curriculum and instruction, diverse learners, early childhood education, reading, special education; elementary education (MAT); family and consumer sciences (MA), including multidisciplinary health communication studies; fine arts (MFA); instructional design and technology (MS); management and leadership (MM); middle school education (MAT); secondary education (MAT); special education (MAT); speech-language pathology (MS); supply chain management (MS); theatre (MA). *Program availability:* Part-time, evening/weekend, online learning. *Degree requirements:* For master's, comprehensive exam (for some programs), thesis (for some programs). *Entrance requirements:* Additional exam requirements/recommendations for international students: Required—TOEFL (minimum score 500 paper-based; 65 iBT). Electronic applications accepted.

Fort Hays State University, Graduate School, College of Arts and Sciences, Department of Art and Design, Hays, KS 67601-4099. Offers studio art (MFA). *Program availability:* Part-time. *Degree requirements:* For master's, comprehensive exam, thesis. *Entrance requirements:* For master's, slides. Additional exam requirements/recommendations for international students: Required—TOEFL (minimum score 550 paper-based; 79 iBT). Electronic applications accepted. *Faculty research:* Migration art of Germanic tribes, iconographic and stylistic development, graphic design, photography, lithography.

Full Sail University, Education Media Design and Technology Master of Science Program - Online, Winter Park, FL 32792-7437. Offers MS. *Program availability:* Online learning. *Entrance requirements:* Additional exam requirements/recommendations for international students: Required—TOEFL (minimum score 550 paper-based; 79 iBT).

Full Sail University, Media Design Master of Fine Arts Program - Online, Winter Park, FL 32792-7437. Offers MFA. *Program availability:* Online learning.

George Mason University, College of Visual and Performing Arts, Program in Visual and Performing Arts, Fairfax, VA 22030. Offers dance (MFA); graphic design (MFA); theater (MFA); visual art (MFA). *Accreditation:* NASAD. *Faculty:* 18 full-time (9 women), 39 part-time/adjunct (20 women). *Students:* 4 full-time (3 women), 7 part-time (3 women); includes 3 minority (1 Hispanic/Latino; 2 Two or more races, non-Hispanic/Latino). Average age 33. 22 applicants, 45% accepted, 5 enrolled. In 2017, 3 master's awarded. *Degree requirements:* For master's, comprehensive experience, studio project or thesis. *Entrance requirements:* For master's, official transcripts; 3 letters of recommendation; letter of intent; resume; professional goals statement. Additional exam requirements/recommendations for international students: Required—TOEFL (minimum score 575 paper-based; 88 iBT), IELTS (minimum score 6.5), PTE (minimum score 59). Application fee: $75 ($80 for international students). Electronic applications accepted. *Expenses:* Tuition, state resident: full-time $11,228; part-time $459.50 per credit. Tuition, nonresident: full-time $30,932; part-time $1280.50 per credit. *Required fees:* $3252;

$135.50 per credit. Part-time tuition and fees vary according to course load and program. *Financial support:* In 2017–18, 2 students received support, including 3 teaching assistantships (averaging $4,123 per year); career-related internships or fieldwork, Federal Work-Study, scholarships/grants, unspecified assistantships, and health care benefits (for full-time research or teaching assistantship recipients) also available. Support available to part-time students. Financial award application deadline: 3/1; financial award applicants required to submit FAFSA. *Faculty research:* Digital arts, painting, photography, print-making, sculpture; combined art forms in in-disciplinary projects including installation, performance, publishing, time or writing-based; combined creative and critical approaches. *Unit head:* Lisa Kahn, Associate Dean, 703-993-4541, E-mail: lkahn2@gmu.edu. *Application contact:* Nikki Brugnoli-Whipkey, Graduate Studies Administrative Assistant, 703-993-5792, Fax: 703-993-8798, E-mail: rbrugnol@gmu.edu. Website: http://soa.gmu.edu

The George Washington University, Columbian College of Arts and Sciences, Department of Fine Arts and Art History, Washington, DC 20052. Offers art history (MA), including art history, museum training; ceramics (MFA); drawing/painting (MFA); interior design (MFA), including interior architecture and design; new media (MFA); photography (MFA); sculpture (MFA). *Accreditation:* CIDA. *Program availability:* Part-time, evening/weekend. *Faculty:* 14 full-time (6 women), 16 part-time/adjunct (10 women). *Students:* 60 full-time (50 women), 13 part-time (11 women); includes 15 minority (5 Black or African American, non-Hispanic/Latino; 3 Asian, non-Hispanic/Latino; 4 Hispanic/Latino; 3 Two or more races, non-Hispanic/Latino), 21 international. Average age 27. 138 applicants, 65% accepted, 31 enrolled. In 2017, 43 master's awarded. *Entrance requirements:* For master's, GRE General Test, bachelor's degree in field, minimum GPA of 3.0. Additional exam requirements/recommendations for international students: Required—TOEFL (minimum score 550 paper-based; 80 iBT). *Application deadline:* For fall admission, 3/1 priority date for domestic students, 1/15 priority date for international students; for spring admission, 10/1 priority date for domestic students, 9/1 priority date for international students. Applications are processed on a rolling basis. Application fee: $75. Electronic applications accepted. *Expenses: Tuition:* Full-time $28,800; part-time $1655 per credit hour. *Required fees:* $45; $2.75 per credit hour. *Financial support:* In 2017–18, 12 students received support. Fellowships, teaching assistantships, career-related internships or fieldwork, Federal Work-Study, and tuition waivers available. Financial award application deadline: 1/15. *Unit head:* Phil Jacks, Chair, 202-994-6085, E-mail: pjacks@gwu.edu. *Application contact:* Information Contact, 202-994-6085, Fax: 202-994-8657, E-mail: art@gwu.edu. Website: http://art.columbian.gwu.edu/

Georgia Southern University, Jack N. Averitt College of Graduate Studies, College of Liberal Arts and Social Sciences, Program in Art, Statesboro, GA 30460. Offers fine arts (MFA), including 2D graphic design, 2D studio art, 3D studio art. *Accreditation:* NASAD. *Program availability:* Part-time. *Faculty:* 19 full-time (9 women). *Students:* 18 full-time (14 women), 2 part-time (0 women); includes 3 minority (2 Black or African American, non-Hispanic/Latino; 1 Hispanic/Latino), 3 international. Average age 33. 4 applicants, 100% accepted, 4 enrolled. *Degree requirements:* For master's, thesis, exhibition. *Entrance requirements:* For master's, minimum GPA of 3.0; 18 semester hours of course work in studio art, 9 in art history; portfolio; letters of reference. Additional exam requirements/ recommendations for international students: Required—TOEFL (minimum score 550 paper-based; 80 iBT), IELTS (minimum score 6). *Application deadline:* For fall admission, 3/1 priority date for domestic and international students; for spring admission, 10/1 priority date for domestic students, 10/1 for international students. Applications are processed on a rolling basis. Application fee: $50. Electronic applications accepted. *Expenses:* Tuition, state resident: full-time $4986; part-time $3324 per year. Tuition, nonresident: full-time $21,982; part-time $15,352 per year. *Required fees:* $2092; $1802 per credit hour. $901 per semester. Tuition and fees vary according to course load, campus/location and program. *Financial support:* In 2017–18, 11 students received support, including 4 fellowships with full tuition reimbursements available (averaging $7,750 per year); career-related internships or fieldwork, Federal Work-Study, scholarships/grants, tuition waivers (full), and unspecified assistantships also available. Support available to part-time students. Financial award application deadline: 4/15; financial award applicants required to submit FAFSA. *Faculty research:* International design trends; graphic design social awareness campaigns; functional design; public sculpture; fine art painting, drawing, printmaking, paper and book arts; folk art; Georgia artists archive, technology, design, contemporary, traditional studio. *Unit head:* Dr. Robert Farber, Department Chair, 912-478-5358, Fax: 912-478-5104, E-mail: rfarber@georgiasouthern.edu. Website: http://class.georgiasouthern.edu/art

Georgia State University, Ernest G. Welch School of Art and Design, Program in Studio Art, Atlanta, GA 30302-3083. Offers ceramics (MFA); drawing and painting (MFA); graphic design (MFA); interior design (MFA); photography (MFA); printmaking (MFA); sculpture (MFA); textiles (MFA). *Accreditation:* NASAD. Application fee: $50. Electronic applications accepted. *Expenses:* Tuition, state resident: full-time $7020. Tuition, nonresident: full-time $22,518. *Required fees:* $2128. Tuition and fees vary according to degree level and program. *Financial support:* Fellowships, research assistantships, teaching assistantships, scholarships/grants, and unspecified assistantships available. Financial award application deadline: 4/15; financial award applicants required to submit FAFSA. *Faculty research:* Advertising and typography, new media, traditional media, three-dimensional art, architectural and environmental design. *Unit head:* Michael White, Director, Welch School of Art and Design, 404-413-5221, Fax: 404-413-5261, E-mail: mwhite@gsu.edu. *Application contact:* Hubert Stanley Anderson, Director of Graduate Studies, 404-413-5229, Fax: 404-413-5261, E-mail: artgrad@gsu.edu. Website: http://artdesign.gsu.edu/graduate/admissions/masters-of-fine-arts-in-studio/

Governors State University, College of Arts and Sciences, Program in Art, University Park, IL 60484. Offers MA. *Program availability:* Part-time. *Faculty:* 60 full-time (34 women), 115 part-time/adjunct (58 women). *Students:* 2 full-time (1 woman), 4 part-time (1 woman); includes 4 minority (3 Black or African American, non-Hispanic/Latino; 1 Hispanic/Latino). Average age 37. In 2017, 4 master's awarded. *Application deadline:* For fall admission, 4/1 for domestic students. Applications are processed on a rolling basis. Application fee: $50. Electronic applications accepted. *Expenses:* Tuition, state resident: full-time $8472; part-time $353 per credit hour. Tuition, nonresident: full-time $16,944; part-time $706 per credit hour. *Required fees:* $1824; $76 per credit hour. $38 per term. Tuition and fees vary according to course load, degree level and program. *Financial support:* Application deadline: 5/1; applicants required to submit FAFSA. *Unit head:* Lori Montalbano, Chair, Division of Arts and Letters, 708-534-5000 Ext. 2802, E-mail: lmontalbano@govst.edu.

Hollins University, Graduate Programs, Program in Liberal Studies, Roanoke, VA 24020. Offers humanities (MALS); interdisciplinary studies (MALS); leadership (MALS); social sciences (MALS); visual and performing arts (MALS). *Program availability:* Part-time, evening/weekend, 100% online, blended/hybrid learning. *Faculty:* 5 part-time/ adjunct (2 women). *Students:* 5 full-time (4 women), 29 part-time (25 women); includes 9 minority (6 Black or African American, non-Hispanic/Latino; 1 Asian, non-Hispanic/ Latino; 1 Hispanic/Latino; 1 Two or more races, non-Hispanic/Latino). Average age 40. 7 applicants, 86% accepted, 3 enrolled. In 2017, 11 master's awarded. *Degree requirements:* For master's, thesis. *Entrance requirements:* For master's, three letters of recommendation, interview, bachelor's degree, undergraduate transcripts, statement of educational objectives. Additional exam requirements/recommendations for

international students: Required—TOEFL (minimum score 550 paper-based; 80 iBT), IELTS (minimum score 6.5). *Application deadline:* Applications are processed on a rolling basis. Application fee: $40. Electronic applications accepted. *Expenses:* Contact institution. *Financial support:* Scholarships/grants available. Financial award application deadline: 7/15; financial award applicants required to submit FAFSA. *Faculty research:* Diversity, gender and women's studies, political science, leadership. *Unit head:* Dr. Lorraine Lange, Director, 540-362-6576, Fax: 540-362-6288, E-mail: hugrad@hollins.edu. *Application contact:* Cathy S. Koon, Manager of Graduate Programs, 540-362-6326, Fax: 540-362-6288, E-mail: hugrad@hollins.edu. Website: http://www.hollins.edu/academics/graduate-degrees/liberal-studies/

Hood College, Graduate School, Program in Ceramic Arts, Frederick, MD 21701-8575. Offers ceramic arts (Certificate); ceramics (MA, MFA). *Program availability:* Part-time, evening/weekend. *Faculty:* 1 (woman) full-time, 3 part-time/adjunct (2 women). *Students:* 5 full-time (3 women), 19 part-time (14 women); includes 3 minority (1 Black or African American, non-Hispanic/Latino; 1 Asian, non-Hispanic/Latino; 1 Hispanic/ Latino), 1 international. Average age 37. 4 applicants, 75% accepted, 3 enrolled. In 2017, 8 master's, 4 other advanced degrees awarded. *Degree requirements:* For master's, thesis (for some programs), capstone project. *Entrance requirements:* For master's, minimum GPA of 2.75, artist statement, resume (MFA), 2 letters of recommendation, portfolio of 20 images; for Certificate, portfolio of 12 images. Additional exam requirements/recommendations for international students: Required—TOEFL (minimum score 575 paper-based; 89 iBT), IELTS (minimum score 6.5). *Application deadline:* For fall admission, 8/15 priority date for domestic students, 8/5 for international students; for spring admission, 12/1 priority date for domestic students, 12/1 for international students; for summer admission, 5/1 priority date for domestic students, 4/ 15 for international students. Applications are processed on a rolling basis. Application fee: $35. Electronic applications accepted. *Expenses:* $465 per credit hour plus $110 comprehensive fee per semester. *Financial support:* Tuition waivers (partial) and unspecified assistantships available. Financial award applicants required to submit FAFSA. *Unit head:* Dr. April M. Boulton, Dean of the Graduate School, 301-696-3600, E-mail: gofurther@hood.edu. *Application contact:* Jan Marcus, Assistant Director of Graduate Admissions, 301-696-3600, E-mail: gofurther@hood.edu. Website: http://www.hood.edu/graduate

Houston Baptist University, School of Fine Arts, Houston, TX 77074-3298. Offers studio art (MFA). *Program availability:* Part-time, evening/weekend. *Faculty:* 7 full-time (1 woman), 2 part-time/adjunct (1 woman). *Students:* 21 full-time (13 women), 2 part-time (both women); includes 5 minority (2 Black or African American, non-Hispanic/Latino; 3 Hispanic/Latino), 2 international. Average age 34. 40 applicants, 43% accepted, 12 enrolled. In 2017, 10 master's awarded. *Degree requirements:* For master's, comprehensive exam. *Entrance requirements:* For master's, minimum GPA of 2.5, essay/ personal statement, resume, bachelor's degree transcript, digital portfolio. Additional exam requirements/recommendations for international students: Required—TOEFL (minimum score 80 iBT), IELTS (minimum score 6.5). *Application deadline:* For fall admission, 4/1 for domestic students, 2/1 for international students. Applications are processed on a rolling basis. Application fee: $0 ($100 for international students). Electronic applications accepted. Application fee is waived when completed online. *Expenses:* $40,000 tuition; $4,500 fees (general, technology and parking). *Financial support:* In 2017–18, 19 students received support. Federal Work-Study and scholarships/grants available. Support available to part-time students. Financial award application deadline: 4/1; financial award applicants required to submit FAFSA. *Unit head:* Dr. Jason Lester, Dean, 281-649-3339, E-mail: jlester@hbu.edu. *Application contact:* Dr. Michael Collins, Program Director, 281-649-3624, E-mail: mcollins@hbu.edu. Website: http://www.hbu.edu/mfa

Howard University, Graduate School, Division of Fine Arts, Department of Art, Program in Fine Arts, Washington, DC 20059-0002. Offers 3D reality (sculpture and ceramics) (MFA); design (MFA); electronic studio (MFA); painting (MFA); photography (MFA). *Accreditation:* NASAD. *Degree requirements:* For master's, comprehensive exam, thesis, exhibit. *Entrance requirements:* For master's, minimum GPA of 3.0, portfolio.

Hunter College of the City University of New York, Graduate School, School of Arts and Sciences, Department of Art and Art History, Program in Studio Art, New York, NY 10013. Offers MFA. *Program availability:* Part-time, evening/weekend. *Degree requirements:* For master's, exhibit, project. *Entrance requirements:* For master's, minimum of 24 credits of course work in studio art, 9 in art history; portfolio; minimum GPA of 3.0 overall and in art courses; statement of purpose; two letters of recommendation. Additional exam requirements/recommendations for international students: Required—TOEFL (minimum score 550 paper-based; 60 iBT). *Faculty research:* Color theory, public printmaking and environmental commissions in painting and sculpture, graphics, ceramics, contemporary film and video.

Idaho State University, Office of Graduate Studies, College of Arts and Letters, Department of Art, Pocatello, ID 83209-8004. Offers MFA. *Program availability:* Part-time. *Degree requirements:* For master's, comprehensive exam, thesis, exhibit, 2 year minimum participation in program, oral exam. *Entrance requirements:* For master's, GRE General Test, GMAT or MAT, minimum GPA of 3.0 in all upper-division classes, portfolio of work, 3 letters of recommendation. Additional exam requirements/ recommendations for international students: Required—TOEFL (minimum score 550 paper-based; 80 iBT). Electronic applications accepted. *Faculty research:* Computerized weaving, anodizing refractory metals, viscosity printing, neon, ceramic shell casting.

Illinois State University, Graduate School, College of Fine Arts, Program in Arts Technology, Normal, IL 61790. Offers MS. *Accreditation:* NASAD. *Degree requirements:* For master's, thesis or alternative.

Illinois State University, Graduate School, College of Fine Arts, School of Art, Normal, IL 61790. Offers art history (MA, MS); ceramics (MFA, MS); drawing (MFA, MS); fibers (MFA, MS); glass (MFA, MS); graphic design (MFA, MS); metals (MFA, MS); painting (MFA, MS); photography (MFA, MS); printmaking (MFA, MS); sculpture (MFA, MS). *Accreditation:* NASAD (one or more programs are accredited). *Degree requirements:* For master's, thesis or alternative, internship. *Entrance requirements:* For master's, portfolio, sample of scholarly writing.

Indiana State University, College of Graduate and Professional Studies, College of Arts and Sciences, Department of Art and Design, Terre Haute, IN 47809. Offers ceramics (MA, MFA); drawing (MA, MFA); graphic design (MA, MFA); painting (MA, MFA); photography (MA, MFA); printmaking (MA, MFA); sculpture (MA, MFA). *Accreditation:* NASAD (one or more programs are accredited). *Program availability:* Part-time. *Degree requirements:* For master's, thesis or alternative, departmental qualifying exam. *Entrance requirements:* For master's, portfolio. Additional exam requirements/recommendations for international students: Required—TOEFL (minimum score 550 paper-based).

Indiana University Bloomington, University Graduate School, College of Arts and Sciences, School of Art and Design, Bloomington, IN 47405-7000. Offers apparel merchandising (MS); studio art (MFA). *Accreditation:* NASAD (one or more programs are accredited). *Entrance requirements:* For master's, portfolio (MFA). Additional exam requirements/recommendations for international students: Required—TOEFL. Electronic applications accepted.

Art/Fine Arts

Indiana University of Pennsylvania, School of Graduate Studies and Research, College of Fine Arts, Department of Art, MA Program in Art, Indiana, PA 15705. Offers MA. *Accreditation:* NASAD. *Program availability:* Part-time. *Faculty:* 6 full-time (3 women), 2 part-time/adjunct (1 woman). *Students:* 3 part-time (2 women). Average age 29. 2 applicants, 100% accepted, 1 enrolled. In 2017, 4 master's awarded. *Degree requirements:* For master's, thesis optional. *Entrance requirements:* For master's, 3 letters of recommendation, portfolio. Additional exam requirements/recommendations for international students: Required—TOEFL (minimum score 540 paper-based). *Application deadline:* For fall admission, 4/15 priority date for domestic students. Applications are processed on a rolling basis. Application fee: $50. Electronic applications accepted. *Expenses:* Tuition, state resident: full-time $12,000; part-time $500 per credit. Tuition, nonresident: full-time $18,000; part-time $750 per credit. *Required fees:* $4073; $165.55 per credit. $64 per term. *Financial support:* In 2017–18, 2 research assistantships with tuition reimbursements (averaging $1,000 per year) were awarded; fellowships, career-related internships or fieldwork, Federal Work-Study, scholarships/grants, and unspecified assistantships also available. Support available to part-time students. Financial award application deadline: 4/15; financial award applicants required to submit FAFSA. *Unit head:* Dr. Susan Palmisano, Graduate Coordinator, 724-357-2530, E-mail: palmisan@iup.edu.
Website: http://www.iup.edu/art/grad/default.aspx

Indiana University of Pennsylvania, School of Graduate Studies and Research, College of Fine Arts, Department of Art, Master of Fine Arts Program, Indiana, PA 15705. Offers MFA. *Program availability:* Part-time. *Faculty:* 6 full-time (3 women), 2 part-time/adjunct (1 woman). *Students:* 13 full-time (7 women), 8 part-time (6 women); includes 3 minority (1 Black or African American, non-Hispanic/Latino; 1 Hispanic/Latino; 1 Two or more races, non-Hispanic/Latino), 2 international. Average age 29. 13 applicants, 92% accepted, 5 enrolled. In 2017, 10 master's awarded. *Degree requirements:* For master's, thesis/exhibition. *Entrance requirements:* For master's, 2 letters of recommendation, art slides. Additional exam requirements/recommendations for international students: Required—TOEFL (minimum score 540 paper-based). *Application deadline:* For fall admission, 2/15 priority date for domestic students. Application fee: $50. Electronic applications accepted. *Expenses:* Tuition, state resident: full-time $12,000; part-time $500 per credit. Tuition, nonresident: full-time $18,000; part-time $750 per credit. *Required fees:* $4073; $165.55 per credit. $64 per term. *Financial support:* In 2017–18, 14 research assistantships with tuition reimbursements (averaging $2,520 per year) were awarded; fellowships with full tuition reimbursements, career-related internships or fieldwork, Federal Work-Study, scholarships/grants, and unspecified assistantships also available. Support available to part-time students. Financial award application deadline: 4/15; financial award applicants required to submit FAFSA. *Unit head:* Dr. Susan Palmisano, Graduate Coordinator, 724-357-2536, E-mail: palmisan@iup.edu.
Website: http://www.iup.edu/art/grad/default.aspx

Indiana University–Purdue University Indianapolis, Herron School of Art and Design, Indianapolis, IN 46202. Offers art therapy (MA); visual art (MFA), including ceramics, furniture design, painting and drawing, photography and intermedia, printmaking, sculpture; visual communication design (MFA). *Degree requirements:* For master's, thesis. *Entrance requirements:* For master's, personal statement, resume, recommendations, portfolio, transcripts (18 credit hours of studio art and 12 credit hours of psychology, including 3 credit hours of developmental psychology and 3 credit hours of abnormal psychology for MA). Additional exam requirements/recommendations for international students: Recommended—TOEFL (minimum score 550 paper-based; 79 iBT), IELTS (minimum score 6.5). Electronic applications accepted. *Expenses:* Contact institution. *Faculty research:* Contemporary digital narratives for the homoerotic trope; sound articulated 3D print; neuroscience, art and related therapeutics; automotive and aeronautical design and fabrication; technological detritus.

Institute for Doctoral Studies in the Visual Arts, PhD Program in Visual Art: Philosophy, Aesthetics, and Art Theory, Portland, ME 04102. Offers aesthetics (PhD); art theory (PhD); philosophy (PhD). *Program availability:* Online learning. *Faculty:* 3 full-time, 7 part-time/adjunct. *Students:* 60 full-time. *Degree requirements:* For doctorate, comprehensive exam, thesis/dissertation, dissertation defense. *Entrance requirements:* For doctorate, curriculum vitae, writing sample, portfolio, interview. *Application deadline:* Applications are processed on a rolling basis. Application fee: $60. Electronic applications accepted. Application fee is waived when completed online. *Financial support:* Fellowships, teaching assistantships, and scholarships/grants available. Financial award applicants required to submit FAFSA. *Faculty research:* Visual culture, cultural studies, feminism, contemporary art. *Application contact:* Molly M. Davis, Director of Administration/Co-Director of Admissions, 207-771-8887, E-mail: info@idsva.edu.
Website: https://www.idsva.edu

Inter American University of Puerto Rico, San Germán Campus, Graduate Studies Center, Program in Fine Arts, San Germán, PR 00683-5008. Offers drawing (MFA); graphic design (MFA); painting (MFA); photography (MFA); printmaking (MFA); sculpture (MFA). *Program availability:* Part-time, evening/weekend. *Degree requirements:* For master's, comprehensive exam, thesis. *Entrance requirements:* For master's, GRE General Test or EXADEP, minimum GPA of 3.0.

Iowa State University of Science and Technology, Program in Integrated Visual Arts, Ames, IA 50011. Offers MFA. *Accreditation:* NASAD. *Entrance requirements:* Additional exam requirements/recommendations for international students: Required—TOEFL (minimum score 550 paper-based; 79 iBT), IELTS (minimum score 6.5).

Ithaca College, Roy H. Park School of Communications, Program in Image Text, Ithaca, NY 14850. Offers MFA. *Program availability:* Part-time-only. *Faculty:* 9 full-time (2 women). *Students:* 18 part-time (9 women); includes 5 minority (3 Hispanic/Latino; 2 Two or more races, non-Hispanic/Latino). Average age 28. 20 applicants, 70% accepted, 10 enrolled. *Degree requirements:* For master's, thesis, field practicum. *Entrance requirements:* Additional exam requirements/recommendations for international students: Required—TOEFL (minimum score 550 paper-based; 80 iBT). *Application deadline:* For fall admission, 3/15 for domestic and international students; for spring admission, 12/1 for domestic and international students. Applications are processed on a rolling basis. Application fee: $40. Electronic applications accepted. *Expenses:* Contact institution. *Financial support:* In 2017–18, 18 students received support, including 18 fellowships (averaging $4,868 per year); career-related internships or fieldwork, Federal Work-Study, and scholarships/grants also available. Support available to part-time students. Financial award application deadline: 3/1; financial award applicants required to submit FAFSA. *Unit head:* Nicholas Muellner, Co-Director, 607-274-1984, E-mail: nmuellner@ithaca.edu. *Application contact:* Nicole Eversley Bradwell, Director, Office of Admission, 607-274-3124, Fax: 607-274-1263, E-mail: admission@ithaca.edu.
Website: http://www.ithaca.edu/gradprograms/image-text

Jacksonville University, College of Fine Arts, MFA in Visual Arts Program, Jacksonville, FL 32211. Offers MFA. *Accreditation:* NASAD. *Program availability:* Blended/hybrid learning. *Faculty:* 1 full-time (0 women), 2 part-time/adjunct (0 women). *Students:* 4 full-time (3 women), 2 part-time (1 woman); includes 2 minority (both Hispanic/Latino). Average age 36. 12 applicants, 58% accepted, 4 enrolled. In 2017, 5 master's awarded. *Degree requirements:* For master's, thesis, portfolio. *Entrance requirements:* For master's, portfolio, artist statement of intent, undergraduate degree, three current references, official transcripts of academic work, sample of selected works (12 minutes maximum). Additional exam requirements/recommendations for international students: Recommended—TOEFL (minimum score 540 paper-based; 76 iBT). *Application deadline:* For spring admission, 5/1 for domestic students, 2/1 for international students. Applications are processed on a rolling basis. Application fee: $50. Electronic applications accepted. *Expenses:* $620 per credit hour. *Financial support:* In 2017–18, 1 fellowship (averaging $35,700 per year) was awarded; institutionally sponsored loans, scholarships/grants, and health care benefits also available. Support available to part-time students. Financial award application deadline: 3/1; financial award applicants required to submit FAFSA. *Faculty research:* Dance for Parkinson's, practice as research, choreographic practices, body politics. *Unit head:* Cari Coble, Professor of Dance and MFA Coordinator, 904-256-7398, E-mail: ccoble@ju.edu. *Application contact:* Rakia Naze, Assistant Director of Graduate Admissions, 904-256-7004, E-mail: rnaze@ju.edu.
Website: https://www.ju.edu/cfa/mfavisualarts/index.php

James Madison University, The Graduate School, College of Visual and Performing Arts, School of Art, Design and Art History, Harrisonburg, VA 22801. Offers art education (MA); studio art (MA, MFA), including ceramics (MFA), drawing/painting (MFA), intermedia (MFA), metal/jewelry (MFA), photography (MFA), sculpture (MFA). *Accreditation:* NASAD. *Program availability:* Part-time. *Students:* 7 full-time (5 women), 1 (woman) part-time. Average age 30. In 2017, 5 master's awarded. Application fee: $55. Electronic applications accepted. *Expenses:* Tuition, state resident: full-time $10,512; part-time $438 per credit hour. Tuition, nonresident: full-time $28,358; part-time $1162 per credit hour. *Required fees:* $1128. *Financial support:* In 2017–18, 7 students received support, including 4 teaching assistantships with full tuition reimbursements available (averaging $9,284 per year); Federal Work-Study and 3 assistantships (averaging $7911) also available. Financial award application deadline: 3/1; financial award applicants required to submit FAFSA. *Unit head:* Dr. Kathy A. Schwartz, Director of School of Art, Design and Art History, 540-568-6216, E-mail: schwarka@jmu.edu. *Application contact:* Lynette D. Michael, Director of Graduate Student Admissions, 540-568-6131 Ext. 6395, Fax: 540-568-7860, E-mail: michaeld@jmu.edu.
Website: http://www.jmu.edu/artandarthistory/

John F. Kennedy University, Graduate School of Holistic Studies, Department of Arts and Consciousness, Program in Studio Arts, Pleasant Hill, CA 94523-4817. Offers MFA. *Program availability:* Part-time, evening/weekend. *Degree requirements:* For master's, thesis or alternative. *Entrance requirements:* For master's, interview, portfolio. Additional exam requirements/recommendations for international students: Required—TOEFL. *Expenses:* Contact institution.

Kansas State University, Graduate School, College of Arts and Sciences, Department of Art, Manhattan, KS 66506. Offers MFA. *Accreditation:* NASAD. *Degree requirements:* For master's, thesis, gallery exhibit. *Entrance requirements:* For master's, slides of artistic work, portfolio, official transcripts, recommendation form/letters, statement of purpose. Additional exam requirements/recommendations for international students: Required—TOEFL (minimum score 550 paper-based; 79 iBT). Electronic applications accepted. *Faculty research:* Drawing, painting, sculpture, metalsmithing, graphic design, digital/experimental media, ceramics, printmaking.

Kent State University, College of the Arts, School of Art, Kent, OH 44242-0001. Offers art education (MA); art history (MA); crafts (MA), including glass (MA, MFA); fine arts (MA), including fashion; studio art (MFA), including ceramics, drawing, glass (MA, MFA), jewelry, metals and enameling, painting, print media and photography, sculpture, textiles. *Accreditation:* NASAD (one or more programs are accredited). *Program availability:* Part-time, online learning. *Faculty:* 24 full-time (13 women), 3 part-time/adjunct (all women). *Students:* 40 full-time (27 women), 22 part-time (19 women); includes 3 minority (2 Black or African American, non-Hispanic/Latino; 1 Two or more races, non-Hispanic/Latino). Average age 31. 40 applicants, 75% accepted, 23 enrolled. In 2017, 22 master's awarded. *Degree requirements:* For master's, comprehensive exam, thesis (for some programs), 1 foreign language (for art history); final project (for crafts and fine arts). *Entrance requirements:* For master's, transcripts, goal statement, 3 letters of recommendation, curriculum vitae, portfolio. Additional exam requirements/recommendations for international students: Required—TOEFL (minimum score 550 paper-based, 79 iBT), Michigan English Language Assessment Battery (minimum score 77), IELTS (minimum score 6.5) or PTE (minimum score 58). *Application deadline:* For fall admission, 2/2 for domestic and international students; for spring admission, 10/15 for domestic and international students. Applications are processed on a rolling basis. Application fee: $45 ($70 for international students). Electronic applications accepted. *Expenses:* Tuition, state resident: full-time $11,310; part-time $515 per credit hour. Tuition, nonresident: full-time $20,396; part-time $928 per credit hour. *International tuition:* $18,544 full-time. *Financial support:* Career-related internships or fieldwork, scholarships/grants, and unspecified assistantships available. Financial award application deadline: 3/16. *Unit head:* Marie Bukowski, Director, 330-672-2192, E-mail: mbukows1@kent.edu. *Application contact:* Linda Hoeptner Poling, Graduate Coordinator and Associate Professor of Art Education, 330-672-7895, E-mail: lhoeptne@kent.edu.
Website: http://www.kent.edu/art

Laguna College of Art & Design, Graduate Program, Laguna Beach, CA 92651-1136. Offers painting (MFA). *Accreditation:* NASAD. *Entrance requirements:* For master's, BA with a studio concentration or BFA, minimum GPA of 3.0 in studio subjects, portfolio, resume. Additional exam requirements/recommendations for international students: Required—TOEFL (minimum score 550 paper-based). Electronic applications accepted.

Lake Forest College, Graduate Program in Liberal Studies, Lake Forest, IL 60045. Offers American studies (MLS); cinema in East Asia (MLS); environmental studies (MLS); history (MLS); Medieval and Renaissance art (MLS); philosophy (MLS); Spanish (MLS); writing (MLS). *Program availability:* Part-time, evening/weekend. *Faculty:* 11 full-time (3 women). *Students:* 34 part-time (19 women); includes 3 minority (1 Asian, non-Hispanic/Latino; 2 Hispanic/Latino). Average age 36. 20 applicants, 55% accepted, 8 enrolled. In 2017, 5 master's awarded. *Degree requirements:* For master's, thesis optional, 8 courses, including at least 3 interdisciplinary seminars. *Entrance requirements:* For master's, transcript, essay, interview. Additional exam requirements/recommendations for international students: Required—TOEFL (minimum score 550 paper-based; 83 iBT); Recommended—IELTS (minimum score 6.5). *Application deadline:* For fall admission, 7/15 priority date for domestic students, 6/1 priority date for international students; for spring admission, 12/1 priority date for domestic students, 10/1 priority date for international students. Applications are processed on a rolling basis. Application fee: $30. Electronic applications accepted. *Expenses:* $2,650 per course. *Financial support:* In 2017–18, 2 students received support. Partial tuition grants (for full-time teachers) available. *Faculty research:* Religion in America, Asian philosophy, cinema studies, theater studies, sociology of religion. *Unit head:* Prof. D. L. LeMahieu, Director, 847-735-5133, Fax: 847-735-6291, E-mail: lemahieu@lakeforest.edu. *Application contact:* Prof. Carol Gayle, Associate Director, 847-735-5083, Fax: 847-735-6291, E-mail: gayle@lakeforest.edu.
Website: http://www.lakeforest.edu/academics/programs/mls/

Lake Forest College, Master of Arts in Teaching Program, Lake Forest, IL 60045. Offers elementary education (MAT); K-12 French (MAT); K-12 music (MAT); K-12 Spanish (MAT); K-12 visual art (MAT); secondary biology (MAT); secondary chemistry (MAT); secondary English (MAT); secondary history (MAT); secondary mathematics

(MAT). *Degree requirements:* For master's, comprehensive exam, portfolio. *Entrance requirements:* For master's, GRE.

Lee University, Program in Education, Cleveland, TN 37320-3450. Offers art (MAT); curriculum and instruction (M Ed, Ed S); early childhood (MAT); educational leadership (M Ed, Ed S); elementary education (MAT); English and math (MAT); English and science (MAT); English and social studies (MAT); higher education administration (MS); history (MAT); history and economics (MAT); math and science (MAT); math and social studies (MAT); middle grades (MAT); science and social studies (MASW); secondary education (MAT); Spanish (MAT); special education (M Ed, MAT); TESOL (MAT). *Accreditation:* NCATE. *Program availability:* Part-time. *Faculty:* 15 full-time (7 women), 8 part-time/adjunct (3 women). *Students:* 28 full-time (21 women), 77 part-time (48 women); includes 12 minority (7 Black or African American, non-Hispanic/Latino; 2 Hispanic/Latino; 3 Two or more races, non-Hispanic/Latino), 1 international. Average age 31. 35 applicants, 83% accepted, 22 enrolled. In 2017, 54 master's, 4 other advanced degrees awarded. *Degree requirements:* For master's, variable foreign language requirement, thesis optional, internship. *Entrance requirements:* For master's, MAT or GRE General Test, minimum undergraduate GPA of 2.75, 3 letters of recommendation, interview, writing sample, official transcripts, background check; for Ed S, minimum undergraduate and master's GPA of 2.75, official transcripts for undergraduate and master's degrees. Additional exam requirements/recommendations for international students: Required—TOEFL (minimum score 61 iBT). *Application deadline:* For fall admission, 6/1 priority date for domestic and international students; for spring admission, 11/1 priority date for domestic and international students; for summer admission, 4/1 priority date for domestic and international students. Applications are processed on a rolling basis. Application fee: $25. Electronic applications accepted. *Expenses: Tuition:* Full-time $12,780; part-time $710 per credit hour. *Required fees:* $60; $60 per term. Tuition and fees vary according to program. *Financial support:* In 2017–18, 32 students received support. Career-related internships or fieldwork, Federal Work-Study, institutionally sponsored loans, scholarships/grants, and unspecified assistantships available. Financial award application deadline: 3/1; financial award applicants required to submit FAFSA. *Unit head:* Dr. William Kamm, Director, 423-614-8544, E-mail: wkamm@leeuniversity.edu. *Application contact:* Crystal Keeter, Graduate Education Secretary, 423-614-8544, E-mail: ckeeter@leeuniversity.edu.
Website: http://www.leeuniversity.edu/academics/graduate/education

Lehman College of the City University of New York, School of Arts and Humanities, Department of Art, Bronx, NY 10468-1589. Offers MA, MFA. *Program availability:* Part-time, evening/weekend. *Entrance requirements:* For master's, 33 undergraduate credits in art, interview, portfolio. *Faculty research:* Graphic art, modern and contemporary art, sculpture, primitive and pre-Columbian art, medieval art.

Lesley University, College of Art and Design, Cambridge, MA 02138-2790. Offers photography (MFA); visual arts (MFA). *Program availability:* Part-time. *Degree requirements:* For master's, thesis, final exhibition of thesis work. *Entrance requirements:* For master's, portfolio, resume, personal statement. Additional exam requirements/recommendations for international students: Required—TOEFL (minimum score 550 paper-based; 80 iBT). Electronic applications accepted. *Faculty research:* Graphic design; Web and multimedia design; book, advertising and editorial illustration; animation; documentary photography; photojournalism; fine arts photography; fine arts; art education.

Lesley University, Graduate School of Education, Cambridge, MA 02138-2790. Offers arts, community, and education (M Ed); autism studies (Certificate); curriculum and instruction (M Ed, CAGS); early childhood education (M Ed); ecological teaching and learning (MS); educational studies (PhD), including adult learning, educational leadership, individually designed; elementary education (M Ed); emergent technologies for educators (Certificate); ESLArts: language learning through the arts (M Ed); high school education (M Ed); individually designed (M Ed); integrated teaching through the arts (M Ed); literacy for K-8 classroom teachers (M Ed); mathematics education (M Ed); middle school education (M Ed); moderate disabilities (M Ed); online learning (Certificate); reading (CAGS); science in education (M Ed); severe disabilities (M Ed); special needs (CAGS); specialist teacher of reading (M Ed); teacher of visual art (M Ed); technology in education (M Ed, CAGS). *Accreditation:* TEAC. *Program availability:* Part-time, evening/weekend, online learning. *Degree requirements:* For master's, practicum; for doctorate, thesis/dissertation. *Entrance requirements:* For master's, Massachusetts Tests for Educator Licensure (MTEL), transcripts, statement of purpose, recommendations; interview (for special education); for doctorate, GRE General Test, transcripts, statement of purpose, recommendations, interview, master's degree, resume; for other advanced degree, interview, master's degree. Additional exam requirements/recommendations for international students: Required—TOEFL (minimum score 550 paper-based; 80 iBT). Electronic applications accepted. *Faculty research:* Assessment in literacy, mathematics and science; autism spectrum disorders; instructional technology and online learning; multicultural education and English language learners.

Liberty University, School of Visual and Performing Arts, Lynchburg, VA 24515. Offers graphic design (MFA); studio art (MFA); visual communication design (MA). *Students:* 37 full-time (19 women), 24 part-time (17 women); includes 9 minority (3 Black or African American, non-Hispanic/Latino; 1 Asian, non-Hispanic/Latino; 1 Hispanic/Latino; 4 Two or more races, non-Hispanic/Latino), 2 international. Average age 31. 109 applicants, 23% accepted, 12 enrolled. In 2017, 12 master's awarded. Application fee: $50. Electronic applications accepted. *Unit head:* Scott Hayes, Dean, E-mail: smhayes@liberty.edu. *Application contact:* Jay Bridge, Director of Admissions, 800-424-9595, Fax: 800-628-7977, E-mail: gradadmissions@liberty.edu.

Long Island University–LIU Post, College of Arts, Communications and Design, Brookville, NY 11548-1300. Offers art (MA); clinical art therapy (MA); clinical art therapy and counseling (MA); digital game design and development (MA); fine arts and design (MFA); interactive multimedia arts (MA); museum studies (MA); music (MA); theatre (MFA). *Faculty:* 22 full-time (10 women), 44 part-time/adjunct (24 women). *Students:* 99 full-time (80 women), 14 part-time (12 women); includes 22 minority (7 Black or African American, non-Hispanic/Latino; 4 Asian, non-Hispanic/Latino; 9 Hispanic/Latino; 2 Two or more races, non-Hispanic/Latino), 23 international. Average age 28. 125 applicants, 70% accepted, 42 enrolled. In 2017, 55 master's awarded. *Degree requirements:* For master's, variable foreign language requirement, comprehensive exam (for some programs), thesis. *Entrance requirements:* For master's, performance audition or portfolio. Additional exam requirements/recommendations for international students: Required—TOEFL (minimum score 550 paper-based; 79 iBT). *Application deadline:* Applications are processed on a rolling basis. Application fee: $50. Electronic applications accepted. *Expenses: Tuition:* Full-time $21,618; part-time $1201 per credit. *Required fees:* $1840; $920 per term. Tuition and fees vary according to course load. *Financial support:* In 2017–18, 78 students received support. Career-related internships or fieldwork, scholarships/grants, tuition waivers (full and partial), and unspecified assistantships available. Support available to part-time students. Financial award application deadline: 2/15; financial award applicants required to submit FAFSA. *Faculty research:* Creative writing, playwriting, music composition, music performance, international impact of art therapy, artistic creation. *Unit head:* Steven Breese, Dean, 516-299-2309, E-mail: steven.breese@liu.edu. *Application contact:* Rita Langdon, Graduate Admissions, 516-299-2334, Fax: 516-299-2137, E-mail: post-enroll@liu.edu.
Website: http://www.liu.edu/CWPost/Academics/School-of-Visual-Arts-Communications-and-Digital-Technologies

Louisiana State University and Agricultural & Mechanical College, Graduate School, College of Art and Design, School of Art, Program in Studio Art, Baton Rouge, LA 70803. Offers ceramics (MFA); graphic design (MFA); painting and drawing (MFA); photography (MFA); printmaking (MFA); sculpture (MFA). *Accreditation:* NASAD. *Students:* 36 full-time (20 women), 1 (woman) part-time; includes 1 minority (Hispanic/Latino), 5 international. Average age 29. 58 applicants, 24% accepted, 13 enrolled. In 2017, 13 master's awarded.

Louisiana Tech University, Graduate School, College of Liberal Arts, Ruston, LA 71272. Offers architecture (M Arch); art (MFA), including graphic design, photography, studio; audiology (Au D); communication (MA), including speech communication, theatre; English (MA), including literature, technical writing; history (MA); speech pathology (MA); technical writing and communication (Graduate Certificate). *Program availability:* Part-time. *Faculty:* 63 full-time (25 women), 5 part-time/adjunct (3 women). *Students:* 114 full-time (29 women), 31 part-time (19 women); includes 12 minority (4 Black or African American, non-Hispanic/Latino; 1 Asian, non-Hispanic/Latino; 3 Hispanic/Latino; 4 Two or more races, non-Hispanic/Latino), 5 international. Average age 30. 146 applicants, 59% accepted, 37 enrolled. In 2017, 49 master's, 3 doctorates awarded. *Degree requirements:* For master's, thesis (for some programs); for doctorate, thesis/dissertation. *Entrance requirements:* For master's, GRE General Test; for doctorate, GRE General Test, bachelor's degree, minimum GPA of 3.0 or 3.2 on last 60 hours attempted. Additional exam requirements/recommendations for international students: Required—TOEFL (minimum score 550 paper-based; 80 iBT), IELTS (minimum score 6.5). *Application deadline:* For fall admission, 8/1 priority date for domestic students, 6/1 for international students; for winter admission, 11/1 priority date for domestic students, 9/1 for international students; for spring admission, 2/1 priority date for domestic students, 12/1 for international students; for summer admission, 5/1 priority date for domestic students, 3/1 for international students. Application fee: $40 ($50 for international students). Electronic applications accepted. *Expenses:* Tuition, state resident: full-time $5146. Tuition, nonresident: full-time $10,147. *International tuition:* $10,267 full-time. *Required fees:* $2273. *Financial support:* In 2017–18, 63 students received support, including 46 research assistantships (averaging $5,229 per year), 7 teaching assistantships (averaging $5,543 per year); fellowships, career-related internships or fieldwork, Federal Work-Study, institutionally sponsored loans, tuition waivers (partial), and unspecified assistantships also available. Financial award application deadline: 2/1. *Faculty research:* Contributing to the expansion of historical and social scientific knowledge and understanding through original research and publication; diverse language, ethnic, cultural, and socioeconomic backgrounds with disorders of speech, language, swallowing, hearing, and cognitive aspects of communication; prevention of communication, swallowing, and hearing disorders. *Unit head:* Dr. Donald P. Kaczvinsky, Dean, 318-257-4805, Fax: 318-257-3935, E-mail: dkaczv@latech.edu. *Application contact:* Mary Green, Administrative Assistant, 318-257-2924, Fax: 318-257-4487, E-mail: meg@latech.edu.
Website: http://liberalarts.latech.edu/

Loyola Marymount University, College of Communication and Fine Arts, Los Angeles, CA 90045-2659. Offers MA. *Faculty:* 5 full-time (4 women), 14 part-time/adjunct (13 women). *Students:* 50 full-time (47 women); includes 24 minority (1 Black or African American, non-Hispanic/Latino; 7 Asian, non-Hispanic/Latino; 13 Hispanic/Latino; 3 Two or more races, non-Hispanic/Latino). Average age 28. 53 applicants, 53% accepted, 23 enrolled. In 2017, 24 master's awarded. *Entrance requirements:* For master's, official transcripts, letters of recommendation. Additional exam requirements/recommendations for international students: Required—TOEFL, IELTS. Application fee: $50. Electronic applications accepted. *Financial support:* Research assistantships, career-related internships or fieldwork, institutionally sponsored loans, scholarships/grants, and unspecified assistantships available. Financial award application deadline: 5/1; financial award applicants required to submit FAFSA. *Unit head:* Dr. Bryant Keith Alexander, Dean, College of Communication and Fine Arts, 310-338-7430, E-mail: bryantkeithalexander@lmu.edu. *Application contact:* Chake H. Kouyoumjian, Associate Dean of Graduate Studies, 310-338-2721, Fax: 310-338-6086, E-mail: graduateinfo@lmu.edu.
Website: http://cfa.lmu.edu

Maine College of Art, Program in Studio Art, Portland, ME 04101. Offers MA, MFA. *Accreditation:* NASAD. *Degree requirements:* For master's, thesis, studio thesis exhibition. *Entrance requirements:* Additional exam requirements/recommendations for international students: Required—TOEFL (minimum score 550 paper-based). Electronic applications accepted.

Maryland Institute College of Art, Graduate Studies, LeRoy E. Hoffberger School of Painting, Baltimore, MD 21201. Offers MFA. *Accreditation:* NASAD. *Degree requirements:* For master's, thesis, exhibit and thesis documentation. *Entrance requirements:* For master's, portfolio, bachelor's degree in any field. Additional exam requirements/recommendations for international students: Required—TOEFL (minimum score 550 paper-based; 80 iBT), IELTS (minimum score 6.5). Electronic applications accepted. *Expenses:* Contact institution.

Maryland Institute College of Art, Graduate Studies, Mount Royal School of Art, Baltimore, MD 21217. Offers painting (MFA). *Degree requirements:* For master's, thesis, exhibit and thesis documentation. *Entrance requirements:* For master's, 40 credits in studio art, bachelor's degree in any field. Additional exam requirements/recommendations for international students: Required—TOEFL (minimum score 550 paper-based; 80 iBT), IELTS (minimum score 6.5). Electronic applications accepted. *Expenses:* Contact institution.

Maryland Institute College of Art, Graduate Studies, MPS Program in Business of Art and Design, Baltimore, MD 21201. Offers MPS. *Program availability:* Part-time. *Degree requirements:* For master's, business plan presentation. *Entrance requirements:* For master's, essay, resume. Additional exam requirements/recommendations for international students: Required—TOEFL (minimum score 550 paper-based; 80 iBT), IELTS (minimum score 6.5). Electronic applications accepted. *Expenses:* Contact institution.

Maryland Institute College of Art, Graduate Studies, Post Baccalaureate Certificate Program in Fine Arts, Baltimore, MD 21201. Offers Postbaccalaureate Certificate. *Degree requirements:* For Postbaccalaureate Certificate, thesis, exhibition and documentation. *Entrance requirements:* For degree, portfolio, 40 studio credits, 6 credits in art history. Additional exam requirements/recommendations for international students: Required—TOEFL (minimum score 550 paper-based; 80 iBT), IELTS (minimum score 6.5). Electronic applications accepted. *Expenses:* Contact institution.

Maryland Institute College of Art, Graduate Studies, Program in Community Arts, Baltimore, MD 21201. Offers MFA. *Program availability:* Part-time. *Degree requirements:* For master's, thesis, exhibition and thesis documentation. *Entrance requirements:* For master's, portfolio, bachelor's degree in any field. Additional exam requirements/recommendations for international students: Required—TOEFL (minimum score 550 paper-based; 80 iBT), IELTS (minimum score 6.5). Electronic applications accepted. *Expenses:* Contact institution.

Maryland Institute College of Art, Graduate Studies, Program in Studio Art, Baltimore, MD 21201. Offers MFA. Offered during summer only. *Degree requirements:* For

master's, thesis, exhibition, final paper. *Entrance requirements:* For master's, portfolio, 40 studio credits, 6 credits in art history, bachelor's degree in any field. Additional exam requirements/recommendations for international students: Required—TOEFL (minimum score 550 paper-based; 80 iBT), IELTS (minimum score 6.5). Electronic applications accepted. *Expenses:* Contact institution.

Maryland Institute College of Art, Graduate Studies, Rinehart School of Sculpture, Baltimore, MD 21201. Offers MFA. *Accreditation:* NASAD. *Degree requirements:* For master's, thesis, exhibition. *Entrance requirements:* For master's, portfolio, bachelor's degree in any field. Additional exam requirements/recommendations for international students: Required—TOEFL (minimum score 550 paper-based; 80 iBT), IELTS (minimum score 6.5). Electronic applications accepted. *Expenses:* Contact institution.

Marywood University, Academic Affairs, Insalaco College of Creative and Performing Arts, Art Department, Program in Studio Art, Scranton, PA 18509-1598. Offers clay (MA); painting (MA); photography (MA); printmaking (MA); sculpture (MA). *Accreditation:* NASAD. Electronic applications accepted. *Faculty research:* Texture and line in clay, cast bronze sculpture, color theories, book art and illustration, sculptural form.

Marywood University, Academic Affairs, Insalaco College of Creative and Performing Arts, Art Department, Program in Visual Arts, Scranton, PA 18509-1598. Offers clay (MFA); graphic design (MFA); illustration (MFA); painting (MFA); photography (MFA); printmaking (MFA); sculpture (MFA). *Accreditation:* NASAD. *Program availability:* Part-time. Electronic applications accepted. *Expenses:* Contact institution.

Massachusetts College of Art and Design, Graduate Programs, MFA Program, Boston, MA 02115-5882. Offers 2D fine arts (MFA), including painting, printmaking; 3D fine arts (MFA), including ceramics, fibers, glass, jewelry and metalsmithing, sculpture; design (MFA, Postbaccalaureate Certificate), including dynamic media; fine arts (MFA), including interdisciplinary; media arts (MFA, Postbaccalaureate Certificate), including film/video (MFA), photography. *Accreditation:* NASAD. *Faculty:* 28 full-time (8 women), 28 part-time/adjunct (17 women). *Students:* 44 full-time (26 women), 28 part-time (17 women); includes 8 minority (5 Asian, non-Hispanic/Latino; 3 Hispanic/Latino), 18 international. 247 applicants, 52% accepted, 47 enrolled. In 2017, 42 master's, 5 other advanced degrees awarded. *Degree requirements:* For master's, thesis, thesis exhibition (for fine arts programs); thesis project and document (for design/dynamic media program). *Entrance requirements:* For master's, portfolio, college transcripts, resume, statement of purpose, letters of reference, interview, 6 credits of art history taken prior to or during MFA program; for Postbaccalaureate Certificate, portfolio, college transcripts, resume, statement of purpose, letters of reference, interview. Additional exam requirements/recommendations for international students: Required—TOEFL (minimum score 550 paper-based, 85 iBT) or IELTS (6). *Application deadline:* For fall admission, 1/4 priority date for domestic and international students; for summer admission, 1/4 priority date for domestic and international students. Applications are processed on a rolling basis. Application fee: $90. Electronic applications accepted. *Expenses:* $780 per credit. *Financial support:* In 2017–18, 51 students received support, including 1 research assistantship (averaging $2,160 per year), 33 teaching assistantships (averaging $2,160 per year); fellowships, career-related internships or fieldwork, scholarships/grants, tuition waivers (partial), unspecified assistantships, and adjunct co-teaching positions also available. Support available to part-time students. Financial award application deadline: 1/4; financial award applicants required to submit FAFSA. *Faculty research:* Painting and printmaking, sculpture, photography, film and video, dynamic media design. *Unit head:* Paul Paturzo, Dean of Graduate Studies, 617-879-7166, E-mail: pjpaturzo@massart.edu. *Application contact:* Lauren O'Neill, Assistant Director of Graduate Admissions, 617-879-7222, E-mail: gradadmissions@massart.edu.
Website: http://www.massart.edu/Admissions/Graduate_Programs.html

Miami University, College of Creative Arts, Department of Art, Oxford, OH 45056. Offers art education (MA); studio art (MFA). *Accreditation:* NASAD (one or more programs are accredited). *Students:* 16 full-time (8 women), 2 part-time (both women); includes 3 minority (1 Black or African American, non-Hispanic/Latino; 1 Asian, non-Hispanic/Latino; 1 Two or more races, non-Hispanic/Latino), 4 international. Average age 33. In 2017, 10 master's awarded. *Expenses:* Tuition, state resident: full-time $13,812; part-time $575 per credit hour. Tuition, nonresident: full-time $30,860; part-time $1286 per credit hour. *Unit head:* Rob Robbins, Chair and Professor, 513-529-2900, E-mail: art@miamioh.edu.
Website: http://www.MiamiOH.edu/art

Michigan State University, The Graduate School, College of Arts and Letters, Department of Art and Art History, East Lansing, MI 48824. Offers studio art (MFA). *Entrance requirements:* For master's, minimum GPA of 3.0, portfolio, resume. Additional exam requirements/recommendations for international students: Required—TOEFL, Michigan State University ELT (minimum score 85), Michigan English Language Assessment Battery (minimum score 83). Electronic applications accepted.

Millersville University of Pennsylvania, College of Graduate Studies and Adult Learning, College of Arts, Humanities and Social Sciences, Department of Art and Design, Millersville, PA 17551-0302. Offers art education (M Ed). *Accreditation:* NASAD; NCATE. *Program availability:* Part-time. *Faculty:* 3 full-time (all women), 3 part-time/adjunct (2 women). *Students:* 3 full-time (2 women), 11 part-time (9 women); includes 3 minority (2 Asian, non-Hispanic/Latino; 1 Hispanic/Latino). Average age 34. 5 applicants, 100% accepted, 1 enrolled. In 2017, 8 master's awarded. *Degree requirements:* For master's, comprehensive exam, thesis optional. *Entrance requirements:* For master's, teaching certificate (unless enrolled in post baccalaureate certificate at same time); portfolio (if not MU graduate); minimum undergraduate and post baccalaureate GPA of 3.0 cumulative, 3.25 in art and art education courses; three letters of recommendation; professional goals as stated by the applicant. Additional exam requirements/recommendations for international students: Required—TOEFL (minimum score 80 iBT), IELTS (minimum score 6.5), PTE (minimum score 60). *Application deadline:* Applications are processed on a rolling basis. Application fee: $40. Electronic applications accepted. *Expenses:* $500 per credit resident tuition and fees; $750 per credit non-resident tuition and fees; $114.75 per credit general fee (maximum of 12 credits); technology fee $27 per credit (resident), $39 per credit (non-resident). *Financial support:* Unspecified assistantships available. Financial award application deadline: 3/15; financial award applicants required to submit FAFSA. *Faculty research:* Ceramics; representational painting; material investigations involving bronze casting, steel forming and fabrication, mold-making, wood working; art educator's professional learning, assessment in the arts, and postmodern; interactive design fundamentals, interdisciplinary design, interaction, visual storytelling and digital narrative forms and choice-based approaches to teaching art. *Unit head:* Deborah S. Sigel, Chairperson, 717-871-7248, Fax: 717-871-2004, E-mail: deborah.sigel@millersville.edu. *Application contact:* Dr. Victor S. DeSantis, Dean of College of Graduate Studies and Adult Learning/Associate Provost for Civic and Community Engagement, 717-871-7619, Fax: 717-871-7954, E-mail: victor.desantis@millersville.edu.
Website: http://www.millersville.edu/art/

Mills College, Graduate Studies, Department of Art, Oakland, CA 94613-1000. Offers art (MFA); ceramics (MFA); intermedia (MFA); painting (MFA); photography (MFA); sculpture (MFA). *Faculty:* 3 full-time (2 women), 5 part-time/adjunct (3 women). *Students:* 20 full-time (11 women); includes 4 minority (1 Asian, non-Hispanic/Latino; 2 Hispanic/Latino; 1

Two or more races, non-Hispanic/Latino). Average age 30. 31 applicants, 74% accepted, 9 enrolled. In 2017, 9 master's awarded. *Degree requirements:* For master's, thesis or alternative, exhibit. *Entrance requirements:* For master's, portfolio, artist statement. Additional exam requirements/recommendations for international students: Required—TOEFL (minimum score 550 paper-based; 80 iBT) or IELTS (minimum score 6). *Application deadline:* For fall admission, 2/1 for domestic students, 12/15 for international students. Application fee: $50. Electronic applications accepted. *Expenses:* Contact institution. *Financial support:* In 2017–18, 21 students received support, including 21 fellowships with partial tuition reimbursements available (averaging $11,386 per year), 8 teaching assistantships with partial tuition reimbursements available; scholarships/grants and unspecified assistantships also available. Financial award application deadline: 2/1; financial award applicants required to submit FAFSA. *Faculty research:* Experimental film and video, public art projects, ecological design, contemporary art philosophy, sound installations. *Unit head:* Catherine Wagner, Professor of Studio Art, 510-430-3288. *Application contact:* Robynne Lofton, Director of Admissions, 510-430-3295, Fax: 510-430-2159, E-mail: grad-admission@mills.edu.
Website: http://www.mills.edu/art

Minneapolis College of Art and Design, Certificate Programs, Minneapolis, MN 55404-4347. Offers graphic design (Certificate); media (Certificate); sustainable design (Certificate). *Program availability:* Part-time, 100% online, blended/hybrid learning. *Faculty:* 42 full-time (29 women). *Students:* 29 full-time (21 women), 5 part-time (all women); includes 6 minority (2 Black or African American, non-Hispanic/Latino; 1 Asian, non-Hispanic/Latino; 3 Hispanic/Latino), 1 international. In 2017, 15 Certificates awarded. *Degree requirements:* For Certificate, final project. *Entrance requirements:* For degree, resume, portfolio, letter of recommendation. Additional exam requirements/recommendations for international students: Required—TOEFL (minimum score 550 paper-based; 79 iBT). *Application deadline:* For fall admission, 1/15 for domestic and international students; for spring admission, 10/15 for domestic and international students. Application fee: $50. Electronic applications accepted. *Expenses:* Tuition: Full-time $38,670. *Required fees:* $450. One-time fee: $300 full-time. *Financial support:* Career-related internships or fieldwork and scholarships/grants available. Financial award application deadline: 3/15; financial award applicants required to submit FAFSA. *Faculty research:* Visual arts. *Unit head:* Lara Roy, Senior Director of Continuing Education, 612-874-3778, E-mail: continuing_education@mcad.edu.
Website: http://www.mcad.edu/showPage.php?pageID-1216

Minneapolis College of Art and Design, Program in Visual Studies, Minneapolis, MN 55404-4347. Offers animation (MFA); comic art (MFA); drawing (MFA); filmmaking (MFA); fine arts (MFA); furniture design (MFA); graphic design (MFA); illustration (MFA); interactive media (MFA); painting (MFA); photography (MFA); printmaking (MFA); sculpture (MFA). *Accreditation:* NASAD. *Program availability:* Part-time. *Faculty:* 42 full-time (13 women). *Students:* 30 full-time (23 women); includes 3 minority (2 Asian, non-Hispanic/Latino; 1 Hispanic/Latino), 13 international. 166 applicants, 28% accepted, 12 enrolled. In 2017, 10 master's awarded. *Degree requirements:* For master's, thesis, thesis exhibit. *Entrance requirements:* For master's, portfolio of visual artwork, resume, 3 letters of recommendation. Additional exam requirements/recommendations for international students: Required—TOEFL (minimum score 550 paper-based; 79 iBT). *Application deadline:* For fall admission, 1/15 for domestic and international students. Application fee: $50. Electronic applications accepted. *Expenses:* Tuition: Full-time $38,670. *Required fees:* $450. One-time fee: $300 full-time. *Financial support:* In 2017–18, 23 students received support, including 15 teaching assistantships (averaging $6,000 per year); career-related internships or fieldwork, Federal Work-Study, scholarships/grants, and unspecified assistantships also available. Support available to part-time students. Financial award application deadline: 3/15; financial award applicants required to submit FAFSA. *Faculty research:* Visual arts: animation, comic art, drawing, filmmaking, furniture design, graphic design, illustration, interactive media, painting, photography, printmaking, sculpture. *Unit head:* Graduate Director, 612-209-1471, E-mail: admissions@mcad.edu. *Application contact:* Mary Kazura, Associate Director of Admissions, 612-874-3760, Fax: 612-874-3701, E-mail: mary_kazura@mcad.edu.
Website: http://mcad.edu/mfa

Minnesota State University Mankato, College of Graduate Studies and Research, College of Arts and Humanities, Department of Art, Mankato, MN 56001. Offers art (MA); art education (MAT). *Accreditation:* NASAD (one or more programs are accredited). *Program availability:* Part-time. *Degree requirements:* For master's, one foreign language, comprehensive exam, thesis or alternative. *Entrance requirements:* For master's, portfolio, three letters of reference. Additional exam requirements/recommendations for international students: Required—TOEFL. Electronic applications accepted.

Mississippi College, Graduate School, College of Arts and Sciences, School of Christian Studies and the Arts, Department of Art, Clinton, MS 39058. Offers M Ed, MA, MFA. *Program availability:* Part-time, evening/weekend. *Degree requirements:* For master's, one foreign language, comprehensive exam, thesis (for some programs). *Entrance requirements:* For master's, GRE or NTE, minimum GPA of 2.5. Additional exam requirements/recommendations for international students: Recommended—TOEFL, IELTS. Electronic applications accepted.

Missouri State University, Graduate College, College of Arts and Letters, Department of Art and Design, Springfield, MO 65897. Offers visual studies (MFA). *Program availability:* Part-time. *Faculty:* 14 full-time (7 women). *Students:* 5 full-time (2 women), 8 part-time (6 women); includes 1 minority (Two or more races, non-Hispanic/Latino), 4 international. Average age 37. 5 applicants, 60% accepted, 3 enrolled. In 2017, 4 master's awarded. *Degree requirements:* For master's, comprehensive exam, thesis, exhibition. *Entrance requirements:* For master's, digital portfolio; 300- to 800-word statement describing reasons and goals behind applicant's interest in graduate study and direction of intended research; at least three letters of recommendation from individuals able to speak of applicant's academic achievements and potential. Additional exam requirements/recommendations for international students: Required—TOEFL (minimum score 550 paper-based; 79 iBT), IELTS (minimum score 6). *Application deadline:* For fall admission, 7/20 priority date for domestic students, 5/1 for international students; for spring admission, 12/20 priority date for domestic students, 9/1 for international students. Applications are processed on a rolling basis. Application fee: $35 ($50 for international students). Electronic applications accepted. *Expenses:* Tuition, state resident: full-time $2915; part-time $2021 per credit hour. Tuition, nonresident: full-time $5354; part-time $3647 per credit hour. *International tuition:* $11,992 full-time. *Required fees:* $173; $173 per credit hour. Tuition and fees vary according to class time, course level, course load, degree level, campus/location and program. *Financial support:* In 2017–18, 5 teaching assistantships with full tuition reimbursements (averaging $8,772 per year) were awarded; Federal Work-Study and unspecified assistantships also available. Financial award application deadline: 3/31; financial award applicants required to submit FAFSA. *Unit head:* Vonda Yarberry, Interim Department Head, 417-837-2330, E-mail: artanddesign@missouristate.edu. *Application contact:* Stephanie Praschan, Director, Graduate Enrollment Management, 417-836-5330, Fax: 417-836-6200, E-mail: stephaniepraschan@missouristate.edu.
Website: http://art.missouristate.edu/

Montana State University, The Graduate School, College of Arts and Architecture, School of Art, Bozeman, MT 59717. Offers art (MFA); art history (MA). *Accreditation:*

NASAD (one or more programs are accredited). *Program availability:* Part-time. *Degree requirements:* For master's, comprehensive exam, thesis. *Entrance requirements:* For master's, GRE General Test, undergraduate degree in art. Additional exam requirements/recommendations for international students: Required—TOEFL (minimum score 550 paper-based). Electronic applications accepted. *Faculty research:* Encaustic painting, wild clay research, environmentally friendly kiln fuel, Roman wall paintings, French revolutionary portraiture.

Montclair State University, The Graduate School, College of the Arts, Program in Fine Art, Montclair, NJ 07043-1624. Offers museum management (MA); studio (MA). *Accreditation:* NASAD. *Program availability:* Part-time, evening/weekend. *Degree requirements:* For master's, project. *Entrance requirements:* For master's, GRE or MAT, 2 letters of recommendation, essay. Electronic applications accepted.

Montclair State University, The Graduate School, College of the Arts, Program in Studio Art, Montclair, NJ 07043-1624. Offers MFA. *Accreditation:* NASAD. *Program availability:* Part-time, evening/weekend. *Degree requirements:* For master's, project. *Entrance requirements:* For master's, 2 letters of recommendation, essay. Additional exam requirements/recommendations for international students: Required—TOEFL (minimum score 83 iBT), IELTS (minimum score 6.5). Electronic applications accepted.

Moore College of Art & Design, Program in Studio Art, Philadelphia, PA 19103. Offers MFA. *Accreditation:* NASAD. *Degree requirements:* For master's, thesis. *Entrance requirements:* For master's, bachelor's degree in visual arts or another field with completion of 15 art history credits; minimum GPA of 3.0; on-site interview; portfolio; 3 letters of recommendation; resume.

Morehead State University, Graduate Programs, Caudill College of Arts, Humanities and Social Sciences, Department of Art and Design, Morehead, KY 40351. Offers art education (MA); graphic design (MA); studio art (MA). *Accreditation:* NASAD. *Program availability:* Part-time, evening/weekend. *Degree requirements:* For master's, comprehensive exam, thesis (for some programs), oral exam during exhibition. *Entrance requirements:* For master's, GRE General Test, minimum undergraduate GPA of 3.0 in major, 2.5 overall; portfolio; bachelor's degree in art. Additional exam requirements/recommendations for international students: Required—TOEFL (minimum score 500 paper-based). Electronic applications accepted. *Faculty research:* Computer art, painting, drawing, ceramics, photography.

New Hampshire Institute of Art, Graduate Studies, Manchester, NH 03104. Offers art education (MA); creative writing (MFA); photography (MFA); teaching visual arts (MAT); visual arts (MFA). *Accreditation:* NASAD. *Faculty:* 31 part-time/adjunct (14 women). *Students:* 59 full-time (42 women), 6 part-time (3 women); includes 2 minority (1 Asian, non-Hispanic/Latino; 1 Hispanic/Latino). Average age 43. 33 applicants, 36% accepted, 5 enrolled. In 2017, 2 master's awarded. *Degree requirements:* For master's, thesis, corresponding exhibition and artist talk. *Entrance requirements:* For master's, writing sample or visual art portfolio; curriculum vitae; transcripts; letters of recommendation. Additional exam requirements/recommendations for international students: Required—TOEFL (minimum score 550 paper-based; 80 iBT), IELTS (minimum score 6.5). *Application deadline:* For fall admission, 5/1 priority date for domestic students; for spring admission, 11/1 priority date for domestic students. Applications are processed on a rolling basis. Application fee: $75. Electronic applications accepted. *Expenses:* Contact institution. *Financial support:* In 2017–18, 2 teaching assistantships (averaging $1,200 per year) were awarded; scholarships/grants and unspecified assistantships also available. Support available to part-time students. Financial award application deadline: 6/1; financial award applicants required to submit FAFSA. *Faculty research:* Fine arts - visual arts, photography, creative writing; art education. *Unit head:* Lucinda Bliss, Dean of Graduate Studies, 603-836-2522, E-mail: lucindabliss@nhia.edu. *Application contact:* Moriah Billups, Graduate Admissions Coordinator, 603-836 2588, E-mail: gradadmissions@nhia.edu.
Website: http://www.nhia.edu/graduate-studies

New Jersey City University, William J. Maxwell College of Arts and Sciences, Department of Art, Jersey City, NJ 07305-1597. Offers art (MFA); art education (MA); studio art (MFA). *Accreditation:* NASAD. *Program availability:* Part-time, evening/weekend. *Degree requirements:* For master's, thesis or alternative, exhibit. *Entrance requirements:* For master's, portfolio. Additional exam requirements/recommendations for international students: Required—TOEFL (minimum score 79 iBT).

New Mexico State University, College of Arts and Sciences, Department of Art, Las Cruces, NM 88003. Offers art history (MA); studio art (MFA). *Program availability:* Part-time. *Faculty:* 10 full-time (8 women), 3 part-time/adjunct (2 women). *Students:* 18 full-time (10 women), 1 (woman) part-time; includes 8 minority (1 Asian, non-Hispanic/Latino; 7 Hispanic/Latino), 1 international. Average age 32. 16 applicants, 44% accepted, 3 enrolled. In 2017, 2 master's awarded. *Degree requirements:* For master's, one foreign language, comprehensive exam (for some programs), thesis, thesis exhibit. *Entrance requirements:* For master's, portfolio (for MFA); 10-20 page paper (for MA). Additional exam requirements/recommendations for international students: Required—TOEFL (minimum score 550 paper-based; 79 iBT), IELTS (minimum score 6.5). *Application deadline:* For fall admission, 1/20 for domestic students; for spring admission, 11/15 for domestic students. Application fee: $40 ($50 for international students). Electronic applications accepted. *Expenses:* Tuition, state resident: full-time $4390. Tuition, nonresident: full-time $15,309. *Required fees:* $853. *Financial support:* In 2017–18, 18 students received support, including 3 fellowships (averaging $4,390 per year), 16 teaching assistantships (averaging $13,089 per year); career-related internships or fieldwork, Federal Work-Study, scholarships/grants, traineeships, health care benefits, and unspecified assistantships also available. Support available to part-time students. Financial award application deadline: 3/1. *Faculty research:* Art history, painting, graphic design, sculpture, ceramics, photography. *Total annual research expenditures:* $5,789. *Unit head:* Dr. Julia Barello, Department Head, 575-646-2728, Fax: 575-646-8036, E-mail: jbarello@nmsu.edu. *Application contact:* 575-646-1705, Fax: 575-646-8036, E-mail: artdept@nmsu.edu.
Website: http://artdepartment.nmsu.edu/

The New School, Parsons School of Design, Program in Fine Arts, New York, NY 10011. Offers MFA. *Program availability:* Part-time. *Faculty:* 7 full-time (4 women), 14 part-time/adjunct (11 women). *Students:* 42 full-time (28 women), 2 part-time (both women); includes 12 minority (2 Black or African American, non-Hispanic/Latino; 2 Asian, non-Hispanic/Latino; 7 Hispanic/Latino; 1 Two or more races, non-Hispanic/Latino), 21 international. Average age 27. 137 applicants, 47% accepted, 20 enrolled. In 2017, 23 master's awarded. *Degree requirements:* For master's, thesis. *Entrance requirements:* For master's, transcripts, resume, statement of purpose, recommendation letters, portfolio, interview. Additional exam requirements/recommendations for international students: Required—TOEFL (minimum score 92 iBT), IELTS (minimum score 7), PTE (minimum score 63). *Application deadline:* For fall admission, 1/1 priority date for domestic and international students; for summer admission, 1/1 priority date for domestic and international students. Applications are processed on a rolling basis. Application fee: $50. Electronic applications accepted. *Expenses:* $24,922 per semester full-time, $1,744 per credit part-time, $100 maintenance of status fee. *Financial support:* In 2017–18, 34 students received support, including 13 teaching assistantships (averaging $2,714 per year); career-related internships or fieldwork, scholarships/grants, and unspecified assistantships also available. Support available to part-time students. Financial award application deadline: 2/1; financial award applicants required to submit FAFSA. *Unit head:* Simone Douglas, Director, 212-229-8950 Ext. 3812, E-mail: douglass@newschool.edu. *Application contact:* Courtney Malenius, Director of Graduate Admissions, 212-229-5150 Ext. 4011, E-mail: maleniuc@newschool.edu.
Website: https://www.newschool.edu/parsons/mfa-fine-arts/

New York Academy of Art, Master of Fine Arts Program, New York, NY 10013-2911. Offers anatomy (MFA); drawing (MFA); fine arts (MFA), including anatomy; painting (MFA); printmaking (MFA); sculpture (MFA). *Accreditation:* NASAD. *Faculty:* 5 full-time (1 woman), 31 part-time/adjunct (13 women). *Students:* 109 full-time (67 women); includes 19 minority (3 Black or African American, non-Hispanic/Latino; 2 American Indian or Alaska Native, non-Hispanic/Latino; 4 Asian, non-Hispanic/Latino; 8 Hispanic/Latino; 1 Native Hawaiian or other Pacific Islander, non-Hispanic/Latino; 1 Two or more races, non-Hispanic/Latino), 33 international. Average age 30. 161 applicants, 57% accepted, 60 enrolled. In 2017, 56 master's awarded. *Degree requirements:* For master's, thesis. *Entrance requirements:* For master's, portfolio, essay, two letters of recommendation, curriculum vitae or resume, official undergraduate transcripts. Additional exam requirements/recommendations for international students: Required—TOEFL (minimum score 550 paper-based; 80 iBT), IELTS (minimum score 6.5). *Application deadline:* For fall admission, 1/17 priority date for domestic and international students. Application fee: $80. Electronic applications accepted. Application fee is waived when completed online. *Expenses:* $37,436 annual tuition, $1,500 annual mandatory fees. *Financial support:* In 2017–18, 88 students received support, including 3 fellowships (averaging $10,000 per year); career-related internships or fieldwork, Federal Work-Study, and scholarships/grants also available. Financial award application deadline: 4/15; financial award applicants required to submit FAFSA. *Faculty research:* Drawing, painting, sculpture, anatomy, printmaking. *Total annual research expenditures:* $27,000. *Unit head:* David Kratz, President, 212-966-0300. *Application contact:* Katie Hemmer, Director of Admissions/Registrar, 212-842-5961, E-mail: khemmer@nyaa.edu.
Website: http://www.nyaa.edu/

New York Institute of Technology, College of Arts and Sciences, Department of Digital Art and Design, Old Westbury, NY 11568-8000. Offers computer graphics (MFA), including animation, fine arts and technology, graphic design. *Program availability:* Part-time, evening/weekend. *Faculty:* 7 full-time (4 women), 6 part-time/adjunct (2 women). *Students:* 35 full-time (24 women), 12 part-time (7 women); includes 7 minority (4 Black or African American, non-Hispanic/Latino; 1 Asian, non-Hispanic/Latino; 2 Hispanic/Latino), 35 international. Average age 26. 37 applicants, 73% accepted, 9 enrolled. In 2017, 27 master's awarded. *Degree requirements:* For master's, thesis. *Entrance requirements:* For master's, BFA or equivalent; minimum undergraduate GPA of 3.0; digital portfolio. Additional exam requirements/recommendations for international students: Required—TOEFL (minimum score 79 iBT), IELTS (minimum score 6). *Application deadline:* For fall admission, 6/1 for domestic and international students. Applications are processed on a rolling basis. Application fee: $50. Electronic applications accepted. *Expenses:* $1,285 per credit plus fees. *Financial support:* Career-related internships or fieldwork, Federal Work-Study, scholarships/grants, tuition waivers (full and partial), and unspecified assistantships available. Support available to part-time students. Financial award application deadline: 2/15; financial award applicants required to submit FAFSA. *Faculty research:* Graphic design, animation, art and technology, virtual reality, sculpture. *Unit head:* Terry Nauheim, Department Chair, 516-686-7881, Fax: 212-261-1742, E-mail: tnauheim@nyit.edu. *Application contact:* Alice Dolitsky, Director, Graduate Admissions, 516-686-7520, Fax: 516-686-1116, E-mail: nyitgrad@nyit.edu.
Website: http://www.nyit.edu/departments/digital_art_and_design

New York Studio School of Drawing, Painting and Sculpture, Certificate Program, New York, NY 10011. Offers studio art (Certificate).

New York Studio School of Drawing, Painting and Sculpture, MFA Program, New York, NY 10011. Offers painting (MFA); sculpture (MFA).

See Display on the next page and Close-Up on page 187.

New York University, Graduate School of Arts and Science, Institute of Fine Arts, New York, NY 10012-1019. Offers art history and archaeology (MA, PhD), including architectural studies (PhD), art history and archaeology, classical art and archaeology (PhD), curatorial studies (PhD), East and South Asian art (PhD), Near Eastern art and archaeology (PhD); MA/Diploma; PhD/Certificate. *Program availability:* Part-time. *Students:* Average age 31. 346 applicants, 43% accepted, 52 enrolled. In 2017, 47 master's, 24 doctorates awarded. Terminal master's awarded for partial completion of doctoral program. *Degree requirements:* For master's, 2 foreign languages, thesis or alternative, 2 qualifying papers; for doctorate, 2 foreign languages, thesis/dissertation. *Entrance requirements:* For master's, GRE General Test; for doctorate, GRE General Test, MA. Additional exam requirements/recommendations for international students: Required—TOEFL. *Application deadline:* For fall admission, 12/18 for domestic and international students. Application fee: $100. *Expenses: Tuition:* Full-time $41,352; part-time $19,968 per year. *Required fees:* $2496; $1628 per unit. $814 per term. Tuition and fees vary according to course load and program. *Financial support:* Fellowships, research assistantships, teaching assistantships, career-related internships or fieldwork, Federal Work-Study, institutionally sponsored loans, and tuition waivers (partial) available. Financial award application deadline: 12/18; financial award applicants required to submit FAFSA. *Unit head:* Patricia Rubin, Chair, 212-992-5800, Fax: 212-992-5807, E-mail: ifa.program@nyu.edu. *Application contact:* Alexander Nagel, Director of Graduate Studies, 212-992-5800, Fax: 212-992-5807, E-mail: ifa.program@nyu.edu.
Website: http://www.nyu.edu/gsas/dept/fineart/

New York University, Steinhardt School of Culture, Education, and Human Development, Department of Art and Art Professions, Program in Studio Art, New York, NY 10003. Offers MA, MFA, Advanced Certificate. *Program availability:* Part-time. *Students:* Average age 48. 159 applicants, 10% accepted, 12 enrolled. In 2017, 24 master's, 3 other advanced degrees awarded. *Entrance requirements:* For master's, portfolio, interview, presentation. Additional exam requirements/recommendations for international students: Required—TOEFL (minimum score 100 iBT). *Application deadline:* For fall admission, 12/1 priority date for domestic and international students. Applications are processed on a rolling basis. Application fee: $75. Electronic applications accepted. *Expenses: Tuition:* Full-time $41,352; part-time $19,968 per year. *Required fees:* $2496; $1628 per unit. $814 per term. Tuition and fees vary according to course load and program. *Financial support:* Teaching assistantships, career-related internships or fieldwork, Federal Work-Study, institutionally sponsored loans, scholarships/grants, tuition waivers (partial), and unspecified assistantships available. Support available to part-time students. Financial award application deadline: 2/1; financial award applicants required to submit FAFSA. *Faculty research:* Media and culture, video art and digital media, multimedia works, critical theory, memory and history, performance and text. *Unit head:* Prof. Maureen Gallace, Program Director, 212-998-5700, Fax: 212-995-4320, E-mail: mag6@nyu.edu. *Application contact:* 212-998-5030, Fax: 212-995-4328, E-mail: steinhardt.gradadmissions@nyu.edu.
Website: http://steinhardt.nyu.edu/art

New York University, Steinhardt School of Culture, Education, and Human Development, Department of Art and Art Professions, Program in Visual Culture, New

Art/Fine Arts

York, NY 10012. Offers costume studies (MA); MA/MS. *Program availability:* Part-time. *Students:* Average age 26. 36 applicants, 53% accepted, 12 enrolled. In 2017, 15 master's awarded. *Entrance requirements:* Additional exam requirements/recommendations for international students: Required—TOEFL (minimum score 100 iBT). *Application deadline:* For fall admission, 12/1 priority date for domestic and international students. Applications are processed on a rolling basis. Application fee: $75. Electronic applications accepted. *Expenses: Tuition:* Full-time $41,352; part-time $19,968 per year. *Required fees:* $2496; $1628 per unit. $814 per term. Tuition and fees vary according to course load and program. *Financial support:* Career-related internships or fieldwork, Federal Work-Study, institutionally sponsored loans, scholarships/grants, and tuition waivers available. Support available to part-time students. Financial award application deadline: 2/1; financial award applicants required to submit FAFSA. *Faculty research:* Textiles as material culture, contemporary visual culture and globalization, cultural theory. *Unit head:* Prof. Nancy Diehl, Director, 212-998-5700, E-mail: nbd2012@nyu.edu. *Application contact:* 212-998-5030, Fax: 212-995-4328, E-mail: steinhardt.gradadmissions@nyu.edu.
Website: http://steinhardt.nyu.edu/art/costume

New York University, Tisch School of the Arts, Program in Arts Politics, New York, NY 10012-1019. Offers MA. *Faculty:* 3 full-time (2 women), 4 part-time/adjunct (3 women). *Students:* 11 full-time (8 women); includes 4 minority (2 Black or African American, non-Hispanic/Latino; 1 Asian, non-Hispanic/Latino; 1 Hispanic/Latino), 4 international. Average age 25. 33 applicants, 97% accepted, 11 enrolled. In 2017, 13 master's awarded. *Entrance requirements:* For master's, professional resume, writing sample, statement of purpose. *Application deadline:* For fall admission, 1/1 for domestic and international students. Application fee: $60. *Expenses: Tuition:* Full-time $41,352; part-time $19,968 per year. *Required fees:* $2496; $1628 per unit. $814 per term. Tuition and fees vary according to course load and program. *Financial support:* In 2017–18, 2 students received support. Federal Work-Study and scholarships/grants available. Financial award application deadline: 2/15; financial award applicants required to submit FAFSA. *Unit head:* Randy Martin, Director, 212-992-8248. *Application contact:* Dan Sandford, Director of Graduate Admissions, 212-998-1918, Fax: 212-995-4060, E-mail: tisch.gradadmissions@nyu.edu.

Norfolk State University, School of Graduate Studies, School of Liberal Arts, Department of Fine Arts, Norfolk, VA 23504. Offers visual studies (MA, MFA). *Program availability:* Part-time. *Degree requirements:* For master's, thesis or alternative. *Entrance requirements:* For master's, portfolio, interview, letters of recommendation. Additional exam requirements/recommendations for international students: Required—TOEFL (minimum score 500 paper-based).

Northeastern University, College of Arts, Media and Design, Boston, MA 02115-5096. Offers architecture (M Arch); game science and design (MS); information design and visualization (MFA); interdisciplinary arts (MFA); journalism (MA); music industry leadership (MS); studio art (MFA); sustainable building systems (MS); sustainable urban environments (M Des). *Faculty:* 145. *Students:* 259. In 2017, 83 master's awarded. Application fee: $75. Electronic applications accepted. *Expenses:* Contact institution. *Financial support:* Applicants required to submit FAFSA. *Unit head:* Dr. Elizabeth Hudson, Dean, 617-373-5088, E-mail: n.elysse@northeastern.edu. *Application contact:* Jane Amidon, Associate Dean for Graduate Programs and Research, 617-373-4614, E-mail: gscamd@northeastern.edu.
Website: http://www.northeastern.edu/camd/

Northern Illinois University, Graduate School, College of Visual and Performing Arts, School of Art, De Kalb, IL 60115-2854. Offers MA, MFA, MS. *Accreditation:* NASAD (one or more programs are accredited). *Program availability:* Part-time, evening/weekend. *Faculty:* 36 full-time (15 women), 1 (woman) part-time/adjunct. *Students:* 41 full-time (29 women), 32 part-time (25 women); includes 12 minority (2 Black or African American, non-Hispanic/Latino; 2 Asian, non-Hispanic/Latino; 6 Hispanic/Latino; 2 Two or more races, non-Hispanic/Latino), 4 international. Average age 32. 44 applicants, 64% accepted, 7 enrolled. In 2017, 21 master's awarded. *Degree requirements:* For master's, variable foreign language requirement, comprehensive exam, thesis (for some programs), show or project. *Entrance requirements:* For master's, GRE General Test, minimum GPA of 2.75, portfolio. Additional exam requirements/recommendations for international students: Required—TOEFL (minimum score 550 paper-based). *Application deadline:* For fall and spring admission, 3/1 for domestic and international students. Applications are processed on a rolling basis. Application fee: $40. Electronic applications accepted. *Financial support:* In 2017–18, 24 teaching assistantships with full tuition reimbursements were awarded; fellowships with full tuition reimbursements, research assistantships with full tuition reimbursements, career-related internships or fieldwork, Federal Work-Study, scholarships/grants, tuition waivers (full), and staff assistantships also available. Support available to part-time students. Financial award applicants required to submit FAFSA. *Faculty research:* Art education, portfolio assessment, central European design history, relationship between modern art and industrialism. *Unit head:* John Siblik, Director, 815-753-7850, Fax: 815-753-7701, E-mail: jsiblik@niu.edu. *Application contact:* Kurt Schultz, Graduate Coordinator, 815-753-1473, E-mail: artgradcoordinator@niu.edu.
Website: http://www.niu.edu/art/

Northern Vermont University–Johnson, Program in Studio Arts, Johnson, VT 05656. Offers ceramics (MFA); digital media (MFA); drawing (MFA); painting (MFA); photography (MFA); printmaking (MFA); sculpture (MFA). *Program availability:* Part-time, online learning. *Faculty:* 3 full-time (1 woman). *Students:* 5 full-time (3 women), 2 part-time (1 woman). In 2017, 2 master's awarded. *Degree requirements:* For master's, thesis. *Entrance requirements:* For master's, portfolio. Additional exam requirements/recommendations for international students: Required—TOEFL. *Application deadline:* For fall admission, 3/1 for domestic students, 2/1 for international students. Applications are processed on a rolling basis. Electronic applications accepted. *Expenses:* Contact institution. *Financial support:* Teaching assistantships and unspecified assistantships available. Support available to part-time students. Financial award application deadline: 3/1; financial award applicants required to submit FAFSA. *Application contact:* Catherine H. Higley, Administrative Assistant, 800-635-2356 Ext. 1244, Fax: 802-635-1248, E-mail: catherine.higley@jsc.edu.
Website: http://www.jsc.edu/academics/fine-arts-department/majors-and-minors/mfa-in-studio-arts/

Northwestern State University of Louisiana, Graduate Studies and Research, School of Creative and Performing Arts, Program in Art, Natchitoches, LA 71497. Offers fine and graphic arts (MA). *Accreditation:* NASAD. *Degree requirements:* For master's, comprehensive exam, thesis or alternative. *Entrance requirements:* For master's, GRE General Test, minimum undergraduate GPA of 2.5. Additional exam requirements/recommendations for international students: Required—TOEFL. Electronic applications accepted.

Northwestern University, The Graduate School, Judd A. and Marjorie Weinberg College of Arts and Sciences, Department of Art Theory and Practice, Evanston, IL 60208. Offers visual arts (MFA). Admissions and degrees offered through The Graduate School. *Degree requirements:* For master's, essay, exhibit. *Entrance requirements:* For master's, 20 slides of recent work. Additional exam requirements/recommendations for international students: Required—TOEFL. Electronic applications accepted.

Nova Southeastern University, College of Arts, Humanities, and Social Sciences, Fort Lauderdale, FL 33314-7796. Offers advanced conflict resolution practice (Graduate Certificate); child protection (MHS); college student affairs (MS); conflict analysis and

resolution (MS, PhD); criminal justice (MS, PhD); cross-disciplinary studies (MA); developmental disabilities (MS); family studies (Graduate Certificate); family systems health care (Graduate Certificate); family therapy (MS, PhD); marriage and family therapy (DMFT); peace studies (Graduate Certificate); qualitative research (Graduate Certificate); solution focused coaching (Graduate Certificate). *Accreditation:* AAMFT/COAMFTE (one or more programs are accredited). *Program availability:* Part-time, evening/weekend, 100% online, blended/hybrid learning. *Faculty:* 29 full-time (18 women), 27 part-time/adjunct (21 women). *Students:* 303 full-time (238 women), 903 part-time (677 women); includes 689 minority (385 Black or African American, non-Hispanic/Latino; 4 American Indian or Alaska Native, non-Hispanic/Latino; 31 Asian, non-Hispanic/Latino; 234 Hispanic/Latino; 1 Native Hawaiian or other Pacific Islander, non-Hispanic/Latino; 34 Two or more races, non-Hispanic/Latino), 60 international. Average age 37. 624 applicants, 61% accepted, 285 enrolled. In 2017, 277 master's, 62 doctorates, 25 other advanced degrees awarded. *Degree requirements:* For master's, thesis optional, comprehensive exams, portfolios (for some programs), table-top exams (for some programs); for doctorate, comprehensive exam, thesis/dissertation, qualifying exams, portfolios (for some programs). *Entrance requirements:* For master's, interview, minimum GPA of 3.0, writing sample; for doctorate, interview, minimum GPA of 3.5, master's degree in related field, writing sample; for Graduate Certificate, minimum GPA of 3.0. Additional exam requirements/recommendations for international students: Required—TOEFL. *Application deadline:* For fall admission, 5/17 priority date for domestic and international students; for winter admission, 12/1 priority date for domestic and international students; for spring admission, 4/1 priority date for domestic and international students. Applications are processed on a rolling basis. Application fee: $50. Electronic applications accepted. *Expenses:* Contact institution. *Financial support:* In 2017–18, 170 students received support. Career-related internships or fieldwork, Federal Work-Study, scholarships/grants, and unspecified assistantships available. Financial award application deadline: 4/1; financial award applicants required to submit CSS PROFILE. *Faculty research:* Conflict resolution, family therapy, peace research, international conflict, multi-disciplinary studies, college student affairs, national security affairs, health care conflict resolution, family systems health care, advanced family systems, qualitative research, solution-focused coaching. *Unit head:* Dr. Honggang Yang, Dean, 954-262-3016, Fax: 954-262-3968, E-mail: yangh@nova.edu. *Application contact:* Marcia Arango, Student Recruitment Coordinator, 954-262-3006, Fax: 954-262-3968, E-mail: marango@nsu.nova.edu.
Website: http://cahss.nova.edu/

NSCAD University, Program in Fine Arts, Halifax, NS B3J 3J6, Canada. Offers craft (MFA); design (M Des); fine and media arts (MFA). *Degree requirements:* For master's, thesis, exhibit. *Entrance requirements:* For master's, portfolio, at least 5 art history classes. Additional exam requirements/recommendations for international students: Required—Michigan English Language Assessment Battery (minimum score: 80), CanTEST (minimum score: 4.5), CAEL (minimum score: 70); Recommended—TOEFL (minimum score 575 paper-based; 90 iBT), IELTS (minimum score 6.5).

The Ohio State University, Graduate School, College of Arts and Sciences, Division of Arts and Humanities, Department of Art, Columbus, OH 43210. Offers MFA. *Accreditation:* NASAD. *Faculty:* 19. *Students:* 41 (23 women). Average age 29. In 2017, 15 master's awarded. *Degree requirements:* For master's, thesis, exhibit, oral exams. *Entrance requirements:* For master's, GRE General Test (if GPA cumulative average is less than 3.0), electronic portfolio. Additional exam requirements/recommendations for international students: Required—Michigan English Language Assessment Battery (minimum score 82); Recommended—TOEFL (minimum score 550 paper-based; 79 iBT), IELTS (minimum score 7). *Application deadline:* For fall admission, 12/31 priority date for domestic students, 11/30 priority date for international students; for spring admission, 3/1 for domestic students, 2/1 for international students. Applications are processed on a rolling basis. Application fee: $60 ($70 for international students). Electronic applications accepted. *Financial support:* Fellowships with tuition reimbursements, teaching assistantships with tuition reimbursements, Federal Work-Study, institutionally sponsored loans, and unspecified assistantships available. Support available to part-time students. *Unit head:* Michael Mercil, Interim Chair, E-mail: mercil.1@osu.edu. *Application contact:* Graduate and Professional Admissions, 614-292-9444, Fax: 614-292-3895, E-mail: gpadmissions@osu.edu.
Website: http://art.osu.edu/

Ohio University, Graduate College, College of Fine Arts, School of Art, Athens, OH 45701-2979. Offers art history (MA); ceramics (MFA); graphic design (MFA); painting (MFA); photography (MFA); printmaking (MFA); sculpture (MFA). *Program availability:* Part-time. *Degree requirements:* For master's, thesis. *Entrance requirements:* For master's, portfolio. Additional exam requirements/recommendations for international students: Required—TOEFL (minimum score 550 paper-based; 80 iBT) or IELTS (minimum score 6.5). Electronic applications accepted. *Faculty research:* Vapor-fired ceramics, video installation, art theory, digital photography, mixed and interdisciplinary media work.

Oregon College of Art and Craft, MFA Program, Portland, OR 97225. Offers craft (MFA). *Accreditation:* NASAD.

Otis College of Art and Design, Program in Fine Arts, Los Angeles, CA 90045-9785. Offers new genres (MFA); painting (MFA); photography (MFA); sculpture (MFA). *Accreditation:* NASAD. *Degree requirements:* For master's, thesis. *Entrance requirements:* For master's, portfolio. Additional exam requirements/recommendations for international students: Required—TOEFL (minimum score 600 paper-based). Electronic applications accepted.

Otis College of Art and Design, Program in Public Practice, Los Angeles, CA 90045-9785. Offers MFA. *Entrance requirements:* Additional exam requirements/recommendations for international students: Required—TOEFL (minimum score 600 paper-based). Electronic applications accepted.

Pacific Northwest College of Art, Program in Visual Studies, Portland, OR 97209. Offers MFA. *Accreditation:* NASAD.

Paris College of Art, Graduate Programs, Paris, France. Offers accessories design (MA); fashion design: new materials and technologies (MA); fashion film and photography (MA); interior design (MA); transdisciplinary new media (MA, MFA). *Entrance requirements:* Additional exam requirements/recommendations for international students: Required—TOEFL or IELTS.

Penn State University Park, Graduate School, College of Arts and Architecture, School of Visual Arts, University Park, PA 16802. Offers art (MFA); art education (MS, PhD, Certificate). *Unit head:* Dr. Barbara O. Korner, Dean, 814-865-2592, Fax: 814-865-2018. *Application contact:* Lori Hawn, Director, Graduate Student Services, 814-865-1795, Fax: 814-863-4627, E-mail: l-gswww@lists.psu.edu.
Website: http://sova.psu.edu/

Pennsylvania Academy of the Fine Arts, Division of Graduate Studies, Philadelphia, PA 19102. Offers drawing (MFA, Postbaccalaureate Certificate); painting (MFA, Postbaccalaureate Certificate); printmaking (MFA, Postbaccalaureate Certificate); sculpture (MFA, Postbaccalaureate Certificate). MFA program also available in a low-residency format. *Accreditation:* NASAD (one or more programs are accredited). *Degree requirements:* For master's, thesis, thesis exhibit. *Entrance requirements:* For master's, 10-20 slides of work and slide list or SlideRoom submission, 3 letters of recommendation, bachelor's degree, statement of purpose. Additional exam requirements/recommendations for international students: Required—TOEFL (minimum score 600 paper-based; 100 iBT), IELTS (minimum score 6). Electronic applications accepted.

Pensacola Christian College, Graduate Studies, Pensacola, FL 32503-2267. Offers business administration (MBA); curriculum and instruction (MS, Ed D, Ed S); dramatics (MFA); educational leadership (MS, Ed D, Ed S); graphic design (MA, MFA); music (MA); nursing (MSN); performance studies (MA); studio art (MA, MFA).

Pontifical Catholic University of Puerto Rico, College of Arts and Humanities, Department of Fine Arts, Ponce, PR 00717-0777. Offers painting and drawing (MA).

Portland State University, Graduate Studies, College of the Arts, School of Art and Design, Portland, OR 97207-0751. Offers contemporary art practice: art and social practice (MFA); contemporary art practice: studio practice (MFA). *Faculty:* 34 full-time (21 women), 48 part-time/adjunct (31 women). *Students:* 17 full-time (10 women), 3 part-time (0 women); includes 2 minority (1 Black or African American, non-Hispanic/Latino; 1 Asian, non-Hispanic/Latino), 4 international. Average age 34. 14 applicants, 57% accepted, 6 enrolled. In 2017, 9 master's awarded. *Degree requirements:* For master's, variable foreign language requirement, thesis, exhibition project. *Entrance requirements:* For master's, minimum GPA of 3.0 in upper-division course work or 2.75 overall, digital portfolio, 3 letters of recommendation, statement of intent. Additional exam requirements/recommendations for international students: Required—TOEFL (minimum score 550 paper-based; 80 iBT), IELTS (minimum score 6.5). *Application deadline:* For fall admission, 3/1 for domestic and international students. Application fee: $65. *Expenses:* Contact institution. *Financial support:* In 2017–18, 16 students received support, including 3 research assistantships with full and partial tuition reimbursements available (averaging $5,325 per year), 7 teaching assistantships with full and partial tuition reimbursements available (averaging $5,325 per year); Federal Work-Study, scholarships/grants, and unspecified assistantships also available. Support available to part-time students. Financial award application deadline: 3/1; financial award applicants required to submit FAFSA. *Unit head:* Patricia Boas, Director, 503-725-8980, Fax: 503-725-4541, E-mail: boasp@pdx.edu. *Application contact:* Ellen Wack, Program Coordinator, 503-725-8450, E-mail: wacke@pdx.edu.
Website: https://www.pdx.edu/art-design/

Pratt Institute, School of Art, Program in Fine Arts, Brooklyn, NY 11205-3899. Offers MFA. *Accreditation:* NASAD. *Program availability:* Part-time. *Students:* 86 full-time (51 women), 2 part-time (both women); includes 19 minority (6 Black or African American, non-Hispanic/Latino; 1 American Indian or Alaska Native, non-Hispanic/Latino; 5 Asian, non-Hispanic/Latino; 4 Hispanic/Latino; 3 Two or more races, non-Hispanic/Latino), 38 international. Average age 28. 343 applicants, 49% accepted, 46 enrolled. In 2017, 36 master's awarded. *Degree requirements:* For master's, thesis, exhibit. *Entrance requirements:* For master's, portfolio, letters of recommendation. Additional exam requirements/recommendations for international students: Required—TOEFL (minimum score 550 paper-based; 79 iBT). *Application deadline:* For fall admission, 1/5 for domestic and international students; for spring admission, 10/1 for domestic and international students. Application fee: $50 ($90 for international students). Electronic applications accepted. *Expenses: Tuition:* Full-time $30,834. *Required fees:* $1974. *Financial support:* Career-related internships or fieldwork, Federal Work-Study, institutionally sponsored loans, scholarships/grants, health care benefits, and unspecified assistantships available. Support available to part-time students. Financial award application deadline: 2/1; financial award applicants required to submit FAFSA. *Unit head:* Jane South, Chairperson, 718-636-3634, E-mail: jsouth@pratt.edu. *Application contact:* Natalie Capannelli, Director of Graduate Admissions, 718-636-3551, Fax: 718-399-4242, E-mail: ncapanne@pratt.edu.
Website: https://www.pratt.edu/academics/school-of-art/graduate-school-of-art/graduate-fine-arts/

See Display on the next page and Close-Up on page 189.

Prescott College, Graduate Programs, Program in Arts and Humanities, Prescott, AZ 86301. Offers humanities (MA); social justice and human rights (MA); student-directed independent study (MA). *Program availability:* Part-time, online learning. *Degree requirements:* For master's, thesis, fieldwork or internship, practicum. *Entrance requirements:* For master's, 2 letters of recommendation, resume, essay. Additional exam requirements/recommendations for international students: Required—TOEFL (minimum score 500 paper-based). Electronic applications accepted.

Purchase College, State University of New York, School of Art and Design, Purchase, NY 10577-1400. Offers art history/visual arts (MA); visual arts (MFA). *Accreditation:* NASAD. *Degree requirements:* For master's, thesis, exhibit. *Entrance requirements:* For master's, portfolio. *Application deadline:* For fall admission, 2/15 for domestic students. Applications are processed on a rolling basis. Application fee: $85. Electronic applications accepted. *Financial support:* Fellowships, teaching assistantships, Federal Work-Study, scholarships/grants, and tuition waivers (partial) available. Support available to part-time students. Financial award application deadline: 3/15; financial award applicants required to submit FAFSA. *Unit head:* Steven Lam, Director, 914-251-6750, Fax: 914-251-6793, E-mail: steven.lam@purchase.edu. *Application contact:* Garrett Marino, Associate Director of Admissions, 914-251-6316, Fax: 914-251-6314, E-mail: admissn@purchase.edu.
Website: https://www.purchase.edu/academics/art-and-design/

Purdue University, Graduate School, College of Liberal Arts, Department of Art and Design, West Lafayette, IN 47907. Offers art education (MA, PhD); industrial design (MFA); integrated studio arts (MFA); interior design (MFA); photography (MFA); visual communications design (MFA). *Accreditation:* NASAD; NAST. *Program availability:* Part-time. *Students:* 20 full-time (14 women), 1 part-time (0 women); includes 1 minority (Two or more races, non-Hispanic/Latino), 16 international. Average age 26. 97 applicants, 26% accepted, 10 enrolled. In 2017, 6 master's awarded. *Degree requirements:* For master's, terminal exhibit, project, or thesis. *Entrance requirements:* For master's, GRE General Test (for art education), minimum undergraduate GPA of 3.0 or equivalent; 9 undergraduate hours in an art or design history; BA in art (for MA in art education); for doctorate, GRE General Test (minimum scores 600 in verbal and 1000 total), master's degree in art education or art with teaching certification; 3 years of teaching experience at the K-12 level. Additional exam requirements/recommendations for international students: Required—TOEFL (minimum score 550 paper-based; 77 iBT). *Application deadline:* For fall admission, 2/1 for domestic students, 2/1 priority date for international students. Applications are processed on a rolling basis. Application fee: $60 ($75 for international students). Electronic applications accepted. *Financial support:* Teaching assistantships with tuition reimbursements and career-related internships or fieldwork available. Support available to part-time students. Financial award applicants required to submit FAFSA. *Faculty research:* Design, fine arts, photography, acting, directing, theatre technology. *Unit head:* Harry T. Bulow, Head of the Graduate Program, 765-494-3056, E-mail: hbulow@purdue.edu. *Application contact:* Sara J. Unser, Graduate Contact, 765-494-8662, E-mail: sunser@purdue.edu.
Website: https://www.cla.purdue.edu/vpa/ad/

Queens College of the City University of New York, Arts and Humanities Division, Department of Art, Queens, NY 11367-1597. Offers art history (MA); studio art (MFA). *Program availability:* Part-time. *Faculty:* 18 full-time (6 women), 56 part-time/adjunct (32 women). *Students:* 13 full-time (7 women), 19 part-time (15 women); includes 9 minority

(1 Black or African American, non-Hispanic/Latino; 2 Asian, non-Hispanic/Latino; 5 Hispanic/Latino; 1 Two or more races, non-Hispanic/Latino), 2 international. Average age 35. 25 applicants, 44% accepted, 8 enrolled. In 2017, 16 master's awarded. *Degree requirements:* For master's, thesis, comprehensive exam (for art history program). *Entrance requirements:* For master's, minimum GPA of 3.0. Additional exam requirements/recommendations for international students: Required—TOEFL (minimum score 600 paper-based), IELTS. *Application deadline:* For fall admission, 4/1 for domestic students; for spring admission, 11/1 for domestic students. Applications are processed on a rolling basis. Application fee: $125. Electronic applications accepted. *Financial support:* Career-related internships or fieldwork available. Financial award application deadline: 4/1; financial award applicants required to submit FAFSA. *Unit head:* Michael Nelson, Chair, 718-997-4800, E-mail: michael.nelson@qc.cuny.edu. *Application contact:* Elizabeth D'Amico-Ramirez, Assistant Director of Graduate Admissions, 718-997-5203, E-mail: elizabeth.damicoramirez@qc.cuny.edu.

Radford University, College of Graduate Studies and Research, Program in Art, Radford, VA 24142. Offers MFA. *Accreditation:* NASAD. *Program availability:* Part-time. *Faculty:* 13 full-time (6 women), 2 part-time/adjunct (1 woman). *Students:* 18 full-time (14 women), 19 part-time (9 women); includes 3 minority (2 Black or African American, non-Hispanic/Latino; 1 Hispanic/Latino), 3 international. Average age 35. 21 applicants, 81% accepted, 11 enrolled. In 2017, 5 master's awarded. *Degree requirements:* For master's, comprehensive exam. *Entrance requirements:* For master's, statement of philosophy; minimum GPA of 2.75, 2 letters of reference, BFA or commensurate collegiate course work, 20 slides or CD of recent work, resume, and official transcripts (for studio art); minimum GPA of 3.0 (preferred) and three letters of reference (for design thinking). Additional exam requirements/recommendations for international students: Required—TOEFL (minimum score 550 paper-based; 79 iBT), IELTS (minimum score 6.5). *Application deadline:* For fall admission, 4/1 priority date for domestic students, 12/1 for international students; for spring admission, 11/1 priority date for domestic students, 7/1 for international students. Applications are processed on a rolling basis. Application fee: $50. Electronic applications accepted. *Expenses:* Contact institution. *Financial support:* In 2017–18, 8 students received support, including 1 research assistantship (averaging $10,000 per year), 6 teaching assistantships (averaging $8,833 per year); scholarships/grants and unspecified assistantships also available. Support available to part-time students. Financial award application deadline: 3/1; financial award applicants required to submit FAFSA. *Unit head:* Dr. Roann Barris, Chair, 540-831-5778, E-mail: rbarris@radford.edu. Website: http://www.radford.edu/content/cvpa/home/art.html

Rensselaer Polytechnic Institute, Graduate School, School of Humanities, Arts, and Social Sciences, Program in Electronic Arts, Troy, NY 12180-3590. Offers PhD. *Faculty:* 25 full-time (10 women), 9 part-time/adjunct (5 women). *Students:* 20 full-time (12 women), 3 part-time (2 women); includes 4 minority (1 Asian, non-Hispanic/Latino; 2 Hispanic/Latino; 1 Two or more races, non-Hispanic/Latino), 4 international. Average age 29. 29 applicants, 24% accepted, 5 enrolled. In 2017, 1 doctorate awarded. *Degree requirements:* For doctorate, comprehensive exam. *Entrance requirements:* For doctorate, portfolio, research proposal, writing sample. Additional exam requirements/recommendations for international students: Required—TOEFL (minimum score 570 paper-based; 88 iBT), IELTS (minimum score 6.5), PTE (minimum score 60). *Application deadline:* For fall admission, 1/1 priority date for domestic and international students. Applications are processed on a rolling basis. Application fee: $75. Electronic applications accepted. *Expenses: Tuition:* Full-time $52,550; part-time $2125 per credit hour. *Required fees:* $2890. *Financial support:* In 2017–18, research assistantships (averaging $23,000 per year), teaching assistantships with full tuition reimbursements (averaging $23,000 per year) were awarded; scholarships/grants also available. Financial award application deadline: 1/1. *Unit head:* Dr. Tomie Hahn, Graduate Program Director, 518-276-2379, E-mail: hahnt@rpi.edu. Website: http://www.arts.rpi.edu/pl/graduate-programs

Rhode Island College, School of Graduate Studies, Faculty of Arts and Sciences, Department of Art, Providence, RI 02908-1991. Offers art education (MA, MAT); media studies (MA). *Accreditation:* NASAD (one or more programs are accredited). *Program availability:* Part-time, evening/weekend. *Faculty:* 3. *Students:* 4 full-time (3 women), 11 part-time (5 women); includes 4 minority (1 Asian, non-Hispanic/Latino; 3 Hispanic/Latino). Average age 33. In 2017, 4 master's awarded. *Degree requirements:* For master's, thesis. *Entrance requirements:* For master's, GRE General Test, portfolio (MA), 3 letters of recommendation, interview. Additional exam requirements/recommendations for international students: Recommended—TOEFL (minimum score 550 paper-based; 79 iBT). *Application deadline:* For fall admission, 3/1 for domestic students. Applications are processed on a rolling basis. Application fee: $50. Electronic applications accepted. *Expenses: Tuition,* state resident: full-time $9768; part-time $407 per credit. Tuition, nonresident: full-time $19,008; part-time $792 per credit. *Required fees:* $696; $29 per credit. One-time fee: $200 full-time; $100 part-time. Tuition and fees vary according to course load. *Financial support:* In 2017–18, 3 teaching assistantships with full tuition reimbursements (averaging $1,500 per year) were awarded; career-related internships or fieldwork, Federal Work-Study, scholarships/grants, health care benefits, and unspecified assistantships also available. Support available to part-time students. Financial award application deadline: 5/15; financial award applicants required to submit FAFSA. *Unit head:* Prof. Richard Whitten, Chair, 401-456-8054. Website: http://www.ric.edu/art/index.php

Rhode Island School of Design, Department of Ceramics, Providence, RI 02903-2784. Offers MFA. *Accreditation:* NASAD. *Faculty:* 2 full-time (1 woman), 5 part-time/adjunct (4 women). *Students:* 10 full-time (6 women), 4 international. Average age 27. 25 applicants, 36% accepted, 6 enrolled. In 2017, 6 master's awarded. *Degree requirements:* For master's, thesis, exhibition. *Entrance requirements:* For master's, portfolio, statement of purpose, 3 letters of recommendation. Additional exam requirements/recommendations for international students: Required—TOEFL (minimum score 580 paper-based; 93 iBT). *Application deadline:* For fall admission, 1/10 for domestic and international students. Application fee: $60. Electronic applications accepted. *Expenses: Tuition:* Full-time $48,210. *Required fees:* $260. *Financial support:* Fellowships, research assistantships, teaching assistantships, Federal Work-Study, scholarships/grants, and unspecified assistantships available. Financial award application deadline: 2/15; financial award applicants required to submit FAFSA. *Unit head:* Katy Schimert, Department Head and Graduate Coordinator, 401-454-6190, Fax: 401-454-6191, E-mail: ceramics@risd.edu. *Application contact:* Molly Pettengill, Assistant Director for Graduate Recruitment, 401-454-6312, Fax: 401-454-6309, E-mail: ceramics@risd.edu. Website: http://www.risd.edu/academics/ceramics/

Rhode Island School of Design, Department of Glass, Providence, RI 02903-2784. Offers MFA. *Accreditation:* NASAD. *Faculty:* 2 full-time (both women), 5 part-time/adjunct (2 women). *Students:* 7 full-time (5 women), 5 international. Average age 26. 17 applicants, 35% accepted, 5 enrolled. In 2017, 2 master's awarded. *Degree requirements:* For master's, thesis, exhibition. *Entrance requirements:* For master's, portfolio, statement of purpose, 3 letters of recommendation. Additional exam requirements/recommendations for international students: Required—TOEFL (minimum score 580 paper-based; 93 iBT). *Application deadline:* For fall admission, 1/10 for domestic and international students. Application fee: $60. Electronic applications accepted. *Expenses: Tuition:* Full-time

$48,210. *Required fees:* $260. *Financial support:* Fellowships, research assistantships, teaching assistantships, Federal Work-Study, scholarships/grants, and unspecified assistantships available. Financial award application deadline: 2/15; financial award applicants required to submit FAFSA. *Unit head:* Rachel Berwick, Department Head and Graduate Program Director, 401-454-6190, Fax: 401-454-6680, E-mail: rberwick@risd.edu. *Application contact:* Molly Pettengill, Assistant Director for Graduate Recruitment, 401-454-6312, Fax: 401-454-6309, E-mail: mpetteng@risd.edu.
Website: http://www.risd.edu/academics/glass/

Rhode Island School of Design, Department of Jewelry and Metalsmithing, Providence, RI 02903-2784. Offers MFA. *Accreditation:* NASAD. *Faculty:* 2 full-time (1 woman), 8 part-time/adjunct (4 women). *Students:* 9 full-time (all women); includes 1 minority (Asian, non-Hispanic/Latino), 5 international. Average age 24. 56 applicants, 16% accepted, 5 enrolled. In 2017, 5 master's awarded. *Degree requirements:* For master's, thesis, exhibition. *Entrance requirements:* For master's, portfolio, statement of purpose, 3 letters of recommendation. Additional exam requirements/recommendations for international students: Required—TOEFL (minimum score 580 paper-based; 93 iBT). *Application deadline:* For fall admission, 1/10 for domestic and international students. Application fee: $60. Electronic applications accepted. *Expenses: Tuition:* Full-time $48,210. *Required fees:* $260. *Financial support:* Fellowships, research assistantships, teaching assistantships, Federal Work-Study, scholarships/grants, and unspecified assistantships available. Financial award application deadline: 2/15; financial award applicants required to submit FAFSA. *Unit head:* Tracy Steepy, Department Head and Graduate Coordinator, 401-454-6190, Fax: 401-454-6191, E-mail: jewelry@risd.edu. *Application contact:* Molly Pettengill, Assistant Director for Graduate Recruitment, 401-454-6312, Fax: 401-454-6309, E-mail: mpetteng@risd.edu.
Website: http://www.risd.edu/academics/jewelry-metalsmithing/

Rhode Island School of Design, Department of Painting, Providence, RI 02903-2784. Offers MFA. *Accreditation:* NASAD. *Faculty:* 4 full-time (1 woman), 9 part-time/adjunct (6 women). *Students:* 20 full-time (12 women); includes 3 minority (all Hispanic/Latino), 6 international. Average age 28. 209 applicants, 10% accepted, 10 enrolled. In 2017, 10 master's awarded. *Degree requirements:* For master's, thesis, exhibition. *Entrance requirements:* For master's, portfolio, statement of purpose, 3 letters of recommendation. Additional exam requirements/recommendations for international students: Required—TOEFL (minimum score 580 paper-based; 93 iBT). *Application deadline:* For fall admission, 1/10 for domestic and international students. Application fee: $60. Electronic applications accepted. *Expenses: Tuition:* Full-time $48,210. *Required fees:* $260. *Financial support:* Fellowships, research assistantships, teaching assistantships, Federal Work-Study, scholarships/grants, and unspecified assistantships available. Financial award application deadline: 2/15; financial award applicants required to submit FAFSA. *Unit head:* Kevin Zucker, Department Head, 401-454-6158, Fax: 401-454-6681, E-mail: painting@risd.edu. *Application contact:* Molly Pettengill, Assistant Director for Graduate Recruitment, 401-454-6312, Fax: 401-454-6309, E-mail: mpetteng@risd.edu.
Website: http://www.risd.edu/academics/painting/

Rhode Island School of Design, Department of Printmaking, Providence, RI 02903-2784. Offers MFA. *Faculty:* 8 full-time (7 women), 7 part-time/adjunct (4 women). *Students:* 14 full-time (12 women); includes 7 minority (2 Black or African American, non-Hispanic/Latino; 1 Asian, non-Hispanic/Latino; 3 Hispanic/Latino; 1 Two or more races, non-Hispanic/Latino), 2 international. Average age 28. 37 applicants, 32% accepted, 6 enrolled. In 2017, 8 master's awarded. *Degree requirements:* For master's, thesis, exhibition. *Entrance requirements:* For master's, portfolio, statement of purpose, 3 letters of recommendation. Additional exam requirements/recommendations for international students: Required—TOEFL (minimum score 580 paper-based; 93 iBT). *Application deadline:* For fall admission, 1/10 for domestic and international students. Application fee: $60. Electronic applications accepted. *Expenses: Tuition:* Full-time $48,210. *Required fees:* $260. *Financial support:* Fellowships, research assistantships, teaching assistantships, Federal Work-Study, scholarships/grants, and unspecified assistantships available. Financial award application deadline: 2/15; financial award applicants required to submit FAFSA. *Unit head:* Cornelia McSheehy, Department Head, 401-454-6224, Fax: 401-454-6707, E-mail: printmaking@risd.edu. *Application contact:* Molly Pettengill, Assistant Director for Graduate Recruitment, 401-454-6312, Fax: 401-454-6309, E-mail: mpetteng@risd.edu.
Website: http://www.risd.edu/academics/printmaking/

Rhode Island School of Design, Department of Sculpture, Providence, RI 02903-2784. Offers MFA. *Accreditation:* NASAD. *Faculty:* 5 full-time (2 women), 10 part-time/adjunct (4 women). *Students:* 13 full-time (9 women); includes 3 minority (1 Asian, non-Hispanic/Latino; 1 Hispanic/Latino; 1 Two or more races, non-Hispanic/Latino), 6 international. Average age 29. 75 applicants, 20% accepted, 9 enrolled. In 2017, 6 master's awarded. *Degree requirements:* For master's, thesis, exhibition. *Entrance requirements:* For master's, portfolio, statement of purpose, 3 letters of recommendation. Additional exam requirements/recommendations for international students: Required—TOEFL (minimum score 580 paper-based; 93 iBT). *Application deadline:* For fall admission, 1/10 for domestic and international students. Application fee: $60. Electronic applications accepted. *Expenses: Tuition:* Full-time $48,210. *Required fees:* $260. *Financial support:* Fellowships, research assistantships, teaching assistantships, Federal Work-Study, scholarships/grants, and unspecified assistantships available. Financial award application deadline: 2/15; financial award applicants required to submit FAFSA. *Unit head:* Lisi Raskin, Department Head, 401-454-6190, Fax: 401-454-6191, E-mail: sculpture@risd.edu. *Application contact:* Molly Pettengill, Assistant Director for Graduate Recruitment, 401-454-6312, Fax: 401-454-6309, E-mail: mpetteng@risd.edu.
Website: http://www.risd.edu/academics/sculpture/

Rochester Institute of Technology, Graduate Enrollment Services, College of Imaging Arts and Sciences, School for American Crafts, MFA Program in Ceramics, Rochester, NY 14623. Offers MFA. *Accreditation:* NASAD. *Program availability:* Part-time. *Students:* 5 full-time (3 women), 4 part-time (2 women); includes 2 minority (1 Asian, non-Hispanic/Latino; 1 Two or more races, non-Hispanic/Latino), 4 international. Average age 31. 10 applicants, 50% accepted, 1 enrolled. In 2017, 2 master's awarded. *Degree requirements:* For master's, thesis. *Entrance requirements:* For master's, GRE, portfolio, minimum GPA of 3.0 (recommended). Additional exam requirements/recommendations for international students: Required—TOEFL (minimum score 550 paper-based; 79 iBT), IELTS (minimum score 6.5), PTE (minimum score 58). *Application deadline:* Applications are processed on a rolling basis. Application fee: $65. Electronic applications accepted. *Expenses:* $1,815 per credit hour. *Financial support:* In 2017–18, 4 students received support. Teaching assistantships with partial tuition reimbursements available, career-related internships or fieldwork, scholarships/grants, and unspecified assistantships available. Support available to part-time students. Financial award applicants required to submit FAFSA. *Faculty research:* Aesthetics, techniques, and theory. *Unit head:* Jane Shellenbarger, Graduate Program Director, 585-475-7562, Fax: 585-475-6447, E-mail: sac@rit.edu. *Application contact:* Diane Ellison, Senior Associate Vice President, Graduate Enrollment Services, 585-475-2229, Fax: 585-475-7164, E-mail: gradinfo@rit.edu.
Website: http://cias.rit.edu/schools/american-crafts/graduate-ceramics-graduate

Rochester Institute of Technology, Graduate Enrollment Services, College of Imaging Arts and Sciences, School for American Crafts, MFA Program in Furniture Design, Rochester, NY 14623-5603. Offers MFA. *Program availability:* Part-time. *Students:* 4 full-time (3 women), 3 part-time (1 woman); includes 1 minority (Asian, non-Hispanic/Latino), 4 international. Average age 31. 15 applicants, 87% accepted, 2 enrolled. In 2017, 2 master's awarded. *Degree requirements:* For master's, thesis, thesis project/exhibition. *Entrance requirements:* For master's, GRE, portfolio, minimum GPA of 3.0 (recommended). Additional exam requirements/recommendations for international students: Required—TOEFL (minimum score 570 paper-based; 80 iBT), IELTS (minimum score 6.5), PTE (minimum score 58). *Application deadline:* Applications are processed on a rolling basis. Application fee: $65. Electronic applications accepted. *Expenses:* $1,815 per credit hour. *Financial support:* In 2017–18, 2 students received support. Teaching assistantships with partial tuition reimbursements available, career-related internships or fieldwork, scholarships/grants, and unspecified assistantships available. Support available to part-time students. Financial award applicants required to submit FAFSA. *Faculty research:* Technology, contemporary art, science, craft; sculptural form in furniture. *Unit head:* Adam Rogers, Graduate Program Director, 585-475-2636, Fax: 585-475-6447, E-mail: sac@rit.edu. *Application contact:* Diane Ellison, Senior Associate Vice President, Graduate Enrollment Services, 585-475-2229, Fax: 585-475-7164, E-mail: gradinfo@rit.edu.
Website: http://cias.rit.edu/schools/american-crafts/graduate-woodworking-graduate

Rochester Institute of Technology, Graduate Enrollment Services, College of Imaging Arts and Sciences, School for American Crafts, MFA Program in Glass, Rochester, NY 14623-5603. Offers MFA. *Accreditation:* NASAD. *Program availability:* Part-time. *Students:* 5 full-time (4 women), 8 part-time (3 women), 3 international. Average age 29. 7 applicants, 86% accepted, 1 enrolled. In 2017, 1 master's awarded. *Degree requirements:* For master's, thesis. *Entrance requirements:* For master's, GRE, portfolio, minimum GPA of 3.0 (recommended). Additional exam requirements/recommendations for international students: Required—TOEFL (minimum score 540 paper-based; 80 iBT), IELTS (minimum score 6), PTE (minimum score 58). *Application deadline:* For fall admission, 2/15 priority date for domestic and international students. Applications are processed on a rolling basis. Application fee: $65. Electronic applications accepted. *Expenses:* $1,815 per credit hour. *Financial support:* In 2017–18, 3 students received support. Teaching assistantships with partial tuition reimbursements available, career-related internships or fieldwork, scholarships/grants, and unspecified assistantships available. Support available to part-time students. Financial award applicants required to submit FAFSA. *Faculty research:* Technology, multi-media sculpture, contemporary art, science, craft. *Unit head:* David Schnuckel, Graduate Program Director, 585-475-7562, Fax: 585-475-6447, E-mail: sac@rit.edu. *Application contact:* Diane Ellison, Senior Associate Vice President, Graduate Enrollment Services, 585-475-2229, Fax: 585-475-7164, E-mail: gradinfo@rit.edu.
Website: http://cias.rit.edu/schools/american-crafts/graduate-glass

Rochester Institute of Technology, Graduate Enrollment Services, College of Imaging Arts and Sciences, School for American Crafts, MFA Program in Metals and Jewelry Design, Rochester, NY 14623-5603. Offers MFA. *Accreditation:* NASAD. *Program availability:* Part-time. *Students:* 16 full-time (12 women), 3 part-time (all women); includes 4 minority (1 Black or African American, non-Hispanic/Latino; 3 Asian, non-Hispanic/Latino), 13 international. Average age 27. 37 applicants, 27% accepted, 5 enrolled. In 2017, 1 master's awarded. *Degree requirements:* For master's, thesis. *Entrance requirements:* For master's, GRE, portfolio, minimum GPA of 3.0 (recommended). Additional exam requirements/recommendations for international students: Required—TOEFL (minimum score 550 paper-based; 79 iBT), IELTS (minimum score 6.5), PTE (minimum score 58). *Application deadline:* For fall admission, 2/15 priority date for domestic and international students. Applications are processed on a rolling basis. Application fee: $65. Electronic applications accepted. *Expenses:* $1,815 per credit hour. *Financial support:* In 2017–18, 11 students received support. Teaching assistantships with partial tuition reimbursements available, career-related internships or fieldwork, scholarships/grants, and unspecified assistantships available. Support available to part-time students. Financial award applicants required to submit FAFSA. *Faculty research:* Computer aided design, computer aided manufacturing, material process research, creation of a body of work. *Unit head:* Juan Carlos Caballero-Perez, Graduate Program Director, 585-475-2654, Fax: 585-475-7562, E-mail: sac@rit.edu. *Application contact:* Diane Ellison, Senior Associate Vice President, Graduate Enrollment Services, 585-475-2229, Fax: 585-475-7164, E-mail: gradinfo@rit.edu.
Website: http://cias.rit.edu/schools/american-crafts/graduate-metalcrafts-graduate

Rochester Institute of Technology, Graduate Enrollment Services, College of Imaging Arts and Sciences, School of Art, MFA Program in Fine Arts Studio, Rochester, NY 14623. Offers fine arts studio (MFA). *Accreditation:* NASAD. *Program availability:* Part-time. *Students:* 10 full-time (8 women), 3 part-time (2 women); includes 2 minority (1 Black or African American, non-Hispanic/Latino; 1 Asian, non-Hispanic/Latino), 5 international. Average age 31. 23 applicants, 43% accepted, 4 enrolled. In 2017, 1 master's awarded. *Degree requirements:* For master's, thesis (for some programs). *Entrance requirements:* For master's, GRE, portfolio, minimum GPA of 3.0 (recommended). Additional exam requirements/recommendations for international students: Required—TOEFL (minimum score 550 paper-based; 79 iBT), IELTS (minimum score 6.5), PTE (minimum score 58). *Application deadline:* For fall admission, 2/15 priority date for domestic and international students. Applications are processed on a rolling basis. Application fee: $65. Electronic applications accepted. *Expenses:* $1,815 per credit hour. *Financial support:* In 2017–18, 5 students received support. Teaching assistantships with partial tuition reimbursements available, career-related internships or fieldwork, scholarships/grants, and unspecified assistantships available. Support available to part-time students. Financial award applicants required to submit FAFSA. *Faculty research:* Art therapy, art criticism, art restoration, gallery and museum management, set and display design, master printmaking, and sculptural casting and foundry fabrication; contemporary and historical art; art education. *Unit head:* Elizabeth Kronfield, Graduate Program Director, 585-475-5762, E-mail: edkfaa@rit.edu. *Application contact:* Diane Ellison, Senior Associate Vice President, Graduate Enrollment Services, 585-475-2229, Fax: 585-475-7164, E-mail: gradinfo@rit.edu.
Website: http://cias.rit.edu/schools/art/graduate-fine-arts-studio

Rutgers University–New Brunswick, Mason Gross School of the Arts, Visual Arts Department, New Brunswick, NJ 08901. Offers drawing (MFA); painting (MFA); sculpture (MFA); visual arts (MFA). *Accreditation:* NASAD. *Degree requirements:* For master's, thesis, exhibit. *Entrance requirements:* For master's, portfolio. Additional exam requirements/recommendations for international students: Required—TOEFL (minimum score 550 paper-based), IELTS (minimum score 7). Electronic applications accepted. *Faculty research:* Media, painting, sculpture, photography, film.

San Diego State University, Graduate and Research Affairs, College of Professional Studies and Fine Arts, School of Art, Design and Art History, San Diego, CA 92182. Offers art history (MA); studio arts (MA, MFA), including applied design, environmental design, graphic design, interior design, painting and printmaking, sculpture. *Accreditation:* NASAD (one or more programs are accredited). *Degree requirements:* For master's, variable foreign language requirement, thesis. *Entrance requirements:* For master's, GRE General Test, bachelor's degree in related field, slide portfolio, typed slide information sheet, 2 letters of recommendation. Additional exam requirements/recommendations for international students: Required—TOEFL. Electronic applications accepted.

San Francisco Art Institute, Master of Fine Arts Programs, San Francisco, CA 94133. Offers studio art (MFA, Certificate), including art and technology (MFA), film (MFA), new

genres (MFA), painting (MFA), photography (MFA), printmaking (MFA), sculpture (MFA); MFA/MA. *Accreditation:* NASAD. *Degree requirements:* For master's, thesis. *Entrance requirements:* For master's and Certificate, portfolio. Additional exam requirements/recommendations for international students: Required—TOEFL (minimum score 580 paper-based; 92 iBT), IELTS (minimum score 7). Electronic applications accepted. *Faculty research:* Studio art, international art exhibitions, neurohumanities, experimental music, virtual reality 360 degree film.

San Francisco State University, Division of Graduate Studies, College of Liberal and Creative Arts, School of Art, San Francisco, CA 94132-1722. Offers art (MFA); museum studies (MA). *Accreditation:* NASAD (one or more programs are accredited). *Unit head:* Mario LaPlante, Interim Director, 415-338-7081, Fax: 415-338-6537, E-mail: laplante@sfsu.edu. *Application contact:* Prof. Chris Finley, Graduate Coordinator, 415-338-6318, Fax: 415-338-6537, E-mail: cfinley@sfsu.edu.
Website: http://www.art.sfsu.edu

Savannah College of Art and Design, Program in Accessory Design, Savannah, GA 31402-3146. Offers MA, MFA. *Program availability:* Part-time. *Faculty:* 5 full-time (4 women). *Students:* 15 full-time (14 women), 4 part-time (all women); includes 5 minority (2 Asian, non-Hispanic/Latino; 3 Hispanic/Latino), 9 international. Average age 27. 11 applicants, 36% accepted, 3 enrolled. In 2017, 5 master's awarded. *Degree requirements:* For master's, final project (for MA); thesis (for MFA). *Entrance requirements:* For master's, GRE (recommended), portfolio (submitted in digital format), audition or writing submission, resume, statement of purpose, two letters of recommendation. Additional exam requirements/recommendations for international students: Recommended—TOEFL (minimum score 550 paper-based; 85 iBT), IELTS (minimum score 6.5). *Application deadline:* For fall admission, 4/1 for domestic and international students. Applications are processed on a rolling basis. Application fee: $40. Electronic applications accepted. *Expenses: Tuition:* Full-time $36,765; part-time $817 per credit hour. One-time fee: $500. *Financial support:* Career-related internships or fieldwork, Federal Work-Study, and scholarships/grants available. Financial award application deadline: 4/1; financial award applicants required to submit FAFSA. *Unit head:* Michael Fink, Dean, School of Fashion. *Application contact:* Jenny Jaquillard, Executive Director of Admissions, Recruitment and Events, 912-525-5100, Fax: 912-525-5985, E-mail: admission@scad.edu.
Website: http://www.scad.edu/academics/programs/accessory-design

Savannah College of Art and Design, Program in Furniture Design, Savannah, GA 31402-3146. Offers MA, MFA. *Program availability:* Part-time. *Faculty:* 5 full-time (1 woman). *Students:* 19 full-time (11 women), 4 part-time (2 women); includes 2 minority (1 Black or African American, non-Hispanic/Latino; 1 Hispanic/Latino), 14 international. Average age 27. 27 applicants, 67% accepted, 8 enrolled. In 2017, 9 master's awarded. *Degree requirements:* For master's, final project (for MA); thesis (for MFA). *Entrance requirements:* For master's, GRE (recommended), portfolio (submitted in digital format), audition or writing submission, resume, statement of purpose, two letters of recommendation. Additional exam requirements/recommendations for international students: Recommended—TOEFL (minimum score 550 paper-based; 85 iBT), IELTS (minimum score 6.5). *Application deadline:* For fall admission, 4/1 for domestic and international students. Applications are processed on a rolling basis. Application fee: $40. Electronic applications accepted. *Expenses: Tuition:* Full-time $36,765; part-time $817 per credit hour. One-time fee: $500. *Financial support:* Career-related internships or fieldwork, Federal Work-Study, and scholarships/grants available. Financial award application deadline: 4/1; financial award applicants required to submit FAFSA. *Unit head:* Fred Spector, Academic Program Coordinator. *Application contact:* Jenny Jaquillard, Executive Director of Admissions, Recruitment and Events, 912-525-5100, Fax: 912-525-5985, E-mail: admission@scad.edu.
Website: http://www.scad.edu/academics/programs/furniture-design

Savannah College of Art and Design, Program in Jewelry, Savannah, GA 31402-3146. Offers MA, MFA. *Program availability:* Part-time. *Faculty:* 4 full-time (all women), 1 part-time/adjunct (0 women). *Students:* 25 full-time (24 women), 2 part-time (both women); includes 1 minority (Black or African American, non-Hispanic/Latino), 24 international. Average age 27. 26 applicants, 73% accepted, 6 enrolled. In 2017, 3 master's awarded. *Degree requirements:* For master's, final project (for MA); thesis (for MFA). *Entrance requirements:* For master's, GRE (recommended), portfolio (submitted in digital format), audition or writing submission, resume, statement of purpose, two letters of recommendation. Additional exam requirements/recommendations for international students: Recommended—TOEFL (minimum score 550 paper-based; 85 iBT), IELTS (minimum score 6.5). *Application deadline:* For fall admission, 4/1 for domestic and international students. Applications are processed on a rolling basis. Application fee: $40. Electronic applications accepted. *Expenses: Tuition:* Full-time $36,765; part-time $817 per credit hour. One-time fee: $500. *Financial support:* Career-related internships or fieldwork, Federal Work-Study, and scholarships/grants available. Financial award application deadline: 4/1; financial award applicants required to submit FAFSA. *Unit head:* Jay Song, Chair, Jewelry. *Application contact:* Jenny Jaquillard, Executive Director of Admissions, Recruitment and Events, 912-525-5100, Fax: 912-525-5985, E-mail: admission@scad.edu.
Website: http://www.scad.edu/academics/programs/jewelry

Savannah College of Art and Design, Program in Painting, Savannah, GA 31402-3146. Offers MA, MFA. *Program availability:* Part-time, 100% online. *Faculty:* 9 full-time (2 women), 1 (woman) part-time/adjunct. *Students:* 61 full-time (42 women), 22 part-time (14 women); includes 12 minority (4 Black or African American, non-Hispanic/Latino; 1 American Indian or Alaska Native, non-Hispanic/Latino; 1 Asian, non-Hispanic/Latino; 6 Hispanic/Latino), 21 international. Average age 34. 93 applicants, 48% accepted, 19 enrolled. In 2017, 18 master's awarded. *Degree requirements:* For master's, final project (for MA); thesis (for MFA). *Entrance requirements:* For master's, GRE (recommended), portfolio (submitted in digital format), audition or writing submission, resume, statement of purpose, two letters of recommendation. Additional exam requirements/recommendations for international students: Recommended—TOEFL (minimum score 550 paper-based; 85 iBT), IELTS (minimum score 6.5). *Application deadline:* For fall admission, 4/1 for domestic and international students. Applications are processed on a rolling basis. Application fee: $40. Electronic applications accepted. *Expenses: Tuition:* Full-time $36,765; part-time $817 per credit hour. One-time fee: $500. *Financial support:* Career-related internships or fieldwork, Federal Work-Study, and scholarships/grants available. Financial award application deadline: 4/1; financial award applicants required to submit FAFSA. *Unit head:* Thomas Francis, Academic Program Coordinator. *Application contact:* Jenny Jaquillard, Executive Director of Admissions, Recruitment and Events, 912-525-5100, Fax: 912-525-5985, E-mail: admission@scad.edu.
Website: http://www.scad.edu/academics/programs/painting

Savannah College of Art and Design, Program in Printmaking, Savannah, GA 31402-3146. Offers MFA. *Program availability:* Part-time. *Faculty:* 3 full-time (2 women). *Students:* 1 (woman) full-time, 1 (woman) part-time. Average age 28. 11 applicants, 27% accepted, 1 enrolled. In 2017, 1 master's awarded. *Degree requirements:* For master's, thesis. *Entrance requirements:* For master's, GRE (recommended), portfolio (submitted in digital format), audition or writing submission, resume, statement of purpose, two letters of recommendation. Additional exam requirements/recommendations for international students: Recommended—TOEFL (minimum score 550 paper-based; 85 iBT), IELTS (minimum score 6.5). *Application deadline:* For fall admission, 4/1 for domestic and international students. Applications are processed on a rolling basis. Application fee: $40. Electronic applications accepted. *Expenses: Tuition:* Full-time $36,765; part-time $817 per credit hour. One-time fee: $500. *Financial support:* Career-related internships or fieldwork, Federal Work-Study, and scholarships/grants available. Financial award application deadline: 4/1; financial award applicants required to submit FAFSA. *Unit head:* Robert Brown, Chair, Printmaking. *Application contact:* Jenny Jaquillard, Executive Director of Admissions, Recruitment and Events, 912-525-5100, Fax: 912-525-5985, E-mail: admission@scad.edu.
Website: http://www.scad.edu/academics/programs/printmaking

Savannah College of Art and Design, Program in Sculpture, Savannah, GA 31402-3146. Offers MA, MFA. *Program availability:* Part-time. *Faculty:* 2 full-time (1 woman), 1 part-time/adjunct (0 women). *Students:* 7 full-time (4 women), 2 part-time (1 woman), 6 international. Average age 34. 17 applicants, 65% accepted, 2 enrolled. In 2017, 3 master's awarded. *Degree requirements:* For master's, final project (for MA); thesis (for MFA). *Entrance requirements:* For master's, GRE (recommended), portfolio (submitted in digital format), audition or writing submission, resume, statement of purpose, two letters of recommendation. Additional exam requirements/recommendations for international students: Recommended—TOEFL (minimum score 550 paper-based; 85 iBT), IELTS (minimum score 6.5). *Application deadline:* For fall admission, 4/1 for domestic and international students. Applications are processed on a rolling basis. Application fee: $40. Electronic applications accepted. *Expenses: Tuition:* Full-time $36,765; part-time $817 per credit hour. One-time fee: $500. *Financial support:* Career-related internships or fieldwork, Federal Work-Study, and scholarships/grants available. Financial award application deadline: 4/1; financial award applicants required to submit FAFSA. *Unit head:* Susan Krause, Chair, Sculpture. *Application contact:* Jenny Jaquillard, Executive Director of Admissions, Recruitment and Events, 912-525-5100, Fax: 912-525-5985, E-mail: admission@scad.edu.
Website: http://www.scad.edu/academics/programs/sculpture

Savannah College of Art and Design, Program in Visual Effects, Savannah, GA 31402-3146. Offers MA, MFA. *Program availability:* Part-time. *Faculty:* 16 full-time (4 women). *Students:* 37 full-time (15 women), 22 part-time (7 women); includes 8 minority (2 Asian, non-Hispanic/Latino; 6 Hispanic/Latino), 36 international. Average age 27. 31 applicants, 61% accepted, 13 enrolled. In 2017, 17 master's awarded. *Degree requirements:* For master's, final project (for MA); thesis (for MFA). *Entrance requirements:* For master's, GRE (recommended), portfolio (submitted in digital format), audition or writing submission, resume, statement of purpose, two letters of recommendation. Additional exam requirements/recommendations for international students: Recommended—TOEFL (minimum score 550 paper-based; 85 iBT), IELTS (minimum score 6.5). *Application deadline:* For fall admission, 4/1 for domestic and international students. Applications are processed on a rolling basis. Application fee: $40. Electronic applications accepted. *Expenses: Tuition:* Full-time $36,765; part-time $817 per credit hour. One-time fee: $500. *Financial support:* Career-related internships or fieldwork, Federal Work-Study, and scholarships/grants available. Financial award application deadline: 4/1; financial award applicants required to submit FAFSA. *Unit head:* Max Almy, Dean, School of Digital Media. *Application contact:* Jenny Jaquillard, Executive Director of Admissions, Recruitment and Events, 912-525-5100, Fax: 912-525-5985, E-mail: admission@scad.edu.
Website: http://www.scad.edu/academics/programs/visual-effects

School of the Art Institute of Chicago, Graduate Division, Department of Art and Technology Studies, Chicago, IL 60603-3103. Offers MFA. *Entrance requirements:* Additional exam requirements/recommendations for international students: Required—TOEFL, IELTS. Electronic applications accepted.

School of the Art Institute of Chicago, Graduate Division, Department of Ceramics, Chicago, IL 60603-3103. Offers MFA. *Accreditation:* NASAD. *Entrance requirements:* Additional exam requirements/recommendations for international students: Required—TOEFL, IELTS. Electronic applications accepted.

School of the Art Institute of Chicago, Graduate Division, Department of Fiber and Material Studies, Chicago, IL 60603-3103. Offers MFA. *Accreditation:* NASAD. *Entrance requirements:* Additional exam requirements/recommendations for international students: Required—TOEFL, IELTS.

School of the Art Institute of Chicago, Graduate Division, Department of Painting and Drawing, Chicago, IL 60603-3103. Offers MFA. *Accreditation:* NASAD. *Entrance requirements:* Additional exam requirements/recommendations for international students: Required—TOEFL, IELTS.

School of the Art Institute of Chicago, Graduate Division, Department of Printmaking, Chicago, IL 60603-3103. Offers MFA. *Accreditation:* NASAD. *Entrance requirements:* Additional exam requirements/recommendations for international students: Required—TOEFL (minimum score 550 paper-based; 80 iBT), IELTS (minimum score 6.5).

School of the Art Institute of Chicago, Graduate Division, Department of Sculpture, Chicago, IL 60603-3103. Offers MFA. *Accreditation:* NASAD. *Entrance requirements:* Additional exam requirements/recommendations for international students: Required—TOEFL, IELTS.

School of the Art Institute of Chicago, Graduate Division, Program in Visual and Critical Studies, Chicago, IL 60603-3103. Offers MA.

School of Visual Arts, Graduate Programs, Art Practice Department, New York, NY 10010-3994. Offers MFA. *Degree requirements:* For master's, thesis. *Entrance requirements:* For master's, portfolio submitted through SlideRoom; 500- to 750-word writing sample. Additional exam requirements/recommendations for international students: Required—TOEFL (minimum score 550 paper-based; 100 iBT), IELTS (minimum score 8). Electronic applications accepted.

School of Visual Arts, Graduate Programs, Computer Art Department, New York, NY 10010-3994. Offers MFA. *Accreditation:* NASAD. *Degree requirements:* For master's, thesis, 60 credits, including all required courses; minimum GPA of 3.0; matriculation of two academic years. *Entrance requirements:* For master's, portfolio; 3-5 minute sample reel showing best work; statement of purpose; official transcript; 3 letters of recommendation; resume/curriculum vitae. Additional exam requirements/recommendations for international students: Required—TOEFL (minimum score 550 paper-based; 79 iBT). Electronic applications accepted. *Expenses:* Contact institution.

School of Visual Arts, Graduate Programs, Design Department, New York, NY 10010-3994. Offers MFA. *Accreditation:* NASAD. *Degree requirements:* For master's, thesis, 60 credits, including all required courses; minimum cumulative GPA of 3.0; residency of two academic years. *Entrance requirements:* For master's, portfolio that reflects wide range of design work and fluency in type and typography. Additional exam requirements/recommendations for international students: Required—TOEFL (minimum score 550 paper-based; 79 iBT). *Expenses:* Contact institution. *Faculty research:* Design, graphic design, multimedia.

School of Visual Arts, Graduate Programs, Illustration as Visual Essay Department, New York, NY 10010-3994. Offers MFA. *Accreditation:* NASAD. *Degree requirements:* For master's, thesis, 60 credits, including all required courses; residency of two academic years. *Entrance requirements:* For master's, portfolio of work (still images)

submitted through SlideRoom. Additional exam requirements/recommendations for international students: Required—TOEFL (minimum score 100 iBT). Electronic applications accepted. *Faculty research:* Illustration, fine arts, computer art, writing, art history, art direction.

School of Visual Arts, Graduate Programs, Program in Fine Arts, New York, NY 10010-3994. Offers MFA. *Accreditation:* NASAD. *Degree requirements:* For master's, thesis, 60 credits, including all required courses; residency of two academic years. *Entrance requirements:* For master's, CD portfolio of work with exactly 12 images. Additional exam requirements/recommendations for international students: Required—TOEFL (minimum score 550 paper-based; 79 iBT). Electronic applications accepted.

School of Visual Arts, Graduate Programs, Program in Photography, Video and Related Media, New York, NY 10010-3994. Offers MFA. *Accreditation:* NASAD. *Degree requirements:* For master's, thesis, 60 credits and all course requirements; minimum GPA of 3.3; thesis project. *Entrance requirements:* For master's, portfolio (still images and/or videos) through SlideRoom. Additional exam requirements/recommendations for international students: Required—TOEFL (minimum score 550 paper-based; 79 iBT). Electronic applications accepted. *Faculty research:* Contemporary and responsible creative initiatives, including experimental, narrative or documentary video, installation and conceptual art, tableau and real-world-witness photography.

Sotheby's Institute of Art–London, Graduate Programs, London, United Kingdom. Offers art business (MA); contemporary art (MA); fine and decorative art and design (MA); modern and contemporary Asian art (MA). *Degree requirements:* For master's, thesis. *Entrance requirements:* Additional exam requirements/recommendations for international students: Required—IELTS (minimum score 7). Electronic applications accepted.

Sotheby's Institute of Art–New York, Graduate Programs, New York, NY 10021. Offers art business (MA); contemporary art (MA); fine and decorative art and design (MA). *Accreditation:* NASAD. *Entrance requirements:* For master's, academic transcripts, two letters of academic reference, personal statement, writing sample, curriculum vitae/resume, interview. Additional exam requirements/recommendations for international students: Required—TOEFL (minimum score 100 iBT), IELTS (minimum score 7). Electronic applications accepted.

Southern Illinois University Carbondale, Graduate School, College of Liberal Arts, School of Art and Design, Carbondale, IL 62901-4701. Offers drawing (MFA); fiber/weaving (MFA); glass (MFA); metalsmithing/blacksmithing (MFA); painting (MFA). *Accreditation:* NASAD. *Degree requirements:* For master's, thesis or alternative. *Entrance requirements:* For master's, minimum GPA of 2.7, portfolio, slides. Additional exam requirements/recommendations for international students: Required—TOEFL. *Faculty research:* Prints/woodcuts, foundry, watercolor.

Southern Illinois University Edwardsville, Graduate School, College of Arts and Sciences, Department of Art and Design, Program in Art Studio, Edwardsville, IL 62026. Offers MFA. *Accreditation:* NASAD. *Program availability:* Part-time. *Degree requirements:* For master's, thesis, exhibition. *Entrance requirements:* For master's, portfolio. Additional exam requirements/recommendations for international students: Required—TOEFL (minimum score 550 paper-based; 79 iBT), IELTS (minimum score 6.5). Electronic applications accepted.

Southern Methodist University, Meadows School of the Arts, Division of Art, Dallas, TX 75275. Offers studio art (MFA), including ceramics, drawing, painting, photography, printmaking, sculpture. *Accreditation:* NASAD. *Degree requirements:* For master's, thesis or alternative, exhibit. *Entrance requirements:* For master's, BFA or equivalent, letters of recommendation, portfolio. Additional exam requirements/recommendations for international students: Required—TOEFL (minimum score 550 paper-based; 80 iBT). *Faculty research:* American stoneware, Southwestern furniture traditions, photographic apparatus and techniques, American ceramists, architecture.

Southwest University of Visual Arts, MFA Programs, Tucson, AZ 85716-2505. Offers motion arts (MFA); painting and drawing (MFA); photography (MFA).

Spring Hill College, Graduate Programs, Program in Liberal Arts, Mobile, AL 36608-1791. Offers fine arts (MLA); leadership and ethics (MLA, Postbaccalaureate Certificate); literature (MLA). *Program availability:* Part-time, evening/weekend. *Faculty:* 11 full-time (1 woman). *Students:* 1 (woman) full-time, 21 part-time (7 women); includes 5 minority (4 Black or African American, non-Hispanic/Latino; 1 Hispanic/Latino), 6 international. Average age 31. In 2017, 12 master's awarded. *Degree requirements:* For master's, capstone course, completion of program within 6 years of initial admittance. *Entrance requirements:* For master's, bachelor's degree with minimum undergraduate GPA of 3.0 or graduate/professional degree. Additional exam requirements/recommendations for international students: Required—TOEFL (minimum score 550 paper-based; 80 iBT), IELTS (minimum score 6.5), CPE or CAE (minimum score C), Michigan English Language Assessment Battery (minimum score 90). *Application deadline:* For fall admission, 8/1 priority date for domestic and international students; for spring admission, 12/1 priority date for domestic and international students. Applications are processed on a rolling basis. Application fee: $25 ($35 for international students). Electronic applications accepted. *Expenses:* Contact institution. *Financial support:* Applicants required to submit FAFSA. *Unit head:* Dr. Thomas J. Hoffman, Director, 251-380-4184, Fax: 251-460-2115, E-mail: thoffman@shc.edu. *Application contact:* Robert Stewart, Vice President of Enrollment, 251-380-3030, Fax: 251-460-2186, E-mail: rstewart@shc.edu. Website: http://ug.shc.edu/graduate-degrees/master-liberal-arts/

Stanford University, School of Humanities and Sciences, Department of Art and Art History, Stanford, CA 94305-2004. Offers art history (PhD); art practice (MFA); design (MFA); documentary film and video (MFA); MS/MFA. *Degree requirements:* For master's, thesis (for some programs), faculty reviews; for doctorate, 2 foreign languages, thesis/dissertation. *Entrance requirements:* For master's and doctorate, GRE General Test. Additional exam requirements/recommendations for international students: Required—TOEFL. Electronic applications accepted. *Expenses: Tuition:* Full-time $48,987; part-time $10,620 per quarter. One-time fee: $400. Tuition and fees vary according to program.

State University of New York at New Paltz, Graduate and Extended Learning School, School of Fine and Performing Arts, Department of Fine Arts, New Paltz, NY 12561. Offers ceramics (MFA); metal (MFA); painting-drawing (MFA); printmaking (MFA); sculpture (MFA). *Accreditation:* NASAD. *Program availability:* Part-time, evening/weekend. *Faculty:* 18 full-time (12 women), 1 (woman) part-time/adjunct. *Students:* 29 full-time (24 women), 2 part-time (1 woman); includes 4 minority (1 Asian, non-Hispanic/Latino; 3 Hispanic/Latino), 4 international. 79 applicants, 43% accepted, 18 enrolled. In 2017, 18 master's awarded. *Degree requirements:* For master's, thesis, portfolio, exhibit (MFA). *Entrance requirements:* For master's, minimum GPA of 3.0, portfolio. Additional exam requirements/recommendations for international students: Required—TOEFL (minimum score 550 paper-based; 80 iBT), IELTS (minimum score 6.5). *Application deadline:* For fall admission, 2/15 priority date for domestic and international students. Applications are processed on a rolling basis. Application fee: $50. Electronic applications accepted. *Financial support:* In 2017–18, 8 research assistantships with partial tuition reimbursements (averaging $5,000 per year), 7 teaching assistantships with partial tuition reimbursements (averaging $5,000 per year) were awarded. Financial

award application deadline: 8/1. *Unit head:* Prof. Anne Galperin, Chair, 845-257-3833, E-mail: galperia@newpaltz.edu. *Application contact:* Prof. Matthew Friday, Graduate Coordinator, 845-257-2609, E-mail: fridaym@newpaltz.edu.
Website: http://www.newpaltz.edu/art/

State University of New York at Oswego, Graduate Studies, Department of Art, Oswego, NY 13126. Offers art (MA); graphic design and digital media (MA). *Accreditation:* NASAD. *Program availability:* Part-time. *Degree requirements:* For master's, exhibit, final presentation. *Entrance requirements:* For master's, slides of previous work. Additional exam requirements/recommendations for international students: Required—TOEFL (minimum score 560 paper-based). *Faculty research:* Ancient and primitive art, nineteenth century art, medieval art, Renaissance art.

Stephen F. Austin State University, Graduate School, College of Fine Arts, School of Art, Nacogdoches, TX 75962. Offers art (MA); design (MFA); drawing (MFA); painting (MFA); sculpture (MFA). *Accreditation:* NASAD. *Program availability:* Part-time. *Degree requirements:* For master's, comprehensive exam, thesis, exhibit. *Entrance requirements:* For master's, GRE General Test, portfolio. Additional exam requirements/recommendations for international students: Required—TOEFL. *Faculty research:* Printmaking, jewelry, photography, ceramics, art history.

Stony Brook University, State University of New York, Graduate School, College of Arts and Sciences, Department of Art, Program in Studio Art, Stony Brook, NY 11794. Offers MFA. *Students:* 9 full-time (7 women); includes 2 minority (both Hispanic/Latino), 1 international. Average age 32. 10 applicants, 30% accepted, 2 enrolled. In 2017, 7 master's awarded. *Degree requirements:* For master's, comprehensive exam, thesis, reading knowledge of German, French, or Italian; exhibition. *Entrance requirements:* For master's, GRE General Test, minimum undergraduate GPA of 3.0. Additional exam requirements/recommendations for international students: Required—TOEFL (minimum score 550 paper-based; 90 iBT), IELTS (minimum score 6.5). *Application deadline:* For fall admission, 1/15 priority date for domestic students; for spring admission, 10/1 for domestic students. Application fee: $100. *Expenses:* Contact institution. *Unit head:* Dr. Barbara Frank, Chair, 631-632-7250, E-mail: barbara.frank@stonybrook.edu. *Application contact:* Lisa Perez, Coordinator, 631-632-7270, Fax: 631-632-7261, E-mail: lisa.perez@stonybrook.edu.
Website: http://art.stonybrook.edu/graduate/g-ars/

Sul Ross State University, College of Arts and Sciences, Department of Fine Arts and Communication, Alpine, TX 79832. Offers art history (MA); studio art (MA), including art education. *Program availability:* Part-time. *Degree requirements:* For master's, oral or written exam. *Entrance requirements:* For master's, GRE General Test, minimum GPA of 2.5 in last 60 hours of undergraduate work. *Faculty research:* Ceramic sculpture, watercolor, wood sculpture, rock art.

Syracuse University, College of Visual and Performing Arts, MFA Program in Studio Arts, Syracuse, NY 13244. Offers MFA. *Accreditation:* NASAD. *Program availability:* Part-time. *Degree requirements:* For master's, thesis or alternative. *Entrance requirements:* For master's, portfolio, three letters of recommendation, resume, personal statement. Additional exam requirements/recommendations for international students: Required—TOEFL (minimum score 100 iBT). *Application deadline:* For fall admission, 2/1 priority date for domestic and international students. Application fee: $75. Electronic applications accepted. *Financial support:* Fellowships with full tuition reimbursements, teaching assistantships with tuition reimbursements, and tuition waivers available. Financial award application deadline: 1/1; financial award applicants required to submit FAFSA. *Faculty research:* Ceramics, drawing, jewelry and metalsmithing, painting, print media and graphic art, sculpture. *Unit head:* Prof. Joanna Spitzner, Associate Professor/Studio Arts Graduate Program Coordinator, 315-443-5698, E-mail: jspitzne@syr.edu. *Application contact:* Caitlin Jarvis, Graduate Recruitment Specialist, 315-443-2769, E-mail: admissg@syr.edu.
Website: http://vpa.syr.edu/academics/art/graduate/studio-arts/

Temple University, Tyler School of Art, Department of Crafts, Philadelphia, PA 19122-6096. Offers ceramics (MFA); fibers and material studies (MFA); glass (MFA); metals/jewelry/CAD-CAM (MFA). *Faculty:* 8 full-time (5 women), 21 part-time/adjunct (18 women). *Students:* 15 full-time (11 women); includes 2 minority (both Hispanic/Latino). 67 applicants, 25% accepted, 8 enrolled. In 2017, 11 master's awarded. *Entrance requirements:* For master's, minimum GPA of 3.0, slide portfolio, 40 credits in studio art, 12 credits in art history, letters of recommendation, resume/curriculum vitae. Additional exam requirements/recommendations for international students: Required—TOEFL (minimum score 550 paper-based; 79 iBT), IELTS (minimum score 6.5). *Application deadline:* For fall admission, 1/15 for domestic students, 12/15 for international students. Application fee: $60. Electronic applications accepted. *Expenses:* Contact institution. *Financial support:* Fellowships, research assistantships, teaching assistantships, and Federal Work-Study available. Support available to part-time students. Financial award application deadline: 1/15; financial award applicants required to submit FAFSA. *Unit head:* Nicholas Kripal, Chair, 215-782-2790, Fax: 215-782-2799, E-mail: nkripal@temple.edu. *Application contact:* Tamryn McDermott, Director of Admissions, 215-777-9090, E-mail: tylerart@temple.edu.

Temple University, Tyler School of Art, Department of Graphic Arts and Design, Philadelphia, PA 19122-6096. Offers graphic and interactive design (MFA); photography (MFA); printmaking (MFA). *Faculty:* 12 full-time (5 women), 31 part-time/adjunct (12 women). *Students:* 19 full-time (12 women); includes 3 minority (2 Asian, non-Hispanic/Latino; 1 Two or more races, non-Hispanic/Latino), 5 international. 117 applicants, 18% accepted, 10 enrolled. In 2017, 8 master's awarded. *Entrance requirements:* For master's, minimum GPA of 3.0, slide portfolio, 40 credits in studio art, 12 credits in art history, letters of recommendation, resume/curriculum vitae. Additional exam requirements/recommendations for international students: Required—TOEFL (minimum score 550 paper-based; 79 iBT), IELTS (minimum score 6.5). *Application deadline:* For fall admission, 1/15 for domestic students, 12/15 for international students. Application fee: $60. Electronic applications accepted. *Expenses:* Contact institution. *Financial support:* Fellowships, research assistantships, teaching assistantships, and Federal Work-Study available. Support available to part-time students. Financial award application deadline: 1/15; financial award applicants required to submit FAFSA. *Unit head:* Dermot Mac Cormack, Chair, 215-777-9179, Fax: 215-782-2799, E-mail: dermot@temple.edu. *Application contact:* Tamryn McDermott, Director of Admissions, 215-777-9090, E-mail: tylerart@temple.edu.
Website: http://tyler.temple.edu/graduate

Temple University, Tyler School of Art, Department of Painting, Drawing, and Sculpture, Philadelphia, PA 19122-6096. Offers painting (MFA); sculpture (MFA). *Faculty:* 8 full-time (3 women), 11 part-time/adjunct (2 women). *Students:* 22 full-time (14 women), 1 (woman) part-time; includes 4 minority (1 Black or African American, non-Hispanic/Latino; 1 Asian, non-Hispanic/Latino; 2 Hispanic/Latino), 4 international. 144 applicants, 9% accepted, 9 enrolled. In 2017, 8 master's awarded. *Degree requirements:* For master's, essay, exhibit. *Entrance requirements:* For master's, minimum GPA of 3.0, slide portfolio, 40 credits in studio art, 12 credits in art history, letters of recommendation, resume/curriculum vitae. Additional exam requirements/recommendations for international students: Required—TOEFL (minimum score 550 paper-based; 79 iBT), IELTS (minimum score 6.5). *Application deadline:* For fall admission, 1/15 for domestic students, 12/15 for international

students. Application fee: $60. Electronic applications accepted. *Expenses:* Contact institution. *Financial support:* Fellowships with full tuition reimbursements, research assistantships with full tuition reimbursements, teaching assistantships with full tuition reimbursements, and Federal Work-Study available. Support available to part-time students. Financial award application deadline: 1/15; financial award applicants required to submit FAFSA. *Unit head:* Mark Shetabi, Chair, 215-777-9176, Fax: 215-782-2799, E-mail: mark.shetabi@temple.edu. *Application contact:* Tamryn McDermott, Director of Admissions, 215-777-9090, E-mail: tylerart@temple.edu.

Texas A&M University, College of Architecture, Department of Visualization, College Station, TX 77843. Offers MFA, MS. *Faculty:* 19. *Students:* 69 full-time (43 women), 25 part-time (8 women); includes 22 minority (3 Black or African American, non-Hispanic/Latino; 10 Asian, non-Hispanic/Latino; 9 Hispanic/Latino), 11 international. Average age 27. 58 applicants, 72% accepted, 28 enrolled. In 2017, 23 master's awarded. *Entrance requirements:* Additional exam requirements/recommendations for international students: Required—TOEFL (minimum score 550 paper-based; 80 iBT), TWE, PTE (minimum score 53). *Application deadline:* For fall admission, 1/5 for domestic students. Application fee: $50 ($90 for international students). *Expenses:* Contact institution. *Financial support:* In 2017–18, 78 students received support, including 19 research assistantships with tuition reimbursements available (averaging $6,345 per year), 51 teaching assistantships with tuition reimbursements available (averaging $5,097 per year); career-related internships or fieldwork, institutionally sponsored loans, scholarships/grants, traineeships, health care benefits, tuition waivers (full and partial), and unspecified assistantships also available. Support available to part-time students. Financial award application deadline: 12/15; financial award applicants required to submit FAFSA. *Unit head:* Dr. Tim McLaughlin, Department Head, 979-845-3465, E-mail: timm@viz.tamu.edu. *Application contact:* Dr. Frederic Parke, Associate Head of Department/Graduate Program Coordinator, 979-845-6596, E-mail: parke@viz.tamu.edu.
Website: http://viz.arch.tamu.edu/

Texas A&M University–Commerce, College of Humanities, Social Sciences and Arts, Commerce, TX 75429. Offers applied criminology (MS); applied linguistics (MA, MS); art (MA, MFA); computational linguistics (Graduate Certificate); creative writing (Graduate Certificate); criminal justice management (Graduate Certificate); criminal justice studies (Graduate Certificate); English (MA, MS, PhD); film studies (Graduate Certificate); history (MA, MS); history of Christianity (Graduate Certificate); Holocaust studies (Graduate Certificate); homeland security (Graduate Certificate); music education (MM); music performance (MM); political science (MA, MS); public history (Graduate Certificate); sociology (MS); Spanish (MA); studies in children's and adolescent literature and culture (Graduate Certificate); teaching English to speakers of other languages (Graduate Certificate); theater (MA, MS); world history (Graduate Certificate). *Program availability:* Part-time. *Faculty:* 56 full-time (26 women), 10 part-time/adjunct (5 women). *Students:* 133 full-time (85 women), 439 part-time (311 women); includes 204 minority (79 Black or African American, non-Hispanic/Latino; 4 American Indian or Alaska Native, non-Hispanic/Latino; 9 Asian, non-Hispanic/Latino; 98 Hispanic/Latino; 14 Two or more races, non-Hispanic/Latino), 26 international. Average age 36. 261 applicants, 50% accepted, 113 enrolled. In 2017, 105 master's, 5 doctorates awarded. *Degree requirements:* For master's, one foreign language, comprehensive exam, thesis (for some programs); for doctorate, one foreign language, comprehensive exam, thesis/dissertation, departmental qualifying exam. *Entrance requirements:* For master's and doctorate, GRE General Test. Additional exam requirements/recommendations for international students: Required—TOEFL (minimum score 550 paper-based; 79 iBT), IELTS (minimum score 6). *Application deadline:* Applications are processed on a rolling basis. Application fee: $50. Electronic applications accepted. *Expenses:* Contact institution. *Financial support:* In 2017–18, 43 students received support, including 9 research assistantships with partial tuition reimbursements available (averaging $9,000 per year), 68 teaching assistantships with partial tuition reimbursements available (averaging $9,000 per year); Federal Work-Study, institutionally sponsored loans, scholarships/grants, health care benefits, and unspecified assistantships also available. Financial award application deadline: 5/1; financial award applicants required to submit FAFSA. *Unit head:* Dr. William F. Kuracina, Interim Dean, 903-886-5166, Fax: 903-886-5774, E-mail: william.kuracina@tamuc.edu. *Application contact:* Vicky Turner, Doctoral Degree and Special Programs Coordinator, 903-886-5167, E-mail: vicky.turner@tamuc.edu.
Website: http://www.tamuc.edu/academics/graduateSchool/programs/humanitiesSocialScienceArts/default.aspx

Texas A&M University–Corpus Christi, College of Graduate Studies, College of Liberal Arts, Program in Studio Art, Corpus Christi, TX 78412. Offers MFA. *Program availability:* Part-time, evening/weekend. *Students:* 6 full-time (4 women), 4 part-time (1 woman); includes 2 minority (both Hispanic/Latino), 1 international. Average age 32. 11 applicants, 18% accepted, 2 enrolled. In 2017, 8 master's awarded. *Degree requirements:* For master's, comprehensive exam, thesis. *Entrance requirements:* For master's, essay (300-500 words); 3 letters of recommendation; portfolio of applicant's works (up to 20 .jpg image files of at least 150 dpi). Additional exam requirements/recommendations for international students: Required—TOEFL (minimum score 550 paper-based; 79 iBT), IELTS (minimum score 6.5). *Application deadline:* For fall admission, 3/15 priority date for domestic and international students. Applications are processed on a rolling basis. Application fee: $50 ($70 for international students). Electronic applications accepted. *Expenses:* Tuition, state resident: full-time $3568; part-time $198.24 per credit hour. Tuition, nonresident: full-time $11,038; part-time $613.24 per credit hour. *Required fees:* $2129; $1422.58 per semester. Tuition and fees vary according to program. *Financial support:* Research assistantships, teaching assistantships, career-related internships or fieldwork, Federal Work-Study, institutionally sponsored loans, scholarships/grants, health care benefits, and unspecified assistantships available. Support available to part-time students. Financial award application deadline: 3/15; financial award applicants required to submit FAFSA. *Unit head:* Ryan O'Malley, Graduate Coordinator, 361-825-5835, E-mail: ryan.omalley@tamucc.edu. *Application contact:* Graduate Admissions Coordinator, 361-825-2177, Fax: 361-825-2755, E-mail: gradweb@tamucc.edu.
Website: http://cla.tamucc.edu/art/Graduate.html

Texas Christian University, College of Fine Arts, School of Art, Fort Worth, TX 76129. Offers art history (MA); studio art (MFA), including painting. *Accreditation:* NASAD. *Faculty:* 11 full-time (5 women). *Students:* 22 full-time (17 women); includes 3 minority (all Hispanic/Latino), 5 international. Average age 28. 31 applicants, 35% accepted, 9 enrolled. In 2017, 3 master's awarded. *Degree requirements:* For master's, variable foreign language requirement, comprehensive exam, thesis. *Entrance requirements:* For master's, GRE General Test (for MA). Additional exam requirements/recommendations for international students: Required—TOEFL (minimum score 550 paper-based; 80 iBT). *Application deadline:* For fall admission, 2/1 for domestic and international students. Application fee: $60. Electronic applications accepted. *Expenses:* Contact institution. *Financial support:* In 2017–18, 18 students received support, including 17 teaching assistantships (averaging $10,000 per year); institutionally sponsored loans, scholarships/grants, health care benefits, tuition waivers (full and partial), and unspecified assistantships also available. Financial award application deadline: 2/15. *Unit head:* Richard Lane, Director, 817-257-7643, E-mail: r.lane@tcu.edu. *Application contact:* Donna Smolik, TCU College of Fine Arts Graduate Office, 817-257-7603, Fax: 817-257-5672, E-mail: cfagradinfo@tcu.edu.
Website: http://www.art.tcu.edu/

Texas Southern University, College of Liberal Arts and Behavioral Sciences, Department of Fine Arts, Houston, TX 77004-4584. Offers fine arts (MA); music (MA). *Program availability:* Part-time. *Degree requirements:* For master's, one foreign language, comprehensive exam, recital. *Entrance requirements:* For master's, GRE General Test, minimum GPA of 2.5. Additional exam requirements/recommendations for international students: Required—TOEFL. Electronic applications accepted. *Faculty research:* Music theory, choral music, composition, percussion composition, ethnic musicology.

Texas Tech University, Graduate School, J.T. and Margaret Talkington College of Visual and Performing Arts, Fine Arts Doctoral Program, Lubbock, TX 79409-5060. Offers PhD. *Accreditation:* NAST. *Students:* 52 full-time (29 women), 40 part-time (25 women); includes 12 minority (2 Black or African American, non-Hispanic/Latino; 1 Asian, non-Hispanic/Latino; 5 Hispanic/Latino; 4 Two or more races, non-Hispanic/Latino), 17 international. Average age 36. 28 applicants, 46% accepted, 9 enrolled. In 2017, 8 doctorates awarded. *Degree requirements:* For doctorate, variable foreign language requirement, comprehensive exam, thesis/dissertation. *Entrance requirements:* For doctorate, GRE General Test (for some tracks). Additional exam requirements/recommendations for international students: Required—TOEFL (minimum score 550 paper-based; 79 iBT). *Application deadline:* For fall admission, 6/1 priority date for domestic students, 1/15 priority date for international students; for spring admission, 9/1 priority date for domestic students, 6/15 priority date for international students. Applications are processed on a rolling basis. Application fee: $60. Electronic applications accepted. *Expenses:* Contact institution. *Financial support:* In 2017–18, 57 students received support, including 57 fellowships (averaging $4,854 per year), 44 teaching assistantships (averaging $12,168 per year); research assistantships, Federal Work-Study, institutionally sponsored loans, scholarships/grants, health care benefits, tuition waivers (partial), unspecified assistantships, and competitive grants to support graduate research also available. Financial award applicants required to submit FAFSA. *Faculty research:* Arts criticism and history, music, theatre arts, arts education, interdisciplinary arts. *Unit head:* Dr. Brian D. Steele, Director/Associate Dean, Talkington College of Visual and Performing Arts, 806-742-0700, Fax: 806-742-0695, E-mail: brian.steele@ttu.edu.
Website: http://www.fadp.vpa.ttu.edu

Texas Tech University, Graduate School, J.T. and Margaret Talkington College of Visual and Performing Arts, School of Art, Lubbock, TX 79409. Offers art (MFA); art education (MAE); art history (MA). *Accreditation:* NASAD (one or more programs are accredited). *Program availability:* Part-time, blended/hybrid learning. *Faculty:* 31 full-time (13 women), 10 part-time/adjunct (6 women). *Students:* 32 full-time (22 women), 18 part-time (14 women); includes 11 minority (1 Black or African American, non-Hispanic/Latino; 1 Asian, non-Hispanic/Latino; 8 Hispanic/Latino; 1 Two or more races, non-Hispanic/Latino), 6 international. Average age 35. 31 applicants, 45% accepted, 9 enrolled. In 2017, 22 master's awarded. *Degree requirements:* For master's, variable foreign language requirement, comprehensive exam, thesis (for some programs), exhibition (for MFA). *Entrance requirements:* For master's, GRE (for MA). Additional exam requirements/recommendations for international students: Required—TOEFL (minimum score 550 paper-based; 79 iBT), IELTS (minimum score 6.5). *Application deadline:* For fall admission, 6/1 priority date for domestic students, 1/15 priority date for international students; for spring admission, 9/1 priority date for domestic students, 6/15 priority date for international students. Applications are processed on a rolling basis. Application fee: $60. Electronic applications accepted. *Expenses:* Contact institution. *Financial support:* In 2017–18, 37 students received support, including 36 fellowships (averaging $3,227 per year), 32 teaching assistantships (averaging $9,937 per year); research assistantships, Federal Work-Study, institutionally sponsored loans, scholarships/grants, health care benefits, tuition waivers (partial), and unspecified assistantships also available. Financial award application deadline: 2/15; financial award applicants required to submit FAFSA. *Faculty research:* Contemporary Chicano/a art; transformation of multidisciplinary approach to printmaking; letter press posters; intersection of art and science; transmedia. *Total annual research expenditures:* $44,636. *Unit head:* Prof. Lydia Thompson, Director and Professor, 806-742-3825 Ext. 255, E-mail: lydia.thompson@ttu.edu. *Application contact:* Linda Rumbelow, Academic Advisor, 806-742-3825 Ext. 222, E-mail: linda.rumbelow@ttu.edu.
Website: http://www.art.ttu.edu

Texas Woman's University, Graduate School, College of Arts and Sciences, School of the Arts, Department of Visual Arts, Denton, TX 76204. Offers art (MA, MAT, MFA), including art education (MA, MAT), art history (MA), ceramics (MFA), graphic design (MA), intermedia (MFA), painting (MFA), photography (MFA), sculpture (MFA). MFA degrees are granted through the Federation of North Texas Area Universities (The University of North Texas, Texas A&M Commerce, and Texas Woman's University). *Faculty:* 6 full-time (3 women). *Students:* 8 full-time (6 women), 9 part-time (8 women); includes 7 minority (1 Black or African American, non-Hispanic/Latino; 1 American Indian or Alaska Native, non-Hispanic/Latino; 4 Hispanic/Latino; 1 Two or more races, non-Hispanic/Latino). Average age 33. 10 applicants, 50% accepted, 2 enrolled. In 2017, 10 master's awarded. *Degree requirements:* For master's, comprehensive exam, thesis (for some programs), exhibit (MFA), oral exam, thesis or professional paper (MA). *Entrance requirements:* For master's, portfolio, interview, current curriculum vitae, letter of intent, 3 letters of recommendation, artist statement, 2 research papers (for art history or art education). Additional exam requirements/recommendations for international students: Required—TOEFL (minimum score 550 paper-based; 79 iBT); Recommended—IELTS (minimum score 6.5), TSE (minimum score 53). *Application deadline:* For fall admission, 1/31 priority date for domestic and international students; for spring admission, 10/15 priority date for domestic students, 7/1 priority date for international students. Applications are processed on a rolling basis. Application fee: $50 ($75 for international students). Electronic applications accepted. *Expenses:* $7,520 per year full-time in-state; $16,820 per year full-time out-of-state. *Financial support:* In 2017–18, 9 students received support, including 5 teaching assistantships (averaging $9,780 per year); career-related internships or fieldwork, Federal Work-Study, institutionally sponsored loans, scholarships/grants, traineeships, health care benefits, and unspecified assistantships also available. Support available to part-time students. Financial award application deadline: 3/1; financial award applicants required to submit FAFSA. *Faculty research:* Art education and electronic technology, film noir, one-of-a kind art books, new media, early video art from 1960-1980. *Unit head:* Dr. Vagner Whitehead, Chair, 940-898-2530, Fax: 940-898-2496, E-mail: visualarts@twu.edu. *Application contact:* Korie Hawkins, Associate Director of Admissions, Graduate Recruitment, 940-898-3188, Fax: 940-898-3081, E-mail: admissions@twu.edu.
Website: http://www.twu.edu/visual-arts/

Thomas Jefferson University, Kanbar College of Design, Engineering and Commerce, Program in Surface Imaging, Philadelphia, PA 19107. Offers MS.

Tiffin University, Program in Humanities, Tiffin, OH 44883-2161. Offers art and visual media (MH); communication (MH); creative writing (MH); English (MH); film studies (MH); humanities (MH); individualized studies (MH). *Program availability:* Part-time, evening/weekend, online only, 100% online, blended/hybrid learning. *Entrance requirements:* For master's, work experience. Additional exam requirements/recommendations for international students: Required—TOEFL (minimum score 550 paper-based; 79 iBT). Electronic applications accepted. Application fee is waived when completed online. *Expenses:* Contact institution.

Towson University, College of Fine Arts and Communication, Program in Studio Art, Towson, MD 21252-0001. Offers MFA. *Students:* 16 full-time (10 women), 5 part-time (1 woman); includes 5 minority (2 Black or African American, non-Hispanic/Latino; 1 Asian, non-Hispanic/Latino; 2 Two or more races, non-Hispanic/Latino), 1 international. *Entrance requirements:* For master's, bachelor's degree, preferably in art; portfolio; minimum GPA of 3.0; letter of intent; current resume; 2 letters of recommendation. *Application deadline:* For fall admission, 1/17 for domestic students, 5/15 for international students; for spring admission, 10/15 for domestic students, 12/1 for international students. Applications are processed on a rolling basis. Application fee: $45. Electronic applications accepted. *Expenses:* Tuition, state resident: full-time $7960; part-time $398 per unit. Tuition, nonresident: full-time $16,480; part-time $824 per unit. *Required fees:* $2600; $130 per year. $390 per term. *Financial support:* Application deadline: 4/1. *Unit head:* Prof. Tonia Matthews, Graduate Program Director, 410-704-2803, E-mail: tmatthews@towson.edu. *Application contact:* Coverley Beidleman, Assistant Director of Graduate Admissions, 410-704-5630, Fax: 410-704-3030, E-mail: cbeidleman@towson.edu.
Website: http://www.towson.edu/cofac/departments/art/grad/studio/index.html

Tufts University, School of the Museum of Fine Arts at Tufts University, Boston, MA 02115. Offers art education (MAT); studio art (MFA, Postbaccalaureate Certificate), including museum studies (MFA). *Faculty:* 31 full-time (19 women), 23 part-time/adjunct (16 women). *Students:* 55 full-time. Average age 25. In 2017, 44 master's, 15 other advanced degrees awarded. Terminal master's awarded for partial completion of doctoral program. *Degree requirements:* For master's, thesis, thesis exhibition. *Entrance requirements:* For master's, BFA (preferred) or bachelor's degree or equivalent in related area; portfolio; for Postbaccalaureate Certificate, portfolio, BFA or equivalent. Additional exam requirements/recommendations for international students: Required—TOEFL (minimum score 85 iBT), IELTS (minimum score 6.5). *Application deadline:* For fall admission, 1/15 priority date for domestic and international students. Applications are processed on a rolling basis. Application fee: $85. Electronic applications accepted. *Expenses:* $45,008 (MFA); $3,995 per credit (Post-Baccalaureate Certificate). *Financial support:* Fellowships, teaching assistantships, Federal Work-Study, and scholarships/grants available. Financial award application deadline: 1/15. *Faculty research:* Public art commissions, National Endowment for the Arts grant recipients, international group and solo exhibitions. *Unit head:* Lisa Bynoe, Associate Director of Graduate Programs, 617-627-0031, E-mail: lisa.bynoe@tufts.edu. *Application contact:* Office of Graduate Admissions, 617-627-3395, E-mail: gradadmissions@tufts.edu.
Website: https://smfa.tufts.edu/

Tulane University, School of Liberal Arts, Department of Art, New Orleans, LA 70118-5669. Offers history of art (MA); studio art (MFA). PhD held jointly with Roger Thayer Stone Center for Latin American Studies. *Degree requirements:* For master's, one foreign language, thesis. *Entrance requirements:* For master's, GRE General Test, minimum B average in undergraduate course work. Additional exam requirements/recommendations for international students: Required—TOEFL. Electronic applications accepted. *Expenses: Tuition:* Full-time $50,920; part-time $2829 per credit hour. *Required fees:* $2040; $44.50 per credit hour. $580 per term. Tuition and fees vary according to course load, degree level and program.

United Theological Seminary of the Twin Cities, Graduate Programs, New Brighton, MN 55112-2598. Offers advanced theological studies (Diploma); justice and peace studies (M Div, MA); leadership toward racial justice (M Div, MA, Certificate); Methodist studies (M Div, MA, Certificate); ministry (D Min); ministry renewal and professional development (Certificate); pastoral care and counseling (M Div, MA, MARL); religion and theology (MA); theological and religious studies (Certificate); theology and the arts (M Div, MA); urban ministry (M Div, MA, MARL); women's studies: religion, theology and ministry (M Div, MA). *Accreditation:* ACIPE; ATS. *Program availability:* Part-time, evening/weekend. *Degree requirements:* For master's, thesis; for doctorate, comprehensive exam, thesis/dissertation. *Entrance requirements:* For master's, minimum GPA of 2.75; strong analytical, reflective thinking and writing skills; vocational and academic goals compatible with those of Seminary; for doctorate, M Div or equivalent, minimum GPA of 3.0, 3 years experience in professional ministry; for other advanced degree, BA or equivalent life experience; strong analytical, reflective thinking and writing skills (Certificate); proficiency in English language, previous study of theology at a theological school, recommendation of student's denomination (Diploma). Additional exam requirements/recommendations for international students: Required—TOEFL (minimum score 550 paper-based).

Universidad del Turabo, Graduate Programs, Programs in Education, Program in Teaching of Fine Arts, Gurabo, PR 00778-3030. Offers M Ed. *Entrance requirements:* For master's, GRE, EXADEP, GMAT, interview, official transcript, essay, recommendation letters. Electronic applications accepted.

Université du Québec à Chicoutimi, Graduate Programs, Program in Fine Arts, Chicoutimi, QC G7H 2B1, Canada. Offers MA. Program offered jointly with Université du Québec à Montréal. *Program availability:* Part-time. *Degree requirements:* For master's, thesis optional. *Entrance requirements:* For master's, appropriate bachelor's degree, proficiency in French.

Université du Québec à Montréal, Graduate Programs, Program in Fine Arts, Montréal, QC H3C 3P8, Canada. Offers MA. Program offered jointly with Université du Québec à Chicoutimi. *Program availability:* Part-time. *Degree requirements:* For master's, thesis optional. *Entrance requirements:* For master's, appropriate bachelor's degree or equivalent, proficiency in French.

Université Laval, Faculty of Architecture, Planning and Visual Arts, School of Visual Arts, Programs in Visual Arts, Québec, QC G1K 7P4, Canada. Offers graphic design and multimedia (MA); visual arts (MA). *Degree requirements:* For master's, thesis (for some programs). *Entrance requirements:* For master's, technical exam, interview, mastery of pertinent software, knowledge of French. Electronic applications accepted.

University at Albany, State University of New York, College of Arts and Sciences, Department of Art and Art History, Albany, NY 12222-0001. Offers art (MA, MFA). *Faculty:* 12 full-time (8 women). *Students:* 26 full-time (19 women), 1 (woman) part-time; includes 3 minority (2 Black or African American, non-Hispanic/Latino; 1 Hispanic/Latino), 1 international. Average age 26. 38 applicants, 58% accepted, 16 enrolled. In 2017, 16 master's awarded. *Degree requirements:* For master's, exhibit. *Entrance requirements:* For master's, portfolio. Additional exam requirements/recommendations for international students: Required—TOEFL (minimum score 550 paper-based). *Application deadline:* For fall admission, 4/15 for domestic and international students; for spring admission, 11/1 for domestic and international students. Application fee: $75. *Expenses:* Tuition, state resident: full-time $10,870; part-time $453 per credit hour. Tuition, nonresident: full-time $22,210; part-time $925 per credit hour. *Required fees:* $84.68 per credit hour. $508.06 per semester. Part-time tuition and fees vary according to course load and program. *Financial support:* Federal Work-Study available. Financial award application deadline: 4/1. *Faculty research:* Art history, sculpture, painting and drawing, photography, digital media. *Unit head:* Rachel Dressler, Chair, 518-442-4020, Fax: 518-442-4807. *Application contact:* Michael DeRensis, Director, Graduate Admissions, 518-442-3980, Fax: 518-442-3922, E-mail: graduate@albany.edu.
Website: http://www.albany.edu/finearts/

University at Buffalo, the State University of New York, Graduate School, College of Arts and Sciences, Department of Art, Program in Studio Art, Buffalo, NY 14260. Offers MFA. *Faculty:* 18 full-time (8 women). *Students:* 21 full-time (11 women); includes 5 minority (2 Black or African American, non-Hispanic/Latino; 1 Asian, non-Hispanic/Latino; 2 Hispanic/Latino). Average age 28. 42 applicants, 50% accepted, 10 enrolled. In 2017, 13 master's awarded. *Degree requirements:* For master's, thesis, thesis exhibition or equivalent public defense. *Entrance requirements:* For master's, portfolio of 20 slides or CD, 3 letters of reference, curriculum vitae. Additional exam requirements/recommendations for international students: Required—TOEFL (minimum score 550 paper-based; 79 iBT). *Application deadline:* For fall admission, 1/15 priority date for domestic and international students; for winter admission, 2/1 for international students. Applications are processed on a rolling basis. Application fee: $75. Electronic applications accepted. *Expenses:* Contact institution. *Financial support:* In 2017–18, 21 students received support, including 23 teaching assistantships with full and partial tuition reimbursements available (averaging $14,161 per year); fellowships with full tuition reimbursements available, career-related internships or fieldwork, Federal Work-Study, institutionally sponsored loans, scholarships/grants, unspecified assistantships, and health benefits (for teaching assistantships/graduate assistanships only) also available. Support available to part-time students. Financial award application deadline: 2/7; financial award applicants required to submit FAFSA. *Faculty research:* Exhibitions and installations, critical theory, communication design, interactive media, curating. *Unit head:* Joan Linder, Chair, 716-645-6878 Ext. 1321, Fax: 716-645-6970, E-mail: joannder@buffalo.edu. *Application contact:* Prof. Stephanie Rothenberg, Director of Graduate Studies, 716-645-6878 Ext. 1367, Fax: 716-645-6970, E-mail: sjr@buffalo.edu.
Website: http://visualstudies.buffalo.edu

The University of Alabama, Graduate School, College of Arts and Sciences, Department of Art and Art History, Tuscaloosa, AL 35487. Offers art history (MA); studio art (MA, MFA), including ceramics, painting, photography, printmaking, sculpture. *Accreditation:* NASAD. *Program availability:* Part-time. *Faculty:* 18 full-time (11 women), 1 part-time/adjunct (0 women). *Students:* 16 full-time (11 women), 1 part-time (0 women); includes 2 minority (1 Black or African American, non-Hispanic/Latino; 1 Hispanic/Latino), 2 international. Average age 31. 22 applicants, 73% accepted, 9 enrolled. In 2017, 10 master's awarded. *Degree requirements:* For master's, one foreign language, comprehensive exam (for some programs), oral exam, thesis statement, exhibit (studio art), thesis (art history). *Entrance requirements:* For master's, GRE General Test or MAT (art history), minimum GPA of 3.0, BFA or equivalent (studio art). Additional exam requirements/recommendations for international students: Required—TOEFL (minimum score 550 paper-based). *Application deadline:* For fall admission, 3/15 for domestic and international students; for spring admission, 10/15 for domestic and international students. Applications are processed on a rolling basis. Application fee: $50 ($60 for international students). Electronic applications accepted. *Financial support:* In 2017–18, 8 students received support, including 2 fellowships with full tuition reimbursements available, 14 teaching assistantships with tuition reimbursements available (averaging $15,427 per year); career-related internships or fieldwork, institutionally sponsored loans, scholarships/grants, and unspecified assistantships also available. Financial award application deadline: 7/14. *Faculty research:* Nineteenth-century American, Medieval Europe, Baroque, twentieth-century, and African American art history. *Unit head:* Jason Guynes, Chair, 205-348-9944, Fax: 205-348-0287, E-mail: jguynes@ua.edu. *Application contact:* Sarah Marshall, Graduate Coordinator, 205-348-1890, Fax: 205-348-5967, E-mail: smarsh@ua.edu.
Website: http://www.art.ua.edu/

University of Alaska Fairbanks, College of Liberal Arts, Department of Art, Fairbanks, AK 99775-5640. Offers art (MFA); ceramics (MFA); computer art (MFA); drawing (MFA); painting (MFA); photography (MFA); printmaking (MFA); sculpture (MFA). *Program availability:* Part-time. *Degree requirements:* For master's, comprehensive exam, oral defense of project or thesis. *Entrance requirements:* For master's, portfolio of work including about 20 slides or appropriate equivalent depending on field of study. Additional exam requirements/recommendations for international students: Required—TOEFL (minimum score 550 paper-based; 79 iBT), IELTS (minimum score 6.5). Electronic applications accepted. *Faculty research:* Computer art, survey of arts in Alaska, found object art, visualization and animation, painting from the wilderness.

University of Alberta, Faculty of Graduate Studies and Research, Department of Art and Design, Edmonton, AB T6G 2E1, Canada. Offers drawing (MFA); history of art, design, and visual culture (MA); industrial design (M Des); painting (MFA); printmaking (MFA); sculpture (MFA); visual communication design (M Des). *Degree requirements:* For master's, thesis. *Entrance requirements:* For master's, portfolio (MFA and MDES). Additional exam requirements/recommendations for international students: Required—TOEFL (minimum score 550 paper-based).

The University of Arizona, College of Fine Arts, School of Art, Program in Art, Tucson, AZ 85721. Offers MFA. *Entrance requirements:* Additional exam requirements/recommendations for international students: Required—TOEFL (minimum score 550 paper-based; 79 iBT). Electronic applications accepted.

University of Arkansas, Graduate School, J. William Fulbright College of Arts and Sciences, Department of Art, Fayetteville, AR 72701. Offers MFA. *Accreditation:* NASAD. In 2017, 6 master's awarded. *Degree requirements:* For master's, exhibit or thesis. *Application deadline:* For fall admission, 8/1 for domestic students, 4/1 for international students; for spring admission, 12/1 for domestic students, 10/1 for international students; for summer admission, 4/15 for domestic students, 3/1 for international students. Applications are processed on a rolling basis. Application fee: $60. Electronic applications accepted. *Expenses:* Tuition, state resident: full-time $3782. Tuition, nonresident: full-time $10,238. *Financial support:* In 2017–18, 11 research assistantships were awarded; fellowships, teaching assistantships, career-related internships or fieldwork, and Federal Work-Study also available. Support available to part-time students. Financial award application deadline: 4/1; financial award applicants required to submit FAFSA. *Unit head:* Jeannie Hulen, Associate Dean of Fine Arts, 479-575-5202, Fax: 479-575-2062, E-mail: jhulen@uark.edu. *Application contact:* Marc Mitchell, Graduate Coordinator, 479-575-2062, Fax: 479-575-2062, E-mail: mmitch@uark.edu.
Website: https://fulbright.uark.edu/departments/art/

University of Arkansas at Little Rock, Graduate School, College of Arts, Letters, and Sciences, Department of Art, Little Rock, AR 72204-1099. Offers art education (MA); art history (MA); studio art (MA). *Accreditation:* NASAD. *Program availability:* Part-time. *Degree requirements:* For master's, 4 foreign languages, oral exam, oral defense of thesis or exhibit. *Entrance requirements:* For master's, portfolio review or term paper evaluation, minimum GPA of 2.7.

The University of British Columbia, Faculty of Arts and Faculty of Graduate Studies, Department of Art History, Visual Art, and Theory, Vancouver, BC V6T 1Z2, Canada. Offers art history (MA, PhD); critical and curatorial studies (MA); visual art (MFA). *Degree requirements:* For master's, one foreign language, thesis, final exhibition (MFA, MA in critical and curatorial studies); for doctorate, 2 foreign languages, comprehensive exam, thesis/dissertation. *Entrance requirements:* For master's, bachelor's degree with minimum B+ average (MFA, MA in critical and curatorial studies), A- (MA in art history); for doctorate, master's degree with minimum A- average. Additional exam requirements/recommendations for international students: Required—TOEFL. Electronic applications

accepted. *Expenses:* Contact institution. *Faculty research:* Conceptual art, Asian art, indigenous North American art, post-second war art, eighteenth- and nineteenth-century art, curatorial, digital art.

University of Calgary, Faculty of Graduate Studies, Faculty of Arts, Department of Art, Calgary, AB T2N 1N4, Canada. Offers MA, MFA. *Degree requirements:* For master's, thesis. *Entrance requirements:* Additional exam requirements/recommendations for international students: Required—TOEFL. *Faculty research:* Painting, sculpture, drawing, photography, printmaking, new media.

University of California, Berkeley, Graduate Division, College of Letters and Science, Department of Art Practice, Berkeley, CA 94720-1500. Offers MFA. *Entrance requirements:* For master's, GRE General Test, minimum GPA of 3.0, sample of work, 3 letters of recommendation. Additional exam requirements/recommendations for international students: Required—TOEFL (minimum score 570 paper-based; 90 iBT). Electronic applications accepted.

University of California, Berkeley, UC Berkeley Extension, Certificate Programs in Art and Design, Berkeley, CA 94720-1500. Offers interior design and interior architecture (Certificate); landscape architecture (Certificate); visual arts (Postbaccalaureate Certificate).

University of California, Davis, Graduate Studies, Program in Art, Davis, CA 95616. Offers MFA. *Degree requirements:* For master's, final exhibit. *Entrance requirements:* For master's, minimum GPA of 3.0, portfolio. Additional exam requirements/recommendations for international students: Required—TOEFL (minimum score 550 paper-based). Electronic applications accepted. *Faculty research:* Drawing, painting, photography, video, interactive art.

University of California, Irvine, Claire Trevor School of the Arts, Department of Art, Irvine, CA 92697. Offers MFA. *Students:* 49 full-time (22 women), 1 (woman) part-time; includes 20 minority (2 Black or African American, non-Hispanic/Latino; 5 Asian, non-Hispanic/Latino; 5 Hispanic/Latino; 8 Two or more races, non-Hispanic/Latino), 5 international. Average age 30. 186 applicants, 21% accepted, 22 enrolled. In 2017, 9 master's awarded. *Degree requirements:* For master's, thesis. *Entrance requirements:* For master's, minimum GPA of 3.0. *Application deadline:* For fall admission, 1/15 for domestic and international students. Applications are processed on a rolling basis. Application fee: $105 ($125 for international students). Electronic applications accepted. *Financial support:* Fellowships with tuition reimbursements, research assistantships with tuition reimbursements, teaching assistantships with tuition reimbursements, institutionally sponsored loans, traineeships, health care benefits, and unspecified assistantships available. Financial award application deadline: 3/1; financial award applicants required to submit FAFSA. *Faculty research:* Experimental concepts, processes relevant to contemporary issues. *Unit head:* John Medina, Department Manager, 949-824-4917, Fax: 949-824-4106, E-mail: jcmedina@uci.edu. *Application contact:* Kevin Appel, Graduate Advisor, Fax: 949-824-5297, E-mail: kappel@uci.edu. Website: http://www.arts.uci.edu/ctsa-academic-departments-art-department

University of California, Irvine, School of Humanities, Department of Art History, Irvine, CA 92697. Offers visual studies (MA, PhD). Program offered jointly with Department of Film and Media Studies. *Students:* 36 full-time (19 women), 2 part-time (both women); includes 13 minority (3 Black or African American, non-Hispanic/Latino; 3 Asian, non-Hispanic/Latino; 4 Hispanic/Latino; 3 Two or more races, non-Hispanic/Latino), 3 international. Average age 31. 85 applicants, 26% accepted, 17 enrolled. In 2017, 4 master's, 4 doctorates awarded. *Entrance requirements:* For master's, GRE, minimum GPA of 3.0; for doctorate, GRE General Test, writing sample. Additional exam requirements/recommendations for international students: Required—TOEFL (minimum score 550 paper-based). *Application deadline:* For fall admission, 12/15 for domestic and international students. Application fee: $105 ($125 for international students). Electronic applications accepted. *Financial support:* Fellowships, teaching assistantships, institutionally sponsored loans, traineeships, health care benefits, and unspecified assistantships available. Financial award application deadline: 3/1; financial award applicants required to submit FAFSA. *Faculty research:* Interdisciplinary study and research in art history, critical theory, women's studies, cultural studies, film studies. *Unit head:* Prof. Cecile Whiting, Chair, 949-824-2464, E-mail: cwhiting@uci.edu. *Application contact:* Lucas Hilderbrand, Director of Graduate Studies for Visual Studies, 949-824-1124, Fax: 949-824-2865, E-mail: lucas.h@uci.edu. Website: http://www.hnet.uci.edu/arthistory/

University of California, Los Angeles, Graduate Division, School of the Arts and Architecture, Department of Art, Los Angeles, CA 90095. Offers MFA. *Degree requirements:* For master's, comprehensive exam. *Entrance requirements:* For master's, bachelor's degree; minimum undergraduate GPA of 3.0 (or its equivalent if letter grade system not used); portfolio. Additional exam requirements/recommendations for international students: Required—TOEFL. Electronic applications accepted. *Expenses:* Contact institution.

University of California, Riverside, Graduate Division, Program in Visual Arts, Riverside, CA 92521-0102. Offers MFA. *Degree requirements:* For master's, thesis. *Entrance requirements:* For master's, portfolio, minimum GPA of 3.2. Additional exam requirements/recommendations for international students: Required—TOEFL (minimum score 550 paper-based; 80 iBT). Electronic applications accepted. *Expenses:* Tuition, state resident: full-time $5746. Tuition, nonresident: full-time $10,780. Tuition and fees vary according to campus/location and program. *Faculty research:* Painting, photography, sculpture, digital art, video.

University of California, San Diego, Graduate Division, Department of Visual Arts, La Jolla, CA 92093. Offers art history, theory, and criticism (PhD); visual arts (MFA). *Students:* 70 full-time (43 women), 3 part-time (all women). 162 applicants, 21% accepted, 19 enrolled. In 2017, 11 master's, 7 doctorates awarded. *Degree requirements:* For master's, comprehensive exam, thesis; for doctorate, 2 foreign languages, comprehensive exam, thesis/dissertation, reading knowledge of at least two of the foreign languages commonly used by scholars engaged in the advanced study in art history, theory, and criticism. *Entrance requirements:* For master's, electronic portfolio; for doctorate, GRE General Test, electronic portfolio. Additional exam requirements/recommendations for international students: Required—TOEFL (minimum score 550 paper-based; 80 iBT), IELTS (minimum score 7). *Application deadline:* For fall admission, 12/12 for domestic students. Application fee: $105 ($125 for international students). Electronic applications accepted. *Financial support:* Fellowships, research assistantships, teaching assistantships, career-related internships or fieldwork, scholarships/grants, and readerships available. Financial award applicants required to submit FAFSA. *Faculty research:* Contemporary art, ancient art, critical design, new media/software/hardware. *Unit head:* Jack Greenstein, Chair, 858-534-0418, E-mail: jgreenstein@ucsd.edu. *Application contact:* Katherine Edwards, Graduate Program Coordinator, 858-822-3882, E-mail: vis-grad@ucsd.edu. Website: http://visarts.ucsd.edu/

University of California, Santa Barbara, Graduate Division, College of Letters and Sciences, Division of Humanities and Fine Arts, Department of Art, Santa Barbara, CA 93106-7120. Offers MFA. *Degree requirements:* For master's, thesis, exhibition. *Entrance requirements:* Additional exam requirements/recommendations for international students: Required—TOEFL (minimum score 550 paper-based; 80 iBT),

IELTS (minimum score 7). Electronic applications accepted. *Faculty research:* Digital media, interactive media, spatial studies, public space art, book arts.

University of California, Santa Cruz, Division of Graduate Studies, Division of the Arts, Program in Digital Arts and New Media, Santa Cruz, CA 95064. Offers MFA. *Degree requirements:* For master's, thesis, written paper. *Entrance requirements:* Additional exam requirements/recommendations for international students: Required—TOEFL (minimum score 550 paper-based; 83 iBT); Recommended—IELTS (minimum score 8). Electronic applications accepted. *Faculty research:* Mechatronics, participatory culture, performative technologies, playable media.

University of California, Santa Cruz, Division of Graduate Studies, Division of the Arts, Program in Visual Studies, Santa Cruz, CA 95064. Offers PhD. *Degree requirements:* For doctorate, one foreign language, thesis/dissertation, qualifying exams. *Entrance requirements:* For doctorate, GRE, writing sample under 20 pages, 3 letters of recommendation. Additional exam requirements/recommendations for international students: Required—TOEFL (minimum score 550 paper-based; 83 iBT); Recommended—IELTS (minimum score 8). Electronic applications accepted. *Faculty research:* Opportunity to consider the role of social and cultural forces in guiding how and what their members see, concentration on cultures in Africa, the Americas, Asia, Europe, and the Pacific Islands.

University of Central Florida, College of Arts and Humanities, School of Visual Arts and Design, Orlando, FL 32816. Offers digital media (MA); emerging media (MFA), including animation and visual effects, digital media, entrepreneurial digital cinema, studio art and the computer. *Program availability:* Part-time. *Students:* 38 full-time (13 women), 9 part-time (3 women); includes 16 minority (6 Black or African American, non-Hispanic/Latino; 2 Asian, non-Hispanic/Latino; 8 Hispanic/Latino), 3 international. Average age 30. 61 applicants, 54% accepted, 20 enrolled. In 2017, 8 master's awarded. *Degree requirements:* For master's, comprehensive exam, thesis or alternative. *Entrance requirements:* For master's, GRE, letter of recommendation. Additional exam requirements/recommendations for international students: Required—TOEFL. *Application deadline:* For fall admission, 7/1 for domestic students. Application fee: $30. Electronic applications accepted. *Expenses:* Tuition, state resident: part-time $288.16 per credit hour. Tuition, nonresident: part-time $1073.31 per credit hour. Tuition and fees vary according to program. *Financial support:* In 2017–18, 17 students received support, including 7 fellowships with partial tuition reimbursements available (averaging $10,000 per year), 3 research assistantships with partial tuition reimbursements available (averaging $6,355 per year), 15 teaching assistantships with partial tuition reimbursements available (averaging $8,208 per year); scholarships/grants, health care benefits, and unspecified assistantships also available. Financial award application deadline: 3/1; financial award applicants required to submit FAFSA. *Unit head:* Dr. Rudy McDaniel, Director, 407-823-3145, E-mail: rudy@ucf.edu. *Application contact:* Associate Director, Graduate Admissions, 407-823-2766, Fax: 407-823-6442, E-mail: gradadmissions@ucf.edu. Website: http://svad.cah.ucf.edu/

University of Chicago, Division of the Humanities, Department of Visual Arts, Chicago, IL 60637. Offers MFA. *Students:* 16 full-time (8 women). 70 applicants, 26% accepted, 8 enrolled. In 2017, 8 master's awarded. *Degree requirements:* For master's, thesis presentation and exhibition. *Entrance requirements:* For master's, portfolio, artist's statement, 3 letters of recommendation, transcripts for all previous degrees and institutions attended. Additional exam requirements/recommendations for international students: Required—TOEFL (minimum score 104 iBT), IELTS (minimum score 7). *Application deadline:* For fall admission, 12/15 for domestic and international students. Application fee: $90. Electronic applications accepted. *Financial support:* Fellowships, Federal Work-Study, institutionally sponsored loans, scholarships/grants, and tuition waivers (full and partial) available. Financial award application deadline: 12/15. *Unit head:* Dr. Jessica Stockholder, Chair, 773-753-4821, E-mail: dova@uchicago.edu. *Application contact:* Michael Beetley, Assistant Dean of Students, Admissions and Fellowships, 773-702-1552, Fax: 773-834-9148, E-mail: humanitiesadmissions@uchicago.edu. Website: http://dova.uchicago.edu/

University of Cincinnati, Graduate School, College of Design, Architecture, Art, and Planning, School of Art, Program in Fine Arts, Cincinnati, OH 45221. Offers MFA. *Accreditation:* NASAD. *Program availability:* Part-time. *Degree requirements:* For master's, thesis, oral exam. *Entrance requirements:* Additional exam requirements/recommendations for international students: Required—TOEFL. Electronic applications accepted. *Expenses:* Tuition, area resident: Full-time $14,468. Tuition, state resident: full-time $14,968; part-time $754 per credit hour. Tuition, nonresident: full-time $24,210; part-time $1311 per credit hour. International tuition: $26,460 full-time. *Required fees:* $3958; $84 per credit hour. One-time fee: $85 full-time. Tuition and fees vary according to course load, degree level and program. *Faculty research:* Painting, drawing, ceramics, printmaking, sculpture.

University of Colorado Boulder, Graduate School, College of Arts and Sciences, Department of Art and Art History, Boulder, CO 80309. Offers art history (MA), including contemporary art criticism, early twentieth-century art, nineteenth-century art, Russian and Soviet art; ceramics (MFA); photography and media arts (MFA); printmaking (MFA); sculpture (MFA). *Faculty:* 23 full-time (10 women). *Students:* 42 full-time (30 women), 3 part-time (2 women); includes 7 minority (4 Hispanic/Latino; 3 Two or more races, non-Hispanic/Latino). Average age 29. 152 applicants, 18% accepted, 15 enrolled. In 2017, 16 master's awarded. Terminal master's awarded for partial completion of doctoral program. *Degree requirements:* For master's, variable foreign language requirement, comprehensive exam, thesis (for some programs). *Entrance requirements:* For master's, GRE General Test, minimum undergraduate GPA of 3.0, portfolio. *Application deadline:* For fall admission, 1/10 for domestic students; for spring admission, 12/1 for domestic students. Application fee: $60 ($80 for international students). Electronic applications accepted. Application fee is waived when completed online. *Financial support:* In 2017–18, 140 students received support, including 43 fellowships (averaging $2,068 per year), 41 teaching assistantships with full and partial tuition reimbursements available (averaging $26,884 per year); institutionally sponsored loans, scholarships/grants, health care benefits, and unspecified assistantships also available. Financial award application deadline: 2/15; financial award applicants required to submit FAFSA. *Faculty research:* Visual arts; sculpture; fine arts; installation art; mixed-media art. *Total annual research expenditures:* $17,000. *Application contact:* E-mail: finearts@colorado.edu. Website: http://www.colorado.edu/arts

University of Colorado Denver, College of Liberal Arts and Sciences, Program in Humanities, Denver, CO 80217. Offers community health science (MSS); humanities (MH); international studies (MSS); philosophy and theory (MH); social justice (MSS); society and the environment (MSS); visual studies (MH); women's and gender studies (MSS). *Program availability:* Part-time, evening/weekend. *Degree requirements:* For master's, 36 credit hours, project or thesis. *Entrance requirements:* For master's, writing sample, statement of purpose/letter of intent, three letters of recommendation. Additional exam requirements/recommendations for international students: Required—TOEFL (minimum score 537 paper-based; 75 iBT); Recommended—IELTS (minimum score 6.5). Electronic applications accepted. *Faculty research:* Women and gender in

the classical Mediterranean, communication theory and democracy, relationship between psychology and philosophy.

University of Dallas, Braniff Graduate School of Liberal Arts, Program in Art, Irving, TX 75062-4736. Offers ceramics (MFA); painting (MFA); printmaking (MFA); sculpture (MFA). *Program availability:* Part-time. *Entrance requirements:* For master's, GRE General Test, portfolio. Additional exam requirements/recommendations for international students: Required—TOEFL (minimum score 550 paper-based). *Application deadline:* For fall admission, 2/15 for domestic students. Applications are processed on a rolling basis. Application fee: $50. *Expenses: Tuition:* Full-time $33,750; part-time $22,500 per year. Tuition and fees vary according to program. *Financial support:* Application deadline: 2/15; applicants required to submit FAFSA. *Faculty research:* Ceramics, printmaking, sculpture, art history, religious imagery and architecture. *Unit head:* Dan Hammett, Chairman, 972-721-5318, Fax: 972-721-5017, E-mail: hammett@udallas.edu.

University of Dayton, Department of Teacher Education, Dayton, OH 45469. Offers adolescence to young adult education (MS Ed); early childhood leadership and advocacy (MS Ed); interdisciplinary education (MS Ed), including visual arts; interdisciplinary education studies (MS Ed); leadership in educational systems (MS Ed); literacy (MS Ed); mathematics education (MS Ed); middle childhood education (MS Ed); multi-age education (MS Ed), including world languages; music education (MS Ed); teacher as leader (MS Ed); teacher education (MS Ed); technology-enhanced learning (MS Ed); trans-disciplinary early childhood education (MS Ed). *Program availability:* Part-time, 100% online. *Faculty:* 23 full-time (20 women), 41 part-time/adjunct (36 women). *Students:* 45 full-time (38 women), 68 part-time (57 women); includes 7 minority (3 Black or African American, non-Hispanic/Latino; 1 Hispanic/Latino; 3 Two or more races, non-Hispanic/Latino), 6 international. Average age 31. 106 applicants, 28% accepted. In 2017, 70 master's awarded. *Degree requirements:* For master's, variable foreign language requirement, thesis or alternative, internship (for teaching licensure or endorsement). *Entrance requirements:* For master's, GRE (minimum score of 149 verbal, 4 on writing) or MAT (minimum score of 396) if undergraduate GPA was under 2.75, minimum GPA of 2.75, 3 letters of recommendation, personal statement or resume, official transcripts. Additional exam requirements/recommendations for international students: Required—TOEFL (minimum score 550 paper-based; 80 iBT); Recommended—IELTS (minimum score 6.5). *Application deadline:* Applications are processed on a rolling basis. Application fee: $0 ($50 for international students). Electronic applications accepted. *Expenses:* Contact institution. *Financial support:* In 2017–18, 5 research assistantships with partial tuition reimbursements (averaging $9,640 per year) were awarded; teaching assistantships, career-related internships or fieldwork, institutionally sponsored loans, and unspecified assistantships also available. Financial award application deadline: 3/1; financial award applicants required to submit FAFSA. *Faculty research:* Social emotional learning, culturally responsive teaching, urban teaching, literacy, instructional strategies, pre-service teacher education preparation. *Unit head:* Dr. Connie L. Bowman, Chair, 937-229-3348, E-mail: cbowman1@udayton.edu. *Application contact:* Gina Seiter, Coordinator of Graduate Programs and Licensing, 937-229-3103, E-mail: gseiter1@udayton.edu. Website: https://www.udayton.edu/education/departments_and_programs/edt

University of Delaware, College of Arts and Sciences, Department of Art, Newark, DE 19716. Offers MA, MFA. *Degree requirements:* For master's, exposition paper final exhibition. *Entrance requirements:* For master's, portfolio of creative work. Electronic applications accepted. *Faculty research:* Painting, printmaking, ceramics, photography, sculpture.

University of Denver, Division of Arts, Humanities and Social Sciences, School of Art and Art History, Denver, CO 80208. Offers art history (MA); museum studies (MA). *Accreditation:* NASAD. *Program availability:* Part-time. *Faculty:* 16 full-time (10 women), 8 part-time/adjunct (7 women). *Students:* 5 full-time (4 women), 14 part-time (all women); includes 1 minority (Hispanic/Latino), 1 international. Average age 24. 33 applicants, 79% accepted, 13 enrolled. In 2017, 7 master's awarded. *Degree requirements:* For master's, one foreign language, comprehensive exam, research paper or thesis project. *Entrance requirements:* For master's, GRE General Test, transcripts, personal statement, writing sample, three letters of recommendation. Additional exam requirements/recommendations for international students: Required—TOEFL (minimum score 550 paper-based; 80 iBT). *Application deadline:* For fall admission, 1/31 priority date for domestic and international students. Applications are processed on a rolling basis. Application fee: $65. Electronic applications accepted. *Expenses:* $31,935 per year full-time. *Financial support:* In 2017–18, 19 students received support. Research assistantships with tuition reimbursements available, teaching assistantships with tuition reimbursements available, career-related internships or fieldwork, Federal Work-Study, institutionally sponsored loans, scholarships/grants, and unspecified assistantships available. Support available to part-time students. Financial award application deadline: 2/15; financial award applicants required to submit FAFSA. *Faculty research:* Abstract expressionist women painters, Chichen Itza, the cult of St. Ursula, rock poster art of the psychedelic era. *Unit head:* Catherine Chauvin, Associate Professor and Director, 303-871-2367, Fax: 303-871-4112, E-mail: catherine.chauvin@du.edu. *Application contact:* Jason Kellermeyer, Coordinator of Academic Programs, 303-871-2846, E-mail: jason.kellermeyer@du.edu. Website: http://www.du.edu/ahss/art/index.html

University of Florida, Graduate School, College of The Arts, School of Art and Art History, Gainesville, FL 32611. Offers art (MA), including digital arts and sciences; art education (MA); art history (MA, PhD); museology (MA), including historic preservation. *Accreditation:* NASAD. *Program availability:* Online learning. *Degree requirements:* For master's, project or thesis (MFA); 1 foreign language (MA in art history); for doctorate, 2 foreign languages, comprehensive exam, thesis/dissertation. *Entrance requirements:* For master's, GRE General Test, portfolio (MFA), writing sample (MA), minimum GPA 3.0; for doctorate, GRE General Test, minimum GPA of 3.0. Additional exam requirements/recommendations for international students: Required—TOEFL (minimum score 550 paper-based; 80 iBT), IELTS (minimum score 6). Electronic applications accepted. *Faculty research:* Studio production, art historical studies of style context.

University of Georgia, Franklin College of Arts and Sciences, Lamar Dodd School of Art, Athens, GA 30602. Offers art (MFA, PhD); art history (MA). *Accreditation:* NASAD (one or more programs are accredited). *Degree requirements:* For doctorate, one foreign language, thesis/dissertation. *Entrance requirements:* For master's and doctorate, GRE General Test. Electronic applications accepted.

University of Guam, Office of Graduate Studies, College of Liberal Arts and Social Sciences, Division of Fine Arts, Mangilao, GU 96923. Offers ceramics (MA); graphics (MA); painting (MA). *Degree requirements:* For master's, thesis or alternative, exhibit, final oral exam. *Entrance requirements:* For master's, GRE General Test, portfolio. Additional exam requirements/recommendations for international students: Required—TOEFL.

University of Guelph, Graduate Studies, College of Arts, School of Fine Art and Music, Guelph, ON N1G 2W1, Canada. Offers studio art (MFA). *Degree requirements:* For master's, exhibition, support paper, oral defense. *Entrance requirements:* For master's, minimum B- average during previous 2 years of course work. Additional exam

requirements/recommendations for international students: Required—TOEFL. Electronic applications accepted. *Faculty research:* Studio practice in painting, sculpture, print, photo, drawing, video.

University of Hartford, Hartford Art School, West Hartford, CT 06117-1599. Offers MFA. *Program availability:* Part-time. *Degree requirements:* For master's, thesis. *Entrance requirements:* For master's, portfolio, 3 letters of recommendation. Additional exam requirements/recommendations for international students: Required—TOEFL (minimum score 550 paper-based). Electronic applications accepted. *Expenses:* Contact institution.

University of Hawaii at Manoa, Office of Graduate Education, College of Arts and Humanities, Department of Art and Art History, Honolulu, HI 96822. Offers art history (MA); visual arts (MFA). *Program availability:* Part-time. *Degree requirements:* For master's, thesis optional. *Entrance requirements:* For master's, GRE General Test, BFA, 18 hours of course work in art history. Additional exam requirements/recommendations for international students: Required—TOEFL (minimum score 550 paper-based; 79 iBT), IELTS (minimum score 7). *Faculty research:* Painting, sculpture, glass, design, printmaking.

University of Houston, Kathrine G. McGovern College of the Arts, School of Art, Houston, TX 77204. Offers art history (MA); interdisciplinary practice and emerging forms (MFA); painting (MFA); studio art (MFA). *Entrance requirements:* For master's, baccalaureate degree, portfolio. Electronic applications accepted. *Faculty research:* Painting, sculpture, photography/installation/video, graphic design and typography, art history (Pre-Columbian to Surrealism).

University of Idaho, College of Graduate Studies, College of Art and Architecture, Moscow, ID 83844. Offers M Arch, MFA, MLA, MS. *Accreditation:* NASAD. *Faculty:* 20 full-time (7 women). *Students:* 67 full-time, 7 part-time. Average age 28. In 2017, 43 master's awarded. *Entrance requirements:* For master's, minimum GPA of 3.0. Additional exam requirements/recommendations for international students: Required—TOEFL (minimum score 79 iBT). *Application deadline:* For fall admission, 8/1 for domestic students; for spring admission, 12/15 for domestic students. Applications are processed on a rolling basis. Application fee: $60. Electronic applications accepted. *Expenses:* Tuition, state resident: full-time $6722; part-time $430 per credit hour. Tuition, nonresident: full-time $23,046; part-time $1337 per credit hour. *Required fees:* $2142; $63 per credit hour. *Financial support:* Applicants required to submit FAFSA. *Faculty research:* Sustainability in communities, urban research, virtual technology, bioregional planning, environment and behavior interaction. *Unit head:* Dr. Shauna Corry, Interim Dean, 208-885-4409, E-mail: caa@uidaho.edu. *Application contact:* Sean Scoggin, Graduate Recruitment Coordinator, 208-885-4001, Fax: 208-885-4406, E-mail: graduateadmissions@uidaho.edu. Website: http://www.uidaho.edu/caa

University of Illinois at Chicago, College of Architecture, Design and the Arts, School of Art and Art History, Chicago, IL 60607-7128. Offers art history (MA); electronic visualization (MFA); museum and exhibition studies (MA); new media arts (MFA). *Program availability:* Part-time, evening/weekend. Terminal master's awarded for partial completion of doctoral program. *Degree requirements:* For master's, one foreign language, thesis or alternative; for doctorate, thesis/dissertation. *Entrance requirements:* For master's, GRE General Test, minimum GPA of 2.75, 3 letters of recommendation; for doctorate, GRE General Test, MA in art history or equivalent, minimum GPA of 3.0. Additional exam requirements/recommendations for international students: Required—TOEFL. Electronic applications accepted. *Expenses:* Contact institution. *Faculty research:* Modern painting and sculpture, history of architecture, city planning and design, history of photography.

University of Illinois at Urbana–Champaign, Graduate College, College of Fine and Applied Arts, School of Art and Design, Program in Design and Media, Champaign, IL 61820. Offers art and design (MFA), including new media; graphic design (MFA); industrial design (MFA). *Accreditation:* NASAD.

University of Illinois at Urbana–Champaign, Graduate College, College of Fine and Applied Arts, School of Art and Design, Program in Studio Arts, Champaign, IL 61820. Offers art and design (MFA); crafts (MFA); metals (MFA); painting (MFA); photography (MFA); sculpture (MFA). *Accreditation:* NASAD. *Entrance requirements:* For master's, minimum GPA of 3.0.

University of Indianapolis, Graduate Programs, College of Arts and Sciences, Department of Art, Indianapolis, IN 46227-3697. Offers MA. *Accreditation:* NASAD. *Program availability:* Part-time, evening/weekend. *Entrance requirements:* For master's, GRE Subject Test, 3 letters of recommendation, portfolio. Additional exam requirements/recommendations for international students: Required—TOEFL.

The University of Iowa, Graduate College, College of Liberal Arts and Sciences, School of Art and Art History, Program in Art, Iowa City, IA 52242-1316. Offers MA, MFA. *Faculty:* 25 full-time (9 women), 5 part-time/adjunct (3 women). *Students:* 56 full-time (40 women), 1 part-time (0 women); includes 8 minority (5 Black or African American, non-Hispanic/Latino; 2 Asian, non-Hispanic/Latino; 1 Two or more races, non-Hispanic/Latino), 7 international. 160 applicants, 26% accepted, 38 enrolled. In 2017, 37 master's awarded. *Degree requirements:* For master's, thesis (for some programs), final exam. *Entrance requirements:* For master's, portfolio. Additional exam requirements/recommendations for international students: Required—TOEFL (minimum score 550 paper-based; 81 iBT). *Application deadline:* For fall admission, 2/1 for domestic and international students. Application fee: $60 ($100 for international students). Electronic applications accepted. *Financial support:* In 2017–18, 50 students received support, including 1 research assistantship with full and partial tuition reimbursement available (averaging $9,510 per year), 50 teaching assistantships with full and partial tuition reimbursements available (averaging $9,510 per year); fellowships, career-related internships or fieldwork, Federal Work-Study, institutionally sponsored loans, scholarships/grants, health care benefits, and unspecified assistantships also available. Support available to part-time students. Financial award application deadline: 2/1. *Faculty research:* Ceramics, painting, design, printmaking, photography, sculpture. *Unit head:* Prof. Isabel Barbuzza, Director of Graduate Studies, 319-335-1789, Fax: 319-384-2715. *Application contact:* Laura Jorgensen, Graduate Program Coordinator, 319-335-1758, Fax: 319-335-1774, E-mail: art@uiowa.edu.

The University of Kansas, Graduate Studies, College of Liberal Arts and Sciences, Department of English, Lawrence, KS 66045. Offers creative writing (MFA), including fine arts/creative writing; English (MA, PhD). *Program availability:* Part-time. *Students:* 86 full-time (49 women), 6 part-time (4 women); includes 16 minority (8 Black or African American, non-Hispanic/Latino; 1 Asian, non-Hispanic/Latino; 4 Hispanic/Latino; 3 Two or more races, non-Hispanic/Latino), 8 international. Average age 30. 165 applicants, 20% accepted, 16 enrolled. In 2017, 9 master's, 9 doctorates awarded. *Entrance requirements:* For master's and doctorate, GRE General Test, two examples of academic writing; resume; statement of approximately 500 words describing interests, training, experience (including teaching experience); academic ability, and goals; three letters of recommendation; official transcripts. Additional exam requirements/recommendations for international students: Required—TOEFL or IELTS. *Application deadline:* For fall admission, 12/31 for domestic and international students. Application fee: $65 ($85 for international students). Electronic applications accepted. Financial

support: Fellowships, research assistantships, teaching assistantships, and unspecified assistantships available. *Faculty research:* Ecocriticism and science/science fiction writing; gender and sexuality studies; U.S. ethnic literatures, race, and diaspora studies; composition, rhetoric, and language studies; creative writing. *Unit head:* Anna Neill, Chair, 785-864-2521, E-mail: aneill@ku.edu. *Application contact:* Lydia Ash, Graduate Secretary, 785-864-2518, E-mail: lash@ku.edu.
Website: http://www.english.ku.edu

The University of Kansas, Graduate Studies, College of Liberal Arts and Sciences, Department of Visual Art, Program in Visual Art Education, Lawrence, KS 66045. Offers MA. *Program availability:* Part-time. *Students:* 2 full-time (both women), 2 part-time (both women). Average age 31. 6 applicants, 33% accepted. *Entrance requirements:* For master's, portfolio, 3 letters of recommendation, minimum GPA of 3.0. Additional exam requirements/recommendations for international students: Required—TOEFL (minimum score 570 paper-based) or IELTS (minimum score 6.5). *Application deadline:* For fall admission, 5/1 for domestic and international students; for spring admission, 12/1 for domestic and international students. Application fee: $65 ($85 for international students). Electronic applications accepted. *Financial support:* Teaching assistantships, Federal Work-Study, scholarships/grants, and unspecified assistantships available. *Faculty research:* Emphasizing a balance of studio, art history, and education courses. *Unit head:* Mary Anne Jordan, Chairperson, 785-864-2952, E-mail: majordan@ku.edu. *Application contact:* Lauren Chaney, Graduate Admissions Contact, 785-864-2306, E-mail: lkchaney@ku.edu.
Website: http://art.ku.edu/programs/visual_art_education/

University of Kentucky, Graduate School, College of Fine Arts, Program in Art Studio, Lexington, KY 40506-0032. Offers MFA. *Accreditation:* NASAD. *Degree requirements:* For master's, comprehensive exam. *Entrance requirements:* For master's, GRE General Test, minimum undergraduate GPA of 2.75. Additional exam requirements/recommendations for international students: Required—TOEFL (minimum score 550 paper-based). Electronic applications accepted.

University of Lethbridge, School of Graduate Studies, Lethbridge, AB T1K 3M4, Canada. Offers addictions counseling (M Sc); agricultural biotechnology (M Sc); agricultural studies (M Sc, MA); anthropology (MA); archaeology (M Sc, MA); art (MA, MFA); biochemistry (M Sc); biological sciences (M Sc); biomolecular science (PhD); biosystems and biodiversity (PhD); Canadian studies (MA); chemistry (M Sc); computer science (M Sc); computer science and geographical information science (M Sc); counseling (MC); counseling psychology (M Ed); dramatic arts (MA); earth, space, and physical science (PhD); economics (MA); education (MA, PhD); educational leadership (M Ed); English (MA); environmental science (M Sc); evolution and behavior (PhD); exercise science (M Sc); French (MA); French/German (MA); French/Spanish (MA); general education (M Ed); geography (M Sc, MA); German (MA); health sciences (M Sc); individualized multidisciplinary (M Sc, MA); kinesiology (M Sc, MA); management (M Sc), including accounting, finance, human resource management and labor relations, information systems, international management, marketing, policy and strategy; mathematics (M Sc); music (M Mus, MA); Native American studies (MA); neuroscience (M Sc, PhD); new media (MA, MFA); nursing (M Sc, MN); philosophy (MA); physics (M Sc); political science (MA); psychology (M Sc, MA); religious studies (MA); sociology (MA); theatre and dramatic arts (MFA); theoretical and computational science (PhD); urban and regional studies (MA); women and gender studies (MA). *Program availability:* Part-time, evening/weekend. *Degree requirements:* For master's, thesis (for some programs); for doctorate, comprehensive exam, thesis/dissertation. *Entrance requirements:* For master's, GMAT (for M Sc in management), bachelor's degree in related field, minimum GPA of 3.0 during previous 20 graded semester courses, 2 years' teaching or related experience (M Ed); for doctorate, master's degree, minimum graduate GPA of 3.5. Additional exam requirements/recommendations for international students: Required—TOEFL (minimum score 580 paper-based; 93 iBT). Electronic applications accepted. *Faculty research:* Movement and brain plasticity, gibberellin physiology, photosynthesis, carbon cycling, molecular properties of main-group ring components.

University of Maine, Graduate School, Intermedia Program, Orono, ME 04469. Offers MFA. *Accreditation:* NASAD. *Faculty:* 9 full-time (4 women), 4 part-time/adjunct (3 women). *Students:* 23 full-time (14 women), 9 part-time (2 women); includes 4 minority (2 American Indian or Alaska Native, non-Hispanic/Latino; 2 Two or more races, non-Hispanic/Latino), 3 international. Average age 39. 16 applicants, 100% accepted, 13 enrolled. In 2017, 4 master's awarded. Terminal master's awarded for partial completion of doctoral program. *Degree requirements:* For master's, comprehensive exam, thesis. *Entrance requirements:* For master's, portfolio. Additional exam requirements/recommendations for international students: Required—TOEFL. Application fee: $65. *Expenses:* Tuition, state resident: full-time $7722; part-time $429 per credit hour. Tuition, nonresident: full-time $25,146; part-time $1397 per credit hour. *Required fees:* $1162; $581 per credit hour. *Financial support:* In 2017–18, 21 students received support, including 1 research assistantship with full tuition reimbursement available (averaging $11,500 per year), 5 teaching assistantships with full tuition reimbursements available (averaging $13,500 per year); Federal Work-Study, scholarships/grants, health care benefits, and unspecified assistantships also available. Financial award application deadline: 3/1; financial award applicants required to submit FAFSA. *Faculty research:* Intermedia, bio-art, art and science, Fluxus, activist art. *Total annual research expenditures:* $4,000. *Unit head:* Dr. Owen Smith, Director, 207-581-4389, E-mail: owen.smith@umit.maine.edu. *Application contact:* Scott G. Delcourt, Assistant Vice President for Graduate Studies and Senior Associate Dean, 207-581-3291, Fax: 207-581-3232, E-mail: graduate@maine.edu.
Website: http://intermediamfa.org

The University of Manchester, School of Arts, Histories and Cultures, Manchester, United Kingdom. Offers anthropology, media and performance (PhD); applied theatre professional (PhD); archaeology (PhD); art history and visual studies (PhD); arts management and cultural policy (PhD); classics and ancient history (PhD); composition (PhD); creative writing (PhD); drama (PhD); economic and social history (PhD); electroacoustic composition (PhD); English and American studies (PhD); history (PhD); humanitarianism and conflict response (PhD); museology (PhD); music (PhD); musicology (PhD); religions and theology (PhD).

The University of Manchester, School of Materials, Manchester, United Kingdom. Offers advanced aerospace materials engineering (M Sc); advanced metallic systems (PhD); biomedical materials (M Phil, M Sc, PhD); ceramics and glass (M Phil, M Sc, PhD); composite materials (M Sc, PhD); corrosion and protection (M Phil, M Sc, PhD); materials (M Phil, PhD); metallic materials (M Phil, M Sc, PhD); nanostructural materials (M Phil, M Sc, PhD); paper science (M Phil, M Sc, PhD); polymer science and engineering (M Phil, M Sc, PhD); technical textiles (M Sc); textile design, fashion and management (M Phil, M Sc, PhD); textile science and technology (M Phil, M Sc, PhD); textiles (M Phil, PhD); textiles and fashion (M Ent).

University of Maryland, College Park, Academic Affairs, College of Arts and Humanities, Department of Art, College Park, MD 20742. Offers MFA. *Degree requirements:* For master's, thesis, oral defense. *Entrance requirements:* For master's, minimum GPA of 3.0, portfolio, 20 digital images, 3 letters of recommendation. Electronic applications accepted. *Faculty research:* Studio art.

University of Massachusetts Amherst, Graduate School, College of Humanities and Fine Arts, Department of Art, Amherst, MA 01003. Offers art (MA, MFA), including art education (MA), studio art (MFA). *Program availability:* Part-time. *Degree requirements:* For master's, comprehensive exam (for some programs), thesis (for some programs). *Entrance requirements:* For master's, portfolio. Additional exam requirements/recommendations for international students: Required—TOEFL (minimum score 550 paper-based; 80 iBT), IELTS (minimum score 6.5). Electronic applications accepted.

University of Massachusetts Dartmouth, Graduate School, College of Visual and Performing Arts, Department of Art and Design, North Dartmouth, MA 02747-2300. Offers artisanry (MFA, Postbaccalaureate Certificate); fine arts (MFA, Postbaccalaureate Certificate); visual design (MFA). *Accreditation:* NASAD. *Program availability:* Part-time. *Faculty:* 27 full-time (12 women), 4 part-time/adjunct (2 women). *Students:* 24 full-time (11 women), 15 part-time (12 women); includes 8 minority (1 Black or African American, non-Hispanic/Latino; 2 Asian, non-Hispanic/Latino; 4 Hispanic/Latino; 1 Two or more races, non-Hispanic/Latino), 8 international. Average age 34. 67 applicants, 54% accepted, 14 enrolled. In 2017, 13 master's, 3 other advanced degrees awarded. *Degree requirements:* For master's, visual and written thesis. *Entrance requirements:* For master's, statement of purpose (minimum of 300 words), resume, 2 letters of recommendation, official transcripts, portfolio (20 images) representing applicant's art work, process of thinking, implementation of concepts and studio production; for Postbaccalaureate Certificate, statement of purpose (minimum of 300 words), resume, 3 letters of recommendation, official transcripts, portfolio (10 images representing applicant's art work, process of thinking, implementation of concepts and studio production). Additional exam requirements/recommendations for international students: Required—TOEFL (minimum score 533 paper-based; 72 iBT), IELTS (minimum score 6). *Application deadline:* For fall admission, 1/11 priority date for domestic students, 12/11 priority date for international students; for spring admission, 10/15 priority date for domestic students, 9/15 priority date for international students. Applications are processed on a rolling basis. Application fee: $60. Electronic applications accepted. *Expenses:* Tuition, state resident: full-time $15,449; part-time $643.71 per credit. Tuition, nonresident: full-time $27,880; part-time $1161.67 per credit. *Required fees:* $405; $25.88 per credit. Tuition and fees vary according to course load and reciprocity agreements. *Financial support:* In 2017–18, 12 fellowships (averaging $5,549 per year), 1 teaching assistantship (averaging $4,600 per year) were awarded; tuition waivers (full and partial), unspecified assistantships, and studio assistantships also available. Support available to part-time students. Financial award application deadline: 3/1; financial award applicants required to submit FAFSA. *Faculty research:* Global textile history and practices, fabrication of jewelry, sculptural objects, slip casting, textile conservation. *Total annual research expenditures:* $27,000. *Unit head:* Laura Franz, Chairperson, Art and Design, 508-999-9285, E-mail: lfranz@umassd.edu. *Application contact:* Steven Briggs, Director of Marketing and Recruitment for Graduate Studies, 508-999-8604, Fax: 508-999-8183, E-mail: graduate@umassd.edu.
Website: http://www.umassd.edu/cvpa/programs

University of Memphis, Graduate School, College of Communication and Fine Arts, Department of Art, Memphis, TN 38152. Offers art history (MA), including Egyptian art and archaeology, general art history; ceramics (MFA); graphic design (MFA); museum studies (Graduate Certificate); painting (MFA); printmaking/photography (MFA); sculpture (MFA). *Accreditation:* NASAD (one or more programs are accredited). *Program availability:* Part-time. *Faculty:* 18 full-time (7 women), 2 part-time/adjunct (1 woman). *Students:* 21 full-time (17 women), 5 part-time (all women); includes 8 minority (2 Black or African American, non-Hispanic/Latino; 1 Asian, non-Hispanic/Latino; 4 Hispanic/Latino; 1 Two or more races, non-Hispanic/Latino). Average age 29. 11 applicants, 73% accepted, 5 enrolled. In 2017, 5 master's, 5 other advanced degrees awarded. *Degree requirements:* For master's, 2 foreign languages, comprehensive exam, thesis, image identification exam, qualifying exam; for Graduate Certificate, internship. *Entrance requirements:* For master's, GRE General Test or MAT, portfolio (MFA), letter of intent, sample of undergraduate writing, two letters of recommendation; for Graduate Certificate, three letters of recommendation, letter of intent. *Application deadline:* For fall admission, 2/15 for domestic students; for spring admission, 11/1 for domestic students. Applications are processed on a rolling basis. Application fee: $35 ($60 for international students). *Expenses:* Contact institution. *Financial support:* In 2017–18, 36 students received support, including 15 research assistantships with full tuition reimbursements available (averaging $11,600 per year); teaching assistantships with full tuition reimbursements available, Federal Work-Study, scholarships/grants, and unspecified assistantships also available. Financial award application deadline: 2/1; financial award applicants required to submit FAFSA. *Faculty research:* Online collaborative learning, advanced art history studies, electronic publishing/design, studio arts, architectural studies. *Unit head:* Prof. Richard Lou, Chair, 901-678-2217, Fax: 901-678-2735, E-mail: ralou@memphis.edu. *Application contact:* Niles Wallice, Coordinator of Graduate Studies, 901-678-4899.
Website: http://memphis.edu/art/

University of Miami, Graduate School, College of Arts and Sciences, Department of Art and Art History, Coral Gables, FL 33124. Offers art history (MA); ceramics/glass (MFA); graphic design/multimedia (MFA); painting (MFA); photography/digital imaging (MFA); printmaking (MFA); sculpture (MFA). *Program availability:* Part-time. *Degree requirements:* For master's, variable foreign language requirement, thesis, exhibit (MFA), comprehensive exam (MA). *Entrance requirements:* For master's, GRE General Test (MA), research paper (MA), slide portfolio (MFA). Additional exam requirements/recommendations for international students: Required—TOEFL. Electronic applications accepted. *Faculty research:* Installation art, public art.

University of Michigan, Rackham Graduate School, Penny W. Stamps School of Art and Design, Ann Arbor, MI 48109-2069. Offers art and design (MFA); integrative design (M Des). *Accreditation:* NASAD. *Faculty:* 37. *Students:* 18 (12 women). 179 applicants, 6% accepted, 10 enrolled. In 2017, 9 master's awarded. *Degree requirements:* For master's, thesis, exhibit (MFA), slide lecture. *Entrance requirements:* For master's, portfolio. Additional exam requirements/recommendations for international students: Required—TOEFL (minimum score 560 paper-based; 84 iBT), IELTS (minimum score 6.5). *Application deadline:* For fall admission, 1/1 for domestic and international students. Application fee: $75 ($90 for international students). Electronic applications accepted. *Expenses:* Tuition, state resident: full-time $22,368; part-time $1201 per credit hour. Tuition, nonresident: full-time $45,156; part-time $2467 per credit hour. *Required fees:* $376 per term. Tuition and fees vary according to course load, degree level and program. *Financial support:* In 2017–18, 19 students received support. Fellowships with full tuition reimbursements available, research assistantships with full tuition reimbursements available, teaching assistantships with full tuition reimbursements available, career-related internships or fieldwork, Federal Work-Study, institutionally sponsored loans, scholarships/grants, health care benefits, tuition waivers (full and partial), and unspecified assistantships available. Support available to part-time students. Financial award application deadline: 1/1. *Faculty research:* Creative expression, social engagement, commercial design, collaborative research, preparation for teaching. *Unit head:* Gunalan Nadarajan, Dean, 734-764-0397, E-mail: artdes-dean@umich.edu. *Application contact:* Meghan Jellema, Graduate Programs

Coordinator, 734-763-5247, E-mail: stamps-graduate-info@umich.edu. Website: http://stamps.umich.edu/

University of Michigan–Flint, Graduate Programs, Program in Arts Administration, Flint, MI 48502-1950. Offers performance (MA), including museum and visual arts, performance. *Program availability:* Part-time. *Faculty:* 5 full-time (3 women), 1 (woman) part-time/adjunct. *Students:* 6 full-time (4 women), 7 part-time (4 women); includes 2 minority (both Black or African American, non-Hispanic/Latino). Average age 43. 12 applicants, 75% accepted, 5 enrolled. In 2017, 3 master's awarded. *Degree requirements:* For master's, thesis, internship. *Entrance requirements:* For master's, bachelor's degree in the arts (visual art, theatre, dance, music, etc.) from regionally-accredited institution; minimum cumulative undergraduate GPA of 3.0. Additional exam requirements/recommendations for international students: Required—TOEFL (minimum score 84 iBT), IELTS (minimum score 6.5). *Application deadline:* For fall admission, 8/1 for domestic students, 5/1 for international students; for winter admission, 11/15 for domestic students, 9/1 for international students. Applications are processed on a rolling basis. Application fee: $55. Electronic applications accepted. *Expenses:* Contact institution. *Financial support:* Federal Work-Study, institutionally sponsored loans, scholarships/grants, and unspecified assistantships available. Support available to part-time students. Financial award application deadline: 3/1; financial award applicants required to submit FAFSA. *Unit head:* Nicole Broughton, Director, 810-237-6522, E-mail: broughn@umflint.edu. *Application contact:* Bradley T. Maki, Director of Graduate Admissions, 810-762-3171, Fax: 810-766-6789, E-mail: bmaki@umflint.edu. Website: http://www.umflint.edu/graduateprograms/arts-administration-ma

University of Minnesota, Duluth, Graduate School, School of Fine Arts, Department of Art and Design, Duluth, MN 55812-2496. Offers graphic design (MFA). *Accreditation:* NASAD. *Program availability:* Part-time. *Degree requirements:* For master's, final exhibit, project, supporting paper. *Entrance requirements:* For master's, minimum GPA of 3.0, writing sample, slide portfolio. Additional exam requirements/recommendations for international students: Required—TOEFL (minimum score 550 paper-based). *Faculty research:* Motion graphics, graphic design history, interactive design, typography, education.

University of Minnesota, Twin Cities Campus, Graduate School, College of Liberal Arts, Department of Art, Minneapolis, MN 55455. Offers MFA. *Degree requirements:* For master's, oral exam, supporting paper, thesis exhibit. *Entrance requirements:* For master's, portfolio, letters of recommendation, minimum GPA of 3.0. Additional exam requirements/recommendations for international students: Required—TOEFL (minimum score 550 paper-based; 79 iBT); Recommended—IELTS (minimum score 6.5). Electronic applications accepted. *Faculty research:* Performed photography, image as code and symbol, cast metal sculpture, performance and installations, high-fired salt glazed and utilitarian ceramic earthenware, contemporary theory, multimedia, video and electronic technology.

University of Mississippi, Graduate School, College of Liberal Arts, University, MS 38677. Offers anthropology (MA); biology (MS, PhD); chemistry (MS, DA, PhD); creative writing (MFA); documentary expression (MFA); economics (MA, PhD); English (MA, PhD); experimental psychology (PhD); history (MA, PhD); mathematics (MS, PhD); modern languages (MA); music (MM); philosophy (MA); physics (MA, MS, PhD); political science (MA, PhD); Southern studies (MA); studio art (MFA). *Program availability:* Part-time. *Faculty:* 465 full-time (207 women), 82 part-time/adjunct (46 women). *Students:* 466 full-time (229 women), 72 part-time (34 women); includes 87 minority (38 Black or African American, non-Hispanic/Latino; 18 Asian, non-Hispanic/Latino; 24 Hispanic/Latino; 7 Two or more races, non-Hispanic/Latino; 121 international. Average age 29. *Degree requirements:* For doctorate, thesis/dissertation. *Entrance requirements:* For master's, GRE General Test, minimum GPA of 3.0; for doctorate, GRE General Test. Additional exam requirements/recommendations for international students: Required—TOEFL. *Application deadline:* For fall admission, 2/1 priority date for domestic students; for spring admission, 10/1 for domestic students. Applications are processed on a rolling basis. Application fee: $50. Electronic applications accepted. *Financial support:* Fellowships, research assistantships, teaching assistantships, career-related internships or fieldwork, Federal Work-Study, institutionally sponsored loans, scholarships/grants, and unspecified assistantships available. Financial award application deadline: 3/1; financial award applicants required to submit FAFSA. *Unit head:* Dr. Lee Michael Cohen, Dean, 662-915-7177, Fax: 662-915-5792, E-mail: libarts@olemiss.edu. *Application contact:* Dr. Christy M. Wyandt, Associate Dean of Graduate School, 662-915-7474, Fax: 662-915-7577, E-mail: cwyandt@olemiss.edu.

University of Missouri, Office of Research and Graduate Studies, College of Arts and Science, Department of Art, Columbia, MO 65211. Offers MFA. *Degree requirements:* For master's, thesis. *Entrance requirements:* For master's, GRE General Test, minimum GPA of 3.0. Additional exam requirements/recommendations for international students: Required—TOEFL (minimum score 550 paper-based; 80 iBT), IELTS (minimum score 6.5). Electronic applications accepted. *Faculty research:* Painting, digital art, new media, photography, ceramics.

University of Missouri–Kansas City, College of Arts and Sciences, Department of Art and Art History, Kansas City, MO 64110-2499. Offers MA, PhD. PhD (interdisciplinary) offered through the School of Graduate Studies. *Program availability:* Part-time. Terminal master's awarded for partial completion of doctoral program. *Degree requirements:* For master's, thesis, qualifying exam; for doctorate, thesis/dissertation, exams. *Entrance requirements:* For master's, good general education in the humanities. Additional exam requirements/recommendations for international students: Required—TOEFL (minimum score 550 paper-based; 80 iBT). Electronic applications accepted. *Faculty research:* Painting, electronic media, Western and non-Western art history, photography.

University of Montana, Graduate School, College of Visual and Performing Arts, School of Art, Missoula, MT 59812. Offers fine arts (MA), including art, art history; photography (MFA). *Accreditation:* NASAD (one or more programs are accredited). *Degree requirements:* For master's, thesis exhibit. *Entrance requirements:* For master's, GRE General Test, portfolio.

University of Nebraska at Omaha, Graduate Studies, College of Communication, Fine Arts and Media, School of the Arts, Omaha, NE 68182. Offers MA. *Accreditation:* NASAD. *Program availability:* Part-time. *Degree requirements:* For master's, comprehensive exam, thesis (for some programs). *Entrance requirements:* For master's, minimum GPA of 3.0, statement of purpose, writing sample, 2 letters of recommendation, transcripts. Additional exam requirements/recommendations for international students: Required—TOEFL, IELTS, PTE. Electronic applications accepted.

University of Nebraska–Lincoln, Graduate College, College of Fine and Performing Arts, Department of Art and Art History, Lincoln, NE 68588. Offers art history (MA); studio art (MFA). *Accreditation:* NASAD. *Degree requirements:* For master's, thesis. *Entrance requirements:* For master's, slide portfolio. Additional exam requirements/recommendations for international students: Required—TOEFL (minimum score 550 paper-based). Electronic applications accepted. *Faculty research:* Classical archaeology, contemporary art, printmaking, photography.

University of Nevada, Las Vegas, Graduate College, College of Fine Arts, Department of Art, Las Vegas, NV 89154-5013. Offers MFA. *Accreditation:* NASAD. *Program availability:* Part-time. *Faculty:* 8 full-time (3 women), 4 part-time/adjunct (2 women). *Students:* 11 full-time (4 women); includes 4 minority (3 Hispanic/Latino; 1 Two or more races, non-Hispanic/Latino). Average age 37. 31 applicants, 10% accepted, 2 enrolled. In 2017, 1 master's awarded. *Degree requirements:* For master's, thesis. *Entrance requirements:* For master's, bachelor's degree, 20 slides of work. Additional exam requirements/recommendations for international students: Required—TOEFL (minimum score 550 paper-based; 80 iBT), IELTS (minimum score 7). *Application deadline:* For fall admission, 3/1 for domestic students. Application fee: $60 ($95 for international students). Electronic applications accepted. *Expenses:* $275 per credit, $850 per course, $7,969 per year resident, $22,157 per year non-resident, $7,094 non-resident fee (7 credits or more), $1,307 annual health insurance fee. *Financial support:* In 2017–18, 10 students received support, including 1 research assistantship with full tuition reimbursement available (averaging $15,000 per year), 9 teaching assistantships with full tuition reimbursements available (averaging $15,000 per year); institutionally sponsored loans, scholarships/grants, health care benefits, and unspecified assistantships also available. Financial award application deadline: 3/15; financial award applicants required to submit FAFSA. *Faculty research:* Studio arts: printmaking, sculpture, mixed media, photography, film and digital; graphic design; art history, theory and criticism. *Unit head:* Dr. Louisa McDonald, Chair/Professor, 702-895-2717, Fax: 702-895-4346, E-mail: louisa.mcdonald@unlv.edu. *Application contact:* Sean Clark, Associate Dean, 702-895-2442, E-mail: sean.clark@unlv.edu. Website: http://art.unlv.edu/

University of Nevada, Reno, Graduate School, College of Liberal Arts, Department of Fine Arts, Reno, NV 89557. Offers MFA. *Degree requirements:* For master's, thesis optional. *Entrance requirements:* For master's, minimum GPA of 2.75. Additional exam requirements/recommendations for international students: Required—TOEFL (minimum score 500 paper-based; 61 iBT), IELTS (minimum score 6). Electronic applications accepted. *Faculty research:* Ceramics; digital-media; drawing; painting; performance; photography; printmaking; sculpture; video; studio program supported by a strong emphasis in the areas of contemporary art, theory and criticism.

University of New Mexico, Graduate Studies, College of Fine Arts, Program in Studio Art, Albuquerque, NM 87131. Offers MFA. *Faculty:* 18 full-time (9 women), 1 (woman) part-time/adjunct. *Students:* 35 full-time (20 women), 13 part-time (9 women); includes 11 minority (2 Black or African American, non-Hispanic/Latino; 1 Asian, non-Hispanic/Latino; 7 Hispanic/Latino; 1 Two or more races, non-Hispanic/Latino), 4 international. Average age 31. 91 applicants, 37% accepted, 22 enrolled. In 2017, 14 master's awarded. *Degree requirements:* For master's, comprehensive exam, thesis or alternative, studio reviews, qualifying exams. *Entrance requirements:* Additional exam requirements/recommendations for international students: Required—TOEFL (minimum score 550 paper-based), IELTS (minimum score 6). *Application deadline:* For fall admission, 1/15 for domestic and international students. Application fee: $50. Electronic applications accepted. *Financial support:* Fellowships, research assistantships, teaching assistantships with partial tuition reimbursements, Federal Work-Study, institutionally sponsored loans, scholarships/grants, health care benefits, and unspecified assistantships available. Support available to part-time students. Financial award application deadline: 3/1; financial award applicants required to submit FAFSA. *Faculty research:* Photography, painting, drawing, print making, sculpture, ceramics, electronic arts, art and ecology. *Unit head:* Prof. Mary Tsiongas, Chair, 505-277-5861, Fax: 505-277-5955, E-mail: tsiongas@unm.edu. *Application contact:* Kat Heatherington, Graduate Advisor, 505-277-6672, Fax: 505-277-5955, E-mail: art255@unm.edu. Website: http://art.unm.edu/graduate-programs/

University of New Orleans, Graduate School, College of Liberal Arts, Department of Fine Arts, New Orleans, LA 70148. Offers MFA. *Accreditation:* NASAD. *Degree requirements:* For master's, thesis. *Entrance requirements:* For master's, GRE General Test, slide review. Additional exam requirements/recommendations for international students: Required—TOEFL (minimum score 550 paper-based; 79 iBT), IELTS (minimum score 6.5). Electronic applications accepted. *Faculty research:* Large-scale painting and sculpture, black-and-white and color photography, computer graphics.

The University of North Carolina at Chapel Hill, Graduate School, College of Arts and Sciences, Department of Art, Studio Art Program, Chapel Hill, NC 27599. Offers MFA. *Degree requirements:* For master's, variable foreign language requirement. *Entrance requirements:* For master's, minimum GPA of 3.0, portfolio. Electronic applications accepted. *Faculty research:* Environmental installation, painting, photography, mixed media, printmaking.

The University of North Carolina at Greensboro, Graduate School, College of Arts and Sciences, Department of Art, Greensboro, NC 27412-5001. Offers studio arts (MFA). *Degree requirements:* For master's, thesis (for some programs). *Entrance requirements:* For master's, GRE General Test, 39 hours of course work in studio art, 15 hours of course work in art history, portfolio. Additional exam requirements/recommendations for international students: Required—TOEFL. Electronic applications accepted.

University of North Dakota, Graduate School, College of Arts and Sciences, Department of Visual Arts, Grand Forks, ND 58202. Offers MFA. *Accreditation:* NASAD. *Degree requirements:* For master's, thesis or alternative, comprehensive evaluation, professional exhibition. *Entrance requirements:* For master's, minimum GPA of 3.0. Additional exam requirements/recommendations for international students: Required—TOEFL (minimum score 550 paper-based; 79 iBT), IELTS (minimum score 6.5). Electronic applications accepted. *Faculty research:* Ceramics, drawing, metalsmithing, printmaking, painting.

University of Northern Colorado, Graduate School, College of Performing and Visual Arts, School of Art and Design, Greeley, CO 80639. Offers art education (MA); art history (MA); studio art (MA). *Accreditation:* NASAD. *Program availability:* Part-time. *Degree requirements:* For master's, comprehensive exam, thesis. *Entrance requirements:* For master's, GRE General Test, portfolio, 3 letters of recommendation, minimum undergraduate GPA of 3.0. Electronic applications accepted.

University of Northern Iowa, Graduate College, College of Humanities, Arts and Sciences, Department of Art, Cedar Falls, IA 50614. Offers art education (MA). *Program availability:* Part-time, evening/weekend. *Degree requirements:* For master's, comprehensive exam (for some programs), thesis or alternative. *Entrance requirements:* For master's, minimum GPA of 3.0, portfolio. Additional exam requirements/recommendations for international students: Required—TOEFL (minimum score 500 paper-based; 61 iBT). Electronic applications accepted.

University of North Texas, Robert B. Toulouse School of Graduate Studies, Denton, TX 76203-5459. Offers accounting (MS); applied anthropology (MA, MS); applied behavior analysis (Certificate); applied geography (MA); applied technology and performance improvement (M Ed, MS); art education (MA); art history (MA); art museum education (Certificate); arts leadership (Certificate); audiology (Au D); behavior analysis (MS); behavioral science (PhD); biochemistry and molecular biology (MS); biology (MA, MS); biomedical engineering (MS); business analysis (MS); chemistry (MS); clinical health psychology (PhD); communication studies (MA, MS); computer engineering (MS);

computer science (MS); counseling (M Ed, MS), including clinical mental health counseling (MS), college and university counseling, elementary school counseling, secondary school counseling; creative writing (MA); criminal justice (MS); curriculum and instruction (M Ed); decision sciences (MBA); design (MA, MFA), including fashion design (MFA), innovation studies, interior design (MFA); early childhood studies (MS); economics (MS); educational leadership (M Ed, Ed D); educational psychology (MS, PhD), including family studies (MS), gifted and talented (MS), human development (MS), learning and cognition (MS), research, measurement and evaluation (MS); electrical engineering (MS); emergency management (MPA); engineering technology (MS); English (MA); English as a second language (MA); environmental science (MS); finance (MBA, MS); financial management (MPA); French (MA); health services management (MBA); higher education (M Ed, Ed D); history (MA, MS); hospitality management (MS); human resources management (MPA); information science (MS); information systems (PhD); information technologies (MBA); interdisciplinary studies (MA, MS); international studies (MA); international sustainable tourism (MS); jazz studies (MM); journalism (MA, MJ, Graduate Certificate), including interactive and virtual digital communication (Graduate Certificate), narrative journalism (Graduate Certificate), public relations (Graduate Certificate); kinesiology (MS); linguistics (MA); local government management (MPA); logistics (PhD); logistics and supply chain management (MBA); long-term care, senior housing, and aging services (MA); management (PhD); marketing (MBA); mathematics (MA, MS); mechanical and energy engineering (MS, PhD); music (MA), including ethnomusicology, music theory, musicology, performance; music composition (PhD); music education (MM Ed, PhD); nonprofit management (MPA); operations and supply chain management (MBA); performance (MM, DMA); philosophy (MA); political science (MA); professional and technical communication (MA); radio, television and film (MA, MFA); rehabilitation counseling (Certificate); sociology (MA); Spanish (MA); special education (M Ed); speech-language pathology (MA); strategic management (MBA); studio art (MFA); teaching (M Ed); MBA/MS. *Program availability:* Part-time, evening/weekend, online learning. Terminal master's awarded for partial completion of doctoral program. *Degree requirements:* For master's, variable foreign language requirement, comprehensive exam (for some programs), thesis (for some programs); for doctorate, variable foreign language requirement, comprehensive exam (for some programs), thesis/dissertation; for other advanced degree, variable foreign language requirement, comprehensive exam (for some programs). *Entrance requirements:* For master's and doctorate, GRE, GMAT. Additional exam requirements/recommendations for international students: Required—TOEFL (minimum score 550 paper-based; 79 iBT). Electronic applications accepted.

University of Notre Dame, Graduate School, College of Arts and Letters, Division of Humanities, Department of Art, Art History, and Design, Notre Dame, IN 46556. Offers art history (MA); design (MFA), including graphic design, industrial design; studio art (MFA), including ceramics, painting, photography, printmaking, sculpture. *Accreditation:* NASAD. *Degree requirements:* For master's, comprehensive exam (for some programs), thesis. *Entrance requirements:* For master's, GRE General Test, minimum GPA of 3.0. Additional exam requirements/recommendations for international students: Required—TOEFL (minimum score 600 paper-based; 80 iBT). Electronic applications accepted. *Faculty research:* Studio art practice in ceramics, printing, photography, printmaking and sculpture, graphic design and industrial design, digital imaging in design and photography, Renaissance and American art history, contemporary art theory and criticism.

University of Oklahoma, Weitzenhoffer Family College of Fine Arts, School of Visual Arts, Program in Art, Norman, OK 73019. Offers art and technology (MFA); ceramics (MFA); painting (MFA); printmaking (MFA); sculpture (MFA); visual communication (MFA). Applicants admitted in fall only. *Students:* 13 full-time (9 women); includes 4 minority (1 Asian, non-Hispanic/Latino; 3 Hispanic/Latino). Average age 33. 24 applicants, 17% accepted, 4 enrolled. In 2017, 3 master's awarded. Terminal master's awarded for partial completion of doctoral program. *Entrance requirements:* Additional exam requirements/recommendations for international students: Required—TOEFL (minimum score 79 iBT) or IELTS (minimum score 6.5). *Application deadline:* For fall admission, 2/1 for domestic and international students. Application fee: $50 ($100 for international students). Electronic applications accepted. *Expenses:* Tuition, state resident: full-time $5119; part-time $213.30 per credit hour. Tuition, nonresident: full-time $19,778; part-time $824.10 per credit hour. *Required fees:* $3458; $133.55 per credit hour. $126.50 per semester. *Financial support:* In 2017–18, 14 students received support. Fellowships with full and partial tuition reimbursements available, research assistantships with full tuition reimbursements available, teaching assistantships with full tuition reimbursements available, Federal Work-Study, institutionally sponsored loans, scholarships/grants, health care benefits, tuition waivers (partial), and unspecified assistantships available. Financial award application deadline: 6/1; financial award applicants required to submit FAFSA. *Faculty research:* 3D printing and sculpture, photography, painting, installation art. *Unit head:* Dr. Bette Talvacchia, Director, 405-325-6210, Fax: 405-325-1668, E-mail: bette.talvacchia-1@ou.edu. *Application contact:* Peter Froslie, MFA Coordinator, E-mail: froslie@ou.edu. Website: http://art.ou.edu

University of Oregon, Graduate School, College of Design, Department of Art, Eugene, OR 97403. Offers MFA. *Accreditation:* NASAD. *Degree requirements:* For master's, thesis or alternative. *Entrance requirements:* For master's, BFA or equivalent. Additional exam requirements/recommendations for international students: Required—TOEFL.

University of Pennsylvania, School of Design, Department of Fine Arts, Philadelphia, PA 19104. Offers emerging design and research (Certificate); fine arts (MFA); time-based and interactive media (Certificate). *Faculty:* 8 full-time (4 women), 1 part-time/adjunct (0 women). *Students:* 25 full-time (11 women); includes 8 minority (3 Black or African American, non-Hispanic/Latino; 1 Asian, non-Hispanic/Latino; 3 Hispanic/Latino; 1 Two or more races, non-Hispanic/Latino), 10 international. Average age 30. 123 applicants, 41% accepted, 15 enrolled. In 2017, 16 master's, 1 other advanced degree awarded. *Degree requirements:* For master's, thesis. *Application deadline:* Applications are processed on a rolling basis. Electronic applications accepted. *Financial support:* In 2017–18, 30 students received support, including teaching assistantships (averaging $6,000 per year); fellowships with full tuition reimbursements available, research assistantships, Federal Work-Study, scholarships/grants, health care benefits, and unspecified assistantships also available. Financial award applicants required to submit FAFSA. *Faculty research:* Performance art, photography and video, drawing and painting, sculpture, animation and creative research. *Unit head:* Joshua Mosley, Professor/Chair/Director of Graduate Program, 215-898-8374, E-mail: jmosley@design.upenn.edu. *Application contact:* Leighann Bogner, Administrative Assistant, 215-898-8374, Fax: 215-573-2459, E-mail: mfa@pobox.upenn.edu. Website: http://www.design.upenn.edu/mfa

University of Regina, Faculty of Graduate Studies and Research, Faculty of Media, Art, and Performance, Department of Visual Arts, Regina, SK S4S 0A2, Canada. Offers ceramics (MFA); drawing (MFA); interdisciplinary studies (MA, MFA); intermedia (MFA); painting (MFA); sculpture (MFA). *Faculty:* 10 full-time (5 women), 3 part-time/adjunct (1 woman). *Students:* 2 part-time (1 woman). 12 applicants, 17% accepted. In 2017, 3 master's awarded. *Degree requirements:* For master's, exhibition, support paper, oral defense. *Entrance requirements:* For master's, portfolio. Additional exam requirements/

recommendations for international students: Required—TOEFL (minimum score 580 paper-based; 80 iBT), IELTS (minimum score 6.5), PTE (minimum score 59). *Application deadline:* For fall admission, 1/15 for domestic and international students. Applications are processed on a rolling basis. Application fee: $100. Electronic applications accepted. *Expenses:* CAD$10,681 per year. *Financial support:* In 2017–18, fellowships (averaging $6,000 per year), teaching assistantships (averaging $2,562 per year) were awarded; research assistantships and scholarships/grants also available. Financial award application deadline: 6/15. *Faculty research:* Contemporary visual art theory and practice; art history; curatorial practice; print media; drawing/painting, sculpture, and ceramics. *Unit head:* Dr. Robert Truszkowski, Department Head, 306-585-5574, Fax: 306-585-5526, E-mail: robert.truszkowski@uregina.ca. *Application contact:* Leesa Streifler, Graduate Coordinator, Visual Arts, 306-585-5529, Fax: 306-585-5526, E-mail: leesa.streifler@uregina.ca.

University of Rochester, School of Arts and Sciences, Department of Art and Art History, Rochester, NY 14627. Offers visual and cultural studies (PhD). *Faculty:* 11 full-time (6 women). *Students:* 28 full-time (17 women); includes 5 minority (1 Black or African American, non-Hispanic/Latino; 2 Asian, non-Hispanic/Latino; 2 Hispanic/Latino), 9 international. Average age 30. 66 applicants, 18% accepted, 4 enrolled. In 2017, 3 doctorates awarded. Terminal master's awarded for partial completion of doctoral program. *Degree requirements:* For doctorate, thesis/dissertation, qualifying exam. *Entrance requirements:* For doctorate, GRE General Test, personal statement, three letters of recommendation, official undergraduate and graduate transcripts, writing sample. Additional exam requirements/recommendations for international students: Required—TOEFL. *Application deadline:* For fall admission, 1/15 for domestic and international students. Application fee: $60. Electronic applications accepted. *Expenses:* $1,596 per credit hour. *Financial support:* In 2017–18, 4 teaching assistantships with full tuition reimbursements (averaging $22,000 per year) were awarded; research assistantships and tuition waivers (full) also available. *Faculty research:* Visual culture from a social-historical perspective. *Unit head:* Rachel Haidu, Director, 585-275-9429, E-mail: rachel.haidu@rochester.edu. *Application contact:* Martin Collier, Administrator, 585-275-7451, E-mail: marty.collier@rochester.edu. Website: http://www.sas.rochester.edu/aah/graduate/index.html

University of Saint Francis, Graduate School, Department of Visual Art and Communication, Fort Wayne, IN 46808-3994. Offers studio art (MA, MFA). *Accreditation:* NASAD. *Program availability:* Part-time, evening/weekend, blended/hybrid learning. *Faculty:* 4 full-time (1 woman). *Students:* 2 part-time (both women); includes 1 minority (Asian, non-Hispanic/Latino). Average age 35. 1 applicant, 100% accepted, 1 enrolled. In 2017, 3 master's awarded. *Degree requirements:* For master's, thesis, exhibit. *Entrance requirements:* For master's, undergraduate degree in art; minimum undergraduate GPA of 3.0; portfolio; essay; resume; three professional recommendations. Additional exam requirements/recommendations for international students: Required—TOEFL (minimum score 550 paper-based) or IELTS (minimum score 6.5). *Application deadline:* For fall admission, 7/1 for international students; for spring admission, 11/1 for international students; for summer admission, 3/1 for international students. Applications are processed on a rolling basis. Application fee: $0. Electronic applications accepted. *Expenses:* $905 per hour. *Financial support:* In 2017–18, 1 student received support. Federal Work-Study, scholarships/grants, and unspecified assistantships available. Financial award application deadline: 4/15; financial award applicants required to submit FAFSA. *Unit head:* Cara Wade, School of Creative Arts Graduate Studies Program Director, 260-399-7700 Ext. 8016, Fax: 260-399-8171, E-mail: cwade@sf.edu. *Application contact:* Kyle Richardson, Associate Director of Enrollment Services for Adult Learning, 260-399-7700 Ext. 6310, Fax: 260-399-8152, E-mail: krichardson@sf.edu. Website: https://art.sf.edu/graduate/

University of Saskatchewan, College of Graduate Studies and Research, College of Arts and Science, Department of Art and Art History, Saskatoon, SK S7N 5A2, Canada. Offers MFA. *Program availability:* Part-time. *Degree requirements:* For master's, thesis. *Entrance requirements:* Additional exam requirements/recommendations for international students: Required—TOEFL (minimum score 80 iBT); Recommended—IELTS (minimum score 6.5).

The University of Scranton, College of Arts and Sciences, Scranton, PA 18510. Offers MA, MS. *Program availability:* Part-time, evening/weekend, 100% online. *Degree requirements:* For master's, comprehensive exam (for some programs), thesis (for some programs), capstone experience. *Entrance requirements:* For master's, GMAT (for MBA), minimum GPA of 3.0, three letters of reference. Additional exam requirements/recommendations for international students: Required—TOEFL (minimum score 500 paper-based; 80 iBT), IELTS (minimum score 6.5). Electronic applications accepted.

University of South Alabama, College of Arts and Sciences, Department of Visual Arts, Mobile, AL 36688. Offers creative technologies and practice (MFA). *Faculty:* 7 full-time (4 women). *Students:* 6 full-time (4 women), 1 (woman) part-time; includes 1 minority (Hispanic/Latino). Average age 28. 11 applicants, 64% accepted, 4 enrolled. *Degree requirements:* For master's, thesis, 4 semesters of residency. *Entrance requirements:* For master's, minimum undergraduate GPA of 3.0, letter of intent, resume, three letters of recommendation, portfolio, artist's statement. Additional exam requirements/recommendations for international students: Required—TOEFL (minimum score 525 paper-based; 71 iBT), IELTS (minimum score 6). *Application deadline:* For fall admission, 2/15 priority date for domestic students. Applications are processed on a rolling basis. Application fee: $35. Electronic applications accepted. *Expenses:* Tuition, state resident: full-time $10,104; part-time $421 per semester hour. Tuition, nonresident: full-time $20,208; part-time $842 per semester hour. *Financial support:* In 2017–18, teaching assistantships with tuition reimbursements (averaging $8,000 per year) were awarded; fellowships, career-related internships or fieldwork, and unspecified assistantships also available. Financial award application deadline: 3/31; financial award applicants required to submit FAFSA. *Faculty research:* Glass vessel and color formation, eighteenth-century art, material culture, and identity through sculptural applications. *Unit head:* Dr. Susan Fitzsimmons, Chairperson, 251-461-1438, E-mail: sgfitzsimmons@southalabama.edu. *Application contact:* Diane Gibbs, Graduate Coordinator, 251-461-1696, Fax: 251-461-1744, E-mail: dgibbs@southalabama.edu. Website: http://www.southalabama.edu/colleges/artsandsci/art/

University of South Carolina, The Graduate School, College of Arts and Sciences, Department of Art, Columbia, SC 29208. Offers art education (IMA, MA, MAT); art history (MA); art studio (MA); media arts (MMA); studio art (MFA). *Accreditation:* NASAD. *Degree requirements:* For master's, comprehensive exam (for some programs), thesis (for some programs). *Entrance requirements:* For master's, GRE General Test or MAT, portfolio. Additional exam requirements/recommendations for international students: Required—TOEFL. Electronic applications accepted. *Faculty research:* Script writing, teaching art at the elementary and secondary levels of education, history of art and architecture.

University of South Dakota, Graduate School, College of Fine Arts, Department of Art, Vermillion, SD 57069. Offers art education (MFA); ceramics (MFA); graphic design (MFA); painting (MFA); photography (MFA); printmaking (MFA); sculpture (MFA). *Accreditation:* NASAD. *Degree requirements:* For master's, thesis or alternative. *Entrance requirements:* For master's, portfolio, minimum GPA of 2.7. Additional exam

requirements/recommendations for international students: Required—TOEFL (minimum score 550 paper-based; 79 iBT). *Application deadline:* Applications are processed on a rolling basis. Application fee: $35. Electronic applications accepted. *Financial support:* Research assistantships with partial tuition reimbursements, teaching assistantships with partial tuition reimbursements, Federal Work-Study, and unspecified assistantships available. Support available to part-time students. Financial award applicants required to submit FAFSA. *Application contact:* Graduate School, 605-658-6140, Fax: 605-677-6118, E-mail: grad@usd.edu.
Website: http://www.usd.edu/fine-arts/art

University of Southern California, Graduate School, Dana and David Dornsife College of Letters, Arts and Sciences, Department of Art History, Los Angeles, CA 90089. Offers art history (MA, PhD); visual studies (Graduate Certificate). *Degree requirements:* For doctorate, 2 foreign languages, comprehensive exam, thesis/dissertation, 60 units. *Entrance requirements:* For doctorate, GRE. Additional exam requirements/recommendations for international students: Required—TOEFL. *Faculty research:* Ancient, medieval, Renaissance, eighteenth-nineteenth century, contemporary.

University of Southern California, Graduate School, Roski School of Fine Arts, Graduate Programs in Fine Arts, Los Angeles, CA 90089. Offers new genres (MFA); painting/drawing (MFA); photography (MFA); sculpture (MFA). *Degree requirements:* For master's, thesis. *Entrance requirements:* For master's, portfolio, artist statement, 3 letters of recommendation. Additional exam requirements/recommendations for international students: Required—TOEFL (minimum score 600 paper-based; 100 iBT). Electronic applications accepted. *Faculty research:* Fine art production in the areas of photography, video, sculpture, drawing, and performance.

University of South Florida, College of The Arts, School of Art and Art History, Tampa, FL 33620-9951. Offers art history (MA); studio art (MFA). *Accreditation:* NASAD. *Program availability:* Part-time. *Faculty:* 21 full-time (11 women). *Students:* 35 full-time (19 women), 2 part-time (1 woman); includes 10 minority (8 Hispanic/Latino; 2 Two or more races, non-Hispanic/Latino), 3 international. Average age 29. 48 applicants, 29% accepted, 13 enrolled. In 2017, 13 master's awarded. *Degree requirements:* For master's, comprehensive exam, thesis, exhibition (for MFA). *Entrance requirements:* For master's, GRE General Test, bachelor's degree from regionally-accredited institution with minimum GPA of 3.0 in upper-division coursework or graduate degree from regionally-accredited institution; portfolio; goals statement (for MA in art history). Additional exam requirements/recommendations for international students: Required—TOEFL (minimum score 550 paper-based; 79 iBT) or IELTS (minimum score 6.5). *Application deadline:* For fall admission, 1/15 priority date for domestic students, 2/1 for international students. Application fee: $30. Electronic applications accepted. *Financial support:* In 2017–18, 33 students received support, including 37 teaching assistantships with partial tuition reimbursements available (averaging $9,440 per year); scholarships/grants, health care benefits, and unspecified assistantships also available. Support available to part-time students. Financial award application deadline: 2/15; financial award applicants required to submit FAFSA. *Faculty research:* Contemporary art and role of the artist, identity strategies, political iconography, art practice and technology, the construction of race in art. *Total annual research expenditures:* $127,255. *Unit head:* Prof. Wallace Wilson, Director, 813-974-2360, Fax: 813-974-9226, E-mail: wwilson2@usf.edu. *Application contact:* Prof. Neil Bender, Associate Professor and Graduate Program Director, 813-974-2360, Fax: 813-974-9226, E-mail: nb2@usf.edu.
Website: http://www.art.usf.edu

The University of Tennessee, Graduate School, College of Arts and Sciences, School of Art, Knoxville, TN 37996. Offers ceramics (MFA); drawing (MFA); graphic design (MFA); inter-area studies (MFA); media arts (MFA); painting (MFA); printmaking (MFA); sculpture (MFA); watercolor (MFA). *Accreditation:* NASAD. *Degree requirements:* For master's, thesis or alternative, exhibit. *Entrance requirements:* For master's, portfolio, minimum GPA of 2.7. Additional exam requirements/recommendations for international students: Required—TOEFL. Electronic applications accepted.

The University of Texas at Arlington, Graduate School, College of Liberal Arts, Department of Art and Art History, Arlington, TX 76019. Offers film and video (MFA); glass (MFA); intermedia (MFA); visual communication (MFA). *Accreditation:* NASAD. *Degree requirements:* For master's, thesis or alternative, mid- and final program reviews; exhibition. *Entrance requirements:* For master's, GRE, minimum GPA of 3.0, 3 letters of recommendation, portfolio, resume. Additional exam requirements/recommendations for international students: Required—TOEFL (minimum score 550 paper-based). Electronic applications accepted.

The University of Texas at Austin, Graduate School, College of Fine Arts, Department of Art and Art History, Program in Studio Art, Austin, TX 78712-1111. Offers MFA. *Accreditation:* NASAD. *Degree requirements:* For master's, thesis, oral exam. *Entrance requirements:* For master's, minimum GPA of 3.0, portfolio of 15 slides. Electronic applications accepted. *Faculty research:* Painting, sculpture, transmedia, photography, printmaking.

The University of Texas at El Paso, Graduate School, College of Liberal Arts, Department of Art, El Paso, TX 79968-0001. Offers art education (MA); studio art (MA). *Program availability:* Part-time, evening/weekend. *Degree requirements:* For master's, thesis optional. *Entrance requirements:* For master's, minimum GPA of 3.0, digital portfolio, letters of recommendation. Additional exam requirements/recommendations for international students: Required—TOEFL; Recommended—IELTS. Electronic applications accepted.

The University of Texas at San Antonio, College of Liberal and Fine Arts, Department of Art and Art History, San Antonio, TX 78249-0617. Offers art (MFA); art history (MA). *Accreditation:* NASAD (one or more programs are accredited). *Faculty:* 14 full-time (6 women), 1 part-time/adjunct (0 women). *Students:* 29 full-time (21 women), 4 part-time (all women); includes 16 minority (1 Asian, non-Hispanic/Latino; 14 Hispanic/Latino; 1 Two or more races, non-Hispanic/Latino), 2 international. Average age 31. 32 applicants, 63% accepted, 14 enrolled. In 2017, 5 master's awarded. *Entrance requirements:* For master's, GRE General Test, portfolio, minimum GPA of 3.0 in last 60 hours, 3 letters of recommendation, statement of purpose. Additional exam requirements/recommendations for international students: Required—TOEFL (minimum score 550 paper-based; 79 iBT), IELTS (minimum score 6.5). *Application deadline:* For fall admission, 6/15 for domestic students, 3/1 for international students; for spring admission, 10/15 for domestic students, 9/15 for international students. Application fee: $50 ($90 for international students). Electronic applications accepted. *Expenses:* Tuition, state resident: full-time $5495. Tuition, nonresident: full-time $21,938. *Required fees:* $1915. Tuition and fees vary according to program. *Unit head:* Dr. Gregory Elliott, Department Chair, 210-458-4352, Fax: 210-458-4356, E-mail: greg.elliott@utsa.edu. *Application contact:* Monica Rodriguez, Director of Graduate Admissions, 210-458-4331, Fax: 210-458-4332, E-mail: graduate.admissions@utsa.edu.
Website: http://art.utsa.edu/

The University of Texas at Tyler, College of Arts and Sciences, Department of Art and Art History, Tyler, TX 75799-0001. Offers art history (MA); interdisciplinary (MAIS); studio art (MFA). *Degree requirements:* For master's, thesis, graduate committee review. *Entrance requirements:* For master's, minimum GPA of 3.0. Additional exam requirements/recommendations for international students: Required—TOEFL. *Faculty research:* Classical myths in contemporary art, social issues in contemporary art, casting methods, Renaissance art.

The University of Texas Rio Grande Valley, College of Fine Arts, School of Art, Edinburg, TX 78539. Offers MFA. *Program availability:* Part-time. *Faculty:* 5 full-time (1 woman). *Students:* 19 full-time (14 women), 11 part-time (9 women); includes 28 minority (all Hispanic/Latino). Average age 33. 11 applicants, 91% accepted, 8 enrolled. In 2017, 7 master's awarded. *Degree requirements:* For master's, thesis, thesis show of artwork. *Entrance requirements:* For master's, bachelor's degree in fine arts, portfolio, minimum GPA of 2.5. Additional exam requirements/recommendations for international students: Required—TOEFL or IELTS. *Application deadline:* Applications are processed on a rolling basis. Application fee: $50 ($100 for international students). *Expenses:* Tuition, state resident: full-time $5550; part-time $417 per credit hour. Tuition, nonresident: full-time $13,020; part-time $832 per credit hour. *Required fees:* $1169. *Financial support:* Unspecified assistantships available. *Faculty research:* Painting, photography, graphic design, sculpture, bronze casting, performance art. *Unit head:* Dr. Susan Fitzsimmons, Director, 956-665-3481, E-mail: susan.fitzsimmons@utrgv.edu. *Application contact:* Stephanie Ozuna, Graduate Student Recruiter, 956-665-3558, E-mail: stephanie.ozuna@utrgv.edu.

The University of the Arts, College of Art, Media and Design, Department of Book Arts/Printmaking, Philadelphia, PA 19102-4944. Offers MFA. *Accreditation:* NASAD. *Degree requirements:* For master's, thesis. *Entrance requirements:* For master's, portfolio of 20-30 digital images showing work that represents applicant's full range of studio experience, preferably including printmaking and book arts; official transcripts from each undergraduate or graduate school attended; three letters of recommendation; one- to two-page statement of professional plans and goals; personal interview. Additional exam requirements/recommendations for international students: Required—TOEFL (minimum score 580 paper-based, 92 iBT) or IELTS (minimum score 6.5).

The University of the Arts, College of Art, Media and Design, Program in Studio Art, Philadelphia, PA 19102-4944. Offers MFA. *Degree requirements:* For master's, thesis, summer residency. *Entrance requirements:* For master's, official transcripts from each undergraduate or graduate school attended, three letters of recommendation, one- to two-page statement of professional plans and goals, personal interview, portfolio. Additional exam requirements/recommendations for international students: Required—TOEFL (minimum score 580 paper-based, 92 iBT) or IELTS (minimum score 6.5).

The University of Tulsa, Graduate School, Kendall College of Arts and Sciences, School of Art, Design, and Art History, Tulsa, OK 74104-3189. Offers MA, MFA, MTA. *Program availability:* Part-time. *Faculty:* 7 full-time (4 women), 6 part-time/adjunct (3 women). *Students:* 6 full-time (5 women), 1 part-time (0 women); includes 1 minority (Asian, non-Hispanic/Latino). Average age 35. 15 applicants, 13% accepted, 2 enrolled. In 2017, 3 master's awarded. *Degree requirements:* For master's, comprehensive exam (for some programs), thesis (for some programs). *Entrance requirements:* For master's, portfolio. Additional exam requirements/recommendations for international students: Required—TOEFL (minimum score 577 paper-based; 91 iBT), IELTS (minimum score 6.5). *Application deadline:* For fall admission, 2/1 for domestic and international students. Application fee: $55. Electronic applications accepted. *Expenses: Tuition:* Full-time $22,230. *Required fees:* $2000. Tuition and fees vary according to course load and program. *Financial support:* In 2017–18, 6 students received support, including 5 fellowships with full tuition reimbursements available (averaging $5,200 per year), 5 teaching assistantships with full tuition reimbursements available (averaging $13,410 per year); career-related internships or fieldwork, Federal Work-Study, scholarships/grants, traineeships, health care benefits, tuition waivers (full and partial), and unspecified assistantships also available. Support available to part-time students. Financial award application deadline: 2/1; financial award applicants required to submit FAFSA. *Faculty research:* Drawing, painting, printmaking, graphic design, photography. *Unit head:* Prof. Teresa Valero, Director, 918-631-3513, Fax: 918-631-3423, E-mail: maria-valero@utulsa.edu. *Application contact:* Prof. Michelle Martin, Program Advisor, 918-631-2736, Fax: 918-631-3423, E-mail: michelle-martin@utulsa.edu.
Website: http://artsandsciences.utulsa.edu/academics/departments-schools/art/

The University of Tulsa, Graduate School, Kendall College of Arts and Sciences, School of Education, Tulsa, OK 74104-3189. Offers mathematics and science education (MSMSE); teaching arts (MTA), including art, biology, English, history, mathematics; urban education (MA). *Accreditation:* TEAC. *Program availability:* Part-time. *Faculty:* 9 full-time (5 women), 2 part-time/adjunct (both women). *Students:* 8 full-time (4 women), 6 part-time (5 women); includes 4 minority (1 Black or African American, non-Hispanic/Latino; 1 American Indian or Alaska Native, non-Hispanic/Latino; 1 Asian, non-Hispanic/Latino; 1 Two or more races, non-Hispanic/Latino). Average age 31. 22 applicants, 9% accepted. In 2017, 10 master's awarded. *Degree requirements:* For master's, thesis optional. *Entrance requirements:* For master's, GRE General Test. Additional exam requirements/recommendations for international students: Required—TOEFL (minimum score 577 paper-based; 91 iBT), IELTS (minimum score 6.5). *Application deadline:* For fall admission, 2/1 priority date for domestic students. Applications are processed on a rolling basis. Application fee: $55. Electronic applications accepted. *Expenses: Tuition:* Full-time $22,230. *Required fees:* $2000. Tuition and fees vary according to course load and program. *Financial support:* In 2017–18, 3 students received support, including 3 teaching assistantships with full tuition reimbursements available (averaging $13,410 per year); fellowships with tuition reimbursements available, research assistantships with tuition reimbursements available, career-related internships or fieldwork, Federal Work-Study, scholarships/grants, health care benefits, tuition waivers (full and partial), and unspecified assistantships also available. Support available to part-time students. Financial award application deadline: 2/1; financial award applicants required to submit FAFSA. *Faculty research:* Elementary/secondary certification, math/science education, teaching arts. *Unit head:* Dr. Elizabeth Smith, Chair, 918-631-2238, Fax: 918-631-3721, E-mail: elizabeth-smith-43@utulsa.edu. *Application contact:* Dr. David Brown, Advisor, 918-631-2719, Fax: 918-631-2133, E-mail: david-brown@utulsa.edu.
Website: http://artsandsciences.utulsa.edu/academics/departments-schools/urban-education/

University of Utah, Graduate School, College of Fine Arts, Department of Art and Art History, Salt Lake City, UT 84112-0380. Offers art history (MA); ceramics (MFA); community-based art education (MFA); drawing (MFA); graphic design (MFA); painting (MFA); photography/digital imaging (MFA); printmaking (MFA); sculpture/intermedia (MFA). *Faculty:* 19 full-time (9 women), 23 part-time/adjunct (11 women). *Students:* 6 full-time (3 women); includes 1 minority (Asian, non-Hispanic/Latino). Average age 24. 48 applicants, 31% accepted, 3 enrolled. In 2017, 6 master's awarded. *Degree requirements:* For master's, variable foreign language requirement, comprehensive exam (for some programs), thesis or alternative, exhibit and final project paper (for MFA). *Entrance requirements:* For master's, CD portfolio (MFA), writing sample (MA), curriculum vitae, letters of recommendation, letter of intent. Additional exam requirements/recommendations for international students: Required—TOEFL (minimum score 575 paper-based; 75 iBT). *Application deadline:* For fall admission, 1/15 priority date for domestic and international students. Application fee: $55 ($65 for international students). Electronic applications accepted. *Expenses:* Contact institution. *Financial support:* In 2017–18, 6 students received support, including 2 fellowships, 6 research assistantships with partial tuition reimbursements available, 34 teaching assistantships

with partial tuition reimbursements available; Federal Work-Study, institutionally sponsored loans, scholarships/grants, tuition waivers (partial), unspecified assistantships, and stipends also available. Financial award application deadline: 1/15; financial award applicants required to submit FAFSA. *Faculty research:* Studio art, European art history, Asian art history, Latin American art history, twentieth-century/contemporary art history. *Total annual research expenditures:* $54,906. *Unit head:* Prof. Brian Snapp, Chair, 801-581-8677, Fax: 801-585-6171, E-mail: b.snapp@utah.edu. *Application contact:* Prof. Kim Martinez, Director of Graduate Studies, 801-581-8677, Fax: 801-585-6171, E-mail: kim.martinez@art.utah.edu.
Website: http://www.art.utah.edu/

University of Victoria, Faculty of Graduate Studies, Faculty of Fine Arts, Department of Visual Arts, Victoria, BC V8W 2Y2, Canada. Offers digital multimedia (MFA); drawing (MFA); painting (MFA); photography (MFA); sculpture (MFA); video (MFA). *Degree requirements:* For master's, exhibit, oral exam. *Entrance requirements:* For master's, portfolio, BFA. Additional exam requirements/recommendations for international students: Required—TOEFL (minimum score 575 paper-based), IELTS (minimum score 7). Electronic applications accepted.

University of Washington, Graduate School, College of Arts and Sciences, School of Art, Division of Art, Seattle, WA 98195. Offers painting and drawing (MFA); photography (MFA). *Degree requirements:* For master's, thesis, exhibit. *Entrance requirements:* For master's, BFA or equivalent academic work in art, 20 slide portfolio. Additional exam requirements/recommendations for international students: Required—TOEFL. Electronic applications accepted.

University of Waterloo, Graduate Studies, Faculty of Arts, Department of Fine Arts, Waterloo, ON N2L 3G1, Canada. Offers studio art (MFA). *Degree requirements:* For master's, thesis exhibit. *Entrance requirements:* For master's, honors degree, minimum A- average, sample of work. Additional exam requirements/recommendations for international students: Required—TOEFL, IELTS, PTE. Electronic applications accepted. *Faculty research:* Ceramic sculpture, computer imaging, painting, drawing, contemporary art theory.

University of Windsor, Faculty of Graduate Studies, Faculty of Arts and Social Sciences, School of Visual Arts, Windsor, ON N9B 3P4, Canada. Offers MFA. *Degree requirements:* For master's, thesis. *Entrance requirements:* For master's, minimum B average, portfolio. Additional exam requirements/recommendations for international students: Required—TOEFL (minimum score 560 paper-based). Electronic applications accepted.

University of Wisconsin–Madison, Graduate School, School of Education, Department of Art, Madison, WI 53706-1380. Offers MFA. *Accreditation:* NASAD. Electronic applications accepted.

University of Wisconsin–River Falls, Outreach and Graduate Studies, College of Arts and Science, Program in Fine Arts, River Falls, WI 54022. Offers MSE.

University of Wisconsin–Stout, Graduate School, College of Arts, Humanities and Social Sciences, Menomonie, WI 54751. Offers design (MFA); technical and professional communication (MS). *Accreditation:* NASAD.

University of Wisconsin–Superior, Graduate Division, Department of Visual Arts, Superior, WI 54880-4500. Offers art education (MA); art history (MA); art therapy (MA); studio arts (MA). *Program availability:* Part-time. *Degree requirements:* For master's, comprehensive exam, exhibit. *Entrance requirements:* For master's, minimum GPA of 2.75, portfolio. Electronic applications accepted.

Utah State University, School of Graduate Studies, Caine College of the Arts, Department of Art and Design, Logan, UT 84322. Offers MFA. *Accreditation:* NASAD. *Degree requirements:* For master's, thesis, exhibit. *Entrance requirements:* For master's, GRE General Test or MAT, minimum GPA of 3.0, slide portfolio of art. Additional exam requirements/recommendations for international students: Required—TOEFL. *Faculty research:* Painting, drawing, sculpture, ceramics, photography.

Vermont College of Fine Arts, MFA in Visual Art Program, Montpelier, VT 05602. Offers MFA. *Accreditation:* NASAD. *Faculty:* 12 part-time/adjunct (6 women). *Students:* 38 full-time (27 women); includes 4 minority (3 Hispanic/Latino; 1 Two or more races, non-Hispanic/Latino), 3 international. Average age 42. 45 applicants, 58% accepted, 16 enrolled. In 2017, 19 master's awarded. *Entrance requirements:* For master's, BFA, BA, or BS from accredited college or university, or Diploma from recognized professional art school; substantial experience in making art; thirty semester hours in undergraduate study (preferred). *Application deadline:* For fall admission, 2/15 priority date for domestic students, 2/15 for international students; for spring admission, 9/15 priority date for domestic students, 9/15 for international students. Applications are processed on a rolling basis. Application fee: $75. Electronic applications accepted. *Expenses:* Contact institution. *Financial support:* In 2017–18, 33 students received support. Scholarships/grants available. Financial award applicants required to submit FAFSA. *Unit head:* Danielle Dahline, Program Director, 802-828-8703, E-mail: danielle.dahline@vcfa.edu. *Application contact:* Thatiana Oliveria, Assistant Director of Admissions, 802-828-8636, E-mail: thatiana.oliveria@vcfa.edu.
Website: http://www.vcfa.edu/visual-art

Virginia Commonwealth University, Graduate School, College of Humanities and Sciences, Richard T. Robertson School of Media and Culture, Program in Media, Art, and Text, Richmond, VA 23284-9005. Offers PhD. *Entrance requirements:* For doctorate, GRE. Additional exam requirements/recommendations for international students: Required—TOEFL (minimum score 600 paper-based; 100 iBT); Recommended—IELTS (minimum score 6.5). Electronic applications accepted.

Virginia Commonwealth University, Graduate School, School of the Arts, Richmond, VA 23284-9005. Offers art education (MAE, PhD); art history (MA, PhD), including curatorial (PhD), historical studies, museum studies (MA); ceramics (MFA); design (MFA), including interior environments, visual communications; fibers (MFA); furniture design (MFA); glassworking (MFA); jewelry/metalworking (MFA); kinetic imaging (MFA); music (MM), including music education; painting (MFA); photography and film (MFA); printmaking (MFA); sculpture (MFA); theatre (MFA), including costume design, pedagogy/literature, pedagogy/performance, scene design/technical theatre. *Program availability:* Part-time. *Entrance requirements:* For doctorate, GRE General Test, writing sample. Additional exam requirements/recommendations for international students: Required—TOEFL (minimum score 600 paper-based; 100 iBT). Electronic applications accepted.

Warren Wilson College, Master of Arts Program in Critical and Historical Craft Studies, Asheville, NC 28815-9000. Offers MA. *Entrance requirements:* For master's, written response to a craft piece, personal essay, letters of reference, official transcripts for previous undergraduate/graduate degrees. Electronic applications accepted.

Washington State University, College of Arts and Sciences, Department of Fine Arts, Pullman, WA 99164. Offers MFA. Programs offered at the Pullman campus. *Degree requirements:* For master's, comprehensive exam (for some programs), thesis, exhibit, oral exam. *Entrance requirements:* For master's, statement of intent, portfolio of no more than 15 images on CD/DVD. Additional exam requirements/recommendations for international students: Required—TOEFL (minimum score 550 paper-based), IELTS. Electronic applications accepted. *Faculty research:* Polynesian art, museum representation, number theory.

Washington University in St. Louis, Sam Fox School of Design and Visual Arts, Graduate School of Art, St. Louis, MO 63130-4899. Offers visual art (MFA). *Accreditation:* NASAD. *Degree requirements:* For master's, thesis, exhibition. *Entrance requirements:* For master's, portfolio, resume, transcripts, 3 letters of recommendation. Additional exam requirements/recommendations for international students: Required—TOEFL (minimum score 577 paper-based; 90 iBT), IELTS (minimum score 7.5). Electronic applications accepted. *Expenses:* Contact institution. *Faculty research:* New media, design, fine arts.

Wayne State University, College of Fine, Performing and Communication Arts, James Pearson Duffy Department of Art and Art History, Detroit, MI 48202. Offers art (MA, MFA), including ceramics, drawing, fashion design and merchandising (MA), fibers, graphic design, industrial design (MA), interior design (MA), metalsmithing, painting, photography, printmaking, sculpture; art history (MA). *Students:* 13 full-time (8 women), 12 part-time (9 women); includes 5 minority (3 Black or African American, non-Hispanic/Latino; 1 Asian, non-Hispanic/Latino; 1 Hispanic/Latino), 2 international. Average age 34. 46 applicants, 24% accepted, 6 enrolled. In 2017, 5 master's awarded. *Degree requirements:* For master's, thesis (for some programs), essay or thesis. *Entrance requirements:* For master's, BFA or another degree and equivalent course work, portfolio, personal interview, reference letters, statement of intent (except for art history program). Additional exam requirements/recommendations for international students: Required—TOEFL (minimum score 550 paper-based; 79 iBT), TWE (minimum score 5.5), Michigan English Language Assessment Battery (minimum score 85); Recommended—IELTS (minimum score 6.5). *Application deadline:* For fall admission, 2/1 for domestic and international students; for winter admission, 10/1 for domestic and international students. Application fee: $50. Electronic applications accepted. *Expenses:* Contact institution. *Financial support:* In 2017–18, 18 students received support, including 1 research assistantship (averaging $22,241 per year), 6 teaching assistantships with tuition reimbursements available (averaging $18,534 per year); fellowships with tuition reimbursements available, scholarships/grants, and unspecified assistantships also available. Support available to part-time students. Financial award applicants required to submit FAFSA. *Unit head:* Dr. John Richardson, Chair, 313-577-2980, Fax: 313-577-3491, E-mail: af5343@wayne.edu. *Application contact:* 313-577-2980, E-mail: art@wayne.edu.
Website: http://art.wayne.edu/

Webster University, Leigh Gerdine College of Fine Arts, Department of Art, Design, and Art History, St. Louis, MO 63119-3194. Offers art history and criticism (MA). *Program availability:* Part-time. *Degree requirements:* For master's, thesis. *Entrance requirements:* For master's, BA or BFA in related field, interview, portfolio. Additional exam requirements/recommendations for international students: Required—TOEFL.

Western Carolina University, Graduate School, College of Fine and Performing Arts, Cullowhee, NC 28723. Offers MFA. *Accreditation:* NASAD. *Program availability:* Part-time. *Degree requirements:* For master's, comprehensive exam, thesis optional. *Entrance requirements:* For master's, GRE, appropriate undergraduate degree, portfolio, letters of recommendation, letter of intent, live audition and/or interview. Additional exam requirements/recommendations for international students: Required—TOEFL (minimum score 550 paper-based; 79 iBT). *Expenses:* Tuition, state resident: full-time $4436. Tuition, nonresident: full-time $14,842. *Required fees:* $2926. *Faculty research:* Vernacular cultural studies and oral history, sound mixing for television, music technology.

Western Connecticut State University, Division of Graduate Studies, School of Visual and Performing Arts, Department of Art, Danbury, CT 06810-6885. Offers illustration (MFA); painting (MFA). *Program availability:* Part-time. *Degree requirements:* For master's, individual exhibition of artwork, review of student's progress prior to admission to final semester, completion of program in 6 years. *Entrance requirements:* For master's, portfolio review, minimum GPA of 2.5. Additional exam requirements/recommendations for international students: Recommended—TOEFL (minimum score 550 paper-based; 79 iBT), IELTS (minimum score 6). *Expenses:* Contact institution. *Faculty research:* Proficiency in both traditional and digital processes.

West Texas A&M University, College of Fine Arts and Humanities, Department of Art, Theatre and Dance, Canyon, TX 79015. Offers studio art (MFA). *Program availability:* Part-time. *Degree requirements:* For master's, comprehensive exam, thesis optional. *Entrance requirements:* For master's, GRE General Test. Additional exam requirements/recommendations for international students: Required—TOEFL (minimum score 550 paper-based). Electronic applications accepted. *Faculty research:* Ceramics, graphic design, woodblock prints, art education, aesthetics.

West Virginia University, College of Creative Arts, Morgantown, WV 26506. Offers acting (MFA); art education (MA); art history (MA); ceramics (MFA); collaborative piano (MM, DMA); composition (MM, DMA); conducting (MM, DMA); costume design and technology (MFA); graphic design (MFA); jazz pedagogy (MM); lighting design and technology (MFA); music (PhD); music education (MM, PhD); music industry (MA); music theory (MM); musicology (MA); painting and printmaking (MFA); performance (MM, DMA); photography (MFA); piano pedagogy (MM); scenic design and technology (MFA); sculpture (MFA); studio art (MA); technical direction (MFA); vocal pedagogy and performance (DMA). *Program availability:* Part-time. *Students:* 114 full-time (64 women), 39 part-time (21 women); includes 19 minority (11 Black or African American, non-Hispanic/Latino; 1 Asian, non-Hispanic/Latino; 6 Hispanic/Latino; 1 Two or more races, non-Hispanic/Latino), 33 international. *Degree requirements:* For master's, thesis, recitals; for doctorate, comprehensive exam, thesis/dissertation, recitals (DMA). *Entrance requirements:* For doctorate, minimum GPA of 3.0, audition. Additional exam requirements/recommendations for international students: Required—TOEFL. *Application deadline:* For fall admission, 3/1 priority date for domestic students, 2/15 for international students; for spring admission, 11/1 for domestic students, 9/15 for international students. Applications are processed on a rolling basis. Application fee: $60. Electronic applications accepted. *Expenses:* Tuition, state resident: full-time $9450. Tuition, nonresident: full-time $24,390. *Financial support:* Research assistantships, teaching assistantships, career-related internships or fieldwork, Federal Work-Study, institutionally sponsored loans, scholarships/grants, health care benefits, tuition waivers (partial), and administrative assistantships available. Financial award applicants required to submit FAFSA. *Faculty research:* Professional directing, consulting, acting design, music education, jazz history. *Unit head:* Dr. Paul Kreider, Dean, 304-293-4841 Ext. 3109, Fax: 304-293-6896, E-mail: paul.kreider@mail.wvu.edu. *Application contact:* Records Officer, 304-293-4841, Fax: 304-293-2533, E-mail: rachel.hanks@mail.wvu.edu.
Website: http://www.ccarts.wvu.edu

Wichita State University, Graduate School, College of Fine Arts, School of Art, Design and Creative Industries, Wichita, KS 67260. Offers studio arts (MFA), including ceramics, painting, photo media, printmaking, sculpture. *Accreditation:* NASAD. *Unit head:* Prof. Jeff Pulaski, Director, 316-978-3555, Fax: 316-978-5418, E-mail: jeff.pulaski1@wichita.edu. *Application contact:* Jordan Oleson, Admissions Coordinator, 316-978-3095, Fax: 316-978-3253, E-mail: jordan.oleson@wichita.edu.
Website: http://www.wichita.edu/artdesign

Wilson College, Graduate Programs, Chambersburg, PA 17201-1285. Offers accounting (M Acc); choreography and visual art (MFA); education (M Ed); educational technology (MET); healthcare administration (MHA); humanities (MA), including art and culture, critical/cultural theory, English language and literature, women's studies; management (MSM); nursing (MSN), including nursing education, nursing leadership and management; special education (MSE). *Program availability:* Evening/weekend. *Degree requirements:* For master's, project. *Entrance requirements:* For master's, PRAXIS, minimum undergraduate cumulative GPA of 3.0, 2 letters of recommendation, current certification for eligibility to teach in grades K-12, resume, personal interview. Electronic applications accepted.

Winthrop University, College of Visual and Performing Arts, Department of Art, Rock Hill, SC 29733. Offers art (MFA); art administration (MA); art education (MA). *Accreditation:* NASAD. *Program availability:* Part-time. *Students:* 6 full-time (5 women), 27 part-time (21 women); includes 10 minority (7 Black or African American, non-Hispanic/Latino; 2 Asian, non-Hispanic/Latino; 1 Hispanic/Latino), 1 international. Average age 38. In 2017, 12 master's awarded. *Degree requirements:* For master's, comprehensive exam (for some programs), thesis (for some programs), documented exhibit, oral exam. *Entrance requirements:* For master's, GRE General Test or MAT, PRAXIS (for MA), minimum GPA of 3.0, resume, slide portfolio, teaching certificate (MA). Additional exam requirements/recommendations for international students: Required—TOEFL (minimum score 550 paper-based; 79 iBT), IELTS (minimum score 6). *Application deadline:* For fall admission,

3/1 priority date for domestic students; for spring admission, 9/1 for domestic students. Applications are processed on a rolling basis. Application fee: $50. Electronic applications accepted. *Financial support:* Research assistantships with full tuition reimbursements, Federal Work-Study, scholarships/grants, and unspecified assistantships available. Support available to part-time students. Financial award application deadline: 2/1; financial award applicants required to submit FAFSA. *Unit head:* Anne Fiala, Interim Chair, 803-323-2653, E-mail: fialaa@winthrop.edu. *Application contact:* 800-411-7041, Fax: 803-323-2292, E-mail: graduatestu@winthrop.edu.
Website: http://www.winthrop.edu/cvpa/finearts

Yale University, School of Art, New Haven, CT 06520-8339. Offers graphic design (MFA); painting/printmaking (MFA); photography (MFA); sculpture (MFA). *Degree requirements:* For master's, thesis (for some programs). *Entrance requirements:* Additional exam requirements/recommendations for international students: Required—TOEFL (minimum score 550 paper-based; 100 iBT). Electronic applications accepted. *Expenses:* Contact institution.

York University, Faculty of Graduate Studies, Faculty of Fine Arts, Program in Visual Arts, Toronto, ON M3J 1P3, Canada. Offers MFA, PhD. *Degree requirements:* For master's, thesis. *Entrance requirements:* For master's, portfolio. Electronic applications accepted.

Art History

Academy of Art University, Graduate Programs, School of Art History, San Francisco, CA 94105-3410. Offers MA. *Program availability:* Part-time, 100% online. *Faculty:* 1 (woman) full-time, 2 part-time/adjunct (1 woman). *Students:* 7 full-time (6 women), 41 part-time (37 women); includes 7 minority (1 Black or African American, non-Hispanic/Latino; 6 Hispanic/Latino), 3 international. Average age 37. 23 applicants, 100% accepted, 8 enrolled. In 2017, 9 master's awarded. *Degree requirements:* For master's, final review. *Entrance requirements:* For master's, statement of intent; resume; portfolio/reel; official college transcripts. *Application deadline:* Applications are processed on a rolling basis. Application fee: $50. Electronic applications accepted. *Expenses:* Tuition: Part-time $982 per unit. *Financial support:* Career-related internships or fieldwork, Federal Work-Study, and scholarships/grants available. Financial award application deadline: 8/10; financial award applicants required to submit FAFSA. *Unit head:* 800-544-ARTS, E-mail: info@academyart.edu. *Application contact:* 800-544-ARTS, E-mail: info@academyart.edu.
Website: http://www.academyart.edu/art-history/

American University, College of Arts and Sciences, Department of Art, Washington, DC 20016-8004. Offers art history (MA); studio art (MFA). *Program availability:* Part-time. *Faculty:* 19 full-time (12 women). *Students:* 27 full-time (22 women), 9 part-time (all women); includes 5 minority (2 Black or African American, non-Hispanic/Latino; 2 Hispanic/Latino; 1 Two or more races, non-Hispanic/Latino), 2 international. Average age 29. 59 applicants, 80% accepted, 20 enrolled. In 2017, 18 master's awarded. *Degree requirements:* For master's, comprehensive exam. *Entrance requirements:* For master's, GRE, portfolio or writing sample, statement of purpose, transcripts, 2 letters of recommendation. Additional exam requirements/recommendations for international students: Required—TOEFL (minimum score 600 paper-based; 100 iBT). *Application deadline:* For fall admission, 2/1 priority date for domestic students; for spring admission, 11/1 priority date for domestic students. Application fee: $55. *Expenses:* Contact institution. *Financial support:* Unspecified assistantships available. Financial award application deadline: 1/15; financial award applicants required to submit FAFSA. *Unit head:* Zoe Charlton, Department Chair, 202-885-3851, Fax: 202-885-1132, E-mail: charlton@american.edu. *Application contact:* Jonathan Harper, Assistant Director, Graduate Recruitment, 202-855-3622, E-mail: jharper@american.edu.
Website: http://www.american.edu/cas/art/

American University of Beirut, Graduate Programs, Faculty of Arts and Sciences, 1107 2020, Lebanon. Offers anthropology (MA); Arab and Middle Eastern history (PhD); Arabic language and literature (MA, PhD); archaeology (MA); art history and curating (MA); biology (MS); cell and molecular biology (PhD); chemistry (MS); clinical psychology (MA); computational sciences (MS); computer science (MS); economics (MA); education (MA), including administration and policy studies, elementary education, mathematics education, psychology school guidance, psychology test and measurements, science education, teaching English as a foreign language; English language (MA); English literature (MA); environmental policy planning (MS); financial economics (MAFE); general psychology (MA); geology (MS); history (MA); Islamic studies (MA); mathematics (MS); media studies (MA); Middle East studies (MA); philosophy (MA); physics (MS); political studies (MA); public administration (MA); public policy and international affairs (MA); sociology (MA); theoretical physics (PhD). *Program availability:* Part-time. *Faculty:* 108 full-time (36 women), 5 part-time/adjunct (4 women). *Students:* 251 full-time (180 women), 233 part-time (172 women). Average age 26. 425 applicants, 65% accepted, 121 enrolled. In 2017, 47 master's, 2 doctorates awarded. *Degree requirements:* For master's, one foreign language, comprehensive exam, thesis (for some programs), project; for doctorate, one foreign language, comprehensive exam, thesis/dissertation. *Entrance requirements:* For master's, GRE General Test (for some programs); for doctorate, GRE General Test (GRE Subject Test for theoretical physics). Additional exam requirements/recommendations for international students: Required—TOEFL (minimum score 583 paper-based; 97 iBT), IELTS (minimum score 7). *Application deadline:* For fall admission, 2/8 for domestic students; for spring admission, 11/3 for domestic students. Application fee: $50. Electronic applications accepted. *Expenses:* Contact institution. *Financial support:* In 2017–18, 29 fellowships, 40 research assistantships were awarded; teaching assistantships, scholarships/grants, tuition waivers (full and partial), and unspecified assistantships also available. Financial award application deadline: 4/4. *Unit head:* Dr. Nadia Maria El Cheikh, Dean, Faculty of Arts and Sciences, 961-1-374374 Ext. 3800, Fax: 961-1-744461, E-mail: nmcheikh@aub.edu.lb. *Application contact:* Rima Rassi, Graduate Studies Officer, 961-1-350000 Ext. 3833, Fax: 961-1-744461, E-mail: rr46@aub.edu.lb.
Website: http://www.aub.edu.lb/fas/pages/default.aspx

Arizona State University at the Tempe campus, Herberger Institute for Design and the Arts, School of Art, Tempe, AZ 85287-1505. Offers art education (MA); art history (MA); ceramics (MFA); design, environment and the arts (PhD), including history, theory and criticism; drawing (MFA); fibers (MFA); intermedia (MFA); metals (MFA); museum studies (MFA); painting (MFA); printmaking (MFA); sculpture (MFA); wood (MFA); MFA/MA. Terminal master's awarded for partial completion of doctoral program. *Degree requirements:* For master's, thesis/exhibition (MFA, MA in art education); interactive

Program of Study (iPOS) submitted before completing 50 percent of required credit hours; for doctorate, comprehensive exam, thesis/dissertation, interactive Program of Study (iPOS) submitted before completing 50 percent of required credit hours. *Entrance requirements:* For master's, GRE or MAT, minimum GPA of 3.0 or equivalent in last 2 years of work leading to bachelor's degree; for doctorate, GRE, master's degree in architecture, graphic design, industrial design, interior design, landscape architecture, or art history or equivalent standing; statement of purpose; 3 letters of recommendation; indication of potential faculty mentor; sample of written work. Additional exam requirements/recommendations for international students: Required—TOEFL, IELTS, or PTE. Electronic applications accepted.

Bard Graduate Center, Graduate Studies, New York, NY 10024-3602. Offers M Phil, MA, PhD. *Program availability:* Part-time. *Degree requirements:* For master's, one foreign language, thesis, internship; for doctorate, 2 foreign languages, thesis/dissertation, 3 field exams. *Entrance requirements:* For master's, GRE General Test, writing sample, 3 letters of recommendation; for doctorate, GRE General Test, MA, master's thesis or equivalent, 3 letters of recommendation. Additional exam requirements/recommendations for international students: Required—TOEFL. *Faculty research:* New York and American material culture; modern design history; history and theory of museums; early Modern Europe; global Middle Ages; archaeology, anthropology, and material culture; cultures of conservation.
See Display on the next page and Close-Up on page 183.

Binghamton University, State University of New York, Graduate School, Harpur College of Arts and Sciences, Department of Art History, Binghamton, NY 13902-6000. Offers MA, PhD. *Program availability:* Part-time. *Faculty:* 8 full-time (4 women). *Students:* 8 full-time (5 women), 24 part-time (19 women); includes 4 minority (3 Asian, non-Hispanic/Latino; 1 Hispanic/Latino), 13 international. Average age 34. 17 applicants, 71% accepted, 2 enrolled. In 2017, 1 master's, 2 doctorates awarded. Terminal master's awarded for partial completion of doctoral program. *Degree requirements:* For master's, one foreign language, comprehensive exam, thesis; for doctorate, 2 foreign languages, comprehensive exam, thesis/dissertation. *Entrance requirements:* For master's and doctorate, GRE General Test, writing sample. Additional exam requirements/recommendations for international students: Required—TOEFL (minimum score 80 iBT). *Application deadline:* Applications are processed on a rolling basis. Application fee: $75. Electronic applications accepted. *Financial support:* In 2017–18, 12 students received support, including 9 teaching assistantships with full tuition reimbursements available (averaging $15,000 per year); career-related internships or fieldwork, Federal Work-Study, institutionally sponsored loans, scholarships/grants, health care benefits, and unspecified assistantships also available. Financial award application deadline: 2/15; financial award applicants required to submit FAFSA. *Faculty research:* History of art and architecture. *Unit head:* Dr. Tom McDonough, Chair, 607-777-2847, E-mail: tmcdonou@binghamton.edu. *Application contact:* Ben Balkaya, Assistant Dean and Director, 607-777-2151, Fax: 607-777-2501, E-mail: balkaya@binghamton.edu.
Website: http://www.binghamton.edu/art-history/

Boston University, Graduate School of Arts and Sciences, Department of History of Art and Architecture, Boston, MA 02215. Offers history of art and architecture (MA, PhD); museum studies (Certificate). *Accreditation:* NASAD. *Students:* 52 full-time (45 women), 3 part-time (1 woman); includes 5 minority (1 Black or African American, non-Hispanic/Latino; 2 Asian, non-Hispanic/Latino; 2 Hispanic/Latino), 8 international. Average age 27. 151 applicants, 32% accepted, 9 enrolled. In 2017, 7 master's, 6 doctorates awarded. Terminal master's awarded for partial completion of doctoral program. *Degree requirements:* For master's, one foreign language, comprehensive exam, thesis or alternative, scholarly paper; for doctorate, 2 foreign languages, comprehensive exam, thesis/dissertation. *Entrance requirements:* For master's and doctorate, GRE General Test, 3 letters of recommendation, transcripts, personal statement, curriculum vitae, writing sample, foreign language proficiency; for Certificate, GRE General Test. Additional exam requirements/recommendations for international students: Required—TOEFL (minimum score 550 paper-based; 84 iBT). *Application deadline:* For fall admission, 1/5 for domestic and international students; for spring admission, 10/15 for domestic and international students. Application fee: $95. Electronic applications accepted. *Financial support:* In 2017–18, 44 students received support, including 16 fellowships with full tuition reimbursements available (averaging $22,000 per year), 11 teaching assistantships with full tuition reimbursements available (averaging $22,000 per year); career-related internships or fieldwork, Federal Work-Study, scholarships/grants, health care benefits, and unspecified assistantships also available. Financial award application deadline: 1/5. *Unit head:* Alice Tseng, Chair, 617-353-1458, Fax: 617-353-3243, E-mail: aytseng@bu.edu. *Application contact:* Cheryl Crombie, Administrative Assistant, 617-353-2522, Fax: 617-353-3243, E-mail: ccrombie@bu.edu.
Website: http://www.bu.edu/AH/

Bowling Green State University, Graduate College, College of Arts and Sciences, School of Art, Bowling Green, OH 43403. Offers 2-D studio art (MA, MFA); 3-D studio art

Art History

(MA, MFA); art education (MA); art history (MA); computer art (MA); design (MFA); digital arts (MFA); graphics (MFA). *Accreditation:* NASAD. *Program availability:* Part-time. *Degree requirements:* For master's, thesis or alternative, final exhibit (MFA). *Entrance requirements:* For master's, GRE General Test (for MA), slide portfolio (15-20 slides). Additional exam requirements/recommendations for international students: Required— TOEFL. Electronic applications accepted. *Faculty research:* Computer animation and virtual reality, Spanish still-life painting from 1600 to 1800, art and psychotherapy, Japanese wood-firing techniques in ceramics, non-toxic printmaking technologies.

Brooklyn College of the City University of New York, School of Visual, Media and Performing Arts, Department of Art, Brooklyn, NY 11210-2889. Offers art history (MA); digital art (MFA); drawing and painting (MFA); photography (MFA); printmaking (MFA); sculpture (MFA). *Program availability:* Part-time. *Degree requirements:* For master's, thesis. *Entrance requirements:* For master's, bachelor's degree in art, portfolio, 2 letters of recommendation. Additional exam requirements/recommendations for international students: Required—TOEFL (minimum score 500 paper-based; 61 iBT). Electronic applications accepted.

Brown University, Graduate School, Department of History of Art and Architecture, Providence, RI 02912. Offers PhD. *Degree requirements:* For doctorate, 2 foreign languages, thesis/dissertation, oral exam. *Entrance requirements:* For doctorate, GRE General Test, MA with distinction.

Brown University, Graduate School, Joukowsky Institute for Archaeology and the Ancient World, Providence, RI 02912. Offers PhD. *Degree requirements:* For doctorate, thesis/dissertation.

Bryn Mawr College, Graduate School of Arts and Sciences, Department of History of Art, Bryn Mawr, PA 19010-2899. Offers MA, PhD. *Program availability:* Part-time. *Faculty:* 7 full-time (4 women). *Students:* 21 full-time (17 women), 1 part-time (0 women); includes 2 minority (1 Hispanic/Latino; 1 Native Hawaiian or other Pacific Islander, non-Hispanic/Latino), 2 international. Average age 31. 33 applicants, 15% accepted, 3 enrolled. In 2017, 2 master's awarded. Terminal master's awarded for partial completion of doctoral program. *Degree requirements:* For master's, 2 foreign languages, thesis; for doctorate, 2 foreign languages, comprehensive exam, thesis/ dissertation. *Entrance requirements:* For master's and doctorate, GRE General Test, transcripts, three letters of recommendation, statement of interest, resume or curriculum vitae. Additional exam requirements/recommendations for international students: Required—TOEFL (minimum score 600 paper-based; 100 iBT), IELTS (minimum score 7). *Application deadline:* For fall admission, 12/15 for domestic and international students. Application fee: $50. Electronic applications accepted. *Financial support:* In 2017–18, 21 students received support, including 14 fellowships with tuition reimbursements available (averaging $16,893 per year), 3 teaching assistantships with tuition reimbursements available (averaging $15,833 per year); Federal Work-Study, scholarships/grants, unspecified assistantships, and tuition awards also available. Support available to part-time students. Financial award application deadline: 12/15. *Unit head:* Maria Dantis, Graduate Program Administrator, 610-526-5074, E-mail: gsas@brynmawr.edu.

California State University, Chico, Office of Graduate Studies, College of Humanities and Fine Arts, Department of Art and Art History, Program in Art History, Chico, CA 95929-0722. Offers MA. *Accreditation:* NASAD. *Degree requirements:* For master's, thesis, examination. *Entrance requirements:* For master's, 2 letters of recommendation; statement of purpose; two upper-division art history papers. Additional exam requirements/recommendations for international students: Required—TOEFL (minimum score 550 paper-based; 80 iBT), IELTS (minimum score 6.5), PTE (minimum score 59). Electronic applications accepted.

California State University, Fullerton, Graduate Studies, College of the Arts, Department of Visual Arts, Fullerton, CA 92831-3599. Offers art (MA, MFA), including art history (MA), ceramics (MFA), crafts, creative photography, exhibition design, glass, graphic design, illustration, sculpture. *Accreditation:* NASAD (one or more programs are accredited). *Program availability:* Part-time. *Faculty:* 17 full-time (7 women), 4 part-time/ adjunct (3 women). *Students:* 35 full-time (22 women), 24 part-time (14 women); includes 26 minority (3 Black or African American, non-Hispanic/Latino; 7 Asian, non-Hispanic/Latino; 14 Hispanic/Latino; 2 Two or more races, non-Hispanic/Latino), 6 international. Average age 33. 81 applicants, 31% accepted, 21 enrolled. In 2017, 17 master's awarded. *Entrance requirements:* For master's, minimum GPA of 2.5 in last 60 units of course work, portfolio. Application fee: $55. *Financial support:* Career-related internships or fieldwork, Federal Work-Study, institutionally sponsored loans, and scholarships/grants available. Support available to part-time students. Financial award application deadline: 3/1; financial award applicants required to submit FAFSA. *Unit head:* Dana Lamb, Chair, 657-278-2076.
Website: http://www.fullerton.edu/arts/art/

California State University, Los Angeles, Graduate Studies, College of Arts and Letters, Department of Art, Los Angeles, CA 90032-8530. Offers art (MA), including art education, art history, art therapy, ceramics, metals, and textiles, design (MA, MFA), painting, sculpture, and graphic arts, photography; fine arts (MFA), including crafts, design (MA, MFA), studio arts. *Accreditation:* NASAD (one or more programs are accredited). *Program availability:* Part-time, evening/weekend. *Degree requirements:* For master's, comprehensive exam, project or thesis. *Entrance requirements:* For master's, portfolio. Additional exam requirements/recommendations for international students: Required—TOEFL (minimum score 500 paper-based). Electronic applications accepted. *Faculty research:* The artist and the book, conceptual art, ceramic processes, computer graphics, architectural graphics.

California State University, Northridge, Graduate Studies, Mike Curb College of Arts, Media, and Communication, Department of Art, Northridge, CA 91330. Offers art education (MA); art history (MA); studio art (MA, MFA); visual communications (MA, MFA). *Accreditation:* NASAD. *Students:* 27 full-time (16 women), 9 part-time (6 women); includes 17 minority (1 Black or African American, non-Hispanic/Latino; 2 Asian, non-Hispanic/Latino; 11 Hispanic/Latino; 3 Two or more races, non-Hispanic/Latino). Average age 31. 58 applicants, 34% accepted, 20 enrolled. In 2017, 11 master's awarded. *Application deadline:* For fall admission, 11/30 for domestic students. Application fee: $55. *Financial support:* Application deadline: 3/1. *Unit head:* Prof. Edward Alfano, Chair, 818-677-2242, E-mail: art.dept@csun.edu.
Website: http://www.csun.edu/art/

Caribbean University, Graduate School, Bayamón, PR 00960-0493. Offers administration and supervision (MA Ed); criminal justice (MA); curriculum and instruction (MA Ed), including elementary education (MA Ed), English education (MA Ed), history education (MA Ed), mathematics education (MA Ed), primary education (MA Ed), science education (MA Ed), Spanish education (MA Ed); educational technology in instructional systems (MA Ed); gerontology (MSN); human resources (MBA); museology, archiving and art history (MA Ed); neonatal pediatrics (MSN); physical education (MA Ed); special education (MA Ed). *Entrance requirements:* For master's, interview, minimum GPA of 2.5.

Carleton University, Faculty of Graduate Studies, Faculty of Arts and Social Sciences, School for Studies in Art and Culture, Program in Art History: Art and its Institutions, Ottawa, ON K1S 5B6, Canada. Offers MA. *Degree requirements:* For master's, thesis. *Entrance requirements:* For master's, honors degree.

Case Western Reserve University, School of Graduate Studies, Department of Art History and Art, Program in Art History, Cleveland, OH 44106. Offers MA, PhD.

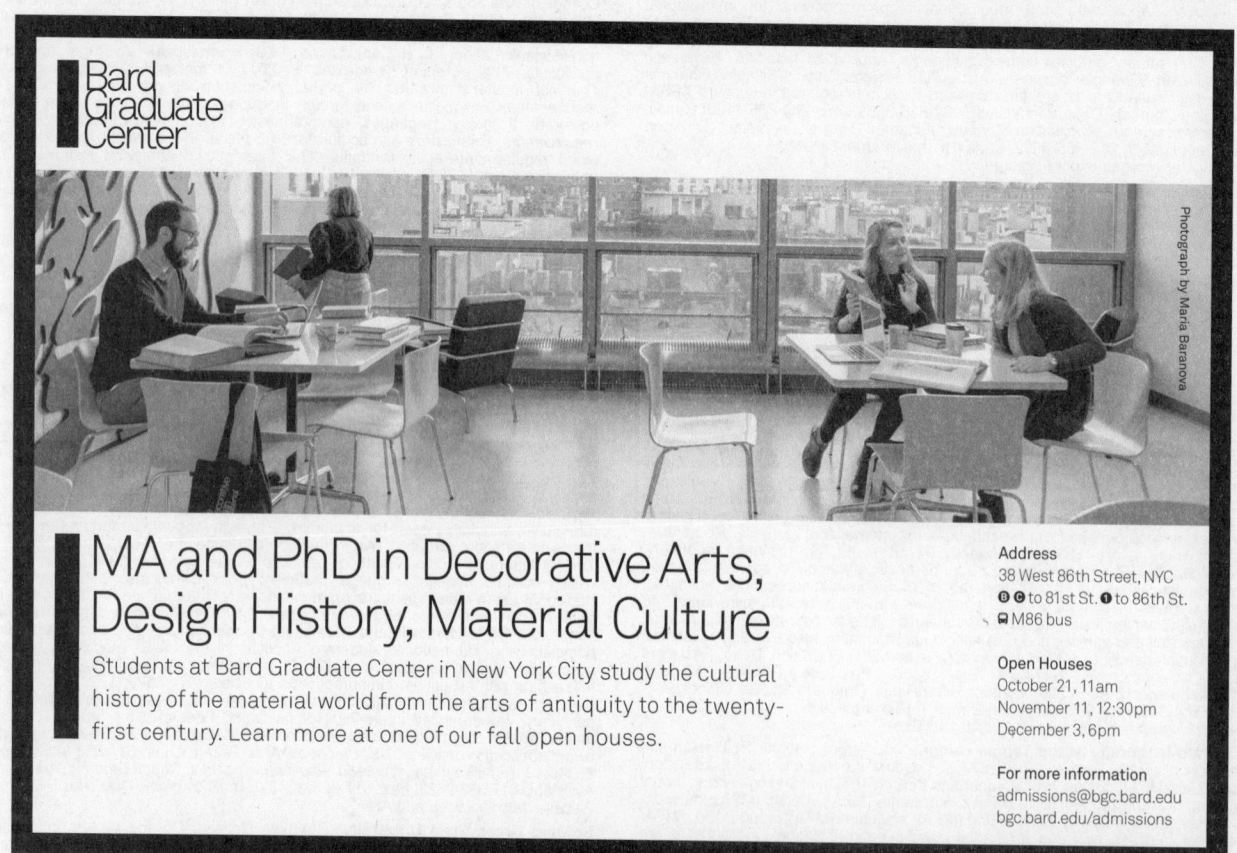

Programs offered jointly with The Cleveland Museum of Art. *Program availability:* Part-time. *Faculty:* 8 full-time (7 women), 2 part-time/adjunct (both women). *Students:* 14 full-time (10 women); includes 2 minority (both Two or more races, non-Hispanic/Latino), 2 international. Average age 28. 19 applicants, 47% accepted, 5 enrolled. In 2017, 3 master's awarded. *Degree requirements:* For master's, one foreign language, comprehensive exam; for doctorate, 2 foreign languages, comprehensive exam, thesis/dissertation. *Entrance requirements:* For master's, GRE General Test, 2 samples of written work; 3 letters of recommendation; for doctorate, GRE General Test, 2 samples of written work, MA thesis. Additional exam requirements/recommendations for international students: Required—TOEFL (minimum score 600 paper-based; 100 iBT). *Application deadline:* For fall admission, 1/1 priority date for domestic students. Applications are processed on a rolling basis. Application fee: $50. Electronic applications accepted. *Expenses: Tuition:* Full-time $43,854; part-time $1827 per credit hour. *Required fees:* $50; $50 per credit hour. Tuition and fees vary according to course load and program. *Financial support:* Fellowships, research assistantships, teaching assistantships, career-related internships or fieldwork, and tuition waivers available. Financial award application deadline: 1/1; financial award applicants required to submit FAFSA. *Faculty research:* Greek art and architecture, Northern Baroque art, Italian Baroque sculpture, abstract expressionism, Indian art, nineteenth-century French art, American and contemporary art. *Unit head:* Catherine Scallen, Associate Professor/Chair, 216-368-2383, Fax: 216-368-4681, E-mail: catherine.scallen@case.edu. *Application contact:* Deborah Tenenbaum, Department Assistant, 216-368-4118, Fax: 216-368-4681, E-mail: deborah.tenenbaum@case.edu.
Website: http://arthistory.case.edu/graduate/art-history/

Christie's Education, MA Program in Modern and Contemporary Art and the Market, New York, NY 10020. Offers MA. *Program availability:* Part-time. *Faculty:* 4 full-time (3 women). *Students:* 23 full-time (21 women), 1 (woman) part-time. In 2017, 25 master's awarded. *Degree requirements:* For master's, one foreign language, thesis, internship. *Entrance requirements:* For master's, writing sample, 3 letters of recommendation. Additional exam requirements/recommendations for international students: Required—TOEFL. *Application deadline:* For fall admission, 1/12 priority date for domestic and international students. Applications are processed on a rolling basis. Application fee: $95. *Expenses:* Contact institution. *Financial support:* In 2017–18, 3 students received support. Scholarships/grants and unspecified assistantships available. Financial award applicants required to submit FAFSA. *Unit head:* Dr. Julie Reiss, Program Director, 212-355-1501 Ext. 3307, Fax: 212-355-7370, E-mail: jreiss@christies.edu. *Application contact:* Hilary Smith, Recruitment and Admissions Officer, 212-355-1501 Ext. 3309, Fax: 212-355-7370, E-mail: hsmith@christies.edu.
Website: https://www.christies.edu/new-york/courses/masters-modern-contemporary-art-markets.aspx

City College of the City University of New York, Graduate School, Division of Humanities and the Arts, Department of Art, Programs in Art History and Museum Studies, New York, NY 10031-9198. Offers art history (MA); art museum education (MA); museum studies (MA). *Program availability:* Part-time. *Degree requirements:* For master's, one foreign language, thesis. *Entrance requirements:* For master's, minimum GPA of 3.0, portfolio, art history paper. Additional exam requirements/recommendations for international students: Required—TOEFL (minimum score 577 paper-based; 90 iBT). Electronic applications accepted. *Faculty research:* Egyptian, Greek, medieval, Romanesque, and Ottoman art.

Cleveland State University, College of Graduate Studies, College of Liberal Arts and Social Sciences, Department of History, Cleveland, OH 44115. Offers art history (MA); museum studies (MA). *Program availability:* Part-time, evening/weekend. *Faculty:* 13 full-time (4 women). *Students:* 12 full-time (8 women), 8 part-time (3 women). Average age 30. 21 applicants, 90% accepted, 6 enrolled. In 2017, 8 master's awarded. *Entrance requirements:* For master's, minimum GPA of 3.0, bachelor's degree in history (or related field for art history). Additional exam requirements/recommendations for international students: Required—TOEFL (minimum score 550 paper-based; 78 iBT). *Application deadline:* Applications are processed on a rolling basis. Application fee: $40. Electronic applications accepted. *Financial support:* In 2017–18, 7 students received support. Research assistantships, career-related internships or fieldwork, tuition waivers (full and partial), and unspecified assistantships available. Financial award application deadline: 4/15. *Faculty research:* Africa and African diaspora, European history, Middle Eastern history, Latin American/Caribbean history, American history, gender and sexuality. *Unit head:* Dr. Elizabeth A. Lehfeldt, Chairperson, 216-687-3920, Fax: 216-687-5592, E-mail: e.lehfeldt@csuohio.edu. *Application contact:* Dr. Karen Sotiropoulos, Graduate Director, 216-687-3940, E-mail: r.s.shelton@csuohio.edu.
Website: http://www.csuohio.edu/history/

Colorado State University, College of Liberal Arts, Department of Art and Art History, Fort Collins, CO 80523-1779. Offers studio art (MFA). *Faculty:* 15 full-time (8 women), 2 part-time/adjunct (1 woman). *Students:* 18 full-time (10 women), 2 part-time (both women); includes 6 minority (1 Black or African American, non-Hispanic/Latino; 1 American Indian or Alaska Native, non-Hispanic/Latino; 3 Hispanic/Latino; 1 Two or more races, non-Hispanic/Latino). Average age 32. 46 applicants, 17% accepted, 6 enrolled. In 2017, 2 master's awarded. *Degree requirements:* For master's, comprehensive exam (for some programs), thesis, exhibition. *Entrance requirements:* For master's, portfolio, three letters of recommendation, transcripts, statement of purpose, resume, artist statement; 20 images of work (including video, if applicable). Additional exam requirements/recommendations for international students: Required—TOEFL (minimum score 550 paper-based; 80 iBT). *Application deadline:* For fall admission, 2/1 priority date for domestic and international students. Applications are processed on a rolling basis. Application fee: $60 ($70 for international students). Electronic applications accepted. *Expenses:* Tuition, state resident: full-time $9917. Tuition, nonresident: full-time $24,312. *Required fees:* $2284. Tuition and fees vary according to course load and program. *Financial support:* In 2017–18, 8 teaching assistantships with full tuition reimbursements (averaging $12,474 per year) were awarded; fellowships with partial tuition reimbursements, scholarships/grants, and unspecified assistantships also available. *Faculty research:* African art history, bronze castings, etching/lithography, pre-Columbian art history, contemporary crafts. *Total annual research expenditures:* $15,357. *Unit head:* Suzanne Faris, Department Chair/Associate Professor, 970-491-6774, Fax: 970-491-0505, E-mail: suzanne.faris@colostate.edu. *Application contact:* Kathleen Chynoweth, Graduate Contact, 970-491-6775, E-mail: kathleen.chynoweth@colostate.edu.
Website: http://art.colostate.edu/

Columbia College Chicago, School of Graduate Studies, Art and Art History Department, Chicago, IL 60605-1996. Offers fine arts (MFA). *Program availability:* Part-time, evening/weekend. *Students:* 17 full-time (13 women), 3 part-time (2 women); includes 4 minority (1 Black or African American, non-Hispanic/Latino; 2 Hispanic/Latino; 1 Two or more races, non-Hispanic/Latino), 4 international. 29 applicants, 69% accepted, 8 enrolled. *Degree requirements:* For master's, thesis. *Entrance requirements:* For master's, self-assessment essay, work sample, interview, letters of recommendation, transcripts. Additional exam requirements/recommendations for international students: Required—TOEFL, IELTS. *Application deadline:* For fall admission, 1/15 priority date for domestic and international students. Applications are processed on a rolling basis. Application fee: $55 ($100 for international students). Electronic applications accepted. *Expenses: Tuition:* Full-time $26,808; part-time $1117 per credit. *Required fees:* $572; $155 per credit. *Financial support:* In 2017–18, 10 students received support. Career-related internships or fieldwork, Federal Work-Study, scholarships/grants, and unspecified assistantships available. Financial award application deadline: 1/15. *Unit head:* Duncan Mackenzie, Chair, 312-369-8663, E-mail: dmackenzie@colum.edu. *Application contact:* David Marts, Graduate Admissions, 312-369-7942, E-mail: dmarts@colum.edu.

Columbia University, Graduate School of Arts and Sciences, New York, NY 10027. Offers African-American studies (MA); American studies (MA); anthropology (MA, PhD); art history and archaeology (MA, PhD); astronomy (PhD); biological sciences (PhD); biotechnology (MA); chemical physics (PhD); chemistry (PhD); classical studies (MA, PhD); classics (MA, PhD); climate and society (MA); conservation biology (MA); earth and environmental sciences (PhD); East Asia: regional studies (MA); East Asian languages and cultures (MA, PhD); ecology, evolution and environmental biology (MA), including conservation biology; ecology, evolution, and environmental biology (PhD), including ecology and evolutionary biology, evolutionary primatology; economics (MA, PhD); English and comparative literature (MA, PhD); French and Romance philology (MA, PhD); Germanic languages (MA, PhD); global French studies (MA); global thought (MA); Hispanic cultural studies (MA); history (PhD); history and literature (MA); human rights studies (MA); Islamic studies (MA); Italian (MA, PhD); Japanese pedagogy (MA); Jewish studies (MA); Latin America and the Caribbean: regional studies (MA); Latin American and Iberian cultures (PhD); mathematics (MA, PhD), including finance (MA); medieval and Renaissance studies (MA); Middle Eastern, South Asian, and African studies (MA, PhD); modern art: critical and curatorial studies (MA); modern European studies (MA); museum anthropology (MA); music (DMA, PhD); oral history (MA); philosophical foundations of physics (MA); philosophy (MA, PhD); physics (PhD); political science (MA, PhD); psychology (PhD); quantitative methods in the social sciences (MA); religion (MA, PhD); Russia, Eurasia and East Europe: regional studies (MA); Russian translation (MA); Slavic cultures (MA); Slavic languages (MA, PhD); sociology (MA, PhD); South Asian studies (MA); statistics (MA, PhD); theatre (PhD). Dual-degree programs require admission to both Graduate School of Arts and Sciences and another Columbia school. *Program availability:* Part-time. Terminal master's awarded for partial completion of doctoral program. *Degree requirements:* For master's, variable foreign language requirement, comprehensive exam (for some programs), thesis (for some programs); for doctorate, variable foreign language requirement, comprehensive exam (for some programs), thesis/dissertation. *Entrance requirements:* For master's and doctorate, GRE General Test, GRE Subject Test (for some programs). Additional exam requirements/recommendations for international students: Required—TOEFL, IELTS. Electronic applications accepted. *Expenses: Tuition:* Full-time $44,864; part-time $1704 per credit. *Required fees:* $2370 per semester. One-time fee: $105.

Concordia University, School of Graduate Studies, Faculty of Fine Arts, Department of Art History, Montréal, QC H3G 1M8, Canada. Offers MA, PhD. PhD program offered jointly with Universityé Laval, Universityé de Montréal, and Universityé du Québec à Montréal. *Degree requirements:* For master's, one foreign language, thesis. *Entrance requirements:* For master's, BFA or equivalent, minimum B average in major. *Faculty research:* Ancient and modern Canadian art and architecture, Canadian decorative arts, museum studies.

Cornell University, Graduate School, Graduate Fields of Arts and Sciences, Field of History of Art, Archaeology and Visual Studies, Ithaca, NY 14853. Offers 19th century art (PhD); African, African American and African diaspora (PhD); American art (PhD); ancient art and archaeology (PhD); Asian American art (PhD); Baroque art (PhD); comparative modernities (PhD); digital art (PhD); East Asian art (PhD); history of photography (PhD); Islamic art (PhD); Latin American art (PhD); medieval art (PhD); modern art (PhD); Renaissance art (PhD); Southeast Asian art (PhD); theory and criticism (PhD); visual studies (PhD). *Degree requirements:* For doctorate, one foreign language, comprehensive exam, thesis/dissertation, general exams in 3 areas. *Entrance requirements:* For doctorate, GRE General Test, sample of written work, 3 letters of recommendation. Additional exam requirements/recommendations for international students: Required—TOEFL (minimum score 550 paper-based; 77 iBT). Electronic applications accepted.

Dominican University of California, School of Liberal Arts and Education, Humanities Program, San Rafael, CA 94901-2298. Offers applied music (MA); art history (MA); creative writing (MA); gender studies (MA); history (MA); philosophy (MA); political theory (MA); religion (MA). *Program availability:* Part-time. *Faculty:* 7 full-time (4 women), 1 (woman) part-time/adjunct. *Students:* 6 full-time (5 women), 16 part-time (12 women); includes 8 minority (3 Black or African American, non-Hispanic/Latino; 4 Hispanic/Latino; 1 Two or more races, non-Hispanic/Latino), 2 international. Average age 45. 7 applicants, 100% accepted, 5 enrolled. In 2017, 14 master's awarded. *Degree requirements:* For master's, thesis or alternative. *Entrance requirements:* For master's, minimum GPA of 3.0, interview. Additional exam requirements/recommendations for international students: Required—TOEFL (minimum score 550 paper-based; 80 iBT), IELTS (minimum score 6.5). *Application deadline:* For fall admission, 5/15 priority date for domestic and international students; for spring admission, 11/15 priority date for domestic and international students. Applications are processed on a rolling basis. Application fee: $0. Electronic applications accepted. *Expenses: Tuition:* Full-time $17,370; part-time $965 per credit. *Required fees:* $150 per semester. Tuition and fees vary according to course load and program. *Financial support:* In 2017–18, 4 students received support. Scholarships/grants available. Support available to part-time students. Financial award application deadline: 3/2; financial award applicants required to submit FAFSA. *Unit head:* Joan Baranow, Program Director, 415-485-3264, E-mail: joan.baranow@dominican.edu. *Application contact:* Michael Lavigna, Assistant Director of Graduate Admissions, 415-485-3253, Fax: 415-485-3214, E-mail: gradmissions@dominican.edu.
Website: https://www.dominican.edu/academics/lae/graduate-programs/ma-in-humanities/index_html

Duke University, Graduate School, Department of Art, Art History and Visual Studies, Durham, NC 27708-0764. Offers historical and cultural visualization (MA); history of art (PhD). *Degree requirements:* For doctorate, thesis/dissertation. *Entrance requirements:* For doctorate, GRE General Test. Additional exam requirements/recommendations for international students: Required—TOEFL (minimum score 577 paper-based; 90 iBT) or IELTS (minimum score 7). Electronic applications accepted.

Emory University, Laney Graduate School, Department of Art History, Atlanta, GA 30322-1100. Offers PhD. *Degree requirements:* For doctorate, 2 foreign languages, comprehensive exam, thesis/dissertation, oral exam. *Entrance requirements:* For doctorate, GRE General Test. Additional exam requirements/recommendations for international students: Required—TOEFL. Electronic applications accepted.

Fashion Institute of Technology, School of Graduate Studies, Program in Art Market Studies, New York, NY 10001-5992. Offers MA. *Accreditation:* NASAD. *Degree requirements:* For master's, thesis or alternative, internship. *Entrance requirements:* For master's, GRE General Test, previous course work in art history, 4 semesters of a foreign language. Additional exam requirements/recommendations for international students: Required—TOEFL (minimum score 550 paper-based). Electronic applications accepted.

Art History

Florida State University, The Graduate School, College of Fine Arts, Department of Art History, Tallahassee, FL 32306-1233. Offers art history (MA, PhD); museum and cultural heritage studies (MA). *Accreditation:* NASAD. *Program availability:* Part-time. *Faculty:* 11 full-time (4 women), 8 part-time/adjunct (6 women). *Students:* 52 full-time (47 women), 6 part-time (5 women); includes 10 minority (2 Black or African American, non-Hispanic/Latino; 2 Asian, non-Hispanic/Latino; 5 Hispanic/Latino; 1 Two or more races, non-Hispanic/Latino). Average age 31. 67 applicants, 73% accepted, 19 enrolled. In 2017, 12 master's, 3 doctorates awarded. Terminal master's awarded for partial completion of doctoral program. *Degree requirements:* For master's, one foreign language, thesis (for some programs), capstone project (for some programs); for doctorate, 2 foreign languages, comprehensive exam, thesis/dissertation. *Entrance requirements:* For master's, GRE General Test, minimum GPA of 3.0; for doctorate, GRE General Test, minimum GPA of 3.5. Additional exam requirements/recommendations for international students: Required—TOEFL (minimum score 550 paper-based; 80 iBT), IELTS (minimum score 6.5). *Application deadline:* For fall admission, 6/1 for domestic and international students. Applications are processed on a rolling basis. Application fee: $35. Electronic applications accepted. *Expenses:* Contact institution. *Financial support:* In 2017–18, 36 students received support, including 15 fellowships with full tuition reimbursements available (averaging $5,801 per year), 14 research assistantships with full tuition reimbursements available (averaging $5,038 per year), 9 teaching assistantships with full tuition reimbursements available (averaging $7,140 per year); career-related internships or fieldwork, Federal Work-Study, institutionally sponsored loans, scholarships/grants, tuition waivers (full), and unspecified assistantships also available. Financial award application deadline: 1/1; financial award applicants required to submit FAFSA. *Faculty research:* Modern art and critical theory, contemporary art, medieval, Renaissance and Baroque, pre-Columbian and Spanish Colonial, visual arts of the Americas. *Unit head:* Dr. Adam Jolles, Associate Professor of Art History/Department Chair, 850-644-7066, E-mail: ajolles@fsu.edu. *Application contact:* Juan Barcelo-Gonzalez, Academic Program Specialist/Graduate Student Advisor, 850-644-8207, Fax: 850-644-7065, E-mail: juan.barcelo@fsu.edu.
Website: http://arthistory.fsu.edu/

George Mason University, College of Humanities and Social Sciences, Department of History and Art History, Program in Art History, Fairfax, VA 22030. Offers MA. *Accreditation:* NASAD. *Faculty:* 10 full-time (7 women). *Students:* 2 full-time (both women), 12 part-time (11 women); includes 2 minority (both Hispanic/Latino). Average age 32. 13 applicants, 85% accepted, 5 enrolled. In 2017, 3 master's awarded. *Degree requirements:* For master's, variable foreign language requirement, comprehensive exam, thesis optional. *Entrance requirements:* For master's, GRE (waived for those who hold another graduate degree or received their undergraduate degree 10 or more years ago), expanded goals statement; 2 letters of recommendation; resume; official transcript. Additional exam requirements/recommendations for international students: Required—TOEFL (minimum score 575 paper-based; 88 iBT), IELTS (minimum score 6.5), PTE (minimum score 59). *Application deadline:* For fall admission, 3/15 for domestic and international students; for spring admission, 11/1 for domestic and international students. Application fee: $75 ($80 for international students). Electronic applications accepted. *Expenses:* Tuition, state resident: full-time $11,228; part-time $459.50 per credit. Tuition, nonresident: full-time $30,932; part-time $1280.50 per credit. *Required fees:* $3252; $135.50 per credit. Part-time tuition and fees vary according to course load and program. *Financial support:* Career-related internships or fieldwork, Federal Work-Study, scholarships/grants, unspecified assistantships, and health care benefits (for full-time research or teaching assistantship recipients) available. Support available to part-time students. Financial award application deadline: 3/1; financial award applicants required to submit FAFSA. *Faculty research:* Exhibit on Pompeii: ancient art, southeast Asia; history on Buddhist art, Twentieth century Latin America interchange, silk road project, American art on visual imagery. *Unit head:* Michele Greet, Director, 703-993-3479, Fax: 703-993-1251, E-mail: mgreet@gmu.edu. *Application contact:* Emily Gibson, Graduate Coordinator, 703-993-1248, Fax: 703-993-1251, E-mail: egibson5@gmu.edu.
Website: http://historyarthistory.gmu.edu/programs/la-ma-ah

The George Washington University, Columbian College of Arts and Sciences, Department of Fine Arts and Art History, Program in Art History, Washington, DC 20052. Offers art history (MA); museum training (MA). *Program availability:* Part-time, evening/weekend. *Faculty:* 7 full-time (4 women). *Students:* 12 full-time (10 women), 7 part-time (all women), 3 international. Average age 25. 50 applicants, 74% accepted, 12 enrolled. In 2017, 6 master's awarded. *Degree requirements:* For master's, one foreign language, comprehensive exam, thesis or alternative. *Entrance requirements:* For master's, GRE General Test, bachelor's degree in field, minimum GPA of 3.0. Additional exam requirements/recommendations for international students: Required—TOEFL (minimum score 550 paper-based; 80 iBT). *Application deadline:* For fall admission, 3/1 priority date for domestic students, 1/15 priority date for international students; for spring admission, 10/1 priority date for domestic students, 9/1 priority date for international students. Applications are processed on a rolling basis. Application fee: $75. Electronic applications accepted. *Expenses: Tuition:* Full-time $28,800; part-time $1655 per credit hour. *Required fees:* $45; $2.75 per credit hour. *Financial support:* In 2017–18, 3 students received support. Fellowships, teaching assistantships, career-related internships or fieldwork, and Federal Work-Study available. Financial award application deadline: 1/15. *Unit head:* Thomas K. Brown, Chair, 202-994-9067, E-mail: thbrown@gwu.edu. *Application contact:* Information Contact, 202-994-6085, Fax: 202-994-8657, E-mail: art@gwu.edu.

Georgia State University, Ernest G. Welch School of Art and Design, Program in Art History, Atlanta, GA 30302-3083. Offers MA. *Accreditation:* NASAD. Application fee: $50. Electronic applications accepted. *Expenses:* Tuition, state resident: full-time $7020. Tuition, nonresident: full-time $22,518. *Required fees:* $2128. Tuition and fees vary according to degree level and program. *Financial support:* Fellowships, research assistantships, scholarships/grants, and unspecified assistantships available. Financial award application deadline: 4/15; financial award applicants required to submit FAFSA. *Faculty research:* Ancient Egyptian tomb painting, nineteenth- and early twentieth-century French representations of primitive mankind, contemporary women artists, early modern images of devotion and death, images of the wet nurse in Afro-Brazilian art. *Unit head:* Michael White, Director, Welch School of Art and Design, 404-413-5221, Fax: 404-413-5261, E-mail: mwhite@gsu.edu. *Application contact:* Hubert Stanley Anderson, Director of Graduate Studies, 404-413-5229, Fax: 404-413-5261, E-mail: artgrad@gsu.edu.
Website: http://artdesign.gsu.edu/graduate/admissions/master-of-arts-in-art-history/

The Graduate Center, City University of New York, Graduate Studies, Program in Art History, New York, NY 10016-4039. Offers architecture (PhD); graphic arts (PhD); painting (PhD); photography (PhD); sculpture (PhD). *Faculty:* 16 full-time (11 women). *Students:* 112 full-time (100 women); includes 11 minority (1 Black or African American, non-Hispanic/Latino; 3 Asian, non-Hispanic/Latino; 5 Hispanic/Latino; 1 Native Hawaiian or other Pacific Islander, non-Hispanic/Latino; 1 Two or more races, non-Hispanic/Latino), 16 international. Average age 34. 104 applicants, 15% accepted, 9 enrolled. In 2017, 13 doctorates awarded. *Degree requirements:* For doctorate, 2 foreign languages, thesis/dissertation. *Entrance requirements:* For doctorate, GRE General Test. Additional exam requirements/recommendations for international students: Required—TOEFL. *Application deadline:* For fall admission, 4/15 for domestic students; for spring admission, 11/15 for domestic students. Application fee: $125. Electronic applications accepted. *Financial support:* In 2017–18, 91 students received support, including 70 fellowships, 4 research assistantships, 12 teaching assistantships; career-related internships or fieldwork, Federal Work-Study, institutionally sponsored loans, and tuition waivers (full and partial) also available. Financial award application deadline: 2/1; financial award applicants required to submit FAFSA. *Unit head:* Dr. Rachel Kousser, Executive Officer, 212-817-8035, Fax: 212-817-1502, E-mail: rkousser@gc.cuny.edu. *Application contact:* Les Gribben, Director of Admissions, 212-817-7470, Fax: 212-817-1624, E-mail: lgribben@gc.cuny.edu.

Graduate Theological Union, Graduate Programs, Berkeley, CA 94709-1212. Offers art and religion (MA, PhD, Th D); biblical languages (MA); biblical studies (MA); Biblical studies (PhD, Th D); Buddhist studies (MA); Christian spirituality (MA, PhD, Th D); cultural and historical studies of religions (MA, PhD, Th D); ethics and social theory (PhD, Th D); history (MA, PhD, Th D); homiletics (MA, PhD, Th D); interdisciplinary studies (PhD, Th D); Jewish studies (MA, PhD, Th D, Certificate); liturgical studies (MA, PhD, Th D); Near Eastern religions (PhD, Th D); Orthodox Christian studies (MA); religion and psychology (MA, PhD, Th D); religion and society/ethics and social theory (MA); systematic and philosophical theology (MA, PhD, Th D). PhD programs in Jewish studies and Near Eastern religions offered jointly with University of California, Berkeley. *Accreditation:* ATS. Terminal master's awarded for partial completion of doctoral program. *Degree requirements:* For master's, one foreign language, thesis; for doctorate, one foreign language, comprehensive exam, thesis/dissertation. *Entrance requirements:* For master's, GRE General Test; for doctorate, GRE General Test, MA or M Div. Additional exam requirements/recommendations for international students: Required—TOEFL. Electronic applications accepted.

Harvard University, Graduate School of Arts and Sciences, Department of History of Art and Architecture, Cambridge, MA 02138. Offers ancient art (PhD); ancient Near Eastern art (PhD); Baroque art (PhD); Byzantine art (PhD); classical art (PhD); Indian art (PhD); Islamic art (PhD); Japanese and Chinese art (PhD); medieval art (PhD); modern art (PhD); Renaissance and modern architecture (PhD); Renaissance art (PhD). *Degree requirements:* For doctorate, variable foreign language requirement, thesis/dissertation, general exams; reading exams in French, German, and Italian. *Entrance requirements:* For doctorate, GRE General Test. Additional exam requirements/recommendations for international students: Required—TOEFL.

Howard University, Graduate School, Division of Fine Arts, Department of Art, Program in Art History, Washington, DC 20059-0002. Offers art history (MA); history of art and visual culture (MA). *Accreditation:* NASAD. *Program availability:* Part-time. *Degree requirements:* For master's, comprehensive exam, thesis. *Entrance requirements:* For master's, GRE General Test, minimum GPA of 3.0, BA in art history or related field, portfolio.

Hunter College of the City University of New York, Graduate School, School of Arts and Sciences, Department of Art and Art History, Program in Art History, New York, NY 10065-5085. Offers MA. *Program availability:* Part-time, evening/weekend. *Degree requirements:* For master's, one foreign language, comprehensive exam, thesis. *Entrance requirements:* For master's, GRE General Test, minimum 12 credits of course work in art history, reading knowledge of a foreign language (Italian, French, German, or Spanish), 2 letters of recommendation, statement of purpose, writing sample. Additional exam requirements/recommendations for international students: Required—TOEFL (minimum score 550 paper-based; 60 iBT). *Faculty research:* Islamic art, Renaissance and Baroque, Impressionism, critical theory, Modernism.

Illinois State University, Graduate School, College of Fine Arts, School of Art, Normal, IL 61790. Offers art history (MA, MS); ceramics (MFA, MS); drawing (MFA, MS); fibers (MFA, MS); glass (MFA, MS); graphic design (MFA, MS); metals (MFA, MS); painting (MFA, MS); photography (MFA, MS); printmaking (MFA, MS); sculpture (MFA, MS). *Accreditation:* NASAD (one or more programs are accredited). *Degree requirements:* For master's, thesis or alternative, internship. *Entrance requirements:* For master's, portfolio, sample of scholarly writing.

James Madison University, The Graduate School, College of Visual and Performing Arts, School of Art, Design and Art History, Harrisonburg, VA 22801. Offers art education (MA); studio art (MA, MFA), including ceramics (MFA), drawing/painting (MFA), intermedia (MFA), metal/jewelry (MFA), photography (MFA), sculpture (MFA). *Accreditation:* NASAD. *Program availability:* Part-time. *Students:* 7 full-time (5 women), 1 (woman) part-time. Average age 30. In 2017, 5 master's awarded. Application fee: $55. Electronic applications accepted. *Expenses:* Tuition, state resident: full-time $10,512; part-time $438 per credit hour. Tuition, nonresident: full-time $28,358; part-time $1162 per credit hour. *Required fees:* $1128. *Financial support:* In 2017–18, 7 students received support, including 4 teaching assistantships with full tuition reimbursements available (averaging $9,284 per year); Federal Work-Study and 3 assistantships (averaging $7911) also available. Financial award application deadline: 3/1; financial award applicants required to submit FAFSA. *Unit head:* Dr. Kathy A. Schwartz, Director of School of Art, Design and Art History, 540-568-6216, E-mail: schwarka@jmu.edu. *Application contact:* Lynette D. Michael, Director of Graduate Student Admissions, 540-568-6131 Ext. 6395, Fax: 540-568-7860, E-mail: michaeld@jmu.edu.
Website: http://www.jmu.edu/artandarthistory/

Johns Hopkins University, Zanvyl Krieger School of Arts and Sciences, Department of History of Art, Baltimore, MD 21218. Offers MA, PhD. *Faculty:* 12 full-time (7 women). *Students:* 26 full-time (17 women); includes 3 minority (1 Black or African American, non-Hispanic/Latino; 2 Asian, non-Hispanic/Latino). Average age 29. 38 applicants, 13% accepted, 3 enrolled. Terminal master's awarded for partial completion of doctoral program. *Degree requirements:* For master's, 2 foreign languages; for doctorate, 2 foreign languages, comprehensive exam, thesis/dissertation. *Entrance requirements:* For doctorate, GRE General Test. Additional exam requirements/recommendations for international students: Required—TOEFL (minimum score 600 paper-based; 100 iBT), IELTS. *Application deadline:* For fall admission, 12/15 for domestic and international students. Application fee: $75. Electronic applications accepted. *Expenses:* Contact institution. *Financial support:* In 2017–18, 18 students received support, including 6 fellowships with full tuition reimbursements available (averaging $29,000 per year), 1 research assistantship with full tuition reimbursement available (averaging $29,000 per year), 10 teaching assistantships with full tuition reimbursements available (averaging $29,000 per year); health care benefits also available. Financial award application deadline: 4/15; financial award applicants required to submit FAFSA. *Faculty research:* Modern art, Renaissance art, medieval art, Greek/Roman art, art of the ancient Near East. *Unit head:* Dr. Marian Feldman, Chair, 410-516-2814, Fax: 410-516-5188, E-mail: mfeldm20@jhu.edu. *Application contact:* Ashley Costello, Senior Administrative Coordinator, 410-516-7117, Fax: 410-516-5188, E-mail: arthist@jhu.edu.
Website: http://arthist.jhu.edu

Kent State University, College of the Arts, School of Art, Kent, OH 44242-0001. Offers art education (MA); art history (MA); crafts (MA), including glass (MA, MFA); fine arts (MA), including fashion; studio art (MFA), including ceramics, drawing, glass (MA, MFA), jewelry, metals and enameling, painting, print media and photography, sculpture,

textiles. *Accreditation:* NASAD (one or more programs are accredited). *Program availability:* Part-time, online learning. *Faculty:* 24 full-time (13 women), 3 part-time/adjunct (all women). *Students:* 40 full-time (27 women), 22 part-time (19 women); includes 3 minority (2 Black or African American, non-Hispanic/Latino; 1 Two or more races, non-Hispanic/Latino). Average age 31. 40 applicants, 75% accepted, 23 enrolled. In 2017, 22 master's awarded. *Degree requirements:* For master's, comprehensive exam, thesis (for some programs), 1 foreign language (for art history); final project (for crafts and fine arts). *Entrance requirements:* For master's, transcripts, goal statement, 3 letters of recommendation, curriculum vitae, portfolio. Additional exam requirements/recommendations for international students: Required—TOEFL (minimum score 550 paper-based, 79 iBT), Michigan English Language Assessment Battery (minimum score 77), IELTS (minimum score 6.5) or PTE (minimum score 58). *Application deadline:* For fall admission, 2/2 for domestic and international students; for spring admission, 10/15 for domestic and international students. Applications are processed on a rolling basis. Application fee: $45 ($70 for international students). Electronic applications accepted. *Expenses:* Tuition, state resident: full-time $11,310; part-time $515 per credit hour. Tuition, nonresident: full-time $20,396; part-time $928 per credit hour. *International tuition:* $18,544 full-time. *Financial support:* Career-related internships or fieldwork, scholarships/grants, and unspecified assistantships available. Financial award application deadline: 3/16. *Unit head:* Marie Bukowski, Director, 330-672-2192, E-mail: mbukows1@kent.edu. *Application contact:* Linda Hoeptner Poling, Graduate Coordinator and Associate Professor of Art Education, 330-672-7895, E-mail: lhoeptne@kent.edu.
Website: http://www.kent.edu/art

Lancaster Theological Seminary, Graduate and Professional Programs, Lancaster, PA 17603-2812. Offers biblical studies (MAR); Christian education (MAR); Christianity and the arts (MAR); church history (MAR); congregational life (MAR); lay leadership (Certificate); theological studies (M Div); theology (D Min); theology and ethics (MAR). *Accreditation:* ACIPE; ATS. *Degree requirements:* For doctorate, thesis/dissertation.

Lindenwood University, Graduate Programs, School of Arts, Media, and Communications, St. Charles, MO 63301-1695. Offers advertising (MA); art history (MA); cinema and media arts (MFA); communications (MA); digital and Web design (MA); fashion and business design (MS); journalism (MA); mass communications (MA); social media and digital content (MS). *Program availability:* Part-time. *Faculty:* 23 full-time (6 women), 8 part-time/adjunct (4 women). *Students:* 26 full-time (13 women), 11 part-time (8 women); includes 3 minority (1 American Indian or Alaska Native, non-Hispanic/Latino; 2 Hispanic/Latino), 7 international. Average age 33. 60 applicants, 45% accepted, 16 enrolled. In 2017, 11 master's awarded. *Degree requirements:* For master's, thesis (for some programs), minimum cumulative GPA of 3.0. *Entrance requirements:* For master's, audition or interview, minimum GPA of 3.0, portfolio, letter of recommendation. Additional exam requirements/recommendations for international students: Required—TOEFL (minimum score 550 paper-based; 80 iBT); Recommended—IELTS (minimum score 6.5). *Application deadline:* For fall admission, 8/27 priority date for domestic and international students; for spring admission, 1/14 for domestic students, 1/14 priority date for international students; for summer admission, 6/4 priority date for domestic and international students. Applications are processed on a rolling basis. Application fee: $30 ($100 for international students). Electronic applications accepted. *Expenses: Tuition:* Full-time $16,300; part-time $460 per credit. *Required fees:* $660; $330 per credit. Tuition and fees vary according to degree level and program. *Financial support:* In 2017–18, 34 students received support. Career-related internships or fieldwork, institutionally sponsored loans, scholarships/grants, tuition waivers (partial), and unspecified assistantships available. Financial award application deadline: 6/30; financial award applicants required to submit FAFSA. *Unit head:* Dr. Joseph Alsobrook, Dean, School of Arts, Media, and Communications, 636-949-4164, Fax: 636-949-4910, E-mail: jalsobrook@lindenwood.edu. *Application contact:* Kara Schilli, Director, Evening and Graduate Admissions, 636-949-4349, Fax: 636-949-4109, E-mail: adultadmissions@lindenwood.edu.
Website: http://www.lindenwood.edu/academics/academic-schools/school-of-arts-media-and-communications/

Louisiana State University and Agricultural & Mechanical College, Graduate School, College of Art and Design, School of Art, Program in Art History, Baton Rouge, LA 70803. Offers MA. *Accreditation:* NASAD. *Students:* 2 full-time (both women), 1 (woman) part-time, 1 international. Average age 29. 2 applicants, 50% accepted, 1 enrolled. In 2017, 3 master's awarded.

Massachusetts Institute of Technology, School of Architecture and Planning, Department of Architecture, Cambridge, MA 02139. Offers architecture (M Arch, PhD), including building technology (PhD), design and computation (PhD), history and theory of architecture (PhD), history and theory of art (PhD); architecture studies (SM Arch S); art, culture and technology (SMACT); building technology (SMBT). *Degree requirements:* For master's, thesis; for doctorate, comprehensive exam, thesis/dissertation. *Entrance requirements:* For master's and doctorate, GRE General Test. Additional exam requirements/recommendations for international students: Required—TOEFL, IELTS. Electronic applications accepted. *Faculty research:* Architecture; urbanism; building technology and sustainability; computation and design; history, theory, and criticism; art, culture, and technology.

McGill University, Faculty of Graduate and Postdoctoral Studies, Faculty of Arts, Department of Art History and Communication Studies, Montréal, QC H3A 2T5, Canada. Offers MA, PhD.

Montana State University, The Graduate School, College of Arts and Architecture, School of Art, Bozeman, MT 59717. Offers art (MFA); art history (MA). *Accreditation:* NASAD (one or more programs are accredited). *Program availability:* Part-time. *Degree requirements:* For master's, comprehensive exam, thesis. *Entrance requirements:* For master's, GRE General Test, undergraduate degree in art. Additional exam requirements/recommendations for international students: Required—TOEFL (minimum score 550 paper-based). Electronic applications accepted. *Faculty research:* Encaustic painting, wild clay research, environmentally friendly kiln fuel, Roman wall paintings, French revolutionary portraiture.

New Mexico State University, College of Arts and Sciences, Department of Art, Las Cruces, NM 88003. Offers art history (MA); studio art (MFA). *Program availability:* Part-time. *Faculty:* 10 full-time (8 women), 3 part-time/adjunct (2 women). *Students:* 18 full-time (10 women), 1 (woman) part-time; includes 8 minority (1 Asian, non-Hispanic/Latino; 7 Hispanic/Latino), 1 international. Average age 32. 16 applicants, 44% accepted, 3 enrolled. In 2017, 2 master's awarded. *Degree requirements:* For master's, one foreign language, comprehensive exam (for some programs), thesis, thesis exhibit. *Entrance requirements:* For master's, portfolio (for MFA); 10-20 page paper (for MA). Additional exam requirements/recommendations for international students: Required—TOEFL (minimum score 550 paper-based; 79 iBT), IELTS (minimum score 6.5). *Application deadline:* For fall admission, 1/20 for domestic students; for spring admission, 11/15 for domestic students. Application fee: $40 ($50 for international students). Electronic applications accepted. *Expenses:* Tuition, state resident: full-time $4390. Tuition, nonresident: full-time $15,309. *Required fees:* $853. *Financial support:* In 2017–18, 18 students received support, including 3 fellowships (averaging $4,390 per year), 16 teaching assistantships (averaging $13,089 per year); career-related internships or fieldwork, Federal Work-Study, scholarships/grants, traineeships, health care benefits, and unspecified assistantships also available. Support available to part-time students. Financial award application deadline: 3/1. *Faculty research:* Art history, painting, graphic design, sculpture, ceramics, photography. *Total annual research expenditures:* $5,789. *Unit head:* Dr. Julia Barello, Department Head, 575-646-2728, Fax: 575-646-8036, E-mail: jbarello@nmsu.edu. *Application contact:* 575-646-1705, Fax: 575-646-8036, E-mail: artdept@nmsu.edu.
Website: http://artdepartment.nmsu.edu/

New York University, Graduate School of Arts and Science, Institute of Fine Arts, Program in Art History and Archaeology, New York, NY 10012-1019. Offers architectural studies (PhD); art history and archaeology (MA, PhD); classical art and archaeology (PhD); curatorial studies (PhD); East and South Asian art (PhD); Near Eastern art and archaeology (PhD); MA/Diploma; PhD/Certificate. *Program availability:* Part-time. *Students:* Average age 31. 346 applicants, 43% accepted, 52 enrolled. In 2017, 47 master's, 24 doctorates awarded. Terminal master's awarded for partial completion of doctoral program. *Degree requirements:* For master's, 2 foreign languages, thesis or alternative, 2 qualifying papers; for doctorate, 2 foreign languages, thesis/dissertation. *Entrance requirements:* For master's, GRE General Test; for doctorate, GRE General Test, MA. Additional exam requirements/recommendations for international students: Required—TOEFL. *Application deadline:* For fall admission, 12/18 for domestic and international students. Application fee: $100. *Expenses: Tuition:* Full-time $41,352; part-time $19,968 per year. *Required fees:* $2496; $1628 per unit. $814 per term. Tuition and fees vary according to course load and program. *Financial support:* Fellowships, research assistantships, teaching assistantships, career-related internships or fieldwork, Federal Work-Study, and institutionally sponsored loans available. Financial award application deadline: 12/18; financial award applicants required to submit FAFSA. *Unit head:* Patricia Rubin, Chair, 212-992-5800, Fax: 212-992-5807, E-mail: ifa.program@nyu.edu. *Application contact:* Alexander Nagel, Director of Graduate Studies, 212-992-5800, Fax: 212-992-5807, E-mail: ifa.program@nyu.edu.
Website: http://www.nyu.edu/gsas/dept/fineart/

Northwestern University, The Graduate School, Judd A. and Marjorie Weinberg College of Arts and Sciences, Department of Art History, Evanston, IL 60208. Offers PhD. Admissions and degrees offered through The Graduate School. *Degree requirements:* For doctorate, 2 foreign languages, comprehensive exam, thesis/dissertation, major and minor field exercises. *Entrance requirements:* For doctorate, GRE General Test. Additional exam requirements/recommendations for international students: Required—TOEFL. Electronic applications accepted. *Faculty research:* Modern American and European art and architecture, prehistoric and ancient art, central Asian art, medieval manuscripts and early printed books, history of museums, art of Western Africa, theory of culture.

The Ohio State University, Graduate School, College of Arts and Sciences, Division of Arts and Humanities, Department of History of Art, Columbus, OH 43210. Offers MA, PhD. *Accreditation:* NASAD. *Faculty:* 12. *Students:* 28 (24 women), 7 international. Average age 30. In 2017, 3 master's, 3 doctorates awarded. Terminal master's awarded for partial completion of doctoral program. *Degree requirements:* For master's, one foreign language, thesis optional; for doctorate, 2 foreign languages, thesis/dissertation. *Entrance requirements:* For master's and doctorate, GRE General Test. Additional exam requirements/recommendations for international students: Required—TOEFL (minimum score 550 paper-based; 79 iBT), Michigan English Language Assessment Battery (minimum score 82); Recommended—IELTS (minimum score 7). *Application deadline:* For fall admission, 12/1 priority date for domestic and international students; for winter admission, 12/1 for domestic students, 11/1 for international students; for spring admission, 3/1 for domestic students, 2/1 for international students. Applications are processed on a rolling basis. Application fee: $60 ($70 for international students). Electronic applications accepted. *Financial support:* Fellowships, teaching assistantships, Federal Work-Study, and institutionally sponsored loans available. Support available to part-time students. *Faculty research:* Western and Oriental art, African art and archaeology. *Unit head:* Dr. Lisa Florman, Chair and Professor, 614-292-7481, E-mail: florman.4@osu.edu. *Application contact:* Graduate and Professional Admissions, 614-292-9444, Fax: 614-292-3895, E-mail: gpadmissions@osu.edu.
Website: http://history-of-art.osu.edu/

Ohio University, Graduate College, College of Fine Arts, School of Art, Athens, OH 45701-2979. Offers art history (MA); ceramics (MFA); graphic design (MFA); painting (MFA); photography (MFA); printmaking (MFA); sculpture (MFA). *Program availability:* Part-time. *Degree requirements:* For master's, thesis. *Entrance requirements:* For master's, portfolio. Additional exam requirements/recommendations for international students: Required—TOEFL (minimum score 550 paper-based; 80 iBT) or IELTS (minimum score 6.5). Electronic applications accepted. *Faculty research:* Vapor-fired ceramics, video installation, art theory, digital photography, mixed and interdisciplinary media work.

Oklahoma State University, College of Arts and Sciences, Department of Art, Graphic Design and Art History, Stillwater, OK 74078. Offers art history (MA); graphic design (MA). *Faculty:* 22 full-time (12 women), 2 part-time/adjunct (1 woman). *Students:* 6 full-time (3 women), 4 part-time (all women); includes 1 minority (Black or African American, non-Hispanic/Latino), 3 international. Average age 29. 16 applicants, 44% accepted, 7 enrolled. In 2017, 5 master's awarded. *Entrance requirements:* Additional exam requirements/recommendations for international students: Required—TOEFL. *Application deadline:* For fall admission, 3/1 for domestic students; for spring admission, 8/1 for domestic students. Application fee: $40 ($75 for international students). Electronic applications accepted. *Expenses:* Tuition, state resident: full-time $4019; part-time $2679.60 per year. Tuition, nonresident: full-time $15,286; part-time $10,190.40 per year. *Required fees:* $2129; $1419 per unit. Tuition and fees vary according to program. *Financial support:* Research assistantships and teaching assistantships available. Financial award applicants required to submit FAFSA. *Unit head:* Dr. Rebecca Brienen, Head, E-mail: rebecca.brienen@okstate.edu.
Website: http://art.okstate.edu/

Penn State University Park, Graduate School, College of Arts and Architecture, Department of Art History, University Park, PA 16802. Offers MA, PhD. *Unit head:* Dr. Barbara O. Korner, Dean, 814-865-2592, Fax: 814-865-2018. *Application contact:* Lori Hawn, Director, Graduate Student Services, 814-865-1795, Fax: 814-863-4627, E-mail: l-gswww@lists.psu.edu.
Website: http://arthistory.psu.edu/

Pratt Institute, School of Liberal Arts and Sciences, History of Art and Design Program, Brooklyn, NY 11205-3899. Offers MA, MA/MFA, MA/MSLIS. *Accreditation:* NASAD. *Program availability:* Part-time. *Students:* 18 full-time (17 women), 8 part-time (7 women); includes 6 minority (1 American Indian or Alaska Native, non-Hispanic/Latino; 3 Hispanic/Latino; 2 Two or more races, non-Hispanic/Latino), 2 international. Average age 27. 38 applicants, 87% accepted, 7 enrolled. In 2017, 10 master's awarded. *Degree requirements:* For master's, one foreign language, thesis. *Entrance requirements:* For master's, GRE General Test, letters of recommendation, writing sample, portfolio. Additional exam requirements/recommendations for international students: Required—TOEFL (minimum score 600 paper-based; 100 iBT). *Application deadline:* For fall admission, 1/5 for domestic and international students; for spring admission, 10/1 for

domestic and international students. Application fee: $50 ($90 for international students). Electronic applications accepted. *Expenses: Tuition:* Full-time $30,834. *Required fees:* $1974. *Financial support:* Career-related internships or fieldwork, Federal Work-Study, institutionally sponsored loans, scholarships/grants, health care benefits, and unspecified assistantships available. Support available to part-time students. Financial award application deadline: 2/1; financial award applicants required to submit FAFSA. *Faculty research:* Conservation techniques, women artists from previous centuries, art of sixteenth-century Veneto, design history, nineteenth-century Germany. *Unit head:* John Decker, Chairperson, 718-636-3598, E-mail: jdecker@pratt.edu. *Application contact:* Natalie Capannelli, Director of Graduate Admissions, 718-636-3551, Fax: 718-399-4242, E-mail: ncapanne@pratt.edu. Website: https://www.pratt.edu/academics/liberal-arts-and-sciences/history-of-art-design-grad/

See Display on page 725 and Close-Up on page 749.

Purchase College, State University of New York, School of Humanities, Purchase, NY 10577-1400. Offers art history (MA). *Accreditation:* NASAD. *Degree requirements:* For master's, one foreign language, thesis. *Entrance requirements:* For master's, BA or BFA, previous course work in art history, three letters of recommendation, personal statement, 1-2 writing samples, official transcripts. *Application deadline:* For fall admission, 3/1 for domestic students. Application fee: $80. Electronic applications accepted. *Financial support:* Fellowships, Federal Work-Study, scholarships/grants, and tuition waivers (partial) available. Support available to part-time students. Financial award application deadline: 3/15; financial award applicants required to submit FAFSA. *Unit head:* Ross Daly, Chair, 914-251-6550. *Application contact:* Garrett Marino, Associate Director of Admissions, 914-251-6316, Fax: 914-251-6314, E-mail: admissn@purchase.edu. Website: https://www.purchase.edu/academics/school-of-humanities/

Queens College of the City University of New York, Arts and Humanities Division, Department of Art, Queens, NY 11367-1597. Offers art history (MA); studio art (MFA). *Program availability:* Part-time. *Faculty:* 18 full-time (6 women), 56 part-time/adjunct (32 women). *Students:* 13 full-time (7 women), 19 part-time (15 women); includes 9 minority (1 Black or African American, non-Hispanic/Latino; 2 Asian, non-Hispanic/Latino; 5 Hispanic/Latino; 1 Two or more races, non-Hispanic/Latino), 2 international. Average age 35. 25 applicants, 44% accepted, 8 enrolled. In 2017, 16 master's awarded. *Degree requirements:* For master's, thesis, comprehensive exam (for art history program). *Entrance requirements:* For master's, minimum GPA of 3.0. Additional exam requirements/recommendations for international students: Required—TOEFL (minimum score 600 paper-based), IELTS. *Application deadline:* For fall admission, 4/1 for domestic students; for spring admission, 11/1 for domestic students. Applications are processed on a rolling basis. Application fee: $125. Electronic applications accepted. *Financial support:* Career-related internships or fieldwork available. Financial award application deadline: 4/1; financial award applicants required to submit FAFSA. *Unit head:* Michael Nelson, Chair, 718-997-4800, E-mail: michael.nelson@qc.cuny.edu. *Application contact:* Elizabeth D'Amico-Ramirez, Assistant Director of Graduate Admissions, 718-997-5203, E-mail: elizabeth.damicoramirez@qc.cuny.edu.

Rice University, Graduate Programs, School of Humanities, Department of Art History, Houston, TX 77251-1892. Offers PhD.

Richmond, The American International University in London, MA in Art History Program, Richmond, United Kingdom. Offers MA. *Program availability:* Part-time. *Degree requirements:* For master's, thesis. *Entrance requirements:* For master's, minimum GPA of 3.0. Additional exam requirements/recommendations for international students: Required—TOEFL, IELTS. Electronic applications accepted. *Expenses:* Contact institution. *Faculty research:* Archaeology of art and representation, contemporary paganisms, nineteenth century modernisms, American twentieth century art, sound media.

Roger Williams University, School of Architecture, Art and Historic Preservation, Bristol, RI 02809. Offers architecture (M Arch); art and architectural history (MA); historical preservation (MS, Certificate); urban and regional planning (Certificate). *Faculty:* 18 full-time (5 women), 9 part-time/adjunct (1 woman). *Students:* 107 full-time (52 women), 9 part-time (5 women); includes 10 minority (1 Asian, non-Hispanic/Latino; 7 Hispanic/Latino; 2 Two or more races, non-Hispanic/Latino), 5 international. Average age 26. 92 applicants, 93% accepted, 58 enrolled. In 2017, 46 master's, 1 other advanced degree awarded. *Degree requirements:* For master's, thesis. *Entrance requirements:* For master's, portfolio, 2 letters of recommendation, college transcript, letter of intent. Additional exam requirements/recommendations for international students: Required—TOEFL (minimum score 85 iBT), IELTS (minimum score 6.5). *Application deadline:* For fall admission, 4/1 for domestic students; for spring admission, 11/15 for domestic students. Application fee: $50. Electronic applications accepted. *Expenses:* $1,463 per credit hour (for M Arch); $876 per credit hour (for MS and MA); $258 graduation fee. *Financial support:* In 2017–18, 116 students received support, including 116 research assistantships (averaging $2,776 per year); career-related internships or fieldwork, scholarships/grants, and unspecified assistantships also available. Financial award application deadline: 4/1; financial award applicants required to submit FAFSA. *Unit head:* Stephen White, Dean, 401-254-3607, E-mail: swhite@rwu.edu. *Application contact:* Marcus Hanscom, Director of Graduate Admissions, 401-254-3345, Fax: 401-254-3557, E-mail: gradadmit@rwu.edu. Website: http://www.rwu.edu/graduate/programs/graduate-programs/architecture

Rutgers University–New Brunswick, Graduate School-New Brunswick, Program in Art History, Piscataway, NJ 08854-8097. Offers art history (MA, PhD); curatorial studies (Certificate); historic preservation (Certificate). *Program availability:* Part-time. Terminal master's awarded for partial completion of doctoral program. *Degree requirements:* For master's, one foreign language, comprehensive exam; for doctorate, 2 foreign languages, comprehensive exam, thesis/dissertation. *Entrance requirements:* For master's and doctorate, GRE General Test, writing sample. Additional exam requirements/recommendations for international students: Required—TOEFL (minimum score 550 paper-based). Electronic applications accepted. *Faculty research:* Ancient and medieval art and architecture; Renaissance and Baroque art and architecture; modern and contemporary art and architecture; Italian studies; the arts of Asia, Africa, and the Americas.

San Diego State University, Graduate and Research Affairs, College of Professional Studies and Fine Arts, School of Art, Design and Art History, San Diego, CA 92182. Offers art history (MA); studio arts (MA, MFA), including applied design, environmental design, graphic design, interior design, painting and printmaking, sculpture. *Accreditation:* NASAD (one or more programs are accredited). *Degree requirements:* For master's, variable foreign language requirement, thesis. *Entrance requirements:* For master's, GRE General Test, bachelor's degree in related field, slide portfolio, typed slide information sheet, 2 letters of recommendation. Additional exam requirements/recommendations for international students: Required—TOEFL. Electronic applications accepted.

San Francisco Art Institute, Master of Arts Programs, San Francisco, CA 94133. Offers exhibition and museum studies (MA); history and theory of contemporary art (MA). *Degree requirements:* For master's, thesis. *Entrance requirements:* For master's,

statement of purpose, writing samples. Additional exam requirements/recommendations for international students: Required—TOEFL (minimum score 600 paper-based; 100 iBT), IELTS (minimum score 7.5). Electronic applications accepted.

San Jose State University, Graduate Studies and Research, College of Humanities and the Arts, San Jose, CA 95192-0088. Offers art (MA, MFA), including digital media art (MFA), history and visual culture (MA), photography (MFA), pictorial art (MFA), spatial art (MFA); English (MA, MFA), including creative writing (MFA); linguistics (MA); music (MM); music education (MA); philosophy (MA); Spanish (MA); teaching English to speakers of other languages (MA). *Program availability:* Part-time. *Faculty:* 35 full-time (17 women), 19 part-time/adjunct (11 women). *Students:* 129 full-time (79 women), 106 part-time (71 women); includes 117 minority (5 Black or African American, non-Hispanic/Latino; 29 Asian, non-Hispanic/Latino; 44 Hispanic/Latino; 39 Two or more races, non-Hispanic/Latino), 28 international. Average age 35. 204 applicants, 65% accepted, 79 enrolled. In 2017, 85 master's awarded. *Degree requirements:* For master's, one foreign language, comprehensive exam (for some programs), thesis (for some programs), graduate writing assessment, special study/project, recital. *Entrance requirements:* Additional exam requirements/recommendations for international students: Required—TOEFL (minimum score 550 paper-based; 80 iBT), IELTS (minimum score 6.5), PTE (minimum score 53). *Application deadline:* For fall admission, 2/1 for domestic and international students. Applications are processed on a rolling basis. Application fee: $55. Electronic applications accepted. *Expenses:* Tuition, state resident: full-time $7176. Tuition, nonresident: full-time $16,680. Tuition and fees vary according to course load and program. *Financial support:* Fellowships, research assistantships, Federal Work-Study, scholarships/grants, traineeships, tuition waivers (full and partial), and unspecified assistantships available. Support available to part-time students. Financial award application deadline: 4/28; financial award applicants required to submit FAFSA. *Unit head:* Dr. Shannon Miller, Dean, 408-924-4300, Fax: 408-924-4365, E-mail: shannon.miller@sjsu.edu. Website: http://www.sjsu.edu/humanitiesandarts/

Savannah College of Art and Design, Program in Art History, Savannah, GA 31402-3146. Offers MA. *Program availability:* Part-time. *Faculty:* 34 full-time (22 women), 6 part-time/adjunct (4 women). *Students:* 6 full-time (5 women), 4 part-time (3 women); includes 2 minority (1 Black or African American, non-Hispanic/Latino; 1 Hispanic/Latino). Average age 30. 21 applicants, 38% accepted, 4 enrolled. In 2017, 3 master's awarded. *Degree requirements:* For master's, one foreign language, comprehensive exam, thesis. *Entrance requirements:* For master's, GRE (recommended), portfolio (submitted in digital format), audition or writing submission, resume, statement of purpose, two letters of recommendation. Additional exam requirements/recommendations for international students: Recommended—TOEFL (minimum score 550 paper-based; 85 iBT), IELTS (minimum score 6.5). *Application deadline:* For fall admission, 4/1 for domestic and international students. Applications are processed on a rolling basis. Application fee: $40. Electronic applications accepted. *Expenses: Tuition:* Full-time $36,765; part-time $817 per credit hour. One-time fee: $500. *Financial support:* Career-related internships or fieldwork, Federal Work-Study, and scholarships/grants available. Financial award application deadline: 4/1; financial award applicants required to submit FAFSA. *Unit head:* Dr. Geoffrey Taylor, Chair, Art History. *Application contact:* Jenny Jaquillard, Executive Director of Admissions, Recruitment and Events, 912-525-5100, Fax: 912-525-5985, E-mail: admission@scad.edu. Website: http://www.scad.edu/academics/programs/art-history

School of the Art Institute of Chicago, Graduate Division, Program in Modern Art History, Theory, and Criticism, Chicago, IL 60603-3103. Offers MA. *Accreditation:* NASAD. *Entrance requirements:* For master's, GRE. Additional exam requirements/recommendations for international students: Required—TOEFL, IELTS.

School of Visual Arts, Graduate Programs, Program in Curatorial Practice, New York, NY 10010-3994. Offers MA.

Southern Methodist University, Meadows School of the Arts, Division of Art History, Dallas, TX 75275. Offers art history (MA); rhetorics of art, space and culture (PhD). *Program availability:* Part-time, evening/weekend. *Degree requirements:* For master's, one foreign language, thesis, translation exam. *Entrance requirements:* For master's, GRE, 12 upper-level hours in art history, sample research paper. Additional exam requirements/recommendations for international students: Required—TOEFL (minimum score 550 paper-based; 80 iBT). *Faculty research:* American art, nineteenth- and twentieth-century art, classical and Byzantine art, Hispanic art, Mesoamerican art, Renaissance-Baroque.

Stony Brook University, State University of New York, Graduate School, College of Arts and Sciences, Department of Art, Program in Art History and Criticism, Stony Brook, NY 11794. Offers MA, PhD. *Program availability:* Part-time. *Students:* 37 full-time (29 women), 1 (woman) part-time; includes 6 minority (1 American Indian or Alaska Native, non-Hispanic/Latino; 3 Asian, non-Hispanic/Latino; 2 Hispanic/Latino), 7 international. Average age 30. 23 applicants, 78% accepted, 9 enrolled. In 2017, 6 master's, 5 doctorates awarded. *Degree requirements:* For master's, comprehensive exam, thesis, reading knowledge of German or French; for doctorate, comprehensive exam, thesis/dissertation, qualifying paper, reading knowledge of German and French, qualifying examination. *Entrance requirements:* For master's, GRE General Test, minimum undergraduate GPA of 3.0; for doctorate, GRE General Test, minimum graduate GPA of 3.0. Additional exam requirements/recommendations for international students: Required—TOEFL (minimum score 550 paper-based), IELTS (minimum score 6.5). *Application deadline:* For fall admission, 1/15 for domestic students; for spring admission, 10/1 for domestic students. Application fee: $100. *Expenses:* Contact institution. *Financial support:* Fellowships, research assistantships, and teaching assistantships available. Financial award applicants required to submit FAFSA. *Unit head:* Dr. Barbara Frank, Director, 631-632-4250, E-mail: barbara.frank@stonybrook.edu. *Application contact:* Lisa Perez, Coordinator, 631-632-7270, E-mail: lisa.a.perez@stonybrook.edu. Website: http://art.stonybrook.edu/graduate/g-arhc/

Sul Ross State University, College of Arts and Sciences, Department of Fine Arts and Communication, Alpine, TX 79832. Offers art history (MA); studio art (MA), including art education. *Program availability:* Part-time. *Degree requirements:* For master's, oral or written exam. *Entrance requirements:* For master's, GRE General Test, minimum GPA of 2.5 in last 60 hours of undergraduate work. *Faculty research:* Ceramic sculpture, watercolor, wood sculpture, rock art.

Syracuse University, College of Arts and Sciences, MA Program in Art History, Syracuse, NY 13207. Offers MA. *Degree requirements:* For master's, one foreign language, symposium presentation. *Entrance requirements:* For master's, GRE, competency exam in the history of art, bachelor's degree, normally as art history major, at accredited institution; academic transcripts of all undergraduate studies. Additional exam requirements/recommendations for international students: Required—TOEFL (minimum score 100 iBT). *Application deadline:* For fall admission, 1/15 for domestic and international students. Application fee: $75. Electronic applications accepted. *Financial support:* Fellowships with full tuition reimbursements, teaching assistantships with tuition reimbursements, career-related internships or fieldwork, scholarships/grants, tuition waivers (full and partial), and partial tuition scholarships, stipends to cover expenses in

Italy available. Financial award application deadline: 1/15; financial award applicants required to submit FAFSA. *Faculty research:* Literature of art criticism, historical methodology, art and culture of various world traditions, cultural management, galleries and the art market. *Unit head:* Sascha Scott, Assistant Professor and Director of Graduate Studies for Art and Music Histories, 315-443-5033, E-mail: sscott04@syr.edu. *Application contact:* Sascha Scott, Assistant Professor and Director of Graduate Studies for Art and Music Histories, 315-443-5033, E-mail: sscott04@syr.edu. Website: http://amh.syr.edu/

Temple University, Tyler School of Art, Department of Art History, Philadelphia, PA 19122-6096. Offers MA, PhD. *Program availability:* Part-time. *Faculty:* 10 full-time (7 women), 8 part-time/adjunct (4 women). *Students:* 47 full-time (41 women), 6 part-time (5 women); includes 10 minority (1 Black or African American, non-Hispanic/Latino; 2 Asian, non-Hispanic/Latino; 5 Hispanic/Latino; 2 Two or more races, non-Hispanic/Latino), 5 international. 36 applicants, 67% accepted, 6 enrolled. In 2017, 6 master's, 4 doctorates awarded. Terminal master's awarded for partial completion of doctoral program. *Entrance requirements:* For master's, GRE General Test, minimum GPA of 3.0, letters of recommendation, resume/curriculum vitae, writing sample; for doctorate, GRE, MA in art history, minimum GPA of 3.0, letters of recommendation, resume/curriculum vitae, writing sample. Additional exam requirements/recommendations for international students: Required—TOEFL (minimum score 550 paper-based; 79 iBT), IELTS (minimum score 6.5). *Application deadline:* For fall admission, 12/15 for domestic and international students; for spring admission, 11/1 for domestic students, 10/1 for international students. Applications are processed on a rolling basis. Application fee: $60. Electronic applications accepted. *Expenses:* Contact institution. *Financial support:* Fellowships, research assistantships, teaching assistantships, career-related internships or fieldwork, institutionally sponsored loans, and technical assistantships available. Financial award application deadline: 1/15. *Faculty research:* Aegean, Greek, and Roman art; early Christian art; medieval art and architecture; Renaissance and Baroque painting, sculpture, and architecture; nineteenth- and twentieth-century painting and sculpture. *Unit head:* Dr. Jane DeRose Evans, Chair, 215-777-9165, Fax: 215-204-6951, E-mail: jevans@temple.edu. *Application contact:* Tamryn McDermott, Director of Admissions, 215-777-9090, E-mail: tylerart@temple.edu. Website: https://tyler.temple.edu/programs/art-history

Texas Christian University, College of Fine Arts, School of Art, Fort Worth, TX 76129. Offers art history (MA); studio art (MFA), including painting. *Accreditation:* NASAD. *Faculty:* 11 full-time (5 women). *Students:* 22 full-time (17 women); includes 3 minority (all Hispanic/Latino), 5 international. Average age 28. 31 applicants, 35% accepted, 9 enrolled. In 2017, 3 master's awarded. *Degree requirements:* For master's, variable foreign language requirement, comprehensive exam, thesis. *Entrance requirements:* For master's, GRE General Test (for MA). Additional exam requirements/recommendations for international students: Required—TOEFL (minimum score 550 paper-based; 80 iBT). *Application deadline:* For fall admission, 2/1 for domestic and international students. Application fee: $60. Electronic applications accepted. *Expenses:* Contact institution. *Financial support:* In 2017–18, 18 students received support, including 17 teaching assistantships (averaging $10,000 per year); institutionally sponsored loans, scholarships/grants, health care benefits, tuition waivers (full and partial), and unspecified assistantships also available. Financial award application deadline: 2/15. *Unit head:* Richard Lane, Director, 817-257-7643, E-mail: r.lane@tcu.edu. *Application contact:* Donna Smolik, TCU College of Fine Arts Graduate Office, 817-257-7603, Fax: 817-257-5672, E-mail: cfagradinfo@tcu.edu. Website: http://www.art.tcu.edu/

Texas Tech University, Graduate School, J.T. and Margaret Talkington College of Visual and Performing Arts, School of Art, Lubbock, TX 79409. Offers art (MFA); art education (MAE); art history (MA). *Accreditation:* NASAD (one or more programs are accredited). *Program availability:* Part-time, blended/hybrid learning. *Faculty:* 31 full-time (13 women), 10 part-time/adjunct (6 women). *Students:* 32 full-time (22 women), 18 part-time (14 women); includes 11 minority (1 Black or African American, non-Hispanic/Latino; 1 Asian, non-Hispanic/Latino; 8 Hispanic/Latino; 1 Two or more races, non-Hispanic/Latino), 6 international. Average age 35. 31 applicants, 45% accepted, 9 enrolled. In 2017, 22 master's awarded. *Degree requirements:* For master's, variable foreign language requirement, comprehensive exam, thesis (for some programs), exhibition (for MFA). *Entrance requirements:* For master's, GRE (for MA). Additional exam requirements/recommendations for international students: Required—TOEFL (minimum score 550 paper-based; 79 iBT), IELTS (minimum score 6.5). *Application deadline:* For fall admission, 6/1 priority date for domestic students, 1/15 priority date for international students; for spring admission, 9/1 priority date for domestic students, 6/15 priority date for international students. Applications are processed on a rolling basis. Application fee: $60. Electronic applications accepted. *Expenses:* Contact institution. *Financial support:* In 2017–18, 37 students received support, including 36 fellowships (averaging $3,227 per year), 32 teaching assistantships (averaging $9,937 per year); research assistantships, Federal Work-Study, institutionally sponsored loans, scholarships/grants, health care benefits, tuition waivers (partial), and unspecified assistantships also available. Financial award application deadline: 2/15; financial award applicants required to submit FAFSA. *Faculty research:* Contemporary Chicano/a art; transformation of multidisciplinary approach to printmaking; letter press posters; intersection of art and science; transmedia. *Total annual research expenditures:* $44,636. *Unit head:* Prof. Lydia Thompson, Director and Professor, 806-742-3825 Ext. 255, E-mail: lydia.thompson@ttu.edu. *Application contact:* Linda Rumbelow, Academic Advisor, 806-742-3825 Ext. 222, E-mail: linda.rumbelow@ttu.edu. Website: http://www.art.ttu.edu

Texas Woman's University, Graduate School, College of Arts and Sciences, School of the Arts, Department of Visual Arts, Denton, TX 76204. Offers art (MA, MAT, MFA), including art education (MA, MAT), art history (MA); ceramics (MFA); graphic design (MA), intermedia (MFA), painting (MFA), photography (MFA), sculpture (MFA). MFA degrees are granted through the Federation of North Texas Area Universities (The University of North Texas, Texas A&M Commerce, and Texas Woman's University). *Faculty:* 6 full-time (3 women). *Students:* 8 full-time (6 women), 9 part-time (8 women); includes 7 minority (1 Black or African American, non-Hispanic/Latino; 1 American Indian or Alaska Native, non-Hispanic/Latino; 4 Hispanic/Latino; 1 Two or more races, non-Hispanic/Latino). Average age 33. 10 applicants, 50% accepted, 2 enrolled. In 2017, 10 master's awarded. *Degree requirements:* For master's, comprehensive exam, thesis (for some programs), exhibit (MFA), oral exam, thesis or professional paper (MA). *Entrance requirements:* For master's, portfolio, interview, current curriculum vitae, letter of intent, 3 letters of recommendation, artist statement, 2 research papers (for art history or art education). Additional exam requirements/recommendations for international students: Required—TOEFL (minimum score 550 paper-based; 79 iBT); Recommended—IELTS (minimum score 6.5), TSE (minimum score 53). *Application deadline:* For fall admission, 1/31 priority date for domestic and international students; for spring admission, 10/15 priority date for domestic students, 7/1 priority date for international students. Applications are processed on a rolling basis. Application fee: $50 ($75 for international students). Electronic applications accepted. *Expenses:* $7,520 per year full-time in-state; $16,820 per year full-time out-of-state. *Financial support:* In 2017–18, 9 students received support, including 5 teaching assistantships (averaging $9,780 per year); career-related internships or fieldwork, Federal Work-Study,

institutionally sponsored loans, scholarships/grants, traineeships, health care benefits, and unspecified assistantships also available. Support available to part-time students. Financial award application deadline: 3/1; financial award applicants required to submit FAFSA. *Faculty research:* Art education and electronic technology, film noir, one-of-a-kind art books, new media, early video art from 1960-1980. *Unit head:* Dr. Vagner Whitehead, Chair, 940-898-2530, Fax: 940-898-2496, E-mail: visualarts@twu.edu. *Application contact:* Korie Hawkins, Associate Director of Admissions, Graduate Recruitment, 940-898-3188, Fax: 940-898-3081, E-mail: admissions@twu.edu. Website: http://www.twu.edu/visual-arts/

Towson University, College of Liberal Arts, Program in Professional Studies, Towson, MD 21252-0001. Offers art history (MA); individualized plan of study (MA). *Program availability:* Part-time, evening/weekend. *Students:* 13 full-time (8 women), 16 part-time (9 women); includes 11 minority (7 Black or African American, non-Hispanic/Latino; 1 Hispanic/Latino; 3 Two or more races, non-Hispanic/Latino). *Degree requirements:* For master's, thesis optional. *Entrance requirements:* For master's, minimum GPA of 3.0, essay. *Application deadline:* For fall admission, 1/17 for domestic students, 5/15 for international students; for spring admission, 10/15 for domestic students, 12/1 for international students. Applications are processed on a rolling basis. Application fee: $45. Electronic applications accepted. *Expenses:* Tuition, state resident: full-time $7960; part-time $398 per unit. Tuition, nonresident: full-time $16,480; part-time $824 per unit. *Required fees:* $2600; $130 per year. $390 per term. *Financial support:* Application deadline: 4/1. *Unit head:* Dr. James Smith, Graduate Program Director, 410-704-4620, E-mail: jmsmith@towson.edu. *Application contact:* Coverley Beidleman, Assistant Director of Graduate Admissions, 410-704-5630, Fax: 410-704-3030, E-mail: cbeidleman@towson.edu. Website: http://www.towson.edu/cla/departments/interdisciplinary/grad/professional/

Tufts University, Graduate School of Arts and Sciences, Department of Art and Art History, Medford, MA 02155. Offers art history (MA); art history and museum studies (MA). *Students:* 14 full-time (10 women); includes 5 minority (1 Black or African American, non-Hispanic/Latino; 2 Asian, non-Hispanic/Latino; 2 Hispanic/Latino). Average age 25. 66 applicants, 42% accepted, 7 enrolled. In 2017, 9 master's awarded. *Degree requirements:* For master's, one foreign language, thesis (for some programs). *Entrance requirements:* For master's, GRE General Test. Additional exam requirements/recommendations for international students: Required—TOEFL (minimum score 550 paper-based; 80 iBT), IELTS (minimum score 6.5). *Application deadline:* For fall admission, 1/15 for domestic and international students. Application fee: $85. Electronic applications accepted. *Expenses:* Contact institution. *Financial support:* Teaching assistantships, Federal Work-Study, scholarships/grants, tuition waivers (full and partial), and unspecified assistantships available. Financial award application deadline: 1/15. *Unit head:* Karen Overbey, Graduate Program Director, 617-627-3395. *Application contact:* Office of Graduate Admissions, 617-627-3395, E-mail: gradadmissions@tufts.edu. Website: http://ase.tufts.edu/art/

Tulane University, School of Liberal Arts, Department of Art, New Orleans, LA 70118-5669. Offers history of art (MA); studio art (MFA). PhD held jointly with Roger Thayer Stone Center for Latin American Studies. *Degree requirements:* For master's, one foreign language, thesis. *Entrance requirements:* For master's, GRE General Test, minimum B average in undergraduate course work. Additional exam requirements/recommendations for international students: Required—TOEFL. Electronic applications accepted. *Expenses:* Tuition: Full-time $50,920; part-time $2829 per credit hour. *Required fees:* $2040; $44.50 per credit hour. $580 per term. Tuition and fees vary according to course load, degree level and program.

Université de Montréal, Faculty of Arts and Sciences, Department of Art History and Film Studies, Montréal, QC H3C 3J7, Canada. Offers art history (MA, PhD); film studies (MA, PhD). Programs offered jointly with Concordia University, Université Laval, and Université du Québec à Montréal. *Degree requirements:* For master's, thesis. Electronic applications accepted. *Faculty research:* Western art from the Middle Ages, classic and modern theory, modern and contemporary art, Canadian art.

Université du Québec à Montréal, Graduate Programs, Program in Art Studies, Montréal, QC H3C 3P8, Canada. Offers art history (PhD); art studies (MA); study and practices of the arts (PhD). *Program availability:* Part-time. *Degree requirements:* For master's, thesis; for doctorate, thesis/dissertation. *Entrance requirements:* For master's, appropriate bachelor's degree or equivalent, proficiency in French; for doctorate, appropriate master's degree or equivalent, proficiency in French.

Université Laval, Faculty of Letters, Department of History, Programs in Art History, Québec, QC G1K 7P4, Canada. Offers MA, PhD. PhD offered jointly with Concordia University, Université de Montréal, and Université du Québec à Montréal. Terminal master's awarded for partial completion of doctoral program. *Degree requirements:* For master's, thesis; for doctorate, comprehensive exam, thesis/dissertation. *Entrance requirements:* For master's, English test (comprehension of written English), knowledge of French; for doctorate, English test (comprehension of written English), knowledge of French and English, knowledge of a third language. Electronic applications accepted.

University at Buffalo, the State University of New York, Graduate School, College of Arts and Sciences, Department of Art, Program in Visual Studies, Buffalo, NY 14260. Offers critical museum studies (MA); visual studies (MA, PhD). *Program availability:* Part-time. *Faculty:* 6 full-time (3 women). *Students:* 13 full-time (9 women), 3 international. Average age 27. 19 applicants, 58% accepted, 6 enrolled. In 2017, 4 master's, 2 doctorates awarded. *Degree requirements:* For master's, thesis, field exam; for doctorate, one foreign language, thesis/dissertation. *Entrance requirements:* Additional exam requirements/recommendations for international students: Required—TOEFL (minimum score 79 iBT). *Application deadline:* For fall admission, 2/1 priority date for domestic students; for spring admission, 10/15 priority date for domestic students. Applications are processed on a rolling basis. Application fee: $50. Electronic applications accepted. *Financial support:* In 2017–18, 9 students received support, including 9 teaching assistantships with full tuition reimbursements available (averaging $13,716 per year); career-related internships or fieldwork, Federal Work-Study, institutionally sponsored loans, tuition waivers (full), and unspecified assistantships also available. Support available to part-time students. Financial award application deadline: 2/28; financial award applicants required to submit FAFSA. *Unit head:* Joan Linder, Chair, 716-645-0539, Fax: 716-645-6970, E-mail: joannder@buffalo.edu. *Application contact:* Dr. Jonathan Katz, Director, 716-645-6878, Fax: 716-645-5978. Website: http://art.buffalo.edu

The University of Alabama, Graduate School, College of Arts and Sciences, Department of Art and Art History, Tuscaloosa, AL 35487. Offers art history (MA); studio art (MA, MFA), including ceramics, painting, photography, printmaking, sculpture. *Accreditation:* NASAD. *Program availability:* Part-time. *Faculty:* 18 full-time (11 women), 1 part-time/adjunct (0 women). *Students:* 16 full-time (11 women), 1 part-time (0 women); includes 2 minority (1 Black or African American, non-Hispanic/Latino; 1 Hispanic/Latino), 2 international. Average age 31. 22 applicants, 73% accepted, 9 enrolled. In 2017, 10 master's awarded. *Degree requirements:* For master's, one foreign language, comprehensive exam (for some programs), oral exam, thesis statement, exhibit (studio art), thesis (art history). *Entrance requirements:* For master's, GRE General Test or MAT (art history), minimum GPA of 3.0, BFA or equivalent (studio art).

Additional exam requirements/recommendations for international students: Required—TOEFL (minimum score 550 paper-based). *Application deadline:* For fall admission, 3/15 for domestic and international students; for spring admission, 10/15 for domestic and international students. Applications are processed on a rolling basis. Application fee: $50 ($60 for international students). Electronic applications accepted. *Financial support:* In 2017–18, 8 students received support, including 2 fellowships with full tuition reimbursements available, 14 teaching assistantships with tuition reimbursements available (averaging $15,427 per year); career-related internships or fieldwork, institutionally sponsored loans, scholarships/grants, and unspecified assistantships also available. Financial award application deadline: 7/14. *Faculty research:* Nineteenth-century American, Medieval Europe, Baroque, twentieth-century, and African American art history. *Unit head:* Jason Guynes, Chair, 205-348-9944, Fax: 205-348-0287, E-mail: jguynes@ua.edu. *Application contact:* Sarah Marshall, Graduate Coordinator, 205-348-1890, Fax: 205-348-5967, E-mail: smarsh@ua.edu.
Website: http://www.art.ua.edu/

The University of Alabama at Birmingham, College of Arts and Sciences, Program in Art History, Birmingham, AL 35294. Offers MA. Program offered jointly with The University of Alabama (Tuscaloosa). *Accreditation:* NASAD. *Program availability:* Part-time, evening/weekend. *Faculty:* 4 full-time (all women). *Students:* 4 full-time (3 women), 4 part-time (3 women); includes 1 minority (Two or more races, non-Hispanic/Latino), 2 international. Average age 29. 4 applicants, 50% accepted, 2 enrolled. In 2017, 4 master's awarded. Terminal master's awarded for partial completion of doctoral program. *Degree requirements:* For master's, one foreign language, comprehensive exam, thesis. *Entrance requirements:* For master's, GRE General Test, minimum GPA of 3.0. Additional exam requirements/recommendations for international students: Required—TOEFL. *Application deadline:* For fall admission, 4/1 for domestic students; for spring admission, 10/1 for domestic students. Applications are processed on a rolling basis. Electronic applications accepted. *Financial support:* In 2017–18, 3 students received support, including 1 fellowship with partial tuition reimbursement available, 2 research assistantships with partial tuition reimbursements available; Federal Work-Study and tuition waivers (partial) also available. Financial award application deadline: 5/1; financial award applicants required to submit FAFSA. *Faculty research:* Race and representation in American art; Hindu temple architecture; the evolving image of the artist in nineteenth-century France through the lens of the artist's studio; animation and realism in early Netherlandish painting; animals in art. *Unit head:* Dr. Cathleen Cummings, Graduate Advisor, 205-934-4941, E-mail: cathleen@uab.edu. *Application contact:* Susan Noblitt Banks, Director of Graduate School Operations, 205-934-8227, Fax: 205-934-8413, E-mail: gradschool@uab.edu.
Website: http://www.uab.edu/cas/art/areas-of-study/ma-art-history

University of Alberta, Faculty of Graduate Studies and Research, Department of Art and Design, Edmonton, AB T6G 2E1, Canada. Offers drawing (MFA); history of art, design, and visual culture (MA); industrial design (M Des); painting (MFA); printmaking (MFA); sculpture (MFA); visual communication design (M Des). *Degree requirements:* For master's, thesis. *Entrance requirements:* For master's, portfolio (MFA and MDES). Additional exam requirements/recommendations for international students: Required—TOEFL (minimum score 550 paper-based).

The University of Arizona, College of Fine Arts, School of Art, Program in Art History, Tucson, AZ 85721. Offers MA. *Accreditation:* NASAD. *Program availability:* Part-time. Terminal master's awarded for partial completion of doctoral program. *Degree requirements:* For master's, one foreign language, thesis. *Entrance requirements:* For master's, GRE, 3 letters of recommendation, resume or curriculum vitae, writing sample. Additional exam requirements/recommendations for international students: Required—TOEFL (minimum score 550 paper-based; 79 iBT). Electronic applications accepted. *Faculty research:* American art, history of photography, Mexican art, contemporary African art.

The University of Arizona, College of Fine Arts, School of Art, Program in Art History and Education, Tucson, AZ 85721. Offers PhD. *Degree requirements:* For doctorate, thesis/dissertation. *Entrance requirements:* Additional exam requirements/recommendations for international students: Required—TOEFL (minimum score 550 paper-based; 79 iBT). Electronic applications accepted.

The University of Arizona, College of Fine Arts, School of Art, Program in History and Theory of Art, Tucson, AZ 85721. Offers PhD. *Entrance requirements:* Additional exam requirements/recommendations for international students: Required—TOEFL (minimum score 550 paper-based; 79 iBT).

University of Arkansas at Little Rock, Graduate School, College of Arts, Letters, and Sciences, Department of Art, Little Rock, AR 72204-1099. Offers art education (MA); art history (MA); studio art (MA). *Accreditation:* NASAD. *Program availability:* Part-time. *Degree requirements:* For master's, 4 foreign languages, oral exam, oral defense of thesis or exhibit. *Entrance requirements:* For master's, portfolio review or term paper evaluation, minimum GPA of 2.7.

The University of British Columbia, Faculty of Arts and Faculty of Graduate Studies, Department of Art History, Visual Art, and Theory, Vancouver, BC V6T 1Z2, Canada. Offers art history (MA, PhD); critical and curatorial studies (MA); visual art (MFA). *Degree requirements:* For master's, one foreign language, thesis, final exhibition (MFA, MA in critical and curatorial studies); for doctorate, 2 foreign languages, comprehensive exam, thesis/dissertation. *Entrance requirements:* For master's, bachelor's degree with minimum B+ average (MFA, MA in critical and curatorial studies), A- (MA in art history); for doctorate, master's degree with minimum A- average. Additional exam requirements/recommendations for international students: Required—TOEFL. Electronic applications accepted. *Expenses:* Contact institution. *Faculty research:* Conceptual art, Asian art, indigenous North American art, post-second war art, eighteenth- and nineteenth-century art, curatorial, digital art.

University of California, Berkeley, Graduate Division, College of Letters and Science, Department of History of Art, Berkeley, CA 94720-1500. Offers PhD. *Degree requirements:* For doctorate, 2 foreign languages, thesis/dissertation, qualifying exam. *Entrance requirements:* For doctorate, GRE General Test, minimum GPA of 3.0, 3 letters of recommendation. Additional exam requirements/recommendations for international students: Required—TOEFL (minimum score 570 paper-based; 90 iBT). Electronic applications accepted. *Faculty research:* Modernism, Italian Renaissance art and architecture, Gothic art and architecture, women artists' representations of the body, the body in ancient Greece.

University of California, Davis, Graduate Studies, Program in Art History, Davis, CA 95616. Offers MA. *Degree requirements:* For master's, thesis. *Entrance requirements:* For master's, GRE, minimum GPA of 3.0, writing sample. Additional exam requirements/recommendations for international students: Required—TOEFL (minimum score 550 paper-based). Electronic applications accepted.

University of California, Los Angeles, Graduate Division, College of Letters and Science, Department of Art History, Los Angeles, CA 90095. Offers MA, PhD. Terminal master's awarded for partial completion of doctoral program. *Degree requirements:* For master's, one foreign language, thesis; for doctorate, one foreign language, thesis/dissertation, oral and written qualifying exams. *Entrance requirements:* For doctorate, GRE General Test, master's degree; minimum undergraduate GPA of 3.0 (or its equivalent if letter grade system not used); thesis or research paper, language survey. Additional exam requirements/recommendations for international students: Required—TOEFL. Electronic applications accepted.

University of California, Riverside, Graduate Division, Department of Art History, Riverside, CA 92521-0102. Offers MA, PhD. *Program availability:* Part-time. *Degree requirements:* For master's, one foreign language, thesis. *Entrance requirements:* For master's, GRE General Test, sample of written work, minimum GPA of 3.2. Additional exam requirements/recommendations for international students: Required—TOEFL (minimum score 550 paper-based; 80 iBT). Electronic applications accepted. *Expenses:* Tuition, state resident: full-time $5746. Tuition, nonresident: full-time $10,780. Tuition and fees vary according to campus/location and program. *Faculty research:* Ancient, medieval, Renaissance, seventeenth and eighteenth century art; modern European art; contemporary art and theory; modern architecture and urbanism; history of photography.

University of California, San Diego, Graduate Division, Department of Visual Arts, La Jolla, CA 92093. Offers art history, theory, and criticism (PhD); visual arts (MFA). *Students:* 70 full-time (43 women), 3 part-time (all women). 162 applicants, 21% accepted, 19 enrolled. In 2017, 11 master's, 7 doctorates awarded. *Degree requirements:* For master's, comprehensive exam, thesis; for doctorate, 2 foreign languages, comprehensive exam, thesis/dissertation, reading knowledge of at least two of the foreign languages commonly used by scholars engaged in the advanced study in art history, theory, and criticism. *Entrance requirements:* For master's, electronic portfolio; for doctorate, GRE General Test, electronic portfolio. Additional exam requirements/recommendations for international students: Required—TOEFL (minimum score 550 paper-based; 80 iBT), IELTS (minimum score 7). *Application deadline:* For fall admission, 12/12 for domestic students. Application fee: $105 ($125 for international students). Electronic applications accepted. *Financial support:* Fellowships, research assistantships, teaching assistantships, career-related internships or fieldwork, scholarships/grants, and readerships available. Financial award applicants required to submit FAFSA. *Faculty research:* Contemporary art, ancient art, critical design, new media/software/hardware. *Unit head:* Jack Greenstein, Chair, 858-534-0418, E-mail: jgreenstein@ucsd.edu. *Application contact:* Katherine Edwards, Graduate Program Coordinator, 858-822-3882, E-mail: vis-grad@ucsd.edu.
Website: http://visarts.ucsd.edu/

University of California, Santa Barbara, Graduate Division, College of Letters and Sciences, Division of Humanities and Fine Arts, Department of History of Art and Architecture, Santa Barbara, CA 93106-2014. Offers art history (PhD), including art history, European medieval studies, feminist studies; MA/PhD. Terminal master's awarded for partial completion of doctoral program. *Degree requirements:* For doctorate, 2 foreign languages, comprehensive exam, thesis/dissertation. *Entrance requirements:* For doctorate, GRE. Additional exam requirements/recommendations for international students: Required—TOEFL (minimum score 550 paper-based; 80 iBT), IELTS (minimum score 7). Electronic applications accepted. *Faculty research:* History of architecture, Renaissance-Italian, Baroque, American, Chinese, Japanese, contemporary, Northern Renaissance.

University of Chicago, Division of the Humanities, Department of Art History, Chicago, IL 60637. Offers PhD. *Students:* 47 full-time (37 women); includes 6 minority (1 Black or African American, non-Hispanic/Latino; 3 Asian, non-Hispanic/Latino; 2 Hispanic/Latino), 17 international. Average age 30. 149 applicants, 7% accepted, 6 enrolled. In 2017, 11 doctorates awarded. Terminal master's awarded for partial completion of doctoral program. *Degree requirements:* For doctorate, variable foreign language requirement, comprehensive exam, thesis/dissertation. *Entrance requirements:* For doctorate, GRE General Test, 15-20 page writing sample, statement of purpose, 3 letters of recommendation, transcripts for all previous degrees and institutions attended. Additional exam requirements/recommendations for international students: Required—TOEFL (minimum score 104 iBT), IELTS (minimum score 7). *Application deadline:* For fall admission, 12/15 for domestic and international students. Application fee: $90. Electronic applications accepted. *Financial support:* In 2017–18, fellowships with full tuition reimbursements (averaging $27,000 per year) were awarded; teaching assistantships with full tuition reimbursements, Federal Work-Study, institutionally sponsored loans, scholarships/grants, and health care benefits also available. Financial award application deadline: 12/15. *Faculty research:* Global ancient art history, Asian art history, modern and contemporary art history, Latin American art history, built environment. *Unit head:* Christine Mehring, Chair, 773-702-0278, E-mail: arth-admissions@lists.uchicago.edu. *Application contact:* Michael Beetley, Assistant Dean of Students, Admissions, 773-702-1552, Fax: 773-834-9148, E-mail: humanitiesadmissions@uchicago.edu.
Website: http://arthistory.uchicago.edu

University of Chicago, Division of the Humanities, Master of Arts Program in the Humanities, Chicago, IL 60637. Offers art history (MA); cinema and media studies (MA); classic languages (MA); comparative literature (MA); creative writing (MA); cultural policy studies (MA); digital humanities (MA); East Asian languages and civilizations (MA); English language and literature (MA); gender and sexuality studies (MA); Germanic studies (MA); linguistics (MA); music (MA); near Eastern languages and civilizations (MA); philosophy (MA); poetics (MA); race, politics and culture (MA); Romance languages and literatures (MA); Slavic languages and literatures (MA); South Asian languages and civilizations (MA); theater and performance studies (MA). *Students:* 95 full-time (50 women), 6 part-time (4 women); includes 22 minority (1 Black or African American, non-Hispanic/Latino; 10 Asian, non-Hispanic/Latino; 11 Hispanic/Latino), 19 international. Average age 26. 708 applicants, 75% accepted, 101 enrolled. In 2017, 91 master's awarded. *Degree requirements:* For master's, thesis. *Entrance requirements:* For master's, GRE General Test, 10-15 page writing sample, statement of purpose, 3 letters of recommendation, transcripts for all previous degrees and institutions attended. Additional exam requirements/recommendations for international students: Required—TOEFL (minimum score 104 iBT), IELTS (minimum score 7). *Application deadline:* For fall admission, 1/3 priority date for domestic and international students. Application fee: $90. Electronic applications accepted. *Expenses:* Contact institution. *Financial support:* In 2017–18, fellowships with partial tuition reimbursements (averaging $12,000 per year) were awarded; Federal Work-Study, institutionally sponsored loans, scholarships/grants, and tuition waivers (partial) also available. Financial award application deadline: 4/30. *Unit head:* Thomas Christensen, Director, 773-834-1201, Fax: 773-834-7526, E-mail: ma-humanities@uchicago.edu. *Application contact:* Michael Beetley, Assistant Dean of Students for Admissions, 773-834-1552, E-mail: humanitiesadmissions@uchicago.edu.
Website: http://maph.uchicago.edu/

University of Cincinnati, Graduate School, College of Design, Architecture, Art, and Planning, School of Art, Program in Art History, Cincinnati, OH 45221. Offers MA. *Accreditation:* NASAD. *Program availability:* Part-time. *Degree requirements:* For master's, one foreign language, comprehensive exam, thesis. Electronic applications accepted. *Expenses: Tuition, area resident:* Full-time $14,468. Tuition, state resident: full-time $14,968; part-time $754 per credit hour. Tuition, nonresident: full-time $24,210; part-time $1311 per credit hour. *International tuition:* $26,460 full-time. *Required fees:* $3958; $84 per credit hour. One-time fee: $85 full-time. Tuition and fees vary according to course load, degree level and program.

University of Colorado Boulder, Graduate School, College of Arts and Sciences, Department of Art and Art History, Boulder, CO 80309. Offers art history (MA), including contemporary art criticism, early twentieth-century art, nineteenth-century art, Russian and Soviet art; ceramics (MFA); photography and media arts (MFA); printmaking (MFA); sculpture (MFA). *Faculty:* 23 full-time (10 women). *Students:* 42 full-time (30 women), 3 part-time (2 women); includes 7 minority (4 Hispanic/Latino; 3 Two or more races, non-Hispanic/Latino). Average age 29. 152 applicants, 18% accepted, 15 enrolled. In 2017, 16 master's awarded. Terminal master's awarded for partial completion of doctoral program. *Degree requirements:* For master's, variable foreign language requirement, comprehensive exam, thesis (for some programs). *Entrance requirements:* For master's, GRE General Test, minimum undergraduate GPA of 3.0, portfolio. *Application deadline:* For fall admission, 1/10 for domestic students; for spring admission, 12/1 for domestic students. Application fee: $60 ($80 for international students). Electronic applications accepted. Application fee is waived when completed online. *Financial support:* In 2017–18, 140 students received support, including 43 fellowships (averaging $2,068 per year), 41 teaching assistantships with full and partial tuition reimbursements available (averaging $26,884 per year); institutionally sponsored loans, scholarships/grants, health care benefits, and unspecified assistantships also available. Financial award application deadline: 2/15; financial award applicants required to submit FAFSA. *Faculty research:* Visual arts; sculpture; fine arts; installation art; mixed-media art. *Total annual research expenditures:* $17,000. *Application contact:* E-mail: finearts@colorado.edu. Website: http://www.colorado.edu/arts

University of Delaware, College of Arts and Sciences, Department of Art History, Newark, DE 19716. Offers MA, PhD. *Program availability:* Part-time. *Degree requirements:* For master's, one foreign language, thesis; for doctorate, 2 foreign languages, comprehensive exam, thesis/dissertation. *Entrance requirements:* For master's and doctorate, GRE General Test, writing sample. Additional exam requirements/recommendations for international students: Required—TOEFL. Electronic applications accepted. *Faculty research:* Art of Europe and the United States, art theory, vernacular architecture, medieval manuscripts, African art and architecture.

University of Denver, Division of Arts, Humanities and Social Sciences, School of Art and Art History, Denver, CO 80208. Offers art history (MA); museum studies (MA). *Accreditation:* NASAD. *Program availability:* Part-time. *Faculty:* 16 full-time (10 women), 8 part-time/adjunct (7 women). *Students:* 5 full-time (4 women), 14 part-time (all women); includes 1 minority (Hispanic/Latino), 1 international. Average age 24. 33 applicants, 79% accepted, 13 enrolled. In 2017, 7 master's awarded. *Degree requirements:* For master's, one foreign language, comprehensive exam, research paper or thesis project. *Entrance requirements:* For master's, GRE General Test, transcripts, personal statement, writing sample, three letters of recommendation. Additional exam requirements/recommendations for international students: Required—TOEFL (minimum score 550 paper-based; 80 iBT). *Application deadline:* For fall admission, 1/31 priority date for domestic and international students. Applications are processed on a rolling basis. Application fee: $65. Electronic applications accepted. *Expenses:* $31,935 per year full-time. *Financial support:* In 2017–18, 19 students received support. Research assistantships with tuition reimbursements available, teaching assistantships with tuition reimbursements available, career-related internships or fieldwork, Federal Work-Study, institutionally sponsored loans, scholarships/grants, and unspecified assistantships available. Support available to part-time students. Financial award application deadline: 2/15; financial award applicants required to submit FAFSA. *Faculty research:* Abstract expressionist women painters, Chichen Itza, the cult of St. Ursula, rock poster art of the psychedelic era. *Unit head:* Catherine Chauvin, Associate Professor and Director, 303-871-2367, Fax: 303-871-4112, E-mail: catherine.chauvin@du.edu. *Application contact:* Jason Kellermeyer, Coordinator of Academic Programs, 303-871-2846, E-mail: jason.kellermeyer@du.edu. Website: http://www.du.edu/ahss/art/index.html

University of Florida, Graduate School, College of The Arts, School of Art and Art History, Gainesville, FL 32611. Offers art (MA), including digital arts and sciences; art education (MA); art history (MA, PhD); museology (MA), including historic preservation. *Accreditation:* NASAD. *Program availability:* Online learning. *Degree requirements:* For master's, project or thesis (MFA); 1 foreign language (MA in art history); for doctorate, 2 foreign languages, comprehensive exam, thesis/dissertation. *Entrance requirements:* For master's, GRE General Test, portfolio (MFA), writing sample (MA), minimum GPA 3.0; for doctorate, GRE General Test, minimum GPA of 3.0. Additional exam requirements/recommendations for international students: Required—TOEFL (minimum score 550 paper-based; 80 iBT), IELTS (minimum score 6). Electronic applications accepted. *Faculty research:* Studio production, art historical studies of style context.

University of Georgia, Franklin College of Arts and Sciences, Lamar Dodd School of Art, Athens, GA 30602. Offers art (MFA, PhD); art history (MA). *Accreditation:* NASAD (one or more programs are accredited). *Degree requirements:* For doctorate, one foreign language, thesis/dissertation. *Entrance requirements:* For master's and doctorate, GRE General Test. Electronic applications accepted.

University of Hawaii at Manoa, Office of Graduate Education, College of Arts and Humanities, Department of Art and Art History, Program in Art History, Honolulu, HI 96822. Offers MA. *Program availability:* Part-time. *Entrance requirements:* Additional exam requirements/recommendations for international students: Required—TOEFL (minimum score 600 paper-based; 100 iBT); Recommended—IELTS.

University of Houston, Kathrine G. McGovern College of the Arts, School of Art, Houston, TX 77204. Offers art history (MA); interdisciplinary practice and emerging forms (MFA); painting (MFA); studio art (MFA). *Entrance requirements:* For master's, baccalaureate degree, portfolio. Electronic applications accepted. *Faculty research:* Painting, sculpture, photography/installation/video, graphic design and typography, art history (Pre-Columbian to Surrealism).

University of Illinois at Chicago, College of Architecture, Design and the Arts, School of Art and Art History, Chicago, IL 60607-7128. Offers art history (MA); electronic visualization (MFA); museum and exhibition studies (MA); new media arts (MFA). *Program availability:* Part-time, evening/weekend. Terminal master's awarded for partial completion of doctoral program. *Degree requirements:* For master's, one foreign language, thesis or alternative; for doctorate, thesis/dissertation. *Entrance requirements:* For master's, GRE General Test, minimum GPA of 2.75, 3 letters of recommendation; for doctorate, GRE General Test, MA in art history or equivalent, minimum GPA of 3.0. Additional exam requirements/recommendations for international students: Required—TOEFL. Electronic applications accepted. *Expenses:* Contact institution. *Faculty research:* Modern painting and sculpture, history of architecture, city planning and design, history of photography.

University of Illinois at Urbana–Champaign, Graduate College, College of Fine and Applied Arts, School of Art and Design, Program in Art History, Champaign, IL 61820. Offers MA, PhD. *Accreditation:* NASAD.

The University of Iowa, Graduate College, College of Liberal Arts and Sciences, School of Art and Art History, Program in Art History, Iowa City, IA 52242-1316. Offers MA, PhD. *Faculty:* 9 full-time (4 women). *Students:* 23 full-time (20 women), 1 (woman) part-time; includes 2 minority (both Hispanic/Latino), 2 international. 16 applicants, 44% accepted, 3 enrolled. In 2017, 1 master's, 3 doctorates awarded. *Degree requirements:* For master's, one foreign language, thesis or alternative, substantial paper and exam; for doctorate, 2 foreign languages, comprehensive exam, thesis/dissertation, final exams. *Entrance requirements:* For master's, GRE General Test; for doctorate, GRE General Test, MA in art history. Additional exam requirements/recommendations for international students: Required—TOEFL (minimum score 550 paper-based; 81 iBT). *Application deadline:* For fall admission, 12/15 for domestic and international students. Application fee: $60 ($100 for international students). Electronic applications accepted. *Financial support:* In 2017–18, 19 students received support, including 4 research assistantships with full and partial tuition reimbursements available (averaging $9,510 per year), 17 teaching assistantships with full and partial tuition reimbursements available (averaging $9,510 per year); fellowships, career-related internships or fieldwork, Federal Work-Study, institutionally sponsored loans, scholarships/grants, health care benefits, and unspecified assistantships also available. Support available to part-time students. Financial award application deadline: 12/15. *Faculty research:* African (Oceanic), Asian, ancient (3000 B.C.-300 A.D.), medieval, Renaissance, Baroque, eighteenth- and nineteenth-century European, American (includes Pre-Columbian, Native American, and African American), and modern/contemporary art history. *Unit head:* Dorothy Johnson, Area Head for Art History, 319-335-1784, E-mail: dorothy-johnson@uiowa.edu. *Application contact:* Laura Jorgensen, Graduate Program Coordinator, 319-335-1758, Fax: 319-335-1774, E-mail: art@uiowa.edu.

The University of Kansas, Graduate Studies, College of Liberal Arts and Sciences, The Kress Foundation Department of Art History, Lawrence, KS 66045. Offers MA, PhD, PhD/MA. *Program availability:* Part-time. *Students:* 45 full-time (40 women), 3 part-time (all women); includes 2 minority (1 Asian, non-Hispanic/Latino; 1 Two or more races, non-Hispanic/Latino), 17 international. Average age 30. 46 applicants, 76% accepted, 9 enrolled. In 2017, 12 master's, 4 doctorates awarded. Terminal master's awarded for partial completion of doctoral program. *Entrance requirements:* For master's and doctorate, GRE, resume or curriculum vitae, one-page statement of educational and career objectives, writing sample (preferably an art history paper), copy or scan of official transcripts. Additional exam requirements/recommendations for international students: Required—TOEFL. *Application deadline:* For fall admission, 1/1 for domestic and international students. Application fee: $65 ($85 for international students). Electronic applications accepted. *Financial support:* Fellowships, research assistantships, teaching assistantships, career-related internships or fieldwork, scholarships/grants, health care benefits, and unspecified assistantships available. Financial award application deadline: 1/1. *Faculty research:* American, Asian, European, and modern art; Medieval/Renaissance. *Unit head:* David Cateforis, Chair, 785-864-1491, E-mail: dcat@ku.edu. *Application contact:* Lisa Cloar, Graduate Admissions Contact, 785-864-4713, Fax: 785-864-5091, E-mail: arthist@ku.edu. Website: http://arthistory.ku.edu/

University of Kentucky, Graduate School, College of Fine Arts, Program in Art History, Lexington, KY 40506-0032. Offers MA. *Accreditation:* NASAD. *Degree requirements:* For master's, 2 foreign languages, comprehensive exam, thesis. *Entrance requirements:* For master's, GRE General Test, minimum undergraduate GPA of 2.75. Additional exam requirements/recommendations for international students: Required—TOEFL (minimum score 550 paper-based). Electronic applications accepted. *Faculty research:* Northern European prints and drawings, nineteenth century French painting and drawing, Roman sarcophagus sculpture, manuscript illumination, history and theory of photography.

University of Louisville, Graduate School, College of Arts and Sciences, Department of Fine Arts, Louisville, KY 40292. Offers art history (MA, PhD); curatorial studies (MA); studio art (MFA), including design. *Program availability:* Online learning. *Faculty:* 23 full-time (9 women), 6 part-time/adjunct (3 women). *Students:* 24 full-time (17 women), 1 (woman) part-time; includes 3 minority (1 Asian, non-Hispanic/Latino; 1 Hispanic/Latino; 1 Two or more races, non-Hispanic/Latino). Average age 35. 16 applicants, 63% accepted, 7 enrolled. In 2017, 5 master's awarded. *Degree requirements:* For master's, one foreign language, thesis. *Entrance requirements:* For doctorate, MA. Additional exam requirements/recommendations for international students: Required—TOEFL (minimum score 550 paper-based; 80 iBT), IELTS (minimum score 6.5). *Application deadline:* For fall admission, 3/1 priority date for domestic and international students. Application fee: $65. *Expenses:* $12,500. *Financial support:* In 2017–18, 7 teaching assistantships with full tuition reimbursements (averaging $14,000 per year) were awarded; research assistantships, scholarships/grants, health care benefits, and unspecified assistantships also available. Financial award application deadline: 3/1. *Faculty research:* Sustainability and environmental design, media theory, cross cultural and critical theories, Installation, urban and public art. *Total annual research expenditures:* $75,000. *Unit head:* Dr. Scott L. Massey, Associate Professor and Chair, 502-852-6794, Fax: 502-852-6791, E-mail: s.massey@louisville.edu. *Application contact:* Theresa Berbet, Senior Advisor, 502-852-6147, Fax: 502-852-6791, E-mail: tberbet@louisville.edu. Website: http://art.louisville.edu

The University of Manchester, School of Arts, Histories and Cultures, Manchester, United Kingdom. Offers anthropology, media and performance (PhD); applied theatre professional (PhD); archaeology (PhD); art history and visual studies (PhD); arts management and cultural policy (PhD); classics and ancient history (PhD); composition (PhD); creative writing (PhD); drama (PhD); economic and social history (PhD); electroacoustic composition (PhD); English and American studies (PhD); history (PhD); humanitarianism and conflict response (PhD); museology (PhD); music (PhD); musicology (PhD); religions and theology (PhD).

University of Maryland, College Park, Academic Affairs, College of Arts and Humanities, Department of Art History and Archaeology, College Park, MD 20742. Offers art history (MA, PhD). *Degree requirements:* For master's, one foreign language, thesis, oral exam; for doctorate, 2 foreign languages, thesis/dissertation, oral exam. *Entrance requirements:* For master's, GRE General Test, minimum GPA of 3.0, writing sample, 3 letters of recommendation. Additional exam requirements/recommendations for international students: Required—TOEFL. Electronic applications accepted. *Faculty research:* Western, African, pre-Columbian, American, and East Asian art.

University of Massachusetts Amherst, Graduate School, College of Humanities and Fine Arts, Department of the History of Art and Architecture, Amherst, MA 01003. Offers MA. *Accreditation:* NASAD. *Program availability:* Part-time. *Degree requirements:* For master's, comprehensive exam, journal-level knowledge of French, German, or Italian. *Entrance requirements:* For master's, GRE General Test, 7-20 page writing sample. Additional exam requirements/recommendations for international students: Required—TOEFL (minimum score 550 paper-based; 80 iBT), IELTS (minimum score 6.5). Electronic applications accepted.

University of Massachusetts Dartmouth, Graduate School, College of Visual and Performing Arts, Department of Art Education, Art History and Media Studies, North Dartmouth, MA 02747-2300. Offers MAE. *Accreditation:* NASAD. *Program availability:* Part-time. *Faculty:* 7 full-time (6 women), 1 (woman) part-time/adjunct. *Students:* 4 full-time (all women), 22 part-time (18 women); includes 2 minority (1 Asian, non-Hispanic/Latino; 1 Hispanic/Latino). Average age 32. 11 applicants, 100% accepted, 9 enrolled. In 2017, 2 master's awarded. *Degree requirements:* For master's, thesis. *Entrance requirements:* For master's, MTEL (Communication Literacy and Visual Arts), statement of purpose (minimum of 300 words), resume, 2 letters of recommendation, official

transcripts, portfolio (20 images representing applicant's art work, process of thinking, implementation of concepts and studio production). Additional exam requirements/ recommendations for international students: Required—TOEFL (minimum score 533 paper-based; 72 iBT), IELTS (minimum score 6). *Application deadline:* For fall admission, 8/1 priority date for domestic students, 7/1 priority date for international students; for spring admission, 10/15 priority date for domestic students, 9/15 priority date for international students. Application fee: $60. Electronic applications accepted. *Expenses:* Tuition, state resident: full-time $15,449; part-time $643.71 per credit. Tuition, nonresident: full-time $27,880; part-time $1161.67 per credit. *Required fees:* $405; $25.88 per credit. Tuition and fees vary according to course load and reciprocity agreements. *Financial support:* In 2017–18, 1 teaching assistantship (averaging $4,000 per year) was awarded; tuition waivers (partial) and unspecified assistantships also available. Support available to part-time students. Financial award application deadline: 3/1; financial award applicants required to submit FAFSA. *Faculty research:* Contemporary art, design and architectural history, curatorial studies, film studies, theory of photography. *Unit head:* Cathy Smilan, Graduate Program Director, 508-910-6594, Fax: 508-999-8901, E-mail: csmilan@umassd.edu. *Application contact:* Steven Briggs, Director of Marketing and Recruitment for Graduate Studies, 508-999-8604, Fax: 508-999-8183, E-mail: graduate@umassd.edu.
Website: http://www.umassd.edu/cvpa/programs

University of Memphis, Graduate School, College of Communication and Fine Arts, Department of Art, Memphis, TN 38152. Offers art history (MA), including Egyptian art and archaeology, general art history; ceramics (MFA); graphic design (MFA); museum studies (Graduate Certificate); painting (MFA); printmaking/photography (MFA); sculpture (MFA). *Accreditation:* NASAD (one or more programs are accredited). *Program availability:* Part-time. *Faculty:* 18 full-time (7 women), 2 part-time/adjunct (1 woman). *Students:* 21 full-time (17 women), 5 part-time (all women); includes 8 minority (2 Black or African American, non-Hispanic/Latino; 1 Asian, non-Hispanic/Latino; 4 Hispanic/Latino; 1 Two or more races, non-Hispanic/Latino). Average age 29. 11 applicants, 73% accepted, 5 enrolled. In 2017, 5 master's, 5 other advanced degrees awarded. *Degree requirements:* For master's, 2 foreign languages, comprehensive exam, thesis, image identification exam, qualifying exam; for Graduate Certificate, internship. *Entrance requirements:* For master's, GRE General Test or MAT, portfolio (MFA), letter of intent, sample of undergraduate writing, two letters of recommendation; for Graduate Certificate, three letters of recommendation, letter of intent. *Application deadline:* For fall admission, 2/15 for domestic students; for spring admission, 11/1 for domestic students. Applications are processed on a rolling basis. Application fee: $35 ($60 for international students). *Expenses:* Contact institution. *Financial support:* In 2017–18, 36 students received support, including 15 research assistantships with full tuition reimbursements available (averaging $11,600 per year); teaching assistantships with full tuition reimbursements available, Federal Work-Study, scholarships/grants, and unspecified assistantships also available. Financial award application deadline: 2/1; financial award applicants required to submit FAFSA. *Faculty research:* Online collaborative learning, advanced art history studies, electronic publishing/design, studio arts, architectural studies. *Unit head:* Prof. Richard Lou, Chair, 901-678-2217, Fax: 901-678-2735, E-mail: ralou@memphis.edu. *Application contact:* Niles Wallice, Coordinator of Graduate Studies, 901-678-4899.
Website: http://memphis.edu/art/

University of Miami, Graduate School, College of Arts and Sciences, Department of Art and Art History, Coral Gables, FL 33124. Offers art history (MA); ceramics/glass (MFA); graphic design/multimedia (MFA); painting (MFA); photography/digital imaging (MFA); printmaking (MFA); sculpture (MFA). *Program availability:* Part-time. *Degree requirements:* For master's, variable foreign language requirement, thesis, exhibit (MFA), comprehensive exam (MA). *Entrance requirements:* For master's, GRE General Test (MA), research paper (MA), slide portfolio (MFA). Additional exam requirements/ recommendations for international students: Required—TOEFL. Electronic applications accepted. *Faculty research:* Installation art, public art.

University of Michigan, Rackham Graduate School, College of Literature, Science, and the Arts, Department of History of Art, Ann Arbor, MI 48109-1357. Offers PhD. *Faculty:* 22 full-time (12 women), 3 part-time/adjunct (2 women). *Students:* 33 full-time (22 women); includes 6 minority (5 Asian, non-Hispanic/Latino; 1 Hispanic/Latino). Average age 26. 81 applicants, 7% accepted, 4 enrolled. In 2017, 3 doctorates awarded. *Degree requirements:* For doctorate, 2 foreign languages, thesis/dissertation, preliminary examinations, oral defense of written dissertation. *Entrance requirements:* For doctorate, GRE General Test. Additional exam requirements/recommendations for international students: Recommended—TOEFL. *Application deadline:* For fall admission, 12/15 for domestic and international students. Application fee: $65 ($75 for international students). Electronic applications accepted. *Expenses:* $45,484. *Financial support:* In 2017–18, 33 students received support, including 19 fellowships with full tuition reimbursements available (averaging $20,000 per year), 25 teaching assistantships with full tuition reimbursements available (averaging $20,400 per year); career-related internships or fieldwork, scholarships/grants, health care benefits, and research funding also available. Financial award application deadline: 1/1. *Faculty research:* Islamic arts and cultures, Medieval Mediterranean and Byzantine arts and cultures, Asian and South Asian arts and cultures, Early Modern and Medieval Europe arts and cultures, art and architecture in Americas and Europe. *Unit head:* Elizabeth Sears, Chair, 734-764-5400, Fax: 734-647-4121, E-mail: esears@umich.edu. *Application contact:* Debbie L. Fitch, Graduate Student Services Coordinator, 734-764-5401, Fax: 734-647-4121, E-mail: dlfitch@umich.edu.
Website: http://www.lsa.umich.edu/histart/

University of Michigan, Rackham Graduate School, College of Literature, Science, and the Arts, Interdepartmental Program in Classical Art and Archaeology, Ann Arbor, MI 48109-1390. Offers MA, PhD. *Degree requirements:* For doctorate, 4 foreign languages, comprehensive exam, thesis/dissertation, ancient history exam, qualifying exam, preliminary exam. *Entrance requirements:* For doctorate, GRE General Test. Additional exam requirements/recommendations for international students: Required—TOEFL (minimum score 560 paper-based; 84 iBT). Electronic applications accepted. *Expenses:* Tuition, state resident: full-time $22,368; part-time $1201 per credit hour. Tuition, nonresident: full-time $45,156; part-time $2467 per credit hour. *Required fees:* $376 per term. Tuition and fees vary according to course load, degree level and program. *Faculty research:* Prehistoric art and archaeology, Greek art and archaeology, Roman art and archaeology, Near Eastern art and archaeology, archaeological theory and methodology.

University of Minnesota, Twin Cities Campus, Graduate School, College of Liberal Arts, Department of Art History, Minneapolis, MN 55455. Offers MA, PhD. *Faculty:* 7 full-time (4 women). *Students:* 22 full-time (18 women); includes 4 minority (2 Black or African American, non-Hispanic/Latino; 1 Hispanic/Latino; 1 Two or more races, non-Hispanic/Latino), 3 international. Average age 27. 30 applicants, 27% accepted, 3 enrolled. In 2017, 3 master's awarded. Terminal master's awarded for partial completion of doctoral program. *Degree requirements:* For master's, one foreign language, comprehensive exam, thesis or alternative; for doctorate, 2 foreign languages, comprehensive exam, thesis/dissertation. *Entrance requirements:* For master's, GRE, 3 letters of recommendation, writing sample, statement of purpose; for doctorate, transcripts, 3 letters of recommendation, writing sample. Additional exam requirements/ recommendations for international students: Required—TOEFL (minimum score 550 paper-based; 79 iBT). *Application deadline:* For fall admission, 1/1 for domestic and international students. Application fee: $75 ($95 for international students). Electronic applications accepted. *Financial support:* In 2017–18, 19 students received support, including 4 fellowships with full tuition reimbursements available (averaging $25,000 per year), 2 research assistantships with full tuition reimbursements available (averaging $19,500 per year), 13 teaching assistantships with full tuition reimbursements available (averaging $19,500 per year); career-related internships or fieldwork, institutionally sponsored loans, scholarships/grants, health care benefits, and unspecified assistantships also available. Financial award application deadline: 1/1. *Faculty research:* Contemporary art, North American art, Early Modern Europe, Islamic art, South Asian art. *Unit head:* Prof. Michael Gaudio, Chair, 612-624-4500, Fax: 612-626-8679, E-mail: gaudio@umn.edu. *Application contact:* Sara Enfield, Graduate Program Coordinator, 612-624-4500, Fax: 612-626-8679, E-mail: arthist@umn.edu.
Website: https://cla.umn.edu/art-history

University of Minnesota, Twin Cities Campus, Graduate School, College of Liberal Arts, Department of Classical and Near Eastern Studies, Minneapolis, MN 55455-0213. Offers ancient and medieval art and archaeology (MA, PhD); classics (MA, PhD); Greek (MA, PhD); Latin (MA, PhD); religions in antiquity (MA). *Program availability:* Part-time. Terminal master's awarded for partial completion of doctoral program. *Degree requirements:* For master's, 2 foreign languages, comprehensive exam, thesis or alternative; for doctorate, variable foreign language requirement, comprehensive exam, thesis/dissertation. *Entrance requirements:* For master's and doctorate, GRE, 3 letters of recommendation, writing sample, copies of transcripts, personal statement. Additional exam requirements/recommendations for international students: Required—TOEFL. Electronic applications accepted. *Faculty research:* Greek and Latin literature, religions in antiquity, ancient Near East.

University of Missouri, Office of Research and Graduate Studies, College of Arts and Science, Department of Art History and Archaeology, Columbia, MO 65211. Offers MA, PhD. Terminal master's awarded for partial completion of doctoral program. *Degree requirements:* For master's, 2 foreign languages, thesis; for doctorate, 2 foreign languages, thesis/dissertation. *Entrance requirements:* For master's, GRE General Test (minimum score 1000 verbal and quantitative, 4.5 analytical), minimum GPA of 3.0, 3.3 in major field; at least 3 semesters in appropriate foreign language; for doctorate, GRE General Test, minimum GPA of 3.0; MA or equivalent in art history or classical archaeology; master's thesis. Additional exam requirements/recommendations for international students: Required—TOEFL (minimum score 500 paper-based; 61 iBT), IELTS (minimum score 5.5). Electronic applications accepted. *Faculty research:* Classical Mediterranean archaeology, medieval and Renaissance art, art and architecture of modern Europe and the Americas.

University of Montana, Graduate School, College of Visual and Performing Arts, School of Art, Missoula, MT 59812. Offers fine arts (MA), including art, art history; photography (MFA). *Accreditation:* NASAD (one or more programs are accredited). *Degree requirements:* For master's, thesis exhibit. *Entrance requirements:* For master's, GRE General Test, portfolio.

University of Nebraska–Lincoln, Graduate College, College of Fine and Performing Arts, Department of Art and Art History, Lincoln, NE 68588. Offers art history (MA); studio art (MFA). *Accreditation:* NASAD. *Degree requirements:* For master's, thesis. *Entrance requirements:* For master's, slide portfolio. Additional exam requirements/ recommendations for international students: Required—TOEFL (minimum score 550 paper-based). Electronic applications accepted. *Faculty research:* Classical archaeology, contemporary art, printmaking, photography.

University of New Mexico, Graduate Studies, College of Fine Arts, Program in Art History, Albuquerque, NM 87131. Offers art history (MA); art of the Americas (MA); history of architecture (PhD); history of graphic arts (PhD); history of photography (PhD); modern Latin American art (PhD); Native American art (PhD); Pre-Columbian art and architecture (PhD); Spanish colonial art (PhD). *Program availability:* Part-time. *Faculty:* 7 full-time (5 women). *Students:* 7 full-time (all women), 18 part-time (15 women); includes 8 minority (2 American Indian or Alaska Native, non-Hispanic/Latino; 5 Hispanic/Latino; 1 Two or more races, non-Hispanic/Latino), 2 international. Average age 41. 21 applicants, 33% accepted, 5 enrolled. In 2017, 5 master's, 1 doctorate awarded. *Degree requirements:* For master's, one foreign language, comprehensive exam (for some programs), thesis, symposium; for doctorate, 2 foreign languages, comprehensive exam, thesis/dissertation, symposium. *Entrance requirements:* Additional exam requirements/recommendations for international students: Required—TOEFL (minimum score 550 paper-based), IELTS (minimum score 6). *Application deadline:* For fall admission, 1/15 for domestic students; for spring admission, 1/15 for domestic students. Application fee: $50. Electronic applications accepted. *Financial support:* Fellowships, research assistantships, teaching assistantships with partial tuition reimbursements, Federal Work-Study, institutionally sponsored loans, scholarships/grants, health care benefits, and unspecified assistantships available. Support available to part-time students. Financial award application deadline: 3/1; financial award applicants required to submit FAFSA. *Faculty research:* Native American, modern Latin American, pre-Columbian, architectural, American, medieval, Spanish Colonial, and Latin American art; history of photography. *Unit head:* Prof. Mary Tsiongas, Chair, 505-277-5861, Fax: 505-277-5955, E-mail: tsiongas@unm.edu. *Application contact:* Kat Heatherington, Graduate Advisor, 505-277-6672, Fax: 505-277-5955, E-mail: art255@unm.edu.
Website: http://art.unm.edu/

The University of North Carolina at Chapel Hill, Graduate School, College of Arts and Sciences, Department of Art, Program in Art History, Chapel Hill, NC 27599. Offers MA, PhD. *Degree requirements:* For master's, one foreign language, comprehensive exam, thesis; for doctorate, one foreign language, comprehensive exam, thesis/dissertation. *Entrance requirements:* For master's and doctorate, GRE General Test, minimum GPA of 3.0.

University of Northern Colorado, Graduate School, College of Performing and Visual Arts, School of Art and Design, Greeley, CO 80639. Offers art education (MA); art history (MA); studio art (MA). *Accreditation:* NASAD. *Program availability:* Part-time. *Degree requirements:* For master's, comprehensive exam, thesis. *Entrance requirements:* For master's, GRE General Test, portfolio, 3 letters of recommendation, minimum undergraduate GPA of 3.0. Electronic applications accepted.

University of North Texas, Robert B. Toulouse School of Graduate Studies, Denton, TX 76203-5459. Offers accounting (MS); applied anthropology (MA, MS); applied behavior analysis (Certificate); applied geography (MA); applied technology and performance improvement (M Ed, MS); art education (MA); art history (MA); art museum education (Certificate); arts leadership (Certificate); audiology (Au D); behavior analysis (MS); behavioral science (PhD); biochemistry and molecular biology (MS); biology (MA, MS); biomedical engineering (MS); business analysis (MS); chemistry (MS); clinical health psychology (PhD); communication studies (MA, MS); computer engineering (MS); computer science (MS); counseling (M Ed, MS), including clinical mental health counseling (MS), college and university counseling, elementary school counseling, secondary school counseling; creative writing (MA); criminal justice (MS); curriculum

and instruction (M Ed); decision sciences (MBA); design (MA, MFA), including fashion design (MFA), innovation studies, interior design (MFA); early childhood studies (MS); economics (MS); educational leadership (M Ed, Ed D); educational psychology (MS, PhD), including family studies (MS), gifted and talented (MS), human development (MS), learning and cognition (MS), research, measurement and evaluation (MS); electrical engineering (MS); emergency management (MPA); engineering technology (MS); English (MA); English as a second language (MA); environmental science (MS); finance (MBA, MS); financial management (MPA); French (MA); health services management (MBA); higher education (M Ed, Ed D); history (MA, MS); hospitality management (MS); human resources management (MPA); information science (MS); information systems (PhD); information technologies (MBA); interdisciplinary studies (MA, MS); international studies (MA); international sustainable tourism (MS); jazz studies (MM); journalism (MA, MJ, Graduate Certificate), including interactive and virtual digital communication (Graduate Certificate), narrative journalism (Graduate Certificate), public relations (Graduate Certificate); kinesiology (MS); linguistics (MA); local government management (MPA); logistics (PhD); logistics and supply chain management (MBA); long-term care, senior housing, and aging services (MA); management (PhD); marketing (MBA); mathematics (MA, MS); mechanical and energy engineering (MS, PhD); music (MA), including ethnomusicology, music theory, musicology, performance; music composition (PhD); music education (MM Ed, PhD); nonprofit management (MPA); operations and supply chain management (MBA); performance (MM, DMA); philosophy (MA); political science (MA); professional and technical communication (MA); radio, television and film (MA, MFA); rehabilitation counseling (Certificate); sociology (MA); Spanish (MA); special education (M Ed); speech-language pathology (MA); strategic management (MBA); studio art (MFA); teaching (M Ed); MBA/MS. *Program availability:* Part-time, evening/weekend, online learning. Terminal master's awarded for partial completion of doctoral program. *Degree requirements:* For master's, variable foreign language requirement, comprehensive exam (for some programs), thesis (for some programs); for doctorate, variable foreign language requirement, comprehensive exam (for some programs), thesis/dissertation; for other advanced degree, variable foreign language requirement, comprehensive exam (for some programs). *Entrance requirements:* For master's and doctorate, GRE, GMAT. Additional exam requirements/recommendations for international students: Required—TOEFL (minimum score 550 paper-based; 79 iBT). Electronic applications accepted.

University of Notre Dame, Graduate School, College of Arts and Letters, Division of Humanities, Department of Art, Art History, and Design, Notre Dame, IN 46556. Offers art history (MA); design (MFA), including graphic design, industrial design; studio art (MFA), including ceramics, painting, photography, printmaking, sculpture. *Accreditation:* NASAD. *Degree requirements:* For master's, comprehensive exam (for some programs), thesis. *Entrance requirements:* For master's, GRE General Test, minimum GPA of 3.0. Additional exam requirements/recommendations for international students: Required—TOEFL (minimum score 600 paper-based; 80 iBT). Electronic applications accepted. *Faculty research:* Studio art practice in ceramics, printing, photography, printmaking and sculpture, graphic design and industrial design, digital imaging in design and photography, Renaissance and American art history, contemporary art theory and criticism.

University of Oklahoma, Weitzenhoffer Family College of Fine Arts, School of Visual Arts, Program in Art History, Norman, OK 73019. Offers art history (MA); art of the American West (PhD); Native American art history (PhD). *Students:* 9 full-time (8 women), 9 part-time (all women); includes 5 minority (1 American Indian or Alaska Native, non-Hispanic/Latino; 1 Hispanic/Latino; 3 Two or more races, non-Hispanic/Latino). Average age 34. 4 applicants, 75% accepted, 2 enrolled. In 2017, 3 master's, 3 doctorates awarded. *Degree requirements:* For master's, 2 foreign languages, comprehensive exam, thesis; for doctorate, 2 foreign languages, comprehensive exam, thesis/dissertation. *Entrance requirements:* For master's and doctorate, GRE. Additional exam requirements/recommendations for international students: Required—TOEFL (minimum score 79 iBT) or IELTS (minimum score 6.5). *Application deadline:* For fall admission, 2/1 for domestic and international students; for spring admission, 10/1 for domestic and international students. Application fee: $50 ($100 for international students). Electronic applications accepted. *Expenses:* Tuition, state resident: full-time $5119; part-time $213.30 per credit hour. Tuition, nonresident: full-time $19,778; part-time $824.10 per credit hour. *Required fees:* $3458; $133.55 per credit hour. $126.50 per semester. *Financial support:* In 2017–18, 16 students received support. Fellowships with full and partial tuition reimbursements available, research assistantships with full tuition reimbursements available, teaching assistantships with full tuition reimbursements available, career-related internships or fieldwork, institutionally sponsored loans, scholarships/grants, health care benefits, tuition waivers (partial), and unspecified assistantships available. Support available to part-time students. Financial award application deadline: 6/1; financial award applicants required to submit FAFSA. *Faculty research:* Medieval, Renaissance, contemporary, 19th century, Native American. *Unit head:* Dr. Bette Talvacchia, Director, 405-325-6210, Fax: 405-325-1668, E-mail: bette.talvacchia-1@ou.edu. *Application contact:* Dr. W. Jackson Rushing, MFA and PhD Graduate Coordinator, 405-325-6919, E-mail: jackson_rushing@ou.edu.
Website: http://art.ou.edu

University of Oregon, Graduate School, College of Design, Department of the History of Art and Architecture, Eugene, OR 97403. Offers art history (MA, PhD). *Degree requirements:* For master's, one foreign language, thesis or alternative; for doctorate, 2 foreign languages, thesis/dissertation. *Entrance requirements:* For master's, GRE General Test, minimum GPA of 3.0; for doctorate, minimum GPA of 3.0. Additional exam requirements/recommendations for international students: Required—TOEFL. *Faculty research:* Scytho-Siberian art, modern Chinese painting, European landscape painting, American architecture, German expressionist graphics.

University of Pennsylvania, School of Arts and Sciences, Graduate Group in the History of Art, Philadelphia, PA 19104. Offers AM, PhD. *Faculty:* 28 full-time (13 women), 12 part-time/adjunct (6 women). *Students:* 47 full-time (38 women), 3 part-time (2 women); includes 9 minority (2 Black or African American, non-Hispanic/Latino; 3 Asian, non-Hispanic/Latino; 3 Hispanic/Latino; 1 Two or more races, non-Hispanic/Latino), 8 international. Average age 29. 174 applicants, 13% accepted, 11 enrolled. In 2017, 3 master's, 5 doctorates awarded. Terminal master's awarded for partial completion of doctoral program.
Website: http://www.sas.upenn.edu/arthistory/graduate/about-the-program

University of Pittsburgh, Kenneth P. Dietrich School of Arts and Sciences, Department of History of Art and Architecture, Pittsburgh, PA 15260. Offers MA, PhD. *Faculty:* 13 full-time (6 women). *Students:* 36 full-time (31 women); includes 7 minority (2 Hispanic/Latino; 1 Native Hawaiian or other Pacific Islander, non-Hispanic/Latino; 4 Two or more races, non-Hispanic/Latino), 7 international. Average age 32. 44 applicants, 20% accepted, 5 enrolled. In 2017, 3 master's, 5 doctorates awarded. *Degree requirements:* For master's, one foreign language, thesis or alternative, paper; for doctorate, 2 foreign languages, comprehensive exam, thesis/dissertation, teaching portfolio. *Entrance requirements:* For master's and doctorate, GRE General Test, 3 letters of recommendation, writing sample, personal statement, transcripts, foreign language questionnaire. Additional exam requirements/recommendations for international students: Required—TOEFL (minimum score 550 paper-based; 90 iBT). *Application deadline:* For fall admission, 12/15 for domestic and international students. Application fee: $50. Electronic applications accepted. *Expenses:* $22,290 full-time resident per year, $36,980 full-time nonresident. *Financial support:* In 2017–18, 24 students received support, including 9 fellowships with full tuition reimbursements available (averaging $22,042 per year), 5 research assistantships with full tuition reimbursements available (averaging $18,620 per year), 6 teaching assistantships with full tuition reimbursements available (averaging $18,620 per year); career-related internships or fieldwork, scholarships/grants, health care benefits, tuition waivers (partial), and unspecified assistantships also available. Financial award application deadline: 12/15. *Faculty research:* Medieval European art and architecture, modern architecture, modern and contemporary art, history of photography, Japanese art, 20th century German art, contemporary Chinese art, art of the United States, ancient Roman art. *Unit head:* Dr. Barbara McCloskey, Chair, 412-648-2417, Fax: 412-648-2792, E-mail: barbara.mccloskey@pitt.edu. *Application contact:* Karoline Swinotek, Graduate Administrator, 412-648-2400, Fax: 412-648-2792, E-mail: karoline@pitt.edu.
Website: http://www.haa.pitt.edu

University of Rochester, School of Arts and Sciences, Department of Art and Art History, Rochester, NY 14627. Offers visual and cultural studies (PhD). *Faculty:* 11 full-time (6 women). *Students:* 28 full-time (17 women); includes 5 minority (1 Black or African American, non-Hispanic/Latino; 2 Asian, non-Hispanic/Latino; 2 Hispanic/Latino), 9 international. Average age 30. 66 applicants, 18% accepted, 4 enrolled. In 2017, 3 doctorates awarded. Terminal master's awarded for partial completion of doctoral program. *Degree requirements:* For doctorate, thesis/dissertation, qualifying exam. *Entrance requirements:* For doctorate, GRE General Test, personal statement, three letters of recommendation, official undergraduate and graduate transcripts, writing sample. Additional exam requirements/recommendations for international students: Required—TOEFL. *Application deadline:* For fall admission, 1/15 for domestic and international students. Application fee: $60. Electronic applications accepted. *Expenses:* $1,596 per credit hour. *Financial support:* In 2017–18, 4 teaching assistantships with full tuition reimbursements (averaging $22,000 per year) were awarded; research assistantships and tuition waivers (full) also available. *Faculty research:* Visual culture from a social-historical perspective. *Unit head:* Rachel Haidu, Director, 585-275-9429, E-mail: rachel.haidu@rochester.edu. *Application contact:* Martin Collier, Administrator, 585-275-7451, E-mail: marty.collier@rochester.edu.
Website: http://www.sas.rochester.edu/aah/graduate/index.html

University of St. Thomas, College of Arts and Sciences, Department of Art History, St. Paul, MN 55105. Offers art history (MA); museum studies (Graduate Certificate). *Program availability:* Part-time, evening/weekend. *Faculty:* 7 full-time (4 women). *Students:* 29 full-time (25 women); includes 3 minority (1 American Indian or Alaska Native, non-Hispanic/Latino; 1 Asian, non-Hispanic/Latino; 1 Hispanic/Latino). Average age 36. 8 applicants, 88% accepted, 6 enrolled. In 2017, 11 master's, 5 other advanced degrees awarded. *Degree requirements:* For master's, one foreign language, thesis, oral exam, reading proficiency in 1 foreign language. *Entrance requirements:* For master's, bachelor's degree in art history or related field; 3 letters of recommendation; writing sample; personal statement. Additional exam requirements/recommendations for international students: Required—TOEFL (minimum score 80 iBT). *Application deadline:* For fall admission, 3/1 priority date for domestic and international students; for spring admission, 11/1 priority date for domestic and international students; for summer admission, 3/1 priority date for domestic and international students. Applications are processed on a rolling basis. Application fee: $0. Electronic applications accepted. *Expenses:* $857.50 per credit tuition ($2,572.50 per course); $55 per semester technology fee ($111 for two or more courses). *Financial support:* In 2017–18, 15 students received support, including 15 fellowships with partial tuition reimbursements available; research assistantships, career-related internships or fieldwork, institutionally sponsored loans, scholarships/grants, and unspecified assistantships also available. Support available to part-time students. Financial award application deadline: 4/1; financial award applicants required to submit FAFSA. *Faculty research:* Pictorial narrative and theory, Mesoamerican art, Chinese manuscript painting, Africa and African diaspora, architectural history, Modernism. *Unit head:* Victoria Young, Chair, 651-962-5855, Fax: 651-962-5861, E-mail: vmyoung@stthomas.edu. *Application contact:* Dr. Heather Shirey, Director of Graduate Studies, 651-962-5572, Fax: 651-962-5861, E-mail: hmshirey@stthomas.edu.
Website: http://www.stthomas.edu/arthistory/

University of South Africa, College of Human Sciences, Pretoria, South Africa. Offers adult education (M Ed); African languages (MA, PhD); African politics (MA, PhD); Afrikaans (MA, PhD); ancient history (MA, PhD); ancient Near Eastern studies (MA, PhD); anthropology (MA, PhD); applied linguistics (MA); Arabic (MA, PhD); archaeology (MA); art history (MA); Biblical archaeology (MA); Biblical studies (M Th, D Th, PhD); Christian spirituality (M Th, D Th); church history (M Th, D Th); classical studies (MA, PhD); clinical psychology (MA); communication (MA, PhD); comparative education (M Ed, Ed D); consulting psychology (D Admin, D Com, PhD); curriculum studies (M Ed, Ed D); development studies (M Admin, MA, D Admin, PhD); didactics (M Ed, Ed D); education (M Tech); education management (M Ed, Ed D); educational psychology (M Ed); English (MA); environmental education (M Ed); French (MA, PhD); German (MA, PhD); Greek (MA); guidance and counseling (M Ed); health studies (MA, PhD), including health sciences education (MA), health services management (MA), medical and surgical nursing science (critical care general) (MA), midwifery and neonatal nursing science (MA), trauma and emergency care (MA); history (MA, PhD); history of education (Ed D); inclusive education (M Ed, Ed D); information and communications technology policy and regulation (MA); information science (MA, MIS, PhD); international politics (MA, PhD); Islamic studies (MA, PhD); Italian (MA, PhD); Judaica (MA, PhD); linguistics (MA, PhD); mathematical education (M Ed); mathematics education (MA); missiology (M Th, D Th); modern Hebrew (MA, PhD); musicology (MA, MMus, D Mus, PhD); natural science education (M Ed); New Testament (M Th, D Th); Old Testament (D Th); pastoral therapy (M Th, D Th); philosophy (MA); philosophy of education (M Ed, Ed D); politics (MA, PhD); Portuguese (MA, PhD); practical theology (M Th, D Th); psychology (MA, MS, PhD); psychology of education (M Ed, Ed D); public health (MA); religious studies (MA, D Th, PhD); Romance languages (MA); Russian (MA, PhD); Semitic languages (MA, PhD); social behavior studies in HIV/AIDS (MA); social science (mental health) (MA); social science in development studies (MA); social science in psychology (MA); social science in social work (MA); social science in sociology (MA); social work (MSW, DSW, PhD); socio-education (M Ed, Ed D); sociolinguistics (MA); sociology (MA, PhD); Spanish (MA, PhD); systematic theology (M Th, D Th); TESOL (teaching English to speakers of other languages) (MA); theological ethics (M Th, D Th); theory of literature (MA, PhD); urban ministries (D Th); urban ministry (M Th).

University of South Carolina, The Graduate School, College of Arts and Sciences, Department of Art, Program in Art History, Columbia, SC 29208. Offers MA. *Accreditation:* NASAD. *Program availability:* Part-time. *Degree requirements:* For master's, one foreign language, comprehensive exam, thesis. *Entrance requirements:* For master's, GRE General Test or MAT, writing sample. Additional exam requirements/recommendations for international students: Required—TOEFL. Electronic applications accepted. *Faculty research:* History of art and architecture.

Art History

University of Southern California, Graduate School, Dana and David Dornsife College of Letters, Arts and Sciences, Department of Art History, Los Angeles, CA 90089. Offers art history (MA, PhD); visual studies (Graduate Certificate). *Degree requirements:* For doctorate, 2 foreign languages, comprehensive exam, thesis/dissertation, 60 units. *Entrance requirements:* For doctorate, GRE. Additional exam requirements/recommendations for international students: Required—TOEFL. *Faculty research:* Ancient, medieval, Renaissance, eighteenth-nineteenth century, contemporary.

University of South Florida, College of The Arts, School of Art and Art History, Tampa, FL 33620-9951. Offers art history (MA); studio art (MFA). *Accreditation:* NASAD. *Program availability:* Part-time. *Faculty:* 21 full-time (11 women). *Students:* 35 full-time (19 women), 2 part-time (1 woman); includes 10 minority (8 Hispanic/Latino; 2 Two or more races, non-Hispanic/Latino), 3 international. Average age 29. 48 applicants, 29% accepted, 13 enrolled. In 2017, 13 master's awarded. *Degree requirements:* For master's, comprehensive exam, thesis, exhibition (for MFA). *Entrance requirements:* For master's, GRE General Test, bachelor's degree from regionally-accredited institution with minimum GPA of 3.0 in upper-division coursework or graduate degree from regionally-accredited institution; portfolio; goals statement (for MA in art history). Additional exam requirements/recommendations for international students: Required—TOEFL (minimum score 550 paper-based; 79 iBT) or IELTS (minimum score 6.5). *Application deadline:* For fall admission, 1/15 priority date for domestic students, 2/1 for international students. Application fee: $30. Electronic applications accepted. *Financial support:* In 2017–18, 33 students received support, including 37 teaching assistantships with partial tuition reimbursements available (averaging $9,440 per year); scholarships/grants, health care benefits, and unspecified assistantships also available. Support available to part-time students. Financial award application deadline: 2/15; financial award applicants required to submit FAFSA. *Faculty research:* Contemporary art and role of the artist, identity strategies, political iconography, art practice and technology, the construction of race in art. *Total annual research expenditures:* $127,255. *Unit head:* Prof. Wallace Wilson, Director, 813-974-2360, Fax: 813-974-9226, E-mail: wwilson2@usf.edu. *Application contact:* Prof. Neil Bender, Associate Professor and Graduate Program Director, 813-974-2360, Fax: 813-974-9226, E-mail: nb2@usf.edu. Website: http://www.art.usf.edu

The University of Texas at Austin, Graduate School, College of Fine Arts, Department of Art and Art History, Program in Art History, Austin, TX 78712-1111. Offers MA, PhD. *Accreditation:* NASAD. *Program availability:* Part-time. *Degree requirements:* For master's, one foreign language, thesis; for doctorate, 2 foreign languages, thesis/dissertation, oral and written qualifying exam. *Entrance requirements:* For master's, GRE General Test, 2 samples of written work; for doctorate, GRE General Test, minimum GPA of 3.0, 2 samples of written work. Electronic applications accepted.

The University of Texas at Dallas, School of Arts and Humanities, Richardson, TX 75080. Offers art history (MA); history (MA); humanities (MA, PhD), including aesthetic studies, history of ideas, studies in literature; Latin American studies (MA). *Program availability:* Part-time, evening/weekend. *Faculty:* 47 full-time (17 women), 4 part-time/adjunct (2 women). *Students:* 132 full-time (83 women), 117 part-time (71 women); includes 62 minority (11 Black or African American, non-Hispanic/Latino; 3 American Indian or Alaska Native, non-Hispanic/Latino; 10 Asian, non-Hispanic/Latino; 25 Hispanic/Latino; 13 Two or more races, non-Hispanic/Latino), 29 international. Average age 40. 127 applicants, 55% accepted, 43 enrolled. In 2017, 17 master's, 18 doctorates awarded. *Degree requirements:* For master's, one foreign language, portfolio; for doctorate, one foreign language, thesis/dissertation. *Entrance requirements:* For master's and doctorate, minimum GPA of 3.0 in undergraduate course work in field. Additional exam requirements/recommendations for international students: Required—TOEFL (minimum score 550 paper-based). *Application deadline:* For fall admission, 7/15 for domestic students, 5/1 priority date for international students; for spring admission, 11/15 for domestic students, 9/1 priority date for international students. Applications are processed on a rolling basis. Application fee: $50 ($100 for international students). Electronic applications accepted. *Expenses:* Tuition, state resident: full-time $12,916; part-time $718 per credit hour. Tuition, nonresident: full-time $25,252; part-time $1403 per credit hour. *Financial support:* In 2017–18, 136 students received support, including 12 research assistantships with partial tuition reimbursements available (averaging $22,710 per year), 71 teaching assistantships with partial tuition reimbursements available (averaging $15,000 per year); fellowships, Federal Work-Study, institutionally sponsored loans, scholarships/grants, and unspecified assistantships also available. Support available to part-time students. Financial award application deadline: 4/30; financial award applicants required to submit FAFSA. *Faculty research:* Science and the arts and humanities, intellectual and philosophical history, cultural studies, translation studies. *Total annual research expenditures:* $183,441. *Unit head:* Dr. Dennis M. Kratz, Dean, 972-883-2984, Fax: 972-883-2989, E-mail: dkratz@utdallas.edu. *Application contact:* Dr. John Gooch, Associate Dean of Graduate Studies, 972-883-2756, Fax: 972-883-2989, E-mail: john.gooch@utdallas.edu. Website: http://www.utdallas.edu/ah/

The University of Texas at San Antonio, College of Liberal and Fine Arts, Department of Art and Art History, San Antonio, TX 78249-0617. Offers art (MFA); art history (MA). *Accreditation:* NASAD (one or more programs are accredited). *Faculty:* 14 full-time (6 women), 1 part-time/adjunct (0 women). *Students:* 29 full-time (21 women), 4 part-time (all women); includes 16 minority (1 Asian, non-Hispanic/Latino; 14 Hispanic/Latino; 1 Two or more races, non-Hispanic/Latino), 2 international. Average age 31. 32 applicants, 63% accepted, 14 enrolled. In 2017, 5 master's awarded. *Entrance requirements:* For master's, GRE General Test, portfolio, minimum GPA of 3.0 in last 60 hours, 3 letters of recommendation, statement of purpose. Additional exam requirements/recommendations for international students: Required—TOEFL (minimum score 550 paper-based; 79 iBT), IELTS (minimum score 6.5). *Application deadline:* For fall admission, 6/15 for domestic students, 3/1 for international students; for spring admission, 10/15 for domestic students, 9/15 for international students. Application fee: $50 ($90 for international students). Electronic applications accepted. *Expenses:* Tuition, state resident: full-time $5495. Tuition, nonresident: full-time $21,938. *Required fees:* $1915. Tuition and fees vary according to program. *Unit head:* Dr. Gregory Elliott, Department Chair, 210-458-4352, Fax: 210-458-4356, E-mail: greg.elliott@utsa.edu. *Application contact:* Monica Rodriguez, Director of Graduate Admissions, 210-458-4331, Fax: 210-458-4332, E-mail: graduate.admissions@utsa.edu. Website: http://art.utsa.edu/

The University of Texas at Tyler, College of Arts and Sciences, Department of Art and Art History, Tyler, TX 75799-0001. Offers art history (MA); interdisciplinary (MAIS); studio art (MFA). *Degree requirements:* For master's, thesis, graduate committee review. *Entrance requirements:* For master's, minimum GPA of 3.0. Additional exam requirements/recommendations for international students: Required—TOEFL. *Faculty research:* Classical myths in contemporary art, social issues in contemporary art, casting methods, Renaissance art.

University of Toronto, School of Graduate Studies, Faculty of Arts and Science, Department of Art, Toronto, ON M5S 1A1, Canada. Offers art history (MA, PhD). *Program availability:* Part-time. *Degree requirements:* For master's, 2 foreign languages, language proficiency exams; for doctorate, 2 foreign languages, comprehensive exam, thesis/dissertation. *Entrance requirements:* For master's, coursework in a foreign language, 3 letters of reference, sample research paper, minimum B+ average in senior art history and/or humanities courses; for doctorate, minimum A- average in senior art history and/or humanities courses, 2 letters of reference, sample research paper. Electronic applications accepted.

The University of Tulsa, Graduate School, Kendall College of Arts and Sciences, School of Art, Design, and Art History, Tulsa, OK 74104-3189. Offers MA, MFA, MTA. *Program availability:* Part-time. *Faculty:* 7 full-time (4 women), 6 part-time/adjunct (3 women). *Students:* 6 full-time (5 women), 1 part-time (0 women); includes 1 minority (Asian, non-Hispanic/Latino). Average age 35. 15 applicants, 13% accepted, 2 enrolled. In 2017, 3 master's awarded. *Degree requirements:* For master's, comprehensive exam (for some programs), thesis (for some programs). *Entrance requirements:* For master's, portfolio. Additional exam requirements/recommendations for international students: Required—TOEFL (minimum score 577 paper-based; 91 iBT), IELTS (minimum score 6.5). *Application deadline:* For fall admission, 2/1 for domestic and international students. Application fee: $55. Electronic applications accepted. *Expenses: Tuition:* Full-time $22,230. *Required fees:* $2000. Tuition and fees vary according to course load and program. *Financial support:* In 2017–18, 6 students received support, including 5 fellowships with full tuition reimbursements available (averaging $5,200 per year), 5 teaching assistantships with full tuition reimbursements available (averaging $13,410 per year); career-related internships or fieldwork, Federal Work-Study, scholarships/grants, traineeships, health care benefits, tuition waivers (full and partial), and unspecified assistantships also available. Support available to part-time students. Financial award application deadline: 2/1; financial award applicants required to submit FAFSA. *Faculty research:* Drawing, painting, printmaking, graphic design, photography. *Unit head:* Prof. Teresa Valero, Director, 918-631-3513, Fax: 918-631-3423, E-mail: maria-valero@utulsa.edu. *Application contact:* Prof. Michelle Martin, Program Advisor, 918-631-2736, Fax: 918-631-3423, E-mail: michelle-martin@utulsa.edu. Website: http://artsandsciences.utulsa.edu/academics/departments-schools/art/

University of Utah, Graduate School, College of Fine Arts, Department of Art and Art History, Program in Art History, Salt Lake City, UT 84112-0380. Offers MA. *Students:* 9 full-time (8 women), 1 part-time (0 women); includes 1 minority (Asian, non-Hispanic/Latino). Average age 27. 9 applicants, 44% accepted, 4 enrolled. In 2017, 4 master's awarded. Terminal master's awarded for partial completion of doctoral program. *Degree requirements:* For master's, one foreign language, comprehensive exam, qualifying paper, thesis or project defense. *Entrance requirements:* For master's, curriculum vitae, academic writing sample, letters of recommendation. Additional exam requirements/recommendations for international students: Required—TOEFL (minimum score 80 iBT). *Application deadline:* For fall admission, 2/1 for domestic and international students. Application fee: $55 ($65 for international students). Electronic applications accepted. *Expenses:* Contact institution. *Financial support:* In 2017–18, 7 students received support, including 5 teaching assistantships with partial tuition reimbursements available (averaging $7,500 per year); scholarships/grants and tuition reduction also available. Financial award application deadline: 2/1; financial award applicants required to submit FAFSA. *Faculty research:* Asian, Latin American, Renaissance/Baroque, European/American, twentieth-century/contemporary, and medieval art. *Unit head:* Prof. Elizabeth A. Peterson, Director, 801-581-8677, Fax: 801-585-6171. *Application contact:* Dr. Jessen Kelly, Director of Graduate Studies, 801-581-8677, Fax: 801-585-6171, E-mail: jessen.kelly@utah.edu. Website: http://www.arthistory.utah.edu/

University of Victoria, Faculty of Graduate Studies, Faculty of Fine Arts, Department of History in Art, Victoria, BC V8W 2Y2, Canada. Offers MA, PhD. *Degree requirements:* For master's, one foreign language, thesis (for some programs), oral defense; for doctorate, 2 foreign languages, comprehensive exam, thesis/dissertation, oral defense. *Entrance requirements:* For master's, minimum B+ average in undergraduate course work; for doctorate, minimum B+ average in graduate course work. Additional exam requirements/recommendations for international students: Required—TOEFL (minimum score 575 paper-based), IELTS (minimum score 7). Electronic applications accepted. *Faculty research:* Europe, Southeast Asia, China and Islamic world, architecture of North America and the Islamic World, film.

University of Virginia, College and Graduate School of Arts and Sciences, Program in Art and Architectural History, Charlottesville, VA 22903. Offers MA, PhD. *Faculty:* 21 full-time (10 women), 2 part-time/adjunct (both women). *Students:* 27 full-time (16 women); includes 6 minority (1 Black or African American, non-Hispanic/Latino; 2 Asian, non-Hispanic/Latino; 2 Hispanic/Latino; 1 Two or more races, non-Hispanic/Latino), 3 international. Average age 31. 56 applicants, 21% accepted, 5 enrolled. In 2017, 7 doctorates awarded. *Degree requirements:* For master's, one foreign language, comprehensive exam, thesis; for doctorate, 2 foreign languages, thesis/dissertation, oral exam. *Entrance requirements:* For master's and doctorate, GRE, 2 letters of recommendation. *Application deadline:* For fall admission, 12/7 for domestic and international students. Applications are processed on a rolling basis. Application fee: $60. Electronic applications accepted. *Financial support:* Application deadline: 12/7. *Unit head:* Larry Goedde, Chair, 434-924-3541, Fax: 434-924-3647, E-mail: artdept@virginia.edu. *Application contact:* Carmenita Higginbotham, Director of Graduate Studies, 434-243-2342, Fax: 434-924-3647, E-mail: artdept@virginia.edu. Website: http://www.virginia.edu/art/phd-program/

University of Washington, Graduate School, College of Arts and Sciences, School of Art, Division of Art History, Seattle, WA 98195. Offers MA, PhD. Terminal master's awarded for partial completion of doctoral program. *Degree requirements:* For master's, 2 foreign languages, practicum or thesis; for doctorate, 2 foreign languages, thesis/dissertation. *Entrance requirements:* For master's, GRE General Test, minimum undergraduate GPA of 3.0, undergraduate major in art history or equivalent; for doctorate, GRE General Test, MA in art history, minimum graduate GPA of 3.0. Additional exam requirements/recommendations for international students: Required—TOEFL (minimum score 580 paper-based). Electronic applications accepted. *Faculty research:* European-American (all periods), Japanese, Chinese, African, and Native American art.

University of Wisconsin–Madison, Graduate School, College of Letters and Science, Department of Art History, Madison, WI 53706-1380. Offers MA, PhD. *Program availability:* Part-time. Terminal master's awarded for partial completion of doctoral program. *Degree requirements:* For master's, one foreign language; for doctorate, 2 foreign languages, thesis/dissertation. *Entrance requirements:* For master's and doctorate, GRE. Additional exam requirements/recommendations for international students: Required—TOEFL. Electronic applications accepted. *Faculty research:* Twentieth-century, African art, Italian Renaissance, Dutch, material culture.

University of Wisconsin–Milwaukee, Graduate School, College of Letters and Science, Department of Art History, Milwaukee, WI 53201-0413. Offers art history (MA); art history and criticism (MA); art museum studies (MA). *Program availability:* Part-time. *Students:* 8 full-time (6 women), 9 part-time (7 women); includes 1 minority (Two or more races, non-Hispanic/Latino), 1 international. Average age 28. 10 applicants, 90% accepted, 9 enrolled. In 2017, 1 master's awarded. *Degree requirements:* For master's, one foreign language, comprehensive exam, thesis or alternative. *Entrance requirements:* For master's, GRE. Additional exam requirements/recommendations for international students: Required—TOEFL (minimum score 550 paper-based; 79 iBT),

IELTS (minimum score 6.5). *Application deadline:* For fall admission, 1/1 priority date for domestic students; for spring admission, 9/1 for domestic students. Application fee: $56 ($96 for international students). Electronic applications accepted. *Financial support:* Fellowships, research assistantships, teaching assistantships, career-related internships or fieldwork, and unspecified assistantships available. Support available to part-time students. Financial award application deadline: 4/15; financial award applicants required to submit FAFSA. *Faculty research:* Ancient Mediterranean art through contemporary Western art, Chinese art, Pre-Columbian art, film, theory. *Unit head:* Tanya Tiffany, Chair, 414-229-3466, E-mail: tanyatif@uwm.edu. *Application contact:* Derek Counts, General Information Contact, 414-229-3466, E-mail: dbc@uwm.edu.
Website: https://uwm.edu/arthistory/

University of Wisconsin–Superior, Graduate Division, Department of Visual Arts, Superior, WI 54880-4500. Offers art education (MA); art history (MA); art therapy (MA); studio arts (MA). *Program availability:* Part-time. *Degree requirements:* For master's, comprehensive exam, exhibit. *Entrance requirements:* For master's, minimum GPA of 2.75, portfolio. Electronic applications accepted.

Virginia Commonwealth University, Graduate School, School of the Arts, Department of Art History, Richmond, VA 23284-9005. Offers curatorial (PhD); historical studies (MA, PhD); museum studies (MA). *Accreditation:* NASAD. *Degree requirements:* For master's, thesis; for doctorate, comprehensive exam, thesis/dissertation. *Entrance requirements:* For master's and doctorate, GRE General Test. Electronic applications accepted. *Faculty research:* Modern, nineteenth-century, Renaissance, American, and medieval art.

Washington University in St. Louis, The Graduate School, Department of Art History and Archaeology, St. Louis, MO 63130-4899. Offers AM, PhD. *Degree requirements:* For doctorate, 2 foreign languages, comprehensive exam, thesis/dissertation. *Entrance requirements:* For master's and doctorate, GRE General Test, sample of written work. Electronic applications accepted. *Faculty research:* Ancient, medieval, Renaissance, early modern European, modern and contemporary European and American, and Asian art history; classical archaeology.

Wayne State University, College of Fine, Performing and Communication Arts, James Pearson Duffy Department of Art and Art History, Detroit, MI 48202. Offers art (MA, MFA), including ceramics, drawing, fashion design and merchandising (MA), fibers, graphic design, industrial design (MA), interior design (MA), metalsmithing, painting, photography, printmaking, sculpture; art history (MA). *Students:* 13 full-time (8 women), 12 part-time (9 women); includes 5 minority (3 Black or African American, non-Hispanic/Latino; 1 Asian, non-Hispanic/Latino; 1 Hispanic/Latino), 2 international. Average age 34. 46 applicants, 24% accepted, 6 enrolled. In 2017, 5 master's awarded. *Degree requirements:* For master's, thesis (for some programs), essay or thesis. *Entrance requirements:* For master's, BFA or another degree and equivalent course work, portfolio, personal interview, reference letters, statement of intent (except for art history program). Additional exam requirements/recommendations for international students: Required—TOEFL (minimum score 550 paper-based; 79 iBT), TWE (minimum score 5.5), Michigan English Language Assessment Battery (minimum score 85); Recommended—IELTS (minimum score 6.5). *Application deadline:* For fall admission, 2/1 for domestic and international students; for winter admission, 10/1 for domestic and international students. Application fee: $50. Electronic applications accepted. *Expenses:* Contact institution. *Financial support:* In 2017–18, 18 students received support, including 1 research assistantship (averaging $22,241 per year), 6 teaching assistantships with tuition reimbursements available (averaging $18,534 per year); fellowships with tuition reimbursements available, scholarships/grants, and unspecified assistantships also available. Support available to part-time students. Financial award applicants required to submit FAFSA. *Unit head:* Dr. John Richardson, Chair, 313-577-2980, Fax: 313-577-3491, E-mail: af5343@wayne.edu. *Application contact:* 313-577-2980, E-mail: art@wayne.edu.
Website: http://art.wayne.edu/

Webster University, Leigh Gerdine College of Fine Arts, Department of Art, Design, and Art History, St. Louis, MO 63119-3194. Offers art history and criticism (MA). *Program availability:* Part-time. *Degree requirements:* For master's, thesis. *Entrance requirements:* For master's, BA or BFA in related field, interview, portfolio. Additional exam requirements/recommendations for international students: Required—TOEFL.

West Virginia University, College of Creative Arts, Morgantown, WV 26506. Offers acting (MFA); art education (MA); art history (MA); ceramics (MFA); collaborative piano (MM, DMA); composition (MM, DMA); conducting (MM, DMA); costume design and technology (MFA); graphic design (MFA); jazz pedagogy (MM); lighting design and technology (MFA); music (PhD); music education (MM, PhD); music industry (MA); music theory (MM); musicology (MA); painting and printmaking (MFA); performance (MM, DMA); photography (MFA); piano pedagogy (MM); scenic design and technology (MFA); sculpture (MFA); studio art (MA); technical direction (MFA); vocal pedagogy and performance (DMA). *Program availability:* Part-time. *Students:* 114 full-time (64 women), 39 part-time (21 women); includes 19 minority (11 Black or African American, non-Hispanic/Latino; 1 Asian, non-Hispanic/Latino; 6 Hispanic/Latino; 1 Two or more races, non-Hispanic/Latino), 33 international. *Degree requirements:* For master's, thesis, recitals; for doctorate, comprehensive exam, thesis/dissertation, recitals (DMA). *Entrance requirements:* For doctorate, minimum GPA of 3.0, audition. Additional exam requirements/recommendations for international students: Required—TOEFL. *Application deadline:* For fall admission, 3/1 priority date for domestic students, 2/15 for international students; for spring admission, 11/1 for domestic students, 9/15 for international students. Applications are processed on a rolling basis. Application fee: $60. Electronic applications accepted. *Expenses:* Tuition, state resident: full-time $9450. Tuition, nonresident: full-time $24,390. *Financial support:* Research assistantships, teaching assistantships, career-related internships or fieldwork, Federal Work-Study, institutionally sponsored loans, scholarships/grants, health care benefits, tuition waivers (partial), and administrative assistantships available. Financial award applicants required to submit FAFSA. *Faculty research:* Professional directing, consulting, acting design, music education, jazz history. *Unit head:* Dr. Paul Kreider, Dean, 304-293-4841 Ext. 3109, Fax: 304-293-6896, E-mail: paul.kreider@mail.wvu.edu. *Application contact:* Records Officer, 304-293-4841, Fax: 304-293-2533, E-mail: rachel.hanks@mail.wvu.edu.
Website: http://www.ccarts.wvu.edu

Williams College, Graduate Program in the History of Art, Williamstown, MA 01267. Offers development economics (MA); history of art (MA). MA in history of art offered jointly with Sterling and Francine Clark Art Institute. *Faculty:* 24. *Students:* 26 full-time (17 women); includes 7 minority (1 Black or African American, non-Hispanic/Latino; 1 American Indian or Alaska Native, non-Hispanic/Latino; 2 Asian, non-Hispanic/Latino; 3 Hispanic/Latino). 124 applicants, 16% accepted, 12 enrolled. In 2017, 12 master's awarded. *Degree requirements:* For master's, 2 foreign languages, symposium paper and lecture. *Entrance requirements:* For master's, GRE General Test. Additional exam requirements/recommendations for international students: Required—TOEFL. *Application deadline:* For fall admission, 1/3 for domestic and international students. Application fee: $75. Electronic applications accepted. *Expenses: Tuition:* Full-time $53,240. *Financial support:* In 2017–18, 18 students received support. Fellowships with full and partial tuition reimbursements available and tuition waivers (full and partial) available. Financial award application deadline: 4/1; financial award applicants required to submit FAFSA. *Application contact:* Karen E. Kowitz, Program Administrator, 413-458-0596, E-mail: kekowitz@williams.edu.
Website: http://gradart.williams.edu

Yale University, Graduate School of Arts and Sciences, Department of History of Art, New Haven, CT 06520. Offers PhD. *Degree requirements:* For doctorate, 2 foreign languages, thesis/dissertation. *Entrance requirements:* For doctorate, GRE General Test.

York University, Faculty of Graduate Studies, Faculty of Fine Arts, Program in Art History, Toronto, ON M3J 1P3, Canada. Offers MA, PhD. *Program availability:* Part-time. *Degree requirements:* For master's, one foreign language, thesis or alternative. Electronic applications accepted.

Arts Administration

American University, College of Arts and Sciences, Department of Performing Arts, Washington, DC 20016-8053. Offers arts management (MA); audio production (Certificate); audio technology (MA); international arts management (Certificate); technology in arts management (Certificate). *Program availability:* Part-time, evening/weekend. *Faculty:* 29 full-time (12 women), 66 part-time/adjunct (29 women). *Students:* 40 full-time (24 women), 31 part-time (17 women); includes 25 minority (16 Black or African American, non-Hispanic/Latino; 2 Asian, non-Hispanic/Latino; 4 Hispanic/Latino; 1 Native Hawaiian or other Pacific Islander, non-Hispanic/Latino; 2 Two or more races, non-Hispanic/Latino), 8 international. Average age 30. 101 applicants, 75% accepted, 24 enrolled. In 2017, 27 master's, 4 other advanced degrees awarded. *Degree requirements:* For master's, comprehensive exam, thesis or alternative. *Entrance requirements:* For master's, GRE, minimum GPA of 3.0, statement of purpose, transcripts, 2 letters of recommendation, resume, art portfolio; for Certificate, bachelor's degree, statement of purpose, transcripts, resume, art portfolio. Additional exam requirements/recommendations for international students: Required—TOEFL (minimum score 600 paper-based; 100 iBT). *Application deadline:* For fall admission, 2/1 priority date for domestic students; for spring admission, 11/1 priority date for domestic students. Application fee: $55. *Expenses:* Contact institution. *Financial support:* Unspecified assistantships available. Financial award application deadline: 2/1; financial award applicants required to submit FAFSA. *Unit head:* Andrew Taylor, Department Chair, 202-885-1601, E-mail: eataylor@american.edu. *Application contact:* Jonathan Harper, Assistant Director, Graduate Recruitment, 202-855-3622, E-mail: jharper@american.edu.
Website: http://www.american.edu/cas/performing-arts/

Arizona State University at the Tempe campus, Herberger Institute for Design and the Arts, School of Film, Dance and Theatre, Tempe, AZ 85287-2002. Offers dance (MFA), including dance, interdisciplinary digital media and performance; theatre (MA, MFA, PhD), including arts entrepreneurship and management (MFA), directing (MFA), dramatic writing (MFA), interdisciplinary digital media and performance (MFA), performance (MFA), performance design (MFA), theatre (MFA), theatre and performance of the Americas (PhD), theatre for youth (MFA, PhD). Terminal master's awarded for partial completion of doctoral program. *Degree requirements:* For master's, comprehensive exam (for some programs), thesis (for some programs), applied project (for some programs); interactive Program of Study (iPOS) submitted before completing 50 percent of required credit hours; for doctorate, comprehensive exam, thesis/dissertation, interactive Program of Study (iPOS) submitted before completing 50 percent of required credit hours. *Entrance requirements:* For master's, GRE or MAT, minimum GPA of 3.0 in last 2 years of work leading to bachelor's degree (depending on program); for doctorate, GRE, minimum GPA of 3.0 or equivalent in last 2 years of work leading to bachelor's degree, 3 letters of recommendation, resume, scholarly writing sample, statement of purpose. Additional exam requirements/recommendations for international students: Required—TOEFL, IELTS, or PTE. Electronic applications accepted.

Baruch College of the City University of New York, Weissman School of Arts and Sciences, Program in Arts Administration, New York, NY 10010-5585. Offers MA. *Program availability:* Part-time, evening/weekend. *Degree requirements:* For master's, thesis or alternative, arts consultancy project. *Entrance requirements:* For master's, GRE/GMAT. Additional exam requirements/recommendations for international students: Required—TOEFL or IELTS. Electronic applications accepted. *Faculty research:* Art policy; art administration; leadership, governance and strategic planning; government-nongovernment relations; immigration policy; policing; twentieth-century and contemporary art; ethics and policymaking; race, politics and social justice; visual culture of the Great War; intersections of dance, theatre, visual art, and technology; spectacle entertainments and strategies of visual display in performance culture.

Boston University, Metropolitan College, Program in Arts Administration, Boston, MA 02215. Offers arts administration (MS, Graduate Certificate); fundraising management (Graduate Certificate). *Program availability:* Part-time, evening/weekend. *Faculty:* 2 full-time (0 women), 8 part-time/adjunct (3 women). *Students:* 26 full-time (25 women), 56 part-time (49 women); includes 7 minority (4 Asian, non-Hispanic/Latino; 2 Hispanic/Latino; 1 Two or more races, non-Hispanic/Latino), 38 international. Average age 27. 134 applicants, 67% accepted, 38 enrolled. In 2017, 28 master's awarded. *Entrance requirements:* Additional exam requirements/recommendations for international students: Required—TOEFL (minimum score 95 iBT). *Application deadline:* For fall admission, 4/1 priority date for domestic students, 2/1 priority date for international students; for spring admission, 11/15 priority date for domestic and international students. Applications are processed on a rolling basis. Application fee: $85. Electronic applications accepted. *Expenses:* Contact institution. *Financial support:* In 2017–18, 3 research assistantships (averaging $8,400 per year) were awarded; career-related internships or fieldwork, unspecified assistantships, and 6 office assistantships (averaging $4200) also available. Support available to part-time students. Financial

award applicants required to submit FAFSA. *Faculty research:* Cultural policy, artists' rights, museum practices, audience development. *Unit head:* Dr. Lanfranco Aceti, Associate Professor of the Practice/Director, 617-353-4064, Fax: 617-353-1230, E-mail: artsad@bu.edu. *Application contact:* Raquel Peula, Program Administrator, 617-353-4064, Fax: 617-358-1230, E-mail: rpeula@bu.edu.
Website: http://www.bu.edu/artsadmin/programs/

Brooklyn College of the City University of New York, School of Visual, Media and Performing Arts, Department of Theater, Brooklyn, NY 11210-2889. Offers acting (MFA); design and technical theater (MFA); directing (MFA); performing arts management (MFA); theater history and criticism (MA). *Program availability:* Part-time. *Degree requirements:* For master's, thesis, professional residency. *Entrance requirements:* For master's, audition or interview, 18 credits in theater, 2 letters of recommendation, essay. Additional exam requirements/recommendations for international students: Required—TOEFL. Electronic applications accepted. *Faculty research:* Multiculturalism and the arts, art education, arts collaboration.

Carnegie Mellon University, Heinz College, School of Public Policy and Management, Master of Arts Management Program, Pittsburgh, PA 15213-3891. Offers MAM. *Degree requirements:* For master's, internship. *Entrance requirements:* For master's, GRE or GMAT, college-level course in advanced algebra/pre-calculus; college-level courses in economics and statistics (recommended). Additional exam requirements/recommendations for international students: Required—TOEFL or IELTS. Electronic applications accepted.

Christie's Education, Certificate Program in Art Business, New York, NY 10020. Offers Certificate. *Application deadline:* Applications are processed on a rolling basis. Electronic applications accepted. *Expenses:* Contact institution. *Unit head:* Dr. Marisa Kayyem, Director of Continuing Education, 212-355-1501, Fax: 212-355-7370, E-mail: mkayyem@christies.edu. *Application contact:* Catherine Warden, Academic Coordinator, 212-355-1501, Fax: 212-355-7370, E-mail: shortcoursesus@christies.edu.
Website: https://www.christies.edu/new-york/courses/certificate-art-business.aspx

Christie's Education, MA Program in Art, Law and Business, New York, NY 10020. Offers MA. *Faculty:* 3 full-time (2 women). *Students:* 17 full-time (15 women). In 2017, 13 master's awarded. *Degree requirements:* For master's, capstone project, internship. *Entrance requirements:* For master's, bachelor's degree or equivalent international degree, official transcripts from all post-secondary institutions attended. Additional exam requirements/recommendations for international students: Required—TOEFL. *Application deadline:* For fall admission, 1/12 priority date for domestic and international students. Applications are processed on a rolling basis. Application fee: $95. *Financial support:* In 2017–18, 1 student received support. Scholarships/grants and unspecified assistantships available. Financial award applicants required to submit FAFSA. *Unit head:* Noah Kupferman, Program Director, 212-355-1501 Ext. 7101, E-mail: nkupferman@christies.edu. *Application contact:* Hilary Smith, Recruitment and Admissions Officer, 212-355-1501 Ext. 3309, Fax: 212-355-7370, E-mail: hsmith@christies.edu.

Claremont Graduate University, Graduate Programs, Peter F. Drucker and Masatoshi Ito Graduate School of Management, Program in Art Business, Claremont, CA 91711-6160. Offers MA. Program offered in conjunction with Sotheby's Institute of Art–Los Angeles. *Degree requirements:* For master's, project seminar. *Entrance requirements:* Additional exam requirements/recommendations for international students: Required—TOEFL (minimum score 75 iBT). Electronic applications accepted.

Claremont Graduate University, Graduate Programs, Program in Arts Management, Claremont, CA 91711. Offers MA. Program offered in conjunction with Sotheby's Institute of Art–Los Angeles. *Entrance requirements:* For master's, GRE General Test. Additional exam requirements/recommendations for international students: Required—TOEFL (minimum score 75 iBT). Electronic applications accepted.

The College at Brockport, State University of New York, School of Business and Management, Department of Public Administration, Brockport, NY 14420-2997. Offers arts administration (AGC); nonprofit management (AGC); public administration (MPA), including health care management, nonprofit management, poverty studies, public management, public safety. *Accreditation:* NASPAA. *Program availability:* Part-time, evening/weekend. *Faculty:* 5 full-time (3 women), 5 part-time/adjunct (1 woman). *Students:* 54 full-time (38 women), 95 part-time (57 women); includes 38 minority (19 Black or African American, non-Hispanic/Latino; 3 Asian, non-Hispanic/Latino; 11 Hispanic/Latino; 5 Two or more races, non-Hispanic/Latino), 4 international. 53 applicants, 91% accepted, 31 enrolled. In 2017, 59 master's, 6 other advanced degrees awarded. *Degree requirements:* For master's, thesis or alternative. *Entrance requirements:* For master's, GRE or minimum GPA of 3.0, letters of recommendation, statement of objectives, current resume. Additional exam requirements/recommendations for international students: Required—TOEFL (minimum score 550 paper-based; 79 iBT), IELTS (minimum score 6.5). *Application deadline:* For fall admission, 8/15 priority date for domestic and international students; for spring admission, 1/15 priority date for domestic and international students; for summer admission, 4/15 priority date for domestic and international students. Application fee: $50. Electronic applications accepted. *Expenses:* Tuition, state resident: full-time $10,870; part-time $453 per credit hour. Tuition, nonresident: full-time $22,210. *Required fees:* $988; $246 per semester. *Financial support:* In 2017–18, 1 fellowship with full tuition reimbursement (averaging $7,500 per year), 1 teaching assistantship with full tuition reimbursement (averaging $6,000 per year) were awarded; Federal Work-Study, scholarships/grants, and unspecified assistantships also available. Support available to part-time students. Financial award application deadline: 3/15; financial award applicants required to submit FAFSA. *Faculty research:* E-government, performance management, nonprofits and policy implementation, Medicaid and disabilities. *Unit head:* Dr. Celia Watt, Graduate Director, 585-395-5538, Fax: 585-395-2172, E-mail: cwatt@brockport.edu. *Application contact:* Danielle A. Welch, Graduate Admissions Counselor, 585-395-2525, Fax: 585-395-2515.
Website: https://www.brockport.edu/academics/public_administration/graduate/masters.html

College of Charleston, Graduate School, School of the Arts, Program in Arts Management, Charleston, SC 29424-0001. Offers Certificate. *Program availability:* Part-time, evening/weekend. *Entrance requirements:* For degree, minimum GPA of 3.0, writing sample. Additional exam requirements/recommendations for international students: Required—TOEFL (minimum score 81 iBT).

Daemen College, Department of Visual and Performing Arts, Amherst, NY 14226-3592. Offers arts administration (MS). *Entrance requirements:* For master's, bachelor's degree from an accredited institution; at least two letters of recommendation; minimum undergraduate GPA of 2.75 or GRE/GMAT.

Drexel University, Westphal College of Media Arts and Design, Program in Arts Administration, Philadelphia, PA 19104-2875. Offers MS. *Accreditation:* NASAD. *Program availability:* Part-time, evening/weekend. *Degree requirements:* For master's, thesis, internship. *Entrance requirements:* For master's, GRE, interview, minimum GPA of 3.0, previous course work in arts and business. Additional exam requirements/recommendations for international students: Required—TOEFL. Electronic applications accepted. *Faculty research:* Evaluation of art administration structures, funding for the arts, impact of politics in the arts, computer applications.

Eastern Michigan University, Graduate School, College of Arts and Sciences, School of Communication, Media and Theatre Arts, Program in Arts Administration, Ypsilanti, MI 48197. Offers MA. *Program availability:* Part-time, evening/weekend, online learning. *Students:* 6 full-time (5 women), 1 (woman) part-time; includes 3 minority (2 Black or African American, non-Hispanic/Latino; 1 Hispanic/Latino), 1 international. Average age 29. 13 applicants, 69% accepted. In 2017, 1 master's awarded. *Entrance requirements:* Additional exam requirements/recommendations for international students: Required—TOEFL. *Application deadline:* Applications are processed on a rolling basis. Application fee: $45. *Financial support:* Fellowships, research assistantships with full tuition reimbursements, teaching assistantships with full tuition reimbursements, career-related internships or fieldwork, Federal Work-Study, institutionally sponsored loans, scholarships/grants, tuition waivers (partial), and unspecified assistantships available. Support available to part-time students. Financial award applicants required to submit FAFSA. *Unit head:* Dr. Susan Booth, Coordinator, 734-487-1220, Fax: 734-487-3443, E-mail: sbooth1@emich.edu.

Fashion Institute of Technology, School of Graduate Studies, Program in Art Market Studies, New York, NY 10001-5992. Offers MA. *Accreditation:* NASAD. *Degree requirements:* For master's, thesis or alternative, internship. *Entrance requirements:* For master's, GRE General Test, previous course work in art history, 4 semesters of a foreign language. Additional exam requirements/recommendations for international students: Required—TOEFL (minimum score 550 paper-based). Electronic applications accepted.

Florida State University, The Graduate School, College of Fine Arts, Department of Art Education, Tallahassee, FL 32306. Offers art education (MA, MS, Ed D, PhD); art therapy (PhD); arts administration (PhD). *Accreditation:* NASAD (one or more programs are accredited). *Program availability:* Part-time, evening/weekend, 100% online. *Faculty:* 9 full-time (6 women), 4 part-time/adjunct (all women). *Students:* 58 full-time (57 women), 20 part-time (15 women); includes 27 minority (8 Black or African American, non-Hispanic/Latino; 1 American Indian or Alaska Native, non-Hispanic/Latino; 1 Asian, non-Hispanic/Latino; 12 Hispanic/Latino; 5 Two or more races, non-Hispanic/Latino), 7 international. Average age 30. 90 applicants, 57% accepted, 38 enrolled. In 2017, 28 master's, 1 doctorate awarded. *Degree requirements:* For master's, comprehensive exam, thesis (for some programs); for doctorate, thesis/dissertation. *Entrance requirements:* For master's, GRE, minimum GPA of 3.0 in last 2 years; for doctorate, GRE. Additional exam requirements/recommendations for international students: Required—TOEFL (minimum score 550 paper-based; 80 iBT). *Application deadline:* For fall admission, 1/15 priority date for domestic and international students; for spring admission, 10/1 priority date for domestic and international students. Application fee: $30. Electronic applications accepted. *Financial support:* In 2017–18, 24 students received support, including 22 research assistantships with full tuition reimbursements available (averaging $5,000 per year), 5 teaching assistantships with full tuition reimbursements available (averaging $8,500 per year); fellowships, career-related internships or fieldwork, scholarships/grants, health care benefits, and unspecified assistantships also available. Financial award application deadline: 1/15; financial award applicants required to submit FAFSA. *Faculty research:* Teaching and learning in art, museum education, art therapy, arts administration, discipline-based art education. *Total annual research expenditures:* $110,000. *Unit head:* Dr. Jeff Broome, Interim Chair, 850-645-9892, Fax: 850-644-5067, E-mail: jbroome@fsu.edu. *Application contact:* Vicki Barr, Academic Support Assistant, 850-644-5473, Fax: 850-644-6067, E-mail: vbarr@fsu.edu.
Website: http://arted.fsu.edu/

Florida State University, The Graduate School, College of Music, Tallahassee, FL 32306. Offers accompanying (MM); arts administration (MA); choral conducting (MM); composition (MM, DM); ethnomusicology (MM); general music (MA); instrumental accompanying (MM); instrumental conducting (MM); jazz studies (MM); music theory (MM, PhD); music therapy (MM); musicology (MM, PhD), including ethnomusicology (PhD), historical musicology; opera (MM); performance (MM, DM); piano pedagogy (MM); piano technology (MA); vocal accompanying (MM). *Accreditation:* NASM. *Program availability:* Part-time. *Students:* 331 full-time (169 women); includes 100 minority (29 Black or African American, non-Hispanic/Latino; 40 Asian, non-Hispanic/Latino; 29 Hispanic/Latino; 2 Native Hawaiian or other Pacific Islander, non-Hispanic/Latino). Average age 26. 760 applicants, 47% accepted, 173 enrolled. In 2017, 94 master's, 45 doctorates awarded. *Degree requirements:* For master's, variable foreign language requirement, comprehensive exam (for some programs), thesis (for some programs), departmental qualifying exam; for doctorate, variable foreign language requirement, comprehensive exam (for some programs), thesis/dissertation, departmental qualifying exam. *Entrance requirements:* For master's, GRE General Test (for some programs), audition, minimum GPA of 3.0; for doctorate, GRE General Test (for some programs), audition, master's degree, minimum GPA of 3.0. Additional exam requirements/recommendations for international students: Required—TOEFL (minimum score 590 paper-based; 97 iBT), IELTS (minimum score 7.5). *Application deadline:* For fall admission, 7/1 for domestic and international students; for spring admission, 11/1 for domestic and international students; for summer admission, 3/1 for domestic students. Applications are processed on a rolling basis. Application fee: $30. Electronic applications accepted. *Financial support:* In 2017–18, 233 students received support, including 2 fellowships with full tuition reimbursements available (averaging $15,000 per year), 14 research assistantships with full and partial tuition reimbursements available (averaging $6,458 per year), 201 teaching assistantships with full and partial tuition reimbursements available (averaging $6,458 per year); career-related internships or fieldwork, scholarships/grants, tuition waivers (full and partial), and unspecified assistantships also available. Support available to part-time students. Financial award application deadline: 2/28; financial award applicants required to submit FAFSA. *Faculty research:* Music therapy in NICU units, music of the Americas, music theory pedagogy, music performance. *Unit head:* Dr. Patricia Flowers, Dean, 850-644-4361, Fax: 850-644-2033, E-mail: pjflowers@fsu.edu. *Application contact:* Kris Watson, Director of Admissions, 850-645-2126, Fax: 850-644-2033, E-mail: krwatson@fsu.edu.
Website: http://www.music.fsu.edu/

George Mason University, College of Visual and Performing Arts, Program in Arts Management, Fairfax, VA 22030. Offers MA. *Accreditation:* NASAD. *Faculty:* 4 full-time (3 women), 7 part-time/adjunct (5 women). *Students:* 52 full-time (45 women), 43 part-time (35 women); includes 14 minority (5 Black or African American, non-Hispanic/Latino; 2 Asian, non-Hispanic/Latino; 4 Hispanic/Latino; 1 Native Hawaiian or other Pacific Islander, non-Hispanic/Latino; 2 Two or more races, non-Hispanic/Latino), 44 international. Average age 27. 69 applicants, 62% accepted, 13 enrolled. In 2017, 31 master's awarded. *Degree requirements:* For master's, internship. *Entrance requirements:* For master's, GRE (recommended), undergraduate degree with minimum GPA of 3.0, official transcripts, 2 letters of recommendation, statement of purpose, resume. Additional exam requirements/recommendations for international students: Required—TOEFL (minimum score 575 paper-based; 88 iBT), IELTS (minimum score 6.5), PTE (minimum score 59). *Application deadline:* For fall admission, 2/15 for domestic and international students. Application fee: $75 ($80 for international

students). Electronic applications accepted. *Expenses:* Tuition, state resident: full-time $11,228; part-time $459.50 per credit. Tuition, nonresident: full-time $30,932; part-time $1280.50 per credit. *Required fees:* $3252; $135.50 per credit. Part-time tuition and fees vary according to course load and program. *Financial support:* In 2017–18, 2 students received support, including 1 research assistantship, 1 teaching assistantship; career-related internships or fieldwork, Federal Work-Study, and scholarships/grants also available. Support available to part-time students. Financial award application deadline: 3/1; financial award applicants required to submit FAFSA. *Faculty research:* Information technology for arts managers, special topics in arts management, directions in gallery management, arts in society, public relations/marketing strategies for art organizations. *Unit head:* Claire Huschle, Program Director, 703-993-8719, Fax: 703-993-9829, E-mail: chuschle@gmu.edu. *Application contact:* Elizabeth Ricks, Program Coordinator, 703-993-8926, Fax: 703-993-9829, E-mail: ericks@gmu.edu.
Website: http://artsmanagement.gmu.edu/arts-management-ma/

Goucher College, MA and MFA Programs, Baltimore, MD 21204-2794. Offers art and technology (MFA); arts administration (MA); cultural sustainability (MA); digital arts (MA); historic preservation (MA); nonfiction (MFA). *Program availability:* Part-time, evening/weekend, blended/hybrid learning. *Degree requirements:* For master's, thesis, e-portfolio. *Entrance requirements:* For master's, digital portfolio (for MA, MFA in digital arts); writing sample (for MFA in creative nonfiction). Additional exam requirements/recommendations for international students: Required—TOEFL (minimum score 550 paper-based; 80 iBT). *Application deadline:* Applications are processed on a rolling basis. Application fee: $75. Electronic applications accepted. *Expenses:* Contact institution. *Financial support:* Scholarships/grants and unspecified assistantships available. Financial award application deadline: 4/15; financial award applicants required to submit FAFSA. *Unit head:* Leslie Rubinkowski, Acting Assistant Provost for Limited Residency Graduate Programs, 410-337-6200, E-mail: leslie.rubinkowski@goucher.edu. *Application contact:* Carlton E. Surbeck, III, Director of Admissions, 410-337-6100, Fax: 410-337-6200, E-mail: admissions@goucher.edu.
Website: http://www.goucher.edu/grad

HEC Montreal, School of Business Administration, Graduate Diploma Programs in Administration, Program in Management of Cultural Organizations, Montréal, QC H3T 2A7, Canada. Offers Graduate Diploma. All courses are given in French. *Program availability:* Part-time, evening/weekend. *Students:* 30 full-time (26 women), 101 part-time (78 women). 76 applicants, 87% accepted, 53 enrolled. In 2017, 73 Graduate Diplomas awarded. *Entrance requirements:* For degree, bachelor's degree (not in administration, preferably cultural field), one year of work experience. *Application deadline:* For fall admission, 4/15 for domestic and international students; for winter admission, 9/15 for domestic and international students. Application fee: $88 Canadian dollars ($184 Canadian dollars for international students). Electronic applications accepted. *Expenses:* Tuition, state resident: full-time $2869 Canadian dollars; part-time $79.70 Canadian dollars per credit. Tuition, nonresident: full-time $8883 Canadian dollars; part-time $246.76 Canadian dollars per credit. International tuition: $19,648 Canadian dollars full-time. *Required fees:* $41.20 Canadian dollars per credit. $67.94 Canadian dollars per term. Tuition and fees vary according to degree level and program. *Financial support:* Research assistantships, teaching assistantships, and scholarships/grants available. Financial award application deadline: 9/2. *Unit head:* Renaud Lachance, Director, 514-340-7165, E-mail: renaud.lachance@hec.ca. *Application contact:* Anny Caron, Administrative Director, 514-340-6151, Fax: 514-340-6411, E-mail: aide@hec.ca.
Website: http://www.hec.ca/programmes/dess/dess-gestion-organismes-culturels/index.html

Indiana University Bloomington, School of Public and Environmental Affairs, Program in Arts Administration, Bloomington, IN 47405-7000. Offers MAAA. *Program availability:* Part-time. *Degree requirements:* For master's, final internship. *Entrance requirements:* For master's, GRE or GMAT. Additional exam requirements/recommendations for international students: Required—TOEFL or IELTS. Electronic applications accepted. *Faculty research:* Cultural policy, nonprofit management, and pricing for the arts.

Kutztown University of Pennsylvania, College of Visual and Performing Arts, Program in Arts Administration, Kutztown, PA 19530-0730. Offers MA. *Program availability:* Evening/weekend, 100% online, blended/hybrid learning. *Students:* 1 (woman) full-time, 9 part-time (8 women); includes 1 minority (Black or African American, non-Hispanic/Latino). Average age 29. 12 applicants, 92% accepted, 9 enrolled. *Entrance requirements:* For master's, official transcripts; professional resume; related work/volunteer experience in arts administration or two reference letters. Additional exam requirements/recommendations for international students: Required—TOEFL (minimum score 550 paper-based, 79 iBT), IELTS (minimum score 6.5), or PTE (minimum score 53). *Application deadline:* For fall admission, 8/1 for domestic and international students; for spring admission, 12/1 for domestic and international students. Application fee: $35. Electronic applications accepted. *Expenses:* Tuition, state resident: part-time $500 per credit. Tuition, nonresident: part-time $750 per credit. *Required fees:* $115 per credit. One-time fee: $50 part-time. Tuition and fees vary according to degree level. *Financial support:* Career-related internships or fieldwork, Federal Work-Study, and unspecified assistantships available. Financial award application deadline: 3/1; financial award applicants required to submit FAFSA. *Application contact:* Jamie VanValkenburgh, Director of Graduate Admissions, 610-683-4203, E-mail: vanvalkenb@kutztown.edu.
Website: https://www.kutztown.edu/academics/graduate-programs/arts-administration.htm

Le Moyne College, Program in Arts Administration, Syracuse, NY 13214. Offers MS. *Program availability:* Part-time, evening/weekend. *Faculty:* 3 part-time/adjunct (2 women). *Students:* 4 full-time (all women), 12 part-time (10 women); includes 1 minority (Black or African American, non-Hispanic/Latino). Average age 29. 16 applicants, 81% accepted, 10 enrolled. In 2017, 9 master's awarded. *Degree requirements:* For master's, capstone consulting project. *Entrance requirements:* For master's, bachelor's degree with minimum GPA of 2.8, two letters of recommendation, résumé, interview. Additional exam requirements/recommendations for international students: Required—TOEFL (minimum score 550 paper-based; 79 iBT); Recommended—IELTS (minimum score 6.5). *Application deadline:* For fall admission, 7/1 priority date for domestic and international students; for spring admission, 11/1 priority date for domestic and international students; for summer admission, 4/1 priority date for domestic and international students. Applications are processed on a rolling basis. Application fee: $50. Electronic applications accepted. *Expenses:* $700 per credit hour. *Financial support:* In 2017–18, 3 students received support. Career-related internships or fieldwork, scholarships/grants, and health care benefits available. Financial award applicants required to submit FAFSA. *Unit head:* Travis Newton, Assistant Professor and Director of Arts Administration, 315-445-4201, E-mail: newtontm@lemoyne.edu. *Application contact:* Kristen P. Richards, Senior Director of Enrollment Management, 315-445-5444, Fax: 315-445-6092, E-mail: trapaskp@lemoyne.edu.
Website: http://www.lemoyne.edu/Learn/Colleges-Schools-Centers/College-of-Arts-Sciences/Majors-Minors/Arts-Administration

London Metropolitan University, Graduate Programs, London, United Kingdom. Offers applied psychology (M Sc); architecture (MA); biomedical science (M Sc); blood science (M Sc); cancer pharmacology (M Sc); computer networking and cyber security (M Sc); computing and information systems (M Sc); conference interpreting (MA); counter-terrorism studies (M Sc); creative, digital and professional writing (MA); crime, violence and prevention (M Sc); criminology (M Sc); curating contemporary art (MA); data analytics (M Sc); digital media (MA); early childhood studies (MA); education (MA, Ed D); financial services law, regulation and compliance (LL M); food science (M Sc); forensic psychology (M Sc); health and social care management and policy (M Sc); human nutrition (M Sc); human resource management (MA); human rights and international conflict (MA); information technology (M Sc); intelligence and security studies (M Sc); international oil, gas and energy law (LL M); international relations (MA); interpreting (MA); learning and teaching in higher education (MA); legal practice (LL M); media and entertainment law (LL M); organizational and consumer psychology (M Sc); psychological therapy (M Sc); psychology of mental health (M Sc); public health (M Sc); public policy and management (MPA); security studies (M Sc); social work (M Sc); spatial planning and urban design (MA); sports therapy (M Sc); supporting older children and young people with dyslexia (MA); teaching languages (MA), including Arabic, English; translation (MA); woman and child abuse (MA).

Montclair State University, The Graduate School, College of the Arts, MA Program in Theatre, Montclair, NJ 07043-1624. Offers arts management (MA); production/stage management (MA); theatre studies (MA). *Accreditation:* NAST. *Program availability:* Part-time, evening/weekend. *Degree requirements:* For master's, comprehensive exam, thesis or alternative. *Entrance requirements:* For master's, GRE General Test, 2 letters of recommendation. Additional exam requirements/recommendations for international students: Required—TOEFL (minimum score 83 iBT) or IELTS (minimum score 6.5). Electronic applications accepted. *Faculty research:* Danceturgy, Arab and Muslim images in American drama, Neil LaBute and playwriting, directing, Robert Edmond Jones.

Moore College of Art & Design, Program in Community Practice, Philadelphia, PA 19103. Offers MFA. *Degree requirements:* For master's, thesis.

New York University, Steinhardt School of Culture, Education, and Human Development, Department of Art and Art Professions, Program in Visual Arts Administration, New York, NY 10003. Offers MA. *Program availability:* Part-time. *Students:* Average age 27. 161 applicants, 47% accepted, 52 enrolled. In 2017, 38 master's awarded. *Entrance requirements:* For master's, interview. Additional exam requirements/recommendations for international students: Required—TOEFL (minimum score 100 iBT). *Application deadline:* For fall admission, 12/1 priority date for domestic and international students. Applications are processed on a rolling basis. Application fee: $75. Electronic applications accepted. *Expenses: Tuition:* Full-time $41,352; part-time $19,968 per year. *Required fees:* $2496; $1628 per unit. $814 per term. Tuition and fees vary according to course load and program. *Financial support:* Career-related internships or fieldwork, Federal Work-Study, institutionally sponsored loans, scholarships/grants, and tuition waivers (partial) available. Support available to part-time students. Financial award application deadline: 2/1; financial award applicants required to submit FAFSA. *Faculty research:* Corporate philanthropy, contemporary art and culture, public art and urban development, cultural policy, arts advocacy. *Unit head:* Prof. Sandra Lang, Director, 212-998-5723, Fax: 212-995-4320, E-mail: sandra.lang@nyu.edu. *Application contact:* 212-998-5030, Fax: 212-995-4328, E-mail: steinhardt.gradadmissions@nyu.edu.
Website: http://steinhardt.nyu.edu/art/admin

New York University, Steinhardt School of Culture, Education, and Human Development, Department of Music and Performing Arts Professions, Program in Performing Arts Administration, New York, NY 10012. Offers MA. *Program availability:* Part-time. *Students:* Average age 27. 132 applicants, 42% accepted, 27 enrolled. In 2017, 26 master's awarded. *Entrance requirements:* For master's, interview. Additional exam requirements/recommendations for international students: Required—TOEFL (minimum score 100 iBT). *Application deadline:* For fall admission, 12/1 priority date for domestic students, 12/1 for international students. Applications are processed on a rolling basis. Application fee: $75. Electronic applications accepted. *Expenses: Tuition:* Full-time $41,352; part-time $19,968 per year. *Required fees:* $2496; $1628 per unit. $814 per term. Tuition and fees vary according to course load and program. *Financial support:* Career-related internships or fieldwork, Federal Work-Study, institutionally sponsored loans, scholarships/grants, and tuition waivers (partial) available. Support available to part-time students. Financial award application deadline: 2/1; financial award applicants required to submit FAFSA. *Faculty research:* Legal dimensions of arts management, global arts management, cultural policy. *Unit head:* Prof. Brann J. Wry, Director, 212-998-5424, E-mail: brann.wry@nyu.edu. *Application contact:* 212-998-5030, Fax: 212-995-4328, E-mail: steinhardt.gradadmissions@nyu.edu.
Website: http://steinhardt.nyu.edu/music/artsadmin

New York University, Tisch School of the Arts, Program in Arts Politics, New York, NY 10012-1019. Offers MA. *Faculty:* 3 full-time (2 women), 4 part-time/adjunct (3 women). *Students:* 11 full-time (8 women); includes 4 minority (2 Black or African American, non-Hispanic/Latino; 1 Asian, non-Hispanic/Latino; 1 Hispanic/Latino), 4 international. Average age 25. 33 applicants, 97% accepted, 11 enrolled. In 2017, 13 master's awarded. *Entrance requirements:* For master's, professional resume, writing sample, statement of purpose. *Application deadline:* For fall admission, 1/1 for domestic and international students. Application fee: $60. *Expenses: Tuition:* Full-time $41,352; part-time $19,968 per year. *Required fees:* $2496; $1628 per unit. $814 per term. Tuition and fees vary according to course load and program. *Financial support:* In 2017–18, 2 students received support. Federal Work-Study and scholarships/grants available. Financial award application deadline: 2/15; financial award applicants required to submit FAFSA. *Unit head:* Randy Martin, Director, 212-992-8248. *Application contact:* Dan Sandford, Director of Graduate Admissions, 212-998-1918, Fax: 212-995-4060, E-mail: tisch.gradadmissions@nyu.edu.

Northwestern University, The Graduate School, School of Communication, Program in Leadership for Creative Enterprises, Evanston, IL 60208. Offers MS.

The Ohio State University, Graduate School, College of Arts and Sciences, Division of Arts and Humanities, Department of Arts Administration, Education and Policy, Program in Arts Policy and Administration, Columbus, OH 43210. Offers MA. *Faculty:* 11. *Students:* 6. Average age 25. In 2017, 3 master's awarded. *Degree requirements:* For master's, thesis. *Entrance requirements:* For master's, GRE General Test. Additional exam requirements/recommendations for international students: Required—TOEFL (minimum score 600 paper-based; 100 iBT); Recommended—IELTS (minimum score 8). *Application deadline:* For fall and spring admission, 11/30 priority date for domestic and international students. Applications are processed on a rolling basis. Application fee: $60 ($70 for international students). Electronic applications accepted. *Financial support:* Fellowships with tuition reimbursements, teaching assistantships with tuition reimbursements, career-related internships or fieldwork, and unspecified assistantships available. Support available to part-time students. Financial award application deadline: 4/5. *Faculty research:* Public policy and advocacy. *Unit head:* Dr. Karen Hutzel, Chair and Associate Professor, 614-292-9852, E-mail: hutzel.4@osu.edu. *Application contact:* Graduate and Professional Admissions, 614-292-6031, Fax: 614-292-3656, E-mail: gpadmissions@osu.edu.
Website: http://aaep.osu.edu/arts-policy-administration-ma-program

Arts Administration

Pratt Institute, School of Art, Program in Arts and Cultural Management, New York, NY 10011. Offers MPS. *Program availability:* Part-time, evening/weekend. *Students:* 18 full-time (14 women), 20 part-time (all women); includes 6 minority (2 Black or African American, non-Hispanic/Latino; 3 Hispanic/Latino; 1 Two or more races, non-Hispanic/Latino), 24 international. Average age 27. 97 applicants, 58% accepted, 18 enrolled. In 2017, 15 master's awarded. *Degree requirements:* For master's, thesis. *Entrance requirements:* For master's, letters of recommendation, portfolio. Additional exam requirements/recommendations for international students: Required—TOEFL (minimum score 600 paper-based; 100 iBT). *Application deadline:* For fall admission, 1/5 for domestic and international students; for spring admission, 10/1 for domestic and international students. Application fee: $50 ($90 for international students). Electronic applications accepted. *Expenses: Tuition:* Full-time $30,834. *Required fees:* $1974. *Financial support:* Career-related internships or fieldwork, Federal Work-Study, institutionally sponsored loans, scholarships/grants, health care benefits, and unspecified assistantships available. Support available to part-time students. Financial award application deadline: 2/1; financial award applicants required to submit FAFSA. *Unit head:* Dr. Mary McBride, Director, 212-647-7538, Fax: 212-367-2480, E-mail: mmcb1033@pratt.edu. *Application contact:* Natalie Capannelli, Director of Graduate Admissions, 718-636-3551, Fax: 718-399-4242, E-mail: ncapanne@pratt.edu.
Website: https://www.pratt.edu/academics/school-of-art/graduate-school-of-art/arts-cultural-management/

Pratt Institute, School of Art, Program in Design Management, New York, NY 10011. Offers MPS. *Program availability:* Part-time. *Students:* 23 full-time (15 women), 18 part-time (17 women); includes 8 minority (4 Black or African American, non-Hispanic/Latino; 2 Asian, non-Hispanic/Latino; 2 Hispanic/Latino), 25 international. Average age 27. 108 applicants, 61% accepted, 22 enrolled. In 2017, 20 master's awarded. *Degree requirements:* For master's, thesis. *Entrance requirements:* For master's, letters of recommendation, portfolio. Additional exam requirements/recommendations for international students: Required—TOEFL (minimum score 600 paper-based; 100 iBT). *Application deadline:* For fall admission, 1/5 for domestic and international students; for spring admission, 10/1 for domestic and international students. Application fee: $50 ($90 for international students). Electronic applications accepted. *Expenses: Tuition:* Full-time $30,834. *Required fees:* $1974. *Financial support:* Career-related internships or fieldwork, Federal Work-Study, institutionally sponsored loans, scholarships/grants, health care benefits, and unspecified assistantships available. Support available to part-time students. Financial award application deadline: 2/1; financial award applicants required to submit FAFSA. *Unit head:* Dr. Mary McBride, Chairperson, 212-647-7538, Fax: 212-367-2480, E-mail: mmcb1033@pratt.edu. *Application contact:* Natalie Capannelli, Director of Graduate Admissions, 718-636-3551, Fax: 718-399-4242, E-mail: ncapanne@pratt.edu.
Website: https://www.pratt.edu/academics/school-of-art/graduate-school-of-art/design-management/

See Display on page 141 and Close-Up on page 189.

Purchase College, State University of New York, School of the Arts, Purchase, NY 10577-1400. Offers entrepreneurship in the arts (MA). *Program availability:* Part-time. *Degree requirements:* For master's, thesis. *Unit head:* Dr. Peggy De Cooke, Acting Dean, 914-251-4455, Fax: 914-251-4457, E-mail: peggy.decooke@purchase.edu.
Website: https://www.purchase.edu/academics/arts/

Rhode Island College, School of Graduate Studies, Faculty of Arts and Sciences, Department of Art, Providence, RI 02908-1991. Offers art education (MA, MAT); media studies (MA). *Accreditation:* NASAD (one or more programs are accredited). *Program availability:* Part-time, evening/weekend. *Faculty:* 3. *Students:* 4 full-time (3 women), 11 part-time (5 women); includes 4 minority (1 Asian, non-Hispanic/Latino; 3 Hispanic/Latino). Average age 33. In 2017, 4 master's awarded. *Degree requirements:* For master's, thesis. *Entrance requirements:* For master's, GRE General Test, portfolio (MA), 3 letters of recommendation, interview. Additional exam requirements/recommendations for international students: Recommended—TOEFL (minimum score 550 paper-based; 79 iBT). *Application deadline:* For fall admission, 3/1 for domestic students. Applications are processed on a rolling basis. Application fee: $50. Electronic applications accepted. *Expenses:* Tuition, state resident: full-time $9768; part-time $407 per credit. Tuition, nonresident: full-time $19,008; part-time $792 per credit. *Required fees:* $696; $29 per credit. One-time fee: $200 full-time; $100 part-time. Tuition and fees vary according to course load. *Financial support:* In 2017–18, 3 teaching assistantships with full tuition reimbursements (averaging $1,500 per year) were awarded; career-related internships or fieldwork, Federal Work-Study, scholarships/grants, health care benefits, and unspecified assistantships also available. Support available to part-time students. Financial award application deadline: 5/15; financial award applicants required to submit FAFSA. *Unit head:* Prof. Richard Whitten, Chair, 401-456-8054.
Website: http://www.ric.edu/art/index.php

Rocky Mountain College of Art + Design, Program in Education, Leadership + Emerging Technologies, Lakewood, CO 80214. Offers MA. *Accreditation:* NASAD. *Program availability:* Online learning.

Roosevelt University, Graduate Division, Chicago College of Performing Arts, Music Conservatory, Chicago, IL 60605. Offers brass (Diploma); brass performance (MM); classical guitar (MM, Diploma); music (MM); music composition (MM); opera (Diploma); orchestral studies (MM, Diploma); percussion (MM, Diploma); performing arts administration (MA); piano (Diploma); piano performance (MM); strings (MM, Diploma); voice (MM); woodwinds (MM, Diploma). *Students:* 116 full-time (70 women), 7 part-time (5 women); includes 10 minority (3 Black or African American, non-Hispanic/Latino; 1 Asian, non-Hispanic/Latino; 3 Hispanic/Latino; 3 Two or more races, non-Hispanic/Latino), 31 international. Average age 25. 139 applicants, 93% accepted, 45 enrolled. In 2017, 36 master's, 13 other advanced degrees awarded. *Application deadline:* Applications are processed on a rolling basis. Application fee: $100. Electronic applications accepted. *Expenses:* Contact institution. *Financial support:* Scholarships/grants available. *Application contact:* Michael Holmes, Interim Assistant Dean for Enrollment Management, 312-341-3797, E-mail: mholmes04@roosevelt.edu.
Website: https://www.roosevelt.edu/colleges/ccpa/music-conservatory

Rowan University, Graduate School, College of Performing Arts, Department of Theatre and Dance, Glassboro, NJ 08028-1701. Offers theatre arts administration (MA). *Accreditation:* NASAD. Electronic applications accepted. *Expenses:* Tuition, state resident: full-time $15,020; part-time $751 per semester hour. Tuition, nonresident: full-time $15,020; part-time $751 per semester hour. *Required fees:* $3158; $157.90 per semester hour. Tuition and fees vary according to course load, campus/location and program.

Ryerson University, School of Graduate Studies, Program in Photographic Preservation and Collections Management, Toronto, ON M5B 2K3, Canada. Offers MA.

St. Thomas University, School of Leadership Studies, Program in Art Management, Miami Gardens, FL 33054-6459. Offers MA.

Savannah College of Art and Design, Program in Business Design and Arts Leadership, Savannah, GA 31402-3146. Offers MA. *Program availability:* Part-time, 100% online. *Faculty:* 5 full-time (1 woman), 3 part-time/adjunct (1 woman). *Students:* 40 full-time (34 women), 53 part-time (46 women); includes 26 minority (21 Black or African American, non-Hispanic/Latino; 2 Asian, non-Hispanic/Latino; 3 Hispanic/Latino), 21 international. Average age 29. 124 applicants, 39% accepted, 27 enrolled. In 2017, 18 master's awarded. *Degree requirements:* For master's, final project. *Entrance requirements:* For master's, GRE (recommended), portfolio (submitted in digital format), audition or writing submission, resume, statement of purpose, two letters of recommendation. Additional exam requirements/recommendations for international students: Recommended—TOEFL (minimum score 550 paper-based; 85 iBT), IELTS (minimum score 6.5). *Application deadline:* For fall admission, 4/1 for domestic and international students. Applications are processed on a rolling basis. Application fee: $40. Electronic applications accepted. *Expenses: Tuition:* Full-time $36,765; part-time $817 per credit hour. One-time fee: $500. *Financial support:* Career-related internships or fieldwork, Federal Work-Study, and scholarships/grants available. Financial award application deadline: 4/1; financial award applicants required to submit FAFSA. *Unit head:* Anita Akella, Academic Program Coordinator. *Application contact:* Jenny Jaquillard, Executive Director of Admissions, Recruitment and Events, 912-525-5100, Fax: 912-525-5985, E-mail: admission@scad.edu.
Website: http://www.scad.edu/academics/programs/business-design-and-arts-leadership

Savannah College of Art and Design, Program in Design Management, Savannah, GA 31402-3146. Offers MA, MFA. *Program availability:* Part-time, 100% online. *Faculty:* 3 full-time (1 woman), 7 part-time/adjunct (4 women). *Students:* 45 full-time (30 women), 64 part-time (45 women); includes 21 minority (7 Black or African American, non-Hispanic/Latino; 5 Asian, non-Hispanic/Latino; 9 Hispanic/Latino), 37 international. Average age 30. 108 applicants, 52% accepted, 24 enrolled. In 2017, 55 master's awarded. *Degree requirements:* For master's, final project (for MA); thesis (for MFA). *Entrance requirements:* For master's, GRE (recommended), portfolio (submitted in digital format), audition or writing submission, resume, statement of purpose, two letters of recommendation. Additional exam requirements/recommendations for international students: Recommended—TOEFL (minimum score 550 paper-based; 85 iBT), IELTS (minimum score 6.5). *Application deadline:* For fall admission, 4/1 for domestic and international students. Applications are processed on a rolling basis. Application fee: $40. Electronic applications accepted. *Expenses: Tuition:* Full-time $36,765; part-time $817 per credit hour. One-time fee: $500. *Financial support:* Career-related internships or fieldwork, Federal Work-Study, and scholarships/grants available. Financial award application deadline: 4/1; financial award applicants required to submit FAFSA. *Unit head:* Bill Lee, Chair, Design Management. *Application contact:* Jenny Jaquillard, Executive Director of Admissions, Recruitment and Events, 912-525-5100, Fax: 912-525-5985, E-mail: admission@scad.edu.
Website: http://www.scad.edu/academics/programs/design-management

School of the Art Institute of Chicago, Graduate Division, Program in Arts Administration and Policy, Chicago, IL 60603-3103. Offers MAAAP. *Accreditation:* NASAD. *Degree requirements:* For master's, thesis, telephone interview. *Entrance requirements:* Additional exam requirements/recommendations for international students: Required—TOEFL, IELTS. *Faculty research:* Latin American artists, activist art, community-based art.

Seattle University, College of Arts and Sciences, Program in Arts Leadership, Seattle, WA 98122-1090. Offers MFA. *Program availability:* Part-time, evening/weekend. *Faculty:* 4 full-time (2 women), 7 part-time/adjunct (4 women). *Students:* 3 full-time (2 women), 60 part-time (47 women); includes 15 minority (3 Black or African American, non-Hispanic/Latino; 4 Asian, non-Hispanic/Latino; 5 Hispanic/Latino; 3 Two or more races, non-Hispanic/Latino), 11 international. Average age 31. 74 applicants, 73% accepted, 32 enrolled. In 2017, 24 master's awarded. *Degree requirements:* For master's, summary capstone project presentation and paper. *Entrance requirements:* For master's, minimum GPA of 3.0; 2 years of management in nonprofit, comparable work, or volunteer experience. Additional exam requirements/recommendations for international students: Required—TOEFL, IELTS. *Application deadline:* For fall admission, 3/15 for domestic students, 4/1 for international students. Applications are processed on a rolling basis. Application fee: $55. Electronic applications accepted. *Expenses: Tuition:* Full-time $12,960. *Required fees:* $570. Tuition and fees vary according to program. *Financial support:* In 2017–18, 23 students received support. Application deadline: 3/15; applicants required to submit FAFSA. *Faculty research:* Leadership succession planning, social media in arts marketing, audience development. *Unit head:* Kevin Maifeld, Director, 206-296-5370, E-mail: maifeldk@seattleu.edu. *Application contact:* Janet Shandley, Associate Dean of Graduate Admissions, 206-296-5900, Fax: 206-298-5656, E-mail: grad_admissions@seattleu.edu.
Website: https://www.seattleu.edu/artsci/mfa/

Sotheby's Institute of Art–London, Graduate Programs, London, United Kingdom. Offers art business (MA); contemporary art (MA); fine and decorative art and design (MA); modern and contemporary Asian art (MA). *Degree requirements:* For master's, thesis. *Entrance requirements:* Additional exam requirements/recommendations for international students: Required—IELTS (minimum score 7). Electronic applications accepted.

Sotheby's Institute of Art–New York, Graduate Programs, New York, NY 10021. Offers art business (MA); contemporary art (MA); fine and decorative art and design (MA). *Accreditation:* NASAD. *Entrance requirements:* For master's, academic transcripts, two letters of academic reference, personal statement, writing sample, curriculum vitae/resume, interview. Additional exam requirements/recommendations for international students: Required—TOEFL (minimum score 100 iBT), IELTS (minimum score 7). Electronic applications accepted.

Southern Methodist University, Meadows School of the Arts, Division of Arts Management and Arts Entrepreneurship, Dallas, TX 75275. Offers international arts management (MM); MA/MBA. MM offered jointly with Bocconi University Graduate School of Management in Milan and HEC Montreal. *Entrance requirements:* For master's, GMAT. Additional exam requirements/recommendations for international students: Required—TOEFL (minimum score 600 paper-based; 100 iBT). Electronic applications accepted.

Southern Utah University, Program in Arts Administration, Cedar City, UT 84720-2498. Offers MA, MFA. *Program availability:* Part-time, 100% online. *Faculty:* 3 full-time (2 women), 5 part-time/adjunct (2 women). *Students:* 13 full-time (7 women), 23 part-time (21 women); includes 5 minority (1 Asian, non-Hispanic/Latino; 4 Hispanic/Latino). Average age 33. 21 applicants, 62% accepted, 13 enrolled. In 2017, 12 master's awarded. *Entrance requirements:* For master's, bachelor's degree, interview, 3 letters of recommendation, resume, minimum undergraduate GPA of 3.0, written statement of purpose, transcripts. Additional exam requirements/recommendations for international students: Required—TOEFL (minimum score 550 paper-based, 79 iBT) or IELTS (minimum score 6). *Application deadline:* For fall admission, 2/15 for domestic and international students. Applications are processed on a rolling basis. Application fee: $60 ($65 for international students). Electronic applications accepted. *Expenses:* Contact institution. *Financial support:* Tuition waivers and unspecified assistantships available. *Unit head:* Rachel Bishop, Program Director/Assistant Professor, 435-586-7873, Fax: 435-865-8657, E-mail: bishopr@suu.edu.
Website: https://www.suu.edu/pva/aa/academic.html

Teachers College, Columbia University, Department of Arts and Humanities, New York, NY 10027. Offers applied linguistics (MA, Ed D); art and art education (Ed M, MA, Ed D, Ed DCT); arts administration (MA); bilingual and bicultural education (MA); global competence (Certificate); history and education (Ed D, PhD); music and music education (Ed DCT); philosophy and education (MA, Ed D, PhD); social studies education (Ed M, PhD); teaching English to speakers of other languages (Ed M); teaching of English and English education (Ed M, MA, Ed D, PhD), including English education (Ed M, Ed D, PhD), teaching of English (MA); teaching of social studies (MA); TESOL (MA, Ed D). *Program availability:* Part-time, evening/weekend. *Students:* 391 full-time (305 women), 418 part-time (283 women); includes 246 minority (62 Black or African American, non-Hispanic/Latino; 3 American Indian or Alaska Native, non-Hispanic/Latino; 94 Asian, non-Hispanic/Latino; 75 Hispanic/Latino; 12 Two or more races, non-Hispanic/Latino), 209 international. Average age 30. 1,053 applicants, 60% accepted, 334 enrolled. Terminal master's awarded for partial completion of doctoral program. *Financial support:* Fellowships, research assistantships, teaching assistantships, career-related internships or fieldwork, Federal Work-Study, institutionally sponsored loans, tuition waivers (full and partial), and unspecified assistantships available. Support available to part-time students. *Unit head:* Prof. William Gaudelli, Department Chair, E-mail: gaudelli@tc.columbia.edu. *Application contact:* David Estrella, Director of Admissions, 212-678-3305, Fax: 212-678-4171, E-mail: estrella@tc.columbia.edu.

Temple University, Tyler School of Art, Department of Art History, Philadelphia, PA 19122-6096. Offers MA, PhD. *Program availability:* Part-time. *Faculty:* 10 full-time (7 women), 8 part-time/adjunct (4 women). *Students:* 47 full-time (41 women), 6 part-time (5 women); includes 10 minority (1 Black or African American, non-Hispanic/Latino; 2 Asian, non-Hispanic/Latino; 5 Hispanic/Latino; 2 Two or more races, non-Hispanic/Latino), 5 international. 36 applicants, 67% accepted, 6 enrolled. In 2017, 6 master's, 4 doctorates awarded. Terminal master's awarded for partial completion of doctoral program. *Entrance requirements:* For master's, GRE General Test, minimum GPA of 3.0, letters of recommendation, resume/curriculum vitae, writing sample; for doctorate, GRE, MA in art history, minimum GPA of 3.0, letters of recommendation, resume/curriculum vitae, writing sample. Additional exam requirements/recommendations for international students: Required—TOEFL (minimum score 550 paper-based; 79 iBT), IELTS (minimum score 6.5). *Application deadline:* For fall admission, 12/15 for domestic and international students; for spring admission, 11/1 for domestic students, 10/1 for international students. Applications are processed on a rolling basis. Application fee: $60. Electronic applications accepted. *Expenses:* Contact institution. *Financial support:* Fellowships, research assistantships, teaching assistantships, career-related internships or fieldwork, institutionally sponsored loans, and technical assistantships available. Financial award application deadline: 1/15. *Faculty research:* Aegean, Greek, and Roman art; early Christian art; medieval art and architecture; Renaissance and Baroque painting, sculpture, and architecture; nineteenth- and twentieth-century painting and sculpture. *Unit head:* Dr. Jane DeRose Evans, Chair, 215-777-9165, Fax: 215-204-6951, E-mail: jevans@temple.edu. *Application contact:* Tamryn McDermott, Director of Admissions, 215-777-9090, E-mail: tylerart@temple.edu. Website: https://tyler.temple.edu/programs/art-history

Universidad del Turabo, Graduate Programs, School of Social Sciences and Humanities, Programs in Public Affairs, Program in Arts Administration, Gurabo, PR 00778-3030. Offers MPA. *Entrance requirements:* For master's, GRE, EXADEP or GMAT, interview, essay, official transcript, recommendation letters. Electronic applications accepted.

University at Buffalo, the State University of New York, Graduate School, College of Arts and Sciences, Arts Management Program, Buffalo, NY 14260. Offers MA. *Program availability:* Part-time. *Faculty:* 3 full-time (2 women), 4 part-time/adjunct (2 women). *Students:* 13 full-time (12 women), 2 part-time (both women), 7 international. Average age 25. 44 applicants, 27% accepted, 7 enrolled. In 2017, 1 master's awarded. *Degree requirements:* For master's, thesis. *Entrance requirements:* For master's, curriculum vitae, academic essay, personal statement, 2 letters of recommendation, official transcripts; bank statements, supporting documentation, and passport (for international students). Additional exam requirements/recommendations for international students: Required—TOEFL or IELTS. *Application deadline:* For fall admission, 3/1 priority date for domestic and international students. Applications are processed on a rolling basis. Application fee: $75. Electronic applications accepted. *Expenses:* Contact institution. *Financial support:* In 2017–18, 1 student received support. Fulbright funding available. Financial award application deadline: 8/15; financial award applicants required to submit FAFSA. *Faculty research:* Cultural policy, arts management, museums and the public space, performing arts and digital media, cultural frameworks. *Unit head:* Prof. Franck Bauchard, Director, 716-645-2437, Fax: 716-645-6737, E-mail: artsmgmt@buffalo.edu. *Application contact:* Anne Gullotti, Assistant to the Director, 716-645-0766, Fax: 716-645-6737, E-mail: artsmgmt@buffalo.edu. Website: http://www.buffalo.edu/cas/arts_management.html

The University of Akron, Graduate School, Buchtel College of Arts and Sciences, School of Dance, Theatre, and Arts Administration, Program in Arts Administration, Akron, OH 44325. Offers MA. *Accreditation:* NASAD. *Students:* 14 full-time (12 women), 4 part-time (all women); includes 3 minority (2 Black or African American, non-Hispanic/Latino; 1 Two or more races, non-Hispanic/Latino), 1 international. Average age 29. 21 applicants, 95% accepted, 8 enrolled. In 2017, 7 master's awarded. *Degree requirements:* For master's, thesis. *Entrance requirements:* For master's, minimum GPA of 2.75, 300-word statement of intent summarizing student background and outlining career goals. Additional exam requirements/recommendations for international students: Required—TOEFL (minimum score 79 iBT), IELTS (minimum score 6.5). *Application deadline:* For fall admission, 3/15 for domestic and international students. Application fee: $45 ($70 for international students). Electronic applications accepted. *Unit head:* Dr. J. Thomas Dukes, Interim Director, 330-972-7948, E-mail: jtdukes@uakron.edu. *Application contact:* James Slowiak, Coordinator, Arts Administration, 330-972-5909, E-mail: jslowiak@uakron.edu. Website: http://www.uakron.edu/dtaa/artsadmin/

University of Cincinnati, Graduate School, College-Conservatory of Music, Division of Theatre Arts, Production and Arts Administration, Cincinnati, OH 45221. Offers arts administration (MA); directing (MFA); theater design and production (MFA); voice and opera (MM, DMA); MBA/MA. *Accreditation:* NAST (one or more programs are accredited). *Degree requirements:* For master's, final project. *Entrance requirements:* For master's, GMAT (MA), audition/interview. Additional exam requirements/recommendations for international students: Required—TOEFL (minimum score 520 paper-based). Electronic applications accepted. *Expenses: Tuition, area resident:* Full-time $14,468. Tuition, state resident: full-time $14,968; part-time $754 per credit hour. Tuition, nonresident: full-time $24,210; part-time $1311 per credit hour. *International tuition:* $26,460 full-time. *Required fees:* $3958; $84 per credit hour. One-time fee: $85 full-time. Tuition and fees vary according to course load, degree level and program.

University of Kentucky, Graduate School, College of Fine Arts, Program in Arts Administration, Lexington, KY 40506-0032. Offers MA.

The University of Manchester, School of Arts, Histories and Cultures, Manchester, United Kingdom. Offers anthropology, media and performance (PhD); applied theatre professional (PhD); archaeology (PhD); art history and visual studies (PhD); arts management and cultural policy (PhD); classics and ancient history (PhD); composition (PhD); creative writing (PhD); drama (PhD); economic and social history (PhD); electroacoustic composition (PhD); English and American studies (PhD); history (PhD); humanitarianism and conflict response (PhD); museology (PhD); music (PhD); musicology (PhD); religions and theology (PhD).

University of Michigan–Flint, Graduate Programs, Program in Arts Administration, Flint, MI 48502-1950. Offers performance (MA), including museum and visual arts, performance. *Program availability:* Part-time. *Faculty:* 5 full-time (3 women), 1 (woman) part-time/adjunct. *Students:* 6 full-time (4 women), 7 part-time (4 women); includes 2 minority (both Black or African American, non-Hispanic/Latino). Average age 43. 12 applicants, 75% accepted, 5 enrolled. In 2017, 3 master's awarded. *Degree requirements:* For master's, thesis, internship. *Entrance requirements:* For master's, bachelor's degree in the arts (visual art, theatre, dance, music, etc.) from regionally-accredited institution; minimum cumulative undergraduate GPA of 3.0. Additional exam requirements/recommendations for international students: Required—TOEFL (minimum score 84 iBT), IELTS (minimum score 6.5). *Application deadline:* For fall admission, 8/1 for domestic students, 5/1 for international students; for winter admission, 11/15 for domestic students, 9/1 for international students. Applications are processed on a rolling basis. Application fee: $55. Electronic applications accepted. *Expenses:* Contact institution. *Financial support:* Federal Work-Study, institutionally sponsored loans, scholarships/grants, and unspecified assistantships available. Support available to part-time students. Financial award application deadline: 3/1; financial award applicants required to submit FAFSA. *Unit head:* Nicole Broughton, Director, 810-237-6522, E-mail: broughn@umflint.edu. *Application contact:* Bradley T. Maki, Director of Graduate Admissions, 810-762-3171, Fax: 810-766-6789, E-mail: bmaki@umflint.edu. Website: http://www.umflint.edu/graduateprograms/arts-administration-ma

University of New Orleans, Graduate School, College of Liberal Arts, Program in Arts Administration, New Orleans, LA 70148. Offers MA. *Program availability:* Part-time. *Degree requirements:* For master's, internship. *Entrance requirements:* For master's, GRE General Test. Additional exam requirements/recommendations for international students: Required—TOEFL (minimum score 550 paper-based; 79 iBT), IELTS (minimum score 6.5). Electronic applications accepted.

The University of North Carolina at Charlotte, College of Liberal Arts and Sciences, Department of Political Science and Public Administration, Charlotte, NC 28223-0001. Offers emergency management (Graduate Certificate); non-profit management (Graduate Certificate); public administration (MPA), including arts administration, emergency management, non-profit management, public budgeting and finance, urban management and policy; public budgeting and finance (Graduate Certificate); urban management and policy (Graduate Certificate). *Accreditation:* NASPAA. *Program availability:* Part-time, evening/weekend. *Faculty:* 19 full-time (9 women), 4 part-time/adjunct (1 woman). *Students:* 20 full-time (11 women), 61 part-time (41 women); includes 21 minority (12 Black or African American, non-Hispanic/Latino; 2 American Indian or Alaska Native, non-Hispanic/Latino; 1 Asian, non-Hispanic/Latino; 4 Hispanic/Latino; 2 Two or more races, non-Hispanic/Latino), 1 international. Average age 28. 48 applicants, 67% accepted, 22 enrolled. In 2017, 25 master's, 15 other advanced degrees awarded. *Degree requirements:* For master's, research project or thesis. *Entrance requirements:* For master's, GRE General Test, bachelor's degree, or its equivalent, from accredited college or university; minimum undergraduate GPA of 3.0; 3 letters of recommendation; statement of purpose; for Graduate Certificate, statement of purpose (1-2 pages in length) explaining applicant's career goals, how the Graduate Certificate fits into achieving those goals, and any relevant work experience; official transcripts; letters of recommendation. Additional exam requirements/recommendations for international students: Required—TOEFL (minimum score 523 paper-based, 70 iBT) or IELTS (6.5). *Application deadline:* For fall admission, 8/1 for domestic and international students; for spring admission, 12/1 for domestic and international students. Applications are processed on a rolling basis. Application fee: $75. Electronic applications accepted. *Expenses:* Tuition, state resident: full-time $4337. Tuition, nonresident: full-time $17,771. *Required fees:* $3211. Tuition and fees vary according to course load and program. *Financial support:* In 2017–18, 14 students received support, including 13 research assistantships (averaging $9,015 per year), 1 teaching assistantship (averaging $19,500 per year); career-related internships or fieldwork, Federal Work-Study, institutionally sponsored loans, scholarships/grants, and unspecified assistantships also available. Support available to part-time students. Financial award application deadline: 3/1; financial award applicants required to submit FAFSA. *Total annual research expenditures:* $419,411. *Unit head:* Dr. Greg Weeks, Chair, 704-687-7574, E-mail: gbweeks@uncc.edu. *Application contact:* Kathy B. Giddings, Director of Graduate Admissions, 704-687-5503, Fax: 704-687-1668, E-mail: gradadm@uncc.edu. Website: http://politicalscience.uncc.edu/

University of Southern California, Graduate School, Roski School of Fine Arts, Art and Curatorial Practices in the Public Sphere Program, Los Angeles, CA 90089. Offers MA. *Degree requirements:* For master's, thesis, practicum exhibition. *Entrance requirements:* For master's, GRE, personal statement, writing sample, three letters of recommendation. Additional exam requirements/recommendations for international students: Required—TOEFL (minimum score 600 paper-based; 100 iBT). Electronic applications accepted. *Faculty research:* Curatorial studies, exhibition histories, modern and contemporary art, public art.

University of Wisconsin–Madison, Graduate School, Wisconsin School of Business, Wisconsin Full-Time MBA Program, Madison, WI 53706. Offers applied security analysis (MBA); arts administration (MBA); brand and product management (MBA); corporate finance and investment banking (MBA); marketing research (MBA); operations and technology management (MBA); real estate (MBA); risk management and insurance (MBA); strategic human resource management (MBA); supply chain management (MBA). *Faculty:* 130 full-time (35 women), 42 part-time/adjunct (13 women). *Students:* 203 full-time (72 women); includes 34 minority (8 Black or African American, non-Hispanic/Latino; 10 Asian, non-Hispanic/Latino; 12 Hispanic/Latino; 4 Two or more races, non-Hispanic/Latino), 41 international. Average age 28. 556 applicants, 30% accepted, 104 enrolled. In 2017, 97 master's awarded. *Entrance requirements:* For master's, GMAT or GRE, bachelor's or equivalent degree, 2 years of work experience, essay, letter of recommendation, resume. Additional exam requirements/recommendations for international students: Required—TOEFL (minimum score 100 iBT), IELTS (minimum score 7.5). *Application deadline:* For fall admission, 11/2 for domestic and international students; for winter admission, 1/11 for domestic and international students; for spring admission, 3/1 for domestic and international students; for summer admission, 4/12 for domestic and international students. Applications are processed on a rolling basis. Application fee: $75 ($81 for international students). Electronic applications accepted. *Expenses:* $9,356 per semester resident, $18,288 non-resident. *Financial support:* In 2017–18, 183 students received support, including 14 fellowships with full tuition reimbursements available (averaging $25,420 per year), 7 research assistantships with full tuition reimbursements available (averaging $13,375 per year), 53 teaching assistantships with full tuition reimbursements available (averaging $13,375 per year); scholarships/grants, health care benefits, tuition waivers

(full), and unspecified assistantships also available. Financial award application deadline: 4/11. *Faculty research:* Forms of competition and outcomes in dual distribution systems; explaining the accuracy of revised forecasts; supply chain planning for random demand surges; advanced demand information in a multi-product system; the effects of presentation salience and measurement subjectivity on nonprofessional investors' fair value judgments. *Unit head:* Dr. Don Hausch, Associate Dean, Full-time MBA Program, 608-262-9731, E-mail: don.hausch@wisc.edu. *Application contact:* Betsy Kacizak, Director of Admissions and Recruiting, Full-time MBA Program, 608-262-4000, E-mail: betsy.kacizak@wisc.edu.
Website: https://wsb.wisc.edu/

Valparaiso University, Graduate School and Continuing Education, Program in Arts and Entertainment Administration, Valparaiso, IN 46383. Offers MA. *Program availability:* Part-time, evening/weekend. *Degree requirements:* For master's, internship or research project. *Entrance requirements:* Additional exam requirements/recommendations for international students: Required—TOEFL (minimum score 550 paper-based; 80 iBT), IELTS (minimum score 6). Electronic applications accepted. *Expenses: Tuition:* Full-time $11,340; part-time $630 per credit hour. *Required fees:* $520; $250 per year. $125 per semester. Tuition and fees vary according to program and reciprocity agreements.

Winthrop University, College of Visual and Performing Arts, Department of Art, Rock Hill, SC 29733. Offers art (MFA); art administration (MA); art education (MA). *Accreditation:* NASAD. *Program availability:* Part-time. *Students:* 6 full-time (5 women), 27 part-time (21 women); includes 10 minority (7 Black or African American, non-Hispanic/Latino; 2 Asian, non-Hispanic/Latino; 1 Hispanic/Latino), 1 international. Average age 38. In 2017, 12 master's awarded. *Degree requirements:* For master's, comprehensive exam (for some programs), thesis (for some programs), documented exhibit, oral exam. *Entrance requirements:* For master's, GRE General Test or MAT, PRAXIS (for MA), minimum GPA of 3.0, resume, slide portfolio, teaching certificate (MA). Additional exam requirements/recommendations for international students: Required—TOEFL (minimum score 550 paper-based; 79 iBT), IELTS (minimum score 6). *Application deadline:* For fall admission, 3/1 priority date for domestic students; for spring admission, 9/1 for domestic students. Applications are processed on a rolling basis. Application fee: $50. Electronic applications accepted. *Financial support:* Research assistantships with full tuition reimbursements, Federal Work-Study, scholarships/grants, and unspecified assistantships available. Support available to part-time students. Financial award application deadline: 2/1; financial award applicants required to submit FAFSA. *Unit head:* Anne Fiala, Interim Chair, 803-323-2653, E-mail: fialaa@winthrop.edu. *Application contact:* 800-411-7041, Fax: 803-323-2292, E-mail: graduatestu@winthrop.edu.
Website: http://www.winthrop.edu/cvpa/finearts

Art Therapy

Adler Graduate School, Program in Adlerian Counseling and Psychotherapy, Richfield, MN 55423. Offers Adlerian studies (MA); art therapy (MA); clinical mental health counseling (MA); co-occurring substance use and mental health disorders (MA); marriage and family therapy (MA); school counseling (MA). *Program availability:* Part-time, evening/weekend. *Faculty:* 71 part-time/adjunct (55 women). *Students:* 317 part-time (259 women); includes 51 minority (40 Black or African American, non-Hispanic/Latino; 6 American Indian or Alaska Native, non-Hispanic/Latino; 5 Hispanic/Latino). *Degree requirements:* For master's, thesis or alternative, 500-700 hour internship (depending on license choice). *Entrance requirements:* For master's, interview, official transcripts, minimum cumulative GPA of 3.0. *Application deadline:* Applications are processed on a rolling basis. Application fee: $50. Electronic applications accepted. *Expenses:* $575 per credit tuition. *Financial support:* Career-related internships or fieldwork and tuition waivers available. Support available to part-time students. Financial award applicants required to submit FAFSA. *Unit head:* Dr. Jeffrey Allen, President, 612-767-7048, Fax: 612-861-7559, E-mail: jeffrey.allen@alfredadler.edu. *Application contact:* Christina Hilpipre-Frischman, Director of Admissions, 612-767-7055, Fax: 612-861-7559, E-mail: christina@alfredadler.edu.
Website: http://alfredadler.edu/programs/masters-level-programs

Adler University, Graduate Programs, MA in Counseling Program: Specialization in Art Therapy, Chicago, IL 60602. Offers MAC.

Adler University, Graduate Programs, Master of Counseling Psychology Program: Art Therapy Concentration, Chicago, IL 60602. Offers MCP. Program offered at Vancouver campus. *Entrance requirements:* For master's, baccalaureate degree, minimum GPA of 3.0, portfolio.

Adler University, Graduate Programs, PhD in Art Therapy Program, Chicago, IL 60602. Offers PhD. *Program availability:* Part-time. *Degree requirements:* For doctorate, comprehensive exam, thesis/dissertation.

Albertus Magnus College, Master of Arts in Art Therapy and Counseling Program, New Haven, CT 06511-1189. Offers MA. *Program availability:* Part-time. *Faculty:* 3 full-time (all women), 13 part-time/adjunct (10 women). *Students:* 20 full-time (19 women), 18 part-time (17 women); includes 2 minority (1 Asian, non-Hispanic/Latino; 1 Hispanic/Latino). Average age 28. 15 applicants, 80% accepted, 10 enrolled. In 2017, 15 master's awarded. *Degree requirements:* For master's, thesis, 725-hour internship; 60 credits. *Entrance requirements:* For master's, interview, writing sample, portfolio (original art), 15 credits in psychology, 18 credits in studio art. Additional exam requirements/recommendations for international students: Required—TOEFL (minimum score 120 iBT). *Application deadline:* For fall admission, 5/1 for domestic students; for spring admission, 11/1 for domestic students. Applications are processed on a rolling basis. Application fee: $50. Electronic applications accepted. *Expenses:* Contact institution. *Financial support:* Federal Work-Study and unspecified assistantships available. Support available to part-time students. Financial award application deadline: 8/15; financial award applicants required to submit FAFSA. *Unit head:* Abbe Miller, Director, 203-773-8543, Fax: 203-773-3117, E-mail: amiller@albertus.edu. *Application contact:* Dr. Sean O'Connell, Vice President for Academic Affairs, 203-777-8539, Fax: 203-777-3701, E-mail: soconnell@albertus.edu.
Website: http://www.albertus.edu/art-therapy/ms/

Athabasca University, Program in Counseling, Athabasca, AB T9S 3A3, Canada. Offers applied psychology (Post Master's Certificate); art therapy (MC); career counseling (MC); counseling (Advanced Certificate); counseling psychology (MC); school counseling (MC).

Caldwell University, School of Psychology and Counseling, Caldwell, NJ 07006-6195. Offers art therapy (MA); counseling (MA), including art therapy, mental health, school counseling; director of school counseling (Post-Master's Certificate); professional counselor (Post-Master's Certificate); school counselor (Post-Master's Certificate). *Accreditation:* ACA. *Program availability:* Part-time. *Faculty:* 16 full-time (13 women), 13 part-time/adjunct (7 women). *Students:* 88 full-time (79 women), 84 part-time (82 women); includes 33 minority (12 Black or African American, non-Hispanic/Latino; 6 Asian, non-Hispanic/Latino; 15 Hispanic/Latino). Average age 30. 104 applicants, 100% accepted, 44 enrolled. In 2017, 31 master's awarded. *Degree requirements:* For master's, comprehensive exam, practicum, internship; for Post-Master's Certificate, comprehensive exam. *Entrance requirements:* For master's, minimum GPA of 3.2; two letters of recommendation; interview; writing sample. Additional exam requirements/recommendations for international students: Required—TOEFL (minimum score 580 paper-based, 92 iBT) or IELTS (7.5). *Application deadline:* For fall admission, 6/1 for domestic students, 7/1 for international students; for spring admission, 12/1 for domestic and international students; for summer admission, 4/1 for domestic and international students. Applications are processed on a rolling basis. Application fee: $50. Electronic applications accepted. *Expenses:* $975 per credit. *Financial support:* 2 general assistantships available. Financial award applicants required to submit FAFSA. *Faculty research:* Mental health counseling, school counseling, art therapy. *Unit head:* Dr. Thomson Ling, Associate Dean, 973-618-3596, E-mail: tling@caldwell.edu. *Application contact:* Tom Disch, Senior Graduate Admissions Counselor, 973-618-3544, E-mail: graduate@caldwell.edu.

California Institute of Integral Studies, School of Professional Psychology and Health, San Francisco, CA 94103. Offers clinical psychology (Psy D); community mental health (MA); drama therapy (MA); expressive arts therapy (MA); integral counseling psychology (MA); integrative health studies (MA); psychological studies (MA); somatic psychology (MA). *Program availability:* Part-time, evening/weekend, 100% online, blended/hybrid learning. *Students:* 507 full-time (401 women), 96 part-time (77 women); includes 167 minority (29 Black or African American, non-Hispanic/Latino; 3 American Indian or Alaska Native, non-Hispanic/Latino; 32 Asian, non-Hispanic/Latino; 62 Hispanic/Latino; 2 Native Hawaiian or other Pacific Islander, non-Hispanic/Latino; 39 Two or more races, non-Hispanic/Latino; 60 international. Average age 34. 302 applicants, 89% accepted, 171 enrolled. In 2017, 194 master's, 18 doctorates awarded. *Degree requirements:* For doctorate, comprehensive exam, thesis/dissertation. *Entrance requirements:* For master's, minimum GPA of 3.0, letters of recommendation, writing sample; for doctorate, GRE, MA in psychology or social work with appropriate practical experience for advanced standing, or BA with a minimum GPA of 3.1; letters of recommendation; writing sample. Additional exam requirements/recommendations for international students: Required—TOEFL. *Application deadline:* For fall admission, 2/1 priority date for domestic and international students; for spring admission, 10/15 priority date for domestic and international students. Applications are processed on a rolling basis. Application fee: $65. Electronic applications accepted. *Expenses:* $21,400 (for MA); $32,734 (for PsyD). *Financial support:* Research assistantships with tuition reimbursements, teaching assistantships with tuition reimbursements, career-related internships or fieldwork, Federal Work-Study, and scholarships/grants available. Support available to part-time students. Financial award application deadline: 4/15; financial award applicants required to submit FAFSA. *Faculty research:* Transpersonal psychology, somatic psychology, expressive arts therapy, drama therapy, community mental health, ecopsychology, integrative health, human sexuality. *Unit head:* Nicolle Zapien, Academic Dean, 415-575-5577, E-mail: nzapien@ciis.edu. *Application contact:* Ellen Durst, Director of Admissions, 415-575-6100, Fax: 415-575-1268, E-mail: admissions@ciis.edu.

California State University, Los Angeles, Graduate Studies, College of Arts and Letters, Department of Art, Los Angeles, CA 90032-8530. Offers art (MA), including art education, art history, art therapy, ceramics, metals, and textiles, design (MA, MFA), painting, sculpture, and graphic arts, photography; fine arts (MFA), including crafts, design (MA, MFA), studio arts. *Accreditation:* NASAD (one or more programs are accredited). *Program availability:* Part-time, evening/weekend. *Degree requirements:* For master's, comprehensive exam, project or thesis. *Entrance requirements:* For master's, portfolio. Additional exam requirements/recommendations for international students: Required—TOEFL (minimum score 500 paper-based). Electronic applications accepted. *Faculty research:* The artist and the book, conceptual art, ceramic processes, computer graphics, architectural graphics.

Cedar Crest College, Program in Art Therapy, Allentown, PA 18104-6196. Offers MA. *Program availability:* Part-time, evening/weekend, blended/hybrid learning. *Faculty:* 2 full-time (both women), 4 part-time/adjunct (all women). *Students:* 12 full-time (all women), 10 part-time (all women); includes 3 minority (1 Black or African American, non-Hispanic/Latino; 1 Asian, non-Hispanic/Latino; 1 Hispanic/Latino). Average age 30. In 2017, 8 master's awarded. *Application deadline:* Applications are processed on a rolling basis. Electronic applications accepted. *Expenses:* Contact institution. *Unit head:* Rebecca Arnold, Director, 610-437-4471 Ext. 3594, E-mail: rarnold@cedarcrest.edu. *Application contact:* Nancy Wunderly, Director of School of Adult and Graduate Education, 610-437-4471, E-mail: sage@cedarcrest.edu.
Website: http://sage.cedarcrest.edu/graduate/master-of-arts-in-art-therapy/

The College of New Rochelle, Graduate School, Division of Art and Communication Studies, Program in Art Therapy, New Rochelle, NY 10805-2308. Offers art therapy (MS); art therapy/counseling (MS). *Program availability:* Part-time, evening/weekend. *Degree requirements:* For master's, thesis, practicum, fieldwork, internship. *Entrance requirements:* For master's, 12 credits in psychology, portfolio. *Expenses: Tuition:* Full-time $17,406. *Required fees:* $1120. *Faculty research:* Phototherapy, assessment and evaluation, developmental stages in art, creativity and mental illness.

Concordia University, School of Graduate Studies, Faculty of Fine Arts, Department of Creative Arts Therapies, Montréal, QC H3G 1M8, Canada. Offers art therapy (MA); drama therapy (MA); music therapy (MA).

Drexel University, College of Nursing and Health Professions, Department of Creative Arts Therapies, Specialization in Art Therapy, Philadelphia, PA 19104-2875. Offers MA, PMC. *Accreditation:* NASAD. *Degree requirements:* For master's, comprehensive exam, thesis. *Entrance requirements:* For master's, GRE General Test or MAT, interview, minimum GPA of 2.75, portfolio. Electronic applications accepted.

Eastern Virginia Medical School, Graduate Art Therapy and Counseling Program, Norfolk, VA 23501-1980. Offers MS. *Degree requirements:* For master's, thesis,

internship. *Entrance requirements:* For master's, 12 credit hours in psychology, including abnormal and developmental; 18 credit hours in studio art; face-to-face interview; portfolio (diverse media preferred). Electronic applications accepted. *Expenses:* Contact institution.

Edinboro University of Pennsylvania, Department of Counseling, School Psychology and Special Education, Edinboro, PA 16444. Offers counseling (MA), including art therapy, clinical mental health counseling, college counseling, rehabilitation counseling, school counseling; educational psychology (M Ed); school psychology (Ed S); special education (M Ed), including autism, behavior management. *Accreditation:* ACA. *Program availability:* Part-time, evening/weekend. *Degree requirements:* For master's, thesis or alternative, competency exam; for Ed S, thesis or alternative. *Entrance requirements:* For master's and Ed S, GRE or MAT, minimum QPA of 2.5. Electronic applications accepted.

Emporia State University, Program in Art Therapy, Emporia, KS 66801-5415. Offers MS. *Accreditation:* NASAD. *Program availability:* Part-time. *Faculty:* 13 full-time (9 women). *Students:* 30 full-time (29 women), 4 part-time (3 women); includes 5 minority (1 American Indian or Alaska Native, non-Hispanic/Latino; 2 Hispanic/Latino; 2 Two or more races, non-Hispanic/Latino), 1 international. 28 applicants, 29% accepted, 5 enrolled. In 2017, 9 master's awarded. *Degree requirements:* For master's, comprehensive exam or thesis, internship. *Entrance requirements:* For master's, GRE General Test or MAT, essay exam, appropriate bachelor's degree. Additional exam requirements/recommendations for international students: Required—TOEFL (minimum score 520 paper-based; 68 iBT). *Application deadline:* For fall admission, 6/1 for domestic students; for spring admission, 10/1 for domestic students. Applications are processed on a rolling basis. Application fee: $30 ($75 for international students). Electronic applications accepted. *Expenses:* Tuition, state resident: full-time $6084; part-time $253.50 per credit hour. Tuition, nonresident: full-time $18,924; part-time $788.50 per credit hour. *Required fees:* $1943; $80.95 per credit hour. Tuition and fees vary according to campus/location. *Financial support:* In 2017–18, 1 research assistantship with full tuition reimbursement (averaging $7,344 per year), 3 teaching assistantships with full tuition reimbursements (averaging $7,344 per year) were awarded; career-related internships or fieldwork, Federal Work-Study, institutionally sponsored loans, health care benefits, and unspecified assistantships also available. Financial award application deadline: 3/15; financial award applicants required to submit FAFSA. *Unit head:* Dr. Katrina Miller, Chair, 620-341-5231, E-mail: kmille12@emporia.edu. *Application contact:* Mary Sewell, Admissions Coordinator, 800-950-GRAD, Fax: 620-341-5909, E-mail: msewell@emporia.edu.

Florida State University, The Graduate School, College of Fine Arts, Department of Art Education, Tallahassee, FL 32306. Offers art education (MA, MS, Ed D, PhD); art therapy (PhD); arts administration (PhD). *Accreditation:* NASAD (one or more programs are accredited). *Program availability:* Part-time, evening/weekend, 100% online. *Faculty:* 9 full-time (6 women), 4 part-time/adjunct (all women). *Students:* 58 full-time (57 women), 20 part-time (15 women); includes 27 minority (8 Black or African American, non-Hispanic/Latino; 1 American Indian or Alaska Native, non-Hispanic/Latino; 1 Asian, non-Hispanic/Latino; 12 Hispanic/Latino; 5 Two or more races, non-Hispanic/Latino), 7 international. Average age 30. 90 applicants, 57% accepted, 38 enrolled. In 2017, 28 master's, 1 doctorate awarded. *Degree requirements:* For master's, comprehensive exam, thesis (for some programs); for doctorate, thesis/dissertation. *Entrance requirements:* For master's, GRE, minimum GPA of 3.0 in last 2 years; for doctorate, GRE. Additional exam requirements/recommendations for international students: Required—TOEFL (minimum score 550 paper-based; 80 iBT). *Application deadline:* For fall admission, 1/15 priority date for domestic and international students; for spring admission, 10/1 priority date for domestic and international students. Application fee: $30. Electronic applications accepted. *Financial support:* In 2017–18, 24 students received support, including 22 research assistantships with full tuition reimbursements available (averaging $5,000 per year), 5 teaching assistantships with full tuition reimbursements available (averaging $8,500 per year); fellowships, career-related internships or fieldwork, scholarships/grants, health care benefits, and unspecified assistantships also available. Financial award application deadline: 1/15; financial award applicants required to submit FAFSA. *Faculty research:* Teaching and learning in art, museum education, art therapy, arts administration, discipline-based art education. *Total annual research expenditures:* $110,000. *Unit head:* Dr. Jeff Broome, Interim Chair, 850-645-9892, Fax: 850-644-5067, E-mail: jbroome@fsu.edu. *Application contact:* Vicki Barr, Academic Support Assistant, 850-644-5473, Fax: 850-644-6067, E-mail: vbarr@fsu.edu.
Website: http://arted.fsu.edu/

The George Washington University, Columbian College of Arts and Sciences, Program in Art Therapy, Washington, DC 20052. Offers MA, Graduate Certificate. *Faculty:* 5 full-time (4 women), 13 part-time/adjunct (all women). *Students:* 49 full-time (48 women), 16 part-time (all women); includes 16 minority (4 Black or African American, non-Hispanic/Latino; 5 Asian, non-Hispanic/Latino; 5 Hispanic/Latino; 2 Two or more races, non-Hispanic/Latino), 8 international. Average age 29. 80 applicants, 65% accepted, 27 enrolled. In 2017, 21 master's awarded. *Entrance requirements:* For master's, GRE General Test, interview, minimum GPA of 3.0; for Graduate Certificate, interview, minimum GPA of 3.0. Additional exam requirements/recommendations for international students: Required—TOEFL (minimum score 550 paper-based; 80 iBT). *Application deadline:* For fall admission, 1/1 priority date for domestic students. Application fee: $75. *Expenses:* Tuition: Full-time $28,800; part-time $1655 per credit hour. *Required fees:* $45; $2.75 per credit hour. *Financial support:* In 2017–18, 11 students received support. Fellowships with partial tuition reimbursements available, career-related internships or fieldwork, Federal Work-Study, institutionally sponsored loans, and tuition waivers available. *Unit head:* Heidi Bardot, Director, 202-994-4148, E-mail: hbardot@gwu.edu. *Application contact:* Information Contact, 202-299-4148, Fax: 202-994-1404, E-mail: artx@gwu.edu.
Website: http://arttherapy.columbian.gwu.edu/program-options

Georgia College & State University, Graduate School, College of Health Sciences, Program in Art Therapy, Milledgeville, GA 31061. Offers MA. *Program availability:* Part-time. *Students:* 8 full-time (6 women), 1 (woman) part-time; includes 3 minority (all Black or African American, non-Hispanic/Latino). Average age 29. 6 applicants, 100% accepted, 5 enrolled. In 2017, 5 master's awarded. *Degree requirements:* For master's, comprehensive exam, minimum GPA of 3.0, thesis or clinical project. *Entrance requirements:* For master's, GRE or MAT, 3 letters of recommendation; minimum undergraduate GPA of 2.75; official transcript; 12 credit hours in psychology, 18 in studio art; 12 pieces of recent artwork; essay; interview (in-person or via Skype). *Application deadline:* For fall admission, 7/1 priority date for domestic students; for spring admission, 11/1 priority date for domestic students; for summer admission, 3/1 priority date for domestic students. Applications are processed on a rolling basis. Application fee: $40. Electronic applications accepted. *Expenses:* $288 per credit hour full-time in-state, $5,187 per semester; $1,027 per credit hour full-time out-of-state, $18,486 per semester; $1,011 per semester fees. *Financial support:* In 2017–18, 2 students received support. Unspecified assistantships available. Financial award application deadline: 3/1; financial award applicants required to submit FAFSA. *Unit head:* Dr. Chesley Mercado, Program Coordinator, Art Therapy, 478-445-2645, Fax: 478-445-

4532, E-mail: chesley.mercado@gcsu.edu. *Application contact:* Kate Marshall, Graduate Admissions Coordinator, 478-445-1184, Fax: 478-445-1336, E-mail: grad-admit@gcsu.edu.
Website: http://catalog.gcsu.edu/en/2015-2016/Graduate-Catalog/College-of-Health-Sciences/Master-of-Arts-with-a-Major-in-Art-Therapy

Goddard College, Graduate Division, Master of Arts in Psychology Program, Plainfield, VT 05667-9432. Offers expressive arts therapy (MA); psychology (MA); sexual orientation (MA). *Program availability:* Part-time, online learning. *Degree requirements:* For master's, thesis or alternative, clinical internship. *Entrance requirements:* For master's, eight specific undergraduate prerequisite courses taken within previous five years (or preparatory semester at Goddard), statement of purpose, 3 letters of recommendation, interview. Electronic applications accepted.

Hofstra University, School of Health Professions and Human Services, Programs in Counseling, Hempstead, NY 11549. Offers counseling (MS Ed, PD); creative arts therapy (MA); interdisciplinary transition specialist (Advanced Certificate); marriage and family therapy (MA); mental health counseling (MA, Advanced Certificate), including alcohol and substance abuse (Advanced Certificate); rehabilitation administration (PD); rehabilitation counseling (MS Ed, Advanced Certificate); rehabilitation counseling in mental health (MS Ed, Advanced Certificate). *Accreditation:* ACA. *Program availability:* Part-time, evening/weekend. *Students:* 103 full-time (87 women), 67 part-time (60 women); includes 50 minority (21 Black or African American, non-Hispanic/Latino; 11 Asian, non-Hispanic/Latino; 15 Hispanic/Latino; 1 Native Hawaiian or other Pacific Islander, non-Hispanic/Latino; 2 Two or more races, non-Hispanic/Latino), 6 international. Average age 30. 131 applicants, 79% accepted, 52 enrolled. In 2017, 66 master's, 4 other advanced degrees awarded. *Degree requirements:* For master's, comprehensive exam (for some programs), thesis (for some programs), internship, practicum, student teaching, seminars, minimum GPA of 3.0. *Entrance requirements:* For master's, GRE, interview, letters of recommendation, portfolio, essay, professional experience, certification; for other advanced degree, GRE, interview, letters of recommendation, essay, professional experience, resume, master's degree. Additional exam requirements/recommendations for international students: Required—TOEFL (minimum score 550 paper-based; 80 iBT). *Application deadline:* Applications are processed on a rolling basis. Application fee: $75. Electronic applications accepted. *Expenses: Tuition:* Full-time $1292. *Required fees:* $970. Tuition and fees vary according to program. *Financial support:* In 2017–18, 78 students received support, including 47 fellowships with full and partial tuition reimbursements available (averaging $3,138 per year), 5 research assistantships with full and partial tuition reimbursements available (averaging $5,702 per year); career-related internships or fieldwork, Federal Work-Study, institutionally sponsored loans, scholarships/grants, traineeships, tuition waivers (full and partial), and unspecified assistantships also available. Support available to part-time students. Financial award applicants required to submit FAFSA. *Faculty research:* Couple and family therapy infidelity; creative arts impact on Parkinson's disease; LGBTQ inclusion; substance abuse/heroin addiction's racial identity, multicultural issues, white privilege, Latinos, school counseling and the intensity of the high school curriculum. *Unit head:* Dr. Jamie Mitus, Chairperson, 516-463-5759, E-mail: jamie.s.mitus@hofstra.edu. *Application contact:* Sunil Samuel, Assistant Vice President of Admissions, 516-463-4723, Fax: 516-463-4664, E-mail: graduateadmission@hofstra.edu.
Website: http://www.hofstra.edu/academics/colleges/healthscienceshumanservices/

Indiana University–Purdue University Indianapolis, Herron School of Art and Design, Indianapolis, IN 46202. Offers art therapy (MA); visual art (MFA), including ceramics, furniture design, painting and drawing, photography and intermedia, printmaking, sculpture; visual communication design (MFA). *Degree requirements:* For master's, thesis. *Entrance requirements:* For master's, personal statement, resume, recommendations, portfolio, transcripts (18 credit hours of studio art and 12 credit hours of psychology, including 3 credit hours of developmental psychology and 3 credit hours of abnormal psychology for MA). Additional exam requirements/recommendations for international students: Recommended—TOEFL (minimum score 550 paper-based; 79 iBT), IELTS (minimum score 6.5). Electronic applications accepted. *Expenses:* Contact institution. *Faculty research:* Contemporary digital narratives for the homoerotic trope; sound articulated 3D print; neuroscience, art and related therapeutics; automotive and aeronautical design and fabrication; technological detritus.

Lesley University, Graduate School of Arts and Social Sciences, Cambridge, MA 02138-2790. Offers clinical mental health counseling (MA), including holistic counseling, school and community counseling, trauma studies; counseling psychology (MA, CAGS), including professional counseling (MA); school counseling (MA); creative writing (MFA); expressive therapies (MA, PhD, CAGS), including art (MA), clinical mental health counseling (MA), dance (MA), expressive therapies (MA), music (MA); independent studies (CAGS); independent study (MA); intercultural relations (MA, CAGS); interdisciplinary studies (MA), including individualized studies, integrative holistic health, mindfulness studies, peace and conflict transformation, trauma sensitive assessment, intervention, and consultation, women's studies; urban environmental leadership (MA). *Program availability:* Part-time, online learning. *Degree requirements:* For master's, internship, practicum, thesis (for expressive therapies); for doctorate, thesis/dissertation, arts apprenticeship, field placement; for CAGS, thesis, internship (for counseling psychology, expressive therapies). *Entrance requirements:* For master's, MAT (counseling psychology), interview, writing samples, art portfolio; for doctorate, GRE or MAT, interview, master's degree; for CAGS, interview, master's degree. Additional exam requirements/recommendations for international students: Required—TOEFL (minimum score 550 paper-based; 80 iBT). Electronic applications accepted. *Faculty research:* Psychotherapy and culture; psychotherapy and psychological trauma; women's issues in art, teaching and psychotherapy; community-based art, psycho-spiritual inquiry.

Long Island University–LIU Post, College of Arts, Communications and Design, Brookville, NY 11548-1300. Offers art (MA); clinical art therapy (MA); clinical art therapy and counseling (MA); digital game design and development (MA); fine arts and design (MFA); interactive multimedia arts (MA); museum studies (MA); music (MA); theatre (MFA). *Faculty:* 22 full-time (10 women), 44 part-time/adjunct (24 women). *Students:* 99 full-time (80 women), 14 part-time (12 women); includes 22 minority (7 Black or African American, non-Hispanic/Latino; 4 Asian, non-Hispanic/Latino; 9 Hispanic/Latino; 2 Two or more races, non-Hispanic/Latino), 23 international. Average age 28. 125 applicants, 70% accepted, 42 enrolled. In 2017, 55 master's awarded. *Degree requirements:* For master's, variable foreign language requirement, comprehensive exam (for some programs), thesis. *Entrance requirements:* For master's, performance audition or portfolio. Additional exam requirements/recommendations for international students: Required—TOEFL (minimum score 550 paper-based; 79 iBT). *Application deadline:* Applications are processed on a rolling basis. Application fee: $50. Electronic applications accepted. *Expenses: Tuition:* Full-time $21,618; part-time $1201 per credit. *Required fees:* $1840; $920 per term. Tuition and fees vary according to course load. *Financial support:* In 2017–18, 78 students received support. Career-related internships or fieldwork, scholarships/grants, tuition waivers (full and partial), and unspecified assistantships available. Support available to part-time students. Financial award application deadline: 2/15; financial award applicants required to submit FAFSA. *Faculty research:* Creative writing, playwriting, music composition, music performance,

international impact of art therapy, artistic creation. *Unit head:* Steven Breese, Dean, 516-299-2309, E-mail: steven.breese@liu.edu. *Application contact:* Rita Langdon, Graduate Admissions, 516-299-2334, Fax: 516-299-2137, E-mail: post-enroll@liu.edu. Website: http://www.liu.edu/CWPost/Academics/School-of-Visual-Arts-Communications-and-Digital-Technologies

Marywood University, Academic Affairs, Insalaco College of Creative and Performing Arts, Art Department, Program in Art Therapy, Scranton, PA 18509-1598. Offers MA, Graduate Certificate. *Accreditation:* NASAD. *Program availability:* Part-time. Electronic applications accepted.

Mount Mary University, Graduate Programs, Program in Art Therapy, Milwaukee, WI 53222-4597. Offers MS, DAT. *Program availability:* Part-time, evening/weekend. *Degree requirements:* For master's, thesis or alternative, internship; for doctorate, culminating project and pre-graduation defense. *Entrance requirements:* For master's, minimum GPA of 3.0; for doctorate, minimum GPA of 3.5. Additional exam requirements/recommendations for international students: Required—TOEFL (minimum score 550 paper-based; 80 iBT); Recommended—IELTS (minimum score 6.5). Electronic applications accepted. *Expenses:* Contact institution. *Faculty research:* Art-based research in art therapy, consensus-group supervision, art therapy in public school programs.

Naropa University, Graduate Programs, Program in Clinical Mental Health Counseling, Concentration in Transpersonal Art Therapy, Boulder, CO 80302-6697. Offers MA. *Faculty:* 10 full-time (7 women), 24 part-time/adjunct (17 women). *Students:* 49 full-time (all women), 2 part-time (1 woman); includes 8 minority (1 American Indian or Alaska Native, non-Hispanic/Latino; 6 Hispanic/Latino; 1 Two or more races, non-Hispanic/Latino), 1 international. Average age 29. 58 applicants, 57% accepted, 19 enrolled. In 2017, 15 master's awarded. *Degree requirements:* For master's, internship, 190 direct art contact hours of studio-based work, counseling practicum. *Entrance requirements:* For master's, interview, visual art portfolio, statement of interest, 2 letters of recommendation, transcripts. Additional exam requirements/recommendations for international students: Required—TOEFL (minimum score 550 paper-based; 80 iBT). *Application deadline:* For fall admission, 1/15 priority date for domestic and international students. Applications are processed on a rolling basis. Application fee: $60. Electronic applications accepted. *Expenses:* $995 per credit. *Financial support:* In 2017–18, 23 students received support, including 3 research assistantships with partial tuition reimbursements available (averaging $1,900 per year); career-related internships or fieldwork, scholarships/grants, tuition waivers (partial), and unspecified assistantships also available. Support available to part-time students. Financial award application deadline: 3/1; financial award applicants required to submit FAFSA. *Unit head:* Dr. Kathleen Gregory, Dean, Graduate School of Counseling and Psychology, 303-546-3559, E-mail: kgregory@naropa.edu. *Application contact:* Office of Admissions, 303-546-3572, Fax: 303-546-3583, E-mail: admissions@naropa.edu. Website: http://www.naropa.edu/academics/masters/clinical-mental-health-counseling/art-therapy/index.php

Nazareth College of Rochester, Graduate Studies, Department of Creative Arts Therapy, Rochester, NY 14618. Offers art therapy (MS); music therapy (MS). *Program availability:* Part-time. *Entrance requirements:* For master's, minimum GPA of 3.0; portfolio review (art therapy); audition (music therapy). Additional exam requirements/recommendations for international students: Required—TOEFL (minimum score 550 paper-based, 79 iBT) or IELTS (6.5). Electronic applications accepted.

New York University, Steinhardt School of Culture, Education, and Human Development, Department of Art and Art Professions, Program in Art Therapy, New York, NY 10003. Offers MA. *Program availability:* Part-time. *Students:* Average age 29. 130 applicants, 23% accepted, 18 enrolled. In 2017, 21 master's awarded. *Entrance requirements:* For master's, interview, portfolio. Additional exam requirements/recommendations for international students: Required—TOEFL (minimum score 100 iBT). *Application deadline:* For fall admission, 12/1 priority date for domestic and international students. Applications are processed on a rolling basis. Application fee: $75. Electronic applications accepted. *Expenses: Tuition:* Full-time $41,352; part-time $19,968 per year. *Required fees:* $2496; $1628 per unit. $814 per term. Tuition and fees vary according to course load and program. *Financial support:* Career-related internships or fieldwork, Federal Work-Study, institutionally sponsored loans, scholarships/grants, and tuition waivers (partial) available. Support available to part-time students. Financial award application deadline: 2/1; financial award applicants required to submit FAFSA. *Faculty research:* Art therapy in non-clinical settings, international art therapy. *Unit head:* Prof. Ikuko Acosta, Director, 212-998-5700, Fax: 212-995-4320, E-mail: ia4@nyu.edu. *Application contact:* 212-998-5030, Fax: 212-995-4328, E-mail: steinhardt.gradadmissions@nyu.edu. Website: http://steinhardt.nyu.edu/art/therapy

Notre Dame de Namur University, Division of Academic Affairs, School of Education and Psychology, Program in Art Therapy, Belmont, CA 94002-1908. Offers art therapy (MA); art therapy psychology (PhD). *Program availability:* Part-time. *Students:* 21 full-time (20 women), 2 part-time (both women). Average age 41. *Degree requirements:* For master's, thesis, oral presentation, portfolio; for doctorate, thesis/dissertation. *Entrance requirements:* For master's, interview, minimum GPA of 2.5; for doctorate, master's degree from accredited university in art therapy or in a related field; minimum of two years of clinical work in the field; portfolio; three professional recommendations; one published article or scholarly academic writing on an art therapy subject in publication-acceptable form; interview. Additional exam requirements/recommendations for international students: Required—TOEFL (minimum score 550 paper-based; 79 iBT). *Application deadline:* For fall admission, 8/1 priority date for domestic students; for spring admission, 12/1 priority date for domestic students. Applications are processed on a rolling basis. Application fee: $60. Electronic applications accepted. *Expenses: Tuition:* Full-time $16,128; part-time $8064 per credit hour. *Required fees:* $80; $80 per credit hour. $40 per semester. *Financial support:* Career-related internships or fieldwork available. Support available to part-time students. Financial award applicants required to submit FAFSA. *Unit head:* Amy Backos, Chair, Art Therapy Program, 650-508-3674, E-mail: abackos@ndnu.edu.

Ottawa University, Graduate Studies-Arizona, Program in Professional Counseling, Ottawa, KS 66067-3399. Offers Christian counseling (MA); expressive arts therapy (MA); marriage and family therapy (MA); treatment of trauma, abuse and deprivation (MA). Programs offered in Mesa, Phoenix, Tempe and West Valley, AZ. *Program availability:* Part-time, evening/weekend, online learning. *Degree requirements:* For master's, comprehensive exam, thesis or alternative, field experience, practicum. *Entrance requirements:* For master's, minimum undergraduate GPA of 3.0; course work in theories of personality, abnormal psychology, and human growth and development. Additional exam requirements/recommendations for international students: Required—TOEFL (minimum score 550 paper-based).

Phillips Graduate University, Master's Program in Psychology, Chatsworth, CA 91311. Offers art therapy (MA); marriage and family therapy (MA); school counseling (MA); school psychology (MA). *Program availability:* Evening/weekend. *Degree requirements:* For master's, comprehensive exam, thesis. *Entrance requirements:* For master's, minimum GPA of 2.5. *Application deadline:* For fall admission, 4/16 priority

date for domestic students; for spring admission, 11/15 for domestic students. Applications are processed on a rolling basis. Application fee: $80. Electronic applications accepted. *Expenses: Tuition:* Part-time $897 per unit. *Required fees:* $375 per semester. Part-time tuition and fees vary according to degree level and program. *Financial support:* Federal Work-Study and tuition waivers (full and partial) available. Financial award application deadline: 8/15; financial award applicants required to submit FAFSA. *Faculty research:* Integration of interpersonal psychological theory, systems approach, firsthand experiential learning. *Application contact:* Christine Montagna, Admissions Advisor, 818-600-4945, Fax: 818-386-5699, E-mail: cmontagna@pgu.edu.

Pratt Institute, School of Art, Programs in Creative Arts Therapy, Brooklyn, NY 11205-3899. Offers art therapy and creativity development (MPS); dance/movement therapy (MS). *Accreditation:* NASAD (one or more programs are accredited). *Program availability:* Part-time. *Students:* 58 full-time (55 women), 49 part-time (all women); includes 44 minority (20 Black or African American, non-Hispanic/Latino; 5 Asian, non-Hispanic/Latino; 15 Hispanic/Latino; 4 Two or more races, non-Hispanic/Latino), 4 international. Average age 30. 124 applicants, 58% accepted, 29 enrolled. In 2017, 32 master's awarded. *Degree requirements:* For master's, thesis. *Entrance requirements:* For master's, letters of recommendation, portfolio. Additional exam requirements/recommendations for international students: Required—TOEFL (minimum score 600 paper-based; 100 iBT). *Application deadline:* For fall admission, 1/5 for domestic and international students; for spring admission, 10/1 for domestic and international students. Applications are processed on a rolling basis. Application fee: $50 ($90 for international students). Electronic applications accepted. *Expenses: Tuition:* Full-time $30,834. *Required fees:* $1974. *Financial support:* Career-related internships or fieldwork, Federal Work-Study, institutionally sponsored loans, scholarships/grants, health care benefits, and unspecified assistantships available. Support available to part-time students. Financial award application deadline: 2/1; financial award applicants required to submit FAFSA. *Faculty research:* Psychology and aesthetic interaction, art therapy and AIDS, art therapy and autism, art diagnosis. *Unit head:* Julie Miller, Chairperson, 718-399-4532, Fax: 718-636-3597, E-mail: jmiller2@pratt.edu. *Application contact:* Natalie Capannelli, Director of Graduate Admissions, 718-636-3551, Fax: 718-399-4242, E-mail: ncapanne@pratt.edu. Website: https://www.pratt.edu/academics/school-of-art/graduate-school-of-art/creative-arts-therapy/

See Display on page 141 and Close-Up on page 189.

Prescott College, Graduate Programs, Program in Counseling and Psychology, Prescott, AZ 86301. Offers adventure-based psychotherapy (MA); counseling psychology (MA); ecopsychology (MA); ecotherapy (MA); equine-assisted mental health (MA); expressive arts therapy (MA); somatic psychology (MA); student-directed independent study (MA). *Program availability:* Part-time, online learning. Terminal master's awarded for partial completion of doctoral program. *Degree requirements:* For master's, thesis, fieldwork or internship, practicum. *Entrance requirements:* For master's, 2 letters of recommendation, resume. Additional exam requirements/recommendations for international students: Required—TOEFL (minimum score 500 paper-based). Electronic applications accepted.

Saint Mary-of-the-Woods College, Master of Arts in Art Therapy Program, Saint Mary of the Woods, IN 47876. Offers MA, Post-Master's Certificate. *Program availability:* Part-time. *Faculty:* 2 full-time (both women). *Students:* 144 full-time (139 women); includes 20 minority (all Two or more races, non-Hispanic/Latino). Average age 37. 88 applicants, 49% accepted, 36 enrolled. In 2017, 24 master's awarded. *Degree requirements:* For master's, thesis, three supervised clinical experiences. *Entrance requirements:* For degree, 12 credit hours each in general psychology, abnormal psychology, theories of personality, and developmental psychology; 18 credit hours in studio art skills. *Application deadline:* For fall admission, 4/30 for domestic and international students; for winter admission, 10/31 for domestic and international students. Application fee: $0. Electronic applications accepted. *Expenses:* $710 per credit hour. *Financial support:* In 2017–18, 92 students received support. Scholarships/grants available. Financial award applicants required to submit FAFSA. *Unit head:* Dr. Jill McNutt, Director, 812-535-5160, E-mail: jmcnutt@smwc.edu. *Application contact:* Marie Elliott, Assistant Director of Admissions, 812-535-5106, E-mail: graduate@smwc.edu. Website: http://www.smwc.edu/graduate/maat/

School of the Art Institute of Chicago, Graduate Division, Program in Art Therapy, Chicago, IL 60603-3103. Offers MAAT. Program offered jointly with Rush University. *Accreditation:* NASAD. *Degree requirements:* For master's, thesis, personal interview. *Entrance requirements:* Additional exam requirements/recommendations for international students: Required—TOEFL, IELTS. *Faculty research:* Migrane, ousider art, community-based practice.

School of Visual Arts, Graduate Programs, Art Therapy Department, New York, NY 10010-3994. Offers MPS. *Degree requirements:* For master's, thesis, 60 credits, including all required courses; minimum cumulative GPA of 3.0; residency of two academic years; internship. *Entrance requirements:* For master's, interview; 18 credits (or equivalent) in studio art and 12 credits in psychology (developmental and abnormal required; courses in introduction to psychology and theories of personality recommended); 15 to 20 digital images on CD. Additional exam requirements/recommendations for international students: Required—TOEFL (minimum score 550 paper-based; 79 iBT). Electronic applications accepted.

Seton Hill University, MA Program in Art Therapy, Greensburg, PA 15601. Offers counseling (MA). *Program availability:* Part-time. *Entrance requirements:* For master's, portfolio; 3 letters of recommendation; letter of intent; transcripts; writing sample (APA style); resume. Additional exam requirements/recommendations for international students: Required—TOEFL (minimum score 650 paper-based; 114 iBT), IELTS (minimum score 7). *Application deadline:* For fall admission, 7/1 for domestic and international students; for spring admission, 11/30 for domestic and international students. Applications are processed on a rolling basis. Application fee: $0. Electronic applications accepted. *Expenses: Tuition:* Part-time $734 per credit. Tuition and fees vary according to class time, course level, course load and program. *Financial support:* Federal Work-Study, scholarships/grants, and tuition discounts available. Financial award application deadline: 8/15; financial award applicants required to submit FAFSA. Website: http://www.setonhill.edu/academics/graduate_programs/art_therapy

Southern Illinois University Edwardsville, Graduate School, College of Arts and Sciences, Department of Art and Design, Program in Art Therapy Counseling, Edwardsville, IL 62026. Offers MA. *Program availability:* Part-time. *Degree requirements:* For master's, thesis or alternative, project. *Entrance requirements:* For master's, MAT, portfolio. Additional exam requirements/recommendations for international students: Required—TOEFL (minimum score 550 paper-based; 79 iBT), IELTS (minimum score 6.5). Electronic applications accepted.

Southwestern College, Program in Art Therapy/Counseling, Santa Fe, NM 87502-4788. Offers MA. *Program availability:* Part-time, evening/weekend. *Degree requirements:* For master's, internship. *Entrance requirements:* For master's, resume, slide portfolio, interview, 3 letters of reference. Additional exam requirements/recommendations for international students: Required—TOEFL.

Springfield College, Graduate Programs, Program in Art Therapy, Springfield, MA 01109-3797. Offers M Ed, MS, CAGS. *Program availability:* Part-time. *Faculty:* 2 full-time (1 woman), 9 part-time/adjunct (8 women). *Students:* 28. Average age 30. 31 applicants, 55% accepted, 11 enrolled. *Degree requirements:* For master's, thesis or alternative, research project, final art exhibition. *Entrance requirements:* For master's, portfolio. Additional exam requirements/recommendations for international students: Required— TOEFL (minimum score 90 iBT); Recommended—IELTS (minimum score 7). *Application deadline:* For fall admission, 7/15 for domestic and international students; for winter admission, 11/1 for domestic and international students; for spring admission, 11/1 for domestic and international students. Applications are processed on a rolling basis. Application fee: $50. Electronic applications accepted. *Financial support:* Fellowships with partial tuition reimbursements, teaching assistantships with partial tuition reimbursements, career-related internships or fieldwork, Federal Work-Study, institutionally sponsored loans, and unspecified assistantships available. Financial award application deadline: 3/1; financial award applicants required to submit FAFSA. *Faculty research:* Cultural terrains of tattoos, art in times of war and political conflict, children's art development, art and the holocaust, art and autism spectrum disorders, language of fine arts pedagogy into art therapy. *Unit head:* Dr. Simone Alter-Muri, Director, 413-748-3752, E-mail: saltermuri@spfldcol.edu. *Application contact:* Anne Griffin, Director of Graduate Admissions, 413-748-3225, Fax: 413-748-3694, E-mail: agriffin2@springfield.edu.

University of Louisville, Graduate School, College of Education and Human Development, Department of Counseling and Human Development, Louisville, KY 40292-0001. Offers counseling and personnel services (M Ed, PhD), including art therapy (M Ed), clinical mental health counseling (M Ed), college student personnel, counseling psychology, counselor education and supervision (PhD), educational psychology, measurement, and evaluation (PhD), school counseling (M Ed). *Accreditation:* APA; NCATE. *Program availability:* Part-time, evening/weekend. *Students:* 144 full-time (107 women), 63 part-time (44 women); includes 49 minority (32 Black or African American, non-Hispanic/Latino; 1 American Indian or Alaska Native, non-Hispanic/Latino; 3 Asian, non-Hispanic/Latino; 7 Hispanic/Latino; 6 Two or more races, non-Hispanic/Latino), 3 international. Average age 28. 178 applicants, 49% accepted, 51 enrolled. In 2017, 35 master's, 3 doctorates awarded. *Degree requirements:* For doctorate, comprehensive exam, thesis/dissertation. *Entrance requirements:* For master's and doctorate, GRE General Test. Application fee: $65. *Expenses:* Tuition, state resident: full-time $12,246; part-time $681 per credit hour. Tuition, nonresident: full-time $25,486; part-time $1417 per credit hour. *Required fees:* $196. Tuition and fees vary according to course load, program and reciprocity agreements. *Financial support:* Fellowships, research assistantships, teaching assistantships, career-related internships or fieldwork, Federal Work-Study, scholarships/grants, health care benefits, and unspecified assistantships available. Financial award application deadline: 6/1; financial award applicants required to submit FAFSA. *Faculty research:* Mental health services and under-served populations; health disparities and outcomes; well-being identity development; measurement and evaluation. *Total annual research expenditures:* $295,684. *Unit head:* Dr. Mark M. Leach, Interim Chair/Professor, 502-852-0588, Fax: 502-852-0629, E-mail: m.leach@louisville.edu. *Application contact:* Betty Hampton, Director of Graduate

Student Services, 502-852-5597, Fax: 502-852-1465, E-mail: edadvise@louisville.edu. Website: http://www.louisville.edu/education/departments/ecpy

University of Maryland, College Park, Academic Affairs, College of Education, Department of Counseling, Higher Education and Special Education, College Park, MD 20742. Offers college student personnel (M Ed, MA); college student personnel administration (PhD); community counseling (CAGS); community/career counseling (M Ed, MA); counseling and personnel services (M Ed, MA, PhD), including art therapy (M Ed), college student personnel (M Ed), counseling and personnel services (PhD), counseling psychology (M Ed), mental health counseling (M Ed); school counseling (M Ed); counseling psychology (PhD); counselor education (PhD); rehabilitation counseling (M Ed, MA, AGSC); school counseling (M Ed, MA); school psychology (M Ed, MA, PhD). *Accreditation:* APA (one or more programs are accredited); NCATE. *Program availability:* Part-time, evening/weekend, online learning. *Degree requirements:* For master's, thesis (for some programs); for doctorate, thesis/dissertation. *Entrance requirements:* For master's, GRE General Test or MAT, minimum GPA of 3.0, 3 letters of recommendation; for doctorate, GRE General Test or MAT, minimum GPA of 3.5, 3 letters of recommendation. Additional exam requirements/recommendations for international students: Required—TOEFL. Electronic applications accepted. *Faculty research:* Educational psychology, counseling, health.

University of Wisconsin–Superior, Graduate Division, Department of Visual Arts, Superior, WI 54880-4500. Offers art education (MA); art history (MA); art therapy (MA); studio arts (MA). *Program availability:* Part-time. *Degree requirements:* For master's, comprehensive exam, exhibit. *Entrance requirements:* For master's, minimum GPA of 2.75, portfolio. Electronic applications accepted.

Ursuline College, School of Graduate and Professional Studies, Program in Counseling and Art Therapy, Pepper Pike, OH 44124-4398. Offers MA. *Program availability:* Part-time. *Faculty:* 5 full-time (4 women), 1 (woman) part-time/adjunct. *Students:* 29 full-time (all women), 39 part-time (36 women); includes 14 minority (9 Black or African American, non-Hispanic/Latino; 3 Hispanic/Latino; 2 Two or more races, non-Hispanic/Latino). Average age 29. 25 applicants, 72% accepted, 15 enrolled. In 2017, 24 master's awarded. *Degree requirements:* For master's, thesis, 700-hour internship. *Entrance requirements:* For master's, BA in psychology, social sciences, or related field; minimum undergraduate GPA of 3.0; portfolio; work experience with human service agency. Additional exam requirements/recommendations for international students: Required—TOEFL (minimum score 500 paper-based; 80 iBT). *Application deadline:* For fall admission, 8/1 priority date for domestic students. Applications are processed on a rolling basis. Application fee: $25. Electronic applications accepted. *Expenses:* $1,094 per credit hour. *Financial support:* In 2017–18, 21 students received support. Scholarships/grants available. Financial award application deadline: 3/1; financial award applicants required to submit FAFSA. *Faculty research:* LGBTQ issues, affirmative counseling, wellness, holistic care, creativity and mental health, creativity and clinical supervision, expressive therapies and counselor education, mindfulness and family therapy. *Unit head:* Gail Rule-Hoffman, Director, 440-646-8138, Fax: 440-684-6135. *Application contact:* Melanie Steele, Director, Graduate Admission, 440-646-8119, Fax: 440-684-6138, E-mail: graduateadmissions@ursuline.edu.

Decorative Arts

Bard Graduate Center, Graduate Studies, New York, NY 10024-3602. Offers M Phil, MA, PhD. *Program availability:* Part-time. *Degree requirements:* For master's, one foreign language, thesis, internship; for doctorate, 2 foreign languages, thesis/dissertation, 3 field exams. *Entrance requirements:* For master's, GRE General Test, writing sample, 3 letters of recommendation; for doctorate, GRE General Test, MA, master's thesis or equivalent, 3 letters of recommendation. Additional exam requirements/recommendations for international students: Required—TOEFL. *Faculty research:* New York and American material culture; modern design history; history and theory of museums; early Modern Europe; global Middle Ages; archaeology, anthropology, and material culture; cultures of conservation.

See Display on page 155 and Close-Up on page 183.

Sotheby's Institute of Art–London, Graduate Programs, London, United Kingdom. Offers art business (MA); contemporary art (MA); fine and decorative art and design (MA); modern and contemporary Asian art (MA). *Degree requirements:* For master's, thesis. *Entrance requirements:* Additional exam requirements/recommendations for international students: Required—IELTS (minimum score 7). Electronic applications accepted.

Sotheby's Institute of Art–New York, Graduate Programs, New York, NY 10021. Offers art business (MA); contemporary art (MA); fine and decorative art and design (MA). *Accreditation:* NASAD. *Entrance requirements:* For master's, academic transcripts, two letters of academic reference, personal statement, writing sample, curriculum vitae/resume, interview. Additional exam requirements/recommendations for international students: Required—TOEFL (minimum score 100 iBT), IELTS (minimum score 7). Electronic applications accepted.

Museum Studies

American Museum of Natural History–Richard Gilder Graduate School, Program in Comparative Biology, New York, NY 10024. Offers PhD. *Degree requirements:* For doctorate, thesis/dissertation, qualifying examination. *Entrance requirements:* For doctorate, GRE General Test (taken within the past five years); GRE Subject Test (recommended), BA, BS, or equivalent degree from accredited institution; official transcripts; essay;. Additional exam requirements/recommendations for international students: Required—TOEFL (minimum score 600 paper-based; 100 iBT), IELTS (minimum score 7).

Arizona State University at the Tempe campus, College of Liberal Arts and Sciences, School of Human Evolution and Social Change, Tempe, AZ 85287-2402. Offers anthropology (MA, PhD), including anthropology (PhD), archaeology (PhD), bioarchaeology (PhD), evolutionary (PhD), museum studies (MA), sociocultural (PhD); applied mathematics for the life and social sciences (PhD); environmental social science (PhD), including environmental social science, urbanism; global health (MA, PhD), including complex adaptive systems science (PhD), evolutionary global health sciences (PhD), health and culture (PhD), urbanism (PhD); immigration studies (Graduate Certificate). Terminal master's awarded for partial completion of doctoral program. *Degree requirements:* For master's, thesis or alternative, interactive Program of Study (iPOS) submitted before completing 50 percent of required credit hours; for doctorate, comprehensive exam, thesis/dissertation, interactive Program of Study (iPOS) submitted before completing 50 percent of required credit hours. *Entrance requirements:* For master's and doctorate, GRE, minimum GPA of 3.0 or equivalent in last 2 years of work leading to bachelor's degree. Additional exam requirements/recommendations for international students: Required—TOEFL, IELTS, or PTE. Electronic applications accepted.

Arizona State University at the Tempe campus, Herberger Institute for Design and the Arts, School of Art, Tempe, AZ 85287-1505. Offers art education (MA); art history (MA); ceramics (MFA); design, environment and the arts (PhD), including history, theory and criticism; drawing (MFA); fibers (MFA); intermedia (MFA); metals (MFA); museum studies (MFA); painting (MFA); printmaking (MFA); sculpture (MFA); wood (MFA); MFA/MA. Terminal master's awarded for partial completion of doctoral program. *Degree requirements:* For master's, thesis/exhibition (MFA, MA in art education); interactive Program of Study (iPOS) submitted before completing 50 percent of required credit hours; for doctorate, comprehensive exam, thesis/dissertation, interactive Program of Study (iPOS) submitted before completing 50 percent of required credit hours. *Entrance requirements:* For master's, GRE or MAT, minimum GPA of 3.0 or equivalent in last 2 years of work leading to bachelor's degree; for doctorate, GRE, master's degree in architecture, graphic design, industrial design, interior design, landscape architecture, or art history or equivalent standing; statement of purpose; 3 letters of recommendation; indication of potential faculty mentor; sample of written work. Additional exam requirements/recommendations for international students: Required—TOEFL, IELTS, or PTE. Electronic applications accepted.

Bard College, Center for Curatorial Studies, Annandale-on-Hudson, NY 12504. Offers MA. *Degree requirements:* For master's, thesis, exhibition. *Entrance requirements:* For master's, exhibition review, 3 letters of recommendation. Additional exam requirements/recommendations for international students: Required—TOEFL (minimum score 550 paper-based). Electronic applications accepted. *Expenses:* Contact institution. *Faculty research:* Contemporary art, history of exhibition, curatorial practice.

Museum Studies

Baylor University, Graduate School, College of Arts and Sciences, Department of Museum Studies, Waco, TX 76798. Offers MA. *Program availability:* Part-time. *Faculty:* 3 full-time (2 women), 4 part-time/adjunct (1 woman). *Students:* 10 full-time (7 women), 5 part-time (all women). Average age 25. 29 applicants, 52% accepted, 9 enrolled. In 2017, 8 master's awarded. *Degree requirements:* For master's, comprehensive exam, thesis or alternative. *Entrance requirements:* For master's, GRE General Test. Additional exam requirements/recommendations for international students: Required—TOEFL (minimum score 550 paper-based; 80 iBT). *Application deadline:* For fall admission, 2/15 priority date for domestic and international students. Applications are processed on a rolling basis. Application fee: $50. Electronic applications accepted. *Financial support:* In 2017–18, 13 students received support, including 13 research assistantships with partial tuition reimbursements available (averaging $26,000 per year); career-related internships or fieldwork, Federal Work-Study, scholarships/grants, tuition waivers (full and partial), and unspecified assistantships also available. Support available to part-time students. Financial award application deadline: 2/15; financial award applicants required to submit FAFSA. *Faculty research:* Material culture, archival collections, 19th-century U.S. history, digitization, American decorative arts. *Unit head:* Dr. Julie Holcomb, Graduate Program Director, 254-710-1233, Fax: 254-710-1173, E-mail: julie_holcomb@baylor.edu. *Application contact:* Lisa Rieger, Administrative Assistant, 254-710-1233, Fax: 254-710-1173, E-mail: lisa_rieger@baylor.edu. Website: http://www.baylor.edu/Museum_Studies/

Boston University, Graduate School of Arts and Sciences, Department of History of Art and Architecture, Boston, MA 02215. Offers history of art and architecture (MA, PhD); museum studies (Certificate). *Accreditation:* NASAD. *Students:* 52 full-time (45 women), 3 part-time (1 woman); includes 5 minority (1 Black or African American, non-Hispanic/Latino; 2 Asian, non-Hispanic/Latino; 2 Hispanic/Latino), 8 international. Average age 27. 151 applicants, 32% accepted, 9 enrolled. In 2017, 7 master's, 6 doctorates awarded. Terminal master's awarded for partial completion of doctoral program. *Degree requirements:* For master's, one foreign language, comprehensive exam, thesis or alternative, scholarly paper; for doctorate, 2 foreign languages, comprehensive exam, thesis/dissertation. *Entrance requirements:* For master's and doctorate, GRE General Test, 3 letters of recommendation, transcripts, personal statement, curriculum vitae, writing sample, foreign language proficiency; for Certificate, GRE General Test. Additional exam requirements/recommendations for international students: Required—TOEFL (minimum score 550 paper-based; 84 iBT). *Application deadline:* For fall admission, 1/5 for domestic and international students; for spring admission, 10/15 for domestic and international students. Application fee: $95. Electronic applications accepted. *Financial support:* In 2017–18, 44 students received support, including 16 fellowships with full tuition reimbursements available (averaging $22,000 per year), 11 teaching assistantships with full tuition reimbursements available (averaging $22,000 per year); career-related internships or fieldwork, Federal Work-Study, scholarships/grants, health care benefits, and unspecified assistantships also available. Financial award application deadline: 1/5. *Unit head:* Alice Tseng, Chair, 617-353-1458, Fax: 617-353-3243, E-mail: aytseng@bu.edu. *Application contact:* Cheryl Crombie, Administrative Assistant, 617-353-2522, Fax: 617-353-3243, E-mail: ccrombie@bu.edu. Website: http://www.bu.edu/AH/

California College of the Arts, Graduate Programs, Curatorial Practice Program, San Francisco, CA 94107. Offers MA. *Faculty:* 2 full-time (0 women), 4 part-time/adjunct (all women). *Students:* 8 full-time (all women); includes 1 minority (Hispanic/Latino), 5 international. Average age 29. 31 applicants, 61% accepted, 2 enrolled. In 2017, 6 master's awarded. *Degree requirements:* For master's, thesis, exhibit. *Entrance requirements:* For master's, appropriate bachelor's degree, portfolio, resume, letters of recommendation, transcript. Additional exam requirements/recommendations for international students: Required—TOEFL, IELTS, or PTE. *Application deadline:* For fall admission, 1/31 priority date for domestic and international students. Applications are processed on a rolling basis. Application fee: $70. Electronic applications accepted. *Expenses:* $39,384 per year full-time tuition, $490 per year fees; $1,641 per unit part-time tuition. *Financial support:* In 2017–18, teaching assistantships (averaging $2,000 per year) were awarded; career-related internships or fieldwork, Federal Work-Study, scholarships/grants, health care benefits, and unspecified assistantships also available. Financial award application deadline: 7/31; financial award applicants required to submit FAFSA. *Unit head:* James Voorhies, Dean of Fine Arts, 415-551-9249, E-mail: jvoorhies@cca.edu. *Application contact:* Wes Fanelli, Assistant Director of Graduate Admissions, 415-703-9533, Fax: 415-703-9539, E-mail: wfanelli@cca.edu.

California State University, Chico, Office of Graduate Studies, College of Behavioral and Social Sciences, Department of Anthropology, Chico, CA 95929-0722. Offers anthropology (MA); museum studies (MA). *Degree requirements:* For master's, comprehensive exam, thesis, oral examination. *Entrance requirements:* For master's, GRE General Test, two letters of recommendation, statement of purpose, curriculum vitae, writing sample. Additional exam requirements/recommendations for international students: Required—TOEFL (minimum score 550 paper-based; 80 iBT), IELTS (minimum score 6.5), PTE (minimum score 59). Electronic applications accepted.

California State University, Fullerton, Graduate Studies, College of the Arts, Department of Visual Arts, Fullerton, CA 92831-3599. Offers art (MA, MFA), including art history (MA), ceramics (MFA), crafts, creative photography, exhibition design, glass, graphic design, illustration, sculpture. *Accreditation:* NASAD (one or more programs are accredited). *Program availability:* Part-time. *Faculty:* 17 full-time (7 women), 4 part-time/adjunct (3 women). *Students:* 35 full-time (22 women), 24 part-time (14 women); includes 26 minority (3 Black or African American, non-Hispanic/Latino; 7 Asian, non-Hispanic/Latino; 14 Hispanic/Latino; 2 Two or more races, non-Hispanic/Latino), 6 international. Average age 33. 81 applicants, 31% accepted, 21 enrolled. In 2017, 17 master's awarded. *Entrance requirements:* For master's, minimum GPA of 2.5 in last 60 units of course work, portfolio. Application fee: $55. *Financial support:* Career-related internships or fieldwork, Federal Work-Study, institutionally sponsored loans, and scholarships/grants available. Support available to part-time students. Financial award application deadline: 3/1; financial award applicants required to submit FAFSA. *Unit head:* Dana Lamb, Chair, 657-278-2076. Website: http://www.fullerton.edu/arts/art/

Caribbean University, Graduate School, Bayamón, PR 00960-0493. Offers administration and supervision (MA Ed); criminal justice (MA); curriculum and instruction (MA Ed, PhD), including elementary education (MA Ed), English education (MA Ed), history education (MA Ed), mathematics education (MA Ed), primary education (MA Ed), science education (MA Ed), Spanish education (MA Ed); educational technology in instructional systems (MA Ed); gerontology (MSN); human resources (MBA); museology, archiving and art history (MA Ed); neonatal pediatrics (MSN); physical education (MA Ed); special education (MA Ed). *Entrance requirements:* For master's, interview, minimum GPA of 2.5.

Case Western Reserve University, School of Graduate Studies, Department of Art History and Art, Program in Art History and Museum Studies, Cleveland, OH 44106. Offers MA. *Program availability:* Part-time. *Faculty:* 8 full-time (7 women), 2 part-time/adjunct (both women). *Students:* 5 full-time (4 women), 1 (woman) part-time. Average age 24. 16 applicants, 56% accepted, 4 enrolled. In 2017, 2 master's awarded. *Degree requirements:* For master's, one foreign language, comprehensive exam. *Entrance*

requirements: For master's, GRE General Test, 2 samples of written work; 3 letters of recommendation. Additional exam requirements/recommendations for international students: Required—TOEFL (minimum score 600 paper-based; 100 iBT). *Application deadline:* For fall admission, 1/1 priority date for domestic students. Applications are processed on a rolling basis. Application fee: $50. Electronic applications accepted. *Expenses: Tuition:* Full-time $43,854; part-time $1827 per credit hour. *Required fees:* $50; $50 per credit hour. Tuition and fees vary according to course load and program. *Financial support:* Fellowships, research assistantships, teaching assistantships, career-related internships or fieldwork, and tuition waivers available. Financial award application deadline: 1/1. *Faculty research:* Greek art and architecture, Northern Baroque art, Italian Renaissance and Baroque, abstract expressionism, East Asian art, nineteenth-century French art, American and contemporary art. *Unit head:* Catherine Scallen, Associate Professor/Chair, 216-368-2383, Fax: 216-368-4681, E-mail: catherine.scallen@case.edu. *Application contact:* Deborah Tenenbaum, Department Assistant, 216-368-4118, Fax: 216-368-4681, E-mail: deborah.tenenbaum@case.edu. Website: http://arthistory.case.edu/graduate/art-history/

Christie's Education, MA Program in Modern and Contemporary Art and the Market, New York, NY 10020. Offers MA. *Program availability:* Part-time. *Faculty:* 4 full-time (3 women). *Students:* 23 full-time (21 women), 1 (woman) part-time. In 2017, 25 master's awarded. *Degree requirements:* For master's, one foreign language, thesis, internship. *Entrance requirements:* For master's, writing sample, 3 letters of recommendation. Additional exam requirements/recommendations for international students: Required—TOEFL. *Application deadline:* For fall admission, 1/12 priority date for domestic and international students. Applications are processed on a rolling basis. Application fee: $95. *Expenses:* Contact institution. *Financial support:* In 2017–18, 3 students received support. Scholarships/grants and unspecified assistantships available. Financial award applicants required to submit FAFSA. *Unit head:* Dr. Julie Reiss, Program Director, 212-355-1501 Ext. 3307, Fax: 212-355-7370, E-mail: jreiss@christies.edu. *Application contact:* Hilary Smith, Recruitment and Admissions Officer, 212-355-1501 Ext. 3309, Fax: 212-355-7370, E-mail: hsmith@christies.edu. Website: https://www.christies.edu/new-york/courses/masters-modern-contemporary-art-markets.aspx

City College of the City University of New York, Graduate School, Division of Humanities and the Arts, Department of Art, Programs in Art History and Museum Studies, New York, NY 10031-9198. Offers art history (MA); art museum education (MA); museum studies (MA). *Program availability:* Part-time. *Degree requirements:* For master's, one foreign language, thesis. *Entrance requirements:* For master's, minimum GPA of 3.0, portfolio, art history paper. Additional exam requirements/recommendations for international students: Required—TOEFL (minimum score 577 paper-based; 90 iBT). Electronic applications accepted. *Faculty research:* Egyptian, Greek, medieval, Romanesque, and Ottoman art.

Claremont Graduate University, Graduate Programs, School of Arts and Humanities, Department of Cultural Studies, Claremont, CA 91711-6160. Offers Africana studies (Certificate); cultural studies (MA, PhD); media studies (MA, PhD); museum studies (MA). *Program availability:* Part-time. *Entrance requirements:* For master's and doctorate, GRE General Test. Additional exam requirements/recommendations for international students: Required—TOEFL (minimum score 75 iBT). Electronic applications accepted.

Cleveland State University, College of Graduate Studies, College of Liberal Arts and Social Sciences, Department of History, Cleveland, OH 44115. Offers art history (MA); museum studies (MA). *Program availability:* Part-time, evening/weekend. *Faculty:* 13 full-time (4 women). *Students:* 12 full-time (8 women), 8 part-time (3 women). Average age 30. 21 applicants, 90% accepted, 6 enrolled. In 2017, 8 master's awarded. *Entrance requirements:* For master's, minimum GPA of 3.0, bachelor's degree in history (or related field for art history). Additional exam requirements/recommendations for international students: Required—TOEFL (minimum score 550 paper-based; 78 iBT). *Application deadline:* Applications are processed on a rolling basis. Application fee: $40. Electronic applications accepted. *Financial support:* In 2017–18, 7 students received support. Research assistantships, career-related internships or fieldwork, tuition waivers (full and partial), and unspecified assistantships available. Financial award application deadline: 4/15. *Faculty research:* Africa and African diaspora, European history, Middle Eastern history, Latin American/Caribbean history, American history, gender and sexuality. *Unit head:* Dr. Elizabeth A. Lehfeldt, Chairperson, 216-687-3920, Fax: 216-687-5592, E-mail: e.lehfeldt@csuohio.edu. *Application contact:* Dr. Karen Sotiropoulos, Graduate Director, 216-687-3940, E-mail: r.s.shelton@csuohio.edu. Website: http://www.csuohio.edu/history/

Columbia University, Graduate School of Arts and Sciences, New York, NY 10027. Offers African-American studies (MA); American studies (MA); anthropology (MA, PhD); art history and archaeology (MA, PhD); astronomy (PhD); biological sciences (PhD); biotechnology (MA); chemical physics (PhD); chemistry (PhD); classical studies (MA, PhD); classics (MA, PhD); climate and society (MA); conservation biology (MA); earth and environmental sciences (PhD); East Asia: regional studies (MA); East Asian languages and cultures (MA, PhD); ecology, evolution and environmental biology (MA), including conservation biology; ecology, evolution, and environmental biology (PhD), including ecology and evolutionary biology, evolutionary primatology; economics (MA, PhD); English and comparative literature (MA, PhD); French and Romance philology (MA, PhD); Germanic languages (MA, PhD); global French studies (MA); global thought (MA); Hispanic cultural studies (MA); history (PhD); history and literature (MA); human rights studies (MA); Islamic studies (MA); Italian (MA, PhD); Japanese pedagogy (MA); Jewish studies (MA); Latin America and the Caribbean: regional studies (MA); Latin American and Iberian cultures (PhD); mathematics (MA, PhD), including finance (MA); medieval and Renaissance studies (MA); Middle Eastern, South Asian, and African studies (MA, PhD); modern art: critical and curatorial studies (MA); modern European studies (MA); museum anthropology (MA); music (DMA, PhD); oral history (MA); philosophical foundations of physics (MA); philosophy (MA, PhD); physics (PhD); political science (MA, PhD); psychology (PhD); quantitative methods in the social sciences (MA); religion (MA, PhD); Russia, Eurasia and East Europe: regional studies (MA); Russian translation (MA); Slavic cultures (MA); Slavic languages (MA, PhD); sociology (MA, PhD); South Asian studies (MA); statistics (MA, PhD); theatre (PhD). Dual-degree programs require admission to both Graduate School of Arts and Sciences and another Columbia school. *Program availability:* Part-time. Terminal master's awarded for partial completion of doctoral program. *Degree requirements:* For master's, variable foreign language requirement, comprehensive exam (for some programs), thesis (for some programs); for doctorate, variable foreign language requirement, comprehensive exam (for some programs), thesis/dissertation. *Entrance requirements:* For master's and doctorate, GRE General Test, GRE Subject Test (for some programs). Additional exam requirements/recommendations for international students: Required—TOEFL, IELTS. Electronic applications accepted. *Expenses: Tuition:* Full-time $44,864; part-time $1704 per credit. *Required fees:* $2370 per semester. One-time fee: $105.

Eastern Michigan University, Graduate School, College of Arts and Sciences, Department of Geography and Geology, Programs in Historic Preservation, Ypsilanti, MI 48197. Offers heritage interpretation and museum practice (MS); historic preservation (Graduate Certificate); preservation planning and administration (MS); recording,

documentation and digital cultural heritage (MS). *Program availability:* Part-time, evening/weekend, online learning. *Students:* 7 full-time (5 women), 39 part-time (28 women); includes 6 minority (1 Black or African American, non-Hispanic/Latino; 3 Hispanic/Latino; 2 Two or more races, non-Hispanic/Latino), 1 international. Average age 37. 19 applicants, 89% accepted, 9 enrolled. In 2017, 18 master's, 2 other advanced degrees awarded. *Entrance requirements:* Additional exam requirements/recommendations for international students: Required—TOEFL. *Application deadline:* Applications are processed on a rolling basis. Application fee: $45. *Financial support:* Fellowships, research assistantships with full tuition reimbursements, teaching assistantships with full tuition reimbursements, career-related internships or fieldwork, Federal Work-Study, institutionally sponsored loans, scholarships/grants, tuition waivers (partial), and unspecified assistantships available. Support available to part-time students. Financial award applicants required to submit FAFSA. *Application contact:* Dr. Ted Ligibel, Program Director, 734-487-0232, Fax: 734-487-6979, E-mail: tligibel@emich.edu.

Fashion Institute of Technology, School of Graduate Studies, Exhibition and Experience Design Program, New York, NY 10001-5992. Offers MA. *Degree requirements:* For master's, qualifying project. *Entrance requirements:* Additional exam requirements/recommendations for international students: Required—TOEFL (minimum score 550 paper-based). Electronic applications accepted.

Fashion Institute of Technology, School of Graduate Studies, Program in Fashion and Textile Studies: History, Theory, Museum Practice, New York, NY 10001-5992. Offers MA. *Accreditation:* NASAD. *Degree requirements:* For master's, one foreign language, thesis, internship. *Entrance requirements:* For master's, GRE General Test or GRE Subject Test, previous course work in art history and chemistry, 4 semesters of a foreign language. Additional exam requirements/recommendations for international students: Required—TOEFL (minimum score 550 paper-based). Electronic applications accepted.

Florida International University, College of Communication, Architecture and The Arts, Department of Art and Art History, Miami, FL 33199. Offers museum studies (Graduate Certificate); studio art (MFA). *Accreditation:* NASAD. *Program availability:* Part-time, evening/weekend. *Faculty:* 13 full-time (6 women), 20 part-time/adjunct (13 women). *Students:* 28 full-time (21 women), 19 part-time (15 women); includes 36 minority (5 Black or African American, non-Hispanic/Latino; 30 Hispanic/Latino; 1 Two or more races, non-Hispanic/Latino), 3 international. Average age 31. 25 applicants, 72% accepted, 15 enrolled. In 2017, 15 master's awarded. *Entrance requirements:* For master's, minimum GPA of 3.0 in upper-level coursework, 3 letters of recommendation, 20 slides of creative work. Additional exam requirements/recommendations for international students: Required—TOEFL (minimum score 550 paper-based; 80 iBT). *Application deadline:* For fall admission, 2/1 for domestic and international students. Application fee: $30. Electronic applications accepted. *Expenses:* Tuition, state resident: full-time $8912; part-time $446 per credit hour. Tuition, nonresident: full-time $21,393; part-time $992 per credit hour. *Required fees:* $390; $195 per semester. *Financial support:* Institutionally sponsored loans and scholarships/grants available. Financial award application deadline: 3/1; financial award applicants required to submit FAFSA. *Unit head:* Dr. Jacek Kolasinski, Chair, 305-348-3362, Fax: 305-348-0513, E-mail: jacek.kolasinski@fiu.edu. *Application contact:* Nanett Rojas, Assistant Director, Graduate Admissions, 305-348-7464, Fax: 305-348-7441, E-mail: gradadm@fiu.edu. Website: http://carta.fiu.edu/arts/

Florida State University, The Graduate School, College of Fine Arts, Department of Art History, Tallahassee, FL 32306-1233. Offers art history (MA, PhD); museum and cultural heritage studies (MA). *Accreditation:* NASAD. *Program availability:* Part-time. *Faculty:* 11 full-time (4 women), 8 part-time/adjunct (6 women). *Students:* 52 full-time (47 women), 6 part-time (5 women); includes 10 minority (2 Black or African American, non-Hispanic/Latino; 2 Asian, non-Hispanic/Latino; 5 Hispanic/Latino; 1 Two or more races, non-Hispanic/Latino). Average age 31. 67 applicants, 73% accepted, 19 enrolled. In 2017, 12 master's, 3 doctorates awarded. Terminal master's awarded for partial completion of doctoral program. *Degree requirements:* For master's, one foreign language, thesis (for some programs), capstone project (for some programs); for doctorate, 2 foreign languages, comprehensive exam, thesis/dissertation. *Entrance requirements:* For master's, GRE General Test, minimum GPA of 3.0; for doctorate, GRE General Test, minimum GPA of 3.5. Additional exam requirements/recommendations for international students: Required—TOEFL (minimum score 550 paper-based; 80 iBT), IELTS (minimum score 6.5). *Application deadline:* For fall admission, 6/1 for domestic and international students. Applications are processed on a rolling basis. Application fee: $35. Electronic applications accepted. *Expenses:* Contact institution. *Financial support:* In 2017–18, 36 students received support, including 15 fellowships with full tuition reimbursements available (averaging $5,801 per year), 14 research assistantships with full tuition reimbursements available (averaging $5,038 per year), 9 teaching assistantships with full tuition reimbursements available (averaging $7,140 per year); career-related internships or fieldwork, Federal Work-Study, institutionally sponsored loans, scholarships/grants, tuition waivers (full), and unspecified assistantships also available. Financial award application deadline: 1/1; financial award applicants required to submit FAFSA. *Faculty research:* Modern art and critical theory, contemporary art, medieval, Renaissance and Baroque, pre-Columbian and Spanish Colonial, visual arts of the Americas. *Unit head:* Dr. Adam Jolles, Associate Professor of Art History/Department Chair, 850-644-7066, E-mail: ajolles@fsu.edu. *Application contact:* Juan Barcelo-Gonzalez, Academic Program Specialist/Graduate Student Advisor, 850-644-8207, Fax: 850-644-7065, E-mail: juan.barcelo@fsu.edu. Website: http://arthistory.fsu.edu/

The George Washington University, Columbian College of Arts and Sciences, Department of Anthropology, Washington, DC 20052. Offers anthropology (MA, PhD); international development (MA); medical anthropology (MA); museum training (MA). *Program availability:* Part-time, evening/weekend. *Faculty:* 3 full-time (2 women), 18 part-time/adjunct (7 women). *Students:* 32 full-time (20 women), 16 part-time (13 women); includes 13 minority (1 Black or African American, non-Hispanic/Latino; 3 Asian, non-Hispanic/Latino; 5 Hispanic/Latino; 4 Two or more races, non-Hispanic/Latino), 9 international. Average age 28. 85 applicants, 42% accepted, 18 enrolled. In 2017, 14 master's awarded. *Degree requirements:* For master's, one foreign language, comprehensive exam, thesis or alternative. *Entrance requirements:* For master's, GRE General Test, minimum GPA of 3.0. Additional exam requirements/recommendations for international students: Required—TOEFL (minimum score 550 paper-based; 80 iBT). *Application deadline:* For fall admission, 1/15 priority date for international students; for spring admission, 9/15 priority date for domestic students, 9/1 priority date for international students. Applications are processed on a rolling basis. Application fee: $75. Electronic applications accepted. *Expenses:* Tuition: Full-time $28,800; part-time $1655 per credit hour. *Required fees:* $45; $2.75 per credit hour. *Financial support:* In 2017–18, 8 students received support. Fellowships, teaching assistantships, career-related internships or fieldwork, and Federal Work-Study available. Financial award application deadline: 1/15. *Unit head:* Richard Grinker, Chair, 202-994-6984, E-mail: rgrink@email.gwu.edu. *Application contact:* Information Contact, 202-994-6075, E-mail: anth@gwu.edu. Website: http://anthropology.columbian.gwu.edu/

The George Washington University, Columbian College of Arts and Sciences, Department of Fine Arts and Art History, Program in Art History, Washington, DC 20052.

Offers art history (MA); museum training (MA). *Program availability:* Part-time, evening/weekend. *Faculty:* 7 full-time (4 women). *Students:* 12 full-time (10 women), 7 part-time (all women), 3 international. Average age 25. 50 applicants, 74% accepted, 12 enrolled. In 2017, 6 master's awarded. *Degree requirements:* For master's, one foreign language, comprehensive exam, thesis or alternative. *Entrance requirements:* For master's, GRE General Test, bachelor's degree in field, minimum GPA of 3.0. Additional exam requirements/recommendations for international students: Required—TOEFL (minimum score 550 paper-based; 80 iBT). *Application deadline:* For fall admission, 3/1 priority date for domestic students, 1/15 priority date for international students; for spring admission, 10/1 priority date for domestic students, 9/1 priority date for international students. Applications are processed on a rolling basis. Application fee: $75. Electronic applications accepted. *Expenses:* Tuition: Full-time $28,800; part-time $1655 per credit hour. *Required fees:* $45; $2.75 per credit hour. *Financial support:* In 2017–18, 3 students received support. Fellowships, teaching assistantships, career-related internships or fieldwork, and Federal Work-Study available. Financial award application deadline: 1/15. *Unit head:* Thomas K. Brown, Chair, 202-994-9067, E-mail: thbrown@gwu.edu. *Application contact:* Information Contact, 202-994-6085, Fax: 202-994-8657, E-mail: art@gwu.edu.

The George Washington University, Columbian College of Arts and Sciences, Program in Museum Studies, Washington, DC 20052. Offers museum collections management and care (Graduate Certificate); museum studies (MA). *Program availability:* Part-time, evening/weekend. *Faculty:* 4 full-time (all women), 8 part-time/adjunct (7 women). *Students:* 90 full-time (83 women), 36 part-time (33 women); includes 22 minority (4 Black or African American, non-Hispanic/Latino; 9 Asian, non-Hispanic/Latino; 5 Hispanic/Latino; 4 Two or more races, non-Hispanic/Latino), 5 international. Average age 27. 176 applicants, 78% accepted, 56 enrolled. In 2017, 58 master's, 11 other advanced degrees awarded. *Degree requirements:* For master's, comprehensive exam, internship. *Entrance requirements:* For master's, GRE General Test, minimum GPA of 3.0. Additional exam requirements/recommendations for international students: Required—TOEFL (minimum score 550 paper-based; 80 iBT). *Application deadline:* For fall admission, 2/1 priority date for domestic students, 1/15 priority date for international students; for spring admission, 10/15 priority date for domestic students, 9/1 priority date for international students. Applications are processed on a rolling basis. Application fee: $75. Electronic applications accepted. *Expenses:* Tuition: Full-time $28,800; part-time $1655 per credit hour. *Required fees:* $45; $2.75 per credit hour. *Financial support:* In 2017–18, 15 students received support. Fellowships with tuition reimbursements available, career-related internships or fieldwork, Federal Work-Study, institutionally sponsored loans, and tuition waivers available. Financial award application deadline: 1/15. *Unit head:* Kym S. Rice, Director, 202-994-0165, Fax: 202-994-7034, E-mail: kym@gwu.edu. *Application contact:* Information Contact, 202-994-7030, Fax: 202-994-7034, E-mail: mstd@gwu.edu. Website: http://museumstudies.columbian.gwu.edu/

Harvard University, Extension School, Cambridge, MA 02138-3722. Offers applied sciences (CAS); biotechnology (ALM); educational technologies (ALM); educational technology (CET); English for graduate and professional studies (DGP); environmental management (ALM, CEM); information technology (ALM); journalism (ALM); liberal arts (ALM); management (ALM, CM); mathematics for teaching (ALM); museum studies (ALM); premedical studies (Diploma); publication and communication (CPC). *Program availability:* Part-time, evening/weekend. *Degree requirements:* For master's, thesis. *Entrance requirements:* For master's, 3 completed graduate courses with grade of B or higher. Additional exam requirements/recommendations for international students: Required—TOEFL (minimum score 600 paper-based), TWE (minimum score 5). *Expenses:* Contact institution.

Indiana University–Purdue University Indianapolis, School of Liberal Arts, Museum Studies Program, Indianapolis, IN 46202. Offers MA, Certificate. *Entrance requirements:* For master's, GRE.

John F. Kennedy University, School of Education and Liberal Arts, Department of Museum Studies, Berkeley, CA 94702. Offers museum studies (MA, Certificate), including administration, collections management, public programming. *Program availability:* Part-time. *Degree requirements:* For master's, project. *Entrance requirements:* For master's, interview. Additional exam requirements/recommendations for international students: Required—TOEFL, TWE. *Faculty research:* Emerging museum philosophies, multicultural diversity issues in museums, trends in collections management and preventive conservation, effective programming techniques and application for diverse audiences.

Johns Hopkins University, Zanvyl Krieger School of Arts and Sciences, Advanced Academic Programs, Program in Museum Studies, Washington, DC 20036. Offers digital curation (Certificate); museum studies (MA). *Program availability:* Part-time, evening/weekend, online learning. *Entrance requirements:* For master's, minimum GPA of 3.0. Additional exam requirements/recommendations for international students: Required—TOEFL (minimum score 100 iBT). Electronic applications accepted.

Long Island University–LIU Post, College of Arts, Communications and Design, Brookville, NY 11548-1300. Offers art (MA); clinical art therapy (MA); clinical art therapy and counseling (MA); digital game design and development (MA); fine arts and design (MFA); interactive multimedia arts (MA); museum studies (MA); music (MA); theatre (MFA). *Faculty:* 22 full-time (10 women), 44 part-time/adjunct (24 women). *Students:* 99 full-time (80 women), 14 part-time (12 women); includes 22 minority (7 Black or African American, non-Hispanic/Latino; 4 Asian, non-Hispanic/Latino; 9 Hispanic/Latino; 2 Two or more races, non-Hispanic/Latino), 23 international. Average age 28. 125 applicants, 70% accepted, 42 enrolled. In 2017, 55 master's awarded. *Degree requirements:* For master's, variable foreign language requirement, comprehensive exam (for some programs), thesis. *Entrance requirements:* For master's, performance audition or portfolio. Additional exam requirements/recommendations for international students: Required—TOEFL (minimum score 550 paper-based; 79 iBT). *Application deadline:* Applications are processed on a rolling basis. Application fee: $50. Electronic applications accepted. *Expenses:* Tuition: Full-time $21,618; part-time $1201 per credit. *Required fees:* $1840; $920 per term. Tuition and fees vary according to course load. *Financial support:* In 2017–18, 78 students received support. Career-related internships or fieldwork, scholarships/grants, tuition waivers (full and partial), and unspecified assistantships available. Support available to part-time students. Financial award application deadline: 2/15; financial award applicants required to submit FAFSA. *Faculty research:* Creative writing, playwriting, music composition, music performance, international impact of art therapy, artistic creation. *Unit head:* Steven Breese, Dean, 516-299-2309, E-mail: steven.breese@liu.edu. *Application contact:* Rita Langdon, Graduate Admissions, 516-299-2334, Fax: 516-299-2137, E-mail: post-enroll@liu.edu. Website: http://www.liu.edu/CWPost/Academics/School-of-Visual-Arts-Communications-and-Digital-Technologies

Marist College, Graduate Programs, School of Communication and the Arts, Poughkeepsie, NY 12601-1387. Offers communication (MA); integrated marketing communication (MA); museum studies (MA). *Program availability:* Part-time, online learning. *Degree requirements:* For master's, thesis or comprehensive exam. *Entrance requirements:* For master's, GRE, minimum undergraduate GPA of 3.0, resume, 3 letters of recommendation. Additional exam requirements/recommendations for

international students: Required—TOEFL (minimum score 550 paper-based; 80 iBT); Recommended—IELTS (minimum score 6.5). Electronic applications accepted.

Maryland Institute College of Art, Graduate Studies, MFA Program in Curatorial Practice, Baltimore, MD 21201. Offers MFA. *Degree requirements:* For master's, thesis, exhibit and thesis documentation. *Entrance requirements:* For master's, portfolio, bachelor's degree in any field. Additional exam requirements/recommendations for international students: Required—TOEFL (minimum score 550 paper-based; 80 iBT), IELTS (minimum score 6.5). Electronic applications accepted. *Expenses:* Contact institution.

Morgan State University, School of Graduate Studies, College of Liberal Arts, Department of History and Geography, Baltimore, MD 21251. Offers African-American studies (MA); history (MA, PhD); museum studies and historic preservation (MA). *Program availability:* Part-time, evening/weekend. *Degree requirements:* For master's, comprehensive exam, thesis; for doctorate, comprehensive exam, thesis/dissertation. *Entrance requirements:* For master's, minimum GPA of 2.5; for doctorate, GRE or MAT. Additional exam requirements/recommendations for international students: Required—TOEFL (minimum score 550 paper-based). *Application deadline:* For fall admission, 2/1 priority date for domestic students; for spring admission, 10/1 priority date for domestic students. Applications are processed on a rolling basis. Application fee: $0. *Expenses:* Tuition, state resident: part-time $433 per credit. Tuition, nonresident: part-time $851 per credit. *Required fees:* $81.50 per credit. *Financial support:* Application deadline: 2/1. *Faculty research:* Women's history, African diaspora history, urban history. *Unit head:* Dr. Jeremiah I. Dibua, Graduate Coordinator, 443-885-3400, Fax: 443-885-8227, E-mail: jeremiah.dibua@morgan.edu. *Application contact:* Dr. Dean Campbell, Graduate Recruitment Specialist, 443-885-3185, Fax: 443-885-8226, E-mail: dean.campbell@morgan.edu.

New Mexico State University, College of Arts and Sciences, Department of Anthropology, Las Cruces, NM 88003. Offers anthropology (MA); cultural resource management (Graduate Certificate); museum studies (Graduate Certificate). *Program availability:* Part-time. *Faculty:* 9 full-time (5 women), 1 part-time/adjunct (0 women). *Students:* 31 full-time (22 women), 19 part-time (12 women); includes 15 minority (2 Black or African American, non-Hispanic/Latino; 2 American Indian or Alaska Native, non-Hispanic/Latino; 9 Hispanic/Latino; 2 Two or more races, non-Hispanic/Latino), 3 international. Average age 34. 28 applicants, 64% accepted, 11 enrolled. In 2017, 12 master's, 17 other advanced degrees awarded. *Degree requirements:* For master's, thesis, internship, or special research project. *Entrance requirements:* For master's, minimum undergraduate GPA of 3.0. Additional exam requirements/recommendations for international students: Required—TOEFL (minimum score 550 paper-based; 79 iBT), IELTS (minimum score 6.5). *Application deadline:* For fall admission, 2/1 priority date for domestic and international students; for spring admission, 10/1 priority date for domestic and international students. Applications are processed on a rolling basis. Application fee: $40 ($50 for international students). Electronic applications accepted. *Expenses:* Tuition, state resident: full-time $4390. Tuition, nonresident: full-time $15,309. *Required fees:* $853. *Financial support:* In 2017–18, 31 students received support, including 3 fellowships (averaging $4,390 per year), 11 teaching assistantships (averaging $9,486 per year); career-related internships or fieldwork, Federal Work-Study, scholarships/grants, traineeships, health care benefits, and unspecified assistantships also available. Support available to part-time students. Financial award application deadline: 3/1. *Unit head:* Dr. Rani Alexander, Department Head, 575-646-5809, E-mail: raalexan@nmsu.edu. *Application contact:* Dr. Lois Stanford, Graduate Advisor, 575-646-6092, E-mail: lstanfor@nmsu.edu.
Website: http://anthropology.nmsu.edu

The New School, Parsons Paris, Program in History of Design and Curatorial Studies, New York, NY 10011. Offers MA. Program offered in cooperation with the Musee des Arts Decoratifs. *Program availability:* Part-time. *Faculty:* 5 full-time (2 women). *Students:* 11 full-time (9 women); includes 4 minority (1 Asian, non-Hispanic/Latino; 3 Hispanic/Latino), 5 international. Average age 29. 14 applicants, 100% accepted, 6 enrolled. In 2017, 6 master's awarded. *Degree requirements:* For master's, one foreign language, thesis optional. *Entrance requirements:* For master's, transcripts, resume, statement of purpose, recommendation letters, interviews. Additional exam requirements/recommendations for international students: Required—TOEFL (minimum score 100 iBT), IELTS (minimum score 7), PTE (minimum score 68). *Application deadline:* For fall admission, 1/1 priority date for domestic and international students. Applications are processed on a rolling basis. Application fee: $50. Electronic applications accepted. *Expenses:* $19,203 per term full-time, $1,339 per credit part-time; $100 fee per term for maintenance of status. *Financial support:* In 2017–18, 9 students received support. Career-related internships or fieldwork and scholarships/grants available. *Unit head:* Emmanuel Guy, Director, 33-176217661, E-mail: guye@newschool.edu. *Application contact:* Mike Fakih, Director of Admissions, Parsons Paris, 33 176 21 76 67, E-mail: thinkparsonsparis@newschool.edu.

The New School, Parsons School of Design, Program in the History of Design and Curatorial Studies, New York, NY 10011. Offers MA. Program offered jointly with the Cooper-Hewitt Museum and the Smithsonian Institution. *Program availability:* Part-time. *Faculty:* 13 full-time (11 women). *Students:* 46 full-time (37 women), 18 part-time (15 women); includes 13 minority (4 Black or African American, non-Hispanic/Latino; 3 Asian, non-Hispanic/Latino; 6 Hispanic/Latino), 13 international. Average age 30. 71 applicants, 82% accepted, 18 enrolled. In 2017, 17 master's awarded. *Degree requirements:* For master's, thesis. *Entrance requirements:* For master's, transcripts, resume, statement of purpose, recommendation letters. Additional exam requirements/recommendations for international students: Required—TOEFL (minimum score 92 iBT), IELTS (minimum score 7), PTE (minimum score 63). *Application deadline:* For fall admission, 1/1 priority date for domestic and international students; for summer admission, 1/1 priority date for domestic and international students. Applications are processed on a rolling basis. Application fee: $50. Electronic applications accepted. *Expenses:* $1,744 per credit. *Financial support:* In 2017–18, 27 students received support, including 10 teaching assistantships (averaging $11,610 per year); career-related internships or fieldwork, scholarships/grants, and unspecified assistantships also available. Support available to part-time students. Financial award application deadline: 2/1; financial award applicants required to submit FAFSA. *Unit head:* Lorraine Karafel, Interim Program Director, 212-229-8916 Ext. 3209, E-mail: karafell@newschool.edu. *Application contact:* Courtney Malenius, Director of Graduate Admissions, 212-229-5150 Ext. 4011, E-mail: maleniuc@newschool.edu.
Website: https://www.newschool.edu/parsons/ma-history-design-curatorial-studies/

New York University, Graduate School of Arts and Science, Program in Museum Studies, New York, NY 10012-1019. Offers museum studies (MA, Advanced Certificate), including Africana studies (MA); Hebrew and Judaic studies (MA); Latin American and Caribbean studies (MA); Near Eastern studies (MA). *Program availability:* Part-time, evening/weekend. *Students:* Average age 26. 123 applicants, 81% accepted, 29 enrolled. In 2017, 35 master's, 1 other advanced degree awarded. *Entrance requirements:* For master's, GRE General Test; for Advanced Certificate, master's degree or PhD. Additional exam requirements/recommendations for international students: Required—TOEFL. *Application deadline:* For fall admission, 2/15 for domestic and international students; for spring admission, 11/1 for domestic and international

students. Application fee: $100. *Expenses: Tuition:* Full-time $41,352; part-time $19,968 per year. *Required fees:* $2496; $1628 per unit. $814 per term. Tuition and fees vary according to course load and program. *Financial support:* Application deadline: 2/15. *Faculty research:* Modern and contemporary art, history of museums and exhibitions, conservation of cultural materials, museum anthropology, ethnography. *Unit head:* Bruce Altshuler, Director, 212-998-8080, Fax: 212-995-4185, E-mail: museum.studies@nyu.edu. *Application contact:* Tatiana Kamorina, Department Administrator, 212-998-8080, Fax: 212-995-4185, E-mail: museum.studies@nyu.edu. Website: http://www.nyu.edu/fas/program/museumstudies/

Penn State Harrisburg, Graduate School, School of Humanities, Middletown, PA 17057. Offers American studies (MA, PhD); communications (MA); folklore and ethnography (Certificate); heritage and museum practice (Certificate); humanities (MA). *Program availability:* Evening/weekend. *Unit head:* Dr. Mukund S. Kulkarni, Chancellor, 717-948-6105, Fax: 717-948-6452. *Application contact:* Robert W. Coffman, Jr., Director of Enrollment Management, Recruitment and Admissions, 717-948-6250, Fax: 717-948-6325, E-mail: hbgadmit@psu.edu.
Website: https://harrisburg.psu.edu/humanities

St. John's University, St. John's College of Liberal Arts and Sciences, Department of Art and Design, Queens, NY 11439. Offers museum administration (MA). *Program availability:* Part-time, evening/weekend, 100% online, blended/hybrid learning. *Faculty:* 14 full-time (6 women), 31 part-time/adjunct (10 women). *Students:* 7 full-time (6 women), 4 part-time (all women); includes 1 minority (Asian, non-Hispanic/Latino), 1 international. Average age 34. 13 applicants, 77% accepted, 3 enrolled. In 2017, 3 master's awarded. *Degree requirements:* For master's, curated exhibition; one-semester internship; 21 credits of required courses and 15 credits of electives. *Entrance requirements:* For master's, GRE General Test, letters of recommendation, transcripts, resume, personal statement. Additional exam requirements/recommendations for international students: Required—TOEFL (minimum score 80 iBT), IELTS (minimum score 6.5). *Application deadline:* For fall admission, 5/1 for domestic students; for spring admission, 11/1 for domestic students. Applications are processed on a rolling basis. Application fee: $70. Electronic applications accepted. *Expenses: Tuition:* Full-time $44,280; part-time $1230 per credit. *Required fees:* $340; $340 per credit. Tuition and fees vary according to course load, degree level and program. *Financial support:* Fellowships, research assistantships, teaching assistantships, scholarships/grants, tuition waivers, and unspecified assistantships available. Support available to part-time students. Financial award application deadline: 2/1; financial award applicants required to submit FAFSA. *Faculty research:* Curatorial practice, history of curating, global contemporary art, historical modern art, 19th century art. *Total annual research expenditures:* $5,000. *Unit head:* Prof. Belenna Lauto, Chair, 718-990-5417, E-mail: lautob@stjohns.edu. *Application contact:* Robert Medrano, Director of Graduate Admission, 718-990-1601, Fax: 718-990-5686, E-mail: gradhelp@stjohns.edu.
Website: http://www.stjohns.edu/academics/schools-and-colleges/st-johns-college-liberal-arts-and-sciences/art-and-design

San Francisco Art Institute, Master of Arts Programs, San Francisco, CA 94133. Offers exhibition and museum studies (MA); history and theory of contemporary art (MA). *Degree requirements:* For master's, thesis. *Entrance requirements:* For master's, statement of purpose, writing samples. Additional exam requirements/recommendations for international students: Required—TOEFL (minimum score 600 paper-based; 100 iBT), IELTS (minimum score 7.5). Electronic applications accepted.

San Francisco State University, Division of Graduate Studies, College of Liberal and Creative Arts, School of Art, Museum Studies Program, San Francisco, CA 94132-1722. Offers MA. *Program availability:* Part-time. *Financial support:* Career-related internships or fieldwork and Federal Work-Study available. *Unit head:* Dr. Edward Luby, Program Director, 415-338-3163, Fax: 415-338-6537, E-mail: emluby@sfsu.edu.
Website: http://museum.sfsu.edu/

Seton Hall University, College of Communication and the Arts, Program in Museum Professions, South Orange, NJ 07079-2697. Offers exhibition development (MA); museum management (MA); museum registration (MA). *Program availability:* Part-time, evening/weekend, online learning. *Degree requirements:* For master's, thesis (for some programs). *Entrance requirements:* For master's, GRE or MAT, official transcripts, resume, personal statement, 3 letters of recommendation. Additional exam requirements/recommendations for international students: Required—TOEFL (minimum iBT score 80) or IELTS (6.5). Electronic applications accepted. *Faculty research:* Art history.

Southern Illinois University Edwardsville, Graduate School, College of Arts and Sciences, Department of Historical Studies, Program in Museum Studies, Edwardsville, IL 62026. Offers Postbaccalaureate Certificate. *Program availability:* Part-time, evening/weekend. *Entrance requirements:* Additional exam requirements/recommendations for international students: Required—TOEFL (minimum score 550 paper-based; 79 iBT), IELTS (minimum score 6.5). Electronic applications accepted.

Southern University at New Orleans, School of Graduate Studies, New Orleans, LA 70126-1009. Offers criminal justice (MA); management information systems (MS); museum studies (MA); social work (MSW). *Accreditation:* CSWE. *Program availability:* Part-time, evening/weekend. *Degree requirements:* For master's, thesis. *Entrance requirements:* For master's, GRE/GMAT. Additional exam requirements/recommendations for international students: Required—TOEFL.

State University of New York College at Oneonta, Graduate Programs, Cooperstown Graduate Program in Museum Studies, Cooperstown, NY 13326. Offers history museum studies (MA); science museum studies (MA). *Degree requirements:* For master's, research paper or thesis. *Entrance requirements:* For master's, GRE General Test. *Expenses:* Contact institution.

Syracuse University, College of Visual and Performing Arts, MA Program in Museum Studies, Syracuse, NY 13244. Offers MA. *Accreditation:* NASAD. In 2017, 15 master's awarded. *Degree requirements:* For master's, thesis or alternative. *Entrance requirements:* For master's, three letters of recommendation, academic transcripts, personal statement/essay, academic writing sample, resume. Additional exam requirements/recommendations for international students: Required—TOEFL (minimum score 100 iBT), IELTS. *Application deadline:* For fall admission, 2/1 priority date for domestic and international students. Application fee: $75. Electronic applications accepted. *Financial support:* Fellowships with full tuition reimbursements and teaching assistantships with tuition reimbursements available. Financial award application deadline: 1/1; financial award applicants required to submit FAFSA. *Faculty research:* Museum preparation and installation, museum graphics and communications, museum development, print history and processes. *Unit head:* Emily Stokes-Rees, Professor/Program Coordinator, Museum Studies, 315-443-2455, Fax: 315-443-1303, E-mail: ewstokes@syr.edu. *Application contact:* Caitlin Jarvis, Graduate Recruitment Specialist, 315-443-2769, E-mail: admissg@syr.edu.
Website: http://vpa.syr.edu/academics/design/graduate/museum-studies/

Texas Tech University, Graduate School, Interdisciplinary Programs, Lubbock, TX 79409. Offers arid land studies (MS); biotechnology (MS); heritage and museum sciences (MA); interdisciplinary studies (MA, MS); wind science and engineering (PhD); JD/MS. *Program availability:* Part-time, blended/hybrid learning. *Faculty:* 11 full-time (5 women). *Students:* 106 full-time (56 women), 85 part-time (52 women); includes 65

minority (23 Black or African American, non-Hispanic/Latino; 2 American Indian or Alaska Native, non-Hispanic/Latino; 3 Asian, non-Hispanic/Latino; 32 Hispanic/Latino; 5 Two or more races, non-Hispanic/Latino), 30 international. Average age 30. 116 applicants, 67% accepted, 55 enrolled. In 2017, 52 master's, 1 doctorate awarded. Terminal master's awarded for partial completion of doctoral program. *Degree requirements:* For master's, comprehensive exam (for some programs), thesis (for some programs); for doctorate, comprehensive exam, thesis/dissertation (for some programs). *Entrance requirements:* Additional exam requirements/recommendations for international students: Required—TOEFL (minimum score 550 paper-based; 79 iBT), IELTS (minimum score 6.5), PTE (minimum score 60), Cambridge advanced (B), Cambridge Proficiency (C), ELS English for Academic Purposes (Level 112). *Application deadline:* For fall admission, 6/1 priority date for domestic students, 1/15 priority date for international students; for spring admission, 9/1 priority date for domestic students, 6/15 priority date for international students. Applications are processed on a rolling basis. Application fee: $60. Electronic applications accepted. *Expenses:* Tuition, state resident: full-time $7632; part-time $318 per credit hour. Tuition, nonresident: full-time $17,424; part-time $726 per credit hour. *Required fees:* $2428; $50.50 per credit hour. $608 per semester. Tuition and fees vary according to program. *Financial support:* In 2017–18, 124 students received support, including 106 fellowships (averaging $4,660 per year), 25 research assistantships (averaging $16,239 per year), 16 teaching assistantships (averaging $10,391 per year); scholarships/grants and unspecified assistantships also available. Financial award application deadline: 4/15; financial award applicants required to submit FAFSA. *Total annual research expenditures:* $2.2 million. *Unit head:* Dr. Mark Sheridan, Vice Provost for Graduate and Postdoctoral Affairs/Dean of the Graduate School, 806-742-2787, Fax: 806-742-1746, E-mail: mark.sheridan@ttu.edu. *Application contact:* Claudia Simon, Senior Academic Advisor, 806-834-8290, Fax: 806-742-4038, E-mail: claudia.simon@ttu.edu.
Website: http://www.depts.ttu.edu/gradschool/

Trinity College, Graduate Programs, Program in American Studies, Hartford, CT 06106-3100. Offers American culture studies (MA); museums and communities (MA). *Program availability:* Part-time, evening/weekend. *Degree requirements:* For master's, thesis or alternative. *Entrance requirements:* For master's, minimum GPA of 3.0.

Tufts University, Graduate School of Arts and Sciences, Department of Art and Art History, Medford, MA 02155. Offers art history (MA); art history and museum studies (MA). *Students:* 14 full-time (10 women); includes 5 minority (1 Black or African American, non-Hispanic/Latino; 2 Asian, non-Hispanic/Latino; 2 Hispanic/Latino). Average age 25. 66 applicants, 42% accepted, 7 enrolled. In 2017, 9 master's awarded. *Degree requirements:* For master's, one foreign language, thesis (for some programs). *Entrance requirements:* For master's, GRE General Test. Additional exam requirements/recommendations for international students: Required—TOEFL (minimum score 550 paper-based; 80 iBT), IELTS (minimum score 6.5). *Application deadline:* For fall admission, 1/15 for domestic and international students. Application fee: $85. Electronic applications accepted. *Expenses:* Contact institution. *Financial support:* Teaching assistantships, Federal Work-Study, scholarships/grants, tuition waivers (full and partial), and unspecified assistantships available. Financial award application deadline: 1/15. *Unit head:* Karen Overbey, Graduate Program Director, 617-627-3395. *Application contact:* Office of Graduate Admissions, 617-627-3395, E-mail: gradadmissions@tufts.edu.
Website: http://ase.tufts.edu/art/

Tufts University, Graduate School of Arts and Sciences, Department of History, Medford, MA 02155. Offers history (MA, PhD), including global history (PhD); history and museum studies (MA). *Students:* 20 full-time (16 women); includes 4 minority (1 Black or African American, non-Hispanic/Latino; 3 Asian, non-Hispanic/Latino), 5 international. Average age 26. 57 applicants, 42% accepted, 7 enrolled. In 2017, 11 master's, 1 doctorate awarded. Terminal master's awarded for partial completion of doctoral program. *Degree requirements:* For master's, one foreign language, thesis optional; for doctorate, 2 foreign languages, comprehensive exam, thesis/dissertation. *Entrance requirements:* For master's and doctorate, GRE General Test, writing sample. Additional exam requirements/recommendations for international students: Required—TOEFL (minimum score 550 paper-based; 80 iBT), IELTS (minimum score 6.5). *Application deadline:* For fall admission, 1/15 for domestic and international students. Applications are processed on a rolling basis. Application fee: $85. Electronic applications accepted. *Expenses:* Contact institution. *Financial support:* Teaching assistantships, Federal Work-Study, scholarships/grants, tuition waivers (full and partial), and unspecified assistantships available. Financial award application deadline: 1/15. *Unit head:* Dr. Steven Marrone, Graduate Program Director, 617-627-2781. *Application contact:* Office of Graduate Admissions, 617-627-3395, E-mail: gradadmissions@tufts.edu.
Website: http://www.ase.tufts.edu/history/

Tufts University, Graduate School of Arts and Sciences, Graduate Certificate Programs, Museum Studies Program, Medford, MA 02155. Offers Certificate. *Program availability:* Part-time, evening/weekend. *Expenses:* Contact institution.

Tufts University, School of the Museum of Fine Arts at Tufts University, Boston, MA 02115. Offers art education (MAT); studio art (MFA, Postbaccalaureate Certificate), including museum studies (MFA). *Faculty:* 31 full-time (19 women), 23 part-time/adjunct (16 women). *Students:* 55 full-time. Average age 25. In 2017, 44 master's, 15 other advanced degrees awarded. Terminal master's awarded for partial completion of doctoral program. *Degree requirements:* For master's, thesis, thesis exhibition. *Entrance requirements:* For master's, BFA (preferred) or bachelor's degree or equivalent in related area; portfolio; for Postbaccalaureate Certificate, portfolio, BFA or equivalent. Additional exam requirements/recommendations for international students: Required—TOEFL (minimum score 85 iBT), IELTS (minimum score 6.5). *Application deadline:* For fall admission, 1/15 priority date for domestic and international students. Applications are processed on a rolling basis. Application fee: $85. Electronic applications accepted. *Expenses:* $45,008 (MFA); $3,995 per credit (Post-Baccalaureate Certificate). *Financial support:* Fellowships, teaching assistantships, Federal Work-Study, and scholarships/grants available. Financial award application deadline: 1/15. *Faculty research:* Public art commissions, National Endowment for the Arts grant recipients, international group and solo exhibitions. *Unit head:* Lisa Bynoe, Associate Director of Graduate Programs, 617-627-0031, E-mail: lisa.bynoe@tufts.edu. *Application contact:* Office of Graduate Admissions, 617-627-3395, E-mail: gradadmissions@tufts.edu.
Website: https://smfa.tufts.edu/

Université de Montréal, Faculty of Arts and Sciences, Program in Museology, Montréal, QC H3C 3J7, Canada. Offers MA. Program offered jointly with Université du Québec à Montréal. Electronic applications accepted. *Faculty research:* Museum exhibits, museum education, natural science and museums, new technologies and museums.

Université du Québec à Montréal, Graduate Programs, Program in Museology, Montréal, QC H3C 3P8, Canada. Offers MA. *Program availability:* Part-time. *Entrance requirements:* For master's, appropriate bachelor's degree or equivalent and proficiency in French.

Université Laval, Faculty of Letters, Department of History, Program in Museology, Québec, QC G1K 7P4, Canada. Offers Diploma. *Program availability:* Part-time. *Entrance requirements:* For degree, English exam (comprehension of English), knowledge of French. Electronic applications accepted.

University at Buffalo, the State University of New York, Graduate School, College of Arts and Sciences, Department of Art, Program in Visual Studies, Buffalo, NY 14260. Offers critical museum studies (MA); visual studies (MA, PhD). *Program availability:* Part-time. *Faculty:* 6 full-time (3 women). *Students:* 13 full-time (9 women), 3 international. Average age 27. 19 applicants, 58% accepted, 6 enrolled. In 2017, 4 master's, 2 doctorates awarded. *Degree requirements:* For master's, thesis, field exam; for doctorate, one foreign language, thesis/dissertation. *Entrance requirements:* Additional exam requirements/recommendations for international students: Required—TOEFL (minimum score 79 iBT). *Application deadline:* For fall admission, 2/1 priority date for domestic students; for spring admission, 10/15 priority date for domestic students. Applications are processed on a rolling basis. Application fee: $50. Electronic applications accepted. *Financial support:* In 2017–18, 9 students received support, including 9 teaching assistantships with full tuition reimbursements available (averaging $13,716 per year); career-related internships or fieldwork, Federal Work-Study, institutionally sponsored loans, tuition waivers (full), and unspecified assistantships also available. Support available to part-time students. Financial award application deadline: 2/28; financial award applicants required to submit FAFSA. *Unit head:* Joan Linder, Chair, 716-645-0539, Fax: 716-645-6970, E-mail: joannder@buffalo.edu. *Application contact:* Dr. Jonathan Katz, Director, 716-645-6878, Fax: 716-645-5978.
Website: http://art.buffalo.edu

The University of British Columbia, Faculty of Arts and Faculty of Graduate Studies, Department of Art History, Visual Art, and Theory, Vancouver, BC V6T 1Z2, Canada. Offers art history (MA, PhD); critical and curatorial studies (MA); visual art (MFA). *Degree requirements:* For master's, one foreign language, thesis, final exhibition (MFA, MA in critical and curatorial studies); for doctorate, 2 foreign languages, comprehensive exam, thesis/dissertation. *Entrance requirements:* For master's, bachelor's degree with minimum B+ average (MFA, MA in critical and curatorial studies), A- (MA in art history); for doctorate, master's degree with minimum A- average. Additional exam requirements/recommendations for international students: Required—TOEFL. Electronic applications accepted. *Expenses:* Contact institution. *Faculty research:* Conceptual art, Asian art, indigenous North American art, post-second war art, eighteenth- and nineteenth-century art, curatorial, digital art.

University of Central Oklahoma, The Jackson College of Graduate Studies, College of Liberal Arts, Department of History, Edmond, OK 73034-5209. Offers museum studies (MA). *Program availability:* Part-time. *Faculty:* 19 full-time (12 women), 2 part-time/adjunct (1 woman). *Students:* 22 full-time (9 women), 30 part-time (18 women); includes 12 minority (3 Black or African American, non-Hispanic/Latino; 4 American Indian or Alaska Native, non-Hispanic/Latino; 3 Hispanic/Latino; 2 Two or more races, non-Hispanic/Latino), 1 international. Average age 33. 13 applicants, 62% accepted, 7 enrolled. In 2017, 8 master's awarded. *Degree requirements:* For master's, one foreign language, comprehensive exam (for some programs), thesis (for some programs). *Entrance requirements:* For master's, writing sample, essay. Additional exam requirements/recommendations for international students: Required—TOEFL (minimum score 550 paper-based; 79 iBT), IELTS (minimum score 6.5). *Application deadline:* For fall admission, 7/15 for international students; for spring admission, 11/15 for international students. Applications are processed on a rolling basis. Application fee: $60. Electronic applications accepted. *Expenses:* Tuition, state resident: full-time $5375; part-time $268.75 per credit hour. Tuition, nonresident: full-time $13,295; part-time $664.75 per credit hour. *Required fees:* $626; $31.30 per credit hour. One-time fee: $50. Tuition and fees vary according to program. *Financial support:* In 2017–18, 14 students received support, including 7 research assistantships with partial tuition reimbursements available (averaging $6,760 per year), 4 teaching assistantships with partial tuition reimbursements available (averaging $6,366 per year); career-related internships or fieldwork, Federal Work-Study, scholarships/grants, tuition waivers (partial), and unspecified assistantships also available. Financial award application deadline: 3/31; financial award applicants required to submit FAFSA. *Unit head:* Dr. Patti Loughlin, Department Chair, 405-974-5540, Fax: 405-974-3823. *Application contact:* Dr. Marc Goulding, Graduate Advisor, 405-974-2838, Fax: 405-974-3823, E-mail: gradcoll@uco.edu.
Website: http://www.uco.edu/la/history-geography/

University of Colorado Boulder, Graduate School, Museum and Field Studies Program, Boulder, CO 80309. Offers MS. *Students:* 20 full-time (19 women), 1 (woman) part-time; includes 5 minority (1 Black or African American, non-Hispanic/Latino; 1 American Indian or Alaska Native, non-Hispanic/Latino; 1 Hispanic/Latino; 2 Two or more races, non-Hispanic/Latino), 1 international. Average age 28. 62 applicants, 16% accepted, 8 enrolled. In 2017, 3 master's awarded. Terminal master's awarded for partial completion of doctoral program. *Degree requirements:* For master's, comprehensive exam, thesis or alternative. *Entrance requirements:* For master's, GRE General Test, GRE Subject Test, minimum undergraduate GPA of 3.0. *Application deadline:* For fall admission, 1/10 for domestic students; for spring admission, 12/1 for domestic students. Application fee: $60 ($80 for international students). Electronic applications accepted. Application fee is waived when completed online. *Financial support:* In 2017–18, 62 students received support, including 20 fellowships (averaging $6,742 per year), 2 research assistantships with full and partial tuition reimbursements available (averaging $20,463 per year), 15 teaching assistantships with full and partial tuition reimbursements available (averaging $28,884 per year); institutionally sponsored loans, scholarships/grants, health care benefits, and unspecified assistantships also available. Financial award application deadline: 2/15; financial award applicants required to submit FAFSA. *Total annual research expenditures:* $270,416. *Application contact:* E-mail: mfsinfo@colorado.edu.
Website: http://cumuseum.colorado.edu/

University of Denver, Division of Arts, Humanities and Social Sciences, Department of Anthropology, Denver, CO 80208. Offers archaeology (MA); cultural anthropology (MA); museum and heritage studies (MA). *Program availability:* Part-time. *Faculty:* 8 full-time (2 women). *Students:* 3 full-time (all women), 23 part-time (20 women); includes 2 minority (1 Black or African American, non-Hispanic/Latino; 1 Hispanic/Latino), 1 international. Average age 25. 49 applicants, 59% accepted, 12 enrolled. In 2017, 9 master's awarded. *Degree requirements:* For master's, one foreign language, comprehensive exam, thesis (for some programs), tool, foreign language literacy, or course work. *Entrance requirements:* For master's, GRE General Test, bachelor's degree, transcripts, personal statement, two letters of recommendation. Additional exam requirements/recommendations for international students: Required—TOEFL (minimum score 550 paper-based; 80 iBT). *Application deadline:* For fall admission, 2/4 priority date for domestic and international students. Applications are processed on a rolling basis. Application fee: $65. Electronic applications accepted. *Expenses:* $31,935 per year full-time. *Financial support:* In 2017–18, 23 students received support. Teaching assistantships with tuition reimbursements available, career-related internships or fieldwork, Federal Work-Study, institutionally sponsored loans, scholarships/grants, and unspecified assistantships available. Support available to part-time students. Financial award application deadline: 2/15; financial award applicants required to submit FAFSA. *Faculty research:* Human diversity, human rights, historic archaeology, museums and

heritage, high-tech field methods. *Unit head:* Dr. Larry Conyers, Professor and Chair, 303-871-2684, Fax: 303-871-2437, E-mail: lconyers@du.edu. Website: http://www.du.edu/ahss/anthropology

University of Denver, Division of Arts, Humanities and Social Sciences, School of Art and Art History, Denver, CO 80208. Offers art history (MA); museum studies (MA). *Accreditation:* NASAD. *Program availability:* Part-time. *Faculty:* 16 full-time (10 women), 8 part-time/adjunct (7 women). *Students:* 5 full-time (4 women), 14 part-time (all women); includes 1 minority (Hispanic/Latino), 1 international. Average age 24. 33 applicants, 79% accepted, 13 enrolled. In 2017, 7 master's awarded. *Degree requirements:* For master's, one foreign language, comprehensive exam, research paper or thesis project. *Entrance requirements:* For master's, GRE General Test, transcripts, personal statement, writing sample, three letters of recommendation. Additional exam requirements/recommendations for international students: Required—TOEFL (minimum score 550 paper-based; 80 iBT). *Application deadline:* For fall admission, 1/31 priority date for domestic and international students. Applications are processed on a rolling basis. Application fee: $65. Electronic applications accepted. *Expenses:* $31,935 per year full-time. *Financial support:* In 2017–18, 19 students received support. Research assistantships with tuition reimbursements available, teaching assistantships with tuition reimbursements available, career-related internships or fieldwork, Federal Work-Study, institutionally sponsored loans, scholarships/grants, and unspecified assistantships available. Support available to part-time students. Financial award application deadline: 2/15; financial award applicants required to submit FAFSA. *Faculty research:* Abstract expressionist women painters, Chichen Itza, the cult of St. Ursula, rock poster art of the psychedelic era. *Unit head:* Catherine Chauvin, Associate Professor and Director, 303-871-2367, Fax: 303-871-4112, E-mail: catherine.chauvin@du.edu. *Application contact:* Jason Kellermeyer, Coordinator of Academic Programs, 303-871-2846, E-mail: jason.kellermeyer@du.edu. Website: http://www.du.edu/ahss/art/index.html

University of Florida, Graduate School, College of The Arts, School of Art and Art History, Gainesville, FL 32611. Offers art (MA), including digital arts and sciences; art education (MA); art history (MA, PhD); museology (MA), including historic preservation. *Accreditation:* NASAD. *Program availability:* Online learning. *Degree requirements:* For master's, project or thesis (MFA); 1 foreign language (MA in art history); for doctorate, 2 foreign languages, comprehensive exam, thesis/dissertation. *Entrance requirements:* For master's, GRE General Test, portfolio (MFA); writing sample (MA), minimum GPA 3.0; for doctorate, GRE General Test, minimum GPA of 3.0. Additional exam requirements/recommendations for international students: Required—TOEFL (minimum score 550 paper-based; 80 iBT), IELTS (minimum score 6). Electronic applications accepted. *Faculty research:* Studio production, art historical studies of style context.

University of Hawaii at Manoa, Office of Graduate Education, College of Arts and Humanities, Department of American Studies, Program in Museum Studies, Honolulu, HI 96822. Offers Graduate Certificate. *Program availability:* Part-time. *Entrance requirements:* Additional exam requirements/recommendations for international students: Required—TOEFL (minimum score 600 paper-based; 100 iBT), IELTS (minimum score 7).

University of Illinois at Chicago, College of Architecture, Design and the Arts, School of Art and Art History, Chicago, IL 60607-7128. Offers art history (MA); electronic visualization (MFA); museum and exhibition studies (MA); new media arts (MFA). *Program availability:* Part-time, evening/weekend. Terminal master's awarded for partial completion of doctoral program. *Degree requirements:* For master's, one foreign language, thesis or alternative; for doctorate, thesis/dissertation. *Entrance requirements:* For master's, GRE General Test, minimum GPA of 2.75, 3 letters of recommendation; for doctorate, GRE General Test, MA in art history or equivalent, minimum GPA of 3.0. Additional exam requirements/recommendations for international students: Required—TOEFL. Electronic applications accepted. *Expenses:* Contact institution. *Faculty research:* Modern painting and sculpture, history of architecture, city planning and design, history of photography.

The University of Kansas, Graduate Studies, College of Liberal Arts and Sciences, Museum Studies Program, Lawrence, KS 66045-7545. Offers MA, Graduate Certificate. *Program availability:* Part-time. *Students:* 18 full-time (15 women), 2 part-time (both women). Average age 28. 37 applicants, 68% accepted, 11 enrolled. In 2017, 6 master's, 1 other advanced degree awarded. *Entrance requirements:* For master's, GRE, 3 letters of recommendation, resume, writing sample, statement of purpose, official transcripts. Additional exam requirements/recommendations for international students: Required—TOEFL. *Application deadline:* For fall admission, 1/1 priority date for domestic and international students. Application fee: $65 ($85 for international students). Electronic applications accepted. *Financial support:* Research assistantships, career-related internships or fieldwork, and unspecified assistantships available. Financial award application deadline: 1/1. *Faculty research:* Museum studies, audience evaluation, community engagement, material culture, anthropology, historical and legal backgrounds by which museums have come to control culturally-sensitive objects. *Unit head:* Dr. Peter H. Welsh, Director, 785-864-5702, E-mail: phwelsh@ku.edu. *Application contact:* Kay Isbell, Graduate Academic Advisor, 785-864-2306, E-mail: kisbell@ku.edu. Website: http://museumstudies.ku.edu/

University of Louisville, Graduate School, College of Arts and Sciences, Department of Fine Arts, Louisville, KY 40292. Offers art history (MA, PhD); curatorial studies (MA); studio art (MFA), including design. *Program availability:* Online learning. *Faculty:* 23 full-time (9 women), 6 part-time/adjunct (3 women). *Students:* 24 full-time (17 women), 1 (woman) part-time; includes 3 minority (1 Asian, non-Hispanic/Latino; 1 Hispanic/Latino; 1 Two or more races, non-Hispanic/Latino). Average age 35. 16 applicants, 63% accepted, 7 enrolled. In 2017, 5 master's awarded. *Degree requirements:* For master's, one foreign language, thesis. *Entrance requirements:* For doctorate, MA. Additional exam requirements/recommendations for international students: Required—TOEFL (minimum score 550 paper-based; 80 iBT), IELTS (minimum score 6.5). *Application deadline:* For fall admission, 3/1 priority date for domestic and international students. Application fee: $65. *Expenses:* $12,500. *Financial support:* In 2017–18, 7 teaching assistantships with full tuition reimbursements (averaging $14,000 per year) were awarded; research assistantships, scholarships/grants, health care benefits, and unspecified assistantships also available. Financial award application deadline: 3/1. *Faculty research:* Sustainability and environmental design, media theory, cross cultural and critical theories, Installation, urban and public art. *Total annual research expenditures:* $75,000. *Unit head:* Dr. Scott L. Massey, Associate Professor and Chair, 502-852-6794, Fax: 502-852-6791, E-mail: s.massey@louisville.edu. *Application contact:* Theresa Berbet, Senior Advisor, 502-852-6147, Fax: 502-852-6791, E-mail: tberbet@louisville.edu. Website: http://art.louisville.edu

The University of Manchester, School of Arts, Histories and Cultures, Manchester, United Kingdom. Offers anthropology, media and performance (PhD); applied theatre professional (PhD); archaeology (PhD); art history and visual studies (PhD); arts management and cultural policy (PhD); classics and ancient history (PhD); composition (PhD); creative writing (PhD); drama (PhD); economic and social history (PhD); electroacoustic composition (PhD); English and American studies (PhD); history (PhD);

humanitarianism and conflict response (PhD); museology (PhD); music (PhD); musicology (PhD); religions and theology (PhD).

University of Memphis, Graduate School, College of Arts and Sciences, Program in Interdisciplinary Studies, Memphis, TN 38152. Offers museum studies (Graduate Certificate); women's and gender studies (Graduate Certificate). *Faculty:* 3 full-time (1 woman). *Students:* 7 full-time (1 woman), 13 part-time (7 women); includes 9 minority (6 Black or African American, non-Hispanic/Latino; 3 Asian, non-Hispanic/Latino), 4 international. Average age 32. 22 applicants, 82% accepted, 14 enrolled. *Degree requirements:* For Graduate Certificate, minimum GPA of 3.0. *Entrance requirements:* For degree, GRE, letter of interest, undergraduate transcript. Additional exam requirements/recommendations for international students: Required—TOEFL (minimum score 550 paper-based). *Application deadline:* For fall admission, 4/3 for domestic students. Application fee: $35 ($60 for international students). *Expenses:* Contact institution. *Financial support:* In 2017–18, 11 students received support, including 13 research assistantships with full tuition reimbursements available (averaging $12,420 per year); teaching assistantships with full tuition reimbursements available, Federal Work-Study, scholarships/grants, and unspecified assistantships also available. Financial award application deadline: 2/1; financial award applicants required to submit FAFSA. *Unit head:* Dr. Henry A. Kurtz, Dean, 901-678-2251, Fax: 901-678-4831, E-mail: hkurtz@memphis.edu. *Application contact:* Dr. Kathy Schultz, Director of Women's and Gender Studies, 901-678-2651, E-mail: klschltz@memphis.edu. Website: http://www.memphis.edu/isc/

University of Memphis, Graduate School, College of Communication and Fine Arts, Department of Art, Memphis, TN 38152. Offers art history (MA), including Egyptian art and archaeology, general art history; ceramics (MFA); graphic design (MFA); museum studies (Graduate Certificate); painting (MFA); printmaking/photography (MFA); sculpture (MFA). *Accreditation:* NASAD (one or more programs are accredited). *Program availability:* Part-time. *Faculty:* 18 full-time (7 women), 2 part-time/adjunct (1 woman). *Students:* 21 full-time (17 women), 5 part-time (all women); includes 8 minority (2 Black or African American, non-Hispanic/Latino; 1 Asian, non-Hispanic/Latino; 4 Hispanic/Latino; 1 Two or more races, non-Hispanic/Latino). Average age 29. 11 applicants, 73% accepted, 5 enrolled. In 2017, 5 master's, 5 other advanced degrees awarded. *Degree requirements:* For master's, 2 foreign languages, comprehensive exam, thesis, image identification exam, qualifying exam; for Graduate Certificate, internship. *Entrance requirements:* For master's, GRE General Test or MAT, portfolio (MFA), letter of intent, sample of undergraduate writing, two letters of recommendation; for Graduate Certificate, three letters of recommendation, letter of intent. *Application deadline:* For fall admission, 2/15 for domestic students; for spring admission, 11/1 for domestic students. Applications are processed on a rolling basis. Application fee: $35 ($60 for international students). *Expenses:* Contact institution. *Financial support:* In 2017–18, 36 students received support, including 15 research assistantships with full tuition reimbursements available (averaging $11,600 per year); teaching assistantships with full tuition reimbursements available, Federal Work-Study, scholarships/grants, and unspecified assistantships also available. Financial award application deadline: 2/1; financial award applicants required to submit FAFSA. *Faculty research:* Online collaborative learning, advanced art history studies, electronic publishing/design, studio arts, architectural studies. *Unit head:* Prof. Richard Lou, Chair, 901-678-2217, Fax: 901-678-2735, E-mail: ralou@memphis.edu. *Application contact:* Niles Wallice, Coordinator of Graduate Studies, 901-678-4899. Website: http://memphis.edu/art/

University of Michigan–Flint, Graduate Programs, Program in Arts Administration, Flint, MI 48502-1950. Offers performance (MA), including museum and visual arts, performance. *Program availability:* Part-time. *Faculty:* 5 full-time (3 women), 1 (woman) part-time/adjunct. *Students:* 6 full-time (4 women), 7 part-time (4 women); includes 2 minority (both Black or African American, non-Hispanic/Latino). Average age 43. 12 applicants, 75% accepted, 5 enrolled. In 2017, 3 master's awarded. *Degree requirements:* For master's, thesis, internship. *Entrance requirements:* For master's, bachelor's degree in the arts (visual art, theatre, dance, music, etc.) from regionally-accredited institution; minimum cumulative undergraduate GPA of 3.0. Additional exam requirements/recommendations for international students: Required—TOEFL (minimum score 84 iBT), IELTS (minimum score 6.5). *Application deadline:* For fall admission, 8/1 for domestic students, 5/1 for international students; for winter admission, 11/15 for domestic students, 9/1 for international students. Applications are processed on a rolling basis. Application fee: $55. Electronic applications accepted. *Expenses:* Contact institution. *Financial support:* Federal Work-Study, institutionally sponsored loans, scholarships/grants, and unspecified assistantships available. Support available to part-time students. Financial award application deadline: 3/1; financial award applicants required to submit FAFSA. *Unit head:* Nicole Broughton, Director, 810-237-6522, E-mail: broughn@umflint.edu. *Application contact:* Bradley T. Maki, Director of Graduate Admissions, 810-762-3171, Fax: 810-766-6789, E-mail: bmaki@umflint.edu. Website: http://www.umflint.edu/graduateprograms/arts-administration-ma

University of Missouri–St. Louis, College of Arts and Sciences, Department of History, St. Louis, MO 63121. Offers history (MA); history education (Certificate); museum studies (MA, Certificate). *Program availability:* Part-time, evening/weekend. *Faculty:* 12 full-time (4 women), 8 part-time/adjunct (0 women). *Students:* 15 full-time (11 women), 31 part-time (13 women); includes 6 minority (2 Black or African American, non-Hispanic/Latino; 1 American Indian or Alaska Native, non-Hispanic/Latino; 3 Asian, non-Hispanic/Latino). 19 applicants, 89% accepted, 12 enrolled. *Degree requirements:* For master's, thesis (for some programs). *Entrance requirements:* For master's, writing sample; minimum GPA of 2.75 (for history), 3.2 (for museum studies). Additional exam requirements/recommendations for international students: Required—TOEFL (minimum score 550 paper-based; 79 iBT), IELTS (minimum score 6.5). *Application deadline:* For fall admission, 3/15 for domestic and international students; for spring admission, 10/15 for domestic and international students. Applications are processed on a rolling basis. Application fee: $50 ($40 for international students). Electronic applications accepted. *Expenses:* Tuition, state resident: part-time $476.50 per credit hour. Tuition, nonresident: part-time $1169.70 per credit hour. *Financial support:* Research assistantships with tuition reimbursements, teaching assistantships with tuition reimbursements, and career-related internships or fieldwork available. Financial award applicants required to submit FAFSA. *Faculty research:* United States, European, East Asian, Latin American, and African history. *Unit head:* Dr. Laura Westhoff, Chair, 314-516-5692, Fax: 314-516-5781, E-mail: westhoffl@msx.umsl.edu. *Application contact:* 314-516-5458, Fax: 314-516-6996, E-mail: gradadm@umsl.edu. Website: http://www.umsl.edu/~umslhistory/

University of New Hampshire, Graduate School, College of Liberal Arts, Department of History, Durham, NH 03824. Offers history (MA, PhD); history: museum studies (MA). *Program availability:* Part-time. *Students:* 23 full-time (13 women), 12 part-time (4 women); includes 2 minority (1 Hispanic/Latino; 1 Two or more races, non-Hispanic/Latino), 1 international. Average age 30. 53 applicants, 51% accepted, 11 enrolled. In 2017, 11 master's, 5 doctorates awarded. *Entrance requirements:* For master's and doctorate, GRE General Test, writing sample. Additional exam requirements/recommendations for international students: Required—TOEFL (minimum score 550 paper-based; 80 iBT). *Application deadline:* For fall admission, 1/15 for domestic and

international students. Application fee: $65. Electronic applications accepted. *Financial support:* In 2017–18, 26 students received support, including 1 fellowship, 13 teaching assistantships; research assistantships, career-related internships or fieldwork, Federal Work-Study, scholarships/grants, and tuition waivers (full and partial) also available. Support available to part-time students. Financial award application deadline: 2/15. *Unit head:* Eliga Gould, Chair, 603-862-3012. *Application contact:* Lara Demarest, Administrative Assistant, 603-862-1765, E-mail: history.grad@unh.edu.
Website: http://cola.unh.edu/history

The University of North Carolina at Greensboro, Graduate School, College of Arts and Sciences, Department of History, Greensboro, NC 27412-5001. Offers historic preservation (Certificate); history (MA); museum studies (Certificate); U.S. history (PhD). *Program availability:* Part-time. *Entrance requirements:* For master's, GRE General Test. Additional exam requirements/recommendations for international students: Required—TOEFL. Electronic applications accepted. *Faculty research:* Simultaneous discovery in science, progressive social reform, Robert Mayer.

The University of North Carolina at Greensboro, Graduate School, College of Arts and Sciences, Department of Interior Architecture, Greensboro, NC 27412-5001. Offers historic preservation (Certificate); interior architecture (MS); museum studies (Certificate). *Degree requirements:* For master's, thesis. *Entrance requirements:* For master's, GRE General Test or MAT, bachelor's degree in interior design, interview, portfolio. Additional exam requirements/recommendations for international students: Required—TOEFL. Electronic applications accepted.

University of North Texas, Robert B. Toulouse School of Graduate Studies, Denton, TX 76203-5459. Offers accounting (MS); applied anthropology (MA, MS); applied behavior analysis (Certificate); applied geography (MA); applied technology and performance improvement (M Ed, MS); art education (MA); art history (MA); art museum education (Certificate); arts leadership (Certificate); audiology (Au D); behavior analysis (MS); behavioral science (PhD); biochemistry and molecular biology (MS); biology (MA, MS); biomedical engineering (MS); business analysis (MS); chemistry (MS); clinical health psychology (PhD); communication studies (MA, MS); computer engineering (MS); computer science (MS); counseling (M Ed, MS), including clinical mental health counseling (MS), college and university counseling, elementary school counseling, secondary school counseling; creative writing (MA); criminal justice (MS); curriculum and instruction (M Ed); decision sciences (MBA); design (MA, MFA), including fashion design (MFA), innovation studies, interior design (MFA); early childhood studies (MS); economics (MS); educational leadership (M Ed, Ed D); educational psychology (MS, PhD), including family studies (MS), gifted and talented (MS), human development (MS), learning and cognition (MS), research, measurement and evaluation (MS); electrical engineering (MS); emergency management (MPA); engineering technology (MS); English (MA); English as a second language (MA); environmental science (MS); finance (MBA, MS); financial management (MPA); French (MA); health services management (MBA); higher education (M Ed, Ed D); history (MA, MS); hospitality management (MS); human resources management (MPA); information science (MS); information systems (PhD); information technologies (MBA); interdisciplinary studies (MA, MS); international studies (MA); international sustainable tourism (MS); jazz studies (MM); journalism (MA, MJ, Graduate Certificate), including interactive and virtual digital communication (Graduate Certificate), narrative journalism (Graduate Certificate), public relations (Graduate Certificate); kinesiology (MS); linguistics (MA); local government management (MPA); logistics (PhD); logistics and supply chain management (MBA); long-term care, senior housing, and aging services (MA); management (PhD); marketing (MBA); mathematics (MA, MS); mechanical and energy engineering (MS, PhD); music (MA), including ethnomusicology, music theory, musicology, performance; music composition (PhD); music education (MM Ed, PhD); nonprofit management (MPA); operations and supply chain management (MBA); performance (MM, DMA); philosophy (MA); political science (MA); professional and technical communication (MA); radio, television and film (MA, MFA); rehabilitation counseling (Certificate); sociology (MA); Spanish (MA); special education (M Ed); speech-language pathology (MA); strategic management (MBA); studio art (MFA); teaching (M Ed); MBA/MS. *Program availability:* Part-time, evening/weekend, online learning. Terminal master's awarded for partial completion of doctoral program. *Degree requirements:* For master's, variable foreign language requirement, comprehensive exam (for some programs), thesis (for some programs); for doctorate, variable foreign language requirement, comprehensive exam (for some programs), thesis/dissertation; for other advanced degree, variable foreign language requirement, comprehensive exam (for some programs). *Entrance requirements:* For master's and doctorate, GRE, GMAT. Additional exam requirements/recommendations for international students: Required—TOEFL (minimum score 550 paper-based; 79 iBT). Electronic applications accepted.

University of Oklahoma, College of Professional and Continuing Studies, Norman, OK 73019. Offers administrative leadership (MA, Graduate Certificate), including government and military leadership (MA), organizational leadership (MA), volunteer and non-profit leadership (MA); corrections management (Graduate Certificate); criminal justice (MS); integrated studies (MA), including human and health services administration, integrated studies; museum studies (MA); prevention science (MPS); restorative justice administration (Graduate Certificate). *Program availability:* Part-time, 100% online, blended/hybrid learning. *Faculty:* 16 full-time (8 women). *Students:* 64 full-time (39 women), 558 part-time (278 women); includes 191 minority (42 Black or African American, non-Hispanic/Latino; 42 American Indian or Alaska Native, non-Hispanic/Latino; 16 Asian, non-Hispanic/Latino; 46 Hispanic/Latino; 1 Native Hawaiian or other Pacific Islander, non-Hispanic/Latino; 44 Two or more races, non-Hispanic/Latino), 4 international. Average age 35. 151 applicants, 95% accepted, 97 enrolled. In 2017, 202 master's, 11 other advanced degrees awarded. *Degree requirements:* For master's, comprehensive exam, thesis optional, 33 credit hours; project/internship (for museum studies program only); for Graduate Certificate, 12 graduate credit hours (for Graduate Certificate). *Entrance requirements:* For master's and Graduate Certificate, minimum GPA of 3.0 in last 60 undergraduate hours; statement of goals; resume. Additional exam requirements/recommendations for international students: Required—TOEFL (minimum score 79 iBT) or IELTS (minimum score 6.5). *Application deadline:* For fall admission, 7/15 for domestic and international students; for winter admission, 12/1 for domestic and international students; for spring admission, 5/1 for domestic and international students. Applications are processed on a rolling basis. Application fee: $50 ($100 for international students). Electronic applications accepted. *Expenses:* Tuition, state resident: full-time $5119; part-time $213.30 per credit hour. Tuition, nonresident: full-time $19,778; part-time $824.10 per credit hour. *Required fees:* $3458; $133.55 per credit hour. $126.50 per semester. *Financial support:* In 2017–18, 92 students received support. Career-related internships or fieldwork, institutionally sponsored loans, scholarships/grants, health care benefits, and tuition waivers available. Support available to part-time students. Financial award application deadline: 6/1; financial award applicants required to submit FAFSA. *Faculty research:* Change management and leadership; policing and corrections management; neuro-psychology of addiction; disproportionate minority contact; ethnic identity and nationalism. *Unit head:* Dr. Martha L. Banz, Associate Provost for Continuing Education/Interim Dean, College of Professional and Continuing Studies, 405-325-4414, Fax: 405-325-7132, E-mail: mlbanz@ou.edu. *Application contact:* Lindsey Gunderson, Graduate Academic Advisor, 405-325-5827, Fax: 405-325-

7132, E-mail: lindsey.gunderson@ou.edu.
Website: https://pacs.ou.edu/

University of St. Thomas, College of Arts and Sciences, Department of Art History, St. Paul, MN 55105. Offers art history (MA); museum studies (Graduate Certificate). *Program availability:* Part-time, evening/weekend. *Faculty:* 7 full-time (4 women). *Students:* 29 full-time (25 women); includes 3 minority (1 American Indian or Alaska Native, non-Hispanic/Latino; 1 Asian, non-Hispanic/Latino; 1 Hispanic/Latino). Average age 36. 8 applicants, 88% accepted, 6 enrolled. In 2017, 11 master's, 5 other advanced degrees awarded. *Degree requirements:* For master's, one foreign language, thesis, oral exam, reading proficiency in 1 foreign language. *Entrance requirements:* For master's, bachelor's degree in art history or related field; 3 letters of recommendation; writing sample; personal statement. Additional exam requirements/recommendations for international students: Required—TOEFL (minimum score 80 iBT). *Application deadline:* For fall admission, 3/1 priority date for domestic and international students; for spring admission, 11/1 priority date for domestic and international students; for summer admission, 3/1 priority date for domestic and international students. Applications are processed on a rolling basis. Application fee: $0. Electronic applications accepted. *Expenses:* $857.50 per credit tuition ($2,572.50 per course); $55 per semester technology fee ($111 for two or more courses). *Financial support:* In 2017–18, 15 students received support, including 15 fellowships with partial tuition reimbursements available; research assistantships, career-related internships or fieldwork, institutionally sponsored loans, scholarships/grants, and unspecified assistantships also available. Support available to part-time students. Financial award application deadline: 4/1; financial award applicants required to submit FAFSA. *Faculty research:* Pictorial narrative and theory, Mesoamerican art, Chinese manuscript painting, Africa and African diaspora, architectural history, Modernism. *Unit head:* Victoria Young, Chair, 651-962-5855, Fax: 651-962-5861, E-mail: vmyoung@stthomas.edu. *Application contact:* Dr. Heather Shirey, Director of Graduate Studies, 651-962-5572, Fax: 651-962-5861, E-mail: hmshirey@stthomas.edu.
Website: http://www.stthomas.edu/arthistory/

University of San Francisco, College of Arts and Sciences, Museum Studies Program, San Francisco, CA 94117-1080. Offers MA. *Program availability:* Part-time. *Entrance requirements:* Additional exam requirements/recommendations for international students: Required—TOEFL, IELTS, PTE. Electronic applications accepted.

University of South Carolina, The Graduate School, College of Arts and Sciences, Department of History, Program in Public History, Columbia, SC 29208. Offers archive management (MA); historic preservation (MA); museum administration (MA); museum management (Certificate); MLIS/MA. *Degree requirements:* For master's, one foreign language, thesis, internship. *Entrance requirements:* For master's, GRE General Test, writing sample. Additional exam requirements/recommendations for international students: Required—TOEFL. Electronic applications accepted. *Faculty research:* Museum studies, historic preservation, archives administration.

University of South Florida, Innovative Education, Tampa, FL 33620-9951. Offers adult, career and higher education (Graduate Certificate), including college teaching, leadership in developing human resources, leadership in higher education; Africana studies (Graduate Certificate), including diasporas and health disparities, genocide and human rights; aging studies (Graduate Certificate), including gerontology; art research (Graduate Certificate), including museum studies; business foundations (Graduate Certificate); chemical and biomedical engineering (Graduate Certificate), including materials science and engineering, water, health and sustainability; child and family studies (Graduate Certificate), including positive behavior support; civil and industrial engineering (Graduate Certificate), including transportation systems analysis; community and family health (Graduate Certificate), including maternal and child health, social marketing and public health, violence and injury: prevention and intervention, women's health; criminology (Graduate Certificate), including criminal justice administration; data science for public administration (Graduate Certificate); digital humanities (Graduate Certificate); educational measurement and research (Graduate Certificate), including evaluation; English (Graduate Certificate), including comparative literary studies, creative writing, professional and technical communication; entrepreneurship (Graduate Certificate); environmental health (Graduate Certificate), including safety management; epidemiology and biostatistics (Graduate Certificate), including applied biostatistics, biostatistics, concepts and tools of epidemiology, epidemiology, epidemiology of infectious diseases; geography, environment and planning (Graduate Certificate), including community development, environmental policy and management, geographical information systems; geology (Graduate Certificate), including hydrogeology; global health (Graduate Certificate), including disaster management, global health and Latin American and Caribbean studies, global health practice, humanitarian assistance, infection control; government and international affairs (Graduate Certificate), including Cuban studies, globalization studies; health policy and management (Graduate Certificate), including health management and leadership, public health policy and programs; hearing specialist: early intervention (Graduate Certificate); industrial and management systems engineering (Graduate Certificate), including systems engineering, technology management; information studies (Graduate Certificate), including school library media specialist; information systems/decision sciences (Graduate Certificate), including analytics and business intelligence; instructional technology (Graduate Certificate), including distance education, Florida digital/virtual educator, instructional design, multimedia design, Web design; internal medicine, bioethics and medical humanities (Graduate Certificate), including biomedical ethics; Latin American and Caribbean studies (Graduate Certificate); leadership for coastal resiliency planning (Graduate Certificate); mass communications (Graduate Certificate), including multimedia journalism; mathematics and statistics (Graduate Certificate), including mathematics; medicine (Graduate Certificate), including aging and neuroscience, bioinformatics, biotechnology, brain fitness and memory management, clinical investigation, hand and upper limb rehabilitation, health informatics, health sciences, integrative weight management, intellectual property, medicine and gender, metabolic and nutritional medicine, metabolic cardiology, pharmacy sciences; national and competitive intelligence (Graduate Certificate); nursing (Graduate Certificate), including simulation based academic fellowship in advanced pain management; psychological and social foundations (Graduate Certificate), including career counseling, college teaching, diversity in education, mental health counseling, school counseling; public affairs (Graduate Certificate), including nonprofit management, public management, research administration; public health (Graduate Certificate), including assessing chemical toxicity and public health risks, health equity, pharmacoepidemiology, public health generalist, toxicology, translational research in adolescent behavioral health; public health practices (Graduate Certificate), including planning for healthy communities; rehabilitation and mental health counseling (Graduate Certificate), including integrative mental health care, marriage and family therapy, rehabilitation technology; secondary education (Graduate Certificate), including ESOL, foreign language education: culture and content, foreign language education: professional; social work (Graduate Certificate), including geriatric social work/clinical gerontology; special education (Graduate Certificate), including autism spectrum disorder, disabilities education: severe/profound; world languages (Graduate Certificate), including teaching English as a second language (TESL) or foreign language. *Unit head:* Dr. Cynthia DeLuca, Associate Vice President and Assistant Vice

Provost, 813-974-3077, Fax: 813-974-7061, E-mail: deluca@usf.edu. *Application contact:* Owen Hooper, Director, Summer and Alternative Calendar Programs, 813-974-6917, E-mail: hooper@usf.edu.
Website: http://www.usf.edu/innovative-education/

The University of the Arts, College of Art, Media and Design, Department of Museum Studies, Philadelphia, PA 19102-4944. Offers museum communication (MA); museum education (MA); museum exhibition planning and design (MFA). *Accreditation:* NASAD. *Degree requirements:* For master's, thesis, internship. *Entrance requirements:* For master's, official transcripts, three letters of recommendation, one- to two-page statement, personal interview; academic writing sample and examples of work (for museum communication); two examples of academic and professional writing (for museum education); portfolio and/or writing samples (for museum exhibition planning and design). Additional exam requirements/recommendations for international students: Required—TOEFL (minimum score 580 paper-based, 92 iBT) or IELTS (minimum score 6.5).

University of Toronto, School of Graduate Studies, Faculty of Information, Program in Museum Studies, Toronto, ON M5S 1A1, Canada. Offers MM St. *Entrance requirements:* Additional exam requirements/recommendations for international students: Required—TOEFL (minimum score 580 paper-based; 93 iBT), TWE (minimum score 5). Electronic applications accepted. *Expenses:* Contact institution.

The University of Tulsa, Graduate School, Program in Museum Science and Management, Tulsa, OK 74104-3189. Offers MA. *Program availability:* Part-time. *Faculty:* 9 full-time (1 woman). *Students:* 12 full-time (11 women), 3 part-time (2 women); includes 3 minority (1 Black or African American, non-Hispanic/Latino; 1 American Indian or Alaska Native, non-Hispanic/Latino; 1 Two or more races, non-Hispanic/Latino), 1 international. Average age 28. 20 applicants, 65% accepted, 10 enrolled. In 2017, 5 master's awarded. *Degree requirements:* For master's, final semester internship or independent research project. *Entrance requirements:* For master's, GRE General Test. Additional exam requirements/recommendations for international students: Required—TOEFL (minimum score 575 paper-based; 91 iBT), IELTS (minimum score 6.5). *Application deadline:* Applications are processed on a rolling basis. Application fee: $55. Electronic applications accepted. *Expenses: Tuition:* Full-time $22,230. *Required fees:* $2000. Tuition and fees vary according to course load and program. *Financial support:* In 2017–18, 11 students received support, including 1 fellowship with full tuition reimbursement available (averaging $234 per year), 11 teaching assistantships with full tuition reimbursements available (averaging $8,602 per year); research assistantships with full tuition reimbursements available, career-related internships or fieldwork, Federal Work-Study, scholarships/grants, health care benefits, tuition waivers (full and partial), and unspecified assistantships also available. Support available to part-time students. Financial award application deadline: 2/1; financial award applicants required to submit FAFSA. *Unit head:* Dr. Bob Pickering, Director, 918-596-2706, Fax: 918-596-2770, E-mail: bob-pickering@utulsa.edu. *Application contact:* Graduate School, 918-631-2336, Fax: 918-631-2156, E-mail: grad@utulsa.edu.
Website: http://graduate.utulsa.edu/academics/museum-science-management-program/

University of Washington, Graduate School, Museology Graduate Program, Seattle, WA 98195. Offers museum evaluation (MA). *Faculty:* 4 full-time (3 women), 14 part-time/adjunct (10 women). *Students:* 71 full-time (61 women); includes 12 minority (1 Black or African American, non-Hispanic/Latino; 4 American Indian or Alaska Native, non-Hispanic/Latino; 4 Asian, non-Hispanic/Latino; 3 Hispanic/Latino), 4 international. Average age 26. 111 applicants, 63% accepted, 34 enrolled. In 2017, 33 master's awarded. *Degree requirements:* For master's, thesis. *Entrance requirements:* For master's, baccalaureate degree; minimum GPA of 3.0 during last 2 years (60 semester credits and 90 quarter credits) of courses. Additional exam requirements/recommendations for international students: Required—TOEFL (minimum score 580 paper-based; 92 iBT). *Application deadline:* For fall admission, 1/15 for domestic and international students. Application fee: $85. Electronic applications accepted. *Expenses:* $6,195 per quarter. *Financial support:* In 2017–18, 3 research assistantships were awarded; career-related internships or fieldwork, Federal Work-Study, institutionally sponsored loans, and scholarships/grants also available. Financial award application deadline: 1/15; financial award applicants required to submit FAFSA. *Faculty research:* Collection management, audience research and evaluation, informal learning, museums and social change, museum administration. *Unit head:* Dr. Jessica Luke, Director, E-mail: uwmuse@uw.edu. *Application contact:* Dylan High, Student Experience Coordinator, 206-221-0713, E-mail: uwmuse@uw.edu.
Website: http://www.washington.edu/museology/

University of West Georgia, College of Arts and Humanities, Carrollton, GA 30118. Offers English (MA); history (MA); museum studies (Postbaccalaureate Certificate); music performance (M Mus); music teacher education (M Mus); public history (Postbaccalaureate Certificate). *Program availability:* Part-time, evening/weekend, 100% online, blended/hybrid learning. *Faculty:* 69 full-time (38 women). *Students:* 25 full-time (15 women), 51 part-time (34 women); includes 16 minority (7 Black or African American, non-Hispanic/Latino; 1 American Indian or Alaska Native, non-Hispanic/Latino; 2 Asian, non-Hispanic/Latino; 5 Hispanic/Latino; 1 Two or more races, non-Hispanic/Latino), 1 international. Average age 30. 23 applicants, 96% accepted, 16 enrolled. In 2017, 29 master's, 6 other advanced degrees awarded. *Entrance requirements:* Additional exam requirements/recommendations for international students: Required—TOEFL (minimum score 523 paper-based; 69 iBT); Recommended—IELTS (minimum score 6.5). *Application deadline:* For fall admission, 8/1 for domestic students, 6/1 for international students; for spring admission, 11/15 for domestic students, 10/15 for international students; for summer admission, 5/15 for domestic students, 3/30 for international students. Applications are processed on a rolling basis. Application fee: $40. Electronic applications accepted. Tuition and fees vary according to degree level and program. *Financial support:* Fellowships, research assistantships, teaching assistantships, career-related internships or fieldwork, Federal Work-Study, institutionally sponsored loans, scholarships/grants, and unspecified assistantships available. Support available to part-time students. Financial award application deadline: 4/1; financial award applicants required to submit FAFSA. *Unit head:* Dr. Pauline D. Gagnon, Dean of Arts and Humanities, 678-839-5450, Fax: 678-839-5451, E-mail: pgagnon@westga.edu. *Application contact:* Dr. Toby Ziglar, Assistant Dean of the Graduate School, 678-839-1394, Fax: 678-839-1395, E-mail: graduate@westga.edu.
Website: http://www.westga.edu/coah

University of Wisconsin–Milwaukee, Graduate School, College of Letters and Science, Department of Anthropology, Milwaukee, WI 53201-0413. Offers anthropology (MS, PhD); museum studies (Graduate Certificate). *Students:* 62 full-time (47 women), 28 part-time (24 women); includes 9 minority (2 American Indian or Alaska Native, non-Hispanic/Latino; 1 Hispanic/Latino; 6 Two or more races, non-Hispanic/Latino). Average age 31. 29 applicants, 79% accepted, 18 enrolled. In 2017, 5 master's, 2 doctorates, 3 other advanced degrees awarded. *Degree requirements:* For master's, thesis or alternative; for doctorate, one foreign language, thesis/dissertation, departmental qualifying exam. *Entrance requirements:* For master's, GRE; for doctorate, GRE, minimum GPA of 3.0, master's degree. Additional exam requirements/recommendations for international students: Required—TOEFL (minimum score 550 paper-based; 79 iBT), IELTS (minimum score 6.5). *Application deadline:* For fall admission, 1/1 priority date for domestic students; for spring admission, 9/1 for domestic students. Application fee: $56 ($96 for international students). Electronic applications accepted. *Financial support:* Fellowships, research assistantships, teaching assistantships, career-related internships or fieldwork, unspecified assistantships, and project assistantships available. Support available to part-time students. Financial award application deadline: 4/15; financial award applicants required to submit FAFSA. *Unit head:* Thomas Malaby, Department Chair, 414-229-5247, E-mail: malaby@uwm.edu. *Application contact:* General Information Contact, 414-229-4982, Fax: 414-229-6967, E-mail: gradschool@uwm.edu.
Website: https://uwm.edu/letters-science/programs/?discipline-Anthropology

Virginia Commonwealth University, Graduate School, School of the Arts, Department of Art History, Richmond, VA 23284-9005. Offers curatorial (PhD); historical studies (MA, PhD); museum studies (MA). *Accreditation:* NASAD. *Degree requirements:* For master's, thesis; for doctorate, comprehensive exam, thesis/dissertation. *Entrance requirements:* For master's and doctorate, GRE General Test. Electronic applications accepted. *Faculty research:* Modern, nineteenth-century, Renaissance, American, and medieval art.

Wayne State University, College of Liberal Arts and Sciences, Department of History, Detroit, MI 48202. Offers history (MA, PhD); public history (MA), including African American history and culture, cultural resource management, gender, sexuality, and women's studies, labor and urban history, museum studies, public policy; world history (Graduate Certificate); JD/MA; M Ed/MA; MLIS/MA. Doctoral program admits for fall only. *Program availability:* Evening/weekend. *Faculty:* 17. *Students:* 21 full-time (7 women), 20 part-time (7 women); includes 9 minority (5 Black or African American, non-Hispanic/Latino; 1 Hispanic/Latino; 3 Two or more races, non-Hispanic/Latino). Average age 40. 50 applicants, 16% accepted, 5 enrolled. In 2017, 11 master's, 2 doctorates awarded. *Degree requirements:* For master's, comprehensive exam, thesis (for some programs), final oral exam on thesis or essay and seminar; internship and project (for public history); for doctorate, variable foreign language requirement, comprehensive exam, thesis/dissertation, qualifying exam in 4 fields of history. *Entrance requirements:* For master's, GRE General Test, minimum undergraduate GPA of 3.25 in history, 3.0 overall; at least 18 credits in history and related subjects at the advanced undergraduate level; foreign language; letter of intent; research paper; at least two letters of recommendation from former instructors; for doctorate, GRE General Test, minimum GPA of 3.0, 3.25 in minimum of 18 semester credits in history and related subjects; letter of intent; research paper; at least three letters of recommendation from former professors; for Graduate Certificate, baccalaureate degree from accredited college or university; minimum GPA of 3.0, 3.25 in a minimum of eighteen semester credits in history and related subjects at the advanced undergraduate level. Additional exam requirements/recommendations for international students: Required—TOEFL (minimum score 550 paper-based; 79 iBT), TWE (minimum score 5.5), Michigan English Language Assessment Battery (minimum score 85); Recommended—IELTS (minimum score 6.5). *Application deadline:* For fall admission, 2/1 priority date for domestic and international students; for winter admission, 11/1 for domestic students, 10/1 priority date for international students; for spring admission, 2/1 for domestic students, 1/1 priority date for international students. Application fee: $50. Electronic applications accepted. *Expenses:* Tuition, state resident: full-time $10,224; part-time $638.98 per credit hour. Tuition, nonresident: full-time $22,145; part-time $1384.04 per credit hour. Tuition and fees vary according to course load and program. *Financial support:* In 2017–18, 17 students received support, including 3 fellowships with tuition reimbursements available (averaging $17,198 per year), 1 research assistantship with tuition reimbursement available (averaging $22,241 per year), 6 teaching assistantships with tuition reimbursements available (averaging $18,534 per year); scholarships/grants, health care benefits, and unspecified assistantships also available. Financial award applicants required to submit FAFSA. *Faculty research:* Urban history, labor, political history, history of gender and women. *Unit head:* Dr. Elizabeth V. Faue, Professor/Chair, 313-577-2525, E-mail: evfaue@wayne.edu. *Application contact:* Dr. Eric Ash, Associate Professor and Director of Graduate Studies, 313-577-2525, E-mail: ericash@wayne.edu.
Website: http://clas.wayne.edu/history/

Western Illinois University, School of Graduate Studies, College of Fine Arts and Communication, Program in Museum Studies, Macomb, IL 61455-1390. Offers MA, Certificate. *Accreditation:* NASAD. *Program availability:* Part-time. *Students:* 27 full-time (21 women), 7 part-time (4 women); includes 1 minority (Two or more races, non-Hispanic/Latino), 2 international. Average age 28. 28 applicants, 93% accepted, 15 enrolled. In 2017, 13 master's awarded. *Entrance requirements:* For master's, minimum GPA of 3.0. Additional exam requirements/recommendations for international students: Required—TOEFL (minimum score 600 paper-based; 100 iBT). *Application deadline:* Applications are processed on a rolling basis. Application fee: $30. Electronic applications accepted. *Financial support:* Unspecified assistantships available. Financial award applicants required to submit FAFSA. *Unit head:* Dr. Pam White, Director, 309-762-9481, E-mail: pj-white@wiu.edu. *Application contact:* Dr. Nancy Parsons, Associate Provost and Director of Graduate Studies, 309-298-1806, Fax: 309-298-2345, E-mail: grad-office@wiu.edu.
Website: http://wiu.edu/museumstudies/

BARD GRADUATE CENTER

Bard
Graduate
Center

Decorative Arts, Design History, Material Culture

Programs of Study

Bard Graduate Center is a graduate institute of Bard College based in New York City that studies the cultural history of the material world. Founded in 1993, it offers the M.A. and Ph.D. degree in Decorative Arts, Design History, Material Culture. Its teaching, research, and exhibitions draw on methodologies and approaches from art and design history, decorative arts, economic history, history of technology, philosophy, anthropology, and archaeology. Areas of particular strength include New York and American material culture, modern design history, history and theory of museums, early modern Europe, global Middle Ages, archaeology, anthropology, and material culture, and cultures of conservation. Hands-on examination of materials and objects is a key part of the curriculum and there is an extensive connection to special programs and exhibition projects with the Metropolitan Museum of Art, the New-York Historical Society, the Brooklyn Museum, the American Museum of Natural History, the Frick Collection, and the Museum of Arts and Design, among other major cultural institutions. As part of their studies, all M.A. students undertake an internship at one of more than 250 institutions around the world and participate in an international study trip. Bard Graduate Center's programs prepare students for careers or career advancement in museums and galleries; auction houses; government agencies; art-related education, research, publishing, and communications; and landscape and historic preservation.

Research and Facilities

Bard Graduate Center occupies two six-story town houses at 18 and 38 West 86th Street in Manhattan. Its facilities include a 55,000-volume research library, a digital media research lab, exhibition galleries, classrooms, faculty offices, outdoor terraces, symposium spaces, and administrative offices.

A semiannual interdisciplinary journal, *West 86th: A Journal of Decorative Arts, Design History, and Material Culture,* which features scholarly articles that focus on the wider crossroads where the decorative arts meet design history and material culture, is published in collaboration with the University of Chicago Press, as is *Source: Notes on the History of Art.* Bard Graduate Center also publishes *Cultural Histories of the Material World,* a book series that is dedicated to showing how attention to materiality can contribute to a more precise historical understanding of specific times, places, ways, and means.

Financial Aid

Bard Graduate Center offers fellowships, scholarships, and student campus employment awards. Aid is awarded on the basis of need and merit. About 85 percent of students receive some financial aid.

Cost of Study

The average annual tuition for incoming full-time students in the 2018–19 academic year is $34,320, based on a cost of $1,430 per credit. Students may contact the Office of Admissions for more detailed and updated fee schedules.

Living and Housing Costs

Bard Hall, located at 410 West 58th Street, provides housing for students, faculty members, and visiting scholars. Nine residential floors offer a variety of furnished studios and one- and two-bedroom suites with kitchens and baths. Apartments are offered year-round. For the 2018–19 academic year, the cost of a studio unit is approximately $1,500 per month, a one-bedroom unit is $1,800 per month, and a two-bedroom unit is $1,300 per month/per student.

Student Group

Bard Graduate Center enrolls approximately 15-20 M.A. students and approximately 3-5 Ph.D. students into the program annually. Applications are received from many countries and from across the United States.

Location

Bard Graduate Center is located on the Upper West Side of Manhattan, near Central Park. It is situated in a landmark neighborhood conveniently served by public transportation, with easy access to the innumerable museums, libraries, auction houses, and galleries of metropolitan New York.

Applying

Students are admitted to the graduate programs annually for fall enrollment. The application deadline for admission is January 4, 2019. Applicants to the M.A. program must have a bachelor's degree or the equivalent; it is recommended that applicants to the Ph.D. program have a master's degree in either the decorative arts or a related field. Because of the interdisciplinary nature of the program, there are no limitations on an applicant's prior field of study. Successful applicants, however, will have had some previous study, training, or work experience in the history of art, architecture, anthropology, archeology, history, the decorative arts, cultural history, or material culture studies.

Applications should include scores on the General Test of the Graduate Record Examinations (GRE), three letters of recommendation, a short resume, a sample of scholarly writing, and a statement of intent describing academic and professional

objectives. International candidates must submit TOEFL scores and a Certification of Finances. An interview is required. The application fee for 2018–19 is $70.

Correspondence and Information

Office of Admissions
Bard Graduate Center
38 West 86th Street
New York, New York 10024
Phone: 212-501-3056
E-mail: admissions@bgc.bard.edu
Website: http://www.bgc.bard.edu/admissions

THE FACULTY AND THEIR RESEARCH

Bard Graduate Center maintains a distinguished core of full-time faculty members, supplemented by visiting faculty, research fellows, and guest lecturers from a broad range of national and international museums and institutions.

Bard Graduate Center Faculty

Susan Weber, Iris Horowitz Professor in the History of the Decorative Arts and Director; Ph.D., Royal College of Art. Eighteenth- and nineteenth-century decorative arts topics.

Peter N. Miller, Professor and Dean; Ph.D., University of Cambridge. History of historical research.

Elissa Auther, Windgate Research Curator, Museum of Arts and Design and Visiting Associate Professor; Ph.D., University of Maryland, College Park.

Jeffrey Collins, Professor; Ph.D., Yale University. Seventeenth- and eighteenth-century art and culture.

Ivan Gaskell, Professor; Ph.D., University of Cambridge. Material culture of North America and Europe, sixteenth through twentieth centuries.

Aaron Glass, Associate Professor; Ph.D., New York University. Native peoples of the Northwest Coast, museums and anthropology.

Freyja Hartzell, Assistant Professor; Ph.D., Yale University. Nineteenth- and twentieth-century European decorative arts and material culture.

Deborah L. Krohn, Associate Professor and Director of Masters Studies; Ph.D., Harvard University. Italian renaissance decorative arts and material culture.

Meredith B. Linn, Assistant Professor; Ph.D., Columbia University. Historical archeology.

François Louis, Associate Professor and Director of Doctoral Studies; Ph.D., University of Zurich. History of Chinese design and visual culture, material culture of Medieval China.

Michele Majer, Assistant Professor; M.A., New York University. European and American clothing and textiles, costume historian.

Jennifer L. Mass, Andrew W. Mellon Professor of Cultural Heritage Science; Ph.D., Cornell University.

Caspar Meyer, Professor; PhD. Oxford University. Greek art and archaeology.

Andrew Morrall, Professor and Chair of Academic Programs; Ph.D., Courtauld Institute of Art, London University. Early modern Northern European fine and applied arts.

Elizabeth Simpson, Professor; Ph.D., University of Pennsylvania. Greek, Roman, Ancient Near Eastern, and Egyptian art and archaeology.

Paul Stirton, Associate Professor; Ph.D. University of Glasgow. Nineteenth- and twentieth-century European design and architecture.

Charlotte Vignon, Curator of Decorative Arts, The Frick Collection and Visiting Assistant Professor; Ph.D., Paris-Sorbonne University.

Ittai Weinryb, Associate Professor; Ph.D., Johns Hopkins University. Medieval European artistic and material culture.

Catherine Whalen, Associate Professor; Ph.D., Yale University. American material culture studies, craft and design history.

Students entering our academic building on Manhattan's Upper West Side.

Classes at Bard Graduate Center are intimate seminars, as in this one taught by our dean Peter Miller.

COLUMBIA UNIVERSITY
School of the Arts
Programs in Film, Theatre, Visual Arts, Writing, and Sound Art

COLUMBIA UNIVERSITY SCHOOL OF THE ARTS

Programs of Study

Columbia University School of the Arts offers M.F.A. degree programs in Film (areas of study include screenwriting/directing, creative producing, and TV writing); Theatre (concentrations in acting, directing, dramaturgy, playwriting, stage management, and theatre management & producing); Visual Arts (areas of study include painting, photography, printmaking, sculpture, new genres, moving image, and a program in Sound Art in association with the Department of Music); Writing (concentrations in fiction, nonfiction, and poetry, with the option of pursuing a joint course of study in writing and literary translation); and an M.A. degree program in Film and Media Studies. In addition, a Ph.D. in Drama and Theatre is available through the Graduate School of Arts and Sciences, and a joint J.D./M.F.A. in Theatre Management & Producing is available in conjunction with Columbia Law School. The School also offers summer programs, including master classes, workshops, and credit and noncredit courses in film, theatre, visual arts, and writing, and an array of international programs in partnership with Columbia University's Global Centers.

The School of the Arts typically enrolls full-time students only, except for the M.A. in Film and Media Studies program, which students can attend part-time. The M.F.A. degree programs require 60 points of completed course work. Once the 60 points of course work are completed, each student completes a thesis and/or internships, often under "research arts" student status.

For all specific program requirements and information, prospective students should visit http://arts.columbia.edu/petersons.

Resources and Facilities

The School of the Arts is located on Columbia's Morningside Campus in the vibrant Upper West Side of Manhattan, with New York City's world-renowned museums, Broadway and Off-Broadway theaters, film centers, galleries, cultural foundations, and literary hubs all nearby. The School is also home to Miller Theatre, the LeRoy Neiman Center for Print Studies, the Columbia University Arts Initiative, and the Office of Public Programs and Engagement. In 2017, the School opened the Lenfest Center for the Arts, a multi-arts venue designed as a hub for the presentation and creation of art across disciplines on the University's new Manhattanville campus. The Lenfest hosts exhibitions, performances, screenings, symposia, readings, and lectures that present new, global voices and perspectives, as well as an exciting, publicly accessible home for Columbia's Miriam and Ira D. Wallach Art Gallery. The University's 22 libraries and countless research centers and institutes are all also available to students.

Financial Aid

The School of the Arts and Columbia University Office of Student Financial Planning work carefully with students to arrange the financing of their degrees. Scholarships, fellowships, federal work-study, on-campus employment, loan packages, and other options are available for eligible students. Students are encouraged to actively explore all options, even before acceptance into the School, to develop a plan to support the costs of graduate study. Each year, the School awards more than $10 million in student financial support.

More information is available at http://arts.columbia.edu/financing-your-degree/petersons.

Cost of Study

M.F.A. tuition and fees for 2017–18 were $58,728 for each of the first two years, based on full-time matriculation of 12 to 18 credits per semester. M.F.A. students who have completed the two-year coursework requirement paid a reduced tuition (in 2017–18) of $2,428 per semester while progressing toward completion of the required thesis. A thesis fee may also be assessed by the student's program (details available at http://arts.columbia.edu/expenses/petersons). The time to completion of the thesis requirement varies by program and by the nature and scope of the student's chosen project. M.A. students paid $54,352 in 2017–18 tuition and fees for the first year, and a reduced tuition during their third and final semester. Historically, tuition and fees have risen each year.

Living and Housing Costs

The University estimates that students need about $30,000 per year to cover living expenses and housing in New York City. Students can find housing around campus in the Morningside Heights neighborhood, in surrounding Manhattan neighborhoods and boroughs, and in the greater New York area. Columbia University apartment housing consists of a limited number of apartment shares; dormitory-style rooms; and one-bedroom, studio, and family units for which priority is given to couples and families. This housing is primarily located within walking distance of campus.

For additional details, visit http://facilities.columbia.edu/housing.

Student Group

In fall 2017, the School enrolled 878 students from 52 countries: 317 in film programs, 156 in theatre programs, 345 in writing programs, 54 in visual arts programs, and 6 in the sound art program.

Location

Columbia University (including Barnard College and Teachers College) occupies approximately 18 square blocks in the Morningside Heights area of Manhattan. The School of the Arts is on the Morningside Campus, at 116th Street and Broadway on the Upper West Side of Manhattan. The School also operates the Lenfest Center for the Arts on Columbia's new Manhattanville Campus, at 129th and Broadway.

The University and the School

Columbia, founded in 1754, is comprised of three undergraduate schools, 14 graduate and professional schools, and affiliates Barnard College and Teachers College.

Additional information is available at http://www.columbia.edu/.

The Faculty

The faculty comprises acclaimed and internationally renowned artists, film and theatre directors, playwrights, producers, poets, writers of fiction and nonfiction, critics, and scholars. Additional information about full-time and adjunct faculty members is available at http://arts.columbia.edu/faculty/petersons.

Columbia University

Applying

Applications are accepted for the fall semester only. The cost for the fall 2018 online application is $110. The GRE is not required for application. TOEFL scores for international students are good for two years from the test date. Applicants whose scores were received over two years ago must retake the test and resubmit their current scores with the admissions application. Applicants should request that TOEFL direct results to school code 2171, department code 15.

Students whose transcripts reflect advanced study at an institution where English is the primary language of instruction may request to have the TOEFL requirement waived by e-mailing admissions-arts@ columbia.edu. An original certified transcript from the institution, in English, will be required to verify the waiver request. If no transcript has been received, the offer of admission will be provisional until the School receives and approves the official transcript.

Deadlines and more information are available at http://arts.columbia. edu/apply/petersons.

Correspondence and Information

Office of Admissions
School of the Arts
Columbia University
305 Dodge Hall, MC 1808
2960 Broadway
New York, New York 10027
United States
Phone: 212-854-2134
E-mail: admissions-arts@columbia.edu
Website: http://arts.columbia.edu/petersons

NEW YORK STUDIO SCHOOL OF DRAWING, PAINTING & SCULPTURE

Master of Fine Arts Program

NEW YORK STUDIO SCHOOL
OF DRAWING, PAINTING & SCULPTURE

 http://petersons.to/nystudioschoolmfa

Programs of Study

The New York Studio School is committed to providing aspiring artists with a significant education that will last a lifetime. Students are encouraged to question rigorously and to think deeply about the practice of drawing, painting, and sculpture. Master of Fine Arts (MFA) students graduate from the program with an ambitious studio practice, a developed understanding of the language of art, and an enlarged imagination stirred by an established work ethic.

During the first year of study, students choose a core faculty member with whom they work alongside within an Atelier model. Faculty members are present in the classrooms two days each week, and students are expected to work on the objectives set by the instructors throughout the week. As students develop independence in their second year. MFA candidates work in private and semi-private studios toward the completion of their individual thesis projects.

The MFA programs are offered with concentrations in painting or in sculpture and are based on maintaining a full-time, rigorous studio practice. Students typically work a minimum of 40 hours per week for the duration of their two years at the School. Studio practice is balanced with Critical Studies courses and instructed critiques. Lectures and seminars are held throughout the semester, as well as small group discussion with current and visiting faculty. Students must complete 60 credits to successfully achieve the Master of Fine Arts degree and credits must include all required courses. A residency of at least two academic years is necessary to complete the degree. Students have access to their studios on a full-time basis. New York City's museums, arts organizations, and culture serve as a profound additional resource to all students.

The School's internationally recognized Marathon Programs were developed in 1988 by Dean Graham Nickson as a way of generating momentum, subject matter, and drawing strategies for the semester to follow. The program has since expanded to become a core component of the School's curriculum. The interest in the Marathon Programs has led to a wider audience of participants outside the full-time student body. Renowned artists, art historians, dealers, collectors, art educators, writers, journalists, and students of all levels and affiliations have since experienced the intensity of the program. The Marathon Sessions are offered three times during the academic year: fall, spring, and summer.

Research Facilities

The John McEnroe Library's mission is to support the New York Studio School's programs and courses by providing materials and information for students, faculty, staff, and visiting lecturers. Holdings include monographs on artists, art historical texts, art periodicals, and exhibition catalogs, as well as an extensive lecture archive, comprising audio and video recordings of lectures from the past thirty years, featuring artists, historians, critics, and philosophers.

The library provides an online catalog to check the holdings of the collection, as well as access to research databases and indexes that aid in scholarly research.

Financial Aid

The financial aid programs are part of the School's desire to attract qualified students from diverse backgrounds. Any student who would like to be considered for financial assistance from the School must complete a financial aid application and submit it to Student Services by the deadline date each year. Financial aid scholarships are contingent on the continuation of satisfactory progress in all enrolled courses and are available to all full-time enrolled students. Scholarships are available for part-time students during the summer session.

Cost of Study

For the 2018–19 academic year, the cost for the MFA program is $12,437.50 per semester. The cost for the Certificate program is $8,425 per semester. For additional, up-to-date cost information, prospective students should visit www.nyss.org/admissions-services/tuition-fees-financial-aid/.

Living and Housing Costs

The School does not have housing facilities. Upon acceptance, students receive information on housing opportunities in New York, including listings of temporary accommodations and help on searching for suitable living situations. The School is easily accessible by public transport from the outer boroughs and New Jersey. Rents in the outer boroughs tend to be lower than in Manhattan. Less expensive situations can be found through sublets or by living with roommates. Students should plan to find proper accommodations prior to enrolling.

Student Group

The Studio School welcomes a diverse demographic of students of varying ages and geographical origins; one third of the full-time student body is composed of international students. All students are encouraged to develop work and cultivate studio skills which will support them and allow them to continue an independent studio practice long after they have graduated from the School. At the School, the pursuit of authenticity tends to subdue the distractions of style or the rush for novelty. Response to the contemporary does not lessen the excitement of discovery within the art of the past. No dichotomy between realism and abstraction is assumed at the School. On the contrary, perceptual experience is encouraged to lead the student to the discovery of abstract equivalents, to a deepening grasp of the plastic means.

Location

The School is located on West 8th Street, between Sixth Avenue/Avenue of the Americas and Fifth Avenue. It is accessible by subway or the PATH train. The School occupies eight historic buildings with an extraordinary cultural and artistic history. Occupied by various artists, and the original site of the Whitney Museum of American Art from 1931 to 1954, the School's physical home has been a place where art has been created, discussed, and displayed for over a century. In the 45 years that the School has been on West 8th Street, artists and students alike have found both inspiration and comfort in continuing the tradition of drawing, painting, and sculpting in the historic spaces that have played such an important role in the history of art in America.

Applying

The application deadline for MFA applicants is February 15. Late applications are reviewed on a case-by-case basis; however late applicants may not be eligible for financial aid. MFA candidates are

New York Studio School of Drawing, Painting & Sculpture

accepted exclusively for enrollment in the fall semester. Applicants must have a bachelor's degree or equivalent to be considered for admission. Forms must be completed online at https://nyss.slideroom.com/#/Login.

Completed applications include the application form, two required essays, a $70 nonrefundable application fee, two letters of recommendation, 20 jpeg images of student work with an image list accompanying the images, and official transcripts from all previous institutions that resulted in the applicant's undergraduate degree. Detailed instructions are available as part of the application form. Partial applications will not be considered. Prospective candidates will be invited for an interview with the Admissions Committee.

For additional information, prospective students should visit http://www.nyss.org/admissions-services/application-requirements/.

Correspondence and Information

New York Studio School
8 West 8th Street
New York, New York 10011
United States
Phone: 212-673-6466
Fax: 212-777-0996
E-mail: info@nyss.org
Website: http://www.nyss.org/programs-courses/mfa-painting-sculpture/

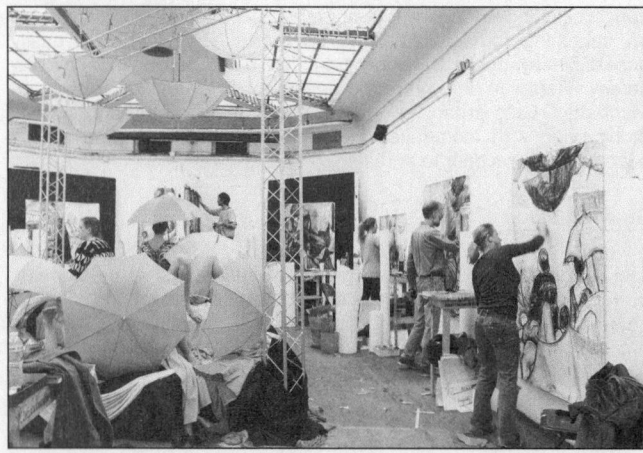

The School's internationally recognized Marathon programs were developed by Dean Graham Nickson, initially as a measure for the rest of the semester at the start of the program year. All MFA and Certificate candidates begin in the fall and spring semesters with either a Drawing or Sculpture Marathon.

THE FACULTY

David Cohen, art critic; publisher of *artcritical.com.*
Garth Evans, sculptor; studied at Manchester Junior and Regional Colleges of Art and the Slade School of Fine Art (London).

Bruce Gagnier, sculptor; M.F.A., Columbia. National Academician represented by Lori Bookstein Fine Art.
Bill Jensen, painter; B.F.A. and M.F.A., University of Minnesota. Represented by Cheim & Read Gallery, New York.
Elisa Jensen, painter; M.A., Smith College and the New York Studio School.
John Lees, painter; B.F.A. and M.F.A., Otis Art Institute. Represented by Betty Cuningham Gallery.
Margrit Lewczuk, painter; studied at Queens College and the Brooklyn Museum Art School.
John Newman, sculptor; B.A., Oberlin College; M.F.A., Yale School of Art.
Graham Nickson, painting and drawing; B.A., Camberwell School of Arts & Crafts; M.A., Royal College of Art (London).
Lee Tribe, sculptor; educated at Saint Martin's School of Art and Birmingham School of Art (England) and the New York Studio School.
Karen Wilkin, art historian and critic; educated at Barnard College and Columbia University. Fulbright and Woodrow Wilson Fellow.

Second-year MFA candidates are provided with semi-private to private studios, allowing for growth and development of their creative practice.

PRATT INSTITUTE
School of Art

Programs of Study

Pratt has been educating professionals for productive careers in the fields of art and design since its founding in 1887. Pratt's School of Art offers an outstanding professional art education taught by a faculty of working professionals that brings high standards and current practices to the classroom. Faculty members have received more than eighteen Tiffany, Fulbright, and Guggenheim awards as well as other prestigious professional awards.

Pratt offers master's degrees in a variety of programs, including Master of Fine Arts in Digital Arts (including animation) or Fine Art (painting and drawing, photography, printmaking, sculpture, and integrated practices); Master of Art in Art and Design Education (teacher certification) and Master of Science in Dance/Movement Therapy; and Master of Professional Studies in Art Therapy and Creativity Development, Arts and Cultural Management, or Design Management. A post-baccalaureate New York State certification program for the teaching of art in grades pre-K–12 is available for fine arts graduate students. Pratt also offers a dual degree in Fine Arts and History of Art and Design, Fine Arts and Library and Information Science and a dual degree in Digital Arts and Library Science.

Art and Design Education graduates are prepared to pursue teaching careers in pre-K–12 schools, museums and cultural institutions, or colleges. Graduates of the Creative Arts Therapy program work in psychiatric, medical rehabilitation, geriatric and family therapy, school, substance abuse, and child-life settings. They also learn to work with a variety of patient populations, including patients with eating disorders and the homeless.

All graduate art curricula include supportive course work in the humanities. Students can choose from a wide array of course offerings, including art and design history, comparative literature, philosophy, foreign languages, and social sciences. The graduate programs require the completion of 30 to 68 credits (75 credits for the M.S./M.F.A. dual-degree program) and last from 1½ to 3 years, depending on the curriculum and the number of prerequisites that have not been met at the time of admission. For the granting of degrees, all of the graduate programs require the submission of a thesis or a comparable effort. For the M.F.A., an exhibition and supporting corollary statement are required. For the M.P.S. in Art Therapy and the M.S. in Dance/Movement Therapy, the thesis project may involve research, an extended case study, the development of a project implementing innovative techniques in therapy, or the opportunity to publish an article. For the M.P.S. in Design Management, the thesis project is the preparation of a business case study.

Research Facilities

The Pratt Library contains 186,589 bound volumes, serial backfiles, and other material (including government documents); 251,603 audiovisual materials; and 3,996 microforms and subscribes to 925 periodicals.

Pratt maintains numerous studios, shops, and technical facilities for work in all media as well as state-of-the-art computer facilities. Digital arts labs include state-of-the-art Macintosh, PC/NT, and UNIX operating systems as well as digital video and audio systems. Pratt also has extensive gallery space for exhibitions.

Financial Aid

Financial aid awards are offered through a variety of institutional, state, and federally funded programs. These include Graduate Scholarships awarded by departments to incoming students on the basis of merit, endowed and restricted scholarships for continuing students, and student employment. Assistantships are awarded on a competitive basis to continuing students in all departments. Special alumni-sponsored fellowships are also available.

Cost of Study

Graduate tuition for 2018–19 is $32,004 per year (full-time 18 credits, $1,778 per credit) and student fees are $1,980 per year. The cost of books and supplies varies widely, depending on the program in which the student is enrolled.

Living and Housing Costs

Campus housing continues to be expanded to meet students' needs and is available for single students on a first-come, first-served basis. Housing costs average $19,550 per academic year. Pratt offers limited graduate student housing two blocks away from the campus. There is a plentiful supply of moderately priced rentals in the immediate area and in adjacent neighborhoods for married students seeking housing and for those students choosing to reside off campus.

Student Group

In educating more than five generations of students to be creative, technically skilled, and adaptable professionals, Pratt has gained an international reputation that attracts over 4,800 undergraduate and graduate students annually from 48 states and 84 countries.

Location

Pratt Institute's 25-acre, parklike main campus is situated among the turn-of-the-century mansions, Victorian brownstones, and wide, tree-lined boulevards of Clinton Hill, one of Brooklyn's historic neighborhoods. Midtown Manhattan, the heart of New York City, is only 25 minutes away by subway and offers students a vast array of professional, cultural, and recreational opportunities. Pratt also maintains a campus in Manhattan's Chelsea district. Pratt Manhattan houses the Institute's graduate arts and cultural management and design management programs.

The Institute

A private, nonsectarian institute of higher education, Pratt Institute was founded by the industrialist and philanthropist Charles Pratt. Changing with the needs and requirements of the professional world for which it prepares its graduates, Pratt today educates 3,439 undergraduate and 1,390 graduate students for careers in art and design, architecture, and library and information science.

Applying

The deadline for applications and all supporting materials, including portfolio, is January 5. Applicants should complete the application process online. Early submission of applications with all necessary credentials is highly desirable. Applications received after these dates are considered if openings exist in a particular program. For applicants who intend to file for financial aid, the FAFSA should be filed by March 1 for fall entrance and by October 1 for spring entrance.

Correspondence and Information

Graduate Admissions Office
Pratt Institute
200 Willoughby Avenue
Brooklyn, New York 11205
United States
Phone: 718-636-3514
      800-331-0834 (toll-free)
Fax: 718-399-4242
E-mail: admissions@pratt.edu
Website: http://www.pratt.edu
      http://www.pratt.edu/admissions/request-information (to request information)

THE FACULTY

Gerry Snyder, Dean
Dianne Bellino, Assistant Dean

Art and Design Education
Heather Lewis, Chair, Professor; Ph.D., NYU.
Caitlin Cahill, Visiting Instructor; M.A., TESOL, City College.
Phillip DeSantis, Visiting Instructor; M.A., Brooklyn College.
Mary Elmer-Dewitt, Adjunct Assistant Professor; M.S., Pratt.
Max Freedman, Visiting Instructor; M.S., The New School.
Borinquen Gallo, Visiting Assistant Professor; M.F.A., CUNY, Hunter.
Sarah Holcomb, Visiting Instructor; M.S., Pratt.
Ann Holt, Visiting Instructor; Ph.D., Penn State.
Sohee Koo, Professor.
Tara Kopp, Visiting Assistant Professor; M.F.A., Pratt.
Rebecca Krucoff, Visiting Assistant Professor; M.S.Ed., Bank Street College.
Monica Marino, Visiting Instructor; M.S., Hunter.
Camille Martin; M. Arch, Washington University–St. Louis.
Phaedra Mastrocola; M.S., Pratt.
Joshua Millis, Visiting Instructor; M.F.A., Art Institute of Chicago.
Ryan Minezzi, Visiting Instructor; M.S., Pratt.
Kelly Normand, Visiting Instructor; M.S., Pratt.
Patrick Rowe, Visiting Instructor; M.F.A., M.S. Pratt.
Theodora Skipitares, Associate Professor; M.F.A., NYU.
Aileen Wilson, Professor, Ed.D., Columbia.

Arts and Cultural Management
Mary McBride, Chair; Professor, Ph.D., NYU.
Christopher Shrum, Associate Professor; Ph.D., Fielding Graduate University.
Catherine Ashcraft, Visiting Assistant Professor; Ph.D., MIT.
Catherine Cacho-Leary, Visiting Assistant Professor; M.B.A., Keller Graduate School of Management.
Laurence DeGaetano, Adjunct Assistant Professor; M.B.A., NYU.
Dyanis De Jesus, Visiting Assistant Professor; M.P.S., Pratt.
Kristen Earls, Visiting Assistant Professor; M.A., NYU.
Scott Fiaschetti, Visiting Associate Professor; M.B.A., Syracuse University.
Monte Gibbs, Visiting Assistant Professor; Appalachian State University.
Richard Green, Professor; B.S., Temple University.
Jeffrey Klein, Visiting Assistant Professor; J.D., Fordham.
Antonio Ponton-Nunez, Visiting Assistant Professor; M.P.S., Pratt.
Christina Rosan, Visiting Assistant Professor; Ph.D., MIT.
Denise Tahara, Visiting Associate Professor; Ph.D., NYU.
Tiffany Townsend, Visiting Assistant Professor; M.S., Columbia.
Kelly Kocinski Trager, Visiting Associate Professor; J.D., Brooklyn Law.
Alicia Whiteman, Visiting Assistant Professor; M.P.S., Pratt.

Creative Arts Therapy
Julie Miller, Chair; M.A./M.S., Hunter.
Dina Schapiro, Assistant Chair, Director Graduate Art Therapy Program; M.P.S., Pratt.
Linda Siegel, Director of Graduate Art Therapy Program, Assistant Professor; M.P.S., Pratt.
Joan Wittig, Director of Graduate Dance/Movement Therapy Program, Associate Professor; M.S., CUNY, Hunter.
Claudia Bader, Visiting Instructor; M.P.S., Pratt.
Shannon Bradley, Visiting Instructor; M.S., Pratt.
Corinna Brown, Visiting Instructor; M.S., CUNY, Hunter.
Kimberly Bush, Adjunct Assistant Professor; M.F.A., Parsons.
Jean Davis, Adjunct Associate Professor; M.P.S., Pratt.
Christina Devereaux, Visiting Assistant Professor; Ph.D., Santa Barbara Graduate Institute.
Ted Ehrhardt, Adjunct Assistant Professor; M.S., CUNY, Hunter.
Cara Gallo, Visiting Instructor; M.S., CUNY, Hunter.
Alison Gigl-George, Adjunct Assistant Professor.
Nancy Herard-Marshall, Visiting Instructor; M.S., Pratt; LCAT, R-DMT.
Valerie Hubbs, Visiting Instructor; M.S., CUNY, Hunter.
Melissa Klay, Adjunct Instructor; Ph.D., Pacifica Graduate.
Judith Luongo, Adjunct Associate Professor; M.P.S., Pratt.
Briana MacWilliam, Visiting Instructor; M.S., Pratt.
Deniz Oktay, Visiting Instructor; M.S., Pratt.
Sean Plunkett, Visiting Instructor; M.P.S., Pratt.
Deborah Rice, Visiting Professor; M.P.S., Pratt.
Sara Rothstein, Visiting Instructor; M.P.S., Pratt.
Jean Seibel, Visiting Instructor; M.S., Hunter College.
Lauren Smith, Visiting Instructor; M.P.S., Pratt.
Elissa White, Visiting Assistant Professor.
Eva Teirstein Young, Visiting Instructor; M.P.S., Pratt.

Pratt Institute

Design Management

Mary McBride, Chair, Professor; Ph.D., NYU.
Catherine Ashcraft, Visiting Assistant Professor; Ph.D., MIT.
Laurence DeGaetano, Adjunct Assistant Professor; M.B.A., NYU.
Dyanis DeJesus, Visiting Assistant Professor; M.P.S., Pratt.
Tyra Nicole Dumars, Visiting Assistant Professor, M.P.S., Pratt.
Scott Fiaschetti, Visiting Associate Professor; M.B.A., Syracuse University.
Monte Gibbs, Visiting Assistant Professor; Appalachian State University.
Richard Green, Professor; B.S., Temple University.
Mung Ki Woo, Visiting Assistant Professor; Ecole Polytechnique and Telecom Paris Tech.
Chinaedu Maduuagwu, Visiting Assistant Professor; M.P.S. Pratt
Jacqueline McCormack, Adjunct Associate Professor; M.P.S., Pratt.
James Murray, Visiting Assistant Professor; M.P.S., Pratt.
Christina Rosan, Visiting Assistant Professor; Ph.D., MIT.
Rachel Starobinsky, Visiting Assistant Professor; M.P.S., Pratt.
Jo Ann Stonier, Visiting Assistant Professor; J.D., St. John's (New York).
Denise Tahara, Visiting Associate Professor; Ph.D., NYU.
Yutaka Takiura, Visiting Assistant Professor; M.Arch., IIT.
Kelly Kocinski Trager, Visiting Associate Professor; J.D., Brooklyn Law.
Marvin Waldman, Visiting Assistant Professor; M.B.A., CUNY, Baruch.

Digital Arts

Peter Patchen, Chair; M.F.A., Oregon.
Carla Gannis, Assistant Chair; M.F.A., Boston University.
Liubomir Borissov, Associate Professor; Ph.D., Columbia.
Michael Bourbeau, Visiting Instructor; M.F.A., School of Visual Arts.
Svjetlana Bukvich-Nichols, Visiting Associate Professor; M.F.A., Rensselaer.
Blake Carrington, Assistant Professor; M.F.A., Syracuse.
Elliot Cowan, Visiting Instructor.
Edward Darino, Adjunct Assistant Professor; Ph.D., UEU on New Technologies.
Marianna Ellenberg, Visiting Instructor; M.A., Slade School of Art.
Mike Enright, Adjunct Assistant Professor; M.F.A., California Institute of the Arts.
Kay Hines, Adjunct Assistant Professor; B.A., Barnard.
Faith Holland, Visiting Instructor; M.F.A., School of Visual Arts.
Kenneth Hughes, Visiting Instructor.
Everett Kane, Assistant Professor; M.F.A., Art Center College of Design.
Jacques Khouri, Visiting Instructor; M.F.A., Savannah College of Art and Design.
Linda Lauro-Lazin, Adjunct Associate Professor, M.A., NYIT.
David Mattingly, Visiting Instructor; M.F.A., Art Center.
Genevieve Okupniak, Visiting Instructor, M.F.A., California Institute of the Arts.
Michael J. O'Rourke, Professor; Ed.M., Harvard.
Mira Scharf, Visiting Instructor; M.F.A., UCLA.
Claudia Tait, Associate Professor; M.F.A., Maryland.
Michael Tanzillo, Visiting Instructor; M.F.A., Savannah College of Art and Design.
Katherine Torn, Visiting Instructor; M.F.A., Art Institute of Chicago.
Lukas Wadya, Visiting Instructor; M.F.A., School of Visual Arts.
Gregory Webb, Adjunct Instructor.
Daniel Weisbard, Visiting Instructor; M.F.A., RIT.
Elizabeth White, Visiting Instructor; M.F.A., School of Visual Arts.

Fine Arts

Jane South, Chair of Fine Arts; M.F.A., UNC Greensboro.
Nat Meade, Assistant Chair of Fine Arts, Visiting Instructor; M.F.A., Pratt.
Dina Weiss, Assistant Chairperson, Visiting Associate Instructor; M.F.A., Parsons.
Ann Agee, Visiting Associate Professor; M.F.A.,Yale.
David Alban, Visiting Assistant Professor; M.F.A., Cranbrook Academy of Art.
Ruby Omyinyechi Amanze, Visiting Assistant Professor; M.F.A., Cranbrook.
Adam Apostolos, Visiting Instructor; Sculpture technician; A.O.S., Pratt.
Karen Bachmann, Visiting Assistant Professor; B.F.A., Pratt.
Lisa Bateman, Adjunct Associate Professor; M.F.A., Virginia Commonwealth.
Michael Brennan, Adjunct Associate Professor; M.F.A., Pratt.
Deborah Bright; M.F.A., University of Chicago.
Mona Brody, Adjunct Associate Professor; M.F.A., Vermont College.
Howard Buchwald, Professor; M.A., CUNY, Hunter.
David Butler, Adjunct Associate Professor; M.F.A., Washington (Seattle).
Kathy Butterly, Visiting Associate Professor; M.F.A., UC Davis.
William Carroll, Visiting Associate Professor; M.F.A., CUNY, Queens.
Nanette Carter, Adjunct Associate Professor, Coordinator for Drawing; M.F.A., Pratt.
Deborah Chaney, Visiting Associate Professor; B.F.A., Tamarind Master Printer.
David Cohen, Visiting Associate Professor; M.A., Courtauld Institute of Art (London).
Angela Conant, Visiting Assistant Professor; M.F.A., SVA.
James Costanzo, Adjunct Associate Professor; M.F.A., Iowa.
Grayson Cox, Visiting Associate Professor; M.F.A., Columbia.
Peggy Cyphers, Adjunct Professor; M.F.A., Pratt.
Pradeep Dalal, Visiting Assistant Director; M.F.A., Bard.
Gregory Drasler, Adjunct Professor; M.F.A., University of Illinois.
Kelly Driscoll, Associate Professor; M.F.A., CUNY, City College.
Samuel Evensen, Visiting Assistant Professor; M.F.A., New York Academy of Art.
Brad Ewing, Visiting Instructor; M.F.A., Rhode Island School of Design.
Patrick Fenton, Visiting Assistant Professor; M.F.A., Stanford.
Allen Frame, Adjunct Associate Professor; B.A., Harvard.
Linda Francis, Adjunct Professor; M.A., CUNY, Hunter.
Michael Fujita, Visiting Assistant Professor; M.F.A., Alfred.
Joseph Fyfe, Adjunct Associate Professor; B.F.A., University of the Arts.
Brice Garrett, Visiting Assistant Professor; M.F.A., Konstfack University, Stockholm, Sweden.
Anne Gilman, Adjunct Professor; M.F.A., CUNY, Brooklyn.
Jonathan Goodman, Visiting Assistant Professor; M.A., Pennsylvania.
David Gothard, Visiting Assistant Professor; B.F.A., Pratt.
Toni Greenbaum, Visiting Associate Professor; M.A., Hunter.
Nancy Grimes, Adjunct Associate Professor; M.F.A., Art Institute of Chicago.
Raphael Griswold, Visiting Assistant Professor; M.F.A., Brooklyn College.

Aubrey Hillman, Visiting Instructor; M.F.A., University of Oregon.
Vera Iliatova, Visiting Assistant Professor; M.F.A., Yale.
Yasu Izaki, Visiting Instructor; M.F.A., Pratt.
Russell Jones, Visiting Assistant Professor; M.A., Metropolitan University of Manchester.
Shirley Kaneda, Professor; B.F.A., Parsons.
Michael Kirk, Adjunct Professor; M.F.A., Pratt.
Ross Knight, Visiting Assistant Professor; B.F.A., Minnesota, Twin Cities.
Vivien Knussi, Adjunct Assistant Professor; Ph.D., Columbia.
Peter Kruty, Visiting Assistant Professor; M.A., Alabama.
Julia Kunin, Visiting Associate Professor; M.F.A., Rutgers.
Alexander Kvares, Visiting Assistant Professor, M.F.A., University of Texas.
Benjamin LaRocco, Visiting Assistant Professor; M.F.A., Pratt.
David Lantow, Visiting Associate Professor; M.F.A., CUNY, Brooklyn.
Catherine Lecleire, Adjunct Associate Professor; M.F.A., USC.
Jenny Lee, Adjunct Professor, B.F.A., Cooper Union.
Frank Lind, Professor; M.F.A., Pratt.
Patricia Madeja, Professor; B.F.A., Pratt, CCE.
Ann Mandelbaum, Adjunct Professor; M.F.A., Pratt.
Mary Mattingly, Visiting Assistant Professor; B.F.A., Pacific Northwest College of Art.
Jen Mazza, Visiting Assistant Professor; M.F.A., Rutgers.
J. Martin Mazzora, Visiting Assistant Professor; M.F.A., American.
Jennifer Melby, Adjunct Associate Professor; M.F.A., Pratt.
Anne Messner, Professor; B.F.A., Pratt.
Curtis Mitchell, Adjunct Professor; M.F.A., Yale.
John Monti, Professor; M.F.A., Pratt.
Donna Moran, Professor; M.F.A., Pratt.
Robert Morgan, Adjunct Professor; Ph.D., NYU.
Dominique Nahas, Adjunct Associate Professor; M.A., NYU.
Mario Naves, Adjunct Assistant Professor; M.F.A., Pratt.
Sarah Nicholls, Visiting Assistant Professor; B.F.A., Sarah Lawrence.
Thirwell Nolen, Adjunct Associate Professor; M.Arch., Georgia Tech.
John O'Connor, Visiting Assistant Professor; M.F.A., Pratt.
Catherine Redmond, Adjunct Associate Professor; B.A., SUNY at Binghamton.
William Richards, Adjunct Associate Professor; M.F.A., New Mexico.
Caitlin Riordan, Visiting Instructor; B.F.A., Maine College of Art.
Mary Beth Rozkewicz, Adjunct Associate Professor; B.F.A., SUNY.
Alan Ruiz, Visiting Assistant Professor; M.F.A., Yale.
Stuart Sachs, Visiting Assistant Professor, Sculptor.
Analia Segal, Adjunct Associate Professor; M.A., NYU.
Jason Segall, Visiting Instructor; M.F.A., Alfred University.
Beverly Semmes, Visiting Professor; M.F.A., Yale.
Steven Sergiovanni, Visiting Assistant Professor; M.A., NYU.
Carla Shapiro, Adjunct Assistant Professor; B.F.A., Syracuse.
Jean Shin, Adjunct Professor; M.S., Pratt.
Robbin Silverberg, Adjunct Associate Professor; B.A., Princeton.
Judith Solodkin, Visiting Associate Professor; M.F.A., Columbia.
Laurel Sparks, Visiting Associate Professor; M.F.A., Bard.
Joseph Stauber, Adjunct Assistant Professor; M.F.A., SUNY Purchase.
Jason Stopa, Visiting Assistant Professor; M.F.A., Pratt.
Irvin Tepper, Adjunct Professor; M.F.A., Washington (Seattle).
Christopher Verstegen, Visiting Instructor, Studio and Gallery Supervisor; M.F.A., Pratt.
Timothy Veske-McMahon, Visiting Assistant Professor; M.F.A., Cranbrook.
Emily Weiner, Visiting Assistant Professor; M.F.A., School of Visual Arts.
Christopher White, Adjunct Associate Professor; B.A., Harvard.
Rachel Wiecking, Visiting Assistant Professor; M.F.A., Purchase, SUNY.
SeoKyeong Yoon, Studio and Gallery Manager; M.F.A., Pratt.
Robert Zakarian, Professor; M.F.A., Pratt.
Katrin Zimmerman, Visiting Assistant Professor; M.A., School of Oriental and African Studies (London).

©2017 Bob Handelman

Section 4
Comparative and Interdisciplinary Arts

This section contains a directory of institutions offering graduate work in comparative and interdisciplinary arts. Additional information about programs listed in the directory may be obtained by writing directly to the dean of a graduate school or chair of a department at the address given in the directory.

For programs offering related work, see also in this book *Applied Arts and Design, Architecture, Art and Art History,* and *Performing Arts.* In another guide in this series:

Graduate Programs in Business, Education, Information Studies, Law & Social Work

See *Subject Areas (Art Education)*

CONTENTS

Program Directory

Comparative and Interdisciplinary Arts

Comparative and Interdisciplinary Arts

Brigham Young University, Graduate Studies, College of Humanities, Department of Comparative Arts and Letters, Provo, UT 84602. Offers comparative studies (MA). *Faculty:* 30 full-time (8 women), 3 part-time/adjunct (1 woman). *Students:* 15 full-time (6 women), 1 part-time (0 women); includes 1 minority (Asian, non-Hispanic/Latino). Average age 29. 12 applicants, 75% accepted, 7 enrolled. In 2017, 10 master's awarded. *Degree requirements:* For master's, 2 foreign languages, comprehensive exam, thesis. *Entrance requirements:* For master's, GRE, minimum GPA of 3.0 in last 60 hours, writing sample, foreign language experience, undergraduate degree or experience in a humanities discipline. Additional exam requirements/recommendations for international students: Required—TOEFL (minimum score 580 paper-based; 85 iBT), IELTS (minimum score 7). *Application deadline:* For fall admission, 3/1 for domestic and international students. Application fee: $50. Electronic applications accepted. *Expenses:* $8,850. *Financial support:* In 2017–18, 15 students received support, including 3 research assistantships (averaging $2,500 per year), 21 teaching assistantships (averaging $5,000 per year); scholarships/grants, tuition waivers, unspecified assistantships, and student instructorships also available. Support available to part-time students. *Faculty research:* Renaissance skepticism, ancient novels, papyrology, Mediterranean piracy, Renaissance devotional art, Seventeenth Century French comedy, representations of chance and probability, Dutch baroque art empowering women, Nineteenth Century Denmark and memory studies. *Unit head:* Dr. Roger Macfarlane, Graduate Coordinator/Professor of Classical Studies, 801-422-9078, Fax: 801-422-0305, E-mail: macfarlane@byu.edu. *Application contact:* Andrea Kristensen, Graduate Program Manager, 801-422-2996, Fax: 801-422-0305, E-mail: andrea_kristensen@byu.edu.
Website: http://cal.byu.edu/

Florida Atlantic University, Dorothy F. Schmidt College of Arts and Letters, Program in Comparative Studies, Boca Raton, FL 33431-0991. Offers PhD. *Program availability:* Part-time. *Students:* 24 full-time (16 women), 20 part-time (16 women); includes 16 minority (4 Black or African American, non-Hispanic/Latino; 11 Hispanic/Latino; 1 Two or more races, non-Hispanic/Latino), 5 international. Average age 41. 16 applicants, 63% accepted, 8 enrolled. In 2017, 4 doctorates awarded. *Degree requirements:* For doctorate, one foreign language, comprehensive exam, thesis/dissertation. *Entrance requirements:* For doctorate, GRE, minimum GPA of 3.5, 3 references. Additional exam requirements/recommendations for international students: Required—TOEFL (minimum score 500 paper-based; 61 iBT), IELTS (minimum score 6). *Application deadline:* For fall admission, 2/1 priority date for domestic and international students. Applications are processed on a rolling basis. Application fee: $30. *Expenses:* Tuition, state resident: full-time $7400; part-time $369.82 per credit. Tuition, nonresident: full-time $20,496; part-time $1042.81 per credit. *Financial support:* Teaching assistantships with tuition reimbursements available. *Faculty research:* Arts, humanities, social sciences. *Unit head:* Dr. Adam Bradford, Director, 561-297-3863, E-mail: letters@fau.edu.
Website: http://www.fau.edu/comparativestudies/

Goddard College, Graduate Division, Master of Fine Arts in Interdisciplinary Arts Program, Plainfield, VT 05667-9432. Offers MFA. *Program availability:* Online learning. *Degree requirements:* For master's, thesis. *Entrance requirements:* For master's, relevant undergraduate degree, 3 letters of recommendation, interview, portfolio, artistic resume. Electronic applications accepted.

John F. Kennedy University, Graduate School of Holistic Studies, Department of Arts and Consciousness, Program in Transformative Arts, Pleasant Hill, CA 94523-4817. Offers MA. *Program availability:* Part-time, evening/weekend. *Degree requirements:* For master's, thesis or alternative. *Entrance requirements:* For master's, interview. Additional exam requirements/recommendations for international students: Required—TOEFL. *Expenses:* Contact institution.

Ohio University, Graduate College, College of Fine Arts, School of Interdisciplinary Arts, Athens, OH 45701-2979. Offers PhD. *Degree requirements:* For doctorate, 2 foreign languages, comprehensive exam, thesis/dissertation. *Entrance requirements:* For doctorate, GRE or MAT, master's degree. Additional exam requirements/recommendations for international students: Required—TOEFL (minimum score 575 paper-based; 91 iBT) or IELTS (minimum score 7). Electronic applications accepted. *Faculty research:* Comparative studies of theater, music, and the visual arts.

Simon Fraser University, Office of Graduate Studies and Postdoctoral Fellows, Faculty of Communication, Art and Technology, School for the Contemporary Arts, Vancouver, BC V6B 5K3, Canada. Offers MA, MFA. *Degree requirements:* For master's, thesis or alternative. *Entrance requirements:* For master's, portfolio; minimum GPA of 3.0 (on scale of 4.33) or 3.33 based on last 60 credits of undergraduate courses. Additional exam requirements/recommendations for international students: Recommended—TOEFL (minimum score 580 paper-based; 93 iBT), IELTS (minimum score 7), TWE (minimum score 5). Electronic applications accepted. *Faculty research:* Dance theory, screenplays, drawing and painting, acting, electroacoustic music.

Section 5
Film, Television, and Video

This section contains a directory of institutions offering graduate work in film, television, and video. Additional information about programs listed in the directory but not augmented by an in-depth entry may be obtained by writing directly to the dean of a graduate school or chair of a department at the address given in the directory.

For programs offering related work, see also in this book *Art and Art History* and *Communication and Media*. In the other guides in this series:

Graduate Programs in Engineering & Applied Sciences
See *Telecommunications*
Graduate Programs in Business, Education, Information Studies, Law & Social Work
See *Advertising and Public Relations*

CONTENTS

Program Directories

Featured School: Display and Close-Up

See:

Film, Television, and Video Production

Academy of Art University, Graduate Programs, School of Animation and Visual Effects, San Francisco, CA 94105-3410. Offers 3D animation (MFA). *Program availability:* Part-time, 100% online. *Faculty:* 18 full-time (5 women), 54 part-time/adjunct (12 women). *Students:* 273 full-time (130 women), 141 part-time (68 women); includes 72 minority (22 Black or African American, non-Hispanic/Latino; 1 American Indian or Alaska Native, non-Hispanic/Latino; 19 Asian, non-Hispanic/Latino; 23 Hispanic/Latino; 1 Native Hawaiian or other Pacific Islander, non-Hispanic/Latino; 6 Two or more races, non-Hispanic/Latino), 254 international. Average age 29. 131 applicants, 100% accepted, 99 enrolled. In 2017, 125 master's awarded. *Degree requirements:* For master's, final review. *Entrance requirements:* For master's, statement of intent; resume; portfolio/reel; official college transcripts. *Application deadline:* Applications are processed on a rolling basis. Application fee: $50. Electronic applications accepted. *Expenses: Tuition:* Part-time $982 per unit. *Financial support:* Career-related internships or fieldwork, Federal Work-Study, and scholarships/grants available. Financial award application deadline: 8/10; financial award applicants required to submit FAFSA. *Unit head:* 800-544-ARTS, E-mail: info@academyart.edu. *Application contact:* 800-544-ARTS, E-mail: info@academyart.edu.
Website: http://www.academyart.edu/animation-school/index.html

Academy of Art University, Graduate Programs, School of Motion Pictures and Television, San Francisco, CA 94105-3410. Offers motion pictures and television (MFA); writing and directing for film (MA). *Program availability:* Part-time, 100% online. *Faculty:* 8 full-time (2 women), 37 part-time/adjunct (10 women). *Students:* 147 full-time (73 women), 69 part-time (27 women); includes 24 minority (10 Black or African American, non-Hispanic/Latino; 1 American Indian or Alaska Native, non-Hispanic/Latino; 4 Asian, non-Hispanic/Latino; 5 Hispanic/Latino; 4 Two or more races, non-Hispanic/Latino), 148 international. Average age 29. 69 applicants, 100% accepted, 44 enrolled. In 2017, 75 master's awarded. *Degree requirements:* For master's, final review. *Entrance requirements:* For master's, statement of intent; resume; portfolio/reel; official college transcripts. *Application deadline:* Applications are processed on a rolling basis. Application fee: $50. Electronic applications accepted. *Expenses: Tuition:* Part-time $982 per unit. *Financial support:* Career-related internships or fieldwork, Federal Work-Study, and scholarships/grants available. Financial award application deadline: 8/10; financial award applicants required to submit FAFSA. *Unit head:* 800-544-ARTS, E-mail: info@academyart.edu. *Application contact:* 800-544-ARTS, E-mail: info@academyart.edu.
Website: http://www.academyart.edu/film-school/index.html

Academy of Art University, Graduate Programs, School of Music Production and Sound Design for Visual Media, San Francisco, CA 94105-3410. Offers music scoring and composition (MA, MFA); sound design (MA, MFA). *Program availability:* Part-time, 100% online. *Faculty:* 4 full-time (0 women), 18 part-time/adjunct (1 woman). *Students:* 73 full-time (36 women), 35 part-time (11 women); includes 13 minority (7 Black or African American, non-Hispanic/Latino; 1 American Indian or Alaska Native, non-Hispanic/Latino; 3 Hispanic/Latino; 1 Native Hawaiian or other Pacific Islander, non-Hispanic/Latino; 1 Two or more races, non-Hispanic/Latino), 71 international. Average age 29. 37 applicants, 100% accepted, 29 enrolled. In 2017, 52 master's awarded. *Degree requirements:* For master's, final review. *Entrance requirements:* For master's, statement of intent; resume; portfolio/reel; official college transcripts. *Application deadline:* Applications are processed on a rolling basis. Application fee: $50. Electronic applications accepted. *Expenses: Tuition:* Part-time $982 per unit. *Financial support:* Career-related internships or fieldwork, Federal Work-Study, and scholarships/grants available. Financial award application deadline: 8/10; financial award applicants required to submit FAFSA. *Unit head:* 800-544-ARTS, E-mail: info@academyart.edu. *Application contact:* 800-544-ARTS, E-mail: info@academyart.edu.
Website: http://www.academyart.edu/music-for-visual-media/index.html

Academy of Art University, Graduate Programs, School of Writing for Film, Television and Digital Media, San Francisco, CA 94105-3410. Offers MFA. *Program availability:* Part-time, 100% online. *Faculty:* 13 part-time/adjunct (4 women). *Students:* 14 full-time (9 women), 23 part-time (19 women); includes 13 minority (5 Black or African American, non-Hispanic/Latino; 1 American Indian or Alaska Native, non-Hispanic/Latino; 4 Hispanic/Latino; 3 Two or more races, non-Hispanic/Latino), 7 international. Average age 36. 15 applicants, 100% accepted, 9 enrolled. In 2017, 3 master's awarded. *Degree requirements:* For master's, final review. *Entrance requirements:* For master's, statement of intent; resume; portfolio/reel; official college transcripts. *Application deadline:* Applications are processed on a rolling basis. Application fee: $50. Electronic applications accepted. *Expenses: Tuition:* Part-time $982 per unit. *Financial support:* Career-related internships or fieldwork, Federal Work-Study, and scholarships/grants available. Financial award application deadline: 8/10; financial award applicants required to submit FAFSA. *Unit head:* 800-544-ARTS, E-mail: info@academyart.edu. *Application contact:* 800-544-ARTS, E-mail: info@academyart.edu.
Website: http://www.academyart.edu/academics/writing-film-television-digital-media

American Film Institute Conservatory, Graduate Program, Los Angeles, CA 90027-1657. Offers cinematography (MFA); directing (MFA); editing (MFA); producing (MFA); production design (MFA); screenwriting (MFA). *Faculty:* 11 full-time (2 women), 64 part-time/adjunct (22 women). *Students:* 341 full-time (159 women); includes 65 minority (13 Black or African American, non-Hispanic/Latino; 2 American Indian or Alaska Native, non-Hispanic/Latino; 15 Asian, non-Hispanic/Latino; 27 Hispanic/Latino; 8 Two or more races, non-Hispanic/Latino), 117 international. Average age 26. *Degree requirements:* For master's, thesis. *Entrance requirements:* For master's, resume, two letters of recommendation, official transcripts. Additional exam requirements/recommendations for international students: Required—TOEFL (minimum score 600 paper-based; 100 iBT), IELTS (minimum score 7). *Application deadline:* For fall admission, 11/30 for domestic and international students. Application fee: $90. Electronic applications accepted. *Expenses: Tuition:* Full-time $54,072. *Required fees:* $3268. *Financial support:* Teaching assistantships, career-related internships or fieldwork, scholarships/grants, and unspecified assistantships available. Financial award applicants required to submit FAFSA. *Faculty research:* Film production, TV production. *Application contact:* Stacy Gaspard, Admissions Counselor, 323-856-7740, Fax: 323-856-7683, E-mail: admissions@afi.com.
Website: http://www.afi.com/conservatory/conservatoryprogram/

American University, School of Communication, Film and Media Arts Division, Washington, DC 20016-8001. Offers art in entertainment (MFA); environmental and wildlife filmmaking (MFA); film and media arts (MFA); game design (MA); games and interactive media (MFA); games and interactivity (MFA); political, cultural, and social impact (MFA); producing film, television and video (MA). *Program availability:* Part-time, evening/weekend. *Faculty:* 16 full-time (6 women), 9 part-time/adjunct (5 women). *Students:* 57 full-time (32 women), 75 part-time (32 women); includes 71 minority (42 Black or African American, non-Hispanic/Latino; 8 Asian, non-Hispanic/Latino; 16 Hispanic/Latino; 5 Two or more races, non-Hispanic/Latino), 7 international. 258 applicants, 29% accepted, 41 enrolled. In 2017, 71 master's awarded. *Degree requirements:* For master's, comprehensive exam, thesis or alternative. *Entrance requirements:* Additional exam requirements/recommendations for international students: Required—TOEFL (minimum score 600 paper-based; 100 iBT), IELTS (minimum score 7). *Application deadline:* For fall admission, 2/1 priority date for domestic and international students. Applications are processed on a rolling basis. Application fee: $50. Electronic applications accepted. *Expenses: Tuition:* Full-time $29,556. *Required fees:* $690. Tuition and fees vary according to course load and program. *Financial support:* In 2017–18, 58 students received support, including 35 teaching assistantships with partial tuition reimbursements available (averaging $10,000 per year); career-related internships or fieldwork, Federal Work-Study, institutionally sponsored loans, scholarships/grants, tuition waivers (partial), and unspecified assistantships also available. Support available to part-time students. Financial award application deadline: 2/1; financial award applicants required to submit FAFSA. *Faculty research:* Documentary film production, social media, media and public policy, visual literacy, new technology. *Unit head:* Prof. Brigid Maher, Director, Film and Media Arts Division, 202-885-2664, Fax: 202-885-2019, E-mail: bmaher@american.edu. *Application contact:* Leila Hernandez, Recruitment Coordinator, Graduate Programs, 202-885-2040, Fax: 202-885-2019, E-mail: leila@american.edu.
Website: https://www.american.edu/soc/film/index.cfm

Arizona State University at the Tempe campus, College of Liberal Arts and Sciences, Department of English, Program in Film and Media Studies, Tempe, AZ 85287-0402. Offers American media and popular culture (MAS). *Program availability:* Part-time, evening/weekend, online learning. *Degree requirements:* For master's, integrated project. *Entrance requirements:* For master's, minimum GPA of 3.0 or equivalent in last 2 years of work leading to bachelor's degree. Additional exam requirements/recommendations for international students: Required—TOEFL, IELTS, or PTE. Electronic applications accepted. *Expenses:* Contact institution.

ArtCenter College of Design, Graduate Film Program, Pasadena, CA 91103. Offers MFA. *Accreditation:* NASAD.

Azusa Pacific University, College of Music and the Arts, Azusa, CA 91702-7000. Offers composition (M Mus); conducting (M Mus); education (M Mus); modern art history, theory, and criticism (MA); music entrepreneurial studies (MA); performance (M Mus); screenwriting (MA); visual art (MFA). *Accreditation:* NASAD; NASM. *Program availability:* Part-time, evening/weekend. *Degree requirements:* For master's, recital. *Entrance requirements:* For master's, interview, audition. Additional exam requirements/recommendations for international students: Required—TOEFL (minimum score 550 paper-based).

Bard College, Milton Avery Graduate School of the Arts, Annandale-on-Hudson, NY 12504. Offers film/video (MFA); music/sound (MFA); painting (MFA); photography (MFA); sculpture (MFA); writing (MFA). *Degree requirements:* For master's, thesis, project, 8-week summer residency, independent study. *Entrance requirements:* For master's, interview, portfolio, 2 letters of recommendation, history of work in the arts. Additional exam requirements/recommendations for international students: Required—TOEFL (minimum score 550 paper-based). Electronic applications accepted. *Expenses:* Contact institution. *Faculty research:* Original work in painting, writing, sculpture, photography, video/film, sound/music.

Bob Jones University, Graduate Programs, Greenville, SC 29614. Offers accountancy (MS); Bible (MA); Bible translation (MA); Biblical studies (Certificate); broadcast management (MS); business administration (MBA); church history (MA, PhD); church ministries (MA); church music (MM); cinema and video production (MA); counseling (MS); curriculum and instruction (Ed D); divinity (M Div); dramatic production (MA); educational leadership (MS, Ed D, Ed S); elementary education (M Ed, MAT); English (M Ed, MA, MAT); fine arts (MA); graphic design (MA); history (M Ed, MA); illustration (MA); interpretative speech (MA); mathematics (M Ed, MAT); medical missions (Certificate); ministry (MM, D Min); multi-categorical special education (M Ed, MAT); music (M Ed); New Testament interpretation (PhD); Old Testament interpretation (PhD); orchestral instrument performance (MM); organ performance (MM); pastoral studies (MA); personnel services (MS, Ed S); piano pedagogy (MM); piano performance (MM); platform arts (MA); radio and television broadcasting (MS); rhetoric and public address (MA); secondary education (M Ed); studio art (MA); teaching Bible (MA); theology (MA, PhD); voice performance (MM); youth ministries (MA); M Div/MM.

Boston University, College of Communication, Department of Film and Television, Boston, MA 02215. Offers MFA, MS. *Program availability:* Part-time. *Faculty:* 17 full-time, 25 part-time/adjunct. *Students:* 97 full-time (63 women), 4 part-time (2 women); includes 30 minority (12 Black or African American, non-Hispanic/Latino; 7 Asian, non-Hispanic/Latino; 7 Hispanic/Latino; 4 Two or more races, non-Hispanic/Latino), 15 international. Average age 25. 340 applicants, 40% accepted, 68 enrolled. In 2017, 41 master's awarded. *Degree requirements:* For master's, thesis. *Entrance requirements:* For master's, GRE General Test, resume, writing and creative samples, letters of recommendation. Additional exam requirements/recommendations for international students: Required—TOEFL (minimum score 600 paper-based; 100 iBT), IELTS (minimum score 7). *Application deadline:* For fall admission, 5/1 for domestic and international students. Applications are processed on a rolling basis. Application fee: $95. Electronic applications accepted. *Financial support:* Research assistantships, teaching assistantships with partial tuition reimbursements, career-related internships or fieldwork, Federal Work-Study, scholarships/grants, and unspecified assistantships available. Support available to part-time students. Financial award application deadline: 5/1; financial award applicants required to submit FAFSA. *Unit head:* Paul Schneider, Chairman, 617-353-3483, Fax: 617-353-1084, E-mail: ftvchair@bu.edu. *Application contact:* Jackie Cummings, Admission and Financial Aid Counselor, 617-353-3481, E-mail: comgrad@bu.edu.
Website: http://www.bu.edu/com/academics/film-tv/

Bowling Green State University, Graduate College, College of Arts and Sciences, Department of Theatre and Film, Bowling Green, OH 43403. Offers MA, PhD. *Accreditation:* NAST. *Program availability:* Part-time. Terminal master's awarded for partial completion of doctoral program. *Degree requirements:* For master's, thesis or alternative; for doctorate, comprehensive exam, thesis/dissertation, 9-hour research tool. *Entrance requirements:* For master's and doctorate, GRE General Test. Additional exam requirements/recommendations for international students: Required—TOEFL. Electronic applications accepted. *Faculty research:* Theatre history, dramatic theory, cultural studies, performance studies, American theatre history.

Brigham Young University, Graduate Studies, College of Fine Arts and Communications, Department of Theatre and Media Arts, Provo, UT 84602-6404. Offers MA. *Accreditation:* NAST. *Faculty:* 18 full-time (6 women). *Students:* 5 full-time (3

women). Average age 32. 4 applicants, 75% accepted, 2 enrolled. In 2017, 1 master's awarded. *Degree requirements:* For master's, comprehensive exam, thesis, 32 hours, oral defense. *Entrance requirements:* For master's, two samples of scholarly writing, letter of intent, three letters of recommendation. Additional exam requirements/recommendations for international students: Required—TOEFL (minimum score 580 paper-based; 85 iBT). *Application deadline:* For fall admission, 3/15 priority date for domestic and international students. Application fee: $50. Electronic applications accepted. *Expenses:* $3,400 per semester, $405 per credit hour for members of the Church of Jesus Christ of Latter-day Saints; $6,880 per semester, $810 per credit hour for those who are not members of the Church. *Financial support:* In 2017–18, 6 students received support, including 6 teaching assistantships with full and partial tuition reimbursements available; research assistantships, career-related internships or fieldwork, scholarships/grants, and unspecified assistantships also available. Support available to part-time students. *Faculty research:* History, literary and screen theory, curatorial studies, critical race theory, popular culture, performance philosophy, women's studies, and media literacy. *Unit head:* Dr. Megan Sanborn Jones, Graduate Coordinator, 801-422-1321, E-mail: msjones@byu.edu. *Application contact:* Lindsi Michelle Neilson, Graduate Secretary, 801-422-3750, E-mail: lindsi_neilson@byu.edu. Website: http://cfac.byu.edu/departments/tma

Brooklyn College of the City University of New York, School of Visual, Media and Performing Arts, Department of Television and Radio, Brooklyn, NY 11210-2889. Offers media studies (MS); television production (MFA). *Program availability:* Part-time, evening/weekend. *Degree requirements:* For master's, comprehensive exam. *Entrance requirements:* For master's, GRE General Test or MAT, 12 credits in television/radio with a minimum B average, 2 letters of recommendation. Additional exam requirements/recommendations for international students: Required—TOEFL (minimum score 580 paper-based; 92 iBT). Electronic applications accepted. *Faculty research:* Criticism, research methods, audience behavior, policy and regulation, program history, international television and radio.

Brooklyn College of the City University of New York, School of Visual, Media and Performing Arts, Feirstein Graduate School of Cinema, Brooklyn, NY 11210-2889. Offers cinema arts (MFA); cinema studies (MA).

California College of the Arts, Graduate Programs, Fine Arts Programs, San Francisco, CA 94107. Offers film (MFA); fine arts (MFA). *Accreditation:* NASAD. *Faculty:* 62 full-time (34 women), 56 part-time/adjunct (34 women). *Students:* 80 full-time (55 women); includes 15 minority (4 Black or African American, non-Hispanic/Latino; 1 American Indian or Alaska Native, non-Hispanic/Latino; 3 Asian, non-Hispanic/Latino; 7 Hispanic/Latino), 33 international. Average age 29. 288 applicants, 57% accepted, 39 enrolled. In 2017, 45 master's awarded. *Degree requirements:* For master's, thesis, exhibit. *Entrance requirements:* For master's, appropriate bachelor's degree, portfolio, resume, 2 letters of recommendation, transcript. Additional exam requirements/recommendations for international students: Required—TOEFL, IELTS, or PTE. *Application deadline:* For fall admission, 1/31 priority date for domestic and international students. Applications are processed on a rolling basis. Application fee: $70. Electronic applications accepted. *Expenses:* $49,230 per year full-time tuition, $490 per year fees; $1,641 per unit part-time tuition. *Financial support:* In 2017–18, fellowships (averaging $42,000 per year), teaching assistantships (averaging $2,000 per year) were awarded; career-related internships or fieldwork, Federal Work-Study, scholarships/grants, health care benefits, and unspecified assistantships also available. Financial award application deadline: 7/31; financial award applicants required to submit FAFSA. *Unit head:* James Gobel, Chair, 415-551-9214, Fax: 415-703-9539, E-mail: jgobel@cca.edu. *Application contact:* Wes Fanelli, Assistant Director of Graduate Admissions, 415-703-9533, Fax: 415-703-9539, E-mail: wfanelli@cca.edu.

California Institute of the Arts, School of Film/Video, Valencia, CA 91355-2340. Offers experimental animation (MFA); film directing (MFA, Adv C); film/video (Adv C). *Entrance requirements:* For master's, portfolio. Additional exam requirements/recommendations for international students: Required—TOEFL. Electronic applications accepted. *Faculty research:* Experimental and character animation, experimental film/video, video graphics.

California State University, Fullerton, Graduate Studies, College of Communications, Department of Cinema and Television Arts, Fullerton, CA 92831-3599. Offers screenwriting (MFA). *Faculty:* 3 full-time (0 women), 2 part-time/adjunct (1 woman). *Students:* 25 full-time (9 women), 2 part-time (both women); includes 11 minority (3 Black or African American, non-Hispanic/Latino; 7 Hispanic/Latino; 1 Native Hawaiian or other Pacific Islander, non-Hispanic/Latino), 1 international. Average age 31. 24 applicants, 63% accepted, 11 enrolled. *Entrance requirements:* For master's, bachelor's degree from accredited university; samples of competent and creative writing, such as original screenplays, teleplays, theatrical plays, or other narrative work; essay; three letters of recommendation. Application fee: $55. Electronic applications accepted. *Unit head:* Garrett Hart, Chair, 657-278-4635, E-mail: gshart@fullerton.edu. *Application contact:* Admissions/Applications, 657-278-2371. Website: http://communications.fullerton.edu/ctva/

California State University, Northridge, Graduate Studies, Mike Curb College of Arts, Media, and Communication, Department of Cinema and Television Arts, Northridge, CA 91330. Offers screenwriting (MA). *Students:* 23 full-time (9 women), 4 part-time (0 women); includes 9 minority (2 Black or African American, non-Hispanic/Latino; 1 American Indian or Alaska Native, non-Hispanic/Latino; 4 Hispanic/Latino; 2 Two or more races, non-Hispanic/Latino), 1 international. Average age 38. 63 applicants, 24% accepted, 12 enrolled. In 2017, 15 master's awarded. *Entrance requirements:* For master's, GRE (if cumulative undergraduate GPA less than 3.0). Application fee: $55. *Unit head:* Thelma Vickroy, Chair, 818-677-3192. Website: http://www.ctva.csun.edu/

Carleton University, Faculty of Graduate Studies, Faculty of Arts and Social Sciences, School for Studies in Art and Culture, Program in Film Studies, Ottawa, ON K1S 5B6, Canada. Offers MA. *Degree requirements:* For master's, thesis. *Entrance requirements:* For master's, honors degree. Additional exam requirements/recommendations for international students: Required—TOEFL.

Carnegie Mellon University, College of Fine Arts, School of Drama, Pittsburgh, PA 15213-3891. Offers design (MFA); directing (MFA); dramatic writing (MFA); production technology and management (MFA); video and media design (MFA). *Degree requirements:* For master's, thesis (for some programs). *Entrance requirements:* For master's, audition, portfolio review, interview. Additional exam requirements/recommendations for international students: Required—TOEFL. *Faculty research:* Developing voice and speech compact disc.

Carnegie Mellon University, School of Computer Science and College of Fine Arts, Program in Entertainment Technology, Pittsburgh, PA 15213-3891. Offers MET.

Central Michigan University, College of Graduate Studies, College of Communication and Fine Arts, School of Broadcasting and Cinematic Arts, Mount Pleasant, MI 48859. Offers electronic media management (MA); electronic media production (MA); electronic media studies (MA); film theory and criticism (MA). *Program availability:* Part-time. *Degree requirements:* For master's, thesis or alternative. *Entrance requirements:* For master's, undergraduate degree in broadcasting, film studies, or an associated

discipline with minimum GPA of 2.7. Electronic applications accepted. *Faculty research:* Multimedia production, film history and criticism, writing and promotions, international broadcasting and media systems, history of American broadcasting.

Chapman University, Dodge College of Film and Media Arts, Orange, CA 92866. Offers documentary filmmaking (MFA); film and television producing (MFA); film production (MFA); film studies (MA); production design (MFA); screenwriting (MFA); television writing and producing (MFA); JD/MFA; MBA/MFA. *Faculty:* 49 full-time (13 women), 95 part-time/adjunct (31 women). *Students:* 273 full-time (129 women), 1 part-time (0 women); includes 58 minority (14 Black or African American, non-Hispanic/Latino; 9 Asian, non-Hispanic/Latino; 21 Hispanic/Latino; 14 Two or more races, non-Hispanic/Latino), 127 international. Average age 26. 467 applicants, 50% accepted, 113 enrolled. In 2017, 82 master's awarded. *Degree requirements:* For master's, thesis. *Entrance requirements:* For master's, GRE (if undergraduate GPA less than 3.0), minimum undergraduate GPA of 2.5, creative portfolio. *Application deadline:* For fall admission, 12/1 for domestic students. Application fee: $60. Electronic applications accepted. *Expenses:* Contact institution. *Financial support:* Fellowships, Federal Work-Study, and scholarships/grants available. Financial award applicants required to submit FAFSA. *Unit head:* Robert Bassett, Dean, 714-997-6715, E-mail: bassett@chapman.edu. *Application contact:* Lauren Kacura, Assistant Director of Admissions, 714-744-7856, E-mail: kacura@chapman.edu.

Chatham University, Program in Film and Digital Technology, Pittsburgh, PA 15232-2826. Offers MFA. *Program availability:* Part-time, evening/weekend. *Faculty:* 3 full-time (2 women), 2 part-time/adjunct (1 woman). *Students:* 7 full-time (3 women), 1 (woman) part-time; includes 3 minority (all Black or African American, non-Hispanic/Latino), 2 international. Average age 28. 10 applicants, 60% accepted, 5 enrolled. In 2017, 4 master's awarded. *Degree requirements:* For master's, thesis, capstone project. *Entrance requirements:* Additional exam requirements/recommendations for international students: Required—TOEFL (minimum score 600 paper-based; 100 iBT), IELTS (minimum score 7), TWE. *Application deadline:* For fall admission, 4/1 priority date for domestic and international students; for spring admission, 11/1 priority date for domestic students, 10/1 priority date for international students. Applications are processed on a rolling basis. Application fee: $45. Electronic applications accepted. Application fee is waived when completed online. *Expenses:* Tuition: Full-time $16,740; part-time $930 per credit. *Required fees:* $486; $27 per credit. $243 per semester. *Financial support:* Applicants required to submit FAFSA. *Unit head:* Dr. Prajna Parasher, Director, 412-365-1182, E-mail: parasher@chatham.edu. *Application contact:* Katie Noel, Assistant Director of Graduate Admission, 412-365-2758, Fax: 412-365-1609, E-mail: gradadmissions@chatham.edu. Website: http://www.chatham.edu/mfafilm

Columbia College Chicago, School of Graduate Studies, Cinema and Television Arts Department, Chicago, IL 60605-1996. Offers cinema directing (MFA); creative producing (MFA). *Students:* 31 full-time (22 women), 9 part-time (3 women); includes 15 minority (7 Black or African American, non-Hispanic/Latino; 3 Asian, non-Hispanic/Latino; 4 Hispanic/Latino; 1 Two or more races, non-Hispanic/Latino), 12 international. 117 applicants, 53% accepted, 26 enrolled. *Degree requirements:* For master's, thesis. *Entrance requirements:* For master's, self-assessment essay, work samples, interview, case study, letters of recommendation, transcripts, resume. Additional exam requirements/recommendations for international students: Required—TOEFL, IELTS. *Application deadline:* For fall admission, 1/15 priority date for domestic and international students. Applications are processed on a rolling basis. Application fee: $55 ($100 for international students). Electronic applications accepted. *Expenses:* Tuition: Full-time $26,808; part-time $1117 per credit. *Required fees:* $572; $155 per credit. *Financial support:* In 2017–18, 16 students received support. Career-related internships or fieldwork, Federal Work-Study, scholarships/grants, and unspecified assistantships available. Financial award application deadline: 1/15. *Unit head:* Eric Scholl, Interim Chair, 312-369-7959, E-mail: escholl@colum.edu. *Application contact:* David Marts, Graduate Admissions, 312-369-7942, E-mail: dmarts@colum.edu. Website: http://www.colum.edu/academics/media-arts/cinema-art-and-science/

Columbia University, School of the Arts, Film Program, New York, NY 10027. Offers film (MFA), including creative producing, screenwriting/directing. *Faculty:* 22 full-time (7 women), 46 part-time/adjunct (14 women). *Students:* 317 full-time (157 women); includes 78 minority (14 Black or African American, non-Hispanic/Latino; 1 American Indian or Alaska Native, non-Hispanic/Latino; 26 Asian, non-Hispanic/Latino; 22 Hispanic/Latino; 15 Two or more races, non-Hispanic/Latino), 124 international. Average age 26. 544 applicants, 28% accepted, 88 enrolled. In 2017, 67 master's awarded. *Degree requirements:* For master's, thesis. *Entrance requirements:* For master's, 3 letters of recommendation, writing sample, complete a scene, feature film treatment (optional visual submission). Additional exam requirements/recommendations for international students: Required—TOEFL (minimum score 600 paper-based; 100 iBT). *Application deadline:* For fall admission, 12/1 for domestic and international students. Application fee: $110. Electronic applications accepted. *Expenses:* Contact institution. *Financial support:* In 2017–18, 235 students received support, including 34 teaching assistantships with full and partial tuition reimbursements available; fellowships, research assistantships, career-related internships or fieldwork, Federal Work-Study, and scholarships/grants also available. Financial award application deadline: 2/1; financial award applicants required to submit FAFSA. *Unit head:* Hilary Brougher, Chair, 212-854-2815, E-mail: film@columbia.edu. *Application contact:* Kenny Wong, Director of Admissions and Financial Aid, 212-854-2134, E-mail: admissions-arts@columbia.edu. Website: http://arts.columbia.edu/film

See Display on page 133 and Close-Up on page 185.

Concordia University, School of Graduate Studies, Faculty of Fine Arts, Department of Studio Arts, Montréal, QC H3G 1M8, Canada. Offers studio arts (MFA), including fibers and material practices, film production, intermedia, painting and drawing, photography, print media, sculpture. *Degree requirements:* For master's, thesis or alternative. *Entrance requirements:* For master's, portfolio.

Concordia University, School of Graduate Studies, Faculty of Fine Arts, Mel Hoppenheim School of Cinema, Montréal, QC H3G 1M8, Canada. Offers film and moving image studies (PhD); film production (MFA); film studies (MA).

DePaul University, College of Computing and Digital Media, Chicago, IL 60604. Offers animation (MA, MFA); applied technology (MS); business information technology (MS); computational finance (MS); computer and information sciences (PhD); computer science (MS); creative producing (MFA); cybersecurity (MS); data science (MS); digital communication and media arts (MA); documentary (MFA); e-commerce technology (MS); experience design (MA); film and television (MS); film and television directing (MFA); game design (MFA); game programming (MS); health informatics (MS); human centered design (PhD); human-computer interaction (MS); information systems (MS); network engineering and security (MS); product innovation and computing (MS); screenwriting (MFA); software engineering (MS); JD/MS. *Program availability:* Part-time, evening/weekend, online learning. *Degree requirements:* For master's, thesis (for some programs); for doctorate, comprehensive exam, thesis/dissertation. *Entrance requirements:* For master's, GRE or GMAT (for MS in computational finance only),

bachelor's degree, resume (MS in predictive analytics only), IT experience (MS in information technology project management only), portfolio review (all MFA programs and MA in animation); for doctorate, GRE, master's degree in computer science. Additional exam requirements/recommendations for international students: Required—TOEFL (minimum score 590 paper-based; 80 iBT), IELTS (minimum score 6.5), PTE (minimum score 53). *Application deadline:* For fall admission, 8/1 priority date for domestic students, 6/15 priority date for international students; for winter admission, 12/1 priority date for domestic students, 10/15 priority date for international students; for spring admission, 3/1 priority date for domestic students, 1/15 priority date for international students; for summer admission, 5/1 for domestic students, 4/15 for international students. Applications are processed on a rolling basis. Application fee: $25. Electronic applications accepted. *Expenses:* Contact institution. *Financial support:* Fellowships with full tuition reimbursements, research assistantships with full and partial tuition reimbursements, teaching assistantships with full and partial tuition reimbursements, Federal Work-Study, scholarships/grants, tuition waivers (full and partial), and unspecified assistantships available. Support available to part-time students. Financial award application deadline: 4/20; financial award applicants required to submit FAFSA. *Faculty research:* Data mining, computer science, human-computer interaction, security, animation and film. *Unit head:* Elly Kafritsas-Wessels, Communications Manager, 312-362-5816, Fax: 312-362-5185, E-mail: ekafrits@cdm.depaul.edu. *Application contact:* Office of Admission, 312-362-8714, E-mail: admission@cdm.depaul.edu.
Website: http://cdm.depaul.edu

Drexel University, Westphal College of Media Arts and Design, Program in Television Management, Philadelphia, PA 19104-2875. Offers MS, MS/MBA.

Florida Atlantic University, Dorothy F. Schmidt College of Arts and Letters, School of Communication and Multimedia Studies, Boca Raton, FL 33431-0991. Offers communication studies (MA); film and video (Certificate); media, technology and entertainment (MFA). *Program availability:* Part-time. *Faculty:* 24 full-time (8 women). *Students:* 21 full-time (15 women), 16 part-time (9 women); includes 19 minority (11 Black or African American, non-Hispanic/Latino; 1 Asian, non-Hispanic/Latino; 6 Hispanic/Latino; 1 Two or more races, non-Hispanic/Latino), 2 international. Average age 32. 29 applicants, 52% accepted, 13 enrolled. In 2017, 15 master's awarded. *Degree requirements:* For master's, one foreign language, comprehensive exam (for some programs), thesis (for some programs). *Entrance requirements:* For master's, GRE General Test, minimum GPA of 3.0, essay, letters of recommendation. *Application deadline:* For fall admission, 7/1 priority date for domestic students, 4/1 for international students; for spring admission, 11/1 for domestic students, 10/1 for international students. Applications are processed on a rolling basis. Application fee: $30. Electronic applications accepted. *Expenses:* Tuition, state resident: full-time $7400; part-time $369.82 per credit. Tuition, nonresident: full-time $20,496; part-time $1042.81 per credit. *Financial support:* Teaching assistantships with partial tuition reimbursements, Federal Work-Study, institutionally sponsored loans, scholarships/grants, and unspecified assistantships available. Support available to part-time students. Financial award application deadline: 3/1; financial award applicants required to submit FAFSA. *Faculty research:* Cultural studies, gender studies, film, communication theory, journalism, new media. *Unit head:* Dr. David Williams, Director, 561-297-0045, Fax: 561-297-2615, E-mail: dcwill@fau.edu. *Application contact:* Dr. Stephen Charbonneau, Graduate Director, 561-297-3856, Fax: 561-297-2615, E-mail: efreedma@fau.edu.
Website: http://www.fau.edu/scms/

Florida State University, The Graduate School, College of Motion Picture Arts, Tallahassee, FL 32306-2350. Offers film production (MFA); screenwriting (MFA). *Faculty:* 28 full-time (8 women), 3 part-time/adjunct (1 woman). *Students:* 62 full-time (26 women); includes 20 minority (10 Black or African American, non-Hispanic/Latino; 1 American Indian or Alaska Native, non-Hispanic/Latino; 4 Asian, non-Hispanic/Latino; 3 Hispanic/Latino; 2 Two or more races, non-Hispanic/Latino), 14 international. Average age 25. 217 applicants, 15% accepted, 32 enrolled. In 2017, 28 master's awarded. *Degree requirements:* For master's, thesis, thesis film project. *Entrance requirements:* For master's, GRE (for MFA in writing), minimum GPA of 3.0, resume, statement of purpose, writing sample, 3 letters of recommendation, creative portfolio. Additional exam requirements/recommendations for international students: Required—TOEFL (minimum score 550 paper-based; 80 iBT). *Application deadline:* For fall admission, 12/1 for domestic and international students. Application fee: $30. Electronic applications accepted. *Expenses:* Contact institution. *Financial support:* In 2017–18, 20 students received support, including 20 teaching assistantships with partial tuition reimbursements available (averaging $5,500 per year); institutionally sponsored loans and unspecified assistantships also available. Financial award application deadline: 12/1; financial award applicants required to submit FAFSA. *Faculty research:* Producing, screenwriting, directing, cinematography, editing. *Unit head:* Reb Braddock, Dean, 850-644-8712, Fax: 850-644-2626. *Application contact:* Gloria McElroy, Staff Director of Admissions and Recruitment, 850-644-8524, Fax: 850-644-2626, E-mail: gmcelroy@fsu.edu.
Website: http://film.fsu.edu/

Georgia State University, College of Arts and Sciences, Department of Communication, Atlanta, GA 30302-3083. Offers film, video, and digital imaging (MA), including critical studies, production, screenwriting; human communication and social influence (MA); mass communication (MA); media and society (PhD); moving image studies (PhD); public communication (PhD); rhetoric and politics (PhD). *Program availability:* Part-time. *Faculty:* 57 full-time (34 women). *Students:* 71 full-time (51 women), 17 part-time (9 women); includes 36 minority (28 Black or African American, non-Hispanic/Latino; 1 Asian, non-Hispanic/Latino; 4 Hispanic/Latino; 1 Native Hawaiian or other Pacific Islander, non-Hispanic/Latino; 2 Two or more races, non-Hispanic/Latino), 15 international. Average age 33. 63 applicants, 54% accepted, 17 enrolled. In 2017, 20 master's, 10 doctorates awarded. *Degree requirements:* For master's, variable foreign language requirement, thesis (for some programs); for doctorate, comprehensive exam, thesis/dissertation. *Entrance requirements:* For master's and doctorate, GRE. Additional exam requirements/recommendations for international students: Required—TOEFL (minimum score 550 paper-based; 80 iBT), IELTS (minimum score 6.5). *Application deadline:* For fall admission, 2/10 for domestic and international students; for spring admission, 10/15 for domestic and international students. Application fee: $50. Electronic applications accepted. *Expenses:* Tuition, state resident: full-time $7020. Tuition, nonresident: full-time $22,518. *Required fees:* $2128. Tuition and fees vary according to degree level and program. *Financial support:* In 2017–18, fellowships with tuition reimbursements (averaging $15,000 per year), teaching assistantships with tuition reimbursements (averaging $15,000 per year) were awarded; career-related internships or fieldwork and unspecified assistantships also available. Financial award applicants required to submit FAFSA. *Faculty research:* New media, mass media and journalism, rhetoric, film and media studies, film production. *Unit head:* Dr. Greg Lisby, Chair, 404-413-5639, Fax: 404-413-5634, E-mail: glisby@gsu.edu.
Website: http://communication.gsu.edu

Governors State University, College of Arts and Sciences, Program in Independent Film and Digital Imaging, University Park, IL 60484. Offers MFA. *Program availability:* Part-time. *Faculty:* 60 full-time (34 women), 115 part-time/adjunct (58 women). *Students:* 11 full-time (7 women), 8 part-time (6 women); includes 11 minority (10 Black or African American, non-Hispanic/Latino; 1 Two or more races, non-Hispanic/Latino), 1 international. Average age 40. 6 applicants, 50% accepted, 3 enrolled. In 2017, 8 master's awarded. *Application deadline:* For fall admission, 4/1 for domestic students. Applications are processed on a rolling basis. Application fee: $50. Electronic applications accepted. *Expenses:* Tuition, state resident: full-time $8472; part-time $353 per credit hour. Tuition, nonresident: full-time $16,944; part-time $706 per credit hour. *Required fees:* $1824; $76 per credit hour. $38 per term. Tuition and fees vary according to course load, degree level and program. *Financial support:* Application deadline: 5/1; applicants required to submit FAFSA. *Unit head:* Lori Montalbano, Chair, Division of Arts and Letters, 708-534-5000 Ext. 2802, E-mail: lmontalbano@govst.edu.

Hollins University, Graduate Programs, Program in Screenwriting and Film Studies, Roanoke, VA 24020. Offers screenwriting (MFA); screenwriting and film studies (MA). Program offered during summer only. *Program availability:* Part-time. *Faculty:* 5 full-time (2 women). *Students:* 23 full-time (14 women), 5 part-time (3 women); includes 5 minority (1 Black or African American, non-Hispanic/Latino; 1 Asian, non-Hispanic/Latino; 2 Hispanic/Latino; 1 Two or more races, non-Hispanic/Latino). Average age 40. 15 applicants, 100% accepted, 7 enrolled. In 2017, 5 master's awarded. *Degree requirements:* For master's, one foreign language, comprehensive exam, thesis. *Entrance requirements:* For master's, letters of recommendation, portfolio, transcript review. Additional exam requirements/recommendations for international students: Required—TOEFL (minimum score 550 paper-based; 80 iBT), IELTS (minimum score 6.5). *Application deadline:* For summer admission, 2/15 priority date for domestic and international students. Application fee: $40. Electronic applications accepted. *Expenses:* Contact institution. *Financial support:* Federal Work-Study and scholarships/grants available. Support available to part-time students. Financial award application deadline: 2/15; financial award applicants required to submit FAFSA. *Faculty research:* Censorship, minorities in film, writing for television, new media. *Unit head:* Dr. Tim Albaugh, Director, 540-362-6575, E-mail: hugrad@hollins.edu. *Application contact:* Cathy S. Koon, Manager of Graduate Programs, 540-362-6326, Fax: 540-362-6288, E-mail: ckoon@hollins.edu.
Website: https://www.hollins.edu/academics/graduate-degrees/mfa-screenwriting-film-studies/

Howard University, Cathy Hughes School of Communications, Department of Media, Journalism and Film, Washington, DC 20059-0002. Offers film (MFA). *Program availability:* Part-time. *Degree requirements:* For master's, thesis optional. *Entrance requirements:* For master's, GRE General Test, minimum GPA of 3.0.

Johns Hopkins University, Zanvyl Krieger School of Arts and Sciences, Advanced Academic Programs, Program in Film and Media, Baltimore, MD 21218. Offers MA. Students choose two concentrations from business, sound, and writing. *Program availability:* Part-time.

Lake Forest College, Graduate Program in Liberal Studies, Lake Forest, IL 60045. Offers American studies (MLS); cinema in East Asia (MLS); environmental studies (MLS); history (MLS); Medieval and Renaissance art (MLS); philosophy (MLS); Spanish (MLS); writing (MLS). *Program availability:* Part-time, evening/weekend. *Faculty:* 11 full-time (3 women). *Students:* 34 part-time (19 women); includes 3 minority (1 Asian, non-Hispanic/Latino; 2 Hispanic/Latino). Average age 36. 20 applicants, 55% accepted, 8 enrolled. In 2017, 5 master's awarded. *Degree requirements:* For master's, thesis optional, 8 courses, including at least 3 interdisciplinary seminars. *Entrance requirements:* For master's, transcript, essay, interview. Additional exam requirements/recommendations for international students: Required—TOEFL (minimum score 550 paper-based; 83 iBT); Recommended—IELTS (minimum score 6.5). *Application deadline:* For fall admission, 7/15 priority date for domestic students, 6/1 priority date for international students; for spring admission, 12/1 priority date for domestic students, 10/1 priority date for international students. Applications are processed on a rolling basis. Application fee: $30. Electronic applications accepted. *Expenses:* $2,650 per course. *Financial support:* In 2017–18, 2 students received support. Partial tuition grants (for full-time teachers) available. *Faculty research:* Religion in America, Asian philosophy, cinema studies, theater studies, sociology of religion. *Unit head:* Prof. D. L. LeMahieu, Director, 847-735-5133, Fax: 847-735-6291, E-mail: lemahieu@lakeforest.edu. *Application contact:* Prof. Carol Gayle, Associate Director, 847-735-5083, Fax: 847-735-6291, E-mail: gayle@lakeforest.edu.
Website: http://www.lakeforest.edu/academics/programs/mls/

Lindenwood University, Graduate Programs, School of Arts, Media, and Communications, St. Charles, MO 63301-1695. Offers advertising (MA); art history (MA); cinema and media arts (MFA); communications (MA); digital and Web design (MA); fashion and business design (MS); journalism (MA); mass communications (MA); social media and digital content (MS). *Program availability:* Part-time. *Faculty:* 23 full-time (6 women), 8 part-time/adjunct (4 women). *Students:* 26 full-time (13 women), 11 part-time (8 women); includes 3 minority (1 American Indian or Alaska Native, non-Hispanic/Latino; 2 Hispanic/Latino), 7 international. Average age 33. 60 applicants, 45% accepted, 16 enrolled. In 2017, 11 master's awarded. *Degree requirements:* For master's, thesis (for some programs), minimum cumulative GPA of 3.0. *Entrance requirements:* For master's, audition or interview, minimum GPA of 3.0, portfolio, letter of recommendation. Additional exam requirements/recommendations for international students: Required—TOEFL (minimum score 550 paper-based; 80 iBT); Recommended—IELTS (minimum score 6.5). *Application deadline:* For fall admission, 8/27 priority date for domestic and international students; for spring admission, 1/14 for domestic students, 1/14 priority date for international students; for summer admission, 6/4 priority date for domestic and international students. Applications are processed on a rolling basis. Application fee: $30 ($100 for international students). Electronic applications accepted. *Expenses: Tuition:* Full-time $16,300; part-time $460 per credit. *Required fees:* $660; $330 per credit. Tuition and fees vary according to degree level and program. *Financial support:* In 2017–18, 34 students received support. Career-related internships or fieldwork, institutionally sponsored loans, scholarships/grants, tuition waivers (partial), and unspecified assistantships available. Financial award application deadline: 6/30; financial award applicants required to submit FAFSA. *Unit head:* Dr. Joseph Alsobrook, Dean, School of Arts, Media, and Communications, 636-949-4164, Fax: 636-949-4910, E-mail: jalsobrook@lindenwood.edu. *Application contact:* Kara Schilli, Director, Evening and Graduate Admissions, 636-949-4349, Fax: 636-949-4109, E-mail: adultadmissions@lindenwood.edu.
Website: http://www.lindenwood.edu/academics/academic-schools/school-of-arts-media-and-communications/

Lipscomb University, Program in Film and Creative Media, Nashville, TN 37204-3951. Offers writer/director (MFA); MFA/MBA. *Program availability:* Part-time, evening/weekend. *Faculty:* 7 full-time (1 woman), 1 part-time/adjunct (0 women). *Students:* 23 full-time (12 women); includes 10 minority (all Black or African American, non-Hispanic/Latino). Average age 32. 26 applicants, 46% accepted, 9 enrolled. In 2017, 12 master's awarded. *Degree requirements:* For master's, professional practicum, portfolio. *Entrance requirements:* For master's, GRE or MAT, 2 references, resume, video portfolio. Additional exam requirements/recommendations for international students: Required—TOEFL (minimum score 570 paper-based; 80 iBT). *Application deadline:* Applications are processed on a rolling basis. Application fee: $50 ($75 for international

students). Electronic applications accepted. *Expenses:* $1,013. *Financial support:* Unspecified assistantships available. Financial award applicants required to submit FAFSA. *Unit head:* David DeBorde, Director, 615-966-7111, E-mail: david.deborde@lipscomb.edu. *Application contact:* Josh Link, Recruiting and Marketing Coordinator, 615-966-6005, E-mail: josh.link@lipscomb.edu.
Website: http://www.lipscomb.edu/cinematicarts/graduate-programs

Loyola Marymount University, School of Film and Television, Program in Film and Television Production, Los Angeles, CA 90045-2659. Offers MFA. *Unit head:* Dr. Eugene Brancolini, Director, Film and Television Production, 310-258-8891, E-mail: ebrancol@lmu.edu. *Application contact:* Chake H. Kouyoumjian, Associate Dean of Graduate Studies, 310-338-2721, Fax: 310-338-6086, E-mail: graduateinfo@lmu.edu.
Website: http://sftv.lmu.edu/academics/graduateprograms/filmandtvproduction

Loyola Marymount University, School of Film and Television, Program in Writing and Producing for Television, Los Angeles, CA 90045-2659. Offers MFA. *Unit head:* Karol Hoeffner, Director, Writing and Producing for Television, 310-338-3033, E-mail: khoeffne@lmu.edu. *Application contact:* Chake H. Kouyoumjian, Associate Dean of Graduate Studies, 310-338-2721, Fax: 310-338-6086, E-mail: graduateinfo@lmu.edu.
Website: http://sftv.lmu.edu/academics/graduateprograms/writingandproducingfortv

Maryland Institute College of Art, Graduate Studies, Program in Filmmaking, Baltimore, MD 21201. Offers MFA. *Degree requirements:* For master's, thesis film and screening, written thesis. *Entrance requirements:* For master's, portfolio, writing samples, bachelor's degree in any field. Additional exam requirements/recommendations for international students: Required—TOEFL (minimum score 550 paper-based; 80 iBT), IELTS (minimum score 6.5). Electronic applications accepted. *Expenses:* Contact institution.

Massachusetts College of Art and Design, Graduate Programs, MFA Program, Boston, MA 02115-5882. Offers 2D fine arts (MFA), including painting, printmaking; 3D fine arts (MFA), including ceramics, fibers, glass, jewelry and metalsmithing, sculpture; design (MFA, Postbaccalaureate Certificate), including dynamic media; fine arts (MFA), including interdisciplinary; media arts (MFA, Postbaccalaureate Certificate), including film/video (MFA), photography. *Accreditation:* NASAD. *Faculty:* 28 full-time (8 women), 28 part-time/adjunct (17 women). *Students:* 44 full-time (26 women), 28 part-time (17 women); includes 8 minority (5 Asian, non-Hispanic/Latino; 3 Hispanic/Latino), 18 international. 247 applicants, 52% accepted, 47 enrolled. In 2017, 42 master's, 5 other advanced degrees awarded. *Degree requirements:* For master's, thesis, thesis exhibition (for fine arts programs); thesis project and document (for design/dynamic media program). *Entrance requirements:* For master's, portfolio, college transcripts, resume, statement of purpose, letters of reference, interview, 6 credits of art history taken prior to or during MFA program; for Postbaccalaureate Certificate, portfolio, college transcripts, resume, statement of purpose, letters of reference, interview. Additional exam requirements/recommendations for international students: Required—TOEFL (minimum score 550 paper-based, 85 iBT) or IELTS (6). *Application deadline:* For fall admission, 1/4 priority date for domestic and international students; for summer admission, 1/4 priority date for domestic and international students. Applications are processed on a rolling basis. Application fee: $90. Electronic applications accepted. *Expenses:* $780 per credit. *Financial support:* In 2017–18, 51 students received support, including 1 research assistantship (averaging $2,160 per year), 33 teaching assistantships (averaging $2,160 per year); fellowships, career-related internships or fieldwork, scholarships/grants, tuition waivers (partial), unspecified assistantships, and adjunct co-teaching positions also available. Support available to part-time students. Financial award application deadline: 1/4; financial award applicants required to submit FAFSA. *Faculty research:* Painting and printmaking, sculpture, photography, film and video, dynamic media design. *Unit head:* Paul Paturzo, Dean of Graduate Studies, 617-879-7166, E-mail: pjpaturzo@massart.edu. *Application contact:* Lauren O'Neill, Assistant Director of Graduate Admissions, 617-879-7222, E-mail: gradadmissions@massart.edu.
Website: http://www.massart.edu/Admissions/Graduate_Programs.html

Miami International University of Art & Design, Program in Film, Miami, FL 33132-1418. Offers MFA. *Program availability:* Online learning.

Minneapolis College of Art and Design, Program in Visual Studies, Minneapolis, MN 55404-4347. Offers animation (MFA); comic art (MFA); drawing (MFA); filmmaking (MFA); fine arts (MFA); furniture design (MFA); graphic design (MFA); illustration (MFA); interactive media (MFA); painting (MFA); photography (MFA); printmaking (MFA); sculpture (MFA). *Accreditation:* NASAD. *Program availability:* Part-time. *Faculty:* 42 full-time (13 women). *Students:* 30 full-time (23 women); includes 3 minority (2 Asian, non-Hispanic/Latino; 1 Hispanic/Latino), 13 international. 166 applicants, 28% accepted, 12 enrolled. In 2017, 10 master's awarded. *Degree requirements:* For master's, thesis, thesis exhibit. *Entrance requirements:* For master's, portfolio of visual artwork, resume, 3 letters of recommendation. Additional exam requirements/recommendations for international students: Required—TOEFL (minimum score 550 paper-based; 79 iBT). *Application deadline:* For fall admission, 1/15 for domestic and international students. Application fee: $50. Electronic applications accepted. *Expenses: Tuition:* Full-time $38,670. *Required fees:* $450. One-time fee: $300 full-time. *Financial support:* In 2017–18, 23 students received support, including 15 teaching assistantships (averaging $6,000 per year); career-related internships or fieldwork, Federal Work-Study, scholarships/grants, and unspecified assistantships also available. Support available to part-time students. Financial award application deadline: 3/15; financial award applicants required to submit FAFSA. *Faculty research:* Visual arts: animation, comic art, drawing, filmmaking, furniture design, graphic design, illustration, interactive media, painting, photography, printmaking, sculpture. *Unit head:* Graduate Director, 612-209-1471, E-mail: admissions@mcad.edu. *Application contact:* Mary Kazura, Associate Director of Admissions, 612-874-3760, Fax: 612-874-3701, E-mail: mary_kazura@mcad.edu.
Website: http://mcad.edu/mfa

Missouri State University, Graduate College, Interdisciplinary Program in Professional Studies, Springfield, MO 65897. Offers administrative studies (Certificate); applied communication (MS); criminal justice (MS); environmental management (MS); homeland security (MS); individualized (MS); professional studies (MS); screenwriting and producing (MS); sports management (MS). *Program availability:* Part-time, evening/weekend, 100% online, blended/hybrid learning. *Students:* 51 full-time (33 women), 95 part-time (41 women); includes 21 minority (8 Black or African American, non-Hispanic/Latino; 1 Asian, non-Hispanic/Latino; 7 Hispanic/Latino; 5 Two or more races, non-Hispanic/Latino), 37 international. Average age 24. 71 applicants, 69% accepted, 35 enrolled. In 2017, 50 master's awarded. *Degree requirements:* For master's, comprehensive exam, thesis or alternative. *Entrance requirements:* For master's, GRE, GMAT (if GPA less than 3.0). Additional exam requirements/recommendations for international students: Required—TOEFL (minimum score 550 paper-based; 79 iBT), IELTS (minimum score 6). *Application deadline:* For fall admission, 7/15 priority date for domestic students; for spring admission, 12/1 priority date for domestic students; for summer admission, 5/1 for domestic students. Applications are processed on a rolling basis. Application fee: $35 ($50 for international students). Electronic applications accepted. *Expenses:* Tuition, state resident: full-time $2915; part-time $2021 per credit hour. Tuition, nonresident: full-time $5354; part-time $3647 per credit hour. *International*

tuition: $11,992 full-time. *Required fees:* $173; $173 per credit hour. Tuition and fees vary according to class time, course level, course load, degree level, campus/location and program. *Financial support:* Career-related internships or fieldwork, Federal Work-Study, institutionally sponsored loans, scholarships/grants, and unspecified assistantships available. Support available to part-time students. Financial award application deadline: 3/31; financial award applicants required to submit FAFSA. *Unit head:* Dr. Gerald Masterson, Program Director, 417-836-5251, Fax: 417-836-6888, E-mail: mps@missouristate.edu. *Application contact:* Stephanie Praschan, Director, Graduate Enrollment Management, 417-836-5330, Fax: 417-836-6200, E-mail: stephaniepraschan@missouristate.edu.
Website: http://mps.missouristate.edu

Montana State University, The Graduate School, College of Arts and Architecture, School of Film and Photography, Bozeman, MT 59717. Offers science and natural history filmmaking (MFA). *Program availability:* Part-time. *Degree requirements:* For master's, comprehensive exam. *Entrance requirements:* For master's, GRE General Test, minimum GPA of 3.0, resume, 3 letters of recommendation. Additional exam requirements/recommendations for international students: Required—TOEFL (minimum score 550 paper-based). Electronic applications accepted. *Faculty research:* Science and natural history filmmaking, science communication, public outreach, new media production, environmental communication.

Mount Saint Mary's University, Graduate Division, Los Angeles, CA 90049. Offers business administration (MBA); counseling psychology (MS); creative writing (MFA); education (MS, Certificate); film and television (MFA); health policy and management (MS); humanities (MA); nursing (MSN, Certificate); physical therapy (DPT); religious studies (MA). *Program availability:* Part-time, evening/weekend. *Faculty:* 50 full-time (35 women), 116 part-time/adjunct (81 women). *Students:* 670 full-time (518 women), 147 part-time (116 women); includes 414 minority (73 Black or African American, non-Hispanic/Latino; 4 American Indian or Alaska Native, non-Hispanic/Latino; 60 Asian, non-Hispanic/Latino; 259 Hispanic/Latino; 7 Native Hawaiian or other Pacific Islander, non-Hispanic/Latino; 11 Two or more races, non-Hispanic/Latino), 4 international. Average age 32. 1,398 applicants, 21% accepted, 242 enrolled. In 2017, 170 master's, 28 doctorates, 35 other advanced degrees awarded. *Entrance requirements:* Additional exam requirements/recommendations for international students: Required—TOEFL. *Application deadline:* For fall admission, 6/30 priority date for domestic and international students; for spring admission, 10/30 priority date for domestic and international students; for summer admission, 3/30 priority date for domestic and international students. Applications are processed on a rolling basis. Application fee: $50. Electronic applications accepted. *Expenses: Tuition:* Part-time $905 per unit. One-time fee: $155 part-time. Tuition and fees vary according to degree level and program. *Financial support:* Career-related internships or fieldwork, Federal Work-Study, institutionally sponsored loans, and tuition waivers (full and partial) available. Support available to part-time students. Financial award application deadline: 3/15; financial award applicants required to submit FAFSA. *Unit head:* Albert Ramos, Director of Graduate Admissions, 213-477-2800, E-mail: gradprograms@msmu.edu. *Application contact:* Shawn Peters, Graduate Admission Counselor, 213-477-2676, E-mail: gradprograms@msmu.edu.
Website: http://www.msmu.edu/graduate-programs/

National University, Academic Affairs, School of Professional Studies, La Jolla, CA 92037-1011. Offers criminal justice (MCJ); digital cinema production (MFA); digital journalism (MA); homeland security and emergency management (MS); juvenile justice (MS); professional screenwriting (MFA); public administration (MPA), including human resource management, organizational leadership. *Program availability:* Part-time, evening/weekend, 100% online, blended/hybrid learning. *Degree requirements:* For master's, thesis (for some programs). *Entrance requirements:* For master's, interview, minimum GPA of 2.5. Additional exam requirements/recommendations for international students: Required—TOEFL (minimum score 550 paper-based; 79 iBT), IELTS (minimum score 6). *Application deadline:* Applications are processed on a rolling basis. Application fee: $60 ($65 for international students). Electronic applications accepted. *Expenses: Tuition:* Part-time $430 per quarter hour. *Financial support:* Career-related internships or fieldwork, institutionally sponsored loans, scholarships/grants, and tuition waivers (partial) available. Support available to part-time students. Financial award application deadline: 6/30; financial award applicants required to submit FAFSA. *Unit head:* Dr. Daniel Donaldson, Dean, 858-642-8480, E-mail: sops@nu.edu. *Application contact:* Brandon Jouganatos, Vice President for Enrollment Services, 800-628-8648, E-mail: advisor@nu.edu.
Website: http://www.nu.edu/OurPrograms/School-of-Professional-Studies.html

New York Film Academy, Program in Filmmaking–Los Angeles, Burbank, CA 91505. Offers acting for film (MFA); cinematography (MFA); documentary film (MFA); film and media production (MA); filmmaking (MFA); game design (MFA); photography (MFA); producing (MA, MFA); screenwriting (MA, MFA). *Accreditation:* NASAD.

New York Film Academy, Program in Filmmaking–South Beach, Florida, Miami Beach, FL 33139. Offers acting for film (MFA); cinematography (MFA); documentary film (MFA); film and media production (MA); filmmaking (MFA); game design (MFA); photography (MFA); producing (MA, MFA); screenwriting (MA, MFA).

New York University, Tisch School of the Arts, Kanbar Institute of Film and Television, New York, NY 10012-1019. Offers MFA. *Faculty:* 19 full-time, 20 part-time/adjunct. *Students:* 115 full-time (55 women); includes 31 minority (12 Black or African American, non-Hispanic/Latino; 9 Asian, non-Hispanic/Latino; 6 Hispanic/Latino; 4 Two or more races, non-Hispanic/Latino), 52 international. 747 applicants, 7% accepted, 38 enrolled. In 2017, 80 master's awarded. *Degree requirements:* For master's, 4 films. *Entrance requirements:* For master's, portfolio. *Application deadline:* For fall admission, 12/1 for domestic and international students. Application fee: $60. Electronic applications accepted. *Expenses: Tuition:* Full-time $41,352; part-time $19,968 per year. *Required fees:* $2496; $1628 per unit. $814 per term. Tuition and fees vary according to course load and program. *Financial support:* In 2017–18, 60 students received support. Fellowships, teaching assistantships, Federal Work-Study, institutionally sponsored loans, scholarships/grants, tuition waivers (full and partial), and unspecified assistantships available. Financial award application deadline: 2/15; financial award applicants required to submit FAFSA. *Unit head:* John Tintori, Chair, 212-998-1780, E-mail: jt42@nyu.edu. *Application contact:* Dan Sandford, Director of Graduate Admissions, 212-998-1918, Fax: 212-995-4060, E-mail: tisch.gradadmissions@nyu.edu.
Website: http://www.filmtv.tisch.nyu.edu/

New York University, Tisch School of the Arts, Program in Moving Image Archiving and Preservation, New York, NY 10012-1019. Offers MA. *Faculty:* 2 full-time, 4 part-time/adjunct. *Students:* 20 full-time (12 women); includes 4 minority (3 Hispanic/Latino; 1 Two or more races, non-Hispanic/Latino), 2 international. Average age 28. 36 applicants, 50% accepted, 10 enrolled. In 2017, 12 master's awarded. *Entrance requirements:* For master's, GRE. Application fee: $60. Electronic applications accepted. *Expenses: Tuition:* Full-time $41,352; part-time $19,968 per year. *Required fees:* $2496; $1628 per unit. $814 per term. Tuition and fees vary according to course load and program. *Financial support:* In 2017–18, 11 students received support. Fellowships and tuition waivers (partial) available. Financial award application deadline: 2/15. *Unit head:*

Richard Allen, Head, 212-998-1618. *Application contact:* Dan Sandford, Director of Graduate Admissions, 212-998-1918, Fax: 212-995-4060, E-mail: tisch.gradadmissions@nyu.edu.
Website: http://www.cinema.tisch.nyu.edu/

Northwestern University, The Graduate School, School of Communication, Department of Radio, Television and Film, Evanston, IL 60208. Offers documentary media (MFA); screen cultures (MA, PhD); writing for the screen and stage (MFA). Admissions and degrees offered through The Graduate School. *Program availability:* Part-time. Terminal master's awarded for partial completion of doctoral program. *Degree requirements:* For master's, comprehensive exam or thesis; for doctorate, thesis/dissertation, qualifying exam. *Entrance requirements:* For master's and doctorate, GRE General Test. Additional exam requirements/recommendations for international students: Required—TOEFL. Electronic applications accepted. *Faculty research:* Art and new media, media theory and criticism, gender, media history, documentary.

Ohio University, Graduate College, College of Fine Arts, School of Film, Athens, OH 45701-2979. Offers film (MFA); film studies (MA). *Degree requirements:* For master's, one foreign language, thesis. *Entrance requirements:* Additional exam requirements/recommendations for international students: Required—TOEFL (minimum score 550 paper-based; 80 iBT) or IELTS (minimum score 6.5). Electronic applications accepted. *Faculty research:* Scriptwriting, sound, editing, cinematography, film theory, digital post production.

Quinnipiac University, School of Communications, Program in Interactive Media and Communications, Hamden, CT 06518-1940. Offers interactive media (MS); media design (MS); social media (MS); UX design (MS). *Program availability:* Part-time, evening/weekend, online only, 100% online. *Faculty:* 2 full-time (1 woman), 10 part-time/adjunct (5 women). *Students:* 5 full-time (3 women), 74 part-time (51 women); includes 23 minority (13 Black or African American, non-Hispanic/Latino; 2 Asian, non-Hispanic/Latino; 6 Hispanic/Latino; 2 Two or more races, non-Hispanic/Latino). 50 applicants, 86% accepted, 38 enrolled. In 2017, 48 master's awarded. *Entrance requirements:* For master's, minimum GPA of 3.0, portfolio or writing sample. Additional exam requirements/recommendations for international students: Required—TOEFL (minimum score 575 paper-based; 90 iBT), IELTS (minimum score 6.5). *Application deadline:* For fall admission, 7/30 priority date for domestic students, 4/30 priority date for international students; for spring admission, 12/30 priority date for domestic students, 9/30 priority date for international students. Applications are processed on a rolling basis. Application fee: $45. Electronic applications accepted. *Expenses:* Contact institution. *Financial support:* Federal Work-Study and unspecified assistantships available. Financial award application deadline: 6/1; financial award applicants required to submit FAFSA. *Faculty research:* User experience, social media, semiotics and communication, online distribution of news, Web-based interventions for research. *Unit head:* Phillip Simon, Director, 203-582-8274, E-mail: phillip.simon@qu.edu. *Application contact:* Quinnipiac University Online Admissions Office, 800-462-1944, E-mail: quonlineadmissions@qu.edu.
Website: https://quonline.quinnipiac.edu/online-programs/online-graduate-programs/ms-in-interactive-media/

Regent University, Graduate School, School of Communication and the Arts, Virginia Beach, VA 23464-9800. Offers acting (MFA); communication (MA, PhD), including media and arts management and promotion (MA), political communication (MA), strategic communication (MA), technical communication (MA); film and TV (MA), including producing (MA, MFA), production, script writing; film-television (MFA), including directing, producing (MA, MFA), script and screenwriting; journalism (MA); theatre (MA). *Program availability:* Part-time, evening/weekend, 100% online, blended/hybrid learning. *Faculty:* 15 full-time (2 women), 66 part-time/adjunct (23 women). *Students:* 101 full-time (65 women), 342 part-time (237 women); includes 177 minority (127 Black or African American, non-Hispanic/Latino; 4 American Indian or Alaska Native, non-Hispanic/Latino; 9 Asian, non-Hispanic/Latino; 25 Hispanic/Latino; 12 Two or more races, non-Hispanic/Latino), 11 international. Average age 37. 498 applicants, 36% accepted, 124 enrolled. In 2017, 93 master's, 22 doctorates awarded. *Degree requirements:* For master's, thesis or alternative; for doctorate, thesis/dissertation. *Entrance requirements:* For master's, transcripts, writing sample, resume, audition (for MFA programs); for doctorate, GRE General Test, resume, writing sample, recommendations, interview, transcripts, personal goals statement. Additional exam requirements/recommendations for international students: Required—TOEFL (minimum score 577 paper-based). *Application deadline:* For fall admission, 3/1 priority date for domestic students; for spring admission, 10/1 priority date for domestic students. Applications are processed on a rolling basis. Application fee: $50. Electronic applications accepted. *Expenses:* $650 per credit (MA, MFA); $885 per credit (PhD); $300 per semester technology fee. *Financial support:* In 2017–18, 234 students received support, including 2 fellowships (averaging $10,000 per year); career-related internships or fieldwork, scholarships/grants, and unspecified assistantships also available. Support available to part-time students. *Faculty research:* Screenwriting, digital media production, communication, acting, directing. *Unit head:* Dr. Robert Herron, Dean, 757-352-4500, E-mail: rherron@regent.edu. *Application contact:* Heidi Cece, Assistant Vice President of Enrollment Management, 800-373-5504, Fax: 757-352-4381, E-mail: admissions@regent.edu.
Website: https://www.regent.edu/school-of-communication-and-the-arts/

Rochester Institute of Technology, Graduate Enrollment Services, College of Imaging Arts and Sciences, School of Film and Animation, MFA Program in Film and Animation, Rochester, NY 14623. Offers MFA. *Program availability:* Part-time. *Students:* 41 full-time (19 women), 12 part-time (6 women); includes 3 minority (1 Asian, non-Hispanic/Latino; 2 Hispanic/Latino), 33 international. Average age 26. 116 applicants, 14% accepted, 11 enrolled. In 2017, 4 master's awarded. *Degree requirements:* For master's, thesis. *Entrance requirements:* For master's, GRE, portfolio, minimum GPA of 3.0 (recommended). Additional exam requirements/recommendations for international students: Required—TOEFL (minimum score 550 paper-based; 82 iBT), IELTS (minimum score 6.5), PTE (minimum score 58). *Application deadline:* For fall admission, 2/15 priority date for domestic and international students. Applications are processed on a rolling basis. Application fee: $65. Electronic applications accepted. *Expenses:* $1,815 per credit hour. *Financial support:* In 2017–18, 31 students received support. Teaching assistantships with partial tuition reimbursements available, career-related internships or fieldwork, scholarships/grants, and unspecified assistantships available. Support available to part-time students. Financial award applicants required to submit FAFSA. *Faculty research:* 3-D printing, super 8 cameras, color and projection, gaming and storytelling, special effects including virtual reality. *Unit head:* Thomas Gasek, Graduate Program Director, 585-475-7403, E-mail: tdgpph@rit.edu. *Application contact:* Diane Ellison, Senior Associate Vice President, Graduate Enrollment Services, 585-475-2229, Fax: 585-475-7164, E-mail: gradinfo@rit.edu.
Website: http://cias.rit.edu/schools/film-animation/graduate-film-and-animation

Rochester Institute of Technology, Graduate Enrollment Services, College of Imaging Arts and Sciences, School of Photographic Arts and Sciences, MFA Program in Photography and Related Media, Rochester, NY 14623-5603. Offers MFA. *Accreditation:* NASAD. *Program availability:* Part-time. *Students:* 15 full-time (8 women), 1 (woman) part-time; includes 5 minority (1 Asian, non-Hispanic/Latino; 3 Hispanic/Latino; 1 Two or more races, non-Hispanic/Latino), 6 international. Average age 28. 63 applicants, 40% accepted, 9 enrolled. In 2017, 5 master's awarded. *Degree requirements:* For master's, thesis, exhibit. *Entrance requirements:* For master's, GRE, portfolio, minimum GPA of 3.0 (recommended). Additional exam requirements/recommendations for international students: Required—TOEFL (minimum score 550 paper-based; 90 iBT), IELTS (minimum score 6.5), PTE (minimum score 58). *Application deadline:* For fall admission, 2/15 priority date for domestic and international students. Applications are processed on a rolling basis. Application fee: $65. Electronic applications accepted. *Expenses:* $1,815 per credit hour. *Financial support:* In 2017–18, 14 students received support. Teaching assistantships with partial tuition reimbursements available, career-related internships or fieldwork, scholarships/grants, and unspecified assistantships available. Support available to part-time students. Financial award applicants required to submit FAFSA. *Faculty research:* Histories and theories of photography, contemporary art, American art and visual culture, and critical theory; photo books, visual narrative and expanded/experimental forms of documentary; contemporary fine art photography practice as personal document; public space, social practice, sensory observation, walking and mapping; relationship between the constructed image, photography as object, and fiction in contemporary practice. *Unit head:* Christine Shank, Graduate Program Director, 585-475-2616, Fax: 585-475-5804, E-mail: crspph@rit.edu. *Application contact:* Diane Ellison, Senior Associate Vice President, Graduate Enrollment Services, 585-475-2229, Fax: 585-475-7164, E-mail: gradinfo@rit.edu.
Website: http://cias.rit.edu/schools/photographic-arts-sciences/graduate-imaging-arts

Sacred Heart University, Graduate Programs, College of Arts and Sciences, Department of Communication, Fairfield, CT 06825. Offers corporate communications and public relations (MA Comm); digital multimedia journalism (MA Comm); digital multimedia production (MA Comm); film and television production (MA); media literacy and digital culture (MA), including children, health and media, media and social justice, political action and media production; sports communication and media (MA), including athletic communications and promotions, sports broadcasting. *Program availability:* Part-time, evening/weekend. *Faculty:* 9 full-time (1 woman), 6 part-time/adjunct (1 woman). *Students:* 70 full-time (36 women), 52 part-time (28 women); includes 36 minority (18 Black or African American, non-Hispanic/Latino; 16 Hispanic/Latino; 2 Two or more races, non-Hispanic/Latino), 20 international. Average age 26. 155 applicants, 89% accepted, 66 enrolled. In 2017, 71 master's awarded. *Degree requirements:* For master's, thesis or alternative. *Entrance requirements:* For master's, bachelor's degree. Additional exam requirements/recommendations for international students: Required—TOEFL (minimum score 570 paper-based, 80 iBT), TWE, or IELTS (6.5). *Application deadline:* Applications are processed on a rolling basis. Application fee: $75. Electronic applications accepted. *Expenses:* Contact institution. *Financial support:* Unspecified assistantships available. Financial award applicants required to submit FAFSA. *Unit head:* Dr. Andrew Miller, Director of Graduate Programs, 203-396-8087, E-mail: millera@sacredheart.edu. *Application contact:* Pam Pillo, Executive Director of Graduate Admissions, 203-365-7619, Fax: 203-365-4732, E-mail: graduatestudies@sacredheart.edu.
Website: http://www.sacredheart.edu/academics/collegeofartssciences/academicdepartments/communicationmediastudies/

St. Thomas University, School of Leadership Studies, Program in Electronic Media, Miami Gardens, FL 33054-6459. Offers MA.

San Diego State University, Graduate and Research Affairs, College of Professional Studies and Fine Arts, School of Theater, Television and Film, Program in Television, Film, and New Media Production, San Diego, CA 92182. Offers MA. *Entrance requirements:* For master's, GRE General Test, 3 letters of recommendation, resume, sample reel, influential book list, influential films list, hobby list. Additional exam requirements/recommendations for international students: Required—TOEFL. Electronic applications accepted. *Faculty research:* Experimental film and television programs, documentary film, television research and production.

San Francisco State University, Division of Graduate Studies, College of Liberal and Creative Arts, School of Cinema, San Francisco, CA 94132-1722. Offers MA, MFA. *Unit head:* Dr. Britta Sjogren, Director, 415-338-1629, Fax: 415-338-0906, E-mail: cinedept@sfsu.edu. *Application contact:* Dr. R. L. Rutsky, MA Coordinator, 415-405-3400, Fax: 415-338-0906, E-mail: rlrutsky@sfsu.edu.
Website: http://www.cinema.sfsu.edu/

Savannah College of Art and Design, Program in Animation, Savannah, GA 31402-3146. Offers MA, MFA. *Program availability:* Part-time, 100% online. *Faculty:* 32 full-time (6 women), 6 part-time/adjunct (3 women). *Students:* 207 full-time (111 women), 72 part-time (38 women); includes 49 minority (29 Black or African American, non-Hispanic/Latino; 8 Asian, non-Hispanic/Latino; 12 Hispanic/Latino), 123 international. Average age 26. 220 applicants, 53% accepted, 64 enrolled. In 2017, 51 master's awarded. *Degree requirements:* For master's, final project (for MA); thesis (for MFA). *Entrance requirements:* For master's, GRE (recommended), portfolio (submitted in digital format), audition or writing submission, resume, statement of purpose, two letters of recommendation. Additional exam requirements/recommendations for international students: Recommended—TOEFL (minimum score 550 paper-based; 85 iBT), IELTS (minimum score 6.5). *Application deadline:* For fall admission, 4/1 for domestic and international students. Applications are processed on a rolling basis. Application fee: $40. Electronic applications accepted. *Expenses: Tuition:* Full-time $36,765; part-time $817 per credit hour. One-time fee: $500. *Financial support:* Career-related internships or fieldwork, Federal Work-Study, and scholarships/grants available. Financial award application deadline: 4/1; financial award applicants required to submit FAFSA. *Unit head:* Greg Araya, Chair, Animation. *Application contact:* Jenny Jaquillard, Executive Director of Admissions, Recruitment and Events, 912-525-5100, Fax: 912-525-5985, E-mail: admission@scad.edu.
Website: http://www.scad.edu/academics/programs/animation

Savannah College of Art and Design, Program in Film and Television, Savannah, GA 31402-3146. Offers MA, MFA. *Program availability:* Part-time. *Faculty:* 14 full-time (2 women), 5 part-time/adjunct (2 women). *Students:* 170 full-time (76 women), 31 part-time (13 women); includes 70 minority (58 Black or African American, non-Hispanic/Latino; 2 American Indian or Alaska Native, non-Hispanic/Latino; 3 Asian, non-Hispanic/Latino; 7 Hispanic/Latino), 89 international. Average age 26. 266 applicants, 66% accepted, 85 enrolled. In 2017, 45 master's awarded. *Degree requirements:* For master's, final project (for MA); thesis (for MFA). *Entrance requirements:* For master's, GRE (recommended), portfolio (submitted in digital format), audition or writing submission, resume, statement of purpose, two letters of recommendation. Additional exam requirements/recommendations for international students: Recommended—TOEFL (minimum score 550 paper-based; 85 iBT), IELTS (minimum score 6.5). *Application deadline:* For fall admission, 4/1 for domestic and international students. Applications are processed on a rolling basis. Application fee: $40. Electronic applications accepted. *Expenses: Tuition:* Full-time $36,765; part-time $817 per credit hour. One-time fee: $500. *Financial support:* Career-related internships or fieldwork, Federal Work-Study, and scholarships/grants available. Financial award application deadline: 4/1; financial award applicants required to submit FAFSA. *Unit head:* Donald Moffett, Chair, Film and Television. *Application contact:* Jenny Jaquillard, Executive

Director of Admissions, Recruitment and Events, 912-525-5100, Fax: 912-525-5985, E-mail: admission@scad.edu.
Website: http://www.scad.edu/academics/programs/film-and-television

Savannah College of Art and Design, Program in Sound Design, Savannah, GA 31402-3146. Offers MA, MFA. *Program availability:* Part-time. *Faculty:* 7 full-time (0 women), 2 part-time/adjunct (0 women). *Students:* 30 full-time (9 women), 2 part-time (1 woman); includes 9 minority (5 Black or African American, non-Hispanic/Latino; 2 Asian, non-Hispanic/Latino; 2 Hispanic/Latino), 12 international. Average age 24. 34 applicants, 62% accepted, 12 enrolled. In 2017, 15 master's awarded. *Degree requirements:* For master's, final project (for MA); thesis (for MFA). *Entrance requirements:* For master's, GRE (recommended), portfolio (submitted in digital format), audition or writing submission, resume, statement of purpose, two letters of recommendation. Additional exam requirements/recommendations for international students: Recommended—TOEFL (minimum score 550 paper-based; 85 iBT), IELTS (minimum score 6.5). *Application deadline:* For fall admission, 4/1 for domestic and international students. Applications are processed on a rolling basis. Application fee: $40. Electronic applications accepted. *Expenses: Tuition:* Full-time $36,765; part-time $817 per credit hour. One-time fee: $500. *Financial support:* Career-related internships or fieldwork, Federal Work-Study, and scholarships/grants available. Financial award application deadline: 4/1; financial award applicants required to submit FAFSA. *Unit head:* Robin Beauchamp, Chair, Sound Design. *Application contact:* Jenny Jaquillard, Executive Director of Admissions, Recruitment and Events, 912-525-5100, Fax: 912-525-5985, E-mail: admission@scad.edu.
Website: http://www.scad.edu/academics/programs/sound-design

School of the Art Institute of Chicago, Graduate Division, Department of Film, Video, and New Media, Chicago, IL 60603-3103. Offers MFA. *Accreditation:* NASAD. *Degree requirements:* For master's, thesis exhibit. *Entrance requirements:* Additional exam requirements/recommendations for international students: Required—TOEFL (minimum score 550 paper-based; 80 iBT), IELTS (minimum score 6.5). Electronic applications accepted.

School of the Art Institute of Chicago, Graduate Division, Department of Sound, Chicago, IL 60603-3103. Offers MFA. *Entrance requirements:* Additional exam requirements/recommendations for international students: Required—TOEFL, IELTS.

School of Visual Arts, Graduate Programs, Directing Department, New York, NY 10010-3994. Offers MPS. *Degree requirements:* For master's, thesis, 36 credits, including all required courses; minimum GPA of 3.0; completion and marketing of his or her thesis film. *Entrance requirements:* For master's, portfolio. Additional exam requirements/recommendations for international students: Required—TOEFL (minimum score 550 paper-based; 79 iBT).

School of Visual Arts, Graduate Programs, Program in Photography, Video and Related Media, New York, NY 10010-3994. Offers MFA. *Accreditation:* NASAD. *Degree requirements:* For master's, thesis, 60 credits and all course requirements; minimum GPA of 3.3; thesis project. *Entrance requirements:* For master's, portfolio (still images and/or videos) through SlideRoom. Additional exam requirements/recommendations for international students: Required—TOEFL (minimum score 550 paper-based; 79 iBT). Electronic applications accepted. *Faculty research:* Contemporary and responsible creative initiatives, including experimental, narrative or documentary video, installation and conceptual art, tableau and real-world-witness photography.

School of Visual Arts, Graduate Programs, Social Documentary Film Department, New York, NY 10010-3994. Offers MFA. *Degree requirements:* For master's, thesis, 60 credits, including all required courses; minimum cumulative GPA of 3.0; residency of two academic years. *Entrance requirements:* For master's, concise treatment for documentary film production; video work or still imagery; visual documentation of a subject (for applicants without prior filmmaking experience). Additional exam requirements/recommendations for international students: Required—TOEFL (minimum score 550 paper-based; 79 iBT). Electronic applications accepted. *Expenses:* Contact institution.

Stanford University, School of Humanities and Sciences, Department of Art and Art History, Stanford, CA 94305-2004. Offers art history (PhD); art practice (MFA); design (MFA); documentary film and video (MFA); MS/MFA. *Degree requirements:* For master's, thesis (for some programs), faculty reviews; for doctorate, 2 foreign languages, thesis/dissertation. *Entrance requirements:* For master's and doctorate, GRE General Test. Additional exam requirements/recommendations for international students: Required—TOEFL. Electronic applications accepted. *Expenses: Tuition:* Full-time $48,987; part-time $10,620 per quarter. One-time fee: $400. Tuition and fees vary according to program.

Stevens Institute of Technology, Graduate School, Charles V. Schaefer Jr. School of Engineering and Science, Interdisciplinary Program in Media and Broadcast Engineering, Hoboken, NJ 07030. Offers MS. *Students:* 3 applicants, 33% accepted. *Degree requirements:* For master's, thesis optional, minimum B average in major field and overall. *Entrance requirements:* Additional exam requirements/recommendations for international students: Required—TOEFL (minimum score 74 iBT), IELTS (minimum score 6). *Application deadline:* For fall admission, 6/1 for domestic students, 4/15 for international students; for spring admission, 11/30 for domestic students, 11/1 for international students. *Expenses: Tuition:* Full-time $34,494; part-time $1554 per credit. *Required fees:* $291 per semester. *Unit head:* Dr. Keith G. Sheppard, Interim Dean, 201-216-5263. *Application contact:* Graduate Admissions, 888-783-8367, Fax: 888-555-1306, E-mail: graduate@stevens.edu.

Stony Brook University, State University of New York, Stony Brook Southampton, Program in Film, Stony Brook, NY 11794. Offers MFA. *Students:* 22 full-time (15 women), 18 part-time (8 women); includes 5 minority (2 Asian, non-Hispanic/Latino; 3 Hispanic/Latino), 1 international. 35 applicants, 71% accepted, 16 enrolled. In 2017, 1 master's awarded. *Entrance requirements:* Additional exam requirements/recommendations for international students: Required—TOEFL (minimum score 85 iBT), IELTS (minimum score 6.5). *Application deadline:* For fall admission, 1/15 for domestic students; for spring admission, 10/1 for domestic students. Application fee: $100. *Expenses:* Contact institution. *Unit head:* Magdalene Brandeis, Director, 631-632-5030, Fax: 631-982-7318, E-mail: magdalene.brandeis@stonybrook.edu. *Application contact:* Margaret S. Grigonis, Administrative Coordinator, 631-632-5028, Fax: 631-982-7318, E-mail: margaret.grigonis@stonybrook.edu.
Website: http://www.stonybrook.edu/southampton/mfa/film/index.html

Syracuse University, College of Visual and Performing Arts, MFA Program in Film, Syracuse, NY 13244. Offers MFA. *Degree requirements:* For master's, thesis or alternative. *Entrance requirements:* For master's, portfolio, artist statement, three letters of recommendation, academic transcripts, personal statement/essay, resume. Additional exam requirements/recommendations for international students: Required—TOEFL (minimum score 100 iBT). *Application deadline:* For fall admission, 2/1 priority date for domestic and international students. Application fee: $75. Electronic applications accepted. *Financial support:* Fellowships with full tuition reimbursements and teaching assistantships with tuition reimbursements available. Financial award application deadline: 1/1; financial award applicants required to submit FAFSA. *Faculty research:* Film production, global cinema, historical, artistic, and international film

contexts. *Unit head:* Owen Shapiro, Professor/Film Program Coordinator, 315-443-2214, E-mail: ojshapir@syr.edu. *Application contact:* Caitlin Jarvis, Graduate Recruitment Specialist, 315-443-2769, E-mail: admissg@syr.edu.
Website: http://vpa.syr.edu/academics/transmedia/graduate/film/

Temple University, Center for the Performing and Cinematic Arts, School of Theater, Film and Media Arts, Department of Film and Media Arts, Philadelphia, PA 19122. Offers MA, MFA. *Program availability:* Part-time. *Faculty:* 17 full-time (6 women), 19 part-time/adjunct (6 women). *Students:* 33 full-time (17 women), 6 part-time (3 women); includes 10 minority (7 Black or African American, non-Hispanic/Latino; 1 Asian, non-Hispanic/Latino; 2 Two or more races, non-Hispanic/Latino), 10 international. 59 applicants, 56% accepted, 19 enrolled. In 2017, 20 master's awarded. *Degree requirements:* For master's, comprehensive exam, project. *Entrance requirements:* For master's, minimum GPA of 3.0; exhibit. Additional exam requirements/recommendations for international students: Required—TOEFL (minimum score 600 paper-based; 100 iBT). *Application deadline:* For fall admission, 2/2 for domestic and international students. Application fee: $60. Electronic applications accepted. *Expenses:* Contact institution. *Financial support:* Fellowships, research assistantships, teaching assistantships, Federal Work-Study, institutionally sponsored loans, and unspecified assistantships available. Financial award application deadline: 3/1; financial award applicants required to submit FAFSA. *Faculty research:* Documentary/experimental film, narrative film, digital media arts, film and media studies, screenwriting. *Unit head:* Jeffrey Rush, Chair, 215-204-3859, Fax: 215-204-5280, E-mail: film@temple.edu. *Application contact:* Leah Dempsey, Assistant Director for Administration, 215-204-8791, E-mail: leahdempsey@temple.edu.
Website: https://tfma.temple.edu/fma

Universidad Autonoma de Guadalajara, Graduate Programs, Guadalajara, Mexico. Offers administrative law and justice (LL M); advertising and corporate communications (MA); architecture (M Arch); business (MBA); computational science (MCC); education (Ed M, Ed D); English-Spanish translation (MA); entrepreneurship and management (MBA); integrated management of digital animation (MA); international business (MIB); international corporate law (LL M); internet technologies (MS); manufacturing systems (MMS); occupational health (MS); philosophy (MA, PhD); power electronics (MS); quality systems (MQS); renewable energy (MS); social evaluation of projects (MBA); strategic market research (MBA); tax law (MA); teaching mathematics (MA).

The University of British Columbia, Faculty of Arts, Creative Writing Program, Vancouver, BC V6T 1Z1, Canada. Offers creative writing (MFA); creative writing and theatre (MFA); film production and creative writing (MFA). *Program availability:* Part-time, online learning. *Degree requirements:* For master's, thesis. *Entrance requirements:* For master's, sample of written work. Additional exam requirements/recommendations for international students: Required—TOEFL. Electronic applications accepted. *Expenses:* Contact institution. *Faculty research:* Writing of fiction; poetry; creative nonfiction, plays for stage, screen, television, radio, writing for children and translation, song lyrics and libretto, new media and graphic novel.

The University of British Columbia, Faculty of Arts and Faculty of Graduate Studies, Department of Theatre and Film, Film Program, Vancouver, BC V6T 1Z2, Canada. Offers film production (MFA); film studies (MA). *Degree requirements:* For master's, variable foreign language requirement, comprehensive exam, thesis (MA); thesis or project (MFA). *Entrance requirements:* For master's, portfolio (MFA). Additional exam requirements/recommendations for international students: Required—TOEFL. *Expenses:* Contact institution. *Faculty research:* Film theory and violence; American and European cinema; cult cinema; Irish cinema.

University of California, Los Angeles, Graduate Division, School of Theater, Film and Television, Department of Film, Television, and Digital Media, Los Angeles, CA 90034. Offers animation (MFA); cinema and media studies (MA, PhD); cinematography (MFA); production (MFA); screenwriting (MFA). *Degree requirements:* For master's, comprehensive exam; for doctorate, one foreign language, thesis/dissertation, oral and written qualifying exams. *Entrance requirements:* For master's, GRE General Test (for MA applicants), bachelor's degree; minimum undergraduate GPA of 3.0 (or its equivalent if letter grade system not used); writing sample (for MA); for doctorate, GRE General Test, master's degree; minimum undergraduate GPA of 3.0 (or its equivalent if letter grade system not used); writing sample. Additional exam requirements/recommendations for international students: Required—TOEFL. Electronic applications accepted. *Expenses:* Contact institution.

University of California, Los Angeles, Graduate Division, School of Theater, Film and Television, Interdepartmental Program in Moving Image Archive Studies, Los Angeles, CA 90095. Offers MA. *Degree requirements:* For master's, comprehensive exam, thesis. *Entrance requirements:* For master's, bachelor's degree; minimum undergraduate GPA of 3.0 (or its equivalent if letter grade system not used); writing sample. Additional exam requirements/recommendations for international students: Required—TOEFL. Electronic applications accepted.

University of California, Santa Barbara, Graduate Division, College of Letters and Sciences, Division of Humanities and Fine Arts, Department of Film and Media Studies, Santa Barbara, CA 93106-4010. Offers PhD, MA/PhD. Terminal master's awarded for partial completion of doctoral program. *Degree requirements:* For doctorate, one foreign language, comprehensive exam, thesis/dissertation. *Entrance requirements:* For doctorate, GRE, MA in film/media studies or equivalent. Additional exam requirements/recommendations for international students: Required—TOEFL (minimum score 600 paper-based; 100 iBT), IELTS (minimum score 7). Electronic applications accepted. *Faculty research:* Classical film theory, film and television history, historiography, cultural studies, global media, media industries, regulation and policy.

University of Central Arkansas, Graduate School, College of Fine Arts and Communication, Program in Digital Filmmaking, Conway, AR 72035-0001. Offers MFA. *Accreditation:* NASAD. *Degree requirements:* For master's, thesis. *Entrance requirements:* For master's, GRE General Test, minimum GPA of 2.7. Additional exam requirements/recommendations for international students: Required—TOEFL (minimum score 550 paper-based). Electronic applications accepted.

University of Central Florida, College of Arts and Humanities, School of Visual Arts and Design, Orlando, FL 32816. Offers digital media (MA); emerging media (MFA), including animation and visual effects, digital media, entrepreneurial digital cinema, studio art and the computer. *Program availability:* Part-time. *Students:* 38 full-time (13 women), 9 part-time (3 women); includes 16 minority (6 Black or African American, non-Hispanic/Latino; 2 Asian, non-Hispanic/Latino; 8 Hispanic/Latino), 3 international. Average age 30. 61 applicants, 54% accepted, 20 enrolled. In 2017, 8 master's awarded. *Degree requirements:* For master's, comprehensive exam, thesis or alternative. *Entrance requirements:* For master's, GRE, letter of recommendation. Additional exam requirements/recommendations for international students: Required—TOEFL. *Application deadline:* For fall admission, 7/1 for domestic students. Application fee: $30. Electronic applications accepted. *Expenses:* Tuition, state resident: part-time $288.16 per credit hour. Tuition, nonresident: part-time $1073.31 per credit hour. Tuition and fees vary according to program. *Financial support:* In 2017–18, 17 students received support, including 7 fellowships with partial tuition reimbursements available (averaging $10,000 per year), 3 research assistantships with partial tuition reimbursements available (averaging $6,355 per year), 15 teaching assistantships with

partial tuition reimbursements available (averaging $8,208 per year); scholarships/grants, health care benefits, and unspecified assistantships also available. Financial award application deadline: 3/1; financial award applicants required to submit FAFSA. *Unit head:* Dr. Rudy McDaniel, Director, 407-823-3145, E-mail: rudy@ucf.edu. *Application contact:* Associate Director, Graduate Admissions, 407-823-2766, Fax: 407-823-6442, E-mail: gradadmissions@ucf.edu.
Website: http://svad.cah.ucf.edu/

University of Colorado Boulder, Graduate School, College of Media, Communication and Information, Program in Critical Media Practices, Boulder, CO 80309. Offers interdisciplinary documentary media practices (MFA). *Faculty:* 5 full-time (3 women). *Students:* 7 full-time (3 women), 1 international. Average age 32. 31 applicants, 16% accepted, 3 enrolled. *Application deadline:* For fall admission, 1/10 for domestic students; for spring admission, 12/1 for domestic students. Application fee: $60 ($80 for international students). Electronic applications accepted. Application fee is waived when completed online. *Financial support:* In 2017–18, 23 students received support, including 5 fellowships (averaging $1,444 per year), 7 teaching assistantships with full and partial tuition reimbursements available (averaging $36,645 per year); research assistantships, institutionally sponsored loans, scholarships/grants, health care benefits, and unspecified assistantships also available. Financial award application deadline: 2/15; financial award applicants required to submit FAFSA. *Faculty research:* Cinema/video; inter-arts—interdisciplinary art forms; media arts; visual arts; arts/humanities/cultural activities. *Application contact:* E-mail: cmci.dcmp@colorado.edu.
Website: http://www.colorado.edu/cmci/academics/critical-media-practices

The University of Iowa, Graduate College, College of Liberal Arts and Sciences, Department of Cinema and Comparative Literature, Program in Film and Video Production, Iowa City, IA 52242-1316. Offers MFA. *Degree requirements:* For master's, thesis (for some programs), exam. *Entrance requirements:* For master's, GRE General Test, minimum GPA of 3.0. Additional exam requirements/recommendations for international students: Required—TOEFL (minimum score 550 paper-based; 81 iBT). Electronic applications accepted.

University of Memphis, Graduate School, College of Communication and Fine Arts, Department of Communication, Memphis, TN 38152. Offers communication (MA); communication arts (PhD); film and video production (MA). *Program availability:* Part-time. *Faculty:* 13 full-time (6 women). *Students:* 18 full-time (11 women), 24 part-time (11 women); includes 11 minority (8 Black or African American, non-Hispanic/Latino; 3 Two or more races, non-Hispanic/Latino), 2 international. Average age 36. 19 applicants, 79% accepted, 9 enrolled. In 2017, 3 master's, 3 doctorates awarded. *Degree requirements:* For master's, comprehensive exam, thesis or alternative, culminating project; for doctorate, comprehensive exam, thesis/dissertation. *Entrance requirements:* For master's and doctorate, GRE General Test, personal goal statement, letters of recommendation, writing sample. Additional exam requirements/recommendations for international students: Required—TOEFL (minimum score 600 paper-based). *Application deadline:* For fall admission, 1/13 priority date for domestic students. Applications are processed on a rolling basis. Application fee: $35 ($60 for international students). *Expenses:* Contact institution. *Financial support:* In 2017–18, 27 students received support, including 2 research assistantships with full tuition reimbursements available (averaging $12,000 per year), 17 teaching assistantships with full tuition reimbursements available (averaging $22,406 per year); Federal Work-Study, scholarships/grants, and unspecified assistantships also available. Financial award application deadline: 2/1; financial award applicants required to submit FAFSA. *Faculty research:* Rhetoric, media studies, applied communication (health communication). *Unit head:* Dr. Sandra Sarkela, Interim Department Chair, 901-678-2565, Fax: 901-678-4331, E-mail: ssarkela@memphis.edu. *Application contact:* Dr. Antonio de Velasco, Coordinator of Graduate Studies, 901-678-3185, Fax: 901-678-4331, E-mail: adevelsc@memphis.edu.
Website: http://www.memphis.edu/ccfa/index.php

University of Miami, Graduate School, School of Communication, Coral Gables, FL 33124. Offers communication (PhD); communication studies (MA); film studies (MA, PhD); motion pictures (MFA), including production, producing, and screenwriting; print journalism (MA); public relations (MA); Spanish language journalism (MA); television broadcast journalism (MA). *Program availability:* Part-time. *Degree requirements:* For master's, comprehensive exam (for some programs), thesis (for some programs); for doctorate, comprehensive exam, thesis/dissertation. *Entrance requirements:* For master's, GRE General Test; for doctorate, GRE General Test, master's thesis or scholarly research. Additional exam requirements/recommendations for international students: Required—TOEFL (minimum score 600 paper-based; 100 iBT). Electronic applications accepted. *Faculty research:* Communication studies, mass communication, international/interpersonal communication, film studies, journalism.

University of Mississippi, Graduate School, College of Liberal Arts, University, MS 38677. Offers anthropology (MA); biology (MS, PhD); chemistry (MS, DA, PhD); creative writing (MFA); documentary expression (MFA); economics (MA, PhD); English (MA, PhD); experimental psychology (PhD); history (MA, PhD); mathematics (MS, PhD); modern languages (MA); music (MM); philosophy (MA); physics (MA, MS, PhD); political science (MA, PhD); Southern studies (MA); studio art (MFA). *Program availability:* Part-time. *Faculty:* 465 full-time (207 women), 82 part-time/adjunct (46 women). *Students:* 466 full-time (229 women), 72 part-time (34 women); includes 87 minority (38 Black or African American, non-Hispanic/Latino; 18 Asian, non-Hispanic/Latino; 24 Hispanic/Latino; 7 Two or more races, non-Hispanic/Latino), 121 international. Average age 29. *Degree requirements:* For doctorate, thesis/dissertation. *Entrance requirements:* For master's, GRE General Test, minimum GPA of 3.0; for doctorate, GRE General Test. Additional exam requirements/recommendations for international students: Required—TOEFL. *Application deadline:* For fall admission, 2/1 priority date for domestic students; for spring admission, 10/1 for domestic students. Applications are processed on a rolling basis. Application fee: $50. Electronic applications accepted. *Financial support:* Fellowships, research assistantships, teaching assistantships, career-related internships or fieldwork, Federal Work-Study, institutionally sponsored loans, scholarships/grants, and unspecified assistantships available. Financial award application deadline: 3/1; financial award applicants required to submit FAFSA. *Unit head:* Dr. Lee Michael Cohen, Dean, 662-915-7177, Fax: 662-915-5792, E-mail: libarts@olemiss.edu. *Application contact:* Dr. Christy M. Wyandt, Associate Dean of Graduate School, 662-915-7474, Fax: 662-915-7577, E-mail: cwyandt@olemiss.edu.

University of Montana, Graduate School, College of Visual and Performing Arts, School of Media Arts, Missoula, MT 59812. Offers digital filmmaking (MFA); integrated digital media (MFA).

University of Nevada, Las Vegas, Graduate College, College of Fine Arts, Department of Film, Las Vegas, NV 89154-5015. Offers film/writing for dramatic media (MFA); writing for dramatic media (Certificate). *Program availability:* Part-time. *Faculty:* 2 full-time (0 women). *Students:* 8 full-time (6 women); includes 1 minority (Asian, non-Hispanic/Latino), 1 international. Average age 32. 5 applicants, 60% accepted, 3 enrolled. In 2017, 3 master's, 1 other advanced degree awarded. *Degree requirements:* For master's, thesis, creative project and defense; for Certificate, creative project and defense. *Entrance requirements:* For master's, writing sample. Additional exam requirements/recommendations for international students: Required—TOEFL (minimum score 550 paper-based; 80 iBT), IELTS (minimum score 7). *Application deadline:* For fall admission, 1/15 for domestic students. Application fee: $60 ($95 for international students). Electronic applications accepted. *Expenses:* $275 per credit, $850 per course, $7,969 per year resident, $22,157 per year non-resident, $7,094 non-resident fee (7 credits or more), $1,307 annual health insurance fee. *Financial support:* In 2017–18, 8 students received support, including 8 teaching assistantships with full tuition reimbursements available (averaging $15,250 per year); institutionally sponsored loans, scholarships/grants, health care benefits, and unspecified assistantships also available. Financial award application deadline: 3/15; financial award applicants required to submit FAFSA. *Faculty research:* Screenplay, stage play, television series, Web entertainment content, production. *Unit head:* Dr. Heather Addison, Chair/Professor, 702-895-3547, Fax: 702-895-4395, E-mail: heather.addison@unlv.edu. *Application contact:* Sean Clark, Graduate Coordinator, 702-895-2442, Fax: 702-895-4395, E-mail: sean.clark@unlv.edu.
Website: http://film.unlv.edu/

University of New Orleans, Graduate School, College of Liberal Arts, Department of Film and Theatre, New Orleans, LA 70148. Offers design (MFA); film production (MFA); theatre performance (MFA), including acting, directing. *Accreditation:* NAST. *Degree requirements:* For master's, comprehensive exam, thesis. *Entrance requirements:* Additional exam requirements/recommendations for international students: Required—TOEFL (minimum score 550 paper-based; 79 iBT), IELTS (minimum score 6.5). Electronic applications accepted. *Faculty research:* Mass communication theory, nineteenth and twentieth century theater history, film criticism and history.

The University of North Carolina at Greensboro, Graduate School, College of Arts and Sciences, Department of Media Studies, Greensboro, NC 27412-5001. Offers film and video production (MFA).

University of North Carolina School of the Arts, School of Filmmaking, Winston-Salem, NC 27127-2738. Offers creative producing (MFA); film music composition (MFA); screenwriting (MFA). *Entrance requirements:* For master's, audition, performance, portfolio, interview. Additional exam requirements/recommendations for international students: Required—TOEFL. Electronic applications accepted.

University of North Texas, Robert B. Toulouse School of Graduate Studies, Denton, TX 76203-5459. Offers accounting (MS); applied anthropology (MA, MS); applied behavior analysis (Certificate); applied geography (MA); applied technology and performance improvement (M Ed, MS); art education (MA); art history (MA); art museum education (Certificate); arts leadership (Certificate); audiology (Au D); behavior analysis (MS); behavioral science (PhD); biochemistry and molecular biology (MS); biology (MA, MS); biomedical engineering (MS); business analysis (MS); chemistry (MS); clinical health psychology (PhD); communication studies (MA, MS); computer engineering (MS); computer science (MS); counseling (M Ed, MS), including clinical mental health counseling (MS), college and university counseling, elementary school counseling, secondary school counseling; creative writing (MA); criminal justice (MS); curriculum and instruction (M Ed); decision sciences (MBA); design (MA, MFA), including fashion design (MFA), innovation studies, interior design (MFA); early childhood studies (MS); economics (MS); educational leadership (M Ed, Ed D); educational psychology (MS, PhD), including family studies (MS), gifted and talented (MS), human development (MS), learning and cognition (MS), research, measurement and evaluation (MS); electrical engineering (MS); emergency management (MPA); engineering technology (MS); English (MA); English as a second language (MA); environmental science (MS); finance (MBA, MS); financial management (MPA); French (MA); health services management (MBA); higher education (M Ed, Ed D); history (MA, MS); hospitality management (MS); human resources management (MPA); information science (MS); information systems (PhD); information technologies (MBA); interdisciplinary studies (MA, MS); international studies (MA); international sustainable tourism (MS); jazz studies (MM); journalism (MA, MJ, Graduate Certificate), including interactive and virtual digital communication (Graduate Certificate), narrative journalism (Graduate Certificate), public relations (Graduate Certificate); kinesiology (MS); linguistics (MA); local government management (MPA); logistics (PhD); logistics and supply chain management (MBA); long-term care, senior housing, and aging services (MA); management (PhD); marketing (MBA); mathematics (MA, MS); mechanical and energy engineering (MS, PhD); music (MA), including ethnomusicology, music theory, musicology, performance; music composition (PhD); music education (MM Ed, PhD); nonprofit management (MPA); operations and supply chain management (MBA); performance (MM, DMA); philosophy (MA); political science (MA); professional and technical communication (MA); radio, television and film (MA, MFA); rehabilitation counseling (Certificate); sociology (MA); Spanish (MA); special education (M Ed); speech-language pathology (MA); strategic management (MBA); studio art (MFA); teaching (M Ed); MBA/MS. *Program availability:* Part-time, evening/weekend, online learning. Terminal master's awarded for partial completion of doctoral program. *Degree requirements:* For master's, variable foreign language requirement, comprehensive exam (for some programs), thesis (for some programs); for doctorate, variable foreign language requirement, comprehensive exam (for some programs), thesis/dissertation; for other advanced degree, variable foreign language requirement, comprehensive exam (for some programs). *Entrance requirements:* For master's and doctorate, GRE, GMAT. Additional exam requirements/recommendations for international students: Required—TOEFL (minimum score 550 paper-based; 79 iBT). Electronic applications accepted.

University of Regina, Faculty of Graduate Studies and Research, Faculty of Media, Art, and Performance, Department of Film, Regina, SK S4S 0A2, Canada. Offers media production (MFA); media studies (MA). *Program availability:* Part-time. *Faculty:* 10 full-time (5 women). *Students:* 1 (woman) part-time. 14 applicants, 14% accepted. In 2017, 4 master's awarded. *Degree requirements:* For master's, thesis (for some programs). *Entrance requirements:* For master's, two writing samples (for MA); media-based support material (for MFA). Additional exam requirements/recommendations for international students: Required—TOEFL (minimum score 600 paper-based; 93 iBT), IELTS (minimum score 7), PTE (minimum score 59). *Application deadline:* For fall admission, 1/15 for domestic and international students. Applications are processed on a rolling basis. Application fee: $100. Electronic applications accepted. *Expenses:* CAD$10,681 per year. *Financial support:* In 2017–18, fellowships (averaging $6,000 per year), teaching assistantships (averaging $2,562 per year) were awarded; research assistantships and scholarships/grants also available. Financial award application deadline: 6/15. *Faculty research:* Dramatic, documentary, and experimental film and video; new and interactive media; animation through a range of artistic, aesthetic, technical, and theoretical skills and knowledge; general and specialized study in media arts production; media arts theory. *Unit head:* Dr. Gerald Saul, Department Head, 306-585-4691, E-mail: gerald.saul@uregina.ca. *Application contact:* Dr. Kathleen Irwin, Associate Dean, Graduate Studies and Research, 306-585-5519, E-mail: kathleen.irwin@uregina.ca.

University of Rhode Island, Graduate School, College of Arts and Sciences, Department of English, Kingston, RI 02881. Offers American literature and culture (PhD); British literature and culture (PhD); creative writing (PhD); critical theories (PhD); English (MA); film (PhD); gender studies (PhD); MLIS/MA. *Program availability:* Part-time. *Faculty:* 17 full-time (10 women). *Students:* 36 full-time (27 women), 7 part-time (4 women); includes 2 minority (both Black or African American, non-Hispanic/Latino), 7

international. 34 applicants, 65% accepted, 10 enrolled. In 2017, 4 master's, 8 doctorates awarded. *Entrance requirements:* Additional exam requirements/recommendations for international students: Required—TOEFL (minimum score 91 iBT). *Application deadline:* For fall admission, 1/15 for domestic and international students. Application fee: $65. Electronic applications accepted. *Expenses:* Tuition, state resident: full-time $12,706; part-time $786 per credit. Tuition, nonresident: full-time $25,216; part-time $1401 per credit. *Required fees:* $1598; $45 per credit. One-time fee: $30 part-time. *Financial support:* In 2017–18, 28 teaching assistantships with tuition reimbursements (averaging $17,158 per year) were awarded. Financial award application deadline: 1/15; financial award applicants required to submit FAFSA. *Unit head:* Dr. Travis Williams, Chair, 401-874-9501, E-mail: tdwilliams@uri.edu. *Application contact:* Dr. David Faflik, Director of Graduate Studies, 401-874-4670, E-mail: faflik@uri.edu.
Website: http://www.uri.edu/artsci/eng/

University of Southern California, Graduate School, School of Cinematic Arts, Division of Animation and Digital Arts, Los Angeles, CA 90089. Offers MFA. *Degree requirements:* For master's, thesis, digital media and research documentation. *Entrance requirements:* Additional exam requirements/recommendations for international students: Recommended—TOEFL. Electronic applications accepted. *Expenses:* Contact institution. *Faculty research:* Character animation, visual effects, motion graphics, documentary animation, experimental animation.

University of Southern California, Graduate School, School of Cinematic Arts, Division of Film and Television Production, Los Angeles, CA 90089. Offers MFA. Terminal master's awarded for partial completion of doctoral program. *Degree requirements:* For master's, advanced project. *Entrance requirements:* Additional exam requirements/recommendations for international students: Required—TOEFL (minimum score 600 paper-based). Electronic applications accepted. *Faculty research:* Documentary filmmaking, narrative filmmaking, initiatives related to health issues, science foundation project, global workshops in China.

University of Southern California, Graduate School, School of Cinematic Arts, The Peter Stark Producing Program, Los Angeles, CA 90089. Offers motion picture producing (MFA). *Degree requirements:* For master's, thesis, set curriculum, oral examination. *Entrance requirements:* For master's, GRE. Additional exam requirements/recommendations for international students: Required—TOEFL (minimum score 600 paper-based; 100 iBT), IELTS (minimum score 7). Electronic applications accepted.

University of Southern California, Graduate School, School of Cinematic Arts, Writing for Screen and Television Division, Los Angeles, CA 90089. Offers MFA. *Degree requirements:* For master's, thesis or alternative. *Entrance requirements:* For master's, GRE. Additional exam requirements/recommendations for international students: Required—TOEFL. Electronic applications accepted. *Faculty research:* Dramatic storytelling, new media content and distribution, television and film character development, theory of storytelling, interactive writing.

The University of Texas at Arlington, Graduate School, College of Liberal Arts, Department of Art and Art History, Arlington, TX 76019. Offers film and video (MFA); glass (MFA); intermedia (MFA); visual communication (MFA). *Accreditation:* NASAD. *Degree requirements:* For master's, thesis or alternative, mid- and final program reviews; exhibition. *Entrance requirements:* For master's, GRE, minimum GPA of 3.0, 3 letters of recommendation, portfolio, resume. Additional exam requirements/recommendations for international students: Required—TOEFL (minimum score 550 paper-based). Electronic applications accepted.

The University of Texas at Austin, Graduate School, College of Communication, Department of Radio-Television-Film, Austin, TX 78712-1111. Offers film and media production (MFA); media studies (MA, PhD); screenwriting (MFA). *Degree requirements:* For master's, thesis (for some programs); for doctorate, thesis/dissertation. *Entrance requirements:* For master's and doctorate, GRE General Test. Electronic applications accepted. *Faculty research:* International communication, film studies, media and culture, telecommunication and new media, gender and sexuality.

The University of Texas at Austin, Graduate School, Michener Center for Writers, Austin, TX 78712-1111. Offers fiction (MFA); playwriting (MFA); poetry (MFA); screenwriting (MFA). Electronic applications accepted.

University of the Sacred Heart, Graduate Programs, Department of Communication, San Juan, PR 00914-0383. Offers contemporary culture and media (MA); digital journalism (MA, Certificate); editing for media (MA, Certificate); public relations (MA, Certificate); publicity (MA, Certificate); scriptwriting (MA, Certificate). *Program availability:* Part-time, evening/weekend. *Degree requirements:* For master's, thesis.

University of Utah, Graduate School, College of Fine Arts, Film and Media Arts Department, Salt Lake City, UT 84112-0380. Offers MFA. *Program availability:* Part-time. *Faculty:* 8 full-time (4 women), 15 part-time/adjunct (5 women). *Students:* 18 full-time (10 women); includes 6 minority (1 Black or African American, non-Hispanic/Latino; 1 American Indian or Alaska Native, non-Hispanic/Latino; 1 Asian, non-Hispanic/Latino; 3 Hispanic/Latino), 3 international. Average age 22. 27 applicants, 15% accepted, 4 enrolled. In 2017, 4 master's awarded. *Entrance requirements:* For master's, minimum GPA of 3.0. Additional exam requirements/recommendations for international students: Required—TOEFL (minimum score 500 paper-based). *Application deadline:* For fall admission, 11/30 for domestic and international students. Application fee: $55 ($65 for international students). *Expenses:* $7,555.48. *Financial support:* In 2017–18, 17 students received support, including 1 research assistantship (averaging $3,750 per year), 17 teaching assistantships with full and partial tuition reimbursements available (averaging $10,588 per year); career-related internships or fieldwork, Federal Work-Study, institutionally sponsored loans, scholarships/grants, health care benefits, and unspecified assistantships also available. Financial award application deadline: 12/31; financial award applicants required to submit FAFSA. *Faculty research:* Film history, criticism, cultural studies, production of narrative and documentary films. *Unit head:* Prof. Kevin D. Hanson, Chair, 801-581-7428, Fax: 801-585-3192, E-mail: kevin.hanson@utah.edu. *Application contact:* Prof. Chris Lippard, Director of Graduate Studies, 801-585-9358, Fax: 801-585-3192, E-mail: chris.lippard@utah.edu.
Website: http://www.film.utah.edu

University of Victoria, Faculty of Graduate Studies, Faculty of Fine Arts, Department of Visual Arts, Victoria, BC V8W 2Y2, Canada. Offers digital multimedia (MFA); drawing (MFA); painting (MFA); photography (MFA); sculpture (MFA); video (MFA). *Degree requirements:* For master's, exhibit, oral exam. *Entrance requirements:* For master's, portfolio, BFA. Additional exam requirements/recommendations for international students: Required—TOEFL (minimum score 575 paper-based), IELTS (minimum score 7). Electronic applications accepted.

Vermont College of Fine Arts, MFA in Film Program, Montpelier, VT 05602. Offers MFA. *Faculty:* 7 part-time/adjunct (3 women). *Students:* 39 full-time (16 women); includes 8 minority (1 Black or African American, non-Hispanic/Latino; 1 American Indian or Alaska Native, non-Hispanic/Latino; 5 Hispanic/Latino; 1 Two or more races, non-Hispanic/Latino), 1 international. Average age 42. 15 applicants, 73% accepted, 8 enrolled. In 2017, 19 master's awarded. *Degree requirements:* For master's, thesis. *Entrance requirements:* For master's, bachelor's degree. *Application deadline:* For fall admission, 8/15 for domestic students; for spring admission, 2/15 for domestic students. Applications are processed on a rolling basis. Application fee: $75. Electronic applications accepted. *Expenses:* Contact institution. *Financial support:* In 2017–18, 35 students received support. Scholarships/grants available. Financial award application deadline: 6/15; financial award applicants required to submit FAFSA. *Unit head:* Stephen Pite, Director, 802-828-8529, E-mail: stephen.pite@vcfa.edu.
Website: http://www.vcfa.edu/film

Virginia Commonwealth University, Graduate School, School of the Arts, Richmond, VA 23284-9005. Offers art education (MAE, PhD); art history (MA, PhD), including curatorial (PhD), historical studies, museum studies (MA); ceramics (MFA); design (MFA), including interior environments, visual communications; fibers (MFA); furniture design (MFA); glassworking (MFA); jewelry/metalworking (MFA); kinetic imaging (MFA); music (MM), including music education; painting (MFA); photography and film (MFA); printmaking (MFA); sculpture (MFA); theatre (MFA), including costume design, pedagogy/literature, pedagogy/performance, scene design/technical theatre. *Program availability:* Part-time. *Entrance requirements:* For doctorate, GRE General Test, writing sample. Additional exam requirements/recommendations for international students: Required—TOEFL (minimum score 600 paper-based; 100 iBT). Electronic applications accepted.

Watkins College of Art, Design, & Film, Program in Film, Nashville, TN 37228. Offers MFA. *Program availability:* Evening/weekend. *Degree requirements:* For master's, thesis.

Western State Colorado University, Program in Creative Writing, Gunnison, CO 81231. Offers mainstream genre fiction (MFA); poetry (MFA); screenwriting (MFA). *Program availability:* Online learning. *Degree requirements:* For master's, thesis.

York University, Faculty of Graduate Studies, Faculty of Fine Arts, Program in Film, Toronto, ON M3J 1P3, Canada. Offers MA, MFA, PhD. *Degree requirements:* For master's, thesis. *Entrance requirements:* For master's, portfolio. Electronic applications accepted.

Film, Television, and Video Theory and Criticism

Brooklyn College of the City University of New York, School of Visual, Media and Performing Arts, Feirstein Graduate School of Cinema, Brooklyn, NY 11210-2889. Offers cinema arts (MFA); cinema studies (MA).

California College of the Arts, Graduate Programs, Visual and Critical Studies Program, San Francisco, CA 94107. Offers MA. *Faculty:* 2 full-time (both women), 3 part-time/adjunct (2 women). *Students:* 3 full-time (2 women); includes 2 minority (both Hispanic/Latino). Average age 40. 9 applicants, 100% accepted, 1 enrolled. In 2017, 1 master's awarded. *Degree requirements:* For master's, thesis. *Entrance requirements:* For master's, portfolio, resume, 2 letters of recommendation, transcripts, essay, interview. Additional exam requirements/recommendations for international students: Required—TOEFL, IELTS, or PTE. *Application deadline:* For fall admission, 1/31 priority date for domestic and international students. Applications are processed on a rolling basis. Application fee: $70. Electronic applications accepted. *Expenses:* $34,461 per year full-time tuition, $490 per year fees; $1,641 per unit part-time tuition. *Financial support:* Fellowships, teaching assistantships, career-related internships or fieldwork, Federal Work-Study, scholarships/grants, and health care benefits available. Financial award application deadline: 7/31; financial award applicants required to submit FAFSA. *Unit head:* Dr. Jacqueline Francis, Chair, E-mail: jfrancis@cca.edu. *Application contact:* Wes Fanelli, Assistant Director of Graduate Admissions, 415-703-9533, Fax: 415-703-9539, E-mail: wfanelli@cca.edu.
Website: https://www.cca.edu/academics/graduate/visual-critical-studies

Central Michigan University, College of Graduate Studies, College of Communication and Fine Arts, School of Broadcasting and Cinematic Arts, Mount Pleasant, MI 48859. Offers electronic media management (MA); electronic media production (MA); electronic media studies (MA); film theory and criticism (MA). *Program availability:* Part-time. *Degree requirements:* For master's, thesis or alternative. *Entrance requirements:* For master's, undergraduate degree in broadcasting, film studies, or an associated discipline with minimum GPA of 2.7. Electronic applications accepted. *Faculty research:* Multimedia production, film history and criticism, writing and promotions, international broadcasting and media systems, history of American broadcasting.

Claremont Graduate University, Graduate Programs, School of Arts and Humanities, Department of English, Claremont, CA 91711-6160. Offers American studies (MA, PhD); critical theory (MA, PhD); early modern studies (MA, PhD); English (M Phil, MA, PhD); literary theory (PhD); literature (MA, PhD); literature and creative writing (MA); literature and film (MA); MBA/MA; MBA/PhD. *Program availability:* Part-time. *Entrance requirements:* For master's and doctorate, GRE General Test. Additional exam requirements/recommendations for international students: Required—TOEFL (minimum score 75 iBT). Electronic applications accepted. *Faculty research:* American, comparative, and English Renaissance literature; modernism; feminist literature and theory.

College of Staten Island of the City University of New York, Graduate Programs, Division of Humanities and Social Sciences, Program in Cinema and Media Studies, Staten Island, NY 10314-6600. Offers MA. *Program availability:* Part-time, evening/weekend. *Faculty:* 3 full-time (all women). *Students:* 7. 12 applicants, 42% accepted, 2 enrolled. In 2017, 1 master's awarded. *Degree requirements:* For master's, comprehensive exam (for some programs), 36 credits in cinema and media studies courses; written thesis, production thesis, or examination. *Entrance requirements:* For master's, bachelor's degree with minimum B average in undergraduate cinema studies or communications courses; 10-12 page writing sample; three letters of recommendation; 1-2 page statement of intent detailing interest in the field, background in film and media studies, and/or research interests; three letters of recommendation. Additional exam requirements/recommendations for international students: Required—

TOEFL (minimum score 550 paper-based; 79 iBT), IELTS (minimum score 6.5). *Application deadline:* For fall admission, 6/15 priority date for domestic and international students; for spring admission, 11/25 priority date for domestic and international students. Applications are processed on a rolling basis. Application fee: $125. Electronic applications accepted. *Expenses:* Tuition, state resident: full-time $10,450; part-time $440 per credit. Tuition, nonresident: full-time $19,320; part-time $440 per credit. *Required fees:* $181.10 per semester. Tuition and fees vary according to program. *Faculty research:* Political communication, Latino/a media and audience, gender and sexuality, representation of race and ethnicity, video surveillance. *Unit head:* Dr. Edward Miller, Graduate Program Coordinator, 718-982-2474, E-mail: edward.miller@csi.cuny.edu. *Application contact:* Sasha Spence, Associate Director for Graduate Admissions, 718-982-2019, Fax: 718-982-2500, E-mail: sasha.spence@csi.cuny.edu.
Website: https://www.csi.cuny.edu/sites/default/files/pdf/admissions/grad/pdf/Cinema%20and%20Media%20Fact%20Sheet.pdf

Columbia University, School of the Arts, Film and Media Studies Program, New York, NY 10027. Offers MA. *Program availability:* Part-time. *Faculty:* 7 full-time (3 women), 3 part-time/adjunct (0 women). *Students:* 36 full-time (19 women); includes 6 minority (1 Black or African American, non-Hispanic/Latino; 2 Asian, non-Hispanic/Latino; 3 Hispanic/Latino), 17 international. Average age 25. 81 applicants, 52% accepted, 14 enrolled. In 2017, 17 master's awarded. Terminal master's awarded for partial completion of doctoral program. *Degree requirements:* For master's, thesis. *Entrance requirements:* Additional exam requirements/recommendations for international students: Required—TOEFL (minimum score 600 paper-based; 100 iBT). *Application deadline:* For fall admission, 2/1 for domestic and international students. Application fee: $110. Electronic applications accepted. *Expenses:* Contact institution. *Financial support:* In 2017–18, 1 student received support, including 2 teaching assistantships with full and partial tuition reimbursements available; fellowships, research assistantships, Federal Work-Study, and scholarships/grants also available. Financial award application deadline: 2/1; financial award applicants required to submit FAFSA. *Unit head:* Carol Becker, Dean, 212-854-9847. *Application contact:* Kenny Wong, Director of Admissions and Financial Aid, 212-854-2134, E-mail: admissions-arts@columbia.edu.
Website: https://arts.columbia.edu/film/ma

Concordia University, School of Graduate Studies, Faculty of Fine Arts, Mel Hoppenheim School of Cinema, Montréal, QC H3G 1M8, Canada. Offers film and moving image studies (PhD); film production (MFA); film studies (MA).

DePaul University, College of Communication, Chicago, IL 60604. Offers digital communication and media arts (MA); health communication (MA); journalism (MA); media and cinema studies (MA); multicultural communication (MA); organizational communication (MA); public relations and advertising (MA); relational communication (MA). *Program availability:* Part-time, evening/weekend. *Entrance requirements:* Additional exam requirements/recommendations for international students: Required—TOEFL (minimum score 590 paper-based; 96 iBT), IELTS (minimum score 7.5) or PTE. *Application deadline:* For fall admission, 6/1 priority date for domestic students; for winter admission, 10/1 priority date for domestic students; for spring admission, 2/15 priority date for domestic students. Applications are processed on a rolling basis. Application fee: $40. Electronic applications accepted. *Financial support:* Applicants required to submit FAFSA. *Unit head:* Salma Ghanem, Dean, 312-362-8600, Fax: 312-362-8620. *Application contact:* Ann Spittle, Director of Graduate Admission, 773-325-7315, Fax: 312-362-8620, E-mail: graddepaul@depaul.edu.
Website: http://communication.depaul.edu/

Emory University, Laney Graduate School, Department of Film Studies, Atlanta, GA 30322-1100. Offers MA, PhD/Certificate. *Degree requirements:* For master's, comprehensive exam, thesis or alternative. *Entrance requirements:* For master's, GRE General Test, 3 letters of reference, 2 writing samples. Additional exam requirements/recommendations for international students: Required—TOEFL. Electronic applications accepted. *Faculty research:* International film history, film theory, film style, feminism and film, reception.

Emory University, Laney Graduate School, Department of Spanish and Portuguese, Atlanta, GA 30322-1100. Offers comparative literature (Certificate); film studies (Certificate); Spanish (PhD); women's studies (Certificate). *Degree requirements:* For doctorate, 2 foreign languages, comprehensive exam, thesis/dissertation. *Entrance requirements:* For doctorate, GRE General Test. Additional exam requirements/recommendations for international students: Required—TOEFL. Electronic applications accepted. *Faculty research:* Spanish literature, Spanish American literature, literary theory, criticism, cultural studies.

Hollins University, Graduate Programs, Program in Screenwriting and Film Studies, Roanoke, VA 24020. Offers screenwriting (MFA); screenwriting and film studies (MA). Program offered during summer only. *Program availability:* Part-time. *Faculty:* 5 full-time (2 women). *Students:* 23 full-time (14 women), 5 part-time (3 women); includes 5 minority (1 Black or African American, non-Hispanic/Latino; 1 Asian, non-Hispanic/Latino; 2 Hispanic/Latino; 1 Two or more races, non-Hispanic/Latino). Average age 40. 15 applicants, 100% accepted, 7 enrolled. In 2017, 5 master's awarded. *Degree requirements:* For master's, one foreign language, comprehensive exam, thesis. *Entrance requirements:* For master's, letters of recommendation, portfolio, transcript review. Additional exam requirements/recommendations for international students: Required—TOEFL (minimum score 550 paper-based; 80 iBT), IELTS (minimum score 6.5). *Application deadline:* For summer admission, 2/15 priority date for domestic and international students. Application fee: $40. Electronic applications accepted. *Expenses:* Contact institution. *Financial support:* Federal Work-Study and scholarships/grants available. Support available to part-time students. Financial award application deadline: 2/15; financial award applicants required to submit FAFSA. *Faculty research:* Censorship, minorities in film, writing for television, new media. *Unit head:* Dr. Tim Albaugh, Director, 540-362-6575, E-mail: hugrad@hollins.edu. *Application contact:* Cathy S. Koon, Manager of Graduate Programs, 540-362-6326, Fax: 540-362-6288, E-mail: ckoon@hollins.edu.
Website: https://www.hollins.edu/academics/graduate-degrees/mfa-screenwriting-film-studies/

National University, Academic Affairs, College of Letters and Sciences, La Jolla, CA 92037-1011. Offers biology (MS); counseling psychology (MA), including licensed professional clinical counseling, marriage and family therapy; creative writing (MFA); english (MA); film studies (MA); forensic and crime scene investigations (Certificate); forensic sciences (MFS); human behavior (MA); mathematics for educators (MS); performance psychology (MA); strategic communications (MA). *Program availability:* Part-time, evening/weekend, 100% online, blended/hybrid learning. *Degree requirements:* For master's, thesis (for some programs). *Entrance requirements:* For master's, interview, minimum GPA of 2.5. Additional exam requirements/recommendations for international students: Required—TOEFL (minimum score 550 paper-based; 79 iBT), IELTS (minimum score 6). *Application deadline:* Applications are processed on a rolling basis. Application fee: $60 ($65 for international students). Electronic applications accepted. *Expenses:* Tuition: Part-time $430 per quarter hour. *Financial support:* Career-related internships or fieldwork, institutionally sponsored loans, scholarships/grants, and tuition waivers (partial) available. Support available to part-time students. Financial award application deadline: 6/30; financial award applicants required to submit FAFSA. *Unit head:* Dr. Carol Richardson, Dean, 858-642-8450, E-mail: cols@nu.edu. *Application contact:* Brandon Jouganatos, Interim Vice President for Enrollment Services, 800-628-8648, E-mail: advisor@nu.edu.
Website: http://www.nu.edu/OurPrograms/CollegeOfLettersAndSciences.html

New York University, Tisch School of the Arts and Graduate School of Arts and Science, Department of Cinema Studies, New York, NY 10012-1019. Offers cinema studies (MA, PhD); moving image archiving and preservation (MA). *Faculty:* 15 full-time, 9 part-time/adjunct. *Students:* 80 full-time (53 women); includes 11 minority (5 Black or African American, non-Hispanic/Latino; 1 Asian, non-Hispanic/Latino; 4 Hispanic/Latino; 1 Two or more races, non-Hispanic/Latino), 45 international. Average age 31. 233 applicants, 42% accepted, 49 enrolled. In 2017, 36 master's, 9 doctorates awarded. *Degree requirements:* For master's, comprehensive exam; for doctorate, one foreign language, thesis/dissertation, 3 comprehensive exams. *Entrance requirements:* For master's, GRE, sample of written work; for doctorate, GRE, master's degree, writing sample. Additional exam requirements/recommendations for international students: Required—TOEFL or IELTS. *Application deadline:* For fall admission, 12/1 for domestic and international students. Application fee: $60. Electronic applications accepted. *Expenses:* Contact institution. *Financial support:* In 2017–18, 59 students received support, including 45 fellowships with full and partial tuition reimbursements available, 10 research assistantships, 4 teaching assistantships; Federal Work-Study, institutionally sponsored loans, tuition waivers (full and partial), and unspecified assistantships also available. Support available to part-time students. Financial award application deadline: 2/15; financial award applicants required to submit FAFSA. *Faculty research:* History and aesthetics of American, European, and Third World cinemas; theory of film and the moving image; cultural studies; gay and lesbian media. *Unit head:* Dr. Richard Allen, Chair, 212-998-1600. *Application contact:* Dan Sandford, Director of Graduate Admissions, 212-998-1918, Fax: 212-995-4060, E-mail: tisch.gradadmissions@nyu.edu.
Website: http://www.cinema.tisch.nyu.edu/

Ohio University, Graduate College, College of Fine Arts, School of Film, Athens, OH 45701-2979. Offers film (MFA); film studies (MA). *Degree requirements:* For master's, one foreign language, thesis. *Entrance requirements:* Additional exam requirements/recommendations for international students: Required—TOEFL (minimum score 550 paper-based; 80 iBT) or IELTS (minimum score 6.5). Electronic applications accepted. *Faculty research:* Scriptwriting, sound, editing, cinematography, film theory, digital post production.

San Francisco State University, Division of Graduate Studies, College of Liberal and Creative Arts, School of Cinema, San Francisco, CA 94132-1722. Offers MA, MFA. *Unit head:* Dr. Britta Sjogren, Director, 415-338-1629, Fax: 415-338-0906, E-mail: cinedept@sfsu.edu. *Application contact:* Dr. R. L. Rutsky, MA Coordinator, 415-405-3400, Fax: 415-338-0906, E-mail: rlrutsky@sfsu.edu.
Website: http://www.cinema.sfsu.edu/

Savannah College of Art and Design, Program in Cinema Studies, Savannah, GA 31402-3146. Offers MA. *Program availability:* Part-time. *Faculty:* 2 full-time (1 woman). *Students:* 6 full-time (3 women), 2 part-time (1 woman); includes 2 minority (both Hispanic/Latino). Average age 28. 11 applicants, 55% accepted, 3 enrolled. In 2017, 3 master's awarded. *Degree requirements:* For master's, thesis. *Entrance requirements:* For master's, GRE (recommended), portfolio (submitted in digital format), audition or writing submission, resume, statement of purpose, two letters of recommendation. Additional exam requirements/recommendations for international students: Recommended—TOEFL (minimum score 550 paper-based; 85 iBT), IELTS (minimum score 6.5). *Application deadline:* For fall admission, 4/1 for domestic and international students. Applications are processed on a rolling basis. Application fee: $40. Electronic applications accepted. *Expenses:* Tuition: Full-time $36,765; part-time $817 per credit hour. One-time fee: $500. *Financial support:* Career-related internships or fieldwork, Federal Work-Study, and scholarships/grants available. Financial award application deadline: 4/1; financial award applicants required to submit FAFSA. *Unit head:* Dr. Geoffrey Taylor, Chair, Art History. *Application contact:* Jenny Jaquillard, Executive Director of Admissions, Recruitment and Events, 912-525-5100, Fax: 912-525-5985, E-mail: admission@scad.edu.
Website: http://www.scad.edu/academics/programs/cinema-studies

Texas A&M University–Commerce, College of Humanities, Social Sciences and Arts, Commerce, TX 75429. Offers applied criminology (MS); applied linguistics (MA, MS); art (MA, MFA); computational linguistics (Graduate Certificate); creative writing (Graduate Certificate); criminal justice management (Graduate Certificate); criminal justice studies (Graduate Certificate); English (MA, MS, PhD); film studies (Graduate Certificate); history (MA, MS); history of Christianity (Graduate Certificate); Holocaust studies (Graduate Certificate); homeland security (Graduate Certificate); music education (MM); music performance (MM); political science (MA, MS); public history (Graduate Certificate); sociology (MS); Spanish (MA); studies in children's and adolescent literature and culture (Graduate Certificate); teaching English to speakers of other languages (Graduate Certificate); theater (MA, MS); world history (Graduate Certificate). *Program availability:* Part-time. *Faculty:* 56 full-time (26 women), 10 part-time/adjunct (5 women). *Students:* 133 full-time (85 women), 439 part-time (311 women); includes 204 minority (79 Black or African American, non-Hispanic/Latino; 4 American Indian or Alaska Native, non-Hispanic/Latino; 9 Asian, non-Hispanic/Latino; 98 Hispanic/Latino; 14 Two or more races, non-Hispanic/Latino), 26 international. Average age 36. 261 applicants, 50% accepted, 113 enrolled. In 2017, 105 master's, 5 doctorates awarded. *Degree requirements:* For master's, one foreign language, comprehensive exam, thesis (for some programs); for doctorate, one foreign language, comprehensive exam, thesis/dissertation, departmental qualifying exam. *Entrance requirements:* For master's and doctorate, GRE General Test. Additional exam requirements/recommendations for international students: Required—TOEFL (minimum score 550 paper-based; 79 iBT), IELTS (minimum score 6). *Application deadline:* Applications are processed on a rolling basis. Application fee: $50. Electronic applications accepted. *Expenses:* Contact institution. *Financial support:* In 2017–18, 43 students received support, including 9 research assistantships with partial tuition reimbursements available (averaging $9,000 per year), 68 teaching assistantships with partial tuition reimbursements available (averaging $9,000 per year); Federal Work-Study, institutionally sponsored loans, scholarships/grants, health care benefits, and unspecified assistantships also available. Financial award application deadline: 5/1; financial award applicants required to submit FAFSA. *Unit head:* Dr. William F. Kuracina, Interim Dean, 903-886-5166, Fax: 903-886-5774, E-mail: william.kuracina@tamuc.edu. *Application contact:* Vicky Turner, Doctoral Degree and Special Programs Coordinator, 903-886-5167, E-mail: vicky.turner@tamuc.edu.
Website: http://www.tamuc.edu/academics/graduateSchool/programs/humanitiesSocialScienceArts/default.aspx

Tiffin University, Program in Humanities, Tiffin, OH 44883-2161. Offers art and visual media (MH); communication (MH); creative writing (MH); English (MH); film studies (MH); humanities (MH); individualized studies (MH). *Program availability:* Part-time, evening/weekend, online only, 100% online, blended/hybrid learning. *Entrance requirements:* For master's, work experience. Additional exam requirements/

recommendations for international students: Required—TOEFL (minimum score 550 paper-based; 79 iBT). Electronic applications accepted. Application fee is waived when completed online. *Expenses:* Contact institution.

Université de Montréal, Faculty of Arts and Sciences, Department of Art History and Film Studies, Montréal, QC H3C 3J7, Canada. Offers art history (MA, PhD); film studies (MA, PhD). Programs offered jointly with Concordia University, Université Laval, and Université du Québec à Montréal. *Degree requirements:* For master's, thesis. Electronic applications accepted. *Faculty research:* Western art from the Middle Ages, classic and modern theory, modern and contemporary art, Canadian art.

Université Laval, Faculty of Letters, Department of Literature, Programs in Literature and Arts of the Screen and Stage, Québec, QC G1K 7P4, Canada. Offers MA, PhD. *Program availability:* Part-time. Terminal master's awarded for partial completion of doctoral program. *Degree requirements:* For master's, thesis; for doctorate, comprehensive exam, thesis/dissertation. *Entrance requirements:* For master's and doctorate, linguistics exams, knowledge of French, knowledge of a second language. Electronic applications accepted.

University at Buffalo, the State University of New York, Graduate School, College of Arts and Sciences, Department of Media Study, Buffalo, NY 14260. Offers film and media study (MAH); media arts production (MFA); media study (PhD); new media design (Certificate); social media (MAH); M Arch/MFA. *Faculty:* 9 full-time (5 women), 3 part-time/adjunct (1 woman). *Students:* 46 full-time (24 women); includes 17 minority (3 Black or African American, non-Hispanic/Latino; 13 Asian, non-Hispanic/Latino; 1 Hispanic/Latino). Average age 32. 84 applicants, 29% accepted, 9 enrolled. In 2017, 5 master's awarded. Terminal master's awarded for partial completion of doctoral program. *Degree requirements:* For master's, thesis, media project; for doctorate, thesis/dissertation, qualifying exam, media project. *Entrance requirements:* For master's, portfolio; for doctorate, GRE, portfolio. Additional exam requirements/recommendations for international students: Required—TOEFL (minimum score 550 paper-based; 79 iBT). *Application deadline:* For fall admission, 1/5 priority date for domestic students, 1/7 priority date for international students. Applications are processed on a rolling basis. Application fee: $75. Electronic applications accepted. *Expenses:* Contact institution. *Financial support:* In 2017–18, 14 students received support, including 11 teaching assistantships with full tuition reimbursements available (averaging $13,733 per year); fellowships, career-related internships or fieldwork, Federal Work-Study, scholarships/grants, health care benefits, and unspecified assistantships also available. Support available to part-time students. Financial award application deadline: 1/5; financial award applicants required to submit FAFSA. *Faculty research:* Digital arts, video, documentary, film, game design, digital poetics, locative media. *Unit head:* Prof. Tom Feeley, Chair, 716-645-6902, Fax: 716-645-6979, E-mail: thfeeley@buffalo.edu. *Application contact:* Bradley Hendricks, Assistant to the Chair for Student Programs, 716-645-0945, Fax: 716-645-6979, E-mail: bhendric@buffalo.edu.
Website: http://mediastudy.buffalo.edu/

The University of Arizona, College of Fine Arts, School of Theatre, Film and Television, Tucson, AZ 85721. Offers MFA. *Accreditation:* NAST. *Degree requirements:* For master's, comprehensive exam (for some programs), thesis (for some programs), production monograph. *Entrance requirements:* For master's, 3 letters of recommendation, portfolio. Additional exam requirements/recommendations for international students: Required—TOEFL (minimum score 550 paper-based; 79 iBT). Electronic applications accepted. *Faculty research:* Modern and contemporary theater, cultural studies, musical theater, women and theater.

The University of British Columbia, Faculty of Arts and Faculty of Graduate Studies, Department of Theatre and Film, Film Program, Vancouver, BC V6T 1Z2, Canada. Offers film production (MFA); film studies (MA). *Degree requirements:* For master's, variable foreign language requirement, comprehensive exam, thesis (MA); thesis or project (MFA). *Entrance requirements:* For master's, portfolio (MFA). Additional exam requirements/recommendations for international students: Required—TOEFL. *Expenses:* Contact institution. *Faculty research:* Film theory and violence; American and European cinema; cult cinema; Irish cinema.

University of California, Berkeley, Graduate Division, College of Letters and Science, Department of Film and Media, Berkeley, CA 94720-2670. Offers PhD. *Degree requirements:* For doctorate, thesis/dissertation, qualifying exam. *Entrance requirements:* Additional exam requirements/recommendations for international students: Required—TOEFL (minimum score 570 paper-based; 90 iBT). Electronic applications accepted.

University of California, Santa Cruz, Division of Graduate Studies, Division of the Arts, Department of Film and Digital Media, Santa Cruz, CA 95064. Offers PhD. *Degree requirements:* For doctorate, one foreign language, thesis/dissertation, qualifying exams. *Entrance requirements:* For doctorate, GRE. Additional exam requirements/recommendations for international students: Required—TOEFL (minimum score 550 paper-based; 83 iBT); Recommended—IELTS (minimum score 8). Electronic applications accepted. *Faculty research:* Integrating critical and creative practice, working across media, pursuing new modes of social and political engagement, fostering global cultural citizenship.

University of Chicago, Division of the Humanities, Department of Cinema and Media Studies, Chicago, IL 60637. Offers PhD. *Students:* 40 full-time (25 women); includes 12 minority (3 Black or African American, non-Hispanic/Latino; 4 Asian, non-Hispanic/Latino; 3 Hispanic/Latino; 2 Two or more races, non-Hispanic/Latino), 14 international. Average age 31. 119 applicants, 5% accepted, 4 enrolled. In 2017, 8 doctorates awarded. *Degree requirements:* For doctorate, 2 foreign languages, comprehensive exam, thesis/dissertation. *Entrance requirements:* For doctorate, GRE General Test, 15-20 page writing sample, statement of purpose, 3 letters of recommendation, transcripts for all previous degrees and institutions attended. Additional exam requirements/recommendations for international students: Required—TOEFL (minimum score 104 iBT), IELTS (minimum score 7). *Application deadline:* For fall admission, 12/15 for domestic and international students. Application fee: $90. Electronic applications accepted. *Financial support:* In 2017–18, fellowships with full tuition reimbursements (averaging $27,000 per year), 4 teaching assistantships with full tuition reimbursements (averaging $27,000 per year) were awarded; Federal Work-Study, institutionally sponsored loans, scholarships/grants, and health care benefits also available. Financial award application deadline: 12/15. *Unit head:* Daniel Morgan, Chair, 773-702-3317, E-mail: cinema@uchicago.edu. *Application contact:* Michael Beetley, Assistant Dean of Students, Admissions and Fellowships, 773-702-1552, Fax: 773-834-9148, E-mail: humanitiesadmissions@uchicago.edu.
Website: https://cms.uchicago.edu/

The University of Iowa, Graduate College, College of Liberal Arts and Sciences, Department of Cinema and Comparative Literature, Program in Film Studies, Iowa City, IA 52242-1316. Offers MA, PhD. *Degree requirements:* For master's, thesis optional, exam; for doctorate, comprehensive exam, thesis/dissertation. *Entrance requirements:* For master's and doctorate, GRE General Test, minimum GPA of 3.0. Additional exam requirements/recommendations for international students: Required—TOEFL (minimum score 550 paper-based; 81 iBT). Electronic applications accepted.

The University of Kansas, Graduate Studies, College of Liberal Arts and Sciences, Department of Film and Media Studies, Lawrence, KS 66045. Offers MA, PhD. *Students:* 16 full-time (6 women), 1 (woman) part-time; includes 5 minority (2 Black or African American, non-Hispanic/Latino; 1 American Indian or Alaska Native, non-Hispanic/Latino; 2 Asian, non-Hispanic/Latino), 3 international. Average age 32. 5 applicants, 40% accepted, 2 enrolled. In 2017, 2 master's, 2 doctorates awarded. *Entrance requirements:* For master's, GRE General Test, three recent letters of recommendation, current resume, statement of personal goals, writing sample; for doctorate, GRE General Test, MA in film or related field; three recent letters of recommendation; current resume; statement of personal goals; writing sample; minimum GPA of 3.2 undergraduate, 3.5 graduate. Additional exam requirements/recommendations for international students: Required—TOEFL or IELTS. *Application deadline:* For fall admission, 1/1 priority date for domestic and international students. Application fee: $65 ($85 for international students). Electronic applications accepted. *Financial support:* Fellowships, research assistantships, teaching assistantships, scholarships/grants, and unspecified assistantships available. Financial award application deadline: 1/1; financial award applicants required to submit FAFSA. *Faculty research:* Latin American cinema, Japanese and East Asian cinema, new media/cultural geography of media, film history, film theory and visual culture. *Unit head:* Dr. Michael Baskett, Chair, 785-864-1384, E-mail: eiga@ku.edu. *Application contact:* Karla Conrad, Graduate Secretary, 785-864-1340, E-mail: kmconrad@ku.edu.
Website: http://film.ku.edu/

University of Miami, Graduate School, School of Communication, Coral Gables, FL 33124. Offers communication (PhD); communication studies (MA); film studies (MA, PhD); motion pictures (MFA), including production, producing, and screenwriting; print journalism (MA); public relations (MA); Spanish language journalism (MA); television broadcast journalism (MA). *Program availability:* Part-time. *Degree requirements:* For master's, comprehensive exam (for some programs), thesis (for some programs); for doctorate, comprehensive exam, thesis/dissertation. *Entrance requirements:* For master's, GRE General Test; for doctorate, GRE General Test, master's thesis or scholarly research. Additional exam requirements/recommendations for international students: Required—TOEFL (minimum score 600 paper-based; 100 iBT). Electronic applications accepted. *Faculty research:* Communication studies, mass communication, international/interpersonal communication, film studies, journalism.

University of Michigan, Rackham Graduate School, College of Literature, Science, and the Arts, Department of Screen Arts and Cultures, Ann Arbor, MI 48109. Offers PhD, Certificate. *Faculty:* 12 full-time (5 women). *Students:* 12 full-time (5 women); includes 3 minority (1 Asian, non-Hispanic/Latino; 2 Hispanic/Latino), 2 international. Average age 28. 37 applicants, 14% accepted, 3 enrolled. In 2017, 2 doctorates awarded. *Degree requirements:* For doctorate, one foreign language, comprehensive exam, thesis/dissertation; for Certificate, 15 credit hours (3 directed study). *Entrance requirements:* For doctorate, GRE. Additional exam requirements/recommendations for international students: Required—TOEFL. *Application deadline:* For fall admission, 12/15 for domestic and international students. Application fee: $75 ($90 for international students). Electronic applications accepted. *Expenses:* Tuition, state resident: full-time $22,368; part-time $1201 per credit hour. Tuition, nonresident: full-time $45,156; part-time $2467 per credit hour. *Required fees:* $376 per term. Tuition and fees vary according to course load, degree level and program. *Financial support:* In 2017–18, 12 students received support, including 4 fellowships with full tuition reimbursements available (averaging $21,000 per year), 20 teaching assistantships with full tuition reimbursements available (averaging $21,000 per year); research assistantships, Federal Work-Study, scholarships/grants, health care benefits, tuition waivers (full), unspecified assistantships, and summer research funds, conference/research travel funds also available. Financial award application deadline: 12/15; financial award applicants required to submit FAFSA. *Faculty research:* New/emerging media studies, media industries, film/media theory, cultural studies, race and media, documentary, television studies, global media, Latina/o film and culture. *Unit head:* Prof. Yeidy Rivero, Chair, 734-763-1314, Fax: 734-936-1846, E-mail: yrivero@umich.edu. *Application contact:* Carrie Moore, Student Services Coordinator, 734-647-6909, Fax: 734-936-1846, E-mail: ctave@umich.edu.
Website: http://www.lsa.umich.edu/sac/

University of Oklahoma, Weitzenhoffer Family College of Fine Arts, School of Visual Arts, Norman, OK 73019. Offers art (MFA), including art and technology, ceramics, film, painting, photography, printmaking, sculpture, video, visual communication; art history (MA, PhD), including art history (MA), art of the American West (PhD), Native American art history (PhD); design (MFA). *Faculty:* 24 full-time (8 women). *Students:* 22 full-time (17 women), 9 part-time (all women); includes 9 minority (1 American Indian or Alaska Native, non-Hispanic/Latino; 1 Asian, non-Hispanic/Latino; 4 Hispanic/Latino; 3 Two or more races, non-Hispanic/Latino). Average age 33. 28 applicants, 25% accepted, 6 enrolled. In 2017, 6 master's, 3 doctorates awarded. *Degree requirements:* For master's, 2 foreign languages, comprehensive exam (for some programs), thesis (for some programs); for doctorate, 2 foreign languages, comprehensive exam, thesis/dissertation. *Entrance requirements:* For master's and doctorate, GRE. Additional exam requirements/recommendations for international students: Required—TOEFL (minimum score 79 iBT) or IELTS (minimum score 6.5). *Application deadline:* For fall admission, 2/1 for domestic and international students. Application fee: $50 ($100 for international students). Electronic applications accepted. *Expenses:* Tuition, state resident: full-time $5119; part-time $213.30 per credit hour. Tuition, nonresident: full-time $19,778; part-time $824.10 per credit hour. *Required fees:* $3458; $133.55 per credit hour. $126.50 per semester. *Financial support:* In 2017–18, 30 students received support, including 1 research assistantship with full tuition reimbursement available (averaging $10,373 per year), 16 teaching assistantships with full tuition reimbursements available (averaging $10,377 per year); fellowships with full tuition reimbursements available, career-related internships or fieldwork, Federal Work-Study, institutionally sponsored loans, scholarships/grants, health care benefits, tuition waivers (full and partial), and unspecified assistantships also available. Support available to part-time students. Financial award application deadline: 6/1; financial award applicants required to submit FAFSA. *Faculty research:* Art history, studio arts, 3D printing, installation art, photography. *Unit head:* Dr. Bette Talvacchia, Director, 405-325-2691, Fax: 405-325-1668, E-mail: bette.talvacchia-1@ou.edu. *Application contact:* Peter Froslie, MFA Coordinator, E-mail: froslie@ou.edu.
Website: http://art.ou.edu

University of Pittsburgh, Kenneth P. Dietrich School of Arts and Sciences, Department of French and Italian Languages and Literatures, Pittsburgh, PA 15260. Offers French (MA, PhD), including film studies (PhD), French (MA), Romance languages and literatures (PhD); Italian (MA). *Program availability:* Part-time. *Faculty:* 12 full-time (6 women). *Students:* 26 full-time (15 women); includes 2 minority (1 Black or African American, non-Hispanic/Latino; 1 Hispanic/Latino), 9 international. Average age 31. 17 applicants, 53% accepted, 6 enrolled. In 2017, 3 master's, 5 doctorates awarded. Terminal master's awarded for partial completion of doctoral program. *Degree requirements:* For master's, one foreign language, comprehensive exam, thesis; for doctorate, variable foreign language requirement, comprehensive exam, thesis/dissertation. *Entrance requirements:* For master's, GRE General Test (for French), phone interview and writing samples in French and English (for French); minimum GPA

of 3.0 and writing sample (for Italian); for doctorate, GRE General Test (for French), phone interview and writing samples in French and English (for French). Additional exam requirements/recommendations for international students: Required—TOEFL (minimum score 600 paper-based; 90 iBT), IELTS. *Application deadline:* For fall admission, 1/10 priority date for domestic and international students. Application fee: $50. Electronic applications accepted. *Expenses:* $22,290 in-state tuition, $36,980 out-of-state, $850 fees. *Financial support:* In 2017–18, 22 students received support, including 5 fellowships with full tuition reimbursements available (averaging $23,262 per year), 1 research assistantship with full tuition reimbursement available (averaging $18,815 per year), 16 teaching assistantships with full tuition reimbursements available (averaging $18,815 per year); traineeships, health care benefits, and unspecified assistantships also available. Financial award application deadline: 1/10. *Faculty research:* Literature and politics; gender and sexuality; Dante and his reception; seventeenth- and eighteenth-century Italian literature and culture; Italian theater; Renaissance studies; culture of the French Caribbean; West Africa and the Maghreb; environmental studies; post-coloniality; French culture from the Middle Ages to the 21st century; poetry and epistolarity; post-unification Italian culture, especially Fascism, World War II, the Holocaust, and Sicilian cultural production. *Total annual research expenditures:* $9,000. *Unit head:* Dr. Lina Insana, Chair, 412-624-6269, E-mail: insana@pitt.edu. *Application contact:* Keanna Cash, Graduate Administrator, 412-624-5227, Fax: 412-624-6263, E-mail: kec176@pitt.edu.
Website: http://frenchanditalian.pitt.edu

University of Pittsburgh, Kenneth P. Dietrich School of Arts and Sciences, Department of Slavic Languages and Literatures, Pittsburgh, PA 15260. Offers film studies (PhD), including Russian literature and culture; Russian literature and culture (MA, PhD). *Program availability:* Part-time. *Faculty:* 9 full-time (2 women), 1 (woman) part-time/adjunct. *Students:* 8 full-time (7 women); includes 2 minority (both Asian, non-Hispanic/Latino), 4 international. Average age 35. 9 applicants, 44% accepted, 1 enrolled. In 2017, 1 master's, 4 doctorates awarded. Terminal master's awarded for partial completion of doctoral program. *Degree requirements:* For master's, 2 foreign languages, comprehensive exam; for doctorate, 2 foreign languages, comprehensive exam, thesis/dissertation. *Entrance requirements:* For master's and doctorate, GRE General Test, writing sample in English or Russian. Additional exam requirements/recommendations for international students: Required—TOEFL (minimum score 600 paper-based; 90 iBT), IELTS. *Application deadline:* For fall admission, 1/15 priority date for domestic and international students. Application fee: $50. Electronic applications accepted. *Expenses:* $22,290 in-state tuition, $36,980 out-of-state, $850 fees. *Financial support:* In 2017–18, 7 students received support, including 4 fellowships with full tuition reimbursements available (averaging $23,262 per year), 3 teaching assistantships with full tuition reimbursements available (averaging $21,412 per year); scholarships/grants, health care benefits, tuition waivers (full), and unspecified assistantships also available. Financial award application deadline: 1/15. *Faculty research:* Russian cinema and media, twentieth-century and contemporary Russian culture, digital humanities, applied linguistics and language pedagogy. *Total annual research expenditures:* $266,000. *Unit head:* Dr. David J. Birnbaum, Co-Chair, 412-624-5712, Fax: 412-624-9714, E-mail: djbpitt@pitt.edu. *Application contact:* Keanna Cash, Graduate Administrator, 412-624-5227, E-mail: kec176@pitt.edu.
Website: http://www.slavic.pitt.edu

University of Pittsburgh, Kenneth P. Dietrich School of Arts and Sciences, Film and Media Studies Program, Pittsburgh, PA 15260. Offers PhD, Certificate. *Faculty:* 29 full-time (16 women). *Students:* 32 full-time (18 women); includes 12 minority (1 Black or African American, non-Hispanic/Latino; 7 Asian, non-Hispanic/Latino; 4 Hispanic/Latino). Average age 32. 67 applicants, 10% accepted, 7 enrolled. Terminal master's awarded for partial completion of doctoral program. *Degree requirements:* For doctorate, variable foreign language requirement, comprehensive exam, thesis/dissertation. *Entrance requirements:* Additional exam requirements/recommendations for international students: Required—TOEFL (minimum score 90 iBT); Recommended—IELTS. Application fee: $50. Electronic applications accepted. *Financial support:* Fellowships, teaching assistantships, and health care benefits available. *Faculty research:* International cinema, film history, media theory, documentary production. *Unit head:* Dr. Randall Halle, Director, 412-648-2164, E-mail: rhalle@pitt.edu. *Application contact:* Kathryn Briar Somerville, Program Assistant, 412-624-6564, E-mail: filmandmedia@pitt.edu.
Website: http://www.filmstudies.pitt.edu/

University of Southern California, Graduate School, School of Cinematic Arts, Division of Critical Studies, Los Angeles, CA 90089. Offers cinema-television (MA); cinema-television (critical studies) (PhD). *Degree requirements:* For master's, comprehensive exam; for doctorate, comprehensive exam, thesis/dissertation. *Entrance requirements:* For master's and doctorate, GRE. Additional exam requirements/recommendations for international students: Required—TOEFL (minimum score 100 iBT). Electronic applications accepted. *Faculty research:* Transnational cinema, race and cultural studies, global media, television studies, digital media, feminist studies.

University of South Florida, College of Arts and Sciences, Department of Humanities and Cultural Studies, Tampa, FL 33620-9951. Offers liberal arts (MA), including American studies, film studies, humanities. *Program availability:* Part-time, evening/weekend. *Faculty:* 8 full-time (2 women). *Students:* 19 full-time (10 women), 3 part-time (2 women); includes 3 minority (2 Black or African American, non-Hispanic/Latino; 1 Hispanic/Latino), 2 international. Average age 29. 25 applicants, 44% accepted, 7 enrolled. In 2017, 8 master's awarded. *Degree requirements:* For master's, comprehensive exam, thesis, language (for humanities subconcentration). *Entrance requirements:* For master's, GRE General Test, minimum GPA of 3.0 in upper-division courses, personal statement, writing sample. Additional exam requirements/recommendations for international students: Required—TOEFL (minimum score 550 paper-based; 79 iBT) or IELTS (minimum score 6.5). *Application deadline:* For fall admission, 2/15 priority date for domestic students, 2/15 for international students; for spring admission, 10/15 priority date for domestic students, 9/15 for international students; for summer admission, 2/15 for domestic students, 1/15 for international students. Application fee: $30. Electronic applications accepted. *Financial support:* In 2017–18, 2 students received support, including 15 teaching assistantships with tuition reimbursements available (averaging $12,437 per year); scholarships/grants also available. Financial award application deadline: 4/1. *Faculty research:* American South, American autobiography, material culture, critical theory, cultural studies, film studies. *Unit head:* Dr. Andrew Berish, Associate Professor and Chair, 813-974-9380, E-mail: aberish@usf.edu. *Application contact:* Dr. Maria Cizmic, Associate Professor and Graduate Program Director, 813-974-9380, E-mail: mcizmic@usf.edu.
Website: http://humanities.usf.edu/

University of Toronto, School of Graduate Studies, Faculty of Arts and Science, Cinema Studies Institute, Toronto, ON M5S 1A1, Canada. Offers MA, PhD. *Entrance requirements:* For master's, minimum B+ in final year or over a year's worth of senior courses, successful completion of minimum of six full-course equivalents in cinema studies or comparable program preparation. Additional exam requirements/recommendations for international students: Required—TOEFL (minimum score 580 paper-based; 93 iBT), TWE (minimum score 5). Electronic applications accepted.

University of Wisconsin–Madison, Graduate School, College of Letters and Science, Department of Communication Arts, Madison, WI 53706-1380. Offers communication science (MA, PhD); film (MA, PhD); media and cultural studies (MA, PhD); rhetoric (MA, PhD). Terminal master's awarded for partial completion of doctoral program. *Degree requirements:* For master's, one foreign language, thesis (for some programs); for doctorate, one foreign language, thesis/dissertation. *Entrance requirements:* For master's and doctorate, GRE General Test, minimum GPA of 3.5. Electronic applications accepted.

University of Wisconsin–Milwaukee, Graduate School, College of Letters and Science, Department of English, Milwaukee, WI 53201-0413. Offers English (MA, PhD), including creative writing, English language and linguistics, English secondary education, literary and critical studies, literature and cultural theory (PhD), literature and language studies, literature, culture, and media, media, cinema and digital studies, professional and technical communication (MA), professional and technical writing, professional writing (PhD), rhetoric and composition (PhD), rhetoric and writing. *Students:* 90 full-time (54 women), 42 part-time (17 women); includes 12 minority (2 Black or African American, non-Hispanic/Latino; 1 American Indian or Alaska Native, non-Hispanic/Latino; 4 Asian, non-Hispanic/Latino; 1 Hispanic/Latino; 4 Two or more races, non-Hispanic/Latino), 9 international. Average age 34. 166 applicants, 21% accepted, 27 enrolled. In 2017, 10 master's, 12 doctorates awarded. *Degree requirements:* For master's, thesis or alternative; for doctorate, one foreign language, thesis/dissertation. *Entrance requirements:* For master's, GRE General Test, GRE Subject Test; for doctorate, GRE. Additional exam requirements/recommendations for international students: Required—TOEFL (minimum score 550 paper-based; 79 iBT), IELTS (minimum score 6.5). *Application deadline:* For fall admission, 1/1 priority date for domestic students; for spring admission, 9/1 for domestic students. Application fee: $56 ($96 for international students). Electronic applications accepted. *Financial support:* Fellowships, research assistantships, teaching assistantships, career-related internships or fieldwork, unspecified assistantships, and project assistantships available. Support available to part-time students. Financial award application deadline: 4/15; financial award applicants required to submit FAFSA. *Unit head:* Mark Netzloff, Department Chair, 414-229-4511, E-mail: netzloff@uwm.edu. *Application contact:* General Information Contact, 414-229-4982, Fax: 414-229-6967, E-mail: gradschool@uwm.edu.
Website: https://uwm.edu/english/

Walla Walla University, Graduate Studies, Center for Cinema, Religion, and Worldview, College Place, WA 99324. Offers Web and interactive media (MA). *Entrance requirements:* For master's, three professional references, transcripts, personal statement. *Application deadline:* For fall admission, 8/15 for domestic students. Application fee: $50. *Unit head:* Lynelle Ellis, Director, 509-527-2843, Fax: 509-527-2237, E-mail: lynelle.ellis@wallawalla.edu. *Application contact:* Rachel Scribner, Coordinator, 509-527-2832, Fax: 509-527-2237, E-mail: rachel.scribner@wallawalla.edu.
Website: https://www.wallawalla.edu/academics/grad-studies/cinema-religion-worldview/

Wayne State University, College of Liberal Arts and Sciences, Department of English, Detroit, MI 48202. Offers English (MA); film and media studies (PhD); literary and cultural studies (PhD); rhetoric and composition studies (PhD). *Faculty:* 23. *Students:* 68 full-time (34 women), 24 part-time (17 women); includes 22 minority (10 Black or African American, non-Hispanic/Latino; 2 Asian, non-Hispanic/Latino; 6 Hispanic/Latino; 4 Two or more races, non-Hispanic/Latino), 5 international. Average age 33. 110 applicants, 35% accepted, 17 enrolled. In 2017, 15 master's, 15 doctorates awarded. Terminal master's awarded for partial completion of doctoral program. *Degree requirements:* For master's, variable foreign language requirement, essay, thesis, or portfolio of work approved by Director of Graduate Studies; for doctorate, one foreign language, comprehensive exam, thesis/dissertation. *Entrance requirements:* For master's, statement of purpose; two academic letters of reference; sample essay from previous English course; for doctorate, GRE General Test, statement of purpose; two academic letters of reference; sample of scholarly or critical writing. Additional exam requirements/recommendations for international students: Required—TOEFL (minimum score 550 paper-based; 79 iBT), TWE (minimum score 5.5), Michigan English Language Assessment Battery (minimum score 85); Recommended—IELTS (minimum score 6.5). *Application deadline:* For fall admission, 1/15 for domestic students. Applications are processed on a rolling basis. Application fee: $50. Electronic applications accepted. *Expenses:* Tuition, state resident: full-time $10,224; part-time $638.98 per credit hour. Tuition, nonresident: full-time $22,145; part-time $1384.04 per credit hour. Tuition and fees vary according to course load and program. *Financial support:* In 2017–18, 61 students received support, including 6 fellowships with tuition reimbursements available (averaging $15,583 per year), 30 teaching assistantships with tuition reimbursements available (averaging $18,534 per year); research assistantships with tuition reimbursements available, scholarships/grants, health care benefits, and unspecified assistantships also available. Financial award applicants required to submit FAFSA. *Faculty research:* Literary and cultural studies, film and new media studies, rhetoric and composition studies, linguistics, and creative writing. *Unit head:* Dr. Kenneth Jackson, Chair and Professor, 313-577-7692, E-mail: ai4054@wayne.edu. *Application contact:* Dr. Carolin Maun, Director of Graduate Studies, 313-577-7694, E-mail: caroline.maun@wayne.edu.
Website: http://clas.wayne.edu/english/

Wilfrid Laurier University, Faculty of Graduate and Postdoctoral Studies, Faculty of Arts, Department of English and Film Studies, Waterloo, ON N2L 3C5, Canada. Offers English (MA); English and film (PhD). *Degree requirements:* For master's, thesis optional; for doctorate, thesis/dissertation. *Entrance requirements:* For master's, honours BA or the equivalent in English, minimum B+ in English courses above first year level; for doctorate, MA in English, minimum A- average in graduate work. Additional exam requirements/recommendations for international students: Recommended—TOEFL (minimum score 89 iBT). Electronic applications accepted. *Faculty research:* Gender and genre, Canadian studies, early modern studies, postcolonial studies, nineteenth century studies.

Yale University, Graduate School of Arts and Sciences, Department of East Asian Languages and Literatures, New Haven, CT 06520. Offers East Asian languages and literatures (PhD); East Asian languages and literatures and film studies (PhD). *Degree requirements:* For doctorate, 2 foreign languages, thesis/dissertation. *Entrance requirements:* For doctorate, GRE General Test.

Yale University, Graduate School of Arts and Sciences, Department of Slavic Languages and Literatures, New Haven, CT 06520. Offers medieval Slavic literature and philology (PhD); Polish literature (PhD); Russian literature (PhD); Slavic languages and literatures and film studies (PhD). *Degree requirements:* For doctorate, 3 foreign languages, thesis/dissertation. *Entrance requirements:* For doctorate, GRE General Test.

Yale University, Graduate School of Arts and Sciences, Interdisciplinary Program in Film Studies, New Haven, CT 06520. Offers PhD.

Section 6
Performing Arts

This section contains a directory of institutions offering graduate work in performing arts, followed by an in-depth entry submitted by an institution that chose to prepare a detailed program description. Additional information about programs listed in the directory but not augmented by an in-depth entry may be obtained by writing directly to the dean of a graduate school or chair of a department at the address given in the directory.

For programs offering related work, see also in this book *Area and Cultural Studies, Art and Art History, Communication and Media,* and *Film, Television, and Video.* In another guide in this series:

Graduate Programs in Business, Education, Information Studies, Law & Social Work

See *Leisure Studies and Recreation, Subject Areas (Music Education),* and *Physical Education and Kinesiology*

CONTENTS

Program Directories

Featured Schools: Displays and Close-Ups

See:

Dance

Arizona State University at the Tempe campus, Herberger Institute for Design and the Arts, School of Film, Dance and Theatre, Department of Dance, Tempe, AZ 85287-0304. Offers dance (MFA); interdisciplinary digital media and performance (MFA). *Degree requirements:* For master's, thesis optional, project, written document and oral defense, interactive Program of Study (iPOS) submitted before completing 50 percent of required credit hours. *Entrance requirements:* For master's, personal statement relating to school's core values, resume, 3 letters of recommendation from professionals in the dance field. Electronic applications accepted.

Bennington College, Graduate Programs, MFA in Dance Program, Bennington, VT 05201. Offers MFA. *Program availability:* Part-time. *Degree requirements:* For master's, performances. *Entrance requirements:* Additional exam requirements/recommendations for international students: Recommended—TOEFL. Electronic applications accepted. *Expenses:* Contact institution. *Faculty research:* Exploration of relationship between emergent improvisation and complex systems.

California Institute of the Arts, The Sharon Disney Lund School of Dance, Valencia, CA 91355-2340. Offers MFA, Adv C. *Accreditation:* NASD. *Degree requirements:* For master's, thesis presentation. *Entrance requirements:* For master's, audition, video of choreography. Additional exam requirements/recommendations for international students: Required—TOEFL.

California State University, Long Beach, Graduate Studies, College of the Arts, Department of Dance, Long Beach, CA 90840. Offers MA, MFA. *Accreditation:* NASD. *Program availability:* Part-time. *Degree requirements:* For master's, thesis. Electronic applications accepted.

Case Western Reserve University, School of Graduate Studies, Department of Dance, Cleveland, OH 44106. Offers MA, MFA. *Faculty:* 3 full-time (2 women), 7 part-time/adjunct (5 women). *Students:* 7 full-time (5 women); includes 1 minority (Black or African American, non-Hispanic/Latino), 3 international. Average age 26. 14 applicants, 36% accepted, 3 enrolled. *Degree requirements:* For master's, thesis, performance thesis. *Entrance requirements:* For master's, professional video, statement of goals and objectives, audition, interview. Additional exam requirements/recommendations for international students: Required—TOEFL (minimum score 577 paper-based; 90 iBT); Recommended—IELTS (minimum score 7). *Application deadline:* For fall admission, 3/1 priority date for domestic students; for spring admission, 11/1 priority date for domestic students. Application fee: $50. Electronic applications accepted. *Expenses: Tuition:* Full-time $43,854; part-time $1827 per credit hour. *Required fees:* $50; $50 per credit hour. Tuition and fees vary according to course load and program. *Financial support:* Fellowships, teaching assistantships, scholarships/grants, and stipends available. Financial award application deadline: 3/1. *Faculty research:* Dance medicine and science, dance/technology. *Unit head:* Karen Potter, Professor and Chair, 216-368-1491, E-mail: karen.potter@case.edu. *Application contact:* Lori Waugh, Department Assistant, 216-368-2854, Fax: 216-368-4250, E-mail: lori.waugh@case.edu. Website: http://dance.case.edu/

The College at Brockport, State University of New York, School of Arts and Sciences, Department of Dance, Brockport, NY 14420-2997. Offers dance (MA, MFA), including choreography/performance, dance studies (MA). *Program availability:* Part-time. *Faculty:* 6 full-time (4 women), 2 part-time/adjunct (both women). *Students:* 12 full-time (all women); includes 1 minority (Black or African American, non-Hispanic/Latino). 24 applicants, 50% accepted, 6 enrolled. In 2017, 4 master's awarded. *Degree requirements:* For master's, thesis or alternative. *Entrance requirements:* For master's, local writing assessment, audition/interview, minimum GPA of 3.0, letters of recommendation. Additional exam requirements/recommendations for international students: Required—TOEFL (minimum score 550 paper-based; 79 iBT), IELTS (minimum score 6.5). *Application deadline:* For fall admission, 4/15 priority date for domestic and international students. Application fee: $50. Electronic applications accepted. *Expenses:* Tuition, state resident: full-time $10,870; part-time $453 per credit hour. Tuition, nonresident: full-time $22,210. *Required fees:* $988; $246 per semester. *Financial support:* In 2017–18, 1 fellowship with full tuition reimbursement (averaging $7,500 per year), 4 teaching assistantships with full tuition reimbursements (averaging $6,000 per year) were awarded; Federal Work-Study, scholarships/grants, and unspecified assistantships also available. Support available to part-time students. Financial award application deadline: 3/15; financial award applicants required to submit FAFSA. *Faculty research:* Choreography and performance, world dance and culture, dance process and theory, dance education, dance science and somatics. *Unit head:* Tamara Carrasco, Graduate Director, 585-395-2413, Fax: 585-395-5134, E-mail: tcarrasc@brockport.edu. *Application contact:* Danielle A. Welch, Graduate Counselor, 585-395-5430, Fax: 585-395-2115, E-mail: dwelch@brockport.edu. Website: https://www.brockport.edu/academics/dance/

Eastern Michigan University, Graduate School, College of Arts and Sciences, School of Music and Dance, Ypsilanti, MI 48197. Offers MM. *Accreditation:* NASM. *Program availability:* Part-time, evening/weekend, online learning. *Faculty:* 24 full-time (11 women). *Students:* 4 full-time (3 women), 12 part-time (7 women); includes 2 minority (1 Asian, non-Hispanic/Latino; 1 Hispanic/Latino), 1 international. Average age 29. 28 applicants, 50% accepted, 6 enrolled. In 2017, 10 master's awarded. *Entrance requirements:* Additional exam requirements/recommendations for international students: Required—TOEFL. *Application deadline:* Applications are processed on a rolling basis. Application fee: $45. *Financial support:* Fellowships, research assistantships with full tuition reimbursements, teaching assistantships with full tuition reimbursements, career-related internships or fieldwork, Federal Work-Study, institutionally sponsored loans, scholarships/grants, tuition waivers (partial), and unspecified assistantships available. Support available to part-time students. Financial award applicants required to submit FAFSA. *Unit head:* Dr. Diane Winder, Director, 734-487-4380, Fax: 734-487-6939, E-mail: dwinder@emich.edu. *Application contact:* Dr. David Pierce, Coordinator of Music Advising, 734-487-4380, Fax: 734-487-6939, E-mail: david.pierce@emich.edu. Website: http://www.emich.edu/musicdance

Florida State University, The Graduate School, College of Fine Arts, School of Dance, Tallahassee, FL 32306-2120. Offers American dance studies (MA); dance (MFA); studio and related studies (MA). *Accreditation:* NASD. *Faculty:* 20 full-time (13 women), 1 (woman) part-time/adjunct. *Students:* 25 full-time (19 women); includes 9 minority (6 Black or African American, non-Hispanic/Latino; 1 Asian, non-Hispanic/Latino; 2 Hispanic/Latino). Average age 28. 21 applicants, 67% accepted, 12 enrolled. In 2017, 12 master's awarded. *Degree requirements:* For master's, comprehensive exam (for some programs), thesis (for some programs), 1 foreign language (for MA in American dance studies). *Entrance requirements:* For master's, GRE General Test or minimum GPA of 3.0 (for MA in American dance studies), letters of recommendation; writing sample, audition and interview (for MFA, MA in studio and related studies); writing

sample (for MA in American dance studies). Additional exam requirements/recommendations for international students: Required—TOEFL (minimum score 550 paper-based, 80 iBT), IELTS (minimum score 6.5) or Michigan English Language Assessment Battery (minimum score 77). *Application deadline:* For fall admission, 1/1 priority date for domestic and international students. Applications are processed on a rolling basis. Application fee: $30. Electronic applications accepted. *Expenses:* Contact institution. *Financial support:* In 2017–18, 44 students received support, including 3 fellowships with full tuition reimbursements available (averaging $15,000 per year), 30 research assistantships with full tuition reimbursements available (averaging $6,558 per year), 14 teaching assistantships with full tuition reimbursements available (averaging $6,558 per year); scholarships/grants, health care benefits, tuition waivers (full), and unspecified assistantships also available. Financial award application deadline: 1/1; financial award applicants required to submit FAFSA. *Faculty research:* Choreography, performance, dance and cultural significance, American dance history, dance technology, critical dance theory. *Unit head:* Prof. Josephine Garibaldi, Associate Professor and Chair, 850-644-1024, Fax: 850-644-1277, E-mail: jgaribaldi@fsu.edu. *Application contact:* Dr. Jeff Bray, Academic Program Manager, 850-644-1023, Fax: 850-644-1277, E-mail: jbray@fsu.edu. Website: http://dance.fsu.edu/

The George Washington University, Columbian College of Arts and Sciences, Department of Theatre and Dance, Washington, DC 20052. Offers classical acting (MFA); dance (MFA); exhibit design (Graduate Certificate); production design (MFA). *Program availability:* Part-time, evening/weekend. *Faculty:* 9 full-time (6 women), 8 part-time/adjunct (5 women). *Students:* 24 full-time (17 women), 18 part-time (12 women); includes 6 minority (4 Black or African American, non-Hispanic/Latino; 1 Hispanic/Latino; 1 Two or more races, non-Hispanic/Latino), 5 international. Average age 33. 70 applicants, 56% accepted, 17 enrolled. In 2017, 19 master's awarded. *Degree requirements:* For master's, thesis. *Entrance requirements:* For master's, minimum GPA of 3.0, portfolio. Additional exam requirements/recommendations for international students: Required—TOEFL (minimum score 550 paper-based; 80 iBT). *Application deadline:* For fall admission, 8/1 priority date for domestic students; for spring admission, 10/1 priority date for domestic students. Applications are processed on a rolling basis. Application fee: $75. Electronic applications accepted. *Expenses: Tuition:* Full-time $28,800; part-time $1655 per credit hour. *Required fees:* $45; $2.75 per credit hour. *Financial support:* In 2017–18, 2 students received support. Fellowships with tuition reimbursements available, teaching assistantships with tuition reimbursements available, career-related internships or fieldwork, Federal Work-Study, and tuition waivers available. *Unit head:* Jodi Kanter, Head, 202-994-6305, E-mail: jikanter@gwu.edu. *Application contact:* Information Contact, 202-994-1700, E-mail: ctad@gwu.edu. Website: http://theatredance.columbian.gwu.edu/

Hollins University, Graduate Programs, Program in Dance, Roanoke, VA 24020. Offers MFA. *Faculty:* 2 full-time (1 woman), 5 part-time/adjunct (2 women). *Students:* 15 full-time (9 women), 15 part-time (12 women); includes 15 minority (6 Black or African American, non-Hispanic/Latino; 3 Asian, non-Hispanic/Latino; 3 Hispanic/Latino; 3 Two or more races, non-Hispanic/Latino). Average age 35. 64 applicants, 70% accepted, 24 enrolled. In 2017, 15 master's awarded. *Degree requirements:* For master's, thesis. *Entrance requirements:* For master's, DVD of selected works, 3 letters of recommendation, bachelor's degree or equivalent dance experience. Additional exam requirements/recommendations for international students: Required—TOEFL (minimum score 550 paper-based; 80 iBT), IELTS (minimum score 6.5). *Application deadline:* For summer admission, 12/1 priority date for domestic and international students. Application fee: $40. Electronic applications accepted. *Expenses:* Contact institution. *Financial support:* Fellowships and institutionally sponsored loans available. Financial award application deadline: 2/2; financial award applicants required to submit FAFSA. *Unit head:* Jeffery Bullock, Director, 540-362-6429, E-mail: hugrad@hollins.edu. *Application contact:* Cathy S. Koon, Manager of Graduate Programs, 540-362-6326, Fax: 540-362-6288, E-mail: ckoon@hollins.edu. Website: http://www.hollins.edu/academics/graduate-degrees/dance-mfa/

Jacksonville University, College of Fine Arts, MFA in Choreography Program, Jacksonville, FL 32211. Offers MFA. *Accreditation:* NASD. *Program availability:* Blended/hybrid learning. *Faculty:* 1 (woman) full-time, 4 part-time/adjunct (2 women). *Students:* 20 full-time (14 women), 10 part-time (all women); includes 12 minority (4 Black or African American, non-Hispanic/Latino; 1 Asian, non-Hispanic/Latino; 6 Hispanic/Latino; 1 Two or more races, non-Hispanic/Latino), 4 international. Average age 36. 59 applicants, 53% accepted, 20 enrolled. In 2017, 6 master's awarded. *Degree requirements:* For master's, thesis. *Entrance requirements:* For master's, portfolio, artist statement of intent, undergraduate degree, three current references, official transcripts of academic work, sample of selected works (12 minutes maximum). Additional exam requirements/recommendations for international students: Recommended—TOEFL (minimum score 540 paper-based; 76 iBT). *Application deadline:* For spring admission, 2/1 for domestic and international students. Applications are processed on a rolling basis. Application fee: $50. Electronic applications accepted. *Expenses:* $620 per credit hour. *Financial support:* In 2017–18, 1 fellowship (averaging $35,700 per year) was awarded; institutionally sponsored loans, scholarships/grants, and health care benefits also available. Support available to part-time students. Financial award application deadline: 3/1; financial award applicants required to submit FAFSA. *Faculty research:* Dance for Parkinson's, practice as research, choreographic practices, body politics. *Unit head:* Cari Coble, Professor of Dance and MFA Coordinator, 904-256-7398, E-mail: ccoble@ju.edu. *Application contact:* Rakia Naze, Assistant Director of Graduate Admissions, 904-256-7004, E-mail: rnaze@ju.edu. Website: https://www.ju.edu/cfa/mfadance/index.php

Mills College, Graduate Studies, Department of Dance, Oakland, CA 94613-1000. Offers MA, MFA. *Program availability:* Part-time. *Faculty:* 4 full-time (2 women), 2 part-time/adjunct (both women). *Students:* 16 full-time (15 women); includes 6 minority (1 Asian, non-Hispanic/Latino; 3 Hispanic/Latino; 2 Two or more races, non-Hispanic/Latino), 3 international. Average age 27. 31 applicants, 68% accepted, 9 enrolled. In 2017, 7 master's awarded. *Degree requirements:* For master's, comprehensive exam, thesis, performance. *Entrance requirements:* For master's, audition, DVD recording of original choreography of up to two choreographic works (for MFA); writing sample with topic related to field of dance studies (for MA). Additional exam requirements/recommendations for international students: Required—TOEFL (minimum score 550 paper-based; 80 iBT) or IELTS (minimum score 6). *Application deadline:* For fall admission, 2/1 priority date for domestic students, 12/15 for international students. Applications are processed on a rolling basis. Application fee: $50. Electronic applications accepted. *Expenses: Tuition:* Full-time $33,480; part-time $1000 per credit. *Required fees:* $1479. Tuition and fees vary according to program. *Financial support:* In

2017–18, 16 students received support, including 16 fellowships with partial tuition reimbursements available (averaging $9,546 per year), 11 teaching assistantships with partial tuition reimbursements available; scholarships/grants and unspecified assistantships also available. Financial award application deadline: 2/1; financial award applicants required to submit FAFSA. *Faculty research:* Modern techniques, movement for actors, choreography, dance criticism and analysis, dance and literature. *Unit head:* Sonya Delawaide-Nichols, Interim Department Head, 510-430-3258, E-mail: sdelwaid@mills.edu. *Application contact:* Robynne Lofton, Director of Admissions, 510-430-3309, Fax: 510-430-2159, E-mail: grad-admission@mills.edu.
Website: http://www.mills.edu/dance

New Mexico State University, College of Education, Department of Curriculum and Instruction, Las Cruces, NM 88003. Offers bilingual education (MA); curriculum and instruction (MA, Ed D, PhD); early childhood education (MA); educational diagnostics (Ed S); language, literacy and culture (MA); learning design and technologies (MA); teaching (MAT), including dance, Spanish; teaching English to speakers of other languages (MA). *Accreditation:* NCATE. *Program availability:* Part-time, evening/weekend, 100% online. *Faculty:* 22 full-time (17 women), 7 part-time/adjunct (2 women). *Students:* 113 full-time (79 women), 194 part-time (138 women); includes 171 minority (15 Black or African American, non-Hispanic/Latino; 3 American Indian or Alaska Native, non-Hispanic/Latino; 4 Asian, non-Hispanic/Latino; 142 Hispanic/Latino; 7 Two or more races, non-Hispanic/Latino), 37 international. Average age 36. 106 applicants, 80% accepted, 56 enrolled. In 2017, 82 master's, 15 doctorates, 1 other advanced degree awarded. *Entrance requirements:* For master's, minimum cumulative GPA of 3.0; for doctorate, portfolio, minimum cumulative GPA of 3.0. Additional exam requirements/recommendations for international students: Required—TOEFL (minimum score 550 paper-based; 79 iBT), IELTS (minimum score 6.5). *Application deadline:* For fall admission, 12/15 priority date for domestic and international students; for spring admission, 11/1 for domestic students. Applications are processed on a rolling basis. Application fee: $40 ($50 for international students). Electronic applications accepted. *Expenses:* Tuition, state resident: full-time $4390. Tuition, nonresident: full-time $15,309. *Required fees:* $853. *Financial support:* In 2017–18, 97 students received support, including 2 fellowships (averaging $4,390 per year), 1 research assistantship (averaging $17,368 per year), 10 teaching assistantships (averaging $17,489 per year); career-related internships or fieldwork, Federal Work-Study, scholarships/grants, traineeships, health care benefits, and unspecified assistantships also available. Support available to part-time students. Financial award application deadline: 3/1. *Faculty research:* STEM education, bilingual and English as a second language education, critical pedagogy/multicultural education, learning design and technology, early childhood education. *Total annual research expenditures:* $13,518. *Unit head:* Dr. David Rutledge, Department Head, 575-646-5411, Fax: 575-646-5436, E-mail: rutledge@nmsu.edu. *Application contact:* Dr. David Rutledge, Associate Department Head for Graduate Programs, 575-646-5411, Fax: 575-646-5436, E-mail: rutledge@nmsu.edu.
Website: http://tpal.nmsu.edu/

New York University, Steinhardt School of Culture, Education, and Human Development, Department of Music and Performing Arts Professions, Program in Dance Education, New York, NY 10012. Offers teaching dance in the professions (MA), including American Ballet Theatre ballet pedagogy, teaching dance in the professions; teaching dance, all grades (MA, Advanced Certificate); MA/MA. *Program availability:* Part-time. *Students:* Average age 28. 34 applicants, 82% accepted, 21 enrolled. In 2017, 25 master's awarded. *Entrance requirements:* For master's, audition, interview. Additional exam requirements/recommendations for international students: Required—TOEFL (minimum score 100 iBT). *Application deadline:* For fall admission, 12/1 priority date for domestic and international students; for spring admission, 10/1 for domestic and international students. Applications are processed on a rolling basis. Application fee: $75. Electronic applications accepted. *Expenses: Tuition:* Full-time $41,352; part-time $19,968 per year. *Required fees:* $2496; $1628 per unit. $814 per term. Tuition and fees vary according to course load and program. *Financial support:* Career-related internships or fieldwork, Federal Work-Study, institutionally sponsored loans, and scholarships/grants available. Support available to part-time students. Financial award application deadline: 2/1; financial award applicants required to submit FAFSA. *Faculty research:* Dance cognition and creativity, technology in dance, development of teacher expertise, ballet pedagogy. *Unit head:* Prof. Susan R. Koff, Director, 212-992-9384, Fax: 212-995-4043, E-mail: susan.koff@nyu.edu. *Application contact:* 212-998-5030, Fax: 212-995-4328, E-mail: steinhardt.gradadmissions@nyu.edu.
Website: http://steinhardt.nyu.edu/music/dance

New York University, Tisch School of the Arts, Department of Dance, New York, NY 10012-1019. Offers MFA. *Faculty:* 11 full-time, 16 part-time/adjunct. *Students:* 30 full-time (19 women); includes 16 minority (6 Black or African American, non-Hispanic/Latino; 7 Hispanic/Latino; 3 Two or more races, non-Hispanic/Latino), 8 international. 61 applicants, 33% accepted, 14 enrolled. In 2017, 14 master's awarded. *Entrance requirements:* For master's, audition. *Application deadline:* For fall admission, 1/1 priority date for domestic students, 1/1 for international students. Application fee: $60. Electronic applications accepted. *Expenses: Tuition:* Full-time $41,352; part-time $19,968 per year. *Required fees:* $2496; $1628 per unit. $814 per term. Tuition and fees vary according to course load and program. *Financial support:* In 2017–18, 19 fellowships with full and partial tuition reimbursements were awarded; Federal Work-Study, institutionally sponsored loans, tuition waivers (partial), and unspecified assistantships also available. Financial award application deadline: 2/15; financial award applicants required to submit FAFSA. *Unit head:* Sean Curran, Chair, 212-998-1980, Fax: 212-995-4644. *Application contact:* Dan Sandford, Director of Graduate Admissions, 212-998-1918, Fax: 212-995-4060, E-mail: tisch.gradadmissions@nyu.edu.
Website: http://dance.tisch.nyu.edu/

New York University, Tisch School of the Arts and Graduate School of Arts and Science, Department of Performance Studies, New York, NY 10012-1019. Offers MA, PhD. *Faculty:* 12 full-time (7 women), 4 part-time/adjunct (3 women). *Students:* 51 full-time (34 women); includes 14 minority (4 Black or African American, non-Hispanic/Latino; 3 Asian, non-Hispanic/Latino; 6 Hispanic/Latino; 1 Two or more races, non-Hispanic/Latino), 13 international. 99 applicants, 90% accepted, 37 enrolled. In 2017, 32 master's, 7 doctorates awarded. *Degree requirements:* For doctorate, one foreign language, comprehensive exam, thesis/dissertation, dissertation defense, qualifying exam. *Entrance requirements:* For master's, sample of written work; for doctorate, master's degree, writing sample. *Application deadline:* For fall admission, 12/1 for domestic and international students. Application fee: $60. Electronic applications accepted. *Expenses:* Contact institution. *Financial support:* In 2017–18, 32 students received support, including 24 fellowships with full and partial tuition reimbursements available, 4 research assistantships, 4 teaching assistantships; Federal Work-Study, institutionally sponsored loans, tuition waivers (partial), and unspecified assistantships also available. Financial award application deadline: 2/15; financial award applicants required to submit CSS PROFILE or FAFSA. *Faculty research:* Performance theory, dance, folklore and festivals, postcolonial theory, anthropology and gender studies. *Unit head:* Karen Shimakawa, Chair, 212-998-1620, Fax: 212-995-4571, E-mail: performance.studies@nyu.edu. *Application contact:* Dan Sandford, Director of Graduate

Admissions, 212-998-1918, Fax: 212-995-4060, E-mail: tisch.gradadmissions@nyu.edu.
Website: http://www.performance.tisch.nyu.edu/

Northern Illinois University, Graduate School, College of Visual and Performing Arts, School of Theatre and Dance, De Kalb, IL 60115-2854. Offers MFA. *Program availability:* Part-time. *Faculty:* 16 full-time (9 women). *Students:* 26 full-time (11 women); includes 3 minority (1 Hispanic/Latino; 2 Two or more races, non-Hispanic/Latino). Average age 28. 9 applicants, 67% accepted, 5 enrolled. In 2017, 14 master's awarded. *Degree requirements:* For master's, comprehensive exam, final project and defense. *Entrance requirements:* For master's, minimum GPA of 2.75, audition or portfolio. Additional exam requirements/recommendations for international students: Required—TOEFL (minimum score 550 paper-based). *Application deadline:* For fall admission, 4/1 priority date for domestic students, 5/1 for international students; for spring admission, 10/15 priority date for domestic students, 10/1 for international students. Applications are processed on a rolling basis. Application fee: $40. Electronic applications accepted. *Financial support:* In 2017–18, 30 teaching assistantships with full tuition reimbursements were awarded; fellowships with full tuition reimbursements, research assistantships with full tuition reimbursements, career-related internships or fieldwork, Federal Work-Study, scholarships/grants, tuition waivers (full), and staff assistantships also available. Support available to part-time students. Financial award applicants required to submit FAFSA. *Faculty research:* Theatre history, choreography, performance art spectacles, storytelling, computer visualization of the ethical space. *Unit head:* Alexander Gelman, Director, 815-753-8253, Fax: 815-753-8415, E-mail: agelman@niu.edu. *Application contact:* Graduate School Office, 815-753-0395, E-mail: gradsch@niu.edu.
Website: http://www.niu.edu/theatre/

The Ohio State University, Graduate School, College of Arts and Sciences, Division of Arts and Humanities, Department of Dance, Columbus, OH 43210. Offers choreography (MFA); dance (MFA, PhD); dance and technology (MFA); dance studies (PhD); history, theory and literature (MFA); lighting and production (MFA); movement analysis, Laban studies, notation and dance documentation (MFA); performance (MFA). *Accreditation:* NASD. *Faculty:* 11. *Students:* 33 (26 women), 5 international. Average age 32. In 2017, 6 master's awarded. *Degree requirements:* For master's, thesis optional. *Entrance requirements:* For master's, GRE General Test (for all applicants with cumulative GPA below 3.0), audition; for doctorate, GRE General Test, invitation-only interview. Additional exam requirements/recommendations for international students: Required—Michigan English Language Assessment Battery (minimum score 82); Recommended—TOEFL (minimum score 550 paper-based; 79 iBT), IELTS (minimum score 7). *Application deadline:* For fall admission, 11/15 priority date for domestic and international students; for spring admission, 3/1 for domestic students, 2/1 for international students. Applications are processed on a rolling basis. Application fee: $60 ($70 for international students). Electronic applications accepted. *Financial support:* Fellowships with tuition reimbursements, teaching assistantships with tuition reimbursements, Federal Work-Study, and institutionally sponsored loans available. Support available to part-time students. *Unit head:* Susan Hadley, Chair, 614-292-0984, E-mail: hadley.4@osu.edu. *Application contact:* Amy Schmidt, Academic Program Coordinator, 614-292-8933, E-mail: schmidt.442@osu.edu.
Website: http://dance.osu.edu/

Saint Mary's College of California, School of Liberal Arts, MFA Program in Dance, Moraga, CA 94575. Offers dance: creative practice (MFA); dance: design and production (MFA).

Sam Houston State University, College of Fine Arts and Mass Communication, Department of Dance, Huntsville, TX 77341. Offers MFA. *Program availability:* Part-time. *Degree requirements:* For master's, comprehensive exam, thesis, project. *Entrance requirements:* For master's, GRE General Test, writing sample, interview, audition, resume, video portfolio, letters of recommendation. Additional exam requirements/recommendations for international students: Required—TOEFL (minimum score 550 paper-based; 79 iBT), IELTS (minimum score 6.5). Electronic applications accepted.

Sarah Lawrence College, Graduate Studies, Program in Dance, Bronxville, NY 10708-5999. Offers MFA. *Degree requirements:* For master's, performance. *Entrance requirements:* For master's, audition, minimum B average in undergraduate course work. Additional exam requirements/recommendations for international students: Required—TOEFL. Electronic applications accepted.

Sarah Lawrence College, Graduate Studies, Program in Dance/Movement Therapy, Bronxville, NY 10708-5999. Offers MS. *Degree requirements:* For master's, thesis, practicum.

Smith College, Graduate and Special Programs, Department of Dance, Northampton, MA 01063. Offers MFA. *Students:* 7 full-time (all women); includes 2 minority (1 Black or African American, non-Hispanic/Latino; 1 Asian, non-Hispanic/Latino). Average age 34. 25 applicants, 32% accepted, 4 enrolled. In 2017, 4 master's awarded. *Degree requirements:* For master's, thesis performance. *Entrance requirements:* For master's, audition. Additional exam requirements/recommendations for international students: Required—TOEFL (minimum score 595 paper-based; 97 iBT), IELTS. *Application deadline:* For fall admission, 1/15 for domestic and international students. Application fee: $60. *Expenses: Tuition:* Full-time $37,440; part-time $1560 per credit. Tuition and fees vary according to course load and program. *Financial support:* In 2017–18, 7 students received support, including 7 teaching assistantships with full tuition reimbursements available (averaging $13,850 per year); institutionally sponsored loans also available. Financial award application deadline: 1/15; financial award applicants required to submit CSS PROFILE or FAFSA. *Unit head:* Rodger Blum, Department Chair, 413-585-3234, E-mail: rblum@smith.edu. *Application contact:* Lester Tome, Graduate Student Adviser, 413-585-3699, E-mail: ltome@smith.edu.
Website: http://www.smith.edu/dance/

Temple University, Center for the Performing and Cinematic Arts, Boyer College of Music and Dance, Department of Dance, Philadelphia, PA 19122. Offers MA, MFA, PhD. *Accreditation:* NASD. *Program availability:* Part-time, online learning. *Faculty:* 9 full-time (7 women). *Students:* 37 full-time (33 women), 5 part-time (all women); includes 10 minority (6 Black or African American, non-Hispanic/Latino; 4 Hispanic/Latino), 9 international. 44 applicants, 52% accepted, 11 enrolled. In 2017, 9 master's, 3 doctorates awarded. *Degree requirements:* For master's, thesis optional, professional project; for doctorate, thesis/dissertation. *Entrance requirements:* For master's and doctorate, minimum GPA of 3.0, audition/interview, academic writing sample, dance questionnaire. Additional exam requirements/recommendations for international students: Required—TOEFL. *Application deadline:* For fall admission, 1/11 for domestic students, 12/1 for international students. Application fee: $60. Electronic applications accepted. *Expenses:* Tuition, state resident: full-time $16,164; part-time $898 per credit hour. Tuition, nonresident: full-time $22,158; part-time $1231 per credit hour. *Required fees:* $890; $445 per semester. Full-time tuition and fees vary according to course load, degree level, campus/location and program. *Financial support:* Fellowships with tuition reimbursements, research assistantships with tuition reimbursements, teaching assistantships with tuition reimbursements, Federal Work-Study, scholarships/grants,

health care benefits, tuition waivers, and unspecified assistantships available. Financial award application deadline: 1/15; financial award applicants required to submit FAFSA. *Faculty research:* Cultural studies, dance technology, aesthetics, choreography, dance research. *Unit head:* Sally Ann Ness, Chair, 215-204-0533. *Application contact:* Norma Porter, Dance Admissions and Recruitment, 215-204-0533, Fax: 215-204-0533, E-mail: norma.porter@temple.edu.
Website: http://www.temple.edu/boyer/academicprograms/dance/

Texas Woman's University, Graduate School, College of Arts and Sciences, School of the Arts, Department of Dance, Denton, TX 76204. Offers MA, MFA, PhD. *Accreditation:* NASD. *Faculty:* 6 full-time (4 women), 2 part-time/adjunct (both women). *Students:* 14 full-time (11 women), 18 part-time (16 women); includes 17 minority (6 Black or African American, non-Hispanic/Latino; 2 Asian, non-Hispanic/Latino; 4 Hispanic/Latino; 5 Two or more races, non-Hispanic/Latino), 1 international. Average age 36. 12 applicants, 75% accepted, 6 enrolled. In 2017, 7 master's, 9 doctorates awarded. *Degree requirements:* For master's, comprehensive exam, thesis, choreography portfolio, professional paper; for doctorate, comprehensive exam, thesis/dissertation. *Entrance requirements:* For master's, audition, 3 letters of recommendation, interview, writing sample, resume, personal essay; for doctorate, interview, 3 letters of reference, personal essay, curriculum vitae, DVD portfolio of artistic work. Additional exam requirements/recommendations for international students: Required—TOEFL (minimum score 550 paper-based; 79 iBT); Recommended—IELTS (minimum score 6.5), TSE (minimum score 53). *Application deadline:* For fall admission, 3/1 priority date for domestic and international students; for spring admission, 11/1 priority date for domestic students, 7/1 priority date for international students; for summer admission, 5/1 priority date for domestic students, 2/1 priority date for international students. Applications are processed on a rolling basis. Application fee: $50 ($75 for international students). Electronic applications accepted. *Expenses:* $7,520 per year full-time in-state; $16,820 per year full-time out-of-state. *Financial support:* In 2017–18, 18 students received support, including 7 teaching assistantships (averaging $16,567 per year); career-related internships or fieldwork, Federal Work-Study, institutionally sponsored loans, scholarships/grants, traineeships, health care benefits, and unspecified assistantships also available. Support available to part-time students. Financial award application deadline: 3/1; financial award applicants required to submit FAFSA. *Faculty research:* Performance, choreography, pedagogy, somatic practices, theorizing artistic practice. *Unit head:* Mary Williford-Shade, Chair/Professor, 940-898-2086, Fax: 940-898-2098, E-mail: dance@twu.edu. *Application contact:* Korie Hawkins, Associate Director of Admissions, Graduate Recruitment, 940-898-3188, Fax: 940-898-3081, E-mail: admissions@twu.edu.
Website: http://www.twu.edu/dance/

Tulane University, School of Liberal Arts, Department of Theatre and Dance, New Orleans, LA 70118-5669. Offers design and technical production (MFA). *Entrance requirements:* For master's, GRE General Test, minimum B average in undergraduate course work. Additional exam requirements/recommendations for international students: Required—TOEFL. Electronic applications accepted. *Expenses: Tuition:* Full-time $50,920; part-time $2829 per credit hour. *Required fees:* $2040; $44.50 per credit hour. $580 per term. Tuition and fees vary according to course load, degree level and program. *Faculty research:* Scene design, stage management, costume design, technical direction, lighting design.

Université du Québec à Montréal, Graduate Programs, Program in Dance, Montréal, QC H3C 3P8, Canada. Offers MA. *Program availability:* Part-time. *Degree requirements:* For master's, thesis optional. *Entrance requirements:* For master's, appropriate bachelor's degree or equivalent and proficiency in French.

University at Buffalo, the State University of New York, Graduate School, College of Arts and Sciences, Department of Theatre and Dance, Buffalo, NY 14260. Offers dance (MFA); theatre and performance (MA, PhD). *Program availability:* Part-time. *Faculty:* 10 full-time (7 women). *Students:* 13 full-time (10 women), 5 part-time (3 women). Average age 36. 31 applicants, 45% accepted, 10 enrolled. *Degree requirements:* For master's, comprehensive exam (for some programs), thesis project or written thesis; for doctorate, one foreign language, comprehensive exam, thesis/dissertation. *Entrance requirements:* For master's, statement of purpose; academic writing sample (e.g., scholarly essay, performance or book review); 3 letters of recommendation (sent electronically); portfolio of creative work; resume; BA, BFA, or BS; audition and sample of choreographic work (for MFA); for doctorate, GRE, statement of purpose; academic writing sample (e.g., scholarly essay, performance or book review); 3 letters of recommendation (sent electronically); portfolio of creative work; resume; master's degree. Additional exam requirements/recommendations for international students: Required—TOEFL (minimum score 550 paper-based). *Application deadline:* For fall admission, 1/1 for domestic and international students. Applications are processed on a rolling basis. Application fee: $75. Electronic applications accepted. *Financial support:* In 2017–18, 1 fellowship (averaging $4,000 per year), 7 teaching assistantships with full tuition reimbursements (averaging $12,400 per year) were awarded; scholarships/grants also available. Financial award application deadline: 12/1. *Faculty research:* Intermediality in theatre and performance; contemporary performance and theory; intersections of technology and performance; digital dramaturgy; interdisciplinary dance making. *Unit head:* Prof. Lynne Koscielniak, Chair, 716-645-6897, Fax: 716-645-6992, E-mail: td-theatredance@buffalo.edu. *Application contact:* Rachel Olszewski, Graduate Studies Staff Assistant, 716-645-6076, E-mail: rachelol@buffalo.edu.
Website: http://www.theatredance.buffalo.edu/

The University of Arizona, College of Fine Arts, School of Dance, Tucson, AZ 85721. Offers MFA. *Accreditation:* NASD. *Entrance requirements:* Additional exam requirements/recommendations for international students: Required—TOEFL (minimum score 550 paper-based; 79 iBT). Electronic applications accepted.

University of California, Irvine, Claire Trevor School of the Arts, Department of Dance, Irvine, CA 92697. Offers MFA. *Students:* 17 full-time (14 women); includes 5 minority (1 Asian, non-Hispanic/Latino; 4 Hispanic/Latino), 1 international. Average age 28. 16 applicants, 63% accepted, 9 enrolled. In 2017, 11 master's awarded. *Degree requirements:* For master's, thesis. *Entrance requirements:* For master's, minimum GPA of 3.0. *Application deadline:* For fall admission, 1/15 priority date for domestic students, 1/15 for international students. Applications are processed on a rolling basis. Application fee: $105 ($125 for international students). Electronic applications accepted. *Financial support:* Fellowships, teaching assistantships, institutionally sponsored loans, traineeships, health care benefits, and unspecified assistantships available. Financial award application deadline: 3/1; financial award applicants required to submit FAFSA. *Faculty research:* Dance science, digital technology, history and theory, choreography. *Unit head:* Lisa Marie Naugle, Chair, 949-824-3209, E-mail: lnaugle@uci.edu. *Application contact:* Alan Terricciano, Graduate Advisor, 949-824-5744, Fax: 949-824-4563, E-mail: aterricc@uci.edu.
Website: http://dance.arts.uci.edu/

University of California, Los Angeles, Graduate Division, School of the Arts and Architecture, Department of World Arts and Cultures, Los Angeles, CA 90095. Offers culture and performance (MA, PhD); dance (MFA). *Degree requirements:* For master's, 1 foreign language, and comprehensive exam or thesis (MA); comprehensive exam (MFA); for doctorate, one foreign language, thesis/dissertation, oral and written qualifying exams. *Entrance requirements:* For master's, bachelor's degree; minimum undergraduate GPA of 3.0 (or its equivalent if letter grade system not used); audition and interview (MFA); writing sample (MA); for doctorate, master's degree; minimum undergraduate GPA of 3.0 (or its equivalent if letter grade system not used); writing sample. Additional exam requirements/recommendations for international students: Required—TOEFL. Electronic applications accepted.

University of California, Riverside, Graduate Division, Department of Dance, Riverside, CA 92521. Offers experimental choreography (MFA). *Entrance requirements:* For master's, stable electronic link (such as Vimeo/YouTube) of a choreographed piece (for MFA program only). Additional exam requirements/recommendations for international students: Required—TOEFL (minimum score 550 paper-based; 80 iBT). Electronic applications accepted. *Expenses:* Tuition, state resident: full-time $5746. Tuition, nonresident: full-time $10,780. Tuition and fees vary according to campus/location and program. *Faculty research:* Movement analysis, cultural postcolonial gender studies of performance, theories of dance, anthropology of dance, history and reconstruction of dance.

University of California, San Diego, Graduate Division, Department of Theatre and Dance, La Jolla, CA 92093. Offers acting (MFA); dance theatre (MFA); design (MFA); directing (MFA); drama and theatre (PhD); playwriting (MFA); stage management (MFA). PhD offered jointly with University of California, Irvine. *Students:* 79 full-time (44 women). 495 applicants, 7% accepted, 29 enrolled. In 2017, 23 master's, 2 doctorates awarded. *Degree requirements:* For master's, thesis; for doctorate, comprehensive exam, thesis/dissertation, 4 quarters of teaching. *Entrance requirements:* For master's, GRE General Test (for playwriting only), minimum GPA of 3.5; audition or interview; for doctorate, GRE General Test, minimum GPA of 3.5, audition and/or interview, two samples of critical writing. Additional exam requirements/recommendations for international students: Required—TOEFL (minimum score 550 paper-based; 80 iBT), IELTS (minimum score 7). *Application deadline:* For fall admission, 1/10 for domestic students. Application fee: $105 ($125 for international students). Electronic applications accepted. *Financial support:* Fellowships, teaching assistantships, and scholarships/grants available. Financial award applicants required to submit FAFSA. *Faculty research:* Theatre of the Americas, European theatre, Asian theatre, gender studies, critical theory. *Unit head:* Judith Dolan, Chair, 858-822-1209, E-mail: jdolan@ucsd.edu. *Application contact:* Marybeth Ward, Graduate Coordinator, 858-534-1046, E-mail: meward@ucsd.edu.
Website: http://theatre.ucsd.edu/

University of Colorado Boulder, Graduate School, College of Arts and Sciences, Department of Theatre and Dance, Boulder, CO 80309. Offers dance (MFA); theatre (MA, PhD). *Faculty:* 16 full-time (8 women). *Students:* 31 full-time (24 women), 3 part-time (1 woman); includes 7 minority (2 Black or African American, non-Hispanic/Latino; 1 Asian, non-Hispanic/Latino; 3 Hispanic/Latino; 1 Two or more races, non-Hispanic/Latino), 2 international. Average age 31. 52 applicants, 37% accepted, 12 enrolled. In 2017, 4 master's, 6 doctorates awarded. Terminal master's awarded for partial completion of doctoral program. *Degree requirements:* For master's, comprehensive exam, thesis; for doctorate, one foreign language, thesis/dissertation. *Entrance requirements:* For master's, GRE General Test (MA), audition (MFA), minimum undergraduate GPA of 2.75. *Application deadline:* For fall admission, 12/1 for domestic students; for spring admission, 12/1 for domestic students. Application fee: $60 ($80 for international students). Electronic applications accepted. Application fee is waived when completed online. *Financial support:* In 2017–18, 90 students received support, including 27 fellowships (averaging $4,365 per year), 27 teaching assistantships with full and partial tuition reimbursements available (averaging $17,551 per year); institutionally sponsored loans, scholarships/grants, health care benefits, and unspecified assistantships also available. Financial award application deadline: 2/15; financial award applicants required to submit FAFSA. *Faculty research:* Performing arts; dramatic/theatre arts; dance; drama; arts/humanities/cultural activities. *Application contact:* E-mail: wendy.franz@colorado.edu.
Website: http://www.colorado.edu/theatredance/

University of Hawaii at Manoa, Office of Graduate Education, College of Arts and Humanities, Department of Theatre and Dance, Honolulu, HI 96822. Offers dance (MA, MFA); theatre (MA, MFA, PhD). *Program availability:* Part-time. *Degree requirements:* For master's, one foreign language, thesis optional; for doctorate, one foreign language, comprehensive exam, thesis/dissertation. *Entrance requirements:* For master's and doctorate, GRE General Test. Additional exam requirements/recommendations for international students: Required—TOEFL (minimum score 600 paper-based; 100 iBT), IELTS (minimum score 7). *Faculty research:* Asian theatre, feminist theatre and dance, Russian theatre, Australian theatre.

University of Illinois at Urbana–Champaign, Graduate College, College of Fine and Applied Arts, Department of Dance, Champaign, IL 61820. Offers MFA. *Accreditation:* NASD.

The University of Iowa, Graduate College, College of Liberal Arts and Sciences, Department of Dance, Iowa City, IA 52242-1316. Offers MFA. *Accreditation:* NASD. *Degree requirements:* For master's, thesis, exam. *Entrance requirements:* For master's, minimum GPA of 3.0. Additional exam requirements/recommendations for international students: Required—TOEFL (minimum score 550 paper-based; 81 iBT). Electronic applications accepted.

University of Maryland, Baltimore County, The Graduate School, College of Arts, Humanities and Social Sciences, Department of Education, Program in Teaching, Baltimore, MD 21250. Offers early childhood education (MAT); elementary education (MAT); teaching (MAT), including art, biology, chemistry, choral music, classical foreign language, dance, earth/space science, English, instrumental music, mathematics, modern foreign language, physical science, physics, social studies, theatre. *Program availability:* Part-time, evening/weekend. *Faculty:* 24 full-time (18 women), 25 part-time/adjunct (19 women). *Students:* 41 full-time (34 women), 27 part-time (18 women); includes 26 minority (6 Black or African American, non-Hispanic/Latino; 9 Asian, non-Hispanic/Latino; 7 Hispanic/Latino; 1 Native Hawaiian or other Pacific Islander, non-Hispanic/Latino; 3 Two or more races, non-Hispanic/Latino), 2 international. Average age 30. 54 applicants, 83% accepted, 35 enrolled. In 2017, 50 master's awarded. *Degree requirements:* For master's, comprehensive exam (for some programs), thesis (for some programs). *Entrance requirements:* For master's, PRAXIS Core Examination or GRE (minimum score of 1000), minimum GPA of 3.0. Additional exam requirements/recommendations for international students: Required—TOEFL. *Application deadline:* For fall admission, 6/1 for domestic and international students; for spring admission, 11/1 for domestic and international students. Applications are processed on a rolling basis. Application fee: $50. Electronic applications accepted. *Expenses: Required fees:* $132. *Financial support:* In 2017–18, 8 students received support, including teaching assistantships with tuition reimbursements available (averaging $12,000 per year); career-related internships or fieldwork, Federal Work-Study, scholarships/grants, tuition waivers, and unspecified assistantships also available. Financial award application deadline: 3/15. *Faculty research:* STEM teacher education, culturally sensitive pedagogy, ESOL/bilingual education, early childhood education, language, literacy and culture. *Total annual research expenditures:* $100,000. *Unit head:* Dr. Susan M. Blunck, Graduate Program Director, 410-455-2869, Fax: 410-455-3986, E-mail:

blunck@umbc.edu. *Application contact:* Cheryl Johnson, MAT Program Specialist, 410-455-3388, E-mail: blackwel@umbc.edu.
Website: http://www.umbc.edu/education/

University of Maryland, College Park, Academic Affairs, College of Arts and Humanities, School of Theatre, Dance and Performance Studies, Program in Dance, College Park, MD 20742. Offers MFA. *Accreditation:* NASD. *Degree requirements:* For master's, final project. *Entrance requirements:* For master's, audition/interview, video tapes/writing sample, 3 letters of recommendation. Additional exam requirements/recommendations for international students: Required—TOEFL. Electronic applications accepted. *Faculty research:* Performance and choreography.

University of Michigan, Rackham Graduate School, School of Music, Theatre, and Dance, Department of Dance, Ann Arbor, MI 48109-2217. Offers modern dance performance and choreography (MFA). Offered through the Rackham Graduate School. *Accreditation:* NASD. *Entrance requirements:* For master's, audition. Additional exam requirements/recommendations for international students: Required—TOEFL. Electronic applications accepted. *Expenses:* Tuition, state resident: full-time $22,368; part-time $1201 per credit hour. Tuition, nonresident: full-time $45,156; part-time $2467 per credit hour. *Required fees:* $376 per term. Tuition and fees vary according to course load, degree level and program.

University of New Mexico, Graduate Studies, College of Fine Arts, Department of Theatre and Dance, Albuquerque, NM 87131-2039. Offers dance (MFA); dance history (MA); dramatic writing (MFA); theatre education and outreach (MA). *Accreditation:* NASD; NAST. *Students:* Average age 36. 15 applicants, 53% accepted, 7 enrolled. In 2017, 4 master's awarded. *Degree requirements:* For master's, comprehensive exam (for some programs), thesis (for some programs). *Entrance requirements:* For master's, minimum GPA of 3.0; undergraduate major in theatre, dance or closely-related field; 3 letters of recommendation; letter of intent; BA, BFA, BS, or MA in dance movement science or related field, or equivalent experience (for MFA in dance). *Application deadline:* For fall admission, 4/15 for domestic students; for spring admission, 11/10 for domestic students. Application fee: $50. Electronic applications accepted. *Financial support:* Fellowships, research assistantships with partial tuition reimbursements, teaching assistantships with partial tuition reimbursements, Federal Work-Study, health care benefits, tuition waivers (partial), and unspecified assistantships available. Financial award application deadline: 3/1; financial award applicants required to submit FAFSA. *Faculty research:* Theater education and outreach, choreography, dramatic writing, dance history/criticism. *Unit head:* Bill Liotta, Chair, 505-277-4332, Fax: 505-277-8921, E-mail: wliotta@unm.edu. *Application contact:* Christina Squire, Administrator II, 505-277-7362, Fax: 505-277-8921, E-mail: csquire@unm.edu.
Website: http://theatredance.unm.edu

The University of North Carolina at Greensboro, Graduate School, School of Music, Theatre and Dance, Department of Dance, Greensboro, NC 27412-5001. Offers MA, MFA. *Accreditation:* NASD. *Degree requirements:* For master's, thesis. *Entrance requirements:* For master's, GRE General Test or MAT, audition or video (MFA). Additional exam requirements/recommendations for international students: Required—TOEFL. Electronic applications accepted. *Faculty research:* Consciousness-raising images, perspectives on ballet.

University of Oklahoma, Weitzenhoffer Family College of Fine Arts, School of Dance, Norman, OK 73019. Offers ballet (MFA); modern dance (MFA). *Faculty:* 4 full-time (2 women). *Students:* 5 full-time (all women); includes 1 minority (Two or more races, non-Hispanic/Latino), 1 international. Average age 41. 1 applicant. *Degree requirements:* For master's, thesis. *Entrance requirements:* For master's, BFA in dance, audition, interview, writing sample, letters of recommendation. Additional exam requirements/recommendations for international students: Required—TOEFL (minimum score 79 iBT) or IELTS (minimum score 6.5). *Application deadline:* For fall admission, 4/15 for domestic students, 3/1 for international students. Applications are processed on a rolling basis. Application fee: $50 ($100 for international students). Electronic applications accepted. *Expenses:* Tuition, state resident: full-time $5119; part-time $213.30 per credit hour. Tuition, nonresident: full-time $19,778; part-time $824.10 per credit hour. *Required fees:* $3458; $133.55 per credit hour. $126.50 per semester. *Financial support:* In 2017–18, 4 students received support, including 1 fellowship with full tuition reimbursement available (averaging $8,000 per year), 4 teaching assistantships (averaging $16,122 per year); health care benefits and unspecified assistantships also available. Financial award application deadline: 6/1; financial award applicants required to submit FAFSA. *Faculty research:* Ballet choreography, modern dance choreography, dance history, teaching methods, body science. *Unit head:* Michael R. Bearden, Director, 405-325-4051, Fax: 405-325-7024, E-mail: mrbearden@ou.edu. *Application contact:* Jeremy Lindberg, Associate Professor, 405-325-0567 Ext. 15, Fax: 405-325-7024, E-mail: jlindberg@ou.edu.
Website: http://www.ou.edu/finearts/dance

University of Oregon, Graduate School, School of Music, Department of Dance, Eugene, OR 97403. Offers MA, MS. *Degree requirements:* For master's, thesis or alternative. *Entrance requirements:* For master's, minimum GPA of 3.0. Additional exam requirements/recommendations for international students: Required—TOEFL. *Faculty research:* Choreography, dance history, dance pedagogy, scientific aspects of dance.

The University of Texas at Austin, Graduate School, College of Fine Arts, Department of Theatre and Dance, Austin, TX 78712-1111. Offers acting (MFA); dance (MFA); directing (MFA); drama and theatre for youth (MFA); performance as public practice (MA, MFA, PhD); playwriting (MFA); theatre technology (MFA); theatrical design (MFA). *Degree requirements:* For master's, thesis; for doctorate, variable foreign language requirement, thesis/dissertation. *Entrance requirements:* For master's and doctorate, GRE General Test.

University of Utah, Graduate School, College of Fine Arts, School of Dance, Salt Lake City, UT 84112-0280. Offers MFA, Certificate. *Accreditation:* NASD. *Faculty:* 13 full-time (7 women), 15 part-time/adjunct (8 women). *Students:* 17 full-time (13 women), 3 part-time (2 women); includes 3 minority (1 Black or African American, non-Hispanic/Latino; 1 Asian, non-Hispanic/Latino; 1 Hispanic/Latino), 2 international. Average age 21. 13 applicants, 54% accepted, 6 enrolled. In 2017, 5 master's awarded. *Entrance requirements:* For master's, audition, interview, minimum GPA of 3.0. Additional exam requirements/recommendations for international students: Required—TOEFL (minimum score 550 paper-based; 80 iBT). *Application deadline:* For fall admission, 3/1 priority date for domestic and international students. Applications are processed on a rolling basis. Application fee: $55 ($65 for international students). Electronic applications accepted. *Expenses:* Contact institution. *Financial support:* In 2017–18, 20 students received support, including 18 teaching assistantships with full tuition reimbursements available (averaging $9,000 per year); fellowships with partial tuition reimbursements available, institutionally sponsored loans, scholarships/grants, health care benefits, and unspecified assistantships also available. Financial award application deadline: 3/1; financial award applicants required to submit FAFSA. *Faculty research:* Choreography, pedagogy, performance, dance for camera, dance technology. *Total annual research expenditures:* $28,926. *Unit head:* Stephen Koester, Chair, 801-581-7327, Fax: 801-581-5442, E-mail: stephen.koester@utah.edu. *Application contact:* Eric Handman, Director of Graduate Studies, 801-587-9813, Fax: 801-581-5442, E-mail: eric.handman@utah.edu.
Website: http://www.dance.utah.edu

University of Washington, Graduate School, College of Arts and Sciences, Program in Dance, Seattle, WA 98195-1150. Offers MFA. *Degree requirements:* For master's, performance, project, course development. *Entrance requirements:* For master's, 8 years of professional dance experience, resume, performance DVD or VHS tape, 3 letters of reference. Additional exam requirements/recommendations for international students: Required—TOEFL. Electronic applications accepted. *Faculty research:* Choreography, history, anatomy, ethnography, integrated dance, social dance.

Washington University in St. Louis, The Graduate School, Department of Performing Arts, St. Louis, MO 63130-4899. Offers dance (MFA); theater and performance studies (MA). *Degree requirements:* For master's, thesis optional. *Entrance requirements:* For master's, GRE General Test, sample of written work. Additional exam requirements/recommendations for international students: Required—TOEFL. Electronic applications accepted. *Faculty research:* Theater and performance studies; dance.

Wayne State University, School of Medicine, Office of Biomedical Graduate Programs, Detroit, MI 48202. Offers anatomy and cell biology (MS, PhD); basic medical sciences (MS); biochemistry and molecular biology (MS, PhD); cancer biology (MS, PhD); clinical and translational science (Graduate Certificate); family medicine and public health sciences (MPH, Graduate Certificate), including public health practice; genetic counseling (MS); immunology and microbiology (MS, PhD); medical physics (MS, PhD, Graduate Certificate); medical research (MS); molecular medicine and genomics (MS, PhD), including molecular genetics and genomics; pathology (PhD); pharmacology (MS, PhD); physiology (MS, PhD), including physiology, reproductive sciences (PhD); psychiatry and behavioral neurosciences (PhD), including translational neuroscience; MD/MPH; MD/PhD; MPH/MA; MSW/MPH. *Program availability:* Part-time, evening/weekend. *Students:* 268 full-time (152 women), 117 part-time (59 women); includes 108 minority (19 Black or African American, non-Hispanic/Latino; 1 American Indian or Alaska Native, non-Hispanic/Latino; 62 Asian, non-Hispanic/Latino; 9 Hispanic/Latino; 17 Two or more races, non-Hispanic/Latino), 48 international. Average age 26. 1,133 applicants, 21% accepted, 151 enrolled. In 2017, 70 master's, 25 doctorates, 10 other advanced degrees awarded. Terminal master's awarded for partial completion of doctoral program. *Degree requirements:* For master's, thesis (for some programs); for doctorate, thesis/dissertation. *Entrance requirements:* For master's, doctorate, and Graduate Certificate, GRE. Additional exam requirements/recommendations for international students: Required—TOEFL (minimum score 550 paper-based; 100 iBT), Michigan English Language Assessment Battery (minimum score 85); Recommended—IELTS (minimum score 6.5), TWE (minimum score 5.5). *Application deadline:* For fall admission, 2/1 for domestic and international students. Applications are processed on a rolling basis. Application fee: $50. Electronic applications accepted. *Expenses:* Contact institution. *Financial support:* In 2017–18, 177 students received support, including 64 fellowships with full tuition reimbursements available (averaging $24,388 per year), 79 research assistantships with full tuition reimbursements available (averaging $26,894 per year); scholarships/grants, traineeships, and health care benefits also available. *Faculty research:* Cancer biology, neurosciences, vision sciences, molecular biology, pathology, physiology, pharmacology, public health, medical physics. *Unit head:* Dr. Daniel A. Walz, Associate Dean for Biomedical Graduate Programs, 313-577-1455, Fax: 313-577-8796, E-mail: gradprogs@med.wayne.edu.
Website: https://www.med.wayne.edu/biomedical-graduate-programs/

Wilson College, Graduate Programs, Chambersburg, PA 17201-1285. Offers accounting (M Acc); choreography and visual art (MFA); education (M Ed); educational technology (MET); healthcare administration (MHA); humanities (MA), including art and culture, critical/cultural theory, English language and literature, women's studies; management (MSM); nursing (MSN), including nursing education, nursing leadership and management; special education (MSE). *Program availability:* Evening/weekend. *Degree requirements:* For master's, project. *Entrance requirements:* For master's, PRAXIS, minimum undergraduate cumulative GPA of 3.0, 2 letters of recommendation, current certification for eligibility to teach in grades K-12, resume, personal interview. Electronic applications accepted.

York University, Faculty of Graduate Studies, Faculty of Fine Arts, Program in Dance, Toronto, ON M3J 1P3, Canada. Offers MA, MFA, PhD. *Degree requirements:* For master's, thesis or alternative. Electronic applications accepted.

Music

Academy of Art University, Graduate Programs, School of Music Production and Sound Design for Visual Media, San Francisco, CA 94105-3410. Offers music scoring and composition (MA, MFA); sound design (MA, MFA). *Program availability:* Part-time, 100% online. *Faculty:* 4 full-time (0 women), 18 part-time/adjunct (1 woman). *Students:* 73 full-time (36 women), 35 part-time (11 women); includes 13 minority (7 Black or African American, non-Hispanic/Latino; 1 American Indian or Alaska Native, non-Hispanic/Latino; 3 Hispanic/Latino; 1 Native Hawaiian or other Pacific Islander, non-Hispanic/Latino; 1 Two or more races, non-Hispanic/Latino), 71 international. Average age 29. 37 applicants, 100% accepted, 29 enrolled. In 2017, 52 master's awarded. *Degree requirements:* For master's, final review. *Entrance requirements:* For master's, statement of intent; resume; portfolio/reel; official college transcripts. *Application deadline:* Applications are processed on a rolling basis. Application fee: $50. Electronic applications accepted. *Expenses: Tuition:* Part-time $982 per unit. *Financial support:* Career-related internships or fieldwork, Federal Work-Study, and scholarships/grants available. Financial award application deadline: 8/10; financial award applicants required to submit FAFSA. *Unit head:* 800-544-ARTS, E-mail: info@academyart.edu. *Application contact:* 800-544-ARTS, E-mail: info@academyart.edu.
Website: http://www.academyart.edu/music-for-visual-media/index.html

American University, College of Arts and Sciences, Department of Performing Arts, Washington, DC 20016-8053. Offers art management (MA); audio production

(Certificate); audio technology (MA); international arts management (Certificate); technology in arts management (Certificate). *Program availability:* Part-time, evening/weekend. *Faculty:* 29 full-time (12 women), 66 part-time/adjunct (29 women). *Students:* 40 full-time (24 women), 31 part-time (17 women); includes 25 minority (16 Black or African American, non-Hispanic/Latino; 2 Asian, non-Hispanic/Latino; 4 Hispanic/Latino; 1 Native Hawaiian or other Pacific Islander, non-Hispanic/Latino; 2 Two or more races, non-Hispanic/Latino), 8 international. Average age 30. 101 applicants, 75% accepted, 24 enrolled. In 2017, 27 master's, 4 other advanced degrees awarded. *Degree requirements:* For master's, comprehensive exam, thesis or alternative. *Entrance requirements:* For master's, GRE, minimum GPA of 3.0, statement of purpose, transcripts, 2 letters of recommendation, resume, art portfolio; for Certificate, bachelor's degree, statement of purpose, transcripts, resume, art portfolio. Additional exam requirements/recommendations for international students: Required—TOEFL (minimum score 600 paper-based; 100 iBT). *Application deadline:* For fall admission, 2/1 priority date for domestic students; for spring admission, 11/1 priority date for domestic students. Application fee: $55. *Expenses:* Contact institution. *Financial support:* Unspecified assistantships available. Financial award application deadline: 2/1; financial award applicants required to submit FAFSA. *Unit head:* Andrew Taylor, Department Chair, 202-885-1601, E-mail: eataylor@american.edu. *Application contact:* Jonathan Harper, Assistant Director, Graduate Recruitment, 202-855-3622, E-mail: jharper@american.edu.
Website: http://www.american.edu/cas/performing-arts/

Andrews University, School of Graduate Studies, College of Arts and Sciences, Department of Music, Berrien Springs, MI 49104. Offers M Mus, MA. *Accreditation:* NASM. *Faculty:* 10 full-time (4 women). *Students:* 6 full-time (4 women), 10 part-time (5 women); includes 1 minority (Hispanic/Latino), 12 international. Average age 28. 15 applicants, 60% accepted, 6 enrolled. In 2017, 6 master's awarded. *Degree requirements:* For master's, variable foreign language requirement. *Entrance requirements:* For master's, GRE Subject Test, minimum undergraduate GPA of 2.6. Additional exam requirements/recommendations for international students: Required—TOEFL (minimum score 550 paper-based). *Application deadline:* Applications are processed on a rolling basis. Application fee: $40. *Unit head:* Dr. Lilinna Doukan, Chairman, 269-471-3555. *Application contact:* Justina Clayburn, Supervisor of Graduate Admission, 800-253-2874, Fax: 269-471-6321, E-mail: graduate@andrews.edu.

Appalachian State University, Cratis D. Williams Graduate School, School of Music, Boone, NC 28608. Offers music performance (MM); music therapy (MMT). *Accreditation:* NASM. *Program availability:* Part-time. *Degree requirements:* For master's, comprehensive exam, thesis or alternative. *Entrance requirements:* For master's, GRE General Test, 3 letters of reference, audition. Additional exam requirements/recommendations for international students: Required—TOEFL (minimum score 550 paper-based; 79 iBT), IELTS (minimum score 6.5). Electronic applications accepted. *Faculty research:* Music of the Holocaust, Celtic folk music, early nineteenth-century performance practice, hypermeter and phase rhythm, world music, music and psychoneuroimmunology.

Aquinas Institute of Theology, Graduate and Professional Programs, St. Louis, MO 63108. Offers biblical studies (Certificate); church music (MM); health care mission (MAHCM); ministry (M Div); pastoral care (Certificate); pastoral ministry (MAPM); pastoral studies (MAPS); preaching (D Min); spiritual direction (Certificate); theology (M Div, MA); Thomistic studies (Certificate); M Div/MA; MA/PhD; MAPS/MSW. *Accreditation:* ATS (one or more programs are accredited). *Program availability:* Part-time, evening/weekend, online learning. *Degree requirements:* For master's, variable foreign language requirement, comprehensive exam (for some programs), thesis (for some programs); for doctorate, thesis/dissertation. *Entrance requirements:* For master's and Certificate, MAT; for doctorate, 3 years of ministerial experience, 6 hours of graduate course work in homiletics, M Div or the equivalent, minimum GPA of 3.0. Additional exam requirements/recommendations for international students: Required—TOEFL. *Expenses:* Contact institution. *Faculty research:* Theology of preaching, hermeneutics, lay ecclesial ministry, pastoral and practical theology.

Arizona State University at the Tempe campus, Herberger Institute for Design and the Arts, School of Film, Dance and Theatre, Tempe, AZ 85287-2002. Offers dance (MFA), including dance, interdisciplinary digital media and performance; theatre (MA, MFA, PhD), including arts entrepreneurship and management (MFA), directing (MFA), dramatic writing (MFA), interdisciplinary digital media and performance (MFA), performance (MFA), performance design (MFA), theatre (MFA), theatre and performance of the Americas (PhD), theatre for youth (MFA, PhD). Terminal master's awarded for partial completion of doctoral program. *Degree requirements:* For master's, comprehensive exam (for some programs), thesis (for some programs), applied project (for some programs); interactive Program of Study (iPOS) submitted before completing 50 percent of required credit hours; for doctorate, comprehensive exam, thesis/dissertation, interactive Program of Study (iPOS) submitted before completing 50 percent of required credit hours. *Entrance requirements:* For master's, GRE or MAT, minimum GPA of 3.0 in last 2 years of work leading to bachelor's degree (depending on program); for doctorate, GRE, minimum GPA of 3.0 or equivalent in last 2 years of work leading to bachelor's degree, 3 letters of recommendation, resume, scholarly writing sample, statement of purpose. Additional exam requirements/recommendations for international students: Required—TOEFL, IELTS, or PTE. Electronic applications accepted.

Arizona State University at the Tempe campus, Herberger Institute for Design and the Arts, School of Music, Tempe, AZ 85287-0405. Offers composition (MM, DMA); conducting (DMA); ethnomusicology (MA); interdisciplinary digital media/performance (DMA); music education (MM, PhD); music history and literature (MA); music therapy (MM); performance (MM, DMA). *Accreditation:* NASM. Terminal master's awarded for partial completion of doctoral program. *Degree requirements:* For master's, thesis (for some programs), interactive Program of Study (iPOS) submitted before completing 50 percent of required credit hours; for doctorate, comprehensive exam, thesis/dissertation, interactive Program of Study (iPOS) submitted before completing 50 percent of required credit hours. *Entrance requirements:* For master's, minimum GPA of 3.0 or equivalent in last 2 years of work leading to bachelor's degree, 3 letters of recommendation, resume; for doctorate, GRE or MAT, minimum GPA of 3.0 or equivalent in last 2 years of work leading to bachelor's degree, 3 letters of recommendation, curriculum vitae, statement of intent. Additional exam requirements/recommendations for international students: Required—TOEFL, IELTS, or PTE. Electronic applications accepted.

Arkansas State University, Graduate School, College of Fine Arts, Department of Music, State University, AR 72467. Offers music education (MME, SCCT); music performance (MM). *Accreditation:* NASM (one or more programs are accredited). *Program availability:* Part-time. *Degree requirements:* For master's, 2 foreign languages, comprehensive exam, thesis or alternative; for SCCT, comprehensive exam. *Entrance requirements:* For master's, GRE General Test or MAT, university entrance exam, appropriate bachelor's degree, audition, letters of recommendation, teaching experience, official transcripts, immunization records, valid teaching certificate; for SCCT, GRE General Test or MAT, interview, master's degree, official transcript, immunization records, letters of recommendation. Additional exam requirements/recommendations for international students: Required—TOEFL (minimum score 550 paper-based; 79 iBT), IELTS (minimum score 6), PTE (minimum score 56). Electronic applications accepted.

Austin Peay State University, College of Graduate Studies, College of Arts and Letters, Department of Music, Clarksville, TN 37044. Offers music education (M Mu); music performance (M Mu). *Accreditation:* NASM. *Program availability:* Part-time. *Faculty:* 17 full-time (7 women), 5 part-time/adjunct (3 women). *Students:* 18 full-time (6 women), 5 part-time (1 woman); includes 1 minority (Black or African American, non-Hispanic/Latino), 3 international. Average age 28. 25 applicants, 72% accepted, 15 enrolled. In 2017, 6 master's awarded. *Degree requirements:* For master's, comprehensive exam, thesis optional. *Entrance requirements:* For master's, GRE General Test, diagnostic exams, audition, interview, bachelor's degree, 3 letters of recommendation. Additional exam requirements/recommendations for international students: Required—TOEFL (minimum score 500 paper-based). *Application deadline:* For fall admission, 8/8 priority date for domestic students. Applications are processed on a rolling basis. Application fee: $45 ($55 for international students). Electronic applications accepted. *Expenses:* Tuition, state resident: full-time $7686; part-time $427 per credit hour. Tuition, nonresident: full-time $20,268; part-time $1126 per credit hour. *Required fees:* $1529; $76.45 per credit hour. *Financial support:* Research assistantships with full tuition reimbursements, career-related internships or fieldwork, Federal Work-Study, institutionally sponsored loans, scholarships/grants, and unspecified assistantships available. Support available to part-time students. Financial award application deadline: 4/1; financial award applicants required to submit FAFSA. *Unit head:* Dr. Eric Branscome, Chair, 931-221-7811, Fax: 931-221-7529, E-mail: branscomee@apsu.edu. *Application contact:* Megan Mitchell, Coordinator of Graduate Admissions, 931-221-6189, Fax: 931-221-7641, E-mail: mitchellm@apsu.edu.
Website: http://www.apsu.edu/music/

Azusa Pacific University, College of Music and the Arts, Azusa, CA 91702-7000. Offers composition (M Mus); conducting (M Mus); education (M Mus); modern art history, theory, and criticism (MA); music entrepreneurial studies (MA); performance (M Mus); screenwriting (MA); visual art (MFA). *Accreditation:* NASAD; NASM. *Program availability:* Part-time, evening/weekend. *Degree requirements:* For master's, recital. *Entrance requirements:* For master's, interview, audition. Additional exam requirements/recommendations for international students: Required—TOEFL (minimum score 550 paper-based).

Ball State University, Graduate School, College of Fine Arts, School of Music, Muncie, IN 47306. Offers music (MA, MM, DA, Artist Diploma), including conducting (MM, DA), music education (MA, MM, DA), music history and musicology (MA, MM, DA), music performance (MA, MM, DA), music theory (MA), music theory and composition (DA), piano chamber music/accompanying (MM, DA), piano performance and pedagogy (MM), woodwinds (MM). *Accreditation:* NASM; NCATE (one or more programs are accredited). *Faculty:* 50 full-time (19 women), 3 part-time/adjunct (2 women). *Students:* 42 full-time, 47 part-time; includes 10 minority (5 Black or African American, non-Hispanic/Latino; 2 Asian, non-Hispanic/Latino; 3 Hispanic/Latino), 27 international. Average age 30. 75 applicants, 56% accepted, 26 enrolled. In 2017, 12 master's, 6 doctorates, 2 other advanced degrees awarded. *Degree requirements:* For doctorate, thesis/dissertation. *Entrance requirements:* For master's, placement tests in history and theory, minimum baccalaureate GPA of 2.75 or 3.0 in latter half of baccalaureate, resume, audition; for doctorate, GRE General Test, minimum graduate GPA of 3.2, interview, audition, resume, three professional letters of reference. Additional exam requirements/recommendations for international students: Required—TOEFL (minimum score 550 paper-based; 79 iBT), IELTS (minimum score 6.5). *Application deadline:* For fall admission, 2/15 for domestic students. Applications are processed on a rolling basis. Application fee: $60. Electronic applications accepted. *Expenses:* Contact institution. *Financial support:* In 2017–18, 58 students received support, including 39 teaching assistantships with partial tuition reimbursements available (averaging $10,361 per year); unspecified assistantships also available. Financial award application deadline: 3/1; financial award applicants required to submit FAFSA. *Unit head:* Dr. Ryan Hourigan, Director, 765-285-5501, Fax: 765-285-5401, E-mail: rmhourigan@bsu.edu. *Application contact:* Dr. Linda Pohly, Graduate Advisor, 765-285-5502, Fax: 765-285-5401, E-mail: lpohly@bsu.edu.
Website: http://www.bsu.edu/music/

The Baptist College of Florida, Graduate Programs, Graceville, FL 32440. Offers Christian ministry (MA); Christian studies (MA), including Biblical studies; music and worship leadership (MA). *Program availability:* Part-time, 100% online, blended/hybrid learning. *Faculty:* 12 full-time (0 women). *Students:* 33 full-time (6 women); includes 2 minority (1 Black or African American, non-Hispanic/Latino; 1 Hispanic/Latino). Average age 28. 10 applicants, 100% accepted, 10 enrolled. In 2017, 3 master's awarded. *Degree requirements:* For master's, variable foreign language requirement, comprehensive exam (for some programs), thesis (for some programs). *Entrance requirements:* For master's, regionally-accredited undergraduate degree, undergraduate courses in field, minimum GPA of 2.5. Additional exam requirements/recommendations for international students: Required—TOEFL. *Application deadline:* For fall admission, 8/15 for domestic students; for spring admission, 1/15 for domestic students. Applications are processed on a rolling basis. Application fee: $25. Electronic applications accepted. *Expenses:* Contact institution. *Financial support:* In 2017–18, 2 students received support. *Faculty research:* Biblical studies, ministry studies. *Unit head:* Dr. Ed Scott, Chair of the Graduate Division, 850-263-3261 Ext. 488, E-mail: eescott@baptistcollege.edu. *Application contact:* Sandra Richards, Director of Student Life and Marketing, 850-263-3261 Ext. 415.
Website: http://www.baptistcollege.edu

Bard College, Conservatory of Music, The Conductors Institute, Annandale-on-Hudson, NY 12504. Offers choral conducting (MM); orchestral conducting (MM). *Entrance requirements:* For master's, resume, 3 letters of recommendation.

Bard College, Conservatory of Music, Graduate Program in Vocal Arts, Annandale-on-Hudson, NY 12504. Offers MM. *Entrance requirements:* For master's, portfolio, 2 letters of recommendation, headshot, repertoire list. *Expenses:* Contact institution.

Bard College, Longy School of Music, Cambridge, MA 02138. Offers chamber music (Artist Diploma); collaborative piano (MM, Artist Diploma, GPD); composition (MM); opera (MM, GPD); organ (MM, Artist Diploma, GPD); piano (MM, Artist Diploma, GPD); voice (MM, Artist Diploma, GPD). MAT offered in partnership with the Los Angeles Philharmonic at the Los Angeles campus only. *Program availability:* Part-time. *Degree requirements:* For master's, thesis (for some programs), recital; for other advanced degree, recital. *Entrance requirements:* For master's and other advanced degree, audition. Additional exam requirements/recommendations for international students: Required—TOEFL (minimum score 550 paper-based; 79 iBT). Electronic applications accepted.

Baylor University, Graduate School, School of Music, Waco, TX 76798. Offers church music (MM, DMA); collaborative piano (MM); composition (MM); conducting (MM); music history and literature (MM); music theory (MM); performance (MM); piano pedagogy and performance (MM); M Div/MM. *Accreditation:* NASM. *Students:* 17 full-time (8 women), 48 part-time (18 women); includes 11 minority (2 Asian, non-Hispanic/Latino; 7 Hispanic/Latino; 2 Two or more races, non-Hispanic/Latino), 17 international.

In 2017, 35 master's awarded. *Entrance requirements:* For master's, GRE General Test. *Application deadline:* Applications are processed on a rolling basis. Application fee: $25. *Financial support:* Teaching assistantships, Federal Work-Study, and institutionally sponsored loans available. *Unit head:* Dr. David Music, Graduate Program Director, 254-710-2360, Fax: 254-710-1191, E-mail: david_music@baylor.edu. *Application contact:* Melinda Coates, Administrative Assistant, 254-710-2360, Fax: 254-710-3870, E-mail: melinda_coats@baylor.edu.
Website: http://www.baylor.edu/music/

Bennington College, Graduate Programs, MFA in Music Program, Bennington, VT 05201. Offers MFA. *Program availability:* Part-time. *Degree requirements:* For master's, thesis, concert performances. *Entrance requirements:* Additional exam requirements/recommendations for international students: Recommended—TOEFL. Electronic applications accepted. *Expenses:* Contact institution.

Berklee College of Music, Berklee Graduate Programs, Boston, MA 46013, Spain. Offers contemporary performance (MM), including global jazz, production; global entertainment and music business (MA); music production, technology, and innovation (MM); scoring for film, television, and video games (MM). Production; global entertainment and music business; music production, technology, and innovation; and scoring for film, television, and video games programs offered at Valencia, Spain campus. *Program availability:* Part-time, blended/hybrid learning. *Faculty:* 45 full-time (12 women), 41 part-time/adjunct (6 women). *Students:* 196 full-time (75 women), 24 part-time (22 women); includes 36 minority (5 Black or African American, non-Hispanic/Latino; 9 Asian, non-Hispanic/Latino; 17 Hispanic/Latino; 5 Two or more races, non-Hispanic/Latino), 109 international. Average age 27. 735 applicants, 38% accepted, 162 enrolled. In 2017, 170 master's awarded. *Degree requirements:* For master's, thesis, culminating experience project. *Entrance requirements:* Additional exam requirements/recommendations for international students: Required—TOEFL (minimum score 600 paper-based; 100 iBT), IELTS (minimum score 7.5), PTE (minimum score 73). *Application deadline:* For fall admission, 1/15 for domestic and international students. Application fee: $150. Electronic applications accepted. *Expenses:* Contact institution. *Financial support:* In 2017–18, 153 students received support, including 123 fellowships with full and partial tuition reimbursements available (averaging $15,943 per year), 30 research assistantships (averaging $5,429 per year); career-related internships or fieldwork, scholarships/grants, and tuition waivers (full and partial) also available. Support available to part-time students. Financial award application deadline: 1/15; financial award applicants required to submit CSS PROFILE or FAFSA. *Faculty research:* Neuroscience, integrative medicine, music therapy practice, music cognition, ethnomusicology. *Unit head:* Camille Colatosti, PhD, Dean, Institutional Research and Assessment/Graduate Studies, 617-536-6340, E-mail: ccolatosti@berklee.edu. *Application contact:* Office of Admissions, 617-747-2221, E-mail: admissions@berklee.edu.
Website: https://www.berklee.edu/graduate

Berklee College of Music, The Boston Conservatory at Berklee, Boston, MA 02215-3693. Offers bassoon performance (MM); cello performance (MM); choral conducting (MM); clarinet performance (MM); collaborative piano (MM); composition (MM); contemporary music performance (MM); double bass performance (MM); flute performance (MM); harp performance (MM); horn performance (MM); marimba performance (MM); music and autism (Certificate); music education (MM); music education and autism (MM); music performance (ADP); musical theater (MFA); oboe performance (MM); opera performance (MM); orchestral conducting (MM); percussion performance (MM); piano performance (MM); saxophone performance (MM); trombone performance (MM); trumpet performance (MM). *Program availability:* Part-time. *Faculty:* 33 full-time (13 women), 19 part-time/adjunct (13 women). *Students:* 237 full-time (141 women), 23 part-time (15 women); includes 43 minority (9 Black or African American, non-Hispanic/Latino; 1 American Indian or Alaska Native, non-Hispanic/Latino; 9 Asian, non-Hispanic/Latino; 13 Hispanic/Latino; 11 Two or more races, non-Hispanic/Latino), 73 international. Average age 25. 668 applicants, 48% accepted, 154 enrolled. In 2017, 85 master's, 31 other advanced degrees awarded. *Degree requirements:* For master's, recital or performance; for other advanced degree, recital. *Entrance requirements:* For master's and other advanced degree, audition. Additional exam requirements/recommendations for international students: Required—TOEFL (minimum score 550 paper-based; 79 iBT), IELTS (minimum score 6.5). *Application deadline:* For fall admission, 12/15 for domestic and international students. Application fee: $110. Electronic applications accepted. *Expenses:* $44,735 per year (master's degrees); $28,020 (diplomas and certificates). *Financial support:* In 2017–18, 247 students received support, including 2 research assistantships (averaging $4,000 per year), 10 teaching assistantships (averaging $2,000 per year); scholarships/grants also available. Financial award application deadline: 12/15; financial award applicants required to submit FAFSA. *Unit head:* Camille Colatosti, PhD, Dean, Institutional Research and Assessment/Graduate Studies, 617-536-6340, E-mail: ccolatosti@berklee.edu. *Application contact:* Director of Admissions, 617-912-9153, Fax: 617-912-9217, E-mail: admissions@bostonconservatory.edu.
Website: http://www.bostonconservatory.edu/

Bethesda University, Graduate and Professional Programs, Anaheim, CA 92801. Offers biblical studies (MA); music (MA); theology (M Div). *Entrance requirements:* For master's, interview. Additional exam requirements/recommendations for international students: Recommended—TOEFL.

Binghamton University, State University of New York, Graduate School, Harpur College of Arts and Sciences, Department of Music, Binghamton, NY 13902-6000. Offers MM. *Accreditation:* NASM. *Program availability:* Part-time. *Faculty:* 12 full-time (3 women). *Students:* 17 full-time (11 women), 1 part-time (0 women); includes 4 minority (2 Black or African American, non-Hispanic/Latino; 1 Hispanic/Latino; 1 Two or more races, non-Hispanic/Latino), 6 international. Average age 26. 38 applicants, 58% accepted, 6 enrolled. In 2017, 7 master's awarded. *Degree requirements:* For master's, variable foreign language requirement, comprehensive exam, thesis (for some programs). *Entrance requirements:* For master's, GRE (for music history and literature applicants), portfolio, writing sample. Additional exam requirements/recommendations for international students: Required—TOEFL (minimum score 550 paper-based; 80 iBT). *Application deadline:* For fall admission, 4/1 priority date for domestic and international students; for spring admission, 10/1 priority date for domestic and international students. Application fee: $75. Electronic applications accepted. *Financial support:* In 2017–18, 13 students received support, including 10 teaching assistantships with full tuition reimbursements available (averaging $9,500 per year); career-related internships or fieldwork, Federal Work-Study, institutionally sponsored loans, scholarships/grants, health care benefits, tuition waivers (full and partial), and unspecified assistantships also available. Financial award application deadline: 2/15; financial award applicants required to submit FAFSA. *Unit head:* Christopher Bartlette, Director of Graduate Studies, 607-777-2559, E-mail: cbartlet@binghamton.edu. *Application contact:* Ben Balkaya, Assistant Dean and Director, 607-777-2151, Fax: 607-777-2501, E-mail: balkaya@binghamton.edu.

Bob Jones University, Graduate Programs, Greenville, SC 29614. Offers accountancy (MS); Bible (MA); Bible translation (MA); Biblical studies (Certificate); broadcast management (MS); business administration (MBA); church history (MA, PhD); church ministries (MA); church music (MM); cinema and video production (MA); counseling (MS); curriculum and instruction (Ed D); divinity (M Div); dramatic production (MA); educational leadership (MS, Ed D, Ed S); elementary education (M Ed, MAT); English (M Ed, MA, MAT); fine arts (MA); graphic design (MA); history (M Ed, MA); illustration (MA); interpretative speech (MA); mathematics (M Ed, MAT); medical missions (Certificate); ministry (MM, D Min); multi-categorical special education (M Ed, MAT); music (M Ed); New Testament interpretation (PhD); Old Testament interpretation (PhD); orchestral instrument performance (MM); organ performance (MM); pastoral studies (MA); personnel services (MS, Ed S); piano pedagogy (MM); piano performance (MM); platform arts (MA); radio and television broadcasting (MS); rhetoric and public address (MA); secondary education (M Ed); studio art (MA); teaching Bible (MA); theology (MA, PhD); voice performance (MM); youth ministries (MA); M Div/MM.

Boise State University, College of Arts and Sciences, Department of Music, Boise, ID 83725-0399. Offers music education (MM); music performance (MM). *Accreditation:* NASM. *Program availability:* Part-time. *Faculty:* 14. *Students:* 11 full-time (3 women), 6 part-time (3 women); includes 2 minority (1 Asian, non-Hispanic/Latino; 1 Hispanic/Latino), 2 international. Average age 27. 9 applicants, 78% accepted, 5 enrolled. In 2017, 10 master's awarded. *Degree requirements:* For master's, thesis optional. *Entrance requirements:* For master's, minimum GPA of 3.0, performance demonstration. Additional exam requirements/recommendations for international students: Required—TOEFL (minimum score 550 paper-based; 80 iBT), IELTS (minimum score 6). *Application deadline:* For fall admission, 2/9 priority date for domestic and international students. Application fee: $65 ($95 for international students). Electronic applications accepted. *Expenses:* Tuition, state resident: full-time $6471; part-time $390 per credit. Tuition, nonresident: full-time $21,787; part-time $685 per credit. *Required fees:* $2283; $100 per term. Part-time tuition and fees vary according to course load and program. *Financial support:* Teaching assistantships, scholarships/grants, and unspecified assistantships available. Financial award application deadline: 2/9; financial award applicants required to submit FAFSA. *Unit head:* Dr. Linda Kline, Chair, 208-426-3665, E-mail: lkline@boisestate.edu. *Application contact:* Dr. Jeanne Belfy, Graduate Program Coordinator, 208-426-1216, E-mail: jbelfy@boisestate.edu.
Website: http://music.boisestate.edu/graduate/

Boston University, College of Fine Arts, Department of Musicology and Ethnomusicology, Boston, MA 02215. Offers ethnomusicology (PhD); historical musicology (PhD); musicology (MA). *Accreditation:* NASM. *Students:* 16 full-time (8 women), 2 international. Average age 28. 29 applicants, 21% accepted, 3 enrolled. In 2017, 1 doctorate awarded. Terminal master's awarded for partial completion of doctoral program. *Degree requirements:* For master's, 2 foreign languages, comprehensive exam, thesis; for doctorate, 2 foreign languages, comprehensive exam, thesis/dissertation. *Entrance requirements:* For master's, GRE General Test, musical composition or research paper, 3 letters of recommendation, transcripts, personal statement, curriculum vitae. Additional exam requirements/recommendations for international students: Required—TOEFL (minimum score 550 paper-based; 84 iBT). Application fee: $95. Electronic applications accepted. *Financial support:* In 2017–18, 16 students received support, including 15 fellowships (averaging $22,000 per year); Federal Work-Study, scholarships/grants, health care benefits, and unspecified assistantships also available. Financial award application deadline: 1/5. *Unit head:* Victor Coelho, Director, 617-358-0628, Fax: 617-353-7455, E-mail: blues@bu.edu. *Application contact:* Melissa Riesgo, Administrative Coordinator, 617-353-6888, Fax: 617-353-7455, E-mail: riesgo@bu.edu.
Website: http://www.bu.edu/musicology/

Boston University, College of Fine Arts, School of Music, Boston, MA 02215. Offers choral conducting (MM); composition and theory (DMA); conducting (Performance Diploma); music education (MM, DMA, CAS); musicology (MA, PhD). *Accreditation:* NASM. *Program availability:* Part-time. *Faculty:* 36 full-time, 21 part-time/adjunct. *Students:* 301 full-time (175 women), 8 part-time (4 women); includes 36 minority (3 Black or African American, non-Hispanic/Latino; 14 Asian, non-Hispanic/Latino; 10 Hispanic/Latino; 9 Two or more races, non-Hispanic/Latino), 151 international. Average age 27. 1,590 applicants, 21% accepted, 101 enrolled. In 2017, 128 master's, 57 doctorates, 10 other advanced degrees awarded. *Degree requirements:* For master's, thesis; for doctorate, 2 foreign languages, thesis/dissertation. *Entrance requirements:* Additional exam requirements/recommendations for international students: Required—TOEFL (minimum score 84 iBT), IELTS (minimum score 7). *Application deadline:* For fall admission, 12/1 priority date for domestic and international students. Application fee: $95. Electronic applications accepted. *Expenses:* Contact institution. *Financial support:* Fellowships, teaching assistantships, scholarships/grants, and unspecified assistantships available. Financial award application deadline: 12/1. *Unit head:* Shiela Kibbe, Director, 617-353-3341, Fax: 617-353-7455, E-mail: cfamusic@bu.edu. *Application contact:* Katie Luellen, Director of Admissions, 617-353-3341, E-mail: arts@bu.edu.

Bowling Green State University, Graduate College, College of Musical Arts, Bowling Green, OH 43403. Offers composition (MM); contemporary music (DMA), including composition, performance; ethnomusicology (MM); music education (MM), including choral music education, comprehensive music education, instrumental music education; music history (MM); music theory (MM); performance (MM). *Accreditation:* NASM. *Program availability:* Part-time. *Degree requirements:* For master's, thesis or alternative, recitals; for doctorate, comprehensive exam, thesis/dissertation. *Entrance requirements:* For master's, GRE General Test, diagnostic placement exams in music history and theory, audition, interview. Additional exam requirements/recommendations for international students: Required—TOEFL. Electronic applications accepted. *Faculty research:* Ethnomusicology.

Brandeis University, Graduate School of Arts and Sciences, Department of Music, Waltham, MA 02454-9110. Offers composition and theory (MA, MFA, PhD); musicology (MA, MFA, PhD). *Program availability:* Part-time. *Faculty:* 6 full-time (2 women), 14 part-time/adjunct (3 women). *Students:* 26 full-time (8 women), 3 part-time (0 women); includes 5 minority (2 Black or African American, non-Hispanic/Latino; 2 Asian, non-Hispanic/Latino; 1 Hispanic/Latino), 5 international. Average age 30. 57 applicants, 26% accepted, 7 enrolled. In 2017, 2 master's, 6 doctorates awarded. Terminal master's awarded for partial completion of doctoral program. *Degree requirements:* For master's, variable foreign language requirement, comprehensive exam (for some programs), thesis (for some programs); for doctorate, one foreign language, comprehensive exam, thesis/dissertation, colloquia. *Entrance requirements:* For master's and doctorate, GRE General Test (recommended), resume, letters of recommendation, transcripts, statement of purpose, writing sample (for musicology applicants), portfolio and composition exam (for composition and theory applicants). Additional exam requirements/recommendations for international students: Required—PTE (minimum score 68), TOEFL (minimum score 600 paper-based, 100 iBT) or IELTS (7). *Application deadline:* For fall admission, 1/15 priority date for domestic students. Applications are processed on a rolling basis. Application fee: $75. Electronic applications accepted. *Expenses: Tuition:* Full-time $48,720. *Required fees:* $88. Tuition and fees vary according to course load, degree level, program and student level. *Financial support:* In 2017–18, 23 students received support, including 17 fellowships with full tuition reimbursements available (averaging $24,480 per year), 1 teaching assistantship with

partial tuition reimbursement available (averaging $3,200 per year); Federal Work-Study, scholarships/grants, health care benefits, and tuition waivers (partial) also available. Support available to part-time students. Financial award application deadline: 4/15; financial award applicants required to submit FAFSA. *Faculty research:* Composition and theory, musicology, music history. *Unit head:* Dr. Karen Desmond, Department Chair, 781-736-3311, E-mail: kdesmond@brandeis.edu. *Application contact:* Mark Kagan, Senior Academic Administrator, 781-736-3311, E-mail: kagan@brandeis.edu.
Website: http://www.brandeis.edu/gsas/programs/music.html

Brandon University, School of Music, Brandon, MB R7A 6A9, Canada. Offers composition (M Mus); music education (M Mus); performance and literature (M Mus), including clarinet, conducting, jazz, low brass, piano, strings, trumpet. *Program availability:* Part-time. *Degree requirements:* For master's, comprehensive exam (for some programs), thesis (for some programs), 2 recitals. *Entrance requirements:* For master's, B Mus. Additional exam requirements/recommendations for international students: Required—TOEFL (minimum score 580 paper-based), IELTS (minimum score 7). Electronic applications accepted. *Expenses:* Contact institution. *Faculty research:* Composition, evaluation and assessment, performance anxiety, philosophy of music, teacher education.

Brigham Young University, Graduate Studies, College of Fine Arts and Communications, School of Music, Provo, UT 84602. Offers composition (MM); conducting (MM), including band and orchestral conducting, choral conducting; music education (MA, MM); performance (MM), including keyboard performance, orchestral instrument, vocal performance. *Accreditation:* NASM. *Faculty:* 51 full-time (10 women), 60 part-time/adjunct (38 women). *Students:* 18 full-time (10 women), 24 part-time (15 women); includes 6 minority (3 Asian, non-Hispanic/Latino; 2 Hispanic/Latino; 1 Native Hawaiian or other Pacific Islander, non-Hispanic/Latino). Average age 24. 44 applicants, 43% accepted, 16 enrolled. In 2017, 16 master's awarded. *Degree requirements:* For master's, comprehensive exam (for some programs), thesis (for some programs), recital, project, or composition (for some programs). *Entrance requirements:* For master's, School of Music Entrance Exam, minimum GPA of 3.0, undergraduate degree in music. Additional exam requirements/recommendations for international students: Required—TOEFL (minimum score 85 iBT), IELTS (minimum score 7). *Application deadline:* For fall admission, 12/15 priority date for domestic and international students. Application fee: $50. Electronic applications accepted. *Expenses:* Contact institution. *Financial support:* In 2017–18, 43 students received support, including 43 research assistantships (averaging $3,000 per year), 43 teaching assistantships (averaging $3,500 per year); career-related internships or fieldwork, institutionally sponsored loans, scholarships/grants, tuition waivers (partial), and unspecified assistantships also available. Support available to part-time students. Financial award application deadline: 12/15; financial award applicants required to submit FAFSA. *Faculty research:* Max Steiner film archive study; liturgical compositions; music education undergraduate curriculum; Mormon music; jazz history. *Unit head:* Dr. Kirt R. Saville, Director, 801-422-6304, Fax: 801-422-0533, E-mail: kirt_saville@byu.edu. *Application contact:* Dr. A. Claudine Bigelow, Graduate Coordinator, 801-422-1315, Fax: 801-422-0533, E-mail: claudine_bigelow@byu.edu.
Website: https://cfac.byu.edu/music/

Brooklyn College of the City University of New York, School of Visual, Media and Performing Arts, Conservatory of Music, Brooklyn, NY 11210-2889. Offers composition (MM); music teacher (MA); musicology (MA); performance (MM). *Program availability:* Part-time. *Degree requirements:* For master's, one foreign language, comprehensive exam, thesis. *Entrance requirements:* For master's, placement exam, 36 credits in music, audition, completed composition, writing sample. Additional exam requirements/recommendations for international students: Required—TOEFL (minimum score 550 paper-based; 79 iBT). Electronic applications accepted. *Faculty research:* American music, computer music.

Brooklyn College of the City University of New York, School of Visual, Media and Performing Arts, Program in Performance and Interactive Media Arts, Brooklyn, NY 11210-2889. Offers MFA. *Entrance requirements:* For master's, 2 letters of recommendation, resume, portfolio, interview. Additional exam requirements/recommendations for international students: Required—TOEFL (minimum score 550 paper-based; 61 iBT). Electronic applications accepted.

Brown University, Graduate School, Department of Music, Providence, RI 02912. Offers computer music and multimedia (PhD); ethnomusicology (PhD). *Degree requirements:* For doctorate, 2 foreign languages, comprehensive exam, thesis/dissertation, departmental qualifying exam. *Entrance requirements:* For doctorate, GRE General Test. *Faculty research:* Ethnomusicology.

Butler University, Jordan College of the Arts, Indianapolis, IN 46208-3485. Offers composition (MM); conducting (MM), including choral, instrumental; music education (MM); musicology (MA); performance (MM); piano pedagogy (MM). *Accreditation:* NASM. *Program availability:* Part-time. *Faculty:* 25 full-time (7 women), 35 part-time/adjunct (18 women). *Students:* 12 full-time (3 women), 25 part-time (9 women); includes 8 minority (3 Black or African American, non-Hispanic/Latino; 2 Asian, non-Hispanic/Latino; 1 Hispanic/Latino; 2 Two or more races, non-Hispanic/Latino), 1 international. Average age 27. 36 applicants, 67% accepted, 14 enrolled. In 2017, 10 master's awarded. *Degree requirements:* For master's, variable foreign language requirement, comprehensive exam, thesis (for some programs). *Entrance requirements:* For master's, GRE General Test (for MA in musicology), audition, interview, three letters of recommendation, transcripts, sample works. Additional exam requirements/recommendations for international students: Required—TOEFL (minimum score 550 paper-based; 79 iBT), IELTS (minimum score 6). *Application deadline:* For fall admission, 2/1 for domestic and international students; for spring admission, 12/15 for domestic and international students; for summer admission, 4/15 for domestic and international students. Applications are processed on a rolling basis. Application fee: $0. Electronic applications accepted. *Expenses:* $560 per credit. *Financial support:* In 2017–18, 19 students received support. Scholarships/grants, tuition waivers (full and partial), and unspecified assistantships available. Financial award application deadline: 7/15; financial award applicants required to submit FAFSA. *Faculty research:* Music neuroscience; woodwind pedagogy and repertoire; Johannes Kepler and Carolus Luython; music criticism in early 20th-century Germany and Austria; Arabic choral music; pedagogy of music theory. *Unit head:* Wendy Meaden, Dean, 317-940-9229, E-mail: wmeaden@butler.edu. *Application contact:* Diane Dubord, Graduate Student Services Specialist, 317-940-8107, E-mail: ddubord@butler.edu.
Website: http://www.butler.edu/jca/

California Baptist University, Program in Music, Riverside, CA 92504-3206. Offers conducting (MM); music education (MM); performance (MM). *Accreditation:* NASM. *Program availability:* Part-time, evening/weekend. *Faculty:* 13 full-time (6 women), 18 part-time/adjunct (9 women). *Students:* 13 full-time (6 women), 6 part-time (5 women); includes 5 minority (2 Black or African American, non-Hispanic/Latino; 2 Asian, non-Hispanic/Latino; 1 Hispanic/Latino), 9 international. Average age 27. 10 applicants, 70% accepted, 5 enrolled. In 2017, 8 master's awarded. *Degree requirements:* For master's, comprehensive exam or thesis. *Entrance requirements:* For master's, minimum undergraduate GPA of 2.75; bachelor's degree in music; three recommendations; comprehensive essay; interview/audition. Additional exam requirements/recommendations for international students: Required—TOEFL (minimum score 80 iBT). *Application deadline:* For fall admission, 8/1 priority date for domestic students, 7/1 for international students; for spring admission, 12/1 priority date for domestic students, 11/1 for international students. Applications are processed on a rolling basis. Application fee: $45. Electronic applications accepted. *Expenses:* Contact institution. *Financial support:* In 2017–18, 8 students received support. Federal Work-Study and scholarships/grants available. Financial award applicants required to submit CSS PROFILE or FAFSA. *Faculty research:* Choral conducting, church music, choir building, hymnology, music technology. *Unit head:* Dr. Joseph Bolin, Dean, School of Music, 951-343-4714, Fax: 951-343-4570, E-mail: jbolin@calbaptist.edu. *Application contact:* Rudy Villarruel, Graduate Admissions Counselor, 951-552-8132, E-mail: rvillarruel@calbaptist.edu.
Website: http://www.calbaptist.edu/masterofmusic/

California Institute of the Arts, The Herb Alpert School of Music, Valencia, CA 91355-2340. Offers African music (MFA, Adv C); composition (MFA, Adv C); composition/new media (MFA, Adv C); Indonesian music (MFA, Adv C); jazz (MFA, Adv C); North Indian music (MFA, Adv C); performance (MFA, Adv C); performer/composer (MFA, Adv C); voice (MFA, Adv C); world music performance (MFA). *Program availability:* Part-time. *Degree requirements:* For master's, composition or recital. *Entrance requirements:* For master's, audition or portfolio. Additional exam requirements/recommendations for international students: Required—TOEFL. Electronic applications accepted. *Faculty research:* Music composition and twentieth century performance practice, interactive multimedia and computer music, music cognition.

California State University, East Bay, Office of Graduate Studies, College of Letters, Arts, and Social Sciences, Department of Music, Hayward, CA 94542-3000. Offers MA. *Accreditation:* NASM. *Program availability:* Part-time. *Faculty:* 7 full-time (1 woman), 26 part-time/adjunct (7 women). *Students:* 8 full-time (4 women), 9 part-time (3 women); includes 9 minority (4 Black or African American, non-Hispanic/Latino; 1 American Indian or Alaska Native, non-Hispanic/Latino; 3 Hispanic/Latino; 1 Two or more races, non-Hispanic/Latino), 4 international. Average age 36. 20 applicants, 55% accepted, 4 enrolled. In 2017, 12 master's awarded. *Degree requirements:* For master's, variable foreign language requirement, comprehensive exam, project, recital, or thesis. *Entrance requirements:* For master's, minimum GPA of 3.0 in field; audition or work sample; 2 letters of recommendation. Additional exam requirements/recommendations for international students: Required—TOEFL (minimum score 550 paper-based). *Application deadline:* For fall admission, 3/2 for domestic and international students. Application fee: $55. Electronic applications accepted. *Financial support:* Fellowships, Federal Work-Study, institutionally sponsored loans, and scholarships/grants available. Support available to part-time students. Financial award application deadline: 3/2. *Unit head:* Buddy James, Chair, 510-885-3149, E-mail: buddy.james@csueastbay.edu. *Application contact:* Prof. Peter Marsh, Graduate Advisor, 510-885-3132, Fax: 510-885-3461, E-mail: peter.marsh@csueastbay.edu.
Website: http://www20.csueastbay.edu/class/departments/music/

California State University, Fresno, Division of Research and Graduate Studies, College of Arts and Humanities, Department of Music, Fresno, CA 93740-8027. Offers music (MA); music education (MA); performance (MA). *Accreditation:* NASM. *Program availability:* Part-time. *Degree requirements:* For master's, thesis or alternative. *Entrance requirements:* For master's, GRE General Test, BA in music, minimum GPA of 3.0. Additional exam requirements/recommendations for international students: Required—TOEFL. Electronic applications accepted. *Faculty research:* Technology transfer, folk art.

California State University, Fullerton, Graduate Studies, College of the Arts, Department of Music, Fullerton, CA 92831-3599. Offers music education (MA); performance (MM). *Accreditation:* NASM. *Program availability:* Part-time. *Faculty:* 13 full-time (3 women), 18 part-time/adjunct (2 women). *Students:* 20 full-time (10 women), 30 part-time (9 women); includes 17 minority (9 Asian, non-Hispanic/Latino; 5 Hispanic/Latino; 3 Two or more races, non-Hispanic/Latino), 8 international. Average age 28. 69 applicants, 46% accepted, 17 enrolled. *Degree requirements:* For master's, comprehensive exam, project or thesis. *Entrance requirements:* For master's, audition, major in music or related field, minimum GPA of 2.5 in last 60 units of course work. Application fee: $55. *Financial support:* Career-related internships or fieldwork, Federal Work-Study, institutionally sponsored loans, and scholarships/grants available. Support available to part-time students. Financial award application deadline: 3/1; financial award applicants required to submit FAFSA. *Unit head:* Dr. Marc Dickey, Chair, 657-278-3511. *Application contact:* Admissions/Applications, 657-278-2371.

California State University, Long Beach, Graduate Studies, College of the Arts, Department of Music, Long Beach, CA 90840. Offers composition (MM); music (MA). *Accreditation:* NASM. *Program availability:* Part-time. *Degree requirements:* For master's, thesis or alternative, departmental qualifying exam. Electronic applications accepted.

California State University, Los Angeles, Graduate Studies, College of Arts and Letters, Department of Music, Los Angeles, CA 90032-8530. Offers music composition (MM); music education (MA); musicology (MA); performance (MM). *Accreditation:* NASM. *Program availability:* Part-time, evening/weekend. *Degree requirements:* For master's, comprehensive exam, project or thesis. *Entrance requirements:* For master's, audition. Additional exam requirements/recommendations for international students: Required—TOEFL (minimum score 500 paper-based). Electronic applications accepted. *Faculty research:* Gregorian semiology, Baroque opera.

California State University, Northridge, Graduate Studies, Mike Curb College of Arts, Media, and Communication, Department of Music, Northridge, CA 91330. Offers composition (MM); conducting (MM); music education (MA); performance (MM). *Accreditation:* NASM. *Students:* 32 full-time (21 women), 35 part-time (18 women); includes 18 minority (1 Black or African American, non-Hispanic/Latino; 7 Asian, non-Hispanic/Latino; 7 Hispanic/Latino; 3 Two or more races, non-Hispanic/Latino), 21 international. Average age 28. 149 applicants, 48% accepted, 23 enrolled. In 2017, 71 master's awarded. *Degree requirements:* For master's, thesis. *Entrance requirements:* For master's, audition, GRE General Test or minimum GPA of 3.0. Additional exam requirements/recommendations for international students: Required—TOEFL. *Application deadline:* For fall admission, 11/30 for domestic students. Application fee: $55. *Financial support:* Application deadline: 3/1. *Unit head:* Ron Borczon, Chair, 816-677-4752. *Application contact:* 818-677-3184.
Website: http://www.csun.edu/music/

California State University, Sacramento, College of Arts and Letters, Department of Music, Sacramento, CA 95819. Offers composition (MM); conducting (MM); performance (MM). *Accreditation:* NASM. *Program availability:* Part-time. *Students:* 17 full-time (8 women), 10 part-time (4 women); includes 7 minority (1 Black or African American, non-Hispanic/Latino; 1 American Indian or Alaska Native, non-Hispanic/Latino; 2 Asian, non-Hispanic/Latino; 3 Hispanic/Latino). Average age 32. 18 applicants, 67% accepted, 12 enrolled. In 2017, 12 master's awarded. *Degree requirements:* For master's, thesis or project, writing proficiency exam. *Entrance requirements:* For master's, GRE, music exam, BA in music or equivalent, minimum GPA of 3.0 during

previous 2 years of course work. Additional exam requirements/recommendations for international students: Required—TOEFL (minimum score 550 paper-based; 80 iBT). *Application deadline:* For fall admission, 3/1 for domestic and international students; for spring admission, 9/15 for domestic students, 9/30 for international students. Applications are processed on a rolling basis. Application fee: $55. Electronic applications accepted. *Expenses:* Contact institution. *Financial support:* Teaching assistantships, career-related internships or fieldwork, Federal Work-Study, and scholarships/grants available. Support available to part-time students. Financial award application deadline: 3/1; financial award applicants required to submit FAFSA. *Unit head:* Dr. Ernie Hills, Chair, 916-278-5191, E-mail: hills@csus.edu. *Application contact:* Jose Martinez, Graduate Admissions Supervisor, 916-278-7871, E-mail: martinj@skymail.csus.edu.
Website: http://www.csus.edu/music

Campbellsville University, School of Music, Campbellsville, KY 42718-2799. Offers music (MA, MM), including conducting (MM), instrumental performance (MM), music education (MM), vocal performance and pedagogy (MM); musicology (MA); worship (MA). *Accreditation:* NASM. *Program availability:* Part-time, 100% online, blended/hybrid learning. *Faculty:* 14 full-time (6 women), 9 part-time/adjunct (4 women). *Students:* 25 part-time (11 women); includes 1 minority (Black or African American, non-Hispanic/ Latino), 6 international. Average age 31. 13 applicants, 38% accepted, 5 enrolled. In 2017, 3 master's awarded. *Degree requirements:* For master's, comprehensive exam, thesis (for some programs), paper or recital. *Entrance requirements:* For master's, GRE General Test or PRAXIS, minimum GPA of 2.75, college transcripts. Additional exam requirements/recommendations for international students: Required—TOEFL (minimum score 550 paper-based; 79 iBT); Recommended—IELTS (minimum score 6). *Application deadline:* Applications are processed on a rolling basis. Application fee: $25. Electronic applications accepted. Application fee is waived when completed online. *Expenses:* $399 per credit hour. *Financial support:* In 2017–18, 14 students received support. Unspecified assistantships and employee tuition waivers available. Financial award application deadline: 6/1; financial award applicants required to submit FAFSA. *Unit head:* Dr. Tony Cunha, Dean, 270-789-5240, Fax: 270-789-5524, E-mail: accunha@campbellsville.edu. *Application contact:* Monica Bamwine, Assistant Director of Graduate Admissions, 270-789-5221, Fax: 270-789-5071, E-mail: mkbamwine@campbellsville.edu.
Website: http://www.campbellsville.edu/music

Capital University, Conservatory of Music, Columbus, OH 43209-2394. Offers music education (MM), including instrumental emphasis, Kodály emphasis. Program offered only in summer. *Accreditation:* NASM. *Program availability:* Part-time. *Degree requirements:* For master's, comprehensive exam, thesis or alternative, chamber performance exam. *Entrance requirements:* For master's, music theory exam, minimum undergraduate GPA of 3.0. Additional exam requirements/recommendations for international students: Required—TOEFL (minimum score 550 paper-based; 80 iBT). Electronic applications accepted. *Expenses:* Contact institution. *Faculty research:* Folk song research, Kodály method, performance, composition.

Carleton University, Faculty of Graduate Studies, Faculty of Arts and Social Sciences, School for Studies in Art and Culture, Program in Music and Culture, Ottawa, ON K1S 5B6, Canada. Offers MA.

Carnegie Mellon University, College of Fine Arts, School of Music, Pittsburgh, PA 15213-3891. Offers collaborative piano (MM); composition (MM); instrumental performance (MM); music and technology (MS); music education (MM); vocal performance (MM). *Accreditation:* NASM. *Program availability:* Part-time. *Degree requirements:* For master's, comprehensive exam, recital. *Entrance requirements:* For master's, audition. *Faculty research:* Computer music, music history.

Case Western Reserve University, School of Graduate Studies, Department of Music, Program in Historical Musicology, Cleveland, OH 44106. Offers historical musicology (PhD); music history (MA). *Faculty:* 7 full-time (2 women). *Students:* 22 full-time (10 women), 1 part-time (0 women), 2 international. Average age 30. 22 applicants, 18% accepted, 4 enrolled. In 2017, 2 doctorates awarded. *Degree requirements:* For master's, thesis. *Entrance requirements:* Additional exam requirements/ recommendations for international students: Required—TOEFL (minimum score 577 paper-based; 90 iBT); Recommended—IELTS (minimum score 7). *Application deadline:* For fall admission, 12/15 for domestic students. Application fee: $50. *Expenses: Tuition:* Full-time $43,854; part-time $1827 per credit hour. *Required fees:* $50; $50 per credit hour. Tuition and fees vary according to course load and program. *Financial support:* Fellowships, teaching assistantships, career-related internships or fieldwork, tuition waivers (full), unspecified assistantships, and stipends available. *Faculty research:* Musicology, historical performance practice. *Unit head:* David J. Rothenberg, Associate Professor/Department Chair, 216-368-6046, Fax: 216-368-6557, E-mail: music@case.edu. *Application contact:* Laura Stauffer, Department Administrator, 216-368-0117, Fax: 216-368-6557, E-mail: music@case.edu.

Case Western Reserve University, School of Graduate Studies, Department of Music, Program in Historical Performance Practice, Cleveland, OH 44106. Offers MA, DMA, PhD. *Faculty:* 2 full-time (both women). *Students:* 10 full-time (5 women); includes 2 minority (1 Hispanic/Latino; 1 Two or more races, non-Hispanic/Latino), 2 international. Average age 26. 10 applicants, 40% accepted, 4 enrolled. In 2017, 2 doctorates awarded. Terminal master's awarded for partial completion of doctoral program. *Degree requirements:* For master's, one foreign language, comprehensive exam (for some programs), ensemble participation; juried lecture-recital; for doctorate, 2 foreign languages, comprehensive exam (for some programs), thesis/dissertation, ensemble participation; juried lecture-recital. *Entrance requirements:* For master's, GRE, statement of purpose; audio/video recording of a performance; two writing samples; three letters of recommendation; live audition; for doctorate, GRE, statement of purpose; two writing samples; curriculum vitae; three letters of recommendation. Additional exam requirements/recommendations for international students: Required—TOEFL (minimum score 577 paper-based; 90 iBT); Recommended—IELTS (minimum score 7). *Application deadline:* For fall admission, 1/1 priority date for domestic students. Application fee: $50. Electronic applications accepted. *Expenses: Tuition:* Full-time $43,854; part-time $1827 per credit hour. *Required fees:* $50; $50 per credit hour. Tuition and fees vary according to course load and program. *Financial support:* Fellowships, tuition waivers (full and partial), and stipends available. Financial award application deadline: 1/1; financial award applicants required to submit FAFSA. *Faculty research:* Early music, music history and historical performance practice. *Unit head:* David J. Rothenberg, Associate Professor/Department Chair, 216-368-6046, Fax: 216-368-6557, E-mail: music@case.edu. *Application contact:* Laura Stauffer, Department Administrator, 216-368-0117, Fax: 216-368-6557, E-mail: music@case.edu.
Website: http://music.case.edu/

The Catholic University of America, Benjamin T. Rome School of Music, Washington, DC 20064. Offers cello (Artist Diploma); chamber music (piano) (MM, DMA); composition (MM, DMA), including concert music (MM), stage music (MM); music (MAT); musicology (MA, PhD); orchestral conducting (MM, DMA, Artist Diploma); orchestral instruments/guitar (MM, DMA); piano (Artist Diploma); piano pedagogy (MM, DMA); piano performance (MM, DMA); sacred music (MMSM, DMA); violin (Artist Diploma); vocal accompanying (MM, DMA); vocal pedagogy (MM, DMA); vocal performance (MM, DMA); voice (Artist Diploma); MA/MSLIS. MA/MSLIS offered in partnership with Department of Library and Information Science. *Accreditation:* NASM. *Program availability:* Part-time. *Faculty:* 19 full-time (4 women), 43 part-time/adjunct (18 women). *Students:* 30 full-time (19 women), 61 part-time (27 women); includes 25 minority (7 Black or African American, non-Hispanic/Latino; 10 Asian, non-Hispanic/ Latino; 5 Hispanic/Latino; 3 Two or more races, non-Hispanic/Latino), 22 international. Average age 33. 104 applicants, 76% accepted, 26 enrolled. In 2017, 14 master's, 18 doctorates awarded. *Degree requirements:* For master's, variable foreign language requirement, comprehensive exam (for some programs), thesis (for some programs), final recital (for some programs); for doctorate, variable foreign language requirement, comprehensive exam (for some programs), thesis/dissertation (for some programs), final recital (for some programs); for Artist Diploma, variable foreign language requirement, final recital (for some programs). *Entrance requirements:* For master's, music theory and music history placement examinations, statement of purpose, 2 letters of recommendation, minimum undergraduate B average, audition (for all performance degrees), official copy of academic transcript showing completed and conferred BM; for doctorate, music theory and music history placement examinations, 2 letters of recommendation, minimum B average in all previous course work and degrees, official copies of academic transcripts showing completion and conferral of all previous degrees, audition (for all performance degrees); for Artist Diploma, music theory and music history placement examinations, statement of purpose, 2 letters of recommendation, minimum B average in all previous course work and degrees, BM, audition, official copies of academic transcripts showing completion and conferral of all previous degrees. Additional exam requirements/recommendations for international students: Required—TOEFL (minimum score 550 paper-based; 80 iBT). *Application deadline:* For fall admission, 7/15 priority date for domestic students, 7/1 for international students; for spring admission, 11/15 priority date for domestic students, 11/1 for international students. Applications are processed on a rolling basis. Application fee: $55. Electronic applications accepted. *Expenses:* Contact institution. *Financial support:* Fellowships, research assistantships, teaching assistantships, Federal Work-Study, scholarships/grants, tuition waivers (full and partial), and unspecified assistantships available. Financial award application deadline: 2/1; financial award applicants required to submit FAFSA. *Faculty research:* Composition, sacred music, orchestral instruments, piano and vocal performance, piano and vocal pedagogy. *Unit head:* Dr. Grayson Wagstaff, Dean, 202-319-5417, Fax: 202-319-6280, E-mail: cua-music@cua.edu. *Application contact:* Dr. Steven Brown, Director of Graduate Admissions, 202-319-5247, Fax: 202-319-6174, E-mail: cua-graduatestudies@cua.edu.
Website: https://music.catholic.edu/

Central Michigan University, College of Graduate Studies, College of Communication and Fine Arts, School of Music, Mount Pleasant, MI 48859. Offers composition (MM); conducting (MM); music education (MM); performance (MM). *Accreditation:* NASM. *Program availability:* Part-time. *Degree requirements:* For master's, thesis or alternative. Electronic applications accepted. *Faculty research:* Music education, music composition, conducting, music performance.

Central Washington University, School of Graduate Studies and Research, College of Arts and Humanities, Department of Music, Ellensburg, WA 98926. Offers composition (MM); conducting (MM); music education (MM); pedagogy (MM); performance (MM). *Accreditation:* NASM. *Entrance requirements:* For master's, minimum GPA of 3.0. Additional exam requirements/recommendations for international students: Required—TOEFL (minimum score 550 paper-based; 79 iBT) or IELTS (minimum score 6.5). *Application deadline:* For fall admission, 2/1 priority date for domestic students; for winter admission, 10/1 for domestic students; for spring admission, 1/1 for domestic students. Applications are processed on a rolling basis. Application fee: $50. Electronic applications accepted. *Financial support:* Application deadline: 3/1; applicants required to submit FAFSA. *Unit head:* Bret P. Smith, Associate Chair, 509-963-1548, E-mail: bpsmith@cwu.edu. *Application contact:* Justine Eason, Admissions Program Coordinator, 509-963-3103, Fax: 509-963-1799, E-mail: masters@cwu.edu.
Website: http://www.cwu.edu/~music/

Claremont Graduate University, Graduate Programs, School of Arts and Humanities, Department of Music, Claremont, CA 91711-6160. Offers church music (MA, DCM); composition (MA, DMA); historical performance practices (MA, DMA); musicology (MA, PhD); performance (MA, DMA); MBA/PhD. *Program availability:* Part-time. Terminal master's awarded for partial completion of doctoral program. *Degree requirements:* For master's, one foreign language, comprehensive exam, thesis (for some programs), oral and written qualifying exams, recitals; for doctorate, 2 foreign languages, comprehensive exam, thesis/dissertation (for some programs), oral and written qualifying exams, oral defense of dissertation, recitals. *Entrance requirements:* For master's and doctorate, GRE General Test, auditions, compositions, or papers. Additional exam requirements/recommendations for international students: Required—TOEFL (minimum score 75 iBT). Electronic applications accepted.

Cleveland Institute of Music, Graduate Programs, Cleveland, OH 44106-1776. Offers MM, DMA, AD, CPS. DMA and MM programs offered jointly with Case Western Reserve University. *Accreditation:* NASM (one or more programs are accredited). *Degree requirements:* For master's, comprehensive exam, recital; for doctorate, comprehensive exam, thesis/dissertation (for some programs), final projects; for other advanced degree, recital. *Entrance requirements:* For master's, theory placement tests, audition; for doctorate, diagnostic exams, theory placement test, audition; for other advanced degree, audition. Additional exam requirements/recommendations for international students: Required—TOEFL (minimum score 550 paper-based). Electronic applications accepted.

Cleveland State University, College of Graduate Studies, College of Liberal Arts and Social Sciences, Department of Music, Cleveland, OH 44115. Offers composition (MM); music education (MM). *Accreditation:* NASM. *Program availability:* Part-time, evening/ weekend. *Faculty:* 9 full-time (2 women), 19 part-time/adjunct (6 women). *Students:* 17 full-time (6 women), 19 part-time (8 women); includes 5 minority (1 Black or African American, non-Hispanic/Latino; 3 Hispanic/Latino; 1 Two or more races, non-Hispanic/ Latino), 8 international. Average age 26. 34 applicants, 91% accepted, 19 enrolled. In 2017, 8 master's awarded. *Entrance requirements:* For master's, departmental assessment in music history, minimum undergraduate GPA of 2.75, audition on primary instrument, or submission of composition portfolio or written samples (for music education). Additional exam requirements/recommendations for international students: Required—TOEFL (minimum score 550 paper-based; 78 iBT). *Application deadline:* For fall admission, 7/1 priority date for domestic students, 5/15 for international students; for spring admission, 11/15 for domestic students, 11/1 for international students; for summer admission, 4/1 for domestic students, 3/15 for international students. Applications are processed on a rolling basis. Application fee: $40. Electronic applications accepted. *Financial support:* In 2017–18, 14 students received support. Scholarships/grants, tuition waivers (partial), and unspecified assistantships available. Financial award application deadline: 3/15; financial award applicants required to submit FAFSA. *Faculty research:* Performance, music education, music composition. *Total annual research expenditures:* $26. *Unit head:* Dr. John Perrine, Chairperson/Associate Professor, 216-687-3959, Fax: 216-687-9279, E-mail: j.m.perrine@csuohio.edu. *Application contact:* Kate Bill, Music Admission Specialist, 216-687-5039, Fax: 216-687-9279, E-mail: m.c.bill@csuohio.edu.
Website: http://www.csuohio.edu/music/

The Colburn School Conservatory of Music, Graduate Programs, Los Angeles, CA 90012. Offers music (AD); performance (MM). *Accreditation:* NASM.

Colorado State University, College of Liberal Arts, School of Music, Theatre and Dance, Fort Collins, CO 80523-1779. Offers collaborative piano (MM). *Accreditation:* NASM. *Program availability:* Part-time. *Faculty:* 24 full-time (6 women), 10 part-time/adjunct (7 women). *Students:* 66 full-time (38 women), 99 part-time (73 women); includes 20 minority (1 Black or African American, non-Hispanic/Latino; 4 Asian, non-Hispanic/Latino; 13 Hispanic/Latino; 2 Two or more races, non-Hispanic/Latino), 16 international. Average age 29. 140 applicants, 57% accepted, 37 enrolled. In 2017, 46 master's awarded. *Degree requirements:* For master's, recital. *Entrance requirements:* For master's, diagnostic exams in music theory and music history, minimum GPA of 3.0; audition. Additional exam requirements/recommendations for international students: Recommended—TOEFL (minimum score 550 paper-based; 80 iBT), IELTS (minimum score 6.5). *Application deadline:* For fall admission, 2/15 for domestic and international students; for summer admission, 2/1 for domestic and international students. Application fee: $60 ($70 for international students). Electronic applications accepted. *Expenses:* Tuition, state resident: full-time $9917. Tuition, nonresident: full-time $24,312. *Required fees:* $2284. Tuition and fees vary according to course load and program. *Financial support:* In 2017–18, 40 students received support, including 25 teaching assistantships with full and partial tuition reimbursements available (averaging $8,839 per year); fellowships with full and partial tuition reimbursements available, scholarships/grants, health care benefits, and unspecified assistantships also available. Financial award application deadline: 2/15. *Total annual research expenditures:* $13,432. *Unit head:* Dr. Daniel Goble, Director, 970-491-5529, E-mail: dan.goble@colostate.edu. *Application contact:* Dr. G. Murray Oliver, Graduate Program Coordinator, 970-491-5193, Fax: 970-491-7541, E-mail: murray.oliver@colostate.edu.
Website: http://smtd.colostate.edu/

Columbia College Chicago, School of Graduate Studies, Music Department, Chicago, IL 60605-1996. Offers MFA. *Students:* 25 full-time (4 women); includes 4 minority (2 Black or African American, non-Hispanic/Latino; 2 Hispanic/Latino), 9 international. 57 applicants, 49% accepted, 13 enrolled. *Entrance requirements:* For master's, self-assessment essay, work samples, resume, letters of recommendation, transcripts. Additional exam requirements/recommendations for international students: Required—TOEFL, IELTS. *Application deadline:* For fall admission, 1/15 for domestic and international students. Application fee: $55 ($100 for international students). Electronic applications accepted. *Expenses:* Contact institution. *Financial support:* In 2017–18, 6 students received support. Research assistantships, career-related internships or fieldwork, Federal Work-Study, scholarships/grants, and unspecified assistantships available. Financial award application deadline: 1/15. *Unit head:* Rosita Sands, Chair, 312-369-6286, E-mail: rsands@colum.edu. *Application contact:* David Marts, Graduate Admissions, 312-369-7942, E-mail: dmarts@colum.edu.
Website: https://www.colum.edu/academics/fine-and-performing-arts/music/index.html

Columbia University, Graduate School of Arts and Sciences, New York, NY 10027. Offers African-American studies (MA); American studies (MA); anthropology (MA, PhD); art history and archaeology (MA, PhD); astronomy (PhD); biological sciences (PhD); biotechnology (MA); chemical physics (PhD); chemistry (PhD); classical studies (MA, PhD); classics (MA, PhD); climate and society (MA); conservation biology (MA); earth and environmental sciences (PhD); East Asia: regional studies (MA); East Asian languages and cultures (MA, PhD); ecology, evolution and environmental biology (MA), including conservation biology; ecology, evolution, and environmental biology (PhD), including ecology and evolutionary biology, evolutionary primatology; economics (MA, PhD); English and comparative literature (MA, PhD); French and Romance philology (MA, PhD); Germanic languages (MA, PhD); global French studies (MA); global thought (MA); Hispanic cultural studies (MA); history (PhD); history and literature (MA); human rights studies (MA); Islamic studies (MA); Italian (MA, PhD); Japanese pedagogy (MA); Jewish studies (MA); Latin America and the Caribbean: regional studies (MA); Latin American and Iberian cultures (PhD); mathematics (MA, PhD), including finance (MA); medieval and Renaissance studies (MA); Middle Eastern, South Asian, and African studies (MA, PhD); modern art: critical and curatorial studies (MA); modern European studies (MA); museum anthropology (MA); music (DMA, PhD); oral history (MA); philosophical foundations of physics (MA); philosophy (MA, PhD); physics (PhD); political science (MA, PhD); psychology (PhD); quantitative methods in the social sciences (MA); religion (MA, PhD); Russia, Eurasia and East Europe: regional studies (MA); Russian translation (MA); Slavic cultures (MA); Slavic languages (MA, PhD); sociology (MA, PhD); South Asian studies (MA); statistics (MA, PhD); theatre (PhD). Dual-degree programs require admission to both Graduate School of Arts and Sciences and another Columbia school. *Program availability:* Part-time. Terminal master's awarded for partial completion of doctoral program. *Degree requirements:* For master's, variable foreign language requirement, comprehensive exam (for some programs), thesis (for some programs); for doctorate, variable foreign language requirement, comprehensive exam (for some programs), thesis/dissertation. *Entrance requirements:* For master's and doctorate, GRE General Test, GRE Subject Test (for some programs). Additional exam requirements/recommendations for international students: Required—TOEFL, IELTS. Electronic applications accepted. *Expenses: Tuition:* Full-time $44,864; part-time $1704 per credit. *Required fees:* $2370 per semester. One-time fee: $105.

Columbia University, School of the Arts, Sound Art Program, New York, NY 10027. Offers MFA. *Expenses: Tuition:* Full-time $44,864; part-time $1704 per credit. *Required fees:* $2370 per semester. One-time fee: $105. *Unit head:* Miya Masaoka, Director, E-mail: soundart@columbia.edu. *Application contact:* Kenny Wong, Director of Admissions and Financial Aid, 212-854-2134, E-mail: admissions-arts@columbia.edu.
Website: https://arts.columbia.edu/sound-art

Columbus State University, Graduate Studies, College of the Arts, Schwob School of Music, Columbus, GA 31907-5645. Offers music (Artist Diploma); music education (MM); music performance (MM). *Accreditation:* NASM; NCATE (one or more programs are accredited). *Program availability:* Part-time. *Faculty:* 25 full-time (10 women), 4 part-time/adjunct (2 women). *Students:* 44 full-time (15 women), 7 part-time (3 women); includes 11 minority (5 Black or African American, non-Hispanic/Latino; 4 Asian, non-Hispanic/Latino; 1 Hispanic/Latino; 1 Native Hawaiian or other Pacific Islander, non-Hispanic/Latino), 20 international. Average age 27. 59 applicants, 44% accepted, 17 enrolled. In 2017, 11 master's, 5 Artist Diplomas awarded. *Degree requirements:* For master's, exit exam. *Entrance requirements:* For master's, audition, letters of recommendation, undergraduate degree in music with minimum GPA of 2.5. Additional exam requirements/recommendations for international students: Required—TOEFL (minimum score 550 paper-based; 79 iBT). *Application deadline:* For fall admission, 6/30 for domestic students, 5/1 for international students; for spring admission, 11/1 for domestic and international students; for summer admission, 3/1 for domestic and international students. Applications are processed on a rolling basis. Application fee: $50. Electronic applications accepted. *Expenses:* Tuition, state resident: full-time $3708; part-time $2472 per year. Tuition, nonresident: full-time $14,418; part-time $9612 per year. *International tuition:* $19,218 full-time. *Required fees:* $1605. Tuition and fees vary according to program. *Financial support:* In 2017–18, 43 students received support, including 26 research assistantships with partial tuition reimbursements available (averaging $3,000 per year); career-related internships or fieldwork, Federal Work-Study, institutionally sponsored loans, scholarships/grants, tuition waivers (partial), and unspecified assistantships also available. Support available to part-time students. Financial award application deadline: 5/1; financial award applicants required to submit FAFSA. *Unit head:* Dr. Edwin Scott Harris, Director, 706-507-8419, E-mail: harris_scott@columbusstate.edu. *Application contact:* Catrina Smith-Edmond, Assistant Director for Graduate and Global Admission, 706-507-8824, Fax: 706-568-5091, E-mail: smithedmond_catrina@columbusstate.edu.
Website: http://music.columbusstate.edu/

Concordia University, School of Graduate Studies, Faculty of Fine Arts, Department of Music, Montréal, QC H3G 1M8, Canada. Offers advanced music performance studies (Diploma). *Degree requirements:* For Diploma, performance, 2 recitals.

Concordia University Chicago, College of Graduate and Innovative Programs, Program in Church Music, River Forest, IL 60305-1499. Offers MCM. *Accreditation:* NASM. *Program availability:* Part-time. *Degree requirements:* For master's, composition, recital, or thesis. *Entrance requirements:* For master's, minimum GPA of 2.9, audition. Additional exam requirements/recommendations for international students: Required—TOEFL (minimum score 550 paper-based). Electronic applications accepted. *Faculty research:* Twentieth-century sacred choral music, liturgical context of sacred music after the Council of Trent, dance and music of J.S. Bach.

Concordia University Chicago, College of Graduate and Innovative Programs, Program in Music, River Forest, IL 60305-1499. Offers MA. *Program availability:* Part-time. *Degree requirements:* For master's, composition, recital, or thesis. *Entrance requirements:* For master's, minimum GPA of 2.9, audition. Additional exam requirements/recommendations for international students: Required—TOEFL (minimum score 550 paper-based). Electronic applications accepted.

Concordia University Wisconsin, Graduate Programs, School of Arts and Sciences, Program in Church Music, Mequon, WI 53097-2402. Offers MCM. *Degree requirements:* For master's, comprehensive exam, thesis or alternative. *Entrance requirements:* For master's, minimum GPA of 3.0. Additional exam requirements/recommendations for international students: Required—TOEFL.

Conservatorio de Musica de Puerto Rico, Program in Musical Performance, San Juan, PR 00907. Offers guitar (Diploma); orchestral instruments (Diploma); piano (Diploma); vocal performance (Diploma). *Entrance requirements:* For degree, 3 letters of recommendation, audition, degree in music, minimum GPA of 2.5.

Converse College, Petrie School of Music, Spartanburg, SC 29302. Offers music education (M Mus); performance (M Mus). *Accreditation:* NASM. *Program availability:* Part-time, evening/weekend. *Degree requirements:* For master's, variable foreign language requirement, comprehensive exam, thesis (for some programs), recitals. *Entrance requirements:* For master's, NTE (music education), audition, 3 letters of recommendation. Additional exam requirements/recommendations for international students: Required—TOEFL. *Application deadline:* For spring admission, 3/1 priority date for domestic and international students. Applications are processed on a rolling basis. Application fee: $40. Electronic applications accepted. *Financial support:* Career-related internships or fieldwork, Federal Work-Study, institutionally sponsored loans, and unspecified assistantships available. Support available to part-time students. Financial award application deadline: 4/15. *Faculty research:* Chamber music, opera, performance, composition, recording. *Unit head:* Chris Vaneman, Head, Petrie School of Music/Associate Professor of Flute and Musicology, 864-596-9038, E-mail: chris.vaneman@converse.edu.
Website: http://www.converse.edu/academics/school-arts/petrie-school-music

Cornell University, Graduate School, Graduate Fields of Arts and Sciences, Field of Music, Ithaca, NY 14853. Offers composition (DMA); musicology (PhD); performance practice (DMA); theory of music (MA). *Degree requirements:* For doctorate, comprehensive exam, thesis/dissertation, 1 foreign language (DMA), 2 foreign languages (PhD). *Entrance requirements:* For doctorate, GRE General Test, 2 music papers (PhD); 2 recent scores with recording and 1 music paper (DMA in composition); 1 music paper, recording and audition (DMA in performance practice). Additional exam requirements/recommendations for international students: Required—TOEFL (minimum score 600 paper-based; 77 iBT). Electronic applications accepted. *Faculty research:* Music history, music theory, performance practice, ethnomusicology, composition.

Curtis Institute of Music, Graduate Studies, Philadelphia, PA 19103-6107. Offers opera (MM). *Accreditation:* NASM. *Entrance requirements:* For master's, audition or performance in 2 or more principal roles or 6 major scenes.

Dalhousie University, Faculty of Arts and Social Science, Department of Musicology, Halifax, NS B3H 4R2, Canada. Offers MA. *Entrance requirements:* Additional exam requirements/recommendations for international students: Required—TOEFL, IELTS, CANTEST, CAEL, or Michigan English Language Assessment Battery. Electronic applications accepted.

Dartmouth College, School of Graduate and Advanced Studies, Department of Music, Hanover, NH 03755. Offers digital music (MA). *Faculty:* 11 full-time (3 women), 23 part-time/adjunct (9 women). *Students:* 6 full-time (2 women); includes 1 minority (Two or more races, non-Hispanic/Latino). Average age 24. 21 applicants, 19% accepted, 3 enrolled. In 2017, 4 master's awarded. *Entrance requirements:* Additional exam requirements/recommendations for international students: Required—TOEFL. *Application deadline:* For fall admission, 2/1 for domestic students. Application fee: $35. Electronic applications accepted. *Financial support:* Fellowships, career-related internships or fieldwork, institutionally sponsored loans, and tuition waivers (full) available. *Faculty research:* Composition and design of computer music software and related topics. *Unit head:* Michael Casey, Chair, 603-646-9609. *Application contact:* Catherine La Touche, Administrative Assistant, 603-646-2520, Fax: 603-646-2551.
Website: http://music.dartmouth.edu/

DePaul University, School of Music, Chicago, IL 60614. Offers composition (MM); jazz studies (MM); music education (MM); music performance (MM); performance (Certificate). *Accreditation:* NASM (one or more programs are accredited). *Program availability:* Part-time, evening/weekend. *Degree requirements:* For master's, comprehensive exam. *Entrance requirements:* For master's, bachelor's degree in music or related field, minimum GPA of 3.0, auditions (performance), scores (composition); for Certificate, master's degree in performance or related field, auditions (for performance majors). Additional exam requirements/recommendations for international students: Required—TOEFL (minimum score 550 paper-based; 80 iBT). *Application deadline:* For fall admission, 12/1 priority date for domestic and international students. Applications are processed on a rolling basis. Application fee: $40. Electronic applications accepted. *Expenses:* Contact institution. *Financial support:* Application deadline: 12/1; applicants required to submit FAFSA. *Unit head:* Ronald Caltabiano, Dean, 773-325-7256, Fax: 773-325-7429, E-mail: rcalt@depaul.edu. *Application contact:* Ross Beacraft, Director of Admission, 773-325-7444, Fax: 773-325-7429, E-mail: musicadmissions@depaul.edu.
Website: http://music.depaul.edu/

Dominican University of California, School of Liberal Arts and Education, Humanities Program, San Rafael, CA 94901-2298. Offers applied music (MA); art history (MA); creative writing (MA); gender studies (MA); history (MA); philosophy (MA); political theory (MA); religion (MA). *Program availability:* Part-time. *Faculty:* 7 full-time (4

women), 1 (woman) part-time/adjunct. *Students:* 6 full-time (5 women), 16 part-time (12 women); includes 8 minority (3 Black or African American, non-Hispanic/Latino; 4 Hispanic/Latino; 1 Two or more races, non-Hispanic/Latino), 2 international. Average age 45. 7 applicants, 100% accepted, 5 enrolled. In 2017, 14 master's awarded. *Degree requirements:* For master's, thesis or alternative. *Entrance requirements:* For master's, minimum GPA of 3.0, interview. Additional exam requirements/recommendations for international students: Required—TOEFL (minimum score 550 paper-based; 80 iBT), IELTS (minimum score 6.5). *Application deadline:* For fall admission, 5/15 priority date for domestic and international students; for spring admission, 11/15 priority date for domestic and international students. Applications are processed on a rolling basis. Application fee: $0. Electronic applications accepted. *Expenses: Tuition:* Full-time $17,370; part-time $965 per credit. *Required fees:* $150 per semester. Tuition and fees vary according to course load and program. *Financial support:* In 2017–18, 4 students received support. Scholarships/grants available. Support available to part-time students. Financial award application deadline: 3/2; financial award applicants required to submit FAFSA. *Unit head:* Joan Baranow, Program Director, 415-485-3264, E-mail: joan.baranow@dominican.edu. *Application contact:* Michael Lavigna, Assistant Director of Graduate Admissions, 415-485-3253, Fax: 415-485-3214, E-mail: gradmissions@dominican.edu.
Website: https://www.dominican.edu/academics/lae/graduate-programs/ma-in-humanities/index_html

Duke University, Graduate School, Department of Music, Durham, NC 27708. Offers music composition (PhD); musicology (PhD); performance practice (PhD). *Program availability:* Part-time. Terminal master's awarded for partial completion of doctoral program. *Degree requirements:* For doctorate, 3 foreign languages, thesis/dissertation. *Entrance requirements:* For doctorate, GRE General Test, paper on musical topic (for musicology); samples of compositions (for music composition). Additional exam requirements/recommendations for international students: Required—TOEFL (minimum score 577 paper-based; 90 iBT) or IELTS (minimum score 7). Electronic applications accepted.

Duquesne University, Mary Pappert School of Music, Pittsburgh, PA 15282-0001. Offers music education (MM). *Accreditation:* NASM. *Program availability:* Part-time. *Faculty:* 26 full-time (9 women), 77 part-time/adjunct (22 women). *Students:* 54 full-time (21 women), 9 part-time (3 women); includes 4 minority (1 Black or African American, non-Hispanic/Latino; 1 Asian, non-Hispanic/Latino; 2 Hispanic/Latino), 23 international. Average age 26. 76 applicants, 95% accepted, 31 enrolled. In 2017, 47 master's, 12 ADs awarded. *Degree requirements:* For master's, comprehensive exam, thesis (for some programs), recital (music performance); for AD, recital. *Entrance requirements:* For master's, audition, minimum undergraduate QPA of 3.0 in music, portfolio of original compositions, or music education experience; for AD, audition. Additional exam requirements/recommendations for international students: Required—TOEFL (minimum score 550 paper-based; 79 iBT), IELTS (minimum score 6.5). *Application deadline:* For fall admission, 7/1 for domestic and international students; for spring admission, 12/1 for domestic and international students; for summer admission, 6/1 for domestic students, 5/1 for international students. Applications are processed on a rolling basis. Application fee: $50. Electronic applications accepted. Application fee is waived when completed online. *Expenses:* $1,525 per credit. *Financial support:* In 2017–18, 76 students received support. Scholarships/grants and unspecified assistantships available. Financial award application deadline: 4/1. *Faculty research:* Assessment of music education and professional dispositions; music philosophy; curricular design, pedagogy, and assessment; music composition; music performance. *Unit head:* Dr. Seth Beckman, Dean/Professor, 412-396-6082, Fax: 412-396-1524, E-mail: beckmans@duq.edu. *Application contact:* Thomas Carsecka, Director of Music Admissions, 412-396-5983, Fax: 412-396-5719, E-mail: carseckat@duq.edu.
Website: http://duq.edu/music

East Carolina University, Graduate School, College of Fine Arts and Communication, School of Music, Greenville, NC 27858-4353. Offers advanced performance studies (Certificate); composition (MM); music education (MM), including choral conducting, instrumental conducting, music theory/composition, music therapy, performance, Suzuki pedagogy; music therapy (MM); Suzuki pedagogy (Certificate); theory (MM); woodwind specialist (MM), including accompanying, choral conducting, instrumental, instrumental conducting, jazz studies, keyboard, organ, piano pedagogy, Suzuki string pedagogy, vocal pedagogy, voice, woodwind specialist. *Accreditation:* NASM. *Program availability:* Part-time. *Students:* 31 full-time (16 women), 18 part-time (8 women); includes 11 minority (4 Black or African American, non-Hispanic/Latino; 5 Asian, non-Hispanic/Latino; 2 Two or more races, non-Hispanic/Latino), 1 international. Average age 28. 39 applicants, 85% accepted, 21 enrolled. In 2017, 10 master's, 2 Certificates awarded. *Degree requirements:* For master's, comprehensive exam, thesis optional. *Application deadline:* For fall admission, 6/1 priority date for domestic students. Applications are processed on a rolling basis. Application fee: $75. *Expenses:* Tuition, state resident: full-time $4749; part-time $297 per credit hour. Tuition, nonresident: full-time $17,898; part-time $1119 per credit hour. *Required fees:* $2691; $224 per credit hour. Part-time tuition and fees vary according to course load and program. *Financial support:* Fellowships, research assistantships, teaching assistantships, and Federal Work-Study available. Support available to part-time students. Financial award application deadline: 6/1. *Unit head:* Christopher Ulffers, Director, 252-328-4270, E-mail: ulffersj@ecu.edu.
Website: http://www.ecu.edu/music/

Eastern Illinois University, Graduate School, College of Liberal Arts and Sciences, Department of Music, Charleston, IL 61920. Offers composition (MA); conducting (MA); music education (MA); performance (MA). *Accreditation:* NASM. *Program availability:* Part-time, evening/weekend, online learning. *Degree requirements:* For master's, comprehensive exam (for some programs), thesis (for some programs). *Entrance requirements:* For master's, personal statement, resume, three letters of recommendation. Additional exam requirements/recommendations for international students: Required—TOEFL (minimum score 500 paper-based; 61 iBT), IELTS (minimum score 6). *Application deadline:* For fall admission, 5/15 for domestic and international students; for spring admission, 10/15 for domestic and international students. Applications are processed on a rolling basis. Application fee: $30. Electronic applications accepted. *Financial support:* Teaching assistantships with full tuition reimbursements, career-related internships or fieldwork, Federal Work-Study, and unspecified assistantships available. Support available to part-time students. Financial award application deadline: 3/1; financial award applicants required to submit FAFSA. *Unit head:* Shellie L. Gregorich, Chair, 217-581-3010, Fax: 217-581-7137, E-mail: slgregorich@eiu.edu. *Application contact:* Shellie L. Gregorich, Chair, 217-581-3010, Fax: 217-581-7137, E-mail: slgregorich@eiu.edu.
Website: http://www.eiu.edu/musicgrad/

Eastern Kentucky University, The Graduate School, College of Arts and Sciences, Department of Music, Richmond, KY 40475-3102. Offers choral conducting (MM); performance (MM); theory/composition (MM). *Accreditation:* NASM. *Program availability:* Part-time. *Degree requirements:* For master's, thesis optional. *Entrance requirements:* For master's, GRE General Test, minimum GPA of 2.5. *Faculty research:* Technology.

Eastern Michigan University, Graduate School, College of Arts and Sciences, School of Music and Dance, Ypsilanti, MI 48197. Offers MM. *Accreditation:* NASM. *Program availability:* Part-time, evening/weekend, online learning. *Faculty:* 24 full-time (11 women). *Students:* 4 full-time (3 women), 12 part-time (7 women); includes 2 minority (1 Asian, non-Hispanic/Latino; 1 Hispanic/Latino), 1 international. Average age 29. 28 applicants, 50% accepted, 6 enrolled. In 2017, 10 master's awarded. *Entrance requirements:* Additional exam requirements/recommendations for international students: Required—TOEFL. *Application deadline:* Applications are processed on a rolling basis. Application fee: $45. *Financial support:* Fellowships, research assistantships with full tuition reimbursements, teaching assistantships with full tuition reimbursements, career-related internships or fieldwork, Federal Work-Study, institutionally sponsored loans, scholarships/grants, tuition waivers (partial), and unspecified assistantships available. Support available to part-time students. Financial award applicants required to submit FAFSA. *Unit head:* Dr. Diane Winder, Director, 734-487-4380, Fax: 734-487-6939, E-mail: dwinder@emich.edu. *Application contact:* Dr. David Pierce, Coordinator of Music Advising, 734-487-4380, Fax: 734-487-6939, E-mail: david.pierce@emich.edu.
Website: http://www.emich.edu/musicdance

Eastern University, Graduate Education Programs, St. Davids, PA 19087-3696. Offers ESL program specialist (K-12) (Certificate); general supervisor (PreK-12) (Certificate); health and physical education (K-12) (Certificate); middle level (4-8) (Certificate); multicultural education (M Ed); music (K-12) (Certificate); Pre K-4 (Certificate); Pre K-4 with special education (Certificate); reading (M Ed); reading specialist (K-12) (Certificate); reading supervisor (K-12) (Certificate); school counseling (MA, CAGS); school principalship (preK-12) (Certificate); school psychology (MS, CAGS); secondary biology education (7-12) (Certificate); secondary chemistry education (7-12) (Certificate); secondary communication education (7-12) (Certificate); secondary English education (7-12) (Certificate); secondary math education (7-12) (Certificate); secondary social studies education (7-12) (Certificate); special education (M Ed); special education (7-12) (Certificate); special education (Pre K-8) (Certificate); special education supervisor (K-12) (Certificate); TESOL (M Ed); world language (Certificate), including Spanish. *Program availability:* Part-time, evening/weekend, online learning. *Students:* 46 full-time (40 women), 115 part-time (93 women); includes 65 minority (42 Black or African American, non-Hispanic/Latino; 3 Asian, non-Hispanic/Latino; 14 Hispanic/Latino; 6 Two or more races, non-Hispanic/Latino), 1 international. Average age 32. In 2017, 72 master's awarded. *Entrance requirements:* Additional exam requirements/recommendations for international students: Required—TOEFL. *Application deadline:* Applications are processed on a rolling basis. Application fee: $35. Electronic applications accepted. Application fee is waived when completed online. *Expenses:* Contact institution. *Unit head:* Michael Dziedziak, Executive Director of Enrollment, 800-452-0996, E-mail: gpsadmissions@eastern.edu.
Website: https://www.eastern.edu/academics/programs/education-department-graduate-programs/graduate-programs

Eastern Washington University, Graduate Studies, College of Arts, Letters and Education, Department of Music, Cheney, WA 99004-2431. Offers composition (MA); instrumental/vocal performance (MA); jazz pedagogy (MA); liberal arts (MA); music education (MA). *Accreditation:* NASM. *Program availability:* Part-time. *Faculty:* 17. *Students:* 10 full-time (4 women), 3 part-time (0 women), 1 international. Average age 31. 12 applicants, 58% accepted, 5 enrolled. In 2017, 7 master's awarded. *Degree requirements:* For master's, comprehensive exam, thesis or alternative. *Entrance requirements:* For master's, GRE General Test, minimum GPA of 3.0. Additional exam requirements/recommendations for international students: Required—TOEFL (minimum score 580 paper-based; 92 iBT), IELTS (minimum score 7), TWE, PTE (minimum score 63). *Application deadline:* For fall admission, 4/1 priority date for domestic students; for spring admission, 1/15 for domestic students. Applications are processed on a rolling basis. Application fee: $75. Electronic applications accepted. *Expenses:* Tuition, state resident: full-time $11,191; part-time $373.06 per credit. Tuition, nonresident: full-time $25,995; part-time $866.52 per credit. *Financial support:* In 2017–18, 8 students received support, including teaching assistantships with partial tuition reimbursements available (averaging $10,000 per year); career-related internships or fieldwork, Federal Work-Study, institutionally sponsored loans, scholarships/grants, health care benefits, tuition waivers (partial), and unspecified assistantships also available. Support available to part-time students. Financial award application deadline: 2/1; financial award applicants required to submit FAFSA. *Unit head:* Dr. Jody Graves, 509-359-6119, E-mail: jgraves@ewu.edu.
Website: http://www.ewu.edu/cale/programs/music.xml

Emory University, Laney Graduate School, Department of Music, Atlanta, GA 30322-1100. Offers choral conducting (MM, MSM); organ performance (MM, MSM). Terminal master's awarded for partial completion of doctoral program. *Degree requirements:* For master's, comprehensive exam, recital or worship service. *Entrance requirements:* For master's, GRE General Test, audition, interview. Additional exam requirements/recommendations for international students: Required—TOEFL. Electronic applications accepted. *Faculty research:* Nineteenth century criticism, Heinrich Schenker, Bach aria styles, contemporary passion music, Louis Andriessen, cross-cultural research, organ performance.

Emporia State University, Department of Music, Emporia, KS 66801-5415. Offers MM. *Accreditation:* NASM. *Program availability:* Part-time. *Faculty:* 13 full-time (4 women), 4 part-time/adjunct (all women). *Students:* 12 full-time (8 women), 8 part-time (1 woman); includes 1 minority (Black or African American, non-Hispanic/Latino), 8 international. 8 applicants, 63% accepted, 5 enrolled. In 2017, 2 master's awarded. *Degree requirements:* For master's, comprehensive exam or thesis. *Entrance requirements:* For master's, music qualifying exam, appropriate undergraduate degree. Additional exam requirements/recommendations for international students: Required—TOEFL (minimum score 520 paper-based; 68 iBT). *Application deadline:* For fall admission, 8/15 priority date for domestic students. Applications are processed on a rolling basis. Application fee: $30 ($75 for international students). Electronic applications accepted. *Expenses:* Tuition, state resident: full-time $6084; part-time $253.50 per credit hour. Tuition, nonresident: full-time $18,924; part-time $788.50 per credit hour. *Required fees:* $1943; $80.95 per credit hour. Tuition and fees vary according to campus/location. *Financial support:* In 2017–18, 4 teaching assistantships with full tuition reimbursements (averaging $6,526 per year) were awarded; Federal Work-Study, institutionally sponsored loans, health care benefits, and unspecified assistantships also available. Financial award application deadline: 3/15; financial award applicants required to submit FAFSA. *Unit head:* Dr. Allan D. Comstock, Chair, 620-341-5431, E-mail: acomstoc@emporia.edu. *Application contact:* Dr. Andrew Houchins, Graduate Coordinator, 620-341-6089, E-mail: ahouchin@emporia.edu.
Website: http://www.emporia.edu/music/

Five Towns College, Graduate Programs, Dix Hills, NY 11746-6055. Offers childhood education (MS Ed); composition and arranging (DMA); jazz/commercial music (MM); music education (MM, DMA); music history and literature (DMA); music performance (DMA). *Program availability:* Part-time. *Faculty:* 12 full-time (3 women), 6 part-time/adjunct (0 women). *Students:* 18 full-time (7 women), 6 part-time (2 women); includes 9 minority (3 Black or African American, non-Hispanic/Latino; 4 Asian, non-Hispanic/

Music

Latino; 1 Hispanic/Latino; 1 Two or more races, non-Hispanic/Latino), 1 international. Average age 35. 63 applicants, 11% accepted, 7 enrolled. In 2017, 4 master's, 2 doctorates awarded. *Degree requirements:* For master's, thesis, exams, major composition or capstone project, recital; for doctorate, comprehensive exam, thesis/dissertation, final oral exam. *Entrance requirements:* For master's, audition (for MM); New York state teaching certification (for MS Ed); personal statement, two letters of recommendation; for doctorate, 3 letters of recommendation, audition, essay. Additional exam requirements/recommendations for international students: Required—TOEFL (minimum score 520 paper-based; 85 iBT); Recommended—IELTS (minimum score 7). *Application deadline:* For fall admission, 9/1 for domestic and international students; for spring admission, 1/25 for domestic and international students. Applications are processed on a rolling basis. Application fee: $50. Electronic applications accepted. *Financial support:* Fellowships with tuition reimbursements, teaching assistantships with tuition reimbursements, and tuition waivers (partial) available. Financial award applicants required to submit FAFSA. *Faculty research:* Teaching methods, teaching strategies and techniques, analysis of modern music, jazz. *Application contact:* Ronnie MacDonald, Director of Admissions, 631-656-2110, Fax: 631-656-2172, E-mail: admissions@ftc.edu.
Website: http://www.ftc.edu

Florida Atlantic University, Dorothy F. Schmidt College of Arts and Letters, Department of Music, Boca Raton, FL 33431-0991. Offers MM. *Accreditation:* NASM. *Program availability:* Part-time. *Faculty:* 13 full-time (7 women), 9 part-time/adjunct (5 women). *Students:* 13 full-time (4 women); includes 3 minority (1 Black or African American, non-Hispanic/Latino; 2 Hispanic/Latino), 3 international. Average age 26. 13 applicants, 69% accepted, 6 enrolled. In 2017, 11 master's awarded. *Degree requirements:* For master's, one foreign language, comprehensive exam, thesis (for some programs), lecture/recital or thesis. *Entrance requirements:* For master's, placement evaluations in music history and theory, audition, minimum GPA of 3.0 in last 60 hours of course work. Additional exam requirements/recommendations for international students: Required—TOEFL (minimum score 500 paper-based; 61 iBT), IELTS (minimum score 6). *Application deadline:* For fall admission, 7/1 priority date for domestic students, 2/15 for international students; for spring admission, 11/1 for domestic students, 7/15 for international students. Applications are processed on a rolling basis. Application fee: $30. *Expenses:* Tuition, state resident: full-time $7400; part-time $369.82 per credit. Tuition, nonresident: full-time $20,496; part-time $1042.81 per credit. *Financial support:* Fellowships with partial tuition reimbursements, teaching assistantships with partial tuition reimbursements, career-related internships or fieldwork, Federal Work-Study, and scholarships/grants available. Financial award application deadline: 5/1. *Faculty research:* Classical guitar history and literature, women composers, Mozart opera, composition, performance. *Unit head:* Dr. Sandra McClain, Graduate Studies Coordinator, 561-297-3820, E-mail: smcclai2@fau.edu.
Website: http://www.fau.edu/music/

Florida International University, College of Communication, Architecture and The Arts, School of Music, Miami, FL 33199. Offers music (MM); music education (MS). *Accreditation:* NASM. *Program availability:* Part-time, evening/weekend. *Faculty:* 22 full-time (4 women), 27 part-time/adjunct (7 women). *Students:* 27 full-time (11 women), 10 part-time (5 women); includes 23 minority (6 Black or African American, non-Hispanic/Latino; 1 Asian, non-Hispanic/Latino; 15 Hispanic/Latino; 1 Two or more races, non-Hispanic/Latino), 4 international. Average age 32. 46 applicants, 61% accepted, 14 enrolled. In 2017, 24 master's awarded. *Degree requirements:* For master's, thesis (for some programs). *Entrance requirements:* For master's, GRE (depending on program), statement of intent; 2 letters of recommendation; audition, interview and/or writing sample (depending on the area). Additional exam requirements/recommendations for international students: Required—TOEFL (minimum score 550 paper-based; 80 iBT). *Application deadline:* For fall admission, 6/1 for domestic students, 4/1 for international students; for spring admission, 10/1 for domestic students, 9/1 for international students. Applications are processed on a rolling basis. Application fee: $30. Electronic applications accepted. *Expenses:* Tuition, state resident: full-time $8912; part-time $446 per credit hour. Tuition, nonresident: full-time $21,393; part-time $992 per credit hour. *Required fees:* $390; $195 per semester. *Financial support:* Institutionally sponsored loans and scholarships/grants available. Financial award application deadline: 3/1; financial award applicants required to submit FAFSA. *Unit head:* Robert Dundas, Interim Chair, 305-348-3587, Fax: 305-348-4073, E-mail: robert.dundas@fiu.edu. *Application contact:* Joel Galand, Graduate Program Director, 305-348-7078, E-mail: galandj@fiu.edu.
Website: http://carta.fiu.edu/music/

Florida State University, The Graduate School, College of Music, Tallahassee, FL 32306. Offers accompanying (MM); arts administration (MA); choral conducting (MM); composition (MM, DM); ethnomusicology (MM); general music (MA); instrumental accompanying (MM); instrumental conducting (MM); jazz studies (MM); music theory (MM, PhD); music therapy (MM); musicology (MM, PhD), including ethnomusicology (PhD), historical musicology; opera (MM); performance (MM, DM); piano pedagogy (MM); piano technology (MA); vocal accompanying (MM). *Accreditation:* NASM. *Program availability:* Part-time. *Students:* 331 full-time (169 women); includes 100 minority (29 Black or African American, non-Hispanic/Latino; 40 Asian, non-Hispanic/Latino; 29 Hispanic/Latino; 2 Native Hawaiian or other Pacific Islander, non-Hispanic/Latino). Average age 26. 760 applicants, 47% accepted, 173 enrolled. In 2017, 94 master's, 45 doctorates awarded. *Degree requirements:* For master's, variable foreign language requirement, comprehensive exam (for some programs), thesis (for some programs), departmental qualifying exam; for doctorate, variable foreign language requirement, comprehensive exam (for some programs), thesis/dissertation, departmental qualifying exam. *Entrance requirements:* For master's, GRE General Test (for some programs), audition, minimum GPA of 3.0; for doctorate, GRE General Test (for some programs), audition, master's degree, minimum GPA of 3.0. Additional exam requirements/recommendations for international students: Required—TOEFL (minimum score 590 paper-based; 97 iBT), IELTS (minimum score 7.5). *Application deadline:* For fall admission, 7/1 for domestic and international students; for spring admission, 11/1 for domestic and international students; for summer admission, 3/1 for domestic students. Applications are processed on a rolling basis. Application fee: $30. Electronic applications accepted. *Financial support:* In 2017–18, 233 students received support, including 2 fellowships with full tuition reimbursements available (averaging $15,000 per year), 14 research assistantships with full and partial tuition reimbursements available (averaging $6,458 per year), 201 teaching assistantships with full and partial tuition reimbursements available (averaging $6,458 per year); career-related internships or fieldwork, scholarships/grants, tuition waivers (full and partial), and unspecified assistantships also available. Support available to part-time students. Financial award application deadline: 2/28; financial award applicants required to submit FAFSA. *Faculty research:* Music therapy in NICU units, music of the Americas, music theory pedagogy, music performance. *Unit head:* Dr. Patricia Flowers, Dean, 850-644-4361, Fax: 850-644-2033, E-mail: pjflowers@fsu.edu. *Application contact:* Kris Watson, Director of Admissions, 850-645-2126, Fax: 850-644-2033, E-mail: krwatson@fsu.edu.
Website: http://www.music.fsu.edu/

Fuller Theological Seminary, Graduate Programs, Pasadena, CA 91182. Offers Christian leadership (MACL); clinical psychology (PhD, Psy D); family studies (MA); global leadership (MA); global ministries (D Min); global ministries (Korean language) (D Min); intercultural studies (MA, Th M, PhD); intercultural studies (Korean language) (MA); marital and family therapy (MS); marriage and family enrichment (Certificate); ministry (M Div, D Min); missiology (D Miss); missiology (Korean language) (Th M); theology (MA, Th M, PhD), including evangelism (MA), family life education (MA), pastoral ministry (MA), recovery ministry (MA), worship music ministry (MA), worship, theology, and the arts (MA), youth, family, and culture (MA); theology and ministry (MA).

Garrett-Evangelical Theological Seminary, Graduate and Professional Programs, Evanston, IL 60201-3298. Offers Bible and culture (PhD); Christian education (MA); Christian education and congregational studies (PhD); contemporary theology and culture (PhD); divinity (M Div); ethics, church, and society (MA); liturgical studies (PhD); ministry (D Min); music ministry (MA); pastoral care and counseling (MA); pastoral theology, personality, and culture (PhD); spiritual formation and evangelism (MA); theological studies (MTS); M Div/MSW. M Div/MSW offered jointly with Loyola University Chicago. *Accreditation:* ACIPE; ATS (one or more programs are accredited). *Program availability:* Part-time. *Degree requirements:* For master's, thesis (for some programs); for doctorate, thesis/dissertation. *Entrance requirements:* For doctorate, GRE (PhD). Additional exam requirements/recommendations for international students: Required—TOEFL (minimum score 560 paper-based). Electronic applications accepted.

George Mason University, College of Visual and Performing Arts, School of Music, Program in Music, Fairfax, VA 22030. Offers composition (MM); conducting (MM); jazz studies (MM); music education (MM); pedagogy (MM); performance (MM). *Accreditation:* NASM. *Faculty:* 21 full-time (10 women), 38 part-time/adjunct (11 women). *Students:* 14 full-time (8 women), 25 part-time (13 women); includes 10 minority (3 Black or African American, non-Hispanic/Latino; 3 Asian, non-Hispanic/Latino; 3 Hispanic/Latino; 1 Two or more races, non-Hispanic/Latino), 1 international. Average age 32. 46 applicants, 59% accepted, 14 enrolled. In 2017, 17 master's awarded. *Degree requirements:* For master's, comprehensive exam. *Entrance requirements:* For master's, expanded goals statement; 2 letters of recommendation; official transcript. Additional exam requirements/recommendations for international students: Required—TOEFL (minimum score 575 paper-based; 88 iBT), IELTS (minimum score 6.5), PTE (minimum score 59). Application fee: $75 ($80 for international students). Electronic applications accepted. *Expenses:* Tuition, state resident: full-time $11,228; part-time $459.50 per credit. Tuition, nonresident: full-time $30,932; part-time $1280.50 per credit. *Required fees:* $3252; $135.50 per credit. Part-time tuition and fees vary according to course load and program. *Financial support:* In 2017–18, 1 student received support, including 1 teaching assistantship; career-related internships or fieldwork, Federal Work-Study, scholarships/grants, and unspecified assistantships also available. Financial award application deadline: 3/1; financial award applicants required to submit FAFSA. *Unit head:* Dr. Linda Apple Monson, Managing Director, 703-993-3580, Fax: 703-993-1394, E-mail: lmonson@gmu.edu. *Application contact:* Dr. Lisa A. Billingham, Director of Graduate Studies, 703-993-3778, Fax: 703-993-1394, E-mail: lbillin1@gmu.edu.
Website: http://music.gmu.edu

George Mason University, College of Visual and Performing Arts, School of Music, Program in Musical Arts, Fairfax, VA 22030. Offers composition (DMA); conducting (DMA); performance (DMA). *Faculty:* 21 full-time (10 women), 38 part-time/adjunct (11 women). *Students:* 10 full-time (3 women), 18 part-time (6 women); includes 6 minority (3 Asian, non-Hispanic/Latino; 2 Hispanic/Latino; 1 Two or more races, non-Hispanic/Latino), 4 international. Average age 34. 31 applicants, 58% accepted, 10 enrolled. In 2017, 3 doctorates awarded. *Degree requirements:* For doctorate, one foreign language, comprehensive exam, thesis/dissertation. *Entrance requirements:* For doctorate, GRE, master's degree in music; minimum GPA of 3.0 in master's coursework, 3.25 in courses related to field of study; 3 letters of recommendation; writing sample; audition or portfolio (depending on area of study). Additional exam requirements/recommendations for international students: Required—TOEFL (minimum score 575 paper-based; 88 iBT), IELTS (minimum score 6.5), PTE (minimum score 59). *Application deadline:* For fall admission, 1/15 for domestic and international students. Application fee: $75 ($80 for international students). Electronic applications accepted. *Expenses:* Tuition, state resident: full-time $11,228; part-time $459.50 per credit. Tuition, nonresident: full-time $30,932; part-time $1280.50 per credit. *Required fees:* $3252; $135.50 per credit. Part-time tuition and fees vary according to course load and program. *Financial support:* In 2017–18, 15 students received support, including 15 teaching assistantships with tuition reimbursements available (averaging $3,183 per year); career-related internships or fieldwork, Federal Work-Study, scholarships/grants, unspecified assistantships, and health care benefits (for full-time research or teaching assistantship recipients) also available. Support available to part-time students. Financial award application deadline: 3/1; financial award applicants required to submit FAFSA. *Unit head:* Dr. Linda Apple Monson, Managing Director, 703-993-3580, Fax: 703-993-1394, E-mail: lmonson@gmu.edu. *Application contact:* Dr. Lisa A. Billingham, Director of Graduate Studies, 703-993-3778, Fax: 703-993-1394, E-mail: lbillin1@gmu.edu.
Website: http://music.gmu.edu

Georgia Institute of Technology, Graduate Studies, College of Design, School of Music, Atlanta, GA 30332-0001. Offers music technology (MS, PhD).

Georgia Southern University, Jack N. Averitt College of Graduate Studies, College of Liberal Arts and Social Sciences, Program in Music, Statesboro, GA 30460. Offers composition (MM); conducting (MM); music education (MM); music technology (MM); performance (MM). *Accreditation:* NASM. *Program availability:* Part-time, evening/weekend. *Faculty:* 26 full-time (10 women), 3 part-time/adjunct (0 women). *Students:* 10 full-time (3 women), 16 part-time (6 women); includes 9 minority (4 Black or African American, non-Hispanic/Latino; 1 Asian, non-Hispanic/Latino; 2 Hispanic/Latino; 2 Two or more races, non-Hispanic/Latino), 3 international. Average age 27. 18 applicants, 94% accepted, 11 enrolled. In 2017, 8 master's awarded. *Degree requirements:* For master's, comprehensive exam, recital or final project. *Entrance requirements:* For master's, minimum GPA of 2.5, audition, letters of recommendation. Additional exam requirements/recommendations for international students: Required—TOEFL (minimum score 550 paper-based; 80 iBT), IELTS (minimum score 6). *Application deadline:* For fall admission, 3/1 priority date for domestic and international students; for spring admission, 10/1 priority date for domestic students, 10/1 for international students. Applications are processed on a rolling basis. Application fee: $50. Electronic applications accepted. *Expenses:* Tuition, state resident: full-time $4986; part-time $3324 per year. Tuition, nonresident: full-time $21,982; part-time $15,352 per year. *Required fees:* $2092; $1802 per credit hour. $901 per semester. Tuition and fees vary according to course load, campus/location and program. *Financial support:* In 2017–18, 19 students received support, including 10 fellowships with full tuition reimbursements available (averaging $7,750 per year), 3 teaching assistantships with full tuition reimbursements available (averaging $7,750 per year); Federal Work-Study, scholarships/grants, tuition waivers (full), and unspecified assistantships also available. Support available to part-time students. Financial award application deadline: 4/15; financial award applicants required to submit FAFSA. *Faculty research:* Performance, conducting, composition, technology, education. *Unit head:* Dr. Greg Harwood, Graduate Director, 912-478-5813, Fax: 912-478-1295, E-mail: gharwood@georgiasouthern.edu.
Website: http://class.georgiasouthern.edu/music/

Georgia State University, School of Music, Atlanta, GA 30303. Offers choral conducting (MM); jazz studies (MM); music (Certificate); music composition (MM); music education (PhD); orchestral conducting (MM); performance (MM), including guitar, orchestral, piano, vocal; piano pedagogy (MM); wind band conducting (MM). *Accreditation:* NASM. *Program availability:* Part-time, evening/weekend. *Faculty:* 40 full-time (13 women). *Students:* 80 full-time (36 women), 10 part-time (4 women); includes 32 minority (19 Black or African American, non-Hispanic/Latino; 5 Asian, non-Hispanic/Latino; 8 Hispanic/Latino), 13 international. Average age 30. 84 applicants, 69% accepted, 42 enrolled. In 2017, 25 master's, 2 other advanced degrees awarded. *Degree requirements:* For master's, comprehensive exam, thesis (for some programs), recital; for doctorate, comprehensive exam, thesis/dissertation; for Certificate, recital. *Entrance requirements:* For master's, GRE (for music education, composition only), BM; for doctorate, GRE, MM; for Certificate, MM. Additional exam requirements/recommendations for international students: Required—TOEFL (minimum score 550 paper-based; 80 iBT). *Application deadline:* For fall admission, 3/1 priority date for domestic and international students; for spring admission, 10/1 priority date for domestic and international students. Applications are processed on a rolling basis. Application fee: $50. Electronic applications accepted. *Expenses:* Tuition, state resident: full-time $7020. Tuition, nonresident: full-time $22,518. *Required fees:* $2128. Tuition and fees vary according to degree level and program. *Financial support:* In 2017–18, research assistantships with full tuition reimbursements (averaging $4,000 per year) were awarded; Federal Work-Study, scholarships/grants, health care benefits, tuition waivers (partial), and unspecified assistantships also available. Financial award application deadline: 3/1; financial award applicants required to submit FAFSA. *Faculty research:* Male changing voice, nineteenth-century chamber music, improvisation and learning, Garibunda, African-American classical musicians. *Unit head:* William Dwight Coleman, Director, School of Music, 404-413-5953, Fax: 404-413-5910, E-mail: wcoleman@gsu.edu. *Application contact:* Dr. Steven Andrew Harper, Graduate Director, 404-413-5943, Fax: 404-413-5910, E-mail: sharper@gsu.edu.
Website: http://www.music.gsu.edu/

The Graduate Center, City University of New York, Graduate Studies, Program in Music, New York, NY 10016-4039. Offers DMA, PhD. *Faculty:* 62 full-time (9 women). *Students:* 169 full-time (89 women), 2 part-time (both women); includes 27 minority (1 Black or African American, non-Hispanic/Latino; 11 Asian, non-Hispanic/Latino; 10 Hispanic/Latino; 5 Two or more races, non-Hispanic/Latino), 49 international. Average age 35. 195 applicants, 15% accepted, 18 enrolled. In 2017, 30 doctorates awarded. *Degree requirements:* For doctorate, 2 foreign languages, thesis/dissertation. *Entrance requirements:* For doctorate, GRE General Test. Additional exam requirements/recommendations for international students: Required—TOEFL. *Application deadline:* For fall admission, 12/1 priority date for domestic students. Application fee: $125. Electronic applications accepted. *Financial support:* In 2017–18, 92 students received support, including 87 fellowships, 3 research assistantships, 6 teaching assistantships; career-related internships or fieldwork, Federal Work-Study, institutionally sponsored loans, and tuition waivers (full and partial) also available. Financial award application deadline: 2/1; financial award applicants required to submit FAFSA. *Unit head:* Dr. Norman Carey, Executive Officer, 212-817-8591, Fax: 212-817-1529, E-mail: ncarey@gc.cuny.edu. *Application contact:* Les Gribben, Director of Admissions, 212-817-7470, Fax: 212-817-1624, E-mail: lgribben@gc.cuny.edu.

Hardin-Simmons University, Graduate School, College of Fine Arts, Abilene, TX 79698-0001. Offers church music (MM); music education (MM); music performance (MM); theory and composition (MM). *Accreditation:* NASM. *Program availability:* Part-time. *Faculty:* 14 full-time (4 women), 1 part-time/adjunct (0 women). *Students:* 4 full-time (2 women), 2 part-time (0 women); includes 3 minority (1 Hispanic/Latino; 2 Two or more races, non-Hispanic/Latino). Average age 29. 2 applicants, 50% accepted, 1 enrolled. In 2017, 3 master's awarded. *Degree requirements:* For master's, comprehensive exam, thesis (for some programs). *Entrance requirements:* For master's, minimum undergraduate GPA of 3.0 in major, 2.7 overall; writing sample; demonstrated knowledge in chosen area. Additional exam requirements/recommendations for international students: Required—TOEFL (minimum score 550 paper-based; 79 iBT). *Application deadline:* For fall admission, 8/15 priority date for domestic students, 4/1 for international students; for spring admission, 1/5 priority date for domestic students, 9/1 for international students. Applications are processed on a rolling basis. Application fee: $50 ($150 for international students). Electronic applications accepted. *Expenses: Tuition:* Full-time $13,500; part-time $750 per semester hour. *Required fees:* $220 per term. One-time fee: $50. Tuition and fees vary according to course load, campus/location and program. *Financial support:* In 2017–18, 6 students received support, including 3 fellowships (averaging $1,213 per year); career-related internships or fieldwork and scholarships/grants also available. Support available to part-time students. Financial award application deadline: 6/30; financial award applicants required to submit FAFSA. *Unit head:* Dr. Lynnette Chambers, Program Director, 325-670-1430, Fax: 325-670-5873, E-mail: lchambers@hsutx.edu. *Application contact:* Dr. Nancy Kucinski, Dean of Graduate Studies, 325-670-1298, Fax: 325-670-1564, E-mail: gradoff@hsutx.edu.
Website: http://www.hsutx.edu/academics/cofa/

Harvard University, Graduate School of Arts and Sciences, Department of Music, Cambridge, MA 02138. Offers composition (AM, PhD); musicology (AM); musicology and ethnomusicology (PhD); theory (AM, PhD). *Degree requirements:* For doctorate, 3 foreign languages, thesis/dissertation, composition, analytical paper. *Entrance requirements:* For master's and doctorate, GRE General Test. Additional exam requirements/recommendations for international students: Required—TOEFL.

Hebrew College, Program in Jewish Studies, Newton Centre, MA 02459. Offers Jewish liturgical music (Certificate); Jewish music education (Certificate); Jewish studies (MA). *Program availability:* Part-time, evening/weekend, online learning. *Degree requirements:* For master's, one foreign language. *Entrance requirements:* For master's, GRE, interview. Additional exam requirements/recommendations for international students: Required—TOEFL.

Hebrew Union College–Jewish Institute of Religion, School of Sacred Music, New York, NY 10012-1186. Offers MSM. *Degree requirements:* For master's, one foreign language, thesis, recital. *Entrance requirements:* For master's, GRE, minimum 2 years of college-level Hebrew, bachelor's degree in music or related area, trained singing voice. Additional exam requirements/recommendations for international students: Required—TOEFL. *Expenses:* Contact institution.

Hollins University, Graduate Programs, Program in Liberal Studies, Roanoke, VA 24020. Offers humanities (MALS); interdisciplinary studies (MALS); leadership (MALS); social sciences (MALS); visual and performing arts (MALS). *Program availability:* Part-time, evening/weekend, 100% online, blended/hybrid learning. *Faculty:* 5 part-time/adjunct (2 women). *Students:* 5 full-time (4 women), 29 part-time (25 women); includes 9 minority (6 Black or African American, non-Hispanic/Latino; 1 Asian, non-Hispanic/Latino; 1 Hispanic/Latino; 1 Two or more races, non-Hispanic/Latino). Average age 40. 7 applicants, 86% accepted, 3 enrolled. In 2017, 11 master's awarded. *Degree requirements:* For master's, thesis. *Entrance requirements:* For master's, three letters of recommendation, interview, bachelor's degree, undergraduate transcripts, statement of educational objectives. Additional exam requirements/recommendations for international students: Required—TOEFL (minimum score 550 paper-based; 80 iBT), IELTS (minimum score 6.5). *Application deadline:* Applications are processed on a rolling basis. Application fee: $40. Electronic applications accepted. *Expenses:* Contact institution. *Financial support:* Scholarships/grants available. Financial award application deadline: 7/15; financial award applicants required to submit FAFSA. *Faculty research:* Diversity, gender and women's studies, political science, leadership. *Unit head:* Dr. Lorraine Lange, Director, 540-362-6576, Fax: 540-362-6288, E-mail: hugrad@hollins.edu. *Application contact:* Cathy S. Koon, Manager of Graduate Programs, 540-362-6326, Fax: 540-362-6288, E-mail: hugrad@hollins.edu.
Website: http://www.hollins.edu/academics/graduate-degrees/liberal-studies/

Holy Names University, Graduate Division, Department of Music, Oakland, CA 94619-1699. Offers Kodaly (Certificate); music education with Kodaly emphasis (MM); piano pedagogy (MM); vocal pedagogy (MM). *Degree requirements:* For master's, comprehensive exam, recital. *Entrance requirements:* For master's, audition; minimum undergraduate GPA of 2.6 overall, 3.0 in major. Additional exam requirements/recommendations for international students: Required—TOEFL (minimum score 550 paper-based; 79 iBT). Electronic applications accepted. *Faculty research:* Performance practice with special interest in Baroque, Romantic, and twentieth-century instrumental and vocal music; choral pedagogy; Hungarian music education.

Hope International University, School of Graduate and Professional Studies, Programs in Ministry, Fullerton, CA 92831-3138. Offers Christian leadership (MCM); church music (MA); church music (Korean track) (MCM); church planting (MCM); intercultural studies (MCM); worship (MCM). *Program availability:* Part-time, evening/weekend, online learning. *Degree requirements:* For master's, thesis (for some programs), project. *Entrance requirements:* For master's, minimum GPA of 3.0, MCM program requires an undergraduate degree in music, 2 references. Additional exam requirements/recommendations for international students: Required—TOEFL (minimum score 550 paper-based; 86 iBT); Recommended—IELTS (minimum score 6.5). Electronic applications accepted. *Expenses:* Contact institution. *Faculty research:* Church dynamics, growth methodologies.

Houghton College, Greatbatch School of Music, Houghton, NY 14744. Offers collaborative performance (MMus); composition (MMus); conducting (MMus); music (MA); performance (MMus); world music with theology and intercultural studies (MA). *Accreditation:* NASM. *Degree requirements:* For master's, comprehensive exam (for some programs), thesis (for some programs), recitals (for some programs). *Entrance requirements:* For master's, B Mus or equivalent. Additional exam requirements/recommendations for international students: Required—TOEFL (minimum score 600 paper-based). Electronic applications accepted. *Faculty research:* Bach Studies; original compositions; professional performance; contemporary women composers; music in Christian worship.

Houston Baptist University, College of Education and Behavioral Sciences, Programs in Education, Houston, TX 77074-3298. Offers bilingual education (M Ed); counselor education (M Ed); curriculum and instruction (M Ed); curriculum and instruction (EC-6 bilingual) (M Ed); curriculum and instruction in all-level art, Spanish, music, or physical education (M Ed); curriculum and instruction in EC-6 and special education (EC-12) (M Ed); curriculum and instruction in instructional technology (M Ed); curriculum and instruction in mathematics, science, or social studies (4-8) (M Ed); curriculum and instruction with EC-6 generalist (M Ed); curriculum and instruction with English language arts and reading (4-8) (M Ed); educational administration (M Ed); educational diagnostician (M Ed); executive educational leadership (Ed D); higher education in business management (M Ed); higher education in Christian studies (M Ed); higher education in counseling (M Ed); higher education in educational technology (M Ed); reading (M Ed); special educational leadership (Ed D). *Program availability:* Part-time, evening/weekend, 100% online, blended/hybrid learning. *Students:* 83 full-time (65 women), 187 part-time (156 women); includes 189 minority (114 Black or African American, non-Hispanic/Latino; 2 American Indian or Alaska Native, non-Hispanic/Latino; 9 Asian, non-Hispanic/Latino; 58 Hispanic/Latino; 6 Two or more races, non-Hispanic/Latino), 7 international. Average age 36. 309 applicants, 31% accepted, 70 enrolled. In 2017, 92 master's awarded. *Degree requirements:* For master's, comprehensive exam; for doctorate, thesis/dissertation. *Entrance requirements:* For master's, minimum GPA of 2.75, two recommendations, resume, bachelor's degree conferred transcript; interview (for non-certified teachers); for doctorate, GRE, 5 letters of recommendation. Additional exam requirements/recommendations for international students: Required—TOEFL (minimum score 80 iBT), IELTS (minimum score 6.5). *Application deadline:* For fall admission, 8/1 for domestic students, 6/1 for international students; for spring admission, 1/1 for domestic students, 11/1 for international students; for summer admission, 5/1 for domestic students, 3/1 for international students. Applications are processed on a rolling basis. Application fee: $0 ($100 for international students). Electronic applications accepted. Application fee is waived when completed online. *Expenses:* $22,000 tuition; $4,500 fees (general, technology and parking). *Financial support:* In 2017–18, 59 students received support. Research assistantships, teaching assistantships, Federal Work-Study, and scholarships/grants available. Support available to part-time students. Financial award application deadline: 4/1; financial award applicants required to submit FAFSA. *Faculty research:* Autism and inclusion, integrating technology into instruction, school change and leadership trust. *Unit head:* Dr. Charlotte Fontenot, Director, Graduate Programs, 281-649-3078, Fax: 281-649-3361, E-mail: cfontenot@hbu.edu. *Application contact:* Kristy Wright, Administrative Assistant for Graduate Programs, 281-649-3094, Fax: 281-649-3361, E-mail: kwright@hbu.edu.
Website: http://www.hbu.edu/MED

Howard University, Graduate School, Division of Fine Arts, Department of Music, Washington, DC 20059-0002. Offers applied music (MM); instrument (MM Ed); jazz studies (MM); organ (MM Ed); piano (MM Ed); voice (MM Ed). *Accreditation:* NASM. *Program availability:* Part-time. *Degree requirements:* For master's, comprehensive exam, thesis or alternative, departmental qualifying exam, recital. *Entrance requirements:* For master's, minimum GPA of 3.0, bachelor's degree in music or music education. Additional exam requirements/recommendations for international students: Required—TOEFL.

Hunter College of the City University of New York, Graduate School, School of Arts and Sciences, Department of Music, New York, NY 10065-5085. Offers composition (MA); ethnomusicology (MA); music history (MA); music theory (MA); performance (MA). *Program availability:* Part-time, evening/weekend. *Degree requirements:* For master's, one foreign language, thesis, composition, essay, or recital; proficiency exam. *Entrance requirements:* For master's, undergraduate major in music (minimum 24 credits) or equivalent, sample of work, research paper. Additional exam requirements/recommendations for international students: Required—TOEFL. *Faculty research:* African and African-American music, Bach, Renaissance music, early romantic music, theory of tonal music.

Illinois State University, Graduate School, College of Fine Arts, School of Music, Normal, IL 61790. Offers MM, MM Ed. *Accreditation:* NASM. *Degree requirements:* For master's, thesis or alternative, performance. *Entrance requirements:* For master's, minimum GPA of 3.0 in music, 2.6 overall; auditions. *Faculty research:* Concerts on the quad summer concert series.

Indiana State University, College of Graduate and Professional Studies, College of Arts and Sciences, School of Music, Terre Haute, IN 47809. Offers conducting (MM); music education (MM); music performance (MM). *Accreditation:* NASM. *Degree requirements:* For master's, comprehensive exam, thesis, qualifying exam. Electronic applications accepted.

Indiana University Bloomington, Jacobs School of Music, Bloomington, IN 47405-7000. Offers MA, MM, MME, MS, DM, DME, PhD, Artist Diploma, Performance Diploma, Spec, MA/MLS, MM/MLS. *Degree requirements:* For master's, comprehensive exam (for some programs); for doctorate, comprehensive exam, thesis/dissertation. *Entrance requirements:* For master's and doctorate, GRE, audition, 3 letters of recommendation. Additional exam requirements/recommendations for international students: Required—TOEFL; Recommended—IELTS. Electronic applications accepted. *Expenses:* Contact institution.

Indiana University Bloomington, University Graduate School, College of Arts and Sciences, Department of Folklore and Ethnomusicology, Bloomington, IN 47405. Offers ethnomusicology (MA, PhD), including folklore. Terminal master's awarded for partial completion of doctoral program. *Degree requirements:* For master's, one foreign language, comprehensive exam, project, thesis, or exam; for doctorate, 2 foreign languages, comprehensive exam, thesis/dissertation. *Entrance requirements:* For master's, GRE General Test (minimum scores: 151 for Verbal, 150 for Quantitative, 4.5 for Analytical), minimum GPA of 3.0, writing sample, curriculum vitae, 3 letters of recommendation, personal statement; for doctorate, GRE General Test (minimum scores: 151 for Verbal, 150 for Quantitative, 4.5 for Analytical), minimum GPA of 3.0, writing sample, curriculum vitae, 3 letters of recommendation, personal statement, MA. Additional exam requirements/recommendations for international students: Required—TOEFL (minimum score 550 paper-based; 79 iBT). Electronic applications accepted. *Expenses:* Contact institution. *Faculty research:* Narrative, performance studies, material culture, popular culture, music, public practice.

Indiana University of Pennsylvania, School of Graduate Studies and Research, College of Fine Arts, Department of Music, Program in Music Performance, Indiana, PA 15705. Offers MA. *Accreditation:* NASM. *Program availability:* Part-time. *Faculty:* 15 full-time (5 women). *Students:* 11 full-time (5 women), 5 part-time (3 women); includes 4 minority (3 Asian, non-Hispanic/Latino; 1 Hispanic/Latino), 2 international. Average age 26. 19 applicants, 95% accepted, 10 enrolled. In 2017, 6 master's awarded. *Degree requirements:* For master's, thesis optional. *Entrance requirements:* For master's, 2 letters of recommendation, audition. Additional exam requirements/recommendations for international students: Required—TOEFL (minimum score 550 paper-based). *Application deadline:* Applications are processed on a rolling basis. Application fee: $50. Electronic applications accepted. *Expenses:* Tuition, state resident: full-time $12,000; part-time $500 per credit. Tuition, nonresident: full-time $18,000; part-time $750 per credit. *Required fees:* $4073; $165.55 per credit. $64 per term. *Financial support:* In 2017–18, 8 research assistantships with tuition reimbursements (averaging $4,205 per year) were awarded; fellowships with full tuition reimbursements, career-related internships or fieldwork, Federal Work-Study, scholarships/grants, and unspecified assistantships also available. Support available to part-time students. Financial award application deadline: 4/15; financial award applicants required to submit FAFSA. *Unit head:* Dr. Stephanie Caulder, Chairperson, 724-357-2391, E-mail: scaulder@iup.edu. Website: http://www.iup.edu/music/grad/default.aspx

Indiana University–Purdue University Indianapolis, School of Engineering and Technology, Department of Music and Arts Technology, Indianapolis, IN 46202. Offers music technology (MS, PhD); music therapy (MS). *Accreditation:* NASM. *Program availability:* Part-time, evening/weekend, online learning. *Degree requirements:* For master's, thesis optional, internship or final project; for doctorate, thesis/dissertation. *Entrance requirements:* For master's, GRE, interview, audition, minimum GPA of 3.0; for doctorate, GRE, three letters of recommendation; research adviser letter; statement of purpose; writing samples; transcripts; portfolio. Additional exam requirements/recommendations for international students: Required—TOEFL (minimum score 550 paper-based; 79 iBT); Recommended—IELTS (minimum score 6.5). Electronic applications accepted. *Expenses:* Contact institution. *Faculty research:* Music-related cross-disciplinary technologies in fine arts, education, business, health care, computer science, and engineering; exploring and creating multi-disciplinary music, dance, and arts performance; developing new recording techniques and emerging technologies.

Indiana University South Bend, Ernestine M. Raclin School of the Arts, South Bend, IN 46615. Offers communication studies (MA); music (MM), including composition, performance; music performance (AD). *Accreditation:* NASM. *Program availability:* Part-time. *Entrance requirements:* For master's, performance audition. Additional exam requirements/recommendations for international students: Required—TOEFL (minimum score 600 paper-based; 90 iBT). Electronic applications accepted. *Expenses:* Contact institution. *Faculty research:* Orchestral conducting.

Inter American University of Puerto Rico, San Germán Campus, Graduate Studies Center, Program in Music Education, San Germán, PR 00683-5008. Offers music (MA); music teacher education (MA). *Accreditation:* TEAC. *Program availability:* Part-time, evening/weekend.

Ithaca College, School of Music, Programs in Music and Music Education, Ithaca, NY 14850. Offers composition (MM); conducting (MM); music education (MM, MS); performance (MM); Suzuki pedagogy (MM). *Accreditation:* NASM. *Program availability:* Part-time. *Faculty:* 66 full-time (22 women), 9 part-time/adjunct (4 women). *Students:* 18 full-time (10 women), 29 part-time (11 women); includes 12 minority (3 Black or African American, non-Hispanic/Latino; 4 Asian, non-Hispanic/Latino; 4 Hispanic/Latino; 1 Two or more races, non-Hispanic/Latino), 5 international. Average age 25. 147 applicants, 44% accepted, 23 enrolled. In 2017, 31 master's awarded. *Degree requirements:* For master's, comprehensive exam (for some programs), thesis (for some programs). *Entrance requirements:* For master's, GRE (for music education applicants). Additional exam requirements/recommendations for international students: Required—TOEFL (minimum score 550 paper-based; 80 iBT). *Application deadline:* For fall admission, 12/1 for domestic and international students. Applications are processed on a rolling basis. Application fee: $40. Electronic applications accepted. *Expenses:* Contact institution. *Financial support:* In 2017–18, 44 students received support, including 43 teaching assistantships (averaging $10,191 per year); career-related internships or fieldwork, Federal Work-Study, scholarships/grants, and unspecified assistantships also available. Support available to part-time students. Financial award application deadline: 12/1; financial award applicants required to submit FAFSA. *Unit head:* Dr. Les Black, Chair, Graduate Studies in Music, 607-274-7997, E-mail: lblack@ithaca.edu. *Application contact:* Nicole Eversley Bradwell, Director, Office of Admission, 607-274-3124, Fax: 607-274-1263, E-mail: admission@ithaca.edu.
Website: http://www.ithaca.edu/gradprograms/music

Jacksonville State University, College of Graduate Studies and Continuing Education, College of Arts and Sciences, Department of Music, Jacksonville, AL 36265-1602. Offers MA. *Accreditation:* NASM. *Program availability:* Part-time, evening/weekend. *Degree requirements:* For master's, comprehensive exam, thesis (for some programs). *Entrance requirements:* For master's, GRE General Test or MAT. Additional exam requirements/recommendations for international students: Required—TOEFL (minimum score 500 paper-based; 61 iBT). Electronic applications accepted.

James Madison University, The Graduate School, College of Visual and Performing Arts, Doctor of Musical Arts Program, Harrisonburg, VA 22801. Offers conducting (DMA); performance (DMA). *Program availability:* Part-time. *Students:* 21 full-time (10 women), 11 part-time (4 women); includes 2 minority (both Hispanic/Latino), 14 international. Average age 30. In 2017, 8 doctorates awarded. Application fee: $55. Electronic applications accepted. *Expenses:* Tuition, state resident: full-time $10,512; part-time $438 per credit hour. Tuition, nonresident: full-time $28,358; part-time $1162 per credit hour. *Required fees:* $1128. *Financial support:* In 2017–18, 17 students received support, including 1 fellowship; Federal Work-Study, unspecified assistantships, and 17 doctoral assistantships (averaging $12,935) also available. Financial award application deadline: 3/1; financial award applicants required to submit FAFSA. *Unit head:* Dr. Jeffrey Bush, Director of the School of Music, 540-568-3614, E-mail: bushje@jmu.edu. *Application contact:* Lynette D. Michael, Director of Graduate Admissions, 540-568-6131 Ext. 6395, Fax: 540-568-7860, E-mail: michaeld@jmu.edu.
Website: http://www.jmu.edu/music/degree-programs/dma.shtml

James Madison University, The Graduate School, College of Visual and Performing Arts, Master of Music Program, Harrisonburg, VA 22801. Offers composition (MM); conducting (MM); music education (MM); performance (MM). *Accreditation:* NASM. *Program availability:* Part-time. *Students:* 18 full-time (9 women), 3 part-time (all women); includes 5 minority (2 Black or African American, non-Hispanic/Latino; 2 Hispanic/Latino; 1 Two or more races, non-Hispanic/Latino), 2 international. Average age 30. In 2017, 11 master's awarded. Application fee: $55. Electronic applications accepted. *Expenses:* Tuition, state resident: full-time $10,512; part-time $438 per credit hour. Tuition, nonresident: full-time $28,358; part-time $1162 per credit hour. *Required fees:* $1128. *Financial support:* In 2017–18, 13 students received support, including 1 teaching assistantship with full tuition reimbursement available (averaging $8,837 per year); fellowships, Federal Work-Study, and 12 assistantships (averaging $7911) also available. Financial award application deadline: 3/1; financial award applicants required to submit FAFSA. *Unit head:* Dr. Jeffrey Bush, Director of the School of Music, 540-568-3614, E-mail: bushje@jmu.edu. *Application contact:* Lynette D. Michael, Director of Graduate Admissions, 540-568-6131 Ext. 6395, Fax: 540-568-7860, E-mail: michaeld@jmu.edu.
Website: http://www.jmu.edu/music/

The Jewish Theological Seminary, H. L. Miller Cantorial School and College of Jewish Music, New York, NY 10027-4649. Offers MSM. *Degree requirements:* For master's, one foreign language, comprehensive exam, departmental qualifying exam, recitals. *Entrance requirements:* For master's, music aptitude test, audition, interview, 3 letters of recommendation. Additional exam requirements/recommendations for international students: Required—TOEFL. *Expenses:* Contact institution.

Johns Hopkins University, Peabody Conservatory, Baltimore, MD 21202. Offers MA, MM, DMA, AD, GPD. *Degree requirements:* For master's, thesis (for some programs), departmental qualifying exam, recital; for doctorate, one foreign language, comprehensive exam, thesis/dissertation (for some programs), departmental qualifying exam, recitals; for other advanced degree, recitals. *Entrance requirements:* For master's and other advanced degree, audition; for doctorate, audition, interview. Additional exam requirements/recommendations for international students: Required—TOEFL (minimum score 550 paper-based; 79 iBT), IELTS (minimum score 6.5). Electronic applications accepted. *Expenses:* Contact institution.

The Juilliard School, Graduate Programs, New York, NY 10023-6588. Offers acting (MFA); jazz studies (Artist Diploma); music (MM, DMA, Diploma); music performance (Artist Diploma); opera studies (Artist Diploma); string quartet (Artist Diploma). *Degree requirements:* For master's and other advanced degree, performance jury, recital; for doctorate, one foreign language, thesis/dissertation, performance jury, 3 recitals. *Entrance requirements:* For master's and other advanced degree, audition; for doctorate, audition, interview. Additional exam requirements/recommendations for international students: Required—TOEFL (minimum score 570 paper-based; 89 iBT). Electronic applications accepted.

Kansas State University, Graduate School, College of Arts and Sciences, School of Music, Theatre and Dance, Manhattan, KS 66506. Offers MA, MM. *Accreditation:* NASM; NAST. *Program availability:* Part-time, online learning. *Degree requirements:* For master's, thesis optional. *Entrance requirements:* For master's, GRE, audition (in person or recording), interview (for music education). Additional exam requirements/recommendations for international students: Required—TOEFL (minimum score 600 paper-based). Electronic applications accepted. *Faculty research:* American music, opera, drama therapy, directing, costume and scenic design, music by women composers.

Kent State University, College of the Arts, Hugh A. Glauser School of Music, Kent, OH 44242-0001. Offers conducting (MM), including choral conducting; ethnomusicology (MA); music composition (MA); music education (MM, PhD); music theory (MA); music theory-composition (PhD); performance (MM), including chamber music. *Accreditation:* NASM. *Program availability:* Part-time, online learning. *Faculty:* 34 full-time (11 women), 22 part-time/adjunct (15 women). *Students:* 64 full-time (36 women), 178 part-time (125 women); includes 22 minority (8 Black or African American, non-Hispanic/Latino; 2 Asian, non-Hispanic/Latino; 6 Hispanic/Latino; 6 Two or more races, non-Hispanic/Latino), 31 international. Average age 31. 106 applicants, 92% accepted, 79 enrolled. In 2017, 78 master's, 2 doctorates awarded. *Degree requirements:* For master's, comprehensive exam (for some programs), thesis (for some programs), capstone project or thesis (for MM in music education); for doctorate, comprehensive exam, thesis/dissertation. *Entrance requirements:* For master's, transcripts; minimum GPA of 3.0; 3 letters of recommendation; goal statement; resume; writing sample (for MA in ethnomusicology); portfolio of original composition (for MA in composition); audition (for MM in conducting, performance); prior degree, teaching certificate, and 1 year of teaching experience (for MM in music education); for doctorate, writing sample; 3 letters of recommendation; curriculum vitae/resume; transcripts; minimum GPA of 3.0; prior degree in music education, teaching license, statement of purpose, video of teaching sample, 3 years of teaching, and interview (for music education); goal statement and 3 original compositions (for music theory-composition). Additional exam requirements/recommendations for international students: Required—TOEFL (minimum score 525 paper-based, 71 iBT), Michigan English Language Assessment Battery (minimum score 74), IELTS (minimum score 6.0) or PTE (minimum score 50). *Application deadline:* Applications are processed on a rolling basis. Application fee: $45 ($70 for international students). Electronic applications accepted. *Expenses:* Tuition, state resident: full-time $11,310; part-time $515 per credit hour. Tuition, nonresident: full-time $20,396; part-time $928 per credit hour. *International tuition:* $18,544 full-time. *Financial support:* Unspecified assistantships available. Financial award application deadline: 4/1. *Unit head:* Jane Dressler, Interim Director, 330-672-2172, E-mail: jdressle@kent.edu. *Application contact:* Michael Chunn, Graduate Coordinator/Trumpet Professor, 330-672-9234, Fax: 330-672-7837, E-mail: mchunn@kent.edu.
Website: http://www.kent.edu/music/

Lamar University, College of Graduate Studies, College of Fine Arts and Communication, Mary Morgan Moore Department of Music, Beaumont, TX 77701. Offers MM. *Accreditation:* NASM. *Faculty:* 19 full-time (7 women), 5 part-time/adjunct (1 woman). *Students:* 3 full-time (1 woman), 4 part-time (0 women); includes 1 minority (Black or African American, non-Hispanic/Latino). Average age 31. 4 applicants, 100% accepted, 2 enrolled. In 2017, 8 master's awarded. *Degree requirements:* For master's, comprehensive exam, thesis optional. *Entrance requirements:* For master's, GRE General Test, theory placement exams, audition. Additional exam requirements/recommendations for international students: Required—TOEFL (minimum score 550 paper-based; 79 iBT), IELTS (minimum score 6.5). *Application deadline:* For fall admission, 8/10 for domestic students, 7/1 for international students; for spring admission, 1/5 for domestic students, 12/1 for international students. Applications are processed on a rolling basis. Application fee: $25 ($50 for international students). Electronic applications accepted. *Expenses:* Contact institution. *Financial support:* In 2017–18, 4 fellowships with tuition reimbursements (averaging $2,000 per year), 3 teaching assistantships were awarded; institutionally sponsored loans and tuition waivers (partial) also available. Support available to part-time students. Financial award application deadline: 4/1; financial award applicants required to submit FAFSA. *Faculty research:* Performance: ensembles and personal. *Unit head:* Dr. Brian Shook, Interim Chair, 409-880-8144, Fax: 409-880-8143. *Application contact:* Deidre Mayer, Interim Director, Admissions and Academic Services, 409-880-8888, Fax: 409-880-7419, E-mail: gradmissions@lamar.edu.
Website: http://fineartscomm.lamar.edu/music

Lee University, Program in Music, Cleveland, TN 37320-3450. Offers conducting (MM); music education (MM); music performance (MM); religious studies (MCM); sacred music (MCM). *Accreditation:* NASM. *Program availability:* Part-time. *Faculty:* 23 full-time (6 women), 6 part-time/adjunct (3 women). *Students:* 24 full-time (10 women), 9 part-time (6 women); includes 3 minority (2 Black or African American, non-Hispanic/Latino; 1 Asian, non-Hispanic/Latino), 5 international. Average age 27. 19 applicants, 89% accepted, 12 enrolled. In 2017, 9 master's awarded. *Degree requirements:* For master's, variable foreign language requirement, comprehensive exam, thesis, internship. *Entrance requirements:* For master's, placement exercises in music theory, music history, diction, and piano proficiency, audition, resume, interview, minimum GPA of 2.75, official transcripts, essay, 3 recommendations, immunization forms. Additional exam requirements/recommendations for international students: Required—TOEFL (minimum score 61 iBT). *Application deadline:* For fall admission, 4/1 priority date for domestic and international students; for spring admission, 10/1 priority date for domestic and international students. Applications are processed on a rolling basis. Application fee: $25. Electronic applications accepted. *Expenses: Tuition:* Full-time $12,780; part-time $710 per credit hour. *Required fees:* $60; $60 per term. Tuition and fees vary according to program. *Financial support:* In 2017–18, 31 students received support. Career-related internships or fieldwork, Federal Work-Study, institutionally sponsored loans, scholarships/grants, and unspecified assistantships available. Financial award application deadline: 3/1; financial award applicants required to submit FAFSA. *Unit head:* Dr. Brad J. Moffett, Director, 423-614-8240, Fax: 423-614-8245, E-mail: gradmusic@leeuniversity.edu.
Website: http://www.leeuniversity.edu/academics/graduate/music

Liberty University, School of Music, Lynchburg, VA 24515. Offers ethnomusicology (MA); music and worship (MA); music education (MA); worship studies (MA, DWS), including ethnomusicology (MA), leadership (MA), pastoral counseling (MA), worship techniques (MA). *Accreditation:* NASM. *Program availability:* Part-time, online learning. *Students:* 93 full-time (43 women), 181 part-time (89 women); includes 69 minority (44 Black or African American, non-Hispanic/Latino; 1 American Indian or Alaska Native, non-Hispanic/Latino; 6 Asian, non-Hispanic/Latino; 12 Hispanic/Latino; 6 Two or more races, non-Hispanic/Latino), 9 international. Average age 37. 307 applicants, 43% accepted, 69 enrolled. In 2017, 26 master's, 2 doctorates awarded. *Entrance requirements:* For master's, minimum GPA of 3.0; interview; letter of recommendation; statement of purpose; bachelor's/master's degree in music, worship, or related field, or 5 years of experience. Additional exam requirements/recommendations for international students: Required—TOEFL (minimum score 600 paper-based; 100 iBT). *Application deadline:* Applications are processed on a rolling basis. Application fee: $50. Electronic applications accepted. *Financial support:* Applicants required to submit FAFSA. *Unit head:* Dr. Vernon Whaley, Dean, 434-592-3463, E-mail: vwhaley@liberty.edu. *Application contact:* Jay Bridge, Director of Admissions, 800-424-9595, Fax: 800-628-7977, E-mail: gradadmissions@liberty.edu.
Website: http://www.liberty.edu/academics/music/

Long Island University–LIU Post, College of Arts, Communications and Design, Brookville, NY 11548-1300. Offers art (MA); clinical art therapy (MA); clinical art therapy and counseling (MA); digital game design and development (MA); fine arts and design (MFA); interactive multimedia arts (MA); museum studies (MA); music (MA); theatre (MFA). *Faculty:* 22 full-time (10 women), 44 part-time/adjunct (24 women). *Students:* 99 full-time (80 women), 14 part-time (12 women); includes 22 minority (7 Black or African American, non-Hispanic/Latino; 4 Asian, non-Hispanic/Latino; 9 Hispanic/Latino; 2 Two or more races, non-Hispanic/Latino), 23 international. Average age 28. 125 applicants, 70% accepted, 42 enrolled. In 2017, 55 master's awarded. *Degree requirements:* For master's, variable foreign language requirement, comprehensive exam (for some programs), thesis. *Entrance requirements:* For master's, performance audition or portfolio. Additional exam requirements/recommendations for international students: Required—TOEFL (minimum score 550 paper-based; 79 iBT). *Application deadline:* Applications are processed on a rolling basis. Application fee: $50. Electronic applications accepted. *Expenses: Tuition:* Full-time $21,618; part-time $1201 per credit. *Required fees:* $1840; $920 per term. Tuition and fees vary according to course load. *Financial support:* In 2017–18, 78 students received support. Career-related internships or fieldwork, scholarships/grants, tuition waivers (full and partial), and unspecified assistantships available. Support available to part-time students. Financial award application deadline: 2/15; financial award applicants required to submit FAFSA. *Faculty research:* Creative writing, playwriting, music composition, music performance, international impact of art therapy, artistic creation. *Unit head:* Steven Breese, Dean, 516-299-2309, E-mail: steven.breese@liu.edu. *Application contact:* Rita Langdon, Graduate Admissions, 516-299-2334, Fax: 516-299-2137, E-mail: post-enroll@liu.edu.
Website: http://www.liu.edu/CWPost/Academics/School-of-Visual-Arts-Communications-and-Digital-Technologies

Louisiana State University and Agricultural & Mechanical College, Graduate School, College of Music and Dramatic Arts, School of Music, Baton Rouge, LA 70803. Offers music (MM, DMA, PhD); music education (PhD). *Accreditation:* NASM. *Faculty:* 54 full-time (16 women), 1 (woman) part-time/adjunct. *Students:* 163 full-time (72 women), 21 part-time (7 women); includes 36 minority (14 Black or African American, non-Hispanic/Latino; 1 American Indian or Alaska Native, non-Hispanic/Latino; 6 Asian, non-Hispanic/Latino; 14 Hispanic/Latino; 1 Two or more races, non-Hispanic/Latino), 53 international. Average age 29. 199 applicants, 45% accepted, 59 enrolled. In 2017, 35 master's, 27 doctorates awarded. *Financial support:* In 2017–18, 2 fellowships (averaging $27,547 per year), 2 research assistantships (averaging $25,682 per year), 107 teaching assistantships (averaging $14,277 per year) were awarded.

Loyola University New Orleans, College of Music and Fine Arts, New Orleans, LA 70118-6195. Offers music therapy (MMT); performance (MM). *Accreditation:* NASM. *Program availability:* Part-time. *Faculty:* 17 full-time (12 women), 9 part-time/adjunct (5 women). *Students:* 20 full-time (12 women), 24 part-time (16 women); includes 18 minority (6 Black or African American, non-Hispanic/Latino; 2 Asian, non-Hispanic/Latino; 6 Hispanic/Latino; 4 Two or more races, non-Hispanic/Latino), 3 international. Average age 29. 31 applicants, 71% accepted, 13 enrolled. In 2017, 9 master's awarded. *Degree requirements:* For master's, comprehensive written and oral exams; thesis (for MMT). *Entrance requirements:* For master's, performance audition, appropriate bachelor's degree, transcripts, minimum GPA of 3.0, 2 letters of recommendation, resume. Additional exam requirements/recommendations for international students: Required—TOEFL (minimum score 550 paper-based; 79 iBT). *Application deadline:* For fall admission, 8/15 priority date for domestic and international students; for spring admission, 1/1 priority date for domestic and international students. Applications are processed on a rolling basis. Application fee: $20. Electronic applications accepted. *Expenses:* $818 per hour tuition; $738 per semester full-time fees, $376.50 part-time. *Financial support:* Career-related internships or fieldwork, Federal Work-Study, institutionally sponsored loans, scholarships/grants, unspecified assistantships, and talent-based music scholarships available. Support available to part-time students. Financial award application deadline: 5/1; financial award applicants required to submit FAFSA. *Faculty research:* Music business, music therapy, musicology, music theory, music education. *Unit head:* Dr. Kern Maass, Dean, 504-865-3039, Fax: 504-865-2852, E-mail: kdmaass@loyno.edu.
Website: http://cmfa.loyno.edu/

Lynn University, Conservatory of Music, Boca Raton, FL 33431-5598. Offers composition (MM); instrumental collaborative piano (MM); performance (MM); professional performance (Certificate). *Accreditation:* NASM. *Program availability:* Part-time, evening/weekend. *Faculty:* 11 full-time (3 women), 17 part-time/adjunct (3 women). *Students:* 36 full-time (13 women), 27 part-time (12 women); includes 9 minority (1 Black or African American, non-Hispanic/Latino; 6 Hispanic/Latino; 2 Two or more races, non-Hispanic/Latino), 32 international. Average age 24. 101 applicants, 72% accepted, 35 enrolled. In 2017, 8 master's, 5 Certificates awarded. *Degree requirements:* For master's, comprehensive exam, completion of program in 4 calendar years, minimum GPA of 3.0, performance forum. *Entrance requirements:* For master's, bachelor's degree from accredited institution, official undergraduate transcripts, two conservatory recommendation forms, audition (for performance and instrumental collaborative piano majors), portfolio of three original compositions and, if available, recordings (for composition majors). Additional exam requirements/recommendations for international students: Required—TOEFL (minimum score 550 paper-based; 80 iBT), IELTS (minimum score 6.5). *Application deadline:* For fall admission, 8/18 for domestic students, 8/4 for international students; for spring admission, 12/15 for domestic students, 12/1 for international students; for summer admission, 4/17 for domestic students, 4/3 for international students. Applications are processed on a rolling basis. Application fee: $50. Electronic applications accepted. *Expenses:* $740 per credit. *Financial support:* Federal Work-Study, scholarships/grants, and unspecified assistantships available. Support available to part-time students. Financial award application deadline: 3/1; financial award applicants required to submit FAFSA. *Unit head:* Dr. Jon Robertson, Dean, 561-237-7702, Fax: 561-237-9002, E-mail: jrobertson@lynn.edu. *Application contact:* Steven Pruitt, Director of Graduate Admissions, 561-237-7834, Fax: 561-237-7100, E-mail: admission@lynn.edu.
Website: http://www.lynn.edu/academics/colleges/conservatory

Manhattan School of Music, Graduate Programs, New York, NY 10027-4698. Offers composition (MM, DMA); jazz (MM, DMA); music performance (MM, DMA); orchestral performance (MM). *Degree requirements:* For master's, recital; for doctorate, variable foreign language requirement, thesis/dissertation, departmental qualifying exam, recitals. *Entrance requirements:* For master's, audition, pre-screen CD, bachelor's degree; for doctorate, departmental exam, audition, interview, pre-screen CD, master's degree. Additional exam requirements/recommendations for international students: Required—TOEFL (minimum score 550 paper-based; 79 iBT). Electronic applications accepted.

Manhattan School of Music, Professional Studies Certificate Program, New York, NY 10027-4698. Offers instrumental music (CPS), including accompanying, brass, composition, guitar, orchestral performance, organ, piano, strings, voice, woodwinds; vocal music (CPS), including accompanying, brass, composition, guitar, orchestral performance, organ, piano, strings, voice, woodwinds. *Degree requirements:* For CPS, recital. *Entrance requirements:* For degree, audition, pre-screen CD. Additional exam requirements/recommendations for international students: Required—TOEFL (minimum score 550 paper-based). Electronic applications accepted.

Mansfield University of Pennsylvania, Graduate Studies, Department of Music, Mansfield, PA 16933. Offers band conducting (MA); choral conducting (MA); performance (MA). *Accreditation:* NASM. *Program availability:* Part-time, evening/weekend. *Degree requirements:* For master's, comprehensive exam, thesis optional. *Entrance requirements:* For master's, minimum GPA of 3.0, audition. Additional exam requirements/recommendations for international students: Required—TOEFL (minimum score 550 paper-based). Electronic applications accepted.

Marshall University, Academic Affairs Division, College of Arts and Media, Program in Music, Huntington, WV 25755. Offers music (MA), including music composition. *Accreditation:* NASM. *Program availability:* Evening/weekend. *Faculty:* 9 full-time (1 woman), 1 (woman) part-time/adjunct. *Students:* 14 full-time (1 woman), 1 part-time (0 women); includes 3 minority (2 Asian, non-Hispanic/Latino; 1 Hispanic/Latino). Average age 30. In 2017, 6 master's awarded. *Degree requirements:* For master's, thesis optional. Application fee: $40. *Unit head:* Dr. Michael Stroeher, Chairperson, 304-696-3109, E-mail: stroeher@marshall.edu. *Application contact:* Information Contact, 304-746-1900, Fax: 304-746-1902, E-mail: services@marshall.edu.
Website: http://www.marshall.edu/somt/

McGill University, Faculty of Graduate and Postdoctoral Studies, Schulich School of Music, Montréal, QC H3A 2T5, Canada. Offers composition (M Mus, D Mus, PhD); music education (MA, PhD); music technology (MA, PhD); musicology (MA, PhD); performance (M Mus); performance studies (D Mus); sound recording (M Mus, PhD); theory (MA, PhD).

Memorial University of Newfoundland, School of Graduate Studies, Interdisciplinary Program in Ethnomusicology, St. John's, NL A1C 5S7, Canada. Offers MA, PhD. *Program availability:* Part-time. *Degree requirements:* For master's, research paper or thesis; for doctorate, one foreign language, comprehensive exam, thesis/dissertation, oral defense of thesis. *Entrance requirements:* For master's, minimum B+ average with B Mus or humanities/social sciences degree; for doctorate, MA in ethnomusicology or a related field. Electronic applications accepted.

Memorial University of Newfoundland, School of Graduate Studies, School of Music, St. John's, NL A1C 5S7, Canada. Offers conducting (MMus); performance pedagogy (MMus); performing (MMus). *Entrance requirements:* For master's, diagnostic exams measuring skills and knowledge in musical literacy, B Mus with first-class standing, audition. Electronic applications accepted.

Mercer University, Graduate Studies, Macon Campus, Townsend School of Music, Macon, GA 31207. Offers choral conducting (MM); church music (MM); collaborative piano (MM), including instrumental, vocal; instrumental conducting (MM); performance (MM). *Faculty:* 9 full-time (3 women), 3 part-time/adjunct (2 women). *Students:* 12 full-time (6 women), 1 (woman) part-time; includes 3 minority (2 Black or African American, non-Hispanic/Latino; 1 Hispanic/Latino). Average age 25. 25 applicants, 48% accepted, 9 enrolled. In 2017, 11 master's awarded. *Degree requirements:* For master's, comprehensive exam, recitals. *Entrance requirements:* For master's, audition. Additional exam requirements/recommendations for international students: Required—TOEFL (minimum score 550 paper-based; 80 iBT). *Application deadline:* For fall admission, 6/1 for domestic students, 5/1 for international students. Applications are processed on a rolling basis. Application fee: $100. *Expenses:* Contact institution. *Financial support:* In 2017–18, 14 students received support. Tuition waivers (full) and unspecified assistantships available. Financial award application deadline: 6/1; financial award applicants required to submit FAFSA. *Faculty research:* Philosophy of church music, performance practices of the Baroque and classical periods, organ repertoire of the high Baroque, choral and instrumental conducting techniques. *Total annual research expenditures:* $5,000. *Unit head:* Dr. Richard G. Kosowski, Director of Graduate Studies, 478-301-4167, Fax: 478-301-5633, E-mail: keith_cd@mercer.edu. *Application contact:* Director, 912-301-2700.
Website: http://music.mercer.edu

Messiah College, Program in Conducting, Mechanicsburg, PA 17055. Offers choral conducting (MM); orchestral conducting (MM); wind conducting (MM). *Accreditation:* NASM. *Program availability:* Part-time, online learning. *Degree requirements:* For master's, advanced conducting project. Electronic applications accepted.

Miami University, College of Creative Arts, Department of Music, Oxford, OH 45056. Offers music education (MM); music performance (MM). *Accreditation:* NASM. *Students:* 15 full-time (8 women), 1 (woman) part-time; includes 2 minority (both Asian, non-Hispanic/Latino), 5 international. Average age 26. In 2017, 12 master's awarded. *Expenses:* Tuition, state resident: full-time $13,812; part-time $575 per credit hour. Tuition, nonresident: full-time $30,860; part-time $1286 per credit hour. *Unit head:* Dr. Chris Tanner, Interim Chair, 513-529-3082, E-mail: tannerc@miamioh.edu. *Application contact:* Dr. Brenda Mitchell, Associate Professor of Music/Director of Graduate Studies, 513-529-1228, E-mail: mitchebs@miamioh.edu.
Website: http://www.miamioh.edu/music

Michigan State University, The Graduate School, College of Music, East Lansing, MI 48824. Offers collaborative piano (M Mus); jazz studies (M Mus); music (PhD); music composition (M Mus, DMA); music conducting (M Mus, DMA); music education (M Mus); music performance (M Mus, DMA); music theory (M Mus); music therapy (M Mus); musicology (MA); piano pedagogy (M Mus). *Accreditation:* NASM. *Entrance requirements:* Additional exam requirements/recommendations for international students: Required—TOEFL. Electronic applications accepted.

Middle Tennessee State University, College of Graduate Studies, College of Liberal Arts, School of Music, Murfreesboro, TN 37132. Offers MA. *Accreditation:* NASM. *Program availability:* Part-time, evening/weekend, online learning. *Degree requirements:* For master's, one foreign language, comprehensive exam, thesis optional. *Entrance requirements:* For master's, GRE or MAT. Additional exam requirements/recommendations for international students: Required—TOEFL (minimum score 525 paper-based; 71 iBT) or IELTS (minimum score 6). Electronic applications accepted.

Middle Tennessee State University, College of Graduate Studies, College of Mass Communication, Department of Recording Industry, Murfreesboro, TN 37132. Offers recording arts and technologies (MFA). *Program availability:* Part-time, evening/weekend, online learning. *Degree requirements:* For master's, comprehensive exam, thesis or alternative. *Entrance requirements:* For master's, GRE. Additional exam requirements/recommendations for international students: Required—TOEFL (minimum score 525 paper-based; 71 iBT) or IELTS (minimum score 6). *Faculty research:* Digital audio, music production.

Midwestern Baptist Theological Seminary, Graduate and Professional Programs, Kansas City, MO 64118-4697. Offers Christian education (MACE); Christian foundations (Graduate Certificate); church music (MCM); counseling (MA); ministry (D Ed Min, D Min); Old or New Testament studies (PhD); theology (M Div). *Accreditation:* ATS. *Program availability:* Part-time, online learning. *Degree requirements:* For doctorate, thesis/dissertation. *Entrance requirements:* For doctorate, MAT. Electronic applications accepted. *Faculty research:* Ministerial studies, Biblical and theological studies, missions, counseling.

Mills College, Graduate Studies, Department of Music, Oakland, CA 94613-1000. Offers composition (MA); electronic music and recording media (MFA); music performance and literature (MFA). *Program availability:* Part-time. *Faculty:* 7 full-time (2 women), 2 part-time/adjunct (1 woman). *Students:* 35 full-time (12 women); includes 11 minority (1 Black or African American, non-Hispanic/Latino; 2 Asian, non-Hispanic/Latino; 5 Hispanic/Latino; 3 Two or more races, non-Hispanic/Latino), 4 international. Average age 30. 54 applicants, 81% accepted, 15 enrolled. In 2017, 16 master's awarded. *Degree requirements:* For master's, variable foreign language requirement, thesis, performance or recital. *Entrance requirements:* For master's, portfolio or audition. Additional exam requirements/recommendations for international students: Required—TOEFL (minimum score 550 paper-based; 80 iBT) or IELTS (minimum score 6). *Application deadline:* For fall admission, 1/15 priority date for domestic students, 12/15 for international students; for spring admission, 11/1 priority date for domestic students, 10/1 for international students. Applications are processed on a rolling basis. Application fee: $50. Electronic applications accepted. *Expenses: Tuition:* Full-time $33,480; part-time $1000 per credit. *Required fees:* $1479. Tuition and fees vary according to program. *Financial support:* In 2017–18, 36 students received support, including 36 fellowships with tuition reimbursements available (averaging $13,992 per year), 23 teaching assistantships with tuition reimbursements available; scholarships/grants also available. Support available to part-time students. Financial award application deadline: 2/1; financial award applicants required to submit FAFSA. *Faculty research:* Composition and songwriting, nineteenth- and twentieth-century Western classical music and opera, interdisciplinary electroacoustic composition and performance, musical instrument building and new instrumental resources, sound installation. *Unit head:* Nalini Ghuman, Head, Center for Contemporary Music, 510-430-2332, Fax: 510-430-3314, E-mail: nalinig@mills.edu. *Application contact:* Robynne Lofton, Director of Admissions, 510-430-3295, Fax: 510-430-2159, E-mail: grad-admission@mills.edu.
Website: http://www.mills.edu/music

Minnesota State University Mankato, College of Graduate Studies and Research, College of Arts and Humanities, Department of Music, Mankato, MN 56001. Offers choral conducting (MM); music education (MAT); piano performance (MM); wind band conducting (MM). *Accreditation:* NASM. *Degree requirements:* For master's, comprehensive exam, thesis or alternative. *Entrance requirements:* For master's, minimum GPA of 3.0 during previous 2 years, audition or test. Additional exam requirements/recommendations for international students: Required—TOEFL. Electronic applications accepted.

Mississippi College, Graduate School, College of Arts and Sciences, School of Christian Studies and the Arts, Department of Music, Clinton, MS 39058. Offers applied music performance (MM); conducting (MM); music education (MM); music performance: organ (MM); vocal pedagogy (MM). *Accreditation:* NASM. *Program availability:* Part-time, evening/weekend. *Degree requirements:* For master's, comprehensive exam, recital. *Entrance requirements:* For master's, GRE, minimum GPA of 2.5. Additional exam requirements/recommendations for international students: Recommended—TOEFL, IELTS. Electronic applications accepted.

Missouri State University, Graduate College, College of Arts and Letters, Department of Music, Springfield, MO 65897. Offers MM, MS Ed. *Accreditation:* NASM. *Program availability:* Part-time. *Faculty:* 27 full-time (11 women), 1 (woman) part-time/adjunct. *Students:* 34 full-time (26 women), 85 part-time (73 women); includes 9 minority (1 Black or African American, non-Hispanic/Latino; 1 Asian, non-Hispanic/Latino; 3 Hispanic/Latino; 1 Native Hawaiian or other Pacific Islander, non-Hispanic/Latino; 3 Two or more races, non-Hispanic/Latino), 14 international. Average age 26. 28 applicants, 39% accepted, 11 enrolled. In 2017, 15 master's awarded. *Degree requirements:* For master's, comprehensive exam, thesis or alternative. *Entrance requirements:* For master's, GRE, interview/audition (MM), 9-12 teaching certification (MS Ed). Additional exam requirements/recommendations for international students: Required—TOEFL (minimum score 550 paper-based; 79 iBT), IELTS (minimum score 6). *Application deadline:* For fall admission, 7/20 for domestic students, 5/1 for international students; for spring admission, 12/20 for domestic students, 9/1 for international students. Applications are processed on a rolling basis. Application fee: $35 ($50 for international students). Electronic applications accepted. *Expenses:* Tuition, state resident: full-time $2915; part-time $2021 per credit hour. Tuition, nonresident: full-time $5354; part-time $3647 per credit hour. *International tuition:* $11,992 full-time. *Required fees:* $173; $173 per credit hour. Tuition and fees vary according to class time, course level, course load, degree level, campus/location and program. *Financial support:* In 2017–18, 14 teaching assistantships with full tuition reimbursements (averaging $8,772 per year) were awarded; Federal Work-Study, institutionally sponsored loans, scholarships/grants, tuition waivers (partial), and unspecified assistantships also available. Financial award application deadline: 3/31; financial award applicants required to submit FAFSA. *Faculty research:* Musical theatre, Ozarks music, carillon, jazz studies. *Unit head:* Dr. Julie Combs, Department Head, 417-836-5648, Fax: 417-836-7665, E-mail: music@missouristate.edu. *Application contact:* Stephanie Praschan, Director, Graduate Enrollment Management, 417-836-5330, Fax: 417-836-6200, E-mail: stephaniepraschan@missouristate.edu.
Website: http://www.missouristate.edu/music/

Montclair State University, The Graduate School, College of the Arts, John J. Cali School of Music, Artist's Diploma Program, Montclair, NJ 07043-1624. Offers AD. *Accreditation:* NASM. *Program availability:* Part-time, evening/weekend. *Entrance requirements:* For degree, essay. Additional exam requirements/recommendations for international students: Required—TOEFL (minimum score 83 iBT), IELTS (minimum score 6.5). Electronic applications accepted.

Montclair State University, The Graduate School, College of the Arts, John J. Cali School of Music, Performer's Certificate Program, Montclair, NJ 07043-1624. Offers Performer's Certificate.

Montclair State University, The Graduate School, College of the Arts, John J. Cali School of Music, Program in Music, Montclair, NJ 07043-1624. Offers music education (MA); music therapy (MA); performance (MA); theory/composition (MA). *Program availability:* Part-time, evening/weekend. *Degree requirements:* For master's, thesis. *Entrance requirements:* For master's, GRE General Test, 2 letters of recommendation, essay. Additional exam requirements/recommendations for international students: Required—TOEFL (minimum score 83 iBT), IELTS (minimum score 6.5). Electronic applications accepted.

Morehead State University, Graduate Programs, Caudill College of Arts, Humanities and Social Sciences, Department of Music, Theatre and Dance, Morehead, KY 40351. Offers music education (MM); music performance (MM). *Accreditation:* NASM. *Program availability:* Part-time, evening/weekend. *Degree requirements:* For master's, comprehensive exam, oral and written exams. *Entrance requirements:* For master's, music entrance exam, BA in music with minimum GPA of 3.0, 2.5 overall; audition. Additional exam requirements/recommendations for international students: Required—TOEFL (minimum score 550 paper-based). Electronic applications accepted. *Faculty research:* Musical instrument digital interface (MIDI) applications, tonal concepts of euphonium and baritone horn, digital synthesis, computer-assisted instruction in music, musical composition.

Morgan State University, School of Graduate Studies, College of Liberal Arts, Department of Fine and Performing Arts, Baltimore, MD 21251. Offers music (MA), including choral, conducting, instrumental, piano, sacred music, vocal. *Accreditation:* NASM. *Program availability:* Part-time, evening/weekend. *Degree requirements:* For master's, comprehensive exam, thesis. *Entrance requirements:* Additional exam requirements/recommendations for international students: Required—TOEFL (minimum score 550 paper-based). *Application deadline:* For fall admission, 2/1 priority date for domestic students; for spring admission, 10/1 priority date for domestic students. Applications are processed on a rolling basis. Application fee: $0. *Expenses:* Tuition, state resident: part-time $433 per credit. Tuition, nonresident: part-time $851 per credit. *Required fees:* $81.50 per credit. *Financial support:* Application deadline: 2/1. *Unit head:* Dr. Eric Conway, Chairperson, 443-885-3598, E-mail: eric.conway@morgan.edu. *Application contact:* Dr. Dean Campbell, Graduate Recruitment Specialist, 443-885-3185, Fax: 443-885-8226, E-mail: dean.campbell@morgan.edu.

Murray State University, College of Humanities and Fine Arts, Department of Music, Murray, KY 42071. Offers music education (MME). *Accreditation:* NASM. *Program availability:* Part-time. *Faculty:* 10 full-time (3 women), 2 part-time/adjunct (1 woman). *Students:* 1 (woman) full-time, 3 part-time (2 women). Average age 27. In 2017, 3 master's awarded. *Entrance requirements:* For master's, GRE or GMAT, minimum university GPA of 2.75. Additional exam requirements/recommendations for international students: Required—TOEFL (minimum score 527 paper-based; 71 iBT). *Application deadline:* Applications are processed on a rolling basis. Application fee: $40 ($50 for international students). Electronic applications accepted. *Expenses:* Tuition, state resident: full-time $9504. Tuition, nonresident: full-time $26,811. *International tuition:* $14,400 full-time. Tuition and fees vary according to course load, degree level and reciprocity agreements. *Financial support:* Federal Work-Study and unspecified assistantships available. Financial award applicants required to submit FAFSA. *Unit head:* Dr. Lucia Unrau, Chair, Department of Music, 270-809-4288, Fax: 270-809-3965, E-mail: lunrauterry@murraystate.edu. *Application contact:* Kaitlyn Burzynski, Interim Assistant Director for Graduate Admission and Records, 270-809-5732, Fax: 270-809-3780, E-mail: msu.graduateadmissions@murraystate.edu.
Website: https://www.murraystate.edu/academics/CollegesDepartments/CollegeOfHumanitiesAndFineArts/Music/index.aspx

Nazareth College of Rochester, Graduate Studies, Department of Music, Rochester, NY 14618. Offers music education (MS Ed); music performance and pedagogy (MM). *Program availability:* Part-time, evening/weekend. *Entrance requirements:* For master's, GRE or

MAT (for music education program), audition, minimum GPA of 3.0. Additional exam requirements/recommendations for international students: Required—TOEFL (minimum score 550 paper-based, 79 iBT) or IELTS (6.5). Electronic applications accepted.

New England Conservatory of Music, Graduate Program in Music, Boston, MA 02115-5000. Offers MM, DMA, Diploma. *Degree requirements:* For master's, variable foreign language requirement, comprehensive exam, thesis (for some programs), recital; for doctorate, one foreign language, comprehensive exam, thesis/dissertation, qualifying exams, recital. *Entrance requirements:* For master's and Diploma, audition; for doctorate, music theory and musicology exam, audition. Additional exam requirements/recommendations for international students: Required—TOEFL (minimum score 550 paper-based; 79 iBT). Electronic applications accepted.

New Jersey City University, William J. Maxwell College of Arts and Sciences, Department of Music, Dance and Theatre, Jersey City, NJ 07305-1597. Offers music education (MA); performance (MM). *Accreditation:* NASM. *Program availability:* Part-time, evening/weekend. *Degree requirements:* For master's, thesis optional, recital. *Entrance requirements:* Additional exam requirements/recommendations for international students: Required—TOEFL (minimum score 79 iBT).

New Mexico State University, College of Arts and Sciences, Department of Music, Las Cruces, NM 88003. Offers conducting (MM); music education (MM); performance (MM). *Accreditation:* NASM. *Program availability:* Part-time-only, online learning. *Faculty:* 16 full-time (5 women), 3 part-time/adjunct (0 women). *Students:* 13 full-time (10 women), 12 part-time (5 women); includes 13 minority (all Hispanic/Latino), 4 international. Average age 31. 10 applicants, 70% accepted, 5 enrolled. In 2017, 3 master's awarded. *Degree requirements:* For master's, comprehensive exam, thesis (for some programs), recital. *Entrance requirements:* For master's, audition, bachelor's degree or equivalent from an accredited institution. Additional exam requirements/recommendations for international students: Required—TOEFL (minimum score 550 paper-based; 79 iBT), IELTS (minimum score 6.5). *Application deadline:* For fall admission, 7/1 priority date for domestic students; for spring admission, 11/1 for domestic students; for summer admission, 3/1 for domestic students. Applications are processed on a rolling basis. Application fee: $40 ($50 for international students). Electronic applications accepted. *Expenses:* Tuition, state resident: full-time $4390. Tuition, nonresident: full-time $15,309. *Required fees:* $853. *Financial support:* In 2017–18, 13 students received support, including 1 fellowship (averaging $788 per year), 8 teaching assistantships (averaging $14,844 per year); career-related internships or fieldwork, Federal Work-Study, scholarships/grants, traineeships, health care benefits, and unspecified assistantships also available. Support available to part-time students. Financial award application deadline: 3/1. *Faculty research:* Music education, contemporary wind band literature, performance, music history, composition. *Total annual research expenditures:* $2,606. *Unit head:* Dr. Lon W. Chaffin, Department Head, 575-646-2421, Fax: 575-646-8199, E-mail: lchaffin@nmsu.edu. *Application contact:* Dr. James Shearer, Coordinator of Graduate Studies, 575-646-2601, Fax: 575-646-8199, E-mail: jshearer@nmsu.edu.
Website: http://music.nmsu.edu

New Orleans Baptist Theological Seminary, Graduate and Professional Programs, Division of Church Music Ministries, New Orleans, LA 70126-4858. Offers M Div, MMCM, DMA. *Accreditation:* NASM. *Program availability:* Online learning. *Degree requirements:* For doctorate, one foreign language, thesis/dissertation. *Entrance requirements:* For doctorate, GRE General Test. Additional exam requirements/recommendations for international students: Required—TOEFL.

The New School, College of Performing Arts, Mannes School of Music, New York, NY 10003. Offers composition (MM, Advanced Diploma); guitar (MM, Advanced Diploma); harpsichord (MM, Advanced Diploma); music theory (MM); orchestral conducting (MM, Advanced Diploma); orchestral instruments (MM, Advanced Diploma); piano (MM, Advanced Diploma); piano and collaborative piano (MM, Advanced Diploma); theory (Advanced Diploma); voice (MM, Advanced Diploma). *Program availability:* Part-time. *Faculty:* 9 full-time (4 women), 128 part-time/adjunct (53 women). *Students:* 305 full-time (189 women), 2 part-time (1 woman); includes 53 minority (7 Black or African American, non-Hispanic/Latino; 1 American Indian or Alaska Native, non-Hispanic/Latino; 16 Asian, non-Hispanic/Latino; 20 Hispanic/Latino; 1 Native Hawaiian or other Pacific Islander, non-Hispanic/Latino; 8 Two or more races, non-Hispanic/Latino), 169 international. Average age 26. 845 applicants, 51% accepted, 157 enrolled. In 2017, 60 master's, 20 Advanced Diplomas awarded. *Degree requirements:* For master's, performance examination. *Entrance requirements:* For master's, transcripts, recommendation letter, essay, live audition. Additional exam requirements/recommendations for international students: Required—TOEFL (minimum score 79 iBT), IELTS (minimum score 6.5), PTE (minimum score 53). *Application deadline:* For fall admission, 12/1 priority date for domestic and international students; for spring admission, 10/15 priority date for domestic and international students. Applications are processed on a rolling basis. Application fee: $50. Electronic applications accepted. *Expenses:* $44,460 per year; $1,560 per credit. *Financial support:* In 2017–18, 256 students received support, including 4 research assistantships (averaging $2,500 per year), 3 teaching assistantships (averaging $2,282 per year); career-related internships or fieldwork, Federal Work-Study, scholarships/grants, and unspecified assistantships also available. Support available to part-time students. Financial award application deadline: 2/1; financial award applicants required to submit FAFSA. *Unit head:* Richard Kessler, Executive Dean, College of Performing Arts, 212-580-0210 Ext. 4848, E-mail: richardkessler@newschool.edu. *Application contact:* Amanda Hosking, Director of Admission, College of Performing Arts, 212-229-5150 Ext. 4805, E-mail: performingarts@newschool.edu.
Website: http://www.newschool.edu/mannes/

New York University, Graduate School of Arts and Science, Department of Music, New York, NY 10012-1019. Offers composition and theory (MA, PhD); early music performance (Advanced Certificate); ethnomusicology (MA, PhD). *Students:* Average age 33. 126 applicants, 5% accepted, 5 enrolled. In 2017, 2 master's, 7 doctorates awarded. Terminal master's awarded for partial completion of doctoral program. *Degree requirements:* For master's, one foreign language, thesis (for some programs), general exam; for doctorate, 2 foreign languages, thesis/dissertation, general and special exams. *Entrance requirements:* For master's, GRE General Test, bachelor's degree in liberal arts or music; for doctorate, GRE General Test, master's degree in music. Additional exam requirements/recommendations for international students: Required—TOEFL. *Application deadline:* For fall admission, 1/4 for domestic and international students. Application fee: $100. *Expenses: Tuition:* Full-time $41,352; part-time $19,968 per year. *Required fees:* $2496; $1628 per unit. $814 per term. Tuition and fees vary according to course load and program. *Financial support:* Fellowships, teaching assistantships, Federal Work-Study, institutionally sponsored loans, scholarships/grants, health care benefits, and unspecified assistantships available. Financial award application deadline: 1/4; financial award applicants required to submit FAFSA. *Faculty research:* Early music (nineteenth century), Wagner, Verdi, performance practice. *Unit head:* David Samuels, Chair, 212-998-8300, Fax: 212-995-4147, E-mail: fas.music.gradadmissions@nyu.edu. *Application contact:* Maureen Mahon, Director of Graduate Studies, 212-998-8300, Fax: 212-995-4147, E-mail: fas.music.gradadmissions@nuy.edu.
Website: http://www.nyu.edu/gsas/dept/music/

New York University, Steinhardt School of Culture, Education, and Human Development, Department of Music and Performing Arts Professions, Program in Music Business, New York, NY 10012. Offers music business (MA); music technology (MA). *Program availability:* Part-time. *Students:* Average age 26. 99 applicants, 64% accepted, 41 enrolled. In 2017, 36 master's awarded. *Entrance requirements:* For master's, interview. Additional exam requirements/recommendations for international students: Required—TOEFL (minimum score 100 iBT). *Application deadline:* For fall admission, 12/1 priority date for domestic and international students. Applications are processed on a rolling basis. Application fee: $75. Electronic applications accepted. *Expenses: Tuition:* Full-time $41,352; part-time $19,968 per year. *Required fees:* $2496; $1628 per unit. $814 per term. Tuition and fees vary according to course load and program. *Financial support:* Career-related internships or fieldwork, Federal Work-Study, scholarships/grants, and tuition waivers (partial) available. Support available to part-time students. Financial award application deadline: 2/1; financial award applicants required to submit FAFSA. *Faculty research:* Strategic marketing, new technologies, intellectual property, entrepreneurship, globalization, music in video games. *Unit head:* Dr. Catherine Moore-Broatman, Director, 212-998-5427, Fax: 212-998-4560, E-mail: catherine.moore@nyu.edu. *Application contact:* 212-998-5030, Fax: 212-995-4328, E-mail: steinhardt.gradadmissions@nyu.edu.
Website: http://steinhardt.nyu.edu/music/business

New York University, Steinhardt School of Culture, Education, and Human Development, Department of Music and Performing Arts Professions, Program in Music Performance and Composition, New York, NY 10012. Offers instrumental performance (MM), including instrumental performance, jazz instrumental performance; music performance and composition (PhD), including music performance and composition; music theory and composition (MM), including composition for film and multimedia, composition for music theater, computer music composition, music theory and composition, songwriting; piano performance (MM), including collaborative piano, solo piano; vocal pedagogy (Advanced Certificate); vocal performance (MM), including classical voice, musical theatre performance. *Program availability:* Part-time. *Students:* Average age 27. 534 applicants, 50% accepted, 141 enrolled. In 2017, 130 master's, 2 doctorates, 12 other advanced degrees awarded. *Entrance requirements:* For master's, audition; for doctorate, GRE General Test, audition, interview. Additional exam requirements/recommendations for international students: Required—TOEFL (minimum score 100 iBT). *Application deadline:* For fall admission, 12/1 priority date for domestic and international students; for spring admission, 10/1 for domestic and international students. Applications are processed on a rolling basis. Application fee: $75. Electronic applications accepted. *Expenses: Tuition:* Full-time $41,352; part-time $19,968 per year. *Required fees:* $2496; $1628 per unit. $814 per term. Tuition and fees vary according to course load and program. *Financial support:* Fellowships with full and partial tuition reimbursements, Federal Work-Study, scholarships/grants, and tuition waivers (partial) available. Support available to part-time students. Financial award application deadline: 2/1; financial award applicants required to submit FAFSA. *Faculty research:* Aesthetics, performance analysis, twentieth century music, music methodologies for arts criticism and analysis. *Unit head:* Dr. Tae Hong Park, Director, 212-998-5424, Fax: 212-995-4043, E-mail: tae.hong.park@nyu.edu. *Application contact:* 212-998-5030, Fax: 212-995-4328, E-mail: steinhardt.gradadmissions@nyu.edu.
Website: http://steinhardt.nyu.edu/music/composition/programs/graduate

New York University, Steinhardt School of Culture, Education, and Human Development, Department of Music and Performing Arts Professions, Program in Music Technology, New York, NY 10012. Offers MM, PhD. *Program availability:* Part-time. *Students:* Average age 30. 126 applicants, 70% accepted, 40 enrolled. In 2017, 24 master's, 2 doctorates awarded. *Entrance requirements:* For master's, portfolio; for doctorate, essay, 3 letters of recommendation, master's degree. Additional exam requirements/recommendations for international students: Required—TOEFL (minimum score 100 iBT). *Application deadline:* For fall admission, 12/1 priority date for domestic and international students; for spring admission, 10/1 for domestic and international students. Applications are processed on a rolling basis. Application fee: $75. Electronic applications accepted. *Expenses: Tuition:* Full-time $41,352; part-time $19,968 per year. *Required fees:* $2496; $1628 per unit. $814 per term. Tuition and fees vary according to course load and program. *Financial support:* Fellowships with full and partial tuition reimbursements, research assistantships with full and partial tuition reimbursements, career-related internships or fieldwork, Federal Work-Study, institutionally sponsored loans, scholarships/grants, and tuition waivers (partial) available. Support available to part-time students. Financial award application deadline: 2/1; financial award applicants required to submit FAFSA. *Faculty research:* Pattern processing in music, computer music, acoustics, music perception, interactive music systems. *Unit head:* Prof. Kenneth J. Peacock, Director, 212-998-5424, Fax: 212-995-4043, E-mail: kp3@nyu.edu. *Application contact:* 212-998-5030, Fax: 212-995-4328, E-mail: steinhardt.gradadmissions@nyu.edu.
Website: http://steinhardt.nyu.edu/music/technology

New York University, Tisch School of the Arts, Graduate Musical Theatre Writing Program, New York, NY 10012-1019. Offers MFA. *Faculty:* 6 full-time, 14 part-time/adjunct. *Students:* 68 full-time (29 women); includes 14 minority (6 Black or African American, non-Hispanic/Latino; 1 Asian, non-Hispanic/Latino; 6 Hispanic/Latino; 1 Two or more races, non-Hispanic/Latino), 18 international. Average age 28. 60 applicants, 82% accepted, 31 enrolled. In 2017, 35 master's awarded. *Degree requirements:* For master's, full-length musical theatre work. *Entrance requirements:* For master's, interview, portfolio. *Application deadline:* For fall admission, 2/1 priority date for domestic and international students. Application fee: $60. Electronic applications accepted. *Expenses: Tuition:* Full-time $41,352; part-time $19,968 per year. *Required fees:* $2496; $1628 per unit. $814 per term. Tuition and fees vary according to course load and program. *Financial support:* In 2017–18, 18 students received support. Fellowships with tuition reimbursements available, career-related internships or fieldwork, Federal Work-Study, tuition waivers (partial), and unspecified assistantships available. Financial award application deadline: 2/15; financial award applicants required to submit FAFSA. *Unit head:* Sarah Schlesinger, Chair, 212-998-1830, Fax: 212-995-4873, E-mail: musical.theatre@nyu.edu. *Application contact:* Dan Sandford, Director of Graduate Admissions, 212-998-1918, Fax: 212-995-4060, E-mail: tisch.gradadmissions@nyu.edu.
Website: http://www.gmtw.tisch.nyu.edu/

Norfolk State University, School of Graduate Studies, School of Liberal Arts, Department of Music, Norfolk, VA 23504. Offers music (MM); music education (MM); performance (MM); theory and composition (MM). *Accreditation:* NASM. *Program availability:* Part-time. *Degree requirements:* For master's, thesis or alternative. *Entrance requirements:* For master's, minimum GPA of 2.7, letters of recommendation. Additional exam requirements/recommendations for international students: Required—TOEFL.

North Carolina Central University, College of Arts and Sciences, Department of Music, Durham, NC 27707-3129. Offers jazz studies (MM). *Expenses:* Tuition, state resident: full-time $2770; part-time $692.50 per credit hour. Tuition, nonresident: full-time $9247; part-time $2311.75 per credit hour. *Unit head:* Ira T. Wiggins, Director of Jazz Studies, 919-530-7214, E-mail: iwiggins@nccu.edu. *Application contact:* Ira T. Wiggins, Director of Jazz Studies, 919-530-7214, E-mail: iwiggins@nccu.edu.
Website: http://www.nccu.edu/music/index.cfm

Music

North Dakota State University, College of Graduate and Interdisciplinary Studies, College of Arts, Humanities and Social Sciences, Challey School of Music, Fargo, ND 58102. Offers conducting (MM, DMA); music education (MM); performance (MM, DMA). *Accreditation:* NASM. *Degree requirements:* For master's, 2 foreign languages, comprehensive exam, thesis or alternative, recitals; for doctorate, 2 foreign languages, comprehensive exam, thesis/dissertation or alternative, recitals. *Entrance requirements:* For master's and doctorate, music history, music theory, performance audition. Additional exam requirements/recommendations for international students: Required—TOEFL (minimum score 525 paper-based; 71 iBT). Electronic applications accepted. *Faculty research:* Performance, conducting.

Northeastern Illinois University, College of Graduate Studies and Research, College of Arts and Sciences, Program in Music, Chicago, IL 60625. Offers music (MA), including applied music pedagogy. *Accreditation:* NASM. *Program availability:* Part-time, evening/weekend. *Degree requirements:* For master's, comprehensive exam, thesis optional. *Entrance requirements:* For master's, departmental exam, audition, minimum GPA of 2.75. Additional exam requirements/recommendations for international students: Required—TOEFL (minimum score 550 paper-based; 79 iBT). *Application deadline:* Applications are processed on a rolling basis. Application fee: $30. Electronic applications accepted. *Expenses:* Tuition, state resident: full-time $7274; part-time $404.11 per credit hour. Tuition, nonresident: full-time $14,548; part-time $808.23 per credit hour. *Required fees:* $1284. *Financial support:* Applicants required to submit FAFSA. *Faculty research:* World music, computers as applied instruments, vocal pedagogy, vocal interpretation, jazz repertory. *Unit head:* Dr. Shayne Cofer, Department Chair, 773-442-5919, E-mail: r-shaynecofer@neiu.edu. *Application contact:* Martha Narvaez, Graduate Admission Representative, 773-442-6006, E-mail: m-narvaez@neiu.edu.

Northern Arizona University, College of Arts and Letters, School of Music, Flagstaff, AZ 86011. Offers music (MM); music performance (Graduate Certificate). *Accreditation:* NASM. *Program availability:* Part-time. *Faculty:* 43 full-time (20 women), 13 part-time/adjunct (11 women). *Students:* 26 full-time (11 women), 1 part-time (0 women); includes 3 minority (1 Black or African American, non-Hispanic/Latino; 1 Asian, non-Hispanic/Latino; 1 Hispanic/Latino), 3 international. Average age 29. 31 applicants, 68% accepted, 21 enrolled. In 2017, 13 master's, 2 other advanced degrees awarded. *Degree requirements:* For master's, variable foreign language requirement, comprehensive exam (for some programs), thesis (for some programs). *Entrance requirements:* For master's, bachelor's degree in music, minimum cumulative GPA of 3.0, audition, major professor and/or area approval for the candidate's sub-plan. Additional exam requirements/recommendations for international students: Required—TOEFL (minimum score 80 iBT), IELTS (minimum score 6.5). *Application deadline:* For fall admission, 3/1 for domestic and international students; for spring admission, 10/1 for domestic and international students. Applications are processed on a rolling basis. Application fee: $65. Electronic applications accepted. *Expenses:* Tuition, state resident: full-time $9240; part-time $458 per credit hour. Tuition, nonresident: full-time $21,588; part-time $1199 per credit hour. *Required fees:* $1021; $14 per credit hour. $646 per semester. Tuition and fees vary according to course load, campus/location and program. *Financial support:* In 2017–18, 18 students received support, including 18 teaching assistantships with partial tuition reimbursements available (averaging $6,000 per year); institutionally sponsored loans, health care benefits, tuition waivers (partial), and unspecified assistantships also available. Financial award application deadline: 2/1; financial award applicants required to submit FAFSA. *Unit head:* Dr. Todd E. Sullivan, Director, 928-523-3731, Fax: 928-523-2562, E-mail: todd.sullivan@nau.edu. *Application contact:* Tina Sutton, Coordinator, Graduate College, 928-523-4348, Fax: 928-523-8950, E-mail: graduate@nau.edu.
Website: https://nau.edu/cal/music/

Northern Illinois University, Graduate School, College of Visual and Performing Arts, School of Music, De Kalb, IL 60115-2854. Offers MM, Performer's Certificate. *Accreditation:* NASM. *Program availability:* Part-time. *Faculty:* 33 full-time (3 women), 14 part-time/adjunct (3 women). *Students:* 38 full-time (14 women), 22 part-time (11 women); includes 9 minority (4 Black or African American, non-Hispanic/Latino; 2 Asian, non-Hispanic/Latino; 3 Hispanic/Latino), 23 international. Average age 28. 86 applicants, 55% accepted, 25 enrolled. In 2017, 44 master's, 5 other advanced degrees awarded. *Degree requirements:* For master's, comprehensive exam, thesis optional, recital or project; for Performer's Certificate, recitals. *Entrance requirements:* For master's, minimum GPA of 2.75, appropriate bachelor's degree, audition, interview; for Performer's Certificate, minimum GPA of 2.75 (undergraduate), 3.2 (graduate); audition. Additional exam requirements/recommendations for international students: Required—TOEFL (minimum score 550 paper-based). *Application deadline:* For fall admission, 4/1 for domestic students, 5/1 for international students; for spring admission, 11/1 for domestic students, 10/1 for international students. Applications are processed on a rolling basis. Application fee: $40. Electronic applications accepted. *Financial support:* In 2017–18, 3 research assistantships with full tuition reimbursements, 24 teaching assistantships with full tuition reimbursements were awarded; fellowships with full tuition reimbursements, Federal Work-Study, scholarships/grants, tuition waivers (full), and staff assistantships also available. Support available to part-time students. Financial award applicants required to submit FAFSA. *Faculty research:* Impact of music on urban children and acquisition of language skills, music in seventeenth-century Madrid, Finnish music and culture, jazz studies. *Unit head:* Dr. Janet Hathaway, Director, 815-753-1551, Fax: 815-753-1759, E-mail: jhathaway@niu.edu. *Application contact:* Lynn Slater, Coordinator of Admissions and Public Relations, 815-753-1546, E-mail: lslater@niu.edu.
Website: http://www.niu.edu/music/

North Park University, School of Music, Chicago, IL 60625-4895. Offers vocal performance (MM). *Accreditation:* NASM.

Northwestern State University of Louisiana, Graduate Studies and Research, School of Creative and Performing Arts, Program in Music, Natchitoches, LA 71497. Offers MM. *Accreditation:* NASM. *Degree requirements:* For master's, comprehensive exam, thesis or alternative. *Entrance requirements:* For master's, GRE General Test, minimum undergraduate GPA of 2.5. Additional exam requirements/recommendations for international students: Required—TOEFL. Electronic applications accepted.

Northwestern University, The Graduate School, School of Communication, Department of Performance Studies, Evanston, IL 60208. Offers MA, PhD. Admissions and degrees offered through The Graduate School. *Program availability:* Part-time. Terminal master's awarded for partial completion of doctoral program. *Degree requirements:* For master's, recital; for doctorate, one foreign language, thesis/dissertation, recital. *Entrance requirements:* For master's and doctorate, GRE General Test. Additional exam requirements/recommendations for international students: Required—TOEFL. *Faculty research:* Adaptation/performance of literature, ethnography of performance, critical cultural studies, performance theory, intercultural performance, gender studies.

Northwestern University, Henry and Leigh Bienen School of Music, Department of Music Performance, Evanston, IL 60208. Offers brass performance (MM, DMA); conducting (MM, DMA); jazz studies (MM); percussion performance (MM, DMA); performance (MM); piano pedagogy (MME); piano performance (MM, DMA); piano performance and collaborative arts (MM, DMA); piano performance and pedagogy (MM, DMA); string performance (MM, DMA); voice and opera performance (MM, DMA); woodwind performance (MM, DMA). *Accreditation:* NASM. *Degree requirements:* For master's, recital; for doctorate, comprehensive exam, thesis/dissertation, 3 recitals. *Entrance requirements:* For master's, audition, prescreening auditions where required; for doctorate, audition, preliminary tapes. Additional exam requirements/recommendations for international students: Required—TOEFL (minimum score 80 iBT).

Northwestern University, Henry and Leigh Bienen School of Music, Department of Music Studies, Evanston, IL 60208. Offers composition (DMA); music education (MME, PhD); music theory and cognition (PhD); musicology (MM, PhD); theory (MM). PhD admissions and degree offered through The Graduate School. *Accreditation:* NASM. *Degree requirements:* For doctorate, comprehensive exam, thesis/dissertation. *Entrance requirements:* For master's, portfolio or research papers; for doctorate, GRE General Test (for PhD), portfolio, research papers. Additional exam requirements/recommendations for international students: Required—TOEFL (minimum score 600 paper-based; 80 iBT). *Faculty research:* Music cognition, cognitive learning, aesthetic education, computer music, technology in education.

Oakland University, Graduate Study and Lifelong Learning, College of Arts and Sciences, Department of Music, Rochester, MI 48309-4401. Offers music (MM); music education (PhD). *Accreditation:* NASM. *Entrance requirements:* For master's, minimum GPA of 3.0. Additional exam requirements/recommendations for international students: Required—TOEFL (minimum score 550 paper-based). Electronic applications accepted. *Expenses:* Contact institution.

Oberlin College, Conservatory of Music, Oberlin, OH 44074-1588. Offers conducting (MM); contemporary chamber music (MM); historical performance (MM); performance (AD); piano technology (AD). *Students:* 26 full-time (8 women). 88 applicants, 25% accepted, 19 enrolled. *Degree requirements:* For master's, 2 recitals. *Entrance requirements:* For master's and AD, audition. Additional exam requirements/recommendations for international students: Recommended—TOEFL, IELTS. *Application deadline:* For fall admission, 12/1 for domestic and international students. Application fee: $100. Electronic applications accepted. *Financial support:* Career-related internships or fieldwork, Federal Work-Study, and scholarships/grants available. Financial award application deadline: 2/15; financial award applicants required to submit CSS PROFILE or FAFSA. *Unit head:* Andrea Kalyn, Dean, 440-775-8200. *Application contact:* Michael Manderen, Director of Conservatory Admissions, 440-775-8413, Fax: 440-775-6972, E-mail: conservatory.admissions@oberlin.edu.
Website: http://new.oberlin.edu/conservatory/

The Ohio State University, Graduate School, College of Arts and Sciences, Division of Arts and Humanities, Department of Dance, Columbus, OH 43210. Offers choreography (MFA); dance (MFA, PhD); dance and technology (MFA); dance studies (PhD); history, theory and literature (MFA); lighting and production (MFA); movement analysis, Laban studies, notation and dance documentation (MFA); performance (MFA). *Accreditation:* NASD. *Faculty:* 11. *Students:* 33 (26 women), 5 international. Average age 32. In 2017, 6 master's awarded. *Degree requirements:* For master's, thesis optional. *Entrance requirements:* For master's, GRE General Test (for all applicants with cumulative GPA below 3.0), audition; for doctorate, GRE General Test, invitation-only interview. Additional exam requirements/recommendations for international students: Required—Michigan English Language Assessment Battery (minimum score 82); Recommended—TOEFL (minimum score 550 paper-based; 79 iBT), IELTS (minimum score 7). *Application deadline:* For fall admission, 11/15 priority date for domestic and international students; for spring admission, 3/1 for domestic students, 2/1 for international students. Applications are processed on a rolling basis. Application fee: $60 ($70 for international students). Electronic applications accepted. *Financial support:* Fellowships with tuition reimbursements, teaching assistantships with tuition reimbursements, Federal Work-Study, and institutionally sponsored loans available. Support available to part-time students. *Unit head:* Susan Hadley, Chair, 614-292-0984, E-mail: hadley.4@osu.edu. *Application contact:* Amy Schmidt, Academic Program Coordinator, 614-292-8933, E-mail: schmidt.442@osu.edu.
Website: http://dance.osu.edu/

The Ohio State University, Graduate School, College of Arts and Sciences, Division of Arts and Humanities, School of Music, Columbus, OH 43210. Offers MA, MM, DMA, PhD. *Accreditation:* NASM. *Program availability:* Part-time. *Faculty:* 47. *Students:* 107 full-time (53 women), 19 part-time (8 women), 24 international. Average age 31. In 2017, 30 master's, 10 doctorates awarded. *Degree requirements:* For master's, thesis optional; for doctorate, 2 foreign languages, thesis/dissertation. *Entrance requirements:* For master's, GRE General Test (for all MA applicants and for MM applicants if GPA is below 3.0), pre-screen video audition (for piano and voice); for doctorate, GRE General Test (for all PhD applicants and for DMA applicants if GPA is below 3.0), pre-screen video audition (for piano and voice). Additional exam requirements/recommendations for international students: Required—TOEFL (minimum score 550 paper-based; 79 iBT), Michigan English Language Assessment Battery (minimum score 82); Recommended—IELTS (minimum score 7). *Application deadline:* For fall admission, 12/13 priority date for domestic students, 11/30 priority date for international students; for spring admission, 12/14 for domestic students, 11/12 for international students; for summer admission, 5/15 for domestic students, 4/14 for international students. Applications are processed on a rolling basis. Application fee: $60 ($70 for international students). Electronic applications accepted. *Financial support:* Fellowships, research assistantships, teaching assistantships, Federal Work-Study, institutionally sponsored loans, and unspecified assistantships available. Support available to part-time students. *Unit head:* William L. Ballenger, Director and Chair, 614-292-7664, E-mail: ballenger.46@osu.edu. *Application contact:* Rebecca Harrah, Graduate Studies Coordinator, 614-292-6389, Fax: 614-292-1102, E-mail: mus-grad@osu.edu.
Website: http://music.osu.edu/

Ohio University, Graduate College, College of Fine Arts, School of Music, Athens, OH 45701-2979. Offers accompanying (MM); composition (MM); conducting (MM); history/literature (MM); music education (MM); music therapy (MM); performance (MM, Certificate); performance/pedagogy (MM); theory (MM). *Accreditation:* NASM. *Program availability:* Part-time, evening/weekend, online learning. *Degree requirements:* For master's, comprehensive exam, thesis (for some programs), oral exam. *Entrance requirements:* For master's, audition, interview, portfolio, recordings (varies by program). Additional exam requirements/recommendations for international students: Required—TOEFL (minimum score 550 paper-based; 80 iBT) or IELTS (minimum score 6.5). Electronic applications accepted.

Oklahoma City University, Wanda L. Bass School of Music, Oklahoma City, OK 73106-1402. Offers composition (MM); conducting (MM); musical theatre (MM); opera performance (MM); performance (MM); vocal coaching (MM). *Accreditation:* NASM. *Program availability:* Part-time. *Faculty:* 26 full-time (10 women), 19 part-time/adjunct (8 women). *Students:* 64 full-time (24 women), 2 part-time (1 woman); includes 17 minority (2 Black or African American, non-Hispanic/Latino; 3 Asian, non-Hispanic/Latino; 8 Hispanic/Latino; 4 Two or more races, non-Hispanic/Latino), 16 international. Average age 25. 95 applicants, 59% accepted, 32 enrolled. In 2017, 22 master's awarded. *Degree requirements:* For master's, thesis, departmental qualifying exam, recital.

Entrance requirements: For master's, audition, bachelor's degree in music from NASM-accredited institution, minimum GPA of 3.0. Additional exam requirements/recommendations for international students: Required—TOEFL (minimum score 550 paper-based; 80 iBT). *Application deadline:* Applications are processed on a rolling basis. Application fee: $50. Electronic applications accepted. *Expenses:* $19,098. *Financial support:* In 2017–18, 67 students received support. Career-related internships or fieldwork, Federal Work-Study, institutionally sponsored loans, scholarships/grants, and tuition waivers (full and partial) available. Support available to part-time students. Financial award application deadline: 6/1; financial award applicants required to submit FAFSA. *Unit head:* Mark Parker, Dean, 405-208-5474, Fax: 405-208-5971, E-mail: mparker@okcu.edu. *Application contact:* Michael Harrington, Director of Graduate Admission, 800-633-7242, Fax: 405-208-5916, E-mail: gadmissions@okcu.edu. Website: http://www.okcu.edu/music/

Oklahoma State University, College of Arts and Sciences, Michael and Anne Greenwood School of Music, Stillwater, OK 74078. Offers pedagogy and performance (MM). *Accreditation:* NASM. *Faculty:* 33 full-time (14 women), 9 part-time/adjunct (2 women). *Students:* 15 full-time (6 women), 7 part-time (2 women); includes 4 minority (2 Black or African American, non-Hispanic/Latino; 1 Hispanic/Latino; 1 Two or more races, non-Hispanic/Latino), 3 international. Average age 26. 37 applicants, 49% accepted, 13 enrolled. In 2017, 5 master's awarded. *Entrance requirements:* For master's, GRE, audition. Additional exam requirements/recommendations for international students: Required—TOEFL (minimum score 550 paper-based; 79 iBT). *Application deadline:* For fall admission, 3/1 priority date for international students; for spring admission, 8/1 priority date for international students. Applications are processed on a rolling basis. Application fee: $40 ($75 for international students). Electronic applications accepted. *Expenses:* Tuition, state resident: full-time $4019; part-time $2679.60 per year. Tuition, nonresident: full-time $15,286; part-time $10,190.40 per year. *Required fees:* $2129; $1419 per unit. Tuition and fees vary according to program. *Financial support:* Teaching assistantships, career-related internships or fieldwork, Federal Work-Study, scholarships/grants, health care benefits, tuition waivers (partial), and unspecified assistantships available. Support available to part-time students. Financial award application deadline: 3/1; financial award applicants required to submit FAFSA. *Faculty research:* Discovery and presentation of music literature of other countries, transportation of ancient music literature to modern notation. *Unit head:* Dr. Howard Potter, Department Head, 405-744-8997, Fax: 405-744-9324, E-mail: osumusic@okstate.edu. Website: http://music.okstate.edu/

Old Dominion University, College of Arts and Letters, Master of Music Education Program, Norfolk, VA 23529. Offers applied studies or conducting (MME); pedagogy (MME); research (MME). *Accreditation:* NASM. *Program availability:* Part-time, evening/weekend. *Faculty:* 13 full-time (2 women), 3 part-time/adjunct (2 women). *Students:* 9 full-time (5 women), 10 part-time (7 women); includes 7 minority (3 Black or African American, non-Hispanic/Latino; 1 Asian, non-Hispanic/Latino; 3 Hispanic/Latino). Average age 35. 8 applicants, 88% accepted, 7 enrolled. In 2017, 11 master's awarded. *Degree requirements:* For master's, comprehensive exam, thesis (for some programs), performance recital (for applied studies or conducting), ePortfolio (for pedagogy). *Entrance requirements:* For master's, music theory exam, diagnostic examination, GRE or MAT, baccalaureate degree in music education, music theory, music history, or applied music; audition (for applied music areas). Additional exam requirements/recommendations for international students: Required—TOEFL. *Application deadline:* Applications are processed on a rolling basis. Application fee: $50. Electronic applications accepted. *Expenses:* Contact institution. *Financial support:* In 2017–18, 6 students received support, including 6 teaching assistantships (averaging $10,000 per year); scholarships/grants and unspecified assistantships also available. Financial award application deadline: 3/30; financial award applicants required to submit FAFSA. *Faculty research:* Performance, composition, conducting, music education research. *Unit head:* Dr. Douglas T. Owens, Graduate Program Director, 757-683-6562, Fax: 757-683-5056, E-mail: dtowens@odu.edu. Website: http://www.odu.edu/musicdept/programs/graduate

Open University, Graduate Programs, Milton Keynes, United Kingdom. Offers business (MBA); education (M Ed); engineering (M Eng); history (MA); music (MA); philosophy (MA).

Park University, School of Graduate and Professional Studies, Kansas City, MO 54105. Offers adult education (M Ed); business and government leadership (Graduate Certificate); business, government, and global society (MPA); communication and leadership (MA); creative and life writing (Graduate Certificate); disaster and emergency management (MPA, Graduate Certificate); educational leadership (M Ed); finance (MBA, Graduate Certificate); general business (MBA); global business (Graduate Certificate); healthcare administration (MHA); healthcare services management and leadership (Graduate Certificate); international business (MBA); language and literacy (M Ed), including English for speakers of other languages, special reading teacher/literacy coach; leadership of international healthcare organizations (Graduate Certificate); management information systems (MBA, Graduate Certificate); music performance (ADP, Graduate Certificate), including cello (MM, ADP), piano (MM, ADP), viola (MM, ADP), violin (MM, ADP); nonprofit and community services management (MPA); nonprofit leadership (Graduate Certificate); performance (MM), including cello (MM, ADP), piano (MM, ADP), viola (MM, ADP), violin (MM, ADP); public management (MPA); social work (MSW); teacher leadership (M Ed), including curriculum and assessment, instructional leader. *Program availability:* Part-time, evening/weekend, online learning. *Degree requirements:* For master's, comprehensive exam (for some programs), thesis (for some programs), internship (for some programs); exam (for some programs). *Entrance requirements:* For master's, GRE or GMAT (for some programs), teacher certification (for some M Ed programs), letters of recommendation, essay, resume (for some programs). Additional exam requirements/recommendations for international students: Required—TOEFL (minimum score 550 paper-based; 79 iBT), IELTS (minimum score 6). Electronic applications accepted.

Penn State University Park, Graduate School, College of Arts and Architecture, School of Music, University Park, PA 16802. Offers composition-theory (M Mus); conducting (M Mus); music (MA); music education (MME, PhD, Certificate); pedagogy and performance (M Mus); performance (M Mus); piano performance (DMA). *Accreditation:* NASM. *Unit head:* Dr. Barbara O. Korner, Dean, 814-865-2592, Fax: 814-865-2018. *Application contact:* Lori Hawn, Director, Graduate Student Services, 814-865-1795, Fax: 814-863-4627, E-mail: l-gswww@lists.psu.edu. Website: http://music.psu.edu/

Pensacola Christian College, Graduate Studies, Pensacola, FL 32503-2267. Offers business administration (MBA); curriculum and instruction (MS, Ed D, Ed S); dramatics (MFA); educational leadership (MS, Ed D, Ed S); graphic design (MA, MFA); music (MA); nursing (MSN); performance studies (MA); studio art (MA, MFA).

Phillips Theological Seminary, Programs in Theology, Tulsa, OK 74116. Offers administration of church agencies (M Div); campus ministry (M Div); church-related social work (M Div); college and seminary teaching (M Div); global mission work (M Div); institutional chaplaincy (M Div); ministerial vocations in Christian education (M Div); ministry (D Min), including parish ministry, pastoral counseling, practices of ministry; ministry and culture (MAMC), including Christian education, congregational leadership,

history and practice of Christian spirituality, theology, ethics, and culture; ministry of music (M Div); pastoral care and counseling (M Div); pastoral ministry (M Div); theological studies (MTS). *Accreditation:* ATS. *Program availability:* Part-time, online learning. *Degree requirements:* For master's, thesis (for some programs); for doctorate, thesis/dissertation. *Entrance requirements:* For master's, minimum GPA of 2.5; for doctorate, M Div, minimum GPA of 3.0. *Faculty research:* Biblical studies, historical studies, theology and culture, practical theology, theology and film.

Pittsburg State University, Graduate School, College of Arts and Sciences, Department of Music, Pittsburg, KS 66762. Offers conducting (MM), including choral, instrumental - orchestral, instrumental - wind, organ, piano, voice; education (MM), including instrumental, vocal; performance (MM), including harpsichord, percussion, strings, winds. *Accreditation:* NASM. *Students:* 8 (3 women); includes 1 minority (Two or more races, non-Hispanic/Latino), 1 international. In 2017, 7 master's awarded. *Degree requirements:* For master's, thesis or alternative. *Entrance requirements:* Additional exam requirements/recommendations for international students: Required—TOEFL (minimum score 520 paper-based; 68 iBT), IELTS (minimum score 6), PTE (minimum score 47). *Application deadline:* For fall admission, 7/15 for domestic students, 6/1 for international students; for spring admission, 12/15 for domestic students, 10/15 for international students; for summer admission, 5/15 for domestic students, 4/1 for international students. Applications are processed on a rolling basis. Application fee: $35 ($60 for international students). Electronic applications accepted. *Expenses:* Contact institution. *Financial support:* In 2017–18, 5 teaching assistantships with full tuition reimbursements (averaging $5,500 per year) were awarded; career-related internships or fieldwork, Federal Work-Study, and unspecified assistantships also available. Financial award application deadline: 2/1; financial award applicants required to submit FAFSA. *Unit head:* Dr. Susan Marchant, Chairperson, 620-235-4466, E-mail: smarchant@pittstate.edu. *Application contact:* Lisa Allen, Assistant Director of Graduate and Continuing Studies, 620-235-4223, Fax: 620-235-4219, E-mail: lallen@pittstate.edu.

Point Park University, Conservatory of Performing Arts, Pittsburgh, PA 15222-1984. Offers screenwriting and playwriting (MFA). *Program availability:* Blended/hybrid learning. *Degree requirements:* For master's, comprehensive exam (for some programs), thesis or alternative. *Entrance requirements:* For master's, interview, undergraduate degree in related field, theatre experience. Additional exam requirements/recommendations for international students: Required—TOEFL (minimum score 550 paper-based; 79 iBT). Electronic applications accepted.

Portland State University, Graduate Studies, College of the Arts, School of Music and Theater, Portland, OR 97207-0751. Offers conducting (Mus M); jazz studies (Mus M); music (Mus M); performance (Mus M). *Accreditation:* NASM. *Program availability:* Part-time. *Faculty:* 27 full-time (9 women), 46 part-time/adjunct (16 women). *Students:* 29 full-time (14 women), 10 part-time (3 women); includes 9 minority (3 Asian, non-Hispanic/Latino; 2 Hispanic/Latino; 4 Two or more races, non-Hispanic/Latino), 6 international. Average age 29. 36 applicants, 86% accepted, 13 enrolled. In 2017, 14 master's awarded. *Degree requirements:* For master's, variable foreign language requirement, exit exam. *Entrance requirements:* For master's, GRE General Test, music diagnostic entrance examination, minimum GPA of 3.0 in graduate coursework or 2.75 overall undergraduate, audition. Additional exam requirements/recommendations for international students: Required—TOEFL (minimum score 550 paper-based). *Application deadline:* For fall admission, 4/15 priority date for domestic students, 4/15 for international students; for winter admission, 10/1 for domestic and international students; for spring admission, 12/1 for domestic and international students; for summer admission, 1/15 for domestic and international students. Application fee: $65. *Expenses:* Contact institution. *Financial support:* In 2017–18, 24 students received support, including 11 teaching assistantships with full and partial tuition reimbursements available (averaging $5,603 per year); Federal Work-Study, scholarships/grants, and unspecified assistantships also available. Support available to part-time students. Financial award application deadline: 3/1; financial award applicants required to submit FAFSA. *Faculty research:* Composition, music analysis, music history, jazz. *Unit head:* Bonnie Miksch, Director, 503-725-3063, Fax: 503-725-8215, E-mail: bonnie@pdx.edu. Website: https://www.pdx.edu/music/

Pratt Institute, School of Liberal Arts and Sciences, Program in Performance and Performance Studies, Brooklyn, NY 11205-3899. Offers MFA. *Students:* 21 full-time (17 women), 1 part-time (0 women); includes 9 minority (7 Black or African American, non-Hispanic/Latino; 2 Hispanic/Latino), 5 international. Average age 33. 38 applicants, 100% accepted, 11 enrolled. *Degree requirements:* For master's, thesis. *Entrance requirements:* Additional exam requirements/recommendations for international students: Required—TOEFL. *Application deadline:* For fall admission, 1/5 for domestic and international students; for spring admission, 10/1 for domestic and international students. Application fee: $50 ($90 for international students). Electronic applications accepted. *Expenses:* Tuition: Full-time $30,834. *Required fees:* $1974. *Financial support:* Career-related internships or fieldwork, Federal Work-Study, institutionally sponsored loans, scholarships/grants, health care benefits, and unspecified assistantships available. Support available to part-time students. Financial award application deadline: 2/1; financial award applicants required to submit FAFSA. *Unit head:* Andrew W. Barnes, Dean, 718-636-3570, Fax: 718-399-4586, E-mail: awbarnes@pratt.edu. *Application contact:* Natalie Capannelli, Director of Graduate Admissions, 718-636-3551, Fax: 718-399-4242, E-mail: ncapanne@pratt.edu. Website: https://www.pratt.edu/academics/liberal-arts-and-sciences/performance-and-performance-studies/

See Display on page 725 and Close-Up on page 749.

Princeton University, Graduate School, Department of Music, Princeton, NJ 08544-1019. Offers composition (PhD); musicology (PhD). *Degree requirements:* For doctorate, variable foreign language requirement, thesis/dissertation. *Entrance requirements:* For doctorate, GRE General Test, sample of written work. Additional exam requirements/recommendations for international students: Required—TOEFL (minimum score 600 paper-based). Electronic applications accepted. *Faculty research:* Computer synthesis, history of Western music, comparative musicology, theory.

Purchase College, State University of New York, Conservatory of Music, Purchase, NY 10577-1400. Offers classical composition (MM); instrumental performance (MM); jazz studies (MM); studio composition (MM); voice and opera studies (MM). *Degree requirements:* For master's, thesis or alternative, composition, performance. *Entrance requirements:* For master's, audition. *Application deadline:* For fall admission, 1/15 for domestic students; for spring admission, 10/15 for domestic students. Application fee: $85. Electronic applications accepted. *Financial support:* Fellowships, teaching assistantships, career-related internships or fieldwork, Federal Work-Study, scholarships/grants, and tuition waivers (partial) available. Support available to part-time students. Financial award application deadline: 3/15; financial award applicants required to submit FAFSA. *Unit head:* Jennifer Undercofler, Director, 914-251-6700, Fax: 914-251-6739, E-mail: jennifer.undercofler@purchase.edu. *Application contact:* Garrett Marino, Associate Director of Admissions, 914-251-6479, Fax: 914-251-6316, E-mail: admissn@purchase.edu. Website: https://www.purchase.edu/academics/music/

Queens College of the City University of New York, Arts and Humanities Division, Aaron Copland School of Music, Queens, NY 11367-1597. Offers classical performance (MM, Advanced Diploma); jazz studies (MM); music (MA); music education (MS Ed, Advanced Certificate). *Program availability:* Part-time. *Students:* 23 full-time (5 women), 162 part-time (72 women); includes 49 minority (8 Black or African American, non-Hispanic/Latino; 16 Asian, non-Hispanic/Latino; 17 Hispanic/Latino; 8 Two or more races, non-Hispanic/Latino), 46 international. Average age 30. *Degree requirements:* For master's, qualifying exams, recital. *Entrance requirements:* For master's, audition, bachelor's degree in music, minimum GPA of 3.0. Additional exam requirements/recommendations for international students: Required—TOEFL, IELTS. *Application deadline:* For fall admission, 4/1 for domestic students; for spring admission, 11/1 for domestic students. Applications are processed on a rolling basis. Application fee: $125. Electronic applications accepted. *Financial support:* Career-related internships or fieldwork, Federal Work-Study, institutionally sponsored loans, and tuition waivers (partial) available. Support available to part-time students. Financial award application deadline: 4/1; financial award applicants required to submit FAFSA. *Unit head:* Dr. David Schober, Chair, 718-997-3800, E-mail: david.schober@qc.cuny.edu. *Application contact:* Elizabeth D'Amico-Ramirez, Assistant Director of Graduate Admissions, 718-997-5203, E-mail: elizabeth.damicoramirez@qc.cuny.edu.
Website: http://qcpages.qc.cuny.edu/music/

Radford University, College of Graduate Studies and Research, Program in Music, Radford, VA 24142. Offers MA, MS. *Accreditation:* NASM. *Program availability:* Part-time. *Faculty:* 11 full-time (5 women), 2 part-time/adjunct (0 women). *Students:* 15 full-time (11 women), 4 part-time (3 women); includes 4 minority (1 Black or African American, non-Hispanic/Latino; 1 Asian, non-Hispanic/Latino; 2 Hispanic/Latino). Average age 32. 10 applicants, 80% accepted, 5 enrolled. In 2017, 5 master's awarded. *Degree requirements:* For master's, comprehensive exam, thesis or alternative. *Entrance requirements:* For master's, GRE or PRAXIS II (music content knowledge); written diagnostic exams in music, minimum GPA of 2.75, 2 letters of reference, resume, official transcripts. Additional exam requirements/recommendations for international students: Required—TOEFL (minimum score 550 paper-based; 79 iBT), IELTS (minimum score 6.5). *Application deadline:* For fall admission, 2/15 priority date for domestic students, 12/1 for international students; for spring admission, 7/1 for international students. Applications are processed on a rolling basis. Application fee: $50. Electronic applications accepted. *Expenses:* Tuition, state resident: full-time $8336; part-time $347 per credit hour. Tuition, nonresident: full-time $16,862; part-time $702 per credit hour. *Required fees:* $3220; $135 per credit hour. Tuition and fees vary according to course load and program. *Financial support:* In 2017–18, 8 students received support, including 5 teaching assistantships (averaging $10,000 per year); scholarships/grants and unspecified assistantships also available. Support available to part-time students. Financial award application deadline: 3/1; financial award applicants required to submit FAFSA. *Unit head:* Dr. Robert Trent, Coordinator, 540-831-5117, E-mail: rstrent@radford.edu.
Website: http://www.radford.edu/content/cvpa/home/music/degree-programs/graduate-programs.html

Rice University, Graduate Programs, Shepherd School of Music, Houston, TX 77251-1892. Offers composition (MM, DMA); conducting (MM); musicology (MM); performance (MM, DMA); theory (MM). *Degree requirements:* For master's, thesis (for some programs), 2 recitals; for doctorate, one foreign language, comprehensive exam, thesis/dissertation, 4 recitals. *Entrance requirements:* For master's, GRE General Test (musicology); for doctorate, GRE General Test. Additional exam requirements/recommendations for international students: Required—TOEFL (minimum score 600 paper-based; 100 iBT), IELTS (minimum score 7). *Faculty research:* Musicology, performance, theory, composition.

Rider University, Westminster Choir College, Programs in Music, Lawrenceville, NJ 08648-3001. Offers American and public musicology (MM); choral conducting (MM); composition (MM); organ performance (MM); piano accompanying and coaching (MM); piano pedagogy and performance (MM); piano performance (MM); sacred music (MM); voice pedagogy and performance (MM, MVP). *Program availability:* Part-time. *Degree requirements:* For master's, variable foreign language requirement, departmental qualifying exam. *Entrance requirements:* For master's, audition, interview, repertoire list, 2 letters of reference, resume. Additional exam requirements/recommendations for international students: Required—TOEFL (minimum score 525 paper-based). Electronic applications accepted.

Roosevelt University, Graduate Division, Chicago College of Performing Arts, Music Conservatory, Chicago, IL 60605. Offers brass (Diploma); brass performance (MM); classical guitar (MM, Diploma); music (MM); music composition (MM); opera (Diploma); orchestral studies (MM, Diploma); percussion (MM, Diploma); performing arts administration (MA); piano (Diploma); piano performance (MM); strings (MM, Diploma); voice (MM); woodwinds (MM, Diploma). *Students:* 116 full-time (70 women), 7 part-time (5 women); includes 10 minority (3 Black or African American, non-Hispanic/Latino; 1 Asian, non-Hispanic/Latino; 3 Hispanic/Latino; 3 Two or more races, non-Hispanic/Latino), 31 international. Average age 25. 139 applicants, 93% accepted, 45 enrolled. In 2017, 36 master's, 13 other advanced degrees awarded. *Application deadline:* Applications are processed on a rolling basis. Application fee: $100. Electronic applications accepted. *Expenses:* Contact institution. *Financial support:* Scholarships/grants available. *Application contact:* Michael Holmes, Interim Assistant Dean for Enrollment Management, 312-341-3797, E-mail: mholmes04@roosevelt.edu.
Website: https://www.roosevelt.edu/colleges/ccpa/music-conservatory

Rowan University, Graduate School, College of Performing Arts, Program in Performance, Glassboro, NJ 08028-1701. Offers MM. *Accreditation:* NASM. *Program availability:* Part-time, evening/weekend. *Degree requirements:* For master's, thesis (for some programs). *Entrance requirements:* For master's, GRE General Test. Additional exam requirements/recommendations for international students: Required—TOEFL. Electronic applications accepted. *Expenses:* Tuition, state resident: full-time $15,020; part-time $751 per semester hour. Tuition, nonresident: full-time $15,020; part-time $751 per semester hour. *Required fees:* $3158; $157.90 per semester hour. Tuition and fees vary according to course load, campus/location and program.

Rutgers University–Newark, Graduate School, Program in Jazz History and Research, Newark, NJ 07102. Offers MA. *Entrance requirements:* For master's, GRE, minimum B average. Electronic applications accepted.

Rutgers University–New Brunswick, Mason Gross School of the Arts, Music Department, New Brunswick, NJ 08901. Offers collaborative piano (MM, DMA); conducting: choral (MM, DMA); conducting: instrumental (MM, DMA); conducting: orchestral (MM, DMA); jazz studies (MM); music (DMA, AD); music education (MM, DMA); music performance (MM). *Accreditation:* NASM. *Degree requirements:* For doctorate, one foreign language. *Entrance requirements:* For master's and doctorate, audition. Additional exam requirements/recommendations for international students: Required—TOEFL (minimum score 550 paper-based), IELTS (minimum score 7). Electronic applications accepted. *Faculty research:* Performance, twentieth-century music, jazz, music education.

St. Cloud State University, School of Graduate Studies, College of Liberal Arts, Department of Music, St. Cloud, MN 56301-4498. Offers conducting and literature (MM); music education (MM); piano pedagogy (MM). *Degree requirements:* For master's, comprehensive exam (for some programs), thesis or alternative. *Entrance requirements:* For master's, GRE General Test, minimum GPA of 2.75. Additional exam requirements/recommendations for international students: Required—TOEFL (minimum score 550 paper-based; 79 iBT), IELTS (minimum score 6.5), Michigan English Language Assessment Battery. Electronic applications accepted.

Saint John's University, Saint John's School of Theology and Seminary, Collegeville, MN 56321. Offers divinity (M Div); liturgical music (MA); liturgical studies (MA); pastoral ministry (MA); theology (MA), including church history, liturgy, monastic studies, scripture, spirituality, systematics; M Div/MA. *Program availability:* Part-time, online learning. *Degree requirements:* For master's, one foreign language, comprehensive exam (for some programs), thesis (for some programs). *Entrance requirements:* For master's, GRE General Test or MAT. Electronic applications accepted. *Faculty research:* Religious education, biblical literature.

Salem College, Graduate Studies, Winston-Salem, NC 27101. Offers art education (MAT); elementary education (M Ed, MAT); language and literacy (M Ed); middle school education (MAT); organ (MM); piano (MM); school counseling (M Ed); second language studies (MAT); secondary education (MAT); special education (M Ed, MAT). *Accreditation:* NCATE. *Program availability:* Part-time, evening/weekend, online learning. *Faculty:* 8 full-time (all women), 11 part-time/adjunct (8 women). In 2017, 17 master's awarded. *Degree requirements:* For master's, practicum (MAT), action research project (M Ed). *Entrance requirements:* For master's, minimum GPA of 3.0, two academic/professional recommendations, acceptable criminal background check. Additional exam requirements/recommendations for international students: Recommended—TOEFL. *Application deadline:* For fall admission, 8/1 for domestic students, 7/15 for international students; for spring admission, 1/15 for domestic students; for summer admission, 5/1 for domestic students. Applications are processed on a rolling basis. Application fee: $30. Electronic applications accepted. *Expenses: Tuition:* Part-time $440 per semester hour. *Financial support:* Scholarships/grants available. Support available to part-time students. Financial award applicants required to submit FAFSA. *Faculty research:* Teacher professional development, adolescent literacy, instructional technology. *Application contact:* Sheryl Long, Director, 336-721-2658, Fax: 336-917-5384, E-mail: sheryl.long@salem.edu.
Website: http://www.salem.edu

Samford University, School of the Arts, Birmingham, AL 35229. Offers church music (MM), including conducting, performance, thesis; instrumental performance (MM); piano performance and pedagogy (MM); vocal performance (MM); vocal/choral or instrumental music (MME). MME program offered in traditional, fifth-year non-traditional, and national board cohort formats. *Accreditation:* NASM. *Program availability:* Part-time. *Faculty:* 13 full-time (4 women), 2 part-time/adjunct (1 woman). *Students:* 13 full-time (5 women), 2 part-time (both women); includes 5 minority (all Black or African American, non-Hispanic/Latino), 1 international. Average age 29. 7 applicants, 86% accepted, 4 enrolled. In 2017, 1 master's awarded. *Degree requirements:* For master's, comprehensive exam, recital. *Entrance requirements:* For master's, 3 letters of recommendation, audition. Additional exam requirements/recommendations for international students: Required—TOEFL (minimum score 550 paper-based; 79 iBT). *Application deadline:* For fall admission, 2/28 priority date for domestic and international students; for winter admission, 10/1 priority date for domestic and international students; for spring admission, 2/28 priority date for domestic and international students; for summer admission, 5/1 priority date for domestic and international students. Applications are processed on a rolling basis. Application fee: $35. Electronic applications accepted. *Expenses: Tuition:* Full-time $19,058; part-time $813 per credit hour. *Required fees:* $550. Tuition and fees vary according to course load, degree level, program and student level. *Financial support:* In 2017–18, 13 students received support. Scholarships/grants available. Financial award application deadline: 2/15; financial award applicants required to submit FAFSA. *Unit head:* Dr. Joseph Hopkin, Dean of the School of the Arts/Professor, 205-726-2778, E-mail: jhopkins@samford.edu. *Application contact:* Dr. Mark Lackey, Assistant Professor, 205-726-4623, Fax: 205-726-2615, E-mail: mlckey@samford.edu.
Website: http://www.samford.edu/arts

Sam Houston State University, College of Fine Arts and Mass Communication, School of Music, Huntsville, TX 77341. Offers MM. *Accreditation:* NASM. *Program availability:* Part-time. *Degree requirements:* For master's, comprehensive exam, thesis, departmental qualifying exam. *Entrance requirements:* For master's, GRE General Test, letters of recommendation, audition/interview. Additional exam requirements/recommendations for international students: Required—TOEFL (minimum score 550 paper-based; 79 iBT), IELTS (minimum score 6.5). Electronic applications accepted.

San Diego State University, Graduate and Research Affairs, College of Professional Studies and Fine Arts, School of Music and Dance, San Diego, CA 92182. Offers composition (acoustic and electronic) (MM); conducting (MM); ethnomusicology (MA); jazz studies (MM); musicology (MA); performance (MM); piano pedagogy (MA); theory (MA). *Degree requirements:* For master's, comprehensive exam (for some programs), thesis (for some programs). *Entrance requirements:* For master's, GRE General Test, bachelor's degree in related field, 2 letters of reference. Additional exam requirements/recommendations for international students: Required—TOEFL. Electronic applications accepted.

San Francisco Conservatory of Music, Graduate Division, San Francisco, CA 94102. Offers brass (MM), including bass trombone, horn, tenor trombone, trumpet, tuba; chamber music (MM, Artist Certificate), including cello (MM, Artist Certificate, Artist Diploma), piano (MM, Artist Certificate, Artist Diploma), preformed string quartet, viola (MM, Artist Certificate, Artist Diploma), violin (MM, Artist Certificate, Artist Diploma); composition (MM); conducting (MM); guitar (MM); harp (MM); historical performance (MM), including harpsichord (MM, MM); percussion (MM), including percussion; piano (MM, MM, Artist Diploma), including collaborative piano (MM), harpsichord (MM, MM), organ (MM), piano (MM, Artist Certificate, Artist Diploma); strings (MM, Artist Diploma), including cello (MM, Artist Certificate, Artist Diploma), double bass (MM), viola (MM, Artist Certificate, Artist Diploma), violin (MM, Artist Certificate, Artist Diploma); voice (MM, Postgraduate Diploma); woodwinds (MM), including bassoon, clarinet, flute, oboe. *Faculty:* 27 full-time (7 women), 107 part-time/adjunct (36 women). *Students:* 208 full-time (120 women), 1 (woman) part-time; includes 37 minority (7 Black or African American, non-Hispanic/Latino; 13 Asian, non-Hispanic/Latino; 7 Hispanic/Latino; 10 Two or more races, non-Hispanic/Latino), 82 international. Average age 25. 709 applicants, 36% accepted, 117 enrolled. In 2017, 74 master's, 41 Artist Diplomas awarded. *Degree requirements:* For master's and other advanced degree, variable foreign language requirement, 1-2 recitals, 1-3 juried performances. *Entrance requirements:* For master's and other advanced degree, recommendations, transcripts, audition. Additional exam requirements/recommendations for international students: Required—TOEFL (minimum score 500 paper-based; 80 iBT). *Application deadline:* For fall admission, 12/1 for domestic and international students; for spring admission, 10/1 for domestic and international students. Application fee: $110. Electronic applications accepted. *Expenses:* $43,700 full-time, $1,924 per credit part-time, $1,110 fees.

Financial support: In 2017–18, 214 students received support. Federal Work-Study, scholarships/grants, tuition waivers (partial), and unspecified assistantships available. Financial award application deadline: 2/15; financial award applicants required to submit FAFSA. *Unit head:* Kate Sheeran, Provost and Dean, 415-503-6251, Fax: 415-503-6205, E-mail: snedel@sfcm.edu. *Application contact:* Melissa Cocco-Mitten, Director of Admission, 415-503-6231, Fax: 415-503-6299, E-mail: admit@sfcm.edu.

San Francisco State University, Division of Graduate Studies, College of Liberal and Creative Arts, School of Music, San Francisco, CA 94132-1722. Offers chamber music (MM); classical performance (MM); composition (MA); conducting (MM); music education (MA); music history (MA). *Accreditation:* NASM. *Unit head:* Dr. Cyrus Ginwala, Director, 415-338-7613, E-mail: cginwala@sfsu.edu. *Application contact:* E-mail: music@sfsu.edu.
Website: http://music.sfsu.edu/

San Jose State University, Graduate Studies and Research, College of Humanities and the Arts, San Jose, CA 95192-0088. Offers art (MA, MFA), including digital media art (MFA), history and visual culture (MA), photography (MFA), pictorial art (MFA), spatial art (MFA); English (MA, MFA), including creative writing (MFA); linguistics (MA); music (MM); music education (MA); philosophy (MA); Spanish (MA); teaching English to speakers of other languages (MA). *Program availability:* Part-time. *Faculty:* 35 full-time (17 women), 19 part-time/adjunct (11 women). *Students:* 129 full-time (79 women), 106 part-time (71 women); includes 117 minority (5 Black or African American, non-Hispanic/Latino; 29 Asian, non-Hispanic/Latino; 44 Hispanic/Latino; 39 Two or more races, non-Hispanic/Latino, 28 international. Average age 35. 204 applicants, 65% accepted, 79 enrolled. In 2017, 85 master's awarded. *Degree requirements:* For master's, one foreign language, comprehensive exam (for some programs), thesis (for some programs), graduate writing assessment, special study/project, recital. *Entrance requirements:* Additional exam requirements/recommendations for international students: Required—TOEFL (minimum score 550 paper-based; 80 iBT), IELTS (minimum score 6.5), PTE (minimum score 53). *Application deadline:* For fall admission, 2/1 for domestic and international students. Applications are processed on a rolling basis. Application fee: $55. Electronic applications accepted. *Expenses:* Tuition, state resident: full-time $7176. Tuition, nonresident: full-time $16,680. Tuition and fees vary according to course load and program. *Financial support:* Fellowships, research assistantships, Federal Work-Study, scholarships/grants, traineeships, tuition waivers (full and partial), and unspecified assistantships available. Support available to part-time students. Financial award application deadline: 4/28; financial award applicants required to submit FAFSA. *Unit head:* Dr. Shannon Miller, Dean, 408-924-4300, Fax: 408-924-4365, E-mail: shannon.miller@sjsu.edu.
Website: http://www.sjsu.edu/humanitiesandarts/

Savannah College of Art and Design, Program in Performing Arts, Savannah, GA 31402-3146. Offers MFA. *Program availability:* Part-time. *Faculty:* 10 full-time (4 women), 7 part-time/adjunct (5 women). *Students:* 45 full-time (30 women), 5 part-time (3 women); includes 25 minority (18 Black or African American, non-Hispanic/Latino; 1 American Indian or Alaska Native, non-Hispanic/Latino; 1 Asian, non-Hispanic/Latino; 5 Hispanic/Latino), 1 international. Average age 27. 97 applicants, 47% accepted, 21 enrolled. In 2017, 14 master's awarded. *Degree requirements:* For master's, thesis. *Entrance requirements:* For master's, GRE (recommended), portfolio (submitted in digital format), audition or writing submission, resume, statement of purpose, two letters of recommendation. Additional exam requirements/recommendations for international students: Recommended—TOEFL (minimum score 550 paper-based; 85 iBT), IELTS (minimum score 6.5). *Application deadline:* For fall admission, 4/1 for domestic and international students. Applications are processed on a rolling basis. Application fee: $40. Electronic applications accepted. *Expenses: Tuition:* Full-time $36,765; part-time $817 per credit hour. One-time fee: $500. *Financial support:* Career-related internships or fieldwork, Federal Work-Study, and scholarships/grants available. Financial award application deadline: 4/1; financial award applicants required to submit FAFSA. *Unit head:* Mark Tymchyshyn, Chair, Performing Arts. *Application contact:* Jenny Jaquillard, Executive Director of Admissions, Recruitment and Events, 912-525-5100, Fax: 912-525-5985, E-mail: admission@scad.edu.
Website: http://www.scad.edu/academics/programs/performing-arts

School of the Art Institute of Chicago, Graduate Division, Department of Performance, Chicago, IL 60603-3103. Offers MFA. *Entrance requirements:* Additional exam requirements/recommendations for international students: Required—TOEFL, IELTS.

Shenandoah University, Shenandoah Conservatory, Winchester, VA 22601-5195. Offers church music (MM, Certificate); collaborative piano (MM); composition (MM); conducting (MM); music (Artist Diploma); music education (MME); music therapy (MMT, Certificate); pedagogy - voice (MM, DMA); performance (MM, DMA); performing arts leadership and management (MS). *Accreditation:* NASM. *Program availability:* Part-time. *Faculty:* 32 full-time (11 women), 12 part-time/adjunct (6 women). *Students:* 70 full-time (38 women), 69 part-time (44 women); includes 20 minority (6 Black or African American, non-Hispanic/Latino; 1 American Indian or Alaska Native, non-Hispanic/Latino; 2 Asian, non-Hispanic/Latino; 11 Hispanic/Latino), 18 international. Average age 30. 135 applicants, 77% accepted, 49 enrolled. In 2017, 32 master's, 13 doctorates, 11 other advanced degrees awarded. *Degree requirements:* For master's, comprehensive exam, minimum GPA of 3.0, internship (MS), recital (MM), research teaching project or thesis (MME), project (MA); for doctorate, comprehensive exam, minimum GPA of 3.0, dissertation or teaching project, recital; for other advanced degree, minimum GPA of 3.0, research project, recital. *Entrance requirements:* For master's, music theory diagnostic exam, bachelor's degree with minimum of GPA of 2.5, performance audition, writing sample, resume, all academic transcripts; for doctorate, music theory diagnostic exam; music history diagnostic exam; vocal diction proficiency exam, master's degree with minimum GPA of 3.25, performance audition, 2 letters of recommendation, writing sample, resume, all academic transcripts; for other advanced degree, bachelor's or master's degree; minimum GPA of 2.5; performance audition (for Artist Diploma). Additional exam requirements/recommendations for international students: Required—TOEFL (minimum score 550 paper-based, 79 iBT) or IELTS (6.5). *Application deadline:* For fall and spring admission, 1/15 for domestic and international students; for summer admission, 4/15 for domestic and international students. Application fee: $30. Electronic applications accepted. *Expenses:* $15,600 tuition, $2,400 fees (applied major lesson fee, conservatory fee, technology fee, and student services fee). *Financial support:* In 2017–18, 42 students received support. Scholarships/grants and unspecified assistantships available. Financial award applicants required to submit FAFSA. *Faculty research:* Brahms, Scriabin, arts as inquiry. *Unit head:* Dr. Michael J. Stepniak, Dean, 540-542-6201, Fax: 540-665-5402, E-mail: mstepnia@su.edu. *Application contact:* Andrew Woodall, Executive Director of Recruitment and Advancement, 540-665-4581, Fax: 540-665-4627, E-mail: admit@su.edu.
Website: http://www.su.edu/conservatory/

Silver Lake College of the Holy Family, Graduate School, Graduate Music Program, Manitowoc, WI 54220-9319. Offers music education-Kodaly emphasis (MM). *Accreditation:* NASM. *Program availability:* Part-time, online learning. *Degree requirements:* For master's, comprehensive exam, thesis, capstone culminating project, comprehensive portfolio, public presentation of skills, or thesis research. *Entrance*

requirements: For master's, ACT (preferred) or SAT, minimum undergraduate GPA of 3.0. Additional exam requirements/recommendations for international students: Required—TOEFL (minimum score 550 paper-based; 89 iBT). Electronic applications accepted. *Expenses:* Contact institution. *Faculty research:* Effects of prenatal music on bonding and stimulation, music and the brain, early childhood music, effective use of smart music for choral and general music areas.

Southeastern Baptist Theological Seminary, Graduate and Professional Programs, Wake Forest, NC 27587. Offers advanced biblical studies (M Div); Christian education (M Div, MACE); Christian ethics (PhD); Christian ministry (M Div); Christian planting (M Div); church music (MACM); counseling (MACO); evangelism (PhD); language (M Div); ministry (D Min); New Testament (PhD); Old Testament (PhD); philosophy (PhD); theology (Th M, PhD); women's studies (M Div). *Accreditation:* ACIPE; ATS (one or more programs are accredited). *Degree requirements:* For master's, thesis (for some programs), oral exam; for doctorate, thesis/dissertation, fieldwork. *Entrance requirements:* For master's, Cooperative English Test, minimum GPA of 2.0, M Div or equivalent (Th M); for doctorate, GRE General Test or MAT, Cooperative English Test, M Div or equivalent, 3 years of professional experience.

Southeastern Louisiana University, College of Arts, Humanities and Social Sciences, Department of Music and Performing Arts, Hammond, LA 70402. Offers choral conducting (M Mus); instrumental conducting (M Mus); music performance (M Mus); music theory (M Mus). *Accreditation:* NASM. *Faculty:* 11 full-time (2 women), 7 part-time/adjunct (3 women). *Students:* 15 full-time (6 women), 3 part-time (2 women); includes 1 minority (Asian, non-Hispanic/Latino), 8 international. Average age 27. 17 applicants, 71% accepted, 10 enrolled. In 2017, 9 master's awarded. *Degree requirements:* For master's, comprehensive exam, thesis (for some programs). *Entrance requirements:* For master's, BM; senior recital (for performance program). Additional exam requirements/recommendations for international students: Required—TOEFL (minimum score 500 paper-based; 61 iBT), IELTS (minimum score 5.5). *Application deadline:* For fall admission, 7/15 priority date for domestic students, 6/1 priority date for international students; for spring admission, 12/1 priority date for domestic students, 10/1 priority date for international students. Applications are processed on a rolling basis. Application fee: $20 ($30 for international students). Electronic applications accepted. *Expenses:* Tuition, state resident: full-time $6684. Tuition, nonresident: full-time $19,162. *Required fees:* $2088. *Financial support:* In 2017–18, 7 students received support, including 2 fellowships (averaging $10,800 per year), 9 teaching assistantships (averaging $9,489 per year); research assistantships, career-related internships or fieldwork, Federal Work-Study, institutionally sponsored loans, scholarships/grants, traineeships, and unspecified assistantships also available. Support available to part-time students. Financial award application deadline: 5/1; financial award applicants required to submit FAFSA. *Faculty research:* Wind band performance and repertoire for young audiences, pedagogical piano music of contemporary American composers, spectral music composition, intonation and extended woodwind techniques. *Unit head:* Dale Newkirk, Interim Department Head, 985-549-2184, Fax: 985-549-2892, E-mail: dale.newkirk@southeastern.edu. *Application contact:* Amanda Harper, Graduate Admissions Analyst, 985-549-5620, Fax: 985-549-5632, E-mail: admissions@southeastern.edu.
Website: https://www.southeastern.edu/acad_research/depts/mus/index.html

Southern Illinois University Carbondale, Graduate School, College of Liberal Arts, School of Music, Carbondale, IL 62901-4701. Offers MM. *Accreditation:* NASM. *Program availability:* Part-time. *Degree requirements:* For master's, one foreign language, thesis or alternative. *Entrance requirements:* For master's, audition, minimum GPA of 2.7. Additional exam requirements/recommendations for international students: Required—TOEFL. *Faculty research:* Performance practices, historical research, operatic development.

Southern Illinois University Edwardsville, Graduate School, College of Arts and Sciences, Department of Music, Program in Music, Edwardsville, IL 62026. Offers music education (MM); music performance (MM). *Accreditation:* NASM. *Program availability:* Part-time. *Degree requirements:* For master's, one foreign language, thesis (for some programs), recital. *Entrance requirements:* Additional exam requirements/recommendations for international students: Required—TOEFL (minimum score 550 paper-based; 79 iBT), IELTS (minimum score 6.5). Electronic applications accepted.

Southern Methodist University, Meadows School of the Arts, Division of Music, Dallas, TX 75275. Offers composition (MM); conducting (MM), including choral, instrumental; music education (MM); music history and literature (MM); performance (MM), including harpsichord, orchestral instrument, organ, piano, voice; piano performance and pedagogy (MM); theory pedagogy (MM). *Accreditation:* NASM. *Program availability:* Part-time. *Degree requirements:* For master's, variable foreign language requirement, comprehensive exam, project, recital, or thesis. *Entrance requirements:* For master's, placement exams in music history and theory, audition; bachelor's degree in music or equivalent; minimum GPA of 3.0; research paper in history, theory, education. Additional exam requirements/recommendations for international students: Required—TOEFL (minimum score 550 paper-based; 80 iBT). Electronic applications accepted. *Faculty research:* Music perception and cognition, computer-based instruction, music medicine and therapy, theoretical and historical analysis-medieval to contemporary.

Southern Oregon University, Graduate Studies, Department of Music, Ashland, OR 97520. Offers performance (MM). *Accreditation:* NASM. *Program availability:* Part-time. *Entrance requirements:* For master's, undergraduate degree with music major, audition, three letters of recommendation.

Southern Utah University, Program in Music, Cedar City, UT 84720-2498. Offers music technology (MMus). *Accreditation:* NASM. *Program availability:* Part-time, online learning. *Faculty:* 4 full-time (1 woman), 6 part-time/adjunct (0 women). *Students:* 16 full-time (5 women), 1 part-time (0 women); includes 3 minority (2 Black or African American, non-Hispanic/Latino; 1 Asian, non-Hispanic/Latino). Average age 32. 16 applicants, 94% accepted, 14 enrolled. *Entrance requirements:* Additional exam requirements/recommendations for international students: Required—TOEFL (minimum score 550 paper-based; 79 iBT), IELTS (minimum score 6). Application fee: $60 ($65 for international students). *Expenses:* Contact institution. *Unit head:* Dr. Keith Bradshaw, Department Chair, 435-586-7891, E-mail: bradshaw@suu.edu.
Website: https://www.suu.edu/pva/music/graduateprograms.html

Southwestern Baptist Theological Seminary, School of Church Music, Fort Worth, TX 76122-0000. Offers MACM, MAWSHP, MM, DMA, PhD. *Accreditation:* NASM. *Program availability:* Part-time. Terminal master's awarded for partial completion of doctoral program. *Degree requirements:* For master's, comprehensive exam, thesis; for doctorate, comprehensive exam, thesis/dissertation. *Entrance requirements:* For master's, audition; for doctorate, MM or equivalent. Additional exam requirements/recommendations for international students: Required—TOEFL. Electronic applications accepted.

Southwestern Oklahoma State University, College of Arts and Sciences, Department of Music, Weatherford, OK 73096-3098. Offers music education (MM); performance (MM). *Accreditation:* NASM. *Program availability:* Part-time. *Degree requirements:* For master's, comprehensive exam, recital (music performance). *Entrance requirements:* For master's, minimum GPA of 2.5. Additional exam requirements/recommendations for international students: Required—TOEFL.

Stanford University, School of Humanities and Sciences, Department of Music, Stanford, CA 94305-2004. Offers composition (DMA); computer-based music theory and acoustics (PhD); music, science, and technology (MA); musicology (PhD). Terminal master's awarded for partial completion of doctoral program. *Degree requirements:* For master's, variable foreign language requirement, thesis or alternative, project; for doctorate, variable foreign language requirement, thesis/dissertation (for some programs), qualifying, special area, and oral exams (PhD); composition project and lecture-demonstration exams (DMA). *Entrance requirements:* For master's and doctorate, GRE General Test, departmental theory/analysis test, samples of work. Additional exam requirements/recommendations for international students: Required—TOEFL. Electronic applications accepted. *Expenses: Tuition:* Full-time $48,987; part-time $10,620 per quarter. One-time fee: $400. Tuition and fees vary according to program.

State University of New York at Fredonia, School of Music, Fredonia, NY 14063-1136. Offers music education (MM); music performance (MM); music theory/composition (MM); music therapy (MM). *Accreditation:* NASM. *Program availability:* Part-time. *Faculty:* 36 full-time (16 women), 14 part-time/adjunct (10 women). *Students:* 34 full-time (17 women), 21 part-time (16 women); includes 6 minority (2 Black or African American, non-Hispanic/Latino; 2 Asian, non-Hispanic/Latino; 2 Hispanic/Latino), 12 international. Average age 25. 46 applicants, 72% accepted, 14 enrolled. In 2017, 25 master's awarded. *Degree requirements:* For master's, comprehensive exam (for some programs), thesis or final project/recital. *Entrance requirements:* For master's, audition. Additional exam requirements/recommendations for international students: Required—TOEFL (minimum score 79 iBT), IELTS (minimum score 6.5). *Application deadline:* For fall admission, 4/1 priority date for domestic and international students; for spring admission, 11/1 priority date for domestic students, 11/1 for international students. Applications are processed on a rolling basis. Application fee: $75. Electronic applications accepted. *Expenses:* Tuition, state resident: full-time $8154. Tuition, nonresident: full-time $16,650. *Required fees:* $1209. *Financial support:* In 2017–18, 14 students received support, including 4 fellowships (averaging $7,314 per year). Financial award application deadline: 3/15; financial award applicants required to submit FAFSA. *Faculty research:* Schenkerian analysis, early American Music, music pedagogy, music therapy, professional performance. *Unit head:* Dr. Melvin Unger, Director, School of Music, 716-673-3151, E-mail: melvin.unger@fredonia.edu. *Application contact:* Dr. Barry Kilpatrick, Admissions Coordinator, School of Music, 716-673-4635, E-mail: barry.kilpatrick@fredonia.edu.
Website: http://www.fredonia.edu/music/

State University of New York at New Paltz, Graduate and Extended Learning School, School of Fine and Performing Arts, Department of Music, New Paltz, NY 12561. Offers music therapy (MS). *Accreditation:* NASM. *Program availability:* Part-time. *Faculty:* 3 full-time (1 woman), 1 part-time/adjunct (0 women). *Students:* 23 full-time (16 women), 10 part-time (7 women); includes 5 minority (1 Black or African American, non-Hispanic/Latino; 1 Asian, non-Hispanic/Latino; 3 Hispanic/Latino), 6 international. 23 applicants, 70% accepted, 9 enrolled. In 2017, 2 master's awarded. *Degree requirements:* For master's, thesis. *Entrance requirements:* For master's, audition, minimum GPA of 3.0. Additional exam requirements/recommendations for international students: Required—TOEFL (minimum score 550 paper-based; 80 iBT), IELTS (minimum score 6.5). *Application deadline:* For fall admission, 5/15 for domestic and international students; for spring admission, 11/15 for domestic and international students. Applications are processed on a rolling basis. Application fee: $50. Electronic applications accepted. *Financial support:* In 2017–18, 4 teaching assistantships with partial tuition reimbursements (averaging $5,000 per year) were awarded. Financial award application deadline: 8/1. *Unit head:* Dr. John Mahoney, Program Director, 845-257-2709, E-mail: mahoneyj@newpaltz.edu.
Website: http://www.newpaltz.edu/music/

State University of New York College at Potsdam, Crane School of Music, Potsdam, NY 13676. Offers music education (MM); music performance (MM). *Program availability:* Part-time. *Degree requirements:* For master's, variable foreign language requirement, thesis (for some programs). *Entrance requirements:* For master's, audition, minimum GPA of 3.0. Additional exam requirements/recommendations for international students: Required—TOEFL (minimum score 550 paper-based; 80 iBT), IELTS (minimum score 6). Electronic applications accepted.

Stephen F. Austin State University, Graduate School, College of Fine Arts, School of Music, Nacogdoches, TX 75962. Offers MA, MM. *Accreditation:* NASM (one or more programs are accredited). *Program availability:* Part-time. *Degree requirements:* For master's, comprehensive exam, thesis optional. *Entrance requirements:* For master's, GRE General Test, audition. Additional exam requirements/recommendations for international students: Required—TOEFL. *Faculty research:* Music classroom methodology, serial music, seventeenth century sacred music, vocal pedagogy, organ duet literature.

Stony Brook University, State University of New York, Graduate School, College of Arts and Sciences, Department of Music, Program in Music History/Theory, Stony Brook, NY 11794. Offers MA, PhD. *Students:* 34 full-time (8 women), 2 part-time (0 women); includes 2 minority (both Hispanic/Latino), 3 international. Average age 30. 51 applicants, 41% accepted, 8 enrolled. In 2017, 1 master's, 3 doctorates awarded. *Degree requirements:* For doctorate, thesis/dissertation. *Entrance requirements:* For master's and doctorate, GRE General Test. Additional exam requirements/recommendations for international students: Required—TOEFL (minimum score 90 iBT). *Application deadline:* For fall admission, 1/15 for domestic students; for spring admission, 10/1 for domestic students. Application fee: $100. Electronic applications accepted. *Expenses:* Contact institution. *Financial support:* Teaching assistantships available. *Unit head:* Dr. Perry Goldstein, Chair, 631-632-7340, E-mail: perry.goldstein@stonybrook.edu. *Application contact:* Monica Gentile, Coordinator, 631-632-7340, Fax: 631-632-7404, E-mail: monica.gentile@stonybrook.edu.

Stony Brook University, State University of New York, Graduate School, College of Arts and Sciences, Department of Music, Program in Music Performance, Stony Brook, NY 11794. Offers MM, DMA. *Students:* 174 full-time (96 women), 6 part-time (4 women); includes 30 minority (2 Black or African American, non-Hispanic/Latino; 17 Asian, non-Hispanic/Latino; 7 Hispanic/Latino; 4 Two or more races, non-Hispanic/Latino), 65 international. 287 applicants, 29% accepted, 41 enrolled. In 2017, 10 master's, 32 doctorates awarded. *Degree requirements:* For doctorate, thesis/dissertation. *Entrance requirements:* For master's and doctorate, GRE General Test. Additional exam requirements/recommendations for international students: Required—TOEFL (minimum score 90 iBT). *Application deadline:* For fall admission, 1/15 for domestic students; for spring admission, 10/1 for domestic students. Application fee: $100. Electronic applications accepted. *Expenses:* Contact institution. *Financial support:* Teaching assistantships available. *Unit head:* Dr. Perry Goldstein, Chair, 631-632-7340, E-mail: perry.goldstein@stonybrook.edu. *Application contact:* Monica Gentile, Coordinator, 631-632-7330, Fax: 631-632-7404, E-mail: monica.gentile@stonybrook.edu.
Website: http://www.stonybrook.edu/commcms/music/degree_programs/graduate/performance.html

Syracuse University, College of Visual and Performing Arts, MM in Music and Performance Program, Syracuse, NY 13244. Offers music and performance (MM), including organ, percussion, piano, strings, voice, wind instruments. *Degree requirements:* For master's, thesis or alternative. *Entrance requirements:* For master's, audition, three letters of recommendation, academic transcript, personal statement/essay, resume. Additional exam requirements/recommendations for international students: Required—TOEFL (minimum score 100 iBT). *Application deadline:* For fall admission, 2/1 priority date for domestic and international students. Application fee: $75. Electronic applications accepted. *Financial support:* Fellowships with full tuition reimbursements and teaching assistantships with tuition reimbursements available. Financial award application deadline: 1/1; financial award applicants required to submit FAFSA. *Faculty research:* Organ, percussion, piano, strings, voice, wind instruments. *Unit head:* Prof. Steven Heyman Jones, Chair, Department of Applied Music and Performance, 315-443-1638, E-mail: sheyman@syr.edu. *Application contact:* Caitlin Jarvis, Graduate Recruitment Specialist, 315-443-2769, E-mail: admissg@syr.edu.
Website: http://vpa.syr.edu/academics/setnor/graduate/performance/

Syracuse University, College of Visual and Performing Arts, MM Program in Composition, Syracuse, NY 13244. Offers MM. *Degree requirements:* For master's, thesis or alternative. *Entrance requirements:* For master's, audition, three letters of recommendation, academic transcript, personal statement/essay, resume. Additional exam requirements/recommendations for international students: Required—TOEFL (minimum score 100 iBT). *Application deadline:* For fall admission, 2/1 priority date for domestic and international students. Application fee: $75. Electronic applications accepted. *Financial support:* Fellowships with full tuition reimbursements and teaching assistantships with tuition reimbursements available. Financial award application deadline: 1/1; financial award applicants required to submit FAFSA. *Faculty research:* Music, tonal analysis, orchestral repertoire, music literature. *Unit head:* Joseph Downing, Associate Professor/Chair, Department of Music Composition, Theory, and History, 315-443-2191, E-mail: jdowning@syr.edu. *Application contact:* Caitlin Jarvis, Graduate Recruitment Specialist, 315-443-2769, E-mail: admissg@syr.edu.
Website: http://vpa.syr.edu/academics/setnor/graduate/composition/

Syracuse University, College of Visual and Performing Arts, MM Program in Conducting, Syracuse, NY 13244. Offers MM. *Accreditation:* NASM. *Degree requirements:* For master's, thesis or alternative. *Entrance requirements:* For master's, audition, interview, three letters of recommendation, transcripts, personal statement, resume. Additional exam requirements/recommendations for international students: Required—TOEFL (minimum score 100 iBT). *Application deadline:* For fall admission, 2/1 priority date for domestic and international students. Application fee: $75. Electronic applications accepted. *Financial support:* Fellowships with full tuition reimbursements, teaching assistantships with tuition reimbursements, Federal Work-Study, and tuition waivers available. Financial award application deadline: 1/1; financial award applicants required to submit FAFSA. *Faculty research:* Choral, orchestral, winds, baton technique and body language, score reading, score study. *Unit head:* Dr. Steven Heyman, Chair, Department of Applied Music and Performance, 315-443-1638, E-mail: sheyman@syr.edu. *Application contact:* Caitlin Jarvis, Graduate Recruitment Specialist, 315-443-2769, E-mail: admissg@syr.edu.
Website: http://vpa.syr.edu/academics/setnor/graduate/conducting/

Temple University, Center for the Performing and Cinematic Arts, Boyer College of Music and Dance, Department of Music, Philadelphia, PA 19122-6096. Offers choral conducting (MM); collaborative piano/chamber music (MM); collaborative piano/opera coaching (MM); composition (MM, PhD); instrumental conducting (MM); music education (MM, PhD); music history (MM); music performance (MM, DMA), including instrumental studies (MM), keyboard (DMA), keyboard studies (MM), voice (DMA), voice and opera (MM); music studies (PhD); music theory (MM, PhD); music therapy (MMT, PhD); musicology (MM, PhD); opera (MM); piano pedagogy (MM); string pedagogy (MM). *Accreditation:* NASM. *Program availability:* Part-time, online learning. *Faculty:* 42 full-time (17 women), 35 part-time/adjunct (13 women). *Students:* 193 full-time (108 women), 51 part-time (33 women); includes 38 minority (13 Black or African American, non-Hispanic/Latino; 8 Asian, non-Hispanic/Latino; 9 Hispanic/Latino; 8 Two or more races, non-Hispanic/Latino), 85 international. 394 applicants, 49% accepted, 77 enrolled. In 2017, 67 master's, 2 doctorates awarded. Terminal master's awarded for partial completion of doctoral program. *Degree requirements:* For doctorate, thesis/dissertation. *Entrance requirements:* Additional exam requirements/recommendations for international students: Required—TOEFL. *Application deadline:* For fall admission, 11/15 for international students; for spring admission, 8/1 for international students. Applications are processed on a rolling basis. Application fee: $60. Electronic applications accepted. *Expenses:* Tuition, state resident: full-time $16,164; part-time $898 per credit hour. Tuition, nonresident: full-time $22,158; part-time $1231 per credit hour. *Required fees:* $890; $445 per semester. Full-time tuition and fees vary according to course load, degree level, campus/location and program. *Financial support:* Fellowships with tuition reimbursements, research assistantships with tuition reimbursements, teaching assistantships with tuition reimbursements, career-related internships or fieldwork, Federal Work-Study, scholarships/grants, health care benefits, and unspecified assistantships available. Financial award application deadline: 3/1; financial award applicants required to submit FAFSA. *Unit head:* Dr. Robert Stroker, Dean, 215-204-8598, Fax: 215-204-4957, E-mail: rstroker@temple.edu. *Application contact:* James Short, Assistant Dean, Undergraduate and Graduate Admissions, 215-204-8301, Fax: 215-204-8598, E-mail: james.short@temple.edu.
Website: http://www.temple.edu/boyer/academicprograms/

Texas A&M University, College of Liberal Arts, Department of Performance Studies, College Station, TX 77843. Offers MA. *Faculty:* 11. *Students:* 6 full-time (2 women); includes 2 minority (both Hispanic/Latino), 2 international. Average age 27. 9 applicants, 78% accepted, 6 enrolled. *Degree requirements:* For master's, comprehensive exam (for some programs), thesis or alternative. *Entrance requirements:* For master's, GRE General Test. Additional exam requirements/recommendations for international students: Required—TOEFL (minimum score 550 paper-based; 80 iBT), IELTS (minimum score 6), PTE (minimum score 53). *Application deadline:* For fall admission, 12/1 for domestic students; for spring admission, 10/15 for domestic students. Applications are processed on a rolling basis. Application fee: $50 ($90 for international students). Electronic applications accepted. *Expenses:* Contact institution. *Financial support:* In 2017–18, 6 students received support, including 6 teaching assistantships (averaging $8,944 per year); unspecified assistantships also available. Financial award application deadline: 3/15; financial award applicants required to submit FAFSA. *Unit head:* Dr. Donnlee Dox, Department Head, 979-458-1870, E-mail: dox@tamu.edu. *Application contact:* Dr. Kirsten Pullen, Director of Graduate Studies, 979-845-2899, Fax: 979-845-5164, E-mail: kpullen@tamu.edu.
Website: http://performancestudies.tamu.edu/

Texas A&M University–Commerce, College of Humanities, Social Sciences and Arts, Commerce, TX 75429. Offers applied criminology (MS); applied linguistics (MA, MS); art (MA, MFA); computational linguistics (Graduate Certificate); creative writing (Graduate Certificate); criminal justice management (Graduate Certificate); criminal justice studies (Graduate Certificate); English (MA, MS, PhD); film studies (Graduate Certificate); history (MA, MS); history of Christianity (Graduate Certificate); Holocaust studies (Graduate Certificate); homeland security (Graduate Certificate); music education (MM); music performance (MM); political science (MA, MS); public history (Graduate

Certificate); sociology (MS); Spanish (MA); studies in children's and adolescent literature and culture (Graduate Certificate); teaching English to speakers of other languages (Graduate Certificate); theater (MA, MS); world history (Graduate Certificate). *Program availability:* Part-time. *Faculty:* 56 full-time (26 women), 10 part-time/adjunct (5 women). *Students:* 133 full-time (85 women), 439 part-time (311 women); includes 204 minority (79 Black or African American, non-Hispanic/Latino; 4 American Indian or Alaska Native, non-Hispanic/Latino; 9 Asian, non-Hispanic/Latino; 98 Hispanic/Latino; 14 Two or more races, non-Hispanic/Latino), 26 international. Average age 36. 261 applicants, 50% accepted, 113 enrolled. In 2017, 105 master's, 5 doctorates awarded. *Degree requirements:* For master's, one foreign language, comprehensive exam, thesis (for some programs); for doctorate, one foreign language, comprehensive exam, thesis/dissertation, departmental qualifying exam. *Entrance requirements:* For master's and doctorate, GRE General Test. Additional exam requirements/recommendations for international students: Required—TOEFL (minimum score 550 paper-based; 79 iBT), IELTS (minimum score 6). *Application deadline:* Applications are processed on a rolling basis. Application fee: $50. Electronic applications accepted. *Expenses:* Contact institution. *Financial support:* In 2017–18, 43 students received support, including 9 research assistantships with partial tuition reimbursements available (averaging $9,000 per year), 68 teaching assistantships with partial tuition reimbursements available (averaging $9,000 per year); Federal Work-Study, institutionally sponsored loans, scholarships/grants, health care benefits, and unspecified assistantships also available. Financial award application deadline: 5/1; financial award applicants required to submit FAFSA. *Unit head:* Dr. William F. Kuracina, Interim Dean, 903-886-5166, Fax: 903-886-5774, E-mail: william.kuracina@tamuc.edu. *Application contact:* Vicky Turner, Doctoral Degree and Special Programs Coordinator, 903-886-5167, E-mail: vicky.turner@tamuc.edu.
Website: http://www.tamuc.edu/academics/graduateSchool/programs/humanitiesSocialScienceArts/default.aspx

Texas A&M University–Kingsville, College of Graduate Studies, College of Arts and Sciences, Department of Music, Progam in Music, Kingsville, TX 78363. Offers instrumental performance (MM); vocal performance (MM).

Texas Christian University, College of Fine Arts, School of Music, Doctoral Programs in Music, Fort Worth, TX 76129. Offers composition (DMA), including music history; conducting (DMA), including music history, music theory; performance (DMA), including music history, music theory, piano pedagogy; piano pedagogy (DMA). *Accreditation:* NASM. *Faculty:* 43 full-time (10 women), 15 part-time/adjunct (7 women). *Students:* 10 full-time (2 women), 3 part-time (1 woman); includes 1 minority (Two or more races, non-Hispanic/Latino), 5 international. Average age 33. 44 applicants, 25% accepted, 2 enrolled. In 2017, 3 doctorates awarded. *Degree requirements:* For doctorate, comprehensive exam, thesis/dissertation. *Entrance requirements:* For doctorate, GRE General Test. Additional exam requirements/recommendations for international students: Required—TOEFL (minimum score 100 iBT). *Application deadline:* For spring admission, 12/1 for domestic and international students. Application fee: $80. Electronic applications accepted. *Financial support:* In 2017–18, 9 students received support, including 10 research assistantships with full tuition reimbursements available (averaging $10,000 per year); career-related internships or fieldwork, institutionally sponsored loans, scholarships/grants, tuition waivers (full and partial), and unspecified assistantships also available. Financial award application deadline: 12/1; financial award applicants required to submit CSS PROFILE or FAFSA. *Unit head:* Dr. Richard C. Gipson, Director, 817-257-6606, Fax: 817-257-5818, E-mail: r.gipson@tcu.edu. *Application contact:* Donna Smolik, TCU College of Fine Arts Graduate Office, 817-257-7603, Fax: 817-257-5672, E-mail: cfagradinfo@tcu.edu.
Website: http://www.music.tcu.edu

Texas Christian University, College of Fine Arts, School of Music, Master's Programs in Music, Fort Worth, TX 76129. Offers conducting (M Mus); music education (MM Ed). *Faculty:* 43 full-time (10 women), 15 part-time/adjunct (7 women). *Students:* 39 full-time (16 women), 1 part-time (0 women); includes 6 minority (4 Hispanic/Latino; 2 Two or more races, non-Hispanic/Latino), 11 international. Average age 24. 62 applicants, 47% accepted, 20 enrolled. In 2017, 21 master's awarded. *Degree requirements:* For master's, comprehensive exam. *Entrance requirements:* For master's, GRE General Test. Additional exam requirements/recommendations for international students: Required—TOEFL (minimum score 80 iBT). *Application deadline:* For fall admission, 3/1 for domestic and international students. Application fee: $80. Electronic applications accepted. *Financial support:* In 2017–18, 41 students received support, including 41 research assistantships with full tuition reimbursements available (averaging $6,000 per year); career-related internships or fieldwork, institutionally sponsored loans, scholarships/grants, tuition waivers (full and partial), and unspecified assistantships also available. Financial award application deadline: 3/1; financial award applicants required to submit CSS PROFILE or FAFSA. *Unit head:* Dr. Richard C. Gipson, Director, 817-257-6606, Fax: 817-257-5818, E-mail: music@tcu.edu. *Application contact:* Donna Smolik, TCU College of Fine Arts Graduate Office, 817-257-7603, Fax: 817-257-5672, E-mail: cfagradinfo@tcu.edu.
Website: http://www.music.tcu.edu

Texas Southern University, College of Liberal Arts and Behavioral Sciences, Department of Fine Arts, Houston, TX 77004-4584. Offers fine arts (MA); music (MA). *Program availability:* Part-time. *Degree requirements:* For master's, one foreign language, comprehensive exam, recital. *Entrance requirements:* For master's, GRE General Test, minimum GPA of 2.5. Additional exam requirements/recommendations for international students: Required—TOEFL. Electronic applications accepted. *Faculty research:* Music theory, choral music, composition, percussion composition, ethnic musicology.

Texas State University, The Graduate College, College of Fine Arts and Communication, Program in Music, San Marcos, TX 78666. Offers MM. *Accreditation:* NASM. *Program availability:* Part-time. *Faculty:* 42 full-time (16 women), 8 part-time/adjunct (3 women). *Students:* 38 full-time (19 women), 17 part-time (9 women); includes 18 minority (3 Black or African American, non-Hispanic/Latino; 15 Hispanic/Latino), 9 international. Average age 28. 55 applicants, 58% accepted, 15 enrolled. In 2017, 28 master's awarded. *Degree requirements:* For master's, comprehensive exam, thesis (for some programs). *Entrance requirements:* For master's, baccalaureate degree in music from regionally-accredited institution with minimum GPA of 2.75 in last 60 hours of undergraduate course work, resume, 3 letters of recommendation; music portfolio (for composition, theory and history concentrations). Additional exam requirements/recommendations for international students: Required—TOEFL (minimum score 550 paper-based; 78 iBT), IELTS (minimum score 6). *Application deadline:* For fall admission, 1/15 priority date for domestic and international students; for spring admission, 10/15 for domestic students, 10/1 for international students; for summer admission, 4/15 for domestic students, 3/15 for international students. Applications are processed on a rolling basis. Application fee: $40 ($90 for international students). Electronic applications accepted. *Expenses:* Tuition, state resident: full-time $7868; part-time $3934 per semester. Tuition, nonresident: full-time $17,828; part-time $8914 per semester. *Required fees:* $2092; $1435 per semester. Tuition and fees vary according to course load. *Financial support:* In 2017–18, 46 students received support, including 26 teaching assistantships (averaging $6,157 per year); research assistantships, career-related internships or fieldwork, Federal Work-Study, institutionally sponsored loans, scholarships/grants, and unspecified assistantships also available. Support available to part-time students. Financial award application deadline: 3/1; financial award applicants required to submit FAFSA. *Unit head:* Dr. Jason Kwak, Graduate Advisor, 512-245-3390, Fax: 512-245-8181, E-mail: jk45@txstate.edu. *Application contact:* Dr. Andrea Golato, Dean of Graduate School, 512-245-2581, Fax: 512-245-8365, E-mail: gradcollege@txstate.edu.
Website: http://www.finearts.txstate.edu/music/

Texas Tech University, Graduate School, J.T. and Margaret Talkington College of Visual and Performing Arts, School of Music, Lubbock, TX 79409-2033. Offers music (MM, DMA); music education (MM Ed). *Accreditation:* NASM. *Program availability:* Part-time. *Faculty:* 56 full-time (22 women), 7 part-time/adjunct (4 women). *Students:* 112 full-time (46 women), 30 part-time (12 women); includes 20 minority (5 Black or African American, non-Hispanic/Latino; 14 Hispanic/Latino; 1 Two or more races, non-Hispanic/Latino), 42 international. Average age 30. 112 applicants, 69% accepted, 43 enrolled. In 2017, 25 master's, 15 doctorates awarded. *Degree requirements:* For master's, thesis or alternative; for doctorate, comprehensive exam (for some programs), thesis/dissertation. *Entrance requirements:* Additional exam requirements/recommendations for international students: Required—TOEFL (minimum score 550 paper-based; 79 iBT). *Application deadline:* For fall admission, 6/1 priority date for domestic students, 1/15 priority date for international students; for spring admission, 9/1 priority date for domestic students, 6/15 priority date for international students. Applications are processed on a rolling basis. Application fee: $60. Electronic applications accepted. *Expenses:* Contact institution. *Financial support:* In 2017–18, 160 students received support, including 142 fellowships (averaging $2,547 per year), 101 teaching assistantships (averaging $10,247 per year); research assistantships, Federal Work-Study, institutionally sponsored loans, scholarships/grants, health care benefits, tuition waivers (partial), and unspecified assistantships also available. Financial award application deadline: 4/15; financial award applicants required to submit FAFSA. *Faculty research:* Strategies for music pedagogy in grades K-12, performance practice of traditional music, role of the woman piano virtuoso, vernacular music center, voice health and culture. *Total annual research expenditures:* $10,747. *Unit head:* Dr. Keith Dye, Interim Director and Professor, 806-834-2497, E-mail: keith.dye@ttu.edu. *Application contact:* Emily Gifford, Graduate Student Coordinator, 806-834-5076, Fax: 806-742-2294, E-mail: emily.gifford@ttu.edu.
Website: http://www.depts.ttu.edu/music

Texas Woman's University, Graduate School, College of Arts and Sciences, School of the Arts, Department of Music and Drama, Denton, TX 76204. Offers drama (MA); music (MA), including music education, music therapy, pedagogy, performance. *Accreditation:* NASM. *Program availability:* Part-time. *Faculty:* 15 full-time (7 women), 8 part-time/adjunct (4 women). *Students:* 54 full-time (41 women), 43 part-time (30 women); includes 32 minority (6 Black or African American, non-Hispanic/Latino; 2 Asian, non-Hispanic/Latino; 21 Hispanic/Latino; 3 Two or more races, non-Hispanic/Latino), 6 international. Average age 30. 42 applicants, 98% accepted, 33 enrolled. In 2017, 21 master's awarded. *Degree requirements:* For master's, comprehensive exam, thesis (for some programs), project recital, professional paper or thesis (for music education). *Entrance requirements:* For master's, music history/theory placement exam (for music only), audition and/or design portfolio, interview, resume, writing sample (for drama only), letter of intent, minimum undergraduate GPA of 3.0. Additional exam requirements/recommendations for international students: Required—TOEFL (minimum score 550 paper-based; 79 iBT); Recommended—IELTS (minimum score 6.5), TSE (minimum score 53). *Application deadline:* For fall admission, 3/1 priority date for domestic and international students; for spring admission, 11/1 priority date for domestic students, 7/1 priority date for international students; for summer admission, 5/1 priority date for domestic students, 2/1 priority date for international students. Applications are processed on a rolling basis. Application fee: $50 ($75 for international students). Electronic applications accepted. *Expenses:* $8,150 per year full-time in-state, $17,450 per year full-time out-of-state (for music). *Financial support:* In 2017–18, 31 students received support, including 5 teaching assistantships (averaging $11,736 per year); career-related internships or fieldwork, Federal Work-Study, institutionally sponsored loans, scholarships/grants, traineeships, health care benefits, and unspecified assistantships also available. Support available to part-time students. Financial award application deadline: 3/1; financial award applicants required to submit FAFSA. *Faculty research:* Musical development in early childhood, little known or neglected compositions for flute (especially by women composers), pedagogical development of the singing voice, music therapy, music and neuroscience technology. *Unit head:* Dr. Pamela Youngblood, Chair of Music and Drama, 940-898-2500, Fax: 940-898-2494, E-mail: music@twu.edu. *Application contact:* Korie Hawkins, Associate Director of Admissions, Graduate Recruitment, 940-898-3188, Fax: 940-898-3081, E-mail: admissions@twu.edu.

Towson University, College of Fine Arts and Communication, Program in Music Performance and Composition, Towson, MD 21252-0001. Offers MM. *Accreditation:* NASM. *Program availability:* Part-time, evening/weekend. *Students:* 5 full-time (4 women), 10 part-time (5 women); includes 6 minority (1 Black or African American, non-Hispanic/Latino; 1 Asian, non-Hispanic/Latino; 1 Hispanic/Latino; 3 Two or more races, non-Hispanic/Latino), 1 international. *Entrance requirements:* For master's, audition, bachelor's degree in music, minimum GPA of 3.0. Additional exam requirements/recommendations for international students: Required—TOEFL (minimum score 550 paper-based). *Application deadline:* For fall admission, 1/17 for domestic students, 5/15 for international students; for spring admission, 10/15 for domestic students, 12/1 for international students. Applications are processed on a rolling basis. Application fee: $45. Electronic applications accepted. *Expenses:* Tuition, state resident: full-time $7960; part-time $398 per unit. Tuition, nonresident: full-time $16,480; part-time $824 per unit. *Required fees:* $2600; $130 per year. $390 per term. *Financial support:* Application deadline: 4/1. *Unit head:* Dr. Terry Ewell, Program Coordinator, 410-704-2824, E-mail: tewell@towson.edu. *Application contact:* Coverley Beidleman, Assistant Director of Graduate Admissions, 410-704-5630, Fax: 410-704-3030, E-mail: cbeidleman@towson.edu.
Website: http://www.towson.edu/cofac/departments/music/grad/performance/

Trinity College, Faculty of Divinity, Toronto, ON M5S 1H8, Canada. Offers ministry (Diploma); ministry for church musicians (Diploma); theology (M Div, MA, MTS, Th M, D Min, PhD, Th D, Diploma, L Th); M Div/MA. *Accreditation:* ATS. *Program availability:* Part-time. *Degree requirements:* For master's, 2 foreign languages, thesis (for some programs); for doctorate, 3 foreign languages, comprehensive exam, thesis/dissertation; for other advanced degree, thesis (for some programs). *Entrance requirements:* For master's, 1 language (modern or ancient), interview; for doctorate, 2 languages (modern and ancient). Additional exam requirements/recommendations for international students: Required—TOEFL, TWE. *Faculty research:* Interreligious dialogue, feminist theology, systematic theology, philosophy of religion, pastoral theology.

Trinity Lutheran Seminary, Graduate and Professional Programs, Columbus, OH 43209-2334. Offers African American studies (MTS); Biblical studies (MTS, STM); Christian education (MA); Christian spirituality (STM); church in the world (MTS); church music (MA); divinity (M Div); general theological studies (MTS); mission and evangelism

(STM); pastoral leadership and practice (STM); youth and family ministry (MA); MSN/MTS; MTS/JD. *Accreditation:* ACIPE; ATS. *Program availability:* Part-time. *Degree requirements:* For master's, variable foreign language requirement, comprehensive exam (for some programs), thesis (for some programs), field experience (for some programs). *Entrance requirements:* For master's, BA or equivalent (for MA, M Div, MTS); M Div, MTS, or equivalent (for STM); audition (for MACM). Additional exam requirements/recommendations for international students: Required—TOEFL. Electronic applications accepted. *Expenses:* Contact institution.

Truman State University, Graduate School, School of Arts and Letters, Program in Music, Kirksville, MO 63501-4221. Offers MA. *Accreditation:* NASM. *Degree requirements:* For master's, comprehensive exam, thesis or alternative. *Entrance requirements:* For master's, GRE General Test, minimum GPA of 3.0. Additional exam requirements/recommendations for international students: Required—TOEFL (minimum score 550 paper-based). Electronic applications accepted.

Tufts University, Graduate School of Arts and Sciences, Department of Music, Medford, MA 02155. Offers composition (MA); ethnomusicology (MA); music theory (MA). *Program availability:* Part-time. *Students:* 11 full-time (2 women); includes 2 minority (1 Asian, non-Hispanic/Latino; 1 Hispanic/Latino). Average age 29. 21 applicants, 52% accepted, 3 enrolled. In 2017, 4 master's awarded. *Degree requirements:* For master's, one foreign language, thesis. *Entrance requirements:* For master's, GRE General Test, writing sample or musical score. Additional exam requirements/recommendations for international students: Required—TOEFL (minimum score 550 paper-based; 80 iBT), IELTS (minimum score 6.5). *Application deadline:* For fall admission, 1/15 for domestic and international students. Applications are processed on a rolling basis. Application fee: $85. Electronic applications accepted. *Expenses:* Contact institution. *Financial support:* Teaching assistantships, Federal Work-Study, scholarships/grants, tuition waivers (full and partial), and unspecified assistantships available. Financial award application deadline: 1/15. *Unit head:* Dr. Stephan Pennington, Graduate Program Director, 617-627-3564. *Application contact:* Office of Graduate Admissions, 617-627-3395, E-mail: gradadmissions@tufts.edu.
Website: http://www.tufts.edu/as/music/

Tulane University, School of Liberal Arts, Department of Music, New Orleans, LA 70118-5669. Offers MA, MFA. *Degree requirements:* For master's, one foreign language, thesis (for some programs), recital or composition (MA). *Entrance requirements:* For master's, GRE General Test, minimum B average in undergraduate course work. Additional exam requirements/recommendations for international students: Required—TOEFL. Electronic applications accepted. *Expenses: Tuition:* Full-time $50,920; part-time $2829 per credit hour. *Required fees:* $2040; $44.50 per credit hour. $580 per term. Tuition and fees vary according to course load, degree level and program. *Faculty research:* New Orleans music, composition, piano, voice, music theatre, classical guitar.

Université de Montréal, Faculty of Music, Montréal, QC H3C 3J7, Canada. Offers composition (M Mus, D Mus); interpretation (M Mus, D Mus, DESS); music (MA, PhD); orchestral repertoire (DESS). *Degree requirements:* For doctorate, thesis/dissertation, general exam. Electronic applications accepted. *Faculty research:* Semiology, music in Creole areas, computer-assisted composition, Argentinean tango.

Université Laval, Faculty of Music, Programs in Music, Québec, QC G1K 7P4, Canada. Offers composition (M Mus); instrumental didactics (M Mus); interpretation (M Mus); music education (M Mus, PhD); musicology (M Mus, PhD). Terminal master's awarded for partial completion of doctoral program. *Degree requirements:* For master's, thesis (for some programs); for doctorate, comprehensive exam, thesis/dissertation. *Entrance requirements:* For master's, English exam, audition, knowledge of French; for doctorate, English exam, knowledge of French, third language. Electronic applications accepted.

University at Buffalo, the State University of New York, Graduate School, College of Arts and Sciences, Department of Music, Buffalo, NY 14260. Offers contemporary performance (Advanced Certificate); historical musicology and music theory (PhD); music composition (MA, PhD); music history (MA); music performance (MM); music theory (MA). *Faculty:* 20 full-time (4 women), 17 part-time/adjunct (3 women). *Students:* 49 full-time (17 women), 3 part-time (1 woman); includes 14 minority (1 Black or African American, non-Hispanic/Latino; 11 Asian, non-Hispanic/Latino; 2 Hispanic/Latino), 4 international. Average age 25. 40 applicants, 48% accepted, 10 enrolled. In 2017, 8 master's, 4 doctorates, 1 other advanced degree awarded. Terminal master's awarded for partial completion of doctoral program. *Degree requirements:* For master's, variable foreign language requirement, comprehensive exam (for some programs), thesis (for some programs), recitals (for MM); projects and/or thesis (for MA); for doctorate, variable foreign language requirement, comprehensive exam, thesis/dissertation; for Advanced Certificate, recitals. *Entrance requirements:* For master's, audition (for MM), compositions, writing sample(s), essay, letters of recommendation; for doctorate, GRE General Test, compositions, writing sample(s), essay, letters of recommendation; for Advanced Certificate, audition. Additional exam requirements/recommendations for international students: Required—TOEFL (minimum score 550 paper-based; 79 iBT), IELTS. *Application deadline:* For fall admission, 1/1 priority date for domestic and international students; for spring admission, 10/1 for domestic students, 9/1 priority date for international students. Applications are processed on a rolling basis. Application fee: $75. Electronic applications accepted. *Financial support:* In 2017–18, 16 students received support, including 11 fellowships with full tuition reimbursements available (averaging $19,580 per year), 5 teaching assistantships with full tuition reimbursements available (averaging $13,580 per year); career-related internships or fieldwork, Federal Work-Study, institutionally sponsored loans, scholarships/grants, health care benefits, and unspecified assistantships also available. Financial award application deadline: 1/1; financial award applicants required to submit FAFSA. *Faculty research:* Music composition, music theory, historical musicology, music performance, contemporary music. *Unit head:* Prof. Jeffrey Stadelman, Chairperson, 716-645-0639, Fax: 716-645-3824, E-mail: stadelm@buffalo.edu. *Application contact:* Karen A. Sausner, Director of Student Programs, 716-645-2758, Fax: 716-645-6196, E-mail: ksausner@buffalo.edu.
Website: http://www.music.buffalo.edu/

The University of Akron, Graduate School, Buchtel College of Arts and Sciences, School of Music, Program in Accompanying, Akron, OH 44325. Offers MM. *Entrance requirements:* For master's, minimum GPA of 2.75, three letters of recommendation, audition. Additional exam requirements/recommendations for international students: Required—TOEFL (minimum score 79 iBT), IELTS (minimum score 6.5). *Application deadline:* Applications are processed on a rolling basis. Application fee: $45 ($70 for international students). *Unit head:* Dr. J. Thomas Dukes, Interim Director, 330-972-5761, E-mail: jtdukes@uakron.edu. *Application contact:* E-mail: ausher@uakron.edu.
Website: http://www.uakron.edu/academics_majors/graduate/programs_detail.dot?programId=52397&pageTitle=Graduate programs&crumbTitle=Music - Accompanying

The University of Akron, Graduate School, Buchtel College of Arts and Sciences, School of Music, Program in Composition, Akron, OH 44325. Offers MM. *Students:* 1 full-time (0 women). Average age 24. 2 applicants, 50% accepted, 1 enrolled. *Degree requirements:* For master's, comprehensive exam, thesis optional. *Entrance requirements:* For master's, theory diagnostic exam, minimum GPA of 2.75, three letters of recommendation, sample of scholarly writing, composition portfolio, interview. Additional exam requirements/recommendations for international students: Required—TOEFL (minimum score 79 iBT), IELTS (minimum score 6.5). *Application deadline:* Applications are processed on a rolling basis. Application fee: $45 ($70 for international students). Electronic applications accepted. *Unit head:* Dr. J. Thomas Dukes, Interim Director, 330-972-5761, E-mail: jtdukes@uakron.edu.
Website: http://www.uakron.edu/academics_majors/graduate/programs_detail.dot?programId=52399&pageTitle=Graduate programs&crumbTitle=Music - Composition

The University of Akron, Graduate School, Buchtel College of Arts and Sciences, School of Music, Program in Music Technology, Akron, OH 44325. Offers MM. *Students:* 2 full-time (0 women). Average age 24. 4 applicants, 50% accepted, 1 enrolled. In 2017, 1 master's awarded. *Degree requirements:* For master's, comprehensive exam, thesis optional. *Entrance requirements:* For master's, minimum GPA of 2.75, three letters of recommendation, interview. Additional exam requirements/recommendations for international students: Required—TOEFL (minimum score 79 iBT), IELTS (minimum score 6.5). *Application deadline:* Applications are processed on a rolling basis. Application fee: $45 ($70 for international students). Electronic applications accepted. *Unit head:* Dr. J. Thomas Dukes, Interim Director, 330-972-5761, E-mail: jtdukes@uakron.edu. *Application contact:* V. Douglas Hicks, Program Coordinator, 330-972-6356, E-mail: dvhicks@uakron.edu.
Website: http://www.uamusictechnology.com/

The University of Akron, Graduate School, Buchtel College of Arts and Sciences, School of Music, Program in Performance, Akron, OH 44325. Offers MM. *Students:* 25 full-time (10 women); includes 3 minority (1 Black or African American, non-Hispanic/Latino; 2 Hispanic/Latino), 4 international. Average age 25. 20 applicants, 95% accepted, 11 enrolled. In 2017, 17 master's awarded. *Degree requirements:* For master's, comprehensive exam. *Entrance requirements:* For master's, minimum GPA of 2.75, three letters of recommendation, audition. Additional exam requirements/recommendations for international students: Required—TOEFL (minimum score 79 iBT), IELTS (minimum score 6.5). *Application deadline:* Applications are processed on a rolling basis. Application fee: $45 ($70 for international students). Electronic applications accepted. *Unit head:* Dr. J. Thomas Dukes, Interim Director, 330-972-5761, E-mail: jtdukes@uakron.edu.
Website: http://www.uakron.edu/academics_majors/graduate/programs_detail.dot?programId=52404&pageTitle=Graduate programs&crumbTitle=Music - Performance

The University of Akron, Graduate School, Buchtel College of Arts and Sciences, School of Music, Program in Theory, Akron, OH 44325. Offers MM. *Students:* 1 part-time (0 women). Average age 49. *Degree requirements:* For master's, comprehensive exam, thesis optional. *Entrance requirements:* For master's, minimum GPA of 2.75, interview, three letters of recommendation. Additional exam requirements/recommendations for international students: Required—TOEFL (minimum score 79 iBT), IELTS (minimum score 6.5). *Application deadline:* Applications are processed on a rolling basis. Application fee: $45 ($70 for international students). Electronic applications accepted. *Unit head:* Dr. J. Thomas Dukes, Interim Director, 330-972-5761, E-mail: jtdukes@uakron.edu.
Website: http://www.uakron.edu/academics_majors/graduate/programs_detail.dot?programId=52409&pageTitle=Graduate programs&crumbTitle=Music - Theory

The University of Alabama, Graduate School, College of Arts and Sciences, School of Music, Tuscaloosa, AL 35487. Offers arranging (MM); choral conducting (MM, DMA); church music (MM); composition (MM, DMA); music education (MA, PhD); musicology (MM); performance (MM, DMA); theory (MM); wind conducting (MM, DMA). *Accreditation:* NASM. *Faculty:* 38 full-time (13 women), 2 part-time/adjunct (both women). *Students:* 56 full-time (26 women), 15 part-time (3 women); includes 15 minority (6 Black or African American, non-Hispanic/Latino; 1 American Indian or Alaska Native, non-Hispanic/Latino; 6 Hispanic/Latino; 2 Two or more races, non-Hispanic/Latino), 11 international. Average age 30. 67 applicants, 64% accepted, 22 enrolled. In 2017, 10 master's, 6 doctorates awarded. *Degree requirements:* For master's, variable foreign language requirement, comprehensive exam (for some programs), thesis (for some programs), recital; for doctorate, variable foreign language requirement, comprehensive exam, thesis/dissertation, oral exam; recital (for some majors). *Entrance requirements:* For master's and doctorate, audition exam, audition in the major instrument or area. Additional exam requirements/recommendations for international students: Required—PTE (minimum score 59), TOEFL (minimum score 550 paper-based, 79 iBT) or IELTS (minimum score 6.5). *Application deadline:* For fall admission, 3/15 priority date for domestic and international students; for winter admission, 9/1 priority date for domestic and international students; for spring admission, 9/1 priority date for domestic and international students. Applications are processed on a rolling basis. Application fee: $50 ($60 for international students). Electronic applications accepted. *Financial support:* In 2017–18, 37 students received support, including fellowships with full tuition reimbursements available (averaging $10,000 per year), teaching assistantships with tuition reimbursements available (averaging $10,161 per year); institutionally sponsored loans, scholarships/grants, health care benefits, and unspecified assistantships also available. Financial award application deadline: 3/15. *Faculty research:* Performance practice, musicology, theory, composition. *Unit head:* Charles G. Snead, Director, 205-348-7110, Fax: 205-348-1473, E-mail: ssnead@music.ua.edu. *Application contact:* Dr. Jon Noffsinger, Director of Graduate Studies, 205-348-1475, Fax: 205-348-1473, E-mail: jnoffsin@ua.edu.
Website: http://music.ua.edu/

University of Alaska Fairbanks, College of Liberal Arts, Department of Music, Fairbanks, AK 99775-5660. Offers MM. *Accreditation:* NASM. *Program availability:* Part-time. *Degree requirements:* For master's, comprehensive exam, thesis or alternative, project, oral defense of project. *Entrance requirements:* For master's, diagnostic examinations in music theory, music history, and music literature, bachelor's degree from accredited institution with minimum cumulative undergraduate and major GPA of 3.0, performance audition. Additional exam requirements/recommendations for international students: Required—TOEFL (minimum score 550 paper-based; 79 iBT), IELTS (minimum score 6.5). Electronic applications accepted.

University of Alberta, Faculty of Graduate Studies and Research, Department of Music, Edmonton, AB T6G 2E1, Canada. Offers applied music (M Mus); choral conducting (M Mus); composition (M Mus); music (PhD); organ and choral conductors (D Mus); piano (D Mus). *Degree requirements:* For master's, one foreign language, thesis; for doctorate, one foreign language, thesis/dissertation. *Entrance requirements:* Additional exam requirements/recommendations for international students: Required—TOEFL (minimum score 550 paper-based). Electronic applications accepted. *Faculty research:* Classical/Indian and West African music, popular music, choral conducting, theory and composition, musicology, applied music.

The University of Arizona, College of Fine Arts, School of Music, Program in Music, Tucson, AZ 85721. Offers composition (MM); ethnomusicology (MM); music education (MM, PhD); music theory (MM, PhD); musicology (MM); performance (MM), including conducting - choral, conducting - instrumental, instrumental, keyboard, piano

accompanying, piano and dance accompanying, vocal. *Entrance requirements:* Additional exam requirements/recommendations for international students: Required—TOEFL (minimum score 550 paper-based; 79 iBT). Electronic applications accepted. *Faculty research:* Music in general education, psychology of music learning, innovation in string music education, Zarzuela, Franz Liszt's work.

The University of Arizona, College of Fine Arts, School of Music, Program in Musical Arts, Tucson, AZ 85721. Offers composition (DMA); conducting (DMA); performance (DMA), including instrumental, keyboard, vocal. *Entrance requirements:* Additional exam requirements/recommendations for international students: Required—TOEFL (minimum score 550 paper-based; 79 iBT). Electronic applications accepted. *Faculty research:* Music in general education, psychology of music learning, innovation in string music education, Zarzuela, Franz Liszt's work.

University of Arkansas, Graduate School, J. William Fulbright College of Arts and Sciences, Department of Music, Fayetteville, AR 72701. Offers MM. *Accreditation:* NASM. In 2017, 15 master's awarded. *Entrance requirements:* For master's, GRE General Test. *Application deadline:* For fall admission, 8/1 for domestic students, 4/1 for international students; for spring admission, 12/1 for domestic students, 10/1 for international students; for summer admission, 4/15 for domestic students, 3/1 for international students. Applications are processed on a rolling basis. Application fee: $60. Electronic applications accepted. *Expenses:* Tuition, state resident: full-time $3782. Tuition, nonresident: full-time $10,238. *Financial support:* In 2017–18, 2 research assistantships, 24 teaching assistantships were awarded; fellowships, career-related internships or fieldwork, and Federal Work-Study also available. Support available to part-time students. Financial award application deadline: 4/1; financial award applicants required to submit FAFSA. *Unit head:* Dr. Ronda M. Mains, Department Chair, 479-575-4701, Fax: 479-575-5409, E-mail: rmains@uark.edu.
Website: https://fulbright.uark.edu/departments/music/

The University of British Columbia, Faculty of Arts and Faculty of Graduate Studies, School of Music, Vancouver, BC V6T 1Z2, Canada. Offers M Mus, MA, DMA, PhD. *Program availability:* Part-time. *Degree requirements:* For master's, recital (M Mus), thesis (MA); for doctorate, one foreign language, comprehensive exam, public performance or composition (DMA), dissertation (PhD). *Entrance requirements:* For master's, audition/performance (M Mus); for doctorate, audition/performance (DMA). Additional exam requirements/recommendations for international students: Required—TOEFL. Electronic applications accepted. *Expenses:* Contact institution. *Faculty research:* Performance, composition, opera, musicology, ethnomusicology, theory.

University of Calgary, Faculty of Graduate Studies, Faculty of Arts, Department of Music, Calgary, AB T2N 1N4, Canada. Offers M Mus, MA, PhD. *Degree requirements:* For master's, one foreign language, thesis; for doctorate, 2 foreign languages, thesis/dissertation. *Entrance requirements:* For master's, audition (performance), 3 compositions. Additional exam requirements/recommendations for international students: Required—TOEFL. Electronic applications accepted. *Faculty research:* Musicology, theory and composition, performance and performance practice, teaching methodology, folk music collection and analyses.

University of California, Berkeley, Graduate Division, College of Letters and Science, Department of Music, Berkeley, CA 94720-1500. Offers composition (PhD); ethnomusicology (PhD); musicology (PhD). *Degree requirements:* For doctorate, 2 foreign languages, thesis/dissertation, qualifying exam. *Entrance requirements:* For doctorate, GRE General Test, minimum GPA of 3.0, examples of work, 3 letters of recommendation. Additional exam requirements/recommendations for international students: Required—TOEFL (minimum score 570 paper-based; 90 iBT). Electronic applications accepted. *Faculty research:* Historical musicology, music criticism, computer music.

University of California, Davis, Graduate Studies, Program in Music, Davis, CA 95616. Offers composition (MA, PhD); conducting (MA, PhD); musicology (MA, PhD). Terminal master's awarded for partial completion of doctoral program. *Degree requirements:* For master's, one foreign language, thesis; for doctorate, 2 foreign languages, thesis/dissertation. *Entrance requirements:* For master's, minimum GPA of 3.0; for doctorate, GRE, minimum GPA of 3.0. Additional exam requirements/recommendations for international students: Required—TOEFL (minimum score 550 paper-based). Electronic applications accepted.

University of California, Davis, Graduate Studies, Program in Performance Studies, Davis, CA 95616. Offers dramatic art (PhD). *Degree requirements:* For doctorate, 2 foreign languages, thesis/dissertation. *Entrance requirements:* For doctorate, GRE, minimum GPA of 3.25. Additional exam requirements/recommendations for international students: Required—TOEFL (minimum score 550 paper-based). Electronic applications accepted.

University of California, Irvine, Claire Trevor School of the Arts, Department of Music, Irvine, CA 92697. Offers accompanying (MFA); choral conducting (MFA); composition and technology (MFA); guitar/lute performance (MFA); instrumental performance (MFA); piano performance (MFA); vocal performance (MFA). *Students:* 9 full-time (6 women), 4 part-time (3 women); includes 7 minority (1 Black or African American, non-Hispanic/Latino; 4 Asian, non-Hispanic/Latino; 1 Hispanic/Latino; 1 Two or more races, non-Hispanic/Latino), 2 international. Average age 29. 20 applicants, 65% accepted, 10 enrolled. In 2017, 4 master's awarded. *Degree requirements:* For master's, one foreign language, thesis. *Entrance requirements:* For master's, minimum GPA of 3.0. *Application deadline:* For fall admission, 1/15 priority date for domestic students, 1/15 for international students. Applications are processed on a rolling basis. Application fee: $105 ($125 for international students). Electronic applications accepted. *Financial support:* Fellowships, teaching assistantships, institutionally sponsored loans, traineeships, health care benefits, and unspecified assistantships available. Financial award application deadline: 3/1; financial award applicants required to submit FAFSA. *Faculty research:* Composition, instrumental and choral performance, African-American music, Italian Baroque music and performance practice. *Unit head:* Michael Dessen, Chair, 949-824-4281, Fax: 949-824-4914, E-mail: mdessen@uci.edu. *Application contact:* Peter Chang, Department Administrator, 949-824-4281, Fax: 949-824-4914, E-mail: pechang@uci.edu.
Website: http://www.arts.uci.edu/ctsa-academic-departments-music

University of California, Los Angeles, Graduate Division, College of Letters and Science, Department of Musicology, Los Angeles, CA 90095. Offers MA, PhD. Terminal master's awarded for partial completion of doctoral program. *Degree requirements:* For master's, one foreign language, comprehensive exam, thesis; for doctorate, one foreign language, thesis/dissertation, oral and written qualifying exams. *Entrance requirements:* For master's and doctorate, GRE General Test (recommended), bachelor's degree; minimum undergraduate GPA of 3.0 (or its equivalent if letter grade system not used); writing sample. Additional exam requirements/recommendations for international students: Required—TOEFL. Electronic applications accepted.

University of California, Los Angeles, Graduate Division, School of the Arts and Architecture, Department of Ethnomusicology, Los Angeles, CA 90095. Offers MA, PhD. *Degree requirements:* For master's, one foreign language, comprehensive exam; for doctorate, 2 foreign languages, thesis/dissertation, oral and written qualifying exams. *Entrance requirements:* For master's, bachelor's degree; minimum undergraduate GPA of 3.0 (or its equivalent if letter grade system not used); writing sample; for doctorate, master's degree; minimum undergraduate GPA of 3.0 (or its equivalent if letter grade system not used); writing sample. Additional exam requirements/recommendations for international students: Required—TOEFL. Electronic applications accepted.

University of California, Los Angeles, Graduate Division, School of the Arts and Architecture, Department of Music, Los Angeles, CA 90095. Offers composition (MA, PhD); performance (MM, DMA). *Degree requirements:* For master's, one foreign language, thesis, final recital (for MM); for doctorate, one foreign language, thesis/dissertation, oral and written qualifying exams; recital (DMA). *Entrance requirements:* For master's, departmental assessment exams, bachelor's degree; minimum undergraduate GPA of 3.0 (or its equivalent if letter grade system not used); portfolio; interview; audition; for doctorate, departmental assessment exams, master's degree; minimum undergraduate GPA of 3.0 (or its equivalent if letter grade system not used); portfolio; interview. Additional exam requirements/recommendations for international students: Required—TOEFL. Electronic applications accepted.

University of California, Riverside, Graduate Division, Department of Music, Riverside, CA 92521-0102. Offers composition (PhD); ethnomusicology (MA). Terminal master's awarded for partial completion of doctoral program. *Degree requirements:* For master's, one foreign language, comprehensive exam, thesis (for some programs), oral exams; for doctorate, 2 foreign languages, comprehensive exam, thesis/dissertation, written and oral qualifying examination. *Entrance requirements:* For master's and doctorate, GRE General Test, minimum GPA of 3.0. Additional exam requirements/recommendations for international students: Required—TOEFL (minimum score 550 paper-based; 80 iBT). Electronic applications accepted. *Expenses:* Tuition, state resident: full-time $5746. Tuition, nonresident: full-time $10,780. Tuition and fees vary according to campus/location and program. *Faculty research:* Composition, ethnomusicology (especially Southeast Asian and Asian-American music), cultural musicology, gender studies, performance practice.

University of California, San Diego, Graduate Division, Department of Music, La Jolla, CA 92093. Offers contemporary music performance (DMA); music (MA, PhD). *Students:* 81 full-time (34 women), 3 part-time (0 women). 140 applicants, 14% accepted, 9 enrolled. In 2017, 4 master's, 12 doctorates awarded. *Degree requirements:* For master's, thesis; for doctorate, comprehensive exam (for some programs), thesis/dissertation (for some programs), 6 credit units of apprentice teaching; major composition (for some programs); major recital (for some programs). *Entrance requirements:* For master's, GRE General Test, musical portfolio; for doctorate, GRE General Test, master's degree; supporting musical portfolio. Additional exam requirements/recommendations for international students: Required—TOEFL (minimum score 550 paper-based; 80 iBT), IELTS (minimum score 7). *Application deadline:* For fall admission, 12/6 for domestic students. Application fee: $105 ($125 for international students). Electronic applications accepted. *Financial support:* Fellowships, research assistantships, teaching assistantships, scholarships/grants, unspecified assistantships, and readerships available. Financial award applicants required to submit FAFSA. *Faculty research:* Composition, computer music, integrative studies, performance. *Unit head:* David Borgo, Chair, 858-822-4957, E-mail: dborgo@ucsd.edu. *Application contact:* Dimple Bhatt, Graduate Coordinator, 858-534-3279, E-mail: mus-grad@ucsd.edu.
Website: http://musicweb.ucsd.edu/

University of California, Santa Barbara, Graduate Division, College of Letters and Sciences, Division of Humanities and Fine Arts, Department of Music, Santa Barbara, CA 93106-2014. Offers brass (MM); composition (MA, PhD); conducting (MM, DMA); ethnomusicology (MA, PhD); keyboard (MM, DMA); musicology (MA, PhD); piano accompanying (MM); strings (MM, DMA); theory (MA, PhD); voice (MM, DMA); woodwinds (MM); MA/PhD; MM/DMA. *Degree requirements:* For master's, variable foreign language requirement, comprehensive exam (for some programs), thesis (for some programs); for doctorate, variable foreign language requirement, comprehensive exam, thesis/dissertation. *Entrance requirements:* For master's and doctorate, GRE. Additional exam requirements/recommendations for international students: Required—TOEFL (minimum score 550 paper-based; 80 iBT), IELTS (minimum score 7). Electronic applications accepted. *Faculty research:* Music theory, ethnomusicology, musicology, music performance, music composition.

University of California, Santa Cruz, Division of Graduate Studies, Division of the Arts, Department of Music, Santa Cruz, CA 95064. Offers ethnomusicology (MA); music (PhD), including cross-cultural and interdisciplinary studies; music composition (MA, DMA), including world music composition (DMA); music composition (DMA), including computer-assisted (algorithmic) composition; performance practice (MA). *Degree requirements:* For master's, one foreign language, thesis, recital; for doctorate, one foreign language, thesis/dissertation, qualifying and final examinations. *Entrance requirements:* For master's, GRE General Test, 3 letters of recommendation, writing or composition sample, 10-20 minute unedited recording; for doctorate, GRE General Test, 3 letters of recommendation, writing sample. Additional exam requirements/recommendations for international students: Required—TOEFL (minimum score 550 paper-based; 83 iBT); Recommended—IELTS (minimum score 8). Electronic applications accepted. *Faculty research:* Western music history, new music, composition, ethnomusicology, musicology.

University of Central Arkansas, Graduate School, College of Fine Arts and Communication, Department of Music, Conway, AR 72035-0001. Offers choral conducting (MM); instrumental conducting (MM); music (PC); music education (MM); music theory (MM); performance (MM). *Accreditation:* NASM. *Program availability:* Part-time. *Degree requirements:* For master's, comprehensive exam, thesis optional. *Entrance requirements:* For master's, GRE General Test, minimum GPA of 2.7. Additional exam requirements/recommendations for international students: Required—TOEFL (minimum score 550 paper-based). Electronic applications accepted.

University of Central Florida, College of Arts and Humanities, School of Performing Arts, Orlando, FL 32816. Offers music (MA); theatre (MA, MFA), including acting (MFA), theatre for young audiences (MFA). *Accreditation:* NASM; NCATE. *Program availability:* Part-time. *Students:* 32 full-time (14 women), 18 part-time (8 women); includes 11 minority (1 Black or African American, non-Hispanic/Latino; 8 Hispanic/Latino; 2 Two or more races, non-Hispanic/Latino), 4 international. Average age 33. 51 applicants, 59% accepted, 18 enrolled. In 2017, 17 master's awarded. *Degree requirements:* For master's, comprehensive exam, thesis or alternative. *Entrance requirements:* For master's, GRE General Test, letters of recommendation, writing sample. Additional exam requirements/recommendations for international students: Required—TOEFL. *Application deadline:* For fall admission, 7/15 for domestic students; for spring admission, 12/1 for domestic students. Application fee: $30. Electronic applications accepted. *Expenses:* Tuition, state resident: part-time $288.16 per credit hour. Tuition, nonresident: part-time $1073.31 per credit hour. Tuition and fees vary according to program. *Financial support:* In 2017–18, 26 students received support, including 7 fellowships with partial tuition reimbursements available (averaging $7,857 per year), 5 research assistantships with partial tuition reimbursements available (averaging $5,539 per year), 21 teaching assistantships with partial tuition reimbursements available (averaging $7,179 per year); career-related internships or fieldwork, Federal Work-Study, institutionally sponsored loans, health care benefits, tuition waivers (partial), and

unspecified assistantships also available. Financial award application deadline: 3/1; financial award applicants required to submit FAFSA. *Unit head:* Dr. Michael Wainstein, Director, 407-823-2519, Fax: 407-823-3378, E-mail: michael.wainstein@ucf.edu. *Application contact:* Associate Director, Graduate Admissions, 407-823-2766, Fax: 407-823-6442, E-mail: gradadmissions@ucf.edu.
Website: http://performingarts.cah.ucf.edu/

University of Central Missouri, The Graduate School, Warrensburg, MO 64093. Offers accountancy (MA); accounting (MBA); applied mathematics (MS); aviation safety (MA); biology (MS); business administration (MBA); career and technical education leadership (MS); college student personnel administration (MS); communication (MA); computer science (MS); counseling (MS); criminal justice (MS); educational leadership (Ed D); educational technology (MS); elementary and early childhood education (MSE); English (MA); environmental studies (MA); finance (MBA); history (MA); human services/educational technology (Ed S); human services/learning resources (Ed S); human services/professional counseling (Ed S); industrial hygiene (MS); industrial management (MS); information systems (MBA); information technology (MS); kinesiology (MS); library science and information services (MS); literacy education (MSE); marketing (MBA); mathematics (MS); music (MA); occupational safety management (MS); psychology (MS); rural family nursing (MS); school administration (MSE); social gerontology (MS); sociology (MA); special education (MSE); speech language pathology (MS); superintendency (Ed S); teaching (MAT); teaching English as a second language (MA); technology (MS); technology management (PhD); theatre (MA). *Program availability:* Part-time, 100% online, blended/hybrid learning. *Faculty:* 337 full-time (145 women), 41 part-time/adjunct (28 women). *Students:* 785 full-time (398 women), 1,633 part-time (1,063 women); includes 231 minority (102 Black or African American, non-Hispanic/Latino; 4 American Indian or Alaska Native, non-Hispanic/Latino; 16 Asian, non-Hispanic/Latino; 52 Hispanic/Latino; 57 Two or more races, non-Hispanic/Latino), 692 international. Average age 30. In 2017, 2,605 master's, 122 other advanced degrees awarded. *Degree requirements:* For master's and Ed S, comprehensive exam (for some programs), thesis (for some programs). *Entrance requirements:* Additional exam requirements/recommendations for international students: Required—TOEFL (minimum score 550 paper-based; 79 iBT). *Application deadline:* For fall admission, 6/1 priority date for domestic and international students; for spring admission, 10/1 priority date for domestic and international students; for summer admission, 4/1 priority date for domestic and international students. Applications are processed on a rolling basis. Application fee: $30 ($75 for international students). Electronic applications accepted. *Expenses:* Tuition, state resident: full-time $8771; part-time $292.35 per credit hour. Tuition, nonresident: full-time $17,541; part-time $584.70 per credit hour. *Required fees:* $372; $24.78 per credit hour. *Financial support:* In 2017–18, 99 students received support. Research assistantships, teaching assistantships, career-related internships or fieldwork, Federal Work-Study, scholarships/grants, and administrative and laboratory assistantships available. Support available to part-time students. Financial award application deadline: 3/1; financial award applicants required to submit FAFSA. *Unit head:* Shellie Hewitt, Director of Graduate and International Student Services, 660-543-4621, Fax: 660-543-4778, E-mail: hewitt@ucmo.edu. *Application contact:* 660-543-4621, E-mail: admit_intl@ucmo.edu.
Website: http://www.ucmo.edu/graduate/

University of Central Oklahoma, The Jackson College of Graduate Studies, College of Fine Arts and Design, Department of Music, Edmond, OK 73034-5209. Offers jazz studies (MM), including music production, performance; music (MM), including collaborative piano, composition, conducting, instrumental performance, music education, musical theatre, piano pedagogy, piano performance, vocal pedagogy, vocal performance. *Accreditation:* NASM. *Program availability:* Part-time. *Faculty:* 25 full-time (10 women), 18 part-time/adjunct (6 women). *Students:* 46 full-time (21 women), 15 part-time (9 women); includes 10 minority (4 Black or African American, non-Hispanic/Latino; 1 American Indian or Alaska Native, non-Hispanic/Latino; 4 Hispanic/Latino; 1 Two or more races, non-Hispanic/Latino), 19 international. Average age 29. 44 applicants, 66% accepted, 21 enrolled. In 2017, 21 master's awarded. *Degree requirements:* For master's, comprehensive exam, recital or project. *Entrance requirements:* For master's, interview, audition. Additional exam requirements/recommendations for international students: Required—TOEFL (minimum score 550 paper-based; 79 iBT), IELTS (minimum score 6.5). *Application deadline:* For fall admission, 7/15 for international students; for spring admission, 11/15 for international students. Applications are processed on a rolling basis. Application fee: $60. Electronic applications accepted. *Expenses:* Tuition, state resident: full-time $5375; part-time $268.75 per credit hour. Tuition, nonresident: full-time $13,295; part-time $664.75 per credit hour. *Required fees:* $626; $31.30 per credit hour. One-time fee: $50. Tuition and fees vary according to program. *Financial support:* In 2017–18, 25 students received support, including 1 research assistantship with partial tuition reimbursement available (averaging $2,958 per year), 16 teaching assistantships with partial tuition reimbursements available (averaging $6,765 per year); career-related internships or fieldwork, Federal Work-Study, scholarships/grants, tuition waivers (partial), and unspecified assistantships also available. Financial award application deadline: 3/31; financial award applicants required to submit FAFSA. *Unit head:* Dr. Brian Lamb, Director of the School of Music, 405-974-5004. *Application contact:* Dr. Samuel Magrill, Graduate Advisor, 405-974-5684, E-mail: gradcoll@uco.edu.
Website: http://sites.uco.edu/cfad/academics/music/index.asp

University of Chicago, Division of the Humanities, Department of Music, Chicago, IL 60637. Offers composition (PhD); ethnomusicology (PhD); music history and theory (PhD). *Students:* 61 full-time (24 women); includes 12 minority (2 Black or African American, non-Hispanic/Latino; 1 Asian, non-Hispanic/Latino; 6 Hispanic/Latino; 3 Two or more races, non-Hispanic/Latino), 18 international. Average age 30. 123 applicants, 11% accepted, 8 enrolled. In 2017, 6 doctorates awarded. Terminal master's awarded for partial completion of doctoral program. *Degree requirements:* For doctorate, 3 foreign languages, comprehensive exam, thesis/dissertation. *Entrance requirements:* For doctorate, GRE General Test, 15-20 page writing sample, statement of purpose, 3 letters of recommendation, transcripts for all previous degrees and institutions attended. Additional exam requirements/recommendations for international students: Required—TOEFL (minimum score 104 iBT), IELTS (minimum score 7). *Application deadline:* For fall admission, 12/15 for domestic and international students. Application fee: $90. Electronic applications accepted. *Financial support:* In 2017–18, fellowships with full tuition reimbursements (averaging $27,000 per year) were awarded; teaching assistantships with full tuition reimbursements, Federal Work-Study, institutionally sponsored loans, scholarships/grants, and health care benefits also available. Financial award application deadline: 12/15. *Faculty research:* Early music, history of music theory, historical anthropology of music, Jewish music, popular and vernacular music. *Unit head:* Berthold Hoeckner, Chair, 773-702-8484. *Application contact:* Michael Beetley, Assistant Dean of Students, Admissions and Fellowships, 773-702-1552, Fax: 773-834-9148, E-mail: humanitiesadmissions@uchicago.edu.
Website: http://music.uchicago.edu/

University of Chicago, Division of the Humanities, Master of Arts Program in the Humanities, Chicago, IL 60637. Offers art history (MA); cinema and media studies (MA); classic languages (MA); comparative literature (MA); creative writing (MA); cultural policy studies (MA); digital humanities (MA); East Asian languages and civilizations (MA); English language and literature (MA); gender and sexuality studies (MA); Germanic studies (MA); linguistics (MA); music (MA); near Eastern languages and civilizations (MA); philosophy (MA); poetics (MA); race, politics and culture (MA); Romance languages and literatures (MA); Slavic languages and literatures (MA); South Asian languages and civilizations (MA); theater and performance studies (MA). *Students:* 95 full-time (50 women), 6 part-time (4 women); includes 22 minority (1 Black or African American, non-Hispanic/Latino; 10 Asian, non-Hispanic/Latino; 11 Hispanic/Latino), 19 international. Average age 26. 708 applicants, 75% accepted, 101 enrolled. In 2017, 91 master's awarded. *Degree requirements:* For master's, thesis. *Entrance requirements:* For master's, GRE General Test, 10-15 page writing sample, statement of purpose, 3 letters of recommendation, transcripts for all previous degrees and institutions attended. Additional exam requirements/recommendations for international students: Required—TOEFL (minimum score 104 iBT), IELTS (minimum score 7). *Application deadline:* For fall admission, 1/3 priority date for domestic and international students. Application fee: $90. Electronic applications accepted. *Expenses:* Contact institution. *Financial support:* In 2017–18, fellowships with partial tuition reimbursements (averaging $12,000 per year) were awarded; Federal Work-Study, institutionally sponsored loans, scholarships/grants, and tuition waivers (partial) also available. Financial award application deadline: 4/30. *Unit head:* Thomas Christensen, Director, 773-834-1201, Fax: 773-834-7526, E-mail: ma-humanities@uchicago.edu. *Application contact:* Michael Beetley, Assistant Dean of Students for Admissions, 773-834-1552, E-mail: humanitiesadmissions@uchicago.edu.
Website: http://maph.uchicago.edu/

University of Cincinnati, Graduate School, College-Conservatory of Music, Division of Composition, Musicology and Theory, Cincinnati, OH 45221. Offers composition (MM, DMA); music history (MM); music theory (MM, PhD); musicology (PhD). *Accreditation:* NASM. *Degree requirements:* For master's, variable foreign language requirement, comprehensive exam, thesis; for doctorate, variable foreign language requirement, comprehensive exam, thesis/dissertation. *Entrance requirements:* For master's and doctorate, GRE General Test, interview. Additional exam requirements/recommendations for international students: Required—TOEFL (minimum score 520 paper-based). Electronic applications accepted. *Expenses: Tuition, area resident:* Full-time $14,468. Tuition, state resident: full-time $14,968; part-time $754 per credit hour. Tuition, nonresident: full-time $24,210; part-time $1311 per credit hour. *International tuition:* $26,460 full-time. *Required fees:* $3958; $84 per credit hour. One-time fee: $85 full-time. Tuition and fees vary according to course load, degree level and program.

University of Cincinnati, Graduate School, College-Conservatory of Music, Division of Ensembles and Conducting, Cincinnati, OH 45221. Offers choral conducting (MM, DMA); orchestral conducting (MM, DMA); wind conducting (MM, DMA). *Accreditation:* NASM. *Degree requirements:* For master's, comprehensive exam, conducting performances; for doctorate, one foreign language, comprehensive exam, thesis/dissertation, conducting performances, lecture recital. *Entrance requirements:* For master's and doctorate, GRE General Test, audition, interview. Additional exam requirements/recommendations for international students: Required—TOEFL (minimum score 520 paper-based). Electronic applications accepted. *Expenses: Tuition, area resident:* Full-time $14,468. Tuition, state resident: full-time $14,968; part-time $754 per credit hour. Tuition, nonresident: full-time $24,210; part-time $1311 per credit hour. *International tuition:* $26,460 full-time. *Required fees:* $3958; $84 per credit hour. One-time fee: $85 full-time. Tuition and fees vary according to course load, degree level and program.

University of Cincinnati, Graduate School, College-Conservatory of Music, Division of Keyboard Studies, Cincinnati, OH 45221. Offers MM, DMA, AD. *Degree requirements:* For master's, comprehensive exam; for doctorate, one foreign language, comprehensive exam, thesis/dissertation. *Entrance requirements:* For master's and doctorate, GRE General Test, audition; for AD, audition. Additional exam requirements/recommendations for international students: Required—TOEFL (minimum score 520 paper-based). Electronic applications accepted. *Expenses: Tuition, area resident:* Full-time $14,468. Tuition, state resident: full-time $14,968; part-time $754 per credit hour. Tuition, nonresident: full-time $24,210; part-time $1311 per credit hour. *International tuition:* $26,460 full-time. *Required fees:* $3958; $84 per credit hour. One-time fee: $85 full-time. Tuition and fees vary according to course load, degree level and program.

University of Cincinnati, Graduate School, College-Conservatory of Music, Division of Performance Studies, Cincinnati, OH 45221. Offers performance (MM, DMA, AD). MM, DMA, and AD are available for every instrument. *Accreditation:* NASM. *Degree requirements:* For master's, comprehensive exam, recitals; for doctorate, one foreign language, comprehensive exam, thesis/dissertation, recitals; for AD, recitals. *Entrance requirements:* For master's and doctorate, GRE General Test, audition. Additional exam requirements/recommendations for international students: Required—TOEFL (minimum score 520 paper-based). Electronic applications accepted. *Expenses: Tuition, area resident:* Full-time $14,468. Tuition, state resident: full-time $14,968; part-time $754 per credit hour. Tuition, nonresident: full-time $24,210; part-time $1311 per credit hour. *International tuition:* $26,460 full-time. *Required fees:* $3958; $84 per credit hour. One-time fee: $85 full-time. Tuition and fees vary according to course load, degree level and program. *Faculty research:* Performance, guest teaching.

University of Cincinnati, Graduate School, College-Conservatory of Music, Division of Theatre Arts, Production and Arts Administration, Cincinnati, OH 45221. Offers arts administration (MA); directing (MFA); theater design and production (MFA); voice and opera (MM, DMA); MBA/MA. *Accreditation:* NAST (one or more programs are accredited). *Degree requirements:* For master's, final project. *Entrance requirements:* For master's, GMAT (MA), audition/interview. Additional exam requirements/recommendations for international students: Required—TOEFL (minimum score 520 paper-based). Electronic applications accepted. *Expenses: Tuition, area resident:* Full-time $14,468. Tuition, state resident: full-time $14,968; part-time $754 per credit hour. Tuition, nonresident: full-time $24,210; part-time $1311 per credit hour. *International tuition:* $26,460 full-time. *Required fees:* $3958; $84 per credit hour. One-time fee: $85 full-time. Tuition and fees vary according to course load, degree level and program.

University of Colorado Boulder, Graduate School, College of Music, Boulder, CO 80309. Offers composition (M Mus, D Mus A); conducting (M Mus); instrumental conducting and literature (D Mus A); literature and performance of choral music (D Mus A); music education (M Mus Ed, PhD), including choral or wind instrument conducting (M Mus Ed), general (M Mus Ed), Kodaly concepts (M Mus Ed), piano pedagogy (M Mus Ed), primary instruments (M Mus Ed), secondary instruments (M Mus Ed), voice pedagogy (M Mus Ed); music theory (M Mus); performance (M Mus, D Mus A); performance and pedagogy (M Mus, D Mus A). *Accreditation:* NASM. *Faculty:* 64 full-time (19 women). *Students:* 165 full-time (79 women), 35 part-time (12 women); includes 22 minority (3 Black or African American, non-Hispanic/Latino; 3 Asian, non-Hispanic/Latino; 10 Hispanic/Latino; 6 Two or more races, non-Hispanic/Latino), 19 international. Average age 29. 459 applicants, 41% accepted, 65 enrolled. In 2017, 46 master's, 22 doctorates awarded. Terminal master's awarded for partial completion of doctoral program. *Degree requirements:* For master's, variable foreign language requirement, comprehensive exam, thesis or alternative, recital; for doctorate, variable foreign language requirement, thesis/dissertation. *Entrance requirements:* For master's, GRE General Test, GRE Subject Test (music literature), minimum

undergraduate GPA of 2.75; for doctorate, GRE General Test, GRE Subject Test, audition, sample of research. *Application deadline:* For fall admission, 12/1 for domestic and international students; for spring admission, 10/1 for domestic and international students. Applications are processed on a rolling basis. Application fee: $60 ($80 for international students). Electronic applications accepted. Application fee is waived when completed online. *Financial support:* In 2017–18, 546 students received support, including 250 fellowships (averaging $2,731 per year), 116 teaching assistantships with full and partial tuition reimbursements available (averaging $19,272 per year); research assistantships, institutionally sponsored loans, scholarships/grants, health care benefits, and unspecified assistantships also available. Financial award application deadline: 2/15; financial award applicants required to submit FAFSA. *Faculty research:* Music; instrumental music; performing arts; chamber music; musicology/music theory. *Total annual research expenditures:* $30,622. *Application contact:* E-mail: gradmusc@colorado.edu.
Website: http://music.colorado.edu/

University of Colorado Denver, College of Arts and Media, Denver, CO 80217. Offers recording arts (MS), including media forensics, recording arts. *Accreditation:* NASM. *Program availability:* Part-time, evening/weekend. *Degree requirements:* For master's, 34 credits, thesis/portfolio. *Entrance requirements:* For master's, GRE General Test (minimum scores higher than 50th percentile for all sections), minimum undergraduate GPA of 3.0, portfolio, resume, interview, 3 letters of recommendation. Additional exam requirements/recommendations for international students: Required—TOEFL (minimum score 70 iBT). Electronic applications accepted. *Expenses:* Contact institution. *Faculty research:* Audio forensics, audio pedagogy, concert recordings, digital audio workstations, music law.

University of Connecticut, Graduate School, School of Fine Arts, Department of Music, Storrs, CT 06269. Offers conducting (M Mus, DMA); historical musicology (MA); music theory (MA); music theory and history (PhD); performance (M Mus, DMA). *Accreditation:* NASM. Terminal master's awarded for partial completion of doctoral program. *Degree requirements:* For master's, comprehensive exam; for doctorate, thesis/dissertation. *Entrance requirements:* For master's, GRE General Test, GRE Subject Test, audition; for doctorate, GRE Subject Test, MAT, audition. Additional exam requirements/recommendations for international students: Required—TOEFL (minimum score 550 paper-based).

University of Delaware, College of Arts and Sciences, Department of Music, Newark, DE 19716. Offers composition (MM); music education (MM); performance (MM). *Accreditation:* NASM. *Program availability:* Part-time. *Entrance requirements:* For master's, audition. Additional exam requirements/recommendations for international students: Required—TOEFL. Electronic applications accepted. *Faculty research:* Teaching of music.

University of Denver, Division of Arts, Humanities and Social Sciences, Lamont School of Music, Denver, CO 80208. Offers composition (MM); composition - jazz emphasis (MM); conducting (MM, Certificate); jazz studies (Certificate); music theory (MA); musicology (MA); orchestral studies (Certificate); pedagogy (MM); performance (MM, Certificate); performance - jazz emphasis (MM); Suzuki teaching (Certificate). *Accreditation:* NASM. *Program availability:* Part-time. *Faculty:* 32 full-time (9 women), 33 part-time/adjunct (15 women). *Students:* 27 full-time (9 women), 76 part-time (38 women); includes 20 minority (3 Black or African American, non-Hispanic/Latino; 3 Asian, non-Hispanic/Latino; 7 Hispanic/Latino; 7 Two or more races, non-Hispanic/Latino), 14 international. Average age 28. 149 applicants, 79% accepted, 54 enrolled. In 2017, 37 master's, 3 other advanced degrees awarded. *Degree requirements:* For master's, one foreign language, comprehensive exam, recital or project (for performance), thesis (for musicology, music theory, piano pedagogy). *Entrance requirements:* For master's, GRE General Test (for MA only), bachelor's degree, transcripts, personal statement, resume, three letters of recommendation, pre-screen audition (for performance), portfolio (for composition), essay or research paper (for MA only); for Certificate, bachelor's degree, transcripts, personal statement, resume, letters of recommendation, pre-screen video recording or music audition. Additional exam requirements/recommendations for international students: Required—TOEFL (minimum score 550 paper-based; 80 iBT). *Application deadline:* For fall admission, 1/15 priority date for domestic and international students. Applications are processed on a rolling basis. Application fee: $65. Electronic applications accepted. *Expenses:* $31,935 per year full-time. *Financial support:* In 2017–18, 89 students received support, including 7 teaching assistantships with tuition reimbursements available (averaging $6,917 per year); career-related internships or fieldwork, Federal Work-Study, institutionally sponsored loans, scholarships/grants, tuition waivers, and unspecified assistantships also available. Support available to part-time students. Financial award application deadline: 2/15; financial award applicants required to submit FAFSA. *Faculty research:* Performance, jazz studies and commercial music, musicology, music theory, composition, music pedagogy, music recording and production. *Unit head:* Dr. Nancy Cochran, Professor and Director, 303-871-6986, Fax: 303-871-3118, E-mail: nancy.cochran@du.edu. *Application contact:* Stephen Campbell, Director of Admission, 303-871-6973, Fax: 303-871-3118, E-mail: stephen.l.campbell@du.edu.
Website: http://www.du.edu/ahss/lamont/index.html

University of Florida, Graduate School, College of The Arts, School of Music, Gainesville, FL 32611. Offers choral conducting (MM); composition (MM, PhD); electronic music (MM); ethnomusicology (MM); instrumental conducting (MM); music (MM, PhD); music education (MM, PhD), including choral conducting (MM), composition (MM), electronic music (MM), ethnomusicology (MM), instrumental conducting (MM), music education (MM), music history and literature (MM), music theory (MM), performance (MM), piano pedagogy (MM); music history and literature (MM, PhD); music theory (MM); performance (MM); sacred music (MM). *Accreditation:* NASM. *Degree requirements:* For master's, variable foreign language requirement, comprehensive exam, thesis, recital; for doctorate, thesis/dissertation. *Entrance requirements:* For master's and doctorate, GRE General Test, audition, minimum GPA of 3.0. Additional exam requirements/recommendations for international students: Required—TOEFL (minimum score 550 paper-based; 80 iBT), IELTS (minimum score 6). Electronic applications accepted.

University of Georgia, Franklin College of Arts and Sciences, Hugh Hodgson School of Music, Athens, GA 30602. Offers composition (MM, DMA); conducting (MM, DMA); music (PhD); music education (MM Ed, Ed D); musicology (MA); performance (MM, DMA). Ed D offered jointly with College of Education. *Accreditation:* NASM. *Degree requirements:* For master's, variable foreign language requirement, thesis (MA); for doctorate, variable foreign language requirement, thesis/dissertation. *Entrance requirements:* For master's and doctorate, GRE General Test. Electronic applications accepted.

University of Hartford, The Hartt School, West Hartford, CT 06117-1599. Offers choral conducting (MM Ed); composition (MM, DMA, Artist Diploma, Diploma); conducting (MM, DMA, Artist Diploma, Diploma), including choral (MM, Diploma), instrumental (MM, Diploma); early childhood education (MM Ed); instrumental conducting (MM Ed); Kodály (MM Ed); music (CAGS); music education (DMA, PhD); music history (MM); music theory (MM); pedagogy (MM Ed); performance (MM, MM Ed, DMA, Artist Diploma, Diploma); research (MM Ed); technology (MM Ed). *Program availability:* Part-time. *Degree requirements:* For master's, variable foreign language requirement, thesis (for some programs), recital; for doctorate, variable foreign language requirement, thesis/dissertation (for some programs), recital; for other advanced degree, recital. *Entrance requirements:* For master's, audition, letters of recommendation; for doctorate, proficiency exam, audition, interview, research paper; for other advanced degree, audition. Additional exam requirements/recommendations for international students: Required—TOEFL. Electronic applications accepted. *Expenses:* Contact institution.

University of Hawaii at Manoa, Office of Graduate Education, College of Arts and Humanities, Department of Music, Honolulu, HI 96822. Offers M Mus, MA, PhD. *Accreditation:* NASM. *Program availability:* Part-time. *Degree requirements:* For master's, variable foreign language requirement, thesis optional; for doctorate, variable foreign language requirement, comprehensive exam, thesis/dissertation. *Entrance requirements:* For master's, GRE General Test, diagnostic exams in acoustics theory; for doctorate, diagnostic exams in music history and theory, GRE General Test. Additional exam requirements/recommendations for international students: Required—TOEFL (minimum score 540 paper-based; 76 iBT), IELTS (minimum score 5). *Faculty research:* Original compositions, nineteenth century German music, Korean and Indonesian music, piano/voice performance, Pacific music.

University of Houston, Kathrine G. McGovern College of the Arts, Moores School of Music, Houston, TX 77204. Offers accompanying and chamber music (MM); applied music (MM); composition (MM); music education (DMA); music theory (MM); performance (DMA). *Accreditation:* NASM. *Program availability:* Part-time. *Degree requirements:* For master's, one foreign language, comprehensive exam, recital; for doctorate, one foreign language, comprehensive exam, thesis/dissertation. *Entrance requirements:* For master's, audition, resume, 3 letters of recommendation; for doctorate, writing sample, audition, statement of purpose, resume. Additional exam requirements/recommendations for international students: Required—TOEFL (minimum score 550 paper-based; 79 iBT), IELTS (minimum score 6.5). Electronic applications accepted. *Faculty research:* Twentieth century music, Baroque music, history of music theory, music analysis.

University of Idaho, College of Graduate Studies, College of Letters, Arts and Social Sciences, Lionel Hampton School of Music, Moscow, ID 83844. Offers M Mus, MA. *Accreditation:* NASM. *Faculty:* 23 full-time. *Students:* 19. Average age 28. In 2017, 3 master's awarded. *Degree requirements:* For master's, thesis or alternative. *Entrance requirements:* For master's, minimum GPA of 3.0. Additional exam requirements/recommendations for international students: Required—TOEFL (minimum score 88 iBT). *Application deadline:* For fall admission, 8/1 for domestic students; for spring admission, 12/15 for domestic students. Applications are processed on a rolling basis. Application fee: $60. Electronic applications accepted. *Expenses:* Tuition, state resident: full-time $6722; part-time $430 per credit hour. Tuition, nonresident: full-time $23,046; part-time $1337 per credit hour. *Required fees:* $2142; $63 per credit hour. *Financial support:* Research assistantships and teaching assistantships available. Financial award applicants required to submit FAFSA. *Unit head:* Dr. Torrey Lawrence, Director, 208-885-6231, E-mail: music@uidaho.edu. *Application contact:* Sean Scoggin, Director of Graduate Admissions, 208-885-4723, Fax: 208-885-4406, E-mail: graduateadmissions@uidaho.edu.
Website: https://www.uidaho.edu/class/music

University of Illinois at Urbana–Champaign, Graduate College, College of Fine and Applied Arts, School of Music, Champaign, IL 61820. Offers music (M Mus, AD, DMA); music education (MME, PhD); musicology (PhD). *Accreditation:* NASM.

The University of Iowa, Graduate College, College of Liberal Arts and Sciences, School of Music, Iowa City, IA 52242-1316. Offers MA, MFA, DMA, PhD. *Accreditation:* NASM. *Degree requirements:* For master's, thesis (for some programs), exam; for doctorate, comprehensive exam, thesis/dissertation. *Entrance requirements:* For master's and doctorate, minimum GPA of 3.0. Additional exam requirements/recommendations for international students: Required—TOEFL (minimum score 550 paper-based; 81 iBT). Electronic applications accepted.

The University of Kansas, Graduate Studies, School of Music, Program in Music, Lawrence, KS 66045. Offers MM, DMA, PhD. *Program availability:* Part-time. *Students:* 131 full-time (55 women), 22 part-time (11 women); includes 11 minority (2 Black or African American, non-Hispanic/Latino; 4 Asian, non-Hispanic/Latino; 5 Two or more races, non-Hispanic/Latino), 48 international. Average age 30. 189 applicants, 57% accepted, 37 enrolled. In 2017, 18 master's, 23 doctorates awarded. *Entrance requirements:* For master's, KU Musicology and Music Theory diagnostic exam, minimum GPA of 3.0, resume/curriculum vitae, 3 letters of reference, official transcripts, statement of purpose; for doctorate, GRE (for PhD); KU Musicology and Music Theory diagnostic exam, minimum GPA of 3.0, audition (for DMA), resume/curriculum vitae, 3 letters of reference, official transcripts, statement of purpose. *Application deadline:* For fall admission, 12/1 priority date for domestic and international students; for summer admission, 4/15 for domestic students, 2/15 for international students. Application fee: $65 ($85 for international students). Electronic applications accepted. *Financial support:* Fellowships, teaching assistantships, institutionally sponsored loans, scholarships/grants, and unspecified assistantships available. Financial award application deadline: 12/1; financial award applicants required to submit FAFSA. *Faculty research:* Musicology, music theory, composition, performance, conducting. *Unit head:* Dr. Martin Bergee, Associate Dean for Academic Affairs, 785-864-3421, Fax: 785-864-5866, E-mail: music@ku.edu. *Application contact:* Michael Austin, Administrative Professional, 785-864-2862, E-mail: michael.austin@ku.edu.
Website: http://www.music.ku.edu

University of Kentucky, Graduate School, College of Fine Arts, Program in Music, Lexington, KY 40506-0032. Offers composition (MM, DMA); conducting (MM, DMA); music education (MM, PhD); music theory (MA, PhD); music therapy (MM); musicology (MA, PhD); performance (MM, DMA); sacred music (MM). *Accreditation:* NASM. *Program availability:* Part-time, evening/weekend. *Degree requirements:* For master's, variable foreign language requirement, comprehensive exam, thesis (for some programs); for doctorate, variable foreign language requirement, comprehensive exam, thesis/dissertation. *Entrance requirements:* For master's, GRE General Test, minimum undergraduate GPA of 2.75; for doctorate, GRE General Test, minimum undergraduate GPA of 2.75, graduate 3.0. Additional exam requirements/recommendations for international students: Required—TOEFL (minimum score 550 paper-based). Electronic applications accepted. *Faculty research:* Musicology, music theory, jazz, music education, performance and conducting.

University of Lethbridge, School of Graduate Studies, Lethbridge, AB T1K 3M4, Canada. Offers addictions counseling (M Sc); agricultural biotechnology (M Sc); agricultural studies (M Sc, MA); anthropology (MA); archaeology (M Sc, MA); art (MA, MFA); biochemistry (M Sc); biological sciences (M Sc); biomolecular science (PhD); biosystems and biodiversity (PhD); Canadian studies (MA); chemistry (M Sc); computer science (M Sc); computer science and geographical information science (M Sc); counseling (MC); counseling psychology (M Ed); dramatic arts (MA); earth, space, and physical science (PhD); economics (MA); education (MA, PhD); educational leadership (M Ed); English (MA); environmental science (M Sc); evolution and behavior (PhD); exercise science (M Sc); French (MA); French/German (MA); French/Spanish (MA);

general education (M Ed); geography (M Sc, MA); German (MA); health sciences (M Sc); individualized multidisciplinary (M Sc, MA); kinesiology (M Sc, MA); management (M Sc), including accounting, finance, human resource management and labor relations, information systems, international management, marketing, policy and strategy; mathematics (M Sc); music (M Mus, MA); Native American studies (MA); neuroscience (M Sc, PhD); new media (MA, MFA); nursing (M Sc, MN); philosophy (MA); physics (M Sc); political science (MA); psychology (M Sc, MA); religious studies (MA); sociology (MA); theatre and dramatic arts (MFA); theoretical and computational science (PhD); urban and regional studies (MA); women and gender studies (MA). *Program availability:* Part-time, evening/weekend. *Degree requirements:* For master's, thesis (for some programs); for doctorate, comprehensive exam, thesis/dissertation. *Entrance requirements:* For master's, GMAT (for M Sc in management), bachelor's degree in related field, minimum GPA of 3.0 during previous 20 graded semester courses, 2 years' teaching or related experience (M Ed); for doctorate, master's degree, minimum graduate GPA of 3.5. Additional exam requirements/recommendations for international students: Required—TOEFL (minimum score 580 paper-based; 93 iBT). Electronic applications accepted. *Faculty research:* Movement and brain plasticity, gibberellin physiology, photosynthesis, carbon cycling, molecular properties of main-group ring components.

University of Louisiana at Lafayette, College of the Arts, School of Music, Lafayette, LA 70504. Offers conducting (MM); pedagogy (MM); vocal and instrumental performance (MM). *Accreditation:* NASM. *Degree requirements:* For master's, thesis or alternative. *Entrance requirements:* For master's, GRE General Test, minimum GPA of 2.75. Additional exam requirements/recommendations for international students: Required—TOEFL (minimum score 550 paper-based). Electronic applications accepted. *Faculty research:* Nineteenth century American music, trumpet pedagogy, fifteenth century Renaissance polyphony, Charles Ives.

University of Louisville, Graduate School, School of Music, Louisville, KY 40292-0001. Offers composition (MM); electronic composition (MM); music education (MME); music history and literature (MM); music performance (MM), including choral conducting, instrumental, jazz composition, jazz performance, orchestral conducting, organ performance, piano pedagogy, piano performance, string pedagogy, vocal performance, wind band performance, wind conducting; music theory (MM). *Accreditation:* NASM. *Program availability:* Part-time. *Faculty:* 38 full-time (11 women), 39 part-time/adjunct (16 women). *Students:* 51 full-time (14 women), 3 part-time (2 women); includes 8 minority (3 Black or African American, non-Hispanic/Latino; 2 Asian, non-Hispanic/Latino; 2 Hispanic/Latino; 1 Two or more races, non-Hispanic/Latino), 7 international. Average age 26. 73 applicants, 53% accepted, 29 enrolled. In 2017, 29 master's awarded. *Degree requirements:* For master's, variable foreign language requirement, comprehensive exam, thesis (for some programs), recital (for performance), paper or thesis (for music education), major composition (for composition). *Entrance requirements:* For master's, music history and theory entrance exams, jazz history and theory entrance exam (for jazz majors), audition, portfolio. Additional exam requirements/recommendations for international students: Required—TOEFL (minimum score 79 iBT) or IELTS (6.5). Application fee: $60. Electronic applications accepted. *Expenses:* Contact institution. *Financial support:* In 2017–18, 1 fellowship with full tuition reimbursement (averaging $12,000 per year), 12 teaching assistantships with full tuition reimbursements (averaging $12,000 per year) were awarded; Federal Work-Study, scholarships/grants, health care benefits, and unspecified assistantships also available. Financial award application deadline: 3/1. *Faculty research:* Composition, musicology, performance, pedagogy, analysis and theoretical application. *Total annual research expenditures:* $87,500. *Unit head:* Dr. Christopher P. Doane, Dean, 502-852-6907, Fax: 502-852-0520, E-mail: c0doan01@louisville.edu. *Application contact:* Laura Angermeier, Admissions Counselor/Senior Advising Counselor, 502-852-1623, Fax: 502-852-0520, E-mail: leange01@louisville.edu.
Website: http://www.louisville.edu/music/

University of Maine, Graduate School, College of Liberal Arts and Sciences, School of Performing Arts, Orono, ME 04469. Offers MM. *Accreditation:* NASM. *Program availability:* Part-time. *Faculty:* 10 full-time (3 women), 5 part-time/adjunct (2 women). *Students:* 5 full-time (2 women), 2 part-time (1 woman), 2 international. Average age 30. 7 applicants, 86% accepted, 3 enrolled. In 2017, 3 master's awarded. *Entrance requirements:* For master's, audition. Additional exam requirements/recommendations for international students: Required—TOEFL. *Application deadline:* For fall admission, 2/1 priority date for domestic students. Applications are processed on a rolling basis. Application fee: $65. Electronic applications accepted. *Expenses:* Tuition, state resident: full-time $7722; part-time $429 per credit hour. Tuition, nonresident: full-time $25,146; part-time $1397 per credit hour. *Required fees:* $1162; $581 per credit hour. *Financial support:* In 2017–18, 3 students received support, including 3 teaching assistantships with full tuition reimbursements available (averaging $10,100 per year); career-related internships or fieldwork, Federal Work-Study, institutionally sponsored loans, scholarships/grants, and tuition waivers (full and partial) also available. Support available to part-time students. Financial award application deadline: 3/1. *Faculty research:* Music education, music performance, musicology, music theory and composition. *Unit head:* Dr. Beth Wiemann, Chair, 207-581-1244, Fax: 207-581-4701. *Application contact:* Scott G. Delcourt, Assistant Vice President for Graduate Studies and Senior Associate Dean, 207-581-3291, Fax: 207-581-3232, E-mail: graduate@maine.edu.
Website: http://umaine.edu/spa/

The University of Manchester, School of Arts, Histories and Cultures, Manchester, United Kingdom. Offers anthropology, media and performance (PhD); applied theatre professional (PhD); archaeology (PhD); art history and visual studies (PhD); arts management and cultural policy (PhD); classics and ancient history (PhD); composition (PhD); creative writing (PhD); drama (PhD); economic and social history (PhD); electroacoustic composition (PhD); English and American studies (PhD); history (PhD); humanitarianism and conflict response (PhD); museology (PhD); music (PhD); musicology (PhD); religions and theology (PhD).

University of Manitoba, Faculty of Graduate Studies, Desautels Faculty of Music, Winnipeg, MB R3T 2N2, Canada. Offers M Mus.

University of Maryland, Baltimore County, The Graduate School, College of Arts, Humanities and Social Sciences, Department of Music, Baltimore, MD 21250-0001. Offers American contemporary music (Postbaccalaureate Certificate). *Accreditation:* NASM. *Program availability:* Part-time. *Faculty:* 3 full-time (2 women). *Students:* 2 full-time (1 woman), 1 (woman) part-time; includes 1 minority (Asian, non-Hispanic/Latino). Average age 22. 3 applicants, 67% accepted, 2 enrolled. In 2017, 1 Postbaccalaureate Certificate awarded. *Degree requirements:* For Postbaccalaureate Certificate, solo recital. *Entrance requirements:* For degree, minimum GPA of 3.0, resume, reference letters, DVD of performance, BM. Additional exam requirements/recommendations for international students: Recommended—TOEFL. *Application deadline:* For fall admission, 12/1 for domestic and international students; for winter admission, 1/30 for domestic and international students; for spring admission, 5/15 priority date for domestic students, 4/15 for international students. Applications are processed on a rolling basis. Application fee: $50. Electronic applications accepted. *Expenses:* Contact institution. *Financial support:* In 2017–18, 1 student received support. Scholarships/grants available. Financial award applicants required to submit FAFSA. *Faculty research:* Music, composition, performance, music technology, contemporary music. *Total annual research expenditures:* $150,000. *Unit head:* Dr. Lisa Cella, Director, 410-455-1405, E-mail: cella@umbc.edu. *Application contact:* Dr. Lisa Cella, Director, Certificate Program in American Contemporary Music, 410-455-1405, Fax: 410-455-1181, E-mail: cella@umbc.edu.
Website: http://music.umbc.edu/degrees-certificates/american-contemporary-music/

University of Maryland, College Park, Academic Affairs, College of Arts and Humanities, School of Music, Program in Ethnomusicology, College Park, MD 20742. Offers MA. *Degree requirements:* For master's, comprehensive exam, thesis optional, oral defense. *Entrance requirements:* Additional exam requirements/recommendations for international students: Required—TOEFL.

University of Maryland, College Park, Academic Affairs, College of Arts and Humanities, School of Music, Program in Music, College Park, MD 20742. Offers M Ed, MA, MM, DMA, Ed D, PhD. *Accreditation:* NASM. *Entrance requirements:* For master's, GRE General Test (for ethnomusicology, historical musicology and music theory), 3 letters of recommendation, audition/interview. Additional exam requirements/recommendations for international students: Required—TOEFL.

University of Massachusetts Amherst, Graduate School, College of Humanities and Fine Arts, Department of Music and Dance, Amherst, MA 01003. Offers collaborative piano (MM); composition (MM); conducting (MM); jazz composition/arranging (MM); music education (MM, PhD); music history (MM); music theory (PhD); performance (MM). *Accreditation:* NASM. *Program availability:* Part-time. Terminal master's awarded for partial completion of doctoral program. *Degree requirements:* For master's, thesis or alternative; for doctorate, comprehensive exam, thesis/dissertation. *Entrance requirements:* For master's and doctorate, placement tests, original scores, research, audition or tape. Additional exam requirements/recommendations for international students: Required—TOEFL (minimum score 550 paper-based; 80 iBT), IELTS (minimum score 6.5). Electronic applications accepted.

University of Massachusetts Lowell, College of Fine Arts, Humanities and Social Sciences, Department of Music, Lowell, MA 01854. Offers music education (MM). *Accreditation:* NASM. *Program availability:* Part-time. *Degree requirements:* For master's, one foreign language, thesis. *Entrance requirements:* For master's, MAT, audition. Electronic applications accepted.

University of Memphis, Graduate School, College of Communication and Fine Arts, Rudi E. Scheidt School of Music, Memphis, TN 38152. Offers composition (M Mu, DMA); conducting (M Mu, DMA); jazz and studio music (M Mu); music education (M Mu, PhD); music theory (DCC); musicology (PhD); Orff-Schulwerk (M Mu); pedagogy (M Mu); performance (M Mu, DMA). *Accreditation:* NASM. *Program availability:* Part-time. *Faculty:* 32 full-time (8 women), 5 part-time/adjunct (1 woman). *Students:* 62 full-time (27 women), 46 part-time (21 women); includes 25 minority (11 Black or African American, non-Hispanic/Latino; 2 Asian, non-Hispanic/Latino; 8 Hispanic/Latino; 4 Two or more races, non-Hispanic/Latino), 10 international. Average age 31. 71 applicants, 82% accepted, 28 enrolled. In 2017, 22 master's, 7 doctorates awarded. Terminal master's awarded for partial completion of doctoral program. *Degree requirements:* For master's, variable foreign language requirement, comprehensive exam, thesis or alternative; for doctorate, one foreign language, comprehensive exam, thesis/dissertation, qualifying exam. *Entrance requirements:* For master's, audition; for doctorate, GRE General Test or MAT, proficiency exam, audition, work sample, master's degree. Additional exam requirements/recommendations for international students: Required—TOEFL (minimum score 550 paper-based; 79 iBT). *Application deadline:* For fall admission, 8/1 for domestic students; for spring admission, 12/1 for domestic students. Applications are processed on a rolling basis. Application fee: $35 ($60 for international students). Electronic applications accepted. *Expenses:* Contact institution. *Financial support:* In 2017–18, 73 students received support, including 26 research assistantships with tuition reimbursements available (averaging $10,250 per year), 26 teaching assistantships with tuition reimbursements available (averaging $11,288 per year); Federal Work-Study, scholarships/grants, and unspecified assistantships also available. Financial award application deadline: 2/1; financial award applicants required to submit FAFSA. *Faculty research:* Spanish Renaissance, twentieth-century music, Project OPTIMUS, composition, musical performance, regional music, performance, performance practice, composition. *Unit head:* Dr. John Chiego, Director, 901-678-3773, Fax: 901-678-3096, E-mail: jchiego@memphis.edu. *Application contact:* Dr. Dave Spencer, Assistant Director for Graduate Studies, 901-678-3779, Fax: 901-678-3096, E-mail: dspencer@memphis.edu.
Website: http://www.memphis.edu/music/

University of Miami, Graduate School, Frost School of Music, Department of Instrumental Performance, Coral Gables, FL 33124. Offers instrumental conducting (MM, DMA); instrumental performance (MM, DMA, AD); multiple woodwinds (MM, DMA). *Accreditation:* NASM. *Degree requirements:* For master's, thesis, recital paper, recital; for doctorate, thesis/dissertation, essay, 2 research tools, 3 recitals. *Entrance requirements:* For master's and doctorate, GRE General Test, audition. Additional exam requirements/recommendations for international students: Required—TOEFL (minimum score 550 paper-based; 59 iBT). Electronic applications accepted. *Faculty research:* Performance, conducting, composition.

University of Miami, Graduate School, Frost School of Music, Department of Keyboard Performance, Coral Gables, FL 33124. Offers accompanying and chamber music (MM, DMA); keyboard performance and pedagogy (MM, DMA); piano performance (MM, DMA, AD). *Accreditation:* NASM. *Degree requirements:* For master's, thesis, recital paper, recital; for doctorate, thesis/dissertation, essay, 2 research tools, 3 recitals. *Entrance requirements:* For master's and doctorate, GRE General Test, audition. Additional exam requirements/recommendations for international students: Required—TOEFL (minimum score 555 paper-based; 59 iBT). Electronic applications accepted.

University of Miami, Graduate School, Frost School of Music, Department of Music Media and Industry, Coral Gables, FL 33124. Offers music business and entertainment industries (MM); music engineering (MS). *Accreditation:* NASM. *Degree requirements:* For master's, thesis, internship (MM), research project (MS). *Entrance requirements:* For master's, GRE General Test. Additional exam requirements/recommendations for international students: Required—TOEFL (minimum score 550 paper-based; 59 iBT). Electronic applications accepted. *Faculty research:* Recording rights and property, digital sound design, recording industry, Internet-based music industries.

University of Miami, Graduate School, Frost School of Music, Department of Musicology, Coral Gables, FL 33124. Offers MM. *Accreditation:* NASM. *Degree requirements:* For master's, thesis. *Entrance requirements:* For master's, GRE General Test. Additional exam requirements/recommendations for international students: Required—TOEFL (minimum score 550 paper-based; 59 iBT). Electronic applications accepted.

University of Miami, Graduate School, Frost School of Music, Department of Music Theory-Composition, Coral Gables, FL 33124. Offers composition (MM, DMA); electronic music (MM); media writing and production (MM); music theory (MM). *Accreditation:* NASM. *Degree requirements:* For master's, thesis; for doctorate, thesis/dissertation, essay. *Entrance requirements:* For master's and doctorate, GRE General

Test, portfolio. Additional exam requirements/recommendations for international students: Required—TOEFL (minimum score 550 paper-based; 59 iBT). Electronic applications accepted. *Faculty research:* Composition, commercial music and media music.

University of Miami, Graduate School, Frost School of Music, Department of Studio Music and Jazz, Coral Gables, FL 33124. Offers jazz composition (DMA); jazz pedagogy (MM); jazz performance (MM, DMA); studio jazz writing (MM). *Accreditation:* NASM. *Degree requirements:* For master's, thesis. *Entrance requirements:* For master's and doctorate, GRE General Test, portfolio. Additional exam requirements/recommendations for international students: Required—TOEFL (minimum score 550 paper-based; 59 iBT). Electronic applications accepted. *Faculty research:* Jazz performance, jazz conducting, jjazz composition.

University of Miami, Graduate School, Frost School of Music, Department of Vocal Performance, Coral Gables, FL 33124. Offers choral conducting (MM, DMA); vocal pedagogy (DMA); vocal performance (MM, DMA, AD). *Accreditation:* NASM. *Degree requirements:* For master's, 2 foreign languages, thesis, recital paper; for doctorate, thesis/dissertation, essay. *Entrance requirements:* For master's and doctorate, GRE General Test, audition. Additional exam requirements/recommendations for international students: Required—TOEFL (minimum score 550 paper-based; 59 iBT). Electronic applications accepted. *Faculty research:* Opera, musical theatre, performance, directing, pedagogy.

University of Michigan, Rackham Graduate School, School of Music, Theatre, and Dance, Program in Composition, Ann Arbor, MI 48109-2217. Offers MA, MM, A Mus D. *Degree requirements:* For doctorate, one foreign language, thesis/dissertation, oral exam, composition. *Entrance requirements:* For master's and doctorate, portfolio. Additional exam requirements/recommendations for international students: Required—TOEFL. *Expenses:* Tuition, state resident: full-time $22,368; part-time $1201 per credit hour. Tuition, nonresident: full-time $45,156; part-time $2467 per credit hour. *Required fees:* $376 per term. Tuition and fees vary according to course load, degree level and program.

University of Michigan, Rackham Graduate School, School of Music, Theatre, and Dance, Program in Composition and Theory, Ann Arbor, MI 48109-2085. Offers PhD. *Degree requirements:* For doctorate, one foreign language, thesis/dissertation, oral exam, composition. *Entrance requirements:* For doctorate, GRE, portfolio. Additional exam requirements/recommendations for international students: Required—TOEFL. Electronic applications accepted. *Expenses:* Tuition, state resident: full-time $22,368; part-time $1201 per credit hour. Tuition, nonresident: full-time $45,156; part-time $2467 per credit hour. *Required fees:* $376 per term. Tuition and fees vary according to course load, degree level and program.

University of Michigan, Rackham Graduate School, School of Music, Theatre, and Dance, Program in Conducting, Ann Arbor, MI 48109-2085. Offers MM, A Mus D. *Degree requirements:* For doctorate, one foreign language, thesis/dissertation, 3 concerts, oral exam. *Entrance requirements:* For doctorate, audition, portfolio. Additional exam requirements/recommendations for international students: Required—TOEFL. Electronic applications accepted. *Expenses:* Tuition, state resident: full-time $22,368; part-time $1201 per credit hour. Tuition, nonresident: full-time $45,156; part-time $2467 per credit hour. *Required fees:* $376 per term. Tuition and fees vary according to course load, degree level and program.

University of Michigan, Rackham Graduate School, School of Music, Theatre, and Dance, Program in Musicology, Ann Arbor, MI 48109-2085. Offers MA, PhD. *Degree requirements:* For doctorate, 2 foreign languages, thesis/dissertation, oral exam. *Entrance requirements:* For master's and doctorate, GRE General Test, writing sample. Additional exam requirements/recommendations for international students: Required—TOEFL. Electronic applications accepted. *Expenses:* Tuition, state resident: full-time $22,368; part-time $1201 per credit hour. Tuition, nonresident: full-time $45,156; part-time $2467 per credit hour. *Required fees:* $376 per term. Tuition and fees vary according to course load, degree level and program.

University of Michigan, Rackham Graduate School, School of Music, Theatre, and Dance, Program in Music Theory, Ann Arbor, MI 48109-2085. Offers PhD. *Degree requirements:* For doctorate, one foreign language, thesis/dissertation, oral exam. *Entrance requirements:* For doctorate, GRE, writing sample. Additional exam requirements/recommendations for international students: Required—TOEFL. Electronic applications accepted. *Expenses:* Tuition, state resident: full-time $22,368; part-time $1201 per credit hour. Tuition, nonresident: full-time $45,156; part-time $2467 per credit hour. *Required fees:* $376 per term. Tuition and fees vary according to course load, degree level and program.

University of Michigan, Rackham Graduate School, School of Music, Theatre, and Dance, Program in Performance, Ann Arbor, MI 48109-2085. Offers MM, A Mus D, Spec M. *Degree requirements:* For doctorate, one foreign language, thesis/dissertation, 3 concerts, oral exam. *Entrance requirements:* For doctorate, audition. Additional exam requirements/recommendations for international students: Required—TOEFL. Electronic applications accepted. *Expenses:* Tuition, state resident: full-time $22,368; part-time $1201 per credit hour. Tuition, nonresident: full-time $45,156; part-time $2467 per credit hour. *Required fees:* $376 per term. Tuition and fees vary according to course load, degree level and program.

University of Michigan–Flint, Graduate Programs, Program in Arts Administration, Flint, MI 48502-1950. Offers performance (MA), including museum and visual arts, performance. *Program availability:* Part-time. *Faculty:* 5 full-time (3 women), 1 (woman) part-time/adjunct. *Students:* 6 full-time (4 women), 7 part-time (4 women); includes 2 minority (both Black or African American, non-Hispanic/Latino). Average age 43. 12 applicants, 75% accepted, 5 enrolled. In 2017, 3 master's awarded. *Degree requirements:* For master's, thesis, internship. *Entrance requirements:* For master's, bachelor's degree in the arts (visual art, theatre, dance, music, etc.) from regionally-accredited institution; minimum cumulative undergraduate GPA of 3.0. Additional exam requirements/recommendations for international students: Required—TOEFL (minimum score 84 iBT), IELTS (minimum score 6.5). *Application deadline:* For fall admission, 8/1 for domestic students, 5/1 for international students; for winter admission, 11/15 for domestic students, 9/1 for international students. Applications are processed on a rolling basis. Application fee: $55. Electronic applications accepted. *Expenses:* Contact institution. *Financial support:* Federal Work-Study, institutionally sponsored loans, scholarships/grants, and unspecified assistantships available. Support available to part-time students. Financial award application deadline: 3/1; financial award applicants required to submit FAFSA. *Unit head:* Nicole Broughton, Director, 810-237-6522, E-mail: broughn@umflint.edu. *Application contact:* Bradley T. Maki, Director of Graduate Admissions, 810-762-3171, Fax: 810-766-6789, E-mail: bmaki@umflint.edu.
Website: http://www.umflint.edu/graduateprograms/arts-administration-ma

University of Minnesota, Duluth, Graduate School, School of Fine Arts, Department of Music, Duluth, MN 55812-2496. Offers music education (MM); performance (MM). *Accreditation:* NASM. *Program availability:* Part-time. *Degree requirements:* For master's, comprehensive exam, thesis (for some programs), recital (MM in performance). *Entrance requirements:* For master's, audition, minimum GPA of 3.0, sample of written work, interview, bachelor's degree in music, video of teaching. Additional exam requirements/recommendations for international students: Required—TOEFL (minimum score 550 paper-based). *Faculty research:* Band composition, music aesthetics, learning theory, value theory, music advocacy.

University of Minnesota, Twin Cities Campus, Graduate School, College of Liberal Arts, School of Music, Minneapolis, MN 55455-0213. Offers MA, MM, DMA, PhD. *Accreditation:* NASM. *Degree requirements:* For master's, comprehensive exam, thesis (for some programs), foreign language (MA), recital (MM); for doctorate, comprehensive exam, 5 recitals (DMA); 2 foreign languages or computer languages, dissertation (PhD). *Entrance requirements:* For master's, GRE (MA); for doctorate, GRE (PhD). Additional exam requirements/recommendations for international students: Required—TOEFL (minimum score 550 paper-based; 79 iBT: 21 writing, 19 reading), IELTS (minimum score 6.5). Electronic applications accepted.

University of Mississippi, Graduate School, College of Liberal Arts, University, MS 38677. Offers anthropology (MA); biology (MS, PhD); chemistry (MS, DA, PhD); creative writing (MFA); documentary expression (MFA); economics (MA, PhD); English (MA, PhD); experimental psychology (PhD); history (MA, PhD); mathematics (MS, PhD); modern languages (MA); music (MM); philosophy (MA); physics (MA, MS, PhD); political science (MA, PhD); Southern studies (MA); studio art (MFA). *Program availability:* Part-time. *Faculty:* 465 full-time (207 women), 82 part-time/adjunct (46 women). *Students:* 466 full-time (229 women), 72 part-time (34 women); includes 87 minority (38 Black or African American, non-Hispanic/Latino; 18 Asian, non-Hispanic/Latino; 24 Hispanic/Latino; 7 Two or more races, non-Hispanic/Latino), 121 international. Average age 29. *Degree requirements:* For doctorate, thesis/dissertation. *Entrance requirements:* For master's, GRE General Test, minimum GPA of 3.0; for doctorate, GRE General Test. Additional exam requirements/recommendations for international students: Required—TOEFL. *Application deadline:* For fall admission, 2/1 priority date for domestic students; for spring admission, 10/1 for domestic students. Applications are processed on a rolling basis. Application fee: $50. Electronic applications accepted. *Financial support:* Fellowships, research assistantships, teaching assistantships, career-related internships or fieldwork, Federal Work-Study, institutionally sponsored loans, scholarships/grants, and unspecified assistantships available. Financial award application deadline: 3/1; financial award applicants required to submit FAFSA. *Unit head:* Dr. Lee Michael Cohen, Dean, 662-915-7177, Fax: 662-915-5792, E-mail: libarts@olemiss.edu. *Application contact:* Dr. Christy M. Wyandt, Associate Dean of Graduate School, 662-915-7474, Fax: 662-915-7577, E-mail: cwyandt@olemiss.edu.

University of Missouri, Office of Research and Graduate Studies, College of Arts and Science, School of Music, Columbia, MO 65211. Offers MA, MM. *Accreditation:* NASM. *Degree requirements:* For master's, 3 foreign languages, thesis. *Entrance requirements:* For master's, minimum GPA of 3.0. Additional exam requirements/recommendations for international students: Required—TOEFL (minimum score 500 paper-based; 61 iBT). Electronic applications accepted.

University of Missouri–Kansas City, Conservatory of Music and Dance, Kansas City, MO 64110-2499. Offers composition (MM, DMA); conducting (MM, DMA); music (MA); music education (MME, PhD); music history and literature (MM); music theory (MM); music therapy (MA); performance (MM, DMA). PhD (interdisciplinary) offered through the School of Graduate Studies. *Accreditation:* NASM. *Program availability:* Part-time. *Degree requirements:* For master's, variable foreign language requirement, comprehensive exam, thesis (for some programs); for doctorate, variable foreign language requirement, comprehensive exam, thesis/dissertation or alternative. *Entrance requirements:* For master's, minimum GPA of 3.0 in major, auditions (for MM in performance); for doctorate, minimum graduate GPA of 3.5, auditions (for DMA in performance), portfolio of compositions. Additional exam requirements/recommendations for international students: Required—TOEFL (minimum score 550 paper-based; 80 iBT). *Faculty research:* Electro-acoustic composition, affective music responses, American music theatre, Russian choral music, music therapy and Alzheimer's.

University of Montana, Graduate School, College of Visual and Performing Arts, School of Music, Missoula, MT 59812. Offers performance (MM). *Accreditation:* NASM. *Entrance requirements:* For master's, GRE General Test, GRE Subject Test, portfolio.

University of Nebraska at Omaha, Graduate Studies, College of Communication, Fine Arts and Media, School of Music, Omaha, NE 68182. Offers MM. *Accreditation:* NASM. *Program availability:* Part-time, evening/weekend. *Degree requirements:* For master's, comprehensive exam (for some programs), thesis (for some programs). *Entrance requirements:* For master's, departmental diagnostic exam, minimum GPA of 3.0, resume, transcripts. Additional exam requirements/recommendations for international students: Required—TOEFL, IELTS, PTE. Electronic applications accepted.

University of Nebraska–Lincoln, Graduate College, College of Fine and Performing Arts, School of Music, Lincoln, NE 68588. Offers composition (MM, DMA); conducting (MM, DMA); music education (MM, PhD); music history (MM); music theory (MM); performance (MM, DMA); piano pedagogy (MM); woodwind specialties (MM). *Accreditation:* NASM. *Degree requirements:* For master's, thesis optional; for doctorate, comprehensive exam, thesis/dissertation. *Entrance requirements:* For master's and doctorate, audition. Additional exam requirements/recommendations for international students: Required—TOEFL. Electronic applications accepted. *Faculty research:* Mozart, Tchaikovsky, Josquin des Prez, practice of J.S. Bach's organ works, instructional strategies in music education.

University of Nevada, Las Vegas, Graduate College, College of Fine Arts, School of Music, Las Vegas, NV 89154-5025. Offers K-12 music (Certificate); music (MM); musical arts (DMA). *Accreditation:* NASM. *Program availability:* Part-time. *Faculty:* 30 full-time (10 women), 17 part-time/adjunct (4 women). *Students:* 67 full-time (37 women), 24 part-time (10 women); includes 20 minority (8 Black or African American, non-Hispanic/Latino; 2 Asian, non-Hispanic/Latino; 8 Hispanic/Latino; 1 Native Hawaiian or other Pacific Islander, non-Hispanic/Latino; 1 Two or more races, non-Hispanic/Latino), 19 international. Average age 34. 59 applicants, 76% accepted, 29 enrolled. In 2017, 18 master's, 17 doctorates awarded. *Degree requirements:* For master's, oral and/or written comprehensive exam; for doctorate, one foreign language, comprehensive exam, thesis/dissertation, lecture-recital and document. *Entrance requirements:* For master's, placement examinations, bachelor's degree with minimum GPA 3.0; statement of purpose; 2 letters of recommendation; portfolio of compositions; for doctorate, music history placement exam, music theory and aural skills/sight-singing placement examination, master's degree in music; for Certificate, PRAXIS I Pre-Professional Skills Test, bachelor's degree. Additional exam requirements/recommendations for international students: Required—TOEFL (minimum score 550 paper-based; 80 iBT), IELTS (minimum score 7). *Application deadline:* For fall admission, 5/1 for domestic students; for spring admission, 11/15 for domestic students; for summer admission, 5/15 for domestic students. Application fee: $60 ($95 for international students). Electronic applications accepted. *Expenses:* $275 per credit, $850 per course, $7,969 per year resident, $22,157 per year non-resident, $7,094 non-resident fee (7 credits or more), $1,307 annual health insurance fee. *Financial support:* In 2017–18, 39 students received support, including 4 research assistantships with full tuition reimbursements available (averaging $13,125 per year), 35 teaching assistantships with full tuition reimbursements available (averaging $13,500 per year);

institutionally sponsored loans, scholarships/grants, health care benefits, and unspecified assistantships also available. Financial award application deadline: 3/15; financial award applicants required to submit FAFSA. *Faculty research:* Technology in preparing future teachers, professional development for music educators, Roman music history, music of Richard Wagner, Baroque music. *Total annual research expenditures:* $71,861. *Unit head:* Dr. Sue Mueller, Chair/Professor, 702-895-5776, Fax: 702-895-4239, E-mail: susan.mueller@unlv.edu. *Application contact:* Dr. Richard Miller, Graduate Coordinator, 702-895-4995, E-mail: richard.miller@unlv.edu.
Website: http://music.unlv.edu/

University of Nevada, Reno, Graduate School, College of Liberal Arts, Department of Music, Reno, NV 89557. Offers MA, MM. *Accreditation:* NASM. *Degree requirements:* For master's, thesis optional. *Entrance requirements:* For master's, minimum GPA of 2.75. Additional exam requirements/recommendations for international students: Required—TOEFL (minimum score 500 paper-based; 61 iBT), IELTS (minimum score 6). Electronic applications accepted. *Faculty research:* Performance, conducting, music composition and arranging.

University of New Hampshire, Graduate School, College of Liberal Arts, Department of Music, Durham, NH 03824. Offers music composition (MA); music conducting (MA); musicology (MA). *Accreditation:* NASM. *Students:* 5 full-time (3 women), 2 part-time (1 woman). Average age 26. 8 applicants, 63% accepted, 4 enrolled. In 2017, 5 master's awarded. *Entrance requirements:* For master's, entrance exam, writing sample, portfolio, audition. Additional exam requirements/recommendations for international students: Required—TOEFL (minimum score 550 paper-based; 80 iBT). *Application deadline:* For fall admission, 4/1 for domestic and international students; for spring admission, 12/1 for domestic students. Application fee: $65. Electronic applications accepted. *Financial support:* In 2017–18, 6 students received support, including 4 teaching assistantships; fellowships, research assistantships, career-related internships or fieldwork, Federal Work-Study, scholarships/grants, and tuition waivers (full and partial) also available. Support available to part-time students. Financial award application deadline: 2/15. *Unit head:* Jenni Cook, Chair, 603-862-1969. *Application contact:* Alexis Saricki, Administrative Assistant, 603-862-2418, E-mail: grad.music@unh.edu.
Website: http://cola.unh.edu/music

University of New Mexico, Graduate Studies, College of Fine Arts, Program in Music, Albuquerque, NM 87131-0001. Offers collaborative piano (M Mu); conducting (M Mu); music education (M Mu); music history and literature (M Mu); performance (M Mu); theory and composition (M Mu). *Accreditation:* NASM. *Program availability:* Part-time. *Students:* Average age 29. 75 applicants, 76% accepted, 36 enrolled. In 2017, 30 master's awarded. *Degree requirements:* For master's, variable foreign language requirement, comprehensive exam, thesis (for some programs), recital (for some programs). *Entrance requirements:* For master's, placement exams in music history and theory. Additional exam requirements/recommendations for international students: Required—TOEFL (minimum score 550 paper-based). *Application deadline:* For fall admission, 7/1 for domestic students, 5/1 for international students; for spring admission, 11/1 for domestic students, 10/1 for international students. Applications are processed on a rolling basis. Application fee: $50. Electronic applications accepted. *Financial support:* Research assistantships, teaching assistantships, Federal Work-Study, scholarships/grants, and unspecified assistantships available. Support available to part-time students. Financial award application deadline: 2/1; financial award applicants required to submit FAFSA. *Faculty research:* Opera, twentieth-century and contemporary music, performance, conducting. *Unit head:* Dr. Steven Block, Chair, 505-277-2127, Fax: 505-277-4202, E-mail: sblock@unm.edu. *Application contact:* Colleen M. Sheinberg, Graduate Coordinator, 505-277-8401, Fax: 505-277-4202, E-mail: colleens@unm.edu.
Website: http://music.unm.edu/

University of New Orleans, Graduate School, College of Liberal Arts, Department of Music, New Orleans, LA 70148. Offers MM. *Accreditation:* NASM. *Program availability:* Evening/weekend. *Degree requirements:* For master's, recital. *Entrance requirements:* For master's, GRE General Test, audition. Additional exam requirements/recommendations for international students: Required—TOEFL (minimum score 550 paper-based; 79 iBT), IELTS (minimum score 6.5). Electronic applications accepted. *Faculty research:* American jazz, Czech music, Hispanic music.

The University of North Carolina at Chapel Hill, Graduate School, College of Arts and Sciences, Department of Music, Chapel Hill, NC 27599. Offers MA, PhD. Terminal master's awarded for partial completion of doctoral program. *Degree requirements:* For master's, one foreign language, thesis, theory and keyboard exams; for doctorate, 2 foreign languages, comprehensive exam, thesis/dissertation, theory and keyboard exams. *Entrance requirements:* For master's and doctorate, GRE General Test, department diagnostic exam, minimum GPA of 3.0. Additional exam requirements/recommendations for international students: Required—TOEFL. Electronic applications accepted. *Expenses:* Contact institution. *Faculty research:* Music theory, ethnomusicology, music history.

The University of North Carolina at Charlotte, College of Arts and Architecture, Department of Music, Charlotte, NC 28223-0001. Offers vocal pedagogy (Graduate Certificate). *Accreditation:* NASM. *Program availability:* Part-time. *Faculty:* 9 full-time (3 women). *Degree requirements:* For Graduate Certificate, thesis or alternative, directed project. *Entrance requirements:* For degree, placement tests in music theory, ear training, and piano; diagnostic vocal pedagogy exam, bachelor's degree in music from accredited university or conservatory; official transcripts; formal audition. Additional exam requirements/recommendations for international students: Required—TOEFL (minimum score 523 paper-based, 70 iBT) or IELTS (6.5). *Application deadline:* For fall admission, 3/1 priority date for domestic and international students; for spring admission, 10/1 priority date for domestic and international students. Applications are processed on a rolling basis. Application fee: $75. Electronic applications accepted. *Expenses:* Tuition, state resident: full-time $4337. Tuition, nonresident: full-time $17,771. *Required fees:* $3211. Tuition and fees vary according to course load and program. *Financial support:* Career-related internships or fieldwork and unspecified assistantships available. Financial award application deadline: 3/1; financial award applicants required to submit FAFSA. *Unit head:* James A. Grymes, Chair, 704-687-0251, E-mail: jagrymes@uncc.edu. *Application contact:* Kathy B. Giddings, Director of Graduate Admissions, 704-687-5503, Fax: 704-687-1668, E-mail: gradadm@uncc.edu.
Website: http://coaa.uncc.edu/academics/department-of-music

The University of North Carolina at Greensboro, Graduate School, School of Music, Theatre and Dance, Greensboro, NC 27412-5001. Offers composition (MM); dance (MA, MFA); education (MM); music education (PhD); performance (MM, DMA); theatre (M Ed, MFA), including acting (MFA), design (MFA), directing (MFA), theatre education (M Ed), theatre for youth (MFA); theory (MM). *Accreditation:* NASM. *Degree requirements:* For master's, variable foreign language requirement, thesis (for some programs), recital; for doctorate, comprehensive exam, thesis/dissertation, diagnostic exam, recital. *Entrance requirements:* For master's, GRE General Test, NTE, audition; for doctorate, GRE General Test, GRE Subject Test (music), audition. Additional exam requirements/recommendations for international students: Required—TOEFL. Electronic applications accepted.

University of North Carolina School of the Arts, School of Filmmaking, Winston-Salem, NC 27127-2738. Offers creative producing (MFA); film music composition (MFA); screenwriting (MFA). *Entrance requirements:* For master's, audition, performance, portfolio, interview. Additional exam requirements/recommendations for international students: Required—TOEFL. Electronic applications accepted.

University of North Carolina School of the Arts, School of Music, Winston-Salem, NC 27127-2738. Offers music (Artist Certificate); music performance (MM), including chamber music performance; vocal performance (MM). *Entrance requirements:* For master's, audition (music performance), interview, original score. Additional exam requirements/recommendations for international students: Required—TOEFL. Electronic applications accepted.

University of North Dakota, Graduate School, College of Arts and Sciences, Department of Music, Grand Forks, ND 58202. Offers music (MM); music education (PhD). *Accreditation:* NASM. *Program availability:* Part-time. *Degree requirements:* For master's, comprehensive exam, thesis or alternative. *Entrance requirements:* For master's, minimum GPA of 3.0. Additional exam requirements/recommendations for international students: Required—TOEFL (minimum score 550 paper-based; 79 iBT), IELTS (minimum score 6.5). Electronic applications accepted.

University of Northern Colorado, Graduate School, College of Performing and Visual Arts, School of Music, Greeley, CO 80639. Offers collaborative piano (MM, DA); composition (DA); conducting (MM, DA); instrumental performance (MM); jazz studies (MM, DA); music education (MM, DA); music history and literature (MM, DA); music theory and composition (MM); performance (DA); vocal performance (MM). *Accreditation:* NASM; NCATE (one or more programs are accredited). *Program availability:* Part-time. *Degree requirements:* For master's, comprehensive exam, thesis or alternative; for doctorate, comprehensive exam, thesis/dissertation. *Entrance requirements:* For master's, audition; for doctorate, GRE General Test, audition, 3 letters of recommendation. Electronic applications accepted.

University of Northern Iowa, Graduate College, College of Humanities, Arts and Sciences, School of Music, MA Program in Music, Cedar Falls, IA 50614. Offers MA. *Accreditation:* NASM. *Degree requirements:* For master's, comprehensive exam, thesis or alternative. *Entrance requirements:* For master's, written diagnostic exam in theory, music history, expository writing skills, and in the area of claimed competency, portfolio, tape recordings of compositions, in-person auditions, minimum GPA of 3.0. Additional exam requirements/recommendations for international students: Required—TOEFL (minimum score 500 paper-based; 61 iBT). Electronic applications accepted.

University of Northern Iowa, Graduate College, College of Humanities, Arts and Sciences, School of Music, MM Program in Composition, Cedar Falls, IA 50614. Offers MM. *Degree requirements:* For master's, comprehensive exam. *Entrance requirements:* For master's, portfolio, recordings of compositions.

University of Northern Iowa, Graduate College, College of Humanities, Arts and Sciences, School of Music, MM Program in Conducting, Cedar Falls, IA 50614. Offers MM. *Degree requirements:* For master's, comprehensive exam. *Entrance requirements:* For master's, audition, interview.

University of Northern Iowa, Graduate College, College of Humanities, Arts and Sciences, School of Music, MM Program in Music History, Cedar Falls, IA 50614. Offers MM. *Entrance requirements:* For master's, scholarly paper.

University of Northern Iowa, Graduate College, College of Humanities, Arts and Sciences, School of Music, MM Program in Performance, Cedar Falls, IA 50614. Offers percussion (MM); piano/organ (MM); strings (MM); voice (MM); woodwind (MM). *Degree requirements:* For master's, comprehensive exam. *Entrance requirements:* For master's, audition.

University of Northern Iowa, Graduate College, College of Humanities, Arts and Sciences, School of Music, MM Program in Piano Performance and Pedagogy, Cedar Falls, IA 50614. Offers MM.

University of North Texas, Robert B. Toulouse School of Graduate Studies, Denton, TX 76203-5459. Offers accounting (MS); applied anthropology (MA, MS); applied behavior analysis (Certificate); applied geography (MA); applied technology and performance improvement (M Ed, MS); art education (MA); art history (MA); art museum education (Certificate); arts leadership (Certificate); audiology (Au D); behavior analysis (MS); behavioral science (PhD); biochemistry and molecular biology (MS); biology (MA, MS); biomedical engineering (MS); business analysis (MS); chemistry (MS); clinical health psychology (PhD); communication studies (MA, MS); computer engineering (MS); computer science (MS); counseling (M Ed, MS), including clinical mental health counseling (MS), college and university counseling, elementary school counseling, secondary school counseling; creative writing (MA); criminal justice (MS); curriculum and instruction (M Ed); decision sciences (MBA); design (MA, MFA), including fashion design (MFA), innovation studies, interior design (MFA); early childhood studies (MS); economics (MS); educational leadership (M Ed, Ed D); educational psychology (MS, PhD), including family studies (MS), gifted and talented (MS), human development (MS), learning and cognition (MS), research, measurement and evaluation (MS); electrical engineering (MS); emergency management (MPA); engineering technology (MS); English (MA); English as a second language (MA); environmental science (MS); finance (MBA, MS); financial management (MPA); French (MA); health services management (MBA); higher education (M Ed, Ed D); history (MA, MS); hospitality management (MS); human resources management (MPA); information science (MS); information systems (PhD); information technologies (MBA); interdisciplinary studies (MA, MS); international studies (MA); international sustainable tourism (MS); jazz studies (MM); journalism (MA, MJ, Graduate Certificate), including interactive and virtual digital communication (Graduate Certificate), narrative journalism (Graduate Certificate), public relations (Graduate Certificate); kinesiology (MS); linguistics (MA); local government management (MPA); logistics (PhD); logistics and supply chain management (MBA); long-term care, senior housing, and aging services (MA); management (PhD); marketing (MBA); mathematics (MA, MS); mechanical and energy engineering (MS, PhD); music (MA), including ethnomusicology, music theory, musicology, performance; music composition (PhD); music education (MM Ed, PhD); nonprofit management (MPA); operations and supply chain management (MBA); performance (MM, DMA); philosophy (MA); political science (MA); professional and technical communication (MA); radio, television and film (MA, MFA); rehabilitation counseling (Certificate); sociology (MA); Spanish (MA); special education (M Ed); speech-language pathology (MA); strategic management (MBA); studio art (MFA); teaching (M Ed); MBA/MS. *Program availability:* Part-time, evening/weekend, online learning. Terminal master's awarded for partial completion of doctoral program. *Degree requirements:* For master's, variable foreign language requirement, comprehensive exam (for some programs), thesis (for some programs); for doctorate, variable foreign language requirement, comprehensive exam (for some programs), thesis/dissertation; for other advanced degree, variable foreign language requirement, comprehensive exam (for some programs). *Entrance requirements:* For master's and doctorate, GRE, GMAT. Additional exam requirements/recommendations for international students: Required—TOEFL (minimum score 550 paper-based; 79 iBT). Electronic applications accepted.

University of Oklahoma, Weitzenhoffer Family College of Fine Arts, School of Music, Norman, OK 73019. Offers choral conducting (M Mus), including church music (M Mus, DMA), standard (M Mus, DMA, PhD); composition (M Mus, DMA); conducting (M Mus Ed, DMA), including choral, church music (M Mus, DMA), instrumental (M Mus Ed), orchestral (DMA), wind (DMA); general (M Mus Ed), including Kodaly concepts (M Mus Ed, PhD), vocal/general; instrumental (M Mus Ed), including primary instrument, secondary instrument; instrumental conducting (M Mus); music education (PhD), including conducting, Kodaly concepts (M Mus Ed, PhD), piano pedagogy, standard (M Mus, DMA, PhD); music performance (Graduate Certificate); music theory (M Mus); musicology (M Mus); organ (M Mus, DMA), including church music, organ technology (M Mus), standard (M Mus, DMA, PhD); piano (M Mus, DMA), including performance, performance and pedagogy; piano pedagogy (M Mus Ed); voice (M Mus, DMA), including opera (M Mus), performance; wind/percussion/string instruments (M Mus, DMA). *Accreditation:* NASM. *Faculty:* 56 full-time (13 women). *Students:* 104 full-time (43 women), 70 part-time (29 women); includes 26 minority (3 Black or African American, non-Hispanic/Latino; 5 American Indian or Alaska Native, non-Hispanic/Latino; 5 Asian, non-Hispanic/Latino; 8 Hispanic/Latino; 5 Two or more races, non-Hispanic/Latino), 26 international. Average age 29. 182 applicants, 42% accepted, 48 enrolled. In 2017, 41 master's, 15 doctorates awarded. *Degree requirements:* For master's, variable foreign language requirement, comprehensive exam (for some programs), thesis (for some programs), final recital (for M Mus performance, conducting, and composition degrees); for doctorate, variable foreign language requirement, comprehensive exam, thesis/dissertation, three recitals and/or workshops (two recitals for DMA in composition); for Graduate Certificate, variable foreign language requirement, two recitals. *Entrance requirements:* For master's, bachelor's degree in music, music education, or the equivalent; transcripts; resume; personal statement; 3 letters of recommendation; audition and/or other practical application materials as appropriate to intended degree; sample of scholarly writing (for M Mus in musicology and in music theory); for doctorate, master's degree in music, music education, or the equivalent; transcripts; resume; personal statement; 3 letters of recommendation; sample of scholarly writing; audition and/or other practical application materials as appropriate to intended degree; for Graduate Certificate, bachelor's degree in music, music education, or the equivalent; transcripts; resume; personal statement; 3 letters of recommendation; audition. Additional exam requirements/recommendations for international students: Required—TOEFL (minimum score 79 iBT) or IELTS (minimum score 6.5). *Application deadline:* For fall admission, 2/1 for domestic and international students; for spring admission, 10/1 for domestic students, 9/1 for international students; for summer admission, 2/1 for domestic and international students. Applications are processed on a rolling basis. Application fee: $50 ($100 for international students). Electronic applications accepted. *Expenses:* Tuition, state resident: full-time $5119; part-time $213.30 per credit hour. Tuition, nonresident: full-time $19,778; part-time $824.10 per credit hour. *Required fees:* $3458; $133.55 per credit hour. $126.50 per semester. *Financial support:* In 2017–18, 123 students received support, including 2 fellowships with full tuition reimbursements available (averaging $5,000 per year), 35 research assistantships with full tuition reimbursements available (averaging $10,515 per year), 62 teaching assistantships with full tuition reimbursements available (averaging $10,452 per year); health care benefits, tuition waivers, and unspecified assistantships also available. Financial award application deadline: 6/1; financial award applicants required to submit FAFSA. *Faculty research:* Piano pedagogy, performance practice, music education, musicology, music theory. *Unit head:* Dr. Roland Barrett, Director, 405-325-2081, Fax: 405-325-7574, E-mail: rcbarrett@ou.edu. *Application contact:* Jan Russell, Graduate Admissions and Recruiting Advisor, 405-325-5393, Fax: 405-325-7574, E-mail: jrussell@ou.edu.
Website: http://music.ou.edu

University of Oregon, Graduate School, School of Music, Program in Music, Eugene, OR 97403. Offers composition (M Mus, DMA, PhD); conducting (M Mus); jazz studies (M Mus); music (MA), including music history, music theory; music history (PhD); music theory (PhD); performance (M Mus, DMA); piano pedagogy (M Mus). *Entrance requirements:* For master's, minimum GPA of 3.0, audition (performance applicants), videotape or interview (conducting applicants); for doctorate, GRE General Test, minimum GPA of 3.0, audition (performance applicants), videotape or interview (conducting applicants). Additional exam requirements/recommendations for international students: Required—TOEFL.

University of Ottawa, Faculty of Graduate and Postdoctoral Studies, Faculty of Arts, Department of Music, Ottawa, ON K1N 6N5, Canada. Offers music (M Mus, MA); orchestral studies (Certificate); piano pedagogy research (Certificate). *Degree requirements:* For master's, thesis optional. *Entrance requirements:* For master's, honors degree or equivalent, minimum B+ average. Electronic applications accepted. *Faculty research:* Performance, theory, musicology.

University of Pennsylvania, School of Arts and Sciences, Graduate Group in Music, Philadelphia, PA 19104. Offers AM, PhD. *Faculty:* 13 full-time (5 women), 3 part-time/adjunct (0 women). *Students:* 54 full-time (8 women); includes 9 minority (1 Black or African American, non-Hispanic/Latino; 4 Asian, non-Hispanic/Latino; 4 Hispanic/Latino), 31 international. Average age 26. 78 applicants, 14% accepted, 8 enrolled. In 2017, 3 master's, 11 doctorates awarded. Terminal master's awarded for partial completion of doctoral program. *Degree requirements:* For doctorate, thesis/dissertation.
Website: http://www.sas.upenn.edu/graduate-division

University of Pittsburgh, Kenneth P. Dietrich School of Arts and Sciences, Department of Music, Pittsburgh, PA 15260. Offers composition and theory (PhD); ethnomusicology (PhD); historical musicology (PhD); jazz studies (PhD); music (MA). *Faculty:* 13 full-time (5 women), 5 part-time/adjunct (2 women). *Students:* 39 full-time (14 women); includes 4 minority (2 Black or African American, non-Hispanic/Latino; 2 Asian, non-Hispanic/Latino), 12 international. Average age 33. 53 applicants, 23% accepted, 5 enrolled. In 2017, 5 master's, 8 doctorates awarded. Terminal master's awarded for partial completion of doctoral program. *Degree requirements:* For master's, thesis; for doctorate, comprehensive exam, thesis/dissertation, 1 foreign language (2 for musicology). *Entrance requirements:* For doctorate, GRE General Test, samples of work, 3 letters of reference, minimum GPA of 3.0, bachelor's degree. Additional exam requirements/recommendations for international students: Required—TOEFL (minimum score 90 iBT), IELTS (minimum score 7). *Application deadline:* For fall admission, 1/5 for domestic and international students. Application fee: $50. Electronic applications accepted. *Expenses:* $22,290 full-time resident, $898 per credit; $36,980 full-time nonresident, $1,512 per credit. *Financial support:* In 2017–18, 33 students received support, including 23 fellowships with full and partial tuition reimbursements available (averaging $18,717 per year), 3 research assistantships with full tuition reimbursements available (averaging $15,060 per year), 8 teaching assistantships with full and partial tuition reimbursements available (averaging $15,391 per year); scholarships/grants, health care benefits, tuition waivers (full and partial), and unspecified assistantships also available. Financial award application deadline: 1/5. *Faculty research:* Composition and theory, ethnomusicology, musicology, jazz studies. *Unit head:* Dr. Deane L. Root, Professor/Chair/Director of Graduate Admissions, 412-624-7775, Fax: 412-624-4186, E-mail: dlr@pitt.edu.
Website: http://www.music.pitt.edu/

University of Redlands, College of Arts and Sciences, School of Music, Redlands, CA 92373-0999. Offers MM. *Accreditation:* NASM. *Program availability:* Part-time. *Degree requirements:* For master's, comprehensive exam, thesis, 3 recitals, major conducted ensemble. *Entrance requirements:* For master's, GRE, bachelor's degree in music, minimum GPA of 2.75, audition, original scores. Additional exam requirements/recommendations for international students: Required—TOEFL (minimum score 550 paper-based). *Expenses:* Contact institution. *Faculty research:* Performance, composition.

University of Regina, Faculty of Graduate Studies and Research, Faculty of Media, Art, and Performance, Department of Music, Regina, SK S4S 0A2, Canada. Offers composition (MMus); conducting (MMus); music theory (MA); musicology (MA); performance (MMus), including piano, organ, voice, and orchestral instruments. *Faculty:* 7 full-time (3 women). *Students:* 4 applicants, 25% accepted. *Degree requirements:* For master's, thesis (for some programs), recital, oral exam, jury examinations. *Entrance requirements:* For master's, B Mus or equivalent; recent compositions (composers only); audition; singing ability in French, Italian, German (vocalists only); DVDs; scores. Additional exam requirements/recommendations for international students: Required—TOEFL (minimum score 580 paper-based; 80 iBT), IELTS (minimum score 6.5), PTE (minimum score 59). *Application deadline:* For fall admission, 1/15 for domestic and international students. Applications are processed on a rolling basis. Application fee: $100. Electronic applications accepted. *Expenses:* CAD$10,681 per year. *Financial support:* In 2017–18, teaching assistantships (averaging $2,562 per year) were awarded; fellowships, research assistantships, and scholarships/grants also available. Financial award application deadline: 6/15. *Faculty research:* Renaissance, Baroque, and Medieval music; music of the Classical and Romantic eras; analysis of music written since 1900; music theory; history of music theory. *Unit head:* Dr. William Hales, Department Head, 306-585-5568, Fax: 306-585-5549, E-mail: william.hales@uregina.ca. *Application contact:* Dr. Kathleen Irwin, Associate Dean, Graduate Studies and Research, 306-585-5519, Fax: 306-585-5544, E-mail: kathleen.irwin@uregina.ca.

University of Rhode Island, Graduate School, College of Arts and Sciences, Department of Music, Kingston, RI 02881. Offers music education (MM), including composition, conducting, performance, thesis; music performance (MM), including composition, conducting, voice or instrument. Program offered in partnership with School of Education. *Accreditation:* NASM. *Program availability:* Part-time. *Faculty:* 12 full-time (6 women). *Students:* 11 full-time (4 women), 1 (woman) part-time; includes 2 minority (both Black or African American, non-Hispanic/Latino). 12 applicants, 75% accepted, 6 enrolled. In 2017, 3 master's awarded. *Entrance requirements:* For master's, 2 letters of recommendation, audition. Additional exam requirements/recommendations for international students: Required—TOEFL. *Application deadline:* For fall admission, 7/15 for domestic students, 2/1 for international students; for spring admission, 11/15 for domestic students, 7/15 for international students. Application fee: $65. Electronic applications accepted. *Expenses:* Tuition, state resident: full-time $12,706; part-time $786 per credit. Tuition, nonresident: full-time $25,216; part-time $1401 per credit. *Required fees:* $1598; $45 per credit. One-time fee: $30 part-time. *Financial support:* In 2017–18, 3 teaching assistantships with tuition reimbursements (averaging $18,054 per year) were awarded. Financial award application deadline: 2/1; financial award applicants required to submit FAFSA. *Unit head:* Dr. Mark Conley, Chair, 401-874-2431, E-mail: mconley@uri.edu. *Application contact:* Dr. Joe Parillo, Director of Graduate Studies, 401-874-2431, E-mail: jmparillo@uri.edu.
Website: https://web.uri.edu/music/

University of Rochester, Eastman School of Music, Program in Ethnomusicology, Rochester, NY 14627. Offers MA.

University of Rochester, Eastman School of Music, Program in Music Theory Pedagogy, Rochester, NY 14627. Offers MA.

University of Rochester, Eastman School of Music, Programs in Music Composition, Rochester, NY 14627. Offers MA, MM, DMA, PhD.

University of Rochester, Eastman School of Music, Programs in Musicology, Rochester, NY 14627. Offers PhD.

University of Rochester, Eastman School of Music, Programs in Music Theory, Rochester, NY 14627. Offers PhD.

University of St. Thomas, College of Arts and Sciences, Graduate Programs in Music Education, St. Paul, MN 55105-1096. Offers choral (MA); instrumental (MA); Kodaly (MA); leadership in music education (Ed D); Orff Schulwerk (MA); piano pedagogy (MA). *Accreditation:* NASM; NCATE. *Program availability:* Part-time. *Faculty:* 11 full-time (5 women), 16 part-time/adjunct (9 women). *Students:* 153 part-time (117 women). 3 applicants, 100% accepted, 3 enrolled. In 2017, 19 master's awarded. *Degree requirements:* For master's, comprehensive exam, thesis, music history theory and diagnostic exam, piano recital (for piano pedagogy students), oral exam. *Entrance requirements:* For master's, performance assessment hearing, interview. Additional exam requirements/recommendations for international students: Required—TOEFL (minimum score 550 paper-based; 80 iBT). *Application deadline:* For fall admission, 7/1 for domestic and international students; for winter admission, 12/1 for domestic and international students; for spring admission, 4/1 for domestic and international students. Applications are processed on a rolling basis. Application fee: $0. Electronic applications accepted. *Expenses:* $875.50 per credit. *Financial support:* In 2017–18, 23 students received support. Federal Work-Study, institutionally sponsored loans, and scholarships/grants available. Financial award application deadline: 4/1; financial award applicants required to submit FAFSA. *Faculty research:* Kodaly, choral, piano pedagogy, Orff, instrumental, world music. *Unit head:* Dr. Douglas C. Orzolek, Director, 651-962-5878, Fax: 651-962-5886, E-mail: dcorzolek@stthomas.edu. *Application contact:* Bev Johnson, Program Coordinator, 651-962-5870, Fax: 651-962-5886, E-mail: bhjohnson@stthomas.edu.
Website: http://www.stthomas.edu/music/graduate

University of St. Thomas, School of Arts and Sciences, Houston, TX 77006-4696. Offers public policy administration (MPPA); sacred music (MSM). *Program availability:* Part-time. *Faculty:* 2 full-time (0 women), 5 part-time/adjunct (3 women). *Students:* 4 full-time (3 women), 21 part-time (13 women); includes 18 minority (8 Black or African American, non-Hispanic/Latino; 10 Hispanic/Latino), 1 international. Average age 34. 8 applicants, 100% accepted, 8 enrolled. In 2017, 8 master's awarded. *Entrance requirements:* Additional exam requirements/recommendations for international students: Required—TOEFL (minimum score 79 iBT), IELTS (minimum score 6.5), PTE (minimum score 53). *Application deadline:* For fall admission, 7/15 priority date for domestic and international students; for spring admission, 12/1 priority date for domestic and international students; for summer admission, 5/1 priority date for domestic and international students. Applications are processed on a rolling basis. Application fee: $35. Electronic applications accepted. *Expenses: Tuition:* Full-time $20,934; part-time $1163 per credit hour. *Required fees:* $250; $210 per semester. *Financial support:* In 2017–18, 6 students received support. Federal Work-Study, scholarships/grants, and state work-study, institutional employment available. Support available to part-time students. Financial award application deadline: 4/15; financial award applicants required to submit FAFSA. *Unit head:* Dr. Christopher Evans, Dean, School of Arts and Sciences, 713-525-7863, E-mail: evanscp@stthom.edu. *Application contact:* Elizabeth Kimes, 713-942-3491, E-mail: kimese@stthom.edu.
Website: http://www.stthom.edu/Academics/School_of_Arts_and_Sciences/Index.aqf

Music

University of Saskatchewan, College of Graduate Studies and Research, College of Arts and Science, Department of Music, Saskatoon, SK S7N 5A2, Canada. Offers M Mus, MA. *Degree requirements:* For master's, thesis. *Entrance requirements:* Additional exam requirements/recommendations for international students: Required—TOEFL (minimum score 80 iBT); Recommended—IELTS (minimum score 6.5). Electronic applications accepted.

University of South Africa, College of Human Sciences, Pretoria, South Africa. Offers adult education (M Ed); African languages (MA, PhD); African politics (MA, PhD); Afrikaans (MA, PhD); ancient history (MA, PhD); ancient Near Eastern studies (MA, PhD); anthropology (MA, PhD); applied linguistics (MA); Arabic (MA, PhD); archaeology (MA); art history (MA); Biblical archaeology (MA); Biblical studies (M Th, D Th, PhD); Christian spirituality (M Th, D Th); church history (M Th, D Th); classical studies (MA, PhD); clinical psychology (MA); communication (MA, PhD); comparative education (M Ed, Ed D); consulting psychology (D Admin, D Com, PhD); curriculum studies (M Ed, Ed D); development studies (M Admin, MA, D Admin, PhD); didactics (M Ed, Ed D); education (M Tech); education management (M Ed, Ed D); educational psychology (M Ed); English (MA); environmental education (M Ed); French (MA, PhD); German (MA, PhD); Greek (MA); guidance and counseling (M Ed); health studies (MA, PhD), including health sciences education (MA), health services management (MA), medical and surgical nursing science (critical care general) (MA), midwifery and neonatal nursing science (MA), trauma and emergency care (MA); history (MA, PhD); history of education (Ed D); inclusive education (M Ed, Ed D); information and communications technology policy and regulation (MA); information science (MA, MIS, PhD); international politics (MA, PhD); Islamic studies (MA, PhD); Italian (MA, PhD); Judaica (MA, PhD); linguistics (MA, PhD); mathematical education (M Ed); mathematics education (MA); missiology (M Th, D Th); modern Hebrew (MA, PhD); musicology (MA, MMus, D Mus, PhD); natural science education (M Ed); New Testament (M Th, D Th); Old Testament (D Th); pastoral therapy (M Th, D Th); philosophy (MA); philosophy of education (M Ed, Ed D); politics (MA, PhD); Portuguese (MA, PhD); practical theology (M Th, D Th); psychology (MA, MS, PhD); psychology of education (M Ed, Ed D); public health (MA); religious studies (MA, D Th, PhD); Romance languages (MA); Russian (MA, PhD); Semitic languages (MA, PhD); social behavior studies in HIV/AIDS (MA); social science (mental health) (MA); social science in development studies (MA); social science in psychology (MA); social science in social work (MA); social science in sociology (MA); social work (MSW, DSW, PhD); socio-education (M Ed, Ed D); sociolinguistics (MA); sociology (MA, PhD); Spanish (MA, PhD); systematic theology (M Th, D Th); TESOL (teaching English to speakers of other languages) (MA); theological ethics (M Th, D Th); theory of literature (MA, PhD); urban ministries (D Th); urban ministry (M Th).

University of South Alabama, College of Arts and Sciences, Department of Music, Mobile, AL 36688. Offers collaborative keyboard (MM); music education (MM); performance (MM). *Faculty:* 4 full-time (1 woman). *Students:* 2 full-time (both women), 2 part-time (0 women). Average age 34. 4 applicants. *Degree requirements:* For master's, comprehensive exam, final project. *Entrance requirements:* For master's, GRE/GMAT, undergraduate degree in music with minimum GPA of 3.0, official transcript, resume, 3 recommendation letters; teaching certificate (for music education). Additional exam requirements/recommendations for international students: Required—TOEFL (minimum score 525 paper-based; 71 iBT). *Application deadline:* For fall admission, 7/1 priority date for domestic students, 6/1 priority date for international students; for spring admission, 12/1 priority date for domestic students, 11/1 priority date for international students; for summer admission, 5/1 priority date for domestic students, 4/1 priority date for international students. Applications are processed on a rolling basis. Application fee: $35. Electronic applications accepted. *Expenses:* Tuition, state resident: full-time $10,104; part-time $421 per semester hour. Tuition, nonresident: full-time $20,208; part-time $842 per semester hour. *Financial support:* Fellowships, research assistantships, teaching assistantships, career-related internships or fieldwork, Federal Work-Study, institutionally sponsored loans, scholarships/grants, and unspecified assistantships available. Support available to part-time students. Financial award application deadline: 3/31; financial award applicants required to submit FAFSA. *Unit head:* Dr. Greg Gruner, Chair, Music, 251-460-6804, Fax: 251-460-7328, E-mail: ggruner@southalabama.edu. *Application contact:* Dr. Jeannette Fresne, Graduate Coordinator, Music, 251-460-6697, Fax: 251-460-7328, E-mail: jfresne@southalabama.edu.
Website: http://www.southalabama.edu/colleges/music/

University of South Carolina, The Graduate School, School of Music, Columbia, SC 29208. Offers composition (MM, DMA); conducting (MM, DMA); jazz studies (MM); music education (MM Ed, PhD); music history (MM); music performance (Certificate); music theory (MM); opera theater (MM); performance (MM, DMA); piano pedagogy (MM, DMA). *Accreditation:* NASM. *Program availability:* Part-time. *Degree requirements:* For master's, 5 foreign languages, comprehensive exam, thesis (for some programs); for doctorate, one foreign language, comprehensive exam, thesis/dissertation; for Certificate, recitals. *Entrance requirements:* For master's and doctorate, GRE General Test or MAT, music diagnostic exam. Additional exam requirements/recommendations for international students: Required—TOEFL (minimum score 570 paper-based). Electronic applications accepted. *Expenses:* Contact institution. *Faculty research:* Music skills in pre-school children, evaluation of school performing ensembles.

University of South Dakota, Graduate School, College of Fine Arts, Department of Music, Vermillion, SD 57069. Offers collaborative piano (MM); conducting (MM); history of musical instruments (MM); music education (MM); music history (MM); music performance (MM). *Accreditation:* NASM. *Degree requirements:* For master's, thesis or alternative. *Entrance requirements:* For master's, minimum GPA of 2.7, audition or performance tape. Additional exam requirements/recommendations for international students: Required—TOEFL (minimum score 550 paper-based; 79 iBT). *Application deadline:* Applications are processed on a rolling basis. Application fee: $35. Electronic applications accepted. *Financial support:* Research assistantships with partial tuition reimbursements, teaching assistantships with partial tuition reimbursements, and scholarships/grants available. Financial award applicants required to submit FAFSA. *Application contact:* Graduate School, 605-658-6140, Fax: 605-677-6118, E-mail: grad@usd.edu.
Website: http://www.usd.edu/fine-arts/music

University of Southern California, Graduate School, Thornton School of Music, Los Angeles, CA 90089. Offers brass performance (MM, DMA, Graduate Certificate); choral and sacred music (MM, DMA); classical guitar (MM, DMA, Graduate Certificate); composition (MM, DMA); early music (MA, DMA); harp performance (MM, DMA, Graduate Certificate); historical musicology (PhD); jazz studies (MM, DMA, Graduate Certificate); keyboard collaborative arts (MM, DMA, Graduate Certificate); music education (MM, DMA); organ performance (MM, DMA, Graduate Certificate); percussion performance (MM, DMA, Graduate Certificate); piano performance (MM, DMA, Graduate Certificate); scoring for motion pictures and television (Graduate Certificate); strings performance (MM, DMA, Graduate Certificate); studio jazz guitar (MM, DMA, Graduate Certificate); teaching music (MA); vocal arts (classical voice/opera) (MM, DMA, Graduate Certificate); woodwind performance (MM, DMA, Graduate Certificate). *Program availability:* Part-time, evening/weekend. Terminal master's awarded for partial completion of doctoral program. *Degree requirements:* For master's, variable foreign language requirement, comprehensive exam (for some programs), thesis (for some programs); for doctorate, variable foreign language requirement, comprehensive exam, thesis/dissertation (for some programs). *Entrance requirements:* For master's, GRE (for MA in early music and MM in music education); for doctorate, GRE (for DMA). Additional exam requirements/recommendations for international students: Required—TOEFL (minimum score 560 paper-based; 83 iBT). Electronic applications accepted. *Expenses:* Contact institution. *Faculty research:* Early Modern musical improvisation and composition, maternal sound stimulation of the premature infant, physiological characteristics of jazz guitarists, the musical experience of the very young child, electronic music.

University of Southern Maine, College of Arts, Humanities, and Social Sciences, School of Music, Portland, ME 04103. Offers composition (MM); conducting (MM); jazz studies (MM); music education (MM); performance (MM). *Accreditation:* NASM.

University of Southern Mississippi, College of Arts and Letters, Department of Theatre, Hattiesburg, MS 39406-0001. Offers costume design (MFA); directing (MFA); lighting and sound design (MFA); performance (MFA); scenic design (MFA). *Accreditation:* NAST. *Program availability:* Part-time. *Students:* 9 full-time (6 women). 13 applicants, 69% accepted, 9 enrolled. In 2017, 2 master's awarded. *Degree requirements:* For master's, comprehensive exam, thesis or alternative, creative project. *Entrance requirements:* For master's, GRE General Test, minimum GPA of 3.0. Additional exam requirements/recommendations for international students: Required—TOEFL, IELTS. *Application deadline:* For fall admission, 3/1 priority date for domestic students, 3/1 for international students; for spring admission, 1/10 priority date for domestic and international students. Applications are processed on a rolling basis. Application fee: $60. Electronic applications accepted. *Expenses:* Tuition, state resident: full-time $3830. *Financial support:* Research assistantships, teaching assistantships with full tuition reimbursements, career-related internships or fieldwork, Federal Work-Study, institutionally sponsored loans, health care benefits, and unspecified assistantships available. Support available to part-time students. Financial award application deadline: 3/15; financial award applicants required to submit FAFSA. *Faculty research:* Technical design, acting. *Unit head:* Louis Rackoff, Chair, 601-266-6907, Fax: 601-266-6423.
Website: http://www.usm.edu/theatre

University of Southern Mississippi, College of Arts and Letters, School of Music, Hattiesburg, MS 39406-0001. Offers conducting (DMA); music education (MME); performance and pedagogy (DMA); piano accompanying (MM); theory (MM); woodwind performance and pedagogy (MM). *Accreditation:* NASM. *Program availability:* Blended/hybrid learning. *Students:* 37 full-time (14 women), 2 part-time (0 women). 89 applicants, 74% accepted, 39 enrolled. In 2017, 3 master's, 1 doctorate awarded. Terminal master's awarded for partial completion of doctoral program. *Degree requirements:* For master's, comprehensive exam, thesis (for some programs); for doctorate, comprehensive exam, thesis/dissertation. *Entrance requirements:* For master's, GRE General Test, minimum GPA of 2.75 in last 60 hours; for doctorate, GRE General Test, minimum GPA of 3.5. Additional exam requirements/recommendations for international students: Required—TOEFL, IELTS. *Application deadline:* For fall admission, 6/1 for domestic students; for spring admission, 11/1 for domestic students; for summer admission, 3/1 for domestic students. Applications are processed on a rolling basis. Application fee: $60. *Expenses:* Tuition, state resident: full-time $3830. *Financial support:* Fellowships with full tuition reimbursements, research assistantships, teaching assistantships with full tuition reimbursements, Federal Work-Study, institutionally sponsored loans, scholarships/grants, health care benefits, tuition waivers (partial), and unspecified assistantships available. Financial award application deadline: 2/1; financial award applicants required to submit FAFSA. *Faculty research:* Music theory, composition, music performance. *Unit head:* Dr. Richard Kravchak, Director, 601-266-5543, Fax: 601-266-6427.
Website: https://www.usm.edu/music

University of South Florida, College of The Arts, School of Music, Tampa, FL 33620-9951. Offers music (MM, PhD), including chamber music (MM), choral conducting (MM), composition (MM), electro-acoustic music (MM), instrumental conducting (MM), jazz composition (MM), jazz performance (MM), music education (PhD), performance (MM), piano pedagogy (MM), theory (MM); music education (MA). *Accreditation:* NASM. *Program availability:* Part-time, evening/weekend. *Faculty:* 27 full-time (8 women), 1 part-time/adjunct (0 women). *Students:* 62 full-time (28 women), 20 part-time (7 women); includes 13 minority (3 Black or African American, non-Hispanic/Latino; 1 Asian, non-Hispanic/Latino; 7 Hispanic/Latino; 2 Two or more races, non-Hispanic/Latino), 21 international. Average age 30. 59 applicants, 61% accepted, 27 enrolled. In 2017, 27 master's, 2 doctorates awarded. *Degree requirements:* For master's, comprehensive exam, thesis optional; for doctorate, comprehensive exam, thesis/dissertation. *Entrance requirements:* For master's, minimum GPA of 3.0 in upper-division courses and music courses for bachelor's degree; resume; three letters of recommendation; at least 2 years of K-12 music teaching experience (for MA in music education); audition or interview (for MM); for doctorate, GRE General Test, master's degree from accredited institution with minimum GPA of 3.5, 3.0 in upper-division undergraduate courses; at least 2 years of K-12 music teaching experience; interview with faculty; 3 letters of recommendation; academic writing sample; curriculum vitae; personal goals statement; 15-20 minute video of applicant teaching music. Additional exam requirements/recommendations for international students: Required—TOEFL (minimum score 550 paper-based; 79 iBT) or IELTS (minimum score 6.5). *Application deadline:* For fall admission, 2/15 priority date for domestic students, 2/1 for international students; for spring admission, 10/15 for domestic students, 9/15 for international students; for summer admission, 2/15 for domestic students, 1/15 for international students. Application fee: $30. Electronic applications accepted. *Financial support:* In 2017–18, 39 students received support, including 1 research assistantship with tuition reimbursement available (averaging $15,724 per year), 46 teaching assistantships with tuition reimbursements available (averaging $10,099 per year); unspecified assistantships also available. Financial award application deadline: 2/15. *Faculty research:* Music education: alternate methods, community collaboration, contemporary changes, early childhood, general music, international perspectives, multicultural issues, technology, teacher behaviors, philosophy, psychology, sociology; music: chamber music, composition, conducting, jazz studies, music performance, music theory, pedagogy, electronic music. *Total annual research expenditures:* $43,461. *Unit head:* Dr. Karen Bryan, Director, 813-974-2311, Fax: 813-974-8721, E-mail: kmbryan@usf.edu. *Application contact:* Dr. David Williams, Associate Director/Associate Professor of Music Education, 813-974-9166, Fax: 813-974-8721, E-mail: davidw@usf.edu.
Website: http://music.arts.usf.edu/

The University of Tennessee, Graduate School, College of Arts and Sciences, Department of Theatre, Knoxville, TN 37996. Offers costume design (MFA); lighting design (MFA); performance (MFA); scene design (MFA); theatre technology (MFA). *Accreditation:* NAST. *Degree requirements:* For master's, thesis or alternative. *Entrance requirements:* For master's, audition, minimum GPA of 2.7. Additional exam requirements/recommendations for international students: Required—TOEFL. Electronic applications accepted.

The University of Tennessee, Graduate School, College of Arts and Sciences, School of Music, Knoxville, TN 37996. Offers accompanying (MM); choral conducting (MM);

composition (MM); instrumental conducting (MM); jazz (MM); music education (MM); music theory (MM); musicology (MM); performance (MM); piano pedagogy and literature (MM). *Accreditation:* NASM. *Program availability:* Part-time. *Degree requirements:* For master's, thesis (for some programs). *Entrance requirements:* For master's, audition, minimum GPA of 2.7. Additional exam requirements/recommendations for international students: Required—TOEFL. Electronic applications accepted.

The University of Tennessee at Chattanooga, Program in Music, Chattanooga, TN 37403. Offers music education (MM); performance (MM). *Accreditation:* NASM. In 2017, 6 master's awarded. *Degree requirements:* For master's, comprehensive exam, thesis or alternative, recital. *Entrance requirements:* For master's, GRE General Test, bachelor's degree in music. Additional exam requirements/recommendations for international students: Required—TOEFL (minimum score 550 paper-based; 79 iBT), IELTS (minimum score 6). *Application deadline:* For fall admission, 6/15 priority date for domestic students, 7/1 for international students; for spring admission, 11/1 priority date for domestic students, 11/1 for international students. Applications are processed on a rolling basis. Application fee: $35 ($40 for international students). Electronic applications accepted. *Expenses:* Contact institution. *Financial support:* Research assistantships, Federal Work-Study, scholarships/grants, and unspecified assistantships available. Financial award application deadline: 7/1; financial award applicants required to submit FAFSA. *Faculty research:* Music education, conducting, opera, vocal instruction, orchestras. *Total annual research expenditures:* $1,400. *Unit head:* Dr. Stuart Benkert, Interim Department Head, 423-425-4614, Fax: 423-425-4603, E-mail: stuart-benkert@utc.edu. *Application contact:* Dr. Joanne Romagni, Dean of the Graduate School, 423-425-4478, Fax: 423-425-5223, E-mail: joanne-romagni@utc.edu.
Website: http://www.utc.edu/music/

The University of Texas at Arlington, Graduate School, College of Liberal Arts, Department of Music, Arlington, TX 76019. Offers education (MM); performance (MM). *Accreditation:* NASM. *Program availability:* Part-time, evening/weekend. *Degree requirements:* For master's, comprehensive exam, thesis optional. *Entrance requirements:* For master's, GRE, 3 letters of recommendation, minimum GPA of 3.0 in last 60 hours of course work. Additional exam requirements/recommendations for international students: Required—TOEFL (minimum score 550 paper-based). Electronic applications accepted.

The University of Texas at Austin, Graduate School, College of Fine Arts, Sarah and Ernest Butler School of Music, Austin, TX 78712-1111. Offers band and wind conducting (M Music, DMA); brass/woodwind/percussion (MM, DMA); chamber music (MM); choral conducting (MM, DMA); collaborative piano (MM, DMA); composition (MM, DMA), including composition, jazz, jazz (DMA); ethnomusicology (MM, PhD); literature and pedagogy (MM); music and human learning (MM, PhD); music and human learning (DMA), including jazz (MM, DMA), piano pedagogy; musicology (MM, PhD); opera performance (MM, DMA); orchestral conducting (MM, DMA); organ (MM), including sacred music; organ performance (MM, DMA); performance (MM), including jazz (MM, DMA); performance (DMA), including jazz (MM, DMA); piano (DMA), including jazz (MM, DMA); piano literature and pedagogy (MM); piano performance (MM, DMA); string performance (MM, DMA); theory (MM, PhD); vocal performance (MM, DMA); voice (DMA), including opera; voice performance pedagogy (DMA); woodwind, brass, percussion performance (MM). *Accreditation:* NASM. *Program availability:* Part-time. *Degree requirements:* For master's, one foreign language, comprehensive exam, thesis (for some programs), recital (performance or composition majors); for doctorate, one foreign language, comprehensive exam, thesis/dissertation (for some programs), recital (for performance or composition majors). *Entrance requirements:* For master's and doctorate, GRE General Test (except for performance or composition majors), audition (performance majors). Electronic applications accepted.

The University of Texas at El Paso, Graduate School, College of Liberal Arts, Department of Music, El Paso, TX 79968-0001. Offers music education (MM); music performance (MM). *Accreditation:* NASM. *Program availability:* Part-time, evening/weekend. *Degree requirements:* For master's, thesis optional. *Entrance requirements:* For master's, audition, interview, letters of recommendation. Additional exam requirements/recommendations for international students: Required—TOEFL; Recommended—IELTS. Electronic applications accepted.

The University of Texas at San Antonio, College of Liberal and Fine Arts, Department of Music, San Antonio, TX 78249-0617. Offers MM. *Accreditation:* NASM. *Program availability:* Part-time. *Faculty:* 15 full-time (6 women), 4 part-time/adjunct (2 women). *Students:* 10 full-time (7 women), 17 part-time (8 women); includes 11 minority (1 Asian, non-Hispanic/Latino; 8 Hispanic/Latino; 2 Two or more races, non-Hispanic/Latino). Average age 33. 8 applicants, 38% accepted, 2 enrolled. In 2017, 8 master's awarded. *Degree requirements:* For master's, comprehensive exam, thesis (for some programs). *Entrance requirements:* For master's, GRE, audition, 3 letters of recommendation. Additional exam requirements/recommendations for international students: Required—TOEFL (minimum score 550 paper-based; 79 iBT), IELTS (minimum score 6.5). *Application deadline:* For fall admission, 2/1 for domestic and international students; for spring admission, 10/15 for domestic students, 9/15 for international students. Application fee: $50 ($90 for international students). Electronic applications accepted. *Expenses:* Tuition, state resident: full-time $5495. Tuition, nonresident: full-time $21,938. *Required fees:* $1915. Tuition and fees vary according to program. *Financial support:* Scholarships/grants and unspecified assistantships available. *Faculty research:* Music cognition and perception, dalcroze eurhythmics in therapy, vocology, music of the Americas, music and film. *Total annual research expenditures:* $4,771. *Unit head:* Dr. Eugene Dowdy, Interim Chair, 210-458-5683, E-mail: eugene.dowdy@utsa.edu.
Website: http://music.utsa.edu

The University of Texas Rio Grande Valley, College of Fine Arts, School of Music, Edinburg, TX 78539. Offers MM. *Accreditation:* NASM. *Program availability:* Part-time. *Faculty:* 14 full-time (4 women), 1 part-time/adjunct (0 women). *Students:* 7 full-time (1 woman), 8 part-time (4 women); includes 9 minority (all Hispanic/Latino), 3 international. Average age 33. 12 applicants, 100% accepted, 6 enrolled. In 2017, 9 master's awarded. *Degree requirements:* For master's, comprehensive exam, thesis optional, recital (performance). *Entrance requirements:* For master's, audition for performance area, bachelor's degree in music. Additional exam requirements/recommendations for international students: Required—TOEFL or IELTS. Application fee: $50 ($100 for international students). *Expenses:* Tuition, state resident: full-time $5550; part-time $417 per credit hour. Tuition, nonresident: full-time $13,020; part-time $832 per credit hour. *Required fees:* $1169. *Faculty research:* Music history, instrumental pedagogy, vocal pedagogy, music education, ethnomusicology. *Unit head:* Kurt Martinez, Director, E-mail: kurt.martinez@utrgv.edu.

The University of the Arts, College of Performing Arts, School of Music, Program in Jazz Studies, Philadelphia, PA 19102-4944. Offers MM. *Degree requirements:* For master's, recital, thesis/project. *Entrance requirements:* For master's, audition consisting of a performance, interview and written examination to measure aural, theoretical, arranging and historical skills and knowledge; official transcripts from each undergraduate or graduate school attended; three letters of recommendation; one- to two-page statement of professional plans and goals. Additional exam requirements/recommendations for international students: Required—TOEFL (minimum score 580 paper-based, 92 iBT) or IELTS (minimum score 6.5).

University of the Pacific, Conservatory of Music, Stockton, CA 95211-0197. Offers music education (MM); music therapy (MA). *Faculty:* 4 full-time (2 women), 3 part-time/adjunct (all women). *Students:* 8 full-time (4 women), 17 part-time (11 women); includes 9 minority (1 Black or African American, non-Hispanic/Latino; 4 Asian, non-Hispanic/Latino; 2 Hispanic/Latino; 2 Two or more races, non-Hispanic/Latino), 3 international. Average age 31. 36 applicants, 42% accepted, 9 enrolled. In 2017, 5 master's awarded. *Entrance requirements:* For master's, GRE General Test. Additional exam requirements/recommendations for international students: Required—TOEFL. *Application deadline:* For fall admission, 3/1 priority date for domestic students; for spring admission, 10/1 priority date for domestic students. Applications are processed on a rolling basis. Application fee: $75. *Financial support:* Teaching assistantships and institutionally sponsored loans available. Support available to part-time students. Financial award application deadline: 3/1; financial award applicants required to submit FAFSA. *Unit head:* Dr. Daniel Ebbers, Interim Dean, 209-946-2415, E-mail: musicdean@pacific.edu. *Application contact:* 209-946-2415, Fax: 209-946-2770.

The University of Toledo, College of Graduate Studies, College of Communication and the Arts, Department of Music, Toledo, OH 43606-3390. Offers music (Certificate); music performance (MMP). *Accreditation:* NASM. *Degree requirements:* For master's, comprehensive exam, diagnostic theory exam. *Entrance requirements:* For master's, GRE if GPA less than 2.7, minimum cumulative point-hour ratio of 2.7 for all previous academic work, audition. Additional exam requirements/recommendations for international students: Required—TOEFL (minimum score 550 paper-based; 80 iBT). Electronic applications accepted.

University of Toronto, School of Graduate Studies, Faculty of Music, Toronto, ON M5S 1A1, Canada. Offers composition (M Mus, DMA); ethnomusicology (MA, PhD); jazz (M Mus); music education (MA, PhD); musicology/theory (MA, PhD); opera (M Mus); performance (M Mus, DMA). *Program availability:* Part-time. *Degree requirements:* For master's, comprehensive exam (for some programs), oral examination (M Mus in composition), 1 foreign language (MA); for doctorate, recital of original works (DMA), thesis (PhD). *Entrance requirements:* For master's, BM in area of specialization with minimum B average in final 2 years, original compositions (M Mus in composition); for doctorate, master's degree in area of specialization, minimum B+ average, at least 2 extended compositions (DMA). Additional exam requirements/recommendations for international students: Required—TOEFL (minimum score 580 paper-based; 93 iBT), TWE (minimum score 5). Electronic applications accepted.

University of Utah, Graduate School, College of Fine Arts, School of Music, Salt Lake City, UT 84112. Offers choral conducting (M Mus, DMA); collaborative piano (M Mus); composition (M Mus, PhD); instrumental conducting (M Mus, DMA); instrumental performance (M Mus, DMA); jazz studies (M Mus); music education (M Mus, PhD); music history and literature (M Mus); musicology (MA); organ performance (M Mus); piano performance (M Mus, DMA); piano performance and pedagogy (M Mus); string performance and pedagogy (M Mus); theory (M Mus); vocal performance (DMA). *Accreditation:* NASM. *Faculty:* 23 full-time (5 women), 59 part-time/adjunct (22 women). *Students:* 68 full-time (31 women), 21 part-time (12 women); includes 12 minority (5 Asian, non-Hispanic/Latino; 4 Hispanic/Latino; 1 Native Hawaiian or other Pacific Islander, non-Hispanic/Latino; 2 Two or more races, non-Hispanic/Latino), 18 international. Average age 25. 121 applicants, 55% accepted, 31 enrolled. In 2017, 28 master's, 10 doctorates awarded. *Entrance requirements:* For master's, placement exams, minimum GPA of 3.0, audition, bachelor's degree in music; for doctorate, placement exams, minimum GPA of 3.0, audition, master's degree in music. Additional exam requirements/recommendations for international students: Required—TOEFL (minimum score 85 iBT). *Application deadline:* For fall admission, 2/15 for domestic students, 1/15 for international students; for spring admission, 10/1 for domestic students, 9/1 for international students; for summer admission, 3/15 for domestic students, 2/15 for international students. Applications are processed on a rolling basis. Application fee: $55 ($65 for international students). Electronic applications accepted. *Expenses:* Contact institution. *Financial support:* In 2017–18, 62 students received support, including 52 teaching assistantships with full and partial tuition reimbursements available (averaging $10,875 per year); scholarships/grants, health care benefits, tuition waivers (full and partial), and unspecified assistantships also available. Financial award application deadline: 2/15. *Faculty research:* Music education, conducting, musicology, composition, performance. *Total annual research expenditures:* $25,000. *Unit head:* Miguel Chuaqui, Director, 801-585-3720, E-mail: m.chauqui@utah.edu. *Application contact:* Cassie Wagstaff, Academic Coordinator, 801-585-6972, Fax: 801-581-5683, E-mail: cassandra.wagstaff@utah.edu.
Website: http://www.music.utah.edu/

University of Valley Forge, Program in Music Technology, Phoenixville, PA 19460. Offers MM. *Program availability:* Online learning.

University of Victoria, Faculty of Graduate Studies, Faculty of Fine Arts, School of Music, Victoria, BC V8W 2Y2, Canada. Offers composition (M Mus); musicology (MA, PhD); musicology with performance (MA); performance (M Mus). *Degree requirements:* For master's, 2 foreign languages, thesis; for doctorate, 2 foreign languages, thesis/dissertation, candidacy exam. *Entrance requirements:* For master's, theory placement test, audition or sample papers and compositions; for doctorate, audition or sample papers and compositions. Additional exam requirements/recommendations for international students: Required—TOEFL (minimum score 575 paper-based), IELTS (minimum score 7). Electronic applications accepted. *Faculty research:* Beethoven, Wagner, metrical structure in tonal music, French baroque, eighteenth-century opera.

University of Virginia, College and Graduate School of Arts and Sciences, Department of Music, Charlottesville, VA 22903. Offers MA, PhD. *Faculty:* 18 full-time (3 women), 14 part-time/adjunct (7 women). *Students:* 26 full-time (11 women); includes 7 minority (1 Black or African American, non-Hispanic/Latino; 1 American Indian or Alaska Native, non-Hispanic/Latino; 2 Hispanic/Latino; 3 Two or more races, non-Hispanic/Latino), 1 international. Average age 30. 44 applicants, 20% accepted, 5 enrolled. In 2017, 7 doctorates awarded. *Degree requirements:* For master's, one foreign language, article-length paper; for doctorate, one foreign language, comprehensive exam, thesis/dissertation. *Entrance requirements:* For master's and doctorate, GRE General Test, 2 writing samples or portfolio. Additional exam requirements/recommendations for international students: Required—TOEFL (minimum score 600 paper-based; 90 iBT), IELTS (minimum score 7). *Application deadline:* For fall admission, 1/1 for domestic students, 1/2 for international students. Applications are processed on a rolling basis. Application fee: $60. Electronic applications accepted. *Financial support:* Teaching assistantships available. Financial award applicants required to submit FAFSA. *Unit head:* Matthew Burtner, Chair, 434-924-3052, Fax: 434-924-6033, E-mail: mburtner@virginia.edu. *Application contact:* Michael Puri, Director of Graduate Studies, 434-924-3052, Fax: 434-924-6033, E-mail: mjp3h@virginia.edu.
Website: http://music.virginia.edu/

University of Washington, Graduate School, College of Arts and Sciences, School of Music, Concentration in Choral Conducting, Seattle, WA 98195. Offers MM, DMA.

Music

University of Washington, Graduate School, College of Arts and Sciences, School of Music, Concentration in Ethnomusicology, Seattle, WA 98195. Offers MA.

University of Washington, Graduate School, College of Arts and Sciences, School of Music, Concentration in Music History, Seattle, WA 98195. Offers MA, PhD.

University of Washington, Graduate School, College of Arts and Sciences, School of Music, Department of Choral Music, Seattle, WA 98195. Offers choral conducting (MM, DMA).

The University of Western Ontario, Faculty of Graduate Studies, Don Wright Faculty of Music, London, ON N6A 5B8, Canada. Offers music (M Mus, PhD); popular music and culture (MA). *Program availability:* Part-time. Terminal master's awarded for partial completion of doctoral program. *Degree requirements:* For master's, 2 foreign languages, thesis (for some programs), recital; for doctorate, 2 foreign languages, thesis/dissertation. *Entrance requirements:* For master's, honors degree in music; minimum A average in proposed area of concentration, B average overall; for doctorate, MA or equivalent. *Faculty research:* Systematic musicology, musicology, theory, music education.

University of West Georgia, College of Arts and Humanities, Carrollton, GA 30118. Offers English (MA); history (MA); museum studies (Postbaccalaureate Certificate); music performance (M Mus); music teacher education (M Mus); public history (Postbaccalaureate Certificate). *Program availability:* Part-time, evening/weekend, 100% online, blended/hybrid learning. *Faculty:* 69 full-time (38 women). *Students:* 25 full-time (15 women), 51 part-time (34 women); includes 16 minority (7 Black or African American, non-Hispanic/Latino; 1 American Indian or Alaska Native, non-Hispanic/Latino; 2 Asian, non-Hispanic/Latino; 5 Hispanic/Latino; 1 Two or more races, non-Hispanic/Latino), 1 international. Average age 30. 23 applicants, 96% accepted, 16 enrolled. In 2017, 29 master's, 6 other advanced degrees awarded. *Entrance requirements:* Additional exam requirements/recommendations for international students: Required—TOEFL (minimum score 523 paper-based; 69 iBT); Recommended—IELTS (minimum score 6.5). *Application deadline:* For fall admission, 8/1 for domestic students, 6/1 for international students; for spring admission, 11/15 for domestic students, 10/15 for international students; for summer admission, 5/15 for domestic students, 3/30 for international students. Applications are processed on a rolling basis. Application fee: $40. Electronic applications accepted. Tuition and fees vary according to degree level and program. *Financial support:* Fellowships, research assistantships, teaching assistantships, career-related internships or fieldwork, Federal Work-Study, institutionally sponsored loans, scholarships/grants, and unspecified assistantships available. Support available to part-time students. Financial award application deadline: 4/1; financial award applicants required to submit FAFSA. *Unit head:* Dr. Pauline D. Gagnon, Dean of Arts and Humanities, 678-839-5450, Fax: 678-839-5451, E-mail: pgagnon@westga.edu. *Application contact:* Dr. Toby Ziglar, Assistant Dean of the Graduate School, 678-839-1394, Fax: 678-839-1395, E-mail: graduate@westga.edu.
Website: http://www.westga.edu/coah

University of Wisconsin–Madison, Graduate School, College of Letters and Science, School of Music, Program in Composition, Madison, WI 53706-1380. Offers MM, DMA. *Accreditation:* NASM. *Degree requirements:* For doctorate, thesis/dissertation.

University of Wisconsin–Madison, Graduate School, College of Letters and Science, School of Music, Program in Conducting, Madison, WI 53706-1380. Offers choral (MM, DMA); instrumental (MM, DMA); orchestral (MM, DMA). *Accreditation:* NASM. *Degree requirements:* For doctorate, thesis/dissertation.

University of Wisconsin–Madison, Graduate School, College of Letters and Science, School of Music, Program in Musicology and Ethnomusicology, Madison, WI 53706-1380. Offers ethnomusicology (MA, PhD); historical musicology (PhD); music history (MA). *Accreditation:* NASM. *Degree requirements:* For doctorate, 2 foreign languages, thesis/dissertation. *Entrance requirements:* For doctorate, GRE General Test.

University of Wisconsin–Madison, Graduate School, College of Letters and Science, School of Music, Program in Music Performance, Madison, WI 53706-1380. Offers MM, DMA. *Accreditation:* NASM. *Degree requirements:* For doctorate, one foreign language, thesis/dissertation.

University of Wisconsin–Madison, Graduate School, College of Letters and Science, School of Music, Program in Music Theory, Madison, WI 53706-1380. Offers MA, PhD. *Accreditation:* NASM. *Degree requirements:* For master's, thesis, 1 foreign language (MA); for doctorate, 2 foreign languages, thesis/dissertation. *Entrance requirements:* For master's, GRE General Test (MA); for doctorate, GRE General Test.

University of Wyoming, College of Arts and Sciences, Department of Music, Laramie, WY 82071. Offers music education (MME); performance (MM). *Accreditation:* NASM. *Degree requirements:* For master's, comprehensive exam, thesis or alternative. *Entrance requirements:* For master's, minimum GPA of 3.0. Additional exam requirements/recommendations for international students: Required—TOEFL (minimum score 540 paper-based). Electronic applications accepted.

Utah State University, School of Graduate Studies, Caine College of the Arts, Department of Music, Logan, UT 84322. Offers guitar performance (MM); piano performance and pedagogy (MM).

Vermont College of Fine Arts, MFA in Music Composition Program, Montpelier, VT 05602. Offers MFA. *Faculty:* 10 part-time/adjunct (1 woman). *Students:* 33 full-time (10 women); includes 5 minority (1 Black or African American, non-Hispanic/Latino; 2 Hispanic/Latino; 2 Two or more races, non-Hispanic/Latino), 1 international. Average age 43. 13 applicants, 77% accepted, 6 enrolled. In 2017, 21 master's awarded. *Entrance requirements:* For master's, resume of education and relevant professional experience, three samples of original compositions, official transcripts of all previous undergraduate and graduate coursework, two letters of recommendation, statement of purpose. *Application deadline:* Applications are processed on a rolling basis. Application fee: $75. *Expenses:* Contact institution. *Financial support:* In 2017–18, 32 students received support. Scholarships/grants available. Financial award applicants required to submit FAFSA. *Unit head:* Carol Beatty, Program Director, 866-934-8232 Ext. 8610, E-mail: carol.beatty@vcfa.edu. *Application contact:* Sarah Madru, Assistant Program Director, 802-828-8534, E-mail: sarah.madru@vcfa.edu.
Website: http://www.vcfa.edu/music-comp

Virginia Commonwealth University, Graduate School, School of the Arts, Department of Music, Richmond, VA 23284-9005. Offers music education (MM). *Accreditation:* NASM. *Degree requirements:* For master's, departmental qualifying exam, recital. *Entrance requirements:* For master's, department examination, audition or tapes, portfolio. Additional exam requirements/recommendations for international students: Required—TOEFL (minimum score 600 paper-based; 100 iBT). Electronic applications accepted. *Faculty research:* Composition, conducting, education, performance.

Washington State University, College of Arts and Sciences, School of Music, Pullman, WA 99164-5300. Offers MA. *Accreditation:* NASM. *Program availability:* Part-time. *Degree requirements:* For master's, one foreign language, comprehensive exam, thesis (for some programs), oral exam. *Entrance requirements:* For master's, audition, minimum GPA of 3.0, 3 letters of recommendation, composition portfolio and recording (for composition); writing sample and written philosophy (for music education); writing sample (for music history); in-depth audition (for performance). Additional exam requirements/recommendations for international students: Required—TOEFL, IELTS. Electronic applications accepted. *Faculty research:* Composition, education.

Washington University in St. Louis, The Graduate School, Department of Music, St. Louis, MO 63130-4899. Offers MA, PhD. Terminal master's awarded for partial completion of doctoral program. *Degree requirements:* For master's, thesis or alternative; for doctorate, thesis/dissertation. *Entrance requirements:* For master's, GRE General Test, departmental exam; for doctorate, departmental exam, GRE General Test. Additional exam requirements/recommendations for international students: Required—TOEFL. Electronic applications accepted. *Faculty research:* Musicology, ethnomusicology; theory.

Wayne State University, College of Fine, Performing and Communication Arts, Department of Music, Detroit, MI 48202. Offers composition/theory (MA, MM); conducting (MA, MM); jazz performance (MA, MM); music education (MA, MM); orchestral studies (Certificate); performance (MA, MM). *Accreditation:* NASM. *Faculty:* 29. *Students:* 13 full-time (2 women), 9 part-time (2 women); includes 4 minority (2 Black or African American, non-Hispanic/Latino; 1 American Indian or Alaska Native, non-Hispanic/Latino; 1 Two or more races, non-Hispanic/Latino), 1 international. Average age 32. 41 applicants, 59% accepted, 10 enrolled. In 2017, 8 master's awarded. *Degree requirements:* For master's, thesis (for some programs), oral examination (for some programs), recital with program notes (for some programs). *Entrance requirements:* For master's, diagnostic exam in theory and history, undergraduate degree in same field as desired field of graduate study or equivalent in course work, private study, or experience; audition/interview; for Certificate, undergraduate degree in same field as desired field of graduate study or equivalent in course work, private study, or experience; audition/interview. Additional exam requirements/recommendations for international students: Required—TOEFL (minimum score 550 paper-based; 79 iBT), Michigan English Language Assessment Battery (minimum score 85); Recommended—IELTS (minimum score 6.5), TWE (minimum score 5.5). *Application deadline:* Applications are processed on a rolling basis. Application fee: $50. Electronic applications accepted. *Expenses:* Contact institution. *Financial support:* In 2017–18, 19 students received support. Career-related internships or fieldwork, institutionally sponsored loans, and scholarships/grants available. Support available to part-time students. Financial award applicants required to submit FAFSA. *Faculty research:* Teacher training, pedagogy, musicology, composition/theory, conducting/performance practice. *Unit head:* Dr. Norah Duncan, Professor and Chair, 313-577-1775, E-mail: norah.duncan@wayne.edu. *Application contact:* E-mail: music@wayne.edu.
Website: http://music.wayne.edu/

Webster University, Leigh Gerdine College of Fine Arts, Department of Music, St. Louis, MO 63119-3194. Offers church music (MM); composition (MM); jazz studies (MM); music (MA); music education (MM); organ (MM); performance (MM); piano (MM); voice (MM). *Accreditation:* NASM. *Entrance requirements:* Additional exam requirements/recommendations for international students: Required—TOEFL.

Wesleyan University, Graduate Studies, Department of Music, Middletown, CT 06459. Offers composition (MA); ethnomusicology (MA, PhD). *Faculty:* 7 full-time (2 women), 1 (woman) part-time/adjunct. *Students:* 21 full-time (8 women). 51 applicants, 16% accepted, 8 enrolled. In 2017, 7 master's, 4 doctorates awarded. *Degree requirements:* For master's, one foreign language, thesis; for doctorate, 2 foreign languages, comprehensive exam, thesis/dissertation. *Entrance requirements:* For master's, undergraduate music major or its equivalent; for doctorate, MA. Additional exam requirements/recommendations for international students: Required—TOEFL. *Application deadline:* For fall admission, 1/15 for domestic and international students. Application fee: $85. Electronic applications accepted. *Financial support:* Tuition waivers (full) and unspecified assistantships available. *Faculty research:* Ethnomusicology, musicology, music theory, composition, performance. *Unit head:* Roger Matthew Grant, Director of Graduate Studies/Professor, 860-685-2588, Fax: 860-685-2651, E-mail: rgrant01@wesleyan.edu. *Application contact:* Deborah Shore, Administrative Assistant, 860-685-2598, Fax: 860-685-2651, E-mail: dshore@wesleyan.edu.
Website: http://www.wesleyan.edu/music/

West Chester University of Pennsylvania, School of Music, Department of Applied Music, West Chester, PA 19383. Offers performance (MM), including conducting, instrumental, keyboard, voice; piano pedagogy (MM, Certificate). *Program availability:* Part-time, evening/weekend. *Students:* 16 full-time (9 women), 14 part-time (4 women); includes 4 minority (1 Asian, non-Hispanic/Latino; 1 Hispanic/Latino; 2 Two or more races, non-Hispanic/Latino), 5 international. Average age 28. 24 applicants, 75% accepted, 15 enrolled. In 2017, 13 master's awarded. *Degree requirements:* For master's, comprehensive exam, thesis optional, recital. *Entrance requirements:* For master's and Certificate, School of Music Graduate Placement Test (GPT), audition, interview. Additional exam requirements/recommendations for international students: Required—TOEFL or IELTS. *Application deadline:* For fall admission, 5/15 for international students; for spring admission, 10/15 for international students. Applications are processed on a rolling basis. Application fee: $50. Electronic applications accepted. *Expenses:* Tuition, state resident: full-time $9000; part-time $500 per credit. Tuition, nonresident: full-time $13,500; part-time $750 per credit. *Required fees:* $2959; $149.79 per credit. *Financial support:* Scholarships/grants and unspecified assistantships available. Financial award application deadline: 2/15; financial award applicants required to submit FAFSA. *Faculty research:* Performance, historical perspective, pedagogy. *Unit head:* Christopher Hanning, Chair, 610-436-4178, Fax: 610-436-2873, E-mail: channing@wcupa.edu. *Application contact:* Dr. M. Gregory Martin, Graduate Coordinator, 610-436-2070, Fax: 610-436-2873, E-mail: mmartin@wcupa.edu.
Website: http://www.wcupa.edu/arts-humanities/music/appliedMusic/

West Chester University of Pennsylvania, School of Music, Department of Music Education, West Chester, PA 19383. Offers Kodaly methodology (Certificate); music education (MM, Teaching Certificate), including Kodaly methodology (MM), music technology (MM), Orff-Schulwerk (MM), performance (MM); music technology (Certificate); Orff-Schulwerk (Certificate). *Accreditation:* NASM; NCATE. *Program availability:* Part-time, evening/weekend. *Students:* 4 full-time (all women), 13 part-time (8 women); includes 1 minority (Asian, non-Hispanic/Latino). Average age 28. 11 applicants, 91% accepted, 6 enrolled. In 2017, 14 master's, 6 Certificates awarded. *Degree requirements:* For master's, comprehensive exam, thesis (for some programs), recital (performance option only). *Entrance requirements:* For master's, School of Music Graduate Placement Test (GPT), audition (performance track only), interview; for other advanced degree, audition, interview. Additional exam requirements/recommendations for international students: Required—TOEFL or IELTS. *Application deadline:* For fall admission, 5/15 for international students; for spring admission, 10/15 for international students. Applications are processed on a rolling basis. Application fee: $50. Electronic applications accepted. *Expenses:* Tuition, state resident: full-time $9000; part-time $500 per credit. Tuition, nonresident: full-time $13,500; part-time $750 per credit. *Required fees:* $2959; $149.79 per credit. *Financial support:* Scholarships/grants and unspecified assistantships available. Financial award application deadline: 2/15; financial award

applicants required to submit FAFSA. *Faculty research:* Music education in other cultures, educational advocacy and pedagogy, research in music education, special needs learners in music education, developing music listening skills. *Unit head:* Dr. Marci Major, Chair, 610-436-3030, Fax: 610-436-2873, E-mail: mmajor@wcupa.edu. *Application contact:* Dr. M. Gregory Martin, Graduate Coordinator, 610-436-2070, E-mail: mmartin@wcupa.edu.
Website: http://www.wcupa.edu/arts-humanities/music/musicEducation/

West Chester University of Pennsylvania, School of Music, Department of Music Theory, History and Composition, West Chester, PA 19383. Offers history and literature (MM), including history and literature; music theory, history, and composition (MM). *Program availability:* Part-time, evening/weekend. *Students:* 2 full-time (0 women), 5 part-time (0 women); includes 1 minority (Black or African American, non-Hispanic/Latino). Average age 30. 5 applicants, 80% accepted, 2 enrolled. In 2017, 1 master's awarded. *Degree requirements:* For master's, comprehensive exam, thesis. *Entrance requirements:* For master's, School of Music Graduate Placement Test (GPT), interview. Additional exam requirements/recommendations for international students: Required—TOEFL or IELTS. *Application deadline:* For fall admission, 5/15 for international students; for spring admission, 10/15 for international students. Applications are processed on a rolling basis. Application fee: $50. Electronic applications accepted. *Expenses:* Tuition, state resident: full-time $9000; part-time $500 per credit. Tuition, nonresident: full-time $13,500; part-time $750 per credit. *Required fees:* $2959; $149.79 per credit. *Financial support:* Scholarships/grants and unspecified assistantships available. Financial award application deadline: 2/15; financial award applicants required to submit FAFSA. *Faculty research:* Musicology, eighteenth century European music, advanced compositional techniques, opera history, current trends in theory and composition. *Unit head:* Dr. Robert Maggio, Chair, 610-436-3157, E-mail: musicinfo@wcupa.edu. *Application contact:* Dr. M. Gregory Martin, Graduate Coordinator, 610-436-2070, E-mail: gmartin@wcupa.edu.
Website: http://www.wcupa.edu/arts-humanities/music/musicTheory/

Western Illinois University, School of Graduate Studies, College of Fine Arts and Communication, School of Music, Macomb, IL 61455-1390. Offers MM. *Accreditation:* NASM. *Program availability:* Part-time. *Students:* 23 full-time (6 women), 3 part-time (1 woman); includes 3 minority (all Hispanic/Latino), 7 international. Average age 28. 28 applicants, 93% accepted, 15 enrolled. In 2017, 14 master's awarded. *Degree requirements:* For master's, comprehensive exam, thesis or alternative. *Entrance requirements:* For master's, audition. Additional exam requirements/recommendations for international students: Required—TOEFL (minimum score 550 paper-based; 80 iBT). *Application deadline:* Applications are processed on a rolling basis. Application fee: $30. Electronic applications accepted. *Financial support:* In 2017–18, teaching assistantships with full tuition reimbursements (averaging $8,688 per year) were awarded; unspecified assistantships also available. Financial award applicants required to submit FAFSA. *Unit head:* Dr. Tammie Walker, Director, 309-298-1544, E-mail: tl-walker4@wiu.edu. *Application contact:* Dr. Nancy Parsons, Associate Provost and Director of Graduate Studies, 309-298-1806, Fax: 309-298-2345, E-mail: grad-office@wiu.edu.
Website: http://wiu.edu/music

Western Michigan University, Graduate College, College of Fine Arts, School of Music, Kalamazoo, MI 49008. Offers music (MA); music composition (MM); music conducting (MM); music education (MM); music performance (MM); music therapy (MM). *Accreditation:* NASM.

Western Oregon University, Graduate Programs, College of Liberal Arts and Sciences, Division of Creative Arts, Monmouth, OR 97361. Offers contemporary music (MM). *Accreditation:* NASM. *Entrance requirements:* Additional exam requirements/recommendations for international students: Required—TOEFL (minimum score 550 paper-based; 79 iBT), IELTS (minimum score 6.5).

Western Washington University, Graduate School, College of Fine and Performing Arts, Department of Music, Bellingham, WA 98225-5996. Offers M Mus. *Accreditation:* NASM. *Program availability:* Part-time. *Degree requirements:* For master's, thesis. *Entrance requirements:* For master's, GRE General Test, department placement exams, audition, portfolio, minimum GPA of 3.0 in last 60 semester hours or last 90 quarter hours of course work. Additional exam requirements/recommendations for international students: Required—TOEFL (minimum score 567 paper-based). Electronic applications accepted. *Faculty research:* Baroque opera, historical music of the Silk Road, original composition, 20th century orchestral music, 13th century polyphony.

West Texas A&M University, College of Fine Arts and Humanities, School of Music, Program in Music, Canyon, TX 79015. Offers MA. *Accreditation:* NASM. *Program availability:* Part-time. *Degree requirements:* For master's, comprehensive exam, thesis optional. *Entrance requirements:* For master's, GRE General Test. Additional exam requirements/recommendations for international students: Required—TOEFL (minimum score 550 paper-based). Electronic applications accepted.

West Texas A&M University, College of Fine Arts and Humanities, School of Music, Program in Performance, Canyon, TX 79015. Offers MM. *Accreditation:* NASM. *Program availability:* Part-time. *Degree requirements:* For master's, comprehensive exam, thesis optional. *Entrance requirements:* For master's, GRE General Test. Additional exam requirements/recommendations for international students: Required—TOEFL (minimum score 550 paper-based). Electronic applications accepted.

West Virginia University, College of Creative Arts, Morgantown, WV 26506. Offers acting (MFA); art education (MA); art history (MA); ceramics (MFA); collaborative piano (MM, DMA); composition (MM, DMA); conducting (MM, DMA); costume design and technology (MFA); graphic design (MFA); jazz pedagogy (MM); lighting design and technology (MFA); music (PhD); music education (MM, PhD); music industry (MA); music theory (MM); musicology (MA); painting and printmaking (MFA); performance (MM, DMA); photography (MFA); piano pedagogy (MM); scenic design and technology (MFA); sculpture (MFA); studio art (MA); technical direction (MFA); vocal pedagogy and performance (DMA). *Program availability:* Part-time. *Students:* 114 full-time (64 women), 39 part-time (21 women); includes 19 minority (11 Black or African American, non-Hispanic/Latino; 1 Asian, non-Hispanic/Latino; 6 Hispanic/Latino; 1 Two or more races, non-Hispanic/Latino), 33 international. *Degree requirements:* For master's, thesis, recitals; for doctorate, comprehensive exam, thesis/dissertation, recitals (DMA). *Entrance requirements:* For doctorate, minimum GPA of 3.0, audition. Additional exam requirements/recommendations for international students: Required—TOEFL. *Application deadline:* For fall admission, 3/1 priority date for domestic students, 2/15 for international students; for spring admission, 11/1 for domestic students, 9/15 for international students. Applications are processed on a rolling basis. Application fee: $60. Electronic applications accepted. *Expenses:* Tuition, state resident: full-time $9450. Tuition, nonresident: full-time $24,390. *Financial support:* Research assistantships, teaching assistantships, career-related internships or fieldwork, Federal Work-Study, institutionally sponsored loans, scholarships/grants, health care benefits, tuition waivers (partial), and administrative assistantships available. Financial award applicants required to submit FAFSA. *Faculty research:* Professional directing, consulting, acting design, music education, jazz history. *Unit head:* Dr. Paul Kreider, Dean, 304-293-4841 Ext. 3109, Fax: 304-293-6896, E-mail: paul.kreider@mail.wvu.edu. *Application contact:* Records Officer, 304-293-4841, Fax: 304-293-2533, E-mail: rachel.hanks@mail.wvu.edu.
Website: http://www.ccarts.wvu.edu

Wichita State University, Graduate School, College of Fine Arts, School of Music, Wichita, KS 67260. Offers music (MM); music education (MME). *Accreditation:* NASM. *Program availability:* Part-time. *Unit head:* Dr. Aleks Sternfeld-Dunn, Director, 316-978-6272, Fax: 316-978-3625, E-mail: aleks.sternfeld-dunn@wichita.edu. *Application contact:* Jordan Oleson, Admissions Coordinator, 316-978-3095, Fax: 316-978-3253, E-mail: jordan.oleson@wichita.edu.
Website: http://www.wichita.edu/music

William Paterson University of New Jersey, College of the Arts and Communication, Wayne, NJ 07470-8420. Offers art (MFA); music (MM); professional communication (MA). *Accreditation:* NASAD. *Program availability:* Part-time. *Faculty:* 21 full-time (10 women), 22 part-time/adjunct (8 women). *Students:* 46 full-time (27 women), 16 part-time (12 women); includes 22 minority (8 Black or African American, non-Hispanic/Latino; 2 Asian, non-Hispanic/Latino; 9 Hispanic/Latino; 3 Two or more races, non-Hispanic/Latino), 12 international. Average age 29. 90 applicants, 53% accepted, 25 enrolled. In 2017, 18 master's awarded. *Degree requirements:* For master's, comprehensive exam (for some programs), thesis (for some programs). *Entrance requirements:* For master's, GRE, minimum GPA of 2.75; audition; 2 letters of recommendation; portfolio with letter of intent. Additional exam requirements/recommendations for international students: Required—TOEFL (minimum score 550 paper-based; 79 iBT), IELTS (minimum score 6). *Application deadline:* For fall admission, 6/1 for domestic students, 3/1 for international students; for spring admission, 11/1 for domestic students, 10/1 for international students. Applications are processed on a rolling basis. Application fee: $50. Electronic applications accepted. *Expenses:* Tuition, state resident: full-time $13,920; part-time $6264 per year. Tuition, nonresident: full-time $21,700; part-time $9765 per year. *Required fees:* $80; $36 per year. Tuition and fees vary according to course load, degree level and program. *Financial support:* Career-related internships or fieldwork, Federal Work-Study, scholarships/grants, and unspecified assistantships available. Support available to part-time students. Financial award application deadline: 3/15; financial award applicants required to submit FAFSA. *Faculty research:* Contemporary culture, mediated social support, photography, development of musicianship, methods for using new technologies for sculpture. *Unit head:* Daryl Moore, Dean, 973-720-2232, E-mail: moored@wpunj.edu. *Application contact:* Christina Aiello, Assistant Director, Graduate Admissions, 973-720-2506, Fax: 973-720-2035, E-mail: aielloc@wpunj.edu.
Website: http://www.wpunj.edu/coac

Winthrop University, College of Visual and Performing Arts, Department of Music, Rock Hill, SC 29733. Offers conducting (MM); music education (MME); performance (MM). *Accreditation:* NASM. *Program availability:* Part-time. *Students:* 8 full-time (4 women), 6 part-time (3 women); includes 4 minority (all Black or African American, non-Hispanic/Latino). Average age 33. In 2017, 8 master's awarded. *Degree requirements:* For master's, comprehensive exam (for some programs), oral and written exams, recital (MM). *Entrance requirements:* For master's, GRE General Test, audition, minimum GPA of 3.0, 2 recitals. Additional exam requirements/recommendations for international students: Required—TOEFL (minimum score 550 paper-based; 79 iBT), IELTS (minimum score 6). *Application deadline:* For fall admission, 7/15 priority date for domestic students; for spring admission, 12/1 for domestic students. Applications are processed on a rolling basis. Application fee: $50. Electronic applications accepted. *Financial support:* Research assistantships with full tuition reimbursements, Federal Work-Study, scholarships/grants, and unspecified assistantships available. Support available to part-time students. Financial award application deadline: 2/1; financial award applicants required to submit FAFSA. *Unit head:* Donald Rogers, Graduate Program Director, E-mail: rogersd@winthrop.edu. *Application contact:* 803-411-7041, E-mail: gradschool@winthrop.edu.
Website: http://www.winthrop.edu/cvpa/music

World Mission University, Graduate Programs, Los Angeles, CA 90020. Offers biblical preaching (M Div); Christian counseling (M Div, MACC); church ministry (M Div); church music (M Div, DCM); ministry (D Min); music (MA); theology (MAT). *Program availability:* Online learning.

Yale University, Graduate School of Arts and Sciences, Department of Music, New Haven, CT 06520. Offers music history (MA); music theory (MA). Terminal master's awarded for partial completion of doctoral program. *Degree requirements:* For master's, one foreign language; for doctorate, 3 foreign languages, thesis/dissertation. *Entrance requirements:* For doctorate, GRE General Test, GRE Subject Test.

Yale University, School of Music, New Haven, CT 06520. Offers MM, MMA, DMA, AD, Certificate. *Faculty:* 28 full-time (9 women), 31 part-time/adjunct (6 women). *Students:* 209 full-time (90 women); includes 47 minority (3 Black or African American, non-Hispanic/Latino; 23 Asian, non-Hispanic/Latino; 10 Hispanic/Latino; 11 Two or more races, non-Hispanic/Latino), 72 international. Average age 24. 1,456 applicants, 11% accepted, 117 enrolled. In 2017, 82 master's, 8 doctorates, 26 ADs awarded. *Degree requirements:* For master's and other advanced degree, one foreign language, recitals; for doctorate, one foreign language, comprehensive exam, thesis/dissertation, oral and written exam, recitals. *Entrance requirements:* For master's and other advanced degree, departmental exams, audition; for doctorate, entrance exam in music history, analysis, and musicianship, audition. Additional exam requirements/recommendations for international students: Required—TOEFL (minimum score 567 paper-based; 86 iBT). *Application deadline:* For fall admission, 12/1 for domestic and international students. Application fee: $150. Electronic applications accepted. *Expenses:* Contact institution. *Financial support:* In 2017–18, 209 students received support, including 209 fellowships (averaging $36,000 per year); Federal Work-Study and scholarships/grants also available. Financial award application deadline: 5/30; financial award applicants required to submit FAFSA. *Faculty research:* Performance, composition, conducting, music history and theory. *Unit head:* Robert Blocker, Dean, 203-432-4160, Fax: 203-432-7542. *Application contact:* Suzanne M. Stringer, Director of Student Services, 203-432-1962, Fax: 203-432-7448, E-mail: suzanne.stringer@yale.edu.
Website: http://music.yale.edu/

York University, Faculty of Graduate Studies, Faculty of Fine Arts, Program in Music, Toronto, ON M3J 1P3, Canada. Offers composition (MA); music (PhD); musicology and ethnomusicology (MA). *Program availability:* Part-time. *Degree requirements:* For master's, one foreign language, thesis optional; for doctorate, 2 foreign languages, comprehensive exam, thesis/dissertation. *Entrance requirements:* For master's, portfolio. Electronic applications accepted.

Youngstown State University, Graduate School, College of Fine and Performing Arts, Dana School of Music, Youngstown, OH 44555-0001. Offers jazz studies (MM); music education (MM); music history and literature (MM); music theory and composition (MM); performance (MM). *Accreditation:* NASM. *Program availability:* Part-time, evening/weekend. *Degree requirements:* For master's, one foreign language, thesis optional, final qualifying exam. *Entrance requirements:* For master's, audition; GRE General Test or minimum GPA of 2.7. Additional exam requirements/recommendations for international students: Required—TOEFL. *Faculty research:* Teaching education, use of computers, conducting.

Theater

Academy of Art University, Graduate Programs, School of Acting, San Francisco, CA 94105-3410. Offers MA, MFA. *Program availability:* Part-time. *Faculty:* 16 part-time/adjunct (10 women). *Students:* 21 full-time (11 women), 1 part-time (0 women); includes 5 minority (3 Black or African American, non-Hispanic/Latino; 1 Asian, non-Hispanic/Latino; 1 Hispanic/Latino), 13 international. Average age 28. 45 applicants, 100% accepted, 13 enrolled. In 2017, 13 master's awarded. *Degree requirements:* For master's, final review. *Entrance requirements:* For master's, statement of intent; resume; portfolio/reel; official college transcripts. *Application deadline:* Applications are processed on a rolling basis. Application fee: $50. Electronic applications accepted. *Expenses: Tuition:* Part-time $982 per unit. *Financial support:* Career-related internships or fieldwork, Federal Work-Study, and scholarships/grants available. Financial award application deadline: 8/10; financial award applicants required to submit FAFSA. *Unit head:* 800-544-ARTS, E-mail: info@academyart.edu. *Application contact:* 800-544-ARTS, E-mail: info@academyart.edu.
Website: http://www.academyart.edu/acting-school/index.html

American Conservatory Theater, Program in Acting, San Francisco, CA 94108-5800. Offers MFA, Certificate. *Degree requirements:* For master's, thesis (for some programs), stage performance. *Entrance requirements:* For master's, audition, interview, bachelor's degree from an accredited institution, 2 confidential letters of recommendation.

Arcadia University, School of Education, Glenside, PA 19038-3295. Offers art education (M Ed); computer education (CAS); curriculum (CAS); curriculum studies (M Ed); early childhood education (M Ed), including individualized, master teacher, research in child development; educational leadership (M Ed, Ed D, CAS); elementary education (M Ed); English education (MA Ed); environmental education (MA Ed); instructional technology (M Ed); language arts (M Ed); library science (M Ed); mathematics education (M Ed, MA Ed); music education (MA Ed); psychology (MA Ed); reading (M Ed, CAS); science education (M Ed, CAS); secondary education (M Ed, CAS); special education (M Ed, Ed D, CAS); theater arts (MA Ed); written communication (MA Ed). *Accreditation:* NASAD. *Program availability:* Part-time, evening/weekend, online learning. Electronic applications accepted. *Expenses:* Contact institution.

Arizona State University at the Tempe campus, Herberger Institute for Design and the Arts, School of Film, Dance and Theatre, Tempe, AZ 85287-2002. Offers dance (MFA), including dance, interdisciplinary digital media and performance; theatre (MA, MFA, PhD), including arts entrepreneurship and management (MFA), directing (MFA), dramatic writing (MFA), interdisciplinary digital media and performance (MFA), performance (MFA), performance design (MFA), theatre (MFA), theatre and performance of the Americas (PhD), theatre for youth (MFA, PhD). Terminal master's awarded for partial completion of doctoral program. *Degree requirements:* For master's, comprehensive exam (for some programs), thesis (for some programs), applied project (for some programs); interactive Program of Study (iPOS) submitted before completing 50 percent of required credit hours; for doctorate, comprehensive exam, thesis/dissertation, interactive Program of Study (iPOS) submitted before completing 50 percent of required credit hours. *Entrance requirements:* For master's, GRE or MAT, minimum GPA of 3.0 in last 2 years of work leading to bachelor's degree (depending on program); for doctorate, GRE, minimum GPA of 3.0 or equivalent in last 2 years of work leading to bachelor's degree, 3 letters of recommendation, resume, scholarly writing sample, statement of purpose. Additional exam requirements/recommendations for international students: Required—TOEFL, IELTS, or PTE. Electronic applications accepted.

Baylor University, Graduate School, College of Arts and Sciences, Department of Theatre Arts, Waco, TX 76798. Offers MA, MFA. *Accreditation:* NAST. *Program availability:* Part-time. *Faculty:* 6 full-time (2 women). *Students:* 6 full-time (1 woman); includes 1 minority (Black or African American, non-Hispanic/Latino). Average age 30. 14 applicants, 21% accepted, 3 enrolled. In 2017, 3 master's awarded. *Degree requirements:* For master's, comprehensive exam, thesis. *Entrance requirements:* For master's, GRE General Test. *Application deadline:* For spring admission, 2/15 for domestic students. Applications are processed on a rolling basis. Application fee: $25. Electronic applications accepted. *Financial support:* In 2017–18, 6 students received support, including 2 research assistantships with full tuition reimbursements available (averaging $12,000 per year), 4 teaching assistantships with full tuition reimbursements available (averaging $13,500 per year); Federal Work-Study, institutionally sponsored loans, health care benefits, tuition waivers (full and partial), and unspecified assistantships also available. Financial award application deadline: 3/15; financial award applicants required to submit FAFSA. *Faculty research:* Military and theatre, World War I theatre, Avant-garde Japanese theatre, Horton Foote, Post-War Japan, Modernism in theatre. *Unit head:* Dr. DeAnna Toten Beard, Chair, 254-710-6486, Fax: 254-710-1765, E-mail: deanna_toten_beard@baylor.edu. *Application contact:* Renee Cluke, Administrative Assistant, 254-710-1861, Fax: 254-710-1765, E-mail: renee_cluke@baylor.edu.
Website: http://www.baylor.edu/Theatre_Arts/

Berklee College of Music, The Boston Conservatory at Berklee, Boston, MA 02215-3693. Offers bassoon performance (MM); cello performance (MM); choral conducting (MM); clarinet performance (MM); collaborative piano (MM); composition (MM); contemporary music performance (MM); double bass performance (MM); flute performance (MM); harp performance (MM); horn performance (MM); marimba performance (MM); music and autism (Certificate); music education (MM); music education and autism (MM); music performance (ADP); musical theater (MFA); oboe performance (MM); opera performance (MM); orchestral conducting (MM); percussion performance (MM); piano performance (MM); saxophone performance (MM); trombone performance (MM); trumpet performance (MM). *Program availability:* Part-time. *Faculty:* 33 full-time (13 women), 19 part-time/adjunct (13 women). *Students:* 237 full-time (141 women), 23 part-time (15 women); includes 43 minority (9 Black or African American, non-Hispanic/Latino; 1 American Indian or Alaska Native, non-Hispanic/Latino; 9 Asian, non-Hispanic/Latino; 13 Hispanic/Latino; 11 Two or more races, non-Hispanic/Latino), 73 international. Average age 25. 668 applicants, 48% accepted, 154 enrolled. In 2017, 85 master's, 31 other advanced degrees awarded. *Degree requirements:* For master's, recital or performance; for other advanced degree, recital. *Entrance requirements:* For master's and other advanced degree, audition. Additional exam requirements/recommendations for international students: Required—TOEFL (minimum score 550 paper-based; 79 iBT), IELTS (minimum score 6.5). *Application deadline:* For fall admission, 12/15 for domestic and international students. Application fee: $110. Electronic applications accepted. *Expenses:* $44,735 per year (master's degrees); $28,020 (diplomas and certificates). *Financial support:* In 2017–18, 247 students received support, including 2 research assistantships (averaging $4,000 per year), 10 teaching assistantships (averaging $2,000 per year); scholarships/grants also available. Financial award application deadline: 12/15; financial award applicants required to submit FAFSA. *Unit head:* Camille Colatosti, PhD, Dean, Institutional Research and Assessment/Graduate Studies, 617-536-6340, E-mail: ccolatosti@berklee.edu. *Application contact:* Director of Admissions, 617-912-9153, Fax: 617-912-9217, E-mail: admissions@bostonconservatory.edu.
Website: http://www.bostonconservatory.edu/

Binghamton University, State University of New York, Graduate School, Harpur College of Arts and Sciences, Department of Theatre, Binghamton, NY 13902-6000. Offers MA. *Program availability:* Part-time. *Faculty:* 9 full-time (4 women). *Students:* 5 full-time (3 women), 2 part-time (both women); includes 1 minority (Asian, non-Hispanic/Latino), 2 international. Average age 28. 6 applicants, 67% accepted, 2 enrolled. In 2017, 1 master's awarded. *Degree requirements:* For master's, thesis. *Entrance requirements:* For master's, GRE General Test, writing sample, portfolio. Additional exam requirements/recommendations for international students: Required—TOEFL (minimum score 550 paper-based; 80 iBT). *Application deadline:* Applications are processed on a rolling basis. Application fee: $75. Electronic applications accepted. *Financial support:* In 2017–18, 5 students received support. Career-related internships or fieldwork, Federal Work-Study, institutionally sponsored loans, scholarships/grants, health care benefits, and unspecified assistantships available. Financial award application deadline: 2/15; financial award applicants required to submit FAFSA. *Unit head:* Dr. Barbara E. Wolfe, Chairperson, 607-777-2360, E-mail: bwolfe@binghamton.edu. *Application contact:* Ben Balkaya, Assistant Dean and Director, 607-777-2151, Fax: 607-777-2501, E-mail: balkaya@binghamton.edu.
Website: http://www2.binghamton.edu/theatre/

Bob Jones University, Graduate Programs, Greenville, SC 29614. Offers accountancy (MS); Bible (MA); Bible translation (MA); Biblical studies (Certificate); broadcast management (MS); business administration (MBA); church history (MA, PhD); church ministries (MA); church music (MM); cinema and video production (MA); counseling (MS); curriculum and instruction (Ed D); divinity (M Div); dramatic production (MA); educational leadership (MS, Ed D, Ed S); elementary education (M Ed, MAT); English (M Ed, MA, MAT); fine arts (MA); graphic design (MA); history (M Ed, MA); illustration (MA); interpretative speech (MA); mathematics (M Ed, MAT); medical missions (Certificate); ministry (MM, D Min); multi-categorical special education (M Ed, MAT); music (M Ed); New Testament interpretation (PhD); Old Testament interpretation (PhD); orchestral instrument performance (MM); organ performance (MM); pastoral studies (MA); personnel services (MS, Ed S); piano pedagogy (MM); piano performance (MM); platform arts (MA); radio and television broadcasting (MS); rhetoric and public address (MA); secondary education (M Ed); studio art (MA); teaching Bible (MA); theology (MA, PhD); voice performance (MM); youth ministries (MA); M Div/MM.

Boston University, College of Fine Arts, School of Theatre, Boston, MA 02215. Offers design (MFA); lighting crafts (Certificate); management (MFA); production (MFA); scenic painting (Certificate). *Faculty:* 16 full-time, 9 part-time/adjunct. *Students:* 53 full-time (35 women), 4 part-time (1 woman); includes 7 minority (1 Black or African American, non-Hispanic/Latino; 1 American Indian or Alaska Native, non-Hispanic/Latino; 3 Asian, non-Hispanic/Latino; 1 Hispanic/Latino; 1 Two or more races, non-Hispanic/Latino), 2 international. Average age 27. 212 applicants, 14% accepted, 17 enrolled. In 2017, 14 master's awarded. *Entrance requirements:* For master's, interview, portfolio. Additional exam requirements/recommendations for international students: Required—TOEFL (minimum score 90 iBT), IELTS (minimum score 7). *Application deadline:* For fall admission, 2/1 priority date for domestic and international students. Application fee: $95. Electronic applications accepted. *Expenses:* Contact institution. *Financial support:* In 2017–18, 16 students received support. Fellowships, teaching assistantships, scholarships/grants, unspecified assistantships, and stipends available. Financial award application deadline: 2/1. *Unit head:* Jim Petosa, Director, 617-353-3390. *Application contact:* Mark Krone, Assistant Director of Graduate Affairs, 617-353-3350, E-mail: arts@bu.edu.

Bowling Green State University, Graduate College, College of Arts and Sciences, Department of Theatre and Film, Bowling Green, OH 43403. Offers MA, PhD. *Accreditation:* NAST. *Program availability:* Part-time. Terminal master's awarded for partial completion of doctoral program. *Degree requirements:* For master's, thesis or alternative; for doctorate, comprehensive exam, thesis/dissertation, 9-hour research tool. *Entrance requirements:* For master's and doctorate, GRE General Test. Additional exam requirements/recommendations for international students: Required—TOEFL. Electronic applications accepted. *Faculty research:* Theatre history, dramatic theory, cultural studies, performance studies, American theatre history.

Brandeis University, Graduate School of Arts and Sciences, Department of Theater Arts: Acting, Waltham, MA 02454-9110. Offers acting (MFA). *Faculty:* 7 full-time (5 women), 7 part-time/adjunct (3 women). *Entrance requirements:* For master's, resume, letters of recommendation, interview, audition, head shot, artistic resume, transcripts, statement of purpose. Additional exam requirements/recommendations for international students: Required—PTE (minimum score 68), TOEFL (minimum score 600 paper-based, 100 iBT) or IELTS (7). *Application deadline:* For fall admission, 3/15 for domestic students. Application fee: $75. Electronic applications accepted. *Expenses: Tuition:* Full-time $48,720. *Required fees:* $88. Tuition and fees vary according to course load, degree level, program and student level. *Financial support:* Application deadline: 4/15; applicants required to submit FAFSA. *Unit head:* Dr. Susan Dibble, Director of Graduate Studies, 781-736-3415, E-mail: dibble@brandeis.edu. *Application contact:* Alicia Hyland, Department Administrator, 781-736-3340, E-mail: adhyland@brandeis.edu.
Website: http://www.brandeis.edu/gsas/programs/theater.html

Brigham Young University, Graduate Studies, College of Fine Arts and Communications, Department of Theatre and Media Arts, Provo, UT 84602-6404. Offers MA. *Accreditation:* NAST. *Faculty:* 18 full-time (6 women). *Students:* 5 full-time (3 women). Average age 32. 4 applicants, 75% accepted, 2 enrolled. In 2017, 1 master's awarded. *Degree requirements:* For master's, comprehensive exam, thesis, 32 hours, oral defense. *Entrance requirements:* For master's, two samples of scholarly writing, letter of intent, three letters of recommendation. Additional exam requirements/recommendations for international students: Required—TOEFL (minimum score 580 paper-based; 85 iBT). *Application deadline:* For fall admission, 3/15 priority date for domestic and international students. Application fee: $50. Electronic applications accepted. *Expenses:* $3,400 per semester, $405 per credit hour for members of the Church of Jesus Christ of Latter-day Saints; $6,880 per semester, $810 per credit hour for those who are not members of the Church. *Financial support:* In 2017–18, 6 students received support, including 6 teaching assistantships with full and partial tuition reimbursements available; research assistantships, career-related internships or fieldwork, scholarships/grants, and unspecified assistantships also available. Support available to part-time students. *Faculty research:* History, literary and screen theory, curatorial studies, critical race theory, popular culture, performance philosophy,

women's studies, and media literacy. *Unit head:* Dr. Megan Sanborn Jones, Graduate Coordinator, 801-422-1321, E-mail: msjones@byu.edu. *Application contact:* Lindsi Michelle Neilson, Graduate Secretary, 801-422-3750, E-mail: lindsi_neilson@byu.edu. Website: http://cfac.byu.edu/departments/tma

Brooklyn College of the City University of New York, School of Visual, Media and Performing Arts, Department of Theater, Brooklyn, NY 11210-2889. Offers acting (MFA); design and technical theater (MFA); directing (MFA); performing arts management (MFA); theater history and criticism (MA). *Program availability:* Part-time. *Degree requirements:* For master's, thesis, professional residency. *Entrance requirements:* For master's, audition or interview, 18 credits in theater, 2 letters of recommendation, essay. Additional exam requirements/recommendations for international students: Required—TOEFL. Electronic applications accepted. *Faculty research:* Multiculturalism and the arts, art education, arts collaboration.

Brown University, Graduate School, Department of Theatre Arts and Performance Studies, Providence, RI 02912. Offers acting and directing (MFA); playwriting (MFA); theatre and performance studies (PhD). *Degree requirements:* For master's, thesis or alternative. *Entrance requirements:* For master's, GRE General Test.

California Institute of the Arts, School of Theater, Valencia, CA 91355-2340. Offers acting (MFA, Adv C); creative producing and management (MFA); design and production (MFA); design and technology (Adv C); directing (MFA); theater management (Adv C). *Degree requirements:* For master's, thesis, (for some programs), faculty review, performance or portfolio. *Entrance requirements:* For master's, audition or portfolio, interview. Additional exam requirements/recommendations for international students: Required—TOEFL. Electronic applications accepted.

California State University, Fullerton, Graduate Studies, College of the Arts, Department of Theatre and Dance, Fullerton, CA 92831-3599. Offers theatre arts (MFA), including acting. *Accreditation:* NAST. *Program availability:* Part-time. *Faculty:* 5 full-time (1 woman), 1 (woman) part-time/adjunct. *Students:* 5 full-time (2 women), 3 part-time (0 women); includes 3 minority (1 Black or African American, non-Hispanic/Latino; 1 American Indian or Alaska Native, non-Hispanic/Latino; 1 Hispanic/Latino). Average age 36. 7 applicants, 43% accepted, 3 enrolled. *Entrance requirements:* For master's, major in theatre or related field, audition or interview, minimum GPA of 2.5 in last 60 units of course work. Application fee: $55. *Financial support:* Career-related internships or fieldwork, Federal Work-Study, institutionally sponsored loans, and scholarships/grants available. Support available to part-time students. Financial award application deadline: 3/1; financial award applicants required to submit FAFSA. *Unit head:* Dr. Bruce Goodrich, Chair, 657-278-3649. *Application contact:* Admissions/Applications, 657-278-2371.
Website: http://www.fullerton.edu/arts/theatredance/

California State University, Long Beach, Graduate Studies, College of the Arts, Department of Theatre Arts, Long Beach, CA 90840. Offers acting (MFA); MBA/MFA. *Accreditation:* NAST. *Program availability:* Part-time. *Degree requirements:* For master's, thesis or alternative. Electronic applications accepted.

California State University, Los Angeles, Graduate Studies, College of Arts and Letters, Department of Theatre Arts and Dance, Los Angeles, CA 90032-8530. Offers theater arts (MA). *Program availability:* Part-time, evening/weekend. *Degree requirements:* For master's, comprehensive exam, project or thesis. *Entrance requirements:* For master's, minimum GPA of 2.5, 30 units of course work in theater. Additional exam requirements/recommendations for international students: Required—TOEFL (minimum score 500 paper-based). Electronic applications accepted. *Faculty research:* Sondheim, Taiwanese theater, Australian theater, absurdism, dramaturgy.

California State University, Northridge, Graduate Studies, Mike Curb College of Arts, Media, and Communication, Department of Theatre, Northridge, CA 91330. Offers MA. *Accreditation:* NAST. *Students:* 5 full-time (3 women), 12 part-time (11 women); includes 6 minority (2 Black or African American, non-Hispanic/Latino; 1 Asian, non-Hispanic/Latino; 2 Hispanic/Latino; 1 Two or more races, non-Hispanic/Latino), 3 international. Average age 33. 10 applicants, 70% accepted, 3 enrolled. In 2017, 1 master's awarded. *Degree requirements:* For master's, thesis. *Entrance requirements:* For master's, GRE General Test or minimum GPA of 3.0. Additional exam requirements/recommendations for international students: Required—TOEFL. *Application deadline:* For fall admission, 11/30 for domestic students. Application fee: $55. *Financial support:* Application deadline: 3/1. *Unit head:* Anamarie Dwyer, Chair, 818-677-3086.
Website: http://www.csun.edu/theatre/

Carnegie Mellon University, College of Fine Arts, School of Drama, Pittsburgh, PA 15213-3891. Offers design (MFA); directing (MFA); dramatic writing (MFA); production technology and management (MFA); video and media design (MFA). *Degree requirements:* For master's, thesis (for some programs). *Entrance requirements:* For master's, audition, portfolio review, interview. Additional exam requirements/recommendations for international students: Required—TOEFL. *Faculty research:* Developing voice and speech compact disc.

Case Western Reserve University, School of Graduate Studies, Department of Theater, Cleveland, OH 44106. Offers acting (MFA); theater (MA). *Faculty:* 6 full-time (3 women), 2 part-time/adjunct (1 woman). *Students:* 15 full-time (6 women), 2 part-time (both women); includes 5 minority (4 Black or African American, non-Hispanic/Latino; 1 Hispanic/Latino). Average age 27. 12 applicants, 83% accepted, 9 enrolled. *Degree requirements:* For master's, comprehensive exam, thesis, oral presentation and defense, portfolio, thesis concert production and presentation (for MFA). *Entrance requirements:* For master's, audition, interview, letter of intent, three recommendations, headshots, resume. Additional exam requirements/recommendations for international students: Required—TOEFL (minimum score 577 paper-based; 90 iBT); Recommended—IELTS (minimum score 7). *Application deadline:* Applications are processed on a rolling basis. Electronic applications accepted. *Expenses: Tuition:* Full-time $43,854; part-time $1827 per credit hour. *Required fees:* $50; $50 per credit hour. Tuition and fees vary according to course load and program. *Financial support:* Fellowships, scholarships/grants, tuition waivers (full and partial), and stipends available. *Faculty research:* Playwriting; history of theater; participation in professional area theaters in performing, design, acting, coaching; choreography, performance and pedagogy, dance wellness medicine and science. *Unit head:* Jerrold Scott, Professor/Chair/Artistic Director, 216-368-6140, Fax: 216-368-5184, E-mail: jerrold.scott@case.edu. *Application contact:* DeBorah Hamilton, Department Assistant, 216-368-4868, Fax: 216-368-5184, E-mail: deborah.hamilton@case.edu.
Website: http://theater.case.edu

The Catholic University of America, School of Arts and Sciences, Department of Drama, Washington, DC 20064. Offers acting (MFA); creative teaching through drama (Certificate); directing (MFA); playwriting (MFA); theatre education (MA); theatre history and criticism (MA). *Program availability:* Part-time. *Faculty:* 8 full-time (4 women), 9 part-time/adjunct (4 women). *Students:* 3 full-time (2 women), 33 part-time (26 women); includes 6 minority (2 Black or African American, non-Hispanic/Latino; 1 Asian, non-Hispanic/Latino; 1 Hispanic/Latino; 2 Two or more races, non-Hispanic/Latino). Average age 32. 20 applicants, 80% accepted, 8 enrolled. In 2017, 5 master's awarded. *Degree requirements:* For master's, variable foreign language requirement, comprehensive exam, thesis or alternative. *Entrance requirements:* For master's, GRE General Test,

statement of purpose, official copies of academic transcripts, three letters of recommendation. Additional exam requirements/recommendations for international students: Required—TOEFL (minimum score 550 paper-based; 80 iBT). *Application deadline:* For fall admission, 7/15 priority date for domestic students, 7/1 for international students; for spring admission, 11/15 priority date for domestic students, 11/1 for international students. Applications are processed on a rolling basis. Application fee: $55. Electronic applications accepted. *Expenses:* Contact institution. *Financial support:* Fellowships, research assistantships, teaching assistantships, Federal Work-Study, scholarships/grants, tuition waivers (full and partial), and unspecified assistantships available. Financial award application deadline: 2/1; financial award applicants required to submit FAFSA. *Faculty research:* Acting, directing, playwriting, costume design, Shakespearean stage history. *Total annual research expenditures:* $204,255. *Unit head:* Dr. Patrick Tuite, Chair, 202-319-5351, Fax: 202-319-5359, E-mail: tuite@cua.edu. *Application contact:* Dr. Steven Brown, Director of Graduate Admissions, 202-319-5057, Fax: 202-319-6533, E-mail: cua-admissions@cua.edu.
Website: http://drama.cua.edu/

Central Washington University, School of Graduate Studies and Research, College of Arts and Humanities, Department of Theatre Arts, Ellensburg, WA 98926. Offers theatre production (MA); theatre studies (MA). *Program availability:* Part-time. *Entrance requirements:* For master's, minimum GPA of 3.0. Additional exam requirements/recommendations for international students: Required—TOEFL (minimum score 550 paper-based; 79 iBT). *Application deadline:* For fall admission, 2/1 for domestic students; for winter admission, 10/1 for domestic students; for spring admission, 1/1 for domestic students. Application fee: $50. Electronic applications accepted. *Financial support:* Application deadline: 3/1; applicants required to submit FAFSA. *Unit head:* Christina Barrigan, Associate Professor, 509-963-1273, E-mail: christina.barrigan@cwu.edu. *Application contact:* Justine Eason, Admissions Program Coordinator, 509-963-3103, Fax: 509-963-1799, E-mail: masters@cwu.edu.

Columbia University, Graduate School of Arts and Sciences, New York, NY 10027. Offers African-American studies (MA); American studies (MA); anthropology (MA, PhD); art history and archaeology (MA, PhD); astronomy (PhD); biological sciences (PhD); biotechnology (MA); chemical physics (PhD); chemistry (PhD); classical studies (MA, PhD); classics (MA, PhD); climate and society (MA); conservation biology (MA); earth and environmental sciences (PhD); East Asia: regional studies (MA); East Asian languages and cultures (MA, PhD); ecology, evolution and environmental biology (MA), including conservation biology; ecology, evolution, and environmental biology (PhD), including ecology and evolutionary biology, evolutionary primatology; economics (MA, PhD); English and comparative literature (MA, PhD); French and Romance philology (MA, PhD); Germanic languages (MA, PhD); global French studies (MA); global thought (MA); Hispanic cultural studies (MA); history (PhD); history and literature (MA); human rights studies (MA); Islamic studies (MA); Italian (MA, PhD); Japanese pedagogy (MA); Jewish studies (MA); Latin America and the Caribbean: regional studies (MA); Latin American and Iberian cultures (PhD); mathematics (MA, PhD), including finance (MA); medieval and Renaissance studies (MA); Middle Eastern, South Asian, and African studies (MA, PhD); modern art: critical and curatorial studies (MA); modern European studies (MA); museum anthropology (MA); music (DMA, PhD); oral history (MA); philosophical foundations of physics (MA); philosophy (MA, PhD); physics (PhD); political science (MA, PhD); psychology (PhD); quantitative methods in the social sciences (MA); religion (MA, PhD); Russia, Eurasia and East Europe: regional studies (MA); Russian translation (MA); Slavic cultures (MA); Slavic languages (MA, PhD); sociology (MA, PhD); South Asian studies (MA); statistics (MA, PhD); theatre (PhD). Dual-degree programs require admission to both Graduate School of Arts and Sciences and another Columbia school. *Program availability:* Part-time. Terminal master's awarded for partial completion of doctoral program. *Degree requirements:* For master's, variable foreign language requirement, comprehensive exam (for some programs), thesis (for some programs); for doctorate, variable foreign language requirement, comprehensive exam (for some programs), thesis/dissertation. *Entrance requirements:* For master's and doctorate, GRE General Test, GRE Subject Test (for some programs). Additional exam requirements/recommendations for international students: Required—TOEFL, IELTS. Electronic applications accepted. *Expenses: Tuition:* Full-time $44,864; part-time $1704 per credit. *Required fees:* $2370 per semester. One-time fee: $105.

Columbia University, School of the Arts, Theatre Program, New York, NY 10027. Offers theatre (MFA), including acting, directing, dramaturgy, playwriting, stage management, theatre management and producing; JD/MFA. JD/MFA offered in cooperation with Columbia Law School. *Faculty:* 15 full-time (3 women), 36 part-time/adjunct (17 women). *Students:* 156 full-time (88 women); includes 45 minority (20 Black or African American, non-Hispanic/Latino; 1 American Indian or Alaska Native, non-Hispanic/Latino; 5 Asian, non-Hispanic/Latino; 15 Hispanic/Latino; 4 Two or more races, non-Hispanic/Latino), 31 international. Average age 27. 365 applicants, 23% accepted, 56 enrolled. In 2017, 59 master's awarded. *Degree requirements:* For master's, thesis, 2 internships (3 for theatre management and producing; none required for acting). *Entrance requirements:* For master's, 3 letters of recommendation, resume. Additional exam requirements/recommendations for international students: Required—TOEFL (minimum score 600 paper-based; 100 iBT). *Application deadline:* For fall admission, 1/5 for domestic and international students. Application fee: $110. Electronic applications accepted. Application fee is waived when completed online. *Expenses:* Contact institution. *Financial support:* In 2017–18, 94 students received support, including 2 teaching assistantships with full and partial tuition reimbursements available; fellowships, research assistantships, career-related internships or fieldwork, Federal Work-Study, and scholarships/grants also available. Financial award application deadline: 2/1; financial award applicants required to submit FAFSA. *Unit head:* Christian Parker, Chair, 212-854-3408, E-mail: theatre@columbia.edu. *Application contact:* Kenny Wong, Director of Admissions and Financial Aid, 212-854-2134, E-mail: admissions-arts@columbia.edu.
Website: http://arts.columbia.edu/theatre

See Display on page 133 and Close-Up on page 185.

Columbus State University, Graduate Studies, College of the Arts, Department of Theatre, Columbus, GA 31907-5645. Offers theatre education (M Ed, MAT). *Accreditation:* NAST. *Faculty:* 2 full-time (1 woman). *Students:* 4 full-time (all women), 12 part-time (9 women); includes 3 minority (2 Black or African American, non-Hispanic/Latino; 1 Hispanic/Latino). Average age 33. 4 applicants, 50% accepted, 1 enrolled. In 2017, 1 master's awarded. *Entrance requirements:* For master's, audition, letters of recommendation, minimum GPA of 2.75. Additional exam requirements/recommendations for international students: Required—TOEFL (minimum score 550 paper-based; 79 iBT). *Application deadline:* For fall admission, 6/1 for domestic and international students; for spring admission, 11/1 for domestic and international students; for summer admission, 3/1 for domestic and international students. Applications are processed on a rolling basis. Application fee: $50. Electronic applications accepted. *Expenses:* Tuition, state resident: full-time $3708; part-time $2472 per year. Tuition, nonresident: full-time $14,418; part-time $9612 per year. *International tuition:* $19,218 full-time. *Required fees:* $1605. Tuition and fees vary according to program. *Financial support:* In 2017–18, 1 research assistantship (averaging $3,000 per year) was awarded; scholarships/grants also available. Financial

award application deadline: 5/1; financial award applicants required to submit FAFSA. *Unit head:* Dr. Larry Dooley, Department Chair, 706-507-8402, E-mail: dooley_larry@columbusstate.edu. *Application contact:* Catrina Smith-Edmond, Assistant Director for Graduate and Global Admission, 706-507-8824, Fax: 706-568-5091, E-mail: smithedmond_catrina@columbusstate.edu.
Website: http://theatre.columbusstate.edu/

Cornell University, Graduate School, Graduate Fields of Arts and Sciences, Field of Theatre Arts, Ithaca, NY 14853. Offers drama and the theatre (PhD); theatre history (PhD); theatre theory and aesthetics (PhD). *Degree requirements:* For doctorate, 2 foreign languages, comprehensive exam, thesis/dissertation. *Entrance requirements:* For doctorate, GRE General Test, sample of written work, 3 letters of recommendation. Additional exam requirements/recommendations for international students: Required—TOEFL (minimum score 600 paper-based; 77 iBT). Electronic applications accepted. *Faculty research:* Cultural studies and critical theory, seventeenth to twenty-first century European and American theater, theory of the performing arts, film history and theory, feminism and theater.

Dell'Arte International School of Physical Theatre, MFA Program, Blue Lake, CA 95525. Offers ensemble based physical theatre (MFA). *Accreditation:* NAST. *Degree requirements:* For master's, thesis. *Entrance requirements:* For master's, undergraduate degree, audition. Electronic applications accepted. *Faculty research:* Physical theatre, international theatre, ensemble, devised.

DePaul University, The Theatre School, Chicago, IL 60614. Offers acting (MFA); arts leadership (MFA); directing (MFA). *Degree requirements:* For master's, comprehensive exam, thesis. *Entrance requirements:* For master's, audition or interview, official transcripts, three letters of recommendation, resume, written statements (for directing program). Additional exam requirements/recommendations for international students: Required—TOEFL (minimum score 550 paper-based; 80 iBT), IELTS (minimum score 6.5). *Application deadline:* For fall admission, 12/15 priority date for domestic students, 1/1 priority date for international students. Application fee: $25. Electronic applications accepted. *Expenses:* Contact institution. *Financial support:* Application deadline: 2/15; applicants required to submit FAFSA. *Unit head:* John Culbert, Dean, 773-325-7917, Fax: 773-325-7920, E-mail: theatreadmissions@depaul.edu. *Application contact:* Tracee Duerson, Director of Admissions, 773-325-7999, Fax: 773-325-7744, E-mail: theatreadmissions@depaul.edu.
Website: http://theatre.depaul.edu/Pages/default.aspx

Eastern Michigan University, Graduate School, College of Arts and Sciences, School of Communication, Media and Theatre Arts, Programs in Applied Drama/Theatre for the Young, Ypsilanti, MI 48197. Offers MA, MFA. *Program availability:* Part-time, online learning. *Students:* 6 full-time (5 women), 2 part-time (both women). Average age 34. 6 applicants, 83% accepted, 3 enrolled. In 2017, 2 master's awarded. *Degree requirements:* For master's, thesis optional. *Entrance requirements:* Additional exam requirements/recommendations for international students: Required—TOEFL. *Application deadline:* Applications are processed on a rolling basis. Application fee: $45. *Financial support:* Fellowships, research assistantships with full tuition reimbursements, teaching assistantships with full tuition reimbursements, career-related internships or fieldwork, Federal Work-Study, institutionally sponsored loans, scholarships/grants, tuition waivers (partial), and unspecified assistantships available. Support available to part-time students. Financial award applicants required to submit FAFSA. *Application contact:* Dr. Christine Tanner, Coordinator, 734-487-0332, Fax: 734-487-3443, E-mail: christine.tanner@emich.edu.

Eastern Michigan University, Graduate School, College of Arts and Sciences, School of Communication, Media and Theatre Arts, Programs in Theatre Arts, Ypsilanti, MI 48197. Offers interpretation/performance studies (MA); theatre arts (MA), including drama/theatre for the young, general. *Program availability:* Part-time, evening/weekend, online learning. *Students:* 2 full-time (both women), 8 part-time (6 women); includes 5 minority (all Black or African American, non-Hispanic/Latino). Average age 31. 8 applicants, 63% accepted. In 2017, 4 master's awarded. *Degree requirements:* For master's, thesis or alternative. *Entrance requirements:* Additional exam requirements/ recommendations for international students: Required—TOEFL. *Application deadline:* Applications are processed on a rolling basis. Application fee: $45. *Financial support:* Fellowships, research assistantships with full tuition reimbursements, teaching assistantships with full tuition reimbursements, career-related internships or fieldwork, Federal Work-Study, institutionally sponsored loans, scholarships/grants, and unspecified assistantships available. Support available to part-time students. Financial award applicants required to submit FAFSA. *Application contact:* Dr. Lee Stille, Coordinator, 734-487-6846, Fax: 734-487-3443, E-mail: lstille@emich.edu.

Florida Atlantic University, Dorothy F. Schmidt College of Arts and Letters, Department of Theatre and Dance, Boca Raton, FL 33431-0991. Offers acting (MFA); design and technology (MFA). *Faculty:* 8 full-time (3 women), 2 part-time/adjunct (1 woman). *Students:* 12 full-time (6 women); includes 6 minority (1 Black or African American, non-Hispanic/Latino; 4 Hispanic/Latino; 1 Two or more races, non-Hispanic/Latino), 1 international. Average age 30. 3 applicants. In 2017, 8 master's awarded. *Degree requirements:* For master's, thesis, production. *Entrance requirements:* For master's, GRE General Test, minimum GPA of 3.0 during last 60 hours of undergraduate course work. *Application deadline:* For fall admission, 8/15 priority date for domestic students, 8/15 for international students. Applications are processed on a rolling basis. Application fee: $30. *Expenses:* Tuition, state resident: full-time $7400; part-time $369.82 per credit. Tuition, nonresident: full-time $20,496; part-time $1042.81 per credit. *Financial support:* Fellowships, teaching assistantships with full tuition reimbursements, career-related internships or fieldwork, Federal Work-Study, and institutionally sponsored loans available. Support available to part-time students. Financial award application deadline: 3/31. *Faculty research:* Contemporary British theatre, Eastern European playwrights, Latin American drama. *Unit head:* Dr. Desmond Gallant, Chair, 561-297-3815, Fax: 561-297-2180, E-mail: dgallant@fau.edu.
Website: http://www.fau.edu/theatre/

Florida State University, The Graduate School, College of Fine Arts, School of Theatre, Tallahassee, FL 32306. Offers acting (MFA); costume design (MFA); directing (MFA); technical production (MFA); theatre (MA, PhD); theatre management (MFA). *Accreditation:* NAST. *Faculty:* 17 full-time (8 women). *Students:* 86 full-time (39 women); includes 17 minority (7 Black or African American, non-Hispanic/Latino; 1 Asian, non-Hispanic/Latino; 7 Hispanic/Latino; 2 Two or more races, non-Hispanic/Latino). Average age 25. 125 applicants, 29% accepted, 31 enrolled. In 2017, 20 master's awarded. *Degree requirements:* For master's, one foreign language, comprehensive exam (for some programs), thesis (for some programs); for doctorate, one foreign language, comprehensive exam, thesis/dissertation. *Entrance requirements:* For master's, GRE General Test, writing sample (MA); interview and portfolio (MFA); minimum undergraduate GPA of 3.0; audition (MFA in acting). Additional exam requirements/ recommendations for international students: Required—TOEFL. *Application deadline:* For fall admission, 2/15 priority date for domestic and international students. Applications are processed on a rolling basis. Application fee: $30. Electronic applications accepted. *Financial support:* In 2017–18, 1 fellowship with full tuition reimbursement (averaging $18,000 per year), 30 research assistantships with full tuition reimbursements (averaging $12,000 per year), 24 teaching assistantships with full

tuition reimbursements (averaging $12,000 per year) were awarded; career-related internships or fieldwork, Federal Work-Study, institutionally sponsored loans, scholarships/grants, health care benefits, and unspecified assistantships also available. Financial award application deadline: 1/1; financial award applicants required to submit FAFSA. *Faculty research:* Gender theatre, performance theory, computers in theatre, dramaturgy, music theatre performance. *Unit head:* Cameron Jackson, Director, 850-644-7257, Fax: 850-644-7408, E-mail: ccjackson@admin.fsu.edu. *Application contact:* Barbara Thomas, Program Assistant, 850-644-7234, Fax: 850-644-7246, E-mail: bgthomas@admin.fsu.edu.
Website: http://theatre.fsu.edu/

Fontbonne University, Graduate Programs, St. Louis, MO 63105-3098. Offers accounting (MBA, MS); art (MA); art (K-12) (MAT); business (MBA); computer science (MS); deaf education (MA); early intervention in deaf education (MA); education (MA), including autism spectrum disorders, curriculum and instruction, diverse learners, early childhood education, reading, special education; elementary education (MAT); family and consumer sciences (MA), including multidisciplinary health communication studies; fine arts (MFA); instructional design and technology (MS); management and leadership (MM); middle school education (MAT); secondary education (MAT); special education (MAT); speech-language pathology (MS); supply chain management (MS); theatre (MA). *Program availability:* Part-time, evening/weekend, online learning. *Degree requirements:* For master's, comprehensive exam (for some programs), thesis (for some programs). *Entrance requirements:* Additional exam requirements/recommendations for international students: Required—TOEFL (minimum score 500 paper-based; 65 iBT). Electronic applications accepted.

Fordham University, Graduate School of Arts and Sciences, Program in Playwriting, New York, NY 10023. Offers MFA. Program offered jointly with Primary Stages theater company. *Students:* 4 full-time (2 women); includes 1 minority (Asian, non-Hispanic/Latino). 19 applicants, 11% accepted, 2 enrolled. In 2017, 2 master's awarded. *Entrance requirements:* For master's, 3 letters of recommendation, resume/curriculum vitae, statement of intent, official transcripts, playwriting portfolio, bachelor's degree. Additional exam requirements/recommendations for international students: Required—TOEFL. *Application deadline:* Applications are processed on a rolling basis. Application fee: $70. Electronic applications accepted. *Unit head:* Matthew Maguire, Director, 212-636-6306, E-mail: mmaguire@fordham.edu. *Application contact:* Bernadette Valentino-Morrison, Director of Graduate Admissions, 718-817-4419, Fax: 718-817-3566, E-mail: valentinomor@fordham.edu.
Website: http://www.fordham.edu/info/21309/playwriting_mfa/2561/playwriting_mfa_application_information

George Mason University, College of Visual and Performing Arts, Program in Visual and Performing Arts, Fairfax, VA 22030. Offers dance (MFA); graphic design (MFA); theater (MFA); visual art (MFA). *Accreditation:* NASAD. *Faculty:* 18 full-time (9 women), 39 part-time/adjunct (20 women). *Students:* 4 full-time (3 women), 7 part-time (3 women); includes 3 minority (1 Hispanic/Latino; 2 Two or more races, non-Hispanic/Latino). Average age 33. 22 applicants, 45% accepted, 5 enrolled. In 2017, 3 master's awarded. *Degree requirements:* For master's, comprehensive experience, studio project or thesis. *Entrance requirements:* For master's, official transcripts; 3 letters of recommendation; letter of intent; resume; professional goals statement. Additional exam requirements/recommendations for international students: Required—TOEFL (minimum score 575 paper-based; 88 iBT), IELTS (minimum score 6.5), PTE (minimum score 59). Application fee: $75 ($80 for international students). Electronic applications accepted. *Expenses:* Tuition, state resident: full-time $11,228; part-time $459.50 per credit. Tuition, nonresident: full-time $30,932; part-time $1280.50 per credit. *Required fees:* $3252; $135.50 per credit. Part-time tuition and fees vary according to course load and program. *Financial support:* In 2017–18, 2 students received support, including 3 teaching assistantships (averaging $4,123 per year); career-related internships or fieldwork, Federal Work-Study, scholarships/grants, unspecified assistantships, and health care benefits (for full-time research or teaching assistantship recipients) also available. Support available to part-time students. Financial award application deadline: 3/1; financial award applicants required to submit FAFSA. *Faculty research:* Digital arts, painting, photography, print-making, sculpture; combined art forms in in-disciplinary projects including installation, performance, publishing, time or writing-based; combined creative and critical approaches. *Unit head:* Lisa Kahn, Associate Dean, 703-993-4541, E-mail: lkahn2@gmu.edu. *Application contact:* Nikki Brugnoli-Whipkey, Graduate Studies Administrative Assistant, 703-993-5792, Fax: 703-993-8798, E-mail: rbrugnol@gmu.edu.
Website: http://soa.gmu.edu

The George Washington University, Columbian College of Arts and Sciences, Department of Theatre and Dance, Washington, DC 20052. Offers classical acting (MFA); dance (MFA); exhibit design (Graduate Certificate); production design (MFA). *Program availability:* Part-time, evening/weekend. *Faculty:* 9 full-time (6 women), 8 part-time/adjunct (5 women). *Students:* 24 full-time (17 women), 18 part-time (12 women); includes 6 minority (4 Black or African American, non-Hispanic/Latino; 1 Hispanic/Latino; 1 Two or more races, non-Hispanic/Latino), 5 international. Average age 33. 70 applicants, 56% accepted, 17 enrolled. In 2017, 19 master's awarded. *Degree requirements:* For master's, thesis. *Entrance requirements:* For master's, minimum GPA of 3.0, portfolio. Additional exam requirements/recommendations for international students: Required—TOEFL (minimum score 550 paper-based; 80 iBT). *Application deadline:* For fall admission, 8/1 priority date for domestic students; for spring admission, 10/1 priority date for domestic students. Applications are processed on a rolling basis. Application fee: $75. Electronic applications accepted. *Expenses:* Tuition: Full-time $28,800; part-time $1655 per credit hour. *Required fees:* $45; $2.75 per credit hour. *Financial support:* In 2017–18, 2 students received support. Fellowships with tuition reimbursements available, teaching assistantships with tuition reimbursements available, career-related internships or fieldwork, Federal Work-Study, and tuition waivers available. *Unit head:* Jodi Kanter, Head, 202-994-6305, E-mail: jikanter@gwu.edu. *Application contact:* Information Contact, 202-994-1700, E-mail: ctad@gwu.edu.
Website: http://theatredance.columbian.gwu.edu/

The Graduate Center, City University of New York, Graduate Studies, Program in Theatre, New York, NY 10016-4039. Offers PhD. *Faculty:* 21 full-time (4 women). *Students:* 59 full-time (36 women), 1 (woman) part-time; includes 6 minority (1 Black or African American, non-Hispanic/Latino; 1 Asian, non-Hispanic/Latino; 2 Hispanic/Latino; 2 Two or more races, non-Hispanic/Latino), 16 international. Average age 36. 31 applicants, 23% accepted, 6 enrolled. In 2017, 6 doctorates awarded. *Degree requirements:* For doctorate, 2 foreign languages, thesis/dissertation. *Entrance requirements:* For doctorate, GRE General Test, writing sample. Additional exam requirements/recommendations for international students: Required—TOEFL. *Application deadline:* For fall admission, 3/1 for domestic students. Application fee: $125. Electronic applications accepted. *Financial support:* In 2017–18, 49 students received support, including 41 fellowships, 8 research assistantships, 12 teaching assistantships; career-related internships or fieldwork, Federal Work-Study, institutionally sponsored loans, and tuition waivers (full and partial) also available. Financial award application deadline: 2/1; financial award applicants required to submit

FAFSA. *Unit head:* Dr. Peter Eckersall, Executive Officer, 212-817-8871, Fax: 212-817-1538. *Application contact:* Les Gribben, Director of Admissions, 212-817-7470, Fax: 212-817-1624, E-mail: lgribben@gc.cuny.edu.

Hollins University, Graduate Programs, Program in Playwriting, Roanoke, VA 24020. Offers new play directing (Certificate); new play performance (Certificate); playwriting (MFA). *Program availability:* Part-time. *Faculty:* 7 full-time (3 women). *Students:* 30 full-time (18 women), 1 (woman) part-time; includes 2 minority (both Black or African American, non-Hispanic/Latino). Average age 35. 18 applicants, 83% accepted, 7 enrolled. In 2017, 4 master's awarded. *Degree requirements:* For master's, comprehensive exam, thesis. *Entrance requirements:* For master's, letters of recommendation, bachelor's degree, undergraduate transcripts, manuscript. Additional exam requirements/recommendations for international students: Required—TOEFL (minimum score 550 paper-based; 80 iBT), IELTS (minimum score 6.5). *Application deadline:* For summer admission, 2/15 priority date for domestic and international students. Application fee: $40. Electronic applications accepted. *Expenses:* Contact institution. *Financial support:* Scholarships/grants available. Support available to part-time students. Financial award application deadline: 2/15; financial award applicants required to submit FAFSA. *Unit head:* Todd Ristau, Director, 540-362-6386, E-mail: tristau@hollins.edu. *Application contact:* Cathy S. Koon, Manager of Graduate Programs, 540-362-6326, Fax: 540-362-6288, E-mail: ckoon@hollins.edu. Website: http://www.hollins.edu/academics/graduate-degrees/playwriting/

Hunter College of the City University of New York, Graduate School, School of Arts and Sciences, Department of Theatre, Program in Theatre, New York, NY 10065-5085. Offers MA.

Idaho State University, Office of Graduate Studies, College of Arts and Letters, Program in Theatre, Pocatello, ID 83209-8006. Offers MA. *Accreditation:* NAST. *Program availability:* Part-time. *Degree requirements:* For master's, comprehensive exam, thesis optional, oral and written exam. *Entrance requirements:* For master's, GRE General Test (35th percentile or above on one of the 3 sections). Additional exam requirements/recommendations for international students: Required—TOEFL (minimum score 550 paper-based; 80 iBT). Electronic applications accepted. *Faculty research:* Theatre history, technical theatre.

Illinois State University, Graduate School, College of Fine Arts, School of Theatre, Normal, IL 61790. Offers MA, MFA, MS. *Accreditation:* NAST. *Program availability:* Part-time. *Degree requirements:* For master's, variable foreign language requirement, thesis or alternative. *Entrance requirements:* For master's, sample of written work, minimum GPA of 3.0 in last 60 hours of course work. *Faculty research:* Illinois Shakespeare festival.

Indiana University Bloomington, University Graduate School, College of Arts and Sciences, Department of Theatre, Drama, and Contemporary Dance, Bloomington, IN 47405. Offers acting (MFA); design and technology (MFA); directing (MFA); playwriting (MFA); theatre history, theory, and literature (MA, PhD). *Accreditation:* NAST. Terminal master's awarded for partial completion of doctoral program. *Degree requirements:* For master's, one foreign language, comprehensive exam, thesis, 30 credit hours; for doctorate, 2 foreign languages, comprehensive exam, thesis/dissertation, 90 credit hours. *Entrance requirements:* For master's, audition, interview, portfolio or script analysis; for doctorate, GRE General Test. Additional exam requirements/recommendations for international students: Required—TOEFL (minimum score 550 paper-based, 80 iBT) or IELTS. Electronic applications accepted. *Expenses:* Contact institution. *Faculty research:* American, Western European, world literature; history and theory; theatrical production, design and technology; acting; directing; playwriting.

The Juilliard School, Graduate Programs, New York, NY 10023-6588. Offers acting (MFA); jazz studies (Artist Diploma); music (MM, DMA, Diploma); music performance (Artist Diploma); opera studies (Artist Diploma); string quartet (Artist Diploma). *Degree requirements:* For master's and other advanced degree, performance jury, recital; for doctorate, one foreign language, thesis/dissertation, performance jury, 3 recitals. *Entrance requirements:* For master's and other advanced degree, audition; for doctorate, audition, interview. Additional exam requirements/recommendations for international students: Required—TOEFL (minimum score 570 paper-based; 89 iBT). Electronic applications accepted.

Kansas State University, Graduate School, College of Arts and Sciences, School of Music, Theatre and Dance, Manhattan, KS 66506. Offers MA, MM. *Accreditation:* NASM; NAST. *Program availability:* Part-time, online learning. *Degree requirements:* For master's, thesis optional. *Entrance requirements:* For master's, GRE, audition (in person or recording), interview (for music education). Additional exam requirements/recommendations for international students: Required—TOEFL (minimum score 600 paper-based). Electronic applications accepted. *Faculty research:* American music, opera, drama therapy, directing, costume and scenic design, music by women composers.

Kent State University, College of the Arts, School of Theatre and Dance, Kent, OH 44242-0001. Offers theatre studies (MFA), including acting, design/technology. *Accreditation:* NAST. *Program availability:* Part-time. *Faculty:* 9 full-time (6 women), 5 part-time/adjunct (2 women). *Students:* 16 full-time (9 women); includes 1 minority (Asian, non-Hispanic/Latino), 2 international. Average age 34. 3 applicants, 100% accepted, 2 enrolled. In 2017, 2 master's awarded. *Degree requirements:* For master's, comprehensive project. *Entrance requirements:* For master's, transcripts, 3 letters of recommendation, goal statement, resume; audition (for acting); portfolio (for design/technology). Additional exam requirements/recommendations for international students: Required—TOEFL (minimum score 525 paper-based, 71 iBT), Michigan English Language Assessment Battery (minimum score 74), IELTS (minimum score 6.0) or PTE (minimum score 50). *Application deadline:* Applications are processed on a rolling basis. Application fee: $45 ($70 for international students). Electronic applications accepted. *Expenses:* Tuition, state resident: full-time $11,310; part-time $515 per credit hour. Tuition, nonresident: full-time $20,396; part-time $928 per credit hour. International tuition: $18,544 full-time. *Financial support:* Teaching assistantships with full tuition reimbursements, career-related internships or fieldwork, Federal Work-Study, scholarships/grants, and unspecified assistantships available. Financial award application deadline: 5/1. *Unit head:* Eric van Baars, Director and Associate Professor, 330-672-0102, E-mail: fvanbaar@kent.edu. *Application contact:* Yuko Kurahashi, Graduate Coordinator and Associate Professor of Theatre, 330-672-9483, E-mail: ykurahas@kent.edu. Website: http://www.kent.edu/theatredance

Long Island University–LIU Post, College of Arts, Communications and Design, Brookville, NY 11548-1300. Offers art (MA); clinical art therapy (MA); clinical art therapy and counseling (MA); digital game design and development (MA); fine arts and design (MFA); interactive multimedia arts (MA); museum studies (MA); music (MA); theatre (MFA). *Faculty:* 22 full-time (10 women), 44 part-time/adjunct (24 women). *Students:* 99 full-time (80 women), 14 part-time (12 women); includes 22 minority (7 Black or African American, non-Hispanic/Latino; 4 Asian, non-Hispanic/Latino; 9 Hispanic/Latino; 2 Two or more races, non-Hispanic/Latino), 23 international. Average age 28. 125 applicants, 70% accepted, 42 enrolled. In 2017, 55 master's awarded. *Degree requirements:* For master's, variable foreign language requirement, comprehensive exam (for some

programs), thesis. *Entrance requirements:* For master's, performance audition or portfolio. Additional exam requirements/recommendations for international students: Required—TOEFL (minimum score 550 paper-based; 79 iBT). *Application deadline:* Applications are processed on a rolling basis. Application fee: $50. Electronic applications accepted. *Expenses: Tuition:* Full-time $21,618; part-time $1201 per credit. *Required fees:* $1840; $920 per term. Tuition and fees vary according to course load. *Financial support:* In 2017–18, 78 students received support. Career-related internships or fieldwork, scholarships/grants, tuition waivers (full and partial), and unspecified assistantships available. Support available to part-time students. Financial award application deadline: 2/15; financial award applicants required to submit FAFSA. *Faculty research:* Creative writing, playwriting, music composition, music performance, international impact of art therapy, artistic creation. *Unit head:* Steven Breese, Dean, 516-299-2309, E-mail: steven.breese@liu.edu. *Application contact:* Rita Langdon, Graduate Admissions, 516-299-2334, Fax: 516-299-2137, E-mail: post-enroll@liu.edu. Website: http://www.liu.edu/CWPost/Academics/School-of-Visual-Arts-Communications-and-Digital-Technologies

Louisiana State University and Agricultural & Mechanical College, Graduate School, College of Music and Dramatic Arts, Department of Theatre, Baton Rouge, LA 70803. Offers acting (MFA); directing (MFA); theatre (PhD); theatre design/technology (MFA). *Accreditation:* NAST. *Faculty:* 18 full-time (6 women). *Students:* 21 full-time (13 women), 3 part-time (all women); includes 5 minority (2 Black or African American, non-Hispanic/Latino; 1 Asian, non-Hispanic/Latino; 2 Hispanic/Latino), 2 international. Average age 33. 18 applicants, 61% accepted, 11 enrolled. In 2017, 7 master's, 2 doctorates awarded. *Financial support:* In 2017–18, 2 fellowships (averaging $23,030 per year), 1 research assistantship (averaging $21,297 per year), 19 teaching assistantships (averaging $15,421 per year) were awarded.

Mary Baldwin University, Graduate Studies, Program in Shakespeare and Renaissance Literature in Performance, Staunton, VA 24401-3610. Offers acting (M Litt); directing (M Litt); Shakespeare and Renaissance literature in performance (MFA); teaching (M Litt). *Entrance requirements:* For master's, GRE (M Litt).

Miami University, College of Creative Arts, Department of Theatre, Oxford, OH 45056. Offers MA. *Accreditation:* NAST. *Students:* 5. In 2017, 3 master's awarded. *Expenses:* Tuition, state resident: full-time $13,812; part-time $575 per credit hour. Tuition, nonresident: full-time $30,860; part-time $1286 per credit hour. *Unit head:* Dr. Julia Guichard, Chair and Associate Professor of Theatre, 513-529-1517, E-mail: theatre@miamioh.edu. *Application contact:* Dr. Ann Elizabeth Armstrong, Associate Professor and Director of Graduate Studies, 513-529-8317, E-mail: armstra2@miamioh.edu. Website: http://www.MiamiOH.edu/theatre

Michigan State University, The Graduate School, College of Arts and Letters, Department of Theatre, East Lansing, MI 48824. Offers MA, MFA. *Entrance requirements:* Additional exam requirements/recommendations for international students: Required—TOEFL. Electronic applications accepted.

Minnesota State University Mankato, College of Graduate Studies and Research, College of Arts and Humanities, Department of Theatre and Dance, Mankato, MN 56001. Offers theatre arts (MA, MFA). *Degree requirements:* For master's, one foreign language, comprehensive exam, thesis. *Entrance requirements:* For master's, minimum GPA of 3.0 during previous 2 years, 3 letters of recommendation, resume of theatre work, audition. Additional exam requirements/recommendations for international students: Required—TOEFL. Electronic applications accepted.

Missouri State University, Graduate College, College of Arts and Letters, Department of Theatre and Dance, Springfield, MO 65897. Offers speech and theatre education (MS Ed). *Accreditation:* NAST. *Program availability:* Part-time. *Faculty:* 9 full-time (5 women). *Students:* 1 (woman) part-time. Average age 49. 1 applicant. In 2017, 1 master's awarded. *Degree requirements:* For master's, comprehensive exam, thesis or alternative. *Entrance requirements:* For master's, 9-12 teaching certification (MS Ed). Additional exam requirements/recommendations for international students: Required—TOEFL (minimum score 550 paper-based; 79 iBT), IELTS (minimum score 6). *Application deadline:* For fall admission, 7/20 for domestic students, 5/1 for international students; for spring admission, 12/20 for domestic students, 9/1 for international students. Applications are processed on a rolling basis. Application fee: $35 ($50 for international students). Electronic applications accepted. *Expenses:* Tuition, state resident: full-time $2915; part-time $2021 per credit hour. Tuition, nonresident: full-time $5354; part-time $3647 per credit hour. International tuition: $11,992 full-time. *Required fees:* $173; $173 per credit hour. Tuition and fees vary according to class time, course level, course load, degree level, campus/location and program. *Financial support:* Federal Work-Study, institutionally sponsored loans, scholarships/grants, and unspecified assistantships available. Financial award application deadline: 3/31; financial award applicants required to submit FAFSA. *Unit head:* Dr. Jeremy Chesman, Interim Department Head, 417-836-4400, Fax: 417-836-4234, E-mail: theatreanddance@missouristate.edu. *Application contact:* Stephanie Praschan, Director, Graduate Enrollment Management, 417-836-5330, Fax: 417-836-6200, E-mail: stephaniepraschan@missouristate.edu. Website: http://theatreanddance.missouristate.edu/

Montclair State University, The Graduate School, College of the Arts, MA Program in Theatre, Montclair, NJ 07043-1624. Offers arts management (MA); production/stage management (MA); theatre studies (MA). *Accreditation:* NAST. *Program availability:* Part-time, evening/weekend. *Degree requirements:* For master's, comprehensive exam, thesis or alternative. *Entrance requirements:* For master's, GRE General Test, 2 letters of recommendation. Additional exam requirements/recommendations for international students: Required—TOEFL (minimum score 83 iBT) or IELTS (minimum score 6.5). Electronic applications accepted. *Faculty research:* Danceturgy, Arab and Muslim images in American drama, Neil LaBute and playwriting, directing, Robert Edmond Jones.

Naropa University, Graduate Programs, Program in Theater: Contemporary Performance, Boulder, CO 80302-6697. Offers MFA. *Faculty:* 1 full-time (0 women), 2 part-time/adjunct (both women). *Students:* 21 full-time (19 women); includes 6 minority (1 Black or African American, non-Hispanic/Latino; 1 Asian, non-Hispanic/Latino; 3 Hispanic/Latino; 1 Two or more races, non-Hispanic/Latino), 2 international. Average age 30. 62 applicants, 98% accepted, 13 enrolled. In 2017, 6 master's awarded. *Degree requirements:* For master's, thesis, culminating projects and performances. *Entrance requirements:* For master's, interview/audition; headshot; resume/curriculum vitae with pertinent academic, employment and volunteer activities; transcripts; 2 letters of recommendation; letter of interest. Additional exam requirements/recommendations for international students: Required—TOEFL (minimum score 550 paper-based; 80 iBT). *Application deadline:* For fall admission, 1/15 priority date for domestic and international students. Applications are processed on a rolling basis. Application fee: $60. Electronic applications accepted. *Expenses:* $995 per credit. *Financial support:* In 2017–18, 19 students received support, including 6 teaching assistantships with partial tuition reimbursements available (averaging $2,250 per year); research assistantships with partial tuition reimbursements available, career-related internships or fieldwork, Federal Work-Study, scholarships/grants, tuition waivers (partial), and unspecified

assistantships also available. Support available to part-time students. Financial award application deadline: 3/1; financial award applicants required to submit FAFSA. *Unit head:* Lorenzo Gonzalez, Chair, MFA in Theater, 303-245-4716, E-mail: lgonzalez@naropa.edu. *Application contact:* Office of Admissions, 303-536-3572, Fax: 303-546-3583, E-mail: admissions@naropa.edu.
Website: http://www.naropa.edu/academics/masters/contemporary-performance/index.php

The New School, College of Performing Arts, School of Drama, New York, NY 10014. Offers acting (MFA); directing (MFA); playwriting (MFA). *Program availability:* Part-time. *Faculty:* 31 part-time/adjunct (19 women). *Students:* 60 full-time (33 women), 1 (woman) part-time; includes 19 minority (9 Black or African American, non-Hispanic/Latino; 2 Asian, non-Hispanic/Latino; 7 Hispanic/Latino; 1 Two or more races, non-Hispanic/Latino), 7 international. Average age 27. 181 applicants, 21% accepted, 21 enrolled. In 2017, 19 master's awarded. *Degree requirements:* For master's, thesis, involvement in theatrical production and presentation. *Entrance requirements:* For master's, official transcripts, recommendation letters, statement of purpose; artistic resume and photograph (for directing and acting); writing sample (for directing); auditions (for acting). Additional exam requirements/recommendations for international students: Required—TOEFL (minimum score 100 iBT), IELTS (minimum score 7), PTE (minimum score 68). *Application deadline:* For fall admission, 12/1 priority date for domestic and international students; for spring admission, 1/15 for domestic students, 1/15 priority date for international students. Applications are processed on a rolling basis. Application fee: $50. Electronic applications accepted. *Expenses:* $45,980 per term; $2,040 per credit. *Financial support:* In 2017–18, 61 students received support, including 2 fellowships (averaging $12,500 per year), 1 teaching assistantship (averaging $4,466 per year); career-related internships or fieldwork, Federal Work-Study, scholarships/grants, and unspecified assistantships also available. Support available to part-time students. Financial award application deadline: 2/1; financial award applicants required to submit FAFSA. *Unit head:* Pippin Parker, Dean, School of Drama, 212-229-5859 Ext. 2636, E-mail: parkerp@newschool.edu. *Application contact:* Marlon Meikle, Assistant Director of Admissions, College of Performing Arts, 212-229-5859 Ext. 4828, E-mail: performingarts@newschool.edu.
Website: https://www.newschool.edu/drama

New York University, Steinhardt School of Culture, Education, and Human Development, Department of Music and Performing Arts Professions, Program in Educational Theatre, New York, NY 10012. Offers educational theatre and English 7-12 (MA); educational theatre and social studies 7-12 (MA); educational theatre in colleges and communities (MA, Ed D, PhD); educational theatre, all grades (MA). *Program availability:* Part-time. *Students:* Average age 28. 90 applicants, 76% accepted, 37 enrolled. In 2017, 47 master's, 5 doctorates awarded. *Entrance requirements:* For master's, audition; for doctorate, GRE General Test, interview. Additional exam requirements/recommendations for international students: Required—TOEFL (minimum score 100 iBT). *Application deadline:* For fall admission, 12/1 priority date for domestic and international students; for spring admission, 10/1 for domestic and international students. Applications are processed on a rolling basis. Application fee: $75. Electronic applications accepted. *Expenses: Tuition:* Full-time $41,352; part-time $19,968 per year. *Required fees:* $2496; $1628 per unit. $814 per term. Tuition and fees vary according to course load and program. *Financial support:* Teaching assistantships with partial tuition reimbursements, career-related internships or fieldwork, Federal Work-Study, institutionally sponsored loans, and scholarships/grants available. Support available to part-time students. Financial award application deadline: 2/1; financial award applicants required to submit FAFSA. *Faculty research:* Theatre for young audiences, drama in education, applied theatre, arts education assessment, reflective praxis. *Unit head:* Prof. David Montgomery, Director, 212-998-5869, Fax: 212-995-4043, E-mail: dm635@nyu.edu. *Application contact:* 212-998-5030, Fax: 212-995-4328, E-mail: steinhardt.gradadmissions@nyu.edu.
Website: http://steinhardt.nyu.edu/music/edtheatre

New York University, Steinhardt School of Culture, Education, and Human Development, Department of Music and Performing Arts Professions, Program in Music Performance and Composition, New York, NY 10012. Offers instrumental performance (MM), including instrumental performance, jazz instrumental performance; music performance and composition (PhD), including music performance and composition; music theory and composition (MM), including composition for film and multimedia, composition for music theater, computer music composition, music theory and composition, songwriting; piano performance (MM), including collaborative piano, solo piano; vocal pedagogy (Advanced Certificate); vocal performance (MM), including classical voice, musical theatre performance. *Program availability:* Part-time. *Students:* Average age 27. 534 applicants, 50% accepted, 141 enrolled. In 2017, 130 master's, 2 doctorates, 12 other advanced degrees awarded. *Entrance requirements:* For master's, audition; for doctorate, GRE General Test, audition, interview. Additional exam requirements/recommendations for international students: Required—TOEFL (minimum score 100 iBT). *Application deadline:* For fall admission, 12/1 priority date for domestic and international students; for spring admission, 10/1 for domestic and international students. Applications are processed on a rolling basis. Application fee: $75. Electronic applications accepted. *Expenses: Tuition:* Full-time $41,352; part-time $19,968 per year. *Required fees:* $2496; $1628 per unit. $814 per term. Tuition and fees vary according to course load and program. *Financial support:* Fellowships with full and partial tuition reimbursements, Federal Work-Study, scholarships/grants, and tuition waivers (partial) available. Support available to part-time students. Financial award application deadline: 2/1; financial award applicants required to submit FAFSA. *Faculty research:* Aesthetics, performance analysis, twentieth century music, music methodologies for arts criticism and analysis. *Unit head:* Dr. Tae Hong Park, Director, 212-998-5424, Fax: 212-995-4043, E-mail: tae.hong.park@nyu.edu. *Application contact:* 212-998-5030, Fax: 212-995-4328, E-mail: steinhardt.gradadmissions@nyu.edu.
Website: http://steinhardt.nyu.edu/music/composition/programs/graduate

New York University, Tisch School of the Arts and Graduate School of Arts and Science, Department of Performance Studies, New York, NY 10012-1019. Offers MA, PhD. *Faculty:* 12 full-time (7 women), 4 part-time/adjunct (3 women). *Students:* 51 full-time (34 women); includes 14 minority (4 Black or African American, non-Hispanic/Latino; 3 Asian, non-Hispanic/Latino; 6 Hispanic/Latino; 1 Two or more races, non-Hispanic/Latino), 13 international. 99 applicants, 90% accepted, 37 enrolled. In 2017, 32 master's, 7 doctorates awarded. *Degree requirements:* For doctorate, one foreign language, comprehensive exam, thesis/dissertation, dissertation defense, qualifying exam. *Entrance requirements:* For master's, sample of written work; for doctorate, master's degree, writing sample. *Application deadline:* For fall admission, 12/1 for domestic and international students. Application fee: $60. Electronic applications accepted. *Expenses:* Contact institution. *Financial support:* In 2017–18, 32 students received support, including 24 fellowships with full and partial tuition reimbursements available, 4 research assistantships, 4 teaching assistantships; Federal Work-Study, institutionally sponsored loans, tuition waivers (partial), and unspecified assistantships also available. Financial award application deadline: 2/15; financial award applicants required to submit CSS PROFILE or FAFSA. *Faculty research:* Performance theory, dance, folklore and festivals, postcolonial theory, anthropology and gender studies. *Unit head:* Karen Shimakawa, Chair, 212-998-1620, Fax: 212-995-4571, E-mail: performance.studies@nyu.edu.

Application contact: Dan Sandford, Director of Graduate Admissions, 212-998-1918, Fax: 212-995-4060, E-mail: tisch.gradadmissions@nyu.edu.
Website: http://www.performance.tisch.nyu.edu/

New York University, Tisch School of the Arts, Graduate Acting Program, New York, NY 10012-1019. Offers MFA. *Faculty:* 9 full-time (6 women), 11 part-time/adjunct (5 women). *Students:* 45 full-time (22 women); includes 18 minority (7 Black or African American, non-Hispanic/Latino; 1 Asian, non-Hispanic/Latino; 9 Hispanic/Latino; 1 Two or more races, non-Hispanic/Latino), 1 international. Average age 26. 731 applicants, 3% accepted, 16 enrolled. In 2017, 16 master's awarded. *Entrance requirements:* For master's, audition. *Application deadline:* For fall admission, 1/1 for domestic and international students. Application fee: $60. Electronic applications accepted. *Expenses: Tuition:* Full-time $41,352; part-time $19,968 per year. *Required fees:* $2496; $1628 per unit. $814 per term. Tuition and fees vary according to course load and program. *Financial support:* In 2017–18, 30 students received support, including 4 fellowships with full and partial tuition reimbursements available; Federal Work-Study, institutionally sponsored loans, scholarships/grants, tuition waivers (full and partial), and unspecified assistantships also available. Financial award application deadline: 2/15; financial award applicants required to submit FAFSA. *Unit head:* Mark Wing-Davey, Chair, 212-998-1964, Fax: 212-995-4067. *Application contact:* Dan Sandford, Director of Graduate Admissions, 212-998-1918, Fax: 212-995-4060, E-mail: tisch.gradadmissions@nyu.edu.
Website: http://www.gradacting.tisch.nyu.edu/

Northern Illinois University, Graduate School, College of Visual and Performing Arts, School of Theatre and Dance, De Kalb, IL 60115-2854. Offers MFA. *Program availability:* Part-time. *Faculty:* 16 full-time (9 women). *Students:* 26 full-time (11 women); includes 3 minority (1 Hispanic/Latino; 2 Two or more races, non-Hispanic/Latino). Average age 28. 9 applicants, 67% accepted, 5 enrolled. In 2017, 14 master's awarded. *Degree requirements:* For master's, comprehensive exam, final project and defense. *Entrance requirements:* For master's, minimum GPA of 2.75, audition or portfolio. Additional exam requirements/recommendations for international students: Required—TOEFL (minimum score 550 paper-based). *Application deadline:* For fall admission, 4/1 priority date for domestic students, 5/1 for international students; for spring admission, 10/15 priority date for domestic students, 10/1 for international students. Applications are processed on a rolling basis. Application fee: $40. Electronic applications accepted. *Financial support:* In 2017–18, 30 teaching assistantships with full tuition reimbursements were awarded; fellowships with full tuition reimbursements, research assistantships with full tuition reimbursements, career-related internships or fieldwork, Federal Work-Study, scholarships/grants, tuition waivers (full), and staff assistantships also available. Support available to part-time students. Financial award applicants required to submit FAFSA. *Faculty research:* Theatre history, choreography, performance art spectacles, storytelling, computer visualization of the ethical space. *Unit head:* Alexander Gelman, Director, 815-753-8253, Fax: 815-753-8415, E-mail: agelman@niu.edu. *Application contact:* Graduate School Office, 815-753-0395, E-mail: gradsch@niu.edu.
Website: http://www.niu.edu/theatre/

Northern Michigan University, Office of Graduate Education and Research, College of Arts and Sciences, Department of English, Marquette, MI 49855-5301. Offers creative writing (MFA); literature (MA); pedagogy (MA); teaching English to speakers of other languages (Graduate Certificate); theater (MA); writing (MA). *Program availability:* Part-time, evening/weekend. Terminal master's awarded for partial completion of doctoral program. *Degree requirements:* For master's, capstone project: thesis, practicum or portfolio (for MA); thesis (for MFA); for Graduate Certificate, one foreign language. *Entrance requirements:* For master's, minimum GPA of 3.0; bachelor's degree in English or minimum of 30 credit hours in undergraduate English; statement of purpose; resume; critical essay; 3 letters of recommendation; for Graduate Certificate, bachelor's degree. Additional exam requirements/recommendations for international students: Required—TOEFL (minimum score 550 paper-based; 79 iBT), IELTS (minimum score 6.5). *Application deadline:* For fall admission, 2/1 for domestic students; for winter admission, 2/1 for domestic students; for spring admission, 3/17 for domestic students. Applications are processed on a rolling basis. Application fee: $50. Electronic applications accepted. *Expenses:* Tuition, state resident: full-time $9417; part-time $542 per credit hour. Tuition, nonresident: full-time $12,873; part-time $758 per credit hour. Tuition and fees vary according to course load, degree level and program. *Financial support:* Research assistantships with full tuition reimbursements, teaching assistantships with full tuition reimbursements, Federal Work-Study, institutionally sponsored loans, and unspecified assistantships available. Support available to part-time students. Financial award application deadline: 3/1; financial award applicants required to submit FAFSA. *Faculty research:* Modern Arabic literature, British literature (medieval to contemporary), postcolonial literature, Native and African-American literature, creative writing, critical theory, pedagogy. *Unit head:* Lynn Domina, Head, 906-227-2711, E-mail: ldomina@nmu.edu. *Application contact:* Dr. Russell Prather, Director of MA Program/Professor, 906-227-2857, E-mail: rprather@nmu.edu.
Website: http://www.nmu.edu/english/

Northwestern University, The Graduate School, School of Communication, Department of Theatre, Evanston, IL 60208. Offers directing (MFA); stage design (MFA); theatre and drama (PhD). Admissions and degrees offered through The Graduate School. *Degree requirements:* For master's, thesis (MFA). *Entrance requirements:* For master's, GRE General Test. Additional exam requirements/recommendations for international students: Required—TOEFL. *Faculty research:* Critical analysis, theory and history of theatre and drama, philosophy of dance and movement, performance in multicultural contexts, storytelling, computer design process.

Northwestern University, The Graduate School, School of Communication, Interdisciplinary PhD Program in Theatre and Drama, Evanston, IL 60208. Offers PhD. Admissions and degree offered through The Graduate School. *Degree requirements:* For doctorate, thesis/dissertation, qualifying and final oral exams. *Entrance requirements:* For doctorate, GRE General Test, sample of written work. Additional exam requirements/recommendations for international students: Required—TOEFL. Electronic applications accepted. *Faculty research:* Theory and history of theatre and drama, performance theory, performance in multicultural contexts, critical analysis drama, theatre historiography.

The Ohio State University, Graduate School, College of Arts and Sciences, Division of Arts and Humanities, Department of Theatre, Columbus, OH 43210. Offers acting (MFA); design (MFA); theatre (PhD); theatre studies (MA). *Accreditation:* NAST. *Faculty:* 16. *Students:* 30 (17 women). Average age 33. In 2017, 1 master's, 4 doctorates awarded. Terminal master's awarded for partial completion of doctoral program. *Degree requirements:* For master's, thesis (for some programs); for doctorate, one foreign language, thesis/dissertation. *Entrance requirements:* For master's, GRE General Test (for all MA applicants and MFA applicants with GPA below 3.0), audition (for MFA in acting); electronic design portfolio (for MFA in design); sample of published or unpublished research work (for MA); for doctorate, GRE General Test. Additional exam requirements/recommendations for international students: Required—Michigan English Language Assessment Battery (minimum score 82); Recommended—TOEFL (minimum score 550 paper-based; 79 iBT), IELTS (minimum score 7). *Application deadline:* For fall

admission, 11/30 priority date for domestic and international students; for spring admission, 3/1 for domestic students, 2/1 for international students. Applications are processed on a rolling basis. Application fee: $60 ($70 for international students). Electronic applications accepted. *Financial support:* Fellowships, teaching assistantships, Federal Work-Study, and institutionally sponsored loans available. Support available to part-time students. Financial award application deadline: 3/1; financial award applicants required to submit FAFSA. *Unit head:* Dr. Janet Parrott, Chair, 614-292-5821, E-mail: parrott.1@osu.edu. *Application contact:* Graduate and Professional Admissions, 614-292-9444, Fax: 614-292-3895, E-mail: gpadmissions@osu.edu.
Website: http://theatre.osu.edu/

Ohio University, Graduate College, College of Fine Arts, School of Theater, Athens, OH 45701-2979. Offers MA, MFA. *Accreditation:* NAST. *Degree requirements:* For master's, thesis or alternative. *Entrance requirements:* For master's, minimum GPA of 3.0. Additional exam requirements/recommendations for international students: Required—TOEFL (minimum score 550 paper-based; 80 iBT) or IELTS (minimum score 6.5). Electronic applications accepted.

Oklahoma State University, College of Arts and Sciences, Department of Theatre, Stillwater, OK 74078. Offers MA. *Accreditation:* NAST. *Faculty:* 9 full-time (5 women), 3 part-time/adjunct (2 women). *Students:* 1 (woman) full-time. Average age 39. In 2017, 4 master's awarded. *Entrance requirements:* For master's, GRE. Additional exam requirements/recommendations for international students: Required—TOEFL (minimum score 550 paper-based; 79 iBT). *Application deadline:* For fall admission, 3/1 priority date for international students; for spring admission, 8/1 priority date for international students. Applications are processed on a rolling basis. Application fee: $40 ($75 for international students). Electronic applications accepted. *Expenses:* Tuition, state resident: full-time $4019; part-time $2679.60 per year. Tuition, nonresident: full-time $15,286; part-time $10,190.40 per year. *Required fees:* $2129; $1419 per unit. Tuition and fees vary according to program. *Financial support:* Research assistantships, teaching assistantships, career-related internships or fieldwork, Federal Work-Study, scholarships/grants, health care benefits, tuition waivers (partial), and unspecified assistantships available. Support available to part-time students. Financial award application deadline: 3/1; financial award applicants required to submit FAFSA. *Faculty research:* Historical scene painting and scenic art, Eastern European stage design, stage direction, voice and diction for the actor, stage choreography and dance. *Unit head:* Andrew Kimbrough, Department Head, 405-744-6094, Fax: 405-744-6509, E-mail: andrew.kimbrough@okstate.edu. *Application contact:* Dr. Maria Beach, Graduate Coordinator, 405-744-2966, Fax: 405-744-6509, E-mail: maria.beach@okstate.edu.
Website: http://theatre.okstate.edu/

Pace University, Dyson College of Arts and Sciences, The Actors Studio MFA Program, New York, NY 10038. Offers acting (MFA); directing (MFA); playwriting (MFA). *Faculty:* 7 full-time (3 women), 11 part-time/adjunct (3 women). *Students:* 107 full-time (59 women); includes 31 minority (14 Black or African American, non-Hispanic/Latino; 3 Asian, non-Hispanic/Latino; 9 Hispanic/Latino; 5 Two or more races, non-Hispanic/Latino), 23 international. Average age 27. In 2017, 38 master's awarded. *Degree requirements:* For master's, thesis. *Entrance requirements:* For master's, artistic resume, 2 letters of recommendation (theater, academic and/or professional), official transcripts; audition (for actors); interview and portfolio (for directors and playwrights). Additional exam requirements/recommendations for international students: Required—TOEFL (minimum score 88 iBT), IELTS (minimum score 7) or PTE (minimum score 60). *Application deadline:* For fall admission, 1/1 for domestic students. Application fee: $70. *Financial support:* Scholarships/grants available. Financial award application deadline: 2/15; financial award applicants required to submit FAFSA. *Unit head:* Andreas Manolikakis, Chair, 212-346-1131, E-mail: actorsstudiomfa@pace.edu. *Application contact:* Susan Ford-Goldschein, Director of Graduate Admissions, 212-346-1531, Fax: 212-346-1585, E-mail: graduateadmission@pace.edu.
Website: http://www.pace.edu/dyson/academic-departments-and-programs/asds

Penn State University Park, Graduate School, College of Arts and Architecture, School of Theatre, University Park, PA 16802. Offers MFA. *Accreditation:* NAST. *Unit head:* Dr. Barbara O. Korner, Dean, 814-865-2592, Fax: 814-865-2018. *Application contact:* Lori Hawn, Director, Graduate Student Services, 814-865-1795, Fax: 814-863-4627, E-mail: l-gswww@lists.psu.edu.
Website: http://theatre.psu.edu/

Pensacola Christian College, Graduate Studies, Pensacola, FL 32503-2267. Offers business administration (MBA); curriculum and instruction (MS, Ed D, Ed S); dramatics (MFA); educational leadership (MS, Ed D, Ed S); graphic design (MA, MFA); music (MA); nursing (MSN); performance studies (MA); studio art (MA, MFA).

Point Park University, Conservatory of Performing Arts, Pittsburgh, PA 15222-1984. Offers screenwriting and playwriting (MFA). *Program availability:* Blended/hybrid learning. *Degree requirements:* For master's, comprehensive exam (for some programs), thesis or alternative. *Entrance requirements:* For master's, interview, undergraduate degree in related field, theatre experience. Additional exam requirements/recommendations for international students: Required—TOEFL (minimum score 550 paper-based; 79 iBT). Electronic applications accepted.

Portland State University, Graduate Studies, College of the Arts, School of Music and Theater, Portland, OR 97207-0751. Offers conducting (Mus M); jazz studies (Mus M); music (Mus M); performance (Mus M). *Accreditation:* NASM. *Program availability:* Part-time. *Faculty:* 27 full-time (9 women), 46 part-time/adjunct (16 women). *Students:* 29 full-time (14 women), 10 part-time (3 women); includes 9 minority (3 Asian, non-Hispanic/Latino; 2 Hispanic/Latino; 4 Two or more races, non-Hispanic/Latino), 6 international. Average age 29. 36 applicants, 86% accepted, 13 enrolled. In 2017, 14 master's awarded. *Degree requirements:* For master's, variable foreign language requirement, exit exam. *Entrance requirements:* For master's, GRE General Test, music diagnostic entrance examination, minimum GPA of 3.0 in graduate coursework or 2.75 overall undergraduate, audition. Additional exam requirements/recommendations for international students: Required—TOEFL (minimum score 550 paper-based). *Application deadline:* For fall admission, 4/15 priority date for domestic students, 4/15 for international students; for winter admission, 10/1 for domestic and international students; for spring admission, 12/1 for domestic and international students; for summer admission, 1/15 for domestic and international students. Application fee: $65. *Expenses:* Contact institution. *Financial support:* In 2017–18, 24 students received support, including 11 teaching assistantships with full and partial tuition reimbursements available (averaging $5,603 per year); Federal Work-Study, scholarships/grants, and unspecified assistantships also available. Support available to part-time students. Financial award application deadline: 3/1; financial award applicants required to submit FAFSA. *Faculty research:* Composition, music analysis, music history, jazz. *Unit head:* Bonnie Miksch, Director, 503-725-3063, Fax: 503-725-8215, E-mail: bonnie@pdx.edu.
Website: https://www.pdx.edu/music/

Purdue University, Graduate School, College of Liberal Arts, Department of Theatre, West Lafayette, IN 47907. Offers MFA. *Accreditation:* NAST. *Students:* 19 full-time (11 women); includes 4 minority (1 Black or African American, non-Hispanic/Latino; 2 Hispanic/Latino; 1 Native Hawaiian or other Pacific Islander, non-Hispanic/Latino), 3 international. Average age 28. 25 applicants, 40% accepted, 10 enrolled. In 2017, 8 master's awarded. *Unit head:* Harry T. Bulow, Head of the Graduate Program, 765-494-3056, E-mail: hbulow@purdue.edu. *Application contact:* Rosina C. Starks, Graduate Contact, 765-494-3080, E-mail: rstarks@purdue.edu.
Website: https://www.cla.purdue.edu/vpa/theatre/

Regent University, Graduate School, School of Communication and the Arts, Virginia Beach, VA 23464-9800. Offers acting (MFA); communication (MA, PhD), including media and arts management and promotion (MA), political communication (MA), strategic communication (MA), technical communication (MA); film and TV (MA), including producing (MA, MFA), production, script writing; film-television (MFA), including directing, producing (MA, MFA), script and screenwriting; journalism (MA); theatre (MA). *Program availability:* Part-time, evening/weekend, 100% online, blended/hybrid learning. *Faculty:* 15 full-time (2 women), 66 part-time/adjunct (23 women). *Students:* 101 full-time (65 women), 342 part-time (237 women); includes 177 minority (127 Black or African American, non-Hispanic/Latino; 4 American Indian or Alaska Native, non-Hispanic/Latino; 9 Asian, non-Hispanic/Latino; 25 Hispanic/Latino; 12 Two or more races, non-Hispanic/Latino), 11 international. Average age 37. 498 applicants, 36% accepted, 124 enrolled. In 2017, 93 master's, 22 doctorates awarded. *Degree requirements:* For master's, thesis or alternative; for doctorate, thesis/dissertation. *Entrance requirements:* For master's, transcripts, writing sample, resume, audition (for MFA programs); for doctorate, GRE General Test, resume, writing sample, recommendations, interview, transcripts, personal goals statement. Additional exam requirements/recommendations for international students: Required—TOEFL (minimum score 577 paper-based). *Application deadline:* For fall admission, 3/1 priority date for domestic students; for spring admission, 10/1 priority date for domestic students. Applications are processed on a rolling basis. Application fee: $50. Electronic applications accepted. *Expenses:* $650 per credit (MA, MFA); $885 per credit (PhD); $300 per semester technology fee. *Financial support:* In 2017–18, 234 students received support, including 2 fellowships (averaging $10,000 per year); career-related internships or fieldwork, scholarships/grants, and unspecified assistantships also available. Support available to part-time students. *Faculty research:* Screenwriting, digital media production, communication, acting, directing. *Unit head:* Dr. Robert Herron, Dean, 757-352-4500, E-mail: rherron@regent.edu. *Application contact:* Heidi Cece, Assistant Vice President of Enrollment Management, 800-373-5504, Fax: 757-352-4381, E-mail: admissions@regent.edu.
Website: https://www.regent.edu/school-of-communication-and-the-arts/

Roosevelt University, Graduate Division, Chicago College of Performing Arts, Theatre Conservatory, Chicago, IL 60605. Offers theatre directing (MA). Special 3-summer program for current teachers and theatre directors only. *Students:* 1 applicant, 100% accepted. In 2017, 9 master's awarded. *Application deadline:* Applications are processed on a rolling basis. Application fee: $100. Electronic applications accepted. *Expenses:* Contact institution. *Financial support:* Scholarships/grants available. *Application contact:* Michael Holmes, Interim Assistant Dean for Enrollment Management, 312-341-3797, E-mail: mholmes04@roosevelt.edu.
Website: https://www.roosevelt.edu/colleges/ccpa/theatre-conservatory

Rowan University, Graduate School, College of Education, Department of Language, Literacy, and Sociocultural Education, Program in Theatre Education, Glassboro, NJ 08028-1701. Offers MST. *Accreditation:* NAST. Electronic applications accepted. *Expenses:* Tuition, state resident: full-time $15,020; part-time $751 per semester hour. Tuition, nonresident: full-time $15,020; part-time $751 per semester hour. *Required fees:* $3158; $157.90 per semester hour. Tuition and fees vary according to course load, campus/location and program.

Rowan University, Graduate School, College of Performing Arts, Department of Theatre and Dance, Glassboro, NJ 08028-1701. Offers theatre arts administration (MA). *Accreditation:* NASAD. Electronic applications accepted. *Expenses:* Tuition, state resident: full-time $15,020; part-time $751 per semester hour. Tuition, nonresident: full-time $15,020; part-time $751 per semester hour. *Required fees:* $3158; $157.90 per semester hour. Tuition and fees vary according to course load, campus/location and program.

Rutgers University–New Brunswick, Mason Gross School of the Arts, Theater Department, New Brunswick, NJ 08901. Offers acting (MFA); design (MFA); playwriting (MFA); stage management (MFA); technical direction (MFA). *Degree requirements:* For master's, thesis (for some programs), performance project. *Entrance requirements:* For master's, audition, interview, portfolio. Additional exam requirements/recommendations for international students: Required—TOEFL (minimum score 550 paper-based), IELTS (minimum score 7). Electronic applications accepted. *Faculty research:* Faculty of working professional.

San Diego State University, Graduate and Research Affairs, College of Professional Studies and Fine Arts, School of Theater, Television and Film, San Diego, CA 92182. Offers television, film, and new media production (MA); theatre arts (MA, MFA). *Accreditation:* NAST. *Program availability:* Part-time. *Degree requirements:* For master's, thesis. *Entrance requirements:* For master's, GRE General Test, 3 letters of recommendation, interview. Additional exam requirements/recommendations for international students: Required—TOEFL. Electronic applications accepted.

San Francisco State University, Division of Graduate Studies, College of Liberal and Creative Arts, School of Theatre and Dance, San Francisco, CA 94132-1722. Offers theatre arts (MA, MFA). *Accreditation:* NAST. *Unit head:* Todd Roehrman, Director, 415-338-2519, Fax: 415-338-6159, E-mail: roehrman@sfsu.edu. *Application contact:* Prof. Bruce Avery, MA Coordinator, 415-338-7582, Fax: 415-338-6159, E-mail: bravery@sfsu.edu.
Website: http://www.theatre.sfsu.edu

Sarah Lawrence College, Graduate Studies, Program in Theater, Bronxville, NY 10708-5999. Offers MFA. *Degree requirements:* For master's, portfolio. *Entrance requirements:* For master's, interview, minimum B average in undergraduate course work. Additional exam requirements/recommendations for international students: Required—TOEFL (minimum score 600 paper-based). Electronic applications accepted.

Savannah College of Art and Design, Program in Dramatic Writing, Savannah, GA 31402-3146. Offers MFA. *Program availability:* Part-time. *Faculty:* 5 full-time (2 women), 1 (woman) part-time/adjunct. *Students:* 18 full-time (11 women), 1 part-time (0 women); includes 7 minority (all Black or African American, non-Hispanic/Latino), 4 international. Average age 25. 28 applicants, 61% accepted, 10 enrolled. In 2017, 10 master's awarded. *Degree requirements:* For master's, thesis. *Entrance requirements:* For master's, GRE (recommended), portfolio (submitted in digital format), audition or writing submission, resume, statement of purpose, two letters of recommendation. Additional exam requirements/recommendations for international students: Recommended—TOEFL (minimum score 550 paper-based; 85 iBT), IELTS (minimum score 6.5). *Application deadline:* For fall admission, 4/1 for domestic and international students. Applications are processed on a rolling basis. Application fee: $40. Electronic applications accepted. *Expenses: Tuition:* Full-time $36,765; part-time $817 per credit hour. One-time fee: $500. *Financial support:* Career-related internships or fieldwork, Federal Work-Study, and scholarships/grants available. Financial award application

deadline: 4/1; financial award applicants required to submit FAFSA. *Unit head:* Averie Storck, Academic Program Coordinator. *Application contact:* Jenny Jaquillard, Executive Director of Admissions, Recruitment and Events, 912-525-5100, Fax: 912-525-5985, E-mail: admission@scad.edu.
Website: http://www.scad.edu/academics/programs/dramatic-writing

Savannah College of Art and Design, Program in Production Design, Savannah, GA 31402-3146. Offers MA, MFA. *Program availability:* Part-time. *Faculty:* 5 full-time (3 women). *Students:* 23 full-time (20 women); includes 3 minority (1 Black or African American, non-Hispanic/Latino; 2 Hispanic/Latino), 9 international. Average age 28. 34 applicants, 44% accepted, 8 enrolled. In 2017, 3 master's awarded. *Degree requirements:* For master's, final project (for MA); thesis (for MFA). *Entrance requirements:* For master's, GRE (recommended), portfolio (submitted in digital format), audition or writing submission, resume, statement of purpose, two letters of recommendation. Additional exam requirements/recommendations for international students: Recommended—TOEFL (minimum score 550 paper-based; 85 iBT), IELTS (minimum score 6.5). *Application deadline:* For fall admission, 4/1 for domestic and international students. Applications are processed on a rolling basis. Application fee: $40. Electronic applications accepted. *Expenses: Tuition:* Full-time $36,765; part-time $817 per credit hour. One-time fee: $500. *Financial support:* Career-related internships or fieldwork, Federal Work-Study, and scholarships/grants available. Financial award application deadline: 4/1; financial award applicants required to submit FAFSA. *Unit head:* Gregory Beck, Chair, Production Design and Themed Entertainment. *Application contact:* Jenny Jaquillard, Executive Director of Admissions, Recruitment and Events, 912-525-5100, Fax: 912-525-5985, E-mail: admission@scad.edu.
Website: http://www.scad.edu/academics/programs/production-design

Smith College, Graduate and Special Programs, Department of Theatre, Northampton, MA 01063. Offers theatre (MFA), including playwriting. *Program availability:* Part-time. *Students:* 2 full-time (both women). Average age 40. 4 applicants, 25% accepted, 1 enrolled. In 2017, 2 master's awarded. *Degree requirements:* For master's, thesis. *Entrance requirements:* For master's, full-length play. Additional exam requirements/ recommendations for international students: Required—TOEFL (minimum score 595 paper-based; 97 iBT), IELTS. *Application deadline:* For fall admission, 4/1 for domestic students, 1/15 for international students; for spring admission, 12/1 for domestic students. Application fee: $60. *Expenses: Tuition:* Full-time $37,440; part-time $1560 per credit. Tuition and fees vary according to course load and program. *Financial support:* In 2017–18, 2 students received support. Scholarships/grants and human resources employee benefit available. Support available to part-time students. Financial award application deadline: 1/15; financial award applicants required to submit CSS PROFILE or FAFSA. *Unit head:* Leonard Berkman, Graduate Student Adviser, 413-585-3206, E-mail: lberkman@smith.edu. *Application contact:* Ruth Morgan, Program Assistant, 413-585-3050, Fax: 413-585-3054, E-mail: rmorgan@smith.edu.
Website: http://www.smith.edu/theatre/

Southern Illinois University Carbondale, Graduate School, College of Liberal Arts, Theater Department, Carbondale, IL 62901-4701. Offers speech/theater (PhD); theater (MFA). *Accreditation:* NAST (one or more programs are accredited). *Program availability:* Part-time. *Degree requirements:* For master's, thesis; for doctorate, thesis/ dissertation. *Entrance requirements:* For master's, minimum GPA of 2.7; for doctorate, minimum GPA of 3.25. Additional exam requirements/recommendations for international students: Required—TOEFL. *Faculty research:* Scenography, theater performance, theater history, dramatic criticism, theater technology, playwriting.

Southern Methodist University, Meadows School of the Arts, Division of Theatre, Dallas, TX 75275. Offers acting (MFA); design (MFA). *Accreditation:* NAST. *Entrance requirements:* For master's, audition or interview. Additional exam requirements/ recommendations for international students: Required—TOEFL (minimum score 550 paper-based; 80 iBT). Electronic applications accepted. *Faculty research:* European lighting techniques.

Southern Oregon University, Graduate Studies, Ashland Center for Theatre Studies, Ashland, OR 97520. Offers MTS. *Program availability:* Part-time. *Degree requirements:* For master's, thesis (for some programs). *Entrance requirements:* For master's, GRE General Test, minimum cumulative GPA of 3.0 in the last 90 quarter credits (60 semester credits) of undergraduate coursework. Additional exam requirements/ recommendations for international students: Required—TOEFL (minimum score 540 paper-based; 76 iBT), IELTS (minimum score 6), ELPT (minimum score 964) or ELS (minimum score 112). Electronic applications accepted.

Stanford University, School of Humanities and Sciences, Department of Theater and Performance Studies, Stanford, CA 94305-2004. Offers PhD. *Degree requirements:* For doctorate, one foreign language, thesis/dissertation, qualifying exams. *Entrance requirements:* For doctorate, GRE General Test, summary of production experience. Additional exam requirements/recommendations for international students: Required— TOEFL. Electronic applications accepted. *Expenses: Tuition:* Full-time $48,987; part-time $10,620 per quarter. One-time fee: $400. Tuition and fees vary according to program.

Stony Brook University, State University of New York, Graduate School, College of Arts and Sciences, Department of Theatre Arts, Program in Dramaturgy, Stony Brook, NY 11794. Offers MFA. *Degree requirements:* For master's, one foreign language, thesis. *Entrance requirements:* For master's, GRE General Test. Additional exam requirements/recommendations for international students: Required—TOEFL. *Application deadline:* For fall admission, 1/15 for domestic students; for spring admission, 10/1 for domestic students. Application fee: $100. *Expenses:* Contact institution. *Unit head:* Dr. John Lutterbie, Chair, 631-632-7245, E-mail: john.lutterbie@stonybrook.edu. *Application contact:* Lisa Perez, Coordinator, 631-632-7270, Fax: 631-632-7261, E-mail: lisa.perez@stonybrook.edu.

Stony Brook University, State University of New York, Graduate School, College of Arts and Sciences, Department of Theatre Arts, Program in Theatre Arts, Stony Brook, NY 11794. Offers MA. *Program availability:* Evening/weekend. *Students:* 1 (woman) full-time, 1 (woman) part-time, 1 international. Average age 35. In 2017, 1 master's awarded. *Degree requirements:* For master's, one foreign language, thesis. *Entrance requirements:* For master's, GRE General Test. Additional exam requirements/ recommendations for international students: Required—TOEFL. *Application deadline:* For fall admission, 1/15 for domestic students; for spring admission, 10/1 for domestic students. Application fee: $100. *Expenses:* Contact institution. *Faculty research:* Theatre arts, theater, dramatic arts, dramatic language and or literature, theatre or film criticism. *Unit head:* Dr. John Lutterbie, Chair, 631-632-7245, E-mail: john.lutterbie@stonybrook.edu. *Application contact:* Lisa Perez, Coordinator, 631-632-7270, Fax: 631-632-7258, E-mail: lisa.perez@stonybrook.edu.
Website: https://www.stonybrook.edu/commcms/theatre-arts/

Temple University, Center for the Performing and Cinematic Arts, School of Theater, Film and Media Arts, Department of Theater, Philadelphia, PA 19122. Offers acting (MFA); design (MFA); directing (MFA); musical theater collaboration (MFA); musical theater studies (MA); playwriting (MFA). *Accreditation:* NAST. *Program availability:* Part-time. *Faculty:* 15 full-time (7 women), 18 part-time/adjunct (13 women). *Students:* 28 full-time (16 women), 1 (woman) part-time; includes 7 minority (4 Black or African American,

non-Hispanic/Latino; 3 Hispanic/Latino), 3 international. 22 applicants, 41% accepted, 8 enrolled. In 2017, 6 master's awarded. *Degree requirements:* For master's, thesis (for some programs). *Entrance requirements:* For master's, minimum GPA of 3.0; audition/ interview, portfolio, or samples of written work. Additional exam requirements/ recommendations for international students: Required—TOEFL (minimum score 550 paper-based; 79 iBT). *Application deadline:* For fall admission, 12/15 for international students. Application fee: $60. Electronic applications accepted. *Expenses:* Contact institution. *Financial support:* Teaching assistantships with full tuition reimbursements, Federal Work-Study, institutionally sponsored loans, and unspecified assistantships available. Financial award application deadline: 3/1; financial award applicants required to submit FAFSA. *Faculty research:* Acting/voice/speech/movement, theatrical design and production, musical theater, directing, playwriting. *Unit head:* Robert Hedley, Chair, 215-204-8413, E-mail: robert.hedley@temple.edu. *Application contact:* Leah Dempsey, Assistant Director for Administration, 215-204-8791, E-mail: leahdempsey@temple.edu.
Website: https://tfma.temple.edu/theater

Texas A&M University–Commerce, College of Humanities, Social Sciences and Arts, Commerce, TX 75429. Offers applied criminology (MS); applied linguistics (MA, MS); art (MA, MFA); computational linguistics (Graduate Certificate); creative writing (Graduate Certificate); criminal justice management (Graduate Certificate); criminal justice studies (Graduate Certificate); English (MA, MS, PhD); film studies (Graduate Certificate); history (MA, MS); history of Christianity (Graduate Certificate); Holocaust studies (Graduate Certificate); homeland security (Graduate Certificate); music education (MM); music performance (MM); political science (MA, MS); public history (Graduate Certificate); sociology (MS); Spanish (MA); studies in children's and adolescent literature and culture (Graduate Certificate); teaching English to speakers of other languages (Graduate Certificate); theater (MA, MS); world history (Graduate Certificate). *Program availability:* Part-time. *Faculty:* 56 full-time (26 women), 10 part-time/adjunct (5 women). *Students:* 133 full-time (85 women), 439 part-time (311 women); includes 204 minority (79 Black or African American, non-Hispanic/Latino; 4 American Indian or Alaska Native, non-Hispanic/Latino; 9 Asian, non-Hispanic/Latino; 98 Hispanic/Latino; 14 Two or more races, non-Hispanic/Latino), 26 international. Average age 36. 261 applicants, 50% accepted, 113 enrolled. In 2017, 105 master's, 5 doctorates awarded. *Degree requirements:* For master's, one foreign language, comprehensive exam, thesis (for some programs); for doctorate, one foreign language, comprehensive exam, thesis/ dissertation, departmental qualifying exam. *Entrance requirements:* For master's and doctorate, GRE General Test. Additional exam requirements/recommendations for international students: Required—TOEFL (minimum score 550 paper-based; 79 iBT), IELTS (minimum score 6). *Application deadline:* Applications are processed on a rolling basis. Application fee: $50. Electronic applications accepted. *Expenses:* Contact institution. *Financial support:* In 2017–18, 43 students received support, including 9 research assistantships with partial tuition reimbursements available (averaging $9,000 per year), 68 teaching assistantships with partial tuition reimbursements available (averaging $9,000 per year); Federal Work-Study, institutionally sponsored loans, scholarships/grants, health care benefits, and unspecified assistantships also available. Financial award application deadline: 5/1; financial award applicants required to submit FAFSA. *Unit head:* Dr. William F. Kuracina, Interim Dean, 903-886-5166, Fax: 903-886-5774, E-mail: william.kuracina@tamuc.edu. *Application contact:* Vicky Turner, Doctoral Degree and Special Programs Coordinator, 903-886-5167, E-mail: vicky.turner@tamuc.edu.
Website: http://www.tamuc.edu/academics/graduateSchool/programs/ humanitiesSocialScienceArts/default.aspx

Texas State University, The Graduate College, College of Fine Arts and Communication, Program in Theatre Arts, San Marcos, TX 78666. Offers design (MFA); directing (MFA); dramatic writing (MFA); theatre history, dramatic criticism and dramaturgy (MA). *Program availability:* Part-time, evening/weekend. *Faculty:* 20 full-time (10 women), 5 part-time/adjunct (3 women). *Students:* 27 full-time (12 women), 1 (woman) part-time; includes 5 minority (2 Black or African American, non-Hispanic/ Latino; 2 Hispanic/Latino; 1 Two or more races, non-Hispanic/Latino). Average age 31. 35 applicants, 40% accepted, 12 enrolled. In 2017, 3 master's awarded. *Degree requirements:* For master's, comprehensive exam, thesis (for some programs). *Entrance requirements:* For master's, GRE General Test with minimum preferred score of 300 verbal and quantitative combined (for MA), baccalaureate degree from regionally-accredited institution with minimum GPA of 2.75 in last 60 hours of undergraduate course work, 2 letters of recommendation, statement of purpose, curriculum vitae/ resume; writing sample (for playwriting applicants only); interview (for directing applicants only). Additional exam requirements/recommendations for international students: Required—TOEFL (minimum score 550 paper-based; 78 iBT), IELTS (minimum score 6). *Application deadline:* For fall admission, 3/15 for domestic and international students. Applications are processed on a rolling basis. Application fee: $40 ($90 for international students). Electronic applications accepted. *Expenses: Tuition,* state resident: full-time $7868; part-time $3934 per semester. *Tuition,* nonresident: full-time $17,828; part-time $8914 per semester. *Required fees:* $2092; $1435 per semester. Tuition and fees vary according to course load. *Financial support:* In 2017–18, 25 teaching assistantships (averaging $12,453 per year) were awarded; research assistantships, Federal Work-Study, institutionally sponsored loans, scholarships/grants, and unspecified assistantships also available. Support available to part-time students. Financial award application deadline: 3/1; financial award applicants required to submit FAFSA. *Faculty research:* Black and Latino playwright conference, creation in motion. *Total annual research expenditures:* $2,900. *Unit head:* Dr. Sandra Mayo, Graduate Advisor, 512-245-7889, Fax: 512-245-8440, E-mail: th_gradadvisor@txstate.edu. *Application contact:* Dr. Andrea Golato, Dean of Graduate School, 512-245-2581, Fax: 512-245-8365, E-mail: gradcollege@txstate.edu.
Website: http://www.theatreanddance.txstate.edu/

Texas Tech University, Graduate School, J.T. and Margaret Talkington College of Visual and Performing Arts, School of Theatre and Dance, Lubbock, TX 79409-2061. Offers dance studies (MA); theatre arts (MA, MFA). *Accreditation:* NAST. *Program availability:* Part-time. *Faculty:* 23 full-time (11 women), 2 part-time/adjunct (both women). *Students:* 28 full-time (16 women), 3 part-time (all women); includes 3 minority (1 Black or African American, non-Hispanic/Latino; 1 Hispanic/Latino; 1 Two or more races, non-Hispanic/Latino), 2 international. Average age 29. 22 applicants, 45% accepted, 6 enrolled. In 2017, 9 master's awarded. *Degree requirements:* For master's, variable foreign language requirement, comprehensive exam (for some programs), thesis (for some programs), direct a production (for some programs). *Entrance requirements:* For master's, GRE, samples of artistic work in area of interest and/or interview/audition with faculty (for MFA). Additional exam requirements/recommendations for international students: Required—TOEFL (minimum score 550 paper-based; 79 iBT), IELTS (minimum score 6.5), PTE (minimum score 60). *Application deadline:* For fall admission, 6/1 priority date for domestic students, 1/15 priority date for international students; for spring admission, 9/1 priority date for domestic students, 6/15 priority date for international students. Applications are processed on a rolling basis. Application fee: $60. Electronic applications accepted. *Expenses:* Contact institution. *Financial support:* In 2017–18, 34 students received support, including 34 fellowships (averaging $3,620 per year), 30 teaching assistantships (averaging $9,794 per year); research assistantships, Federal Work-Study, scholarships/grants, tuition waivers (partial), and unspecified

assistantships also available. Financial award application deadline: 4/15; financial award applicants required to submit FAFSA. *Faculty research:* Translation/adaptation, early modern theatre studies, arts in medicine, Bertolt Brecht studies, devised theatre, working with diverse populations including people on the spectrum. *Total annual research expenditures:* $46,349. *Unit head:* Dr. Mark Charney, Director of Theatre and Dance, 806-742-3601, Fax: 806-742-1338, E-mail: mark.charney@ttu.edu. *Application contact:* Abigail Chowning, Graduate Admissions and Recruitment Coordinator, 806-834-7679, Fax: 806-742-1338, E-mail: abigail.chowning@ttu.edu.
Website: http://www.depts.ttu.edu/theatreanddance/

Texas Woman's University, Graduate School, College of Arts and Sciences, School of the Arts, Department of Music and Drama, Denton, TX 76204. Offers drama (MA); music (MA), including music education, music therapy, pedagogy, performance. *Accreditation:* NASM. *Program availability:* Part-time. *Faculty:* 15 full-time (7 women), 8 part-time/adjunct (4 women). *Students:* 54 full-time (41 women), 43 part-time (30 women); includes 32 minority (6 Black or African American, non-Hispanic/Latino; 2 Asian, non-Hispanic/Latino; 21 Hispanic/Latino; 3 Two or more races, non-Hispanic/Latino), 6 international. Average age 30. 42 applicants, 98% accepted, 33 enrolled. In 2017, 21 master's awarded. *Degree requirements:* For master's, comprehensive exam, thesis (for some programs), project recital, professional paper or thesis (for music education). *Entrance requirements:* For master's, music history/theory placement exam (for music only), audition and/or design portfolio, interview, resume, writing sample (for drama only), letter of intent, minimum undergraduate GPA of 3.0. Additional exam requirements/recommendations for international students: Required—TOEFL (minimum score 550 paper-based; 79 iBT); Recommended—IELTS (minimum score 6.5), TSE (minimum score 53). *Application deadline:* For fall admission, 3/1 priority date for domestic and international students; for spring admission, 11/1 priority date for domestic students, 7/1 priority date for international students; for summer admission, 5/1 priority date for domestic students, 2/1 priority date for international students. Applications are processed on a rolling basis. Application fee: $50 ($75 for international students). Electronic applications accepted. *Expenses:* $8,150 per year full-time in-state, $17,450 per year full-time out-of-state (for music). *Financial support:* In 2017–18, 31 students received support, including 5 teaching assistantships (averaging $11,736 per year); career-related internships or fieldwork, Federal Work-Study, institutionally sponsored loans, scholarships/grants, traineeships, health care benefits, and unspecified assistantships also available. Support available to part-time students. Financial award application deadline: 3/1; financial award applicants required to submit FAFSA. *Faculty research:* Musical development in early childhood, little known or neglected compositions for flute (especially by women composers), pedagogical development of the singing voice, music therapy, music and neuroscience technology. *Unit head:* Dr. Pamela Youngblood, Chair of Music and Drama, 940-898-2500, Fax: 940-898-2494, E-mail: music@twu.edu. *Application contact:* Korie Hawkins, Associate Director of Admissions, Graduate Recruitment, 940-898-3188, Fax: 940-898-3081, E-mail: admissions@twu.edu.

Towson University, College of Fine Arts and Communication, Program in Theatre, Towson, MD 21252-0001. Offers MFA. *Accreditation:* NAST. *Students:* 5 full-time (4 women), 1 international. *Degree requirements:* For master's, thesis. *Entrance requirements:* For master's, minimum GPA of 3.0, bachelor's degree, 3 letters of recommendation, artistic statement, current professional resume, 3 references, portfolio, interview. *Application deadline:* For fall admission, 1/17 for domestic students, 5/15 for international students; for spring admission, 10/15 for domestic students, 12/1 for international students. Applications are processed on a rolling basis. Application fee: $45. Electronic applications accepted. *Expenses:* Tuition, state resident: full-time $7960; part-time $398 per unit. Tuition, nonresident: full-time $16,480; part-time $824 per unit. *Required fees:* $2600; $130 per year. $390 per term. *Financial support:* Application deadline: 4/1. *Unit head:* Prof. Naoko Maeshiba, Graduate Program Director, 410-704-2791, E-mail: nmaeshiba@towson.edu. *Application contact:* Coverley Beidleman, Assistant Director of Graduate Admissions, 410-704-5630, Fax: 410-704-3030, E-mail: cbeidleman@towson.edu.
Website: http://www.towson.edu/cofac/departments/theatre/gradtheatre/

Tufts University, Graduate School of Arts and Sciences, Department of Drama and Dance, Medford, MA 02155. Offers theatre and performance studies (MA, PhD). *Students:* 24 full-time (14 women); includes 2 minority (1 Black or African American, non-Hispanic/Latino; 1 Hispanic/Latino), 5 international. Average age 31. 25 applicants, 40% accepted, 4 enrolled. In 2017, 3 doctorates awarded. Terminal master's awarded for partial completion of doctoral program. *Degree requirements:* For master's, one foreign language, thesis; for doctorate, one foreign language, thesis/dissertation, oral exam, written general exam. *Entrance requirements:* For master's and doctorate, GRE General Test, writing sample. Additional exam requirements/recommendations for international students: Required—TOEFL (minimum score 600 paper-based; 80 iBT), IELTS (minimum score 6.5). *Application deadline:* For fall admission, 1/15 for domestic and international students. Applications are processed on a rolling basis. Application fee: $85. Electronic applications accepted. *Expenses:* Contact institution. *Financial support:* Fellowships, teaching assistantships, Federal Work-Study, scholarships/grants, tuition waivers (full and partial), and unspecified assistantships available. Financial award application deadline: 1/15. *Unit head:* Dr. Noe Montez, Graduate Program Director. *Application contact:* Office of Graduate Admissions, 617-627-3395, E-mail: gradadmissions@tufts.edu.
Website: http://www.tufts.edu/as/drama/

Tulane University, School of Liberal Arts, Department of Theatre and Dance, New Orleans, LA 70118-5669. Offers design and technical production (MFA). *Entrance requirements:* For master's, GRE General Test, minimum B average in undergraduate course work. Additional exam requirements/recommendations for international students: Required—TOEFL. Electronic applications accepted. *Expenses: Tuition:* Full-time $50,920; part-time $2829 per credit hour. *Required fees:* $2040; $44.50 per credit hour. $580 per term. Tuition and fees vary according to course load, degree level and program. *Faculty research:* Scene design, stage management, costume design, technical direction, lighting design.

Université de Sherbrooke, Faculty of Letters and Human Sciences, Department of Letters and Communications, Sherbrooke, QC J1K 2R1, Canada. Offers comparative Canadian literature (MA, PhD); French literature (MA, PhD); linguistics (MA); theatre (MA). *Degree requirements:* For master's, thesis or alternative; for doctorate, thesis/dissertation. *Entrance requirements:* For master's, minimum GPA of 2.8; for doctorate, minimum GPA of 3.0.

Université Laval, Faculty of Letters, Department of Literature, Programs in Literature and Arts of the Screen and Stage, Québec, QC G1K 7P4, Canada. Offers MA, PhD. *Program availability:* Part-time. Terminal master's awarded for partial completion of doctoral program. *Degree requirements:* For master's, thesis; for doctorate, comprehensive exam, thesis/dissertation. *Entrance requirements:* For master's and doctorate, linguistics exams, knowledge of French, knowledge of a second language. Electronic applications accepted.

University at Buffalo, the State University of New York, Graduate School, College of Arts and Sciences, Department of Theatre and Dance, Buffalo, NY 14260. Offers dance (MFA); theatre and performance (MA, PhD). *Program availability:* Part-time. *Faculty:* 10 full-time (7 women). *Students:* 13 full-time (10 women), 5 part-time (3 women). Average age 36. 31 applicants, 45% accepted, 10 enrolled. *Degree requirements:* For master's, comprehensive exam (for some programs), thesis project or written thesis; for doctorate, one foreign language, comprehensive exam, thesis/dissertation. *Entrance requirements:* For master's, statement of purpose; academic writing sample (e.g., scholarly essay, performance or book review); 3 letters of recommendation (sent electronically); portfolio of creative work; resume; BA, BFA, or BS; audition and sample of choreographic work (for MFA); for doctorate, GRE, statement of purpose; academic writing sample (e.g., scholarly essay, performance or book review); 3 letters of recommendation (sent electronically); portfolio of creative work; resume; master's degree. Additional exam requirements/recommendations for international students: Required—TOEFL (minimum score 550 paper-based). *Application deadline:* For fall admission, 1/1 for domestic and international students. Applications are processed on a rolling basis. Application fee: $75. Electronic applications accepted. *Financial support:* In 2017–18, 1 fellowship (averaging $4,000 per year), 7 teaching assistantships with full tuition reimbursements (averaging $12,400 per year) were awarded; scholarships/grants also available. Financial award application deadline: 12/1. *Faculty research:* Intermediality in theatre and performance; contemporary performance and theory; intersections of technology and performance; digital dramaturgy; interdisciplinary dance making. *Unit head:* Prof. Lynne Koscielniak, Chair, 716-645-6897, Fax: 716-645-6992, E-mail: td-theatredance@buffalo.edu. *Application contact:* Rachel Olszewski, Graduate Studies Staff Assistant, 716-645-6076, E-mail: rachelol@buffalo.edu.
Website: http://www.theatredance.buffalo.edu/

The University of Akron, Graduate School, Buchtel College of Arts and Sciences, School of Dance, Theatre, and Arts Administration, Akron, OH 44325. Offers arts administration (MA); theatre arts (MA). *Program availability:* Part-time, evening/weekend. *Faculty:* 2 full-time (0 women), 5 part-time/adjunct (3 women). *Students:* 14 full-time (12 women), 4 part-time (all women); includes 3 minority (2 Black or African American, non-Hispanic/Latino; 1 Two or more races, non-Hispanic/Latino), 1 international. Average age 29. 21 applicants, 95% accepted, 8 enrolled. In 2017, 7 master's awarded. *Degree requirements:* For master's, thesis. *Entrance requirements:* For master's, minimum GPA of 2.75, 300-word statement of intent summarizing student background and outlining career goals. Additional exam requirements/recommendations for international students: Required—TOEFL (minimum score 79 iBT), IELTS (minimum score 6.5). *Application deadline:* For fall admission, 3/15 for domestic and international students. Application fee: $45 ($70 for international students). Electronic applications accepted. *Financial support:* In 2017–18, 13 teaching assistantships with full and partial tuition reimbursements were awarded. *Faculty research:* Theatre history; technical theatre; set, costume, and design; lighting; playwriting. *Total annual research expenditures:* $5,908. *Unit head:* Dr. J. Thomas Dukes, Interim Director, 330-972-7948, E-mail: jtdukes@uakron.edu. *Application contact:* James Slowiak, Coordinator, Arts Administration, 330-972-5909, E-mail: jslowiak@uakron.edu.
Website: http://www.uakron.edu/dtaa/

The University of Alabama, Graduate School, College of Arts and Sciences, Department of Theatre and Dance, Tuscaloosa, AL 35487. Offers acting (MFA); costume design (MFA); directing (MFA); scene design/technical production (MFA); stage management (MFA); theatre (MFA); theatre management/administration (MFA). *Accreditation:* NAST. *Faculty:* 16 full-time (9 women). *Students:* 37 full-time (17 women), 1 part-time (0 women); includes 7 minority (3 Black or African American, non-Hispanic/Latino; 4 Hispanic/Latino). Average age 29. 24 applicants, 67% accepted, 12 enrolled. In 2017, 12 master's awarded. *Degree requirements:* For master's, thesis project. *Entrance requirements:* For master's, audition and/or portfolio review. *Application deadline:* For fall admission, 4/1 priority date for domestic students, 3/1 priority date for international students. Applications are processed on a rolling basis. Application fee: $50 ($60 for international students). Electronic applications accepted. *Financial support:* In 2017–18, 38 students received support, including research assistantships with full tuition reimbursements available (averaging $13,140 per year), teaching assistantships with full tuition reimbursements available (averaging $13,140 per year); career-related internships or fieldwork, health care benefits, and unspecified assistantships also available. Financial award application deadline: 4/15. *Faculty research:* Acting, theatre history, directing, design practice and production (scenery, costumes, and lighting), technical direction and production, theatre management. *Unit head:* Prof. William Teague, Chair and Professor, 205-348-5283, Fax: 205-348-9048, E-mail: wteague@ua.edu. *Application contact:* Nancy Calvert, Recruiting Contact, 205-348-5283, Fax: 205-348-9048, E-mail: ncalvert@ua.edu.
Website: http://www.as.ua.edu/theatre/

University of Alberta, Faculty of Graduate Studies and Research, Department of Drama, Edmonton, AB T6G 2E1, Canada. Offers design (MFA); directing (MFA); drama (MA). *Degree requirements:* For master's, one foreign language, production thesis. *Faculty research:* Dramaturgy, history, theory and criticism, design.

The University of Arizona, College of Fine Arts, School of Theatre, Film and Television, Tucson, AZ 85721. Offers MFA. *Accreditation:* NAST. *Degree requirements:* For master's, comprehensive exam (for some programs), thesis (for some programs), production monograph. *Entrance requirements:* For master's, 3 letters of recommendation, portfolio. Additional exam requirements/recommendations for international students: Required—TOEFL (minimum score 550 paper-based; 79 iBT). Electronic applications accepted. *Faculty research:* Modern and contemporary theater, cultural studies, musical theater, women and theater.

University of Arkansas, Graduate School, J. William Fulbright College of Arts and Sciences, Department of Theatre, Fayetteville, AR 72701. Offers MA, MFA. In 2017, 9 master's awarded. *Degree requirements:* For master's, thesis optional. *Application deadline:* For fall admission, 8/1 for domestic students, 4/1 for international students; for spring admission, 12/1 for domestic students, 10/1 for international students; for summer admission, 4/15 for domestic students, 3/1 for international students. Applications are processed on a rolling basis. Application fee: $60. Electronic applications accepted. *Expenses:* Tuition, state resident: full-time $3782. Tuition, nonresident: full-time $10,238. *Financial support:* In 2017–18, 9 research assistantships, 11 teaching assistantships were awarded; fellowships with tuition reimbursements, career-related internships or fieldwork, and Federal Work-Study also available. Support available to part-time students. Financial award application deadline: 4/1; financial award applicants required to submit FAFSA. *Unit head:* Dr. Michael Riha, Department Chair, 479-575-2953, Fax: 479-575-7602, E-mail: mriha@uark.edu. *Application contact:* Les Wade, Professor, 479-575-2293, Fax: 479-575-7602, E-mail: law018@uark.edu.
Website: https://fulbright.uark.edu/departments/theatre/

The University of British Columbia, Faculty of Arts, Creative Writing Program, Vancouver, BC V6T 1Z1, Canada. Offers creative writing (MFA); creative writing and theatre (MFA); film production and creative writing (MFA). *Program availability:* Part-time, online learning. *Degree requirements:* For master's, thesis. *Entrance requirements:* For master's, sample of written work. Additional exam requirements/recommendations for international students: Required—TOEFL. Electronic applications accepted. *Expenses:* Contact institution. *Faculty research:* Writing of fiction; poetry, creative nonfiction, plays for stage, screen, television, radio, writing for children and translation, song lyrics and libretto, new media and graphic novel.

Theater

The University of British Columbia, Faculty of Arts and Faculty of Graduate Studies, Department of Theatre and Film, Theatre Program, Vancouver, BC V6T 1Z2, Canada. Offers theatre (MA, PhD); theatre design (MFA); theatre directing (MFA). Terminal master's awarded for partial completion of doctoral program. *Degree requirements:* For master's, variable foreign language requirement, comprehensive exam, thesis; for doctorate, one foreign language, comprehensive exam, thesis/dissertation. *Entrance requirements:* For master's, portfolio (MFA); for doctorate, MA or equivalent. Additional exam requirements/recommendations for international students: Required—TOEFL (minimum score 550 paper-based for MFA; 600 for MA and PhD). *Expenses:* Contact institution. *Faculty research:* Devising theatre; Canadian theatre; multicultural and theatre arts; stage lighting and costume design.

University of Calgary, Faculty of Graduate Studies, Faculty of Arts, Department of Drama, Calgary, AB T2N 1N4, Canada. Offers design and technical theatre (MFA); directing (MFA); playwriting (MFA); theatre studies (MFA). *Degree requirements:* For master's, thesis. *Entrance requirements:* For master's, bachelor's degree in drama, minimum GPA of 3.0, portfolio (design and playwriting). Additional exam requirements/recommendations for international students: Required—TOEFL. *Faculty research:* Popular theatre, collective creation, technical design, dramaturgy, directing styles.

University of California, Berkeley, Graduate Division, College of Letters and Science, Group in Performance Studies, Berkeley, CA 94720-1500. Offers PhD. *Degree requirements:* For doctorate, one foreign language, thesis/dissertation, qualifying exam. *Entrance requirements:* For doctorate, GRE General Test, sample of critical writing, 3 letters of recommendation. Additional exam requirements/recommendations for international students: Required—TOEFL. Electronic applications accepted. *Faculty research:* Postcolonial performance; gender, sexuality, and performance; political performance; dramatic literature and theory; race, ethnicity, performance.

University of California, Davis, Graduate Studies, Program in Dramatic Art, Davis, CA 95616. Offers acting (MFA); dramatic art (PhD). *Entrance requirements:* For master's, minimum GPA of 3.0, portfolio. Additional exam requirements/recommendations for international students: Required—TOEFL (minimum score 550 paper-based). Electronic applications accepted. *Faculty research:* Twentieth century performance and culture.

University of California, Davis, Graduate Studies, Program in Performance Studies, Davis, CA 95616. Offers dramatic art (PhD). *Degree requirements:* For doctorate, 2 foreign languages, thesis/dissertation. *Entrance requirements:* For doctorate, GRE, minimum GPA of 3.25. Additional exam requirements/recommendations for international students: Required—TOEFL (minimum score 550 paper-based). Electronic applications accepted.

University of California, Irvine, Claire Trevor School of the Arts, Department of Drama, Irvine, CA 92697. Offers acting (MFA); design and stage management (MFA); directing (MFA); drama (MFA); drama and theatre (PhD). *Students:* 69 full-time (34 women), 3 part-time (2 women); includes 28 minority (3 Black or African American, non-Hispanic/Latino; 5 Asian, non-Hispanic/Latino; 12 Hispanic/Latino; 8 Two or more races, non-Hispanic/Latino), 4 international. Average age 28. 210 applicants, 13% accepted, 23 enrolled. In 2017, 21 master's, 1 doctorate awarded. *Degree requirements:* For master's, comprehensive exam, thesis; for doctorate, one foreign language, thesis/dissertation. *Entrance requirements:* For master's, audition, interview, or portfolio; minimum GPA of 3.0; for doctorate, GRE, minimum GPA of 3.5, critical writing samples. *Application deadline:* For fall admission, 1/15 priority date for domestic students, 1/15 for international students. Applications are processed on a rolling basis. Application fee: $105 ($125 for international students). Electronic applications accepted. *Financial support:* Fellowships, teaching assistantships, institutionally sponsored loans, traineeships, health care benefits, and unspecified assistantships available. Financial award application deadline: 3/1; financial award applicants required to submit FAFSA. *Faculty research:* Costume, scenery, and lighting design; production; theatre history, literature, and criticism. *Unit head:* Daniel Gary Busby, Department Chair, 949-824-8243, Fax: 949-824-3475, E-mail: dgbusby@uci.edu. *Application contact:* Prof. Stephen F. Barker, Interim Dean, 949-824-5684, Fax: 949-824-2450, E-mail: barker@uci.edu. Website: http://www.arts.uci.edu/ctsa-academic-departments-drama

University of California, Los Angeles, Graduate Division, School of Theater, Film and Television, Department of Theater, Los Angeles, CA 90095. Offers theater (MA, MFA); theater and performance studies (PhD). *Accreditation:* NAST. *Degree requirements:* For master's, comprehensive exam or thesis; for doctorate, one foreign language, thesis/dissertation, oral and written qualifying exams. *Entrance requirements:* For master's, bachelor's degree; minimum undergraduate GPA of 3.0 (or its equivalent if letter grade system not used); portfolio (MFA); writing sample (MA); for doctorate, GRE General Test, bachelor's degree; minimum undergraduate GPA of 3.0 (or its equivalent if letter grade system not used); writing sample. Additional exam requirements/recommendations for international students: Required—TOEFL. Electronic applications accepted. *Expenses:* Contact institution.

University of California, San Diego, Graduate Division, Department of Theatre and Dance, La Jolla, CA 92093. Offers acting (MFA); dance theatre (MFA); design (MFA); directing (MFA); drama and theatre (PhD); playwriting (MFA); stage management (MFA). PhD offered jointly with University of California, Irvine. *Students:* 79 full-time (44 women). 495 applicants, 7% accepted, 29 enrolled. In 2017, 23 master's, 2 doctorates awarded. *Degree requirements:* For master's, thesis; for doctorate, comprehensive exam, thesis/dissertation, 4 quarters of teaching. *Entrance requirements:* For master's, GRE General Test (for playwriting only), minimum GPA of 3.5; audition or interview; for doctorate, GRE General Test, minimum GPA of 3.5, audition and/or interview, two samples of critical writing. Additional exam requirements/recommendations for international students: Required—TOEFL (minimum score 550 paper-based; 80 iBT), IELTS (minimum score 7). *Application deadline:* For fall admission, 1/10 for domestic students. Application fee: $105 ($125 for international students). Electronic applications accepted. *Financial support:* Fellowships, teaching assistantships, and scholarships/grants available. Financial award applicants required to submit FAFSA. *Faculty research:* Theatre of the Americas, European theatre, Asian theatre, gender studies, critical theory. *Unit head:* Judith Dolan, Chair, 858-822-1209, E-mail: jdolan@ucsd.edu. *Application contact:* Marybeth Ward, Graduate Coordinator, 858-534-1046, E-mail: meward@ucsd.edu.
Website: http://theatre.ucsd.edu/

University of California, Santa Barbara, Graduate Division, College of Letters and Sciences, Division of Humanities and Fine Arts, Department of Theater and Dance, Santa Barbara, CA 93106-7060. Offers theater studies (MA, PhD), including European medieval studies (PhD), feminist studies (PhD), theatre studies (PhD); MA/PhD. Terminal master's awarded for partial completion of doctoral program. *Degree requirements:* For master's, comprehensive exam, thesis; for doctorate, one foreign language, comprehensive exam, thesis/dissertation. *Entrance requirements:* For master's and doctorate, GRE. Additional exam requirements/recommendations for international students: Required—TOEFL (minimum score 550 paper-based; 80 iBT), IELTS (minimum score 7). Electronic applications accepted. *Faculty research:* English and American theater and Ancient Greek; Spanish, Latin American and Caribbean performance; Renaissance and Baroque drama and intercultural theory; East Asian performance, gender and nationalism; Korean cultural studies, Russian literature, and

Slavic folklore; history of German theater, Shakespeare, and European opera; postcolonialism, performance-based ethnography, globalism and national identity formation in Africa.

University of California, Santa Cruz, Division of Graduate Studies, Division of the Arts, Department of Theater Arts, Santa Cruz, CA 95064. Offers Certificate. *Entrance requirements:* Additional exam requirements/recommendations for international students: Required—TOEFL (minimum score 550 paper-based; 83 iBT); Recommended—IELTS (minimum score 8). Electronic applications accepted.

University of Central Florida, College of Arts and Humanities, School of Performing Arts, Orlando, FL 32816. Offers music (MA); theatre (MA, MFA), including acting (MFA), theatre for young audiences (MFA). *Accreditation:* NASM; NCATE. *Program availability:* Part-time. *Students:* 32 full-time (14 women), 18 part-time (8 women); includes 11 minority (1 Black or African American, non-Hispanic/Latino; 8 Hispanic/Latino; 2 Two or more races, non-Hispanic/Latino), 4 international. Average age 33. 51 applicants, 59% accepted, 18 enrolled. In 2017, 17 master's awarded. *Degree requirements:* For master's, comprehensive exam, thesis or alternative. *Entrance requirements:* For master's, GRE General Test, letters of recommendation, writing sample. Additional exam requirements/recommendations for international students: Required—TOEFL. *Application deadline:* For fall admission, 7/15 for domestic students; for spring admission, 12/1 for domestic students. Application fee: $30. Electronic applications accepted. *Expenses:* Tuition, state resident: part-time $288.16 per credit hour. Tuition, nonresident: part-time $1073.31 per credit hour. Tuition and fees vary according to program. *Financial support:* In 2017–18, 26 students received support, including 7 fellowships with partial tuition reimbursements available (averaging $7,857 per year), 5 research assistantships with partial tuition reimbursements available (averaging $5,539 per year), 21 teaching assistantships with partial tuition reimbursements available (averaging $7,179 per year); career-related internships or fieldwork, Federal Work-Study, institutionally sponsored loans, health care benefits, tuition waivers (partial), and unspecified assistantships also available. Financial award application deadline: 3/1; financial award applicants required to submit FAFSA. *Unit head:* Dr. Michael Wainstein, Director, 407-823-2519, Fax: 407-823-3378, E-mail: michael.wainstein@ucf.edu. *Application contact:* Associate Director, Graduate Admissions, 407-823-2766, Fax: 407-823-6442, E-mail: gradadmissions@ucf.edu.
Website: http://performingarts.cah.ucf.edu/

University of Central Missouri, The Graduate School, Warrensburg, MO 64093. Offers accountancy (MA); accounting (MBA); applied mathematics (MS); aviation safety (MA); biology (MS); business administration (MBA); career and technical education leadership (MS); college student personnel administration (MS); communication (MA); computer science (MS); counseling (MS); criminal justice (MS); educational leadership (Ed D); educational technology (MS); elementary and early childhood education (MSE); English (MA); environmental studies (MA); finance (MBA); history (MA); human services/educational technology (Ed S); human services/learning resources (Ed S); human services/professional counseling (Ed S); industrial hygiene (MS); industrial management (MS); information systems (MBA); information technology (MS); kinesiology (MS); library science and information services (MS); literacy education (MSE); marketing (MBA); mathematics (MS); music (MA); occupational safety management (MS); psychology (MS); rural family nursing (MS); school administration (MSE); social gerontology (MS); sociology (MA); special education (MSE); speech language pathology (MS); superintendency (Ed S); teaching (MAT); teaching English as a second language (MA); technology (MS); technology management (PhD); theatre (MA). *Program availability:* Part-time, 100% online, blended/hybrid learning. *Faculty:* 337 full-time (145 women), 41 part-time/adjunct (28 women). *Students:* 785 full-time (398 women), 1,633 part-time (1,063 women); includes 231 minority (102 Black or African American, non-Hispanic/Latino; 4 American Indian or Alaska Native, non-Hispanic/Latino; 16 Asian, non-Hispanic/Latino; 52 Hispanic/Latino; 57 Two or more races, non-Hispanic/Latino), 692 international. Average age 30. In 2017, 2,605 master's, 122 other advanced degrees awarded. *Degree requirements:* For master's and Ed S, comprehensive exam (for some programs), thesis (for some programs). *Entrance requirements:* Additional exam requirements/recommendations for international students: Required—TOEFL (minimum score 550 paper-based; 79 iBT). *Application deadline:* For fall admission, 6/1 priority date for domestic and international students; for spring admission, 10/1 priority date for domestic and international students; for summer admission, 4/1 priority date for domestic and international students. Applications are processed on a rolling basis. Application fee: $30 ($75 for international students). Electronic applications accepted. *Expenses:* Tuition, state resident: full-time $8771; part-time $292.35 per credit hour. Tuition, nonresident: full-time $17,541; part-time $584.70 per credit hour. *Required fees:* $372; $24.78 per credit hour. *Financial support:* In 2017–18, 99 students received support. Research assistantships, teaching assistantships, career-related internships or fieldwork, Federal Work-Study, scholarships/grants, and administrative and laboratory assistantships available. Support available to part-time students. Financial award application deadline: 3/1; financial award applicants required to submit FAFSA. *Unit head:* Shellie Hewitt, Director of Graduate and International Student Services, 660-543-4621, Fax: 660-543-4778, E-mail: hewitt@ucmo.edu. *Application contact:* 660-543-4621, E-mail: admit_intl@ucmo.edu.
Website: http://www.ucmo.edu/graduate/

University of Chicago, Division of the Humanities, Master of Arts Program in the Humanities, Chicago, IL 60637. Offers art history (MA); cinema and media studies (MA); classic languages (MA); comparative literature (MA); creative writing (MA); cultural policy studies (MA); digital humanities (MA); East Asian languages and civilizations (MA); English language and literature (MA); gender and sexuality studies (MA); Germanic studies (MA); linguistics (MA); music (MA); near Eastern languages and civilizations (MA); philosophy (MA); poetics (MA); race, politics and culture (MA); Romance languages and literatures (MA); Slavic languages and literatures (MA); South Asian languages and civilizations (MA); theater and performance studies (MA). *Students:* 95 full-time (50 women), 6 part-time (4 women); includes 22 minority (1 Black or African American, non-Hispanic/Latino; 10 Asian, non-Hispanic/Latino; 11 Hispanic/Latino), 19 international. Average age 26. 708 applicants, 75% accepted, 101 enrolled. In 2017, 91 master's awarded. *Degree requirements:* For master's, thesis. *Entrance requirements:* For master's, GRE General Test, 10-15 page writing sample, statement of purpose, 3 letters of recommendation, transcripts for all previous degrees and institutions attended. Additional exam requirements/recommendations for international students: Required—TOEFL (minimum score 104 iBT), IELTS (minimum score 7). *Application deadline:* For fall admission, 1/3 priority date for domestic and international students. Application fee: $90. Electronic applications accepted. *Expenses:* Contact institution. *Financial support:* In 2017–18, fellowships with partial tuition reimbursements (averaging $12,000 per year) were awarded; Federal Work-Study, institutionally sponsored loans, scholarships/grants, and tuition waivers (partial) also available. Financial award application deadline: 4/30. *Unit head:* Thomas Christensen, Director, 773-834-1201, Fax: 773-834-7526, E-mail: ma-humanities@uchicago.edu. *Application contact:* Michael Beetley, Assistant Dean of Students for Admissions, 773-834-1552, E-mail: humanitiesadmissions@uchicago.edu.
Website: http://maph.uchicago.edu/

University of Cincinnati, Graduate School, College-Conservatory of Music, Division of Theatre Arts, Production and Arts Administration, Cincinnati, OH 45221. Offers arts administration (MA); directing (MFA); theater design and production (MFA); voice and opera (MM, DMA); MBA/MA. *Accreditation:* NAST (one or more programs are accredited). *Degree requirements:* For master's, final project. *Entrance requirements:* For master's, GMAT (MA), audition/interview. Additional exam requirements/ recommendations for international students: Required—TOEFL (minimum score 520 paper-based). Electronic applications accepted. *Expenses: Tuition, area resident:* Full-time $14,468. Tuition, state resident: full-time $14,968; part-time $754 per credit hour. Tuition, nonresident: full-time $24,210; part-time $1311 per credit hour. *International tuition:* $26,460 full-time. *Required fees:* $3958; $84 per credit hour. One-time fee: $85 full-time. Tuition and fees vary according to course load, degree level and program.

University of Colorado Boulder, Graduate School, College of Arts and Sciences, Department of Theatre and Dance, Boulder, CO 80309. Offers dance (MFA); theatre (MA, PhD). *Faculty:* 16 full-time (8 women). *Students:* 31 full-time (24 women), 3 part-time (1 woman); includes 7 minority (2 Black or African American, non-Hispanic/Latino; 1 Asian, non-Hispanic/Latino; 3 Hispanic/Latino; 1 Two or more races, non-Hispanic/Latino), 2 international. Average age 31. 52 applicants, 37% accepted, 12 enrolled. In 2017, 4 master's, 6 doctorates awarded. Terminal master's awarded for partial completion of doctoral program. *Degree requirements:* For master's, comprehensive exam, thesis; for doctorate, one foreign language, thesis/dissertation. *Entrance requirements:* For master's, GRE General Test (MA), audition (MFA), minimum undergraduate GPA of 2.75. *Application deadline:* For fall admission, 12/1 for domestic students; for spring admission, 12/1 for domestic students. Application fee: $60 ($80 for international students). Electronic applications accepted. Application fee is waived when completed online. *Financial support:* In 2017–18, 90 students received support, including 27 fellowships (averaging $4,365 per year), 27 teaching assistantships with full and partial tuition reimbursements available (averaging $17,551 per year); institutionally sponsored loans, scholarships/grants, health care benefits, and unspecified assistantships also available. Financial award application deadline: 2/15; financial award applicants required to submit FAFSA. *Faculty research:* Performing arts; dramatic/ theatre arts; dance; drama; arts/humanities/cultural activities. *Application contact:* E-mail: wendy.franz@colorado.edu.
Website: http://www.colorado.edu/theatredance/

University of Connecticut, Graduate School, School of Fine Arts, Department of Dramatic Arts, Storrs, CT 06269. Offers acting (MA, MFA); design (MA, MFA); puppetry (MA, MFA); technical direction (MA, MFA). *Degree requirements:* For master's, comprehensive exam. *Entrance requirements:* Additional exam requirements/ recommendations for international students: Required—TOEFL (minimum score 550 paper-based). Electronic applications accepted.

University of Delaware, College of Arts and Sciences, Professional Theatre Training Program, Newark, DE 19716. Offers acting (MFA); stage management (MFA); technical production (MFA). Students are matriculated into program once every three years. *Entrance requirements:* For master's, audition, interview. Electronic applications accepted. *Faculty research:* Theatre training, acting, technical production, stage management.

University of Florida, Graduate School, College of The Arts, School of Theatre and Dance, Gainesville, FL 32611. Offers theatre (MFA), including acting, costume design, lighting design, scene design. *Accreditation:* NAST. *Program availability:* Online learning. *Degree requirements:* For master's, thesis, creative project. *Entrance requirements:* For master's, GRE General Test, audition/portfolio, bachelor's degree in theatre, interview, minimum GPA 3.0. Additional exam requirements/recommendations for international students: Required—TOEFL (minimum score 550 paper-based; 80 iBT), IELTS (minimum score 6). Electronic applications accepted. *Faculty research:* Aesthetics of lighting design for the theater, production, history of theatre, criticism.

University of Georgia, Franklin College of Arts and Sciences, Department of Theatre and Film Studies, Athens, GA 30602. Offers theatre (MFA, PhD). *Accreditation:* NAST. *Degree requirements:* For master's, comprehensive exam; for doctorate, one foreign language, comprehensive exam, thesis/dissertation. *Entrance requirements:* For master's and doctorate, GRE General Test. Additional exam requirements/ recommendations for international students: Required—TOEFL (minimum score 550 paper-based). Electronic applications accepted. *Faculty research:* Digital media, African-American theatre, Indian theatre, history of animation, Vaudeville and popular culture history.

University of Guelph, Graduate Studies, College of Arts, School of English and Theatre Studies, Program in Drama, Guelph, ON N1G 2W1, Canada. Offers MA. *Program availability:* Part-time. *Degree requirements:* For master's, thesis (for some programs). *Entrance requirements:* For master's, 2 letters of reference, 4 year honours undergraduate degree in English or drama. Additional exam requirements/ recommendations for international students: Required—TOEFL. Electronic applications accepted. *Faculty research:* Canadian theatre, Renaissance, nineteenth- and twentieth-century drama and theatre, Shaw, theatre history, dramatic literature, performance theory.

University of Hawaii at Manoa, Office of Graduate Education, College of Arts and Humanities, Department of Theatre and Dance, Honolulu, HI 96822. Offers dance (MA, MFA); theatre (MA, MFA, PhD). *Program availability:* Part-time. *Degree requirements:* For master's, one foreign language, thesis optional; for doctorate, one foreign language, comprehensive exam, thesis/dissertation. *Entrance requirements:* For master's and doctorate, GRE General Test. Additional exam requirements/recommendations for international students: Required—TOEFL (minimum score 600 paper-based; 100 iBT), IELTS (minimum score 7). *Faculty research:* Asian theatre, feminist theatre and dance, Russian theatre, Australian theatre.

University of Houston, Kathrine G. McGovern College of the Arts, School of Theatre and Dance, Houston, TX 77204. Offers theatre (MA, MFA). *Program availability:* Part-time. *Degree requirements:* For master's, thesis optional. *Entrance requirements:* For master's, GRE General Test, audition/interview (for MFA). Electronic applications accepted.

University of Idaho, College of Graduate Studies, College of Letters, Arts and Social Sciences, Department of Theatre Arts, Moscow, ID 83844. Offers MFA. *Faculty:* 7 full-time. *Students:* 31 full-time (7 women). Average age 39. In 2017, 12 master's awarded. *Entrance requirements:* For master's, minimum GPA of 3.0. Additional exam requirements/recommendations for international students: Required—TOEFL (minimum score 79 iBT). *Application deadline:* For fall admission, 8/1 for domestic students; for spring admission, 12/15 for domestic students. Applications are processed on a rolling basis. Application fee: $60. Electronic applications accepted. *Expenses:* Tuition, state resident: full-time $6722; part-time $430 per credit hour. Tuition, nonresident: full-time $23,046; part-time $1337 per credit hour. *Required fees:* $2142; $63 per credit hour. *Financial support:* Research assistantships and teaching assistantships available. Financial award applicants required to submit FAFSA. *Unit head:* Dr. Ann Hoste, Chair, 208-885-5182, E-mail: theatre@uidaho.edu. *Application contact:* Sean Scoggin, Graduate Recruitment Coordinator, 208-885-4723, E-mail: graduateadmissions@uidaho.edu.
Website: https://www.uidaho.edu/class/theatre

University of Illinois at Urbana–Champaign, Graduate College, College of Fine and Applied Arts, Department of Theatre, Champaign, IL 61820. Offers MA, MFA, PhD.

The University of Iowa, Graduate College, College of Liberal Arts and Sciences, Department of Theatre Arts, Iowa City, IA 52242-1316. Offers MFA. *Accreditation:* NAST. *Degree requirements:* For master's, thesis, exam. *Entrance requirements:* For master's, minimum GPA of 3.0. Additional exam requirements/recommendations for international students: Required—TOEFL (minimum score 550 paper-based; 81 iBT). Electronic applications accepted.

The University of Kansas, Graduate Studies, College of Liberal Arts and Sciences, Department of Theatre, Lawrence, KS 66045. Offers theatre (MA, PhD); theatre design (MFA), including scenography. *Program availability:* Part-time. *Students:* 18 full-time (13 women), 1 (woman) part-time; includes 5 minority (2 Black or African American, non-Hispanic/Latino; 1 American Indian or Alaska Native, non-Hispanic/Latino; 1 Hispanic/ Latino; 1 Two or more races, non-Hispanic/Latino), 1 international. Average age 31. 16 applicants, 50% accepted, 7 enrolled. In 2017, 2 master's, 2 doctorates awarded. *Entrance requirements:* For master's and doctorate, GRE General Test, official transcript, three recent letters of recommendation, current resume, statement of personal goals, writing sample. Additional exam requirements/recommendations for international students: Required—TOEFL. *Application deadline:* For fall admission, 1/1 priority date for domestic and international students. Application fee: $65 ($85 for international students). Electronic applications accepted. *Financial support:* Fellowships, research assistantships, teaching assistantships, Federal Work-Study, scholarships/grants, and unspecified assistantships available. Financial award application deadline: 1/1. *Faculty research:* Theatre history, performance studies, scenography, theatre historiography, cultural studies. *Unit head:* Nicole Hodges Persley, Acting Chair/Director of Graduate Studies, 785-864-2820, E-mail: hodgespersley@ku.edu. *Application contact:* Karen Hummel, Graduate Secretary, 785-864-3511, E-mail: kuthr@ku.edu.
Website: http://www.theatre.ku.edu/

University of Lethbridge, School of Graduate Studies, Lethbridge, AB T1K 3M4, Canada. Offers addictions counseling (M Sc); agricultural biotechnology (M Sc); agricultural studies (M Sc, MA); anthropology (MA); archaeology (M Sc, MA); art (MA, MFA); biochemistry (M Sc); biological sciences (M Sc); biomolecular science (PhD); biosystems and biodiversity (PhD); Canadian studies (MA); chemistry (M Sc); computer science (M Sc); computer science and geographical information science (M Sc); counseling (MC); counseling psychology (M Ed); dramatic arts (MA); earth, space, and physical science (PhD); economics (MA); education (MA, PhD); educational leadership (M Ed); English (MA); environmental science (M Sc); evolution and behavior (PhD); exercise science (M Sc); French (MA); French/German (MA); French/Spanish (MA); general education (M Ed); geography (M Sc, MA); German (MA); health sciences (M Sc); individualized multidisciplinary (M Sc, MA); kinesiology (M Sc, MA); management (M Sc), including accounting, finance, human resource management and labor relations, information systems, international management, marketing, policy and strategy; mathematics (M Sc); music (M Mus, MA); Native American studies (MA); neuroscience (M Sc, PhD); new media (MA, MFA); nursing (M Sc, MN); philosophy (MA); physics (M Sc); political science (MA); psychology (M Sc, MA); religious studies (MA); sociology (MA); theatre and dramatic arts (MFA); theoretical and computational science (PhD); urban and regional studies (MA); women and gender studies (MA). *Program availability:* Part-time, evening/weekend. *Degree requirements:* For master's, thesis (for some programs); for doctorate, comprehensive exam, thesis/dissertation. *Entrance requirements:* For master's, GMAT (for M Sc in management), bachelor's degree in related field, minimum GPA of 3.0 during previous 20 graded semester courses, 2 years' teaching or related experience (M Ed); for doctorate, master's degree, minimum graduate GPA of 3.5. Additional exam requirements/recommendations for international students: Required—TOEFL (minimum score 580 paper-based; 93 iBT). Electronic applications accepted. *Faculty research:* Movement and brain plasticity, gibberellin physiology, photosynthesis, carbon cycling, molecular properties of main-group ring components.

University of Louisville, Graduate School, College of Arts and Sciences, Department of Theatre Arts, Louisville, KY 40292-0001. Offers design (MFA); performance (MFA). *Accreditation:* NAST. *Program availability:* Part-time. *Faculty:* 11 full-time (5 women), 4 part-time/adjunct (3 women). *Students:* 11 full-time (7 women); includes 6 minority (5 Black or African American, non-Hispanic/Latino; 1 Hispanic/Latino), 1 international. Average age 30. 6 applicants, 100% accepted, 4 enrolled. In 2017, 3 master's awarded. *Degree requirements:* For master's, variable foreign language requirement, performance project and monograph. *Entrance requirements:* For master's, audition. Additional exam requirements/recommendations for international students: Required— TOEFL. *Application deadline:* For spring admission, 4/15 for domestic and international students. Application fee: $65. Electronic applications accepted. *Expenses:* Contact institution. *Financial support:* In 2017–18, 3 teaching assistantships (averaging $12,000 per year) were awarded; health care benefits also available. Financial award application deadline: 2/15; financial award applicants required to submit FAFSA. *Faculty research:* Social justice, African American theatre, African diaspora theatre, costume history and design, lighting design, scenic design. *Unit head:* Dr. Kevin Gawley, Chair, 502-852-8683, Fax: 502-852-7235, E-mail: kevin.gawley@louisville.edu. *Application contact:* Latonia Craig, Director of Graduate Recruitment and Diversity Retention, 502-852-5207, Fax: 502-852-6536, E-mail: gradadm@louisville.edu.
Website: http://louisville.edu/theatrearts/

The University of Manchester, School of Arts, Histories and Cultures, Manchester, United Kingdom. Offers anthropology, media and performance (PhD); applied theatre professional (PhD); archaeology (PhD); art history and visual studies (PhD); arts management and cultural policy (PhD); classics and ancient history (PhD); composition (PhD); creative writing (PhD); drama (PhD); economic and social history (PhD); electroacoustic composition (PhD); English and American studies (PhD); history (PhD); humanitarianism and conflict response (PhD); museology (PhD); music (PhD); musicology (PhD); religions and theology (PhD).

University of Maryland, Baltimore County, The Graduate School, College of Arts, Humanities and Social Sciences, Department of Education, Program in Teaching, Baltimore, MD 21250. Offers early childhood education (MAT); elementary education (MAT); teaching (MAT), including art, biology, chemistry, choral music, classical foreign language, dance, earth/space science, English, instrumental music, mathematics, modern foreign language, physical science, physics, social studies, theatre. *Program availability:* Part-time, evening/weekend. *Faculty:* 24 full-time (18 women), 25 part-time/ adjunct (19 women). *Students:* 41 full-time (34 women), 27 part-time (18 women); includes 26 minority (6 Black or African American, non-Hispanic/Latino; 9 Asian, non-Hispanic/Latino; 7 Hispanic/Latino; 1 Native Hawaiian or other Pacific Islander, non-Hispanic/Latino; 3 Two or more races, non-Hispanic/Latino), 2 international. Average age 30. 54 applicants, 83% accepted, 35 enrolled. In 2017, 50 master's awarded. *Degree requirements:* For master's, comprehensive exam (for some programs), thesis (for some programs). *Entrance requirements:* For master's, PRAXIS Core Examination or GRE (minimum score of 1000), minimum GPA of 3.0. Additional exam requirements/

recommendations for international students: Required—TOEFL. *Application deadline:* For fall admission, 6/1 for domestic and international students; for spring admission, 11/1 for domestic and international students. Applications are processed on a rolling basis. Application fee: $50. Electronic applications accepted. *Expenses: Required fees:* $132. *Financial support:* In 2017–18, 8 students received support, including teaching assistantships with tuition reimbursements available (averaging $12,000 per year); career-related internships or fieldwork, Federal Work-Study, scholarships/grants, tuition waivers, and unspecified assistantships also available. Financial award application deadline: 3/15. *Faculty research:* STEM teacher education, culturally sensitive pedagogy, ESOL/bilingual education, early childhood education, language, literacy and culture. *Total annual research expenditures:* $100,000. *Unit head:* Dr. Susan M. Blunck, Graduate Program Director, 410-455-2869, Fax: 410-455-3986, E-mail: blunck@umbc.edu. *Application contact:* Cheryl Johnson, MAT Program Specialist, 410-455-3388, E-mail: blackwel@umbc.edu.
Website: http://www.umbc.edu/education/

University of Maryland, College Park, Academic Affairs, College of Arts and Humanities, School of Theatre, Dance and Performance Studies, Theatre Program, College Park, MD 20742. Offers performance (MFA); theatre and performance studies (MA, PhD); theatre design (MFA). *Degree requirements:* For master's, comprehensive exam, thesis optional. *Entrance requirements:* For master's, GRE General Test, portfolio, writing sample, 3 letters of recommendation. Additional exam requirements/recommendations for international students: Required—TOEFL. Electronic applications accepted.

University of Massachusetts Amherst, Graduate School, College of Humanities and Fine Arts, Department of Theater, Amherst, MA 01003. Offers costume design (MFA); directing (MFA); dramaturgy (MFA); lighting design (MFA); scenic design (MFA). *Program availability:* Part-time. *Degree requirements:* For master's, thesis. *Entrance requirements:* For master's, GRE (for dramaturgy and costume design only), two critical essays or design portfolios, resume of production experience. Additional exam requirements/recommendations for international students: Required—TOEFL (minimum score 550 paper-based; 80 iBT), IELTS (minimum score 6.5). Electronic applications accepted.

University of Memphis, Graduate School, College of Communication and Fine Arts, Department of Theatre and Dance, Memphis, TN 38152. Offers theatre (MFA). *Accreditation:* NAST. *Faculty:* 10 full-time (4 women). *Students:* 16 full-time (6 women), 2 part-time (1 woman); includes 3 minority (1 Black or African American, non-Hispanic/Latino; 1 Hispanic/Latino; 1 Two or more races, non-Hispanic/Latino), 1 international. Average age 39. 22 applicants, 36% accepted, 6 enrolled. In 2017, 7 master's awarded. *Degree requirements:* For master's, comprehensive exam, practicum, internship. *Entrance requirements:* For master's, minimum GPA of 3.0 in major, 2.5 overall, interview/audition. *Application deadline:* For fall admission, 8/1 priority date for domestic students; for spring admission, 12/1 priority date for domestic students. Applications are processed on a rolling basis. Application fee: $35 ($60 for international students). Electronic applications accepted. *Expenses:* Contact institution. *Financial support:* In 2017–18, 12 students received support, including 11 research assistantships with full tuition reimbursements available (averaging $10,546 per year), 7 teaching assistantships with full tuition reimbursements available (averaging $2,500 per year); career-related internships or fieldwork, Federal Work-Study, institutionally sponsored loans, scholarships/grants, and unspecified assistantships also available. Financial award application deadline: 2/1; financial award applicants required to submit FAFSA. *Faculty research:* Theatre design, production management, Lessac vocal training, movement styles, directing. *Unit head:* Prof. Holly C. Lau, Chair, 901-678-2523, Fax: 901-678-4331, E-mail: hclau@memphis.edu. *Application contact:* Sarah Brown, Director of Graduate Studies, 901-678-2523, Fax: 901-678-5118, E-mail: kshupe@memphis.edu.
Website: http://www.memphis.edu/theatre/

University of Minnesota, Twin Cities Campus, Graduate School, College of Liberal Arts, Department of Theatre Arts and Dance, Minneapolis, MN 55455. Offers design technology (MFA); theatre arts (MA, PhD). Terminal master's awarded for partial completion of doctoral program. *Degree requirements:* For master's, thesis (for some programs), final creative project (MFA), foreign language (MA); for doctorate, one foreign language, thesis/dissertation, oral defense, written exams. *Entrance requirements:* For master's, GRE General Test (for MA), minimum GPA of 3.0 or portfolio; for doctorate, GRE General Test, minimum GPA of 3.0, writing sample, 1 foreign language. Additional exam requirements/recommendations for international students: Required—TOEFL (minimum score 550 paper-based; 79 iBT). Electronic applications accepted. *Faculty research:* Theatre historiography, theatre for social change, dance and performance studies, performance politics of ethnicity, migration, globalization, European avant-garde; theatre design and technology: costume, scenography, lighting, sound, multimedia.

University of Missouri, Office of Research and Graduate Studies, College of Arts and Science, Department of Theatre, Columbia, MO 65211. Offers MA, PhD. *Program availability:* Part-time. *Degree requirements:* For doctorate, thesis/dissertation. *Entrance requirements:* For master's, GRE General Test, minimum GPA of 3.0 overall and in last 60 hours; for doctorate, GRE General Test, minimum GPA of 3.0 overall and in last 60 hours, 3.5 in master's program. Additional exam requirements/recommendations for international students: Required—TOEFL (minimum score 650 paper-based; 114 iBT). Electronic applications accepted.

University of Missouri–Kansas City, College of Arts and Sciences, Theatre Department, Kansas City, MO 64110-2499. Offers MA, MFA. *Accreditation:* NAST. *Degree requirements:* For master's, thesis. *Entrance requirements:* For master's, audition or portfolio, interview. Additional exam requirements/recommendations for international students: Required—TOEFL (minimum score 550 paper-based; 80 iBT). Electronic applications accepted. *Faculty research:* Contemporary Russian theatre, Shakespeare in performance, subtle energies in actor training, multi-channel sound, renovation of Zuni Pueblo historic Spanish mission.

University of Montana, Graduate School, College of Visual and Performing Arts, School of Theatre and Dance, Missoula, MT 59812. Offers design/technology (MFA); theatre (MA). *Accreditation:* NAST (one or more programs are accredited). *Degree requirements:* For master's, thesis or alternative. *Entrance requirements:* For master's, GRE General Test, audition, portfolio, production notebook.

University of Nebraska–Lincoln, Graduate College, College of Fine and Performing Arts, Johnny Carson School of Theatre and Film, Lincoln, NE 68588. Offers acting (MFA); costume (MFA); directing (MFA); stage design (MFA). *Accreditation:* NAST. *Degree requirements:* For master's, thesis. *Entrance requirements:* For master's, audition, portfolio. Additional exam requirements/recommendations for international students: Required—TOEFL (minimum score 500 paper-based). Electronic applications accepted. *Faculty research:* American theatre history, British theatre history, modern American drama, contemporary performance, Elizabethan theatre history.

University of Nevada, Las Vegas, Graduate College, College of Fine Arts, Department of Theatre, Las Vegas, NV 89154-5036. Offers MA, MFA. *Program availability:* Part-time. *Faculty:* 11 full-time (5 women), 5 part-time/adjunct (2 women). *Students:* 29 full-

time (16 women), 3 part-time (all women); includes 10 minority (4 Black or African American, non-Hispanic/Latino; 4 Hispanic/Latino; 2 Two or more races, non-Hispanic/Latino), 1 international. Average age 31. 18 applicants, 39% accepted, 7 enrolled. In 2017, 4 master's awarded. *Degree requirements:* For master's, comprehensive exam (for some programs), thesis (for some programs), creative project, oral exam. *Entrance requirements:* For master's, sample research paper or research statement; statement of purpose; 2 letters of recommendation. Additional exam requirements/recommendations for international students: Required—TOEFL (minimum score 550 paper-based; 80 iBT), IELTS (minimum score 7). *Application deadline:* For fall admission, 8/1 for domestic students, 5/1 for international students. Application fee: $60 ($95 for international students). Electronic applications accepted. *Expenses:* $275 per credit, $850 per course, $7,969 per year resident, $22,157 per year non-resident, $7,094 non-resident fee (7 credits or more), $1,307 annual health insurance fee. *Financial support:* In 2017–18, 29 students received support, including 14 research assistantships with full tuition reimbursements available (averaging $15,000 per year), 15 teaching assistantships with full tuition reimbursements available (averaging $14,667 per year); institutionally sponsored loans, scholarships/grants, health care benefits, and unspecified assistantships also available. Financial award application deadline: 3/15; financial award applicants required to submit FAFSA. *Faculty research:* Designing scenery, costumes or lighting, directing or stage managing, serving as technical director/consultant, or acting for a production for a regional theatre. *Unit head:* Norma Saldivar, Chair/Professor, 702-895-3666, E-mail: norma.saldivar@unlv.edu. *Application contact:* Nate Bynum, Graduate Coordinator, 702-895-4248, Fax: 702-895-0833, E-mail: joe.bynum@unlv.edu.
Website: http://theatre.unlv.edu/

University of New Mexico, Graduate Studies, College of Fine Arts, Department of Theatre and Dance, Albuquerque, NM 87131-2039. Offers dance (MFA); dance history (MA); dramatic writing (MFA); theatre education and outreach (MA). *Accreditation:* NASD; NAST. *Students:* Average age 36. 15 applicants, 53% accepted, 7 enrolled. In 2017, 4 master's awarded. *Degree requirements:* For master's, comprehensive exam (for some programs), thesis (for some programs). *Entrance requirements:* For master's, minimum GPA of 3.0; undergraduate major in theatre, dance or closely-related field; 3 letters of recommendation; letter of intent; BA, BFA, BS, or MA in dance movement science or related field, or equivalent experience (for MFA in dance). *Application deadline:* For fall admission, 4/15 for domestic students; for spring admission, 11/10 for domestic students. Application fee: $50. Electronic applications accepted. *Financial support:* Fellowships, research assistantships with partial tuition reimbursements, teaching assistantships with partial tuition reimbursements, Federal Work-Study, health care benefits, tuition waivers (partial), and unspecified assistantships available. Financial award application deadline: 3/1; financial award applicants required to submit FAFSA. *Faculty research:* Theater education and outreach, choreography, dramatic writing, dance history/criticism. *Unit head:* Bill Liotta, Chair, 505-277-4332, Fax: 505-277-8921, E-mail: wliotta@unm.edu. *Application contact:* Christina Squire, Administrator II, 505-277-7362, Fax: 505-277-8921, E-mail: csquire@unm.edu.
Website: http://theatredance.unm.edu/

University of New Orleans, Graduate School, College of Liberal Arts, Department of Film and Theatre, New Orleans, LA 70148. Offers design (MFA); film production (MFA); theatre performance (MFA), including acting, directing. *Accreditation:* NAST. *Degree requirements:* For master's, comprehensive exam, thesis. *Entrance requirements:* Additional exam requirements/recommendations for international students: Required—TOEFL (minimum score 550 paper-based; 79 iBT), IELTS (minimum score 6.5). Electronic applications accepted. *Faculty research:* Mass communication theory, nineteenth and twentieth century theater history, film criticism and history.

The University of North Carolina at Chapel Hill, Graduate School, College of Arts and Sciences, Department of Dramatic Art, Chapel Hill, NC 27599. Offers acting (MFA); costume production (MFA); technical production (MFA). *Entrance requirements:* For master's, audition or portfolio.

The University of North Carolina at Charlotte, Cato College of Education, Interdisciplinary Education Programs, Charlotte, NC 28223-0001. Offers art education (Graduate Certificate); child and family development: early childhood education (MAT); curriculum and instruction (PhD); elementary education (MAT); foreign language education (MAT); middle grades education (MAT); secondary education (MAT); special education (MAT); teaching (Graduate Certificate); teaching English as a second language (MAT); theatre education (Graduate Certificate). *Program availability:* Part-time, 100% online, blended/hybrid learning. *Students:* 86 full-time (63 women), 533 part-time (423 women); includes 229 minority (169 Black or African American, non-Hispanic/Latino; 1 American Indian or Alaska Native, non-Hispanic/Latino; 7 Asian, non-Hispanic/Latino; 39 Hispanic/Latino; 13 Two or more races, non-Hispanic/Latino), 13 international. Average age 32. 382 applicants, 91% accepted, 253 enrolled. In 2017, 182 master's, 10 doctorates, 172 other advanced degrees awarded. *Degree requirements:* For master's, thesis or alternative, research project/portfolio. *Entrance requirements:* For master's, GRE or MAT, bachelor's degree, or its U.S. equivalent, from regionally-accredited college or university; minimum overall GPA of 3.0 on all previous work beyond high school; statement of purpose (essay); at least three recommendation forms; for doctorate, GRE or MAT, bachelor's degree (or its U.S. equivalent) from regionally-accredited college or university; minimum overall GPA of 3.5 in master's degree program; for Graduate Certificate, bachelor's degree from regionally-accredited university; minimum GPA of 2.75 on all post-secondary work attempted; transcripts; personal statement outlining why the applicant seeks admission to the program. Additional exam requirements/recommendations for international students: Required—TOEFL (minimum score 523 paper-based, 70 iBT) or IELTS (6.5). *Application deadline:* For fall admission, 3/1 priority date for domestic and international students; for spring admission, 10/1 priority date for domestic and international students; for summer admission, 4/1 priority date for domestic and international students. Applications are processed on a rolling basis. Application fee: $75. Electronic applications accepted. *Expenses:* Tuition, state resident: full-time $4337. Tuition, nonresident: full-time $17,771. *Required fees:* $3211. Tuition and fees vary according to course load and program. *Financial support:* Career-related internships or fieldwork, institutionally sponsored loans, scholarships/grants, and unspecified assistantships available. Support available to part-time students. Financial award application deadline: 3/1; financial award applicants required to submit FAFSA. *Unit head:* Dr. Ellen McIntyre, Dean, 704-687-8722, E-mail: ellen.mcintyre@uncc.edu. *Application contact:* Kathy B. Giddings, Director of Graduate Admissions, 704-687-5503, Fax: 704-687-1668, E-mail: gradadm@uncc.edu.
Website: http://education.uncc.edu/academic-programs

The University of North Carolina at Greensboro, Graduate School, School of Music, Theatre and Dance, Department of Theatre, Greensboro, NC 27412-5001. Offers acting (MFA); design (MFA); directing (MFA); theater education (M Ed); theater for youth (MFA). *Accreditation:* NAST. *Entrance requirements:* For master's, portfolio, interviews. Electronic applications accepted.

University of North Carolina School of the Arts, School of Design and Production, Winston-Salem, NC 27127-2738. Offers costume design (MFA); costume technology (MFA); scene design (MFA); scenic art (MFA); sound design (MFA); stage automation (MFA); stage properties (MFA); technical direction (MFA); wig and makeup design

(MFA). *Degree requirements:* For master's, thesis (for some programs), project. *Entrance requirements:* For master's, interview, portfolio. Additional exam requirements/recommendations for international students: Required—TOEFL. Electronic applications accepted.

University of Oregon, Graduate School, College of Arts and Sciences, Department of Theater Arts, Eugene, OR 97403. Offers MA, MFA, MS, PhD. *Degree requirements:* For master's, variable foreign language requirement, thesis or alternative; for doctorate, variable foreign language requirement, thesis/dissertation. *Entrance requirements:* For master's and doctorate, minimum GPA of 3.0. Additional exam requirements/recommendations for international students: Required—TOEFL.

University of Ottawa, Faculty of Graduate and Postdoctoral Studies, Faculty of Arts, Department of Theatre, Ottawa, ON K1N 6N5, Canada. Offers directing for theatre (MA). Electronic applications accepted.

University of Pittsburgh, Kenneth P. Dietrich School of Arts and Sciences, Department of Theatre Arts, Pittsburgh, PA 15260. Offers MA, MFA, PhD. *Accreditation:* NAST. *Faculty:* 6 full-time (5 women). *Students:* 15 full-time (11 women); includes 5 minority (2 Black or African American, non-Hispanic/Latino; 1 Asian, non-Hispanic/Latino; 2 Hispanic/Latino). Average age 30. 37 applicants, 8% accepted, 2 enrolled. In 2017, 2 master's, 1 doctorate awarded. Terminal master's awarded for partial completion of doctoral program. *Degree requirements:* For master's, comprehensive exam (for some programs), thesis (for some programs); for doctorate, one foreign language, comprehensive exam, thesis/dissertation, diagnostic exam. *Entrance requirements:* For master's and doctorate, GRE General Test, samples of written work. Additional exam requirements/recommendations for international students: Required—TOEFL (minimum score 500 paper-based; 90 iBT). *Application deadline:* For fall admission, 1/15 priority date for domestic and international students. Application fee: $50. Electronic applications accepted. *Financial support:* In 2017–18, 13 students received support, including 10 fellowships with full tuition reimbursements available (averaging $18,620 per year), 2 teaching assistantships with full tuition reimbursements available (averaging $17,910 per year). Financial award application deadline: 1/15; financial award applicants required to submit FAFSA. *Faculty research:* American theatre and popular entertainment, performance pedagogy, theatre historiography, Latin American theatre and performance, performance studies. *Unit head:* Prof. Annmarie Duggan, Chairman, 412-624-7284, Fax: 412-624-6338, E-mail: duggan@pitt.edu. *Application contact:* Margaret Bupp, Graduate Student Services Administrator, 412-624-6568, Fax: 412-624-6338, E-mail: maggiebupp@pitt.edu.
Website: http://www.play.pitt.edu/

University of Portland, Department of Performing and Fine Arts, Portland, OR 97203-5798. Offers directing (MFA). *Program availability:* Part-time, evening/weekend. *Degree requirements:* For master's, thesis optional. *Entrance requirements:* For master's, GRE General Test, minimum GPA of 3.0, resume, 3 letters of recommendation, statement of goals, official transcripts. Additional exam requirements/recommendations for international students: Required—TOEFL (minimum score 600 paper-based; 100 iBT), IELTS (minimum score 7.5).

University of San Diego, College of Arts and Sciences, The Old Globe and University of San Diego Shiley Graduate Theatre Program, San Diego, CA 92110-2492. Offers MFA. *Faculty:* 3 full-time (1 woman), 1 part-time/adjunct (0 women). *Students:* 14 full-time (6 women); includes 6 minority (2 Black or African American, non-Hispanic/Latino; 1 Asian, non-Hispanic/Latino; 3 Hispanic/Latino), 1 international. Average age 28. 353 applicants, 2% accepted, 7 enrolled. In 2017, 6 master's awarded. *Entrance requirements:* For master's, audition. Additional exam requirements/recommendations for international students: Required—TOEFL (minimum score 580 paper-based; 83 iBT), TWE. *Application deadline:* For fall admission, 1/5 for domestic and international students. Application fee: $55. *Financial support:* In 2017–18, 14 students received support, including 14 fellowships with full tuition reimbursements available; career-related internships or fieldwork, Federal Work-Study, and institutionally sponsored loans also available. Financial award applicants required to submit FAFSA. *Faculty research:* Voice and dialect coaching, directing, stage combat, movement choreography, acting. *Unit head:* Ray Chambers, Interim Graduate Program Director, 619-260-7934, Fax: 619-260-8810, E-mail: theatrearts@sandiego.edu. *Application contact:* Monica Mahon, Associate Director of Graduate Admissions, 619-260-4524, Fax: 619-260-4158, E-mail: grads@sandiego.edu.
Website: http://www.graduateacting.com/

University of Saskatchewan, College of Graduate Studies and Research, College of Arts and Science, Department of Drama, Saskatoon, SK S7N 5A2, Canada. Offers MA. *Degree requirements:* For master's, thesis. *Entrance requirements:* Additional exam requirements/recommendations for international students: Required—TOEFL (minimum score 80 iBT); Recommended—IELTS (minimum score 6.5). Electronic applications accepted.

University of South Carolina, The Graduate School, College of Arts and Sciences, Department of Theatre and Dance, Columbia, SC 29208. Offers theatre (MA, MAT, MFA). MA and MAT offered in cooperation with the College of Education. *Accreditation:* NAST (one or more programs are accredited). *Degree requirements:* For master's, comprehensive exam, thesis. *Entrance requirements:* For master's, GRE General Test, GRE or MAT (MAT), audition, interview (for MFA). Additional exam requirements/recommendations for international students: Required—TOEFL. Electronic applications accepted. *Faculty research:* Computer assisted design, rhetoric of science and technology, Alexander Technique, script analysis, Lessac Method.

University of South Carolina, The Graduate School, College of Education, Department of Instruction and Teacher Education, Program in Secondary Education, Columbia, SC 29208. Offers art education (IMA, MAT); business education (IMA, MAT); English (MAT); foreign language (MAT); health education (MAT); mathematics (MAT); science (IMA, MAT); secondary (Ed D); secondary education (MT, PhD); social studies (MAT); theatre and speech (MAT). IMA and MT offered jointly with the subject areas. *Accreditation:* NCATE. *Degree requirements:* For master's, comprehensive exam, thesis (for some programs), foreign language (MA); for doctorate, one foreign language, comprehensive exam, thesis/dissertation. *Entrance requirements:* For master's, GRE General Test or MAT, teaching certificate (IMA, M Ed), interview; for doctorate, GRE General Test or MAT, interview. *Faculty research:* Middle school programs, professional development, school collaboration.

University of South Dakota, Graduate School, College of Fine Arts, Department of Theatre, Vermillion, SD 57069. Offers design/technology (MFA); directing (MFA); theatre (MA). *Accreditation:* NAST. *Degree requirements:* For master's, thesis or alternative. *Entrance requirements:* For master's, GRE (for MA), minimum GPA of 2.7, portfolio. Additional exam requirements/recommendations for international students: Required—TOEFL (minimum score 550 paper-based; 79 iBT). *Application deadline:* Applications are processed on a rolling basis. Application fee: $35. Electronic applications accepted. *Financial support:* Research assistantships with partial tuition reimbursements, teaching assistantships with partial tuition reimbursements, and unspecified assistantships available. Financial award applicants required to submit FAFSA. *Application contact:* Graduate School, 605-658-6140, Fax: 605-677-6118, E-mail: grad@usd.edu.
Website: http://www.usd.edu/fine-arts/theatre

University of Southern California, Graduate School, School of Dramatic Arts, Los Angeles, CA 90089. Offers acting (MFA); dramatic writing (MFA). *Degree requirements:* For master's, comprehensive exam. *Entrance requirements:* For master's, GRE. Additional exam requirements/recommendations for international students: Required—TOEFL. Electronic applications accepted.

University of Southern Mississippi, College of Arts and Letters, Department of Theatre, Hattiesburg, MS 39406-0001. Offers costume design (MFA); directing (MFA); lighting and sound design (MFA); performance (MFA); scenic design (MFA). *Accreditation:* NAST. *Program availability:* Part-time. *Students:* 9 full-time (6 women). 13 applicants, 69% accepted, 9 enrolled. In 2017, 2 master's awarded. *Degree requirements:* For master's, comprehensive exam, thesis or alternative, creative project. *Entrance requirements:* For master's, GRE General Test, minimum GPA of 3.0. Additional exam requirements/recommendations for international students: Required—TOEFL, IELTS. *Application deadline:* For fall admission, 3/1 priority date for domestic students, 3/1 for international students; for spring admission, 1/10 priority date for domestic and international students. Applications are processed on a rolling basis. Application fee: $60. Electronic applications accepted. *Expenses:* Tuition, state resident: full-time $3830. *Financial support:* Research assistantships, teaching assistantships with full tuition reimbursements, career-related internships or fieldwork, Federal Work-Study, institutionally sponsored loans, health care benefits, and unspecified assistantships available. Support available to part-time students. Financial award application deadline: 3/15; financial award applicants required to submit FAFSA. *Faculty research:* Technical design, acting. *Unit head:* Louis Rackoff, Chair, 601-266-6907, Fax: 601-266-6423.
Website: http://www.usm.edu/theatre

The University of Tennessee, Graduate School, College of Arts and Sciences, Department of Theatre, Knoxville, TN 37996. Offers costume design (MFA); lighting design (MFA); performance (MFA); scene design (MFA); theatre technology (MFA). *Accreditation:* NAST. *Degree requirements:* For master's, thesis or alternative. *Entrance requirements:* For master's, audition, minimum GPA of 2.7. Additional exam requirements/recommendations for international students: Required—TOEFL. Electronic applications accepted.

The University of Texas at Austin, Graduate School, College of Fine Arts, Department of Theatre and Dance, Austin, TX 78712-1111. Offers acting (MFA); dance (MFA); directing (MFA); drama and theatre for youth (MFA); performance as public practice (MA, MFA, PhD); playwriting (MFA); theatre technology (MFA); theatrical design (MFA). *Degree requirements:* For master's, thesis; for doctorate, variable foreign language requirement, thesis/dissertation. *Entrance requirements:* For master's and doctorate, GRE General Test.

The University of Texas at Austin, Graduate School, Michener Center for Writers, Austin, TX 78712-1111. Offers fiction (MFA); playwriting (MFA); poetry (MFA); screenwriting (MFA). Electronic applications accepted.

University of the Cumberlands, Graduate Programs in Education, Williamsburg, KY 40769-1372. Offers all grades (P-12) (M Ed); business and marketing (MA Ed, MAT); counselor education and supervision (Ed D); director of pupil personnel (Certificate); director of special education (Certificate); educational administration and supervision (Ed S); educational leadership (Ed D); elementary education (MA Ed, MAT); instructional leadership - principalship (MA Ed); instructional leadership - school principal (Certificate); middle school education (MA Ed, MAT); reading and writing (MA Ed); school counseling (MA Ed); school superintendent (Certificate); secondary education (MA Ed, MAT); special education (MAT); supervisor of instruction (Certificate); teacher leader (MA Ed). *Program availability:* Part-time, evening/weekend, online learning. *Degree requirements:* For master's, comprehensive exam. Electronic applications accepted.

University of Toronto, School of Graduate Studies, Faculty of Arts and Science, Centre for Drama, Theatre and Performance Studies, Toronto, ON M5S 1A1, Canada. Offers MA, PhD. *Program availability:* Part-time. *Entrance requirements:* For master's, minimum B+ average, significant coursework in drama and related disciplines, resume, 2 letters of recommendation. Additional exam requirements/recommendations for international students: Required—TOEFL (minimum score 580 paper-based; 93 iBT), TWE (minimum score 5). Electronic applications accepted.

University of Victoria, Faculty of Graduate Studies, Faculty of Fine Arts, Department of Theatre, Victoria, BC V8W 2Y2, Canada. Offers design (MFA); directing (MFA); theatre history (MA). *Degree requirements:* For master's, thesis. *Entrance requirements:* Additional exam requirements/recommendations for international students: Required—TOEFL (minimum score 575 paper-based), IELTS (minimum score 7). Electronic applications accepted.

University of Virginia, College and Graduate School of Arts and Sciences, Department of Drama, Charlottesville, VA 22903. Offers MFA. *Faculty:* 18 full-time (11 women), 2 part-time/adjunct (both women). *Students:* 19 full-time (10 women); includes 3 minority (1 Black or African American, non-Hispanic/Latino; 1 Hispanic/Latino; 1 Two or more races, non-Hispanic/Latino), 1 international. Average age 30. 7 applicants, 86% accepted, 6 enrolled. In 2017, 5 master's awarded. *Degree requirements:* For master's, thesis project. *Entrance requirements:* For master's, GRE General Test, resume; 3 letters of recommendation. Additional exam requirements/recommendations for international students: Required—TOEFL (minimum score 600 paper-based; 90 iBT), IELTS (minimum score 7). *Application deadline:* For fall admission, 2/20 for domestic and international students. Applications are processed on a rolling basis. Application fee: $60. Electronic applications accepted. *Financial support:* Fellowships and teaching assistantships available. Financial award applicants required to submit FAFSA. *Faculty research:* Acting, scenic design, lighting design, technical direction, costume design/technology. *Unit head:* Colleen Kelly, Chair, 434-924-3326, Fax: 434-924-1447, E-mail: drama@virginia.edu.
Website: http://drama.virginia.edu//

University of Washington, Graduate School, College of Arts and Sciences, School of Drama, Seattle, WA 98195. Offers acting (MFA); costume design (MFA); directing (MFA); dramatic theory (PhD); lighting design (MFA); scenic design (MFA); theatre and performance history (PhD). *Degree requirements:* For master's, thesis; for doctorate, one foreign language, comprehensive exam, thesis/dissertation. *Entrance requirements:* For master's, interview, minimum GPA of 3.0, portfolio; for doctorate, GRE General Test, minimum GPA of 3.0, writing sample. Additional exam requirements/recommendations for international students: Required—TOEFL. *Faculty research:* Semiotics, Suzuki actor training, modern American theatre, ethnic American theatre.

University of Wisconsin–Madison, Graduate School, College of Letters and Science, Department of Theatre and Drama, Madison, WI 53706-1380. Offers MA, MFA, PhD. *Accreditation:* NAST. *Program availability:* Part-time. *Degree requirements:* For master's, thesis; for doctorate, thesis/dissertation. *Entrance requirements:* For master's and doctorate, GRE. Electronic applications accepted. *Faculty research:* Theories and histories of dance, theatre and performance studies; Russian theatre and dance; postmodern performance; Holocaust drama; race and representation.

University of Wisconsin–Superior, Graduate Division, Department of Communicating Arts, Superior, WI 54880-4500. Offers mass communication (MA); speech communication (MA); theater (MA). *Program availability:* Part-time. *Degree requirements:* For master's, comprehensive exam, thesis or alternative, position paper or project. *Entrance requirements:* For master's, minimum GPA of 2.75. Electronic applications accepted. *Faculty research:* Multimedia technology, ethics in journalism, diversity, electronic portfolio assessment.

Utah State University, School of Graduate Studies, Caine College of the Arts, Department of Theatre Arts, Logan, UT 84322. Offers design (MFA). *Degree requirements:* For master's, variable foreign language requirement, thesis (for some programs), summer internship. *Entrance requirements:* For master's, GRE General Test or MAT, portfolio, minimum GPA of 3.0, interview, BS or 20 semester credits. Additional exam requirements/recommendations for international students: Required—TOEFL. *Faculty research:* Seventeenth and eighteenth century Spanish theatre, Greek and Roman theatre, interpretation of literature for performance.

Villanova University, Graduate School of Liberal Arts and Sciences, Department of Theatre, Villanova, PA 19085-1699. Offers MA. *Program availability:* Part-time, evening/weekend. *Faculty:* 6. *Students:* 30 full-time (23 women), 6 part-time (1 woman); includes 8 minority (6 Black or African American, non-Hispanic/Latino; 1 Hispanic/Latino; 1 Two or more races, non-Hispanic/Latino), 1 international. Average age 32. 15 applicants, 100% accepted, 10 enrolled. In 2017, 15 master's awarded. *Degree requirements:* For master's, comprehensive exam. *Entrance requirements:* For master's, GRE, minimum GPA of 3.0, resume, statement of goals, headshot. Additional exam requirements/recommendations for international students: Required—TOEFL. *Application deadline:* For fall admission, 3/1 for domestic students, 5/1 priority date for international students; for spring admission, 11/15 for domestic students, 10/15 priority date for international students; for summer admission, 5/1 for domestic students. Applications are processed on a rolling basis. Application fee: $50. Electronic applications accepted. *Financial support:* Research assistantships, teaching assistantships, scholarships/grants, and unspecified assistantships available. Financial award applicants required to submit FAFSA. *Unit head:* Valerie Joyce, Program Director, 610-519-7174. *Application contact:* Dean, Graduate School of Liberal Arts and Sciences.
Website: http://www1.villanova.edu/villanova/artsci/theatre.html

Virginia Commonwealth University, Graduate School, School of the Arts, Department of Theatre, Richmond, VA 23284-9005. Offers costume design (MFA); pedagogy/literature (MFA); pedagogy/performance (MFA); scene design/technical theatre (MFA). *Accreditation:* NAST. *Degree requirements:* For master's, thesis (for some programs). *Entrance requirements:* For master's, audition, portfolio. Additional exam requirements/recommendations for international students: Required—TOEFL (minimum score 600 paper-based; 100 iBT). Electronic applications accepted. *Faculty research:* Dramatic literature, speech.

Washington University in St. Louis, The Graduate School, Department of Performing Arts, St. Louis, MO 63130-4899. Offers dance (MFA); theater and performance studies (MA). *Degree requirements:* For master's, thesis optional. *Entrance requirements:* For master's, GRE General Test, sample of written work. Additional exam requirements/recommendations for international students: Required—TOEFL. Electronic applications accepted. *Faculty research:* Theater and performance studies; dance.

Wayne State University, College of Fine, Performing and Communication Arts, Maggie Allesee Department of Theatre and Dance, Detroit, MI 48202. Offers theatre (MFA), including acting, stage costume design, stage lighting design, stage management, theatre management, theatre stage design; theatre and dance (MA). Application deadline for MA is June 1. *Accreditation:* NAST. *Program availability:* 100% online, blended/hybrid learning. *Faculty:* 3. *Students:* 38 full-time (25 women), 11 part-time (all women); includes 12 minority (11 Black or African American, non-Hispanic/Latino; 1 Two or more races, non-Hispanic/Latino), 1 international. Average age 29. 182 applicants, 14% accepted, 25 enrolled. In 2017, 13 master's awarded. *Degree requirements:* For master's, comprehensive exam, thesis (for some programs), final project (for MFA). *Entrance requirements:* For master's, minimum GPA of 3.0; auditions and head shots (for MFA in acting only); interviews, resume, letters of recommendation, samples of work (except for MFA in acting and MA). Additional exam requirements/recommendations for international students: Required—TOEFL (minimum score 550 paper-based; 79 iBT), TWE (minimum score 5.5), Michigan English Language Assessment Battery (minimum score 85); Recommended—IELTS (minimum score 6.5). *Application deadline:* For fall admission, 1/15 for domestic and international students. Applications are processed on a rolling basis. Application fee: $50. Electronic applications accepted. *Expenses:* Contact institution. *Financial support:* In 2017–18, 42 students received support, including 36 research assistantships with tuition reimbursements available (averaging $18,534 per year); fellowships with tuition reimbursements available, teaching assistantships with tuition reimbursements available, scholarships/grants, and unspecified assistantships also available. Financial award applicants required to submit FAFSA. *Unit head:* Dr. John Wolf, Chair, 313-577-4273, E-mail: fe3828@wayne.edu. *Application contact:* E-mail: theatreanddance@wayne.edu.
Website: http://theatreanddance.wayne.edu/

Western Illinois University, School of Graduate Studies, College of Fine Arts and Communication, Department of Theatre and Dance, Macomb, IL 61455-1390. Offers theatre (MFA), including acting, design, directing. *Accreditation:* NAST. *Program availability:* Part-time. *Students:* 14 full-time (5 women), 1 (woman) part-time; includes 3 minority (2 Black or African American, non-Hispanic/Latino; 1 Two or more races, non-Hispanic/Latino). Average age 30. 30 applicants, 67% accepted, 12 enrolled. In 2017, 10 master's awarded. *Degree requirements:* For master's, comprehensive exam, thesis or alternative, creative project, written exam. *Entrance requirements:* For master's, audition or interview. Additional exam requirements/recommendations for international students: Required—TOEFL (minimum score 550 paper-based; 80 iBT). *Application deadline:* Applications are processed on a rolling basis. Application fee: $30. Electronic applications accepted. *Financial support:* In 2017–18, teaching assistantships with full tuition reimbursements (averaging $8,688 per year) were awarded; unspecified assistantships also available. Financial award applicants required to submit FAFSA. *Unit head:* Dr. Sharon Evans, Chairperson, 309-298-1618. *Application contact:* Dr. Nancy Parsons, Associate Provost and Director of Graduate Studies, 309-298-1806, Fax: 309-298-2345, E-mail: grad-office@wiu.edu.
Website: http://wiu.edu/theatre/

West Virginia University, College of Creative Arts, Morgantown, WV 26506. Offers acting (MFA); art education (MA); art history (MA); ceramics (MFA); collaborative piano (MM, DMA); composition (MM, DMA); conducting (MM, DMA); costume design and technology (MFA); graphic design (MFA); jazz pedagogy (MM); lighting design and technology (MFA); music (PhD); music education (MM, PhD); music industry (MA); music theory (MM); musicology (MA); painting and printmaking (MFA); performance (MM, DMA); photography (MFA); piano pedagogy (MM); scenic design and technology (MFA); sculpture (MFA); studio art (MA); technical direction (MFA); vocal pedagogy and performance (DMA). *Program availability:* Part-time. *Students:* 114 full-time (64 women), 39 part-time (21 women); includes 19 minority (11 Black or African American, non-Hispanic/Latino; 1 Asian, non-Hispanic/Latino; 6 Hispanic/Latino; 1 Two or more races, non-Hispanic/Latino), 33 international. *Degree requirements:* For master's, thesis, recitals; for doctorate, comprehensive exam, thesis/dissertation, recitals (DMA). *Entrance requirements:* For doctorate, minimum GPA of 3.0, audition. Additional exam requirements/recommendations for international students: Required—TOEFL. *Application deadline:* For fall admission, 3/1 priority date for domestic students, 2/15 for international students; for spring admission, 11/1 for domestic students, 9/15 for international students. Applications are processed on a rolling basis. Application fee: $60. Electronic applications accepted. *Expenses:* Tuition, state resident: full-time $9450. Tuition, nonresident: full-time $24,390. *Financial support:* Research assistantships, teaching assistantships, career-related internships or fieldwork, Federal Work-Study, institutionally sponsored loans, scholarships/grants, health care benefits, tuition waivers (partial), and administrative assistantships available. Financial award applicants required to submit FAFSA. *Faculty research:* Professional directing, consulting, acting design, music education, jazz history. *Unit head:* Dr. Paul Kreider, Dean, 304-293-4841 Ext. 3109, Fax: 304-293-6896, E-mail: paul.kreider@mail.wvu.edu. *Application contact:* Records Officer, 304-293-4841, Fax: 304-293-2533, E-mail: rachel.hanks@mail.wvu.edu.
Website: http://www.ccarts.wvu.edu

Yale University, School of Drama, New Haven, CT 06520. Offers acting (MFA, Certificate); design (MFA, Certificate), including costume design, lighting design, projection design, set design; directing (MFA, Certificate); dramaturgy and dramatic criticism (MFA, DFA); playwriting (MFA, Certificate); sound design (MFA, Certificate); stage management (MFA, Certificate); technical design and production (MFA, Certificate); theater management (MFA); MFA/MBA. *Degree requirements:* For master's, comprehensive exam (for some programs), thesis (for some programs); for doctorate, thesis/dissertation, oral and written comprehensive exams. *Entrance requirements:* For master's, GRE (verbal, quantitative, and analytical), in-person audition (for acting); portfolio review (for design). Additional exam requirements/recommendations for international students: Required—TOEFL. Electronic applications accepted.

York University, Faculty of Graduate Studies, Faculty of Fine Arts, Program in Theatre, Toronto, ON M3J 1P3, Canada. Offers MFA. *Degree requirements:* For master's, thesis. Electronic applications accepted.

York University, Faculty of Graduate Studies, Faculty of Fine Arts, Program in Theatre and Performance Studies, Toronto, ON M3J 1P3, Canada. Offers MA, PhD.

Therapies—Dance, Drama, and Music

Antioch University New England, Graduate School, Department of Applied Psychology, Program in Dance/Movement Therapy and Counseling, Keene, NH 03431-3552. Offers M Ed, MA, PMC. *Degree requirements:* For master's, thesis, internship, practicum. *Entrance requirements:* For master's, previous course work and work experience in psychology, experience in dance or movement. Additional exam requirements/recommendations for international students: Required—TOEFL (minimum score 550 paper-based). Electronic applications accepted. *Expenses:* Contact institution. *Faculty research:* Research attitudes and needs of dance/movement therapists.

Antioch University Seattle, Program in Education, Seattle, WA 98121. Offers adult education (MA); drama therapy (MA); individualized studies (MA); leadership in edible education (MA); teaching (MAT); urban environmental education (MA). *Program availability:* Part-time, evening/weekend. *Students:* 58 full-time (40 women), 15 part-time (12 women); includes 12 minority (2 Asian, non-Hispanic/Latino; 6 Hispanic/Latino; 4 Two or more races, non-Hispanic/Latino). Average age 36. *Degree requirements:* For master's, comprehensive exam (for some programs), thesis. *Entrance requirements:* For master's, WEST-B, WEST-E, current resume, transcripts of undergraduate degree and coursework (or for highest degree completed), two letters of recommendation, proof of fingerprinting and background check, moral character with fitness statement of understanding, documentation of 40 hours' experience in school classroom(s). *Application deadline:* Applications are processed on a rolling basis. *Expenses:* Contact institution. *Financial support:* Research assistantships, Federal Work-Study, scholarships/grants, and unspecified assistantships available. Financial award application deadline: 6/15. *Faculty research:* Visual thinking and science education, K-8 equity and engaged pedagogy in science education, K-12 inquiry-based mathematics education, education in prisons and other institutions of confinement. *Unit head:* Ed Mikel, Interim Dean, 206-268-4617, E-mail: emikel@antioch.edu. *Application contact:* Eileen Knight, Recruitment and Admissions Director, 206-268-4200, E-mail: eknight@antioch.edu.
Website: https://www.antioch.edu/seattle/degrees-programs/education-degrees/

Appalachian State University, Cratis D. Williams Graduate School, School of Music, Boone, NC 28608. Offers music performance (MM); music therapy (MMT). *Accreditation:* NASM. *Program availability:* Part-time. *Degree requirements:* For master's, comprehensive exam, thesis or alternative. *Entrance requirements:* For master's, GRE General Test, 3 letters of reference, audition. Additional exam requirements/recommendations for international students: Required—TOEFL (minimum score 550 paper-based; 79 iBT), IELTS (minimum score 6.5). Electronic applications accepted. *Faculty research:* Music of the Holocaust, Celtic folk music, early nineteenth-century performance practice, hypermeter and phase rhythm, world music, music and psychoneuroimmunology.

Arizona State University at the Tempe campus, Herberger Institute for Design and the Arts, School of Music, Tempe, AZ 85287-0405. Offers composition (MM, DMA); conducting (DMA); ethnomusicology (MA); interdisciplinary digital media/performance (DMA); music education (MM, PhD); music history and literature (MA); music therapy (MM); performance (MM, DMA). *Accreditation:* NASM. Terminal master's awarded for partial completion of doctoral program. *Degree requirements:* For master's, thesis (for some programs), interactive Program of Study (iPOS) submitted before completing 50

percent of required credit hours; for doctorate, comprehensive exam, thesis/dissertation, interactive Program of Study (iPOS) submitted before completing 50 percent of required credit hours. *Entrance requirements:* For master's, minimum GPA of 3.0 or equivalent in last 2 years of work leading to bachelor's degree, 3 letters of recommendation, resume; for doctorate, GRE or MAT, minimum GPA of 3.0 or equivalent in last 2 years of work leading to bachelor's degree, 3 letters of recommendation, curriculum vitae, statement of intent. Additional exam requirements/recommendations for international students: Required—TOEFL, IELTS, or PTE. Electronic applications accepted.

California Institute of Integral Studies, School of Professional Psychology and Health, San Francisco, CA 94103. Offers clinical psychology (Psy D); community mental health (MA); drama therapy (MA); expressive arts therapy (MA); integral counseling psychology (MA); integrative health studies (MA); psychological studies (MA); somatic psychology (MA). *Program availability:* Part-time, evening/weekend, 100% online, blended/hybrid learning. *Students:* 507 full-time (401 women), 96 part-time (77 women); includes 167 minority (29 Black or African American, non-Hispanic/Latino; 3 American Indian or Alaska Native, non-Hispanic/Latino; 32 Asian, non-Hispanic/Latino; 62 Hispanic/Latino; 2 Native Hawaiian or other Pacific Islander, non-Hispanic/Latino; 39 Two or more races, non-Hispanic/Latino), 60 international. Average age 34. 302 applicants, 89% accepted, 171 enrolled. In 2017, 194 master's, 18 doctorates awarded. *Degree requirements:* For doctorate, comprehensive exam, thesis/dissertation. *Entrance requirements:* For master's, minimum GPA of 3.0, letters of recommendation, writing sample; for doctorate, GRE, MA in psychology or social work with appropriate practical experience for advanced standing, or BA with a minimum GPA of 3.1; letters of recommendation; writing sample. Additional exam requirements/recommendations for international students: Required—TOEFL. *Application deadline:* For fall admission, 2/1 priority date for domestic and international students; for spring admission, 10/15 priority date for domestic and international students. Applications are processed on a rolling basis. Application fee: $65. Electronic applications accepted. *Expenses:* $21,400 (for MA); $32,734 (for PsyD). *Financial support:* Research assistantships with tuition reimbursements, teaching assistantships with tuition reimbursements, career-related internships or fieldwork, Federal Work-Study, and scholarships/grants available. Support available to part-time students. Financial award application deadline: 4/15; financial award applicants required to submit FAFSA. *Faculty research:* Transpersonal psychology, somatic psychology, expressive arts therapy, drama therapy, community mental health, ecopsychology, integrative health, human sexuality. *Unit head:* Nicolle Zapien, Academic Dean, 415-575-5577, E-mail: nzapien@ciis.edu. *Application contact:* Ellen Durst, Director of Admissions, 415-575-6100, Fax: 415-575-1268, E-mail: admissions@ciis.edu.

Concordia University, School of Graduate Studies, Faculty of Fine Arts, Department of Creative Arts Therapies, Montréal, QC H3G 1M8, Canada. Offers art therapy (MA); drama therapy (MA); music therapy (MA).

Drexel University, College of Nursing and Health Professions, Department of Creative Arts Therapies, Specialization in Dance/Movement Therapy, Philadelphia, PA 19104-2875. Offers MA, PMC. *Program availability:* Part-time. *Degree requirements:* For master's, comprehensive exam, thesis. *Entrance requirements:* For master's, GRE General Test or MAT, audition, interview, minimum GPA of 2.75. Electronic applications accepted. *Faculty research:* Family nonverbal communication, early intervention, sexual abuse.

Drexel University, College of Nursing and Health Professions, Department of Creative Arts Therapies, Specialization in Music Therapy, Philadelphia, PA 19104-2875. Offers MA, PMC. *Program availability:* Part-time. *Degree requirements:* For master's, comprehensive exam, thesis. *Entrance requirements:* For master's, GRE General Test or MAT, audition, interview, minimum GPA of 2.75. Electronic applications accepted. *Faculty research:* Early childhood intervention through creative art therapies, rhythm and dementia, music therapy and bulimia, assessment of adolescent suicide.

East Carolina University, Graduate School, College of Fine Arts and Communication, School of Music, Greenville, NC 27858-4353. Offers advanced performance studies (Certificate); composition (MM); music education (MM), including choral conducting, instrumental conducting, music theory/composition, music therapy, performance, Suzuki pedagogy; music therapy (MM); Suzuki pedagogy (Certificate); theory (MM); woodwind specialist (MM), including accompanying, choral conducting, instrumental, instrumental conducting, jazz studies, keyboard, organ, piano pedagogy, Suzuki string pedagogy, vocal pedagogy, voice, woodwind specialist. *Accreditation:* NASM. *Program availability:* Part-time. *Students:* 31 full-time (16 women), 18 part-time (8 women); includes 11 minority (4 Black or African American, non-Hispanic/Latino; 5 Asian, non-Hispanic/Latino; 2 Two or more races, non-Hispanic/Latino), 1 international. Average age 28. 39 applicants, 85% accepted, 21 enrolled. In 2017, 10 master's, 2 Certificates awarded. *Degree requirements:* For master's, comprehensive exam, thesis optional. *Application deadline:* For fall admission, 6/1 priority date for domestic students. Applications are processed on a rolling basis. Application fee: $75. *Expenses:* Tuition, state resident: full-time $4749; part-time $297 per credit hour. Tuition, nonresident: full-time $17,898; part-time $1119 per credit hour. *Required fees:* $2691; $224 per credit hour. Part-time tuition and fees vary according to course load and program. *Financial support:* Fellowships, research assistantships, teaching assistantships, and Federal Work-Study available. Support available to part-time students. Financial award application deadline: 6/1. *Unit head:* Christopher Ulffers, Director, 252-328-4270, E-mail: ulffersj@ecu.edu.
Website: http://www.ecu.edu/music/

Florida State University, The Graduate School, College of Music, Tallahassee, FL 32306. Offers accompanying (MM); arts administration (MA); choral conducting (MM); composition (MM, DM); ethnomusicology (MM); general music (MA); instrumental accompanying (MM); instrumental conducting (MM); jazz studies (MM); music theory (MM, PhD); music therapy (MM); musicology (MM, PhD), including ethnomusicology (PhD), historical musicology; opera (MM); performance (MM, DM); piano pedagogy (MM); piano technology (MA); vocal accompanying (MM). *Accreditation:* NASM. *Program availability:* Part-time. *Students:* 331 full-time (169 women); includes 100 minority (29 Black or African American, non-Hispanic/Latino; 40 Asian, non-Hispanic/Latino; 29 Hispanic/Latino; 2 Native Hawaiian or other Pacific Islander, non-Hispanic/Latino). Average age 26. 760 applicants, 47% accepted, 173 enrolled. In 2017, 94 master's, 45 doctorates awarded. *Degree requirements:* For master's, variable foreign language requirement, comprehensive exam (for some programs), thesis (for some programs), departmental qualifying exam; for doctorate, variable foreign language requirement, comprehensive exam (for some programs), thesis/dissertation, departmental qualifying exam. *Entrance requirements:* For master's, GRE General Test (for some programs), audition, minimum GPA of 3.0; for doctorate, GRE General Test (for some programs), audition, master's degree, minimum GPA of 3.0. Additional exam requirements/recommendations for international students: Required—TOEFL (minimum score 590 paper-based; 97 iBT), IELTS (minimum score 7.5). *Application deadline:* For fall admission, 7/1 for domestic and international students; for spring admission, 11/1 for domestic and international students; for summer admission, 3/1 for domestic students. Applications are processed on a rolling basis. Application fee: $30. Electronic applications accepted. *Financial support:* In 2017–18, 233 students received support, including 2 fellowships with full tuition reimbursements available (averaging $15,000 per year), 14 research assistantships with full and partial tuition reimbursements available (averaging $6,458 per year), 201 teaching assistantships with full and partial tuition reimbursements available (averaging $6,458 per year); career-related internships or fieldwork, scholarships/grants, tuition waivers (full and partial), and unspecified assistantships also available. Support available to part-time students. Financial award application deadline: 2/28; financial award applicants required to submit FAFSA. *Faculty research:* Music therapy in NICU units, music of the Americas, music theory pedagogy, music performance. *Unit head:* Dr. Patricia Flowers, Dean, 850-644-4361, Fax: 850-644-2033, E-mail: pjflowers@fsu.edu. *Application contact:* Kris Watson, Director of Admissions, 850-645-2126, Fax: 850-644-2033, E-mail: krwatson@fsu.edu.
Website: http://www.music.fsu.edu/

Georgia College & State University, Graduate School, College of Health Sciences, Program in Music Therapy, Milledgeville, GA 31061. Offers MMT. *Program availability:* Part-time, evening/weekend. *Students:* 9 full-time (5 women), 3 part-time (all women); includes 4 minority (3 Black or African American, non-Hispanic/Latino; 1 Hispanic/Latino). Average age 31. 4 applicants, 100% accepted, 3 enrolled. In 2017, 1 master's awarded. *Degree requirements:* For master's, comprehensive exam, thesis or alternative, minimum GPA of 3.0, complete program within 6 years from starting. *Entrance requirements:* For master's, bachelor's degree in music therapy or equivalent, minimum undergraduate GPA of 2.75, 2 letters of recommendation, essay, interview, audition. *Application deadline:* For fall admission, 7/1 priority date for domestic students; for spring admission, 11/1 priority date for domestic students; for summer admission, 4/1 priority date for domestic students. Applications are processed on a rolling basis. Application fee: $40. Electronic applications accepted. *Expenses:* $338 per credit hour full-time, $3,042 per semester; $343 per term fees. *Financial support:* In 2017–18, 3 students received support. Unspecified assistantships available. Support available to part-time students. Financial award application deadline: 3/1; financial award applicants required to submit FAFSA. *Unit head:* Dr. Chesley Mercado, Director, 478-445-2645, Fax: 478-445-2645, E-mail: chesley.mercado@gcsu.edu. *Application contact:* Kate Marshall, Graduate Admissions Coordinator, 478-445-1184, Fax: 478-445-1336, E-mail: grad-admit@gcsu.edu.
Website: http://gcsu.edu/health/therapy/music-therapy-mmt

Immaculata University, College of Graduate Studies, Program in Music Therapy, Immaculata, PA 19345. Offers MA. *Accreditation:* NASM. *Program availability:* Part-time, evening/weekend. *Degree requirements:* For master's, comprehensive exam, thesis optional. *Entrance requirements:* For master's, GRE General Test or MAT, minimum GPA of 3.0. Additional exam requirements/recommendations for international students: Required—TOEFL. Electronic applications accepted. *Faculty research:* Biofeedback music laboratory, experimental music therapy, virtual arts therapies, sound beam.

Indiana University–Purdue University Indianapolis, School of Engineering and Technology, Department of Music and Arts Technology, Indianapolis, IN 46202. Offers music technology (MS, PhD); music therapy (MS). *Accreditation:* NASM. *Program availability:* Part-time, evening/weekend, online learning. *Degree requirements:* For master's, thesis optional, internship or final project; for doctorate, thesis/dissertation. *Entrance requirements:* For master's, GRE, interview, audition, minimum GPA of 3.0; for doctorate, GRE, three letters of recommendation; research adviser letter; statement of purpose; writing samples; transcripts; portfolio. Additional exam requirements/recommendations for international students: Required—TOEFL (minimum score 550 paper-based; 79 iBT); Recommended—IELTS (minimum score 6.5). Electronic applications accepted. *Expenses:* Contact institution. *Faculty research:* Music-related cross-disciplinary technologies in fine arts, education, business, health care, computer science, and engineering; exploring and creating multi-disciplinary music, dance, and arts performance; developing new recording techniques and emerging technologies.

Lesley University, Graduate School of Arts and Social Sciences, Cambridge, MA 02138-2790. Offers clinical mental health counseling (MA), including holistic counseling, school and community counseling, trauma studies; counseling psychology (MA, CAGS), including professional counseling (MA), school counseling (MA); creative writing (MFA); expressive therapies (MA, PhD, CAGS), including art (MA), clinical mental health counseling (MA), dance (MA), expressive therapies (MA), music (MA); independent studies (CAGS); independent study (MA); intercultural relations (MA, CAGS); interdisciplinary studies (MA), including individualized studies, integrative holistic health, mindfulness studies, peace and conflict transformation, trauma sensitive assessment, intervention, and consultation, women's studies; urban environmental leadership (MA). *Program availability:* Part-time, online learning. *Degree requirements:* For master's, internship, practicum, thesis (for expressive therapies); for doctorate, thesis/dissertation, arts apprenticeship, field placement; for CAGS, thesis, internship (for counseling psychology, expressive therapies). *Entrance requirements:* For master's, MAT (counseling psychology), interview, writing samples, art portfolio; for doctorate, GRE or MAT, interview, master's degree; for CAGS, interview, master's degree. Additional exam requirements/recommendations for international students: Required—TOEFL (minimum score 550 paper-based; 80 iBT). Electronic applications accepted. *Faculty research:* Psychotherapy and culture; psychotherapy and psychological trauma; women's issues in art, teaching and psychotherapy; community-based art, psycho-spiritual inquiry.

Loyola University New Orleans, College of Music and Fine Arts, New Orleans, LA 70118-6195. Offers music therapy (MMT); performance (MM). *Accreditation:* NASM. *Program availability:* Part-time. *Faculty:* 17 full-time (12 women), 9 part-time/adjunct (5 women). *Students:* 20 full-time (12 women), 24 part-time (16 women); includes 18 minority (6 Black or African American, non-Hispanic/Latino; 2 Asian, non-Hispanic/Latino; 6 Hispanic/Latino; 4 Two or more races, non-Hispanic/Latino), 3 international. Average age 29. 31 applicants, 71% accepted, 13 enrolled. In 2017, 9 master's awarded. *Degree requirements:* For master's, comprehensive written and oral exams; thesis (for MMT). *Entrance requirements:* For master's, performance audition, appropriate bachelor's degree, transcripts, minimum GPA of 3.0, 2 letters of recommendation, resume. Additional exam requirements/recommendations for international students: Required—TOEFL (minimum score 550 paper-based; 79 iBT). *Application deadline:* For fall admission, 8/15 priority date for domestic and international students; for spring admission, 1/1 priority date for domestic and international students. Applications are processed on a rolling basis. Application fee: $20. Electronic applications accepted. *Expenses:* $818 per hour tuition; $738 per semester full-time fees, $376.50 part-time. *Financial support:* Career-related internships or fieldwork, Federal Work-Study, institutionally sponsored loans, scholarships/grants, unspecified assistantships, and talent-based music scholarships available. Support available to part-time students. Financial award application deadline: 5/1; financial award applicants required to submit FAFSA. *Faculty research:* Music business, music therapy, musicology, music theory, music education. *Unit head:* Dr. Kern Maass, Dean, 504-865-3039, Fax: 504-865-2852, E-mail: kdmaass@loyno.edu.
Website: http://cmfa.loyno.edu/

Maryville University of Saint Louis, Myrtle E. and Earl E. Walker College of Health Professions, Program in Music Therapy, St. Louis, MO 63141-7299. Offers MMT. *Accreditation:* NASM. *Program availability:* Part-time. *Faculty:* 2 full-time (both women). *Students:* 7 full-time (6 women), 4 part-time (all women); includes 3 minority (2 Black or African American, non-Hispanic/Latino; 1 Two or more races, non-Hispanic/Latino), 1 international. Average age 27. In 2017, 1 master's awarded. *Entrance requirements:* For

master's, music audition, interview, minimum undergraduate GPA of 3.0, 3 letters of recommendation. Additional exam requirements/recommendations for international students: Required—TOEFL (minimum score 550 paper-based). *Application deadline:* Applications are processed on a rolling basis. Electronic applications accepted. *Expenses:* Contact institution. *Financial support:* Application deadline: 4/1; applicants required to submit FAFSA. *Unit head:* Dr. Cynthia Briggs, Director, 314-529-9441, Fax: 314-529-9495, E-mail: cbriggs@maryville.edu. *Application contact:* Jeannie DeLuca, Director, Admissions and Advising, 314-529-9355, Fax: 314-529-9927, E-mail: jdeluca@maryville.edu.
Website: http://www.maryville.edu/hp/music-therapy/

Michigan State University, The Graduate School, College of Music, East Lansing, MI 48824. Offers collaborative piano (M Mus); jazz studies (M Mus); music (PhD); music composition (M Mus, DMA); music conducting (M Mus, DMA); music education (M Mus); music performance (M Mus, DMA); music theory (M Mus); music therapy (M Mus); musicology (MA); piano pedagogy (M Mus). *Accreditation:* NASM. *Entrance requirements:* Additional exam requirements/recommendations for international students: Required—TOEFL. Electronic applications accepted.

Molloy College, Graduate Music Therapy Program, Rockville Centre, NY 11571-5002. Offers MS. *Program availability:* Part-time, evening/weekend. *Faculty:* 4 full-time (3 women), 3 part-time/adjunct (all women). *Students:* 6 full-time (5 women), 24 part-time (13 women); includes 4 minority (1 Asian, non-Hispanic/Latino; 2 Hispanic/Latino; 1 Two or more races, non-Hispanic/Latino), 7 international. Average age 34. 28 applicants, 46% accepted, 8 enrolled. In 2017, 10 master's awarded. *Entrance requirements:* Additional exam requirements/recommendations for international students: Required—TOEFL (minimum score 550 paper-based; 79 iBT). *Application deadline:* Applications are processed on a rolling basis. Application fee: $60. Electronic applications accepted. *Expenses: Tuition:* Full-time $19,980; part-time $1110 per credit. *Required fees:* $1040. Tuition and fees vary according to course load and degree level. *Financial support:* Application deadline: 3/1; applicants required to submit FAFSA. *Faculty research:* Children's behavioral style and parents' needs toward developing a temperament profile of children with ASD; effects of music therapy on cortisol levels and EEG outcomes of children with ASD; effectiveness of improvisational music therapy techniques on levels of engagement for children with Autism: A Microanalysis Study; Stress management with parents who have a child with developmental disabilities in music therapy; the use of improv. *Unit head:* Suzanne Sorel, Associate Dean/Director of Graduate Music Therapy, 516-323-3322, E-mail: ssorel@molloy.edu. *Application contact:* Jaclyn Machowicz, Assistant Director for Admissions, 516-323-4010, E-mail: jmachowicz@molloy.edu.

Montclair State University, The Graduate School, College of the Arts, John J. Cali School of Music, Post Baccalaureate Certificate Program in Music Therapy, Montclair, NJ 07043-1624. Offers Postbaccalaureate Certificate. *Program availability:* Part-time, evening/weekend. *Entrance requirements:* For degree, 2 letters of recommendation, essay. Additional exam requirements/recommendations for international students: Required—TOEFL (minimum score 83 iBT), IELTS (minimum score 6.5). Electronic applications accepted.

Montclair State University, The Graduate School, College of the Arts, John J. Cali School of Music, Program in Music, Montclair, NJ 07043-1624. Offers music education (MA); music therapy (MA); performance (MA); theory/composition (MA). *Program availability:* Part-time, evening/weekend. *Degree requirements:* For master's, thesis. *Entrance requirements:* For master's, GRE General Test, 2 letters of recommendation, essay. Additional exam requirements/recommendations for international students: Required—TOEFL (minimum score 83 iBT), IELTS (minimum score 6.5). Electronic applications accepted.

Naropa University, Graduate Programs, Program in Clinical Mental Health Counseling, Concentration in Somatic Counseling: Dance/Movement Therapy, Boulder, CO 80302-6697. Offers MA. *Faculty:* 3 full-time (2 women), 9 part-time/adjunct (all women). *Students:* 20 full-time (all women), 6 part-time (all women); includes 12 minority (4 Black or African American, non-Hispanic/Latino; 1 American Indian or Alaska Native, non-Hispanic/Latino; 2 Asian, non-Hispanic/Latino; 4 Hispanic/Latino; 1 Two or more races, non-Hispanic/Latino), 1 international. Average age 28. 24 applicants, 79% accepted, 12 enrolled. In 2017, 12 master's awarded. *Degree requirements:* For master's, internship, clinical practicum. *Entrance requirements:* For master's, BA (preferably in field related to the helping professions); minimum of 100 hours of paid or volunteer experience in mental health field or community facility/service organization; interview; state of interest essay; supplemental essays; 2 letters of recommendation; transcripts. Additional exam requirements/recommendations for international students: Required—TOEFL (minimum score 550 paper-based; 80 iBT). *Application deadline:* For fall admission, 1/15 priority date for domestic and international students. Applications are processed on a rolling basis. Application fee: $60. Electronic applications accepted. *Expenses:* $995 per credit. *Financial support:* In 2017–18, 11 students received support, including 1 research assistantship with partial tuition reimbursement available (averaging $1,500 per year); teaching assistantships with partial tuition reimbursements available, career-related internships or fieldwork, Federal Work-Study, scholarships/grants, tuition waivers (partial), and unspecified assistantships also available. Support available to part-time students. Financial award application deadline: 3/1; financial award applicants required to submit FAFSA. *Unit head:* Dr. Kathleen Gregory, Dean, Graduate School of Counseling and Psychology, 303-245-4706, E-mail: kgregory@naropa.edu. *Application contact:* Office of Admissions, 303-546-3572, Fax: 303-546-3583, E-mail: admissions@naropa.edu.
Website: http://www.naropa.edu/academics/masters/clinical-mental-health-counseling/somatic-counseling/dance-movement-therapy/index.php

Nazareth College of Rochester, Graduate Studies, Department of Creative Arts Therapy, Rochester, NY 14618. Offers art therapy (MS); music therapy (MS). *Program availability:* Part-time. *Entrance requirements:* For master's, minimum GPA of 3.0; portfolio review (art therapy); audition (music therapy). Additional exam requirements/recommendations for international students: Required—TOEFL (minimum score 550 paper-based, 79 iBT) or IELTS (6.5). Electronic applications accepted.

New York University, Steinhardt School of Culture, Education, and Human Development, Department of Music and Performing Arts Professions, Program in Drama Therapy, New York, NY 10012. Offers MA. *Program availability:* Part-time. *Students:* Average age 29. 41 applicants, 73% accepted, 18 enrolled. In 2017, 17 master's awarded. *Entrance requirements:* For master's, audition, interview. Additional exam requirements/recommendations for international students: Required—TOEFL (minimum score 100 iBT). *Application deadline:* For fall admission, 12/1 priority date for domestic and international students; for spring admission, 10/1 for domestic and international students. Applications are processed on a rolling basis. Application fee: $75. Electronic applications accepted. *Expenses: Tuition:* Full-time $41,352; part-time $19,968 per year. *Required fees:* $2496; $1628 per unit. $814 per term. Tuition and fees vary according to course load and program. *Financial support:* Career-related internships or fieldwork, Federal Work-Study, institutionally sponsored loans, scholarships/grants, and tuition waivers (partial) available. Support available to part-time students. Financial award application deadline: 2/1; financial award applicants required to submit FAFSA. *Faculty research:* Meaning of role in drama, therapy, and everyday life; clinical approaches to

drama therapy; trauma effects on children. *Unit head:* Prof. Robert Landy, Director, 212-998-5258, E-mail: rjl1@nyu.edu. *Application contact:* 212-998-5030, Fax: 212-995-4328, E-mail: steinhardt.gradadmissions@nyu.edu.
Website: http://steinhardt.nyu.edu/music/dramatherapy

New York University, Steinhardt School of Culture, Education, and Human Development, Department of Music and Performing Arts Professions, Program in Music Therapy, New York, NY 10012. Offers MA. *Program availability:* Part-time. *Students:* Average age 30. 70 applicants, 31% accepted, 18 enrolled. In 2017, 17 master's awarded. *Entrance requirements:* For master's, audition, interview. Additional exam requirements/recommendations for international students: Required—TOEFL (minimum score 100 iBT). *Application deadline:* For fall admission, 12/1 priority date for domestic and international students. Applications are processed on a rolling basis. Application fee: $75. Electronic applications accepted. *Expenses: Tuition:* Full-time $41,352; part-time $19,968 per year. *Required fees:* $2496; $1628 per unit. $814 per term. Tuition and fees vary according to course load and program. *Financial support:* Career-related internships or fieldwork, Federal Work-Study, institutionally sponsored loans, scholarships/grants, and tuition waivers (partial) available. Support available to part-time students. Financial award application deadline: 2/1; financial award applicants required to submit FAFSA. *Faculty research:* Music therapy in special education, including autism and emotional disabilities; guided imagery. *Unit head:* Prof. Barbara Hesser, Director, 212-998-5452, Fax: 212-995-4043, E-mail: barbara.hesser@nyu.edu. *Application contact:* 212-998-5030, Fax: 212-995-4328, E-mail: steinhardt.gradadmissions@nyu.edu.
Website: http://steinhardt.nyu.edu/music/therapy

Ohio University, Graduate College, College of Fine Arts, School of Music, Athens, OH 45701-2979. Offers accompanying (MM); composition (MM); conducting (MM); history/literature (MM); music education (MM); music therapy (MM); performance (MM, Certificate); performance/pedagogy (MM); theory (MM). *Accreditation:* NASM. *Program availability:* Part-time, evening/weekend, online learning. *Degree requirements:* For master's, comprehensive exam, thesis (for some programs), oral exam. *Entrance requirements:* For master's, audition, interview, portfolio, recordings (varies by program). Additional exam requirements/recommendations for international students: Required—TOEFL (minimum score 550 paper-based; 80 iBT) or IELTS (minimum score 6.5). Electronic applications accepted.

Pratt Institute, School of Art, Programs in Creative Arts Therapy, Brooklyn, NY 11205-3899. Offers art therapy and creativity development (MPS); dance/movement therapy (MS). *Accreditation:* NASAD (one or more programs are accredited). *Program availability:* Part-time. *Students:* 58 full-time (55 women), 49 part-time (all women); includes 44 minority (20 Black or African American, non-Hispanic/Latino; 5 Asian, non-Hispanic/Latino; 15 Hispanic/Latino; 4 Two or more races, non-Hispanic/Latino), 4 international. Average age 30. 124 applicants, 58% accepted, 29 enrolled. In 2017, 32 master's awarded. *Degree requirements:* For master's, thesis. *Entrance requirements:* For master's, letters of recommendation, portfolio. Additional exam requirements/recommendations for international students: Required—TOEFL (minimum score 600 paper-based; 100 iBT). *Application deadline:* For fall admission, 1/5 for domestic and international students; for spring admission, 10/1 for domestic and international students. Applications are processed on a rolling basis. Application fee: $50 ($90 for international students). Electronic applications accepted. *Expenses: Tuition:* Full-time $30,834. *Required fees:* $1974. *Financial support:* Career-related internships or fieldwork, Federal Work-Study, institutionally sponsored loans, scholarships/grants, health care benefits, and unspecified assistantships available. Support available to part-time students. Financial award application deadline: 2/1; financial award applicants required to submit FAFSA. *Faculty research:* Psychology and aesthetic interaction, art therapy and AIDS, art therapy and autism, art diagnosis. *Unit head:* Julie Miller, Chairperson, 718-399-4532, Fax: 718-636-3597, E-mail: jmiller2@pratt.edu. *Application contact:* Natalie Capannelli, Director of Graduate Admissions, 718-636-3551, Fax: 718-399-4242, E-mail: ncapanne@pratt.edu.
Website: https://www.pratt.edu/academics/school-of-art/graduate-school-of-art/creative-arts-therapy/

See Display on page 141 and Close-Up on page 189.

Saint Mary-of-the-Woods College, Master of Arts in Music Therapy Program, Saint Mary of the Woods, IN 47876. Offers MA. *Accreditation:* NASM. *Program availability:* Part-time, blended/hybrid learning. *Students:* 24 full-time (22 women). Average age 32. 20 applicants, 55% accepted, 9 enrolled. In 2017, 7 master's awarded. *Degree requirements:* For master's, thesis, qualifying exam, portfolio. *Entrance requirements:* For master's, diagnostic music exam, audition. *Application deadline:* For fall admission, 4/30 for domestic and international students; for winter admission, 10/31 for domestic students, 10/30 for international students. Application fee: $0. Electronic applications accepted. *Expenses:* $710 per credit hour. *Financial support:* In 2017–18, 16 students received support. Career-related internships or fieldwork, scholarships/grants, and unspecified assistantships available. Financial award applicants required to submit FAFSA. *Unit head:* Dr. Tracy Richardson, Director, 812-535-5154, E-mail: trichardson@smwc.edu. *Application contact:* Marie Elliott, Assistant Director of Admissions, 800-926-7692, E-mail: graduate@smwc.edu.
Website: http://www.smwc.edu

Shenandoah University, Shenandoah Conservatory, Winchester, VA 22601-5195. Offers church music (MM, Certificate); collaborative piano (MM); composition (MM); conducting (MM); music (Artist Diploma); music education (MME); music therapy (MMT, Certificate); pedagogy - voice (MM, DMA); performance (MM, DMA); performing arts leadership and management (MS). *Accreditation:* NASM. *Program availability:* Part-time. *Faculty:* 32 full-time (11 women), 12 part-time/adjunct (6 women). *Students:* 70 full-time (38 women), 69 part-time (44 women); includes 20 minority (6 Black or African American, non-Hispanic/Latino; 1 American Indian or Alaska Native, non-Hispanic/Latino; 2 Asian, non-Hispanic/Latino; 11 Hispanic/Latino), 18 international. Average age 30. 135 applicants, 77% accepted, 49 enrolled. In 2017, 32 master's, 13 doctorates, 11 other advanced degrees awarded. *Degree requirements:* For master's, comprehensive exam, minimum GPA of 3.0, internship (MS), recital (MM), research teaching project or thesis (MME), project (MA); for doctorate, comprehensive exam, minimum GPA of 3.0, dissertation or teaching project, recital; for other advanced degree, minimum GPA of 3.0, research project, recital. *Entrance requirements:* For master's, music theory diagnostic exam, bachelor's degree with minimum of GPA of 2.5, performance audition, writing sample, resume, all academic transcripts; for doctorate, music theory diagnostic exam; music history diagnostic exam; vocal diction proficiency exam, master's degree with minimum GPA of 3.25, performance audition, 2 letters of recommendation, writing sample, resume, all academic transcripts; for other advanced degree, bachelor's or master's degree; minimum GPA of 2.5; performance audition (for Artist Diploma). Additional exam requirements/recommendations for international students: Required—TOEFL (minimum score 550 paper-based, 79 iBT) or IELTS (6.5). *Application deadline:* For fall and spring admission, 1/15 for domestic and international students; for summer admission, 4/15 for domestic and international students. Application fee: $30. Electronic applications accepted. *Expenses:* $15,600 tuition, $2,400 fees (applied major lesson fee, conservatory fee, technology fee, and student services fee). *Financial support:* In 2017–18, 42 students received support. Scholarships/grants and unspecified

assistantships available. Financial award applicants required to submit FAFSA. *Faculty research:* Brahms, Scriabin, arts as inquiry. *Unit head:* Dr. Michael J. Stepniak, Dean, 540-542-6201, Fax: 540-665-5402, E-mail: mstepnia@su.edu. *Application contact:* Andrew Woodall, Executive Director of Recruitment and Advancement, 540-665-4581, Fax: 540-665-4627, E-mail: admit@su.edu.
Website: http://www.su.edu/conservatory/

Slippery Rock University of Pennsylvania, Graduate Studies (Recruitment), College of Liberal Arts, Department of Music, Slippery Rock, PA 16057-1383. Offers music therapy (MMT). *Program availability:* Part-time, blended/hybrid learning, interactive online classes and face-to-face intensives. *Degree requirements:* For master's, thesis or alternative. *Entrance requirements:* For master's, bachelor's degree in music therapy with minimum GPA of 3.0, resume, statement of professional goals, video-recording of three songs accompanied on piano and three songs accompanied on guitar, video interview, official transcripts. Additional exam requirements/recommendations for international students: Required—TOEFL (minimum score 550 paper-based; 80 iBT). Electronic applications accepted. *Expenses:* Contact institution.

State University of New York at New Paltz, Graduate and Extended Learning School, School of Fine and Performing Arts, Department of Music, New Paltz, NY 12561. Offers music therapy (MS). *Accreditation:* NASM. *Program availability:* Part-time. *Faculty:* 3 full-time (1 woman), 1 part-time/adjunct (0 women). *Students:* 23 full-time (16 women), 10 part-time (7 women); includes 5 minority (1 Black or African American, non-Hispanic/Latino; 1 Asian, non-Hispanic/Latino; 3 Hispanic/Latino), 6 international. 23 applicants, 70% accepted, 9 enrolled. In 2017, 2 master's awarded. *Degree requirements:* For master's, thesis. *Entrance requirements:* For master's, audition, minimum GPA of 3.0. Additional exam requirements/recommendations for international students: Required—TOEFL (minimum score 550 paper-based; 80 iBT), IELTS (minimum score 6.5). *Application deadline:* For fall admission, 5/15 for domestic and international students; for spring admission, 11/15 for domestic and international students. Applications are processed on a rolling basis. Application fee: $50. Electronic applications accepted. *Financial support:* In 2017–18, 4 teaching assistantships with partial tuition reimbursements (averaging $5,000 per year) were awarded. Financial award application deadline: 8/1. *Unit head:* Dr. John Mahoney, Program Director, 845-257-2709, E-mail: mahoneyj@newpaltz.edu.
Website: http://www.newpaltz.edu/music/

Temple University, Center for the Performing and Cinematic Arts, Boyer College of Music and Dance, Department of Music, Philadelphia, PA 19122-6096. Offers choral conducting (MM); collaborative piano/chamber music (MM); collaborative piano/opera coaching (MM); composition (MM, PhD); instrumental conducting (MM); music education (MM, PhD); music history (MM); music performance (MM, DMA), including instrumental studies (MM), keyboard (DMA), keyboard studies (MM), voice (DMA), voice and opera (MM); music studies (PhD); music theory (MM, PhD); music therapy (MMT, PhD); musicology (MM, PhD); opera (MM); piano pedagogy (MM); string pedagogy (MM). *Accreditation:* NASM. *Program availability:* Part-time, online learning. *Faculty:* 42 full-time (17 women), 35 part-time/adjunct (13 women). *Students:* 193 full-time (108 women), 51 part-time (33 women); includes 38 minority (13 Black or African American, non-Hispanic/Latino; 8 Asian, non-Hispanic/Latino; 9 Hispanic/Latino; 8 Two or more races, non-Hispanic/Latino), 85 international. 394 applicants, 49% accepted, 77 enrolled. In 2017, 67 master's, 2 doctorates awarded. Terminal master's awarded for partial completion of doctoral program. *Degree requirements:* For doctorate, thesis/dissertation. *Entrance requirements:* Additional exam requirements/recommendations for international students: Required—TOEFL. *Application deadline:* For fall admission, 11/15 for international students; for spring admission, 8/1 for international students. Applications are processed on a rolling basis. Application fee: $60. Electronic applications accepted. *Expenses:* Tuition, state resident: full-time $16,164; part-time $898 per credit hour. Tuition, nonresident: full-time $22,158; part-time $1231 per credit hour. *Required fees:* $890; $445 per semester. Full-time tuition and fees vary according to course load, degree level, campus/location and program. *Financial support:* Fellowships with tuition reimbursements, research assistantships with tuition reimbursements, teaching assistantships with tuition reimbursements, career-related internships or fieldwork, Federal Work-Study, scholarships/grants, health care benefits, and unspecified assistantships available. Financial award application deadline: 3/1; financial award applicants required to submit FAFSA. *Unit head:* Dr. Robert Stroker, Dean, 215-204-8598, Fax: 215-204-4957, E-mail: rstroker@temple.edu. *Application contact:* James Short, Assistant Dean, Undergraduate and Graduate Admissions, 215-204-8301, Fax: 215-204-8598, E-mail: james.short@temple.edu.
Website: http://www.temple.edu/boyer/academicprograms/

Texas Woman's University, Graduate School, College of Arts and Sciences, School of the Arts, Department of Music and Drama, Denton, TX 76204. Offers drama (MA); music (MA), including music education, music therapy, pedagogy, performance. *Accreditation:* NASM. *Program availability:* Part-time. *Faculty:* 15 full-time (7 women), 8 part-time/adjunct (4 women). *Students:* 54 full-time (41 women), 43 part-time (30 women); includes 32 minority (6 Black or African American, non-Hispanic/Latino; 2 Asian, non-Hispanic/Latino; 21 Hispanic/Latino; 3 Two or more races, non-Hispanic/Latino), 6 international. Average age 30. 42 applicants, 98% accepted, 33 enrolled. In 2017, 21 master's awarded. *Degree requirements:* For master's, comprehensive exam, thesis (for some programs), project recital, professional paper or thesis (for music education). *Entrance requirements:* For master's, music history/theory placement exam (for music only), audition and/or design portfolio, interview, resume, writing sample (for drama only), letter of intent, minimum undergraduate GPA of 3.0. Additional exam requirements/recommendations for international students: Required—TOEFL (minimum score 550 paper-based; 79 iBT); Recommended—IELTS (minimum score 6.5), TSE (minimum score 53). *Application deadline:* For fall admission, 3/1 priority date for domestic and international students; for spring admission, 11/1 priority date for domestic students, 7/1 priority date for international students; for summer admission, 5/1 priority date for domestic students, 2/1 priority date for international students. Applications are processed on a rolling basis. Application fee: $50 ($75 for international students). Electronic applications accepted. *Expenses:* $8,150 per year full-time in-state, $17,450 per year full-time out-of-state (for music). *Financial support:* In 2017–18, 31 students received support, including 5 teaching assistantships (averaging $11,736 per year); career-related internships or fieldwork, Federal Work-Study, institutionally sponsored loans, scholarships/grants, traineeships, health care benefits, and unspecified assistantships also available. Support available to part-time students. Financial award application deadline: 3/1; financial award applicants required to submit FAFSA. *Faculty*

research: Musical development in early childhood, little known or neglected compositions for flute (especially by women composers), pedagogical development of the singing voice, music therapy, music and neuroscience technology. *Unit head:* Dr. Pamela Youngblood, Chair of Music and Drama, 940-898-2500, Fax: 940-898-2494, E-mail: music@twu.edu. *Application contact:* Korie Hawkins, Associate Director of Admissions, Graduate Recruitment, 940-898-3188, Fax: 940-898-3081, E-mail: admissions@twu.edu.

The University of Kansas, Graduate Studies, School of Music, Program in Music Therapy, Lawrence, KS 66045. Offers MME, PhD. *Program availability:* Part-time. *Students:* 11 full-time (all women), 9 part-time (7 women); includes 1 minority (Black or African American, non-Hispanic/Latino), 3 international. Average age 26. 10 applicants, 50% accepted, 4 enrolled. In 2017, 10 master's awarded. *Entrance requirements:* For master's, GRE General Test, minimum undergraduate GPA of 3.0, video, reference letters, transcripts; for doctorate, GRE General Test, MEMT Diagnostic Exam, minimum graduate GPA of 3.5, video, reference letters, transcripts, writing sample, proof of professional experience. *Application deadline:* For fall admission, 12/1 priority date for domestic and international students. Application fee: $65 ($85 for international students). Electronic applications accepted. *Financial support:* Fellowships, research assistantships, teaching assistantships, institutionally sponsored loans, scholarships/grants, and unspecified assistantships available. Financial award application deadline: 12/1; financial award applicants required to submit FAFSA. *Faculty research:* Orff-based music therapy; music therapy in health, wellness, autism and hospice; changing attitudes toward individuals with disabilities; music therapy in medical settings; music therapy in pediatrics, early intervention. *Unit head:* Dr. Christopher Johnson, Director, 785-864-9633, E-mail: cmj@ku.edu. *Application contact:* Lois Elmer, Administrative Professional for Music, 785-864-2862, Fax: 785-864-9640, E-mail: elmer@ku.edu.
Website: http://www.memt.ku.edu

University of Kentucky, Graduate School, College of Fine Arts, Program in Music, Lexington, KY 40506-0032. Offers composition (MM, DMA); conducting (MM, DMA); music education (MM, PhD); music theory (MA, PhD); music therapy (MM); musicology (MA, PhD); performance (MM, DMA); sacred music (MM). *Accreditation:* NASM. *Program availability:* Part-time, evening/weekend. *Degree requirements:* For master's, variable foreign language requirement, comprehensive exam, thesis (for some programs); for doctorate, variable foreign language requirement, comprehensive exam, thesis/dissertation. *Entrance requirements:* For master's, GRE General Test, minimum undergraduate GPA of 2.75; for doctorate, GRE General Test, minimum undergraduate GPA of 2.75, graduate 3.0. Additional exam requirements/recommendations for international students: Required—TOEFL (minimum score 550 paper-based). Electronic applications accepted. *Faculty research:* Musicology, music theory, jazz, music education, performance and conducting.

University of Miami, Graduate School, Frost School of Music, Department of Music Education and Music Therapy, Coral Gables, FL 33124. Offers music education (MM, PhD, Spec M); music therapy (MM). *Accreditation:* NASM. *Degree requirements:* For master's, thesis; for doctorate, thesis/dissertation, 2 research tools; for Spec M, thesis, research project. *Entrance requirements:* For master's and doctorate, GRE General Test. Additional exam requirements/recommendations for international students: Required—TOEFL (minimum score 550 paper-based; 59 iBT). Electronic applications accepted. *Faculty research:* Motivation, quantitative research, early childhood, instrumental music, elementary music.

University of Missouri–Kansas City, Conservatory of Music and Dance, Kansas City, MO 64110-2499. Offers composition (MM, DMA); conducting (MM, DMA); music (MA); music education (MME, PhD); music history and literature (MM); music theory (MM); music therapy (MA); performance (MM, DMA). PhD (interdisciplinary) offered through the School of Graduate Studies. *Accreditation:* NASM. *Program availability:* Part-time. *Degree requirements:* For master's, variable foreign language requirement, comprehensive exam, thesis (for some programs); for doctorate, variable foreign language requirement, comprehensive exam, thesis/dissertation or alternative. *Entrance requirements:* For master's, minimum GPA of 3.0 in major, auditions (for MM in performance); for doctorate, minimum graduate GPA of 3.5, auditions (for DMA in performance), portfolio of compositions. Additional exam requirements/recommendations for international students: Required—TOEFL (minimum score 550 paper-based; 80 iBT). *Faculty research:* Electro-acoustic composition, affective music responses, American music theatre, Russian choral music, music therapy and Alzheimer's.

University of the Pacific, Conservatory of Music, Stockton, CA 95211-0197. Offers music education (MM); music therapy (MA). *Faculty:* 4 full-time (2 women), 3 part-time/adjunct (all women). *Students:* 8 full-time (4 women), 17 part-time (11 women); includes 9 minority (1 Black or African American, non-Hispanic/Latino; 4 Asian, non-Hispanic/Latino; 2 Hispanic/Latino; 2 Two or more races, non-Hispanic/Latino), 3 international. Average age 31. 36 applicants, 42% accepted, 9 enrolled. In 2017, 5 master's awarded. *Entrance requirements:* For master's, GRE General Test. Additional exam requirements/recommendations for international students: Required—TOEFL. *Application deadline:* For fall admission, 3/1 priority date for domestic students; for spring admission, 10/1 priority date for domestic students. Applications are processed on a rolling basis. Application fee: $75. *Financial support:* Teaching assistantships and institutionally sponsored loans available. Support available to part-time students. Financial award application deadline: 3/1; financial award applicants required to submit FAFSA. *Unit head:* Dr. Daniel Ebbers, Interim Dean, 209-946-2415, E-mail: musicdean@pacific.edu. *Application contact:* 209-946-2415, Fax: 209-946-2770.

Western Michigan University, Graduate College, College of Fine Arts, School of Music, Kalamazoo, MI 49008. Offers music (MA); music composition (MM); music conducting (MM); music education (MM); music performance (MM); music therapy (MM). *Accreditation:* NASM.

Wilfrid Laurier University, Faculty of Graduate and Postdoctoral Studies, Faculty of Music, Waterloo, ON N2L 3C5, Canada. Offers MMT. *Entrance requirements:* For master's, 4-year honours BA in music therapy with minimum B average in final year, grade 6 RCM and grade 10 performance ability (for 1-year program); 4-year honours BA in allied area (music or psychology) with minimum B average in final year, grade 6 RCM, grade 10 performance ability (for 2-year program). Additional exam requirements/recommendations for international students: Required—TOEFL (minimum score 89 iBT). Electronic applications accepted. *Faculty research:* Group analytic music therapy, music psychotherapy, low frequency sound wave, aesthetic music therapy.

ACADEMIC AND PROFESSIONAL
PROGRAMS IN THE HUMANITIES

Section 7
History

This section contains a directory of institutions offering graduate work in history. Additional information about programs listed in the directory may be obtained by writing directly to the dean of a graduate school or chair of a department at the address given in the directory.

For programs offering related work, see also in this book *Area and Cultural Studies, Architecture, Humanities, Political Science and International Affairs,* and *Sociology, Anthropology, and Archaeology.*

CONTENTS

Program Directories

History

Adams State University, Office of Graduate Studies, Department of History, Government and Philosophy, Alamosa, CO 81101. Offers humanities (MA), including cultural resource management, public administration, U.S. history. Application fee: $30. *Expenses:* Tuition, state resident: full-time $4800; part-time $2400 per credit. Tuition, nonresident: full-time $7100; part-time $3550 per credit. *Required fees:* $213; $106 per credit. One-time fee: $100. Tuition and fees vary according to campus/location and program. *Unit head:* Dr. Edward Crowther, Chair, 719-587-7771, Fax: 719-587-7176, E-mail: ascgrad@adams.edu. *Application contact:* Eileen Tilton, Administrative Assistant III, 719-587-7771, Fax: 719-587-7176, E-mail: ascgrad@adams.edu. Website: http://www2.adams.edu/academics/hgp/

Alabama State University, College of Liberal Arts and Social Sciences, Department of History and Political Science, Montgomery, AL 36101-0271. Offers history (MA). *Program availability:* Part-time. *Faculty:* 2 full-time (1 woman), 1 part-time/adjunct (0 women). *Students:* 1 full-time (0 women), 1 part-time (0 women), 1 international. Average age 33. 4 applicants, 25% accepted. *Degree requirements:* For master's, one foreign language, comprehensive exam, thesis. *Entrance requirements:* For master's, GRE General Test, writing competency test or MAT. Additional exam requirements/recommendations for international students: Recommended—TOEFL (minimum score 500 paper-based). *Application deadline:* For fall admission, 7/15 for domestic students; for spring admission, 12/15 for domestic students. Applications are processed on a rolling basis. Application fee: $25. Electronic applications accepted. *Expenses:* Tuition, state resident: part-time $412 per credit hour. Tuition, nonresident: part-time $824 per credit hour. *Required fees:* $685 per semester. *Financial support:* In 2017–18, 2 research assistantships (averaging $9,000 per year) were awarded. *Faculty research:* NAACP in Alabama, race relations in Alabama, confrontation at Cassville in 1864. *Unit head:* Dr. Derryn Moten, Acting Chair, 334-229-5130.

American Public University System, AMU/APU Graduate Programs, Charles Town, WV 25414. Offers accounting (MS); applied business analytics (MS); business administration (MBA); criminal justice (MA); cybersecurity studies (MS); educational leadership (M Ed); environmental policy and management (MS); global security (DGS); health information management (MS); history (MA), including American military history, American Revolution, civil war, war since 1945, World War II; information technology (MS); international relations and conflict resolution (MA), including American politics and government, comparative government and development, general, international relations, public policy; national security studies (MA); nursing (MSN); political science (MA); public policy (MPP); reverse logistics management (MA), including comparative and security issues, conflict resolution, international and transnational security issues, peacekeeping; space studies (MS); sports management (MS); strategic intelligence (DSI); teaching (M Ed), including secondary social studies; transportation and logistics management (MA). *Program availability:* Part-time, evening/weekend, online only, 100% online. *Students:* 455 full-time (227 women), 7,939 part-time (3,353 women); includes 2,793 minority (1,429 Black or African American, non-Hispanic/Latino; 48 American Indian or Alaska Native, non-Hispanic/Latino; 205 Asian, non-Hispanic/Latino; 766 Hispanic/Latino; 62 Native Hawaiian or other Pacific Islander, non-Hispanic/Latino; 283 Two or more races, non-Hispanic/Latino), 101 international. Average age 37. In 2017, 2,977 master's awarded. *Degree requirements:* For master's, comprehensive exam or practicum. *Entrance requirements:* For master's, official transcript showing earned bachelor's degree from institution accredited by recognized accrediting body. Additional exam requirements/recommendations for international students: Required—TOEFL (minimum score 550 paper-based), IELTS (minimum score 6.5). *Application deadline:* Applications are processed on a rolling basis. Application fee: $0. Electronic applications accepted. *Expenses:* Tuition: Full-time $6300; part-time $350 per credit. *Required fees:* $300; $50 per course. *Financial support:* Scholarships/grants available. Financial award applicants required to submit FAFSA. *Unit head:* Dr. Wallace Boston, President, 877-468-6268, Fax: 304-728-2348, E-mail: president@apus.edu. *Application contact:* Yoci Deal, Associate Vice President, Graduate and International Admissions, 877-468-6268, Fax: 304-724-3764, E-mail: info@apus.edu. Website: http://www.apus.edu

American University, College of Arts and Sciences, Department of History, Washington, DC 20016-8038. Offers MA, PhD. *Program availability:* Part-time, evening/weekend. *Faculty:* 24 full-time (10 women), 3 part-time/adjunct (2 women). *Students:* 63 full-time (37 women), 21 part-time (13 women); includes 9 minority (2 Black or African American, non-Hispanic/Latino; 1 Asian, non-Hispanic/Latino; 3 Hispanic/Latino; 3 Two or more races, non-Hispanic/Latino), 7 international. Average age 31. 131 applicants, 63% accepted, 25 enrolled. In 2017, 18 master's, 4 doctorates awarded. *Degree requirements:* For master's, comprehensive exam, thesis or alternative; for doctorate, thesis/dissertation. *Entrance requirements:* For master's, GRE, personal statement, transcripts, 2 letters of recommendation, resume, writing sample; for doctorate, GRE, sample of written work, personal statement, transcripts, 3 letters of recommendation, resume. Additional exam requirements/recommendations for international students: Required—TOEFL (minimum score 600 paper-based; 100 iBT). *Application deadline:* For fall admission, 2/1 priority date for domestic students. Application fee: $55. Electronic applications accepted. *Expenses:* Contact institution. *Financial support:* Institutionally sponsored loans and unspecified assistantships available. Financial award application deadline: 2/1; financial award applicants required to submit FAFSA. *Unit head:* Dr. Eric J. Lohr, Department Chair, 202-885-2464, Fax: 202-885-1098, E-mail: elohr@american.edu. *Application contact:* Jonathan Harper, Assistant Director, Graduate Recruitment, 202-855-3622, E-mail: jharper@american.edu. Website: http://www.american.edu/cas/history/

American University of Beirut, Graduate Programs, Faculty of Arts and Sciences, 1107 2020, Lebanon. Offers anthropology (MA); Arab and Middle Eastern history (PhD); Arabic language and literature (MA, PhD); archaeology (MA); art history and curating (MA); biology (MS); cell and molecular biology (PhD); chemistry (MS); clinical psychology (MA); computational sciences (MS); computer science (MS); economics (MA); education (MA), including administration and policy studies, elementary education, mathematics education, psychology school guidance, psychology test and measurements, science education, teaching English as a foreign language; English language (MA); English literature (MA); environmental policy planning (MS); financial economics (MAFE); general psychology (MA); geology (MS); history (MA); Islamic studies (MA); mathematics (MS); media studies (MA); Middle East studies (MA); philosophy (MA); physics (MS); political studies (MA); public administration (MA); public policy and international affairs (MA); sociology (MA); theoretical physics (PhD). *Program availability:* Part-time. *Faculty:* 108 full-time (36 women), 5 part-time/adjunct (4 women). *Students:* 251 full-time (180 women), 233 part-time (172 women). Average age 26. 425 applicants, 65% accepted, 121 enrolled. In 2017, 47 master's, 2 doctorates awarded. *Degree requirements:* For master's, one foreign language, comprehensive exam, thesis (for some programs), project; for doctorate, one foreign language, comprehensive exam,

thesis/dissertation. *Entrance requirements:* For master's, GRE General Test (for some programs); for doctorate, GRE General Test (GRE Subject Test for theoretical physics). Additional exam requirements/recommendations for international students: Required—TOEFL (minimum score 583 paper-based; 97 iBT), IELTS (minimum score 7). *Application deadline:* For fall admission, 2/8 for domestic students; for spring admission, 11/3 for domestic students. Application fee: $50. Electronic applications accepted. *Expenses:* Contact institution. *Financial support:* In 2017–18, 29 fellowships, 40 research assistantships were awarded; teaching assistantships, scholarships/grants, tuition waivers (full and partial), and unspecified assistantships also available. Financial award application deadline: 4/4. *Unit head:* Dr. Nadia Maria El Cheikh, Dean, Faculty of Arts and Sciences, 961-1-374374 Ext. 3800, Fax: 961-1-744461, E-mail: nmcheikh@aub.edu.lb. *Application contact:* Rima Rassi, Graduate Studies Officer, 961-1-350000 Ext. 3833, Fax: 961-1-744461, E-mail: rr46@aub.edu.lb. Website: http://www.aub.edu.lb/fas/pages/default.aspx

Appalachian State University, Cratis D. Williams Graduate School, Department of History, Boone, NC 28608. Offers general history (MA). *Program availability:* Part-time, online learning. *Degree requirements:* For master's, one foreign language, comprehensive exam, thesis (for some programs). *Entrance requirements:* For master's, GRE General Test, 3 letters of recommendation. Additional exam requirements/recommendations for international students: Required—TOEFL (minimum score 570 paper-based; 79 iBT), IELTS (minimum score 6.5). Electronic applications accepted. *Faculty research:* Women's history, social/cultural history, U.S. history, Latin America, medieval studies.

Arizona State University at the Tempe campus, College of Liberal Arts and Sciences, School of Historical, Philosophical and Religious Studies, Tempe, AZ 85287-4301. Offers European history (MA, PhD); medieval studies (Graduate Certificate); North American history (MA, PhD); philosophy (MA, PhD); public history (MA); religious studies (MA, PhD); Renaissance studies (Graduate Certificate); scholarly publishing (Graduate Certificate). *Program availability:* Part-time. Terminal master's awarded for partial completion of doctoral program. *Degree requirements:* For master's, thesis or alternative, interactive Program of Study (iPOS) submitted before completing 50 percent of required credit hours; for doctorate, variable foreign language requirement, comprehensive exam, thesis/dissertation, interactive Program of Study (iPOS) submitted before completing 50 percent of required credit hours. *Entrance requirements:* For master's and doctorate, GRE, minimum GPA of 3.0 or equivalent in last 2 years of work leading to bachelor's degree. Additional exam requirements/recommendations for international students: Required—TOEFL, IELTS, or PTE. Electronic applications accepted.

Arkansas State University, Graduate School, College of Humanities and Social Sciences, Department of History, State University, AR 72467. Offers history (MA); history education (SCCT); social science education (MSE). *Program availability:* Part-time. *Degree requirements:* For master's, comprehensive exam, thesis or alternative; for SCCT, comprehensive exam. *Entrance requirements:* For master's, GRE General Test or MAT, GMAT, appropriate bachelor's degree, letters of reference, official transcript, valid teaching certificate (for MSE), immunization records; for SCCT, GRE General Test or MAT, interview, master's degree, letters of reference, official transcript, immunization records. Additional exam requirements/recommendations for international students: Required—TOEFL (minimum score 550 paper-based; 79 iBT), IELTS (minimum score 6), PTE (minimum score 56). Electronic applications accepted.

Arkansas Tech University, College of Arts and Humanities, Russellville, AR 72801. Offers applied sociology (MS); English (M Ed, MA); history (MA); liberal arts (MLA); multi-media journalism (MA); psychology (MS); teaching English as a second language (MA). *Program availability:* Part-time, 100% online, blended/hybrid learning. *Students:* 35 full-time (22 women), 122 part-time (94 women); includes 34 minority (11 Black or African American, non-Hispanic/Latino; 2 Asian, non-Hispanic/Latino; 19 Hispanic/Latino; 2 Two or more races, non-Hispanic/Latino), 19 international. Average age 34. In 2017, 85 master's awarded. *Degree requirements:* For master's, comprehensive exam (for some programs), thesis (for some programs), project. *Entrance requirements:* Additional exam requirements/recommendations for international students: Required—TOEFL (minimum score 550 paper-based; 79 iBT), IELTS (minimum score 6.5), PTE (minimum score 58). *Application deadline:* For fall admission, 3/1 priority date for domestic students, 5/1 priority date for international students; for spring admission, 10/1 priority date for domestic and international students. Applications are processed on a rolling basis. Application fee: $40 ($90 for international students). Electronic applications accepted. *Expenses:* Tuition, state resident: full-time $6816; part-time $284 per credit hour. Tuition, nonresident: full-time $13,632; part-time $568 per credit hour. *Required fees:* $420 per semester. Tuition and fees vary according to course load. *Financial support:* In 2017–18, research assistantships with full and partial tuition reimbursements (averaging $4,800 per year), teaching assistantships with full and partial tuition reimbursements (averaging $4,800 per year) were awarded; career-related internships or fieldwork, Federal Work-Study, scholarships/grants, health care benefits, and unspecified assistantships also available. Support available to part-time students. Financial award application deadline: 4/15; financial award applicants required to submit FAFSA. *Unit head:* Dr. Jeffrey Woods, Dean, 479-968-0274, Fax: 479-964-0812, E-mail: jwoods@atu.edu. *Application contact:* Dr. Mary B. Gunter, Dean of Graduate College, 479-968-0398, Fax: 479-964-0542, E-mail: gradcollege@atu.edu. Website: http://www.atu.edu/humanities/

Ashland University, College of Arts and Sciences, Program in American History and Government, Ashland, OH 44805-3702. Offers American history and government (MAHG). *Program availability:* Part-time, evening/weekend, 100% online, blended/hybrid learning. *Faculty:* 6 full-time (1 woman), 31 part-time/adjunct (4 women). *Students:* 16 full-time (4 women), 159 part-time (96 women); includes 15 minority (11 Black or African American, non-Hispanic/Latino; 1 American Indian or Alaska Native, non-Hispanic/Latino; 2 Hispanic/Latino; 1 Two or more races, non-Hispanic/Latino). Average age 39. 104 applicants, 87% accepted, 65 enrolled. In 2017, 54 master's awarded. *Degree requirements:* For master's, capstone project, thesis, or comprehensive exam. *Entrance requirements:* For master's, minimum undergraduate GPA of 2.75, 3.0 graduate. *Application deadline:* Applications are processed on a rolling basis. Application fee: $30. Electronic applications accepted. *Expenses:* $561 per semester hour tuition (on-campus), $412 per semester hour (online). *Financial support:* In 2017–18, 92 students received support. Scholarships/grants available. Financial award application deadline: 4/1. *Faculty research:* American founding, United States Civil War, Progressive Era, twentieth-century America, religion in America. *Unit head:* Dr. John E. Moser, Chair, 419-289-5411, Fax: 419-289-5425, E-mail: jmoser1@ashland.edu. *Application contact:* Christian A. Pascarella, Director, 419-289-5411, Fax: 419-289-5425, E-mail: cpascare@ashland.edu. Website: http://mahg.ashland.edu

Auburn University, Graduate School, College of Liberal Arts, Department of History, Auburn University, AL 36849. Offers MA, PhD, Graduate Certificate. *Program availability:* Part-time. *Faculty:* 27 full-time (12 women), 3 part-time/adjunct (0 women). *Students:* 25 full-time (11 women), 20 part-time (3 women); includes 3 minority (1 Black or African American, non-Hispanic/Latino; 1 Hispanic/Latino; 1 Two or more races, non-Hispanic/Latino). Average age 34. 32 applicants, 56% accepted, 9 enrolled. In 2017, 3 master's, 6 doctorates, 4 other advanced degrees awarded. *Degree requirements:* For master's, thesis, oral exam; for doctorate, 2 foreign languages, thesis/dissertation. *Entrance requirements:* For master's, GRE General Test; for doctorate, GRE General Test, master's degree with thesis. *Application deadline:* Applications are processed on a rolling basis. Application fee: $50 ($60 for international students). Electronic applications accepted. *Expenses:* Tuition, state resident: full-time $10,974; part-time $519 per credit hour. Tuition, nonresident: full-time $29,658; part-time $1557 per credit hour. *Required fees:* $816 per semester. Tuition and fees vary according to degree level and program. *Financial support:* Teaching assistantships and Federal Work-Study available. Support available to part-time students. Financial award application deadline: 3/15; financial award applicants required to submit FAFSA. *Unit head:* David Lucsko, Chair, 334-844-4360. *Application contact:* Dr. George Flowers, Dean of the Graduate School, 334-844-2125.

Ball State University, Graduate School, College of Sciences and Humanities, Department of History, Muncie, IN 47306. Offers MA. *Program availability:* Part-time. *Faculty:* 11 full-time (4 women). *Students:* 8 full-time (2 women), 17 part-time (7 women); includes 2 minority (1 Asian, non-Hispanic/Latino; 1 Two or more races, non-Hispanic/Latino). Average age 30. 12 applicants, 92% accepted, 9 enrolled. In 2017, 5 master's awarded. *Entrance requirements:* For master's, minimum baccalaureate GPA of 2.75 or 3.0 in latter half of baccalaureate, resume or curriculum vitae, two letters of recommendation, undergraduate transcripts, writing sample, goal statement. Additional exam requirements/recommendations for international students: Required—TOEFL (minimum score 550 paper-based; 79 iBT), IELTS (minimum score 6.5). *Application deadline:* For fall admission, 7/1 for domestic students; for spring admission, 11/1 for domestic students. Applications are processed on a rolling basis. Application fee: $60. Electronic applications accepted. *Financial support:* In 2017-18, 6 students received support, including 2 research assistantships with partial tuition reimbursements available (averaging $10,816 per year), 3 teaching assistantships with partial tuition reimbursements available (averaging $11,977 per year); unspecified assistantships also available. Financial award application deadline: 3/1; financial award applicants required to submit FAFSA. *Faculty research:* European, British, and American history. *Unit head:* Dr. Abel Alves, Chairperson/Professor, 765-285-3376, E-mail: aalves@bsu.edu. *Application contact:* Dr. Daniel Ingram, Associate Professor/Graduate Director, 765-285-8739, Fax: 765-285-5612, E-mail: dpingram@bsu.edu. Website: http://www.bsu.edu/history

Bard College, Master of Arts in Teaching Program, Annandale-on-Hudson, NY 12504. Offers secondary education (MAT), including biology, history, literature, mathematics, Spanish; MS/MAT. *Program availability:* Part-time. *Degree requirements:* For master's, year-long teaching residencies in area middle and high schools. *Entrance requirements:* For master's, GRE General Test, resume, 3 letters of recommendation, personal statement, official transcripts. Additional exam requirements/recommendations for international students: Required—TOEFL. Electronic applications accepted. Application fee is waived when completed online.

Baylor University, Graduate School, College of Arts and Sciences, Department of History, Waco, TX 76798. Offers MA, PhD. *Students:* 19 full-time (9 women), 4 part-time (2 women); includes 1 minority (Hispanic/Latino). 20 applicants, 35% accepted, 5 enrolled. In 2017, 4 master's, 1 doctorate awarded. Terminal master's awarded for partial completion of doctoral program. *Entrance requirements:* For master's and doctorate, GRE General Test, 18 semester hours in history. Additional exam requirements/recommendations for international students: Required—TOEFL. Application fee: $25. Electronic applications accepted. *Financial support:* In 2017-18, 20 students received support. Fellowships, research assistantships, tuition waivers (full), and unspecified assistantships available. Financial award application deadline: 12/30. *Faculty research:* American religion and culture, British religion and culture, American higher education and religion, medieval women and religion. *Unit head:* Dr. Beth Allison Barr, Graduate Program Director, 254-710-3512, Fax: 254-710-2551, E-mail: beth_barr@baylor.edu. Website: http://www.baylor.edu/history/

Binghamton University, State University of New York, Graduate School, Harpur College of Arts and Sciences, Department of History, Binghamton, NY 13902-6000. Offers MA, PhD. *Program availability:* Part-time. *Faculty:* 25 full-time (13 women). *Students:* 33 full-time (18 women), 35 part-time (20 women); includes 1 minority (Black or African American, non-Hispanic/Latino), 24 international. Average age 31. 60 applicants, 65% accepted, 13 enrolled. In 2017, 11 master's, 2 doctorates awarded. Terminal master's awarded for partial completion of doctoral program. *Degree requirements:* For master's, variable foreign language requirement, comprehensive exam, thesis; for doctorate, variable foreign language requirement, comprehensive exam, thesis/dissertation. *Entrance requirements:* For master's and doctorate, GRE General Test, writing sample. Additional exam requirements/recommendations for international students: Required—TOEFL (minimum score 550 paper-based; 80 iBT). *Application deadline:* For fall admission, 4/1 priority date for domestic and international students; for spring admission, 11/1 priority date for domestic and international students. Application fee: $75. Electronic applications accepted. *Financial support:* In 2017-18, 40 students received support, including 40 teaching assistantships with full tuition reimbursements available (averaging $15,000 per year); career-related internships or fieldwork, Federal Work-Study, institutionally sponsored loans, scholarships/grants, health care benefits, tuition waivers (full and partial), and unspecified assistantships also available. Financial award application deadline: 1/15; financial award applicants required to submit FAFSA. *Unit head:* Heather DeHaan, Chairperson, 607-777-2625, E-mail: hdehaan@binghamton.edu. *Application contact:* Ben Balkaya, Assistant Dean and Director, 607-777-2151, Fax: 607-777-2501, E-mail: balkaya@binghamton.edu.

Bob Jones University, Graduate Programs, Greenville, SC 29614. Offers accountancy (MS); Bible (MA); Bible translation (MA); Biblical studies (Certificate); broadcast management (MS); business administration (MBA); church history (MA, PhD); church ministries (MA); church music (MM); cinema and video production (MA); counseling (MS); curriculum and instruction (Ed D); divinity (M Div); dramatic production (MA); educational leadership (MS, Ed D, Ed S); elementary education (M Ed, MAT); English (M Ed, MA, MAT); fine arts (MA); graphic design (MA); history (M Ed, MA); illustration (MA); interpretative speech (MA); mathematics (M Ed, MAT); medical missions (Certificate); ministry (MM, D Min); multi-categorical special education (M Ed, MAT); music (M Ed); New Testament interpretation (PhD); Old Testament interpretation (PhD); orchestral instrument performance (MM); organ performance (MM); pastoral studies (MA); personnel services (MS, Ed S); piano pedagogy (MM); piano performance (MM); platform arts (MA); radio and television broadcasting (MS); rhetoric and public address (MA); secondary education (M Ed); studio art (MA); teaching Bible (MA); theology (MA, PhD); voice performance (MM); youth ministries (MA); M Div/MM.

Boise State University, College of Arts and Sciences, Department of History, Boise, ID 83725-0399. Offers applied historical research (MAHR); history (MA). *Program availability:* Part-time. *Faculty:* 12. *Students:* 12 full-time (5 women), 11 part-time (7 women); includes 1 minority (Hispanic/Latino). Average age 38. 19 applicants, 63% accepted, 6 enrolled. In 2017, 7 master's awarded. *Degree requirements:* For master's, thesis (for MA); applied research project (for MAHR). *Entrance requirements:* For master's, GRE General Test, minimum GPA of 3.0. Additional exam requirements/recommendations for international students: Required—TOEFL (minimum score 550 paper-based; 80 iBT), IELTS (minimum score 6). *Application deadline:* For fall admission, 4/1 for domestic and international students; for spring admission, 9/15 for domestic and international students. Application fee: $65 ($95 for international students). Electronic applications accepted. *Expenses:* Tuition, state resident: full-time $6471; part-time $390 per credit. Tuition, nonresident: full-time $21,787; part-time $685 per credit. *Required fees:* $2283; $100 per term. Part-time tuition and fees vary according to course load and program. *Financial support:* Research assistantships, teaching assistantships, scholarships/grants, and unspecified assistantships available. Financial award application deadline: 1/15; financial award applicants required to submit FAFSA. *Faculty research:* Public history, American social and cultural history, European history, Third World history. *Unit head:* Dr. Nick Miller, Department Chair, 208-426-3902, E-mail: nmiller@boisestate.edu. *Application contact:* Dr. Lisa McClain, Graduate Coordinator, 208-426-1985, E-mail: lisamcclain@boisestate.edu. Website: http://history.boisestate.edu/

Boston College, Graduate School of Arts and Sciences, Department of History, Chestnut Hill, MA 02467-3800. Offers European national studies (MA); history (MA, PhD); medieval studies (MA). Terminal master's awarded for partial completion of doctoral program. *Degree requirements:* For master's, one foreign language, comprehensive exam, thesis optional; for doctorate, 2 foreign languages, comprehensive exam, thesis/dissertation. *Entrance requirements:* For master's and doctorate, GRE General Test, writing sample. Additional exam requirements/recommendations for international students: Required—TOEFL (minimum score 600 paper-based; 100 iBT), IELTS (minimum score 8). Electronic applications accepted. *Faculty research:* U.S. history, medieval history, early modern European history, modern European history, British and Irish history, Latin American history, Asian history, Middle eastern history, international and global history, transnational history.

Boston University, Graduate School of Arts and Sciences, Department of History, Boston, MA 02215. Offers MA, PhD, JD/MA. *Students:* 37 full-time (16 women), 2 part-time (1 woman); includes 5 minority (2 Black or African American, non-Hispanic/Latino; 1 Hispanic/Latino; 2 Two or more races, non-Hispanic/Latino), 1 international. Average age 27. 106 applicants, 21% accepted, 4 enrolled. In 2017, 5 master's, 3 doctorates awarded. Terminal master's awarded for partial completion of doctoral program. *Degree requirements:* For master's, one foreign language, thesis or alternative, major research paper; for doctorate, 2 foreign languages, comprehensive exam, thesis/dissertation. *Entrance requirements:* For master's and doctorate, GRE General Test, 3 letters of recommendation, writing sample, transcripts, personal statement, curriculum vitae, foreign language proficiency. Additional exam requirements/recommendations for international students: Required—TOEFL (minimum score 550 paper-based; 84 iBT). *Application deadline:* For fall admission, 1/15 for domestic and international students. Application fee: $95. Electronic applications accepted. *Financial support:* In 2017-18, 38 students received support, including 9 fellowships with full tuition reimbursements available (averaging $22,000 per year), 6 research assistantships with full tuition reimbursements available (averaging $22,000 per year), 11 teaching assistantships with full tuition reimbursements available (averaging $21,500 per year); Federal Work-Study, scholarships/grants, health care benefits, and unspecified assistantships also available. Financial award application deadline: 1/15. *Unit head:* Louis Ferleger, Chairman, 617-353-2550, Fax: 617-353-2556, E-mail: ferleger@bu.edu. *Application contact:* Carrie Mountain, Department Administrator, 617-353-2555, Fax: 617-353-2556, E-mail: cmount@bu.edu. Website: http://www.bu.edu/history/

Bowling Green State University, Graduate College, College of Arts and Sciences, Department of History, Bowling Green, OH 43403. Offers history (MA, MAT, PhD); public history (MA); MA/MA. *Program availability:* Part-time. *Degree requirements:* For master's, thesis or alternative; for doctorate, one foreign language, comprehensive exam, thesis/dissertation. *Entrance requirements:* For master's and doctorate, GRE General Test. Additional exam requirements/recommendations for international students: Required—TOEFL. Electronic applications accepted. *Faculty research:* Policy history, modern Europe, recent United States history, East Asia, Latin America.

Brandeis University, Graduate School of Arts and Sciences, Department of History, Waltham, MA 02454-9110. Offers MA, PhD. *Faculty:* 14 full-time (4 women), 4 part-time/adjunct (1 woman). *Students:* 29 full-time (15 women), 3 part-time (all women); includes 6 minority (3 Black or African American, non-Hispanic/Latino; 1 Asian, non-Hispanic/Latino; 1 Hispanic/Latino; 1 Two or more races, non-Hispanic/Latino), 4 international. Average age 31. 98 applicants, 18% accepted, 7 enrolled. In 2017, 8 master's, 4 doctorates awarded. Terminal master's awarded for partial completion of doctoral program. *Degree requirements:* For master's, thesis or capstone; seminars; for doctorate, one foreign language, comprehensive exam, thesis/dissertation, regional colloquia; seminars; directed research analyzing primary sources. *Entrance requirements:* For master's and doctorate, GRE General Test, resume, critical writing sample, letters of recommendation, statement of purpose, transcripts. Additional exam requirements/recommendations for international students: Required—PTE (minimum score 68), TOEFL (minimum score 600 paper-based, 100 iBT) or IELTS (7). *Application deadline:* For fall admission, 1/15 priority date for domestic students. Applications are processed on a rolling basis. Application fee: $75. Electronic applications accepted. *Expenses:* Tuition: Full-time $48,720. *Required fees:* $88. Tuition and fees vary according to course load, degree level, program and student level. *Financial support:* In 2017-18, 24 students received support, including 20 fellowships with full tuition reimbursements available (averaging $29,580 per year), 3 teaching assistantships with partial tuition reimbursements available (averaging $3,200 per year); Federal Work-Study, scholarships/grants, health care benefits, and tuition waivers (partial) also available. Financial award application deadline: 4/15; financial award applicants required to submit FAFSA. *Faculty research:* American and European history, world history, regional and national history, medieval history, modern history, international and cultural history. *Unit head:* Dr. Govind Sreenivasan, Director of Graduate Studies, 781-736-2270, E-mail: engerman@brandeis.edu. *Application contact:* Dona DeLorenzo, Senior Academic Administrator, 781-736-2270, E-mail: delorenz@brandeis.edu. Website: http://www.brandeis.edu/gsas/programs/history.html

Brock University, Faculty of Graduate Studies, Faculty of Humanities, Program in History, St. Catharines, ON L2S 3A1, Canada. Offers MA. *Program availability:* Part-time. *Degree requirements:* For master's, thesis optional. *Entrance requirements:* For master's, honors degree in history. Additional exam requirements/recommendations for international students: Required—TOEFL (minimum score 550 paper-based; 80 iBT), IELTS (minimum score 6.5), TWE (minimum score 4). Electronic applications accepted.

Brooklyn College of the City University of New York, School of Humanities and Social Sciences, Department of History, Brooklyn, NY 11210-2889. Offers MA. *Program*

availability: Part-time, evening/weekend. *Degree requirements:* For master's, 30 credits. *Entrance requirements:* For master's, 12 credits in history, minimum GPA of 3.0 in major, 2 letters of recommendation. Additional exam requirements/recommendations for international students: Required—TOEFL (minimum score 650 paper-based; 114 iBT). Electronic applications accepted. *Faculty research:* Modern European, U.S., medieval, women's, Asian, and Caribbean history.

Brown University, Graduate School, Department of History, Providence, RI 02912. Offers MA, PhD. *Degree requirements:* For master's, thesis or alternative; for doctorate, variable foreign language requirement, thesis/dissertation, preliminary exam.

Buffalo State College, State University of New York, The Graduate School, Faculty of Natural and Social Sciences, Department of History and Social Studies, Buffalo, NY 14222-1095. Offers history (MA); secondary education (MS Ed), including social studies. *Program availability:* Part-time, evening/weekend. *Degree requirements:* For master's, one foreign language, thesis (for some programs), project (MS Ed). *Entrance requirements:* For master's, minimum GPA of 2.75, 30 hours in history (MA), 36 hours in history or social sciences (MS Ed). Additional exam requirements/recommendations for international students: Required—TOEFL (minimum score 550 paper-based).

Butler University, College of Liberal Arts and Sciences, Department of History, Indianapolis, IN 46208-3485. Offers MA. *Program availability:* Part-time. *Faculty:* 10 full-time (2 women). *Students:* 1 full-time (0 women), 3 part-time (2 women), 1 international. Average age 45. 7 applicants. *Degree requirements:* For master's, thesis (for some programs). *Entrance requirements:* For master's, GRE General Test. Additional exam requirements/recommendations for international students: Required—TOEFL (minimum score 550 paper-based; 79 iBT), IELTS (minimum score 6). *Application deadline:* For fall admission, 3/1 for domestic and international students; for spring admission, 12/15 for domestic and international students; for summer admission, 4/1 for domestic and international students. Applications are processed on a rolling basis. Application fee: $0. Electronic applications accepted. *Expenses:* $560 per credit. *Financial support:* In 2017–18, 1 student received support. Scholarships/grants, tuition waivers (full and partial), and unspecified assistantships available. Financial award application deadline: 7/15; financial award applicants required to submit FAFSA. *Faculty research:* European history, U.S. history, Latin American history, East Asian history, cultural geography. *Unit head:* Dr. Elise Edwards, Chair, 317-940-9743, E-mail: emedwar1@butler.edu. *Application contact:* Diane Dubord, Student Services Specialist, 317-940-8100, Fax: 317-940-8250, E-mail: ddubord@butler.edu.
Website: https://www.butler.edu/history-anthropology/graduate

Cabrini University, Academic Affairs, Radnor, PA 19087. Offers accounting (M Acc); autism spectrum disorder (M Ed); biological sciences (MS), including civic leadership; criminology and criminal justice (MA); curriculum, instruction, and assessment (M Ed); educational leadership (M Ed, Ed D), including curriculum and instructional leadership (Ed D), preK-12 leadership (Ed D); English as a second language (M Ed); organizational leadership (DBA, PhD); preK to 4 (M Ed); reading specialist (M Ed); secondary education (M Ed), including biology, chemistry, English, English/communication, mathematics, social studies; special education grades 7-12 (M Ed); special education preK-8 (M Ed); teaching and learning (M Ed). *Program availability:* Part-time, evening/weekend. *Faculty:* 23 full-time (17 women), 46 part-time/adjunct (38 women). *Students:* 60 full-time (35 women), 559 part-time (435 women); includes 93 minority (66 Black or African American, non-Hispanic/Latino; 1 American Indian or Alaska Native, non-Hispanic/Latino; 8 Asian, non-Hispanic/Latino; 15 Hispanic/Latino; 3 Two or more races, non-Hispanic/Latino), 4 international. Average age 33. 290 applicants, 82% accepted, 154 enrolled. In 2017, 283 master's awarded. *Degree requirements:* For master's, comprehensive exam (for some programs), thesis (for some programs); for doctorate, comprehensive exam (for some programs), thesis/dissertation. *Entrance requirements:* For master's, professional resume, personal statement, two recommendations, official transcripts; for doctorate, official transcripts, minimum master's GPA of 3.0, two recommendations, interview with admissions committee. Additional exam requirements/recommendations for international students: Required—TOEFL (minimum score 80 iBT). *Application deadline:* For fall admission, 8/26 for domestic students, 8/1 for international students; for winter admission, 1/13 for domestic students, 12/20 for international students; for spring admission, 1/13 for domestic students, 12/20 for international students; for summer admission, 5/20 for domestic students, 4/30 for international students. Applications are processed on a rolling basis. Application fee: $50. Electronic applications accepted. Application fee is waived when completed online. *Expenses:* Contact institution. *Financial support:* In 2017–18, 1,459 students received support. Tuition waivers and unspecified assistantships available. Financial award application deadline: 5/1; financial award applicants required to submit FAFSA. *Unit head:* Dr. Maliha Zaman, 610-902-8502, Fax: 610-902-8797, E-mail: msz37@cabrini.edu. *Application contact:* Diane Greenwood, Director of Graduate Admissions, 610-902-8291, E-mail: diane.l.greenwood@cabrini.edu.
Website: http://cabrini.edu/graduate

California Polytechnic State University, San Luis Obispo, College of Liberal Arts, Department of History, San Luis Obispo, CA 93407. Offers MA. *Program availability:* Part-time. *Faculty:* 5 full-time (2 women). *Students:* 4 full-time (2 women), 12 part-time (4 women); includes 3 minority (2 Hispanic/Latino; 1 Two or more races, non-Hispanic/Latino). Average age 29. 13 applicants, 62% accepted, 6 enrolled. In 2017, 4 master's awarded. *Degree requirements:* For master's, comprehensive exam (for some programs), thesis (for some programs). *Entrance requirements:* For master's, GRE. Additional exam requirements/recommendations for international students: Required—TOEFL (minimum score 80 iBT). *Application deadline:* For fall admission, 4/1 for domestic students, 3/1 for international students. Applications are processed on a rolling basis. Application fee: $55. Electronic applications accepted. *Expenses:* Tuition, state resident: full-time $7176; part-time $4164 per year. *Required fees:* $3690; $3219 per year. $1073 per trimester. *Financial support:* Federal Work-Study and scholarships/grants available. Support available to part-time students. Financial award application deadline: 3/2; financial award applicants required to submit FAFSA. *Faculty research:* American history, European history, Asian history, African history, comparative world history. *Unit head:* Dr. Kathleen Murphy, Graduate Coordinator, 805-756-2839, E-mail: ksmurphy@calpoly.edu.
Website: http://cla.calpoly.edu/hist.html

California State Polytechnic University, Pomona, Program in History, Pomona, CA 91768-2557. Offers MA. *Program availability:* Part-time, evening/weekend. *Students:* 1 full-time (0 women), 15 part-time (6 women); includes 9 minority (1 Asian, non-Hispanic/Latino; 7 Hispanic/Latino; 1 Two or more races, non-Hispanic/Latino). Average age 34. 12 applicants, 58% accepted, 6 enrolled. In 2017, 4 master's awarded. *Entrance requirements:* Additional exam requirements/recommendations for international students: Required—TOEFL (minimum score 550 paper-based). *Application deadline:* Applications are processed on a rolling basis. Application fee: $55. Electronic applications accepted. *Expenses:* Contact institution. *Financial support:* Application deadline: 3/2; applicants required to submit FAFSA. *Unit head:* Dr. Amanda H. Podany, Professor/Graduate Coordinator, 909-869-3875, Fax: 909-869-4724, E-mail: ahpodany@cpp.edu. *Application contact:* Deborah L. Brandon, Executive Director of Admissions and Enrollment Planning, 909-869-3427, Fax: 909-869-5315, E-mail: dlbrandon@cpp.edu.
Website: http://www.cpp.edu/~class/history/graduate-students/

California State University, Bakersfield, Division of Graduate Studies, School of Arts and Humanities, Program in History, Bakersfield, CA 93311. Offers MA. *Faculty:* 5 full-time (2 women). *Students:* 13 applicants, 77% accepted. In 2017, 9 master's awarded. *Degree requirements:* For master's, comprehensive exam or thesis. *Entrance requirements:* For master's, 2 letters of recommendation, letter of intent, writing sample, undergraduate transcripts. *Application deadline:* For fall admission, 7/15 for domestic students; for winter admission, 11/1 for domestic students; for spring admission, 2/1 for domestic students. Applications are processed on a rolling basis. Application fee: $55. *Expenses:* Tuition, state resident: full-time $7176; part-time $4164 per year. *Financial support:* In 2017–18, fellowships (averaging $1,850 per year) were awarded; Federal Work-Study, scholarships/grants, and tuition waivers (full and partial) also available. Financial award application deadline: 3/2; financial award applicants required to submit FAFSA. *Faculty research:* American, European, Latin American, and modern Chinese history. *Unit head:* Dr. Douglas Dodd, Coordinator, 661-654-6815, Fax: 661-654-6906, E-mail: ddodd@csub.edu. *Application contact:* Debbie Blowers, Assistant Director of Admissions and Evaluations, 661-654-3381, E-mail: dblowers@csub.edu.
Website: https://www.csub.edu/history/M.A.%20Program/index.html

California State University, Chico, Office of Graduate Studies, College of Humanities and Fine Arts, Department of History, Chico, CA 95929-0722. Offers MA. *Program availability:* Part-time. *Degree requirements:* For master's, thesis, oral exam. *Entrance requirements:* For master's, GRE General Test, 2 letters of recommendation, statement of purpose, writing sample. Additional exam requirements/recommendations for international students: Required—TOEFL (minimum score 550 paper-based; 80 iBT), IELTS (minimum score 6.5), PTE (minimum score 59). Electronic applications accepted.

California State University, East Bay, Office of Graduate Studies, College of Letters, Arts, and Social Sciences, Department of History, Hayward, CA 94542-3000. Offers history (MA); public history (MA); teaching (MA). *Program availability:* Part-time, evening/weekend. *Faculty:* 9 full-time (6 women), 11 part-time/adjunct (4 women). *Students:* 1 (woman) full-time, 17 part-time (9 women); includes 4 minority (1 Black or African American, non-Hispanic/Latino; 2 Hispanic/Latino; 1 Two or more races, non-Hispanic/Latino). Average age 39. 17 applicants, 47% accepted, 4 enrolled. In 2017, 6 master's awarded. *Degree requirements:* For master's, one foreign language, comprehensive exam, project, thesis, or exam. *Entrance requirements:* For master's, GRE (strongly recommended), minimum GPA of 3.0 in field, 3.3 in history; 2 letters of recommendation; writing sample. Additional exam requirements/recommendations for international students: Required—TOEFL (minimum score 550 paper-based). *Application deadline:* For fall admission, 5/19 for domestic and international students. Applications are processed on a rolling basis. Application fee: $55. Electronic applications accepted. *Financial support:* Fellowships, teaching assistantships, career-related internships or fieldwork, Federal Work-Study, institutionally sponsored loans, and scholarships/grants available. Support available to part-time students. Financial award application deadline: 3/2; financial award applicants required to submit FAFSA. *Faculty research:* Digital history, American women, early America, Native Americans, medieval colonial India. *Unit head:* Dr. Linda L. Ivey, Chair, 510-885-4015, E-mail: linda.ivey@csueastbay.edu. *Application contact:* Dr. Khal Schneider, Graduate Coordinator, 510-885-3237, Fax: 510-885-4791, E-mail: khal.schneider@csueastbay.edu.
Website: http://www20.csueastbay.edu/class/departments/history/

California State University, Fresno, Division of Research and Graduate Studies, College of Social Sciences, Department of History, Fresno, CA 93740-8027. Offers history (MA); history teaching (MA). *Program availability:* Part-time, evening/weekend. *Degree requirements:* For master's, project; thesis or comprehensive examination. *Entrance requirements:* For master's, GRE General Test, minimum GPA of 3.0. Additional exam requirements/recommendations for international students: Required—TOEFL. Electronic applications accepted. *Faculty research:* International education, classical art history, improving teacher quality.

California State University, Fullerton, Graduate Studies, College of Humanities and Social Sciences, Department of History, Fullerton, CA 92831-3599. Offers MA. *Program availability:* Part-time. *Faculty:* 14 full-time (10 women). *Students:* 13 full-time (6 women), 82 part-time (36 women); includes 40 minority (2 Black or African American, non-Hispanic/Latino; 6 Asian, non-Hispanic/Latino; 30 Hispanic/Latino; 2 Two or more races, non-Hispanic/Latino). Average age 32. 40 applicants, 73% accepted, 21 enrolled. *Degree requirements:* For master's, comprehensive exam, project or thesis. *Entrance requirements:* For master's, undergraduate major in history or related field, minimum GPA of 3.0. Application fee: $55. *Financial support:* Career-related internships or fieldwork, Federal Work-Study, institutionally sponsored loans, and scholarships/grants available. Support available to part-time students. Financial award application deadline: 3/1; financial award applicants required to submit FAFSA. *Unit head:* Dr. Jochen Burgtorf, Chair, 657-278-3474. *Application contact:* Admissions/Applications, 657-278-2371.

California State University, Long Beach, Graduate Studies, College of Liberal Arts, Department of History, Long Beach, CA 90840. Offers Africa and the Middle East (MA). *Program availability:* Part-time, evening/weekend. *Degree requirements:* For master's, one foreign language, comprehensive exam or thesis. Electronic applications accepted. *Faculty research:* All periods of European and American history, recent Asian and African history.

California State University, Los Angeles, Graduate Studies, College of Natural and Social Sciences, Department of History, Los Angeles, CA 90032-8530. Offers MA. *Program availability:* Part-time, evening/weekend. *Degree requirements:* For master's, one foreign language, comprehensive exam or thesis. *Entrance requirements:* For master's, minimum GPA of 3.0, undergraduate major in history. Additional exam requirements/recommendations for international students: Required—TOEFL (minimum score 500 paper-based). Electronic applications accepted. *Faculty research:* Ancient and modern Europe, the Middle East, Latin America, U.S. history: Bill of Rights.

California State University, Northridge, Graduate Studies, College of Social and Behavioral Sciences, Department of History, Northridge, CA 91330. Offers MA. *Students:* 19 full-time (9 women), 35 part-time (14 women); includes 15 minority (1 Black or African American, non-Hispanic/Latino; 1 American Indian or Alaska Native, non-Hispanic/Latino; 1 Asian, non-Hispanic/Latino; 10 Hispanic/Latino; 2 Two or more races, non-Hispanic/Latino), 2 international. Average age 33. 49 applicants, 82% accepted, 30 enrolled. In 2017, 18 master's awarded. *Degree requirements:* For master's, one foreign language. *Entrance requirements:* For master's, GRE General Test or minimum GPA of 3.0, 2 letters of recommendation. Additional exam requirements/recommendations for international students: Required—TOEFL. *Application deadline:* For fall admission, 5/15 for domestic students; for spring admission, 11/1 for domestic students. Application fee: $55. *Financial support:* Fellowships and scholarships/grants available. Financial award application deadline: 3/1. *Unit head:* Dr. Susan Fitzpatrick-Behrens, Chair, 818-677-3566.
Website: http://www.csun.edu/csbs/departments/history/index.html

California State University, San Marcos, College of Humanities, Arts, Behavioral and Social Sciences, Program in History, San Marcos, CA 92096-0001. Offers MA. *Entrance requirements:* For master's, GRE General Test, three letters of recommendation, minimum GPA of 3.0 overall and in major, academic writing sample. Additional exam requirements/recommendations for international students: Required—TOEFL (minimum score 500 paper-based). *Application deadline:* For fall admission, 2/1 priority date for domestic students; for spring admission, 8/30 priority date for domestic students. *Expenses:* Tuition, state resident: full-time $7176. Tuition, nonresident: full-time $9504. *Unit head:* Jill Watts, Coordinator, 760-750-4093, E-mail: jwatts@csusm.edu.
Website: http://www.csusm.edu/history/masters/

California State University, Stanislaus, College of the Arts, Humanities and Social Sciences, Master of Arts in History Program, Turlock, CA 95382. Offers MA. *Program availability:* Part-time. *Degree requirements:* For master's, comprehensive exam, thesis or alternative. *Entrance requirements:* For master's, GRE, minimum GPA of 3.0, personal statement. Additional exam requirements/recommendations for international students: Required—TOEFL (minimum score 575 paper-based). Electronic applications accepted. *Faculty research:* History of Ancient Greece, history and ecology of the Central Valley, acculturation and gender.

Carleton University, Faculty of Graduate Studies, Faculty of Arts and Social Sciences, Department of History, Ottawa, ON K1S 5B6, Canada. Offers MA, PhD. *Degree requirements:* For master's, one foreign language, thesis; for doctorate, one foreign language, thesis/dissertation. *Entrance requirements:* For master's, honors degree; for doctorate, master's degree. Additional exam requirements/recommendations for international students: Required—TOEFL. *Faculty research:* Canadian, American, British, modern French, and modern Russian history; international, medieval, and European intellectual history; women's history.

Carnegie Mellon University, Dietrich College of Humanities and Social Sciences, Department of History, Pittsburgh, PA 15213-3891. Offers African and African-American diaspora (PhD); culture and power (PhD); labor, politics and social movements (PhD); technology, environment, science and health (PhD); women, gender and the family (PhD). *Program availability:* Part-time. *Degree requirements:* For doctorate, oral and written comprehensive exams, dissertation defense. *Entrance requirements:* For doctorate, GRE General Test. Additional exam requirements/recommendations for international students: Required—TOEFL. Electronic applications accepted. *Faculty research:* Anthropology and history, African-American history, technology/environment, cultural history analysis.

Case Western Reserve University, School of Graduate Studies, Department of History, Cleveland, OH 44106. Offers MA, PhD. *Program availability:* Part-time. *Faculty:* 13 full-time (4 women), 2 part-time/adjunct (1 woman). *Students:* 22 full-time (11 women), 2 part-time (both women); includes 1 minority (Black or African American, non-Hispanic/Latino), 3 international. Average age 34. 11 applicants, 45% accepted, 2 enrolled. In 2017, 2 master's, 3 doctorates awarded. Terminal master's awarded for partial completion of doctoral program. *Degree requirements:* For master's, thesis; for doctorate, thesis/dissertation. *Entrance requirements:* For master's and doctorate, GRE General Test, statement of objectives; three letters of recommendation; curriculum vitae; writing sample; short essay. Additional exam requirements/recommendations for international students: Required—TOEFL (minimum score 577 paper-based; 90 iBT); Recommended—IELTS (minimum score 7). *Application deadline:* For fall admission, 1/31 priority date for domestic students. Application fee: $50. Electronic applications accepted. *Expenses: Tuition:* Full-time $43,854; part-time $1827 per credit hour. *Required fees:* $50; $50 per credit hour. Tuition and fees vary according to course load and program. *Financial support:* Fellowships, research assistantships, teaching assistantships, career-related internships or fieldwork, tuition waivers (full and partial), and unspecified assistantships available. Financial award application deadline: 1/31; financial award applicants required to submit FAFSA. *Faculty research:* American social history, social policy history, history of technology, environment, science, medicine. *Unit head:* Kenneth Ledford, Associate Professor and Chair, 216-368-4144, Fax: 216-368-4681, E-mail: kenneth.ledford@case.edu. *Application contact:* Daniel Cohen, Associate Professor, 216-368-4165, Fax: 216-368-4681, E-mail: daniel.a.cohen@case.edu.
Website: http://history.case.edu/

The Catholic University of America, School of Arts and Sciences, Department of History, Washington, DC 20064. Offers history (MA, PhD), including early modern European history, medieval history, modern European history, U.S. history; religion and society in the late medieval and early modern world (MA); MA/JD; MSLS/MA. *Program availability:* Part-time. *Faculty:* 15 full-time (6 women), 1 part-time/adjunct (0 women). *Students:* 6 full-time (0 women), 19 part-time (7 women); includes 3 minority (all Two or more races, non-Hispanic/Latino), 2 international. Average age 31. 11 applicants, 82% accepted, 3 enrolled. In 2017, 4 master's, 2 doctorates awarded. Terminal master's awarded for partial completion of doctoral program. *Degree requirements:* For master's, one foreign language, comprehensive exam, thesis optional, 2 languages (for medievalists), one of which must be Latin; for doctorate, 2 foreign languages, comprehensive exam, thesis/dissertation, 3 languages (for medievalists), one of which must be Latin. *Entrance requirements:* For master's and doctorate, GRE General Test, statement of purpose, official copies of academic transcripts, three letters of recommendation, writing sample. Additional exam requirements/recommendations for international students: Required—TOEFL (minimum score 550 paper-based; 80 iBT). *Application deadline:* For fall admission, 7/15 priority date for domestic students, 7/1 for international students; for spring admission, 11/15 priority date for domestic students, 11/1 for international students. Applications are processed on a rolling basis. Application fee: $55. Electronic applications accepted. *Expenses:* Contact institution. *Financial support:* Fellowships, research assistantships, teaching assistantships, Federal Work-Study, scholarships/grants, tuition waivers (full and partial), and unspecified assistantships available. Financial award application deadline: 2/1; financial award applicants required to submit FAFSA. *Faculty research:* Medieval history, including the Islamic Middle East, with particular expertise in later medieval religious, social, and economic history and early medieval and late antique history; European and American intellectual history; renaissance, reformation, catholic reformation; U.S. Catholic history; history of immigration. *Unit head:* Dr. Katherine Jansen, Chair, 202-319-5484, Fax: 202-319-5569, E-mail: jansen@cua.edu. *Application contact:* Dr. Steven Brown, Director of Graduate Admissions, 202-319-5057, Fax: 202-319-6533, E-mail: cua-admissions@cua.edu.
Website: http://history.cua.edu/

Central Connecticut State University, School of Graduate Studies, College of Liberal Arts and Social Sciences, Department of History, New Britain, CT 06050-4010. Offers MA, Certificate. *Program availability:* Part-time, evening/weekend. *Faculty:* 12 full-time (7 women), 1 part-time/adjunct (0 women). *Students:* 22 full-time (9 women), 23 part-time (12 women); includes 4 minority (2 Black or African American, non-Hispanic/Latino; 1 Hispanic/Latino; 1 Two or more races, non-Hispanic/Latino). Average age 30. 30 applicants, 67% accepted, 13 enrolled. In 2017, 17 master's, 2 other advanced degrees awarded. *Degree requirements:* For master's, comprehensive exam, thesis or alternative; for Certificate, qualifying exam. *Entrance requirements:* For master's, minimum undergraduate GPA of 3.0, essays, letters of recommendation. Additional exam requirements/recommendations for international students: Required—TOEFL (minimum score 550 paper-based; 79 iBT); Recommended—IELTS (minimum score 6.5). *Application deadline:* For fall admission, 5/1 for domestic and international students; for spring admission, 11/1 for domestic and international students. Applications are processed on a rolling basis. Application fee: $50. Electronic applications accepted. *Expenses: Tuition, area resident:* Full-time $6757. Tuition, state resident: full-time $9750; part-time $374 per credit. Tuition, nonresident: full-time $18,102; part-time $374 per credit. *Required fees:* $4635; $255 per credit. *Financial support:* In 2017–18, 7 students received support. Career-related internships or fieldwork, Federal Work-Study, scholarships/grants, and unspecified assistantships available. Support available to part-time students. Financial award application deadline: 3/1; financial award applicants required to submit FAFSA. *Faculty research:* American West, African history, Eastern Europe, modern Middle East, East Asia. *Unit head:* Dr. Katherine Hermes, Chair, 860-832-2800, E-mail: hermesk@ccsu.edu. *Application contact:* Patricia Gardner, Associate Director of Graduate Studies, 860-832-2350, Fax: 860-832-2362.
Website: http://www.ccsu.edu/history/

Central European University, Department of History, 1051, Hungary. Offers MA, PhD. *Faculty:* 13 full-time (3 women), 8 part-time/adjunct (2 women). *Students:* 92 full-time (41 women). Average age 28. 169 applicants, 41% accepted, 41 enrolled. In 2017, 34 master's, 5 doctorates awarded. Terminal master's awarded for partial completion of doctoral program. *Degree requirements:* For master's, one foreign language, thesis; for doctorate, one foreign language, comprehensive exam, thesis/dissertation. *Entrance requirements:* For master's and doctorate, essay, statement of purpose, interview. Additional exam requirements/recommendations for international students: Required—TOEFL (minimum score 570 paper-based); Recommended—IELTS (minimum score 6.5). *Application deadline:* For fall admission, 2/4 for domestic and international students. Application fee: $30. Electronic applications accepted. *Expenses: Tuition:* Full-time 12,000 euros. *Required fees:* 230 euros. One-time fee: 30 euros full-time. Tuition and fees vary according to course level, course load, degree level and program. *Financial support:* Fellowships, career-related internships or fieldwork, institutionally sponsored loans, scholarships/grants, and tuition waivers (full and partial) available. *Faculty research:* History of central, Southeastern and Eastern Europe and the Eastern Mediterranean from the 16th century to the present. *Unit head:* Dr. Balazs Trencsenyi, Head, 36 1 327-3022, Fax: 36-1-327-3191, E-mail: history@ceu.edu. *Application contact:* Agnes Bendik, Coordinator, 361-327-3000 Ext. 2591, Fax: 361-235-6145, E-mail: history@ceu.edu.
Website: http://history.ceu.edu/

Central Michigan University, College of Graduate Studies, College of Humanities and Social and Behavioral Sciences, Department of History, Mount Pleasant, MI 48859. Offers European history (Graduate Certificate); history (MA); modern history (Graduate Certificate); United States history (Graduate Certificate); MA/PhD. *Program availability:* Part-time. *Degree requirements:* For master's, thesis or alternative. Electronic applications accepted. *Faculty research:* Colonial and revolutionary United States history, modern European history, Latin American and transatlantic history, transnational and comparative history, United States social history.

Central Washington University, School of Graduate Studies and Research, College of Arts and Humanities, Department of History, Ellensburg, WA 98926. Offers MA. *Entrance requirements:* For master's, GRE General Test, minimum GPA of 3.0, writing sample. Additional exam requirements/recommendations for international students: Required—TOEFL (minimum score 550 paper-based; 79 iBT). *Application deadline:* For fall admission, 2/1 priority date for domestic students; for winter admission, 10/1 for domestic students; for spring admission, 1/1 for domestic students. Application fee: $50. Electronic applications accepted. *Financial support:* Application deadline: 3/1; applicants required to submit FAFSA. *Unit head:* Dr. Jason Knirk, Chair, 509-963-2422, E-mail: jason.knirk@cwu.edu. *Application contact:* Justine Eason, Admissions Program Coordinator, 509-963-3103, Fax: 509-963-1799, E-mail: masters@cwu.edu.

Centro de Estudios Avanzados de Puerto Rico y el Caribe, Graduate Program in Puerto Rican and Caribbean Studies, Old San Juan, PR 00902-3970. Offers Puerto Rican and Caribbean history (MA, PhD); Puerto Rican and Caribbean literature (MA, PhD); Puerto Rican studies (MA). *Program availability:* Part-time, evening/weekend. *Degree requirements:* For master's, comprehensive exam, thesis; for doctorate, 2 foreign languages, comprehensive exam, thesis/dissertation. *Entrance requirements:* For master's and doctorate, interview. *Faculty research:* Literature, history, art, folklore, and culture of Puerto Rico and Caribbean countries.

Chicago State University, School of Graduate and Professional Studies, College of Arts and Sciences, Department of Geography, Sociology, History, African-American Studies and Anthropology, Chicago, IL 60628. Offers geographic information systems (MA); history (MA). *Entrance requirements:* For master's, minimum GPA of 3.0. *Application deadline:* For fall admission, 3/15 for domestic students; for spring admission, 10/15 for domestic students. Application fee: $30. *Unit head:* Dr. Arthur Redman, Chair, 773-995-2186, Fax: 773-995-2030. *Application contact:* Anika Miller, Graduate Studies Office, 773-995-2404, E-mail: g-studies1@csu.edu.
Website: http://www.csu.edu/gsea/

The Citadel, The Military College of South Carolina, Citadel Graduate College, School of Humanities and Social Sciences, Department of History, Charleston, SC 29409. Offers history (MA); history and teaching content (Graduate Certificate). Program offered jointly with The Graduate School of the College of Charleston. *Program availability:* Part-time, evening/weekend. *Degree requirements:* For master's, variable foreign language requirement, thesis optional. *Entrance requirements:* For master's, GRE (minimum verbal score of 152) taken within the last 5 years, minimum undergraduate GPA of 2.5 (3.0 in major); 3 letters of recommendation; evidence of ability to conduct research and present findings; at least 15 hours of history course work; for Graduate Certificate, no more than 2 page letter of intent that answers specific questions listed on the Department of History website and academic course catalog; 3 references familiar with work; baccalaureate degree in specified fields. Additional exam requirements/recommendations for international students: Required—TOEFL (minimum score 550 paper-based). Electronic applications accepted. *Expenses:* Tuition, state resident: part-time $587 per credit hour. Tuition, nonresident: part-time $988 per credit hour. *Required fees:* $90 per term.

City College of the City University of New York, Graduate School, Division of Humanities and the Arts, Department of History, New York, NY 10031-9198. Offers MA. *Program availability:* Part-time. *Degree requirements:* For master's, one foreign language, comprehensive exam, thesis. *Entrance requirements:* Additional exam requirements/recommendations for international students: Required—TOEFL (minimum score 600 paper-based; 100 iBT). Electronic applications accepted. *Faculty research:* Latin American, European, Asian, urban, and architectural history.

Claremont Graduate University, Graduate Programs, School of Arts and Humanities, Department of History, Claremont, CA 91711-6160. Offers Africana history (Certificate); American studies and U.S. history (MA, PhD); archival studies (MA); early modern studies (MA, PhD); European studies (MA, PhD); oral history (MA, PhD); MBA/MA; MBA/PhD. Terminal master's awarded for partial completion of doctoral program. *Entrance requirements:* For master's and doctorate, GRE General Test. Additional exam requirements/recommendations for international students: Required—TOEFL (minimum score 75 iBT). Electronic applications accepted. *Faculty research:* Intellectual and social history, cultural studies, gender studies, Western history, Chicano history.

History

Clark University, Graduate School, Department of History, Program in United States and Atlantic History, Worcester, MA 01610-1477. Offers history of the Atlantic world (PhD); history of the United States (PhD). *Students:* 14 full-time (4 women), 1 international. Average age 36. 14 applicants, 43% accepted, 6 enrolled. In 2017, 1 doctorate awarded. *Application deadline:* For fall admission, 1/15 for domestic students. Application fee: $75. *Financial support:* Fellowships, research assistantships, and teaching assistantships available. *Faculty research:* American political history, comparative history, American family history. *Unit head:* Dr. Nina Kushner, Professor, 508-421-3797, E-mail: nkushner@clarku.edu. *Application contact:* Diane Fenner, Department Assistant, 508-793-7288, Fax: 508-793-8816, E-mail: dfenner@clarku.edu.

Clayton State University, School of Graduate Studies, College of Arts and Sciences, Program in Education, Morrow, GA 30260-0285. Offers biology (MAT); English (MAT); history (MAT); mathematics (MAT). *Accreditation:* NCATE. *Entrance requirements:* For master's, GRE, GACE, 2 official copies of transcripts, 3 recommendation letters, statement of purpose. Additional exam requirements/recommendations for international students: Required—TOEFL (minimum score 550 paper-based). Electronic applications accepted.

Clemson University, Graduate School, College of Architecture, Arts, and Humanities, Department of History, Clemson, SC 29634. Offers MA. *Program availability:* Part-time. *Faculty:* 25 full-time (10 women). *Students:* 28 full-time (16 women), 8 part-time (4 women); includes 6 minority (2 Black or African American, non-Hispanic/Latino; 4 Hispanic/Latino). Average age 30. 18 applicants, 72% accepted, 5 enrolled. In 2017, 12 master's awarded. *Degree requirements:* For master's, one foreign language, thesis. *Entrance requirements:* For master's, GRE General Test, unofficial transcripts, letters of recommendation, personal statement, sample term paper. Additional exam requirements/recommendations for international students: Required—TOEFL (minimum score 80 iBT), IELTS (minimum score 6.5). *Application deadline:* For fall admission, 1/20 priority date for domestic and international students. Application fee: $80 ($90 for international students). Electronic applications accepted. *Expenses:* $5,767 per semester full-time resident, $10,918 per semester full-time non-resident, $656 per credit hour part-time resident, $1,310 per credit hour part-time non-resident, $915 per credit hour online; other fees may apply per session. *Financial support:* In 2017–18, 9 students received support. Unspecified assistantships available. Financial award application deadline: 1/20. *Faculty research:* U.S., U.S. South, British and European history. *Total annual research expenditures:* $35,625. *Unit head:* Dr. James Burns, Department Chair, 864-656-3153, E-mail: burnsj@clemson.edu. *Application contact:* Dr. Paul Anderson, Graduate Program Coordinator, 864-656-3153, E-mail: pcander@clemson.edu.
Website: https://www.clemson.edu/caah/departments/history/

Cleveland State University, College of Graduate Studies, College of Liberal Arts and Social Sciences, Department of History, Cleveland, OH 44115. Offers art history (MA); museum studies (MA). *Program availability:* Part-time, evening/weekend. *Faculty:* 13 full-time (4 women). *Students:* 12 full-time (8 women), 8 part-time (3 women). Average age 30. 21 applicants, 90% accepted, 6 enrolled. In 2017, 8 master's awarded. *Entrance requirements:* For master's, minimum GPA of 3.0, bachelor's degree in history (or related field for art history). Additional exam requirements/recommendations for international students: Required—TOEFL (minimum score 550 paper-based; 78 iBT). *Application deadline:* Applications are processed on a rolling basis. Application fee: $40. Electronic applications accepted. *Financial support:* In 2017–18, 7 students received support. Research assistantships, career-related internships or fieldwork, tuition waivers (full and partial), and unspecified assistantships available. Financial award application deadline: 4/15. *Faculty research:* Africa and African diaspora, European history, Middle Eastern history, Latin American/Caribbean history, American history, gender and sexuality. *Unit head:* Dr. Elizabeth A. Lehfeldt, Chairperson, 216-687-3920, Fax: 216-687-5592, E-mail: e.lehfeldt@csuohio.edu. *Application contact:* Dr. Karen Sotiropoulos, Graduate Director, 216-687-3940, E-mail: r.s.shelton@csuohio.edu.
Website: http://www.csuohio.edu/history/

The College at Brockport, State University of New York, School of Arts and Sciences, Department of History, Brockport, NY 14420-2997. Offers history (MA), including American and world history, American history, American public history, world history. *Program availability:* Part-time, evening/weekend. *Faculty:* 9 full-time (5 women). *Students:* 15 full-time (5 women), 19 part-time (10 women); includes 1 minority (Black or African American, non-Hispanic/Latino). 20 applicants, 75% accepted, 10 enrolled. In 2017, 10 master's awarded. *Degree requirements:* For master's, thesis or alternative. *Entrance requirements:* For master's, minimum GPA of 3.0, writing sample, letters of recommendation, statement of objectives. Additional exam requirements/recommendations for international students: Required—TOEFL (minimum score 550 paper-based; 79 iBT), IELTS (minimum score 6.5). *Application deadline:* For fall admission, 7/1 priority date for domestic and international students; for spring admission, 11/15 priority date for domestic and international students; for summer admission, 4/15 for domestic and international students. Application fee: $50. Electronic applications accepted. *Expenses:* Tuition, state resident: full-time $10,870; part-time $453 per credit hour. Tuition, nonresident: full-time $22,210. *Required fees:* $988; $246 per semester. *Financial support:* In 2017–18, 1 fellowship with tuition reimbursement (averaging $3,750 per year), 2 teaching assistantships with full tuition reimbursements (averaging $6,000 per year) were awarded; Federal Work-Study, scholarships/grants, and unspecified assistantships also available. Support available to part-time students. Financial award application deadline: 3/15; financial award applicants required to submit FAFSA. *Faculty research:* American history, women's history, European history, world history, cultural history. *Unit head:* Dr. Owen Steve Ireland, Chairperson, 585-395-5627, Fax: 585-395-2620, E-mail: oireland@brockport.edu. *Application contact:* Dr. Morag Martin, Graduate Director, 585-395-5690, Fax: 585-395-2620, E-mail: mmartin@brockport.edu.
Website: https://www.brockport.edu/academics/history/graduate/masters.html

College of Charleston, Graduate School, School of Humanities and Social Sciences, Program in History, Charleston, SC 29424-0001. Offers MA. Program offered jointly with The Citadel, The Military College of South Carolina. *Program availability:* Part-time, evening/weekend. *Degree requirements:* For master's, comprehensive exam, thesis optional. *Entrance requirements:* For master's, GRE General Test or MAT, writing sample. Additional exam requirements/recommendations for international students: Required—TOEFL (minimum score 81 iBT). Electronic applications accepted. *Faculty research:* Modern West Africa, labor history, Southern women's' education, Native Americans, the Atlantic world.

College of Staten Island of the City University of New York, Graduate Programs, Division of Humanities and Social Sciences, Program in History, Staten Island, NY 10314-6600. Offers history (MA), including Africa and the Middle East, Asia, Europe, Latin America and the Caribbean, United States. *Program availability:* Part-time, evening/weekend. *Faculty:* 2 full-time (1 woman). *Students:* 18. 19 applicants, 79% accepted, 11 enrolled. In 2017, 3 master's awarded. *Degree requirements:* For master's, comprehensive exam (for some programs), 32 credits (total of eight courses); thesis or portfolio. *Entrance requirements:* For master's, bachelor's degree with minimum GPA of 3.0 overall and in undergraduate history courses, two letters of recommendation, letter of interest, research-based writing sample. Additional exam requirements/

recommendations for international students: Required—TOEFL (minimum score 550 paper-based; 79 iBT), IELTS (minimum score 6.5). *Application deadline:* For fall admission, 5/10 priority date for domestic and international students; for spring admission, 12/2 priority date for domestic and international students. Applications are processed on a rolling basis. Application fee: $125. Electronic applications accepted. *Expenses:* Tuition, state resident: full-time $10,450; part-time $440 per credit. Tuition, nonresident: full-time $19,320; part-time $440 per credit. *Required fees:* $181.10 per semester. Tuition and fees vary according to program. *Faculty research:* African and African diaspora history, South Asian history, Middle Eastern history, U.S. history, environmental history. *Unit head:* Dr. John Dixon, Graduate Program Coordinator, 718-982-3307, E-mail: john.dixon@csi.cuny.edu. *Application contact:* Sasha Spence, Associate Director for Graduate Admissions, 718-982-2019, Fax: 718-982-2500, E-mail: sasha.spence@csi.cuny.edu.
Website: https://www.csi.cuny.edu/sites/default/files/pdf/admissions/grad/pdf/History%20Fact%20Sheet.pdf

College of Staten Island of the City University of New York, Graduate Programs, School of Education, Program in Adolescence Education, Staten Island, NY 10314-6600. Offers adolescence education (MS Ed), including biology, English, mathematics, social studies. *Program availability:* Part-time, evening/weekend. *Faculty:* 23 full-time, 6 part-time/adjunct. *Students:* 87. 45 applicants, 67% accepted, 23 enrolled. In 2017, 21 master's awarded. *Degree requirements:* For master's, thesis, educational research project supervised by faculty. *Entrance requirements:* For master's, GRE General Test or an approved equivalent examination, relevant bachelor's degree, minimum overall GPA of 3.0, two letters of recommendation, one- or two-page personal statement. Additional exam requirements/recommendations for international students: Required—TOEFL (minimum score 550 paper-based; 79 iBT), IELTS (minimum score 6.5). *Application deadline:* For fall admission, 4/25 for domestic and international students; for spring admission, 11/25 for domestic and international students. Applications are processed on a rolling basis. Application fee: $125. Electronic applications accepted. *Expenses:* Tuition, state resident: full-time $10,450; part-time $440 per credit. Tuition, nonresident: full-time $19,320; part-time $440 per credit. *Required fees:* $181.10 per semester. Tuition and fees vary according to program. *Faculty research:* Development and assessment of TPACK (technological pedagogical content knowledge), technology and differentiation in stem classrooms, teacher effectiveness and student achievement, teacher knowledge, knowledge transfer from college to classroom. *Unit head:* Diane Brescia, 718-982-3877, E-mail: diane.brescia@csi.cuny.edu. *Application contact:* Sasha Spence, Associate Director for Graduate Admissions, 718-982-2019, Fax: 718-982-2500, E-mail: sasha.spence@csi.cuny.edu.
Website: http://www.csi.cuny.edu/catalog/graduate/graduate-programs-in-education.htm#o2608

The College of William and Mary, Faculty of Arts and Sciences, Lyon Gardiner Tyler Department of History, Williamsburg, VA 23187-8795. Offers MA, PhD. *Faculty:* 37 full-time (15 women), 2 part-time/adjunct (1 woman). *Students:* 51 full-time (29 women); includes 4 minority (1 Black or African American, non-Hispanic/Latino; 1 Hispanic/Latino; 2 Two or more races, non-Hispanic/Latino), 3 international. Average age 27. 103 applicants, 25% accepted, 18 enrolled. In 2017, 16 master's, 9 doctorates awarded. Terminal master's awarded for partial completion of doctoral program. *Degree requirements:* For master's, one foreign language, comprehensive exam, thesis; for doctorate, one foreign language, comprehensive exam, thesis/dissertation. *Entrance requirements:* For master's and doctorate, GRE General Test, minimum GPA of 3.0. Additional exam requirements/recommendations for international students: Required—TOEFL. *Application deadline:* For fall admission, 12/5 for domestic and international students. Application fee: $50. Electronic applications accepted. *Financial support:* In 2017–18, 32 students received support, including 3 fellowships with full tuition reimbursements available (averaging $25,000 per year), 18 research assistantships with full tuition reimbursements available (averaging $22,800 per year), 9 teaching assistantships with full tuition reimbursements available (averaging $22,800 per year); career-related internships or fieldwork also available. Financial award application deadline: 12/5; financial award applicants required to submit FAFSA. *Faculty research:* Early America and the Atlantic world; comparative and transnational; race and ethnicity; gender and sexuality; imperialism and colonialism. *Total annual research expenditures:* $191,575. *Unit head:* Dr. Frederick Corney, Chair, 757-221-6285, Fax: 757-221-2111, E-mail: fccorn@wm.edu. *Application contact:* Dr. Kathrin Levitan, Director of Graduate Studies, 757-221-3724, Fax: 757-221-2111, E-mail: khlevi@wm.edu.
Website: http://www.wm.edu/as/history/gradprogram/index.php

The College of William and Mary, School of Education, Program in Curriculum and Instruction, Williamsburg, VA 23187-8795. Offers elementary education (MA Ed); English as a second language/bilingual education (MA Ed); gifted education (MA Ed); literacy leadership (MA Ed); math specialist (MA Ed); secondary education (MA Ed), including English, foreign language, math, science, social studies; special education (MA Ed). *Accreditation:* NCATE. *Program availability:* Part-time. *Faculty:* 23 full-time (16 women), 40 part-time/adjunct (32 women). *Students:* 85 full-time (63 women), 16 part-time (15 women); includes 18 minority (5 Black or African American, non-Hispanic/Latino; 4 Asian, non-Hispanic/Latino; 7 Hispanic/Latino; 2 Two or more races, non-Hispanic/Latino), 1 international. Average age 27. 152 applicants, 83% accepted, 90 enrolled. In 2017, 67 master's awarded. *Degree requirements:* For master's, project. *Entrance requirements:* For master's, GRE, MAT, PRAXIS Core Academic Skills for Educators, minimum GPA of 2.5. Additional exam requirements/recommendations for international students: Required—TOEFL (minimum score 100 iBT), IELTS (minimum score 7). *Application deadline:* For fall admission, 1/15 for domestic and international students; for spring admission, 10/1 for domestic and international students. Application fee: $50. Electronic applications accepted. *Expenses:* $9,630 resident full-time, $535 resident part-time per credit hour; $25,920 nonresident full-time, $1,265 nonresident part-time per credit hour; $5,944 full-time fees. *Financial support:* In 2017–18, 35 students received support, including 7 research assistantships (averaging $6,678 per year); scholarships/grants and unspecified assistantships also available. Financial award application deadline: 1/15; financial award applicants required to submit FAFSA. *Faculty research:* Educational technology, professional development and evaluation, inclusive education, rural education, education policy. *Unit head:* Dr. Jeremy D. Stoddard, Department Chair, 757-221-2348, E-mail: jdstod@wm.edu. *Application contact:* Dorothy Smith Osborne, Assistant Dean for Academic Programs and Student Services, 757-221-2317, E-mail: dsosbo@wm.edu.
Website: http://education.wm.edu

Colorado State University, College of Liberal Arts, Department of History, Fort Collins, CO 80523-1776. Offers liberal arts (MA). *Program availability:* Part-time. *Faculty:* 7 full-time (4 women), 1 (woman) part-time/adjunct. *Students:* 23 full-time (13 women), 3 part-time (0 women); includes 1 minority (Hispanic/Latino). Average age 27. 34 applicants, 56% accepted, 11 enrolled. In 2017, 16 master's awarded. *Degree requirements:* For master's, variable foreign language requirement, comprehensive exam, thesis (for some programs). *Entrance requirements:* For master's, GRE, 21 undergraduate credits in history; minimum undergraduate GPA of 3.0; personal statement; 3 letters of reference. Additional exam requirements/recommendations for international students: Required—TOEFL, IELTS. *Application deadline:* For winter admission, 2/1 for domestic and international students. Application fee: $60 ($70 for international students). Electronic

applications accepted. *Expenses:* Tuition, state resident: full-time $9917. Tuition, nonresident: full-time $24,312. *Required fees:* $2284. Tuition and fees vary according to course load and program. *Financial support:* In 2017–18, 22 students received support, including 22 teaching assistantships (averaging $14,256 per year); health care benefits also available. Financial award application deadline: 2/1; financial award applicants required to submit FAFSA. *Faculty research:* Environment, gender, public history, United States West. *Total annual research expenditures:* $303,063. *Unit head:* Dr. Doug Yarrington, Department Chair, 970-491-6801, Fax: 970-491-2941, E-mail: doug.yarrington@colostate.edu. *Application contact:* Nancy Rehe, Administrative Assistant, 970-491-6334, E-mail: nancy.rehe@colostate.edu.
Website: http://history.colostate.edu/

Columbia University, Graduate School of Arts and Sciences, New York, NY 10027. Offers African-American studies (MA); American studies (MA); anthropology (MA, PhD); art history and archaeology (MA, PhD); astronomy (PhD); biological sciences (PhD); biotechnology (MA); chemical physics (PhD); chemistry (PhD); classical studies (MA, PhD); classics (MA, PhD); climate and society (MA); conservation biology (MA); earth and environmental sciences (PhD); East Asia: regional studies (MA); East Asian languages and cultures (MA, PhD); ecology, evolution and environmental biology (MA), including conservation biology; ecology, evolution, and environmental biology (PhD), including ecology and evolutionary biology, evolutionary primatology; economics (MA, PhD); English and comparative literature (MA, PhD); French and Romance philology (MA, PhD); Germanic languages (MA, PhD); global French studies (MA); global thought (MA); Hispanic cultural studies (MA); history (PhD); history and literature (MA); human rights studies (MA); Islamic studies (MA); Italian (MA, PhD); Japanese pedagogy (MA); Jewish studies (MA); Latin America and the Caribbean: regional studies (MA); Latin American and Iberian cultures (PhD); mathematics (MA, PhD), including finance (MA); medieval and Renaissance studies (MA); Middle Eastern, South Asian, and African studies (MA, PhD); modern art: critical and curatorial studies (MA); modern European studies (MA); museum anthropology (MA); music (DMA, PhD); oral history (MA); philosophical foundations of physics (MA); philosophy (MA, PhD); physics (PhD); political science (MA, PhD); psychology (PhD); quantitative methods in the social sciences (MA); religion (MA, PhD); Russia, Eurasia and East Europe: regional studies (MA); Russian translation (MA); Slavic cultures (MA); Slavic languages (MA, PhD); sociology (MA, PhD); South Asian studies (MA); statistics (MA, PhD); theatre (PhD). Dual-degree programs require admission to both Graduate School of Arts and Sciences and another Columbia school. *Program availability:* Part-time. Terminal master's awarded for partial completion of doctoral program. *Degree requirements:* For master's, variable foreign language requirement, comprehensive exam (for some programs), thesis (for some programs); for doctorate, variable foreign language requirement, comprehensive exam (for some programs), thesis/dissertation. *Entrance requirements:* For master's and doctorate, GRE General Test, GRE Subject Test (for some programs). Additional exam requirements/recommendations for international students: Required—TOEFL, IELTS. Electronic applications accepted. *Expenses: Tuition:* Full-time $44,864; part-time $1704 per credit. *Required fees:* $2370 per semester. One-time fee: $105.

Columbus State University, Graduate Studies, College of Education and Health Professions, Department of Teacher Education, Columbus, GA 31907-5645. Offers curriculum and instruction in accomplished teaching (M Ed); early childhood education (M Ed, MAT, Ed S); middle grades education (M Ed, MAT, Ed S); secondary education (M Ed, MAT, Ed S), including biology (MAT), chemistry (MAT), earth and space science (MAT), English/language arts, general science (M Ed), history (MAT), mathematics, science (Ed S), social science (M Ed, Ed S); special education (M Ed, MAT, Ed S), including general curriculum (M Ed, MAT); teacher leadership (M Ed). *Accreditation:* NCATE. *Program availability:* Part-time, evening/weekend, 100% online, blended/hybrid learning. *Faculty:* 19 full-time (12 women), 24 part-time/adjunct (18 women). *Students:* 99 full-time (76 women), 181 part-time (143 women); includes 109 minority (94 Black or African American, non-Hispanic/Latino; 1 American Indian or Alaska Native, non-Hispanic/Latino; 1 Asian, non-Hispanic/Latino; 6 Hispanic/Latino; 7 Two or more races, non-Hispanic/Latino). Average age 34. 136 applicants, 63% accepted, 56 enrolled. In 2017, 119 master's, 8 other advanced degrees awarded. *Degree requirements:* For Ed S, thesis or alternative. *Entrance requirements:* For master's, GRE General Test, minimum undergraduate GPA of 2.75; for Ed S, GRE General Test, minimum undergraduate GPA of 2.75, graduate 3.0. Additional exam requirements/recommendations for international students: Required—TOEFL (minimum score 550 paper-based; 79 iBT). *Application deadline:* For fall admission, 6/30 for domestic students, 5/1 for international students; for spring admission, 11/1 for domestic and international students; for summer admission, 3/1 for domestic and international students. Applications are processed on a rolling basis. Application fee: $50. Electronic applications accepted. *Expenses:* Tuition, state resident: full-time $3708; part-time $2472 per year. Tuition, nonresident: full-time $14,418; part-time $9612 per year. *International tuition:* $19,218 full-time. *Required fees:* $1605. Tuition and fees vary according to program. *Financial support:* In 2017–18, 45 students received support, including 9 research assistantships with partial tuition reimbursements available (averaging $3,000 per year); career-related internships or fieldwork, Federal Work-Study, institutionally sponsored loans, scholarships/grants, tuition waivers (partial), and unspecified assistantships also available. Support available to part-time students. Financial award application deadline: 5/1; financial award applicants required to submit FAFSA. *Unit head:* Dr. Jan Burcham, Department Chair, 706-507-8519, Fax: 706-568-3134, E-mail: burcham_jan@columbusstate.edu. *Application contact:* Catrina Smith-Edmond, Assistant Director for Graduate and Global Admission, 706-507-8824, Fax: 706-568-5091, E-mail: smithedmond_catrina@columbusstate.edu.
Website: http://te.columbusstate.edu/

Columbus State University, Graduate Studies, College of Letters and Sciences, Department of History and Geography, Columbus, GA 31907-5645. Offers history (MA), including race, ethnicity and society. *Program availability:* Evening/weekend. *Faculty:* 2 full-time (1 woman). *Students:* 4 part-time (3 women); includes 2 minority (1 Black or African American, non-Hispanic/Latino; 1 American Indian or Alaska Native, non-Hispanic/Latino). Average age 34. 3 applicants, 100% accepted, 2 enrolled. In 2017, 2 master's awarded. *Degree requirements:* For master's, thesis. *Entrance requirements:* For master's, GRE, minimum GPA of 3.0, writing sample, statement of purpose, two letters of recommendation. Additional exam requirements/recommendations for international students: Required—TOEFL (minimum score 550 paper-based; 79 iBT). *Application deadline:* For fall admission, 6/30 for domestic students, 5/1 for international students; for spring admission, 11/1 for domestic and international students; for summer admission, 3/1 for domestic and international students. Applications are processed on a rolling basis. Application fee: $50. Electronic applications accepted. *Expenses:* Tuition, state resident: full-time $3708; part-time $2472 per year. Tuition, nonresident: full-time $14,418; part-time $9612 per year. *International tuition:* $19,218 full-time. *Required fees:* $1605. Tuition and fees vary according to program. *Financial support:* In 2017–18, 1 student received support. Research assistantships, teaching assistantships, tuition waivers (partial), and unspecified assistantships available. Financial award application deadline: 5/1; financial award applicants required to submit FAFSA. *Unit head:* Dr. Doug Tompson, Department Chair, 706-507-8356, E-mail: tompson_doug@columbusstate.edu. *Application contact:* Catrina Smith-Edmond, Assistant Director for Graduate and Global Admission, 706-507-8824, Fax: 706-568-5091, E-mail: smithedmond_catrina@columbusstate.edu.
Website: http://history.columbusstate.edu/

Concordia University, School of Graduate Studies, Faculty of Arts and Science, Department of History, Montréal, QC H3G 1M8, Canada. Offers MA, PhD. *Degree requirements:* For master's, one foreign language, thesis optional; for doctorate, one foreign language, comprehensive exam, thesis/dissertation. *Entrance requirements:* For master's, honors degree in history or equivalent. *Faculty research:* Canadian history, European social history, Canadian-American relations.

Converse College, Program in Liberal Arts, Spartanburg, SC 29302. Offers English (MLA); history (MLA); political science (MLA). *Degree requirements:* For master's, capstone paper. *Entrance requirements:* For master's, minimum GPA of 3.0, 2 recommendations. *Application deadline:* For fall admission, 5/1 priority date for domestic students; for spring admission, 1/30 for domestic students. Application fee: $40. *Unit head:* Lienne Medford, Dean of Graduate Studies and Distance Education, 864-596-9082, E-mail: lienne.medford@converse.edu.

Cornell University, Graduate School, Graduate Fields of Arts and Sciences, Field of History, Ithaca, NY 14853. Offers African history (MA, PhD); American history (MA, PhD); ancient Greek history (PhD); ancient history (MA, PhD); ancient Roman history (PhD); early modern European history (MA, PhD); English history (MA, PhD); French history (MA, PhD); German history (MA, PhD); history of science (MA, PhD); Korean history (PhD); Latin American history (MA, PhD); medieval Chinese history (MA, PhD); medieval history (MA, PhD); modern Chinese history (MA, PhD); modern European history (MA, PhD); modern Japanese history (MA, PhD); modern Middle Eastern history (PhD); premodern Islamic history (MA, PhD); premodern Japanese history (MA, PhD); Renaissance history (MA, PhD); Russian history (MA, PhD); South Asian history (PhD); Southeast Asian history (MA, PhD). Terminal master's awarded for partial completion of doctoral program. *Degree requirements:* For master's, thesis; for doctorate, 2 foreign languages, comprehensive exam, thesis/dissertation, 1 year of teaching experience. *Entrance requirements:* For master's and doctorate, GRE General Test, writing sample, 3 letters of recommendation. Additional exam requirements/recommendations for international students: Required—TOEFL (minimum score 550 paper-based; 77 iBT). Electronic applications accepted.

Dalhousie University, Faculty of Arts and Social Science, Department of History, Halifax, NS B3H 4R2, Canada. Offers MA, PhD. *Entrance requirements:* Additional exam requirements/recommendations for international students: Required—TOEFL, IELTS, CANTEST, CAEL, or Michigan English Language Assessment Battery. Electronic applications accepted. *Faculty research:* African, British, Russian, Canadian and medieval history.

DePaul University, College of Liberal Arts and Social Sciences, Chicago, IL 60614. Offers Arabic (MA); Chinese (MA); critical ethnic studies (MA); English (MA); French (MA); German (MA); history (MA); interdisciplinary studies (MA, MS); international public service (MS); international studies (MA); Italian (MA); Japanese (MA); liberal studies (MA); nonprofit management (MNM); public administration (MPA); public health (MPH); public policy (MPP); public service management (MS); refugee and forced migration studies (MS); social work (MSW); sociology (MA); Spanish (MA); sustainable urban development (MA); women's and gender studies (MA); writing and publishing (MA); writing, rhetoric and discourse (MA); MA/PhD. *Program availability:* Part-time, evening/weekend, online learning. Terminal master's awarded for partial completion of doctoral program. *Degree requirements:* For master's, variable foreign language requirement, comprehensive exam (for some programs), thesis (for some programs). *Application deadline:* Applications are processed on a rolling basis. Application fee: $40. Electronic applications accepted. *Financial support:* Applicants required to submit FAFSA. *Unit head:* Dr. Guillermo Vasquez de Velasco, Dean, 773-325-7305. *Application contact:* Ann Spittle, Director of Graduate Admission, 773-325-8369, Fax: 312-476-3244, E-mail: graddepaul@depaul.edu.
Website: http://las.depaul.edu/

Dominican University of California, School of Liberal Arts and Education, Humanities Program, San Rafael, CA 94901-2298. Offers applied music (MA); art history (MA); creative writing (MA); gender studies (MA); history (MA); philosophy (MA); political theory (MA); religion (MA). *Program availability:* Part-time. *Faculty:* 7 full-time (4 women), 1 (woman) part-time/adjunct. *Students:* 6 full-time (5 women), 16 part-time (12 women); includes 8 minority (3 Black or African American, non-Hispanic/Latino; 4 Hispanic/Latino; 1 Two or more races, non-Hispanic/Latino), 2 international. Average age 45. 7 applicants, 100% accepted, 5 enrolled. In 2017, 14 master's awarded. *Degree requirements:* For master's, thesis or alternative. *Entrance requirements:* For master's, minimum GPA of 3.0, interview. Additional exam requirements/recommendations for international students: Required—TOEFL (minimum score 550 paper-based; 80 iBT), IELTS (minimum score 6.5). *Application deadline:* For fall admission, 5/15 priority date for domestic and international students; for spring admission, 11/15 priority date for domestic and international students. Applications are processed on a rolling basis. Application fee: $0. Electronic applications accepted. *Expenses: Tuition:* Full-time $17,370; part-time $965 per credit. *Required fees:* $150 per semester. Tuition and fees vary according to course load and program. *Financial support:* In 2017–18, 4 students received support. Scholarships/grants available. Support available to part-time students. Financial award application deadline: 3/2; financial award applicants required to submit FAFSA. *Unit head:* Joan Baranow, Program Director, 415-485-3264, E-mail: joan.baranow@dominican.edu. *Application contact:* Michael Lavigna, Assistant Director of Graduate Admissions, 415-485-3253, Fax: 415-485-3214, E-mail: gradmissions@dominican.edu.
Website: https://www.dominican.edu/academics/lae/graduate-programs/ma-in-humanities/index_html

Drew University, Caspersen School of Graduate Studies, Madison, NJ 07940-1493. Offers conflict resolution and leadership (Certificate), including community leadership, moderation, peace building; education (M Ed); finance (MA); history and culture (MA, PhD), including American history, book history, British history, European history, Holocaust and genocide (M Litt, MA, D Litt, PhD), intellectual history, Irish history, print culture, public history; K-12 education (MAT), including art, biology, chemistry, elementary education, English, French, Italian, math, secondary education, special education, teacher of students with disabilities; liberal studies (M Litt, D Litt), including history, Holocaust and genocide (M Litt, MA, D Litt, PhD), Irish/Irish-American studies, literature (M Litt, MMH, D Litt, DMH, CMH), religion, spirituality, teaching in the two-year college, writing; medical humanities (MMH, DMH, CMH), including arts, health, healthcare, literature (M Litt, MMH, D Litt, DMH, CMH), scientific research; poetry (MFA). *Program availability:* Part-time, evening/weekend. *Faculty:* 4 full-time (2 women), 29 part-time/adjunct (15 women). *Students:* 77 full-time (42 women), 175 part-time (114 women); includes 39 minority (12 Black or African American, non-Hispanic/Latino; 6 Asian, non-Hispanic/Latino; 16 Hispanic/Latino; 5 Two or more races, non-Hispanic/Latino), 11 international. Average age 41. 126 applicants, 75% accepted, 52 enrolled. In 2017, 38 master's, 23 doctorates, 35 other advanced degrees awarded. Terminal master's awarded for partial completion of doctoral program. *Degree requirements:* For master's and other advanced degree, thesis (for some programs); for doctorate, one foreign language, comprehensive exam (for some programs), thesis/dissertation. *Entrance requirements:* For master's, PRAXIS Core and Subject Area tests (for MAT),

GRE/GMAT (for M Fin), resume, transcripts, writing sample, personal statement, letters of recommendation; for doctorate, GRE (PhD in history and culture), resume, transcripts, writing sample, personal statement, letters of recommendation; for other advanced degree, resume, transcripts, personal statement. Additional exam requirements/recommendations for international students: Required—TOEFL (minimum score 587 paper-based; 80 iBT), IELTS (minimum score 6), TWE (minimum score 4). *Application deadline:* For fall admission, 8/1 for domestic students, 6/1 for international students; for spring admission, 12/1 for domestic students, 10/1 for international students. Applications are processed on a rolling basis. Application fee: $35. Electronic applications accepted. *Financial support:* Fellowships, research assistantships, teaching assistantships, career-related internships or fieldwork, Federal Work-Study, scholarships/grants, and unspecified assistantships available. Support available to part-time students. Financial award applicants required to submit FAFSA. *Faculty research:* Irish history and culture, conflict resolution and leadership. *Application contact:* Leanne Horinko, Director of Caspersen Admissions, 973-408-3280, E-mail: gradm@drew.edu. Website: http://www.drew.edu/caspersen

Duke University, Graduate School, Department of History, Durham, NC 27708. Offers history (AM, PhD); Latin American studies (PhD); JD/AM. *Degree requirements:* For doctorate, 2 foreign languages, thesis/dissertation. *Entrance requirements:* For doctorate, GRE General Test. Additional exam requirements/recommendations for international students: Required—TOEFL (minimum score 577 paper-based; 90 iBT) or IELTS (minimum score 7). Electronic applications accepted.

Duquesne University, Graduate School of Liberal Arts, Department of History, Pittsburgh, PA 15282-0001. Offers historical studies (MA); public history (MA). *Program availability:* Part-time, evening/weekend. *Faculty:* 15 full-time (5 women), 5 part-time/adjunct (3 women). *Students:* 34 full-time (21 women), 5 part-time (1 woman); includes 2 minority (1 Black or African American, non-Hispanic/Latino; 1 Two or more races, non-Hispanic/Latino). Average age 26. 22 applicants, 100% accepted, 14 enrolled. In 2017, 13 master's awarded. *Degree requirements:* For master's, comprehensive exam (for some programs), thesis optional. *Entrance requirements:* For master's, GRE General Test, writing sample. Additional exam requirements/recommendations for international students: Required—TOEFL. *Application deadline:* For fall admission, 8/15 for domestic students, 5/1 for international students; for spring admission, 11/1 priority date for domestic students. Applications are processed on a rolling basis. Application fee: $0. Electronic applications accepted. *Expenses:* $1,259 per credit. *Financial support:* In 2017–18, 30 students received support, including 7 teaching assistantships with full tuition reimbursements available (averaging $8,000 per year); career-related internships or fieldwork, Federal Work-Study, scholarships/grants, tuition waivers (full and partial), and unspecified assistantships also available. Support available to part-time students. Financial award application deadline: 5/1. *Faculty research:* American studies, immigration history, local social history, applied history, Eastern European history. *Unit head:* Dr. John Dwyer, Chair, 412-396-6470, E-mail: dwyer@duq.edu. *Application contact:* Linda Rendulic, Assistant to the Dean, 412-396-6400, Fax: 412-396-5265, E-mail: rendulic@duq.edu.
Website: http://www.duq.edu/academics/schools/liberal-arts/graduate-school/programs/history

East Carolina University, Graduate School, Thomas Harriot College of Arts and Sciences, Department of History, Greenville, NC 27858-4353. Offers American history (MA); Atlantic world (MA); European history (MA); maritime studies (MA); military history (MA); public history (MA). *Program availability:* Part-time. *Students:* 39 full-time (16 women), 49 part-time (21 women); includes 11 minority (2 Black or African American, non-Hispanic/Latino; 1 Asian, non-Hispanic/Latino; 5 Hispanic/Latino; 3 Two or more races, non-Hispanic/Latino), 1 international. Average age 29. 35 applicants, 83% accepted, 19 enrolled. In 2017, 15 master's awarded. *Degree requirements:* For master's, one foreign language, comprehensive exam, thesis. *Entrance requirements:* For master's, GRE General Test. Additional exam requirements/recommendations for international students: Recommended—TOEFL (minimum score 78 iBT), IELTS (minimum score 6.5). *Application deadline:* For fall admission, 4/1 priority date for domestic and international students; for spring admission, 10/15 priority date for domestic and international students. Applications are processed on a rolling basis. Application fee: $75. Electronic applications accepted. *Expenses:* Tuition, state resident: full-time $4749; part-time $297 per credit hour. Tuition, nonresident: full-time $17,898; part-time $1119 per credit hour. *Required fees:* $2691; $224 per credit hour. Part-time tuition and fees vary according to course load and program. *Financial support:* Fellowships, research assistantships with partial tuition reimbursements, teaching assistantships with partial tuition reimbursements, and Federal Work-Study available. Support available to part-time students. Financial award application deadline: 1/15. *Unit head:* Dr. Christopher Oakley, Chair, 252-328-1025, E-mail: oakleyc@ecu.edu. *Application contact:* Dean of Graduate School, 252-328-6012, E-mail: gradschool@ecu.edu.
Website: http://www.ecu.edu/cs-cas/history/

Eastern Illinois University, Graduate School, College of Liberal Arts and Sciences, Department of History, Charleston, IL 61920. Offers history (MA). *Program availability:* Part-time, evening/weekend. *Degree requirements:* For master's, comprehensive exam (for some programs), thesis (for some programs). *Entrance requirements:* For master's, GMAT or GRE. Additional exam requirements/recommendations for international students: Required—TOEFL (minimum score 500 paper-based; 61 iBT), IELTS (minimum score 6). *Application deadline:* For fall admission, 5/15 for domestic and international students; for spring admission, 10/15 for domestic and international students. Applications are processed on a rolling basis. Application fee: $30. Electronic applications accepted. *Financial support:* Research assistantships with full tuition reimbursements, career-related internships or fieldwork, Federal Work-Study, and unspecified assistantships available. Support available to part-time students. Financial award application deadline: 3/1; financial award applicants required to submit FAFSA. *Unit head:* Sace E. Elder, Interim Chair, 217-581-6380, Fax: 217-581-7233, E-mail: seelder@eiu.edu. *Application contact:* Lee Patterson, Graduate Coordinator, 217-581-6372, Fax: 217-581-7233, E-mail: lepatterson2@eiu.edu.
Website: http://www.eiu.edu/history/

Eastern Kentucky University, The Graduate School, College of Arts and Sciences, Department of History, Richmond, KY 40475-3102. Offers MA. *Program availability:* Part-time. *Degree requirements:* For master's, comprehensive exam, thesis optional. *Entrance requirements:* For master's, GRE General Test, GRE Subject Test, minimum GPA of 2.5. *Faculty research:* Twentieth-century U.S. history, Kentucky history, British history, world history, Eastern Europe.

Eastern Michigan University, Graduate School, College of Arts and Sciences, Department of History and Philosophy, Program in History, Ypsilanti, MI 48197. Offers MA. *Program availability:* Part-time, evening/weekend, online learning. *Students:* 9 full-time (3 women), 34 part-time (18 women); includes 12 minority (5 Black or African American, non-Hispanic/Latino; 1 Asian, non-Hispanic/Latino; 4 Hispanic/Latino; 2 Two or more races, non-Hispanic/Latino), 1 international. Average age 34. 22 applicants, 91% accepted, 7 enrolled. In 2017, 14 master's awarded. *Degree requirements:* For master's, thesis optional. *Entrance requirements:* Additional exam requirements/recommendations for international students: Required—TOEFL. *Application deadline:* Applications are processed on a rolling basis. Application fee: $45. *Financial support:* Fellowships, research assistantships with full tuition reimbursements, teaching assistantships with full tuition reimbursements, career-related internships or fieldwork, Federal Work-Study, institutionally sponsored loans, scholarships/grants, tuition waivers (partial), and unspecified assistantships available. Support available to part-time students. Financial award applicants required to submit FAFSA. *Application contact:* Dr. Ronald Delph, Director, 734-487-1018, Fax: 734-487-6835, E-mail: rdelph@emich.edu.

Eastern Washington University, Graduate Studies, College of Social Sciences, Department of History, Cheney, WA 99004-2431. Offers MA. *Faculty:* 5. *Students:* 13 full-time (9 women), 1 part-time (0 women); includes 2 minority (both Hispanic/Latino). Average age 30. 10 applicants, 80% accepted, 6 enrolled. In 2017, 6 master's awarded. *Degree requirements:* For master's, comprehensive exam, thesis optional. *Entrance requirements:* For master's, minimum GPA of 3.0. Additional exam requirements/recommendations for international students: Required—TOEFL (minimum score 580 paper-based; 92 iBT), IELTS (minimum score 7), TWE, PTE (minimum score 63). *Application deadline:* For fall admission, 4/1 priority date for domestic students; for spring admission, 1/15 for domestic students. Applications are processed on a rolling basis. Application fee: $50. *Expenses:* Tuition, state resident: full-time $11,191; part-time $373.06 per credit. Tuition, nonresident: full-time $25,995; part-time $866.52 per credit. *Financial support:* In 2017–18, 6 students received support. Teaching assistantships with partial tuition reimbursements available, career-related internships or fieldwork, Federal Work-Study, institutionally sponsored loans, scholarships/grants, health care benefits, tuition waivers (partial), and unspecified assistantships available. Support available to part-time students. Financial award application deadline: 2/1; financial award applicants required to submit FAFSA. *Unit head:* Dr. Liping Zhu, Chair, 509-359-6086, E-mail: lzhu@ewu.edu. *Application contact:* Dr. Michael Conlin, Director of Graduate Programs, 509-359-7851.

East Stroudsburg University of Pennsylvania, Graduate and Extended Studies, College of Arts and Sciences, Department of History and Geography, East Stroudsburg, PA 18301-2999. Offers M Ed, MA. *Program availability:* Part-time, evening/weekend. *Faculty:* 6 full-time (4 women). *Students:* 13 full-time (4 women), 8 part-time (1 woman), 7 international. Average age 30. 15 applicants, 87% accepted, 10 enrolled. In 2017, 6 master's awarded. *Degree requirements:* For master's, comprehensive exam, thesis, thesis defense. *Entrance requirements:* For master's, Commonwealth of Pennsylvania Department of Education certification requirements (M Ed). Additional exam requirements/recommendations for international students: Recommended—TOEFL (minimum score 560 paper-based; 83 iBT), IELTS. *Application deadline:* For fall admission, 7/31 priority date for domestic students, 6/30 priority date for international students; for spring admission, 11/30 for domestic students, 10/31 for international students. Applications are processed on a rolling basis. Application fee: $50. Electronic applications accepted. *Expenses:* Tuition, state resident: full-time $4500; part-time $3000 per credit. Tuition, nonresident: full-time $6750; part-time $4500 per credit. *Required fees:* $2642; $1756 per credit. $878 per semester. Tuition and fees vary according to course load, campus/location and program. *Financial support:* Research assistantships with tuition reimbursements, Federal Work-Study, and unspecified assistantships available. Support available to part-time students. Financial award application deadline: 3/1; financial award applicants required to submit FAFSA. *Unit head:* Martin Wilson, Graduate Coordinator, 570-422-3536, Fax: 570-422-3937, E-mail: mwilson@esu.edu. *Application contact:* Kevin Quintero, Associate Director, Graduate and Extended Studies, 570-422-3890, Fax: 570-422-2711, E-mail: kquintero@esu.edu.

East Tennessee State University, School of Graduate Studies, College of Arts and Sciences, Department of Appalachian Studies, Johnson City, TN 37614. Offers Appalachian communities (MA); Appalachian heritage and culture (MA); Appalachian studies (Postbaccalaureate Certificate). *Program availability:* Part-time. *Degree requirements:* For master's, thesis optional. *Entrance requirements:* For master's, GRE General Test, minimum undergraduate GPA of 3.0, writing sample, 3 letters of recommendation; for Postbaccalaureate Certificate, minimum undergraduate GPA of 3.0, writing sample. Additional exam requirements/recommendations for international students: Required—TOEFL (minimum score 550 paper-based; 79 iBT). *Application deadline:* For fall admission, 6/1 for domestic students, 4/29 for international students; for spring admission, 11/1 for domestic students, 9/30 for international students. Applications are processed on a rolling basis. Application fee: $55 ($65 for international students). Electronic applications accepted. *Financial support:* Research assistantships with full tuition reimbursements, career-related internships or fieldwork, institutionally sponsored loans, scholarships/grants, and unspecified assistantships available. Financial award applicants required to submit FAFSA. *Faculty research:* Appalachian culture, history, literature, art, environmental studies; bluegrass, old time, Celtic, and country music; community development and sustainability. *Unit head:* Dr. Ron Roach, Chair, 423-439-7494, Fax: 423-439-7870. *Application contact:* Dr. Ron Roach, Chair, 423-439-7494, Fax: 423-439-7870.
Website: http://www.etsu.edu/cas/das/

East Tennessee State University, School of Graduate Studies, College of Arts and Sciences, Department of History, Johnson City, TN 37614. Offers MA. *Program availability:* Part-time, evening/weekend. *Degree requirements:* For master's, comprehensive exam, thesis optional. *Entrance requirements:* For master's, bachelor's degree in history, minimum GPA of 3.0, three letters of recommendation, minimum of 27 credit hours of study in history. Additional exam requirements/recommendations for international students: Required—TOEFL (minimum score 550 paper-based; 79 iBT). *Application deadline:* For fall admission, 3/1 for domestic students, 1/29 for international students; for spring admission, 11/1 for domestic students, 9/29 for international students. Application fee: $55 ($65 for international students). Electronic applications accepted. *Financial support:* Research assistantships with full tuition reimbursements, teaching assistantships with full tuition reimbursements, career-related internships or fieldwork, institutionally sponsored loans, scholarships/grants, and unspecified assistantships available. Financial award application deadline: 7/1; financial award applicants required to submit FAFSA. *Faculty research:* Post-World War II German occupation, biographies of Eleanor Copenhaver Anderson and Harry M. Candill, the Miss America Pageant, encyclopedia of colonialism, the new Georgia campaign in the Pacific war. *Unit head:* Dr. William Douglas Burgess, Jr., Chair, 423-439-6691, Fax: 423-439-5373, E-mail: burgessw@etsu.edu. *Application contact:* Dr. William Douglas Burgess, Jr., Chair, 423-439-6691, Fax: 423-439-5373, E-mail: burgessw@etsu.edu.
Website: http://www.etsu.edu/cas/history/

Edinboro University of Pennsylvania, Department of History, Politics, Languages and Cultures, Edinboro, PA 16444. Offers social sciences (MA), including anthropology, history. *Program availability:* Part-time, evening/weekend. *Degree requirements:* For master's, thesis or alternative, competency exam. *Entrance requirements:* For master's, GRE or MAT, minimum QPA of 2.5. Electronic applications accepted.

Emory & Henry College, Graduate Programs, Emory, VA 24327. Offers American history (MA Ed); education professional studies (M Ed); occupational therapy (MOT); organizational leadership (MCOL); physical therapy (DPT); physician assistant studies (MPAS); reading specialist (MA Ed). *Program availability:* Part-time. *Faculty:* 7 full-time (3 women). *Students:* 194 full-time (128 women), 4 part-time (2 women); includes 6 minority (2 Black or African American, non-Hispanic/Latino; 1 American Indian or Alaska

Native, non-Hispanic/Latino; 1 Asian, non-Hispanic/Latino; 2 Hispanic/Latino). Average age 25. 525 applicants, 21% accepted, 74 enrolled. In 2017, 24 master's awarded. *Degree requirements:* For master's, thesis optional; for doctorate, thesis/dissertation optional. *Entrance requirements:* For master's, GRE or PRAXIS I, official transcripts from all colleges previously attended, three professional recommendations, essay. Additional exam requirements/recommendations for international students: Recommended—TOEFL, IELTS (minimum score 6). *Application deadline:* Applications are processed on a rolling basis. Electronic applications accepted. *Expenses:* Contact institution. *Financial support:* Application deadline: 10/15; applicants required to submit FAFSA. *Unit head:* Dr. Michael Puglisi, Associate Dean for Academic Affairs, 276-944-6662, E-mail: mpuglisi@ehc.edu. *Application contact:* Mary Bolt, Director of Transfer and Graduate Admission, 276-944-6135, E-mail: mbolt@ehc.edu.

Emory University, Laney Graduate School, Department of History, Atlanta, GA 30322-1100. Offers PhD. *Degree requirements:* For doctorate, 2 foreign languages, comprehensive exam, thesis/dissertation. *Entrance requirements:* For doctorate, GRE General Test, minimum GPA of 3.0. Additional exam requirements/recommendations for international students: Recommended—TOEFL. Electronic applications accepted. *Faculty research:* United States, modern Europe, early modern Europe, medieval Europe, Latin America, Africa.

Emporia State University, Program in History, Emporia, KS 66801-5415. Offers American history (MA); world history (MA). *Program availability:* Part-time. *Faculty:* 13 full-time (6 women), 1 part-time/adjunct (0 women). *Students:* 5 full-time (0 women), 23 part-time (11 women); includes 2 minority (1 Black or African American, non-Hispanic/Latino; 1 Two or more races, non-Hispanic/Latino). 9 applicants, 100% accepted, 9 enrolled. In 2017, 8 master's awarded. *Degree requirements:* For master's, comprehensive exam or thesis. *Entrance requirements:* For master's, 12 credit hours in history, minimum undergraduate GPA of 2.5, writing sample. Additional exam requirements/recommendations for international students: Required—TOEFL (minimum score 520 paper-based; 68 iBT). *Application deadline:* For fall admission, 8/15 priority date for domestic students. Applications are processed on a rolling basis. Application fee: $30 ($75 for international students). Electronic applications accepted. *Expenses:* Tuition, state resident: full-time $6084; part-time $253.50 per credit hour. Tuition, nonresident: full-time $18,924; part-time $788.50 per credit hour. *Required fees:* $1943; $80.95 per credit hour. Tuition and fees vary according to campus/location. *Financial support:* In 2017–18, 1 research assistantship with full tuition reimbursement (averaging $7,344 per year), 4 teaching assistantships with full tuition reimbursements (averaging $6,426 per year) were awarded; Federal Work-Study, institutionally sponsored loans, health care benefits, and unspecified assistantships also available. Financial award application deadline: 3/15; financial award applicants required to submit FAFSA. *Faculty research:* Great Plains history. *Unit head:* Dr. Michael Smith, Chair, 620-341-5566, E-mail: msmith3@emporia.edu.

Fairleigh Dickinson University, Metropolitan Campus, University College: Arts, Sciences, and Professional Studies, School of History, Political and International Studies, Program in History, Teaneck, NJ 07666-1914. Offers MA.

Fitchburg State University, Division of Graduate and Continuing Education, Program in Middle School Education, Fitchburg, MA 01420-2697. Offers English (M Ed); general science (M Ed); history (M Ed); math (M Ed). *Accreditation:* NCATE. *Program availability:* Part-time, evening/weekend. *Students:* 15 full-time (7 women), 5 part-time (2 women); includes 3 minority (2 Black or African American, non-Hispanic/Latino; 1 Two or more races, non-Hispanic/Latino). Average age 32. 11 applicants, 100% accepted, 10 enrolled. In 2017, 4 master's awarded. *Entrance requirements:* Additional exam requirements/recommendations for international students: Required—TOEFL (minimum score 550 paper-based; 79 iBT). *Application deadline:* For fall admission, 7/15 for international students; for spring admission, 12/1 for international students. Applications are processed on a rolling basis. Application fee: $50. Electronic applications accepted. *Expenses:* Contact institution. *Financial support:* In 2017–18, research assistantships with partial tuition reimbursements (averaging $5,500 per year) were awarded; Federal Work-Study, scholarships/grants, and unspecified assistantships also available. Support available to part-time students. Financial award application deadline: 3/1; financial award applicants required to submit FAFSA. *Unit head:* William Cortezia, Chair, 978-665-3193, Fax: 978-665-3658, E-mail: gce@fitchburgstate.edu. *Application contact:* Jinawa McNeil, Director of Admissions, 978-665-3140, Fax: 978-665-4540, E-mail: admissions@fitchburgstate.edu.
Website: http://www.fitchburgstate.edu

Fitchburg State University, Division of Graduate and Continuing Education, Programs in History and Teaching History (Secondary Level), Fitchburg, MA 01420-2697. Offers MA. *Accreditation:* NCATE. *Program availability:* Part-time, evening/weekend. *Faculty:* 4 full-time (0 women). *Students:* 1 (woman) full-time, 8 part-time (2 women). Average age 31. 3 applicants, 100% accepted, 2 enrolled. In 2017, 2 master's awarded. *Entrance requirements:* Additional exam requirements/recommendations for international students: Required—TOEFL (minimum score 550 paper-based; 79 iBT). *Application deadline:* For fall admission, 7/15 for international students; for spring admission, 12/1 for international students. Applications are processed on a rolling basis. Application fee: $50. Electronic applications accepted. *Expenses:* Contact institution. *Financial support:* In 2017–18, research assistantships with partial tuition reimbursements (averaging $5,500 per year) were awarded; Federal Work-Study, scholarships/grants, and unspecified assistantships also available. Support available to part-time students. Financial award application deadline: 3/1; financial award applicants required to submit FAFSA. *Unit head:* Dr. Daniel Sarefield, Chair, 978-665-3379, Fax: 978-665-3658, E-mail: gce@fitchburgstate.edu. *Application contact:* Jinawa McNeil, Director of Admissions, 978-665-3140, Fax: 978-665-4540, E-mail: admissions@fitchburgstate.edu.

Florida Agricultural and Mechanical University, Division of Graduate Studies, Research, and Continuing Education, College of Social Sciences, Arts and Humanities, Department of History and Political Science, Program in Applied Social Science, Tallahassee, FL 32307-3200. Offers criminal justice (MASS); history (MASS); political science (MASS); public administration (MASS). *Program availability:* Part-time. *Degree requirements:* For master's, thesis optional. *Entrance requirements:* For master's, GRE General Test, minimum GPA of 3.0. *Faculty research:* Southern history, black history, election trends, Presidential history.

Florida Atlantic University, Dorothy F. Schmidt College of Arts and Letters, Department of History, Boca Raton, FL 33431-0991. Offers MA. *Program availability:* Part-time. *Faculty:* 17 full-time (6 women). *Students:* 15 full-time (4 women), 9 part-time (1 woman); includes 5 minority (1 Asian, non-Hispanic/Latino; 4 Hispanic/Latino). Average age 30. 8 applicants, 75% accepted, 6 enrolled. In 2017, 7 master's awarded. *Degree requirements:* For master's, one foreign language, thesis optional. *Entrance requirements:* For master's, GRE General Test, minimum GPA of 3.0. Additional exam requirements/recommendations for international students: Required—TOEFL (minimum score 500 paper-based; 61 iBT), IELTS (minimum score 6). *Application deadline:* For fall admission, 6/1 priority date for domestic students, 2/15 for international students; for spring admission, 10/15 for domestic students, 8/15 for international students. Applications are processed on a rolling basis. Application fee: $30. Electronic applications accepted. *Expenses:* Tuition, state resident: full-time $7400; part-time $369.82 per credit. Tuition, nonresident: full-time $20,496; part-time $1042.81 per credit. *Financial support:* Fellowships, research assistantships, teaching assistantships with tuition reimbursements, career-related internships or fieldwork, Federal Work-Study, and tuition waivers (partial) available. Support available to part-time students. Financial award application deadline: 3/1. *Faculty research:* Twentieth-century America, U.S. urban history, Florida history, history of socialism, Latin America. *Unit head:* Dr. Douglas Kanter, Director, Graduate Studies Program, 561-297-3593, E-mail: dkanter1@fau.edu.
Website: http://www.fau.edu/history/

Florida Gulf Coast University, College of Arts and Sciences, Program in History, Fort Myers, FL 33965-6565. Offers MA. *Program availability:* Part-time, evening/weekend. *Faculty:* 245 full-time (104 women), 155 part-time/adjunct (71 women). *Students:* 7 full-time (5 women), 7 part-time (2 women). Average age 32. 6 applicants, 100% accepted, 4 enrolled. In 2017, 9 master's awarded. *Entrance requirements:* Additional exam requirements/recommendations for international students: Required—TOEFL (minimum score 550 paper-based). *Application deadline:* For fall admission, 2/15 priority date for domestic students, 5/1 for international students; for spring admission, 12/1 for domestic students, 9/15 for international students. Applications are processed on a rolling basis. Application fee: $30. Electronic applications accepted. *Expenses:* Tuition, state resident: part-time $290 per credit hour. Tuition, nonresident: part-time $1173 per credit hour. *Required fees:* $127 per credit hour. Tuition and fees vary according to course load. *Financial support:* Application deadline: 6/30; applicants required to submit FAFSA. *Unit head:* Eric Strahorn, Head, 239-590-7214, E-mail: estraho@fgcu.edu. *Application contact:* Patricia Rice, Executive Secretary, 239-590-7196, Fax: 239-590-7200, E-mail: price@fgcu.edu.

Florida International University, Steven J. Green School of International and Public Affairs, Department of History, Miami, FL 33199. Offers Atlantic history (PhD); history (MA). *Program availability:* Part-time, evening/weekend. *Faculty:* 20 full-time (13 women), 9 part-time/adjunct (7 women). *Students:* 38 full-time (17 women), 26 part-time (8 women); includes 38 minority (6 Black or African American, non-Hispanic/Latino; 31 Hispanic/Latino; 1 Two or more races, non-Hispanic/Latino), 6 international. Average age 36. 28 applicants, 79% accepted, 16 enrolled. In 2017, 12 master's, 5 doctorates awarded. *Degree requirements:* For master's, one foreign language, thesis optional; for doctorate, 2 foreign languages, comprehensive exam, thesis/dissertation. *Entrance requirements:* For master's, 12 credits of history courses (non-history majors), 2 letters of recommendation, writing sample, minimum GPA of 3.25; for doctorate, GRE General Test (minimum score of 1120), two letters of recommendation, statement of purpose, curriculum vitae, writing sample, minimum GPA of 3.25. Additional exam requirements/recommendations for international students: Required—TOEFL (minimum score 575 paper-based; 90 iBT). *Application deadline:* For fall admission, 1/15 priority date for domestic students, 1/15 for international students. Application fee: $30. Electronic applications accepted. *Expenses:* Tuition, state resident: full-time $8912; part-time $446 per credit hour. Tuition, nonresident: full-time $21,393; part-time $992 per credit hour. *Required fees:* $390; $195 per semester. *Financial support:* Institutionally sponsored loans, scholarships/grants, and unspecified assistantships available. Financial award application deadline: 3/1; financial award applicants required to submit FAFSA. *Faculty research:* European social history, American culture, social and labor history, Latin American culture and social history, military history, Diaspora studies. *Unit head:* Dr. Victor Uribe, Chair, 305-348-2961, Fax: 305-348-3561, E-mail: victor.uribe@fiu.edu. *Application contact:* Nanett Rojas, Manager, Admissions Operations, 305-348-7464, E-mail: gradadm@fiu.edu.
Website: http://history.fiu.edu/

Florida State University, The Graduate School, College of Arts and Sciences, Department of Classics, Tallahassee, FL 32306-1510. Offers ancient history (MA); classical archaeology (MA); classical civilization (MA); classics (PhD), including classical archaeology, classics; Greek (MA); Greek and Latin (MA); Latin (MA). *Faculty:* 17 full-time (7 women), 2 part-time/adjunct (1 woman). *Students:* 41 full-time (30 women); includes 4 minority (2 Black or African American, non-Hispanic/Latino; 1 Asian, non-Hispanic/Latino; 1 Hispanic/Latino). Average age 25. 50 applicants, 40% accepted, 12 enrolled. In 2017, 8 master's, 6 doctorates awarded. Terminal master's awarded for partial completion of doctoral program. *Degree requirements:* For master's, 2 foreign languages, comprehensive exam, thesis or alternative; for doctorate, 4 foreign languages, comprehensive exam, thesis/dissertation. *Entrance requirements:* For master's, GRE General Test, minimum GPA of 3.0; for doctorate, GRE General Test, minimum GPA of 3.5. Additional exam requirements/recommendations for international students: Required—TOEFL (minimum score 550 paper-based; 80 iBT). *Application deadline:* For fall admission, 12/15 priority date for domestic students, 12/15 for international students. Applications are processed on a rolling basis. Application fee: $30. Electronic applications accepted. *Financial support:* In 2017–18, 39 students received support, including 1 fellowship with full tuition reimbursement available (averaging $18,000 per year), 2 research assistantships with full tuition reimbursements available (averaging $12,000 per year), 24 teaching assistantships with full tuition reimbursements available (averaging $12,400 per year); Federal Work-Study, scholarships/grants, tuition waivers (full), and unspecified assistantships also available. Financial award application deadline: 1/15; financial award applicants required to submit FAFSA. *Faculty research:* Greek and Latin literature, classical archaeology, mythology, ancient history, religion. *Total annual research expenditures:* $100,000. *Unit head:* Dr. Daniel J. Pullen, Chairman, 850-644-0304, Fax: 850-644-4073, E-mail: dpullen@fsu.edu. *Application contact:* Dr. Timothy Stover, Admissions Director, 850-644-4259, Fax: 850-644-4073, E-mail: tstover@fsu.edu.
Website: http://classics.fsu.edu/

Florida State University, The Graduate School, College of Arts and Sciences, Department of History, Tallahassee, FL 32306. Offers history (MA, MS, PhD); public history (MA). *Program availability:* Part-time. *Faculty:* 31 full-time (14 women). *Students:* 61 full-time (24 women), 21 part-time (5 women); includes 4 minority (2 Black or African American, non-Hispanic/Latino; 2 Asian, non-Hispanic/Latino), 3 international. Average age 30. 53 applicants, 60% accepted, 15 enrolled. In 2017, 13 master's, 7 doctorates awarded. *Degree requirements:* For master's, one foreign language, comprehensive exam (for some programs), thesis (for some programs), internships; for doctorate, one foreign language, comprehensive exam, thesis/dissertation. *Entrance requirements:* For master's, GRE General Test, minimum GPA of 3.3, minimum 18 hours of course work in history; for doctorate, GRE General Test, master's degree, minimum graduate GPA of 3.65. Additional exam requirements/recommendations for international students: Required—TOEFL (minimum score 550 paper-based; 80 iBT). *Application deadline:* For fall admission, 12/1 for domestic and international students. Applications are processed on a rolling basis. Application fee: $30. Electronic applications accepted. *Financial support:* In 2017–18, 49 students received support, including 7 fellowships with full tuition reimbursements available (averaging $19,000 per year), 5 research assistantships with full tuition reimbursements available (averaging $15,500 per year), 5 teaching assistantships with full tuition reimbursements available (averaging $18,000 per year); Federal Work-Study, institutionally sponsored loans, scholarships/grants, tuition waivers (full and partial), and unspecified assistantships also available. Financial award application deadline: 12/1; financial award applicants required to submit FAFSA. *Faculty research:* Napoleon and the French Revolution, modern Europe, early modern

History

Europe, Middle East, Latin America, Hispanic Caribbean, 20th-century Cuba, modern Britain, gender and sexuality, Atlantic world, modern Germany, Medieval Europe, World War II, U.S. 19th century, early U.S., Native American, science, medicine and technology, Russia, East Asia. *Unit head:* Dr. Edward Gray, Chair, 850-644-5888, Fax: 850-644-6402, E-mail: egray@fsu.edu. *Application contact:* Anne Kozar, Academic Program Specialist, 850-644-4494, E-mail: mkozar@fsu.edu.
Website: http://history.fsu.edu/

Fordham University, Graduate School of Arts and Sciences, Department of History, New York, NY 10458. Offers MA, PhD. *Program availability:* Part-time, evening/weekend. *Faculty:* 32 full-time (14 women). *Students:* 28 full-time (12 women), 16 part-time (7 women); includes 6 minority (2 Black or African American, non-Hispanic/Latino; 1 Asian, non-Hispanic/Latino; 3 Hispanic/Latino), 3 international. Average age 33. 51 applicants, 59% accepted, 8 enrolled. In 2017, 9 master's, 5 doctorates awarded. Terminal master's awarded for partial completion of doctoral program. *Degree requirements:* For master's, one foreign language, thesis optional; for doctorate, 2 foreign languages, comprehensive exam, thesis/dissertation. *Entrance requirements:* For master's and doctorate, GRE General Test. Additional exam requirements/recommendations for international students: Required—TOEFL (minimum score 650 paper-based). *Application deadline:* For fall admission, 1/4 priority date for domestic students; for spring admission, 11/1 for domestic students. Application fee: $70. Electronic applications accepted. *Financial support:* In 2017–18, 23 students received support, including 3 fellowships with tuition reimbursements available (averaging $27,622 per year), 16 teaching assistantships with tuition reimbursements available (averaging $16,806 per year); research assistantships with tuition reimbursements available, institutionally sponsored loans, tuition waivers (full and partial), and unspecified assistantships also available. Financial award application deadline: 1/4; financial award applicants required to submit FAFSA. *Unit head:* Dr. Grace Shen, Director of Graduate Studies, 718-817-3925, Fax: 718-817-4680, E-mail: gshen1@fordham.edu. *Application contact:* Travis Strattion, Interim Director of Graduate Admissions, 718-817-4417, Fax: 718-817-3566, E-mail: tstrattion@fordham.edu.

Fort Hays State University, Graduate School, College of Arts and Sciences, Department of History, Hays, KS 67601-4099. Offers MA. *Degree requirements:* For master's, comprehensive exam, thesis or alternative. *Entrance requirements:* For master's, minimum undergraduate GPA of 3.0. Additional exam requirements/recommendations for international students: Required—TOEFL (minimum score 550 paper-based). Electronic applications accepted. *Faculty research:* Seventeenth century English legal history, Native American history, immigration history, Volga German settlement.

George Mason University, College of Education and Human Development, Programs in Curriculum and Instruction, Fairfax, VA 22030. Offers advanced international baccalaureate (M Ed); assistive technology (M Ed); designing digital learning in schools (M Ed); early childhood education (M Ed); early childhood education for diverse learners (M Ed); elementary education (M Ed); English as a second language (M Ed); gifted child education (M Ed); history (M Ed); literacy (M Ed), including PK-12 classroom teachers, reading specialist; literacy leadership for diverse schools (M Ed), including K-12 reading; physical education (M Ed); science K-12 (M Ed); secondary education (M Ed), including biology, chemistry, earth science, English, history/social science, math, physics; special education (M Ed); teacher leadership (M Ed); teaching culturally, linguistically diverse and exceptional learners (M Ed); transformative teaching (M Ed). *Program availability:* Part-time, evening/weekend, 100% online, blended/hybrid learning. *Faculty:* 41 full-time (36 women), 45 part-time/adjunct (37 women). *Students:* 173 full-time (151 women), 729 part-time (611 women); includes 271 minority (65 Black or African American, non-Hispanic/Latino; 5 American Indian or Alaska Native, non-Hispanic/Latino; 88 Asian, non-Hispanic/Latino; 94 Hispanic/Latino; 1 Native Hawaiian or other Pacific Islander, non-Hispanic/Latino; 18 Two or more races, non-Hispanic/Latino), 28 international. Average age 32. 426 applicants, 91% accepted, 289 enrolled. In 2017, 349 master's awarded. *Degree requirements:* For master's, thesis. *Entrance requirements:* For master's, PRAXIS Core (for some programs), 2 letters of recommendation, interview, program goals statement; 9 hours of complete licensure endorsement requirements (for elementary education); minimum GPA of 3.0 in applicant's last 60 hours of undergraduate coursework (for secondary education); at least 1 year of teaching experience (for literacy). Additional exam requirements/recommendations for international students: Required—TOEFL (minimum score 575 paper-based; 88 iBT), IELTS (minimum score 6.5), PTE (minimum score 59). *Application deadline:* For fall admission, 4/2 priority date for domestic and international students; for spring admission, 11/1 for domestic and international students. Application fee: $75 ($80 for international students). Electronic applications accepted. *Expenses:* Tuition, state resident: full-time $11,228; part-time $459.50 per credit. Tuition, nonresident: full-time $30,932; part-time $1280.50 per credit. *Required fees:* $3252; $135.50 per credit. Part-time tuition and fees vary according to course load and program. *Financial support:* In 2017–18, 2 students received support, including 2 teaching assistantships; career-related internships or fieldwork, Federal Work-Study, scholarships/grants, unspecified assistantships, and health care benefits (for full-time research or teaching assistantship recipients) also available. Support available to part-time students. Financial award application deadline: 3/1; financial award applicants required to submit FAFSA. *Faculty research:* Teacher preparation and professional development; adaptive teaching; wonder in science teacher preparation; literacy (digital, adolescent); site based course instruction. *Unit head:* Rebecca Fox, Professor and Academic Program Coordinator, 703-993-4123, E-mail: rfox@gmu.edu.
Website: http://gse.gmu.edu/programs/gsemasters

George Mason University, College of Humanities and Social Sciences, Department of History and Art History, Program in History, Fairfax, VA 22030. Offers digital public humanities (Certificate); history (MA, PhD). *Faculty:* 44 full-time (16 women), 16 part-time/adjunct (9 women). *Students:* 57 full-time (31 women), 103 part-time (41 women); includes 16 minority (1 Black or African American, non-Hispanic/Latino; 1 American Indian or Alaska Native, non-Hispanic/Latino; 2 Asian, non-Hispanic/Latino; 7 Hispanic/Latino; 2 Native Hawaiian or other Pacific Islander, non-Hispanic/Latino; 3 Two or more races, non-Hispanic/Latino), 1 international. Average age 34. 136 applicants, 75% accepted, 50 enrolled. In 2017, 36 master's, 8 doctorates awarded. *Degree requirements:* For master's, comprehensive exam, thesis or alternative, translation language exam; for doctorate, comprehensive exam, thesis/dissertation; for Certificate, comprehensive exam, thesis or alternative, internship in applied history. *Entrance requirements:* For master's, goals statement, writing sample, letters of recommendation; for doctorate, GRE, goals statement, writing sample, letters of recommendation. Additional exam requirements/recommendations for international students: Required—TOEFL (minimum score 575 paper-based; 88 iBT), IELTS (minimum score 6.5), PTE (minimum score 59). Application fee: $75 ($80 for international students). Electronic applications accepted. *Expenses:* Tuition, state resident: full-time $11,228; part-time $459.50 per credit. Tuition, nonresident: full-time $30,932; part-time $1280.50 per credit. *Required fees:* $3252; $135.50 per credit. Part-time tuition and fees vary according to course load and program. *Financial support:* In 2017–18, 33 students received support, including 13 research assistantships with tuition reimbursements available (averaging $18,325 per year), 20 teaching assistantships with tuition reimbursements available (averaging $10,716 per year); career-related internships or fieldwork, Federal Work-Study, scholarships/grants, unspecified assistantships, and health care benefits (for full-time research or teaching assistantship recipients) also available. Support available to part-time students. Financial award application deadline: 3/1; financial award applicants required to submit FAFSA. *Faculty research:* U.S. history, digital history, global history, colonial U.S. history, European history. *Unit head:* Brian Platt, Chair, 703-993-1253, Fax: 703-993-1251, E-mail: bplatt1@gmu.edu. *Application contact:* Emily Gibson, Graduate Program Coordinator, 703-993-1248, Fax: 703-993-1251, E-mail: egibson5@gmu.edu.
Website: http://historyarthistory.gmu.edu/programs/la-ma-hist

Georgetown University, Graduate School of Arts and Sciences, Department of History, Washington, DC 20057-1305. Offers global history (MA); global, international and comparative history (MA); history (MA, PhD); MA/PhD; MS/MA. MA in global history offered jointly with the history department at King's College London. *Degree requirements:* For master's, thesis (for some programs); for doctorate, 2 foreign languages, comprehensive exam, thesis/dissertation. *Entrance requirements:* For master's and doctorate, GRE General Test. Additional exam requirements/recommendations for international students: Required—TOEFL.

Georgetown University, Graduate School of Arts and Sciences, School of Continuing Studies, Washington, DC 20057. Offers American studies (MALS); applied intelligence (MPS); Catholic studies (MALS); classical civilizations (MALS); emergency and disaster management (MPS); ethics and the professions (MALS); global strategic communications (MPS); hospitality management (MPS); human resources management (MPS); humanities (MALS); individualized study (MALS); integrated marketing communications (MPS); international affairs (MALS); Islam and Muslim-Christian relations (MALS); journalism (MPS); liberal studies (DLS); literature and society (MALS); medieval and early modern European studies (MALS); public relations and corporate communications (MPS); real estate (MPS); religious studies (MALS); social and public policy (MALS); sports industry management (MPS); systems engineering management (MPS); technology management (MPS); the theory and practice of American democracy (MALS); urban and regional planning (MPS); visual culture (MALS). MPS in systems engineering management offered jointly with Stevens Institute of Technology. *Entrance requirements:* Additional exam requirements/recommendations for international students: Required—TOEFL.

The George Washington University, Columbian College of Arts and Sciences, Department of History, Washington, DC 20052. Offers MA, PhD. *Program availability:* Part-time, evening/weekend. *Faculty:* 25 full-time (8 women), 10 part-time/adjunct (4 women). *Students:* 26 full-time (9 women), 29 part-time (10 women); includes 10 minority (4 Black or African American, non-Hispanic/Latino; 2 Asian, non-Hispanic/Latino; 3 Hispanic/Latino; 1 Two or more races, non-Hispanic/Latino), 6 international. Average age 30. 143 applicants, 29% accepted, 12 enrolled. In 2017, 14 master's, 4 doctorates awarded. Terminal master's awarded for partial completion of doctoral program. *Degree requirements:* For master's, one foreign language, comprehensive exam, thesis or alternative; for doctorate, 2 foreign languages, thesis/dissertation, general exam. *Entrance requirements:* For master's and doctorate, GRE General Test, minimum GPA of 3.0. Additional exam requirements/recommendations for international students: Required—TOEFL (minimum score 550 paper-based; 80 iBT). *Application deadline:* For fall admission, 1/15 priority date for domestic and international students; for spring admission, 10/1 priority date for domestic students, 9/1 priority date for international students. Applications are processed on a rolling basis. Application fee: $75. Electronic applications accepted. *Expenses: Tuition:* Full-time $28,800; part-time $1655 per credit hour. *Required fees:* $45; $2.75 per credit hour. *Financial support:* In 2017–18, 28 students received support. Fellowships with full tuition reimbursements available, teaching assistantships with tuition reimbursements available, career-related internships or fieldwork, Federal Work-Study, and tuition waivers available. Financial award application deadline: 1/15. *Unit head:* Katrin Schultheiss, Chair, 202-994-6232, E-mail: kschulth@gwu.edu. *Application contact:* Information Contact, 202-994-6230, Fax: 202-994-6231, E-mail: history@gwu.edu.
Website: http://www.gwu.edu/~history/

Georgia Southern University, Jack N. Averitt College of Graduate Studies, College of Liberal Arts and Social Sciences, Program in History, Statesboro, GA 30460. Offers history (MA); public history (Graduate Certificate). *Program availability:* Part-time. *Faculty:* 24 full-time (7 women). *Students:* 11 full-time (7 women), 7 part-time (3 women); includes 2 minority (1 American Indian or Alaska Native, non-Hispanic/Latino; 1 Hispanic/Latino). Average age 30. 14 applicants, 93% accepted, 11 enrolled. In 2017, 12 master's awarded. *Degree requirements:* For master's, one foreign language, thesis optional, terminal exams. *Entrance requirements:* For master's, GRE General Test, minimum GPA of 3.0, undergraduate major in history or equivalent, letters of reference. Additional exam requirements/recommendations for international students: Required—TOEFL (minimum score 550 paper-based; 80 iBT), IELTS (minimum score 6). *Application deadline:* For fall admission, 3/1 priority date for domestic and international students; for spring admission, 10/1 priority date for domestic students, 10/1 for international students. Applications are processed on a rolling basis. Application fee: $50. Electronic applications accepted. *Expenses:* Tuition, state resident: full-time $4986; part-time $3324 per year. Tuition, nonresident: full-time $21,982; part-time $15,352 per year. *Required fees:* $2092; $1802 per credit hour. $901 per semester. Tuition and fees vary according to course load, campus/location and program. *Financial support:* In 2017–18, 15 students received support, including 14 fellowships with full tuition reimbursements available (averaging $7,750 per year), 1 teaching assistantship with full tuition reimbursement available (averaging $7,750 per year); career-related internships or fieldwork, Federal Work-Study, scholarships/grants, tuition waivers (full), and unspecified assistantships also available. Support available to part-time students. Financial award application deadline: 4/15; financial award applicants required to submit FAFSA. *Faculty research:* Women's/gender history, the American South, military history, public history, modern Europe. *Unit head:* Dr. Timothy Teeter, Graduate Program Director, 912-478-0239, Fax: 912-478-0377, E-mail: tmteeter@georgiasouthern.edu.
Website: http://class.georgiasouthern.edu/history/

Georgia Southern University–Armstrong Campus, College of Graduate Studies, Program in History, Savannah, GA 31419-1997. Offers American and European history (MA); public history (MA). *Program availability:* Part-time, evening/weekend. *Faculty:* 11 full-time (3 women), 1 (woman) part-time/adjunct. *Students:* 7 full-time (3 women), 10 part-time (5 women); includes 3 minority (all Black or African American, non-Hispanic/Latino). Average age 43. 14 applicants, 43% accepted, 5 enrolled. In 2017, 5 master's awarded. *Degree requirements:* For master's, one foreign language, comprehensive exam (for some programs), thesis (for some programs), thesis, internship, or advanced fieldwork. *Entrance requirements:* For master's, GRE General Test, minimum GPA of 3.0, letters of recommendation, BA in history or equivalent. Additional exam requirements/recommendations for international students: Required—TOEFL (minimum score 523 paper-based; 70 iBT). *Application deadline:* For fall admission, 6/30 priority date for domestic students, 5/1 priority date for international students; for spring admission, 11/15 priority date for domestic students, 9/15 priority date for international students; for summer admission, 4/15 priority date for domestic students, 9/15 for international students. Applications are processed on a rolling basis. Application fee:

$30. Electronic applications accepted. *Expenses:* Tuition, state resident: part-time $211 per credit hour. Tuition, nonresident: part-time $782 per credit hour. *Required fees:* $737 per semester. Tuition and fees vary according to course load, degree level, campus/location and program. *Financial support:* In 2017–18, research assistantships with full tuition reimbursements (averaging $5,000 per year) were awarded; career-related internships or fieldwork, Federal Work-Study, and unspecified assistantships also available. Support available to part-time students. Financial award application deadline: 3/15; financial award applicants required to submit FAFSA. *Faculty research:* Public history; European, Latin American, African, and United States history. *Unit head:* Dr. Christopher Hendricks, Interim Department Head, 912-344-2725, Fax: 912-344-3451, E-mail: chris.hendricks@armstrong.edu. *Application contact:* McKenzie Peterman, Graduate Admissions Specialist, 912-478-5678, Fax: 912-478-0740, E-mail: mpeterman@georgiasouthern.edu.
Website: http://www.armstrong.edu/Liberal_Arts/history/history_graduate_program

Georgia State University, College of Arts and Sciences, Department of History, Program in History, Atlanta, GA 30302-3083. Offers historic preservation (MA); history (PhD); public history (MA); world history (MA). *Program availability:* Part-time, evening/weekend. Terminal master's awarded for partial completion of doctoral program. *Entrance requirements:* For master's, GRE, BA in history; statement of purpose; writing sample; three letters of recommendation; official transcripts; for doctorate, GRE, MA in history; master's thesis; statement of purpose; writing sample; three letters of recommendation; official transcripts; appropriate language skills. Additional exam requirements/recommendations for international students: Required—TOEFL (minimum score 550 paper-based; 80 iBT). *Application deadline:* Applications are processed on a rolling basis. Application fee: $50. Electronic applications accepted. *Expenses:* Tuition, state resident: full-time $7020. Tuition, nonresident: full-time $22,518. *Required fees:* $2128. Tuition and fees vary according to degree level and program. *Financial support:* Research assistantships, teaching assistantships, and scholarships/grants available. Financial award application deadline: 2/15; financial award applicants required to submit FAFSA. *Faculty research:* Nineteenth- and twentieth-century U.S. history, early modern European history, modern European history, world history, public history. *Unit head:* Dr. Michelle Brattain, Chair, 404-413-6352, Fax: 404-413-6384, E-mail: mbrattain@gsu.edu. *Application contact:* Dr. Joe Perry, Director of Graduate Studies, 404-413-6374, Fax: 404-413-6384, E-mail: jbperry@gsu.edu.
Website: http://www.gsu.edu/~wwwhis/

Georgia State University, College of Education and Human Development, Department of Middle and Secondary Education, Atlanta, GA 30302-3083. Offers curriculum and instruction (Ed D); English education (MAT); mathematics education (M Ed, MAT); middle level education (MAT); reading, language and literacy education (M Ed, MAT), including reading instruction (M Ed); science education (M Ed, MAT), including biology (MAT), broad field science (MAT), chemistry (MAT), earth science (MAT), physics (MAT); social studies education (M Ed, MAT), including economics (MAT), geography (MAT), history (MAT), political science (MAT); teaching and learning (PhD), including language and literacy, mathematics education, music education, science education, social studies education, teaching and teacher education. *Accreditation:* NCATE. *Program availability:* Part-time, evening/weekend, online learning. *Faculty:* 24 full-time (18 women). *Students:* 179 full-time (110 women), 192 part-time (133 women); includes 193 minority (130 Black or African American, non-Hispanic/Latino; 1 American Indian or Alaska Native, non-Hispanic/Latino; 23 Asian, non-Hispanic/Latino; 25 Hispanic/Latino; 14 Two or more races, non-Hispanic/Latino), 6 international. Average age 33. 175 applicants, 58% accepted, 83 enrolled. In 2017, 81 master's, 17 doctorates awarded. *Entrance requirements:* For master's, GRE; GACE I (for initial teacher preparation programs), baccalaureate degree or equivalent, resume, goals statement, two letters of recommendation, minimum undergraduate GPA of 2.5; proof of initial teacher certification in the content area (for M Ed); for doctorate, GRE, resume, goals statement, writing sample, two letters of recommendation, minimum graduate GPA of 3.3, interview. *Application deadline:* For fall admission, 1/15 priority date for domestic and international students; for spring admission, 10/1 for domestic and international students. Application fee: $50. Electronic applications accepted. *Expenses:* Tuition, state resident: full-time $7020. Tuition, nonresident: full-time $22,518. *Required fees:* $2128. Tuition and fees vary according to degree level and program. *Financial support:* In 2017–18, fellowships with full tuition reimbursements (averaging $19,667 per year), research assistantships with full tuition reimbursements (averaging $5,436 per year), teaching assistantships with full tuition reimbursements (averaging $2,779 per year) were awarded; career-related internships or fieldwork, Federal Work-Study, scholarships/grants, health care benefits, tuition waivers (full and partial), and unspecified assistantships also available. Financial award application deadline: 3/15. *Faculty research:* Teacher education in language and literacy, mathematics, science, and social studies in urban middle and secondary school settings; learning technologies in school, community, and corporate settings; multicultural education and education for social justice; urban education; international education. *Unit head:* Dr. Dana L. Fox, Chair, 404-413-8060, Fax: 404-413-8063, E-mail: dfox@gsu.edu. *Application contact:* Bobbie Turner, Administrative Coordinator, 404-413-8405, Fax: 404-413-8063, E-mail: bnturner@gsu.edu.
Website: http://mse.education.gsu.edu/

The Graduate Center, City University of New York, Graduate Studies, Program in History, New York, NY 10016-4039. Offers PhD. *Faculty:* 75 full-time (18 women). *Students:* 105 full-time (47 women), 3 part-time (2 women); includes 7 minority (1 Black or African American, non-Hispanic/Latino; 3 Asian, non-Hispanic/Latino; 2 Hispanic/Latino; 1 Two or more races, non-Hispanic/Latino), 10 international. Average age 36. 112 applicants, 14% accepted, 11 enrolled. In 2017, 20 doctorates awarded. *Degree requirements:* For doctorate, one foreign language, thesis/dissertation. *Entrance requirements:* For doctorate, GRE General Test, writing sample (15 pages). Additional exam requirements/recommendations for international students: Required—TOEFL. *Application deadline:* For fall admission, 1/15 priority date for domestic students. Application fee: $125. Electronic applications accepted. *Financial support:* In 2017–18, 86 students received support, including 90 fellowships, 12 research assistantships, 13 teaching assistantships; career-related internships or fieldwork, Federal Work-Study, institutionally sponsored loans, and tuition waivers (full and partial) also available. Financial award application deadline: 2/1; financial award applicants required to submit FAFSA. *Unit head:* Prof. Helena Rosenblatt, Executive Officer, 212-817-8430, Fax: 212-817-1523, E-mail: hrosenblatt@gc.cuny.edu. *Application contact:* Les Gribben, Director of Admissions, 212-817-7470, Fax: 212-817-1624, E-mail: lgribben@gc.cuny.edu.

Hardin-Simmons University, Graduate School, Cynthia Ann Parker College of Liberal Arts, Department of History, Abilene, TX 79698-0001. Offers MA. *Program availability:* Part-time. *Faculty:* 1 full-time (0 women). *Students:* 1 part-time (0 women). Average age 35. In 2017, 1 master's awarded. *Degree requirements:* For master's, comprehensive exam, thesis or alternative. *Entrance requirements:* For master's, GRE, minimum undergraduate GPA of 3.0 in history, 2.7 overall; 18 upper-level hours of course work in history; letters of recommendation; resume; writing sample. Additional exam requirements/recommendations for international students: Required—TOEFL (minimum score 550 paper-based; 79 iBT). *Application deadline:* For fall admission, 8/15 priority date for domestic students, 4/1 for international students; for spring admission, 1/5 priority date for domestic students, 9/1 for international students. Applications are processed on a rolling basis. Application fee: $50 ($150 for international students).

Electronic applications accepted. *Expenses: Tuition:* Full-time $13,500; part-time $750 per semester hour. *Required fees:* $220 per term. One-time fee: $50. Tuition and fees vary according to course load, campus/location and program. *Financial support:* Fellowships and scholarships/grants available. Support available to part-time students. Financial award application deadline: 6/30; financial award applicants required to submit FAFSA. *Faculty research:* Vietnam, diplomatic history, Texas politics, Mexico and NAFTA, classical warfare. *Unit head:* Dr. Don Taylor, Program Director, 325-670-1294, Fax: 325-670-1526, E-mail: mbeasley@hsutx.edu. *Application contact:* Dr. Nancy Kucinski, Dean of Graduate Studies, 325-670-1298, Fax: 325-670-1564, E-mail: gradoff@hsutx.edu.
Website: http://www.hsutx.edu/academics/cap/graduate/history

Harvard University, Graduate School of Arts and Sciences, Department of History, Cambridge, MA 02138. Offers African history (PhD); American history (PhD); ancient, medieval, early modern, and modern Europe (PhD), including Central Europe, Russia, Southeastern Europe, Western Europe; diplomatic history (PhD); East Asian history (PhD); economic and social history (PhD); intellectual history (PhD); Latin American history (PhD); Near Eastern history (PhD); oceanic history (PhD). *Degree requirements:* For doctorate, variable foreign language requirement, thesis/dissertation, oral general exam. *Entrance requirements:* For doctorate, GRE General Test, proficiency in 2 languages. Additional exam requirements/recommendations for international students: Required—TOEFL.

Howard University, Graduate School, Department of History, Washington, DC 20059-0002. Offers African diaspora (MA, PhD); African history (MA, PhD); Latin America and the Caribbean (MA, PhD); public history (MA); United States history (MA, PhD). *Program availability:* Part-time. Terminal master's awarded for partial completion of doctoral program. *Degree requirements:* For master's, one foreign language, thesis optional; for doctorate, 2 foreign languages, comprehensive exam, thesis/dissertation. *Entrance requirements:* For master's, GRE General Test, minimum GPA of 3.0, 3 letters of recommendation; for doctorate, GRE General Test, minimum GPA of 3.5, 3 letters of recommendation. Additional exam requirements/recommendations for international students: Required—TOEFL. Electronic applications accepted. *Faculty research:* Africa diaspora, U.S. diplomatic relations, Caribbean economic history.

Hunter College of the City University of New York, Graduate School, School of Arts and Sciences, Department of History, New York, NY 10065-5085. Offers MA. *Degree requirements:* For master's, one foreign language, comprehensive exam, thesis, essay, language exam. *Entrance requirements:* For master's, GRE General Test, minimum of 18 credits in undergraduate history or related field. Additional exam requirements/recommendations for international students: Required—TOEFL.

Idaho State University, Office of Graduate Studies, College of Arts and Letters, Department of History, Pocatello, ID 83209-8079. Offers historical resources management (MA). *Program availability:* Part-time. *Degree requirements:* For master's, comprehensive exam, thesis optional, internship. *Entrance requirements:* For master's, GRE, 3 letters of recommendation, minimum of 18 upper division history credits. Additional exam requirements/recommendations for international students: Required—TOEFL (minimum score 550 paper-based; 80 iBT). Electronic applications accepted. *Faculty research:* Historical geographic information systems, historical and urban geography, environmental history and environmental policy, United States political history, womens' and gender history.

Illinois State University, Graduate School, College of Arts and Sciences, Department of History, Normal, IL 61790. Offers MA, MS. *Degree requirements:* For master's, thesis or alternative. *Entrance requirements:* For master's, GRE General Test, minimum GPA of 2.6 in last 60 hours of course work.

Indiana State University, College of Graduate and Professional Studies, College of Arts and Sciences, Department of History, Terre Haute, IN 47809. Offers MA, MS. *Program availability:* Part-time, evening/weekend. *Degree requirements:* For master's, comprehensive exam (for some programs), thesis or alternative. *Entrance requirements:* For master's, GRE, equivalent of minor in geography or geology. Additional exam requirements/recommendations for international students: Required—TOEFL (minimum score 550 paper-based).

Indiana University Bloomington, School of Education, Department of Educational Leadership and Policy Studies, Bloomington, IN 47405. Offers educational leadership (MS, Ed D, Ed S); higher education (Ed D, PhD); higher education and student affairs (MS); history and philosophy of education (MS); history, philosophy, and policy in education (PhD), including education policy studies, history of education, philosophy of education; international and comparative education (MS). *Accreditation:* NCATE. *Degree requirements:* For master's, thesis optional; for doctorate, comprehensive exam, thesis/dissertation; for Ed S, comprehensive exam or project. *Entrance requirements:* For master's, doctorate, and Ed S, GRE General Test. Additional exam requirements/recommendations for international students: Required—TOEFL (minimum score 79 iBT). Electronic applications accepted. *Faculty research:* Culturally engaging campus environments, school choice policy analysis, democracy and education in the national and international context, and principal leadership.

Indiana University Bloomington, University Graduate School, College of Arts and Sciences, Department of Art History, Bloomington, IN 47405-7000. Offers MA, PhD, MA/MLS. *Accreditation:* NASAD. *Degree requirements:* For master's, one foreign language, thesis; for doctorate, 2 foreign languages, comprehensive exam, thesis/dissertation. *Entrance requirements:* For master's, GRE, writing sample, 3 letters of recommendation, transcript; for doctorate, GRE, transcript, writing samples, 3 letters of recommendation. Additional exam requirements/recommendations for international students: Required—TOEFL (minimum score 550 paper-based). *Faculty research:* Art and social history, consumer culture, feminist art and theory, classical revivals.

Indiana University Bloomington, University Graduate School, College of Arts and Sciences, Department of History, Bloomington, IN 47405. Offers MA, MAT, PhD, MA/MLS. Terminal master's awarded for partial completion of doctoral program. *Degree requirements:* For master's, one foreign language, thesis optional; for doctorate, variable foreign language requirement, comprehensive exam, thesis/dissertation. *Entrance requirements:* For master's and doctorate, GRE General Test. Additional exam requirements/recommendations for international students: Required—TOEFL. Electronic applications accepted. *Faculty research:* Medieval and early modern Europe, Russia, Latin America, Middle East, Great Britain, United States, Africa, African Diaspora, Europe, eastern Europe, gender and sexuality.

Indiana University of Pennsylvania, School of Graduate Studies and Research, College of Humanities and Social Sciences, Department of History, Program in History, Indiana, PA 15705. Offers MA. *Program availability:* Part-time. *Faculty:* 4 full-time (2 women). *Students:* 6 full-time (3 women). Average age 26. 12 applicants, 67% accepted, 3 enrolled. In 2017, 5 master's awarded. *Degree requirements:* For master's, thesis optional. *Entrance requirements:* For master's, GRE, 2 letters of recommendation. Additional exam requirements/recommendations for international students: Required—TOEFL (minimum score 540 paper-based). *Application deadline:* Applications are processed on a rolling basis. Application fee: $50. Electronic applications accepted. *Expenses:* Tuition, state resident: full-time $12,000; part-time $500 per credit. Tuition, nonresident: full-time $18,000; part-time $750 per credit.

Required fees: $4073; $165.55 per credit. $64 per term. *Financial support:* In 2017–18, 3 research assistantships with tuition reimbursements (averaging $2,870 per year) were awarded; fellowships, career-related internships or fieldwork, Federal Work-Study, scholarships/grants, and unspecified assistantships also available. Support available to part-time students. Financial award application deadline: 4/15; financial award applicants required to submit FAFSA. *Unit head:* Dr. Jeanine Mazak-Kahne, Graduate Coordinator, 724-357-2436, E-mail: j.mkahne@iup.edu.
Website: http://www.iup.edu/grad/history/default.aspx

Indiana University–Purdue University Indianapolis, School of Liberal Arts, Department of History, Indianapolis, IN 46202. Offers European history (MA); public history (MA); United States history (MA); MA/MA; MA/MLS. *Program availability:* Part-time, evening/weekend. *Degree requirements:* For master's, one foreign language, thesis. *Entrance requirements:* For master's, GRE General Test, minimum GPA of 3.0. Electronic applications accepted.

Inter American University of Puerto Rico, Barranquitas Campus, Program in Education, Barranquitas, PR 00794. Offers curriculum and teaching (M Ed), including biology, English as a second language, history, Spanish; educational leadership and management (MA); elementary education (M Ed); information and library service technology (M Ed); special education (MA). *Accreditation:* TEAC. *Program availability:* Part-time, evening/weekend. *Faculty:* 1 full-time (0 women), 3 part-time/adjunct (2 women). *Students:* 17 full-time (16 women), 2 part-time (both women); all minorities (all Hispanic/Latino). Average age 34. 9 applicants, 89% accepted, 8 enrolled. In 2017, 5 master's awarded. *Degree requirements:* For master's, 2 foreign languages, comprehensive exam, thesis (for some programs). *Entrance requirements:* For master's, GRE or EXADEP, bachelor's degree or its equivalent from accredited institution, official academic transcript from institution that conferred bachelor's degree, minimum GPA of 2.5, two recommendation letters, interview (for some programs), essay (for some programs). *Application deadline:* Applications are processed on a rolling basis. Application fee: $31. Electronic applications accepted. *Expenses:* $3,392 full-time tuition plus $652 fees. *Financial support:* Applicants required to submit FAFSA. *Unit head:* Juan A. Negron-Berrios, PhD, Chancellor, 787-857-3600 Ext. 2002, Fax: 787-857-2125, E-mail: janegron@br.inter.edu. *Application contact:* Aramilda Cartagena-Santiago, Dean of Students, 787-857-3600 Ext. 2009, Fax: 787-857-2125, E-mail: aramildacartagena@br.inter.edu.

Inter American University of Puerto Rico, Metropolitan Campus, Graduate Programs, Program in History, San Juan, PR 00919-1293. Offers American history (PhD); history (MA, PhD).

Inter American University of Puerto Rico, Metropolitan Campus, Graduate Programs, Program in History Education, San Juan, PR 00919-1293. Offers MA.

Iona College, School of Arts and Science, Department of History, New Rochelle, NY 10801-1890. Offers MA. *Program availability:* Part-time, evening/weekend. *Faculty:* 2 full-time (1 woman). *Students:* 1 (woman) full-time, 4 part-time (0 women); includes 1 minority (Hispanic/Latino). Average age 44. 1 applicant, 100% accepted. In 2017, 9 master's awarded. *Degree requirements:* For master's, one foreign language, comprehensive exam, 27 credits of coursework and culminating project or 24 credits of coursework and thesis. *Entrance requirements:* For master's, undergraduate major in history or related field, minimum GPA of 3.0. Additional exam requirements/recommendations for international students: Required—TOEFL (minimum score 550 paper-based; 80 iBT), IELTS (minimum score 6.5). *Application deadline:* For fall admission, 8/1 priority date for domestic students, 5/1 priority date for international students; for spring admission, 1/1 priority date for domestic students, 8/1 priority date for international students. Applications are processed on a rolling basis. Electronic applications accepted. Tuition and fees vary according to program. *Financial support:* In 2017–18, 3 students received support. Unspecified assistantships available. Financial award application deadline: 4/15; financial award applicants required to submit FAFSA. *Faculty research:* Military history, Asian economies, American diplomacy, Catholic education, Armenian history, the history of violence, French Revolution, medieval religion. *Unit head:* Daniel Thiery, PhD, Chairman, 914-633-2694, E-mail: dthiery@iona.edu. *Application contact:* Katelyn Brunck, Assistant Director of Graduate Admissions, 914-633-2492, Fax: 914-633-2277, E-mail: kbrunck@iona.edu.
Website: http://www.iona.edu/Academics/School-of-Arts-Science/Departments/History/Graduate-Programs.aspx

Iowa State University of Science and Technology, Department of History, Ames, IA 50011. Offers history (MA); rural, agricultural, technological, and environmental history (PhD). *Degree requirements:* For master's, thesis or alternative; for doctorate, thesis/dissertation. *Entrance requirements:* For master's and doctorate, GRE General Test. Additional exam requirements/recommendations for international students: Required—TOEFL (minimum score 600 paper-based; 79 iBT), IELTS (minimum score 7). Electronic applications accepted.

Jackson State University, Graduate School, College of Liberal Arts, Department of History and Philosophy, Jackson, MS 39217. Offers history (MA). *Program availability:* Part-time, evening/weekend, 100% online, blended/hybrid learning. *Degree requirements:* For master's, comprehensive exam, thesis or alternative. *Entrance requirements:* For master's, GRE General Test. Additional exam requirements/recommendations for international students: Required—TOEFL (minimum score 520 paper-based; 67 iBT). Electronic applications accepted. *Expenses:* Contact institution.

Jacksonville State University, College of Graduate Studies and Continuing Education, College of Arts and Sciences, Department of History, Jacksonville, AL 36265-1602. Offers MA. *Program availability:* Part-time, evening/weekend. *Degree requirements:* For master's, comprehensive exam, thesis (for some programs). *Entrance requirements:* For master's, GRE General Test or MAT. Additional exam requirements/recommendations for international students: Required—TOEFL (minimum score 500 paper-based; 61 iBT). Electronic applications accepted.

James Madison University, The Graduate School, College of Arts and Letters, Program in History, Harrisonburg, VA 22801. Offers public history (MA); U.S. history (MA); world history (MA). *Program availability:* Part-time. *Students:* 16 full-time (6 women), 10 part-time (4 women). Average age 30. In 2017, 8 master's awarded. *Degree requirements:* For master's, one foreign language, comprehensive exam, thesis. Application fee: $55. Electronic applications accepted. *Expenses:* Tuition, state resident: full-time $10,512; part-time $438 per credit hour. Tuition, nonresident: full-time $28,358; part-time $1162 per credit hour. *Required fees:* $1128. *Financial support:* In 2017–18, 10 students received support, including 7 fellowships, 3 teaching assistantships with full tuition reimbursements available (averaging $9,284 per year); Federal Work-Study and assistantships (averaging $7911) also available. Financial award application deadline: 3/1; financial award applicants required to submit FAFSA. *Unit head:* Dr. Gabrielle Lanier, Department Head, 540-568-6132, E-mail: laniergm@jmu.edu. *Application contact:* Lynette D. Michael, Director of Graduate Admissions, 540-568-6131 Ext. 6395, Fax: 540-568-7860, E-mail: michaeld@jmu.edu.
Website: http://www.jmu.edu/history

Johns Hopkins University, Zanvyl Krieger School of Arts and Sciences, Department of History, Baltimore, MD 21218. Offers PhD. *Faculty:* 27 full-time (11 women). *Students:* 74 full-time (41 women); includes 16 minority (7 Black or African American, non-Hispanic/Latino; 5 Asian, non-Hispanic/Latino; 4 Hispanic/Latino), 8 international. Average age 28. 120 applicants, 15% accepted, 10 enrolled. In 2017, 8 doctorates awarded. *Degree requirements:* For doctorate, variable foreign language requirement, comprehensive exam, thesis/dissertation. *Entrance requirements:* For doctorate, GRE General Test. Additional exam requirements/recommendations for international students: Required—TOEFL (minimum score 600 paper-based; 100 iBT), IELTS. *Application deadline:* For fall admission, 12/15 for domestic and international students. Application fee: $75. Electronic applications accepted. *Financial support:* Fellowships with full tuition reimbursements, research assistantships with full tuition reimbursements, teaching assistantships with full tuition reimbursements, Federal Work-Study, and institutionally sponsored loans available. Financial award application deadline: 4/15; financial award applicants required to submit FAFSA. *Faculty research:* American, European, Latin American, East Asian, and African history. *Unit head:* Dr. Michael Kwass, Chair, 410-516-5789, Fax: 410-516-7586, E-mail: kwass@jhu.edu. *Application contact:* Megan B. Zeller, Senior Academic Program Coordinator, 410-516-5296, Fax: 410-516-7586, E-mail: mzeller4@jhu.edu.
Website: http://history.jhu.edu/

Kansas State University, Graduate School, College of Arts and Sciences, Department of History, Manhattan, KS 66506. Offers MA, PhD. *Program availability:* Part-time. *Degree requirements:* For master's, thesis (for some programs); for doctorate, one foreign language, thesis/dissertation, qualifying exam. *Entrance requirements:* For master's, GRE General Test, minimum undergraduate GPA of 3.0; for doctorate, GRE General Test. Additional exam requirements/recommendations for international students: Required—TOEFL (minimum score 600 paper-based). Electronic applications accepted. *Faculty research:* Environmental history, religious history, American social history, history of war and society, history of international relations and diplomacy, gender and women's history.

Kent State University, College of Arts and Sciences, Department of History, Kent, OH 44242-0001. Offers history (MA, PhD), including history (MA), history for teachers (MA). *Program availability:* Part-time. *Faculty:* 13 full-time (5 women), 1 part-time/adjunct (0 women). *Students:* 23 full-time (6 women), 3 part-time (2 women); includes 4 minority (2 Black or African American, non-Hispanic/Latino; 1 Hispanic/Latino; 1 Two or more races, non-Hispanic/Latino). Average age 35. 12 applicants, 50% accepted, 3 enrolled. In 2017, 5 master's, 1 doctorate awarded. *Degree requirements:* For master's, one foreign language, thesis (for some programs); for doctorate, one foreign language, comprehensive exam, thesis/dissertation. *Entrance requirements:* For master's, GRE General Test, official transcript(s), statement of purpose describing professional objectives and proposed field of study, significant piece of written work, three letters of recommendation (preferably academic); for doctorate, GRE General Test, official transcript(s), master's degree in history or related discipline, statement of purpose describing professional objectives and proposed field of study, significant piece of written work, three letters of recommendation (preferably academic). Additional exam requirements/recommendations for international students: Required—TOEFL (minimum score 550 paper-based, 79 iBT), Michigan English Language Assessment Battery (minimum score 77), IELTS (minimum score 6.5) or PTE (minimum score 58). *Application deadline:* For fall admission, 2/1 for domestic and international students. Applications are processed on a rolling basis. Application fee: $45 ($70 for international students). Electronic applications accepted. *Expenses:* Tuition, state resident: full-time $11,310; part-time $515 per credit hour. Tuition, nonresident: full-time $20,396; part-time $928 per credit hour. *International tuition:* $18,544 full-time. *Financial support:* Teaching assistantships with full tuition reimbursements and unspecified assistantships available. Financial award application deadline: 2/1. *Unit head:* Dr. Brian Hayashi, Professor and Chair, 330-672-8914, E-mail: bhayashi@kent.edu. *Application contact:* Kevin Adams, Associate Professor and Graduate Coordinator, 330-672-8902, E-mail: kadams9@kent.edu.
Website: https://www.kent.edu/history/

Lake Forest College, Graduate Program in Liberal Studies, Lake Forest, IL 60045. Offers American studies (MLS); cinema in East Asia (MLS); environmental studies (MLS); history (MLS); Medieval and Renaissance art (MLS); philosophy (MLS); Spanish (MLS); writing (MLS). *Program availability:* Part-time, evening/weekend. *Faculty:* 11 full-time (3 women). *Students:* 34 part-time (19 women); includes 3 minority (1 Asian, non-Hispanic/Latino; 2 Hispanic/Latino). Average age 36. 20 applicants, 55% accepted, 8 enrolled. In 2017, 5 master's awarded. *Degree requirements:* For master's, thesis optional, 8 courses, including at least 3 interdisciplinary seminars. *Entrance requirements:* For master's, transcript, essay, interview. Additional exam requirements/recommendations for international students: Required—TOEFL (minimum score 550 paper-based; 83 iBT); Recommended—IELTS (minimum score 6.5). *Application deadline:* For fall admission, 7/15 priority date for domestic students, 6/1 priority date for international students; for spring admission, 12/1 priority date for domestic students, 10/1 priority date for international students. Applications are processed on a rolling basis. Application fee: $30. Electronic applications accepted. *Expenses:* $2,650 per course. *Financial support:* In 2017–18, 2 students received support. Partial tuition grants (for full-time teachers) available. *Faculty research:* Religion in America, Asian philosophy, cinema studies, theater studies, sociology of religion. *Unit head:* Prof. D. L. LeMahieu, Director, 847-735-5133, Fax: 847-735-6291, E-mail: lemahieu@lakeforest.edu. *Application contact:* Prof. Carol Gayle, Associate Director, 847-735-5083, Fax: 847-735-6291, E-mail: gayle@lakeforest.edu.
Website: http://www.lakeforest.edu/academics/programs/mls/

Lakehead University, Graduate Studies, Department of History, Thunder Bay, ON P7B 5E1, Canada. Offers gerontology (MA); history (MA); women's studies (MA). *Program availability:* Part-time. *Degree requirements:* For master's, one foreign language, thesis. *Entrance requirements:* For master's, minimum B average. Additional exam requirements/recommendations for international students: Required—TOEFL. *Faculty research:* Canadian history, British history, Russian/German history, women's studies.

Lamar University, College of Graduate Studies, College of Arts and Sciences, Department of History, Beaumont, TX 77701. Offers MA. *Program availability:* Part-time. *Faculty:* 12 full-time (7 women), 4 part-time/adjunct (2 women). *Students:* 4 full-time (2 women), 5 part-time (3 women); includes 1 minority (Black or African American, non-Hispanic/Latino). Average age 33. 4 applicants, 100% accepted, 1 enrolled. In 2017, 2 master's awarded. *Degree requirements:* For master's, comprehensive exam (for some programs), thesis (for some programs). *Entrance requirements:* For master's, GRE General Test, minimum GPA of 2.5 in last 60 hours of undergraduate course work. Additional exam requirements/recommendations for international students: Required—TOEFL (minimum score 550 paper-based; 79 iBT), IELTS (minimum score 6.5). *Application deadline:* For fall admission, 8/11 for domestic students, 7/1 for international students; for spring admission, 1/5 for domestic students, 12/1 for international students. Applications are processed on a rolling basis. Application fee: $25 ($50 for international students). Electronic applications accepted. *Expenses:* Contact institution. *Financial support:* In 2017–18, fellowships (averaging $1,000 per year), teaching assistantships (averaging $2,000 per year) were awarded. Financial award application deadline: 4/1. *Faculty research:* Old South, nineteenth-century reform, twentieth-century U.S., religion in America's South, Renaissance/early modern Europe. *Unit head:* Dr. Mary L. Scheer, Chair, 409-880-8511, Fax: 409-880-8710. *Application contact:* Deidre Mayer, Interim

Director, Admissions and Academic Services, 409-880-8888, Fax: 409-880-7419, E-mail: gradmissions@lamar.edu. Website: http://artssciences.lamar.edu/history/

La Salle University, School of Arts and Sciences, Program in History, Philadelphia, PA 19141-1199. Offers American history (Certificate); European history (Certificate); history (MA); history for educators (MA); public history (MA); teaching advanced placement history (Certificate); world history (Certificate). *Program availability:* Part-time. *Faculty:* 4 full-time (1 woman), 2 part-time/adjunct (0 women). *Students:* 2 full-time (0 women), 10 part-time (5 women); includes 1 minority (Asian, non-Hispanic/Latino). Average age 37. 9 applicants, 78% accepted, 2 enrolled. In 2017, 7 master's awarded. *Degree requirements:* For master's, thesis or comprehensive exam. *Entrance requirements:* For master's, GRE or MAT, 18 hours of undergraduate coursework in history or a related discipline with minimum GPA of 3.0; two letters of recommendation; brief personal statement (250 to 500 words); writing sample (preferably from an undergraduate research paper). Additional exam requirements/recommendations for international students: Required—TOEFL. *Application deadline:* For fall admission, 8/15 priority date for domestic students, 7/15 for international students; for spring admission, 12/15 priority date for domestic students, 11/15 for international students; for summer admission, 4/15 priority date for domestic students, 3/15 for international students. Applications are processed on a rolling basis. Application fee: $35. Electronic applications accepted. Application fee is waived when completed online. *Expenses:* Contact institution. *Financial support:* In 2017–18, 1 student received support. Scholarships/grants available. Support available to part-time students. Financial award application deadline: 8/31; financial award applicants required to submit FAFSA. *Unit head:* Dr. George B. Stow, Director, 215-951-1097, E-mail: grahis@lasalle.edu. *Application contact:* Elizabeth Heenan, Director, Graduate and Adult Enrollment, 215-951-1100, Fax: 215-951-1462, E-mail: heenan@lasalle.edu. Website: http://www.lasalle.edu/master-history/

Laurentian University, School of Graduate Studies and Research, Programme in History, Sudbury, ON P3E 2C6, Canada. Offers European history (MA); history of Northern Ontario (MA); North American history (MA). *Program availability:* Part-time. *Degree requirements:* For master's, thesis or alternative. *Entrance requirements:* For master's, honors degree with minimum second class. *Faculty research:* Franco-Ontarian history, northern Ontarian history, Canadian social history, European social history, Franco-Canadian history.

Lee University, Program in Education, Cleveland, TN 37320-3450. Offers art (MAT); curriculum and instruction (M Ed, Ed S); early childhood (MAT); educational leadership (M Ed, Ed S); elementary education (MAT); English and math (MAT); English and science (MAT); English and social studies (MAT); higher education administration (MS); history (MAT); history and economics (MAT); math and science (MAT); math and social studies (MAT); middle grades (MAT); science and social studies (MASW); secondary education (MAT); Spanish (MAT); special education (M Ed, MAT); TESOL (MAT). *Accreditation:* NCATE. *Program availability:* Part-time. *Faculty:* 15 full-time (7 women), 8 part-time/adjunct (3 women). *Students:* 28 full-time (21 women), 77 part-time (48 women); includes 12 minority (7 Black or African American, non-Hispanic/Latino; 2 Hispanic/Latino; 3 Two or more races, non-Hispanic/Latino), 1 international. Average age 31. 35 applicants, 83% accepted, 22 enrolled. In 2017, 54 master's, 4 other advanced degrees awarded. *Degree requirements:* For master's, variable foreign language requirement, thesis optional, internship. *Entrance requirements:* For master's, MAT or GRE General Test, minimum undergraduate GPA of 2.75, 3 letters of recommendation, interview, writing sample, official transcripts, background check; for Ed S, minimum undergraduate and master's GPA of 2.75, official transcripts for undergraduate and master's degrees. Additional exam requirements/recommendations for international students: Required—TOEFL (minimum score 61 iBT). *Application deadline:* For fall admission, 6/1 priority date for domestic and international students; for spring admission, 11/1 priority date for domestic and international students; for summer admission, 4/1 priority date for domestic and international students. Applications are processed on a rolling basis. Application fee: $25. Electronic applications accepted. *Expenses:* Tuition: Full-time $12,780; part-time $710 per credit hour. *Required fees:* $60; $60 per term. Tuition and fees vary according to program. *Financial support:* In 2017–18, 32 students received support. Career-related internships or fieldwork, Federal Work-Study, institutionally sponsored loans, scholarships/grants, and unspecified assistantships available. Financial award application deadline: 3/1; financial award applicants required to submit FAFSA. *Unit head:* Dr. William Kamm, Director, 423-614-8544, E-mail: wkamm@leeuniversity.edu. *Application contact:* Crystal Keeter, Graduate Education Secretary, 423-614-8544, E-mail: ckeeter@leeuniversity.edu. Website: http://www.leeuniversity.edu/academics/graduate/education

Lehigh University, College of Arts and Sciences, Department of History, Bethlehem, PA 18015. Offers Atlantic world (PhD); British history (PhD); history (MA); industrial and modern America (PhD); public history (MA). *Program availability:* Part-time. *Faculty:* 14 full-time (7 women). *Students:* 19 full-time (6 women), 15 part-time (2 women); includes 2 minority (1 Black or African American, non-Hispanic/Latino; 1 Two or more races, non-Hispanic/Latino), 2 international. Average age 35. 12 applicants, 58% accepted, 1 enrolled. In 2017, 3 master's, 2 doctorates awarded. Terminal master's awarded for partial completion of doctoral program. *Degree requirements:* For master's, comprehensive exam (for some programs), thesis (for some programs), comprehensive exam or thesis; for doctorate, comprehensive exam, thesis/dissertation. *Entrance requirements:* For master's, GRE General Test, recommendations, writing sample; for doctorate, GRE General Test, recommendations, writing samples. Additional exam requirements/recommendations for international students: Required—TOEFL. *Application deadline:* For fall admission, 2/15 for domestic and international students. Application fee: $75. *Financial support:* In 2017–18, 2 fellowships with full tuition reimbursements (averaging $22,500 per year), 10 teaching assistantships with full tuition reimbursements (averaging $10,000 per year) were awarded; research assistantships, institutionally sponsored loans, scholarships/grants, tuition waivers (full and partial), and unspecified assistantships also available. Financial award application deadline: 1/15. *Faculty research:* Colonial America, modern America, history of technology, Atlantic world, French Atlantic, Spanish Atlantic, British empire, gender, intellectual history, African diaspora history. *Unit head:* Prof. John Pettegrew, Chairman, 610-758-3360, Fax: 610-758-6554, E-mail: jcp5@lehigh.edu. *Application contact:* Dr. John Savage, Graduate Coordinator, 610-758-3363, Fax: 610-758-6554, E-mail: jms8@lehigh.edu. Website: http://history.cas2.lehigh.edu/

Lehman College of the City University of New York, School of Arts and Humanities, Department of History, Bronx, NY 10468-1589. Offers MA. *Program availability:* Part-time, evening/weekend. *Degree requirements:* For master's, comprehensive exam, thesis. *Entrance requirements:* For master's, 18 undergraduate credits in history, minimum GPA of 2.7.

Liberty University, College of Arts and Sciences, Lynchburg, VA 24515. Offers English (MA); history (MA); professional writing (MA). *Accreditation:* AACN. *Program availability:* Part-time, online learning. *Students:* 176 full-time (110 women), 302 part-time (170 women); includes 101 minority (67 Black or African American, non-Hispanic/Latino; 5 American Indian or Alaska Native, non-Hispanic/Latino; 1 Asian, non-Hispanic/Latino;

14 Hispanic/Latino; 14 Two or more races, non-Hispanic/Latino), 10 international. Average age 38. 476 applicants, 57% accepted, 150 enrolled. In 2017, 82 master's awarded. *Degree requirements:* For master's, comprehensive exam (for some programs), thesis (for some programs). *Entrance requirements:* For master's, GRE, minimum undergraduate GPA of 3.0, letters of recommendation, statement of purpose. Additional exam requirements/recommendations for international students: Required—TOEFL (minimum score 600 paper-based; 100 iBT). *Application deadline:* For fall admission, 6/1 for domestic students; for spring admission, 11/1 for domestic students. Applications are processed on a rolling basis. Application fee: $50. Electronic applications accepted. *Financial support:* Teaching assistantships with tuition reimbursements and Federal Work-Study available. *Faculty research:* God concept and adult attachment, building marital strength, image of God and gender, breastfeeding behavior among adolescent mothers, osteoporosis. *Unit head:* Dr. Roger Schultz, Dean, 434-592-4031, Fax: 434-522-0430, E-mail: rschultz@liberty.edu. *Application contact:* Dr. Terry Elam, Director of Graduate Admissions, 434-592-3966, Fax: 434-522-0430, E-mail: gradadmissions@liberty.edu.

Lincoln University, Graduate Studies, Jefferson City, MO 65101. Offers business administration (MBA), including accounting, management, management information systems, public administration/policy; elementary teaching (M Ed); environmental science (MS); guidance and counseling (M Ed), including community/agency counseling, elementary school, secondary school; higher education (MA); history (MA); integrated agricultural systems (MS); middle school (M Ed); natural sciences (MS); secondary teaching (M Ed); sociology (MA); sociology/criminal justice (MA). *Program availability:* Part-time, evening/weekend, 100% online, blended/hybrid learning. *Students:* 40 full-time (23 women), 64 part-time (32 women); includes 33 minority (30 Black or African American, non-Hispanic/Latino; 2 Hispanic/Latino; 1 Two or more races, non-Hispanic/Latino), 12 international. Average age 33. 48 applicants, 81% accepted, 22 enrolled. In 2017, 46 master's awarded. *Degree requirements:* For master's, comprehensive exam, thesis optional. *Entrance requirements:* For master's, GRE, MAT, or GMAT, minimum GPA of 2.75 overall, 3.0 in courses related to specialization; 3 letters of recommendation; minimum C average in English composition; personal statement of purpose. Additional exam requirements/recommendations for international students: Required—TOEFL (minimum score 500 paper-based; 61 iBT), IELTS (minimum score 5.5), Michigan English Language Assessment Battery (minimum score 80). *Application deadline:* For fall admission, 7/1 priority date for domestic students, 5/1 priority date for international students; for spring admission, 11/1 priority date for domestic students, 10/1 priority date for international students; for summer admission, 6/1 priority date for domestic students. Applications are processed on a rolling basis. Application fee: $30. Electronic applications accepted. *Expenses:* Tuition, state resident: part-time $291 per credit hour. Tuition, nonresident: part-time $541.50 per credit hour. *Financial support:* In 2017–18, 2 fellowships with tuition reimbursements, 3 research assistantships with tuition reimbursements were awarded; Federal Work-Study, scholarships/grants, and unspecified assistantships also available. Support available to part-time students. Financial award application deadline: 3/1; financial award applicants required to submit FAFSA. *Unit head:* Dr. Debra F. Greene, Interim Provost, 573-681-5247, Fax: 573-681-5106, E-mail: gradschool@lincolnu.edu. *Application contact:* Irasema Steck, Administrative Assistant, 573-681-5247, Fax: 573-681-5106, E-mail: gradschool@lincolnu.edu. Website: http://www.lincolnu.edu/web/graduate-studies/graduate-studies

Long Island University–LIU Post, College of Liberal Arts and Sciences, Brookville, NY 11548-1300. Offers applied mathematics (MS); behavior analysis (MA); biology (MS); criminal justice (MS); earth science (MS); English (MA); environmental sustainability (MS); genetic counseling (MS); history (MA); interdisciplinary studies (MA, MS); political science (MA); psychology (MA). *Program availability:* Part-time, evening/weekend, blended/hybrid learning. *Faculty:* 41 full-time (21 women), 24 part-time/adjunct (13 women). *Students:* 173 full-time (124 women), 62 part-time (35 women); includes 54 minority (11 Black or African American, non-Hispanic/Latino; 13 Asian, non-Hispanic/Latino; 23 Hispanic/Latino; 7 Two or more races, non-Hispanic/Latino), 12 international. Average age 28. 368 applicants, 54% accepted, 74 enrolled. In 2017, 89 master's, 15 other advanced degrees awarded. Terminal master's awarded for partial completion of doctoral program. *Degree requirements:* For master's, comprehensive exam (for some programs), thesis (for some programs). *Entrance requirements:* Additional exam requirements/recommendations for international students: Required—TOEFL, IELTS, or PTE. *Application deadline:* Applications are processed on a rolling basis. Application fee: $50. Electronic applications accepted. *Expenses:* Tuition: Full-time $21,618; part-time $1201 per credit. *Required fees:* $1840; $920 per term. Tuition and fees vary according to course load. *Financial support:* In 2017–18, 165 students received support. Fellowships, research assistantships, teaching assistantships, career-related internships or fieldwork, Federal Work-Study, scholarships/grants, tuition waivers (partial), and unspecified assistantships available. Support available to part-time students. Financial award application deadline: 2/15; financial award applicants required to submit FAFSA. *Faculty research:* Biology, environmental sustainability, mathematics, psychology, genetic counseling. *Unit head:* Dr. Nathaniel Bowditch, Dean, 516-299-2234, Fax: 516-299-4140, E-mail: nathaniel.bowditch@liu.edu. *Application contact:* Rita Langdon, Graduate Admissions, 516-299-2900, Fax: 516-299-2137, E-mail: post-enroll@liu.edu. Website: http://liu.edu/CWPost/Academics/Schools/CLAS

Louisiana State University and Agricultural & Mechanical College, Graduate School, College of Humanities and Social Sciences, Department of History, Baton Rouge, LA 70803. Offers MA, PhD. *Faculty:* 22 full-time (11 women). *Students:* 43 full-time (19 women), 7 part-time (4 women); includes 13 minority (2 Black or African American, non-Hispanic/Latino; 8 Hispanic/Latino; 3 Two or more races, non-Hispanic/Latino). Average age 32. 34 applicants, 79% accepted, 9 enrolled. In 2017, 6 master's, 4 doctorates awarded. *Financial support:* In 2017–18, 1 fellowship (averaging $34,642 per year), 31 teaching assistantships (averaging $20,331 per year) were awarded. *Total annual research expenditures:* $62,911.

Louisiana Tech University, Graduate School, College of Liberal Arts, Ruston, LA 71272. Offers architecture (M Arch); art (MFA), including graphic design, photography, studio; audiology (Au D); communication (MA), including speech communication, theatre; English (MA), including literature, technical writing; history (MA); speech pathology (MA); technical writing and communication (Graduate Certificate). *Program availability:* Part-time. *Faculty:* 63 full-time (25 women), 5 part-time/adjunct (3 women). *Students:* 114 full-time (29 women), 31 part-time (19 women); includes 12 minority (4 Black or African American, non-Hispanic/Latino; 1 Asian, non-Hispanic/Latino; 3 Hispanic/Latino; 4 Two or more races, non-Hispanic/Latino), 5 international. Average age 30. 146 applicants, 59% accepted, 37 enrolled. In 2017, 49 master's, 3 doctorates awarded. *Degree requirements:* For master's, thesis (for some programs); for doctorate, thesis/dissertation. *Entrance requirements:* For master's, GRE General Test; for doctorate, GRE General Test, bachelor's degree, minimum GPA of 3.0 or 3.2 on last 60 hours attempted. Additional exam requirements/recommendations for international students: Required—TOEFL (minimum score 550 paper-based; 80 iBT), IELTS (minimum score 6.5). *Application deadline:* For fall admission, 8/1 priority date for domestic students, 6/1 for international students; for winter admission, 11/1 priority date for domestic students, 9/1 for international students; for spring admission, 2/1 priority

date for domestic students, 12/1 for international students; for summer admission, 5/1 priority date for domestic students, 3/1 for international students. Application fee: $40 ($50 for international students). Electronic applications accepted. *Expenses:* Tuition, state resident: full-time $5146. Tuition, nonresident: full-time $10,147. *International tuition:* $10,267 full-time. *Required fees:* $2273. *Financial support:* In 2017–18, 63 students received support, including 46 research assistantships (averaging $5,229 per year), 7 teaching assistantships (averaging $5,543 per year); fellowships, career-related internships or fieldwork, Federal Work-Study, institutionally sponsored loans, tuition waivers (partial), and unspecified assistantships also available. Financial award application deadline: 2/1. *Faculty research:* Contributing to the expansion of historical and social scientific knowledge and understanding through original research and publication; diverse language, ethnic, cultural, and socioeconomic backgrounds with disorders of speech, language, swallowing, hearing, and cognitive aspects of communication; prevention of communication, swallowing, and hearing disorders. *Unit head:* Dr. Donald P. Kaczvinsky, Dean, 318-257-4805, Fax: 318-257-3935, E-mail: dkaczv@latech.edu. *Application contact:* Mary Green, Administrative Assistant, 318-257-2924, Fax: 318-257-4487, E-mail: meg@latech.edu.
Website: http://liberalarts.latech.edu/

Loyola University Chicago, Graduate School, Department of History, Chicago, IL 60611. Offers history (MA, PhD); public history (MA). *Program availability:* Part-time, evening/weekend. *Faculty:* 38 full-time (21 women), 9 part-time/adjunct (6 women). *Students:* 38 full-time (21 women), 9 part-time (6 women); includes 5 minority (1 Black or African American, non-Hispanic/Latino; 1 Asian, non-Hispanic/Latino; 2 Hispanic/Latino; 1 Two or more races, non-Hispanic/Latino), 1 international. Average age 30. 77 applicants, 57% accepted, 13 enrolled. In 2017, 14 master's, 8 doctorates awarded. Terminal master's awarded for partial completion of doctoral program. *Degree requirements:* For master's, one foreign language, comprehensive exam, thesis optional, portfolio (for public history program); for doctorate, 2 foreign languages, comprehensive exam, thesis/dissertation. *Entrance requirements:* For master's, GRE General Test, research paper/writing sample; for doctorate, GRE General Test, seminar paper or master's thesis. Additional exam requirements/recommendations for international students: Required—TOEFL (minimum score 550 paper-based), IELTS. *Application deadline:* For fall admission, 5/1 for domestic students; for spring admission, 10/1 for domestic students. Applications are processed on a rolling basis. Application fee: $50. Electronic applications accepted. Application fee is waived when completed online. *Expenses:* $19,026 full-time. *Financial support:* In 2017–18, 20 students received support, including 1 fellowship with full tuition reimbursement available (averaging $20,000 per year), 1 research assistantship with full tuition reimbursement available (averaging $18,000 per year), 16 teaching assistantships with full tuition reimbursements available (averaging $18,000 per year); Federal Work-Study, scholarships/grants, traineeships, health care benefits, and unspecified assistantships also available. Financial award application deadline: 1/1; financial award applicants required to submit FAFSA. *Faculty research:* Medieval and early modern Europe, U.S. public history, U.S. urban history, gender history, transnational history. *Unit head:* Dr. Stephen Schloesser, Chair, 773-508-2221, Fax: 773-508-3693, E-mail: sschloesser@luc.edu. *Application contact:* Dr. Patricia Mooney-Melvin, Director, Graduate Programs, 773-508-2228, Fax: 773-508-3693, E-mail: pmooney@luc.edu.
Website: http://www.luc.edu/history/

Marquette University, Graduate School, College of Arts and Sciences, Department of History, Milwaukee, WI 53201-1881. Offers European history (MA, PhD); global studies (MA); United States history (MA, PhD). *Program availability:* Part-time. *Degree requirements:* For master's, comprehensive exam, essay, 2 classes of research seminars (6 hours); for doctorate, one foreign language, comprehensive exam, thesis/dissertation, 2 research seminars, dissertation seminar. *Entrance requirements:* For master's, GRE General Test, official transcripts from all current and previous colleges/universities except Marquette, one-page statement of purpose, three letters of recommendation from former teachers; for doctorate, GRE General Test, official transcripts from all current and previous colleges/universities except Marquette, one-page statement of purpose, three letters of recommendation from former teachers, writing sample. Additional exam requirements/recommendations for international students: Required—TOEFL. Electronic applications accepted. *Faculty research:* Children's history, Soviet and post-Soviet history, modern Ireland and Britain, Japan and martial arts, American Catholicism.

Marshall University, Academic Affairs Division, College of Liberal Arts, Department of History, Huntington, WV 25755. Offers MA, Certificate. *Students:* 17 full-time (10 women), 2 part-time (1 woman); includes 1 minority (Two or more races, non-Hispanic/Latino). Average age 29. In 2017, 6 master's awarded. *Entrance requirements:* For master's, GRE. Application fee: $40. *Unit head:* Dr. Dan Holbrook, Chair, 304-696-2417, Fax: 304-696-2957, E-mail: holbrook@marshall.edu. *Application contact:* Graduate Admissions, 304-746-1900, Fax: 304-746-1902, E-mail: services@marshall.edu.

McGill University, Faculty of Graduate and Postdoctoral Studies, Faculty of Arts, Department of History and Classical Studies, Montréal, QC H3A 2T5, Canada. Offers history (MA, PhD); history of medicine (MA).

McMaster University, School of Graduate Studies, Faculty of Humanities, Department of History, Hamilton, ON L8S 4M2, Canada. Offers MA, PhD. *Program availability:* Part-time. *Degree requirements:* For master's, one foreign language, thesis or alternative; for doctorate, one foreign language, comprehensive exam, thesis/dissertation. *Entrance requirements:* For master's, honors BA in history, minimum B+ average. Additional exam requirements/recommendations for international students: Required—TOEFL (minimum score 580 paper-based). *Faculty research:* Canadian, European, British, U.S. history; ancient history.

Memorial University of Newfoundland, School of Graduate Studies, Department of History, St. John's, NL A1C 5S7, Canada. Offers MA, PhD. *Program availability:* Part-time. *Degree requirements:* For master's, thesis or comprehensive exam; for doctorate, one foreign language, comprehensive exam, thesis/dissertation, oral defense of thesis. *Entrance requirements:* For master's, honors degree or equivalent; for doctorate, master's degree. Electronic applications accepted. *Faculty research:* Canadian history, maritime history, Newfoundland history, social history, labor history.

Miami University, College of Arts and Science, Department of History, Oxford, OH 45056. Offers MA. *Students:* 13 full-time (7 women), 1 international. Average age 26. In 2017, 5 master's awarded. *Expenses:* Tuition, state resident: full-time $13,812; part-time $575 per credit hour. Tuition, nonresident: full-time $30,860; part-time $1286 per credit hour. *Unit head:* Dr. Weitse de Boer, Department Chair, 513-529-5146, E-mail: deboerwt@miamioh.edu. *Application contact:* Dr. Daniel Prior, Director of Graduate Studies, 513-529-7148, E-mail: priordg@miamioh.edu.
Website: http://www.MiamiOH.edu/history/

Michigan State University, The Graduate School, College of Social Science, Department of History, East Lansing, MI 48824. Offers history (MA, PhD); history-secondary school teaching (MA). *Entrance requirements:* Additional exam requirements/recommendations for international students: Required—TOEFL. Electronic applications accepted.

Middle Tennessee State University, College of Graduate Studies, College of Liberal Arts, Department of History, Program in History, Murfreesboro, TN 37132. Offers MA. *Program availability:* Part-time, evening/weekend, online learning. *Degree requirements:* For master's, one foreign language, comprehensive exam, thesis optional. *Entrance requirements:* For master's, GRE. Additional exam requirements/recommendations for international students: Required—TOEFL (minimum score 525 paper-based; 71 iBT) or IELTS (minimum score 6).

Midwestern State University, Billie Doris McAda Graduate School, Prothro-Yeager College of Humanities and Social Sciences, Department of History, Wichita Falls, TX 76308. Offers MA. *Program availability:* Part-time. *Degree requirements:* For master's, one foreign language, thesis. *Entrance requirements:* For master's, GRE General Test. Additional exam requirements/recommendations for international students: Required—TOEFL (minimum score 550 paper-based). Electronic applications accepted. *Faculty research:* Early modern England, Spanish borderlands, Jacksonian era, New Deal, Texas and the Southwest.

Millersville University of Pennsylvania, College of Graduate Studies and Adult Learning, College of Arts, Humanities and Social Sciences, Department of History, Millersville, PA 17551-0302. Offers MA. *Program availability:* Part-time. *Faculty:* 6 full-time (4 women). *Students:* 1 full-time (0 women), 8 part-time (5 women). Average age 37. 6 applicants, 67% accepted. In 2017, 9 master's awarded. *Degree requirements:* For master's, comprehensive exam, thesis optional. *Entrance requirements:* For master's, GRE if undergraduate GPA is lower than 2.85, 8-12 page academic writing sample; minimum of 18 semester hours in history; minimum overall GPA of 2.85, history 3.0. Additional exam requirements/recommendations for international students: Required—TOEFL (minimum score 80 iBT), IELTS (minimum score 6.5), PTE (minimum score 60). *Application deadline:* Applications are processed on a rolling basis. Application fee: $40. Electronic applications accepted. *Expenses:* $500 per credit resident tuition and fees; $750 per credit non-resident tuition and fees; $114.75 per credit general fee (maximum of 12 credits); technology fee $27 per credit (resident), $39 per credit (non-resident). *Financial support:* In 2017–18, 2 students received support. Unspecified assistantships available. Financial award application deadline: 3/15; financial award applicants required to submit FAFSA. *Faculty research:* Modern and early American history, modern and early European history, genocide and Holocaust studies, women's history, military and diplomacy. *Unit head:* Dr. John M. MacLarnon, III, Department Chair, 717-871-7193, Fax: 717-871-7939, E-mail: john.mclarnon@millersville.edu. *Application contact:* Dr. Victor S. DeSantis, Dean of College of Graduate Studies and Adult Learning/Associate Provost for Civic and Community Engagement, 717-871-7619, Fax: 717-871-7954, E-mail: victor.desantis@millersville.edu.
Website: http://www.millersville.edu/history/graduate-program.php

Minnesota State University Mankato, College of Graduate Studies and Research, College of Social and Behavioral Sciences, Department of History, Mankato, MN 56001. Offers history (MA, MS); social studies (MAT). *Degree requirements:* For master's, one foreign language, comprehensive exam, thesis or alternative. *Entrance requirements:* For master's, minimum GPA of 3.0, statement of purpose. Additional exam requirements/recommendations for international students: Required—TOEFL (minimum score 600 paper-based). Electronic applications accepted.

Mississippi College, Graduate School, College of Arts and Sciences, School of Humanities and Social Sciences, Department of History, Political Science, Administration of Justice, and Paralegal Studies, Clinton, MS 39058. Offers administration of justice (MSS); history (M Ed, MA, MSS); paralegal studies (Certificate); political science (MSS); social sciences (M Ed, MSS). *Program availability:* Part-time. *Degree requirements:* For master's, one foreign language, comprehensive exam, thesis (for some programs). *Entrance requirements:* For master's, GRE or NTE, minimum GPA of 2.5. Additional exam requirements/recommendations for international students: Recommended—TOEFL, IELTS. Electronic applications accepted.

Mississippi State University, College of Arts and Sciences, Department of History, Mississippi State, MS 39762. Offers Africa (MA, PhD); Asia (MA, PhD); Europe (MA, PhD); Latin America (MA, PhD); United States (MA, PhD); world history (MA, PhD). *Program availability:* Part-time. *Faculty:* 20 full-time (8 women). *Students:* 47 full-time (18 women), 11 part-time (2 women); includes 7 minority (5 Black or African American, non-Hispanic/Latino; 2 Two or more races, non-Hispanic/Latino), 2 international. Average age 29. 27 applicants, 78% accepted, 15 enrolled. In 2017, 4 master's, 5 doctorates awarded. *Degree requirements:* For master's, one foreign language, comprehensive exam, thesis optional; for doctorate, 2 foreign languages, thesis/dissertation, comprehensive oral and written exam. *Entrance requirements:* For master's, minimum GPA of 3.0 on last two years of undergraduate courses; for doctorate, GRE, writing sample, minimum graduate GPA of 3.0. Additional exam requirements/recommendations for international students: Required—TOEFL (minimum score 550 paper-based). *Application deadline:* For fall admission, 4/1 for domestic students, 5/1 for international students; for spring admission, 11/1 for domestic students, 9/1 for international students. Applications are processed on a rolling basis. Application fee: $60 ($80 for international students). Electronic applications accepted. *Expenses:* Tuition, state resident: full-time $8318; part-time $462.12 per credit hour. Tuition, nonresident: full-time $22,358; part-time $1242.12 per credit hour. *Required fees:* $110; $12.24 per credit hour. $6.12 per semester. *Financial support:* In 2017–18, 41 teaching assistantships with full tuition reimbursements (averaging $12,345 per year) were awarded; Federal Work-Study, institutionally sponsored loans, scholarships/grants, and unspecified assistantships also available. Financial award application deadline: 4/1; financial award applicants required to submit FAFSA. *Faculty research:* U.S. political, diplomatic, military, social, and cultural history; modern Europe; Latin America; Asian history; African history. *Unit head:* Dr. Alan I. Marcus, Professor and Head, 662-325-7075, Fax: 662-325-1139, E-mail: aim10@msstate.edu. *Application contact:* Marina Hunt, Admissions and Enrollment Assistant, 662-325-5188, E-mail: mhunt@grad.msstate.edu.
Website: http://www.history.msstate.edu

Missouri State University, Graduate College, College of Humanities and Public Affairs, Department of History, Springfield, MO 65897. Offers history (MA); history education (MS Ed); history for teachers (Certificate). *Program availability:* Part-time, 100% online, blended/hybrid learning. *Faculty:* 18 full-time (7 women). *Students:* 10 full-time (5 women), 37 part-time (17 women); includes 1 minority (Asian, non-Hispanic/Latino), 2 international. Average age 33. 31 applicants, 39% accepted, 8 enrolled. In 2017, 16 master's awarded. *Degree requirements:* For master's, comprehensive exam, thesis or alternative. *Entrance requirements:* For master's, minimum GPA of 2.75, 24 hours of undergraduate course work in history (MA), 9-12 teaching certification (MS Ed). Additional exam requirements/recommendations for international students: Required—TOEFL (minimum score 550 paper-based; 79 iBT), IELTS (minimum score 6). *Application deadline:* For fall admission, 7/20 priority date for domestic students, 5/1 for international students; for spring admission, 12/20 priority date for domestic students, 9/1 for international students. Applications are processed on a rolling basis. Application fee: $35 ($50 for international students). Electronic applications accepted. *Expenses:* Tuition, state resident: full-time $2915; part-time $2021 per credit hour. Tuition, nonresident: full-time $5354; part-time $3647 per credit hour. *International tuition:* $11,992 full-time. *Required fees:* $173; $173 per credit hour. Tuition and fees vary

according to class time, course level, course load, degree level, campus/location and program. *Financial support:* Federal Work-Study, scholarships/grants, and unspecified assistantships available. Support available to part-time students. Financial award application deadline: 3/31; financial award applicants required to submit FAFSA. *Faculty research:* Early modern France, cultural history of modern Britain, Latin American history, women's history, American Civil War in Missouri. *Unit head:* Dr. Kathleen Kennedy, Department Head, 417-836-5511, Fax: 417-836-5523, E-mail: history@missouristate.edu. *Application contact:* Stephanie Praschan, Director, Graduate Enrollment Management, 417-836-5330, Fax: 417-836-6200, E-mail: stephaniepraschan@missouristate.edu.
Website: http://history.missouristate.edu/

Monmouth University, Graduate Studies, Program in History, West Long Branch, NJ 07764-1898. Offers European history (MA); United States history (MA); world history (MA). *Program availability:* Part-time, evening/weekend. *Faculty:* 4 full-time (2 women). *Students:* 3 full-time (2 women), 22 part-time (7 women); includes 4 minority (all Hispanic/Latino). Average age 33. In 2017, 14 master's awarded. *Degree requirements:* For master's, comprehensive exam (for some programs), thesis (for some programs). *Entrance requirements:* For master's, minimum GPA of 3.0 in major, 2.5 overall; two letters of recommendation; statement describing historical areas of interest and how graduate study will contribute to professional and academic goals. Additional exam requirements/recommendations for international students: Required—TOEFL (minimum score 550 paper-based; 79 iBT), IELTS (minimum score 6) or Michigan English Language Assessment Battery (minimum score 77). *Application deadline:* For fall admission, 7/15 priority date for domestic students, 6/1 for international students; for spring admission, 12/15 priority date for domestic students, 11/1 for international students. Applications are processed on a rolling basis. Application fee: $50. Electronic applications accepted. *Expenses: Tuition:* Full-time $21,366; part-time $7122 per credit. *Required fees:* $700; $175 per term. *Financial support:* In 2017–18, 4 students received support. Institutionally sponsored loans, scholarships/grants, and unspecified assistantships available. Support available to part-time students. Financial award applicants required to submit FAFSA. *Faculty research:* British, German, and French Revolutions; Soviet Union; Africa; English history; U.S. military; women's history. *Unit head:* Dr. Maryann Rhett, Director, 732-263-5768, Fax: 732-263-5112, E-mail: mrhett@monmouth.edu. *Application contact:* Andrea Thompson, Graduate Admission Counselor, 732-571-3452, Fax: 732-263-5123, E-mail: gradadm@monmouth.edu.
Website: https://www.monmouth.edu/graduate/ma-history/

Montana State University, The Graduate School, College of Letters and Science, Department of History, Bozeman, MT 59717. Offers MA, PhD. *Program availability:* Part-time. *Degree requirements:* For master's, comprehensive exam; for doctorate, comprehensive exam, thesis/dissertation. *Entrance requirements:* For master's, GRE General Test, transcripts, 3 letters of recommendation, writing sample, statement of interest; for doctorate, GRE General Test, MA, transcripts, 3 letters of recommendation, writing sample, statement of interest. Additional exam requirements/recommendations for international students: Required—TOEFL (minimum score 550 paper-based). Electronic applications accepted. *Faculty research:* Science, environment, technology, American West, science and technology, environmental history, Asian studies.

Morgan State University, School of Graduate Studies, College of Liberal Arts, Department of History and Geography, Baltimore, MD 21251. Offers African-American studies (MA); history (MA, PhD); museum studies and historic preservation (MA). *Program availability:* Part-time, evening/weekend. *Degree requirements:* For master's, comprehensive exam, thesis; for doctorate, comprehensive exam, thesis/dissertation. *Entrance requirements:* For master's, minimum GPA of 2.5; for doctorate, GRE or MAT. Additional exam requirements/recommendations for international students: Required—TOEFL (minimum score 550 paper-based). *Application deadline:* For fall admission, 2/1 priority date for domestic students; for spring admission, 10/1 priority date for domestic students. Applications are processed on a rolling basis. Application fee: $0. *Expenses:* Tuition, state resident: part-time $433 per credit. Tuition, nonresident: part-time $851 per credit. *Required fees:* $81.50 per credit. *Financial support:* Application deadline: 2/1. *Faculty research:* Women's history, African diaspora history, urban history. *Unit head:* Dr. Jeremiah I. Dibua, Graduate Coordinator, 443-885-3400, Fax: 443-885-8227, E-mail: jeremiah.dibua@morgan.edu. *Application contact:* Dr. Dean Campbell, Graduate Recruitment Specialist, 443-885-3185, Fax: 443-885-8226, E-mail: dean.campbell@morgan.edu.

Murray State University, College of Humanities and Fine Arts, Department of History, Murray, KY 42071. Offers MA. *Program availability:* Part-time. *Faculty:* 9 full-time (4 women). *Students:* 5 full-time (0 women), 3 part-time (1 woman). Average age 31. 2 applicants, 100% accepted, 2 enrolled. In 2017, 2 master's awarded. *Entrance requirements:* For master's, GRE or GMAT, minimum university GPA of 2.75. Additional exam requirements/recommendations for international students: Required—TOEFL (minimum score 527 paper-based; 71 iBT). *Application deadline:* Applications are processed on a rolling basis. Application fee: $40 ($50 for international students). Electronic applications accepted. *Expenses:* Tuition, state resident: full-time $9504. Tuition, nonresident: full-time $26,811. *International tuition:* $14,400 full-time. Tuition and fees vary according to course load, degree level and reciprocity agreements. *Financial support:* In 2017–18, 4 research assistantships were awarded; Federal Work-Study and unspecified assistantships also available. Financial award applicants required to submit FAFSA. *Faculty research:* Modern Europe, African history, Chinese history, early American history, diasporas. *Unit head:* Dr. Kathy Callahan, Chair, Department of History, 270-809-6580, Fax: 270-809-6587, E-mail: kcallahan@murraystate.edu. *Application contact:* Kaitlyn Burzynski, Interim Assistant Director for Graduate Admission and Records, 270-809-5732, Fax: 270-809-3780, E-mail: msu.graduateadmissions@murraystate.edu.
Website: http://www.murraystate.edu/academics/CollegesDepartments/CollegeOfHumanitiesAndFineArts/History/index.aspx

Nebraska Wesleyan University, University College, Program in Historical Studies, Lincoln, NE 68504-2796. Offers MA. *Program availability:* Part-time. *Expenses:* Contact institution.

New Jersey Institute of Technology, College of Science and Liberal Arts, Newark, NJ 07102. Offers applied mathematics (MS); applied physics (MS, PhD); applied statistics (MS, Certificate); biology (MS, PhD); biostatistics (MS); chemistry (MS, PhD); environmental and sustainability policy (MS); environmental science (MS, PhD); history (MA, MAT); materials science and engineering (MS, PhD); mathematical and computational finance (MS); mathematical sciences (PhD); pharmaceutical chemistry (MS); professional and technical communications (MS); technical communication essentials (Certificate). *Program availability:* Part-time, evening/weekend. *Students:* Average age 28. 504 applicants, 64% accepted, 65 enrolled. In 2017, 81 master's, 18 doctorates, 1 other advanced degree awarded. Terminal master's awarded for partial completion of doctoral program. *Entrance requirements:* For master's, GRE General Test; for doctorate, GRE General Test, minimum graduate GPA of 3.5. Additional exam requirements/recommendations for international students: Required—TOEFL (minimum score 550 paper-based; 79 iBT). *Application deadline:* For fall admission, 6/1 priority date for domestic students, 5/1 priority date for international students; for spring admission, 11/15 priority date for domestic and international students. Applications are processed on a rolling basis. Application fee: $75. Electronic applications accepted. *Expenses:* Contact institution. *Financial support:* In 2017–18, 106 students received support, including 8 fellowships (averaging $3,436 per year), 51 research assistantships (averaging $23,452 per year), 91 teaching assistantships (averaging $25,553 per year); scholarships/grants, traineeships, and unspecified assistantships also available. Financial award application deadline: 1/15. *Faculty research:* Biophotonics and bioimaging, morphogenetic patterning, embryogenesis, biological fluid dynamics, applied research in the mathematical sciences. *Unit head:* Dr. Kevin Belfield, Dean, 973-596-3676, Fax: 973-565-0586, E-mail: kevin.d.belfield@njit.edu. *Application contact:* Stephen Eck, Director of Admissions, 973-596-3300, Fax: 973-596-3461, E-mail: admissions@njit.edu.
Website: http://csla.njit.edu/

New Mexico Highlands University, Graduate Studies, College of Arts and Sciences, Department of History, Political Science, and Languages and Culture, Las Vegas, NM 87701. Offers public affairs (MA), including historical and cross-cultural perspectives, history/political science, political and governmental processes. *Degree requirements:* For master's, comprehensive exam, thesis or alternative. *Entrance requirements:* Additional exam requirements/recommendations for international students: Required—TOEFL (minimum score 540 paper-based).

New Mexico State University, College of Arts and Sciences, Department of History, Las Cruces, NM 88003. Offers history (MA); public history (MA). *Program availability:* Part-time. *Faculty:* 12 full-time (5 women). *Students:* 16 full-time (4 women), 7 part-time (3 women); includes 9 minority (8 Hispanic/Latino; 1 Two or more races, non-Hispanic/Latino). Average age 36. 13 applicants, 77% accepted, 5 enrolled. In 2017, 12 master's awarded. *Degree requirements:* For master's, comprehensive exam, thesis (for some programs). *Entrance requirements:* For master's, minimum of 12 upper-division history credits, writing sample, minimum GPA of 3.0. Additional exam requirements/recommendations for international students: Required—TOEFL (minimum score 550 paper-based; 79 iBT), IELTS (minimum score 6.5). *Application deadline:* For fall admission, 7/1 priority date for domestic students; for spring admission, 11/1 for domestic students. Applications are processed on a rolling basis. Application fee: $40 ($50 for international students). Electronic applications accepted. *Expenses:* Tuition, state resident: full-time $4390. Tuition, nonresident: full-time $15,309. *Required fees:* $853. *Financial support:* In 2017–18, 10 students received support, including 7 teaching assistantships (averaging $16,964 per year); career-related internships or fieldwork, Federal Work-Study, scholarships/grants, traineeships, health care benefits, and unspecified assistantships also available. Support available to part-time students. Financial award application deadline: 3/1. *Faculty research:* European history, U.S. history (early and recent), history of science, public history, east Asian history, U.S. Southwestern and border history, new Mexico history, Latin American history, environmental history. *Total annual research expenditures:* $48,853. *Unit head:* Dr. Mark Cioc-Ortega, Department Head, 575-646-4601, Fax: 575-646-6096, E-mail: mcioc@nmsu.edu. *Application contact:* Dr. Margaret Malamud, Director of Graduate Studies, 575-646-4310, Fax: 575-646-6096, E-mail: mmalamud@nmsu.edu.
Website: http://history.nmsu.edu

The New School, The New School for Social Research, Department of Historical Studies, New York, NY 10011. Offers historical studies (MA); politics (PhD), including historical studies; sociology (PhD), including historical studies. *Program availability:* Part-time, evening/weekend. *Faculty:* 1 (woman) full-time. *Students:* 8 full-time (3 women), 3 part-time (2 women); includes 2 minority (1 Asian, non-Hispanic/Latino; 1 Hispanic/Latino), 1 international. Average age 28. 19 applicants, 95% accepted, 6 enrolled. In 2017, 3 master's awarded. *Degree requirements:* For master's, thesis. *Entrance requirements:* For master's, GRE, two letters of recommendation, writing sample, essays, transcripts. Additional exam requirements/recommendations for international students: Required—TOEFL (minimum score 100 iBT), IELTS (minimum score 7), PTE (minimum score 68). *Application deadline:* For fall admission, 1/15 priority date for domestic and international students; for spring admission, 10/15 priority date for domestic and international students. Applications are processed on a rolling basis. Application fee: $50. Electronic applications accepted. *Expenses:* $2,180 per credit. *Financial support:* In 2017–18, 8 students received support, including 5 teaching assistantships (averaging $5,520 per year); Federal Work-Study, scholarships/grants, health care benefits, and tuition waivers (full and partial) also available. Support available to part-time students. Financial award application deadline: 2/1; financial award applicants required to submit FAFSA. *Unit head:* Dr. William Milberg, Dean, The New School for Social Research, 212-229-5777, E-mail: milbergw@newschool.edu. *Application contact:* Dana Messinger, Director of Graduate Admission, 212-229-5150 Ext. 2300, E-mail: messingd@newschool.edu.
Website: http://www.newschool.edu/nssr/historical-studies/

The New School, The New School for Social Research, Department of Sociology, New York, NY 10003. Offers historical studies (PhD); sociology (M Phil, MA). *Program availability:* Part-time. *Faculty:* 11 full-time (6 women), 2 part-time/adjunct (0 women). *Students:* 91 full-time (36 women), 5 part-time (4 women); includes 12 minority (7 Hispanic/Latino; 5 Two or more races, non-Hispanic/Latino), 55 international. Average age 33. 100 applicants, 76% accepted, 21 enrolled. In 2017, 23 master's, 8 doctorates awarded. Terminal master's awarded for partial completion of doctoral program. *Degree requirements:* For master's, comprehensive exam; for doctorate, one foreign language, thesis/dissertation. *Entrance requirements:* For master's and doctorate, GRE, letters of recommendation, writing sample, essays, transcripts. Additional exam requirements/recommendations for international students: Required—TOEFL (minimum score 92 iBT), IELTS (minimum score 7), PTE (minimum score 68). *Application deadline:* For fall admission, 5/5 priority date for domestic students, 6/15 priority date for international students; for spring admission, 10/15 priority date for domestic and international students. Applications are processed on a rolling basis. Application fee: $50. Electronic applications accepted. *Expenses:* $2,180 per credit. *Financial support:* In 2017–18, 62 students received support, including 15 fellowships (averaging $18,567 per year), 14 teaching assistantships (averaging $10,057 per year); Federal Work-Study, scholarships/grants, and tuition waivers (full and partial) also available. Support available to part-time students. Financial award application deadline: 2/1; financial award applicants required to submit FAFSA. *Unit head:* Eiko Ikegami, Program Chair, 212-229-5376 Ext. 4925, E-mail: ikegame1@newschool.edu. *Application contact:* Dana Messinger, Director of Graduate Admission, 212-229-5150 Ext. 2300, E-mail: socialresearchadmit@newschool.edu.
Website: https://www.newschool.edu/nssr/sociology/

New York University, Graduate School of Arts and Science, Department of History, New York, NY 10012-1019. Offers African diaspora (PhD); African history (PhD); archival management (Advanced Certificate); Atlantic history (PhD); French studies/history (PhD); Hebrew and Judaic studies/history (PhD); history (MA, PhD), including Europe (PhD), Latin America and the Caribbean (PhD), United States (PhD), women's history (MA); Middle Eastern history (MA); Middle Eastern studies/history (PhD); public history (Advanced Certificate); world history (MA); JD/MA; MA/Advanced Certificate. *Program availability:* Part-time. *Students:* Average age 29. 401 applicants, 31% accepted, 38 enrolled. In 2017, 24 master's, 16 doctorates awarded. Terminal master's awarded for partial completion of doctoral program. *Degree requirements:* For master's,

seminar paper; for doctorate, one foreign language, thesis/dissertation, oral and written exams; for Advanced Certificate, internship. *Entrance requirements:* For master's, GRE General Test, minimum GPA of 3.0, writing sample; for doctorate, GRE. Additional exam requirements/recommendations for international students: Required—TOEFL. *Application deadline:* For fall admission, 12/18 for domestic and international students. Application fee: $100. *Expenses: Tuition:* Full-time $41,352; part-time $19,968 per year. *Required fees:* $2496; $1628 per unit. $814 per term. Tuition and fees vary according to course load and program. *Financial support:* Fellowships, research assistantships, teaching assistantships, career-related internships or fieldwork, Federal Work-Study, institutionally sponsored loans, scholarships/grants, health care benefits, and unspecified assistantships available. Financial award application deadline: 12/18; financial award applicants required to submit FAFSA. *Faculty research:* African, East Asian, medieval, early modern, and modern European history; U.S. history; African and African diaspora; Latin American history; Atlantic world. *Unit head:* Barbara Weinstein, Chair, 212-998-8600, Fax: 212-995-4017, E-mail: history.admissions@nyu.edu. *Application contact:* Stepfanos Geroulanos, Director of Graduate Studies, 212-998-8600, Fax: 212-995-4017, E-mail: history.admissions@nyu.edu.
Website: http://history.as.nyu.edu/

New York University, Graduate School of Arts and Science, Institute for the Study of the Ancient World, New York, NY 10012-1019. Offers PhD. *Students:* Average age 31. 50 applicants, 10% accepted, 1 enrolled. *Degree requirements:* For doctorate, 4 foreign languages, comprehensive exam, thesis/dissertation, fieldwork, teaching experience. *Entrance requirements:* For doctorate, GRE General Test. *Application deadline:* For fall admission, 1/4 for domestic and international students. Application fee: $100. Electronic applications accepted. *Expenses: Tuition:* Full-time $41,352; part-time $19,968 per year. *Required fees:* $2496; $1628 per unit. $814 per term. Tuition and fees vary according to course load and program. *Financial support:* Fellowships and stipends available. Financial award application deadline: 1/4; financial award applicants required to submit FAFSA. *Unit head:* Dr. Roger Bagnall, Director, 212-992-7843, Fax: 212-992-7809, E-mail: isaw@nyu.edu. *Application contact:* Marc Leblanc, Graduate Department Administrator, 212-992-7843, Fax: 212-992-7809, E-mail: isaw@nyu.edu.

North Carolina Central University, College of Arts and Sciences, Department of History, Durham, NC 27707-3129. Offers MA. *Program availability:* Part-time, evening/weekend. *Degree requirements:* For master's, one foreign language, comprehensive exam, thesis. *Entrance requirements:* For master's, GRE, minimum GPA of 3.0 in major, 2.5 overall. Additional exam requirements/recommendations for international students: Required—TOEFL. *Application deadline:* For fall admission, 8/1 for domestic students. Application fee: $30. *Expenses:* Tuition, state resident: full-time $2770; part-time $692.50 per credit hour. Tuition, nonresident: full-time $9247; part-time $2311.75 per credit hour. *Financial support:* Application deadline: 5/1; applicants required to submit FAFSA. *Unit head:* Jim C. Harper, II, Chair, 919-530-6271, E-mail: jcharper@nccu.edu. *Application contact:* Jim C. Harper, II, Chair, 919-530-6271, E-mail: jcharper@nccu.edu.

North Carolina State University, Graduate School, College of Humanities and Social Sciences, Department of History, Raleigh, NC 27695. Offers history (MA); public history (MA). *Program availability:* Part-time, evening/weekend. *Degree requirements:* For master's, thesis. *Entrance requirements:* For master's, GRE General Test. Electronic applications accepted. *Faculty research:* History of the United States, Europe, Asia Africa and the Middle East; history of science; intellectual, cultural, social, environmental and political history.

North Dakota State University, College of Graduate and Interdisciplinary Studies, College of Arts, Humanities and Social Sciences, Department of History, Philosophy, and Religious Studies, Fargo, ND 58102. Offers history (MA, MS, PhD). *Program availability:* Part-time, evening/weekend. *Degree requirements:* For master's, one foreign language, comprehensive exam, thesis optional; for doctorate, 2 foreign languages, comprehensive exam, thesis/dissertation. *Entrance requirements:* For master's and doctorate, GRE General Test. Additional exam requirements/recommendations for international students: Required—TOEFL (minimum score 600 paper-based; 100 iBT). Electronic applications accepted. *Faculty research:* Recent U.S., modern English, early modern European, North Dakota, Latin American, and Great Plains history.

Northeastern Illinois University, College of Graduate Studies and Research, College of Arts and Sciences, Program in History, Chicago, IL 60625. Offers MA. *Program availability:* Part-time, evening/weekend. *Degree requirements:* For master's, comprehensive exam, thesis optional. *Entrance requirements:* For master's, 24 undergraduate hours in history, minimum GPA of 2.75. Additional exam requirements/recommendations for international students: Required—TOEFL (minimum score 550 paper-based; 79 iBT). *Application deadline:* For fall admission, 4/1 priority date for domestic students; for spring admission, 8/15 for domestic students. Applications are processed on a rolling basis. Application fee: $3. Electronic applications accepted. *Expenses:* Tuition, state resident: full-time $7274; part-time $404.11 per credit hour. Tuition, nonresident: full-time $14,548; part-time $808.23 per credit hour. *Required fees:* $1284. *Financial support:* Applicants required to submit FAFSA. *Faculty research:* Africa; East Asia; European medieval, early-modern, and modern history; U.S. social, cultural, and intellectual history. *Unit head:* Dr. Michael Tuck, Department Chair, 773-442-5606, E-mail: m-tuck@neiu.edu. *Application contact:* Martha Narvaez, Graduate Admission Representative, 773-442-6006, E-mail: m-narvaez@neiu.edu.

Northeastern University, College of Social Sciences and Humanities, Boston, MA 02115. Offers criminology and criminal justice (MSCJ); criminology and justice policy (PhD); economics (MA, PhD); English (MA, PhD); international affairs (MA); law and public policy (PhD); political science (MA, PhD); public administration (MPA); public policy (MPP); security and resilience studies (MS); sociology (MA, PhD); urban and regional policy (MS); urban informatics (MS); world history (MA, PhD). *Program availability:* Online learning. *Faculty:* 242. *Students:* 491. In 2017, 143 master's, 38 doctorates awarded. *Degree requirements:* For doctorate, variable foreign language requirement, comprehensive exam, thesis/dissertation. *Entrance requirements:* For master's and doctorate, GRE. Additional exam requirements/recommendations for international students: Required—TOEFL, IELTS. Application fee: $75. Electronic applications accepted. *Expenses:* Contact institution. *Financial support:* Teaching assistantships, career-related internships or fieldwork, scholarships/grants, health care benefits, tuition waivers (full and partial), and unspecified assistantships available. Support available to part-time students. Financial award applicants required to submit FAFSA. *Unit head:* Dr. Uta Poiger, Dean, 617-373-5173, E-mail: college_of_social_sciences_and_humanities@neu.edu. *Application contact:* 617-373-5990, E-mail: gradcssh@northeastern.edu.
Website: http://www.northeastern.edu/cssh/

Northern Arizona University, College of Arts and Letters, Department of History, Flagstaff, AZ 86011. Offers MA. *Program availability:* Part-time. *Faculty:* 17 full-time (7 women). *Students:* 10 full-time (2 women), 3 part-time (all women); includes 2 minority (both Hispanic/Latino). Average age 31. 9 applicants, 89% accepted, 6 enrolled. In 2017, 9 master's awarded. *Degree requirements:* For master's, variable foreign language requirement, comprehensive exam (for some programs), thesis (for some programs). *Entrance requirements:* For master's, GRE General Test. Additional exam requirements/recommendations for international students: Required—TOEFL (minimum score 80 iBT), IELTS (minimum score 6.5). *Application deadline:* For fall admission, 2/15 for domestic students, 2/1 for international students; for spring admission, 10/1 for domestic and international students. Applications are processed on a rolling basis. Application fee: $65. Electronic applications accepted. *Expenses:* Tuition, state resident: full-time $9240; part-time $458 per credit hour. Tuition, nonresident: full-time $21,588; part-time $1199 per credit hour. *Required fees:* $1021; $14 per credit hour. $646 per semester. Tuition and fees vary according to course load, campus/location and program. *Financial support:* In 2017–18, 8 students received support, including 8 teaching assistantships with full and partial tuition reimbursements available (averaging $12,000 per year); institutionally sponsored loans, health care benefits, tuition waivers (full and partial), and unspecified assistantships also available. Financial award application deadline: 2/1; financial award applicants required to submit FAFSA. *Unit head:* Derek Heng, Chair, 928-523-4378, Fax: 928-523-1277, E-mail: derek.heng@nau.edu. *Application contact:* Tina Sutton, Coordinator, Graduate College, 928-523-4348, Fax: 928-523-8950, E-mail: graduate@nau.edu.
Website: https://nau.edu/cal/history/

Northern Illinois University, Graduate School, College of Liberal Arts and Sciences, Department of History, De Kalb, IL 60115-2854. Offers MA, PhD. *Program availability:* Part-time. *Faculty:* 18 full-time (8 women), 2 part-time/adjunct (0 women). *Students:* 17 full-time (9 women), 20 part-time (9 women); includes 7 minority (1 Black or African American, non-Hispanic/Latino; 3 Asian, non-Hispanic/Latino; 3 Hispanic/Latino), 2 international. Average age 32. 33 applicants, 76% accepted, 10 enrolled. In 2017, 7 master's, 3 doctorates awarded. Terminal master's awarded for partial completion of doctoral program. *Degree requirements:* For master's, variable foreign language requirement, comprehensive exam, thesis optional, research seminars; for doctorate, variable foreign language requirement, thesis/dissertation, candidacy exam, dissertation defense, research seminars. *Entrance requirements:* For master's, GRE General Test, minimum GPA of 2.75; for doctorate, GRE General Test, minimum undergraduate GPA of 2.75, graduate 3.2. Additional exam requirements/recommendations for international students: Required—TOEFL (minimum score 550 paper-based). *Application deadline:* For fall admission, 6/1 for domestic students, 5/1 for international students; for spring admission, 11/1 for domestic students, 10/1 for international students. Applications are processed on a rolling basis. Application fee: $40. Electronic applications accepted. *Financial support:* In 2017–18, 6 research assistantships with full tuition reimbursements, 16 teaching assistantships with full tuition reimbursements were awarded; fellowships with full tuition reimbursements, career-related internships or fieldwork, Federal Work-Study, scholarships/grants, tuition waivers (full), and unspecified assistantships also available. Support available to part-time students. Financial award applicants required to submit FAFSA. *Faculty research:* History of the Carolingian empire, history of early modern Europe, modern Irish history, history of the Ming dynasty. *Unit head:* Dr. James Schmidt, Chair, 815-753-6810, Fax: 815-753-6302, E-mail: jschmidt@niu.edu. *Application contact:* Dr. Anne G. Hanley, Assistant Chair/ Director of Graduate Studies, 815-753-6695, E-mail: ahanley@niu.edu.
Website: http://www.niu.edu/history/

Northwestern University, The Graduate School, Judd A. and Marjorie Weinberg College of Arts and Sciences, Department of History, Evanston, IL 60208. Offers PhD, JD/PhD. Admissions and degrees offered through The Graduate School. *Degree requirements:* For doctorate, variable foreign language requirement, thesis/dissertation, major and minor field exams. *Entrance requirements:* For doctorate, sample of written work. Additional exam requirements/recommendations for international students: Required—TOEFL. Electronic applications accepted. *Faculty research:* Medieval and early modern Europe, Africa, race and slavery, Atlantic history, gender.

Northwestern University, School of Professional Studies, Program in Liberal Studies, Evanston, IL 60208. Offers American studies (MA); history (MA); religious and ethical studies (MA). *Program availability:* Part-time, evening/weekend.
Website: https://sps.northwestern.edu/masters/liberal-studies/index.php

Norwich University, College of Graduate and Continuing Studies, Master of Arts in History Program, Northfield, VT 05663. Offers history (MA), including American history, world history. *Program availability:* Evening/weekend, online only, mostly all online with a week-long residency requirement. *Degree requirements:* For master's, thesis optional, capstone. *Entrance requirements:* For master's, minimum undergraduate GPA of 2.75. Additional exam requirements/recommendations for international students: Required—TOEFL (minimum score 550 paper-based; 80 iBT), IELTS (minimum score 6.5). Electronic applications accepted. *Expenses:* Contact institution.

Oakland University, Graduate Study and Lifelong Learning, College of Arts and Sciences, Department of History, Rochester, MI 48309-4401. Offers MA. *Program availability:* Part-time, evening/weekend. *Entrance requirements:* For master's, minimum GPA of 3.0. Additional exam requirements/recommendations for international students: Required—TOEFL (minimum score 550 paper-based). Electronic applications accepted. *Expenses:* Tuition, state resident: full-time $16,950; part-time $706.25 per credit. Tuition, nonresident: full-time $24,648; part-time $1027 per credit.

The Ohio State University, Graduate School, College of Arts and Sciences, Division of Arts and Humanities, Department of History, Columbus, OH 43210. Offers MA, PhD. *Faculty:* 52. *Students:* 89 (33 women); includes 8 minority (all Hispanic/Latino), 10 international. Average age 30. In 2017, 10 master's, 20 doctorates awarded. Terminal master's awarded for partial completion of doctoral program. *Degree requirements:* For master's, thesis optional; for doctorate, variable foreign language requirement, thesis/dissertation. *Entrance requirements:* For master's and doctorate, GRE General Test. Additional exam requirements/recommendations for international students: Required—TOEFL (minimum score 550 paper-based; 79 iBT), GRE General Test (strongly recommended). *Application deadline:* For fall admission, 12/1 priority date for domestic students, 11/30 priority date for international students; for spring admission, 3/1 for domestic students, 2/1 for international students. Applications are processed on a rolling basis. Application fee: $60 ($70 for international students). Electronic applications accepted. *Financial support:* Fellowships, research assistantships, teaching assistantships, Federal Work-Study, institutionally sponsored loans, and unspecified assistantships available. Support available to part-time students. *Unit head:* Dr. Nathan Rosenstein, Chair and Professor, 614-292-7645, E-mail: rosenstein.1@osu.edu. *Application contact:* Graduate and Professional Admissions, 614-292-9444, Fax: 614-292-3895, E-mail: gpadmissions@osu.edu.
Website: http://history.osu.edu/

Ohio University, Graduate College, College of Arts and Sciences, Department of History, Athens, OH 45701-2979. Offers MA, PhD. *Degree requirements:* For master's, one foreign language, thesis optional; for doctorate, 2 foreign languages, comprehensive exam, thesis/dissertation. *Entrance requirements:* For master's, GRE, minimum GPA of 3.0; for doctorate, GRE, minimum GPA of 3.0, MA. Additional exam requirements/recommendations for international students: Required—TOEFL (minimum score 550 paper-based; 80 iBT) or IELTS (minimum score 6.5). Electronic applications accepted. *Faculty research:* U.S. foreign relations, modern Europe, Latin America, southeast Asia, U.S. women.

Oklahoma State University, College of Arts and Sciences, Department of History, Stillwater, OK 74078. Offers MA, PhD. *Faculty:* 21 full-time (8 women), 4 part-time/

adjunct (2 women). *Students:* 5 full-time (1 woman), 27 part-time (10 women); includes 7 minority (2 Black or African American, non-Hispanic/Latino; 1 Hispanic/Latino; 4 Two or more races, non-Hispanic/Latino). Average age 35. 20 applicants, 55% accepted, 9 enrolled. In 2017, 7 master's, 8 doctorates awarded. *Entrance requirements:* For master's and doctorate, GRE. Additional exam requirements/recommendations for international students: Required—TOEFL (minimum score 550 paper-based; 79 iBT). *Application deadline:* For fall admission, 3/1 priority date for international students; for spring admission, 8/1 priority date for international students. Applications are processed on a rolling basis. Application fee: $40 ($75 for international students). Electronic applications accepted. *Expenses:* Tuition, state resident: full-time $4019; part-time $2679.60 per year. Tuition, nonresident: full-time $15,286; part-time $10,190.40 per year. *Required fees:* $2129; $1419 per unit. Tuition and fees vary according to program. *Financial support:* Teaching assistantships, career-related internships or fieldwork, Federal Work-Study, scholarships/grants, health care benefits, tuition waivers (partial), and unspecified assistantships available. Support available to part-time students. Financial award application deadline: 3/1; financial award applicants required to submit FAFSA. *Faculty research:* U.S. history, the American West, Native American history, modern European history, women's history. *Unit head:* Dr. Laura Belmonte, Head, 405-744-8182, Fax: 405-744-5400, E-mail: laura.belmonte@okstate.edu.
Website: http://history.okstate.edu/

Old Dominion University, College of Arts and Letters, Program in History, Norfolk, VA 23529. Offers MA. *Program availability:* Part-time, evening/weekend. *Faculty:* 16 full-time (9 women), 1 part-time/adjunct (0 women). *Students:* 11 full-time (7 women), 7 part-time (2 women); includes 2 minority (1 Black or African American, non-Hispanic/Latino; 1 Hispanic/Latino). Average age 30. 41 applicants, 80% accepted, 20 enrolled. In 2017, 19 master's awarded. *Degree requirements:* For master's, comprehensive exam, thesis optional. *Entrance requirements:* For master's, GRE General Test, 24 credits in history with minimum GPA of 3.0. Additional exam requirements/recommendations for international students: Recommended—TOEFL. *Application deadline:* For fall admission, 4/1 for domestic students; for spring admission, 11/1 for domestic students. Applications are processed on a rolling basis. Application fee: $50. Electronic applications accepted. *Expenses:* Tuition, state resident: full-time $8928; part-time $496 per credit. Tuition, nonresident: full-time $22,482; part-time $1249 per credit. *Required fees:* $66 per semester. *Financial support:* In 2017–18, 6 students received support, including 1 research assistantship (averaging $10,000 per year), 5 teaching assistantships (averaging $10,000 per year); career-related internships or fieldwork, scholarships/grants, and unspecified assistantships also available. Support available to part-time students. Financial award application deadline: 2/15; financial award applicants required to submit FAFSA. *Faculty research:* History: maritime, American, European, modern Asian, and African. *Unit head:* Dr. Michael C. Carhart, Graduate Program Director, 757-683-3949, Fax: 757-683-5644, E-mail: histgpd@odu.edu. *Application contact:* Dr. David C. Earnest, Associate Dean, 757-683-6077, Fax: 757-683-5746, E-mail: dearnest@odu.edu.
Website: http://al.odu.edu/history/

Open University, Graduate Programs, Milton Keynes, United Kingdom. Offers business (MBA); education (M Ed); engineering (M Eng); history (MA); music (MA); philosophy (MA).

Penn State University Park, Graduate School, College of the Liberal Arts, Department of History, University Park, PA 16802. Offers MA, PhD. *Unit head:* Dr. Susan Welch, Dean, 814-865-7691, Fax: 814-863-2085. *Application contact:* Lori Hawn, Director, Graduate Student Services, 814-865-1795, Fax: 814-863-4627, E-mail: l-gswww@lists.psu.edu.
Website: http://history.psu.edu/

Pittsburg State University, Graduate School, College of Arts and Sciences, Department of History, Pittsburg, KS 66762. Offers MA. *Program availability:* Part-time, 100% online, blended/hybrid learning. *Students:* 29 (16 women); includes 1 minority (Hispanic/Latino), 1 international. In 2017, 15 master's awarded. *Degree requirements:* For master's, thesis or alternative. *Entrance requirements:* Additional exam requirements/recommendations for international students: Required—TOEFL (minimum score 520 paper-based; 68 iBT), IELTS (minimum score 6), PTE (minimum score 47). *Application deadline:* For fall admission, 6/1 for international students; for spring admission, 10/15 for international students; for summer admission, 4/1 for international students. Applications are processed on a rolling basis. Application fee: $35 ($60 for international students). Electronic applications accepted. *Expenses:* Contact institution. *Financial support:* In 2017–18, 2 teaching assistantships with full tuition reimbursements (averaging $5,500 per year) were awarded; career-related internships or fieldwork, Federal Work-Study, and unspecified assistantships also available. Financial award application deadline: 2/1; financial award applicants required to submit FAFSA. *Unit head:* Dr. Barbara Bonnekessen, Chairperson, 620-235-4325, E-mail: bbonnekessen@pittstate.edu. *Application contact:* Lisa Allen, Assistant Director of Graduate and Continuing Studies, 620-235-4223, Fax: 620-235-4219, E-mail: lallen@pittstate.edu.

Pontifical Catholic University of Puerto Rico, College of Arts and Humanities, Department of History, Ponce, PR 00717-0777. Offers MA. *Entrance requirements:* For master's, GRE General Test, minimum GPA of 2.75, 2 letters of recommendation.

Portland State University, Graduate Studies, College of Liberal Arts and Sciences, Department of History, Portland, OR 97207-0751. Offers MA. *Program availability:* Part-time. *Faculty:* 22 full-time (6 women), 1 (woman) part-time/adjunct. *Students:* 14 full-time (5 women), 20 part-time (13 women); includes 2 minority (1 Asian, non-Hispanic/Latino; 1 Two or more races, non-Hispanic/Latino). Average age 35. 18 applicants, 56% accepted, 6 enrolled. In 2017, 7 master's awarded. *Degree requirements:* For master's, one foreign language, comprehensive exam, thesis, oral and written exams. *Entrance requirements:* For master's, GRE General Test, minimum GPA of 3.5 in upper-division history courses, overall 3.25; 2 letters of recommendation; BA/BS in history; statement of intent; writing samples. Additional exam requirements/recommendations for international students: Required—TOEFL (minimum score 550 paper-based; 80 iBT). *Application deadline:* For fall admission, 2/15 for domestic and international students; for winter admission, 9/1 for domestic students, 6/1 for international students; for spring admission, 11/1 for domestic and international students; for summer admission, 2/1 for domestic and international students. Application fee: $65. Electronic applications accepted. *Expenses:* Tuition, state resident: full-time $14,436; part-time $401 per credit. Tuition, nonresident: full-time $21,780; part-time $605 per credit. *Required fees:* $1380; $22 per credit. $119 per quarter. One-time fee: $325. Tuition and fees vary according to program. *Financial support:* In 2017–18, 10 students received support, including 2 research assistantships with full and partial tuition reimbursements available (averaging $11,183 per year), 5 teaching assistantships with full and partial tuition reimbursements available (averaging $7,056 per year); career-related internships or fieldwork, Federal Work-Study, scholarships/grants, and unspecified assistantships also available. Support available to part-time students. Financial award application deadline: 3/1; financial award applicants required to submit FAFSA. *Faculty research:* Germany and modern Europe, early modern France and England, Mexico in the 1920's, eighteenth-century France, Reformation, U.S. cultural history. *Total annual research expenditures:* $107,061. *Unit head:* Dr. Tim Garrison, Chair, 503-725-3978, Fax: 503-725-3953, E-mail: timgarrison@pdx.edu. *Application contact:* Dr. Richard Beyler, Graduate Coordinator, 503-725-3996, Fax: 503-725-3953, E-mail: r.beyler@pdx.edu.
Website: https://www.pdx.edu/history/

Princeton University, Graduate School, Department of Classics, Princeton, NJ 08544-1019. Offers classical and hellenic studies (PhD); classical philosophy (PhD); history (the ancient world) (PhD); literature and philology (PhD). *Degree requirements:* For doctorate, thesis/dissertation. *Entrance requirements:* For doctorate, GRE General Test, sample of written work. Additional exam requirements/recommendations for international students: Required—TOEFL (minimum score 600 paper-based). Electronic applications accepted.

Princeton University, Graduate School, Department of History, Princeton, NJ 08544-1019. Offers history (PhD); history of science (PhD). *Degree requirements:* For doctorate, variable foreign language requirement, comprehensive exam, thesis/dissertation. *Entrance requirements:* For doctorate, GRE General Test, sample of written work. Additional exam requirements/recommendations for international students: Required—TOEFL (minimum score 600 paper-based). Electronic applications accepted. *Faculty research:* World comparative, Europe-early modern, modern, late antique, medieval.

Providence College, Department of History, Providence, RI 02918. Offers American history (MA); modern European history (MA). *Program availability:* Part-time, evening/weekend. *Degree requirements:* For master's, comprehensive exam, thesis optional. *Entrance requirements:* Additional exam requirements/recommendations for international students: Required—TOEFL (minimum score 577 paper-based; 90 iBT). *Expenses:* Contact institution. *Faculty research:* American history, modern European history, Medieval history, Native American history, religion, slavery, western civilization, labor movements, Japanese and Asian history, early modern Europe.

Purdue University, Graduate School, College of Liberal Arts, Department of History, West Lafayette, IN 47907. Offers MA, PhD. *Program availability:* Part-time. *Faculty:* 32 full-time (14 women), 1 (woman) part-time/adjunct. *Students:* 36 full-time (17 women), 13 part-time (7 women); includes 2 minority (1 Hispanic/Latino; 1 Two or more races, non-Hispanic/Latino), 5 international. Average age 35. 41 applicants, 46% accepted, 11 enrolled. In 2017, 7 master's, 7 doctorates awarded. *Degree requirements:* For master's, thesis optional; for doctorate, one foreign language, thesis/dissertation. *Entrance requirements:* For master's, GRE General Test, minimum undergraduate GPA of 3.0 or equivalent; for doctorate, GRE General Test, minimum undergraduate GPA of 3.0 or equivalent; master's degree with minimum GPA of 3.0 or equivalent. Additional exam requirements/recommendations for international students: Required—TOEFL (minimum score 550 paper-based; 77 iBT), TWE. *Application deadline:* For fall admission, 1/1 priority date for domestic and international students; for spring admission, 9/1 for domestic and international students. Applications are processed on a rolling basis. Application fee: $60 ($75 for international students). Electronic applications accepted. *Financial support:* In 2017–18, 37 students received support. Fellowships with full tuition reimbursements available and teaching assistantships with full tuition reimbursements available available. Support available to part-time students. Financial award application deadline: 1/15; financial award applicants required to submit FAFSA. *Faculty research:* U.S. history, early modern and modern European history, global women's history, U.S. minority history, medieval history. *Unit head:* Dr. R. Douglas Hurt, Head, 765-494-4132, E-mail: doughurt@purdue.edu. *Application contact:* Fay M. Chan, Graduate Contact, 765-494-4126, E-mail: chanf@purdue.edu.
Website: http://www.cla.purdue.edu/history/

Purdue University Northwest, Graduate Studies Office, School of Liberal Arts and Social Sciences, Department of History and Political Science, Hammond, IN 46323-2094. Offers history (MA). *Program availability:* Part-time, evening/weekend. *Entrance requirements:* Additional exam requirements/recommendations for international students: Required—TOEFL. *Faculty research:* The Middle East, German history, U.S. regional history, U.S. social history, the Holocaust.

Queens College of the City University of New York, Division of Social Sciences, Department of History, Queens, NY 11367-1597. Offers MA. *Program availability:* Part-time, evening/weekend. *Students:* 3 full-time (2 women), 46 part-time (18 women); includes 13 minority (3 Black or African American, non-Hispanic/Latino; 3 Asian, non-Hispanic/Latino; 7 Hispanic/Latino). Average age 32. *Degree requirements:* For master's, comprehensive exam, thesis optional. *Entrance requirements:* For master's, minimum GPA of 3.0. Additional exam requirements/recommendations for international students: Required—TOEFL (minimum score 90 iBT), IELTS (minimum score 6.5). *Application deadline:* For fall admission, 4/1 for domestic students; for spring admission, 11/1 for domestic students. Applications are processed on a rolling basis. Application fee: $125. Electronic applications accepted. *Financial support:* Career-related internships or fieldwork, tuition waivers (partial), and unspecified assistantships available. Financial award application deadline: 4/1; financial award applicants required to submit FAFSA. *Unit head:* Dr. Joel W. Allen, Chairperson, 718-997-5350, E-mail: joel.allen@qc.cuny.edu. *Application contact:* Elizabeth D'Amico-Ramirez, Assistant Director of Graduate Admissions, 718-997-5203, E-mail: elizabeth.damicoramirez@qc.cuny.edu.

Rhode Island College, School of Graduate Studies, Faculty of Arts and Sciences, Department of History, Providence, RI 02908-1991. Offers MA. *Program availability:* Part-time, evening/weekend. *Faculty:* 8. *Students:* 1 (woman) full-time, 3 part-time (2 women). Average age 30. In 2017, 2 master's awarded. *Degree requirements:* For master's, oral exam or thesis. *Entrance requirements:* For master's, GRE General and Subject Tests, 3 letters of recommendation, interview. Additional exam requirements/recommendations for international students: Recommended—TOEFL (minimum score 550 paper-based; 79 iBT). *Application deadline:* For fall admission, 3/1 for domestic students; for spring admission, 11/1 for domestic students. Applications are processed on a rolling basis. Application fee: $50. Electronic applications accepted. *Expenses:* Tuition, state resident: full-time $9768; part-time $407 per credit. Tuition, nonresident: full-time $19,008; part-time $792 per credit. *Required fees:* $696; $29 per credit. One-time fee: $200 full-time; $100 part-time. Tuition and fees vary according to course load. *Financial support:* In 2017–18, 1 teaching assistantship with full tuition reimbursement (averaging $3,000 per year) was awarded; Federal Work-Study, scholarships/grants, health care benefits, and unspecified assistantships also available. Support available to part-time students. Financial award application deadline: 5/15; financial award applicants required to submit FAFSA. *Unit head:* Dr. David Espinosa, Chair, 401-456-8039.
Website: http://www.ric.edu/history/index.php

Rice University, Graduate Programs, School of Humanities, Department of History, Houston, TX 77251-1892. Offers MA, PhD. Terminal master's awarded for partial completion of doctoral program. *Degree requirements:* For doctorate, variable foreign language requirement, comprehensive exam, thesis/dissertation, 4 semesters of coursework. *Entrance requirements:* For doctorate, GRE, writing samples, letters of recommendation, personal statement, transcripts. Additional exam requirements/recommendations for international students: Required—TOEFL (minimum score 600 paper-based; 90 iBT) or IELTS (minimum score 7). Electronic applications accepted. *Faculty research:* U.S. Southern, Caribbean, African-American, world, Latin American.

History

Roosevelt University, Graduate Division, College of Arts and Sciences, Department of History and Philosophy, Chicago, IL 60605. Offers history (MA). *Program availability:* Part-time, evening/weekend. *Students:* 1 full-time (0 women), 10 part-time (7 women); includes 4 minority (all Black or African American, non-Hispanic/Latino). Average age 36. 5 applicants, 100% accepted, 3 enrolled. In 2017, 3 master's awarded. *Application deadline:* Applications are processed on a rolling basis. Application fee: $40. Electronic applications accepted. *Financial support:* Scholarships/grants and unspecified assistantships available. *Application contact:* Sivling Lam, Graduate Admission Counselor, 312-281-3252, E-mail: slam02@roosevelt.edu.

Rowan University, Graduate School, College of Humanities and Social Sciences, Department of History, Glassboro, NJ 08028-1701. Offers history (MA, CGS). *Expenses:* Tuition, state resident: full-time $15,020; part-time $751 per semester hour. Tuition, nonresident: full-time $15,020; part-time $751 per semester hour. *Required fees:* $3158; $157.90 per semester hour. Tuition and fees vary according to course load, campus/location and program.

Rowan University, Graduate School, College of Humanities and Social Sciences, Program in History, Glassboro, NJ 08028-1701. Offers MA, CGS. *Degree requirements:* For master's, thesis optional. *Entrance requirements:* For master's, GRE, statement of objectives; current resume; official transcript demonstrating that applicant has earned undergraduate degree from accredited institution with minimum GPA of 3.0; two letters of recommendation from undergraduate professors or other qualified professionals; writing sample. Additional exam requirements/recommendations for international students: Required—TOEFL (minimum score 90 iBT). Electronic applications accepted. *Expenses:* Tuition, state resident: full-time $15,020; part-time $751 per semester hour. Tuition, nonresident: full-time $15,020; part-time $751 per semester hour. *Required fees:* $3158; $157.90 per semester hour. Tuition and fees vary according to course load, campus/location and program.

Rutgers University–Camden, Graduate School of Arts and Sciences, Program in American and Public History, Camden, NJ 08102. Offers MA. *Program availability:* Part-time, evening/weekend. *Degree requirements:* For master's, comprehensive exam, thesis optional, 30 credits. *Entrance requirements:* For master's, GRE General Test (for full-time applicants), 3 letters of recommendation; history or related undergraduate degree (preferred). Additional exam requirements/recommendations for international students: Required—TOEFL, IELTS. Electronic applications accepted. *Faculty research:* Women's history, military history, Afro-American history, urban history, history of technology.

Rutgers University–Newark, Graduate School, Program in History, Newark, NJ 07102. Offers MA, MAT. MA, MAT offered jointly with New Jersey Institute of Technology. *Program availability:* Part-time, evening/weekend. *Degree requirements:* For master's, one foreign language, comprehensive exam, thesis optional. *Entrance requirements:* For master's, GRE, minimum undergraduate B average. *Faculty research:* Global history, American history, American diplomatic and legal history, women's history, history of technology, environment and medicine.

Rutgers University–New Brunswick, Graduate School-New Brunswick, Program in History, Piscataway, NJ 08854-8097. Offers African-American history (PhD); early American history (PhD); early modern European history (PhD); east Asian history (PhD); global and comparative history (PhD); history (PhD); history of diplomacy and foreign relations (PhD); history of technology, environment and health (PhD); history of the Atlantic cultures and African diaspora (PhD); Latin American history (PhD); medieval history (PhD); modern European history (PhD); nineteenth and twentieth century American history (PhD); women's and gender history (PhD). *Degree requirements:* For doctorate, thesis/dissertation. *Entrance requirements:* For doctorate, GRE General Test, sample of written work. Electronic applications accepted. *Faculty research:* American history, European history, Afro-American history, women's history, Latin American history.

St. Cloud State University, School of Graduate Studies, College of Liberal Arts, Department of History, St. Cloud, MN 56301-4498. Offers MA, MS. *Program availability:* Part-time. *Degree requirements:* For master's, thesis or alternative. *Entrance requirements:* For master's, GRE General Test, GRE Subject Test, minimum GPA of 2.75. Additional exam requirements/recommendations for international students: Required—Michigan English Language Assessment Battery; Recommended—TOEFL (minimum score 550 paper-based), IELTS (minimum score 6.5).

St. John's University, St. John's College of Liberal Arts and Sciences, Department of History, Queens, NY 11439. Offers history (MA, PhD); public history (MA). *Program availability:* Part-time, evening/weekend. *Faculty:* 17 full-time (8 women), 13 part-time/adjunct (10 women). *Students:* 25 full-time (9 women), 23 part-time (5 women); includes 13 minority (4 Black or African American, non-Hispanic/Latino; 4 Asian, non-Hispanic/Latino; 3 Hispanic/Latino; 2 Two or more races, non-Hispanic/Latino), 3 international. Average age 34. 37 applicants, 95% accepted, 17 enrolled. In 2017, 8 master's, 4 doctorates awarded. Terminal master's awarded for partial completion of doctoral program. *Degree requirements:* For master's, variable foreign language requirement, comprehensive exam, thesis optional; for doctorate, variable foreign language requirement, thesis/dissertation, annual portfolio, internships. *Entrance requirements:* For master's, letters of recommendation, transcripts, resume, personal statement; for doctorate, GRE General Test, letters of recommendation, transcripts, resume, personal statement. Additional exam requirements/recommendations for international students: Required—TOEFL (minimum score 80 iBT), IELTS (minimum score 6.5). *Application deadline:* For fall admission, 4/1 for domestic students; for spring admission, 11/1 for domestic students. Applications are processed on a rolling basis. Application fee: $70. Electronic applications accepted. *Expenses: Tuition:* Full-time $44,280; part-time $1230 per credit. *Required fees:* $340; $340 per credit. Tuition and fees vary according to course load, degree level and program. *Financial support:* Fellowships, research assistantships, teaching assistantships, scholarships/grants, tuition waivers, and unspecified assistantships available. Support available to part-time students. Financial award application deadline: 2/1; financial award applicants required to submit FAFSA. *Faculty research:* World history, gender and cultural history, public history, history of science and technology, social history and business history. *Unit head:* Dr. Nerina Rustomji, Chair, 718-990-6229, E-mail: rustomjn@stjohns.edu. *Application contact:* Robert Medrano, Director of Graduate Admission, 718-990-1601, Fax: 718-990-5686, E-mail: gradhelp@stjohns.edu.
Website: https://www.stjohns.edu/academics/schools-and-colleges/st-johns-college-liberal-arts-and-sciences/history

Saint Louis University, Graduate Programs, College of Arts and Sciences and Graduate Programs, Department of History, St. Louis, MO 63103. Offers MA, MA-R, PhD. *Program availability:* Part-time. *Degree requirements:* For master's, one foreign language, comprehensive exam, thesis optional, comprehensive oral exam; for doctorate, 2 foreign languages, comprehensive exam, thesis/dissertation, preliminary oral and written exams. *Entrance requirements:* For master's, GRE General Test, letters of recommendation, resume, writing sample; for doctorate, GRE General Test, letters of recommendation, resumé, writing sample, goal statement, transcripts. Additional exam requirements/recommendations for international students: Required—TOEFL (minimum score 525 paper-based). Electronic applications accepted. *Faculty research:* Medieval Europe, Crusades, Byzantine Empire, U.S. West and Borderlands, Early Modern Europe.

Saint Mary's University, Faculty of Arts, Department of History, Halifax, NS B3H 3C3, Canada. Offers MA. *Program availability:* Part-time. *Degree requirements:* For master's, one foreign language, comprehensive exam, thesis. *Entrance requirements:* For master's, honors degree. *Expenses:* Contact institution. *Faculty research:* Atlantic Canada, British Empire, history of science, South Africa.

Salem State University, School of Graduate Studies, Program in History, Salem, MA 01970-5353. Offers MA, MAT. *Program availability:* Part-time, evening/weekend. *Entrance requirements:* For master's, GRE or MAT. Additional exam requirements/recommendations for international students: Required—TOEFL (minimum score 550 paper-based; 80 iBT) or IELTS (minimum score 5.5).

Salisbury University, Department of History, Salisbury, MD 21801-6837. Offers history (MA), including Colonial and Revolutionary American history, history of the Chesapeake Bay region, United States history in the 19th and 20th centuries, world history. *Program availability:* Part-time, evening/weekend. *Faculty:* 7 full-time (3 women). *Students:* 5 full-time (2 women), 6 part-time (1 woman); includes 1 minority (Two or more races, non-Hispanic/Latino). Average age 31. 7 applicants, 86% accepted, 6 enrolled. In 2017, 10 master's awarded. *Degree requirements:* For master's, comprehensive exam, thesis optional. *Entrance requirements:* For master's, three letters of recommendation; transcripts for colleges and universities attended; personal statement; writing sample; minimum GPA of 3.0. Additional exam requirements/recommendations for international students: Required—TOEFL (minimum score 587 paper-based, 94 iBT), Michigan English Language Assessment Battery (82), IELTS (7.0), or PTE (65). *Application deadline:* For fall admission, 4/15 priority date for domestic and international students; for spring admission, 10/15 priority date for domestic and international students. Applications are processed on a rolling basis. Application fee: $65. Electronic applications accepted. *Expenses:* $392 per credit hour resident; $703 per credit hour non-resident; $92 per credit hour fees. *Financial support:* In 2017–18, 5 students received support, including 1 teaching assistantship with full tuition reimbursement available (averaging $8,000 per year); career-related internships or fieldwork and scholarships/grants also available. Support available to part-time students. Financial award application deadline: 3/1; financial award applicants required to submit FAFSA. *Faculty research:* Chesapeake studies (regional focus 17th-20th century), African American history, Native American history (minorities/ethnic focus), Afro-Asia (transitional topic), 20th century U.S. history. *Unit head:* Dr. Celine Carayon, Graduate Program Director, 410-677-3251, E-mail: cxcarayon@salisbury.edu.
Website: http://www.salisbury.edu/gsr/gradstudies/HISTpage.html

Sam Houston State University, College of Humanities and Social Sciences, Department of History, Huntsville, TX 77341. Offers MA. *Program availability:* Part-time, evening/weekend. *Degree requirements:* For master's, comprehensive exam, thesis optional. *Entrance requirements:* For master's, GRE General Test. Additional exam requirements/recommendations for international students: Required—TOEFL (minimum score 550 paper-based; 79 iBT), IELTS (minimum score 6.5). Electronic applications accepted.

San Diego State University, Graduate and Research Affairs, College of Arts and Letters, Department of History, San Diego, CA 92182. Offers MA. *Degree requirements:* For master's, one foreign language. *Entrance requirements:* For master's, GRE General Test, bachelor's degree in related field. Additional exam requirements/recommendations for international students: Required—TOEFL. Electronic applications accepted. *Faculty research:* Latin American history, Filipino history.

San Francisco State University, Division of Graduate Studies, College of Liberal and Creative Arts, Department of History, San Francisco, CA 94132-1722. Offers MA. *Unit head:* Dr. Trevor R. Getz, Chair, 415-338-1604, Fax: 415-338-6159, E-mail: tgetz@sfsu.edu. *Application contact:* Dr. Sarah Curtis, Graduate Coordinator, 415-338-2250, Fax: 415-338-6159, E-mail: scurtis@sfsu.edu.
Website: http://history.sfsu.edu/

San Jose State University, Graduate Studies and Research, College of Social Sciences, San Jose, CA 95192-0107. Offers applied anthropology (MA); communication studies (MA); economics (MA), including applied economics, economics; environmental studies (MS); geography (MA); history (MA), including history, history education; Mexican American studies (MA); psychology (MA, MS), including clinical psychology (MS), industrial/organizational psychology (MS), research and experimental psychology (MA); public administration (MPA); social sciences (MS); sociology (MA). *Faculty:* 59 full-time (29 women), 18 part-time/adjunct (5 women). *Students:* 181 full-time (126 women), 221 part-time (127 women); includes 228 minority (15 Black or African American, non-Hispanic/Latino; 48 Asian, non-Hispanic/Latino; 112 Hispanic/Latino; 3 Native Hawaiian or other Pacific Islander, non-Hispanic/Latino; 50 Two or more races, non-Hispanic/Latino), 38 international. Average age 30. 532 applicants, 44% accepted, 156 enrolled. In 2017, 139 master's awarded. *Degree requirements:* For master's, one foreign language, comprehensive exam, thesis (for some programs), project, field work, professional work experience. *Entrance requirements:* Additional exam requirements/recommendations for international students: Required—TOEFL (minimum score 550 paper-based; 80 iBT), IELTS (minimum score 6.5), PTE (minimum score 53). *Application deadline:* For fall admission, 2/1 for domestic and international students. Applications are processed on a rolling basis. Application fee: $55. Electronic applications accepted. *Expenses:* Tuition, state resident: full-time $7176. Tuition, nonresident: full-time $16,680. Tuition and fees vary according to course load and program. *Financial support:* Fellowships, research assistantships, career-related internships or fieldwork, Federal Work-Study, scholarships/grants, tuition waivers (full and partial), and unspecified assistantships available. Support available to part-time students. Financial award application deadline: 4/28; financial award applicants required to submit FAFSA. *Unit head:* Dr. Walt Jacobs, Dean, 408-924-5300, Fax: 408-924-5303, E-mail: walter.jacobs@sjsu.edu.
Website: http://www.sjsu.edu/socialsciences/

Sarah Lawrence College, Graduate Studies, Program in Women's History, Bronxville, NY 10708-5999. Offers MA. *Program availability:* Part-time. *Degree requirements:* For master's, thesis. *Entrance requirements:* For master's, previous course work in history, minimum B average in undergraduate course work. Additional exam requirements/recommendations for international students: Required—TOEFL (minimum score 600 paper-based). Electronic applications accepted.

Seton Hall University, College of Arts and Sciences, Department of History, South Orange, NJ 07079-2697. Offers history (MA), including Catholic history, European history, global history, United States history. *Program availability:* Part-time. *Degree requirements:* For master's, thesis or comprehensive exam. *Entrance requirements:* For master's, GRE. Additional exam requirements/recommendations for international students: Required—TOEFL. Electronic applications accepted. *Faculty research:* Catholic history, European history, global history, United States history, African-American history.

Shippensburg University of Pennsylvania, School of Graduate Studies, College of Arts and Sciences, Department of History and Philosophy, Shippensburg, PA 17257-2299. Offers applied history (MA). *Program availability:* Part-time, evening/weekend.

Faculty: 5 full-time (1 woman). *Students:* 14 full-time (7 women), 12 part-time (3 women); includes 2 minority (1 Black or African American, non-Hispanic/Latino; 1 Two or more races, non-Hispanic/Latino). Average age 29. 24 applicants, 88% accepted, 12 enrolled. In 2017, 10 master's awarded. *Degree requirements:* For master's, thesis, internship, or student teaching and professional practicum. *Entrance requirements:* For master's, 500-word statement of purpose; interview or minimum GPA of 2.75. Additional exam requirements/recommendations for international students: Required—TOEFL (minimum score 550 paper-based, 68 iBT) or IELTS (minimum score 6). *Application deadline:* For fall admission, 2/15 for domestic and international students; for spring admission, 9/15 for domestic and international students; for summer admission, 2/15 for domestic and international students. Applications are processed on a rolling basis. Application fee: $45. Electronic applications accepted. *Expenses:* Tuition, state resident: part-time $500 per credit. Tuition, nonresident: part-time $750 per credit. *Required fees:* $145 per credit. *Financial support:* In 2017–18, 8 students received support. Career-related internships or fieldwork, scholarships/grants, unspecified assistantships, and resident hall director and student payroll positions available. Support available to part-time students. Financial award application deadline: 3/1; financial award applicants required to submit FAFSA. *Unit head:* Dr. John D. Bloom, Associate Professor and Program Coordinator, 717-477-1621, Fax: 717-477-4062, E-mail: jdbloo@ship.edu. *Application contact:* Maya T. Mapp, Director of Admissions, 717-477-1231, Fax: 717-477-4016, E-mail: mtmapp@ship.edu.
Website: http://www.ship.edu/history/

Shippensburg University of Pennsylvania, School of Graduate Studies, College of Education and Human Services, Department of Teacher Education, Shippensburg, PA 17257-2299. Offers curriculum and instruction (M Ed), including biology, early childhood education, elementary education, geography/earth science, history, mathematics, middle school education, modern languages; reading (M Ed). *Accreditation:* NCATE. *Program availability:* Part-time, evening/weekend, 100% online, blended/hybrid learning. *Faculty:* 13 full-time (8 women), 1 (woman) part-time/adjunct. *Students:* 10 full-time (7 women), 94 part-time (81 women); includes 10 minority (3 Black or African American, non-Hispanic/Latino; 2 Asian, non-Hispanic/Latino; 5 Hispanic/Latino), 1 international. Average age 34. 71 applicants, 86% accepted, 35 enrolled. In 2017, 23 master's awarded. *Degree requirements:* For master's, comprehensive exam (for some programs), thesis optional, practicum or internship; capstone seminar (for some programs). *Entrance requirements:* For master's, MAT or GRE (if GPA less than 2.75), interview, 3 letters of reference, questionnaire of teaching background and future goals, resume. Additional exam requirements/recommendations for international students: Required—TOEFL (minimum score 550 paper-based, 68 iBT) or IELTS (minimum score 6). *Application deadline:* For fall admission, 4/1 priority date for domestic students, 4/30 for international students; for spring admission, 9/1 priority date for domestic students, 9/30 for international students; for summer admission, 2/1 priority date for domestic students. Applications are processed on a rolling basis. Application fee: $45. Electronic applications accepted. *Expenses:* Tuition, state resident: part-time $500 per credit. Tuition, nonresident: part-time $750 per credit. *Required fees:* $145 per credit. *Financial support:* In 2017–18, 1 student received support. Career-related internships or fieldwork, scholarships/grants, unspecified assistantships, and resident hall director and student payroll positions available. Support available to part-time students. Financial award application deadline: 3/1; financial award applicants required to submit FAFSA. *Unit head:* Dr. Christine A. Royce, Chairperson, 717-477-1688, Fax: 717-477-4046, E-mail: caroyc@ship.edu. *Application contact:* Maya T. Mapp, Director of Admissions, 717-477-1231, Fax: 717-477-4016, E-mail: mtmapp@ship.edu.
Website: http://www.ship.edu/teacher/

Simmons College, College of Arts and Sciences, Boston, MA 02115. Offers English (MA); gender/cultural studies (MA); history (MA); public health (MPH); public policy (MPP). *Program availability:* Part-time. *Faculty:* 19 full-time (13 women), 2 part-time/adjunct (both women). *Students:* 4 full-time (3 women), 39 part-time (34 women); includes 11 minority (7 Black or African American, non-Hispanic/Latino; 1 Hispanic/Latino; 3 Two or more races, non-Hispanic/Latino). Average age 26. 99 applicants, 57% accepted, 27 enrolled. In 2017, 23 master's awarded. Terminal master's awarded for partial completion of doctoral program. *Degree requirements:* For master's, thesis optional. *Entrance requirements:* For master's, GRE, bachelor's degree from accredited college or university; minimum B average (preferred). Additional exam requirements/recommendations for international students: Required—TOEFL (minimum score 600 paper-based; 100 iBT). *Application deadline:* For fall admission, 8/1 for domestic and international students; for spring admission, 12/15 for domestic and international students; for summer admission, 5/1 for domestic and international students. Applications are processed on a rolling basis. Application fee: $35. Electronic applications accepted. *Expenses:* $1,052 per credit, $55 activity fee per semester. *Financial support:* In 2017–18, 4 fellowships with partial tuition reimbursements, 22 teaching assistantships with partial tuition reimbursements were awarded; scholarships/grants and unspecified assistantships also available. Support available to part-time students. Financial award applicants required to submit FAFSA. *Faculty research:* Film and media studies, postcolonial literature, critical theory, arts and culture. *Unit head:* Dr. Leanne Doherty, Dean, 617-521-2581, E-mail: leanne.doherty@simmons.edu. *Application contact:* Patricia Flaherty, Director, Graduate Studies Admission, 617-521-3902, Fax: 617-521-3058, E-mail: gsa@simmons.edu.
Website: http://www.simmons.edu/gradstudies/

Simon Fraser University, Office of Graduate Studies and Postdoctoral Fellows, Faculty of Arts and Social Sciences, Department of History, Burnaby, BC V5A 1S6, Canada. Offers MA, PhD. *Degree requirements:* For master's, one foreign language, thesis, language exam; for doctorate, one foreign language, comprehensive exam, thesis/dissertation, language exam. *Entrance requirements:* For master's, minimum GPA of 3.0 (on scale of 4.33) or 3.33 based on last 60 credits of undergraduate courses; for doctorate, minimum GPA of 3.5 (on scale of 4.33). Additional exam requirements/recommendations for international students: Recommended—TOEFL (minimum score 580 paper-based; 93 iBT), IELTS (minimum score 7), TWE (minimum score 5). Electronic applications accepted. *Faculty research:* Colonialism and imperialism Asian history, labor history, race, gender and sexuality, political and social history, cultural and urban history.

Slippery Rock University of Pennsylvania, Graduate Studies (Recruitment), College of Liberal Arts, Department of History, Slippery Rock, PA 16057-1383. Offers MA. *Program availability:* Part-time, evening/weekend, online only, 100% online. *Degree requirements:* For master's, comprehensive exam, thesis (for some programs). *Entrance requirements:* For master's, transcripts (undergraduate/graduate), minimum GPA of 3.0, personal statement. Additional exam requirements/recommendations for international students: Required—TOEFL (minimum score 550 paper-based; 80 iBT). Electronic applications accepted. *Expenses:* Contact institution.

Smith College, Graduate and Special Programs, Department of History, Northampton, MA 01063. Offers secondary education (MAT), including history education. *Program availability:* Part-time. *Students:* 2 full-time (both women), 1 part-time (0 women); includes 1 minority (Hispanic/Latino). Average age 30. 3 applicants, 100% accepted, 1 enrolled. In 2017, 2 master's awarded. *Entrance requirements:* Additional exam requirements/recommendations for international students: Required—TOEFL (minimum

score 595 paper-based; 97 iBT), IELTS. *Application deadline:* For fall admission, 4/15 for domestic students, 1/15 for international students; for spring admission, 12/1 for domestic students. Applications are processed on a rolling basis. Application fee: $60. *Expenses:* Contact institution. *Financial support:* In 2017–18, 3 students received support, including 1 fellowship with full tuition reimbursement available; scholarships/grants also available. Support available to part-time students. Financial award application deadline: 4/15; financial award applicants required to submit CSS PROFILE or FAFSA. *Unit head:* Joshua Birk, Graduate Student Adviser, 413-585-3740, E-mail: jbirk@smith.edu. *Application contact:* Ruth Morgan, Program Assistant, 413-585-3050, Fax: 413-585-3054, E-mail: gradstdy@smith.edu.
Website: http://www.smith.edu/history/

Sonoma State University, School of Social Sciences, Department of History, Rohnert Park, CA 94928. Offers MA. *Program availability:* Part-time. *Entrance requirements:* For master's, GRE General Test or GRE Subject Test, minimum GPA of 3.0. Additional exam requirements/recommendations for international students: Required—TOEFL (minimum score 500 paper-based). *Application deadline:* For fall admission, 11/30 for domestic students; for spring admission, 8/31 for domestic students. Application fee: $55. *Financial support:* Fellowships, research assistantships, teaching assistantships, career-related internships or fieldwork, and Federal Work-Study available. Financial award application deadline: 3/2; financial award applicants required to submit FAFSA. *Unit head:* Kathleen Noonan, Chair, 707-664-2313, E-mail: noonan@sonoma.edu.
Website: http://www.sonoma.edu/history/

Southeastern Louisiana University, College of Arts, Humanities and Social Sciences, Department of History and Political Science, Hammond, LA 70402. Offers history (MA). *Program availability:* Part-time. *Faculty:* 9 full-time (2 women). *Students:* 1 (woman) full-time, 30 part-time (8 women); includes 3 minority (2 Hispanic/Latino; 1 Two or more races, non-Hispanic/Latino). Average age 27. 11 applicants, 73% accepted, 7 enrolled. In 2017, 7 master's awarded. *Degree requirements:* For master's, comprehensive exam, thesis optional. *Entrance requirements:* For master's, GRE General Test (minimum score of 290 combined verbal and quantitative), at least 30 undergraduate hours of history. Additional exam requirements/recommendations for international students: Required—TOEFL (minimum score 500 paper-based; 61 iBT). *Application deadline:* For fall admission, 7/15 priority date for domestic students, 6/1 priority date for international students; for spring admission, 12/1 priority date for domestic students, 10/1 priority date for international students. Applications are processed on a rolling basis. Application fee: $20 ($30 for international students). Electronic applications accepted. *Expenses:* Tuition, state resident: full-time $6684. Tuition, nonresident: full-time $19,162. *Required fees:* $2088. *Financial support:* In 2017–18, 13 students received support, including 3 teaching assistantships (averaging $4,030 per year); research assistantships, career-related internships or fieldwork, Federal Work-Study, institutionally sponsored loans, scholarships/grants, and unspecified assistantships also available. Support available to part-time students. Financial award application deadline: 5/1; financial award applicants required to submit FAFSA. *Faculty research:* American, British and European, and Southern and Louisiana history; American and international politics; philosophy. *Unit head:* Dr. William Robison, Department Head, 985-549-2109, Fax: 985-549-2012, E-mail: wrobison@southeastern.edu. *Application contact:* Amanda Harper, Graduate Admissions Analyst, 985-549-5620, Fax: 985-549-5632, E-mail: admissions@southeastern.edu.
Website: http://www.southeastern.edu/acad_research/depts/hist_ps/index.html

Southeast Missouri State University, School of Graduate Studies, Department of History, Cape Girardeau, MO 63701-4799. Offers heritage interpretation (Certificate); historic preservation (Certificate); history (MA); public history (MA), including heritage education, historic preservation. *Program availability:* Part-time, evening/weekend. *Faculty:* 10 full-time (4 women). *Students:* 12 full-time (7 women), 14 part-time (5 women); includes 3 minority (2 Black or African American, non-Hispanic/Latino; 1 Hispanic/Latino). Average age 32. 12 applicants, 100% accepted, 10 enrolled. In 2017, 8 master's awarded. *Degree requirements:* For master's, comprehensive exam (for some programs), thesis or comprehensive exams plus a capstone project/paper (for history); thesis or internship plus advanced project in applied history and comprehensive exams (for public history). *Entrance requirements:* For master's, minimum GPA of 2.75; 24 semester hours of undergraduate credit in history; letter of intent indicating how past experiences have prepared the candidate for graduate study and what the candidate expects to achieve through graduate study; two letters of recommendation; academic or professional writing sample; for Certificate, minimum GPA of 2.75; letter of intent indicating how past experiences have prepared the candidate for graduate study and what the candidate expects to achieve through graduate study; two letters of recommendation; academic or professional writing sample. Additional exam requirements/recommendations for international students: Required—TOEFL (minimum score 550 paper-based; 79 iBT), IELTS (minimum score 6), PTE (minimum score 53). *Application deadline:* For fall admission, 8/1 for domestic students, 6/1 for international students; for spring admission, 11/21 for domestic students, 10/1 for international students; for summer admission, 5/15 for domestic students. Applications are processed on a rolling basis. Application fee: $30 ($40 for international students). Electronic applications accepted. *Expenses:* $270.35 per credit hour in-state tuition, $33.40 per credit hour fees. *Financial support:* In 2017–18, 4 students received support, including 4 teaching assistantships with full tuition reimbursements available; career-related internships or fieldwork, Federal Work-Study, scholarships/grants, traineeships, tuition waivers (full), and unspecified assistantships also available. Financial award application deadline: 6/30; financial award applicants required to submit FAFSA. *Faculty research:* Medieval Europe; modern Europe including Britain, Germany, France, Russia, and Spain; colonial and nineteenth-century America; twentieth-century America and American West; public history and medieval Europe; modern Europe including Britain, Germany, France, Russia, and Spain; colonial and nineteenth-century America; twentieth-century America and American West; public history and historic preservation; Latin America. *Unit head:* Dr. Toni Alexander, Chairperson/Professor of History, 573-651-2179, Fax: 573-651-5114, E-mail: talexander@semo.edu. *Application contact:* Dr. Vicky McAlister, Graduate Coordinator/Assistant Professor of History, 573-651-2763, Fax: 573-651-5114, E-mail: vmcalister@semo.edu.

Southern Connecticut State University, School of Graduate Studies, School of Arts and Sciences, Department of History, New Haven, CT 06515-1355. Offers MA, MS. *Program availability:* Part-time, evening/weekend. *Degree requirements:* For master's, one foreign language, thesis. *Entrance requirements:* For master's, interview, undergraduate major or minor in history. Electronic applications accepted.

Southern Illinois University Carbondale, Graduate School, College of Liberal Arts, Department of History, Carbondale, IL 62901-4701. Offers MA, PhD. *Program availability:* Part-time. *Degree requirements:* For master's, one foreign language, research papers or thesis, written exams; for doctorate, 2 foreign languages, thesis/dissertation. *Entrance requirements:* For master's, GRE General Test, minimum GPA of 3.0; for doctorate, GRE General Test, minimum GPA of 3.25. Additional exam requirements/recommendations for international students: Required—TOEFL. *Faculty research:* American, Asian, European, and Latin American history; global history.

Southern Illinois University Edwardsville, Graduate School, College of Arts and Sciences, Department of Historical Studies, Program in History, Edwardsville, IL 62026.

Offers MA. *Program availability:* Part-time, evening/weekend. *Degree requirements:* For master's, one foreign language, thesis (for some programs), final exam. *Entrance requirements:* For master's, GRE. Additional exam requirements/recommendations for international students: Required—TOEFL (minimum score 550 paper-based; 79 iBT), IELTS (minimum score 6.5). Electronic applications accepted.

Southern Methodist University, Dedman College of Humanities and Sciences, Clements Department of History, Dallas, TX 75275. Offers classical/medieval history (MA); European history (MA); history (PhD); Ibero-American history (MA); United States history (MA). PhD offered jointly with the Clements Center for Southwest Studies. *Program availability:* Part-time. Terminal master's awarded for partial completion of doctoral program. *Degree requirements:* For master's, one foreign language, thesis, oral exam, thesis defense; for doctorate, one foreign language, thesis/dissertation, oral exam, dissertation defense. *Entrance requirements:* For master's and doctorate, GRE General Test, minimum GPA of 3.0, 12 undergraduate hours in advanced level history, writing sample. Additional exam requirements/recommendations for international students: Required—TOEFL. Electronic applications accepted. *Faculty research:* U.S. history, European history, Latin America, Africa/Middle East, China.

Southern New Hampshire University, School of Arts and Sciences, Manchester, NH 03106-1045. Offers clinical mental health counseling (MS); creative writing (MA); criminal justice (MS); cyber security (MS); English (MA); fiction and nonfiction (MFA); history (MA); political science (MS); psychology (MS). *Program availability:* Part-time, evening/weekend. *Degree requirements:* For master's, one foreign language, thesis. *Entrance requirements:* For master's, minimum GPA of 2.75 (for MS in teaching English as a foreign language), 3.0 (for MFA). Additional exam requirements/recommendations for international students: Required—TOEFL (minimum score 550 paper-based; 79 iBT), IELTS (minimum score 6.5), TWE (minimum score 5). *Application deadline:* For fall admission, 7/1 priority date for domestic students; for winter admission, 11/1 priority date for domestic students; for spring admission, 6/1 priority date for domestic students. Applications are processed on a rolling basis. Application fee: $40. Electronic applications accepted. *Expenses:* Contact institution. *Financial support:* Research assistantships, career-related internships or fieldwork, and scholarships/grants available. Financial award applicants required to submit FAFSA. *Faculty research:* Action research, state of the art practice in behavioral health services, wraparound approaches to working with youth, learning styles. *Unit head:* Steven K. Johnson, Dean, 603-629-4626. *Application contact:* Office of Graduate Admission, 888-327-SNHU, Fax: 603-644-3144, E-mail: enroll@snhu.edu.

Southern University and Agricultural and Mechanical College, Graduate School, College of Arts and Humanities, Department of History, Baton Rouge, LA 70813. Offers social sciences (MA). *Program availability:* Part-time. *Degree requirements:* For master's, thesis. *Entrance requirements:* For master's, GRE General Test. Additional exam requirements/recommendations for international students: Required—TOEFL (minimum score 525 paper-based).

Southwestern Assemblies of God University, Thomas F. Harrison School of Graduate Studies, Program in History, Waxahachie, TX 75165-5735. Offers MA.

Stanford University, School of Humanities and Sciences, Department of History, Stanford, CA 94305-2004. Offers MA, PhD. Terminal master's awarded for partial completion of doctoral program. *Degree requirements:* For doctorate, variable foreign language requirement, thesis/dissertation, oral exam. *Entrance requirements:* For master's and doctorate, GRE General Test. Additional exam requirements/recommendations for international students: Required—TOEFL. Electronic applications accepted. *Expenses: Tuition:* Full-time $48,987; part-time $10,620 per quarter. One-time fee: $400. Tuition and fees vary according to program.

State University of New York at Oswego, Graduate Studies, College of Liberal Arts and Sciences, Department of History, Oswego, NY 13126. Offers MA. *Program availability:* Part-time. *Degree requirements:* For master's, thesis optional. *Entrance requirements:* For master's, writing sample. Additional exam requirements/recommendations for international students: Required—TOEFL (minimum score 560 paper-based).

State University of New York College at Cortland, Graduate Studies, School of Arts and Sciences, Department of History, Cortland, NY 13045. Offers MA. *Program availability:* Part-time, evening/weekend. *Degree requirements:* For master's, one foreign language, comprehensive exam, thesis optional. *Entrance requirements:* Additional exam requirements/recommendations for international students: Required—TOEFL.

Stephen F. Austin State University, Graduate School, College of Liberal Arts, Department of History, Nacogdoches, TX 75962. Offers MA. *Program availability:* Part-time, evening/weekend. *Degree requirements:* For master's, comprehensive exam. *Entrance requirements:* For master's, GRE General Test. Additional exam requirements/recommendations for international students: Required—TOEFL. *Faculty research:* U.S.-Third World foreign policy, racial attitudes of antebellum Southern whites, naval warfare in World War II, demography of East Texas, medieval sermons.

Stony Brook University, State University of New York, Graduate School, College of Arts and Sciences, Department of History, Stony Brook, NY 11794. Offers MA, PhD. *Program availability:* Evening/weekend. *Faculty:* 30 full-time (15 women), 3 part-time/adjunct (1 woman). *Students:* 51 full-time (23 women), 2 part-time (0 women); includes 5 minority (1 Black or African American, non-Hispanic/Latino; 3 Hispanic/Latino; 1 Two or more races, non-Hispanic/Latino), 12 international. Average age 33. 34 applicants, 53% accepted, 7 enrolled. In 2017, 4 master's, 5 doctorates awarded. *Degree requirements:* For doctorate, thesis/dissertation. *Entrance requirements:* For master's and doctorate, GRE General Test. Additional exam requirements/recommendations for international students: Required—TOEFL. *Application deadline:* For fall admission, 1/15 for domestic students; for spring admission, 10/1 for domestic students. Application fee: $100. Electronic applications accepted. *Expenses:* Contact institution. *Financial support:* In 2017–18, 19 teaching assistantships were awarded; fellowships and research assistantships also available. *Total annual research expenditures:* $17,446. *Unit head:* Dr. Paul Gootenberg, Chair, 631-632-7507, Fax: 631-632-7367, E-mail: paul.gootenberg@stonybrook.edu. *Application contact:* Roxanne Fernandez, Coordinator, 631-632-7490, Fax: 631-632-7367, E-mail: roxanne.fernandez@stonybrook.edu.
Website: http://www.sunysb.edu/history/

Sul Ross State University, College of Arts and Sciences, Department of Behavioral and Social Sciences, Program in History, Alpine, TX 79832. Offers MA. *Program availability:* Part-time, evening/weekend. *Degree requirements:* For master's, thesis optional. *Entrance requirements:* For master's, GRE General Test, minimum GPA of 2.5 in last 60 hours of undergraduate work. *Faculty research:* Borderland/Southwestern studies, British studies, women's history, Native American studies, local history.

Syracuse University, Maxwell School of Citizenship and Public Affairs, Programs in History, Syracuse, NY 13244. Offers MA, PhD. *Program availability:* Part-time. Terminal master's awarded for partial completion of doctoral program. *Degree requirements:* For master's, comprehensive exam, thesis or alternative; for doctorate, 2 foreign languages, comprehensive exam, thesis/dissertation. *Entrance requirements:* For master's and doctorate, GRE General Test, sample of written work, resume, personal statement, three letters of recommendation. Additional exam requirements/recommendations for international students: Required—TOEFL (minimum score 100 iBT). *Application deadline:* For fall admission, 1/1 priority date for domestic and international students. Application fee: $75. Electronic applications accepted. *Financial support:* Fellowships with full tuition reimbursements, research assistantships, and teaching assistantships available. Financial award application deadline: 1/1; financial award applicants required to submit FAFSA. *Faculty research:* American, medieval, European, South East Asian, and Russian history. *Unit head:* Dr. Norman Kutcher, Department Chair, 315-443-2210, E-mail: mebner@maxwell.syr.edu. *Application contact:* Erin Borchik, Information Contact, 315-443-2210, E-mail: eborchik@syr.edu.
Website: https://www.maxwell.syr.edu/hist.aspx?id=757

Tarleton State University, College of Graduate Studies, College of Liberal and Fine Arts, Department of Social Sciences, Stephenville, TX 76402. Offers history (MA). *Program availability:* Part-time, evening/weekend. *Faculty:* 5 full-time (4 women), 1 part-time/adjunct (0 women). *Students:* 2 full-time (1 woman), 10 part-time (7 women); includes 1 minority (Hispanic/Latino). Average age 34. 7 applicants, 71% accepted, 2 enrolled. In 2017, 1 master's awarded. *Degree requirements:* For master's, comprehensive exam, thesis optional. *Entrance requirements:* For master's, GRE General Test, minimum GPA of 3.0. Additional exam requirements/recommendations for international students: Required—TOEFL (minimum score 550 paper-based; 80 iBT), IELTS (minimum score 6). *Application deadline:* For fall admission, 8/15 priority date for domestic students; for spring admission, 1/7 for domestic students. Applications are processed on a rolling basis. Application fee: $45 ($145 for international students). Electronic applications accepted. *Expenses:* Contact institution. *Financial support:* Research assistantships, teaching assistantships, career-related internships or fieldwork, and Federal Work-Study available. Support available to part-time students. Financial award application deadline: 5/1; financial award applicants required to submit FAFSA. *Unit head:* Dr. Eric Morrow, Department Head, 254-968-9626, E-mail: morrow@tarleton.edu. *Application contact:* Information Contact, 254-968-9104, Fax: 254-968-9670, E-mail: gradoffice@tarleton.edu.

Temple University, College of Liberal Arts, Department of History, Philadelphia, PA 19122-6096. Offers MA, PhD. *Program availability:* Part-time, evening/weekend. *Faculty:* 22 full-time (8 women), 11 part-time/adjunct (3 women). *Students:* 62 full-time (17 women), 10 part-time (4 women); includes 7 minority (2 Black or African American, non-Hispanic/Latino; 2 Hispanic/Latino; 3 Two or more races, non-Hispanic/Latino), 5 international. 63 applicants, 43% accepted, 8 enrolled. In 2017, 10 master's, 9 doctorates awarded. Terminal master's awarded for partial completion of doctoral program. *Degree requirements:* For doctorate, one foreign language, thesis/dissertation. *Entrance requirements:* For master's and doctorate, GRE General Test, minimum GPA of 3.0, 3 letters of recommendation. Additional exam requirements/recommendations for international students: Required—TOEFL (minimum score 550 paper-based; 79 iBT). *Application deadline:* For fall admission, 2/15 priority date for domestic students, 12/15 for international students; for spring admission, 10/15 for domestic students, 8/1 for international students. Application fee: $60. Electronic applications accepted. *Expenses:* Tuition, state resident: full-time $16,164; part-time $898 per credit hour. Tuition, nonresident: full-time $22,158; part-time $1231 per credit hour. *Required fees:* $890; $445 per semester. Full-time tuition and fees vary according to course load, degree level, campus/location and program. *Financial support:* Fellowships with tuition reimbursements, teaching assistantships with tuition reimbursements, career-related internships or fieldwork, and tuition waivers (partial) available. Support available to part-time students. Financial award application deadline: 1/15; financial award applicants required to submit FAFSA. *Faculty research:* American history, foreign relations, transnational and international history, military history, urban history, environmental history. *Unit head:* Andrew Isenberg, Graduate Director, 215-384-6419, E-mail: aisenber@temple.edu. *Application contact:* Jessica Roney, MA Coordinator, 215-204-4997, E-mail: jessica.roney@temple.edu.
Website: http://www.cla.temple.edu/history/

Texas A&M International University, Office of Graduate Studies and Research, College of Arts and Sciences, Department of Humanities, Laredo, TX 78041. Offers English (MA); Hispanic studies (PhD); history and political thought (MA); language, literature and translation (MA). *Degree requirements:* For master's, comprehensive exam (for some programs), thesis (for some programs). *Entrance requirements:* For master's, GRE General Test. Additional exam requirements/recommendations for international students: Required—TOEFL (minimum score 550 paper-based; 79 iBT).

Texas A&M International University, Office of Graduate Studies and Research, College of Arts and Sciences, Department of Public Affairs and Social Research, Laredo, TX 78041. Offers criminal justice (MS); history and political thought (MA); political science (MA); public administration (MPA). *Degree requirements:* For master's, comprehensive exam (for some programs), thesis (for some programs). *Entrance requirements:* For master's, GRE General Test. Additional exam requirements/recommendations for international students: Required—TOEFL (minimum score 550 paper-based; 79 iBT).

Texas A&M University, College of Liberal Arts, Department of History, College Station, TX 77843. Offers MA, PhD. *Program availability:* Part-time. *Faculty:* 35. *Students:* 32 full-time (12 women), 20 part-time (4 women); includes 7 minority (all Hispanic/Latino). Average age 35. 23 applicants, 70% accepted, 7 enrolled. In 2017, 3 master's, 10 doctorates awarded. Terminal master's awarded for partial completion of doctoral program. *Degree requirements:* For master's, one foreign language, thesis optional; for doctorate, 2 foreign languages, thesis/dissertation. *Entrance requirements:* For master's and doctorate, GRE General Test. Additional exam requirements/recommendations for international students: Required—TOEFL (minimum score 550 paper-based; 80 iBT), IELTS (minimum score 6), PTE (minimum score 53). *Application deadline:* For fall admission, 12/15 for domestic students. Application fee: $50 ($90 for international students). *Expenses:* Contact institution. *Financial support:* In 2017–18, 35 students received support, including 4 fellowships with tuition reimbursements available (averaging $19,500 per year), 2 research assistantships with tuition reimbursements available (averaging $9,510 per year), 30 teaching assistantships with tuition reimbursements available (averaging $11,933 per year); career-related internships or fieldwork, institutionally sponsored loans, scholarships/grants, traineeships, health care benefits, tuition waivers (full and partial), and unspecified assistantships also available. Support available to part-time students. Financial award application deadline: 3/15; financial award applicants required to submit FAFSA. *Faculty research:* Recent U.S. history, Southwest, border studies, military history, Europe. *Unit head:* Dr. David Vaught, Department Head, 979-845-2571, Fax: 979-862-4314, E-mail: d-vaught@tamu.edu. *Application contact:* Adam Seipp, Director of Graduate Studies, 979-845-5996, Fax: 979-862-4314, E-mail: aseipp@tamu.edu.
Website: http://history.tamu.edu/

Texas A&M University–Central Texas, Graduate Studies and Research, Killeen, TX 76549. Offers accounting (MS); business administration (MBA); clinical mental health counseling (MS); criminal justice (MCJ); curriculum and instruction (M Ed); educational administration (M Ed); educational psychology - experimental psychology (MS); history (MA); human resource management (MS); information systems (MS); liberal studies

(MS); management and leadership (MS); marriage and family therapy (MS); mathematics (MS); political science (MA); school counseling (M Ed); school psychology (Ed S).

Texas A&M University–Commerce, College of Humanities, Social Sciences and Arts, Commerce, TX 75429. Offers applied criminology (MS); applied linguistics (MA, MS); art (MA, MFA); computational linguistics (Graduate Certificate); creative writing (Graduate Certificate); criminal justice management (Graduate Certificate); criminal justice studies (Graduate Certificate); English (MA, MS, PhD); film studies (Graduate Certificate); history (MA, MS); history of Christianity (Graduate Certificate); Holocaust studies (Graduate Certificate); homeland security (Graduate Certificate); music education (MM); music performance (MM); political science (MA, MS); public history (Graduate Certificate); sociology (MS); Spanish (MA); studies in children's and adolescent literature and culture (Graduate Certificate); teaching English to speakers of other languages (Graduate Certificate); theater (MA, MS); world history (Graduate Certificate). *Program availability:* Part-time. *Faculty:* 56 full-time (26 women), 10 part-time/adjunct (5 women). *Students:* 133 full-time (85 women), 439 part-time (311 women); includes 204 minority (79 Black or African American, non-Hispanic/Latino; 4 American Indian or Alaska Native, non-Hispanic/Latino; 9 Asian, non-Hispanic/Latino; 98 Hispanic/Latino; 14 Two or more races, non-Hispanic/Latino), 26 international. Average age 36. 261 applicants, 50% accepted, 113 enrolled. In 2017, 105 master's, 5 doctorates awarded. *Degree requirements:* For master's, one foreign language, comprehensive exam, thesis (for some programs); for doctorate, one foreign language, comprehensive exam, thesis/dissertation, departmental qualifying exam. *Entrance requirements:* For master's and doctorate, GRE General Test. Additional exam requirements/recommendations for international students: Required—TOEFL (minimum score 550 paper-based; 79 iBT), IELTS (minimum score 6). *Application deadline:* Applications are processed on a rolling basis. Application fee: $50. Electronic applications accepted. *Expenses:* Contact institution. *Financial support:* In 2017–18, 43 students received support, including 9 research assistantships with partial tuition reimbursements available (averaging $9,000 per year), 68 teaching assistantships with partial tuition reimbursements available (averaging $9,000 per year); Federal Work-Study, institutionally sponsored loans, scholarships/grants, health care benefits, and unspecified assistantships also available. Financial award application deadline: 5/1; financial award applicants required to submit FAFSA. *Unit head:* Dr. William F. Kuracina, Interim Dean, 903-886-5166, Fax: 903-886-5774, E-mail: william.kuracina@tamuc.edu. *Application contact:* Vicky Turner, Doctoral Degree and Special Programs Coordinator, 903-886-5167, E-mail: vicky.turner@tamuc.edu.
Website: http://www.tamuc.edu/academics/graduateSchool/programs/humanitiesSocialScienceArts/default.aspx

Texas A&M University–Corpus Christi, College of Graduate Studies, College of Liberal Arts, Corpus Christi, TX 78412. Offers communication (MA); English (MA); history (MA); psychology (MA), including clinical psychology, general psychology; public administration (MPA); studio art (MFA). *Program availability:* Part-time, evening/weekend. *Faculty:* 76 full-time (39 women), 9 part-time/adjunct (4 women). *Students:* 83 full-time (56 women), 109 part-time (78 women); includes 112 minority (9 Black or African American, non-Hispanic/Latino; 100 Hispanic/Latino; 3 Two or more races, non-Hispanic/Latino). Average age 32. 119 applicants, 67% accepted, 65 enrolled. In 2017, 65 master's awarded. *Degree requirements:* For master's, comprehensive exam (for some programs). *Entrance requirements:* For master's, portfolio. Additional exam requirements/recommendations for international students: Required—TOEFL (minimum score 550 paper-based; 79 iBT), IELTS (minimum score 6.5). *Application deadline:* For fall admission, 7/15 for domestic students, 5/1 for international students; for spring admission, 11/15 priority date for domestic students, 9/1 priority date for international students. Applications are processed on a rolling basis. Application fee: $50 ($70 for international students). Electronic applications accepted. *Expenses:* Tuition, state resident: full-time $3568; part-time $198.24 per credit hour. Tuition, nonresident: full-time $11,038; part-time $613.24 per credit hour. *Required fees:* $2129; $1422.58 per semester. Tuition and fees vary according to program. *Financial support:* Research assistantships, teaching assistantships, career-related internships or fieldwork, Federal Work-Study, institutionally sponsored loans, scholarships/grants, health care benefits, and unspecified assistantships available. Support available to part-time students. Financial award application deadline: 3/15; financial award applicants required to submit FAFSA. *Unit head:* Dr. Mark Hartlaub, Dean, 361-825-2659, Fax: 361-825-5844, E-mail: mark.hartlaub@tamucc.edu. *Application contact:* Graduate Admissions Coordinator, 361-825-2177, Fax: 361-825-2755, E-mail: gradweb@tamucc.edu.
Website: http://cla.tamucc.edu/

Texas Christian University, AddRan College of Liberal Arts, Department of History, Fort Worth, TX 76129. Offers Latin America (MA, PhD); United States (MA, PhD). *Faculty:* 18 full-time (6 women). *Students:* 50 full-time (20 women); includes 6 minority (5 Hispanic/Latino; 1 Two or more races, non-Hispanic/Latino), 1 international. Average age 34. 21 applicants, 57% accepted, 9 enrolled. In 2017, 1 master's, 6 doctorates awarded. Terminal master's awarded for partial completion of doctoral program. *Degree requirements:* For master's, comprehensive exam, thesis or alternative; for doctorate, one foreign language, comprehensive exam, thesis/dissertation. *Entrance requirements:* For master's and doctorate, GRE General Test. Additional exam requirements/recommendations for international students: Recommended—TOEFL. *Application deadline:* 2/1 for domestic and international students; for summer admission, 2/1 for domestic and international students. Application fee: $60. Electronic applications accepted. *Financial support:* In 2017–18, 50 students received support, including 3 fellowships with full tuition reimbursements available (averaging $20,000 per year), 15 research assistantships with full tuition reimbursements available (averaging $17,500 per year), 5 teaching assistantships with full tuition reimbursements available (averaging $17,500 per year); tuition waivers (full) also available. Financial award application deadline: 2/1. *Faculty research:* U.S. South, Latin American history, Atlantic World history, American West. *Total annual research expenditures:* $140,000. *Unit head:* Dr. Jodi Campbell, Professor, 817-257-5882, Fax: 817-257-5650, E-mail: j.campbell@tcu.edu. *Application contact:* Heather Confessore, Administrative Assistant, 817-257-7288, Fax: 817-257-5650, E-mail: h.confessore@tcu.edu.
Website: http://www.his.tcu.edu/graduate.asp

Texas Southern University, College of Liberal Arts and Behavioral Sciences, Department of History and Geography, Houston, TX 77004-4584. Offers history (MA). *Program availability:* Part-time, evening/weekend. *Degree requirements:* For master's, comprehensive exam, thesis optional. *Entrance requirements:* For master's, GRE General Test, minimum GPA of 2.5. Additional exam requirements/recommendations for international students: Required—TOEFL. Electronic applications accepted. *Faculty research:* American, Colonial, African, Asian, and African-American history.

Texas State University, The Graduate College, College of Liberal Arts, Program in History, San Marcos, TX 78666. Offers M Ed, MA. *Program availability:* Part-time. *Faculty:* 34 full-time (17 women), 4 part-time/adjunct (0 women). *Students:* 45 full-time (26 women), 27 part-time (15 women); includes 18 minority (2 Black or African American, non-Hispanic/Latino; 1 Asian, non-Hispanic/Latino; 14 Hispanic/Latino; 1 Two or more races, non-Hispanic/Latino). Average age 29. 41 applicants, 83% accepted, 25 enrolled. In 2017, 22 master's awarded. *Degree requirements:* For master's, comprehensive exam, thesis optional. *Entrance requirements:* For master's, GRE General Test (minimum preferred score 156 verbal reasoning/500 old test), baccalaureate degree from regionally-accredited university with minimum GPA of 2.75 on last 60 undergraduate semester hours, 3.25 on 24 hours of undergraduate history course work; description of foreign language competencies; resume; statement of purpose describing interest in history and work experience; 2 letters of recommendation. Additional exam requirements/recommendations for international students: Required—TOEFL (minimum score 550 paper-based; 78 iBT), IELTS (minimum score 6.5). *Application deadline:* For fall admission, 2/15 priority date for domestic and international students; for spring admission, 10/15 for domestic students, 10/1 for international students; for summer admission, 4/15 for domestic students, 3/15 for international students. Applications are processed on a rolling basis. Application fee: $40 ($90 for international students). Electronic applications accepted. *Expenses:* Tuition, state resident: full-time $7868; part-time $3934 per semester. Tuition, nonresident: full-time $17,828; part-time $8914 per semester. *Required fees:* $2092; $1435 per semester. Tuition and fees vary according to course load. *Financial support:* In 2017–18, 42 students received support, including 2 research assistantships (averaging $11,855 per year), 30 teaching assistantships (averaging $12,457 per year); Federal Work-Study, institutionally sponsored loans, scholarships/grants, health care benefits, and unspecified assistantships also available. Support available to part-time students. Financial award application deadline: 3/1; financial award applicants required to submit FAFSA. *Faculty research:* Race and the art of tourist promotion in Bahia, Brazil: crafting an urban landscape. *Total annual research expenditures:* $36,918. *Unit head:* Dr. Rebecca Montgomery, Graduate Advisor, 512-245-2116, Fax: 512-245-3043, E-mail: rm53@txstate.edu. *Application contact:* Dr. Andrea Golato, Dean of the Graduate College, 512-245-2581, E-mail: gradcollege@txstate.edu.
Website: http://www.txstate.edu/history/graduate.html

Texas Tech University, Graduate School, College of Arts and Sciences, Department of History, Lubbock, TX 79409. Offers MA, PhD. *Program availability:* Part-time, evening/weekend. *Faculty:* 31 full-time (10 women), 6 part-time/adjunct (1 woman). *Students:* 51 full-time (24 women), 20 part-time (6 women); includes 12 minority (1 Black or African American, non-Hispanic/Latino; 1 American Indian or Alaska Native, non-Hispanic/Latino; 1 Asian, non-Hispanic/Latino; 7 Hispanic/Latino; 1 Native Hawaiian or other Pacific Islander, non-Hispanic/Latino; 1 Two or more races, non-Hispanic/Latino), 6 international. Average age 35. 29 applicants, 21% accepted, 4 enrolled. In 2017, 15 master's, 4 doctorates awarded. *Degree requirements:* For master's, one foreign language, comprehensive exam (for some programs), thesis optional; for doctorate, one foreign language, comprehensive exam, thesis/dissertation. *Entrance requirements:* For master's and doctorate, GRE, statement of purpose, 3 letters of reference, writing sample. Additional exam requirements/recommendations for international students: Required—TOEFL (minimum score 550 paper-based; 79 iBT). *Application deadline:* For fall admission, 6/1 priority date for domestic students, 1/15 priority date for international students; for spring admission, 9/1 priority date for domestic students, 6/15 priority date for international students. Applications are processed on a rolling basis. Application fee: $60. Electronic applications accepted. *Expenses:* Contact institution. *Financial support:* In 2017–18, 57 students received support, including 56 fellowships (averaging $2,467 per year), 53 teaching assistantships (averaging $13,818 per year); research assistantships, scholarships/grants, health care benefits, and unspecified assistantships also available. Financial award application deadline: 3/15; financial award applicants required to submit FAFSA. *Faculty research:* International politics and political culture; U.S. in global context; Texas, borderlands, and the West; race and national identity; gender and sexuality. *Total annual research expenditures:* $9,272. *Unit head:* Dr. Sean P. Cunningham, Chair, 806-742-3744, Fax: 806-742-1060, E-mail: sean.cunningham@ttu.edu. *Application contact:* Dr. Laura Calkins, Director of Graduate Studies, 806-742-3744, Fax: 806-742-1060, E-mail: laura.calkins@ttu.edu.
Website: http://www.history.ttu.edu

Texas Woman's University, Graduate School, College of Arts and Sciences, Department of History and Government, Denton, TX 76204. Offers government (MA); history (MA). *Program availability:* Part-time, evening/weekend. *Faculty:* 8 full-time (4 women), 2 part-time/adjunct (0 women). *Students:* 4 full-time (0 women), 24 part-time (20 women); includes 9 minority (3 Black or African American, non-Hispanic/Latino; 2 Asian, non-Hispanic/Latino; 4 Hispanic/Latino), 2 international. Average age 33. 9 applicants, 67% accepted, 5 enrolled. In 2017, 4 master's awarded. *Degree requirements:* For master's, comprehensive exam, thesis (for some programs), professional paper or thesis. *Entrance requirements:* For master's, minimum GPA of 3.25, written statement of purpose, 2 letters of recommendation. Additional exam requirements/recommendations for international students: Required—TOEFL (minimum score 550 paper-based; 79 iBT); Recommended—IELTS (minimum score 6.5), TSE (minimum score 53). *Application deadline:* For fall admission, 3/1 priority date for domestic and international students; for spring admission, 11/1 priority date for domestic students, 7/1 priority date for international students. Applications are processed on a rolling basis. Application fee: $50 ($75 for international students). Electronic applications accepted. *Expenses:* $7,520 per year full-time in-state; $16,820 per year full-time out-of-state. *Financial support:* In 2017–18, 12 students received support, including 1 research assistantship (averaging $23,270 per year); teaching assistantships, career-related internships or fieldwork, Federal Work-Study, institutionally sponsored loans, scholarships/grants, traineeships, health care benefits, and unspecified assistantships also available. Support available to part-time students. Financial award application deadline: 3/1; financial award applicants required to submit FAFSA. *Faculty research:* U.S. history politics and law, global history politics and law, Latin American and Caribbean history; legal studies. *Total annual research expenditures:* $219,734. *Unit head:* Dr. Jonathan Olsen, Chair, 940-898-2133, Fax: 940-898-2130, E-mail: historygov@twu.edu. *Application contact:* Korie Hawkins, Associate Director of Admissions, Graduate Recruitment, 940-898-3188, Fax: 940-898-3081, E-mail: admissions@twu.edu.
Website: http://www.twu.edu/history-government/

Trinity Western University, School of Graduate Studies, Program in Interdisciplinary Humanities, Langley, BC V2Y 1Y1, Canada. Offers general humanities (MAIH); specialized (MAIH), including English, history, philosophy. *Program availability:* Part-time. *Degree requirements:* For master's, thesis or alternative, 36 semester hours. *Entrance requirements:* For master's, strong undergraduate degree in humanities or English, history or philosophy. Additional exam requirements/recommendations for international students: Recommended—TOEFL. Electronic applications accepted. *Faculty research:* Literary theory, gender, medieval and early modern literature, philosophy of religion, Thomas Merton's poetics.

Troy University, Graduate School, College of Arts and Sciences, Program in History, Troy, AL 36082. Offers American history (MA); European history (MA). *Program availability:* Part-time, evening/weekend. *Faculty:* 7 full-time (3 women). *Students:* 1 full-time (0 women), 12 part-time (4 women); includes 1 minority (Hispanic/Latino). Average age 35. 22 applicants, 91% accepted, 4 enrolled. *Degree requirements:* For master's, variable foreign language requirement, comprehensive exam, thesis optional. *Entrance requirements:* For master's, GRE (minimum score of 850 on old exam or 290 on new exam), MAT (minimum score of 385), or GMAT (minimum score of 380), bachelor's degree, minimum undergraduate GPA of 2.5 or 3.0 on last 30 semester hours, letter of

recommendation. Additional exam requirements/recommendations for international students: Required—TOEFL (minimum score 523 paper-based; 70 iBT), IELTS (minimum score 6); Recommended—TWE. *Application deadline:* For fall admission, 6/1 for international students; for spring admission, 10/15 for international students. Applications are processed on a rolling basis. Application fee: $50. Electronic applications accepted. *Expenses:* Tuition, state resident: part-time $417 per credit hour. Tuition, nonresident: part-time $834 per credit hour. *Required fees:* $42 per credit hour. $50 per semester. Tuition and fees vary according to campus/location. *Financial support:* Fellowships, career-related internships or fieldwork, and scholarships/grants available. Support available to part-time students. Financial award applicants required to submit FAFSA. *Unit head:* Dr. Allen E. Jones, Jr., Chairman, 334-340-3512, E-mail: ajones@troy.edu. *Application contact:* Jessica Campbell, Director of Graduate Admissions, 334-670-3178, Fax: 334-670-3733, E-mail: jacord@troy.edu.

Tufts University, Graduate School of Arts and Sciences, Department of History, Medford, MA 02155. Offers history (MA, PhD), including global history (PhD); history and museum studies (MA). *Students:* 20 full-time (16 women); includes 4 minority (1 Black or African American, non-Hispanic/Latino; 3 Asian, non-Hispanic/Latino), 5 international. Average age 26. 57 applicants, 42% accepted, 7 enrolled. In 2017, 11 master's, 1 doctorate awarded. Terminal master's awarded for partial completion of doctoral program. *Degree requirements:* For master's, one foreign language, thesis optional; for doctorate, 2 foreign languages, comprehensive exam, thesis/dissertation. *Entrance requirements:* For master's and doctorate, GRE General Test, writing sample. Additional exam requirements/recommendations for international students: Required—TOEFL (minimum score 550 paper-based; 80 iBT), IELTS (minimum score 6.5). *Application deadline:* For fall admission, 1/15 for domestic and international students. Applications are processed on a rolling basis. Application fee: $85. Electronic applications accepted. *Expenses:* Contact institution. *Financial support:* Teaching assistantships, Federal Work-Study, scholarships/grants, tuition waivers (full and partial), and unspecified assistantships available. Financial award application deadline: 1/15. *Unit head:* Dr. Steven Marrone, Graduate Program Director, 617-627-2781. *Application contact:* Office of Graduate Admissions, 617-627-3395, E-mail: gradadmissions@tufts.edu.
Website: http://www.ase.tufts.edu/history/

Tulane University, School of Liberal Arts, Department of History, New Orleans, LA 70118-5669. Offers MA, PhD. *Degree requirements:* For master's, one foreign language, thesis; for doctorate, variable foreign language requirement, thesis/dissertation. *Entrance requirements:* For master's, GRE General Test, minimum B average in undergraduate course work; for doctorate, GRE General Test. Additional exam requirements/recommendations for international students: Required—TOEFL. Electronic applications accepted. *Expenses: Tuition:* Full-time $50,920; part-time $2829 per credit hour. *Required fees:* $2040; $44.50 per credit hour. $580 per term. Tuition and fees vary according to course load, degree level and program.

Union Institute & University, Master of Arts Program, Cincinnati, OH 45206-1925. Offers creativity studies (MA); health and wellness (MA); history and culture (MA); leadership, public policy, and social issues (MA); literature and writing (MA). *Program availability:* Part-time, online only, 100% online. *Students:* 9 full-time (7 women), 70 part-time (56 women); includes 33 minority (22 Black or African American, non-Hispanic/Latino; 1 American Indian or Alaska Native, non-Hispanic/Latino; 6 Hispanic/Latino; 4 Two or more races, non-Hispanic/Latino). Average age 40. *Degree requirements:* For master's, thesis. *Entrance requirements:* For master's, transcript, essay, 3 letters of recommendation, resume. Additional exam requirements/recommendations for international students: Recommended—TOEFL. *Application deadline:* For spring admission, 3/13 for domestic students. Applications are processed on a rolling basis. Application fee: $50. Electronic applications accepted. *Expenses:* Contact institution. *Financial support:* Career-related internships or fieldwork and tuition waivers available. Financial award applicants required to submit FAFSA. *Unit head:* Elden Golden, Director, 513-487-1153, E-mail: elden.golden@myunion.edu. *Application contact:* Director of Admissions, 800-861-6400.

Université de Moncton, Faculty of Arts and Social Sciences, Department of History and Geography, Moncton, NB E1A 3E9, Canada. Offers history (MA). *Degree requirements:* For master's, thesis, proficiency in English and French. *Entrance requirements:* For master's, honors degree in history, minimum GPA of 2.7. Electronic applications accepted. *Faculty research:* Economic and social history (Canada, France, Acadia), sociocultural history, women's history, labor history, history of the press.

Université de Montréal, Faculty of Arts and Sciences, Department of History, Montréal, QC H3C 3J7, Canada. Offers MA, PhD. *Degree requirements:* For master's, thesis; for doctorate, thesis/dissertation, general exam. *Entrance requirements:* For doctorate, master's degree in related field. Electronic applications accepted. *Faculty research:* Preindustrial Quebec, Quebec working class, Quebec intellectual, diffusion of scientific thought, history of medicine.

Université de Sherbrooke, Faculty of Letters and Human Sciences, Department of Human Sciences, Sherbrooke, QC J1K 2R1, Canada. Offers history (MA); philosophy (MA). *Degree requirements:* For master's, thesis. *Entrance requirements:* For master's, minimum GPA of 2.75. *Faculty research:* Political, social, and urban history; history of women.

Université du Québec à Montréal, Graduate Programs, Program in History, Montréal, QC H3C 3P8, Canada. Offers MA, PhD. *Program availability:* Part-time. *Degree requirements:* For master's, thesis; for doctorate, thesis/dissertation. *Entrance requirements:* For master's, appropriate bachelor's degree or equivalent, proficiency in French; for doctorate, appropriate master's degree or equivalent, proficiency in French.

Université Laval, Faculty of Letters, Department of History, Programs in History, Québec, QC G1K 7P4, Canada. Offers MA, PhD. Terminal master's awarded for partial completion of doctoral program. *Degree requirements:* For master's, thesis (for some programs); for doctorate, comprehensive exam, thesis/dissertation. *Entrance requirements:* For master's and doctorate, English exam (comprehension of written English), knowledge of French. Electronic applications accepted.

Université Laval, Faculty of Letters, Department of Literature, Programs in Ancient Civilization, Québec, QC G1K 7P4, Canada. Offers MA, PhD. *Program availability:* Part-time. Terminal master's awarded for partial completion of doctoral program. *Degree requirements:* For master's, thesis; for doctorate, comprehensive exam, thesis/dissertation. *Entrance requirements:* For master's and doctorate, English test (comprehension of written English), knowledge of French, knowledge of an ancient language. Electronic applications accepted.

University at Albany, State University of New York, College of Arts and Sciences, Department of History, Albany, NY 12222-0001. Offers history (MA, PhD); public history (Certificate). *Program availability:* Part-time. *Faculty:* 19 full-time (6 women). *Students:* 16 full-time (4 women), 60 part-time (26 women); includes 4 minority (1 Black or African American, non-Hispanic/Latino; 1 Hispanic/Latino; 2 Two or more races, non-Hispanic/Latino), 4 international. 49 applicants, 61% accepted, 17 enrolled. In 2017, 12 master's, 4 doctorates awarded. *Degree requirements:* For master's, variable foreign language requirement, exam, research paper or thesis; for doctorate, thesis/dissertation. *Entrance requirements:* For master's, minimum GPA of 3.0; for doctorate, GRE General Test, minimum GPA of 3.0. Additional exam requirements/recommendations for international students: Required—TOEFL (minimum score 550 paper-based). *Application deadline:* For fall admission, 3/1 for domestic students, 5/1 for international students; for spring admission, 11/1 for international students. Applications are processed on a rolling basis. Application fee: $75. Electronic applications accepted. *Expenses:* Tuition, state resident: full-time $10,870; part-time $453 per credit hour. Tuition, nonresident: full-time $22,210; part-time $925 per credit hour. *Required fees:* $84.68 per credit hour. $508.06 per semester. Part-time tuition and fees vary according to course load and program. *Financial support:* Teaching assistantships and career-related internships or fieldwork available. Financial award application deadline: 3/1. *Faculty research:* American history (all phases); public policy; European history (Medieval to modern); Asian, African, and Latin American history. *Unit head:* Richard Hamm, Chair, 518-442-5300, Fax: 518-442-5301, E-mail: rhamm@albany.edu. *Application contact:* Michael DeRensis, Director, Graduate Admissions, 518-442-3980, Fax: 518-442-3922, E-mail: graduate@albany.edu.
Website: http://www.albany.edu/history/

University at Buffalo, the State University of New York, Graduate School, College of Arts and Sciences, Department of History, Buffalo, NY 14260. Offers history (MA, PhD, Advanced Certificate); public history (MA). *Program availability:* Part-time. *Faculty:* 26 full-time (11 women). *Students:* 54 full-time (21 women), 2 part-time (1 woman); includes 6 minority (all Asian, non-Hispanic/Latino). Average age 29. 60 applicants, 57% accepted, 16 enrolled. In 2017, 10 master's, 3 doctorates awarded. Terminal master's awarded for partial completion of doctoral program. *Degree requirements:* For master's, project; for doctorate, one foreign language, comprehensive exam, thesis/dissertation. *Entrance requirements:* For doctorate, GRE General Test. Additional exam requirements/recommendations for international students: Required—TOEFL (minimum score 550 paper-based; 79 iBT). *Application deadline:* For fall admission, 1/5 priority date for domestic and international students; for spring admission, 10/1 priority date for domestic students, 10/1 for international students. Applications are processed on a rolling basis. Application fee: $75. Electronic applications accepted. *Expenses:* Contact institution. *Financial support:* In 2017–18, 40 students received support, including 5 fellowships (averaging $14,000 per year), 4 research assistantships (averaging $600 per year), 26 teaching assistantships with full tuition reimbursements available (averaging $16,500 per year); career-related internships or fieldwork, institutionally sponsored loans, scholarships/grants, health care benefits, unspecified assistantships, and conference travel support also available. Financial award application deadline: 1/5; financial award applicants required to submit FAFSA. *Faculty research:* Geographical areas: Africa, Asia, early modern Europe, Latin America and Caribbean, modern Europe (Britain, France, Germany, Spain), North and South Atlantic, world, United States and Colonial America; thematic areas: African-American, gender, imperialism and colonialism, intellectual/cultural/religious, political, public history, medicine/disability/science/knowledge, slavery, transnational/international, urban. *Total annual research expenditures:* $35,000. *Unit head:* Dr. Victoria Wolcott, Chair, 716-645-3435, Fax: 716-645-5954, E-mail: vwwolcot@buffalo.edu. *Application contact:* Sarah Handley-Cousins, Staff Assistant, 716-645-3433, Fax: 716-645-5954, E-mail: handley2@buffalo.edu.
Website: https://www.history.buffalo.edu

The University of Akron, Graduate School, Buchtel College of Arts and Sciences, Department of History, Akron, OH 44325. Offers MA, PhD. *Program availability:* Part-time. *Faculty:* 14 full-time (4 women), 1 (woman) part-time/adjunct. *Students:* 16 full-time (8 women), 8 part-time (3 women); includes 1 minority (Two or more races, non-Hispanic/Latino). Average age 32. 15 applicants, 87% accepted, 10 enrolled. In 2017, 5 master's, 2 doctorates awarded. *Entrance requirements:* For master's, GRE General Test, minimum GPA of 3.0, writing sample, three letters of recommendation, letter of intent; for doctorate, GRE General Test, minimum GPA of 3.5, three letters of recommendation, personal statement, writing sample, evidence of reading knowledge in one foreign language. Additional exam requirements/recommendations for international students: Required—TOEFL (minimum score 92 iBT). *Application deadline:* For fall admission, 2/1 priority date for domestic and international students. Application fee: $45 ($70 for international students). Electronic applications accepted. *Financial support:* In 2017–18, 1 fellowship with full tuition reimbursement, 10 teaching assistantships with full tuition reimbursements were awarded. Financial award application deadline: 2/1. *Faculty research:* European, American, and world history. *Total annual research expenditures:* $15,444. *Unit head:* Dr. A. Martin Wainwright, Chair, 330-972-6512, E-mail: amartin@uakron.edu. *Application contact:* Dr. Martha Santos, Graduate Director, 330-972-2686, E-mail: santos@uakron.edu.
Website: http://www.uakron.edu/history/

The University of Alabama, Graduate School, College of Arts and Sciences, Department of History, Tuscaloosa, AL 35487. Offers MA, PhD. *Faculty:* 25 full-time (12 women). *Students:* 42 full-time (17 women), 5 part-time (1 woman); includes 6 minority (5 Black or African American, non-Hispanic/Latino; 1 Two or more races, non-Hispanic/Latino). Average age 30. 52 applicants, 71% accepted, 13 enrolled. In 2017, 6 master's, 7 doctorates awarded. Terminal master's awarded for partial completion of doctoral program. *Degree requirements:* For master's, one foreign language, thesis optional, oral exam; for doctorate, 2 foreign languages, comprehensive exam, thesis/dissertation, oral exams, written exam. *Entrance requirements:* For master's and doctorate, GRE General Test. *Application deadline:* For fall admission, 12/15 for domestic and international students. Applications are processed on a rolling basis. Application fee: $50 ($60 for international students). *Financial support:* In 2017–18, 37 students received support, including fellowships with full tuition reimbursements available (averaging $10,000 per year), research assistantships (averaging $10,000 per year), teaching assistantships with full tuition reimbursements available (averaging $10,200 per year); institutionally sponsored loans and unspecified assistantships also available. Financial award application deadline: 12/15. *Faculty research:* United States, modern European, Latin American, military, and southern U.S. history. *Unit head:* Dr. Joshua Rothman, Professor/Department Chair, 205-348-3818, E-mail: jrothman@ua.edu. *Application contact:* Dr. Daniel Riches, 205-348-1825, E-mail: dlriches@ua.edu.

The University of Alabama at Birmingham, College of Arts and Sciences, Program in History, Birmingham, AL 35294. Offers MA. *Program availability:* Part-time. *Degree requirements:* For master's, variable foreign language requirement, thesis or alternative. *Entrance requirements:* For master's, GRE General Test. Additional exam requirements/recommendations for international students: Required—TOEFL, TWE. Electronic applications accepted. *Faculty research:* History of Europe, United States, Latin America, American South.

The University of Alabama in Huntsville, School of Graduate Studies, College of Arts, Humanities, and Social Sciences, Department of History, Huntsville, AL 35899. Offers MA. *Program availability:* Part-time, evening/weekend. *Degree requirements:* For master's, one foreign language, comprehensive exam, thesis or alternative, oral and written exams. *Entrance requirements:* For master's, GRE General Test, minimum GPA of 3.0, bachelor's degree in history or related area. Additional exam requirements/recommendations for international students: Required—TOEFL (minimum score 500 paper-based; 80 iBT), IELTS (minimum score 6.5). Electronic applications accepted. *Faculty research:* Public history, history of the U.S. space program, military history, history of science and technology, women in history.

University of Alaska Fairbanks, College of Liberal Arts, Department of Arctic and Northern Studies, Fairbanks, AK 99775-6460. Offers Arctic policy (MA); environmental politics and policy (MA); Northern history (MA). *Program availability:* Part-time. *Degree requirements:* For master's, comprehensive exam, oral defense of project or thesis. *Entrance requirements:* For master's, bachelor's degree from accredited institution with minimum cumulative undergraduate and major GPA of 3.0. Additional exam requirements/recommendations for international students: Required—TOEFL (minimum score 550 paper-based; 79 iBT), IELTS (minimum score 6.5). Electronic applications accepted.

University of Alberta, Faculty of Graduate Studies and Research, Department of History and Classics, Edmonton, AB T6G 2E1, Canada. Offers ancient history (PhD); classical archaeology (MA, PhD); classical literature (PhD); classics (MA); history (MA, PhD). *Program availability:* Part-time, evening/weekend. *Degree requirements:* For master's, one foreign language, thesis (for some programs); for doctorate, one foreign language, thesis/dissertation. *Entrance requirements:* For master's, minimum B+ average; for doctorate, minimum A- average. Additional exam requirements/ recommendations for international students: Required—TOEFL (minimum score 580 paper-based). Electronic applications accepted. *Faculty research:* Western Canada, classical archaeology, Britain, Eastern Europe, East Asia.

The University of Arizona, College of Social and Behavioral Sciences, Department of History, Tucson, AZ 85721. Offers MA, PhD, Graduate Certificate. *Program availability:* Part-time. Terminal master's awarded for partial completion of doctoral program. *Degree requirements:* For master's, one foreign language, comprehensive exam, thesis optional; for doctorate, 2 foreign languages, comprehensive exam, thesis/dissertation. *Entrance requirements:* For master's, GRE General Test, 3 letters of recommendation, writing sample; for doctorate, GRE General Test, 3 letters of recommendation, statement of purpose, 2 writing samples. Additional exam requirements/ recommendations for international students: Required—TOEFL (minimum score 550 paper-based; 79 iBT). Electronic applications accepted. *Faculty research:* Latin American history, European history, U.S. history, women's history, global/environmental history.

University of Arkansas, Graduate School, J. William Fulbright College of Arts and Sciences, Department of History, Fayetteville, AR 72701. Offers MA, PhD. *Program availability:* Part-time. In 2017, 7 master's, 7 doctorates awarded. *Degree requirements:* For master's, thesis optional; for doctorate, 2 foreign languages, thesis/dissertation. *Entrance requirements:* For master's, GRE General Test; for doctorate, GRE General Test, GRE Subject Test. *Application deadline:* For fall admission, 8/1 for domestic students, 4/1 for international students; for spring admission, 12/1 for domestic students, 10/1 for international students; for summer admission, 4/15 for domestic students, 3/1 for international students. Applications are processed on a rolling basis. Application fee: $60. Electronic applications accepted. *Expenses:* Tuition, state resident: full-time $3782. Tuition, nonresident: full-time $10,238. *Financial support:* In 2017–18, 9 research assistantships, 9 teaching assistantships were awarded; fellowships with tuition reimbursements, career-related internships or fieldwork, and Federal Work-Study also available. Support available to part-time students. Financial award application deadline: 4/1; financial award applicants required to submit FAFSA. *Unit head:* Dr. Calvin White, Jr., Department Chair, 479-575-3001, Fax: 479-575-2775, E-mail: calvinwh@uark.edu. *Application contact:* Dr. Jim Gigantino, II, Graduate Coordinator, 479-575-3001, Fax: 479-575-2775, E-mail: jgiganti@uark.edu.
Website: https://fulbright.uark.edu/departments/history/

The University of British Columbia, Faculty of Arts, Department of History, Vancouver, BC V6T 1Z1, Canada. Offers finance (MA). *Faculty:* 35 full-time (12 women). *Students:* 60 full-time (21 women). 99 applicants, 19% accepted, 11 enrolled. In 2017, 7 master's, 3 doctorates awarded. *Degree requirements:* For master's, one foreign language, thesis, six 3-credit courses; for doctorate, one foreign language, comprehensive exam, thesis/dissertation, five 3-credit courses. *Entrance requirements:* For master's, four-year bachelor's degree; for doctorate, master's degree (or equivalent) in history, first-class (A) standing in graduate courses, language relevant to dissertation research. Additional exam requirements/recommendations for international students: Required—TOEFL (minimum score 90 iBT). *Application deadline:* For fall admission, 12/15 for domestic and international students. Application fee: $100 Canadian dollars ($165 Canadian dollars for international students). Electronic applications accepted. *Financial support:* In 2017–18, 40 students received support, including 12 fellowships with partial tuition reimbursements available (averaging $18,000 per year), 3 research assistantships with tuition reimbursements available (averaging $3,310 per year), 32 teaching assistantships with tuition reimbursements available (averaging $10,914 per year); scholarships/grants, tuition waivers (partial), and unspecified assistantships also available. Financial award application deadline: 9/19. *Faculty research:* Canadian, British, European, modern Chinese and Japanese history; international relations. *Unit head:* Dr. Eagle Glassheim, Department Head, 604-822-4101, Fax: 604-822-6658, E-mail: eagle.g@ubc.ca. *Application contact:* Jason Wu, Graduate Program Assistant, 604-822-6070, Fax: 604-822-6658, E-mail: hist.grad@ubc.ca.
Website: http://www.history.ubc.ca/

University of Calgary, Faculty of Graduate Studies, Faculty of Arts, Department of History, Calgary, AB T2N 1N4, Canada. Offers MA, PhD. *Program availability:* Part-time. *Degree requirements:* For master's, one foreign language, thesis; for doctorate, one foreign language, thesis/dissertation, 3 written comprehensive exams, oral candidacy exam. *Entrance requirements:* For master's, minimum GPA of 3.4, writing sample; for doctorate, sample of written work, master's degree in history. Additional exam requirements/recommendations for international students: Recommended—TOEFL. Electronic applications accepted. *Faculty research:* Military history, Canadian history, Latin American history, gender/women's history, native history.

University of California, Berkeley, Graduate Division, College of Letters and Science, Department of History, Berkeley, CA 94720-2550. Offers PhD. *Degree requirements:* For doctorate, variable foreign language requirement, comprehensive exam, thesis/ dissertation. *Entrance requirements:* For doctorate, GRE General Test, minimum GPA of 3.0, 3 letters of recommendation, writing sample (not to exceed 10 pages), academic transcripts, 2 essays (statement of purpose, personal statement). Additional exam requirements/recommendations for international students: Required—TOEFL (minimum score 570 paper-based; 68 iBT). Electronic applications accepted. *Faculty research:* African, British, Byzantine, European (Ancient Greece and Rome, Medieval, Early Modern, Late Modern), Asian (China, Japan, South, Southeast), Jewish, Latin American, Middle Eastern, science, and United States history.

University of California, Berkeley, Graduate Division, College of Letters and Science, Group in Ancient History and Mediterranean Archaeology, Berkeley, CA 94720-1500. Offers MA, PhD. Terminal master's awarded for partial completion of doctoral program. *Degree requirements:* For master's, one foreign language, exam or thesis; for doctorate, 2 foreign languages, thesis/dissertation, qualifying exam. *Entrance requirements:* For master's and doctorate, GRE General Test, minimum GPA of 3.0, 3 letters of recommendation. Additional exam requirements/recommendations for international students: Required—TOEFL (minimum score 570 paper-based; 90 iBT), TWE. Electronic applications accepted.

University of California, Davis, Graduate Studies, Program in History, Davis, CA 95616. Offers MA, PhD. Terminal master's awarded for partial completion of doctoral program. *Degree requirements:* For master's, one foreign language, comprehensive exam (for some programs), thesis (for some programs); for doctorate, 2 foreign languages, thesis/dissertation. *Entrance requirements:* For master's, GRE General Test, minimum GPA of 3.0, writing sample; for doctorate, GRE General Test, master's degree, writing sample. Additional exam requirements/recommendations for international students: Required—TOEFL (minimum score 550 paper-based). Electronic applications accepted. *Faculty research:* American social, cultural, and western history; modern and early history; modern European, East Asian, and Latin American history; history of science and medicine; cross-cultural history of women.

University of California, Irvine, School of Humanities, Department of History, Irvine, CA 92697. Offers MA, PhD. *Students:* 42 full-time (24 women), 2 part-time (1 woman); includes 17 minority (2 Black or African American, non-Hispanic/Latino; 3 Asian, non-Hispanic/Latino; 6 Hispanic/Latino; 6 Two or more races, non-Hispanic/Latino), 9 international. Average age 33. 64 applicants, 31% accepted, 10 enrolled. In 2017, 1 master's, 5 doctorates awarded. *Entrance requirements:* For master's and doctorate, GRE General Test, minimum GPA of 3.0. Additional exam requirements/ recommendations for international students: Required—TOEFL (minimum score 550 paper-based). *Application deadline:* For fall admission, 1/2 priority date for domestic students, 1/2 for international students. Application fee: $105 ($125 for international students). Electronic applications accepted. *Financial support:* Fellowships, research assistantships with full tuition reimbursements, teaching assistantships, institutionally sponsored loans, traineeships, health care benefits, and unspecified assistantships available. Financial award application deadline: 3/1; financial award applicants required to submit FAFSA. *Faculty research:* European, U.S., Latin American, ancient, and East Asian history. *Unit head:* Prof. David Igler, Chair, 949-824-9313, E-mail: digler@uci.edu. *Application contact:* Yuting Wu, Graduate Coordinator, 949-824-5891, E-mail: yutingw6@uci.edu.
Website: http://www.hnet.uci.edu/history/

University of California, Los Angeles, Graduate Division, College of Letters and Science, Department of History, Los Angeles, CA 90095. Offers MA, PhD, MLIS/MA. Terminal master's awarded for partial completion of doctoral program. *Degree requirements:* For master's, one foreign language, comprehensive exam; for doctorate, variable foreign language requirement, thesis/dissertation, oral and written qualifying exams. *Entrance requirements:* For doctorate, GRE General Test, bachelor's degree; minimum undergraduate GPA of 3.0, 3.5 graduate (or its equivalent if letter grade system not used). Additional exam requirements/recommendations for international students: Required—TOEFL. Electronic applications accepted.

University of California, Riverside, Graduate Division, Department of History, Riverside, CA 92521-0102. Offers archival management (MA); history (PhD). *Program availability:* Part-time. Terminal master's awarded for partial completion of doctoral program. *Degree requirements:* For master's, one foreign language, comprehensive exam, internship report and oral exams, or thesis; for doctorate, 2 foreign languages, thesis/dissertation, qualifying exams. *Entrance requirements:* For master's and doctorate, GRE General Test, minimum GPA of 3.2. Additional exam requirements/ recommendations for international students: Required—TOEFL (minimum score 550 paper-based; 80 iBT). Electronic applications accepted. *Expenses:* Tuition, state resident: full-time $5746. Tuition, nonresident: full-time $10,780. Tuition and fees vary according to campus/location and program. *Faculty research:* Native American history, United States, public history, Europe, Latin America.

University of California, San Diego, Graduate Division, Department of History, La Jolla, CA 92093. Offers history (MA, PhD); Judaic studies (MA). *Students:* 83 full-time (34 women), 3 part-time (2 women). 114 applicants, 15% accepted, 8 enrolled. In 2017, 9 master's, 5 doctorates awarded. *Degree requirements:* For master's, one foreign language, comprehensive exam; for doctorate, one foreign language, comprehensive exam, thesis/dissertation. *Entrance requirements:* For master's, GRE General Test, minimum GPA of 3.0; for doctorate, GRE General Test, writing sample (7-15 pages long), preferably in a history course. Additional exam requirements/recommendations for international students: Required—TOEFL (minimum score 550 paper-based; 80 iBT), IELTS (minimum score 7). *Application deadline:* For fall admission, 1/12 for domestic students. Application fee: $105 ($125 for international students). Electronic applications accepted. *Financial support:* Fellowships, research assistantships, teaching assistantships, career-related internships or fieldwork, scholarships/grants, and readerships available. Financial award applicants required to submit FAFSA. *Faculty research:* Ancient history, east Asian history, history of science, Jewish studies, global transnational studies. *Unit head:* Pamela Radcliff, Chair, 858-534-8919, E-mail: pradcliff@ucsd.edu. *Application contact:* Sally Hargate, Graduate Coordinator, 858-822-0664, E-mail: shargate@ucsd.edu.
Website: http://history.ucsd.edu

University of California, Santa Barbara, Graduate Division, College of Letters and Sciences, Division of Humanities and Fine Arts, Department of History, Santa Barbara, CA 93106-9410. Offers European medieval studies (PhD); global studies (PhD); public historical studies (PhD); technology and society (PhD); women's studies (PhD); MA/ PhD. *Degree requirements:* For doctorate, variable foreign language requirement, comprehensive exam, thesis/dissertation. *Entrance requirements:* For doctorate, GRE. Additional exam requirements/recommendations for international students: Required—TOEFL (minimum score 550 paper-based; 80 iBT), IELTS (minimum score 7). Electronic applications accepted. *Faculty research:* Europe, United States, Latin America, Africa, Middle East, East Asia.

University of California, Santa Cruz, Division of Graduate Studies, Division of Humanities, Department of History, Santa Cruz, CA 95064. Offers MA, PhD. *Degree requirements:* For doctorate, variable foreign language requirement, comprehensive exam, thesis/dissertation, qualifying exam. *Entrance requirements:* For master's and doctorate, GRE, writing sample of up to 30 pages. Additional exam requirements/ recommendations for international students: Required—TOEFL (minimum score 550 paper-based; 83 iBT); Recommended—IELTS (minimum score 8). Electronic applications accepted. *Faculty research:* Comparative, interdisciplinary approach to history; the Americas, Asia, the Islamic world, and Europe since 1500; society history.

University of Central Arkansas, Graduate School, College of Liberal Arts, Department of History, Conway, AR 72035-0001. Offers MA. *Program availability:* Part-time. *Degree requirements:* For master's, one foreign language, comprehensive exam, thesis optional. *Entrance requirements:* For master's, GRE General Test, minimum GPA of 2.7. Additional exam requirements/recommendations for international students: Required—TOEFL (minimum score 550 paper-based). Electronic applications accepted. *Faculty research:* History Day, Russian culture.

University of Central Florida, College of Arts and Humanities, Department of History, Orlando, FL 32816. Offers MA. *Program availability:* Part-time, evening/weekend. *Students:* 28 full-time (6 women), 22 part-time (6 women); includes 14 minority (4 Black or African American, non-Hispanic/Latino; 1 Asian, non-Hispanic/Latino; 7 Hispanic/ Latino; 2 Two or more races, non-Hispanic/Latino). Average age 29. 14 applicants, 86% accepted, 8 enrolled. In 2017, 4 master's awarded. *Degree requirements:* For master's,

thesis, written exam. *Entrance requirements:* For master's, GRE General Test, minimum GPA of 3.0 in last 60 hours. Additional exam requirements/recommendations for international students: Required—TOEFL. *Application deadline:* For fall admission, 6/1 for domestic students; for spring admission, 12/1 for domestic students; for summer admission, 4/15 for domestic students. Application fee: $30. Electronic applications accepted. *Expenses:* Tuition, state resident: part-time $288.16 per credit hour. Tuition, nonresident: part-time $1073.31 per credit hour. Tuition and fees vary according to program. *Financial support:* In 2017–18, 13 students received support, including 7 fellowships with partial tuition reimbursements available (averaging $3,800 per year), 7 research assistantships with partial tuition reimbursements available (averaging $4,650 per year), 8 teaching assistantships with partial tuition reimbursements available (averaging $6,243 per year); career-related internships or fieldwork, Federal Work-Study, institutionally sponsored loans, health care benefits, tuition waivers (partial), and unspecified assistantships also available. Financial award application deadline: 3/1; financial award applicants required to submit FAFSA. *Unit head:* Dr. Peter Larson, Chair, 407-823-6466, E-mail: peter.larson@ucf.edu. *Application contact:* Associate Director, Graduate Admissions, 407-823-2766, Fax: 407-823-6442, E-mail: gradadmissions@ucf.edu.
Website: http://history.cah.ucf.edu/

University of Central Missouri, The Graduate School, Warrensburg, MO 64093. Offers accountancy (MA); accounting (MBA); applied mathematics (MS); aviation safety (MA); biology (MS); business administration (MBA); career and technical education leadership (MS); college student personnel administration (MS); communication (MA); computer science (MS); counseling (MS); criminal justice (MS); educational leadership (Ed D); educational technology (MS); elementary and early childhood education (MSE); English (MA); environmental studies (MA); finance (MBA); history (MA); human services/educational technology (Ed S); human services/learning resources (Ed S); human services/professional counseling (Ed S); industrial hygiene (MS); industrial management (MS); information systems (MBA); information technology (MS); kinesiology (MS); library science and information services (MS); literacy education (MSE); marketing (MBA); mathematics (MS); music (MA); occupational safety management (MS); psychology (MS); rural family nursing (MS); school administration (MSE); social gerontology (MS); sociology (MA); special education (MSE); speech language pathology (MS); superintendency (Ed S); teaching (MAT); teaching English as a second language (MA); technology (MS); technology management (PhD); theatre (MA). *Program availability:* Part-time, 100% online, blended/hybrid learning. *Faculty:* 337 full-time (145 women), 41 part-time/adjunct (28 women). *Students:* 785 full-time (398 women), 1,633 part-time (1,063 women); includes 231 minority (102 Black or African American, non-Hispanic/Latino; 4 American Indian or Alaska Native, non-Hispanic/Latino; 16 Asian, non-Hispanic/Latino; 52 Hispanic/Latino; 57 Two or more races, non-Hispanic/Latino), 692 international. Average age 30. In 2017, 2,605 master's, 122 other advanced degrees awarded. *Degree requirements:* For master's and Ed S, comprehensive exam (for some programs), thesis (for some programs). *Entrance requirements:* Additional exam requirements/recommendations for international students: Required—TOEFL (minimum score 550 paper-based; 79 iBT). *Application deadline:* For fall admission, 6/1 priority date for domestic and international students; for spring admission, 10/1 priority date for domestic and international students; for summer admission, 4/1 priority date for domestic and international students. Applications are processed on a rolling basis. Application fee: $30 ($75 for international students). Electronic applications accepted. *Expenses:* Tuition, state resident: full-time $8771; part-time $292.35 per credit hour. Tuition, nonresident: full-time $17,541; part-time $584.70 per credit hour. *Required fees:* $372; $24.78 per credit hour. *Financial support:* In 2017–18, 99 students received support. Research assistantships, teaching assistantships, career-related internships or fieldwork, Federal Work-Study, scholarships/grants, and administrative and laboratory assistantships available. Support available to part-time students. Financial award application deadline: 3/1; financial award applicants required to submit FAFSA. *Unit head:* Shellie Hewitt, Director of Graduate and International Student Services, 660-543-4621, Fax: 660-543-4778, E-mail: hewitt@ucmo.edu. *Application contact:* 660-543-4621, E-mail: admit_intl@ucmo.edu.
Website: http://www.ucmo.edu/graduate/

University of Central Oklahoma, The Jackson College of Graduate Studies, College of Liberal Arts, Department of History, Edmond, OK 73034-5209. Offers museum studies (MA). *Program availability:* Part-time. *Faculty:* 19 full-time (12 women), 2 part-time/adjunct (1 woman). *Students:* 22 full-time (9 women), 30 part-time (18 women); includes 12 minority (3 Black or African American, non-Hispanic/Latino; 4 American Indian or Alaska Native, non-Hispanic/Latino; 3 Hispanic/Latino; 2 Two or more races, non-Hispanic/Latino), 1 international. Average age 33. 13 applicants, 62% accepted, 7 enrolled. In 2017, 8 master's awarded. *Degree requirements:* For master's, one foreign language, comprehensive exam (for some programs), thesis (for some programs). *Entrance requirements:* For master's, writing sample, essay. Additional exam requirements/recommendations for international students: Required—TOEFL (minimum score 550 paper-based; 79 iBT), IELTS (minimum score 6.5). *Application deadline:* For fall admission, 7/15 for international students; for spring admission, 11/15 for international students. Applications are processed on a rolling basis. Application fee: $60. Electronic applications accepted. *Expenses:* Tuition, state resident: full-time $5375; part-time $268.75 per credit hour. Tuition, nonresident: full-time $13,295; part-time $664.75 per credit hour. *Required fees:* $626; $31.30 per credit hour. One-time fee: $50. Tuition and fees vary according to program. *Financial support:* In 2017–18, 14 students received support, including 7 research assistantships with partial tuition reimbursements available (averaging $6,760 per year), 4 teaching assistantships with partial tuition reimbursements available (averaging $6,366 per year); career-related internships or fieldwork, Federal Work-Study, scholarships/grants, tuition waivers (partial), and unspecified assistantships also available. Financial award application deadline: 3/31; financial award applicants required to submit FAFSA. *Unit head:* Dr. Patti Loughlin, Department Chair, 405-974-5540, Fax: 405-974-3823. *Application contact:* Dr. Marc Goulding, Graduate Advisor, 405-974-2838, Fax: 405-974-3823, E-mail: gradcoll@uco.edu.
Website: http://www.uco.edu/la/history-geography/

University of Chicago, Division of the Social Sciences, Department of History, Chicago, IL 60637. Offers PhD. *Faculty:* 49. *Students:* 158 full-time (67 women); includes 49 minority (8 Black or African American, non-Hispanic/Latino; 9 Asian, non-Hispanic/Latino; 26 Hispanic/Latino; 6 Two or more races, non-Hispanic/Latino), 28 international. Average age 31. 343 applicants, 8% accepted, 14 enrolled. In 2017, 17 doctorates awarded. *Degree requirements:* For doctorate, variable foreign language requirement, thesis/dissertation, oral exams in 3 fields. *Entrance requirements:* For doctorate, GRE General Test, 3 letters of recommendation, statement of purpose, transcripts, resume or curriculum vitae, writing sample (dependent on department). Additional exam requirements/recommendations for international students: Required—TOEFL (minimum score 104 iBT), IELTS (minimum score 7). *Application deadline:* For fall admission, 12/10 priority date for domestic and international students. Application fee: $90. Electronic applications accepted. *Financial support:* In 2017–18, 21 students received support, including 21 fellowships with full tuition reimbursements available (averaging $27,000 per year); Federal Work-Study, institutionally sponsored loans, scholarships/grants, and health care benefits also available. Financial award application deadline: 12/10. *Unit head:* Dr. Emilio Kouri, Chair, 773-834-4769, Fax: 773-702-7550, E-mail: kouri@uchicago.edu. *Application contact:* Office of the Dean of Students, 773-702-8415, E-mail: ssd-admissions@uchicago.edu.
Website: http://history.uchicago.edu

University of Cincinnati, Graduate School, McMicken College of Arts and Sciences, Department of History, Cincinnati, OH 45221. Offers MA, PhD. Terminal master's awarded for partial completion of doctoral program. *Degree requirements:* For master's, comprehensive exam, thesis optional; for doctorate, comprehensive exam, thesis/dissertation. *Entrance requirements:* For master's, GRE General Test, BA in history; for doctorate, GRE General Test, MA in history. Additional exam requirements/recommendations for international students: Required—TOEFL (minimum score 600 paper-based). Electronic applications accepted. *Expenses: Tuition, area resident:* Full-time $14,468. Tuition, state resident: full-time $14,968; part-time $754 per credit hour. Tuition, nonresident: full-time $24,210; part-time $1311 per credit hour. *International tuition:* $26,460 full-time. *Required fees:* $3958; $84 per credit hour. One-time fee: $85 full-time. Tuition and fees vary according to course load, degree level and program. *Faculty research:* U.S. cultural and social history, women's history, U.S. and British intellectual history, modern Europe.

University of Colorado Boulder, Graduate School, College of Arts and Sciences, Department of History, Boulder, CO 80309. Offers MA, PhD. *Faculty:* 35 full-time (14 women). *Students:* 43 full-time (20 women), 3 part-time (1 woman); includes 7 minority (1 Black or African American, non-Hispanic/Latino; 1 American Indian or Alaska Native, non-Hispanic/Latino; 2 Asian, non-Hispanic/Latino; 3 Two or more races, non-Hispanic/Latino), 2 international. Average age 33. 68 applicants, 26% accepted, 6 enrolled. In 2017, 4 master's, 11 doctorates awarded. Terminal master's awarded for partial completion of doctoral program. *Degree requirements:* For master's, comprehensive exam, thesis optional; for doctorate, one foreign language, thesis/dissertation. *Entrance requirements:* For master's, GRE General Test, minimum undergraduate GPA of 2.75; for doctorate, GRE General Test. *Application deadline:* For fall admission, 12/1 for domestic students; for spring admission, 12/1 for domestic students. Application fee: $60 ($80 for international students). Electronic applications accepted. Application fee is waived when completed online. *Financial support:* In 2017–18, 105 students received support, including 30 fellowships (averaging $8,995 per year), 1 research assistantship with full and partial tuition reimbursement available (averaging $27,639 per year), 29 teaching assistantships with full and partial tuition reimbursements available (averaging $27,356 per year); institutionally sponsored loans, scholarships/grants, health care benefits, and unspecified assistantships also available. Financial award application deadline: 2/15; financial award applicants required to submit FAFSA. *Faculty research:* History; social history; American history; cultural history; modern history. *Total annual research expenditures:* $286,643. *Application contact:* E-mail: history@colorado.edu.
Website: http://www.colorado.edu/history/

University of Colorado Colorado Springs, College of Letters, Arts and Sciences, Department of History, Colorado Springs, CO 80918. Offers MA. *Program availability:* Part-time, evening/weekend. *Faculty:* 9 full-time (5 women), 10 part-time/adjunct (5 women). *Students:* 3 full-time (0 women), 38 part-time (14 women); includes 12 minority (3 Black or African American, non-Hispanic/Latino; 7 Hispanic/Latino; 2 Two or more races, non-Hispanic/Latino). Average age 36. 27 applicants, 81% accepted, 12 enrolled. In 2017, 16 master's awarded. *Degree requirements:* For master's, portfolio of 3-4 research projects, oral exam. *Entrance requirements:* For master's, minimum GPA of 3.0, writing sample. Additional exam requirements/recommendations for international students: Recommended—TOEFL (minimum score 550 paper-based; 80 iBT), IELTS (minimum score 6.5). *Application deadline:* Applications are processed on a rolling basis. Application fee: $60 ($100 for international students). Electronic applications accepted. *Expenses:* $10,350 per year resident tuition, $20,935 nonresident, $11,961 nonresidential online; annual costs vary depending on program, course-load, and residency status. *Financial support:* In 2017–18, 8 students received support. Federal Work-Study, scholarships/grants, and unspecified assistantships available. Support available to part-time students. Financial award application deadline: 3/1; financial award applicants required to submit FAFSA. *Faculty research:* Greek and Roman history; late antiquity; historiography; Greek and Latin languages/stylistics; ancient and Renaissance cultural history; early medieval history; Native American Indian ethno history east of the Mississippi; U.S. social history, 1865-1980; traditional West African (Yoruba) religion and syncretism; U.S. religious, political, economic, and cultural history; environmental history of modern India; Latin American history; Mexican history; history of cities, citizenship. *Unit head:* Dr. Robert Sackett, Professor/Graduate Director, 719-255-4079, Fax: 719-255-4068, E-mail: rsackett@uccs.edu. *Application contact:* Ian Smith, Administrative Assistant, 719-255-4069, Fax: 719-255-4068, E-mail: ismith2@uccs.edu.
Website: http://www.uccs.edu/~history/

University of Colorado Denver, College of Liberal Arts and Sciences, Department of History, Denver, CO 80217. Offers European history (MA); global history (MA); public history (MA); U.S. history (MA). *Program availability:* Part-time, evening/weekend. *Degree requirements:* For master's, comprehensive exam, thesis optional, 36 semester hours (12 courses). *Entrance requirements:* For master's, GRE General Test, writing sample, minimum undergraduate GPA of 3.25, three letters of recommendation, statement of purpose addressing any weaknesses in academic record. Additional exam requirements/recommendations for international students: Required—TOEFL (minimum score 537 paper-based; 75 iBT); Recommended—IELTS (minimum score 6.5). Electronic applications accepted. *Faculty research:* Uses of pre-modern Islamic heritage in modern India; relationship between liberal understandings of democracy, crime, and police discretion; relationships between gender, class, health, and welfare in nineteenth and early twentieth century England; U.S. business cultures and their influences on marketing and personnel practices; intersection of business and political ideologies; social and environmental history of the Rocky Mountain West.

University of Connecticut, Graduate School, College of Liberal Arts and Sciences, Department of History, Storrs, CT 06269. Offers MA, PhD. Terminal master's awarded for partial completion of doctoral program. *Degree requirements:* For master's, comprehensive exam; for doctorate, thesis/dissertation. *Entrance requirements:* For master's and doctorate, GRE General Test, GRE Subject Test. Additional exam requirements/recommendations for international students: Required—TOEFL (minimum score 550 paper-based). Electronic applications accepted.

University of Delaware, College of Arts and Sciences, Department of History, Hagley Program in the History of Technology and Industrialization, Newark, DE 19716. Offers MA, PhD. *Degree requirements:* For master's, thesis optional; for doctorate, comprehensive exam, thesis/dissertation. *Entrance requirements:* For master's and doctorate, interview. Electronic applications accepted.

University of Denver, University College, Denver, CO 80208. Offers arts and culture (MA, Certificate); communication management (MS, Certificate), including translation studies (Certificate), world history and culture (Certificate); environmental policy and management (MS); geographic information systems (MS); global affairs (MA, Certificate), including human capital in organizations (Certificate), philanthropic leadership (Certificate), project management (Certificate), strategic innovation and change (Certificate); healthcare leadership (MS); information communications and

technology (MS); leadership and organizations (MS); professional creative writing (MA, Certificate), including emergency planning and response (Certificate), organizational security (Certificate); security management (MS, Certificate); strategic human resources (Certificate). *Program availability:* Part-time, evening/weekend, online learning. *Faculty:* 118 part-time/adjunct (62 women). *Students:* 56 full-time (32 women), 1,287 part-time (707 women); includes 330 minority (99 Black or African American, non-Hispanic/Latino; 7 American Indian or Alaska Native, non-Hispanic/Latino; 43 Asian, non-Hispanic/Latino; 141 Hispanic/Latino; 3 Native Hawaiian or other Pacific Islander, non-Hispanic/Latino; 37 Two or more races, non-Hispanic/Latino), 84 international. Average age 34. 783 applicants, 86% accepted, 420 enrolled. In 2017, 461 master's, 173 other advanced degrees awarded. *Degree requirements:* For master's, capstone project. *Entrance requirements:* For master's, transcripts, two letters of recommendation, personal statement, resume. Additional exam requirements/recommendations for international students: Required—TOEFL (minimum score 550 paper-based; 80 iBT). *Application deadline:* For fall admission, 6/21 priority date for domestic students, 5/1 priority date for international students; for winter admission, 9/14 priority date for domestic students, 9/19 priority date for international students; for spring admission, 1/11 priority date for domestic students, 12/12 priority date for international students; for summer admission, 3/29 priority date for domestic students, 3/6 priority date for international students. Applications are processed on a rolling basis. Application fee: $75. Electronic applications accepted. *Expenses:* $7,968 per year half-time. *Financial support:* In 2017–18, 29 students received support. Teaching assistantships available. Financial award applicants required to submit FAFSA. *Unit head:* Dr. Michael McGuire, Dean, 303-871-3518, Fax: 303-871-3303, E-mail: mmcguire@du.edu. *Application contact:* Information Contact, 303-871-2291, E-mail: ucoladm@du.edu.
Website: http://universitycollege.du.edu/

University of Florida, Graduate School, College of Liberal Arts and Sciences, Department of History, Gainesville, FL 32611. Offers historic preservation (MA, PhD); history (MA, PhD); Jewish studies (MA); women's and gender studies (PhD); JD/MA; JD/PhD. *Program availability:* Part-time. Terminal master's awarded for partial completion of doctoral program. *Degree requirements:* For master's, variable foreign language requirement, thesis optional, 30 credit hours; for doctorate, variable foreign language requirement, comprehensive exam, thesis/dissertation, 90 credit hours. *Entrance requirements:* For master's and doctorate, GRE General Test, minimum GPA of 3.0. Additional exam requirements/recommendations for international students: Required—TOEFL (minimum score 550 paper-based; 80 iBT), IELTS (minimum score 6). Electronic applications accepted. *Faculty research:* Latin American and Caribbean history, nineteenth century U.S. history, medieval European history, African history and Atlantic world history.

University of Georgia, Franklin College of Arts and Sciences, Department of History, Athens, GA 30602. Offers MA, PhD. *Degree requirements:* For master's, one foreign language, thesis; for doctorate, one foreign language, thesis/dissertation. *Entrance requirements:* For master's and doctorate, GRE General Test. Electronic applications accepted.

University of Guelph, Graduate Studies, College of Arts, Department of History, Guelph, ON N1G 2W1, Canada. Offers MA, PhD. MA, PhD offered jointly with University of Waterloo, Wilfrid Laurier University. *Program availability:* Part-time. *Degree requirements:* For master's, one foreign language, thesis (for some programs); for doctorate, one foreign language, thesis/dissertation, 3 qualifying fields. *Entrance requirements:* For master's, minimum B+ average during previous 2 years of course work; for doctorate, minimum A- average in MA. Additional exam requirements/recommendations for international students: Required—TOEFL (minimum score 550 paper-based). Electronic applications accepted. *Faculty research:* Gender and family, Scottish history, rural and urban community studies, eighteenth century England, Canadian legal and social history, modern Europe.

University of Hawaii at Manoa, Office of Graduate Education, College of Arts and Humanities, Department of History, Honolulu, HI 96822. Offers MA, PhD. *Program availability:* Part-time. *Degree requirements:* For master's, 2 foreign languages, thesis optional; for doctorate, 2 foreign languages, comprehensive exam, thesis/dissertation. *Entrance requirements:* For master's, GRE, minimum GPA of 3.0, writing sample; for doctorate, GRE, MA, sample of written work. Additional exam requirements/recommendations for international students: Required—TOEFL (minimum score 580 paper-based; 92 iBT), IELTS (minimum score 5). *Faculty research:* Asian, Pacific, world, American and European history.

University of Houston, College of Liberal Arts and Social Sciences, Department of History, Houston, TX 77204. Offers MA, PhD. *Program availability:* Part-time. Terminal master's awarded for partial completion of doctoral program. *Degree requirements:* For master's, one foreign language, thesis (for some programs); for doctorate, one foreign language, comprehensive exam, thesis/dissertation. *Entrance requirements:* For master's, GRE General Test, minimum GPA of 3.3; for doctorate, GRE General Test, minimum GPA of 3.67. Additional exam requirements/recommendations for international students: Required—TOEFL. Electronic applications accepted. *Faculty research:* U.S., Latin American, European, social, and women's history.

University of Houston–Clear Lake, School of Human Sciences and Humanities, Programs in Humanities and Fine Arts, Houston, TX 77058-1002. Offers history (MA); humanities (MA); literature (MA). *Program availability:* Part-time, evening/weekend, online learning. *Degree requirements:* For master's, thesis or alternative. *Entrance requirements:* For master's, GRE General Test. Additional exam requirements/recommendations for international students: Required—TOEFL (minimum score 550 paper-based). *Faculty research:* Digital media studies, Latin American history, labor history, Chaucer evolution versus creationism debate.

University of Idaho, College of Graduate Studies, College of Letters, Arts and Social Sciences, Department of History, Moscow, ID 83844. Offers MA, PhD. *Faculty:* 2. *Students:* 10. Average age 36. In 2017, 5 master's awarded. *Degree requirements:* For doctorate, thesis/dissertation. *Entrance requirements:* For master's and doctorate, minimum GPA of 3.0. Additional exam requirements/recommendations for international students: Required—TOEFL (minimum score 88 iBT). *Application deadline:* For fall admission, 8/1 for domestic students; for spring admission, 12/15 for domestic students. Applications are processed on a rolling basis. Application fee: $60. Electronic applications accepted. *Expenses:* Tuition, state resident: full-time $6722; part-time $430 per credit hour. Tuition, nonresident: full-time $23,046; part-time $1337 per credit hour. *Required fees:* $2142; $63 per credit hour. *Financial support:* Research assistantships and teaching assistantships available. Financial award applicants required to submit FAFSA. *Unit head:* Dr. Sean Quinlan, Chair, 208-885-6253, E-mail: history@uidaho.edu. *Application contact:* Sean Scoggin, Graduate Recruitment Coordinator, 208-885-4723, Fax: 208-885-4406, E-mail: graduateadmissions@uidaho.edu.
Website: https://www.uidaho.edu/class/history

University of Illinois at Chicago, College of Liberal Arts and Sciences, Department of History, Chicago, IL 60607-7128. Offers MA, MAT, PhD. *Program availability:* Part-time, evening/weekend. *Degree requirements:* For master's, one foreign language, comprehensive exam; for doctorate, 2 foreign languages, comprehensive exam, thesis/

dissertation. *Entrance requirements:* For master's and doctorate, GRE General Test, previous course work in a foreign language, minimum GPA of 3.0. Additional exam requirements/recommendations for international students: Required—TOEFL. Electronic applications accepted. *Faculty research:* American urban and immigration history, early modern European history, Eastern European history.

University of Illinois at Springfield, Graduate Programs, College of Liberal Arts and Sciences, Program in History, Springfield, IL 62703-5407. Offers MA. *Program availability:* Part-time, evening/weekend. *Faculty:* 9 full-time (4 women). *Students:* 9 full-time (3 women), 17 part-time (5 women); includes 1 minority (Two or more races, non-Hispanic/Latino), 1 international. Average age 32. 16 applicants, 88% accepted, 8 enrolled. In 2017, 7 master's awarded. *Degree requirements:* For master's, internship; closure exercise; position paper and historiography; thesis or project. *Entrance requirements:* For master's, BA in history or related field, minimum undergraduate GPA of 3.0, writing sample, statement of purpose. Additional exam requirements/recommendations for international students: Required—TOEFL (minimum score 500 paper-based; 61 iBT). *Application deadline:* Applications are processed on a rolling basis. Application fee: $60 ($75 for international students). Electronic applications accepted. *Expenses:* Tuition, state resident: full-time $7896; part-time $329 per credit hour. Tuition, nonresident: full-time $16,200; part-time $675 per credit hour. Tuition and fees vary according to program. *Financial support:* In 2017–18, research assistantships with full tuition reimbursements (averaging $10,249 per year), teaching assistantships with full tuition reimbursements (averaging $10,303 per year) were awarded; fellowships, career-related internships or fieldwork, Federal Work-Study, scholarships/grants, health care benefits, and unspecified assistantships also available. Support available to part-time students. Financial award application deadline: 11/15; financial award applicants required to submit FAFSA. *Unit head:* Dr. David Bertaina, Program Administrator, 217-206-8412, Fax: 217-206-6217, E-mail: dbert3@uis.edu.
Website: http://www.uis.edu/history/curriculum/ma/

University of Illinois at Urbana–Champaign, Graduate College, College of Liberal Arts and Sciences, Department of History, Champaign, IL 61820. Offers MA, PhD.

University of Indianapolis, Graduate Programs, College of Arts and Sciences, Department of History and Political Science, Indianapolis, IN 46227-3697. Offers history (MA); international relations (MA). *Program availability:* Part-time, evening/weekend. *Degree requirements:* For master's, thesis optional. *Entrance requirements:* For master's, GRE Subject Test, minimum GPA of 3.0, 3 letters of recommendation. Additional exam requirements/recommendations for international students: Required—TOEFL (minimum score 550 paper-based). Electronic applications accepted.

The University of Iowa, Graduate College, College of Liberal Arts and Sciences, Department of History, Iowa City, IA 52242-1316. Offers MA, PhD. *Degree requirements:* For master's, thesis optional, exam; for doctorate, comprehensive exam, thesis/dissertation. *Entrance requirements:* For master's and doctorate, GRE General Test, minimum GPA of 3.0. Additional exam requirements/recommendations for international students: Required—TOEFL (minimum score 550 paper-based; 81 iBT). Electronic applications accepted.

The University of Kansas, Graduate Studies, College of Liberal Arts and Sciences, Department of History, Lawrence, KS 66045. Offers MA, PhD. *Program availability:* Part-time. *Students:* 47 full-time (17 women), 1 part-time (0 women); includes 4 minority (1 Hispanic/Latino; 3 Two or more races, non-Hispanic/Latino), 7 international. Average age 34. 48 applicants, 21% accepted, 7 enrolled. In 2017, 2 master's, 9 doctorates awarded. *Entrance requirements:* For master's and doctorate, GRE General Test, two-page statement of objectives, writing sample (20-25 pages maximum), three letters of reference, transcripts, curriculum vitae. Additional exam requirements/recommendations for international students: Required—TOEFL or IELTS. *Application deadline:* For fall admission, 1/1 for domestic and international students. Application fee: $65 ($85 for international students). Electronic applications accepted. *Financial support:* Fellowships, research assistantships, teaching assistantships, and unspecified assistantships available. Financial award application deadline: 1/1. *Faculty research:* Environmental history, early American history, modern European history. *Unit head:* Eve Levin, Chair, 785-864-9463, E-mail: evelevin@ku.edu. *Application contact:* Emily Lowrance-Floyd, Graduate Program Administrator, 785-864-9438, E-mail: lowrance@ku.edu.
Website: http://www.history.ku.edu/

University of Kentucky, Graduate School, College of Arts and Sciences, Program in History, Lexington, KY 40506-0032. Offers MA, PhD. *Program availability:* Part-time. *Degree requirements:* For master's, one foreign language, comprehensive exam, thesis optional; for doctorate, variable foreign language requirement, comprehensive exam, thesis/dissertation. *Entrance requirements:* For master's, GRE General Test, minimum undergraduate GPA of 2.75; for doctorate, GRE General Test, minimum graduate GPA of 3.0. Additional exam requirements/recommendations for international students: Required—TOEFL (minimum score 550 paper-based). Electronic applications accepted. *Faculty research:* English, British, European history; U.S. social, political and diplomatic history; U.S. early national history; U.S. Southern history; Native American and African-American history.

University of Louisiana at Lafayette, College of Liberal Arts, Department of History and Geography, Lafayette, LA 70504. Offers history (MA). *Program availability:* Part-time. *Degree requirements:* For master's, one foreign language, thesis or alternative. *Entrance requirements:* For master's, GRE General Test, minimum GPA of 2.75. Additional exam requirements/recommendations for international students: Required—TOEFL (minimum score 550 paper-based). Electronic applications accepted.

University of Louisiana at Monroe, Graduate School, College of Arts, Education, and Sciences, Department of History, Monroe, LA 71209-0001. Offers MA. *Program availability:* Part-time, evening/weekend. *Faculty:* 4 full-time (0 women). *Students:* 6 full-time (4 women), 3 part-time (0 women), 1 international. Average age 34. 12 applicants, 58% accepted, 4 enrolled. In 2017, 3 master's awarded. *Degree requirements:* For master's, thesis (for some programs). *Entrance requirements:* For master's, GRE General Test, minimum undergraduate GPA of 2.5. Additional exam requirements/recommendations for international students: Required—TOEFL (minimum score 500 paper-based; 61 iBT). *Application deadline:* For fall admission, 8/24 priority date for domestic students, 7/1 for international students; for winter admission, 12/14 priority date for domestic students; for spring admission, 1/19 for domestic students, 11/1 for international students. Applications are processed on a rolling basis. Application fee: $20 ($30 for international students). Electronic applications accepted. *Expenses:* Tuition, state resident: full-time $6489; part-time $479 per hour. Tuition, nonresident: full-time $12,100; part-time $479 per hour. *Required fees:* $8860; $802 per hour. $3273 per semester. *Financial support:* In 2017–18, 7 students received support. Research assistantships, career-related internships or fieldwork, Federal Work-Study, and unspecified assistantships available. Financial award application deadline: 4/1; financial award applicants required to submit FAFSA. *Faculty research:* Early Louisiana settlements, Soviet history, Anglo-American relations, U.S./East European relations. *Unit head:* Dr. Monica Bontty, Head, 318-342-1542, E-mail: bontty@ulm.edu.
Website: http://www.ulm.edu/history/

History

University of Louisville, Graduate School, College of Arts and Sciences, Department of History, Louisville, KY 40292-0001. Offers history (MA); public history (Certificate). *Program availability:* Part-time. *Faculty:* 20 full-time (8 women), 2 part-time/adjunct (1 woman). *Students:* 7 full-time (6 women), 15 part-time (6 women); includes 4 minority (1 Black or African American, non-Hispanic/Latino; 1 Hispanic/Latino; 2 Two or more races, non-Hispanic/Latino). Average age 37. 14 applicants, 86% accepted, 6 enrolled. In 2017, 2 master's awarded. *Degree requirements:* For master's, variable foreign language requirement, comprehensive exam (for some programs), thesis. *Entrance requirements:* For master's, GRE General Test, statement of purpose, not to exceed 500 words, which describes in reasonably specific terms, academic and career objectives and how they can be advanced through work in program. Additional exam requirements/recommendations for international students: Required—TOEFL. *Application deadline:* For fall admission, 2/15 for domestic and international students; for winter admission, 12/1 for domestic students; for spring admission, 12/1 for domestic and international students. Application fee: $65. Electronic applications accepted. *Expenses:* Contact institution. *Financial support:* In 2017–18, 1 teaching assistantship with full tuition reimbursement (averaging $12,000 per year) was awarded; scholarships/grants also available. Financial award application deadline: 2/15. *Faculty research:* Ancient and Medieval Europe, U.S. social and constitutional history, U.S. foreign relations and military, public history, Latin American and Borderlands. *Unit head:* Dr. Blake Beattie, Chairperson/Associate Professor, 502-852-6818, Fax: 502-852-0770, E-mail: history@louisville.edu. *Application contact:* Jennifer T. Westerfeld, Associate Professor, 502-852-3756, Fax: 502-852-0770, E-mail: histgrad@louisville.edu. Website: http://louisville.edu/history/

University of Maine, Graduate School, College of Liberal Arts and Sciences, Department of History, Orono, ME 04469. Offers MA, PhD. *Faculty:* 14 full-time (3 women), 9 part-time/adjunct (2 women). *Students:* 20 full-time (9 women), 20 part-time (9 women); includes 2 minority (both Two or more races, non-Hispanic/Latino), 2 international. Average age 38. 15 applicants, 73% accepted, 6 enrolled. In 2017, 1 master's, 3 doctorates awarded. *Degree requirements:* For master's, variable foreign language requirement, thesis optional; for doctorate, one foreign language, comprehensive exam, thesis/dissertation. *Entrance requirements:* For master's and doctorate, GRE General Test. Additional exam requirements/recommendations for international students: Required—TOEFL (minimum score 79 iBT). *Application deadline:* For fall admission, 1/15 priority date for domestic and international students; for spring admission, 10/15 for domestic students, 10/15 priority date for international students. Applications are processed on a rolling basis. Application fee: $65. Electronic applications accepted. *Expenses:* Tuition, state resident: full-time $7722; part-time $429 per credit hour. Tuition, nonresident: full-time $25,146; part-time $1397 per credit hour. *Required fees:* $1162; $581 per credit hour. *Financial support:* In 2017–18, 22 students received support, including 4 fellowships (averaging $16,300 per year), 12 teaching assistantships with tuition reimbursements available (averaging $15,200 per year); career-related internships or fieldwork, Federal Work-Study, scholarships/grants, tuition waivers (full and partial), and unspecified assistantships also available. Support available to part-time students. Financial award application deadline: 3/1. *Faculty research:* Borderlands, loyalism, trans-Atlantic, environmental, modern U.S (culture, labor, and foreign relations). *Total annual research expenditures:* $45,000. *Unit head:* Dr. Stephen Miller, Chair, 207-581-1905, Fax: 207-581-1817, E-mail: stephen.miller@maine.edu. *Application contact:* Scott G. Delcourt, Assistant Vice President for Graduate Studies and Senior Associate Dean, 207-581-3291, Fax: 207-581-3232, E-mail: graduate@maine.edu. Website: http://www.umaine.edu/history/

The University of Manchester, School of Arts, Histories and Cultures, Manchester, United Kingdom. Offers anthropology, media and performance (PhD); applied theatre professional (PhD); archaeology (PhD); art history and visual studies (PhD); arts management and cultural policy (PhD); classics and ancient history (PhD); composition (PhD); creative writing (PhD); drama (PhD); economic and social history (PhD); electroacoustic composition (PhD); English and American studies (PhD); history (PhD); humanitarianism and conflict response (PhD); museology (PhD); music (PhD); musicology (PhD); religions and theology (PhD).

University of Manitoba, Faculty of Graduate Studies, Faculty of Arts, Department of History, Winnipeg, MB R3T 2N2, Canada. Offers archival studies (MA); history (MA, PhD). MA offered jointly with The University of Winnipeg. *Degree requirements:* For master's, thesis; for doctorate, one foreign language, thesis/dissertation.

University of Maryland, Baltimore County, The Graduate School, College of Arts, Humanities and Social Sciences, Department of History, Program in Historical Studies, Baltimore, MD 21250. Offers MA. *Program availability:* Part-time, evening/weekend. *Faculty:* 16 full-time (10 women), 8 part-time/adjunct (5 women). *Students:* 9 full-time (3 women), 14 part-time (7 women); includes 8 minority (3 Black or African American, non-Hispanic/Latino; 3 Asian, non-Hispanic/Latino; 2 Hispanic/Latino), 1 international. Average age 30. 22 applicants, 91% accepted, 14 enrolled. In 2017, 7 master's awarded. *Degree requirements:* For master's, thesis. *Entrance requirements:* For master's, GRE General Test, minimum GPA of 3.0. Additional exam requirements/recommendations for international students: Required—TOEFL. *Application deadline:* For fall admission, 2/15 priority date for domestic students, 1/1 for international students. Application fee: $50. Electronic applications accepted. *Expenses:* $743 per credit. *Financial support:* In 2017–18, 7 students received support, including 1 research assistantship with full tuition reimbursement available (averaging $12,874 per year), 6 teaching assistantships with tuition reimbursements available (averaging $12,874 per year); career-related internships or fieldwork, health care benefits, tuition waivers (partial), and unspecified assistantships also available. Financial award application deadline: 2/15; financial award applicants required to submit FAFSA. *Faculty research:* U.S. history, European history, public history, community engagement. *Total annual research expenditures:* $50,000. *Unit head:* Dr. Daniel Ritschel, Graduate Program Director, 410-455-2034, Fax: 410-455-1045, E-mail: ritschel@umbc.edu. *Application contact:* Carla S. Ison, Graduate Program Coordinator, 410-455-2049, Fax: 410-455-1045, E-mail: ison@umbc.edu. Website: http://www.umbc.edu/history

University of Maryland, College Park, Academic Affairs, College of Arts and Humanities, Department of History, College Park, MD 20742. Offers MA, PhD. *Degree requirements:* For master's, comprehensive exam, thesis optional; for doctorate, one foreign language, thesis/dissertation, oral and written exams. *Entrance requirements:* For master's, GRE General Test, minimum GPA of 3.25, writing sample, 3 letters of recommendation, statements of goals and research interests and experiences; for doctorate, GRE General Test, minimum GPA of 3.5. Additional exam requirements/recommendations for international students: Required—TOEFL. Electronic applications accepted. *Faculty research:* Ancient, British, East Asian, Latin American, and diplomatic history; papers of Samuel Gompers; Freedman and Southern Society; Caesarea excavations; Folger Institute.

University of Maryland, College Park, Academic Affairs, Program in History, Library, and Information Services, College Park, MD 20742. Offers MA/MLS. *Entrance requirements:* Additional exam requirements/recommendations for international students: Required—TOEFL. Electronic applications accepted.

University of Massachusetts Amherst, Graduate School, College of Humanities and Fine Arts, Department of History, Amherst, MA 01003. Offers MA, PhD. *Program availability:* Part-time. Terminal master's awarded for partial completion of doctoral program. *Degree requirements:* For master's, one foreign language, thesis or alternative; for doctorate, one foreign language, comprehensive exam, thesis/dissertation. *Entrance requirements:* For master's and doctorate, GRE General Test, writing sample. Additional exam requirements/recommendations for international students: Required—TOEFL (minimum score 550 paper-based; 80 iBT), IELTS (minimum score 6.5). Electronic applications accepted. *Faculty research:* Ancient and medieval history; global and comparative history; public history; history of science, technology, medicine and the environment; history of women, gender, sexuality and family.

University of Massachusetts Boston, College of Liberal Arts, Program in History, Boston, MA 02125-3393. Offers archival methods (MA). *Program availability:* Part-time, evening/weekend. *Faculty:* 18 full-time (11 women), 9 part-time/adjunct (5 women). *Students:* 16 full-time (9 women), 58 part-time (33 women); includes 8 minority (3 Black or African American, non-Hispanic/Latino; 1 Asian, non-Hispanic/Latino; 4 Hispanic/Latino). Average age 34. 55 applicants, 85% accepted, 22 enrolled. In 2017, 22 master's awarded. *Entrance requirements:* For master's, minimum GPA of 2.75. *Application deadline:* For fall admission, 3/1 for domestic students; for spring admission, 11/1 for domestic students. *Expenses:* Tuition, state resident: full-time $17,375. Tuition, nonresident: full-time $33,915. *Required fees:* $355. *Financial support:* Research assistantships, teaching assistantships, career-related internships or fieldwork, Federal Work-Study, and unspecified assistantships available. Support available to part-time students. Financial award application deadline: 3/1; financial award applicants required to submit FAFSA. *Faculty research:* European intellectual history, American labor and social history in nineteenth century, colonial American Revolution, Afro-American Cold War. *Unit head:* Dr. Spencer DiScala, Director, 617-287-6860, E-mail: spencer.discala@umb.edu. *Application contact:* Graduate Admissions Coordinator, 617-287-6400, Fax: 617-287-6236, E-mail: bos.gadm@dpc.umassp.edu.

University of Memphis, Graduate School, College of Arts and Sciences, Department of History, Memphis, TN 38152. Offers ancient Egyptian history (MA, PhD). *Program availability:* 100% online. *Faculty:* 20 full-time (8 women), 1 (woman) part-time/adjunct. *Students:* 31 full-time (20 women), 46 part-time (26 women); includes 16 minority (11 Black or African American, non-Hispanic/Latino; 2 Hispanic/Latino; 3 Two or more races, non-Hispanic/Latino), 2 international. Average age 35. 33 applicants, 82% accepted, 22 enrolled. In 2017, 7 master's, 3 doctorates awarded. *Degree requirements:* For master's, comprehensive exam, thesis optional; for doctorate, one foreign language, comprehensive exam, thesis/dissertation, 60 credits plus 12 dissertation credits, 2 research seminars. *Entrance requirements:* For master's, GRE General Test or MAT, 18 undergraduate hours of course work in history with minimum GPA of 3.0, 2 letters of recommendation, writing sample, statement of research interest; for doctorate, GRE General Test, GRE Subject Test, MA in history or related field, three letters of recommendation, writing sample, statement of purpose. Additional exam requirements/recommendations for international students: Required—TOEFL (minimum score 550 paper-based; 79 iBT). *Application deadline:* For fall admission, 1/15 for domestic students; for spring admission, 9/15 for domestic students. Applications are processed on a rolling basis. Application fee: $35 ($60 for international students). Electronic applications accepted. *Expenses:* Contact institution. *Financial support:* In 2017–18, 54 students received support, including 4 research assistantships with full tuition reimbursements available (averaging $12,000 per year), 21 teaching assistantships with full tuition reimbursements available (averaging $18,142 per year); career-related internships or fieldwork, Federal Work-Study, scholarships/grants, and unspecified assistantships also available. Financial award application deadline: 2/1; financial award applicants required to submit FAFSA. *Faculty research:* African/African-American history; U.S. history; ancient Egyptian history; modern European history; women, gender, and family studies. *Unit head:* Dr. Aram Goudsouzian, Chair, 901-678-2516, Fax: 901-678-2720, E-mail: agoudszn@memphis.edu. *Application contact:* Dr. Daniel Unowsky, Coordinator of Graduate Studies, 901-678-3385, Fax: 901-678-2720, E-mail: dunowsky@memphis.edu. Website: http://history.memphis.edu/

University of Miami, Graduate School, College of Arts and Sciences, Department of History, Coral Gables, FL 33124. Offers MA, PhD. *Program availability:* Part-time. Terminal master's awarded for partial completion of doctoral program. *Degree requirements:* For master's, one foreign language, comprehensive exam, thesis optional; for doctorate, one foreign language, comprehensive exam, thesis/dissertation. *Entrance requirements:* For master's and doctorate, GRE General Test, GRE Subject Test. Additional exam requirements/recommendations for international students: Required—TOEFL (minimum score 550 paper-based; 59 iBT). Electronic applications accepted. *Faculty research:* Latin American, European, U.S., and public history.

University of Michigan, Rackham Graduate School, College of Literature, Science, and the Arts, Department of History, Ann Arbor, MI 48109. Offers PhD. *Faculty:* 70 full-time (24 women), 14 part-time/adjunct (2 women). *Students:* 152 full-time (74 women); includes 32 minority (13 Black or African American, non-Hispanic/Latino; 2 American Indian or Alaska Native, non-Hispanic/Latino; 9 Asian, non-Hispanic/Latino; 8 Hispanic/Latino), 29 international. Average age 30. 343 applicants, 13% accepted, 20 enrolled. In 2017, 18 doctorates awarded. *Degree requirements:* For doctorate, 2 foreign languages, thesis/dissertation, oral defense of dissertation, preliminary exam. *Entrance requirements:* For doctorate, GRE General Test, writing sample. Additional exam requirements/recommendations for international students: Required—TOEFL. *Application deadline:* For fall admission, 12/1 for domestic and international students. Application fee: $65 ($75 for international students). Electronic applications accepted. *Expenses:* Tuition, state resident: full-time $22,368; part-time $1201 per credit hour. Tuition, nonresident: full-time $45,156; part-time $2467 per credit hour. *Required fees:* $376 per term. Tuition and fees vary according to course load, degree level and program. *Financial support:* In 2017–18, 106 students received support, including 57 fellowships with full and partial tuition reimbursements available (averaging $19,300 per year), 1 research assistantship with full tuition reimbursement available (averaging $19,300 per year), 48 teaching assistantships with full tuition reimbursements available (averaging $19,300 per year); institutionally sponsored loans and scholarships/grants also available. Financial award application deadline: 3/1. *Faculty research:* Europe, Latin America, Africa, Asia, Middle East/Near East, United States, world/global history, science/medicine/technology, topical/thematic history. *Total annual research expenditures:* $101,628. *Unit head:* Prof. Jay Cook, Chair, 734-763-1460, Fax: 734-647-4881, E-mail: jwcook@umich.edu. *Application contact:* Susan Kaiser, Graduate Program Coordinator, 734-764-6358, Fax: 734-647-4881, E-mail: smkaiser@umich.edu. Website: http://www.lsa.umich.edu/history/

University of Michigan, Rackham Graduate School, College of Literature, Science, and the Arts, Department of Women's Studies, Ann Arbor, MI 48109. Offers English and women's studies (PhD); history and women's studies (PhD); LGBTQ studies (Certificate); psychology and women's studies (PhD); women's studies (Certificate). *Degree requirements:* For doctorate, variable foreign language requirement, comprehensive exam (for some programs), thesis/dissertation. *Entrance requirements:*

For doctorate, GRE General Test, previous undergraduate coursework in women's studies. Electronic applications accepted. *Expenses:* Tuition, state resident: full-time $22,368; part-time $1201 per credit hour. Tuition, nonresident: full-time $45,156; part-time $2467 per credit hour. *Required fees:* $376 per term. Tuition and fees vary according to course load, degree level and program. *Faculty research:* LGBTQ studies, sexuality studies, feminist science studies, global feminism, health studies, international studies, cultural studies.

University of Michigan, Rackham Graduate School, College of Literature, Science, and the Arts, Doctoral Program in Anthropology and History, Ann Arbor, MI 48109. Offers PhD. *Degree requirements:* For doctorate, 2 foreign languages, thesis/dissertation, oral defense of dissertation, preliminary exam. *Entrance requirements:* For doctorate, GRE General Test, writing sample. Additional exam requirements/recommendations for international students: Required—TOEFL. Electronic applications accepted. *Expenses:* Tuition, state resident: full-time $22,368; part-time $1201 per credit hour. Tuition, nonresident: full-time $45,156; part-time $2467 per credit hour. *Required fees:* $376 per term. Tuition and fees vary according to course load, degree level and program. *Faculty research:* Historical anthropology.

University of Michigan, Rackham Graduate School, College of Literature, Science, and the Arts, Interdepartmental Program in Greek and Roman History, Ann Arbor, MI 48109. Offers PhD, Certificate. Certificate program only open to students already studying in another PhD program at University of Michigan. *Degree requirements:* For doctorate, 4 foreign languages, comprehensive exam, thesis/dissertation, oral defense of dissertation, dissertation prospectus, preliminary exams, qualifying exams. *Entrance requirements:* For doctorate, GRE, strict minimum of 2 years each of classical Greek and Latin. Additional exam requirements/recommendations for international students: Required—TOEFL (minimum score 560 paper-based). Electronic applications accepted. *Expenses:* Tuition, state resident: full-time $22,368; part-time $1201 per credit hour. Tuition, nonresident: full-time $45,156; part-time $2467 per credit hour. *Required fees:* $376 per term. Tuition and fees vary according to course load, degree level and program. *Faculty research:* Greek history, Roman history, history of ancient Mediterranean cultures.

University of Minnesota, Twin Cities Campus, Graduate School, College of Liberal Arts, Department of Classical and Near Eastern Studies, Minneapolis, MN 55455-0213. Offers ancient and medieval art and archaeology (MA, PhD); classics (MA, PhD); Greek (MA, PhD); Latin (MA, PhD); religions in antiquity (MA). *Program availability:* Part-time. Terminal master's awarded for partial completion of doctoral program. *Degree requirements:* For master's, 2 foreign languages, comprehensive exam, thesis or alternative; for doctorate, variable foreign language requirement, comprehensive exam, thesis/dissertation. *Entrance requirements:* For master's and doctorate, GRE, 3 letters of recommendation, writing sample, copies of transcripts, personal statement. Additional exam requirements/recommendations for international students: Required—TOEFL. Electronic applications accepted. *Faculty research:* Greek and Latin literature, religions in antiquity, ancient Near East.

University of Minnesota, Twin Cities Campus, Graduate School, College of Liberal Arts, Department of History, Minneapolis, MN 55455-0213. Offers MA, PhD. *Degree requirements:* For master's, one foreign language, comprehensive exam, thesis or alternative; for doctorate, 2 foreign languages, comprehensive exam, thesis/dissertation. *Entrance requirements:* For doctorate, GRE General Test, writing sample, letters of recommendation. Additional exam requirements/recommendations for international students: Required—TOEFL (minimum score 550 paper-based). Electronic applications accepted. *Faculty research:* Early and modern United States; medieval, early modern and modern Europe; Africa; East and South Asia; Latin America.

University of Mississippi, Graduate School, College of Liberal Arts, University, MS 38677. Offers anthropology (MA); biology (MS, PhD); chemistry (MS, DA, PhD); creative writing (MFA); documentary expression (MFA); economics (MA, PhD); English (MA, PhD); experimental psychology (PhD); history (MA, PhD); mathematics (MS, PhD); modern languages (MA); music (MM); philosophy (MA); physics (MA, MS, PhD); political science (MA, PhD); Southern studies (MA); studio art (MFA). *Program availability:* Part-time. *Faculty:* 465 full-time (207 women), 82 part-time/adjunct (46 women). *Students:* 466 full-time (229 women), 72 part-time (34 women); includes 87 minority (38 Black or African American, non-Hispanic/Latino; 18 Asian, non-Hispanic/Latino; 24 Hispanic/Latino; 7 Two or more races, non-Hispanic/Latino), 121 international. Average age 29. *Degree requirements:* For doctorate, thesis/dissertation. *Entrance requirements:* For master's, GRE General Test, minimum GPA of 3.0; for doctorate, GRE General Test. Additional exam requirements/recommendations for international students: Required—TOEFL. *Application deadline:* For fall admission, 2/1 priority date for domestic students; for spring admission, 10/1 for domestic students. Applications are processed on a rolling basis. Application fee: $50. Electronic applications accepted. *Financial support:* Fellowships, research assistantships, teaching assistantships, career-related internships or fieldwork, Federal Work-Study, institutionally sponsored loans, scholarships/grants, and unspecified assistantships available. Financial award application deadline: 3/1; financial award applicants required to submit FAFSA. *Unit head:* Dr. Lee Michael Cohen, Dean, 662-915-7177, Fax: 662-915-5792, E-mail: libarts@olemiss.edu. *Application contact:* Dr. Christy M. Wyandt, Associate Dean of Graduate School, 662-915-7474, Fax: 662-915-7577, E-mail: cwyandt@olemiss.edu.

University of Missouri, Office of Research and Graduate Studies, College of Arts and Science, Department of History, Columbia, MO 65211. Offers MA, PhD. *Degree requirements:* For master's, thesis; for doctorate, 2 foreign languages, comprehensive exam, thesis/dissertation. *Entrance requirements:* For master's, GRE General Test, minimum GPA of 3.0 in last 60 hours, 3.3 in undergraduate history courses; at least 18 hours in history; BA or BS; for doctorate, GRE General Test, minimum GPA of 3.0; MA in history (strongly preferred); master's thesis or research seminar paper. Additional exam requirements/recommendations for international students: Required—TOEFL (minimum score 500 paper-based; 61 iBT). Electronic applications accepted. *Faculty research:* U.S. history, African-American history, ancient history, Latin American history, Asian history.

University of Missouri–Kansas City, College of Arts and Sciences, Department of History, Kansas City, MO 64110-2499. Offers MA, PhD. PhD (interdisciplinary) offered through the School of Graduate Studies. *Program availability:* Part-time. *Degree requirements:* For master's, thesis optional; for doctorate, one foreign language, thesis/dissertation. *Entrance requirements:* For master's, GRE General Test, minimum GPA of 3.0, 2 writing samples, 3 letters of recommendation; for doctorate, GRE General Test. Additional exam requirements/recommendations for international students: Required—TOEFL (minimum score 550 paper-based; 80 iBT). Electronic applications accepted. *Faculty research:* U.S. history, Europe, women and gender, religious studies, history of science.

University of Missouri–St. Louis, College of Arts and Sciences, Department of History, St. Louis, MO 63121. Offers history (MA); history education (Certificate); museum studies (MA, Certificate). *Program availability:* Part-time, evening/weekend. *Faculty:* 12 full-time (4 women), 8 part-time/adjunct (0 women). *Students:* 15 full-time (11 women), 31 part-time (13 women); includes 6 minority (2 Black or African American, non-Hispanic/Latino; 1 American Indian or Alaska Native, non-Hispanic/Latino; 3 Asian, non-Hispanic/Latino). 19 applicants, 89% accepted, 12 enrolled. *Degree requirements:* For master's, thesis (for some programs). *Entrance requirements:* For master's, writing sample; minimum GPA of 2.75 (for history), 3.2 (for museum studies). Additional exam requirements/recommendations for international students: Required—TOEFL (minimum score 550 paper-based; 79 iBT), IELTS (minimum score 6.5). *Application deadline:* For fall admission, 3/15 for domestic and international students; for spring admission, 10/15 for domestic and international students. Applications are processed on a rolling basis. Application fee: $50 ($40 for international students). Electronic applications accepted. *Expenses:* Tuition, state resident: part-time $476.50 per credit hour. Tuition, nonresident: part-time $1169.70 per credit hour. *Financial support:* Research assistantships with tuition reimbursements, teaching assistantships with tuition reimbursements, and career-related internships or fieldwork available. Financial award applicants required to submit FAFSA. *Faculty research:* United States, European, East Asian, Latin American, and African history. *Unit head:* Dr. Laura Westhoff, Chair, 314-516-5692, Fax: 314-516-5781, E-mail: westhoffl@msx.umsl.edu. *Application contact:* 314-516-5458, Fax: 314-516-6996, E-mail: gradadm@umsl.edu.
Website: http://www.umsl.edu/~umslhistory/

University of Montana, Graduate School, College of Humanities and Sciences, Department of History, Missoula, MT 59812. Offers MA, PhD. *Degree requirements:* For master's, thesis or additional course work/professional paper. *Entrance requirements:* For master's, GRE General Test. Additional exam requirements/recommendations for international students: Required—TOEFL.

University of Nebraska at Kearney, College of Natural and Social Sciences, Department of History, Kearney, NE 68849-0001. Offers MA. *Program availability:* Part-time, evening/weekend, 100% online. *Degree requirements:* For master's, comprehensive exam, thesis optional. *Entrance requirements:* For master's, letters of recommendation, writing sample, letter of interest. Additional exam requirements/recommendations for international students: Recommended—TOEFL (minimum score 550 paper-based; 79 iBT), IELTS (minimum score 6.5). Electronic applications accepted. *Faculty research:* Military history, labor history/labor and the law, state formation and nationalism, American intellectual history, Civil War and Reconstruction, South Asia, Africa, Medieval England, American West, Plains Indians, Soviet Union, cemeteries, gender, history of Christian mission.

University of Nebraska at Omaha, Graduate Studies, College of Arts and Sciences, Department of History, Omaha, NE 68182. Offers MA. *Program availability:* Part-time, evening/weekend. *Degree requirements:* For master's, comprehensive exam, thesis (for some programs). *Entrance requirements:* For master's, minimum GPA of 3.0, 21 hours of course work in history, 2 letters of recommendation, resume, statement of purpose, writing sample, official transcripts. Additional exam requirements/recommendations for international students: Required—TOEFL, IELTS, PTE. Electronic applications accepted.

University of Nebraska–Lincoln, Graduate College, College of Arts and Sciences, Department of History, Lincoln, NE 68588. Offers MA, PhD. *Degree requirements:* For master's, thesis optional; for doctorate, one foreign language, comprehensive exam, thesis/dissertation. *Entrance requirements:* For master's and doctorate, GRE General Test, GRE Subject Test, writing sample. Additional exam requirements/recommendations for international students: Required—TOEFL (minimum score 575 paper-based). Electronic applications accepted. *Faculty research:* Military history, indigenous peoples, German history, American history (American West society and culture).

University of Nevada, Las Vegas, Graduate College, College of Liberal Arts, Department of History, Las Vegas, NV 89154-5020. Offers MA, PhD. *Program availability:* Part-time. *Faculty:* 19 full-time (8 women). *Students:* 23 full-time (7 women), 16 part-time (9 women); includes 6 minority (2 Black or African American, non-Hispanic/Latino; 1 American Indian or Alaska Native, non-Hispanic/Latino; 1 Hispanic/Latino; 2 Two or more races, non-Hispanic/Latino), 2 international. Average age 37. 29 applicants, 52% accepted, 8 enrolled. In 2017, 6 master's, 1 doctorate awarded. *Degree requirements:* For master's, one foreign language, comprehensive exam (for some programs), thesis (for some programs); for doctorate, 2 foreign languages, comprehensive exam, thesis/dissertation, written and oral examinations. *Entrance requirements:* For master's, minimum overall GPA of 3.0, 3.3 in history courses; 2 recommendations; statement of purpose; writing sample; for doctorate, GRE General Test, completion of significant course work at upper-division or graduate level in history; 3 recommendations; minimum overall GPA of 3.75 undergraduate, 3.5 graduate; statement of purpose; writing sample. Additional exam requirements/recommendations for international students: Required—TOEFL (minimum score 550 paper-based; 80 iBT), IELTS (minimum score 7). *Application deadline:* For fall admission, 4/15 for domestic students; for spring admission, 11/1 for domestic students. Application fee: $60 ($95 for international students). Electronic applications accepted. *Expenses:* $275 per credit, $850 per course, $7,969 per year resident, $22,157 per year non-resident, $7,094 non-resident fee (7 credits or more), $1,307 annual health insurance fee. *Financial support:* In 2017–18, 20 students received support, including 1 research assistantship with full tuition reimbursement available (averaging $12,000 per year), 19 teaching assistantships with full tuition reimbursements available (averaging $14,276 per year); institutionally sponsored loans, scholarships/grants, health care benefits, and unspecified assistantships also available. Financial award application deadline: 3/15; financial award applicants required to submit FAFSA. *Faculty research:* North American West, North American culture and society, European culture and society, American urban history, American gender and sexuality. *Total annual research expenditures:* $35,944. *Unit head:* Dr. Paul Werth, Chair/Professor, 702-895-3344, Fax: 702-895-1782, E-mail: paul.werth@unlv.edu. *Application contact:* Dr. William Bauer, Graduate Coordinator, 702-895-0918, Fax: 702-895-1782, E-mail: wbauer@unlv.edu.
Website: http://history.unlv.edu/graduate.html

University of Nevada, Reno, Graduate School, College of Liberal Arts, Department of History, Reno, NV 89557. Offers MA, PhD. Terminal master's awarded for partial completion of doctoral program. *Degree requirements:* For master's, thesis optional; for doctorate, one foreign language, thesis/dissertation. *Entrance requirements:* For master's, GRE General Test, minimum GPA of 2.75; for doctorate, GRE General Test, minimum GPA of 3.0. Additional exam requirements/recommendations for international students: Required—TOEFL (minimum score 500 paper-based; 61 iBT), IELTS (minimum score 6). Electronic applications accepted. *Faculty research:* History of medicine, science, environmental history, western America, social/cultural history.

University of New Brunswick Fredericton, School of Graduate Studies, Faculty of Arts, Department of History, Fredericton, NB E3B 5A3, Canada. Offers MA, PhD. *Program availability:* Part-time. *Degree requirements:* For master's, thesis; for doctorate, thesis/dissertation. *Entrance requirements:* For master's, minimum GPA of 3.0, resume, writing sample, statement of research interests, honors degree in history or equivalent; for doctorate, minimum GPA of 3.0, statement of research interests, writing sample, master's degree in history. Additional exam requirements/recommendations for international students: Required—TWE (minimum score 5.5), TOEFL (minimum paper-based score 600) or IELTS (minimum score 7). Electronic applications accepted. *Faculty research:* Atlantic Canada, military, early modern-modern Europe, colonial North America, women's and gender history, history of medicine.

History

University of New Hampshire, Graduate School, College of Liberal Arts, Department of History, Durham, NH 03824. Offers history (MA, PhD); history: museum studies (MA). *Program availability:* Part-time. *Students:* 23 full-time (13 women), 12 part-time (4 women); includes 2 minority (1 Hispanic/Latino; 1 Two or more races, non-Hispanic/Latino), 1 international. Average age 30. 53 applicants, 51% accepted, 11 enrolled. In 2017, 11 master's, 5 doctorates awarded. *Entrance requirements:* For master's and doctorate, GRE General Test, writing sample. Additional exam requirements/recommendations for international students: Required—TOEFL (minimum score 550 paper-based; 80 iBT). *Application deadline:* For fall admission, 1/15 for domestic and international students. Application fee: $65. Electronic applications accepted. *Financial support:* In 2017–18, 26 students received support, including 1 fellowship, 13 teaching assistantships; research assistantships, career-related internships or fieldwork, Federal Work-Study, scholarships/grants, and tuition waivers (full and partial) also available. Support available to part-time students. Financial award application deadline: 2/15. *Unit head:* Eliga Gould, Chair, 603-862-3012. *Application contact:* Lara Demarest, Administrative Assistant, 603-862-1765, E-mail: history.grad@unh.edu.
Website: http://cola.unh.edu/history

University of New Mexico, Graduate Studies, College of Arts and Sciences, Program in History, Albuquerque, NM 87131-2039. Offers MA, PhD. *Program availability:* Part-time. *Faculty:* 18 full-time (6 women). *Students:* 22 full-time (11 women), 34 part-time (15 women); includes 14 minority (1 Black or African American, non-Hispanic/Latino; 3 American Indian or Alaska Native, non-Hispanic/Latino; 8 Hispanic/Latino; 2 Two or more races, non-Hispanic/Latino). Average age 38. 40 applicants, 70% accepted, 9 enrolled. In 2017, 13 master's, 9 doctorates awarded. Terminal master's awarded for partial completion of doctoral program. *Degree requirements:* For master's, one foreign language, comprehensive exam, thesis optional; for doctorate, 2 foreign languages, comprehensive exam, thesis/dissertation. *Entrance requirements:* For master's, GRE, BA in history or equivalent; for doctorate, GRE, MA in history or equivalent. Additional exam requirements/recommendations for international students: Required—TOEFL. *Application deadline:* For fall admission, 12/15 for domestic students; for spring admission, 10/15 for domestic students. Application fee: $50. Electronic applications accepted. *Financial support:* Fellowships, research assistantships, teaching assistantships with full tuition reimbursements, institutionally sponsored loans, scholarships/grants, and health care benefits available. Financial award application deadline: 12/15. *Faculty research:* American Western history, Asian history, environmental history, European history, frontiers and borderlands, gender and sexuality, Latin American history, politics and economy, race and ethnicity, religion, United States history, war and society. *Unit head:* Dr. Charlie Steen, Chair, 505-277-2451, Fax: 505-277-6023, E-mail: csteen@unm.edu. *Application contact:* Yolanda Martinez, Department Administrator, 505-277-2451, Fax: 505-277-6023, E-mail: history@unm.edu.
Website: http://www.unm.edu/~hist/

University of New Orleans, Graduate School, College of Liberal Arts, Department of History, New Orleans, LA 70148. Offers MA. *Degree requirements:* For master's, one foreign language, thesis (for some programs). *Entrance requirements:* For master's, GRE General Test. Additional exam requirements/recommendations for international students: Required—TOEFL (minimum score 550 paper-based; 79 iBT), IELTS (minimum score 6.5). Electronic applications accepted. *Faculty research:* Recent U.S. political, military, urban, regional, and legal history.

University of North Alabama, College of Arts and Sciences, Department of History, Program in History, Florence, AL 35632-0001. Offers MA. *Program availability:* Part-time, 100% online. *Faculty:* 9 full-time (3 women), 3 part-time/adjunct (2 women). *Students:* 2 full-time (0 women), 10 part-time (6 women). Average age 31. 6 applicants, 100% accepted, 3 enrolled. In 2017, 1 master's awarded. *Degree requirements:* For master's, comprehensive exam (for some programs), thesis optional. *Entrance requirements:* For master's, GRE, three letters of recommendation; essay; writing sample. Additional exam requirements/recommendations for international students: Required—TOEFL (minimum score 79 iBT), IELTS (minimum score 6), PTE (minimum score 54). *Application deadline:* Applications are processed on a rolling basis. Application fee: $50 ($100 for international students). Electronic applications accepted. *Expenses:* Tuition, state resident: full-time $7824; part-time $5943 per year. Tuition, nonresident: full-time $15,648; part-time $11,736 per year. *Required fees:* $3064; $2298 per unit. Tuition and fees vary according to course load and reciprocity agreements. *Financial support:* In 2017–18, 1 student received support. Federal Work-Study, scholarships/grants, and unspecified assistantships available. Financial award application deadline: 2/1; financial award applicants required to submit FAFSA. *Unit head:* Dr. Jeffrey Bibbee, Chair, 256-765-4306, E-mail: jrbibbee@una.edu. *Application contact:* Hillary N. Coats, Graduate Admissions Coordinator, 256-765-4447, E-mail: graduate@una.edu.
Website: https://www.una.edu/history/graduate-students/master-of-arts-degree-program.html

The University of North Carolina at Chapel Hill, Graduate School, College of Arts and Sciences, Department of History, Chapel Hill, NC 27599. Offers MA, PhD. Terminal master's awarded for partial completion of doctoral program. *Degree requirements:* For master's, one foreign language, thesis, oral thesis defense; for doctorate, 2 foreign languages, comprehensive exam, thesis/dissertation, oral dissertation defense. *Entrance requirements:* For master's and doctorate, GRE General Test, minimum GPA of 3.0. Electronic applications accepted.

The University of North Carolina at Charlotte, College of Liberal Arts and Sciences, Department of History, Charlotte, NC 28223-0001. Offers MA. *Program availability:* Part-time, evening/weekend. *Faculty:* 30 full-time (14 women), 1 part-time/adjunct (0 women). *Students:* 19 full-time (9 women), 31 part-time (14 women); includes 7 minority (2 Black or African American, non-Hispanic/Latino; 1 Asian, non-Hispanic/Latino; 4 Hispanic/Latino), 1 international. Average age 31. 35 applicants, 86% accepted, 17 enrolled. In 2017, 12 master's awarded. *Degree requirements:* For master's, thesis or comprehensive exam. *Entrance requirements:* For master's, GRE General Test, minimum undergraduate GPA of 3.0 in history or related discipline; personal statement (1-2 pages) detailing experiences, interests, and goals in history; three letters of recommendation, at least two of which should be from professors in history or related field; writing sample; curriculum vitae/resume. Additional exam requirements/recommendations for international students: Required—TOEFL (minimum score 523 paper-based, 70 iBT) or IELTS (6.5). *Application deadline:* For fall admission, 2/1 priority date for domestic and international students; for spring admission, 10/1 priority date for domestic and international students. Applications are processed on a rolling basis. Application fee: $75. Electronic applications accepted. *Expenses:* Tuition, state resident: full-time $4337. Tuition, nonresident: full-time $17,771. *Required fees:* $3211. Tuition and fees vary according to course load and program. *Financial support:* In 2017–18, 17 students received support, including 4 research assistantships (averaging $9,500 per year), 13 teaching assistantships (averaging $9,308 per year); career-related internships or fieldwork, Federal Work-Study, institutionally sponsored loans, scholarships/grants, and unspecified assistantships also available. Support available to part-time students. Financial award application deadline: 3/1; financial award applicants required to submit FAFSA. *Total annual research expenditures:* $5,536. *Unit head:* Dr.

Jurgen Buchenau, Chair, 704-687-5125, E-mail: jbuchenau@uncc.edu. *Application contact:* Kathy B. Giddings, Director of Graduate Admissions, 704-687-5530, Fax: 704-687-1668, E-mail: gradadm@uncc.edu.
Website: http://history.uncc.edu/

The University of North Carolina at Greensboro, Graduate School, College of Arts and Sciences, Department of History, Greensboro, NC 27412-5001. Offers historic preservation (Certificate); history (MA); museum studies (Certificate); U.S. history (PhD). *Program availability:* Part-time. *Entrance requirements:* For master's, GRE General Test. Additional exam requirements/recommendations for international students: Required—TOEFL. Electronic applications accepted. *Faculty research:* Simultaneous discovery in science, progressive social reform, Robert Mayer.

The University of North Carolina Wilmington, College of Arts and Sciences, Department of History, Wilmington, NC 28403-3297. Offers MA. *Program availability:* Part-time, 100% online. *Faculty:* 17 full-time (4 women). *Students:* 10 full-time (6 women), 21 part-time (14 women); includes 3 minority (all Black or African American, non-Hispanic/Latino). Average age 29. 19 applicants, 63% accepted, 9 enrolled. In 2017, 21 master's awarded. *Degree requirements:* For master's, comprehensive exam, thesis (for some programs). *Entrance requirements:* For master's, GRE General Test, 3 recommendations, essay, writing sample (research paper preferred). Additional exam requirements/recommendations for international students: Required—TOEFL (minimum score 550 paper-based; 79 iBT), IELTS (minimum score 6.5). *Application deadline:* For fall admission, 3/15 for domestic students. Applications are processed on a rolling basis. Application fee: $75. Electronic applications accepted. *Expenses:* Tuition, state resident: full-time $4626; part-time $226.76 per credit hour. Tuition, nonresident: full-time $17,834; part-time $874.22 per credit hour. *Required fees:* $2124. Tuition and fees vary according to program. *Financial support:* Teaching assistantships, scholarships/grants, and out-of-state tuition remission available. Financial award application deadline: 1/1; financial award applicants required to submit FAFSA. *Unit head:* Dr. Lynn Mollenauer, Chair, 910-962-3308, Fax: 910-962-7011, E-mail: mollenauerl@uncw.edu. *Application contact:* Dr. W. Taylor Fain, Graduate Director, 910-962-3305, Fax: 910-962-7011, E-mail: fainwt@uncw.edu.
Website: http://www.uncw.edu/hst/graduate/index.html

University of North Dakota, Graduate School, College of Arts and Sciences, Department of History, Grand Forks, ND 58202. Offers M Ed, MA, DA, PhD. *Program availability:* Part-time. *Degree requirements:* For master's, comprehensive exam (for some programs), thesis (for some programs), final exam; for doctorate, comprehensive exam, thesis/dissertation, final exam. *Entrance requirements:* For master's, minimum GPA of 3.0; for doctorate, minimum GPA of 3.5. Additional exam requirements/recommendations for international students: Required—TOEFL (minimum score 550 paper-based; 79 iBT), IELTS (minimum score 6.5). Electronic applications accepted. *Faculty research:* U.S. history, Latin America, Russia, modern Europe, women studies.

University of Northern British Columbia, Office of Graduate Studies, Prince George, BC V2N 4Z9, Canada. Offers business administration (Diploma); community health science (M Sc); disability management (MA); education (M Ed); first nations studies (MA); gender studies (MA); history (MA); interdisciplinary studies (MA); international studies (MA); mathematical, computer and physical sciences (M Sc); natural resources and environmental studies (M Sc, MA, MNRES, PhD); political science (MA); psychology (M Sc, PhD); social work (MSW). *Program availability:* Part-time, evening/weekend, online learning. *Degree requirements:* For master's, thesis; for doctorate, thesis/dissertation. *Entrance requirements:* For master's, GRE, minimum B average in undergraduate course work; for doctorate, candidacy exam, minimum A average in graduate course work.

University of Northern Colorado, Graduate School, College of Humanities and Social Sciences, Department of History, Greeley, CO 80639. Offers MA. *Program availability:* Part-time. *Degree requirements:* For master's, comprehensive exam; thesis or alternative. *Entrance requirements:* For master's, GRE, 3 letters of recommendation. Electronic applications accepted.

University of Northern Iowa, Graduate College, College of Social and Behavioral Sciences, Department of History, Cedar Falls, IA 50614. Offers history (MA); public history (MA). *Program availability:* Part-time. *Degree requirements:* For master's, comprehensive exam (for some programs), thesis or alternative. *Entrance requirements:* For master's, minimum GPA of 3.2. Additional exam requirements/recommendations for international students: Required—TOEFL (minimum score 500 paper-based; 61 iBT). Electronic applications accepted.

University of North Florida, College of Arts and Sciences, Department of History, Jacksonville, FL 32224. Offers European history (MA); U.S. history (MA). *Program availability:* Part-time. *Degree requirements:* For master's, comprehensive exam (for some programs), thesis optional. *Entrance requirements:* For master's, GRE General Test, 3 letters of recommendation, minimum GPA of 3.0 in last 60 hours of course work. Additional exam requirements/recommendations for international students: Required—TOEFL (minimum score 500 paper-based; 61 iBT). Electronic applications accepted.

University of North Georgia, Department of History, Anthropology and Philosophy, Dahlonega, GA 30597. Offers history (MA), including American history, military history, world history. *Program availability:* Part-time, evening/weekend. *Faculty:* 10 full-time (5 women), 1 part-time/adjunct (0 women). *Students:* 2 full-time (0 women), 13 part-time (4 women); includes 1 minority (Hispanic/Latino). Average age 34. 9 applicants, 78% accepted, 3 enrolled. In 2017, 2 master's awarded. *Degree requirements:* For master's, thesis optional. *Entrance requirements:* For master's, GRE, 3 recommendations, writing sample, letter of intent, minimum GPA of 3.0. Additional exam requirements/recommendations for international students: Required—TOEFL (minimum score 550 paper-based; 79 iBT), IELTS (minimum score 6.5). *Application deadline:* For fall admission, 4/1 priority date for domestic students. Applications are processed on a rolling basis. Application fee: $40. Electronic applications accepted. *Expenses:* Contact institution. *Financial support:* Unspecified assistantships available. Financial award application deadline: 3/17; financial award applicants required to submit FAFSA. *Unit head:* Dr. Jeff Pardue, Department Head, 678-717-3867. *Application contact:* Melinda Maxwell, Director of Graduate Admissions, 706-864-1543, E-mail: melinda.maxwell@ung.edu.
Website: http://ung.edu/history-anthropology-philosophy/

University of North Texas, Robert B. Toulouse School of Graduate Studies, Denton, TX 76203-5459. Offers accounting (MS); applied anthropology (MA, MS); applied behavior analysis (Certificate); applied geography (MA); applied technology and performance improvement (M Ed, MS); art education (MA); art history (MA); art museum education (Certificate); arts leadership (Certificate); audiology (Au D); behavior analysis (MS); behavioral science (PhD); biochemistry and molecular biology (MS); biology (MA, MS); biomedical engineering (MS); business analysis (MS); chemistry (MS); clinical health psychology (PhD); communication studies (MA, MS); computer engineering (MS); computer science (MS); counseling (M Ed, MS), including clinical mental health counseling (MS), college and university counseling, elementary school counseling, secondary school counseling; creative writing (MA); criminal justice (MS); curriculum and instruction (M Ed); decision sciences (MBA); design (MA, MFA), including fashion design (MFA), innovation studies, interior design (MFA); early childhood studies (MS);

economics (MS); educational leadership (M Ed, Ed D); educational psychology (MS, PhD), including family studies (MS), gifted and talented (MS), human development (MS), learning and cognition (MS), research, measurement and evaluation (MS); electrical engineering (MS); emergency management (MPA); engineering technology (MS); English (MA); English as a second language (MA); environmental science (MS); finance (MBA, MS); financial management (MPA); French (MA); health services management (MBA); higher education (M Ed, Ed D); history (MA, MS); hospitality management (MS); human resources management (MPA); information science (MS); information systems (PhD); information technologies (MBA); interdisciplinary studies (MA, MS); international studies (MA); international sustainable tourism (MS); jazz studies (MM); journalism (MA, MJ, Graduate Certificate), including interactive and virtual digital communication (Graduate Certificate), narrative journalism (Graduate Certificate), public relations (Graduate Certificate); kinesiology (MS); linguistics (MA); local government management (MPA); logistics (PhD); logistics and supply chain management (MBA); long-term care, senior housing, and aging services (MA); management (PhD); marketing (MBA); mathematics (MA, MS); mechanical and energy engineering (MS, PhD); music (MA), including ethnomusicology, music theory, musicology, performance; music composition (PhD); music education (MM Ed, PhD); nonprofit management (MPA); operations and supply chain management (MBA); performance (MM, DMA); philosophy (MA); political science (MA); professional and technical communication (MA); radio, television and film (MA, MFA); rehabilitation counseling (Certificate); sociology (MA); Spanish (MA); special education (M Ed); speech-language pathology (MA); strategic management (MBA); studio art (MFA); teaching (M Ed); MBA/MS. *Program availability:* Part-time, evening/weekend, online learning. Terminal master's awarded for partial completion of doctoral program. *Degree requirements:* For master's, variable foreign language requirement, comprehensive exam (for some programs), thesis (for some programs); for doctorate, variable foreign language requirement, comprehensive exam (for some programs), thesis/dissertation; for other advanced degree, variable foreign language requirement, comprehensive exam (for some programs). *Entrance requirements:* For master's and doctorate, GRE, GMAT. Additional exam requirements/recommendations for international students: Required—TOEFL (minimum score 550 paper-based; 79 iBT). Electronic applications accepted.

University of Notre Dame, Graduate School, College of Arts and Letters, Division of Humanities, Department of History, Notre Dame, IN 46556. Offers MA, PhD. *Degree requirements:* For doctorate, one foreign language, thesis/dissertation, candidacy exam. *Entrance requirements:* For doctorate, GRE General Test. Additional exam requirements/recommendations for international students: Required—TOEFL (minimum score 600 paper-based; 80 iBT). Electronic applications accepted. *Faculty research:* U.S., modern European and medieval history; history of European and U.S. religions; U.S. and European intellectual and cultural history; history of Central Europe.

University of Oklahoma, College of Arts and Sciences, Department of History, Norman, OK 73019. Offers MA, PhD. *Faculty:* 38 full-time (16 women), 1 part-time/adjunct (0 women). *Students:* 23 full-time (9 women), 30 part-time (11 women); includes 9 minority (1 Black or African American, non-Hispanic/Latino; 1 American Indian or Alaska Native, non-Hispanic/Latino; 4 Hispanic/Latino; 3 Two or more races, non-Hispanic/Latino). Average age 31. 24 applicants, 33% accepted, 3 enrolled. In 2017, 3 master's, 2 doctorates awarded. *Degree requirements:* For master's, comprehensive exam (for some programs), thesis (for some programs), 30 hours for thesis option; 34 hours for non-thesis option plus a 4-hour written exam; for doctorate, one foreign language, comprehensive exam, thesis/dissertation. *Entrance requirements:* For master's, GRE, 3 letters of reference, preferably from applicant's professors; statement of purpose; writing sample; minimum GPA of 3.5; for doctorate, GRE, 3 letters of reference, preferably from applicant's history professors; statement of purpose; writing sample; minimum GPA of 3.5. Additional exam requirements/recommendations for international students: Required—TOEFL (minimum score 79 iBT) or IELTS (minimum score 6.5). *Application deadline:* For fall admission, 12/1 for domestic and international students. Application fee: $50 ($100 for international students). Electronic applications accepted. *Expenses:* Tuition, state resident: full-time $5119; part-time $213.30 per credit hour. Tuition, nonresident: full-time $19,778; part-time $824.10 per credit hour. *Required fees:* $3458; $133.55 per credit hour. $126.50 per semester. *Financial support:* In 2017–18, 38 students received support, including 11 fellowships with full tuition reimbursements available (averaging $5,376 per year), 8 research assistantships with full tuition reimbursements available (averaging $17,766 per year), 25 teaching assistantships with full tuition reimbursements available (averaging $17,002 per year); health care benefits and unspecified assistantships also available. Financial award application deadline: 6/1; financial award applicants required to submit FAFSA. *Faculty research:* American West, Native American studies, Latin American studies, environmental history, Judaic studies. *Total annual research expenditures:* $31,087. *Unit head:* Dr. James Hart, Jr., Professor/Chair of History, 405-325-6305, Fax: 405-325-4503, E-mail: jshart@ou.edu. *Application contact:* Dr. Judith S. Lewis, Professor of History/Director of Graduate Studies, 405-325-6383, Fax: 405-325-4503, E-mail: judith.s.lewis-1@ou.edu.
Website: http://history.ou.edu

University of Oregon, Graduate School, College of Arts and Sciences, Department of History, Eugene, OR 97403. Offers MA, PhD. *Degree requirements:* For master's, one foreign language, thesis or alternative, written exam; for doctorate, 2 foreign languages, thesis/dissertation, oral and written exams. *Entrance requirements:* For master's and doctorate, GRE General Test, minimum GPA of 3.0. Additional exam requirements/recommendations for international students: Required—TOEFL. *Faculty research:* U.S., European, East and Southeast Asian, Latin American, and ancient history.

University of Ottawa, Faculty of Graduate and Postdoctoral Studies, Faculty of Arts, Department of History, Ottawa, ON K1N 6N5, Canada. Offers MA, PhD. *Degree requirements:* For master's, 2 foreign languages, thesis or alternative; for doctorate, 2 foreign languages, thesis/dissertation, oral exam. *Entrance requirements:* For master's, honors degree or equivalent, minimum B average; for doctorate, master's degree, minimum B+ average. Electronic applications accepted. *Faculty research:* Canadian history.

University of Pennsylvania, School of Arts and Sciences, Graduate Group in Ancient History, Philadelphia, PA 19104. Offers AM, PhD. *Faculty:* 20 full-time (7 women), 2 part-time/adjunct (0 women). *Students:* 14 full-time (3 women); includes 1 minority (Hispanic/Latino), 3 international. Average age 29. 22 applicants, 14% accepted, 2 enrolled. In 2017, 2 doctorates awarded. Application fee: $80.
Website: http://www.sas.upenn.edu/graduate-division

University of Pennsylvania, School of Arts and Sciences, Graduate Group in History, Philadelphia, PA 19104. Offers AM, PhD. *Faculty:* 45 full-time (21 women), 10 part-time/adjunct (3 women). *Students:* 73 full-time (33 women), 3 part-time (all women); includes 10 minority (1 Black or African American, non-Hispanic/Latino; 2 Asian, non-Hispanic/Latino; 5 Hispanic/Latino; 2 Two or more races, non-Hispanic/Latino), 22 international. Average age 30. 234 applicants, 11% accepted, 13 enrolled. In 2017, 7 master's, 7 doctorates awarded. Terminal master's awarded for partial completion of doctoral program.
Website: http://www.sas.upenn.edu/graduate-division

University of Pittsburgh, Kenneth P. Dietrich School of Arts and Sciences, Department of History, Pittsburgh, PA 15260. Offers MA, PhD. *Faculty:* 21 full-time (9 women). *Students:* 30 full-time (10 women); includes 7 minority (2 Black or African American, non-Hispanic/Latino; 5 Hispanic/Latino). Average age 25. 56 applicants, 14% accepted, 8 enrolled. In 2017, 5 master's, 3 doctorates awarded. Terminal master's awarded for partial completion of doctoral program. *Degree requirements:* For master's, one foreign language, thesis, oral exam, seminar paper; for doctorate, one foreign language, comprehensive exam, thesis/dissertation. *Entrance requirements:* For master's and doctorate, GRE General Test, writing sample. Additional exam requirements/recommendations for international students: Required—TOEFL (minimum score 550 paper-based, 90 iBT) or IELTS (minimum score 7.0). *Application deadline:* For fall admission, 1/15 for domestic and international students. Application fee: $50. Electronic applications accepted. *Financial support:* In 2017–18, 30 students received support, including 15 fellowships with full tuition reimbursements available (averaging $22,000 per year), 13 teaching assistantships with full tuition reimbursements available (averaging $18,000 per year); scholarships/grants, health care benefits, tuition waivers (full and partial), and unspecified assistantships also available. Financial award application deadline: 1/15. *Faculty research:* Europe, Latin America, Atlantic, United States, East Asia. *Unit head:* Dr. Lara Putnam, Chair, 412-648-7452, Fax: 412-648-9074, E-mail: lep22@pitt.edu. *Application contact:* Patty Landon, Academic Administrator, 412-687-7450, Fax: 412-648-9074, E-mail: pal24@pitt.edu.
Website: http://www.history.pitt.edu

University of Puerto Rico–Río Piedras, College of Humanities, Department of History, San Juan, PR 00931-3300. Offers Caribbean history (PhD); history (MA); Puerto Rican history (PhD). *Program availability:* Part-time. *Degree requirements:* For master's, one foreign language, comprehensive exam, thesis; for doctorate, one foreign language, comprehensive exam, thesis/dissertation. *Entrance requirements:* For master's, PAEG or GRE, interview, minimum GPA of 3.0, 2 letters of recommendation; for doctorate, PAEG or GRE, interview, master's degree, minimum GPA of 3.0, 2 letters of recommendation.

University of Regina, Faculty of Graduate Studies and Research, Faculty of Arts, Department of History, Regina, SK S4S 0A2, Canada. Offers MA. *Program availability:* Part-time. *Faculty:* 11 full-time (4 women). *Students:* 3 full-time (2 women), 5 part-time (2 women). 4 applicants. In 2017, 2 master's awarded. *Degree requirements:* For master's, thesis. *Entrance requirements:* Additional exam requirements/recommendations for international students: Required—TOEFL (minimum score 580 paper-based; 80 iBT), IELTS (minimum score 6.5), PTE (minimum score 59). *Application deadline:* For fall admission, 3/31 for domestic and international students. Application fee: $100. Electronic applications accepted. *Expenses:* Tuition, nonresident: full-time $21,330 Canadian dollars; part-time $18,165 Canadian dollars per year. *International tuition:* $24,713 Canadian dollars full-time. *Required fees:* $5136 Canadian dollars; $3118 Canadian dollars per credit hour. $1008 Canadian dollars per semester. Tuition and fees vary according to program. *Financial support:* In 2017–18, 2 fellowships (averaging $6,000 per year), 2 teaching assistantships (averaging $2,562 per year) were awarded; research assistantships and scholarships/grants also available. Financial award application deadline: 6/15. *Faculty research:* Canadian, European, Asian, British, and the Americas history. *Unit head:* Dr. Raymond Blake, Department Head, 306-585-5431, Fax: 306-585-4827, E-mail: raymond.blake@uregina.ca. *Application contact:* Dr. Philip Charrier, Graduate Program Coordinator, 306-585-4215, Fax: 306-585-4827, E-mail: philip.charrier@uregina.ca.
Website: http://www.uregina.ca/arts/history

University of Rhode Island, Graduate School, College of Arts and Sciences, Department of History, Kingston, RI 02881. Offers archaeology and anthropology (MA); European history (MA), including European history, United States history; MLIS/MA. *Program availability:* Part-time. *Faculty:* 17 full-time (8 women). *Students:* 7 full-time (1 woman), 6 part-time (3 women). 12 applicants, 92% accepted, 5 enrolled. In 2017, 5 master's awarded. *Entrance requirements:* Additional exam requirements/recommendations for international students: Required—TOEFL. *Application deadline:* For fall admission, 7/15 for domestic students; for spring admission, 11/15 for domestic students. Application fee: $65. Electronic applications accepted. *Expenses:* Tuition, state resident: full-time $12,706; part-time $786 per credit. Tuition, nonresident: full-time $25,216; part-time $1401 per credit. *Required fees:* $1598; $45 per credit. One-time fee: $30 part-time. *Financial support:* In 2017–18, 3 teaching assistantships with tuition reimbursements (averaging $17,724 per year) were awarded. Financial award application deadline: 2/1; financial award applicants required to submit FAFSA. *Unit head:* Dr. Rod Mather, Chair, 401-874-4093, E-mail: rodmather@uri.edu. *Application contact:* Dr. Evelyn Sterne, Director of Graduate Studies, 401-874-4074, E-mail: sterne@uri.edu.
Website: http://www.uri.edu/artsci/his/

University of Rochester, School of Arts and Sciences, Department of History, Rochester, NY 14627. Offers MA, PhD. *Faculty:* 20 full-time (5 women). *Students:* 33 full-time (16 women), 1 part-time (0 women); includes 5 minority (1 Asian, non-Hispanic/Latino; 2 Hispanic/Latino; 2 Two or more races, non-Hispanic/Latino), 2 international. Average age 31. 59 applicants, 25% accepted, 8 enrolled. In 2017, 16 master's, 2 doctorates awarded. Terminal master's awarded for partial completion of doctoral program. *Degree requirements:* For master's, thesis optional, essay; for doctorate, 2 foreign languages, comprehensive exam, thesis/dissertation, first- and second-year essays, teaching assistant for two semesters. *Entrance requirements:* For master's and doctorate, GRE General Test, statement of purpose, transcripts, three letters of recommendation, writing sample. *Application deadline:* For fall admission, 1/15 for domestic and international students. Application fee: $60. Electronic applications accepted. *Expenses:* $1,596 per credit hour. *Financial support:* In 2017–18, 27 students received support, including 11 fellowships (averaging $22,000 per year), 5 teaching assistantships (averaging $20,000 per year); tuition waivers (full and partial) and unspecified assistantships also available. *Faculty research:* Contemporary American culture, intellectual history, urban history, east Asian history, environmental history. *Total annual research expenditures:* $48,099. *Unit head:* Stewart Weaver, Interim Chair, 585-275-9348, E-mail: stewart.weaver@rochester.edu. *Application contact:* Kristina Pakusch, Secretary and Graduate Coordinator, 585-275-2053, E-mail: kristina.pakusch@rochester.edu.
Website: https://www.sas.rochester.edu/his/graduate/index.html

University of Saskatchewan, College of Graduate Studies and Research, College of Arts and Science, Department of History, Saskatoon, SK S7N 5A2, Canada. Offers MA, PhD. *Program availability:* Part-time. *Degree requirements:* For master's, thesis; for doctorate, comprehensive exam (for some programs), thesis/dissertation. *Entrance requirements:* Additional exam requirements/recommendations for international students: Required—TOEFL (minimum score 80 iBT); Recommended—IELTS (minimum score 6.5). Electronic applications accepted.

University of South Africa, College of Human Sciences, Pretoria, South Africa. Offers adult education (M Ed); African languages (MA, PhD); African politics (MA, PhD); Afrikaans (MA, PhD); ancient history (MA, PhD); ancient Near Eastern studies (MA, PhD); anthropology (MA, PhD); applied linguistics (MA); Arabic (MA, PhD); archaeology (MA); art history (MA); Biblical archaeology (MA); Biblical studies (M Th, D Th, PhD);

Christian spirituality (M Th, D Th); church history (M Th, D Th); classical studies (MA, PhD); clinical psychology (MA); communication (MA, PhD); comparative education (M Ed, Ed D); consulting psychology (D Admin, D Com, PhD); curriculum studies (M Ed, Ed D); development studies (M Admin, MA, D Admin, PhD); didactics (M Ed, Ed D); education (M Tech); education management (M Ed, Ed D); educational psychology (M Ed); English (MA); environmental education (M Ed); French (MA, PhD); German (MA, PhD); Greek (MA); guidance and counseling (M Ed); health studies (MA, PhD), including health sciences education (MA), health services management (MA), medical and surgical nursing science (critical care general) (MA), midwifery and neonatal nursing science (MA), trauma and emergency care (MA); history (MA, PhD); history of education (Ed D); inclusive education (M Ed, Ed D); information and communications technology policy and regulation (MA); information science (MA, MIS, PhD); international politics (MA, PhD); Islamic studies (MA, PhD); Italian (MA, PhD); Judaica (MA, PhD); linguistics (MA, PhD); mathematical education (M Ed); mathematics education (MA); missiology (M Th, D Th); modern Hebrew (MA, PhD); musicology (MA, MMus, D Mus, PhD); natural science education (M Ed); New Testament (M Th, D Th); Old Testament (D Th); pastoral therapy (M Th, D Th); philosophy (MA); philosophy of education (M Ed, Ed D); politics (MA, PhD); Portuguese (MA, PhD); practical theology (M Th, D Th); psychology (MA, MS, PhD); psychology of education (M Ed, Ed D); public health (MA); religious studies (MA, D Th, PhD); Romance languages (MA); Russian (MA, PhD); Semitic languages (MA, PhD); social behavior studies in HIV/AIDS (MA); social science (mental health) (MA); social science in development studies (MA); social science in psychology (MA); social science in social work (MA); social science in sociology (MA); social work (MSW, DSW, PhD); socio-education (M Ed, Ed D); sociolinguistics (MA); sociology (MA, PhD); Spanish (MA, PhD); systematic theology (M Th, D Th); TESOL (teaching English to speakers of other languages) (MA); theological ethics (M Th, D Th); theory of literature (MA, PhD); urban ministries (D Th); urban ministry (M Th).

University of South Alabama, College of Arts and Sciences, Department of History, Mobile, AL 36688. Offers MA. *Program availability:* Part-time, evening/weekend. *Faculty:* 5 full-time (3 women). *Students:* 8 full-time (5 women), 6 part-time (3 women). Average age 31. 8 applicants, 50% accepted, 4 enrolled. In 2017, 4 master's awarded. *Degree requirements:* For master's, comprehensive exam, thesis optional, 30 credit hours of course work. *Entrance requirements:* For master's, GRE General Test, 21 hours of course work in history, minimum GPA of 3.0. Additional exam requirements/recommendations for international students: Required—TOEFL (minimum score 525 paper-based; 71 iBT). *Application deadline:* For fall admission, 7/10 priority date for domestic students, 6/15 priority date for international students; for spring admission, 11/20 priority date for domestic students, 11/1 priority date for international students; for summer admission, 4/20 for domestic students. Applications are processed on a rolling basis. Application fee: $35. Electronic applications accepted. *Expenses:* Tuition, state resident: full-time $10,104; part-time $421 per semester hour. Tuition, nonresident: full-time $20,208; part-time $842 per semester hour. *Financial support:* Fellowships, research assistantships, teaching assistantships, career-related internships or fieldwork, Federal Work-Study, institutionally sponsored loans, scholarships/grants, and unspecified assistantships available. Support available to part-time students. Financial award application deadline: 3/31; financial award applicants required to submit FAFSA. *Unit head:* David Messenger, Chair, History, 251-460-6210, E-mail: davidamessenger@southalabama.edu. *Application contact:* Dr. Martha J. Brazy, Graduate Coordinator, History, 251-460-7540, E-mail: mjbrazy@southalabama.edu.
Website: http://www.southalabama.edu/colleges/artsandsci/history/gradprogram.html

University of South Carolina, The Graduate School, College of Arts and Sciences, Department of History, Columbia, SC 29208. Offers history (MA, PhD); public history (MA, Certificate), including archive management (MA), historic preservation (MA), museum administration (MA), museum management (Certificate); MLIS/MA. IMA and MAT offered in cooperation with the College of Education. *Program availability:* Part-time. Terminal master's awarded for partial completion of doctoral program. *Degree requirements:* For master's, one foreign language, thesis; for doctorate, one foreign language, thesis/dissertation. *Entrance requirements:* For master's and doctorate, GRE General Test. Additional exam requirements/recommendations for international students: Required—TOEFL. Electronic applications accepted. *Faculty research:* U.S. history; European history; Latin American history; history of science and technology.

University of South Dakota, Graduate School, College of Arts and Sciences, Department of History, Vermillion, SD 57069. Offers MA, JD/MA. *Program availability:* Part-time. *Degree requirements:* For master's, thesis (for some programs). *Entrance requirements:* For master's, GRE General Test, minimum GPA of 2.7. Additional exam requirements/recommendations for international students: Required—TOEFL (minimum score 550 paper-based; 79 iBT). *Application deadline:* Applications are processed on a rolling basis. Application fee: $35. Electronic applications accepted. *Financial support:* Research assistantships with partial tuition reimbursements, teaching assistantships with partial tuition reimbursements, Federal Work-Study, scholarships/grants, and unspecified assistantships available. Financial award applicants required to submit FAFSA. *Application contact:* Graduate School, 605-658-6140, Fax: 605-677-6118, E-mail: grad@usd.edu.
Website: http://www.usd.edu/history/

University of Southern California, Graduate School, Dana and David Dornsife College of Letters, Arts and Sciences, Department of History, Los Angeles, CA 90089. Offers PhD. *Degree requirements:* For doctorate, 2 foreign languages, comprehensive exam, thesis/dissertation, 60 semester units of acceptable coursework. *Entrance requirements:* For doctorate, GRE General Test. Additional exam requirements/recommendations for international students: Recommended—TOEFL. Electronic applications accepted. *Faculty research:* U.S. North American and Latin American history, California and Western American history (including Borderlands), European history from the early Middle Ages to present, East Asian (Chinese, Japanese, Korean) history, early modern Atlantic world/world history.

University of Southern Mississippi, College of Arts and Letters, Department of History, Hattiesburg, MS 39406-0001. Offers MA, MS, PhD. *Program availability:* Part-time. *Students:* 9 full-time (3 women). 24 applicants, 79% accepted, 10 enrolled. In 2017, 56 master's, 5 doctorates awarded. *Degree requirements:* For master's, one foreign language, comprehensive exam, thesis (for some programs); for doctorate, 2 foreign languages, comprehensive exam, thesis/dissertation. *Entrance requirements:* For master's, GRE General Test, minimum GPA of 3.0 in field of study, 2.75 in last 2 years; for doctorate, GRE General Test, minimum GPA of 3.5. Additional exam requirements/recommendations for international students: Required—TOEFL, IELTS. *Application deadline:* For fall admission, 3/1 priority date for domestic students, 3/1 for international students. Applications are processed on a rolling basis. Application fee: $60. *Expenses:* Tuition, state resident: full-time $3830. *Financial support:* Fellowships with full tuition reimbursements, research assistantships with full tuition reimbursements, teaching assistantships with full tuition reimbursements, Federal Work-Study, institutionally sponsored loans, scholarships/grants, health care benefits, and unspecified assistantships available. Financial award application deadline: 3/15; financial award applicants required to submit FAFSA. *Faculty research:* Civil War, civil rights, modern European history, war history. *Unit head:* Dr. Kyle F. Zelner, Chair, 601-266-6196, Fax: 601-266-4334. *Application contact:* Dr. Ken Swope, Program Coordinator, E-mail: kenneth.swope@usm.edu.
Website: https://www.usm.edu/history

University of South Florida, College of Arts and Sciences, Department of History, Tampa, FL 33620-9951. Offers history (MA, PhD), including American history (MA), ancient history (MA), European history (MA), Latin American history (MA), Medieval history (MA). *Program availability:* Part-time, evening/weekend. *Faculty:* 17 full-time (8 women), 1 (woman) part-time/adjunct. *Students:* 39 full-time (9 women), 19 part-time (9 women); includes 5 minority (1 American Indian or Alaska Native, non-Hispanic/Latino; 4 Hispanic/Latino). Average age 33. 41 applicants, 80% accepted, 24 enrolled. In 2017, 10 master's, 1 doctorate awarded. *Degree requirements:* For master's, one foreign language, comprehensive exam, thesis optional; for doctorate, one foreign language, comprehensive exam, thesis/dissertation. *Entrance requirements:* For master's, GRE General Test, minimum GPA of 3.0, two letters of recommendation, 2-page statement of purpose, writing sample; for doctorate, GRE General Test, minimum GPA of 3.5 in master's degree coursework, three letters of recommendation, statement of purpose, writing sample, foreign language proficiency in the field of study. Additional exam requirements/recommendations for international students: Required—TOEFL (minimum score 550 paper-based; 79 iBT) or IELTS (minimum score 6.5). *Application deadline:* For fall admission, 12/1 priority date for domestic students, 12/1 for international students. Applications are processed on a rolling basis. Application fee: $30. Electronic applications accepted. *Financial support:* In 2017–18, 3 students received support, including 17 teaching assistantships with tuition reimbursements available (averaging $12,750 per year); unspecified assistantships also available. Financial award application deadline: 1/15. *Faculty research:* North American and U.S. history, European history, nineteenth- and twentieth-centuries/modern world, early modern world, ancient history, history of gender/sexuality, Latin American history, history of science and medicine. *Total annual research expenditures:* $194,096. *Unit head:* Dr. Fraser Ottanelli, Professor and Chair, 813-974-6209, Fax: 813-974-6228, E-mail: ottanelli@usf.edu. *Application contact:* Dr. Kees Boterbloem, Professor and Graduate Program Director, 813-974-2807, E-mail: cboterbl@usf.edu.
Website: http://history.usf.edu

The University of Tennessee, Graduate School, College of Arts and Sciences, Department of History, Knoxville, TN 37996. Offers American history (PhD); European history (PhD); history (MA). *Program availability:* Part-time. *Degree requirements:* For master's, thesis or alternative; for doctorate, one foreign language, thesis/dissertation. *Entrance requirements:* For master's and doctorate, GRE General Test, minimum GPA of 2.7. Additional exam requirements/recommendations for international students: Required—TOEFL. Electronic applications accepted.

The University of Texas at Arlington, Graduate School, College of Liberal Arts, Department of History, Arlington, TX 76019. Offers history (MA); transatlantic history (PhD). *Program availability:* Part-time, evening/weekend. *Degree requirements:* For master's, one foreign language, comprehensive exam (for some programs), thesis (for some programs); for doctorate, one foreign language, comprehensive exam, thesis/dissertation. *Entrance requirements:* For master's, GRE General Test, minimum GPA of 3.0 in last 60 hours, 3 letters of recommendation; for doctorate, GRE General Test, minimum graduate GPA of 3.5, 3 letters of recommendation, academic writing sample. Additional exam requirements/recommendations for international students: Required—TOEFL (minimum score 550 paper-based). Electronic applications accepted.

The University of Texas at Austin, Graduate School, College of Liberal Arts, Department of History, Austin, TX 78712-1111. Offers MA, PhD. *Degree requirements:* For doctorate, thesis/dissertation. *Entrance requirements:* For master's and doctorate, GRE General Test. Electronic applications accepted. *Faculty research:* United States, Latin American, European, African, Asian, and Middle Eastern history.

The University of Texas at Dallas, School of Arts and Humanities, Richardson, TX 75080. Offers art history (MA); history (MA); humanities (MA, PhD), including aesthetic studies, history of ideas, studies in literature; Latin American studies (MA). *Program availability:* Part-time, evening/weekend. *Faculty:* 47 full-time (17 women), 4 part-time/adjunct (2 women). *Students:* 132 full-time (83 women), 117 part-time (71 women); includes 62 minority (11 Black or African American, non-Hispanic/Latino; 3 American Indian or Alaska Native, non-Hispanic/Latino; 10 Asian, non-Hispanic/Latino; 25 Hispanic/Latino; 13 Two or more races, non-Hispanic/Latino), 29 international. Average age 40. 127 applicants, 55% accepted, 43 enrolled. In 2017, 17 master's, 18 doctorates awarded. *Degree requirements:* For master's, one foreign language, portfolio; for doctorate, one foreign language, thesis/dissertation. *Entrance requirements:* For master's and doctorate, minimum GPA of 3.0 in undergraduate course work in field. Additional exam requirements/recommendations for international students: Required—TOEFL (minimum score 550 paper-based). *Application deadline:* For fall admission, 7/15 for domestic students, 5/1 priority date for international students; for spring admission, 11/15 for domestic students, 9/1 priority date for international students. Applications are processed on a rolling basis. Application fee: $50 ($100 for international students). Electronic applications accepted. *Expenses:* Tuition, state resident: full-time $12,916; part-time $718 per credit hour. Tuition, nonresident: full-time $25,252; part-time $1403 per credit hour. *Financial support:* In 2017–18, 136 students received support, including 12 research assistantships with partial tuition reimbursements available (averaging $22,710 per year), 71 teaching assistantships with partial tuition reimbursements available (averaging $15,000 per year); fellowships, Federal Work-Study, institutionally sponsored loans, scholarships/grants, and unspecified assistantships also available. Support available to part-time students. Financial award application deadline: 4/30; financial award applicants required to submit FAFSA. *Faculty research:* Science and the arts and humanities, intellectual and philosophical history, cultural studies, translation studies. *Total annual research expenditures:* $183,441. *Unit head:* Dr. Dennis M. Kratz, Dean, 972-883-2984, Fax: 972-883-2989, E-mail: dkratz@utdallas.edu. *Application contact:* Dr. John Gooch, Associate Dean of Graduate Studies, 972-883-2756, Fax: 972-883-2989, E-mail: john.gooch@utdallas.edu.
Website: http://www.utdallas.edu/ah/

The University of Texas at El Paso, Graduate School, College of Liberal Arts, Department of History, El Paso, TX 79968-0001. Offers border history (MA); borderlands history (PhD); history (MA). *Program availability:* Part-time. *Degree requirements:* For master's, thesis optional; for doctorate, 2 foreign languages, thesis/dissertation. *Entrance requirements:* For master's, GRE, minimum GPA of 3.0, writing sample, letters of recommendation, transcripts; for doctorate, GRE, statement of purpose, writing sample, letters of recommendation, transcripts. Additional exam requirements/recommendations for international students: Required—TOEFL; Recommended—IELTS.

The University of Texas at San Antonio, College of Liberal and Fine Arts, Department of History, San Antonio, TX 78249-0617. Offers MA. *Program availability:* Part-time. *Faculty:* 10 full-time (5 women). *Students:* 9 full-time (4 women), 21 part-time (12 women); includes 15 minority (3 Black or African American, non-Hispanic/Latino; 1 Asian, non-Hispanic/Latino; 10 Hispanic/Latino; 1 Two or more races, non-Hispanic/Latino), 1 international. Average age 31. 18 applicants, 67% accepted, 8 enrolled. In 2017, 10 master's awarded. *Degree requirements:* For master's, comprehensive exam, thesis optional, minimum of 30 credit hours. *Entrance requirements:* For master's, GRE, bachelor's degree with 18 credit hours in field of study or in another appropriate field of

study (12 of these hours must be at the upper-division level with minimum GPA of 3.0 in last 60 hours), statement of purpose. Additional exam requirements/recommendations for international students: Required—TOEFL (minimum score 550 paper-based; 79 iBT), IELTS (minimum score 6.5). *Application deadline:* For fall admission, 6/15 for domestic students, 3/1 for international students; for spring admission, 10/15 for domestic students, 9/15 for international students. Application fee: $50 ($90 for international students). Electronic applications accepted. *Expenses:* Contact institution. *Financial support:* Research assistantships and Federal Work-Study available. *Faculty research:* Borderlands and empires, Latin American history, early American history, Chinese history, Latina/o studies. *Total annual research expenditures:* $64,586. *Unit head:* Dr. Kirsten Gardner, Department Chair, 210-458-4033, E-mail: kirsten.gardner@utsa.edu. *Application contact:* Roschelle Kelly, Administrative Associate II, 210-458-5716, E-mail: roschelle.kelly@utsa.edu.
Website: http://colfa.utsa.edu/history/

The University of Texas at Tyler, College of Arts and Sciences, Department of History, Tyler, TX 75799-0001. Offers MA. *Program availability:* Part-time, evening/weekend. *Degree requirements:* For master's, one foreign language, comprehensive exam, thesis optional. *Entrance requirements:* For master's, GRE General Test, minimum GPA of 3.0. Additional exam requirements/recommendations for international students: Required—TOEFL. Electronic applications accepted. *Faculty research:* Early and modern U.S. history, early modern and modern European history.

The University of Texas of the Permian Basin, Office of Graduate Studies, College of Arts and Sciences, Department of History, Odessa, TX 79762-0001. Offers MA. *Program availability:* Part-time, evening/weekend. *Degree requirements:* For master's, comprehensive exam (for some programs), thesis (for some programs). *Entrance requirements:* For master's, GRE General Test. Additional exam requirements/recommendations for international students: Required—TOEFL (minimum score 550 paper-based).

The University of Texas Rio Grande Valley, College of Liberal Arts, Department of History, Edinburg, TX 78539. Offers MA, MAIS. *Program availability:* Part-time. *Faculty:* 5 full-time (3 women). *Students:* 3 full-time (1 woman), 37 part-time (11 women); includes 32 minority (all Hispanic/Latino). Average age 34. 10 applicants, 80% accepted, 7 enrolled. In 2017, 3 master's awarded. *Degree requirements:* For master's, comprehensive exam, thesis or alternative. *Entrance requirements:* For master's, GRE General Test, minimum GPA of 3.0. Additional exam requirements/recommendations for international students: Required—TOEFL or IELTS. *Application deadline:* For fall admission, 4/15 priority date for domestic students; for spring admission, 11/5 priority date for domestic students. Applications are processed on a rolling basis. Application fee: $50 ($100 for international students). *Expenses:* Tuition, state resident: full-time $5550; part-time $417 per credit hour. Tuition, nonresident: full-time $13,020; part-time $832 per credit hour. *Required fees:* $1169. *Financial support:* Application deadline: 6/1. *Faculty research:* Texas-Mexican legacy, modern America, Southwest, labor, modern Europe. *Unit head:* Thomas Britten, Chair, 956-882-5130, E-mail: thomas.britten@utrgv.edu.

The University of Toledo, College of Graduate Studies, College of Languages, Literature and Social Sciences, Department of History, Toledo, OH 43606-3390. Offers MA, PhD. *Program availability:* Part-time. *Degree requirements:* For master's, comprehensive exam (for some programs), thesis or comprehensive exam; for doctorate, thesis/dissertation, oral and written exams. *Entrance requirements:* For master's and doctorate, GRE General Test, minimum cumulative point-hour ratio of 2.7 for all previous academic work, three letters of recommendation. Additional exam requirements/recommendations for international students: Required—TOEFL (minimum score 550 paper-based; 80 iBT). Electronic applications accepted. *Faculty research:* U.S. diplomatic history, U.S. history, urban history, public history, European history.

University of Toronto, School of Graduate Studies, Faculty of Arts and Science, Department of History, Toronto, ON M5S 1A1, Canada. Offers MA, PhD. *Program availability:* Part-time. *Degree requirements:* For master's, one foreign language, thesis or research essay, French language exam; for doctorate, comprehensive exam, thesis/dissertation, oral examination/thesis defense. *Entrance requirements:* For master's, minimum B+ average or GPA of 3.3, 6 full academic year history courses; for doctorate, MA in history, minimum A- average or GPA of 3.7. Additional exam requirements/recommendations for international students: Required—TOEFL (minimum score 580 paper-based; 93 iBT), TWE (minimum score 5). Electronic applications accepted.

The University of Tulsa, Graduate School, Kendall College of Arts and Sciences, Department of History, Tulsa, OK 74104-3189. Offers MA, MTA, JD/MA. *Program availability:* Part-time. *Faculty:* 8 full-time (2 women). *Students:* 4 full-time (1 woman), 13 part-time (7 women); includes 6 minority (1 Black or African American, non-Hispanic/Latino; 5 American Indian or Alaska Native, non-Hispanic/Latino). Average age 33. 6 applicants, 50% accepted, 3 enrolled. In 2017, 1 master's awarded. *Degree requirements:* For master's, thesis (for some programs), public presentation or oral defense of thesis. *Entrance requirements:* For master's, GRE General Test, writing sample. Additional exam requirements/recommendations for international students: Required—TOEFL (minimum score 577 paper-based; 91 iBT), IELTS (minimum score 6.5). *Application deadline:* Applications are processed on a rolling basis. Application fee: $55. Electronic applications accepted. *Expenses:* Tuition: Full-time $22,230. *Required fees:* $2000. Tuition and fees vary according to course load and program. *Financial support:* In 2017–18, 13 students received support, including 3 fellowships with full tuition reimbursements available (averaging $6,519 per year), 6 teaching assistantships with full tuition reimbursements available (averaging $10,750 per year); research assistantships, Federal Work-Study, scholarships/grants, health care benefits, tuition waivers (full and partial), and unspecified assistantships also available. Support available to part-time students. Financial award application deadline: 2/1; financial award applicants required to submit FAFSA. *Faculty research:* United States history, modern European history, Native American history, comparative history. *Unit head:* Dr. Kristen Oertel, Chairperson, 918-631-2825, Fax: 918-631-2057, E-mail: kristen-oertel@utulsa.edu. *Application contact:* Dr. Jan Wilson, Adviser, 918-631-2410, Fax: 918-631-2057, E-mail: jan-wilson@utulsa.edu.
Website: http://artsandsciences.utulsa.edu/academics/departments-schools/history/

The University of Tulsa, Graduate School, Kendall College of Arts and Sciences, School of Education, Tulsa, OK 74104-3189. Offers mathematics and science education (MSMSE); teaching arts (MTA), including art, biology, English, history, mathematics; urban education (MA). *Accreditation:* TEAC. *Program availability:* Part-time. *Faculty:* 9 full-time (5 women), 2 part-time/adjunct (both women). *Students:* 8 full-time (4 women), 6 part-time (5 women); includes 4 minority (1 Black or African American, non-Hispanic/Latino; 1 American Indian or Alaska Native, non-Hispanic/Latino; 1 Asian, non-Hispanic/Latino; 1 Two or more races, non-Hispanic/Latino). Average age 31. 22 applicants, 9% accepted. In 2017, 10 master's awarded. *Degree requirements:* For master's, thesis optional. *Entrance requirements:* For master's, GRE General Test. Additional exam requirements/recommendations for international students: Required—TOEFL (minimum score 577 paper-based; 91 iBT), IELTS (minimum score 6.5). *Application deadline:* For fall admission, 2/1 priority date for domestic students. Applications are processed on a rolling basis. Application fee: $55. Electronic applications accepted. *Expenses:* Tuition: Full-time $22,230. *Required fees:* $2000. Tuition and fees vary according to course load

and program. *Financial support:* In 2017–18, 3 students received support, including 3 teaching assistantships with full tuition reimbursements available (averaging $13,410 per year); fellowships with tuition reimbursements available, research assistantships with tuition reimbursements available, career-related internships or fieldwork, Federal Work-Study, scholarships/grants, health care benefits, tuition waivers (full and partial), and unspecified assistantships also available. Support available to part-time students. Financial award application deadline: 2/1; financial award applicants required to submit FAFSA. *Faculty research:* Elementary/secondary certification, math/science education, teaching arts. *Unit head:* Dr. Elizabeth Smith, Chair, 918-631-2238, Fax: 918-631-3721, E-mail: elizabeth-smith-43@utulsa.edu. *Application contact:* Dr. David Brown, Advisor, 918-631-2719, Fax: 918-631-2133, E-mail: david-brown@utulsa.edu.
Website: http://artsandsciences.utulsa.edu/academics/departments-schools/urban-education/

University of Utah, Graduate School, College of Humanities, Department of History, Salt Lake City, UT 84112. Offers MA, MS, PhD. *Program availability:* Part-time. *Faculty:* 27 full-time (14 women), 4 part-time/adjunct (0 women). *Students:* 19 full-time (9 women), 19 part-time (5 women); includes 9 minority (1 Black or African American, non-Hispanic/Latino; 1 American Indian or Alaska Native, non-Hispanic/Latino; 1 Asian, non-Hispanic/Latino; 3 Hispanic/Latino; 3 Two or more races, non-Hispanic/Latino), 1 international. Average age 28. 45 applicants, 33% accepted, 14 enrolled. In 2017, 12 master's, 1 doctorate awarded. *Degree requirements:* For master's, one foreign language, comprehensive exam (for some programs), thesis (for some programs); for doctorate, one foreign language, comprehensive exam, thesis/dissertation. *Entrance requirements:* For master's, GRE General Test, minimum GPA of 3.2; for doctorate, GRE General Test, minimum graduate GPA of 3.6. Additional exam requirements/recommendations for international students: Required—TOEFL (minimum score 500 paper-based). *Application deadline:* For fall admission, 1/15 for domestic and international students. Application fee: $55 ($65 for international students). Electronic applications accepted. *Expenses:* $7,254 resident per year; $22,988 nonresident per year. *Financial support:* In 2017–18, 17 students received support, including 3 fellowships with full tuition reimbursements available (averaging $17,000 per year), 14 teaching assistantships with full tuition reimbursements available (averaging $16,200 per year); health care benefits and unspecified assistantships also available. Financial award application deadline: 1/15. *Faculty research:* U.S. history, European history, Asian history, Middle East, Latin America. *Unit head:* Prof. Isabel Moreira, Chair, 801-581-5685, Fax: 801-585-0580, E-mail: isabel.moreira@utah.edu. *Application contact:* Amarilys Scott, Academic Advisor, 801-581-6121, Fax: 801-585-0580, E-mail: amarilys.scott@utah.edu.
Website: http://history.utah.edu

University of Utah, Graduate School, College of Humanities, Program in Middle East Studies, Salt Lake City, UT 84112. Offers Arabic (MA, PhD); Hebrew (MA); history (MA, PhD); Persian (MA, PhD); political science (MA, PhD). *Students:* 2 part-time (1 woman); includes 1 minority (Asian, non-Hispanic/Latino). In 2017, 1 doctorate awarded. *Entrance requirements:* For master's, GRE General Test, minimum GPA of 3.2; for doctorate, GRE General Test, MA in Middle East studies or equivalent, minimum GPA of 3.2. Additional exam requirements/recommendations for international students: Required—TOEFL (minimum score 580 paper-based; 92 iBT); Recommended—IELTS (minimum score 7). Application fee: $55 ($65 for international students). Electronic applications accepted. *Financial support:* In 2017–18, 5 students received support, including 2 teaching assistantships with full tuition reimbursements available (averaging $13,500 per year); fellowships and unspecified assistantships also available. Financial award application deadline: 1/15. *Faculty research:* Islamic studies; Middle Eastern history; political science; Judaic studies; anthropology; Arabic, Persian, Hebrew, and Turkish language and literature. *Unit head:* Johanna Watzinger-Tharp, Director, 801-581-7148, Fax: 801-581-6105, E-mail: j.tharp@utah.edu. *Application contact:* Kellie Hubbard, Academic Advisor, 801-581-5362, Fax: 801-581-6105, E-mail: kellie.hubbard@utah.edu.
Website: http://www.mec.utah.edu

University of Vermont, Graduate College, College of Arts and Sciences, Program in History, Burlington, VT 05405. Offers MA. *Students:* 13 (4 women). 22 applicants, 77% accepted, 6 enrolled. In 2017, 5 master's awarded. *Degree requirements:* For master's, thesis. *Entrance requirements:* For master's, GRE General Test, writing sample (10 pages using primary sources). Additional exam requirements/recommendations for international students: Required—TOEFL (minimum score 550 paper-based, 90 iBT) or IELTS (6.5). *Application deadline:* For fall admission, 2/15 priority date for domestic and international students; for spring admission, 11/1 for domestic and international students. Applications are processed on a rolling basis. Application fee: $65. Electronic applications accepted. *Expenses:* $646 per credit in-state, $1,130 per credit out-of-state. *Financial support:* In 2017–18, 8 students received support, including 1 research assistantship with full tuition reimbursement available (averaging $16,000 per year), 6 teaching assistantships with partial tuition reimbursements available (averaging $8,000 per year); fellowships, career-related internships or fieldwork, scholarships/grants, and health care benefits also available. Financial award application deadline: 2/15. *Faculty research:* American, European, and Asian history. *Unit head:* Dr. Dona Brown, Acting Director, 802-656-3180, E-mail: dona.brown@uvm.edu.
Website: https://www.uvm.edu/cas/history/graduate-programs

University of Victoria, Faculty of Graduate Studies, Faculty of Humanities, Department of History, Victoria, BC V8W 2Y2, Canada. Offers MA, PhD. *Program availability:* Part-time. *Degree requirements:* For master's, one foreign language, thesis; for doctorate, one foreign language, comprehensive exam, thesis/dissertation. *Entrance requirements:* Additional exam requirements/recommendations for international students: Required—TOEFL (minimum score 600 paper-based), TWE. Electronic applications accepted. *Faculty research:* Canadian social history, Canadian gender history, Canadian native history, Canadian military history, British Columbian history, Western history, medieval history, world history.

University of Virginia, College and Graduate School of Arts and Sciences, Corcoran Department of History, Charlottesville, VA 22903. Offers MA, PhD, JD/MA. *Faculty:* 35 full-time (9 women). *Students:* 65 full-time (30 women); includes 4 minority (1 Black or African American, non-Hispanic/Latino; 1 Asian, non-Hispanic/Latino; 2 Hispanic/Latino), 11 international. Average age 27. 180 applicants, 18% accepted, 17 enrolled. In 2017, 7 master's, 12 doctorates awarded. *Degree requirements:* For master's, one foreign language, essay; for doctorate, variable foreign language requirement, comprehensive exam, thesis/dissertation. *Entrance requirements:* For master's and doctorate, GRE General Test, 2 or more letters of recommendation. Additional exam requirements/recommendations for international students: Required—TOEFL (minimum score 600 paper-based; 90 iBT), IELTS (minimum score 7). *Application deadline:* For fall admission, 12/1 for domestic and international students. Applications are processed on a rolling basis. Application fee: $60. Electronic applications accepted. *Financial support:* Fellowships and teaching assistantships available. Financial award application deadline: 12/1; financial award applicants required to submit FAFSA. *Unit head:* Karen Parshall, Chair, 434-924-6397, Fax: 434-924-7891, E-mail: history@virginia.edu.
Website: http://history.as.virginia.edu/

History

University of Washington, Graduate School, College of Arts and Sciences, Department of History, Seattle, WA 98195. Offers MA, PhD. *Program availability:* Part-time. *Degree requirements:* For master's, one foreign language, comprehensive exam, thesis optional; for doctorate, one foreign language, comprehensive exam, thesis/dissertation. *Entrance requirements:* For master's and doctorate, GRE, minimum GPA of 3.0. Additional exam requirements/recommendations for international students: Required—TOEFL. Electronic applications accepted. *Faculty research:* United States, Asia, Europe, comparative history.

University of Waterloo, Graduate Studies, Faculty of Arts, Department of Classical Studies, Waterloo, ON N2L 3G1, Canada. Offers ancient Mediterranean cultures (MA). *Degree requirements:* For master's, one foreign language. *Faculty research:* Ancient history, philosophy, anthropology, religion, culture.

University of Waterloo, Graduate Studies, Faculty of Arts, Department of History, Waterloo, ON N2L 3G1, Canada. Offers MA, PhD. PhD offered jointly with University of Guelph and Wilfrid Laurier University. *Program availability:* Part-time, evening/weekend. *Degree requirements:* For master's, one foreign language, thesis optional; for doctorate, one foreign language, thesis/dissertation. *Entrance requirements:* For master's, honors degree, minimum B+ average, resume; for doctorate, master's degree, minimum A average, resume, writing sample. Additional exam requirements/recommendations for international students: Required—TOEFL, IELTS, PTE. Electronic applications accepted. *Faculty research:* Canadian, British, international, modern, European, and U.S. history; women's history; imperialism and slavery.

The University of West Alabama, School of Graduate Studies, College of Education, Program in Secondary Education, Livingston, AL 35470. Offers biology (MAT); English language arts (MAT); high school 6-12 (M Ed); history (MAT); mathematics (MAT); science (MAT); social science (MAT). *Program availability:* Part-time, evening/weekend, 100% online. *Faculty:* 21 full-time (7 women), 5 part-time/adjunct (1 woman). *Students:* 259 (183 women); includes 61 minority (51 Black or African American, non-Hispanic/Latino; 2 American Indian or Alaska Native, non-Hispanic/Latino; 3 Asian, non-Hispanic/Latino; 2 Hispanic/Latino; 3 Two or more races, non-Hispanic/Latino). Average age 32. 58 applicants, 93% accepted, 45 enrolled. In 2017, 80 master's awarded. *Degree requirements:* For master's, comprehensive exam, thesis optional. *Entrance requirements:* For master's, GRE, minimum GPA of 2.75, verification of background clearance/fingerprints, valid bachelor's-level Professional Educator Certificate in same teaching field. Additional exam requirements/recommendations for international students: Required—TOEFL (minimum score 500 paper-based; 61 iBT). *Application deadline:* Applications are processed on a rolling basis. Application fee: $40. Electronic applications accepted. *Expenses:* Tuition, state resident: part-time $371 per credit hour. Tuition, nonresident: part-time $742 per credit hour. *Required fees:* $130 per semester. *Financial support:* Teaching assistantships, Federal Work-Study, scholarships/grants, and unspecified assistantships available. Support available to part-time students. Financial award application deadline: 3/1; financial award applicants required to submit FAFSA. *Unit head:* Dr. Jodie Winship, Chair of Teaching and Learning, 205-652-5415, Fax: 205-652-3706, E-mail: jwinship@uwa.edu. *Application contact:* Dr. B. J. Kimbrough, Dean of Graduate Studies, 205-652-3647, Fax: 205-652-3670, E-mail: bkimbrough@uwa.edu.

The University of Western Ontario, Faculty of Graduate Studies, Social Sciences Division, Department of History, London, ON N6A 5B8, Canada. Offers MA, PhD. *Program availability:* Part-time. *Degree requirements:* For master's, one foreign language, thesis (for some programs); for doctorate, one foreign language, thesis/dissertation. *Entrance requirements:* For master's, minimum B+ average on last 10 senior courses; for doctorate, minimum A- average on MA or last year honors degree. Additional exam requirements/recommendations for international students: Required—TOEFL. *Faculty research:* Canadian, U.S., Britain, Modern Europe, British Empire and Commonwealth Latin America.

University of West Florida, College of Arts, Social Sciences, and Humanities, Department of History, Pensacola, FL 32514-5750. Offers early American studies (MA); public history (MA); traditional history (MA). *Program availability:* Part-time, evening/weekend. *Degree requirements:* For master's, thesis or alternative. *Entrance requirements:* For master's, GRE (minimum score: verbal 500, writing 3.5) or MAT (minimum score 415), minimum GPA of 3.0; minimum 15 hours of upper-level history courses; official transcripts; letter of intent; writing sample (undergraduate research paper preferred). Additional exam requirements/recommendations for international students: Required—TOEFL (minimum score 550 paper-based).

University of West Georgia, College of Arts and Humanities, Carrollton, GA 30118. Offers English (MA); history (MA); museum studies (Postbaccalaureate Certificate); music performance (M Mus); music teacher education (M Mus); public history (Postbaccalaureate Certificate). *Program availability:* Part-time, evening/weekend, 100% online, blended/hybrid learning. *Faculty:* 69 full-time (38 women). *Students:* 25 full-time (15 women), 51 part-time (34 women); includes 16 minority (7 Black or African American, non-Hispanic/Latino; 1 American Indian or Alaska Native, non-Hispanic/Latino; 2 Asian, non-Hispanic/Latino; 5 Hispanic/Latino; 1 Two or more races, non-Hispanic/Latino), 1 international. Average age 30. 23 applicants, 96% accepted, 16 enrolled. In 2017, 29 master's, 6 other advanced degrees awarded. *Entrance requirements:* Additional exam requirements/recommendations for international students: Required—TOEFL (minimum score 523 paper-based; 69 iBT); Recommended—IELTS (minimum score 6.5). *Application deadline:* For fall admission, 8/1 for domestic students, 6/1 for international students; for spring admission, 11/15 for domestic students, 10/15 for international students; for summer admission, 5/15 for domestic students, 3/30 for international students. Applications are processed on a rolling basis. Application fee: $40. Electronic applications accepted. Tuition and fees vary according to degree level and program. *Financial support:* Fellowships, research assistantships, teaching assistantships, career-related internships or fieldwork, Federal Work-Study, institutionally sponsored loans, scholarships/grants, and unspecified assistantships available. Support available to part-time students. Financial award application deadline: 4/1; financial award applicants required to submit FAFSA. *Unit head:* Dr. Pauline D. Gagnon, Dean of Arts and Humanities, 678-839-5450, Fax: 678-839-5451, E-mail: pgagnon@westga.edu. *Application contact:* Dr. Toby Ziglar, Assistant Dean of the Graduate School, 678-839-1394, Fax: 678-839-1395, E-mail: graduate@westga.edu. Website: http://www.westga.edu/coah

University of Windsor, Faculty of Graduate Studies, Faculty of Arts and Social Sciences, Department of History, Windsor, ON N9B 3P4, Canada. Offers MA. *Program availability:* Part-time. *Degree requirements:* For master's, thesis (for some programs). *Entrance requirements:* For master's, minimum B average. Additional exam requirements/recommendations for international students: Required—TOEFL (minimum score 600 paper-based). Electronic applications accepted. *Faculty research:* Gender history, social-history questions about class gender and national identity, divorce in France: 1792-1816, gender and sexuality in Western Europe during the high and later Middle Ages, U.S.-Canadian comparisons in women's history.

The University of Winnipeg, Graduate Studies, Department of History, Winnipeg, MB R3B 2E9, Canada. Offers MA. Program offered jointly with University of Manitoba. *Program availability:* Part-time, evening/weekend. *Degree requirements:* For master's, one foreign language, comprehensive exam or thesis. *Faculty research:* Canadian social history, European diplomacy, Indian history, colonial America, medieval history.

University of Wisconsin–Eau Claire, College of Arts and Sciences, Department of History, Eau Claire, WI 54702-4004. Offers public history (MA). *Program availability:* Part-time. *Degree requirements:* For master's, comprehensive exam, thesis optional, oral and written exams. *Entrance requirements:* For master's, minimum GPA of 3.15 during last 2 years, 3.3 in history, or 3.0 overall; research paper; bachelor's degree with minimum of 24 credits in history. Additional exam requirements/recommendations for international students: Required—TOEFL (minimum score 79 iBT).

University of Wisconsin–Madison, Graduate School, College of Letters and Science, Department of History, Madison, WI 53706-1380. Offers African history (MA, PhD); Central Asian history (MA, PhD); comparative world history (MA, PhD); East Asian history (MA, PhD); European history (MA, PhD); gender and women's history (MA, PhD); Latin American and Caribbean history (MA, PhD); Middle Eastern history (MA, PhD); South Asian history (MA, PhD); Southeast Asian history (MA, PhD); United States history (MA, PhD). Terminal master's awarded for partial completion of doctoral program. *Degree requirements:* For master's, thesis (for some programs); for doctorate, variable foreign language requirement, thesis/dissertation. *Entrance requirements:* For master's and doctorate, GRE General Test. Additional exam requirements/recommendations for international students: Required—Michigan English Language Assessment Battery or TOEFL. Electronic applications accepted. *Faculty research:* American, African, European, Asian, Latin American, and Middle Eastern history.

University of Wisconsin–Milwaukee, Graduate School, College of Letters and Science, Department of History, Milwaukee, WI 53201-0413. Offers MA, PhD. *Program availability:* Part-time. *Students:* 30 full-time (19 women), 33 part-time (10 women); includes 5 minority (1 Black or African American, non-Hispanic/Latino; 1 Asian, non-Hispanic/Latino; 3 Two or more races, non-Hispanic/Latino). Average age 31. 57 applicants, 60% accepted, 26 enrolled. In 2017, 11 master's, 2 doctorates awarded. *Degree requirements:* For master's, comprehensive exam, thesis or alternative; for doctorate, thesis/dissertation. *Entrance requirements:* For master's and doctorate, GRE General Test. Additional exam requirements/recommendations for international students: Required—TOEFL (minimum score 550 paper-based; 79 iBT), IELTS (minimum score 6.5). *Application deadline:* For fall admission, 1/1 priority date for domestic students; for spring admission, 9/1 for domestic students. Application fee: $56 ($96 for international students). Electronic applications accepted. *Financial support:* Teaching assistantships, career-related internships or fieldwork, and unspecified assistantships available. Support available to part-time students. Financial award application deadline: 4/15; financial award applicants required to submit FAFSA. *Unit head:* Merry Weisner-Hanks, Department Chair, 414-229-4529, E-mail: merryh@uwm.edu. *Application contact:* General Information Contact, 414-229-4982, Fax: 414-229-6967, E-mail: gradschool@uwm.edu. Website: http://www.uwm.edu/dept/history/

University of Wisconsin–Stevens Point, College of Letters and Science, Department of History, Stevens Point, WI 54481-3897. Offers MST. *Degree requirements:* For master's, thesis or alternative.

University of Wyoming, College of Arts and Sciences, Department of History, Laramie, WY 82071. Offers MA, MAT. *Program availability:* Part-time. *Degree requirements:* For master's, one foreign language, thesis (for some programs). *Entrance requirements:* For master's, GRE General Test, minimum GPA of 3.0, 12 semester hours of undergraduate course work in history. Additional exam requirements/recommendations for international students: Required—TOEFL. Electronic applications accepted. *Faculty research:* American West, Native American history, nineteenth and twentieth century U.S. history, European history, Asian studies.

Utah State University, School of Graduate Studies, College of Humanities and Social Sciences, Department of History, Logan, UT 84322. Offers MA, MS. *Program availability:* Part-time, evening/weekend. *Degree requirements:* For master's, one foreign language, thesis. *Entrance requirements:* For master's, GRE General Test, minimum GPA of 3.0. Additional exam requirements/recommendations for international students: Required—TOEFL. Electronic applications accepted. *Faculty research:* U.S. race and ethnicity, early modern and modern Europe, environmental history, Western regional history.

Vanderbilt University, Department of History, Nashville, TN 37240-1001. Offers MA, MAT, PhD. *Faculty:* 41 full-time (12 women). *Students:* 56 full-time (32 women), 1 (woman) part-time; includes 10 minority (2 Black or African American, non-Hispanic/Latino; 1 Asian, non-Hispanic/Latino; 4 Hispanic/Latino; 3 Two or more races, non-Hispanic/Latino), 12 international. Average age 30. 175 applicants, 11% accepted, 7 enrolled. In 2017, 10 master's, 7 doctorates awarded. Terminal master's awarded for partial completion of doctoral program. *Degree requirements:* For doctorate, one foreign language, comprehensive exam, thesis/dissertation, final and qualifying exams. *Entrance requirements:* For doctorate, GRE General Test, sample of written work (recommended). Additional exam requirements/recommendations for international students: Required—TOEFL (minimum score 570 paper-based; 88 iBT). *Application deadline:* For fall admission, 1/15 for domestic and international students. Application fee: $0. Electronic applications accepted. *Financial support:* Fellowships with full tuition reimbursements, teaching assistantships with full tuition reimbursements, Federal Work-Study, institutionally sponsored loans, scholarships/grants, and health care benefits available. Financial award application deadline: 1/15; financial award applicants required to submit CSS PROFILE or FAFSA. *Faculty research:* Southern American history, recent U.S. history, intellectual and cultural history, European history, Latin American history. *Unit head:* Dr. Joel Harrington, Chair, 615-322-2575, Fax: 615-343-6002, E-mail: joel.harrington@vanderbilt.edu. *Application contact:* Catherine Molineux, Director of Graduate Studies, 615-322-2575, Fax: 615-343-6002, E-mail: catherine.a.molineux@vanderbilt.edu. Website: http://www.vanderbilt.edu/historydept/graduate.html

Villanova University, Graduate School of Liberal Arts and Sciences, Department of History, Villanova, PA 19085-1699. Offers MA. *Program availability:* Part-time, evening/weekend. *Faculty:* 6. *Students:* 30 full-time (14 women), 13 part-time (2 women); includes 5 minority (1 Black or African American, non-Hispanic/Latino; 1 Asian, non-Hispanic/Latino; 2 Hispanic/Latino; 1 Two or more races, non-Hispanic/Latino), 2 international. Average age 27. 19 applicants, 100% accepted, 16 enrolled. In 2017, 24 master's awarded. *Degree requirements:* For master's, comprehensive exam, thesis optional. *Entrance requirements:* For master's, GRE General Test, minimum GPA of 3.0, 3 letters of recommendation, personal statement. Additional exam requirements/recommendations for international students: Required—TOEFL. *Application deadline:* For fall admission, 3/1 for domestic students, 5/1 priority date for international students; for spring admission, 11/15 for domestic students, 10/15 priority date for international students; for summer admission, 5/1 for domestic students. Applications are processed on a rolling basis. Application fee: $50. Electronic applications accepted. *Financial support:* Research assistantships, Federal Work-Study, scholarships/grants, and unspecified assistantships available. Financial award applicants required to submit FAFSA. *Unit head:* Dr. Judith Giesberg, Director, 610-519-4668. Website: http://www1.villanova.edu/villanova/artsci/history/academic-programs/graduate.html

Virginia Commonwealth University, Graduate School, College of Humanities and Sciences, Department of History, Richmond, VA 23284-9005. Offers MA. *Program availability:* Part-time. *Degree requirements:* For master's, thesis optional. *Entrance requirements:* For master's, GRE General Test, 30 undergraduate credits in history. Additional exam requirements/recommendations for international students: Required—TOEFL (minimum score 600 paper-based; 100 iBT); Recommended—IELTS (minimum score 6.5). Electronic applications accepted. *Faculty research:* United States history, history of the South, urban history, African American history, colonial American history, the Civil War, twentieth-century American history, European history, trans-Atlantic history.

Washington State University, College of Arts and Sciences, Department of History, Pullman, WA 99164. Offers MA, PhD. Program applications must be made through the Pullman campus. *Program availability:* Part-time. *Degree requirements:* For master's, comprehensive exam, thesis optional, oral exam; for doctorate, one foreign language, comprehensive exam, thesis/dissertation, oral and written exam. *Entrance requirements:* For master's and doctorate, GRE General Test, official transcripts from all universities attended; three letters of recommendation; statement of purpose; writing sample; Preferred Fields of Study form; Language Background form. Additional exam requirements/recommendations for international students: Required—TOEFL (minimum score 550 paper-based), IELTS. Electronic applications accepted. *Faculty research:* Public, world, environmental, women's and U.S. history.

Washington University in St. Louis, The Graduate School, Department of History, St. Louis, MO 63130-4899. Offers PhD. *Degree requirements:* For doctorate, 2 foreign languages, thesis/dissertation. *Entrance requirements:* For doctorate, GRE General Test. Additional exam requirements/recommendations for international students: Required—TOEFL. Electronic applications accepted. *Faculty research:* Seventeenth-through nineteenth-century America, twentieth-century America, African history, Central Europe, East Asian history, history of American political culture, international urban history, Middle East, Medieval and Early Modern Europe.

Wayland Baptist University, Graduate Programs, Programs in Behavioral and Social Sciences, Plainview, TX 79072-6998. Offers counseling (MA); criminal justice (MACJ); government administration (MPA); history (MA); homeland security (MPA); humanities (MAH); justice administration (MPA). *Program availability:* Part-time, evening/weekend, 100% online, blended/hybrid learning. *Faculty:* 19 full-time (5 women), 18 part-time/ adjunct (8 women). *Students:* 16 full-time (10 women), 322 part-time (183 women); includes 207 minority (82 Black or African American, non-Hispanic/Latino; 8 American Indian or Alaska Native, non-Hispanic/Latino; 8 Asian, non-Hispanic/Latino; 84 Hispanic/ Latino; 5 Native Hawaiian or other Pacific Islander, non-Hispanic/Latino; 20 Two or more races, non-Hispanic/Latino), 1 international. Average age 40. 56 applicants, 93% accepted, 39 enrolled. In 2017, 141 master's awarded. *Degree requirements:* For master's, comprehensive exam. *Entrance requirements:* For master's, GRE, MAT. Additional exam requirements/recommendations for international students: Required— TOEFL (minimum score 500 paper-based; 61 iBT). *Application deadline:* Applications are processed on a rolling basis. Application fee: $50. Electronic applications accepted. *Expenses: Tuition:* Full-time $11,250; part-time $625 per credit hour. *Required fees:* $1200. *Financial support:* Federal Work-Study, institutionally sponsored loans, and scholarships/grants available. Support available to part-time students. Financial award application deadline: 5/1; financial award applicants required to submit FAFSA. *Unit head:* Dr. Peter Bowen, Dean, 806-291-1179, Fax: 806-291-1972, E-mail: pbowen@wbu.edu. *Application contact:* Amanda Stanton, Graduate Studies, 806-291-3423, Fax: 806-291-1950, E-mail: stanton@wbu.edu.

Wayne State University, College of Liberal Arts and Sciences, Department of History, Detroit, MI 48202. Offers history (MA, PhD); public history (MA), including African American history and culture, cultural resource management, gender, sexuality, and women's studies, labor and urban history, museum studies, public policy; world history (Graduate Certificate); JD/MA; M Ed/MA; MLIS/MA. Doctoral program admits for fall only. *Program availability:* Evening/weekend. *Faculty:* 17. *Students:* 21 full-time (7 women), 20 part-time (7 women); includes 9 minority (5 Black or African American, non-Hispanic/Latino; 1 Hispanic/Latino; 3 Two or more races, non-Hispanic/Latino). Average age 40. 50 applicants, 16% accepted, 5 enrolled. In 2017, 11 master's, 2 doctorates awarded. *Degree requirements:* For master's, comprehensive exam, thesis (for some programs), final oral exam on thesis or essay and seminar; internship and project (for public history); for doctorate, variable foreign language requirement, comprehensive exam, thesis/dissertation, qualifying exam in 4 fields of history. *Entrance requirements:* For master's, GRE General Test, minimum undergraduate GPA of 3.25 in history, 3.0 overall; at least 18 credits in history and related subjects at the advanced undergraduate level; foreign language; letter of intent; research paper; at least two letters of recommendation from former instructors; for doctorate, GRE General Test, minimum GPA of 3.0, 3.25 in minimum of 18 semester credits in history and related subjects; letter of intent; research paper; at least three letters of recommendation from former professors; for Graduate Certificate, baccalaureate degree from accredited college or university; minimum GPA of 3.0, 3.25 in a minimum of eighteen semester credits in history and related subjects at the advanced undergraduate level. Additional exam requirements/recommendations for international students: Required—TOEFL (minimum score 550 paper-based; 79 iBT), TWE (minimum score 5.5), Michigan English Language Assessment Battery (minimum score 85); Recommended—IELTS (minimum score 6.5). *Application deadline:* For fall admission, 2/1 priority date for domestic and international students; for winter admission, 11/1 for domestic students, 10/1 priority date for international students; for spring admission, 2/1 for domestic students, 1/1 priority date for international students. Application fee: $50. Electronic applications accepted. *Expenses:* Tuition, state resident: full-time $10,224; part-time $638.98 per credit hour. Tuition, nonresident: full-time $22,145; part-time $1384.04 per credit hour. Tuition and fees vary according to course load and program. *Financial support:* In 2017–18, 17 students received support, including 3 fellowships with tuition reimbursements available (averaging $17,198 per year), 1 research assistantship with tuition reimbursement available (averaging $22,241 per year), 6 teaching assistantships with tuition reimbursements available (averaging $18,534 per year); scholarships/grants, health care benefits, and unspecified assistantships also available. Financial award applicants required to submit FAFSA. *Faculty research:* Urban history, labor, political history, history of gender and women. *Unit head:* Dr. Elizabeth V. Faue, Professor/Chair, 313-577-2525, E-mail: evfaue@wayne.edu. *Application contact:* Dr. Eric Ash, Associate Professor and Director of Graduate Studies, 313-577-2525, E-mail: ericash@wayne.edu.
Website: http://clas.wayne.edu/history/

West Chester University of Pennsylvania, College of Arts and Humanities, Department of History, West Chester, PA 19383. Offers history (M Ed, MA). *Program availability:* Part-time, evening/weekend. *Students:* 3 full-time (0 women), 15 part-time (8 women); includes 2 minority (1 Hispanic/Latino; 1 Two or more races, non-Hispanic/ Latino). Average age 28. 22 applicants, 77% accepted, 9 enrolled. In 2017, 7 master's awarded. *Degree requirements:* For master's, comprehensive exam, thesis optional. *Entrance requirements:* For master's, statement of professional goals, writing sample, minimum GPA of 3.0 in history, two letters of recommendation. Additional exam requirements/recommendations for international students: Required—TOEFL or IELTS.

Application deadline: For fall admission, 5/15 for international students; for spring admission, 10/15 for international students. Applications are processed on a rolling basis. Application fee: $50. Electronic applications accepted. *Expenses:* Tuition, state resident: full-time $9000; part-time $500 per credit. Tuition, nonresident: full-time $13,500; part-time $750 per credit. *Required fees:* $2959; $149.79 per credit. *Financial support:* Scholarships/grants and unspecified assistantships available. Financial award application deadline: 2/15; financial award applicants required to submit FAFSA. *Unit head:* Dr. Robert Kodosky, Chair, 610-436-2201, E-mail: rkodosky@wcupa.edu. *Application contact:* Dr. Brenda L. Gaydosh, Graduate Coordinator, 610-436-0734, E-mail: bgaydosh@wcupa.edu.
Website: http://www.wcupa.edu/arts-humanities/history/

Western Carolina University, Graduate School, College of Arts and Sciences, Department of History, Cullowhee, NC 28723. Offers MA. *Program availability:* Part-time, evening/weekend. *Students:* 16. *Degree requirements:* For master's, comprehensive exam, thesis or alternative. *Entrance requirements:* For master's, GRE General Test, appropriate undergraduate degree, 3 letters of recommendation, statement of purpose. Additional exam requirements/recommendations for international students: Required—TOEFL (minimum score 550 paper-based; 79 iBT) or IELTS (6.5). *Application deadline:* For fall admission, 4/15 priority date for domestic and international students; for spring admission, 10/15 priority date for domestic and international students. Applications are processed on a rolling basis. Application fee: $65. *Expenses:* $10,000 per year, in-state full-time; $20,308 per year out-of-state full-time. *Financial support:* In 2017–18, 5 research assistantships with full and partial tuition reimbursements (averaging $9,000 per year), 5 teaching assistantships with full and partial tuition reimbursements (averaging $9,000 per year) were awarded; career-related internships or fieldwork, institutionally sponsored loans, scholarships/grants, and unspecified assistantships also available. Financial award application deadline: 4/15; financial award applicants required to submit FAFSA. *Faculty research:* Social and economic history of the American South, Islamic world history, German history, social and political protest, medieval social history. *Unit head:* Dr. Mary Ella Engel, Department Head, E-mail: mengel@email.wcu.edu. *Application contact:* Bobbi Smith, Graduate Admissions Coordinator, E-mail: bobbismith@email.wcu.edu.
Website: http://www.wcu.edu/as/history/

Western Connecticut State University, Division of Graduate Studies, Maricostas School of Arts and Sciences, Department of History and Non-Western Cultures, Danbury, CT 06810-6885. Offers MA. *Program availability:* Part-time. *Degree requirements:* For master's, thesis or research project, completion of program in 6 years. *Entrance requirements:* For master's, minimum GPA of 2.5. Additional exam requirements/recommendations for international students: Recommended—TOEFL (minimum score 550 paper-based; 79 iBT), IELTS (minimum score 6). *Expenses:* Tuition, state resident: full-time $6757; part-time $374 per credit hour. Tuition, nonresident: full-time $18,102; part-time $374 per credit hour. *Required fees:* $4994; $190 per credit hour. $60 per term. Tuition and fees vary according to degree level and program. *Faculty research:* History of jazz, music and leisure, African-American musicians.

Western Illinois University, School of Graduate Studies, College of Arts and Sciences, Department of History, Macomb, IL 61455-1390. Offers MA. *Program availability:* Part-time. *Students:* 11 full-time (2 women), 5 part-time (3 women); includes 3 minority (2 Black or African American, non-Hispanic/Latino; 1 American Indian or Alaska Native, non-Hispanic/Latino). Average age 30. 11 applicants, 100% accepted, 7 enrolled. In 2017, 12 master's awarded. *Degree requirements:* For master's, thesis or alternative. *Entrance requirements:* Additional exam requirements/recommendations for international students: Required—TOEFL (minimum score 550 paper-based; 80 iBT). *Application deadline:* Applications are processed on a rolling basis. Application fee: $30. Electronic applications accepted. *Financial support:* In 2017–18, 9 students received support. Unspecified assistantships available. Financial award applicants required to submit FAFSA. *Unit head:* Dr. Jennifer McNabb, Chairperson, 309-298-1053. *Application contact:* Dr. Nancy Parsons, Associate Provost and Director of Graduate Studies, 309-298-1806, Fax: 309-298-2345, E-mail: grad-office@wiu.edu.
Website: http://wiu.edu/history

Western Kentucky University, Graduate Studies, Potter College of Arts and Letters, Department of History, Bowling Green, KY 42101. Offers MA, MA Ed. *Program availability:* Part-time, evening/weekend, online learning. *Degree requirements:* For master's, comprehensive exam, thesis optional, final exam. *Entrance requirements:* For master's, GRE General Test, minimum GPA of 2.75. Additional exam requirements/ recommendations for international students: Required—TOEFL (minimum score 555 paper-based; 79 iBT). *Faculty research:* United States, Europe, China, India, Latin America.

Western Michigan University, Graduate College, College of Arts and Sciences, Department of History, Kalamazoo, MI 49008. Offers MA, PhD. *Degree requirements:* For master's, thesis optional; for doctorate, thesis/dissertation.

Western Washington University, Graduate School, College of Humanities and Social Sciences, Department of History, Bellingham, WA 98225-5996. Offers MA. *Program availability:* Part-time. *Degree requirements:* For master's, one foreign language, comprehensive exam, thesis (for some programs). *Entrance requirements:* For master's, GRE General Test, minimum GPA of 3.0 in last 60 semester hours or last 90 quarter hours. Additional exam requirements/recommendations for international students: Required—TOEFL (minimum score 567 paper-based). Electronic applications accepted.

West Texas A&M University, College of Fine Arts and Humanities, Department of History, Canyon, TX 79015. Offers MA. *Program availability:* Part-time, evening/ weekend. *Degree requirements:* For master's, comprehensive exam, thesis optional. *Entrance requirements:* For master's, GRE General Test. Additional exam requirements/ recommendations for international students: Required—TOEFL (minimum score 550 paper-based). Electronic applications accepted. *Faculty research:* Latin America, Middle and Far East, Southern Asia, Western Europe, United States.

West Virginia University, Eberly College of Arts and Sciences, Morgantown, WV 26506. Offers biology (MS, PhD); chemistry (MS, PhD); communication studies (MA, PhD); computational statistics (PhD); creative writing (MFA); English (MA, PhD); forensic and investigative science (MS); forensic science (PhD); geography (MA); geology (MA, PhD); history (MA, PhD); legal studies (MLS); math (MS); physics (MS, PhD); political science (MA, PhD); professional writing and editing (MA); psychology (MA); public administration (MPA); social work (MSW); sociology (MA, PhD); statistics (MS). *Program availability:* Part-time, evening/weekend, online learning. *Students:* 831 full-time (437 women), 236 part-time (142 women); includes 112 minority (35 Black or African American, non-Hispanic/Latino; 15 Asian, non-Hispanic/Latino; 29 Hispanic/ Latino; 33 Two or more races, non-Hispanic/Latino), 235 international. Terminal master's awarded for partial completion of doctoral program. *Degree requirements:* For master's, thesis (for some programs); for doctorate, comprehensive exam, thesis/ dissertation. *Entrance requirements:* For master's and doctorate, GRE. Additional exam requirements/recommendations for international students: Required—TOEFL (minimum score 600 paper-based); Recommended—TWE. *Application deadline:* For spring admission, 2/15 priority date for domestic and international students. Applications are

processed on a rolling basis. Application fee: $45. Electronic applications accepted. *Expenses:* Tuition, state resident: full-time $9450. Tuition, nonresident: full-time $24,390. *Financial support:* Fellowships with full tuition reimbursements, research assistantships with full tuition reimbursements, teaching assistantships with full tuition reimbursements, career-related internships or fieldwork, Federal Work-Study, institutionally sponsored loans, scholarships/grants, health care benefits, tuition waivers (full and partial), unspecified assistantships, and administrative assistantships available. Financial award application deadline: 2/1; financial award applicants required to submit FAFSA. *Faculty research:* Humanities, social sciences, life science, physical sciences, mathematics. *Unit head:* Dr. Mary Ellen Mazey, Dean, 304-293-4611, Fax: 304-293-6858, E-mail: mary.mazey@mail.wvu.edu. *Application contact:* Dr. Fred L. King, Associate Dean for Graduate Studies, 304-293-4611 Ext. 5205, Fax: 304-293-6858, E-mail: fred.king@mail.wvu.edu.
Website: http://www.as.wvu.edu/

Wichita State University, Graduate School, Fairmount College of Liberal Arts and Sciences, Department of History, Wichita, KS 67260. Offers MA. *Program availability:* Part-time. *Unit head:* Dr. Jay Price, Chair, 316-978-3150, Fax: 316-978-3473, E-mail: jay.price@wichita.edu. *Application contact:* Jordan Oleson, Admissions Coordinator, 316-978-3150, Fax: 316-978-3473, E-mail: jordan.oleson@wichita.edu.
Website: http://www.wichita.edu/history

Wilfrid Laurier University, Faculty of Graduate and Postdoctoral Studies, Faculty of Arts, Department of History, Waterloo, ON N2L 3C5, Canada. Offers MA, PhD. *Program availability:* Part-time. *Degree requirements:* For master's, thesis optional; for doctorate, thesis/dissertation. *Entrance requirements:* For master's, honors BA or the equivalent in history; minimum B+ average in undergraduate course work, exclusive of first year level courses; for doctorate, MA in history, minimum A- average. Additional exam requirements/recommendations for international students: Required—TOEFL (minimum score 89 iBT). Electronic applications accepted. *Faculty research:* Canadian, early modern European, modern European, Scottish, race, class, imperialism, slavery, British, urban and rural, science/medicine/technology, gender/women's/family, international, United States.

William Paterson University of New Jersey, College of Humanities and Social Sciences, Wayne, NJ 07470-8420. Offers applied sociology (MA); assessment and evaluation research (Certificate); bilingual education (Certificate); clinical and counseling psychology (MA); clinical psychology (Psy D); creative and professional writing (MFA); English (MA); history (MA); public policy and international affairs (MA); teaching English as a second language (Certificate). *Program availability:* Part-time. *Faculty:* 36 full-time (21 women), 10 part-time/adjunct (5 women). *Students:* 62 full-time (44 women), 102 part-time (71 women); includes 76 minority (12 Black or African American, non-Hispanic/Latino; 8 Asian, non-Hispanic/Latino; 50 Hispanic/Latino; 6 Two or more races, non-Hispanic/Latino), 6 international. Average age 33. 156 applicants, 51% accepted, 52 enrolled. In 2017, 39 master's awarded. *Degree requirements:* For master's, thesis (for some programs), internship (for some programs). *Entrance requirements:* For master's, GRE/MAT, minimum GPA of 3.0; 2 letters of recommendation; writing sample/personal statement. Additional exam requirements/recommendations for international students: Required—TOEFL (minimum score 550 paper-based; 79 iBT), IELTS (minimum score 6). *Application deadline:* For fall admission, 6/1 for domestic students, 3/1 for international students; for spring admission, 11/1 for domestic students, 10/1 for international students. Applications are processed on a rolling basis. Application fee: $50. Electronic applications accepted. *Expenses:* Tuition, state resident: full-time $13,920; part-time $6264 per year. Tuition, nonresident: full-time $21,700; part-time $9765 per year. *Required fees:* $80; $36 per year. Tuition and fees vary according to course load, degree level and program. *Financial support:* In 2017–18, 3,480 students received support. Career-related internships or fieldwork, Federal Work-Study, scholarships/grants, and unspecified assistantships available. Support available to part-time students. Financial award application deadline: 3/15; financial award applicants required to submit FAFSA. *Faculty research:* Relationship violence, work-family balance, social development of Japan, theories justifying war, reactions to trauma. *Total annual research expenditures:* $32,300. *Unit head:* Dr. Kara Rabbitt, Dean, 973-720-2180, Fax: 973-720-2955, E-mail: rabbittk@wpunj.edu. *Application contact:* Tinu Adeniran, Associate Director, Graduate Admissions, 973-720-2764, Fax: 973-720-2035, E-mail: adenirant@wpunj.edu.
Website: http://www.wpunj.edu/cohss

Winthrop University, College of Arts and Sciences, Department of History, Rock Hill, SC 29733. Offers MA. *Program availability:* Part-time. *Students:* 5 full-time (2 women), 12 part-time (4 women); includes 5 minority (3 Black or African American, non-Hispanic/Latino; 1 Hispanic/Latino; 1 Two or more races, non-Hispanic/Latino). Average age 35. In 2017, 7 master's awarded. *Degree requirements:* For master's, one foreign language. *Entrance requirements:* For master's, GRE General Test or PRAXIS, 24 hours of history at the undergraduate level. Additional exam requirements/recommendations for international students: Required—TOEFL (minimum score 550 paper-based; 79 iBT), IELTS (minimum score 6). *Application deadline:* For fall admission, 7/15 priority date for domestic students; for spring admission, 12/1 for domestic students. Applications are processed on a rolling basis. Application fee: $50. Electronic applications accepted. *Financial support:* In 2017–18, 1 research assistantship with full tuition reimbursement (averaging $3,600 per year) was awarded; Federal Work-Study, scholarships/grants, and unspecified assistantships also available. Support available to part-time students. Financial award application deadline: 2/1; financial award applicants required to submit FAFSA. *Unit head:* Dr. Gregory Crider, Department Chair, 803-323-4816, E-mail: criderg@winthrop.edu. *Application contact:* 800-411-7041, Fax: 580-323-2292, E-mail: graduatestu@winthrop.edu.
Website: https://www.winthrop.edu/history/

Worcester State University, Graduate School, Program in History, Worcester, MA 01602-2597. Offers MA. *Program availability:* Part-time. *Faculty:* 12 full-time, 2 part-time/adjunct. *Students:* 7 full-time (3 women), 13 part-time (9 women); includes 2 minority (1 Black or African American, non-Hispanic/Latino; 1 American Indian or Alaska Native, non-Hispanic/Latino). Average age 39. 17 applicants, 94% accepted, 6 enrolled. In 2017, 12 master's awarded. *Degree requirements:* For master's, comprehensive exam (for some programs), thesis (for some programs), portfolio. *Entrance requirements:* For master's, GRE General Test or MAT, 18 undergraduate credits in history, including U.S. history and Western civilizations. Additional exam requirements/recommendations for international students: Required—TOEFL (minimum score 550 paper-based; 79 iBT). *Application deadline:* For fall admission, 6/15 for domestic and international students; for spring admission, 11/1 for domestic and international students; for summer admission, 4/1 for domestic and international students. Applications are processed on a rolling basis. Application fee: $50. Electronic applications accepted. *Expenses:* Tuition, state resident: full-time $3042; part-time $169 per credit hour. Tuition, nonresident: full-time $3042; part-time $169 per credit hour. *Required fees:* $2754; $153 per credit hour. *Financial support:* Career-related internships or fieldwork, scholarships/grants, and unspecified assistantships available. Financial award application deadline: 3/1; financial award applicants required to submit FAFSA. *Unit head:* Dr. Erika Briesacher, Coordinator, 508-929-8692, E-mail: ebriesacher@worcester.edu. *Application contact:* Sara Grady, Associate Dean, Graduate Studies and Professional Development, 508-929-8130, Fax: 508-929-8100, E-mail: sara.grady@worcester.edu.

Wright State University, Graduate School, College of Liberal Arts, Department of History, Dayton, OH 45435. Offers MA. *Degree requirements:* For master's, thesis optional. *Entrance requirements:* For master's, GRE General Test, minimum GPA of 3.0 in history, 2.7 overall. Additional exam requirements/recommendations for international students: Required—TOEFL. *Faculty research:* U.S. religions; women's, Southern, European, and archival history.

Yale University, Graduate School of Arts and Sciences, Department of History, New Haven, CT 06520. Offers history (M Phil, MA, PhD); history of science and medicine (MA, PhD). Terminal master's awarded for partial completion of doctoral program. *Degree requirements:* For master's, one foreign language; for doctorate, 2 foreign languages, thesis/dissertation. *Entrance requirements:* For doctorate, GRE General Test.

York University, Faculty of Graduate Studies, Faculty of Liberal Arts and Professional Studies, Program in History, Toronto, ON M3J 1P3, Canada. Offers MA, PhD. *Program availability:* Part-time. *Degree requirements:* For master's, thesis or alternative; for doctorate, one foreign language, comprehensive exam, thesis/dissertation, qualifying exam. Electronic applications accepted.

Youngstown State University, Graduate School, College of Liberal Arts and Social Sciences, Department of History, Youngstown, OH 44555-0001. Offers MA. *Program availability:* Part-time. *Degree requirements:* For master's, thesis optional, oral and written exams. *Entrance requirements:* For master's, minimum GPA of 2.75. Additional exam requirements/recommendations for international students: Required—TOEFL. *Faculty research:* Holocaust, Marxism, nineteenth- and twentieth-century United States, historic preservation, revolutionary France.

History of Medicine

The College at Brockport, State University of New York, School of Education, Health, and Human Services, Department of Education and Human Development, Brockport, NY 14420-2997. Offers adolescence education (MS Ed), including adolescence biology education, adolescence chemistry education, adolescence English, adolescence mathematics, adolescence physics education, adolescence social studies education; bilingual education (MS Ed, AGC); childhood curriculum specialist (MS Ed); inclusive generalist education (MS Ed, AGC, Advanced Certificate), including biology (MS Ed, AGC), chemistry (MS Ed), English (MS Ed, Advanced Certificate), mathematics (MS Ed, Advanced Certificate), science (MS Ed, Advanced Certificate), social studies (MS Ed, Advanced Certificate); literacy education B-12 (MS Ed). *Accreditation:* NCATE. *Faculty:* 14 full-time (9 women), 12 part-time/adjunct (11 women). *Students:* 57 full-time (26 women), 168 part-time (130 women); includes 8 minority (3 Black or African American, non-Hispanic/Latino; 1 American Indian or Alaska Native, non-Hispanic/Latino; 1 Asian, non-Hispanic/Latino; 3 Hispanic/Latino). 107 applicants, 83% accepted, 63 enrolled. In 2017, 88 master's awarded. *Degree requirements:* For master's, thesis or alternative. *Entrance requirements:* For master's, minimum GPA of 3.0, letters of recommendation, interview (for some programs); statement of objectives, current resume. Additional exam requirements/recommendations for international students: Required—TOEFL (minimum score 550 paper-based; 79 iBT), IELTS (minimum score 6.5). *Application deadline:* For fall admission, 3/15 priority date for domestic and international students; for spring admission, 10/15 priority date for domestic and international students; for summer admission, 3/15 priority date for domestic and international students. Application fee: $80. Electronic applications accepted. *Expenses:* Tuition, state resident: full-time $10,870; part-time $453 per credit hour. Tuition, nonresident: full-time $22,210. *Required fees:* $988; $246 per semester. *Financial support:* In 2017–18, 1 fellowship with full tuition reimbursement (averaging $7,500 per year), 1 teaching assistantship with full tuition reimbursement (averaging $6,000 per year) were awarded; Federal Work-Study, scholarships/grants, and unspecified assistantships also available. Support available to part-time students. Financial award application deadline: 3/15; financial award applicants required to submit FAFSA. *Faculty research:* Educational assessment, literacy education, inclusive education, teacher preparation, qualitative methodology. *Unit head:* Dr. Sue Robb, Chairperson, 585-395-5550, Fax: 585-395-2172, E-mail: srobb@brockport.edu. *Application contact:* Anne Walton, Coordinator of Certification and Graduate Advisement, 585-395-2326, Fax: 585-395-2172, E-mail: awalton@brockport.edu.
Website: https://www.brockport.edu/academics/education_human_development/department.html

McGill University, Faculty of Graduate and Postdoctoral Studies, Faculty of Arts, Department of History and Classical Studies, Montréal, QC H3A 2T5, Canada. Offers history (MA, PhD); history of medicine (MA).

McGill University, Faculty of Graduate and Postdoctoral Studies, Faculty of Medicine, Department of Social Studies in Medicine, Montréal, QC H3A 2T5, Canada. Offers medical anthropology (MA, PhD); medical history (MA, PhD); medical sociology (MA, PhD).

Rutgers University–New Brunswick, Graduate School-New Brunswick, Program in History, Piscataway, NJ 08854-8097. Offers African-American history (PhD); early American history (PhD); early modern European history (PhD); east Asian history (PhD); global and comparative history (PhD); history (PhD); history of diplomacy and foreign relations (PhD); history of technology, environment and health (PhD); history of the Atlantic cultures and African diaspora (PhD); Latin American history (PhD); medieval history (PhD); modern European history (PhD); nineteenth and twentieth century American history (PhD); women's and gender history (PhD). *Degree requirements:* For doctorate, thesis/dissertation. *Entrance requirements:* For doctorate, GRE General Test, sample of written work. Electronic applications accepted. *Faculty research:* American history, European history, Afro-American history, women's history, Latin American history.

The University of Manchester, Faculty of Life Sciences, Manchester, United Kingdom. Offers adaptive organismal biology (M Phil, PhD); animal biology (M Phil, PhD); biochemistry (M Phil, PhD); bioinformatics (M Phil, PhD); biomolecular sciences (M Phil, PhD); biotechnology (M Phil, PhD); cell biology (M Phil, PhD); cell matrix research (M Phil, PhD); channels and transporters (M Phil, PhD); developmental biology (M Phil, PhD); Egyptology (M Phil, PhD); environmental biology (M Phil, PhD); evolutionary biology (M Phil, PhD); gene expression (M Phil, PhD); genetics (M Phil, PhD); history of science, technology and medicine (M Phil, PhD); immunology (M Phil, PhD); integrative neurobiology and behavior (M Phil, PhD); membrane trafficking (M Phil, PhD); microbiology (M Phil, PhD); molecular and cellular neuroscience (M Phil, PhD); molecular biology (M Phil, PhD); molecular cancer studies (M Phil, PhD); neuroscience (M Phil, PhD); ophthalmology (M Phil, PhD); optometry (M Phil, PhD); organelle function (M Phil, PhD); pharmacology (M Phil, PhD); physiology (M Phil, PhD); plant sciences (M Phil, PhD); stem cell research (M Phil, PhD); structural biology (M Phil, PhD); systems neuroscience (M Phil, PhD); toxicology (M Phil, PhD).

University of Minnesota, Twin Cities Campus, Graduate School, Program in the History of Science, Technology and Medicine, Minneapolis, MN 55455-0213. Offers MA, PhD. *Program availability:* Part-time. *Degree requirements:* For master's, one foreign language, thesis or alternative; for doctorate, 2 foreign languages, thesis/dissertation. *Entrance requirements:* For master's and doctorate, GRE General Test. *Faculty research:* History of infectious diseases, history of public health, history of evolutionary biology, history of infertility, women in science.

Yale University, Graduate School of Arts and Sciences, Department of History, Program in the History of Science and Medicine, New Haven, CT 06520. Offers MS, PhD. *Degree requirements:* For doctorate, 2 foreign languages, thesis/dissertation. *Entrance requirements:* For doctorate, GRE General Test.

History of Science and Technology

Arizona State University at the Tempe campus, College of Liberal Arts and Sciences, School of Life Sciences, Tempe, AZ 85287-4601. Offers animal behavior (PhD); applied ethics (biomedical and health ethics) (MA); biology (MS, PhD), including biology, biology and society, complex adaptive systems science (PhD), plant biology and conservation (MS); environmental life sciences (PhD); evolutionary biology (PhD); history and philosophy of science (PhD); human and social dimensions of science and technology (PhD); microbiology (PhD); molecular and cellular biology (PhD); neuroscience (PhD). Terminal master's awarded for partial completion of doctoral program. *Degree requirements:* For master's, thesis (for some programs), interactive Program of Study (iPOS) submitted before completing 50 percent of required credit hours; for doctorate, variable foreign language requirement, comprehensive exam, thesis/dissertation, interactive Program of Study (iPOS) submitted before completing 50 percent of required credit hours. *Entrance requirements:* For master's and doctorate, GRE, minimum GPA of 3.0 or equivalent in last 2 years of work leading to bachelor's degree. Additional exam requirements/recommendations for international students: Required—TOEFL (minimum score 600 paper-based; 100 iBT). Electronic applications accepted.

Arizona State University at the Tempe campus, Graduate College, Program in Human and Social Dimensions of Science and Technology, Tempe, AZ 85287-5603. Offers PhD. *Degree requirements:* For doctorate, comprehensive exam, thesis/dissertation, interactive Program of Study (iPOS) submitted before completing 50 percent of required credit hours. *Entrance requirements:* For doctorate, GRE, minimum GPA of 3.0 in the last 2 years of work leading to the bachelor's degree, 3 letters of recommendation, statement of research interests and goals, curriculum vitae or resume, completed academic record form, 10-25 page writing sample. Additional exam requirements/recommendations for international students: Required—TOEFL (minimum score 550 paper-based; 80 iBT), IELTS (minimum score 6.5). Electronic applications accepted.

Brown University, Graduate School, Department of Egyptology and Assyriology, Providence, RI 02912. Offers ancient western Asian studies (PhD); Egyptology (PhD); history of the exact sciences in antiquity (PhD). *Degree requirements:* For doctorate, 2 foreign languages, comprehensive exam, thesis/dissertation. *Entrance requirements:* For doctorate, GRE General Test.

Carnegie Mellon University, Dietrich College of Humanities and Social Sciences, Department of History, Pittsburgh, PA 15213-3891. Offers African and African-American diaspora (PhD); culture and power (PhD); labor, politics and social movements (PhD); technology, environment, science and health (PhD); women, gender and the family (PhD). *Program availability:* Part-time. *Degree requirements:* For doctorate, oral and written comprehensive exams, dissertation defense. *Entrance requirements:* For doctorate, GRE General Test. Additional exam requirements/recommendations for international students: Required—TOEFL. Electronic applications accepted. *Faculty research:* Anthropology and history, African-American history, technology/environment, cultural history analysis.

Cornell University, Graduate School, Graduate Fields of Arts and Sciences, Field of History, Ithaca, NY 14853. Offers African history (MA, PhD); American history (MA, PhD); ancient Greek history (PhD); ancient history (MA, PhD); ancient Roman history (PhD); early modern European history (MA, PhD); English history (MA, PhD); French history (MA, PhD); German history (MA, PhD); history of science (MA, PhD); Korean history (PhD); Latin American history (MA, PhD); medieval Chinese history (MA, PhD); medieval history (MA, PhD); modern Chinese history (MA, PhD); modern European history (MA, PhD); modern Japanese history (MA, PhD); modern Middle Eastern history (PhD); premodern Islamic history (MA, PhD); premodern Japanese history (MA, PhD); Renaissance history (MA, PhD); Russian history (MA, PhD); South Asian history (PhD); Southeast Asian history (MA, PhD). Terminal master's awarded for partial completion of doctoral program. *Degree requirements:* For master's, thesis; for doctorate, 2 foreign languages, comprehensive exam, thesis/dissertation, 1 year of teaching experience. *Entrance requirements:* For master's and doctorate, GRE General Test, writing sample, 3 letters of recommendation. Additional exam requirements/recommendations for international students: Required—TOEFL (minimum score 550 paper-based; 77 iBT). Electronic applications accepted.

Cornell University, Graduate School, Graduate Fields of Arts and Sciences, Field of Science and Technology Studies, Ithaca, NY 14853. Offers history and philosophy of science and technology (MA, PhD); social studies of science and technology (MA, PhD). Terminal master's awarded for partial completion of doctoral program. *Degree requirements:* For master's, one foreign language, thesis; for doctorate, one foreign language, comprehensive exam, thesis/dissertation. *Entrance requirements:* For master's and doctorate, GRE General Test, writing sample, 3 letters of recommendation. Additional exam requirements/recommendations for international students: Required—TOEFL (minimum score 550 paper-based; 77 iBT). Electronic applications accepted. *Faculty research:* History, philosophy, sociology, politics, and policy of science and technology; gender, legal order, environment, and communication.

Drexel University, College of Arts and Sciences, Department of History and Politics, Philadelphia, PA 19104-2875. Offers science, technology and society (MS). *Program availability:* Part-time. *Entrance requirements:* For master's, GRE. Additional exam requirements/recommendations for international students: Required—TOEFL. Electronic applications accepted.

Georgia Institute of Technology, Graduate Studies, Ivan Allen College of Liberal Arts, School of History, Technology, and Society, Atlanta, GA 30332-0001. Offers history and sociology of technology and science (MS, PhD). *Program availability:* Part-time. Terminal master's awarded for partial completion of doctoral program. *Degree requirements:* For master's, research paper; for doctorate, one foreign language, comprehensive exam, thesis/dissertation. *Entrance requirements:* For master's and doctorate, GRE, college transcripts, three letters of recommendation, biographical statement. Additional exam requirements/recommendations for international students: Required—TOEFL (minimum score 550 paper-based; 79 iBT). Electronic applications accepted. *Faculty research:* Industrialization, labor history, modern Europe, social history, sociology of science.

Harvard University, Graduate School of Arts and Sciences, Department of the History of Science, Cambridge, MA 02138. Offers AM, PhD. Terminal master's awarded for partial completion of doctoral program. *Degree requirements:* For master's, one foreign language; for doctorate, 2 foreign languages, thesis/dissertation. *Entrance requirements:* For master's and doctorate, GRE General Test. Additional exam requirements/recommendations for international students: Required—TOEFL.

Indiana University Bloomington, University Graduate School, College of Arts and Sciences, Department of History and Philosophy of Science, Bloomington, IN 47405-7000. Offers MA, PhD, MLS/MA. *Program availability:* Part-time. Terminal master's awarded for partial completion of doctoral program. *Degree requirements:* For master's, one foreign language, thesis optional; for doctorate, 2 foreign languages, thesis/dissertation. *Entrance requirements:* For master's and doctorate, GRE General Test. Additional exam requirements/recommendations for international students: Required—TOEFL. Electronic applications accepted. *Faculty research:* History of scientific ideas, instruments, and institutions; foundations of physics; history of philosophy of science; history and philosophy of biology; early modern science and medicine.

Johns Hopkins University, Zanvyl Krieger School of Arts and Sciences, Department of the History of Science and Technology, Baltimore, MD 21218. Offers MA, PhD. *Faculty:* 7 full-time (3 women), 1 part-time/adjunct (0 women). *Students:* 9 full-time (3 women), 3 international. Average age 29. 14 applicants, 36% accepted, 4 enrolled. In 2017, 1 master's, 1 doctorate awarded. Terminal master's awarded for partial completion of doctoral program. *Degree requirements:* For master's, one foreign language, thesis; for doctorate, 2 foreign languages, thesis/dissertation. *Entrance requirements:* For doctorate, GRE General Test. Additional exam requirements/recommendations for international students: Required—TOEFL (minimum score 600 paper-based; 100 iBT), IELTS. *Application deadline:* For fall admission, 1/15 for domestic and international students. Application fee: $75. Electronic applications accepted. *Financial support:* In 2017–18, 9 students received support, including 4 fellowships with full tuition reimbursements available (averaging $28,375 per year), 5 teaching assistantships with full tuition reimbursements available (averaging $26,800 per year); career-related internships or fieldwork and health care benefits also available. Financial award application deadline: 1/15. *Faculty research:* History of physical and biological sciences, history of technology, history of medicine (sixteenth-twentieth centuries), environmental science (nineteenth-twentieth century). *Unit head:* Dr. Maria Portuondo, Chair, 410-516-7503, Fax: 410-516-7502, E-mail: mportuondo@jhu.edu. *Application contact:* Danielle Stout, Senior Administrative Coordinator, 410-516-7501, Fax: 410-516-7502, E-mail: danielle@jhu.edu.
Website: http://host.jhu.edu

Massachusetts Institute of Technology, School of Humanities, Arts, and Social Sciences, Program in Science, Technology, and Society, Cambridge, MA 02139. Offers history, anthropology, and science, technology and society (PhD). *Degree requirements:* For doctorate, one foreign language, comprehensive exam, thesis/dissertation. *Entrance requirements:* For doctorate, GRE General Test. Additional exam requirements/recommendations for international students: Required—TOEFL, IELTS. Electronic applications accepted. *Faculty research:* History of science; history of technology; sociology of science and technology; anthropology of science and technology; science, technology, and society.

Oregon State University, College of Liberal Arts, Program in History of Science, Corvallis, OR 97331. Offers development of the physical, biological, and environmental sciences (MA, MS, PhD). *Program availability:* Part-time. *Degree requirements:* For master's, variable foreign language requirement, thesis optional; for doctorate, one foreign language, thesis/dissertation. *Entrance requirements:* For master's and doctorate, GRE. Additional exam requirements/recommendations for international students: Required—TOEFL (minimum score 80 iBT), IELTS (minimum score 6.5). *Application deadline:* For fall admission, 1/1 for domestic and international students. Application fee: $75 ($85 for international students). *Financial support:* Application deadline: 1/1. *Unit head:* Dr. Jacob Hamblin, Director of Graduate Studies, 541-737-3503, E-mail: jacob.hamblin@oregonstate.edu. *Application contact:* Dr. Allen Thompson, Director of Graduate Studies/Associate Professor, 541-737-5654, E-mail: allen.thompson@oregonstate.edu.
Website: http://liberalarts.oregonstate.edu/history/graduate-history-of-science

Princeton University, Graduate School, Department of History, Program in History of Science, Princeton, NJ 08544-1019. Offers PhD. *Degree requirements:* For doctorate, 2 foreign languages, thesis/dissertation. *Entrance requirements:* For doctorate, GRE General Test, sample of written work, 3 letters of recommendation. Additional exam requirements/recommendations for international students: Required—TOEFL (minimum score 600 paper-based). Electronic applications accepted. *Faculty research:* Early modern science, history of modern life sciences, history of physical sciences, history of modern technology, science and medicine in European expansion and colonialism.

Rensselaer Polytechnic Institute, Graduate School, School of Humanities, Arts, and Social Sciences, Program in Science and Technology Studies, Troy, NY 12180-3590. Offers MS, PhD. *Faculty:* 15 full-time (5 women), 1 part-time/adjunct (0 women).

History of Science and Technology

Students: 17 full-time (8 women), 1 part-time (0 women); includes 2 minority (1 Asian, non-Hispanic/Latino; 1 Hispanic/Latino), 2 international. Average age 31. 14 applicants, 50% accepted, 2 enrolled. In 2017, 1 master's, 6 doctorates awarded. Terminal master's awarded for partial completion of doctoral program. *Degree requirements:* For master's, thesis (for some programs); for doctorate, comprehensive exam, thesis/dissertation. *Entrance requirements:* For master's and doctorate, GRE, writing sample. Additional exam requirements/recommendations for international students: Required—TOEFL (minimum score 600 paper-based; 100 iBT), IELTS (minimum score 7), PTE (minimum score 68). *Application deadline:* For fall admission, 1/1 priority date for domestic and international students; for spring admission, 8/15 priority date for domestic and international students. Applications are processed on a rolling basis. Application fee: $75. Electronic applications accepted. *Expenses: Tuition:* Full-time $52,550; part-time $2125 per credit hour. *Required fees:* $2890. *Financial support:* In 2017–18, research assistantships (averaging $23,000 per year), teaching assistantships (averaging $23,000 per year) were awarded; fellowships also available. Financial award application deadline: 1/1. *Faculty research:* Policy studies, science studies, technology studies. *Total annual research expenditures:* $30,324. *Unit head:* Dr. Atsushi Akera, Graduate Program Director, 518-276-2314, E-mail: akeraa@rpi.edu.
Website: http://www.sts.rpi.edu/pl/graduate-programs-sts

Rutgers University–New Brunswick, Graduate School-New Brunswick, Program in History, Piscataway, NJ 08854-8097. Offers African-American history (PhD); early American history (PhD); early modern European history (PhD); east Asian history (PhD); global and comparative history (PhD); history (PhD); history of diplomacy and foreign relations (PhD); history of technology, environment and health (PhD); history of the Atlantic cultures and African diaspora (PhD); Latin American history (PhD); medieval history (PhD); modern European history (PhD); nineteenth and twentieth century American history (PhD); women's and gender history (PhD). *Degree requirements:* For doctorate, thesis/dissertation. *Entrance requirements:* For doctorate, GRE General Test, sample of written work. Electronic applications accepted. *Faculty research:* American history, European history, Afro-American history, women's history, Latin American history.

University of California, Berkeley, Graduate Division, College of Letters and Science, Group in Logic and the Methodology of Science, Berkeley, CA 94720-1500. Offers PhD. *Degree requirements:* For doctorate, qualifying exam, oral defense of dissertation. *Entrance requirements:* For doctorate, GRE General Test, minimum GPA of 3.5, 3 letters of recommendation. Electronic applications accepted. *Faculty research:* Set theory, recursion theory, theoretical computer science, philosophy of mathematics, philosophy of language.

University of California, San Diego, Graduate Division, Program in Science Studies, La Jolla, CA 92093. Offers communication of science (PhD); history of science (PhD); philosophy of science (PhD); sociology of science (PhD). *Students:* 2 full-time (both women). In 2017, 1 doctorate awarded. *Degree requirements:* For doctorate, one foreign language, comprehensive exam, thesis/dissertation, internship. *Entrance requirements:* For doctorate, GRE General Test, 3 letters of recommendation. Additional exam requirements/recommendations for international students: Required—TOEFL (minimum score 550 paper-based; 80 iBT), IELTS (minimum score 7). Electronic applications accepted. *Financial support:* Fellowships, research assistantships, teaching assistantships, and scholarships/grants available. Financial award applicants required to submit FAFSA. *Unit head:* Cathy Gere, Director, 858-534-6051, E-mail: cgere@ucsd.edu. *Application contact:* Jennifer Dieli, Program Coordinator, 858-534-0491, E-mail: ssadmin@ucsd.edu.
Website: http://sciencestudies.ucsd.edu/

University of California, San Francisco, Graduate Division, Program in History of Health Sciences, San Francisco, CA 94143. Offers MA, PhD, MD/PhD. Program admits students biennially. Terminal master's awarded for partial completion of doctoral program. *Degree requirements:* For master's, 2 foreign languages, thesis; for doctorate, 2 foreign languages, thesis/dissertation. *Entrance requirements:* For master's and doctorate, GRE General Test.

University of Delaware, College of Arts and Sciences, Department of History, Hagley Program in the History of Technology and Industrialization, Newark, DE 19716. Offers MA, PhD. *Degree requirements:* For master's, thesis optional; for doctorate, comprehensive exam, thesis/dissertation. *Entrance requirements:* For master's and doctorate, interview. Electronic applications accepted.

The University of Manchester, Faculty of Life Sciences, Manchester, United Kingdom. Offers adaptive organismal biology (M Phil, PhD); animal biology (M Phil, PhD); biochemistry (M Phil, PhD); bioinformatics (M Phil, PhD); biomolecular sciences (M Phil, PhD); biotechnology (M Phil, PhD); cell biology (M Phil, PhD); cell matrix research (M Phil, PhD); channels and transporters (M Phil, PhD); developmental biology (M Phil, PhD); Egyptology (M Phil, PhD); environmental biology (M Phil, PhD); evolutionary biology (M Phil, PhD); gene expression (M Phil, PhD); genetics (M Phil, PhD); history of science, technology and medicine (M Phil, PhD); immunology (M Phil, PhD); integrative neurobiology and behavior (M Phil, PhD); membrane trafficking (M Phil, PhD); microbiology (M Phil, PhD); molecular and cellular neuroscience (M Phil, PhD); molecular biology (M Phil, PhD); molecular cancer studies (M Phil, PhD); neuroscience (M Phil, PhD); ophthalmology (M Phil, PhD); optometry (M Phil, PhD); organelle function (M Phil, PhD); pharmacology (M Phil, PhD); physiology (M Phil, PhD); plant sciences (M Phil, PhD); stem cell research (M Phil, PhD); structural biology (M Phil, PhD); systems neuroscience (M Phil, PhD); toxicology (M Phil, PhD).

University of Minnesota, Twin Cities Campus, College of Science and Engineering, Program in History of Science, Technology and Medicine, Minneapolis, MN 55455-0213. Offers MA, PhD. Terminal master's awarded for partial completion of doctoral program. *Degree requirements:* For master's, one foreign language; for doctorate, 2 foreign languages, thesis/dissertation. *Entrance requirements:* For master's and doctorate, GRE General Test. Additional exam requirements/recommendations for international students: Required—TOEFL. Electronic applications accepted. *Faculty research:* History of physical sciences, biological sciences, technology, and medicine.

University of Notre Dame, Graduate School, College of Arts and Letters, Division of Humanities, Program in History and Philosophy of Science, Notre Dame, IN 46556. Offers history and philosophy of science (MA, PhD); theology and science (PhD). *Degree requirements:* For doctorate, 2 foreign languages, comprehensive exam, thesis/dissertation, candidacy exam. *Entrance requirements:* For doctorate, GRE General Test. Additional exam requirements/recommendations for international students: Required—TOEFL (minimum score 600 paper-based; 80 iBT). Electronic applications accepted. *Faculty research:* Philosophy of physics, science and ethics, history and philosophy of biology, history of medicine and technology, history and philosophy of economics.

University of Oklahoma, College of Arts and Sciences, Department of History of Science, Norman, OK 73019. Offers history of science, technology and medicine (MA, PhD); MLIS/MA. *Program availability:* Part-time. *Faculty:* 13 full-time (5 women). *Students:* 9 full-time (5 women), 10 part-time (5 women), 2 international. Average age 31. 5 applicants, 60% accepted, 1 enrolled. In 2017, 2 master's awarded. Terminal master's awarded for partial completion of doctoral program. *Degree requirements:* For master's, one foreign language, comprehensive exam (for some programs), thesis (for some programs); for doctorate, 2 foreign languages, comprehensive exam, thesis/dissertation. *Entrance requirements:* For master's, GRE General Test, transcripts, statement of purpose, 3 letters of recommendation, writing sample; for doctorate, GRE General Test, MA in the history of science or related field, transcripts, statement of purpose, 3 letters of recommendation, writing sample. Additional exam requirements/recommendations for international students: Required—TOEFL (minimum score 79 iBT) or IELTS (minimum score 6.5). *Application deadline:* For fall admission, 1/15 for domestic and international students. Application fee: $50 ($100 for international students). Electronic applications accepted. *Expenses:* Tuition, state resident: full-time $5119; part-time $213.30 per credit hour. Tuition, nonresident: full-time $19,778; part-time $824.10 per credit hour. *Required fees:* $3458; $133.55 per credit hour. $126.50 per semester. *Financial support:* In 2017–18, 14 students received support, including 2 fellowships with full tuition reimbursements available (averaging $2,823 per year), 4 research assistantships with full tuition reimbursements available (averaging $15,438 per year), 7 teaching assistantships with full tuition reimbursements available (averaging $16,264 per year); career-related internships or fieldwork, Federal Work-Study, institutionally sponsored loans, scholarships/grants, traineeships, and health care benefits also available. Financial award application deadline: 6/1; financial award applicants required to submit FAFSA. *Faculty research:* Premodern science; medicine, public health, and social sciences; science, the public, and popular culture; science and religion; history of technology. *Total annual research expenditures:* $31,477. *Unit head:* Dr. Hunter Heyck, Professor/Department Chair, 405-325-2213, Fax: 405-325-2363, E-mail: hheyck@ou.edu. *Application contact:* Stella L. Graves Stuart, Graduate Studies Coordinator, 405-325-6026, Fax: 405-325-2363, E-mail: slgstuart@ou.edu.
Website: http://cas.ou.edu/hsci

University of Pennsylvania, School of Arts and Sciences, Graduate Group in the History and Sociology of Science, Philadelphia, PA 19104. Offers AM, PhD. *Faculty:* 25 full-time (13 women), 9 part-time/adjunct (6 women). *Students:* 26 full-time (17 women); includes 1 minority (Hispanic/Latino), 8 international. Average age 32. 47 applicants, 21% accepted, 6 enrolled. In 2017, 2 master's, 4 doctorates awarded. *Financial support:* Application deadline: 12/1.
Website: http://hss.sas.upenn.edu/hssc

University of Pittsburgh, Kenneth P. Dietrich School of Arts and Sciences, Department of History and Philosophy of Science, Pittsburgh, PA 15260. Offers PhD. *Faculty:* 8 full-time (2 women). *Students:* 32 full-time (14 women); includes 3 minority (1 American Indian or Alaska Native, non-Hispanic/Latino; 1 Native Hawaiian or other Pacific Islander, non-Hispanic/Latino; 1 Two or more races, non-Hispanic/Latino), 10 international. Average age 28. 52 applicants, 13% accepted, 6 enrolled. In 2017, 1 doctorate awarded. Terminal master's awarded for partial completion of doctoral program. *Degree requirements:* For doctorate, one foreign language, comprehensive exam, thesis/dissertation, minimum of 72 credit hours, proficiency in logic. *Entrance requirements:* For doctorate, GRE General Test, curriculum vitae, statement of career objective, 3 letters of recommendation, sample of written work. Additional exam requirements/recommendations for international students: Required—TOEFL (minimum score 577 paper-based; 90 iBT), IELTS (minimum score 7). *Application deadline:* For fall admission, 1/10 for domestic and international students. Application fee: $50. Electronic applications accepted. *Financial support:* In 2017–18, 26 students received support, including 14 fellowships with full tuition reimbursements available (averaging $24,710 per year), 11 teaching assistantships with full tuition reimbursements available (averaging $24,710 per year); health care benefits and tuition waivers (full) also available. Financial award application deadline: 1/10. *Faculty research:* History and philosophy of biology, psychology, and neuroscience; history and philosophy of physics; early modern science; cognitive science; philosophy of social science; philosophy of mind and perception. *Unit head:* Dr. John D. Norton, Chair, 412-624-1051, E-mail: jdnorton@pitt.edu. *Application contact:* Kathleen U. Labuda, Graduate Administrator, 412-624-5774, Fax: 412-624-5377, E-mail: kathleenlabuda@pitt.edu.
Website: http://www.hps.pitt.edu/

University of Toronto, School of Graduate Studies, Faculty of Arts and Science, Institute for the History and Philosophy of Science and Technology, Toronto, ON M5S 1A1, Canada. Offers MA, PhD. *Program availability:* Part-time. *Degree requirements:* For master's, one foreign language, thesis optional, reading ability in French or German; for doctorate, 2 foreign languages, thesis/dissertation, reading knowledge examinations, thesis defense. *Entrance requirements:* For master's, 2 letters of reference, B+ in the final two years of undergraduate work; for doctorate, 2 letters of reference, MA in history and philosophy of science and technology, minimum A- average. Additional exam requirements/recommendations for international students: Required—TOEFL (minimum score 580 paper-based; 93 iBT), TWE (minimum score 5). Electronic applications accepted.

University of Wisconsin–Madison, Graduate School, College of Letters and Science, Department of History of Science, Madison, WI 53706-1380. Offers history of medicine (MA); history of science (MA, PhD). Terminal master's awarded for partial completion of doctoral program. *Degree requirements:* For master's, thesis; for doctorate, 2 foreign languages, thesis/dissertation. *Entrance requirements:* For master's and doctorate, GRE General Test. Electronic applications accepted. *Faculty research:* History of biology, physical sciences, technology, medicine.

Yale University, Graduate School of Arts and Sciences, Department of History, Program in the History of Science and Medicine, New Haven, CT 06520. Offers MS, PhD. *Degree requirements:* For doctorate, 2 foreign languages, thesis/dissertation. *Entrance requirements:* For doctorate, GRE General Test.

Medieval and Renaissance Studies

Arizona State University at the Tempe campus, College of Liberal Arts and Sciences, Department of English, Tempe, AZ 85287-0302. Offers applied linguistics (PhD); creative writing (MFA); English (MA, PhD), including comparative literature (MA), linguistics (MA), literature, rhetoric and composition (MA), rhetoric, composition, and linguistics (PhD); film and media studies (MAS), including American media and popular culture; linguistics (Graduate Certificate); teaching English to speakers of other languages (MTESOL); translation studies (Graduate Certificate). Terminal master's awarded for partial completion of doctoral program. *Degree requirements:* For master's, variable foreign language requirement, comprehensive exam (for some programs), thesis (for some programs), interactive Program of Study (iPOS) submitted before completing 50 percent of required credit hours; for doctorate, variable foreign language requirement, comprehensive exam, thesis/dissertation, interactive Program of Study (iPOS) submitted before completing 50 percent of required credit hours. *Entrance requirements:* For master's and doctorate, GRE, minimum GPA of 3.0 or equivalent in last 2 years of work leading to bachelor's degree. Additional exam requirements/recommendations for international students: Required—TOEFL, IELTS, or PTE. Electronic applications accepted.

Arizona State University at the Tempe campus, College of Liberal Arts and Sciences, School of Historical, Philosophical and Religious Studies, Tempe, AZ 85287-4301. Offers European history (MA, PhD); medieval studies (Graduate Certificate); North American history (MA, PhD); philosophy (MA, PhD); public history (MA); religious studies (MA, PhD); Renaissance studies (Graduate Certificate); scholarly publishing (Graduate Certificate). *Program availability:* Part-time. Terminal master's awarded for partial completion of doctoral program. *Degree requirements:* For master's, thesis or alternative, interactive Program of Study (iPOS) submitted before completing 50 percent of required credit hours; for doctorate, variable foreign language requirement, comprehensive exam, thesis/dissertation, interactive Program of Study (iPOS) submitted before completing 50 percent of required credit hours. *Entrance requirements:* For master's and doctorate, GRE, minimum GPA of 3.0 or equivalent in last 2 years of work leading to bachelor's degree. Additional exam requirements/recommendations for international students: Required—TOEFL, IELTS, or PTE. Electronic applications accepted.

The Catholic University of America, School of Arts and Sciences, Department of History, Washington, DC 20064. Offers history (MA, PhD), including early modern European history, medieval history, modern European history, U.S. history; religion and society in the late medieval and early modern world (MA); MA/JD; MSLS/MA. *Program availability:* Part-time. *Faculty:* 15 full-time (6 women), 1 part-time/adjunct (0 women). *Students:* 6 full-time (0 women), 19 part-time (7 women); includes 3 minority (all Two or more races, non-Hispanic/Latino), 2 international. Average age 31. 11 applicants, 82% accepted, 3 enrolled. In 2017, 4 master's, 2 doctorates awarded. Terminal master's awarded for partial completion of doctoral program. *Degree requirements:* For master's, one foreign language, comprehensive exam, thesis optional, 2 languages (for medievalists), one of which must be Latin; for doctorate, 2 foreign languages, comprehensive exam, thesis/dissertation, 3 languages (for medievalists), one of which must be Latin. *Entrance requirements:* For master's and doctorate, GRE General Test, statement of purpose, official copies of academic transcripts, three letters of recommendation, writing sample. Additional exam requirements/recommendations for international students: Required—TOEFL (minimum score 550 paper-based; 80 iBT). *Application deadline:* For fall admission, 7/15 priority date for domestic students, 7/1 for international students; for spring admission, 11/15 priority date for domestic students, 11/1 for international students. Applications are processed on a rolling basis. Application fee: $55. Electronic applications accepted. *Expenses:* Contact institution. *Financial support:* Fellowships, research assistantships, teaching assistantships, Federal Work-Study, scholarships/grants, tuition waivers (full and partial), and unspecified assistantships available. Financial award application deadline: 2/1; financial award applicants required to submit FAFSA. *Faculty research:* Medieval history, including the Islamic Middle East, with particular expertise in later medieval religious, social, and economic history and early medieval and late antique history; European and American intellectual history; renaissance, reformation, catholic reformation; U.S. Catholic history; history of immigration. *Unit head:* Dr. Katherine Jansen, Chair, 202-319-5484, Fax: 202-319-5569, E-mail: jansen@cua.edu. *Application contact:* Dr. Steven Brown, Director of Graduate Admissions, 202-319-5057, Fax: 202-319-6533, E-mail: cua-admissions@cua.edu.
Website: http://history.cua.edu/

The Catholic University of America, School of Arts and Sciences, Program in Medieval and Byzantine Studies, Washington, DC 20064. Offers Byzantine and Orthodox studies (MA); Medieval and Byzantine studies (PhD, Certificate); the Islamic world (MA); the Medieval West (MA). *Program availability:* Part-time. *Students:* Average age 31. 13 applicants, 54% accepted, 3 enrolled. In 2017, 2 master's awarded. *Degree requirements:* For master's, one foreign language, comprehensive exam, thesis or alternative; for doctorate, 2 foreign languages, comprehensive exam, thesis/dissertation. *Entrance requirements:* For master's and doctorate, GRE General Test, statement of purpose, official copies of academic transcripts, three letters of recommendation, writing sample; for Certificate, bachelor's degree. Additional exam requirements/recommendations for international students: Required—TOEFL (minimum score 550 paper-based; 80 iBT). *Application deadline:* For fall admission, 7/15 priority date for domestic students, 7/1 for international students; for spring admission, 11/15 priority date for domestic students, 11/1 for international students. Applications are processed on a rolling basis. Application fee: $55. Electronic applications accepted. *Expenses:* Contact institution. *Financial support:* Fellowships, research assistantships, teaching assistantships, Federal Work-Study, scholarships/grants, tuition waivers (full and partial), and unspecified assistantships available. Financial award application deadline: 2/1; financial award applicants required to submit FAFSA. *Faculty research:* Scholasticism and medieval theology; early and late medieval history; medieval philosophy; liturgical studies; medieval English literature. *Unit head:* Dr. Lilla Kopar, Director, 202-319-5794, Fax: 202-319-6609, E-mail: kopar@cua.edu. *Application contact:* Director of Graduate Admissions, 202-319-5057, Fax: 202-319-6533, E-mail: cua-admissions@cua.edu.
Website: http://mbs.cua.edu/

Central European University, Department of Medieval Studies, Budapest, Hungary. Offers comparative history: interdisciplinary Medieval studies (MA); cultural heritage studies (MA); Medieval studies (MA, PhD). *Faculty:* 14 full-time (4 women), 7 part-time/adjunct (2 women). *Students:* 89 full-time (50 women). Average age 30. 132 applicants, 38% accepted, 34 enrolled. In 2017, 32 master's, 6 doctorates awarded. *Degree requirements:* For master's, one foreign language, thesis; for doctorate, variable foreign language requirement, comprehensive exam, thesis/dissertation. *Entrance requirements:* For master's and doctorate, interview. Additional exam requirements/recommendations for international students: Required—TOEFL (minimum score 570 paper-based); Recommended—IELTS (minimum score 6.5). *Application deadline:* For fall admission, 2/4 for domestic and international students. Application fee: $30. Electronic applications accepted. *Expenses: Tuition:* Full-time 12,000 euros. *Required fees:* 230 euros. One-time fee: 30 euros full-time. Tuition and fees vary according to course level, course load, degree level and program. *Financial support:* In 2017–18, 74 students received support. Fellowships, scholarships/grants, health care benefits, and tuition waivers (full and partial) available. *Faculty research:* Late antique and medieval civilization in Europe (c. 300-1550 AD), dealing with different methods of communication, migration of peoples, mobility of objects, texts, and ideas in the larger medieval oikumene, including Asia and North Africa. *Unit head:* Dr. Katalin Szende, Head, 36 1 327-3046, E-mail: medstud@ceu.edu. *Application contact:* Zsuzsanna Jaszberenyi, Admissions Officer, 361-324-3009, Fax: 367-327-3211, E-mail: admissions@ceu.edu.
Website: http://medievalstudies.ceu.edu/

Columbia University, Graduate School of Arts and Sciences, New York, NY 10027. Offers African-American studies (MA); American studies (MA); anthropology (MA, PhD); art history and archaeology (MA, PhD); astronomy (PhD); biological sciences (PhD); biotechnology (MA); chemical physics (PhD); chemistry (PhD); classical studies (MA, PhD); classics (MA, PhD); climate and society (MA); conservation biology (MA); earth and environmental sciences (PhD); East Asia: regional studies (MA); East Asian languages and cultures (MA, PhD); ecology, evolution and environmental biology (MA), including conservation biology; ecology, evolution, and environmental biology (PhD), including ecology and evolutionary biology, evolutionary primatology; economics (MA, PhD); English and comparative literature (MA, PhD); French and Romance philology (MA, PhD); Germanic languages (MA, PhD); global French studies (MA); global thought (MA); Hispanic cultural studies (MA); history (PhD); history and literature (MA); human rights studies (MA); Islamic studies (MA); Italian (MA, PhD); Japanese pedagogy (MA); Jewish studies (MA); Latin America and the Caribbean: regional studies (MA); Latin American and Iberian cultures (PhD); mathematics (MA, PhD), including finance (MA); medieval and Renaissance studies (MA); Middle Eastern, South Asian, and African studies (MA, PhD); modern art: critical and curatorial studies (MA); modern European studies (MA); museum anthropology (MA); music (DMA, PhD); oral history (MA); philosophical foundations of physics (MA); philosophy (MA, PhD); physics (PhD); political science (MA, PhD); psychology (PhD); quantitative methods in the social sciences (MA); religion (MA, PhD); Russia, Eurasia and East Europe: regional studies (MA); Russian translation (MA); Slavic cultures (MA); Slavic languages (MA, PhD); sociology (MA, PhD); South Asian studies (MA); statistics (MA, PhD); theatre (PhD). Dual-degree programs require admission to both Graduate School of Arts and Sciences and another Columbia school. *Program availability:* Part-time. Terminal master's awarded for partial completion of doctoral program. *Degree requirements:* For master's, variable foreign language requirement, comprehensive exam (for some programs), thesis (for some programs); for doctorate, variable foreign language requirement, comprehensive exam (for some programs), thesis/dissertation. *Entrance requirements:* For master's and doctorate, GRE General Test, GRE Subject Test (for some programs). Additional exam requirements/recommendations for international students: Required—TOEFL, IELTS. Electronic applications accepted. *Expenses: Tuition:* Full-time $44,864; part-time $1704 per credit. *Required fees:* $2370 per semester. One-time fee: $105.

Cornell University, Graduate School, Graduate Fields of Arts and Sciences, Field of Archaeology, Ithaca, NY 14853. Offers environmental archaeology (MA); historical archaeology (MA); Latin American archaeology (MA); medieval archaeology (MA); Mediterranean and Near Eastern archaeology (MA); Stone Age archaeology (MA). *Degree requirements:* For master's, one foreign language, thesis. *Entrance requirements:* For master's, GRE General Test, 3 letters of recommendation, sample of written work. Additional exam requirements/recommendations for international students: Required—TOEFL (minimum score 550 paper-based; 77 iBT). Electronic applications accepted. *Faculty research:* Anatolia, Lydia, Sardis, classical and Hellenistic Greece, science in archaeology, North American Indians, Stone Age Africa, Mayan trade.

Cornell University, Graduate School, Graduate Fields of Arts and Sciences, Field of English Language and Literature, Ithaca, NY 14853. Offers African-American literature (PhD); American literature after 1865 (PhD); American literature to 1865 (PhD); American studies (PhD); colonial and postcolonial literatures (PhD); creative writing (MFA); cultural studies (PhD); dramatic literature (PhD); English poetry (PhD); English Renaissance to 1660 (PhD); lesbian, bisexual, and gay literary studies (PhD); literary criticism and theory (PhD); Old and Middle English (PhD); prose fiction (PhD); Restoration and the eighteenth-century (PhD); the nineteenth century (PhD); the twentieth century (PhD); women's literature (PhD); MFA/PhD. Terminal master's awarded for partial completion of doctoral program. *Degree requirements:* For master's, one foreign language, thesis; for doctorate, one foreign language, comprehensive exam, thesis/dissertation, teaching experience. *Entrance requirements:* For master's, GRE General Test, 3 letters of recommendation, creative writing sample; for doctorate, GRE General Test, GRE Subject Test (English), 3 letters of recommendation, writing sample. Additional exam requirements/recommendations for international students: Required—TOEFL (minimum score 600 paper-based; 77 iBT). Electronic applications accepted. *Faculty research:* English and American literature, women's writing, ethnic and post-colonial literature, critical theory, medievalism.

Cornell University, Graduate School, Graduate Fields of Arts and Sciences, Field of History, Ithaca, NY 14853. Offers African history (MA, PhD); American history (MA, PhD); ancient Greek history (PhD); ancient history (MA, PhD); ancient Roman history (PhD); early modern European history (MA, PhD); English history (MA, PhD); French history (MA, PhD); German history (MA, PhD); history of science (MA, PhD); Korean history (PhD); Latin American history (MA, PhD); medieval Chinese history (MA, PhD); medieval history (MA, PhD); modern Chinese history (MA, PhD); modern European history (MA, PhD); modern Japanese history (MA, PhD); modern Middle Eastern history (PhD); premodern Islamic history (MA, PhD); premodern Japanese history (MA, PhD); Renaissance history (MA, PhD); Russian history (MA, PhD); South Asian history (PhD); Southeast Asian history (MA, PhD). Terminal master's awarded for partial completion of doctoral program. *Degree requirements:* For master's, thesis; for doctorate, 2 foreign languages, comprehensive exam, thesis/dissertation, 1 year of teaching experience. *Entrance requirements:* For master's and doctorate, GRE General Test, writing sample, 3 letters of recommendation. Additional exam requirements/recommendations for international students: Required—TOEFL (minimum score 550 paper-based; 77 iBT). Electronic applications accepted.

Cornell University, Graduate School, Graduate Fields of Arts and Sciences, Field of History of Art, Archaeology and Visual Studies, Ithaca, NY 14853. Offers 19th century art (PhD); African, African American and African diaspora (PhD); American art (PhD); ancient art and archaeology (PhD); Asian American art (PhD); Baroque art (PhD);

comparative modernities (PhD); digital art (PhD); East Asian art (PhD); history of photography (PhD); Islamic art (PhD); Latin American art (PhD); medieval art (PhD); modern art (PhD); Renaissance art (PhD); Southeast Asian art (PhD); theory and criticism (PhD); visual studies (PhD). *Degree requirements:* For doctorate, one foreign language, comprehensive exam, thesis/dissertation, general exams in 3 areas. *Entrance requirements:* For doctorate, GRE General Test, sample of written work, 3 letters of recommendation. Additional exam requirements/recommendations for international students: Required—TOEFL (minimum score 550 paper-based; 77 iBT). Electronic applications accepted.

Cornell University, Graduate School, Graduate Fields of Arts and Sciences, Field of Medieval Studies, Ithaca, NY 14853. Offers medieval archaeology (PhD); medieval art (PhD); medieval history (PhD); medieval literature (PhD); medieval music (PhD); medieval philology and linguistics (PhD); medieval philosophy (PhD). *Degree requirements:* For doctorate, 3 foreign languages, comprehensive exam, thesis/dissertation, teaching experience. *Entrance requirements:* For doctorate, GRE General Test, 3 letters of recommendation, proficiency in Latin (recommended), 20-page writing sample on a Medieval topic. Additional exam requirements/recommendations for international students: Required—TOEFL (minimum score 600 paper-based; 77 iBT). Electronic applications accepted. *Faculty research:* Interdisciplinary study of medieval culture, languages, literatures, history, archaeology.

Fordham University, Graduate School of Arts and Sciences, Program in Medieval Studies, New York, NY 10458. Offers MA, Certificate. *Program availability:* Part-time, evening/weekend. *Students:* 9 full-time (7 women), 14 part-time (7 women); includes 2 minority (both Hispanic/Latino). Average age 27. 17 applicants, 94% accepted, 9 enrolled. In 2017, 8 master's, 2 other advanced degrees awarded. *Degree requirements:* For master's, thesis. *Entrance requirements:* For master's, GRE General Test. Additional exam requirements/recommendations for international students: Required—TOEFL (minimum score 650 paper-based). *Application deadline:* For fall admission, 1/4 priority date for domestic students; for spring admission, 11/1 for domestic students. Applications are processed on a rolling basis. Application fee: $70. Electronic applications accepted. *Financial support:* In 2017–18, 4 students received support. Institutionally sponsored loans, tuition waivers (full and partial), and unspecified assistantships available. Financial award application deadline: 1/4; financial award applicants required to submit FAFSA. *Faculty research:* Medieval literature, history, philosophy, theology, and fine arts; Anglo-Norman. *Unit head:* Dr. Susanne Hafner, Director, 718-817-4655, E-mail: hafner@fordham.edu. *Application contact:* Bernadette Valentino-Morrison, Director of Graduate Admissions, 718-817-4419, Fax: 718-817-3566, E-mail: valentinomor@fordham.edu.

Georgetown University, Graduate School of Arts and Sciences, School of Continuing Studies, Washington, DC 20057. Offers American studies (MALS); applied intelligence (MPS); Catholic studies (MALS); classical civilizations (MALS); emergency and disaster management (MPS); ethics and the professions (MALS); global strategic communications (MPS); hospitality management (MPS); human resources management (MPS); humanities (MALS); individualized study (MALS); integrated marketing communications (MPS); international affairs (MALS); Islam and Muslim-Christian relations (MALS); journalism (MPS); liberal studies (DLS); literature and society (MALS); medieval and early modern European studies (MALS); public relations and corporate communications (MPS); real estate (MPS); religious studies (MALS); social and public policy (MALS); sports industry management (MPS); systems engineering management (MPS); technology management (MPS); the theory and practice of American democracy (MALS); urban and regional planning (MPS); visual culture (MALS). MPS in systems engineering management offered jointly with Stevens Institute of Technology. *Entrance requirements:* Additional exam requirements/recommendations for international students: Required—TOEFL.

Harvard University, Graduate School of Arts and Sciences, Department of English and American Literature and Language, Cambridge, MA 02138. Offers critical theory (PhD); eighteenth-century literature (PhD); literature: nineteenth-century to the present (PhD); medieval literature and language (PhD); modern British and American literature (PhD); Renaissance literature (PhD). Terminal master's awarded for partial completion of doctoral program. *Degree requirements:* For doctorate, 2 foreign languages, thesis/dissertation, oral exam. *Entrance requirements:* For doctorate, GRE General Test, GRE Subject Test, writing sample. Additional exam requirements/recommendations for international students: Required—TOEFL. *Faculty research:* Old and Middle English language and literature, drama, creative writing, transition to Romanticism, history and theory of criticism.

Indiana University Bloomington, University Graduate School, College of Arts and Sciences, Department of Germanic Studies, Bloomington, IN 47405-7000. Offers German philology and linguistics (PhD); German studies (MA, PhD), including German (MA), German literature and culture (MA), German literature and linguistics (MA); medieval German studies (PhD); teaching German (MAT). *Degree requirements:* For master's, one foreign language, project; for doctorate, one foreign language, comprehensive exam, thesis/dissertation. *Entrance requirements:* For master's, GRE General Test, BA in German or equivalent; for doctorate, GRE General Test, MA in German or equivalent. Additional exam requirements/recommendations for international students: Required—TOEFL. Electronic applications accepted. *Faculty research:* German and other European literature: medieval to modern/postmodern, German and culture studies, Germanic philology, literary theory, literature and the other arts.

Loyola University Chicago, Graduate School, Department of English, Chicago, IL 60660. Offers 19th century studies (PhD); English (MA); Medieval and Renaissance literature (PhD); modern literature and culture (PhD); textual studies and digital humanities (PhD). *Program availability:* Part-time, evening/weekend. *Faculty:* 24 full-time (11 women). *Students:* 36 full-time (23 women), 3 part-time (all women); includes 4 minority (1 Black or African American, non-Hispanic/Latino; 2 Hispanic/Latino; 1 Two or more races, non-Hispanic/Latino). Average age 29. 65 applicants, 37% accepted, 7 enrolled. In 2017, 5 master's, 2 doctorates awarded. Terminal master's awarded for partial completion of doctoral program. *Degree requirements:* For master's, comprehensive exam, thesis or alternative; for doctorate, one foreign language, comprehensive exam, thesis/dissertation. *Entrance requirements:* For master's and doctorate, GRE General Test. Additional exam requirements/recommendations for international students: Required—TOEFL, IELTS. *Application deadline:* For fall admission, 6/1 for domestic students. Applications are processed on a rolling basis. Application fee: $0. Electronic applications accepted. *Expenses:* $1,004 per credit hour tuition. *Financial support:* In 2017–18, 26 students received support, including 5 fellowships with full tuition reimbursements available (averaging $18,000 per year), research assistantships with full tuition reimbursements available (averaging $10,000 per year), 21 teaching assistantships with full tuition reimbursements available (averaging $18,000 per year); Federal Work-Study, institutionally sponsored loans, tuition waivers (partial), and unspecified assistantships also available. Support available to part-time students. Financial award application deadline: 1/15; financial award applicants required to submit FAFSA. *Faculty research:* Medieval and renaissance studies, 19th century studies, American and British modernism and postmodernism, African American and Anglophone literatures, textual studies and digital humanities. *Unit head:* Dr. James Knapp, Graduate Program Director, 773-508-2241, Fax: 773-508-8696, E-mail: jknapp3@luc.edu.
Website: http://www.luc.edu/english/

Rutgers University–New Brunswick, Graduate School-New Brunswick, Program in History, Piscataway, NJ 08854-8097. Offers African-American history (PhD); early American history (PhD); early modern European history (PhD); east Asian history (PhD); global and comparative history (PhD); history (PhD); history of diplomacy and foreign relations (PhD); history of technology, environment and health (PhD); history of the Atlantic cultures and African diaspora (PhD); Latin American history (PhD); medieval history (PhD); modern European history (PhD); nineteenth and twentieth century American history (PhD); women's and gender history (PhD). *Degree requirements:* For doctorate, thesis/dissertation. *Entrance requirements:* For doctorate, GRE General Test, sample of written work. Electronic applications accepted. *Faculty research:* American history, European history, Afro-American history, women's history, Latin American history.

Southern Methodist University, Dedman College of Humanities and Sciences, Program in Medieval Studies, Dallas, TX 75275. Offers MA. *Program availability:* Part-time. *Degree requirements:* For master's, 2 foreign languages, thesis. *Entrance requirements:* For master's, GRE General Test, minimum GPA of 3.0. Electronic applications accepted. *Faculty research:* Byzantine culture, medieval Europe, Arthurian literature, Chaucer, Romance.

University of California, Santa Barbara, Graduate Division, College of Letters and Sciences, Division of Humanities and Fine Arts, Department of English, Santa Barbara, CA 93106-3170. Offers English (PhD), including environment and society, European medieval studies, feminist studies, global studies, technology and society, translation studies, writing studies; MA/PhD. Terminal master's awarded for partial completion of doctoral program. *Degree requirements:* For doctorate, one foreign language, comprehensive exam, thesis/dissertation. *Entrance requirements:* For doctorate, GRE General Test, GRE Subject Test (English literature). Additional exam requirements/recommendations for international students: Required—TOEFL (minimum score 550 paper-based; 80 iBT), IELTS (minimum score 7). Electronic applications accepted. *Faculty research:* Medieval, Romantic and Victorian studies; gender studies and feminist theory; literature and the mind; American literature; literature and new media/information culture.

University of California, Santa Barbara, Graduate Division, College of Letters and Sciences, Division of Humanities and Fine Arts, Department of History, Santa Barbara, CA 93106-9410. Offers European medieval studies (PhD); global studies (PhD); public historical studies (PhD); technology and society (PhD); women's studies (PhD); MA/PhD. *Degree requirements:* For doctorate, variable foreign language requirement, comprehensive exam, thesis/dissertation. *Entrance requirements:* For doctorate, GRE. Additional exam requirements/recommendations for international students: Required—TOEFL (minimum score 550 paper-based; 80 iBT), IELTS (minimum score 7). Electronic applications accepted. *Faculty research:* Europe, United States, Latin America, Africa, Middle East, East Asia.

University of California, Santa Barbara, Graduate Division, College of Letters and Sciences, Division of Humanities and Fine Arts, Department of History of Art and Architecture, Santa Barbara, CA 93106-2014. Offers art history (PhD), including art history, European medieval studies, feminist studies; MA/PhD. Terminal master's awarded for partial completion of doctoral program. *Degree requirements:* For doctorate, 2 foreign languages, comprehensive exam, thesis/dissertation. *Entrance requirements:* For doctorate, GRE. Additional exam requirements/recommendations for international students: Required—TOEFL (minimum score 550 paper-based; 80 iBT), IELTS (minimum score 7). Electronic applications accepted. *Faculty research:* History of architecture, Renaissance-Italian, Baroque, American, Chinese, Japanese, contemporary, Northern Renaissance.

University of California, Santa Barbara, Graduate Division, College of Letters and Sciences, Division of Humanities and Fine Arts, Department of Religious Studies, Santa Barbara, CA 93106-3130. Offers ancient Mediterranean studies (PhD); cognitive science (PhD); European medieval studies (PhD); feminist studies (PhD); global studies (PhD); religious studies (MA, PhD); translation studies (PhD); MA/PhD. Terminal master's awarded for partial completion of doctoral program. *Degree requirements:* For master's, one foreign language, comprehensive exam (for some programs), thesis (for some programs); for doctorate, 2 foreign languages, thesis/dissertation, methodology. *Entrance requirements:* For master's and doctorate, GRE General Test. Additional exam requirements/recommendations for international students: Required—TOEFL (minimum score 550 paper-based; 80 iBT), IELTS (minimum score 7). Electronic applications accepted. *Faculty research:* Area studies; religious traditions; theory and method in the study of religion; religion, culture, and politics; spirituality and religious experience.

University of California, Santa Barbara, Graduate Division, College of Letters and Sciences, Division of Humanities and Fine Arts, Department of Spanish and Portuguese, Santa Barbara, CA 93106-4150. Offers Hispanic languages and literatures (PhD), including European medieval studies, feminist studies, Hispanic linguistics, Hispanic literature, Luso-Brazilian literature; Hispanic linguistics (MA); Luso-Brazilian literature (MA); Spanish or Spanish-American literature (MA); MA/PhD. Terminal master's awarded for partial completion of doctoral program. *Degree requirements:* For master's, 2 foreign languages, comprehensive exam (for some programs), thesis optional; for doctorate, 3 foreign languages, comprehensive exam, thesis/dissertation. *Entrance requirements:* For master's and doctorate, GRE. Additional exam requirements/recommendations for international students: Required—TOEFL (minimum score 550 paper-based; 80 iBT), IELTS (minimum score 7). Electronic applications accepted. *Faculty research:* Nineteenth-century Spanish and Portuguese literature, Spanish and Spanish-American literature, nineteenth- and twentieth-century Portuguese and Brazilian literatures, Hispanic linguistics, Catalan language and culture.

University of California, Santa Barbara, Graduate Division, College of Letters and Sciences, Division of Humanities and Fine Arts, Department of Theater and Dance, Santa Barbara, CA 93106-7060. Offers theater studies (MA, PhD), including European medieval studies (PhD), feminist studies (PhD), theatre studies (PhD); MA/PhD. Terminal master's awarded for partial completion of doctoral program. *Degree requirements:* For master's, comprehensive exam, thesis; for doctorate, one foreign language, comprehensive exam, thesis/dissertation. *Entrance requirements:* For master's and doctorate, GRE. Additional exam requirements/recommendations for international students: Required—TOEFL (minimum score 550 paper-based; 80 iBT), IELTS (minimum score 7). Electronic applications accepted. *Faculty research:* English and American theater and Ancient Greek; Spanish, Latin American and Caribbean performance; Renaissance and Baroque drama and intercultural theory; East Asian performance, gender and nationalism; Korean cultural studies, Russian literature, and Slavic folklore; history of German theater, Shakespeare, and European opera; postcolonialism, performance-based ethnography, globalism and national identity formation in Africa.

University of Chicago, Division of the Humanities, Department of Romance Languages and Literatures, Chicago, IL 60637. Offers French and Francophone studies (PhD); Hispanic and Luso-Brazilian studies (PhD); Italian studies (PhD); Renaissance and early modern studies (PhD). *Students:* 50 full-time (28 women); includes 12 minority (2 Asian,

non-Hispanic/Latino; 9 Hispanic/Latino; 1 Two or more races, non-Hispanic/Latino), 25 international. Average age 30. 52 applicants, 31% accepted, 7 enrolled. In 2017, 4 doctorates awarded. Terminal master's awarded for partial completion of doctoral program. *Degree requirements:* For doctorate, 3 foreign languages, comprehensive exam, thesis/dissertation. *Entrance requirements:* For doctorate, GRE General Test, 15-20 page writing sample, statement of purpose, 3 letters of recommendation, transcripts for all previous degrees and institutions attended. Additional exam requirements/recommendations for international students: Required—TOEFL (minimum score 104 iBT), IELTS (minimum score 7). *Application deadline:* For fall admission, 12/15 for domestic and international students. Application fee: $90. Electronic applications accepted. *Financial support:* In 2017–18, fellowships with full tuition reimbursements (averaging $27,000 per year) were awarded; teaching assistantships with full tuition reimbursements, Federal Work-Study, institutionally sponsored loans, scholarships/grants, and health care benefits also available. Financial award application deadline: 12/15. *Unit head:* Daisy Delogu, Chair, 773-702-8481, E-mail: romance-languages@uchicago.edu. *Application contact:* Michael Beetley, Assistant Dean of Students, Admissions and Fellowships, 773-702-1552, Fax: 773-834-9148, E-mail: humanitiesadmissions@uchicago.edu.
Website: http://rll.uchicago.edu

University of Connecticut, Graduate School, College of Liberal Arts and Sciences, Field of Medieval Studies, Storrs, CT 06269. Offers MA, PhD. Terminal master's awarded for partial completion of doctoral program. *Degree requirements:* For master's, comprehensive exam; for doctorate, 3 foreign languages, thesis/dissertation. *Entrance requirements:* For master's and doctorate, GRE General Test, GRE Subject Test. Additional exam requirements/recommendations for international students: Required—TOEFL (minimum score 550 paper-based). Electronic applications accepted.

University of Guelph, Graduate Studies, College of Arts, School of English and Theatre Studies, Joint Program in Literary Studies/Theatre Studies in English, Guelph, ON N1G 2W1, Canada. Offers PhD. *Program availability:* Part-time. *Degree requirements:* For doctorate, one foreign language, comprehensive exam, thesis/dissertation. *Entrance requirements:* For doctorate, MA, 3 letters of reference, writing samples, resume, minimum A- average in graduate course work. Additional exam requirements/recommendations for international students: Required—TOEFL. Electronic applications accepted. *Faculty research:* Canadian studies, Early Modern studies, Postcolonial studies, studies in gender and genre, 19th Century studies.

University of Minnesota, Twin Cities Campus, Graduate School, College of Liberal Arts, Department of German, Scandinavian, and Dutch, Minneapolis, MN 55455. Offers Germanic studies (MA, PhD), including German, Germanic medieval studies, Scandinavian studies (MA). *Program availability:* Part-time. Terminal master's awarded for partial completion of doctoral program. *Degree requirements:* For doctorate, 2 foreign languages, thesis/dissertation. *Entrance requirements:* For master's, GRE General Test, BA in German, Scandinavian, or equivalent; for doctorate, MA in German, Scandinavian, or equivalent. Additional exam requirements/recommendations for international

students: Required—TOEFL (minimum score 550 paper-based; 79 iBT). Electronic applications accepted. *Faculty research:* Cultural studies, literary theory, feminist criticism, film, Germanic medieval studies.

University of Notre Dame, Graduate School, College of Arts and Letters, Division of Humanities, Medieval Institute, Notre Dame, IN 46556. Offers MMS, PhD. Terminal master's awarded for partial completion of doctoral program. *Degree requirements:* For master's, 3 foreign languages, comprehensive exam; for doctorate, 3 foreign languages, thesis/dissertation, candidacy exam. *Entrance requirements:* For master's and doctorate, GRE General Test. Additional exam requirements/recommendations for international students: Required—TOEFL (minimum score 600 paper-based; 80 iBT). Electronic applications accepted. *Faculty research:* Medieval history, vernacular literatures, theology, philosophy, Ambrosiana manuscripts and drawings.

University of Pittsburgh, Kenneth P. Dietrich School of Arts and Sciences, Program in Medieval and Renaissance Studies, Pittsburgh, PA 15260. Offers Doctoral Certificate, Master's Certificate. *Faculty:* 40 full-time (17 women). *Students:* 7 full-time (4 women). Average age 25. 1 applicant, 100% accepted, 1 enrolled. In 2017, 1 Master's Certificate awarded. *Degree requirements:* For other advanced degree, thesis. *Entrance requirements:* For degree, good academic standing in a University of Pittsburgh graduate degree-granting department. *Application deadline:* Applications are processed on a rolling basis. Application fee: $0. Electronic applications accepted. *Financial support:* Scholarships/grants available. *Faculty research:* History, French writing, Medieval and Renaissance art and architecture, Shakespeare. *Unit head:* Prof. Jennifer Waldron, Director, 412-624-6564, Fax: 412-383-6999, E-mail: jwaldron@pitt.edu. *Application contact:* Kathryn Briar Somerville, Graduate Administrator, 412-624-6564, E-mail: kbs47@pitt.edu.
Website: http://www.medren.pitt.edu/

University of Toronto, School of Graduate Studies, Faculty of Arts and Science, Centre for Medieval Studies, Toronto, ON M5S 1A1, Canada. Offers MA, PhD. *Program availability:* Part-time. *Degree requirements:* For master's, one foreign language, 4 courses or 3 courses and thesis; for doctorate, 3 foreign languages, thesis/dissertation, proficiency in Latin, German and French. *Entrance requirements:* For master's, letters of reference, minimum B+ average, course work in the Medieval period; for doctorate, letters of reference. Additional exam requirements/recommendations for international students: Required—TOEFL (minimum score 580 paper-based; 93 iBT), TWE (minimum score 5). Electronic applications accepted.

Yale University, Graduate School of Arts and Sciences, Interdisciplinary Program in Medieval Studies, New Haven, CT 06520. Offers M Phil, PhD. *Entrance requirements:* For doctorate, GRE General Test.

Yale University, Graduate School of Arts and Sciences, Program in Renaissance Studies, New Haven, CT 06520. Offers PhD. *Degree requirements:* For doctorate, 3 foreign languages. *Entrance requirements:* For doctorate, GRE General Test.

Public History

Arizona State University at the Tempe campus, College of Liberal Arts and Sciences, School of Historical, Philosophical and Religious Studies, Tempe, AZ 85287-4301. Offers European history (MA, PhD); medieval studies (Graduate Certificate); North American history (MA, PhD); philosophy (MA, PhD); public history (MA); religious studies (MA, PhD); Renaissance studies (Graduate Certificate); scholarly publishing (Graduate Certificate). *Program availability:* Part-time. Terminal master's awarded for partial completion of doctoral program. *Degree requirements:* For master's, thesis or alternative, interactive Program of Study (iPOS) submitted before completing 50 percent of required credit hours; for doctorate, variable foreign language requirement, comprehensive exam, thesis/dissertation, interactive Program of Study (iPOS) submitted before completing 50 percent of required credit hours. *Entrance requirements:* For master's and doctorate, GRE, minimum GPA of 3.0 or equivalent in last 2 years of work leading to bachelor's degree. Additional exam requirements/recommendations for international students: Required—TOEFL, IELTS, or PTE. Electronic applications accepted.

California State University, East Bay, Office of Graduate Studies, College of Letters, Arts, and Social Sciences, Department of History, Hayward, CA 94542-3000. Offers history (MA); public history (MA); teaching (MA). *Program availability:* Part-time, evening/weekend. *Faculty:* 9 full-time (6 women), 11 part-time/adjunct (4 women). *Students:* 1 (woman) full-time, 17 part-time (9 women); includes 4 minority (1 Black or African American, non-Hispanic/Latino; 2 Hispanic/Latino; 1 Two or more races, non-Hispanic/Latino). Average age 39. 17 applicants, 47% accepted, 4 enrolled. In 2017, 6 master's awarded. *Degree requirements:* For master's, one foreign language, comprehensive exam, project, thesis, or exam. *Entrance requirements:* For master's, GRE (strongly recommended), minimum GPA of 3.0 in field, 3.3 in history; 2 letters of recommendation; writing sample. Additional exam requirements/recommendations for international students: Required—TOEFL (minimum score 550 paper-based). *Application deadline:* For fall admission, 5/19 for domestic and international students. Applications are processed on a rolling basis. Application fee: $55. Electronic applications accepted. *Financial support:* Fellowships, teaching assistantships, career-related internships or fieldwork, Federal Work-Study, institutionally sponsored loans, and scholarships/grants available. Support available to part-time students. Financial award application deadline: 3/2; financial award applicants required to submit FAFSA. *Faculty research:* Digital history, American women, early America, Native Americans, medieval colonial India. *Unit head:* Dr. Linda L. Ivey, Chair, 510-885-4015, E-mail: linda.ivey@csueastbay.edu. *Application contact:* Dr. Khal Schneider, Graduate Coordinator, 510-885-3237, Fax: 510-885-4791, E-mail: khal.schneider@csueastbay.edu.
Website: http://www20.csueastbay.edu/class/departments/history/

California State University, Sacramento, College of Arts and Letters, Department of History, Sacramento, CA 95819. Offers history (MA); public historical studies (PhD); public history (MA). PhD held jointly with University of California, Santa Barbara. *Program availability:* Part-time. *Students:* 26 full-time (13 women), 36 part-time (14 women); includes 12 minority (1 Black or African American, non-Hispanic/Latino; 1 American Indian or Alaska Native, non-Hispanic/Latino; 2 Asian, non-Hispanic/Latino; 8 Hispanic/Latino). Average age 29. 44 applicants, 80% accepted, 28 enrolled. In 2017, 21 master's awarded. *Degree requirements:* For master's, thesis, project or comprehensive exam; writing proficiency exam. *Entrance requirements:* For master's, minimum GPA of 3.25 in history, 3.0 overall during previous 2 years; BA in history or equivalent. Additional exam requirements/recommendations for international students:

Required—TOEFL (minimum score 550 paper-based; 80 iBT). *Application deadline:* For fall admission, 2/3 for domestic students, 3/1 for international students; for spring admission, 9/15 for domestic students, 9/30 for international students. Applications are processed on a rolling basis. Application fee: $55. Electronic applications accepted. *Expenses:* Contact institution. *Financial support:* Career-related internships or fieldwork, Federal Work-Study, and scholarships/grants available. Support available to part-time students. Financial award application deadline: 3/1; financial award applicants required to submit FAFSA. *Unit head:* Dr. Jeffrey Wilson, Chair, 916-278-6136, Fax: 916-278-7476, E-mail: jkwilson@saclink.csus.edu. *Application contact:* Jose Martinez, Outreach and Graduate Diversity Coordinator, 916-278-6470, Fax: 916-278-5669, E-mail: martinj@skymail.csus.edu.
Website: http://www.csus.edu/hist

The College at Brockport, State University of New York, School of Arts and Sciences, Department of History, Brockport, NY 14420-2997. Offers history (MA), including American and world history, American history, American public history, world history. *Program availability:* Part-time, evening/weekend. *Faculty:* 9 full-time (5 women). *Students:* 15 full-time (5 women), 19 part-time (10 women); includes 1 minority (Black or African American, non-Hispanic/Latino). 20 applicants, 75% accepted, 10 enrolled. In 2017, 10 master's awarded. *Degree requirements:* For master's, thesis or alternative. *Entrance requirements:* For master's, minimum GPA of 3.0, writing sample, letters of recommendation, statement of objectives. Additional exam requirements/recommendations for international students: Required—TOEFL (minimum score 550 paper-based; 79 iBT), IELTS (minimum score 6.5). *Application deadline:* For fall admission, 7/1 priority date for domestic and international students; for spring admission, 11/15 priority date for domestic and international students; for summer admission, 4/15 for domestic and international students. Application fee: $50. Electronic applications accepted. *Expenses:* Tuition, state resident: full-time $10,870; part-time $453 per credit hour. Tuition, nonresident: full-time $22,210. *Required fees:* $988; $246 per semester. *Financial support:* In 2017–18, 1 fellowship with tuition reimbursement (averaging $3,750 per year), 2 teaching assistantships with full tuition reimbursements (averaging $6,000 per year) were awarded; Federal Work-Study, scholarships/grants, and unspecified assistantships also available. Support available to part-time students. Financial award application deadline: 3/15; financial award applicants required to submit FAFSA. *Faculty research:* American history, women's history, European history, world history, cultural history. *Unit head:* Dr. Owen Steve Ireland, Chairperson, 585-395-5627, Fax: 585-395-2620, E-mail: oireland@brockport.edu. *Application contact:* Dr. Morag Martin, Graduate Director, 585-395-5690, Fax: 585-395-2620, E-mail: mmartin@brockport.edu.
Website: https://www.brockport.edu/academics/history/graduate/masters.html

College of Staten Island of the City University of New York, Graduate Programs, Division of Humanities and Social Sciences, Program in Public History, Staten Island, NY 10314-6600. Offers Advanced Certificate. *Program availability:* Part-time, evening/weekend. *Degree requirements:* For Advanced Certificate, 20 credits. *Entrance requirements:* For degree, baccalaureate or graduate degree in history or related field with minimum GPA of 3.0, two letters of recommendation, current resume, academic or professional writing sample of up to 25 pages. Additional exam requirements/recommendations for international students: Required—TOEFL (minimum score 79 iBT), IELTS (minimum score 6.5). *Application deadline:* For fall admission, 5/10 priority date for domestic students, 4/25 for international students; for spring admission, 12/2 priority date for domestic students, 11/25 for international students. Applications are

processed on a rolling basis. Application fee: $125. Electronic applications accepted. *Expenses:* Tuition, state resident: full-time $10,450; part-time $440 per credit. Tuition, nonresident: full-time $19,320; part-time $440 per credit. *Required fees:* $181.10 per semester. Tuition and fees vary according to program. *Unit head:* Prof. John M. Dixon, Program Coordinator, 718-982-3307, E-mail: john.dixon@csi.cuny.edu. *Application contact:* Sasha Spence, Associate Director for Graduate Admissions, 718-982-2019, Fax: 718-982-2500, E-mail: sasha.spence@csi.cuny.edu.
Website: http://csicuny.smartcatalogiq.com/current/Graduate-Catalog/Graduate-Programs-Disciplines-and-Offerings-in-Selected-Disciplines/Public-History

Drew University, Caspersen School of Graduate Studies, Madison, NJ 07940-1493. Offers conflict resolution and leadership (Certificate), including community leadership, moderation, peace building; education (M Ed); finance (MA); history and culture (MA, PhD), including American history, book history, British history, European history, Holocaust and genocide (M Litt, MA, D Litt, PhD), intellectual history, Irish history, print culture, public history; K-12 education (MAT), including art, biology, chemistry, elementary education, English, French, Italian, math, secondary education, special education, teacher of students with disabilities; liberal studies (M Litt, D Litt), including history, Holocaust and genocide (M Litt, MA, D Litt, PhD), Irish/Irish-American studies, literature (M Litt, MMH, D Litt, DMH, CMH), religion, spirituality, teaching in the two-year college, writing; medical humanities (MMH, DMH, CMH), including arts, health, healthcare, literature (M Litt, MMH, D Litt, DMH, CMH), scientific research; poetry (MFA). *Program availability:* Part-time, evening/weekend. *Faculty:* 4 full-time (2 women), 29 part-time/adjunct (15 women). *Students:* 77 full-time (42 women), 175 part-time (114 women); includes 39 minority (12 Black or African American, non-Hispanic/Latino; 6 Asian, non-Hispanic/Latino; 16 Hispanic/Latino; 5 Two or more races, non-Hispanic/Latino), 11 international. Average age 41. 126 applicants, 75% accepted, 52 enrolled. In 2017, 38 master's, 23 doctorates, 35 other advanced degrees awarded. Terminal master's awarded for partial completion of doctoral program. *Degree requirements:* For master's and other advanced degree, thesis (for some programs); for doctorate, one foreign language, comprehensive exam (for some programs), thesis/dissertation. *Entrance requirements:* For master's, PRAXIS Core and Subject Area tests (for MAT), GRE/GMAT (for M Fin), resume, transcripts, writing sample, personal statement, letters of recommendation; for doctorate, GRE (PhD in history and culture), resume, transcripts, writing sample, personal statement, letters of recommendation; for other advanced degree, resume, transcripts, personal statement. Additional exam requirements/recommendations for international students: Required—TOEFL (minimum score 587 paper-based; 80 iBT), IELTS (minimum score 6), TWE (minimum score 4). *Application deadline:* For fall admission, 8/1 for domestic students, 6/1 for international students; for spring admission, 12/1 for domestic students, 10/1 for international students. Applications are processed on a rolling basis. Application fee: $35. Electronic applications accepted. *Financial support:* Fellowships, research assistantships, teaching assistantships, career-related internships or fieldwork, Federal Work-Study, scholarships/grants, and unspecified assistantships available. Support available to part-time students. Financial award applicants required to submit FAFSA. *Faculty research:* Irish history and culture, conflict resolution and leadership. *Application contact:* Leanne Horinko, Director of Caspersen Admissions, 973-408-3280, E-mail: gradm@drew.edu.
Website: http://www.drew.edu/caspersen

Duquesne University, Graduate School of Liberal Arts, Department of History, Pittsburgh, PA 15282-0001. Offers historical studies (MA); public history (MA). *Program availability:* Part-time, evening/weekend. *Faculty:* 15 full-time (5 women), 5 part-time/adjunct (3 women). *Students:* 34 full-time (21 women), 5 part-time (1 woman); includes 2 minority (1 Black or African American, non-Hispanic/Latino; 1 Two or more races, non-Hispanic/Latino). Average age 26. 22 applicants, 100% accepted, 14 enrolled. In 2017, 13 master's awarded. *Degree requirements:* For master's, comprehensive exam (for some programs), thesis optional. *Entrance requirements:* For master's, GRE General Test, writing sample. Additional exam requirements/recommendations for international students: Required—TOEFL. *Application deadline:* For fall admission, 8/15 for domestic students, 5/1 for international students; for spring admission, 11/1 priority date for domestic students. Applications are processed on a rolling basis. Application fee: $0. Electronic applications accepted. *Expenses:* $1,259 per credit. *Financial support:* In 2017–18, 30 students received support, including 7 teaching assistantships with full tuition reimbursements available (averaging $8,000 per year); career-related internships or fieldwork, Federal Work-Study, scholarships/grants, tuition waivers (full and partial), and unspecified assistantships also available. Support available to part-time students. Financial award application deadline: 5/1. *Faculty research:* American studies, immigration history, local social history, applied history, Eastern European history. *Unit head:* Dr. John Dwyer, Chair, 412-396-6470, E-mail: dwyer@duq.edu. *Application contact:* Linda Rendulic, Assistant to the Dean, 412-396-6400, Fax: 412-396-5265, E-mail: rendulic@duq.edu.
Website: http://www.duq.edu/academics/schools/liberal-arts/graduate-school/programs/history

East Carolina University, Graduate School, Thomas Harriot College of Arts and Sciences, Department of History, Greenville, NC 27858-4353. Offers American history (MA); Atlantic world (MA); European history (MA); maritime studies (MA); military history (MA); public history (MA). *Program availability:* Part-time. *Students:* 39 full-time (16 women), 49 part-time (21 women); includes 11 minority (2 Black or African American, non-Hispanic/Latino; 1 Asian, non-Hispanic/Latino; 5 Hispanic/Latino; 3 Two or more races, non-Hispanic/Latino), 1 international. Average age 29. 35 applicants, 83% accepted, 19 enrolled. In 2017, 15 master's awarded. *Degree requirements:* For master's, one foreign language, comprehensive exam, thesis. *Entrance requirements:* For master's, GRE General Test. Additional exam requirements/recommendations for international students: Recommended—TOEFL (minimum score 78 iBT), IELTS (minimum score 6.5). *Application deadline:* For fall admission, 4/1 priority date for domestic and international students; for spring admission, 10/15 priority date for domestic and international students. Applications are processed on a rolling basis. Application fee: $75. Electronic applications accepted. *Expenses:* Tuition, state resident: full-time $4749; part-time $297 per credit hour. Tuition, nonresident: full-time $17,898; part-time $1119 per credit hour. *Required fees:* $2691; $224 per credit hour. Part-time tuition and fees vary according to course load and program. *Financial support:* Fellowships, research assistantships with partial tuition reimbursements, teaching assistantships with partial tuition reimbursements, and Federal Work-Study available. Support available to part-time students. Financial award application deadline: 1/15. *Unit head:* Dr. Christopher Oakley, Chair, 252-328-1025, E-mail: oakleyc@ecu.edu. *Application contact:* Dean of Graduate School, 252-328-6012, E-mail: gradschool@ecu.edu.
Website: http://www.ecu.edu/cs-cas/history/

Florida State University, The Graduate School, College of Arts and Sciences, Department of History, Tallahassee, FL 32306. Offers history (MA, MS, PhD); public history (MA). *Program availability:* Part-time. *Faculty:* 31 full-time (14 women). *Students:* 61 full-time (24 women), 21 part-time (5 women); includes 4 minority (2 Black or African American, non-Hispanic/Latino; 2 Asian, non-Hispanic/Latino), 3 international. Average age 30. 53 applicants, 60% accepted, 15 enrolled. In 2017, 13 master's, 7 doctorates awarded. *Degree requirements:* For master's, one foreign language, comprehensive exam (for some programs), thesis (for some programs), internships; for doctorate, one foreign language, comprehensive exam, thesis/dissertation. *Entrance requirements:* For master's, GRE General Test, minimum GPA of 3.3, minimum 18 hours of course work in history; for doctorate, GRE General Test, master's degree, minimum graduate GPA of 3.65. Additional exam requirements/recommendations for international students: Required—TOEFL (minimum score 550 paper-based; 80 iBT). *Application deadline:* For fall admission, 12/1 for domestic and international students. Applications are processed on a rolling basis. Application fee: $30. Electronic applications accepted. *Financial support:* In 2017–18, 49 students received support, including 7 fellowships with full tuition reimbursements available (averaging $19,000 per year), 5 research assistantships with full tuition reimbursements available (averaging $15,500 per year), 5 teaching assistantships with full tuition reimbursements available (averaging $18,000 per year); Federal Work-Study, institutionally sponsored loans, scholarships/grants, tuition waivers (full and partial), and unspecified assistantships also available. Financial award application deadline: 12/1; financial award applicants required to submit FAFSA. *Faculty research:* Napoleon and the French Revolution, modern Europe, early modern Europe, Middle East, Latin America, Hispanic Caribbean, 20th-century Cuba, modern Britain, gender and sexuality, Atlantic world, modern Germany, Medieval Europe, World War II, U.S. 19th century, early U.S., Native American, science, medicine and technology, Russia, East Asia. *Unit head:* Dr. Edward Gray, Chair, 850-644-5888, Fax: 850-644-6402, E-mail: egray@fsu.edu. *Application contact:* Anne Kozar, Academic Program Specialist, 850-644-4494, E-mail: mkozar@fsu.edu.
Website: http://history.fsu.edu/

Georgia Southern University, Jack N. Averitt College of Graduate Studies, College of Liberal Arts and Social Sciences, Program in History, Statesboro, GA 30460. Offers history (MA); public history (Graduate Certificate). *Program availability:* Part-time. *Faculty:* 24 full-time (7 women). *Students:* 11 full-time (7 women), 7 part-time (3 women); includes 2 minority (1 American Indian or Alaska Native, non-Hispanic/Latino; 1 Hispanic/Latino). Average age 30. 14 applicants, 93% accepted, 11 enrolled. In 2017, 12 master's awarded. *Degree requirements:* For master's, one foreign language, thesis optional, terminal exams. *Entrance requirements:* For master's, GRE General Test, minimum GPA of 3.0, undergraduate major in history or equivalent, letters of reference. Additional exam requirements/recommendations for international students: Required—TOEFL (minimum score 550 paper-based; 80 iBT), IELTS (minimum score 6). *Application deadline:* For fall admission, 3/1 priority date for domestic and international students; for spring admission, 10/1 priority date for domestic students, 10/1 for international students. Applications are processed on a rolling basis. Application fee: $50. Electronic applications accepted. *Expenses:* Tuition, state resident: full-time $4986; part-time $3324 per year. Tuition, nonresident: full-time $21,982; part-time $15,352 per year. *Required fees:* $2092; $1802 per credit hour. $901 per semester. Tuition and fees vary according to course load, campus/location and program. *Financial support:* In 2017–18, 15 students received support, including 14 fellowships with full tuition reimbursements available (averaging $7,750 per year), 1 teaching assistantship with full tuition reimbursement available (averaging $7,750 per year); career-related internships or fieldwork, Federal Work-Study, scholarships/grants, tuition waivers (full), and unspecified assistantships also available. Support available to part-time students. Financial award application deadline: 4/15; financial award applicants required to submit FAFSA. *Faculty research:* Women's/gender history, the American South, military history, public history, modern Europe. *Unit head:* Dr. Timothy Teeter, Graduate Program Director, 912-478-0239, Fax: 912-478-0377, E-mail: tmteeter@georgiasouthern.edu.
Website: http://class.georgiasouthern.edu/history/

Georgia Southern University–Armstrong Campus, College of Graduate Studies, Program in History, Savannah, GA 31419-1997. Offers American and European history (MA); public history (MA). *Program availability:* Part-time, evening/weekend. *Faculty:* 11 full-time (3 women), 1 (woman) part-time/adjunct. *Students:* 7 full-time (3 women), 10 part-time (5 women); includes 3 minority (all Black or African American, non-Hispanic/Latino). Average age 43. 14 applicants, 43% accepted, 5 enrolled. In 2017, 5 master's awarded. *Degree requirements:* For master's, one foreign language, comprehensive exam (for some programs), thesis (for some programs), thesis, internship, or advanced fieldwork. *Entrance requirements:* For master's, GRE General Test, minimum GPA of 3.0, letters of recommendation, BA in history or equivalent. Additional exam requirements/recommendations for international students: Required—TOEFL (minimum score 523 paper-based; 70 iBT). *Application deadline:* For fall admission, 6/30 priority date for domestic students, 5/1 priority date for international students; for spring admission, 11/15 priority date for domestic students, 9/15 priority date for international students; for summer admission, 4/15 priority date for domestic students, 9/15 for international students. Applications are processed on a rolling basis. Application fee: $30. Electronic applications accepted. *Expenses:* Tuition, state resident: part-time $211 per credit hour. Tuition, nonresident: part-time $782 per credit hour. *Required fees:* $737 per semester. Tuition and fees vary according to course load, degree level, campus/location and program. *Financial support:* In 2017–18, research assistantships with full tuition reimbursements (averaging $5,000 per year) were awarded; career-related internships or fieldwork, Federal Work-Study, and unspecified assistantships also available. Support available to part-time students. Financial award application deadline: 3/15; financial award applicants required to submit FAFSA. *Faculty research:* Public history; European, Latin American, African, and United States history. *Unit head:* Dr. Christopher Hendricks, Interim Department Head, 912-344-2725, Fax: 912-344-3451, E-mail: chris.hendricks@armstrong.edu. *Application contact:* McKenzie Peterman, Graduate Admissions Specialist, 912-478-5678, Fax: 912-478-0740, E-mail: mpeterman@georgiasouthern.edu.
Website: http://www.armstrong.edu/Liberal_Arts/history/history_graduate_program

Georgia State University, College of Arts and Sciences, Department of History, Program in History, Atlanta, GA 30302-3083. Offers historic preservation (MA); history (PhD); public history (MA); world history (MA). *Program availability:* Part-time, evening/weekend. Terminal master's awarded for partial completion of doctoral program. *Entrance requirements:* For master's, GRE, BA in history; statement of purpose; writing sample; three letters of recommendation; official transcripts; for doctorate, GRE, MA in history; master's thesis; statement of purpose; writing sample; three letters of recommendation; official transcripts; appropriate language skills. Additional exam requirements/recommendations for international students: Required—TOEFL (minimum score 550 paper-based; 80 iBT). *Application deadline:* Applications are processed on a rolling basis. Application fee: $50. Electronic applications accepted. *Expenses:* Tuition, state resident: full-time $7020. Tuition, nonresident: full-time $22,518. *Required fees:* $2128. Tuition and fees vary according to degree level and program. *Financial support:* Research assistantships, teaching assistantships, and scholarships/grants available. Financial award application deadline: 2/15; financial award applicants required to submit FAFSA. *Faculty research:* Nineteenth- and twentieth-century U.S. history, early modern European history, modern European history, world history, public history. *Unit head:* Dr. Michelle Brattain, Chair, 404-413-6352, Fax: 404-413-6384, E-mail: mbrattain@gsu.edu. *Application contact:* Dr. Joe Perry, Director of Graduate Studies, 404-413-6374, Fax: 404-413-6384, E-mail: jbperry@gsu.edu.
Website: http://www.gsu.edu/~wwwhis/

Indiana University of Pennsylvania, School of Graduate Studies and Research, College of Humanities and Social Sciences, Department of History, Indiana, PA 15705. Offers history (MA); public history (MA). *Program availability:* Part-time. *Faculty:* 4 full-

time (2 women). *Students:* 6 full-time (3 women). Average age 26. 12 applicants, 67% accepted, 3 enrolled. In 2017, 5 master's awarded. *Degree requirements:* For master's, thesis optional. *Entrance requirements:* For master's, GRE, 2 letters of recommendation. Additional exam requirements/recommendations for international students: Required—TOEFL (minimum score 540 paper-based). *Application deadline:* Applications are processed on a rolling basis. Application fee: $50. Electronic applications accepted. *Expenses:* Tuition, state resident: full-time $12,000; part-time $500 per credit. Tuition, nonresident: full-time $18,000; part-time $750 per credit. *Required fees:* $4073; $165.55 per credit. $64 per term. *Financial support:* In 2017–18, 6 research assistantships with tuition reimbursements (averaging $3,827 per year) were awarded; fellowships with partial tuition reimbursements, career-related internships or fieldwork, Federal Work-Study, scholarships/grants, and unspecified assistantships also available. Support available to part-time students. Financial award application deadline: 4/15; financial award applicants required to submit FAFSA. *Unit head:* Dr. R. Scott Moore, Chairperson, 724-357-2573, E-mail: rsmoore@iup.edu. *Application contact:* Dr. Jeanine Mazak-Kahne, Graduate Coordinator, 724-357-2436, E-mail: jmkahne@iup.edu.
Website: http://www.iup.edu/history

Indiana University–Purdue University Indianapolis, School of Liberal Arts, Department of History, Indianapolis, IN 46202. Offers European history (MA); public history (MA); United States history (MA); MA/MA; MA/MLS. *Program availability:* Part-time, evening/weekend. *Degree requirements:* For master's, one foreign language, thesis. *Entrance requirements:* For master's, GRE General Test, minimum GPA of 3.0. Electronic applications accepted.

James Madison University, The Graduate School, College of Arts and Letters, Program in History, Harrisonburg, VA 22801. Offers public history (MA); U.S. history (MA); world history (MA). *Program availability:* Part-time. *Students:* 16 full-time (6 women), 10 part-time (4 women). Average age 30. In 2017, 8 master's awarded. *Degree requirements:* For master's, one foreign language, comprehensive exam, thesis. Application fee: $55. Electronic applications accepted. *Expenses:* Tuition, state resident: full-time $10,512; part-time $438 per credit hour. Tuition, nonresident: full-time $28,358; part-time $1162 per credit hour. *Required fees:* $1128. *Financial support:* In 2017–18, 10 students received support, including 7 fellowships, 3 teaching assistantships with full tuition reimbursements available (averaging $9,284 per year); Federal Work-Study and assistantships (averaging $7911) also available. Financial award application deadline: 3/1; financial award applicants required to submit FAFSA. *Unit head:* Dr. Gabrielle Lanier, Department Head, 540-568-6132, E-mail: laniergm@jmu.edu. *Application contact:* Lynette D. Michael, Director of Graduate Admissions, 540-568-6131 Ext. 6395, Fax: 540-568-7860, E-mail: michaeld@jmu.edu.
Website: http://www.jmu.edu/history

La Salle University, School of Arts and Sciences, Program in History, Philadelphia, PA 19141-1199. Offers American history (Certificate); European history (Certificate); history (MA); history for educators (MA); public history (MA); teaching advanced placement history (Certificate); world history (Certificate). *Program availability:* Part-time. *Faculty:* 4 full-time (1 woman), 2 part-time/adjunct (0 women). *Students:* 2 full-time (0 women), 10 part-time (5 women); includes 1 minority (Asian, non-Hispanic/Latino). Average age 37. 9 applicants, 78% accepted, 2 enrolled. In 2017, 7 master's awarded. *Degree requirements:* For master's, thesis or comprehensive exam. *Entrance requirements:* For master's, GRE or MAT, 18 hours of undergraduate coursework in history or a related discipline with minimum GPA of 3.0; two letters of recommendation; brief personal statement (250 to 500 words); writing sample (preferably from an undergraduate research paper). Additional exam requirements/recommendations for international students: Required—TOEFL. *Application deadline:* For fall admission, 8/15 priority date for domestic students, 7/15 for international students; for spring admission, 12/15 priority date for domestic students, 11/15 for international students; for summer admission, 4/15 priority date for domestic students, 3/15 for international students. Applications are processed on a rolling basis. Application fee: $35. Electronic applications accepted. Application fee is waived when completed online. *Expenses:* Contact institution. *Financial support:* In 2017–18, 1 student received support. Scholarships/grants available. Support available to part-time students. Financial award application deadline: 8/31; financial award applicants required to submit FAFSA. *Unit head:* Dr. George B. Stow, Director, 215-951-1097, E-mail: grahis@lasalle.edu. *Application contact:* Elizabeth Heenan, Director, Graduate and Adult Enrollment, 215-951-1100, Fax: 215-951-1462, E-mail: heenan@lasalle.edu.
Website: http://www.lasalle.edu/master-history/

Lehigh University, College of Arts and Sciences, Department of History, Bethlehem, PA 18015. Offers Atlantic world (PhD); British history (PhD); history (MA); industrial and modern America (PhD); public history (MA). *Program availability:* Part-time. *Faculty:* 14 full-time (7 women). *Students:* 19 full-time (6 women), 15 part-time (2 women); includes 2 minority (1 Black or African American, non-Hispanic/Latino; 1 Two or more races, non-Hispanic/Latino), 2 international. Average age 35. 12 applicants, 58% accepted, 1 enrolled. In 2017, 3 master's, 2 doctorates awarded. Terminal master's awarded for partial completion of doctoral program. *Degree requirements:* For master's, comprehensive exam (for some programs), thesis (for some programs), comprehensive exam or thesis; for doctorate, comprehensive exam, thesis/dissertation. *Entrance requirements:* For master's, GRE General Test, recommendations, writing sample; for doctorate, GRE General Test, recommendations, writing samples. Additional exam requirements/recommendations for international students: Required—TOEFL. *Application deadline:* For fall admission, 2/15 for domestic and international students. Application fee: $75. *Financial support:* In 2017–18, 2 fellowships with full tuition reimbursements (averaging $22,500 per year), 10 teaching assistantships with full tuition reimbursements (averaging $10,000 per year) were awarded; research assistantships, institutionally sponsored loans, scholarships/grants, tuition waivers (full and partial), and unspecified assistantships also available. Financial award application deadline: 1/15. *Faculty research:* Colonial America, modern America, history of technology, Atlantic world, French Atlantic, Spanish Atlantic, British empire, gender, intellectual history, African diaspora history. *Unit head:* Prof. John Pettegrew, Chairman, 610-758-3360, Fax: 610-758-6554, E-mail: jcp5@lehigh.edu. *Application contact:* Dr. John Savage, Graduate Coordinator, 610-758-3363, Fax: 610-758-6554, E-mail: jms8@lehigh.edu.
Website: http://history.cas2.lehigh.edu/

Loyola University Chicago, Graduate School, Department of History, Chicago, IL 60611. Offers history (MA, PhD); public history (MA). *Program availability:* Part-time, evening/weekend. *Faculty:* 38 full-time (21 women), 9 part-time/adjunct (6 women). *Students:* 38 full-time (21 women), 9 part-time (6 women); includes 5 minority (1 Black or African American, non-Hispanic/Latino; 1 Asian, non-Hispanic/Latino; 2 Hispanic/Latino; 1 Two or more races, non-Hispanic/Latino), 1 international. Average age 30. 77 applicants, 57% accepted, 13 enrolled. In 2017, 14 master's, 8 doctorates awarded. Terminal master's awarded for partial completion of doctoral program. *Degree requirements:* For master's, one foreign language, comprehensive exam, thesis optional, portfolio (for public history program); for doctorate, 2 foreign languages, comprehensive exam, thesis/dissertation. *Entrance requirements:* For master's, GRE General Test, research paper/writing sample; for doctorate, GRE General Test, seminar

paper or master's thesis. Additional exam requirements/recommendations for international students: Required—TOEFL (minimum score 550 paper-based), IELTS. *Application deadline:* For fall admission, 5/1 for domestic students; for spring admission, 10/1 for domestic students. Applications are processed on a rolling basis. Application fee: $50. Electronic applications accepted. Application fee is waived when completed online. *Expenses:* $19,026 full-time. *Financial support:* In 2017–18, 20 students received support, including 1 fellowship with full tuition reimbursement available (averaging $20,000 per year), 1 research assistantship with full tuition reimbursement available (averaging $18,000 per year), 16 teaching assistantships with full tuition reimbursements available (averaging $18,000 per year); Federal Work-Study, scholarships/grants, traineeships, health care benefits, and unspecified assistantships also available. Financial award application deadline: 1/1; financial award applicants required to submit FAFSA. *Faculty research:* Medieval and early modern Europe, U.S. public history, U.S. urban history, gender history, transnational history. *Unit head:* Dr. Stephen Schloesser, Chair, 773-508-2221, Fax: 773-508-3693, E-mail: sschloesser@luc.edu. *Application contact:* Dr. Patricia Mooney-Melvin, Director, Graduate Programs, 773-508-2228, Fax: 773-508-3693, E-mail: pmooney@luc.edu.
Website: http://www.luc.edu/history/

Middle Tennessee State University, College of Graduate Studies, College of Liberal Arts, Department of History, Program in Public History, Murfreesboro, TN 37132. Offers PhD. *Program availability:* Part-time, evening/weekend, online learning. *Degree requirements:* For doctorate, one foreign language, comprehensive exam, thesis/dissertation. *Entrance requirements:* For doctorate, GRE. Additional exam requirements/recommendations for international students: Required—TOEFL (minimum score 525 paper-based; 71 iBT) or IELTS (minimum score 6).

New York University, Graduate School of Arts and Science, Department of History, New York, NY 10012-1019. Offers African diaspora (PhD); African history (PhD); archival management (Advanced Certificate); Atlantic history (PhD); French studies/history (PhD); Hebrew and Judaic studies/history (PhD); history (MA, PhD), including Europe (PhD), Latin America and the Caribbean (PhD), United States (PhD), women's history (MA); Middle Eastern history (MA); Middle Eastern studies/history (PhD); public history (Advanced Certificate); world history (MA); JD/MA; MA/Advanced Certificate. *Program availability:* Part-time. *Students:* Average age 29. 401 applicants, 31% accepted, 38 enrolled. In 2017, 24 master's, 16 doctorates awarded. Terminal master's awarded for partial completion of doctoral program. *Degree requirements:* For master's, seminar paper; for doctorate, one foreign language, thesis/dissertation, oral and written exams; for Advanced Certificate, internship. *Entrance requirements:* For master's, GRE General Test, minimum GPA of 3.0, writing sample; for doctorate, GRE. Additional exam requirements/recommendations for international students: Required—TOEFL. *Application deadline:* For fall admission, 12/18 for domestic and international students. Application fee: $100. *Expenses:* Tuition: Full-time $41,352; part-time $19,968 per year. *Required fees:* $2496; $1628 per unit. $814 per term. Tuition and fees vary according to course load and program. *Financial support:* Fellowships, research assistantships, teaching assistantships, career-related internships or fieldwork, Federal Work-Study, institutionally sponsored loans, scholarships/grants, health care benefits, and unspecified assistantships available. Financial award application deadline: 12/18; financial award applicants required to submit FAFSA. *Faculty research:* African, East Asian, medieval, early modern, and modern European history; U.S. history; African and African diaspora; Latin American history; Atlantic world. *Unit head:* Barbara Weinstein, Chair, 212-998-8600, Fax: 212-995-4017, E-mail: history.admissions@nyu.edu. *Application contact:* Stepfanos Geroulanos, Director of Graduate Studies, 212-998-8600, Fax: 212-995-4017, E-mail: history.admissions@nyu.edu.
Website: http://history.as.nyu.edu/

North Carolina State University, Graduate School, College of Humanities and Social Sciences, Department of History, Program in Public History, Raleigh, NC 27695. Offers MA. *Degree requirements:* For master's, thesis optional. *Entrance requirements:* For master's, GRE General Test. Electronic applications accepted.

Northern Kentucky University, Office of Graduate Programs, College of Arts and Sciences, Program in Public History, Highland Heights, KY 41099. Offers MA. *Program availability:* Part-time, evening/weekend. *Degree requirements:* For master's, comprehensive exam, final capstone project. *Entrance requirements:* Additional exam requirements/recommendations for international students: Required—TOEFL (minimum score 550 paper-based; 79 iBT); Recommended—IELTS (minimum score 6.5). Electronic applications accepted. *Faculty research:* Local history.

Rutgers University–Camden, Graduate School of Arts and Sciences, Program in American and Public History, Camden, NJ 08102. Offers MA. *Program availability:* Part-time, evening/weekend. *Degree requirements:* For master's, comprehensive exam, thesis optional, 30 credits. *Entrance requirements:* For master's, GRE General Test (for full-time applicants), 3 letters of recommendation; history or related undergraduate degree (preferred). Additional exam requirements/recommendations for international students: Required—TOEFL, IELTS. Electronic applications accepted. *Faculty research:* Women's history, military history, Afro-American history, urban history, history of technology.

St. John's University, St. John's College of Liberal Arts and Sciences, Department of History, Queens, NY 11439. Offers history (MA, PhD); public history (MA). *Program availability:* Part-time, evening/weekend. *Faculty:* 17 full-time (8 women), 13 part-time/adjunct (10 women). *Students:* 25 full-time (9 women), 23 part-time (5 women); includes 13 minority (4 Black or African American, non-Hispanic/Latino; 4 Asian, non-Hispanic/Latino; 3 Hispanic/Latino; 2 Two or more races, non-Hispanic/Latino), 3 international. Average age 34. 37 applicants, 95% accepted, 17 enrolled. In 2017, 8 master's, 4 doctorates awarded. Terminal master's awarded for partial completion of doctoral program. *Degree requirements:* For master's, variable foreign language requirement, comprehensive exam, thesis optional; for doctorate, variable foreign language requirement, thesis/dissertation, annual portfolio, internships. *Entrance requirements:* For master's, letters of recommendation, transcripts, resume, personal statement; for doctorate, GRE General Test, letters of recommendation, transcripts, resume, personal statement. Additional exam requirements/recommendations for international students: Required—TOEFL (minimum score 80 iBT), IELTS (minimum score 6.5). *Application deadline:* For fall admission, 4/1 for domestic students; for spring admission, 11/1 for domestic students. Applications are processed on a rolling basis. Application fee: $70. Electronic applications accepted. *Expenses:* Tuition: Full-time $44,280; part-time $1230 per credit. *Required fees:* $340; $340 per credit. Tuition and fees vary according to course load, degree level and program. *Financial support:* Fellowships, research assistantships, teaching assistantships, scholarships/grants, tuition waivers, and unspecified assistantships available. Support available to part-time students. Financial award application deadline: 2/1; financial award applicants required to submit FAFSA. *Faculty research:* World history, gender and cultural history, public history, history of science and technology, social history and business history. *Unit head:* Dr. Nerina Rustomji, Chair, 718-990-6229, E-mail: rustomjn@stjohns.edu. *Application contact:* Robert Medrano, Director of Graduate Admission, 718-990-1601, Fax: 718-990-5686, E-mail: gradhelp@stjohns.edu.
Website: https://www.stjohns.edu/academics/schools-and-colleges/st-johns-college-liberal-arts-and-sciences/history

Public History

Shippensburg University of Pennsylvania, School of Graduate Studies, College of Arts and Sciences, Department of History and Philosophy, Shippensburg, PA 17257-2299. Offers applied history (MA). *Program availability:* Part-time, evening/weekend. *Faculty:* 5 full-time (1 woman). *Students:* 14 full-time (7 women), 12 part-time (3 women); includes 2 minority (1 Black or African American, non-Hispanic/Latino; 1 Two or more races, non-Hispanic/Latino). Average age 29. 24 applicants, 88% accepted, 12 enrolled. In 2017, 10 master's awarded. *Degree requirements:* For master's, thesis, internship, or student teaching and professional practicum. *Entrance requirements:* For master's, 500-word statement of purpose; interview or minimum GPA of 2.75. Additional exam requirements/recommendations for international students: Required—TOEFL (minimum score 550 paper-based, 68 iBT) or IELTS (minimum score 6). *Application deadline:* For fall admission, 2/15 for domestic and international students; for spring admission, 9/15 for domestic and international students; for summer admission, 2/15 for domestic and international students. Applications are processed on a rolling basis. Application fee: $45. Electronic applications accepted. *Expenses:* Tuition, state resident: part-time $500 per credit. Tuition, nonresident: part-time $750 per credit. *Required fees:* $145 per credit. *Financial support:* In 2017–18, 8 students received support. Career-related internships or fieldwork, scholarships/grants, unspecified assistantships, and resident hall director and student payroll positions available. Support available to part-time students. Financial award application deadline: 3/1; financial award applicants required to submit FAFSA. *Unit head:* Dr. John D. Bloom, Associate Professor and Program Coordinator, 717-477-1621, Fax: 717-477-4062, E-mail: jdbloo@ship.edu. *Application contact:* Maya T. Mapp, Director of Admissions, 717-477-1231, Fax: 717-477-4016, E-mail: mtmapp@ship.edu.
Website: http://www.ship.edu/history/

Shippensburg University of Pennsylvania, School of Graduate Studies, College of Arts and Sciences, Department of Sociology and Anthropology, Shippensburg, PA 17257-2299. Offers organizational development and leadership (MS), including business, higher education structure and policy, historical administration, leadership in society, management information systems, public organizations. *Program availability:* Part-time, evening/weekend. *Faculty:* 4 full-time (2 women). *Students:* 14 full-time (6 women), 19 part-time (11 women); includes 7 minority (4 Black or African American, non-Hispanic/Latino; 2 Hispanic/Latino; 1 Two or more races, non-Hispanic/Latino), 1 international. Average age 26. 31 applicants, 81% accepted, 15 enrolled. In 2017, 22 master's awarded. *Degree requirements:* For master's, capstone experience including internship. *Entrance requirements:* For master's, interview (if GPA less than 2.75), current resume, personal goals statement. Additional exam requirements/recommendations for international students: Required—TOEFL (minimum score 550 paper-based, 68 iBT) or IELTS (minimum score 6). *Application deadline:* For fall admission, 4/30 for international students; for spring admission, 9/30 for international students. Applications are processed on a rolling basis. Application fee: $45. Electronic applications accepted. *Expenses:* Tuition, state resident: part-time $500 per credit. Tuition, nonresident: part-time $750 per credit. *Required fees:* $145 per credit. *Financial support:* In 2017–18, 12 students received support. Career-related internships or fieldwork, scholarships/grants, unspecified assistantships, and resident hall director and student payroll positions available. Support available to part-time students. Financial award application deadline: 3/1; financial award applicants required to submit FAFSA. *Unit head:* Dr. Barbara J. Denison, Departmental Chair and Program Coordinator, 717-477-1735, Fax: 717-477-4011, E-mail: bjdeni@ship.edu. *Application contact:* Maya T. Mapp, Director of Admissions, 717-477-1231, Fax: 717-477-4016, E-mail: mtmapp@ship.edu.
Website: http://www.ship.edu/odl/

Sonoma State University, School of Social Sciences, Program in Cultural Resources Management, Rohnert Park, CA 94928. Offers MA. *Program availability:* Part-time. *Entrance requirements:* For master's, minimum GPA of 3.0. Additional exam requirements/recommendations for international students: Required—TOEFL (minimum score 500 paper-based). *Application deadline:* For fall admission, 1/31 for domestic students. Application fee: $55. *Financial support:* Career-related internships or fieldwork, scholarships/grants, traineeships, and unspecified assistantships available. Financial award application deadline: 3/2; financial award applicants required to submit FAFSA. *Unit head:* Alexis Boutin, Chair, Anthropology Department, 707-664-2312, Fax: 707-664-2505, E-mail: alexis.boutin@sonoma.edu.
Website: http://www.sonoma.edu/anthropology/graduate/master.html

Southeast Missouri State University, School of Graduate Studies, Department of History, Cape Girardeau, MO 63701-4799. Offers heritage interpretation (Certificate); historic preservation (Certificate); history (MA); public history (MA), including heritage education, historic preservation. *Program availability:* Part-time, evening/weekend. *Faculty:* 10 full-time (4 women). *Students:* 12 full-time (7 women), 14 part-time (5 women); includes 3 minority (2 Black or African American, non-Hispanic/Latino; 1 Hispanic/Latino). Average age 32. 12 applicants, 100% accepted, 10 enrolled. In 2017, 8 master's awarded. *Degree requirements:* For master's, comprehensive exam (for some programs), thesis or comprehensive exams plus a capstone project/paper (for history); thesis or internship plus advanced project in applied history and comprehensive exams (for public history). *Entrance requirements:* For master's, minimum GPA of 2.75; 24 semester hours of undergraduate credit in history; letter of intent indicating how past experiences have prepared the candidate for graduate study and what the candidate expects to achieve through graduate study; two letters of recommendation; academic or professional writing sample; for Certificate, minimum GPA of 2.75; letter of intent indicating how past experiences have prepared the candidate for graduate study and what the candidate expects to achieve through graduate study; two letters of recommendation; academic or professional writing sample. Additional exam requirements/recommendations for international students: Required—TOEFL (minimum score 550 paper-based; 79 iBT), IELTS (minimum score 6), PTE (minimum score 53). *Application deadline:* For fall admission, 8/1 for domestic students, 6/1 for international students; for spring admission, 11/21 for domestic students, 10/1 for international students; for summer admission, 5/15 for domestic students. Applications are processed on a rolling basis. Application fee: $30 ($40 for international students). Electronic applications accepted. *Expenses:* $270.35 per credit hour in-state tuition, $33.40 per credit hour fees. *Financial support:* In 2017–18, 4 students received support, including 4 teaching assistantships with full tuition reimbursements available; career-related internships or fieldwork, Federal Work-Study, scholarships/grants, traineeships, tuition waivers (full), and unspecified assistantships also available. Financial award application deadline: 6/30; financial award applicants required to submit FAFSA. *Faculty research:* Medieval Europe; modern Europe including Britain, Germany, France, Russia, and Spain; colonial and nineteenth-century America; twentieth-century America and American West; public history and medieval Europe; modern Europe including Britain, Germany, France, Russia, and Spain; colonial and nineteenth-century America; twentieth-century America and American West; public history and historic preservation; Latin America. *Unit head:* Dr. Toni Alexander, Chairperson/Professor of History, 573-651-2179, Fax: 573-651-5114, E-mail: talexander@semo.edu. *Application contact:* Dr. Vicky McAlister, Graduate Coordinator/Assistant Professor of History, 573-651-2763, Fax: 573-651-5114, E-mail: vmcalister@semo.edu.

Texas A&M University–Commerce, College of Humanities, Social Sciences and Arts, Commerce, TX 75429. Offers applied criminology (MS); applied linguistics (MA, MS); art (MA, MFA); computational linguistics (Graduate Certificate); creative writing (Graduate Certificate); criminal justice management (Graduate Certificate); criminal justice studies (Graduate Certificate); English (MA, MS, PhD); film studies (Graduate Certificate); history (MA, MS); history of Christianity (Graduate Certificate); Holocaust studies (Graduate Certificate); homeland security (Graduate Certificate); music education (MM); music performance (MM); political science (MA, MS); public history (Graduate Certificate); sociology (MS); Spanish (MA); studies in children's and adolescent literature and culture (Graduate Certificate); teaching English to speakers of other languages (Graduate Certificate); theater (MA, MS); world history (Graduate Certificate). *Program availability:* Part-time. *Faculty:* 56 full-time (26 women), 10 part-time/adjunct (5 women). *Students:* 133 full-time (85 women), 439 part-time (311 women); includes 204 minority (79 Black or African American, non-Hispanic/Latino; 4 American Indian or Alaska Native, non-Hispanic/Latino; 9 Asian, non-Hispanic/Latino; 98 Hispanic/Latino; 14 Two or more races, non-Hispanic/Latino), 26 international. Average age 36. 261 applicants, 50% accepted, 113 enrolled. In 2017, 105 master's, 5 doctorates awarded. *Degree requirements:* For master's, one foreign language, comprehensive exam, thesis (for some programs); for doctorate, one foreign language, comprehensive exam, thesis/dissertation, departmental qualifying exam. *Entrance requirements:* For master's and doctorate, GRE General Test. Additional exam requirements/recommendations for international students: Required—TOEFL (minimum score 550 paper-based; 79 iBT), IELTS (minimum score 6). *Application deadline:* Applications are processed on a rolling basis. Application fee: $50. Electronic applications accepted. *Expenses:* Contact institution. *Financial support:* In 2017–18, 43 students received support, including 9 research assistantships with partial tuition reimbursements available (averaging $9,000 per year), 68 teaching assistantships with partial tuition reimbursements available (averaging $9,000 per year); Federal Work-Study, institutionally sponsored loans, scholarships/grants, health care benefits, and unspecified assistantships also available. Financial award application deadline: 5/1; financial award applicants required to submit FAFSA. *Unit head:* Dr. William F. Kuracina, Interim Dean, 903-886-5166, Fax: 903-886-5774, E-mail: william.kuracina@tamuc.edu. *Application contact:* Vicky Turner, Doctoral Degree and Special Programs Coordinator, 903-886-5167, E-mail: vicky.turner@tamuc.edu.
Website: http://www.tamuc.edu/academics/graduateSchool/programs/humanitiesSocialScienceArts/default.aspx

University at Albany, State University of New York, College of Arts and Sciences, Department of History, Albany, NY 12222-0001. Offers history (MA, PhD); public history (Certificate). *Program availability:* Part-time. *Faculty:* 19 full-time (6 women). *Students:* 16 full-time (4 women), 60 part-time (26 women); includes 4 minority (1 Black or African American, non-Hispanic/Latino; 1 Hispanic/Latino; 2 Two or more races, non-Hispanic/Latino), 4 international. 49 applicants, 61% accepted, 17 enrolled. In 2017, 12 master's, 4 doctorates awarded. *Degree requirements:* For master's, variable foreign language requirement, exam, research paper or thesis; for doctorate, thesis/dissertation. *Entrance requirements:* For master's, minimum GPA of 3.0; for doctorate, GRE General Test, minimum GPA of 3.0. Additional exam requirements/recommendations for international students: Required—TOEFL (minimum score 550 paper-based). *Application deadline:* For fall admission, 3/1 for domestic students, 5/1 for international students; for spring admission, 11/1 for international students. Applications are processed on a rolling basis. Application fee: $75. Electronic applications accepted. *Expenses:* Tuition, state resident: full-time $10,870; part-time $453 per credit hour. Tuition, nonresident: full-time $22,210; part-time $925 per credit hour. *Required fees:* $84.68 per credit hour. $508.06 per semester. Part-time tuition and fees vary according to course load and program. *Financial support:* Teaching assistantships and career-related internships or fieldwork available. Financial award application deadline: 3/1. *Faculty research:* American history (all phases); public policy; European history (Medieval to modern); Asian, African, and Latin American history. *Unit head:* Richard Hamm, Chair, 518-442-5300, Fax: 518-442-5301, E-mail: rhamm@albany.edu. *Application contact:* Michael DeRensis, Director, Graduate Admissions, 518-442-3980, Fax: 518-442-3922, E-mail: graduate@albany.edu.
Website: http://www.albany.edu/history/

University at Buffalo, the State University of New York, Graduate School, College of Arts and Sciences, Department of History, Buffalo, NY 14260. Offers history (MA, PhD, Advanced Certificate); public history (MA). *Program availability:* Part-time. *Faculty:* 26 full-time (11 women). *Students:* 54 full-time (21 women), 2 part-time (1 woman); includes 6 minority (all Asian, non-Hispanic/Latino). Average age 29. 60 applicants, 57% accepted, 16 enrolled. In 2017, 10 master's, 3 doctorates awarded. Terminal master's awarded for partial completion of doctoral program. *Degree requirements:* For master's, project; for doctorate, one foreign language, comprehensive exam, thesis/dissertation. *Entrance requirements:* For doctorate, GRE General Test. Additional exam requirements/recommendations for international students: Required—TOEFL (minimum score 550 paper-based; 79 iBT). *Application deadline:* For fall admission, 1/5 priority date for domestic and international students; for spring admission, 10/1 priority date for domestic students, 10/1 for international students. Applications are processed on a rolling basis. Application fee: $75. Electronic applications accepted. *Expenses:* Contact institution. *Financial support:* In 2017–18, 40 students received support, including 5 fellowships (averaging $14,000 per year), 4 research assistantships (averaging $600 per year), 26 teaching assistantships with full tuition reimbursements available (averaging $16,500 per year); career-related internships or fieldwork, institutionally sponsored loans, scholarships/grants, health care benefits, unspecified assistantships, and conference travel support also available. Financial award application deadline: 1/5; financial award applicants required to submit FAFSA. *Faculty research:* Geographical areas: Africa, Asia, early modern Europe, Latin America and Caribbean, modern Europe (Britain, France, Germany, Spain), North and South Atlantic, world, United States and Colonial America; thematic areas: African-American, gender, imperialism and colonialism, intellectual/cultural/religious, political, public history, medicine/disability/science/knowledge, slavery, transnational/international, urban. *Total annual research expenditures:* $35,000. *Unit head:* Dr. Victoria Wolcott, Chair, 716-645-3435, Fax: 716-645-5954, E-mail: vwwolcot@buffalo.edu. *Application contact:* Sarah Handley-Cousins, Staff Assistant, 716-645-3433, Fax: 716-645-5954, E-mail: handley2@buffalo.edu.
Website: https://www.history.buffalo.edu

University of Arkansas at Little Rock, Graduate School, College of Arts, Letters, and Sciences, Department of History, Little Rock, AR 72204-1099. Offers public history (MA). *Program availability:* Part-time. *Degree requirements:* For master's, oral exam. *Entrance requirements:* For master's, GRE General Test, minimum GPA of 3.25 in history, 2.7 overall; 15 hours of undergraduate history; two letters of recommendation. *Faculty research:* Historic preservation and restoration, museum studies, archives.

University of California, Santa Barbara, Graduate Division, College of Letters and Sciences, Division of Humanities and Fine Arts, Department of History, Santa Barbara, CA 93106-9410. Offers European medieval studies (PhD); global studies (PhD); public historical studies (PhD); technology and society (PhD); women's studies (PhD); MA/PhD. *Degree requirements:* For doctorate, variable foreign language requirement, comprehensive exam, thesis/dissertation. *Entrance requirements:* For doctorate, GRE. Additional exam requirements/recommendations for international students: Required—TOEFL (minimum score 550 paper-based; 80 iBT), IELTS (minimum score 7). Electronic

applications accepted. *Faculty research:* Europe, United States, Latin America, Africa, Middle East, East Asia.

University of Colorado Denver, College of Liberal Arts and Sciences, Department of History, Denver, CO 80217. Offers European history (MA); global history (MA); public history (MA); U.S. history (MA). *Program availability:* Part-time, evening/weekend. *Degree requirements:* For master's, comprehensive exam, thesis optional, 36 semester hours (12 courses). *Entrance requirements:* For master's, GRE General Test, writing sample, minimum undergraduate GPA of 3.25, three letters of recommendation, statement of purpose addressing any weaknesses in academic record. Additional exam requirements/recommendations for international students: Required—TOEFL (minimum score 537 paper-based; 75 iBT); Recommended—IELTS (minimum score 6.5). Electronic applications accepted. *Faculty research:* Uses of pre-modern Islamic heritage in modern India; relationship between liberal understandings of democracy, crime, and police discretion; relationships between gender, class, health, and welfare in nineteenth and early twentieth century England; U.S. business cultures and their influences on marketing and personnel practices; intersection of business and political ideologies; social and environmental history of the Rocky Mountain West.

University of Illinois at Springfield, Graduate Programs, College of Liberal Arts and Sciences, Program in History, Springfield, IL 62703-5407. Offers MA. *Program availability:* Part-time, evening/weekend. *Faculty:* 9 full-time (4 women). *Students:* 9 full-time (3 women), 17 part-time (5 women); includes 1 minority (Two or more races, non-Hispanic/Latino), 1 international. Average age 32. 16 applicants, 88% accepted, 8 enrolled. In 2017, 7 master's awarded. *Degree requirements:* For master's, internship; closure exercise; position paper and historiography; thesis or project. *Entrance requirements:* For master's, BA in history or related field, minimum undergraduate GPA of 3.0, writing sample, statement of purpose. Additional exam requirements/recommendations for international students: Required—TOEFL (minimum score 500 paper-based; 61 iBT). *Application deadline:* Applications are processed on a rolling basis. Application fee: $60 ($75 for international students). Electronic applications accepted. *Expenses:* Tuition, state resident: full-time $7896; part-time $329 per credit hour. Tuition, nonresident: full-time $16,200; part-time $675 per credit hour. Tuition and fees vary according to program. *Financial support:* In 2017–18, research assistantships with full tuition reimbursements (averaging $10,249 per year), teaching assistantships with full tuition reimbursements (averaging $10,303 per year) were awarded; fellowships, career-related internships or fieldwork, Federal Work-Study, scholarships/grants, health care benefits, and unspecified assistantships also available. Support available to part-time students. Financial award application deadline: 11/15; financial award applicants required to submit FAFSA. *Unit head:* Dr. David Bertaina, Program Administrator, 217-206-8412, Fax: 217-206-6217, E-mail: dbert3@uis.edu. Website: http://www.uis.edu/history/curriculum/ma/

University of Louisville, Graduate School, College of Arts and Sciences, Department of History, Louisville, KY 40292-0001. Offers history (MA); public history (Certificate). *Program availability:* Part-time. *Faculty:* 20 full-time (8 women), 2 part-time/adjunct (1 woman). *Students:* 7 full-time (6 women), 15 part-time (6 women); includes 4 minority (1 Black or African American, non-Hispanic/Latino; 1 Hispanic/Latino; 2 Two or more races, non-Hispanic/Latino). Average age 37. 14 applicants, 86% accepted, 6 enrolled. In 2017, 2 master's awarded. *Degree requirements:* For master's, variable foreign language requirement, comprehensive exam (for some programs), thesis. *Entrance requirements:* For master's, GRE General Test, statement of purpose, not to exceed 500 words, which describes in reasonably specific terms, academic and career objectives and how they can be advanced through work in program. Additional exam requirements/recommendations for international students: Required—TOEFL. *Application deadline:* For fall admission, 2/15 for domestic and international students; for winter admission, 12/1 for domestic students; for spring admission, 12/1 for domestic and international students. Application fee: $65. Electronic applications accepted. *Expenses:* Contact institution. *Financial support:* In 2017–18, 1 teaching assistantship with full tuition reimbursement (averaging $12,000 per year) was awarded; scholarships/grants also available. Financial award application deadline: 2/15. *Faculty research:* Ancient and Medieval Europe, U.S. social and constitutional history, U.S. foreign relations and military, public history, Latin American and Borderlands. *Unit head:* Dr. Blake Beattie, Chairperson/Associate Professor, 502-852-6818, Fax: 502-852-0770, E-mail: history@louisville.edu. *Application contact:* Jennifer T. Westerfeld, Associate Professor, 502-852-3756, Fax: 502-852-0770, E-mail: histgrad@louisville.edu. Website: http://louisville.edu/history/

University of Maryland, Baltimore County, The Graduate School, College of Arts, Humanities and Social Sciences, School of Public Policy, Baltimore, MD 21250. Offers public policy (MPP, PhD), including economics (PhD), educational policy, emergency services (PhD), environmental policy (MPP), evaluation and analytical methods, health policy, policy history (PhD), public management, urban policy. *Program availability:* Part-time, evening/weekend. *Faculty:* 10 full-time (5 women). *Students:* 50 full-time (24 women), 69 part-time (37 women); includes 35 minority (17 Black or African American, non-Hispanic/Latino; 1 American Indian or Alaska Native, non-Hispanic/Latino; 8 Asian, non-Hispanic/Latino; 5 Hispanic/Latino; 1 Native Hawaiian or other Pacific Islander, non-Hispanic/Latino; 3 Two or more races, non-Hispanic/Latino), 6 international. Average age 37. 60 applicants, 68% accepted, 25 enrolled. In 2017, 15 master's, 3 doctorates awarded. Terminal master's awarded for partial completion of doctoral program. *Degree requirements:* For master's, thesis, policy analysis paper, internship for pre-service; for doctorate, comprehensive exam, thesis/dissertation, comprehensive and field qualifying exams. *Entrance requirements:* For master's, GRE General Test, 3 academic letters of reference, resume, official transcripts; for doctorate, GRE General Test, 3 academic letters of reference, resume, research paper, official transcripts. Additional exam requirements/recommendations for international students: Required—TOEFL (minimum score 550 paper-based; 80 iBT), IELTS (minimum score 6.5). *Application deadline:* For fall admission, 1/15 priority date for domestic students, 1/1 priority date for international students; for spring admission, 11/1 priority date for domestic students, 5/1 priority date for international students. Applications are processed on a rolling basis. Application fee: $50. Electronic applications accepted. *Expenses:* $28,061 in-state, $39,356 out-of-state to complete the degree (for MPP); $43,823 in-state, $61,508 out-of-state to complete the degree (for PhD). *Financial support:* In 2017–18, 26 students received support, including 26 research assistantships with full tuition reimbursements available (averaging $20,000 per year); Federal Work-Study, scholarships/grants, health care benefits, and unspecified assistantships also available. Financial award application deadline: 1/1; financial award applicants required to submit FAFSA. *Faculty research:* Education policy, health policy, urban and environmental policy, public management, evaluation and analytical method. *Unit head:* Dr. Susan Sterett, Director, 410-455-2140, Fax: 410-455-1172, E-mail: ssterett@umbc.edu. *Application contact:* Sally F. Helms, Administrator of Academic Affairs, 410-455-3202, Fax: 410-455-1172, E-mail: gradpubpol@umbc.edu. Website: http://publicpolicy.umbc.edu/

University of North Alabama, College of Arts and Sciences, Department of History, Program in Public History, Florence, AL 35632-0001. Offers historic preservation (MA); historical administration (MA). *Program availability:* Part-time. *Faculty:* 9 full-time (3 women), 3 part-time/adjunct (2 women). *Students:* 5 full-time (3 women), 3 part-time (2

women). Average age 35. 4 applicants, 100% accepted, 4 enrolled. In 2017, 3 master's awarded. *Degree requirements:* For master's, comprehensive exam (for some programs), thesis optional. *Entrance requirements:* For master's, GRE, three letters of recommendation; essay; writing sample. Additional exam requirements/recommendations for international students: Required—TOEFL (minimum score 79 iBT), IELTS (minimum score 6), TWE, PTE (minimum score 54). *Application deadline:* Applications are processed on a rolling basis. Application fee: $50 ($100 for international students). Electronic applications accepted. *Expenses:* Tuition, state resident: full-time $7824; part-time $5943 per year. Tuition, nonresident: full-time $15,648; part-time $11,736 per year. *Required fees:* $3064; $2298 per unit. Tuition and fees vary according to course load and reciprocity agreements. *Financial support:* In 2017–18, 5 students received support. Federal Work-Study, scholarships/grants, and unspecified assistantships available. Financial award application deadline: 2/1; financial award applicants required to submit FAFSA. *Unit head:* Dr. Jeffrey Bibbee, Chair, 256-765-4306, E-mail: jrbibbee@una.edu. *Application contact:* Hillary N. Coats, Graduate Admissions Coordinator, 256-765-4447, E-mail: graduate@una.edu. Website: https://www.una.edu/history/graduate-students/master-of-arts-in-public-history.html

University of Northern Iowa, Graduate College, College of Social and Behavioral Sciences, Department of History, Cedar Falls, IA 50614. Offers history (MA); public history (MA). *Program availability:* Part-time. *Degree requirements:* For master's, comprehensive exam (for some programs), thesis or alternative. *Entrance requirements:* For master's, minimum GPA of 3.2. Additional exam requirements/recommendations for international students: Required—TOEFL (minimum score 500 paper-based; 61 iBT). Electronic applications accepted.

University of South Carolina, The Graduate School, College of Arts and Sciences, Department of History, Program in Public History, Columbia, SC 29208. Offers archive management (MA); historic preservation (MA); museum administration (MA); museum management (Certificate); MLIS/MA. *Degree requirements:* For master's, one foreign language, thesis, internship. *Entrance requirements:* For master's, GRE General Test, writing sample. Additional exam requirements/recommendations for international students: Required—TOEFL. Electronic applications accepted. *Faculty research:* Museum studies, historic preservation, archives administration.

The University of Texas at Austin, Graduate School, College of Liberal Arts, Department of Anthropology, Austin, TX 78712-1111. Offers archaeology (MA, PhD); cultural forms (MA, PhD); linguistic anthropology (MA, PhD); physical anthropology (MA, PhD); social anthropology (MA, PhD). *Program availability:* Part-time. Terminal master's awarded for partial completion of doctoral program. *Degree requirements:* For master's, thesis; for doctorate, one foreign language, thesis/dissertation. *Entrance requirements:* For master's and doctorate, GRE General Test. Additional exam requirements/recommendations for international students: Required—TOEFL. Electronic applications accepted.

University of West Florida, College of Arts, Social Sciences, and Humanities, Department of History, Pensacola, FL 32514-5750. Offers early American studies (MA); public history (MA); traditional history (MA). *Program availability:* Part-time, evening/weekend. *Degree requirements:* For master's, thesis or alternative. *Entrance requirements:* For master's, GRE (minimum score: verbal 500, writing 3.5) or MAT (minimum score 415), minimum GPA of 3.0; minimum 15 hours of upper-level history courses; official transcripts; letter of intent; writing sample (undergraduate research paper preferred). Additional exam requirements/recommendations for international students: Required—TOEFL (minimum score 550 paper-based).

University of West Georgia, College of Arts and Humanities, Carrollton, GA 30118. Offers English (MA); history (MA); museum studies (Postbaccalaureate Certificate); music performance (M Mus); music teacher education (M Mus); public history (Postbaccalaureate Certificate). *Program availability:* Part-time, evening/weekend, 100% online, blended/hybrid learning. *Faculty:* 69 full-time (38 women). *Students:* 25 full-time (15 women), 51 part-time (34 women); includes 16 minority (7 Black or African American, non-Hispanic/Latino; 1 American Indian or Alaska Native, non-Hispanic/Latino; 2 Asian, non-Hispanic/Latino; 5 Hispanic/Latino; 1 Two or more races, non-Hispanic/Latino), 1 international. Average age 30. 23 applicants, 96% accepted, 16 enrolled. In 2017, 29 master's, 6 other advanced degrees awarded. *Entrance requirements:* Additional exam requirements/recommendations for international students: Required—TOEFL (minimum score 523 paper-based; 69 iBT); Recommended—IELTS (minimum score 6.5). *Application deadline:* For fall admission, 8/1 for domestic students, 6/1 for international students; for spring admission, 11/15 for domestic students, 10/15 for international students; for summer admission, 5/15 for domestic students, 3/30 for international students. Applications are processed on a rolling basis. Application fee: $40. Electronic applications accepted. Tuition and fees vary according to degree level and program. *Financial support:* Fellowships, research assistantships, teaching assistantships, career-related internships or fieldwork, Federal Work-Study, institutionally sponsored loans, scholarships/grants, and unspecified assistantships available. Support available to part-time students. Financial award application deadline: 4/1; financial award applicants required to submit FAFSA. *Unit head:* Dr. Pauline D. Gagnon, Dean of Arts and Humanities, 678-839-5450, Fax: 678-839-5451, E-mail: pgagnon@westga.edu. *Application contact:* Dr. Toby Ziglar, Assistant Dean of the Graduate School, 678-839-1394, Fax: 678-839-1395, E-mail: graduate@westga.edu. Website: http://www.westga.edu/coah

Wayne State University, College of Liberal Arts and Sciences, Department of History, Detroit, MI 48202. Offers history (MA, PhD); public history (MA), including African American history and culture, cultural resource management, gender, sexuality, and women's studies, labor and urban history, museum studies, public policy; world history (Graduate Certificate); JD/MA; M Ed/MA; MLIS/MA. Doctoral program admits for fall only. *Program availability:* Evening/weekend. *Faculty:* 17. *Students:* 21 full-time (7 women), 20 part-time (7 women); includes 9 minority (5 Black or African American, non-Hispanic/Latino; 1 Hispanic/Latino; 3 Two or more races, non-Hispanic/Latino). Average age 40. 50 applicants, 16% accepted, 5 enrolled. In 2017, 11 master's, 2 doctorates awarded. *Degree requirements:* For master's, comprehensive exam, thesis (for some programs), final oral exam on thesis or essay and seminar; internship and project (for public history); for doctorate, variable foreign language requirement, comprehensive exam, thesis/dissertation, qualifying exam in 4 fields of history. *Entrance requirements:* For master's, GRE General Test, minimum undergraduate GPA of 3.25 in history, 3.0 overall; at least 18 credits in history and related subjects at the advanced undergraduate level; foreign language; letter of intent; research paper; at least two letters of recommendation from former instructors; for doctorate, GRE General Test, minimum GPA of 3.0, 3.25 in minimum of 18 semester credits in history and related subjects; letter of intent; research paper; at least three letters of recommendation from former professors; for Graduate Certificate, baccalaureate degree from accredited college or university; minimum GPA of 3.0, 3.25 in a minimum of eighteen semester credits in history and related subjects at the advanced undergraduate level. Additional exam requirements/recommendations for international students: Required—TOEFL (minimum score 550 paper-based; 79 iBT), TWE (minimum score 5.5), Michigan English Language Assessment Battery (minimum score 85); Recommended—IELTS (minimum score 6.5).

Public History

Application deadline: For fall admission, 2/1 priority date for domestic and international students; for winter admission, 11/1 for domestic students, 10/1 priority date for international students; for spring admission, 2/1 for domestic students, 1/1 priority date for international students. Application fee: $50. Electronic applications accepted. *Expenses:* Tuition, state resident: full-time $10,224; part-time $638.98 per credit hour. Tuition, nonresident: full-time $22,145; part-time $1384.04 per credit hour. Tuition and fees vary according to course load and program. *Financial support:* In 2017–18, 17 students received support, including 3 fellowships with tuition reimbursements available (averaging $17,198 per year), 1 research assistantship with tuition reimbursement available (averaging $22,241 per year), 6 teaching assistantships with tuition reimbursements available (averaging $18,534 per year); scholarships/grants, health care benefits, and unspecified assistantships also available. Financial award applicants required to submit FAFSA. *Faculty research:* Urban history, labor, political history, history of gender and women. *Unit head:* Dr. Elizabeth V. Faue, Professor/Chair, 313-577-2525, E-mail: evfaue@wayne.edu. *Application contact:* Dr. Eric Ash, Associate Professor and Director of Graduate Studies, 313-577-2525, E-mail: ericash@wayne.edu.
Website: http://clas.wayne.edu/history/

Section 8
Humanities

This section contains a directory of institutions offering graduate work in humanities. Additional information about programs listed in the directory may be obtained by writing directly to the dean of a graduate school or chair of a department at the address given in the directory.

For programs offering related work, see also in this book *Area and Cultural Studies, Geography, Interdisciplinary Studies, Philosophy, Political Science and International Affairs, Religious Studies,* and *Sociology, Anthropology, and Archaeology.*

CONTENTS

Humanities

Adams State University, Office of Graduate Studies, Department of History, Government and Philosophy, Alamosa, CO 81101. Offers humanities (MA), including cultural resource management, public administration, U.S. history. Application fee: $30. *Expenses:* Tuition, state resident: full-time $4800; part-time $2400 per credit. Tuition, nonresident: full-time $7100; part-time $3550 per credit. *Required fees:* $213; $106 per credit. One-time fee: $100. Tuition and fees vary according to campus/location and program. *Unit head:* Dr. Edward Crowther, Chair, 719-587-7771, Fax: 719-587-7176, E-mail: ascgrad@adams.edu. *Application contact:* Eileen Tilton, Administrative Assistant III, 719-587-7771, Fax: 719-587-7176, E-mail: ascgrad@adams.edu. Website: http://www2.adams.edu/academics/hgp/

The American University in Cairo, School of Humanities and Social Sciences, Cairo, Egypt. Offers Arab and Islamic civilizations (Graduate Diploma); Arabic studies (MA); comparative literary studies (Graduate Diploma); Egyptology and Coptology (MA); English and comparative literature (MA); humanities and social sciences (Graduate Diploma); philosophy (MA); psychology (MA); sociology and anthropology (MA); teaching Arabic as a foreign language (MA); teaching English to speakers of other languages (MA). *Program availability:* Part-time, evening/weekend. *Faculty:* 52 full-time (27 women), 7 part-time/adjunct (3 women). *Students:* 52 full-time (41 women), 159 part-time (119 women), 38 international. Average age 31. 209 applicants, 36% accepted, 39 enrolled. In 2017, 73 master's awarded. *Degree requirements:* For master's, comprehensive exam (for some programs), thesis (for some programs). *Entrance requirements:* Additional exam requirements/recommendations for international students: Required—TOEFL (minimum score 450 paper-based; 45 iBT), IELTS (minimum score 5). *Application deadline:* For fall admission, 2/1 priority date for domestic and international students; for spring admission, 10/15 priority date for domestic and international students. Applications are processed on a rolling basis. Application fee: $85. Electronic applications accepted. *Financial support:* Fellowships with partial tuition reimbursements, scholarships/grants, tuition waivers (partial), and unspecified assistantships available. Financial award application deadline: 3/10. *Faculty research:* English literature, political science, psychology, sociology, anthropology and Egyptology, philosophy, Arabic studies, history, teaching Arabic as a foreign language, teaching English to speakers of other languages. *Unit head:* Dr. Robert Switzer, Interim Dean, 20-2-2615-1068, E-mail: nbowditch@aucegypt.edu. *Application contact:* Maha Hegazi, Director for Graduate Admissions, 20-2-2615-1462, E-mail: mahahegazi@aucegypt.edu. Website: http://www.aucegypt.edu/huss/Pages/default.aspx

Antioch University New England, Graduate School, Department of Education, Integrated Learning Program, Keene, NH 03431-3552. Offers early childhood education (M Ed); elementary education (M Ed), including arts and humanities, science and environmental education; special education (M Ed). *Degree requirements:* For master's, internship. *Entrance requirements:* For master's, previous course work or work experience in education. Additional exam requirements/recommendations for international students: Required—TOEFL (minimum score 550 paper-based). Electronic applications accepted. *Expenses:* Contact institution. *Faculty research:* Problem-based learning, place-based education, mathematics education, democratic classrooms, art education.

Arcadia University, College of Arts and Sciences, Program in Humanities, Glenside, PA 19038-3295. Offers MAH. *Program availability:* Part-time. *Degree requirements:* For master's, thesis or alternative. *Expenses:* Contact institution.

Brandeis University, Graduate School of Arts and Sciences, Program in Comparative Humanities, Waltham, MA 02454-9110. Offers MA. *Program availability:* Part-time. *Faculty:* 27 full-time (11 women), 1 (woman) part-time/adjunct. *Students:* 2 full-time (both women), 1 international. Average age 31. 10 applicants, 70% accepted, 2 enrolled. In 2017, 7 master's awarded. *Degree requirements:* For master's, one foreign language, thesis or alternative, capstone project. *Entrance requirements:* For master's, GRE General Test, transcripts, letters of recommendation, resume, statement of purpose, writing sample. Additional exam requirements/recommendations for international students: Required—PTE (minimum score 68), TOEFL (minimum score 600 paper-based, 100 iBT) or IELTS (7). *Application deadline:* For fall admission, 5/1 for domestic students. Applications are processed on a rolling basis. Application fee: $75. Electronic applications accepted. *Expenses: Tuition:* Full-time $48,720. *Required fees:* $88. Tuition and fees vary according to course load, degree level, program and student level. *Financial support:* In 2017–18, 3 students received support. Federal Work-Study, scholarships/grants, and tuition waivers (partial) available. Support available to part-time students. Financial award application deadline: 5/1; financial award applicants required to submit FAFSA. *Faculty research:* Humanities, cross-cultural comparison, trans-regional studies. *Unit head:* Dr. Matthew Fraleigh, Director of Graduate Study, 781-736-3229, E-mail: fraleigh@brandeis.edu. *Application contact:* Dr. Matthew Fraleigh, Director of Graduate Study, 781-736-3229, E-mail: mach@brandeis.edu. Website: http://www.brandeis.edu/gsas/programs/humanities.html

Brigham Young University, Graduate Studies, College of Humanities, Department of Comparative Arts and Letters, Provo, UT 84602. Offers comparative studies (MA). *Faculty:* 30 full-time (8 women), 3 part-time/adjunct (1 woman). *Students:* 15 full-time (6 women), 1 part-time (0 women); includes 1 minority (Asian, non-Hispanic/Latino). Average age 29. 12 applicants, 75% accepted, 7 enrolled. In 2017, 10 master's awarded. *Degree requirements:* For master's, 2 foreign languages, comprehensive exam, thesis. *Entrance requirements:* For master's, GRE, minimum GPA of 3.0 in last 60 hours, writing sample, foreign language experience, undergraduate degree or experience in a humanities discipline. Additional exam requirements/recommendations for international students: Required—TOEFL (minimum score 580 paper-based; 85 iBT), IELTS (minimum score 7). *Application deadline:* For fall admission, 3/1 for domestic and international students. Application fee: $50. Electronic applications accepted. *Expenses:* $8,850. *Financial support:* In 2017–18, 15 students received support, including 3 research assistantships (averaging $2,500 per year), 21 teaching assistantships (averaging $5,000 per year); scholarships/grants, tuition waivers, unspecified assistantships, and student instructorships also available. Support available to part-time students. *Faculty research:* Renaissance skepticism, ancient novels, papyrology, Mediterranean piracy, Renaissance devotional art, Seventeenth Century French comedy, representations of chance and probability, Dutch baroque art empowering women, Nineteenth Century Denmark and memory studies. *Unit head:* Dr. Roger Macfarlane, Graduate Coordinator/Professor of Classical Studies, 801-422-9078, Fax: 801-422-0305, E-mail: macfarlane@byu.edu. *Application contact:* Andrea Kristensen, Graduate Program Manager, 801-422-2996, Fax: 801-422-0305, E-mail: andrea_kristensen@byu.edu. Website: http://cal.byu.edu/

California Institute of Integral Studies, School of Consciousness and Transformation, San Francisco, CA 94103. Offers anthropology and social change (MA, PhD); Asian philosophies and cultures (MA); creative inquiry/interdisciplinary arts (MFA); East-West psychology (MA, PhD); integral and transpersonal psychology (PhD); philosophy and religion (PhD), including ecology, spirituality, and religion, philosophy, cosmology, and consciousness, women's spirituality; philosophy, cosmology, and consciousness (Certificate); transformative leadership (MA); transformative studies (PhD); women, gender, spirituality and social justice (MA); writing and consciousness (MFA). *Program availability:* Part-time, evening/weekend, 100% online, blended/hybrid learning. *Students:* 392 full-time (265 women), 141 part-time (98 women); includes 145 minority (40 Black or African American, non-Hispanic/Latino; 1 American Indian or Alaska Native, non-Hispanic/Latino; 19 Asian, non-Hispanic/Latino; 54 Hispanic/Latino; 31 Two or more races, non-Hispanic/Latino), 61 international. Average age 43. 212 applicants, 96% accepted, 153 enrolled. In 2017, 49 master's, 36 doctorates awarded. Terminal master's awarded for partial completion of doctoral program. *Degree requirements:* For master's, thesis optional; for doctorate, comprehensive exam, thesis/dissertation, 1 foreign language (for Asian philosophies and cultures). *Entrance requirements:* For master's, minimum GPA of 3.0, letters of recommendation, writing sample; for doctorate, master's degree, minimum GPA of 3.0, letters of recommendation, writing sample. Additional exam requirements/recommendations for international students: Required—TOEFL. *Application deadline:* For fall admission, 2/1 priority date for domestic and international students; for spring admission, 10/15 priority date for domestic and international students. Applications are processed on a rolling basis. Application fee: $65. Electronic applications accepted. *Expenses:* $21,400 tuition and fees (for MA); $28,390 (for MFA); $24,658 (for PhD). *Financial support:* Fellowships, research assistantships, teaching assistantships, career-related internships or fieldwork, Federal Work-Study, and scholarships/grants available. Support available to part-time students. Financial award application deadline: 4/15; financial award applicants required to submit FAFSA. *Faculty research:* Ecology and sustainability, philosophy and religion, East-West psychology, integrative health, social and cultural anthropology, transformative leadership. *Unit head:* Kathy Littles, Academic Dean, 415-575-6100, E-mail: klittles@ciis.edu. *Application contact:* Ellen Durst, Director of Admissions, 415-575-6100, Fax: 415-575-1268, E-mail: admissions@ciis.edu. Website: http://www.ciis.edu/

California State University, Dominguez Hills, College of Arts and Humanities, Program in Arts and Humanities, Carson, CA 90747-0001. Offers MA. *Program availability:* Part-time, evening/weekend. *Degree requirements:* For master's, thesis or alternative. *Entrance requirements:* For master's, minimum GPA of 3.0. Additional exam requirements/recommendations for international students: Required—TOEFL (minimum score 550 paper-based; 80 iBT). *Faculty research:* African-American music, postmodernism, cities of antiquity, Faust, African studies.

California State University, Dominguez Hills, College of Extended and International Education, Humanities Program, Carson, CA 90747-0001. Offers MA. *Program availability:* Part-time, evening/weekend, 100% online. *Degree requirements:* For master's, thesis, advancement to candidacy essays. *Entrance requirements:* For master's, minimum GPA of 3.0 in last 60 undergraduate units. Additional exam requirements/recommendations for international students: Required—TOEFL. Electronic applications accepted. *Expenses:* Contact institution. *Faculty research:* Nineteenth- and twentieth-century literature, Arab history, Greek philosophy, ancient history, East Asian history, Soviet cultural history, Native American history and culture, feminist studies.

Central Michigan University, College of Graduate Studies, College of Humanities and Social and Behavioral Sciences, Program in Humanities, Mount Pleasant, MI 48859. Offers humanities (MA), including contemporary issues in the humanities: race, class, and gender, images and ideas of self, Native American issues in modern culture, popular culture studies, the rise of industrial society. *Program availability:* Part-time, evening/weekend. *Degree requirements:* For master's, thesis or alternative. Electronic applications accepted. *Faculty research:* Rise of industrial society; images and ideas of self; contemporary issues of race, class, and gender; popular culture; Native American issues in modern culture.

Claremont Graduate University, Graduate Programs, School of Arts and Humanities, Claremont, CA 91711-6160. Offers M Phil, MA, MFA, DCM, DMA, PhD, Certificate, MA/PhD, MBA/MA, MBA/PhD. *Program availability:* Part-time. *Degree requirements:* For doctorate, 2 foreign languages, comprehensive exam, thesis/dissertation, oral and written qualifying exams, oral defense of dissertation, recitals. *Entrance requirements:* For master's and doctorate, GRE General Test. Additional exam requirements/recommendations for international students: Required—TOEFL (minimum score 75 iBT). Electronic applications accepted.

The Colorado College, Education Department, Experienced Teacher Program, Colorado Springs, CO 80903-3294. Offers arts and humanities (MAT); integrated natural sciences (MAT); liberal arts (MAT); Southwest studies (MAT). Programs offered during summer only. *Program availability:* Part-time. *Degree requirements:* For master's, thesis, oral exam, 50-page paper. *Expenses:* Contact institution.

Colorado School of Mines, Office of Graduate Studies, Division of Humanities, Arts and Social Sciences, Golden, CO 80401. Offers international political economy (Graduate Certificate); science and technology policy (Graduate Certificate). *Program availability:* Part-time. *Students:* 2 full-time (1 woman); includes 1 minority (Hispanic/Latino), 1 international. Average age 37. 1 applicant, 100% accepted, 1 enrolled. *Entrance requirements:* Additional exam requirements/recommendations for international students: Required—TOEFL (minimum score 550 paper-based; 79 iBT). *Application deadline:* For fall admission, 12/15 priority date for domestic and international students; for spring admission, 9/1 priority date for domestic and international students. Application fee: $60 ($80 for international students). Electronic applications accepted. *Expenses:* Tuition, state resident: full-time $16,170. Tuition, nonresident: full-time $35,220. *Required fees:* $2216. *Financial support:* Fellowships, research assistantships, teaching assistantships, scholarships/grants, health care benefits, and unspecified assistantships available. Financial award application deadline: 12/15. *Unit head:* Dr. Hussain Amery, Department Head, 303-273-3339, E-mail: hamery@mines.edu. *Application contact:* Jody Lowther, Program Assistant, 303-384-2509, E-mail: jlowther@mines.edu. Website: https://hass.mines.edu/

Concordia University, School of Graduate Studies, Faculty of Arts and Science, Program in Humanities, Montréal, QC H3G 1M8, Canada. Offers PhD. *Degree requirements:* For doctorate, one foreign language, comprehensive exam, thesis/dissertation.

Dominican University of California, School of Liberal Arts and Education, Humanities Program, San Rafael, CA 94901-2298. Offers applied music (MA); art history (MA); creative writing (MA); gender studies (MA); history (MA); philosophy (MA); political theory (MA); religion (MA). *Program availability:* Part-time. *Faculty:* 7 full-time (4 women), 1 (woman) part-time/adjunct. *Students:* 6 full-time (5 women), 16 part-time (12 women); includes 8 minority (3 Black or African American, non-Hispanic/Latino; 4 Hispanic/Latino; 1 Two or more races, non-Hispanic/Latino), 2 international. Average age 45. 7 applicants, 100% accepted, 5 enrolled. In 2017, 14 master's awarded. *Degree requirements:* For master's, thesis or alternative. *Entrance requirements:* For master's, minimum GPA of 3.0, interview. Additional exam requirements/recommendations for international students: Required—TOEFL (minimum score 550 paper-based; 80 iBT), IELTS (minimum score 6.5). *Application deadline:* For fall admission, 5/15 priority date for domestic and international students; for spring admission, 11/15 priority date for domestic and international students. Applications are processed on a rolling basis. Application fee: $0. Electronic applications accepted. *Expenses: Tuition:* Full-time $17,370; part-time $965 per credit. *Required fees:* $150 per semester. Tuition and fees vary according to course load and program. *Financial support:* In 2017–18, 4 students received support. Scholarships/grants available. Support available to part-time students. Financial award application deadline: 3/2; financial award applicants required to submit FAFSA. *Unit head:* Joan Baranow, Program Director, 415-485-3264, E-mail: joan.baranow@dominican.edu. *Application contact:* Michael Lavigna, Assistant Director of Graduate Admissions, 415-485-3253, Fax: 415-485-3214, E-mail: gradmissions@dominican.edu.
Website: https://www.dominican.edu/academics/lae/graduate-programs/ma-in-humanities/index_html

Duke University, Graduate School, Program in Humanities, Durham, NC 27708. Offers AM, JD/AM. *Program availability:* Part-time. *Entrance requirements:* For master's, GRE General Test. Additional exam requirements/recommendations for international students: Required—TOEFL (minimum score 577 paper-based; 90 iBT) or IELTS (minimum score 7). Electronic applications accepted.

Faulkner University, Alabama Christian College of Arts and Sciences, Department of Humanities, Montgomery, AL 36109-3398. Offers MA, PhD. *Program availability:* Part-time, evening/weekend, online only, 100% online. *Faculty:* 3 full-time (0 women), 4 part-time/adjunct (0 women). *Students:* 21 full-time (11 women), 61 part-time (17 women); includes 9 minority (3 Black or African American, non-Hispanic/Latino; 1 American Indian or Alaska Native, non-Hispanic/Latino; 4 Hispanic/Latino; 1 Two or more races, non-Hispanic/Latino), 1 international. Average age 42. 35 applicants, 51% accepted, 12 enrolled. In 2017, 4 doctorates awarded. *Degree requirements:* For master's, thesis; for doctorate, thesis/dissertation. *Entrance requirements:* For master's, MAT with minimum score of 400 (if taken within last five years) or GRE with minimum revised score of 297 (if taken within last five years), bachelor's degree from regionally-accredited college or university, minimum cumulative GPA of 3.0, official transcripts from all colleges and universities attended, three recommendation letters or emails, goal statement (300-word minimum), approval by director; for doctorate, MAT with minimum score of 400 (if taken within last five years), GRE with minimum revised score of 297 (if taken within last five years), or master's degree in related field, minimum cumulative GPA of 3.0, master's degree from regionally-accredited college or university, official transcripts from all colleges and universities attended, three recommendation letters or emails, goal statement (400-500 words), scholarly postgraduate writing sample, approval by director. Additional exam requirements/recommendations for international students: Required—TOEFL (minimum score 500 paper-based). *Application deadline:* For fall admission, 6/1 for domestic students; for spring admission, 11/1 for domestic students; for summer admission, 4/1 for domestic students. Applications are processed on a rolling basis. Application fee: $35. Electronic applications accepted. *Expenses:* $460 per hour tuition (for MA); $640 per hour tuition (for PhD); $220 per semester fees. *Financial support:* Applicants required to submit FAFSA. *Unit head:* Dr. Jason E. Jewell, Chairman, Humanities Department, 334-386-7919, Fax: 334-386-7673, E-mail: jjewell@faulkner.edu.
Website: http://www.faulkner.edu/Academics/artsandsciences/humanities/

Georgetown University, Graduate School of Arts and Sciences, School of Continuing Studies, Washington, DC 20057. Offers American studies (MALS); applied intelligence (MPS); Catholic studies (MALS); classical civilizations (MALS); emergency and disaster management (MPS); ethics and the professions (MALS); global strategic communications (MPS); hospitality management (MPS); human resources management (MPS); humanities (MALS); individualized study (MALS); integrated marketing communications (MPS); international affairs (MALS); Islam and Muslim-Christian relations (MALS); journalism (MPS); liberal studies (DLS); literature and society (MALS); medieval and early modern European studies (MALS); public relations and corporate communications (MPS); real estate (MPS); religious studies (MALS); social and public policy (MALS); sports industry management (MPS); systems engineering management (MPS); technology management (MPS); the theory and practice of American democracy (MALS); urban and regional planning (MPS); visual culture (MALS). MPS in systems engineering management offered jointly with Stevens Institute of Technology. *Entrance requirements:* Additional exam requirements/recommendations for international students: Required—TOEFL.

Harrison Middleton University, Graduate Program, Tempe, AZ 85282. Offers education (MA, Ed D); humanities (MA); imaginative literature (MA); interdisciplinary studies (DA); jurisprudence (MA); natural science (MA); philosophy and religion (MA); social science (MA). *Program availability:* Part-time, evening/weekend, online learning. *Degree requirements:* For master's and doctorate, capstone project. *Entrance requirements:* For master's, interview; for doctorate, 2 academic letters of reference, interview, essay. Additional exam requirements/recommendations for international students: Required—TOEFL (minimum score 550 paper-based; 80 iBT). Electronic applications accepted. *Faculty research:* Japanese animation, educational leadership, war art, John Muir's wilderness.

Hofstra University, School of Education, Programs in Teacher Education, Hempstead, NY 11549. Offers bilingual education (MA); bilingual extension (Advanced Certificate), including education/speech language pathology, intensive teacher institute; business education (MS Ed); curriculum studies (MS Ed); early childhood and childhood education (MS Ed); early childhood education (MA, MS Ed); educational technology (Advanced Certificate); elementary education (MA, MS Ed), including science, technology, engineering, and mathematics (STEM) (MA); English education (MS Ed); family and consumer science (MS Ed); fine arts and music education (Advanced Certificate); fine arts education (MS Ed); foreign language and TESOL (MS Ed); foreign language education (MA, MS Ed), including Arabic (MS Ed), biology, chemistry, Chinese (MS Ed), earth science, French, German, Italian (MS Ed), Mandarin (MS Ed), physics, Russian, Spanish; foundations of education (Advanced Certificate), including grades 5-6, grades 7-9; languages other than English and teaching English as a second language (MA); learning and teaching (Ed D), including applied linguistics, art education, arts and humanities, early childhood education, English education, human development, math education, math, science, and technology, multicultural education, physical education, science education, social studies education, special education; mathematics education (MA, MS Ed); music education (MA, MS Ed); science education (MA), including biology (MA, MS Ed), chemistry (MA, MS Ed), earth science (MA, MS Ed), physics (MA, MS Ed); secondary education (Advanced Certificate); social studies education (MA, MS Ed); teaching languages other than English and TESOL (MS Ed); technology for learning (MA); TESOL (MS Ed, Advanced Certificate); TESOL with specialization in STEM (MA); work based learning extension (Advanced Certificate). *Program availability:* Part-time, evening/weekend, blended/hybrid learning. *Students:* 119 full-time (83 women), 124 part-time (90 women); includes 54 minority (15 Black or African American, non-Hispanic/Latino; 9 Asian, non-Hispanic/Latino; 29 Hispanic/Latino; 1 Native Hawaiian or other Pacific Islander, non-Hispanic/Latino), 12 international. Average age 29. 205 applicants, 88% accepted, 93 enrolled. In 2017, 103 master's, 4 doctorates, 32 other advanced degrees awarded. *Degree requirements:* For master's, comprehensive exam, thesis (for some programs), exit project, student teaching, fieldwork, electronic portfolio, curriculum project, minimum GPA of 3.0; for doctorate, thesis/dissertation; for Advanced Certificate, 3 foreign languages, comprehensive exam (for some programs), thesis project. *Entrance requirements:* For master's, GRE, 2 letters of recommendation, portfolio, teacher certification (MA), interview, essay; for doctorate, GMAT, GRE, LSAT, or MAT; for Advanced Certificate, 2 letters of recommendation, essay, interview and/or portfolio, teaching certificate. Additional exam requirements/recommendations for international students: Required—TOEFL (minimum score 550 paper-based; 80 iBT). *Application deadline:* Applications are processed on a rolling basis. Application fee: $75. Electronic applications accepted. *Expenses: Tuition:* Full-time $1292. *Required fees:* $970. Tuition and fees vary according to program. *Financial support:* In 2017–18, 112 students received support, including 56 fellowships with full and partial tuition reimbursements available (averaging $4,998 per year), 2 research assistantships with full and partial tuition reimbursements available (averaging $8,753 per year); career-related internships or fieldwork, Federal Work-Study, institutionally sponsored loans, scholarships/grants, traineeships, tuition waivers (full and partial), and unspecified assistantships also available. Support available to part-time students. Financial award applicants required to submit FAFSA. *Faculty research:* Educational interventions that foster critical-thinking skills; teachers' attitudes about professional development; threats to teacher quality. *Unit head:* Dr. Eustace Thompson, Chairperson, 516-463-5749, Fax: 516-463-6275, E-mail: eustace.g.thompson@hofstra.edu. *Application contact:* Sunil Samuel, Assistant Vice President of Admissions, 516-463-4723, Fax: 516-463-4664, E-mail: graduateadmission@hofstra.edu.
Website: http://www.hofstra.edu/education/

Hollins University, Graduate Programs, Program in Liberal Studies, Roanoke, VA 24020. Offers humanities (MALS); interdisciplinary studies (MALS); leadership (MALS); social sciences (MALS); visual and performing arts (MALS). *Program availability:* Part-time, evening/weekend, 100% online, blended/hybrid learning. *Faculty:* 5 part-time/adjunct (2 women). *Students:* 5 full-time (4 women), 29 part-time (25 women); includes 9 minority (6 Black or African American, non-Hispanic/Latino; 1 Asian, non-Hispanic/Latino; 1 Hispanic/Latino; 1 Two or more races, non-Hispanic/Latino). Average age 40. 7 applicants, 86% accepted, 3 enrolled. In 2017, 11 master's awarded. *Degree requirements:* For master's, thesis. *Entrance requirements:* For master's, three letters of recommendation, interview, bachelor's degree, undergraduate transcripts, statement of educational objectives. Additional exam requirements/recommendations for international students: Required—TOEFL (minimum score 550 paper-based; 80 iBT), IELTS (minimum score 6.5). *Application deadline:* Applications are processed on a rolling basis. Application fee: $40. Electronic applications accepted. *Expenses:* Contact institution. *Financial support:* Scholarships/grants available. Financial award application deadline: 7/15; financial award applicants required to submit FAFSA. *Faculty research:* Diversity, gender and women's studies, political science, leadership. *Unit head:* Dr. Lorraine Lange, Director, 540-362-6576, Fax: 540-362-6288, E-mail: hugrad@hollins.edu. *Application contact:* Cathy S. Koon, Manager of Graduate Programs, 540-362-6326, Fax: 540-362-6288, E-mail: hugrad@hollins.edu.
Website: http://www.hollins.edu/academics/graduate-degrees/liberal-studies/

Hood College, Graduate School, Program in Humanities, Frederick, MD 21701-8575. Offers MA. *Program availability:* Part-time,. evening/weekend. *Faculty:* 5 full-time (4 women). *Students:* 4 full-time (3 women), 17 part-time (13 women); includes 2 minority (1 American Indian or Alaska Native, non-Hispanic/Latino; 1 Asian, non-Hispanic/Latino), 4 international. Average age 32. 3 applicants, 100% accepted, 2 enrolled. In 2017, 5 master's awarded. *Degree requirements:* For master's, thesis or alternative, capstone or portfolio. *Entrance requirements:* For master's, minimum GPA of 2.75, essay. Additional exam requirements/recommendations for international students: Required—TOEFL (minimum score 575 paper-based; 89 iBT), IELTS (minimum score 6.5). *Application deadline:* For fall admission, 8/15 priority date for domestic students, 8/5 for international students; for spring admission, 12/1 priority date for domestic students, 12/1 for international students; for summer admission, 5/1 priority date for domestic students, 4/15 for international students. Applications are processed on a rolling basis. Application fee: $35. Electronic applications accepted. *Expenses:* $465 per credit hour plus $110 comprehensive fee per semester. *Financial support:* Tuition waivers (partial) and unspecified assistantships available. Financial award applicants required to submit FAFSA. *Unit head:* Dr. April M. Boulton, Dean of the Graduate School, 301-696-3600, E-mail: gofurther@hood.edu. *Application contact:* Jan Marcus, Assistant Director of Graduate Admissions, 301-696-3600, E-mail: gofurther@hood.edu.
Website: http://www.hood.edu/graduate

Illinois Institute of Technology, Graduate College, Lewis College of Human Sciences, Department of Humanities, Chicago, IL 60616. Offers information architecture (MS); technical communication (PhD); technical communication and information design (MS). *Program availability:* Part-time. *Degree requirements:* For master's, comprehensive exam, thesis or alternative; for doctorate, comprehensive exam, thesis/dissertation. *Entrance requirements:* For master's, GRE General Test (minimum score 144 Quantitative, 153 Verbal, and 4.0 Analytical Writing), minimum undergraduate GPA of 3.0; 2 letters of recommendation from faculty or supervisors; professional statement discussing academic goals; for doctorate, GRE General Test (minimum score 144 Quantitative, 153 Verbal, and 4.0 Analytical Writing), bachelor's or master's degree in a field that, in combination with the 27-credit hour technical core, would provide a solid basis for advanced academic work leading to original research in the field; 3 letters of recommendation from faculty or supervisors; professional statement discussing academic goals. Additional exam requirements/recommendations for international students: Required—TOEFL (minimum score 95 iBT); Recommended—IELTS (minimum score 7). Electronic applications accepted. *Faculty research:* Linguistics, punishment theory, political communication, gender and technology, philosophical and ethical issues in neuroscience.

Instituto Tecnologico de Santo Domingo, Graduate School, Area of Humanities and Social Sciences, Santo Domingo, Dominican Republic. Offers accounting (Certificate); adult education (Certificate); applied linguistics (MA); economics (MA); education (M Ed); educational psychology (MA, Certificate); gender and development (MA, Certificate); humanistic studies (MA); international marketing management (Certificate); international relations in the Caribbean basin (Certificate); intervention systems in family therapy (MA); linguistic and literary communication (Certificate); pedagogical support (MA); social science education (M Ed); sustainable human development (MA); terminal illness and death psychology (Certificate); youth and adult education (M Ed).

Humanities

Instituto Tecnológico y de Estudios Superiores de Monterrey, Campus Central de Veracruz, Graduate Programs, Córdoba, Mexico. Offers administration (MA); administration of information technologies (MTI); computer sciences (MCC); education (MEE); educational institution administration (MAD); educational technology (MTE); electronic commerce (MCE); finance (MAF); humanistic studies (MEH); international business for Latin America (MNL); marketing (MMT); science (MCP). *Program availability:* Part-time, evening/weekend, online learning. *Degree requirements:* For master's, thesis (for some programs). *Entrance requirements:* For master's, PAEP College Board. Electronic applications accepted.

Instituto Tecnológico y de Estudios Superiores de Monterrey, Campus Ciudad de México, Virtual University Division, Ciudad de Mexico, Mexico. Offers administration of information technologies (MA); computer sciences (MA); education (MA, PhD); educational technology (MA); environmental engineering (MA); environmental systems (MA); humanistic studies (MA); industrial engineering (MA); international business for Latin America (MA); quality systems (MA); quality systems and productivity (MA). *Program availability:* Part-time, evening/weekend, online learning. *Entrance requirements:* For master's and doctorate, Instituto entrance exam. Additional exam requirements/recommendations for international students: Required—TOEFL.

Instituto Tecnológico y de Estudios Superiores de Monterrey, Campus Ciudad Juárez, Program in Humanistic Studies, Ciudad Juárez, Mexico. Offers MEH.

Instituto Tecnológico y de Estudios Superiores de Monterrey, Campus Estado de México, Professional and Graduate Division, Estado de Mexico, Mexico. Offers administration of information technologies (MITA); architecture (M Arch); business administration (GMBA, MBA); computer sciences (MCS, PhD); education (M Ed); educational institution administration (MAD); educational technology and innovation (PhD); electronic commerce (MEC); environmental systems (MS); finance (MAF); humanistic studies (MHS); information sciences and knowledge management (MISKM); information systems (MS); manufacturing systems (MS); marketing (MEM); quality systems and productivity (MS); science and materials engineering (PhD); telecommunications management (MTM). *Program availability:* Part-time, online learning. *Degree requirements:* For master's, one foreign language, thesis (for some programs); for doctorate, one foreign language, thesis/dissertation. *Entrance requirements:* For master's, E-PAEP 500, interview; for doctorate, E-PAEP 500, research proposal. Additional exam requirements/recommendations for international students: Required—TOEFL (minimum score 550 paper-based). *Faculty research:* Surface treatments by plasmas, mechanical properties, robotics, graphical computing, mechatronics security protocols.

Instituto Tecnológico y de Estudios Superiores de Monterrey, Campus Irapuato, Graduate Programs, Irapuato, Mexico. Offers administration (MBA); administration of information technology (MAIT); administration of telecommunications (MAT); architecture (M Arch); computer science (MCS); education (M Ed); educational administration (MEA); educational innovation and technology (DEIT); educational technology (MET); electronic commerce (MBA); environmental administration and planning (MEAP); environmental systems (MES); finances (MBA); humanistic studies (MHS); international management for Latin American executives (MIMLAE); library and information science (MLIS); manufacturing quality management (MMQM); marketing research (MBA).

John Carroll University, Graduate Studies, Program in Humanities, University Heights, OH 44118. Offers MA. *Program availability:* Part-time, evening/weekend. *Faculty:* 3 full-time (1 woman). *Students:* 3 full-time (2 women), 15 part-time (6 women); includes 3 minority (2 Black or African American, non-Hispanic/Latino; 1 Two or more races, non-Hispanic/Latino). Average age 38. In 2017, 6 master's awarded. *Degree requirements:* For master's, thesis optional, comprehensive research essay. *Entrance requirements:* For master's, minimum GPA of 2.75, interview. *Application deadline:* For fall admission, 8/15 priority date for domestic students; for spring admission, 1/3 for domestic students. Applications are processed on a rolling basis. Application fee: $25 ($35 for international students). Electronic applications accepted. *Expenses: Tuition:* Full-time $16,238; part-time $788 per credit hour. One-time fee: $200. Part-time tuition and fees vary according to course load and program. *Financial support:* Application deadline: 3/1; applicants required to submit FAFSA. *Faculty research:* Modern French history, modern American Catholic history. *Unit head:* Dr. Maria N. Marsilli, Coordinator, 216-397-4174, Fax: 216-397-4175, E-mail: mmarsilli@jcu.edu. *Application contact:* Jennifer L. Tucker, Records Management Assistant, 216-397-1925, Fax: 216-397-1835, E-mail: jtucker@jcu.edu.

Laurentian University, School of Graduate Studies and Research, Programme in Humanities: Interpretation and Values, Sudbury, ON P3E 2C6, Canada. Offers MA. *Program availability:* Part-time. *Faculty research:* Modern Canadian literature; aboriginal languages and cultures; relation between ethics, religion, and the arts; narrative conventions; Renaissance drama and Reformation literature, Biblical and philosophical hermeneutics.

Loyola University Chicago, Graduate School, Program in Digital Humanities, Chicago, IL 60660. Offers MA. *Program availability:* Part-time. *Faculty:* 11 full-time (6 women). *Students:* 5 full-time (3 women), 3 part-time (2 women); includes 3 minority (1 Asian, non-Hispanic/Latino; 2 Hispanic/Latino). Average age 31. 5 applicants, 100% accepted, 4 enrolled. In 2017, 2 master's awarded. *Entrance requirements:* For master's, GRE General Test, BS or BA, transcripts, 2 letters of recommendation, letter of intent. Additional exam requirements/recommendations for international students: Required—TOEFL. *Expenses:* $1,033 per credit, $432 per semester mandatory fees. *Financial support:* In 2017–18, 4 students received support, including 4 fellowships with partial tuition reimbursements available (averaging $9,000 per year); health care benefits also available. Financial award application deadline: 2/1. *Faculty research:* Archiving, computational analytics, digital humanities, public history, textual editing. *Total annual research expenditures:* $15,000. *Unit head:* Dr. Kyle Roberts, Director, Center for Textual Studies and Digital Humanities, 773-508-2215, Fax: 773-508-2153, E-mail: kroberts2@luc.edu. *Application contact:* Jill Schur, Director of Graduate Enrollment Management, 312-915-8902, E-mail: gradinfo@luc.edu.
Website: http://luc.edu/ctsdh

Marshall University, Academic Affairs Division, College of Liberal Arts, Program in Humanities, Huntington, WV 25755. Offers MA, Certificate. *Program availability:* Part-time, evening/weekend. *Students:* 4 part-time (1 woman). Average age 29. In 2017, 5 master's awarded. *Degree requirements:* For master's, thesis, comprehensive assessment. *Entrance requirements:* For master's, GRE General Test, MAT, bachelor's degree in humanities, minimum undergraduate GPA of 3.0. Application fee: $40. *Financial support:* Applicants required to submit FAFSA. *Unit head:* Dr. Luke Eric Lassiter, Chairperson, 304-746-1923, E-mail: lassiter@marshall.edu. *Application contact:* Information Contact, 304-746-1900, Fax: 304-746-1902, E-mail: services@marshall.edu.

Memorial University of Newfoundland, School of Graduate Studies, Interdisciplinary Programs in Humanities, St. John's, NL A1C 5S7, Canada. Offers M Phil. *Program availability:* Part-time. *Degree requirements:* For master's, comprehensive exam, journal. *Entrance requirements:* For master's, honors bachelor's degree. Electronic applications accepted. *Faculty research:* Western language, philosophy, literature, and history.

Mount Saint Mary's University, Graduate Division, Los Angeles, CA 90049. Offers business administration (MBA); counseling psychology (MS); creative writing (MFA); education (MS, Certificate); film and television (MFA); health policy and management (MS); humanities (MA); nursing (MSN, Certificate); physical therapy (DPT); religious studies (MA). *Program availability:* Part-time, evening/weekend. *Faculty:* 50 full-time (35 women), 116 part-time/adjunct (81 women). *Students:* 670 full-time (518 women), 147 part-time (116 women); includes 414 minority (73 Black or African American, non-Hispanic/Latino; 4 American Indian or Alaska Native, non-Hispanic/Latino; 60 Asian, non-Hispanic/Latino; 259 Hispanic/Latino; 7 Native Hawaiian or other Pacific Islander, non-Hispanic/Latino; 11 Two or more races, non-Hispanic/Latino), 4 international. Average age 32. 1,398 applicants, 21% accepted, 242 enrolled. In 2017, 170 master's, 28 doctorates, 35 other advanced degrees awarded. *Entrance requirements:* Additional exam requirements/recommendations for international students: Required—TOEFL. *Application deadline:* For fall admission, 6/30 priority date for domestic and international students; for spring admission, 10/30 priority date for domestic and international students; for summer admission, 3/30 priority date for domestic and international students. Applications are processed on a rolling basis. Application fee: $50. Electronic applications accepted. *Expenses: Tuition:* Part-time $905 per unit. One-time fee: $155 part-time. Tuition and fees vary according to degree level and program. *Financial support:* Career-related internships or fieldwork, Federal Work-Study, institutionally sponsored loans, and tuition waivers (full and partial) available. Support available to part-time students. Financial award application deadline: 3/15; financial award applicants required to submit FAFSA. *Unit head:* Albert Ramos, Director of Graduate Admissions, 213-477-2800, E-mail: gradprograms@msmu.edu. *Application contact:* Shawn Peters, Graduate Admission Counselor, 213-477-2676, E-mail: gradprograms@msmu.edu.
Website: http://www.msmu.edu/graduate-programs/

New York University, Graduate School of Arts and Science, Draper Interdisciplinary Program in Humanities and Social Thought, New York, NY 10012-1019. Offers humanities and social thought (MA); religion (Advanced Certificate); social theory (Advanced Certificate). *Program availability:* Part-time. *Students:* Average age 29. 118 applicants, 67% accepted, 38 enrolled. In 2017, 50 master's awarded. *Degree requirements:* For master's, thesis, comprehensive exam or essay. *Entrance requirements:* For master's, GRE General Test; for Advanced Certificate, master's degree. Additional exam requirements/recommendations for international students: Required—TOEFL. *Application deadline:* For fall admission, 7/1 for domestic and international students; for spring admission, 12/1 for domestic and international students. Applications are processed on a rolling basis. Application fee: $100. *Expenses: Tuition:* Full-time $41,352; part-time $19,968 per year. *Required fees:* $2496; $1628 per unit. $814 per term. Tuition and fees vary according to course load and program. *Financial support:* Teaching assistantships, Federal Work-Study, institutionally sponsored loans, and tuition waivers (partial) available. Financial award application deadline: 7/1; financial award applicants required to submit FAFSA. *Faculty research:* Art world, gender politics, global histories, literary cultures, the city. *Unit head:* Robin Nagle, Director, 212-998-8070, Fax: 212-995-4691, E-mail: draper.program@nyu.edu. *Application contact:* Robert Dimit, Director of Graduate Studies, 212-998-8070, Fax: 212-995-4691, E-mail: draper.program@nyu.edu.
Website: http://www.nyu.edu/gsas/dept/draper/

New York University, Tandon School of Engineering, Department of Technology, Culture and Society, New York, NY 10012-1019. Offers integrated digital media (MS). *Program availability:* Part-time, evening/weekend. *Faculty:* 18 full-time (9 women), 58 part-time/adjunct (19 women). *Students:* 55 full-time (31 women), 25 part-time (16 women); includes 16 minority (5 Black or African American, non-Hispanic/Latino; 4 Asian, non-Hispanic/Latino; 5 Hispanic/Latino; 2 Two or more races, non-Hispanic/Latino), 44 international. Average age 27. 189 applicants, 41% accepted, 37 enrolled. In 2017, 23 master's awarded. *Degree requirements:* For master's, comprehensive exam (for some programs), thesis (for some programs). *Entrance requirements:* Additional exam requirements/recommendations for international students: Required—TOEFL (minimum score 550 paper-based; 90 iBT); Recommended—IELTS (minimum score 7). *Application deadline:* For fall admission, 2/15 priority date for domestic and international students; for spring admission, 11/1 priority date for domestic and international students. Applications are processed on a rolling basis. Application fee: $75. Electronic applications accepted. *Expenses:* $1,720 per credit tuition plus $89 per credit fees. *Financial support:* Fellowships, research assistantships, teaching assistantships, career-related internships or fieldwork, institutionally sponsored loans, scholarships/grants, and unspecified assistantships available. Support available to part-time students. Financial award applicants required to submit FAFSA. *Faculty research:* Trade magazine journalism, technical writing, financial reporting, medical and science reporting, industrial advertising and public relations. *Total annual research expenditures:* $255,171. *Unit head:* Dr. Jonathan M. Soffer, Head, 646-997-3999, E-mail: jonathan.soffer@nyu.edu. *Application contact:* Elizabeth Ensweiler, Senior Director of Graduate Enrollment and Graduate Admissions, 646-997-3182, E-mail: elizabeth.ensweiler@nyu.edu.

Northeast Ohio Medical University, College of Graduate Studies, Rootstown, OH 44272-0095. Offers bioethics (Certificate); health-system pharmacy administration (MS); integrated pharmaceutical medicine (MS, PhD); medical ethics and humanities (MS); public health (MPH). MPH offered as part of consortium with The University of Akron, Youngstown State University, Ohio University, and Cleveland State University. *Program availability:* Part-time, evening/weekend. *Faculty:* 23 part-time/adjunct (14 women). *Students:* 22 full-time (13 women), 21 part-time (13 women); includes 10 minority (1 Black or African American, non-Hispanic/Latino; 8 Asian, non-Hispanic/Latino; 1 Two or more races, non-Hispanic/Latino). In 2017, 3 master's, 1 doctorate awarded. *Degree requirements:* For master's, thesis (for MS in medical ethics and humanities, integrated pharmaceutical medicine); for doctorate, thesis/dissertation. *Application deadline:* For fall admission, 5/1 priority date for domestic students; for winter admission, 1/5 priority date for domestic students. Applications are processed on a rolling basis. Application fee: $95. Electronic applications accepted. *Expenses:* Contact institution. *Financial support:* Institutionally sponsored loans and tuition waivers available. Financial award application deadline: 3/15; financial award applicants required to submit FAFSA. *Unit head:* Dr. Steven Schmidt, Dean, 330-325-6290. *Application contact:* Heidi Terry, Executive Director, Enrollment Services, 330-325-6479, E-mail: hterry@neomed.edu.
Website: https://www.neomed.edu/graduatestudies/

Nova Southeastern University, College of Arts, Humanities, and Social Sciences, Fort Lauderdale, FL 33314-7796. Offers advanced conflict resolution practice (Graduate Certificate); child protection (MHS); college student affairs (MS); conflict analysis and resolution (MS, PhD); criminal justice (MS, PhD); cross-disciplinary studies (MA); developmental disabilities (MS); family studies (Graduate Certificate); family systems health care (Graduate Certificate); family therapy (MS, PhD); marriage and family therapy (DMFT); peace studies (Graduate Certificate); qualitative research (Graduate Certificate); solution focused coaching (Graduate Certificate). *Accreditation:* AAMFT/COAMFTE (one or more programs are accredited). *Program availability:* Part-time, evening/weekend, 100% online, blended/hybrid learning. *Faculty:* 29 full-time (18 women), 27 part-time/adjunct (21 women). *Students:* 303 full-time (238 women), 903 part-time (677 women); includes 689 minority (385 Black or African American, non-

Hispanic/Latino; 4 American Indian or Alaska Native, non-Hispanic/Latino; 31 Asian, non-Hispanic/Latino; 234 Hispanic/Latino; 1 Native Hawaiian or other Pacific Islander, non-Hispanic/Latino; 34 Two or more races, non-Hispanic/Latino), 60 international. Average age 37. 624 applicants, 61% accepted, 285 enrolled. In 2017, 277 master's, 62 doctorates, 25 other advanced degrees awarded. *Degree requirements:* For master's, thesis optional, comprehensive exams, portfolios (for some programs), table-top exams (for some programs); for doctorate, comprehensive exam, thesis/dissertation, qualifying exams, portfolios (for some programs). *Entrance requirements:* For master's, interview, minimum GPA of 3.0, writing sample; for doctorate, interview, minimum GPA of 3.5, master's degree in related field, writing sample; for Graduate Certificate, minimum GPA of 3.0. Additional exam requirements/recommendations for international students: Required—TOEFL. *Application deadline:* For fall admission, 5/17 priority date for domestic and international students; for winter admission, 12/1 priority date for domestic and international students; for spring admission, 4/1 priority date for domestic and international students. Applications are processed on a rolling basis. Application fee: $50. Electronic applications accepted. *Expenses:* Contact institution. *Financial support:* In 2017–18, 170 students received support. Career-related internships or fieldwork, Federal Work-Study, scholarships/grants, and unspecified assistantships available. Financial award application deadline: 4/1; financial award applicants required to submit CSS PROFILE. *Faculty research:* Conflict resolution, family therapy, peace research, international conflict, multi-disciplinary studies, college student affairs, national security affairs, health care conflict resolution, family systems health care, advanced family systems, qualitative research, solution-focused coaching. *Unit head:* Dr. Honggang Yang, Dean, 954-262-3016, Fax: 954-262-3968, E-mail: yangh@nova.edu. *Application contact:* Marcia Arango, Student Recruitment Coordinator, 954-262-3006, Fax: 954-262-3968, E-mail: marango@nsu.nova.edu.
Website: http://cahss.nova.edu/

Old Dominion University, College of Arts and Letters, Institute for the Humanities, Norfolk, VA 23529. Offers arts and entrepreneurship (Certificate); cultural and human geography (MA); cultural studies (MA); gender and sexuality studies (MA); health, communication and culture (Certificate); media and popular culture studies (MA); philosophy and religious studies (MA); social justice and entrepreneurship (Certificate); visual studies (MA); world cultures (MA). *Program availability:* Part-time, evening/weekend. *Faculty:* 1 full-time (0 women), 1 part-time/adjunct (0 women). *Students:* 20 full-time (16 women), 13 part-time (8 women); includes 15 minority (8 Black or African American, non-Hispanic/Latino; 2 Asian, non-Hispanic/Latino; 2 Hispanic/Latino; 3 Two or more races, non-Hispanic/Latino), 2 international. Average age 35. 27 applicants, 96% accepted, 22 enrolled. In 2017, 3 master's awarded. *Degree requirements:* For master's, thesis optional, project. *Entrance requirements:* For master's, GRE General Test, minimum GPA of 3.25. *Application deadline:* For fall admission, 6/15 for domestic students; for spring admission, 11/15 for domestic students; for summer admission, 4/15 for domestic students. Applications are processed on a rolling basis. Application fee: $50. Electronic applications accepted. *Expenses:* Tuition, state resident: full-time $8928; part-time $496 per credit. Tuition, nonresident: full-time $22,482; part-time $1249 per credit. *Required fees:* $66 per semester. *Financial support:* In 2017–18, 3 students received support, including 5 research assistantships (averaging $10,000 per year); career-related internships or fieldwork, scholarships/grants, and unspecified assistantships also available. Financial award application deadline: 3/15; financial award applicants required to submit FAFSA. *Faculty research:* Media studies, cultural studies, gender studies, American literature, philosophy, art history, cultural geography. *Unit head:* Dr. Avi D. Santo, Graduate Program Director, 757-683-3719, Fax: 757-683-6191, E-mail: humgpd@odu.edu. *Application contact:* Dr. David C. Earnest, Associate Dean, 757-683-6077, Fax: 757-683-5746, E-mail: dearnest@odu.edu.
Website: http://al.odu.edu/hum/

Penn State Harrisburg, Graduate School, School of Humanities, Middletown, PA 17057. Offers American studies (MA, PhD); communications (MA); folklore and ethnography (Certificate); heritage and museum practice (Certificate); humanities (MA). *Program availability:* Evening/weekend. *Unit head:* Dr. Mukund S. Kulkarni, Chancellor, 717-948-6105, Fax: 717-948-6452. *Application contact:* Robert W. Coffman, Jr., Director of Enrollment Management, Recruitment and Admissions, 717-948-6250, Fax: 717-948-6325, E-mail: hbgadmit@psu.edu.
Website: https://harrisburg.psu.edu/humanities

Pepperdine University, Seaver College, Division of Humanities, Malibu, CA 90263. Offers American studies (MA); writing for screen and television (MFA). *Program availability:* Part-time. *Students:* 9 full-time (7 women), 41 part-time (23 women); includes 10 minority (4 Black or African American, non-Hispanic/Latino; 1 Asian, non-Hispanic/Latino; 3 Hispanic/Latino; 2 Two or more races, non-Hispanic/Latino), 2 international. Average age 31. In 2017, 13 master's awarded. *Degree requirements:* For master's, oral and written exams. *Entrance requirements:* For master's, GRE General Test, writing sample, letters of recommendation. Additional exam requirements/recommendations for international students: Required—TOEFL. *Application deadline:* For fall admission, 2/1 priority date for domestic students. Applications are processed on a rolling basis. Application fee: $65. *Financial support:* Applicants required to submit FAFSA. *Unit head:* Dr. Michael G. Ditmore, Chair/Professor of English, 310-506-4182, Fax: 310-506-7307, E-mail: michael.ditmore@pepperdine.edu. *Application contact:* Hayley Wolf, Director of Admission, 310-506-4392, E-mail: hayley.wolf@pepperdine.edu.
Website: http://seaver.pepperdine.edu/humanities/default.htm

Prescott College, Graduate Programs, Program in Arts and Humanities, Prescott, AZ 86301. Offers humanities (MA); social justice and human rights (MA); student-directed independent study (MA). *Program availability:* Part-time, online learning. *Degree requirements:* For master's, thesis, fieldwork or internship, practicum. *Entrance requirements:* For master's, 2 letters of recommendation, resume, essay. Additional exam requirements/recommendations for international students: Required—TOEFL (minimum score 500 paper-based). Electronic applications accepted.

Roosevelt University, Graduate Division, College of Arts and Sciences, Department of Humanities, Chicago, IL 60605. Offers creative writing (MFA). *Students:* 19 full-time (13 women), 5 part-time (3 women); includes 12 minority (5 Black or African American, non-Hispanic/Latino; 1 Asian, non-Hispanic/Latino; 3 Hispanic/Latino; 3 Two or more races, non-Hispanic/Latino). Average age 28. 11 applicants, 100% accepted, 9 enrolled. In 2017, 11 master's awarded. *Application deadline:* Applications are processed on a rolling basis. Application fee: $40. Electronic applications accepted. *Expenses:* Contact institution. *Financial support:* Scholarships/grants and unspecified assistantships available. *Application contact:* Sivling Lam, Graduate Admission Counselor, 312-281-3252, E-mail: slam02@roosevelt.edu.

St. Edward's University, School of Education, Master of Liberal Arts Program, Austin, TX 78704. Offers humanities (MLA); liberal arts (MLA, Certificate). *Program availability:* Part-time, evening/weekend. *Students:* 5 full-time (4 women), 21 part-time (12 women); includes 8 minority (all Hispanic/Latino). Average age 36. 19 applicants, 58% accepted, 7 enrolled. In 2017, 19 master's awarded. *Entrance requirements:* Additional exam requirements/recommendations for international students: Required—TOEFL, IELTS. *Application deadline:* For fall admission, 6/1 priority date for domestic and international students; for spring admission, 10/1 priority date for domestic and international students. Applications are processed on a rolling basis. Application fee: $50. Electronic applications accepted. *Expenses: Tuition:* Full-time $26,406; part-time $1467 per hour. *Required fees:* $75 per trimester. Full-time tuition and fees vary according to course load and program. *Unit head:* Dr. Ramsey Fowler, MLA Program Director/Associate Professor of English, 512-448-8736, E-mail: ramseyf@stewards.edu. *Application contact:* Mike Leveriza, Graduate Recruiter, 512-448-8745, E-mail: mleveriz@stedwards.edu.

Salve Regina University, Program in Humanities, Newport, RI 02840-4192. Offers humanitarian assistance (MA); humanities (PhD); public humanities (MA); religion, peace and justice (MA). *Program availability:* Part-time, evening/weekend, online learning. *Degree requirements:* For master's, thesis optional; for doctorate, one foreign language, comprehensive exam, thesis/dissertation. *Entrance requirements:* For master's, GMAT, GRE General Test, or MAT; for doctorate, GRE General Test. Additional exam requirements/recommendations for international students: Required—TOEFL (minimum score 600 paper-based; 100 iBT) or IELTS. Electronic applications accepted.

Sam Houston State University, College of Humanities and Social Sciences, Huntsville, TX 77341. Offers MA, MFA, MPA, PhD, SSP. *Program availability:* Part-time, online learning. Terminal master's awarded for partial completion of doctoral program. *Degree requirements:* For master's, comprehensive exam (for some programs), thesis optional, internship, portfolio; for doctorate, comprehensive exam, thesis/dissertation. *Entrance requirements:* For master's, GRE General Test, personal essay, letters of recommendation, writing sample; for doctorate, GRE General Test, GRE Subject Test (advanced psychology), personal essay, letters of recommendation, resume. Additional exam requirements/recommendations for international students: Required—TOEFL (minimum score 550 paper-based; 79 iBT), IELTS (minimum score 6.5). Electronic applications accepted.

San Francisco State University, Division of Graduate Studies, College of Liberal and Creative Arts, School of Humanities and Liberal Studies, San Francisco, CA 94132-1722. Offers MA. *Program availability:* Part-time, evening/weekend. *Unit head:* Dr. Christina Ruotolo, Director, 415-338-1099, E-mail: ruotolo@sfsu.edu. *Application contact:* Prof. Mary Scott, Graduate Advisor, 415-338-7412, E-mail: mscott@sfsu.edu.
Website: http://humanities.sfsu.edu/

Simon Fraser University, Office of Graduate Studies and Postdoctoral Fellows, Faculty of Arts and Social Sciences, Department of Humanities, Burnaby, BC V5A 1S6, Canada. Offers MA. *Degree requirements:* For master's, thesis. *Entrance requirements:* Additional exam requirements/recommendations for international students: Required—TOEFL (minimum score 580 paper-based; 93 iBT), IELTS (minimum score 7), TWE (minimum score 5). Electronic applications accepted. *Faculty research:* Classic and medieval studies, modern thought and culture, Renaissance humanism, Eastern and Western religions.

Tiffin University, Program in Humanities, Tiffin, OH 44883-2161. Offers art and visual media (MH); communication (MH); creative writing (MH); English (MH); film studies (MH); humanities (MH); individualized studies (MH). *Program availability:* Part-time, evening/weekend, online only, 100% online, blended/hybrid learning. *Entrance requirements:* For master's, work experience. Additional exam requirements/recommendations for international students: Required—TOEFL (minimum score 550 paper-based; 79 iBT). Electronic applications accepted. Application fee is waived when completed online. *Expenses:* Contact institution.

Towson University, College of Liberal Arts, Program in Global Humanities, Towson, MD 21252-0001. Offers MA. *Program availability:* Part-time, evening/weekend. *Students:* 9 part-time (5 women); includes 1 minority (Two or more races, non-Hispanic/Latino). *Degree requirements:* For master's, thesis or alternative. *Entrance requirements:* For master's, bachelor's degree, 2 letters of recommendation, minimum GPA of 3.0, research paper, statement of intent. *Application deadline:* For fall admission, 1/17 for domestic students, 5/15 for international students; for spring admission, 10/15 for domestic students, 12/1 for international students. Applications are processed on a rolling basis. Application fee: $45. Electronic applications accepted. *Expenses:* Tuition, state resident: full-time $7960; part-time $398 per unit. Tuition, nonresident: full-time $16,480; part-time $824 per unit. *Required fees:* $2600; $130 per year. $390 per term. *Financial support:* Application deadline: 4/1. *Unit head:* Dr. Jennifer Ballengee, Graduate Program Director, 410-704-5213, E-mail: jballengee@towson.edu. *Application contact:* Coverley Beidleman, Assistant Director of Graduate Admissions, 410-704-5630, Fax: 410-704-3030, E-mail: cbeidleman@towson.edu.
Website: http://www.towson.edu/cla/departments/interdisciplinary/grad/humanities/

Trinity Western University, School of Graduate Studies, Program in Interdisciplinary Humanities, Langley, BC V2Y 1Y1, Canada. Offers general humanities (MAIH); specialized (MAIH), including English, history, philosophy. *Program availability:* Part-time. *Degree requirements:* For master's, thesis or alternative, 36 semester hours. *Entrance requirements:* For master's, strong undergraduate degree in humanities or English, history or philosophy. Additional exam requirements/recommendations for international students: Recommended—TOEFL. Electronic applications accepted. *Faculty research:* Literary theory, gender, medieval and early modern literature, philosophy of religion, Thomas Merton's poetics.

Union Institute & University, PhD Program in Interdisciplinary Studies, Cincinnati, OH 45206-1925. Offers educational studies (PhD), including Martin Luther King studies; ethical and creative leadership (PhD); humanities and culture (PhD); public policy and social change (PhD). Program requires participation in brief on-campus residencies twice each year (January and July). *Program availability:* Part-time, online only, blended/hybrid learning. *Degree requirements:* For doctorate, comprehensive exam, thesis/dissertation. *Entrance requirements:* For doctorate, master's degree, three letters of recommendation, statement of purpose. Additional exam requirements/recommendations for international students: Required—TOEFL. *Application deadline:* Applications are processed on a rolling basis. Application fee: $50. Electronic applications accepted. *Expenses:* Contact institution. *Financial support:* Federal Work-Study and scholarships/grants available. Financial award application deadline: 5/1; financial award applicants required to submit FAFSA. *Faculty research:* Social responsibility, ethical leadership, Martin Luther King studies. *Unit head:* Dr. Michael Raffanti, Dean of Graduate College, 800-641-6400 Ext. 1237, E-mail: michael.raffanti@myunion.edu. *Application contact:* Admissions Counselor, 800-486-3116.
Website: https://myunion.edu/academics/doctoral/

United Theological Seminary of the Twin Cities, Graduate Programs, New Brighton, MN 55112-2598. Offers advanced theological studies (Diploma); justice and peace studies (M Div, MA); leadership toward racial justice (M Div, MA, Certificate); Methodist studies (M Div, MA, Certificate); ministry (D Min); ministry renewal and professional development (Certificate); pastoral care and counseling (M Div, MA, MARL); religion and theology (MA); theological and religious studies (Certificate); theology and the arts (M Div, MA); urban ministry (M Div, MA, MARL); women's studies: religion, theology and ministry (M Div, MA). *Accreditation:* ACIPE; ATS. *Program availability:* Part-time, evening/weekend. *Degree requirements:* For master's, thesis; for doctorate, comprehensive exam, thesis/dissertation. *Entrance requirements:* For master's,

minimum GPA of 2.75; strong analytical, reflective thinking and writing skills; vocational and academic goals compatible with those of Seminary; for doctorate, M Div or equivalent, minimum GPA of 3.0, 3 years experience in professional ministry; for other advanced degree, BA or equivalent life experience; strong analytical, reflective thinking and writing skills (Certificate); proficiency in English language, previous study of theology at a theological school, recommendation of student's denomination (Diploma). Additional exam requirements/recommendations for international students: Required—TOEFL (minimum score 550 paper-based).

University at Buffalo, the State University of New York, Graduate School, College of Arts and Sciences, Program in Interdisciplinary Studies, Buffalo, NY 14260. Offers humanities (MA); natural sciences (MS); social sciences (MS). *Program availability:* Part-time. *Entrance requirements:* Additional exam requirements/recommendations for international students: Required—TOEFL (minimum score 550 paper-based; 79 iBT). *Application deadline:* For fall admission, 6/1 priority date for domestic students, 1/1 priority date for international students; for spring admission, 12/1 priority date for domestic students, 10/1 priority date for international students. Applications are processed on a rolling basis. Electronic applications accepted. *Financial support:* Fellowships, research assistantships, teaching assistantships, and unspecified assistantships available. *Unit head:* Danielle Lewis, Assistant Director, Strategic Programs, 716-645-1457, E-mail: dvegas@buffalo.edu.
Website: http://gradidp.buffalo.edu/

University of California, Merced, Graduate Division, School of Social Sciences, Humanities and Arts, Merced, CA 95343. Offers cognitive and information sciences (PhD); interdisciplinary humanities (MA, PhD); psychological sciences (MA, PhD); social sciences (MA, PhD); sociology (MA, PhD). *Faculty:* 101 full-time (49 women), 3 part-time/adjunct (1 woman). *Students:* 197 full-time (131 women), 2 part-time (1 woman); includes 86 minority (7 Black or African American, non-Hispanic/Latino; 17 Asian, non-Hispanic/Latino; 55 Hispanic/Latino; 1 Native Hawaiian or other Pacific Islander, non-Hispanic/Latino; 6 Two or more races, non-Hispanic/Latino), 33 international. Average age 31. 190 applicants, 41% accepted, 49 enrolled. In 2017, 7 master's, 10 doctorates awarded. Terminal master's awarded for partial completion of doctoral program. *Degree requirements:* For master's, variable foreign language requirement, comprehensive exam, thesis or alternative; for doctorate, variable foreign language requirement, comprehensive exam, thesis/dissertation. *Entrance requirements:* For master's and doctorate, GRE. Additional exam requirements/recommendations for international students: Required—TOEFL (minimum score 550 paper-based; 80 iBT); Recommended—IELTS (minimum score 7). *Application deadline:* For fall admission, 1/15 for domestic and international students. Application fee: $90 ($110 for international students). Electronic applications accepted. *Expenses:* Tuition, state resident: full-time $11,502; part-time $5751 per semester. Tuition, nonresident: full-time $26,604; part-time $13,302 per semester. *Required fees:* $564 per semester. *Financial support:* In 2017–18, 167 students received support, including 17 fellowships with full tuition reimbursements available (averaging $23,250 per year), 13 research assistantships with full tuition reimbursements available (averaging $15,387 per year), 162 teaching assistantships with full tuition reimbursements available (averaging $16,103 per year); scholarships/grants, traineeships, and health care benefits also available. Financial award application deadline: 1/15. *Faculty research:* Social inequality, critical race and ethnic studies, public health and health sciences, cognitive science and language acquisition, political institutions, literature, cultural studies, anthropology, art history, ethnomusicology, history. *Total annual research expenditures:* $1.2 million. *Unit head:* Dr. Jill Robbins, Dean, 209-228-7843, E-mail: jillrobbins@ucmerced.edu. *Application contact:* Tsu Ya, Director of Admissions and Academic Services, 209-228-4521, Fax: 209-228-6906, E-mail: tya@ucmerced.edu.

University of California, Santa Cruz, Division of Graduate Studies, Division of Humanities, Program in the History of Consciousness, Santa Cruz, CA 95064. Offers PhD. *Degree requirements:* For doctorate, one foreign language, thesis/dissertation, qualifying exam. *Entrance requirements:* For doctorate, GRE General Test. Additional exam requirements/recommendations for international students: Required—TOEFL (minimum score 550 paper-based; 83 iBT); Recommended—IELTS (minimum score 8). Electronic applications accepted. *Faculty research:* Interdisciplinary humanities and social sciences, political theory, cultural theory, feminist studies, literary theory.

University of Chicago, Division of the Humanities, Master of Arts Program in the Humanities, Chicago, IL 60637. Offers art history (MA); cinema and media studies (MA); classic languages (MA); comparative literature (MA); creative writing (MA); cultural policy studies (MA); digital humanities (MA); East Asian languages and civilizations (MA); English language and literature (MA); gender and sexuality studies (MA); Germanic studies (MA); linguistics (MA); music (MA); near Eastern languages and civilizations (MA); philosophy (MA); poetics (MA); race, politics and culture (MA); Romance languages and literatures (MA); Slavic languages and literatures (MA); South Asian languages and civilizations (MA); theater and performance studies (MA). *Students:* 95 full-time (50 women), 6 part-time (4 women); includes 22 minority (1 Black or African American, non-Hispanic/Latino; 10 Asian, non-Hispanic/Latino; 11 Hispanic/Latino), 19 international. Average age 26. 708 applicants, 75% accepted, 101 enrolled. In 2017, 91 master's awarded. *Degree requirements:* For master's, thesis. *Entrance requirements:* For master's, GRE General Test, 10-15 page writing sample, statement of purpose, 3 letters of recommendation, transcripts for all previous degrees and institutions attended. Additional exam requirements/recommendations for international students: Required—TOEFL (minimum score 104 iBT), IELTS (minimum score 7). *Application deadline:* For fall admission, 1/3 priority date for domestic and international students. Application fee: $90. Electronic applications accepted. *Expenses:* Contact institution. *Financial support:* In 2017–18, fellowships with partial tuition reimbursements (averaging $12,000 per year) were awarded; Federal Work-Study, institutionally sponsored loans, scholarships/grants, and tuition waivers (partial) also available. Financial award application deadline: 4/30. *Unit head:* Thomas Christensen, Director, 773-834-1201, Fax: 773-834-7526, E-mail: ma-humanities@uchicago.edu. *Application contact:* Michael Beetley, Assistant Dean of Students for Admissions, 773-834-1552, E-mail: humanitiesadmissions@uchicago.edu.
Website: http://maph.uchicago.edu/

University of Colorado Denver, College of Liberal Arts and Sciences, Program in Humanities, Denver, CO 80217. Offers community health science (MSS); humanities (MH); international studies (MSS); philosophy and theory (MH); social justice (MSS); society and the environment (MSS); visual studies (MH); women's and gender studies (MSS). *Program availability:* Part-time, evening/weekend. *Degree requirements:* For master's, 36 credit hours, project or thesis. *Entrance requirements:* For master's, writing sample, statement of purpose/letter of intent, three letters of recommendation. Additional exam requirements/recommendations for international students: Required—TOEFL (minimum score 537 paper-based; 75 iBT); Recommended—IELTS (minimum score 6.5). Electronic applications accepted. *Faculty research:* Women and gender in the classical Mediterranean, communication theory and democracy, relationship between psychology and philosophy.

University of Dallas, Braniff Graduate School of Liberal Arts, Program in Humanities, Irving, TX 75062-4736. Offers M Hum, MA. *Program availability:* Part-time. *Degree requirements:* For master's, one foreign language, comprehensive exam, thesis (for some programs). *Entrance requirements:* For master's, GRE General Test. Additional exam requirements/recommendations for international students: Required—TOEFL. *Application deadline:* For fall admission, 2/15 priority date for domestic students; for spring admission, 11/15 for domestic students. Applications are processed on a rolling basis. Application fee: $50. *Expenses: Tuition:* Full-time $33,750; part-time $22,500 per year. Tuition and fees vary according to program. *Financial support:* Application deadline: 2/15. *Faculty research:* Classical epic poetry, scholastic poetry, Renaissance drama, nineteenth- and twentieth-century Continental philosophy. *Unit head:* Dr. Sally F. Hicks, Interim Dean, 972-721-5215, Fax: 972-721-5280, E-mail: constantindean@udallas.edu.

University of Houston–Clear Lake, School of Human Sciences and Humanities, Programs in Humanities and Fine Arts, Houston, TX 77058-1002. Offers history (MA); humanities (MA); literature (MA). *Program availability:* Part-time, evening/weekend, online learning. *Degree requirements:* For master's, thesis or alternative. *Entrance requirements:* For master's, GRE General Test. Additional exam requirements/recommendations for international students: Required—TOEFL (minimum score 550 paper-based). *Faculty research:* Digital media studies, Latin American history, labor history, Chaucer evolution versus creationism debate.

University of Louisville, Graduate School, College of Arts and Sciences, Department of Comparative Humanities, Louisville, KY 40292-0001. Offers civic leadership (MA); culture, criticism, and contemporary thought (PhD); linguistics (MA); public arts and letters (PhD); traditional humanities (MA); MA/JD; MA/MBA. *Program availability:* Part-time. *Faculty:* 14 full-time (6 women), 8 part-time/adjunct (4 women). *Students:* 33 full-time (21 women), 22 part-time (9 women); includes 7 minority (1 Black or African American, non-Hispanic/Latino; 1 Hispanic/Latino; 5 Two or more races, non-Hispanic/Latino), 4 international. Average age 39. 14 applicants, 79% accepted, 9 enrolled. In 2017, 3 master's, 10 doctorates awarded. *Degree requirements:* For master's, one foreign language, thesis or alternative, directed study culminating project; for doctorate, 2 foreign languages, comprehensive exam, thesis/dissertation, internship. *Entrance requirements:* For master's, GRE General Test, two letters of recommendation, transcripts from all institutions attended; for doctorate, GRE General Test, three letters of recommendation, statement of intent, scholarly writing sample, transcripts from all institutions attended. Additional exam requirements/recommendations for international students: Recommended—TOEFL. *Application deadline:* For fall admission, 1/15 for domestic and international students. Application fee: $65. Electronic applications accepted. *Expenses:* Contact institution. *Financial support:* In 2017–18, 1 fellowship with full tuition reimbursement (averaging $18,000 per year), 10 teaching assistantships with full tuition reimbursements (averaging $18,000 per year) were awarded. Financial award application deadline: 1/15. *Faculty research:* Literary studies, medieval studies, religious studies, linguistics, translation studies. *Total annual research expenditures:* $7,733. *Unit head:* Dr. Ann Hall, Chair, 502-852-6805, Fax: 502-852-0078, E-mail: ann.hall@louisville.edu. *Application contact:* Latonia Craig, Director of Graduate Recruitment and Diversity Retention, 502-852-5207, Fax: 502-852-6536, E-mail: gradadm@louisville.edu.
Website: http://louisville.edu/humanities/

University of Louisville, Graduate School, College of Arts and Sciences, Department of Philosophy, Louisville, KY 40292-0001. Offers humanities (MA, PhD). *Faculty:* 11 full-time (3 women), 5 part-time/adjunct (2 women). *Students:* 7 part-time (6 women); includes 6 minority (all Black or African American, non-Hispanic/Latino). Average age 37. *Degree requirements:* For master's, one foreign language, thesis or alternative. *Entrance requirements:* For master's, GRE General Test. Additional exam requirements/recommendations for international students: Required—TOEFL (minimum score 550 paper-based; 79 iBT), IELTS (minimum score 6.5). *Application deadline:* Applications are processed on a rolling basis. Application fee: $65. Electronic applications accepted. *Expenses:* Tuition, state resident: full-time $12,246; part-time $681 per credit hour. Tuition, nonresident: full-time $25,486; part-time $1417 per credit hour. *Required fees:* $196. Tuition and fees vary according to course load, program and reciprocity agreements. *Faculty research:* Philosophy of race; feminist philosophy; political philosophy, bioethics, ethics. *Unit head:* Dr. David S. Owen, Chair and Professor, 502-852-0488, Fax: 502-852-0459, E-mail: david.owen@louisville.edu. *Application contact:* Latonia Craig, Director of Graduate Recruitment and Diversity Retention, 502-852-5207, Fax: 502-852-6536, E-mail: gradadm@louisville.edu.
Website: http://louisville.edu/philosophy

University of South Florida, College of Arts and Sciences, Department of Humanities and Cultural Studies, Tampa, FL 33620-9951. Offers liberal arts (MA), including American studies, film studies, humanities. *Program availability:* Part-time, evening/weekend. *Faculty:* 8 full-time (2 women). *Students:* 19 full-time (10 women), 3 part-time (2 women); includes 3 minority (2 Black or African American, non-Hispanic/Latino; 1 Hispanic/Latino), 2 international. Average age 29. 25 applicants, 44% accepted, 7 enrolled. In 2017, 8 master's awarded. *Degree requirements:* For master's, comprehensive exam, thesis, language (for humanities subconcentration). *Entrance requirements:* For master's, GRE General Test, minimum GPA of 3.0 in upper-division courses, personal statement, writing sample. Additional exam requirements/recommendations for international students: Required—TOEFL (minimum score 550 paper-based; 79 iBT) or IELTS (minimum score 6.5). *Application deadline:* For fall admission, 2/15 priority date for domestic students, 2/15 for international students; for spring admission, 10/15 priority date for domestic students, 9/15 for international students; for summer admission, 2/15 for domestic students, 1/15 for international students. Application fee: $30. Electronic applications accepted. *Financial support:* In 2017–18, 2 students received support, including 15 teaching assistantships with tuition reimbursements available (averaging $12,437 per year); scholarships/grants also available. Financial award application deadline: 4/1. *Faculty research:* American South, American autobiography, material culture, critical theory, cultural studies, film studies. *Unit head:* Dr. Andrew Berish, Associate Professor and Chair, 813-974-9380, E-mail: aberish@usf.edu. *Application contact:* Dr. Maria Cizmic, Associate Professor and Graduate Program Director, 813-974-9380, E-mail: mcizmic@usf.edu.
Website: http://humanities.usf.edu/

The University of Texas at Dallas, School of Arts and Humanities, Richardson, TX 75080. Offers art history (MA); history (MA); humanities (MA, PhD), including aesthetic studies, history of ideas, studies in literature; Latin American studies (MA). *Program availability:* Part-time, evening/weekend. *Faculty:* 47 full-time (17 women), 4 part-time/adjunct (2 women). *Students:* 132 full-time (83 women), 117 part-time (71 women); includes 62 minority (11 Black or African American, non-Hispanic/Latino; 3 American Indian or Alaska Native, non-Hispanic/Latino; 10 Asian, non-Hispanic/Latino; 25 Hispanic/Latino; 13 Two or more races, non-Hispanic/Latino), 29 international. Average age 40. 127 applicants, 55% accepted, 43 enrolled. In 2017, 17 master's, 18 doctorates awarded. *Degree requirements:* For master's, one foreign language, portfolio; for doctorate, one foreign language, thesis/dissertation. *Entrance requirements:* For master's and doctorate, minimum GPA of 3.0 in undergraduate course work in field. Additional exam requirements/recommendations for international students: Required—TOEFL (minimum score 550 paper-based). *Application deadline:* For fall admission, 7/15 for domestic students, 5/1 priority date for international students; for spring admission, 11/15 for domestic students, 9/1 priority date for international students.

Applications are processed on a rolling basis. Application fee: $50 ($100 for international students). Electronic applications accepted. *Expenses:* Tuition, state resident: full-time $12,916; part-time $718 per credit hour. Tuition, nonresident: full-time $25,252; part-time $1403 per credit hour. *Financial support:* In 2017–18, 136 students received support, including 12 research assistantships with partial tuition reimbursements available (averaging $22,710 per year), 71 teaching assistantships with partial tuition reimbursements available (averaging $15,000 per year); fellowships, Federal Work-Study, institutionally sponsored loans, scholarships/grants, and unspecified assistantships also available. Support available to part-time students. Financial award application deadline: 4/30; financial award applicants required to submit FAFSA. *Faculty research:* Science and the arts and humanities, intellectual and philosophical history, cultural studies, translation studies. *Total annual research expenditures:* $183,441. *Unit head:* Dr. Dennis M. Kratz, Dean, 972-883-2984, Fax: 972-883-2989, E-mail: dkratz@utdallas.edu. *Application contact:* Dr. John Gooch, Associate Dean of Graduate Studies, 972-883-2756, Fax: 972-883-2989, E-mail: john.gooch@utdallas.edu.
Website: http://www.utdallas.edu/ah/

The University of Texas Medical Branch, Graduate School of Biomedical Sciences, Program in Medical Humanities, Galveston, TX 77555. Offers MA, PhD. *Degree requirements:* For master's, thesis; for doctorate, thesis/dissertation. *Entrance requirements:* For master's and doctorate, GRE General Test, writing sample. Additional exam requirements/recommendations for international students: Required—TOEFL (minimum score 550 paper-based). Electronic applications accepted.

University of Utah, Graduate School, College of Humanities, Environmental Humanities Graduate Program, Salt Lake City, UT 84112. Offers MA, MS. *Faculty:* 11 full-time (5 women). *Students:* 14 full-time (12 women), 1 (woman) part-time; includes 2 minority (1 Asian, non-Hispanic/Latino; 1 Hispanic/Latino), 1 international. Average age 26. 31 applicants, 23% accepted, 6 enrolled. In 2017, 5 master's awarded. *Entrance requirements:* For master's, minimum GPA of 3.0; undergraduate degree. Additional exam requirements/recommendations for international students: Required—TOEFL (minimum score 500 paper-based; 80 iBT). Application fee: $55 ($65 for international students). Electronic applications accepted. *Financial support:* In 2017–18, 14 students received support, including 14 teaching assistantships with full tuition reimbursements available (averaging $16,100 per year); scholarships/grants also available. Financial award application deadline: 1/15. *Faculty research:* Environmental writing, history/philosophy of science, environmental rhetoric and communication, American environmental history, urban environmentalism. *Unit head:* Jeffrey McCarthy, Director, 801-585-7052, Fax: 801-585-5190, E-mail: j.mccarthy@utah.edu. *Application contact:* Cory Pike, Graduate Advisor, 801-581-6156, E-mail: cory.pike@utah.edu.
Website: http://environmental-humanities.utah.edu/

Virginia Polytechnic Institute and State University, Graduate School, College of Liberal Arts and Human Sciences, Blacksburg, VA 24061. Offers career and technical education (MS Ed, Ed S); communication (MA); counselor education (MA); creative writing (MFA); curriculum and instruction (MA Ed, Ed S); educational leadership and policy studies (Ed S); educational research and evaluation (PhD); English (MA); social, political, ethical, and cultural thought (PhD); Ed D/PhD. *Faculty:* 411 full-time (213 women), 3 part-time/adjunct (all women). *Students:* 623 full-time (427 women), 431 part-time (278 women); includes 203 minority (115 Black or African American, non-Hispanic/Latino; 4 American Indian or Alaska Native, non-Hispanic/Latino; 29 Asian, non-Hispanic/Latino; 33 Hispanic/Latino; 2 Native Hawaiian or other Pacific Islander, non-Hispanic/Latino; 20 Two or more races, non-Hispanic/Latino), 87 international. Average age 34. 898 applicants, 50% accepted, 329 enrolled. In 2017, 314 master's, 102 doctorates awarded. *Degree requirements:* For master's, comprehensive exam (for some programs), thesis (for some programs); for doctorate, comprehensive exam (for some programs), thesis/dissertation (for some programs). *Entrance requirements:* For master's and doctorate, GRE/GMAT. Additional exam requirements/recommendations for international students: Required—TOEFL (minimum score 80 iBT). *Application deadline:* For fall admission, 8/1 for domestic students, 4/1 for international students; for spring admission, 1/1 for domestic students, 9/1 for international students. Applications are processed on a rolling basis. Application fee: $75. Electronic applications accepted. *Expenses:* Tuition, state resident: full-time $15,072; part-time $718.50 per credit hour. Tuition, nonresident: full-time $28,810; part-time $1448.25 per credit hour. *Required fees:* $2741; $502 per semester. Tuition and fees vary according to course load, campus/location and program. *Financial support:* In 2017–18, 19 research assistantships with full tuition reimbursements (averaging $19,611 per year), 226 teaching assistantships with full tuition reimbursements (averaging $16,220 per year) were awarded. Financial award application deadline: 3/1; financial award applicants required to submit FAFSA. *Total annual research expenditures:* $7.9 million. *Unit head:* Dr. Rosemary Blieszner, Dean, 540-231-6779, Fax: 540-231-7157, E-mail: rmb@vt.edu. *Application contact:* Chelsea Blanchet, Executive Assistant, 540-231-6779, Fax: 540-231-7157, E-mail: bchels1@vt.edu.
Website: http://www.liberalarts.vt.edu/

Wayland Baptist University, Graduate Programs, Programs in Behavioral and Social Sciences, Plainview, TX 79072-6998. Offers counseling (MA); criminal justice (MACJ); government administration (MPA); history (MA); homeland security (MPA); humanities (MAH); justice administration (MPA). *Program availability:* Part-time, evening/weekend, 100% online, blended/hybrid learning. *Faculty:* 19 full-time (5 women), 18 part-time/adjunct (8 women). *Students:* 16 full-time (10 women), 322 part-time (183 women); includes 207 minority (82 Black or African American, non-Hispanic/Latino; 8 American Indian or Alaska Native, non-Hispanic/Latino; 8 Asian, non-Hispanic/Latino; 84 Hispanic/Latino; 5 Native Hawaiian or other Pacific Islander, non-Hispanic/Latino; 20 Two or more races, non-Hispanic/Latino), 1 international. Average age 40. 56 applicants, 93% accepted, 39 enrolled. In 2017, 141 master's awarded. *Degree requirements:* For master's, comprehensive exam. *Entrance requirements:* For master's, GRE, MAT. Additional exam requirements/recommendations for international students: Required—TOEFL (minimum score 500 paper-based; 61 iBT). *Application deadline:* Applications are processed on a rolling basis. Application fee: $50. Electronic applications accepted. *Expenses: Tuition:* Full-time $11,250; part-time $625 per credit hour. *Required fees:* $1200. *Financial support:* Federal Work-Study, institutionally sponsored loans, and scholarships/grants available. Support available to part-time students. Financial award application deadline: 5/1; financial award applicants required to submit FAFSA. *Unit head:* Dr. Peter Bowen, Dean, 806-291-1179, Fax: 806-291-1972, E-mail: pbowen@wbu.edu. *Application contact:* Amanda Stanton, Graduate Studies, 806-291-3423, Fax: 806-291-1950, E-mail: stanton@wbu.edu.

Wilson College, Graduate Programs, Chambersburg, PA 17201-1285. Offers accounting (M Acc); choreography and visual art (MFA); education (M Ed); educational technology (MET); healthcare administration (MHA); humanities (MA), including art and culture, critical/cultural theory, English language and literature, women's studies; management (MSM); nursing (MSN), including nursing education, nursing leadership and management; special education (MSE). *Program availability:* Evening/weekend. *Degree requirements:* For master's, project. *Entrance requirements:* For master's, PRAXIS, minimum undergraduate cumulative GPA of 3.0, 2 letters of recommendation, current certification for eligibility to teach in grades K-12, resume, personal interview. Electronic applications accepted.

Wright State University, Graduate School, College of Liberal Arts, Interdisciplinary Program in Humanities, Dayton, OH 45435. Offers M Hum. *Degree requirements:* For master's, thesis or alternative. *Entrance requirements:* Additional exam requirements/recommendations for international students: Required—TOEFL.

York University, Faculty of Graduate Studies, Faculty of Liberal Arts and Professional Studies, Program in Humanities, Toronto, ON M3J 1P3, Canada. Offers MA, PhD. *Program availability:* Part-time. *Degree requirements:* For master's, thesis or alternative; for doctorate, comprehensive exam, thesis/dissertation. *Entrance requirements:* Additional exam requirements/recommendations for international students: Required—TOEFL (minimum score 600 paper-based). Electronic applications accepted.

Liberal Studies

Abilene Christian University, Graduate Programs, College of Arts and Sciences, Interdisciplinary Program in the Liberal Arts, Abilene, TX 79699. Offers MLA. *Program availability:* Part-time. *Students:* 1 part-time (0 women). 2 applicants, 50% accepted, 1 enrolled. In 2017, 1 master's awarded. *Degree requirements:* For master's, comprehensive exam, thesis or alternative. *Entrance requirements:* For master's, GRE General Test. Additional exam requirements/recommendations for international students: Required—TOEFL (minimum score 80 iBT), IELTS (minimum score 6), PTE. *Application deadline:* For fall admission, 4/1 priority date for domestic students; for spring admission, 11/1 for domestic students. Applications are processed on a rolling basis. Application fee: $50. Electronic applications accepted. *Expenses:* $1,148 per hour. *Financial support:* Federal Work-Study available. Support available to part-time students. Financial award application deadline: 4/1; financial award applicants required to submit FAFSA. *Unit head:* Dr. Joe Cardot, Graduate Advisor, 325-674-2136, Fax: 325-674-6966, E-mail: cardotj@acu.edu. *Application contact:* Graduate Admissions, 325-674-6911, Fax: 325-674-6717, E-mail: gradinfo@acu.edu.
Website: http://www.acu.edu/graduate/academics/liberal-arts.html

Alaska Pacific University, Graduate Programs, Liberal Studies Department, Anchorage, AK 99508-4672. Offers self-designed study (MA).

Albertus Magnus College, Master of Arts in Liberal Studies Program, New Haven, CT 06511-1189. Offers MALS. *Program availability:* Part-time, evening/weekend, blended/hybrid learning. *Degree requirements:* For master's, thesis, completion of all credits within six years from time when student begins program; minimum cumulative GPA of 3.9; final project. *Entrance requirements:* For master's, interview, 500-word essay detailing applicant's intellectual and professional interests, minimum GPA of 2.8, transcripts. Additional exam requirements/recommendations for international students: Required—TOEFL (minimum score 550 paper-based; 80 iBT). *Application deadline:* For fall admission, 8/31 for domestic students; for spring admission, 1/10 for domestic students. Applications are processed on a rolling basis. Application fee: $50. Electronic applications accepted. *Expenses:* Contact institution. *Financial support:* Federal Work-Study and unspecified assistantships available. Support available to part-time students. Financial award application deadline: 8/15; financial award applicants required to submit FAFSA. *Unit head:* Prof. Julia A. Coash, Director, 203-773-8973, Fax: 203-773-5257, E-mail: jcoash@albertus.edu. *Application contact:* Anthony Reich, Director of Admission, Division of Professional and Graduate Studies, 203-773-5032, Fax: 203-773-5257, E-mail: arreich@albertus.edu.
Website: http://www.albertus.edu/liberal-studies/ma/

Alvernia University, School of Graduate Studies, Program in Liberal Studies, Reading, PA 19607-1799. Offers MALS. *Program availability:* Part-time, evening/weekend. *Degree requirements:* For master's, thesis optional. *Entrance requirements:* For master's, MAT or GRE (alumni excluded). Electronic applications accepted.

Arizona State University at the Tempe campus, College of Liberal Arts and Sciences, Program in Liberal Studies, Tempe, AZ 85287-6505. Offers MLS. *Program availability:* Part-time, evening/weekend. *Degree requirements:* For master's, thesis or alternative, integrated/capstone project, interactive Program of Study (iPOS) submitted before completing 50 percent of required credit hours. *Entrance requirements:* For master's, minimum GPA of 3.0 or equivalent in last 2 years of work leading to bachelor's degree, resume or biographical statement, personal letter expressing liberal studies concentration interest, official college transcripts, 2 letters of recommendation, interview with program director (recommended). Additional exam requirements/recommendations for international students: Required—TOEFL, IELTS, or PTE. Electronic applications accepted. *Expenses:* Contact institution.

Arkansas Tech University, College of Arts and Humanities, Russellville, AR 72801. Offers applied sociology (MS); English (M Ed, MA); history (MA); liberal arts (MLA); multi-media journalism (MA); psychology (MS); teaching English as a second language (MA). *Program availability:* Part-time, 100% online, blended/hybrid learning. *Students:* 35 full-time (22 women), 122 part-time (94 women); includes 34 minority (11 Black or African American, non-Hispanic/Latino; 2 Asian, non-Hispanic/Latino; 19 Hispanic/Latino; 2 Two or more races, non-Hispanic/Latino), 19 international. Average age 34. In 2017, 85 master's awarded. *Degree requirements:* For master's, comprehensive exam (for some programs), thesis (for some programs), project. *Entrance requirements:* Additional exam requirements/recommendations for international students: Required—TOEFL (minimum score 550 paper-based; 79 iBT), IELTS (minimum score 6.5), PTE (minimum score 58). *Application deadline:* For fall admission, 3/1 priority date for domestic students, 5/1 priority date for international students; for spring admission, 10/1 priority date for domestic and international students. Applications are processed on a rolling basis. Application fee: $40 ($90 for international students). Electronic applications accepted. *Expenses:* Tuition, state resident: full-time $6816; part-time $284 per credit hour. Tuition, nonresident: full-time $13,632; part-time $568 per credit hour. *Required fees:* $420 per semester. Tuition and fees vary according to course load. *Financial support:* In 2017–18, research assistantships with full and partial tuition reimbursements (averaging $4,800 per year), teaching assistantships with full and partial tuition reimbursements (averaging $4,800 per year) were awarded; career-related internships

or fieldwork, Federal Work-Study, scholarships/grants, health care benefits, and unspecified assistantships also available. Support available to part-time students. Financial award application deadline: 4/15; financial award applicants required to submit FAFSA. *Unit head:* Dr. Jeffrey Woods, Dean, 479-968-0274, Fax: 479-964-0812, E-mail: jwoods@atu.edu. *Application contact:* Dr. Mary B. Gunter, Dean of Graduate College, 479-968-0398, Fax: 479-964-0542, E-mail: gradcollege@atu.edu.
Website: http://www.atu.edu/humanities/

Auburn University at Montgomery, College of Arts and Sciences, Program in Liberal Arts, Montgomery, AL 36124-4023. Offers MLA. *Faculty:* 9 full-time (5 women). *Students:* 11 full-time (8 women), 39 part-time (27 women); includes 14 minority (all Black or African American, non-Hispanic/Latino), 1 international. Average age 35. 23 applicants, 100% accepted, 12 enrolled. In 2017, 16 master's awarded. *Degree requirements:* For master's, thesis. *Entrance requirements:* For master's, official transcripts; minimum undergraduate GPA of 2.75 or MAT. Additional exam requirements/recommendations for international students: Recommended—TOEFL (minimum score 500 paper-based; 61 iBT), IELTS (minimum score 5.5), TSE (minimum score 44). *Application deadline:* For fall admission, 7/15 for international students; for spring admission, 11/15 for international students; for summer admission, 4/15 for international students. Applications are processed on a rolling basis. Application fee: $25. Electronic applications accepted. *Expenses:* Tuition, state resident: full-time $6930; part-time $385 per credit hour. Tuition, nonresident: full-time $15,588; part-time $866 per credit hour. *Required fees:* $640. *Financial support:* Scholarships/grants and unspecified assistantships available. Financial award application deadline: 3/1; financial award applicants required to submit FAFSA. *Unit head:* Dr. Matthew Ragland, Acting Dean, 334-244-3138, E-mail: mragland@aum.edu. *Application contact:* Dr. Eric Sterling, Director of MLA Program, 334-244-3760, E-mail: esterlin@aum.edu.
Website: http://www.cas.aum.edu/academic-programs/graduate-programs/mla

Baker University, School of Professional and Graduate Studies, Program in Liberal Arts, Baldwin City, KS 66006-0065. Offers MLA. *Program availability:* Part-time, evening/weekend, online learning. *Students:* 38 part-time (31 women); includes 10 minority (4 Black or African American, non-Hispanic/Latino; 1 American Indian or Alaska Native, non-Hispanic/Latino; 1 Asian, non-Hispanic/Latino; 4 Hispanic/Latino). Average age 38. In 2017, 21 master's awarded. *Degree requirements:* For master's, portfolio of learning. *Entrance requirements:* Additional exam requirements/recommendations for international students: Required—TOEFL (minimum score 600 paper-based; 100 iBT). *Application deadline:* Applications are processed on a rolling basis. Electronic applications accepted. *Financial support:* Applicants required to submit FAFSA. *Unit head:* Dr. Emily Ford, Interim Dean of the School of Professional and Graduate Studies, 785-594-8475, E-mail: emily.ford@bakeru.edu. *Application contact:* Kelly Belk, Vice President of Enrollment Management, 913-491-4432, E-mail: kelly.belk@learn.bakeru.edu.
Website: https://www.bakeru.edu/spgs/mla/

Barry University, College of Arts and Sciences, Interdisciplinary Program, Miami Shores, FL 33161-6695. Offers MA.

Binghamton University, State University of New York, Graduate School, Harpur College of Arts and Sciences, Program in Applied Liberal Studies, Binghamton, NY 13902-6000. Offers MA. *Students:* 3 full-time (0 women); includes 1 minority (Black or African American, non-Hispanic/Latino), 1 international. Average age 25. 4 applicants, 75% accepted, 3 enrolled. *Unit head:* Dr. Terrence Deak, Dean, 607-777-2145, E-mail: tdeak@binghamton.edu. *Application contact:* Ben Balkaya, Assistant Dean and Director, 607-777-2151, Fax: 607-777-2501, E-mail: balkaya@binghamton.edu.

Brooklyn College of the City University of New York, School of Education, Program in Childhood Education, Brooklyn, NY 11210-2889. Offers bilingual education (MS Ed); liberal arts (MS Ed); mathematics (MS Ed); science and environmental education (MS Ed). *Program availability:* Part-time, evening/weekend. *Entrance requirements:* For master's, LAST, interview, previous course work in education, writing sample, resume, 2 letters of recommendation. Additional exam requirements/recommendations for international students: Required—TOEFL (minimum score 500 paper-based; 61 iBT). Electronic applications accepted. *Faculty research:* Emotional intelligence, multiculturalism, arts immersion, the Holocaust.

Cardinal Stritch University, College of Arts and Sciences, Milwaukee, WI 53217-3985. Offers MA, MS. *Program availability:* Part-time, evening/weekend. *Students:* 23 full-time (17 women), 38 part-time (23 women); includes 14 minority (7 Black or African American, non-Hispanic/Latino; 2 American Indian or Alaska Native, non-Hispanic/Latino; 1 Asian, non-Hispanic/Latino; 2 Hispanic/Latino; 1 Native Hawaiian or other Pacific Islander, non-Hispanic/Latino; 1 Two or more races, non-Hispanic/Latino), 12 international. Average age 31. 70 applicants, 100% accepted, 14 enrolled. In 2017, 32 master's awarded. *Degree requirements:* For master's, thesis. *Entrance requirements:* Additional exam requirements/recommendations for international students: Required—TOEFL (minimum score 79 iBT), IELTS (minimum score 6.5). *Application deadline:* For fall admission, 7/15 priority date for domestic students; for spring admission, 12/15 priority date for domestic students. Applications are processed on a rolling basis. Application fee: $0. Electronic applications accepted. *Expenses:* $782 per credit hour. *Financial support:* Research assistantships with partial tuition reimbursements, career-related internships or fieldwork, Federal Work-Study, scholarships/grants, and unspecified assistantships available. Financial award applicants required to submit FAFSA. *Unit head:* Dr. Carl D. Mueller, Interim Dean, 414-410-4376, E-mail: cd2mueller@stritch.edu. *Application contact:* 800-347-8822 Ext. 4042, E-mail: admissions@stritch.edu.

Clayton State University, School of Graduate Studies, College of Arts and Sciences, Program in Liberal Studies, Morrow, GA 30260-0285. Offers MA. *Program availability:* Part-time. *Degree requirements:* For master's, thesis optional. *Entrance requirements:* For master's, official transcripts, 3 letters of recommendation, statement of purpose, on-campus interview. Additional exam requirements/recommendations for international students: Required—TOEFL (minimum score 550 paper-based; 80 iBT). Electronic applications accepted.

Coastal Carolina University, Thomas W. and Robin W. Edwards College of Humanities and Fine Arts, Conway, SC 29528-6054. Offers liberal studies (MA); writing (MA). *Program availability:* Part-time, evening/weekend. *Faculty:* 20 full-time (12 women), 1 (woman) part-time/adjunct. *Students:* 29 full-time (17 women), 13 part-time (8 women); includes 7 minority (6 Black or African American, non-Hispanic/Latino; 1 Two or more races, non-Hispanic/Latino), 2 international. Average age 32. 32 applicants, 72% accepted, 19 enrolled. In 2017, 18 master's awarded. *Entrance requirements:* For master's, GRE, official transcripts, 2 letters of recommendation, writing sample; 2-page statement of interest, minimum GPA of 3.3 in 18 hours of undergraduate and graduate coursework in English or related discipline. Additional exam requirements/recommendations for international students: Required—TOEFL (minimum score 550 paper-based; 79 iBT), IELTS (minimum score 6.5). *Application deadline:* For fall admission, 5/15 priority date for domestic and international students; for spring admission, 11/15 priority date for domestic and international students. Applications are processed on a rolling basis. Application fee: $45. Electronic applications accepted. *Expenses:* Tuition, state resident: full-time $5184; part-time $576 per credit hour. Tuition, nonresident: full-time $9369; part-time $1041 per credit hour. *Required fees:* $90; $5 per credit hour. *Financial support:* Fellowships, research assistantships, teaching assistantships, and tuition waivers available. Financial award application deadline: 3/1; financial award applicants required to submit FAFSA. *Unit head:* Dr. Daniel J. Ennis, Dean/Vice President for Academic Outreach, 843-349-2746, E-mail: dennis@coastal.edu. *Application contact:* Dr. James O. Luken, Associate Provost for Graduate Program/Vice-Dean of the Coastal Environment, 843-349-2235, Fax: 843-349-6444, E-mail: joluken@coastal.edu.
Website: https://www.coastal.edu/humanities/

The College at Brockport, State University of New York, School of Arts and Sciences, Program in Liberal Studies, Brockport, NY 14420-2997. Offers MA. *Program availability:* Part-time, 100% online, blended/hybrid learning. *Students:* 1 (woman) full-time, 18 part-time (13 women); includes 4 minority (3 Black or African American, non-Hispanic/Latino; 1 Hispanic/Latino). 11 applicants, 64% accepted, 6 enrolled. In 2017, 10 master's awarded. *Degree requirements:* For master's, thesis. *Entrance requirements:* Additional exam requirements/recommendations for international students: Required—TOEFL (minimum score 550 paper-based; 79 iBT), IELTS (minimum score 6.5). *Application deadline:* For fall admission, 6/15 for domestic and international students; for spring admission, 10/15 for domestic and international students; for summer admission, 3/15 for domestic and international students. Application fee: $50. Electronic applications accepted. *Expenses:* Tuition, state resident: full-time $10,870; part-time $453 per credit hour. Tuition, nonresident: full-time $22,210. *Required fees:* $988; $246 per semester. *Financial support:* Fellowships, research assistantships, teaching assistantships, scholarships/grants, and unspecified assistantships available. Financial award applicants required to submit FAFSA. *Unit head:* Dr. Jose Maliekal, Dean, School of Arts and Sciences, 585-395-5806. *Application contact:* Kulathur Rajasethupathy, Director of Liberal Studies, 585-395-5760, E-mail: kraja@brockport.edu.

College of Staten Island of the City University of New York, Graduate Programs, Division of Humanities and Social Sciences, Program in Liberal Studies, Staten Island, NY 10314-6600. Offers MA. *Program availability:* Part-time, evening/weekend. *Faculty:* 3 full-time, 1 part-time/adjunct. *Students:* 21. 25 applicants, 64% accepted, 9 enrolled. *Degree requirements:* For master's, comprehensive exam, 30 credits; essay that will be extended reflection on problem of contemporary social and/or cultural interest drawing on the intellectual tradition of the liberal arts and on student's own values and analysis. *Entrance requirements:* For master's, BA or BS with minimum cumulative GPA of 3.0. Additional exam requirements/recommendations for international students: Required—TOEFL (minimum score 550 paper-based; 79 iBT), IELTS (minimum score 6.5). *Application deadline:* For fall admission, 8/15 priority date for domestic and international students; for spring admission, 1/15 priority date for domestic and international students. Applications are processed on a rolling basis. Application fee: $125. Electronic applications accepted. *Expenses:* Tuition, state resident: full-time $10,450; part-time $440 per credit. Tuition, nonresident: full-time $19,320; part-time $440 per credit. *Required fees:* $181.10 per semester. Tuition and fees vary according to program. *Faculty research:* Latin-American studies, historical and political anthropology, sociological theory, political economy. *Unit head:* Dr. Ismael Garcia Colon, Graduate Program Coordinator, 718-982-3766, E-mail: ismael.garcia@csi.cuny.edu. *Application contact:* Sasha Spence, Associate Director for Graduate Admissions, 718-982-2019, Fax: 718-982-2500, E-mail: sasha.spence@csi.cuny.edu.
Website: https://www.csi.cuny.edu/sites/default/files/pdf/admissions/grad/pdf/Liberal%20Studies%20Fact%20Sheet.pdf

The Colorado College, Education Department, Experienced Teacher Program, Colorado Springs, CO 80903-3294. Offers arts and humanities (MAT); integrated natural sciences (MAT); liberal arts (MAT); Southwest studies (MAT). Programs offered during summer only. *Program availability:* Part-time. *Degree requirements:* For master's, thesis, oral exam, 50-page paper. *Expenses:* Contact institution.

Colorado State University, College of Liberal Arts, College of Liberal Arts, Fort Collins, CO 80523-1778. Offers MALCM. *Program availability:* Part-time, evening/weekend, 100% online. *Faculty:* 6 part-time/adjunct (3 women). *Students:* 4 full-time (all women), 65 part-time (53 women); includes 14 minority (2 Black or African American, non-Hispanic/Latino; 4 Asian, non-Hispanic/Latino; 6 Hispanic/Latino; 2 Two or more races, non-Hispanic/Latino), 6 international. Average age 31. 50 applicants, 82% accepted, 24 enrolled. In 2017, 9 master's awarded. *Degree requirements:* For master's, comprehensive exam, internship. *Entrance requirements:* For master's, official transcripts, 3 letters of recommendation, personal statement, resume. Additional exam requirements/recommendations for international students: Required—TOEFL (minimum score 550 paper-based; 80 iBT). *Application deadline:* For fall admission, 6/30 for domestic and international students; for spring admission, 11/15 for domestic and international students; for summer admission, 4/1 for domestic and international students. Applications are processed on a rolling basis. Application fee: $60 ($70 for international students). Electronic applications accepted. *Expenses:* $642 per credit hour (for online program), $750 per semester (for on-campus program). *Financial support:* Career-related internships or fieldwork, scholarships/grants, and unspecified assistantships available. Financial award application deadline: 1/1; financial award applicants required to submit FAFSA. *Faculty research:* Cultural citizenship and the arts, culturally sustainable entrepreneurship, arts management practices, and everyday aesthetics. *Unit head:* Dr. Constance DeVereaux, Director, 970-491-3902, E-mail: constance.devereaux@colostate.edu. *Application contact:* Erica Pepmeyer, Recruitment Coordinator, 970-491-1194, E-mail: erika.pepmeyer@colostate.edu.
Website: http://leap.colostate.edu/

Colorado State University, College of Liberal Arts, Department of History, Fort Collins, CO 80523-1776. Offers liberal arts (MA). *Program availability:* Part-time. *Faculty:* 7 full-time (4 women), 1 (woman) part-time/adjunct. *Students:* 23 full-time (13 women), 3 part-time (0 women); includes 1 minority (Hispanic/Latino). Average age 27. 34 applicants, 56% accepted, 11 enrolled. In 2017, 16 master's awarded. *Degree requirements:* For master's, variable foreign language requirement, comprehensive exam, thesis (for some programs). *Entrance requirements:* For master's, GRE, 21 undergraduate credits in history; minimum undergraduate GPA of 3.0; personal statement; 3 letters of reference. Additional exam requirements/recommendations for international students: Required—TOEFL, IELTS. *Application deadline:* For winter admission, 2/1 for domestic and international students. Application fee: $60 ($70 for international students). Electronic applications accepted. *Expenses:* Tuition, state resident: full-time $9917. Tuition, nonresident: full-time $24,312. *Required fees:* $2284. Tuition and fees vary according to course load and program. *Financial support:* In 2017–18, 22 students received support, including 22 teaching assistantships (averaging $14,256 per year); health care benefits also available. Financial award application deadline: 2/1; financial award applicants required to submit FAFSA. *Faculty research:* Environment, gender, public history, United States West. *Total annual research expenditures:* $303,063. *Unit head:* Dr. Doug Yarrington, Department Chair, 970-491-6801, Fax: 970-491-2941, E-mail: doug.yarrington@colostate.edu. *Application contact:* Nancy Rehe, Administrative Assistant, 970-491-6334, E-mail: nancy.rehe@colostate.edu.
Website: http://history.colostate.edu/

Concordia University Chicago, College of Graduate and Innovative Programs, Program in Liberal Studies, River Forest, IL 60305-1499. Offers MA. *Entrance requirements:* Additional exam requirements/recommendations for international students: Required—TOEFL (minimum score 550 paper-based). Electronic applications accepted.

Converse College, Program in Liberal Arts, Spartanburg, SC 29302. Offers English (MLA); history (MLA); political science (MLA). *Degree requirements:* For master's, capstone paper. *Entrance requirements:* For master's, minimum GPA of 3.0, 2 recommendations. *Application deadline:* For fall admission, 5/1 priority date for domestic students; for spring admission, 1/30 for domestic students. Application fee: $40. *Unit head:* Lienne Medford, Dean of Graduate Studies and Distance Education, 864-596-9082, E-mail: lienne.medford@converse.edu.

Dallas Baptist University, Liberal Arts Program, Dallas, TX 75211-9299. Offers art (MLA); Christian studies (MLA); commercial art (MLA); East Asian studies (MLA); English (MLA); English as a second language (MLA); fine arts (MLA); history (MLA); missions (MLA); political science (MLA). *Program availability:* Part-time, evening/weekend. *Application deadline:* Applications are processed on a rolling basis. Application fee: $25. Electronic applications accepted. Application fee is waived when completed online. *Expenses: Tuition:* Full-time $16,308; part-time $906 per credit hour. *Required fees:* $900; $450 per semester. Tuition and fees vary according to course load and degree level. *Unit head:* Jared Ingram, Director, 214-333-5584, E-mail: jaredi@dbu.edu. *Application contact:* Bobby Soto, Director of Admissions, 214-333-5242, E-mail: bobby@dbu.edu.
Website: http://www3.dbu.edu/graduate/mla.asp

Dartmouth College, School of Graduate and Advanced Studies, Master of Arts in Liberal Studies Program, Hanover, NH 03755. Offers MALS. *Program availability:* Part-time. *Faculty:* 10 full-time (4 women), 12 part-time/adjunct (5 women). *Students:* 31 full-time (17 women), 31 part-time (17 women); includes 10 minority (1 Black or African American, non-Hispanic/Latino; 2 Asian, non-Hispanic/Latino; 5 Hispanic/Latino; 2 Two or more races, non-Hispanic/Latino), 11 international. Average age 32. 91 applicants, 76% accepted, 36 enrolled. In 2017, 51 master's awarded. *Entrance requirements:* Additional exam requirements/recommendations for international students: Required—TOEFL. *Application deadline:* For fall admission, 2/15 for domestic students; for winter admission, 7/15 for domestic students; for spring admission, 7/15 for domestic students; for summer admission, 2/15 for domestic students. Application fee: $50. Electronic applications accepted. *Financial support:* Institutionally sponsored loans available. Financial award application deadline: 4/1; financial award applicants required to submit FAFSA. *Unit head:* Ronald Edsforth, Chair, 603-646-1738. *Application contact:* Wole Ojurongbe, Director, 603-646-3592, E-mail: mals.program@dartmouth.edu.
Website: http://mals.dartmouth.edu/

See Display below and Close-Up on page 319.

Delta State University, Graduate Programs, College of Arts and Sciences, Program in Liberal Studies, Cleveland, MS 38733-0001. Offers evolving human voices (MALS); gender and diversity studies (MALS); globalization studies (MALS); Mississippi Delta studies (MALS); philosophy (MALS); religious studies (MALS). *Degree requirements:* For master's, oral and/or written comprehensive exam.

DePaul University, College of Liberal Arts and Social Sciences, Chicago, IL 60614. Offers Arabic (MA); Chinese (MA); critical ethnic studies (MA); English (MA); French (MA); German (MA); history (MA); interdisciplinary studies (MA, MS); international public service (MS); international studies (MA); Italian (MA); Japanese (MA); liberal studies (MA); nonprofit management (MNM); public administration (MPA); public health (MPH); public policy (MPP); public service management (MS); refugee and forced migration studies (MS); social work (MSW); sociology (MA); Spanish (MA); sustainable urban

development (MA); women's and gender studies (MA); writing and publishing (MA); writing, rhetoric and discourse (MA); MA/PhD. *Program availability:* Part-time, evening/weekend, online learning. Terminal master's awarded for partial completion of doctoral program. *Degree requirements:* For master's, variable foreign language requirement, comprehensive exam (for some programs), thesis (for some programs). *Application deadline:* Applications are processed on a rolling basis. Application fee: $40. Electronic applications accepted. *Entrance requirements:* For master's, minimum GPA of 3.0. Required—TOEFL (minimum score 550 paper-based; 80 iBT), IELTS (minimum score 6.5). *Application contact:* Ann Spittle, Director of Graduate Admission, 773-325-8369, Fax: 312-476-3244, E-mail: graddepaul@depaul.edu.
Website: http://las.depaul.edu/

Dominican University of California, School of Liberal Arts and Education, San Rafael, CA 94901-2298. Offers MA. *Program availability:* Part-time, evening/weekend. *Faculty:* 17 full-time (11 women), 11 part-time/adjunct (10 women). *Students:* 57 full-time (43 women), 99 part-time (75 women); includes 37 minority (4 Black or African American, non-Hispanic/Latino; 1 American Indian or Alaska Native, non-Hispanic/Latino; 4 Asian, non-Hispanic/Latino; 20 Hispanic/Latino; 2 Native Hawaiian or other Pacific Islander, non-Hispanic/Latino; 6 Two or more races, non-Hispanic/Latino), 2 international. Average age 37. 63 applicants, 98% accepted, 41 enrolled. In 2017, 51 master's awarded. *Degree requirements:* For master's, comprehensive exam (for some programs), thesis (for some programs). *Entrance requirements:* For master's, minimum GPA of 3.0. Additional exam requirements/recommendations for international students: Required—TOEFL (minimum score 550 paper-based; 80 iBT), IELTS (minimum score 6.5). *Application deadline:* For fall admission, 5/15 for domestic and international students; for spring admission, 11/15 for domestic and international students. Applications are processed on a rolling basis. Application fee: $0. Electronic applications accepted. *Expenses: Tuition:* Full-time $17,370; part-time $965 per credit. *Required fees:* $150 per semester. Tuition and fees vary according to course load and program. *Financial support:* In 2017–18, 69 students received support. Scholarships/grants available. Support available to part-time students. Financial award application deadline: 3/2; financial award applicants required to submit FAFSA. *Unit head:* Laura Stivers, Dean, 415-458-3734, E-mail: laura.stivers@dominican.edu. *Application contact:* Michael Lavigna, Assistant Director of Graduate Admissions, 415-485-3253, Fax: 415-485-3214, E-mail: gradmissions@dominican.edu.
Website: https://www.dominican.edu/academics/lae/index_html

Drew University, Caspersen School of Graduate Studies, Madison, NJ 07940-1493. Offers conflict resolution and leadership (Certificate), including community leadership, moderation, peace building; education (M Ed); finance (MA); history and culture (MA, PhD), including American history, book history, British history, European history, Holocaust and genocide (M Litt, MA, D Litt, PhD), intellectual history, Irish history, print culture, public history; K-12 education (MAT), including art, biology, chemistry, elementary education, English, French, Italian, math, secondary education, special education, teacher of students with disabilities; liberal studies (M Litt, D Litt), including history, Holocaust and genocide (M Litt, MA, D Litt, PhD), Irish/Irish-American studies, literature (M Litt, MMH, D Litt, DMH, CMH), religion, spirituality, teaching in the two-year college, writing; medical humanities (MMH, DMH, CMH), including arts, health, healthcare, literature (M Litt, MMH, D Litt, DMH, CMH), scientific research; poetry (MFA). *Program availability:* Part-time, evening/weekend. *Faculty:* 4 full-time (2 women), 29 part-time/adjunct (15 women). *Students:* 77 full-time (42 women), 175 part-time (114 women); includes 39 minority (12 Black or African American, non-Hispanic/Latino; 6 Asian, non-Hispanic/Latino; 16 Hispanic/Latino; 5 Two or more races, non-Hispanic/Latino), 11 international. Average age 41. 126 applicants, 75% accepted, 52 enrolled. In 2017, 38 master's, 23 doctorates, 35 other advanced degrees awarded. Terminal master's awarded for partial completion of doctoral program. *Degree requirements:* For

DARTMOUTH COLLEGE MASTER OF ARTS IN LIBERAL STUDIES

ESTABLISHED IN 1970, THE MALS PROGRAM AT DARTMOUTH is part of Dartmouth's School of Graduate and Advanced Studies, and offers an intensive and immersive, master's degree program in liberal arts.

MALS at Dartmouth is a highly selective program and awards the Master of Arts degree in the following concentrations: Cultural Studies, Creative Writing, Globalization Studies, and General Liberal Studies. With access to Dartmouth's world renowned faculty and all of Dartmouth's graduate and undergraduate schools, students are able to pursue comprehensive, interdisciplinary study of the liberal arts at the graduate level from one of the top liberal arts colleges in the world.

Through this interdisciplinary approach, and by working closely with our award-winning faculty, students create an individualized plan-of-study that significantly enhances their academic and professional credentials. This unique MALS at Dartmouth interdisciplinary experience prepares our graduates to advance in their chosen field; pursue doctoral programs across all disciplines; as well as, gain entrance into the professional schools of law, business, and medicine.

Learn more at: mals.dartmouth.edu

"The MALS program at Dartmouth is everything graduate school ought to be: intellectually vigorous and challenging, yet without the narrowness of vision that too often folds the act of learning into tiny boxes. Graduate liberal studies has a range as broad as the student's own desire to chase down the truth, wherever it lies."

- Tom Zoellner, MALS 2011
Author of *A Safeway in Arizona*

PHOTOS: ELI BURAKIAN

603.646.3592 | 6092 Wentworth Hall, Hanover, NH 03755-3526 | MALS.Program@Dartmouth.edu

master's and other advanced degree, thesis (for some programs); for doctorate, one foreign language, comprehensive exam (for some programs), thesis/dissertation. *Entrance requirements:* For master's, PRAXIS Core and Subject Area tests (for MAT), GRE/GMAT (for M Fin), resume, transcripts, writing sample, personal statement, letters of recommendation; for doctorate, GRE (PhD in history and culture), resume, transcripts, writing sample, personal statement, letters of recommendation; for other advanced degree, resume, transcripts, personal statement. Additional exam requirements/recommendations for international students: Required—TOEFL (minimum score 587 paper-based; 80 iBT), IELTS (minimum score 6), TWE (minimum score 4). *Application deadline:* For fall admission, 8/1 for domestic students, 6/1 for international students; for spring admission, 12/1 for domestic students, 10/1 for international students. Applications are processed on a rolling basis. Application fee: $35. Electronic applications accepted. *Financial support:* Fellowships, research assistantships, teaching assistantships, career-related internships or fieldwork, Federal Work-Study, scholarships/grants, and unspecified assistantships available. Support available to part-time students. Financial award applicants required to submit FAFSA. *Faculty research:* Irish history and culture, conflict resolution and leadership. *Application contact:* Leanne Horinko, Director of Caspersen Admissions, 973-408-3280, E-mail: gradm@drew.edu.
Website: http://www.drew.edu/caspersen

Duke University, Graduate School, Program in Liberal Studies, Durham, NC 27708. Offers AM. *Program availability:* Part-time, evening/weekend. *Degree requirements:* For master's, thesis or alternative, final project. *Entrance requirements:* For master's, interview. Additional exam requirements/recommendations for international students: Required—IELTS (preferred) or TOEFL. Electronic applications accepted.

Eastern Washington University, Graduate Studies, College of Arts, Letters and Education, Department of Music, Cheney, WA 99004-2431. Offers composition (MA); instrumental/vocal performance (MA); jazz pedagogy (MA); liberal arts (MA); music education (MA). *Accreditation:* NASM. *Program availability:* Part-time. *Faculty:* 17. *Students:* 10 full-time (4 women), 3 part-time (0 women), 1 international. Average age 31. 12 applicants, 58% accepted, 5 enrolled. In 2017, 7 master's awarded. *Degree requirements:* For master's, comprehensive exam, thesis or alternative. *Entrance requirements:* For master's, GRE General Test, minimum GPA of 3.0. Additional exam requirements/recommendations for international students: Required—TOEFL (minimum score 580 paper-based; 92 iBT), IELTS (minimum score 7), TWE, PTE (minimum score 63). *Application deadline:* For fall admission, 4/1 priority date for domestic students; for spring admission, 1/15 for domestic students. Applications are processed on a rolling basis. Application fee: $75. Electronic applications accepted. *Expenses:* Tuition, state resident: full-time $11,191; part-time $373.06 per credit. Tuition, nonresident: full-time $25,995; part-time $866.52 per credit. *Financial support:* In 2017–18, 8 students received support, including teaching assistantships with partial tuition reimbursements available (averaging $10,000 per year); career-related internships or fieldwork, Federal Work-Study, institutionally sponsored loans, scholarships/grants, health care benefits, tuition waivers (partial), and unspecified assistantships also available. Support available to part-time students. Financial award application deadline: 2/1; financial award applicants required to submit FAFSA. *Unit head:* Dr. Jody Graves, 509-359-6119, E-mail: jgraves@ewu.edu.
Website: http://www.ewu.edu/cale/programs/music.xml

East Tennessee State University, School of Graduate Studies, School of Continuing Studies and Academic Outreach, Johnson City, TN 37614. Offers archival studies (Postbaccalaureate Certificate); liberal studies (MALS); reinforcing education through artistic learning (Postbaccalaureate Certificate); strategic leadership (MPS); training and development (MPS). *Program availability:* Part-time, online learning. In 2017, 9 master's, 1 other advanced degree awarded. *Degree requirements:* For master's, comprehensive exam, thesis (for some programs), professional project. *Entrance requirements:* For master's, GRE General Test, minimum GPA of 2.75, professional portfolio, three letters of recommendation, interview, writing sample; for Postbaccalaureate Certificate, minimum GPA of 2.5, three letters of recommendation, interview. Additional exam requirements/recommendations for international students: Required—TOEFL (minimum score 550 paper-based; 79 iBT). *Application deadline:* For fall admission, 6/1 for domestic students, 4/29 for international students; for spring admission, 11/1 for domestic students, 9/29 for international students. Application fee: $55 ($65 for international students). Electronic applications accepted. *Financial support:* Research assistantships with full tuition reimbursements, teaching assistantships with full tuition reimbursements, institutionally sponsored loans, scholarships/grants, tuition waivers, and unspecified assistantships available. Financial award application deadline: 7/1; financial award applicants required to submit FAFSA. *Faculty research:* Appalachian studies, women's and gender studies, interdisciplinary theory, regional and Southern cultures. *Unit head:* Dr. Rick E. Osborn, Dean, 423-439-4223, Fax: 423-439-7091, E-mail: osbornr@etsu.edu. *Application contact:* Dr. Rick E. Osborn, Dean, 423-439-4223, Fax: 423-439-7091, E-mail: osbornr@etsu.edu.
Website: http://www.etsu.edu/academicaffairs/scs/

Excelsior College, School of Liberal Arts, Albany, NY 12203-5159. Offers liberal studies (MA). *Program availability:* Part-time, evening/weekend, online learning. *Faculty:* 25 part-time/adjunct (17 women). *Students:* 76 part-time (34 women); includes 34 minority (19 Black or African American, non-Hispanic/Latino; 2 American Indian or Alaska Native, non-Hispanic/Latino; 1 Asian, non-Hispanic/Latino; 5 Hispanic/Latino; 7 Two or more races, non-Hispanic/Latino). Average age 45. In 2017, 16 master's awarded. *Degree requirements:* For master's, thesis or alternative. *Application deadline:* Applications are processed on a rolling basis. Application fee: $50. Electronic applications accepted. *Expenses: Tuition:* Part-time $645 per credit. *Required fees:* $265 per credit. *Financial support:* Scholarships/grants available. *Unit head:* Dr. George Timmons, Dean, 518-464-8500, Fax: 518-464-8777, E-mail: mlsadmin@excelsior.edu. *Application contact:* Admissions Counselor, 518-464-8500, Fax: 518-464-8777, E-mail: gradadmissions@excelsior.edu.
Website: http://www.excelsior.edu/programs/liberal-arts

Florida International University, College of Arts, Sciences, and Education, Program in Liberal Studies, Miami, FL 33199. Offers MA. *Program availability:* Part-time, evening/weekend. *Faculty:* 2 part-time/adjunct (both women). *Students:* 4 part-time (2 women); includes 2 minority (1 Black or African American, non-Hispanic/Latino; 1 Hispanic/Latino). Average age 40. In 2017, 1 master's awarded. *Degree requirements:* For master's, thesis optional. *Entrance requirements:* For master's, minimum GPA of 3.0, 2-3 letters of recommendation, writing sample, curriculum vitae. Additional exam requirements/recommendations for international students: Required—TOEFL (minimum score 550 paper-based; 80 iBT). *Application deadline:* For fall admission, 6/1 for domestic students, 4/1 for international students; for spring admission, 10/1 for domestic students, 9/1 for international students. Applications are processed on a rolling basis. Application fee: $30. Electronic applications accepted. *Expenses:* Tuition, state resident: full-time $8912; part-time $446 per credit hour. Tuition, nonresident: full-time $21,393; part-time $992 per credit hour. *Required fees:* $390; $195 per semester. *Financial support:* Institutionally sponsored loans and scholarships/grants available. Financial award application deadline: 3/1; financial award applicants required to submit FAFSA. *Unit head:* Dr. Paul Warren, Chair, 305-348-2498, Fax: 305-348-1799, E-mail: paul.warren@fiu.edu. *Application contact:* Nanett Rojas, Assistant Director, Graduate Admissions, 305-348-7464, Fax: 305-348-7441, E-mail: gradadm@fiu.edu.

Fort Hays State University, Graduate School, College of Arts and Sciences, Center for Interdisciplinary Studies, Hays, KS 67601-4099. Offers liberal studies (MLS). *Program availability:* Online learning. *Degree requirements:* For master's, comprehensive exam, thesis or alternative. *Entrance requirements:* Additional exam requirements/recommendations for international students: Required—TOEFL (minimum score 550 paper-based). Electronic applications accepted.

Georgetown University, Graduate School of Arts and Sciences, School of Continuing Studies, Washington, DC 20057. Offers American studies (MALS); applied intelligence (MPS); Catholic studies (MALS); classical civilizations (MALS); emergency and disaster management (MPS); ethics and the professions (MALS); global strategic communications (MPS); hospitality management (MPS); human resources management (MPS); humanities (MALS); individualized study (MALS); integrated marketing communications (MPS); international affairs (MALS); Islam and Muslim-Christian relations (MALS); journalism (MPS); liberal studies (DLS); literature and society (MALS); medieval and early modern European studies (MALS); public relations and corporate communications (MPS); real estate (MPS); religious studies (MALS); social and public policy (MALS); sports industry management (MPS); systems engineering management (MPS); technology management (MPS); the theory and practice of American democracy (MALS); urban and regional planning (MPS); visual culture (MALS). MPS in systems engineering management offered jointly with Stevens Institute of Technology. *Entrance requirements:* Additional exam requirements/recommendations for international students: Required—TOEFL.

The Graduate Center, City University of New York, Graduate Studies, Program in Liberal Studies, New York, NY 10016-4039. Offers MA. *Students:* 6 full-time (3 women), 354 part-time (230 women); includes 155 minority (49 Black or African American, non-Hispanic/Latino; 29 Asian, non-Hispanic/Latino; 69 Hispanic/Latino; 8 Two or more races, non-Hispanic/Latino), 32 international. Average age 34. 270 applicants, 67% accepted, 101 enrolled. In 2017, 15 master's awarded. *Degree requirements:* For master's, thesis. *Entrance requirements:* For master's, GRE General Test. Additional exam requirements/recommendations for international students: Required—TOEFL. *Application deadline:* For fall admission, 4/15 for domestic students; for spring admission, 11/15 for domestic students. Application fee: $125. Electronic applications accepted. *Financial support:* In 2017–18, 24 students received support, including 2 fellowships; Federal Work-Study, institutionally sponsored loans, and tuition waivers (full and partial) also available. Financial award application deadline: 2/1; financial award applicants required to submit FAFSA. *Unit head:* Dr. Elizabeth Macaulay-Lewis, Acting Executive Officer, 212-817-8481, Fax: 212-817-1525, E-mail: emacaulay_lewis@gc.cuny.edu. *Application contact:* Les Gribben, Director of Admissions, 212-817-7470, Fax: 212-817-1624, E-mail: lgribben@gc.cuny.edu.

Hampton University, School of Liberal Arts and Education, Hampton, VA 23668. Offers MA, MS, MT, PhD, Ed S. *Accreditation:* NCATE. *Program availability:* Part-time, evening/weekend. *Students:* 85 full-time (52 women), 75 part-time (52 women); includes 144 minority (all Black or African American, non-Hispanic/Latino), 1 international. Average age 33. 79 applicants, 41% accepted, 4 enrolled. In 2017, 37 master's, 10 doctorates awarded. *Degree requirements:* For master's, comprehensive exam, thesis (for some programs); for doctorate, comprehensive exam, thesis/dissertation. *Entrance requirements:* For master's, GRE General Test, PRAXIS; for doctorate, GRE General Test, GMAT. *Application deadline:* For fall admission, 6/1 priority date for domestic students, 4/1 priority date for international students; for winter admission, 9/1 priority date for international students; for spring admission, 11/1 for domestic students; for summer admission, 4/15 for domestic students, 2/1 priority date for international students. Applications are processed on a rolling basis. Application fee: $35. Electronic applications accepted. *Expenses: Tuition:* Full-time $22,630; part-time $575 per semester hour. *Required fees:* $70. Tuition and fees vary according to program. *Financial support:* Fellowships, research assistantships, teaching assistantships, career-related internships or fieldwork, Federal Work-Study, institutionally sponsored loans, and scholarships/grants available. Support available to part-time students. Financial award application deadline: 5/1; financial award applicants required to submit FAFSA. *Unit head:* Dr. Linda Malone-Colon, Dean, 757-727-5400. *Application contact:* Dr. Michelle Penn-Marshall, Dean, Graduate College, 757-727-5454, E-mail: hugrad@hamptonu.edu.
Website: http://edhd.hamptonu.edu/

Harvard University, Extension School, Cambridge, MA 02138-3722. Offers applied sciences (CAS); biotechnology (ALM); educational technologies (ALM); educational technology (CET); English for graduate and professional studies (DGP); environmental management (ALM, CEM); information technology (ALM); journalism (ALM); liberal arts (ALM); management (ALM, CM); mathematics for teaching (ALM); museum studies (ALM); premedical studies (Diploma); publication and communication (CPC). *Program availability:* Part-time, evening/weekend. *Degree requirements:* For master's, thesis. *Entrance requirements:* For master's, 3 completed graduate courses with grade of B or higher. Additional exam requirements/recommendations for international students: Required—TOEFL (minimum score 600 paper-based), TWE (minimum score 5). *Expenses:* Contact institution.

Hawai`i Pacific University, College of Liberal Arts, Honolulu, HI 96813. Offers MA. *Program availability:* Part-time, evening/weekend. *Faculty:* 24 full-time (9 women), 7 part-time/adjunct (3 women). *Students:* 110 full-time (62 women), 69 part-time (35 women); includes 82 minority (13 Black or African American, non-Hispanic/Latino; 22 Asian, non-Hispanic/Latino; 19 Hispanic/Latino; 28 Two or more races, non-Hispanic/Latino), 27 international. Average age 32. 134 applicants, 72% accepted, 69 enrolled. In 2017, 61 master's awarded. *Entrance requirements:* Additional exam requirements/recommendations for international students: Recommended—TOEFL (minimum score 550 paper-based; 80 iBT), IELTS (minimum score 6), TWE (minimum score 5). *Application deadline:* For fall admission, 1/15 priority date for domestic students; for spring admission, 10/15 priority date for domestic students. Applications are processed on a rolling basis. Application fee: $50. Electronic applications accepted. *Expenses: Tuition:* Full-time $18,000; part-time $1000 per credit. *Required fees:* $200; $26 per credit. Tuition and fees vary according to course load and program. *Financial support:* In 2017–18, 33 students received support. Career-related internships or fieldwork, Federal Work-Study, scholarships/grants, tuition waivers (partial), and unspecified assistantships available. Financial award application deadline: 3/1; financial award applicants required to submit FAFSA. *Unit head:* Dr. Allison Gough, Dean, 808-544-1109, E-mail: agough@hpu.edu. *Application contact:* Danny Lam, Assistant Director of Graduate Admissions, 808-544-1135, E-mail: graduate@hpu.edu.
Website: https://www.hpu.edu/cla/index.html

Henderson State University, Graduate Studies, Ellis College of Arts and Sciences, Arkadelphia, AR 71999-0001. Offers MLA. *Program availability:* Part-time. *Degree requirements:* For master's, thesis. *Entrance requirements:* For master's, MAT or GRE, minimum GPA of 2.7, interview, essay. Additional exam requirements/recommendations for international students: Required—TOEFL (minimum score 600 paper-based); Recommended—IELTS (minimum score 6.5).

Hollins University, Graduate Programs, Program in Liberal Studies, Roanoke, VA 24020. Offers humanities (MALS); interdisciplinary studies (MALS); leadership (MALS); social sciences (MALS); visual and performing arts (MALS). *Program availability:* Part-time, evening/weekend, 100% online, blended/hybrid learning. *Faculty:* 5 part-time/adjunct (2 women). *Students:* 5 full-time (4 women), 29 part-time (25 women); includes 9 minority (6 Black or African American, non-Hispanic/Latino; 1 Asian, non-Hispanic/Latino; 1 Hispanic/Latino; 1 Two or more races, non-Hispanic/Latino). Average age 40. 7 applicants, 86% accepted, 3 enrolled. In 2017, 11 master's awarded. *Degree requirements:* For master's, thesis. *Entrance requirements:* For master's, three letters of recommendation, interview, bachelor's degree, undergraduate transcripts, statement of educational objectives. Additional exam requirements/recommendations for international students: Required—TOEFL (minimum score 550 paper-based; 80 iBT), IELTS (minimum score 6.5). *Application deadline:* Applications are processed on a rolling basis. Application fee: $40. Electronic applications accepted. *Expenses:* Contact institution. *Financial support:* Scholarships/grants available. Financial award application deadline: 7/15; financial award applicants required to submit FAFSA. *Faculty research:* Diversity, gender and women's studies, political science, leadership. *Unit head:* Dr. Lorraine Lange, Director, 540-362-6576, Fax: 540-362-6288, E-mail: hugrad@hollins.edu. *Application contact:* Cathy S. Koon, Manager of Graduate Programs, 540-362-6326, Fax: 540-362-6288, E-mail: hugrad@hollins.edu.
Website: http://www.hollins.edu/academics/graduate-degrees/liberal-studies/

Houston Baptist University, School of Humanities, Program in Liberal Arts, Houston, TX 77074-3298. Offers education (EC-12 art, music, physical education, or Spanish) (MLA); education (EC-6 generalist) (MLA); general liberal arts (MLA); specialization in education (4-8 or 7-12) (MLA). *Program availability:* Part-time, evening/weekend. *Students:* 11 full-time (7 women), 13 part-time (9 women); includes 12 minority (5 Black or African American, non-Hispanic/Latino; 2 Asian, non-Hispanic/Latino; 5 Hispanic/Latino). Average age 31. 26 applicants, 73% accepted, 12 enrolled. In 2017, 15 master's awarded. *Entrance requirements:* For master's, minimum GPA of 2.5, essay/personal statement, resume, bachelor's degree transcript. Additional exam requirements/recommendations for international students: Required—TOEFL (minimum score 80 iBT), IELTS (minimum score 6.5). *Application deadline:* For fall admission, 8/1 for domestic students, 6/1 for international students; for spring admission, 1/1 for domestic students, 11/1 for international students; for summer admission, 5/1 for domestic students, 3/1 for international students. Applications are processed on a rolling basis. Application fee: $0 ($100 for international students). Electronic applications accepted. Application fee is waived when completed online. *Expenses:* $18,000 tuition; $4,500 fees (general, technology and parking). *Financial support:* In 2017–18, 12 students received support. Federal Work-Study and scholarships/grants available. Support available to part-time students. Financial award application deadline: 4/1; financial award applicants required to submit FAFSA. *Unit head:* Dr. Collin Garbarino, Graduate Programs Director, 281-649-3679, E-mail: cgarbarino@hbu.edu. *Application contact:* Kathy Holston, Administrative Assistant to the Dean, 281-649-3404, E-mail: kholston@hbu.edu.
Website: http://www.hbu.edu/mla

Indiana University Northwest, College of Arts and Sciences, Gary, IN 46408. Offers clinical counseling (MS), including drug and alcohol counseling; community development/urban studies (Graduate Certificate); computer information systems (Graduate Certificate); liberal studies (MLS); race-ethnic studies (Graduate Certificate); women's and gender studies (Graduate Certificate). *Program availability:* Part-time, evening/weekend. *Entrance requirements:* For master's, GRE (recommended for MS), minimum undergraduate GPA of 3.0, bachelor's degree from accredited university (for MS). Electronic applications accepted. *Expenses:* Contact institution.

Indiana University–Purdue University Indianapolis, School of Liberal Arts, Indianapolis, IN 46202. Offers MA, MS, PhD, Certificate, JD/MA, MA/MA, MA/MLS, MD/MA.

Indiana University South Bend, College of Liberal Arts and Sciences, South Bend, IN 46615. Offers advanced computer programming (Graduate Certificate); applied informatics (Graduate Certificate); applied mathematics and computer science (MS); behavior modification (Graduate Certificate); computer applications (Graduate Certificate); computer programming (Graduate Certificate); correctional management and supervision (Graduate Certificate); English (MA); health systems management (Graduate Certificate); international studies (Graduate Certificate); liberal studies (MLS); nonprofit management (Graduate Certificate); paralegal studies (Graduate Certificate); professional writing (Graduate Certificate); public affairs (MPA); public management (Graduate Certificate); social and cultural diversity (Graduate Certificate); strategic sustainability leadership (Graduate Certificate); technology for administration (Graduate Certificate). *Program availability:* Part-time, evening/weekend. *Degree requirements:* For master's, variable foreign language requirement, thesis (for some programs). *Entrance requirements:* For master's, minimum GPA of 3.0. Additional exam requirements/recommendations for international students: Required—TOEFL (minimum score 550 paper-based; 80 iBT). *Expenses:* Contact institution. *Faculty research:* Artificial intelligence, bioinformatics, English language and literature, creative writing, computer networks.

Jacksonville State University, College of Graduate Studies and Continuing Education, College of Arts and Sciences, Department of Liberal Studies, Jacksonville, AL 36265-1602. Offers MA. *Program availability:* Part-time, evening/weekend. *Degree requirements:* For master's, comprehensive exam, thesis (for some programs). *Entrance requirements:* Additional exam requirements/recommendations for international students: Required—TOEFL (minimum score 500 paper-based; 61 iBT). Electronic applications accepted.

Johns Hopkins University, Zanvyl Krieger School of Arts and Sciences, Advanced Academic Programs, Program in Liberal Arts, Washington, DC 20036. Offers MA, Certificate. *Program availability:* Part-time, evening/weekend, online learning. *Degree requirements:* For master's, thesis. *Entrance requirements:* For master's, minimum GPA of 3.0. Additional exam requirements/recommendations for international students: Required—TOEFL (minimum score 100 iBT). Electronic applications accepted.

Kean University, College of Liberal Arts, Union, NJ 07083. Offers MA. *Program availability:* Part-time. *Faculty:* 84 full-time (44 women). *Students:* 152 full-time (122 women), 118 part-time (85 women); includes 140 minority (61 Black or African American, non-Hispanic/Latino; 17 Asian, non-Hispanic/Latino; 54 Hispanic/Latino; 2 Native Hawaiian or other Pacific Islander, non-Hispanic/Latino; 6 Two or more races, non-Hispanic/Latino), 5 international. Average age 30. 180 applicants, 89% accepted, 109 enrolled. In 2017, 75 master's awarded. *Degree requirements:* For master's, comprehensive exam, thesis, exhibition, practicum, internship. *Entrance requirements:* Additional exam requirements/recommendations for international students: Required—TOEFL (minimum score 550 paper-based; 79 iBT), IELTS (minimum score 6.5). *Application deadline:* For fall admission, 6/30 for domestic and international students; for spring admission, 12/1 for domestic and international students. Applications are processed on a rolling basis. Application fee: $75. Electronic applications accepted. *Expenses:* Tuition, state resident: full-time $13,419; part-time $653 per credit. Tuition, nonresident: full-time $18,188; part-time $801 per credit. *Required fees:* $3382; $154 per credit. Tuition and fees vary according to course level, course load, degree level and program. *Financial support:* Scholarships/grants and unspecified assistantships available. Financial award applicants required to submit FAFSA. *Unit head:* Dr. Jonathan Mercantini, Acting Dean, 908-737-0430, Fax: 908-737-0435, E-mail: jmercant@kean.edu. *Application contact:* Amy Clark, Program Assistant, 908-737-7100, E-mail: gradadmissions@kean.edu.
Website: http://www.kean.edu/academics/college-liberal-arts

Kent State University, College of Arts and Sciences, Center for Comparative and Integrative Programs, Kent, OH 44242-0001. Offers MLS. *Program availability:* Part-time, online learning. *Faculty:* 1 full-time (0 women), 1 part-time/adjunct (0 women). *Students:* 3 part-time (all women); includes 1 minority (Black or African American, non-Hispanic/Latino). Average age 37. 6 applicants, 83% accepted, 1 enrolled. *Degree requirements:* For master's, capstone essay. *Entrance requirements:* For master's, official transcript(s), goal statement, three letters of recommendation. Additional exam requirements/recommendations for international students: Required—TOEFL (minimum score 610 paper-based, 102 iBT), Michigan English Language Assessment Battery (minimum score 86), IELTS (minimum score 7.5) or PTE (minimum score 73). *Application deadline:* For fall admission, 6/15 for domestic and international students; for spring admission, 11/29 for domestic and international students. Applications are processed on a rolling basis. Application fee: $45 ($70 for international students). Electronic applications accepted. *Expenses:* Tuition, state resident: full-time $11,310; part-time $515 per credit hour. Tuition, nonresident: full-time $20,396; part-time $928 per credit hour. *International tuition:* $18,544 full-time. *Financial support:* Career-related internships or fieldwork and Federal Work-Study available. Financial award application deadline: 2/1; financial award applicants required to submit FAFSA. *Unit head:* Dr. David W. Odell-Scott, Director of Center for Comparative and Integrative Programs, 330-672-0271, E-mail: dodellsc@kent.edu.
Website: http://www.kent.edu/ccip/graduate-degree-programs

Lake Forest College, Graduate Program in Liberal Studies, Lake Forest, IL 60045. Offers American studies (MLS); cinema in East Asia (MLS); environmental studies (MLS); history (MLS); Medieval and Renaissance art (MLS); philosophy (MLS); Spanish (MLS); writing (MLS). *Program availability:* Part-time, evening/weekend. *Faculty:* 11 full-time (3 women). *Students:* 34 part-time (19 women); includes 3 minority (1 Asian, non-Hispanic/Latino; 2 Hispanic/Latino). Average age 36. 20 applicants, 55% accepted, 8 enrolled. In 2017, 5 master's awarded. *Degree requirements:* For master's, thesis optional, 8 courses, including at least 3 interdisciplinary seminars. *Entrance requirements:* For master's, transcript, essay, interview. Additional exam requirements/recommendations for international students: Required—TOEFL (minimum score 550 paper-based; 83 iBT); Recommended—IELTS (minimum score 6.5). *Application deadline:* For fall admission, 7/15 priority date for domestic students, 6/1 priority date for international students; for spring admission, 12/1 priority date for domestic students, 10/1 priority date for international students. Applications are processed on a rolling basis. Application fee: $30. Electronic applications accepted. *Expenses:* $2,650 per course. *Financial support:* In 2017–18, 2 students received support. Partial tuition grants (for full-time teachers) available. *Faculty research:* Religion in America, Asian philosophy, cinema studies, theater studies, sociology of religion. *Unit head:* Prof. D. L. LeMahieu, Director, 847-735-5133, Fax: 847-735-6291, E-mail: lemahieu@lakeforest.edu. *Application contact:* Prof. Carol Gayle, Associate Director, 847-735-5083, Fax: 847-735-6291, E-mail: gayle@lakeforest.edu.
Website: http://www.lakeforest.edu/academics/programs/mls/

Louisiana State University and Agricultural & Mechanical College, Graduate School, College of Humanities and Social Sciences, Interdepartmental Program in the Liberal Arts, Baton Rouge, LA 70803. Offers MALA. *Faculty:* 9 full-time (1 woman). *Students:* 19 full-time (13 women), 13 part-time (6 women); includes 11 minority (10 Black or African American, non-Hispanic/Latino; 1 Hispanic/Latino), 9 international. Average age 34. 13 applicants, 69% accepted, 5 enrolled. In 2017, 6 master's awarded.

Louisiana State University in Shreveport, College of Arts and Sciences, Program in Liberal Arts, Shreveport, LA 71115-2399. Offers MA. *Program availability:* Part-time, evening/weekend. *Students:* 5 full-time (3 women), 19 part-time (11 women); includes 6 minority (5 Black or African American, non-Hispanic/Latino; 1 Two or more races, non-Hispanic/Latino), 1 international. Average age 40. 15 applicants, 93% accepted, 7 enrolled. In 2017, 6 master's awarded. *Degree requirements:* For master's, comprehensive exam, thesis or alternative. *Entrance requirements:* For master's, interview, minimum GPA of 3.0 during final 2 years of course work, statement of purpose. Additional exam requirements/recommendations for international students: Required—TOEFL (minimum score 550 paper-based; 61 iBT). *Application deadline:* For fall admission, 6/30 for domestic and international students; for spring admission, 11/30 for domestic and international students; for summer admission, 4/30 for domestic and international students. Applications are processed on a rolling basis. Application fee: $20 ($30 for international students). Electronic applications accepted. *Expenses:* Tuition, state resident: full-time $3098; part-time $344 per credit hour. Tuition, nonresident: full-time $9923; part-time $1103 per credit hour. *Required fees:* $384 per semester. Tuition and fees vary according to program. *Financial support:* In 2017–18, 3 students received support, including 2 research assistantships (averaging $3,750 per year). Financial award applicants required to submit FAFSA. *Unit head:* Dr. Helen Taylor, Program Director, 318-797-5211, Fax: 318-797-5358, E-mail: helen.taylor@lsus.edu. *Application contact:* Mary Catherine Harvison, Director of Admissions, 318-797-2400, Fax: 318-797-5286, E-mail: mary.harvison@lsus.edu.

Madonna University, Program in Liberal Studies, Livonia, MI 48150-1173. Offers MALS.

McDaniel College, Graduate and Professional Studies, Program in Liberal Arts, Westminster, MD 21157-4390. Offers liberal arts (MLA); writing for children and young adults (Postbaccalaureate Certificate). *Program availability:* Part-time, evening/weekend, 100% online. *Faculty:* 2 full-time (both women), 6 part-time/adjunct (4 women). *Students:* 2 full-time (both women), 10 part-time (all women). Average age 35. 4 applicants, 50% accepted. In 2017, 6 master's awarded. *Degree requirements:* For master's, final project. *Entrance requirements:* For master's, 3 recommendations. Additional exam requirements/recommendations for international students: Required—TOEFL (minimum score 79 iBT), IELTS (minimum score 6). *Application deadline:* For fall admission, 6/1 priority date for domestic students; for spring admission, 11/1 priority date for domestic students; for summer admission, 3/1 priority date for domestic students. Applications are processed on a rolling basis. Application fee: $75. Electronic applications accepted. *Expenses: Tuition:* Full-time $11,760; part-time $490 per credit hour. Tuition and fees vary according to course load and program. *Financial support:* Application deadline: 3/1; applicants required to submit FAFSA. *Unit head:* E-mail: gradadms@mcdaniel.edu. *Application contact:* Crystal L. Perry, Assistant Director, Graduate Enrollment Management, 410-857-2516, Fax: 410-857-2515, E-mail: cperry@mcdaniel.edu.

Metropolitan State University, College of Liberal Arts, St. Paul, MN 55106-5000. Offers liberal studies (MA); technical communication (MS). *Program availability:* Part-time, evening/weekend. *Entrance requirements:* For master's, minimum GPA of 2.75, resume. Additional exam requirements/recommendations for international students: Required—TOEFL (minimum score 550 paper-based). *Application deadline:* For fall admission, 8/1 priority date for domestic students, 3/15 for international students; for

winter admission, 10/15 for international students; for spring admission, 12/1 priority date for domestic students, 3/15 for international students. Applications are processed on a rolling basis. Application fee: $20. Electronic applications accepted. *Expenses:* Tuition, state resident: part-time $388.55 per credit. Tuition, nonresident: part-time $777.11 per credit. *Required fees:* $35.11 per credit. Part-time tuition and fees vary according to campus/location and program. *Financial support:* Research assistantships available. Financial award applicants required to submit FAFSA. *Application contact:* Susan Honsvall, Office and Administrative Specialist, 651-793-1445, E-mail: susan.honsvall@metrostate.edu.
Website: https://www.metrostate.edu/academics/liberal-arts

Mississippi College, Graduate School, Program in Liberal Studies, Clinton, MS 39058. Offers MLS. *Program availability:* Part-time. *Degree requirements:* For master's, comprehensive exam, thesis optional. *Entrance requirements:* For master's, GRE, minimum GPA of 2.5. Additional exam requirements/recommendations for international students: Recommended—TOEFL, IELTS.

The New School, The New School for Social Research, Department of Liberal Studies, New York, NY 10003. Offers MA. *Program availability:* Part-time. *Faculty:* 16 full-time (9 women), 3 part-time/adjunct (1 woman). *Students:* 25 full-time (11 women), 9 part-time (6 women); includes 5 minority (2 Black or African American, non-Hispanic/Latino; 2 Asian, non-Hispanic/Latino; 1 Hispanic/Latino), 10 international. Average age 28. 39 applicants, 90% accepted, 16 enrolled. In 2017, 11 master's awarded. *Degree requirements:* For master's, thesis. *Entrance requirements:* For master's, GRE, letters of recommendation, writing sample, essays, transcript. Additional exam requirements/recommendations for international students: Required—TOEFL (minimum score 100 iBT), IELTS (minimum score 7), PTE (minimum score 68). *Application deadline:* For fall admission, 1/5 priority date for domestic students, 1/1 priority date for international students; for spring admission, 10/15 priority date for domestic and international students. Applications are processed on a rolling basis. Application fee: $50. Electronic applications accepted. *Expenses:* $2,180 per credit. *Financial support:* In 2017–18, 26 students received support, including 6 teaching assistantships (averaging $4,184 per year); career-related internships or fieldwork, Federal Work-Study, and scholarships/grants also available. Support available to part-time students. Financial award application deadline: 2/1; financial award applicants required to submit FAFSA. *Unit head:* Dr. William Milberg, Dean, The New School for Social Research, 212-229-5777, E-mail: milbergw@newschool.edu. *Application contact:* Dana Messinger, Director of Graduate Admissions, 212-229-5150 Ext. 2300, E-mail: messingd@newschool.edu.
Website: http://www.newschool.edu/nssr/liberal-studies/

North Carolina State University, Graduate School, College of Humanities and Social Sciences, Program in Liberal Studies, Raleigh, NC 27695. Offers MA. *Program availability:* Part-time, evening/weekend. *Degree requirements:* For master's, thesis optional. Electronic applications accepted. *Faculty research:* Humanities, social sciences, sciences.

North Central College, School of Graduate and Professional Studies, Program in Liberal Studies, Naperville, IL 60566-7063. Offers culture and society (MALS). *Program availability:* Part-time, evening/weekend. *Degree requirements:* For master's, thesis optional, project. *Entrance requirements:* For master's, interview. Additional exam requirements/recommendations for international students: Required—TOEFL (minimum score 550 paper-based; 80 iBT), IELTS (minimum score 6.5). Electronic applications accepted. Application fee is waived when completed online. *Expenses:* Contact institution.

Northern Arizona University, College of Social and Behavioral Sciences, Sustainable Communities Program, Flagstaff, AZ 86011. Offers MA. *Program availability:* Part-time. *Faculty:* 4 full-time (3 women), 3 part-time/adjunct (2 women). *Students:* 27 full-time (19 women), 10 part-time (7 women); includes 11 minority (4 American Indian or Alaska Native, non-Hispanic/Latino; 7 Hispanic/Latino), 2 international. Average age 32. 18 applicants, 72% accepted, 12 enrolled. In 2017, 8 master's awarded. *Degree requirements:* For master's, variable foreign language requirement, comprehensive exam (for some programs), thesis, fieldwork experience/internship, oral defense. *Entrance requirements:* Additional exam requirements/recommendations for international students: Required—TOEFL (minimum score 80 iBT), IELTS (minimum score 6.5). *Application deadline:* For fall admission, 3/1 for domestic and international students; for spring admission, 10/1 for domestic and international students. Applications are processed on a rolling basis. Application fee: $65. Electronic applications accepted. *Expenses:* Tuition, state resident: full-time $9240; part-time $458 per credit hour. Tuition, nonresident: full-time $21,588; part-time $1199 per credit hour. *Required fees:* $1021; $14 per credit hour. $646 per semester. Tuition and fees vary according to course load, campus/location and program. *Financial support:* In 2017–18, 6 students received support, including 4 research assistantships with partial tuition reimbursements available (averaging $9,000 per year), 1 teaching assistantship with partial tuition reimbursement available (averaging $9,000 per year); institutionally sponsored loans, health care benefits, tuition waivers (full and partial), and unspecified assistantships also available. Financial award application deadline: 2/1; financial award applicants required to submit FAFSA. *Unit head:* Luis Fernandez, Director, 928-523-2382, Fax: 928-523-2020, E-mail: luis.fernandez@nau.edu. *Application contact:* Ginger Christenson, Program Coordinator, 928-523-0499, Fax: 928-523-2020, E-mail: sustainable.communities@nau.edu.
Website: http://nau.edu/sbs/sus/

Northern Kentucky University, Office of Graduate Programs, College of Arts and Sciences, Program in Integrative Studies, Highland Heights, KY 41099. Offers MA. *Program availability:* Part-time, evening/weekend. *Degree requirements:* For master's, thesis or capstone. *Entrance requirements:* For master's, statement of purpose, three letters of reference, resume, minimum GPA of 3.0. Additional exam requirements/recommendations for international students: Required—TOEFL (minimum score 79 iBT); Recommended—IELTS (minimum score 6.5). Electronic applications accepted. *Faculty research:* Industrial/organizational psychology, truancy, athletic health training, motivation, compassion and stress.

Northwestern University, School of Professional Studies, Program in Liberal Studies, Evanston, IL 60208. Offers American studies (MA); history (MA); religious and ethical studies (MA). *Program availability:* Part-time, evening/weekend.
Website: https://sps.northwestern.edu/masters/liberal-studies/index.php

Notre Dame of Maryland University, Graduate Studies, Program in Liberal Studies, Baltimore, MD 21210-2476. Offers MA. *Program availability:* Part-time, evening/weekend. *Degree requirements:* For master's, thesis or alternative. *Entrance requirements:* For master's, minimum GPA of 3.0. Additional exam requirements/recommendations for international students: Required—TOEFL (minimum score 500 paper-based; 61 iBT). Electronic applications accepted.

Oakland University, Graduate Study and Lifelong Learning, College of Arts and Sciences, Program in Liberal Studies, Rochester, MI 48309-4401. Offers MA. *Entrance requirements:* For master's, minimum GPA of 3.0. Additional exam requirements/recommendations for international students: Required—TOEFL (minimum score 550 paper-based). Electronic applications accepted. *Expenses:* Tuition, state resident: full-time $16,950; part-time $706.25 per credit. Tuition, nonresident: full-time $24,648; part-time $1027 per credit.

Queens College of the City University of New York, Division of Social Sciences, Program in Liberal Studies, Queens, NY 11367-1597. Offers MA. *Program availability:* Part-time, evening/weekend. *Degree requirements:* For master's, thesis. *Entrance requirements:* For master's, minimum GPA of 3.0. Additional exam requirements/recommendations for international students: Required—TOEFL (minimum score 61 iBT), IELTS (minimum score 5). *Application deadline:* For fall admission, 8/15 for domestic students; for spring admission, 1/15 for domestic students. Applications are processed on a rolling basis. Application fee: $125. Electronic applications accepted. *Financial support:* Career-related internships or fieldwork available. Financial award application deadline: 4/1; financial award applicants required to submit FAFSA. *Application contact:* James Jordan, Academic Advisor, 718-997-5280, E-mail: james.jordan@qc.cuny.edu.

Reed College, Graduate Program in Liberal Studies, Portland, OR 97202-8199. Offers MALS. *Program availability:* Part-time-only, evening/weekend. *Faculty:* 10 part-time/adjunct (1 woman). *Students:* 29 part-time (17 women); includes 2 minority (both Black or African American, non-Hispanic/Latino). Average age 43. 5 applicants, 80% accepted, 4 enrolled. In 2017, 1 master's awarded. *Degree requirements:* For master's, thesis, oral defense of thesis. *Entrance requirements:* For master's, interview, letters of recommendation, critical essay. Additional exam requirements/recommendations for international students: Recommended—TOEFL. *Application deadline:* For fall admission, 7/1 priority date for domestic students, 5/1 for international students; for spring admission, 12/1 priority date for domestic students, 9/1 for international students; for summer admission, 4/1 for domestic students, 2/1 for international students. Applications are processed on a rolling basis. Application fee: $75. Electronic applications accepted. *Expenses:* $2,380 per course. *Financial support:* In 2017–18, 7 students received support. Scholarships/grants and health care benefits available. Support available to part-time students. Financial award application deadline: 5/1; financial award applicants required to submit CSS PROFILE or FAFSA. *Faculty research:* American climate change policy, The Reformation, geometry of color/light, Joyce's "Ulysses", Apollonius' "Argonautica". *Unit head:* Barbara A. Amen, Director, Graduate Studies, 503-777-7259, Fax: 503-517-7345, E-mail: bamen@reed.edu.
Website: http://www.reed.edu/mals

Rice University, Graduate Programs, Susanne M. Glasscock School of Continuing Studies, Houston, TX 77251-1892. Offers MLS. *Program availability:* Part-time, evening/weekend. *Degree requirements:* For master's, thesis or alternative, capstone paper/project. *Entrance requirements:* For master's, bachelor's degree from accredited institution; minimum GPA of 3.0; two letters of recommendation; personal statement; 3 writing samples; current resume. Additional exam requirements/recommendations for international students: Required—TOEFL (minimum score 600 paper-based; 90 iBT). *Expenses:* Contact institution.

Rollins College, Hamilton Holt School, Master of Liberal Studies Program, Winter Park, FL 32789. Offers MLS. *Program availability:* Part-time, evening/weekend. *Faculty:* 5 full-time (1 woman), 1 (woman) part-time/adjunct. *Students:* 1 full-time (0 women), 48 part-time (28 women); includes 12 minority (4 Black or African American, non-Hispanic/Latino; 1 American Indian or Alaska Native, non-Hispanic/Latino; 6 Hispanic/Latino; 1 Two or more races, non-Hispanic/Latino), 1 international. Average age 39. In 2017, 4 master's awarded. *Degree requirements:* For master's, thesis. *Entrance requirements:* For master's, official transcripts, two letters of recommendation, essay. Additional exam requirements/recommendations for international students: Required—TOEFL (minimum score 550 paper-based; 80 iBT). *Application deadline:* For fall admission, 4/1 for domestic students; for spring admission, 12/1 for domestic students. Application fee: $50. *Expenses:* $1,916 per course. *Financial support:* Scholarships/grants and unspecified assistantships available. Support available to part-time students. Financial award applicants required to submit FAFSA. *Unit head:* Dr. Thomas Cook, Faculty Director, 407-646-2037, Fax: 407-646-2363. *Application contact:* Graduate Coordinator, 407-646-2653, Fax: 407-646-1551, E-mail: eveningadmission@rollins.edu.
Website: http://www.rollins.edu/holt/graduate/mls.html

Rutgers University–Camden, Graduate School of Arts and Sciences, Program in Liberal Studies, Camden, NJ 08102. Offers MALS. *Program availability:* Part-time, evening/weekend. *Degree requirements:* For master's, thesis, 30 credits. *Entrance requirements:* For master's, 2 letters of recommendation, writing sample, statement of personal, professional and academic goals. Additional exam requirements/recommendations for international students: Required—TOEFL, IELTS. Electronic applications accepted. *Faculty research:* Psychology, English, history, philosophy, religion.

St. Edward's University, School of Education, Master of Liberal Arts Program, Austin, TX 78704. Offers humanities (MLA); liberal arts (MLA, Certificate). *Program availability:* Part-time, evening/weekend. *Students:* 5 full-time (4 women), 21 part-time (12 women); includes 8 minority (all Hispanic/Latino). Average age 36. 19 applicants, 58% accepted, 7 enrolled. In 2017, 19 master's awarded. *Entrance requirements:* Additional exam requirements/recommendations for international students: Required—TOEFL, IELTS. *Application deadline:* For fall admission, 6/1 priority date for domestic and international students; for spring admission, 10/1 priority date for domestic and international students. Applications are processed on a rolling basis. Application fee: $50. Electronic applications accepted. *Expenses: Tuition:* Full-time $26,406; part-time $1467 per hour. *Required fees:* $75 per trimester. Full-time tuition and fees vary according to course load and program. *Unit head:* Dr. Ramsey Fowler, MLA Program Director/Associate Professor of English, 512-448-8736, E-mail: ramseyf@stewards.edu. *Application contact:* Mike Leveriza, Graduate Recruiter, 512-448-8745, E-mail: mleveriz@stedwards.edu.

St. John's College, Graduate Institute, Annapolis, MD 21401. Offers MALA. *Program availability:* Evening/weekend. *Degree requirements:* For master's, thesis optional. *Entrance requirements:* For master's, bachelor's degree. Additional exam requirements/recommendations for international students: Required—TOEFL (minimum score 650 paper-based; 112 iBT), TWE (minimum score 5). Electronic applications accepted.

St. John's College, Graduate Institute in Liberal Education, Program in Liberal Arts, Santa Fe, NM 87505. Offers MA. *Program availability:* Evening/weekend. *Entrance requirements:* For master's, 2 letters of recommendation. Additional exam requirements/recommendations for international students: Required—TOEFL, TWE.

St. John's University, St. John's College of Liberal Arts and Sciences, Program in Liberal Studies, Queens, NY 11439. Offers MA. *Program availability:* Part-time, evening/weekend. *Students:* 7 part-time (4 women); includes 3 minority (2 Black or African American, non-Hispanic/Latino; 1 Asian, non-Hispanic/Latino), 1 international. Average age 39. 10 applicants, 80% accepted, 1 enrolled. In 2017, 5 master's awarded. *Degree requirements:* For master's, capstone project. *Entrance requirements:* For master's, letters of recommendation, transcripts, resume, personal statement. Additional exam requirements/recommendations for international students: Required—TOEFL (minimum score 80 iBT), IELTS (minimum score 6.5). *Application deadline:* For fall admission, 5/1 for domestic students; for spring admission, 11/1 for domestic students. Applications are processed on a rolling basis. Application fee: $70. Electronic applications accepted.

Expenses: Tuition: Full-time $44,280; part-time $1230 per credit. *Required fees:* $340; $340 per credit. Tuition and fees vary according to course load, degree level and program. *Financial support:* Fellowships, research assistantships, teaching assistantships, scholarships/grants, tuition waivers, and unspecified assistantships available. Support available to part-time students. Financial award application deadline: 2/1; financial award applicants required to submit FAFSA. *Faculty research:* Women's and gender studies, immigration culture studies, urban studies. *Unit head:* Rev. Jean-Pierre Ruiz, Director, 718-990-5038, E-mail: ruizj@stjohns.edu. *Application contact:* Robert Medrano, Director of Graduate Admission, 718-990-1601, Fax: 718-990-5686, E-mail: gradhelp@stjohns.edu.
Website: https://www.stjohns.edu/academics/schools-and-colleges/st-johns-college-liberal-arts-and-sciences/liberal-studies

St. Norbert College, Master of Arts in Liberal Studies Program, De Pere, WI 54115-2099. Offers MA. *Program availability:* Part-time-only, evening/weekend. *Faculty:* 2 part-time/adjunct (0 women). *Students:* 10 part-time (8 women); includes 1 minority (Hispanic/Latino). Average age 38. 1 applicant, 100% accepted, 1 enrolled. In 2017, 3 master's awarded. *Degree requirements:* For master's, thesis. *Application deadline:* Applications are processed on a rolling basis. Application fee: $50. Electronic applications accepted. *Expenses: Tuition:* Part-time $675 per credit. Tuition and fees vary according to program. *Financial support:* Applicants required to submit FAFSA. *Unit head:* Dr. Howard Ebert, Director, 920-403-3956, E-mail: howard.ebert@snc.edu. *Application contact:* Dinah Grassel, Program Coordinator, 920-403-3957, E-mail: dinah.grassel@snc.edu.
Website: http://www.snc.edu/mls/

San Diego State University, Graduate and Research Affairs, College of Arts and Letters, Program in Liberal Arts and Sciences, San Diego, CA 92182. Offers MA. *Program availability:* Part-time, evening/weekend. *Degree requirements:* For master's, thesis. *Entrance requirements:* For master's, GRE General Test. Additional exam requirements/recommendations for international students: Required—TOEFL. Electronic applications accepted.

San Francisco State University, Division of Graduate Studies, College of Liberal and Creative Arts, School of Humanities and Liberal Studies, San Francisco, CA 94132-1722. Offers MA. *Program availability:* Part-time, evening/weekend. *Unit head:* Dr. Christina Ruotolo, Director, 415-338-1099, E-mail: ruotolo@sfsu.edu. *Application contact:* Prof. Mary Scott, Graduate Advisor, 415-338-7412, E-mail: mscott@sfsu.edu.
Website: http://humanities.sfsu.edu/

Simon Fraser University, Office of Graduate Studies and Postdoctoral Fellows, Faculty of Arts and Social Sciences, Program in Liberal Studies, Vancouver, BC V6B 5K3, Canada. Offers MALS. *Program availability:* Part-time, evening/weekend, online learning. *Degree requirements:* For master's, thesis or alternative. *Entrance requirements:* For master's, minimum GPA of 3.0 (on scale of 4.33) or 3.33 based on last 60 credits of undergraduate courses. Additional exam requirements/recommendations for international students: Recommended—TOEFL (minimum score 580 paper-based; 93 iBT), IELTS (minimum score 7), TWE (minimum score 5). Electronic applications accepted. *Faculty research:* Humanities, art history and culture, women's studies, literature, philosophy.

Southern Methodist University, Annette Caldwell Simmons School of Education and Human Development, Program in Liberal Studies, Dallas, TX 75275. Offers MLS.

Spring Hill College, Graduate Programs, Program in Liberal Arts, Mobile, AL 36608-1791. Offers fine arts (MLA); leadership and ethics (MLA, Postbaccalaureate Certificate); literature (MLA). *Program availability:* Part-time, evening/weekend. *Faculty:* 11 full-time (1 woman). *Students:* 1 (woman) full-time, 21 part-time (7 women); includes 5 minority (4 Black or African American, non-Hispanic/Latino; 1 Hispanic/Latino), 6 international. Average age 31. In 2017, 12 master's awarded. *Degree requirements:* For master's, capstone course, completion of program within 6 years of initial admittance. *Entrance requirements:* For master's, bachelor's degree with minimum undergraduate GPA of 3.0 or graduate/professional degree. Additional exam requirements/recommendations for international students: Required—TOEFL (minimum score 550 paper-based; 80 iBT), IELTS (minimum score 6.5), CPE or CAE (minimum score C), Michigan English Language Assessment Battery (minimum score 90). *Application deadline:* For fall admission, 8/1 priority date for domestic and international students; for spring admission, 12/1 priority date for domestic and international students. Applications are processed on a rolling basis. Application fee: $25 ($35 for international students). Electronic applications accepted. *Expenses:* Contact institution. *Financial support:* Applicants required to submit FAFSA. *Unit head:* Dr. Thomas J. Hoffman, Director, 251-380-4184, Fax: 251-460-2115, E-mail: thoffman@shc.edu. *Application contact:* Robert Stewart, Vice President of Enrollment, 251-380-3030, Fax: 251-460-2186, E-mail: rstewart@shc.edu.
Website: http://ug.shc.edu/graduate-degrees/master-liberal-arts/

State University of New York College at Old Westbury, Program in Liberal Studies, Old Westbury, NY 11568-0210. Offers MA. *Program availability:* Part-time, evening/weekend. *Faculty:* 2 full-time (both women). *Students:* 5 full-time (1 woman), 4 part-time (3 women); includes 4 minority (1 Black or African American, non-Hispanic/Latino; 1 Asian, non-Hispanic/Latino; 2 Hispanic/Latino). Average age 38. 10 applicants, 80% accepted, 5 enrolled. In 2017, 1 master's awarded. *Degree requirements:* For master's, thesis project or internship. *Application deadline:* Applications are processed on a rolling basis. Application fee: $50. Electronic applications accepted. *Financial support:* Applicants required to submit FAFSA. *Unit head:* Dr. Amanda Frisken, Associate Professor, American Studies, 516-876-4853, E-mail: friskena@oldwestbury.edu. *Application contact:* Philip D'Angelo, Graduate Admissions Office, 516-876-3073, E-mail: enroll@oldwestbury.edu.

State University of New York Empire State College, School for Graduate Studies, Program in Liberal Studies, Saratoga Springs, NY 12866-4391. Offers MA. *Program availability:* Part-time, evening/weekend, online learning. *Degree requirements:* For master's, thesis, final project. *Entrance requirements:* Additional exam requirements/recommendations for international students: Required—TOEFL (minimum score 600 paper-based). Electronic applications accepted.

Stony Brook University, State University of New York, School of Professional Development, Stony Brook, NY 11794. Offers biology (MAT); chemistry (MAT); coaching (Graduate Certificate); earth science (MAT); educational computing (Graduate Certificate); educational leadership (Advanced Certificate); English (MAT); environmental management (MPS, Graduate Certificate); French (MAT); German (MAT); higher education administration (MA, Certificate); human resource management (MS, Graduate Certificate); industrial management (Graduate Certificate); information systems management (Graduate Certificate); Italian (MAT); liberal studies (MA); mathematics (MAT); operations research (Graduate Certificate); physics (MAT); school district business leadership (Advanced Certificate); social studies (MAT); Spanish (MAT). *Program availability:* Part-time, evening/weekend, online learning. *Faculty:* 3 full-time (2 women), 101 part-time/adjunct (45 women). *Students:* 190 full-time (126 women), 974 part-time (708 women); includes 255 minority (88 Black or African American, non-Hispanic/Latino; 2 American Indian or Alaska Native, non-Hispanic/Latino; 31 Asian, non-Hispanic/Latino; 113 Hispanic/Latino; 1 Native Hawaiian or other

Pacific Islander, non-Hispanic/Latino; 20 Two or more races, non-Hispanic/Latino), 6 international. Average age 33. 411 applicants, 91% accepted, 288 enrolled. In 2017, 333 master's, 180 other advanced degrees awarded. *Entrance requirements:* Additional exam requirements/recommendations for international students: Required—TOEFL (minimum score 85 iBT). *Application deadline:* For fall admission, 1/15 for domestic students, 6/1 for international students; for spring admission, 10/1 for domestic and international students. Applications are processed on a rolling basis. Application fee: $100. *Expenses:* Contact institution. *Financial support:* Fellowships, research assistantships, teaching assistantships, and career-related internships or fieldwork available. Support available to part-time students. *Unit head:* Dr. Ken Lindblom, Dean, 631-632-7049, Fax: 631-632-9046, E-mail: kenneth.lindblom@stonybrook.edu. *Application contact:* Melissa Jordan, Assistant Dean, 631-632-7751, E-mail: melissa.jordan@stonybrook.edu.
Website: http://www.stonybrook.edu/spd/

Texas A&M University–Central Texas, Graduate Studies and Research, Killeen, TX 76549. Offers accounting (MS); business administration (MBA); clinical mental health counseling (MS); criminal justice (MCJ); curriculum and instruction (M Ed); educational administration (M Ed); educational psychology - experimental psychology (MS); history (MA); human resource management (MS); information systems (MS); liberal studies (MS); management and leadership (MS); marriage and family therapy (MS); mathematics (MS); political science (MA); school counseling (M Ed); school psychology (Ed S).

Texas Christian University, Master of Liberal Arts Program, Fort Worth, TX 76129. Offers MLA. *Program availability:* Part-time, evening/weekend, 100% online. *Faculty:* 5 part-time/adjunct (0 women). *Students:* 81 full-time (33 women), 30 part-time (22 women); includes 37 minority (21 Black or African American, non-Hispanic/Latino; 2 American Indian or Alaska Native, non-Hispanic/Latino; 8 Hispanic/Latino; 1 Native Hawaiian or other Pacific Islander, non-Hispanic/Latino; 5 Two or more races, non-Hispanic/Latino), 3 international. Average age 32. 85 applicants, 93% accepted, 57 enrolled. In 2017, 33 master's awarded. *Entrance requirements:* Additional exam requirements/recommendations for international students: Required—TOEFL (minimum score 550 paper-based; 80 iBT), IELTS (minimum score 6.5). *Application deadline:* For fall admission, 8/15 for domestic students, 6/1 for international students; for spring admission, 1/15 for domestic students, 11/1 for international students. Applications are processed on a rolling basis. Application fee: $60. Electronic applications accepted. *Expenses:* $890 per credit hour, $125 online course fee. *Financial support:* In 2017–18, 60 students received support. Scholarships/grants, unspecified assistantships, and employee tuition benefits available. Financial award applicants required to submit FAFSA. *Unit head:* Dr. Tim Barth, Interim Associate Provost/Dean of University Programs, 817-257-7104, Fax: 817-257-7484, E-mail: t.barth@tcu.edu. *Application contact:* Anita Unger, Graduate Program Coordinator, 817-257-7515, Fax: 817-257-7484, E-mail: a.unger@tcu.edu.
Website: https://universityprograms.tcu.edu/mla

Thomas Edison State University, Heavin School of Arts and Sciences, Program in Liberal Studies, Trenton, NJ 08608. Offers digital humanities (MALS, Graduate Certificate); geropsychology (MALS, Graduate Certificate); industrial-organizational psychology (MALS, Graduate Certificate); learner-designed area of study (MALS); professional communications (MALS, Graduate Certificate). *Program availability:* Part-time, online learning. *Degree requirements:* For master's, final project. *Entrance requirements:* For master's, bachelor's degree from a regionally-accredited college or university; minimum 2 letters of recommendation; 3-5 years of related working experience; current resume. Additional exam requirements/recommendations for international students: Required—TOEFL (minimum score 550 paper-based; 79 iBT). Electronic applications accepted.

Towson University, College of Liberal Arts, Program in Professional Studies, Towson, MD 21252-0001. Offers art history (MA); individualized plan of study (MA). *Program availability:* Part-time, evening/weekend. *Students:* 13 full-time (8 women), 16 part-time (9 women); includes 11 minority (7 Black or African American, non-Hispanic/Latino; 1 Hispanic/Latino; 3 Two or more races, non-Hispanic/Latino). *Degree requirements:* For master's, thesis optional. *Entrance requirements:* For master's, minimum GPA of 3.0, essay. *Application deadline:* For fall admission, 1/17 for domestic students, 5/15 for international students; for spring admission, 10/15 for domestic students, 12/1 for international students. Applications are processed on a rolling basis. Application fee: $45. Electronic applications accepted. *Expenses:* Tuition, state resident: full-time $7960; part-time $398 per unit. Tuition, nonresident: full-time $16,480; part-time $824 per unit. *Required fees:* $2600; $130 per year. $390 per term. *Financial support:* Application deadline: 4/1. *Unit head:* Dr. James Smith, Graduate Program Director, 410-704-4620, E-mail: jmsmith@towson.edu. *Application contact:* Coverley Beidleman, Assistant Director of Graduate Admissions, 410-704-5630, Fax: 410-704-3030, E-mail: cbeidleman@towson.edu.
Website: http://www.towson.edu/cla/departments/interdisciplinary/grad/professional/

Tulane University, School of Professional Advancement, New Orleans, LA 70118-5669. Offers health and wellness management (MPS); homeland security studies (MPS); information technology management (MPS); liberal arts (MLA). *Program availability:* Part-time. *Degree requirements:* For master's, thesis. *Entrance requirements:* For master's, GRE General Test, minimum B average in undergraduate course work. Additional exam requirements/recommendations for international students: Required—TOEFL. *Expenses: Tuition:* Full-time $50,920; part-time $2829 per credit hour. *Required fees:* $2040; $44.50 per credit hour. $580 per term. Tuition and fees vary according to course load, degree level and program.

University at Albany, State University of New York, College of Arts and Sciences, Liberal Studies Program, Albany, NY 12222-0001. Offers MALS. *Faculty:* 4 full-time (1 woman), 1 part-time/adjunct (0 women). *Entrance requirements:* Additional exam requirements/recommendations for international students: Required—TOEFL (minimum score 550 paper-based). *Application deadline:* For fall admission, 4/1 for domestic students, 5/1 for international students. Applications are processed on a rolling basis. Application fee: $75. Electronic applications accepted. *Expenses:* Tuition, state resident: full-time $10,870; part-time $453 per credit hour. Tuition, nonresident: full-time $22,210; part-time $925 per credit hour. *Required fees:* $84.68 per credit hour. $508.06 per semester. Part-time tuition and fees vary according to course load and program. *Financial support:* Application deadline: 4/1. *Unit head:* Dr. Kir Kuiken, Jr., Interim Director, 518-442-4069, E-mail: kkuiken@albany.edu. *Application contact:* Michael DeRensis, Director, Graduate Admissions, 518-442-3980, Fax: 518-442-3922, E-mail: graduate@albany.edu.
Website: http://www.albany.edu/liberal_studies/

University of Central Oklahoma, The Jackson College of Graduate Studies, College of Liberal Arts, Department of Humanities and Philosophy, Edmond, OK 73034-5209. Offers liberal studies (MA). *Faculty:* 2 full-time (1 woman). *Students:* 1 (woman) full-time, 3 part-time (1 woman); includes 3 minority (1 Black or African American, non-Hispanic/Latino; 2 American Indian or Alaska Native, non-Hispanic/Latino). Average age 57. 8 applicants, 63% accepted, 3 enrolled. In 2017, 1 master's awarded. *Degree requirements:* For master's, comprehensive exam (for some programs), thesis (for some programs). *Entrance requirements:* Additional exam requirements/recommendations for

international students: Required—TOEFL (minimum score 550 paper-based; 79 iBT), IELTS (minimum score 6.5). *Application deadline:* For fall admission, 7/15 for international students; for spring admission, 11/15 for international students. Applications are processed on a rolling basis. Application fee: $60. Electronic applications accepted. *Expenses:* Tuition, state resident: full-time $5375; part-time $268.75 per credit hour. Tuition, nonresident: full-time $13,295; part-time $664.75 per credit hour. *Required fees:* $626; $31.30 per credit hour. One-time fee: $50. Tuition and fees vary according to program. *Financial support:* In 2017–18, 1 student received support. Research assistantships, teaching assistantships, career-related internships or fieldwork, scholarships/grants, tuition waivers (partial), and unspecified assistantships available. Financial award application deadline: 3/31; financial award applicants required to submit FAFSA. *Unit head:* Dr. Mark Silcox, Chairperson, 405-974-5540, Fax: 405-974-3823. *Application contact:* Dr. Theresa Vaughan, Graduate Advisor, 405-974-3434, Fax: 405-974-3823, E-mail: gradcoll@uco.edu.
Website: http://sites.uco.edu/la/humanities-philosophy/index.asp

University of Chicago, Graham School of Continuing Liberal and Professional Studies, Program in Liberal Arts, Chicago, IL 60637. Offers MLA. *Program availability:* Part-time, evening/weekend. *Faculty:* 22. *Students:* 6 full-time (2 women), 36 part-time (16 women); includes 9 minority (3 Black or African American, non-Hispanic/Latino; 3 Asian, non-Hispanic/Latino; 2 Hispanic/Latino; 1 Two or more races, non-Hispanic/Latino), 4 international. Average age 39. 25 applicants, 92% accepted, 19 enrolled. In 2017, 20 master's awarded. *Entrance requirements:* For master's, writing sample, transcripts, 2 letters of recommendation, resume or curriculum vitae. Additional exam requirements/recommendations for international students: Required—TOEFL (minimum score 104 iBT), IELTS (minimum score 7). *Application deadline:* For fall admission, 9/15 for domestic students, 8/15 for international students; for spring admission, 3/3 for domestic students, 2/3 for international students. Application fee: $75. Electronic applications accepted. *Unit head:* Tim Murphy, Assistant Director, 773-834-3233, E-mail: timmurphy@uchicago.edu. *Application contact:* Bonni Van Eck, Admissions Coordinator, E-mail: mla@uchicago.edu.
Website: https://grahamschool.uchicago.edu/credit/master-liberal-arts/index

University of Delaware, College of Arts and Sciences, Program in Liberal Studies, Newark, DE 19716. Offers MALS. *Program availability:* Part-time, evening/weekend. *Degree requirements:* For master's, thesis. Electronic applications accepted. *Faculty research:* British Raj, medical and scientific ethics, Jewish-American novelists, intellectual freedom.

University of Detroit Mercy, College of Liberal Arts and Education, Detroit, MI 48221. Offers addiction counseling (MA); addiction studies (Certificate); clinical mental health counseling (MA); clinical psychology (MA, PhD); computer and information systems (MS); criminal justice (MA); curriculum and instruction (MA); economics (MA); educational administration (MA); financial economics (MA); industrial/organizational psychology (MA); information assurance (MS); intelligence analysis (MA); liberal studies (MALS); religious studies (MA); school counseling (MA, Certificate); school psychology (Spec); security administration (MS); special education: emotionally impaired/behaviorally disordered (MA); special education: learning disabilities (MA). *Program availability:* Part-time, evening/weekend. *Degree requirements:* For doctorate, departmental qualifying exam. *Faculty research:* Psychology of aging, history of technology, Renaissance humanism, U.S. and Japanese economic relations.

University of Memphis, Graduate School, University College, Memphis, TN 38152. Offers human resources leadership (MPS); liberal studies (MALS, Graduate Certificate); strategic leadership (MPS, Graduate Certificate); training and development (MPS). *Program availability:* Part-time, evening/weekend. *Faculty:* 3 full-time (1 woman), 1 part-time/adjunct (0 women). *Students:* 27 full-time (16 women), 105 part-time (79 women); includes 86 minority (78 Black or African American, non-Hispanic/Latino; 1 Asian, non-Hispanic/Latino; 2 Hispanic/Latino; 1 Native Hawaiian or other Pacific Islander, non-Hispanic/Latino; 4 Two or more races, non-Hispanic/Latino), 4 international. Average age 38. 70 applicants, 76% accepted, 39 enrolled. *Degree requirements:* For master's, comprehensive exam, thesis (for some programs). *Entrance requirements:* For master's, GRE (for MPS), resume, letters of recommendation, personal essay, interview, minimum undergraduate GPA of 2.75 (for MALS); portfolio in lieu of GRE (for MPS applicants with substantial professional work experience); for Graduate Certificate, essay, letter of recommendation. Additional exam requirements/recommendations for international students: Required—TOEFL (minimum score 550 paper-based; 79 iBT). *Application deadline:* For fall admission, 7/1 for domestic students, 5/1 for international students; for spring admission, 11/1 for domestic students, 9/15 for international students. Applications are processed on a rolling basis. Application fee: $35 ($60 for international students). Electronic applications accepted. *Expenses:* Contact institution. *Financial support:* In 2017–18, 123 students received support, including 4 teaching assistantships with tuition reimbursements available (averaging $13,000 per year); research assistantships with full tuition reimbursements available, Federal Work-Study, scholarships/grants, and unspecified assistantships also available. Financial award application deadline: 2/3; financial award applicants required to submit FAFSA. *Faculty research:* Media ethics, history of psychiatry, public relations. *Unit head:* Dr. Joanne Gikas, Interim Dean, 901-678-2716, E-mail: jgikas@memphis.edu. *Application contact:* Dr. Colin Chapell, Graduate Studies Coordinator, 901-678-3066, Fax: 901-678-2971, E-mail: cbchpell@memphis.edu.
Website: http://www.memphis.edu/univcoll/

University of Miami, Graduate School, College of Arts and Sciences, Program in Liberal Studies, Coral Gables, FL 33124. Offers MALS. *Program availability:* Part-time, evening/weekend. *Degree requirements:* For master's, thesis or alternative. *Entrance requirements:* For master's, minimum GPA of 3.0. Additional exam requirements/recommendations for international students: Required—TOEFL. Electronic applications accepted. *Expenses:* Contact institution.

University of Minnesota, Duluth, Graduate School, College of Liberal Arts, Department of Sociology/Anthropology, Liberal Studies Program, Duluth, MN 55812-2496. Offers MLS. *Program availability:* Part-time, evening/weekend. *Faculty research:* Nature of knowledge, cultural studies, language, literature, sociology.

University of New Hampshire, Graduate School, College of Liberal Arts, Program in Liberal Studies, Durham, NH 03824. Offers MALS. *Students:* 12 part-time (6 women); includes 2 minority (1 Asian, non-Hispanic/Latino; 1 Hispanic/Latino). Average age 44. 5 applicants, 40% accepted, 2 enrolled. In 2017, 1 master's awarded. *Entrance requirements:* For master's, GRE General Test. Additional exam requirements/recommendations for international students: Required—TOEFL (minimum score 550 paper-based; 80 iBT). *Application deadline:* For fall admission, 4/1 for domestic and international students; for spring admission, 12/1 for domestic students; for summer admission, 4/1 for domestic students. Application fee: $65. Electronic applications accepted. *Financial support:* Fellowships, research assistantships, and teaching assistantships available. Financial award application deadline: 2/15. *Unit head:* Catherine Peebles, Director, 603-862-3638, E-mail: liberal.studies@unh.edu. *Application contact:* Tama Andrews, Coordinator, 603-862-2321, E-mail: liberal.studies@unh.edu.
Website: http://www.cola.unh.edu/liberal-studies

University of North Carolina at Asheville, Master of Liberal Arts and Sciences Program, Asheville, NC 28804-3299. Offers climate change and society (Graduate Certificate); environmental and cultural sustainability (Graduate Certificate). *Program availability:* Part-time, evening/weekend. *Faculty:* 7 full-time (1 woman), 3 part-time/adjunct (1 woman). *Students:* 1 full-time (0 women), 24 part-time (12 women); includes 3 minority (2 Black or African American, non-Hispanic/Latino; 1 Two or more races, non-Hispanic/Latino). Average age 44. 18 applicants, 83% accepted, 8 enrolled. In 2017, 19 master's awarded. *Degree requirements:* For master's, thesis or alternative. *Entrance requirements:* For master's and Graduate Certificate, essay, 3 letters of recommendation, transcript. Additional exam requirements/recommendations for international students: Required—TOEFL (minimum score 85 iBT), IELTS (minimum score 6.5). *Application deadline:* For fall admission, 4/15 priority date for domestic students; for spring admission, 11/15 priority date for domestic students. Applications are processed on a rolling basis. Application fee: $60. Electronic applications accepted. *Expenses:* $4,914. *Financial support:* Application deadline: 5/1; applicants required to submit FAFSA. *Unit head:* Gerard Voos, Director, Master of Liberal Arts and Sciences Program and the Asheville Graduate Center, 828-232-5040, E-mail: gvoos@unca.edu. *Application contact:* Jordan Dolfi, Program Coordinator, Master of Liberal Arts and Sciences Program and the Asheville Graduate Center, 828-251-6099, E-mail: jdolfi@unca.edu.
Website: https://mlas.unca.edu/

The University of North Carolina at Charlotte, College of Liberal Arts and Sciences, Interdisciplinary Liberal Arts and Sciences Programs, Charlotte, NC 28223-0001. Offers gender, sexuality, and women's studies (Graduate Certificate); gerontology (MA, Graduate Certificate); Latin American studies (MA); liberal studies (MA); organizational science (PhD); public policy (PhD). *Program availability:* Part-time, evening/weekend. *Faculty:* 1 full-time (0 women). *Students:* 66 full-time (48 women), 66 part-time (52 women); includes 41 minority (14 Black or African American, non-Hispanic/Latino; 2 Asian, non-Hispanic/Latino; 24 Hispanic/Latino; 1 Two or more races, non-Hispanic/Latino), 16 international. Average age 27. 129 applicants, 53% accepted, 43 enrolled. In 2017, 22 master's, 10 doctorates, 9 other advanced degrees awarded. *Degree requirements:* For master's, comprehensive exam (for some programs), thesis (for some programs), practicum, project; for doctorate, comprehensive exam, thesis/dissertation; for Graduate Certificate, practicum (for gerontology). *Entrance requirements:* For master's, GRE General Test or MAT, bachelor's degree from accredited college or university; official transcripts of all previous academic work attempted beyond high school with minimum overall GPA of 3.0; statement of purpose; recommendation letters; for doctorate, GRE or GMAT, statement of purpose discussing interest in program and objectives for pursuing degree, current resume or curriculum vitae, unofficial transcripts; for Graduate Certificate, bachelor's degree from accredited university and either enrolled and in good standing in a graduate degree program at UNC Charlotte or have a minimum undergraduate GPA of 3.0. Additional exam requirements/recommendations for international students: Required—TOEFL (minimum score 523 paper-based, 70 iBT) or IELTS (6.5). *Application deadline:* For fall admission, 2/15 for domestic and international students; for spring admission, 10/1 for domestic and international students; for summer admission, 4/1 for domestic and international students. Applications are processed on a rolling basis. Application fee: $75. Electronic applications accepted. *Expenses:* Tuition, state resident: full-time $4337. Tuition, nonresident: full-time $17,771. *Required fees:* $3211. Tuition and fees vary according to course load and program. *Financial support:* In 2017–18, 21 students received support, including 19 research assistantships (averaging $12,011 per year), 1 teaching assistantship (averaging $18,600 per year); career-related internships or fieldwork, institutionally sponsored loans, scholarships/grants, unspecified assistantships, and administrative assistantships also available. Support available to part-time students. Financial award application deadline: 3/1; financial award applicants required to submit FAFSA. *Unit head:* Dr. Nancy A. Gutierrez, Dean, 704-687-0081, E-mail: ngutierr@uncc.edu. *Application contact:* Kathy B. Giddings, Director of Graduate Admissions, 704-687-5503, Fax: 704-687-3279, E-mail: gradadm@uncc.edu.
Website: http://clas.uncc.edu/academics

The University of North Carolina at Greensboro, Graduate School, Program in Liberal Studies, Greensboro, NC 27412-5001. Offers MALS. Electronic applications accepted.

The University of North Carolina Wilmington, College of Arts and Sciences, Graduate Liberal Studies Program, Wilmington, NC 28403-3297. Offers MA. *Program availability:* Part-time, 100% online. *Faculty:* 1 (woman) full-time, 2 part-time/adjunct (1 woman). *Students:* 12 full-time (11 women), 29 part-time (21 women); includes 8 minority (5 Black or African American, non-Hispanic/Latino; 2 Hispanic/Latino; 1 Two or more races, non-Hispanic/Latino). Average age 40. 8 applicants, 88% accepted, 6 enrolled. In 2017, 8 master's awarded. *Degree requirements:* For master's, final project. *Entrance requirements:* For master's, essay, 3 letters of recommendation. Additional exam requirements/recommendations for international students: Required—TOEFL (minimum score 550 paper-based; 79 iBT), IELTS (minimum score 6.5). *Application deadline:* For fall admission, 6/13 for domestic students; for spring admission, 11/5 for domestic students; for summer admission, 3/14 for domestic students. Applications are processed on a rolling basis. Application fee: $75. Electronic applications accepted. *Expenses:* Tuition, state resident: full-time $4626; part-time $226.76 per credit hour. Tuition, nonresident: full-time $17,834; part-time $874.22 per credit hour. *Required fees:* $2124. Tuition and fees vary according to program. *Financial support:* Scholarships/grants and unspecified assistantships available. Financial award application deadline: 1/1; financial award applicants required to submit FAFSA. *Unit head:* Dr. Patricia Turrisi, Director, 910-962-3299, Fax: 910-962-3542, E-mail: turrisip@uncw.edu. *Application contact:* Dr. Ashley Hudson, Assistant Director, 910-962-2427, Fax: 910-962-3542, E-mail: hudsona@uncw.edu.
Website: http://www.uncw.edu/gls/

University of Pennsylvania, School of Arts and Sciences, College of Liberal and Professional Studies, Philadelphia, PA 19104. Offers applied geosciences (MSAG); applied positive psychology (MAP); chemical sciences (MCS); environmental studies (MES); individualized study (MLA); liberal arts (M Phil); medical physics (MMP); organization dynamics (M Phil). *Students:* 191 full-time (112 women), 311 part-time (178 women); includes 99 minority (34 Black or African American, non-Hispanic/Latino; 2 American Indian or Alaska Native, non-Hispanic/Latino; 28 Asian, non-Hispanic/Latino; 24 Hispanic/Latino; 11 Two or more races, non-Hispanic/Latino), 83 international. Average age 34. 633 applicants, 52% accepted, 249 enrolled. In 2017, 141 master's awarded. *Unit head:* Nora Lewis, Vice Dean, Professional and Liberal Education, 215-898-7326, E-mail: nlewis@sas.upenn.edu.
Website: http://www.sas.upenn.edu/lps/graduate

University of St. Thomas, Program in Liberal Arts, Houston, TX 77006-4696. Offers MLA. *Program availability:* Part-time, evening/weekend. *Faculty:* 23 full-time (10 women), 13 part-time/adjunct (8 women). *Students:* 11 full-time (9 women), 56 part-time (39 women); includes 26 minority (11 Black or African American, non-Hispanic/Latino; 1 Asian, non-Hispanic/Latino; 13 Hispanic/Latino; 1 Two or more races, non-Hispanic/Latino), 4 international. Average age 38. 27 applicants, 100% accepted, 25 enrolled. In 2017, 23 master's awarded. *Degree requirements:* For master's, thesis optional,

capstone, minimum cumulative GPA of 3.0. *Entrance requirements:* For master's, 4-year undergraduate degree with minimum GPA of 2.5, essay, 2 letters of recommendation, interview. Additional exam requirements/recommendations for international students: Required—TOEFL (minimum score 100 iBT), IELTS (minimum score 7), PTE (minimum score 68). *Application deadline:* Applications are processed on a rolling basis. Application fee: $35. Electronic applications accepted. *Expenses: Tuition:* Full-time $20,934; part-time $1163 per credit hour. *Required fees:* $250; $210 per semester. *Financial support:* In 2017–18, 3 students received support. Federal Work-Study, scholarships/grants, and state work-study, institutional employment available. Support available to part-time students. Financial award application deadline: 4/15; financial award applicants required to submit FAFSA. *Unit head:* Dr. Ravi Srinivas, Associate Vice President for Academic Affairs/Dean of Extended Programs/MLA Director, 713-525-3804, Fax: 713-525-6924, E-mail: mla@stthom.edu. *Application contact:* Kate Henderson, Program Coordinator, 713-525-3556, Fax: 713-525-6924, E-mail: mla@stthom.edu.
Website: http://www.stthom.edu/Academics/School_of_Arts_and_Sciences/Graduate/Master_of_Liberal_Arts/Index.aqf

University of Southern Indiana, Graduate Studies, College of Liberal Arts, Program in Liberal Studies, Evansville, IN 47712-3590. Offers MALS. *Program availability:* Part-time, evening/weekend. *Faculty:* 8 full-time (6 women). *Students:* 4 part-time (3 women); includes 1 minority (Black or African American, non-Hispanic/Latino). Average age 43. *Entrance requirements:* For master's, minimum GPA of 2.5, resume, interview, written statement of interest, three professional references. Additional exam requirements/recommendations for international students: Required—TOEFL (minimum score 550 paper-based; 79 iBT), IELTS (minimum score 6). *Application deadline:* For fall admission, 8/15 priority date for domestic students, 3/1 priority date for international students. Applications are processed on a rolling basis. Application fee: $40. Electronic applications accepted. *Expenses:* Tuition, state resident: full-time $9394. Tuition, nonresident: full-time $17,917. *Required fees:* $510. *Financial support:* Federal Work-Study, scholarships/grants, tuition waivers (full and partial), and unspecified assistantships available. Financial award application deadline: 3/1; financial award applicants required to submit FAFSA. *Unit head:* Dr. Tamara Hunt, Program Director, 812-465-1202, E-mail: tlhunt@usi.edu. *Application contact:* Dr. Mayola Rowser, Director, Graduate Studies, 812-465-7015, E-mail: mrowser@usi.edu.
Website: http://www.usi.edu/liberalarts/master-of-arts-in-liberal-studies

University of South Florida, College of Arts and Sciences, Department of Humanities and Cultural Studies, Tampa, FL 33620-9951. Offers liberal arts (MA), including American studies, film studies, humanities. *Program availability:* Part-time, evening/weekend. *Faculty:* 8 full-time (2 women). *Students:* 19 full-time (10 women), 3 part-time (2 women); includes 3 minority (2 Black or African American, non-Hispanic/Latino; 1 Hispanic/Latino), 2 international. Average age 29. 25 applicants, 44% accepted, 7 enrolled. In 2017, 8 master's awarded. *Degree requirements:* For master's, comprehensive exam, thesis, language (for humanities subconcentration). *Entrance requirements:* For master's, GRE General Test, minimum GPA of 3.0 in upper-division courses, personal statement, writing sample. Additional exam requirements/recommendations for international students: Required—TOEFL (minimum score 550 paper-based; 79 iBT) or IELTS (minimum score 6.5). *Application deadline:* For fall admission, 2/15 priority date for domestic students, 2/15 for international students; for spring admission, 10/15 priority date for domestic students, 9/15 for international students; for summer admission, 2/15 for domestic students, 1/15 for international students. Application fee: $30. Electronic applications accepted. *Financial support:* In 2017–18, 2 students received support, including 15 teaching assistantships with tuition reimbursements available (averaging $12,437 per year); scholarships/grants also available. Financial award application deadline: 4/1. *Faculty research:* American South, American autobiography, material culture, critical theory, cultural studies, film studies. *Unit head:* Dr. Andrew Berish, Associate Professor and Chair, 813-974-9380, E-mail: aberish@usf.edu. *Application contact:* Dr. Maria Cizmic, Associate Professor and Graduate Program Director, 813-974-9380, E-mail: mcizmic@usf.edu.
Website: http://humanities.usf.edu/

University of South Florida, College of Arts and Sciences, Department of Philosophy, Tampa, FL 33620-9951. Offers liberal arts (MA), including social and political thought; philosophy (MA, PhD), including philosophy and religion. *Program availability:* Part-time, evening/weekend. *Faculty:* 14 full-time (2 women). *Students:* 41 full-time (7 women), 15 part-time (3 women); includes 10 minority (2 Black or African American, non-Hispanic/Latino; 3 Asian, non-Hispanic/Latino; 4 Hispanic/Latino; 1 Two or more races, non-Hispanic/Latino), 1 international. Average age 35. 29 applicants, 76% accepted, 9 enrolled. In 2017, 7 master's, 7 doctorates awarded. Terminal master's awarded for partial completion of doctoral program. *Degree requirements:* For master's, comprehensive exam, thesis optional; for doctorate, comprehensive exam, thesis/dissertation. *Entrance requirements:* For master's and doctorate, GRE General Test, minimum GPA of 3.0, three letters of recommendation, 10-page philosophy writing sample, statement of philosophical interests. Additional exam requirements/recommendations for international students: Required—TOEFL (minimum score 550 paper-based; 79 iBT) or IELTS (minimum score 6.5). *Application deadline:* For fall admission, 1/2 priority date for domestic students, 2/15 for international students; for spring admission, 10/15 priority date for domestic students, 8/1 for international students. Application fee: $30. Electronic applications accepted. *Financial support:* In 2017–18, 5 students received support, including 32 teaching assistantships with tuition reimbursements available (averaging $11,025 per year); unspecified assistantships also available. Financial award application deadline: 1/1. *Faculty research:* Medieval philosophy, early modern philosophy (seventeenth-, eighteenth-, and twentieth-century Continental philosophy), feminist philosophy, social philosophy, ethics, philosophy of science. *Total annual research expenditures:* $10,921. *Unit head:* Dr. Alex Levine, Professor and Chairperson, 813-974-5508, E-mail: levineat@usf.edu. *Application contact:* Dr. William Goodwin, Associate Professor, 813-974-5670, E-mail: wgoodwin@usf.edu.
Website: http://philosophy.usf.edu/

University of South Florida, College of Arts and Sciences, School of Interdisciplinary Global Studies, Tampa, FL 33620-9951. Offers government (PhD); Latin American, Caribbean and Latino studies (MA); liberal arts (MA), including Africana studies; political science (MA), including comparative government and politics. *Accreditation:* NASPAA. *Program availability:* Part-time, evening/weekend. *Faculty:* 14 full-time (2 women). *Students:* 3 applicants. In 2017, 9 master's, 1 doctorate awarded. *Degree requirements:* For master's, comprehensive exam, thesis; for doctorate, comprehensive exam, thesis/dissertation. *Entrance requirements:* For master's, GRE General Test, minimum GPA of 3.0 in upper-division undergraduate course work; letters of recommendation (2 for MPA, 3 for MS); 500-word personal statement and undergraduate background in political science or related fields (for MS); one-page career statement (for MPA); for doctorate, GRE General Test, 500-word personal statement, three letters of recommendation, transcripts of MA/BA coursework, writing sample. Additional exam requirements/recommendations for international students: Required—TOEFL (minimum score 550 paper-based; 79 iBT) or IELTS (minimum score 6.5). *Application deadline:* For fall admission, 1/5 for domestic and international students; for spring admission, 10/15 for domestic students, 9/15 for international students. Applications are processed on a rolling basis. Application fee: $30. Electronic applications accepted. *Financial support:* In 2017–18, 3 students received support, including 18 teaching assistantships with tuition reimbursements available (averaging $12,390 per year); unspecified assistantships also available. Financial award application deadline: 4/1. *Faculty research:* Citizenship and identity, social movements, global governance, American politics, public policy. *Total annual research expenditures:* $195,426. *Unit head:* Dr. Steven Tauber, Associate Professor/Interim Chair, 813-974-2278, Fax: 813-974-0832, E-mail: stauber@usf.edu. *Application contact:* Dr. Bernd Reiter, Associate Professor and Director of Graduate Studies, 813-974-3583, Fax: 813-974-0832, E-mail: breiter@usf.edu.
Website: http://gia.usf.edu/

University of South Florida, St. Petersburg, College of Arts and Sciences, St. Petersburg, FL 33701. Offers digital journalism and design (MA); environmental science and policy (MA, MS); Florida studies (MLA); journalism and media studies (MA); liberal studies (MLA); psychology (MA). *Program availability:* Part-time, online learning. *Degree requirements:* For master's, comprehensive exam, thesis or project. *Entrance requirements:* For master's, GRE, LSAT, MCAT (varies by program), letter of intent, 3 letters of recommendation, writing samples, bachelor's degree from regionally-accredited institution with minimum GPA of 3.0 overall or in upper two years. Additional exam requirements/recommendations for international students: Required—TOEFL (minimum score 550 paper-based; 79 iBT); Recommended—IELTS. Electronic applications accepted.

University of South Florida Sarasota-Manatee, College of Liberal Arts and Social Sciences, Sarasota, FL 34243. Offers criminal justice (MA); education (MA); educational leadership (M Ed), including curriculum leadership, K-12 public school leadership, non-public/charter school leadership; elementary education (MAT); English education (MA); social work (MSW). *Program availability:* Part-time, 100% online, blended/hybrid learning. *Faculty:* 15 full-time (12 women), 8 part-time/adjunct (6 women). *Students:* 11 full-time (10 women), 43 part-time (37 women); includes 17 minority (7 Black or African American, non-Hispanic/Latino; 2 Asian, non-Hispanic/Latino; 8 Hispanic/Latino), 1 international. Average age 35. 62 applicants, 27% accepted, 14 enrolled. In 2017, 32 master's awarded. *Degree requirements:* For master's, comprehensive exam (for some programs). *Entrance requirements:* For master's, GRE. Additional exam requirements/recommendations for international students: Required—TOEFL (minimum score 550 paper-based; 79 iBT), IELTS (minimum score 6.5). *Application deadline:* For fall admission, 3/1 priority date for domestic students, 3/1 for international students; for spring admission, 10/1 priority date for domestic students, 10/1 for international students. Applications are processed on a rolling basis. Application fee: $30. Electronic applications accepted. *Expenses:* Tuition, state resident: full-time $8350; part-time $418 per credit hour. Tuition, nonresident: full-time $19,047; part-time $863 per credit hour. *Required fees:* $1689. Tuition and fees vary according to degree level and program. *Financial support:* In 2017–18, 1 student received support. Career-related internships or fieldwork, institutionally sponsored loans, scholarships/grants, health care benefits, and unspecified assistantships available. Support available to part-time students. Financial award application deadline: 3/1; financial award applicants required to submit FAFSA. *Faculty research:* Educational leadership, secondary education, elementary education, criminal justice, social work. *Total annual research expenditures:* $72,000. *Unit head:* Dr. Jane Rose, Dean, 941-359-4469, Fax: 941-359-4778, E-mail: jane.rose@sar.usf.edu. *Application contact:* Brandon Avery, Assistant Director, Admissions, 941-359-4331, E-mail: bavery@sar.usf.edu.

The University of Texas at El Paso, Graduate School, College of Liberal Arts, Master of Arts in Interdisciplinary Studies Program, El Paso, TX 79968-0001. Offers MAIS. *Program availability:* Part-time, evening/weekend. *Entrance requirements:* For master's, GRE, minimum GPA of 3.0, letters of recommendation. Additional exam requirements/recommendations for international students: Required—TOEFL; Recommended—IELTS. Electronic applications accepted.

University of the Virgin Islands, College of Liberal Arts and Social Sciences, St. Thomas, VI 00802. Offers M Psych, MPA. *Program availability:* Part-time, evening/weekend. *Degree requirements:* For master's, comprehensive exam, thesis or alternative. *Entrance requirements:* For master's, GRE, minimum GPA of 2.5. Additional exam requirements/recommendations for international students: Required—TOEFL (minimum score 550 paper-based). Electronic applications accepted. *Expenses:* Contact institution. *Faculty research:* Ethical issues of arbitration, spiritual leadership, accountability.

The University of Toledo, College of Graduate Studies, College of Languages, Literature and Social Sciences, Master of Liberal Studies Program, Toledo, OH 43606-3390. Offers MLS. *Program availability:* Part-time, evening/weekend. *Degree requirements:* For master's, thesis. *Entrance requirements:* For master's, GRE if cumulative GPA is less than 3.0, minimum cumulative point-hour ratio of 2.7 for all previous academic work, three letters of recommendation, statement of purpose, transcripts from all prior institutions attended. Additional exam requirements/recommendations for international students: Required—TOEFL (minimum score 550 paper-based; 80 iBT). Electronic applications accepted.

University of Wisconsin–Milwaukee, Graduate School, College of Letters and Science, Program in Liberal Studies, Milwaukee, WI 53201-0413. Offers MLS. *Entrance requirements:* For master's, interview, bachelor's degree. Additional exam requirements/recommendations for international students: Required—TOEFL (minimum score 600 paper-based; 79 iBT), IELTS (minimum score 7). Application fee: $56 ($96 for international students). Electronic applications accepted. *Financial support:* Fellowships, research assistantships, teaching assistantships, health care benefits, unspecified assistantships, and project assistantships available. Financial award applicants required to submit FAFSA. *Application contact:* General Information Contact, 414-229-4982, Fax: 414-229-6967, E-mail: gradschool@uwm.edu.
Website: https://uwm.edu/liberal-studies/

Ursuline College, School of Graduate and Professional Studies, Program in Liberal Studies, Pepper Pike, OH 44124-4398. Offers MALS. *Program availability:* Part-time. *Faculty:* 1 full-time (0 women). *Students:* 1 (woman) full-time, 5 part-time (all women); includes 4 minority (3 Black or African American, non-Hispanic/Latino; 1 Two or more races, non-Hispanic/Latino). Average age 51. 1 applicant, 100% accepted, 1 enrolled. In 2017, 3 master's awarded. *Degree requirements:* For master's, thesis. *Entrance requirements:* For master's, minimum undergraduate GPA of 3.0. Additional exam requirements/recommendations for international students: Required—TOEFL (minimum score 500 paper-based; 80 iBT). *Application deadline:* For fall admission, 8/1 priority date for domestic students. Applications are processed on a rolling basis. Application fee: $25. Electronic applications accepted. *Expenses:* $1,094 per credit hour. *Financial support:* In 2017–18, 3 students received support. Scholarships/grants available. Financial award application deadline: 3/1; financial award applicants required to submit FAFSA. *Faculty research:* The city in history, values and their expressions, the 1960s, globalization. *Unit head:* Dr. Tim Kinsella, Director, 440-646-8389, Fax: 440-684-6088, E-mail: tkinsell@ursuline.edu. *Application contact:* Melanie Steele, Director, Graduate Admissions, 440-646-8119, Fax: 440-684-6138, E-mail: graduateadmissions@ursuline.edu.

Liberal Studies

Vanderbilt University, Program in Liberal Arts and Science, Nashville, TN 37240-1001. Offers MLAS. *Program availability:* Part-time. *Students:* 1 full-time (0 women), 34 part-time (22 women); includes 5 minority (3 Black or African American, non-Hispanic/Latino; 1 Asian, non-Hispanic/Latino; 1 Two or more races, non-Hispanic/Latino). Average age 42. 16 applicants, 75% accepted, 9 enrolled. In 2017, 12 master's awarded. *Entrance requirements:* For master's, GRE General Test. Additional exam requirements/recommendations for international students: Required—TOEFL (minimum score 570 paper-based; 88 iBT). *Application deadline:* For fall admission, 1/15 priority date for domestic students, 1/15 for international students; for spring admission, 11/15 for domestic and international students. Applications are processed on a rolling basis. *Financial support:* Institutionally sponsored loans and tuition waivers (partial) available. *Unit head:* Dr. Martin Rapisarda, Associate Dean and Director of Graduate Studies, 615-343-3140, Fax: 615-343-8702, E-mail: martin.rapisarda@vanderbilt.edu. *Application contact:* Lisa Poynter, Coordinator, 615-343-3140, Fax: 615-343-8702, E-mail: lisa.poynter@vanderbilt.edu.
Website: http://www.vanderbilt.edu/mlas/

Villanova University, Graduate School of Liberal Arts and Sciences, Graduate Liberal Studies Program, Villanova, PA 19085-1699. Offers MA. *Program availability:* Part-time, evening/weekend. *Faculty:* 4. *Students:* 8 full-time (5 women), 8 part-time (5 women); includes 3 minority (2 Black or African American, non-Hispanic/Latino; 1 Two or more races, non-Hispanic/Latino). Average age 38. 7 applicants, 100% accepted, 4 enrolled. In 2017, 4 master's awarded. *Degree requirements:* For master's, comprehensive exam. *Entrance requirements:* For master's, GRE, statement of objectives, 2 letters of recommendation, writing sample. Additional exam requirements/recommendations for international students: Required—TOEFL. *Application deadline:* For fall admission, 5/1 priority date for international students; for spring admission, 10/15 priority date for international students. Applications are processed on a rolling basis. Application fee: $50. Electronic applications accepted. *Financial support:* Research assistantships, scholarships/grants, and unspecified assistantships available. Financial award applicants required to submit FAFSA. *Unit head:* Dr. Marylu Hill, Program Director, 610-519-7325.
Website: http://www1.villanova.edu/villanova/artsci/liberalstudies.html

Virginia Polytechnic Institute and State University, VT Online, Blacksburg, VA 24061. Offers advanced transportation systems (Certificate); aerospace engineering (MS); agricultural and life sciences (MSLFS); business information systems (Graduate Certificate); career and technical education (MS); civil engineering (MS); computer engineering (M Eng, MS); decision support systems (Graduate Certificate); eLearning leadership (MA); electrical engineering (M Eng, MS); engineering administration (MEA); environmental engineering (Certificate); environmental politics and policy (Graduate Certificate); environmental sciences and engineering (MS); foundations of political analysis (Graduate Certificate); health product risk management (Graduate Certificate); industrial and systems engineering (MS); information policy and society (Graduate Certificate); information security (Graduate Certificate); information technology (MIT); instructional technology (MA); integrative STEM education (MA Ed); liberal arts (Graduate Certificate); life sciences: health product risk management (MS); natural resources (MNR, Graduate Certificate); networking (Graduate Certificate); nonprofit and nongovernmental organization management (Graduate Certificate); ocean engineering (MS); political science (MA); security studies (Graduate Certificate); software development (Graduate Certificate). *Expenses:* Tuition, state resident: full-time $15,072; part-time $718.50 per credit hour. Tuition, nonresident: full-time $28,810; part-time $1448.25 per credit hour. *Required fees:* $2741; $502 per semester. Tuition and fees vary according to course load, campus/location and program.

Wake Forest University, Graduate School of Arts and Sciences, Liberal Studies Program, Winston-Salem, NC 27109. Offers MALS. *Program availability:* Part-time. *Degree requirements:* For master's, thesis. *Entrance requirements:* Additional exam requirements/recommendations for international students: Required—TOEFL (minimum score 79 iBT). Electronic applications accepted.

Washburn University, College of Arts and Sciences, Program in Liberal Studies, Topeka, KS 66621. Offers MLS. *Program availability:* Part-time, evening/weekend. *Degree requirements:* For master's, thesis, 15 seminar hours. *Entrance requirements:* For master's, minimum GPA of 3.0 in the last 60 hours of undergraduate coursework. Additional exam requirements/recommendations for international students: Required—TOEFL (minimum score 80 iBT). *Faculty research:* European architecture/history, British cultural studies movement, American military strategy/history.

Wesleyan University, Graduate Liberal Studies Program, Middletown, CT 06459. Offers liberal arts (M Phil); liberal studies (MALS); writing (Graduate Certificate). *Program availability:* Part-time, evening/weekend. *Degree requirements:* For master's, thesis optional; for Graduate Certificate, thesis. *Entrance requirements:* For master's, statement of intent, essay, undergraduate transcripts, two letters of recommendation. Additional exam requirements/recommendations for international students: Required—TOEFL (minimum score 100 iBT), IELTS (minimum score 7). *Application deadline:* For fall admission, 7/16 for domestic students; for spring admission, 11/14 for domestic students; for summer admission, 4/15 for domestic students. Applications are processed on a rolling basis. Application fee: $100. Electronic applications accepted. *Expenses:* Contact institution. *Financial support:* Scholarships/grants available. Support available to part-time students. *Faculty research:* Interdisciplinary studies. *Unit head:* Jennifer Curran, Director, 860-685-3338, Fax: 860-685-2901, E-mail: jcurran@wesleyan.edu. *Application contact:* Sarah-Jane Ripa, Associate Director, Student Services and Outreach, 860-685-3345, Fax: 860-685-2901, E-mail: sripa@wesleyan.edu.
Website: http://www.wesleyan.edu/masters/

Western Illinois University, School of Graduate Studies, College of Arts and Sciences, Program in Liberal Arts and Sciences, Macomb, IL 61455-1390. Offers MLAS. *Program availability:* Part-time. *Degree requirements:* For master's, thesis, project, or internship. *Entrance requirements:* For master's, minimum GPA of 2.75, official transcripts, 1- to 2-page personal statement, academic paper, 3 letters of recommendation. Additional exam requirements/recommendations for international students: Required—TOEFL (minimum score 580 paper-based; 92 iBT). *Application deadline:* Applications are processed on a rolling basis. Application fee: $30. Electronic applications accepted. *Financial support:* Unspecified assistantships available. Financial award applicants required to submit FAFSA. *Unit head:* Dr. Sarah Haynes, Director, 309-298-2214. *Application contact:* Dr. Nancy Parsons, Associate Provost and Director of Graduate Studies, 309-298-1806, Fax: 309-298-2345, E-mail: grad-office@wiu.edu.
Website: http://wiu.edu/cas/liberal_arts_and_sciences/

Wichita State University, Graduate School, Fairmount College of Liberal Arts and Sciences, Interdisciplinary Program in Liberal Studies, Wichita, KS 67260. Offers MA. *Program availability:* Part-time. *Unit head:* Dr. Jeffrey Herschfield, Graduate Coordinator, 316-978-3125, E-mail: jeffrey.hershfield@wichita.edu. *Application contact:* Jordan Oleson, Admissions Coordinator, 316-978-3095, Fax: 316-978-3253, E-mail: jordan.oleson@wichita.edu.
Website: http://www.wichita.edu/mals

Winthrop University, College of Arts and Sciences, Program in Liberal Arts, Rock Hill, SC 29733. Offers MLA. *Program availability:* Part-time. *Students:* 1 (woman) full-time, 7 part-time (5 women). Average age 43. In 2017, 5 master's awarded. *Entrance requirements:* For master's, interview, minimum GPA of 3.0. Additional exam requirements/recommendations for international students: Required—TOEFL (minimum score 550 paper-based; 79 iBT), IELTS (minimum score 6). *Application deadline:* For fall admission, 7/15 priority date for domestic students; for spring admission, 12/1 for domestic students. Applications are processed on a rolling basis. Application fee: $50. Electronic applications accepted. *Financial support:* Federal Work-Study, scholarships/grants, and unspecified assistantships available. Support available to part-time students. Financial award application deadline: 2/1; financial award applicants required to submit FAFSA. *Unit head:* Dr. Siobhan Brownson, Graduate Program Director, 803-323-4572, Fax: 803-323-3012, E-mail: mla@winthrop.edu. *Application contact:* 800-411-7041, Fax: 803-323-2292, E-mail: graduatestu@winthrop.edu.
Website: http://www.winthrop.edu/cas/mla/default.aspx?id-23091

DARTMOUTH COLLEGE
Master of Arts in Liberal Studies

 For more information, visit http://petersons.to/dartmouthliberalstudies

Programs of Study

Interdisciplinary, immersive, and flexible graduate-level study—the Master of Arts in Liberal Studies (MALS) program is part of the Guarini School of Graduate and Advanced Studies at Dartmouth, which offers graduate programs in the natural sciences, social sciences, and humanities.

MALS at Dartmouth is a highly selective, inclusive, and diverse program and awards the Master of Arts degree in the following concentrations:

- Cultural Studies
- Creative Writing
- Globalization Studies
- General Liberal Studies

Students enter MALS at Dartmouth from different stages in their academic or professional careers. They come from a wide array of backgrounds and include recent college graduates, scholars, doctors, business leaders, and artists, as well as military personnel, writers, educators, and lawyers.

MALS at Dartmouth is designed for individuals who want to engage in self-directed graduate study in the liberal arts at the Ivy League level. The program affords students full access to both Dartmouth's graduate and undergraduate schools in order to pursue comprehensive, interdisciplinary study. Students create an individualized plan-of-study that significantly enhances their academic and professional credentials. During the past few years, students have received prestigious awards such as the Fulbright Fellowship, the J.B. Reynolds Scholarship, and the MacArthur Genius Grant. The unique MALS at Dartmouth interdisciplinary experience prepares graduates to advance in their chosen field, pursue doctoral programs across all disciplines, as well as gain entrance into the professional schools of law, business, and medicine.

Candidates for the MALS at Dartmouth program may attend on a full-time, part-time, or summers-only basis (for teachers and other professionals) or in a combination of these patterns. The Dartmouth College academic year operates on a four-term/quarter system. The program generally takes seven to eight terms (2 years) with full-time attendance, including thesis research and writing; students have six years from the time of entry to complete the requirements and earn their degree.

The Application Process

The academic program at Dartmouth is intensive, so applications are evaluated carefully. A student's motivation, initiative, maturity, and ability to do graduate-level work are critical. The program typically enrolls 75 to 90 students during the academic year, and approximately 100 to 120 in the summer session.

The MALS at Dartmouth Admissions Committee requires the completion of an application form, three letters of professional/academic reference, an essay, and academic transcripts; GRE scores are not required. The application is available online through a link on the MALS at Dartmouth website.

An interview is required prior to the application deadline. Skype or telephone interviews are also acceptable for individuals living outside the immediate area. Application deadlines are February 15 (for summer or fall enrollment) and July 15 (for winter or spring entry). Successful applicants must enroll during the academic year for which they were accepted into the program.

Resources and History Provide Extraordinary Access

Dartmouth College's reach and reputation as a member of the Ivy League provides students opportunities to engage with the world's leaders and intellectuals. The College's extensive facilities are available to all graduate students year-round including the College library's collection of more than a million volumes, the Hopkins Center for the Performing Arts, the Hood Museum, Alumni Gym, and numerous other facilities and services.

Dartmouth also provides many other resources for students to engage in additional areas of academic and personal interest including community activism, international and public affairs, and intellectual forums with guest speakers, debates, discussion groups, and student organizations. Some of these resources include the Montgomery Fellows Program, the Tucker Center, the John Sloan Dickey Center for International Understanding, the Nelson A. Rockefeller Center for Public Policy, the Ethics Institute, the Leslie Center for the Humanities, and the Gender Research Institute at Dartmouth—among many others.

Cost of Study

For 2018–19, full-time tuition (2 credits) is $12,482 per term (3 months), plus activity and document fees of $110. Room and board are estimated at $6,950 per term, while books and supplies are $350.

Faculty

For details on the extraordinary faculty members of MALS at Dartmouth, visit http://mals.dartmouth.edu/people.

Rural Setting Balances the Fast Pace of Academic Life

Dartmouth College is located in Hanover, New Hampshire, a small New England town dating back to a few years before the college's founding in 1769. Situated in the Upper Valley of the Connecticut River between the White Mountains of New Hampshire and the Green Mountains of Vermont, Hanover combines the advantages of a spectacular rural setting with the extraordinary resources of a university.

The Dartmouth College campus is approximately 2.5 hours by car from Boston and 3 hours from Montreal. Surrounding airports include Lebanon, Manchester (75 miles), Burlington (96 miles), Boston-Logan (126 miles) and Bradley International (150 miles) airports. There are Amtrak and Greyhound stations approximately 15 minutes from campus in White River Junction, Vermont. The Dartmouth Coach runs daily from Logan Airport and South Station to Hanover.

Correspondence and Information

Master of Arts in Liberal Studies
Dartmouth College
116 Wentworth Hall, HB 6092
Hanover, New Hampshire 03755
United States
Phone: 603-646-3592
E-mail: mals.admissions@dartmouth.edu
Website: http://mals.dartmouth.edu/

MALS at Dartmouth College in Hanover, NH combines the advantages of a spectacular rural setting with the extraordinary resources of a university.

Section 9
Language and Literature

This section contains a directory of institutions offering graduate work in language and literature. Additional information about programs listed in the directory may be obtained by writing directly to the dean of a graduate school or chair of a department at the address given in the directory.

For programs offering related work, see also in this book *Area and Cultural Studies, Communication and Media, Political Science and International Affairs,* and *Sociology, Anthropology, and Archaeology.* In another guide in this series:

Graduate Programs in Business, Education, Information Studies, Law & Social Work

See *Special Focus* and *Subject Areas*

CONTENTS

Program Directories

Featured Schools: Displays and Close-Ups

See also:

Asian Languages

Cornell University, Graduate School, Graduate Fields of Arts and Sciences, Field of Linguistics, Ithaca, NY 14853. Offers applied linguistics (MA, PhD); East Asian linguistics (MA, PhD); English linguistics (MA, PhD); general linguistics (MA, PhD); Germanic linguistics (MA, PhD); Indo-European linguistics (MA, PhD); phonetics (MA, PhD); phonological theory (MA, PhD); Romance linguistics (MA, PhD); second language acquisition (MA, PhD); semantics (MA, PhD); Slavic linguistics (MA, PhD); sociolinguistics (MA, PhD); South Asian linguistics (MA, PhD); Southeast Asian linguistics (MA, PhD); syntactic theory (MA, PhD). Terminal master's awarded for partial completion of doctoral program. *Degree requirements:* For master's, one foreign language, thesis; for doctorate, one foreign language, comprehensive exam, thesis/dissertation. *Entrance requirements:* For master's and doctorate, GRE General Test, 2 letters of recommendation. Additional exam requirements/recommendations for international students: Required—TOEFL (minimum score 600 paper-based; 77 iBT). Electronic applications accepted. *Faculty research:* Phonology and phonetics, syntax and semantics, historical linguistics, philosophy of language, language acquisition.

Harvard University, Graduate School of Arts and Sciences, Department of East Asian Languages and Civilizations, Cambridge, MA 02138. Offers Chinese (PhD); Japanese (PhD); Korean (PhD); Mongolian (PhD); Vietnamese (PhD). Terminal master's awarded for partial completion of doctoral program. *Degree requirements:* For doctorate, 3 foreign languages, thesis/dissertation, general exams. *Entrance requirements:* For doctorate, GRE General Test. Additional exam requirements/recommendations for international students: Required—TOEFL. *Faculty research:* Central Asian literature, religion, and premodern history.

Harvard University, Graduate School of Arts and Sciences, Department of Sanskrit and Indian Studies, Cambridge, MA 02138. Offers Indian philosophy (AM, PhD); Pali (AM, PhD); Sanskrit (AM, PhD); Tibetan (AM, PhD); Urdu (AM, PhD). Terminal master's awarded for partial completion of doctoral program. *Degree requirements:* For master's, 3 foreign languages; for doctorate, 3 foreign languages, thesis/dissertation. *Entrance requirements:* For master's, GRE General Test; for doctorate, GRE General Test, proficiency in French and German. Additional exam requirements/recommendations for international students: Required—TOEFL.

Indiana University Bloomington, University Graduate School, College of Arts and Sciences, School of Global and International Studies, Department of East Asian Languages and Cultures, Bloomington, IN 47408. Offers Chinese (MA, PhD); Chinese language pedagogy (MA); East Asian studies (MA); Japanese (MA, PhD); Japanese language pedagogy (MA). *Program availability:* Part-time. *Degree requirements:* For master's, one foreign language, thesis; for doctorate, 2 foreign languages, comprehensive exam, thesis/dissertation. *Entrance requirements:* Additional exam requirements/recommendations for international students: Required—TOEFL (minimum score 93 iBT). Electronic applications accepted. *Faculty research:* Modern East Asian history; politics and society; traditional Chinese thought and society; medieval and premodern Japanese history, literature and society; modern Chinese and Japanese film and literature; Chinese, Japanese, Korean language and linguistics.

The Ohio State University, Graduate School, College of Arts and Sciences, Division of Arts and Humanities, Department of East Asian Languages and Literatures, Columbus, OH 43210. Offers Chinese (MA, PhD); Japanese (MA, PhD). *Faculty:* 19. *Students:* 50 full-time (32 women), 4 part-time (2 women); includes 5 minority (all Asian, non-Hispanic/Latino), 24 international. Average age 30. In 2017, 9 master's, 6 doctorates awarded. Terminal master's awarded for partial completion of doctoral program. *Entrance requirements:* For master's and doctorate, GRE General Test (if applying for financial aid). Additional exam requirements/recommendations for international students: Required—TOEFL (minimum score 577 paper-based; 90 iBT); Recommended—IELTS (minimum score 7.5). *Application deadline:* For fall admission, 11/30 priority date for domestic and international students; for spring admission, 3/1 for domestic students, 2/1 for international students. Applications are processed on a rolling basis. Application fee: $60 ($70 for international students). Electronic applications accepted. *Financial support:* Fellowships, research assistantships, teaching assistantships, Federal Work-Study, institutionally sponsored loans, and unspecified assistantships available. Support available to part-time students. *Unit head:* Dr. Mark Bender, Chair and Professor, 614-688-5737, E-mail: bender.4@osu.edu. *Application contact:* Graduate and Professional Admissions, 614-292-9444, Fax: 614-292-3895, E-mail: gpadmissions@osu.edu.
Website: http://deall.osu.edu/

St. John's College, Graduate Institute in Liberal Education, Program in Eastern Classics, Santa Fe, NM 87505. Offers MA. *Program availability:* Part-time, evening/weekend. *Entrance requirements:* For master's, 2 letters of recommendation. Additional exam requirements/recommendations for international students: Required—TOEFL, TWE. *Expenses:* Contact institution.

Stanford University, School of Humanities and Sciences, Department of East Asian Languages and Cultures, Stanford, CA 94305-2004. Offers Chinese (MA, PhD); Japanese (MA, PhD). Terminal master's awarded for partial completion of doctoral program. *Degree requirements:* For master's, one foreign language, thesis or an annotated translation of a literary or historical text; for doctorate, 2 foreign languages, thesis/dissertation, field exams. *Entrance requirements:* For master's and doctorate, GRE General Test. Additional exam requirements/recommendations for international students: Required—TOEFL. Electronic applications accepted. *Expenses: Tuition:* Full-time $48,987; part-time $10,620 per quarter. One-time fee: $400. Tuition and fees vary according to program.

University of California, Berkeley, Graduate Division, College of Letters and Science, Department of South and Southeast Asian Studies, Berkeley, CA 94720-1500. Offers Hindi (MA, PhD); Indonesian (MA, PhD); Sanskrit (MA, PhD); Tamil (MA, PhD). Terminal master's awarded for partial completion of doctoral program. *Degree requirements:* For master's, 2 foreign languages, thesis; for doctorate, 2 foreign languages, thesis/dissertation, oral qualifying exam. *Entrance requirements:* For master's and doctorate, GRE General Test, minimum GPA of 3.0, 3 letters of recommendation. Electronic applications accepted.

University of California, Irvine, School of Humanities, Department of East Asian Languages and Literatures, Irvine, CA 92697. Offers Chinese (MA, PhD); East Asian languages and literatures (MA, PhD); Japanese (MA, PhD). *Students:* 9 full-time (7 women), 3 part-time (2 women); includes 4 minority (all Asian, non-Hispanic/Latino), 4 international. Average age 31. 46 applicants, 9% accepted, 2 enrolled. In 2017, 2 doctorates awarded. *Entrance requirements:* For master's and doctorate, GRE General Test, minimum GPA of 3.0. Additional exam requirements/recommendations for international students: Required—TOEFL (minimum score 550 paper-based). *Application deadline:* For fall admission, 1/15 priority date for domestic students, 1/15 for international students. Application fee: $105 ($125 for international students). Electronic applications accepted. *Financial support:* Fellowships with tuition reimbursements, research assistantships with full tuition reimbursements, teaching assistantships with partial tuition reimbursements, institutionally sponsored loans, traineeships, health care benefits, and unspecified assistantships available. Financial award application deadline: 3/1; financial award applicants required to submit FAFSA. *Faculty research:* Chinese, Japanese, and Korean literature and culture; language and textual analysis; historical, social, and cultural dimensions of literary study. *Unit head:* Michael A. Fuller, Chair, 949-824-2802 Ext. 2227, Fax: 949-824-3248, E-mail: mafuller@uci.edu. *Application contact:* Hu Ying, Graduate Faculty Advisor, 949-824-6312, Fax: 949-824-3248, E-mail: huying@uci.edu.
Website: http://www.hnet.uci.edu/eastasian/

University of California, Los Angeles, Graduate Division, College of Letters and Science, Department of Asian Languages and Cultures, Los Angeles, CA 90095. Offers MA, PhD. Terminal master's awarded for partial completion of doctoral program. *Degree requirements:* For master's, one foreign language, comprehensive exam or thesis; for doctorate, 2 foreign languages, thesis/dissertation, oral and written qualifying exams. *Entrance requirements:* For master's, GRE General Test, bachelor's degree; minimum undergraduate GPA of 3.0 (or its equivalent if letter grade system not used); writing sample; for doctorate, GRE General Test, master's degree; minimum undergraduate GPA of 3.0 (or its equivalent if letter grade system not used); writing sample. Additional exam requirements/recommendations for international students: Required—TOEFL. Electronic applications accepted.

University of California, Santa Barbara, Graduate Division, College of Letters and Sciences, Division of Humanities and Fine Arts, Department of East Asian Languages and Cultural Studies, Santa Barbara, CA 93106-7075. Offers applied linguistics (PhD); East Asian languages and cultural studies (MA); translation studies (PhD). *Degree requirements:* For master's, one foreign language, comprehensive exam (for some programs), thesis (for some programs); for doctorate, 2 foreign languages, thesis/dissertation, methodology. *Entrance requirements:* For master's and doctorate, GRE General Test. Additional exam requirements/recommendations for international students: Required—TOEFL (minimum score 550 paper-based; 80 iBT), IELTS (minimum score 7). Electronic applications accepted. *Faculty research:* Chinese literature, Chinese film, Japanese society, Japanese literature, East Asian cultural studies.

University of California, Santa Barbara, Graduate Division, College of Letters and Sciences, Division of Humanities and Fine Arts, Program in Comparative Literature, Santa Barbara, CA 93106-4130. Offers comparative literature (PhD); East Asian literatures (PhD); feminist studies (PhD); French (PhD); global studies (PhD); translation studies (PhD); MA/PhD. *Degree requirements:* For doctorate, 2 foreign languages, comprehensive exam, thesis/dissertation. *Entrance requirements:* For doctorate, GRE. Additional exam requirements/recommendations for international students: Required—TOEFL (minimum score 550 paper-based; 80 iBT), IELTS (minimum score 7). Electronic applications accepted. *Faculty research:* Comparative literary studies in global context, critical theory, translation studies, media technological studies, trauma studies.

University of Chicago, Division of the Humanities, Department of East Asian Languages and Civilizations, Chicago, IL 60637. Offers PhD. *Students:* 28 full-time (17 women); includes 5 minority (4 Asian, non-Hispanic/Latino; 1 Two or more races, non-Hispanic/Latino), 16 international. Average age 30. 98 applicants, 7% accepted, 3 enrolled. In 2017, 6 doctorates awarded. Terminal master's awarded for partial completion of doctoral program. *Degree requirements:* For doctorate, 2 foreign languages, comprehensive exam, thesis/dissertation, qualifying exam. *Entrance requirements:* For doctorate, GRE General Test, 15-20 page writing sample, statement of purpose, 3 letters of recommendation, transcripts for all previous degrees and institutions attended. Additional exam requirements/recommendations for international students: Required—TOEFL (minimum score 104 iBT), IELTS (minimum score 7). *Application deadline:* For fall admission, 12/15 for domestic and international students. Application fee: $90. Electronic applications accepted. *Financial support:* In 2017–18, fellowships with full tuition reimbursements (averaging $27,000 per year) were awarded; teaching assistantships with full tuition reimbursements, Federal Work-Study, institutionally sponsored loans, scholarships/grants, traineeships, and health care benefits also available. Financial award application deadline: 12/15. *Faculty research:* East Asian literature, material culture, religious and intellectual history, paleography of early China, performance studies. *Unit head:* Dr. Jacob Eyferth, Chair, 773-834-1323, E-mail: ealc@uchicago.edu. *Application contact:* Michael Beetley, Assistant Dean of Students, Admissions and Fellowships, 773-702-1552, Fax: 773-834-9148, E-mail: humanitiesadmissions@uchicago.edu.
Website: http://ealc.uchicago.edu/

University of Chicago, Division of the Humanities, Department of South Asian Languages and Civilizations, Chicago, IL 60637. Offers South Asian languages and civilizations (PhD), including Bengali, Hindi, Sanskrit, Tamil, Urdu. *Students:* 33 full-time (17 women); includes 5 minority (1 Black or African American, non-Hispanic/Latino; 3 Asian, non-Hispanic/Latino; 1 Two or more races, non-Hispanic/Latino), 19 international. Average age 31. 34 applicants, 15% accepted, 4 enrolled. In 2017, 2 doctorates awarded. Terminal master's awarded for partial completion of doctoral program. *Degree requirements:* For doctorate, 3 foreign languages, comprehensive exam, thesis/dissertation. *Entrance requirements:* For doctorate, GRE General Test, 15-20 page writing sample, statement of purpose, 3 letters of recommendation, transcripts for all previous degrees and institutions attended. Additional exam requirements/recommendations for international students: Required—TOEFL (minimum score 104 iBT), IELTS (minimum score 7). *Application deadline:* For fall admission, 12/15 for domestic and international students. Application fee: $90. Electronic applications accepted. *Financial support:* In 2017–18, fellowships with full tuition reimbursements (averaging $27,000 per year) were awarded; teaching assistantships with full tuition reimbursements, Federal Work-Study, institutionally sponsored loans, scholarships/grants, and health care benefits also available. Financial award application deadline: 12/15. *Unit head:* Gary Tubb, Chair, 773-834-2825, E-mail: salc@lists.uchicago.edu. *Application contact:* Michael Beetley, Assistant Dean of Students, Admissions and Fellowships, 773-702-1552, Fax: 773-834-9148, E-mail: humanitiesadmissions@uchicago.edu.
Website: http://salc.uchicago.edu

University of Hawaii at Manoa, Office of Graduate Education, College of Languages, Linguistics and Literature, Department of East Asian Languages and Literatures, Program in Korean, Honolulu, HI 96822. Offers MA, PhD. *Program availability:* Part-time. *Degree requirements:* For master's, 2 foreign languages, thesis optional; for doctorate, 2 foreign languages, comprehensive exam, thesis/dissertation. *Entrance requirements:* For master's and doctorate, GRE General Test. Additional exam

requirements/recommendations for international students: Required—TOEFL (minimum score 560 paper-based; 83 iBT), IELTS (minimum score 5).

University of Illinois at Urbana–Champaign, Graduate College, College of Liberal Arts and Sciences, School of Literatures, Cultures and Linguistics, Department of East Asian Languages and Cultures, Champaign, IL 61820. Offers East Asian languages and cultures (PhD); East Asian studies (MA).

The University of Iowa, Graduate College, College of Liberal Arts and Sciences, Program in Asian Civilizations, Iowa City, IA 52242-1316. Offers Chinese (MA); Hindi (MA); Sanskrit (MA); South Asian studies (MA). *Degree requirements:* For master's, thesis optional, exam. *Entrance requirements:* For master's, GRE General Test, minimum GPA of 3.0. Additional exam requirements/recommendations for international students: Required—TOEFL (minimum score 590 paper-based; 96 iBT). Electronic applications accepted.

The University of Kansas, Graduate Studies, College of Liberal Arts and Sciences, Department of East Asian Languages and Cultures, Lawrence, KS 66045. Offers MA, Graduate Certificate. *Program availability:* Part-time. *Students:* 3 full-time (1 woman); includes 1 minority (Two or more races, non-Hispanic/Latino), 1 international. Average age 26. 3 applicants, 67% accepted, 1 enrolled. In 2017, 3 master's, 2 other advanced degrees awarded. *Entrance requirements:* For master's, GRE, current curriculum vitae, statement of purpose explaining academic objectives, writing sample that demonstrates writing skills and basic research capacity, three letters of recommendation, transcripts. Additional exam requirements/recommendations for international students: Required—TOEFL. *Application deadline:* For fall admission, 2/1 priority date for domestic and international students. Application fee: $65 ($85 for international students). Electronic applications accepted. *Financial support:* Fellowships, teaching assistantships, and unspecified assistantships available. *Faculty research:* Gender relations in literature, ancient Chinese law, visual culture of modern Japan, Japanese language pedagogy, Chinese paleography, Korean shamanism, folklore, traditional Chinese and Japanese literature, Chinese linguistics and language pedagogy. *Unit head:* Dr. Maggie Childs, Chair, 785-864-9128, E-mail: mgchilds@ku.edu. *Application contact:* Cari Ann Kreienhop, Graduate Programs and Admissions Contact, 785-864-3665, E-mail: ckreienhop@ku.edu.
Website: http://ealc.ku.edu/

University of Michigan, Rackham Graduate School, College of Literature, Science, and the Arts, Department of Asian Languages and Cultures, Ann Arbor, MI 48104. Offers PhD. *Faculty:* 26 full-time (10 women). *Students:* 18 full-time (11 women); includes 4 minority (3 Asian, non-Hispanic/Latino; 1 Two or more races, non-Hispanic/Latino), 6 international. Average age 32. 79 applicants, 9% accepted, 3 enrolled. In 2017, 3 doctorates awarded. Terminal master's awarded for partial completion of doctoral program. *Degree requirements:* For doctorate, 2 foreign languages, comprehensive exam, thesis/dissertation, preliminary exams, oral defense of dissertation. *Entrance requirements:* Additional exam requirements/recommendations for international students: Required—TOEFL (minimum score 560 paper-based; 84 iBT), IELTS (minimum score 6.5). *Application deadline:* For fall admission, 12/1 for domestic and international students. Application fee: $75 ($90 for international students). Electronic applications accepted. *Expenses:* Tuition, state resident: full-time $22,368; part-time $1201 per credit hour. Tuition, nonresident: full-time $45,156; part-time $2467 per credit hour. *Required fees:* $376 per term. Tuition and fees vary according to course load, degree level and program. *Financial support:* In 2017–18, 18 students received support. Fellowships with full tuition reimbursements available, teaching assistantships with full tuition reimbursements available, scholarships/grants, health care benefits, and spring/summer stipends available. Financial award application deadline: 12/1. *Faculty research:* Literature, religion, visual culture, history, modern culture, languages. *Unit head:* Prof. Donald S. Lopez, Jr., Chair, 734-615-6571, Fax: 734-647-0157, E-mail: umalc@umich.edu. *Application contact:* ALC Student Services, 734-734-8286, Fax: 734-647-0157, E-mail: alc-gradservices@umich.edu.
Website: http://www.lsa.umich.edu/asian/

University of Minnesota, Twin Cities Campus, Graduate School, College of Liberal Arts, Department of Asian Languages and Literatures, Minneapolis, MN 55455-0213. Offers Asian literatures, cultures, and media (PhD). *Degree requirements:* For doctorate, comprehensive exam, thesis/dissertation. *Entrance requirements:* For doctorate, GRE, 3 letters of recommendation. Additional exam requirements/recommendations for international students: Required—TOEFL (minimum score 550 paper-based), IELTS (minimum score 6.5). Electronic applications accepted. *Faculty research:* Gender studies, post-colonial theory, poetics and poetic theory, film studies, post modernist thought.

University of Oregon, Graduate School, College of Arts and Sciences, Department of East Asian Languages and Literature, Eugene, OR 97403. Offers Chinese (MA, PhD); Japanese (MA, PhD). *Entrance requirements:* Additional exam requirements/recommendations for international students: Required—TOEFL. *Faculty research:* Linguistics, pedagogy.

University of Southern California, Graduate School, Dana and David Dornsife College of Letters, Arts and Sciences, Department of East Asian Languages and Cultures, Los Angeles, CA 90089. Offers classical Chinese literature (MA, PhD); classical Japanese literature (MA, PhD); linguistics (MA, PhD); modern Chinese literature (MA, PhD); modern Japanese literature (MA, PhD); modern Korean literature (MA, PhD). *Degree requirements:* For master's, thesis; for doctorate, 2 foreign languages, comprehensive exam, thesis/dissertation. *Entrance requirements:* For master's and doctorate, GRE, BA in relevant field. Additional exam requirements/recommendations for international students: Required—TOEFL. Electronic applications accepted. *Faculty research:* Gender, visual studies, multimedia, ecocriticism, second language acquisition.

University of Southern California, Graduate School, Dana and David Dornsife College of Letters, Arts and Sciences, Department of Linguistics, Los Angeles, CA 90089. Offers East Asian linguistics (PhD); Hispanic linguistics (PhD); linguistics (PhD); Slavic linguistics (PhD). *Degree requirements:* For doctorate, comprehensive exam, thesis/dissertation. *Entrance requirements:* For doctorate, GRE. Additional exam requirements/recommendations for international students: Required—TOEFL (minimum score 100 iBT). Electronic applications accepted. *Faculty research:* Syntax, phonology, phonetics, semantics, sociolinguistics, psycholinguistics.

The University of Texas at Austin, Graduate School, College of Liberal Arts, Department of Asian Studies, Austin, TX 78712-1111. Offers Asian cultures and languages (MA, PhD); Asian studies (MA). *Program availability:* Part-time. *Degree requirements:* For master's, thesis; for doctorate, 3 foreign languages, thesis/dissertation. *Entrance requirements:* For master's and doctorate, GRE General Test. Electronic applications accepted. *Faculty research:* Modern Taiwanese fiction, modern Japanese literature, religious studies in South Asia during classical period.

University of Washington, Graduate School, College of Arts and Sciences, Department of Asian Languages and Literature, Seattle, WA 98195. Offers Buddhist studies (MA, PhD); Chinese language and literature (MA, PhD); Japanese language and literature (MA, PhD); Korean language and literature (MA, PhD); South Asian language and literature (MA, PhD). *Degree requirements:* For master's, 2 foreign languages, general exam, thesis or 2 research papers; for doctorate, 3 foreign languages, thesis/dissertation, general exam. *Entrance requirements:* For master's, GRE, minimum GPA of 3.0; for doctorate, GRE, master's degree in related field, minimum GPA of 3.0. Additional exam requirements/recommendations for international students: Required—TOEFL. Electronic applications accepted. *Faculty research:* Textual, linguistic, philological, and literary study of languages and literatures of Asia.

University of Wisconsin–Madison, Graduate School, College of Letters and Science, Department of Languages and Cultures of Asia, Madison, WI 53706-1380. Offers civilizations and cultures (PhD); languages and cultures of Asia (MA); languages and literatures (PhD); religions of Asia (PhD). *Program availability:* Part-time. Terminal master's awarded for partial completion of doctoral program. *Degree requirements:* For master's, one foreign language, thesis or alternative; for doctorate, 2 foreign languages, thesis/dissertation. *Entrance requirements:* For master's, minimum GPA of 3.0; for doctorate, minimum GPA of 3.25, master's degree. Electronic applications accepted. *Faculty research:* Literature, folklore, religion.

Washington University in St. Louis, The Graduate School, Department of East Asian Languages and Cultures, St. Louis, MO 63130-4899. Offers Chinese (MA); Chinese and comparative literature (PhD); Chinese language and literature (PhD); East Asian studies (MA); Japanese (MA); Japanese and comparative literature (PhD); Japanese language and literature (PhD). Terminal master's awarded for partial completion of doctoral program. *Degree requirements:* For master's, thesis optional; for doctorate, thesis/dissertation. *Entrance requirements:* For master's and doctorate, GRE General Test. Additional exam requirements/recommendations for international students: Required—TOEFL. Electronic applications accepted. *Faculty research:* Chinese; Japanese; Chinese fiction, theater, poetry, modern literature; Japanese modern and classical fiction, translation theory.

Yale University, Graduate School of Arts and Sciences, Department of East Asian Languages and Literatures, New Haven, CT 06520. Offers East Asian languages and literatures (PhD); East Asian languages and literatures and film studies (PhD). *Degree requirements:* For doctorate, 2 foreign languages, thesis/dissertation. *Entrance requirements:* For doctorate, GRE General Test.

Celtic Languages

Harvard University, Graduate School of Arts and Sciences, Department of Celtic Languages and Literatures, Cambridge, MA 02138. Offers Irish (PhD); Welsh (PhD). *Degree requirements:* For doctorate, thesis/dissertation, proficiency in 2 Celtic languages; reading knowledge of French, German, and Latin. *Entrance requirements:* For doctorate, GRE General Test. Additional exam requirements/recommendations for international students: Required—TOEFL.

Chinese

Arizona State University at the Tempe campus, College of Liberal Arts and Sciences, School of International Letters and Cultures, Program in Chinese, Tempe, AZ 85287-0202. Offers Asian languages and civilizations: Chinese (MA); Chinese (PhD). *Program availability:* Part-time, evening/weekend. Terminal master's awarded for partial completion of doctoral program. *Degree requirements:* For master's, thesis, oral defense, interactive Program of Study (iPOS) submitted no later than beginning of third semester of study; for doctorate, comprehensive exam, thesis/dissertation, interactive Program of Study (iPOS) submitted before completing 50 percent of required credit hours. *Entrance requirements:* For master's, GRE, minimum GPA of 3.0 in the last two years of work leading to the bachelor's degree, BA in Chinese studies (preferred), personal statement, writing sample, 3 letters of recommendation; for doctorate, GRE, minimum GPA of 3.5 in the last two years of work leading to the bachelor's degree, completion of 3 years of modern Chinese and 1 year of classical Chinese, personal statement, writing sample, 3 letters of recommendation. Additional exam requirements/recommendations for international students: Required—TOEFL (minimum score 550 paper-based; 83 iBT), IELTS (minimum score 6.5). Electronic applications accepted.

Brandeis University, Graduate School of Arts and Sciences, Program in Teaching Chinese Language and Culture, Waltham, MA 02454-9110. Offers MA. *Students:* 5 full-time (all women), all international. Average age 24. 15 applicants, 80% accepted, 12 enrolled. In 2017, 6 master's awarded. *Degree requirements:* For master's, one foreign language. *Entrance requirements:* For master's, transcripts, letters of recommendation, resume, video of teaching in the classroom, statement of purpose. Additional exam requirements/recommendations for international students: Required—PTE (minimum score 68), TOEFL (minimum score 600 paper-based, 100 iBT) or IELTS (7). *Application deadline:* For fall admission, 1/15 priority date for domestic students. Applications are processed on a rolling basis. Application fee: $75. Electronic applications accepted.

Chinese

Expenses: Tuition: Full-time $48,720. *Required fees:* $88. Tuition and fees vary according to course load, degree level, program and student level. *Financial support:* In 2017–18, 2 students received support, including 4 teaching assistantships (averaging $3,200 per year); scholarships/grants also available. Financial award application deadline: 4/15; financial award applicants required to submit FAFSA. *Unit head:* Dr. Yu Feng, Director of Graduate Studies, 781-736-2961, E-mail: yfeng@brandeis.edu. Website: http://www.brandeis.edu/gsas/programs/chinese.html

DePaul University, College of Liberal Arts and Social Sciences, Chicago, IL 60614. Offers Arabic (MA); Chinese (MA); critical ethnic studies (MA); English (MA); French (MA); German (MA); history (MA); interdisciplinary studies (MA, MS); international public service (MS); international studies (MA); Italian (MA); Japanese (MA); liberal studies (MA); nonprofit management (MNM); public administration (MPA); public health (MPH); public policy (MPP); public service management (MS); refugee and forced migration studies (MS); social work (MSW); sociology (MA); Spanish (MA); sustainable urban development (MA); women's and gender studies (MA); writing and publishing (MA); writing, rhetoric and discourse (MA); MA/PhD. *Program availability:* Part-time, evening/weekend, online learning. Terminal master's awarded for partial completion of doctoral program. *Degree requirements:* For master's, variable foreign language requirement, comprehensive exam (for some programs), thesis (for some programs). *Application deadline:* Applications are processed on a rolling basis. Application fee: $40. Electronic applications accepted. *Financial support:* Applicants required to submit FAFSA. *Unit head:* Dr. Guillermo Vasquez de Velasco, Dean, 773-325-7305. *Application contact:* Ann Spittle, Director of Graduate Admission, 773-325-8369, Fax: 312-476-3244, E-mail: graddepaul@depaul.edu.
Website: http://las.depaul.edu/

Harvard University, Graduate School of Arts and Sciences, Department of East Asian Languages and Civilizations, Cambridge, MA 02138. Offers Chinese (PhD); Japanese (PhD); Korean (PhD); Mongolian (PhD); Vietnamese (PhD). Terminal master's awarded for partial completion of doctoral program. *Degree requirements:* For doctorate, 3 foreign languages, thesis/dissertation, general exams. *Entrance requirements:* For doctorate, GRE General Test. Additional exam requirements/recommendations for international students: Required—TOEFL. *Faculty research:* Central Asian literature, religion, and premodern history.

Hofstra University, School of Education, Programs in Teacher Education, Hempstead, NY 11549. Offers bilingual education (MA); bilingual extension (Advanced Certificate), including education/speech language pathology, intensive teacher institute; business education (MS Ed); curriculum studies (MS Ed); early childhood and childhood education (MS Ed); early childhood education (MA, MS Ed); educational technology (Advanced Certificate); elementary education (MA, MS Ed), including science, technology, engineering, and mathematics (STEM) (MA); English education (MS Ed); family and consumer science (MS Ed); fine arts and music education (Advanced Certificate); fine arts education (MS Ed); foreign language and TESOL (MS Ed); foreign language education (MA, MS Ed), including Arabic (MS Ed), biology, chemistry, Chinese (MS Ed), earth science, French, German, Italian (MS Ed), Mandarin (MS Ed), physics, Russian, Spanish; foundations of education (Advanced Certificate), including grades 5-6, grades 7-9; languages other than English and teaching English as a second language (MA); learning and teaching (Ed D), including applied linguistics, art education, arts and humanities, early childhood education, English education, human development, math education, math, science, and technology, multicultural education, physical education, science education, social studies education, special education; mathematics education (MA, MS Ed); music education (MA, MS Ed); science education (MA), including biology (MA, MS Ed), chemistry (MA, MS Ed), earth science (MA, MS Ed), physics (MA, MS Ed); secondary education (Advanced Certificate); social studies education (MA, MS Ed); teaching languages other than English and TESOL (MS Ed); technology for learning (MA); TESOL (MS Ed, Advanced Certificate); TESOL with specialization in STEM (MA); work based learning extension (Advanced Certificate). *Program availability:* Part-time, evening/weekend, blended/hybrid learning. *Students:* 119 full-time (83 women), 124 part-time (90 women); includes 54 minority (15 Black or African American, non-Hispanic/Latino; 9 Asian, non-Hispanic/Latino; 29 Hispanic/Latino; 1 Native Hawaiian or other Pacific Islander, non-Hispanic/Latino), 12 international. Average age 29. 205 applicants, 88% accepted, 93 enrolled. In 2017, 103 master's, 4 doctorates, 32 other advanced degrees awarded. *Degree requirements:* For master's, comprehensive exam, thesis (for some programs), exit project, student teaching, fieldwork, electronic portfolio, curriculum project, minimum GPA of 3.0; for doctorate, thesis/dissertation; for Advanced Certificate, 3 foreign languages, comprehensive exam (for some programs), thesis project. *Entrance requirements:* For master's, GRE, 2 letters of recommendation, portfolio, teacher certification (MA), interview, essay; for doctorate, GMAT, GRE, LSAT, or MAT; for Advanced Certificate, 2 letters of recommendation, essay, interview and/or portfolio, teaching certificate. Additional exam requirements/recommendations for international students: Required—TOEFL (minimum score 550 paper-based; 80 iBT). *Application deadline:* Applications are processed on a rolling basis. Application fee: $75. Electronic applications accepted. *Expenses: Tuition:* Full-time $1292. *Required fees:* $970. Tuition and fees vary according to program. *Financial support:* In 2017–18, 112 students received support, including 56 fellowships with full and partial tuition reimbursements available (averaging $4,998 per year), 2 research assistantships with full and partial tuition reimbursements available (averaging $8,753 per year); career-related internships or fieldwork, Federal Work-Study, institutionally sponsored loans, scholarships/grants, traineeships, tuition waivers (full and partial), and unspecified assistantships also available. Support available to part-time students. Financial award applicants required to submit FAFSA. *Faculty research:* Educational interventions that foster critical-thinking skills; teachers' attitudes about professional development; threats to teacher quality. *Unit head:* Dr. Eustace Thompson, Chairperson, 516-463-5749, Fax: 516-463-6275, E-mail: eustace.g.thompson@hofstra.edu. *Application contact:* Sunil Samuel, Assistant Vice President of Admissions, 516-463-4723, Fax: 516-463-4664, E-mail: graduateadmission@hofstra.edu.
Website: http://www.hofstra.edu/education/

Hunter College of the City University of New York, Graduate School, School of Arts and Sciences, Department of Classical and Oriental Studies, Program in Teaching Chinese, New York, NY 10065-5085. Offers MA.

Indiana University Bloomington, University Graduate School, College of Arts and Sciences, School of Global and International Studies, Department of East Asian Languages and Cultures, Bloomington, IN 47408. Offers Chinese (MA, PhD); Chinese language pedagogy (MA); East Asian studies (MA); Japanese (MA, PhD); Japanese language pedagogy (MA). *Program availability:* Part-time. *Degree requirements:* For master's, one foreign language, thesis; for doctorate, 2 foreign languages, comprehensive exam, thesis/dissertation. *Entrance requirements:* Additional exam requirements/recommendations for international students: Required—TOEFL (minimum score 93 iBT). Electronic applications accepted. *Faculty research:* Modern East Asian history; politics and society; traditional Chinese thought and society; medieval and premodern Japanese history, literature and society; modern Chinese and Japanese film and literature; Chinese, Japanese, Korean language and linguistics.

Middlebury College, Language Schools, Chinese School, Middlebury, VT 05753-6002. Offers MA. *Degree requirements:* For master's, one foreign language, teaching

practicum. *Entrance requirements:* For master's, placement test, 3 letters of recommendation, writing sample, curriculum vitae, official transcripts of undergraduate coursework. Additional exam requirements/recommendations for international students: Required—TOEFL (minimum score 600 paper-based; 100 iBT), IELTS (minimum score 7.5). *Application deadline:* Applications are processed on a rolling basis. Application fee: $75. Electronic applications accepted. *Expenses:* Contact institution. *Financial support:* Fellowships and scholarships/grants available. Financial award application deadline: 3/15; financial award applicants required to submit FAFSA. *Unit head:* Dr. Jianhua Bai, Director, 802-443-5520, Fax: 802-443-2075, E-mail: jbai@middlebury.edu. *Application contact:* Mimi Clark, Coordinator, 802-443-5520, Fax: 802-443-2075, E-mail: chineseschool@middlebury.edu.
Website: http://www.middlebury.edu/ls/grad_programs/chinese

New York University, Steinhardt School of Culture, Education, and Human Development, Department of Teaching and Learning, Program in Multilingual/Multicultural Studies, New York, NY 10012. Offers bilingual education (MA, PhD, Advanced Certificate); foreign language education (MA); teaching English to speakers of other languages (MA, PhD); teaching foreign languages, 7-12 (MA), including Chinese, French, Italian, Japanese, Spanish; teaching French as a foreign language (MA), including teaching English to speakers of other languages; teaching Spanish as a foreign language (MA), including teaching English to speakers of other languages. MA in teaching English to speakers of other languages also offered in collaboration with NYU Shanghai. *Accreditation:* TEAC. *Program availability:* Part-time, evening/weekend. *Students:* Average age 29. 431 applicants, 61% accepted, 92 enrolled. In 2017, 121 master's, 1 doctorate, 2 other advanced degrees awarded. *Entrance requirements:* For doctorate, GRE General Test, interview; for Advanced Certificate, master's degree. Additional exam requirements/recommendations for international students: Required—TOEFL (minimum score 100 iBT). *Application deadline:* For fall admission, 12/1 priority date for domestic and international students; for spring admission, 10/1 for domestic and international students. Applications are processed on a rolling basis. Application fee: $75. Electronic applications accepted. *Expenses: Tuition:* Full-time $41,352; part-time $19,968 per year. *Required fees:* $2496; $1628 per unit. $814 per term. Tuition and fees vary according to course load and program. *Financial support:* Fellowships with full and partial tuition reimbursements, career-related internships or fieldwork, Federal Work-Study, institutionally sponsored loans, scholarships/grants, and tuition waivers (partial) available. Support available to part-time students. Financial award application deadline: 2/1; financial award applicants required to submit FAFSA. *Faculty research:* Second language acquisition, cross-cultural communication, technology-enhanced language learning, language variation, action learning. *Unit head:* Prof. Shondel Nero, Director, 212-998-5757, E-mail: shondel.nero@nyu.edu. *Application contact:* 212-998-5030, Fax: 212-995-4328, E-mail: steinhardt.gradadmissions@nyu.edu.
Website: http://steinhardt.nyu.edu/teachlearn/mms

The Ohio State University, Graduate School, College of Arts and Sciences, Division of Arts and Humanities, Department of East Asian Languages and Literatures, Columbus, OH 43210. Offers Chinese (MA, PhD); Japanese (MA, PhD). *Faculty:* 19. *Students:* 50 full-time (32 women), 4 part-time (2 women); includes 5 minority (all Asian, non-Hispanic/Latino), 24 international. Average age 30. In 2017, 9 master's, 6 doctorates awarded. Terminal master's awarded for partial completion of doctoral program. *Entrance requirements:* For master's and doctorate, GRE General Test (if applying for financial aid). Additional exam requirements/recommendations for international students: Required—TOEFL (minimum score 577 paper-based; 90 iBT); Recommended—IELTS (minimum score 7.5). *Application deadline:* For fall admission, 11/30 priority date for domestic and international students; for spring admission, 3/1 for domestic students, 2/1 for international students. Applications are processed on a rolling basis. Application fee: $60 ($70 for international students). Electronic applications accepted. *Financial support:* Fellowships, research assistantships, teaching assistantships, Federal Work-Study, institutionally sponsored loans, and unspecified assistantships available. Support available to part-time students. *Unit head:* Dr. Mark Bender, Chair and Professor, 614-688-5737, E-mail: bender.4@osu.edu. *Application contact:* Graduate and Professional Admissions, 614-292-9444, Fax: 614-292-3895, E-mail: gpadmissions@osu.edu.
Website: http://deall.osu.edu/

Saginaw Valley State University, College of Education, Program in Teaching Chinese as a Foreign Language, University Center, MI 48710. Offers MAT. *Program availability:* Part-time, evening/weekend. *Students:* 10 full-time (6 women), all international. Average age 26. 10 applicants, 90% accepted, 8 enrolled. In 2017, 4 master's awarded. *Entrance requirements:* For master's, minimum GPA of 3.0. Additional exam requirements/recommendations for international students: Required—TOEFL (minimum score 550 paper-based; 79 iBT). *Application deadline:* For fall admission, 7/15 for international students; for winter admission, 11/15 for international students; for spring admission, 4/15 for international students. Applications are processed on a rolling basis. Application fee: $30 ($90 for international students). Electronic applications accepted. *Expenses:* Tuition, state resident: full-time $10,156; part-time $564.20 per credit hour. Tuition, nonresident: full-time $19,336; part-time $1074.20 per credit hour. *Required fees:* $263; $14.60 per credit hour. Tuition and fees vary according to degree level and program. *Financial support:* Federal Work-Study and scholarships/grants available. Support available to part-time students. Financial award application deadline: 4/1; financial award applicants required to submit FAFSA. *Unit head:* Dr. Craig Douglas, Dean, 989-964-4057, Fax: 989-964-4563, E-mail: coeconnect@svsu.edu. *Application contact:* Jenna Briggs, Director, Graduate and International Admissions, 989-964-6096, Fax: 989-964-2788, E-mail: gradadm@svsu.edu.

San Francisco State University, Division of Graduate Studies, College of Liberal and Creative Arts, Department of Modern Languages and Literatures, Program in Chinese, San Francisco, CA 94132-1722. Offers MA. *Application deadline:* Applications are processed on a rolling basis. *Unit head:* Dr. Chris Wen-Chao Li, Program Coordinator and Graduate Advisor, 415-338-1034, Fax: 415-338-6159, E-mail: wenchao@sfsu.edu. Website: http://chinese.sfsu.edu/

Stanford University, School of Humanities and Sciences, Department of East Asian Languages and Cultures, Stanford, CA 94305-2004. Offers Chinese (MA, PhD); Japanese (MA, PhD). Terminal master's awarded for partial completion of doctoral program. *Degree requirements:* For master's, one foreign language, thesis or an annotated translation of a literary or historical text; for doctorate, 2 foreign languages, thesis/dissertation, field exams. *Entrance requirements:* For master's and doctorate, GRE General Test. Additional exam requirements/recommendations for international students: Required—TOEFL. Electronic applications accepted. *Expenses: Tuition:* Full-time $48,987; part-time $10,620 per quarter. One-time fee: $400. Tuition and fees vary according to program.

University of Alberta, Faculty of Graduate Studies and Research, Department of East Asian Studies, Edmonton, AB T6G 2E1, Canada. Offers Chinese literature (MA); East Asian interdisciplinary studies (MA); Japanese literature (MA). *Program availability:* Part-time. *Degree requirements:* For master's, one foreign language, thesis. *Entrance requirements:* Additional exam requirements/recommendations for international students: Required—TOEFL. Electronic applications accepted. *Faculty research:*

Classical Chinese poetry and poetics, Chinese philosophy, modern/contemporary Chinese literature, modern Japanese literature and culture, Japanese women's writing.

University of California, Berkeley, Graduate Division, College of Letters and Science, Department of East Asian Languages and Cultures, Berkeley, CA 94720-1500. Offers Chinese language (PhD); Japanese language (PhD). *Degree requirements:* For doctorate, one foreign language, thesis/dissertation, oral qualifying exam. *Entrance requirements:* For doctorate, GRE General Test, minimum GPA of 3.0, MA thesis, 3 letters of recommendation. Electronic applications accepted. *Faculty research:* Chinese and Japanese modern and classical texts, prose, and poetry; Chinese and Japanese linguistics.

University of California, Irvine, School of Humanities, Department of East Asian Languages and Literatures, Irvine, CA 92697. Offers Chinese (MA, PhD); East Asian languages and literatures (MA, PhD); Japanese (MA, PhD). *Students:* 9 full-time (7 women), 3 part-time (2 women); includes 4 minority (all Asian, non-Hispanic/Latino), 4 international. Average age 31. 46 applicants, 9% accepted, 2 enrolled. In 2017, 2 doctorates awarded. *Entrance requirements:* For master's and doctorate, GRE General Test, minimum GPA of 3.0. Additional exam requirements/recommendations for international students: Required—TOEFL (minimum score 550 paper-based). *Application deadline:* For fall admission, 1/15 priority date for domestic students, 1/15 for international students. Application fee: $105 ($125 for international students). Electronic applications accepted. *Financial support:* Fellowships with tuition reimbursements, research assistantships with full tuition reimbursements, teaching assistantships with partial tuition reimbursements, institutionally sponsored loans, traineeships, health care benefits, and unspecified assistantships available. Financial award application deadline: 3/1; financial award applicants required to submit FAFSA. *Faculty research:* Chinese, Japanese, and Korean literature and culture; language and textual analysis; historical, social, and cultural dimensions of literary study. *Unit head:* Michael A. Fuller, Chair, 949-824-2802 Ext. 2227, Fax: 949-824-3248, E-mail: mafuller@uci.edu. *Application contact:* Hu Ying, Graduate Faculty Advisor, 949-824-6312, Fax: 949-824-3248, E-mail: huying@uci.edu.
Website: http://www.hnet.uci.edu/eastasian/

University of Colorado Boulder, Graduate School, College of Arts and Sciences, Department of Asian Languages and Civilizations, Boulder, CO 80309. Offers MA, PhD. *Faculty:* 12 full-time (5 women). *Students:* 20 full-time (13 women), 1 (woman) part-time; includes 6 minority (3 Asian, non-Hispanic/Latino; 2 Hispanic/Latino; 1 Two or more races, non-Hispanic/Latino), 9 international. Average age 28. 53 applicants, 40% accepted, 6 enrolled. In 2017, 7 master's awarded. Terminal master's awarded for partial completion of doctoral program. *Degree requirements:* For master's, comprehensive exam. *Entrance requirements:* For master's, BA in Chinese or Japanese, minimum undergraduate GPA of 3.0. Additional exam requirements/recommendations for international students: Required—TOEFL. *Application deadline:* For fall admission, 12/1 for domestic and international students; for spring admission, 10/1 for domestic and international students. Applications are processed on a rolling basis. Application fee: $60 ($80 for international students). Electronic applications accepted. Application fee is waived when completed online. *Financial support:* In 2017–18, 90 students received support, including 41 fellowships (averaging $1,708 per year), 16 teaching assistantships with full and partial tuition reimbursements available (averaging $28,844 per year); institutionally sponsored loans, scholarships/grants, health care benefits, and unspecified assistantships also available. Financial award application deadline: 2/15; financial award applicants required to submit FAFSA. *Faculty research:* Asian languages/literature; Chinese language/literature; Asian religions; literary criticism; religious literature. *Application contact:* E-mail: dalc@colorado.edu.
Website: http://alc.colorado.edu/

University of Delaware, College of Arts and Sciences, Department of Foreign Languages and Literatures, Newark, DE 19716. Offers foreign languages and literatures (MA), including French, German, Spanish; foreign languages pedagogy (MA), including French, German, Spanish; technical Chinese translation (MA). *Degree requirements:* For master's, one foreign language, comprehensive exam, thesis optional. *Entrance requirements:* For master's, GRE General Test, letters of recommendation, writing sample. Additional exam requirements/recommendations for international students: Required—TOEFL. Electronic applications accepted. *Faculty research:* Medieval to Modern French and Spanish literature, twentieth-century German, French, Spanish literature by women, computer-assisted instruction.

University of Hawaii at Manoa, Office of Graduate Education, College of Languages, Linguistics and Literature, Department of East Asian Languages and Literatures, Program in Chinese, Honolulu, HI 96822. Offers MA, PhD. *Program availability:* Part-time. *Degree requirements:* For master's, 2 foreign languages, thesis optional; for doctorate, 2 foreign languages, comprehensive exam, thesis/dissertation. *Entrance requirements:* For master's and doctorate, GRE General Test. Additional exam requirements/recommendations for international students: Required—TOEFL (minimum score 560 paper-based; 83 iBT), IELTS (minimum score 5).

University of Hawaii at Manoa, Office of Graduate Education, School of Pacific and Asian Studies, Program in Asian Studies, Concentration in Chinese Studies, Honolulu, HI 96822. Offers Graduate Certificate. *Program availability:* Part-time. *Degree requirements:* For Graduate Certificate, one foreign language. *Entrance requirements:* For degree, GRE. Additional exam requirements/recommendations for international students: Required—TOEFL (minimum score 560 paper-based; 83 iBT), IELTS (minimum score 5).

The University of Iowa, Graduate College, College of Liberal Arts and Sciences, Program in Asian Civilizations, Iowa City, IA 52242-1316. Offers Chinese (MA); Hindi (MA); Sanskrit (MA); South Asian studies (MA). *Degree requirements:* For master's,

thesis optional, exam. *Entrance requirements:* For master's, GRE General Test, minimum GPA of 3.0. Additional exam requirements/recommendations for international students: Required—TOEFL (minimum score 590 paper-based; 96 iBT). Electronic applications accepted.

The University of Manchester, School of Languages, Linguistics and Cultures, Manchester, United Kingdom. Offers Arab world studies (PhD); Chinese studies (M Phil, PhD); East Asian studies (M Phil, PhD); English language (PhD); French studies (M Phil, PhD); German studies (M Phil, PhD); interpreting studies (PhD); Italian studies (M Phil, PhD); Japanese studies (M Phil, PhD); Latin American cultural studies (M Phil, PhD); linguistics (M Phil, PhD); Middle Eastern studies (M Phil, PhD); Polish studies (M Phil, PhD); Portuguese studies (M Phil, PhD); Russian studies (M Phil, PhD); Spanish studies (M Phil, PhD); translation and intercultural studies (M Phil, PhD).

University of Massachusetts Amherst, Graduate School, College of Humanities and Fine Arts, Department of Languages, Literatures, and Cultures, Programs in Asian Languages and Literatures, Amherst, MA 01003. Offers Chinese (MA); Japanese (MA). *Program availability:* Part-time. *Degree requirements:* For master's, thesis, general exam. *Entrance requirements:* For master's, GRE General Test. Additional exam requirements/recommendations for international students: Required—TOEFL (minimum score 550 paper-based; 80 iBT), IELTS (minimum score 6.5). Electronic applications accepted.

University of Oregon, Graduate School, College of Arts and Sciences, Department of East Asian Languages and Literature, Eugene, OR 97403. Offers Chinese (MA, PhD); Japanese (MA, PhD). *Entrance requirements:* Additional exam requirements/recommendations for international students: Required—TOEFL. *Faculty research:* Linguistics, pedagogy.

University of Pittsburgh, Kenneth P. Dietrich School of Arts and Sciences, Department of East Asian Languages and Literatures, Pittsburgh, PA 15260. Offers Chinese (MA); Japanese (MA). *Program availability:* Part-time. *Faculty:* 18 full-time (11 women), 11 part-time/adjunct (all women). *Students:* 4 full-time (all women); includes 2 minority (both Asian, non-Hispanic/Latino). Average age 24. 13 applicants, 31% accepted, 3 enrolled. In 2017, 4 master's awarded. *Degree requirements:* For master's, one foreign language, thesis, oral comprehensive exam. *Entrance requirements:* For master's, GRE General Test, 2 years of college-level Chinese or Japanese, minimum QPA of 3.0, writing sample in English. Additional exam requirements/recommendations for international students: Required—TOEFL (minimum score 600 paper-based; 90 iBT), IELTS. *Application deadline:* For fall admission, 1/15 for domestic and international students. Application fee: $50. Electronic applications accepted. *Expenses:* $22,290 tuition; $850 fees. *Financial support:* In 2017–18, 5 students received support, including 1 fellowship with full tuition reimbursement available (averaging $23,262 per year); scholarships/grants and tuition waivers (full and partial) also available. Financial award application deadline: 1/15. *Faculty research:* Chinese literature, film, and poetry; Japanese literature, film, and theater; Chinese society and culture; East Asian foreign policy, security studies, and economic history; Japanese performing arts and fine arts translation studies; cultural studies; intellectual history; language and linguistics; second language acquisition; Japanese government; Japanese and Chinese history; ethnomusicology; religious studies. *Unit head:* Dr. Hiroshi Nara, Chair, 412-624-5579, Fax: 412-624-3458, E-mail: hnara@pitt.edu. *Application contact:* Keanna Cash, Graduate Administrator, 412-624-5227, E-mail: kec176@pitt.edu.
Website: http://deall.pitt.edu/

University of Washington, Graduate School, College of Arts and Sciences, Department of Asian Languages and Literature, Seattle, WA 98195. Offers Buddhist studies (MA, PhD); Chinese language and literature (MA, PhD); Japanese language and literature (MA, PhD); Korean language and literature (MA, PhD); South Asian language and literature (MA, PhD). *Degree requirements:* For master's, 2 foreign languages, general exam, thesis or 2 research papers; for doctorate, 3 foreign languages, thesis/dissertation, general exam. *Entrance requirements:* For master's, GRE, minimum GPA of 3.0; for doctorate, GRE, master's degree in related field, minimum GPA of 3.0. Additional exam requirements/recommendations for international students: Required—TOEFL. Electronic applications accepted. *Faculty research:* Textual, linguistic, philological, and literary study of languages and literatures of Asia.

University of Wisconsin–Madison, Graduate School, College of Letters and Science, Department of East Asian Languages and Literature, Program in Chinese Literature, Madison, WI 53706-1380. Offers MA, PhD. *Program availability:* Part-time. Terminal master's awarded for partial completion of doctoral program. *Degree requirements:* For master's, one foreign language, seminars, written exam; for doctorate, 3 foreign languages, thesis/dissertation, seminars, preliminary exams, oral exam. *Entrance requirements:* For master's, bachelor's degree or equivalent in Chinese; for doctorate, master's degree or equivalent in Chinese. Electronic applications accepted. *Faculty research:* Chinese historical and modern linguistics, classical Chinese literary and cultural history, modern Chinese literary and cultural history, Chinese paleography.

Washington University in St. Louis, The Graduate School, Department of East Asian Languages and Cultures, St. Louis, MO 63130-4899. Offers Chinese (MA); Chinese and comparative literature (PhD); Chinese language and literature (PhD); East Asian studies (MA); Japanese (MA); Japanese and comparative literature (PhD); Japanese language and literature (PhD). Terminal master's awarded for partial completion of doctoral program. *Degree requirements:* For master's, thesis optional; for doctorate, thesis/dissertation. *Entrance requirements:* For master's and doctorate, GRE General Test. Additional exam requirements/recommendations for international students: Required—TOEFL. Electronic applications accepted. *Faculty research:* Chinese; Japanese; Chinese fiction, theater, poetry, modern literature; Japanese modern and classical fiction, translation theory.

Classics

Asbury University, School of Graduate and Professional Studies, Wilmore, KY 40390-1198. Offers biology: alternative certificate (MA Ed); chemistry: alternative certificate (MA Ed); English (MA Ed); English as a second language (MA Ed); ESL (MA Ed); French (MA Ed); Latin: alternative certificate (MA Ed); mathematics: alternative certificate (MA Ed); reading/writing endorsement (MA Ed); social studies (MA Ed); social work (MSW), including child and family services; Spanish (MA Ed); special education (MA Ed); special education: alternative certificate (MA Ed); teacher as leader endorsement (MA Ed). *Accreditation:* NCATE. *Program availability:* Part-time. *Degree requirements:* For master's, action research project, portfolio. *Entrance requirements:* For master's, PRAXIS/NTE, minimum GPA of 2.75, letters of recommendation.

Additional exam requirements/recommendations for international students: Required—TOEFL (minimum score 550 paper-based). Electronic applications accepted.

Bethel Seminary, Graduate and Professional Programs, St. Paul, MN 55112-6998. Offers Anglican studies (Certificate); children's and family ministry (MA); Christian studies (Certificate); Christian thought (MA); church planting (Certificate); Greek and Hebrew language (M Div); Greek language (M Div); Hebrew language (M Div); marriage and family therapy (MA, Certificate); mental health counseling (MA); ministry (MA, D Min); ministry practice (Certificate); theological studies (MA, Certificate); transformational leadership (MA); young life youth ministry (Certificate). *Accreditation:* ACIPE. *Program availability:* Part-time, evening/weekend, 100% online, blended/hybrid learning. *Faculty:* 16 full-time (4 women), 31 part-time/adjunct (15 women). *Students:*

380 full-time (170 women), 167 part-time (55 women); includes 161 minority (65 Black or African American, non-Hispanic/Latino; 52 Asian, non-Hispanic/Latino; 31 Hispanic/Latino; 1 Native Hawaiian or other Pacific Islander, non-Hispanic/Latino; 12 Two or more races, non-Hispanic/Latino), 5 international. Average age 38. 356 applicants, 62% accepted, 156 enrolled. In 2017, 120 master's, 15 doctorates, 4 other advanced degrees awarded. *Degree requirements:* For master's, variable foreign language requirement, thesis (for some programs); for doctorate, thesis/dissertation. *Entrance requirements:* For master's, letters of reference, transcripts, personal statement; for doctorate, M Div, letters of reference, organizational support; for Certificate, letters of reference, family essay, personal statement, and family of origin paper (for marriage and family therapy). Additional exam requirements/recommendations for international students: Required—TOEFL (minimum score 550 paper-based; 87 iBT). *Application deadline:* For fall admission, 8/1 priority date for domestic students, 8/1 for international students; for winter admission, 12/1 priority date for domestic students; for spring admission, 1/1 priority date for domestic students. Applications are processed on a rolling basis. Application fee: $0. Electronic applications accepted. *Expenses:* Contact institution. *Financial support:* Teaching assistantships, career-related internships or fieldwork, Federal Work-Study, and scholarships/grants available. Financial award applicants required to submit FAFSA. *Faculty research:* Nature of theology, ethics, Biblical commentaries, nature of God, science and theology. *Unit head:* Dr. Randy Bergen, Associate Provost, 651-635-8000, E-mail: r-bergen@bethel.edu. *Application contact:* Director of Admissions, 651-638-8000, Fax: 651-638-6002, E-mail: seminary-admissions@bethel.edu.
Website: https://www.bethel.edu/seminary

Boston College, Graduate School of Arts and Sciences, Department of Classics, Chestnut Hill, MA 02467-3800. Offers classics (MA); Greek (MA); Latin (MA). *Degree requirements:* For master's, one foreign language, thesis optional. *Entrance requirements:* For master's, GRE. Additional exam requirements/recommendations for international students: Required—TOEFL (minimum score 600 paper-based; 100 iBT), IELTS (minimum score 8). Electronic applications accepted. *Faculty research:* Latin, Greek, classical philology, ancient history, modern Greek.

Boston University, Graduate School of Arts and Sciences, Department of Classical Studies, Boston, MA 02215. Offers MA, PhD, MA/PhD. *Students:* 20 full-time (9 women), 2 part-time (1 woman); includes 4 minority (1 Hispanic/Latino; 3 Two or more races, non-Hispanic/Latino), 1 international. Average age 27. 33 applicants, 24% accepted, 5 enrolled. In 2017, 5 master's awarded. Terminal master's awarded for partial completion of doctoral program. *Degree requirements:* For master's, one foreign language, comprehensive exam; for doctorate, 2 foreign languages, comprehensive exam, thesis/dissertation. *Entrance requirements:* For master's and doctorate, GRE General Test, 3 letters of recommendation, transcripts, scholarly writing sample, personal statement. Additional exam requirements/recommendations for international students: Required—TOEFL (minimum score 550 paper-based; 84 iBT). *Application deadline:* For fall admission, 1/15 for domestic and international students; for spring admission, 10/15 for domestic and international students. Application fee: $95. Electronic applications accepted. *Financial support:* In 2017–18, 24 students received support, including 7 fellowships with full tuition reimbursements available (averaging $22,000 per year), 11 teaching assistantships with full tuition reimbursements available (averaging $22,000 per year); career-related internships or fieldwork, Federal Work-Study, institutionally sponsored loans, and health care benefits also available. Financial award application deadline: 1/15. *Faculty research:* Homer and Hesiod, tragedy and comedy, classical tradition, fifth-century Athenian history, empire literature and history. *Unit head:* Stephen Scully, Chair, 617-353-4572, Fax: 617-353-1610, E-mail: sscully@bu.edu. *Application contact:* Meghan Kelly, Department Administrator, 617-353-2426, Fax: 617-353-1610, E-mail: mekel@bu.edu.
Website: http://www.bu.edu/classics/

Brandeis University, Graduate School of Arts and Sciences, Department of Ancient Greek and Roman Studies (Classical Studies), Waltham, MA 02454-9110. Offers MA. *Program availability:* Part-time. *Faculty:* 6 full-time (4 women), 1 part-time/adjunct (0 women). *Students:* 23 full-time (12 women), 3 part-time (2 women); includes 2 minority (both Hispanic/Latino), 1 international. Average age 26. 31 applicants, 81% accepted, 9 enrolled. In 2017, 3 master's awarded. *Degree requirements:* For master's, variable foreign language requirement, thesis or alternative, capstone course, paper. *Entrance requirements:* For master's, recommendation letters, resume, statement of purpose, transcripts. Additional exam requirements/recommendations for international students: Required—PTE (minimum score 68), TOEFL (minimum score 600 paper-based, 100 iBT) or IELTS (7). *Application deadline:* For fall admission, 2/15 for domestic students; for spring admission, 10/15 for domestic students. Application fee: $75. Electronic applications accepted. *Expenses: Tuition:* Full-time $48,720. *Required fees:* $88. Tuition and fees vary according to course load, degree level, program and student level. *Financial support:* In 2017–18, 21 students received support, including 13 teaching assistantships with partial tuition reimbursements available (averaging $3,200 per year); scholarships/grants and tuition waivers (partial) also available. Support available to part-time students. Financial award application deadline: 4/15; financial award applicants required to submit FAFSA. *Faculty research:* Languages, literatures, history, and archaeology of ancient Greece and ancient Rome. *Unit head:* Dr. Ann Olga Koloski-Ostrow, Chair, Graduate Program, 781-736-2183, E-mail: aoko@brandeis.edu. *Application contact:* Sybil Schlesinger, Department Administrator, 781-736-2668, E-mail: sybilsch@brandeis.edu.
Website: http://www.brandeis.edu/gsas/programs/greek_roman.html

Brigham Young University, Graduate Studies, College of Humanities, Department of Comparative Arts and Letters, Provo, UT 84602. Offers comparative studies (MA). *Faculty:* 30 full-time (8 women), 3 part-time/adjunct (1 woman). *Students:* 15 full-time (6 women), 1 part-time (0 women); includes 1 minority (Asian, non-Hispanic/Latino). Average age 29. 12 applicants, 75% accepted, 7 enrolled. In 2017, 10 master's awarded. *Degree requirements:* For master's, 2 foreign languages, comprehensive exam, thesis. *Entrance requirements:* For master's, GRE, minimum GPA of 3.0 in last 60 hours, writing sample, foreign language experience, undergraduate degree or experience in a humanities discipline. Additional exam requirements/recommendations for international students: Required—TOEFL (minimum score 580 paper-based; 85 iBT), IELTS (minimum score 7). *Application deadline:* For fall admission, 3/1 for domestic and international students. Application fee: $50. Electronic applications accepted. *Expenses:* $8,850. *Financial support:* In 2017–18, 15 students received support, including 3 research assistantships (averaging $2,500 per year), 21 teaching assistantships (averaging $5,000 per year); scholarships/grants, tuition waivers, unspecified assistantships, and student instructorships also available. Support available to part-time students. *Faculty research:* Renaissance skepticism, ancient novels, papyrology, Mediterranean piracy, Renaissance devotional art, Seventeenth Century French comedy, representations of chance and probability, Dutch baroque art empowering women, Nineteenth Century Denmark and memory studies. *Unit head:* Dr. Roger Macfarlane, Graduate Coordinator/Professor of Classical Studies, 801-422-9078, Fax: 801-422-0305, E-mail: macfarlane@byu.edu. *Application contact:* Andrea Kristensen, Graduate Program Manager, 801-422-2996, Fax: 801-422-0305, E-mail: andrea_kristensen@byu.edu.
Website: http://cal.byu.edu/

Brock University, Faculty of Graduate Studies, Faculty of Humanities, Program in Classics, St. Catharines, ON L2S 3A1, Canada. Offers MA. *Program availability:* Part-time. *Degree requirements:* For master's, one foreign language, major research paper or thesis. *Entrance requirements:* For master's, honors degree, 3 letters of reference, written work (no more than 20 pages). Additional exam requirements/recommendations for international students: Required—TOEFL (minimum score 550 paper-based; 80 iBT), IELTS (minimum score 6.5), TWE (minimum score 4). Electronic applications accepted.

Brown University, Graduate School, Department of Classics, Providence, RI 02912. Offers MA, PhD. Terminal master's awarded for partial completion of doctoral program. *Degree requirements:* For master's, one foreign language, thesis; for doctorate, 2 foreign languages, thesis/dissertation. *Entrance requirements:* For master's and doctorate, GRE General Test. *Faculty research:* Philology, archaeology, Sanskrit.

Bryn Mawr College, Graduate School of Arts and Sciences, Department of Greek, Latin, and Classical Studies, Bryn Mawr, PA 19010-2899. Offers MA, PhD. *Program availability:* Part-time. *Faculty:* 5 full-time (3 women), 1 part-time/adjunct (0 women). *Students:* 9 full-time (6 women), 8 part-time (6 women); includes 1 minority (Black or African American, non-Hispanic/Latino). Average age 29. 18 applicants, 39% accepted, 3 enrolled. In 2017, 5 master's, 3 doctorates awarded. Terminal master's awarded for partial completion of doctoral program. *Degree requirements:* For master's, 2 foreign languages, thesis; for doctorate, 4 foreign languages, comprehensive exam, thesis/dissertation. *Entrance requirements:* For master's and doctorate, GRE General Test, transcripts, three letters of recommendation, statement of interest, resume or curriculum vitae, writing sample. Additional exam requirements/recommendations for international students: Required—TOEFL (minimum score 600 paper-based; 100 iBT), IELTS (minimum score 7). *Application deadline:* For fall admission, 12/15 for domestic and international students. Application fee: $50. Electronic applications accepted. *Financial support:* In 2017–18, 16 students received support, including 11 fellowships with tuition reimbursements available (averaging $18,591 per year), 3 teaching assistantships with tuition reimbursements available (averaging $15,833 per year); Federal Work-Study, scholarships/grants, and tuition awards also available. Support available to part-time students. Financial award application deadline: 12/15. *Unit head:* Maria Dantis, Graduate Program Administrator, 610-526-5074, E-mail: gsas@brynmawr.edu.

The Catholic University of America, School of Arts and Sciences, Department of Greek and Latin, Washington, DC 20064. Offers Greek (MA, Certificate); Greek and Latin (MA, PhD, Certificate); Latin (MA, Certificate). *Program availability:* Part-time. *Faculty:* 5 full-time (1 woman), 2 part-time/adjunct (1 woman). *Students:* 20 part-time (9 women); includes 2 minority (both Two or more races, non-Hispanic/Latino), 1 international. Average age 38. 6 applicants, 83% accepted, 1 enrolled. In 2017, 1 master's awarded. *Degree requirements:* For master's, one foreign language, comprehensive exam; for doctorate, 2 foreign languages, comprehensive exam, thesis/dissertation. *Entrance requirements:* For master's and doctorate, GRE General Test, statement of purpose, official copies of academic transcripts, three letters of recommendation; for Certificate, bachelor's degree. Additional exam requirements/recommendations for international students: Required—TOEFL (minimum score 550 paper-based; 80 iBT). *Application deadline:* For fall admission, 7/15 priority date for domestic students, 7/1 for international students; for spring admission, 11/15 priority date for domestic students, 11/1 for international students. Applications are processed on a rolling basis. Application fee: $55. Electronic applications accepted. *Expenses:* Contact institution. *Financial support:* Fellowships, research assistantships, teaching assistantships, Federal Work-Study, scholarships/grants, tuition waivers (full and partial), and unspecified assistantships available. Financial award application deadline: 2/1; financial award applicants required to submit FAFSA. *Faculty research:* Greek and Latin history and literature; classical, late antique and patristic history and literature. *Total annual research expenditures:* $721. *Unit head:* Dr. Sarah Ferrario, Chair, 202-319-5216, Fax: 202-319-5297, E-mail: ferrario@cua.edu. *Application contact:* Dr. Steven Brown, Director of Graduate Admissions, 202-319-5057, Fax: 202-319-6533, E-mail: cua-admissions@cua.edu.
Website: http://greeklatin.cua.edu/

City College of the City University of New York, Graduate School, Division of Humanities and the Arts, Department of Classical and Modern Languages and Literatures, New York, NY 10031-9198. Offers Spanish (MA). *Degree requirements:* For master's, one foreign language, comprehensive exam, thesis or alternative. *Entrance requirements:* For master's, minimum GPA of 3.0. Additional exam requirements/recommendations for international students: Required—TOEFL (minimum score 500 paper-based; 61 iBT). Electronic applications accepted.

Columbia University, Graduate School of Arts and Sciences, New York, NY 10027. Offers African-American studies (MA); American studies (MA); anthropology (MA, PhD); art history and archaeology (MA, PhD); astronomy (PhD); biological sciences (PhD); biotechnology (MA); chemical physics (PhD); chemistry (PhD); classical studies (MA, PhD); classics (MA, PhD); climate and society (MA); conservation biology (MA); earth and environmental sciences (PhD); East Asia: regional studies (MA); East Asian languages and cultures (MA, PhD); ecology, evolution and environmental biology (MA), including conservation biology; ecology, evolution, and environmental biology (PhD), including ecology and evolutionary biology, evolutionary primatology; economics (MA, PhD); English and comparative literature (MA, PhD); French and Romance philology (MA, PhD); Germanic languages (MA, PhD); global French studies (MA); global thought (MA); Hispanic cultural studies (MA); history (PhD); history and literature (MA); human rights studies (MA); Islamic studies (MA); Italian (MA, PhD); Japanese pedagogy (MA); Jewish studies (MA); Latin America and the Caribbean: regional studies (MA); Latin American and Iberian cultures (PhD); mathematics (MA, PhD), including finance (MA); medieval and Renaissance studies (MA); Middle Eastern, South Asian, and African studies (MA, PhD); modern art: critical and curatorial studies (MA); modern European studies (MA); museum anthropology (MA); music (DMA, PhD); oral history (MA); philosophical foundations of physics (MA); philosophy (MA, PhD); physics (PhD); political science (MA, PhD); psychology (PhD); quantitative methods in the social sciences (MA); religion (MA, PhD); Russia, Eurasia and East Europe: regional studies (MA); Russian translation (MA); Slavic cultures (MA); Slavic languages (MA, PhD); sociology (MA, PhD); South Asian studies (MA); statistics (MA, PhD); theatre (PhD). Dual-degree programs require admission to both Graduate School of Arts and Sciences and another Columbia school. *Program availability:* Part-time. Terminal master's awarded for partial completion of doctoral program. *Degree requirements:* For master's, variable foreign language requirement, comprehensive exam (for some programs), thesis (for some programs); for doctorate, variable foreign language requirement, comprehensive exam (for some programs), thesis/dissertation. *Entrance requirements:* For master's and doctorate, GRE General Test, GRE Subject Test (for some programs). Additional exam requirements/recommendations for international students: Required—TOEFL, IELTS. Electronic applications accepted. *Expenses: Tuition:* Full-time $44,864; part-time $1704 per credit. *Required fees:* $2370 per semester. One-time fee: $105.

Cornell University, Graduate School, Graduate Fields of Arts and Sciences, Field of Classics, Ithaca, NY 14853. Offers ancient history (PhD); ancient philosophy (PhD); classical archaeology (PhD); classical literature and philology (PhD); classical myth (PhD); classical rhetoric (PhD); Greek and Latin language and linguistics (PhD); Indo-European linguistics (PhD); medieval and Renaissance Latin literature (PhD). *Degree*

requirements: For doctorate, 2 foreign languages, comprehensive exam, thesis/dissertation. *Entrance requirements:* For doctorate, GRE General Test, 3 letters of recommendation, sample of written work. Additional exam requirements/recommendations for international students: Required—TOEFL (minimum score 550 paper-based; 77 iBT). Electronic applications accepted. *Faculty research:* Greek and Roman literature, ancient philosophy, Greek and Roman archaeology, ancient history, Indo-European linguistics.

Dalhousie University, Faculty of Arts and Social Science, Department of Classics, Halifax, NS B3H 4R2, Canada. Offers MA, PhD. *Entrance requirements:* Additional exam requirements/recommendations for international students: Required—TOEFL, IELTS, CANTEST, CAEL, or Michigan English Language Assessment Battery. Electronic applications accepted.

Duke University, Graduate School, Department of Classical Studies, Durham, NC 27708-0103. Offers PhD. *Degree requirements:* For doctorate, 2 foreign languages, thesis/dissertation. *Entrance requirements:* For doctorate, GRE General Test. Additional exam requirements/recommendations for international students: Required—TOEFL (minimum score 577 paper-based; 90 iBT) or IELTS (minimum score 7). Electronic applications accepted. *Faculty research:* Greek Bronze Age; classical and Roman archaeology; Pompeii and Hadrian; epigraphy, papyrology, and Latin paleography.

Duquesne University, School of Education, Department of Instruction and Leadership, Program in Secondary Education, Pittsburgh, PA 15282-0001. Offers biology (MS Ed); chemistry (MS Ed); English (MS Ed); K-12 education (MS Ed), including Latin; mathematics (MS Ed); physics (MS Ed); social studies (MS Ed). *Program availability:* Part-time, evening/weekend. *Faculty:* 5 full-time (4 women). *Students:* 22 full-time (10 women); includes 3 minority (2 Black or African American, non-Hispanic/Latino; 1 Two or more races, non-Hispanic/Latino). Average age 26. 8 applicants, 100% accepted, 5 enrolled. In 2017, 9 master's awarded. *Entrance requirements:* For master's, two letters of recommendation, letter of intent, interview, bachelor's degree. Additional exam requirements/recommendations for international students: Required—TOEFL (minimum score 550 paper-based), IELTS (minimum score 7). *Application deadline:* For fall admission, 9/1 for domestic students; for spring admission, 1/2 for domestic students. Applications are processed on a rolling basis. Application fee: $0. Electronic applications accepted. *Expenses:* $1,259 per credit. *Financial support:* Research assistantships and Federal Work-Study available. Support available to part-time students. *Faculty research:* Factors that create highly effective teachers; how to best support teachers to support students in reform-oriented environments; urban education; models of teacher leadership; improving instruction in mathematics/science/social studies/English. *Unit head:* Dr. Melissa Boston, Associate Dean for Teacher Education/Professor, 412-396.6109, Fax: 412-396-5585, E-mail: bostonm@duq.edu. *Application contact:* Kelly McGinley, Graduate Admissions Assistant, 412-396-1559, Fax: 412-396-5585, E-mail: mcginleyk@duq.edu.
Website: http://www.duq.edu/academics/schools/education/graduate-programs-education/ms-ed-secondary-education

Florida State University, The Graduate School, College of Arts and Sciences, Department of Classics, Tallahassee, FL 32306-1510. Offers ancient history (MA); classical archaeology (MA); classical civilization (MA); classics (PhD), including classical archaeology, classics; Greek (MA); Greek and Latin (MA); Latin (MA). *Faculty:* 17 full-time (7 women), 2 part-time/adjunct (1 woman). *Students:* 41 full-time (30 women); includes 4 minority (2 Black or African American, non-Hispanic/Latino; 1 Asian, non-Hispanic/Latino; 1 Hispanic/Latino). Average age 25. 50 applicants, 40% accepted, 12 enrolled. In 2017, 8 master's, 6 doctorates awarded. Terminal master's awarded for partial completion of doctoral program. *Degree requirements:* For master's, 2 foreign languages, comprehensive exam, thesis or alternative; for doctorate, 4 foreign languages, comprehensive exam, thesis/dissertation. *Entrance requirements:* For master's, GRE General Test, minimum GPA of 3.0; for doctorate, GRE General Test, minimum GPA of 3.5. Additional exam requirements/recommendations for international students: Required—TOEFL (minimum score 550 paper-based; 80 iBT). *Application deadline:* For fall admission, 12/15 priority date for domestic students, 12/15 for international students. Applications are processed on a rolling basis. Application fee: $30. Electronic applications accepted. *Financial support:* In 2017–18, 39 students received support, including 1 fellowship with full tuition reimbursement available (averaging $18,000 per year), 2 research assistantships with full tuition reimbursements available (averaging $12,000 per year), 24 teaching assistantships with full tuition reimbursements available (averaging $12,400 per year); Federal Work-Study, scholarships/grants, tuition waivers (full), and unspecified assistantships also available. Financial award application deadline: 1/15; financial award applicants required to submit FAFSA. *Faculty research:* Greek and Latin literature, classical archaeology, mythology, ancient history, religion. *Total annual research expenditures:* $100,000. *Unit head:* Dr. Daniel J. Pullen, Chairman, 850-644-0304, Fax: 850-644-4073, E-mail: dpullen@fsu.edu. *Application contact:* Dr. Timothy Stover, Admissions Director, 850-644-4259, Fax: 850-644-4073, E-mail: tstover@fsu.edu.
Website: http://classics.fsu.edu/

Fordham University, Graduate School of Arts and Sciences, Department of Classical Languages and Literatures, New York, NY 10458. Offers MA, PhD. *Program availability:* Part-time, evening/weekend. *Faculty:* 7 full-time (1 woman). *Students:* 7 full-time (2 women), 4 part-time (2 women), 1 international. Average age 31. 9 applicants, 33% accepted, 1 enrolled. In 2017, 1 master's, 2 doctorates awarded. Terminal master's awarded for partial completion of doctoral program. *Degree requirements:* For master's, one foreign language, comprehensive exam; for doctorate, 2 foreign languages, comprehensive exam, thesis/dissertation. *Entrance requirements:* For master's and doctorate, GRE General Test. Additional exam requirements/recommendations for international students: Required—TOEFL (minimum score 650 paper-based). *Application deadline:* For fall admission, 1/4 priority date for domestic students; for spring admission, 11/1 for domestic students. Application fee: $70. Electronic applications accepted. *Financial support:* In 2017–18, 11 students received support, including 2 fellowships with tuition reimbursements available (averaging $27,000 per year), 4 teaching assistantships with tuition reimbursements available (averaging $21,000 per year); Federal Work-Study, institutionally sponsored loans, scholarships/grants, tuition waivers (full and partial), and unspecified assistantships also available. Support available to part-time students. Financial award application deadline: 1/4; financial award applicants required to submit FAFSA. *Unit head:* Dr. Matthew McGowan, Chair, 718-817-3140, Fax: 718-817-3134, E-mail: mamcgowan@fordham.edu. *Application contact:* Travis Strattion, Interim Director of Graduate Admissions, 718-817-4417, Fax: 718-817-3566, E-mail: valentinomor@fordham.edu.

The Graduate Center, City University of New York, Graduate Studies, Program in Classics, New York, NY 10016-4039. Offers MA, PhD. *Faculty:* 14 full-time (5 women). *Students:* 18 full-time (5 women), 2 part-time (1 woman); includes 2 minority (1 Black or African American, non-Hispanic/Latino; 1 Hispanic/Latino), 3 international. Average age 40. 13 applicants, 54% accepted, 2 enrolled. In 2017, 1 master's, 1 doctorate awarded. *Degree requirements:* For master's, 2 foreign languages, thesis; for doctorate, 2 foreign languages, thesis/dissertation. *Entrance requirements:* For master's and doctorate, GRE General Test. Additional exam requirements/recommendations for international students: Required—TOEFL. *Application deadline:* For fall admission, 4/15 for domestic

students. Application fee: $125. Electronic applications accepted. *Financial support:* In 2017–18, 9 students received support, including 10 fellowships, 1 teaching assistantship; research assistantships, career-related internships or fieldwork, Federal Work-Study, institutionally sponsored loans, and tuition waivers (full and partial) also available. Financial award application deadline: 2/1; financial award applicants required to submit FAFSA. *Unit head:* Dr. Dee Clayman, Executive Officer, 212-817-8151, Fax: 212-817-1508. *Application contact:* Les Gribben, Director of Admissions, 212-817-7470, Fax: 212-817-1624, E-mail: lgribben@gc.cuny.edu.
Website: http://web.gc.cuny.edu/Classics/

Harvard University, Graduate School of Arts and Sciences, Department of the Classics, Cambridge, MA 02138. Offers Byzantine Greek (PhD); classical archaeology (PhD); classical philology (PhD); classical philosophy (PhD); medieval Latin (PhD). *Degree requirements:* For doctorate, 4 foreign languages, thesis/dissertation, preliminary and special exams. *Entrance requirements:* For doctorate, GRE General Test. Additional exam requirements/recommendations for international students: Required—TOEFL.

Heritage Christian University, Graduate Programs, Florence, AL 35630. Offers counseling (MM); Greek (MA); ministry (MM); New Testament (MA). *Degree requirements:* For master's, practicum (MM), major research paper (MA). *Entrance requirements:* For master's, MAT or GRE, bachelor's degree in Bible from an accredited college or university, minimum GPA of 2.75, 3 letters of recommendation.

Hunter College of the City University of New York, Graduate School, School of Arts and Sciences, Department of Classical and Oriental Studies, Program in Teaching Latin, New York, NY 10065-5085. Offers MA. *Program availability:* Part-time, evening/weekend. *Degree requirements:* For master's, one foreign language. *Entrance requirements:* For master's, undergraduate major in Latin or equivalent with minimum GPA of 3.0; 2 letters of recommendation; personal statement. Additional exam requirements/recommendations for international students: Required—TOEFL. *Faculty research:* Late antique religion and social history, women in antiquity, Horace and lyric poetry, Roman comedy, Latin prose.

Indiana University Bloomington, University Graduate School, College of Arts and Sciences, Department of Classical Studies, Bloomington, IN 47405. Offers MA, MAT, PhD. *Program availability:* Part-time. *Degree requirements:* For master's, 2 foreign languages, comprehensive exam; for doctorate, 3 foreign languages, thesis/dissertation. *Entrance requirements:* For master's and doctorate, GRE, minimum GPA of 3.0. Additional exam requirements/recommendations for international students: Required—TOEFL. Electronic applications accepted. *Faculty research:* Roman literature (particularly Empire and late Latin), Greek drama, Homer, history of ideas, papyrology.

Johns Hopkins University, Zanvyl Krieger School of Arts and Sciences, Department of Classics, Baltimore, MD 21218. Offers PhD. *Faculty:* 6 full-time (2 women). *Students:* 16 full-time (6 women). Average age 31. 20 applicants, 15% accepted, 2 enrolled. In 2017, 1 doctorate awarded. Terminal master's awarded for partial completion of doctoral program. *Degree requirements:* For doctorate, 4 foreign languages, thesis/dissertation. *Entrance requirements:* For doctorate, GRE General Test. Additional exam requirements/recommendations for international students: Required—TOEFL (minimum score 600 paper-based), IELTS (minimum score 7). *Application deadline:* For fall admission, 1/15 for domestic and international students. Application fee: $75. Electronic applications accepted. *Expenses:* $50,410 tuition; $1,800 health insurance; $500 matriculation fee. *Financial support:* In 2017–18, 11 students received support, including 6 fellowships with full tuition reimbursements available (averaging $30,500 per year), 4 teaching assistantships with full tuition reimbursements available (averaging $29,500 per year); career-related internships or fieldwork, institutionally sponsored loans, scholarships/grants, and health care benefits also available. Financial award application deadline: 1/15. *Faculty research:* Greek culture, mythology, language and literature; ancient Greek vase inscriptions and vase painting; Aegean and Eastern Mediterranean Bronze Age art and archaeology; Latin literature (ancient, Medieval, Renaissance); Roman social and cultural history. *Unit head:* Dr. Shane Butler, Professor and Chair, 410-516-3835, Fax: 410-516-4848, E-mail: shane.butler@jhu.edu. *Application contact:* Ginnie Miller, Senior Administrative Coordinator, 410-516-7556, Fax: 410-516-4848, E-mail: gmiller@jhu.edu.
Website: http://classics.jhu.edu

Knox Theological Seminary, Graduate Programs, Master of Arts Programs, Fort Lauderdale, FL 33308. Offers Biblical and theological studies (MA); Christian and classical studies (MA). *Accreditation:* ATS. *Program availability:* Part-time, evening/weekend. *Entrance requirements:* Additional exam requirements/recommendations for international students: Required—TOEFL (minimum score 520 paper-based; 83 iBT), TWE (minimum score 5).

Manhattanville College, School of Education, Program in Teaching of Languages Other than English, Purchase, NY 10577-2132. Offers adolescence education (grades 7-12) foreign language (MAT, Advanced Certificate), including French, Italian, Latin (Advanced Certificate), Latin (MAT), Spanish. *Program availability:* Part-time, evening/weekend. *Faculty:* 2 full-time (1 woman). *Students:* 3 part-time (2 women); includes 1 minority (Hispanic/Latino). Average age 31. In 2017, 4 master's, 1 other advanced degree awarded. *Degree requirements:* For master's, comprehensive exam (for some programs), thesis (for some programs), student teaching, research seminars, portfolios, internships, writing assessment; for Advanced Certificate, comprehensive exam (for some programs). *Entrance requirements:* For master's, GRE or MAT (for programs leading to certification), minimum GPA of 3.0, 2 letters of recommendation, interview, essay (2-3 page personal statement that describes reasons for choosing teaching or educational leadership as profession and philosophy of education), proof of immunization (for those born after 1957). Additional exam requirements/recommendations for international students: Required—TOEFL (minimum score 600 paper-based; 110 iBT); Recommended—IELTS (minimum score 8). *Application deadline:* Applications are processed on a rolling basis. Application fee: $75. Electronic applications accepted. *Expenses:* $915 per credit. *Financial support:* Teaching assistantships, career-related internships or fieldwork, Federal Work-Study, institutionally sponsored loans, scholarships/grants, and unspecified assistantships available. Financial award application deadline: 3/15; financial award applicants required to submit FAFSA. *Faculty research:* Changing suburbs institute and community schools. *Unit head:* Dr. Shelly Wepner, Dean, 914-323-3153, Fax: 914-323-5493. *Application contact:* Alissa Wilson, Director, Graduate Admissions, 914-323-3150, Fax: 914-694-1732, E-mail: edschool@mville.edu.
Website: https://www.mville.edu/programs/teaching-languages-other-english

McMaster University, School of Graduate Studies, Faculty of Humanities, Department of Classics, Hamilton, ON L8S 4M2, Canada. Offers MA, PhD. *Degree requirements:* For master's, one foreign language, thesis or alternative; for doctorate, 2 foreign languages, comprehensive exam, thesis/dissertation. *Entrance requirements:* For master's, honors degree, minimum B+ average. Additional exam requirements/recommendations for international students: Required—TOEFL (minimum score 580 paper-based). *Faculty research:* Ancient history, art and archaeology, Latin language and literature, Greek language and literature.

Classics

Memorial University of Newfoundland, School of Graduate Studies, Department of Classics, St. John's, NL A1C 5S7, Canada. Offers MA. *Program availability:* Part-time. *Degree requirements:* For master's, one foreign language, thesis, language exam, translation exam, research essay. *Entrance requirements:* For master's, honors degree in related field, course work in Greek and Latin. Electronic applications accepted. *Faculty research:* Ancient history, historiography, literature, drama, philosophy, paleography, epigraphy, and textual criticism.

New York University, Graduate School of Arts and Science, Department of Classics, New York, NY 10012-1019. Offers classics (MA, PhD); poetics and theory (Advanced Certificate). *Program availability:* Part-time. *Students:* Average age 29. 47 applicants, 21% accepted, 6 enrolled. In 2017, 2 doctorates awarded. *Degree requirements:* For master's, 4 foreign languages, exam or specialized project; for doctorate, 4 foreign languages, thesis/dissertation, exams. *Entrance requirements:* For master's, GRE General Test, knowledge of Greek and Latin history and literature, proficiency in Greek and Latin translation; for doctorate, GRE General Test. Additional exam requirements/recommendations for international students: Required—TOEFL. *Application deadline:* For fall admission, 1/4 priority date for domestic students, 1/4 for international students. Application fee: $100. *Expenses: Tuition:* Full-time $41,352; part-time $19,968 per year. *Required fees:* $2496; $1628 per unit. $814 per term. Tuition and fees vary according to course load and program. *Financial support:* Fellowships, teaching assistantships, Federal Work-Study, institutionally sponsored loans, scholarships/grants, health care benefits, and unspecified assistantships available. Financial award application deadline: 1/4; financial award applicants required to submit FAFSA. *Faculty research:* Greek and Latin literature, Greek and Roman history, epigraphy, Greek and Roman philosophy, classical archeology. *Unit head:* David Levene, Chair, 212-998-8590, Fax: 212-995-4209, E-mail: gsas.classic@nyu.edu. *Application contact:* Barbara Kowalzig, Director of Graduate Studies, 212-998-8590, Fax: 212-995-4209, E-mail: gsas.classics@nyu.edu.
Website: http://classics.as.nyu.edu/

The Ohio State University, Graduate School, College of Arts and Sciences, Division of Arts and Humanities, Department of Classics, Columbus, OH 43210. Offers ancient Greek and Latin (MA, PhD); Greek studies (MA); Latin studies (MA, PhD); modern Greek (MA, PhD). *Faculty:* 14. *Students:* 22 (13 women). Average age 28. In 2017, 1 doctorate awarded. *Degree requirements:* For master's, 2 foreign languages, thesis or alternative; for doctorate, 2 foreign languages, thesis/dissertation. *Entrance requirements:* For master's and doctorate, GRE General Test. Additional exam requirements/recommendations for international students: Required—TOEFL (minimum score 550 paper-based; 79 iBT), Michigan English Language Assessment Battery (minimum score 82); Recommended—IELTS (minimum score 7). *Application deadline:* For fall admission, 11/30 priority date for domestic and international students; for winter admission, 12/1 for domestic students, 11/1 for international students; for spring admission, 3/1 for domestic students, 2/1 for international students. Applications are processed on a rolling basis. Application fee: $60 ($70 for international students). Electronic applications accepted. *Financial support:* Fellowships with tuition reimbursements, research assistantships with tuition reimbursements, teaching assistantships with tuition reimbursements, Federal Work-Study, and institutionally sponsored loans available. Support available to part-time students. *Unit head:* Dr. Anthony Kaldellis, Chair and Professor, E-mail: kaldellis.1@osu.edu. *Application contact:* Graduate and Professional Admissions, 614-292-9444, Fax: 614-292-3895, E-mail: gpadmissions@osu.edu.
Website: http://classics.osu.edu/

Princeton University, Graduate School, Department of Classics, Princeton, NJ 08544-1019. Offers classical and hellenic studies (PhD); classical philosophy (PhD); history (the ancient world) (PhD); literature and philology (PhD). *Degree requirements:* For doctorate, thesis/dissertation. *Entrance requirements:* For doctorate, GRE General Test, sample of written work. Additional exam requirements/recommendations for international students: Required—TOEFL (minimum score 600 paper-based). Electronic applications accepted.

Queen's University at Kingston, School of Graduate Studies, Faculty of Arts and Sciences, Department of Classics, Kingston, ON K7L 3N6, Canada. Offers classics, Greek, Latin (MA). *Program availability:* Part-time. *Degree requirements:* For master's, one foreign language, thesis (for some programs). *Entrance requirements:* For master's, 3 years of Latin, 2 years of Greek. Additional exam requirements/recommendations for international students: Required—TOEFL. Electronic applications accepted. *Faculty research:* Greek and Latin literature, Greek and Roman history, ancient philosophy, Greek archaeology.

Rutgers University–New Brunswick, Graduate School-New Brunswick, Department of Classics, Piscataway, NJ 08854-8097. Offers classics (MA, MAT, PhD); interdisciplinary classical studies and ancient history (MA, PhD). *Program availability:* Part-time, evening/weekend. Terminal master's awarded for partial completion of doctoral program. *Degree requirements:* For master's, 3 foreign languages, comprehensive exam, thesis or alternative; for doctorate, 3 foreign languages, comprehensive exam, thesis/dissertation. *Entrance requirements:* For master's and doctorate, GRE General Test. *Faculty research:* Greek and Latin literature, Greek and Roman social and political history, mythology, religion, ancient philosophy.

San Francisco State University, Division of Graduate Studies, College of Liberal and Creative Arts, Department of Classics, San Francisco, CA 94132-1722. Offers MA. *Program availability:* Part-time. *Application deadline:* Applications are processed on a rolling basis. *Unit head:* Dr. David Leitao, Chair, 415-338-2068, Fax: 415-338-2664, E-mail: dleitao@sfsu.edu. *Application contact:* Dr. Gillian McIntosh, Graduate Coordinator, 415-338-1537, Fax: 415-338-2664, E-mail: gillianm@sfsu.edu.
Website: http://classics.sfsu.edu/

Stanford University, School of Humanities and Sciences, Department of Classics, Stanford, CA 94305-2004. Offers MA, PhD. *Degree requirements:* For master's, 2 foreign languages, thesis or alternative; for doctorate, 4 foreign languages, thesis/dissertation, general exams. *Entrance requirements:* For master's and doctorate, GRE General Test. Additional exam requirements/recommendations for international students: Required—TOEFL. Electronic applications accepted. *Expenses: Tuition:* Full-time $48,987; part-time $10,620 per quarter. One-time fee: $400. Tuition and fees vary according to program.

Tufts University, Graduate School of Arts and Sciences, Department of Classics, Medford, MA 02155. Offers classics (MA); classics with teaching licensure (MA); digital tools for premodern studies (MA). *Program availability:* Part-time. *Students:* 17 full-time (9 women); includes 3 minority (1 Black or African American, non-Hispanic/Latino; 1 Asian, non-Hispanic/Latino; 1 Hispanic/Latino), 3 international. Average age 26. 32 applicants, 53% accepted, 7 enrolled. In 2017, 3 master's awarded. *Degree requirements:* For master's, 2 foreign languages, comprehensive exam, thesis or alternative. *Entrance requirements:* For master's, GRE General Test, writing sample. Additional exam requirements/recommendations for international students: Required—TOEFL (minimum score 550 paper-based; 80 iBT), IELTS (minimum score 6.5). *Application deadline:* For fall admission, 2/15 for domestic and international students; for spring admission, 10/15 for domestic and international students. Applications are processed on a rolling basis. Application fee: $85. Electronic applications accepted. *Expenses:* Contact institution. *Financial support:* Teaching assistantships, Federal Work-Study, scholarships/grants, tuition waivers (full and partial), and unspecified assistantships available. Financial award application deadline: 1/15; financial award applicants required to submit FAFSA. *Unit head:* Dr. Marie-Claire Beaulieu, Graduate Program Director, 617-627-2438. *Application contact:* Office of Graduate Admissions, 617-627-3395, E-mail: gradadmissions@tufts.edu.
Website: http://www.ase.tufts.edu/classics/

Tulane University, School of Liberal Arts, Department of Classical Studies, New Orleans, LA 70118-5669. Offers MA. *Degree requirements:* For master's, 2 foreign languages, thesis or alternative. *Entrance requirements:* For master's, GRE General Test, minimum B average in undergraduate course work. Additional exam requirements/recommendations for international students: Required—TOEFL. Electronic applications accepted. *Expenses: Tuition:* Full-time $50,920; part-time $2829 per credit hour. *Required fees:* $2040; $44.50 per credit hour. $580 per term. Tuition and fees vary according to course load, degree level and program.

Université de Montréal, Faculty of Arts and Sciences, Program in Classical Studies, Montréal, QC H3C 3J7, Canada. Offers MA. Electronic applications accepted.

University at Buffalo, the State University of New York, Graduate School, College of Arts and Sciences, Department of Classics, Buffalo, NY 14261. Offers classics (MA, PhD); Latin (MA). *Faculty:* 10 full-time (3 women), 3 part-time/adjunct (1 woman). *Students:* 27 full-time (14 women); includes 2 minority (both Asian, non-Hispanic/Latino). Average age 25. 21 applicants, 48% accepted, 5 enrolled. In 2017, 6 master's, 2 doctorates awarded. Terminal master's awarded for partial completion of doctoral program. *Degree requirements:* For master's, 3 foreign languages, project; for doctorate, 4 foreign languages, comprehensive exam, thesis/dissertation, general and 2 special exams. *Entrance requirements:* For master's and doctorate, GRE General Test. Additional exam requirements/recommendations for international students: Required—TOEFL, IELTS. *Application deadline:* For fall admission, 1/15 priority date for domestic and international students. Application fee: $75. Electronic applications accepted. *Expenses:* Contact institution. *Financial support:* In 2017–18, 16 students received support, including 3 fellowships with full tuition reimbursements available (averaging $4,000 per year), 16 teaching assistantships with full tuition reimbursements available (averaging $14,500 per year); Federal Work-Study, institutionally sponsored loans, and unspecified assistantships also available. Financial award application deadline: 1/15. *Faculty research:* Greek and Latin literature, historiography, and epigraphy; Greek archaeology, mythology, and ancient philosophy; ancient and Roman religion and women's studies. *Total annual research expenditures:* $37,616. *Unit head:* Dr. Bradley Ault, Chair, 716-645-0458, Fax: 716-645-2225, E-mail: clarbrad@buffalo.edu. *Application contact:* Dr. Martha Malamud, Director of Graduate Studies, 716-645-0459, Fax: 716-645-2225, E-mail: malamud@buffalo.edu.
Website: http://www.classics.buffalo.edu/

University at Buffalo, the State University of New York, Graduate School, Graduate School of Education, Department of Learning and Instruction, Buffalo, NY 14260. Offers biology education (Ed M, Certificate); chemistry education (Ed M, Certificate); childhood education (Ed M); childhood education with bilingual extension (Ed M); college teaching (Advanced Certificate); curriculum, instruction and the science of learning (PhD); early childhood education (Ed M); early childhood education with bilingual extension (Ed M); earth science education (Ed M, Certificate); education and technology (Ed M); education studies (Ed M); educational technology and new literacies (Certificate); educational technology and new literacies (Advanced Certificate); elementary education (Ed D); English education (Ed M, Certificate); English education studies (Ed M); English for speakers of other languages (Ed M); foreign and second language education (PhD); French education (Ed M, Certificate); German education (Ed M, Certificate); gifted education (Certificate); Latin education (Ed M, Certificate); literacy education studies (Ed M); literacy specialist (Ed M); literacy teaching and learning (Certificate); mathematics education (Ed M, Certificate); music education (Ed M, Certificate); music education studies (Ed M); music learning theory (Advanced Certificate); online education (Advanced Certificate); physics education (Ed M, Certificate); science and the public (Ed M); social studies education (Ed M, Certificate); Spanish education (Ed M, Certificate); special education (PhD); teaching English to speakers of other languages (Ed M). *Program availability:* Part-time, evening/weekend, 100% online. *Faculty:* 26 full-time (19 women), 74 part-time/adjunct (52 women). *Students:* 172 full-time (122 women), 325 part-time (226 women); includes 44 minority (25 Black or African American, non-Hispanic/Latino; 5 American Indian or Alaska Native, non-Hispanic/Latino; 14 Asian, non-Hispanic/Latino), 57 international. Average age 33. 316 applicants, 78% accepted, 174 enrolled. In 2017, 109 master's, 34 doctorates, 15 other advanced degrees awarded. *Degree requirements:* For master's, comprehensive exam; for doctorate, thesis/dissertation, research analysis exam, research experience. *Entrance requirements:* For master's, letters of reference; for doctorate, GRE General Test or MAT, interview, writing sample, letters of recommendation. Additional exam requirements/recommendations for international students: Required—TOEFL (minimum score 600 paper-based; 96 iBT). *Application deadline:* For fall admission, 2/1 priority date for domestic and international students; for spring admission, 11/15 priority date for domestic students, 10/1 for international students. Applications are processed on a rolling basis. Application fee: $50. Electronic applications accepted. *Financial support:* In 2017–18, 42 fellowships (averaging $5,181 per year), 44 research assistantships with tuition reimbursements (averaging $10,908 per year) were awarded; teaching assistantships, career-related internships or fieldwork, Federal Work-Study, institutionally sponsored loans, scholarships/grants, tuition waivers (full and partial), and unspecified assistantships also available. Financial award application deadline: 2/28; financial award applicants required to submit FAFSA. *Faculty research:* Science assessment, foreign language teaching and learning, early learning, new literacies, gender and education. *Total annual research expenditures:* $413,233. *Unit head:* Dr. David Bruce, Chair, 716-645-4069, Fax: 716-645-3161, E-mail: gse-info@buffalo.edu. *Application contact:* Luann Zak, Admissions Assistant, 716-645-2110, Fax: 716-645-7937, E-mail: luannzak@buffalo.edu.
Website: http://gse.buffalo.edu/lai

University of Alberta, Faculty of Graduate Studies and Research, Department of History and Classics, Edmonton, AB T6G 2E1, Canada. Offers ancient history (PhD); classical archaeology (MA, PhD); classical literature (PhD); classics (MA); history (MA, PhD). *Program availability:* Part-time, evening/weekend. *Degree requirements:* For master's, one foreign language, thesis (for some programs); for doctorate, one foreign language, thesis/dissertation. *Entrance requirements:* For master's, minimum B+ average; for doctorate, minimum A- average. Additional exam requirements/recommendations for international students: Required—TOEFL (minimum score 580 paper-based). Electronic applications accepted. *Faculty research:* Western Canada, classical archaeology, Britain, Eastern Europe, East Asia.

The University of Arizona, College of Humanities, Department of Classics, Tucson, AZ 85721. Offers MA. *Program availability:* Part-time. *Degree requirements:* For master's, one foreign language, comprehensive exam, thesis. *Entrance requirements:* For master's, GRE General Test (minimum combined score of 1000 verbal and quantitative), 2 letters of recommendation. Additional exam requirements/recommendations for international students: Required—TOEFL (minimum score 550 paper-based; 79 iBT).

Electronic applications accepted. *Faculty research:* Greek and Roman archaeology, ancient Greek, modern Greek, Latin, Greek and Roman religion, women in antiquity.

The University of British Columbia, Faculty of Arts, Department of Classical, Near Eastern and Religious Studies, Program in Classics, Vancouver, BC V6T 1Z1, Canada. Offers classics (MA, PhD). *Program availability:* Part-time. *Degree requirements:* For master's, one foreign language, thesis or comprehensive exam; for doctorate, 2 foreign languages, comprehensive exam, thesis/dissertation. *Entrance requirements:* For doctorate, MA. Additional exam requirements/recommendations for international students: Required—TOEFL, IELTS. Electronic applications accepted. *Expenses:* Contact institution. *Faculty research:* Classical archaeology, ancient historians, late antiquity, ancient prose fiction, epigraphy.

University of Calgary, Faculty of Graduate Studies, Faculty of Arts, Department of Greek and Roman Studies, Calgary, AB T2N 1N4, Canada. Offers MA, PhD. *Program availability:* Part-time. *Degree requirements:* For master's, one foreign language; for doctorate, 2 foreign languages, comprehensive exam, thesis/dissertation. *Entrance requirements:* For master's, BA in classics or related field, knowledge of Latin and/or Greek, minimum GPA of 3.7; for doctorate, MA in classics or related field, knowledge of Latin and Greek, GPA 3.7. Additional exam requirements/recommendations for international students: Required—TOEFL. Electronic applications accepted. *Faculty research:* Greek literature, Latin literature, Greek history, Roman history, classical archaeology.

University of California, Berkeley, Graduate Division, College of Letters and Science, Department of Classics, Berkeley, CA 94720-1500. Offers classical archaeology (MA, PhD); classics (MA, PhD); Greek (MA); Latin (MA). Terminal master's awarded for partial completion of doctoral program. *Degree requirements:* For master's, one foreign language, exams; for doctorate, 2 foreign languages, thesis/dissertation, qualifying exam. *Entrance requirements:* For master's and doctorate, GRE General Test, minimum GPA of 3.0, 3 letters of recommendation. Additional exam requirements/recommendations for international students: Required—TOEFL (minimum score 570 paper-based; 90 iBT), TWE. Electronic applications accepted. *Faculty research:* Greek and Latin literature, textual criticism, history, archaeology and philosophy.

University of California, Irvine, School of Humanities, Department of Classics, Irvine, CA 92697. Offers MA, PhD. *Students:* 3 full-time (1 woman). Average age 36. In 2017, 1 master's, 1 doctorate awarded. Terminal master's awarded for partial completion of doctoral program. *Degree requirements:* For master's, one foreign language, thesis or alternative; for doctorate, 2 foreign languages, thesis/dissertation. *Entrance requirements:* For master's and doctorate, GRE General Test, minimum GPA of 3.0. Additional exam requirements/recommendations for international students: Required—TOEFL (minimum score 550 paper-based). *Application deadline:* For fall admission, 1/15 priority date for domestic students, 1/15 for international students. Applications are processed on a rolling basis. Application fee: $105 ($125 for international students). Electronic applications accepted. *Financial support:* Fellowships, research assistantships with full tuition reimbursements, teaching assistantships, institutionally sponsored loans, traineeships, health care benefits, and unspecified assistantships available. Financial award application deadline: 3/1; financial award applicants required to submit FAFSA. *Faculty research:* Greek literature, computer application to Greek literature, Latin literature. *Unit head:* Susan Jarratt, Interim Chair, 949-824-6406, E-mail: sjarratt@uci.edu. *Application contact:* Zina Giannopoulou, Graduate Advisor, 949-824-2641, Fax: 949-824-1966, E-mail: zgiannop@uci.edu.
Website: http://www.humanities.uci.edu/classics/

University of California, Los Angeles, Graduate Division, College of Letters and Science, Department of Classics, Los Angeles, CA 90095. Offers classics (MA, PhD); Greek (MA); Latin (MA). Terminal master's awarded for partial completion of doctoral program. *Degree requirements:* For master's, 2 foreign languages, comprehensive exam; for doctorate, 2 foreign languages, thesis/dissertation, oral and written qualifying exams. *Entrance requirements:* For doctorate, GRE General Test, bachelor's degree; minimum undergraduate GPA of 3.0 (or its equivalent if letter grade system not used); Greek and Latin. Additional exam requirements/recommendations for international students: Required—TOEFL. Electronic applications accepted.

University of California, Riverside, Graduate Division, Tri-Campus Program in Classics, Riverside, CA 92521-0102. Offers PhD. Program offered jointly with University of California, Irvine and University of California, San Diego. *Degree requirements:* For doctorate, 3 foreign languages, comprehensive exam, thesis/dissertation. *Entrance requirements:* For doctorate, GRE, MA in classics. Additional exam requirements/recommendations for international students: Required—TOEFL (minimum score 550 paper-based; 80 iBT). Electronic applications accepted. *Expenses:* Tuition, state resident: full-time $5746. Tuition, nonresident: full-time $10,780. Tuition and fees vary according to campus/location and program. *Faculty research:* Rhetoric, Greek and Latin drama, Hellenistic poetry, Anglo-Latin literature, Greek and Latin prose.

University of California, Santa Barbara, Graduate Division, College of Letters and Sciences, Division of Humanities and Fine Arts, Department of Classics, Santa Barbara, CA 93106-2014. Offers ancient history (PhD); classics (MA, PhD); literature and theory (MA); MA/PhD. Terminal master's awarded for partial completion of doctoral program. *Degree requirements:* For master's, 3 foreign languages, comprehensive exam; for doctorate, 4 foreign languages, comprehensive exam, thesis/dissertation. *Entrance requirements:* For master's and doctorate, GRE. Additional exam requirements/recommendations for international students: Required—TOEFL (minimum score 550 paper-based; 80 iBT), IELTS (minimum score 7). Electronic applications accepted. *Faculty research:* Literary theory and cultural history, gender studies, Greek and Latin literature, Greek and Roman history, Greek and Roman drama and performance.

University of Chicago, Division of the Humanities, Department of Classics, Chicago, IL 60637. Offers ancient Greek and Roman philosophy (PhD); ancient Mediterranean world (PhD); classical languages and literatures (PhD); transformations in the classical tradition (PhD). *Students:* 25 full-time (12 women); includes 3 minority (1 Asian, non-Hispanic/Latino; 2 Hispanic/Latino), 4 international. Average age 30. 70 applicants, 11% accepted, 1 enrolled. In 2017, 3 doctorates awarded. Terminal master's awarded for partial completion of doctoral program. *Degree requirements:* For doctorate, 3 foreign languages, comprehensive exam (for some programs), thesis/dissertation. *Entrance requirements:* For doctorate, GRE General Test, 15-20 page writing sample, statement of purpose, 3 letters of recommendation, transcripts for all previous degrees and institutions attended. Additional exam requirements/recommendations for international students: Required—TOEFL (minimum score 104 iBT), IELTS (minimum score 7). *Application deadline:* For fall admission, 12/15 for domestic and international students. Application fee: $90. Electronic applications accepted. *Financial support:* In 2017–18, fellowships with full tuition reimbursements (averaging $27,000 per year) were awarded; teaching assistantships with full tuition reimbursements, Federal Work-Study, institutionally sponsored loans, scholarships/grants, and health care benefits also available. Financial award application deadline: 12/15. *Unit head:* Dr. Cliff Ando, Chair, 773-702-8514, E-mail: classics-department@uchicago.edu. *Application contact:* Michael Beetley, Assistant Dean of Students, Admissions and Fellowships, 773-702-1552, Fax: 773-834-9148, E-mail: humanitiesadmissions@uchicago.edu.
Website: http://classics.uchicago.edu/

University of Chicago, Division of the Humanities, Master of Arts Program in the Humanities, Chicago, IL 60637. Offers art history (MA); cinema and media studies (MA); classic languages (MA); comparative literature (MA); creative writing (MA); cultural policy studies (MA); digital humanities (MA); East Asian languages and civilizations (MA); English language and literature (MA); gender and sexuality studies (MA); Germanic studies (MA); linguistics (MA); music (MA); near Eastern languages and civilizations (MA); philosophy (MA); poetics (MA); race, politics and culture (MA); Romance languages and literatures (MA); Slavic languages and literatures (MA); South Asian languages and civilizations (MA); theater and performance studies (MA). *Students:* 95 full-time (50 women), 6 part-time (4 women); includes 22 minority (1 Black or African American, non-Hispanic/Latino; 10 Asian, non-Hispanic/Latino; 11 Hispanic/Latino), 19 international. Average age 26. 708 applicants, 75% accepted, 101 enrolled. In 2017, 91 master's awarded. *Degree requirements:* For master's, thesis. *Entrance requirements:* For master's, GRE General Test, 10-15 page writing sample, statement of purpose, 3 letters of recommendation, transcripts for all previous degrees and institutions attended. Additional exam requirements/recommendations for international students: Required—TOEFL (minimum score 104 iBT), IELTS (minimum score 7). *Application deadline:* For fall admission, 1/3 priority date for domestic and international students. Application fee: $90. Electronic applications accepted. *Expenses:* Contact institution. *Financial support:* In 2017–18, fellowships with partial tuition reimbursements (averaging $12,000 per year) were awarded; Federal Work-Study, institutionally sponsored loans, scholarships/grants, and tuition waivers (partial) also available. Financial award application deadline: 4/30. *Unit head:* Thomas Christensen, Director, 773-834-1201, Fax: 773-834-7526, E-mail: ma-humanities@uchicago.edu. *Application contact:* Michael Beetley, Assistant Dean of Students for Admissions, 773-834-1552, E-mail: humanitiesadmissions@uchicago.edu.
Website: http://maph.uchicago.edu/

University of Cincinnati, Graduate School, McMicken College of Arts and Sciences, Department of Classics, Cincinnati, OH 45221. Offers MA, PhD. *Program availability:* Part-time. Terminal master's awarded for partial completion of doctoral program. *Degree requirements:* For master's, comprehensive exam (for some programs), thesis (for some programs); for doctorate, 2 foreign languages, comprehensive exam, thesis/dissertation. *Entrance requirements:* For master's and doctorate, GRE. Additional exam requirements/recommendations for international students: Required—TOEFL. Electronic applications accepted. *Expenses: Tuition, area resident:* Full-time $14,468. Tuition, state resident: full-time $14,968; part-time $754 per credit hour. Tuition, nonresident: full-time $24,210; part-time $1311 per credit hour. *International tuition:* $26,460 full-time. *Required fees:* $3958; $84 per credit hour. One-time fee: $85 full-time. Tuition and fees vary according to course load, degree level and program. *Faculty research:* Archaeology (bronze age and classical), philosophy (Greek and Latin), ancient history (Greek and Roman).

University of Colorado Boulder, Graduate School, College of Arts and Sciences, Department of Classics, Boulder, CO 80309. Offers MA, PhD. *Faculty:* 13 full-time (8 women). *Students:* 19 full-time (9 women); includes 2 minority (1 Hispanic/Latino; 1 Two or more races, non-Hispanic/Latino). Average age 26. 70 applicants, 50% accepted, 5 enrolled. In 2017, 7 master's, 1 doctorate awarded. Terminal master's awarded for partial completion of doctoral program. *Degree requirements:* For master's, one foreign language, comprehensive exam, thesis or alternative, oral exam; for doctorate, 4 foreign languages, comprehensive exam, thesis/dissertation. *Entrance requirements:* For master's, minimum undergraduate GPA of 2.75; for doctorate, master's degree in classics or related field. *Application deadline:* For fall admission, 2/15 for domestic students; for spring admission, 2/15 for domestic students. Applications are processed on a rolling basis. Application fee: $60 ($80 for international students). Electronic applications accepted. Application fee is waived when completed online. *Financial support:* In 2017–18, 61 students received support, including 22 fellowships (averaging $3,306 per year), 15 teaching assistantships with full and partial tuition reimbursements available (averaging $28,888 per year); research assistantships, institutionally sponsored loans, scholarships/grants, health care benefits, and unspecified assistantships also available. Financial award application deadline: 2/15; financial award applicants required to submit FAFSA. *Faculty research:* Ancient/classical history; classical/ancient language/literature; classical Greek language/literature; arts/humanities/cultural activities; classical Latin language/literature. *Application contact:* E-mail: classics@colorado.edu.
Website: http://www.colorado.edu/classics/

University of Dallas, Braniff Graduate School of Liberal Arts, Program in Classics, Irving, TX 75062-4736. Offers MA, MC. *Degree requirements:* For master's, comprehensive exam, thesis (for MA). *Expenses: Tuition:* Full-time $33,750; part-time $22,500 per year. Tuition and fees vary according to program. *Unit head:* Dr. David Sweet, Dean, 972-721-5288, Fax: 972-721-5280, E-mail: dsweet@udallas.edu.

University of Florida, Graduate School, College of Liberal Arts and Sciences, Department of Classics, Gainesville, FL 32611. Offers classical studies (MA, PhD); Latin (MA, MAT, ML). *Program availability:* Part-time, online learning. *Degree requirements:* For master's, one foreign language, thesis (for some programs); for doctorate, 2 foreign languages, comprehensive exam, thesis/dissertation. *Entrance requirements:* For master's, GRE General Test, minimum GPA of 3.0; for doctorate, GRE General Test, minimum GPA of 3.25 in both graduate and undergraduate work; MA in classical studies or equivalent. Additional exam requirements/recommendations for international students: Required—TOEFL (minimum score 550 paper-based; 80 iBT), IELTS (minimum score 6). Electronic applications accepted. *Faculty research:* Augustan Age Rome, ancient archaeology, Athenian democracy, Roman historiography and satire, Modern Greek studies.

University of Georgia, Franklin College of Arts and Sciences, Department of Classics, Athens, GA 30602. Offers classical languages (MA); Greek (MA); Latin (MA). *Degree requirements:* For master's, one foreign language, thesis. *Entrance requirements:* For master's, GRE General Test. Electronic applications accepted.

University of Illinois at Urbana–Champaign, Graduate College, College of Liberal Arts and Sciences, School of Literatures, Cultures and Linguistics, Department of the Classics, Champaign, IL 61820. Offers classical philology (PhD); classics (MA); teaching of Latin (MA).

The University of Iowa, Graduate College, College of Liberal Arts and Sciences, Department of Classics, Iowa City, IA 52242-1316. Offers classics (MA, PhD); Greek (MA); Latin (MA). *Degree requirements:* For master's, exam; for doctorate, comprehensive exam, thesis/dissertation. *Entrance requirements:* For master's and doctorate, GRE General Test, minimum GPA of 3.0. Additional exam requirements/recommendations for international students: Required—TOEFL (minimum score 550 paper-based; 81 iBT). Electronic applications accepted.

The University of Kansas, Graduate Studies, College of Liberal Arts and Sciences, Department of Classics, Lawrence, KS 66045. Offers MA. *Students:* 11 full-time (6 women), 1 (woman) part-time. Average age 25. 19 applicants, 42% accepted, 6 enrolled. In 2017, 4 master's awarded. *Entrance requirements:* For master's, GRE (recommended), resume (suggested one-page in length), writing sample (25-page maximum), statement of purpose, three letters of reference, official transcripts.

Classics

Additional exam requirements/recommendations for international students: Required—TOEFL. *Application deadline:* For fall admission, 1/15 priority date for domestic and international students; for spring admission, 10/25 priority date for domestic and international students. Application fee: $65 ($85 for international students). Electronic applications accepted. *Financial support:* Fellowships, teaching assistantships, career-related internships or fieldwork, Federal Work-Study, scholarships/grants, traineeships, and unspecified assistantships available. Support available to part-time students. Financial award application deadline: 1/15; financial award applicants required to submit FAFSA. *Faculty research:* Greek and Roman gender and sexuality, Roman literature (Cicero, Virgil, Horace, elegy, post-Virgilian epic), Greek literature (archaic epic, tragedy, Second Sophistic), Greek art and archaeology (the Bronze Age), Roman art and archaeology (imperial painting and architecture). *Unit head:* Prof. Tara Welch, Chair, 785-864-2395, E-mail: tswelch@ku.edu. *Application contact:* Cari Ann Kreienhop, Graduate Admissions Contact, 785-864-3665, Fax: 785-864-5566, E-mail: ckreienhop@ku.edu.
Website: http://classics.drupal.ku.edu/

University of Kentucky, Graduate School, College of Arts and Sciences, Program in Modern and Classical Languages and Literatures, Lexington, KY 40506-0032. Offers MA. *Program availability:* Part-time. *Degree requirements:* For master's, one foreign language, comprehensive exam, thesis optional. *Entrance requirements:* For master's, GRE General Test, minimum undergraduate GPA of 2.75. Additional exam requirements/recommendations for international students: Required—TOEFL (minimum score 550 paper-based). Electronic applications accepted. *Faculty research:* Erasmus, Renaissance Latin, Greek and Roman epic, Greek biography, early Christian literature, classical philosophy.

The University of Manchester, School of Arts, Histories and Cultures, Manchester, United Kingdom. Offers anthropology, media and performance (PhD); applied theatre professional (PhD); archaeology (PhD); art history and visual studies (PhD); arts management and cultural policy (PhD); classics and ancient history (PhD); composition (PhD); creative writing (PhD); drama (PhD); economic and social history (PhD); electroacoustic composition (PhD); English and American studies (PhD); history (PhD); humanitarianism and conflict response (PhD); museology (PhD); music (PhD); musicology (PhD); religions and theology (PhD).

University of Manitoba, Faculty of Graduate Studies, Faculty of Arts, Department of Classics, Winnipeg, MB R3T 2N2, Canada. Offers MA. *Degree requirements:* For master's, thesis.

University of Maryland, College Park, Academic Affairs, College of Arts and Humanities, Department of Classics, College Park, MD 20742. Offers MA. *Degree requirements:* For master's, 2 foreign languages, thesis or alternative. *Entrance requirements:* For master's, writing sample, 3 letters of recommendation. Additional exam requirements/recommendations for international students: Required—TOEFL. Electronic applications accepted. *Faculty research:* Latin, Greek, and Roman culture.

University of Massachusetts Amherst, Graduate School, College of Humanities and Fine Arts, Department of Classics, Amherst, MA 01003. Offers Latin and classical humanities (MAT). *Program availability:* Part-time. *Degree requirements:* For master's, thesis or alternative. *Entrance requirements:* For master's, GRE General Test. Additional exam requirements/recommendations for international students: Required—TOEFL (minimum score 550 paper-based; 80 iBT), IELTS (minimum score 6.5). Electronic applications accepted.

University of Massachusetts Boston, College of Liberal Arts, Program in Latin and Classical Humanities, Boston, MA 02125-3393. Offers MA. *Faculty:* 9 full-time (8 women), 7 part-time/adjunct (4 women). *Students:* 4 full-time (3 women), 12 part-time (4 women). Average age 29. 6 applicants, 67% accepted, 3 enrolled. In 2017, 6 master's awarded. *Expenses:* Tuition, state resident: full-time $17,375. Tuition, nonresident: full-time $33,915. *Required fees:* $355. *Unit head:* Dr. Jacqueline Carlon, 617-287-6121, E-mail: jacqueline.carlon@umb.edu. *Application contact:* Graduate Admissions Coordinator, 617-287-6400, Fax: 617-287-6236, E-mail: bos.gadm@dpc.umassp.edu.

University of Michigan, Rackham Graduate School, College of Literature, Science, and the Arts, Department of Classical Studies, Ann Arbor, MI 48109. Offers classical studies (MA, PhD); Greek and Roman history (PhD); Latin (MA); Latin with teaching certification (MAT). *Faculty:* 26 full-time (15 women), 3 part-time/adjunct (2 women). *Students:* 41 full-time (16 women); includes 4 minority (2 Asian, non-Hispanic/Latino; 2 Two or more races, non-Hispanic/Latino), 6 international. Average age 27. 72 applicants, 19% accepted, 10 enrolled. In 2017, 1 master's, 4 doctorates awarded. Terminal master's awarded for partial completion of doctoral program. *Degree requirements:* For master's, one foreign language, comprehensive exam; for doctorate, 4 foreign languages, comprehensive exam, thesis/dissertation, oral defense of dissertation, preliminary exams, qualifying exams. *Entrance requirements:* For master's, GRE General Test, 2-3 years of Latin (for the Latin MAT); for doctorate, GRE General Test, strict minimum of 3 years of college-level Latin and 2 years of college-level Greek. Additional exam requirements/recommendations for international students: Required—TOEFL (minimum score 560 paper-based). *Application deadline:* For fall admission, 12/15 for domestic and international students. Application fee: $75 ($90 for international students). Electronic applications accepted. *Expenses:* Tuition and fees for PhD programs are waived. *Financial support:* In 2017–18, 41 students received support, including 23 fellowships with full tuition reimbursements available (averaging $20,850 per year), 1 research assistantship with full tuition reimbursement available (averaging $20,850 per year), 15 teaching assistantships with full tuition reimbursements available (averaging $20,850 per year); career-related internships or fieldwork, institutionally sponsored loans, scholarships/grants, traineeships, tuition waivers (full), unspecified assistantships, and summer stipends, year-round health care also available. Financial award application deadline: 3/15. *Faculty research:* Greek and Latin literature, ancient history, papyrology, archaeology. *Unit head:* Prof. Artemis Leontis, Chair and Professor, 734-764-0360, Fax: 734-763-4959, E-mail: classics@umich.edu. *Application contact:* Sarah Kandell-Gritzmaker, Student Services Coordinator, 734-615-3181, Fax: 734-763-4959, E-mail: skandell@umich.edu.
Website: http://www.lsa.umich.edu/classics

University of Michigan, Rackham Graduate School, College of Literature, Science, and the Arts, Interdepartmental Program in Greek and Roman History, Ann Arbor, MI 48109. Offers PhD, Certificate. Certificate program only open to students already studying in another PhD program at University of Michigan. *Degree requirements:* For doctorate, 4 foreign languages, comprehensive exam, thesis/dissertation, oral defense of dissertation, dissertation prospectus, preliminary exams, qualifying exams. *Entrance requirements:* For doctorate, GRE, strict minimum of 2 years each of classical Greek and Latin. Additional exam requirements/recommendations for international students: Required—TOEFL (minimum score 560 paper-based). Electronic applications accepted. *Expenses:* Tuition, state resident: full-time $22,368; part-time $1201 per credit hour. Tuition, nonresident: full-time $45,156; part-time $2467 per credit hour. *Required fees:* $376 per term. Tuition and fees vary according to course load, degree level and program. *Faculty research:* Greek history, Roman history, history of ancient Mediterranean cultures.

University of Minnesota, Twin Cities Campus, Graduate School, College of Liberal Arts, Department of Classical and Near Eastern Studies, Minneapolis, MN 55455-0213. Offers ancient and medieval art and archaeology (MA, PhD); classics (MA, PhD); Greek (MA, PhD); Latin (MA, PhD); religions in antiquity (MA). *Program availability:* Part-time. Terminal master's awarded for partial completion of doctoral program. *Degree requirements:* For master's, 2 foreign languages, comprehensive exam, thesis or alternative; for doctorate, variable foreign language requirement, comprehensive exam, thesis/dissertation. *Entrance requirements:* For master's and doctorate, GRE, 3 letters of recommendation, writing sample, copies of transcripts, personal statement. Additional exam requirements/recommendations for international students: Required—TOEFL. Electronic applications accepted. *Faculty research:* Greek and Latin literature, religions in antiquity, ancient Near East.

University of Missouri, Office of Research and Graduate Studies, College of Arts and Science, Department of Classical Studies, Columbia, MO 65211. Offers classical languages (MA, PhD); classical studies (MA, PhD). Terminal master's awarded for partial completion of doctoral program. *Degree requirements:* For master's, one foreign language; for doctorate, 2 foreign languages, comprehensive exam, thesis/dissertation. *Entrance requirements:* For master's, GRE General Test, minimum GPA of 3.0 during last 2 years; BA from accredited college/university; reading knowledge of Greek and/or Latin; for doctorate, GRE General Test, minimum GPA of 3.0; MA with major in Greek, Latin, or classics, or equivalent minimum of 21 hours of graduate work; reading knowledge of Greek, Latin, German, and French (or Italian). Additional exam requirements/recommendations for international students: Required—TOEFL (minimum score 500 paper-based; 61 iBT), IELTS (minimum score 5.5). Electronic applications accepted. *Faculty research:* Studies in the oral tradition, ancient Mediterranean religion, archaeology of the Ancient World, ancient political culture, late antiquity, rhetoric, the Classical Tradition.

University of Nebraska–Lincoln, Graduate College, College of Arts and Sciences, Department of Classics and Religious Studies, Lincoln, NE 68588. Offers MA. *Degree requirements:* For master's, thesis optional. *Entrance requirements:* For master's, GRE. Additional exam requirements/recommendations for international students: Required—TOEFL (minimum score 550 paper-based). Electronic applications accepted. *Faculty research:* Greek and Latin poetry and prose, Greek and Latin linguistics, patristics, gnosticism, religion of late antiquity.

University of New Brunswick Fredericton, School of Graduate Studies, Faculty of Arts, Department of Classics and Ancient History, Fredericton, NB E3B 5A3, Canada. Offers classics (MA). *Program availability:* Part-time. *Degree requirements:* For master's, thesis. *Entrance requirements:* For master's, minimum GPA of 3.0, minimum of 18 credit hours or equivalent in either Greek or Latin. Additional exam requirements/recommendations for international students: Required—TOEFL, TWE. Electronic applications accepted. *Faculty research:* Roman history, Silver Age Latin poetry, stamped roof tiles, Plato, early Christianity, Greek and Roman archaeology, late Antiquity and Byzantium.

The University of North Carolina at Chapel Hill, Graduate School, College of Arts and Sciences, Department of Classics, Chapel Hill, NC 27599. Offers classical archaeology (MA, PhD); classics (MA, PhD). Terminal master's awarded for partial completion of doctoral program. *Degree requirements:* For master's, one foreign language, comprehensive exam, thesis; for doctorate, 2 foreign languages, comprehensive exam, thesis/dissertation. *Entrance requirements:* For master's and doctorate, GRE General Test, minimum GPA of 3.0. Electronic applications accepted.

The University of North Carolina at Greensboro, Graduate School, College of Arts and Sciences, Department of Classical Studies, Greensboro, NC 27412-5001. Offers Latin (M Ed). *Entrance requirements:* For master's, GRE General Test, MAT, or PRAXIS. Additional exam requirements/recommendations for international students: Required—TOEFL. Electronic applications accepted.

University of Oregon, Graduate School, College of Arts and Sciences, Department of Classics, Eugene, OR 97403. Offers classical civilization (MA); classics (MA), including Greek, Latin; Greek (MA); Latin (MA). *Program availability:* Part-time. *Degree requirements:* For master's, 2 foreign languages, thesis or alternative. *Entrance requirements:* For master's, GRE General Test, minimum GPA of 3.0. Additional exam requirements/recommendations for international students: Required—TOEFL. *Faculty research:* Roman religion, Greek philosophy, archaeology, Greek and Roman literature.

University of Ottawa, Faculty of Graduate and Postdoctoral Studies, Faculty of Arts, Department of Classics and Religious Studies, Ottawa, ON K1N 6N5, Canada. Offers classical studies (MA); religious studies (PhD). *Degree requirements:* For master's, comprehensive exam, thesis or alternative; for doctorate, comprehensive exam, thesis/dissertation. *Entrance requirements:* For master's, honors degree or equivalent, minimum B average; for doctorate, master's degree, minimum B+ average. Electronic applications accepted. *Faculty research:* Religions in Canada, including Amerindian and Inuit religions; religion and culture; late antiquity.

University of Pennsylvania, School of Arts and Sciences, Graduate Group in Classical Studies, Philadelphia, PA 19104. Offers AM, PhD. *Faculty:* 17 full-time (8 women), 1 part-time/adjunct (0 women). *Students:* 17 full-time (11 women); includes 3 minority (all Two or more races, non-Hispanic/Latino), 4 international. Average age 27. 53 applicants, 19% accepted, 4 enrolled. In 2017, 2 master's awarded. Terminal master's awarded for partial completion of doctoral program. Application fee: $70.

University of South Africa, College of Human Sciences, Pretoria, South Africa. Offers adult education (M Ed); African languages (MA, PhD); African politics (MA, PhD); Afrikaans (MA, PhD); ancient history (MA, PhD); ancient Near Eastern studies (MA, PhD); anthropology (MA, PhD); applied linguistics (MA); Arabic (MA, PhD); archaeology (MA); art history (MA); Biblical archaeology (MA); Biblical studies (M Th, D Th, PhD); Christian spirituality (M Th, D Th); church history (M Th, D Th); classical studies (MA, PhD); clinical psychology (MA); communication (MA, PhD); comparative education (M Ed, Ed D); consulting psychology (D Admin, D Com, PhD); curriculum studies (M Ed, Ed D); development studies (M Admin, MA, D Admin, PhD); didactics (M Ed, Ed D); education (M Tech); education management (M Ed, Ed D); educational psychology (M Ed); English (MA); environmental education (M Ed); French (MA, PhD); German (MA, PhD); Greek (MA); guidance and counseling (M Ed); health studies (MA, PhD), including health sciences education (MA), health services management (MA), medical and surgical nursing science (critical care general) (MA), midwifery and neonatal nursing science (MA), trauma and emergency care (MA); history (MA, PhD); history of education (Ed D); inclusive education (M Ed, Ed D); information and communications technology policy and regulation (MA); information science (MA, MIS, PhD); international politics (MA, PhD); Islamic studies (MA, PhD); Italian (MA, PhD); Judaica (MA, PhD); linguistics (MA, PhD); mathematical education (M Ed); mathematics education (MA); missiology (M Th, D Th); modern Hebrew (MA, PhD); musicology (MA, MMus, D Mus, PhD); natural science education (M Ed); New Testament (M Th, D Th); Old Testament (D Th); pastoral therapy (M Th, D Th); philosophy (MA); philosophy of education (M Ed, Ed D); politics (MA, PhD); Portuguese (MA, PhD); practical theology (M Th, D Th); psychology (MA, MS, PhD); psychology of education (M Ed, Ed D); public health (MA); religious studies (MA, D Th, PhD); Romance languages (MA); Russian (MA, PhD); Semitic languages (MA, PhD); social behavior studies in HIV/AIDS (MA); social science (mental

health) (MA); social science in development studies (MA); social science in psychology (MA); social science in social work (MA); social science in sociology (MA); social work (MSW, DSW, PhD); socio-education (M Ed, Ed D); sociolinguistics (MA); sociology (MA, PhD); Spanish (MA, PhD); systematic theology (M Th, D Th); TESOL (teaching English to speakers of other languages) (MA); theological ethics (M Th, D Th); theory of literature (MA, PhD); urban ministries (D Th); urban ministry (M Th).

University of Southern California, Graduate School, Dana and David Dornsife College of Letters, Arts and Sciences, Department of Classics, Los Angeles, CA 90089. Offers MA, PhD. Terminal master's awarded for partial completion of doctoral program. *Degree requirements:* For master's, 2 foreign languages, comprehensive exam, thesis or alternative, Greek and Latin; for doctorate, 2 foreign languages, comprehensive exam, thesis/dissertation, Greek and Latin. *Entrance requirements:* Additional exam requirements/recommendations for international students: Required—TOEFL. Electronic applications accepted. *Faculty research:* Roman literature, Roman history, Greek tragedy, ancient rhetoric and oratory, Greek philosophy.

The University of Texas at Austin, Graduate School, College of Liberal Arts, Department of Classics, Austin, TX 78712-1111. Offers MA, PhD. *Degree requirements:* For master's, 2 foreign languages, comprehensive exam, thesis; for doctorate, 4 foreign languages, comprehensive exam, thesis/dissertation. *Entrance requirements:* For master's, GRE General Test, proficiency in classics; for doctorate, GRE General Test, master's degree in classics. Electronic applications accepted.

University of Toronto, School of Graduate Studies, Faculty of Arts and Science, Department of Classics, Toronto, ON M5S 1A1, Canada. Offers MA, PhD. *Program availability:* Part-time. *Degree requirements:* For master's, qualifying examinations, sight translation exams in Greek and Latin; for doctorate, thesis/dissertation, qualifying examinations, sight translation exams in Greek and Latin. *Entrance requirements:* For master's, minimum B+ average in final year of an undergraduate program in classics, 3-4 years of course work in Greek and Latin; for doctorate, minimum B+ average with at least one A–; MA in classics. Electronic applications accepted.

University of Vermont, Graduate College, College of Arts and Sciences, Department of Classics, Burlington, VT 05404. Offers Greek and Latin (MA); Greek and Latin languages (Graduate Certificate); Latin (MAT). *Students:* 4 (3 women). 6 applicants, 83% accepted, 2 enrolled. In 2017, 3 master's awarded. *Degree requirements:* For master's, one foreign language, thesis. *Entrance requirements:* For master's, GRE General Test, writing sample (for MA). Additional exam requirements/recommendations for international students: Required—TOEFL (minimum score 550 paper-based, 90 iBT) or IELTS (6.5). *Application deadline:* For fall admission, 2/15 priority date for domestic and international students. Applications are processed on a rolling basis. Application fee: $65. Electronic applications accepted. *Expenses:* Tuition, state resident: full-time $11,628; part-time $646 per credit. Tuition, nonresident: full-time $29,340; part-time $1630 per credit. *Required fees:* $1994; $10 per credit. Tuition and fees vary according to course load and program. *Financial support:* In 2017–18, 4 students received support, including 4 teaching assistantships with full tuition reimbursements available (averaging $8,000 per year); fellowships and health care benefits also available. Financial award application deadline: 3/1. *Faculty research:* Early Greek literature. *Unit head:* Dr. John C. Franklin, Chair, 802-656-0649, E-mail: john.franklin@uvm.edu. *Application contact:* Prof. Jacques Bailly, Coordinator, 802-656-3210, E-mail: jacques.bailly@uvm.edu. Website: http://www.uvm.edu/~classics/

University of Victoria, Faculty of Graduate Studies, Faculty of Humanities, Department of Greek and Roman Studies, Victoria, BC V8W 2Y2, Canada. Offers MA, PhD. PhD offered by special arrangement. *Program availability:* Part-time. *Degree requirements:* For master's, 3 foreign languages, thesis. *Entrance requirements:* For master's, knowledge of Greek and Latin. Additional exam requirements/recommendations for international students: Required—TOEFL (minimum score 575 paper-based), IELTS (minimum score 7). Electronic applications accepted. *Faculty research:* Roman social history, Roman archaeology and technology, Roman literature, Greek literature, Homer and tragedy, Greek historiography.

University of Virginia, College and Graduate School of Arts and Sciences, Department of Classics, Charlottesville, VA 22903. Offers MA, PhD. *Faculty:* 9 full-time (3 women), 1 (woman) part-time/adjunct. *Students:* 17 full-time (7 women); includes 1 minority (Hispanic/Latino), 2 international. Average age 27. 32 applicants, 34% accepted, 4 enrolled. In 2017, 1 master's, 2 doctorates awarded. *Degree requirements:* For master's, one foreign language, comprehensive exam, thesis, oral exam; for doctorate, 2 foreign languages, comprehensive exam, thesis/dissertation, oral exam. *Entrance requirements:* For master's and doctorate, GRE General Test, 2 letters of recommendation. Additional exam requirements/recommendations for international students: Required—TOEFL (minimum score 600 paper-based; 90 iBT), IELTS (minimum score 7). *Application deadline:* Applications are processed on a rolling basis. Application fee: $60. Electronic applications accepted. *Financial support:* Fellowships, teaching assistantships, and unspecified assistantships available. Financial award application deadline: 1/3; financial award applicants required to submit FAFSA. *Unit head:* K. Sara Myers, Chair, 434-924-3008, Fax: 434-924-3062, E-mail: classics@virginia.edu. *Application contact:* John Miller, Director of Graduate Studies, 434-924-3008, Fax: 434-924-3062, E-mail: jfm4j@virginia.edu. Website: http://classics.virginia.edu/

University of Washington, Graduate School, College of Arts and Sciences, Department of Classics, Seattle, WA 98195-3110. Offers classics (MA, PhD), including ancient philosophy (PhD), classics (PhD), textual studies (PhD), theory and criticism (PhD). *Program availability:* Part-time. *Faculty:* 11 full-time (7 women). *Students:* 15 full-time (9 women), 2 part-time (both women); includes 3 minority (1 Black or African American, non-Hispanic/Latino; 1 American Indian or Alaska Native, non-Hispanic/Latino; 1 Hispanic/Latino), 4 international. Average age 29. 45 applicants, 42% accepted. In 2017, 3 doctorates awarded. Terminal master's awarded for partial completion of doctoral program. *Degree requirements:* For master's, one foreign language, thesis or alternative; for doctorate, 2 foreign languages, comprehensive exam, thesis/dissertation. *Entrance requirements:* For master's, GRE, bachelor's degree in classics, Greek, or Latin; minimum GPA of 3.0; for doctorate, GRE, minimum GPA of 3.0. Additional exam requirements/recommendations for international students: Required—TOEFL (minimum score 82 iBT). *Application deadline:* For fall admission, 1/5 for domestic students. Application fee: $75. Electronic applications accepted. *Financial support:* In 2017–18, 12 students received support, including 3 fellowships with full tuition reimbursements available (averaging $23,850 per year), research assistantships with full tuition reimbursements available (averaging $23,850 per year), 10 teaching assistantships with full tuition reimbursements available (averaging $23,148 per year); Federal Work-Study, institutionally sponsored loans, health care benefits, and tuition waivers (partial) also available. Financial award application deadline: 1/5; financial

award applicants required to submit FAFSA. *Faculty research:* Greek and Latin poetry, Greek and Roman cultural institutions, Greek and Latin historiography, Greek tragedy. *Unit head:* Prof. Catherine M. Connors, Chair, 206-543-2266, Fax: 206-543-2267, E-mail: cconnors@uw.edu. *Application contact:* Prof. Deborah Kamen, Graduate Program Coordinator, 206-543-2526, Fax: 206-543-2267, E-mail: dkamen@uw.edu. Website: http://classics.washington.edu

University of Washington, Graduate School, College of Arts and Sciences, Department of Philosophy, Seattle, WA 98195. Offers classics and philosophy (PhD); philosophy (MA, PhD). Terminal master's awarded for partial completion of doctoral program. *Degree requirements:* For master's, 3 papers; for doctorate, thesis/dissertation, general exam. *Entrance requirements:* For master's and doctorate, GRE, minimum GPA of 3.0. Additional exam requirements/recommendations for international students: Required—TOEFL. *Faculty research:* History and philosophy of science, epistemology, Aristotle's metaphysics, ethics and politics, causation in modern philosophy.

The University of Western Ontario, Faculty of Graduate Studies, Faculty of Arts and Humanities, Department of Classical Studies, London, ON N6A 5B8, Canada. Offers MA. *Program availability:* Part-time. *Degree requirements:* For master's, one foreign language. *Entrance requirements:* For master's, honors degree, minimum B+ average. Additional exam requirements/recommendations for international students: Required—TOEFL. *Faculty research:* Greek literature, Roman history and law, ancient sport, Byzantine literature, Bronze Age archaeology.

University of Wisconsin–Madison, Graduate School, College of Letters and Science, Department of Classics, Madison, WI 53706-1380. Offers classics (MA, PhD); Greek (MA); Latin (MA). *Program availability:* Part-time. Terminal master's awarded for partial completion of doctoral program. *Degree requirements:* For master's, 3 foreign languages, oral and written exams; for doctorate, 4 foreign languages, thesis/dissertation, written exams. *Entrance requirements:* For master's, GRE; for doctorate, master's degree. Electronic applications accepted. *Faculty research:* Greek tragedy, Latin elegy, historiography, Homer, Greek lyric poetry.

University of Wisconsin–Milwaukee, Graduate School, College of Letters and Science, Department of Foreign Languages and Literature, Milwaukee, WI 53201-0413. Offers foreign languages and literature (MA), including classic Greek, classics, comparative literature, French/Francophone language, literature, and culture, German language, literature, and culture, interpreting, Latin, linguistics, Spanish language, literature, and culture, translation; interpreting (Graduate Certificate); language, literature, and translation (MA, MALLT); translation (Graduate Certificate). *Program availability:* Part-time. *Students:* 11 full-time (6 women), 40 part-time (29 women); includes 10 minority (2 Black or African American, non-Hispanic/Latino; 3 Hispanic/Latino; 5 Two or more races, non-Hispanic/Latino), 4 international. Average age 35. 37 applicants, 68% accepted, 20 enrolled. In 2017, 5 master's awarded. *Degree requirements:* For master's, 2 foreign languages, thesis or alternative. *Entrance requirements:* Additional exam requirements/recommendations for international students: Required—TOEFL (minimum score 550 paper-based; 79 iBT), IELTS (minimum score 6.5). *Application deadline:* For fall admission, 1/1 priority date for domestic students; for spring admission, 9/1 for domestic students. Application fee: $56 ($96 for international students). Electronic applications accepted. *Financial support:* Fellowships, research assistantships, teaching assistantships, career-related internships or fieldwork, health care benefits, unspecified assistantships, and project assistantships available. Support available to part-time students. Financial award application deadline: 4/15; financial award applicants required to submit FAFSA. *Unit head:* Kevin Muse, Department Chair, 414-229-5213, E-mail: kmuse@uwm.edu. *Application contact:* General Information Contact, 414-229-4982, Fax: 414-229-6967, E-mail: gradschool@uwm.edu. Website: http://uwm.edu/foreign-languages-literature/

Vanderbilt University, Department of Classical Studies, Nashville, TN 37240-1001. Offers classics (MA). *Faculty:* 2 full-time (1 woman). *Degree requirements:* For master's, 2 foreign languages, thesis. *Entrance requirements:* For master's, GRE General Test. Additional exam requirements/recommendations for international students: Required—TOEFL (minimum score 570 paper-based; 88 iBT). *Application deadline:* For fall admission, 1/15 for domestic and international students. Electronic applications accepted. *Financial support:* Fellowships with tuition reimbursements, teaching assistantships with tuition reimbursements, Federal Work-Study, institutionally sponsored loans, scholarships/grants, and health care benefits available. Financial award application deadline: 1/15; financial award applicants required to submit CSS PROFILE or FAFSA. *Faculty research:* Greek and Latin literature and language, Greek and Roman history, classical archaeology, philosophy, religion. *Unit head:* Dr. Barbara Tsakirgis, Director of Graduate Studies, 615-322-2516, Fax: 615-343-7261, E-mail: barbara.tsakirgis@vanderbilt.edu. *Application contact:* Walter B. Bieschke, Program Coordinator for Graduate Admissions, 615-322-0236, Fax: 615-343-9936, E-mail: vandygrad@vanderbilt.edu. Website: http://www.vanderbilt.edu/classics/

Villanova University, Graduate School of Liberal Arts and Sciences, Program in Classical Studies, Villanova, PA 19085-1699. Offers MA. *Program availability:* Part-time, evening/weekend, blended/hybrid learning. *Faculty:* 2 full-time (both women). *Students:* 8 full-time (3 women), 3 part-time (1 woman). Average age 30. 12 applicants, 58% accepted, 3 enrolled. In 2017, 3 master's awarded. *Degree requirements:* For master's, comprehensive exam, thesis optional. *Entrance requirements:* For master's, minimum GPA of 3.0. *Application deadline:* Applications are processed on a rolling basis. Application fee: $50. Electronic applications accepted. *Financial support:* Research assistantships, Federal Work-Study, and scholarships/grants available. Financial award applicants required to submit FAFSA. *Unit head:* Dr. Valentina DeNardis, Director, 610-519-4735. Website: http://www1.villanova.edu/villanova/artsci/classical.html

Washington University in St. Louis, The Graduate School, Department of Classics, St. Louis, MO 63130-4899. Offers MA, PhD. Terminal master's awarded for partial completion of doctoral program. *Degree requirements:* For master's, thesis or alternative. *Entrance requirements:* For master's and doctorate, GRE General Test. Additional exam requirements/recommendations for international students: Required—TOEFL. Electronic applications accepted. *Faculty research:* Greek and Latin language and literature; ancient history, philosophy, performance, music, and material culture.

Yale University, Graduate School of Arts and Sciences, Department of Classics, New Haven, CT 06520. Offers M Phil, MA, PhD. *Degree requirements:* For doctorate, 2 foreign languages, thesis/dissertation. *Entrance requirements:* For doctorate, GRE General Test.

Comparative Literature

American University, College of Arts and Sciences, Department of Literature, Washington, DC 20016-8047. Offers creative writing (MFA); literature (MA). *Program availability:* Part-time, evening/weekend. *Faculty:* 53 full-time (36 women), 14 part-time/adjunct (9 women). *Students:* 39 full-time (22 women), 22 part-time (13 women); includes 22 minority (10 Black or African American, non-Hispanic/Latino; 5 Asian, non-Hispanic/Latino; 6 Hispanic/Latino; 1 Two or more races, non-Hispanic/Latino), 3 international. Average age 34. 136 applicants, 77% accepted, 21 enrolled. In 2017, 17 master's awarded. *Degree requirements:* For master's, comprehensive exam. *Entrance requirements:* For master's, GRE, writing sample, statement of purpose, transcripts, 2 letters of recommendation, resume. Additional exam requirements/recommendations for international students: Required—TOEFL (minimum score 600 paper-based; 100 iBT). *Application deadline:* For fall admission, 2/1 priority date for domestic students; for spring admission, 11/1 priority date for domestic students. Application fee: $55. *Expenses:* Contact institution. *Financial support:* Institutionally sponsored loans and unspecified assistantships available. Financial award application deadline: 2/1; financial award applicants required to submit FAFSA. *Unit head:* Dr. David Pike, Department Chair, 202-885-2996, E-mail: dpike@american.edu. *Application contact:* Jonathan Harper, Assistant Director, Graduate Recruitment, 202-855-3622, E-mail: jharper@american.edu.
Website: http://www.american.edu/cas/literature/

The American University in Cairo, School of Humanities and Social Sciences, Cairo, Egypt. Offers Arab and Islamic civilizations (Graduate Diploma); Arabic studies (MA); comparative literary studies (Graduate Diploma); Egyptology and Coptology (MA); English and comparative literature (MA); humanities and social sciences (Graduate Diploma); philosophy (MA); psychology (MA); sociology and anthropology (MA); teaching Arabic as a foreign language (MA); teaching English to speakers of other languages (MA). *Program availability:* Part-time, evening/weekend. *Faculty:* 52 full-time (27 women), 7 part-time/adjunct (3 women). *Students:* 52 full-time (41 women), 159 part-time (119 women), 38 international. Average age 31. 209 applicants, 36% accepted, 39 enrolled. In 2017, 73 master's awarded. *Degree requirements:* For master's, comprehensive exam (for some programs), thesis (for some programs). *Entrance requirements:* Additional exam requirements/recommendations for international students: Required—TOEFL (minimum score 450 paper-based; 45 iBT), IELTS (minimum score 5). *Application deadline:* For fall admission, 2/1 priority date for domestic and international students; for spring admission, 10/15 priority date for domestic and international students. Applications are processed on a rolling basis. Application fee: $85. Electronic applications accepted. *Financial support:* Fellowships with partial tuition reimbursements, scholarships/grants, tuition waivers (partial), and unspecified assistantships available. Financial award application deadline: 3/10. *Faculty research:* English literature, political science, psychology, sociology, anthropology and Egyptology, philosophy, Arabic studies, history, teaching Arabic as a foreign language, teaching English to speakers of other languages. *Unit head:* Dr. Robert Switzer, Interim Dean, 20-2-2615-1068, E-mail: nbowditch@aucegypt.edu. *Application contact:* Maha Hegazi, Director for Graduate Admissions, 20-2-2615-1462, E-mail: mahahegazi@aucegypt.edu.
Website: http://www.aucegypt.edu/huss/Pages/default.aspx

Arizona State University at the Tempe campus, College of Liberal Arts and Sciences, Department of English, Tempe, AZ 85287-0302. Offers applied linguistics (PhD); creative writing (MFA); English (MA, PhD), including comparative literature (MA), linguistics (MA), literature, rhetoric and composition (MA), rhetoric, composition, and linguistics (PhD); film and media studies (MAS), including American media and popular culture; linguistics (Graduate Certificate); teaching English to speakers of other languages (MTESOL); translation studies (Graduate Certificate). Terminal master's awarded for partial completion of doctoral program. *Degree requirements:* For master's, variable foreign language requirement, comprehensive exam (for some programs), thesis (for some programs), interactive Program of Study (iPOS) submitted before completing 50 percent of required credit hours; for doctorate, variable foreign language requirement, comprehensive exam, thesis/dissertation, interactive Program of Study (iPOS) submitted before completing 50 percent of required credit hours. *Entrance requirements:* For master's and doctorate, GRE, minimum GPA of 3.0 or equivalent in last 2 years of work leading to bachelor's degree. Additional exam requirements/recommendations for international students: Required—TOEFL, IELTS, or PTE. Electronic applications accepted.

Binghamton University, State University of New York, Graduate School, Harpur College of Arts and Sciences, Department of Comparative Literature, Binghamton, NY 13902-6000. Offers MA, PhD. *Program availability:* Part-time. *Faculty:* 8 full-time (6 women), 6 part-time/adjunct (4 women). *Students:* 23 full-time (13 women), 38 part-time (25 women); includes 10 minority (1 Black or African American, non-Hispanic/Latino; 3 Asian, non-Hispanic/Latino; 5 Hispanic/Latino; 1 Two or more races, non-Hispanic/Latino), 32 international. Average age 34. 32 applicants, 84% accepted, 9 enrolled. In 2017, 2 master's, 4 doctorates awarded. Terminal master's awarded for partial completion of doctoral program. *Degree requirements:* For master's, 2 foreign languages, comprehensive exam, thesis or alternative; for doctorate, 2 foreign languages, comprehensive exam, thesis/dissertation. *Entrance requirements:* For master's and doctorate, GRE General Test, writing sample. Additional exam requirements/recommendations for international students: Required—TOEFL (minimum score 550 paper-based; 80 iBT). *Application deadline:* For fall admission, 1/1 priority date for domestic and international students; for spring admission, 10/15 priority date for domestic and international students. Application fee: $75. Electronic applications accepted. *Financial support:* In 2017–18, 23 students received support, including 21 teaching assistantships with full tuition reimbursements available (averaging $14,500 per year); career-related internships or fieldwork, Federal Work-Study, institutionally sponsored loans, scholarships/grants, health care benefits, tuition waivers (full and partial), and unspecified assistantships also available. Financial award applicants required to submit FAFSA. *Unit head:* Dr. Luiza Franco Moreira, Chairperson, 607-777-3673, E-mail: lmoreira@binghamton.edu. *Application contact:* Ben Balkaya, Assistant Dean and Director, 607-777-2151, Fax: 607-777-2501, E-mail: balkaya@binghamton.edu.

Brigham Young University, Graduate Studies, College of Humanities, Department of Comparative Arts and Letters, Provo, UT 84602. Offers comparative studies (MA). *Faculty:* 30 full-time (8 women), 3 part-time/adjunct (1 woman). *Students:* 15 full-time (6 women), 1 part-time (0 women); includes 1 minority (Asian, non-Hispanic/Latino). Average age 29. 12 applicants, 75% accepted, 7 enrolled. In 2017, 10 master's awarded. *Degree requirements:* For master's, 2 foreign languages, comprehensive exam, thesis. *Entrance requirements:* For master's, GRE, minimum GPA of 3.0 in last 60 hours, writing sample, foreign language experience, undergraduate degree or experience in a humanities discipline. Additional exam requirements/recommendations for international students: Required—TOEFL (minimum score 580 paper-based; 85 iBT), IELTS (minimum score 7). *Application deadline:* For fall admission, 3/1 for domestic and international students. Application fee: $50. Electronic applications accepted. *Expenses:* $8,850. *Financial support:* In 2017–18, 15 students received support, including 3 research assistantships (averaging $2,500 per year), 21 teaching assistantships (averaging $5,000 per year); scholarships/grants, tuition waivers, unspecified assistantships, and student instructorships also available. Support available to part-time students. *Faculty research:* Renaissance skepticism, ancient novels, papyrology, Mediterranean piracy, Renaissance devotional art, Seventeenth Century French comedy, representations of chance and probability, Dutch baroque art empowering women, Nineteenth Century Denmark and memory studies. *Unit head:* Dr. Roger Macfarlane, Graduate Coordinator/Professor of Classical Studies, 801-422-9078, Fax: 801-422-0305, E-mail: macfarlane@byu.edu. *Application contact:* Andrea Kristensen, Graduate Program Manager, 801-422-2996, Fax: 801-422-0305, E-mail: andrea_kristensen@byu.edu.
Website: http://cal.byu.edu/

Brock University, Faculty of Graduate Studies, Faculty of Humanities, Program in Studies in Comparative Literatures and Arts, St. Catharines, ON L2S 3A1, Canada. Offers MA. *Degree requirements:* For master's, thesis optional. *Entrance requirements:* For master's, honors degree. Additional exam requirements/recommendations for international students: Required—TOEFL (minimum score 550 paper-based; 80 iBT), IELTS (minimum score 6.5), TWE (minimum score 4). Electronic applications accepted.

Brown University, Graduate School, Department of Comparative Literature, Providence, RI 02912. Offers PhD. *Degree requirements:* For doctorate, 2 foreign languages, thesis/dissertation, preliminary exam. *Entrance requirements:* For doctorate, GRE General Test, GRE Subject Test.

California State University, Northridge, Graduate Studies, College of Humanities, Department of English, Northridge, CA 91330. Offers creative writing (MA); literature (MA); rhetoric and composition theory (MA). *Program availability:* Part-time, evening/weekend. *Students:* 24 full-time (19 women), 66 part-time (40 women); includes 39 minority (4 Black or African American, non-Hispanic/Latino; 5 Asian, non-Hispanic/Latino; 23 Hispanic/Latino; 1 Native Hawaiian or other Pacific Islander, non-Hispanic/Latino; 6 Two or more races, non-Hispanic/Latino), 1 international. Average age 34. 74 applicants, 77% accepted, 33 enrolled. In 2017, 42 master's awarded. *Degree requirements:* For master's, thesis or alternative. *Entrance requirements:* For master's, writing proficiency test, GRE General Test or minimum GPA of 3.0. Additional exam requirements/recommendations for international students: Required—TOEFL. *Application deadline:* For fall admission, 11/30 for domestic students. Application fee: $55. *Financial support:* Teaching assistantships available. Financial award application deadline: 3/1. *Faculty research:* Reading improvement, professional writing, Dickens, Shaw, English as a second language. *Unit head:* Kent Baxter, Chair, 818-677-3431.
Website: http://www.csun.edu/english/index.php

Carleton University, Faculty of Graduate Studies, Faculty of Arts and Social Sciences, School for Languages, Literatures, and Comparative Literary Studies, Ottawa, ON K1S 5B6, Canada. Offers cultural mediations (PhD). *Entrance requirements:* Additional exam requirements/recommendations for international students: Required—TOEFL. *Faculty research:* Literary history, theory of literature, cross-cultural studies, modernism/postmodernism, comparative Canadian literature.

Carnegie Mellon University, Dietrich College of Humanities and Social Sciences, Department of English, Pittsburgh, PA 15213-3891. Offers communication planning and design (M Des); literary and cultural studies (MA, PhD); professional writing (MAPW), including editing and publishing, policy and non-profit communication, public and media relations / corporate communications, science or healthcare communication, technical writing, writing for new media, writing for print media; rhetoric (MA, PhD). *Program availability:* Part-time. Terminal master's awarded for partial completion of doctoral program. *Degree requirements:* For doctorate, 2 foreign languages, comprehensive exam, thesis/dissertation. *Entrance requirements:* For master's and doctorate, GRE General Test. Additional exam requirements/recommendations for international students: Required—TOEFL, TWE. *Faculty research:* Cognitive processes in discourse with emphasis on writing, testing, and evaluation.

Case Western Reserve University, School of Graduate Studies, Department of Modern Languages and Literatures and Department of English, Program in World Literature, Cleveland, OH 44106. Offers MA. *Faculty:* 16 full-time (11 women). *Students:* 2 full-time (1 woman); includes 1 minority (Hispanic/Latino). Average age 36. 1 applicant, 100% accepted, 1 enrolled. *Degree requirements:* For master's, 2 foreign languages, thesis, written exam. *Entrance requirements:* For master's, GRE General Test, sample of written work; project proposal. Additional exam requirements/recommendations for international students: Required—TOEFL (minimum score 577 paper-based; 90 iBT); Recommended—IELTS (minimum score 7). *Application deadline:* For fall admission, 3/1 priority date for domestic students. Applications are processed on a rolling basis. Application fee: $50. Electronic applications accepted. *Expenses: Tuition:* Full-time $43,854; part-time $1827 per credit hour. *Required fees:* $50; $50 per credit hour. Tuition and fees vary according to course load and program. *Financial support:* Fellowships, career-related internships or fieldwork, institutionally sponsored loans, and tuition waivers (partial) available. Financial award application deadline: 3/1; financial award applicants required to submit CSS PROFILE or FAFSA. *Faculty research:* Literary theory and translation, Middle Ages, Renaissance, Baroque, Enlightenment, Romanticism, Modernism. *Unit head:* Prof. Cheryl Toman, Professor of French/Chair, 216-368-2233, Fax: 216-368-2216. *Application contact:* Prof. Marie Lathers, Professor of French and Humanities, 216-368-8983, Fax: 216-368-2216, E-mail: marie.lathers@case.edu.
Website: http://artsci.case.edu/world-literature/

Claremont Graduate University, Graduate Programs, School of Arts and Humanities, Department of English, Claremont, CA 91711-6160. Offers American studies (MA, PhD); critical theory (MA, PhD); early modern studies (MA, PhD); English (M Phil, MA, PhD); literary theory (PhD); literature (MA, PhD); literature and creative writing (MA); literature and film (MA); MBA/MA; MBA/PhD. *Program availability:* Part-time. *Entrance requirements:* For master's and doctorate, GRE General Test. Additional exam requirements/recommendations for international students: Required—TOEFL (minimum score 75 iBT). Electronic applications accepted. *Faculty research:* American, comparative, and English Renaissance literature; modernism; feminist literature and theory.

Columbia University, Graduate School of Arts and Sciences, New York, NY 10027. Offers African-American studies (MA); American studies (MA); anthropology (MA, PhD); art history and archaeology (MA, PhD); astronomy (PhD); biological sciences (PhD); biotechnology (MA); chemical physics (PhD); chemistry (PhD); classical studies (MA, PhD); classics (MA, PhD); climate and society (MA); conservation biology (MA); earth and environmental sciences (PhD); East Asia: regional studies (MA); East Asian

languages and cultures (MA, PhD); ecology, evolution and environmental biology (MA), including conservation biology; ecology, evolution, and environmental biology (PhD), including ecology and evolutionary biology, evolutionary primatology; economics (MA, PhD); English and comparative literature (MA, PhD); French and Romance philology (MA, PhD); Germanic languages (MA, PhD); global French studies (MA); global thought (MA); Hispanic cultural studies (MA); history (PhD); history and literature (MA); human rights studies (MA); Islamic studies (MA); Italian (MA, PhD); Japanese pedagogy (MA); Jewish studies (MA); Latin America and the Caribbean: regional studies (MA); Latin American and Iberian cultures (PhD); mathematics (MA, PhD), including finance (MA); medieval and Renaissance studies (MA); Middle Eastern, South Asian, and African studies (MA, PhD); modern art: critical and curatorial studies (MA); modern European studies (MA); museum anthropology (MA); music (DMA, PhD); oral history (MA); philosophical foundations of physics (MA); philosophy (MA, PhD); physics (PhD); political science (MA, PhD); psychology (PhD); quantitative methods in the social sciences (MA); religion (MA, PhD); Russia, Eurasia and East Europe: regional studies (MA); Russian translation (MA); Slavic cultures (MA); Slavic languages (MA, PhD); sociology (MA, PhD); South Asian studies (MA); statistics (MA, PhD); theatre (PhD). Dual-degree programs require admission to both Graduate School of Arts and Sciences and another Columbia school. *Program availability:* Part-time. Terminal master's awarded for partial completion of doctoral program. *Degree requirements:* For master's, variable foreign language requirement, comprehensive exam (for some programs), thesis (for some programs); for doctorate, variable foreign language requirement, comprehensive exam (for some programs), thesis/dissertation. *Entrance requirements:* For master's and doctorate, GRE General Test, GRE Subject Test (for some programs). Additional exam requirements/recommendations for international students: Required—TOEFL, IELTS. Electronic applications accepted. *Expenses: Tuition:* Full-time $44,864; part-time $1704 per credit. *Required fees:* $2370 per semester. One-time fee: $105.

Cornell University, Graduate School, Graduate Fields of Arts and Sciences, Field of Comparative Literature, Ithaca, NY 14853. Offers PhD. *Degree requirements:* For doctorate, 2 foreign languages, comprehensive exam, thesis/dissertation, teaching experience. *Entrance requirements:* For doctorate, GRE General Test, proficiency in 2 foreign literatures, writing sample, 3 letters of recommendation. Additional exam requirements/recommendations for international students: Required—TOEFL (minimum score 550 paper-based; 77 iBT). Electronic applications accepted. *Faculty research:* Critical theory, European studies, Latin American studies, Asian studies.

Dartmouth College, School of Graduate and Advanced Studies, Comparative Literature Program, Hanover, NH 03755. Offers MA. *Faculty:* 25 full-time (16 women), 2 part-time/adjunct (1 woman). *Students:* 11 full-time (6 women); includes 1 minority (Two or more races, non-Hispanic/Latino), 7 international. Average age 24. 22 applicants, 68% accepted, 11 enrolled. In 2017, 5 master's awarded. *Entrance requirements:* For master's, proficiency in 2 languages. Additional exam requirements/recommendations for international students: Required—TOEFL. *Application deadline:* For fall admission, 1/15 for domestic students. Application fee: $40. Electronic applications accepted. *Financial support:* Fellowships, teaching assistantships, career-related internships or fieldwork, institutionally sponsored loans, scholarships/grants, and tuition waivers (full) available. Support available to part-time students. Financial award application deadline: 4/1; financial award applicants required to submit CSS PROFILE or FAFSA. *Unit head:* Dr. Dennis Washburn, Chair, 603-646-1287. *Application contact:* Elizabeth Cassell, Program Administrator, 603-646-0470, E-mail: liz.cassell@dartmouth.edu. Website: http://complit.dartmouth.edu/

Duke University, Graduate School, Program in Literature, Durham, NC 27708. Offers PhD, JD/MA. *Degree requirements:* For doctorate, 2 foreign languages, thesis/dissertation. *Entrance requirements:* For doctorate, GRE General Test, writing sample. Additional exam requirements/recommendations for international students: Required—TOEFL (minimum score 577 paper-based; 90 iBT) or IELTS (minimum score 7).

East Carolina University, Graduate School, Thomas Harriot College of Arts and Sciences, Department of English, Greenville, NC 27858-4353. Offers creative writing (MA); English studies (MA); linguistics (MA); literature (MA); multicultural and transnational literatures (MA, Certificate); professional communication (Certificate); rhetoric and composition (MA); rhetoric, writing, and professional communication (PhD); teaching English in the two-year college (Certificate); teaching English to speakers of other languages (MA, Certificate); technical and professional communication (MA). *Program availability:* Part-time, evening/weekend, online learning. *Students:* 40 full-time (27 women), 74 part-time (57 women); includes 33 minority (23 Black or African American, non-Hispanic/Latino; 2 Asian, non-Hispanic/Latino; 4 Hispanic/Latino; 4 Two or more races, non-Hispanic/Latino). Average age 35. 36 applicants, 94% accepted, 25 enrolled. In 2017, 23 master's, 4 doctorates, 24 other advanced degrees awarded. *Degree requirements:* For master's, comprehensive exam, thesis optional; for doctorate, comprehensive exam, thesis/dissertation. *Entrance requirements:* For master's, GRE General Test or MAT; for doctorate, GRE General Test or MAT, writing samples. Additional exam requirements/recommendations for international students: Recommended—TOEFL (minimum score 78 iBT), IELTS (minimum score 6.5), TWE. *Application deadline:* For fall admission, 7/31 priority date for domestic students, 2/1 priority date for international students; for spring admission, 11/30 priority date for domestic students, 10/1 priority date for international students. Applications are processed on a rolling basis. Application fee: $75. Electronic applications accepted. *Expenses:* Tuition, state resident: full-time $4749; part-time $297 per credit hour. Tuition, nonresident: full-time $17,898; part-time $1119 per credit hour. *Required fees:* $2691; $224 per credit hour. Part-time tuition and fees vary according to course load and program. *Financial support:* Research assistantships with partial tuition reimbursements, teaching assistantships with partial tuition reimbursements, and Federal Work-Study available. Support available to part-time students. Financial award application deadline: 3/1. *Faculty research:* Technical and professional communication, rhetoric/composition, multicultural and transnational literature, creative writing, film studies. *Unit head:* Dr. Marianne Montgomery, Chair, 252-328-6687, E-mail: montgomerym@ecu.edu. *Application contact:* Dean of Graduate School, 252-328-6012, Fax: 252-328-6071, E-mail: gradschool@ecu.edu.
Website: http://www.ecu.edu/cs-cas/engl/

Emory University, Laney Graduate School, Department of Comparative Literature, Atlanta, GA 30322-1100. Offers comparative literature (PhD); philosophy (Certificate); psychoanalytic studies (PhD); women's studies (Certificate). *Degree requirements:* For doctorate, 2 foreign languages, comprehensive exam, thesis/dissertation. *Entrance requirements:* For doctorate, GRE General Test, minimum GPA of 3.0. Additional exam requirements/recommendations for international students: Required—TOEFL. Electronic applications accepted. *Faculty research:* Literary theory, psychoanalysis trauma and testimony, literature and religion, literature and technology, literature and philosophy, politics and global culture, literature and aesthetics.

Emory University, Laney Graduate School, Department of Spanish and Portuguese, Atlanta, GA 30322-1100. Offers comparative literature (Certificate); film studies (Certificate); Spanish (PhD); women's studies (Certificate). *Degree requirements:* For doctorate, 2 foreign languages, comprehensive exam, thesis/dissertation. *Entrance requirements:* For doctorate, GRE General Test. Additional exam requirements/recommendations for international students: Required—TOEFL. Electronic applications

accepted. *Faculty research:* Spanish literature, Spanish American literature, literary theory, criticism, cultural studies.

Fairleigh Dickinson University, Metropolitan Campus, University College: Arts, Sciences, and Professional Studies, Department of English, Philosophy, and Humanities, Program in English and Literature, Teaneck, NJ 07666-1914. Offers MA.

Florida Atlantic University, Dorothy F. Schmidt College of Arts and Letters, Department of Languages, Linguistics, and Comparative Literature, Boca Raton, FL 33431-0991. Offers comparative literature (MA); French (MA); linguistics (MA); Spanish (MA). *Program availability:* Part-time. *Faculty:* 21 full-time (13 women). *Students:* 25 full-time (19 women), 16 part-time (12 women); includes 16 minority (5 Black or African American, non-Hispanic/Latino; 1 Asian, non-Hispanic/Latino; 10 Hispanic/Latino), 12 international. Average age 36. 42 applicants, 60% accepted, 18 enrolled. In 2017, 19 master's awarded. *Degree requirements:* For master's, one foreign language, comprehensive exam, thesis optional. *Entrance requirements:* For master's, GRE General Test, minimum GPA of 3.0. Additional exam requirements/recommendations for international students: Required—TOEFL (minimum score 500 paper-based; 61 iBT), IELTS (minimum score 6). *Application deadline:* For fall admission, 7/1 priority date for domestic students, 2/15 for international students; for spring admission, 11/1 for domestic students, 7/15 for international students. Applications are processed on a rolling basis. Application fee: $30. *Expenses:* Tuition, state resident: full-time $7400; part-time $369.82 per credit. Tuition, nonresident: full-time $20,496; part-time $1042.81 per credit. *Financial support:* Fellowships, research assistantships, teaching assistantships with partial tuition reimbursements, Federal Work-Study, and tuition waivers (partial) available. Support available to part-time students. Financial award application deadline: 4/1. *Faculty research:* Modern European studies, modern Latin America, medieval Europe. *Unit head:* Dr. Marcella Munson, Chair, 561-297-2118, Fax: 561-297-2756, E-mail: mmunson@fau.edu. *Application contact:* Dr. Linda Johnson, Associate Dean, 561-297-0928, Fax: 561-297-2744.
Website: http://www.fau.edu/LLCL/

Georgetown University, Graduate School of Arts and Sciences, School of Continuing Studies, Washington, DC 20057. Offers American studies (MALS); applied intelligence (MPS); Catholic studies (MALS); classical civilizations (MALS); emergency and disaster management (MPS); ethics and the professions (MALS); global strategic communications (MPS); hospitality management (MPS); human resources management (MPS); humanities (MALS); individualized study (MALS); integrated marketing communications (MPS); international affairs (MALS); Islam and Muslim-Christian relations (MALS); journalism (MPS); liberal studies (DLS); literature and society (MALS); medieval and early modern European studies (MALS); public relations and corporate communications (MPS); real estate (MPS); religious studies (MALS); social and public policy (MALS); sports industry management (MPS); systems engineering management (MPS); technology management (MPS); the theory and practice of American democracy (MALS); urban and regional planning (MPS); visual culture (MALS). MPS in systems engineering management offered jointly with Stevens Institute of Technology. *Entrance requirements:* Additional exam requirements/recommendations for international students: Required—TOEFL.

The Graduate Center, City University of New York, Graduate Studies, Program in Comparative Literature, New York, NY 10016-4039. Offers comparative literature (MA, PhD), including Italian (PhD). *Faculty:* 16 full-time (3 women). *Students:* 97 full-time (51 women), 4 part-time (3 women); includes 8 minority (4 Asian, non-Hispanic/Latino; 4 Hispanic/Latino), 39 international. Average age 37. 74 applicants, 27% accepted, 14 enrolled. In 2017, 13 master's, 7 doctorates awarded. Terminal master's awarded for partial completion of doctoral program. *Degree requirements:* For master's, 2 foreign languages, comprehensive exam, thesis; for doctorate, 3 foreign languages, comprehensive exam, thesis/dissertation. *Entrance requirements:* For master's and doctorate, GRE General Test. Additional exam requirements/recommendations for international students: Required—TOEFL. *Application deadline:* For fall admission, 4/15 for domestic students; for spring admission, 11/15 for domestic students. Application fee: $125. Electronic applications accepted. *Financial support:* In 2017–18, 63 students received support, including 60 fellowships, 5 research assistantships, 14 teaching assistantships; career-related internships or fieldwork, Federal Work-Study, institutionally sponsored loans, and tuition waivers (full and partial) also available. Financial award application deadline: 2/1; financial award applicants required to submit FAFSA. *Unit head:* Dr. Giancarlo Lombardi, Executive Officer, 212-817-8170, Fax: 212-817-1509, E-mail: glombardi@gc.cuny.edu. *Application contact:* Les Gribben, Director of Admissions, 212-817-7470, Fax: 212-817-1624, E-mail: lgribben@gc.cuny.edu.

Harrison Middleton University, Graduate Program, Tempe, AZ 85282. Offers education (MA, Ed D); humanities (MA); imaginative literature (MA); interdisciplinary studies (DA); jurisprudence (MA); natural science (MA); philosophy and religion (MA); social science (MA). *Program availability:* Part-time, evening/weekend, online learning. *Degree requirements:* For master's and doctorate, capstone project. *Entrance requirements:* For master's, interview; for doctorate, 2 academic letters of reference, interview, essay. Additional exam requirements/recommendations for international students: Required—TOEFL (minimum score 550 paper-based; 80 iBT). Electronic applications accepted. *Faculty research:* Japanese animation, educational leadership, war art, John Muir's wilderness.

Harvard University, Graduate School of Arts and Sciences, Department of Comparative Literature, Cambridge, MA 02138. Offers comparative literature (PhD); oral literature (PhD). *Degree requirements:* For doctorate, 4 foreign languages, thesis/dissertation, written and oral exams. *Entrance requirements:* For doctorate, GRE General Test, GRE Subject Test (recommended), sample of written work. Additional exam requirements/recommendations for international students: Required—TOEFL.

Hunter College of the City University of New York, Graduate School, School of Arts and Sciences, Department of English, Program in Literature, Language, and Theory, New York, NY 10065-5085. Offers MA. *Program availability:* Part-time, evening/weekend. *Degree requirements:* For master's, one foreign language, comprehensive exam, thesis. *Entrance requirements:* For master's, GRE General Test, minimum 18 credits of course work in English, excluding journalism and writing; statement of purpose. Additional exam requirements/recommendations for international students: Required—TOEFL.

Indiana University Bloomington, University Graduate School, College of Arts and Sciences, Department of Comparative Literature, Bloomington, IN 47405. Offers MA, MAT, PhD. *Program availability:* Part-time. *Degree requirements:* For master's, 2 foreign languages, comprehensive exam (for some programs), thesis (for some programs); for doctorate, 3 foreign languages, comprehensive exam, thesis/dissertation. *Entrance requirements:* For master's, GRE, proficiency in 1 foreign language, 25-page writing sample, 3 letters of recommendation, transcripts, statement of purpose; for doctorate, GRE, proficiency in 2 foreign languages, 25-page writing sample, 3 letters of recommendation, transcripts, statement of purpose. Additional exam requirements/recommendations for international students: Required—TOEFL (minimum score 550 paper-based; 79 iBT). Electronic applications accepted. *Faculty research:* Literary theory, translation, African studies, medieval studies, comparative arts, East-West literary relations.

Comparative Literature

Johns Hopkins University, Zanvyl Krieger School of Arts and Sciences, Department of Comparative Thought and Literature, Baltimore, MD 21218. Offers comparative literature (PhD); intellectual history (PhD). *Faculty:* 4 full-time (3 women). *Students:* 15 full-time (6 women); includes 1 minority (Hispanic/Latino). Average age 27. 26 applicants, 12% accepted, 3 enrolled. In 2017, 2 doctorates awarded. *Degree requirements:* For doctorate, 2 foreign languages, thesis/dissertation. *Entrance requirements:* For doctorate, samples of written work. Additional exam requirements/recommendations for international students: Required—TOEFL (minimum score 600 paper-based; 100 iBT), IELTS (minimum score 7). *Application deadline:* For fall admission, 12/1 for domestic and international students. Application fee: $75. Electronic applications accepted. *Expenses:* Contact institution. *Financial support:* In 2017–18, 15 students received support, including 7 fellowships with full tuition reimbursements available (averaging $29,000 per year), 8 teaching assistantships with full tuition reimbursements available (averaging $29,000 per year); institutionally sponsored loans, tuition waivers (full), and unspecified assistantships also available. Financial award application deadline: 12/1. *Faculty research:* European literature, modern and contemporary French philosophy, American pragmatism and skepticism, moral perfectionism, cinema and philosophy, gender studies, 19th- and 20th-century literature and philosophy, the novel, modernism, existentialism, ethics and justice in contemporary anglophone literature, Russian literature and cinema, film theory and history, gender studies, philosophies of community, theories of spectatorship. *Unit head:* Prof. Betsy Bryan, Acting Chair, 410-516-7619, Fax: 410-516-4897, E-mail: betsy.bryan@jhu.edu. *Application contact:* Marva Philip, Administrator, 410-516-7619, Fax: 410-516-4897, E-mail: mphilip@jhu.edu.
Website: http://www.jhu.edu/~humctr/

Louisiana State University and Agricultural & Mechanical College, Graduate School, College of Humanities and Social Sciences, Interdepartmental Program in Comparative Literature, Baton Rouge, LA 70803. Offers MA, PhD. *Students:* 19 full-time (13 women), 13 part-time (6 women); includes 11 minority (10 Black or African American, non-Hispanic/Latino; 1 Hispanic/Latino), 9 international. Average age 34. 13 applicants, 69% accepted, 5 enrolled. In 2017, 6 master's, 5 doctorates awarded. *Financial support:* In 2017–18, 1 fellowship (averaging $46,705 per year), 1 research assistantship (averaging $20,067 per year), 9 teaching assistantships (averaging $20,067 per year) were awarded.

New York University, Graduate School of Arts and Science, Department of Comparative Literature, New York, NY 10012-1019. Offers MA, PhD. *Program availability:* Part-time. *Students:* Average age 30. 175 applicants, 7% accepted, 7 enrolled. In 2017, 3 master's, 3 doctorates awarded. *Degree requirements:* For master's, 2 foreign languages, thesis; for doctorate, 3 foreign languages, thesis/dissertation. *Entrance requirements:* For master's and doctorate, GRE General Test. Additional exam requirements/recommendations for international students: Required—TOEFL. *Application deadline:* For fall admission, 12/18 for domestic and international students. Application fee: $100. *Expenses: Tuition:* Full-time $41,352; part-time $19,968 per year. *Required fees:* $2496; $1628 per unit. $814 per term. Tuition and fees vary according to course load and program. *Financial support:* Fellowships, teaching assistantships, Federal Work-Study, institutionally sponsored loans, scholarships/grants, health care benefits, and unspecified assistantships available. Financial award application deadline: 12/18; financial award applicants required to submit FAFSA. *Faculty research:* European and non-European literature and culture, comparative poetics, cultural studies, Colonial and Post-Colonial literature and theory, philosophical issues and literary theory. *Unit head:* Avital Ronell, Acting Chair, 212-998-8790, Fax: 212-995-4377, E-mail: complit.grad.admissions@nyu.edu. *Application contact:* Richard Sieburth, Acting Director of Graduate Studies, 212-998-8790, Fax: 212-995-4377, E-mail: complit.grad.admissions@nyu.edu.
Website: http://www.nyu.edu/gsas/dept/complit/

Northwestern University, The Graduate School, Judd A. and Marjorie Weinberg College of Arts and Sciences, Program in Comparative Literary Studies, Evanston, IL 60208. Offers PhD. Admissions and degrees offered through The Graduate School. *Program availability:* Part-time. *Degree requirements:* For doctorate, 2 foreign languages, thesis/dissertation, preliminary exams. *Entrance requirements:* For doctorate, GRE General Test, sample of written work. Additional exam requirements/recommendations for international students: Required—TOEFL. *Faculty research:* The novel, modernism, post-colonial literature and theory, literature and the arts, Middle Ages and Renaissance, literature and philosophy.

Northwestern University, School of Professional Studies, Program in Literature, Evanston, IL 60208. Offers American literature (MA); British literature (MA); comparative and world literature (MA). *Program availability:* Part-time, evening/weekend.
Website: https://sps.northwestern.edu/masters/literature/index.php

Penn State University Park, Graduate School, College of the Liberal Arts, Department of Comparative Literature, University Park, PA 16802. Offers comparative literature (MA, PhD); Russian and comparative literature (MA). *Unit head:* Dr. Susan Welch, Dean, 814-865-7691, Fax: 814-863-2085. *Application contact:* Lori Hawn, Director, Graduate Student Services, 814-865-1795, Fax: 814-863-4627, E-mail: l-gswww@lists.psu.edu.
Website: http://complit.la.psu.edu/

Princeton University, Graduate School, Department of Comparative Literature, Princeton, NJ 08544. Offers PhD. *Faculty:* 9 full-time (5 women), 1 (woman) part-time/adjunct. *Students:* 92 applicants, 11% accepted, 7 enrolled. In 2017, 4 doctorates awarded. *Degree requirements:* For doctorate, variable foreign language requirement, thesis/dissertation. *Entrance requirements:* For doctorate, GRE General Test, GRE Subject Test, sample of written work. Additional exam requirements/recommendations for international students: Required—TOEFL (minimum score 600 paper-based). *Application deadline:* For fall admission, 12/31 for domestic students, 12/1 for international students. Electronic applications accepted. *Financial support:* Fellowships with full tuition reimbursements, teaching assistantships with full tuition reimbursements, Federal Work-Study, and institutionally sponsored loans available. Financial award application deadline: 1/2. *Unit head:* Prof. Benjamin Conisbee Baer, Director of Graduate Studies, 609-258-6127, Fax: 609-258-1873, E-mail: bencbaer@princeton.edu. *Application contact:* Graduate Admissions Office, 609-258-3034, Fax: 609-258-7262, E-mail: gsadmit@princeton.edu.
Website: http://www.princeton.edu/complit/

Purdue University, Graduate School, College of Liberal Arts, Program in Comparative Literature, West Lafayette, IN 47907. Offers MA, PhD. *Program availability:* Part-time. *Students:* 12 full-time (8 women), 9 part-time (6 women), 16 international. Average age 33. 15 applicants, 7% accepted. In 2017, 1 master's, 3 doctorates awarded. *Degree requirements:* For master's, comprehensive exam (for some programs), thesis optional; for doctorate, comprehensive exam, thesis/dissertation. *Entrance requirements:* For master's, GRE General Test, minimum undergraduate GPA of 3.0 or equivalent; for doctorate, GRE General Test, minimum undergraduate GPA of 3.0 or equivalent; master's degree with minimum GPA of 3.0 or equivalent. Additional exam requirements/recommendations for international students: Required—TOEFL (minimum score 550 paper-based; 77 iBT); Recommended—TWE. *Application deadline:* For fall admission, 1/10 priority date for domestic and international students; for spring admission, 10/1 for domestic and international students. Applications are processed on a rolling basis. Application fee: $60 ($75 for international students). Electronic applications accepted. *Financial support:* In 2017–18, teaching assistantships with tuition reimbursements (averaging $12,000 per year) were awarded; fellowships also available. Support available to part-time students. Financial award application deadline: 4/1; financial award applicants required to submit FAFSA. *Faculty research:* Theory and criticism, philosophy and aesthetics, East Asian literature, postcolonial literature, classics. *Unit head:* Dr. Charles S. Ross, Head, 765-494-3749, E-mail: cross@purdue.edu. *Application contact:* Elsa Schirmer, Graduate Contact, 765-496-9629, Fax: 765-496-1700, E-mail: eschirme@purdue.edu.
Website: https://www.cla.purdue.edu/complit/

Rutgers University–New Brunswick, Graduate School-New Brunswick, Program in Comparative Literature, Piscataway, NJ 08854-8097. Offers MA, PhD. *Program availability:* Part-time. Terminal master's awarded for partial completion of doctoral program. *Degree requirements:* For master's, comprehensive exam; for doctorate, 3 foreign languages, thesis/dissertation, written and oral exams. *Entrance requirements:* For doctorate, GRE General Test, GRE Subject Test (recommended). Additional exam requirements/recommendations for international students: Required—TOEFL. Electronic applications accepted. *Faculty research:* Genres and periods, modern literary theory, psychoanalytic approaches to literature, literature and gender, cultural studies.

San Francisco State University, Division of Graduate Studies, College of Liberal and Creative Arts, Department of Comparative and World Literature, San Francisco, CA 94132-1722. Offers comparative literature (MA). *Program availability:* Part-time. *Degree requirements:* For master's, one foreign language. *Application deadline:* Applications are processed on a rolling basis. *Unit head:* Dr. Dane Johnson, Chair, 415-338-3072, Fax: 415-338-6159, E-mail: danej@sfsu.edu. *Application contact:* Dr. Shirin Khanmohamadi, Graduate Coordinator, 415-338-7035, Fax: 415-338-6159, E-mail: shirin1@sfsu.edu.
Website: http://complit.sfsu.edu/

Stanford University, School of Humanities and Sciences, Department of Comparative Literature, Stanford, CA 94305-2004. Offers PhD. *Degree requirements:* For doctorate, 3 foreign languages, thesis/dissertation. *Entrance requirements:* For doctorate, GRE General Test, GRE Subject Test. Additional exam requirements/recommendations for international students: Required—TOEFL. Electronic applications accepted. *Expenses: Tuition:* Full-time $48,987; part-time $10,620 per quarter. One-time fee: $400. Tuition and fees vary according to program.

Stanford University, School of Humanities and Sciences, Program in Modern Thought and Literature, Stanford, CA 94305-2004. Offers PhD. *Degree requirements:* For doctorate, 2 foreign languages, thesis/dissertation, qualifying paper, oral exam. *Entrance requirements:* For doctorate, GRE General Test. Additional exam requirements/recommendations for international students: Required—TOEFL. Electronic applications accepted. *Expenses: Tuition:* Full-time $48,987; part-time $10,620 per quarter. One-time fee: $400. Tuition and fees vary according to program.

Stony Brook University, State University of New York, Graduate School, College of Arts and Sciences, Department of Cultural Studies and Comparative Literature, Stony Brook, NY 11794. Offers comparative literature (MA, PhD); cultural studies (PhD, Certificate). *Program availability:* Evening/weekend. *Faculty:* 10 full-time (3 women). *Students:* 49 full-time (35 women), 4 part-time (all women); includes 9 minority (1 Black or African American, non-Hispanic/Latino; 4 Asian, non-Hispanic/Latino; 4 Hispanic/Latino), 17 international. Average age 34. 65 applicants, 29% accepted, 6 enrolled. In 2017, 6 master's, 5 doctorates, 5 other advanced degrees awarded. Terminal master's awarded for partial completion of doctoral program. *Degree requirements:* For master's, 2 foreign languages, exam; for doctorate, 3 foreign languages, comprehensive exam, thesis/dissertation. *Entrance requirements:* For master's and doctorate, GRE General Test, minimum GPA of 3.5 in major, 3.0 overall. Additional exam requirements/recommendations for international students: Required—TOEFL. *Application deadline:* For fall admission, 1/15 for domestic students; for spring admission, 10/1 for domestic students. Application fee: $100. Electronic applications accepted. *Expenses:* Contact institution. *Financial support:* In 2017–18, 17 teaching assistantships were awarded; fellowships and research assistantships also available. *Faculty research:* Humanities, women's studies, literary criticism, gender studies, philosophy. *Unit head:* 631-632-7464, Fax: 631-632-5707. *Application contact:* Mary Moran-Luba, Coordinator, 631-632-7460, Fax: 631-632-5707, E-mail: mary.moran-luba@stonybrook.edu.
Website: http://www.stonybrook.edu/commcms/cat/index.html

Université de Montréal, Faculty of Arts and Sciences, Department of Comparative Literature, Montréal, QC H3C 3J7, Canada. Offers comparative literature (MA); literature (PhD). *Degree requirements:* For master's, 2 foreign languages, thesis; for doctorate, 3 foreign languages, thesis/dissertation, general exam. *Entrance requirements:* For doctorate, MA with minimum B+ average. Electronic applications accepted.

Université de Sherbrooke, Faculty of Letters and Human Sciences, Department of Letters and Communications, Sherbrooke, QC J1K 2R1, Canada. Offers comparative Canadian literature (MA, PhD); French literature (MA, PhD); linguistics (MA); theatre (MA). *Degree requirements:* For master's, thesis or alternative; for doctorate, thesis/dissertation. *Entrance requirements:* For master's, minimum GPA of 2.8; for doctorate, minimum GPA of 3.0.

Université du Québec à Chicoutimi, Graduate Programs, Program in Literary Studies, Chicoutimi, QC G7H 2B1, Canada. Offers MA. Program offered jointly with Université du Québec à Rimouski and Université du Québec à Trois-Rivières. *Program availability:* Part-time. *Degree requirements:* For master's, thesis optional. *Entrance requirements:* For master's, appropriate bachelor's degree, proficiency in French.

Université du Québec à Montréal, Graduate Programs, Program in Literary Studies, Montréal, QC H3C 3P8, Canada. Offers MA, PhD. *Program availability:* Part-time. *Degree requirements:* For master's, thesis; for doctorate, thesis/dissertation. *Entrance requirements:* For master's, appropriate bachelor's degree or equivalent, proficiency in French; for doctorate, appropriate master's degree or equivalent, proficiency in French.

Université du Québec à Montréal, Graduate Programs, Program in Semiology, Montréal, QC H3C 3P8, Canada. Offers PhD. *Program availability:* Part-time. *Degree requirements:* For doctorate, thesis/dissertation. *Entrance requirements:* For doctorate, appropriate master's degree or equivalent, proficiency in French.

Université du Québec à Rimouski, Graduate Programs, Program in Literary Studies, Rimouski, QC G5L 3A1, Canada. Offers MA, PhD. Programs offered jointly with Université du Québec à Chicoutimi and Université du Québec à Trois-Rivières. *Program availability:* Part-time. *Degree requirements:* For master's, thesis or alternative. *Entrance requirements:* For master's, appropriate bachelor's degree, proficiency in French.

Université du Québec à Trois-Rivières, Graduate Programs, Program in Literary Studies, Trois-Rivières, QC G9A 5H7, Canada. Offers MA. Program offered jointly with Université du Québec à Chicoutimi and Université du Québec à Rimouski. *Program availability:* Part-time. *Degree requirements:* For master's, thesis optional. *Entrance requirements:* For master's, appropriate bachelor's degree, proficiency in French.

Université Laval, Faculty of Letters, Department of Literature, Programs in Literary Studies, Québec, QC G1K 7P4, Canada. Offers MA, PhD. *Program availability:* Part-time. Terminal master's awarded for partial completion of doctoral program. *Degree requirements:* For master's, thesis; for doctorate, comprehensive exam, thesis/

dissertation. *Entrance requirements:* For master's and doctorate, linguistics exams, knowledge of French, knowledge of a second language. Electronic applications accepted.

University at Buffalo, the State University of New York, Graduate School, College of Arts and Sciences, Department of Comparative Literature, Buffalo, NY 14260. Offers MA, PhD. *Program availability:* Part-time. *Faculty:* 7 full-time (2 women). *Students:* 28 full-time (13 women), 12 international. Average age 25. 35 applicants, 54% accepted, 4 enrolled. In 2017, 2 master's, 5 doctorates awarded. Terminal master's awarded for partial completion of doctoral program. *Degree requirements:* For master's, one foreign language, exam or project; for doctorate, 2 foreign languages, comprehensive exam, thesis/dissertation. *Entrance requirements:* For master's, writing sample, 3 letters of recommendation, statement of purpose, undergraduate transcripts; for doctorate, GRE General Test, writing sample, 3 letters of recommendation, statement of purpose, undergraduate transcripts. Additional exam requirements/recommendations for international students: Required—TOEFL (minimum score 550 paper-based; 79 iBT). *Application deadline:* For fall admission, 1/1 for domestic and international students. Applications are processed on a rolling basis. Application fee: $75. Electronic applications accepted. *Financial support:* In 2017–18, 15 students received support, including fellowships with full tuition reimbursements available (averaging $4,150 per year), 15 teaching assistantships with full tuition reimbursements available (averaging $14,700 per year); health care benefits and unspecified assistantships also available. Financial award application deadline: 1/1; financial award applicants required to submit FAFSA. *Faculty research:* Theory; interaction between literature and philosophy; European, Francophone, African, American, and South American literature; postmodernism; post colonialism. *Unit head:* Dr. Krzysztof Ziarek, Chair, 716-645-0858, Fax: 716-645-5979, E-mail: kziarek@buffalo.edu. *Application contact:* Dr. Kalliopi Nikolopoulou, Director of Graduate Studies, 716-645-0857, Fax: 716-645-5979, E-mail: kn34@buffalo.edu.
Website: http://www.complit.buffalo.edu/

University of Arkansas, Graduate School, Interdisciplinary Program in Comparative Literature and Cultural Studies, Fayetteville, AR 72701. Offers MA, PhD. *Degree requirements:* For doctorate, 2 foreign languages, comprehensive exam, thesis/ dissertation optional. *Entrance requirements:* For doctorate, GRE General Test, official transcripts of all undergraduate and graduate work, three letters of recommendation, writing sample, statement of purpose. Additional exam requirements/recommendations for international students: Required—TOEFL (minimum score 550 paper-based; 80 iBT) or IELTS (minimum score 6.5). *Application deadline:* For fall admission, 8/1 for domestic students, 4/1 for international students; for spring admission, 12/1 for domestic students, 10/1 for international students; for summer admission, 4/15 for domestic students, 3/1 for international students. Application fee: $60. Electronic applications accepted. *Expenses:* Tuition, state resident: full-time $3782. Tuition, nonresident: full-time $10,238. *Financial support:* In 2017–18, 1 research assistantship, 13 teaching assistantships were awarded; fellowships, Federal Work-Study, and institutionally sponsored loans also available. *Faculty research:* Literary and cultural theory, cultural studies, postcolonial theory, gender studies, world literature. *Unit head:* Prof. Luis Fernando Restrepo, Director, 479-575-7580, Fax: 479-575-6795, E-mail: lrestr@uark.edu.
Website: http://www.uark.edu/ua/cplt/

University of California, Berkeley, Graduate Division, College of Letters and Science, Department of Comparative Literature, Berkeley, CA 94720-1500. Offers PhD. *Degree requirements:* For doctorate, 3 foreign languages, thesis/dissertation, qualifying exam. *Entrance requirements:* For doctorate, GRE General Test, fluency in 1 foreign language (2 preferred), minimum GPA of 3.0, writing sample, 3 letters of recommendation. Additional exam requirements/recommendations for international students: Recommended—TOEFL (minimum score 570 paper-based; 90 iBT). Electronic applications accepted.

University of California, Davis, Graduate Studies, Graduate Group in Comparative Literature, Davis, CA 95616. Offers PhD. *Degree requirements:* For doctorate, 3 foreign languages, thesis/dissertation. *Entrance requirements:* For doctorate, GRE General Test, minimum GPA of 3.0. Additional exam requirements/recommendations for international students: Required—TOEFL (minimum score 550 paper-based). Electronic applications accepted. *Faculty research:* Literary criticism, literary theory, gender history and literature, genre.

University of California, Irvine, School of Humanities, Department of Comparative Literature, Irvine, CA 92697. Offers MA, PhD. *Students:* 33 full-time (19 women), 4 part-time (2 women); includes 7 minority (3 Asian, non-Hispanic/Latino; 2 Hispanic/Latino; 2 Two or more races, non-Hispanic/Latino), 10 international. Average age 31. 57 applicants, 26% accepted, 9 enrolled. In 2017, 6 master's, 4 doctorates awarded. *Degree requirements:* For master's, one foreign language; for doctorate, 2 foreign languages, thesis/dissertation. *Entrance requirements:* For doctorate, GRE General Test, minimum GPA of 3.5, sample of written work, 3 letters of recommendation. Additional exam requirements/recommendations for international students: Required—TOEFL (minimum score 550 paper-based). *Application deadline:* For fall admission, 12/15 for domestic and international students. Application fee: $105 ($125 for international students). Electronic applications accepted. *Financial support:* Fellowships with full tuition reimbursements, research assistantships with full tuition reimbursements, teaching assistantships with partial tuition reimbursements, institutionally sponsored loans, and tuition waivers (partial) available. Financial award application deadline: 3/1; financial award applicants required to submit FAFSA. *Faculty research:* Critical theory, feminist studies, Asian-American studies. *Unit head:* Gabriele Schwab, Department Chair, 949-824-6406, Fax: 949-824-6416, E-mail: gmschwab@uci.edu. *Application contact:* Bindya Baliga, Graduate Coordinator, 949-824-7968, E-mail: bbaliga@uci.edu.

University of California, Los Angeles, Graduate Division, College of Letters and Science, Department of Comparative Literature, Los Angeles, CA 90095. Offers MA, PhD. Terminal master's awarded for partial completion of doctoral program. *Degree requirements:* For master's, 2 foreign languages; for doctorate, 2 foreign languages, thesis/dissertation, oral and written qualifying exams. *Entrance requirements:* For doctorate, GRE General Test, bachelor's degree; minimum undergraduate GPA of 3.0, 3.4 in upper-division literature courses (or its equivalent if letter grade system not used); literary proficiency in one foreign language and elementary knowledge of another; writing sample. Additional exam requirements/recommendations for international students: Required—TOEFL. Electronic applications accepted.

University of California, Riverside, Graduate Division, Department of Comparative Literature and Foreign Languages, Riverside, CA 92521-0102. Offers comparative literature (MA, PhD). Terminal master's awarded for partial completion of doctoral program. *Degree requirements:* For master's, 3 foreign languages, comprehensive exam; for doctorate, 3 foreign languages, thesis/dissertation, qualifying exams. *Entrance requirements:* For master's and doctorate, GRE General Test, minimum GPA of 3.0. Additional exam requirements/recommendations for international students: Required—TOEFL (minimum score 550 paper-based; 80 iBT). Electronic applications accepted. *Expenses:* Tuition, state resident: full-time $5746. Tuition, nonresident: full-time $10,780. Tuition and fees vary according to campus/location and program. *Faculty research:* French and German Enlightenment, modern drama and theatre,

contemporary critical theory, East-West comparative studies, science fiction and fantasy.

University of California, Santa Barbara, Graduate Division, College of Letters and Sciences, Division of Humanities and Fine Arts, Program in Comparative Literature, Santa Barbara, CA 93106-4130. Offers comparative literature (PhD); East Asian literatures (PhD); feminist studies (PhD); French (PhD); global studies (PhD); translation studies (PhD); MA/PhD. *Degree requirements:* For doctorate, 2 foreign languages, comprehensive exam, thesis/dissertation. *Entrance requirements:* For doctorate, GRE. Additional exam requirements/recommendations for international students: Required—TOEFL (minimum score 550 paper-based; 80 iBT), IELTS (minimum score 7). Electronic applications accepted. *Faculty research:* Comparative literary studies in global context, critical theory, translation studies, media technological studies, trauma studies.

University of California, Santa Cruz, Division of Graduate Studies, Division of Humanities, Department of Literature, Santa Cruz, CA 95064. Offers MA, PhD. Terminal master's awarded for partial completion of doctoral program. *Degree requirements:* For master's, thesis; for doctorate, one foreign language, thesis/dissertation, qualifying exam. *Entrance requirements:* For master's, GRE General Test, writing sample, minimum GPA of 3.5; for doctorate, GRE General Test, minimum GPA of 3.5, writing sample. Additional exam requirements/recommendations for international students: Required—TOEFL (minimum score 550 paper-based; 83 iBT); Recommended—IELTS (minimum score 8). Electronic applications accepted. *Faculty research:* Technologies of narrative; trans/post/emergent nationalisms; poetics, poetry, and experimental writing; materialism and material culture; critical theories.

University of Chicago, Division of the Humanities, Department of Comparative Literature, Chicago, IL 60637. Offers PhD. *Students:* 22 full-time (10 women). 86 applicants, 9% accepted, 2 enrolled. In 2017, 5 doctorates awarded. Terminal master's awarded for partial completion of doctoral program. *Degree requirements:* For doctorate, 2 foreign languages, comprehensive exam, thesis/dissertation. *Entrance requirements:* For doctorate, GRE General Test, 15-20 page writing sample, statement of purpose, 3 letters of recommendation, transcripts for all previous degrees and institutions attended. Additional exam requirements/recommendations for international students: Required—TOEFL (minimum score 104 iBT), IELTS (minimum score 7). *Application deadline:* For fall admission, 12/15 for domestic and international students. Application fee: $90. Electronic applications accepted. *Financial support:* In 2017–18, fellowships with full tuition reimbursements (averaging $27,000 per year) were awarded; teaching assistantships with full tuition reimbursements, Federal Work-Study, institutionally sponsored loans, scholarships/grants, and health care benefits also available. Financial award application deadline: 12/15. *Unit head:* Francoise Meltzer, Chair, E-mail: mltz@uchicago.edu. *Application contact:* Michael Beetley, Assistant Dean of Students, Admissions and Fellowships, 773-702-1552, Fax: 773-834-9148, E-mail: humanitiesadmissions@uchicago.edu.
Website: http://complit.uchicago.edu/

University of Chicago, Division of the Humanities, Master of Arts Program in the Humanities, Chicago, IL 60637. Offers art history (MA); cinema and media studies (MA); classic languages (MA); comparative literature (MA); creative writing (MA); cultural policy studies (MA); digital humanities (MA); East Asian languages and civilizations (MA); English language and literature (MA); gender and sexuality studies (MA); Germanic studies (MA); linguistics (MA); music (MA); near Eastern languages and civilizations (MA); philosophy (MA); poetics (MA); race, politics and culture (MA); Romance languages and literatures (MA); Slavic languages and literatures (MA); South Asian languages and civilizations (MA); theater and performance studies (MA). *Students:* 95 full-time (50 women), 6 part-time (4 women); includes 22 minority (1 Black or African American, non-Hispanic/Latino; 10 Asian, non-Hispanic/Latino; 11 Hispanic/ Latino), 19 international. Average age 26. 708 applicants, 75% accepted, 101 enrolled. In 2017, 91 master's awarded. *Degree requirements:* For master's, thesis. *Entrance requirements:* For master's, GRE General Test, 10-15 page writing sample, statement of purpose, 3 letters of recommendation, transcripts for all previous degrees and institutions attended. Additional exam requirements/recommendations for international students: Required—TOEFL (minimum score 104 iBT), IELTS (minimum score 7). *Application deadline:* For fall admission, 1/3 priority date for domestic and international students. Application fee: $90. Electronic applications accepted. *Expenses:* Contact institution. *Financial support:* In 2017–18, fellowships with partial tuition reimbursements (averaging $12,000 per year) were awarded; Federal Work-Study, institutionally sponsored loans, scholarships/grants, and tuition waivers (partial) also available. Financial award application deadline: 4/30. *Unit head:* Thomas Christensen, Director, 773-834-1201, Fax: 773-834-7526, E-mail: ma-humanities@uchicago.edu. *Application contact:* Michael Beetley, Assistant Dean of Students for Admissions, 773-834-1552, E-mail: humanitiesadmissions@uchicago.edu.
Website: http://maph.uchicago.edu/

University of Dallas, Braniff Graduate School of Liberal Arts, Institute of Philosophic Studies, Program in Literature, Irving, TX 75062-4736. Offers PhD. *Degree requirements:* For doctorate, 2 foreign languages, comprehensive exam, thesis/ dissertation, qualifying exams. *Entrance requirements:* For doctorate, GRE General Test. Additional exam requirements/recommendations for international students: Required—TOEFL. *Application deadline:* For fall admission, 2/15 priority date for domestic students. Application fee: $50. *Expenses: Tuition:* Full-time $33,750; part-time $22,500 per year. Tuition and fees vary according to program. *Financial support:* Application deadline: 2/15. *Faculty research:* Medieval studies, modern literature, Renaissance, Shakespeare. *Unit head:* Dr. Theresa Kenney, Director, 972-721-4069, Fax: 972-721-4007, E-mail: tereska@udallas.edu.

University of Georgia, Franklin College of Arts and Sciences, Department of Comparative Literature, Athens, GA 30602. Offers MA, PhD. *Degree requirements:* For master's, 2 foreign languages, thesis; for doctorate, one foreign language, thesis/ dissertation. *Entrance requirements:* For master's and doctorate, GRE General Test. Electronic applications accepted.

University of Guelph, Graduate Studies, College of Arts, School of English and Theatre Studies, Joint Program in Literary Studies/Theatre Studies in English, Guelph, ON N1G 2W1, Canada. Offers PhD. *Program availability:* Part-time. *Degree requirements:* For doctorate, one foreign language, comprehensive exam, thesis/ dissertation. *Entrance requirements:* For doctorate, MA, 3 letters of reference, writing samples, resume, minimum A- average in graduate course work. Additional exam requirements/recommendations for international students: Required—TOEFL. Electronic applications accepted. *Faculty research:* Canadian studies, Early Modern studies, Postcolonial studies, studies in gender and genre, 19th Century studies.

University of Houston, College of Liberal Arts and Social Sciences, Department of Modern and Classical Languages, Houston, TX 77204. Offers world cultures and literatures (MA). *Degree requirements:* For master's, one foreign language, thesis optional. *Entrance requirements:* For master's, GRE General Test, minimum GPA of 3.0 in last 60 hours of course work. Additional exam requirements/recommendations for international students: Required—TOEFL (minimum score 500 paper-based). Electronic applications accepted.

Comparative Literature

University of Illinois at Urbana–Champaign, Graduate College, College of Liberal Arts and Sciences, School of Literatures, Cultures and Linguistics, Program in Comparative and World Literature, Champaign, IL 61820. Offers comparative literature (MA, PhD). *Entrance requirements:* For master's, minimum GPA of 3.0; writing sample.

University of Maryland, College Park, Academic Affairs, College of Arts and Humanities, Department of English, Program in Comparative Literature, College Park, MD 20742. Offers MA, PhD. *Degree requirements:* For master's, thesis, oral defense; for doctorate, 3 foreign languages, thesis/dissertation, comprehensive exams in 4 areas. *Entrance requirements:* For master's, GRE General Test, foreign language, writing sample, 3 letters of recommendation; for doctorate, GRE General Test, minimum GPA of 3.0, foreign language, writing sample. Additional exam requirements/recommendations for international students: Required—TOEFL. Electronic applications accepted. *Faculty research:* Renaissance studies, drama, modern literature, postcolonial studies, feminist scholarship.

University of Massachusetts Amherst, Graduate School, College of Humanities and Fine Arts, Department of Languages, Literatures, and Cultures, Program in Comparative Literature, Amherst, MA 01003. Offers MA, PhD. *Program availability:* Part-time. Terminal master's awarded for partial completion of doctoral program. *Degree requirements:* For master's, thesis or alternative; for doctorate, comprehensive exam, thesis/dissertation. *Entrance requirements:* For master's and doctorate, GRE General Test, writing samples. Additional exam requirements/recommendations for international students: Required—TOEFL (minimum score 550 paper-based; 80 iBT), IELTS (minimum score 6.5). Electronic applications accepted.

University of Memphis, Graduate School, College of Arts and Sciences, Department of English, Memphis, TN 38152. Offers African-American literature (Graduate Certificate); applied linguistics (PhD); composition studies (PhD); creative writing (MFA); English as a second language (MA); linguistics (MA); literary and cultural studies (PhD), including African-American literature; literature (MA); professional writing (MA, PhD); teaching English as a second/foreign language (Graduate Certificate). *Program availability:* Part-time, evening/weekend, 100% online. *Faculty:* 30 full-time (15 women). *Students:* 73 full-time (34 women), 80 part-time (52 women); includes 35 minority (20 Black or African American, non-Hispanic/Latino; 3 Asian, non-Hispanic/Latino; 9 Hispanic/Latino; 3 Two or more races, non-Hispanic/Latino), 36 international. Average age 35. 78 applicants, 88% accepted, 35 enrolled. In 2017, 27 master's, 15 doctorates, 10 other advanced degrees awarded. Terminal master's awarded for partial completion of doctoral program. *Degree requirements:* For master's, one foreign language, comprehensive exam, thesis optional; for doctorate, 2 foreign languages, comprehensive exam, thesis/dissertation, qualifying exam. *Entrance requirements:* For master's, GRE, minimum undergraduate GPA of 3.0, statement of purpose, two letters of recommendation; for doctorate, GRE, minimum undergraduate and graduate GPA of 3.25, statement of purpose, writing sample, three letters of recommendation. Additional exam requirements/recommendations for international students: Required—TOEFL. *Application deadline:* For fall admission, 1/15 for domestic students; for spring admission, 10/15 for domestic students. Applications are processed on a rolling basis. Application fee: $35 ($60 for international students). Electronic applications accepted. *Expenses:* Contact institution. *Financial support:* In 2017–18, 123 students received support, including 16 research assistantships with full tuition reimbursements available (averaging $15,704 per year), 23 teaching assistantships with full tuition reimbursements available (averaging $22,076 per year); Federal Work-Study, scholarships/grants, and unspecified assistantships also available. Financial award application deadline: 2/1; financial award applicants required to submit FAFSA. *Faculty research:* Applied linguistics, British and American literature, professional writing, composition studies. *Unit head:* Dr. Joshua Phillips, Chair, 901-678-2651, Fax: 901-678-2226, E-mail: jsphllps@memphis.edu. *Application contact:* Dr. Jeffrey Scraba, Coordinator of Graduate Studies, 901-678-4768, Fax: 901-678-2226, E-mail: jscraba@memphis.edu.
Website: http://www.memphis.edu/english

University of Michigan, Rackham Graduate School, College of Literature, Science, and the Arts, Department of Comparative Literature, Ann Arbor, MI 48109. Offers PhD. *Faculty:* 15 full-time (9 women). *Students:* 30 full-time (18 women); includes 6 minority (2 Black or African American, non-Hispanic/Latino; 1 Asian, non-Hispanic/Latino; 3 Hispanic/Latino). Average age 26. 40 applicants, 25% accepted, 5 enrolled. In 2017, 3 doctorates awarded. *Degree requirements:* For doctorate, thesis/dissertation, 2 languages at advanced level in addition to language of instruction, preliminary exam, topics paper, prospectus, oral defense of dissertation. *Entrance requirements:* For doctorate, GRE General Test. Additional exam requirements/recommendations for international students: Required—TOEFL (minimum score 560 paper-based; 84 iBT), Michigan English Language Assessment Battery, or IELTS (minimum score 6.5). *Application deadline:* For fall admission, 1/7 for domestic and international students. Application fee: $75 ($90 for international students). Electronic applications accepted. *Expenses:* Tuition, state resident: full-time $22,368; part-time $1201 per credit hour. Tuition, nonresident: full-time $45,156; part-time $2467 per credit hour. *Required fees:* $376 per term. Tuition and fees vary according to course load, degree level and program. *Financial support:* In 2017–18, 31 students received support, including 10 fellowships with full tuition reimbursements available (averaging $48,257 per year), 1 research assistantship with full tuition reimbursement available (averaging $33,780 per year), 20 teaching assistantships with full tuition reimbursements available (averaging $39,283 per year); scholarships/grants, health care benefits, and unspecified assistantships also available. Financial award application deadline: 4/15. *Faculty research:* Postcolonial theory, cultural studies, critical translation studies, comparative poetics, classical reception studies, gender studies/queer theory, animal studies, medieval literature. *Unit head:* Yopie Prins, Chair, 734-763-2351, Fax: 734-764-8503, E-mail: chair-complit@umich.edu. *Application contact:* Joe Johnson, Student Services Coordinator, 734-647-4894, Fax: 734-764-8503, E-mail: joecjohn@umich.edu.
Website: http://www.lsa.umich.edu/complit/

University of Minnesota, Twin Cities Campus, Graduate School, College of Liberal Arts, Department of Cultural Studies and Comparative Literature, Program in Comparative Literature, Minneapolis, MN 55455-0213. Offers PhD. *Degree requirements:* For doctorate, 3 foreign languages, comprehensive exam, thesis/dissertation. *Entrance requirements:* For doctorate, GRE General Test, sample of written work. Additional exam requirements/recommendations for international students: Required—TOEFL. *Faculty research:* Literary theory, emergent literatures, popular culture, postcolonial literature, gender and sexuality.

University of Missouri, Office of Research and Graduate Studies, College of Arts and Science, Department of Romance Languages and Literatures, Columbia, MO 65211. Offers French (MA, PhD); literature (MA); Spanish (MA, PhD); teaching (MA). Terminal master's awarded for partial completion of doctoral program. *Degree requirements:* For master's, one foreign language; for doctorate, 4 foreign languages, comprehensive exam, thesis/dissertation. *Entrance requirements:* For master's, GRE General Test, minimum GPA of 3.0 in field of major; bachelor's degree; for doctorate, GRE General Test, minimum GPA of 3.0 in field of major; master's degree. Additional exam requirements/recommendations for international students: Required—TOEFL (minimum score 500 paper-based; 61 iBT). Electronic applications accepted.

University of Nebraska–Lincoln, Graduate College, College of Arts and Sciences, Department of English, Lincoln, NE 68588-0333. Offers composition and rhetoric (MA, PhD); creative writing (MA, PhD); literature studies (MA, PhD). *Degree requirements:* For master's, thesis optional; for doctorate, one foreign language, comprehensive exam, thesis/dissertation. *Entrance requirements:* For master's, writing sample; for doctorate, GRE General Test, writing sample. Additional exam requirements/recommendations for international students: Required—TOEFL (minimum score 600 paper-based). Electronic applications accepted. *Faculty research:* Creative writing, composition and rhetoric, women's studies, North American literature, medieval/Renaissance studies.

University of New Mexico, Graduate Studies, College of Arts and Sciences, Program in Foreign Languages and Literatures, Albuquerque, NM 87131-2039. Offers comparative literature and cultural studies (MA); French (MA); French studies (PhD); German studies (MA). *Program availability:* Part-time. *Faculty:* 10 full-time (6 women), 1 (woman) part-time/adjunct. *Students:* 19 full-time (11 women), 10 part-time (6 women); includes 6 minority (4 Hispanic/Latino; 2 Two or more races, non-Hispanic/Latino), 7 international. Average age 29. 22 applicants, 59% accepted, 12 enrolled. In 2017, 9 master's awarded. *Degree requirements:* For master's, one foreign language, thesis optional; for doctorate, 2 foreign languages, thesis/dissertation. *Entrance requirements:* For master's and doctorate, transcript, writing sample, 3 letters of recommendation. Additional exam requirements/recommendations for international students: Required—TOEFL. *Application deadline:* For fall admission, 2/1 priority date for domestic students; for spring admission, 10/1 priority date for domestic students. Application fee: $50. Electronic applications accepted. *Financial support:* Research assistantships, teaching assistantships with tuition reimbursements, Federal Work-Study, health care benefits, and unspecified assistantships available. Financial award application deadline: 3/1; financial award applicants required to submit FAFSA. *Faculty research:* German, Russian, Italian, Japanese, French, comparative literature, culture studies, classics. *Unit head:* Dr. Walter Putnam, Chair, 505-277-4771, Fax: 505-277-3599, E-mail: wputnam@unm.edu. *Application contact:* Jacqueline Ochoa, Application and Graduation Advisor, 505-277-4471, Fax: 505-277-3599, E-mail: jochoa@unm.edu.
Website: http://www.unm.edu/~fll/

University of Notre Dame, Graduate School, College of Arts and Letters, Division of Humanities, PhD Program in Literature, Notre Dame, IN 46556. Offers PhD. *Degree requirements:* For doctorate, 3 foreign languages, thesis/dissertation, candidacy exam. *Entrance requirements:* For doctorate, GRE General Test. Additional exam requirements/recommendations for international students: Required—TOEFL (minimum score 600 paper-based; 80 iBT). Electronic applications accepted. *Faculty research:* Interdisciplinary study of literature from a transitional and intercultural perspective; classics, East Asian, French, German, Irish, Italian, Iberian and Latin American (Portuguese, Spanish).

University of Oregon, Graduate School, College of Arts and Sciences, Program in Comparative Literature, Eugene, OR 97403. Offers MA, PhD. *Program availability:* Part-time. Terminal master's awarded for partial completion of doctoral program. *Degree requirements:* For master's, 2 foreign languages, field exam; for doctorate, 2 foreign languages, thesis/dissertation, field exam. *Entrance requirements:* For master's, previous course work in English and literature, proficiency in 3 foreign languages, writing sample; for doctorate, previous course work in English and literature, proficiency in 2 foreign languages, writing sample. Additional exam requirements/recommendations for international students: Required—TOEFL. *Faculty research:* Critical theory, historical periods, interdisciplinary approach, Feminist studies.

University of Pennsylvania, School of Arts and Sciences, Graduate Group in Comparative Literature and Literary Theory, Philadelphia, PA 19104. Offers comparative literature (AM, PhD); literary theory (AM, PhD). *Faculty:* 20 full-time (7 women), 6 part-time/adjunct (3 women). *Students:* 27 full-time (13 women), 3 part-time (2 women); includes 5 minority (2 Black or African American, non-Hispanic/Latino; 3 Hispanic/Latino), 9 international. Average age 30. 96 applicants, 13% accepted, 5 enrolled. In 2017, 4 master's, 3 doctorates awarded. *Entrance requirements:* Additional exam requirements/recommendations for international students: Required—TOEFL.
Website: http://ccat.sas.upenn.edu/Complit

University of Puerto Rico–Río Piedras, College of Humanities, Department of Comparative Literature, San Juan, PR 00931-3300. Offers MA. *Program availability:* Part-time. *Degree requirements:* For master's, comprehensive exam, thesis. *Entrance requirements:* For master's, EXADEP, interview, minimum GPA of 3.0, letter of recommendation.

University of Rochester, School of Arts and Sciences, Department of Modern Languages and Cultures, Rochester, NY 14627. Offers comparative literature (MA). *Faculty:* 15 full-time (8 women). *Students:* 2 full-time (1 woman), both international. Average age 26. 2 applicants, 100% accepted, 2 enrolled. In 2017, 2 master's awarded. *Degree requirements:* For master's, comprehensive exam, thesis, comparative literature (for German students from Cologne only). *Entrance requirements:* For master's, GRE General Test. *Application deadline:* Applications are processed on a rolling basis. Application fee: $0. *Expenses:* $1,596 per credit hour. *Financial support:* Application deadline: 2/1. Total annual research expenditures: $5,085. *Unit head:* John Givens, Chair, 585-275-4253, E-mail: john.givens@rochester.edu. *Application contact:* Joanna Drexel, Department Manager, 585-275-4253, E-mail: joanna.drexel@rochester.edu.
Website: https://www.sas.rochester.edu/mlc/

University of South Carolina, The Graduate School, College of Arts and Sciences, Department of Languages, Literatures, and Cultures, Columbia, SC 29208. Offers comparative literature (MA, PhD); foreign languages (MAT), including French, German, Spanish; French (MA); German (MA); Spanish (MA). MAT offered in cooperation with the College of Education. *Program availability:* Part-time. *Degree requirements:* For master's, one foreign language, comprehensive exam, thesis optional; for doctorate, 2 foreign languages, comprehensive exam, thesis/dissertation. *Entrance requirements:* For master's and doctorate, GRE General Test, writing sample. Additional exam requirements/recommendations for international students: Required—TOEFL (minimum score 75 iBT). Electronic applications accepted. *Faculty research:* Modern literature, linguistics, literature and culture, medieval literature, literary theory.

University of Southern California, Graduate School, Dana and David Dornsife College of Letters, Arts and Sciences, Comparative Studies in Literature and Culture Doctoral Program, Los Angeles, CA 90089. Offers comparative literature (PhD); comparative media and culture (PhD); Spanish and Latin American studies (PhD). *Degree requirements:* For doctorate, 2 foreign languages, comprehensive exam, thesis/dissertation. *Entrance requirements:* For doctorate, GRE, competence in language other than English (highly recommended). Additional exam requirements/recommendations for international students: Required—TOEFL. Electronic applications accepted. *Faculty research:* Literary theory, Japanese film and contemporary fiction, Francophone literature and cinema, Latin American and Caribbean literature, Spanish literature and film, nineteenth and twentieth century British and American literature.

University of South Florida, Innovative Education, Tampa, FL 33620-9951. Offers adult, career and higher education (Graduate Certificate), including college teaching, leadership in developing human resources, leadership in higher education; Africana studies (Graduate Certificate), including diasporas and health disparities, genocide and

human rights; aging studies (Graduate Certificate), including gerontology; art research (Graduate Certificate), including museum studies; business foundations (Graduate Certificate); chemical and biomedical engineering (Graduate Certificate), including materials science and engineering, water, health and sustainability; child and family studies (Graduate Certificate), including positive behavior support; civil and industrial engineering (Graduate Certificate), including transportation systems analysis; community and family health (Graduate Certificate), including maternal and child health, social marketing and public health, violence and injury: prevention and intervention, women's health; criminology (Graduate Certificate), including criminal justice administration; data science for public administration (Graduate Certificate); digital humanities (Graduate Certificate); educational measurement and research (Graduate Certificate), including evaluation; English (Graduate Certificate), including comparative literary studies, creative writing, professional and technical communication; entrepreneurship (Graduate Certificate); environmental health (Graduate Certificate), including safety management; epidemiology and biostatistics (Graduate Certificate), including applied biostatistics, biostatistics, concepts and tools of epidemiology, epidemiology, epidemiology of infectious diseases; geography, environment and planning (Graduate Certificate), including community development, environmental policy and management, geographical information systems; geology (Graduate Certificate), including hydrogeology; global health (Graduate Certificate), including disaster management, global health and Latin American and Caribbean studies, global health practice, humanitarian assistance, infection control; government and international affairs (Graduate Certificate), including Cuban studies, globalization studies; health policy and management (Graduate Certificate), including health management and leadership, public health policy and programs; hearing specialist: early intervention (Graduate Certificate); industrial and management systems engineering (Graduate Certificate), including systems engineering, technology management; information studies (Graduate Certificate), including school library media specialist; information systems/decision sciences (Graduate Certificate), including analytics and business intelligence; instructional technology (Graduate Certificate), including distance education, Florida digital/virtual educator, instructional design, multimedia design, Web design; internal medicine, bioethics and medical humanities (Graduate Certificate), including biomedical ethics; Latin American and Caribbean studies (Graduate Certificate); leadership for coastal resiliency planning (Graduate Certificate); mass communications (Graduate Certificate), including multimedia journalism; mathematics and statistics (Graduate Certificate), including mathematics; medicine (Graduate Certificate), including aging and neuroscience, bioinformatics, biotechnology, brain fitness and memory management, clinical investigation, hand and upper limb rehabilitation, health informatics, health sciences, integrative weight management, intellectual property, medicine and gender, metabolic and nutritional medicine, metabolic cardiology, pharmacy sciences; national and competitive intelligence (Graduate Certificate); nursing (Graduate Certificate), including simulation based academic fellowship in advanced pain management; psychological and social foundations (Graduate Certificate), including career counseling, college teaching, diversity in education, mental health counseling, school counseling; public affairs (Graduate Certificate), including nonprofit management, public management, research administration; public health (Graduate Certificate), including assessing chemical toxicity and public health risks, health equity, pharmacoepidemiology, public health generalist, toxicology, translational research in adolescent behavioral health; public health practices (Graduate Certificate), including planning for healthy communities; rehabilitation and mental health counseling (Graduate Certificate), including integrative mental health care, marriage and family therapy, rehabilitation technology; secondary education (Graduate Certificate), including ESOL, foreign language education: culture and content, foreign language education: professional; social work (Graduate Certificate), including geriatric social work/clinical gerontology; special education (Graduate Certificate), including autism spectrum disorder, disabilities education: severe/profound; world languages (Graduate Certificate), including teaching English as a second language (TESL) or foreign language. *Unit head:* Dr. Cynthia DeLuca, Associate Vice President and Assistant Vice Provost, 813-974-3077, Fax: 813-974-7061, E-mail: deluca@usf.edu. *Application contact:* Owen Hooper, Director, Summer and Alternative Calendar Programs, 813-974-6917, E-mail: hooper@usf.edu.
Website: http://www.usf.edu/innovative-education/

The University of Texas at Austin, Graduate School, College of Liberal Arts, Program in Comparative Literature, Austin, TX 78712-1111. Offers MA, PhD. *Degree requirements:* For master's, 2 foreign languages, report or thesis; for doctorate, 3 foreign languages, thesis/dissertation. *Entrance requirements:* For master's and doctorate, GRE General Test. Electronic applications accepted.

The University of Texas at Dallas, School of Arts and Humanities, Richardson, TX 75080. Offers art history (MA); history (MA); humanities (MA, PhD), including aesthetic studies, history of ideas, studies in literature; Latin American studies (MA). *Program availability:* Part-time, evening/weekend. *Faculty:* 47 full-time (17 women), 4 part-time/adjunct (2 women). *Students:* 132 full-time (83 women), 117 part-time (71 women); includes 62 minority (11 Black or African American, non-Hispanic/Latino; 3 American Indian or Alaska Native, non-Hispanic/Latino; 10 Asian, non-Hispanic/Latino; 25 Hispanic/Latino; 13 Two or more races, non-Hispanic/Latino), 29 international. Average age 40. 127 applicants, 55% accepted, 43 enrolled. In 2017, 17 master's, 18 doctorates awarded. *Degree requirements:* For master's, one foreign language, portfolio; for doctorate, one foreign language, thesis/dissertation. *Entrance requirements:* For master's and doctorate, minimum GPA of 3.0 in undergraduate course work in field. Additional exam requirements/recommendations for international students: Required—TOEFL (minimum score 550 paper-based). *Application deadline:* For fall admission, 7/15 for domestic students, 5/1 priority date for international students; for spring admission, 11/15 for domestic students, 9/1 priority date for international students. Applications are processed on a rolling basis. Application fee: $50 ($100 for international students). Electronic applications accepted. *Expenses:* Tuition, state resident: full-time $12,916; part-time $718 per credit hour. Tuition, nonresident: full-time $25,252; part-time $1403 per credit hour. *Financial support:* In 2017–18, 136 students received support, including 12 research assistantships with partial tuition reimbursements available (averaging $22,710 per year), 71 teaching assistantships with partial tuition reimbursements available (averaging $15,000 per year); fellowships, Federal Work-Study, institutionally sponsored loans, scholarships/grants, and unspecified assistantships also available. Support available to part-time students. Financial award application deadline: 4/30; financial award applicants required to submit FAFSA. *Faculty research:* Science and the arts and humanities, intellectual and philosophical history, cultural studies, translation studies. *Total annual research expenditures:* $183,441. *Unit head:* Dr. Dennis M. Kratz, Dean, 972-883-2984, Fax: 972-883-2989, E-mail: dkratz@utdallas.edu. *Application contact:* Dr. John Gooch, Associate Dean of Graduate Studies, 972-883-2756, Fax: 972-883-2989, E-mail: john.gooch@utdallas.edu.
Website: http://www.utdallas.edu/ah/

University of Toronto, School of Graduate Studies, Faculty of Arts and Science, Centre for Comparative Literature, Toronto, ON M5S 1A1, Canada. Offers MA, PhD. *Program availability:* Part-time. *Degree requirements:* For doctorate, thesis/dissertation. *Entrance requirements:* For master's, 2 letters of recommendation, sample of work (short essay on a literary topic preferred), resume, bachelor's degree with a B+ average; for doctorate, 2 letters of recommendation, sample of work (short essay on a literary topic preferred), resume, master's degree with average grade of at least A-. Additional exam requirements/recommendations for international students: Required—TOEFL (minimum score 580 paper-based; 93 iBT), TWE (minimum score 5). Electronic applications accepted.

University of Utah, Graduate School, College of Humanities, Department of World Languages and Cultures, Salt Lake City, UT 84112. Offers comparative literary and cultural studies (MA, PhD); French (MA); Spanish (MA, MALP); world languages (MA). *Program availability:* Part-time. *Faculty:* 36 full-time (22 women). *Students:* 27 full-time (19 women), 8 part-time (6 women); includes 5 minority (4 Hispanic/Latino; 1 Two or more races, non-Hispanic/Latino), 10 international. Average age 27. 17 applicants, 76% accepted, 9 enrolled. In 2017, 13 master's, 2 doctorates awarded. Terminal master's awarded for partial completion of doctoral program. *Degree requirements:* For master's, variable foreign language requirement, comprehensive exam (for some programs), thesis (for some programs); for doctorate, 2 foreign languages, comprehensive exam, thesis/dissertation. *Entrance requirements:* For master's, bachelor's degree from regionally-accredited college or university with minimum undergraduate overall GPA of 3.0; for doctorate, MA from regionally-accredited college or university, advanced proficiency in target language. Additional exam requirements/recommendations for international students: Required—TOEFL (minimum score 550 paper-based; 80 iBT), IELTS (minimum score 6.5). *Application deadline:* For fall admission, 1/15 priority date for domestic students, 12/15 priority date for international students. Application fee: $55 ($65 for international students). Electronic applications accepted. *Financial support:* In 2017–18, 24 students received support, including 24 teaching assistantships with full and partial tuition reimbursements available (averaging $17,200 per year); unspecified assistantships also available. Financial award application deadline: 1/15. *Faculty research:* Literary study, literary theory, linguistics, cultural studies, comparative studies. *Unit head:* Dr. Katharina Gerstenberger, Chair, 801-585-7908, Fax: 801-581-7581, E-mail: katharina.gerstenberger@utah.edu. *Application contact:* Mackenzie Buie, Academic Coordinator, 801-581-7748, Fax: 801-581-7581, E-mail: mackenzie.buie@utah.edu.
Website: http://languages.utah.edu/

University of Washington, Graduate School, College of Arts and Sciences, Department of Comparative Literature, Seattle, WA 98195. Offers MA, PhD. *Program availability:* Part-time. Terminal master's awarded for partial completion of doctoral program. *Degree requirements:* For master's, 2 foreign languages, thesis optional; for doctorate, 3 foreign languages, thesis/dissertation. *Entrance requirements:* For master's, GRE General Test, BA in comparative literature or equivalent, minimum GPA of 3.0, proficiency in 1 foreign language; for doctorate, GRE General Test, MA in comparative literature or equivalent, minimum GPA of 3.0, proficiency in 2 foreign languages. Additional exam requirements/recommendations for international students: Required—TOEFL. Electronic applications accepted. *Faculty research:* Literature and culture from classical antiquity to twentieth-century, literary theory and criticism.

The University of Western Ontario, Faculty of Graduate Studies, Faculty of Arts and Humanities, Department of Modern Languages and Literatures, London, ON N6A 5B8, Canada. Offers comparative literature (MA, PhD); Hispanic studies (MA, PhD). *Program availability:* Part-time. *Degree requirements:* For master's, 2 foreign languages, thesis (for some programs). *Entrance requirements:* For master's, honors degree in Spanish or equivalent, minimum B average. Additional exam requirements/recommendations for international students: Required—TOEFL (comparative literature). *Faculty research:* Spanish golden age, Latin-American, romance, medieval, film.

University of Wisconsin–Madison, Graduate School, College of Letters and Science, Department of Comparative Literature, Madison, WI 53706-1380. Offers MA, PhD. *Program availability:* Part-time. Terminal master's awarded for partial completion of doctoral program. *Degree requirements:* For master's, one foreign language, second-year exam; for doctorate, 3 foreign languages, thesis/dissertation, 3 preliminary exams. *Entrance requirements:* For master's, GRE General Test, writing sample; for doctorate, GRE General Test. Electronic applications accepted. *Faculty research:* Literary theory, cultural criticism, classics through early modern literature, postmodernity, gender studies.

University of Wisconsin–Madison, Graduate School, College of Letters and Science, Department of East Asian Languages and Literature, Program in Chinese Literature, Madison, WI 53706-1380. Offers MA, PhD. *Program availability:* Part-time. Terminal master's awarded for partial completion of doctoral program. *Degree requirements:* For master's, one foreign language, seminars, written exam; for doctorate, 3 foreign languages, thesis/dissertation, seminars, preliminary exams, oral exam. *Entrance requirements:* For master's, bachelor's degree or equivalent in Chinese; for doctorate, master's degree or equivalent in Chinese. Electronic applications accepted. *Faculty research:* Chinese historical and modern linguistics, classical Chinese literary and cultural history, modern Chinese literary and cultural history, Chinese paleography.

University of Wisconsin–Madison, Graduate School, College of Letters and Science, Department of Scandinavian Studies, Madison, WI 53706-1380. Offers area studies (MA); folklore (PhD); literature (MA, PhD); philology (PhD). *Program availability:* Part-time. *Degree requirements:* For master's, 2 foreign languages, exam; for doctorate, thesis/dissertation, exam. *Entrance requirements:* For master's, minimum GPA of 3.25; for doctorate, minimum GPA of 3.5. Electronic applications accepted. *Faculty research:* Historical fiction, Icelandic poetry, nineteenth-century literature, theater, gender studies, folklore.

University of Wisconsin–Milwaukee, Graduate School, College of Letters and Science, Department of Foreign Languages and Literature, Milwaukee, WI 53201-0413. Offers foreign languages and literature (MA), including classic Greek, classics, comparative literature, French/Francophone language, literature, and culture, German language, literature, and culture, interpreting, Latin, linguistics, Spanish language, literature, and culture, translation; interpreting (Graduate Certificate); language, literature, and translation (MA, MALLT); translation (Graduate Certificate). *Program availability:* Part-time. *Students:* 11 full-time (6 women), 40 part-time (29 women); includes 10 minority (2 Black or African American, non-Hispanic/Latino; 3 Hispanic/Latino; 5 Two or more races, non-Hispanic/Latino), 4 international. Average age 35. 37 applicants, 68% accepted, 20 enrolled. In 2017, 5 master's awarded. *Degree requirements:* For master's, 2 foreign languages, thesis or alternative. *Entrance requirements:* Additional exam requirements/recommendations for international students: Required—TOEFL (minimum score 550 paper-based; 79 iBT), IELTS (minimum score 6.5). *Application deadline:* For fall admission, 1/1 priority date for domestic students; for spring admission, 9/1 for domestic students. Application fee: $56 ($96 for international students). Electronic applications accepted. *Financial support:* Fellowships, research assistantships, teaching assistantships, career-related internships or fieldwork, health care benefits, unspecified assistantships, and project assistantships available. Support available to part-time students. Financial award application deadline: 4/15; financial award applicants required to submit FAFSA. *Unit head:* Kevin Muse, Department Chair, 414-229-5213, E-mail: kmuse@uwm.edu. *Application contact:* General Information Contact, 414-229-4982, Fax: 414-229-6967, E-mail: gradschool@uwm.edu.
Website: http://uwm.edu/foreign-languages-literature/

Comparative Literature

Washington University in St. Louis, The Graduate School, Department of East Asian Languages and Cultures, St. Louis, MO 63130-4899. Offers Chinese (MA); Chinese and comparative literature (PhD); Chinese language and literature (PhD); East Asian studies (MA); Japanese (MA); Japanese and comparative literature (PhD); Japanese language and literature (PhD). Terminal master's awarded for partial completion of doctoral program. *Degree requirements:* For master's, thesis optional; for doctorate, thesis/dissertation. *Entrance requirements:* For master's and doctorate, GRE General Test. Additional exam requirements/recommendations for international students: Required—TOEFL. Electronic applications accepted. *Faculty research:* Chinese; Japanese; Chinese fiction, theater, poetry, modern literature; Japanese modern and classical fiction, translation theory.

Washington University in St. Louis, The Graduate School, Department of Romance Languages and Literatures, Program in French, St. Louis, MO 63130-4899. Offers French and comparative literature (PhD); French language and literature (PhD). Terminal master's awarded for partial completion of doctoral program. *Degree requirements:* For doctorate, thesis/dissertation. *Entrance requirements:* For doctorate, GRE General Test. Additional exam requirements/recommendations for international students: Required—TOEFL. Electronic applications accepted. *Faculty research:* French language and literature.

Washington University in St. Louis, The Graduate School, Department of Romance Languages and Literatures, Program in Spanish, St. Louis, MO 63130-4899. Offers Hispanic languages and literatures (PhD); Spanish and comparative literature (PhD). Terminal master's awarded for partial completion of doctoral program. *Degree requirements:* For doctorate, thesis/dissertation. *Entrance requirements:* For doctorate, GRE General Test. Additional exam requirements/recommendations for international

students: Required—TOEFL. Electronic applications accepted. *Faculty research:* Latin American and Iberian literatures and languages, Spanish and comparative literature.

Washington University in St. Louis, The Graduate School, Program in Comparative Literature, St. Louis, MO 63130-4899. Offers PhD. Terminal master's awarded for partial completion of doctoral program. *Degree requirements:* For doctorate, thesis/dissertation. *Entrance requirements:* For doctorate, GRE General Test. Additional exam requirements/recommendations for international students: Required—TOEFL. Electronic applications accepted. *Faculty research:* World literature; literary theory; translation studies; global and multicultural theory; comparative drama; comparative arts; studies in literature, politics and society; narrative theory; media ecologies, histories, and poetics.

Western Kentucky University, Graduate Studies, Potter College of Arts and Letters, Department of English, Bowling Green, KY 42101. Offers education (MA); English (MA Ed); literature (MA), including American literature, British literature, literary theory, women writers, world literature; teaching English as a second language (MA); writing (MA). *Program availability:* Part-time, evening/weekend. *Degree requirements:* For master's, comprehensive exam, thesis optional, final exam. *Entrance requirements:* For master's, GRE General Test, minimum GPA of 2.75. Additional exam requirements/recommendations for international students: Required—TOEFL (minimum score 555 paper-based; 79 iBT). *Faculty research:* Improving writing, linking teacher knowledge and performance, Victorian women writers, Kentucky women writers, Kentucky poets.

Yale University, Graduate School of Arts and Sciences, Department of Comparative Literature, New Haven, CT 06520. Offers PhD. *Degree requirements:* For doctorate, 2 foreign languages, thesis/dissertation. *Entrance requirements:* For doctorate, GRE General Test.

English

Abilene Christian University, Graduate Programs, College of Arts and Sciences, Department of English, Abilene, TX 79699. Offers composition/rhetoric (MA); literature (MA); writing (MA). *Program availability:* Part-time. *Faculty:* 16 part-time/adjunct (6 women). *Students:* 4 full-time (3 women), 1 (woman) part-time. 8 applicants, 50% accepted, 1 enrolled. In 2017, 8 master's awarded. *Degree requirements:* For master's, one foreign language, comprehensive exam (for some programs), thesis (for some programs). *Entrance requirements:* For master's, GRE General Test. Additional exam requirements/recommendations for international students: Required—TOEFL (minimum score 80 iBT), IELTS (minimum score 6), PTE. *Application deadline:* For fall admission, 8/11 for domestic students; for spring admission, 11/1 for domestic students. Applications are processed on a rolling basis. Application fee: $50. Electronic applications accepted. *Expenses:* $1,148 per hour. *Financial support:* In 2017–18, 4 students received support, including 4 teaching assistantships with partial tuition reimbursements available (averaging $5,800 per year); Federal Work-Study and scholarships/grants also available. Support available to part-time students. Financial award application deadline: 4/1; financial award applicants required to submit FAFSA. *Faculty research:* Feminism, Shakespearean dimensions of new literature, poetic consciousness, deconstruction myths. *Unit head:* Dr. William Carroll, Graduate Director, 325-674-2556, Fax: 325-674-2408, E-mail: william.carroll@acu.edu. *Application contact:* Graduate Admissions, 325-674-6911, Fax: 325-674-6717, E-mail: gradinfo@acu.edu. Website: http://www.acu.edu/graduate/academics/english.html

Acadia University, Faculty of Arts, Department of English, Wolfville, NS B4P 2R6, Canada. Offers MA. *Entrance requirements:* For master's, honors degree in English, minimum A- average. Additional exam requirements/recommendations for international students: Required—TOEFL (minimum score 630 paper-based; 93 iBT), IELTS (minimum score 6.5). *Application deadline:* For fall admission, 2/1 priority date for domestic and international students; for spring admission, 3/30 for domestic students. Applications are processed on a rolling basis. Application fee: $50. *Financial support:* Application deadline: 2/1. *Faculty research:* Renaissance, Canadian, medieval, Victorian, and Romantic literature. *Unit head:* Dr. Lisa Narbeshuber, Graduate Advisor, 902-585-1251, E-mail: lisa.narbeshuber@acadiau.ca. *Application contact:* Christine Kendrick, Secretary, 902-585-1502, Fax: 902-585-1070, E-mail: christine.kendrick@acadiau.ca.
Website: http://english.acadiau.ca/

The American University in Cairo, School of Humanities and Social Sciences, Cairo, Egypt. Offers Arab and Islamic civilizations (Graduate Diploma); Arabic studies (MA); comparative literary studies (Graduate Diploma); Egyptology and Coptology (MA); English and comparative literature (MA); humanities and social sciences (Graduate Diploma); philosophy (MA); psychology (MA); sociology and anthropology (MA); teaching Arabic as a foreign language (MA); teaching English to speakers of other languages (MA). *Program availability:* Part-time, evening/weekend. *Faculty:* 52 full-time (27 women), 7 part-time/adjunct (3 women). *Students:* 52 full-time (41 women), 159 part-time (119 women), 38 international. Average age 31. 209 applicants, 36% accepted, 39 enrolled. In 2017, 73 master's awarded. *Degree requirements:* For master's, comprehensive exam (for some programs), thesis (for some programs). *Entrance requirements:* Additional exam requirements/recommendations for international students: Required—TOEFL (minimum score 450 paper-based; 45 iBT), IELTS (minimum score 5). *Application deadline:* For fall admission, 2/1 priority date for domestic and international students; for spring admission, 10/15 priority date for domestic and international students. Applications are processed on a rolling basis. Application fee: $85. Electronic applications accepted. *Financial support:* Fellowships with partial tuition reimbursements, scholarships/grants, tuition waivers (partial), and unspecified assistantships available. Financial award application deadline: 3/10. *Faculty research:* English literature, political science, psychology, sociology, anthropology and Egyptology, philosophy, Arabic studies, history, teaching Arabic as a foreign language, teaching English to speakers of other languages. *Unit head:* Dr. Robert Switzer, Interim Dean, 20-2-2615-1068, E-mail: nbowditch@aucegypt.edu. *Application contact:* Maha Hegazi, Director for Graduate Admissions, 20-2-2615-1462, E-mail: mahahegazi@aucegypt.edu.
Website: http://www.aucegypt.edu/huss/Pages/default.aspx

American University of Beirut, Graduate Programs, Faculty of Arts and Sciences, 1107 2020, Lebanon. Offers anthropology (MA); Arab and Middle Eastern history (PhD); Arabic language and literature (MA, PhD); archaeology (MA); art history and curating (MA); biology (MS); cell and molecular biology (PhD); chemistry (MS); clinical psychology (MA); computational sciences (MS); computer science (MS); economics (MA); education (MA), including administration and policy studies, elementary education, mathematics education, psychology school guidance, psychology test and measurements, science education, teaching English as a foreign language; English

language (MA); English literature (MA); environmental policy planning (MS); financial economics (MAFE); general psychology (MA); geology (MS); history (MA); Islamic studies (MA); mathematics (MS); media studies (MA); Middle East studies (MA); philosophy (MA); physics (MS); political studies (MA); public administration (MA); public policy and international affairs (MA); sociology (MA); theoretical physics (PhD). *Program availability:* Part-time. *Faculty:* 108 full-time (36 women), 5 part-time/adjunct (4 women). *Students:* 251 full-time (180 women), 233 part-time (172 women). Average age 26. 425 applicants, 65% accepted, 121 enrolled. In 2017, 47 master's, 2 doctorates awarded. *Degree requirements:* For master's, one foreign language, comprehensive exam, thesis (for some programs), project; for doctorate, one foreign language, comprehensive exam, thesis/dissertation. *Entrance requirements:* For master's, GRE General Test (for some programs); for doctorate, GRE General Test (GRE Subject Test for theoretical physics). Additional exam requirements/recommendations for international students: Required—TOEFL (minimum score 583 paper-based; 97 iBT), IELTS (minimum score 7). *Application deadline:* For fall admission, 2/8 for domestic students; for spring admission, 11/3 for domestic students. Application fee: $50. Electronic applications accepted. *Expenses:* Contact institution. *Financial support:* In 2017–18, 29 fellowships, 40 research assistantships were awarded; teaching assistantships, scholarships/grants, tuition waivers (full and partial), and unspecified assistantships also available. Financial award application deadline: 4/4. *Unit head:* Dr. Nadia Maria El Cheikh, Dean, Faculty of Arts and Sciences, 961-1-374374 Ext. 3800, Fax: 961-1-744461, E-mail: nmcheikh@aub.edu.lb. *Application contact:* Rima Rassi, Graduate Studies Officer, 961-1-350000 Ext. 3833, Fax: 961-1-744461, E-mail: rr46@aub.edu.lb.
Website: http://www.aub.edu.lb/fas/pages/default.aspx

Andrews University, School of Graduate Studies, College of Arts and Sciences, Department of English, Berrien Springs, MI 49104. Offers MA, MAT. *Program availability:* Part-time. *Faculty:* 8 full-time (4 women), 2 part-time/adjunct (1 woman). *Students:* 5 full-time (3 women), 7 part-time (6 women); includes 5 minority (2 Black or African American, non-Hispanic/Latino; 3 Hispanic/Latino), 1 international. Average age 33. 5 applicants, 80% accepted, 4 enrolled. In 2017, 2 master's awarded. *Degree requirements:* For master's, one foreign language, thesis optional. *Entrance requirements:* For master's, GRE Subject Test. Additional exam requirements/recommendations for international students: Required—TOEFL (minimum score 550 paper-based). *Application deadline:* For fall admission, 8/15 for domestic students. Applications are processed on a rolling basis. Application fee: $40. *Financial support:* Fellowships, research assistantships, teaching assistantships, career-related internships or fieldwork, and Federal Work-Study available. *Faculty research:* Shakespearean studies. *Unit head:* Dr. Meredith Jones-Gray, Chairperson, 269-471-3298. *Application contact:* Justina Clayburn, Supervisor of Graduate Admission, 800-253-2874, Fax: 269-471-6321, E-mail: graduate@andrews.edu.

Angelo State University, College of Graduate Studies and Research, College of Arts and Humanities, Department of English and Modern Languages, San Angelo, TX 76909. Offers English (MA); TESOL (MA). *Program availability:* Part-time, evening/weekend. *Students:* 8 full-time (7 women), 11 part-time (9 women); includes 5 minority (1 Asian, non-Hispanic/Latino; 4 Hispanic/Latino), 2 international. Average age 29. *Degree requirements:* For master's, comprehensive exam. *Entrance requirements:* For master's, essay. Additional exam requirements/recommendations for international students: Required—TOEFL or IELTS. *Application deadline:* For fall admission, 7/15 priority date for domestic students, 6/10 for international students; for spring admission, 12/1 priority date for domestic students, 11/1 for international students. Applications are processed on a rolling basis. Application fee: $40 ($50 for international students). Electronic applications accepted. *Expenses:* Tuition, state resident: full-time $3856. Tuition, nonresident: full-time $11,324. *Required fees:* $2650. *Financial support:* Teaching assistantships, Federal Work-Study, scholarships/grants, and unspecified assistantships available. Support available to part-time students. Financial award application deadline: 3/1; financial award applicants required to submit FAFSA. *Unit head:* Dr. Laurence E. Musgrove, Chair, 325-486-6138, Fax: 325-942-2208, E-mail: laurence.musgrove@angelo.edu.
Website: http://www.angelo.edu/dept/english_modern_languages/

Appalachian State University, Cratis D. Williams Graduate School, Department of English, Boone, NC 28608. Offers English (MA). *Program availability:* Part-time, online learning. *Degree requirements:* For master's, one foreign language, comprehensive exam, thesis (for some programs). *Entrance requirements:* For master's, GRE General Test, 3 letters of recommendation. Additional exam requirements/recommendations for international students: Required—TOEFL (minimum score 570 paper-based; 79 iBT), IELTS (minimum score 6.5). Electronic applications accepted. *Faculty research:* Contemporary Irish literature, Romantic psychology, cultural practices of everyday life, Gullah linguistics, Renaissance women's writing.

Arcadia University, College of Arts and Sciences, Department of English, Program in English, Glenside, PA 19038-3295. Offers MA. *Expenses:* Contact institution.

Arizona State University at the Tempe campus, College of Liberal Arts and Sciences, Department of English, Tempe, AZ 85287-0302. Offers applied linguistics (PhD); creative writing (MFA); English (MA, PhD), including comparative literature (MA), linguistics (MA), literature, rhetoric and composition (MA), rhetoric, composition, and linguistics (PhD); film and media studies (MAS), including American media and popular culture; linguistics (Graduate Certificate); teaching English to speakers of other languages (MTESOL); translation studies (Graduate Certificate). Terminal master's awarded for partial completion of doctoral program. *Degree requirements:* For master's, variable foreign language requirement, comprehensive exam (for some programs), thesis (for some programs), interactive Program of Study (iPOS) submitted before completing 50 percent of required credit hours; for doctorate, variable foreign language requirement, comprehensive exam, thesis/dissertation, interactive Program of Study (iPOS) submitted before completing 50 percent of required credit hours. *Entrance requirements:* For master's and doctorate, GRE, minimum GPA of 3.0 or equivalent in last 2 years of work leading to bachelor's degree. Additional exam requirements/recommendations for international students: Required—TOEFL, IELTS, or PTE. Electronic applications accepted.

Arkansas State University, Graduate School, College of Humanities and Social Sciences, Department of English and Philosophy, State University, AR 72467. Offers English (MA); English education (MSE, SCCT). *Program availability:* Part-time. *Degree requirements:* For master's, variable foreign language requirement, comprehensive exam, thesis or alternative, preliminary exam; for SCCT, comprehensive exam. *Entrance requirements:* For master's, GRE General Test or MAT, appropriate bachelor's degree, official transcript, valid teaching certificate (for MSE), immunization records; for SCCT, GRE General Test or MAT, interview, master's degree, official transcript, immunization records. Additional exam requirements/recommendations for international students: Required—TOEFL (minimum score 550 paper-based; 79 iBT), IELTS (minimum score 6), PTE (minimum score 56). Electronic applications accepted.

Arkansas Tech University, College of Arts and Humanities, Russellville, AR 72801. Offers applied sociology (MS); English (M Ed, MA); history (MA); liberal arts (MLA); multi-media journalism (MA); psychology (MS); teaching English as a second language (MA). *Program availability:* Part-time, 100% online, blended/hybrid learning. *Students:* 35 full-time (22 women), 122 part-time (94 women); includes 34 minority (11 Black or African American, non-Hispanic/Latino; 2 Asian, non-Hispanic/Latino; 19 Hispanic/Latino; 2 Two or more races, non-Hispanic/Latino), 19 international. Average age 34. In 2017, 85 master's awarded. *Degree requirements:* For master's, comprehensive exam (for some programs), thesis (for some programs), project. *Entrance requirements:* Additional exam requirements/recommendations for international students: Required—TOEFL (minimum score 550 paper-based; 79 iBT), IELTS (minimum score 6.5), PTE (minimum score 58). *Application deadline:* For fall admission, 3/1 priority date for domestic students, 5/1 priority date for international students; for spring admission, 10/1 priority date for domestic and international students. Applications are processed on a rolling basis. Application fee: $40 ($90 for international students). Electronic applications accepted. *Expenses:* Tuition, state resident: full-time $6816; part-time $284 per credit hour. Tuition, nonresident: full-time $13,632; part-time $568 per credit hour. *Required fees:* $420 per semester. Tuition and fees vary according to course load. *Financial support:* In 2017–18, research assistantships with full and partial tuition reimbursements (averaging $4,800 per year), teaching assistantships with full and partial tuition reimbursements (averaging $4,800 per year) were awarded; career-related internships or fieldwork, Federal Work-Study, scholarships/grants, health care benefits, and unspecified assistantships also available. Support available to part-time students. Financial award application deadline: 4/15; financial award applicants required to submit FAFSA. *Unit head:* Dr. Jeffrey Woods, Dean, 479-968-0274, Fax: 479-964-0812, E-mail: jwoods@atu.edu. *Application contact:* Dr. Mary B. Gunter, Dean of Graduate College, 479-968-0398, Fax: 479-964-0542, E-mail: gradcollege@atu.edu. Website: http://www.atu.edu/humanities/

Asbury University, School of Graduate and Professional Studies, Wilmore, KY 40390-1198. Offers biology: alternative certificate (MA Ed); chemistry: alternative certificate (MA Ed); English (MA Ed); English as a second language (MA Ed); ESL (MA Ed); French (MA Ed); Latin: alternative certificate (MA Ed); mathematics: alternative certificate (MA Ed); reading/writing endorsement (MA Ed); social studies (MA Ed); social work (MSW), including child and family services; Spanish (MA Ed); special education (MA Ed); special education: alternative certificate (MA Ed); teacher as leader endorsement (MA Ed). *Accreditation:* NCATE. *Program availability:* Part-time. *Degree requirements:* For master's, action research project, portfolio. *Entrance requirements:* For master's, PRAXIS/NTE, minimum GPA of 2.75, letters of recommendation. Additional exam requirements/recommendations for international students: Required—TOEFL (minimum score 550 paper-based). Electronic applications accepted.

⭐ **Auburn University,** Graduate School, College of Liberal Arts, Department of English, Auburn University, AL 36849. Offers MA, MTPC, PhD, Graduate Certificate. *Program availability:* Part-time. *Faculty:* 66 full-time (33 women), 8 part-time/adjunct (4 women). *Students:* 25 full-time (14 women), 29 part-time (18 women); includes 6 minority (5 Black or African American, non-Hispanic/Latino; 1 Hispanic/Latino), 1 international. Average age 30. 57 applicants, 60% accepted, 17 enrolled. In 2017, 14 master's, 7 doctorates, 1 other advanced degree awarded. *Degree requirements:* For master's, one foreign language, thesis optional, written exam; for doctorate, 2 foreign languages, thesis/dissertation, oral and written exams. *Entrance requirements:* For master's, GRE General Test, sample of written work; for doctorate, GRE General Test, GRE Subject Test, sample of written work. *Application deadline:* Applications are processed on a rolling basis. Application fee: $50 ($60 for international students). Electronic applications accepted. *Expenses:* Tuition, state resident: full-time $10,974; part-time $519 per credit hour. Tuition, nonresident: full-time $29,658; part-time $1557 per credit hour. *Required fees:* $816 per semester. Tuition and fees vary according to degree level and program. *Financial support:* Fellowships, teaching assistantships, and Federal Work-Study available. Support available to part-time students. Financial award application deadline: 3/15; financial award applicants required to submit FAFSA. *Faculty research:* English literature, American literature, linguistics, rhetoric and composition, literary theory. *Unit head:* Dr. Jeremy M. Downes, Chair, 334-844-9079. *Application contact:* Dr. George Flowers, Dean of the Graduate School, 334-844-2125.

See Display on this page and Close-Up on page 433.

Austin Peay State University, College of Graduate Studies, College of Arts and Letters, Department of Languages and Literature, Clarksville, TN 37044. Offers English (MA). *Program availability:* Part-time. *Faculty:* 8 full-time (5 women). *Students:* 5 full-time (3 women), 8 part-time (5 women); includes 1 minority (Two or more races, non-Hispanic/Latino). Average age 29. 7 applicants, 86% accepted, 3 enrolled. In 2017, 3 master's awarded. *Degree requirements:* For master's, comprehensive exam, thesis optional. *Entrance requirements:* For master's, GRE General Test, 2 letters of recommendation, minimum undergraduate GPA of 2.9. Additional exam requirements/recommendations for international students: Required—TOEFL (minimum score 500

paper-based). *Application deadline:* For fall admission, 8/8 priority date for domestic students. Applications are processed on a rolling basis. Application fee: $45 ($55 for international students). Electronic applications accepted. *Expenses:* Tuition, state resident: full-time $7686; part-time $427 per credit hour. Tuition, nonresident: full-time $20,268; part-time $1126 per credit hour. *Required fees:* $1529; $76.45 per credit hour. *Financial support:* Research assistantships with full tuition reimbursements, career-related internships or fieldwork, Federal Work-Study, institutionally sponsored loans, scholarships/grants, and unspecified assistantships available. Support available to part-time students. Financial award application deadline: 4/1; financial award applicants required to submit FAFSA. *Faculty research:* American literature, British literature, linguistics, composition, technical writing. *Unit head:* Dr. David Guest, Chair, 931-221-7891, Fax: 931-221-7219, E-mail: guestd@apsu.edu. *Application contact:* Megan Mitchell, Coordinator of Graduate Admissions, 931-221-6189, Fax: 931-221-7641, E-mail: mitchellm@apsu.edu.
Website: http://www.apsu.edu/langlit/index.php

Azusa Pacific University, College of Liberal Arts and Sciences, Department of English, Azusa, CA 91702-7000. Offers MA. *Program availability:* Part-time. *Expenses:* Contact institution.

Ball State University, Graduate School, College of Sciences and Humanities, Department of English, Muncie, IN 47306. Offers English (MA, PhD), including composition (MA), creative writing (MA), literature, rhetoric and composition; linguistics (MA), including linguistics, teaching English to speakers of other languages (TESOL) and linguistics. *Program availability:* Part-time. *Faculty:* 20 full-time (15 women), 2 part-time/adjunct (both women). *Students:* 45 full-time (30 women), 30 part-time (17 women); includes 5 minority (2 Asian, non-Hispanic/Latino; 3 Hispanic/Latino), 17 international. Average age 29. 93 applicants, 61% accepted, 32 enrolled. In 2017, 20 master's, 7 doctorates awarded. *Degree requirements:* For doctorate, variable foreign language requirement, thesis/dissertation. *Entrance requirements:* For master's, GRE General Test, minimum baccalaureate GPA of 2.75 or 3.0 in latter half of baccalaureate, statement of purpose, writing sample, three letters of recommendation; for doctorate, GRE General Test, GRE Subject Test, minimum graduate GPA of 3.2, statement of purpose, writing sample, three letters of recommendation. Additional exam requirements/recommendations for international students: Required—TOEFL (minimum score 550 paper-based; 79 iBT), IELTS (minimum score 6.5). *Application deadline:* Applications are processed on a rolling basis. Application fee: $60. Electronic applications accepted. *Financial support:* In 2017–18, 46 students received support, including 5 research assistantships with partial tuition reimbursements available (averaging $15,132 per year), 28 teaching assistantships with partial tuition reimbursements available (averaging $13,595 per year); unspecified assistantships also available. Financial award application deadline: 3/1; financial award applicants required to submit FAFSA. *Faculty research:* American literature; literary editing; medieval, Renaissance, and eighteenth-century British literature; rhetoric. *Unit head:* Dr. Deborah Mix, Assistant Chair of Programs, 765-285-8401, Fax: 765-285-3765, E-mail: dmmix@bsu.edu. *Application contact:* Dr. Deborah Mix, Assistant Chair of Programs, 765-285-8401, Fax: 765-285-3765, E-mail: dmmix@bsu.edu.
Website: http://www.bsu.edu/english/

Bard College, Master of Arts in Teaching Program, Annandale-on-Hudson, NY 12504. Offers secondary education (MAT), including biology, history, literature, mathematics, Spanish; MS/MAT. *Program availability:* Part-time. *Degree requirements:* For master's, year-long teaching residencies in area middle and high schools. *Entrance requirements:* For master's, GRE General Test, resume, 3 letters of recommendation, personal statement, official transcripts. Additional exam requirements/recommendations for international students: Required—TOEFL. Electronic applications accepted. Application fee is waived when completed online.

Baylor University, Graduate School, College of Arts and Sciences, Department of English, Waco, TX 76798. Offers MA, PhD. *Students:* 39 full-time (22 women), 20 part-time (10 women); includes 2 minority (both Two or more races, non-Hispanic/Latino), 1 international. 57 applicants, 12% accepted, 6 enrolled. In 2017, 4 master's, 10 doctorates awarded. Terminal master's awarded for partial completion of doctoral program. *Entrance requirements:* For master's and doctorate, GRE (Verbal and Quantitative), 18 hours of upper-level course work in English. Additional exam requirements/recommendations for international students: Required—TOEFL. *Application deadline:* Applications are processed on a rolling basis. Application fee: $75. Electronic applications accepted. *Financial support:* In 2017–18, 70 students received support. Fellowships, research assistantships, teaching assistantships, Federal Work-Study, and institutionally sponsored loans available. Financial award application deadline: 1/15. *Faculty research:* Nineteenth-century British literature, literature and religion, Irish literature, Renaissance studies, rhetoric and composition. *Total annual research expenditures:* $48,400. *Unit head:* Dr. Richard R. Russell, Graduate Program Director, 254-710-1768 Ext. 4815, Fax: 254-710-4815, E-mail: richard_russell@baylor.edu. *Application contact:* Julie Sherrod, Administrative Assistant, 254-710-1768, Fax: 254-710-3870, E-mail: julie_sherrod@baylor.edu.
Website: http://www.baylor.edu/english/

Bemidji State University, School of Graduate Studies, Bemidji, MN 56601. Offers biology (MS); education (MS); English (MA, MS); environmental studies (MS); mathematics (MS); mathematics (elementary and middle level education) (MS); special education (M Sp Ed). *Program availability:* Part-time, online learning. *Degree requirements:* For master's, comprehensive exam, thesis (for some programs). *Entrance requirements:* For master's, GRE; GMAT, letters of recommendation, letters of interest. Additional exam requirements/recommendations for international students: Required—TOEFL (minimum score 550 paper-based; 80 iBT). Electronic applications accepted. *Expenses:* Contact institution. *Faculty research:* Human performance, sport, and health: physical education teacher education, continuum models, spiritual health, intellectual health, resiliency, health priorities; psychology: health psychology, college student drinking behavior, micro-aggressions, infant cognition, false memories, leadership assessment; biology: structure and dynamics of forest communities, aquatic and riverine ecology, interaction between animal populations and aquatic environments, cellular motility.

Binghamton University, State University of New York, Graduate School, Harpur College of Arts and Sciences, Department of English, Binghamton, NY 13902-6000. Offers creative writing (MA); English (PhD); English/American literature (MA). *Program availability:* Part-time. *Faculty:* 33 full-time (20 women). *Students:* 36 full-time (25 women), 47 part-time (26 women); includes 12 minority (3 Black or African American, non-Hispanic/Latino; 1 American Indian or Alaska Native, non-Hispanic/Latino; 4 Asian, non-Hispanic/Latino; 3 Hispanic/Latino; 1 Two or more races, non-Hispanic/Latino), 21 international. Average age 32. 74 applicants, 57% accepted, 16 enrolled. In 2017, 12 master's, 10 doctorates awarded. Terminal master's awarded for partial completion of doctoral program. *Degree requirements:* For master's, one foreign language, thesis; for doctorate, one foreign language, comprehensive exam, thesis/dissertation. *Entrance requirements:* For master's and doctorate, GRE General Test, writing sample. Additional exam requirements/recommendations for international students: Required—TOEFL (minimum score 550 paper-based; 80 iBT). *Application deadline:* For fall admission, 2/15 priority date for domestic and international students; for spring admission, 11/15 priority

date for domestic and international students. Application fee: $75. Electronic applications accepted. *Financial support:* In 2017–18, 38 students received support, including 1 fellowship with full tuition reimbursement available (averaging $15,000 per year), 1 research assistantship (averaging $9,000 per year), 30 teaching assistantships with full tuition reimbursements available (averaging $15,000 per year); career-related internships or fieldwork, Federal Work-Study, institutionally sponsored loans, scholarships/grants, health care benefits, tuition waivers (full and partial), and unspecified assistantships also available. Financial award applicants required to submit FAFSA. *Unit head:* Praseeda Gopinath, Graduate Director, 607-777-2033, Fax: 607-777-2408, E-mail: gopinath@binghamton.edu. *Application contact:* Ben Balkaya, Assistant Dean and Director, 607-777-2151, Fax: 607-777-2501, E-mail: balkaya@binghamton.edu.
Website: http://www2.binghamton.edu/english/

Bob Jones University, Graduate Programs, Greenville, SC 29614. Offers accountancy (MS); Bible (MA); Bible translation (MA); Biblical studies (Certificate); broadcast management (MS); business administration (MBA); church history (MA, PhD); church ministries (MA); church music (MM); cinema and video production (MA); counseling (MS); curriculum and instruction (Ed D); divinity (M Div); dramatic production (MA); educational leadership (MS, Ed D, Ed S); elementary education (M Ed, MAT); English (M Ed, MA, MAT); fine arts (MA); graphic design (MA); history (M Ed, MA); illustration (MA); interpretative speech (MA); mathematics (M Ed, MAT); medical missions (Certificate); ministry (MM, D Min); multi-categorical special education (M Ed, MAT); music (M Ed); New Testament interpretation (PhD); Old Testament interpretation (PhD); orchestral instrument performance (MM); organ performance (MM); pastoral studies (MA); personnel services (MS, Ed S); piano pedagogy (MM); piano performance (MM); platform arts (MA); radio and television broadcasting (MS); rhetoric and public address (MA); secondary education (M Ed); studio art (MA); teaching Bible (MA); theology (MA, PhD); voice performance (MM); youth ministries (MA); M Div/MM.

Boston College, Graduate School of Arts and Sciences, Department of English, Chestnut Hill, MA 02467-3800. Offers English (MA, PhD); Irish studies (MA, PhD). Terminal master's awarded for partial completion of doctoral program. *Degree requirements:* For master's, one foreign language, thesis optional; for doctorate, 2 foreign languages, thesis/dissertation. *Entrance requirements:* For master's and doctorate, GRE General Test, GRE Subject Test. Additional exam requirements/recommendations for international students: Required—TOEFL (minimum score 600 paper-based; 100 iBT), IELTS (minimum score 8). Electronic applications accepted. *Faculty research:* English and American literature, Irish literature, British literature, early modern and modern literature, critical theory.

Boston University, Graduate School of Arts and Sciences, Department of English, Boston, MA 02215. Offers MA, PhD, JD/MA. *Students:* 50 full-time (24 women), 4 part-time (all women); includes 6 minority (2 Black or African American, non-Hispanic/Latino; 4 Hispanic/Latino), 4 international. Average age 25. 193 applicants, 39% accepted, 19 enrolled. In 2017, 8 master's, 4 doctorates awarded. Terminal master's awarded for partial completion of doctoral program. *Degree requirements:* For master's, one foreign language; for doctorate, 2 foreign languages, comprehensive exam, thesis/dissertation, qualifying/oral exam. *Entrance requirements:* For master's, GRE General Test, GRE Subject Test in literature (strongly recommended), 3 letters of recommendation, transcripts, personal statement, scholarly writing sample, curriculum vitae; for doctorate, GRE General Test, GRE Subject Test in literature, 3 letters of recommendation, transcripts, personal statement, scholarly writing sample, curriculum vitae. Additional exam requirements/recommendations for international students: Required—TOEFL (minimum score 550 paper-based; 84 iBT). *Application deadline:* For fall admission, 1/5 for domestic and international students. Application fee: $95. Electronic applications accepted. *Financial support:* In 2017–18, 39 students received support, including 10 fellowships with full tuition reimbursements available (averaging $22,000 per year), 22 teaching assistantships with full tuition reimbursements available (averaging $22,000 per year); Federal Work-Study, scholarships/grants, health care benefits, and unspecified assistantships also available. Financial award application deadline: 1/5. *Unit head:* Robert Chodat, Chair, 617-353-2509, Fax: 617-353-3653, E-mail: rchodat@bu.edu. *Application contact:* Anne Austin, Administrative Assistant, 617-353-2509, Fax: 617-353-3653, E-mail: akaustin@bu.edu.
Website: http://www.bu.edu/english/

Bowie State University, Graduate Programs, Program in English, Bowie, MD 20715-9465. Offers MA. *Program availability:* Part-time, evening/weekend. *Entrance requirements:* For master's, minimum GPA of 2.5, English degree. Electronic applications accepted.

Bowling Green State University, Graduate College, College of Arts and Sciences, Department of English, Program in English, Bowling Green, OH 43403. Offers English (MA, PhD); literature (MA); rhetoric and writing (PhD); scientific and technical communication (MA). *Program availability:* Part-time. *Degree requirements:* For master's, thesis or alternative; for doctorate, comprehensive exam, thesis/dissertation, foreign language or proficiency in Old English. *Entrance requirements:* For master's and doctorate, GRE General Test. Additional exam requirements/recommendations for international students: Required—TOEFL. Electronic applications accepted. *Faculty research:* Postmodern literary theory, rhetorical theory, ethnic American literature, literature and culture, composition pedagogy.

Bradley University, The Graduate School, College of Liberal Arts and Sciences, Department of English, Peoria, IL 61625-0002. Offers MA. *Program availability:* Part-time. *Degree requirements:* For master's, comprehensive exam, thesis optional. *Entrance requirements:* For master's, writing sample, 2 letters of recommendation. Additional exam requirements/recommendations for international students: Required—TOEFL (minimum score 550 paper-based; 79 iBT), IELTS (minimum score 6.5). Electronic applications accepted.

Brandeis University, Graduate School of Arts and Sciences, Department of English, Waltham, MA 02454-9110. Offers English (MA, PhD); English/women's, gender, and sexuality studies (MA). *Program availability:* Part-time. *Faculty:* 18 full-time (9 women), 12 part-time/adjunct (6 women). *Students:* 40 full-time (22 women), 3 part-time (2 women); includes 8 minority (2 Black or African American, non-Hispanic/Latino; 1 Asian, non-Hispanic/Latino; 3 Hispanic/Latino; 2 Two or more races, non-Hispanic/Latino), 8 international. Average age 33. 134 applicants, 27% accepted, 6 enrolled. In 2017, 3 master's, 5 doctorates awarded. Terminal master's awarded for partial completion of doctoral program. *Degree requirements:* For master's, one foreign language, thesis or alternative; for doctorate, 2 foreign languages, thesis/dissertation, field exam, symposium presentation, prospectus defense. *Entrance requirements:* For master's, GRE, resume, critical writing sample, letters of recommendation, statement of purpose, transcripts; for doctorate, GRE General Test, GRE Subject Test, resume, critical writing sample, letters of recommendation, statement of purpose, transcripts. Additional exam requirements/recommendations for international students: Required—PTE (minimum score 68), TOEFL (minimum score 600 paper-based, 100 iBT) or IELTS (7). *Application deadline:* For fall admission, 1/5 for domestic students. Application fee: $75. Electronic applications accepted. *Expenses: Tuition:* Full-time $48,720. *Required fees:* $88. Tuition and fees vary according to course load, degree level, program and student level. *Financial support:* In 2017–18, 31 students received support, including 24 fellowships

with full tuition reimbursements available (averaging $24,480 per year), 3 teaching assistantships with partial tuition reimbursements available (averaging $3,200 per year); Federal Work-Study, scholarships/grants, health care benefits, and tuition waivers (partial) also available. Support available to part-time students. Financial award application deadline: 4/15; financial award applicants required to submit FAFSA. *Faculty research:* Feminist and gender theory, American literature and post-Colonial theory, early modern (Renaissance) English literature, modernism, literature and science, literary theory and philosophy, contemporary poetry. *Unit head:* Dr. David Sherman, Director of Graduate Studies, 781-736-2130, E-mail: chaucer@brandeis.edu. *Application contact:* Lisa Pannella, Department Academic Administrator, 781-736-2130, E-mail: pannella@brandeis.edu.
Website: http://www.brandeis.edu/gsas/programs/english.html

Bridgewater State University, College of Graduate Studies, College of Humanities and Social Sciences, Department of English, Bridgewater, MA 02325. Offers MA, MAT. *Program availability:* Part-time, evening/weekend. *Degree requirements:* For master's, one foreign language, comprehensive exam, thesis optional. *Entrance requirements:* For master's, GRE General Test.

Brigham Young University, Graduate Studies, College of Humanities, Department of English, Provo, UT 84602. Offers creative writing (MFA); literature (MA); rhetoric/composition (MA). *Faculty:* 53 full-time (15 women). *Students:* 68 full-time (44 women), 1 part-time (0 women); includes 3 minority (1 Asian, non-Hispanic/Latino; 2 Hispanic/Latino). Average age 28. 44 applicants, 64% accepted, 24 enrolled. In 2017, 31 master's awarded. *Degree requirements:* For master's, variable foreign language requirement, comprehensive exam, thesis. *Entrance requirements:* For master's, GRE General Test, creative portfolio (for MFA). *Application deadline:* For fall admission, 1/15 for domestic and international students. Application fee: $50. Electronic applications accepted. *Expenses: Tuition:* Full-time $6880; part-time $405 per credit hour. Tuition and fees vary according to course load, program and student's religious affiliation. *Financial support:* In 2017–18, 67 students received support, including 10 research assistantships (averaging $4,000 per year), 62 teaching assistantships (averaging $6,700 per year); career-related internships or fieldwork, institutionally sponsored loans, and scholarships/grants also available. Support available to part-time students. Financial award application deadline: 3/15. *Faculty research:* English literature, American literature, rhetoric, creative writing. *Unit head:* Prof. Phillip Snyder, Head, 801-422-2487, Fax: 801-422-0221, E-mail: phillip_snyder@byu.edu. *Application contact:* Danielle N. Steed, Graduate Secretary and English Program Manager, 801-422-8673, Fax: 801-422-0221, E-mail: danielle-steed@byu.edu.
Website: http://english.byu.edu/

Brock University, Faculty of Graduate Studies, Faculty of Humanities, Program in English, St. Catharines, ON L2S 3A1, Canada. Offers MA. *Program availability:* Part-time. *Degree requirements:* For master's, thesis optional. *Entrance requirements:* For master's, honours in English. Additional exam requirements/recommendations for international students: Required—TOEFL (minimum score 550 paper-based; 80 iBT), IELTS (minimum score 6.5), TWE (minimum score 4). Electronic applications accepted. *Faculty research:* Literary theory, Canadian literature, Milton and 17th century American literature, 19th century American literature, British Romantic literature and culture.

Brooklyn College of the City University of New York, School of Humanities and Social Sciences, Department of English, Brooklyn, NY 11210-2889. Offers creative writing (MFA), including fiction, playwriting, poetry; English (MA). *Program availability:* Part-time, evening/weekend. *Degree requirements:* For master's, one foreign language, comprehensive exam (for some programs), thesis (for some programs). *Entrance requirements:* For master's, advanced undergraduate courses in English, 2 letters of recommendation, writing sample, statement of purpose. Additional exam requirements/recommendations for international students: Required—TOEFL. Electronic applications accepted. *Faculty research:* Cultural studies, medieval literature, Virginia Woolf.

Brown University, Graduate School, Department of English, Providence, RI 02912. Offers English (PhD); literary arts (MFA). *Degree requirements:* For doctorate, thesis/dissertation. *Entrance requirements:* For master's and doctorate, GRE General Test, GRE Subject Test.

Bucknell University, Graduate Studies, College of Arts and Sciences, Department of English, Lewisburg, PA 17837. Offers MA. *Program availability:* Part-time. *Degree requirements:* For master's, one foreign language, thesis. *Entrance requirements:* For master's, GRE General Test, GRE Subject Test, minimum GPA of 3.0. Additional exam requirements/recommendations for international students: Required—TOEFL (minimum score 600 paper-based).

Buffalo State College, State University of New York, The Graduate School, Faculty of Arts and Humanities, Department of English, Buffalo, NY 14222-1095. Offers English (MA); secondary education (MS Ed), including English. *Program availability:* Part-time, evening/weekend. *Degree requirements:* For master's, thesis or project, 1 foreign language (MS Ed). *Entrance requirements:* For master's, minimum GPA of 2.75, 36 hours in English, New York teaching certificate (MS Ed). Additional exam requirements/recommendations for international students: Required—TOEFL (minimum score 550 paper-based).

Butler University, College of Liberal Arts and Sciences, Department of English, Indianapolis, IN 46208-3485. Offers creative writing (MFA); English (MA). *Program availability:* Part-time, evening/weekend. *Faculty:* 7 full-time (3 women), 5 part-time/adjunct (2 women). *Students:* 6 full-time (2 women), 44 part-time (26 women); includes 7 minority (3 Black or African American, non-Hispanic/Latino; 1 Hispanic/Latino; 3 Two or more races, non-Hispanic/Latino). Average age 33. 48 applicants, 79% accepted, 14 enrolled. In 2017, 20 master's awarded. *Degree requirements:* For master's, thesis (for some programs). *Entrance requirements:* For master's, minimum GPA of 3.0, 350-word statement of purpose, and 7-12 page sample essay (for MA); writing sample in intended genre (12 pages of poetry or 30 pages of prose), statement of interest (1-2 pages), two letters of recommendation, and transcripts from all undergraduate and graduate institutions attended (for MFA). Additional exam requirements/recommendations for international students: Required—TOEFL (minimum score 550 paper-based; 79 iBT), IELTS (minimum score 6). *Application deadline:* For fall admission, 2/15 for domestic and international students; for spring admission, 9/15 for domestic and international students. Applications are processed on a rolling basis. Application fee: $0. Electronic applications accepted. *Expenses:* $560 per credit (for MA); $820 per credit (for MFA). *Financial support:* In 2017–18, 19 students received support. Scholarships/grants, tuition waivers (full and partial), and unspecified assistantships available. Financial award application deadline: 7/15; financial award applicants required to submit FAFSA. *Faculty research:* Novel, poetry, screenplay and creative nonfiction writing; literary and cultural theory; American literature and culture; British and Postcolonial literature. *Unit head:* Dr. Dan Barden, Director of MFA Program, Department of English Language and Literature, 317-940-9688, E-mail: dbarden@butler.edu. *Application contact:* Diane Dubord, Graduate Student Services Specialist, 317-940-8107, Fax: 317-940-8250, E-mail: ddubord@butler.edu.
Website: https://www.butler.edu/english/graduate-studies/ma-english

Cabrini University, Academic Affairs, Radnor, PA 19087. Offers accounting (M Acc); autism spectrum disorder (M Ed); biological sciences (MS), including civic leadership; criminology and criminal justice (MA); curriculum, instruction, and assessment (M Ed); educational leadership (M Ed, Ed D), including curriculum and instructional leadership (Ed D), preK-12 leadership (Ed D); English as a second language (M Ed); organizational leadership (DBA, PhD); preK to 4 (M Ed); reading specialist (M Ed); secondary education (M Ed), including biology, chemistry, English, English/communication, mathematics, social studies; special education grades 7-12 (M Ed); special education preK-8 (M Ed); teaching and learning (M Ed). *Program availability:* Part-time, evening/weekend. *Faculty:* 23 full-time (17 women), 46 part-time/adjunct (38 women). *Students:* 60 full-time (35 women), 559 part-time (435 women); includes 93 minority (66 Black or African American, non-Hispanic/Latino; 1 American Indian or Alaska Native, non-Hispanic/Latino; 8 Asian, non-Hispanic/Latino; 15 Hispanic/Latino; 3 Two or more races, non-Hispanic/Latino), 4 international. Average age 33. 290 applicants, 82% accepted, 154 enrolled. In 2017, 283 master's awarded. *Degree requirements:* For master's, comprehensive exam (for some programs), thesis (for some programs); for doctorate, comprehensive exam (for some programs), thesis/dissertation. *Entrance requirements:* For master's, professional resume, personal statement, two recommendations, official transcripts; for doctorate, official transcripts, minimum master's GPA of 3.0, two recommendations, interview with admissions committee. Additional exam requirements/recommendations for international students: Required—TOEFL (minimum score 80 iBT). *Application deadline:* For fall admission, 8/26 for domestic students, 8/1 for international students; for winter admission, 1/13 for domestic students, 12/20 for international students; for spring admission, 1/13 for domestic students, 12/20 for international students; for summer admission, 5/20 for domestic students, 4/30 for international students. Applications are processed on a rolling basis. Application fee: $50. Electronic applications accepted. Application fee is waived when completed online. *Expenses:* Contact institution. *Financial support:* In 2017–18, 1,459 students received support. Tuition waivers and unspecified assistantships available. Financial award application deadline: 5/1; financial award applicants required to submit FAFSA. *Unit head:* Dr. Maliha Zaman, 610-902-8502, Fax: 610-902-8797, E-mail: msz37@cabrini.edu. *Application contact:* Diane Greenwood, Director of Graduate Admissions, 610-902-8291, E-mail: diane.l.greenwood@cabrini.edu.
Website: http://cabrini.edu/graduate

California Baptist University, Program in English, Riverside, CA 92504-3206. Offers English pedagogy (MA); literature (MA); teaching English to speakers of other languages (TESOL) (MA). *Program availability:* Part-time, evening/weekend. *Faculty:* 13 full-time (8 women), 1 (woman) part-time/adjunct. *Students:* 3 full-time (2 women), 26 part-time (19 women); includes 14 minority (4 Black or African American, non-Hispanic/Latino; 1 Asian, non-Hispanic/Latino; 9 Hispanic/Latino), 3 international. Average age 28. 11 applicants, 45% accepted, 4 enrolled. In 2017, 8 master's awarded. *Degree requirements:* For master's, comprehensive exam, project, or thesis. *Entrance requirements:* For master's, GRE (for applicants with a GPA below 2.75) or CSET, minimum undergraduate GPA of 2.75; 18 semester hours of course work in English beyond freshman level; three recommendations; essay; demonstration of writing; interview. Additional exam requirements/recommendations for international students: Required—TOEFL (minimum score 80 iBT). *Application deadline:* For fall admission, 8/1 priority date for domestic students, 7/1 for international students; for spring admission, 12/1 priority date for domestic students, 11/1 for international students. Applications are processed on a rolling basis. Application fee: $45. Electronic applications accepted. *Expenses:* Contact institution. *Financial support:* In 2017–18, 5 students received support. Federal Work-Study and scholarships/grants available. Financial award applicants required to submit CSS PROFILE or FAFSA. *Faculty research:* Classical mythology and folklore, multicultural literature, genre studies, science fiction and fantasy literature, intercultural rhetoric. *Unit head:* Dr. Gayne Anacker, Dean, College of Arts and Sciences, 951-343-4682, E-mail: ganacker@calbaptist.edu. *Application contact:* Dr. Laura Veltman, Director, Master of Arts Program in English, 951-343-4276, Fax: 951-343-4661, E-mail: lveltman@calbaptist.edu.
Website: http://www.calbaptist.edu/maenglish/

California Polytechnic State University, San Luis Obispo, College of Liberal Arts, Department of English, San Luis Obispo, CA 93407. Offers MA. *Program availability:* Part-time. *Faculty:* 5 full-time (1 woman). *Students:* 4 full-time (2 women), 18 part-time (13 women); includes 3 minority (2 Hispanic/Latino; 1 Two or more races, non-Hispanic/Latino). Average age 28. 16 applicants, 69% accepted, 8 enrolled. In 2017, 8 master's awarded. *Degree requirements:* For master's, one foreign language, comprehensive exam. *Entrance requirements:* For master's, GRE. Additional exam requirements/recommendations for international students: Required—TOEFL (minimum score 80 iBT). *Application deadline:* For fall admission, 4/1 for domestic students, 3/1 for international students. Applications are processed on a rolling basis. Application fee: $55. *Expenses:* Tuition, state resident: full-time $7176; part-time $4164 per year. *Required fees:* $3690; $3219 per year. $1073 per trimester. *Financial support:* Fellowships, teaching assistantships, career-related internships or fieldwork, Federal Work-Study, institutionally sponsored loans, and tutorships, writing laboratory assistantships available. Support available to part-time students. Financial award application deadline: 3/2; financial award applicants required to submit FAFSA. *Faculty research:* Feminist literary criticism, literary theory, British and American literature, linguistics, composition theory. *Unit head:* Dr. Dustin Stegner, Graduate Coordinator, 805-756-1277, E-mail: pstegner@calpoly.edu.
Website: http://cla.calpoly.edu/engl.html

California State Polytechnic University, Pomona, Program in English, Pomona, CA 91768-2557. Offers MA. *Program availability:* Part-time, evening/weekend. *Students:* 12 full-time (7 women), 60 part-time (42 women); includes 34 minority (2 Black or African American, non-Hispanic/Latino; 1 American Indian or Alaska Native, non-Hispanic/Latino; 8 Asian, non-Hispanic/Latino; 21 Hispanic/Latino; 2 Two or more races, non-Hispanic/Latino), 1 international. Average age 29. 33 applicants, 88% accepted, 16 enrolled. In 2017, 19 master's awarded. *Degree requirements:* For master's, thesis or alternative. *Entrance requirements:* Additional exam requirements/recommendations for international students: Required—TOEFL (minimum score 585 paper-based). *Application deadline:* Applications are processed on a rolling basis. Application fee: $55. Electronic applications accepted. *Expenses:* Contact institution. *Financial support:* Application deadline: 3/2; applicants required to submit FAFSA. *Unit head:* Dr. Lise-Hélène V. Smith, Associate Professor/Graduate Coordinator, 909-869-3979, Fax: 909-869-4896, E-mail: lvtrouilloud@cpp.edu. *Application contact:* Deborah L. Brandon, Executive Director of Admissions and Enrollment Planning, 909-869-3427, Fax: 909-869-5315, E-mail: dlbrandon@cpp.edu.
Website: http://www.cpp.edu/~class/english-foreign-languages/graduate-programs/

California State University, Bakersfield, Division of Graduate Studies, School of Arts and Humanities, Program in English, Bakersfield, CA 93311. Offers MA. *Faculty:* 3 full-time (1 woman). *Students:* 8 full-time (7 women), 11 part-time (6 women); includes 12 minority (3 Asian, non-Hispanic/Latino; 9 Hispanic/Latino). Average age 34. 8 applicants, 75% accepted, 4 enrolled. In 2017, 17 master's awarded. *Degree requirements:* For master's, comprehensive exam or thesis. *Entrance requirements:* For master's, GRE General Test, GRE Subject Test (literature), minimum GPA of 2.5 for last 90 quarter units. Additional exam requirements/recommendations for international students: Required—TOEFL (minimum score 550 paper-based). *Application deadline:* Applications are processed on a rolling basis. Application fee: $55. Electronic

applications accepted. *Expenses:* Tuition, state resident: full-time $7176; part-time $4164 per year. *Financial support:* In 2017–18, fellowships (averaging $1,850 per year) were awarded; Federal Work-Study, scholarships/grants, and tuition waivers (full and partial) also available. Financial award application deadline: 3/2; financial award applicants required to submit FAFSA. *Unit head:* Dr. Robert Carlisle, Graduate Studies Coordinator, 661-654-2127, Fax: 661-654-2063, E-mail: rcarlisle@csub.edu. *Application contact:* Debbie Blowers, Assistant Director of Admissions and Evaluations, 661-654-3381, E-mail: dblowers@csub.edu.

California State University, Chico, Office of Graduate Studies, College of Humanities and Fine Arts, English Department, Chico, CA 95929-0722. Offers MA. *Degree requirements:* For master's, thesis, project, or comprehensive exam. *Entrance requirements:* For master's, GRE, two letters of recommendation, statement of purpose, writing sample. Additional exam requirements/recommendations for international students: Required—TOEFL (minimum score 550 paper-based; 80 iBT), IELTS (minimum score 6.5), PTE (minimum score 59). Electronic applications accepted.

California State University, Dominguez Hills, College of Arts and Humanities, Department of English, Carson, CA 90747-0001. Offers English literature (MA); rhetoric and composition (Certificate); teaching English as a second language (MA, Certificate). *Program availability:* Part-time, evening/weekend. *Degree requirements:* For master's, comprehensive exam (for some programs), thesis or alternative. *Entrance requirements:* For master's, minimum GPA of 3.0 in last 60 units. Additional exam requirements/recommendations for international students: Required—TOEFL (minimum score 550 paper-based). Electronic applications accepted. *Faculty research:* Gender studies, transnationalism, discourse analysis, visual culture, Shakespeare.

California State University, East Bay, Office of Graduate Studies, College of Letters, Arts, and Social Sciences, Department of English, Hayward, CA 94542-3000. Offers English (MA); teaching English to speaker of other languages (MA). *Program availability:* Part-time. *Faculty:* 20 full-time (10 women), 26 part-time/adjunct (18 women). *Students:* 14 full-time (8 women), 30 part-time (20 women); includes 19 minority (3 Black or African American, non-Hispanic/Latino; 4 Asian, non-Hispanic/Latino; 10 Hispanic/Latino; 2 Two or more races, non-Hispanic/Latino), 8 international. Average age 34. 34 applicants, 74% accepted, 17 enrolled. In 2017, 19 master's awarded. *Degree requirements:* For master's, one foreign language, comprehensive exam, thesis optional. *Entrance requirements:* For master's, minimum GPA of 3.0 in field; 2 letters of recommendation; academic or professional writing sample; teaching experience and some degree of bilingualism (preferred for TESOL). Additional exam requirements/recommendations for international students: Required—TOEFL (minimum score 550 paper-based); Recommended—IELTS (minimum score 6.5). *Application deadline:* For fall admission, 6/1 for domestic and international students. Applications are processed on a rolling basis. Application fee: $55. Electronic applications accepted. *Financial support:* Fellowships, teaching assistantships, career-related internships or fieldwork, Federal Work-Study, institutionally sponsored loans, and scholarships/grants available. Support available to part-time students. Financial award application deadline: 3/2; financial award applicants required to submit FAFSA. *Unit head:* Dr. Sarah Nielsen, Acting Chair, 510-885-3151, Fax: 510-885-4797. *Application contact:* Philip Cole-Regis, Administrative Support Coordinator, 510-885-3286, E-mail: philip.coleregis@csueastbay.edu.
Website: http://www20.csueastbay.edu/class/departments/english/index.html

California State University, Fresno, Division of Research and Graduate Studies, College of Arts and Humanities, Department of English, Fresno, CA 93740-8027. Offers creative writing (MFA); literature (MA); rhetoric and writing studies (MA). *Program availability:* Part-time, evening/weekend. *Degree requirements:* For master's, one foreign language, thesis. *Entrance requirements:* For master's, GRE General Test, minimum GPA of 3.0, writing sample. Additional exam requirements/recommendations for international students: Required—TOEFL. Electronic applications accepted. *Faculty research:* American literature, Renaissance literature, foreign literature.

California State University, Fullerton, Graduate Studies, College of Humanities and Social Sciences, Department of English, Comparative Literature, and Linguistics, Fullerton, CA 92831-3599. Offers English (MA); linguistics (MA). *Program availability:* Part-time. *Faculty:* 9 full-time (4 women), 1 (woman) part-time/adjunct. *Students:* 44 full-time (30 women), 40 part-time (22 women); includes 38 minority (10 Asian, non-Hispanic/Latino; 24 Hispanic/Latino; 4 Two or more races, non-Hispanic/Latino), 14 international. Average age 29. 76 applicants, 58% accepted, 24 enrolled. *Degree requirements:* For master's, one foreign language, thesis or alternative, project. *Entrance requirements:* For master's, minimum GPA of 3.0, undergraduate major in linguistics or related field. Application fee: $55. *Financial support:* Career-related internships or fieldwork, Federal Work-Study, institutionally sponsored loans, and scholarships/grants available. Support available to part-time students. Financial award application deadline: 3/1; financial award applicants required to submit FAFSA. *Unit head:* Dr. Stephen J. Mexal, Chair, 657-278-3163.

California State University, Long Beach, Graduate Studies, College of Liberal Arts, Department of English, Long Beach, CA 90840. Offers creative writing (MFA); English (MA). *Program availability:* Part-time. *Degree requirements:* For master's, one foreign language, comprehensive exam or thesis. *Entrance requirements:* For master's, GRE Subject Test, minimum GPA of 3.0 in English. Electronic applications accepted. *Faculty research:* English and American literature, literary theory, linguistics, rhetoric and composition.

California State University, Los Angeles, Graduate Studies, College of Arts and Letters, Department of English, Los Angeles, CA 90032-8530. Offers MA, Certificate. *Program availability:* Part-time, evening/weekend. *Degree requirements:* For master's, comprehensive exam or thesis. *Entrance requirements:* Additional exam requirements/recommendations for international students: Required—TOEFL (minimum score 500 paper-based). Electronic applications accepted. *Faculty research:* English and American literature, linguistics, composition.

California State University, Northridge, Graduate Studies, College of Humanities, Department of English, Northridge, CA 91330. Offers creative writing (MA); literature (MA); rhetoric and composition theory (MA). *Program availability:* Part-time, evening/weekend. *Students:* 24 full-time (19 women), 66 part-time (40 women); includes 39 minority (4 Black or African American, non-Hispanic/Latino; 5 Asian, non-Hispanic/Latino; 23 Hispanic/Latino; 1 Native Hawaiian or other Pacific Islander, non-Hispanic/Latino; 6 Two or more races, non-Hispanic/Latino), 1 international. Average age 34. 74 applicants, 77% accepted, 33 enrolled. In 2017, 42 master's awarded. *Degree requirements:* For master's, thesis or alternative. *Entrance requirements:* For master's, writing proficiency test, GRE General Test or minimum GPA of 3.0. Additional exam requirements/recommendations for international students: Required—TOEFL. *Application deadline:* For fall admission, 11/30 for domestic students. Application fee: $55. *Financial support:* Teaching assistantships available. Financial award application deadline: 3/1. *Faculty research:* Reading improvement, professional writing, Dickens, Shaw, English as a second language. *Unit head:* Kent Baxter, Chair, 818-677-3431.
Website: http://www.csun.edu/english/index.php

California State University, Sacramento, College of Arts and Letters, Department of English, Sacramento, CA 95819. Offers composition (MA); creative writing (MA); literature (MA); teaching English to speakers of other languages (MA). *Program availability:* Part-time. *Students:* 25 full-time (15 women), 36 part-time (27 women); includes 18 minority (4 Black or African American, non-Hispanic/Latino; 3 Asian, non-Hispanic/Latino; 11 Hispanic/Latino). Average age 30. 47 applicants, 81% accepted, 31 enrolled. In 2017, 19 master's awarded. *Degree requirements:* For master's, thesis, project, or comprehensive exam; TESOL exam; writing proficiency exam. *Entrance requirements:* For master's, portfolio (creative writing); minimum GPA of 3.0 in English and overall during previous 2 years. Additional exam requirements/recommendations for international students: Required—TOEFL (minimum score 600 paper-based; 100 iBT). *Application deadline:* For fall admission, 2/15 for domestic students, 3/1 for international students; for spring admission, 9/30 for international students. Applications are processed on a rolling basis. Application fee: $55. Electronic applications accepted. *Expenses:* Contact institution. *Financial support:* Teaching assistantships, career-related internships or fieldwork, Federal Work-Study, and scholarships/grants available. Support available to part-time students. Financial award application deadline: 3/1; financial award applicants required to submit FAFSA. *Faculty research:* Teaching composition, remedial writing. *Unit head:* Dr. David Toise, Chair, 916-278-6586, E-mail: dwtoise@csus.edu. *Application contact:* Jose Martinez, Graduate Admissions Supervisor, 916-278-7871, E-mail: martinj@skymail.csus.edu.
Website: http://www.csus.edu/engl

California State University, San Bernardino, Graduate Studies, College of Arts and Letters, Program in English, San Bernardino, CA 92407. Offers creative writing (MFA), including fiction; English composition (MA), including composition. *Program availability:* Part-time, evening/weekend. *Faculty:* 6 full-time (all women), 1 (woman) part-time/adjunct. *Students:* 2 full-time (both women), 59 part-time (44 women); includes 38 minority (6 Black or African American, non-Hispanic/Latino; 1 Asian, non-Hispanic/Latino; 29 Hispanic/Latino; 2 Two or more races, non-Hispanic/Latino). Average age 31. 18 applicants, 72% accepted, 11 enrolled. In 2017, 16 master's awarded. *Degree requirements:* For master's, one foreign language, thesis. *Entrance requirements:* Additional exam requirements/recommendations for international students: Required—TOEFL. *Application deadline:* For fall admission, 7/16 for domestic students. Application fee: $55. *Financial support:* Application deadline: 3/1. *Unit head:* Dr. David Carlson, Chair, 909-537-5834, Fax: 909-537-7086, E-mail: dajcarls@csusb.edu. *Application contact:* Dr. Dorota Huizinga, Dean of Graduate Studies, 909-537-3064, Fax: 909-537-5078, E-mail: dorota.huizinga@csusb.edu.

California State University, San Marcos, College of Humanities, Arts, Behavioral and Social Sciences, Program in Literature and Writing Studies, San Marcos, CA 92096-0001. Offers MA. *Program availability:* Part-time, evening/weekend. *Degree requirements:* For master's, one foreign language, thesis. *Entrance requirements:* For master's, GRE General Test, minimum GPA of 3.0, writing sample. *Application deadline:* For fall admission, 3/15 priority date for domestic students; for spring admission, 11/15 for domestic students. Applications are processed on a rolling basis. Application fee: $55. *Expenses:* Tuition, state resident: full-time $7176. Tuition, nonresident: full-time $9504. *Faculty research:* Postcolonialism, feminism rhetoric, cultural studies, creative writing, critical theory. *Unit head:* Salah Moukhlis, Department Chair, 760-750-8081, E-mail: smoukhli@csusm.edu.

California State University, Stanislaus, College of the Arts, Humanities and Social Sciences, MA Program in English, Turlock, CA 95382. Offers literature (Certificate); rhetoric and teaching writing (MA); teaching English to speakers of other languages (MA). *Program availability:* Part-time. *Degree requirements:* For master's, comprehensive exam, thesis or alternative. *Entrance requirements:* For master's, GRE, minimum GPA of 3.0, 2 letters of reference, personal statement. Additional exam requirements/recommendations for international students: Required—TOEFL (minimum score 575 paper-based), TWE (minimum score 4). Electronic applications accepted. *Faculty research:* Transnational literacies, Renaissance and medieval literature, abolition writings and slave narratives, qualitative writing.

Carleton University, Faculty of Graduate Studies, Faculty of Arts and Social Sciences, Department of English Language and Literature, Ottawa, ON K1S 5B6, Canada. Offers MA, PhD. *Degree requirements:* For master's, thesis optional. *Entrance requirements:* For master's, honors degree. Additional exam requirements/recommendations for international students: Required—TOEFL. *Faculty research:* British, Canadian, American, and Commonwealth literatures; English language and writing; literary criticism; social and historical context of literature.

Carnegie Mellon University, Dietrich College of Humanities and Social Sciences, Department of English, Pittsburgh, PA 15213-3891. Offers communication planning and design (M Des); literary and cultural studies (MA, PhD); professional writing (MAPW), including editing and publishing, policy and non-profit communication, public and media relations / corporate communications, science or healthcare communication, technical writing, writing for new media, writing for print media; rhetoric (MA, PhD). *Program availability:* Part-time. Terminal master's awarded for partial completion of doctoral program. *Degree requirements:* For doctorate, 2 foreign languages, comprehensive exam, thesis/dissertation. *Entrance requirements:* For master's and doctorate, GRE General Test. Additional exam requirements/recommendations for international students: Required—TOEFL, TWE. *Faculty research:* Cognitive processes in discourse with emphasis on writing, testing, and evaluation.

Case Western Reserve University, School of Graduate Studies, Department of English, Cleveland, OH 44106. Offers MA, PhD. *Program availability:* Part-time. *Faculty:* 20 full-time (11 women), 2 part-time/adjunct (0 women). *Students:* 21 full-time (12 women), 5 part-time (all women); includes 3 minority (1 Black or African American, non-Hispanic/Latino; 1 Hispanic/Latino; 1 Two or more races, non-Hispanic/Latino), 2 international. Average age 30. 33 applicants, 21% accepted, 7 enrolled. In 2017, 2 master's, 5 doctorates awarded. *Degree requirements:* For master's, one foreign language, comprehensive exam, thesis or alternative, written exam; for doctorate, one foreign language, thesis/dissertation, oral and written exams. *Entrance requirements:* For master's and doctorate, GRE General Test, sample of written work, three letters of recommendation. Additional exam requirements/recommendations for international students: Required—TOEFL (minimum score 577 paper-based; 90 iBT); Recommended—IELTS (minimum score 7). *Application deadline:* For fall admission, 1/15 priority date for domestic students. Applications are processed on a rolling basis. Application fee: $50. Electronic applications accepted. *Expenses: Tuition:* Full-time $43,854; part-time $1827 per credit hour. *Required fees:* $50; $50 per credit hour. Tuition and fees vary according to course load and program. *Financial support:* Fellowships, teaching assistantships, institutionally sponsored loans, and tuition waivers (partial) available. Financial award application deadline: 1/15; financial award applicants required to submit FAFSA. *Faculty research:* Sixteenth- to twentieth-century English literature, rhetorical and critical theory, women's studies, genre studies, Renaissance, America modernism, authorship. *Unit head:* Christopher Flint, Associate Professor and Chair, 216-368-3342, Fax: 216-368-4681, E-mail: christopher.flint@case.edu. *Application contact:* Prof. Kurt Koenigsberger, Associate Professor and Graduate Director, 216-368-6994, Fax: 216-368-4367, E-mail: kurt.koenigsberger@case.edu.
Website: http://english.case.edu/

The Catholic University of America, School of Arts and Sciences, Department of English Language and Literature, Washington, DC 20064. Offers English (MA, PhD);

rhetoric (Certificate). *Program availability:* Part-time. *Faculty:* 14 full-time (6 women), 2 part-time/adjunct (1 woman). *Students:* 7 full-time (6 women), 29 part-time (14 women); includes 4 minority (3 Hispanic/Latino; 1 Two or more races, non-Hispanic/Latino), 3 international. Average age 30. 35 applicants, 49% accepted. In 2017, 2 master's, 6 doctorates awarded. *Degree requirements:* For master's, one foreign language, comprehensive exam; for doctorate, 2 foreign languages, comprehensive exam, thesis/dissertation. *Entrance requirements:* For master's and doctorate, GRE General Test, statement of purpose, official copies of academic transcripts, three letters of recommendation, writing sample. Additional exam requirements/recommendations for international students: Required—TOEFL (minimum score 550 paper-based; 80 iBT). *Application deadline:* For fall admission, 7/15 priority date for domestic students, 7/1 for international students; for spring admission, 11/15 priority date for domestic students, 11/1 for international students. Applications are processed on a rolling basis. Application fee: $55. Electronic applications accepted. *Expenses:* Contact institution. *Financial support:* Fellowships, research assistantships, teaching assistantships, Federal Work-Study, scholarships/grants, tuition waivers (full and partial), and unspecified assistantships available. Financial award application deadline: 2/1; financial award applicants required to submit FAFSA. *Faculty research:* Medieval literature, theory and history of rhetoric, Renaissance literature, religion and literature, English and American drama. *Total annual research expenditures:* $4,035. *Unit head:* Dr. Ernest Suarez, Chair, 202-319-5488, Fax: 202-319-4188, E-mail: johnsong@cua.edu. *Application contact:* Dr. Steven Brown, Director of Graduate Admissions, 202-319-5057, Fax: 202-319-6533, E-mail: cua-admissions@cua.edu.
Website: http://english.cua.edu/

Central Connecticut State University, School of Graduate Studies, College of Liberal Arts and Social Sciences, Department of English, New Britain, CT 06050-4010. Offers English (MA); English education (MAT); teaching English to speakers of other languages (MS, Certificate). *Program availability:* Part-time, evening/weekend. *Faculty:* 6 full-time (4 women), 1 part-time/adjunct (0 women). *Students:* 17 full-time (12 women), 43 part-time (37 women); includes 16 minority (5 Black or African American, non-Hispanic/Latino; 1 Asian, non-Hispanic/Latino; 8 Hispanic/Latino; 2 Two or more races, non-Hispanic/Latino), 2 international. Average age 33. 35 applicants, 77% accepted, 16 enrolled. In 2017, 17 master's, 3 other advanced degrees awarded. *Degree requirements:* For master's, comprehensive exam, thesis or alternative; for Certificate, qualifying exam. *Entrance requirements:* For master's, minimum undergraduate GPA of 3.0, writing sample, letters of recommendation, essay. Additional exam requirements/recommendations for international students: Required—TOEFL (minimum score 550 paper-based; 79 iBT); Recommended—IELTS (minimum score 6.5). *Application deadline:* For fall admission, 8/1 for domestic students, 5/1 for international students; for spring admission, 11/1 for domestic and international students. Applications are processed on a rolling basis. Application fee: $50. Electronic applications accepted. *Expenses: Tuition, area resident:* Full-time $6757. Tuition, state resident: full-time $9750; part-time $374 per credit. Tuition, nonresident: full-time $18,102; part-time $374 per credit. *Required fees:* $4635; $255 per credit. *Financial support:* In 2017–18, 9 students received support. Career-related internships or fieldwork, Federal Work-Study, scholarships/grants, and unspecified assistantships available. Support available to part-time students. Financial award application deadline: 3/1; financial award applicants required to submit FAFSA. *Unit head:* Dr. Stephen Cohen, Chair, 860-832-2795, E-mail: cohens@ccsu.edu. *Application contact:* Patricia Gardner, Associate Director of Graduate Studies, 860-832-2350, Fax: 860-832-2362.
Website: http://www.ccsu.edu/english

Central Michigan University, College of Graduate Studies, College of Humanities and Social and Behavioral Sciences, Department of English Language and Literature, Mount Pleasant, MI 48859. Offers English composition and communication (MA); English language and literature (MA), including children's and young adult literature, creative writing, English language and literature; TESOL: teaching English to speakers of other languages (MA). *Program availability:* Part-time, evening/weekend. *Degree requirements:* For master's, thesis or alternative. Electronic applications accepted. *Faculty research:* Composition theory, science fiction history and bibliography, children's and young adult literature, nineteenth century American literature, applied linguistics.

Central Washington University, School of Graduate Studies and Research, College of Arts and Humanities, Department of English, Ellensburg, WA 98926. Offers literature (MA); professional and creative writing (MA); teaching English to speakers of other languages (MA). *Program availability:* Part-time. *Entrance requirements:* For master's, GRE General Test, minimum GPA of 3.0, writing sample. Additional exam requirements/recommendations for international students: Required—TOEFL (minimum score 550 paper-based; 79 iBT) or IELTS (minimum score 6.5). *Application deadline:* For fall admission, 2/1 priority date for domestic students; for winter admission, 10/1 for domestic students; for spring admission, 1/1 for domestic students. Applications are processed on a rolling basis. Application fee: $50. Electronic applications accepted. *Financial support:* Application deadline: 3/1; applicants required to submit FAFSA. *Unit head:* Dr. Bobby Cummings, Graduate Coordinator, 509-963-1075, E-mail: bobby.cummings@cwu.edu. *Application contact:* Justine Eason, Admissions Program Coordinator, 509-963-3103, Fax: 509-963-1799, E-mail: masters@cwu.edu.
Website: http://www.cwu.edu/~english

Chapman University, Wilkinson College of Arts, Humanities, and Social Sciences, Department of English, Orange, CA 92866. Offers creative writing (MFA); English (MA). *Program availability:* Part-time, evening/weekend. *Faculty:* 23 full-time (11 women), 43 part-time/adjunct (28 women). *Students:* 48 full-time (29 women), 17 part-time (12 women); includes 17 minority (1 Black or African American, non-Hispanic/Latino; 5 Asian, non-Hispanic/Latino; 9 Hispanic/Latino; 2 Two or more races, non-Hispanic/Latino), 5 international. Average age 30. 88 applicants, 90% accepted, 23 enrolled. In 2017, 24 master's awarded. *Degree requirements:* For master's, thesis. *Entrance requirements:* For master's, GRE (if undergraduate GPA less than 3.0), minimum undergraduate GPA of 2.5. *Application deadline:* For fall admission, 2/1 priority date for domestic students. Applications are processed on a rolling basis. Application fee: $60. Electronic applications accepted. *Expenses:* Contact institution. *Financial support:* Fellowships, teaching assistantships, Federal Work-Study, and scholarships/grants available. Financial award applicants required to submit FAFSA. *Unit head:* Dr. Joanna Levin, Director, 714-997-6534, E-mail: jlevin@chapman.edu. *Application contact:* Sharnique Dow, Graduate Admission Counselor, 714-997-6770, E-mail: sdow@chapman.edu.
Website: https://www.chapman.edu/wilkinson/english/index.aspx

Chicago State University, School of Graduate and Professional Studies, College of Arts and Sciences, Department of English, Foreign Languages and Literatures, Chicago, IL 60628. Offers creative writing (MFA); English (MA). *Degree requirements:* For master's, comprehensive exam (for some programs), thesis (for some programs). *Entrance requirements:* For master's, minimum GPA of 3.0. *Application deadline:* For fall admission, 7/1 for domestic students; for spring admission, 11/10 for domestic students. Application fee: $25. *Unit head:* Dr. Brenda Aghahowa, Graduate Advisor, 773-995-2203, E-mail: baghahow@csu.edu. *Application contact:* Anika Miller, Graduate Studies Office, 773-995-2404, E-mail: g-studies1@csu.edu.
Website: http://www.csu.edu/cas/englishforeignlanguageliterature/

The Citadel, The Military College of South Carolina, Citadel Graduate College, School of Humanities and Social Sciences, Department of English, Fine Arts and Communications, Charleston, SC 29409. Offers English (MA). Program offered jointly with The Graduate School of the College of Charleston. *Program availability:* Part-time, evening/weekend. *Degree requirements:* For master's, one foreign language, comprehensive exam, thesis optional. *Entrance requirements:* For master's, GRE (minimum combined verbal and quantitative score of 300, 4 on writing assessment section) or MAT (minimum score of 400); GRE Subject Test (for applicants without undergraduate degree in English), minimum undergraduate GPA of 2.5 (3.0 in major); 2 letters of recommendation preferably from former professors; writing sample that demonstrates ability to perform literary analysis and to conduct research; 2-page statement about educational goals and interest in a graduate program in English. Additional exam requirements/recommendations for international students: Required—TOEFL (minimum score 550 paper-based). Electronic applications accepted. *Expenses:* Tuition, state resident: part-time $587 per credit hour. Tuition, nonresident: part-time $988 per credit hour. *Required fees:* $90 per term.

City College of the City University of New York, Graduate School, Division of Humanities and the Arts, Department of Classical and Modern Languages and Literatures, New York, NY 10031-9198. Offers Spanish (MA). *Degree requirements:* For master's, one foreign language, comprehensive exam, thesis or alternative. *Entrance requirements:* For master's, minimum GPA of 3.0. Additional exam requirements/recommendations for international students: Required—TOEFL (minimum score 500 paper-based; 61 iBT). Electronic applications accepted.

City College of the City University of New York, Graduate School, Division of Humanities and the Arts, Department of English, Program in Literature, New York, NY 10031-9198. Offers MA. *Degree requirements:* For master's, one foreign language, comprehensive exam, thesis. *Entrance requirements:* For master's, minimum GPA of 3.0. Additional exam requirements/recommendations for international students: Required—TOEFL (minimum score 600 paper-based; 100 iBT). Electronic applications accepted.

Claremont Graduate University, Graduate Programs, School of Arts and Humanities, Department of English, Claremont, CA 91711-6160. Offers American studies (MA, PhD); critical theory (MA, PhD); early modern studies (MA, PhD); English (M Phil, MA, PhD); literary theory (PhD); literature (MA, PhD); literature and creative writing (MA); literature and film (MA); MBA/MA; MBA/PhD. *Program availability:* Part-time. *Entrance requirements:* For master's and doctorate, GRE General Test. Additional exam requirements/recommendations for international students: Required—TOEFL (minimum score 75 iBT). Electronic applications accepted. *Faculty research:* American, comparative, and English Renaissance literature; modernism; feminist literature and theory.

Clark Atlanta University, School of Arts and Sciences, Department of English and Modern Languages, Atlanta, GA 30314. Offers MA, PhD. *Program availability:* Part-time. *Faculty:* 15 full-time (7 women), 16 part-time/adjunct (11 women). *Students:* 11 full-time (7 women), 16 part-time (13 women); includes 21 minority (all Black or African American, non-Hispanic/Latino), 5 international. Average age 34. 3 applicants, 100% accepted, 2 enrolled. In 2017, 6 master's, 1 doctorate awarded. *Degree requirements:* For master's, one foreign language, comprehensive exam, thesis; for doctorate, 2 foreign languages, comprehensive exam, thesis/dissertation. *Entrance requirements:* For master's, GRE General Test, minimum GPA of 2.5. Additional exam requirements/recommendations for international students: Required—TOEFL (minimum score 500 paper-based; 61 iBT). *Application deadline:* For fall admission, 4/1 for domestic and international students; for spring admission, 11/1 for domestic and international students. Applications are processed on a rolling basis. Application fee: $40 ($55 for international students). *Financial support:* Career-related internships or fieldwork, Federal Work-Study, scholarships/grants, and unspecified assistantships available. Support available to part-time students. Financial award application deadline: 4/30; financial award applicants required to submit FAFSA. *Unit head:* Dr. Georgene Bess Montgomery, Chairperson, 404-880-8174, E-mail: gmontgomery@cau.edu.

Clarks Summit University, Online Master's Programs, South Abington Township, PA 18411. Offers Bible (MA); counseling (MA, MS); curriculum and instruction (M Ed); educational administration (M Ed); literature (MA); organizational leadership (MA). *Program availability:* Part-time, evening/weekend, online learning. *Entrance requirements:* Additional exam requirements/recommendations for international students: Required—TOEFL (minimum score 500 paper-based). *Application deadline:* Applications are processed on a rolling basis. Application fee: $30. *Financial support:* Institutionally sponsored loans and scholarships/grants available. Financial award application deadline: 8/20; financial award applicants required to submit FAFSA. *Unit head:* Dr. James Lytle, President, 570-586-2400 Ext. 9222, Fax: 570-586-1753. *Application contact:* Drew Whipple, Vice President for Enrollment Management, 570-585-9370, Fax: 570-585-9299, E-mail: awhipple@clarkssummitu.edu.
Website: https://www.clarkssummitu.edu/online-masters-degrees/

Clark University, Graduate School, Department of English, Worcester, MA 01610-1477. Offers MA. *Program availability:* Part-time. *Faculty:* 8 full-time (4 women), 16 part-time/adjunct (10 women). *Students:* 15 full-time (8 women); includes 1 minority (Hispanic/Latino), 3 international. Average age 27. 33 applicants, 30% accepted, 6 enrolled. In 2017, 12 master's awarded. *Degree requirements:* For master's, thesis, oral exam. *Entrance requirements:* For master's, GRE Subject Test, 2 references, resume or curriculum vitae, personal statement. Additional exam requirements/recommendations for international students: Required—TOEFL (minimum score 575 paper-based; 90 iBT), IELTS (minimum score 6.5). *Application deadline:* For fall admission, 1/15 priority date for domestic students. Application fee: $75. Electronic applications accepted. *Expenses:* $5,685 tuition per 14-week course; $40 activity fee (full-time students only); $80 miscellaneous one-time fee. *Financial support:* Fellowships, research assistantships, teaching assistantships, career-related internships or fieldwork, and tuition waivers (partial) available. Support available to part-time students. *Faculty research:* Renaissance literature, American literature, medieval literature, Victorian literature. *Unit head:* Dr. Lisa Kasmer, 508-793-7136, E-mail: lkasmer@clarku.edu.
Website: http://www.clarku.edu/departments/english/

Cleveland State University, College of Graduate Studies, College of Liberal Arts and Social Sciences, Department of English, Cleveland, OH 44115. Offers creative writing (MFA), including fiction, non-fiction, playwriting, poetry. *Program availability:* Part-time, evening/weekend. *Faculty:* 14 full-time (8 women), 14 part-time/adjunct (4 women). *Students:* 22 full-time (17 women), 26 part-time (17 women); includes 8 minority (6 Black or African American, non-Hispanic/Latino; 1 Asian, non-Hispanic/Latino; 1 Two or more races, non-Hispanic/Latino). Average age 34. 38 applicants, 68% accepted, 9 enrolled. In 2017, 21 master's awarded. *Entrance requirements:* For master's, minimum GPA of 2.75, undergraduate concentration in English, writing sample, portfolio. Additional exam requirements/recommendations for international students: Required—TOEFL (minimum score 550 paper-based; 78 iBT). *Application deadline:* Applications are processed on a rolling basis. Application fee: $40. Electronic applications accepted. *Financial support:* In 2017–18, 20 students received support. Teaching assistantships, tuition waivers (full and partial), and unspecified assistantships available. Financial award application deadline: 2/1; financial award applicants required to submit FAFSA. *Faculty research:*

English

Literary history and criticism, literature, creative writing. *Total annual research expenditures:* $5,000. *Application contact:* Dr. James J. Marino, Associate Professor/Director of Graduate Studies, 216-687-6874, Fax: 216-687-6943, E-mail: j.marino22@csuohio.edu.
Website: http://www.csuohio.edu/class/english/english

The College at Brockport, State University of New York, School of Arts and Sciences, Department of English, Brockport, NY 14420-2997. Offers creative writing (AGC); English (MA), including creative writing, literature. *Program availability:* Part-time. *Faculty:* 8 full-time (3 women). *Students:* 17 full-time (13 women), 13 part-time (7 women); includes 2 minority (1 Hispanic/Latino; 1 Two or more races, non-Hispanic/Latino), 1 international. 13 applicants, 92% accepted, 5 enrolled. In 2017, 10 master's, 1 other advanced degree awarded. *Degree requirements:* For master's, thesis. *Entrance requirements:* For master's, minimum GPA of 3.0, letters of recommendation, writing sample. Additional exam requirements/recommendations for international students: Required—TOEFL (minimum score 550 paper-based; 79 iBT), IELTS (minimum score 6.5). *Application deadline:* For fall admission, 4/15 priority date for domestic and international students; for spring admission, 11/15 priority date for domestic and international students; for summer admission, 4/15 priority date for domestic and international students. Application fee: $50. Electronic applications accepted. *Expenses:* Tuition, state resident: full-time $10,870; part-time $453 per credit hour. Tuition, nonresident: full-time $22,210. *Required fees:* $988; $246 per semester. *Financial support:* In 2017–18, 3 teaching assistantships with full tuition reimbursements (averaging $6,000 per year) were awarded; Federal Work-Study, scholarships/grants, and unspecified assistantships also available. Support available to part-time students. Financial award application deadline: 3/15; financial award applicants required to submit FAFSA. *Faculty research:* British and American literature, creative writing, film studies, children's literature, ancient and modern world literature. *Unit head:* Dr. Jennifer Haytock, Chairperson, 585-395-5832, Fax: 585-395-2391, E-mail: jhaytock@brockport.edu. *Application contact:* Dr. Gregory Garvey, Graduate Program Director, 585-395-5712, Fax: 585-395-5487, E-mail: tgarvey@brockport.edu.
Website: https://www.brockport.edu/academics/english/

The College at Brockport, State University of New York, School of Education, Health, and Human Services, Department of Education and Human Development, Program in Inclusive Generalist Education, Brockport, NY 14420-2997. Offers biology (MS Ed, AGC); chemistry (MS Ed, AGC); English (MS Ed, Advanced Certificate); mathematics (MS Ed, Advanced Certificate); science (MS Ed, Advanced Certificate); social studies (MS Ed, Advanced Certificate). *Students:* 61 part-time (30 women); includes 2 minority (1 Black or African American, non-Hispanic/Latino; 1 Asian, non-Hispanic/Latino). 41 applicants, 78% accepted, 25 enrolled. In 2017, 12 master's, 3 AGCs awarded. *Degree requirements:* For master's, thesis or alternative. *Entrance requirements:* For master's, edTPA, GRE or MAT, minimum GPA of 3.0, letters of recommendation, statement of objectives, academic major (or equivalent) in program discipline, current resume. Additional exam requirements/recommendations for international students: Required—TOEFL (minimum score 550 paper-based; 79 iBT), IELTS (minimum score 6.5). *Application deadline:* For fall admission, 3/15 priority date for domestic and international students; for spring admission, 10/15 priority date for domestic and international students; for summer admission, 3/15 for domestic and international students. Application fee: $80. Electronic applications accepted. *Expenses:* Tuition, state resident: full-time $10,870; part-time $453 per credit hour. Tuition, nonresident: full-time $22,210. *Required fees:* $988; $246 per semester. *Financial support:* Federal Work-Study, scholarships/grants, and unspecified assistantships available. Support available to part-time students. Financial award application deadline: 3/15; financial award applicants required to submit FAFSA. *Unit head:* Dr. Sue Robb, Chairperson, 585-395-5935, Fax: 585-395-2171, E-mail: srobb@brockport.edu. *Application contact:* Anne Walton, Coordinator of Graduate Advisement, 585-395-2326, Fax: 585-395-2172, E-mail: awalton@brockport.edu.
Website: https://www.brockport.edu/academics/education_human_development/department.html

College of Charleston, Graduate School, School of Humanities and Social Sciences, Program in English, Charleston, SC 29424-0001. Offers MA. Program offered jointly with The Citadel, The Military College of South Carolina. *Program availability:* Part-time, evening/weekend. *Degree requirements:* For master's, one foreign language, comprehensive exam, thesis optional. *Entrance requirements:* For master's, GRE General Test or MAT, minimum GPA of 2.5 overall, 3.0 in major; 2 letters of recommendation; writing sample. Additional exam requirements/recommendations for international students: Required—TOEFL (minimum score 81 iBT). Electronic applications accepted.

The College of New Jersey, Office of Graduate and Advancing Education, School of Humanities and Social Sciences, Department of English, Program in English, Ewing, NJ 08628. Offers MA. *Program availability:* Part-time. *Degree requirements:* For master's, comprehensive exam. *Entrance requirements:* For master's, GRE, minimum GPA of 3.0 in field or 2.75 overall. Additional exam requirements/recommendations for international students: Required—TOEFL. Electronic applications accepted.

College of Staten Island of the City University of New York, Graduate Programs, Division of Humanities and Social Sciences, Program in English, Staten Island, NY 10314-6600. Offers English (MA), including literature, rhetoric. *Program availability:* Part-time, evening/weekend. *Faculty:* 2 full-time, 1 part-time/adjunct. *Students:* 47. 29 applicants, 55% accepted, 13 enrolled. In 2017, 2 master's awarded. *Degree requirements:* For master's, comprehensive exam, minimum overall GPA of 3.0. *Entrance requirements:* For master's, BA with minimum GPA of 3.0 or in English courses, 32 undergraduate credits in English, two letters of recommendation, one- to two-page personal statement (500-700 words), minimum 8-10 page paper written for an English course. Additional exam requirements/recommendations for international students: Required—TOEFL (minimum score 550 paper-based; 79 iBT), IELTS (minimum score 6.5). *Application deadline:* For fall admission, 4/30 priority date for domestic and international students; for spring admission, 10/31 for domestic and international students. Applications are processed on a rolling basis. Application fee: $125. Electronic applications accepted. *Expenses:* Tuition, state resident: full-time $10,450; part-time $440 per credit. Tuition, nonresident: full-time $19,320; part-time $440 per credit. *Required fees:* $181.10 per semester. Tuition and fees vary according to program. *Faculty research:* Renaissance drama, 18th and 19th century British fiction and poetry, 19th and 20th century American literature, 20th century Chinese literature, queer studies. *Unit head:* Dr. Katharine Goodland, Graduate Program Coordinator, 718-982-3639, E-mail: katharine.goodland@csi.cuny.edu. *Application contact:* Sasha Spence, Associate Director for Graduate Admissions, 718-982-2019, Fax: 718-982-2500, E-mail: sasha.spence@csi.cuny.edu.
Website: https://www.csi.cuny.edu/sites/default/files/pdf/admissions/grad/pdf/English%20Fact%20Sheet.pdf

The College of William and Mary, School of Education, Program in Curriculum and Instruction, Williamsburg, VA 23187-8795. Offers elementary education (MA Ed); English as a second language/bilingual education (MA Ed); gifted education (MA Ed); literacy leadership (MA Ed); math specialist (MA Ed); secondary education (MA Ed), including English, foreign language, math, science, social studies; special education

(MA Ed). *Accreditation:* NCATE. *Program availability:* Part-time. *Faculty:* 23 full-time (16 women), 40 part-time/adjunct (32 women). *Students:* 85 full-time (63 women), 16 part-time (15 women); includes 18 minority (5 Black or African American, non-Hispanic/Latino; 4 Asian, non-Hispanic/Latino; 7 Hispanic/Latino; 2 Two or more races, non-Hispanic/Latino), 1 international. Average age 27. 152 applicants, 83% accepted, 90 enrolled. In 2017, 67 master's awarded. *Degree requirements:* For master's, project. *Entrance requirements:* For master's, GRE, MAT, PRAXIS Core Academic Skills for Educators, minimum GPA of 2.5. Additional exam requirements/recommendations for international students: Required—TOEFL (minimum score 100 iBT), IELTS (minimum score 7). *Application deadline:* For fall admission, 1/15 for domestic and international students; for spring admission, 10/1 for domestic and international students. Application fee: $50. Electronic applications accepted. *Expenses:* $9,630 resident full-time, $535 resident part-time per credit hour; $25,920 nonresident full-time, $1,265 nonresident part-time per credit hour; $5,944 full-time fees. *Financial support:* In 2017–18, 35 students received support, including 7 research assistantships (averaging $6,678 per year); scholarships/grants and unspecified assistantships also available. Financial award application deadline: 1/15; financial award applicants required to submit FAFSA. *Faculty research:* Educational technology, professional development and evaluation, inclusive education, rural education, education policy. *Unit head:* Dr. Jeremy D. Stoddard, Department Chair, 757-221-2348, E-mail: jdstod@wm.edu. *Application contact:* Dorothy Smith Osborne, Assistant Dean for Academic Programs and Student Services, 757-221-2317, E-mail: dsosbo@wm.edu.
Website: http://education.wm.edu

Colorado State University, College of Liberal Arts, Department of English, Fort Collins, CO 80523-1773. Offers creative writing (MFA); rhetoric and composition (MA). *Faculty:* 17 full-time (7 women), 10 part-time/adjunct (9 women). *Students:* 64 full-time (44 women), 33 part-time (28 women); includes 6 minority (2 Black or African American, non-Hispanic/Latino; 1 Asian, non-Hispanic/Latino; 3 Hispanic/Latino), 12 international. Average age 30. 207 applicants, 38% accepted, 23 enrolled. In 2017, 33 master's awarded. *Degree requirements:* For master's, thesis (for some programs), portfolio, project or thesis. *Entrance requirements:* For master's, BA/BS or equivalent with minimum cumulative undergraduate GPA of 3.0, transcripts, writing sample, statement of purpose, 3 letters of recommendation. Additional exam requirements/recommendations for international students: Recommended—TOEFL (minimum score 550 paper-based; 80 iBT), IELTS (minimum score 6.5). Application fee: $60 ($70 for international students). Electronic applications accepted. *Expenses:* Tuition, state resident: full-time $9917. Tuition, nonresident: full-time $24,312. *Required fees:* $2284. Tuition and fees vary according to course load and program. *Financial support:* In 2017–18, 1 fellowship with full and partial tuition reimbursement (averaging $14,256 per year), 40 teaching assistantships with full and partial tuition reimbursements (averaging $14,678 per year) were awarded; scholarships/grants and unspecified assistantships also available. *Faculty research:* Narratives written in new media; racial, gender, and sexual identity in the United States; the rhetoric of social change; pedagogical potential of graphic narratives. *Total annual research expenditures:* $134,319. *Unit head:* Louann Reid, Professor, 970-491-6428, E-mail: louann.reid@colostate.edu. *Application contact:* Marnie Leonard, Administrative Assistant, 970-491-2403, E-mail: marnie.leonard@colostate.edu.
Website: http://english.colostate.edu/

Columbia College Chicago, School of Graduate Studies, English and Creative Writing Department, Chicago, IL 60605-1996. Offers fiction (MFA); nonfiction (MFA); poetry (MFA). *Program availability:* Part-time, evening/weekend. *Students:* 45 full-time (24 women), 21 part-time (12 women); includes 18 minority (11 Black or African American, non-Hispanic/Latino; 3 Asian, non-Hispanic/Latino; 3 Hispanic/Latino; 1 Two or more races, non-Hispanic/Latino). 118 applicants, 88% accepted, 28 enrolled. *Degree requirements:* For master's, thesis. *Entrance requirements:* For master's, self-assessment essay, work samples, letters of recommendation, transcripts. Additional exam requirements/recommendations for international students: Required—TOEFL, IELTS. *Application deadline:* For fall admission, 1/15 priority date for domestic and international students. Applications are processed on a rolling basis. Application fee: $55 ($100 for international students). Electronic applications accepted. *Expenses:* Tuition: Full-time $26,808; part-time $1117 per credit. *Required fees:* $572; $155 per credit. *Financial support:* In 2017–18, 18 students received support. Teaching assistantships, career-related internships or fieldwork, Federal Work-Study, scholarships/grants, and unspecified assistantships available. Financial award application deadline: 1/15. *Unit head:* Kenneth Daley, Chair, 312-369-8121, E-mail: kdaley@colum.edu. *Application contact:* Emily Schmidt, Graduate Admissions, 312-369-7298, E-mail: eschmidt@colum.edu.
Website: https://www.colum.edu/academics/liberal-arts-and-sciences/english-and-creative-writing/index.html

Columbia University, Graduate School of Arts and Sciences, New York, NY 10027. Offers African-American studies (MA); American studies (MA); anthropology (MA, PhD); art history and archaeology (MA, PhD); astronomy (PhD); biological sciences (PhD); biotechnology (MA); chemical physics (PhD); chemistry (PhD); classical studies (MA, PhD); classics (MA, PhD); climate and society (MA); conservation biology (MA); earth and environmental sciences (PhD); East Asia: regional studies (MA); East Asian languages and cultures (MA, PhD); ecology, evolution and environmental biology (MA), including conservation biology; ecology, evolution, and environmental biology (PhD), including ecology and evolutionary biology, evolutionary primatology; economics (MA, PhD); English and comparative literature (MA, PhD); French and Romance philology (MA, PhD); Germanic languages (MA, PhD); global French studies (MA); global thought (MA); Hispanic cultural studies (MA); history (PhD); history and literature (MA); human rights studies (MA); Islamic studies (MA); Italian (MA, PhD); Japanese pedagogy (MA); Jewish studies (MA); Latin America and the Caribbean: regional studies (MA); Latin American and Iberian cultures (PhD); mathematics (MA, PhD), including finance (MA); medieval and Renaissance studies (MA); Middle Eastern, South Asian, and African studies (MA, PhD); modern art: critical and curatorial studies (MA); modern European studies (MA); museum anthropology (MA); music (DMA, PhD); oral history (MA); philosophical foundations of physics (MA); philosophy (MA, PhD); physics (PhD); political science (MA, PhD); psychology (PhD); quantitative methods in the social sciences (MA); religion (MA, PhD); Russia, Eurasia and East Europe: regional studies (MA); Russian translation (MA); Slavic cultures (MA); Slavic languages (MA, PhD); sociology (MA, PhD); South Asian studies (MA); statistics (MA, PhD); theatre (PhD). Dual-degree programs require admission to both Graduate School of Arts and Sciences and another Columbia school. *Program availability:* Part-time. Terminal master's awarded for partial completion of doctoral program. *Degree requirements:* For master's, variable foreign language requirement, comprehensive exam (for some programs), thesis (for some programs); for doctorate, variable foreign language requirement, comprehensive exam (for some programs), thesis/dissertation. *Entrance requirements:* For master's and doctorate, GRE General Test, GRE Subject Test (for some programs). Additional exam requirements/recommendations for international students: Required—TOEFL, IELTS. Electronic applications accepted. *Expenses: Tuition:* Full-time $44,864; part-time $1704 per credit. *Required fees:* $2370 per semester. One-time fee: $105.

Concordia University, School of Graduate Studies, Faculty of Arts and Science, Department of English, Program in English Literature, Montréal, QC H3G 1M8, Canada.

Offers MA, PhD. *Degree requirements:* For master's, one foreign language, thesis optional. *Entrance requirements:* For master's, honors degree in English, minimum GPA of 3.3 in English literature.

Converse College, Program in Liberal Arts, Spartanburg, SC 29302. Offers English (MLA); history (MLA); political science (MLA). *Degree requirements:* For master's, capstone paper. *Entrance requirements:* For master's, minimum GPA of 3.0, 2 recommendations. *Application deadline:* For fall admission, 5/1 priority date for domestic students; for spring admission, 1/30 for domestic students. Application fee: $40. *Unit head:* Lienne Medford, Dean of Graduate Studies and Distance Education, 864-596-9082, E-mail: lienne.medford@converse.edu.

Converse College, Program in Middle Level Education, Spartanburg, SC 29302. Offers language arts/English (MAT); mathematics (MAT); middle level education (M Ed); science (MAT); social studies (MAT). *Unit head:* Lienne Medford, Dean of Graduate Studies and Distance Education, 864-596-9082, E-mail: lienne.medford@converse.edu. *Application contact:* 864-596-9404, E-mail: graduate@converse.edu.

Cornell University, Graduate School, Graduate Fields of Arts and Sciences, Field of English Language and Literature, Ithaca, NY 14853. Offers African-American literature (PhD); American literature after 1865 (PhD); American literature to 1865 (PhD); American studies (PhD); colonial and postcolonial literatures (PhD); creative writing (MFA); cultural studies (PhD); dramatic literature (PhD); English poetry (PhD); English Renaissance to 1660 (PhD); lesbian, bisexual, and gay literary studies (PhD); literary criticism and theory (PhD); Old and Middle English (PhD); prose fiction (PhD); Restoration and the eighteenth-century (PhD); the nineteenth century (PhD); the twentieth century (PhD); women's literature (PhD); MFA/PhD. Terminal master's awarded for partial completion of doctoral program. *Degree requirements:* For master's, one foreign language, thesis; for doctorate, one foreign language, comprehensive exam, thesis/dissertation, teaching experience. *Entrance requirements:* For master's, GRE General Test, 3 letters of recommendation, creative writing sample; for doctorate, GRE General Test, GRE Subject Test (English), 3 letters of recommendation, writing sample. Additional exam requirements/recommendations for international students: Required—TOEFL (minimum score 600 paper-based; 77 iBT). Electronic applications accepted. *Faculty research:* English and American literature, women's writing, ethnic and post-colonial literature, critical theory, medievalism.

Cornell University, Graduate School, Graduate Fields of Arts and Sciences, Field of Linguistics, Ithaca, NY 14853. Offers applied linguistics (MA, PhD); East Asian linguistics (MA, PhD); English linguistics (MA, PhD); general linguistics (MA, PhD); Germanic linguistics (MA, PhD); Indo-European linguistics (MA, PhD); phonetics (MA, PhD); phonological theory (MA, PhD); Romance linguistics (MA, PhD); second language acquisition (MA, PhD); semantics (MA, PhD); Slavic linguistics (MA, PhD); sociolinguistics (MA, PhD); South Asian linguistics (MA, PhD); Southeast Asian linguistics (MA, PhD); syntactic theory (MA, PhD). Terminal master's awarded for partial completion of doctoral program. *Degree requirements:* For master's, one foreign language, thesis; for doctorate, one foreign language, comprehensive exam, thesis/dissertation. *Entrance requirements:* For master's and doctorate, GRE General Test, 2 letters of recommendation. Additional exam requirements/recommendations for international students: Required—TOEFL (minimum score 600 paper-based; 77 iBT). Electronic applications accepted. *Faculty research:* Phonology and phonetics, syntax and semantics, historical linguistics, philosophy of language, language acquisition.

Creighton University, Graduate School, College of Arts and Sciences, Department of English, Omaha, NE 68178-0001. Offers creative writing (MA, MFA). *Program availability:* Part-time. *Faculty:* 15 full-time (8 women), 1 part-time/adjunct (0 women). *Students:* 6 full-time (4 women), 1 (woman) part-time, 1 international. Average age 27. 31 applicants, 87% accepted, 6 enrolled. In 2017, 1 master's awarded. *Degree requirements:* For master's, thesis optional. *Entrance requirements:* For master's, 10-15 page writing sample, 3 letters of recommendation. Additional exam requirements/recommendations for international students: Required—TOEFL (minimum score 90 iBT). *Application deadline:* For fall admission, 3/15 priority date for domestic and international students. Application fee: $50. Electronic applications accepted. Part-time tuition and fees vary according to course load, degree level, campus/location and program. *Financial support:* In 2017–18, 5 fellowships with tuition reimbursements (averaging $11,465 per year) were awarded; scholarships/grants, tuition waivers (full and partial), and unspecified assistantships also available. Financial award applicants required to submit FAFSA. *Faculty research:* Henry James letters. *Unit head:* Dr. Robert Whipple, Director, 402-280-2520, E-mail: whippl@creighton.edu. *Application contact:* Lindsay Johnson, Director of Graduate and Adult Recruitment, 402-280-2703, Fax: 402-280-2423, E-mail: gradschool@creighton.edu.

Dalhousie University, Faculty of Arts and Social Science, Department of English, Halifax, NS B3H 4R2, Canada. Offers MA, PhD. *Entrance requirements:* Additional exam requirements/recommendations for international students: Required—TOEFL, IELTS, CANTEST, CAEL, or Michigan English Language Assessment Battery. Electronic applications accepted. *Faculty research:* Victorian, Canadian, Renaissance, eighteenth-century, and modern literature.

DePaul University, College of Liberal Arts and Social Sciences, Chicago, IL 60614. Offers Arabic (MA); Chinese (MA); critical ethnic studies (MA); English (MA); French (MA); German (MA); history (MA); interdisciplinary studies (MA, MS); international public service (MS); international studies (MA); Italian (MA); Japanese (MA); liberal studies (MA); nonprofit management (MNM); public administration (MPA); public health (MPH); public policy (MPP); public service management (MS); refugee and forced migration studies (MS); social work (MSW); sociology (MA); Spanish (MA); sustainable urban development (MA); women's and gender studies (MA); writing and publishing (MA); writing, rhetoric and discourse (MA); MA/PhD. *Program availability:* Part-time, evening/weekend, online learning. Terminal master's awarded for partial completion of doctoral program. *Degree requirements:* For master's, variable foreign language requirement, comprehensive exam (for some programs), thesis (for some programs). *Application deadline:* Applications are processed on a rolling basis. Application fee: $40. Electronic applications accepted. *Financial support:* Applicants required to submit FAFSA. *Unit head:* Dr. Guillermo Vasquez de Velasco, Dean, 773-325-7305. *Application contact:* Ann Spittle, Director of Graduate Admission, 773-325-8369, Fax: 312-476-3244, E-mail: graddepaul@depaul.edu.
Website: http://las.depaul.edu/

Drew University, Caspersen School of Graduate Studies, Madison, NJ 07940-1493. Offers conflict resolution and leadership (Certificate), including community leadership, moderation, peace building; education (M Ed); finance (MA); history and culture (MA, PhD), including American history, book history, British history, European history, Holocaust and genocide (M Litt, MA, D Litt, PhD), intellectual history, Irish history, print culture, public history; K-12 education (MAT), including art, biology, chemistry, elementary education, English, French, Italian, math, secondary education, special education, teacher of students with disabilities; liberal studies (M Litt, D Litt), including history, Holocaust and genocide (M Litt, MA, D Litt, PhD), Irish/Irish-American studies, literature (M Litt, MMH, D Litt, DMH, CMH), religion, spirituality, teaching in the two-year college, writing; medical humanities (MMH, DMH, CMH), including arts, health, healthcare, literature (M Litt, MMH, D Litt, DMH, CMH), scientific research; poetry (MFA). *Program availability:* Part-time, evening/weekend. *Faculty:* 4 full-time (2 women), 29 part-time/adjunct (15 women). *Students:* 77 full-time (42 women), 175 part-time (114 women); includes 39 minority (12 Black or African American, non-Hispanic/Latino; 6 Asian, non-Hispanic/Latino; 16 Hispanic/Latino; 5 Two or more races, non-Hispanic/Latino), 11 international. Average age 41. 126 applicants, 75% accepted, 52 enrolled. In 2017, 38 master's, 23 doctorates, 35 other advanced degrees awarded. Terminal master's awarded for partial completion of doctoral program. *Degree requirements:* For master's and other advanced degree, thesis (for some programs); for doctorate, one foreign language, comprehensive exam (for some programs), thesis/dissertation. *Entrance requirements:* For master's, PRAXIS Core and Subject Area tests (for MAT), GRE/GMAT (for M Fin), resume, transcripts, writing sample, personal statement, letters of recommendation; for doctorate, GRE (PhD in history and culture), resume, transcripts, writing sample, personal statement, letters of recommendation; for other advanced degree, resume, transcripts, personal statement. Additional exam requirements/recommendations for international students: Required—TOEFL (minimum score 587 paper-based; 80 iBT), IELTS (minimum score 6), TWE (minimum score 4). *Application deadline:* For fall admission, 8/1 for domestic students, 6/1 for international students; for spring admission, 12/1 for domestic students, 10/1 for international students. Applications are processed on a rolling basis. Application fee: $35. Electronic applications accepted. *Financial support:* Fellowships, research assistantships, teaching assistantships, career-related internships or fieldwork, Federal Work-Study, scholarships/grants, and unspecified assistantships available. Support available to part-time students. Financial award applicants required to submit FAFSA. *Faculty research:* Irish history and culture, conflict resolution and leadership. *Application contact:* Leanne Horinko, Director of Caspersen Admissions, 973-408-3280, E-mail: gradm@drew.edu.
Website: http://www.drew.edu/caspersen

Duke University, Graduate School, Department of English, Durham, NC 27708. Offers PhD, JD/AM. *Degree requirements:* For doctorate, 2 foreign languages, thesis/dissertation. *Entrance requirements:* For doctorate, GRE General Test, writing sample. Additional exam requirements/recommendations for international students: Required—TOEFL (minimum score 577 paper-based; 90 iBT) or IELTS (minimum score 7). Electronic applications accepted.

Duquesne University, Graduate School of Liberal Arts, Department of English, Pittsburgh, PA 15282-0001. Offers MA, PhD. *Program availability:* Part-time, evening/weekend. *Faculty:* 16 full-time (10 women), 8 part-time/adjunct (4 women). *Students:* 44 full-time (31 women), 3 part-time (2 women); includes 3 minority (1 Black or African American, non-Hispanic/Latino; 2 Hispanic/Latino), 4 international. Average age 29. 41 applicants, 68% accepted, 13 enrolled. In 2017, 5 master's, 4 doctorates awarded. Terminal master's awarded for partial completion of doctoral program. *Entrance requirements:* For master's and doctorate, GRE General Test, bachelor's degree in English, writing sample. Additional exam requirements/recommendations for international students: Required—TOEFL. *Application deadline:* For fall admission, 2/1 priority date for domestic and international students. Applications are processed on a rolling basis. Application fee: $0. Electronic applications accepted. *Expenses:* $1,259 per credit. *Financial support:* In 2017–18, 33 students received support. Research assistantships, teaching assistantships, Federal Work-Study, scholarships/grants, tuition waivers (full), and unspecified assistantships available. Support available to part-time students. Financial award application deadline: 5/1. *Unit head:* Dr. Greg Barnhisel, Chair, 412-396-6432, E-mail: barnhiselg@duq.edu. *Application contact:* Linda Rendulic, Assistant to the Dean, 412-396-6400, Fax: 412-396-5265, E-mail: rendulic@duq.edu.
Website: http://www.duq.edu/academics/schools/liberal-arts/graduate-school/programs/english

East Carolina University, Graduate School, Thomas Harriot College of Arts and Sciences, Department of English, Greenville, NC 27858-4353. Offers creative writing (MA); English studies (MA); linguistics (MA); literature (MA); multicultural and transnational literatures (MA, Certificate); professional communication (Certificate); rhetoric and composition (MA); rhetoric, writing, and professional communication (PhD); teaching English in the two-year college (Certificate); teaching English to speakers of other languages (MA, Certificate); technical and professional communication (MA). *Program availability:* Part-time, evening/weekend, online learning. *Students:* 40 full-time (27 women), 74 part-time (57 women); includes 33 minority (23 Black or African American, non-Hispanic/Latino; 2 Asian, non-Hispanic/Latino; 4 Hispanic/Latino; 4 Two or more races, non-Hispanic/Latino). Average age 35. 36 applicants, 94% accepted, 25 enrolled. In 2017, 23 master's, 4 doctorates, 24 other advanced degrees awarded. *Degree requirements:* For master's, comprehensive exam, thesis optional; for doctorate, comprehensive exam, thesis/dissertation. *Entrance requirements:* For master's, GRE General Test or MAT; for doctorate, GRE General Test or MAT, writing samples. Additional exam requirements/recommendations for international students: Recommended—TOEFL (minimum score 78 iBT), IELTS (minimum score 6.5), TWE. *Application deadline:* For fall admission, 7/31 priority date for domestic students, 2/1 priority date for international students; for spring admission, 11/30 priority date for domestic students, 10/1 priority date for international students. Applications are processed on a rolling basis. Application fee: $75. Electronic applications accepted. *Expenses:* Tuition, state resident: full-time $4749; part-time $297 per credit hour. Tuition, nonresident: full-time $17,898; part-time $1119 per credit hour. *Required fees:* $2691; $224 per credit hour. Part-time tuition and fees vary according to course load and program. *Financial support:* Research assistantships with partial tuition reimbursements, teaching assistantships with partial tuition reimbursements, and Federal Work-Study available. Support available to part-time students. Financial award application deadline: 3/1. *Faculty research:* Technical and professional communication, rhetoric/composition, multicultural and transnational literature, creative writing, film studies. *Unit head:* Dr. Marianne Montgomery, Chair, 252-328-6687, E-mail: montgomerym@ecu.edu. *Application contact:* Dean of Graduate School, 252-328-6012, Fax: 252-328-6071, E-mail: gradschool@ecu.edu.
Website: http://www.ecu.edu/cs-cas/engl/

Eastern Illinois University, Graduate School, College of Liberal Arts and Sciences, Department of English, Charleston, IL 61920. Offers MA. *Program availability:* Part-time, evening/weekend. *Degree requirements:* For master's, comprehensive exam (for some programs), thesis (for some programs). *Entrance requirements:* For master's, GMAT or GRE. Additional exam requirements/recommendations for international students: Required—TOEFL (minimum score 500 paper-based; 61 iBT), IELTS (minimum score 6). *Application deadline:* For fall admission, 5/15 for domestic and international students; for spring admission, 10/15 for domestic and international students. Applications are processed on a rolling basis. Application fee: $30. Electronic applications accepted. *Financial support:* Teaching assistantships with full tuition reimbursements, career-related internships or fieldwork, Federal Work-Study, and unspecified assistantships available. Support available to part-time students. Financial award application deadline: 3/1; financial award applicants required to submit FAFSA. *Unit head:* Dana Ringuette, Chair, 217-581-2428, Fax: 217-581-7209, E-mail: dringuette@eiu.edu. *Application contact:* Randall Beebe, Director of Graduate Studies, 217-581-2428, Fax: 217-581-7209, E-mail: rlbeebe@eiu.edu.
Website: http://www.eiu.edu/englishgrad/

Eastern Kentucky University, The Graduate School, College of Arts and Sciences, Department of English and Theatre, Richmond, KY 40475-3102. Offers creative writing (MFA); English (MA). *Program availability:* Part-time, evening/weekend. *Degree requirements:* For master's, thesis optional. *Entrance requirements:* For master's, GRE General Test, minimum GPA of 2.5, minor in English with 3.0 GPA. *Faculty research:* Old English, Victorian studies, women's studies, rhetoric, popular culture, novel studies.

Eastern Michigan University, Graduate School, College of Arts and Sciences, Department of English Language and Literature, Program in Children's Literature, Ypsilanti, MI 48197. Offers MA. *Program availability:* Part-time, evening/weekend, online learning. *Students:* 3 full-time (2 women), 10 part-time (9 women); includes 2 minority (1 Black or African American, non-Hispanic/Latino; 1 Asian, non-Hispanic/Latino). Average age 30. 8 applicants, 75% accepted, 1 enrolled. In 2017, 2 master's awarded. *Entrance requirements:* Additional exam requirements/recommendations for international students: Required—TOEFL. *Application deadline:* Applications are processed on a rolling basis. Application fee: $45. *Financial support:* Fellowships, research assistantships with full tuition reimbursements, teaching assistantships with full tuition reimbursements, and tuition waivers (partial) available. Financial award applicants required to submit FAFSA. *Application contact:* Dr. Ian Wojcik-Andrews, Program Advisor, 734-487-0138, Fax: 734-483-9744, E-mail: iwojcika@emich.edu.

Eastern Michigan University, Graduate School, College of Arts and Sciences, Department of English Language and Literature, Program in Literature, Ypsilanti, MI 48197. Offers MA. *Program availability:* Part-time, evening/weekend, online learning. *Students:* 3 full-time (all women), 11 part-time (5 women); includes 1 minority (Hispanic/Latino), 1 international. Average age 29. 6 applicants, 67% accepted, 2 enrolled. In 2017, 2 master's awarded. *Entrance requirements:* Additional exam requirements/recommendations for international students: Required—TOEFL. *Application deadline:* Applications are processed on a rolling basis. Application fee: $45. *Financial support:* Fellowships, research assistantships with full tuition reimbursements, teaching assistantships with full tuition reimbursements, career-related internships or fieldwork, Federal Work-Study, institutionally sponsored loans, scholarships/grants, tuition waivers (partial), and unspecified assistantships available. Support available to part-time students. Financial award applicants required to submit FAFSA. *Application contact:* Dr. Natasa Kovacevic, Program Coordinator, 734-487-0976, Fax: 734-483-9744, E-mail: nkovacev@emich.edu.

Eastern New Mexico University, Graduate School, College of Liberal Arts and Sciences, Department of Languages and Literature, Portales, NM 88130. Offers English (MA), including English. *Program availability:* Part-time. *Degree requirements:* For master's, one foreign language, thesis, oral and written comprehensive exams. *Entrance requirements:* For master's, minimum GPA of 3.0, foreign language proficiency, interview. Additional exam requirements/recommendations for international students: Required—TOEFL (minimum score 550 paper-based; 79 iBT), IELTS (minimum score 6). *Application deadline:* For fall admission, 7/20 priority date for domestic students, 6/20 priority date for international students; for spring admission, 12/15 priority date for domestic students, 11/15 priority date for international students. Applications are processed on a rolling basis. Application fee: $10. Electronic applications accepted. *Financial support:* Applicants required to submit FAFSA. *Unit head:* Dr. Carol Erwin, Graduate Coordinator, 575-562-2135, E-mail: carol.erwin@enmu.edu. *Application contact:* Sharon Johnson, Department Secretary, 575-562-2423, Fax: 575-562-2142, E-mail: sharon.johnson@enmu.edu. Website: https://www.enmu.edu/academics/colleges-departments/college-liberal-arts-sciences/department-languages-literature

Eastern Washington University, Graduate Studies, College of Arts, Letters and Education, Department of English, Cheney, WA 99004-2431. Offers literature (MA); rhetoric, composition, and technical communication (MA); teaching English as a second language (MA). *Faculty:* 14. *Students:* 61 full-time (40 women), 11 part-time (9 women); includes 3 minority (1 Asian, non-Hispanic/Latino; 2 Hispanic/Latino), 7 international. Average age 34. 91 applicants, 52% accepted, 33 enrolled. In 2017, 32 master's awarded. *Degree requirements:* For master's, comprehensive exam, thesis or alternative. *Entrance requirements:* For master's, GRE General Test, minimum GPA of 3.0. Additional exam requirements/recommendations for international students: Required—TOEFL (minimum score 580 paper-based; 92 iBT), IELTS (minimum score 7), PTE (minimum score 6). *Application deadline:* For fall admission, 4/1 priority date for domestic students; for spring admission, 1/15 for domestic students. Applications are processed on a rolling basis. Application fee: $50. *Expenses:* Tuition, state resident: full-time $11,191; part-time $373.06 per credit. Tuition, nonresident: full-time $25,995; part-time $866.52 per credit. *Financial support:* Teaching assistantships with partial tuition reimbursements, career-related internships or fieldwork, Federal Work-Study, institutionally sponsored loans, scholarships/grants, health care benefits, tuition waivers (partial), and unspecified assistantships available. Support available to part-time students. Financial award application deadline: 2/1; financial award applicants required to submit FAFSA. *Application contact:* Kathy White, Advisor/Recruiter for Graduate Studies, 509-359-2491, E-mail: gradprograms@ewu.edu. Website: http://www.ewu.edu/CALE/Programs/English.xml

East Tennessee State University, School of Graduate Studies, College of Arts and Sciences, Department of Literature and Language, Johnson City, TN 37614. Offers healthcare translation and interpreting (Postbaccalaureate Certificate); literature (MA); teaching English to speakers of other languages (Postbaccalaureate Certificate). *Program availability:* Part-time, evening/weekend. *Degree requirements:* For master's, comprehensive exam, thesis optional; for Postbaccalaureate Certificate, one foreign language. *Entrance requirements:* For master's, GRE General Test, minimum undergraduate GPA of 3.0 in English, writing sample, three letters of recommendation; for Postbaccalaureate Certificate, GRE General Test, speaking and listening assessment, resume, three letters of recommendation, two years of coursework or basic proficiency in a foreign language. Additional exam requirements/recommendations for international students: Required—TOEFL (minimum score 550 paper-based; 79 iBT). *Application deadline:* For fall admission, 6/1 for domestic students, 4/29 for international students; for spring admission, 11/1 for domestic students, 9/29 for international students. Application fee: $55 ($65 for international students). Electronic applications accepted. *Financial support:* Research assistantships with full tuition reimbursements, teaching assistantships with full tuition reimbursements, career-related internships or fieldwork, institutionally sponsored loans, scholarships/grants, and unspecified assistantships available. Financial award application deadline: 7/1; financial award applicants required to submit FAFSA. *Faculty research:* Linguistics and dialectology, English education, critical literary theory, literary biography, environmental literature, modern and ancient languages. *Unit head:* Dr. Katherine Weiss, Chair, 423-439-4347, Fax: 423-439-7193, E-mail: weisk01@etsu.edu. *Application contact:* Dr. Michael A. Cody, Assistant Chair for Graduate Studies, 423-439-6676, Fax: 423-439-5624, E-mail: codym@etsu.edu. Website: http://www.etsu.edu/cas/litlang/

Emory University, Laney Graduate School, Department of English, Atlanta, GA 30322-1100. Offers PhD, Graduate Certificate. *Degree requirements:* For doctorate, one foreign language, comprehensive exam, thesis/dissertation. *Entrance requirements:* For doctorate, GRE General Test, minimum GPA of 3.0. Additional exam requirements/

recommendations for international students: Required—TOEFL. Electronic applications accepted. *Faculty research:* American literature, Renaissance literature, twentieth-century poetry, Irish literature, cultural studies.

Emporia State University, Program in English, Emporia, KS 66801-5415. Offers MA. *Program availability:* Part-time. *Faculty:* 17 full-time (10 women), 8 part-time/adjunct (6 women). *Students:* 10 full-time (5 women), 39 part-time (25 women); includes 2 minority (1 Black or African American, non-Hispanic/Latino; 1 Hispanic/Latino), 5 international. 26 applicants, 54% accepted, 7 enrolled. In 2017, 7 master's awarded. *Degree requirements:* For master's, comprehensive exam, thesis optional. *Entrance requirements:* For master's, minimum undergraduate GPA of 2.75 in last 60 hours. Additional exam requirements/recommendations for international students: Required—TOEFL (minimum score 550 paper-based; 68 iBT). *Application deadline:* For fall admission, 8/15 for domestic students. Application fee: $30 ($75 for international students). *Expenses:* Tuition, state resident: full-time $6084; part-time $253.50 per credit hour. Tuition, nonresident: full-time $18,924; part-time $788.50 per credit hour. *Required fees:* $1943; $80.95 per credit hour. Tuition and fees vary according to campus/location. *Financial support:* In 2017–18, 3 research assistantships with full tuition reimbursements (averaging $7,344 per year), 4 teaching assistantships with full tuition reimbursements (averaging $7,344 per year) were awarded; Federal Work-Study, health care benefits, and unspecified assistantships also available. Financial award application deadline: 2/15; financial award applicants required to submit FAFSA. *Unit head:* Dr. Kevin Rabas, Chair, 620-341-5216, E-mail: krabas@emporia.edu. *Application contact:* Mary Sewell, Admissions Coordinator, 800-950-GRAD, Fax: 620-341-5909, E-mail: msewell@emporia.edu. Website: http://www.emporia.edu/info/degrees-courses/grad/english

Fairleigh Dickinson University, Metropolitan Campus, University College: Arts, Sciences, and Professional Studies, Department of English, Philosophy, and Humanities, Program in English and Literature, Teaneck, NJ 07666-1914. Offers MA.

Fitchburg State University, Division of Graduate and Continuing Education, Program in Middle School Education, Fitchburg, MA 01420-2697. Offers English (M Ed); general science (M Ed); history (M Ed); math (M Ed). *Accreditation:* NCATE. *Program availability:* Part-time, evening/weekend. *Students:* 15 full-time (7 women), 5 part-time (2 women); includes 3 minority (2 Black or African American, non-Hispanic/Latino; 1 Two or more races, non-Hispanic/Latino). Average age 32. 11 applicants, 100% accepted, 10 enrolled. In 2017, 4 master's awarded. *Entrance requirements:* Additional exam requirements/recommendations for international students: Required—TOEFL (minimum score 550 paper-based; 79 iBT). *Application deadline:* For fall admission, 7/15 for international students; for spring admission, 12/1 for international students. Applications are processed on a rolling basis. Application fee: $50. Electronic applications accepted. *Expenses:* Contact institution. *Financial support:* In 2017–18, research assistantships with partial tuition reimbursements (averaging $5,500 per year) were awarded; Federal Work-Study, scholarships/grants, and unspecified assistantships also available. Support available to part-time students. Financial award application deadline: 3/1; financial award applicants required to submit FAFSA. *Unit head:* William Cortezia, Chair, 978-665-3193, Fax: 978-665-3658, E-mail: gce@fitchburgstate.edu. *Application contact:* Jinawa McNeil, Director of Admissions, 978-665-3140, Fax: 978-665-4540, E-mail: admissions@fitchburgstate.edu. Website: http://www.fitchburgstate.edu

Fitchburg State University, Division of Graduate and Continuing Education, Programs in English and Teaching English (Secondary Level), Fitchburg, MA 01420-2697. Offers MA, MAT, Certificate. *Accreditation:* NCATE. *Program availability:* Part-time, evening/weekend. *Faculty:* 4 full-time (2 women). *Students:* 6 full-time (4 women), 10 part-time (9 women); includes 1 minority (Asian, non-Hispanic/Latino). Average age 28. 6 applicants, 100% accepted, 6 enrolled. In 2017, 5 master's awarded. *Entrance requirements:* Additional exam requirements/recommendations for international students: Required—TOEFL (minimum score 550 paper-based; 79 iBT). *Application deadline:* For fall admission, 7/15 for international students; for spring admission, 12/1 for international students. Applications are processed on a rolling basis. Application fee: $50. Electronic applications accepted. *Expenses:* Contact institution. *Financial support:* In 2017–18, research assistantships with partial tuition reimbursements (averaging $5,500 per year) were awarded; Federal Work-Study, scholarships/grants, and unspecified assistantships also available. Support available to part-time students. Financial award application deadline: 3/1; financial award applicants required to submit FAFSA. *Unit head:* Dr. Chola Chisunka, Chair, 978-665-3445, Fax: 978-665-3658, E-mail: gce@fitchburgstate.edu. *Application contact:* Jinawa McNeil, Director of Admissions, 978-665-3140, Fax: 978-665-4540, E-mail: admissions@fitchburgstate.edu.

Florida Atlantic University, Dorothy F. Schmidt College of Arts and Letters, Department of English, Boca Raton, FL 33431-0991. Offers American literature (MA). *Program availability:* Part-time. *Faculty:* 22 full-time (11 women). *Students:* 34 full-time (19 women), 27 part-time (19 women); includes 15 minority (3 Black or African American, non-Hispanic/Latino; 1 Asian, non-Hispanic/Latino; 10 Hispanic/Latino; 1 Two or more races, non-Hispanic/Latino), 3 international. Average age 33. 51 applicants, 47% accepted, 18 enrolled. In 2017, 17 master's awarded. *Degree requirements:* For master's, one foreign language, thesis. *Entrance requirements:* For master's, GRE General Test, minimum GPA of 3.0, writing samples, 2 letters of recommendation. Additional exam requirements/recommendations for international students: Required—TOEFL (minimum score 500 paper-based; 61 iBT), IELTS (minimum score 6). *Application deadline:* For fall admission, 3/1 for domestic students, 2/15 for international students; for spring admission, 11/1 for domestic students, 7/15 for international students. Applications are processed on a rolling basis. Application fee: $30. Electronic applications accepted. *Expenses:* Tuition, state resident: full-time $7400; part-time $369.82 per credit. Tuition, nonresident: full-time $20,496; part-time $1042.81 per credit. *Financial support:* Fellowships, teaching assistantships with partial tuition reimbursements, Federal Work-Study, and tuition waivers available. Support available to part-time students. Financial award application deadline: 3/1. *Faculty research:* African-American writers, critical theory, British-American, Asian-American. *Unit head:* Mary Sheffield, Senior Instructor, 561-297-2974, E-mail: msheffi3@fau.edu. Website: http://www.fau.edu/english/

Florida Gulf Coast University, College of Arts and Sciences, Program in English, Fort Myers, FL 33965-6565. Offers MA. *Program availability:* Part-time. *Faculty:* 245 full-time (104 women), 155 part-time/adjunct (71 women). *Students:* 4 full-time (2 women), 14 part-time (11 women); includes 2 minority (1 Black or African American, non-Hispanic/Latino; 1 Hispanic/Latino). Average age 34. 10 applicants, 80% accepted, 7 enrolled. In 2017, 10 master's awarded. *Entrance requirements:* For master's, GRE General Test, minimum GPA of 3.0. Additional exam requirements/recommendations for international students: Required—TOEFL (minimum score 550 paper-based). *Application deadline:* For fall admission, 2/15 priority date for domestic students, 5/1 for international students; for spring admission, 12/1 for domestic students, 9/15 for international students. Applications are processed on a rolling basis. Application fee: $30. Electronic applications accepted. *Expenses:* Tuition, state resident: part-time $290 per credit hour. Tuition, nonresident: part-time $1173 per credit hour. *Required fees:* $127 per credit hour. Tuition and fees vary according to course load. *Financial support:* In 2017–18, 2 students received support. Application deadline: 6/30; applicants required to submit

FAFSA. *Unit head:* Fiona Tolhurst, Program Coordinator, 239-590-7262, E-mail: ftolhurst@fgcu.edu. *Application contact:* Patricia Rice, Executive Secretary, 239-590-7196, Fax: 239-590-7200, E-mail: price@fgcu.edu.

Florida International University, College of Arts, Sciences, and Education, Department of English, Miami, FL 33199. Offers creative writing (MFA); English (MA), including literature; linguistics (MA). *Program availability:* Part-time, evening/weekend. *Faculty:* 53 full-time (26 women), 38 part-time/adjunct (24 women). *Students:* 40 full-time (24 women), 33 part-time (19 women); includes 40 minority (6 Black or African American, non-Hispanic/Latino; 33 Hispanic/Latino; 1 Two or more races, non-Hispanic/Latino), 4 international. Average age 31. 50 applicants, 50% accepted, 20 enrolled. In 2017, 31 master's awarded. *Degree requirements:* For master's, thesis. *Entrance requirements:* For master's, GRE General Test, minimum undergraduate GPA of 3.0 (upper-level coursework), letter of intent, two letters of recommendation. Additional exam requirements/recommendations for international students: Required—TOEFL (minimum score 550 paper-based; 80 iBT). *Application deadline:* For fall admission, 2/1 for domestic and international students; for spring admission, 10/1 for domestic students, 9/1 for international students. Applications are processed on a rolling basis. Application fee: $30. Electronic applications accepted. *Expenses:* Tuition, state resident: full-time $8912; part-time $446 per credit hour. Tuition, nonresident: full-time $21,393; part-time $992 per credit hour. *Required fees:* $390; $195 per semester. *Financial support:* Institutionally sponsored loans and scholarships/grants available. Financial award application deadline: 3/1; financial award applicants required to submit FAFSA. *Unit head:* Dr. Heather Russell, Chair, 305-348-3369, Fax: 305-348-3878, E-mail: heather.russell@fiu.edu. *Application contact:* Nanett Rojas, Assistant Director, Graduate Admissions, 305-348-7464, Fax: 305-348-7441, E-mail: gradadm@fiu.edu.

Florida State University, The Graduate School, College of Arts and Sciences, Department of English, Tallahassee, FL 32312. Offers English (MA, MFA, PhD), including creative writing (MFA, PhD), literature (MA, PhD), rhetoric and composition (MA, PhD). *Program availability:* Part-time. *Faculty:* 47 full-time (24 women), 2 part-time/adjunct (1 woman). *Students:* 142 full-time (80 women), 31 part-time (23 women); includes 44 minority (17 Black or African American, non-Hispanic/Latino; 1 American Indian or Alaska Native, non-Hispanic/Latino; 12 Asian, non-Hispanic/Latino; 5 Hispanic/Latino; 9 Two or more races, non-Hispanic/Latino), 9 international. Average age 30. 307 applicants, 22% accepted, 47 enrolled. In 2017, 21 master's, 24 doctorates awarded. *Degree requirements:* For master's, one foreign language, 33 hours of coursework including capstone essay, thesis or portfolio (MA); 45 hours of coursework including 9-12 thesis hours (MFA); for doctorate, one foreign language, comprehensive exam, thesis/dissertation, 27 hours of coursework, 24 hours of dissertation work. *Entrance requirements:* For master's and doctorate, GRE General Test, sample of written work, 3 letters of recommendation, resume. Additional exam requirements/recommendations for international students: Required—TOEFL. *Application deadline:* For fall admission, 12/17 priority date for domestic and international students. Application fee: $30. Electronic applications accepted. *Financial support:* In 2017–18, 132 students received support, including 5 fellowships with tuition reimbursements available, teaching assistantships with tuition reimbursements available (averaging $13,500 per year); career-related internships or fieldwork, Federal Work-Study, and institutionally sponsored loans also available. Financial award application deadline: 8/1; financial award applicants required to submit FAFSA. *Faculty research:* British and Irish literature, American literature, creative writing, rhetoric and composition, multiethnic transnational literature, history of text technologies. *Unit head:* Dr. Gary Taylor, Chair, 850-644-4230, Fax: 850-644-0811, E-mail: gtaylor@fsu.edu. *Application contact:* Ginger Martin, Senior Graduate Academic Coordinator, 850-644-1081, Fax: 850-644-9656, E-mail: vmartin@fsu.edu.
Website: http://english.fsu.edu/

Fordham University, Graduate School of Arts and Sciences, Department of English Language and Literature, New York, NY 10458. Offers MA, PhD. *Program availability:* Part-time, evening/weekend. *Faculty:* 37 full-time (23 women). *Students:* 56 full-time (34 women), 11 part-time (6 women); includes 5 minority (1 American Indian or Alaska Native, non-Hispanic/Latino; 4 Asian, non-Hispanic/Latino), 4 international. Average age 31. 184 applicants, 37% accepted, 14 enrolled. In 2017, 14 master's, 11 doctorates awarded. Terminal master's awarded for partial completion of doctoral program. *Degree requirements:* For master's, one foreign language, comprehensive exam, thesis optional; for doctorate, 2 foreign languages, comprehensive exam, thesis/dissertation. *Entrance requirements:* For master's, GRE General Test; for doctorate, GRE General Test, GRE Subject Test. Additional exam requirements/recommendations for international students: Required—TOEFL (minimum score 650 paper-based). *Application deadline:* For fall admission, 1/4 priority date for domestic students; for spring admission, 11/1 for domestic students. Application fee: $70. Electronic applications accepted. *Financial support:* In 2017–18, 63 students received support, including 1 fellowship with tuition reimbursement available (averaging $25,390 per year), 49 teaching assistantships with tuition reimbursements available (averaging $19,311 per year); institutionally sponsored loans, tuition waivers (full and partial), and unspecified assistantships also available. Financial award application deadline: 1/4; financial award applicants required to submit FAFSA. *Faculty research:* Nineteenth century British and American literature, Shakespeare and early modern drama, Aesthetic Theory, Old Norse, poetics of race and gender, Anglo-Norman. *Unit head:* Dr. Julie Chun Kim, Director, Graduate Studies, 718-817-4017, Fax: 718-817-4013, E-mail: jukim@fordham.edu. *Application contact:* Travis Strattion, Interim Director of Graduate Admissions, 718-817-4417, Fax: 718-817-3566, E-mail: tstrattion@fordham.edu.

Fort Hays State University, Graduate School, College of Arts and Sciences, Department of English, Hays, KS 67601-4099. Offers MA. *Degree requirements:* For master's, comprehensive exam, thesis or alternative. *Entrance requirements:* Additional exam requirements/recommendations for international students: Required—TOEFL (minimum score 550 paper-based). Electronic applications accepted. *Faculty research:* Eisenhower and Hansen papers, Celtic literature and culture, poetry of Robert Frost.

Framingham State University, Graduate Studies, Program in English, Framingham, MA 01701-9101. Offers MA. *Unit head:* Dr. Julia Scandrett, Coordinator, 508-626-4550, Fax: 508-626-4030, E-mail: jscande@frc.mass.edu. *Application contact:* 508-626-4550, Fax: 508-626-4030, E-mail: dgce@frc.mass.edu.

Gannon University, School of Graduate Studies, College of Humanities, Education, and Social Sciences, School of Humanities, Program in English, Erie, PA 16541-0001. Offers MA. *Program availability:* Part-time, evening/weekend. *Degree requirements:* For master's, thesis. *Entrance requirements:* For master's, undergraduate degree in English. Additional exam requirements/recommendations for international students: Required—TOEFL (minimum score 79 iBT). Electronic applications accepted. Application fee is waived when completed online.

Gardner-Webb University, Graduate School, Department of English, Boiling Springs, NC 28017. Offers English (MA); English education (MA). *Program availability:* Part-time, evening/weekend. *Faculty:* 4 full-time (all women). *Students:* 27 part-time (19 women); includes 3 minority (2 Black or African American, non-Hispanic/Latino; 1 Two or more races, non-Hispanic/Latino). Average age 31. 27 applicants, 37% accepted, 6 enrolled. In 2017, 6 master's awarded. *Degree requirements:* For master's, comprehensive exam. *Entrance requirements:* For master's, GRE General Test, MAT, or NTE; PRAXIS, minimum GPA of 2.5. *Application deadline:* For fall admission, 8/1 priority date for domestic students. Applications are processed on a rolling basis. Application fee: $0. Electronic applications accepted. *Expenses:* Contact institution. *Financial support:* Unspecified assistantships available. *Unit head:* Jennifer Buckner, Chair, 704-406-4394, E-mail: jbuckner@gardner-webb.edu. *Application contact:* Office of Graduate Admissions, 877-498-4723, Fax: 704-406-3895, E-mail: gradinfo@gardner-webb.edu.

George Mason University, College of Humanities and Social Sciences, Department of English, Fairfax, VA 22030. Offers college teaching (Certificate), including higher education pedagogy; creative writing (MFA), including fiction, nonfiction writing, poetry; English (MA), including cultural studies, linguistics, literature, professional writing and rhetoric, teaching of writing and literature; English pedagogy (Certificate); folklore studies (Certificate); linguistics (PhD); writing and rhetoric (PhD). *Program availability:* Part-time. *Faculty:* 78 full-time (40 women), 45 part-time/adjunct (30 women). *Students:* 120 full-time (84 women), 116 part-time (94 women); includes 43 minority (13 Black or African American, non-Hispanic/Latino; 8 Asian, non-Hispanic/Latino; 14 Hispanic/Latino; 1 Native Hawaiian or other Pacific Islander, non-Hispanic/Latino; 7 Two or more races, non-Hispanic/Latino), 19 international. Average age 32. 224 applicants, 61% accepted, 68 enrolled. In 2017, 60 master's, 1 doctorate, 17 other advanced degrees awarded. *Degree requirements:* For master's, thesis (for some programs), proficiency in a foreign language by course work or translation test; for doctorate, comprehensive exam, thesis/dissertation, 2 papers. *Entrance requirements:* For master's, official transcripts; expanded goals statement; writing sample; portfolio; 2 letters of recommendation; resume; for doctorate, GRE (for linguistics), expanded goals statement; 2 letters of recommendation (writing and rhetoric); 3 letters of recommendation (linguistics); writing sample; introductory course in linguistics; official transcripts; master's degree in relevant field; for Certificate, official transcripts; expanded goals statement; 2 letters of recommendation; writing sample; resume. Additional exam requirements/recommendations for international students: Required—TOEFL (minimum score 575 paper-based; 88 iBT), IELTS (minimum score 6.5), PTE (minimum score 59). *Application deadline:* For fall admission, 3/15 for domestic and international students; for spring admission, 10/15 for domestic and international students. Application fee: $75 ($80 for international students). Electronic applications accepted. *Expenses:* Tuition, state resident: full-time $11,228; part-time $459.50 per credit. Tuition, nonresident: full-time $30,932; part-time $1280.50 per credit. *Required fees:* $3252; $135.50 per credit. Part-time tuition and fees vary according to course load and program. *Financial support:* In 2017–18, 84 students received support, including 9 research assistantships with tuition reimbursements available (averaging $17,199 per year), 76 teaching assistantships with tuition reimbursements available (averaging $11,917 per year); career-related internships or fieldwork, Federal Work-Study, scholarships/grants, unspecified assistantships, and health care benefits (for full-time research or teaching assistantship recipients) also available. Support available to part-time students. Financial award application deadline: 3/1; financial award applicants required to submit FAFSA. *Faculty research:* Literature, professional writing and editing, writing of fiction or poetry. *Total annual research expenditures:* $68,592. *Unit head:* Debra Lattanzi-Shutika, Chair, 703-993-1170, Fax: 703-993-1161, E-mail: dshutika@gmu.edu. *Application contact:* Alex Walsh, Graduate Admissions Coordinator, 703-993-1185, Fax: 703-993-1161, E-mail: awalsh7@gmu.edu.
Website: http://english.gmu.edu

Georgetown University, Graduate School of Arts and Sciences, Department of English, Washington, DC 20057. Offers British and American literature (MA). *Degree requirements:* For master's, thesis or alternative, independent study, oral exam. *Entrance requirements:* For master's, GRE General Test. Additional exam requirements/recommendations for international students: Required—TOEFL.

The George Washington University, Columbian College of Arts and Sciences, Department of English, Washington, DC 20052. Offers MA, PhD. *Program availability:* Part-time, evening/weekend. *Faculty:* 31 full-time (17 women), 13 part-time/adjunct (7 women). *Students:* 28 full-time (20 women), 25 part-time (16 women); includes 7 minority (2 Black or African American, non-Hispanic/Latino; 2 Asian, non-Hispanic/Latino; 2 Hispanic/Latino; 1 Two or more races, non-Hispanic/Latino), 6 international. Average age 30. 149 applicants, 42% accepted, 22 enrolled. In 2017, 6 master's, 6 doctorates awarded. Terminal master's awarded for partial completion of doctoral program. *Degree requirements:* For master's, one foreign language, comprehensive exam, thesis or alternative; for doctorate, 2 foreign languages, thesis/dissertation, general exam. *Entrance requirements:* For master's and doctorate, GRE General Test, GRE Subject Test, minimum GPA of 3.0, writing sample. Additional exam requirements/recommendations for international students: Required—TOEFL (minimum score 550 paper-based; 80 iBT). *Application deadline:* For fall admission, 1/15 priority date for domestic and international students; for spring admission, 10/1 priority date for domestic students, 9/1 priority date for international students. Applications are processed on a rolling basis. Application fee: $75. Electronic applications accepted. *Expenses: Tuition:* Full-time $28,800; part-time $1655 per credit hour. *Required fees:* $45; $2.75 per credit hour. *Financial support:* In 2017–18, 18 students received support. Fellowships with tuition reimbursements available, teaching assistantships with tuition reimbursements available, and Federal Work-Study available. Financial award application deadline: 1/15. *Unit head:* Robert McRuer, Chair, 202-994-6180, E-mail: rmcruer@gwu.edu. *Application contact:* 202-994-6210, Fax: 202-994-6213, E-mail: askccas@gwu.edu.
Website: http://departments.columbian.gwu.edu/english/

Georgia College & State University, Graduate School, College of Arts and Sciences, Department of English, Program in English, Milledgeville, GA 31061. Offers MA. *Program availability:* Part-time. *Students:* 8 full-time (5 women), 5 part-time (3 women). Average age 27. 7 applicants, 100% accepted, 6 enrolled. In 2017, 4 master's awarded. *Degree requirements:* For master's, variable foreign language requirement, comprehensive exam, thesis optional. *Entrance requirements:* For master's, GRE (minimum score 156 on revised verbal section, 550 on previous version), undergraduate major in English. *Application deadline:* For fall admission, 7/1 priority date for domestic students, 4/1 priority date for international students; for spring admission, 11/1 priority date for domestic students, 9/1 priority date for international students; for summer admission, 4/1 priority date for domestic students. Applications are processed on a rolling basis. Application fee: $40. Electronic applications accepted. *Expenses:* $288 per credit hour full-time in-state, $2,592 per semester; $1,027 per credit hour full-time out-of-state, $9,243 per semester; $343 per semester fees. *Financial support:* In 2017–18, 3 students received support. Unspecified assistantships available. Support available to part-time students. Financial award applicants required to submit FAFSA. *Unit head:* Dr. Jennifer Flaherty, MA Program Coordinator, 478-445-3180, Fax: 478-445-4581, E-mail: jennifer.flaherty@gcsu.edu. *Application contact:* Kate Marshall, Graduate Admissions Coordinator, 478-445-1184, Fax: 478-445-1336, E-mail: grad-admit@gcsu.edu.
Website: http://gcsu.edu/artsandsciences/english/english-ma

Georgia Southern University, Jack N. Averitt College of Graduate Studies, College of Liberal Arts and Social Sciences, Program in English, Statesboro, GA 30460. Offers MA. *Program availability:* Part-time. *Students:* 13 full-time (9 women), 9 part-time (5 women); includes 5 minority (3 Black or African American, non-Hispanic/Latino; 2 Two or more races, non-Hispanic/Latino), 1 international. Average age 30. 8 applicants, 88% accepted, 5 enrolled. In 2017, 6 master's awarded. *Degree requirements:* For master's, one foreign language, thesis optional, terminal exams. *Entrance requirements:* For

master's, GRE General Test, minimum GPA of 3.0, letters of reference. Additional exam requirements/recommendations for international students: Required—TOEFL (minimum score 550 paper-based; 80 iBT), IELTS (minimum score 6). *Application deadline:* For fall admission, 3/1 priority date for domestic and international students; for spring admission, 10/1 priority date for domestic students, 10/1 for international students. Applications are processed on a rolling basis. Application fee: $50. Electronic applications accepted. *Expenses:* Tuition, state resident: full-time $4986; part-time $3324 per year. Tuition, nonresident: full-time $21,982; part-time $15,352 per year. *Required fees:* $2092; $1802 per credit hour. $901 per semester. Tuition and fees vary according to course load, campus/location and program. *Financial support:* In 2017–18, 17 students received support, including 4 fellowships with full tuition reimbursements available (averaging $7,750 per year); career-related internships or fieldwork, Federal Work-Study, scholarships/grants, tuition waivers (full), and unspecified assistantships also available. Support available to part-time students. Financial award application deadline: 4/15; financial award applicants required to submit FAFSA. *Faculty research:* Irish literature, Gothic literature, modern British drama, American short story, children's literature. *Unit head:* Dr. Dustin Anderson, Graduate Program Director, 912-478-1354, E-mail: danderson@georgiasouthern.edu.
Website: http://class.georgiasouthern.edu/litphi/

Georgia State University, College of Arts and Sciences, Department of English, Atlanta, GA 30302-3083. Offers creative writing (MA, MFA, PhD), including creative writing (PhD), fiction (MA, MFA), poetry (MA, MFA); English (MA, PhD); literary studies (MA, PhD); rhetoric and composition (MA, PhD). *Program availability:* Part-time. *Faculty:* 47 full-time (24 women). *Students:* 122 full-time (77 women), 63 part-time (39 women); includes 26 minority (16 Black or African American, non-Hispanic/Latino; 4 Asian, non-Hispanic/Latino; 1 Hispanic/Latino; 5 Two or more races, non-Hispanic/Latino), 12 international. Average age 36. 168 applicants, 58% accepted, 38 enrolled. In 2017, 16 master's, 18 doctorates awarded. *Entrance requirements:* For master's and doctorate, GRE. Additional exam requirements/recommendations for international students: Required—TOEFL (minimum score 550 paper-based; 80 iBT). *Application deadline:* For fall admission, 1/15 for domestic and international students. Application fee: $50. Electronic applications accepted. *Expenses:* Tuition, state resident: full-time $7020. Tuition, nonresident: full-time $22,518. *Required fees:* $2128. Tuition and fees vary according to degree level and program. *Financial support:* In 2017–18, research assistantships with full tuition reimbursements (averaging $6,000 per year), teaching assistantships with full tuition reimbursements (averaging $15,000 per year) were awarded; career-related internships or fieldwork, traineeships, and health care benefits also available. Financial award application deadline: 2/15. *Faculty research:* British and American literature and transnational literatures in English, literary theory and cultural studies, creative writing (fiction and poetry), rhetoric and composition, new media and digital humanities. *Unit head:* Dr. Lynnee Lewis Gaillet, Chair, 404-413-5842, Fax: 404-413-5830, E-mail: lgaillet@gsu.edu.
Website: http://www.english.gsu.edu

Governors State University, College of Arts and Sciences, Program in English, University Park, IL 60484. Offers MA. *Program availability:* Part-time. *Faculty:* 60 full-time (34 women), 115 part-time/adjunct (58 women). *Students:* 3 full-time (2 women), 11 part-time (7 women); includes 4 minority (3 Black or African American, non-Hispanic/Latino; 1 Hispanic/Latino). Average age 34. 7 applicants, 71% accepted, 3 enrolled. In 2017, 4 master's awarded. *Application deadline:* For fall admission, 4/1 for domestic students. Applications are processed on a rolling basis. Application fee: $50. Electronic applications accepted. *Expenses:* Tuition, state resident: full-time $8472; part-time $353 per credit hour. Tuition, nonresident: full-time $16,944; part-time $706 per credit hour. *Required fees:* $1824; $76 per credit hour. $38 per term. Tuition and fees vary according to course load, degree level and program. *Financial support:* Application deadline: 5/1; applicants required to submit FAFSA. *Unit head:* Lori Montalbano, Chair, Division of Arts and Letters, 708-534-5000 Ext. 2802, E-mail: lmontalbano@govst.edu.

The Graduate Center, City University of New York, Graduate Studies, Program in English, New York, NY 10016-4039. Offers PhD. *Faculty:* 51 full-time (13 women). *Students:* 200 full-time (112 women); includes 33 minority (6 Black or African American, non-Hispanic/Latino; 2 American Indian or Alaska Native, non-Hispanic/Latino; 2 Asian, non-Hispanic/Latino; 16 Hispanic/Latino; 7 Two or more races, non-Hispanic/Latino), 19 international. Average age 35. 309 applicants, 13% accepted, 21 enrolled. In 2017, 23 doctorates awarded. *Degree requirements:* For doctorate, 2 foreign languages, thesis/dissertation. *Entrance requirements:* For doctorate, GRE General Test, GRE Subject Test, writing sample, curriculum vitae. Additional exam requirements/recommendations for international students: Required—TOEFL. *Application deadline:* For fall admission, 1/1 for domestic students. Application fee: $125. Electronic applications accepted. *Financial support:* In 2017–18, 201 students received support, including 163 fellowships, 29 research assistantships, 27 teaching assistantships; career-related internships or fieldwork, Federal Work-Study, institutionally sponsored loans, and tuition waivers (full and partial) also available. Financial award application deadline: 2/1; financial award applicants required to submit FAFSA. *Unit head:* Prof. Eric Lott, Executive Officer, 212-817-8352, Fax: 212-817-1518, E-mail: elott@gc.cuny.edu. *Application contact:* Les Gribben, Director of Admissions, 212-817-7470, Fax: 212-817-1624, E-mail: lgribben@gc.cuny.edu.

Grambling State University, School of Graduate Studies and Research, College of Education, Department of Educational Leadership, Grambling, LA 71245. Offers developmental education (MS, Ed D, PMC), including curriculum and instructional design (Ed D), English (MS), guidance and counseling (MS), higher education administration and management (Ed D), mathematics (MS), reading (MS), science (MS), student development and personnel services (Ed D); educational leadership (M Ed). *Program availability:* Part-time, evening/weekend. *Degree requirements:* For master's, comprehensive exam, thesis (for some programs); for doctorate, comprehensive exam, thesis/dissertation. *Entrance requirements:* For master's, GRE, minimum GPA of 2.5 on last degree; for doctorate, GRE (minimum score 1000, 500 on Verbal), master's degree, minimum GPA of 3.0 on last degree. Additional exam requirements/recommendations for international students: Required—TOEFL (minimum score 500 paper-based; 62 iBT). Electronic applications accepted.

Grand Valley State University, College of Liberal Arts and Sciences, English Department, Allendale, MI 49401-9403. Offers MA. *Program availability:* Part-time, evening/weekend. *Faculty:* 20 full-time (10 women). *Students:* 4 full-time (all women), 22 part-time (18 women); includes 2 minority (1 Asian, non-Hispanic/Latino; 1 Hispanic/Latino), 3 international. Average age 33. 6 applicants, 83% accepted, 2 enrolled. In 2017, 8 master's awarded. *Degree requirements:* For master's, comprehensive exam (for some programs), thesis (for some programs), thesis or project. *Entrance requirements:* For master's, GRE General Test, brief statement of purpose, original essay (writing sample). Additional exam requirements/recommendations for international students: Required—TOEFL (minimum iBT score of 80), IELTS (6.5), or Michigan English Language Assessment Battery (77). *Application deadline:* Applications are processed on a rolling basis. Application fee: $30. Electronic applications accepted. *Expenses:* $627 per credit hour. *Financial support:* In 2017–18, 5 students received support, including 1 fellowship, 5 research assistantships with full and partial tuition reimbursements available (averaging $4,000 per year); unspecified assistantships also available. *Faculty research:* Literary history, philosophy and literature, feminist issues in literature. *Unit head:* Dr. Corinna McLeod, Chair, 616-331-8576, Fax: 616-331-3430, E-mail: mcleodc@gvsu.edu. *Application contact:* Dr. Jo Miller, Graduate Program Co-Director, 616-331-3552, Fax: 616-331-3430, E-mail: millerj@gvsu.edu.

Hardin-Simmons University, Graduate School, Cynthia Ann Parker College of Liberal Arts, Department of English, Abilene, TX 79698-0001. Offers MA. *Program availability:* Part-time. *Faculty:* 3 full-time (0 women). *Students:* 4 part-time (2 women). Average age 33. 1 applicant, 100% accepted. In 2017, 2 master's awarded. *Degree requirements:* For master's, comprehensive exam, thesis or alternative. *Entrance requirements:* For master's, minimum undergraduate GPA of 3.0 in English, 2.7 overall; writing sample; letters of recommendation; interview. Additional exam requirements/recommendations for international students: Required—TOEFL (minimum score 550 paper-based; 79 iBT). *Application deadline:* For fall admission, 8/15 priority date for domestic students, 4/1 for international students; for spring admission, 1/5 priority date for domestic students, 9/1 for international students. Applications are processed on a rolling basis. Application fee: $50 ($150 for international students). Electronic applications accepted. *Expenses: Tuition:* Full-time $13,500; part-time $750 per semester hour. *Required fees:* $220 per term. One-time fee: $50. Tuition and fees vary according to course load, campus/location and program. *Financial support:* In 2017–18, 4 students received support, including 1 fellowship (averaging $2,000 per year); scholarships/grants also available. Support available to part-time students. Financial award application deadline: 6/30; financial award applicants required to submit FAFSA. *Faculty research:* Milton, Tennyson, American Romantic period, Derek Walcott, women's literature. *Unit head:* Dr. Jason King, Program Director, 325-670-1303, Fax: 325-671-5764, E-mail: jking@hsutx.edu. *Application contact:* Dr. Nancy Kucinski, Dean of Graduate Studies, 325-670-1298, Fax: 325-670-1564, E-mail: gradoff@hsutx.edu.
Website: http://www.hsutx.edu/academics/cap/graduate/english

Harvard University, Extension School, Cambridge, MA 02138-3722. Offers applied sciences (CAS); biotechnology (ALM); educational technologies (ALM); educational technology (CET); English for graduate and professional studies (DGP); environmental management (ALM, CEM); information technology (ALM); journalism (ALM); liberal arts (ALM); management (ALM, CM); mathematics for teaching (ALM); museum studies (ALM); premedical studies (Diploma); publication and communication (CPC). *Program availability:* Part-time, evening/weekend. *Degree requirements:* For master's, thesis. *Entrance requirements:* For master's, 3 completed graduate courses with grade of B or higher. Additional exam requirements/recommendations for international students: Required—TOEFL (minimum score 600 paper-based), TWE (minimum score 5). *Expenses:* Contact institution.

Harvard University, Graduate School of Arts and Sciences, Department of English and American Literature and Language, Cambridge, MA 02138. Offers critical theory (PhD); eighteenth-century literature (PhD); literature: nineteenth-century to the present (PhD); medieval literature and language (PhD); modern British and American literature (PhD); Renaissance literature (PhD). Terminal master's awarded for partial completion of doctoral program. *Degree requirements:* For doctorate, 2 foreign languages, thesis/dissertation, oral exam. *Entrance requirements:* For doctorate, GRE General Test, GRE Subject Test, writing sample. Additional exam requirements/recommendations for international students: Required—TOEFL. *Faculty research:* Old and Middle English language and literature, drama, creative writing, transition to Romanticism, history and theory of criticism.

Heritage University, Graduate Programs in Education, Program in Professional Studies, Toppenish, WA 98948-9599. Offers bilingual education/ESL (M Ed); biology (M Ed); English and literature (M Ed); reading/literacy (M Ed); special education (M Ed). *Program availability:* Part-time, evening/weekend. *Degree requirements:* For master's, comprehensive exam (for some programs), thesis (for some programs).

Hofstra University, College of Liberal Arts and Sciences, Programs in Creative Writing and English Literature, Hempstead, NY 11549. Offers creative writing (MFA), including Spanish. *Program availability:* Part-time. *Students:* 8 full-time (4 women), 10 part-time (6 women); includes 3 minority (1 Asian, non-Hispanic/Latino; 2 Hispanic/Latino), 1 international. Average age 33. 14 applicants, 100% accepted, 4 enrolled. In 2017, 12 master's awarded. *Degree requirements:* For master's, thesis optional, minimum GPA of 3.0. *Entrance requirements:* For master's, writing sample, essay, minimum GPA of 3.0 in literature courses. Additional exam requirements/recommendations for international students: Required—TOEFL (minimum score 550 paper-based; 80 iBT). *Application deadline:* Applications are processed on a rolling basis. Application fee: $75. Electronic applications accepted. *Expenses: Tuition:* Full-time $1292. *Required fees:* $970. Tuition and fees vary according to program. *Financial support:* In 2017–18, 10 students received support, including 10 fellowships with full and partial tuition reimbursements available (averaging $4,338 per year); research assistantships with full and partial tuition reimbursements available, career-related internships or fieldwork, Federal Work-Study, institutionally sponsored loans, scholarships/grants, tuition waivers (full and partial), and unspecified assistantships also available. Support available to part-time students. Financial award applicants required to submit FAFSA. *Faculty research:* "The Penguin of Sonnets", Phillis Levin; "Lady Byron and Her Daughters", Julia Markus; "Gorgeous Lies", Martha McPhee; "This is the Place", Kelly McMasters; "Faces in the Crowd", Valeria Luiselli. *Unit head:* Dr. Craig Rustici, Chairperson, 516-463-5455, E-mail: craig.m.rustici@hofstra.edu. *Application contact:* Sunil Samuel, Assistant Vice President of Admissions, 516-463-4723, Fax: 516-463-4664, E-mail: graduateadmission@hofstra.edu.
Website: http://www.hofstra.edu/hclas

Hollins University, Graduate Programs, Program in Children's Literature, Roanoke, VA 24020. Offers children's book illustration (Certificate); children's book writing and illustrating (MFA); children's literature (MA, MFA). Program offered during summer only. *Program availability:* Part-time. *Faculty:* 2 full-time (both women), 8 part-time/adjunct (7 women). *Students:* 40 full-time (38 women), 6 part-time (5 women); includes 6 minority (1 Black or African American, non-Hispanic/Latino; 1 Asian, non-Hispanic/Latino; 3 Hispanic/Latino; 1 Two or more races, non-Hispanic/Latino). Average age 35. 24 applicants, 96% accepted, 10 enrolled. In 2017, 11 master's awarded. *Degree requirements:* For master's, one foreign language, comprehensive exam, thesis. *Entrance requirements:* For master's, transcripts, letters of recommendation, portfolio, personal statement of educational objectives. Additional exam requirements/recommendations for international students: Required—TOEFL (minimum score 550 paper-based; 79 iBT), IELTS (minimum score 6.5). *Application deadline:* For summer admission, 2/15 priority date for domestic and international students. Application fee: $40. Electronic applications accepted. *Expenses:* Contact institution. *Financial support:* Federal Work-Study and scholarships/grants available. Support available to part-time students. Financial award application deadline: 2/15; financial award applicants required to submit FAFSA. *Faculty research:* Fantasy, children's film, young adult fiction, picture books, mythology and folk tales. *Unit head:* Amanda Cockrell, Director, 540-362-6024, Fax: 540-362-6642, E-mail: acockrell@hollins.edu. *Application contact:* Cathy S. Koon, Manager of Graduate Services, 540-362-6326, Fax: 540-362-6288, E-mail: ckoon@hollins.edu.

Houston Baptist University, College of Education and Behavioral Sciences, Programs in Education, Houston, TX 77074-3298. Offers bilingual education (M Ed); counselor

education (M Ed); curriculum and instruction (M Ed); curriculum and instruction (EC-6 bilingual) (M Ed); curriculum and instruction in all-level art, Spanish, music, or physical education (M Ed); curriculum and instruction in EC-6 and special education (EC-12) (M Ed); curriculum and instruction in instructional technology (M Ed); curriculum and instruction in mathematics, science, or social studies (4-8) (M Ed); curriculum and instruction with EC-6 generalist (M Ed); curriculum and instruction with English language arts and reading (4-8) (M Ed); educational administration (M Ed); educational diagnostician (M Ed); executive educational leadership (Ed D); higher education in business management (M Ed); higher education in Christian studies (M Ed); higher education in counseling (M Ed); higher education in educational technology (M Ed); reading (M Ed); special educational leadership (Ed D). *Program availability:* Part-time, evening/weekend, 100% online, blended/hybrid learning. *Students:* 83 full-time (65 women), 187 part-time (156 women); includes 189 minority (114 Black or African American, non-Hispanic/Latino; 2 American Indian or Alaska Native, non-Hispanic/Latino; 9 Asian, non-Hispanic/Latino; 58 Hispanic/Latino; 6 Two or more races, non-Hispanic/Latino), 7 international. Average age 36. 309 applicants, 31% accepted, 70 enrolled. In 2017, 92 master's awarded. *Degree requirements:* For master's, comprehensive exam; for doctorate, thesis/dissertation. *Entrance requirements:* For master's, minimum GPA of 2.75, two recommendations, resume, bachelor's degree conferred transcript; interview (for non-certified teachers); for doctorate, GRE, 5 letters of recommendation. Additional exam requirements/recommendations for international students: Required—TOEFL (minimum score 80 iBT), IELTS (minimum score 6.5). *Application deadline:* For fall admission, 8/1 for domestic students, 6/1 for international students; for spring admission, 1/1 for domestic students, 11/1 for international students; for summer admission, 5/1 for domestic students, 3/1 for international students. Applications are processed on a rolling basis. Application fee: $0 ($100 for international students). Electronic applications accepted. Application fee is waived when completed online. *Expenses:* $22,000 tuition; $4,500 fees (general, technology and parking). *Financial support:* In 2017–18, 59 students received support. Research assistantships, teaching assistantships, Federal Work-Study, and scholarships/grants available. Support available to part-time students. Financial award application deadline: 4/1; financial award applicants required to submit FAFSA. *Faculty research:* Autism and inclusion, integrating technology into instruction, school change and leadership trust. *Unit head:* Dr. Charlotte Fontenot, Director, Graduate Programs, 281-649-3078, Fax: 281-649-3361, E-mail: cfontenot@hbu.edu. *Application contact:* Kristy Wright, Administrative Assistant for Graduate Programs, 281-649-3094, Fax: 281-649-3361, E-mail: kwright@hbu.edu.
Website: http://www.hbu.edu/MED

Howard University, Graduate School, Department of English, Washington, DC 20059-0002. Offers MA, PhD. *Program availability:* Part-time. *Degree requirements:* For master's, one foreign language, comprehensive exam, thesis; for doctorate, 2 foreign languages, comprehensive exam, thesis/dissertation, qualifying exam. *Entrance requirements:* For master's, GRE General Test, minimum GPA of 3.0; for doctorate, GRE General Test.

Humboldt State University, Academic Programs, College of Arts, Humanities, and Social Sciences, Department of English, Arcata, CA 95521-8299. Offers English (MA), including composition studies and pedagogy, literary and cultural studies, teaching English as a second language. *Degree requirements:* For master's, variable foreign language requirement, thesis or alternative, qualifying exam. *Entrance requirements:* For master's, GRE, minimum GPA of 3.0, 3 letters of recommendation, sample of writing. Additional exam requirements/recommendations for international students: Required—TOEFL (minimum score 500 paper-based). *Faculty research:* Teaching of writing, literature.

Idaho State University, Office of Graduate Studies, College of Arts and Letters, Department of English and Philosophy, Pocatello, ID 83209-8056. Offers English (MA); English and the teaching of English (PhD); TESOL (Post-Master's Certificate). *Program availability:* Part-time. *Degree requirements:* For master's, one foreign language, comprehensive exam, thesis optional; for doctorate, one foreign language, comprehensive exam, thesis/dissertation, 2 papers, 2 teaching internships; for Post-Master's Certificate, 6 credits of elective linguistics, practicum. *Entrance requirements:* For master's, GRE General Test (minimum 50th percentile verbal), general literature exam, minimum GPA of 3.0, 3 letters of recommendation, 5-page writing sample; for doctorate, GRE General Test, GRE Subject Test, minimum GPA of 3.5, writing examples, 3 letters of recommendation, master's degree in English; for Post-Master's Certificate, GRE (minimum 35th percentile on verbal section), bachelor's degree, minimum undergraduate GPA of 3.0 in last 2 years, 3 letters of recommendation, knowledge of second language. Additional exam requirements/recommendations for international students: Required—TOEFL (minimum score 550 paper-based; 80 iBT). Electronic applications accepted. *Faculty research:* American literature, Renaissance literature, composition and rhetoric, Intermountain West studies, ethics.

Illinois State University, Graduate School, College of Arts and Sciences, Department of English, Program in English, Normal, IL 61790. Offers English (MA, MS); English studies (PhD). *Degree requirements:* For doctorate, thesis/dissertation, 2 terms of residency. *Entrance requirements:* For master's, GRE General Test, minimum GPA of 3.0 in last 60 hours; for doctorate, GRE General Test.

Indiana State University, College of Graduate and Professional Studies, College of Arts and Sciences, Department of English, Terre Haute, IN 47809. Offers British and American literature (MA); English (MA); writing (MA). *Program availability:* Part-time, evening/weekend. *Degree requirements:* For master's, one foreign language, thesis optional. *Entrance requirements:* For master's, minimum GPA of 2.75 in all English courses above freshman level. Additional exam requirements/recommendations for international students: Required—TOEFL (minimum score 550 paper-based). Electronic applications accepted.

Indiana University Bloomington, University Graduate School, College of Arts and Sciences, Department of English, Bloomington, IN 47405. Offers creative writing (MA, MFA), including fiction (MFA), poetry (MFA); literature (PhD); rhetoric (PhD). *Degree requirements:* For master's, 30-36 credit hours plus one language proficiency (for MA); 60 credit hours plus thesis (for MFA); for doctorate, thesis/dissertation, qualifying exam. 90 credit hours; 2nd language proficiency or one language only if acquired at in-depth level. *Entrance requirements:* For master's, GRE General Test, GRE Subject Test (for all but MFA and MA in creative writing), minimum GPA of 3.5; for doctorate, GRE General Test, GRE Subject Test, minimum GPA of 3.7. Additional exam requirements/recommendations for international students: Required—TOEFL (minimum score 550 paper-based; 79 iBT), IELTS (minimum score 6.5). Electronic applications accepted.

Indiana University of Pennsylvania, School of Graduate Studies and Research, College of Humanities and Social Sciences, Department of English, PhD Program in Composition and Teaching English to Speakers of Other Languages, Indiana, PA 15705. Offers PhD. *Program availability:* Part-time. *Faculty:* 22 full-time (10 women). *Students:* 18 full-time (11 women), 79 part-time (48 women); includes 9 minority (2 Black or African American, non-Hispanic/Latino; 4 Asian, non-Hispanic/Latino; 2 Hispanic/Latino; 1 Two or more races, non-Hispanic/Latino), 38 international. Average age 38. 108 applicants, 57% accepted, 7 enrolled. In 2017, 22 doctorates awarded. *Degree requirements:* For doctorate, one foreign language, comprehensive exam, thesis/dissertation. *Entrance requirements:* For doctorate, 2 letters of recommendation. Additional exam requirements/recommendations for international students: Required—TOEFL (minimum score 600 paper-based). *Application deadline:* For fall admission, 2/1 priority date for domestic students; for summer admission, 11/1 priority date for domestic students. Applications are processed on a rolling basis. Application fee: $50. Electronic applications accepted. *Expenses:* Contact institution. *Financial support:* In 2017–18, 18 research assistantships with tuition reimbursements (averaging $6,398 per year), 5 teaching assistantships with partial tuition reimbursements (averaging $11,652 per year) were awarded; fellowships with full tuition reimbursements, career-related internships or fieldwork, Federal Work-Study, scholarships/grants, and unspecified assistantships also available. Support available to part-time students. Financial award application deadline: 4/15; financial award applicants required to submit FAFSA. *Unit head:* Dr. Sharon Deckert, Graduate Coordinator, 724-357-2261, E-mail: sharon.deckert@iup.edu.
Website: http://www.iup.edu/english/grad/composition-tesol-phd/default.aspx

Indiana University of Pennsylvania, School of Graduate Studies and Research, College of Humanities and Social Sciences, Department of English, Program in Composition and Literature, Indiana, PA 15705. Offers MA. *Faculty:* 22 full-time (10 women). *Students:* 11 full-time (7 women), 6 part-time (5 women); includes 1 minority (Hispanic/Latino), 3 international. Average age 28. 6 applicants, 100% accepted, 4 enrolled. In 2017, 6 master's awarded. Application fee: $50. *Expenses:* Tuition, state resident: full-time $12,000; part-time $500 per credit. Tuition, nonresident: full-time $18,000; part-time $750 per credit. *Required fees:* $4073; $165.55 per credit. $64 per term. *Financial support:* In 2017–18, 4 research assistantships with tuition reimbursements (averaging $1,000 per year) were awarded. *Unit head:* Dr. Todd Thompson, Coordinator, 724-357-2267, E-mail: todd.thompson@iup.edu.
Website: http://www.iup.edu/english/grad/composition-literature-ma/

Indiana University of Pennsylvania, School of Graduate Studies and Research, College of Humanities and Social Sciences, Department of English, Program in English: Generalist, Indiana, PA 15705. Offers MA. *Program availability:* Part-time. *Faculty:* 22 full-time (10 women). *Degree requirements:* For master's, thesis optional. *Entrance requirements:* Additional exam requirements/recommendations for international students: Required—TOEFL (minimum score 540 paper-based). *Application deadline:* Applications are processed on a rolling basis. Application fee: $50. Electronic applications accepted. *Expenses:* Tuition, state resident: full-time $12,000; part-time $500 per credit. Tuition, nonresident: full-time $18,000; part-time $750 per credit. *Required fees:* $4073; $165.55 per credit. $64 per term. *Financial support:* Research assistantships with tuition reimbursements, career-related internships or fieldwork, Federal Work-Study, scholarships/grants, and unspecified assistantships available. Financial award application deadline: 4/15; financial award applicants required to submit FAFSA. *Unit head:* Dr. Todd Thompson, Coordinator, 724-357-4931, E-mail: todd.thompson@iup.edu.
Website: http://www.iup.edu/grad/englishgeneralist/default.aspx

Indiana University of Pennsylvania, School of Graduate Studies and Research, College of Humanities and Social Sciences, Department of English, Program in English: Literature, Indiana, PA 15705. Offers MA. *Program availability:* Part-time. *Faculty:* 22 full-time (10 women). *Students:* 7 full-time (all women), 3 part-time (all women); includes 2 minority (both Two or more races, non-Hispanic/Latino), 2 international. Average age 31. 15 applicants, 60% accepted, 4 enrolled. In 2017, 11 master's awarded. *Degree requirements:* For master's, thesis optional. *Entrance requirements:* For master's, two letters of recommendation. Additional exam requirements/recommendations for international students: Required—TOEFL (minimum score 540 paper-based). *Application deadline:* Applications are processed on a rolling basis. Application fee: $50. Electronic applications accepted. *Expenses:* Tuition, state resident: full-time $12,000; part-time $500 per credit. Tuition, nonresident: full-time $18,000; part-time $750 per credit. *Required fees:* $4073; $165.55 per credit. $64 per term. *Financial support:* Fellowships, research assistantships with tuition reimbursements, teaching assistantships with tuition reimbursements, Federal Work-Study, scholarships/grants, and unspecified assistantships available. Financial award application deadline: 4/15; financial award applicants required to submit FAFSA. *Unit head:* Dr. Todd Thompson, Coordinator, 724-357-4931, E-mail: todd.thompson@iup.edu.
Website: http://www.iup.edu/grad/literature/default.aspx

Indiana University of Pennsylvania, School of Graduate Studies and Research, College of Humanities and Social Sciences, Department of English, Program in Literature and Criticism, Indiana, PA 15705. Offers PhD. *Program availability:* Part-time. *Faculty:* 22 full-time (10 women). *Students:* 24 full-time (13 women), 104 part-time (65 women); includes 17 minority (9 Black or African American, non-Hispanic/Latino; 1 Asian, non-Hispanic/Latino; 3 Hispanic/Latino; 4 Two or more races, non-Hispanic/Latino), 35 international. Average age 36. 58 applicants, 72% accepted, 4 enrolled. In 2017, 14 doctorates awarded. *Degree requirements:* For doctorate, one foreign language, comprehensive exam, thesis/dissertation. *Entrance requirements:* For doctorate, 2 letters of recommendation. Additional exam requirements/recommendations for international students: Required—TOEFL (minimum score 540 paper-based). *Application deadline:* Applications are processed on a rolling basis. Application fee: $50. Electronic applications accepted. *Expenses:* Tuition, state resident: full-time $12,000; part-time $500 per credit. Tuition, nonresident: full-time $18,000; part-time $750 per credit. *Required fees:* $4073; $165.55 per credit. $64 per term. *Financial support:* In 2017–18, 2 fellowships with full tuition reimbursements (averaging $1,021 per year), 14 research assistantships with tuition reimbursements (averaging $6,733 per year), 5 teaching assistantships with partial tuition reimbursements (averaging $11,652 per year) were awarded; career-related internships or fieldwork, Federal Work-Study, scholarships/grants, and unspecified assistantships also available. Support available to part-time students. Financial award application deadline: 4/15; financial award applicants required to submit FAFSA. *Unit head:* Dr. David Downing, Graduate Coordinator, 724-357-3963, E-mail: david.downing@iup.edu.
Website: http://www.iup.edu/english/grad/literature-criticism-phd/default.aspx

Indiana University–Purdue University Fort Wayne, College of Arts and Sciences, Department of English and Linguistics, Fort Wayne, IN 46805-1499. Offers English (MA, MAT); TENL (teaching English as a new language) (Certificate). *Program availability:* Part-time. *Degree requirements:* For master's, one foreign language, thesis (for some programs), teaching certificate (for MAT). *Entrance requirements:* For master's, GRE General Test, minimum GPA of 3.0, major or minor in English, 3 letters of recommendation; for Certificate, bachelor's degree with minimum GPA of 2.5. Additional exam requirements/recommendations for international students: Required—TOEFL (minimum score 600 paper-based; 79 iBT). *Faculty research:* Hebrew names and the vernacular Savior in Anglo-Saxon England.

Indiana University–Purdue University Indianapolis, School of Liberal Arts, Department of English, Indianapolis, IN 46202. Offers English (MA); teaching English to speakers of other languages (TESOL) (MA, Certificate); teaching literature (Certificate); teaching writing (Certificate). *Entrance requirements:* For master's, GRE. Additional exam requirements/recommendations for international students: Required—TOEFL.

Indiana University South Bend, College of Liberal Arts and Sciences, South Bend, IN 46615. Offers advanced computer programming (Graduate Certificate); applied informatics (Graduate Certificate); applied mathematics and computer science (MS);

behavior modification (Graduate Certificate); computer applications (Graduate Certificate); computer programming (Graduate Certificate); correctional management and supervision (Graduate Certificate); English (MA); health systems management (Graduate Certificate); international studies (Graduate Certificate); liberal studies (MLS); nonprofit management (Graduate Certificate); paralegal studies (Graduate Certificate); professional writing (Graduate Certificate); public affairs (MPA); public management (Graduate Certificate); social and cultural diversity (Graduate Certificate); strategic sustainability leadership (Graduate Certificate); technology for administration (Graduate Certificate). *Program availability:* Part-time, evening/weekend. *Degree requirements:* For master's, variable foreign language requirement, thesis (for some programs). *Entrance requirements:* For master's, minimum GPA of 3.0. Additional exam requirements/recommendations for international students: Required—TOEFL (minimum score 550 paper-based; 80 iBT). *Expenses:* Contact institution. *Faculty research:* Artificial intelligence, bioinformatics, English language and literature, creative writing, computer networks.

Inter American University of Puerto Rico, Metropolitan Campus, Graduate Programs, Program in English, San Juan, PR 00919-1293. Offers MA.

Iona College, School of Arts and Science, Department of English, New Rochelle, NY 10801-1890. Offers MA. *Program availability:* Part-time. *Faculty:* 7 full-time (2 women). *Students:* 6 full-time (4 women), 3 part-time (all women); includes 4 minority (1 Black or African American, non-Hispanic/Latino; 1 Asian, non-Hispanic/Latino; 2 Hispanic/Latino), 2 international. Average age 28. 6 applicants, 100% accepted, 4 enrolled. In 2017, 4 master's awarded. *Degree requirements:* For master's, one foreign language, thesis optional, foreign language competency for use in research. *Entrance requirements:* For master's, minimum GPA of 3.0. Additional exam requirements/recommendations for international students: Required—TOEFL (minimum score 550 paper-based; 80 iBT), IELTS (minimum score 6.5). *Application deadline:* For fall admission, 8/1 priority date for domestic students, 5/1 priority date for international students; for spring admission, 1/1 priority date for domestic students, 9/1 priority date for international students. Applications are processed on a rolling basis. Electronic applications accepted. Tuition and fees vary according to program. *Financial support:* In 2017–18, 1 student received support. Scholarships/grants, tuition waivers (partial), and unspecified assistantships available. Support available to part-time students. Financial award application deadline: 4/15; financial award applicants required to submit FAFSA. *Faculty research:* Victorian fiction, women's studies, nineteenth-century American literature, Irish literature, Shakespeare. *Unit head:* Dean DeFino, PhD, Chair, 914-637-2160, E-mail: ddefino@iona.edu. *Application contact:* Katelyn Brunck, Graduate Admissions, 914-633-2420, Fax: 914-633-2451, E-mail: kbrunck@iona.edu.
Website: http://www.iona.edu/Academics/School-of-Arts-Science/Departments/English/Graduate-Programs.aspx

Iowa State University of Science and Technology, Department of English, Ames, IA 50011. Offers creative writing (MFA); English (MA); rhetoric and professional communication (PhD). *Degree requirements:* For master's, thesis or alternative; for doctorate, thesis/dissertation. *Entrance requirements:* For master's, GRE General Test, sample of written work, resume, portfolio in creative writing; for doctorate, GRE General Test, sample of written work, resume. Additional exam requirements/recommendations for international students: Required—TOEFL (minimum score 600 paper-based; 100 iBT), IELTS (minimum score 7). Electronic applications accepted. *Faculty research:* Creative writing, literature, rhetoric, composition and professional communication, teaching English as a second language, applied linguistics.

Jackson State University, Graduate School, College of Liberal Arts, Department of English and Modern Foreign Languages, Jackson, MS 39217. Offers English (MA); teaching English (MAT). *Program availability:* Part-time, evening/weekend. *Degree requirements:* For master's, comprehensive exam, thesis or alternative. *Entrance requirements:* For master's, GRE General Test. Additional exam requirements/recommendations for international students: Required—TOEFL (minimum score 520 paper-based; 67 iBT). Electronic applications accepted. *Expenses:* Contact institution.

Jacksonville State University, College of Graduate Studies and Continuing Education, College of Arts and Sciences, Department of English, Jacksonville, AL 36265-1602. Offers MA. *Program availability:* Part-time, evening/weekend. *Degree requirements:* For master's, comprehensive exam, thesis (for some programs). *Entrance requirements:* For master's, GRE General Test or MAT. Additional exam requirements/recommendations for international students: Required—TOEFL (minimum score 500 paper-based; 61 iBT). Electronic applications accepted.

James Madison University, The Graduate School, College of Arts and Letters, Program in English, Harrisonburg, VA 22801. Offers MA. *Program availability:* Part-time. *Students:* 6 full-time (4 women); includes 1 minority (Two or more races, non-Hispanic/Latino). Average age 30. In 2017, 8 master's awarded. *Degree requirements:* For master's, one foreign language, thesis. Application fee: $55. Electronic applications accepted. *Expenses:* Tuition, state resident: full-time $10,512; part-time $438 per credit hour. Tuition, nonresident: full-time $28,358; part-time $1162 per credit hour. *Required fees:* $1128. *Financial support:* In 2017–18, 5 students received support, including 5 teaching assistantships with full tuition reimbursements available (averaging $9,284 per year); fellowships, Federal Work-Study, and 2 assistantships (averaging $7911) also available. Financial award application deadline: 3/1; financial award applicants required to submit FAFSA. *Unit head:* Dr. Dabney A. Bankert, Department Head, 540-568-6797, E-mail: bankerda@jmu.edu. *Application contact:* Lynette D. Michael, Director of Graduate Admissions, 540-568-6131 Ext. 6395, Fax: 540-568-7860, E-mail: michaeld@jmu.edu.
Website: http://www.jmu.edu/english

John Carroll University, Graduate Studies, Department of English, University Heights, OH 44118. Offers MA. *Program availability:* Part-time, evening/weekend. *Faculty:* 4 full-time (0 women), 1 (woman) part-time/adjunct. *Students:* 7 full-time (6 women), 7 part-time (5 women). Average age 26. In 2017, 5 master's awarded. *Degree requirements:* For master's, comprehensive exam, research essay or thesis. *Entrance requirements:* For master's, GRE General Test, GRE Subject Test, minimum GPA of 3.0, writing sample. Additional exam requirements/recommendations for international students: Required—TOEFL. *Application deadline:* For fall admission, 8/15 priority date for domestic students; for spring admission, 3/15 for domestic students. Applications are processed on a rolling basis. Application fee: $25 ($35 for international students). Electronic applications accepted. *Expenses: Tuition:* Full-time $16,238; part-time $788 per credit hour. One-time fee: $200. Part-time tuition and fees vary according to course load and program. *Financial support:* Teaching assistantships with full tuition reimbursements available. Financial award application deadline: 3/15; financial award applicants required to submit FAFSA. *Faculty research:* Post-colonial literature, African-American literature, Renaissance poetry, Anglo-Saxon literature, American literature. *Unit head:* Dr. Debra J. Rosenthal, Chair, 216-397-4746, Fax: 216-397-1723. *Application contact:* Dr. George Bilgere, Program Coordinator, 216-397-4746, E-mail: gbilgere@jcu.edu.

Johns Hopkins University, School of Education, Master's Programs in Education, Baltimore, MD 21218. Offers counseling (MS), including clinical mental health counseling, school counseling; education (MS), including educational studies, gifted education, reading, school administration and supervision, technology for educators; elementary education (MAT); health professions (M Ed); intelligence analysis (MS); organizational leadership (MS); secondary education (MAT), including biology, chemistry, earth/space science, English, physics, social studies; special education (MS), including early childhood special education, general special education studies, mild to moderate disabilities, severe disabilities. *Program availability:* Part-time, evening/weekend, 100% online, blended/hybrid learning. *Degree requirements:* For master's, comprehensive exam (for some programs), portfolio, capstone project and/or internship; PRAXIS II (subject area assessments) for initial teacher preparation programs that lead to licensure. *Entrance requirements:* For master's, GRE (for full-time programs only); PRAXIS I/core or state-approved alternative (for initial teacher preparation programs that lead to licensure), minimum of bachelor's degree from regionally- or nationally-accredited institution; minimum GPA of 3.0 in all previous programs of study; official transcripts from all post-secondary institutions attended; essay; curriculum vitae/resume; letters of recommendation (3 for full-time programs, 2 for part-time programs); dispositions survey. Additional exam requirements/recommendations for international students: Required—TOEFL (minimum score 600 paper-based; 100 iBT), IELTS (minimum score 7). Electronic applications accepted. *Expenses:* Contact institution.

Johns Hopkins University, Zanvyl Krieger School of Arts and Sciences, Department of English, Baltimore, MD 21218. Offers English and American literature (PhD). *Faculty:* 13 full-time (4 women). *Students:* 33 full-time (13 women), 6 international. Average age 29. 75 applicants, 16% accepted, 3 enrolled. In 2017, 6 doctorates awarded. *Degree requirements:* For doctorate, 2 foreign languages, comprehensive exam, thesis/dissertation, 10 seminars, 2 oral exams. *Entrance requirements:* For doctorate, GRE General and Subject Tests. Additional exam requirements/recommendations for international students: Required—TOEFL (minimum score 600 paper-based; 100 iBT), IELTS. *Application deadline:* For fall admission, 12/15 priority date for domestic and international students. Application fee: $75. Electronic applications accepted. *Financial support:* In 2017–18, 27 students received support, including 10 fellowships with full tuition reimbursements available (averaging $32,930 per year), 16 teaching assistantships with full tuition reimbursements available (averaging $32,100 per year); research assistantships, Federal Work-Study, institutionally sponsored loans, and unspecified assistantships also available. Financial award application deadline: 4/15; financial award applicants required to submit FAFSA. *Faculty research:* Nineteenth-century British, eighteenth-century, Renaissance, Modernity, and cultural studies. *Total annual research expenditures:* $1,859. *Unit head:* Dr. Mark Thompson, Chair, 410-516-6237, Fax: 410-516-4757, E-mail: mthomp59@jhu.edu. *Application contact:* Tracy Glink, Senior Academic Program Coordinator, 410-516-4311, Fax: 410-516-4757, E-mail: tglink1@jhu.edu.
Website: http://english.jhu.edu/

Kansas State University, Graduate School, College of Arts and Sciences, Department of English, Manhattan, KS 66506. Offers English (MA); technical writing and professional communication (Graduate Certificate). *Program availability:* Part-time. *Degree requirements:* For master's, one foreign language, thesis optional. *Entrance requirements:* For master's, GRE, minimum B average in English. Additional exam requirements/recommendations for international students: Required—TOEFL. Electronic applications accepted. *Faculty research:* Cultural studies, children's literature, American literature, rhetorical and composition theory, British literature.

Kent State University, College of Arts and Sciences, Department of English, Kent, OH 44242-0001. Offers creative writing (MFA); English (MA, PhD); English for teachers (MA); literature and writing (MA); rhetoric and composition (PhD); teaching English as a second language (MA). MFA program offered jointly with Cleveland State University, The University of Akron, and Youngstown State University. *Program availability:* Part-time. *Faculty:* 25 full-time (13 women), 2 part-time/adjunct (1 woman). *Students:* 101 full-time (69 women), 19 part-time (11 women); includes 10 minority (4 Black or African American, non-Hispanic/Latino; 1 Asian, non-Hispanic/Latino; 2 Hispanic/Latino; 3 Two or more races, non-Hispanic/Latino), 20 international. Average age 34. 63 applicants, 76% accepted, 18 enrolled. In 2017, 37 master's, 6 doctorates awarded. *Degree requirements:* For master's, one foreign language, thesis (for some programs), final portfolio, final exam, or thesis (for MA in teaching English as a second language); for doctorate, one foreign language, comprehensive exam, thesis/dissertation. *Entrance requirements:* For master's, GRE General Test, goal statement, 3 letters of recommendation, 8-15 page writing sample relevant to the field of study (waived for MA in English for teachers concentration), transcripts; for doctorate, GRE General Test, statement of purpose, 3 letters of recommendation, 8-15 page writing sample relevant to field of study, transcripts. Additional exam requirements/recommendations for international students: Required—TOEFL (minimum score 587 paper-based, 94 iBT), Michigan English Language Assessment Battery (minimum score 82), IELTS (minimum score 7.0) or PTE (minimum score 65). *Application deadline:* For fall admission, 1/15 for domestic and international students. Applications are processed on a rolling basis. Application fee: $45 ($70 for international students). Electronic applications accepted. *Expenses:* Tuition, state resident: full-time $11,310; part-time $515 per credit hour. Tuition, nonresident: full-time $20,396; part-time $928 per credit hour. *International tuition:* $18,544 full-time. *Financial support:* Fellowships with full tuition reimbursements, teaching assistantships with full tuition reimbursements, and unspecified assistantships available. Financial award application deadline: 1/15. *Unit head:* Dr. Robert Trogdon, Chair, 330-672-2676, E-mail: rtrogdon@kent.edu. *Application contact:* Wesley Raabe, Graduate Studies Coordinator, E-mail: wraabe@kent.edu.
Website: http://www.kent.edu/english/

Kutztown University of Pennsylvania, College of Liberal Arts and Sciences, Program in English, Kutztown, PA 19530-0730. Offers MA. *Program availability:* Part-time, evening/weekend. *Faculty:* 9 full-time (4 women). *Students:* 6 full-time (2 women), 14 part-time (9 women); includes 3 minority (2 Black or African American, non-Hispanic/Latino; 1 Two or more races, non-Hispanic/Latino), 1 international. Average age 32. 13 applicants, 77% accepted, 6 enrolled. In 2017, 4 master's awarded. *Degree requirements:* For master's, comprehensive exam, thesis optional. *Entrance requirements:* For master's, brief statement of purpose, short writing example, 3 letters of recommendation. Additional exam requirements/recommendations for international students: Required—TOEFL (minimum score 550 paper-based, 79 iBT), IELTS (minimum score 6.5), or PTE (minimum score 53). *Application deadline:* For fall admission, 8/1 for domestic and international students; for spring admission, 12/1 for domestic and international students. Application fee: $35. Electronic applications accepted. *Expenses:* Tuition, state resident: part-time $500 per credit. Tuition, nonresident: part-time $750 per credit. *Required fees:* $115 per credit. One-time fee: $50 part-time. Tuition and fees vary according to degree level. *Financial support:* Career-related internships or fieldwork, Federal Work-Study, and unspecified assistantships available. Financial award application deadline: 3/1; financial award applicants required to submit FAFSA. *Faculty research:* Women science fiction writers, Joyce Cary, myth and symbol, folklore, Victorian revision modes. *Unit head:* Dr. Andrew Vogel, Department Chair, 610-683-4353, Fax: 610-683-4355, E-mail: vogel@kutztown.edu.
Website: https://www.kutztown.edu/academics/graduate-programs/english.htm

Lakehead University, Graduate Studies, Faculty of Social Sciences and Humanities, Department of English, Thunder Bay, ON P7B 5E1, Canada. Offers English (MA); women's studies (MA). *Program availability:* Part-time, evening/weekend. *Degree requirements:* For master's, one foreign language, thesis optional. *Entrance requirements:* For master's, minimum B average. Additional exam requirements/recommendations for international students: Required—TOEFL. *Faculty research:* Rhetoric and literary studies, children's literature, nineteenth- and twentieth-century American literature, modern literature, women's studies.

Lamar University, College of Graduate Studies, College of Arts and Sciences, Department of English and Modern Languages, Beaumont, TX 77701. Offers English (MA); teaching Spanish (MA). *Program availability:* Part-time, evening/weekend. *Faculty:* 30 full-time (18 women), 4 part-time/adjunct (3 women). *Students:* 9 full-time (7 women), 21 part-time (18 women); includes 17 minority (2 Black or African American, non-Hispanic/Latino; 15 Hispanic/Latino), 1 international. Average age 40. 18 applicants, 100% accepted, 10 enrolled. In 2017, 12 master's awarded. *Degree requirements:* For master's, one foreign language, thesis optional, practicum. *Entrance requirements:* For master's, GRE General Test, minimum GPA of 2.5 in last 60 hours of undergraduate course work. Additional exam requirements/recommendations for international students: Required—TOEFL (minimum score 550 paper-based; 79 iBT), IELTS (minimum score 6.5). *Application deadline:* For fall admission, 8/10 for domestic students, 7/1 for international students; for spring admission, 1/5 for domestic students, 12/1 for international students. Applications are processed on a rolling basis. Application fee: $25 ($50 for international students). Electronic applications accepted. *Expenses:* Contact institution. *Financial support:* In 2017–18, 4 teaching assistantships (averaging $8,000 per year) were awarded; career-related internships or fieldwork, Federal Work-Study, and institutionally sponsored loans also available. Support available to part-time students. Financial award application deadline: 4/1; financial award applicants required to submit FAFSA. *Faculty research:* British, Renaissance, nineteenth-century, and American literature; creative writing; modern literature; African-American literature. *Unit head:* Dr. Jim Sanderson, Chair, 409-880-8558, Fax: 409-880-8591. *Application contact:* Deidre Mayer, Interim Director, Admissions and Academic Services, 409-880-8888, Fax: 409-880-7419, E-mail: gradmissions@lamar.edu.
Website: http://artssciences.lamar.edu/english-and-modern-languages

La Salle University, School of Arts and Sciences, Program in Education, Philadelphia, PA 19141-1199. Offers autism spectrum disorders (MA, Certificate); bilingual/bicultural studies (MA); classroom management (MA); dual early childhood and special education (MA); dual middle-level science and math and special education (MA); education (MA); English (MA); English as a second language (Certificate); history (MA); instructional coach (Certificate); instructional leadership (MA); reading specialist (MA, Certificate); secondary education (MA); special education (MA, Certificate). *Program availability:* Part-time, evening/weekend. *Faculty:* 5 full-time (4 women), 8 part-time/adjunct (5 women). *Students:* 2 full-time (1 woman), 110 part-time (81 women); includes 23 minority (11 Black or African American, non-Hispanic/Latino; 1 Asian, non-Hispanic/Latino; 7 Hispanic/Latino; 4 Two or more races, non-Hispanic/Latino). Average age 33. 137 applicants, 70% accepted, 63 enrolled. In 2017, 148 master's awarded. *Degree requirements:* For master's, comprehensive exam. *Entrance requirements:* For master's, MAT or GRE, 2 letters of recommendation; for Certificate, GMAT or GRE, 2 letters of recommendation. Additional exam requirements/recommendations for international students: Required—TOEFL. *Application deadline:* For fall admission, 8/15 priority date for domestic students, 7/15 for international students; for spring admission, 12/15 priority date for domestic students, 11/15 for international students; for summer admission, 4/15 priority date for domestic students, 3/15 for international students. Applications are processed on a rolling basis. Application fee: $35. Electronic applications accepted. Application fee is waived when completed online. *Expenses:* Contact institution. *Financial support:* In 2017–18, 19 students received support. Scholarships/grants available. Support available to part-time students. Financial award application deadline: 8/31; financial award applicants required to submit FAFSA. *Unit head:* Dr. Greer Richardson, Director, 215-951-1806, Fax: 215-951-1843, E-mail: graded@lasalle.edu. *Application contact:* Elizabeth Heenan, Director, Graduate and Adult Enrollment, 215-951-1100, Fax: 215-951-1462, E-mail: heenan@lasalle.edu.
Website: http://www.lasalle.edu/grad-education-programs/

La Sierra University, College of Arts and Sciences, Department of English and Communication, Riverside, CA 92505. Offers communication (MA), including public relations/advertising, theory emphasis; English (MA), including literary emphasis, writing emphasis. *Program availability:* Part-time. *Degree requirements:* For master's, one foreign language. *Entrance requirements:* For master's, GRE General Test.

Lee University, Program in Education, Cleveland, TN 37320-3450. Offers art (MAT); curriculum and instruction (M Ed, Ed S); early childhood (MAT); educational leadership (M Ed, Ed S); elementary education (MAT); English and math (MAT); English and science (MAT); English and social studies (MAT); higher education administration (MS); history (MAT); history and economics (MAT); math and science (MAT); math and social studies (MAT); middle grades (MAT); science and social studies (MASW); secondary education (MAT); Spanish (MAT); special education (M Ed, MAT); TESOL (MAT). *Accreditation:* NCATE. *Program availability:* Part-time. *Faculty:* 15 full-time (7 women), 8 part-time/adjunct (3 women). *Students:* 28 full-time (21 women), 77 part-time (48 women); includes 12 minority (7 Black or African American, non-Hispanic/Latino; 2 Hispanic/Latino; 3 Two or more races, non-Hispanic/Latino), 1 international. Average age 31. 35 applicants, 83% accepted, 22 enrolled. In 2017, 54 master's, 4 other advanced degrees awarded. *Degree requirements:* For master's, variable foreign language requirement, thesis optional, internship. *Entrance requirements:* For master's, MAT or GRE General Test, minimum undergraduate GPA of 2.75, 3 letters of recommendation, interview, writing sample, official transcripts, background check; for Ed S, minimum undergraduate and master's GPA of 2.75, official transcripts for undergraduate and master's degrees. Additional exam requirements/recommendations for international students: Required—TOEFL (minimum score 61 iBT). *Application deadline:* For fall admission, 6/1 priority date for domestic and international students; for spring admission, 11/1 priority date for domestic and international students; for summer admission, 4/1 priority date for domestic and international students. Applications are processed on a rolling basis. Application fee: $25. Electronic applications accepted. *Expenses: Tuition:* Full-time $12,780; part-time $710 per credit hour. *Required fees:* $60; $60 per term. Tuition and fees vary according to program. *Financial support:* In 2017–18, 32 students received support. Career-related internships or fieldwork, Federal Work-Study, institutionally sponsored loans, scholarships/grants, and unspecified assistantships available. Financial award application deadline: 3/1; financial award applicants required to submit FAFSA. *Unit head:* Dr. William Kamm, Director, 423-614-8544, E-mail: wkamm@leeuniversity.edu. *Application contact:* Crystal Keeter, Graduate Education Secretary, 423-614-8544, E-mail: ckeeter@leeuniversity.edu.
Website: http://www.leeuniversity.edu/academics/graduate/education

Lehigh University, College of Arts and Sciences, Department of English, Bethlehem, PA 18015. Offers MA, PhD. *Program availability:* Part-time. *Faculty:* 21 full-time (10 women). *Students:* 30 full-time (20 women), 2 part-time (both women); includes 2 minority (1 Black or African American, non-Hispanic/Latino; 1 Hispanic/Latino), 2 international. Average age 30. 40 applicants, 50% accepted, 8 enrolled. In 2017, 7 master's, 4 doctorates awarded. Terminal master's awarded for partial completion of doctoral program. *Degree requirements:* For master's, thesis optional; for doctorate, one foreign language, comprehensive exam, thesis/dissertation. *Entrance requirements:* For master's, GRE General Test, minimum GPA of 3.0 in undergraduate English courses; for doctorate, GRE General Test, minimum GPA of 3.5 in MA coursework. Additional exam requirements/recommendations for international students: Required—TOEFL (minimum score 620 paper-based; 96 iBT). *Application deadline:* For fall admission, 1/1 priority date for domestic and international students. Application fee: $75. Electronic applications accepted. *Expenses:* $1,460 per credit. *Financial support:* In 2017–18, 34 students received support, including 4 fellowships with full tuition reimbursements available (averaging $26,040 per year), 25 teaching assistantships with full tuition reimbursements available (averaging $21,843 per year); scholarships/grants and tuition waivers (full and partial) also available. Support available to part-time students. Financial award application deadline: 1/1. *Faculty research:* Literature and social justice, English literature, American literature, literature and medicine, postcolonial literature. *Total annual research expenditures:* $11,376. *Unit head:* Dr. Dawn Keetley, Chairperson, 610-758-3311, Fax: 610-758-6616, E-mail: dek7@lehigh.edu. *Application contact:* Dr. Jenna Lay, Director of Graduate Studies, 610-758-3308, Fax: 610-758-6616, E-mail: jdl210@lehigh.edu.
Website: http://cas.lehigh.edu/casweb/English

Lehman College of the City University of New York, School of Arts and Humanities, Department of English, Bronx, NY 10468-1589. Offers MA. *Degree requirements:* For master's, thesis. *Entrance requirements:* For master's, GRE, 18 upper-level credits in U. S. or English literature.

Liberty University, College of Arts and Sciences, Lynchburg, VA 24515. Offers English (MA); history (MA); professional writing (MA). *Accreditation:* AACN. *Program availability:* Part-time, online learning. *Students:* 176 full-time (110 women), 302 part-time (170 women); includes 101 minority (67 Black or African American, non-Hispanic/Latino; 5 American Indian or Alaska Native, non-Hispanic/Latino; 1 Asian, non-Hispanic/Latino; 14 Hispanic/Latino; 14 Two or more races, non-Hispanic/Latino), 10 international. Average age 38. 476 applicants, 57% accepted, 150 enrolled. In 2017, 82 master's awarded. *Degree requirements:* For master's, comprehensive exam (for some programs), thesis (for some programs). *Entrance requirements:* For master's, GRE, minimum undergraduate GPA of 3.0, letters of recommendation, statement of purpose. Additional exam requirements/recommendations for international students: Required—TOEFL (minimum score 600 paper-based; 100 iBT). *Application deadline:* For fall admission, 6/1 for domestic students; for spring admission, 11/1 for domestic students. Applications are processed on a rolling basis. Application fee: $50. Electronic applications accepted. *Financial support:* Teaching assistantships with tuition reimbursements and Federal Work-Study available. *Faculty research:* God concept and adult attachment, building marital strength, image of God and gender, breastfeeding behavior among adolescent mothers, osteoporosis. *Unit head:* Dr. Roger Schultz, Dean, 434-592-4031, Fax: 434-522-0430, E-mail: rschultz@liberty.edu. *Application contact:* Dr. Terry Elam, Director of Graduate Admissions, 434-592-3966, Fax: 434-522-0430, E-mail: gradadmissions@liberty.edu.

Lipscomb University, College of Education, Nashville, TN 37204-3951. Offers applied behavior analysis (MS, Certificate); coaching for learning (M Ed, Certificate, Ed S); educational leadership (M Ed, Ed S); English language learning (M Ed, Ed S); instructional coaching (M Ed, Certificate, Ed S); instructional practice (M Ed); learning organizations and strategic change (Ed D); literacy coaching (Certificate, Ed S); reading specialty (M Ed, Ed S); school counseling (M Ed, Ed S); special education (M Ed); teaching, learning, and leading (M Ed); technology integration (M Ed, Ed S); technology integration specialist (Certificate). *Accreditation:* NCATE. *Program availability:* Part-time, evening/weekend, 100% online. *Faculty:* 21 full-time (14 women), 42 part-time/adjunct (29 women). *Students:* 565 full-time (452 women), 59 part-time (45 women); includes 154 minority (102 Black or African American, non-Hispanic/Latino; 2 American Indian or Alaska Native, non-Hispanic/Latino; 8 Asian, non-Hispanic/Latino; 26 Hispanic/Latino; 16 Two or more races, non-Hispanic/Latino). Average age 32. 395 applicants, 54% accepted, 196 enrolled. In 2017, 162 master's, 30 doctorates, 54 other advanced degrees awarded. *Degree requirements:* For master's, comprehensive exam, portfolio, research project and presentation; for doctorate, practical capstone project in experiential setting. *Entrance requirements:* For master's, MAT (minimum score 31) or GRE General Test (minimum score 294), 2 reference letters, goals statement, writing sample, interview; for doctorate, MAT or GRE General Test, 3 reference letters, artifact of demonstrated academic excellence, written personal statements, interview. Additional exam requirements/recommendations for international students: Required—TOEFL (minimum score 570 paper-based; 80 iBT). *Application deadline:* For fall admission, 8/29 priority date for domestic students; for spring admission, 1/15 priority date for domestic students. Applications are processed on a rolling basis. Application fee: $50 ($75 for international students). Electronic applications accepted. *Expenses:* Contact institution. *Financial support:* Scholarships/grants, unspecified assistantships, and partnerships with local school districts available. Financial award applicants required to submit FAFSA. *Faculty research:* Facilitative learning styles, leadership, student assessment, interactive multimedia inclusion, learning organizations and strategic change. *Unit head:* Dr. Deborah Boyd, Director of Graduate Studies, 615-966-6263, E-mail: deborah.boyd@lipscomb.edu. *Application contact:* Amanda Logsdon, Director of Enrollment and Outreach, 615-966-7199, E-mail: amanda.logsdon@lipscomb.edu.
Website: http://www.lipscomb.edu/education/graduate-programs

Long Island University–LIU Brooklyn, Richard L. Conolly College of Liberal Arts and Sciences, Brooklyn, NY 11201-8423. Offers biology (MS); chemistry (MS); clinical psychology (PhD); creative writing (MFA); English (MA); media arts (MA, MFA); political science (MA); psychology (MA); social science (MS); United Nations (Advanced Certificate); urban studies (MA); writing and production for television (MFA). *Program availability:* Part-time. *Faculty:* 32 full-time (13 women), 17 part-time/adjunct (6 women). *Students:* 178 full-time (123 women), 143 part-time (96 women); includes 128 minority (65 Black or African American, non-Hispanic/Latino; 22 Asian, non-Hispanic/Latino; 31 Hispanic/Latino; 10 Two or more races, non-Hispanic/Latino), 54 international. Average age 30. 629 applicants, 38% accepted, 74 enrolled. In 2017, 147 master's, 9 doctorates, 8 other advanced degrees awarded. Terminal master's awarded for partial completion of doctoral program. *Degree requirements:* For master's, comprehensive exam (for some programs), thesis (for some programs); for doctorate, thesis/dissertation. *Entrance requirements:* For doctorate, GRE. Additional exam requirements/recommendations for international students: Required—TOEFL (minimum score 550 paper-based, 79 iBT) or IELTS. *Application deadline:* Applications are processed on a rolling basis. Application fee: $50. Electronic applications accepted. *Expenses: Tuition:* Full-time $21,618; part-time $1201 per credit. *Required fees:* $1840; $920 per term. Tuition and fees vary according to course load. *Financial support:* In 2017–18, 214 students received support, including 120 fellowships with full and partial tuition reimbursements available (averaging $915 per year), 5 research assistantships with full and partial tuition reimbursements available (averaging $2,300 per year), 136 teaching assistantships with full and partial tuition reimbursements available (averaging $2,300 per year); career-related internships or fieldwork, Federal Work-Study, institutionally sponsored loans, scholarships/grants, and unspecified assistantships also available. Support available to part-time students. Financial award application deadline: 2/15; financial award

applicants required to submit FAFSA. *Faculty research:* Quantum gravity and astrophysics; string theory; pharmaceutical biotechnology with a focus on molecular details of drug susceptibility/resistance mechanisms; entomology, population and community ecology, agroecology, and biodiversity; psychotherapy process-outcome, particularly therapeutic alliance development, the role of common factors, and the study of treatment failures; personality pathology, borderline personality disorder and pathological narcissism. *Unit head:* Dr. Scott Krawczyk, Dean, 718-488-1003, E-mail: scott.krawczyk@liu.edu. *Application contact:* Bayu Sutrisno, Graduate Admissions Counselor, 718-488-1564, Fax: 718-780-6110, E-mail: bayu.sutrisno@liu.edu.

Long Island University–LIU Post, College of Liberal Arts and Sciences, Brookville, NY 11548-1300. Offers applied mathematics (MS); behavior analysis (MA); biology (MS); criminal justice (MS); earth science (MS); English (MA); environmental sustainability (MS); genetic counseling (MS); history (MA); interdisciplinary studies (MA, MS); political science (MA); psychology (MA). *Program availability:* Part-time, evening/weekend, blended/hybrid learning. *Faculty:* 41 full-time (21 women), 24 part-time/adjunct (13 women). *Students:* 173 full-time (124 women), 62 part-time (35 women); includes 54 minority (11 Black or African American, non-Hispanic/Latino; 13 Asian, non-Hispanic/Latino; 23 Hispanic/Latino; 7 Two or more races, non-Hispanic/Latino), 12 international. Average age 28. 368 applicants, 54% accepted, 74 enrolled. In 2017, 89 master's, 15 other advanced degrees awarded. Terminal master's awarded for partial completion of doctoral program. *Degree requirements:* For master's, comprehensive exam (for some programs), thesis (for some programs). *Entrance requirements:* Additional exam requirements/recommendations for international students: Required—TOEFL, IELTS, or PTE. *Application deadline:* Applications are processed on a rolling basis. Application fee: $50. Electronic applications accepted. *Expenses: Tuition:* Full-time $21,618; part-time $1201 per credit. *Required fees:* $1840; $920 per term. Tuition and fees vary according to course load. *Financial support:* In 2017–18, 165 students received support. Fellowships, research assistantships, teaching assistantships, career-related internships or fieldwork, Federal Work-Study, scholarships/grants, tuition waivers (partial), and unspecified assistantships available. Support available to part-time students. Financial award application deadline: 2/15; financial award applicants required to submit FAFSA. *Faculty research:* Biology, environmental sustainability, mathematics, psychology, genetic counseling. *Unit head:* Dr. Nathaniel Bowditch, Dean, 516-299-2234, Fax: 516-299-4140, E-mail: nathaniel.bowditch@liu.edu. *Application contact:* Rita Langdon, Graduate Admissions, 516-299-2900, Fax: 516-299-2137, E-mail: post-enroll@liu.edu.
Website: http://liu.edu/CWPost/Academics/Schools/CLAS

Louisiana State University and Agricultural & Mechanical College, Graduate School, College of Humanities and Social Sciences, Department of English, Baton Rouge, LA 70803. Offers creative writing (MFA); English (MA, PhD). *Faculty:* 43 full-time (23 women). *Students:* 77 full-time (48 women), 12 part-time (8 women); includes 16 minority (8 Black or African American, non-Hispanic/Latino; 2 Asian, non-Hispanic/Latino; 5 Hispanic/Latino; 1 Two or more races, non-Hispanic/Latino), 10 international. Average age 30. 191 applicants, 13% accepted, 2 enrolled. In 2017, 11 master's, 9 doctorates awarded. *Financial support:* In 2017–18, 3 fellowships (averaging $28,784 per year), 1 research assistantship (averaging $25,000 per year), 65 teaching assistantships (averaging $23,755 per year) were awarded. *Total annual research expenditures:* $80,469.

Louisiana Tech University, Graduate School, College of Education, Ruston, LA 71272. Offers counseling and guidance (MA), including clinical mental health counseling, human services, orientation and mobility; counseling psychology (PhD); curriculum and instruction (M Ed); cyber education (Graduate Certificate); dynamics of domestic and family violence (Graduate Certificate); early childhood education - PreK-3 (MAT); educational leadership (M Ed, Ed D); elementary education and special education mild/moderate grades 1-5 (MAT); higher education administration (Graduate Certificate); industrial/organizational psychology (MA, PhD); kinesiology (MS); middle school education (MAT), including mathematics; orientation and mobility (Graduate Certificate); rehabilitation teaching for the blind (Graduate Certificate); secondary education (MAT), including agriculture, biology, business, chemistry, English; special education: visually impaired (MAT); teacher leader education (Graduate Certificate); visual impairments - blind education (Graduate Certificate). *Accreditation:* NCATE. *Program availability:* Part-time. *Faculty:* 28 full-time (16 women), 23 part-time/adjunct (22 women). *Students:* 269 full-time (192 women), 194 part-time (150 women); includes 127 minority (94 Black or African American, non-Hispanic/Latino; 2 American Indian or Alaska Native, non-Hispanic/Latino; 6 Asian, non-Hispanic/Latino; 16 Hispanic/Latino; 1 Native Hawaiian or other Pacific Islander, non-Hispanic/Latino; 8 Two or more races, non-Hispanic/Latino), 8 international. Average age 34. 226 applicants, 74% accepted, 60 enrolled. In 2017, 5 master's, 2 doctorates, 1 other advanced degree awarded. *Degree requirements:* For master's, thesis; for doctorate, thesis/dissertation. *Entrance requirements:* For master's and doctorate, GRE General Test. Additional exam requirements/recommendations for international students: Required—TOEFL (minimum score 550 paper-based; 80 iBT), IELTS (minimum score 6.5). *Application deadline:* For fall admission, 9/1 priority date for domestic students, 6/1 for international students; for winter admission, 11/1 priority date for domestic students, 9/1 for international students; for spring admission, 2/1 priority date for domestic students, 12/1 for international students; for summer admission, 5/1 priority date for domestic students, 3/1 for international students. Application fee: $40. Electronic applications accepted. *Expenses:* Tuition, state resident: full-time $5146. Tuition, nonresident: full-time $10,147. International tuition: $10,267 full-time. *Required fees:* $2273. *Financial support:* In 2017–18, 40 students received support, including 23 research assistantships (averaging $10,346 per year), 15 teaching assistantships (averaging $6,887 per year); fellowships and career-related internships or fieldwork also available. Financial award application deadline: 2/1. *Faculty research:* Blindness and the best methods for increasing independence for individuals who are blind or visually impaired; educating and investigating factors contributing to improvements in human performance across the lifespan and a reduction in injury rates during training. *Total annual research expenditures:* $2.1 million. *Unit head:* Dr. Don Schillinger, Dean, 318-257-3712, E-mail: dschill@latech.edu. *Application contact:* Dr. Dawn Basinger, Associate Dean of Academic Affairs, 318-257-2977, Fax: 318-257-2379, E-mail: dbasing@latech.edu.
Website: http://education.latech.edu/

Louisiana Tech University, Graduate School, College of Liberal Arts, Ruston, LA 71272. Offers architecture (M Arch); art (MFA), including graphic design, photography, studio; audiology (Au D); communication (MA), including speech communication, theatre; English (MA), including literature, technical writing; history (MA); speech pathology (MA); technical writing and communication (Graduate Certificate). *Program availability:* Part-time. *Faculty:* 63 full-time (25 women), 5 part-time/adjunct (3 women). *Students:* 114 full-time (29 women), 31 part-time (19 women); includes 12 minority (4 Black or African American, non-Hispanic/Latino; 1 Asian, non-Hispanic/Latino; 3 Hispanic/Latino; 4 Two or more races, non-Hispanic/Latino), 5 international. Average age 30. 146 applicants, 59% accepted, 37 enrolled. In 2017, 49 master's, 3 doctorates awarded. *Degree requirements:* For master's, thesis (for some programs); for doctorate, thesis/dissertation. *Entrance requirements:* For master's, GRE General Test; for doctorate, GRE General Test, bachelor's degree, minimum GPA of 3.0 or 3.2 on last 60 hours attempted. Additional exam requirements/recommendations for international

students: Required—TOEFL (minimum score 550 paper-based; 80 iBT), IELTS (minimum score 6.5). *Application deadline:* For fall admission, 8/1 priority date for domestic students, 6/1 for international students; for winter admission, 11/1 priority date for domestic students, 9/1 for international students; for spring admission, 2/1 priority date for domestic students, 12/1 for international students; for summer admission, 5/1 priority date for domestic students, 3/1 for international students. Application fee: $40 ($50 for international students). Electronic applications accepted. *Expenses:* Tuition, state resident: full-time $5146. Tuition, nonresident: full-time $10,147. *International tuition:* $10,267 full-time. *Required fees:* $2273. *Financial support:* In 2017–18, 63 students received support, including 46 research assistantships (averaging $5,229 per year), 7 teaching assistantships (averaging $5,543 per year); fellowships, career-related internships or fieldwork, Federal Work-Study, institutionally sponsored loans, tuition waivers (partial), and unspecified assistantships also available. Financial award application deadline: 2/1. *Faculty research:* Contributing to the expansion of historical and social scientific knowledge and understanding through original research and publication; diverse language, ethnic, cultural, and socioeconomic backgrounds with disorders of speech, language, swallowing, hearing, and cognitive aspects of communication; prevention of communication, swallowing, and hearing disorders. *Unit head:* Dr. Donald P. Kaczvinsky, Dean, 318-257-4805, Fax: 318-257-3935, E-mail: dkaczv@latech.edu. *Application contact:* Mary Green, Administrative Assistant, 318-257-2924, Fax: 318-257-4487, E-mail: meg@latech.edu.
Website: http://liberalarts.latech.edu/

Loyola Marymount University, Bellarmine College of Liberal Arts, Program in English, Los Angeles, CA 90045-2659. Offers MA. *Unit head:* Dr. Gail Wronsky, Director, English Program, 310-338-7668, Fax: 310-338-7727, E-mail: gwronsky@lmu.edu. *Application contact:* Chake H. Kouyoumjian, Associate Dean of Graduate Studies, 310-338-2721, Fax: 310-338-6086, E-mail: graduateinfo@lmu.edu.
Website: http://bellarmine.lmu.edu/english/graduateprogram

Loyola University Chicago, Graduate School, Department of English, Chicago, IL 60660. Offers 19th century studies (PhD); English (MA); Medieval and Renaissance literature (PhD); modern literature and culture (PhD); textual studies and digital humanities (PhD). *Program availability:* Part-time, evening/weekend. *Faculty:* 24 full-time (11 women). *Students:* 36 full-time (23 women), 3 part-time (all women); includes 4 minority (1 Black or African American, non-Hispanic/Latino; 2 Hispanic/Latino; 1 Two or more races, non-Hispanic/Latino). Average age 29. 65 applicants, 37% accepted, 7 enrolled. In 2017, 5 master's, 2 doctorates awarded. Terminal master's awarded for partial completion of doctoral program. *Degree requirements:* For master's, comprehensive exam, thesis or alternative; for doctorate, one foreign language, comprehensive exam, thesis/dissertation. *Entrance requirements:* For master's and doctorate, GRE General Test. Additional exam requirements/recommendations for international students: Required—TOEFL, IELTS. *Application deadline:* For fall admission, 6/1 for domestic students. Applications are processed on a rolling basis. Application fee: $0. Electronic applications accepted. *Expenses:* $1,004 per credit hour tuition. *Financial support:* In 2017–18, 26 students received support, including 5 fellowships with full tuition reimbursements available (averaging $18,000 per year), research assistantships with full tuition reimbursements available (averaging $10,000 per year), 21 teaching assistantships with full tuition reimbursements available (averaging $18,000 per year); Federal Work-Study, institutionally sponsored loans, tuition waivers (partial), and unspecified assistantships also available. Support available to part-time students. Financial award application deadline: 1/15; financial award applicants required to submit FAFSA. *Faculty research:* Medieval and renaissance studies, 19th century studies, American and British modernism and postmodernism, African American and Anglophone literatures, textual studies and digital humanities. *Unit head:* Dr. James Knapp, Graduate Program Director, 773-508-2241, Fax: 773-508-8696, E-mail: jknapp3@luc.edu.
Website: http://www.luc.edu/english/

Manhattan College, Graduate Programs, School of Education and Health, Program in Special Education, Riverdale, NY 10471. Offers adolescence education students with disabilities generalist extension in English or math or social studies - grades 7-12 (MS Ed); bilingual education (Advanced Certificate); dual childhood/students with disabilities - grades 1-6 (MS Ed); students with disabilities - grades 1-6 (MS Ed). *Program availability:* Part-time, evening/weekend. *Degree requirements:* For master's, thesis, internship (if not certified). *Entrance requirements:* For master's, GRE, minimum GPA of 3.0. Additional exam requirements/recommendations for international students: Required—TOEFL (minimum score 550 paper-based; 80 iBT), IELTS (minimum score 6). Electronic applications accepted. Application fee is waived when completed online. *Expenses:* Contact institution.

Manhattanville College, School of Education, Jump Start Program, Purchase, NY 10577-2132. Offers childhood education and special education (grades 1-6) (MPS); early childhood education (birth-grade 2) (MAT); education (Advanced Certificate); English and special education (grades 5-12) (MPS); mathematics and special education (grades 5-12) (MPS); science and special education (grades 5-12) (MPS); social studies and special education (grades 5-12) (MPS); Spanish (grades 7-12) (MAT); TESOL (all grades) (MPS). *Program availability:* Part-time, evening/weekend. *Faculty:* 10 full-time (7 women), 39 part-time/adjunct (27 women). *Students:* 3 full-time (2 women), 40 part-time (24 women); includes 11 minority (3 Black or African American, non-Hispanic/Latino; 6 Hispanic/Latino; 1 Native Hawaiian or other Pacific Islander, non-Hispanic/Latino; 1 Two or more races, non-Hispanic/Latino). Average age 33. 25 applicants, 60% accepted, 7 enrolled. In 2017, 17 master's, 2 other advanced degrees awarded. *Degree requirements:* For master's, comprehensive exam (for some programs), thesis (for some programs), student teaching, research seminars, portfolios, internships, writing assessment; for Advanced Certificate, comprehensive exam (for some programs). *Entrance requirements:* For master's, GRE or MAT (for programs leading to certification), minimum GPA of 3.0, 2 letters of recommendation, interview, essay (2-3 page personal statement that describes reasons for choosing teaching or educational leadership as profession and philosophy of education), proof of immunization (for those born after 1957). Additional exam requirements/recommendations for international students: Required—TOEFL (minimum score 600 paper-based; 110 iBT); Recommended—IELTS (minimum score 8). *Application deadline:* Applications are processed on a rolling basis. Application fee: $75. Electronic applications accepted. *Expenses:* $915 per credit. *Financial support:* Teaching assistantships, career-related internships or fieldwork, Federal Work-Study, institutionally sponsored loans, scholarships/grants, and unspecified assistantships available. Financial award application deadline: 3/15; financial award applicants required to submit FAFSA. *Faculty research:* Early childhood and technology, professional development schools and community schools, students with emotional difficulties, literacy and adolescents, mindfulness, changing suburbs institute, and community schools, studying the effects of the environment on special populations, the most difficult cases, students who are presented with multiple challenges: learning, behavioral and ACE experiences who see criminal behavior as a way to cope; working on giving them the tools they need to succeed. *Unit head:* Dr. Shelly Wepner, Dean, 914-323-3153, E-mail: shelly.wepner@mville.edu. *Application contact:* Alissa Wilson, Director, Graduate Admissions, 914-323-3150, Fax: 914-694-1732, E-mail: edschool@mville.edu.
Website: http://www.mville.edu/programs/jump-start

Manhattanville College, School of Education, Program in Middle Childhood/ Adolescence Education (Grades 5-12), Purchase, NY 10577-2132. Offers biology (MAT, Advanced Certificate); biology and special education (MPS); chemistry (MAT, Advanced Certificate); chemistry and special education (MPS); earth science (Advanced Certificate); education for sustainability (Advanced Certificate); English (MAT, Advanced Certificate); English and special education (MPS); literacy and special education (MPS); literacy specialist (MPS); math and special education (MPS); mathematics (MAT, Advanced Certificate); physics (MAT, Advanced Certificate); social studies (MAT); social studies and special education (MPS); special education generalist (MPS). *Program availability:* Part-time, evening/weekend. *Faculty:* 2 full-time (both women), 5 part-time/ adjunct (1 woman). *Students:* 8 full-time (7 women), 28 part-time (16 women); includes 4 minority (1 Asian, non-Hispanic/Latino; 2 Hispanic/Latino; 1 Two or more races, non-Hispanic/Latino). Average age 31. 7 applicants, 86% accepted, 4 enrolled. In 2017, 13 master's, 1 other advanced degree awarded. *Degree requirements:* For master's, comprehensive exam (for some programs), thesis (for some programs), student teaching, research seminars, portfolios, internships, writing assessment; for Advanced Certificate, comprehensive exam (for some programs). *Entrance requirements:* For master's, GRE or MAT (for programs leading to certification), minimum GPA of 3.0, 2 letters of recommendation, interview, essay (2-3 page personal statement that describes reasons for choosing teaching or educational leadership as profession and philosophy of education), proof of immunization (for those born after 1957). Additional exam requirements/recommendations for international students: Required—TOEFL (minimum score 600 paper-based; 110 iBT); Recommended—IELTS (minimum score 8). *Application deadline:* Applications are processed on a rolling basis. Application fee: $75. Electronic applications accepted. *Expenses:* $915 per credit. *Financial support:* Teaching assistantships, career-related internships or fieldwork, Federal Work-Study, institutionally sponsored loans, scholarships/grants, and unspecified assistantships available. Financial award application deadline: 3/15; financial award applicants required to submit FAFSA. *Faculty research:* Education for sustainability. *Unit head:* Dr. Shelly Wepner, Dean, 914-323-3153, Fax: 914-323-5493, E-mail: shelly.wepner@mville.edu. *Application contact:* Alissa Wilson, Director, Graduate Admissions, 914-323-3150, Fax: 914-694-1732, E-mail: edschool@mville.edu.
Website: http://www.mville.edu/programs#/search/19

Marquette University, Graduate School, College of Arts and Sciences, Department of English, Milwaukee, WI 53201-1881. Offers American literature (PhD); British and American literature (MA); British literature (PhD). *Program availability:* Part-time. Terminal master's awarded for partial completion of doctoral program. *Degree requirements:* For master's, comprehensive exam, thesis or alternative; for doctorate, one foreign language, thesis/dissertation, qualifying exam. *Entrance requirements:* For master's and doctorate, GRE General Test, GRE Subject Test, official transcripts from all current and previous colleges/universities except Marquette, three letters of recommendation, statement of purpose, one or two writing samples. Additional exam requirements/recommendations for international students: Required—TOEFL. Electronic applications accepted. *Faculty research:* Discourse analysis, American literature, British literature, textual criticism, literary history.

Marshall University, Academic Affairs Division, College of Liberal Arts, Department of English, Huntington, WV 25755. Offers MA, Graduate Certificate. *Students:* 27 full-time (21 women), 4 part-time (3 women); includes 4 minority (2 Asian, non-Hispanic/Latino; 2 Two or more races, non-Hispanic/Latino). Average age 28. In 2017, 16 master's awarded. *Degree requirements:* For master's, one foreign language, thesis optional. *Entrance requirements:* For master's, GRE General Test. Application fee: $40. *Unit head:* Dr. Jane Hill, Chair, 304-696-6638, E-mail: hillj@marshall.edu. *Application contact:* Dr. Kristen Lillvis, Information Contact, 304-696-6269, E-mail: lillvis@marshall.edu.

Mary Baldwin University, Graduate Studies, Program in Shakespeare and Renaissance Literature in Performance, Staunton, VA 24401-3610. Offers acting (M Litt); directing (M Litt); Shakespeare and Renaissance literature in performance (MFA); teaching (M Litt). *Entrance requirements:* For master's, GRE (M Litt).

Marymount University, School of Arts and Sciences, Program in English and the Humanities, Arlington, VA 22207-4299. Offers English and humanities (MA); teaching English at the community college (Certificate). *Program availability:* Part-time, evening/ weekend. *Faculty:* 3 full-time (0 women). *Students:* 2 full-time (both women), 10 part-time (6 women); includes 5 minority (2 Black or African American, non-Hispanic/Latino; 1 Asian, non-Hispanic/Latino; 1 Hispanic/Latino; 1 Two or more races, non-Hispanic/ Latino). Average age 34. 8 applicants, 100% accepted, 5 enrolled. In 2017, 7 master's, 1 other advanced degree awarded. *Degree requirements:* For master's, thesis, capstone. *Entrance requirements:* For master's, 2 letters of recommendation, resume, bachelor's degree in English or other humanities discipline, writing sample of 8-10 pages. Additional exam requirements/recommendations for international students: Required—TOEFL (minimum score 600 paper-based; 96 iBT), IELTS (minimum score 6.5). *Application deadline:* Applications are processed on a rolling basis. Application fee: $40. Electronic applications accepted. *Expenses: Tuition:* Full-time $17,550; part-time $975 per credit hour. *Required fees:* $198; $11 per credit hour. One-time fee: $250. Tuition and fees vary according to program. *Financial support:* In 2017–18, 1 student received support, including 1 research assistantship with full and partial tuition reimbursement available (averaging $11,700 per year); teaching assistantships with full and partial tuition reimbursements available, career-related internships or fieldwork, Federal Work-Study, scholarships/grants, and unspecified assistantships also available. Support available to part-time students. Financial award application deadline: 3/1; financial award applicants required to submit FAFSA. *Unit head:* Dr. David Brown, Director, English and the Humanities, 703-284-5762, Fax: 703-284-3859, E-mail: david.brown@marymount.edu. *Application contact:* Francesca Reed, Director, Graduate Admissions, 703-284-5901, Fax: 703-527-3815, E-mail: grad.admissions@marymount.edu.
Website: http://www.marymount.edu/Academics/School-of-Arts-Sciences/Graduate-Programs/English-Humanities-(M-A-)

McGill University, Faculty of Graduate and Postdoctoral Studies, Faculty of Arts, Department of English, Montréal, QC H3A 2T5, Canada. Offers MA, PhD. Electronic applications accepted.

McMaster University, School of Graduate Studies, Faculty of Humanities, Department of English and Cultural Studies, Hamilton, ON L8S 4M2, Canada. Offers cultural studies and critical theory (MA); English (MA, PhD). *Program availability:* Part-time. *Degree requirements:* For master's, one foreign language, thesis; for doctorate, one foreign language, comprehensive exam, thesis/dissertation. *Entrance requirements:* For master's, honors degree, minimum B+ average in at least 6 full courses of English beyond year 1; for doctorate, MA; minimum A- average in two of three courses. Additional exam requirements/recommendations for international students: Required—TOEFL (minimum score 580 paper-based). *Faculty research:* Literary theory, feminist theory, literature of migration, Bakhting globalization.

McNeese State University, Doré School of Graduate Studies, College of Liberal Arts, Department of English and Foreign Languages, Program in Literature, Lake Charles, LA 70609. Offers MA. *Program availability:* Evening/weekend. *Degree requirements:* For master's, one foreign language, thesis or alternative. *Entrance requirements:* For master's, GRE. *Application deadline:* For fall admission, 5/15 priority date for domestic and international students; for spring admission, 10/15 priority date for domestic and international students. Applications are processed on a rolling basis. Application fee: $20 ($30 for international students). *Financial support:* Application deadline: 5/1. *Faculty research:* Textual criticism, seventeenth century literature, American women writers, Romanticism and the origins of diplomacy. *Unit head:* Dr. Scott E. Goins, Head, 337-475-5456, Fax: 337-475-5327, E-mail: sgoins@mcneese.edu. *Application contact:* Dr. Dustin M. Hebert, Director of Dore' School of Graduate Studies, 337-475-5396, Fax: 337-475-5397, E-mail: admissions@mcneese.edu.

Memorial University of Newfoundland, School of Graduate Studies, Department of English, St. John's, NL A1C 5S7, Canada. Offers MA, PhD. *Program availability:* Part-time. *Degree requirements:* For master's, thesis optional; for doctorate, one foreign language, comprehensive exam, thesis/dissertation, oral thesis defense, minimum 3 semesters of full-time study. *Entrance requirements:* For master's, honors degree. Electronic applications accepted. *Faculty research:* American, British, Canadian, and Anglo-Irish literature; Newfoundland literature.

Mercy College, School of Liberal Arts, Program in English Literature, Dobbs Ferry, NY 10522-1189. Offers MA. *Program availability:* Part-time, evening/weekend, 100% online, blended/hybrid learning. *Students:* 5 full-time (all women), 53 part-time (46 women); includes 17 minority (10 Black or African American, non-Hispanic/Latino; 1 Asian, non-Hispanic/Latino; 6 Hispanic/Latino). Average age 35. 25 applicants, 80% accepted, 10 enrolled. In 2017, 19 master's awarded. *Degree requirements:* For master's, comprehensive exam, thesis. *Entrance requirements:* For master's, essay, 2 letters of recommendation, undergraduate transcripts. Additional exam requirements/ recommendations for international students: Required—TOEFL (minimum score 600 paper-based; 100 iBT), IELTS (minimum score 8). *Application deadline:* For fall admission, 8/1 for international students. Applications are processed on a rolling basis. Application fee: $40. Electronic applications accepted. *Expenses: Tuition:* Full-time $15,426; part-time $857 per credit hour. *Required fees:* $630; $158 per term. Tuition and fees vary according to course load, degree level and program. *Financial support:* Career-related internships or fieldwork, Federal Work-Study, scholarships/grants, and unspecified assistantships available. Support available to part-time students. Financial award applicants required to submit FAFSA. *Unit head:* Dean, School of Liberal Arts, 914-674-7593. *Application contact:* Allison Gurdineer, Senior Director of Admissions, 877-637-2946, Fax: 914-674-7382, E-mail: admissions@mercy.edu.
Website: https://www.mercy.edu/degrees-programs/ma-english-literature

Miami University, College of Arts and Science, Department of English, Oxford, OH 45056. Offers MA, MAT, PhD. *Students:* 82 full-time (46 women), 59 part-time (43 women); includes 18 minority (4 Black or African American, non-Hispanic/Latino; 2 Asian, non-Hispanic/Latino; 6 Hispanic/Latino; 6 Two or more races, non-Hispanic/ Latino), 10 international. Average age 32. In 2017, 34 master's, 8 doctorates awarded. *Expenses:* Tuition, state resident: full-time $13,812; part-time $575 per credit hour. Tuition, nonresident: full-time $30,860; part-time $1286 per credit hour. *Unit head:* Dr. LuMing Mao, Chair, 513-529-5221, Fax: 513-529-5221, E-mail: maolr@miamioh.edu. *Application contact:* Cynthia Klestinec, Director of Graduate Program, 513-529-5221, E-mail: klestic@miamioh.edu.
Website: http://www.MiamiOH.edu/english/

Michigan State University, The Graduate School, College of Arts and Letters, Department of English, East Lansing, MI 48824. Offers English (PhD); literature in English (MA). *Entrance requirements:* For master's, GRE General Test, minimum GPA of 3.25, 2 years of foreign language or American Sign Language study, 3 letters of recommendation; for doctorate, GRE General Test, master's degree in English, 2 years of foreign language study, 3 letters of recommendation. Additional exam requirements/recommendations for international students: Required—TOEFL. Electronic applications accepted.

Middlebury College, Middlebury Bread Loaf School of English, Middlebury, VT 05753. Offers M Litt, MA. Offered during summer only. *Program availability:* Part-time. *Entrance requirements:* For master's, 2 letters of recommendation; statement of purpose; official transcripts (both undergraduate and graduate); 3-to 10-page writing sample. Electronic applications accepted. *Expenses:* Contact institution.

Middle Tennessee State University, College of Graduate Studies, College of Liberal Arts, Department of English, Murfreesboro, TN 37132. Offers MA, PhD. *Program availability:* Part-time, evening/weekend, online learning. *Degree requirements:* For master's, one foreign language, comprehensive exam, thesis optional; for doctorate, one foreign language, comprehensive exam, thesis/dissertation. *Entrance requirements:* For master's and doctorate, GRE. Additional exam requirements/recommendations for international students: Required—TOEFL (minimum score 525 paper-based; 71 iBT) or IELTS (minimum score 6). Electronic applications accepted.

Midwestern State University, Billie Doris McAda Graduate School, Prothro-Yeager College of Humanities and Social Sciences, Department of English, Humanities, and Philosophy, Wichita Falls, TX 76308. Offers English (MA); philosophy (PhD). *Program availability:* Part-time, evening/weekend. *Degree requirements:* For master's, one foreign language, thesis optional. *Entrance requirements:* For master's, GRE General Test, MAT or GMAT. Additional exam requirements/recommendations for international students: Required—TOEFL (minimum score 550 paper-based). Electronic applications accepted. *Faculty research:* Mythology, Shakespeare, Oscar Hahn, origins of language, modern American literature.

Millersville University of Pennsylvania, College of Graduate Studies and Adult Learning, College of Arts, Humanities and Social Sciences, Department of English, Millersville, PA 17551-0302. Offers English (M Ed, MA); writing (Postbaccalaureate Certificate). *Program availability:* Part-time, evening/weekend. *Faculty:* 7 full-time (3 women). *Students:* 5 full-time (2 women), 20 part-time (15 women); includes 2 minority (1 Black or African American, non-Hispanic/Latino; 1 Asian, non-Hispanic/Latino), 6 international. Average age 32. 16 applicants, 94% accepted, 8 enrolled. In 2017, 9 master's awarded. *Degree requirements:* For master's, one foreign language, thesis optional. *Entrance requirements:* For master's, GRE or MAT. Additional exam requirements/recommendations for international students: Required—TOEFL (minimum score 80 iBT), IELTS (minimum score 6.5), PTE (minimum score 60). *Application deadline:* Applications are processed on a rolling basis. Application fee: $40. Electronic applications accepted. *Expenses:* $500 per credit resident tuition and fees; $750 per credit non-resident tuition and fees; $114.75 per credit general fee (maximum of 12 credits); technology fee $27 per credit (resident), $39 per credit (non-resident). *Financial support:* In 2017–18, 4 students received support. Unspecified assistantships available. Financial award application deadline: 3/15; financial award applicants required to submit FAFSA. *Faculty research:* Film studies; critical theory; narrative studies; literacy narratives; multicultural issues surrounding literacy; African American literature and rhetorical traditions; writing pedagogy; public and civic discourse; civic engagement; academic, workplace, and community literacy; grounded theory; critical discourse analysis; rhetorical theory; composition theory; science writing; technical writing; environmental rhetoric; rhetoric of place; public sphere theory. *Unit head:* Dr. Jill R. Craven, Chair, 717-871-7385, Fax: 717-871-7933, E-mail: jill.craven@millersville.edu. *Application contact:* Dr. Victor S. DeSantis, Dean of College of Graduate Studies and Adult Learning/Associate Provost for Civic and Community Engagement, 717-871-7619, Fax: 717-871-7954, E-mail: victor.desantis@millersville.edu.
Website: http://www.millersville.edu/english/graduate/index.php

Mills College, Graduate Studies, Department of English, Oakland, CA 94613-1000. Offers book art and creative writing (MFA); literature (MA); poetry (MFA); prose (MFA); Spanish creative writing (Certificate); translation (MFA). *Program availability:* Part-time. *Faculty:* 6 full-time (5 women), 4 part-time/adjunct (all women). *Students:* 36 full-time (29 women), 21 part-time (14 women); includes 26 minority (9 Black or African American, non-Hispanic/Latino; 3 Asian, non-Hispanic/Latino; 9 Hispanic/Latino; 5 Two or more races, non-Hispanic/Latino). Average age 32. 100 applicants, 95% accepted, 27 enrolled. In 2017, 18 master's awarded. *Degree requirements:* For master's, comprehensive exam, thesis. *Entrance requirements:* For master's, 15-20 page writing sample. Additional exam requirements/recommendations for international students: Required—TOEFL (minimum score 600 paper-based; 100 iBT), IELTS (minimum score 7). *Application deadline:* For fall admission, 12/15 priority date for domestic students, 12/15 for international students. Applications are processed on a rolling basis. Application fee: $50. Electronic applications accepted. *Expenses:* Contact institution. *Financial support:* In 2017–18, 23 students received support, including 23 fellowships with partial tuition reimbursements available (averaging $6,327 per year), 21 teaching assistantships with tuition reimbursements available; research assistantships and scholarships/grants also available. Support available to part-time students. Financial award application deadline: 2/1; financial award applicants required to submit FAFSA. *Faculty research:* Creative writing, African-American literature, Victorian women writers, theories of sexuality, Shakespeare. *Unit head:* Dr. Thomas Strychacz, Chair of the English Department, 510-430-2208, E-mail: toms@mills.edu. *Application contact:* Robynne Lofton, Director of Admissions, 510-430-3295, Fax: 510-430-2159, E-mail: grad-admission@mills.edu.
Website: http://www.mills.edu/english/

Minnesota State University Mankato, College of Graduate Studies and Research, College of Arts and Humanities, Department of English, Mankato, MN 56001. Offers communication and composition (MA); creative writing (MFA); English studies (MA); teaching English as a second language (MA, Certificate); technical communication (MA, Certificate). *Program availability:* Part-time. *Degree requirements:* For master's, one foreign language, comprehensive exam, thesis or alternative. *Entrance requirements:* For master's, minimum GPA of 3.0 during previous 2 years, writing sample (MFA). Additional exam requirements/recommendations for international students: Required—TOEFL (minimum score 500 paper-based; 61 iBT). Electronic applications accepted.

Mississippi College, Graduate School, College of Arts and Sciences, School of Humanities and Social Sciences, Department of English, Clinton, MS 39058. Offers M Ed, MA. *Program availability:* Part-time, evening/weekend. *Degree requirements:* For master's, one foreign language, comprehensive exam, thesis or alternative. *Entrance requirements:* For master's, GRE or NTE, minimum GPA of 2.5. Additional exam requirements/recommendations for international students: Recommended—TOEFL, IELTS. Electronic applications accepted.

Mississippi State University, College of Arts and Sciences, Department of English, Mississippi State, MS 39762. Offers MA. *Program availability:* Part-time. *Faculty:* 25 full-time (12 women), 1 part-time/adjunct (0 women). *Students:* 23 full-time (16 women), 4 part-time (3 women); includes 10 minority (6 Black or African American, non-Hispanic/Latino; 2 Asian, non-Hispanic/Latino; 2 Hispanic/Latino), 1 international. Average age 26. 20 applicants, 75% accepted, 10 enrolled. In 2017, 13 master's awarded. *Degree requirements:* For master's, thesis optional, comprehensive oral or written exam. *Entrance requirements:* For master's, GRE General Test, minimum GPA of 2.75 on last two years of undergraduate courses. Additional exam requirements/recommendations for international students: Required—TOEFL (minimum score 625 paper-based; 106 iBT); Recommended—IELTS (minimum score 8). *Application deadline:* For fall admission, 7/1 for domestic students, 5/1 for international students; for spring admission, 11/1 for domestic students, 9/1 for international students. Applications are processed on a rolling basis. Application fee: $60 ($80 for international students). Electronic applications accepted. *Expenses:* Tuition, state resident: full-time $8318; part-time $462.12 per credit hour. Tuition, nonresident: full-time $22,358; part-time $1242.12 per credit hour. *Required fees:* $110; $12.24 per credit hour. $6.12 per semester. *Financial support:* In 2017–18, 14 teaching assistantships with partial tuition reimbursements (averaging $10,000 per year) were awarded; Federal Work-Study, institutionally sponsored loans, scholarships/grants, and unspecified assistantships also available. Financial award application deadline: 4/1; financial award applicants required to submit FAFSA. *Faculty research:* Literary criticism, linguistics, textual editing, editing quot; Mississippi Quarterly quot;, Southern literature. *Unit head:* Dr. Daniel Punday, Professor and Head, 662-325-3644, Fax: 662-325-3645, E-mail: dp1525@msstate.edu. *Application contact:* Lakan Drinker, Admissions and Enrollment Assistant, 662-325-8951, E-mail: ldrinker@grad.msstate.edu.
Website: http://www.english.msstate.edu

Missouri State University, Graduate College, College of Arts and Letters, Department of English, Springfield, MO 65897. Offers applied second language acquisition (MASLA); English (MA); English education (MS Ed); teaching English to speakers of other languages (Certificate); writing (MA). MASLA offered with the Department of Modern and Classical Languages. *Program availability:* Part-time, evening/weekend. *Faculty:* 25 full-time (18 women), 5 part-time/adjunct (2 women). *Students:* 34 full-time (26 women), 85 part-time (73 women); includes 9 minority (1 Black or African American, non-Hispanic/Latino; 1 Asian, non-Hispanic/Latino; 3 Hispanic/Latino; 1 Native Hawaiian or other Pacific Islander, non-Hispanic/Latino; 3 Two or more races, non-Hispanic/Latino), 14 international. Average age 26. 97 applicants, 65% accepted, 56 enrolled. In 2017, 57 master's awarded. *Degree requirements:* For master's, one foreign language, comprehensive exam, thesis or alternative. *Entrance requirements:* For master's, GRE (for MA), 9-12 teacher certification (MS Ed); minimum GPA of 3.0 (MA); personal statement (200- to 250-word description of reasons and goals behind interest in English graduate studies); at least two letters of recommendation from individuals able to speak of the applicant's academic achievements and potential; writing sample. Additional exam requirements/recommendations for international students: Required—TOEFL (minimum score 550 paper-based; 79 iBT), IELTS (minimum score 6). *Application deadline:* For fall admission, 3/1 priority date for domestic students, 3/1 for international students; for spring admission, 10/1 priority date for domestic students, 10/1 for international students. Applications are processed on a rolling basis. Application fee: $35 ($50 for international students). Electronic applications accepted. *Expenses:* Tuition, state resident: full-time $2915; part-time $2021 per credit hour. Tuition, nonresident: full-time $5354; part-time $3647 per credit hour. *International tuition:* $11,992 full-time. *Required fees:* $173; $173 per credit hour. Tuition and fees vary according to class time, course level, course load, degree level, campus/location and program. *Financial support:* In 2017–18, 23 teaching assistantships with full tuition reimbursements (averaging $8,772 per year) were awarded; Federal Work-Study, institutionally sponsored loans, scholarships/grants, and unspecified assistantships also available. Financial award application deadline: 3/31; financial award applicants required to submit FAFSA. *Faculty research:* History of rhetoric, modern poetry, African-American literature, digital writing, teaching English to speakers of other languages. *Unit head:* Dr. W. D. Blackmon, Department Head, 417-836-5107, Fax: 417-836-6940, E-mail: english@missouristate.edu. *Application contact:* Stephanie Praschan, Director, Graduate Enrollment Management, 417-836-5330, Fax: 417-836-6200, E-mail: stephaniepraschan@missouristate.edu.
Website: http://english.missouristate.edu/

Monmouth University, Graduate Studies, Department of English, West Long Branch, NJ 07764-1898. Offers creative writing (MA); literature (MA); rhetoric and writing (MA). *Program availability:* Part-time, evening/weekend. *Faculty:* 5 full-time (3 women). *Students:* 1 full-time (0 women), 28 part-time (21 women); includes 2 minority (1 Hispanic/Latino; 1 Two or more races, non-Hispanic/Latino). Average age 30. In 2017, 9 master's awarded. *Degree requirements:* For master's, comprehensive exam (for some programs), thesis. *Entrance requirements:* For master's, minimum overall GPA of 2.75, fifteen or more credits in literature or related field, essay of 1000 words describing interest and goals, two letters of recommendation, creative writing sample. Additional exam requirements/recommendations for international students: Required—TOEFL (minimum score 550 paper-based, 79 iBT), IELTS (minimum score 6), Michigan English Language Assessment Battery (minimum score 77) or Certificate of Advanced English (minimum score of 160). *Application deadline:* For fall admission, 7/15 for domestic students, 6/1 for international students; for spring admission, 12/1 for domestic students, 11/1 for international students; for summer admission, 5/1 for domestic students. Applications are processed on a rolling basis. Application fee: $50. Electronic applications accepted. *Expenses: Tuition:* Full-time $21,366; part-time $7122 per credit. *Required fees:* $700; $175 per term. *Financial support:* In 2017–18, 7 students received support. Institutionally sponsored loans, scholarships/grants, and unspecified assistantships available. Support available to part-time students. Financial award applicants required to submit FAFSA. *Faculty research:* Renaissance and medieval literature, nineteenth-century American literature, eighteenth-century British literature and women's studies, Old and Middle English, African diaspora and African post-colonial literature. *Unit head:* Dr. Kristin Bluemel, Program Director, 732-571-3622, Fax: 732-263-5242, E-mail: kbluemel@monmouth.edu. *Application contact:* Andrea Thompson, Graduate Admission Counselor, 732-571-3452, Fax: 732-263-5123, E-mail: gradadm@monmouth.edu.
Website: https://www.monmouth.edu/graduate/ma-english/

Montana State University, The Graduate School, College of Letters and Science, Department of English, Bozeman, MT 59717. Offers MA. *Program availability:* Part-time. *Degree requirements:* For master's, comprehensive exam. *Entrance requirements:* For master's, GRE General Test, minimum GPA of 3.0, 3 recommendations. Additional exam requirements/recommendations for international students: Required—TOEFL (minimum score 550 paper-based). Electronic applications accepted. *Faculty research:* Writing studies, writing in the disciplines, contemporary literature, Renaissance, Shakespeare, American studies, global studies, urban studies, Victorian literature, popular culture gender and sexuality studies, pedagogy, queer theory, English education, literacy education, literary theory.

Montclair State University, The Graduate School, College of Humanities and Social Sciences, Program in English, Montclair, NJ 07043-1624. Offers MA. *Program availability:* Part-time, evening/weekend. *Degree requirements:* For master's, thesis. *Entrance requirements:* For master's, GRE General Test, 2 letters of recommendation, essay. Additional exam requirements/recommendations for international students: Required—TOEFL (minimum score 83 iBT), IELTS (minimum score 6.5). Electronic applications accepted. *Faculty research:* Shakespeare and aging, nineteenth-century Gothic and Catholicism, African-American poetry and poetics, modern Irish and British culture, Darwin and literary modernism.

Morehead State University, Graduate Programs, Caudill College of Arts, Humanities and Social Sciences, Department of English, Morehead, KY 40351. Offers MA. *Program availability:* Part-time, evening/weekend. *Degree requirements:* For master's, comprehensive exam, thesis optional. *Entrance requirements:* For master's, GRE General Test, minimum GPA of 3.0 in English; undergraduate major or minor in English. Additional exam requirements/recommendations for international students: Required—TOEFL (minimum score 500 paper-based). Electronic applications accepted. *Faculty research:* Nineteenth and twentieth century American literature, linguistics, Victorian literature, modern British literature, creative writing.

Morgan State University, School of Graduate Studies, College of Liberal Arts, Department of English, Baltimore, MD 21251. Offers MA, PhD. *Program availability:* Part-time. *Degree requirements:* For master's, comprehensive exam, thesis; for doctorate, comprehensive exam, thesis/dissertation. *Entrance requirements:* For master's, GRE, minimum GPA of 2.5; for doctorate, GRE. Additional exam requirements/recommendations for international students: Required—TOEFL (minimum score 550 paper-based). *Application deadline:* For fall admission, 2/1 priority date for domestic students; for spring admission, 10/1 priority date for domestic students. Applications are processed on a rolling basis. Application fee: $0. *Expenses:* Tuition, state resident: part-time $433 per credit. Tuition, nonresident: part-time $851 per credit. *Required fees:* $81.50 per credit. *Financial support:* Application deadline: 2/1. *Faculty research:* African and African-American studies, nineteenth-century American literature, rhetoric, women's studies, children's literature. *Unit head:* Dr. Julie Cary Nerad, Coordinator, 443-885-3165, E-mail: julie.nerad@morgan.edu. *Application contact:* Dr. Dean Campbell, Graduate Recruitment Specialist, 443-885-3185, Fax: 443-885-8226, E-mail: dean.campbell@morgan.edu.

Mount Mary University, Graduate Programs, Program in English, Milwaukee, WI 53222-4597. Offers creative writing (MA); professional and new media writing (MA). *Program availability:* Part-time, evening/weekend. *Degree requirements:* For master's, comprehensive exam, thesis or alternative. *Entrance requirements:* For master's, minimum GPA of 2.75. Additional exam requirements/recommendations for international students: Required—TOEFL (minimum score 550 paper-based; 80 iBT); Recommended—IELTS (minimum score 6.5). Electronic applications accepted. *Expenses:* Contact institution.

Mount Saint Mary's University, Graduate Division, Los Angeles, CA 90049. Offers business administration (MBA); counseling psychology (MS); creative writing (MFA); education (MS, Certificate); film and television (MFA); health policy and management (MS); humanities (MA); nursing (MSN, Certificate); physical therapy (DPT); religious studies (MA). *Program availability:* Part-time, evening/weekend. *Faculty:* 50 full-time (35 women), 116 part-time/adjunct (81 women). *Students:* 670 full-time (518 women), 147 part-time (116 women); includes 414 minority (73 Black or African American, non-Hispanic/Latino; 4 American Indian or Alaska Native, non-Hispanic/Latino; 60 Asian, non-Hispanic/Latino; 259 Hispanic/Latino; 7 Native Hawaiian or other Pacific Islander, non-Hispanic/Latino; 11 Two or more races, non-Hispanic/Latino), 4 international. Average age 32. 1,398 applicants, 21% accepted, 242 enrolled. In 2017, 170 master's, 28 doctorates, 35 other advanced degrees awarded. *Entrance requirements:* Additional exam requirements/recommendations for international students: Required—TOEFL. *Application deadline:* For fall admission, 6/30 priority date for domestic and international students; for spring admission, 10/30 priority date for domestic and international students; for summer admission, 3/30 priority date for domestic and international students. Applications are processed on a rolling basis. Application fee: $50. Electronic applications accepted. *Expenses: Tuition:* Part-time $905 per unit. One-time fee: $155 part-time. Tuition and fees vary according to degree level and program. *Financial support:* Career-related internships or fieldwork, Federal Work-Study, institutionally sponsored loans, and tuition waivers (full and partial) available. Support available to

part-time students. Financial award application deadline: 3/15; financial award applicants required to submit FAFSA. *Unit head:* Albert Ramos, Director of Graduate Admissions, 213-477-2800, E-mail: gradprograms@msmu.edu. *Application contact:* Shawn Peters, Graduate Admission Counselor, 213-477-2676, E-mail: gradprograms@msmu.edu.
Website: http://www.msmu.edu/graduate-programs/

Murray State University, College of Humanities and Fine Arts, Department of English and Philosophy, Murray, KY 42071. Offers creative writing (MFA); English (MA); English pedagogy and technology (DA); gender studies (Certificate); teaching English to speakers of other languages (TESOL) (MA). *Program availability:* Part-time, 100% online, blended/hybrid learning. *Faculty:* 26 full-time (14 women), 1 part-time/adjunct (0 women). *Students:* 31 full-time (12 women), 91 part-time (61 women); includes 11 minority (5 Black or African American, non-Hispanic/Latino; 2 American Indian or Alaska Native, non-Hispanic/Latino; 2 Asian, non-Hispanic/Latino; 2 Two or more races, non-Hispanic/Latino), 23 international. Average age 36. 55 applicants, 95% accepted, 30 enrolled. In 2017, 21 master's awarded. *Entrance requirements:* For master's, doctorate, and Certificate, GRE or GMAT, minimum university GPA of 2.75. Additional exam requirements/recommendations for international students: Required—TOEFL (minimum score 527 paper-based; 71 iBT). *Application deadline:* Applications are processed on a rolling basis. Application fee: $40 ($50 for international students). Electronic applications accepted. *Expenses:* Tuition, state resident: full-time $9504. Tuition, nonresident: full-time $26,811. *International tuition:* $14,400 full-time. Tuition and fees vary according to course load, degree level and reciprocity agreements. *Financial support:* In 2017–18, 3 teaching assistantships were awarded; Federal Work-Study and unspecified assistantships also available. Financial award applicants required to submit FAFSA. *Unit head:* Dr. Sue Sroda, Chair, Department of English and Philosophy, 270-809-4715, Fax: 270-809-4545, E-mail: msroda@murraystate.edu. *Application contact:* Kaitlyn Burzynski, Interim Assistant Director for Graduate Admission and Records, 270-809-5732, Fax: 270-809-3780, E-mail: msu.graduateadmissions@murraystate.edu.
Website: https://www.murraystate.edu/academics/CollegesDepartments/CollegeOfHumanitiesAndFineArts/EnglishAndPhilosophy/index.aspx

National University, Academic Affairs, College of Letters and Sciences, La Jolla, CA 92037-1011. Offers biology (MS); counseling psychology (MA), including licensed professional clinical counseling, marriage and family therapy; creative writing (MFA); english (MA); film studies (MA); forensic and crime scene investigations (Certificate); forensic sciences (MFS); human behavior (MA); mathematics for educators (MS); performance psychology (MA); strategic communications (MA). *Program availability:* Part-time, evening/weekend, 100% online, blended/hybrid learning. *Degree requirements:* For master's, thesis (for some programs). *Entrance requirements:* For master's, interview, minimum GPA of 2.5. Additional exam requirements/recommendations for international students: Required—TOEFL (minimum score 550 paper-based; 79 iBT), IELTS (minimum score 6). *Application deadline:* Applications are processed on a rolling basis. Application fee: $60 ($65 for international students). Electronic applications accepted. *Expenses:* Tuition: Part-time $430 per quarter hour. *Financial support:* Career-related internships or fieldwork, institutionally sponsored loans, scholarships/grants, and tuition waivers (partial) available. Support available to part-time students. Financial award application deadline: 6/30; financial award applicants required to submit FAFSA. *Unit head:* Dr. Carol Richardson, Dean, 858-642-8450, E-mail: cols@nu.edu. *Application contact:* Brandon Jouganatos, Interim Vice President for Enrollment Services, 800-628-8648, E-mail: advisor@nu.edu.
Website: http://www.nu.edu/OurPrograms/CollegeOfLettersAndSciences.html

New Mexico Highlands University, Graduate Studies, College of Arts and Sciences, Department of English, Las Vegas, NM 87701. Offers English (MA), including creative writing, language, rhetoric and composition, literature. *Degree requirements:* For master's, comprehensive exam, thesis. *Entrance requirements:* For master's, minimum undergraduate GPA of 3.0. Additional exam requirements/recommendations for international students: Required—TOEFL (minimum score 540 paper-based). *Faculty research:* Twentieth-century literature, life path writing in homeless shelters, native American philosophy, medieval intellectual and cultural history, creating pedagogical tools for teaching law.

New Mexico State University, College of Arts and Sciences, Department of English, Las Cruces, NM 88003. Offers creative writing (MFA); English (MA), including creative writing, English studies for teachers, literature, rhetoric and professional communication; rhetoric and professional communication (PhD). *Program availability:* Part-time. *Faculty:* 17 full-time (9 women), 3 part-time/adjunct (1 woman). *Students:* 50 full-time (32 women), 21 part-time (14 women); includes 19 minority (2 Black or African American, non-Hispanic/Latino; 2 Asian, non-Hispanic/Latino; 14 Hispanic/Latino; 1 Two or more races, non-Hispanic/Latino), 8 international. Average age 35. 68 applicants, 50% accepted, 12 enrolled. In 2017, 13 master's, 1 doctorate awarded. *Entrance requirements:* For master's and doctorate, sample of written work. Additional exam requirements/recommendations for international students: Required—TOEFL (minimum score 550 paper-based; 79 iBT), IELTS (minimum score 6.5). *Application deadline:* For fall admission, 2/1 for domestic and international students. Application fee: $40 ($50 for international students). Electronic applications accepted. *Expenses:* Tuition, state resident: full-time $4390. Tuition, nonresident: full-time $15,309. *Required fees:* $853. *Financial support:* In 2017–18, 49 students received support, including 6 fellowships (averaging $4,390 per year), 41 teaching assistantships (averaging $17,317 per year); career-related internships or fieldwork, Federal Work-Study, scholarships/grants, traineeships, health care benefits, and unspecified assistantships also available. Support available to part-time students. Financial award application deadline: 3/1. *Faculty research:* Composition research, history and theory of rhetoric, technical/professional communication, creative writing, English and American literature. *Total annual research expenditures:* $10,666. *Unit head:* Dr. Elizabeth Schirmer, Interim Department Head, 575-646-3931, Fax: 575-646-7725, E-mail: eschirme@nmsu.edu. *Application contact:* Dr. Tracey Eileen Miller-Tomlinson, Director of Graduate Studies, 575-646-2213, Fax: 575-646-7725, E-mail: tomlin@nmsu.edu.
Website: http://english.nmsu.edu

New York University, Graduate School of Arts and Science, Program in English and American Literature, New York, NY 10012-1019. Offers MA, PhD. *Students:* Average age 28. 411 applicants, 26% accepted, 14 enrolled. In 2017, 20 master's, 9 doctorates awarded. *Degree requirements:* For master's, one foreign language, thesis or alternative, qualifying exams, special project; for doctorate, one foreign language, thesis/dissertation. *Entrance requirements:* For master's, GRE General Test; GRE Subject Test in English (recommended). Additional exam requirements/recommendations for international students: Required—TOEFL. *Application deadline:* For fall admission, 12/1 for domestic and international students. Application fee: $100. *Expenses: Tuition:* Full-time $41,352; part-time $19,968 per year. *Required fees:* $2496; $1628 per unit. $814 per term. Tuition and fees vary according to course load and program. *Financial support:* Fellowships, teaching assistantships, Federal Work-Study, institutionally sponsored loans, scholarships/grants, health care benefits, and unspecified assistantships available. Financial award application deadline: 12/1; financial award applicants required to submit FAFSA. *Unit head:* Chris Cannon, Chair, 212-998-8800, Fax: 212-995-4019, E-mail: gsas.english.admissions@nyu.edu.

Application contact: Crystal Parikh, Director of Graduate Studies, 212-998-8800, Fax: 212-995-4019, E-mail: gsas.english.admissions@nyu.edu.

North Carolina Agricultural and Technical State University, School of Graduate Studies, College of Arts and Sciences, Department of English, Greensboro, NC 27411. Offers English (MA); English and African-American literature (MA); English education (MAT, MS). *Program availability:* Part-time, evening/weekend. *Degree requirements:* For master's, comprehensive exam, qualifying exam. *Entrance requirements:* For master's, GRE General Test, minimum GPA of 3.0.

North Carolina Central University, College of Arts and Sciences, Department of Language and Literature, Durham, NC 27707-3129. Offers English (MA). *Program availability:* Part-time, evening/weekend. *Degree requirements:* For master's, one foreign language, comprehensive exam, thesis. *Entrance requirements:* For master's, GRE, minimum GPA of 3.0 in major, 2.5 overall. Additional exam requirements/recommendations for international students: Required—TOEFL. *Application deadline:* For fall admission, 8/1 for domestic students. Application fee: $30. *Expenses:* Tuition, state resident: full-time $2770; part-time $692.50 per credit hour. Tuition, nonresident: full-time $9247; part-time $2311.75 per credit hour. *Financial support:* Application deadline: 5/1; applicants required to submit FAFSA. *Unit head:* Wendy Rountree, Chairperson, 919-530-7461, E-mail: wrountree@nccu.edu. *Application contact:* Wendy Rountree, Chairperson, 919-530-7461, E-mail: wrountree@nccu.edu.

North Carolina State University, Graduate School, College of Humanities and Social Sciences, Department of English, Program in English, Raleigh, NC 27695. Offers MA. *Degree requirements:* For master's, thesis. *Entrance requirements:* For master's, GRE General Test. Electronic applications accepted. *Faculty research:* Creative writing, linguistics, rhetoric and composition, rhetoric and technical communication, film studies.

North Dakota State University, College of Graduate and Interdisciplinary Studies, College of Arts, Humanities and Social Sciences, Department of English, Fargo, ND 58102. Offers composition (MA); literature (MA); rhetoric, writing and culture (PhD). *Program availability:* Part-time. *Degree requirements:* For master's, one foreign language, thesis. *Entrance requirements:* Additional exam requirements/recommendations for international students: Required—TOEFL (minimum score 600 paper-based; 100 iBT), IELTS (minimum score 7). Electronic applications accepted. *Faculty research:* American and English literature, women's studies, language attitudes, composition practices, computers and composition.

See Display on page 736 and Close-Up on page 747.

Northeastern Illinois University, College of Graduate Studies and Research, College of Arts and Sciences, Programs in English, Chicago, IL 60625. Offers English (MA), including composition, literature. *Program availability:* Part-time, evening/weekend. *Degree requirements:* For master's, comprehensive exam, thesis optional. *Entrance requirements:* For master's, 30 hours of undergraduate course work in literature and composition (literature), BA in English or approval (composition/writing), minimum GPA of 2.75. Additional exam requirements/recommendations for international students: Required—TOEFL (minimum score 550 paper-based; 79 iBT). *Application deadline:* Applications are processed on a rolling basis. Application fee: $30. Electronic applications accepted. *Expenses:* Tuition, state resident: full-time $7274; part-time $404.11 per credit hour. Tuition, nonresident: full-time $14,548; part-time $808.23 per credit hour. *Required fees:* $1284. *Financial support:* Applicants required to submit FAFSA. *Faculty research:* Arthurian literature, Southern American literature, rhetoric and theories of authorship. *Unit head:* Dr. Timothy R. Libretti, Department Chair, 773-442-5820, Fax: 773-442-5490, E-mail: t-libretti@neiu.edu. *Application contact:* Martha Narvaez, Graduate Admission Representative, 773-442-6006, E-mail: m-narvaez@neiu.edu.

Northeastern State University, College of Liberal Arts, Department of Languages and Literature, Tahlequah, OK 74464-2399. Offers English (MA), including literature. *Faculty:* 8 full-time (1 woman). *Students:* 7 full-time (5 women), 22 part-time (12 women); includes 5 minority (1 American Indian or Alaska Native, non-Hispanic/Latino; 1 Hispanic/Latino; 3 Two or more races, non-Hispanic/Latino). Average age 32. In 2017, 8 master's awarded. *Degree requirements:* For master's, thesis. *Entrance requirements:* For master's, GRE or MAT, minimum GPA of 2.5. Additional exam requirements/recommendations for international students: Required—TOEFL. *Application deadline:* For fall admission, 6/1 priority date for domestic students. Applications are processed on a rolling basis. Application fee: $25. Electronic applications accepted. *Expenses:* Tuition, state resident: part-time $222 per credit hour. Tuition, nonresident: part-time $501.75 per credit hour. *Required fees:* $37.40 per credit hour. Tuition and fees vary according to degree level. *Financial support:* Application deadline: 3/1. *Unit head:* Dr. Mike Chanslor, Interim Department Chair, 918-456-3627, E-mail: chanslor@nsuok.edu. *Application contact:* Josh McCollum, Graduate Coordinator, 918-444-2093, E-mail: mccolluj@nsuok.edu.
Website: http://academics.nsuok.edu/languagesliterature/DegreePrograms/English,MA.aspx

Northeastern University, College of Social Sciences and Humanities, Boston, MA 02115. Offers criminology and criminal justice (MSCJ); criminology and justice policy (PhD); economics (MA, PhD); English (MA, PhD); international affairs (MA); law and public policy (PhD); political science (MA, PhD); public administration (MPA); public policy (MPP); security and resilience studies (MS); sociology (MA, PhD); urban and regional policy (MS); urban informatics (MS); world history (MA, PhD). *Program availability:* Online learning. *Faculty:* 242. *Students:* 491. In 2017, 143 master's, 38 doctorates awarded. *Degree requirements:* For doctorate, variable foreign language requirement, comprehensive exam, thesis/dissertation. *Entrance requirements:* For master's and doctorate, GRE. Additional exam requirements/recommendations for international students: Required—TOEFL, IELTS. Application fee: $75. Electronic applications accepted. *Expenses:* Contact institution. *Financial support:* Teaching assistantships, career-related internships or fieldwork, scholarships/grants, health care benefits, tuition waivers (full and partial), and unspecified assistantships available. Support available to part-time students. Financial award applicants required to submit FAFSA. *Unit head:* Dr. Uta Poiger, Dean, 617-373-5173, E-mail: college_of_social_sciences_and_humanities@neu.edu. *Application contact:* 617-373-5990, E-mail: gradcssh@northeastern.edu.
Website: http://www.northeastern.edu/cssh/

Northern Arizona University, College of Arts and Letters, Department of English, Flagstaff, AZ 86011. Offers applied linguistics (PhD); creative writing (MFA), including creative writing; English (MA), including literature, professional writing, rhetoric, writing, and digital media studies, secondary education; professional writing (Graduate Certificate); rhetoric, writing and digital media studies (Graduate Certificate); teaching English as a second language (MA, Graduate Certificate). *Program availability:* Part-time, 100% online, blended/hybrid learning. *Faculty:* 62 full-time (43 women), 3 part-time/adjunct (2 women). *Students:* 115 full-time (78 women), 115 part-time (89 women); includes 57 minority (11 Black or African American, non-Hispanic/Latino; 3 American Indian or Alaska Native, non-Hispanic/Latino; 4 Asian, non-Hispanic/Latino; 26 Hispanic/Latino; 13 Two or more races, non-Hispanic/Latino), 19 international. Average age 35. 189 applicants, 56% accepted, 92 enrolled. In 2017, 82 master's, 5 doctorates, 15 other advanced degrees awarded. *Degree requirements:* For master's, variable foreign

language requirement, comprehensive exam (for some programs), thesis (for some programs); for doctorate, variable foreign language requirement, comprehensive exam (for some programs), thesis/dissertation (for some programs); for Graduate Certificate, comprehensive exam (for some programs). *Entrance requirements:* Additional exam requirements/recommendations for international students: Required—TOEFL (minimum score 80 iBT), IELTS (minimum score 6.5). *Application deadline:* For fall admission, 1/30 for domestic and international students; for spring admission, 10/1 for domestic and international students. Application fee: $65. Electronic applications accepted. *Expenses:* Tuition, state resident: full-time $9240; part-time $458 per credit hour. Tuition, nonresident: full-time $21,588; part-time $1199 per credit hour. *Required fees:* $1021; $14 per credit hour. $646 per semester. Tuition and fees vary according to course load, campus/location and program. *Financial support:* In 2017–18, 69 students received support, including 4 fellowships with full and partial tuition reimbursements available (averaging $16,250 per year), 2 research assistantships with full and partial tuition reimbursements available (averaging $16,250 per year), 65 teaching assistantships with full and partial tuition reimbursements available (averaging $16,250 per year); institutionally sponsored loans, health care benefits, tuition waivers (full and partial), and unspecified assistantships also available. Financial award application deadline: 2/1; financial award applicants required to submit FAFSA. *Unit head:* Dr. Steven Rosendale, Chair, 928-523-4911, Fax: 928-523-7074, E-mail: steven.rosendale@nau.edu. *Application contact:* Tina Sutton, Coordinator, Graduate College, 928-523-4348, Fax: 928-523-8950, E-mail: graduate@nau.edu.
Website: https://nau.edu/cal/english/

Northern Illinois University, Graduate School, College of Liberal Arts and Sciences, Department of English, De Kalb, IL 60115-2854. Offers MA, PhD. *Program availability:* Part-time. *Faculty:* 32 full-time (13 women), 2 part-time/adjunct (both women). *Students:* 33 full-time (24 women), 61 part-time (35 women); includes 9 minority (1 Black or African American, non-Hispanic/Latino; 3 Hispanic/Latino; 5 Two or more races, non-Hispanic/Latino), 3 international. Average age 35. 44 applicants, 77% accepted, 11 enrolled. In 2017, 18 master's, 10 doctorates awarded. Terminal master's awarded for partial completion of doctoral program. *Degree requirements:* For master's, variable foreign language requirement, comprehensive exam, thesis optional; for doctorate, variable foreign language requirement, thesis/dissertation, candidacy exam, dissertation defense. *Entrance requirements:* For master's, GRE General Test, minimum GPA of 2.75; for doctorate, GRE General Test, minimum GPA of 2.75 (undergraduate), 3.2 (graduate). Additional exam requirements/recommendations for international students: Required—TOEFL (minimum score 550 paper-based). *Application deadline:* For fall admission, 6/1 for domestic students, 5/1 for international students; for spring admission, 11/1 for domestic students, 10/1 for international students. Applications are processed on a rolling basis. Application fee: $40. Electronic applications accepted. *Financial support:* In 2017–18, 48 teaching assistantships with full tuition reimbursements were awarded; fellowships with full tuition reimbursements, research assistantships with full tuition reimbursements, career-related internships or fieldwork, Federal Work-Study, scholarships/grants, tuition waivers (full), and unspecified assistantships also available. Support available to part-time students. Financial award applicants required to submit FAFSA. *Faculty research:* Nineteenth-century English literature, linguistic programs, portfolio assembly, Mideast literature, old English folklore. *Unit head:* Dr. Kathleen Renk, Chair, 815-753-0615, Fax: 815-753-0606, E-mail: krenk@niu.edu. *Application contact:* Graduate School Office, 815-753-0395, E-mail: gradsch@niu.edu.
Website: http://www.engl.niu.edu/

Northern Kentucky University, Office of Graduate Programs, College of Arts and Sciences, Program in English, Highland Heights, KY 41099. Offers composition and rhetoric (Certificate); creative writing (Certificate); cultural studies and discourses (Certificate); English (MA); professional writing (Certificate). *Program availability:* Part-time, evening/weekend. *Degree requirements:* For master's, comprehensive exam (for some programs), capstone (thesis, portfolio, project, or exams); 30 hours of credit; for Certificate, 18 hours of credit. *Entrance requirements:* For master's, bachelor's degree in English or related field from regionally-accredited institution with minimum GPA of 3.0 in major or cognate area coursework; official transcripts for all undergraduate and graduate work; two letters of reference; for Certificate, official transcripts for all undergraduate and graduate work; bachelor's degree from regionally-accredited institution; minimum undergraduate GPA of 2.5. Additional exam requirements/recommendations for international students: Required—TOEFL (minimum score 79 iBT); Recommended—IELTS (minimum score 6.5). Electronic applications accepted.

Northern Michigan University, Office of Graduate Education and Research, College of Arts and Sciences, Department of English, Marquette, MI 49855-5301. Offers creative writing (MFA); literature (MA); pedagogy (MA); teaching English to speakers of other languages (Graduate Certificate); theater (MA); writing (MA). *Program availability:* Part-time, evening/weekend. Terminal master's awarded for partial completion of doctoral program. *Degree requirements:* For master's, capstone project: thesis, practicum or portfolio (for MA); thesis (for MFA); for Graduate Certificate, one foreign language. *Entrance requirements:* For master's, minimum GPA of 3.0; bachelor's degree in English or minimum of 30 credit hours in undergraduate English; statement of purpose; resume; critical essay; 3 letters of recommendation; for Graduate Certificate, bachelor's degree. Additional exam requirements/recommendations for international students: Required—TOEFL (minimum score 550 paper-based; 79 iBT), IELTS (minimum score 6.5). *Application deadline:* For fall admission, 2/1 for domestic students; for winter admission, 2/1 for domestic students; for spring admission, 3/17 for domestic students. Applications are processed on a rolling basis. Application fee: $50. Electronic applications accepted. *Expenses:* Tuition, state resident: full-time $9417; part-time $542 per credit hour. Tuition, nonresident: full-time $12,873; part-time $758 per credit hour. Tuition and fees vary according to course load, degree level and program. *Financial support:* Research assistantships with full tuition reimbursements, teaching assistantships with full tuition reimbursements, Federal Work-Study, institutionally sponsored loans, and unspecified assistantships available. Support available to part-time students. Financial award application deadline: 3/1; financial award applicants required to submit FAFSA. *Faculty research:* Modern Arabic literature, British literature (medieval to contemporary), postcolonial literature, Native and African-American literature, creative writing, critical theory, pedagogy. *Unit head:* Lynn Domina, Head, 906-227-2711, E-mail: ldomina@nmu.edu. *Application contact:* Dr. Russell Prather, Director of MA Program/ Professor, 906-227-2857, E-mail: rprather@nmu.edu.
Website: http://www.nmu.edu/english/

Northwestern State University of Louisiana, Graduate Studies and Research, Department of Language and Communication, Natchitoches, LA 71497. Offers English (MA). *Degree requirements:* For master's, one foreign language, comprehensive exam, thesis or alternative. *Entrance requirements:* For master's, GRE General Test, minimum undergraduate GPA of 2.5. Additional exam requirements/recommendations for international students: Required—TOEFL. Electronic applications accepted.

Northwestern University, The Graduate School, Judd A. and Marjorie Weinberg College of Arts and Sciences, Department of English, Evanston, IL 60208. Offers MA, PhD. Admissions and degrees offered through The Graduate School. Terminal master's awarded for partial completion of doctoral program. *Degree requirements:* For master's, thesis; for doctorate, one foreign language, thesis/dissertation, oral and written qualifying exam. *Entrance requirements:* For master's and doctorate, GRE General Test, sample of written work. Additional exam requirements/recommendations for international students: Required—TOEFL. Electronic applications accepted. *Faculty research:* Renaissance literature, theatre and drama, American literature, modern European contemporary literature, poetry, cultural history.

Northwestern University, School of Professional Studies, Program in Literature, Evanston, IL 60208. Offers American literature (MA); British literature (MA); comparative and world literature (MA). *Program availability:* Part-time, evening/weekend.
Website: https://sps.northwestern.edu/masters/literature/index.php

Northwest Missouri State University, Graduate School, College of Arts and Sciences, Maryville, MO 64468-6001. Offers biology (MS); elementary mathematics specialist (MS Ed); English (MA); English education (MS Ed); English pedagogy (MA); geographic information science (MS, Certificate); history (MS Ed); mathematics (MS); mathematics education (MS Ed); teaching: science (MS Ed). *Program availability:* Part-time. *Faculty:* 67 full-time (21 women). *Students:* 11 full-time (5 women), 70 part-time (39 women); includes 9 minority (2 Black or African American, non-Hispanic/Latino; 1 American Indian or Alaska Native, non-Hispanic/Latino; 3 Hispanic/Latino; 3 Two or more races, non-Hispanic/Latino). Average age 34. 33 applicants, 42% accepted, 10 enrolled. In 2017, 19 master's, 7 other advanced degrees awarded. *Degree requirements:* For master's, comprehensive exam. *Entrance requirements:* For master's, GRE General Test, writing sample. Additional exam requirements/recommendations for international students: Required—TOEFL (minimum score 550 paper-based). *Application deadline:* For fall admission, 7/1 for domestic and international students; for spring admission, 11/15 for domestic and international students. Applications are processed on a rolling basis. Application fee: $0 ($50 for international students). Electronic applications accepted. *Expenses:* Tuition, state resident: full-time $4551; part-time $252.86 per credit hour. Tuition, nonresident: full-time $9103; part-time $505.72 per credit hour. *Required fees:* $2453; $136.25 per credit hour. Tuition and fees vary according to course load and program. *Financial support:* Research assistantships with full tuition reimbursements, teaching assistantships with full tuition reimbursements, and administrative assistantships, tutorial assistantships available. Financial award application deadline: 4/1; financial award applicants required to submit FAFSA. *Unit head:* Dr. Michael Steiner, Dean, 660-562-1197.
Website: https://www.nwmissouri.edu/academics/undergraduate/majors/liberal-arts-sciences.htm

Oakland University, Graduate Study and Lifelong Learning, College of Arts and Sciences, Department of English, Rochester, MI 48309-4401. Offers MA. *Program availability:* Part-time, evening/weekend. *Entrance requirements:* For master's, minimum GPA of 3.0. Additional exam requirements/recommendations for international students: Required—TOEFL (minimum score 550 paper-based). Electronic applications accepted. *Expenses:* Tuition, state resident: full-time $16,950; part-time $706.25 per credit. Tuition, nonresident: full-time $24,648; part-time $1027 per credit.

Ohio Dominican University, Division of Arts and Letters, Program in English, Columbus, OH 43219-2099. Offers MA. *Program availability:* Part-time, evening/weekend, online only, 100% online. *Faculty:* 4 full-time (2 women). *Students:* 2 full-time (both women), 31 part-time (25 women). Average age 33. 21 applicants, 48% accepted, 8 enrolled. In 2017, 5 master's awarded. *Degree requirements:* For master's, thesis or alternative. *Entrance requirements:* For master's, minimum undergraduate GPA of 3.0, 3 letters of recommendation, transcripts. Additional exam requirements/recommendations for international students: Required—TOEFL (minimum score 550 paper-based), IELTS (minimum score 6.5). *Application deadline:* For fall admission, 8/15 for domestic students, 6/10 for international students; for spring admission, 1/4 for domestic students, 11/2 for international students; for summer admission, 5/30 for domestic students. Applications are processed on a rolling basis. Application fee: $25. Electronic applications accepted. *Expenses:* $600 per credit hour; $175 technology fee per semester. *Financial support:* Applicants required to submit FAFSA. *Faculty research:* James Joyce, poetry, African literature. *Unit head:* Dr. Martin Brick, Director, 614-251-4519, E-mail: brickm@ohiodominican.edu. *Application contact:* John W. Naughton, Associate Vice President for Enrollment Management, 614-251-4721, Fax: 614-251-6654, E-mail: grad@ohiodominican.edu.
Website: http://www.ohiodominican.edu/academics/graduate/ma-in-english

The Ohio State University, Graduate School, College of Arts and Sciences, Division of Arts and Humanities, Department of English, Columbus, OH 43210. Offers MA, MFA, PhD. *Faculty:* 64. *Students:* 163 (100 women); includes 27 minority (9 Black or African American, non-Hispanic/Latino; 18 Hispanic/Latino), 6 international. Average age 29. In 2017, 25 master's, 11 doctorates awarded. *Degree requirements:* For master's, one foreign language, thesis or written exam; for doctorate, one foreign language, thesis/ dissertation. *Entrance requirements:* For master's and doctorate, GRE General Test. Additional exam requirements/recommendations for international students: Required— TOEFL (minimum score 600 paper-based; 100 iBT), IELTS (minimum score 8), Michigan English Language Assessment Battery (minimum score 86). *Application deadline:* For fall admission, 12/6 priority date for domestic students, 11/30 priority date for international students; for spring admission, 3/1 for domestic students, 2/1 for international students. Applications are processed on a rolling basis. Application fee: $60 ($70 for international students). Electronic applications accepted. *Financial support:* Fellowships, research assistantships, teaching assistantships, Federal Work-Study, institutionally sponsored loans, and unspecified assistantships available. Support available to part-time students. *Unit head:* Dr. Robyn Warhol, Chair/Arts and Humanities Professor, 614-292-6065, E-mail: warhol.1@osu.edu. *Application contact:* Graduate and Professional Admissions, 614-292-9444, Fax: 614-292-3895, E-mail: gpadmissions@osu.edu.
Website: http://english.osu.edu/

Ohio University, Graduate College, College of Arts and Sciences, Department of English Language and Literature, Athens, OH 45701-2979. Offers MA, PhD. *Program availability:* Part-time. *Degree requirements:* For master's, one foreign language, thesis or alternative; for doctorate, one foreign language, comprehensive exam, thesis/ dissertation, oral exam, public lecture. *Entrance requirements:* For master's, GRE General Test, minimum GPA of 3.0, writing sample; for doctorate, GRE General Test, minimum GPA of 3.0, master's degree in English, writing sample. Additional exam requirements/recommendations for international students: Required—TOEFL (minimum score 550 paper-based; 80 iBT) or IELTS (minimum score 6.5). Electronic applications accepted. *Faculty research:* Environmental literature, post-colonial studies, print culture, film in popular culture, computers in pedagogy.

Oklahoma State University, College of Arts and Sciences, Department of English, Stillwater, OK 74078. Offers creative writing (MFA); English (MA, PhD). *Faculty:* 60 full-time (33 women), 7 part-time/adjunct (3 women). *Students:* 7 full-time (4 women), 106 part-time (59 women); includes 18 minority (6 Black or African American, non-Hispanic/ Latino; 4 American Indian or Alaska Native, non-Hispanic/Latino; 2 Asian, non-Hispanic/ Latino; 4 Hispanic/Latino; 2 Two or more races, non-Hispanic/Latino), 21 international. Average age 32. 99 applicants, 34% accepted, 21 enrolled. In 2017, 21 master's, 12 doctorates awarded. *Entrance requirements:* For master's, GRE General Test, minimum GPA of 3.0, writing sample; for doctorate, GRE General Test, minimum GPA of 3.5,

writing sample. Additional exam requirements/recommendations for international students: Required—TOEFL (minimum score 550 paper-based; 79 iBT). *Application deadline:* For fall admission, 3/1 priority date for international students; for spring admission, 8/1 priority date for international students. Applications are processed on a rolling basis. Application fee: $40 ($75 for international students). Electronic applications accepted. *Expenses:* Tuition, state resident: full-time $4019; part-time $2679.60 per year. Tuition, nonresident: full-time $15,286; part-time $10,190.40 per year. *Required fees:* $2129; $1419 per unit. Tuition and fees vary according to program. *Financial support:* Research assistantships, teaching assistantships, career-related internships or fieldwork, Federal Work-Study, scholarships/grants, health care benefits, tuition waivers (partial), and unspecified assistantships available. Support available to part-time students. Financial award application deadline: 3/1; financial award applicants required to submit FAFSA. *Faculty research:* American and British novels, poetry, and autobiography; Native American languages and literature; institutional history of American film, history, and adaptations; rhetoric and theories of human communication; learning strategies of second language learners. *Unit head:* Dr. Richard Frohock, Department Head, 405-744-9474, Fax: 405-744-6326, E-mail: richard.frohock@okstate.edu.
Website: http://english.okstate.edu/

Old Dominion University, College of Arts and Letters, Doctoral Program in English, Norfolk, VA 23529. Offers PhD. *Program availability:* Part-time, evening/weekend, online learning. *Faculty:* 24 full-time (14 women), 1 (woman) part-time/adjunct. *Students:* 7 full-time (6 women), 54 part-time (37 women); includes 8 minority (5 Black or African American, non-Hispanic/Latino; 1 Hispanic/Latino; 1 Native Hawaiian or other Pacific Islander, non-Hispanic/Latino; 1 Two or more races, non-Hispanic/Latino). Average age 39. 83 applicants, 22% accepted, 10 enrolled. In 2017, 3 doctorates awarded. *Degree requirements:* For doctorate, comprehensive exam, thesis/dissertation, research competency in foreign language, statistics, or new media. *Entrance requirements:* For doctorate, GRE General Test, MA in English or related field with minimum GPA of 3.5, writing sample, resume, goals statement, letter of recommendation. Additional exam requirements/recommendations for international students: Required—TOEFL; Recommended—IELTS. *Application deadline:* For fall admission, 2/1 for domestic students. Application fee: $80. Electronic applications accepted. *Expenses:* Tuition, state resident: full-time $8928; part-time $496 per credit. Tuition, nonresident: full-time $22,482; part-time $1249 per credit. *Required fees:* $66 per semester. *Financial support:* In 2017–18, 12 students received support, including 8 research assistantships with full tuition reimbursements available (averaging $15,000 per year), 4 teaching assistantships with full tuition reimbursements available (averaging $15,000 per year); career-related internships or fieldwork, scholarships/grants, and unspecified assistantships also available. Support available to part-time students. Financial award application deadline: 2/15; financial award applicants required to submit FAFSA. *Faculty research:* New media studies, rhetoric, teaching and learning of writing, literature, cultural studies. *Unit head:* Dr. Kevin Eric DePew, Graduate Program Director, 757-683-4019, Fax: 757-683-3241, E-mail: kdepew@odu.edu. *Application contact:* Dr. David C. Earnest, Associate Dean, 757-683-6077, Fax: 757-683-5746, E-mail: dearnest@odu.edu.
Website: https://www.odu.edu/academics/programs/doctoral/english

Old Dominion University, College of Arts and Letters, Master of Arts in English Program, Norfolk, VA 23529. Offers literature (MA); professional writing (MA); rhetoric and composition (MA). *Program availability:* Part-time, evening/weekend. *Faculty:* 15 full-time (7 women). *Students:* 7 full-time (4 women), 16 part-time (13 women); includes 9 minority (2 Black or African American, non-Hispanic/Latino; 1 American Indian or Alaska Native, non-Hispanic/Latino; 3 Hispanic/Latino; 3 Two or more races, non-Hispanic/Latino). Average age 34. 12 applicants, 67% accepted, 7 enrolled. In 2017, 11 master's awarded. Terminal master's awarded for partial completion of doctoral program. *Degree requirements:* For master's, comprehensive exam, thesis optional. *Entrance requirements:* For master's, GRE General Test, 24 hours in English, sample of written work, BA. Additional exam requirements/recommendations for international students: Required—TOEFL. *Application deadline:* For fall admission, 3/15 priority date for domestic and international students; for winter admission, 11/1 for domestic students, 10/1 for international students; for spring admission, 11/1 priority date for domestic students, 11/1 for international students. Applications are processed on a rolling basis. Application fee: $50. Electronic applications accepted. *Expenses:* Tuition, state resident: full-time $8928; part-time $496 per credit. Tuition, nonresident: full-time $22,482; part-time $1249 per credit. *Required fees:* $66 per semester. *Financial support:* In 2017–18, 9 students received support, including 4 research assistantships (averaging $10,000 per year), 6 teaching assistantships (averaging $10,000 per year); career-related internships or fieldwork and unspecified assistantships also available. Financial award application deadline: 2/15; financial award applicants required to submit FAFSA. *Faculty research:* Literary theory, composition theory, professional writing, rhetoric, British and American literature. *Total annual research expenditures:* $3,451. *Unit head:* Dr. Drew Lopenzina, Graduate Program Director, 757-683-4033, E-mail: alopenzi@odu.edu. *Application contact:* Dr. Dale Miller, Associate Dean, 757-683-6077, Fax: 757-683-5746, E-mail: demiller@odu.edu.

Old Dominion University, Darden College of Education, Programs in Secondary Education, Norfolk, VA 23529. Offers chemistry (MS Ed); English (MS Ed); secondary education (MS Ed). *Accreditation:* NCATE. *Program availability:* Part-time, evening/weekend, online learning. *Faculty:* 13 full-time (7 women), 10 part-time/adjunct (7 women). *Students:* 52 full-time (35 women), 88 part-time (71 women); includes 31 minority (13 Black or African American, non-Hispanic/Latino; 1 American Indian or Alaska Native, non-Hispanic/Latino; 3 Asian, non-Hispanic/Latino; 6 Hispanic/Latino; 2 Native Hawaiian or other Pacific Islander, non-Hispanic/Latino; 6 Two or more races, non-Hispanic/Latino). Average age 34. 75 applicants, 71% accepted, 53 enrolled. In 2017, 56 master's awarded. *Degree requirements:* For master's, comprehensive exam, thesis. *Entrance requirements:* For master's, GRE General Test or MAT, PRAXIS I (for licensure), minimum GPA of 2.8, teaching certificate. Additional exam requirements/recommendations for international students: Required—TOEFL. *Application deadline:* For fall admission, 6/1 for domestic and international students; for winter admission, 11/1 for domestic and international students; for spring admission, 3/1 for domestic and international students. Applications are processed on a rolling basis. Application fee: $50. Electronic applications accepted. *Expenses:* Tuition, state resident: full-time $8928; part-time $496 per credit. Tuition, nonresident: full-time $22,482; part-time $1249 per credit. *Required fees:* $66 per semester. *Financial support:* In 2017–18, 56 students received support, including fellowships (averaging $15,000 per year), research assistantships with tuition reimbursements available (averaging $9,000 per year), teaching assistantships with tuition reimbursements available (averaging $15,000 per year). Financial award application deadline: 2/15; financial award applicants required to submit FAFSA. *Faculty research:* Use of technology, writing project for teachers, geography teaching, reading. *Unit head:* Dr. KaaVonia Hinton, Department Chair, 757-683-5958, Fax: 757-683-5862, E-mail: khintonj@odu.edu. *Application contact:* William Heffelfinger, Director of Graduate Admissions, 757-683-5554, Fax: 757-683-3255, E-mail: gradadmit@odu.edu.
Website: http://education.odu.edu/eci/secondary/

Oregon State University, College of Liberal Arts, Program in English, Corvallis, OR 97331. Offers film and visual studies (MA); literature and culture (MA); rhetoric, writing and composition (MA). *Program availability:* Part-time. *Entrance requirements:* For master's, GRE (recommended). Additional exam requirements/recommendations for international students: Required—TOEFL (minimum score 80 iBT), IELTS (minimum score 6.5). *Application deadline:* For fall admission, 1/3 for domestic and international students. Application fee: $75 ($85 for international students). *Financial support:* Application deadline: 1/3. *Unit head:* Molly McFerran, Office Specialist, 541-737-1635, E-mail: molly.mcferran@oregonstate.edu. *Application contact:* Dr. Raymond Malewitz, Assistant Professor and Director, 541-737-1656, E-mail: raymond.malewitz@oregonstate.edu.
Website: http://liberalarts.oregonstate.edu/wlf/ma

Our Lady of the Lake University, College of Arts and Sciences, Programs in English, San Antonio, TX 78207-4689. Offers literature, creative writing, and social justice (MA); MA/MFA. Program offered jointly with University of the Incarnate Word and St. Mary's University. *Program availability:* Part-time, evening/weekend. *Faculty:* 2 part-time/adjunct (1 woman). *Students:* 15 full-time (12 women), 7 part-time (all women); includes 17 minority (1 Black or African American, non-Hispanic/Latino; 16 Hispanic/Latino). Average age 33. 7 applicants, 100% accepted, 5 enrolled. In 2017, 2 master's awarded. *Degree requirements:* For master's, comprehensive exam, thesis optional. *Entrance requirements:* For master's, GRE General Test or MAT taken within the last 5 years, bachelor's degree with at least 18 hours of advanced course work in English and/or communication arts with minimum cumulative GPA of 2.5; 2 letters of recommendation; samples of creative and scholarly writing (25 pages total); personal statement. Additional exam requirements/recommendations for international students: Required—TOEFL. *Application deadline:* For fall admission, 6/15 for domestic and international students; for spring admission, 11/15 for domestic and international students; for summer admission, 4/15 for domestic and international students. Applications are processed on a rolling basis. Application fee: $40 ($50 for international students). Electronic applications accepted. Application fee is waived when completed online. *Expenses: Tuition:* Full-time $10,668; part-time $5334 per year. *Required fees:* $816; $816 per year. $408 per semester. *Financial support:* In 2017–18, 8 students received support. Federal Work-Study, scholarships/grants, unspecified assistantships, and tuition discounts available. Support available to part-time students. Financial award application deadline: 5/1; financial award applicants required to submit FAFSA. *Unit head:* Dr. Candance Zepeda, Chair of the English, Mass Communications and Drama Department, 210-431-4166, E-mail: llarson@ollusa.edu. *Application contact:* Office of Graduate Admissions, 210-431-3995, Fax: 210-431-3945, E-mail: gradadm@ollusa.edu.
Website: http://www.ollusa.edu/s/1190/hybrid/default-hybrid-ollu.aspx?sid-1190&gid-1&pgid-7884

Pace University, School of Education, New York, NY 10038. Offers adolescent education (MST), including biology, chemistry, earth science, English, foreign languages, mathematics, physics, social studies; childhood education (MST); early childhood development, learning and intervention (MST); educational technology studies (MS); inclusive adolescent education (MST), including biology, chemistry, earth science, English, foreign languages, mathematics, physics, social studies; integrated instruction for educational technology (Certificate); integrated instruction for literacy and technology (Certificate); literacy (MS Ed); special education (MS Ed). *Accreditation:* NCATE. *Program availability:* Part-time, evening/weekend, 100% online, blended/hybrid learning. *Faculty:* 19 full-time (13 women), 86 part-time/adjunct (49 women). *Students:* 91 full-time (76 women), 548 part-time (401 women); includes 247 minority (112 Black or African American, non-Hispanic/Latino; 2 American Indian or Alaska Native, non-Hispanic/Latino; 31 Asian, non-Hispanic/Latino; 93 Hispanic/Latino; 1 Native Hawaiian or other Pacific Islander, non-Hispanic/Latino; 8 Two or more races, non-Hispanic/Latino), 6 international. Average age 30. 188 applicants, 86% accepted, 114 enrolled. In 2017, 213 master's, 8 other advanced degrees awarded. *Degree requirements:* For master's and Certificate, certification exams. *Entrance requirements:* For master's, GRE (for initial certification programs only), teaching certificate (for MS Ed in literacy and special education programs only). Additional exam requirements/recommendations for international students: Required—TOEFL (minimum score 88 iBT), IELTS or PTE. *Application deadline:* For fall admission, 8/1 priority date for domestic students, 6/1 for international students; for spring admission, 12/1 priority date for domestic students, 10/1 for international students. Applications are processed on a rolling basis. Application fee: $70. Electronic applications accepted. *Expenses:* Contact institution. *Financial support:* In 2017–18, 17 students received support, including 17 research assistantships with partial tuition reimbursements available (averaging $6,020 per year); career-related internships or fieldwork, Federal Work-Study, scholarships/grants, and unspecified assistantships also available. Financial award application deadline: 9/1; financial award applicants required to submit FAFSA. *Faculty research:* STEM education, TESOL, teacher education, special education, language and literary development. *Total annual research expenditures:* $29,706. *Unit head:* Dr. Xiao-Lei Wang, Dean, School of Education, 914-773-3876, E-mail: xwang@pace.edu. *Application contact:* Susan Ford-Goldschein, Director of Graduate Admissions, 212-346-1531, Fax: 212-346-1585, E-mail: graduateadmission@pace.edu.
Website: http://www.pace.edu/school-of-education

Penn State University Park, Graduate School, College of the Liberal Arts, Department of English, University Park, PA 16802. Offers MA, MFA, PhD. *Unit head:* Dr. Susan Welch, Dean, 814-865-7691, Fax: 814-863-2085. *Application contact:* Lori Hawn, Director, Graduate Student Services, 814-865-1795, Fax: 814-863-4627, E-mail: l-gswww@lists.psu.edu.
Website: http://english.la.psu.edu/

Pittsburg State University, Graduate School, College of Arts and Sciences, Department of English and Modern Languages, Pittsburg, KS 66762. Offers English (MA), including creative writing, literature, professional writing. *Program availability:* Part-time. *Students:* 16 (12 women). In 2017, 9 master's awarded. *Degree requirements:* For master's, thesis or alternative. *Entrance requirements:* Additional exam requirements/recommendations for international students: Required—TOEFL (minimum score 550 paper-based; 79 iBT), IELTS (minimum score 6.5), PTE (minimum score 53). *Application deadline:* For fall admission, 7/15 for domestic students, 6/1 for international students; for spring admission, 12/15 for domestic students, 10/15 for international students; for summer admission, 5/15 for domestic students, 4/1 for international students. Applications are processed on a rolling basis. Application fee: $35 ($60 for international students). Electronic applications accepted. *Expenses:* Contact institution. *Financial support:* In 2017–18, 10 teaching assistantships with full tuition reimbursements (averaging $8,000 per year) were awarded; career-related internships or fieldwork, Federal Work-Study, and unspecified assistantships also available. Financial award application deadline: 2/1; financial award applicants required to submit FAFSA. *Faculty research:* American fiction, American poetry, British fiction, British poetry, composition theory, creative writing. *Unit head:* Dr. Celia Patterson, Chairperson, 620-235-4689, E-mail: cpatterson@pittstate.edu. *Application contact:* Lisa Allen, Assistant Director of Graduate and Continuing Studies, 620-235-4223, Fax: 620-235-4219, E-mail: lallen@pittstate.edu.

English

Portland State University, Graduate Studies, College of Liberal Arts and Sciences, Department of English, Portland, OR 97207-0751. Offers creative writing (MFA); English (MA); MA/MS. *Program availability:* Part-time, evening/weekend. *Faculty:* 37 full-time (22 women), 35 part-time/adjunct (20 women). *Students:* 88 full-time (61 women), 47 part-time (25 women); includes 20 minority (2 Black or African American, non-Hispanic/Latino; 1 American Indian or Alaska Native, non-Hispanic/Latino; 2 Asian, non-Hispanic/Latino; 7 Hispanic/Latino; 1 Native Hawaiian or other Pacific Islander, non-Hispanic/Latino; 7 Two or more races, non-Hispanic/Latino), 2 international. Average age 32. 181 applicants, 43% accepted, 45 enrolled. In 2017, 67 master's awarded. *Degree requirements:* For master's, one foreign language, comprehensive exam (for some programs), thesis (for some programs), oral and written exams. *Entrance requirements:* For master's, GRE (for some programs), statement of purpose, 2 letters of recommendation, transcripts, critical writing sample. Additional exam requirements/recommendations for international students: Required—TOEFL (minimum score 600 paper-based; 100 iBT). *Application deadline:* For fall admission, 1/3 for domestic and international students; for winter admission, 9/1 for domestic and international students; for spring admission, 11/1 for domestic and international students. Application fee: $65. *Expenses:* Tuition, state resident: full-time $14,436; part-time $401 per credit. Tuition, nonresident: full-time $21,780; part-time $605 per credit. *Required fees:* $1380; $22 per credit. $119 per quarter. One-time fee: $325. Tuition and fees vary according to program. *Financial support:* In 2017–18, 40 students received support, including 18 teaching assistantships with full and partial tuition reimbursements available (averaging $8,289 per year); career-related internships or fieldwork, Federal Work-Study, scholarships/grants, tuition waivers (full and partial), and unspecified assistantships also available. Support available to part-time students. Financial award application deadline: 3/1; financial award applicants required to submit FAFSA. *Faculty research:* American literature and cultural studies, medieval and British literature, writing prose fiction and poetry, rhetoric and composition, women's literature. *Total annual research expenditures:* $28,767. *Unit head:* Dr. Paul Collins, Chair, 503-725-9777, Fax: 503-725-3561, E-mail: pcollins@pdx.edu. *Application contact:* Matt Swetnam, Academic and Program Coordinator, 503-725-3623, Fax: 503-725-3561, E-mail: grdstudy@pdx.edu. Website: http://www.pdx.edu/english/

Princeton University, Graduate School, Department of English, Princeton, NJ 08544-1019. Offers PhD. *Degree requirements:* For doctorate, 2 foreign languages, thesis/dissertation. *Entrance requirements:* For doctorate, GRE General Test, GRE Subject Test, sample of written work. Additional exam requirements/recommendations for international students: Required—TOEFL (minimum score 600 paper-based). Electronic applications accepted.

Purdue University, Graduate School, College of Liberal Arts, Department of English, West Lafayette, IN 47907. Offers creative writing (MFA); literature (MA, PhD), including linguistics, literature and philosophy (PhD); rhetoric and composition, theory and cultural studies (PhD). *Program availability:* Part-time. *Faculty:* 57 full-time (26 women), 3 part-time/adjunct (all women). *Students:* 130 full-time (82 women), 50 part-time (28 women); includes 21 minority (6 Black or African American, non-Hispanic/Latino; 5 Asian, non-Hispanic/Latino; 7 Hispanic/Latino; 3 Two or more races, non-Hispanic/Latino), 31 international. Average age 31. 299 applicants, 14% accepted, 29 enrolled. In 2017, 19 master's, 26 doctorates awarded. *Degree requirements:* For master's, one foreign language, comprehensive exam (for some programs), thesis (for some programs); for doctorate, one foreign language, comprehensive exam, thesis/dissertation. *Entrance requirements:* For master's, GRE General Test; GRE Subject Test in English literature (recommended for students applying to literary studies), minimum undergraduate GPA of 3.0 or equivalent; for doctorate, GRE General Test; GRE Subject Test in English literature (recommended for students applying to literary studies), master's degree. Additional exam requirements/recommendations for international students: Required—TOEFL (minimum score 620 paper-based; 77 iBT). *Application deadline:* For fall admission, 1/15 for domestic and international students. Applications are processed on a rolling basis. Application fee: $60 ($75 for international students). Electronic applications accepted. *Financial support:* Fellowships with tuition reimbursements and teaching assistantships with tuition reimbursements available. Support available to part-time students. Financial award application deadline: 1/15; financial award applicants required to submit FAFSA. *Faculty research:* Cultural studies, postmodern narrative, contemporary women writers, composition theory, slave narratives. *Unit head:* Dorsey Armstrong, Head, 765-494-6478, E-mail: darmstrong@purdue.edu. *Application contact:* Jill M. Quirk, Graduate Contact, 765-494-3748, Fax: 765-494-1700, E-mail: griff@purdue.edu.
Website: https://www.cla.purdue.edu/english/

Purdue University, Graduate School, Program in Philosophy and Literature, West Lafayette, IN 47907. Offers PhD. Program offered jointly with Department of English, School of Languages and Cultures, and Department of Philosophy. *Faculty:* 19 full-time (4 women), 1 part-time/adjunct (0 women). *Students:* 36 full-time (5 women), 9 part-time (5 women); includes 4 minority (1 American Indian or Alaska Native, non-Hispanic/Latino; 2 Hispanic/Latino; 1 Two or more races, non-Hispanic/Latino), 6 international. Average age 29. 66 applicants, 14% accepted, 4 enrolled. In 2017, 5 doctorates awarded. *Degree requirements:* For doctorate, one foreign language, comprehensive exam, thesis/dissertation. *Entrance requirements:* For doctorate, GRE, master's degree in either English, philosophy or foreign languages. Additional exam requirements/recommendations for international students: Required—TOEFL. *Application deadline:* For fall admission, 1/10 priority date for domestic students, 1/10 for international students. Application fee: $60 ($75 for international students). Electronic applications accepted. *Financial support:* In 2017–18, teaching assistantships (averaging $1,415 per year) were awarded; fellowships and research assistantships also available. *Unit head:* Venetria K. Patton, Head of the Graduate Program, 765-496-1848, E-mail: vpatton@purdue.edu. *Application contact:* Elsa Schirmer, Graduate Contact, 765-496-9629, E-mail: eschirme@purdue.edu.
Website: http://www.cla.purdue.edu/phil-lit/graduate/

Purdue University Northwest, Graduate Studies Office, School of Liberal Arts and Social Sciences, Department of English and Philosophy, Hammond, IN 46323-2094. Offers English (MA). *Program availability:* Part-time, evening/weekend, online learning. *Degree requirements:* For master's, comprehensive exam, thesis optional. *Entrance requirements:* Additional exam requirements/recommendations for international students: Required—TOEFL. Electronic applications accepted. *Faculty research:* English literature, American literature, critical theory, women's studies, historical philosophy.

Queens College of the City University of New York, Arts and Humanities Division, Department of English, Queens, NY 11367-1597. Offers creative writing and literary translation (MFA); English (MA). *Program availability:* Part-time, evening/weekend. *Faculty:* 36 full-time (17 women), 1 (woman) part-time/adjunct. *Students:* 1 (woman) full-time, 99 part-time (57 women); includes 31 minority (10 Black or African American, non-Hispanic/Latino; 4 Asian, non-Hispanic/Latino; 14 Hispanic/Latino; 3 Two or more races, non-Hispanic/Latino), 3 international. Average age 31. 188 applicants, 35% accepted, 32 enrolled. In 2017, 41 master's awarded. *Degree requirements:* For master's, thesis, oral exam/thesis defense. *Entrance requirements:* For master's, minimum GPA of 3.0; minimum 24 undergraduate credits in English or related field and 10-15 page writing sample (for MA); manuscript (for MFA). Additional exam requirements/recommendations for international students: Required—TOEFL (minimum score 100 iBT), IELTS (minimum score 7). *Application deadline:* For fall admission, 4/1 for domestic students; for spring admission, 11/1 for domestic students. Applications are processed on a rolling basis. Application fee: $125. Electronic applications accepted. *Expenses:* $2,640 to $10,450 range (depending on number of credits). *Financial support:* In 2017–18, 6 students received support, including 2 fellowships (averaging $20,801 per year), 1 research assistantship (averaging $988 per year); career-related internships or fieldwork and scholarships/grants also available. Financial award application deadline: 4/1; financial award applicants required to submit FAFSA. *Faculty research:* Global Anglophone literature; race and ethnic studies; gender and sexuality studies; creative writing; literary translation. *Unit head:* Glenn Burger, Chair, 718-997-4658, E-mail: glenn.burger@qc.cuny.edu. *Application contact:* Elizabeth D'Amico-Ramirez, Assistant Director of Graduate Admissions, 718-997-5203, E-mail: elizabeth.damicoramirez@qc.cuny.edu.

Queen's University at Kingston, School of Graduate Studies, Faculty of Arts and Sciences, Department of English Language and Literature, Kingston, ON K7L 3N6, Canada. Offers MA, PhD. *Degree requirements:* For master's, one foreign language, thesis optional; for doctorate, 2 foreign languages, comprehensive exam, thesis/dissertation. *Entrance requirements:* For master's, B.A.H. upper 2nd class standing, 10 full courses in English; for doctorate, M.A. upper 2nd class standing. Additional exam requirements/recommendations for international students: Required—TOEFL, TWE. *Faculty research:* Renaissance, 18th century, post colonial, Canadian, 19th century.

Radford University, College of Graduate Studies and Research, Program in English, Radford, VA 24142. Offers MA, MS. *Program availability:* Part-time. *Faculty:* 9 full-time (4 women). *Students:* 14 full-time (9 women), 1 (woman) part-time; includes 1 minority (Native Hawaiian or other Pacific Islander, non-Hispanic/Latino). Average age 23. 13 applicants, 92% accepted, 11 enrolled. In 2017, 10 master's awarded. *Degree requirements:* For master's, comprehensive exam, thesis (for some programs). *Entrance requirements:* For master's, GRE, minimum GPA of 2.75, 2 letters of reference, sample of expository writing, resume, official transcripts. Additional exam requirements/recommendations for international students: Required—TOEFL (minimum score 550 paper-based; 79 iBT), IELTS (minimum score 6.5). *Application deadline:* For fall admission, 2/15 priority date for domestic students, 12/1 for international students; for spring admission, 7/1 for international students. Applications are processed on a rolling basis. Application fee: $50. Electronic applications accepted. *Expenses:* Tuition, state resident: full-time $8336; part-time $347 per credit hour. Tuition, nonresident: full-time $16,862; part-time $702 per credit hour. *Required fees:* $3220; $135 per credit hour. Tuition and fees vary according to course load and program. *Financial support:* In 2017–18, 12 students received support, including 12 teaching assistantships (averaging $10,333 per year); scholarships/grants and unspecified assistantships also available. Support available to part-time students. Financial award application deadline: 3/1; financial award applicants required to submit FAFSA. *Faculty research:* Effect of translation on the works of James Joyce, life and work of Olive Moore, southern trajectory of the works of Phillis Wheatley after her death, influence of French feminism on the poetry of Anne Bradstreet, postmodern theory and Native American fiction. *Unit head:* Dr. Amanda Kellogg, Coordinator, 540-831-5541, E-mail: akellogg1@radford.edu. Website: http://www.radford.edu/content/chbs/home/english/graduate-programs.html

Rhode Island College, School of Graduate Studies, Faculty of Arts and Sciences, Department of English, Providence, RI 02908-1991. Offers creative writing (MA, CGS); English (MA); literature (CGS). *Program availability:* Part-time, evening/weekend. *Faculty:* 6 full-time (2 women). *Students:* 3 full-time (1 woman), 5 part-time (1 woman); includes 1 minority (Hispanic/Latino). Average age 31. In 2017, 5 master's awarded. *Degree requirements:* For master's, thesis (for some programs). *Entrance requirements:* For master's, GRE General Test, 3 letters of recommendation, interview. Additional exam requirements/recommendations for international students: Recommended—TOEFL (minimum score 550 paper-based; 79 iBT). *Application deadline:* For fall admission, 3/1 for domestic students; for spring admission, 11/1 for domestic students. Applications are processed on a rolling basis. Application fee: $50. *Expenses:* Tuition, state resident: full-time $9768; part-time $407 per credit. Tuition, nonresident: full-time $19,008; part-time $792 per credit. *Required fees:* $696; $29 per credit. One-time fee: $200 full-time; $100 part-time. Tuition and fees vary according to course load. *Financial support:* In 2017–18, 1 teaching assistantship with full tuition reimbursement (averaging $3,000 per year) was awarded; career-related internships or fieldwork, Federal Work-Study, scholarships/grants, health care benefits, and unspecified assistantships also available. Support available to part-time students. Financial award application deadline: 5/15; financial award applicants required to submit FAFSA. *Unit head:* Dr. Stephen Brown, Co-Chair, 401-456-8028.
Website: http://www.ric.edu/english/index.php

Rice University, Graduate Programs, School of Humanities, Department of English, Houston, TX 77251-1892. Offers MA, PhD. Terminal master's awarded for partial completion of doctoral program. *Degree requirements:* For master's, comprehensive exam, thesis (for some programs); for doctorate, comprehensive exam, thesis/dissertation. *Entrance requirements:* For master's and doctorate, GRE General Test, minimum GPA of 3.0. Additional exam requirements/recommendations for international students: Required—TOEFL (minimum score 600 paper-based; 90 iBT). Electronic applications accepted. *Faculty research:* Traditional periods and genres (excluding Old English), literary criticism and theory, Victorian literature, feminist literature, Renaissance literature, American literature, African-American literature.

Rivier University, School of Graduate Studies, Department of English, Nashua, NH 03060. Offers English (MAT); writing and literature (MA). *Program availability:* Part-time, evening/weekend. *Degree requirements:* For master's, comprehensive exam (for some programs). *Entrance requirements:* For master's, GRE Subject Test.

Rutgers University–Camden, Graduate School of Arts and Sciences, Program in English, Camden, NJ 08102. Offers MA. *Program availability:* Part-time, evening/weekend. *Degree requirements:* For master's, comprehensive exam, thesis optional, 30 credits. *Entrance requirements:* For master's, GRE General Test, 3 letters of recommendation, writing sample, statement of personal, professional, and academic goals. Additional exam requirements/recommendations for international students: Required—TOEFL, IELTS. Electronic applications accepted. *Faculty research:* British literature; American literature; women's studies; literary, poetic, and rhetorical theory; creative writing.

Rutgers University–Newark, Graduate School, Program in English, Newark, NJ 07102. Offers MA. *Program availability:* Part-time, evening/weekend. *Degree requirements:* For master's, one foreign language, comprehensive exam, thesis optional. *Entrance requirements:* For master's, GRE, minimum undergraduate B average. Electronic applications accepted. *Faculty research:* British and American literature, cultural studies, literary theory, minority literatures.

Rutgers University–New Brunswick, Graduate School-New Brunswick, Program of Literatures in English, Piscataway, NJ 08854-8097. Offers PhD. *Degree requirements:* For doctorate, one foreign language, thesis/dissertation, qualifying exam. *Entrance requirements:* For doctorate, GRE General Test, GRE Subject Test, writing sample, 3

letters of recommendation. Additional exam requirements/recommendations for international students: Required—TOEFL. Electronic applications accepted. *Faculty research:* Medieval literature; Renaissance; African American literature; 18th-century British literature; feminism, gender, and sexuality; postcolonial studies.

St. Cloud State University, School of Graduate Studies, College of Liberal Arts, Department of English, St. Cloud, MN 56301-4498. Offers English (MA, MS); teaching English as a second language (MA). *Program availability:* Part-time. *Degree requirements:* For master's, thesis or alternative. *Entrance requirements:* For master's, GRE General Test, minimum GPA of 2.75. Additional exam requirements/recommendations for international students: Required—Michigan English Language Assessment Battery; Recommended—TOEFL (minimum score 550 paper-based), IELTS (minimum score 6.5). Electronic applications accepted.

St. John's University, St. John's College of Liberal Arts and Sciences, Department of English, Queens, NY 11439. Offers MA, PhD. *Program availability:* Part-time, evening/weekend. *Faculty:* 27 full-time (13 women), 27 part-time/adjunct (8 women). *Students:* 45 full-time (35 women), 44 part-time (27 women); includes 30 minority (10 Black or African American, non-Hispanic/Latino; 8 Asian, non-Hispanic/Latino; 7 Hispanic/Latino; 5 Two or more races, non-Hispanic/Latino), 3 international. Average age 33. 64 applicants, 73% accepted, 24 enrolled. In 2017, 15 master's, 9 doctorates awarded. *Degree requirements:* For master's, comprehensive exam, thesis optional, portfolio; for doctorate, comprehensive exam, thesis/dissertation. *Entrance requirements:* For master's and doctorate, GRE, letters of recommendation, transcripts, resume, personal statement. Additional exam requirements/recommendations for international students: Required—TOEFL (minimum score 80 iBT), IELTS (minimum score 6.5). *Application deadline:* For fall admission, 5/1 for domestic students; for spring admission, 11/1 for domestic students. Applications are processed on a rolling basis. Application fee: $70. Electronic applications accepted. *Expenses: Tuition:* Full-time $44,280; part-time $1230 per credit. *Required fees:* $340; $340 per credit. Tuition and fees vary according to course load, degree level and program. *Financial support:* Fellowships, research assistantships, teaching assistantships, scholarships/grants, tuition waivers, and unspecified assistantships available. Support available to part-time students. Financial award application deadline: 2/1; financial award applicants required to submit FAFSA. *Faculty research:* Literary, cultural, and composition theory; writing studies; postcolonial and ethnic studies; British and American literature; creative writing. *Unit head:* Dr. Stephen Sicari, Chair, 718-990-6390, E-mail: sicaris@stjohns.edu. *Application contact:* Robert Medrano, Director of Graduate Admission, 718-990-1601, Fax: 718-990-5686, E-mail: gradhelp@stjohns.edu.
Website: https://www.stjohns.edu/academics/schools-and-colleges/st-johns-college-liberal-arts-and-sciences/english

Saint Louis University, Graduate Programs, College of Arts and Sciences and Graduate Programs, Department of English, St. Louis, MO 63103. Offers MA, MA-R, PhD. *Program availability:* Part-time. *Degree requirements:* For master's, one foreign language, comprehensive exam, thesis optional, comprehensive oral exam; for doctorate, 2 foreign languages, comprehensive exam, thesis/dissertation, preliminary oral and written exams. *Entrance requirements:* For master's, GRE General Test, GRE Subject Test, letters of recommendation, resume, writing sample, interview; for doctorate, GRE General Test, GRE Subject Test, letters of recommendation, resumé, writing sample, interview, goal statement, writing sample. Additional exam requirements/recommendations for international students: Required—TOEFL (minimum score 550 paper-based). *Faculty research:* English literature, American literature, post-colonial literature, composition, literary theory.

Saint Louis University–Madrid Campus, Graduate Programs, Master of Arts in English Program, Madrid, Spain. Offers MA. *Program availability:* Part-time. *Degree requirements:* For master's, one foreign language, comprehensive exam, thesis optional. *Entrance requirements:* For master's, GRE General Test, transcripts, 3 letters of recommendation, writing sample, personal statement, curriculum vitae. Additional exam requirements/recommendations for international students: Required—TOEFL (minimum score 550 paper-based; 80 iBT). Electronic applications accepted. *Faculty research:* English, Irish and American literature; literary theory; translation; linguistics.

St. Mary's University, Graduate Studies, Program in English Literature and Language, San Antonio, TX 78228. Offers MA, JD/MA. *Program availability:* Part-time, evening/weekend. *Students:* 6 full-time (5 women), 10 part-time (9 women); includes 6 minority (all Hispanic/Latino), 6 international. Average age 32. 13 applicants, 69% accepted, 6 enrolled. In 2017, 6 master's awarded. *Degree requirements:* For master's, thesis (for some programs). *Entrance requirements:* For master's, GRE (minimum score within top 35% of verbal section and top 35% of analytical section), minimum GPA of 3.0. Additional exam requirements/recommendations for international students: Required—TOEFL (minimum score 550 paper-based; 80 iBT), IELTS (minimum score 6). *Application deadline:* For fall admission, 7/1 for domestic students; for spring admission, 11/15 for domestic students; for summer admission, 4/1 for domestic students. Applications are processed on a rolling basis. Application fee: $0. Electronic applications accepted. *Expenses: Tuition:* Full-time $16,200; part-time $900 per credit hour. *Required fees:* $810; $405 per semester. *Financial support:* Application deadline: 3/31; applicants required to submit FAFSA. *Faculty research:* Interpersonal communication, rhetorical communication. *Unit head:* Dr. Mary Lynne Gasaway Hill, Director of English Literature and Language Graduate Program, 210-431-2006, E-mail: mhill@stmarytx.edu. *Application contact:* Kim Thornton, Director of Graduate Admission, 210-436-3101, E-mail: kthornton@stmarytx.edu.
Website: https://www.stmarytx.edu/academics/programs/master-english-literature-language/

Salem State University, School of Graduate Studies, Program in English, Salem, MA 01970-5353. Offers MA, MAT, MA/MAT. *Program availability:* Part-time, evening/weekend. *Entrance requirements:* For master's, GRE or MAT. Additional exam requirements/recommendations for international students: Required—TOEFL (minimum score 550 paper-based; 80 iBT) or IELTS (minimum score 5.5).

Salisbury University, Department of English, Salisbury, MD 21801-6837. Offers English (MA), including TESOL. *Program availability:* Part-time. *Faculty:* 10 full-time (6 women). *Students:* 15 full-time (12 women), 14 part-time (11 women); includes 1 minority (Black or African American, non-Hispanic/Latino), 2 international. Average age 34. 27 applicants, 37% accepted, 10 enrolled. In 2017, 26 master's awarded. *Degree requirements:* For master's, comprehensive exam, thesis optional. *Entrance requirements:* For master's, GRE/MAT/PRAXIS I, two letters of recommendation; transcripts from all colleges and universities attended; bachelor's degree in English or related field; personal statement; minimum GPA of 3.0. Additional exam requirements/recommendations for international students: Required—TOEFL (minimum score 550 paper-based; 79 iBT), IELTS (minimum score 6.5). *Application deadline:* For fall admission, 8/1 for domestic and international students; for spring admission, 1/1 for domestic and international students. Application fee: $65. Electronic applications accepted. *Expenses:* $392 per credit hour resident; $703 per credit hour non-resident; $92 per credit hour fees. *Financial support:* In 2017–18, 8 students received support, including 11 teaching assistantships with full tuition reimbursements available (averaging $11,275 per year); career-related internships or fieldwork and scholarships/grants also available. Support available to part-time students. Financial award application deadline: 3/1; financial award applicants required to submit FAFSA. *Faculty research:* Literature; linguistics; film studies; rhetoric and composition; TESOL. *Unit head:* Dr. Christopher Vilmar, Graduate Program Director, English, 410-677-6511, E-mail: csvilmar@salisbury.edu.
Website: http://www.salisbury.edu/gsr/gradstudies/ENGpage.html

Sam Houston State University, College of Humanities and Social Sciences, Department of English, Huntsville, TX 77341. Offers creative writing, editing, and publishing (MFA); English (MA). *Program availability:* Part-time. *Degree requirements:* For master's, comprehensive exam, thesis optional. *Entrance requirements:* For master's, GRE General Test, creative writing sample, letters of recommendation. Additional exam requirements/recommendations for international students: Required—TOEFL (minimum score 550 paper-based; 79 iBT), IELTS (minimum score 6.5). Electronic applications accepted.

San Diego State University, Graduate and Research Affairs, College of Arts and Letters, Department of English and Comparative Literature, San Diego, CA 92182. Offers creative writing (MFA); English (MA). *Degree requirements:* For master's, one foreign language, comprehensive exam (for some programs), thesis (for some programs). *Entrance requirements:* For master's, GRE General Test, minimum GPA of 2.85, writing sample, 3 letters of recommendation. Additional exam requirements/recommendations for international students: Required—TOEFL. Electronic applications accepted.

San Francisco State University, Division of Graduate Studies, College of Liberal and Creative Arts, Department of English Language and Literature, Program in Composition, San Francisco, CA 94132-1722. Offers MA, Certificate. *Program availability:* Part-time. *Degree requirements:* For master's, comprehensive exam. *Entrance requirements:* Additional exam requirements/recommendations for international students: Required—TOEFL, TWE. *Application deadline:* Applications are processed on a rolling basis. *Unit head:* Dr. Sugie Goen-Salter, Chair, 415-338-7582, Fax: 415-338-6159, E-mail: sgoen@sfsu.edu. *Application contact:* Prof. Mark Roberge, Graduate Coordinator, 415-338-7457, Fax: 415-338-6159, E-mail: roberge@sfsu.edu.
Website: http://english.sfsu.edu/graduate-composition

San Francisco State University, Division of Graduate Studies, College of Liberal and Creative Arts, Department of English Language and Literature, Program in Literature, San Francisco, CA 94132-1722. Offers MA. *Program availability:* Part-time. *Application deadline:* Applications are processed on a rolling basis. *Unit head:* Dr. Sugie Goen-Salter, Chair, 415-338-7582, Fax: 415-338-6159, E-mail: sgoen@sfsu.edu. *Application contact:* Dr. Julie Paulson, Graduate Coordinator, 415-338-3107, Fax: 415-338-6159, E-mail: jpaulson@sfsu.edu.
Website: http://english.sfsu.edu/graduate-literature

San Jose State University, Graduate Studies and Research, College of Humanities and the Arts, San Jose, CA 95192-0088. Offers art (MA, MFA), including digital media art (MFA), history and visual culture (MA), photography (MFA), pictorial art (MFA), spatial art (MFA); English (MA, MFA), including creative writing (MFA); linguistics (MA); music (MM); music education (MA); philosophy (MA); Spanish (MA); teaching English to speakers of other languages (MA). *Program availability:* Part-time. *Faculty:* 35 full-time (17 women), 19 part-time/adjunct (11 women). *Students:* 129 full-time (79 women), 106 part-time (71 women); includes 117 minority (5 Black or African American, non-Hispanic/Latino; 29 Asian, non-Hispanic/Latino; 44 Hispanic/Latino; 39 Two or more races, non-Hispanic/Latino), 28 international. Average age 35. 204 applicants, 65% accepted, 79 enrolled. In 2017, 85 master's awarded. *Degree requirements:* For master's, one foreign language, comprehensive exam (for some programs), thesis (for some programs), graduate writing assessment, special study/project, recital. *Entrance requirements:* Additional exam requirements/recommendations for international students: Required—TOEFL (minimum score 550 paper-based; 80 iBT), IELTS (minimum score 6.5), PTE (minimum score 53). *Application deadline:* For fall admission, 2/1 for domestic and international students. Applications are processed on a rolling basis. Application fee: $55. Electronic applications accepted. *Expenses:* Tuition, state resident: full-time $7176. Tuition, nonresident: full-time $16,680. Tuition and fees vary according to course load and program. *Financial support:* Fellowships, research assistantships, Federal Work-Study, scholarships/grants, traineeships, tuition waivers (full and partial), and unspecified assistantships available. Support available to part-time students. Financial award application deadline: 4/28; financial award applicants required to submit FAFSA. *Unit head:* Dr. Shannon Miller, Dean, 408-924-4300, Fax: 408-924-4365, E-mail: shannon.miller@sjsu.edu.
Website: http://www.sjsu.edu/humanitiesandarts/

Seton Hall University, College of Arts and Sciences, Department of English, South Orange, NJ 07079-2697. Offers literature (MA). *Program availability:* Part-time, evening/weekend. *Degree requirements:* For master's, one foreign language, comprehensive exam, thesis (for some programs). *Entrance requirements:* For master's, GRE, minimum of 21 undergraduate credits in English. Additional exam requirements/recommendations for international students: Required—TOEFL. Electronic applications accepted. *Faculty research:* The essay, modern poetry, the novel, medieval poetry, Renaissance drama.

Simmons College, College of Arts and Sciences, Boston, MA 02115. Offers English (MA); gender/cultural studies (MA); history (MA); public health (MPH); public policy (MPP). *Program availability:* Part-time. *Faculty:* 19 full-time (13 women), 2 part-time/adjunct (both women). *Students:* 4 full-time (3 women), 39 part-time (34 women); includes 11 minority (7 Black or African American, non-Hispanic/Latino; 1 Hispanic/Latino; 3 Two or more races, non-Hispanic/Latino). Average age 26. 99 applicants, 57% accepted, 27 enrolled. In 2017, 23 master's awarded. Terminal master's awarded for partial completion of doctoral program. *Degree requirements:* For master's, thesis optional. *Entrance requirements:* For master's, GRE, bachelor's degree from accredited college or university; minimum B average (preferred). Additional exam requirements/recommendations for international students: Required—TOEFL (minimum score 600 paper-based; 100 iBT). *Application deadline:* For fall admission, 8/1 for domestic and international students; for spring admission, 12/15 for domestic and international students; for summer admission, 5/1 for domestic and international students. Applications are processed on a rolling basis. Application fee: $35. Electronic applications accepted. *Expenses:* $1,052 per credit, $55 activity fee per semester. *Financial support:* In 2017–18, 4 fellowships with partial tuition reimbursements, 22 teaching assistantships with partial tuition reimbursements were awarded; scholarships/grants and unspecified assistantships also available. Support available to part-time students. Financial award applicants required to submit FAFSA. *Faculty research:* Film and media studies, postcolonial literature, critical theory, arts and culture. *Unit head:* Dr. Leanne Doherty, Dean, 617-521-2581, E-mail: leanne.doherty@simmons.edu. *Application contact:* Patricia Flaherty, Director, Graduate Studies Admission, 617-521-3902, Fax: 617-521-3058, E-mail: gsa@simmons.edu.
Website: http://www.simmons.edu/gradstudies/

Simon Fraser University, Office of Graduate Studies and Postdoctoral Fellows, Faculty of Arts and Social Sciences, Department of English, Burnaby, BC V5A 1S6, Canada. Offers English (MA, PhD); teachers of English (MA). *Program availability:* Part-time. *Degree requirements:* For master's, one foreign language, thesis or alternative; for doctorate, one foreign language, thesis/dissertation, field exams. *Entrance*

requirements: For master's, minimum GPA of 3.0 (on scale of 4.33) or 3.33 based on last 60 credits of undergraduate courses; for doctorate, minimum GPA of 3.5 (on scale of 4.33). Additional exam requirements/recommendations for international students: Recommended—TOEFL (minimum score 580 paper-based; 93 iBT), IELTS (minimum score 7), TWE (minimum score 5). Electronic applications accepted. *Faculty research:* Literary criticism, literature and psychoanalysis, Renaissance drama and poetry, Shakespeare, Canadian and American literature.

Slippery Rock University of Pennsylvania, Graduate Studies (Recruitment), College of Liberal Arts, Department of English, Slippery Rock, PA 16057-1383. Offers MA. *Program availability:* Part-time, evening/weekend, online only, 100% online. *Degree requirements:* For master's, comprehensive exam (for some programs), thesis (for some programs). *Entrance requirements:* For master's, official transcripts, essay, two letters of recommendation. Additional exam requirements/recommendations for international students: Required—TOEFL (minimum score 550 paper-based; 80 iBT). Electronic applications accepted. *Expenses:* Contact institution.

Sonoma State University, Department of English, Rohnert Park, CA 94928. Offers American literature (MA); creative writing (MA); English literature (MA); world literature (MA). *Program availability:* Part-time, evening/weekend. *Degree requirements:* For master's, one foreign language, thesis or alternative. *Entrance requirements:* For master's, minimum GPA of 2.5. Additional exam requirements/recommendations for international students: Required—TOEFL (minimum score 500 paper-based). *Application deadline:* For fall admission, 11/30 priority date for domestic students. Application fee: $55. *Financial support:* Fellowships, teaching assistantships, career-related internships or fieldwork, and Federal Work-Study available. Financial award application deadline: 3/2; financial award applicants required to submit FAFSA. *Unit head:* Brantley L. Bryant, Chair, 707-664-2164, E-mail: brantley.bryant@sonoma.edu. *Application contact:* Dr. Stefan Kiesbye, Chair of Graduate Studies, 707-664-2403, Fax: 707-664-6040, E-mail: kiesbye@sonoma.edu.
Website: http://www.sonoma.edu/english/programs/ma-program.html

South Carolina State University, College of Graduate and Professional Studies, Department of Education, Orangeburg, SC 29117-0001. Offers early childhood education (MAT); education (M Ed); elementary education (M Ed, MAT); English (MAT); general science/biology (MAT); mathematics (MAT); secondary education (M Ed), including biology education, business education, counselor education, English education, home economics education, industrial education, mathematics education, science education, social studies education; special education (M Ed), including emotionally handicapped, learning disabilities, mentally handicapped. *Accreditation:* NCATE. *Program availability:* Part-time, evening/weekend. *Faculty:* 11 full-time (6 women), 4 part-time/adjunct (2 women). *Students:* 26 full-time (18 women), 22 part-time (17 women); includes 41 minority (all Black or African American, non-Hispanic/Latino), 1 international. Average age 33. 25 applicants, 100% accepted, 19 enrolled. In 2017, 6 master's awarded. *Degree requirements:* For master's, thesis optional, departmental qualifying exam. *Entrance requirements:* For master's, GRE General Test, NTE, interview, teaching certificate. *Application deadline:* For fall admission, 6/15 priority date for domestic students, 6/15 for international students; for spring admission, 11/1 for domestic and international students. Application fee: $25. Electronic applications accepted. *Expenses:* Tuition, state resident: full-time $9388; part-time $607 per credit hour. Tuition, nonresident: full-time $19,968; part-time $1194 per credit hour. *Required fees:* $766; $766 per credit hour. *Financial support:* Fellowships, career-related internships or fieldwork, Federal Work-Study, and scholarships/grants available. Financial award application deadline: 6/1. *Unit head:* Dr. Charlie Spell, Interim Chair, Department of Education, 803-536-8963, Fax: 803-516-4568, E-mail: cspell@scsu.edu. *Application contact:* Curtis Foskey, Coordinator of Graduate Studies, 803-536-8419, Fax: 803-536-8812, E-mail: cfoskey@scsu.edu.

South Dakota State University, Graduate School, College of Arts and Science, Department of English, Brookings, SD 57007. Offers MA. *Program availability:* Part-time. *Degree requirements:* For master's, comprehensive exam (for some programs), thesis (for some programs), oral and written exams. *Entrance requirements:* For master's, minimum GPA of 2.75. Additional exam requirements/recommendations for international students: Required—TOEFL (minimum score 600 paper-based; 100 iBT). *Faculty research:* English and American literature topics, regional literature (Midwestern), women's literature, Lakota literature and culture, rhetoric and writing.

Southeastern Louisiana University, College of Arts, Humanities and Social Sciences, Department of English, Hammond, LA 70402. Offers creative writing (MA); language and theory (MA); professional writing (MA); publishing studies (MA). *Program availability:* Part-time. *Faculty:* 10 full-time (2 women). *Students:* 11 full-time (9 women), 11 part-time (10 women); includes 5 minority (2 Black or African American, non-Hispanic/Latino; 2 Hispanic/Latino; 1 Two or more races, non-Hispanic/Latino). Average age 25. 8 applicants, 38% accepted, 3 enrolled. In 2017, 8 master's awarded. *Degree requirements:* For master's, comprehensive exam, thesis optional. *Entrance requirements:* For master's, GRE (minimum score of 290 combined verbal and quantitative). Additional exam requirements/recommendations for international students: Required—TOEFL (minimum score 500 paper-based; 61 iBT), IELTS (minimum score 5.5). *Application deadline:* For fall admission, 7/15 priority date for domestic students, 6/1 priority date for international students; for spring admission, 12/1 priority date for domestic students, 10/1 priority date for international students. Applications are processed on a rolling basis. Application fee: $20 ($30 for international students). Electronic applications accepted. *Expenses:* Tuition, state resident: full-time $6684. Tuition, nonresident: full-time $19,162. *Required fees:* $2088. *Financial support:* In 2017–18, 16 students received support, including 7 teaching assistantships (averaging $5,415 per year); research assistantships, institutionally sponsored loans, scholarships/grants, and unspecified assistantships also available. Support available to part-time students. Financial award application deadline: 5/1; financial award applicants required to submit FAFSA. *Faculty research:* John Ruskin, animal studies, linguistics, film studies. *Unit head:* Dr. David Hanson, Department Head, 985-549-2100, Fax: 985-549-5021, E-mail: dhanson@southeastern.edu. *Application contact:* Amanda Harper, Graduate Admissions Analyst, 985-549-5620, Fax: 985-549-5632, E-mail: admissions@southeastern.edu.
Website: http://www.southeastern.edu/acad_research/depts/engl

Southeast Missouri State University, School of Graduate Studies, Department of English, Cape Girardeau, MO 63701-4799. Offers teaching English to speakers of other languages (MA). *Program availability:* Part-time, evening/weekend, online learning. *Faculty:* 17 full-time (8 women). *Students:* 44 full-time (33 women), 36 part-time (27 women); includes 1 minority (Hispanic/Latino), 28 international. Average age 31. 35 applicants, 94% accepted, 28 enrolled. In 2017, 42 master's awarded. *Degree requirements:* For master's, comprehensive exam (for some programs), thesis optional. *Entrance requirements:* Additional exam requirements/recommendations for international students: Required—TOEFL (minimum score 550 paper-based; 79 iBT), IELTS (minimum score 6), PTE (minimum score 53). *Application deadline:* For fall admission, 8/1 for domestic students, 6/1 for international students; for spring admission, 11/21 for domestic students, 10/1 for international students; for summer admission, 5/15 for domestic students. Applications are processed on a rolling basis. Application fee: $30 ($40 for international students). Electronic applications accepted. *Expenses:* $270.35 per credit hour in-state tuition, $33.40 per credit hour fees. *Financial support:* In 2017–18, 17 students received support, including 25 teaching assistantships with full tuition reimbursements available; career-related internships or fieldwork, Federal Work-Study, scholarships/grants, traineeships, tuition waivers (full), and unspecified assistantships also available. Financial award application deadline: 6/30; financial award applicants required to submit FAFSA. *Faculty research:* Literature, creative writing, technical writing, secondary English education, teaching English as a second language. *Unit head:* Dr. Susan Kendrick, Department of English Chair, 573-651-2156, Fax: 573-651-5188, E-mail: skendrick@semo.edu. *Application contact:* 573-651-2590, E-mail: admissions@semo.edu.
Website: http://www.semo.edu/english/

Southern Connecticut State University, School of Graduate Studies, School of Arts and Sciences, Department of English, New Haven, CT 06515-1355. Offers MA, MS, MLS/MS. *Program availability:* Part-time, evening/weekend. *Degree requirements:* For master's, one foreign language, thesis or alternative. *Entrance requirements:* For master's, interview. Electronic applications accepted.

Southern Illinois University Carbondale, Graduate School, College of Liberal Arts, Department of English, Carbondale, IL 62901-4701. Offers composition (MA, PhD), including composition, literature, rhetoric; creative writing (MFA). *Degree requirements:* For master's, one foreign language, thesis; for doctorate, 2 foreign languages, thesis/dissertation. *Entrance requirements:* For master's, GRE General Test, GRE Subject Test, minimum GPA of 2.7; for doctorate, GRE General Test, GRE Subject Test, minimum GPA of 3.25. Additional exam requirements/recommendations for international students: Required—TOEFL. *Faculty research:* British literature, English literature, modern Continental literature, literary criticism and theory, film studies, Irish studies.

Southern Illinois University Edwardsville, Graduate School, College of Arts and Sciences, Department of English Language and Literature, Program in Literature, Edwardsville, IL 62026. Offers MA, Postbaccalaureate Certificate. *Program availability:* Part-time. *Degree requirements:* For master's, one foreign language, thesis (for some programs), written papers, oral examination. *Entrance requirements:* Additional exam requirements/recommendations for international students: Required—TOEFL (minimum score 550 paper-based, 79 iBT), IELTS (minimum score 6.5), Michigan Test of English Language Proficiency or PTE. Electronic applications accepted.

Southern Methodist University, Dedman College of Humanities and Sciences, Department of English, Dallas, TX 75275. Offers MA, PhD. Terminal master's awarded for partial completion of doctoral program. *Degree requirements:* For master's, one foreign language, comprehensive exam, thesis optional, oral exam; for doctorate, one foreign language, comprehensive exam, thesis/dissertation. *Entrance requirements:* For master's, GRE General Test, minimum GPA of 3.0; for doctorate, GRE General Test, minimum GPA of 3.5, BA in English or other appropriate field. Additional exam requirements/recommendations for international students: Required—TOEFL (minimum score 550 paper-based). Electronic applications accepted. *Faculty research:* British/American literature, critical theory, medieval studies, gender studies, book history.

Southern New Hampshire University, School of Arts and Sciences, Manchester, NH 03106-1045. Offers clinical mental health counseling (MS); creative writing (MA); criminal justice (MS); cyber security (MS); English (MA); fiction and nonfiction (MFA); history (MA); political science (MS); psychology (MS). *Program availability:* Part-time, evening/weekend. *Degree requirements:* For master's, one foreign language, thesis. *Entrance requirements:* For master's, minimum GPA of 2.75 (for MS in teaching English as a foreign language), 3.0 (for MFA). Additional exam requirements/recommendations for international students: Required—TOEFL (minimum score 550 paper-based; 79 iBT), IELTS (minimum score 6.5), TWE (minimum score 5). *Application deadline:* For fall admission, 7/1 priority date for domestic students; for winter admission, 11/1 priority date for domestic students; for spring admission, 6/1 priority date for domestic students. Applications are processed on a rolling basis. Application fee: $40. Electronic applications accepted. *Expenses:* Contact institution. *Financial support:* Research assistantships, career-related internships or fieldwork, and scholarships/grants available. Financial award applicants required to submit FAFSA. *Faculty research:* Action research, state of the art practice in behavioral health services, wraparound approaches to working with youth, learning styles. *Unit head:* Steven K. Johnson, Dean, 603-629-4626. *Application contact:* Office of Graduate Admission, 888-327-SNHU, Fax: 603-644-3144, E-mail: enroll@snhu.edu.

Spring Hill College, Graduate Programs, Program in Liberal Arts, Mobile, AL 36608-1791. Offers fine arts (MLA); leadership and ethics (MLA, Postbaccalaureate Certificate); literature (MLA). *Program availability:* Part-time, evening/weekend. *Faculty:* 11 full-time (1 woman). *Students:* 1 (woman) full-time, 21 part-time (7 women); includes 5 minority (4 Black or African American, non-Hispanic/Latino; 1 Hispanic/Latino), 6 international. Average age 31. In 2017, 12 master's awarded. *Degree requirements:* For master's, capstone course, completion of program within 6 years of initial admittance. *Entrance requirements:* For master's, bachelor's degree with minimum undergraduate GPA of 3.0 or graduate/professional degree. Additional exam requirements/recommendations for international students: Required—TOEFL (minimum score 550 paper-based; 80 iBT), IELTS (minimum score 6.5), CPE or CAE (minimum score C), Michigan English Language Assessment Battery (minimum score 90). *Application deadline:* For fall admission, 8/1 priority date for domestic and international students; for spring admission, 12/1 priority date for domestic and international students. Applications are processed on a rolling basis. Application fee: $25 ($35 for international students). Electronic applications accepted. *Expenses:* Contact institution. *Financial support:* Applicants required to submit FAFSA. *Unit head:* Dr. Thomas J. Hoffman, Director, 251-380-4184, Fax: 251-460-2115, E-mail: thoffman@shc.edu. *Application contact:* Robert Stewart, Vice President of Enrollment, 251-380-3030, Fax: 251-460-2186, E-mail: rstewart@shc.edu.
Website: http://ug.shc.edu/graduate-degrees/master-liberal-arts/

Stanford University, School of Humanities and Sciences, Department of English, Stanford, CA 94305-2004. Offers MA, PhD. Terminal master's awarded for partial completion of doctoral program. *Degree requirements:* For master's, one foreign language, thesis (for some programs); for doctorate, 2 foreign languages, thesis/dissertation, oral exam. *Entrance requirements:* For master's and doctorate, GRE General Test, GRE Subject Test. Additional exam requirements/recommendations for international students: Required—TOEFL. Electronic applications accepted. *Expenses:* *Tuition:* Full-time $48,987; part-time $10,620 per quarter. One-time fee: $400. Tuition and fees vary according to program.

State University of New York at Fredonia, College of Liberal Arts and Sciences, Fredonia, NY 14063-1136. Offers biology (MS); English (MA); English education 7-12 (MA); interdisciplinary studies (MA, MS); math education (MS Ed); professional writing (CAS); speech pathology (MS); MA/MS. *Program availability:* Part-time, evening/weekend. *Students:* 73 full-time (62 women), 9 part-time (6 women); includes 7 minority (1 Black or African American, non-Hispanic/Latino; 1 Asian, non-Hispanic/Latino; 2 Hispanic/Latino; 1 Native Hawaiian or other Pacific Islander, non-Hispanic/Latino; 2 Two or more races, non-Hispanic/Latino). Average age 24. 200 applicants, 25% accepted, 43 enrolled. In 2017, 41 master's, 1 other advanced degree awarded. *Degree requirements:* For master's, comprehensive exam (for some programs), thesis (for some

programs). *Entrance requirements:* For master's, GRE. Additional exam requirements/recommendations for international students: Required—TOEFL (minimum score 79 iBT), IELTS (minimum score 6.5). *Application deadline:* Applications are processed on a rolling basis. Application fee: $75. Electronic applications accepted. *Expenses:* Tuition, state resident: full-time $8154. Tuition, nonresident: full-time $16,650. *Required fees:* $1209. *Financial support:* In 2017–18, 5 students received support, including 14 teaching assistantships with full and partial tuition reimbursements available (averaging $5,957 per year); tuition waivers (full and partial) and unspecified assistantships also available. *Faculty research:* Immunology/microbiology, applied human physiology, ecology and evolution, invertebrate biology, molecular biology, biochemistry, physiology, animal behavior, science education, vertebrate physiology, cell biology, plant biology, developmental biology, aquatic ecology, bilingual language acquisition, bilingual language acquisition and disorders, augmentative and alternate communication with ALS, World War I, Zweig, environmental literature, editing, adolescent literature, pedagogy. *Unit head:* Dr. Andy Karafa, Dean, 716-673-3173, Fax: 716-673-3338, E-mail: andy.karafa@gmail.com. *Application contact:* Wendy S. Dunst, Interim Graduate Recruitment and Admissions Associate, 716-673-3808, Fax: 716-673-3712, E-mail: wendy.dunst@fredonia.edu.
Website: http://www.fredonia.edu/clas/

State University of New York at New Paltz, Graduate and Extended Learning School, School of Liberal Arts and Sciences, Department of English, New Paltz, NY 12561. Offers MA. *Program availability:* Part-time, evening/weekend. *Faculty:* 9 full-time (2 women). *Students:* 9 full-time (4 women), 29 part-time (17 women); includes 3 minority (1 Black or African American, non-Hispanic/Latino; 2 Hispanic/Latino), 1 international. 16 applicants, 94% accepted, 15 enrolled. In 2017, 15 master's awarded. *Degree requirements:* For master's, comprehensive exam, thesis (for some programs), foreign language proficiency exam. *Entrance requirements:* For master's, minimum GPA of 3.0, 10-15 page writing sample. Additional exam requirements/recommendations for international students: Required—TOEFL (minimum score 563 paper-based; 85 iBT), IELTS (minimum score 7). *Application deadline:* For fall admission, 3/15 priority date for domestic students, 3/15 for international students; for spring admission, 10/15 for domestic and international students. Application fee: $50. Electronic applications accepted. *Financial support:* In 2017–18, 1 research assistantship with partial tuition reimbursement (averaging $5,000 per year), 17 teaching assistantships with partial tuition reimbursements (averaging $5,000 per year) were awarded. Financial award application deadline: 8/1. *Faculty research:* Twentieth-century British literature, Hemingway and modernism, British modernist fiction, Faulkner and the Southern Renaissance, revisionary approaches to early twentieth-century literature. *Unit head:* Dr. Nancy Johnson, Chair, 845-257-2720, E-mail: english@newpaltz.edu. *Application contact:* Dr. Cy Mulready, Director of Graduate Studies, 845-257-2739, E-mail: mulreadc@newpaltz.edu.
Website: http://www.newpaltz.edu/english/

State University of New York at Oswego, Graduate Studies, College of Liberal Arts and Sciences, Department of English, Oswego, NY 13126. Offers MA. *Program availability:* Part-time. *Degree requirements:* For master's, thesis optional. *Entrance requirements:* Additional exam requirements/recommendations for international students: Required—TOEFL (minimum score 560 paper-based).

State University of New York College at Cortland, Graduate Studies, School of Arts and Sciences, Department of English, Cortland, NY 13045. Offers MA. *Program availability:* Part-time, evening/weekend. *Degree requirements:* For master's, one foreign language, comprehensive exam, thesis. *Entrance requirements:* For master's, GRE General Test.

State University of New York College at Potsdam, School of Arts and Sciences, Department of English and Communication, Potsdam, NY 13676. Offers MA. *Program availability:* Part-time, evening/weekend. *Degree requirements:* For master's, one foreign language, thesis or alternative. *Entrance requirements:* For master's, minimum GPA of 3.0 in last 60 hours of undergraduate course work. Additional exam requirements/recommendations for international students: Required—TOEFL (minimum score 550 paper-based; 80 iBT), IELTS (minimum score 6). Electronic applications accepted.

Stephen F. Austin State University, Graduate School, College of Liberal Arts, Department of English and Philosophy, Nacogdoches, TX 75962. Offers English (MA). *Degree requirements:* For master's, comprehensive exam. *Entrance requirements:* For master's, GRE General Test. Additional exam requirements/recommendations for international students: Required—TOEFL. *Faculty research:* Creative writing, Latin American literature, modern American literature, modern British literature, literature for children.

Stony Brook University, State University of New York, Graduate School, College of Arts and Sciences, Department of Cultural Studies and Comparative Literature, Stony Brook, NY 11794. Offers comparative literature (MA, PhD); cultural studies (PhD, Certificate). *Program availability:* Evening/weekend. *Faculty:* 10 full-time (3 women). *Students:* 49 full-time (35 women), 4 part-time (all women); includes 9 minority (1 Black or African American, non-Hispanic/Latino; 4 Asian, non-Hispanic/Latino; 4 Hispanic/Latino), 17 international. Average age 34. 65 applicants, 29% accepted, 6 enrolled. In 2017, 6 master's, 5 doctorates, 5 other advanced degrees awarded. Terminal master's awarded for partial completion of doctoral program. *Degree requirements:* For master's, 2 foreign languages, exam; for doctorate, 3 foreign languages, comprehensive exam, thesis/dissertation. *Entrance requirements:* For master's and doctorate, GRE General Test, minimum GPA of 3.5 in major, 3.0 overall. Additional exam requirements/recommendations for international students: Required—TOEFL. *Application deadline:* For fall admission, 1/15 for domestic students; for spring admission, 10/1 for domestic students. Application fee: $100. Electronic applications accepted. *Expenses:* Contact institution. *Financial support:* In 2017–18, 17 teaching assistantships were awarded; fellowships and research assistantships also available. *Faculty research:* Humanities, women's studies, literary criticism, gender studies, philosophy. *Unit head:* 631-632-7464, Fax: 631-632-5707. *Application contact:* Mary Moran-Luba, Coordinator, 631-632-7460, Fax: 631-632-5707, E-mail: mary.moran-luba@stonybrook.edu.
Website: http://www.stonybrook.edu/commcms/cat/index.html

Stony Brook University, State University of New York, Graduate School, College of Arts and Sciences, Department of English, Stony Brook, NY 11794. Offers English (MA, PhD); English education (MAT). MAT offered through the School of Professional Development. *Faculty:* 20 full-time (10 women), 5 part-time/adjunct (2 women). *Students:* 45 full-time (23 women), 10 part-time (8 women); includes 10 minority (3 Asian, non-Hispanic/Latino; 5 Hispanic/Latino; 2 Two or more races, non-Hispanic/Latino), 4 international. Average age 31. 69 applicants, 38% accepted, 10 enrolled. In 2017, 9 master's, 8 doctorates awarded. Terminal master's awarded for partial completion of doctoral program. *Degree requirements:* For doctorate, thesis/dissertation. *Entrance requirements:* For master's and doctorate, GRE General Test. Additional exam requirements/recommendations for international students: Required—TOEFL. *Application deadline:* For fall admission, 1/15 for domestic students; for spring admission, 10/1 for domestic students. Application fee: $100. Electronic applications accepted. *Expenses:* Contact institution. *Financial support:* In 2017–18, 25 teaching assistantships were awarded; fellowships and research assistantships also available. *Faculty research:* Humanities, poetry, literary theory, rhetoric, American literature. *Unit head:* Dr. Celia Marshik, Chair, 631-632-7356, E-mail: celia.marshik@stonybrook.edu. *Application contact:* Theresa Spadola, Coordinator, 631-632-7373, E-mail: theresa.spadola@stonybrook.edu.
Website: http://www.stonybrook.edu/english/

Sul Ross State University, College of Arts and Sciences, Department of Languages and Literature, Alpine, TX 79832. Offers English (MA). *Program availability:* Part-time, evening/weekend. *Degree requirements:* For master's, thesis optional. *Entrance requirements:* For master's, GRE General Test, minimum GPA of 2.5 in last 60 hours of undergraduate work. *Faculty research:* Narrative theory, feminist literary criticism, autobiography studies, multiculturalism, biblical narrative.

Syracuse University, College of Arts and Sciences, English Department, Syracuse, NY 13244. Offers MA, PhD. *Degree requirements:* For master's, thesis; for doctorate, comprehensive exam, thesis/dissertation. *Entrance requirements:* For master's and doctorate, GRE General Test, transcript from undergraduate/graduate institution, intellectual statement, three letters of recommendation, writing sample, teaching statement. Additional exam requirements/recommendations for international students: Required—TOEFL (minimum score 100 iBT). *Application deadline:* For fall admission, 1/9 for domestic and international students. Application fee: $75. Electronic applications accepted. *Financial support:* Fellowships with full tuition reimbursements, teaching assistantships with full tuition reimbursements, scholarships/grants, and tuition waivers available. Financial award application deadline: 1/1. *Faculty research:* Critical theory, early modern studies, American studies, literary and filmic periods, reception and book history. *Unit head:* Harvey Teres, Professor/Director of Graduate Studies, English, 315-443-4891, E-mail: hmteres@syr.edu. *Application contact:* Terri Zollo, Graduate Coordinator, 315-443-2174, E-mail: tazollo@syr.edu.
Website: http://english.syr.edu/graduate/graduate-programs.html

Tarleton State University, College of Graduate Studies, College of Liberal and Fine Arts, Department of English and Languages, Stephenville, TX 76402. Offers English (MA). *Program availability:* Part-time, evening/weekend, 100% online, blended/hybrid learning. *Faculty:* 6 full-time (4 women). *Students:* 4 full-time (2 women), 14 part-time (12 women); includes 3 minority (1 Asian, non-Hispanic/Latino; 1 Hispanic/Latino; 1 Two or more races, non-Hispanic/Latino). Average age 34. 14 applicants, 86% accepted, 7 enrolled. In 2017, 1 master's awarded. *Degree requirements:* For master's, comprehensive exam, thesis (for some programs). *Entrance requirements:* For master's, GRE General Test, minimum GPA of 3.0. Additional exam requirements/recommendations for international students: Required—TOEFL (minimum score 550 paper-based; 80 iBT), IELTS (minimum score 6). *Application deadline:* For fall admission, 8/15 priority date for domestic students; for spring admission, 1/7 for domestic students. Applications are processed on a rolling basis. Application fee: $45 ($145 for international students). Electronic applications accepted. *Expenses:* Contact institution. *Financial support:* Research assistantships, teaching assistantships, career-related internships or fieldwork, and Federal Work-Study available. Support available to part-time students. Financial award application deadline: 5/1; financial award applicants required to submit FAFSA. *Unit head:* Dr. Jeanelle Barrett, Head, 254-968-9039, Fax: 254-968-1931, E-mail: jbarrett@tarleton.edu. *Application contact:* Information Contact, 254-968-9104, Fax: 254-968-9670, E-mail: gradoffice@tarleton.edu.
Website: https://www.tarleton.edu/english/

Temple University, College of Liberal Arts, Department of English, Philadelphia, PA 19122-6096. Offers creative writing (MFA); English (MA, PhD). *Program availability:* Part-time. *Faculty:* 22 full-time (9 women), 14 part-time/adjunct (4 women). *Students:* 71 full-time (39 women), 8 part-time (7 women); includes 17 minority (4 Black or African American, non-Hispanic/Latino; 1 American Indian or Alaska Native, non-Hispanic/Latino; 7 Asian, non-Hispanic/Latino; 5 Hispanic/Latino), 5 international. 107 applicants, 67% accepted, 17 enrolled. In 2017, 9 master's, 8 doctorates awarded. *Degree requirements:* For doctorate, 2 foreign languages, thesis/dissertation. *Entrance requirements:* For master's and doctorate, GRE General Test, minimum GPA of 3.0; 3 letters of recommendation. Additional exam requirements/recommendations for international students: Required—TOEFL (minimum score 620 paper-based; 105 iBT). *Application deadline:* For fall admission, 12/15 for domestic and international students. Application fee: $60. Electronic applications accepted. *Expenses:* Tuition, state resident: full-time $16,164; part-time $898 per credit hour. Tuition, nonresident: full-time $22,158; part-time $1231 per credit hour. *Required fees:* $890; $445 per semester. Full-time tuition and fees vary according to course load, degree level, campus/location and program. *Financial support:* Fellowships, teaching assistantships, and Federal Work-Study available. Financial award application deadline: 1/15; financial award applicants required to submit FAFSA. *Faculty research:* Early modern British literature, American literature, modernism, critical theory, rhetoric, composition. *Unit head:* Don Lee, MFA Program Director, 215-204-1796, Fax: 215-204-9620, E-mail: don.lee@temple.edu. *Application contact:* Sharon Logan, Coordinator, 215-204-1796, Fax: 215-204-9620, E-mail: logansd@temple.edu.
Website: http://www.cla.temple.edu/english/

Tennessee Technological University, College of Graduate Studies, College of Arts and Sciences, Department of English, Cookeville, TN 38505. Offers MA. *Program availability:* Part-time. *Faculty:* 23 full-time (8 women). *Students:* 4 full-time (3 women), 5 part-time (3 women). 7 applicants, 86% accepted, 5 enrolled. In 2017, 4 master's awarded. *Degree requirements:* For master's, comprehensive exam, thesis or alternative. *Entrance requirements:* For master's, GRE General Test. Additional exam requirements/recommendations for international students: Required—TOEFL (minimum score 527 paper-based; 71 iBT), IELTS (minimum score 5.5), PTE (minimum score 48), or TOEIC (Test of English as an International Communication). *Application deadline:* For fall admission, 8/1 for domestic students, 5/1 for international students; for spring admission, 12/1 for domestic students, 10/1 for international students; for summer admission, 5/1 for domestic students, 2/1 for international students. Applications are processed on a rolling basis. Application fee: $35 ($40 for international students). Electronic applications accepted. *Expenses:* Tuition, state resident: full-time $9925; part-time $565 per credit hour. Tuition, nonresident: full-time $22,993; part-time $1291 per credit hour. *Financial support:* In 2017–18, 8 teaching assistantships (averaging $8,000 per year) were awarded; fellowships and research assistantships also available. Financial award application deadline: 4/1. *Unit head:* Dr. Ted Pelton, Chairperson, 931-372-3343, Fax: 931-372-6142, E-mail: tpelton@tntech.edu. *Application contact:* Shelia K. Kendrick, Coordinator of Graduate Studies, 931-372-3808, Fax: 931-372-3497, E-mail: skendrick@tntech.edu.

Texas A&M International University, Office of Graduate Studies and Research, College of Arts and Sciences, Department of Humanities, Laredo, TX 78041. Offers English (MA); Hispanic studies (PhD); history and political thought (MA); language, literature and translation (MA). *Degree requirements:* For master's, comprehensive exam (for some programs), thesis (for some programs). *Entrance requirements:* For master's, GRE General Test. Additional exam requirements/recommendations for international students: Required—TOEFL (minimum score 550 paper-based; 79 iBT).

Texas A&M University, College of Liberal Arts, Department of English, College Station, TX 77843. Offers MA, PhD. *Faculty:* 42. *Students:* 61 full-time (47 women), 26 part-time (17 women); includes 14 minority (2 Black or African American, non-Hispanic/Latino; 1

American Indian or Alaska Native, non-Hispanic/Latino; 2 Asian, non-Hispanic/Latino; 7 Hispanic/Latino; 2 Two or more races, non-Hispanic/Latino), 25 international. Average age 32. 61 applicants, 56% accepted, 23 enrolled. In 2017, 11 master's, 5 doctorates awarded. Terminal master's awarded for partial completion of doctoral program. *Degree requirements:* For master's, one foreign language, thesis optional; for doctorate, 2 foreign languages, thesis/dissertation. *Entrance requirements:* For master's and doctorate, GRE General Test, sample of written work. Additional exam requirements/recommendations for international students: Required—TOEFL (minimum score 550 paper-based; 80 iBT), IELTS (minimum score 6), PTE (minimum score 53). *Application deadline:* For fall admission, 1/16 for domestic students, 2/1 for international students. Applications are processed on a rolling basis. Application fee: $50 ($90 for international students). Electronic applications accepted. *Expenses:* Contact institution. *Financial support:* In 2017–18, 64 students received support, including 5 fellowships with tuition reimbursements available (averaging $27,520 per year), 7 research assistantships with tuition reimbursements available (averaging $6,643 per year), 59 teaching assistantships with tuition reimbursements available (averaging $9,433 per year); career-related internships or fieldwork, institutionally sponsored loans, scholarships/grants, traineeships, health care benefits, tuition waivers (full and partial), and unspecified assistantships also available. Support available to part-time students. Financial award application deadline: 3/15; financial award applicants required to submit FAFSA. *Faculty research:* American, Renaissance, medieval, textual, and discourse studies. *Unit head:* Dr. Maura Ives, Interim Department Head, 979-845-8319, E-mail: m-ives@tamu.edu. *Application contact:* Director of Graduate Studies, 979-845-9836, Fax: 979-862-2292, E-mail: grad-program@tamuenglish.org.
Website: http://www.english.tamu.edu/

Texas A&M University–Commerce, College of Humanities, Social Sciences and Arts, Commerce, TX 75429. Offers applied criminology (MS); applied linguistics (MA, MS); art (MA, MFA); computational linguistics (Graduate Certificate); creative writing (Graduate Certificate); criminal justice management (Graduate Certificate); criminal justice studies (Graduate Certificate); English (MA, MS, PhD); film studies (Graduate Certificate); history (MA, MS); history of Christianity (Graduate Certificate); Holocaust studies (Graduate Certificate); homeland security (Graduate Certificate); music education (MM); music performance (MM); political science (MA, MS); public history (Graduate Certificate); sociology (MS); Spanish (MA); studies in children's and adolescent literature and culture (Graduate Certificate); teaching English to speakers of other languages (Graduate Certificate); theater (MA, MS); world history (Graduate Certificate). *Program availability:* Part-time. *Faculty:* 56 full-time (26 women), 10 part-time/adjunct (5 women). *Students:* 133 full-time (85 women), 439 part-time (311 women); includes 204 minority (79 Black or African American, non-Hispanic/Latino; 4 American Indian or Alaska Native, non-Hispanic/Latino; 9 Asian, non-Hispanic/Latino; 98 Hispanic/Latino; 14 Two or more races, non-Hispanic/Latino), 26 international. Average age 36. 261 applicants, 50% accepted, 113 enrolled. In 2017, 105 master's, 5 doctorates awarded. *Degree requirements:* For master's, one foreign language, comprehensive exam, thesis (for some programs); for doctorate, one foreign language, comprehensive exam, thesis/dissertation, departmental qualifying exam. *Entrance requirements:* For master's and doctorate, GRE General Test. Additional exam requirements/recommendations for international students: Required—TOEFL (minimum score 550 paper-based; 79 iBT), IELTS (minimum score 6). *Application deadline:* Applications are processed on a rolling basis. Application fee: $50. Electronic applications accepted. *Expenses:* Contact institution. *Financial support:* In 2017–18, 43 students received support, including 9 research assistantships with partial tuition reimbursements available (averaging $9,000 per year), 68 teaching assistantships with partial tuition reimbursements available (averaging $9,000 per year); Federal Work-Study, institutionally sponsored loans, scholarships/grants, health care benefits, and unspecified assistantships also available. Financial award application deadline: 5/1; financial award applicants required to submit FAFSA. *Unit head:* Dr. William F. Kuracina, Interim Dean, 903-886-5166, Fax: 903-886-5774, E-mail: william.kuracina@tamuc.edu. *Application contact:* Vicky Turner, Doctoral Degree and Special Programs Coordinator, 903-886-5167, E-mail: vicky.turner@tamuc.edu.
Website: http://www.tamuc.edu/academics/graduateSchool/programs/humanitiesSocialScienceArts/default.aspx

Texas A&M University–Corpus Christi, College of Graduate Studies, College of Liberal Arts, Program in English, Corpus Christi, TX 78412. Offers MA. *Program availability:* Part-time, evening/weekend. *Students:* 8 full-time (5 women), 15 part-time (13 women); includes 11 minority (1 Black or African American, non-Hispanic/Latino; 10 Hispanic/Latino). Average age 32. 12 applicants, 75% accepted, 7 enrolled. In 2017, 11 master's awarded. *Degree requirements:* For master's, comprehensive exam, thesis optional, capstone experience. *Entrance requirements:* For master's, essay (500-1,000 words), writing sample (minimum of 2,000 words), 3 letters of recommendation. Additional exam requirements/recommendations for international students: Required—TOEFL (minimum score 550 paper-based; 79 iBT), IELTS (minimum score 6.5). *Application deadline:* For fall admission, 8/13 for domestic students, 5/1 for international students; for spring admission, 1/1 for domestic students, 11/1 for international students; for summer admission, 5/15 for domestic students. Applications are processed on a rolling basis. Application fee: $50 ($70 for international students). Electronic applications accepted. *Expenses:* Tuition, state resident: full-time $3568; part-time $198.24 per credit hour. Tuition, nonresident: full-time $11,038; part-time $613.24 per credit hour. *Required fees:* $2129; $1422.58 per semester. Tuition and fees vary according to program. *Financial support:* Research assistantships, career-related internships or fieldwork, Federal Work-Study, institutionally sponsored loans, scholarships/grants, health care benefits, and unspecified assistantships available. Support available to part-time students. Financial award application deadline: 3/15; financial award applicants required to submit FAFSA. *Unit head:* Dr. Kathryn Santos, Graduate Coordinator, 361-825-3826, E-mail: kathryn.santos@tamucc.edu. *Application contact:* Graduate Admissions Coordinator, 361-825-2177, Fax: 361-825-2755, E-mail: gradweb@tamucc.edu.
Website: http://cla.tamucc.edu/english/pages/graduate.html

Texas A&M University–Kingsville, College of Graduate Studies, College of Arts and Sciences, Department of Language and Literature, Kingsville, TX 78363. Offers cultural studies (MA); English (MA, MS); Spanish (MA). *Entrance requirements:* Additional exam requirements/recommendations for international students: Required—TOEFL (minimum score 550 paper-based; 79 iBT); Recommended—IELTS. Electronic applications accepted.

Texas A&M University–San Antonio, School of Arts and Sciences, San Antonio, TX 78224. Offers English (MA). *Program availability:* Part-time, evening/weekend, online learning. *Faculty:* 6 full-time (4 women). *Students:* 6 full-time (all women), 13 part-time (9 women); includes 13 minority (1 Black or African American, non-Hispanic/Latino; 11 Hispanic/Latino; 1 Two or more races, non-Hispanic/Latino). Average age 31. 20 applicants, 40% accepted, 4 enrolled. In 2017, 5 master's awarded. *Degree requirements:* For master's, comprehensive exam, thesis. *Entrance requirements:* For master's, GRE (Verbal and Writing), analytical writing sample of 6-10 pages; two letters of recommendation, at least one from former professor. Additional exam requirements/recommendations for international students: Required—TOEFL (minimum score 550 paper-based; 79 iBT), IELTS (minimum score 6). *Application deadline:* For fall admission, 3/15 priority date for domestic and international students; for spring admission, 11/1 priority date for domestic and international students; for summer admission, 4/1 priority date for domestic and international students. Applications are processed on a rolling basis. Application fee: $35 ($50 for international students). Electronic applications accepted. *Expenses:* Tuition, state resident: full-time $3475; part-time $1930 per semester. Tuition, nonresident: full-time $10,945; part-time $6080 per semester. *Required fees:* $2148; $1412 per year. $706 per semester. Tuition and fees vary according to course load. *Financial support:* Federal Work-Study, scholarships/grants, and tuition waivers available. Financial award application deadline: 3/15; financial award applicants required to submit FAFSA. *Unit head:* Dr. Katherine Gillen, Graduate Coordinator. *Application contact:* Caitie Garza, Graduate Admissions Coordinator, 210-784-1300, E-mail: beajaguar@tamusa.edu.
Website: http://www.tamusa.edu/collegeofartsandsciences/artsandhumanities/english/GradProgram.html

Texas A&M University–Texarkana, Graduate Studies and Research, College of Education and Liberal Arts, Texarkana, TX 75503. Offers adult education (MS); curriculum and instruction (M Ed); education (MS); educational administration (M Ed); English (MA); instructional technology (MS); interdisciplinary studies (MA, MS); special education (MS). *Program availability:* Part-time, evening/weekend. *Degree requirements:* For master's, comprehensive exam (for some programs), thesis optional. *Entrance requirements:* For master's, minimum GPA of 2.5 on last 60 hours of bachelor's degree. Additional exam requirements/recommendations for international students: Required—TOEFL. Electronic applications accepted.

Texas Christian University, AddRan College of Liberal Arts, Department of English, Fort Worth, TX 76129. Offers English (MA, PhD); rhetoric and composition (PhD). *Faculty:* 16 full-time (11 women), 1 (woman) part-time/adjunct. *Students:* 60 full-time (48 women); includes 12 minority (3 Black or African American, non-Hispanic/Latino; 6 Hispanic/Latino; 3 Two or more races, non-Hispanic/Latino), 3 international. Average age 29. 29 applicants, 34% accepted, 10 enrolled. In 2017, 1 master's, 5 doctorates awarded. *Degree requirements:* For master's, one foreign language, thesis; for doctorate, one foreign language, comprehensive exam, thesis/dissertation. *Entrance requirements:* For master's and doctorate, GRE General Test. Additional exam requirements/recommendations for international students: Required—TOEFL. *Application deadline:* 1/10 for domestic and international students. Application fee: $60. Electronic applications accepted. *Expenses:* Contact institution. *Financial support:* In 2017–18, 55 students received support, including 4 fellowships with full tuition reimbursements available (averaging $21,000 per year), 6 research assistantships with full tuition reimbursements available, 25 teaching assistantships with full tuition reimbursements available (averaging $17,000 per year); Federal Work-Study, tuition waivers (full and partial), and unspecified assistantships also available. Financial award application deadline: 1/10; financial award applicants required to submit FAFSA. *Faculty research:* Literary studies, rhetoric and composition, new media and digital humanities, print culture, women and gender studies. *Total annual research expenditures:* $10,000. *Unit head:* Dr. Brad E. Lucas, Director of Graduate Studies, 817-257-6981, Fax: 817-257-6238, E-mail: b.e.lucas2@tcu.edu. *Application contact:* Merry Roberts, English Department Office Manager, 817-257-6890, Fax: 817-257-6238, E-mail: m.roberts@tcu.edu.
Website: http://www.eng.tcu.edu/

Texas Southern University, College of Liberal Arts and Behavioral Sciences, Department of English, Houston, TX 77004-4584. Offers MA. *Program availability:* Part-time. *Degree requirements:* For master's, one foreign language, comprehensive exam, thesis. *Entrance requirements:* For master's, GRE General Test, minimum GPA of 2.5. Additional exam requirements/recommendations for international students: Required—TOEFL. Electronic applications accepted. *Faculty research:* Linguistics, teaching of English, African-American literature, African literature, developmental English.

Texas State University, The Graduate College, College of Liberal Arts, Program in Literature, San Marcos, TX 78666. Offers MA. *Program availability:* Part-time, evening/weekend. *Faculty:* 24 full-time (11 women), 1 part-time/adjunct (0 women). *Students:* 24 full-time (20 women), 21 part-time (16 women); includes 17 minority (1 Black or African American, non-Hispanic/Latino; 1 Asian, non-Hispanic/Latino; 14 Hispanic/Latino; 1 Two or more races, non-Hispanic/Latino), 2 international. Average age 29. 35 applicants, 74% accepted, 14 enrolled. In 2017, 19 master's awarded. *Degree requirements:* For master's, comprehensive exam, thesis optional. *Entrance requirements:* For master's, baccalaureate degree from regionally-accredited university with minimum GPA of 2.75 on last 60 undergraduate semester hours, 3.25 in minimum of 24 hours of undergraduate English including at least 12 advanced hours; minimum of 6 hours in a foreign language; 2 letters of recommendation; writing sample of non-fiction prose. Additional exam requirements/recommendations for international students: Required—TOEFL (minimum score 550 paper-based; 78 iBT), IELTS (minimum score 6.5). *Application deadline:* For fall admission, 1/15 priority date for domestic and international students; for spring admission, 10/15 for domestic students, 10/1 for international students; for summer admission, 4/15 for domestic students, 3/15 for international students. Applications are processed on a rolling basis. Application fee: $40 ($90 for international students). Electronic applications accepted. *Expenses:* Tuition, state resident: full-time $7868; part-time $3934 per semester. Tuition, nonresident: full-time $17,828; part-time $8914 per semester. *Required fees:* $2092; $1435 per semester. Tuition and fees vary according to course load. *Financial support:* In 2017–18, 28 students received support, including 19 teaching assistantships (averaging $14,241 per year); research assistantships, Federal Work-Study, institutionally sponsored loans, scholarships/grants, health care benefits, and unspecified assistantships also available. Support available to part-time students. Financial award application deadline: 3/1; financial award applicants required to submit FAFSA. *Faculty research:* Bilingual adaptation of and quote; the comedy of errors and quote. *Total annual research expenditures:* $10,000. *Unit head:* Dr. Paul Cohen, Acting Graduate Adviser, 512-245-7685, Fax: 512-245-8546, E-mail: pc06@txstate.edu. *Application contact:* Dr. Andrea Golato, Dean of Graduate School, 512-245-2581, Fax: 512-245-8365, E-mail: gradcollege@txstate.edu.
Website: http://malit.english.txstate.edu/

Texas Tech University, Graduate School, College of Arts and Sciences, Department of English, Lubbock, TX 79409-3091. Offers English (MA, PhD); technical communication (MA); technical communication and rhetoric (PhD). *Program availability:* Part-time, 100% online, blended/hybrid learning. *Faculty:* 79 full-time (46 women), 9 part-time/adjunct (4 women). *Students:* 80 full-time (46 women), 88 part-time (60 women); includes 32 minority (9 Black or African American, non-Hispanic/Latino; 1 American Indian or Alaska Native, non-Hispanic/Latino; 3 Asian, non-Hispanic/Latino; 13 Hispanic/Latino; 6 Two or more races, non-Hispanic/Latino), 8 international. Average age 35. 136 applicants, 32% accepted, 32 enrolled. In 2017, 28 master's, 16 doctorates awarded. Terminal master's awarded for partial completion of doctoral program. *Degree requirements:* For master's, variable foreign language requirement, comprehensive exam, thesis optional; for doctorate, variable foreign language requirement, comprehensive exam, thesis/dissertation. *Entrance requirements:* For master's and doctorate, GRE General Test. Additional exam requirements/recommendations for international students: Required—TOEFL (minimum score 550 paper-based; 79 iBT),

IELTS (minimum score 6.5). *Application deadline:* For fall admission, 6/1 priority date for domestic students, 1/15 priority date for international students; for spring admission, 9/1 priority date for domestic students, 6/15 priority date for international students. Applications are processed on a rolling basis. Application fee: $60. Electronic applications accepted. *Expenses:* Contact institution. *Financial support:* In 2017–18, 101 students received support, including 84 fellowships (averaging $2,712 per year), 6 research assistantships (averaging $17,139 per year), 76 teaching assistantships (averaging $15,638 per year); career-related internships or fieldwork, Federal Work-Study, scholarships/grants, and unspecified assistantships also available. Financial award application deadline: 1/8; financial award applicants required to submit FAFSA. *Faculty research:* American, British, and comparative literature; creative writing; linguistics; film; technical communication and rhetoric. *Total annual research expenditures:* $21,274. *Unit head:* Dr. Brian Still, Department Chair, 806-834-6439, Fax: 806-742-0989, E-mail: brian.still@ttu.edu. *Application contact:* Dr. Julie Nelson Couch, Director of Graduate Studies, 806-834-1742, Fax: 806-742-0989, E-mail: english.gradadvisor@ttu.edu.
Website: http://www.english.ttu.edu/

Texas Woman's University, Graduate School, College of Arts and Sciences, Department of English, Speech, and Foreign Languages, Denton, TX 76204. Offers English (MA, MAT); rhetoric (PhD). *Program availability:* Part-time. *Faculty:* 9 full-time (4 women). *Students:* 6 full-time (5 women), 38 part-time (30 women); includes 10 minority (4 Black or African American, non-Hispanic/Latino; 2 Asian, non-Hispanic/Latino; 2 Hispanic/Latino; 2 Two or more races, non-Hispanic/Latino), 1 international. Average age 39. 8 applicants, 63% accepted, 4 enrolled. In 2017, 7 master's, 4 doctorates awarded. *Degree requirements:* For master's, comprehensive exam, thesis (for some programs), professional paper, thesis or coursework; for doctorate, comprehensive exam, thesis/dissertation, residency for at least 2 consecutive semesters (strongly encouraged). *Entrance requirements:* For master's, GRE General Test (preferred minimum score 153 [500 old version] verbal, 138 [350 old version] quantitative), 3 letters of reference, minimum GPA of 3.0 on previous upper-division and graduate work, writing sample, statement of purpose; for doctorate, GRE General Test (preferred minimum score 153 [500 old version] verbal, 138 [350 old version] quantitative), writing sample, 3 letters of reference, interview (for graduate assistants), minimum GPA of 3.0 on previous upper-division and graduate work, statement of purpose. Additional exam requirements/recommendations for international students: Required—TOEFL (minimum score 600 paper-based; 79 iBT); Recommended—IELTS (minimum score 6.5). *Application deadline:* For fall admission, 7/1 for domestic students, 3/1 priority date for international students; for spring admission, 11/1 for domestic students, 7/1 priority date for international students; for summer admission, 4/1 for domestic students, 2/1 priority date for international students. Applications are processed on a rolling basis. Application fee: $50 ($75 for international students). Electronic applications accepted. *Expenses:* $7,520 per year full-time in-state; $16,820 per year full-time out-of-state. *Financial support:* In 2017–18, 20 students received support, including 13 teaching assistantships (averaging $23,215 per year); career-related internships or fieldwork, Federal Work-Study, institutionally sponsored loans, scholarships/grants, traineeships, health care benefits, and unspecified assistantships also available. Support available to part-time students. Financial award application deadline: 3/1; financial award applicants required to submit FAFSA. *Faculty research:* American literature, medieval literature, history of the English language, rhetoric, world literature. *Unit head:* Dr. Genevieve West, Chair, 940-898-2324, Fax: 940-898-2297, E-mail: engspfl@twu.edu. *Application contact:* Korie Hawkins, Associate Director of Admissions, Graduate Recruitment, 940-898-3188, Fax: 940-898-3081, E-mail: admissions@twu.edu.
Website: http://www.twu.edu/english-speech-foreign-languages/

Tiffin University, Program in Humanities, Tiffin, OH 44883-2161. Offers art and visual media (MH); communication (MH); creative writing (MH); English (MH); film studies (MH); humanities (MH); individualized studies (MH). *Program availability:* Part-time, evening/weekend, online only, 100% online, blended/hybrid learning. *Entrance requirements:* For master's, work experience. Additional exam requirements/recommendations for international students: Required—TOEFL (minimum score 550 paper-based; 79 iBT). Electronic applications accepted. Application fee is waived when completed online. *Expenses:* Contact institution.

Trinity College, Graduate Programs, Program in English, Hartford, CT 06106-3100. Offers literary studies (MA); writing, rhetoric, and media arts (MA). *Program availability:* Part-time, evening/weekend. *Degree requirements:* For master's, thesis (for some programs). *Entrance requirements:* For master's, minimum GPA of 3.0.

Trinity Western University, School of Graduate Studies, Program in Interdisciplinary Humanities, Langley, BC V2Y 1Y1, Canada. Offers general humanities (MAIH); specialized (MAIH), including English, history, philosophy. *Program availability:* Part-time. *Degree requirements:* For master's, thesis or alternative, 36 semester hours. *Entrance requirements:* For master's, strong undergraduate degree in humanities or English, history or philosophy. Additional exam requirements/recommendations for international students: Recommended—TOEFL. Electronic applications accepted. *Faculty research:* Literary theory, gender, medieval and early modern literature, philosophy of religion, Thomas Merton's poetics.

Truman State University, Graduate School, School of Arts and Letters, Program in English, Kirksville, MO 63501-4221. Offers MA. *Degree requirements:* For master's, thesis. *Entrance requirements:* For master's, GRE General Test, minimum GPA of 3.0. Additional exam requirements/recommendations for international students: Required—TOEFL (minimum score 550 paper-based). Electronic applications accepted.

Tufts University, Graduate School of Arts and Sciences, Department of English, Medford, MA 02155. Offers MA, PhD. *Students:* 60 full-time (32 women); includes 10 minority (2 Black or African American, non-Hispanic/Latino; 4 Asian, non-Hispanic/Latino; 1 Hispanic/Latino; 3 Two or more races, non-Hispanic/Latino), 3 international. Average age 31. 68 applicants, 29% accepted, 8 enrolled. In 2017, 2 master's, 5 doctorates awarded. Terminal master's awarded for partial completion of doctoral program. *Degree requirements:* For master's, one foreign language, thesis; for doctorate, 2 foreign languages, thesis/dissertation. *Entrance requirements:* For master's and doctorate, GRE General Test, GRE Subject Test, writing sample. Additional exam requirements/recommendations for international students: Required—TOEFL (minimum score 550 paper-based; 80 iBT), IELTS (minimum score 6.5). *Application deadline:* For fall admission, 1/15 for domestic and international students. Applications are processed on a rolling basis. Application fee: $85. Electronic applications accepted. *Expenses:* Contact institution. *Financial support:* Fellowships, teaching assistantships, Federal Work-Study, scholarships/grants, tuition waivers (full and partial), and unspecified assistantships available. Financial award application deadline: 1/15. *Unit head:* Dr. Elizabeth Ammons, Graduate Program Director, 617-627-2047. *Application contact:* Office of Graduate Admissions, 617-627-3395, E-mail: gradadmissions@tufts.edu.
Website: http://www.ase.tufts.edu/english/

Tulane University, School of Liberal Arts, Department of English, New Orleans, LA 70118-5669. Offers MA. *Degree requirements:* For master's, one foreign language, thesis or alternative. *Entrance requirements:* For master's, GRE General Test, minimum B average in undergraduate course work. Additional exam requirements/recommendations for international students: Required—TOEFL. Electronic applications accepted. *Expenses: Tuition:* Full-time $50,920; part-time $2829 per credit hour. *Required fees:* $2040; $44.50 per credit hour. $580 per term. Tuition and fees vary according to course load, degree level and program.

Universidad de las Américas Puebla, Division of Graduate Studies, School of Humanities, Program in Literature, Puebla, Mexico. Offers MA. *Program availability:* Part-time, evening/weekend. *Degree requirements:* For master's, one foreign language, thesis. *Entrance requirements:* Additional exam requirements/recommendations for international students: Required—TOEFL. *Faculty research:* Women in literature, Mexican and Hispanic literature.

Université de Montréal, Faculty of Arts and Sciences, Department of English Studies, Montréal, QC H3C 3J7, Canada. Offers MA, PhD. *Degree requirements:* For doctorate, thesis/dissertation, general exam. *Entrance requirements:* For master's, BA in English with minimum B+ average; for doctorate, MA in English with minimum B+ average. Electronic applications accepted. *Faculty research:* British, Canadian, and American literature.

Université Laval, Faculty of Letters, Department of Literature, Programs in Ancient Civilization, Québec, QC G1K 7P4, Canada. Offers MA, PhD. *Program availability:* Part-time. Terminal master's awarded for partial completion of doctoral program. *Degree requirements:* For master's, thesis; for doctorate, comprehensive exam, thesis/dissertation. *Entrance requirements:* For master's and doctorate, English test (comprehension of written English), knowledge of French, knowledge of an ancient language. Electronic applications accepted.

Université Laval, Faculty of Letters, Department of Literature, Programs in English Literatures, Québec, QC G1K 7P4, Canada. Offers MA, PhD. *Program availability:* Part-time. Terminal master's awarded for partial completion of doctoral program. *Degree requirements:* For master's, thesis (for some programs); for doctorate, comprehensive exam, thesis/dissertation. *Entrance requirements:* For master's, French exam, knowledge of English; for doctorate, French exam, knowledge of English, knowledge of a third language. Electronic applications accepted.

University at Albany, State University of New York, College of Arts and Sciences, Department of English, Albany, NY 12222-0001. Offers MA, PhD. *Faculty:* 28 full-time (10 women), 1 (woman) part-time/adjunct. *Students:* 21 full-time (14 women), 60 part-time (33 women); includes 14 minority (3 Black or African American, non-Hispanic/Latino; 1 Asian, non-Hispanic/Latino; 6 Hispanic/Latino; 4 Two or more races, non-Hispanic/Latino), 14 international. 99 applicants, 38% accepted, 13 enrolled. In 2017, 8 master's, 2 doctorates awarded. *Degree requirements:* For master's, one foreign language; for doctorate, one foreign language, comprehensive exam, thesis/dissertation, residency. *Entrance requirements:* For master's and doctorate, GRE General Test, GRE Subject Test. Additional exam requirements/recommendations for international students: Required—TOEFL (minimum score 550 paper-based). *Application deadline:* For fall admission, 6/15 for domestic students, 1/15 for international students; for spring admission, 11/1 for international students. Applications are processed on a rolling basis. Application fee: $75. Electronic applications accepted. *Expenses:* Tuition, state resident: full-time $10,870; part-time $453 per credit hour. Tuition, nonresident: full-time $22,210; part-time $925 per credit hour. *Required fees:* $84.68 per credit hour. $508.06 per semester. Part-time tuition and fees vary according to course load and program. *Financial support:* Fellowships and career-related internships or fieldwork available. Financial award application deadline: 2/15. *Faculty research:* Women playwrights; critical literary theory; poetry and poetics; media history, writing and reporting; creative non-fiction. *Unit head:* Randall Craig, Chair, 518-442-4056, Fax: 518-442-4599. *Application contact:* Michael DeRensis, Director, Graduate Admissions, 518-442-3980, Fax: 518-442-3922, E-mail: graduate@albany.edu.
Website: http://www.albany.edu/english/

University at Buffalo, the State University of New York, Graduate School, College of Arts and Sciences, Department of English, Buffalo, NY 14260. Offers MA, PhD. *Program availability:* Part-time. *Faculty:* 32 full-time (15 women). *Students:* 94 full-time (40 women), 1 (woman) part-time; includes 14 minority (4 Black or African American, non-Hispanic/Latino; 7 Asian, non-Hispanic/Latino; 3 Hispanic/Latino), 33 international. Average age 29. 193 applicants, 31% accepted, 24 enrolled. In 2017, 17 master's, 14 doctorates awarded. Terminal master's awarded for partial completion of doctoral program. *Degree requirements:* For master's, thesis or alternative; for doctorate, thesis/dissertation, departmental qualifying exam. *Entrance requirements:* For master's and doctorate, GRE General Test, sample of written work. Additional exam requirements/recommendations for international students: Required—TOEFL (minimum score 79 iBT). *Application deadline:* For fall admission, 12/15 for domestic and international students. Application fee: $75. Electronic applications accepted. *Financial support:* In 2017–18, 63 students received support, including 17 fellowships with full tuition reimbursements available (averaging $19,000 per year), 65 teaching assistantships with full tuition reimbursements available (averaging $15,000 per year); research assistantships, career-related internships or fieldwork, Federal Work-Study, institutionally sponsored loans, and unspecified assistantships also available. Financial award application deadline: 12/15; financial award applicants required to submit FAFSA. *Faculty research:* Psychoanalysis, early modern British literature, poetics, nineteenth-century American literature, British and Irish Modernism. *Total annual research expenditures:* $38,000. *Unit head:* Dr. Rachel Ablow, Chair, 716-645-0674, Fax: 716-645-5980, E-mail: rablow@buffalo.edu. *Application contact:* Dr. Carla Mazzio, Director of Graduate Admissions, 716-645-2575, Fax: 716-645-5980, E-mail: eng-grad@buffalo.edu.
Website: http://www.buffalo.edu/cas/english.html

University at Buffalo, the State University of New York, Graduate School, Graduate School of Education, Department of Learning and Instruction, Buffalo, NY 14260. Offers biology education (Ed M, Certificate); chemistry education (Ed M, Certificate); childhood education (Ed M); childhood education with bilingual extension (Ed M); college teaching (Advanced Certificate); curriculum, instruction and the science of learning (PhD); early childhood education (Ed M); early childhood education with bilingual extension (Ed M); earth science education (Ed M, Certificate); education and technology (Ed M); education studies (Ed M); educational technology and new literacies (Certificate); educational technology and new literacies (Advanced Certificate); elementary education (Ed D); English education (Ed M, Certificate); English education studies (Ed M); English for speakers of other languages (Ed M); foreign and second language education (PhD); French education (Ed M, Certificate); German education (Ed M, Certificate); gifted education (Certificate); Latin education (Ed M, Certificate); literacy education studies (Ed M); literacy specialist (Ed M); literacy teaching and learning (Certificate); mathematics education (Ed M, Certificate); music education (Ed M, Certificate); music education studies (Ed M); music learning theory (Advanced Certificate); online education (Advanced Certificate); physics education (Ed M, Certificate); science and the public (Ed M); social studies education (Ed M, Certificate); Spanish education (Ed M, Certificate); special education (PhD); teaching English to speakers of other languages (Ed M). *Program availability:* Part-time, evening/weekend, 100% online. *Faculty:* 26 full-time (19 women), 74 part-time/adjunct (52 women). *Students:* 172 full-time (122 women), 325 part-time (226 women); includes 44 minority (25 Black or African American, non-Hispanic/Latino; 5 American Indian or Alaska Native, non-Hispanic/Latino; 14 Asian, non-Hispanic/Latino), 57 international. Average age 33. 316

applicants, 78% accepted, 174 enrolled. In 2017, 109 master's, 34 doctorates, 15 other advanced degrees awarded. *Degree requirements:* For master's, comprehensive exam; for doctorate, thesis/dissertation, research analysis exam, research experience. *Entrance requirements:* For master's, letters of reference; for doctorate, GRE General Test or MAT, interview, writing sample, letters of recommendation. Additional exam requirements/recommendations for international students: Required—TOEFL (minimum score 600 paper-based; 96 iBT). *Application deadline:* For fall admission, 2/1 priority date for domestic and international students; for spring admission, 11/15 priority date for domestic students, 10/1 for international students. Applications are processed on a rolling basis. Application fee: $50. Electronic applications accepted. *Financial support:* In 2017–18, 42 fellowships (averaging $5,181 per year), 44 research assistantships with tuition reimbursements (averaging $10,908 per year) were awarded; teaching assistantships, career-related internships or fieldwork, Federal Work-Study, institutionally sponsored loans, scholarships/grants, tuition waivers (full and partial), and unspecified assistantships also available. Financial award application deadline: 2/28; financial award applicants required to submit FAFSA. *Faculty research:* Science assessment, foreign language teaching and learning, early learning, new literacies, gender and education. *Total annual research expenditures:* $413,233. *Unit head:* Dr. David Bruce, Chair, 716-645-4069, Fax: 716-645-3161, E-mail: gse-info@buffalo.edu. *Application contact:* Luann Zak, Admissions Assistant, 716-645-2110, Fax: 716-645-7937, E-mail: luannzak@buffalo.edu.
Website: http://gse.buffalo.edu/lai

The University of Akron, Graduate School, Buchtel College of Arts and Sciences, Department of English, Program in Literature, Akron, OH 44325. Offers MA. *Students:* 6 full-time (5 women), 10 part-time (9 women); includes 1 minority (Hispanic/Latino), 2 international. Average age 36. 6 applicants, 100% accepted, 6 enrolled. In 2017, 7 master's awarded. *Degree requirements:* For master's, thesis optional. *Entrance requirements:* For master's, statement of purpose. Additional exam requirements/recommendations for international students: Required—TOEFL (minimum score 92 iBT). *Application deadline:* Applications are processed on a rolling basis. *Financial support:* Fellowships, institutionally sponsored loans, and unspecified assistantships available. *Unit head:* Dr. Sheldon Wrice, Interim Chair, 330-972-6023, E-mail: swrice1@uakron.edu. *Application contact:* David Giffels, Director of Graduate Studies, 330-972-6604, E-mail: dg36@uakron.edu.

The University of Alabama, Graduate School, College of Arts and Sciences, Department of English, Tuscaloosa, AL 35487. Offers composition and rhetoric (PhD); creative writing (MFA), including fiction, poetry; literature (MA, PhD); rhetoric and composition (MA); teaching English as a second language (MATESOL). *Faculty:* 37 full-time (21 women). *Students:* 123 full-time (71 women), 11 part-time (8 women); includes 22 minority (10 Black or African American, non-Hispanic/Latino; 1 Asian, non-Hispanic/Latino; 6 Hispanic/Latino; 5 Two or more races, non-Hispanic/Latino), 2 international. Average age 29. 378 applicants, 17% accepted, 44 enrolled. In 2017, 32 master's, 7 doctorates awarded. *Degree requirements:* For master's, one foreign language, comprehensive exam, thesis; for doctorate, 2 foreign languages, comprehensive exam, thesis/dissertation. *Entrance requirements:* For master's, GRE (minimum score of 300, except for MFA), minimum GPA of 3.0, critical writing sample; for doctorate, GRE (minimum score of 300), minimum GPA of 3.5 on master's or equivalent graduate work, critical writing sample. Additional exam requirements/recommendations for international students: Recommended—TOEFL (minimum score 550 paper-based; 79 iBT). *Application deadline:* For fall admission, 12/20 for domestic and international students. Application fee: $50 ($60 for international students). Electronic applications accepted. *Financial support:* In 2017–18, 113 students received support, including fellowships with full tuition reimbursements available (averaging $15,000 per year), research assistantships with full tuition reimbursements available (averaging $13,500 per year), teaching assistantships with full tuition reimbursements available (averaging $13,500 per year); career-related internships or fieldwork, scholarships/grants, health care benefits, and unspecified assistantships also available. Financial award application deadline: 12/20. *Faculty research:* American literature, British literature, composition/rhetoric, applied linguistics, creative writing. *Unit head:* Prof. Joel Brouwer, Department Chair, 205-348-5065, Fax: 205-348-1388, E-mail: joel.brouwer@ua.edu. *Application contact:* Jennifer Fuqua, Graduate Coordinator, 205-348-0766, Fax: 205-348-1388, E-mail: jfuqua@ua.edu.

The University of Alabama at Birmingham, College of Arts and Sciences, Program in English, Birmingham, AL 35294. Offers creative writing (MA); literature (MA); rhetoric and composition (MA). *Program availability:* Part-time. *Degree requirements:* For master's, one foreign language, comprehensive exam, thesis or alternative. *Entrance requirements:* For master's, GRE General Test or MAT, minimum GPA of 2.75. Electronic applications accepted.

The University of Alabama in Huntsville, School of Graduate Studies, College of Arts, Humanities, and Social Sciences, Department of English, Huntsville, AL 35899. Offers education (MA); English (MA); technical writing (Certificate); TESOL (Certificate). *Program availability:* Part-time, evening/weekend. *Degree requirements:* For master's, one foreign language, comprehensive exam, thesis or alternative, oral and written exams. *Entrance requirements:* For master's and Certificate, GRE General Test, minimum GPA of 3.0. Additional exam requirements/recommendations for international students: Required—TOEFL (minimum score 500 paper-based; 80 iBT), IELTS (minimum score 6.5). Electronic applications accepted. *Faculty research:* Fiction and identity, Shakespeare, science fiction, eighteenth-century literature, technical writing.

University of Alaska Anchorage, College of Arts and Sciences, Department of English, Anchorage, AK 99508. Offers MA. *Program availability:* Part-time. *Degree requirements:* For master's, comprehensive exam, thesis or alternative. *Entrance requirements:* For master's, GRE General Test, GRE Subject Test, portfolio, minimum GPA of 3.5, writing sample. Additional exam requirements/recommendations for international students: Required—TOEFL (minimum score 550 paper-based). *Faculty research:* The rhetoric of essays, American and American Indian literature, linguistics, Shakespeare, literature of war.

University of Alaska Fairbanks, College of Liberal Arts, Department of English, Fairbanks, AK 99775-5720. Offers creative writing (MFA); literature (MA); MA/MFA. *Program availability:* Part-time. *Degree requirements:* For master's, comprehensive exam, oral defense of project or thesis. *Entrance requirements:* For master's, GRE General Test, bachelor's degree from accredited institution with minimum cumulative undergraduate and major GPA of 3.0, academic writing sample. Additional exam requirements/recommendations for international students: Required—TOEFL (minimum score 550 paper-based; 79 iBT), IELTS (minimum score 6.5). Electronic applications accepted.

University of Alberta, Faculty of Graduate Studies and Research, Department of English and Film Studies, Edmonton, AB T6G 2E1, Canada. Offers English (MA, PhD). *Program availability:* Part-time, evening/weekend. *Degree requirements:* For master's, one foreign language, thesis optional; for doctorate, 2 foreign languages, thesis/dissertation. *Entrance requirements:* For master's, honors BA or equivalent; for doctorate, honors BA and MA. Additional exam requirements/recommendations for international students: Required—TOEFL (minimum score 600 paper-based). Electronic

applications accepted. *Faculty research:* Women's writing, postcolonial theory, Victorian literature, Renaissance literature, Canadian literature.

The University of Arizona, College of Humanities, Department of English, English Language/Linguistics Program, Tucson, AZ 85721. Offers English (MA, PhD); ESL (MA). *Entrance requirements:* Additional exam requirements/recommendations for international students: Required—TOEFL (minimum score 550 paper-based; 79 iBT); Recommended—IELTS (minimum score 7). Electronic applications accepted.

University of Arkansas, Graduate School, J. William Fulbright College of Arts and Sciences, Department of English, Program in English, Fayetteville, AR 72701. Offers MA, PhD. In 2017, 14 master's, 11 doctorates awarded. *Degree requirements:* For master's, thesis; for doctorate, thesis/dissertation. *Entrance requirements:* For master's, GRE General Test; for doctorate, GRE General Test, GRE Subject Test. *Application deadline:* For fall admission, 8/1 for domestic students, 4/1 for international students; for spring admission, 12/1 for domestic students, 10/1 for international students; for summer admission, 4/15 for domestic students, 3/1 for international students. Applications are processed on a rolling basis. Application fee: $60. Electronic applications accepted. *Expenses:* Tuition, state resident: full-time $3782. Tuition, nonresident: full-time $10,238. *Financial support:* In 2017–18, 3 research assistantships, 44 teaching assistantships were awarded; fellowships with tuition reimbursements, career-related internships or fieldwork, and Federal Work-Study also available. Support available to part-time students. Financial award application deadline: 4/1; financial award applicants required to submit FAFSA. *Faculty research:* Creative writing, seventeenth-century literature, twentieth-century literature, American literature. *Unit head:* Dr. Dorothy Stephens, Department Chair, 479-575-4301, Fax: 479-575-5919, E-mail: dstephen@uark.edu. *Application contact:* Dr. William Quinn, Graduate Coordinator, 479-575-4301, E-mail: wquinn@uark.edu.
Website: https://fulbright.uark.edu/departments/english/

The University of British Columbia, Faculty of Arts and Faculty of Graduate Studies, Department of English, Vancouver, BC V6T 1Z1, Canada. Offers MA, PhD. *Degree requirements:* For master's, thesis or alternative; for doctorate, one foreign language, comprehensive exam, thesis/dissertation. *Entrance requirements:* For master's, BA or equivalent; for doctorate, MA. Additional exam requirements/recommendations for international students: Required—TOEFL, IELTS. Electronic applications accepted. *Expenses:* Contact institution. *Faculty research:* English, American, Canadian, and Commonwealth post-colonial literature; English language; rhetoric.

The University of British Columbia, Faculty of Arts, School of Library, Archival and Information Studies, Master of Arts Program in Children's Literature, Vancouver, BC V6T 1Z1, Canada. Offers MA. *Program availability:* Part-time. *Degree requirements:* For master's, thesis. *Entrance requirements:* For master's, minimum GPA of 3.3 in undergraduate upper-division courses. Additional exam requirements/recommendations for international students: Required—TOEFL. Electronic applications accepted. *Expenses:* Contact institution. *Faculty research:* Children's and young adult literature; children's and young adult public library services; Canadian children's and young adult literature; publishing for youth.

University of Calgary, Faculty of Graduate Studies, Faculty of Arts, Department of English, Calgary, AB T2N 1N4, Canada. Offers MA, PhD. *Program availability:* Part-time. *Degree requirements:* For master's, one foreign language, comprehensive exam (for some programs), thesis; for doctorate, one foreign language, thesis/dissertation, candidacy exam. *Entrance requirements:* Additional exam requirements/recommendations for international students: Required—TOEFL (minimum score 600 paper-based). Electronic applications accepted. *Faculty research:* Various national and period literatures, creative writing, literary theory, gender and women's studies, postcolonial literatures.

University of California, Berkeley, Graduate Division, College of Letters and Science, Department of English, Berkeley, CA 94720-1500. Offers PhD. *Degree requirements:* For doctorate, 2 foreign languages, thesis/dissertation, qualifying exam. *Entrance requirements:* For doctorate, GRE General Test, GRE Subject Test, minimum GPA of 3.0, writing sample, 3 letters of recommendation. Electronic applications accepted.

University of California, Davis, Graduate Studies, Program in English, Davis, CA 95616. Offers creative writing (MA); English (MA, PhD). Terminal master's awarded for partial completion of doctoral program. *Degree requirements:* For master's, one foreign language, thesis optional; for doctorate, 2 foreign languages, thesis/dissertation. *Entrance requirements:* For master's and doctorate, GRE General Test, GRE Subject Test, minimum GPA of 3.0, writing sample. Additional exam requirements/recommendations for international students: Required—TOEFL (minimum score 550 paper-based). Electronic applications accepted. *Faculty research:* Feminist theory, ethnic literature, literary theory, history of literature, literature of nature.

University of California, Irvine, School of Humanities, Department of English, Program in English, Irvine, CA 92697. Offers English (MA); English and American literature (PhD). *Students:* 61 full-time (26 women); includes 18 minority (5 Asian, non-Hispanic/Latino; 5 Hispanic/Latino; 8 Two or more races, non-Hispanic/Latino), 4 international. Average age 31. 144 applicants, 27% accepted, 17 enrolled. In 2017, 24 master's, 3 doctorates awarded. Terminal master's awarded for partial completion of doctoral program. *Degree requirements:* For master's, one foreign language, comprehensive exam; for doctorate, 2 foreign languages, comprehensive exam, thesis/dissertation. *Entrance requirements:* For doctorate, GRE General Test, GRE Subject Test, minimum GPA of 3.5, sample of written work, 3 letters of recommendation. Additional exam requirements/recommendations for international students: Required—TOEFL (minimum score 550 paper-based). *Application deadline:* For fall admission, 12/1 for domestic and international students. Application fee: $105 ($125 for international students). Electronic applications accepted. *Financial support:* In 2017–18, 59 students received support. Fellowships with full tuition reimbursements available, research assistantships, teaching assistantships with partial tuition reimbursements available, institutionally sponsored loans, health care benefits, tuition waivers (full and partial), and unspecified assistantships available. Financial award application deadline: 3/1; financial award applicants required to submit FAFSA. *Faculty research:* Critical theory, literary history, cultural studies. *Unit head:* Martin Harries, Department Chair, 949-824-6715, Fax: 949-824-2916, E-mail: martin.harries@uci.edu. *Application contact:* Jerome Christensen, Graduate Faculty Advisor, 949-824-9046, Fax: 949-824-2916, E-mail: jchris@uci.edu.

University of California, Los Angeles, Graduate Division, College of Letters and Science, Department of English, Los Angeles, CA 90095. Offers MA, PhD. Terminal master's awarded for partial completion of doctoral program. *Degree requirements:* For master's, one foreign language, comprehensive exam, thesis; for doctorate, 2 foreign languages, thesis/dissertation, oral and written qualifying exams. *Entrance requirements:* For doctorate, GRE General Test, GRE Subject Test (literature), bachelor's degree; minimum undergraduate GPA of 3.0, 3.5 in upper-division English courses (or its equivalent if letter grade system not used), 3.7 in graduate courses for applicant with master's degree; writing sample. Additional exam requirements/recommendations for international students: Required—TOEFL. Electronic applications accepted.

University of California, Riverside, Graduate Division, Department of English, Riverside, CA 92521-0102. Offers MA, PhD. *Degree requirements:* For master's, one

foreign language, comprehensive exam; for doctorate, 2 foreign languages, thesis/dissertation, qualifying exams. *Entrance requirements:* For doctorate, GRE General Test, minimum GPA of 3.5. Additional exam requirements/recommendations for international students: Required—TOEFL (minimum score 550 paper-based; 80 iBT). Electronic applications accepted. *Expenses:* Tuition, state resident: full-time $5746. Tuition, nonresident: full-time $10,780. Tuition and fees vary according to campus/location and program. *Faculty research:* Critical theory, cultural and film studies, lesbian and gay studies, minority and feminist discourses, rhetoric and composition.

University of California, San Diego, Graduate Division, Department of Literature, La Jolla, CA 92093. Offers literature (PhD); writing (MFA). *Students:* 73 full-time (50 women), 2 part-time (both women). 195 applicants, 28% accepted, 22 enrolled. In 2017, 10 master's, 9 doctorates awarded. *Degree requirements:* For master's, thesis; for doctorate, one foreign language, comprehensive exam, thesis/dissertation, 3 quarters of teaching assistantship. *Entrance requirements:* For master's, writing sample; for doctorate, GRE General Test, writing sample. Additional exam requirements/recommendations for international students: Required—TOEFL (minimum score 550 paper-based; 80 iBT), IELTS (minimum score 7); Recommended—TSE. *Application deadline:* For fall admission, 12/15 for domestic students. Application fee: $105 ($125 for international students). Electronic applications accepted. *Financial support:* Fellowships, research assistantships, teaching assistantships, scholarships/grants, and readerships available. Financial award applicants required to submit FAFSA. *Faculty research:* Chicano/a-Latino/a studies, European studies, film studies and visual culture, Latin American literary and cultural studies, medieval/early modern studies, transnational Africa/African diaspora studies, transnational Asia/Asian diaspora studies. *Unit head:* Yingjin Zhang, Chair, 858-534-5991, E-mail: litchair@ucsd.edu. *Application contact:* Graduate Coordinator, 858-534-3217, E-mail: litgrad@ucsd.edu.
Website: http://literature.ucsd.edu

University of California, Santa Barbara, Graduate Division, College of Letters and Sciences, Division of Humanities and Fine Arts, Department of English, Santa Barbara, CA 93106-3170. Offers English (PhD), including environment and society, European medieval studies, feminist studies, global studies, technology and society, translation studies, writing studies; MA/PhD. Terminal master's awarded for partial completion of doctoral program. *Degree requirements:* For doctorate, one foreign language, comprehensive exam, thesis/dissertation. *Entrance requirements:* For doctorate, GRE General Test, GRE Subject Test (English literature). Additional exam requirements/recommendations for international students: Required—TOEFL (minimum score 550 paper-based; 80 iBT), IELTS (minimum score 7). Electronic applications accepted. *Faculty research:* Medieval, Romantic and Victorian studies; gender studies and feminist theory; literature and the mind; American literature; literature and new media/information culture.

University of California, Santa Cruz, Division of Graduate Studies, Division of Humanities, Department of Literature, Santa Cruz, CA 95064. Offers MA, PhD. Terminal master's awarded for partial completion of doctoral program. *Degree requirements:* For master's, thesis; for doctorate, one foreign language, thesis/dissertation, qualifying exam. *Entrance requirements:* For master's, GRE General Test, writing sample, minimum GPA of 3.5; for doctorate, GRE General Test, minimum GPA of 3.5, writing sample. Additional exam requirements/recommendations for international students: Required—TOEFL (minimum score 550 paper-based; 83 iBT); Recommended—IELTS (minimum score 8). Electronic applications accepted. *Faculty research:* Technologies of narrative; trans/post/emergent nationalisms; poetics, poetry, and experimental writing; materialism and material culture; critical theories.

University of Central Arkansas, Graduate School, College of Liberal Arts, Department of English, Conway, AR 72035-0001. Offers MA. *Program availability:* Part-time. *Degree requirements:* For master's, comprehensive exam, thesis optional. *Entrance requirements:* For master's, GRE General Test, minimum GPA of 2.7. Additional exam requirements/recommendations for international students: Required—TOEFL (minimum score 550 paper-based). Electronic applications accepted. *Faculty research:* Writing project.

University of Central Florida, College of Arts and Humanities, Department of English, Orlando, FL 32816. Offers creative writing (MFA); English (MA, Certificate); texts and technology (PhD). *Program availability:* Part-time, evening/weekend. *Students:* 72 full-time (53 women), 87 part-time (62 women); includes 36 minority (2 Black or African American, non-Hispanic/Latino; 3 Asian, non-Hispanic/Latino; 27 Hispanic/Latino; 4 Two or more races, non-Hispanic/Latino), 5 international. Average age 33. 117 applicants, 65% accepted, 53 enrolled. In 2017, 37 master's, 6 doctorates, 5 other advanced degrees awarded. *Degree requirements:* For master's, one foreign language, thesis or alternative; for doctorate, thesis/dissertation. *Entrance requirements:* For master's, GRE General Test, letters of recommendation, goal statement. Additional exam requirements/recommendations for international students: Required—TOEFL. *Application deadline:* For fall admission, 3/30 for domestic students; for spring admission, 11/1 for domestic students. Application fee: $30. Electronic applications accepted. *Expenses:* Tuition, state resident: part-time $288.16 per credit hour. Tuition, nonresident: part-time $1073.31 per credit hour. Tuition and fees vary according to program. *Financial support:* In 2017–18, 56 students received support, including 18 fellowships with partial tuition reimbursements available (averaging $6,500 per year), 18 research assistantships with partial tuition reimbursements available (averaging $8,328 per year), 35 teaching assistantships with partial tuition reimbursements available (averaging $10,144 per year); career-related internships or fieldwork, Federal Work-Study, institutionally sponsored loans, tuition waivers (partial), and unspecified assistantships also available. Financial award application deadline: 3/1; financial award applicants required to submit FAFSA. *Unit head:* Dr. Trey Philpotts, Chair, 407-823-1159, E-mail: trey.philpotts@ucf.edu. *Application contact:* Associate Director, Graduate Admissions, 407-823-2766, Fax: 407-823-6442, E-mail: gradadmissions@ucf.edu.
Website: http://www.english.cah.ucf.edu/

University of Central Missouri, The Graduate School, Warrensburg, MO 64093. Offers accountancy (MA); accounting (MBA); applied mathematics (MS); aviation safety (MA); biology (MS); business administration (MBA); career and technical education leadership (MS); college student personnel administration (MS); communication (MA); computer science (MS); counseling (MS); criminal justice (MS); educational leadership (Ed D); educational technology (MS); elementary and early childhood education (MSE); English (MA); environmental studies (MA); finance (MBA); history (MA); human services/educational technology (Ed S); human services/learning resources (Ed S); human services/professional counseling (Ed S); industrial hygiene (MS); industrial management (MS); information systems (MBA); information technology (MS); kinesiology (MS); library science and information services (MS); literacy education (MSE); marketing (MBA); mathematics (MS); music (MA); occupational safety management (MS); psychology (MS); rural family nursing (MS); school administration (MSE); social gerontology (MS); sociology (MA); special education (MSE); speech language pathology (MS); superintendency (Ed S); teaching (MAT); teaching English as a second language (MA); technology (MS); technology management (PhD); theatre (MA). *Program availability:* Part-time, 100% online, blended/hybrid learning. *Faculty:* 337 full-time (145 women), 41 part-time/adjunct (28 women). *Students:* 785 full-time (398 women), 1,633 part-time (1,063 women); includes 231 minority (102 Black or African American, non-Hispanic/

Latino; 4 American Indian or Alaska Native, non-Hispanic/Latino; 16 Asian, non-Hispanic/Latino; 52 Hispanic/Latino; 57 Two or more races, non-Hispanic/Latino), 692 international. Average age 30. In 2017, 2,605 master's, 122 other advanced degrees awarded. *Degree requirements:* For master's and Ed S, comprehensive exam (for some programs), thesis (for some programs). *Entrance requirements:* Additional exam requirements/recommendations for international students: Required—TOEFL (minimum score 550 paper-based; 79 iBT). *Application deadline:* For fall admission, 6/1 priority date for domestic and international students; for spring admission, 10/1 priority date for domestic and international students; for summer admission, 4/1 priority date for domestic and international students. Applications are processed on a rolling basis. Application fee: $30 ($75 for international students). Electronic applications accepted. *Expenses:* Tuition, state resident: full-time $8771; part-time $292.35 per credit hour. Tuition, nonresident: full-time $17,541; part-time $584.70 per credit hour. *Required fees:* $372; $24.78 per credit hour. *Financial support:* In 2017–18, 99 students received support. Research assistantships, teaching assistantships, career-related internships or fieldwork, Federal Work-Study, scholarships/grants, and administrative and laboratory assistantships available. Support available to part-time students. Financial award application deadline: 3/1; financial award applicants required to submit FAFSA. *Unit head:* Shellie Hewitt, Director of Graduate and International Student Services, 660-543-4621, Fax: 660-543-4778, E-mail: hewitt@ucmo.edu. *Application contact:* 660-543-4621, E-mail: admit_intl@ucmo.edu.
Website: http://www.ucmo.edu/graduate/

University of Central Oklahoma, The Jackson College of Graduate Studies, College of Liberal Arts, Department of English, Edmond, OK 73034-5209. Offers composition and rhetoric (MA); creative writing (MA); literature (MA); teaching English as a second language (MA). *Program availability:* Part-time. *Faculty:* 21 full-time (14 women). *Students:* 30 full-time (17 women), 45 part-time (23 women); includes 17 minority (3 Black or African American, non-Hispanic/Latino; 3 American Indian or Alaska Native, non-Hispanic/Latino; 2 Asian, non-Hispanic/Latino; 3 Hispanic/Latino; 2 Native Hawaiian or other Pacific Islander, non-Hispanic/Latino; 4 Two or more races, non-Hispanic/Latino), 13 international. Average age 32. 34 applicants, 76% accepted, 18 enrolled. In 2017, 30 master's awarded. *Degree requirements:* For master's, variable foreign language requirement, comprehensive exam (for some programs), thesis (for some programs), portfolio. *Entrance requirements:* For master's, 18-24 hours of course work in English language and literature; writing sample; essay. Additional exam requirements/recommendations for international students: Required—TOEFL (minimum score 550 paper-based; 79 iBT), IELTS (minimum score 6.5). *Application deadline:* For fall admission, 7/15 for international students; for spring admission, 11/15 for international students. Applications are processed on a rolling basis. Application fee: $60. Electronic applications accepted. *Expenses:* Tuition, state resident: full-time $5375; part-time $268.75 per credit hour. Tuition, nonresident: full-time $13,295; part-time $664.75 per credit hour. *Required fees:* $626; $31.30 per credit hour. One-time fee: $50. Tuition and fees vary according to program. *Financial support:* In 2017–18, 22 students received support, including 4 research assistantships with partial tuition reimbursements available (averaging $11,830 per year), 8 teaching assistantships with partial tuition reimbursements available (averaging $11,830 per year); career-related internships or fieldwork, Federal Work-Study, scholarships/grants, tuition waivers (partial), and unspecified assistantships also available. Financial award application deadline: 3/31; financial award applicants required to submit FAFSA. *Unit head:* Dr. Matt Hollrah, Chairperson, 405-974-5540, Fax: 405-974-3823, E-mail: gradcoll@uco.edu.
Website: http://www.uco.edu/la/english/

University of Chicago, Division of the Humanities, Department of English Language and Literature, Chicago, IL 60637. Offers PhD. *Students:* 81 full-time (44 women); includes 18 minority (5 Black or African American, non-Hispanic/Latino; 4 Asian, non-Hispanic/Latino; 6 Hispanic/Latino; 3 Two or more races, non-Hispanic/Latino), 17 international. Average age 30. 487 applicants, 5% accepted, 13 enrolled. In 2017, 13 doctorates awarded. Terminal master's awarded for partial completion of doctoral program. *Degree requirements:* For doctorate, 2 foreign languages, comprehensive exam, thesis/dissertation. *Entrance requirements:* For doctorate, GRE General Test, 15-20 page writing sample, statement of purpose, 3 letters of recommendation, transcripts for all previous degrees and institutions attended. Additional exam requirements/recommendations for international students: Required—TOEFL (minimum score 104 iBT), IELTS (minimum score 7). *Application deadline:* For fall admission, 12/15 for domestic and international students. Application fee: $90. Electronic applications accepted. *Financial support:* In 2017–18, fellowships with full tuition reimbursements (averaging $27,000 per year) were awarded; teaching assistantships with full tuition reimbursements, Federal Work-Study, institutionally sponsored loans, scholarships/grants, and health care benefits also available. Financial award application deadline: 12/15. *Unit head:* Dr. Deborah Nelson, Chair, 773-702-8024, E-mail: dnelson@uchicago.edu. *Application contact:* Michael Beetley, Assistant Dean of Students, Admissions and Fellowships, 773-702-1552, Fax: 773-834-9148, E-mail: humanitiesadmissions@uchicago.edu.
Website: http://english.uchicago.edu/

University of Chicago, Division of the Humanities, Master of Arts Program in the Humanities, Chicago, IL 60637. Offers art history (MA); cinema and media studies (MA); classic languages (MA); comparative literature (MA); creative writing (MA); cultural policy studies (MA); digital humanities (MA); East Asian languages and civilizations (MA); English language and literature (MA); gender and sexuality studies (MA); Germanic studies (MA); linguistics (MA); music (MA); near Eastern languages and civilizations (MA); philosophy (MA); poetics (MA); race, politics and culture (MA); Romance languages and literatures (MA); Slavic languages and literatures (MA); South Asian languages and civilizations (MA); theater and performance studies (MA). *Students:* 95 full-time (50 women), 6 part-time (4 women); includes 22 minority (1 Black or African American, non-Hispanic/Latino; 10 Asian, non-Hispanic/Latino; 11 Hispanic/Latino), 19 international. Average age 26. 708 applicants, 75% accepted, 101 enrolled. In 2017, 91 master's awarded. *Degree requirements:* For master's, thesis. *Entrance requirements:* For master's, GRE General Test, 10-15 page writing sample, statement of purpose, 3 letters of recommendation, transcripts for all previous degrees and institutions attended. Additional exam requirements/recommendations for international students: Required—TOEFL (minimum score 104 iBT), IELTS (minimum score 7). *Application deadline:* For fall admission, 1/3 priority date for domestic and international students. Application fee: $90. Electronic applications accepted. *Expenses:* Contact institution. *Financial support:* In 2017–18, fellowships with partial tuition reimbursements (averaging $12,000 per year) were awarded; Federal Work-Study, institutionally sponsored loans, scholarships/grants, and tuition waivers (partial) also available. Financial award application deadline: 4/30. *Unit head:* Thomas Christensen, Director, 773-834-1201, Fax: 773-834-7526, E-mail: ma-humanities@uchicago.edu. *Application contact:* Michael Beetley, Assistant Dean of Students for Admissions, 773-834-1552, E-mail: humanitiesadmissions@uchicago.edu.
Website: http://maph.uchicago.edu/

University of Cincinnati, Graduate School, McMicken College of Arts and Sciences, Department of English and Comparative Literature, Cincinnati, OH 45221. Offers MA, MAT, PhD. *Program availability:* Part-time. Terminal master's awarded for partial completion of doctoral program. *Degree requirements:* For master's, one foreign

language, thesis (for some programs); for doctorate, 2 foreign languages, thesis/dissertation. *Entrance requirements:* For master's, GRE General Test, letters of recommendation (3), writing samples; for doctorate, GRE General Test, GRE Subject Test, letters of recommendation (3), writing samples. Additional exam requirements/recommendations for international students: Required—TOEFL. Electronic applications accepted. *Expenses: Tuition, area resident:* Full-time $14,468. Tuition, state resident: full-time $14,968; part-time $754 per credit hour. Tuition, nonresident: full-time $24,210; part-time $1311 per credit hour. *International tuition:* $26,460 full-time. *Required fees:* $3958; $84 per credit hour. One-time fee: $85 full-time. Tuition and fees vary according to course load, degree level and program. *Faculty research:* Literature/theory, creative writing, composition, professional writing/editing, linguistics.

University of Colorado Boulder, Graduate School, College of Arts and Sciences, Department of English, Boulder, CO 80309. Offers literature (MA, PhD), including creative writing (MA). *Faculty:* 44 full-time (26 women). *Students:* 86 full-time (58 women), 3 part-time (1 woman); includes 20 minority (4 Black or African American, non-Hispanic/Latino; 3 American Indian or Alaska Native, non-Hispanic/Latino; 3 Asian, non-Hispanic/Latino; 9 Hispanic/Latino; 1 Two or more races, non-Hispanic/Latino), 2 international. Average age 29. 328 applicants, 28% accepted, 26 enrolled. In 2017, 26 master's, 11 doctorates awarded. Terminal master's awarded for partial completion of doctoral program. *Degree requirements:* For master's, one foreign language, comprehensive exam, thesis or alternative; for doctorate, 2 foreign languages, comprehensive exam, thesis/dissertation. *Entrance requirements:* For master's, GRE General Test, GRE Subject Test, minimum undergraduate GPA of 3.0; for doctorate, GRE General Test, GRE Subject Test. *Application deadline:* For fall admission, 1/10 for domestic students; for spring admission, 12/1 for domestic students. Application fee: $60 ($80 for international students). Electronic applications accepted. Application fee is waived when completed online. *Financial support:* In 2017–18, 195 students received support, including 36 fellowships (averaging $3,412 per year), 5 research assistantships with full and partial tuition reimbursements available (averaging $32,381 per year), 51 teaching assistantships with full and partial tuition reimbursements available (averaging $18,748 per year); institutionally sponsored loans, scholarships/grants, health care benefits, and unspecified assistantships also available. Financial award application deadline: 2/15; financial award applicants required to submit FAFSA. *Faculty research:* Literary criticism; English language/literature; literary history; fiction; fiction language/literature. *Total annual research expenditures:* $808,950. *Application contact:* E-mail: gsengl@colorado.edu.
Website: http://english.colorado.edu/

University of Colorado Boulder, Graduate School, College of Arts and Sciences, Department of Spanish and Portuguese, Boulder, CO 80309. Offers Hispanic linguistics (MA); medieval and early modern Hispanic literatures (PhD); peninsular and Latin American literature (MA). *Faculty:* 13 full-time (5 women). *Students:* 33 full-time (22 women), 3 part-time (all women); includes 7 minority (all Hispanic/Latino), 15 international. Average age 31. 31 applicants, 48% accepted, 8 enrolled. In 2017, 5 master's, 2 doctorates awarded. Terminal master's awarded for partial completion of doctoral program. *Degree requirements:* For master's, one foreign language, comprehensive exam, thesis or alternative; for doctorate, 2 foreign languages, thesis/dissertation. *Entrance requirements:* For master's, minimum undergraduate GPA of 2.75. *Application deadline:* For fall admission, 1/10 for domestic students; for spring admission, 1/10 for domestic students. Applications are processed on a rolling basis. Application fee: $60 ($80 for international students). Electronic applications accepted. Application fee is waived when completed online. *Financial support:* In 2017–18, 119 students received support, including 33 fellowships (averaging $583 per year), 31 teaching assistantships with full and partial tuition reimbursements available (averaging $33,436 per year); institutionally sponsored loans, scholarships/grants, health care benefits, and unspecified assistantships also available. Financial award application deadline: 2/15; financial award applicants required to submit FAFSA. *Faculty research:* Literary criticism, Spanish language/literature, Latin American languages/literature, cultural history. *Total annual research expenditures:* $40,777. *Application contact:* E-mail: spanport@colorado.edu.
Website: http://spanish.colorado.edu/

University of Colorado Denver, College of Liberal Arts and Sciences, Department of English, Denver, CO 80217. Offers applied linguistics (MA); literature (MA); rhetoric and teaching of writing (MA). *Program availability:* Part-time, evening/weekend. *Degree requirements:* For master's, variable foreign language requirement, comprehensive exam (for some programs), thesis (for some programs), minimum of 33 credit hours (for literature program), 30 (for rhetoric and teaching of writing and applied linguistics programs). *Entrance requirements:* For master's, GRE General Test, minimum GPA of 3.0 in undergraduate courses, critical writing sample, letters of recommendation, completion of 24 semester hours in English courses (at least 16 at the upper-division level), statement of purpose. Additional exam requirements/recommendations for international students: Required—TOEFL (minimum score 537 paper-based; 75 iBT); Recommended—IELTS (minimum score 6.5). Electronic applications accepted. *Faculty research:* Literature, rhetoric, teaching of writing, applied linguistics.

University of Connecticut, Graduate School, College of Liberal Arts and Sciences, Department of English, Storrs, CT 06269. Offers MA, PhD. Terminal master's awarded for partial completion of doctoral program. *Degree requirements:* For master's, comprehensive exam; for doctorate, thesis/dissertation. *Entrance requirements:* For master's and doctorate, GRE General Test, GRE Subject Test. Additional exam requirements/recommendations for international students: Required—TOEFL (minimum score 550 paper-based). Electronic applications accepted.

University of Dallas, Braniff Graduate School of Liberal Arts, Program in English, Irving, TX 75062-4736. Offers MA. *Program availability:* Part-time. *Entrance requirements:* For master's, GRE General Test. *Application deadline:* For fall admission, 2/15 priority date for domestic students; for spring admission, 11/15 for domestic students. Applications are processed on a rolling basis. Application fee: $50. *Expenses: Tuition:* Full-time $33,750; part-time $22,500 per year. Tuition and fees vary according to program. *Financial support:* Application deadline: 2/15. *Faculty research:* Modern literature, Renaissance, Shakespeare, medieval studies. *Unit head:* Dr. Sally F. Hicks, Interim Dean, 972-721-5215, Fax: 972-721-4007, E-mail: constantindean@udallas.edu.
Website: http://www.udallas.edu/academics/braniff/mastersenglish/englishprogram

University of Dayton, Department of English, Dayton, OH 45469. Offers literary and cultural studies (MA); teaching English to speakers of other languages (TESOL) (MA); writing and rhetoric (MA). *Program availability:* Part-time. *Faculty:* 22 full-time (11 women). *Students:* 20 full-time (14 women), 1 (woman) part-time; includes 2 minority (both Black or African American, non-Hispanic/Latino), 7 international. Average age 26. 35 applicants, 34% accepted. In 2017, 9 master's awarded. *Degree requirements:* For master's, thesis optional. *Entrance requirements:* For master's, 24 undergraduate-level semester hours in literature and/or writing; minimum GPA of 3.0; transcripts; personal statement; 8-10 page writing sample; three professional letters of recommendation. Additional exam requirements/recommendations for international students: Required—TOEFL (minimum score 550 paper-based, 80 iBT) or IELTS. *Application deadline:* For fall admission, 6/15 priority date for domestic and international students; for spring admission, 12/15 priority date for domestic and international students. Applications are processed on a rolling basis. Application fee: $0 ($50 for international students). Electronic applications accepted. Tuition and fees vary according to degree level and program. *Financial support:* In 2017–18, 9 teaching assistantships with full tuition reimbursements (averaging $11,105 per year) were awarded; institutionally sponsored loans also available. Financial award application deadline: 3/1; financial award applicants required to submit FAFSA. *Faculty research:* Gender and Victorian periodicals; literature and human rights; Paul Lawrence Dunbar; the archetype of the Indian princess; Amish country. *Unit head:* Dr. Andrew Slade, Chair, 937-229-3434, Fax: 937-229-3563, E-mail: aslade1@udayton.edu. *Application contact:* Dr. Tereza Szeghi, Director of Graduate Studies, 937-229-3443, E-mail: tszeghi1@udayton.edu.
Website: https://www.udayton.edu/artssciences/academics/english/welcome/index.php

University of Delaware, College of Arts and Sciences, Department of English, Newark, DE 19716. Offers English and American literature (MA, PhD); MA/PhD. Terminal master's awarded for partial completion of doctoral program. *Degree requirements:* For master's, one foreign language, thesis optional; for doctorate, 2 foreign languages, comprehensive exam, thesis/dissertation, specialty exam. *Entrance requirements:* For master's and doctorate, GRE General Test, GRE Subject Test. Additional exam requirements/recommendations for international students: Required—TOEFL (minimum score 550 paper-based). Electronic applications accepted. *Faculty research:* Significant strengths in American literature and culture, material cultural studies, Renaissance studies, archival studies.

University of Denver, Division of Arts, Humanities and Social Sciences, Department of English, Denver, CO 80208. Offers creative writing (PhD); literary studies (MA, PhD). *Program availability:* Part-time. *Students:* Average age 33. 165 applicants, 13% accepted, 10 enrolled. In 2017, 3 master's, 9 doctorates awarded. *Degree requirements:* For master's, one foreign language, comprehensive exam, thesis; for doctorate, 2 foreign languages, comprehensive exam, thesis/dissertation. *Entrance requirements:* For master's, GRE General Test, GRE Subject Test (advanced literature), bachelor's degree, transcripts, academic essay, statement of intent, three letters of recommendation; for doctorate, GRE General Test, GRE Subject Test (advanced literature), master's degree, transcripts, academic essay, statement of intent, three letters of recommendation, and a writing sample (creative writing program only). Additional exam requirements/recommendations for international students: Required—TOEFL (minimum score 570 paper-based; 88 iBT). *Application deadline:* For fall admission, 1/1 priority date for domestic and international students. Applications are processed on a rolling basis. Application fee: $65. Electronic applications accepted. *Expenses:* Contact institution. *Financial support:* In 2017–18, 34 students received support, including 21 teaching assistantships with tuition reimbursements available (averaging $17,500 per year); Federal Work-Study, institutionally sponsored loans, scholarships/grants, and unspecified assistantships also available. Support available to part-time students. Financial award application deadline: 2/15; financial award applicants required to submit FAFSA. *Faculty research:* African diaspora semiotics, Susan Howe's poetics, Renaissance drama and emblematic culture, New England Colonial literature, postmodern literature. *Unit head:* Dr. Clark Davis, Professor and Chair, 303-871-2900, Fax: 303-871-2853, E-mail: cldavis@du.edu. *Application contact:* Dr. Adam Rovner, Associate Professor and Director of Graduate Studies, 303-871-2861, Fax: 303-871-2853, E-mail: adam.rovner@du.edu.
Website: http://www.du.edu/ahss/english

University of Florida, Graduate School, College of Liberal Arts and Sciences, Department of English, Gainesville, FL 32611. Offers creative writing (MFA); English (MA, PhD). *Degree requirements:* For master's, one foreign language, comprehensive exam, thesis or alternative; for doctorate, one foreign language, comprehensive exam, thesis/dissertation. *Entrance requirements:* For master's and doctorate, GRE General Test, minimum GPA of 3.0. Additional exam requirements/recommendations for international students: Required—TOEFL (minimum score 550 paper-based; 80 iBT), IELTS (minimum score 6). Electronic applications accepted. *Faculty research:* Modern global literatures in English, film and media studies, cultural studies and critical theory, American literature, English literature.

University of Georgia, Franklin College of Arts and Sciences, Department of English, Athens, GA 30602. Offers English (MA, MAT, PhD). *Degree requirements:* For master's, one foreign language, thesis (MA); for doctorate, 2 foreign languages, thesis/dissertation. *Entrance requirements:* For master's and doctorate, GRE General Test. Additional exam requirements/recommendations for international students: Required—TWE. Electronic applications accepted.

University of Guam, Office of Graduate Studies, College of Liberal Arts and Social Sciences, Department of English, Mangilao, GU 96923. Offers MA. *Entrance requirements:* For master's, GRE. Additional exam requirements/recommendations for international students: Required—TOEFL.

University of Guelph, Graduate Studies, College of Arts, School of English and Theatre Studies, Program in English, Guelph, ON N1G 2W1, Canada. Offers MA. *Program availability:* Part-time. *Degree requirements:* For master's, thesis (for some programs). *Entrance requirements:* For master's, letters of reference, 4-year honours undergraduate degree in English or drama. Additional exam requirements/recommendations for international students: Required—TOEFL. Electronic applications accepted. *Faculty research:* Post-colonial literature, Canadian literature, children's literature, Scottish literature, American literature, cultural studies.

University of Hawaii at Manoa, Office of Graduate Education, College of Languages, Linguistics and Literature, Department of English, Honolulu, HI 96822. Offers MA, PhD. *Program availability:* Part-time. *Degree requirements:* For master's, 2 foreign languages, thesis optional; for doctorate, 2 foreign languages, comprehensive exam, thesis/dissertation. *Entrance requirements:* For master's, GRE General Test; for doctorate, GRE General Test, GRE Subject Test. Additional exam requirements/recommendations for international students: Required—TOEFL (minimum score 600 paper-based; 100 iBT), IELTS (minimum score 7). *Faculty research:* British and American literature, creative writing, cultural studies, rhetoric and composition.

University of Houston–Clear Lake, School of Human Sciences and Humanities, Programs in Humanities and Fine Arts, Houston, TX 77058-1002. Offers history (MA); humanities (MA); literature (MA). *Program availability:* Part-time, evening/weekend, online learning. *Degree requirements:* For master's, thesis or alternative. *Entrance requirements:* For master's, GRE General Test. Additional exam requirements/recommendations for international students: Required—TOEFL (minimum score 550 paper-based). *Faculty research:* Digital media studies, Latin American history, labor history, Chaucer evolution versus creationism debate.

University of Houston–Downtown, College of Humanities and Social Sciences, Department of English, Houston, TX 77002. Offers rhetoric and composition (MA); technical communication (MS). *Program availability:* Part-time, evening/weekend. *Faculty:* 9 full-time (3 women). *Students:* 17 full-time (9 women), 44 part-time (31 women); includes 31 minority (12 Black or African American, non-Hispanic/Latino; 1 American Indian or Alaska Native, non-Hispanic/Latino; 2 Asian, non-Hispanic/Latino; 16 Hispanic/Latino), 1 international. Average age 39. 16 applicants, 81% accepted, 12 enrolled. In 2017, 10 master's awarded. *Entrance requirements:* Additional exam requirements/recommendations for international students: Required—TOEFL.

Application deadline: For fall admission, 4/1 for domestic and international students; for spring admission, 11/15 for domestic and international students. Application fee: $35 ($60 for international students). Electronic applications accepted. *Expenses:* $335 per credit resident; $700 per credit non-resident. *Financial support:* Federal Work-Study and scholarships/grants available. Financial award application deadline: 4/1; financial award applicants required to submit FAFSA. *Faculty research:* Environmental rhetoric, instructional design, usability, assessment, presentation slides. *Unit head:* Dr. Paul Kintzele, Chair, 713-221-8254, Fax: 713-221-8090, E-mail: kintzelep@uhd.edu. *Application contact:* Ceshia Love, Director of Admissions, 713-221-8093, Fax: 713-223-7408, E-mail: gradadmissions@uhd.edu.
Website: https://www.uhd.edu/academics/humanities/undergraduate-programs/english/Pages/english-english.aspx

University of Illinois at Chicago, College of Liberal Arts and Sciences, Department of English, Chicago, IL 60607-7128. Offers MA, PhD. *Program availability:* Part-time, evening/weekend. *Degree requirements:* For doctorate, variable foreign language requirement, thesis/dissertation, written and oral exams. *Entrance requirements:* For master's, GRE General Test, GRE Subject Test; for doctorate, GRE General Test, GRE Subject Test, minimum GPA of 2.0. Additional exam requirements/recommendations for international students: Required—TOEFL. Electronic applications accepted. *Faculty research:* Literary history and theory.

University of Illinois at Springfield, Graduate Programs, College of Liberal Arts and Sciences, Department of English and Modern Languages, Springfield, IL 62703-5407. Offers English (MA); teaching English (Graduate Certificate). *Program availability:* Part-time, evening/weekend. *Faculty:* 12 full-time (11 women). *Students:* 7 full-time (5 women), 13 part-time (6 women); includes 1 minority (Asian, non-Hispanic/Latino), 1 international. Average age 33. 9 applicants, 56% accepted, 5 enrolled. In 2017, 2 master's awarded. *Degree requirements:* For master's, thesis, critical project, or creative project. *Entrance requirements:* For master's, GRE General Test, minimum overall undergraduate GPA of 3.0; analytical writing sample or sample of creative work; curriculum vitae/academic resume; three references, two of which must be academic references. Additional exam requirements/recommendations for international students: Required—TOEFL (minimum score 500 paper-based; 61 iBT). *Application deadline:* Applications are processed on a rolling basis. Application fee: $60 ($75 for international students). Electronic applications accepted. *Expenses:* Tuition, state resident: full-time $7896; part-time $329 per credit hour. Tuition, nonresident: full-time $16,200; part-time $675 per credit hour. Tuition and fees vary according to program. *Financial support:* In 2017–18, research assistantships with full tuition reimbursements (averaging $10,249 per year), teaching assistantships with full tuition reimbursements (averaging $10,303 per year) were awarded; fellowships, career-related internships or fieldwork, Federal Work-Study, scholarships/grants, health care benefits, and unspecified assistantships also available. Support available to part-time students. Financial award application deadline: 11/15; financial award applicants required to submit FAFSA. *Unit head:* Dr. Lan Dong, Program Administrator, 217-206-6779, Fax: 217-206-6217, E-mail: ldong4@uis.edu.

University of Illinois at Urbana–Champaign, Graduate College, College of Liberal Arts and Sciences, Department of English, Champaign, IL 61820. Offers creative writing (MFA); English (MA, PhD).

University of Indianapolis, Graduate Programs, College of Arts and Sciences, Department of English Language and Literature, Indianapolis, IN 46227-3697. Offers English (MA). *Program availability:* Part-time, evening/weekend. *Entrance requirements:* For master's, GRE Subject Test, minimum GPA of 2.5. Additional exam requirements/recommendations for international students: Required—TOEFL (minimum score 550 paper-based). Electronic applications accepted.

The University of Iowa, Graduate College, College of Liberal Arts and Sciences, Department of English, Iowa City, IA 52242-1316. Offers English (PhD); literary studies (MA); nonfiction writing (MFA). *Degree requirements:* For master's, thesis (for some programs), exam; for doctorate, comprehensive exam, thesis/dissertation. *Entrance requirements:* For master's and doctorate, GRE General Test, minimum GPA of 3.0. Additional exam requirements/recommendations for international students: Required—TOEFL (minimum score 640 paper-based; 111 iBT). Electronic applications accepted.

The University of Kansas, Graduate Studies, College of Liberal Arts and Sciences, Department of English, Lawrence, KS 66045. Offers creative writing (MFA), including fine arts/creative writing; English (MA, PhD). *Program availability:* Part-time. *Students:* 86 full-time (49 women), 6 part-time (4 women); includes 16 minority (8 Black or African American, non-Hispanic/Latino; 1 Asian, non-Hispanic/Latino; 4 Hispanic/Latino; 3 Two or more races, non-Hispanic/Latino), 8 international. Average age 30. 165 applicants, 20% accepted, 16 enrolled. In 2017, 9 master's, 9 doctorates awarded. *Entrance requirements:* For master's and doctorate, GRE General Test, two examples of academic writing; resume; statement of approximately 500 words describing interests, training, experience (including teaching experience), academic ability, and goals; three letters of recommendation; official transcripts. Additional exam requirements/recommendations for international students: Required—TOEFL or IELTS. *Application deadline:* For fall admission, 12/31 for domestic and international students. Application fee: $65 ($85 for international students). Electronic applications accepted. *Financial support:* Fellowships, research assistantships, teaching assistantships, and unspecified assistantships available. *Faculty research:* Ecocriticism and science/science fiction writing; gender and sexuality studies; U.S. ethnic literatures, race, and diaspora studies; composition, rhetoric, and language studies; creative writing. *Unit head:* Anna Neill, Chair, 785-864-2521, E-mail: aneill@ku.edu. *Application contact:* Lydia Ash, Graduate Secretary, 785-864-2518, E-mail: lash@ku.edu.
Website: http://www.english.ku.edu

University of Kentucky, Graduate School, College of Arts and Sciences, Program in English, Lexington, KY 40506-0032. Offers MA, PhD. *Degree requirements:* For master's, one foreign language, comprehensive exam, thesis optional; for doctorate, one foreign language, comprehensive exam, thesis/dissertation. *Entrance requirements:* For master's, GRE General Test, minimum undergraduate GPA of 2.75; for doctorate, GRE General Test, minimum graduate GPA of 3.0. Additional exam requirements/recommendations for international students: Required—TOEFL (minimum score 550 paper-based). Electronic applications accepted.

University of La Verne, Regional and Online Campuses, Graduate Credential Program in Education, California Statewide Campus, La Verne, CA 91750-4443. Offers administration services (preliminary) (Credential); education specialist: mild/moderate (Credential); English (Certificate); multiple subject teaching (Credential); pupil personnel services: school counseling (Credential); single subject teaching (Credential); special education (MS); special emphasis (M Ed). *Accreditation:* NCATE. *Program availability:* Part-time. *Faculty:* 3 full-time (2 women), 25 part-time/adjunct (19 women). *Students:* 120 full-time (95 women), 62 part-time (47 women); includes 47 minority (3 Black or African American, non-Hispanic/Latino; 2 American Indian or Alaska Native, non-Hispanic/Latino; 2 Asian, non-Hispanic/Latino; 40 Hispanic/Latino). Average age 31. In 2017, 25 master's, 61 other advanced degrees awarded. *Entrance requirements:* For degree, California Basic Educational Skills Test, minimum undergraduate GPA of 2.75, 3 letters of recommendation, interview. *Application deadline:* Applications are processed

on a rolling basis. Application fee: $50. *Expenses:* Contact institution. *Financial support:* Application deadline: 3/2; applicants required to submit FAFSA. *Unit head:* Pam Bergovoy, Assistant Dean, Regional and Online Campuses/Director, Center for Educators, 909-448-4953, E-mail: pbergovoy@laverne.edu. *Application contact:* 877-468-6858, E-mail: gradadmission@laverne.edu.
Website: https://laverne.edu/locations/

University of Lethbridge, School of Graduate Studies, Lethbridge, AB T1K 3M4, Canada. Offers addictions counseling (M Sc); agricultural biotechnology (M Sc); agricultural studies (M Sc, MA); anthropology (MA); archaeology (M Sc, MA); art (MA, MFA); biochemistry (M Sc); biological sciences (M Sc); biomolecular science (PhD); biosystems and biodiversity (PhD); Canadian studies (MA); chemistry (M Sc); computer science (M Sc); computer science and geographical information science (M Sc); counseling (MC); counseling psychology (M Ed); dramatic arts (MA); earth, space, and physical science (PhD); economics (MA); education (MA, PhD); educational leadership (M Ed); English (MA); environmental science (M Sc); evolution and behavior (PhD); exercise science (M Sc); French (MA); French/German (MA); French/Spanish (MA); general education (M Ed); geography (M Sc, MA); German (MA); health sciences (M Sc); individualized multidisciplinary (M Sc, MA); kinesiology (M Sc, MA); management (M Sc), including accounting, finance, human resource management and labor relations, information systems, international management, marketing, policy and strategy; mathematics (M Sc); music (M Mus, MA); Native American studies (MA); neuroscience (M Sc, PhD); new media (MA, MFA); nursing (M Sc, MN); philosophy (MA); physics (M Sc); political science (MA); psychology (M Sc, MA); religious studies (MA); sociology (MA); theatre and dramatic arts (MFA); theoretical and computational science (PhD); urban and regional studies (MA); women and gender studies (MA). *Program availability:* Part-time, evening/weekend. *Degree requirements:* For master's, thesis (for some programs); for doctorate, comprehensive exam, thesis/dissertation. *Entrance requirements:* For master's, GMAT (for M Sc in management), bachelor's degree in related field, minimum GPA of 3.0 during previous 20 graded semester courses, 2 years' teaching or related experience (M Ed); for doctorate, master's degree, minimum graduate GPA of 3.5. Additional exam requirements/recommendations for international students: Required—TOEFL (minimum score 580 paper-based; 93 iBT). Electronic applications accepted. *Faculty research:* Movement and brain plasticity, gibberellin physiology, photosynthesis, carbon cycling, molecular properties of maingroup ring components.

University of Louisiana at Lafayette, College of Liberal Arts, Department of English, Lafayette, LA 70504. Offers British and American literature (MA), including creative writing, folklore, rhetoric; creative writing (PhD); literature (PhD); rhetoric (PhD). *Program availability:* Part-time. Terminal master's awarded for partial completion of doctoral program. *Degree requirements:* For master's, one foreign language, thesis or alternative; for doctorate, 2 foreign languages, comprehensive exam, thesis/dissertation. *Entrance requirements:* For master's, GRE General Test, minimum GPA of 2.75; for doctorate, GRE General Test, minimum GPA of 3.0. Additional exam requirements/recommendations for international students: Required—TOEFL (minimum score 550 paper-based). Electronic applications accepted. *Faculty research:* Composition theory, Southern literature, medieval literature.

University of Louisiana at Monroe, Graduate School, College of Arts, Education, and Sciences, Department of English, Monroe, LA 71209-0001. Offers MA. *Program availability:* Part-time, evening/weekend. *Faculty:* 6 full-time (4 women). *Students:* 12 full-time (8 women), 1 (woman) part-time; includes 3 minority (1 Black or African American, non-Hispanic/Latino; 1 Hispanic/Latino; 1 Two or more races, non-Hispanic/Latino). Average age 26. 11 applicants, 82% accepted, 7 enrolled. In 2017, 8 master's awarded. *Degree requirements:* For master's, one foreign language, thesis (for some programs). *Entrance requirements:* For master's, GRE General Test (minimum score 900 verbal and quantitative), minimum GPA of 3.0 in English, 2.5 overall. Additional exam requirements/recommendations for international students: Required—TOEFL (minimum score 500 paper-based; 61 iBT) or Michigan English Language Assessment Battery. *Application deadline:* For fall admission, 8/24 priority date for domestic students, 7/1 for international students; for winter admission, 12/14 priority date for domestic students; for spring admission, 1/19 for domestic students, 11/1 for international students. Applications are processed on a rolling basis. Application fee: $20 ($30 for international students). Electronic applications accepted. *Expenses:* Tuition, state resident: full-time $6489; part-time $479 per hour. Tuition, nonresident: full-time $12,100; part-time $479 per hour. *Required fees:* $8860; $802 per hour. $3273 per semester. *Financial support:* In 2017–18, 10 students received support. Teaching assistantships, career-related internships or fieldwork, Federal Work-Study, institutionally sponsored loans, and unspecified assistantships available. Financial award application deadline: 4/1; financial award applicants required to submit FAFSA. *Faculty research:* Creative writing, American literature, British literature, multicultural literature, literary theory. *Unit head:* Dr. Mary Adams, Program Coordinator, 318-342-1500, Fax: 318-342-1755, E-mail: madams@ulm.edu. *Application contact:* Dr. Julia Guernsey-Pitchford, Associate Professor, 318-342-1496, E-mail: pitchford@ulm.edu.
Website: http://www.ulm.edu/english

University of Louisville, Graduate School, College of Arts and Sciences, Department of English, Louisville, KY 40292. Offers English (MA), including creative writing, literature, rhetoric and composition (MA, PhD); rhetoric and composition (PhD), including rhetoric and composition (MA, PhD). *Program availability:* Part-time, evening/weekend. *Faculty:* 37 full-time (20 women), 3 part-time/adjunct (2 women). *Students:* 43 full-time (24 women), 12 part-time (9 women); includes 5 minority (2 Black or African American, non-Hispanic/Latino; 1 Asian, non-Hispanic/Latino; 1 Hispanic/Latino; 1 Two or more races, non-Hispanic/Latino). Average age 31. 47 applicants, 66% accepted, 15 enrolled. In 2017, 12 master's, 6 doctorates awarded. *Degree requirements:* For master's, one foreign language, thesis optional, culminating project of 25-30 pages; for doctorate, one foreign language, comprehensive exam, thesis/dissertation. *Entrance requirements:* For master's and doctorate, GRE General Test. Additional exam requirements/recommendations for international students: Required—TOEFL (minimum score 600 paper-based) or IELTS (6.5). *Application deadline:* Applications are processed on a rolling basis. Application fee: $65. Electronic applications accepted. *Expenses:* Contact institution. *Financial support:* In 2017–18, 3 fellowships with full tuition reimbursements (averaging $20,000 per year), 2 research assistantships (averaging $17,750 per year), 34 teaching assistantships with full tuition reimbursements (averaging $17,750 per year) were awarded; health care benefits and unspecified assistantships also available. Financial award application deadline: 1/5. *Faculty research:* Rhetoric and composition, creative writing, Eighteenth- and Nineteenth-Century British literature, Nineteenth-Century American literature, critical theory. Total annual research expenditures: $124,449. *Unit head:* Dr. Glynis Ridley, Chair, 502-852-6803, E-mail: glynis.ridley@louisville.edu. *Application contact:* Annelise Gray, Senior Program Assistant, 502-852-0505, E-mail: annelise.gray@louisville.edu.
Website: http://www.louisville.edu/english/graduate

University of Maine, Graduate School, College of Liberal Arts and Sciences, Department of English, Orono, ME 04469. Offers MA. *Program availability:* Part-time, evening/weekend. *Faculty:* 23 full-time (12 women). *Students:* 23 full-time (13 women), 4 part-time (all women); includes 3 minority (2 Black or African American, non-Hispanic/

Latino; 1 Two or more races, non-Hispanic/Latino), 1 international. Average age 30. 20 applicants, 80% accepted, 8 enrolled. In 2017, 12 master's awarded. *Degree requirements:* For master's, one foreign language, thesis optional. *Entrance requirements:* For master's, GRE General Test, minimum GPA of 3.0. Additional exam requirements/recommendations for international students: Required—TOEFL (minimum score 80 iBT). *Application deadline:* For fall admission, 1/15 priority date for domestic and international students. Applications are processed on a rolling basis. Application fee: $65. Electronic applications accepted. *Expenses:* Tuition, state resident: full-time $7722; part-time $429 per credit hour. Tuition, nonresident: full-time $25,146; part-time $1397 per credit hour. *Required fees:* $1162; $581 per credit hour. *Financial support:* In 2017–18, 24 students received support, including 20 teaching assistantships with full tuition reimbursements available (averaging $15,200 per year); Federal Work-Study, scholarships/grants, tuition waivers (full and partial), and unspecified assistantships also available. Financial award application deadline: 3/1. *Unit head:* Dr. Steve Evans, Chair, 207-581-3823, Fax: 207-581-1604, E-mail: steven.evans@maine.edu. *Application contact:* Scott G. Delcourt, Assistant Vice President for Graduate Studies and Senior Associate Dean, 207-581-3291, Fax: 207-581-3232, E-mail: graduate@maine.edu. Website: http://english.umaine.edu/

The University of Manchester, School of Arts, Histories and Cultures, Manchester, United Kingdom. Offers anthropology, media and performance (PhD); applied theatre professional (PhD); archaeology (PhD); art history and visual studies (PhD); arts management and cultural policy (PhD); classics and ancient history (PhD); composition (PhD); creative writing (PhD); drama (PhD); economic and social history (PhD); electroacoustic composition (PhD); English and American studies (PhD); history (PhD); humanitarianism and conflict response (PhD); museology (PhD); music (PhD); musicology (PhD); religions and theology (PhD).

University of Manitoba, Faculty of Graduate Studies, Faculty of Arts, Department of English, Film, and Theatre, Winnipeg, MB R3T 2N2, Canada. Offers English (MA, PhD). *Degree requirements:* For master's, one foreign language, thesis; for doctorate, one foreign language, thesis/dissertation.

University of Maryland, Baltimore County, The Graduate School, College of Arts, Humanities and Social Sciences, Program in English: Texts, Technologies, and Literature, Baltimore, MD 21250. Offers MA. *Program availability:* Part-time, evening/weekend. *Faculty:* 14 full-time (11 women). *Students:* 11 full-time (8 women), 7 part-time (5 women); includes 9 minority (6 Black or African American, non-Hispanic/Latino; 2 Asian, non-Hispanic/Latino; 1 Hispanic/Latino). Average age 29. 12 applicants, 83% accepted, 9 enrolled. In 2017, 3 master's awarded. *Degree requirements:* For master's, thesis or portfolio. *Entrance requirements:* For master's, GRE. Additional exam requirements/recommendations for international students: Required—TOEFL. *Application deadline:* For fall admission, 5/1 for domestic students; for spring admission, 5/1 for domestic students. Applications are processed on a rolling basis. Electronic applications accepted. *Expenses: Required fees:* $132. *Financial support:* In 2017–18, 4 students received support. Unspecified assistantships available. Financial award application deadline: 5/1. *Faculty research:* British and American literature, post colonial and Islamic literature, digital media, electronic literacies, rhetoric and composition. *Unit head:* Dr. Orianne Smith, English Department Chair, 410-455-2384, Fax: 410-455-3010, E-mail: osmith@umbc.edu. *Application contact:* Dr. Lucille McCarthy, Graduate Program Director, 410-455-2384, Fax: 410-455-3010, E-mail: mccarthy@umbc.edu. Website: http://www.umbc.edu/english/ma.html

University of Maryland, College Park, Academic Affairs, College of Arts and Humanities, Department of English, Program in English Language and Literature, College Park, MD 20742. Offers MA, PhD. *Degree requirements:* For master's, thesis optional; for doctorate, one foreign language, thesis/dissertation, oral and written exams. *Entrance requirements:* For master's, GRE General Test, minimum GPA of 3.5, writing sample, 3 letters of recommendation; for doctorate, GRE General Test, minimum GPA of 3.7, writing sample. Additional exam requirements/recommendations for international students: Required—TOEFL. Electronic applications accepted.

University of Massachusetts Amherst, Graduate School, College of Humanities and Fine Arts, Department of English, Amherst, MA 01003. Offers American studies (PhD); composition and rhetoric (PhD); creative writing (MFA); English and American literature (MA, PhD). *Program availability:* Part-time. Terminal master's awarded for partial completion of doctoral program. *Degree requirements:* For master's, one foreign language, thesis optional; for doctorate, one foreign language, comprehensive exam, thesis/dissertation. *Entrance requirements:* For master's, manuscript; for doctorate, GRE General Test, manuscript. Additional exam requirements/recommendations for international students: Required—TOEFL (minimum score 550 paper-based; 80 iBT), IELTS (minimum score 6.5). Electronic applications accepted.

University of Massachusetts Boston, College of Liberal Arts, Program in English, Boston, MA 02125-3393. Offers MA. *Program availability:* Part-time, evening/weekend. *Faculty:* 67 full-time (31 women), 17 part-time/adjunct (7 women). *Students:* 20 full-time (13 women), 38 part-time (21 women); includes 10 minority (3 Black or African American, non-Hispanic/Latino; 5 Hispanic/Latino; 2 Two or more races, non-Hispanic/Latino), 3 international. Average age 33. 37 applicants, 70% accepted, 15 enrolled. In 2017, 26 master's awarded. *Entrance requirements:* For master's, minimum GPA of 2.75. *Application deadline:* For fall admission, 3/1 for domestic students; for spring admission, 11/1 for domestic students. *Expenses:* Tuition, state resident: full-time $17,375. Tuition, nonresident: full-time $33,915. *Required fees:* $355. *Financial support:* Research assistantships, teaching assistantships, career-related internships or fieldwork, Federal Work-Study, and unspecified assistantships available. Support available to part-time students. Financial award application deadline: 3/1; financial award applicants required to submit FAFSA. *Faculty research:* Working class literature, women writers, British fiction, composition theory, modern American literature. *Application contact:* Graduate Admissions Coordinator, 617-287-6400, Fax: 617-287-6236, E-mail: bos.gadm@dpc.umassp.edu.

University of Memphis, Graduate School, College of Arts and Sciences, Department of English, Memphis, TN 38152. Offers African-American literature (Graduate Certificate); applied linguistics (PhD); composition studies (PhD); creative writing (MFA); English as a second language (MA); linguistics (MA); literary and cultural studies (PhD), including African-American literature; literature (MA); professional writing (MA, PhD); teaching English as a second/foreign language (Graduate Certificate). *Program availability:* Part-time, evening/weekend, 100% online. *Faculty:* 30 full-time (15 women). *Students:* 73 full-time (34 women), 80 part-time (52 women); includes 35 minority (20 Black or African American, non-Hispanic/Latino; 3 Asian, non-Hispanic/Latino; 9 Hispanic/Latino; 3 Two or more races, non-Hispanic/Latino), 36 international. Average age 35. 78 applicants, 88% accepted, 35 enrolled. In 2017, 27 master's, 15 doctorates, 10 other advanced degrees awarded. Terminal master's awarded for partial completion of doctoral program. *Degree requirements:* For master's, one foreign language, comprehensive exam, thesis optional; for doctorate, 2 foreign languages, comprehensive exam, thesis/dissertation, qualifying exam. *Entrance requirements:* For master's, GRE, minimum undergraduate GPA of 3.0, statement of purpose, two letters of recommendation; for doctorate, GRE, minimum undergraduate and graduate GPA of 3.25, statement of purpose, writing sample, three letters of recommendation. Additional exam requirements/recommendations for international students: Required—TOEFL. *Application deadline:* For fall admission, 1/15 for domestic students; for spring admission, 10/15 for domestic students. Applications are processed on a rolling basis. Application fee: $35 ($60 for international students). Electronic applications accepted. *Expenses:* Contact institution. *Financial support:* In 2017–18, 123 students received support, including 16 research assistantships with full tuition reimbursements available (averaging $15,704 per year), 23 teaching assistantships with full tuition reimbursements available (averaging $22,076 per year); Federal Work-Study, scholarships/grants, and unspecified assistantships also available. Financial award application deadline: 2/1; financial award applicants required to submit FAFSA. *Faculty research:* Applied linguistics, British and American literature, professional writing, composition studies. *Unit head:* Dr. Joshua Phillips, Chair, 901-678-2651, Fax: 901-678-2226, E-mail: jsphllps@memphis.edu. *Application contact:* Dr. Jeffrey Scraba, Coordinator of Graduate Studies, 901-678-4768, Fax: 901-678-2226, E-mail: jscraba@memphis.edu.
Website: http://www.memphis.edu/english

University of Miami, Graduate School, College of Arts and Sciences, Department of English, Coral Gables, FL 33124. Offers creative writing (MFA); English (MA, PhD). *Program availability:* Part-time. Terminal master's awarded for partial completion of doctoral program. *Degree requirements:* For master's, one foreign language, thesis optional; for doctorate, one foreign language, thesis/dissertation. *Entrance requirements:* For master's and doctorate, GRE General Test. Electronic applications accepted. *Faculty research:* Anglo-Irish literature, feminist criticism and theory, Caribbean literature, early modern literature and culture, postcolonial and ethnic studies.

University of Michigan, Rackham Graduate School, College of Literature, Science, and the Arts, Department of English Language and Literature, Ann Arbor, MI 48109. Offers creative writing (MFA); English and education (PhD); English and women's studies (PhD); English language and literature (PhD). *Faculty:* 51 full-time (28 women). *Students:* 85 full-time (54 women); includes 20 minority (4 Black or African American, non-Hispanic/Latino; 5 Asian, non-Hispanic/Latino; 8 Hispanic/Latino; 3 Two or more races, non-Hispanic/Latino), 2 international. Average age 29. 302 applicants, 8% accepted, 13 enrolled. In 2017, 10 doctorates awarded. *Degree requirements:* For doctorate, 2 foreign languages, comprehensive exam, thesis/dissertation, oral defense of dissertation, preliminary exam. *Entrance requirements:* For doctorate, GRE General Test, writing sample. Additional exam requirements/recommendations for international students: Required—TOEFL (minimum score 620 paper-based; 106 iBT). *Application deadline:* For fall admission, 12/10 for domestic and international students. Application fee: $75 ($90 for international students). Electronic applications accepted. *Expenses:* Tuition, state resident: full-time $22,368; part-time $1201 per credit hour. Tuition, nonresident: full-time $45,156; part-time $2467 per credit hour. *Required fees:* $376 per term. Tuition and fees vary according to course load, degree level and program. *Financial support:* In 2017–18, 73 students received support. Fellowships with full tuition reimbursements available, teaching assistantships with full tuition reimbursements available, and health care benefits available. Financial award application deadline: 12/10. *Faculty research:* Post colonialism, modernism, early modern, American literature, British literature. *Application contact:* Graduate Admissions, 734-763-4139, Fax: 734-763-3128, E-mail: graduate.english@umich.edu.
Website: https://www.lsa.umich.edu/english/

University of Michigan, Rackham Graduate School, College of Literature, Science, and the Arts, Department of Women's Studies, Ann Arbor, MI 48109. Offers English and women's studies (PhD); history and women's studies (PhD); LGBTQ studies (Certificate); psychology and women's studies (PhD); women's studies (Certificate). *Degree requirements:* For doctorate, variable foreign language requirement, comprehensive exam (for some programs), thesis/dissertation. *Entrance requirements:* For doctorate, GRE General Test, previous undergraduate coursework in women's studies. Electronic applications accepted. *Expenses:* Tuition, state resident: full-time $22,368; part-time $1201 per credit hour. Tuition, nonresident: full-time $45,156; part-time $2467 per credit hour. *Required fees:* $376 per term. Tuition and fees vary according to course load, degree level and program. *Faculty research:* LGBTQ studies, sexuality studies, feminist science studies, global feminism, health studies, international studies, cultural studies.

University of Michigan–Flint, College of Arts and Sciences, Program in English Language and Literature, Flint, MI 48502-1950. Offers literature (MA); writing and rhetoric (MA). *Program availability:* Part-time. *Faculty:* 26 full-time (17 women), 3 part-time/adjunct (2 women). *Students:* 7 full-time (6 women), 16 part-time (13 women); includes 6 minority (1 Black or African American, non-Hispanic/Latino; 3 Hispanic/Latino; 2 Two or more races, non-Hispanic/Latino), 1 international. Average age 37. 16 applicants, 69% accepted, 9 enrolled. In 2017, 4 master's awarded. *Degree requirements:* For master's, thesis optional. *Entrance requirements:* For master's, bachelor's degree with major or significant coursework in English or related fields from regionally-accredited institution; minimum overall undergraduate GPA of 3.0. Additional exam requirements/recommendations for international students: Required—TOEFL (minimum score 84 iBT), IELTS (minimum score 6.5). *Application deadline:* For fall admission, 8/1 for domestic students, 5/1 for international students; for winter admission, 11/15 for domestic students, 9/1 for international students; for spring admission, 3/15 for domestic students, 1/1 for international students; for summer admission, 5/15 for domestic students. Applications are processed on a rolling basis. Application fee: $55. Electronic applications accepted. *Expenses:* Contact institution. *Financial support:* Career-related internships or fieldwork, Federal Work-Study, scholarships/grants, and unspecified assistantships available. Support available to part-time students. Financial award application deadline: 3/1; financial award applicants required to submit FAFSA. *Unit head:* Dr. Suzanne Knight, Director, 810-762-0145, E-mail: suknight@umflint.edu. *Application contact:* Bradley T. Maki, Director of Graduate Admissions, 810-762-3171, Fax: 810-766-6789, E-mail: bmaki@umflint.edu.
Website: http://www.umflint.edu/graduateprograms/english-language-and-literature-ma

University of Minnesota, Duluth, Graduate School, College of Liberal Arts, Department of English, Duluth, MN 55812-2496. Offers MA. *Program availability:* Part-time. *Degree requirements:* For master's, one foreign language, comprehensive exam, 2 extended papers or projects. *Entrance requirements:* For master's, GRE General Test, minimum GPA of 3.0. Additional exam requirements/recommendations for international students: Required—TOEFL. *Faculty research:* British cultural studies, Irish literature, American studies, linguistics, information design.

University of Minnesota, Twin Cities Campus, Graduate School, College of Liberal Arts, Department of English, Minneapolis, MN 55455. Offers MA, PhD. Terminal master's awarded for partial completion of doctoral program. *Degree requirements:* For master's, one foreign language, thesis or alternative; for doctorate, 2 foreign languages, thesis/dissertation. *Entrance requirements:* For master's and doctorate, GRE General Test. Additional exam requirements/recommendations for international students: Required—TOEFL (minimum score 620 paper-based, 105 iBT) or IELTS (minimum score 7.5). Electronic applications accepted. *Faculty research:* British and American literature, medieval and early modern literature, postcolonial and contemporary literature, feminist studies, film and cultural studies.

University of Mississippi, Graduate School, College of Liberal Arts, University, MS 38677. Offers anthropology (MA); biology (MS, PhD); chemistry (MS, DA, PhD); creative

writing (MFA); documentary expression (MFA); economics (MA, PhD); English (MA, PhD); experimental psychology (PhD); history (MA, PhD); mathematics (MS, PhD); modern languages (MA); music (MM); philosophy (MA); physics (MA, MS, PhD); political science (MA, PhD); Southern studies (MA); studio art (MFA). *Program availability:* Part-time. *Faculty:* 465 full-time (207 women), 82 part-time/adjunct (46 women). *Students:* 466 full-time (229 women), 72 part-time (34 women); includes 87 minority (38 Black or African American, non-Hispanic/Latino; 18 Asian, non-Hispanic/Latino; 24 Hispanic/Latino; 7 Two or more races, non-Hispanic/Latino), 121 international. Average age 29. *Degree requirements:* For doctorate, thesis/dissertation. *Entrance requirements:* For master's, GRE General Test, minimum GPA of 3.0; for doctorate, GRE General Test. Additional exam requirements/recommendations for international students: Required—TOEFL. *Application deadline:* For fall admission, 2/1 priority date for domestic students; for spring admission, 10/1 for domestic students. Applications are processed on a rolling basis. Application fee: $50. Electronic applications accepted. *Financial support:* Fellowships, research assistantships, teaching assistantships, career-related internships or fieldwork, Federal Work-Study, institutionally sponsored loans, scholarships/grants, and unspecified assistantships available. Financial award application deadline: 3/1; financial award applicants required to submit FAFSA. *Unit head:* Dr. Lee Michael Cohen, Dean, 662-915-7177, Fax: 662-915-5792, E-mail: libarts@olemiss.edu. *Application contact:* Dr. Christy M. Wyandt, Associate Dean of Graduate School, 662-915-7474, Fax: 662-915-7577, E-mail: cwyandt@olemiss.edu.

University of Missouri, Office of Research and Graduate Studies, College of Arts and Science, Department of English, Columbia, MO 65211. Offers MA, PhD. Terminal master's awarded for partial completion of doctoral program. *Degree requirements:* For doctorate, 2 foreign languages, comprehensive exam, thesis/dissertation. *Entrance requirements:* For master's, GRE General Test, minimum GPA of 3.0; for doctorate, GRE General Test, minimum GPA of 3.0; MA in English or equivalent. Additional exam requirements/recommendations for international students: Required—TOEFL (minimum score 500 paper-based; 61 iBT). Electronic applications accepted. *Faculty research:* British and American literature and culture, African Diaspora studies, creative writing, folklore, linguistics, rhetoric and composition.

University of Missouri–Kansas City, College of Arts and Sciences, Department of English Language and Literature, Kansas City, MO 64110-2499. Offers English (MA, PhD). PhD (interdisciplinary) offered through the School of Graduate Studies. *Program availability:* Part-time, evening/weekend. *Degree requirements:* For master's, one foreign language; for doctorate, 2 foreign languages, comprehensive exam, thesis/dissertation. *Entrance requirements:* For master's, GRE General Test, 3 letters of recommendation. Additional exam requirements/recommendations for international students: Required—TOEFL (minimum score 550 paper-based; 80 iBT). Electronic applications accepted. *Faculty research:* Creative writing: poetry and prose, computational linguistics, rhetoric and composition, African-American and British literature, print culture.

University of Missouri–St. Louis, College of Arts and Sciences, Department of English, St. Louis, MO 63121. Offers creative writing (MFA); English (MA). *Program availability:* Part-time, evening/weekend. *Faculty:* 19 full-time (7 women), 4 part-time/adjunct (2 women). *Students:* 16 full-time (9 women), 48 part-time (33 women); includes 12 minority (6 Black or African American, non-Hispanic/Latino; 2 Asian, non-Hispanic/Latino; 1 Hispanic/Latino; 3 Two or more races, non-Hispanic/Latino), 1 international. 37 applicants, 84% accepted, 17 enrolled. *Degree requirements:* For master's, thesis optional. *Entrance requirements:* For master's, two letters of recommendation; writing sample (MFA). Additional exam requirements/recommendations for international students: Required—TOEFL (minimum score 550 paper-based; 79 iBT), IELTS (minimum score 6.5). *Application deadline:* For fall admission, 7/1 priority date for domestic and international students; for spring admission, 12/1 priority date for domestic and international students. Applications are processed on a rolling basis. Application fee: $50 ($40 for international students). Electronic applications accepted. *Expenses:* Tuition, state resident: part-time $476.50 per credit hour. Tuition, nonresident: part-time $1169.70 per credit hour. *Financial support:* Teaching assistantships with tuition reimbursements available. Financial award applicants required to submit FAFSA. *Faculty research:* Victorian literature, Shakespeare and Renaissance literature, eighteenth-century literature, composition theory. *Unit head:* Dr. Frank Grady, Chair, 314-516-5510, Fax: 314-516-5781, E-mail: fgrady@umsl.edu. *Application contact:* 314-516-5458, Fax: 314-516-5310, E-mail: gradadm@umsl.edu.
Website: http://www.umsl.edu/divisions/artscience/english/

University of Montana, Graduate School, College of Humanities and Sciences, Department of English, Program in Literature, Missoula, MT 59812. Offers MA. *Degree requirements:* For master's, thesis optional. *Entrance requirements:* For master's, GRE General Test, sample of written work. Additional exam requirements/recommendations for international students: Required—TOEFL. *Faculty research:* Literary history, cultural studies, criticism and theory, Western studies.

University of Montevallo, College of Arts and Sciences, Department of English, Montevallo, AL 35115. Offers MA. *Program availability:* Part-time. *Students:* 1 (woman) full-time, 5 part-time (4 women). *Degree requirements:* For master's, comprehensive exam, thesis optional. *Entrance requirements:* For master's, GRE General Test, MAT, minimum undergraduate GPA of 2.75 in last 60 hours or 2.5 overall, bachelor's degree in English or equivalent. Additional exam requirements/recommendations for international students: Required—TOEFL (minimum score 550 paper-based). *Application deadline:* For fall admission, 7/15 for domestic students; for spring admission, 11/15 for domestic students. Application fee: $30. *Expenses:* Tuition, state resident: full-time $9888. Tuition, nonresident: full-time $21,144. *Required fees:* $1920. *Financial support:* Federal Work-Study, scholarships/grants, and unspecified assistantships available. *Unit head:* Dr. Paul Mahaffey, Chair, 205-665-6420, E-mail: mahaffey@montevallo.edu. *Application contact:* Alexander Beringer, 205-665-6420, E-mail: aberinger@montevallo.edu.
Website: http://www.montevallo.edu/english/

University of Nebraska at Kearney, College of Fine Arts and Humanities, Department of English, Kearney, NE 68849-0001. Offers creative writing (MA); literature (MA); writing (MA). *Program availability:* Part-time, evening/weekend, online learning. *Degree requirements:* For master's, comprehensive exam (for some programs), thesis optional, thesis or exam (for literature option). *Entrance requirements:* For master's, writing sample, three letters of recommendation, letter of interest. Additional exam requirements/recommendations for international students: Recommended—TOEFL (minimum score 550 paper-based; 79 iBT), IELTS (minimum score 6.5). Electronic applications accepted. *Faculty research:* Narrative theory, popular culture, western and plains literature, women's studies, media studies, children's literature, poetry, speculative fiction, creative writing, comics, composition and rhetoric, renaissance drama, film studies, ecocriticism.

University of Nebraska at Omaha, Graduate Studies, College of Arts and Sciences, Department of English, Omaha, NE 68182. Offers advanced writing (Certificate); English (MA); teaching English to speakers of other languages (Certificate); technical communication (Certificate). *Program availability:* Part-time, evening/weekend. *Degree requirements:* For master's, comprehensive exam, thesis (for some programs). *Entrance requirements:* For master's, GRE or MAT, minimum GPA of 3.0, transcripts, 3 letters of recommendation, statement of purpose, writing sample; for Certificate, minimum GPA of 3.0, transcripts, statement of purpose. Additional exam requirements/recommendations for international students: Required—TOEFL, IELTS, PTE. Electronic applications accepted.

University of Nebraska–Lincoln, Graduate College, College of Arts and Sciences, Department of English, Lincoln, NE 68588-0333. Offers composition and rhetoric (MA, PhD); creative writing (MA, PhD); literature studies (MA, PhD). *Degree requirements:* For master's, thesis optional; for doctorate, one foreign language, comprehensive exam, thesis/dissertation. *Entrance requirements:* For master's, writing sample; for doctorate, GRE General Test, writing sample. Additional exam requirements/recommendations for international students: Required—TOEFL (minimum score 600 paper-based). Electronic applications accepted. *Faculty research:* Creative writing, composition and rhetoric, women's studies, North American literature, medieval/Renaissance studies.

University of Nevada, Las Vegas, Graduate College, College of Liberal Arts, Department of English, Las Vegas, NV 89154-5011. Offers creative writing (MFA); English (MA, PhD). *Program availability:* Part-time. *Faculty:* 23 full-time (10 women), 1 (woman) part-time/adjunct. *Students:* 69 full-time (38 women), 16 part-time (7 women); includes 24 minority (1 Black or African American, non-Hispanic/Latino; 7 Asian, non-Hispanic/Latino; 9 Hispanic/Latino; 1 Native Hawaiian or other Pacific Islander, non-Hispanic/Latino; 6 Two or more races, non-Hispanic/Latino), 2 international. Average age 33. 141 applicants, 22% accepted, 24 enrolled. In 2017, 14 master's, 5 doctorates awarded. *Degree requirements:* For master's, one foreign language, comprehensive exam (for some programs), thesis, creative thesis; for doctorate, one foreign language, comprehensive exam, thesis/dissertation. *Entrance requirements:* For master's, GRE General Test, GRE Subject Test, writing sample; statement of purpose; 2 letters of recommendation; transcripts from all colleges; for doctorate, GRE General Test, GRE Subject Test, MA in English with minimum GPA of 3.5; writing sample; 3 letters of recommendation; statement of purpose. Additional exam requirements/recommendations for international students: Required—TOEFL (minimum score 550 paper-based; 80 iBT), IELTS (minimum score 7). *Application deadline:* For fall admission, 1/15 for domestic students; for spring admission, 11/1 for domestic students. Application fee: $60 ($95 for international students). Electronic applications accepted. *Expenses:* Contact institution. *Financial support:* In 2017–18, 63 students received support, including 2 research assistantships with full tuition reimbursements available (averaging $17,500 per year), 61 teaching assistantships with full tuition reimbursements available (averaging $15,512 per year); institutionally sponsored loans, scholarships/grants, health care benefits, and unspecified assistantships also available. Financial award application deadline: 3/15; financial award applicants required to submit FAFSA. *Faculty research:* Creative writing, poetry, fiction. *Total annual research expenditures:* $22,954. *Unit head:* Dr. Gary Totten, Chair/Professor, 702-895-1258, Fax: 702-895-4801, E-mail: gary.totten@unlv.edu. *Application contact:* Anne Stevens, Graduate Coordinator, 702-895-3500, E-mail: anne.stevens@unlv.edu.
Website: http://english.unlv.edu/

University of Nevada, Reno, Graduate School, College of Liberal Arts, Department of English, Reno, NV 89557. Offers MA, MATE, PhD. Terminal master's awarded for partial completion of doctoral program. *Degree requirements:* For master's, variable foreign language requirement, thesis optional; for doctorate, variable foreign language requirement, thesis/dissertation. *Entrance requirements:* For master's, GRE General Test, minimum GPA of 2.75; for doctorate, GRE General Test, minimum GPA of 3.0. Additional exam requirements/recommendations for international students: Required—TOEFL (minimum score 500 paper-based; 61 iBT), IELTS (minimum score 6). Electronic applications accepted. *Faculty research:* Translating Persian/Iraqi literature, Shakespearean literature, modern American literature, composition and rhetoric.

University of New Brunswick Fredericton, School of Graduate Studies, Faculty of Arts, Department of English, Fredericton, NB E3B 5A3, Canada. Offers MA, PhD. *Program availability:* Part-time. *Degree requirements:* For master's, thesis, 18 credit hours; for doctorate, one foreign language, comprehensive exam, thesis/dissertation. *Entrance requirements:* For master's, BA with minimum GPA of 3.5, honors English (preferred); for doctorate, minimum GPA of 3.7; MA in English. Additional exam requirements/recommendations for international students: Required—TWE (minimum score 4), TOEFL (minimum paper-based score 600) or IELTS (minimum score 7). Electronic applications accepted. *Faculty research:* Creative writing, Canadian and maritime literature, post-Colonial/Commonwealth literature, early modern/Renaissance literature, scholarly editing and textual studies, American literature, British literature, film.

University of New Hampshire, Graduate School, College of Liberal Arts, Department of English, Durham, NH 03824. Offers English (MST, PhD); language and linguistics (MA); literature (MA); writing (MFA). *Program availability:* Part-time. *Students:* 57 full-time (39 women), 39 part-time (28 women); includes 9 minority (4 Black or African American, non-Hispanic/Latino; 4 Hispanic/Latino; 1 Two or more races, non-Hispanic/Latino), 4 international. Average age 31. 117 applicants, 60% accepted, 27 enrolled. In 2017, 29 master's, 3 doctorates awarded. *Entrance requirements:* For master's, GRE General Test, sample of written work; for doctorate, GRE General Test, GRE Subject Test, sample of written work. Additional exam requirements/recommendations for international students: Required—TOEFL (minimum score 550 paper-based; 80 iBT). *Application deadline:* For fall admission, 1/15 for domestic and international students; for spring admission, 12/1 for domestic students. Application fee: $65. Electronic applications accepted. *Financial support:* In 2017–18, 64 students received support, including 2 fellowships, 37 teaching assistantships; research assistantships, career-related internships or fieldwork, Federal Work-Study, scholarships/grants, and tuition waivers (full and partial) also available. Support available to part-time students. Financial award application deadline: 2/15. *Unit head:* Dr. Rachel Trubowitz, Chair, 603-862-0254. *Application contact:* Janine Wilks, Administrative Assistant, 603-862-3963, E-mail: engl.grad@unh.edu.
Website: http://cola.unh.edu/english

University of New Mexico, Graduate Studies, College of Arts and Sciences, Program in English, Albuquerque, NM 87131. Offers MA, PhD. *Faculty:* 14 full-time (8 women). *Students:* 39 full-time (27 women), 24 part-time (16 women); includes 12 minority (1 American Indian or Alaska Native, non-Hispanic/Latino; 8 Hispanic/Latino; 3 Two or more races, non-Hispanic/Latino), 5 international. Average age 34. 51 applicants, 33% accepted, 16 enrolled. In 2017, 16 master's, 7 doctorates awarded. *Degree requirements:* For master's, one foreign language, comprehensive exam (for some programs), thesis or alternative, portfolio; for doctorate, 2 foreign languages, comprehensive exam, thesis/dissertation. *Entrance requirements:* For master's, GRE General Test; for doctorate, GRE General Test, GRE Subject Test (literature). *Application deadline:* For fall admission, 1/15 for domestic and international students. Application fee: $50. Electronic applications accepted. *Financial support:* Teaching assistantships with full tuition reimbursements and health care benefits available. Financial award application deadline: 1/15. *Faculty research:* American, Native American, Chicano, and British and Irish literature; rhetoric and writing; medieval studies. *Unit head:* Dr. Gail Turley Houston, Chair, 505-277-6347, Fax: 505-277-0021, E-mail: ghouston@unm.edu. *Application contact:* N. Ezra Meier, Graduate Advisor, 505-277-4437, Fax: 505-277-0021, E-mail: nezra@unm.edu.
Website: http://english.unm.edu/graduate/index.html

English

University of New Orleans, Graduate School, College of Liberal Arts, Department of English, Program in English, New Orleans, LA 70148. Offers MA. *Program availability:* Part-time, evening/weekend. *Degree requirements:* For master's, one foreign language, thesis (for some programs). *Entrance requirements:* For master's, GRE General Test. Additional exam requirements/recommendations for international students: Required—TOEFL (minimum score 550 paper-based; 79 iBT), IELTS (minimum score 6.5). Electronic applications accepted. *Faculty research:* British and American Literature, professional writing.

University of North Alabama, College of Arts and Sciences, Department of English, Program in English, Florence, AL 35632-0001. Offers MA. *Program availability:* Part-time. *Faculty:* 12 full-time (8 women). *Students:* 6 full-time (3 women), 6 part-time (4 women). Average age 29. 5 applicants, 80% accepted, 3 enrolled. In 2017, 4 master's awarded. *Degree requirements:* For master's, comprehensive exam (for some programs), thesis optional. *Entrance requirements:* For master's, GRE, MAT. Additional exam requirements/recommendations for international students: Required—TOEFL (minimum score 79 iBT), IELTS (minimum score 6), PTE (minimum score 54). *Application deadline:* Applications are processed on a rolling basis. Application fee: $50 ($100 for international students). Electronic applications accepted. *Expenses:* Tuition, state resident: full-time $7824; part-time $5943 per year. Tuition, nonresident: full-time $15,648; part-time $11,736 per year. *Required fees:* $3064; $2298 per unit. Tuition and fees vary according to course load and reciprocity agreements. *Financial support:* In 2017–18, 5 students received support. Federal Work-Study, scholarships/grants, and unspecified assistantships available. Financial award application deadline: 2/1; financial award applicants required to submit FAFSA. *Unit head:* Dr. Cynthia Burkhead, Chair, 256-765-4238, E-mail: english@una.edu. *Application contact:* Hillary N. Coats, Graduate Admissions Coordinator, 256-765-4447, E-mail: graduate@una.edu.
Website: https://www.una.edu/english/master-of-arts-in-english.html

The University of North Carolina at Chapel Hill, Graduate School, College of Arts and Sciences, Department of English, Chapel Hill, NC 27599. Offers MA, PhD. *Degree requirements:* For master's, one foreign language, comprehensive exam, thesis; for doctorate, 2 foreign languages, comprehensive exam, thesis/dissertation. *Entrance requirements:* For master's and doctorate, GRE General Test, GRE Subject Test, minimum GPA of 3.0 for last 2 undergraduate years, writing sample. Additional exam requirements/recommendations for international students: Required—TOEFL. Electronic applications accepted. *Faculty research:* African-American, Southern, period, genre, critical theory/culture studies.

The University of North Carolina at Charlotte, College of Liberal Arts and Sciences, Department of English, Charlotte, NC 28223-0001. Offers applied linguistics (Graduate Certificate); English (MA); technical and professional writing (Graduate Certificate). *Program availability:* Part-time, evening/weekend. *Faculty:* 33 full-time (19 women), 2 part-time/adjunct (1 woman). *Students:* 33 full-time (25 women), 20 part-time (14 women); includes 9 minority (1 Black or African American, non-Hispanic/Latino; 2 Asian, non-Hispanic/Latino; 5 Hispanic/Latino; 1 Two or more races, non-Hispanic/Latino), 2 international. Average age 30. 38 applicants, 87% accepted, 18 enrolled. In 2017, 19 master's, 2 other advanced degrees awarded. *Degree requirements:* For master's, comprehensive exam (for some programs), thesis, comprehensive exam, or project. *Entrance requirements:* For master's, GRE, MAT, minimum undergraduate GPA of 3.0, statement of purpose, recommendation letters; for Graduate Certificate, statement of purpose, three letters of recommendation, writing sample, minimum GPA of 2.75. Additional exam requirements/recommendations for international students: Required—TOEFL (minimum score 523 paper-based, 70 iBT) or IELTS (6.5). *Application deadline:* For fall admission, 3/1 priority date for domestic and international students; for spring admission, 10/1 priority date for domestic and international students; for summer admission, 4/1 priority date for domestic and international students. Applications are processed on a rolling basis. Application fee: $75. Electronic applications accepted. *Expenses:* Tuition, state resident: full-time $4337. Tuition, nonresident: full-time $17,771. *Required fees:* $3211. Tuition and fees vary according to course load and program. *Financial support:* In 2017–18, 17 students received support, including 17 teaching assistantships (averaging $8,118 per year); career-related internships or fieldwork, institutionally sponsored loans, scholarships/grants, and unspecified assistantships also available. Support available to part-time students. Financial award application deadline: 3/1; financial award applicants required to submit FAFSA. *Total annual research expenditures:* $30,460. *Unit head:* Dr. Mark West, Chair, 704-687-0618, E-mail: miwest@uncc.edu. *Application contact:* Kathy B. Giddings, Director of Graduate Admissions, 704-687-5503, Fax: 704-687-1668, E-mail: gradadm@uncc.edu.
Website: http://english.uncc.edu/

The University of North Carolina at Greensboro, Graduate School, College of Arts and Sciences, Department of English, Program in English, Greensboro, NC 27412-5001. Offers American literature (PhD); English (M Ed, MA); English literature (PhD); rhetoric and composition (PhD). *Degree requirements:* For master's, comprehensive exam, thesis or alternative; for doctorate, variable foreign language requirement, thesis/dissertation, preliminary exam. *Entrance requirements:* For master's, GRE General Test, GRE Subject Test, minimum GPA of 3.0; for doctorate, GRE General Test, GRE Subject Test, critical writing sample, minimum GPA of 3.0. Additional exam requirements/recommendations for international students: Required—TOEFL. Electronic applications accepted.

The University of North Carolina Wilmington, College of Arts and Sciences, Department of English, Wilmington, NC 28403-3297. Offers MA. *Program availability:* Part-time. *Faculty:* 16 full-time (10 women). *Students:* 17 full-time (11 women), 6 part-time (all women); includes 1 minority (Black or African American, non-Hispanic/Latino). Average age 28. 17 applicants, 47% accepted, 7 enrolled. In 2017, 8 master's awarded. *Degree requirements:* For master's, comprehensive exam, thesis (for some programs). *Entrance requirements:* For master's, GRE General Test, 3 recommendations, statement of interest, writing sample. Additional exam requirements/recommendations for international students: Required—TOEFL (minimum score 550 paper-based; 79 iBT), IELTS (minimum score 6.5). *Application deadline:* For fall admission, 5/1 for domestic students; for spring admission, 11/1 for domestic students; for summer admission, 5/1 for domestic students. Applications are processed on a rolling basis. Application fee: $75. Electronic applications accepted. *Expenses:* Tuition, state resident: full-time $4626; part-time $226.76 per credit hour. Tuition, nonresident: full-time $17,834; part-time $874.22 per credit hour. *Required fees:* $2124. Tuition and fees vary according to program. *Financial support:* Teaching assistantships and scholarships/grants available. Financial award application deadline: 1/1; financial award applicants required to submit FAFSA. *Unit head:* Dr. Tiffany Gilbert, Chair, 910-962-7746, Fax: 910-962-7186, E-mail: gilbertt@uncw.edu. *Application contact:* Dr. Meghan Sweeney, Graduate Coordinator, 910-962-3054, Fax: 910-962-7186, E-mail: sweeneym@uncw.edu.
Website: http://www.uncw.edu/english/graduate/index.html

University of North Dakota, Graduate School, College of Arts and Sciences, Department of English, Grand Forks, ND 58202. Offers MA, PhD. *Degree requirements:* For master's, one foreign language, comprehensive exam, thesis or alternative; for doctorate, one foreign language, comprehensive exam, thesis/dissertation. *Entrance requirements:* For master's and doctorate, GRE General Test, minimum GPA of 3.0. Additional exam requirements/recommendations for international students: Required—TOEFL (minimum score 550 paper-based; 79 iBT), IELTS (minimum score 6.5). Electronic applications accepted. *Faculty research:* Creative writing, rhetorical theory, cinema, American literature, European literature.

University of Northern Colorado, Graduate School, College of Humanities and Social Sciences, Department of English, Greeley, CO 80639. Offers MA. *Program availability:* Part-time. *Degree requirements:* For master's, comprehensive exam. *Entrance requirements:* For master's, GRE General Test, 2 letters of recommendation. Electronic applications accepted.

University of Northern Iowa, Graduate College, College of Humanities, Arts and Sciences, Department of Languages and Literatures, MA Program in English, Cedar Falls, IA 50614. Offers creative writing (MA); English (MA); literature (MA). *Program availability:* Part-time, evening/weekend. *Degree requirements:* For master's, one foreign language, comprehensive exam, thesis or alternative, portfolio. *Entrance requirements:* Additional exam requirements/recommendations for international students: Required—TOEFL (minimum score 600 paper-based; 100 iBT). Electronic applications accepted.

University of North Florida, College of Arts and Sciences, Department of English, Jacksonville, FL 32224. Offers MA. *Program availability:* Part-time, evening/weekend. *Degree requirements:* For master's, comprehensive exam, thesis optional. *Entrance requirements:* For master's, GRE General Test, minimum GPA of 3.0 in last 60 hours, writing sample. Additional exam requirements/recommendations for international students: Required—TOEFL (minimum score 500 paper-based; 61 iBT). Electronic applications accepted.

University of North Texas, Robert B. Toulouse School of Graduate Studies, Denton, TX 76203-5459. Offers accounting (MS); applied anthropology (MA, MS); applied behavior analysis (Certificate); applied geography (MA); applied technology and performance improvement (M Ed, MS); art education (MA); art history (MA); art museum education (Certificate); arts leadership (Certificate); audiology (Au D); behavior analysis (MS); behavioral science (PhD); biochemistry and molecular biology (MS); biology (MA, MS); biomedical engineering (MS); business analysis (MS); chemistry (MS); clinical health psychology (PhD); communication studies (MA, MS); computer engineering (MS); computer science (MS); counseling (M Ed, MS), including clinical mental health counseling (MS), college and university counseling, elementary school counseling, secondary school counseling; creative writing (MA); criminal justice (MS); curriculum and instruction (M Ed); decision sciences (MBA); design (MA, MFA), including fashion design (MFA), innovation studies, interior design (MFA); early childhood studies (MS); economics (MS); educational leadership (M Ed, Ed D); educational psychology (MS, PhD), including family studies (MS), gifted and talented (MS), human development (MS), learning and cognition (MS), research, measurement and evaluation (MS); electrical engineering (MS); emergency management (MPA); engineering technology (MS); English (MA); English as a second language (MA); environmental science (MS); finance (MBA, MS); financial management (MPA); French (MA); health services management (MBA); higher education (M Ed, Ed D); history (MA, MS); hospitality management (MS); human resources management (MPA); information science (MS); information systems (PhD); information technologies (MBA); interdisciplinary studies (MA, MS); international studies (MA); international sustainable tourism (MS); jazz studies (MM); journalism (MA, MJ, Graduate Certificate), including interactive and virtual digital communication (Graduate Certificate), narrative journalism (Graduate Certificate), public relations (Graduate Certificate); kinesiology (MS); linguistics (MA); local government management (MPA); logistics (PhD); logistics and supply chain management (MBA); long-term care, senior housing, and aging services (MA); management (PhD); marketing (MBA); mathematics (MA, MS); mechanical and energy engineering (MS, PhD); music (MA), including ethnomusicology, music theory, musicology, performance; music composition (PhD); music education (MM Ed, PhD); nonprofit management (MPA); operations and supply chain management (MBA); performance (MM, DMA); philosophy (MA); political science (MA); professional and technical communication (MA); radio, television and film (MA, MFA); rehabilitation counseling (Certificate); sociology (MA); Spanish (MA); special education (M Ed); speech-language pathology (MA); strategic management (MBA); studio art (MFA); teaching (M Ed); MBA/MS. *Program availability:* Part-time, evening/weekend, online learning. Terminal master's awarded for partial completion of doctoral program. *Degree requirements:* For master's, variable foreign language requirement, comprehensive exam (for some programs), thesis (for some programs); for doctorate, variable foreign language requirement, comprehensive exam (for some programs), thesis/dissertation; for other advanced degree, variable foreign language requirement, comprehensive exam (for some programs). *Entrance requirements:* For master's and doctorate, GRE, GMAT. Additional exam requirements/recommendations for international students: Required—TOEFL (minimum score 550 paper-based; 79 iBT). Electronic applications accepted.

University of Notre Dame, Graduate School, College of Arts and Letters, Division of Humanities, Department of English, Notre Dame, IN 46556. Offers creative writing (MFA); English (MA, PhD). *Degree requirements:* For doctorate, one foreign language, thesis/dissertation, candidacy exam. *Entrance requirements:* For master's, GRE General Test, minimum GPA of 3.0; for doctorate, GRE General Test, GRE Subject Test, minimum GPA of 3.0. Additional exam requirements/recommendations for international students: Required—TOEFL (minimum score 600 paper-based; 80 iBT). Electronic applications accepted. *Faculty research:* Early modern studies (medieval/Renaissance), modern British studies (eighteenth-twentieth centuries), American Studies, literature and philosophy, Irish studies.

University of Oklahoma, College of Arts and Sciences, Department of English, Norman, OK 73019. Offers literary and cultural studies (MA, PhD); writing and rhetoric studies (MA, PhD). *Program availability:* Part-time. *Faculty:* 25 full-time (13 women), 1 part-time/adjunct (0 women). *Students:* 29 full-time (21 women), 17 part-time (8 women); includes 9 minority (1 American Indian or Alaska Native, non-Hispanic/Latino; 2 Asian, non-Hispanic/Latino; 5 Hispanic/Latino; 1 Two or more races, non-Hispanic/Latino), 2 international. Average age 31. 34 applicants, 71% accepted, 18 enrolled. In 2017, 7 master's, 4 doctorates awarded. *Degree requirements:* For master's, one foreign language, comprehensive exam (for some programs), thesis (for some programs), exam or thesis; for doctorate, one foreign language, comprehensive exam, thesis/dissertation. *Entrance requirements:* For master's, GRE, BA in English or related field; for doctorate, GRE, MA in English or related field. Additional exam requirements/recommendations for international students: Required—TOEFL (minimum score 79 iBT) or IELTS (minimum score 6.5). *Application deadline:* For fall admission, 1/5 priority date for domestic and international students. Application fee: $50 ($100 for international students). Electronic applications accepted. *Expenses:* Tuition, state resident: full-time $5119; part-time $213.30 per credit hour. Tuition, nonresident: full-time $19,778; part-time $824.10 per credit hour. *Required fees:* $3458; $133.55 per credit hour. $126.50 per semester. *Financial support:* In 2017–18, 40 students received support, including 6 research assistantships with full tuition reimbursements available (averaging $14,515 per year), 31 teaching assistantships with full tuition reimbursements available (averaging $12,496 per year); fellowships with full tuition reimbursements available, scholarships/grants, health care benefits, and unspecified assistantships also available. Financial award application deadline: 6/1; financial award applicants required to submit FAFSA. *Faculty research:* American Indian literature and culture; composition and rhetoric; American

literature; British literature; postcolonial literature and culture. *Total annual research expenditures:* $101. *Unit head:* Dr. Daniela Garofalo, Professor and Chair, 405-325-4661, Fax: 405-325-0831, E-mail: dg@ou.edu. *Application contact:* Sara Day, Graduate Assistant, 405-325-0489, Fax: 405-325-0831, E-mail: redpanda@ou.edu.
Website: http://cas.ou.edu/english

University of Oregon, Graduate School, College of Arts and Sciences, Department of English, Eugene, OR 97403. Offers MA, PhD. Terminal master's awarded for partial completion of doctoral program. *Degree requirements:* For master's, one foreign language; for doctorate, 2 foreign languages, thesis/dissertation. *Entrance requirements:* For master's, GRE General Test; for doctorate, GRE Subject Test (English literature), minimum GPA of 3.5. Additional exam requirements/recommendations for international students: Required—TOEFL. *Faculty research:* Old and Middle English, women writers, critical theory, literature and the environment, rhetoric and composition.

University of Ottawa, Faculty of Graduate and Postdoctoral Studies, Faculty of Arts, Department of English, Ottawa, ON K1N 6N5, Canada. Offers MA, PhD. *Program availability:* Part-time, evening/weekend. *Degree requirements:* For master's, one foreign language, thesis optional; for doctorate, 2 foreign languages, comprehensive exam, thesis/dissertation. *Entrance requirements:* For master's, honors degree or equivalent, minimum B average; for doctorate, master's degree, minimum B+ average. Electronic applications accepted. *Faculty research:* Anglo-Saxon and medieval literature.

University of Pennsylvania, School of Arts and Sciences, Graduate Group in English, Philadelphia, PA 19104. Offers AM, PhD. *Faculty:* 52 full-time (25 women), 12 part-time/adjunct (5 women). *Students:* 68 full-time (38 women), 1 part-time (0 women); includes 24 minority (8 Black or African American, non-Hispanic/Latino; 10 Asian, non-Hispanic/Latino; 3 Hispanic/Latino; 3 Two or more races, non-Hispanic/Latino), 13 international. Average age 28. 554 applicants, 4% accepted, 15 enrolled. In 2017, 4 master's, 10 doctorates awarded. Terminal master's awarded for partial completion of doctoral program.
Website: http://www.english.upenn.edu

University of Pittsburgh, Kenneth P. Dietrich School of Arts and Sciences, Department of English, Pittsburgh, PA 15260. Offers English (MA, PhD); writing (MFA). *Faculty:* 59 full-time (27 women). *Students:* 108 full-time (76 women); includes 43 minority (11 Black or African American, non-Hispanic/Latino; 1 American Indian or Alaska Native, non-Hispanic/Latino; 17 Asian, non-Hispanic/Latino; 12 Hispanic/Latino; 2 Two or more races, non-Hispanic/Latino). Average age 29. 285 applicants, 14% accepted, 24 enrolled. In 2017, 16 master's, 8 doctorates awarded. Terminal master's awarded for partial completion of doctoral program. *Degree requirements:* For master's, variable foreign language requirement, thesis; for doctorate, variable foreign language requirement, comprehensive exam, thesis/dissertation. *Entrance requirements:* For master's and doctorate, GRE General Test, writing sample. Additional exam requirements/recommendations for international students: Required—TOEFL (minimum score 550 paper-based, 90 iBT) or IELTS (7.0). *Application deadline:* For fall admission, 12/10 for domestic and international students. Application fee: $50. Electronic applications accepted. *Financial support:* In 2017–18, 22 fellowships with full tuition reimbursements (averaging $22,896 per year), 11 research assistantships with full and partial tuition reimbursements (averaging $15,060 per year), 56 teaching assistantships with full and partial tuition reimbursements (averaging $18,815 per year) were awarded; Federal Work-Study, institutionally sponsored loans, scholarships/grants, health care benefits, tuition waivers (full and partial), and unspecified assistantships also available. Support available to part-time students. Financial award application deadline: 12/10. *Faculty research:* Cultural studies, literary studies, film and media studies, composition and rhetoric. *Unit head:* Dr. Don Bialostosky, Chair, 412-624-6509, Fax: 412-624-6639, E-mail: dhb2@pitt.edu. *Application contact:* Jesse Daugherty, Graduate Administrator, 412-624-6549, Fax: 412-624-6639, E-mail: jed110@pitt.edu.
Website: http://www.english.pitt.edu

University of Puerto Rico–Mayagüez, Graduate Studies, College of Arts and Sciences, Department of English, Mayagüez, PR 00681-9000. Offers English education (MA). *Program availability:* Part-time. *Degree requirements:* For master's, one foreign language, comprehensive exam, thesis. *Entrance requirements:* For master's, minimum GPA of 3.0; course work in linguistics or language, American literature, British literature, and structure/grammar or syntax. Additional exam requirements/recommendations for international students: Required—TOEFL (minimum score 550 paper-based; 79 iBT). Electronic applications accepted. *Faculty research:* Multiliteracies and multimodality theorizing and practice, second language writing, Afro-Puerto Rican studies, modern poetry, Puerto Rican culture and folklore.

University of Puerto Rico–Río Piedras, College of Humanities, Department of English, San Juan, PR 00931-3300. Offers Caribbean linguistics (PhD); Caribbean literature (PhD); English (MA). *Program availability:* Part-time. *Degree requirements:* For master's, one foreign language, comprehensive exam, thesis; for doctorate, residency. *Entrance requirements:* For master's, PAEG or GRE, interview, minimum GPA of 3.0, 2 letters of recommendation; for doctorate, PAEG or GRE, minimum GPA of 3.0, 3 letters of recommendation, interview.

University of Regina, Faculty of Graduate Studies and Research, Faculty of Arts, Department of English, Regina, SK S4S 0A2, Canada. Offers creative writing (MA); English (MA, PhD). PhD program is a special case provision. *Program availability:* Part-time. *Faculty:* 21 full-time (9 women), 1 part-time/adjunct (0 women). *Students:* 11 full-time (8 women), 4 part-time (3 women). 19 applicants, 16% accepted. In 2017, 5 master's awarded. *Degree requirements:* For master's, thesis (for some programs); for doctorate, thesis/dissertation. *Entrance requirements:* For master's, writing sample and portfolio of creative material (for creative writing). Additional exam requirements/recommendations for international students: Required—TOEFL (minimum score 600 paper-based; 100 iBT), IELTS (minimum score 7.5), PTE (minimum score 59). *Application deadline:* For fall admission, 4/15 for domestic and international students; for winter admission, 10/15 for domestic and international students; for spring admission, 2/15 for domestic and international students. Application fee: $100. Electronic applications accepted. *Expenses:* $10,681. *Financial support:* In 2017–18, 2 fellowships (averaging $6,000 per year), 4 teaching assistantships (averaging $2,562 per year) were awarded; research assistantships and scholarships/grants also available. Financial award application deadline: 6/15. *Faculty research:* British, American, and Canadian literature; sixteenth-, eighteenth-, nineteenth-, and twentieth-century literature; literary theory. *Unit head:* Dr. Marcel DeCoste, Department Head, 306-585-4691, Fax: 306-585-5429, E-mail: marcel.decoste@uregina.ca. *Application contact:* Dr. Susan Johnston, Graduate Chair, 306-585-4672, Fax: 306-585-5429, E-mail: susan.johnston@uregina.ca.
Website: http://www.uregina.ca/arts/english

University of Rhode Island, Graduate School, College of Arts and Sciences, Department of English, Kingston, RI 02881. Offers American literature and culture (PhD); British literature and culture (PhD); creative writing (PhD); critical theories (PhD); English (MA); film (PhD); gender studies (PhD); MLIS/MA. *Program availability:* Part-time. *Faculty:* 17 full-time (10 women). *Students:* 36 full-time (27 women), 7 part-time (4 women); includes 2 minority (both Black or African American, non-Hispanic/Latino), 7 international. 34 applicants, 65% accepted, 10 enrolled. In 2017, 4 master's, 8 doctorates awarded. *Entrance requirements:* Additional exam requirements/recommendations for international students: Required—TOEFL (minimum score 91 iBT). *Application deadline:* For fall admission, 1/15 for domestic and international students. Application fee: $65. Electronic applications accepted. *Expenses:* Tuition, state resident: full-time $12,706; part-time $786 per credit. Tuition, nonresident: full-time $25,216; part-time $1401 per credit. *Required fees:* $1598; $45 per credit. One-time fee: $30 part-time. *Financial support:* In 2017–18, 28 teaching assistantships with tuition reimbursements (averaging $17,158 per year) were awarded. Financial award application deadline: 1/15; financial award applicants required to submit FAFSA. *Unit head:* Dr. Travis Williams, Chair, 401-874-9501, E-mail: tdwilliams@uri.edu. *Application contact:* Dr. David Faflik, Director of Graduate Studies, 401-874-4670, E-mail: faflik@uri.edu.
Website: http://www.uri.edu/artsci/eng/

University of Rochester, School of Arts and Sciences, Department of English, Rochester, NY 14627-0451. Offers MA, PhD. *Faculty:* 21 full-time (7 women). *Students:* 61 full-time (35 women), 5 part-time (all women); includes 7 minority (1 Black or African American, non-Hispanic/Latino; 2 Asian, non-Hispanic/Latino; 3 Hispanic/Latino; 1 Two or more races, non-Hispanic/Latino), 5 international. Average age 29. 137 applicants, 35% accepted, 19 enrolled. In 2017, 16 master's, 7 doctorates awarded. Terminal master's awarded for partial completion of doctoral program. *Degree requirements:* For master's, comprehensive exam or comprehensive essay; for doctorate, one foreign language, comprehensive exam, thesis/dissertation, qualifying exam. *Entrance requirements:* For master's and doctorate, GRE, personal statement (two to three pages, double spaced), writing sample, two to three letters of recommendation. *Application deadline:* For fall admission, 1/15 for domestic and international students. Application fee: $60. Electronic applications accepted. *Expenses:* $1,596 per credit hour. *Financial support:* In 2017–18, 12 fellowships with full and partial tuition reimbursements (averaging $21,600 per year), 6 teaching assistantships with full and partial tuition reimbursements (averaging $18,000 per year) were awarded; health care benefits also available. Support available to part-time students. *Faculty research:* English, American, and Anglophone literature, poetry, fiction, non-fiction, and drama. *Total annual research expenditures:* $297,687. *Unit head:* Rosemary Kegl, Chair, 585-275-4092, E-mail: rosemary.kegl@rochester.edu. *Application contact:* Carrie Morriss, Graduate Coordinator, 585-275-9256, E-mail: carrie.morriss@rochester.edu.
Website: https://www.sas.rochester.edu/eng/graduate/index.html

University of St. Thomas, College of Arts and Sciences, Graduate Program in English, St. Paul, MN 55105. Offers creative writing and publishing (MA); English literature (MA); teaching college English (Certificate). *Program availability:* Part-time, evening/weekend. *Faculty:* 24 full-time (15 women). *Students:* 41 full-time (29 women); includes 4 minority (3 Black or African American, non-Hispanic/Latino; 1 Asian, non-Hispanic/Latino). Average age 30. 9 applicants, 89% accepted, 8 enrolled. In 2017, 16 master's awarded. *Degree requirements:* For master's, essay. *Entrance requirements:* For master's, minimum GPA of 3.0, minimum 5 upper-level undergraduate courses in literature, sample of written work, personal statement, BA from accredited university, transcripts. Additional exam requirements/recommendations for international students: Required—TOEFL (minimum score 80 iBT), IELTS (minimum score 6.5). *Application deadline:* For fall admission, 3/1 priority date for domestic and international students; for spring admission, 10/1 priority date for domestic and international students; for summer admission, 3/1 priority date for domestic and international students. Applications are processed on a rolling basis. Application fee: $0. Electronic applications accepted. *Expenses:* $2,572.50 per course, $857.50 per credit; $55 technology fee per semester part-time, $111 full-time. *Financial support:* In 2017–18, 23 students received support, including 18 fellowships with partial tuition reimbursements available (averaging $5,145 per year), 3 research assistantships (averaging $2,000 per year), 4 teaching assistantships (averaging $750 per year); institutionally sponsored loans, scholarships/grants, traineeships, and unspecified assistantships also available. Support available to part-time students. Financial award application deadline: 3/1; financial award applicants required to submit FAFSA. *Faculty research:* Multicultural literature, literature and theory, regional writers, creative writing, 19th-century American literature. *Unit head:* Dr. Alexis Easley, Director, 651-962-5653, Fax: 651-962-5623, E-mail: maeasley@stthomas.edu. *Application contact:* Soren Hoeger-Lerdal, Coordinator, 651-962-5628, Fax: 651-962-5623, E-mail: gradenglish@stthomas.edu.
Website: http://www.stthomas.edu/english/graduate/

University of Saskatchewan, College of Graduate Studies and Research, College of Arts and Science, Department of English, Saskatoon, SK S7N 5A2, Canada. Offers MA, PhD. *Degree requirements:* For master's, one foreign language, thesis; for doctorate, one foreign language, comprehensive exam (for some programs), thesis/dissertation. *Entrance requirements:* Additional exam requirements/recommendations for international students: Required—TOEFL (minimum score 80 iBT); Recommended—IELTS (minimum score 6.5). Electronic applications accepted.

University of South Africa, College of Human Sciences, Pretoria, South Africa. Offers adult education (M Ed); African languages (MA, PhD); African politics (MA, PhD); Afrikaans (MA, PhD); ancient history (MA, PhD); ancient Near Eastern studies (MA, PhD); anthropology (MA, PhD); applied linguistics (MA); Arabic (MA, PhD); archaeology (MA); art history (MA); Biblical archaeology (MA); Biblical studies (M Th, D Th, PhD); Christian spirituality (M Th, D Th); church history (M Th, D Th); classical studies (MA, PhD); clinical psychology (MA); communication (MA, PhD); comparative education (M Ed, Ed D); consulting psychology (D Admin, D Com, PhD); curriculum studies (M Ed, Ed D); development studies (M Admin, MA, D Admin, PhD); didactics (M Ed, Ed D); education (M Tech); education management (M Ed, Ed D); educational psychology (M Ed); English (MA); environmental education (M Ed); French (MA, PhD); German (MA, PhD); Greek (MA); guidance and counseling (M Ed); health studies (MA, PhD), including health sciences education (MA), health services management (MA), medical and surgical nursing science (critical care general) (MA), midwifery and neonatal nursing science (MA), trauma and emergency care (MA); history (MA, PhD); history of education (Ed D); inclusive education (M Ed, Ed D); information and communications technology policy and regulation (MA); information science (MA, MIS, PhD); international politics (MA, PhD); Islamic studies (MA, PhD); Italian (MA, PhD); Judaica (MA, PhD); linguistics (MA, PhD); mathematical education (M Ed); mathematics education (MA); missiology (M Th, D Th); modern Hebrew (MA, PhD); musicology (MA, MMus, D Mus, PhD); natural science education (M Ed); New Testament (M Th, D Th); Old Testament (D Th); pastoral therapy (M Th, D Th); philosophy (MA); philosophy of education (M Ed, Ed D); politics (MA, PhD); Portuguese (MA, PhD); practical theology (M Th, D Th); psychology (MA, MS, PhD); psychology of education (M Ed, Ed D); public health (MA); religious studies (MA, D Th, PhD); Romance languages (MA); Russian (MA, PhD); Semitic languages (MA, PhD); social behavior studies in HIV/AIDS (MA); social science (mental health) (MA); social science in development studies (MA); social science in psychology (MA); social science in social work (MA); social science in sociology (MA); social work (MSW, DSW, PhD); socio-education (M Ed, Ed D); sociolinguistics (MA); sociology (MA, PhD); Spanish (MA, PhD); systematic theology (M Th, D Th); TESOL (teaching English to speakers of other languages) (MA); theological ethics (M Th, D Th); theory of literature (MA, PhD); urban ministries (D Th); urban ministry (M Th).

English

University of South Alabama, College of Arts and Sciences, Department of English, Mobile, AL 36688. Offers creative writing (MA); literature (MA). *Program availability:* Part-time, evening/weekend. *Faculty:* 9 full-time (3 women). *Students:* 15 full-time (8 women), 10 part-time (6 women); includes 4 minority (2 Black or African American, non-Hispanic/Latino; 2 Two or more races, non-Hispanic/Latino). Average age 31. 13 applicants, 54% accepted, 7 enrolled. In 2017, 5 master's awarded. *Degree requirements:* For master's, one foreign language, comprehensive exam, thesis optional. *Entrance requirements:* For master's, GRE General Test, BA in English or 30 hours of course work in English, minimum GPA of 3.0, personal statement. Additional exam requirements/recommendations for international students: Required—TOEFL (minimum score 535 paper-based; 79 iBT), IELTS (minimum score 6.5). *Application deadline:* For fall admission, 7/15 priority date for domestic students, 5/15 priority date for international students; for spring admission, 12/1 priority date for domestic students, 11/1 priority date for international students; for summer admission, 5/1 for domestic students, 4/1 for international students. Applications are processed on a rolling basis. Application fee: $35. Electronic applications accepted. *Expenses:* Tuition, state resident: full-time $10,104; part-time $421 per semester hour. Tuition, nonresident: full-time $20,208; part-time $842 per semester hour. *Financial support:* Fellowships, research assistantships, teaching assistantships, career-related internships or fieldwork, Federal Work-Study, institutionally sponsored loans, scholarships/grants, and unspecified assistantships available. Support available to part-time students. Financial award application deadline: 3/31; financial award applicants required to submit FAFSA. *Unit head:* Dr. Steven Trout, Chair, English, 251-460-6439, E-mail: strout@southalabama.edu. *Application contact:* Dr. Ellen B. Harrington, Graduate Coordinator, English, 251-460-7326, E-mail: eharrington@southalabama.edu.
Website: http://www.southalabama.edu/colleges/artsandsci/english/

University of South Carolina, The Graduate School, College of Arts and Sciences, Department of English Language and Literature, Columbia, SC 29208. Offers creative writing (MFA); English (MA, PhD); English education (MAT); MLIS/MA. MAT offered in cooperation with the College of Education. *Program availability:* Part-time. *Degree requirements:* For master's, one foreign language, comprehensive exam, thesis; for doctorate, 2 foreign languages, comprehensive exam, thesis/dissertation. *Entrance requirements:* For master's, GRE General Test (MFA), GRE Subject Test (MA, MAT), sample of written work; for doctorate, GRE General Test, GRE Subject Test, sample of written work. Additional exam requirements/recommendations for international students: Required—TOEFL. Electronic applications accepted. *Faculty research:* American literature, British literature, composition and rhetoric, linguistics, speech communication.

University of South Dakota, Graduate School, College of Arts and Sciences, Department of English, Vermillion, SD 57069. Offers MA, PhD. *Degree requirements:* For master's, comprehensive exam (for some programs), thesis (for some programs); for doctorate, comprehensive exam, thesis/dissertation. *Entrance requirements:* For master's, minimum GPA of 3.0, writing sample; for doctorate, GRE, minimum GPA of 3.0, writing sample. Additional exam requirements/recommendations for international students: Required—TOEFL (minimum score 620 paper-based; 105 iBT). *Application deadline:* For fall admission, 1/15 priority date for domestic students, 2/1 priority date for international students. Applications are processed on a rolling basis. Application fee: $35. Electronic applications accepted. *Financial support:* Research assistantships with partial tuition reimbursements, teaching assistantships with partial tuition reimbursements, career-related internships or fieldwork, Federal Work-Study, and scholarships/grants available. Financial award applicants required to submit FAFSA. *Application contact:* Graduate School, 605-658-6140, Fax: 605-677-6118.
Website: http://www.usd.edu/english

University of Southern California, Graduate School, Dana and David Dornsife College of Letters, Arts and Sciences, Department of English, Los Angeles, CA 90089. Offers English (MA, PhD); literature and creative writing (PhD). Terminal master's awarded for partial completion of doctoral program. *Degree requirements:* For doctorate, one foreign language, comprehensive exam, thesis/dissertation. *Entrance requirements:* For doctorate, GRE General Test, GRE Subject Test (English literature). Additional exam requirements/recommendations for international students: Required—TOEFL. Electronic applications accepted. *Faculty research:* Creative writing and literature; early modern studies; gender and sexuality; narrative studies; poetry and poetics; media, film, and popular culture; studies in race and minority literature.

University of Southern Indiana, Graduate Studies, College of Liberal Arts, Program in English, Evansville, IN 47712-3590. Offers MA. *Program availability:* Part-time, evening/weekend. *Faculty:* 8 full-time (6 women). *Students:* 7 full-time (5 women), 16 part-time (14 women); includes 1 minority (Black or African American, non-Hispanic/Latino). Average age 37. In 2017, 5 master's awarded. *Entrance requirements:* For master's, writing sample, three letters of recommendation. Additional exam requirements/recommendations for international students: Required—TOEFL (minimum score 550 paper-based; 79 iBT), IELTS (minimum score 6). *Application deadline:* For fall admission, 8/1 for domestic and international students; for spring admission, 11/15 for domestic and international students. Applications are processed on a rolling basis. Application fee: $40. Electronic applications accepted. *Expenses:* Tuition, state resident: full-time $9394. Tuition, nonresident: full-time $17,917. *Required fees:* $510. *Financial support:* In 2017–18, 5 students received support. Federal Work-Study, scholarships/grants, and unspecified assistantships available. Financial award application deadline: 3/1; financial award applicants required to submit FAFSA. *Unit head:* Dr. Charles A. Conaway, Program Director, 812-461-5435, E-mail: conaway@usi.edu. *Application contact:* Dr. Mayola Rowser, Director, Graduate Studies, 812-465-7015, E-mail: mrowser@usi.edu.
Website: http://www.usi.edu/liberal-arts/master-of-arts-in-english/

University of Southern Mississippi, College of Arts and Letters, Department of English, Hattiesburg, MS 39406-0001. Offers creative writing (MA, PhD); English education (MA); literature (MA, PhD). *Students:* 16 full-time (12 women), 2 part-time (both women). 48 applicants, 65% accepted, 18 enrolled. In 2017, 73 master's, 16 doctorates awarded. *Degree requirements:* For master's, one foreign language, comprehensive exam, thesis; for doctorate, 2 foreign languages, comprehensive exam, thesis/dissertation. *Entrance requirements:* For master's, GRE General Test, minimum GPA of 3.0 in field of study, 2.75 in last 2 years; for doctorate, GRE General Test, minimum GPA of 3.5. Additional exam requirements/recommendations for international students: Required—TOEFL, IELTS. *Application deadline:* For fall admission, 3/15 priority date for domestic students, 3/15 for international students. Application fee: $60. Electronic applications accepted. *Expenses:* Tuition, state resident: full-time $3830. *Financial support:* Fellowships, research assistantships with full tuition reimbursements, teaching assistantships with full tuition reimbursements, Federal Work-Study, institutionally sponsored loans, scholarships/grants, and unspecified assistantships available. Financial award application deadline: 3/15; financial award applicants required to submit FAFSA. *Faculty research:* English and American literature, critical theory and cultural studies, creative writing. *Unit head:* Dr. Luis Iglesias, Chair, 601-266-4060, Fax: 601-266-5757, E-mail: luis.iglesias@usm.edu. *Application contact:* Dr. Alexandra Valint, Director, Graduate Studies, 601-266-4070.
Website: https://www.usm.edu/english

University of South Florida, College of Arts and Sciences, Department of English, Tampa, FL 33620-9951. Offers creative writing (MFA), including fiction, poetry; English (MA, PhD), including literature, rhetoric and composition. *Program availability:* Part-time, evening/weekend. *Faculty:* 24 full-time (13 women). *Students:* 70 full-time (51 women), 17 part-time (15 women); includes 14 minority (6 Black or African American, non-Hispanic/Latino; 3 Asian, non-Hispanic/Latino; 3 Hispanic/Latino; 2 Two or more races, non-Hispanic/Latino). Average age 32. 74 applicants, 54% accepted, 25 enrolled. In 2017, 22 master's, 10 doctorates awarded. *Degree requirements:* For master's, comprehensive exam, thesis (for MFA); thesis or portfolio (for MA); for doctorate, one foreign language, comprehensive exam, thesis/dissertation. *Entrance requirements:* For master's, GRE General Test, minimum undergraduate GPA of 3.5 (for MA), 3.2 (for MFA); three letters of recommendation; personal statement; writing sample from 10 to 20 pages (depending on genre); for doctorate, GRE General Test, minimum graduate GPA of 3.7; three letters of recommendation; 2-3 page personal statement; 2500-word writing sample from English coursework. Additional exam requirements/recommendations for international students: Required—TOEFL minimum score 550 paper-based; 79 iBT or IELTS minimum score 6.5 (for MA and PhD); TOEFL minimum score 600 paper-based (for MFA). *Application deadline:* For fall admission, 1/1 for domestic and international students. Applications are processed on a rolling basis. Application fee: $30. Electronic applications accepted. *Financial support:* In 2017–18, 20 students received support, including 2 research assistantships (averaging $17,221 per year), 79 teaching assistantships with tuition reimbursements available (averaging $11,576 per year); unspecified assistantships also available. Financial award application deadline: 6/30; financial award applicants required to submit FAFSA. *Faculty research:* British and American literature, rhetoric and composition, world and comparative literatures, creative writing, gender and sexuality studies, women's literature, film and genre studies, literary theory, popular and visual culture, textual and translation studies. *Total annual research expenditures:* $202,166. *Unit head:* Dr. Laura Runge, Professor and Chairperson, 813-974-9496, E-mail: runge@usf.edu. *Application contact:* Dr. John Lennon, Associate Professor and Graduate Director, 813-974-2663, Fax: 813-974-2270, E-mail: jflennon@usf.edu.
Website: http://english.usf.edu/

University of South Florida, Innovative Education, Tampa, FL 33620-9951. Offers adult, career and higher education (Graduate Certificate), including college teaching, leadership in developing human resources, leadership in higher education; Africana studies (Graduate Certificate), including diasporas and health disparities, genocide and human rights; aging studies (Graduate Certificate), including gerontology; art research (Graduate Certificate), including museum studies; business foundations (Graduate Certificate); chemical and biomedical engineering (Graduate Certificate), including materials science and engineering, water, health and sustainability; child and family studies (Graduate Certificate), including positive behavior support; civil and industrial engineering (Graduate Certificate), including transportation systems analysis; community and family health (Graduate Certificate), including maternal and child health, social marketing and public health, violence and injury: prevention and intervention, women's health; criminology (Graduate Certificate), including criminal justice administration; data science for public administration (Graduate Certificate); digital humanities (Graduate Certificate); educational measurement and research (Graduate Certificate), including evaluation; English (Graduate Certificate), including comparative literary studies, creative writing, professional and technical communication; entrepreneurship (Graduate Certificate); environmental health (Graduate Certificate), including safety management; epidemiology and biostatistics (Graduate Certificate), including applied biostatistics, biostatistics, concepts and tools of epidemiology, epidemiology, epidemiology of infectious diseases; geography, environment and planning (Graduate Certificate), including community development, environmental policy and management, geographical information systems; geology (Graduate Certificate), including hydrogeology; global health (Graduate Certificate), including disaster management, global health and Latin American and Caribbean studies, global health practice, humanitarian assistance, infection control; government and international affairs (Graduate Certificate), including Cuban studies, globalization studies; health policy and management (Graduate Certificate), including health management and leadership, public health policy and programs; hearing specialist: early intervention (Graduate Certificate); industrial and management systems engineering (Graduate Certificate), including systems engineering, technology management; information studies (Graduate Certificate), including school library media specialist; information systems/decision sciences (Graduate Certificate), including analytics and business intelligence; instructional technology (Graduate Certificate), including distance education, Florida digital/virtual educator, instructional design, multimedia design, Web design; internal medicine, bioethics and medical humanities (Graduate Certificate), including biomedical ethics; Latin American and Caribbean studies (Graduate Certificate); leadership for coastal resiliency planning (Graduate Certificate); mass communications (Graduate Certificate), including multimedia journalism; mathematics and statistics (Graduate Certificate), including mathematics; medicine (Graduate Certificate), including aging and neuroscience, bioinformatics, biotechnology, brain fitness and memory management, clinical investigation, hand and upper limb rehabilitation, health informatics, health sciences, integrative weight management, intellectual property, medicine and gender, metabolic and nutritional medicine, metabolic cardiology, pharmacy sciences; national and competitive intelligence (Graduate Certificate); nursing (Graduate Certificate), including simulation based academic fellowship in advanced pain management; psychological and social foundations (Graduate Certificate), including career counseling, college teaching, diversity in education, mental health counseling, school counseling; public affairs (Graduate Certificate), including nonprofit management, public management, research administration; public health (Graduate Certificate), including assessing chemical toxicity and public health risks, health equity, pharmacoepidemiology, public health generalist, toxicology, translational research in adolescent behavioral health; public health practices (Graduate Certificate), including planning for healthy communities; rehabilitation and mental health counseling (Graduate Certificate), including integrative mental health care, marriage and family therapy, rehabilitation technology; secondary education (Graduate Certificate), including ESOL, foreign language education: culture and content, foreign language education: professional; social work (Graduate Certificate), including geriatric social work/clinical gerontology; special education (Graduate Certificate), including autism spectrum disorder, disabilities education: severe/profound; world languages (Graduate Certificate), including teaching English as a second language (TESL) or foreign language. *Unit head:* Dr. Cynthia DeLuca, Associate Vice President and Assistant Vice Provost, 813-974-3077, Fax: 813-974-7061, E-mail: deluca@usf.edu. *Application contact:* Owen Hooper, Director, Summer and Alternative Calendar Programs, 813-974-6917, E-mail: hooper@usf.edu.
Website: http://www.usf.edu/innovative-education/

The University of Tennessee, Graduate School, College of Arts and Sciences, Department of English, Knoxville, TN 37996. Offers MA, PhD. *Program availability:* Part-time. *Degree requirements:* For master's, one foreign language, thesis or alternative; for doctorate, one foreign language, thesis/dissertation. *Entrance requirements:* For master's, GRE General Test, minimum GPA of 2.7; for doctorate, GRE General Test, GRE Subject Test, minimum GPA of 2.7. Additional exam requirements/

recommendations for international students: Required—TOEFL. Electronic applications accepted.

The University of Tennessee at Chattanooga, Program in English, Chattanooga, TN 37403. Offers creative writing (MA); literary study (MA); rhetoric and writing (MA). *Program availability:* Part-time. *Students:* 12 full-time (8 women), 14 part-time (11 women); includes 4 minority (1 Black or African American, non-Hispanic/Latino; 1 Asian, non-Hispanic/Latino; 1 Hispanic/Latino; 1 Two or more races, non-Hispanic/Latino). Average age 27. 10 applicants, 100% accepted, 7 enrolled. In 2017, 12 master's awarded. *Degree requirements:* For master's, comprehensive exam, thesis. *Entrance requirements:* For master's, minimum GPA of 3.0 in English, two letters of recommendation. Additional exam requirements/recommendations for international students: Required—TOEFL (minimum score 550 paper-based; 79 iBT), IELTS (minimum score 6). *Application deadline:* For fall admission, 6/15 priority date for domestic students, 7/1 for international students; for spring admission, 11/1 priority date for domestic students, 11/1 for international students. Applications are processed on a rolling basis. Application fee: $35 ($40 for international students). Electronic applications accepted. *Expenses:* Contact institution. *Financial support:* Research assistantships, teaching assistantships, career-related internships or fieldwork, scholarships/grants, health care benefits, and unspecified assistantships available. Support available to part-time students. Financial award application deadline: 7/1; financial award applicants required to submit FAFSA. *Faculty research:* Technical writing, African-American literature, Milton, creative writing and poetry, American modernism and gender theory. *Total annual research expenditures:* $6,000. *Unit head:* Dr. Christopher Stuart, Department Head, 423-425-2140, Fax: 423-425-2282, E-mail: chris-stuart@utc.edu. *Application contact:* Dr. Joanne Romagni, Dean of the Graduate School, 423-425-4478, Fax: 423-425-5223, E-mail: joanne-romagni@utc.edu. Website: http://www.utc.edu/english/

The University of Texas at Arlington, Graduate School, College of Liberal Arts, Department of English, Arlington, TX 76019. Offers English (MA); literature (PhD). *Program availability:* Part-time, evening/weekend. *Degree requirements:* For master's, thesis or comprehensive exam; for doctorate, one foreign language, comprehensive exam, thesis/dissertation. *Entrance requirements:* For master's, GRE General Test, minimum 5-page writing sample, minimum GPA of 3.0, 3 letters of recommendation; for doctorate, GRE General Test, minimum graduate GPA of 3.5, writing sample, 3 letters of recommendation. Additional exam requirements/recommendations for international students: Required—TOEFL (minimum score 550 paper-based). *Faculty research:* Rhetoric composition, American literature, British literature, cultural studies, women's studies.

The University of Texas at Austin, Graduate School, College of Liberal Arts, Department of English, Austin, TX 78712-1111. Offers creative writing (MFA); English (MA, PhD). *Program availability:* Part-time. Terminal master's awarded for partial completion of doctoral program. *Degree requirements:* For master's, 2 foreign languages; for doctorate, variable foreign language requirement. *Entrance requirements:* For master's and doctorate, GRE General Test. Electronic applications accepted.

The University of Texas at El Paso, Graduate School, College of Liberal Arts, Department of English, El Paso, TX 79968-0001. Offers bilingual professional writing (Certificate); English and American literature (MA); rhetoric and composition (PhD); rhetoric and writing studies (MA); teaching English (MAT). *Program availability:* Part-time, evening/weekend. *Degree requirements:* For master's, thesis optional. *Entrance requirements:* For master's, GRE General Test, minimum GPA of 3.0. Additional exam requirements/recommendations for international students: Required—TOEFL. Electronic applications accepted. *Faculty research:* Literature, creative writing, literary theory.

The University of Texas at San Antonio, College of Liberal and Fine Arts, Department of English, San Antonio, TX 78249-0617. Offers MA, PhD. *Program availability:* Part-time, evening/weekend. *Faculty:* 13 full-time (8 women), 1 (woman) part-time/adjunct. *Students:* 27 full-time (17 women), 31 part-time (24 women); includes 24 minority (2 Black or African American, non-Hispanic/Latino; 19 Hispanic/Latino; 3 Two or more races, non-Hispanic/Latino), 2 international. Average age 33. 29 applicants, 76% accepted, 10 enrolled. In 2017, 11 master's, 3 doctorates awarded. Terminal master's awarded for partial completion of doctoral program. *Degree requirements:* For master's, comprehensive exam, thesis optional; for doctorate, one foreign language, comprehensive exam, thesis/dissertation. *Entrance requirements:* For master's, GRE General Test, minimum GPA of 3.3 on all upper-division English courses, 18 hours of English of which 12 hours must be upper-division English literature; for doctorate, GRE General Test, GRE Subject Test (English literature), 18 hours of upper-division and/or graduate English, minimum GPA of 3.5, statement of purpose, writing sample, 3 letters of recommendation. Additional exam requirements/recommendations for international students: Required—TOEFL (minimum score 550 paper-based; 79 iBT), IELTS (minimum score 6.5). *Application deadline:* For fall admission, 6/15 for domestic students, 3/1 for international students; for spring admission, 10/15 for domestic students, 9/15 for international students. Applications are processed on a rolling basis. Application fee: $50 ($90 for international students). Electronic applications accepted. *Expenses:* Tuition, state resident: full-time $5495. Tuition, nonresident: full-time $21,938. *Required fees:* $1915. Tuition and fees vary according to program. *Financial support:* Unspecified assistantships available. *Faculty research:* Transnational, cross-cultural studies in literature. *Total annual research expenditures:* $24,415. *Unit head:* Dr. Mark Bayer, Department Chair, 210-458-4374, Fax: 210-458-5366, E-mail: mark.bayer@utsa.edu. Website: http://colfa.utsa.edu/English/

The University of Texas at Tyler, College of Arts and Sciences, Department of Literature and Languages, Tyler, TX 75799-0001. Offers English (MA); interdisciplinary studies (MAIS). *Program availability:* Part-time, evening/weekend. *Degree requirements:* For master's, one foreign language, comprehensive exam, thesis optional. *Entrance requirements:* For master's, GRE General Test, minimum GPA of 3.0; four semesters or the equivalent of one foreign language. Additional exam requirements/recommendations for international students: Required—TOEFL. Electronic applications accepted. *Faculty research:* Medieval and Tudor drama, Shakespeare, British Romanticism, British and Irish modernism, American realism, Greek drama, nineteenth-century American literature.

The University of Texas of the Permian Basin, Office of Graduate Studies, College of Arts and Sciences, Department of Literature and Languages, Program in English, Odessa, TX 79762-0001. Offers MA. *Program availability:* Part-time, evening/weekend. *Degree requirements:* For master's, comprehensive exam (for some programs), thesis (for some programs). *Entrance requirements:* For master's, GRE General Test. Additional exam requirements/recommendations for international students: Required—TOEFL (minimum score 550 paper-based).

The University of Texas Rio Grande Valley, College of Liberal Arts, Department of Literatures and Cultural Studies, Edinburg, TX 78539. Offers English (MA); Spanish (MA). MA in Spanish conducted in conjunction with Department of Writing and Language Studies. *Program availability:* Part-time, evening/weekend. *Faculty:* 11 full-time (6 women). *Students:* 14 full-time (9 women), 78 part-time (60 women); includes 85 minority (all Hispanic/Latino), 2 international. Average age 33. 26 applicants, 100% accepted, 22 enrolled. In 2017, 32 master's awarded. *Degree requirements:* For master's, comprehensive exam, thesis optional. *Entrance requirements:* For master's, GRE General Test, minimum GPA of 3.0. Additional exam requirements/recommendations for international students: Required—TOEFL or IELTS. *Application deadline:* For fall admission, 2/1 priority date for domestic students; for spring admission, 9/1 priority date for domestic students. Applications are processed on a rolling basis. Application fee: $50 ($100 for international students). *Expenses:* Tuition, state resident: full-time $5550; part-time $417 per credit hour. Tuition, nonresident: full-time $13,020; part-time $832 per credit hour. *Required fees:* $1169. *Financial support:* Application deadline: 4/15. *Faculty research:* Oral vs. literary culture, Borderland literature, Mexican-American literature, topics in British and American literature, discourse analysis. *Unit head:* Steve Wilson, Interim Chair, E-mail: steve.wilson@utrgv.edu.

The University of the South, Sewanee School of Letters, Sewanee, TN 37383-1000. Offers American and English literature (MA); creative writing (MFA). *Program availability:* Part-time. *Faculty:* 1 full-time (0 women), 10 part-time/adjunct (7 women). *Students:* 53 part-time (33 women); includes 4 minority (1 Black or African American, non-Hispanic/Latino; 3 Two or more races, non-Hispanic/Latino), 1 international. Average age 41. In 2017, 13 master's awarded. *Degree requirements:* For master's, thesis (for some programs). *Entrance requirements:* For master's, writing sample, two letters of recommendation, official transcripts. *Application deadline:* Applications are processed on a rolling basis. Application fee: $40. Electronic applications accepted. *Expenses:* Contact institution. *Financial support:* Institutionally sponsored loans and scholarships/grants available. *Unit head:* Dr. John Gatta, Interim Director, 931-598-1636, E-mail: sletters@sewanee.edu. *Application contact:* April R. Alvarez, Administrator, 931-598-1636, E-mail: sletters@sewanee.edu. Website: http://letters.sewanee.edu/

The University of Toledo, College of Graduate Studies, College of Languages, Literature and Social Sciences, Department of English Language and Literature, Toledo, OH 43606-3390. Offers English as a second language (MA); teaching of writing (Certificate). *Program availability:* Part-time. *Degree requirements:* For master's, thesis. *Entrance requirements:* For master's, GRE if GPA is less than 3.0, minimum cumulative point-hour ratio of 2.7 for all previous academic work, three letters of recommendation, transcripts from all prior institutions attended, critical essay; for Certificate, statement of purpose, transcripts from all prior institutions attended, 2 letters of recommendation. Additional exam requirements/recommendations for international students: Required—TOEFL (minimum score 550 paper-based; 80 iBT). Electronic applications accepted. *Faculty research:* Literary criticism, linguistics, creative writing, folklore and cultural studies.

University of Toronto, School of Graduate Studies, Faculty of Arts and Science, Department of English, Toronto, ON M5S 1A1, Canada. Offers creative writing (MA); English (MA, PhD); JD/MA. *Program availability:* Part-time. *Degree requirements:* For master's, thesis optional; for doctorate, 2 foreign languages, thesis/dissertation. *Entrance requirements:* For master's, minimum B+ average, 2 letters of reference, portfolio (creative writing program); for doctorate, minimum A- average, 2 letters of reference, writing sample. Additional exam requirements/recommendations for international students: Required—TOEFL (minimum score 580 paper-based; 93 iBT), TWE (minimum score 5). Electronic applications accepted.

The University of Tulsa, Graduate School, Kendall College of Arts and Sciences, Department of English, Tulsa, OK 74104-3189. Offers English language and literature (MA, PhD); JD/MA. *Program availability:* Part-time, evening/weekend. *Faculty:* 14 full-time (6 women). *Students:* 17 full-time (9 women), 16 part-time (10 women); includes 4 minority (1 Black or African American, non-Hispanic/Latino; 1 American Indian or Alaska Native, non-Hispanic/Latino; 2 Hispanic/Latino), 1 international. Average age 34. 24 applicants, 50% accepted, 6 enrolled. In 2017, 4 master's, 4 doctorates awarded. Terminal master's awarded for partial completion of doctoral program. *Degree requirements:* For master's, independent research project; for doctorate, one foreign language, comprehensive exam, thesis/dissertation. *Entrance requirements:* For master's, GRE General Test, writing sample; for doctorate, GRE General Test, writing sample, list of language proficiencies. Additional exam requirements/recommendations for international students: Required—TOEFL (minimum score 577 paper-based; 91 iBT), IELTS (minimum score 6.5). *Application deadline:* For fall admission, 1/15 priority date for domestic students, 1/15 for international students. Applications are processed on a rolling basis. Application fee: $55. Electronic applications accepted. *Expenses: Tuition:* Full-time $22,230. *Required fees:* $2000. Tuition and fees vary according to course load and program. *Financial support:* In 2017–18, 52 students received support, including 16 fellowships with full tuition reimbursements available (averaging $2,032 per year), 1 research assistantship with full tuition reimbursement available (averaging $13,908 per year), 25 teaching assistantships with full tuition reimbursements available (averaging $12,350 per year); career-related internships or fieldwork, Federal Work-Study, scholarships/grants, health care benefits, tuition waivers (full and partial), and unspecified assistantships also available. Support available to part-time students. Financial award application deadline: 1/15; financial award applicants required to submit FAFSA. *Faculty research:* Twentieth-century literature; modern and contemporary British, Irish, and American literatures; Victorian literature; American studies; cultural and gender studies; African-American literature; women's literature, nineteenth century American literature. *Unit head:* Dr. Lars Engle, Chairperson, 918-631-2807, Fax: 918-631-3033, E-mail: lars-engle@utulsa.edu. *Application contact:* Dr. Jennifer Airey, Advisor, 918-631-2854, Fax: 918-631-3033, E-mail: jennifer-airey@utulsa.edu. Website: http://artsandsciences.utulsa.edu/academics/departments-schools/english/

The University of Tulsa, Graduate School, Kendall College of Arts and Sciences, School of Education, Tulsa, OK 74104-3189. Offers mathematics and science education (MSMSE); teaching arts (MTA), including art, biology, English, history, mathematics; urban education (MA). *Accreditation:* TEAC. *Program availability:* Part-time. *Faculty:* 9 full-time (5 women), 2 part-time/adjunct (both women). *Students:* 8 full-time (4 women), 6 part-time (5 women); includes 4 minority (1 Black or African American, non-Hispanic/Latino; 1 American Indian or Alaska Native, non-Hispanic/Latino; 1 Asian, non-Hispanic/Latino; 1 Two or more races, non-Hispanic/Latino). Average age 31. 22 applicants, 9% accepted. In 2017, 10 master's awarded. *Degree requirements:* For master's, thesis optional. *Entrance requirements:* For master's, GRE General Test. Additional exam requirements/recommendations for international students: Required—TOEFL (minimum score 577 paper-based; 91 iBT), IELTS (minimum score 6.5). *Application deadline:* For fall admission, 2/1 priority date for domestic students. Applications are processed on a rolling basis. Application fee: $55. Electronic applications accepted. *Expenses: Tuition:* Full-time $22,230. *Required fees:* $2000. Tuition and fees vary according to course load and program. *Financial support:* In 2017–18, 3 students received support, including 3 teaching assistantships with full tuition reimbursements available (averaging $13,410 per year); fellowships with tuition reimbursements available, research assistantships with tuition reimbursements available, career-related internships or fieldwork, Federal Work-Study, scholarships/grants, health care benefits, tuition waivers (full and partial), and unspecified assistantships also available. Support available to part-time students. Financial award application deadline: 2/1; financial award applicants required to submit

FAFSA. *Faculty research:* Elementary/secondary certification, math/science education, teaching arts. *Unit head:* Dr. Elizabeth Smith, Chair, 918-631-2238, Fax: 918-631-3721, E-mail: elizabeth-smith-43@utulsa.edu. *Application contact:* Dr. David Brown, Advisor, 918-631-2719, Fax: 918-631-2133, E-mail: david-brown@utulsa.edu.
Website: http://artsandsciences.utulsa.edu/academics/departments-schools/urban-education/

University of Utah, Graduate School, College of Humanities, Department of English, Salt Lake City, UT 84112. Offers English (MA, MFA, PhD), including creative writing (MFA, PhD), literary and cultural studies (MA, PhD), rhetoric and composition (MA, PhD). *Program availability:* Part-time. *Faculty:* 31 full-time (13 women), 5 part-time/adjunct (2 women). *Students:* 43 full-time (24 women), 25 part-time (15 women); includes 13 minority (5 Asian, non-Hispanic/Latino; 5 Hispanic/Latino; 3 Two or more races, non-Hispanic/Latino), 3 international. Average age 26. 225 applicants, 17% accepted, 14 enrolled. In 2017, 1 master's, 8 doctorates awarded. Terminal master's awarded for partial completion of doctoral program. *Entrance requirements:* For master's and doctorate, GRE General Test, minimum GPA of 3.2. Additional exam requirements/recommendations for international students: Required—TOEFL (minimum score 650 paper-based; 115 iBT); Recommended—IELTS (minimum score 9), TSE. *Application deadline:* For fall admission, 12/15 for domestic and international students. Application fee: $55 ($65 for international students). Electronic applications accepted. *Financial support:* In 2017–18, 39 students received support, including 10 fellowships (averaging $18,600 per year), 29 teaching assistantships with full tuition reimbursements available (averaging $18,600 per year); health care benefits also available. Financial award application deadline: 12/15; financial award applicants required to submit FAFSA. *Faculty research:* Creative writing including poetics and modern poetry, fiction, and experimental forms; nineteenth- and twentieth-century British and American literature; American Studies, the American West, and environmental studies; critical theory and practice; race and gender studies. *Total annual research expenditures:* $126,500. *Unit head:* Prof. Barry L. Weller, Department Chair, 801-581-6168, Fax: 801-585-5167, E-mail: barry.weller@utah.edu. *Application contact:* Prof. Andrew Franta, Director of Graduate Studies, 801-581-7850, Fax: 801-585-5167, E-mail: a.franta@utah.edu.
Website: http://english.utah.edu/

University of Vermont, Graduate College, College of Arts and Sciences, Department of English, Burlington, VT 05405. Offers MA. *Students:* 18 (11 women). 37 applicants, 86% accepted, 7 enrolled. In 2017, 6 master's awarded. *Degree requirements:* For master's, one foreign language, thesis. *Entrance requirements:* For master's, GRE General Test, writing sample. Additional exam requirements/recommendations for international students: Required—TOEFL (minimum score 550 paper-based, 90 iBT) or IELTS (6.5). *Application deadline:* For fall admission, 2/1 for domestic and international students. Application fee: $65. Electronic applications accepted. *Expenses:* Tuition, state resident: full-time $11,628; part-time $646 per credit. Tuition, nonresident: full-time $29,340; part-time $1630 per credit. *Required fees:* $1994; $10 per credit. Tuition and fees vary according to course load and program. *Financial support:* In 2017–18, 13 students received support, including 1 research assistantship with full tuition reimbursement available (averaging $16,000 per year), 12 teaching assistantships with full tuition reimbursements available (averaging $16,000 per year); fellowships and health care benefits also available. Financial award application deadline: 3/1. *Unit head:* Dr. Jennifer Sisk, Graduate Program Director, 802-656-3056, E-mail: jennifer.sisk@uvm.edu.
Website: http://www.uvm.edu/~english/?Page=graduate.html&SM=gradsubmenu.html

University of Victoria, Faculty of Graduate Studies, Faculty of Humanities, Department of English, Victoria, BC V8W 2Y2, Canada. Offers MA, PhD. *Program availability:* Part-time. *Degree requirements:* For master's, one foreign language, thesis (for some programs); for doctorate, 2 foreign languages, comprehensive exam, thesis/dissertation, candidacy exam. *Entrance requirements:* For master's, minimum A- average in last 2 years of undergraduate course work, writing sample, resume; for doctorate, minimum A- average in graduate course work, writing sample, resumé. Additional exam requirements/recommendations for international students: Required—TOEFL (minimum score 630 paper-based). Electronic applications accepted. *Faculty research:* Critical theory, nineteenth century literature, postcolonialism/multiculturalism, medieval and Renaissance literature, cultural theory.

University of Virginia, College and Graduate School of Arts and Sciences, Department of English Language and Literature, Program in English, Charlottesville, VA 22903. Offers MA, PhD, JD/MA. *Faculty:* 73 full-time (35 women), 4 part-time/adjunct (2 women). *Students:* 96 full-time (59 women), 1 (woman) part-time; includes 12 minority (5 Black or African American, non-Hispanic/Latino; 3 Asian, non-Hispanic/Latino; 4 Two or more races, non-Hispanic/Latino), 7 international. Average age 27. 222 applicants, 33% accepted, 31 enrolled. In 2017, 16 master's, 7 doctorates awarded. *Degree requirements:* For master's, one foreign language, oral exam or thesis; for doctorate, 2 foreign languages, comprehensive exam, thesis/dissertation. *Entrance requirements:* For master's, GRE General Test, GRE Subject Test, 3 letters of recommendation, 2 writing samples; for doctorate, GRE General Test, GRE Subject Test, 3 letters of recommendation; 2 writing samples. Additional exam requirements/recommendations for international students: Required—TOEFL (minimum score 600 paper-based; 90 iBT), IELTS (minimum score 7). *Application deadline:* For fall admission, 1/1 for domestic students, 1/2 for international students. Applications are processed on a rolling basis. Application fee: $60. Electronic applications accepted. *Financial support:* Fellowships and teaching assistantships available. Financial award applicants required to submit FAFSA. *Unit head:* Stephen Arata, Chair, 434-924-7105, Fax: 434-924-1478, E-mail: sda2e@virginia.edu. *Application contact:* Victoria Olwell, Director of Graduate Studies, 434-924-7105, Fax: 434-924-1478, E-mail: vjo2f@virginia.edu.
Website: http://www.engl.virginia.edu/

University of Washington, Graduate School, College of Arts and Sciences, Department of English, Seattle, WA 98195. Offers creative writing (MFA); English as a second language (MAT); English literature and language (MA, MAT, PhD). *Program availability:* Part-time. Terminal master's awarded for partial completion of doctoral program. *Degree requirements:* For master's, one foreign language, thesis (for some programs); for doctorate, one foreign language, thesis/dissertation. *Entrance requirements:* For master's, GRE General Test, GRE Subject Test (MA and MAT in English), minimum GPA of 3.0; for doctorate, GRE General Test, GRE Subject Test. Additional exam requirements/recommendations for international students: Required—TOEFL. Electronic applications accepted. *Faculty research:* English and American literature, critical theory, creative writing, language theory.

University of Waterloo, Graduate Studies, Faculty of Arts, Department of English Language and Literature, Waterloo, ON N2L 3G1, Canada. Offers English language and literature (PhD); literary studies (MA); rhetoric and communication design (MA). *Program availability:* Part-time. *Degree requirements:* For master's, one foreign language, thesis optional; for doctorate, 2 foreign languages, thesis/dissertation. *Entrance requirements:* For master's, honors degree, minimum B+ average; for doctorate, master's degree, minimum A- average. Additional exam requirements/recommendations for international students: Required—TOEFL, IELTS, PTE. Electronic applications accepted. *Faculty research:* Shakespeare, American literature, rhetoric, Romantics, moderns.

The University of Western Ontario, Faculty of Graduate Studies, Faculty of Arts and Humanities, Department of English, London, ON N6A 5B8, Canada. Offers Canadian literature (MA); English (PhD); English literature (MA). *Degree requirements:* For master's, one foreign language, thesis or alternative; for doctorate, 2 foreign languages, thesis/dissertation, qualifying exam. *Entrance requirements:* For master's, minimum A average in appropriate field; for doctorate, MA or equivalent, minimum A average. Additional exam requirements/recommendations for international students: Required—TOEFL (minimum score 630 paper-based). *Faculty research:* Renaissance, nineteenth-century, modern, and postcolonial literature.

University of West Florida, College of Arts, Social Sciences, and Humanities, Department of English, Pensacola, FL 32514-5750. Offers creative writing (MA); literature (MA). *Program availability:* Part-time, evening/weekend. *Degree requirements:* For master's, thesis. *Entrance requirements:* For master's, GRE (minimum score: verbal 500, writing 4.5) or MAT (minimum score 413), official transcripts; two-page statement of purpose; writing sample (2500 words of literary analysis for literature track, or 2500 words of fiction/non-fiction prose or 10 poems for creative writing track); three letters of recommendation from instructors; 20 hours' upper-division undergraduate coursework in English. Additional exam requirements/recommendations for international students: Required—TOEFL (minimum score 550 paper-based). *Faculty research:* Faulkner, Shakespeare, American humor, women's studies, poetry.

University of West Georgia, College of Arts and Humanities, Carrollton, GA 30118. Offers English (MA); history (MA); museum studies (Postbaccalaureate Certificate); music performance (M Mus); music teacher education (M Mus); public history (Postbaccalaureate Certificate). *Program availability:* Part-time, evening/weekend, 100% online, blended/hybrid learning. *Faculty:* 69 full-time (38 women). *Students:* 25 full-time (15 women), 51 part-time (34 women); includes 16 minority (7 Black or African American, non-Hispanic/Latino; 1 American Indian or Alaska Native, non-Hispanic/Latino; 2 Asian, non-Hispanic/Latino; 5 Hispanic/Latino; 1 Two or more races, non-Hispanic/Latino), 1 international. Average age 30. 23 applicants, 96% accepted, 16 enrolled. In 2017, 29 master's, 6 other advanced degrees awarded. *Entrance requirements:* Additional exam requirements/recommendations for international students: Required—TOEFL (minimum score 523 paper-based; 69 iBT); Recommended—IELTS (minimum score 6.5). *Application deadline:* For fall admission, 8/1 for domestic students, 6/1 for international students; for spring admission, 11/15 for domestic students, 10/15 for international students; for summer admission, 5/15 for domestic students, 3/30 for international students. Applications are processed on a rolling basis. Application fee: $40. Electronic applications accepted. Tuition and fees vary according to degree level and program. *Financial support:* Fellowships, research assistantships, teaching assistantships, career-related internships or fieldwork, Federal Work-Study, institutionally sponsored loans, scholarships/grants, and unspecified assistantships available. Support available to part-time students. Financial award application deadline: 4/1; financial award applicants required to submit FAFSA. *Unit head:* Dr. Pauline D. Gagnon, Dean of Arts and Humanities, 678-839-5450, Fax: 678-839-5451, E-mail: pgagnon@westga.edu. *Application contact:* Dr. Toby Ziglar, Assistant Dean of the Graduate School, 678-839-1394, Fax: 678-839-1395, E-mail: graduate@westga.edu.
Website: http://www.westga.edu/coah

University of Windsor, Faculty of Graduate Studies, Faculty of Arts and Social Sciences, Department of English Language, Literature and Creative Writing, Windsor, ON N9B 3P4, Canada. Offers English: creative writing and language and literature (MA); English: language and literature (MA). *Program availability:* Part-time. *Degree requirements:* For master's, thesis. *Entrance requirements:* For master's, minimum B average, portfolio. Additional exam requirements/recommendations for international students: Required—TOEFL (minimum score 600 paper-based). Electronic applications accepted. *Faculty research:* Use of gender-related terms in popular culture; international and Aboriginal literatures: expression of cultural identity; critical analysis of authors: Pope, Munroe, Lady Morgan, Orwell, Thomas; the "feminine" voice in literature and contemporary culture.

University of Wisconsin–Eau Claire, College of Arts and Sciences, Program in English, Eau Claire, WI 54702-4004. Offers literature and textual interpretation (MA); writing (MA). *Program availability:* Part-time. *Degree requirements:* For master's, oral defense with thesis. *Entrance requirements:* For master's, minimum GPA of 3.25 in English, 3.0 overall; bachelor's degree with minimum of 24 credits in English. Additional exam requirements/recommendations for international students: Required—TOEFL (minimum score 79 iBT).

University of Wisconsin–Madison, Graduate School, College of Letters and Science, Department of English, Madison, WI 53706-1380. Offers applied English linguistics (MA); composition and rhetoric (PhD); creative writing (MFA); English language and linguistics (PhD); literary studies (MA, PhD). *Degree requirements:* For doctorate, thesis/dissertation.

University of Wisconsin–Milwaukee, Graduate School, College of Letters and Science, Department of English, Milwaukee, WI 53201-0413. Offers English (MA, PhD), including creative writing, English language and linguistics, English secondary education, literary and critical studies, literature and cultural theory (PhD), literature and language studies, literature, culture, and media, media, cinema and digital studies, professional and technical communication (MA), professional and technical writing, professional writing (PhD), rhetoric and composition (PhD), rhetoric and writing. *Students:* 90 full-time (54 women), 42 part-time (17 women); includes 12 minority (2 Black or African American, non-Hispanic/Latino; 1 American Indian or Alaska Native, non-Hispanic/Latino; 4 Asian, non-Hispanic/Latino; 1 Hispanic/Latino; 4 Two or more races, non-Hispanic/Latino), 9 international. Average age 34. 166 applicants, 21% accepted, 27 enrolled. In 2017, 10 master's, 12 doctorates awarded. *Degree requirements:* For master's, thesis or alternative; for doctorate, one foreign language, thesis/dissertation. *Entrance requirements:* For master's, GRE General Test, GRE Subject Test; for doctorate, GRE. Additional exam requirements/recommendations for international students: Required—TOEFL (minimum score 550 paper-based; 79 iBT), IELTS (minimum score 6.5). *Application deadline:* For fall admission, 1/1 priority date for domestic students; for spring admission, 9/1 for domestic students. Application fee: $56 ($96 for international students). Electronic applications accepted. *Financial support:* Fellowships, research assistantships, teaching assistantships, career-related internships or fieldwork, unspecified assistantships, and project assistantships available. Support available to part-time students. Financial award application deadline: 4/15; financial award applicants required to submit FAFSA. *Unit head:* Mark Netzloff, Department Chair, 414-229-4511, E-mail: netzloff@uwm.edu. *Application contact:* General Information Contact, 414-229-4982, Fax: 414-229-6967, E-mail: gradschool@uwm.edu.
Website: https://uwm.edu/english/

University of Wisconsin–Oshkosh, Graduate Studies, College of Letters and Science, Department of English, Oshkosh, WI 54901. Offers MA. *Program availability:* Part-time. *Degree requirements:* For master's, thesis or alternative. *Entrance requirements:* For master's, GRE. Additional exam requirements/recommendations for international students: Required—TOEFL (minimum score 550 paper-based; 79 iBT). Electronic applications accepted.

University of Wisconsin–Stevens Point, College of Letters and Science, Department of English, Stevens Point, WI 54481-3897. Offers MST. *Degree requirements:* For master's, thesis or alternative.

University of Wyoming, College of Arts and Sciences, Department of English, Laramie, WY 82071. Offers creative writing (MFA); English (MA). *Program availability:* Part-time. *Degree requirements:* For master's, thesis or alternative, internship. *Entrance requirements:* For master's, GRE General Test, minimum GPA of 3.0. Electronic applications accepted. *Faculty research:* Literature and theory, creative writing, English as a second language, ethnic and women's studies, composition.

Utah State University, School of Graduate Studies, College of Humanities and Social Sciences, Department of English, Logan, UT 84322. Offers American studies (MA, MS), including folklore, western American literature and culture; English (MA, MS), including literature and writing, technical writing. *Program availability:* Part-time, evening/weekend. *Degree requirements:* For master's, thesis or alternative. *Entrance requirements:* For master's, GRE General Test or MAT, minimum GPA of 3.0, recommendation letters, writing samples. Additional exam requirements/recommendations for international students: Required—TOEFL. *Faculty research:* Scottish enlightenment, material culture, composition theory, creative nonfiction, literary criticism.

Valdosta State University, Department of English, Valdosta, GA 31698. Offers English (MA); English studies for language arts teachers (MA). *Program availability:* Part-time, 100% online, blended/hybrid learning. *Degree requirements:* For master's, one foreign language, thesis, comprehensive written and/or oral exams. *Entrance requirements:* For master's, GRE General Test, minimum GPA of 3.0. Additional exam requirements/recommendations for international students: Required—TOEFL (minimum score 523 paper-based); Recommended—IELTS. *Application deadline:* For fall admission, 7/1 for domestic and international students; for spring admission, 11/1 for domestic and international students. Applications are processed on a rolling basis. Application fee: $45. Electronic applications accepted. *Expenses:* Contact institution. *Financial support:* Research assistantships with full tuition reimbursements, teaching assistantships with full tuition reimbursements, institutionally sponsored loans, scholarships/grants, and unspecified assistantships available. Support available to part-time students. Financial award application deadline: 7/1; financial award applicants required to submit FAFSA. *Faculty research:* American literature, creative writing. *Unit head:* Dr. Maren Clegg Hyer, Graduate Program Adviser, 229-333-7347, E-mail: mclegghyer@valdosta.edu. *Application contact:* Jessica Powers, Admission Specialist, 229-333-5694, Fax: 229-245-3853, E-mail: jldevane@valdosta.edu. Website: https://www.valdosta.edu/english/

Valparaiso University, Graduate School and Continuing Education, Program in English Studies and Communication, Valparaiso, IN 46383. Offers English studies and communication (MA). *Program availability:* Part-time, evening/weekend. *Entrance requirements:* For master's, minimum GPA of 3.0. Additional exam requirements/recommendations for international students: Required—TOEFL (minimum score 550 paper-based; 80 iBT), IELTS (minimum score 6). Electronic applications accepted. *Expenses: Tuition:* Full-time $11,340; part-time $630 per credit hour. *Required fees:* $520; $250 per year. $125 per semester. Tuition and fees vary according to program and reciprocity agreements.

Vanderbilt University, Department of English, Nashville, TN 37240-1001. Offers MA, MAT, PhD. *Faculty:* 31 full-time (21 women). *Students:* 35 full-time (26 women), 1 (woman) part-time; includes 15 minority (12 Black or African American, non-Hispanic/Latino; 2 Asian, non-Hispanic/Latino; 1 Two or more races, non-Hispanic/Latino), 4 international. Average age 28. 242 applicants, 7% accepted, 7 enrolled. In 2017, 13 master's, 7 doctorates awarded. *Degree requirements:* For master's, thesis; for doctorate, one foreign language, comprehensive exam, thesis/dissertation, final and qualifying exams. *Entrance requirements:* For master's and doctorate, GRE General Test, sample of written work. Additional exam requirements/recommendations for international students: Required—TOEFL (minimum score 570 paper-based; 88 iBT). *Application deadline:* For fall admission, 1/15 for domestic and international students. Electronic applications accepted. *Financial support:* Fellowships with tuition reimbursements, research assistantships with tuition reimbursements, teaching assistantships with full tuition reimbursements, Federal Work-Study, institutionally sponsored loans, scholarships/grants, and health care benefits available. Financial award application deadline: 1/15; financial award applicants required to submit CSS PROFILE or FAFSA. *Faculty research:* British, American, and Anglophone literature, film, cultural studies, literary theory. *Unit head:* Dr. Dana Nelson, Chair, 615-322-2541, Fax: 615-343-8028, E-mail: dana.d.nelson@vanderbilt.edu. *Application contact:* Vera Kutzinski, Director of Graduate Studies, 615-322-2541, Fax: 615-343-8028, E-mail: vera.kutzinski@vanderbilt.edu. Website: http://as.vanderbilt.edu/english/graduate/

Villanova University, Graduate School of Liberal Arts and Sciences, Department of English, Villanova, PA 19085-1699. Offers MA. *Program availability:* Part-time, evening/weekend. *Faculty:* 5. *Students:* 26 full-time (15 women), 11 part-time (7 women); includes 6 minority (1 Asian, non-Hispanic/Latino; 3 Hispanic/Latino; 2 Two or more races, non-Hispanic/Latino), 1 international. Average age 29. 29 applicants, 79% accepted, 14 enrolled. In 2017, 14 master's awarded. *Degree requirements:* For master's, comprehensive exam, thesis optional. *Entrance requirements:* For master's, GRE General Test, minimum GPA of 3.0, writing sample, 3 recommendation letters. Additional exam requirements/recommendations for international students: Required—TOEFL. *Application deadline:* For fall admission, 3/1 priority date for domestic students, 5/1 for international students; for spring admission, 11/15 priority date for domestic students, 10/15 for international students; for summer admission, 5/1 for domestic students. Applications are processed on a rolling basis. Application fee: $50. Electronic applications accepted. *Financial support:* Research assistantships, Federal Work-Study, scholarships/grants, and unspecified assistantships available. Financial award applicants required to submit FAFSA. *Unit head:* Dr. Evan Radcliffe, Program Director, 610-519-4648. Website: http://www1.villanova.edu/villanova/artsci/english/gradenglish.html

Virginia Commonwealth University, Graduate School, College of Humanities and Sciences, Department of English, Program in English, Richmond, VA 23284-9005. Offers literature (MA). *Program availability:* Part-time. *Entrance requirements:* For master's, GRE General Test. Additional exam requirements/recommendations for international students: Required—TWE, TOEFL (minimum score 600 paper-based; 100 iBT) or IELTS (minimum score 6.5). Electronic applications accepted. *Faculty research:* Literature, writing, rhetoric.

Virginia Polytechnic Institute and State University, Graduate School, College of Liberal Arts and Human Sciences, Blacksburg, VA 24061. Offers career and technical education (MS Ed, Ed S); communication (MA); counselor education (MA); creative writing (MFA); curriculum and instruction (MA Ed, Ed S); educational leadership and policy studies (Ed S); educational research and evaluation (PhD); English (MA); social, political, ethical, and cultural thought (PhD); Ed D/PhD. *Faculty:* 411 full-time (213 women), 3 part-time/adjunct (all women). *Students:* 623 full-time (427 women), 431 part-time (278 women); includes 203 minority (115 Black or African American, non-Hispanic/

Latino; 4 American Indian or Alaska Native, non-Hispanic/Latino; 29 Asian, non-Hispanic/Latino; 33 Hispanic/Latino; 2 Native Hawaiian or other Pacific Islander, non-Hispanic/Latino; 20 Two or more races, non-Hispanic/Latino), 87 international. Average age 34. 898 applicants, 50% accepted, 329 enrolled. In 2017, 314 master's, 102 doctorates awarded. *Degree requirements:* For master's, comprehensive exam (for some programs), thesis (for some programs); for doctorate, comprehensive exam (for some programs), thesis/dissertation (for some programs). *Entrance requirements:* For master's and doctorate, GRE/GMAT. Additional exam requirements/recommendations for international students: Required—TOEFL (minimum score 80 iBT). *Application deadline:* For fall admission, 8/1 for domestic students, 4/1 for international students; for spring admission, 1/1 for domestic students, 9/1 for international students. Applications are processed on a rolling basis. Application fee: $75. Electronic applications accepted. *Expenses: Tuition,* state resident: full-time $15,072; part-time $718.50 per credit hour. Tuition, nonresident: full-time $28,810; part-time $1448.25 per credit hour. *Required fees:* $2741; $502 per semester. Tuition and fees vary according to course load, campus/location and program. *Financial support:* In 2017–18, 19 research assistantships with full tuition reimbursements (averaging $19,611 per year), 226 teaching assistantships with full tuition reimbursements (averaging $16,220 per year) were awarded. Financial award application deadline: 3/1; financial award applicants required to submit FAFSA. *Total annual research expenditures:* $7.9 million. *Unit head:* Dr. Rosemary Blieszner, Dean, 540-231-6779, Fax: 540-231-7157, E-mail: rmb@vt.edu. *Application contact:* Chelsea Blanchet, Executive Assistant, 540-231-6779, Fax: 540-231-7157, E-mail: bchels1@vt.edu. Website: http://www.liberalarts.vt.edu/

Wake Forest University, Graduate School of Arts and Sciences, Department of English, Winston-Salem, NC 27109. Offers MA. *Program availability:* Part-time. *Degree requirements:* For master's, one foreign language, thesis. *Entrance requirements:* For master's, GRE General Test, writing sample. Additional exam requirements/recommendations for international students: Required—TOEFL (minimum score 79 iBT). Electronic applications accepted. *Faculty research:* Modern and contemporary poetry, feminist criticism and theory, Irish literature, British Commonwealth literature, medieval poetry.

Washington State University, College of Arts and Sciences, Department of English, Pullman, WA 99164. Offers MA, PhD. Program applications must be made through the Pullman campus. *Degree requirements:* For master's, one foreign language, comprehensive exam (for some programs), thesis (for some programs), oral exam; for doctorate, 2 foreign languages, comprehensive exam, thesis/dissertation, oral exam, written exam. *Entrance requirements:* For master's and doctorate, GRE General Test, GRE Subject Test, official transcripts; writing sample (approximately 10 pages); three letters of recommendation; statement of purpose (approximately 500 words); undergraduate major in English or other appropriate discipline. Additional exam requirements/recommendations for international students: Required—TOEFL, IELTS. Electronic applications accepted. *Faculty research:* Nationalism and gender in the American West, slavery and exploitation in nineteenth-century Britain, photography and the color line, D.H. Lawrence and Mexico, social movement cultures and the arts.

Washington University in St. Louis, The Graduate School, Department of English, St. Louis, MO 63130-4899. Offers English and American literature (PhD); writing (MFA). Terminal master's awarded for partial completion of doctoral program. *Degree requirements:* For master's, thesis or written exam; for doctorate, 2 foreign languages, thesis/dissertation. *Entrance requirements:* For master's and doctorate, GRE General Test, sample of written work. Additional exam requirements/recommendations for international students: Required—TOEFL. Electronic applications accepted. *Faculty research:* Medieval, early modern, early American, eighteenth-century British, nineteenth-century British, nineteenth-century American, twentieth- and twenty-first century British, and twentieth- and twenty-first century American literature; African American literature and culture; Irish literature; Anglophone Postcolonial literature; gender and sexuality studies; Modernism; poetry and poetics; theory.

Wayne State University, College of Liberal Arts and Sciences, Department of English, Detroit, MI 48202. Offers English (MA); film and media studies (PhD); literary and cultural studies (PhD); rhetoric and composition studies (PhD). *Faculty:* 23. *Students:* 68 full-time (34 women), 24 part-time (17 women); includes 22 minority (10 Black or African American, non-Hispanic/Latino; 2 Asian, non-Hispanic/Latino; 6 Hispanic/Latino; 4 Two or more races, non-Hispanic/Latino), 5 international. Average age 33. 110 applicants, 35% accepted, 17 enrolled. In 2017, 15 master's, 15 doctorates awarded. Terminal master's awarded for partial completion of doctoral program. *Degree requirements:* For master's, variable foreign language requirement, essay, thesis, or portfolio of work approved by Director of Graduate Studies; for doctorate, one foreign language, comprehensive exam, thesis/dissertation. *Entrance requirements:* For master's, statement of purpose, two academic letters of reference; sample essay from previous English course; for doctorate, GRE General Test, statement of purpose; two academic letters of reference; sample of scholarly or critical writing. Additional exam requirements/recommendations for international students: Required—TOEFL (minimum score 550 paper-based; 79 iBT), TWE (minimum score 5.5), Michigan English Language Assessment Battery (minimum score 85); Recommended—IELTS (minimum score 6.5). *Application deadline:* For fall admission, 1/15 for domestic students. Applications are processed on a rolling basis. Application fee: $50. Electronic applications accepted. *Expenses: Tuition,* state resident: full-time $10,224; part-time $638.98 per credit hour. Tuition, nonresident: full-time $22,145; part-time $1384.04 per credit hour. Tuition and fees vary according to course load and program. *Financial support:* In 2017–18, 61 students received support, including 6 fellowships with tuition reimbursements available (averaging $15,583 per year), 30 teaching assistantships with tuition reimbursements available (averaging $18,534 per year); research assistantships with tuition reimbursements available, scholarships/grants, health care benefits, and unspecified assistantships also available. Financial award applicants required to submit FAFSA. *Faculty research:* Literary and cultural studies, film and new media studies, rhetoric and composition studies, linguistics, and creative writing. *Unit head:* Dr. Kenneth Jackson, Chair and Professor, 313-577-7692, E-mail: ai4054@wayne.edu. *Application contact:* Dr. Carolin Maun, Director of Graduate Studies, 313-577-7694, E-mail: caroline.maun@wayne.edu. Website: http://clas.wayne.edu/english

Weber State University, Telitha E. Lindquist College of Arts and Humanities, Program in English, Ogden, UT 84408-1001. Offers MA. *Program availability:* Part-time, evening/weekend. *Faculty:* 16 full-time (9 women). *Students:* 2 full-time (1 woman), 42 part-time (36 women); includes 4 minority (1 Asian, non-Hispanic/Latino; 1 Hispanic/Latino; 2 Two or more races, non-Hispanic/Latino), 1 international. Average age 34. In 2017, 16 master's awarded. *Degree requirements:* For master's, one foreign language. *Entrance requirements:* For master's, 3 letters of recommendation, 5- to 8-page writing sample. Additional exam requirements/recommendations for international students: Required—TOEFL (minimum score 550 paper-based; 79 iBT). *Application deadline:* For fall admission, 3/15 for domestic students; for spring admission, 3/15 for domestic students; for summer admission, 10/15 for domestic students. Application fee: $60 ($90 for international students). Electronic applications accepted. *Expenses: Tuition,* state resident: full-time $7283. Tuition, nonresident: full-time $17,166. *Required fees:* $898.

Tuition and fees vary according to program. *Financial support:* In 2017–18, 14 students received support. Scholarships/grants available. Financial award application deadline: 4/1; financial award applicants required to submit FAFSA. *Unit head:* Dr. Mali Subbiah, Program Director, 801-626-6335, Fax: 801-626-7760, E-mail: msubbiah@weber.edu. *Application contact:* Rami Collins, Administrative Specialist, 801-626-7179, Fax: 801-626-7760, E-mail: masterofenglish@weber.edu.
Website: http://weber.edu/maenglish

West Chester University of Pennsylvania, College of Arts and Humanities, Department of English, West Chester, PA 19383. Offers English (MA), including creative writing, literature, writing, teaching, and criticism; publishing (Certificate); secondary English (Teaching Certificate). *Program availability:* Part-time, evening/weekend. *Students:* 25 full-time (17 women), 47 part-time (27 women); includes 5 minority (1 Black or African American, non-Hispanic/Latino; 1 Asian, non-Hispanic/Latino; 3 Two or more races, non-Hispanic/Latino), 2 international. Average age 29. 43 applicants, 88% accepted, 25 enrolled. In 2017, 10 master's, 1 other advanced degree awarded. *Degree requirements:* For master's, thesis optional; for other advanced degree, capstone internship and e-portfolio (for Certificate in publishing). *Entrance requirements:* For master's, minimum GPA of 2.8, two letters of recommendation, writing sample, goals statement, official transcripts; for other advanced degree, two letters of recommendation, statement of goals, official transcripts; undergraduate degree (for Certificate); minimum GPA of 2.85 and writing sample (for Teaching Certificate). Additional exam requirements/recommendations for international students: Required—TOEFL or IELTS. *Application deadline:* For fall admission, 5/15 for international students; for spring admission, 10/15 for international students. Applications are processed on a rolling basis. Application fee: $50. Electronic applications accepted. *Expenses:* Tuition, state resident: full-time $9000; part-time $500 per credit. Tuition, nonresident: full-time $13,500; part-time $750 per credit. *Required fees:* $2959; $149.79 per credit. *Financial support:* Scholarships/grants and unspecified assistantships available. Financial award application deadline: 2/15; financial award applicants required to submit FAFSA. *Faculty research:* Critical theory, cultural studies, literature, rhetoric and composition, creative writing. *Unit head:* Dr. Rodney Mader, Chair, 610-436-2822, Fax: 610-738-0516, E-mail: rmader@wcupa.edu. *Application contact:* Dr. Eleanor Shevlin, Graduate Coordinator for English, 610-436-2745, Fax: 610-738-0516, E-mail: eshevlin@wcupa.edu.
Website: http://www.wcupa.edu/arts-humanities/english/

Western Carolina University, Graduate School, College of Arts and Sciences, Department of English, Cullowhee, NC 28723. Offers literature (MA); professional writing (MA); rhetoric and composition (MA); teaching English to speakers of other languages (Certificate); technical and professional writing (Certificate). *Program availability:* Part-time, evening/weekend. *Students:* 31. *Degree requirements:* For master's, one foreign language, comprehensive exam, thesis (for some programs). *Entrance requirements:* For master's, appropriate undergraduate degree, writing sample, 3 letters of recommendation. Additional exam requirements/recommendations for international students: Required—TOEFL (minimum score 550 paper-based, 79 iBT) or IELTS (6.5). *Application deadline:* For fall admission, 2/15 priority date for domestic and international students; for spring admission, 11/15 priority date for domestic students, 10/15 priority date for international students. Applications are processed on a rolling basis. Application fee: $65. Electronic applications accepted. *Expenses:* $10,000 per year in-state full-time; $20,308 per year out-of-state full-time. *Financial support:* In 2017–18, 1 research assistantship with full and partial tuition reimbursement (averaging $9,000 per year), 16 teaching assistantships with full and partial tuition reimbursements (averaging $9,500 per year) were awarded; career-related internships or fieldwork, institutionally sponsored loans, scholarships/grants, and unspecified assistantships also available. Financial award application deadline: 2/15; financial award applicants required to submit FAFSA. *Faculty research:* Teaching English to speakers of other languages (TESOL), language assessment, applied linguistics, poetry, folk and fairy tales, post World War II British literature, Appalachian and Southern literature. *Unit head:* Dr. Brent Kinser, Department Head, E-mail: bkinser@wcu.edu. *Application contact:* Bobbi Smith, Graduate Admissions Coordinator, E-mail: bobbismith@email.wcu.edu.
Website: https://www.wcu.edu/learn/departments-schools-colleges/cas/humanities/english/enggrad/index.aspx

Western Connecticut State University, Division of Graduate Studies, Maricostas School of Arts and Sciences, Department of English, Danbury, CT 06810-6885. Offers literature (MA). *Program availability:* Part-time. *Degree requirements:* For master's, completion of program in 6 years. *Entrance requirements:* For master's, minimum GPA of 2.5, writing sample. Additional exam requirements/recommendations for international students: Recommended—TOEFL (minimum score 550 paper-based; 79 iBT), IELTS (minimum score 6). *Expenses:* Tuition, state resident: full-time $6757; part-time $374 per credit hour. Tuition, nonresident: full-time $18,102; part-time $374 per credit hour. *Required fees:* $4994; $190 per credit hour. $60 per term. Tuition and fees vary according to degree level and program. *Faculty research:* Developing inquiry in teachers and students, encouraging talent development, analyzing program development and assessment techniques, developing student learning outcomes, encouraging teachers as researchers, assessing the impact of computer technologies.

Western Illinois University, School of Graduate Studies, College of Arts and Sciences, Department of English and Journalism, Macomb, IL 61455-1390. Offers English (MA); literary studies (Certificate). *Program availability:* Part-time. *Students:* 7 full-time (5 women), 30 part-time (16 women); includes 4 minority (2 Black or African American, non-Hispanic/Latino; 1 Asian, non-Hispanic/Latino; 1 Hispanic/Latino), 2 international. Average age 30. 18 applicants, 89% accepted, 14 enrolled. In 2017, 9 master's awarded. *Degree requirements:* For master's, thesis or alternative. *Entrance requirements:* Additional exam requirements/recommendations for international students: Required—TOEFL (minimum score 575 paper-based; 88 iBT). *Application deadline:* Applications are processed on a rolling basis. Application fee: $30. Electronic applications accepted. *Financial support:* In 2017–18, 17 students received support, including 5 teaching assistantships with full tuition reimbursements available (averaging $8,688 per year). Financial award applicants required to submit FAFSA. *Unit head:* Dr. Mark Mossman, Chairperson, 309-298-1103. *Application contact:* Dr. Nancy Parsons, Associate Provost and Director of Graduate Studies, 309-298-1806, Fax: 309-298-2345, E-mail: grad-office@wiu.edu.
Website: http://wiu.edu/English

Western Kentucky University, Graduate Studies, Potter College of Arts and Letters, Department of English, Bowling Green, KY 42101. Offers education (MA); English (MA Ed); literature (MA), including American literature, British literature, literary theory, women writers, world literature; teaching English as a second language (MA); writing (MA). *Program availability:* Part-time, evening/weekend. *Degree requirements:* For master's, comprehensive exam, thesis optional, final exam. *Entrance requirements:* For master's, GRE General Test, minimum GPA of 2.75. Additional exam requirements/recommendations for international students: Required—TOEFL (minimum score 555 paper-based; 79 iBT). *Faculty research:* Improving writing, linking teacher knowledge and performance, Victorian women writers, Kentucky women writers, Kentucky poets.

Western Michigan University, Graduate College, College of Arts and Sciences, Department of English, Kalamazoo, MI 49008. Offers creative writing (MFA, PhD); English (MA, PhD); English teaching (MA). *Degree requirements:* For doctorate, one foreign language, thesis/dissertation.

Western Washington University, Graduate School, College of Humanities and Social Sciences, Department of English, Bellingham, WA 98225-5996. Offers MA. *Program availability:* Part-time. *Degree requirements:* For master's, one foreign language, comprehensive exam, thesis (for some programs). *Entrance requirements:* For master's, GRE General Test, writing sample, minimum GPA of 3.0 in last 60 semester hours or last 90 quarter hours of course work. Additional exam requirements/recommendations for international students: Required—TOEFL (minimum score 567 paper-based). Electronic applications accepted. *Faculty research:* Literature and technology, film, composition and rhetoric, technical writing, critical and cultural theory.

Westfield State University, College of Graduate and Continuing Education, Department of English, Westfield, MA 01086. Offers MA. *Program availability:* Part-time, evening/weekend. *Faculty:* 3 full-time (1 woman). *Students:* 1 (woman) full-time, 12 part-time (6 women); includes 1 minority (Hispanic/Latino). Average age 28. 1 applicant, 100% accepted, 1 enrolled. In 2017, 5 master's awarded. *Degree requirements:* For master's, one foreign language, thesis. *Entrance requirements:* For master's, GRE General Test, MAT, minimum undergraduate GPA of 2.8, 3.0 in all English classes; undergraduate course work in English. Additional exam requirements/recommendations for international students: Recommended—TOEFL (minimum score 550 paper-based; 79 iBT). *Application deadline:* For fall admission, 7/1 for domestic students; for spring admission, 11/1 for domestic students; for summer admission, 4/1 for domestic students. Applications are processed on a rolling basis. Application fee: $50. *Expenses:* Tuition, state resident: part-time $332 per credit. Tuition, nonresident: part-time $332 per credit. *Required fees:* $75 per semester. Tuition and fees vary according to program. *Financial support:* Unspecified assistantships and SOS scholarships (for education majors only) available. Financial award application deadline: 3/1; financial award applicants required to submit FAFSA. *Unit head:* Dr. Emily Todd, Director, 413-572-5337, E-mail: etodd@westfield.ma.edu. *Application contact:* Shelly Henrichon, Admissions Coordinator, 413-572-8022, Fax: 413-572-5227, E-mail: mhenrichon@westfield.ma.edu.
Website: http://www.westfield.ma.edu/academics/degrees/english-masters-degree

West Texas A&M University, College of Fine Arts and Humanities, Department of English, Philosophy and Modern Languages, Canyon, TX 79015. Offers English (MA). *Program availability:* Part-time, evening/weekend. *Degree requirements:* For master's, comprehensive exam, thesis optional. *Entrance requirements:* For master's, GRE General Test. Additional exam requirements/recommendations for international students: Required—TOEFL (minimum score 550 paper-based). Electronic applications accepted. *Faculty research:* Medieval studies, composition theory, literary criticism, Evelyn Scott, transformation of literacy in computer mediated communication.

West Virginia University, Eberly College of Arts and Sciences, Morgantown, WV 26506. Offers biology (MS, PhD); chemistry (MS, PhD); communication studies (MA, PhD); computational statistics (PhD); creative writing (MFA); English (MA, PhD); forensic and investigative science (MS); forensic science (PhD); geography (MA); geology (MA, PhD); history (MA, PhD); legal studies (MLS); math (MS); physics (MS, PhD); political science (MA, PhD); professional writing and editing (MA); psychology (MA); public administration (MPA); social work (MSW); sociology (MA, PhD); statistics (MS). *Program availability:* Part-time, evening/weekend, online learning. *Students:* 831 full-time (437 women), 236 part-time (142 women); includes 112 minority (35 Black or African American, non-Hispanic/Latino; 15 Asian, non-Hispanic/Latino; 29 Hispanic/Latino; 33 Two or more races, non-Hispanic/Latino), 235 international. Terminal master's awarded for partial completion of doctoral program. *Degree requirements:* For master's, thesis (for some programs); for doctorate, comprehensive exam, thesis/dissertation. *Entrance requirements:* For master's and doctorate, GRE. Additional exam requirements/recommendations for international students: Required—TOEFL (minimum score 600 paper-based); Recommended—TWE. *Application deadline:* For spring admission, 2/15 priority date for domestic and international students. Applications are processed on a rolling basis. Application fee: $45. Electronic applications accepted. *Expenses:* Tuition, state resident: full-time $9450. Tuition, nonresident: full-time $24,390. *Financial support:* Fellowships with full tuition reimbursements, research assistantships with full tuition reimbursements, teaching assistantships with full tuition reimbursements, career-related internships or fieldwork, Federal Work-Study, institutionally sponsored loans, scholarships/grants, health care benefits, tuition waivers (full and partial), unspecified assistantships, and administrative assistantships available. Financial award application deadline: 2/1; financial award applicants required to submit FAFSA. *Faculty research:* Humanities, social sciences, life science, physical sciences, mathematics. *Unit head:* Dr. Mary Ellen Mazey, Dean, 304-293-4611, Fax: 304-293-6858, E-mail: mary.mazey@mail.wvu.edu. *Application contact:* Dr. Fred L. King, Associate Dean for Graduate Studies, 304-293-4611 Ext. 5205, Fax: 304-293-6858, E-mail: fred.king@mail.wvu.edu.
Website: http://www.as.wvu.edu/

Wichita State University, Graduate School, Fairmount College of Liberal Arts and Sciences, Department of English, Wichita, KS 67260. Offers creative writing (MFA); English (MA). *Program availability:* Part-time, evening/weekend. *Entrance requirements:* For master's, writing sample (MFA). *Unit head:* Dr. Mary Waters, Chair, 316-978-3130, Fax: 316-978-3548, E-mail: mary.waters@wichita.edu. *Application contact:* Jordan Oleson, Admissions Coordinator, 316-978-3095, Fax: 316-978-3253, E-mail: jordan.oleson@wichita.edu.
Website: http://www.wichita.edu/english

Wilfrid Laurier University, Faculty of Graduate and Postdoctoral Studies, Faculty of Arts, Department of English and Film Studies, Waterloo, ON N2L 3C5, Canada. Offers English (MA); English and film (PhD). *Degree requirements:* For master's, thesis optional; for doctorate, thesis/dissertation. *Entrance requirements:* For master's, honours BA or the equivalent in English, minimum B+ in English courses above first year level; for doctorate, MA in English, minimum A- average in graduate work. Additional exam requirements/recommendations for international students: Recommended—TOEFL (minimum score 89 iBT). Electronic applications accepted. *Faculty research:* Gender and genre, Canadian studies, early modern studies, postcolonial studies, nineteenth century studies.

William Paterson University of New Jersey, College of Humanities and Social Sciences, Wayne, NJ 07470-8420. Offers applied sociology (MA); assessment and evaluation research (Certificate); bilingual education (Certificate); clinical and counseling psychology (MA); clinical psychology (Psy D); creative and professional writing (MFA); English (MA); history (MA); public policy and international affairs (MA); teaching English as a second language (Certificate). *Program availability:* Part-time. *Faculty:* 36 full-time (21 women), 10 part-time/adjunct (5 women). *Students:* 62 full-time (44 women), 102 part-time (71 women); includes 76 minority (12 Black or African American, non-Hispanic/Latino; 8 Asian, non-Hispanic/Latino; 50 Hispanic/Latino; 6 Two or more races, non-Hispanic/Latino), 6 international. Average age 33. 156 applicants, 51% accepted, 52 enrolled. In 2017, 39 master's awarded. *Degree requirements:* For master's, thesis (for some programs), internship (for some programs). *Entrance requirements:* For master's, GRE/MAT, minimum GPA of 3.0; 2 letters of recommendation; writing sample/personal statement. Additional exam requirements/recommendations for international students:

Required—TOEFL (minimum score 550 paper-based; 79 iBT), IELTS (minimum score 6). *Application deadline:* For fall admission, 6/1 for domestic students, 3/1 for international students; for spring admission, 11/1 for domestic students, 10/1 for international students. Applications are processed on a rolling basis. Application fee: $50. Electronic applications accepted. *Expenses:* Tuition, state resident: full-time $13,920; part-time $6264 per year. Tuition, nonresident: full-time $21,700; part-time $9765 per year. *Required fees:* $80; $36 per year. Tuition and fees vary according to course load, degree level and program. *Financial support:* In 2017–18, 3,480 students received support. Career-related internships or fieldwork, Federal Work-Study, scholarships/grants, and unspecified assistantships available. Support available to part-time students. Financial award application deadline: 3/15; financial award applicants required to submit FAFSA. *Faculty research:* Relationship violence, work-family balance, social development of Japan, theories justifying war, reactions to trauma. *Total annual research expenditures:* $32,300. *Unit head:* Dr. Kara Rabbitt, Dean, 973-720-2180, Fax: 973-720-2955, E-mail: rabbittk@wpunj.edu. *Application contact:* Tinu Adeniran, Associate Director, Graduate Admissions, 973-720-2764, Fax: 973-720-2035, E-mail: adenirant@wpunj.edu.
Website: http://www.wpunj.edu/cohss

Wilson College, Graduate Programs, Chambersburg, PA 17201-1285. Offers accounting (M Acc); choreography and visual art (MFA); education (M Ed); educational technology (MET); healthcare administration (MHA); humanities (MA), including art and culture, critical/cultural theory, English language and literature, women's studies; management (MSM); nursing (MSN), including nursing education, nursing leadership and management; special education (MSE). *Program availability:* Evening/weekend. *Degree requirements:* For master's, project. *Entrance requirements:* For master's, PRAXIS, minimum undergraduate cumulative GPA of 3.0, 2 letters of recommendation, current certification for eligibility to teach in grades K-12, resume, personal interview. Electronic applications accepted.

Winona State University, College of Liberal Arts, Department of English, Winona, MN 55987. Offers English (MS); literature and language (MA); TESOL (MA). *Program availability:* Part-time. *Degree requirements:* For master's, thesis or alternative.

Winthrop University, College of Arts and Sciences, Department of English, Rock Hill, SC 29733. Offers MA. *Program availability:* Part-time, evening/weekend. *Students:* 15 full-time (9 women), 4 part-time (3 women); includes 4 minority (3 Black or African American, non-Hispanic/Latino; 1 Hispanic/Latino). Average age 34. In 2017, 8 master's awarded. *Degree requirements:* For master's, one foreign language, comprehensive exam, thesis optional. *Entrance requirements:* For master's, GRE General Test, MAT or PRAXIS, 24 undergraduate hours of course work in English. Additional exam requirements/recommendations for international students: Required—TOEFL (minimum score 550 paper-based; 79 iBT). *Application deadline:* For fall admission, 7/15 priority date for domestic students; for spring admission, 12/1 for domestic students. Applications are processed on a rolling basis. Application fee: $50. Electronic applications accepted.

Financial support: Research assistantships with full tuition reimbursements, Federal Work-Study, scholarships/grants, and unspecified assistantships available. Support available to part-time students. Financial award application deadline: 2/1; financial award applicants required to submit FAFSA. *Unit head:* Gregg Hecimovich, Chair, 803-323-2171, Fax: 803-323-4837, E-mail: hecimovichg@winthrop.edu. *Application contact:* 800-411-7041, E-mail: gradschool@winthrop.edu.
Website: http://winthrop.edu/graduate-studies/english.htm

Wright State University, Graduate School, College of Liberal Arts, Department of English Language and Literatures, Dayton, OH 45435. Offers English (MA). *Degree requirements:* For master's, thesis optional, portfolio. *Entrance requirements:* For master's, 20 hours in upper-level English. Additional exam requirements/recommendations for international students: Required—TOEFL. *Faculty research:* American literature, world literature in English, applied linguistics, writing theory and pedagogy.

Xavier University, College of Arts and Sciences, Department of English, Cincinnati, OH 45207. Offers MA. *Program availability:* Part-time, evening/weekend. *Degree requirements:* For master's, one foreign language, comprehensive exam, thesis optional. *Entrance requirements:* For master's, GRE, writing sample; minimum GPA of 3.2 in undergraduate English courses, 3.0 for all undergraduate coursework; official transcript; intent/purpose statement. Additional exam requirements/recommendations for international students: Required—TOEFL (minimum score 550 paper-based; 79 iBT). Electronic applications accepted. Application fee is waived when completed online. *Expenses:* Contact institution. *Faculty research:* British literature, American literature, linguistics, literary theory, composition studies.

Yale University, Graduate School of Arts and Sciences, Department of English Language and Literature, New Haven, CT 06520. Offers MA, PhD. Terminal master's awarded for partial completion of doctoral program. *Degree requirements:* For master's, 2 foreign languages; for doctorate, 3 foreign languages, thesis/dissertation. *Entrance requirements:* For master's and doctorate, GRE General Test, GRE Subject Test.

York University, Faculty of Graduate Studies, Faculty of Liberal Arts and Professional Studies, Program in English, Toronto, ON M3J 1P3, Canada. Offers MA, PhD. *Program availability:* Part-time. *Degree requirements:* For master's, thesis or alternative; for doctorate, one foreign language, comprehensive exam, thesis/dissertation. Electronic applications accepted.

Youngstown State University, Graduate School, College of Liberal Arts and Social Sciences, Department of English, Youngstown, OH 44555-0001. Offers MA. *Program availability:* Part-time. *Degree requirements:* For master's, portfolio. *Entrance requirements:* For master's, bachelor's degree in English, minimum GPA of 2.7. Additional exam requirements/recommendations for international students: Required—TOEFL. *Faculty research:* Technical communications, multicultural literacy, children's literature, women's literature, film study, linguistics.

French

American University, College of Arts and Sciences, Department of World Languages and Cultures, Washington, DC 20016-8045. Offers Spanish: Latin American studies (MA); teaching English as a foreign language (MA); teaching English to speakers of other languages (MA, Certificate); translation: French (Certificate); translation: Russian (Certificate); translation: Spanish (Certificate). *Program availability:* Part-time, evening/weekend. *Faculty:* 43 full-time (33 women), 23 part-time/adjunct (17 women). *Students:* 17 full-time (14 women), 19 part-time (15 women); includes 10 minority (2 Black or African American, non-Hispanic/Latino; 6 Hispanic/Latino; 2 Two or more races, non-Hispanic/Latino), 5 international. Average age 32. 39 applicants, 97% accepted, 9 enrolled. In 2017, 16 master's, 11 other advanced degrees awarded. *Degree requirements:* For master's, one foreign language, comprehensive exam, thesis or alternative. *Entrance requirements:* For master's, GRE, writing sample, statement of purpose, transcripts, 2 letters of recommendation, resume; for Certificate, bachelor's degree, statement of purpose, transcripts, resume. Additional exam requirements/recommendations for international students: Required—TOEFL (minimum score 600 paper-based; 100 iBT). *Application deadline:* For fall admission, 2/1 priority date for domestic students; for spring admission, 11/1 priority date for domestic students. Application fee: $55. *Expenses:* Contact institution. *Financial support:* Institutionally sponsored loans, scholarships/grants, and unspecified assistantships available. Financial award application deadline: 2/1; financial award applicants required to submit FAFSA. *Unit head:* Henry Gerfen, Chair, 202-885-2385, Fax: 202-885-1076, E-mail: gerfen@american.edu. *Application contact:* Jonathan Harper, Director of Graduate Recruitment, 202-885-3622, E-mail: jharper@american.edu.
Website: http://www.american.edu/cas/wlc/

Arizona State University at the Tempe campus, College of Liberal Arts and Sciences, School of International Letters and Cultures, Program in French, Tempe, AZ 85287-0202. Offers comparative literature (MA); linguistics (MA); literature (MA). *Program availability:* Part-time, evening/weekend. *Degree requirements:* For master's, thesis or applied project, interactive Program of Study (iPOS) submitted no later than beginning of third semester of study or before completing 50 percent of coursework towards completion of degree. *Entrance requirements:* For master's, GRE, minimum GPA of 3.25 in the last two years of work leading to the bachelor's degree in French major, personal statement, writing sample (preferably written in French), 3 letters of recommendation. Additional exam requirements/recommendations for international students: Required—TOEFL (minimum score 550 paper-based; 83 iBT), IELTS (minimum score 6.5). Electronic applications accepted.

Asbury University, School of Graduate and Professional Studies, Wilmore, KY 40390-1198. Offers biology: alternative certificate (MA Ed); chemistry: alternative certificate (MA Ed); English (MA Ed); English as a second language (MA Ed); ESL (MA Ed); French (MA Ed); Latin: alternative certificate (MA Ed); mathematics: alternative certificate (MA Ed); reading/writing endorsement (MA Ed); social studies (MA Ed); social work (MSW), including child and family services; Spanish (MA Ed); special education (MA Ed); special education: alternative certificate (MA Ed); teacher as leader endorsement (MA Ed). *Accreditation:* NCATE. *Program availability:* Part-time. *Degree requirements:* For master's, action research project, portfolio. *Entrance requirements:* For master's, PRAXIS/NTE, minimum GPA of 2.75, letters of recommendation. Additional exam requirements/recommendations for international students: Required—TOEFL (minimum score 550 paper-based). Electronic applications accepted.

Binghamton University, State University of New York, Graduate School, Harpur College of Arts and Sciences, Department of Romance Languages and Literatures, Program in French, Binghamton, NY 13902-6000. Offers MA. *Program availability:* Part-time. *Students:* 1 full-time (0 women), 2 part-time (1 woman); includes 1 minority (Black or African American, non-Hispanic/Latino). Average age 41. 1 applicant, 100% accepted, 1 enrolled. *Degree requirements:* For master's, one foreign language, comprehensive exam, thesis or alternative. *Entrance requirements:* For master's, GRE General Test. Additional exam requirements/recommendations for international students: Required—TOEFL (minimum score 550 paper-based; 80 iBT). *Application deadline:* For fall admission, 2/15 priority date for domestic and international students; for spring admission, 11/15 priority date for domestic and international students. Application fee: $75. Electronic applications accepted. *Financial support:* Career-related internships or fieldwork, Federal Work-Study, institutionally sponsored loans, and unspecified assistantships available. Support available to part-time students. Financial award applicants required to submit FAFSA. *Unit head:* Dr. Dana Stewart, Chairperson, 607-777-2645, E-mail: stewart@binghamton.edu. *Application contact:* Ben Balkaya, Assistant Dean and Director, 607-777-2151, Fax: 607-777-2501, E-mail: balkaya@binghamton.edu.

Boston College, Graduate School of Arts and Sciences, Department of Romance Languages and Literatures, Chestnut Hill, MA 02467-3800. Offers French (MA); Italian (MA); Spanish (MA). *Program availability:* Part-time. Terminal master's awarded for partial completion of doctoral program. *Degree requirements:* For master's, one foreign language. *Entrance requirements:* Additional exam requirements/recommendations for international students: Required—TOEFL (minimum score 600 paper-based; 100 iBT), IELTS (minimum score 8). Electronic applications accepted. *Faculty research:* Spanish-American literature, philology, medieval French romance and troubadour lyrics, Golden Age Peninsular literature, secondary language acquisition and pedagogy, Hispanic studies, French language and literature, Italian language and literature.

Bowling Green State University, Graduate College, College of Arts and Sciences, Department of Romance and Classical Studies, Program in French, Bowling Green, OH 43403. Offers French (MA). *Program availability:* Part-time. *Degree requirements:* For master's, one foreign language, thesis or alternative. *Entrance requirements:* For master's, GRE General Test. Additional exam requirements/recommendations for international students: Required—TOEFL. Electronic applications accepted. *Faculty research:* Francophone literature, French cinema, business French, nineteenth- and twentieth-century literature.

Brigham Young University, Graduate Studies, College of Humanities, Department of French and Italian, Provo, UT 84602. Offers French studies (MA). In 2017, 1 master's awarded. *Degree requirements:* For master's, one foreign language, thesis. *Entrance requirements:* For master's, GRE General Test, BA in French. Additional exam requirements/recommendations for international students: Required—TOEFL. *Application deadline:* For fall admission, 2/28 for domestic and international students. Application fee: $50. Electronic applications accepted. *Expenses: Tuition:* Full-time $6880; part-time $405 per credit hour. Tuition and fees vary according to course load, program and student's religious affiliation. *Financial support:* Research assistantships, teaching assistantships, career-related internships or fieldwork, institutionally sponsored loans, scholarships/grants, and tuition waivers (full and partial) available. Support available to part-time students. *Faculty research:* Francophone studies, medieval literature, Provencal literature, existentialism, second language acquisition, cultural studies, the sacred, Renaissance poetry, satire. *Unit head:* Dr. Corry L. Cropper, Department Chair, 801-422-4484, Fax: 801-422-0260, E-mail: corrycropper@gmail.com. *Application contact:* Nicolas G. Unlandt, Graduate Coordinator, 801-422-2895, Fax: 801-422-0260, E-mail: nicolas_unlandt@byu.edu.
Website: http://frenital.byu.edu/department.html

French

Brooklyn College of the City University of New York, School of Humanities and Social Sciences, Department of Modern Languages and Literatures, Brooklyn, NY 11210-2889. Offers French (MA); Spanish (MA). *Degree requirements:* For master's, comprehensive exam or research paper. *Entrance requirements:* For master's, 18 credits in advanced courses in Spanish, 2 letters of recommendation. Additional exam requirements/recommendations for international students: Required—TOEFL (minimum score 500 paper-based; 61 iBT). Electronic applications accepted. *Faculty research:* Latin American contemporary novel, Caribbean female contemporary literature, nineteenth- and twentieth-century Spanish novel, twentieth-century Mexican poetry.

Brown University, Graduate School, Department of French Studies, Providence, RI 02912. Offers PhD. *Degree requirements:* For doctorate, variable foreign language requirement, thesis/dissertation, preliminary exam.

California State University, Long Beach, Graduate Studies, College of Liberal Arts, Department of Romance, German, Russian Languages and Literatures, Program in French and Francophone Studies, Long Beach, CA 90840. Offers MA. *Program availability:* Part-time. *Degree requirements:* For master's, one foreign language, comprehensive exam, thesis optional. *Entrance requirements:* For master's, BA in French. Electronic applications accepted. *Faculty research:* Eighteenth-century encyclopedism, development of the novel, La Chanson de Roland.

California State University, Los Angeles, Graduate Studies, College of Arts and Letters, Department of Modern Languages and Literatures, Los Angeles, CA 90032-8530. Offers French (MA); Spanish (MA). *Program availability:* Part-time, evening/weekend. *Degree requirements:* For master's, comprehensive exam. *Entrance requirements:* Additional exam requirements/recommendations for international students: Required—TOEFL (minimum score 500 paper-based). Electronic applications accepted. *Faculty research:* French literature, language teaching and methodology, Spanish poetry, Spanish American fiction and poetry.

Carleton University, Faculty of Graduate Studies, Faculty of Arts and Social Sciences, Department of French, Ottawa, ON K1S 5B6, Canada. Offers MA. *Degree requirements:* For master's, thesis optional. *Entrance requirements:* For master's, honors degree. *Faculty research:* French, French Canadian and Acadian literatures and linguistics, Francophone studies, rhetorical studies.

Case Western Reserve University, School of Graduate Studies, Department of Modern Languages and Literatures, Program in French, Cleveland, OH 44106. Offers MA. *Program availability:* Part-time. *Faculty:* 4 full-time (3 women), 2 part-time/adjunct (both women). In 2017, 1 master's awarded. Terminal master's awarded for partial completion of doctoral program. *Degree requirements:* For master's, one foreign language, comprehensive exam. *Entrance requirements:* For master's, GRE General Test, writing sample, three letters of recommendation. Additional exam requirements/recommendations for international students: Required—TOEFL (minimum score 577 paper-based; 90 iBT); Recommended—IELTS (minimum score 7). *Application deadline:* Applications are processed on a rolling basis. Application fee: $50. Electronic applications accepted. *Expenses: Tuition:* Full-time $43,854; part-time $1827 per credit hour. *Required fees:* $50; $50 per credit hour. Tuition and fees vary according to course load and program. *Financial support:* Fellowships, institutionally sponsored loans, and tuition waivers (full) available. Financial award applicants required to submit CSS PROFILE or FAFSA. *Faculty research:* Eighteenth- and nineteenth-century literature (novel, poetry, drama), literary theory, women's studies, cultural criticism. *Unit head:* Prof. Cheryl Toman, Professor of French/Chair, 216-368-2233, Fax: 216-368-2216. *Application contact:* Prof. Marie Lathers, Professor of French and Humanities, 216-368-8983, Fax: 216-368-2216, E-mail: marie.lathers@case.edu.
Website: http://dmll.case.edu/graduate/

Central Connecticut State University, School of Graduate Studies, College of Liberal Arts and Social Sciences, Department of Modern Languages, New Britain, CT 06050-4010. Offers modern language (MA, Certificate), including French, German (Certificate), Italian, Spanish (MA); Spanish (MS, Certificate). *Program availability:* Part-time, evening/weekend. *Faculty:* 7 full-time (6 women). *Students:* 6 full-time (5 women), 16 part-time (12 women); includes 9 minority (all Hispanic/Latino), 1 international. Average age 32. 8 applicants, 88% accepted, 5 enrolled. In 2017, 12 master's awarded. *Degree requirements:* For master's, one foreign language, comprehensive exam, thesis or alternative; for Certificate, qualifying exam. *Entrance requirements:* For master's, minimum undergraduate GPA of 2.7, 24 credits of undergraduate courses in each language in which graduate work will be undertaken. Additional exam requirements/recommendations for international students: Required—TOEFL (minimum score 550 paper-based; 79 iBT); Recommended—IELTS (minimum score 6.5). *Application deadline:* For fall admission, 8/1 for domestic students, 5/1 for international students; for spring admission, 11/1 for domestic and international students. Applications are processed on a rolling basis. Application fee: $50. Electronic applications accepted. *Expenses: Tuition, area resident:* Full-time $6757. Tuition, state resident: full-time $9750; part-time $374 per credit. Tuition, nonresident: full-time $18,102; part-time $374 per credit. *Required fees:* $4635; $255 per credit. *Financial support:* In 2017–18, 3 students received support. Career-related internships or fieldwork, Federal Work-Study, scholarships/grants, and unspecified assistantships available. Support available to part-time students. Financial award application deadline: 3/1; financial award applicants required to submit FAFSA. *Faculty research:* Quebecois literature, Caribbean literature, modern French/Spanish drama, Puerto Rican novel and drama. *Unit head:* Dr. Carmela Pesca, Chair, 860-832-2875, E-mail: pescac@ccsu.edu. *Application contact:* Patricia Gardner, Associate Director of Graduate Studies, 860-832-2350, Fax: 860-832-2362.
Website: http://www.ccsu.edu/modlang/

Colorado State University, College of Liberal Arts, Department of Languages, Literatures and Cultures, Fort Collins, CO 80523-1774. Offers French (MA). *Program availability:* Part-time, evening/weekend. *Faculty:* 9 full-time (7 women), 2 part-time/adjunct (both women). *Students:* 13 full-time (9 women), 2 part-time (1 woman); includes 3 minority (all Hispanic/Latino), 7 international. Average age 32. 8 applicants, 63% accepted, 4 enrolled. In 2017, 4 master's awarded. *Degree requirements:* For master's, one foreign language, comprehensive exam, thesis, teaching portfolio or additional coursework. *Entrance requirements:* For master's, BA in the language object of study, or having studied in a country in which that language was the language of instruction (French or Spanish). Additional exam requirements/recommendations for international students: Required—TOEFL (minimum score 550 paper-based; 79 iBT); Recommended—IELTS (minimum score 6.5), TSE (minimum score 58). *Application deadline:* For fall admission, 2/1 priority date for domestic and international students; for spring admission, 11/1 priority date for domestic and international students. Applications are processed on a rolling basis. Application fee: $60 ($70 for international students). Electronic applications accepted. *Expenses:* Tuition, state resident: full-time $9917. Tuition, nonresident: full-time $24,312. *Required fees:* $2284. Tuition and fees vary according to course load and program. *Financial support:* In 2017–18, 11 students received support, including 12 teaching assistantships with full tuition reimbursements available (averaging $14,256 per year); unspecified assistantships also available. Financial award application deadline: 2/1. *Faculty research:* Hispanic/French literature, Hispanic/French culture, second language acquisition, Hispanic/French linguistics, translation and interpretation. *Unit head:* Dr. Mary Vogl, Department Chair, 970-491-6100, Fax: 970-491-2822, E-mail: mary.vogl@colostate.edu. *Application contact:* Antonio Pedros-Gascon, Graduate Studies Coordinator, 970-491-5421, E-mail: cla_llcgradstudies@colostate.edu.
Website: http://languages.colostate.edu/

Columbia University, Graduate School of Arts and Sciences, New York, NY 10027. Offers African-American studies (MA); American studies (MA); anthropology (MA, PhD); art history and archaeology (MA, PhD); astronomy (PhD); biological sciences (PhD); biotechnology (MA); chemical physics (PhD); chemistry (PhD); classical studies (MA, PhD); classics (MA, PhD); climate and society (MA); conservation biology (MA); earth and environmental sciences (PhD); East Asia: regional studies (MA); East Asian languages and cultures (MA, PhD); ecology, evolution and environmental biology (MA), including conservation biology; ecology, evolution, and environmental biology (PhD), including ecology and evolutionary biology, evolutionary primatology; economics (MA, PhD); English and comparative literature (MA, PhD); French and Romance philology (MA, PhD); Germanic languages (MA, PhD); global French studies (MA); global thought (MA); Hispanic cultural studies (MA); history (PhD); history and literature (MA); human rights studies (MA); Islamic studies (MA); Italian (MA, PhD); Japanese pedagogy (MA); Jewish studies (MA); Latin America and the Caribbean: regional studies (MA); Latin American and Iberian cultures (PhD); mathematics (MA, PhD), including finance (MA); medieval and Renaissance studies (MA); Middle Eastern, South Asian, and African studies (MA, PhD); modern art: critical and curatorial studies (MA); modern European studies (MA); museum anthropology (MA); music (DMA, PhD); oral history (MA); philosophical foundations of physics (MA); philosophy (MA, PhD); physics (PhD); political science (MA, PhD); psychology (PhD); quantitative methods in the social sciences (MA); religion (MA, PhD); Russia, Eurasia and East Europe: regional studies (MA); Russian translation (MA); Slavic cultures (MA); Slavic languages (MA, PhD); sociology (MA, PhD); South Asian studies (MA); statistics (MA, PhD); theatre (PhD). Dual-degree programs require admission to both Graduate School of Arts and Sciences and another Columbia school. *Program availability:* Part-time. Terminal master's awarded for partial completion of doctoral program. *Degree requirements:* For master's, variable foreign language requirement, comprehensive exam (for some programs), thesis (for some programs); for doctorate, variable foreign language requirement, comprehensive exam (for some programs), thesis/dissertation. *Entrance requirements:* For master's and doctorate, GRE General Test, GRE Subject Test (for some programs). Additional exam requirements/recommendations for international students: Required—TOEFL, IELTS. Electronic applications accepted. *Expenses: Tuition:* Full-time $44,864; part-time $1704 per credit. *Required fees:* $2370 per semester. One-time fee: $105.

Concordia University, School of Graduate Studies, Faculty of Arts and Science, Department of Études Françaises, Montréal, QC H3G 1M8, Canada. Offers Anglais-Français en langue et techniques de localization (Certificate); littératures Francophones et résonances médiatiques (MA); translation (Diploma); translation studies (MA). *Degree requirements:* For other advanced degree, one foreign language.

Cornell University, Graduate School, Graduate Fields of Arts and Sciences, Field of Romance Studies, Ithaca, NY 14853. Offers French linguistics (PhD); French literature (PhD); Hispanic literature (PhD); Italian linguistics (PhD); Italian literature (PhD); Romance linguistics (PhD); Spanish linguistics (PhD). *Degree requirements:* For doctorate, 2 foreign languages, comprehensive exam, thesis/dissertation. *Entrance requirements:* For doctorate, GRE General Test, sample of written work, 3 letters of recommendation. Additional exam requirements/recommendations for international students: Required—TOEFL (minimum score 550 paper-based; 77 iBT). Electronic applications accepted. *Faculty research:* Literary theory, Hispanic studies, French studies, gender studies.

Dalhousie University, Faculty of Arts and Social Science, Department of French, Halifax, NS B3H 4R2, Canada. Offers MA, PhD. *Entrance requirements:* Additional exam requirements/recommendations for international students: Required—TOEFL, IELTS, CANTEST, CAEL, or Michigan English Language Assessment Battery. Electronic applications accepted. *Faculty research:* Literature, linguistics, French civilization, French and Francophone literature of all periods, translation and cultural studies.

DePaul University, College of Liberal Arts and Social Sciences, Chicago, IL 60614. Offers Arabic (MA); Chinese (MA); critical ethnic studies (MA); English (MA); French (MA); German (MA); history (MA); interdisciplinary studies (MA, MS); international public service (MS); international studies (MA); Italian (MA); Japanese (MA); liberal studies (MA); nonprofit management (MNM); public administration (MPA); public health (MPH); public policy (MPP); public service management (MS); refugee and forced migration studies (MS); social work (MSW); sociology (MA); Spanish (MA); sustainable urban development (MA); women's and gender studies (MA); writing and publishing (MA); writing, rhetoric and discourse (MA); MA/PhD. *Program availability:* Part-time, evening/weekend, online learning. Terminal master's awarded for partial completion of doctoral program. *Degree requirements:* For master's, variable foreign language requirement, comprehensive exam (for some programs), thesis (for some programs). *Application deadline:* Applications are processed on a rolling basis. Application fee: $40. Electronic applications accepted. *Financial support:* Applicants required to submit FAFSA. *Unit head:* Dr. Guillermo Vasquez de Velasco, Dean, 773-325-7305. *Application contact:* Ann Spittle, Director of Graduate Admission, 773-325-8369, Fax: 312-476-3244, E-mail: graddepaul@depaul.edu.
Website: http://las.depaul.edu/

Drew University, Caspersen School of Graduate Studies, Madison, NJ 07940-1493. Offers conflict resolution and leadership (Certificate), including community leadership, moderation, peace building; education (M Ed); finance (MA); history and culture (MA, PhD), including American history, book history, British history, European history, Holocaust and genocide (M Litt, MA, D Litt, PhD), intellectual history, Irish history, print culture, public history; K-12 education (MAT), including art, biology, chemistry, elementary education, English, French, Italian, math, secondary education, special education, teacher of students with disabilities; liberal studies (M Litt, D Litt), including history, Holocaust and genocide (M Litt, MA, D Litt, PhD), Irish/Irish-American studies, literature (M Litt, MMH, D Litt, DMH, CMH), religion, spirituality, teaching in the two-year college, writing; medical humanities (MMH, DMH, CMH), including arts, health, healthcare, literature (M Litt, MMH, D Litt, DMH, CMH), scientific research; poetry (MFA). *Program availability:* Part-time, evening/weekend. *Faculty:* 4 full-time (2 women), 29 part-time/adjunct (15 women). *Students:* 77 full-time (42 women), 175 part-time (114 women); includes 39 minority (12 Black or African American, non-Hispanic/Latino; 6 Asian, non-Hispanic/Latino; 16 Hispanic/Latino; 5 Two or more races, non-Hispanic/Latino), 11 international. Average age 41. 126 applicants, 75% accepted, 52 enrolled. In 2017, 38 master's, 23 doctorates, 35 other advanced degrees awarded. Terminal master's awarded for partial completion of doctoral program. *Degree requirements:* For master's and other advanced degree, thesis (for some programs); for doctorate, one foreign language, comprehensive exam (for some programs), thesis/dissertation. *Entrance requirements:* For master's, PRAXIS Core and Subject Area tests (for MAT), GRE/GMAT (for M Fin), resume, transcripts, writing sample, personal statement, letters of recommendation; for doctorate, GRE (PhD in history and culture), resume, transcripts, writing sample, personal statement, letters of recommendation; for other advanced degree, resume, transcripts, personal statement. Additional exam requirements/recommendations for international students: Required—TOEFL (minimum

score 587 paper-based; 80 iBT), IELTS (minimum score 6), TWE (minimum score 4). *Application deadline:* For fall admission, 8/1 for domestic students, 6/1 for international students; for spring admission, 12/1 for domestic students, 10/1 for international students. Applications are processed on a rolling basis. Application fee: $35. Electronic applications accepted. *Financial support:* Fellowships, research assistantships, teaching assistantships, career-related internships or fieldwork, Federal Work-Study, scholarships/grants, and unspecified assistantships available. Support available to part-time students. Financial award applicants required to submit FAFSA. *Faculty research:* Irish history and culture, conflict resolution and leadership. *Application contact:* Leanne Horinko, Director of Caspersen Admissions, 973-408-3280, E-mail: gradm@drew.edu.
Website: http://www.drew.edu/caspersen

Duke University, Graduate School, Department of Romance Studies, Durham, NC 27708. Offers French (PhD); Italian (PhD); Spanish (PhD); JD/AM. *Degree requirements:* For doctorate, 2 foreign languages, thesis/dissertation. *Entrance requirements:* For doctorate, GRE General Test. Additional exam requirements/recommendations for international students: Required—TOEFL (minimum score 577 paper-based; 90 iBT) or IELTS (minimum score 7). Electronic applications accepted.

Emory University, Laney Graduate School, Department of French and Italian, Atlanta, GA 30322-1100. Offers French (PhD); French and educational studies (PhD). *Degree requirements:* For doctorate, one foreign language, comprehensive exam, thesis/dissertation. *Entrance requirements:* For doctorate, GRE General Test. Additional exam requirements/recommendations for international students: Recommended—TOEFL. Electronic applications accepted. *Faculty research:* French literature through multidisciplinary critical approaches, second language acquisition theory.

Florida Atlantic University, College of Education, Department of Teaching and Learning, Boca Raton, FL 33431-0991. Offers curriculum and instruction (M Ed), including art, biology, chemistry, English, French, German, mathematics, music, physics, Pre-K and primary education, reading, social sciences, Spanish; elementary education (M Ed); environmental education (M Ed); reading education (M Ed); social foundations of education (M Ed), including educational psychology, educational technology, multilingual education. *Accreditation:* NCATE. *Program availability:* Part-time, evening/weekend. *Faculty:* 13 full-time (10 women), 1 part-time/adjunct (0 women). *Students:* 26 full-time (22 women), 43 part-time (39 women); includes 19 minority (9 Black or African American, non-Hispanic/Latino; 1 Asian, non-Hispanic/Latino; 8 Hispanic/Latino; 1 Two or more races, non-Hispanic/Latino), 3 international. Average age 30. 91 applicants, 57% accepted, 33 enrolled. In 2017, 25 master's awarded. *Entrance requirements:* For master's, GRE General Test, minimum GPA of 3.0 in last 2 years of undergraduate course work. Additional exam requirements/recommendations for international students: Required—TOEFL (minimum score 500 paper-based; 61 iBT), IELTS (minimum score 6). *Application deadline:* For fall admission, 7/1 for domestic students, 2/15 for international students; for spring admission, 11/1 for domestic students, 7/15 for international students. Applications are processed on a rolling basis. Application fee: $30. *Expenses:* Tuition, state resident: full-time $7400; part-time $369.82 per credit. Tuition, nonresident: full-time $20,496; part-time $1042.81 per credit. *Financial support:* Fellowships with partial tuition reimbursements, research assistantships with partial tuition reimbursements, teaching assistantships with partial tuition reimbursements, career-related internships or fieldwork, scholarships/grants, and unspecified assistantships available. *Faculty research:* Technology, teaching English to speakers of other languages, math teaching, electronic portfolio assessment, global perspectives through social studies. *Unit head:* Dr. Barbara Ridener, Chairperson, 561-297-3588, E-mail: bridener@fau.edu. *Application contact:* Dr. Eliah Watlington, Associate Dean, 561-296-8520, Fax: 261-297-2991, E-mail: ewatling@fau.edu.
Website: http://www.coe.fau.edu/academicdepartments/tl/

Florida Atlantic University, Dorothy F. Schmidt College of Arts and Letters, Department of Languages, Linguistics, and Comparative Literature, Boca Raton, FL 33431-0991. Offers comparative literature (MA); French (MA); linguistics (MA); Spanish (MA). *Program availability:* Part-time. *Faculty:* 21 full-time (13 women). *Students:* 25 full-time (19 women), 16 part-time (12 women); includes 16 minority (5 Black or African American, non-Hispanic/Latino; 1 Asian, non-Hispanic/Latino; 10 Hispanic/Latino), 12 international. Average age 36. 42 applicants, 60% accepted, 18 enrolled. In 2017, 19 master's awarded. *Degree requirements:* For master's, one foreign language, comprehensive exam, thesis optional. *Entrance requirements:* For master's, GRE General Test, minimum GPA of 3.0. Additional exam requirements/recommendations for international students: Required—TOEFL (minimum score 500 paper-based; 61 iBT), IELTS (minimum score 6). *Application deadline:* For fall admission, 7/1 priority date for domestic students, 2/15 for international students; for spring admission, 11/1 for domestic students, 7/15 for international students. Applications are processed on a rolling basis. Application fee: $30. *Expenses:* Tuition, state resident: full-time $7400; part-time $369.82 per credit. Tuition, nonresident: full-time $20,496; part-time $1042.81 per credit. *Financial support:* Fellowships, research assistantships, teaching assistantships with partial tuition reimbursements, Federal Work-Study, and tuition waivers (partial) available. Support available to part-time students. Financial award application deadline: 4/1. *Faculty research:* Modern European studies, modern Latin America, medieval Europe. *Unit head:* Dr. Marcella Munson, Chair, 561-297-2118, Fax: 561-297-2756, E-mail: mmunson@fau.edu. *Application contact:* Dr. Linda Johnson, Associate Dean, 561-297-0928, Fax: 561-297-2744.
Website: http://www.fau.edu/LLCL/

Florida State University, The Graduate School, College of Arts and Sciences, Department of Modern Languages and Linguistics, Program in French, Tallahassee, FL 32306. Offers MA, PhD. *Faculty:* 7 full-time (4 women), 1 (woman) part-time/adjunct. *Students:* 17 full-time (10 women); includes 5 minority (4 Black or African American, non-Hispanic/Latino; 1 Hispanic/Latino). Average age 25. 15 applicants, 87% accepted, 4 enrolled. In 2017, 4 master's awarded. Terminal master's awarded for partial completion of doctoral program. *Degree requirements:* For master's, comprehensive exam, thesis optional; for doctorate, 2 foreign languages, thesis/dissertation, reading knowledge of French and 2 other languages. *Entrance requirements:* For master's and doctorate, GRE General Test, minimum GPA of 3.0. Additional exam requirements/recommendations for international students: Required—TOEFL (minimum score 550 paper-based; 80 iBT). *Application deadline:* For fall admission, 1/15 for domestic and international students. Applications are processed on a rolling basis. Application fee: $30. Electronic applications accepted. *Financial support:* In 2017–18, fellowships with partial tuition reimbursements (averaging $16,500 per year), research assistantships with partial tuition reimbursements (averaging $9,500 per year), 9 teaching assistantships with partial tuition reimbursements (averaging $14,500 per year) were awarded. Financial award application deadline: 1/15; financial award applicants required to submit FAFSA. *Faculty research:* Twentieth-century European novel, Renaissance and Middle Ages literature, second language acquisition. *Unit head:* Dr. Mark Pietralunga, Chair, 850-644-8600, Fax: 850-644-0524, E-mail: mpietralunga@fsu.edu. *Application contact:* Wendy E. Pigott, Graduate Academic Coordinator, 850-644-8397, Fax: 850-644-0524, E-mail: wpigott@fsu.edu.
Website: http://www.modlang.fsu.edu/Programs2/French/Graduate-Programs

George Mason University, College of Humanities and Social Sciences, Department of Modern and Classical Languages, Fairfax, VA 22030. Offers foreign languages (MA), including French, Spanish, Spanish and French, Spanish/bilingual-multicultural education. *Faculty:* 33 full-time (23 women), 38 part-time/adjunct (26 women). *Students:* 7 full-time (5 women), 17 part-time (11 women); includes 17 minority (3 Black or African American, non-Hispanic/Latino; 13 Hispanic/Latino; 1 Two or more races, non-Hispanic/Latino), 1 international. Average age 35. 12 applicants, 92% accepted, 6 enrolled. In 2017, 8 master's awarded. *Degree requirements:* For master's, one foreign language, thesis optional, take-home exit exam. *Entrance requirements:* For master's, goals statement, language proficiency statement. Additional exam requirements/recommendations for international students: Required—TOEFL (minimum score 575 paper-based; 88 iBT), IELTS (minimum score 6.5), PTE (minimum score 59). *Application deadline:* For fall admission, 4/15 for domestic students. Application fee: $75 ($80 for international students). Electronic applications accepted. *Expenses:* Tuition, state resident: full-time $11,228; part-time $459.50 per credit. Tuition, nonresident: full-time $30,932; part-time $1280.50 per credit. *Required fees:* $3252; $135.50 per credit. Part-time tuition and fees vary according to course load and program. *Financial support:* In 2017–18, 6 students received support, including 6 teaching assistantships with tuition reimbursements available (averaging $8,415 per year); career-related internships or fieldwork, Federal Work-Study, scholarships/grants, unspecified assistantships, and health care benefits (for full-time research or teaching assistantship recipients) also available. Support available to part-time students. Financial award application deadline: 3/1; financial award applicants required to submit FAFSA. *Faculty research:* Film and media studies; literary analysis, criticism, and theory; applied linguistics and pedagogy, sociolinguistics, interdisciplinary approaches. *Unit head:* Rei Berroa, Chair, 703-993-1220, Fax: 703-993-1245, E-mail: rberroa@gmu.edu. *Application contact:* Jen Barnard, Office Manager, 703-993-1230, Fax: 703-993-1245, E-mail: jbarnard@gmu.edu.
Website: http://mcl.gmu.edu/

Georgia State University, College of Arts and Sciences, Department of World Languages and Cultures, Program in French, Atlanta, GA 30302-3083. Offers applied linguistics and pedagogy (MA); French studies (MA); literature and culture (MA). *Program availability:* Part-time. *Entrance requirements:* For master's, GRE, statement of purpose, writing sample in the target language, 2 letters of recommendation, official transcripts. Additional exam requirements/recommendations for international students: Required—TOEFL (minimum score 79 iBT). Application fee: $50. Electronic applications accepted. *Expenses:* Tuition, state resident: full-time $7020. Tuition, nonresident: full-time $22,518. *Required fees:* $2128. Tuition and fees vary according to degree level and program. *Financial support:* Institutionally sponsored loans available. Financial award applicants required to submit FAFSA. *Faculty research:* The nineteenth-century novel, narratology, genetic criticism, poetics, semiotics, and intertextuality; Francophone and transnational studies; early modern travel literature; post/colonial and Diaspora studies; film studies; social and gender studies; eighteenth century French literature and history of ideas; history of civilization; Enlightenment, encyclopedism. *Unit head:* Dr. Fernando Reati, Department Chair, 404-413-5984, Fax: 404-413-5982, E-mail: freati@gsu.edu. *Application contact:* Lita Malveaux, Administrative Academic Specialist, 404-413-5046, Fax: 404-413-5036, E-mail: lmalveaux@gsu.edu.
Website: http://www.gsu.edu/~wwwmcl/

Georgia State University, College of Arts and Sciences, Department of World Languages and Cultures, Program in Translation and Interpretation, Atlanta, GA 30302-3083. Offers interpretation (Certificate), including Spanish; translation (Certificate), including French, German, Spanish. *Program availability:* Part-time. *Entrance requirements:* For degree, entrance examination involving translating one passage from English to the target language and one passage from the target language to English, 3 letters of recommendation, resume/curriculum vitae, official transcripts. Additional exam requirements/recommendations for international students: Required—TOEFL (minimum score 79 iBT). Application fee: $50. Electronic applications accepted. *Expenses:* Tuition, state resident: full-time $7020. Tuition, nonresident: full-time $22,518. *Required fees:* $2128. Tuition and fees vary according to degree level and program. *Faculty research:* Romance linguistics and translation; theory and practice of translation; medical and legal interpretation. *Unit head:* Dr. Fernando Reati, Chair, 404-413-5984, Fax: 404-413-5982, E-mail: freati@gsu.edu. *Application contact:* Lita Malveaux, Administrative Academic Specialist, 404-413-5046, Fax: 404-413-5036, E-mail: lmalveaux@gsu.edu.
Website: http://wlc.gsu.edu/home/graduate/graduate-certificate/

The Graduate Center, City University of New York, Graduate Studies, Program in French, New York, NY 10016-4039. Offers PhD. *Faculty:* 20 full-time (11 women). *Students:* 34 full-time (23 women); includes 7 minority (3 Black or African American, non-Hispanic/Latino; 1 Asian, non-Hispanic/Latino; 3 Hispanic/Latino), 8 international. Average age 37. 19 applicants, 37% accepted, 4 enrolled. In 2017, 5 doctorates awarded. *Degree requirements:* For doctorate, 2 foreign languages, thesis/dissertation. *Entrance requirements:* For doctorate, GRE General Test. Additional exam requirements/recommendations for international students: Required—TOEFL. *Application deadline:* For fall admission, 1/15 for domestic students. Application fee: $125. Electronic applications accepted. *Financial support:* In 2017–18, 35 students received support, including 28 fellowships, 5 research assistantships, 6 teaching assistantships; career-related internships or fieldwork, Federal Work-Study, institutionally sponsored loans, and tuition waivers (full and partial) also available. Financial award application deadline: 2/1; financial award applicants required to submit FAFSA. *Unit head:* Dr. Francesca Sautman, Executive Officer, 212-817-8366, Fax: 212-817-1520, E-mail: fsautman@gc.cuny.edu. *Application contact:* Les Gribben, Director of Admissions, 212-817-7470, Fax: 212-817-1624, E-mail: lgribben@gc.cuny.edu.

Harvard University, Graduate School of Arts and Sciences, Department of Romance Languages and Literatures, Cambridge, MA 02138. Offers French (AM, PhD); Italian (AM, PhD); Portuguese (AM, PhD); Spanish (AM, PhD). Terminal master's awarded for partial completion of doctoral program. *Degree requirements:* For master's, 2 foreign languages; for doctorate, 2 foreign languages, thesis/dissertation. *Entrance requirements:* For master's and doctorate, GRE General Test, sample of written work. Additional exam requirements/recommendations for international students: Required—TOEFL.

Hofstra University, School of Education, Programs in Teacher Education, Hempstead, NY 11549. Offers bilingual education (MA); bilingual extension (Advanced Certificate), including education/speech language pathology, intensive teacher institute; business education (MS Ed); curriculum studies (MS Ed); early childhood and childhood education (MS Ed); early childhood education (MA, MS Ed); educational technology (Advanced Certificate); elementary education (MA, MS Ed), including science, technology, engineering, and mathematics (STEM) (MA); English education (MS Ed); family and consumer science (MS Ed); fine arts and music education (Advanced Certificate); fine arts education (MS Ed); foreign language and TESOL (MS Ed); foreign language education (MA, MS Ed), including Arabic (MS Ed), biology, chemistry, Chinese (MS Ed), earth science, French, German, Italian (MS Ed), Mandarin (MS Ed), physics, Russian, Spanish; foundations of education (Advanced Certificate), including grades 5-6, grades 7-9; languages other than English and teaching English as a second language (MA); learning and teaching (Ed D), including applied linguistics, art education, arts and

humanities, early childhood education, English education, human development, math education, math, science, and technology, multicultural education, physical education, science education, social studies education, special education; mathematics education (MA, MS Ed); music education (MA, MS Ed); science education (MA), including biology (MA, MS Ed), chemistry (MA, MS Ed), earth science (MA, MS Ed), physics (MA, MS Ed); secondary education (Advanced Certificate); social studies education (MA, MS Ed); teaching languages other than English and TESOL (MS Ed); technology for learning (MA); TESOL (MS Ed, Advanced Certificate); TESOL with specialization in STEM (MA); work based learning extension (Advanced Certificate). *Program availability:* Part-time, evening/weekend, blended/hybrid learning. *Students:* 119 full-time (83 women), 124 part-time (90 women); includes 54 minority (15 Black or African American, non-Hispanic/Latino; 9 Asian, non-Hispanic/Latino; 29 Hispanic/Latino; 1 Native Hawaiian or other Pacific Islander, non-Hispanic/Latino), 12 international. Average age 29. 205 applicants, 88% accepted, 93 enrolled. In 2017, 103 master's, 4 doctorates, 32 other advanced degrees awarded. *Degree requirements:* For master's, comprehensive exam, thesis (for some programs), exit project, student teaching, fieldwork, electronic portfolio, curriculum project, minimum GPA of 3.0; for doctorate, thesis/dissertation; for Advanced Certificate, 3 foreign languages, comprehensive exam (for some programs), thesis project. *Entrance requirements:* For master's, GRE, 2 letters of recommendation, portfolio, teacher certification (MA), interview, essay; for doctorate, GMAT, GRE, LSAT, or MAT; for Advanced Certificate, 2 letters of recommendation, essay, interview and/or portfolio, teaching certificate. Additional exam requirements/recommendations for international students: Required—TOEFL (minimum score 550 paper-based; 80 iBT). *Application deadline:* Applications are processed on a rolling basis. Application fee: $75. Electronic applications accepted. *Expenses: Tuition:* Full-time $1292. *Required fees:* $970. Tuition and fees vary according to program. *Financial support:* In 2017–18, 112 students received support, including 56 fellowships with full and partial tuition reimbursements available (averaging $4,998 per year), 2 research assistantships with full and partial tuition reimbursements available (averaging $8,753 per year); career-related internships or fieldwork, Federal Work-Study, institutionally sponsored loans, scholarships/grants, traineeships, tuition waivers (full and partial), and unspecified assistantships also available. Support available to part-time students. Financial award applicants required to submit FAFSA. *Faculty research:* Educational interventions that foster critical-thinking skills; teachers' attitudes about professional development; threats to teacher quality. *Unit head:* Dr. Eustace Thompson, Chairperson, 516-463-5749, Fax: 516-463-6275, E-mail: eustace.g.thompson@hofstra.edu. *Application contact:* Sunil Samuel, Assistant Vice President of Admissions, 516-463-4723, Fax: 516-463-4664, E-mail: graduateadmission@hofstra.edu.
Website: http://www.hofstra.edu/education/

Howard University, Graduate School, Department of Modern Languages and Literatures, Washington, DC 20059-0002. Offers French (MA); Spanish (MA). *Program availability:* Part-time. *Degree requirements:* For master's, one foreign language, comprehensive exam, thesis. *Entrance requirements:* For master's, GRE General Test, writing samples in English and French or Spanish. *Faculty research:* African literature in French, Spanish linguistics, Spanish Peninsular literature, Spanish sociolinguistics.

Hunter College of the City University of New York, Graduate School, School of Arts and Sciences, Department of Romance Languages, Program in French, New York, NY 10065-5085. Offers MA. *Program availability:* Part-time, evening/weekend. *Degree requirements:* For master's, 2 foreign languages, comprehensive exam, thesis optional. *Entrance requirements:* For master's, GRE General Test, GRE Subject Test, ability to read, speak, and write French; interview. Additional exam requirements/recommendations for international students: Required—TOEFL. *Faculty research:* Contemporary French theater, Villiers de l'Isle-Adam, Voltaire, medieval folklore, fin-de-siècle.

Illinois State University, Graduate School, College of Arts and Sciences, Department of Foreign Languages, Literatures and Cultures, Normal, IL 61790. Offers French (MA); French and German (MA); French and Spanish (MA); German (MA); German and Spanish (MA); Spanish (MA). *Degree requirements:* For master's, variable foreign language requirement, comprehensive exam, 1 term of residency. *Entrance requirements:* For master's, GRE General Test, minimum GPA of 2.8 in last 60 hours of course work.

Indiana University Bloomington, University Graduate School, College of Arts and Sciences, Department of French and Italian, Bloomington, IN 47405. Offers French (MA, PhD), including French and Francophone studies (MA), French instruction (MA), French linguistics; Italian (MA, PhD). *Program availability:* Part-time. Terminal master's awarded for partial completion of doctoral program. *Degree requirements:* For master's, variable foreign language requirement, comprehensive exam (for some programs), thesis or alternative; for doctorate, variable foreign language requirement, comprehensive exam, thesis/dissertation. *Entrance requirements:* For master's, GRE General Test, BA or equivalent undergraduate preparation in French or Italian; for doctorate, GRE General Test, MA from degree program at IU; MA in the specific field. Additional exam requirements/recommendations for international students: Required—TOEFL (minimum score 550 paper-based; 79 iBT), GRE General Test (recommended). Electronic applications accepted. *Faculty research:* French and Italian literature, French linguistics, including the novel and political theory, literature and fine arts, literary theory, postcolonialism, French-Creole studies, French literature of Africa and its Diaspora, humanism, Medieval folklore and mythology, humor in Medieval and Renaissance literature, emigration, second language acquisition, syntax, sociolinguistics, phonology, lexicography, media and cultural studies, cinema, drama.

Johns Hopkins University, Zanvyl Krieger School of Arts and Sciences, Department of German and Romance Languages and Literatures, Baltimore, MD 21218. Offers German (MA, PhD); romance languages (PhD), including French, Italian, Spanish. *Faculty:* 49 full-time (30 women), 1 part-time/adjunct (0 women). *Students:* 55 full-time (31 women); includes 4 minority (3 Hispanic/Latino; 1 Two or more races, non-Hispanic/Latino), 24 international. Average age 29. 39 applicants, 46% accepted, 8 enrolled. In 2017, 2 master's, 10 doctorates awarded. Terminal master's awarded for partial completion of doctoral program. *Degree requirements:* For master's, comprehensive exam; for doctorate, 2 foreign languages, comprehensive exam, thesis/dissertation. *Entrance requirements:* For doctorate, GRE General Test. Additional exam requirements/recommendations for international students: Required—TOEFL (minimum score 600 paper-based; 100 iBT), IELTS. *Application deadline:* For fall admission, 1/15 for domestic and international students. Application fee: $75. Electronic applications accepted. *Expenses:* Contact institution. *Financial support:* In 2017–18, 80 students received support, including 12 fellowships with full tuition reimbursements available (averaging $29,000 per year), 21 teaching assistantships with full tuition reimbursements available (averaging $29,000 per year); research assistantships, institutionally sponsored loans, and health care benefits also available. *Faculty research:* Nineteenth-century French prose and poetry, genetic theory and criticism; twentieth-century Latin American literature and film; medieval and Renaissance Italian literature; gender and queer theory in German literature; the ideology of Baroque and neo-Baroque aesthetics. *Unit head:* Dr. Derek Schilling, Chair, 410-516-4626, Fax: 410-516-5358, E-mail: dschill4@jhu.edu. *Application contact:* Kathy Loehmer, Senior

Academic Coordinator, 410-516-7226, Fax: 410-516-5358, E-mail: kathy.grll@jhu.edu. Website: http://grll.jhu.edu/

Kansas State University, Graduate School, College of Arts and Sciences, Department of Modern Languages, Manhattan, KS 66506. Offers literature (MA), including French, German, Spanish; second language acquisition (MA), including French, German, Spanish, teaching English as a foreign language. *Program availability:* Part-time, evening/weekend, blended/hybrid learning. *Degree requirements:* For master's, thesis optional. *Entrance requirements:* For master's, teaching certificate. Additional exam requirements/recommendations for international students: Required—TOEFL (minimum score 550 paper-based; 83 iBT), TOEFL (minimum speaking-portion score of 26). Electronic applications accepted. *Faculty research:* Second language acquisitions; U.S. Latino literature; Francophone literature; German, French, Spanish, and Spanish-American literature from the Middle Ages to the modern era; teaching English as a foreign language; linguistics.

Kent State University, College of Arts and Sciences, Department of Modern and Classical Language Studies, Kent, OH 44242-0001. Offers French (MA), including applied linguistics and pedagogy, literature; German (MA), including applied linguistics and pedagogy, literature; Latin (MA), including applied linguistics and pedagogy, literature; Spanish (MA), including applied linguistics and pedagogy, literature; translation (MA), including Arabic, French, German, Japanese, Russian, Spanish; translation studies (PhD); MA/MBA. *Program availability:* Part-time. *Faculty:* 21 full-time (13 women), 5 part-time/adjunct (3 women). *Students:* 78 full-time (50 women), 20 part-time (13 women); includes 18 minority (3 Black or African American, non-Hispanic/Latino; 1 Asian, non-Hispanic/Latino; 9 Hispanic/Latino; 5 Two or more races, non-Hispanic/Latino), 44 international. Average age 31. 95 applicants, 55% accepted, 27 enrolled. In 2017, 30 master's awarded. *Degree requirements:* For master's, variable foreign language requirement, comprehensive exam (for some programs), thesis (for some programs); for doctorate, variable foreign language requirement, comprehensive exam, thesis/dissertation. *Entrance requirements:* For master's, transcripts, goal statement, 3 letters of recommendation, CD/MP3 with oral sample of first and second languages, writing sample of second language; for doctorate, transcripts; MA in translation, a foreign language, or similar field; proficiency in a foreign language; minimum GPA of 3.5 from MA; goal statement; 3 letters of recommendation; essay or writing sample. Additional exam requirements/recommendations for international students: Required—TOEFL (minimum score 550 paper-based, 79 iBT), Michigan English Language Assessment Battery (minimum score 77), IELTS (minimum score 6.5) or PTE (minimum score 58). *Application deadline:* For fall admission, 2/1 for domestic and international students. Applications are processed on a rolling basis. Application fee: $45 ($70 for international students). Electronic applications accepted. *Expenses:* Tuition, state resident: full-time $11,310; part-time $515 per credit hour. Tuition, nonresident: full-time $20,396; part-time $928 per credit hour. *International tuition:* $18,544 full-time. *Financial support:* Fellowships with full tuition reimbursements, teaching assistantships with full tuition reimbursements, and unspecified assistantships available. Financial award application deadline: 2/1. *Unit head:* Dr. Keiran Dunne, Professor of French Translation/Chair, 330-672-2150, E-mail: kdunne@kent.edu. *Application contact:* Said Shiyab, Professor of Translation Studies/Graduate Coordinator, 330-672-1864, E-mail: sshiyab@kent.edu. Website: http://www.kent.edu/mcls/

Lake Forest College, Master of Arts in Teaching Program, Lake Forest, IL 60045. Offers elementary education (MAT); K-12 French (MAT); K-12 music (MAT); K-12 Spanish (MAT); K-12 visual art (MAT); secondary biology (MAT); secondary chemistry (MAT); secondary English (MAT); secondary history (MAT); secondary mathematics (MAT). *Degree requirements:* For master's, comprehensive exam, portfolio. *Entrance requirements:* For master's, GRE.

Louisiana State University and Agricultural & Mechanical College, Graduate School, College of Humanities and Social Sciences, Department of French Studies, Baton Rouge, LA 70803. Offers French literature and linguistics (MA, PhD). *Faculty:* 13 full-time (5 women). *Students:* 18 full-time (13 women), 2 part-time (both women); includes 2 minority (1 Black or African American, non-Hispanic/Latino; 1 Hispanic/Latino), 8 international. Average age 33. 18 applicants, 22% accepted, 4 enrolled. In 2017, 1 master's, 3 doctorates awarded. *Financial support:* In 2017–18, 1 fellowship (averaging $34,642 per year), 3 research assistantships (averaging $25,680 per year), 14 teaching assistantships (averaging $23,304 per year) were awarded. *Total annual research expenditures:* $69,165.

Manhattanville College, School of Education, Program in Teaching of Languages Other than English, Purchase, NY 10577-2132. Offers adolescence education (grades 7-12) foreign language (MAT, Advanced Certificate), including French, Italian, Latin (Advanced Certificate), Latin (MAT), Spanish. *Program availability:* Part-time, evening/weekend. *Faculty:* 2 full-time (1 woman). *Students:* 3 part-time (2 women); includes 1 minority (Hispanic/Latino). Average age 31. In 2017, 4 master's, 1 other advanced degree awarded. *Degree requirements:* For master's, comprehensive exam (for some programs), thesis (for some programs), student teaching, research seminars, portfolios, internships, writing assessment; for Advanced Certificate, comprehensive exam (for some programs). *Entrance requirements:* For master's, GRE or MAT (for programs leading to certification), minimum GPA of 3.0, 2 letters of recommendation, interview, essay (2-3 page personal statement that describes reasons for choosing teaching or educational leadership as profession and philosophy of education), proof of immunization (for those born after 1957). Additional exam requirements/recommendations for international students: Required—TOEFL (minimum score 600 paper-based; 110 iBT); Recommended—IELTS (minimum score 8). *Application deadline:* Applications are processed on a rolling basis. Application fee: $75. Electronic applications accepted. *Expenses:* $915 per credit. *Financial support:* Teaching assistantships, career-related internships or fieldwork, Federal Work-Study, institutionally sponsored loans, scholarships/grants, and unspecified assistantships available. Financial award application deadline: 3/15; financial award applicants required to submit FAFSA. *Faculty research:* Changing suburbs institute and community schools. *Unit head:* Dr. Shelly Wepner, Dean, 914-323-3153, Fax: 914-323-5493. *Application contact:* Alissa Wilson, Director, Graduate Admissions, 914-323-3150, Fax: 914-694-1732, E-mail: edschool@mville.edu. Website: https://www.mville.edu/programs/teaching-languages-other-english

McGill University, Faculty of Graduate and Postdoctoral Studies, Faculty of Arts, Department of French Language and Literature, Montréal, QC H3A 2T5, Canada. Offers MA, PhD.

McMaster University, School of Graduate Studies, Faculty of Humanities, Department of French, Hamilton, ON L8S 4M2, Canada. Offers MA. *Program availability:* Part-time, evening/weekend. *Degree requirements:* For master's, thesis or alternative. *Entrance requirements:* For master's, honors degree in French, minimum B+ average. Additional exam requirements/recommendations for international students: Required—TOEFL (minimum score 580 paper-based). *Faculty research:* Medieval literature, eighteenth- and nineteenth-century literature, twentieth-century French and Francophone literature, linguistics.

Memorial University of Newfoundland, School of Graduate Studies, Department of French and Spanish, St. John's, NL A1C 5S7, Canada. Offers French studies (MA). *Program availability:* Part-time. *Degree requirements:* For master's, one foreign language, thesis. *Entrance requirements:* For master's, honors degree (minimum 2nd class standing). Electronic applications accepted. *Faculty research:* French and French-Canadian literature, literary theory, linguistics, philosophy, translation, Francophone culture.

Miami University, College of Arts and Science, Department of French and Italian, Oxford, OH 45056. Offers French (MA). *Students:* 6. In 2017, 3 master's awarded. *Expenses:* Tuition, state resident: full-time $13,812; part-time $575 per credit hour. Tuition, nonresident: full-time $30,860; part-time $1286 per credit hour. *Unit head:* Dr. Jonathan Strauss, Chair, 513-529-7508, E-mail: strausja@miamioh.edu. *Application contact:* Dr. Elisabeth Hodges, Graduate Director, 513-529-5809, E-mail: hodgesed@miamioh.edu.
Website: http://www.MiamiOH.edu/frenchitalian/

Michigan State University, The Graduate School, College of Arts and Letters, Department of French, Classics, and Italian, East Lansing, MI 48824. Offers French (MA); French language and literature (PhD). *Entrance requirements:* Additional exam requirements/recommendations for international students: Required—TOEFL. Electronic applications accepted.

Middlebury College, Language Schools, French School, Middlebury, VT 05753-6002. Offers MA, DML. *Degree requirements:* For master's, one foreign language; for doctorate, 2 foreign languages, comprehensive exam, thesis/dissertation, residence abroad, teaching experience. *Entrance requirements:* For master's, online placement test, 3 letters of recommendation, critical essay, transcripts, personal statement; for doctorate, 1st and 2nd language online placement exam, 3 letters of recommendation, critical essay, transcripts, personal statement, MA in first language, oral interview. *Application deadline:* Applications are processed on a rolling basis. Application fee: $75. Electronic applications accepted. *Expenses:* Contact institution. *Financial support:* Fellowships and scholarships/grants available. Financial award application deadline: 3/10; financial award applicants required to submit FAFSA. *Unit head:* Dr. Philippe France, Director, 802-443-5526, Fax: 802-443-2075. *Application contact:* Sheila Schwaneflugel, Coordinator, 802-443-5526, Fax: 802-443-2075, E-mail: sschwaneflugel@middlebury.edu.
Website: http://www.middlebury.edu/ls/grad_programs/french

Middle Tennessee State University, College of Graduate Studies, College of Liberal Arts, Department of Foreign Languages and Literatures, Murfreesboro, TN 37132. Offers foreign languages (MAT), including French, German, Spanish. *Program availability:* Part-time, evening/weekend, online learning. *Degree requirements:* For master's, one foreign language, comprehensive exam, thesis optional. *Entrance requirements:* For master's, GRE. Additional exam requirements/recommendations for international students: Required—TOEFL (minimum score 525 paper-based; 71 iBT) or IELTS (minimum score 6). Electronic applications accepted.

Millersville University of Pennsylvania, College of Graduate Studies and Adult Learning, College of Arts, Humanities and Social Sciences, Department of Foreign Languages, Program in Languages and Cultures: French Option, Millersville, PA 17551-0302. Offers MA. *Program availability:* Part-time. *Faculty:* 3 full-time (1 woman). *Students:* 1 (woman) part-time. Average age 26. *Degree requirements:* For master's, one foreign language, comprehensive exam (for some programs), thesis optional, exam, portfolio, or research project and presentation. *Entrance requirements:* For master's, ACTFL, OPI, OPIc and WPT, baccalaureate degree from regionally-accredited four-year college or university, 24 undergraduate credits in selected language. Additional exam requirements/recommendations for international students: Required—TOEFL (minimum score 80 iBT), IELTS (minimum score 6.5), PTE (minimum score 60). *Application deadline:* Applications are processed on a rolling basis. Application fee: $40. Electronic applications accepted. *Expenses:* $500 per credit resident tuition and fees; $750 per credit non-resident tuition and fees; $114.75 per credit general fee (maximum of 12 credits); technology fee $27 per credit (resident), $39 per credit (non-resident). *Financial support:* Unspecified assistantships available. Financial award application deadline: 3/15; financial award applicants required to submit FAFSA. *Faculty research:* Detective fiction and women's literature. *Unit head:* Dr. Christine M. Gaudry, Associate Professor/Program Contact, 717-871-7152, Fax: 717-871-7935, E-mail: christine.gaudry@millersville.edu. *Application contact:* Dr. Victor S. DeSantis, Dean of College of Graduate Studies and Adult Learning/Associate Provost for Civic and Community Engagement, 717-871-7619, Fax: 717-871-7954, E-mail: victor.desantis@millersville.edu.
Website: http://www.millersville.edu/forlang/

Minnesota State University Mankato, College of Graduate Studies and Research, College of Arts and Humanities, Department of World Languages and Cultures, Program in French, Mankato, MN 56001. Offers French (MS); French education (MS). *Degree requirements:* For master's, one foreign language, comprehensive exam, thesis or alternative. *Entrance requirements:* For master's, minimum GPA of 3.0 during previous 2 years. Additional exam requirements/recommendations for international students: Required—TOEFL. Electronic applications accepted.

Montclair State University, The Graduate School, College of Education and Human Services, MAT Program in Teaching, Montclair, NJ 07043-1624. Offers art (MAT); biology (MAT); chemistry (MAT); earth science (MAT); English (MAT); French (MAT); health and physical education (MAT); health education (MAT); mathematics (MAT); music (MAT); physical education (MAT); physical science (MAT); social studies (MAT); Spanish (MAT); teacher of English as a second language (MAT). *Degree requirements:* For master's, comprehensive exam, thesis or alternative. *Entrance requirements:* For master's, interview, 2 letters of recommendation. Additional exam requirements/recommendations for international students: Required—TOEFL (minimum score 83 iBT), IELTS (minimum score 6.5). Electronic applications accepted.

Montclair State University, The Graduate School, College of Humanities and Social Sciences, Program in French, Montclair, NJ 07043-1624. Offers French literature (MA); French studies (MA). *Program availability:* Part-time, evening/weekend. *Degree requirements:* For master's, comprehensive exam, thesis optional. *Entrance requirements:* Additional exam requirements/recommendations for international students: Required—TOEFL (minimum score 83 iBT), IELTS (minimum score 6.5). Electronic applications accepted. *Faculty research:* Medieval to twentieth-century French literature, Francophone studies, critical theory, language pedagogy.

New York University, Graduate School of Arts and Science, Center for French Civilization and Culture, Department of French, New York, NY 10012-1019. Offers French (PhD); French language and civilization (MA); French literature (MA); Romance languages and literatures (MA). *Program availability:* Part-time. *Faculty:* 18 full-time (7 women), 2 part-time/adjunct (both women). *Students:* 52 full-time (36 women), 3 part-time (2 women); includes 10 minority (3 Black or African American, non-Hispanic/Latino; 2 Asian, non-Hispanic/Latino; 5 Hispanic/Latino), 12 international. Average age 29. 67 applicants, 58% accepted, 20 enrolled. In 2017, 15 master's, 15 doctorates awarded. Terminal master's awarded for partial completion of doctoral program. *Degree requirements:* For master's, one foreign language, thesis (for some programs); for doctorate, one foreign language, thesis/dissertation. *Entrance requirements:* For master's and doctorate, GRE General Test, proficiency in French. Additional exam requirements/recommendations for international students: Required—TOEFL. *Application deadline:* For fall admission, 1/4 for domestic and international students; for spring admission, 11/1 for domestic students. Application fee: $100. *Expenses: Tuition:* Full-time $41,352; part-time $19,968 per year. *Required fees:* $2496; $1628 per unit. $814 per term. Tuition and fees vary according to course load and program. *Financial support:* Fellowships, teaching assistantships, Federal Work-Study, institutionally sponsored loans, scholarships/grants, traineeships, health care benefits, unspecified assistantships, and instructorships available. Financial award application deadline: 1/4; financial award applicants required to submit FAFSA. *Faculty research:* French and Francophone literature, literary theory, and history; rhetoric and poetics; cultural history; theater and cinema. *Unit head:* Lucien Nouis, Director of Graduate Studies, 212-998-8700, Fax: 212-995-4187, E-mail: french.grad@nyu.edu. *Application contact:* Erin Brau, Graduate Administrator, 212-998-8700, Fax: 212-995-4187, E-mail: french.grad@nyu.edu.
Website: http://www.nyu.edu/gsas/dept/french/

New York University, Graduate School of Arts and Science, Center for French Civilization and Culture, Institute of French Studies, New York, NY 10012-1019. Offers French civilization (PhD); French studies (MA, PhD, Advanced Certificate); French studies and anthropology (PhD); French studies and history (PhD); French studies and journalism (MA); French studies and sociology (PhD); JD/MA; MBA/MA. *Program availability:* Part-time. *Students:* 36 full-time (26 women), 4 part-time (2 women); includes 8 minority (2 Black or African American, non-Hispanic/Latino; 1 American Indian or Alaska Native, non-Hispanic/Latino; 1 Asian, non-Hispanic/Latino; 2 Hispanic/Latino; 2 Two or more races, non-Hispanic/Latino), 9 international. Average age 29. 56 applicants, 57% accepted, 19 enrolled. In 2017, 16 master's, 2 doctorates, 1 other advanced degree awarded. Terminal master's awarded for partial completion of doctoral program. *Degree requirements:* For master's, one foreign language, comprehensive exam; for doctorate, one foreign language, thesis/dissertation, qualifying exam. *Entrance requirements:* For master's and doctorate, GRE General Test, knowledge of French. Additional exam requirements/recommendations for international students: Required—TOEFL. *Application deadline:* For fall admission, 1/4 for domestic and international students. Application fee: $100. *Expenses: Tuition:* Full-time $41,352; part-time $19,968 per year. *Required fees:* $2496; $1628 per unit. $814 per term. Tuition and fees vary according to course load and program. *Financial support:* Fellowships with tuition reimbursements, teaching assistantships with tuition reimbursements, Federal Work-Study, institutionally sponsored loans, scholarships/grants, health care benefits, and unspecified assistantships available. Financial award application deadline: 1/4; financial award applicants required to submit FAFSA. *Faculty research:* Contemporary French society, politics, economy, and culture; French history since 1789; French cultural studies, French colonialism and the post-colonial world; France and the European community. *Unit head:* Edward Berenson, Director, 212-988-8740, Fax: 212-995-4142, E-mail: institute.french@nyu.edu. *Application contact:* Frederic Viguier, Acting Director of Graduate Studies, 212-988-8740, Fax: 212-995-4142, E-mail: institute.french@nyu.edu.
Website: http://www.nyu.edu/fas/program/frenchstudies/

New York University, Steinhardt School of Culture, Education, and Human Development, Department of Teaching and Learning, Program in Multilingual/Multicultural Studies, New York, NY 10012. Offers bilingual education (MA, PhD, Advanced Certificate); foreign language education (MA); teaching English to speakers of other languages (MA, PhD); teaching foreign languages, 7-12 (MA), including Chinese, French, Italian, Japanese, Spanish; teaching French as a foreign language (MA), including teaching English to speakers of other languages; teaching Spanish as a foreign language (MA), including teaching English to speakers of other languages. MA in teaching English to speakers of other languages also offered in collaboration with NYU Shanghai. *Accreditation:* TEAC. *Program availability:* Part-time, evening/weekend. *Students:* Average age 29. 431 applicants, 61% accepted, 92 enrolled. In 2017, 121 master's, 1 doctorate, 2 other advanced degrees awarded. *Entrance requirements:* For doctorate, GRE General Test, interview; for Advanced Certificate, master's degree. Additional exam requirements/recommendations for international students: Required—TOEFL (minimum score 100 iBT). *Application deadline:* For fall admission, 12/1 priority date for domestic and international students; for spring admission, 10/1 for domestic and international students. Applications are processed on a rolling basis. Application fee: $75. Electronic applications accepted. *Expenses: Tuition:* Full-time $41,352; part-time $19,968 per year. *Required fees:* $2496; $1628 per unit. $814 per term. Tuition and fees vary according to course load and program. *Financial support:* Fellowships with full and partial tuition reimbursements, career-related internships or fieldwork, Federal Work-Study, institutionally sponsored loans, scholarships/grants, and tuition waivers (partial) available. Support available to part-time students. Financial award application deadline: 2/1; financial award applicants required to submit FAFSA. *Faculty research:* Second language acquisition, cross-cultural communication, technology-enhanced language learning, language variation, action learning. *Unit head:* Prof. Shondel Nero, Director, 212-998-5757, E-mail: shondel.nero@nyu.edu. *Application contact:* 212-998-5030, Fax: 212-995-4328, E-mail: steinhardt.gradadmissions@nyu.edu.
Website: http://steinhardt.nyu.edu/teachlearn/mms

North Carolina State University, Graduate School, College of Humanities and Social Sciences, Department of Foreign Languages and Literatures, Program in French Language and Literature, Raleigh, NC 27695. Offers MA. *Degree requirements:* For master's, thesis optional. *Entrance requirements:* For master's, fluency in French. Electronic applications accepted. *Faculty research:* 19th-century visual culture, translation, cinema, modern theater, linguistics.

Northern Illinois University, Graduate School, College of Liberal Arts and Sciences, Department of Foreign Languages and Literatures, De Kalb, IL 60115-2854. Offers French (MA); Spanish (MA). *Program availability:* Part-time. *Faculty:* 25 full-time (11 women). *Students:* 5 full-time (2 women), 12 part-time (8 women); includes 11 minority (1 Black or African American, non-Hispanic/Latino; 10 Hispanic/Latino). Average age 32. 8 applicants, 88% accepted, 5 enrolled. In 2017, 2 master's awarded. *Degree requirements:* For master's, one foreign language, comprehensive exam, thesis or alternative, language proficiency exam. *Entrance requirements:* For master's, GRE General Test, interview, minimum GPA of 2.75, undergraduate major in French or Spanish. Additional exam requirements/recommendations for international students: Required—TOEFL (minimum score 550 paper-based). *Application deadline:* For fall admission, 6/1 for domestic students, 5/1 for international students; for spring admission, 11/1 for domestic students, 10/1 for international students. Applications are processed on a rolling basis. Application fee: $40. Electronic applications accepted. *Financial support:* In 2017–18, 7 teaching assistantships with full tuition reimbursements were awarded; fellowships with full tuition reimbursements, research assistantships with full tuition reimbursements, career-related internships or fieldwork, Federal Work-Study, scholarships/grants, tuition waivers (full), and unspecified assistantships also available. Support available to part-time students. Financial award applicants required to submit FAFSA. *Faculty research:* Francophone women writers, prosodies of French and Italian, early Spanish drama, business German, history of Burmese literature. *Unit head:* Dr. Katharina Barbe, Chair, 815-753-1559, Fax: 815-753-5989, E-mail: kbarbe@niu.edu. *Application contact:* Graduate School Office, 815-753-0395, E-mail: gradsch@niu.edu.
Website: http://www.forlangs.net/

French

Northwestern University, The Graduate School, Judd A. and Marjorie Weinberg College of Arts and Sciences, Department of French and Italian, Evanston, IL 60208. Offers French/Francophone studies (PhD); Italian studies (Graduate Certificate). Admissions and degrees offered through The Graduate School. *Degree requirements:* For doctorate, one foreign language, thesis/dissertation, written and oral exams. *Entrance requirements:* For doctorate, GRE, writing sample, cassette recording. Additional exam requirements/recommendations for international students: Required—TOEFL. *Faculty research:* Francophone studies, eighteenth century contemporary theory.

The Ohio State University, Graduate School, College of Arts and Sciences, Division of Arts and Humanities, Department of French and Italian, Columbus, OH 43210. Offers French (MA, PhD); Italian (MA); Italian studies (PhD). *Faculty:* 11. *Students:* 18 full-time (10 women), 7 international. Average age 30. In 2017, 5 master's, 4 doctorates awarded. Terminal master's awarded for partial completion of doctoral program. *Degree requirements:* For master's, variable foreign language requirement, thesis optional; for doctorate, variable foreign language requirement, thesis/dissertation. *Entrance requirements:* For master's and doctorate, GRE General Test. Additional exam requirements/recommendations for international students: Required—TOEFL (minimum score 550 paper-based; 79 iBT), IELTS (minimum score 7), Michigan English Language Assessment Battery (minimum score 82). *Application deadline:* For fall admission, 12/15 priority date for domestic students, 11/30 priority date for international students; for spring admission, 3/1 for domestic students, 2/1 for international students. Applications are processed on a rolling basis. Application fee: $60 ($70 for international students). Electronic applications accepted. *Financial support:* Fellowships, research assistantships, teaching assistantships, Federal Work-Study, institutionally sponsored loans, and unspecified assistantships available. Support available to part-time students. *Faculty research:* Italian and Romance linguistics. *Unit head:* Dr. Dana Renga, Chair, 614-292-4938, E-mail: renga.1@osu.edu. *Application contact:* Graduate and Professional Admissions, 614-292-9444, Fax: 614-292-3895, E-mail: gpadmissions@osu.edu.
Website: http://frit.osu.edu/

Ohio University, Graduate College, College of Arts and Sciences, Department of Modern Languages, Athens, OH 45701-2979. Offers French (MA); Spanish (MA). *Program availability:* Part-time. *Degree requirements:* For master's, 2 foreign languages, comprehensive exam, thesis optional. *Entrance requirements:* For master's, oral and written samples. Additional exam requirements/recommendations for international students: Required—TOEFL (minimum score 550 paper-based; 80 iBT) or IELTS (minimum score 6.5). Electronic applications accepted. *Faculty research:* French and Spanish language and literature.

Penn State University Park, Graduate School, College of the Liberal Arts, Department of French and Francophone Studies, University Park, PA 16802. Offers French (MA, PhD). *Unit head:* Dr. Susan Welch, Dean, 814-865-7691, Fax: 814-863-2085. *Application contact:* Lori Hawn, Director, Graduate Student Services, 814-865-1795, Fax: 814-863-4627, E-mail: l-gswww@lists.psu.edu.
Website: http://french.psu.edu/

Portland State University, Graduate Studies, College of Liberal Arts and Sciences, Department of World Languages and Literatures, Portland, OR 97207-0751. Offers French (MA); German (MA); Japanese (MA); Spanish (MA); world literature and language (MA). *Program availability:* Part-time. *Faculty:* 61 full-time (37 women), 26 part-time/adjunct (20 women). *Students:* 22 full-time (13 women), 11 part-time (5 women); includes 7 minority (1 Asian, non-Hispanic/Latino; 6 Hispanic/Latino), 8 international. Average age 30. 26 applicants, 73% accepted, 16 enrolled. In 2017, 9 master's awarded. *Degree requirements:* For master's, variable foreign language requirement, thesis (for some programs). *Entrance requirements:* For master's, ACTFL, BA in the major language, minimum GPA of 3.0 in all coursework. Additional exam requirements/recommendations for international students: Required—TOEFL (minimum score 550 paper-based; 80 iBT), IELTS (minimum score 6.5). *Application deadline:* For fall admission, 4/1 for domestic students, 3/1 for international students; for winter admission, 9/1 for domestic students, 7/1 for international students; for spring admission, 11/1 for domestic and international students. Applications are processed on a rolling basis. Application fee: $65. *Expenses:* Tuition, state resident: full-time $14,436; part-time $401 per credit. Tuition, nonresident: full-time $21,780; part-time $605 per credit. *Required fees:* $1380; $22 per credit. $119 per quarter. One-time fee: $325. Tuition and fees vary according to program. *Financial support:* In 2017–18, 22 teaching assistantships with full and partial tuition reimbursements (averaging $11,431 per year) were awarded; research assistantships, Federal Work-Study, scholarships/grants, and unspecified assistantships also available. Support available to part-time students. Financial award application deadline: 3/1; financial award applicants required to submit FAFSA. *Faculty research:* Foreign language pedagogy, applied and social linguistics, literary history and criticism. *Total annual research expenditures:* $522,357. *Unit head:* Dr. Gina Greco, Chair, 503-725-5287, E-mail: grecog@pdx.edu. *Application contact:* Kelli Martin, Graduate Admissions Coordinator, 503-725-3243, E-mail: kmarti@pdx.edu.
Website: http://www.pdx.edu/wll/

Princeton University, Graduate School, Department of French and Italian, Princeton, NJ 08544. Offers French language and literature (PhD). *Faculty:* 10 full-time (4 women). *Students:* 28 full-time (21 women); includes 1 minority (Hispanic/Latino), 7 international. Average age 26. 28 applicants, 29% accepted, 4 enrolled. In 2017, 3 doctorates awarded. *Degree requirements:* For doctorate, 2 foreign languages, thesis/dissertation. *Entrance requirements:* For doctorate, GRE General Test, sample of written work. Additional exam requirements/recommendations for international students: Required—TOEFL (minimum score 600 paper-based). *Application deadline:* For fall admission, 12/31 for domestic students, 12/1 for international students. Electronic applications accepted. *Financial support:* In 2017–18, 26 students received support, including 9 fellowships with full tuition reimbursements available (averaging $13,131 per year), 8 teaching assistantships with full tuition reimbursements available (averaging $19,182 per year); Federal Work-Study and institutionally sponsored loans also available. Financial award application deadline: 1/2; financial award applicants required to submit FAFSA. *Faculty research:* Renaissance studies; Classical Age; The Enlightenment; nineteenth- to twenty-first century French Modernism; Francophone studies. *Unit head:* Prof. Thomas Trezise, Director of Graduate Studies, 609-258-4525, Fax: 609-258-4535, E-mail: ttrezise@princeton.edu. *Application contact:* Graduate Admissions Office, 609-258-3034, Fax: 609-258-7262, E-mail: gsadmit@princeton.edu.
Website: http://web.princeton.edu/sites/fit/

Purdue University, Graduate School, College of Liberal Arts, School of Languages and Cultures, West Lafayette, IN 47907. Offers French (MA, MAT, PhD), including French (MA, PhD), French education (MAT); German (MA, MAT, PhD), including German (MA, PhD), German education (MAT); Japanese pedagogy (MA); Spanish (MA, MAT, PhD), including Spanish (MA, PhD), Spanish education (MAT). *Faculty:* 44 full-time (22 women), 1 (woman) part-time/adjunct. *Students:* 37 full-time (18 women), 41 part-time (30 women); includes 9 minority (1 Asian, non-Hispanic/Latino; 8 Hispanic/Latino), 52 international. Average age 32. 49 applicants, 39% accepted, 14 enrolled. In 2017, 11 master's, 5 doctorates awarded. Terminal master's awarded for partial completion of doctoral program. *Degree requirements:* For master's, one foreign language; for doctorate, 2 foreign languages, thesis/dissertation. *Entrance requirements:* For master's, GRE General Test (minimum score 600, 160 for new scoring), two writing samples, one in English, one in language (French, German, Japanese, or Spanish); sample recording of English and language of study; for doctorate, GRE General Test (minimum score 600, 160 for new scoring), master's degree with minimum GPA of 3.5 or equivalent; two writing samples, one in English, one in language (French, German, Japanese, or Spanish); sample recording of English and language of study. Additional exam requirements/recommendations for international students: Required—TOEFL (minimum score 550 paper-based; 77 iBT); Recommended—TWE. *Application deadline:* For fall admission, 12/12 for domestic and international students; for spring admission, 10/1 for domestic and international students. Applications are processed on a rolling basis. Application fee: $60 ($75 for international students). Electronic applications accepted. *Financial support:* In 2017–18, fellowships with tuition reimbursements (averaging $15,750 per year), teaching assistantships with tuition reimbursements (averaging $13,463 per year) were awarded. Support available to part-time students. Financial award applicants required to submit FAFSA. *Faculty research:* Linguistics, semiotics, literary criticism, pedagogy. *Unit head:* Jennifer M. William, Head, 765-494-3834, E-mail: jmwilliam@purdue.edu. *Application contact:* Joni L. Hipsher, Graduate Contact, 765-494-3841, E-mail: jlhipshe@purdue.edu.
Website: http://www.cla.purdue.edu/slc/main/

Queens College of the City University of New York, Arts and Humanities Division, Department of European Languages and Literatures, Queens, NY 11367-1597. Offers French (MA); Italian (MA). *Program availability:* Part-time-only, evening/weekend. *Faculty:* 10 full-time (5 women), 1 part-time/adjunct (0 women). *Students:* 1 full-time (0 women), 11 part-time (6 women); includes 6 minority (5 Black or African American, non-Hispanic/Latino; 1 Hispanic/Latino). Average age 42. 11 applicants, 82% accepted, 6 enrolled. In 2017, 4 master's awarded. *Degree requirements:* For master's, 2 foreign languages, thesis optional, oral exam. *Entrance requirements:* For master's, minimum GPA of 3.0. Additional exam requirements/recommendations for international students: Required—TOEFL (minimum score 61 iBT), IELTS (minimum score 5). *Application deadline:* For fall admission, 4/1 for domestic students; for spring admission, 11/1 for domestic students. Applications are processed on a rolling basis. Application fee: $125. Electronic applications accepted. *Financial support:* Career-related internships or fieldwork, Federal Work-Study, institutionally sponsored loans, and tuition waivers (partial) available. Financial award application deadline: 4/1; financial award applicants required to submit FAFSA. *Faculty research:* Italian literature and culture, French and Francophone literature and theory, Romance linguistics, French and Italian cinema. *Unit head:* Dr. David Andrew Jones, Chair, 718-997-5980, E-mail: david.jones@qc.cuny.edu. *Application contact:* Elizabeth D'Amico-Ramirez, Assistant Director of Graduate Admissions, 718-997-5203, E-mail: elizabeth.damicoramirez@qc.cuny.edu.

Queen's University at Kingston, School of Graduate Studies, Faculty of Arts and Sciences, Department of French Studies, Kingston, ON K7L 3N6, Canada. Offers MA, PhD. *Program availability:* Part-time. *Degree requirements:* For master's, thesis or 4 credits and oral exam; for doctorate, one foreign language, comprehensive exam, thesis/dissertation. *Entrance requirements:* For master's, minimum B+ average; for doctorate, minimum 80% average. Additional exam requirements/recommendations for international students: Required—TOEFL (minimum score 550 paper-based). Electronic applications accepted. *Faculty research:* Reception of Quebec literature in English Canada, autobiography and postcolonialism, irony in women's writing, critical editions of renaissance authors, aspectual systems and grammatical categories.

Rider University, College of Education and Human Services, Teacher Certification Program, Lawrenceville, NJ 08648-3001. Offers bilingual education (Certificate); business education (Certificate); early childhood education (Certificate); elementary education (Certificate); English as a second language (Certificate); English education (Certificate); mathematics education (Certificate); science education (Certificate); secondary education (Certificate); social studies education (Certificate); world languages (Certificate), including French, German, Spanish. *Program availability:* Part-time, online learning. *Degree requirements:* For Certificate, internship, professional portfolio. *Entrance requirements:* For degree, PRAXIS, resume. Additional exam requirements/recommendations for international students: Required—TOEFL (minimum score 550 paper-based). Electronic applications accepted. *Faculty research:* Conceptual foundations for optimal development of creativity; creative theory, cognitive processes in mathematics learning, teacher collaboration.

Rutgers University–New Brunswick, Graduate School-New Brunswick, Program in French, Piscataway, NJ 08854-8097. Offers French (MA, PhD); French studies (MAT). *Program availability:* Part-time, evening/weekend. Terminal master's awarded for partial completion of doctoral program. *Degree requirements:* For master's, one foreign language, written and oral exams (MA); for doctorate, 3 foreign languages, thesis/dissertation, qualifying exam. *Entrance requirements:* For master's and doctorate, GRE General Test. *Faculty research:* Literatures in French, literary history and theory, rhetoric and poetics.

St. John Fisher College, Ralph C. Wilson Jr. School of Education, Program in Adolescence Education and Special Education, Rochester, NY 14618-3597. Offers adolescence education: biology with special education (MS Ed); adolescence education: chemistry with special education (MS Ed); adolescence education: English with special education (MS Ed); adolescence education: French with special education (MS Ed); adolescence education: math with special education (MS Ed); adolescence education: physics with special education (MS Ed); adolescence education: social studies with special education (MS Ed); adolescence education: Spanish with special education (MS Ed). *Program availability:* Part-time, evening/weekend. *Faculty:* 5 full-time (4 women), 7 part-time/adjunct (6 women). *Students:* 15 full-time (3 women), 4 part-time (all women); includes 4 minority (2 Black or African American, non-Hispanic/Latino; 1 Hispanic/Latino; 1 Two or more races, non-Hispanic/Latino). Average age 27. 34 applicants, 85% accepted, 12 enrolled. In 2017, 19 master's awarded. *Degree requirements:* For master's, field experiences, student teaching. *Entrance requirements:* For master's, LAST, 2 letters of recommendation, personal statement, current resume. Additional exam requirements/recommendations for international students: Required—TOEFL (minimum score 575 paper-based; 80 iBT). *Application deadline:* Applications are processed on a rolling basis. Application fee: $30. Electronic applications accepted. *Expenses:* Contact institution. *Financial support:* Scholarships/grants available. Financial award applicants required to submit FAFSA. *Faculty research:* Arts and humanities, urban schools, constructivist learning, at-risk students, mentoring. *Unit head:* Dr. Susan Hildenbrand, Program Director, 585-385-7297, E-mail: shildenbrand@sjfc.edu. *Application contact:* Michelle Gosier, Director of Transfer and Graduate Admissions, 585-385-8064, E-mail: mgosier@sjfc.edu.

Saint Louis University, Graduate Programs, College of Arts and Sciences, Department of Languages, Literatures, and Cultures, St. Louis, MO 63103. Offers French (MA); Spanish (MA). *Program availability:* Part-time. *Degree requirements:* For master's, one foreign language, comprehensive exam, thesis/dissertation (Spanish). *Entrance requirements:* For master's, GRE General Test or MAT, letters of recommendation, resume, interview. Additional exam requirements/recommendations for international students: Required—TOEFL (minimum score 525 paper-based). Electronic applications

accepted. *Faculty research:* Culture studies, literature studies, foreign language acquisition.

San Francisco State University, Division of Graduate Studies, College of Liberal and Creative Arts, Department of Modern Languages and Literatures, Program in French, San Francisco, CA 94132-1722. Offers MA. *Application deadline:* Applications are processed on a rolling basis. *Unit head:* Dr. Berenice Le Marchand, Program Coordinator and Graduate Advisor, 415-338-7419, Fax: 415-338-6159, E-mail: blemarch@sfsu.edu.
Website: http://mll.sfsu.edu/french-program/

Simon Fraser University, Office of Graduate Studies and Postdoctoral Fellows, Faculty of Arts and Social Sciences, Department of French, Burnaby, BC V5A 1S6, Canada. Offers MA. *Degree requirements:* For master's, one foreign language, thesis or alternative. *Entrance requirements:* For master's, minimum GPA of 3.0 (on scale of 4.33) or 3.33 based on last 60 credits of undergraduate courses. Additional exam requirements/recommendations for international students: Recommended—TOEFL (minimum score 580 paper-based; 93 iBT), IELTS (minimum score 7), TWE (minimum score 5). Electronic applications accepted. *Faculty research:* French linguistics, Creole linguistics, French literature of the Middle Ages and Ancient Regime, modern and contemporary French literature, French Canadian language and literature.

Southern Oregon University, Graduate Studies, Department of Foreign Languages and Literatures, Ashland, OR 97520. Offers French language teaching (MA); Spanish language teaching (MA). *Program availability:* Part-time, online learning. *Degree requirements:* For master's, thesis (for some programs). *Entrance requirements:* For master's, GRE General Test, minimum cumulative GPA of 3.0 in the last 90 quarter credits (60 semester credits) of undergraduate coursework. Additional exam requirements/recommendations for international students: Required—TOEFL (minimum score 540 paper-based; 76 iBT), IELTS (minimum score 6), ELPT (minimum score 964) or ELS (minimum score 112). Electronic applications accepted.

Stanford University, School of Humanities and Sciences, Department of French and Italian, Stanford, CA 94305-2004. Offers French (MA, PhD); French and Italian (PhD); Italian (MA, PhD). Terminal master's awarded for partial completion of doctoral program. *Degree requirements:* For master's, one foreign language, written exam; for doctorate, 2 foreign languages, thesis/dissertation, oral exam. *Entrance requirements:* For master's and doctorate, GRE General Test. Additional exam requirements/recommendations for international students: Required—TOEFL. Electronic applications accepted. *Expenses: Tuition:* Full-time $48,987; part-time $10,620 per quarter. One-time fee: $400. Tuition and fees vary according to program.

State University of New York at New Paltz, Graduate and Extended Learning School, School of Education, Department of Teaching and Learning, New Paltz, NY 12561. Offers adolescence education: biology (MAT, MS Ed); adolescence education: chemistry (MAT, MS Ed); adolescence education: earth science (MAT, MS Ed); adolescence education: English (MAT, MS Ed); adolescence education: French (MAT, MS Ed); adolescence education: social studies (MAT, MS Ed); adolescence education: Spanish (MAT, MS Ed); second language education (MS Ed, AC), including second language education (MS Ed), teaching English language learners (AC). *Accreditation:* NCATE. *Program availability:* Part-time, evening/weekend. *Faculty:* 6 full-time (5 women), 10 part-time/adjunct (6 women). *Students:* 48 full-time (27 women), 54 part-time (41 women); includes 24 minority (2 Black or African American, non-Hispanic/Latino; 4 Asian, non-Hispanic/Latino; 15 Hispanic/Latino; 3 Two or more races, non-Hispanic/Latino). 33 applicants, 64% accepted, 12 enrolled. In 2017, 49 master's awarded. *Degree requirements:* For master's, comprehensive exam (for some programs), portfolio. *Entrance requirements:* For master's, minimum GPA of 3.0, New York state teaching certificate (MS Ed). Additional exam requirements/recommendations for international students: Required—TOEFL (minimum score 550 paper-based; 80 iBT), IELTS (minimum score 6.5). *Application deadline:* For fall admission, 3/1 priority date for domestic students, 3/1 for international students; for spring admission, 10/1 priority date for domestic students, 10/1 for international students. Application fee: $50. Electronic applications accepted. *Financial support:* Application deadline: 8/1. *Unit head:* Dr. Laura Dull, Chair, 845-257-2849, E-mail: dullj@newpaltz.edu. *Application contact:* Vika Shock, Director of Graduate Admissions, 845-257-3285, Fax: 845-257-3284, E-mail: gradschool@newpaltz.edu.
Website: http://www.newpaltz.edu/secondaryed/

State University of New York College at Geneseo, Graduate Studies, School of Education, Program in Adolescence Education, Geneseo, NY 14454-1401. Offers English 7-12 (MS Ed); French 7-12 (MS Ed); social studies 7-12 (MS Ed); Spanish 7-12 (MS Ed). *Program availability:* Part-time, evening/weekend. *Faculty:* 8 full-time (6 women), 1 (woman) part-time/adjunct. *Students:* 3 full-time (2 women), 2 part-time (1 woman). Average age 27. 9 applicants, 56% accepted, 3 enrolled. In 2017, 6 master's awarded. *Degree requirements:* For master's, 2 foreign languages, comprehensive examination, thesis or research project. *Entrance requirements:* For master's, GRE, MAT, EAS, edTPA, PRAXIS, or another substantially equivalent test, proof of New York State initial certification or equivalent certification from another state. Additional exam requirements/recommendations for international students: Required—TOEFL (minimum score 525 paper-based; 71 iBT), IELTS (minimum score 6.5), PTE, iTEP. *Application deadline:* For fall admission, 4/1 priority date for domestic students; for spring admission, 11/1 priority date for domestic students; for summer admission, 4/1 priority date for domestic students. Applications are processed on a rolling basis. Application fee: $50. Electronic applications accepted. *Expenses:* Contact institution. *Financial support:* In 2017–18, 3 students received support. Fellowships, research assistantships, scholarships/grants, health care benefits, tuition waivers (full and partial), and unspecified assistantships available. Support available to part-time students. Financial award application deadline: 4/1; financial award applicants required to submit FAFSA. *Unit head:* Dr. Anjoo Sikka, Dean of School of Education, 585-245-5151, Fax: 585-245-5220, E-mail: sikka@geneseo.edu. *Application contact:* Michael R. George, Director of Graduate Admissions, 585-245-5148, Fax: 585-245-5550, E-mail: georgem@geneseo.edu.

Stony Brook University, State University of New York, Graduate School, College of Arts and Sciences, Department of European Languages, Literatures, and Cultures, Program in French, Stony Brook, NY 11794. Offers Romance languages (MA). *Program availability:* Evening/weekend. *Students:* 2 part-time (both women). 1 applicant, 100% accepted. In 2017, 2 master's awarded. *Degree requirements:* For master's, one foreign language. *Entrance requirements:* For master's, GRE General Test. Additional exam requirements/recommendations for international students: Required—TOEFL. *Application deadline:* For fall admission, 1/15 for domestic students; for spring admission, 10/1 for domestic students. Application fee: $100. *Expenses:* Contact institution. *Unit head:* Dr. Prosper Sanou, Coordinator, 631-632-7440, Fax: 631-632-9612, E-mail: prosper.sanou@stonybrook.edu. *Application contact:* Elizabeth Tolson, Coordinator, 631-632-7440, Fax: 631-632-9612, E-mail: elizabeth-a.tolson@stonybrook.edu.

Syracuse University, College of Arts and Sciences, MA Program in French and Francophone Studies, Syracuse, NY 13207. Offers MA. *Program availability:* Part-time. *Students:* Average age 27. *Degree requirements:* For master's, comprehensive exam, thesis or alternative. *Entrance requirements:* For master's, GRE General Test, writing sample of 5 to 15 pages in French (e.g., paper written for undergraduate French course, honors or senior thesis), personal statement, three letters of recommendation, transcripts. Additional exam requirements/recommendations for international students: Required—TOEFL (minimum score 100 iBT). *Application deadline:* For fall admission, 2/1 for domestic and international students. Application fee: $75. Electronic applications accepted. *Financial support:* Teaching assistantships with tuition reimbursements available. Financial award application deadline: 2/1; financial award applicants required to submit FAFSA. *Faculty research:* French, Francophone literature, French culture, literary analysis, critical theory. *Unit head:* Jean Jonassaint, Professor, French and Francophone Studies/French Program Coordinator, 315-443-5382, E-mail: jjonassa@syr.edu. *Application contact:* Jean Jonassaint, Professor, French and Francophone Studies/French Program Coordinator, 315-443-5382, E-mail: jjonassa@syr.edu.
Website: http://lang.syr.edu/academics/French/MA-French.html

Tufts University, Graduate School of Arts and Sciences, Program in French, Medford, MA 02155. Offers MA. *Students:* 1 applicant. In 2017, 1 master's awarded. *Degree requirements:* For master's, one foreign language. *Entrance requirements:* For master's, GRE General Test, writing sample. Additional exam requirements/recommendations for international students: Required—TOEFL (minimum score 550 paper-based; 80 iBT), IELTS (minimum score 6.5). *Application deadline:* For fall admission, 2/15 for domestic and international students; for spring admission, 10/15 for domestic and international students. Applications are processed on a rolling basis. Application fee: $85. Electronic applications accepted. *Expenses:* Contact institution. *Financial support:* Federal Work-Study, scholarships/grants, and tuition waivers (full and partial) available. Support available to part-time students. Financial award application deadline: 1/15. *Unit head:* Dr. Vincent Pollina, Graduate Program Director, 617-627-2751. *Application contact:* Office of Graduate Admissions, 617-627-3395, E-mail: gradadmissions@tufts.edu.

Tulane University, School of Liberal Arts, Department of French and Italian, New Orleans, LA 70118-5669. Offers French (MA, PhD). *Degree requirements:* For master's, one foreign language, thesis or alternative; for doctorate, 2 foreign languages, thesis/dissertation. *Entrance requirements:* For master's, GRE General Test, minimum B average in undergraduate course work; for doctorate, GRE General Test. Additional exam requirements/recommendations for international students: Required—TOEFL. Electronic applications accepted. *Expenses: Tuition:* Full-time $50,920; part-time $2829 per credit hour. *Required fees:* $2040; $44.50 per credit hour. $580 per term. Tuition and fees vary according to course load, degree level and program.

Université de Moncton, Faculty of Arts and Social Sciences, Department of French Studies, Moncton, NB E1A 3E9, Canada. Offers MA, PhD. *Program availability:* Part-time. Terminal master's awarded for partial completion of doctoral program. *Degree requirements:* For master's, thesis, proficiency in French; for doctorate, thesis/dissertation, proficiency in French. *Entrance requirements:* For master's, honors degree in French; for doctorate, MA in French. Electronic applications accepted. *Faculty research:* Language, linguistics, literature, ethnology, Acadian studies.

Université de Montréal, Faculty of Arts and Sciences, Department of French Literature, Montréal, QC H3C 3J7, Canada. Offers MA, PhD. *Degree requirements:* For master's, one foreign language, thesis; for doctorate, one foreign language, thesis/dissertation, general exam. Electronic applications accepted. *Faculty research:* Literary history, literary genres, critical edition, creative writing, Quebecois literature.

Université de Sherbrooke, Faculty of Letters and Human Sciences, Department of Letters and Communications, Sherbrooke, QC J1K 2R1, Canada. Offers comparative Canadian literature (MA, PhD); French literature (MA, PhD); linguistics (MA); theatre (MA). *Degree requirements:* For master's, thesis or alternative; for doctorate, thesis/dissertation. *Entrance requirements:* For master's, minimum GPA of 2.8; for doctorate, minimum GPA of 3.0.

Université du Québec à Chicoutimi, Graduate Programs, Program in Didactics of French-Mother Tongue, Chicoutimi, QC G7H 2B1, Canada. Offers Diploma. *Program availability:* Part-time. *Entrance requirements:* For degree, appropriate bachelor's degree, proficiency in French.

University at Buffalo, the State University of New York, Graduate School, College of Arts and Sciences, Department of Romance Languages and Literatures, Buffalo, NY 14260-4620. Offers French (MA, PhD); Spanish (MA, PhD). *Program availability:* Part-time. Terminal master's awarded for partial completion of doctoral program. *Degree requirements:* For master's, one foreign language, comprehensive exam, thesis (for some programs); for doctorate, 2 foreign languages, comprehensive exam (for some programs), thesis/dissertation. *Entrance requirements:* For doctorate, GRE. Additional exam requirements/recommendations for international students: Required—TOEFL (minimum score 550 paper-based; 79 iBT), IELTS (minimum score 6.5), PTE (minimum score 55). Electronic applications accepted. *Faculty research:* Romance linguistics, cultural studies, literary studies, literature, philosophy and poetry.

University at Buffalo, the State University of New York, Graduate School, Graduate School of Education, Department of Learning and Instruction, Buffalo, NY 14260. Offers biology education (Ed M, Certificate); chemistry education (Ed M, Certificate); childhood education (Ed M); childhood education with bilingual extension (Ed M); college teaching (Advanced Certificate); curriculum, instruction and the science of learning (PhD); early childhood education (Ed M); early childhood education with bilingual extension (Ed M); earth science education (Ed M, Certificate); education and technology (Ed M); education studies (Ed M); educational technology and new literacies (Certificate); educational technology and new literacies (Advanced Certificate); elementary education (Ed D); English education (Ed M, Certificate); English education studies (Ed M); English for speakers of other languages (Ed M); foreign and second language education (PhD); French education (Ed M, Certificate); German education (Ed M, Certificate); gifted education (Certificate); Latin education (Ed M, Certificate); literacy education studies (Ed M); literacy specialist (Ed M); literacy teaching and learning (Certificate); mathematics education (Ed M, Certificate); music education (Ed M, Certificate); music education studies (Ed M); music learning theory (Advanced Certificate); online education (Advanced Certificate); physics education (Ed M, Certificate); science and the public (Ed M); social studies education (Ed M, Certificate); Spanish education (Ed M, Certificate); special education (PhD); teaching English to speakers of other languages (Ed M). *Program availability:* Part-time, evening/weekend, 100% online. *Faculty:* 26 full-time (19 women), 74 part-time/adjunct (52 women). *Students:* 172 full-time (122 women), 325 part-time (226 women); includes 44 minority (25 Black or African American, non-Hispanic/Latino; 5 American Indian or Alaska Native, non-Hispanic/Latino; 14 Asian, non-Hispanic/Latino), 57 international. Average age 33. 316 applicants, 78% accepted, 174 enrolled. In 2017, 109 master's, 34 doctorates, 15 other advanced degrees awarded. *Degree requirements:* For master's, comprehensive exam; for doctorate, thesis/dissertation, research analysis exam, research experience. *Entrance requirements:* For master's, letters of reference; for doctorate, GRE General Test or MAT, interview, writing sample, letters of recommendation. Additional exam requirements/recommendations for international students: Required—TOEFL (minimum score 600 paper-based; 96 iBT). *Application deadline:* For fall admission, 2/1 priority date for domestic and international students; for spring admission, 11/15 priority date for

domestic students, 10/1 for international students. Applications are processed on a rolling basis. Application fee: $50. Electronic applications accepted. *Financial support:* In 2017–18, 42 fellowships (averaging $5,181 per year), 44 research assistantships with tuition reimbursements (averaging $10,908 per year) were awarded; teaching assistantships, career-related internships or fieldwork, Federal Work-Study, institutionally sponsored loans, scholarships/grants, tuition waivers (full and partial), and unspecified assistantships also available. Financial award application deadline: 2/28; financial award applicants required to submit FAFSA. *Faculty research:* Science assessment, foreign language teaching and learning, early learning, new literacies, gender and education. *Total annual research expenditures:* $413,233. *Unit head:* Dr. David Bruce, Chair, 716-645-4069, Fax: 716-645-3161, E-mail: gse-info@buffalo.edu. *Application contact:* Luann Zak, Admissions Assistant, 716-645-2110, Fax: 716-645-7937, E-mail: luannzak@buffalo.edu.
Website: http://gse.buffalo.edu/lai

The University of Alabama, Graduate School, College of Arts and Sciences, Department of Modern Languages and Classics, Tuscaloosa, AL 35487. Offers French (MA, PhD); French and Spanish (PhD); German (MA); Romance languages (MA, PhD); Spanish (MA, PhD). *Program availability:* Part-time. *Faculty:* 30 full-time (18 women). *Students:* 45 full-time (27 women), 4 part-time (1 woman); includes 11 minority (5 Black or African American, non-Hispanic/Latino; 1 Asian, non-Hispanic/Latino; 3 Hispanic/Latino; 2 Two or more races, non-Hispanic/Latino), 14 international. Average age 32. 26 applicants, 88% accepted, 11 enrolled. In 2017, 18 master's awarded. *Degree requirements:* For master's, comprehensive exam, thesis optional; for doctorate, one foreign language, thesis/dissertation, preliminary exam. *Entrance requirements:* For master's and doctorate, minimum GPA of 3.0, writing sample. *Application deadline:* For fall admission, 7/6 priority date for domestic students, 1/15 priority date for international students; for spring admission, 12/5 priority date for domestic students, 6/1 priority date for international students. Applications are processed on a rolling basis. Application fee: $50 ($60 for international students). Electronic applications accepted. *Financial support:* In 2017–18, 40 students received support, including research assistantships with full tuition reimbursements available (averaging $10,291 per year), teaching assistantships with full tuition reimbursements available (averaging $10,291 per year); fellowships, career-related internships or fieldwork, Federal Work-Study, institutionally sponsored loans, and scholarships/grants also available. Financial award application deadline: 7/14. *Faculty research:* Non-English literature, linguistics, culture, film. *Unit head:* Dr. Douglas Lightfoot, Department Chair, 205-348-5059, E-mail: lightfoot@ua.edu. *Application contact:* Michael Picone, Graduate Director, 205-348-8473, E-mail: picone@ua.edu.
Website: http://bama.ua.edu/~mlc

University of Alberta, Faculty of Graduate Studies and Research, Department of Modern Languages and Cultural Studies, Edmonton, AB T6G 2E1, Canada. Offers applied linguistics (Germanic, Romance, Slavic) (MA); French language, literatures and linguistics (PhD); French language, literatures, and linguistics (MA); Germanic languages, literatures and linguistics (PhD); Germanic languages, literatures, and linguistics (MA); Italian studies (MA); Slavic languages and literatures (Russian, Ukrainian) (MA, PhD); Slavic linguistics (Russian, Ukrainian) (MA, PhD); Spanish and Latin American studies (MA, PhD); Ukrainian folklore (MA, PhD). *Program availability:* Part-time. *Degree requirements:* For master's, one foreign language, thesis; for doctorate, 2 foreign languages, comprehensive exam, thesis/dissertation. *Entrance requirements:* For master's and doctorate, 1 language other than English. Additional exam requirements/recommendations for international students: Required—Michigan English Language Assessment Battery or TOEFL (minimum score 550 paper-based). Electronic applications accepted. *Faculty research:* Russian/Ukrainian studies; German studies; contemporary Latin American, French and Francophone studies; Italian studies.

The University of Arizona, College of Humanities, Department of French and Italian, Tucson, AZ 85721. Offers French (MA). *Program availability:* Part-time. *Entrance requirements:* For master's, 3 letters of reference, writing sample in French, audio recording. Additional exam requirements/recommendations for international students: Required—TOEFL (minimum score 550 paper-based; 79 iBT). Electronic applications accepted. *Faculty research:* French literature (history, criticism, and theory), Francophone literature and culture, second language acquisition and teaching.

University of Arkansas, Graduate School, J. William Fulbright College of Arts and Sciences, Department of World Languages, Literatures and Cultures, Program in French, Fayetteville, AR 72701. Offers MA. In 2017, 1 master's awarded. *Degree requirements:* For master's, variable foreign language requirement. *Application deadline:* For fall admission, 4/1 for international students; for spring admission, 10/1 for international students. Applications are processed on a rolling basis. Application fee: $60. Electronic applications accepted. *Expenses:* Tuition, state resident: full-time $3782. Tuition, nonresident: full-time $10,238. *Financial support:* In 2017–18, 7 teaching assistantships were awarded; fellowships, research assistantships, career-related internships or fieldwork, and Federal Work-Study also available. Support available to part-time students. Financial award application deadline: 4/1; financial award applicants required to submit FAFSA. *Unit head:* Dr. Steven Bell, Departmental Chair, 479-575-2951, Fax: 479-575-6795, E-mail: sbell@uark.edu. *Application contact:* Dr. Hope Christiansen, Graduate Coordinator, 479-575-2951, Fax: 479-575-6795, E-mail: hopec@uark.edu.
Website: https://fulbright.uark.edu/departments/world-languages/

The University of British Columbia, Faculty of Arts and Faculty of Graduate Studies, Department of French, Hispanic and Italian Studies, Vancouver, BC V6T 1Z1, Canada. Offers French (MA, PhD); Hispanic studies (MA, PhD). *Program availability:* Part-time. *Degree requirements:* For master's, thesis optional; for doctorate, 2 foreign languages, comprehensive exam, thesis/dissertation. *Entrance requirements:* For doctorate, MA. Additional exam requirements/recommendations for international students: Required—TOEFL. Electronic applications accepted. *Expenses:* Contact institution. *Faculty research:* Medieval and Renaissance literature, modern literature, romance philology and linguistics, cultural studies, women's literature.

University of Calgary, Faculty of Graduate Studies, Faculty of Arts, Department of French, Italian and Spanish, Calgary, AB T2N 1N4, Canada. Offers French (MA, PhD); Spanish (MA, PhD). PhD offered in special cases only. *Program availability:* Part-time. *Degree requirements:* For master's, one foreign language, thesis, exam; for doctorate, 2 foreign languages, comprehensive exam, thesis/dissertation, candidacy exam. *Entrance requirements:* Additional exam requirements/recommendations for international students: Required—TOEFL (minimum score 550 paper-based; 80 iBT) or IELTS (minimum score 7). Electronic applications accepted. *Faculty research:* French and French-Canadian language and literature, Hispanic language and literature, comparative literature, language instruction, literary theory.

University of California, Berkeley, Graduate Division, College of Letters and Science, Department of French, Berkeley, CA 94720-1500. Offers PhD. *Degree requirements:* For doctorate, one foreign language, thesis/dissertation, qualifying exam. *Entrance requirements:* For doctorate, minimum GPA of 3.0, 3 letters of recommendation. Electronic applications accepted.

University of California, Berkeley, Graduate Division, College of Letters and Science, Group in Romance Languages and Literatures, Berkeley, CA 94720-1500. Offers French (PhD); Italian (PhD); Spanish (PhD). *Degree requirements:* For doctorate, thesis/dissertation, qualifying exam. *Entrance requirements:* For doctorate, GRE General Test, minimum GPA of 3.0, 3 letters of recommendation. Additional exam requirements/recommendations for international students: Required—TOEFL (minimum score 570 paper-based; 90 iBT). Electronic applications accepted.

University of California, Davis, Graduate Studies, Program in French, Davis, CA 95616. Offers PhD. *Program availability:* Part-time. *Degree requirements:* For doctorate, thesis/dissertation. *Entrance requirements:* For doctorate, GRE General Test, minimum GPA of 3.0. Additional exam requirements/recommendations for international students: Required—TOEFL (minimum score 550 paper-based). Electronic applications accepted. *Faculty research:* Art and art criticism, Francophone literature, travel narrative, colonial and postcolonial studies and romance linguistics.

University of California, Irvine, School of Humanities, Department of European Languages and Studies, Irvine, CA 92697. Offers French (MA, PhD); German (MA, PhD). *Students:* 8 full-time (4 women); includes 1 minority (Hispanic/Latino), 3 international. Average age 29. 12 applicants, 42% accepted, 2 enrolled. In 2017, 2 master's awarded. *Entrance requirements:* For master's and doctorate, GRE General Test, minimum GPA of 3.0. Additional exam requirements/recommendations for international students: Required—TOEFL (minimum score 550 paper-based). *Application deadline:* For fall admission, 1/15 for domestic and international students. Applications are processed on a rolling basis. Application fee: $105 ($125 for international students). Electronic applications accepted. *Financial support:* Fellowships, research assistantships with full tuition reimbursements, teaching assistantships, institutionally sponsored loans, traineeships, health care benefits, and unspecified assistantships available. Financial award application deadline: 3/1; financial award applicants required to submit FAFSA. *Faculty research:* Montaigne, psychoanalysis, feminism and the problem of repression, aesthetics of nationalism and the limits of culture. *Unit head:* Prof. David Pan, Chair, 949-824-6406, Fax: 949-824-6416, E-mail: dtpan@uci.edu. *Application contact:* Bindya Baliga, Graduate Program Coordinator, 949-824-7968, Fax: 949-824-6416, E-mail: bbaliga@uci.edu.
Website: http://www.humanities.uci.edu/els/

University of California, Los Angeles, Graduate Division, College of Letters and Science, Department of French and Francophone Studies, Los Angeles, CA 90095. Offers MA, PhD. Terminal master's awarded for partial completion of doctoral program. *Degree requirements:* For master's, one foreign language, comprehensive exam; for doctorate, 2 foreign languages, thesis/dissertation, oral and written qualifying exams. *Entrance requirements:* For doctorate, GRE General Test, bachelor's degree; minimum undergraduate GPA of 3.0 (or its equivalent if letter grade system not used); writing sample in French. Additional exam requirements/recommendations for international students: Required—TOEFL. Electronic applications accepted.

University of California, Santa Barbara, Graduate Division, College of Letters and Sciences, Division of Humanities and Fine Arts, Program in Comparative Literature, Santa Barbara, CA 93106-4130. Offers comparative literature (PhD); East Asian literatures (PhD); feminist studies (PhD); French (PhD); global studies (PhD); translation studies (PhD); MA/PhD. *Degree requirements:* For doctorate, 2 foreign languages, comprehensive exam, thesis/dissertation. *Entrance requirements:* For doctorate, GRE. Additional exam requirements/recommendations for international students: Required—TOEFL (minimum score 550 paper-based; 80 iBT), IELTS (minimum score 7). Electronic applications accepted. *Faculty research:* Comparative literary studies in global context, critical theory, translation studies, media technological studies, trauma studies.

University of Chicago, Division of the Humanities, Department of Romance Languages and Literatures, Chicago, IL 60637. Offers French and Francophone studies (PhD); Hispanic and Luso-Brazilian studies (PhD); Italian studies (PhD); Renaissance and early modern studies (PhD). *Students:* 50 full-time (28 women); includes 12 minority (2 Asian, non-Hispanic/Latino; 9 Hispanic/Latino; 1 Two or more races, non-Hispanic/Latino), 25 international. Average age 30. 52 applicants, 31% accepted, 7 enrolled. In 2017, 4 doctorates awarded. Terminal master's awarded for partial completion of doctoral program. *Degree requirements:* For doctorate, 3 foreign languages, comprehensive exam, thesis/dissertation. *Entrance requirements:* For doctorate, GRE General Test, 15-20 page writing sample, statement of purpose, 3 letters of recommendation, transcripts for all previous degrees and institutions attended. Additional exam requirements/recommendations for international students: Required—TOEFL (minimum score 104 iBT), IELTS (minimum score 7). *Application deadline:* For fall admission, 12/15 for domestic and international students. Application fee: $90. Electronic applications accepted. *Financial support:* In 2017–18, fellowships with full tuition reimbursements (averaging $27,000 per year) were awarded; teaching assistantships with full tuition reimbursements, Federal Work-Study, institutionally sponsored loans, scholarships/grants, and health care benefits also available. Financial award application deadline: 12/15. *Unit head:* Daisy Delogu, Chair, 773-702-8481, E-mail: romance-languages@uchicago.edu. *Application contact:* Michael Beetley, Assistant Dean of Students, Admissions and Fellowships, 773-702-1552, Fax: 773-834-9148, E-mail: humanitiesadmissions@uchicago.edu.
Website: http://rll.uchicago.edu

University of Cincinnati, Graduate School, McMicken College of Arts and Sciences, Department of Romance Languages and Literatures, Program in French, Cincinnati, OH 45221. Offers MA, PhD. Terminal master's awarded for partial completion of doctoral program. *Degree requirements:* For master's, thesis optional; for doctorate, 2 foreign languages, thesis/dissertation. *Entrance requirements:* For master's, minimum GPA of 3.0. Electronic applications accepted. *Expenses: Tuition, area resident:* Full-time $14,468. Tuition, state resident: full-time $14,968; part-time $754 per credit hour. Tuition, nonresident: full-time $24,210; part-time $1311 per credit hour. *International tuition:* $26,460 full-time. *Required fees:* $3958; $84 per credit hour. One-time fee: $85 full-time. Tuition and fees vary according to course load, degree level and program.

University of Colorado Boulder, Graduate School, College of Arts and Sciences, Department of French and Italian, Boulder, CO 80309. Offers MA, PhD. *Faculty:* 9 full-time (5 women). *Students:* 23 full-time (16 women); includes 2 minority (both Hispanic/Latino), 4 international. Average age 32. 17 applicants, 41% accepted, 6 enrolled. In 2017, 4 doctorates awarded. Terminal master's awarded for partial completion of doctoral program. *Degree requirements:* For master's, 2 foreign languages, comprehensive exam, thesis or alternative; for doctorate, 3 foreign languages, thesis/dissertation. *Entrance requirements:* For master's, GRE General Test, minimum undergraduate GPA of 3.0; for doctorate, GRE General Test. *Application deadline:* For fall admission, 1/10 for domestic students; for spring admission, 1/10 for domestic students. Applications are processed on a rolling basis. Application fee: $60 ($80 for international students). Electronic applications accepted. Application fee is waived when completed online. *Financial support:* In 2017–18, 57 students received support, including 7 fellowships (averaging $5,991 per year), 1 research assistantship with full and partial tuition reimbursement available (averaging $34,989 per year), 18 teaching assistantships with full and partial tuition reimbursements available (averaging $25,649 per year); institutionally sponsored loans, scholarships/grants, health care benefits, and unspecified assistantships also available. Financial award application deadline: 2/15;

financial award applicants required to submit FAFSA. *Faculty research:* Literary criticism; French language/literature; arts/humanities/cultural activities; culture; fiction language/literature. *Application contact:* E-mail: frenital@colorado.edu. Website: http://www.colorado.edu/FRIT/

University of Delaware, College of Arts and Sciences, Department of Foreign Languages and Literatures, Newark, DE 19716. Offers foreign languages and literatures (MA), including French, German, Spanish; foreign languages pedagogy (MA), including French, German, Spanish; technical Chinese translation (MA). *Degree requirements:* For master's, one foreign language, comprehensive exam, thesis optional. *Entrance requirements:* For master's, GRE General Test, letters of recommendation, writing sample. Additional exam requirements/recommendations for international students: Required—TOEFL. Electronic applications accepted. *Faculty research:* Medieval to Modern French and Spanish literature, twentieth-century German, French, Spanish literature by women, computer-assisted instruction.

University of Florida, Graduate School, College of Liberal Arts and Sciences, Department of Languages, Literatures and Cultures, Gainesville, FL 32611. Offers French and Francophone studies (MA, PhD); German (MA, PhD), including women's and gender studies (PhD). *Degree requirements:* For master's, comprehensive exam, thesis optional; for doctorate, one foreign language, comprehensive exam, thesis/dissertation. *Entrance requirements:* For master's and doctorate, GRE General Test, minimum GPA of 3.0. Additional exam requirements/recommendations for international students: Required—TOEFL (minimum score 550 paper-based; 80 iBT), IELTS (minimum score 6). Electronic applications accepted. *Faculty research:* Medieval epic, romance, and allegory; Renaissance and Baroque poetry; the eighteenth-century novel; nineteenth-century prose, poetry, and poetics; the twentieth-century novel, theater, and poetry; the literatures of the Francophone world; French and Francophone film; the literatures in Breton and Occitan; criticism and critical theory; applied linguistics; the history of French; phonology; sociolinguistics; the structure of French; French and Haitian Creole linguistics.

University of Georgia, Franklin College of Arts and Sciences, Department of Romance Languages, Athens, GA 30602. Offers French (PhD); Italian (MA, PhD); Portuguese (MA, PhD); romance linguistics (MA); Spanish (PhD). *Degree requirements:* For master's, one foreign language; for doctorate, 2 foreign languages, thesis/dissertation. *Entrance requirements:* For master's and doctorate, GRE General Test. Electronic applications accepted.

University of Guelph, Graduate Studies, College of Arts, School of Languages and Literatures, Guelph, ON N1G 2W1, Canada. Offers European studies (MA); French studies (MA). *Entrance requirements:* For master's, honours BA or equivalent. Electronic applications accepted. *Faculty research:* Sociolinguistics, poetics and politics of literature, language acquisition.

University of Hawaii at Manoa, Office of Graduate Education, College of Languages, Linguistics and Literature, Department of Languages and Literatures of Europe and the Americas, Program in French, Honolulu, HI 96822. Offers MA. *Program availability:* Part-time. *Degree requirements:* For master's, one foreign language, thesis optional. *Entrance requirements:* Additional exam requirements/recommendations for international students: Required—TOEFL (minimum score 580 paper-based; 92 iBT), IELTS (minimum score 5).

University of Illinois at Chicago, College of Liberal Arts and Sciences, School of Literatures, Cultural Studies and Linguistics, Department of French and Francophone Studies, Chicago, IL 60607-7128. Offers MA. *Program availability:* Part-time. *Degree requirements:* For master's, one foreign language, thesis optional, exam. *Entrance requirements:* For master's, minimum GPA of 2.75. Additional exam requirements/ recommendations for international students: Required—TOEFL. Electronic applications accepted. *Faculty research:* French civilization, feminist theory, French theater, sociology of literature, narrative theory.

University of Illinois at Urbana–Champaign, Graduate College, College of Liberal Arts and Sciences, School of Literatures, Cultures and Linguistics, Department of French, Champaign, IL 61820. Offers MA, PhD.

The University of Iowa, Graduate College, College of Liberal Arts and Sciences, Department of French and Italian, Iowa City, IA 52242-1316. Offers French (MA, PhD). *Degree requirements:* For master's, thesis optional, exam; for doctorate, comprehensive exam, thesis/dissertation. *Entrance requirements:* For master's and doctorate, GRE General Test, minimum GPA of 3.0. Additional exam requirements/recommendations for international students: Required—TOEFL (minimum score 550 paper-based; 81 iBT). Electronic applications accepted.

The University of Kansas, Graduate Studies, College of Liberal Arts and Sciences, Department of French and Italian, Lawrence, KS 66045-7590. Offers French (MA, PhD). *Students:* 13 full-time (11 women), 1 part-time (0 women); includes 1 minority (Two or more races, non-Hispanic/Latino), 3 international. Average age 29. 12 applicants, 67% accepted, 6 enrolled. In 2017, 1 master's awarded. *Entrance requirements:* For master's and doctorate, GRE, statement of academic purpose and goals, resume, sample essay, three letters of recommendation, official transcripts. Additional exam requirements/ recommendations for international students: Required—TOEFL (minimum score 80 iBT). *Application deadline:* For fall admission, 1/15 priority date for domestic and international students; for spring admission, 11/15 for domestic and international students. Application fee: $65 ($85 for international students). Electronic applications accepted. *Financial support:* Fellowships, teaching assistantships, and unspecified assistantships available. Financial award application deadline: 1/15; financial award applicants required to submit FAFSA. *Faculty research:* French literature and cultural studies; Francophone literature, film. *Unit head:* Dr. Bruce Hayes, Chair, 785-864-9062, E-mail: bhayes@ku.edu. *Application contact:* Cari Ann Kreienhop, Academic Advisor, 785-864-3665, E-mail: ckreienhop@ku.edu. Website: http://www.frenchitalian.ku.edu/

University of Lethbridge, School of Graduate Studies, Lethbridge, AB T1K 3M4, Canada. Offers addictions counseling (M Sc); agricultural biotechnology (M Sc); agricultural studies (M Sc, MA); anthropology (MA); archaeology (M Sc, MA); art (MA, MFA); biochemistry (M Sc); biological sciences (M Sc); biomolecular science (PhD); biosystems and biodiversity (PhD); Canadian studies (MA); chemistry (M Sc); computer science (M Sc); computer science and geographical information science (M Sc); counseling (MC); counseling psychology (M Ed); dramatic arts (MA); earth, space, and physical science (PhD); economics (MA); education (MA, PhD); educational leadership (M Ed); English (MA); environmental science (M Sc); evolution and behavior (PhD); exercise science (M Sc); French (MA); French/German (MA); French/Spanish (MA); general education (M Ed); geography (M Sc, MA); German (MA); health sciences (M Sc); individualized multidisciplinary (M Sc, MA); kinesiology (M Sc, MA); management (M Sc), including accounting, finance, human resource management and labor relations, information systems, international management, marketing, policy and strategy; mathematics (M Sc); music (M Mus, MA); Native American studies (MA); neuroscience (M Sc, PhD); new media (MA, MFA); nursing (M Sc, MN); philosophy (MA); physics (M Sc); political science (MA); psychology (M Sc, MA); religious studies (MA); sociology (MA); theatre and dramatic arts (MFA); theoretical and computational science (PhD); urban and regional studies (MA); women and gender studies (MA).

Program availability: Part-time, evening/weekend. *Degree requirements:* For master's, thesis (for some programs); for doctorate, comprehensive exam, thesis/dissertation. *Entrance requirements:* For master's, GMAT (for M Sc in management), bachelor's degree in related field, minimum GPA of 3.0 during previous 20 graded semester courses, 2 years' teaching or related experience (M Ed); for doctorate, master's degree, minimum graduate GPA of 3.5. Additional exam requirements/recommendations for international students: Required—TOEFL (minimum score 580 paper-based; 93 iBT). Electronic applications accepted. *Faculty research:* Movement and brain plasticity, gibberellin physiology, photosynthesis, carbon cycling, molecular properties of main-group ring components.

University of Louisiana at Lafayette, College of Liberal Arts, Department of Modern Languages, Program in Francophone Studies, Lafayette, LA 70504. Offers PhD. *Degree requirements:* For doctorate, 2 foreign languages, comprehensive exam, thesis/dissertation. *Entrance requirements:* For doctorate, GRE General Test, minimum GPA of 2.75. Additional exam requirements/recommendations for international students: Required—TOEFL (minimum score 550 paper-based). Electronic applications accepted. *Faculty research:* Louisiana folklore, eighteenth-century French literature, contemporary criticism.

University of Louisiana at Lafayette, College of Liberal Arts, Department of Modern Languages, Program in French, Lafayette, LA 70504. Offers MA. *Program availability:* Part-time. *Degree requirements:* For master's, 2 foreign languages, thesis or alternative. *Entrance requirements:* For master's, GRE General Test, minimum GPA of 2.75. Additional exam requirements/recommendations for international students: Required—TOEFL (minimum score 550 paper-based). Electronic applications accepted. *Faculty research:* Louisiana studies, nineteenth-century French literature, Francophone studies.

University of Louisville, Graduate School, College of Arts and Sciences, Department of Classical and Modern Languages, Louisville, KY 40292-0001. Offers French (MA); Spanish (MA); translation and interpretation (Certificate). *Program availability:* Part-time, evening/weekend. *Faculty:* 31 full-time (15 women), 14 part-time/adjunct (13 women). *Students:* 13 full-time (10 women), 14 part-time (10 women); includes 13 minority (2 Black or African American, non-Hispanic/Latino; 10 Hispanic/Latino; 1 Two or more races, non-Hispanic/Latino), 1 international. Average age 33. 17 applicants, 76% accepted, 11 enrolled. In 2017, 8 master's, 1 other advanced degree awarded. *Degree requirements:* For master's, one foreign language, thesis (for some programs). *Entrance requirements:* For master's, GRE General Test (recommended), letters of recommendation, transcripts, curriculum vitae, personal statement; for Certificate, GRE, letters of recommendation, transcripts, curriculum vitae, personal statement. Additional exam requirements/recommendations for international students: Required—TOEFL (minimum score 550 paper-based; 79 iBT); Recommended—IELTS (minimum score 6.5). *Application deadline:* Applications are processed on a rolling basis. Application fee: $65. *Expenses:* Tuition, state resident: full-time $12,246; part-time $681 per credit hour. Tuition, nonresident: full-time $25,486; part-time $1417 per credit hour. *Required fees:* $196. Tuition and fees vary according to course load, program and reciprocity agreements. *Financial support:* In 2017–18, 12 teaching assistantships with full tuition reimbursements (averaging $14,000 per year) were awarded; scholarships/grants, health care benefits, and unspecified assistantships also available. Financial award applicants required to submit FAFSA. *Faculty research:* Medieval Spanish literature and culture, Modern Spanish literature and culture, translation and interpreting, film studies, Medieval French literature and culture, Modern, French literature and culture, American Sign Language studies. *Unit head:* Dr. Alan Leidner, Chair, 502-852-0483, Fax: 502-852-8885, E-mail: alan.leidner@louisville.edu. *Application contact:* Travis Henretty, Administrative Assistant, 502-852-6686, Fax: 502-852-8885, E-mail: travis.henretty@louisville.edu. Website: http://louisville.edu/modernlanguages/

University of Maine, Graduate School, College of Liberal Arts and Sciences, Department of Modern Languages and Classics, Orono, ME 04469. Offers French (MA, MAT); Spanish (MAT). *Program availability:* Part-time. *Faculty:* 7 full-time (4 women). *Students:* 4 full-time (3 women), 2 part-time (both women); includes 2 minority (1 Black or African American, non-Hispanic/Latino; 1 Hispanic/Latino). Average age 38. 6 applicants, 100% accepted, 3 enrolled. In 2017, 3 master's awarded. *Degree requirements:* For master's, one foreign language, thesis (for some programs). *Entrance requirements:* For master's, GRE General Test; PRAXIS II (for MAT). Additional exam requirements/ recommendations for international students: Required—TOEFL, PRAXIS II. *Application deadline:* For fall admission, 2/1 priority date for domestic and international students. Applications are processed on a rolling basis. Application fee: $65. Electronic applications accepted. *Expenses:* Tuition, state resident: full-time $7722; part-time $429 per credit hour. Tuition, nonresident: full-time $25,146; part-time $1397 per credit hour. *Required fees:* $1162; $581 per credit hour. *Financial support:* In 2017–18, 4 students received support, including 2 fellowships (averaging $15,000 per year), 2 teaching assistantships with tuition reimbursements available (averaging $15,200 per year); Federal Work-Study and tuition waivers (full and partial) also available. Financial award application deadline: 3/1. *Faculty research:* Contemporary Latin American literature and culture, modern and contemporary Spanish peninsular literature, North American French linguistics, 20th-century Quebec literature and culture, contemporary French philosophy. *Unit head:* Dr. Jane Smith, Chair, 207-581-2075, Fax: 207-581-1832. *Application contact:* Scott G. Delcourt, Assistant Vice President for Graduate Studies/Senior Associate Dean, 207-581-3291, Fax: 207-581-3232, E-mail: graduate@maine.edu. Website: https://umaine.edu/mlandc/graduate-programs/

The University of Manchester, School of Languages, Linguistics and Cultures, Manchester, United Kingdom. Offers Arab world studies (PhD); Chinese studies (M Phil, PhD); East Asian studies (M Phil, PhD); English language (PhD); French studies (M Phil, PhD); German studies (M Phil, PhD); interpreting studies (PhD); Italian studies (M Phil, PhD); Japanese studies (M Phil, PhD); Latin American cultural studies (M Phil, PhD); linguistics (M Phil, PhD); Middle Eastern studies (M Phil, PhD); Polish studies (M Phil, PhD); Portuguese studies (M Phil, PhD); Russian studies (M Phil, PhD); Spanish studies (M Phil, PhD); translation and intercultural studies (M Phil, PhD).

University of Manitoba, Faculty of Graduate Studies, Faculty of Arts, Department of French, Spanish and Italian, Winnipeg, MB R3T 2N2, Canada. Offers French (MA, PhD). *Degree requirements:* For master's, one foreign language, thesis; for doctorate, 2 foreign languages, thesis/dissertation.

University of Maryland, College Park, Academic Affairs, College of Arts and Humanities, School of Languages, Literatures, and Cultures, Modern French Studies Program, College Park, MD 20742. Offers PhD. *Entrance requirements:* For doctorate, GRE, letters of recommendation, writing sample. Additional exam requirements/ recommendations for international students: Required—TOEFL.

University of Maryland, College Park, Academic Affairs, College of Arts and Humanities, School of Languages, Literatures, and Cultures, Program in French Language and Literature, College Park, MD 20742. Offers MA. *Degree requirements:* For master's, one foreign language, comprehensive exam, thesis or alternative. *Entrance requirements:* For master's, GRE General Test, GRE Subject Test, minimum GPA of 3.0, 3 letters of recommendation. Additional exam requirements/ recommendations for international students: Required—TOEFL. Electronic applications accepted.

French

University of Massachusetts Amherst, Graduate School, College of Humanities and Fine Arts, Department of Languages, Literatures, and Cultures, Program in French and Francophone Studies, Amherst, MA 01003. Offers French (MAT); French and Francophone studies (MA). *Program availability:* Part-time. *Degree requirements:* For master's, thesis or alternative. *Entrance requirements:* For master's, GRE General Test. Additional exam requirements/recommendations for international students: Required—TOEFL (minimum score 550 paper-based; 80 iBT), IELTS (minimum score 6.5). Electronic applications accepted.

University of Memphis, Graduate School, College of Arts and Sciences, Department of Foreign Languages and Literatures, Memphis, TN 38152. Offers romance languages (MA), including French, Spanish. *Program availability:* Part-time. *Faculty:* 6 full-time (2 women). *Students:* 15 full-time (13 women), 4 part-time (3 women); includes 11 minority (3 Black or African American, non-Hispanic/Latino; 8 Hispanic/Latino), 1 international. Average age 32. 13 applicants, 92% accepted, 9 enrolled. In 2017, 5 master's awarded. *Degree requirements:* For master's, 2 foreign languages, comprehensive exam. *Entrance requirements:* For master's, GRE, interview in language of concentration, writing sample, letter of intent, two letters of recommendation. Additional exam requirements/recommendations for international students: Required—TOEFL (minimum score 94 iBT). *Application deadline:* For fall admission, 5/15 for domestic students, 4/5 for international students; for spring admission, 11/30 for domestic students, 10/5 for international students. Applications are processed on a rolling basis. Application fee: $35 ($60 for international students). Electronic applications accepted. *Expenses:* Contact institution. *Financial support:* In 2017–18, 11 students received support, including 13 teaching assistantships with full tuition reimbursements available (averaging $12,846 per year); research assistantships with full tuition reimbursements available, Federal Work-Study, scholarships/grants, and unspecified assistantships also available. Financial award application deadline: 2/1; financial award applicants required to submit FAFSA. *Faculty research:* Latin American studies, Brazilian culture and literature, modernity and postmodernity, Hispanic studies, French studies, French and Hispanic culture and literature, Hispanic linguistics, applied linguistics. *Unit head:* Dr. William Thompson, Chair, 901-678-2507, E-mail: wjthmpsn@memphis.edu. *Application contact:* Dr. Fernando Burgos, Coordinator of Graduate Studies, 901-678-3158, E-mail: fburgos@memphis.edu.
Website: http://www.memphis.edu/fl/

University of Miami, Graduate School, College of Arts and Sciences, Department of Modern Languages and Literatures, Coral Gables, FL 33124. Offers romance studies (PhD), including French, Spanish. *Degree requirements:* For doctorate, 2 foreign languages, thesis/dissertation, area exam, qualifying exam. *Entrance requirements:* For doctorate, 1 writing sample in English and 1 writing sample in French or Spanish, minimum GPA of 3.0, oral interview, letters of recommendation. Additional exam requirements/recommendations for international students: Required—TOEFL (minimum score 550 paper-based; 59 iBT). Electronic applications accepted. *Faculty research:* Transatlantic studies, Caribbean studies, comparative literature, gender theory, cultural studies.

University of Michigan, Rackham Graduate School, College of Literature, Science, and the Arts, Department of Romance Languages and Literatures, Program in French, Ann Arbor, MI 48109. Offers PhD. *Degree requirements:* For doctorate, 2 foreign languages, thesis/dissertation, oral defense of dissertation, preliminary exams in essay format. *Entrance requirements:* Additional exam requirements/recommendations for international students: Required—TOEFL or Michigan English Language Assessment Battery. Electronic applications accepted. *Expenses:* Tuition, state resident: full-time $22,368; part-time $1201 per credit hour. Tuition, nonresident: full-time $45,156; part-time $2467 per credit hour. *Required fees:* $376 per term. Tuition and fees vary according to course load, degree level and program. *Faculty research:* Comparative Romance studies, medieval and early modern studies, postcolonial and minority literatures, culture and materiality, reflection on the nature and function of scholarship.

University of Minnesota, Twin Cities Campus, Graduate School, College of Liberal Arts, Department of French and Italian, Minneapolis, MN 55455-0213. Offers French (MA, PhD). *Program availability:* Part-time. *Degree requirements:* For master's, one foreign language, comprehensive exam, thesis optional; for doctorate, one foreign language, thesis/dissertation, individualized exam on topic areas. *Entrance requirements:* For master's and doctorate, GRE, minimum GPA of 3.25 (recommended). Additional exam requirements/recommendations for international students: Required—TOEFL (minimum score 550 paper-based). Electronic applications accepted. *Faculty research:* Francophone literature, cultural studies, feminism, critical theory, medieval studies.

University of Missouri, Office of Research and Graduate Studies, College of Arts and Science, Department of Romance Languages and Literatures, Columbia, MO 65211. Offers French (MA, PhD); literature (MA); Spanish (MA, PhD); teaching (MA). Terminal master's awarded for partial completion of doctoral program. *Degree requirements:* For master's, one foreign language; for doctorate, 4 foreign languages, comprehensive exam, thesis/dissertation. *Entrance requirements:* For master's, GRE General Test, minimum GPA of 3.0 in field of major; bachelor's degree; for doctorate, GRE General Test, minimum GPA of 3.0 in field of major; master's degree. Additional exam requirements/recommendations for international students: Required—TOEFL (minimum score 500 paper-based; 61 iBT). Electronic applications accepted.

University of Missouri–Kansas City, College of Arts and Sciences, Department of Foreign Languages and Literatures, Kansas City, MO 64110-2499. Offers romance languages and literatures (MA), including French, Spanish. *Program availability:* Part-time. *Degree requirements:* For master's, 2 foreign languages. *Entrance requirements:* For master's, GRE General Test, minimum GPA of 2.75, 2 letters of recommendation. Additional exam requirements/recommendations for international students: Required—TOEFL (minimum score 550 paper-based; 80 iBT). Electronic applications accepted. *Faculty research:* Literary analyses; psychology and literature; narrative techniques, poetic structure, and style; literature, politics, and society (especially in Latin America).

University of Montana, Graduate School, College of Humanities and Sciences, Department of Modern and Classical Languages and Literatures, Missoula, MT 59812. Offers French (MA); German (MA); Spanish (MA). *Degree requirements:* For master's, one foreign language. *Entrance requirements:* For master's, GRE General Test. Additional exam requirements/recommendations for international students: Required—TOEFL.

University of Nebraska–Lincoln, Graduate College, College of Arts and Sciences, Department of Modern Languages and Literatures, Lincoln, NE 68588. Offers French (MA, PhD); German (MA, PhD); Spanish (MA, PhD). *Degree requirements:* For master's, thesis optional; for doctorate, comprehensive exam, thesis/dissertation. *Entrance requirements:* For master's and doctorate, writing sample in target language. Additional exam requirements/recommendations for international students: Required—TOEFL (minimum score 550 paper-based). Electronic applications accepted. *Faculty research:* French, German, and Spanish language, literature, and culture.

University of Nevada, Reno, Graduate School, College of Liberal Arts, Department of Foreign Languages and Literatures, Reno, NV 89557. Offers French (MA); German (MA); Spanish (MA). *Degree requirements:* For master's, one foreign language, thesis optional. *Entrance requirements:* For master's, GRE General Test, minimum GPA of 2.75. Additional exam requirements/recommendations for international students: Required—TOEFL (minimum score 500 paper-based; 61 iBT), IELTS (minimum score 6). *Faculty research:* Thirteenth century mysticism, contemporary Spanish and Latin American poetry and theater, French interrelation between narration and photography, exile literature and Holocaust.

University of New Mexico, Graduate Studies, College of Arts and Sciences, Program in Foreign Languages and Literatures, Albuquerque, NM 87131-2039. Offers comparative literature and cultural studies (MA); French (MA); French studies (PhD); German studies (MA). *Program availability:* Part-time. *Faculty:* 10 full-time (6 women), 1 (woman) part-time/adjunct. *Students:* 19 full-time (11 women), 10 part-time (6 women); includes 6 minority (4 Hispanic/Latino; 2 Two or more races, non-Hispanic/Latino), 7 international. Average age 29. 22 applicants, 59% accepted, 12 enrolled. In 2017, 9 master's awarded. *Degree requirements:* For master's, one foreign language, thesis optional; for doctorate, 2 foreign languages, thesis/dissertation. *Entrance requirements:* For master's and doctorate, transcript, writing sample, 3 letters of recommendation. Additional exam requirements/recommendations for international students: Required—TOEFL. *Application deadline:* For fall admission, 2/1 priority date for domestic students; for spring admission, 10/1 priority date for domestic students. Application fee: $50. Electronic applications accepted. *Financial support:* Research assistantships, teaching assistantships with tuition reimbursements, Federal Work-Study, health care benefits, and unspecified assistantships available. Financial award application deadline: 3/1; financial award applicants required to submit FAFSA. *Faculty research:* German, Russian, Italian, Japanese, French, comparative literature, culture studies, classics. *Unit head:* Dr. Walter Putnam, Chair, 505-277-4771, Fax: 505-277-3599, E-mail: wputnam@unm.edu. *Application contact:* Jacqueline Ochoa, Application and Graduation Advisor, 505-277-4471, Fax: 505-277-3599, E-mail: jochoa@unm.edu.
Website: http://www.unm.edu/~fll/

The University of North Carolina at Chapel Hill, Graduate School, College of Arts and Sciences, Department of Romance Languages and Literatures, Chapel Hill, NC 27599. Offers French (MA, PhD); Italian (MA, PhD); Portuguese (MA, PhD); Romance languages (MA, PhD); Romance philology (MA, PhD); Spanish (MA, PhD). *Degree requirements:* For master's, one foreign language, comprehensive exam, thesis; for doctorate, 2 foreign languages, comprehensive exam, thesis/dissertation. *Entrance requirements:* For master's and doctorate, GRE General Test, minimum GPA of 3.0. Additional exam requirements/recommendations for international students: Required—TOEFL (minimum score 550 paper-based). Electronic applications accepted.

The University of North Carolina at Greensboro, Graduate School, College of Arts and Sciences, Department of Languages, Literatures, and Cultures, Program in French, Greensboro, NC 27412-5001. Offers MA. *Degree requirements:* For master's, one foreign language, comprehensive exam, thesis or alternative. *Entrance requirements:* For master's, GRE General Test, 3-5 minute tape demonstrating foreign language proficiency, composition in French, sample paper in English. Additional exam requirements/recommendations for international students: Required—TOEFL. Electronic applications accepted.

University of North Texas, Robert B. Toulouse School of Graduate Studies, Denton, TX 76203-5459. Offers accounting (MS); applied anthropology (MA, MS); applied behavior analysis (Certificate); applied geography (MA); applied technology and performance improvement (M Ed, MS); art education (MA); art history (MA); art museum education (Certificate); arts leadership (Certificate); audiology (Au D); behavior analysis (MS); behavioral science (PhD); biochemistry and molecular biology (MS); biology (MA, MS); biomedical engineering (MS); business analysis (MS); chemistry (MS); clinical health psychology (PhD); communication studies (MA, MS); computer engineering (MS); computer science (MS); counseling (M Ed, MS), including clinical mental health counseling (MS), college and university counseling, elementary school counseling, secondary school counseling; creative writing (MA); criminal justice (MS); curriculum and instruction (M Ed); decision sciences (MBA); design (MA, MFA), including fashion design (MFA), innovation studies, interior design (MFA); early childhood studies (MS); economics (MS); educational leadership (M Ed, Ed D); educational psychology (MS, PhD), including family studies (MS), gifted and talented (MS), human development (MS), learning and cognition (MS), research, measurement and evaluation (MS); electrical engineering (MS); emergency management (MPA); engineering technology (MS); English (MA); English as a second language (MA); environmental science (MS); finance (MBA, MS); financial management (MPA); French (MA); health services management (MBA); higher education (M Ed, Ed D); history (MA, MS); hospitality management (MS); human resources management (MPA); information science (MS); information systems (PhD); information technologies (MBA); interdisciplinary studies (MA, MS); international studies (MA); international sustainable tourism (MS); jazz studies (MM); journalism (MA, MJ, Graduate Certificate), including interactive and virtual digital communication (Graduate Certificate), narrative journalism (Graduate Certificate), public relations (Graduate Certificate); kinesiology (MS); linguistics (MA); local government management (MPA); logistics (PhD); logistics and supply chain management (MBA); long-term care, senior housing, and aging services (MA); management (PhD); marketing (MBA); mathematics (MA, MS); mechanical and energy engineering (MS, PhD); music (MA), including ethnomusicology, music theory, musicology, performance; music composition (PhD); music education (MM Ed, PhD); nonprofit management (MPA); operations and supply chain management (MBA); performance (MM, DMA); philosophy (MA); political science (MA); professional and technical communication (MA); radio, television and film (MA, MFA); rehabilitation counseling (Certificate); sociology (MA); Spanish (MA); special education (M Ed); speech-language pathology (MA); strategic management (MBA); studio art (MFA); teaching (M Ed); MBA/MS. *Program availability:* Part-time, evening/weekend, online learning. Terminal master's awarded for partial completion of doctoral program. *Degree requirements:* For master's, variable foreign language requirement, comprehensive exam (for some programs), thesis (for some programs); for doctorate, variable foreign language requirement, comprehensive exam (for some programs), thesis/dissertation; for other advanced degree, variable foreign language requirement, comprehensive exam (for some programs). *Entrance requirements:* For master's and doctorate, GRE, GMAT. Additional exam requirements/recommendations for international students: Required—TOEFL (minimum score 550 paper-based; 79 iBT). Electronic applications accepted.

University of Notre Dame, Graduate School, College of Arts and Letters, Division of Humanities, Department of Romance Languages and Literatures, Notre Dame, IN 46556. Offers French and Francophone studies (MA); Iberian and Latin American studies (MA); Italian studies (MA); Romance literatures (MA). *Degree requirements:* For master's, 2 foreign languages, comprehensive exam, thesis optional. *Entrance requirements:* For master's, GRE General Test, BA in target language. Additional exam requirements/recommendations for international students: Required—TOEFL (minimum score 600 paper-based; 80 iBT). Electronic applications accepted. *Faculty research:* Literature of discovery and exploration, modern literature, literary criticism, medieval literature, feminist critical theory.

University of Oklahoma, College of Arts and Sciences, Department of Modern Languages, Literatures, and Linguistics, Program in French, Norman, OK 73019-2032. Offers MA, PhD, MBA/MA. *Program availability:* Part-time. *Students:* 6 full-time (5

women), 4 part-time (3 women); includes 2 minority (1 Hispanic/Latino; 1 Two or more races, non-Hispanic/Latino), 2 international. Average age 31. 4 applicants, 50% accepted, 2 enrolled. In 2017, 1 master's, 1 doctorate awarded. Terminal master's awarded for partial completion of doctoral program. *Degree requirements:* For master's, comprehensive exam, thesis optional, two languages (one must be French); for doctorate, comprehensive exam, thesis/dissertation, two languages (one must be French). *Entrance requirements:* For master's, BA (or equivalent) in French, or equivalent hours in the major; for doctorate, MA (or equivalent) in French. Additional exam requirements/recommendations for international students: Required—TOEFL (minimum score 79 iBT) or IELTS (minimum score 6.5). *Application deadline:* For fall admission, 2/1 for domestic and international students; for spring admission, 10/1 for domestic and international students. Application fee: $50 ($100 for international students). Electronic applications accepted. *Expenses:* Tuition, state resident: full-time $5119; part-time $213.30 per credit hour. Tuition, nonresident: full-time $19,778; part-time $824.10 per credit hour. *Required fees:* $3458; $133.55 per credit hour. $126.50 per semester. *Financial support:* In 2017–18, 9 students received support. Fellowships, teaching assistantships with full tuition reimbursements available, scholarships/grants, health care benefits, and unspecified assistantships available. Support available to part-time students. Financial award application deadline: 6/1; financial award applicants required to submit FAFSA. *Faculty research:* Medieval literature and culture, 17th century literature, 18th century literature and culture, 19th century literature and culture, 20th and 21st century literature and culture. *Unit head:* Dr. Logan Whalen, Associate Professor of French, E-mail: lwhalen@ou.edu. *Application contact:* Pamela Genova, Professor of French/Graduate Liaison, 405-325-6181, E-mail: genova@ou.edu. Website: http://mlll.publishpath.com/graduate

University of Oregon, Graduate School, College of Arts and Sciences, Department of Romance Languages, Program in French, Eugene, OR 97403. Offers MA. *Program availability:* Part-time. *Degree requirements:* For master's, one foreign language. *Entrance requirements:* For master's, GRE General Test, minimum GPA of 3.0. Additional exam requirements/recommendations for international students: Required—TOEFL.

University of Ottawa, Faculty of Graduate and Postdoctoral Studies, Faculty of Arts, Department of Lettres Françaises, Ottawa, ON K1N 6N5, Canada. Offers MA, PhD. *Degree requirements:* For master's, thesis or alternative; for doctorate, thesis/dissertation, oral exam. *Entrance requirements:* For master's, honors degree or equivalent, minimum B average; for doctorate, master's degree, minimum B+ average. Electronic applications accepted. *Faculty research:* Littérature française, du Moyen-Âge á nos jours; littérature québécoise, des origines au XXe sie&,cle; création littéraire.

University of Pennsylvania, School of Arts and Sciences, Graduate Group in Romance Languages, Philadelphia, PA 19104. Offers French (AM, PhD); Italian (AM, PhD); Spanish (AM, PhD). *Faculty:* 20 full-time (7 women), 6 part-time/adjunct (3 women). *Students:* 61 full-time (29 women); includes 7 minority (6 Hispanic/Latino; 1 Two or more races, non-Hispanic/Latino), 34 international. Average age 31. 82 applicants, 32% accepted, 13 enrolled. In 2017, 12 master's, 8 doctorates awarded. Terminal master's awarded for partial completion of doctoral program. Application fee: $70.
Website: http://www.sas.upenn.edu/graduate-division

University of Pittsburgh, Kenneth P. Dietrich School of Arts and Sciences, Department of French and Italian Languages and Literatures, Pittsburgh, PA 15260. Offers French (MA, PhD), including film studies (PhD), French (MA), Romance languages and literatures (PhD); Italian (MA). *Program availability:* Part-time. *Faculty:* 12 full-time (6 women). *Students:* 26 full-time (15 women); includes 2 minority (1 Black or African American, non-Hispanic/Latino; 1 Hispanic/Latino), 9 international. Average age 31. 17 applicants, 53% accepted, 6 enrolled. In 2017, 3 master's, 5 doctorates awarded. Terminal master's awarded for partial completion of doctoral program. *Degree requirements:* For master's, one foreign language, comprehensive exam, thesis; for doctorate, variable foreign language requirement, comprehensive exam, thesis/dissertation. *Entrance requirements:* For master's, GRE General Test (for French), phone interview and writing samples in French and English (for French); minimum GPA of 3.0 and writing sample (for Italian); for doctorate, GRE General Test (for French), phone interview and writing samples in French and English (for French). Additional exam requirements/recommendations for international students: Required—TOEFL (minimum score 600 paper-based; 90 iBT), IELTS. *Application deadline:* For fall admission, 1/10 priority date for domestic and international students. Application fee: $50. Electronic applications accepted. *Expenses:* $22,290 in-state tuition, $36,980 out-of-state, $850 fees. *Financial support:* In 2017–18, 22 students received support, including 5 fellowships with full tuition reimbursements available (averaging $23,262 per year), 1 research assistantship with full tuition reimbursement available (averaging $18,815 per year), 16 teaching assistantships with full tuition reimbursements available (averaging $18,815 per year); traineeships, health care benefits, and unspecified assistantships also available. Financial award application deadline: 1/10. *Faculty research:* Literature and politics; gender and sexuality; Dante and his reception; seventeenth- and eighteenth-century Italian literature and culture; Italian theater; Renaissance studies; culture of the French Caribbean; West Africa and the Maghreb; environmental studies; post-coloniality; French culture from the Middle Ages to the 21st century; poetry and epistolarity; post-unification Italian culture, especially Fascism, World War II, the Holocaust, and Sicilian cultural production. *Total annual research expenditures:* $9,000. *Unit head:* Dr. Lina Insana, Chair, 412-624-6269, E-mail: insana@pitt.edu. *Application contact:* Keanna Cash, Graduate Administrator, 412-624-5227, Fax: 412-624-6263, E-mail: kec176@pitt.edu.
Website: http://frenchanditalian.pitt.edu

University of Regina, Faculty of Graduate Studies and Research, Faculty of Arts, Department of French, Regina, SK S4S 0A2, Canada. Offers MA. *Program availability:* Part-time. *Faculty:* 6 full-time (0 women). *Students:* 7 full-time (5 women), 3 part-time (2 women). 12 applicants, 58% accepted. *Degree requirements:* For master's, thesis, seminar presentation. *Entrance requirements:* Additional exam requirements/recommendations for international students: Required—TOEFL (minimum score 580 paper-based; 80 iBT), IELTS (minimum score 6.5), PTE (minimum score 59). *Application deadline:* Applications are processed on a rolling basis. Application fee: $100. Electronic applications accepted. *Expenses:* Tuition, nonresident: full-time $21,330 Canadian dollars; part-time $18,165 Canadian dollars per year. *International tuition:* $24,713 Canadian dollars full-time. *Required fees:* $5136 Canadian dollars; $3118 Canadian dollars per credit hour. $1008 Canadian dollars per semester. Tuition and fees vary according to program. *Financial support:* In 2017–18, 1 teaching assistantship (averaging $2,562 per year) was awarded; fellowships, research assistantships, and scholarships/grants also available. Financial award application deadline: 6/15. *Faculty research:* French literature, French linguistics, rhetoric, translation and terminology, lexicography. *Unit head:* Dr. Emmanuel Aito, Department Head and Graduate Program Coordinator, 306-337-2576, Fax: 306-585-4827, E-mail: emmanuel.aito@uregina.ca.
Website: http://www.uregina.ca/arts/french

University of Saskatchewan, College of Graduate Studies and Research, College of Arts and Science, Department of Languages and Linguistics, Saskatoon, SK S7N 5A2,

Canada. Offers MA. *Degree requirements:* For master's, 2 foreign languages, thesis. *Entrance requirements:* Additional exam requirements/recommendations for international students: Required—TOEFL (minimum score 80 iBT); Recommended—IELTS (minimum score 6.5). Electronic applications accepted.

University of South Africa, College of Human Sciences, Pretoria, South Africa. Offers adult education (M Ed); African languages (MA, PhD); African politics (MA, PhD); Afrikaans (MA, PhD); ancient history (MA, PhD); ancient Near Eastern studies (MA, PhD); anthropology (MA, PhD); applied linguistics (MA); Arabic (MA, PhD); archaeology (MA); art history (MA); Biblical archaeology (MA); Biblical studies (M Th, D Th, PhD); Christian spirituality (M Th, D Th); church history (M Th, D Th); classical studies (MA, PhD); clinical psychology (MA); communication (MA, PhD); comparative education (M Ed, Ed D); consulting psychology (D Admin, D Com, PhD); curriculum studies (M Ed, Ed D); development studies (M Admin, MA, D Admin, PhD); didactics (M Ed, Ed D); education (M Tech); education management (M Ed, Ed D); educational psychology (M Ed); English (MA); environmental education (M Ed); French (MA, PhD); German (MA, PhD); Greek (MA); guidance and counseling (M Ed); health studies (MA, PhD), including health sciences education (MA), health services management (MA), medical and surgical nursing science (critical care general) (MA), midwifery and neonatal nursing science (MA), trauma and emergency care (MA); history (MA, PhD); history of education (Ed D); inclusive education (M Ed, Ed D); information and communications technology policy and regulation (MA); information science (MA, MIS, PhD); international politics (MA, PhD); Islamic studies (MA, PhD); Italian (MA, PhD); Judaica (MA, PhD); linguistics (MA, PhD); mathematical education (M Ed); mathematics education (MA); missiology (M Th, D Th); modern Hebrew (MA, PhD); musicology (MA, MMus, D Mus, PhD); natural science education (M Ed); New Testament (M Th, D Th); Old Testament (D Th); pastoral therapy (M Th, D Th); philosophy (MA); philosophy of education (M Ed, Ed D); politics (MA, PhD); Portuguese (MA, PhD); practical theology (M Th, D Th); psychology (MA, MS, PhD); psychology of education (M Ed, Ed D); public health (MA); religious studies (MA, D Th, PhD); Romance languages (MA); Russian (MA, PhD); Semitic languages (MA, PhD); social behavior studies in HIV/AIDS (MA); social science (mental health) (MA); social science in development studies (MA); social science in psychology (MA); social science in social work (MA); social science in sociology (MA); social work (MSW, DSW, PhD); socio-education (M Ed, Ed D); sociolinguistics (MA); sociology (MA, PhD); Spanish (MA, PhD); systematic theology (M Th, D Th); TESOL (teaching English to speakers of other languages) (MA); theological ethics (M Th, D Th); theory of literature (MA, PhD); urban ministries (D Th); urban ministry (M Th).

University of South Carolina, The Graduate School, College of Arts and Sciences, Department of Languages, Literatures, and Cultures, Columbia, SC 29208. Offers comparative literature (MA, PhD); foreign languages (MAT), including French, German, Spanish; French (MA); German (MA); Spanish (MA). MAT offered in cooperation with the College of Education. *Program availability:* Part-time. *Degree requirements:* For master's, one foreign language, comprehensive exam, thesis optional; for doctorate, 2 foreign languages, comprehensive exam, thesis/dissertation. *Entrance requirements:* For master's and doctorate, GRE General Test, writing sample. Additional exam requirements/recommendations for international students: Required—TOEFL (minimum score 75 iBT). Electronic applications accepted. *Faculty research:* Modern literature, linguistics, literature and culture, medieval literature, literary theory.

University of South Florida, College of Arts and Sciences, Department of World Languages, Tampa, FL 33620-9951. Offers French (MA); linguistics (MA); linguistics and applied linguistics studies (PhD); linguistics: English as a second language (MA); Spanish (MA). *Program availability:* Part-time, evening/weekend. *Faculty:* 18 full-time (14 women). *Students:* 40 full-time (34 women), 9 part-time (7 women); includes 20 minority (1 Black or African American, non-Hispanic/Latino; 1 Asian, non-Hispanic/Latino; 16 Hispanic/Latino; 2 Two or more races, non-Hispanic/Latino), 16 international. Average age 33. 65 applicants, 62% accepted, 18 enrolled. In 2017, 30 master's awarded. *Degree requirements:* For master's, one foreign language, comprehensive exam, thesis optional; for doctorate, one foreign language, comprehensive exam, thesis/dissertation. *Entrance requirements:* For master's, GRE General Test, minimum undergraduate GPA of 3.0 and 2-3 letters of recommendation; two-page statement of purpose written in Spanish (for Spanish program); oral interview (for Spanish and French programs); writing sample (for French program); for doctorate, GRE General Test, minimum GPA of 3.5 or international equivalent; master's degree or equivalent academic level; statement of purpose; current curriculum vitae; three letters of recommendation; personal interview with faculty; evidence of research experience or scholarly promise. Additional exam requirements/recommendations for international students: Required—TOEFL minimum score 600 paper-based; 80 iBT or IELTS minimum score 6.5 (for MA); TOEFL minimum score 550 paper-based; 80 iBT or IELTS minimum score 6.5 (for PhD). *Application deadline:* For fall admission, 1/15 for domestic and international students; for spring admission, 10/15 for domestic students, 9/15 for international students. Application fee: $30. Electronic applications accepted. *Financial support:* In 2017–18, 10 students received support, including 43 teaching assistantships with tuition reimbursements available (averaging $10,152 per year); tuition waivers (partial) and unspecified assistantships also available. Financial award application deadline: 6/30. *Faculty research:* Second language acquisition, instructional technology, foreign language education, English for speakers of other languages, distance learning. *Total annual research expenditures:* $7,706. *Unit head:* Dr. Stephan Schindler, Chair and Professor, 813-974-2548, Fax: 813-905-9937, E-mail: skschindler@usf.edu. *Application contact:* Patricia Garcia, Academic Program Specialist, 813-974-2548, Fax: 813-905-9937, E-mail: pgarcia@usf.edu.
Website: http://languages.usf.edu/

The University of Tennessee, Graduate School, College of Arts and Sciences, Department of Modern Foreign Languages and Literatures, Program in French, Knoxville, TN 37996. Offers MA. *Degree requirements:* For master's, one foreign language, thesis or alternative. *Entrance requirements:* For master's, minimum GPA of 2.7. Additional exam requirements/recommendations for international students: Required—TOEFL. Electronic applications accepted.

The University of Tennessee, Graduate School, College of Arts and Sciences, Department of Modern Foreign Languages and Literatures, Program in Modern Foreign Languages, Knoxville, TN 37996. Offers applied linguistics (PhD); French (PhD); German (PhD); Italian (PhD); Portuguese (PhD); Russian (PhD); Spanish (PhD). *Degree requirements:* For doctorate, 2 foreign languages, thesis/dissertation. *Entrance requirements:* For doctorate, minimum GPA of 2.7. Additional exam requirements/recommendations for international students: Required—TOEFL. Electronic applications accepted.

The University of Texas at Arlington, Graduate School, College of Liberal Arts, Department of Modern Languages, Arlington, TX 76019. Offers French (MA); Spanish (MA). *Program availability:* Part-time, evening/weekend. *Degree requirements:* For master's, 2 foreign languages, comprehensive exam, thesis optional. *Entrance requirements:* For master's, GRE General Test, minimum GPA of 3.0, 3 letters of recommendation. Additional exam requirements/recommendations for international students: Required—TOEFL (minimum score 550 paper-based).

The University of Texas at Austin, Graduate School, College of Liberal Arts, Department of French and Italian, Austin, TX 78712-1111. Offers French linguistics (MA,

PhD); French studies (MA, PhD); Italian studies (MA, PhD); Romance linguistics (PhD). *Program availability:* Part-time. *Degree requirements:* For master's, one foreign language, thesis; for doctorate, 2 foreign languages, thesis/dissertation. *Entrance requirements:* For master's, GRE General Test, minimum GPA of 3.0, bachelor's degree in French or equivalent; for doctorate, GRE General Test, minimum GPA of 3.0, master's degree in French. Additional exam requirements/recommendations for international students: Required—TOEFL. Electronic applications accepted. *Faculty research:* Nineteenth-century Italian literature, Italian Renaissance, twentieth-century French literature, Francophone literature, fifteenth-century literature and culture.

The University of Toledo, College of Graduate Studies, College of Languages, Literature and Social Sciences, Department of Foreign Languages, Toledo, OH 43606-3390. Offers French (MA); German (MA); Spanish (MA). *Program availability:* Part-time. *Degree requirements:* For master's, one foreign language, comprehensive exam, comprehensive reading exam in 1 additional foreign language. *Entrance requirements:* For master's, minimum cumulative point-hour ratio of 2.7 for all previous academic work. Additional exam requirements/recommendations for international students: Required—TOEFL (minimum score 550 paper-based; 80 iBT). Electronic applications accepted.

University of Toronto, School of Graduate Studies, Faculty of Arts and Science, Department of French, Toronto, ON M5S 1A1, Canada. Offers French language and literature (MA, PhD). *Program availability:* Part-time. *Degree requirements:* For master's, research essay; for doctorate, one foreign language, thesis/dissertation, field exam. *Entrance requirements:* For master's, 2 letters of reference, writing sample, minimum B+ average overall and in French, undergraduate major in French; for doctorate, 7 courses in French language and literature, minimum A- average, writing sample. Additional exam requirements/recommendations for international students: Required—TOEFL (minimum score 580 paper-based; 93 iBT), TWE (minimum score 5). Electronic applications accepted.

University of Utah, Graduate School, College of Humanities, Department of World Languages and Cultures, Salt Lake City, UT 84112. Offers comparative literary and cultural studies (MA, PhD); French (MA); Spanish (MA, MALP); world languages (MA). *Program availability:* Part-time. *Faculty:* 36 full-time (22 women). *Students:* 27 full-time (19 women), 8 part-time (6 women); includes 5 minority (4 Hispanic/Latino; 1 Two or more races, non-Hispanic/Latino), 10 international. Average age 27. 17 applicants, 76% accepted, 9 enrolled. In 2017, 13 master's, 2 doctorates awarded. Terminal master's awarded for partial completion of doctoral program. *Degree requirements:* For master's, variable foreign language requirement, comprehensive exam (for some programs), thesis (for some programs); for doctorate, 2 foreign languages, comprehensive exam, thesis/dissertation. *Entrance requirements:* For master's, bachelor's degree from regionally-accredited college or university with minimum undergraduate overall GPA of 3.0; for doctorate, MA from regionally-accredited college or university, advanced proficiency in target language. Additional exam requirements/recommendations for international students: Required—TOEFL (minimum score 550 paper-based; 80 iBT), IELTS (minimum score 6.5). *Application deadline:* For fall admission, 1/15 priority date for domestic students, 12/15 priority date for international students. Application fee: $55 ($65 for international students). Electronic applications accepted. *Financial support:* In 2017–18, 24 students received support, including 24 teaching assistantships with full and partial tuition reimbursements available (averaging $17,200 per year); unspecified assistantships also available. Financial award application deadline: 1/15. *Faculty research:* Literary study, literary theory, linguistics, cultural studies, comparative studies. *Unit head:* Dr. Katharina Gerstenberger, Chair, 801-585-7908, Fax: 801-581-7581, E-mail: katharina.gerstenberger@utah.edu. *Application contact:* Mackenzie Buie, Academic Coordinator, 801-581-7748, Fax: 801-581-7581, E-mail: mackenzie.buie@utah.edu.
Website: http://languages.utah.edu/

University of Victoria, Faculty of Graduate Studies, Faculty of Humanities, Department of French, Victoria, BC V8W 2Y2, Canada. Offers literature (MA); teaching emphasis (MA). *Program availability:* Part-time, evening/weekend. *Degree requirements:* For master's, 2 foreign languages, thesis optional. *Entrance requirements:* For master's, BA in French. Additional exam requirements/recommendations for international students: Required—TOEFL (minimum score 575 paper-based), IELTS (minimum score 7). Electronic applications accepted. *Faculty research:* French-Canadian literature, stylistics, comparative literature, Francophone literature.

University of Virginia, College and Graduate School of Arts and Sciences, Department of French, Charlottesville, VA 22903. Offers MA, PhD. *Faculty:* 20 full-time (16 women), 3 part-time/adjunct (1 woman). *Students:* 23 full-time (16 women); includes 2 minority (1 Asian, non-Hispanic/Latino; 1 Hispanic/Latino), 10 international. Average age 30. 47 applicants, 32% accepted, 11 enrolled. In 2017, 7 master's, 6 doctorates awarded. *Degree requirements:* For master's, one foreign language, comprehensive exam; for doctorate, one foreign language, comprehensive exam, thesis/dissertation. *Entrance requirements:* For master's and doctorate, GRE General Test, minimum GPA of 3.0 in major and overall; 2 letters of recommendation; writing sample. Additional exam requirements/recommendations for international students: Required—TOEFL (minimum score 600 paper-based; 90 iBT), IELTS (minimum score 7). *Application deadline:* For fall admission, 12/1 for domestic and international students. Applications are processed on a rolling basis. Application fee: $60. Electronic applications accepted. *Financial support:* Fellowships and teaching assistantships available. Financial award applicants required to submit FAFSA. *Unit head:* Gary Ferguson, Chair, 434-924-4632, Fax: 434-924-7157, E-mail: rgf3y@virginia.edu. *Application contact:* Amy Ogden, Director of Graduate Studies, 434-924-7158, Fax: 434-924-7157, E-mail: avo2n@virginia.edu.
Website: http://french.as.virginia.edu/

University of Washington, Graduate School, College of Arts and Sciences, Division of French and Italian Studies, Seattle, WA 98195. Offers French (MA, PhD); Italian (MA). Terminal master's awarded for partial completion of doctoral program. *Degree requirements:* For master's, 2 foreign languages, exam; for doctorate, 3 foreign languages, thesis/dissertation, exam. *Entrance requirements:* For master's and doctorate, GRE General Test, minimum GPA of 3.0. Additional exam requirements/recommendations for international students: Required—TOEFL. Electronic applications accepted. *Faculty research:* Interdisciplinary studies, literary theory and criticism, film, major periods of French and Italian literature, Francophonie.

University of Waterloo, Graduate Studies, Faculty of Arts, Department of French Studies, Waterloo, ON N2L 3G1, Canada. Offers French (MA, PhD). *Program availability:* Part-time. *Entrance requirements:* For master's, honors degree, minimum B average, course work and assignments in French, resume. Additional exam requirements/recommendations for international students: Required—TOEFL, IELTS. Electronic applications accepted. *Faculty research:* French and Quebec literature: Middle Ages through twentieth century, phonology of Acadian dialect, computerized scholarly editions of medieval and Renaissance texts.

The University of Western Ontario, Faculty of Graduate Studies, Faculty of Arts and Humanities, Department of French Studies, London, ON N6A 5B8, Canada. Offers MA, PhD. *Degree requirements:* For master's, thesis or alternative; for doctorate, one foreign language, thesis/dissertation. *Entrance requirements:* For master's, minimum B average, honors degree, 2 years of teaching experience (MAT); for doctorate, MA or equivalent, minimum B average in French. Additional exam requirements/recommendations for international students: Required—TOEFL. Electronic applications accepted.

University of Wisconsin–Madison, Graduate School, College of Letters and Science, Department of French and Italian, Program in French, Madison, WI 53706-1380. Offers MA, PhD. *Program availability:* Part-time. *Degree requirements:* For master's, one foreign language; for doctorate, one foreign language, thesis/dissertation. *Entrance requirements:* For master's and doctorate, GRE. Electronic applications accepted. *Faculty research:* Francophone literature; French literature, culture, linguistics, and language pedagogy.

University of Wisconsin–Madison, Graduate School, College of Letters and Science, Department of French and Italian, Program in French Studies, Madison, WI 53706-1380. Offers MFS, Certificate. *Program availability:* Part-time. *Degree requirements:* For master's, one foreign language, thesis, internship; for Certificate, one foreign language, internship. *Entrance requirements:* For master's, GRE. Electronic applications accepted. *Faculty research:* International development, European citizenship, French and business, foreign language education, agricultural economics.

University of Wisconsin–Milwaukee, Graduate School, College of Letters and Science, Department of Foreign Languages and Literature, Milwaukee, WI 53201-0413. Offers foreign languages and literature (MA), including classic Greek, classics, comparative literature, French/Francophone language, literature, and culture, German language, literature, and culture, interpreting, Latin, linguistics, Spanish language, literature, and culture, translation; interpreting (Graduate Certificate); language, literature, and translation (MA, MALLT); translation (Graduate Certificate). *Program availability:* Part-time. *Students:* 11 full-time (6 women), 40 part-time (29 women); includes 10 minority (2 Black or African American, non-Hispanic/Latino; 3 Hispanic/Latino; 5 Two or more races, non-Hispanic/Latino), 4 international. Average age 35. 37 applicants, 68% accepted, 20 enrolled. In 2017, 5 master's awarded. *Degree requirements:* For master's, 2 foreign languages, thesis or alternative. *Entrance requirements:* Additional exam requirements/recommendations for international students: Required—TOEFL (minimum score 550 paper-based; 79 iBT), IELTS (minimum score 6.5). *Application deadline:* For fall admission, 1/1 priority date for domestic students; for spring admission, 9/1 for domestic students. Application fee: $56 ($96 for international students). Electronic applications accepted. *Financial support:* Fellowships, research assistantships, teaching assistantships, career-related internships or fieldwork, health care benefits, unspecified assistantships, and project assistantships available. Support available to part-time students. Financial award application deadline: 4/15; financial award applicants required to submit FAFSA. *Unit head:* Kevin Muse, Department Chair, 414-229-5213, E-mail: kmuse@uwm.edu. *Application contact:* General Information Contact, 414-229-4982, Fax: 414-229-6967, E-mail: gradschool@uwm.edu.
Website: http://uwm.edu/foreign-languages-literature/

University of Wyoming, College of Arts and Sciences, Department of Modern and Classical Languages, Program in French, Laramie, WY 82071. Offers MA. *Program availability:* Part-time. *Degree requirements:* For master's, one foreign language, thesis or alternative. *Entrance requirements:* For master's, GRE General Test, minimum GPA of 3.0. *Faculty research:* Poetry, Asian literature, medieval literature, nineteenth- and twentieth century literature.

Vanderbilt University, Department of French and Italian, Nashville, TN 37240-1001. Offers French (MA, MAT, PhD). *Faculty:* 12 full-time (7 women). *Students:* 13 full-time (8 women); includes 2 minority (1 Hispanic/Latino; 1 Two or more races, non-Hispanic/Latino), 2 international. Average age 28. 17 applicants, 29% accepted, 3 enrolled. In 2017, 1 doctorate awarded. Terminal master's awarded for partial completion of doctoral program. *Degree requirements:* For master's, one foreign language, comprehensive exam; for doctorate, 2 foreign languages, comprehensive exam, thesis/dissertation, final and qualifying exams. *Entrance requirements:* For master's and doctorate, GRE General Test. Additional exam requirements/recommendations for international students: Required—TOEFL (minimum score 570 paper-based; 88 iBT). *Application deadline:* For fall admission, 1/15 for domestic and international students. Electronic applications accepted. *Financial support:* Fellowships, teaching assistantships, career-related internships or fieldwork, Federal Work-Study, institutionally sponsored loans, scholarships/grants, and health care benefits available. Financial award application deadline: 1/15; financial award applicants required to submit CSS PROFILE or FAFSA. *Faculty research:* Baudelaire, Rabelais, voyage literature, postcolonial literature, medieval epic. *Unit head:* Dr. Laura Schneider, Chair, 615-322-6900, Fax: 615-343-6909, E-mail: laura.c.schneider@vanderbilt.edu. *Application contact:* Paul Miller, Director of Graduate Studies, 615-322-6900, Fax: 615-343-6909, E-mail: paul.miller@vanderbilt.edu.
Website: http://as.vanderbilt.edu/french-italian/

Washington University in St. Louis, The Graduate School, Department of Romance Languages and Literatures, Program in French, St. Louis, MO 63130-4899. Offers French and comparative literature (PhD); French language and literature (PhD). Terminal master's awarded for partial completion of doctoral program. *Degree requirements:* For doctorate, thesis/dissertation. *Entrance requirements:* For doctorate, GRE General Test. Additional exam requirements/recommendations for international students: Required—TOEFL. Electronic applications accepted. *Faculty research:* French language and literature.

Wayne State University, College of Liberal Arts and Sciences, Department of Classical and Modern Languages, Literatures, and Cultures, Detroit, MI 48202. Offers classics (MA), including ancient Greek and Latin, ancient studies, classics, Latin; German (MA); language learning (MALL), including Arabic (MA, MALL), French (MA, MALL, PhD), German (MALL, PhD), Italian (MA, MALL), Spanish (MA, MALL, PhD); modern languages (PhD), including French (MA, MALL, PhD), German (MALL, PhD), Spanish (MA, MALL, PhD); Near Eastern languages (MA), including Arabic (MA, MALL), Hebrew; Romance languages (MA), including French (MA, MALL, PhD), Italian (MA, MALL), Spanish (MA, MALL, PhD). *Faculty:* 22. *Students:* 24 full-time (18 women), 21 part-time (15 women); includes 11 minority (4 Black or African American, non-Hispanic/Latino; 1 American Indian or Alaska Native, non-Hispanic/Latino; 2 Asian, non-Hispanic/Latino; 2 Hispanic/Latino; 2 Two or more races, non-Hispanic/Latino), 3 international. Average age 37. 32 applicants, 63% accepted, 14 enrolled. In 2017, 10 master's awarded. *Degree requirements:* For master's, variable foreign language requirement, comprehensive exam (for some programs), thesis (for some programs); for doctorate, one foreign language, comprehensive exam, thesis/dissertation. *Entrance requirements:* Additional exam requirements/recommendations for international students: Required—TOEFL (minimum score 550 paper-based; 79 iBT), TWE (minimum score 5.5), Michigan English Language Assessment Battery (minimum score 85); Recommended—IELTS (minimum score 6.5). Application fee: $50. Electronic applications accepted. *Expenses:* Tuition, state resident: full-time $10,224; part-time $638.98 per credit hour. Tuition, nonresident: full-time $22,145; part-time $1384.04 per credit hour. Tuition and fees vary according to course load and program. *Financial support:* In 2017–18, 25 students received support, including 4 fellowships with tuition reimbursements available (averaging $13,500 per year), 17 teaching assistantships with tuition reimbursements available (averaging $18,591 per year); research assistantships, scholarships/grants,

health care benefits, and unspecified assistantships also available. Financial award applicants required to submit FAFSA. *Faculty research:* Classical and modern literature and culture (Greek, Latin, Arabic, Chinese, French, German, Russian, Spanish) including colonial studies and exile and Holocaust studies; critical theory (French, German, Slavic, Spanish); theoretical and applied linguistics (Arabic, Chinese, French, Spanish); area studies (Arabic, Near Eastern, classical, Islamic, and Judaic studies). *Unit head:* Dr. Anne Duggan, Department Chair, 313-577-6244, Fax: 313-577-6243, E-mail: a.duggan@wayne.edu.
Website: http://clas.wayne.edu/languages/

West Chester University of Pennsylvania, College of Arts and Humanities, Department of Languages and Cultures, West Chester, PA 19383. Offers French (Teaching Certificate); German (Teaching Certificate); languages and cultures (MA), including French, German, Spanish; Spanish (Teaching Certificate). *Program availability:* Part-time, evening/weekend, minimal on-campus study. *Students:* 8 full-time (all women), 24 part-time (19 women); includes 10 minority (all Hispanic/Latino), 1 international. Average age 30. 8 applicants, 88% accepted, 7 enrolled. In 2017, 10 master's awarded. *Degree requirements:* For master's, one foreign language, comprehensive exam, portfolio defended at oral exit exam, capstone project; for Teaching Certificate, one foreign language. *Entrance requirements:* For master's and Teaching Certificate, ACTFL OPI and WPT. Additional exam requirements/recommendations for international students: Required—TOEFL or IELTS. *Application deadline:* For fall admission, 5/15 for international students; for spring admission, 10/15 for international students. Applications are processed on a rolling basis. Application fee: $50. Electronic applications accepted. *Expenses:* Tuition, state resident: full-time $9000; part-time $500 per credit. Tuition, nonresident: full-time $13,500; part-time $750 per credit. *Required fees:* $2959; $149.79 per credit. *Financial support:* Scholarships/grants and unspecified assistantships available. Financial award application deadline: 2/15; financial award applicants required to submit FAFSA. *Faculty research:* Language structure, literature, film, culture, pedagogy, technology. *Unit head:* Dr. Mahmoud Amer, Chair, 610-430-5077, Fax: 610-436-3048, E-mail: mamer@wcupa.edu. *Application contact:* Dr. Maria Van Liew, Graduate Coordinator, 610-436-4746, Fax: 610-436-3048, E-mail: mvanliew@wcupa.edu.
Website: http://www.wcupa.edu/arts-humanities/languagesCultures/

Western Kentucky University, Graduate Studies, Potter College of Arts and Letters, Department of Modern Languages, Bowling Green, KY 42101. Offers French (MA Ed); German (MA Ed); Spanish (MA Ed).

Yale University, Graduate School of Arts and Sciences, Department of French, New Haven, CT 06520. Offers M Phil, MA, PhD. *Degree requirements:* For doctorate, 3 foreign languages, thesis/dissertation. *Entrance requirements:* For doctorate, GRE General Test.

York University, Faculty of Graduate Studies, Glendon Campus, Program in French Studies, Toronto, ON M3J 1P3, Canada. Offers MA, PhD. *Degree requirements:* For master's, thesis or alternative. Electronic applications accepted.

German

Arizona State University at the Tempe campus, College of Liberal Arts and Sciences, School of International Letters and Cultures, Program in German, Tempe, AZ 85287-0202. Offers comparative literature (MA); language and culture (MA); literature (MA). *Degree requirements:* For master's, thesis, applied pedagogical project, or paper portfolio consisting of 2 seminar papers; interactive Program of Study (iPOS) submitted no later than beginning of third semester of study or before completing 50 percent of coursework. *Entrance requirements:* For master's, minimum GPA of 3.0 in the last two years of work leading to the bachelor's degree, personal statement, writing sample (preferably written in German), 3 letters of recommendation. Additional exam requirements/recommendations for international students: Required—TOEFL (minimum score 550 paper-based; 83 iBT), IELTS (minimum score 6.5). Electronic applications accepted.

Bowling Green State University, Graduate College, College of Arts and Sciences, Department of German, Russian, and East Asian Languages, Bowling Green, OH 43403. Offers German (MA); MA/MA. *Program availability:* Part-time. *Degree requirements:* For master's, one foreign language, thesis or alternative. *Entrance requirements:* For master's, GRE General Test. Additional exam requirements/recommendations for international students: Required—TOEFL. Electronic applications accepted.

Brown University, Graduate School, Department of German Studies, Providence, RI 02912. Offers PhD. *Degree requirements:* For doctorate, 2 foreign languages, thesis/dissertation, preliminary exam. *Entrance requirements:* For doctorate, GRE General Test.

California State University, Long Beach, Graduate Studies, College of Liberal Arts, Department of Romance, German, Russian Languages and Literatures, Program in German, Long Beach, CA 90840. Offers MA. *Program availability:* Part-time. *Degree requirements:* For master's, one foreign language, comprehensive exam or thesis. Electronic applications accepted. *Faculty research:* Contemporary German society, Baroque, Goethe, Wagner.

Central Connecticut State University, School of Graduate Studies, College of Liberal Arts and Social Sciences, Department of Modern Languages, New Britain, CT 06050-4010. Offers modern language (MA, Certificate), including French, German (Certificate), Italian, Spanish (MA); Spanish (MS, Certificate). *Program availability:* Part-time, evening/weekend. *Faculty:* 7 full-time (6 women). *Students:* 6 full-time (5 women), 16 part-time (12 women); includes 9 minority (all Hispanic/Latino), 1 international. Average age 32. 8 applicants, 88% accepted, 5 enrolled. In 2017, 12 master's awarded. *Degree requirements:* For master's, one foreign language, comprehensive exam, thesis or alternative; for Certificate, qualifying exam. *Entrance requirements:* For master's, minimum undergraduate GPA of 2.7, 24 credits of undergraduate courses in each language in which graduate work will be undertaken. Additional exam requirements/recommendations for international students: Required—TOEFL (minimum score 550 paper-based; 79 iBT); Recommended—IELTS (minimum score 6.5). *Application deadline:* For fall admission, 8/1 for domestic students, 5/1 for international students; for spring admission, 11/1 for domestic and international students. Applications are processed on a rolling basis. Application fee: $50. Electronic applications accepted. *Expenses: Tuition, area resident:* Full-time $6757. Tuition, state resident: full-time $9750; part-time $374 per credit. Tuition, nonresident: full-time $18,102; part-time $374 per credit. *Required fees:* $4635; $255 per credit. *Financial support:* In 2017–18, 3 students received support. Career-related internships or fieldwork, Federal Work-Study, scholarships/grants, and unspecified assistantships available. Support available to part-time students. Financial award application deadline: 3/1; financial award applicants required to submit FAFSA. *Faculty research:* Quebecois literature, Caribbean literature, modern French/Spanish drama, Puerto Rican novel and drama. *Unit head:* Dr. Carmela Pesca, Chair, 860-832-2875, E-mail: pescac@ccsu.edu. *Application contact:* Patricia Gardner, Associate Director of Graduate Studies, 860-832-2350, Fax: 860-832-2362.
Website: http://www.ccsu.edu/modlang/

Columbia University, Graduate School of Arts and Sciences, New York, NY 10027. Offers African-American studies (MA); American studies (MA); anthropology (MA, PhD); art history and archaeology (MA, PhD); astronomy (PhD); biological sciences (PhD); biotechnology (MA); chemical physics (PhD); chemistry (PhD); classical studies (MA, PhD); classics (MA, PhD); climate and society (MA); conservation biology (MA); earth and environmental sciences (PhD); East Asia: regional studies (MA); East Asian languages and cultures (MA, PhD); ecology, evolution and environmental biology (MA), including conservation biology; ecology, evolution, and environmental biology (PhD), including ecology and evolutionary biology, evolutionary primatology; economics (MA, PhD); English and comparative literature (MA, PhD); French and Romance philology (MA, PhD); Germanic languages (MA, PhD); global French studies (MA); global thought (MA); Hispanic cultural studies (MA); history (PhD); history and literature (MA); human rights studies (MA); Islamic studies (MA); Italian (MA, PhD); Japanese pedagogy (MA); Jewish studies (MA); Latin America and the Caribbean: regional studies (MA); Latin American and Iberian cultures (PhD); mathematics (MA, PhD), including finance (MA); medieval and Renaissance studies (MA); Middle Eastern, South Asian, and African studies (MA, PhD); modern art: critical and curatorial studies (MA); modern European studies (MA); museum anthropology (MA); music (DMA, PhD); oral history (MA); philosophical foundations of physics (MA); philosophy (MA, PhD); physics (PhD); political science (MA, PhD); psychology (PhD); quantitative methods in the social sciences (MA); religion (MA, PhD); Russia, Eurasia and East Europe: regional studies (MA); Russian translation (MA); Slavic cultures (MA); Slavic languages (MA, PhD); sociology (MA, PhD); South Asian studies (MA); statistics (MA, PhD); theatre (PhD). Dual-degree programs require admission to both Graduate School of Arts and Sciences and another Columbia school. *Program availability:* Part-time. Terminal master's awarded for partial completion of doctoral program. *Degree requirements:* For master's, variable foreign language requirement, comprehensive exam (for some programs), thesis (for some programs); for doctorate, variable foreign language requirement, comprehensive exam (for some programs), thesis/dissertation. *Entrance requirements:* For master's and doctorate, GRE General Test, GRE Subject Test (for some programs). Additional exam requirements/recommendations for international students: Required—TOEFL, IELTS. Electronic applications accepted. *Expenses: Tuition:* Full-time $44,864; part-time $1704 per credit. *Required fees:* $2370 per semester. One-time fee: $105.

Cornell University, Graduate School, Graduate Fields of Arts and Sciences, Field of Germanic Studies, Ithaca, NY 14853. Offers German area studies (MA, PhD); German intellectual history (MA, PhD); Germanic linguistics (MA, PhD); Germanic literature (MA, PhD); old Norse (MA, PhD). Terminal master's awarded for partial completion of doctoral program. *Degree requirements:* For master's, one foreign language, thesis; for doctorate, 2 foreign languages, comprehensive exam, thesis/dissertation. *Entrance requirements:* For master's and doctorate, GRE General Test, fluency in German, writing sample, 2 letters of recommendation. Additional exam requirements/recommendations for international students: Required—TOEFL (minimum score 550 paper-based; 77 iBT). Electronic applications accepted. *Faculty research:* Women's studies, minority literature, literature and intellectual history, theater and film studies, Continental philosophy.

Cornell University, Graduate School, Graduate Fields of Arts and Sciences, Field of Linguistics, Ithaca, NY 14853. Offers applied linguistics (MA, PhD); East Asian linguistics (MA, PhD); English linguistics (MA, PhD); general linguistics (MA, PhD); Germanic linguistics (MA, PhD); Indo-European linguistics (MA, PhD); phonetics (MA, PhD); phonological theory (MA, PhD); Romance linguistics (MA, PhD); second language acquisition (MA, PhD); semantics (MA, PhD); Slavic linguistics (MA, PhD); sociolinguistics (MA, PhD); South Asian linguistics (MA, PhD); Southeast Asian linguistics (MA, PhD); syntactic theory (MA, PhD). Terminal master's awarded for partial completion of doctoral program. *Degree requirements:* For master's, one foreign language, thesis; for doctorate, one foreign language, comprehensive exam, thesis/dissertation. *Entrance requirements:* For master's and doctorate, GRE General Test, 2 letters of recommendation. Additional exam requirements/recommendations for international students: Required—TOEFL (minimum score 600 paper-based; 77 iBT). Electronic applications accepted. *Faculty research:* Phonology and phonetics, syntax and semantics, historical linguistics, philosophy of language, language acquisition.

Dalhousie University, Faculty of Arts and Social Science, Department of German, Halifax, NS B3H 4R2, Canada. Offers MA. *Entrance requirements:* Additional exam requirements/recommendations for international students: Required—TOEFL, IELTS, CANTEST, CAEL, or Michigan English Language Assessment Battery. Electronic applications accepted. *Faculty research:* Baroque age in Germany, literature and philosophy of German idealism, twentieth-century German culture, aesthetics, reception of the Islamic Orient, reception of Greek and Roman antiquity, realism and ornament.

DePaul University, College of Liberal Arts and Social Sciences, Chicago, IL 60614. Offers Arabic (MA); Chinese (MA); critical ethnic studies (MA); English (MA); French (MA); German (MA); history (MA); interdisciplinary studies (MA, MS); international public service (MS); international studies (MA); Italian (MA); Japanese (MA); liberal studies (MA); nonprofit management (MNM); public administration (MPA); public health (MPH); public policy (MPP); public service management (MS); refugee and forced migration studies (MS); social work (MSW); sociology (MA); Spanish (MA); sustainable urban development (MA); women's and gender studies (MA); writing and publishing (MA); writing, rhetoric and discourse (MA); MA/PhD. *Program availability:* Part-time, evening/weekend, online learning. Terminal master's awarded for partial completion of doctoral program. *Degree requirements:* For master's, variable foreign language requirement, comprehensive exam (for some programs), thesis (for some programs). *Application deadline:* Applications are processed on a rolling basis. Application fee: $40. Electronic applications accepted. *Financial support:* Applicants required to submit FAFSA. *Unit head:* Dr. Guillermo Vasquez de Velasco, Dean, 773-325-7305. *Application contact:* Ann Spittle, Director of Graduate Admission, 773-325-8369, Fax: 312-476-3244, E-mail: graddepaul@depaul.edu.
Website: http://las.depaul.edu/

German

Duke University, Graduate School, Carolina-Duke Graduate Program in German Studies, Durham, NC 27708-0256. Offers PhD. Program offered jointly with The University of North Carolina Chapel Hill. *Program availability:* Part-time. *Degree requirements:* For doctorate, thesis/dissertation. *Entrance requirements:* For doctorate, GRE General Test, writing sample. Additional exam requirements/recommendations for international students: Required—TOEFL (minimum score 577 paper-based; 90 iBT) or IELTS (minimum score 7). Electronic applications accepted.

Florida Atlantic University, College of Education, Department of Teaching and Learning, Boca Raton, FL 33431-0991. Offers curriculum and instruction (M Ed), including art, biology, chemistry, English, French, German, mathematics, music, physics, Pre-K and primary education, reading, social sciences, Spanish; elementary education (M Ed); environmental education (M Ed); reading education (M Ed); social foundations of education (M Ed), including educational psychology, educational technology, multilingual education. *Accreditation:* NCATE. *Program availability:* Part-time, evening/weekend. *Faculty:* 13 full-time (10 women), 1 part-time/adjunct (0 women). *Students:* 26 full-time (22 women), 43 part-time (39 women); includes 19 minority (9 Black or African American, non-Hispanic/Latino; 1 Asian, non-Hispanic/Latino; 8 Hispanic/Latino; 1 Two or more races, non-Hispanic/Latino), 3 international. Average age 30. 91 applicants, 57% accepted, 33 enrolled. In 2017, 25 master's awarded. *Entrance requirements:* For master's, GRE General Test, minimum GPA of 3.0 in last 2 years of undergraduate course work. Additional exam requirements/recommendations for international students: Required—TOEFL (minimum score 500 paper-based; 61 iBT), IELTS (minimum score 6). *Application deadline:* For fall admission, 7/1 for domestic students, 2/15 for international students; for spring admission, 11/1 for domestic students, 7/15 for international students. Applications are processed on a rolling basis. Application fee: $30. *Expenses:* Tuition, state resident: full-time $7400; part-time $369.82 per credit. Tuition, nonresident: full-time $20,496; part-time $1042.81 per credit. *Financial support:* Fellowships with partial tuition reimbursements, research assistantships with partial tuition reimbursements, teaching assistantships with partial tuition reimbursements, career-related internships or fieldwork, scholarships/grants, and unspecified assistantships available. *Faculty research:* Technology, teaching English to speakers of other languages, math teaching, electronic portfolio assessment, global perspectives through social studies. *Unit head:* Dr. Barbara Ridener, Chairperson, 561-297-3588, E-mail: bridener@fau.edu. *Application contact:* Dr. Eliah Watlington, Associate Dean, 561-296-8520, Fax: 261-297-2991, E-mail: ewatling@fau.edu.
Website: http://www.coe.fau.edu/academicdepartments/tl/

Florida State University, The Graduate School, College of Arts and Sciences, Department of Modern Languages and Linguistics, Program in German, Tallahassee, FL 32306. Offers MA. *Faculty:* 4 full-time (3 women), 1 part-time/adjunct (0 women). *Students:* 6 full-time (4 women); includes 1 minority (Two or more races, non-Hispanic/Latino). Average age 25. 4 applicants, 100% accepted, 2 enrolled. In 2017, 4 master's awarded. *Degree requirements:* For master's, thesis optional. *Entrance requirements:* For master's, GRE General Test, minimum GPA of 3.0. Additional exam requirements/recommendations for international students: Required—TOEFL (minimum score 550 paper-based; 80 iBT). *Application deadline:* For fall admission, 1/15 for domestic students, 2/15 for international students. Electronic applications accepted. *Financial support:* In 2017–18, 4 students received support, including research assistantships (averaging $12,000 per year), 8 teaching assistantships with partial tuition reimbursements available (averaging $14,500 per year). Financial award application deadline: 2/1; financial award applicants required to submit FAFSA. *Unit head:* Dr. Christian Weber, Divisional Coordinator, 850-644-8194, Fax: 850-644-0524, E-mail: cweber@fsu.edu. *Application contact:* Wendy E. Pigott, Graduate Academic Coordinator, 850-644-8397, Fax: 850-644-0524, E-mail: wpigott@fsu.edu.
Website: http://www.modlang.fsu.edu/Programs2/German/Graduate-program

Georgetown University, Graduate School of Arts and Sciences, Department of German, Washington, DC 20057. Offers MA, PhD, MA/PhD. *Degree requirements:* For master's, 2 foreign languages, research project; for doctorate, 3 foreign languages, thesis/dissertation. *Entrance requirements:* For master's, GRE General Test. Additional exam requirements/recommendations for international students: Required—TOEFL.

Georgetown University, Graduate School of Arts and Sciences, Walsh School of Foreign Service, BMW Center for German and European Studies, Washington, DC 20057. Offers MA, MA/JD, MA/PhD. *Degree requirements:* For master's, 2 foreign languages, comprehensive exam. *Entrance requirements:* For master's, GRE General Test. Additional exam requirements/recommendations for international students: Required—TOEFL. Electronic applications accepted. *Faculty research:* Transatlantic relations, European Union, German and European Studies.

Georgia State University, College of Arts and Sciences, Department of World Languages and Cultures, Program in Translation and Interpretation, Atlanta, GA 30302-3083. Offers interpretation (Certificate), including Spanish; translation (Certificate), including French, German, Spanish. *Program availability:* Part-time. *Entrance requirements:* For degree, entrance examination involving translating one passage from English to the target language and one passage from the target language to English, 3 letters of recommendation, resume/curriculum vitae, official transcripts. Additional exam requirements/recommendations for international students: Required—TOEFL (minimum score 79 iBT). Application fee: $50. Electronic applications accepted. *Expenses:* Tuition, state resident: full-time $7020. Tuition, nonresident: full-time $22,518. *Required fees:* $2128. Tuition and fees vary according to degree level and program. *Faculty research:* Romance linguistics and translation; theory and practice of translation; medical and legal interpretation. *Unit head:* Dr. Fernando Reati, Chair, 404-413-5984, Fax: 404-413-5982, E-mail: freati@gsu.edu. *Application contact:* Lita Malveaux, Administrative Academic Specialist, 404-413-5046, Fax: 404-413-5036, E-mail: lmalveaux@gsu.edu.
Website: http://wlc.gsu.edu/home/graduate/graduate-certificate/

Harvard University, Graduate School of Arts and Sciences, Department of Germanic Languages and Literatures, Cambridge, MA 02138. Offers German (PhD); Scandinavian (PhD). Terminal master's awarded for partial completion of doctoral program. *Degree requirements:* For doctorate, 2 foreign languages, thesis/dissertation, exams. *Entrance requirements:* For doctorate, GRE General Test, German writing sample. Additional exam requirements/recommendations for international students: Required—TOEFL.

Hofstra University, School of Education, Programs in Teacher Education, Hempstead, NY 11549. Offers bilingual education (MA); bilingual extension (Advanced Certificate), including education/speech language pathology, intensive teacher institute; business education (MS Ed); curriculum studies (MS Ed); early childhood and childhood education (MS Ed); early childhood education (MA, MS Ed); educational technology (Advanced Certificate); elementary education (MA, MS Ed), including science, technology, engineering, and mathematics (STEM) (MA); English education (MS Ed); family and consumer science (MS Ed); fine arts and music education (Advanced Certificate); fine arts education (MS Ed); foreign language and TESOL (MS Ed); foreign language education (MA, MS Ed), including Arabic (MS Ed), biology, chemistry, Chinese (MS Ed), earth science, French, German, Italian (MS Ed), Mandarin (MS Ed), physics, Russian, Spanish; foundations of education (Advanced Certificate), including grades 5-6, grades 7-9; languages other than English and teaching English as a second language

(MA); learning and teaching (Ed D), including applied linguistics, art education, arts and humanities, early childhood education, English education, human development, math education, math, science, and technology, multicultural education, physical education, science education, social studies education, special education; mathematics education (MA, MS Ed); music education (MA, MS Ed); science education (MA), including biology (MA, MS Ed), chemistry (MA, MS Ed), earth science (MA, MS Ed), physics (MA, MS Ed); secondary education (Advanced Certificate); social studies education (MA, MS Ed); teaching languages other than English and TESOL (MS Ed); technology for learning (MA); TESOL (MS Ed, Advanced Certificate); TESOL with specialization in STEM (MA); work based learning extension (Advanced Certificate). *Program availability:* Part-time, evening/weekend, blended/hybrid learning. *Students:* 119 full-time (83 women), 124 part-time (90 women); includes 54 minority (15 Black or African American, non-Hispanic/Latino; 9 Asian, non-Hispanic/Latino; 29 Hispanic/Latino; 1 Native Hawaiian or other Pacific Islander, non-Hispanic/Latino), 12 international. Average age 29. 205 applicants, 88% accepted, 93 enrolled. In 2017, 103 master's, 4 doctorates, 32 other advanced degrees awarded. *Degree requirements:* For master's, comprehensive exam, thesis (for some programs), exit project, student teaching, fieldwork, electronic portfolio, curriculum project, minimum GPA of 3.0; for doctorate, thesis/dissertation; for Advanced Certificate, 3 foreign languages, comprehensive exam (for some programs), thesis project. *Entrance requirements:* For master's, GRE, 2 letters of recommendation, portfolio, teacher certification (MA), interview, essay; for doctorate, GMAT, GRE, LSAT, or MAT; for Advanced Certificate, 2 letters of recommendation, essay, interview and/or portfolio, teaching certificate. Additional exam requirements/recommendations for international students: Required—TOEFL (minimum score 550 paper-based; 80 iBT). *Application deadline:* Applications are processed on a rolling basis. Application fee: $75. Electronic applications accepted. *Expenses:* Tuition: Full-time $1292. *Required fees:* $970. Tuition and fees vary according to program. *Financial support:* In 2017–18, 112 students received support, including 56 fellowships with full and partial tuition reimbursements available (averaging $4,998 per year), 2 research assistantships with full and partial tuition reimbursements available (averaging $8,753 per year); career-related internships or fieldwork, Federal Work-Study, institutionally sponsored loans, scholarships/grants, traineeships, tuition waivers (full and partial), and unspecified assistantships also available. Support available to part-time students. Financial award applicants required to submit FAFSA. *Faculty research:* Educational interventions that foster critical-thinking skills; teachers' attitudes about professional development; threats to teacher quality. *Unit head:* Dr. Eustace Thompson, Chairperson, 516-463-5749, Fax: 516-463-6275, E-mail: eustace.g.thompson@hofstra.edu. *Application contact:* Sunil Samuel, Assistant Vice President of Admissions, 516-463-4723, Fax: 516-463-4664, E-mail: graduateadmission@hofstra.edu.
Website: http://www.hofstra.edu/education/

Illinois State University, Graduate School, College of Arts and Sciences, Department of Foreign Languages, Literatures and Cultures, Normal, IL 61790. Offers French (MA); French and German (MA); French and Spanish (MA); German (MA); German and Spanish (MA); Spanish (MA). *Degree requirements:* For master's, variable foreign language requirement, comprehensive exam, 1 term of residency. *Entrance requirements:* For master's, GRE General Test, minimum GPA of 2.8 in last 60 hours of course work.

Indiana University Bloomington, University Graduate School, College of Arts and Sciences, Department of Germanic Studies, Bloomington, IN 47405-7000. Offers German philology and linguistics (PhD); German studies (MA, PhD), including German (MA), German literature and culture (MA), German literature and linguistics (MA); medieval German studies (PhD); teaching German (MAT). *Degree requirements:* For master's, one foreign language, project; for doctorate, one foreign language, comprehensive exam, thesis/dissertation. *Entrance requirements:* For master's, GRE General Test, BA in German or equivalent; for doctorate, GRE General Test, MA in German or equivalent. Additional exam requirements/recommendations for international students: Required—TOEFL. Electronic applications accepted. *Faculty research:* German and other European literature: medieval to modern/postmodern, German and culture studies, Germanic philology, literary theory, literature and the other arts.

Johns Hopkins University, Zanvyl Krieger School of Arts and Sciences, Department of German and Romance Languages and Literatures, Baltimore, MD 21218. Offers German (MA, PhD); romance languages (PhD), including French, Italian, Spanish. *Faculty:* 49 full-time (30 women), 1 part-time/adjunct (0 women). *Students:* 55 full-time (31 women); includes 4 minority (3 Hispanic/Latino; 1 Two or more races, non-Hispanic/Latino), 24 international. Average age 29. 39 applicants, 46% accepted, 8 enrolled. In 2017, 2 master's, 10 doctorates awarded. Terminal master's awarded for partial completion of doctoral program. *Degree requirements:* For master's, comprehensive exam; for doctorate, 2 foreign languages, comprehensive exam, thesis/dissertation. *Entrance requirements:* For doctorate, GRE General Test. Additional exam requirements/recommendations for international students: Required—TOEFL (minimum score 600 paper-based; 100 iBT), IELTS. *Application deadline:* For fall admission, 1/15 for domestic and international students. Application fee: $75. Electronic applications accepted. *Expenses:* Contact institution. *Financial support:* In 2017–18, 80 students received support, including 12 fellowships with full tuition reimbursements available (averaging $29,000 per year), 21 teaching assistantships with full tuition reimbursements available (averaging $29,000 per year); research assistantships, institutionally sponsored loans, and health care benefits also available. *Faculty research:* Nineteenth-century French prose and poetry, genetic theory and criticism; twentieth-century Latin American literature and film; medieval and Renaissance Italian literature; gender and queer theory in German literature; the ideology of Baroque and neo-Baroque aesthetics. *Unit head:* Dr. Derek Schilling, Chair, 410-516-4626, Fax: 410-516-5358, E-mail: dschill4@jhu.edu. *Application contact:* Kathy Loehmer, Senior Academic Coordinator, 410-516-7226, Fax: 410-516-5358, E-mail: kathy.grll@jhu.edu.
Website: http://grll.jhu.edu/

Kansas State University, Graduate School, College of Arts and Sciences, Department of Modern Languages, Manhattan, KS 66506. Offers literature (MA), including French, German, Spanish; second language acquisition (MA), including French, German, Spanish, teaching English as a foreign language. *Program availability:* Part-time, evening/weekend, blended/hybrid learning. *Degree requirements:* For master's, thesis optional. *Entrance requirements:* For master's, teaching certificate. Additional exam requirements/recommendations for international students: Required—TOEFL (minimum score 550 paper-based; 83 iBT), TOEFL (minimum speaking-portion score of 26). Electronic applications accepted. *Faculty research:* Second language acquisitions; U.S. Latino literature; Francophone literature; German, French, Spanish, and Spanish-American literature from the Middle Ages to the modern era; teaching English as a foreign language; linguistics.

Kent State University, College of Arts and Sciences, Department of Modern and Classical Language Studies, Kent, OH 44242-0001. Offers French (MA), including applied linguistics and pedagogy, literature; German (MA), including applied linguistics and pedagogy, literature; Latin (MA), including applied linguistics and pedagogy, literature; Spanish (MA), including applied linguistics and pedagogy, literature; translation (MA), including Arabic, French, German, Japanese, Russian, Spanish; translation studies (PhD); MA/MBA. *Program availability:* Part-time. *Faculty:* 21 full-time

(13 women), 5 part-time/adjunct (3 women). *Students:* 78 full-time (50 women), 20 part-time (13 women); includes 18 minority (3 Black or African American, non-Hispanic/Latino; 1 Asian, non-Hispanic/Latino; 9 Hispanic/Latino; 5 Two or more races, non-Hispanic/Latino), 44 international. Average age 31. 95 applicants, 55% accepted, 27 enrolled. In 2017, 30 master's awarded. *Degree requirements:* For master's, variable foreign language requirement, comprehensive exam (for some programs), thesis (for some programs); for doctorate, variable foreign language requirement, comprehensive exam, thesis/dissertation. *Entrance requirements:* For master's, transcripts, goal statement, 3 letters of recommendation, CD/MP3 with oral sample of first and second languages, writing sample of second language; for doctorate, transcripts; MA in translation, a foreign language, or similar field; proficiency in a foreign language; minimum GPA of 3.5 from MA; goal statement; 3 letters of recommendation; essay or writing sample. Additional exam requirements/recommendations for international students: Required—TOEFL (minimum score 550 paper-based, 79 iBT), Michigan English Language Assessment Battery (minimum score 77), IELTS (minimum score 6.5) or PTE (minimum score 58). *Application deadline:* For fall admission, 2/1 for domestic and international students. Applications are processed on a rolling basis. Application fee: $45 ($70 for international students). Electronic applications accepted. *Expenses:* Tuition, state resident: full-time $11,310; part-time $515 per credit hour. Tuition, nonresident: full-time $20,396; part-time $928 per credit hour. *International tuition:* $18,544 full-time. *Financial support:* Fellowships with full tuition reimbursements, teaching assistantships with full tuition reimbursements, and unspecified assistantships available. Financial award application deadline: 2/1. *Unit head:* Dr. Keiran Dunne, Professor of French Translation/Chair, 330-672-2150, E-mail: kdunne@kent.edu. *Application contact:* Said Shiyab, Professor of Translation Studies/Graduate Coordinator, 330-672-1864, E-mail: sshiyab@kent.edu.
Website: http://www.kent.edu/mcls/

McGill University, Faculty of Graduate and Postdoctoral Studies, Faculty of Arts, Department of German Studies, Montréal, QC H3A 2T5, Canada. Offers MA, PhD.

Memorial University of Newfoundland, School of Graduate Studies, Department of German and Russian, St. John's, NL A1C 5S7, Canada. Offers German language and literature (M Phil, MA). *Program availability:* Part-time. *Degree requirements:* For master's, one foreign language, thesis (for some programs), comprehensive exam (M Phil). *Entrance requirements:* For master's, honors degree (minimum 2nd class standing). Electronic applications accepted. *Faculty research:* German literature from the Middle Ages to the twentieth century, German studies.

Michigan State University, The Graduate School, College of Arts and Letters, Department of Linguistics and Germanic, Slavic, Asian, and African Languages, East Lansing, MI 48824. Offers German studies (MA, PhD); linguistics (MA, PhD); teaching English to speakers of other languages (MA). *Program availability:* Part-time, evening/weekend. *Entrance requirements:* For master's, GRE General Test, minimum GPA of 3.2 in last 2 undergraduate years, 2 years of college-level foreign language, 3 letters of recommendation, portfolio (German studies); for doctorate, GRE General Test, minimum graduate GPA of 3.5, 3 letters of recommendation, master's degree or sufficient graduate course work in linguistics or language of study, master's thesis or major research paper. Additional exam requirements/recommendations for international students: Required—TOEFL. Electronic applications accepted.

Middlebury College, Language Schools, German School, Middlebury, VT 05753-6002. Offers MA, DML. *Degree requirements:* For master's, one foreign language; for doctorate, 2 foreign languages, comprehensive exam, thesis/dissertation, residence abroad, teaching experience. *Entrance requirements:* For master's, placement exam, 3 letters of recommendation, transcripts, personal statement; for doctorate, 1st and 2nd language placement exams, 3 letters of recommendation, transcripts, personal statement, MA in German. *Application deadline:* Applications are processed on a rolling basis. Application fee: $75. Electronic applications accepted. *Expenses:* Contact institution. *Financial support:* Fellowships and scholarships/grants available. Financial award application deadline: 3/9; financial award applicants required to submit FAFSA. *Unit head:* Dr. Bettina Matthias, Director, 802-443-3527, Fax: 802-443-2075, E-mail: bmatthia@middlebury.edu. *Application contact:* Christina Ellison, Coordinator, 802-443-5203, Fax: 802-443-2075, E-mail: germanschool@middlebury.edu.
Website: http://www.middlebury.edu/ls/grad_programs/german

Middle Tennessee State University, College of Graduate Studies, College of Liberal Arts, Department of Foreign Languages and Literatures, Murfreesboro, TN 37132. Offers foreign languages (MAT), including French, German, Spanish. *Program availability:* Part-time, evening/weekend, online learning. *Degree requirements:* For master's, one foreign language, comprehensive exam, thesis optional. *Entrance requirements:* For master's, GRE. Additional exam requirements/recommendations for international students: Required—TOEFL (minimum score 525 paper-based; 71 iBT) or IELTS (minimum score 6). Electronic applications accepted.

Millersville University of Pennsylvania, College of Graduate Studies and Adult Learning, College of Arts, Humanities and Social Sciences, Department of Foreign Languages, Program in Languages and Cultures: German Option, Millersville, PA 17551-0302. Offers MA. *Program availability:* Part-time. *Faculty:* 3 full-time (1 woman). *Students:* 2 part-time (1 woman). Average age 36. 1 applicant, 100% accepted. In 2017, 2 master's awarded. *Degree requirements:* For master's, one foreign language, comprehensive exam (for some programs), thesis optional, exam, portfolio, or research project and presentation. *Entrance requirements:* For master's, ACTFL, OPI, OPIc and WPT, baccalaureate degree from regionally-accredited four-year college or university, 24 undergraduate credits in selected language. Additional exam requirements/recommendations for international students: Required—TOEFL (minimum score 80 iBT), IELTS (minimum score 6.5), PTE (minimum score 60). *Application deadline:* Applications are processed on a rolling basis. Application fee: $40. Electronic applications accepted. *Expenses:* $500 per credit resident tuition and fees; $750 per credit non-resident tuition and fees; $114.75 per credit general fee (maximum of 12 credits); technology fee $27 per credit (resident), $39 per credit (non-resident). *Financial support:* In 2017–18, 1 student received support. Unspecified assistantships available. Financial award application deadline: 3/15; financial award applicants required to submit FAFSA. *Faculty research:* Second language acquisition, teaching methodology. *Unit head:* Dr. Susanne J. Nimmrichter, Associate Professor/Program Contact, 717-871-7153, Fax: 717-871-7935, E-mail: susanne.nimmrichter@millersville.edu. *Application contact:* Dr. Victor S. DeSantis, Dean of College of Graduate Studies and Adult Learning/Associate Provost for Civic and Community Engagement, 717-871-7619, Fax: 717-871-7954, E-mail: victor.desantis@millersville.edu.
Website: http://www.millersville.edu/forlang/

New York University, Graduate School of Arts and Science, Department of German, New York, NY 10012-1019. Offers German studies and critical thought (MA, PhD). *Program availability:* Part-time. *Students:* Average age 32. 15 applicants, 20% accepted, 2 enrolled. In 2017, 1 master's, 2 doctorates awarded. Terminal master's awarded for partial completion of doctoral program. *Degree requirements:* For master's, one foreign language, thesis; for doctorate, 2 foreign languages, thesis/dissertation. *Entrance requirements:* For master's, GRE; for doctorate, GRE, sample of written work. Additional exam requirements/recommendations for international students: Required—TOEFL. *Application deadline:* For fall admission, 1/4 priority date for domestic students, 1/4 for international students. Application fee: $100. *Expenses: Tuition:* Full-time $41,352; part-time $19,968 per year. *Required fees:* $2496; $1628 per unit. $814 per term. Tuition and fees vary according to course load and program. *Financial support:* Fellowships, teaching assistantships, Federal Work-Study, institutionally sponsored loans, scholarships/grants, health care benefits, and unspecified assistantships available. Financial award application deadline: 1/4; financial award applicants required to submit FAFSA. *Faculty research:* Eighteenth- to twentieth-century literature, culture and critical thought, film and visual culture, philosophy, critical theory. *Unit head:* Leif Weatherby, Director of Graduate Studies, 212-998-8650, Fax: 212-995-4823, E-mail: german.dept@nyu.edu. *Application contact:* Lindsay O'Connor, Department Administrator, 212-998-8650, Fax: 212-995-4823, E-mail: german.dept@nyu.edu.
Website: http://www.nyu.edu/gsas/dept/german/

Northwestern University, The Graduate School, Judd A. and Marjorie Weinberg College of Arts and Sciences, Department of German, Evanston, IL 60208. Offers German literature and critical thought (PhD). Admissions and degrees offered through The Graduate School. *Degree requirements:* For doctorate, one foreign language, thesis/dissertation. *Entrance requirements:* For doctorate, GRE General Test. Additional exam requirements/recommendations for international students: Required—TOEFL. Electronic applications accepted. *Faculty research:* Eighteenth through twentieth century German literature, comparative literature, theory, philosophy, language pedagogy.

The Ohio State University, Graduate School, College of Arts and Sciences, Division of Arts and Humanities, Department of Germanic Languages and Literatures, Columbus, OH 43210. Offers MA, PhD. *Faculty:* 11. *Students:* 13 full-time (8 women). Average age 29. In 2017, 10 master's, 1 doctorate awarded. *Degree requirements:* For master's, one foreign language, thesis optional; for doctorate, 2 foreign languages, thesis/dissertation. *Entrance requirements:* For master's and doctorate, GRE General Test. Additional exam requirements/recommendations for international students: Required—TOEFL (minimum score 550 paper-based; 79 iBT), Michigan English Language Assessment Battery (minimum score 82); Recommended—IELTS (minimum score 7). *Application deadline:* For fall admission, 12/13 priority date for domestic students, 11/30 priority date for international students; for spring admission, 3/1 for domestic students, 2/1 for international students. Applications are processed on a rolling basis. Application fee: $60 ($70 for international students). Electronic applications accepted. *Financial support:* Fellowships, research assistantships, teaching assistantships, Federal Work-Study, and institutionally sponsored loans available. Support available to part-time students. *Faculty research:* German literature, Germanic philology, linguistics. *Unit head:* Dr. Robert C. Holub, Chair/Professor, 614-292-6985, E-mail: holub.5@osu.edu. *Application contact:* Graduate and Professional Admissions, 614-292-9444, Fax: 614-292-3895, E-mail: gpadmissions@osu.edu.
Website: http://germanic.osu.edu/

Penn State University Park, Graduate School, College of the Liberal Arts, Department of Germanic and Slavic Languages and Literatures, University Park, PA 16802. Offers German (MA, PhD). *Faculty research:* Literature, literary theory, culture, language pedagogy. *Unit head:* Dr. Susan Welch, Dean, 814-865-7691, Fax: 814-863-2085. *Application contact:* Lori Hawn, Director, Graduate Student Services, 814-865-1795, Fax: 814-863-4627, E-mail: l-gswww@lists.psu.edu.
Website: http://german.la.psu.edu/

Portland State University, Graduate Studies, College of Liberal Arts and Sciences, Department of World Languages and Literatures, Portland, OR 97207-0751. Offers French (MA); German (MA); Japanese (MA); Spanish (MA); world literature and language (MA). *Program availability:* Part-time. *Faculty:* 61 full-time (37 women), 26 part-time/adjunct (20 women). *Students:* 22 full-time (13 women), 11 part-time (5 women); includes 7 minority (1 Asian, non-Hispanic/Latino; 6 Hispanic/Latino), 8 international. Average age 30. 26 applicants, 73% accepted, 16 enrolled. In 2017, 9 master's awarded. *Degree requirements:* For master's, variable foreign language requirement, thesis (for some programs). *Entrance requirements:* For master's, ACTFL, BA in the major language, minimum GPA of 3.0 in all coursework. Additional exam requirements/recommendations for international students: Required—TOEFL (minimum score 550 paper-based; 80 iBT), IELTS (minimum score 6.5). *Application deadline:* For fall admission, 4/1 for domestic students, 3/1 for international students; for winter admission, 9/1 for domestic students, 7/1 for international students; for spring admission, 11/1 for domestic and international students. Applications are processed on a rolling basis. Application fee: $65. *Expenses:* Tuition, state resident: full-time $14,436; part-time $401 per credit. Tuition, nonresident: full-time $21,780; part-time $605 per credit. *Required fees:* $1380; $22 per credit. $119 per quarter. One-time fee: $325. Tuition and fees vary according to program. *Financial support:* In 2017–18, 22 teaching assistantships with full and partial tuition reimbursements (averaging $11,431 per year) were awarded; research assistantships, Federal Work-Study, scholarships/grants, and unspecified assistantships also available. Support available to part-time students. Financial award application deadline: 3/1; financial award applicants required to submit FAFSA. *Faculty research:* Foreign language pedagogy, applied and social linguistics, literary history and criticism. *Total annual research expenditures:* $522,357. *Unit head:* Dr. Gina Greco, Chair, 503-725-5287, E-mail: grecog@pdx.edu. *Application contact:* Kelli Martin, Graduate Admissions Coordinator, 503-725-3243, E-mail: kmarti@pdx.edu.
Website: http://www.pdx.edu/wll/

Princeton University, Graduate School, Department of German, Princeton, NJ 08544-1019. Offers PhD. *Degree requirements:* For doctorate, 2 foreign languages, thesis/dissertation. *Entrance requirements:* For doctorate, GRE General Test. Additional exam requirements/recommendations for international students: Required—TOEFL (minimum score 600 paper-based). Electronic applications accepted.

Purdue University, Graduate School, College of Liberal Arts, School of Languages and Cultures, West Lafayette, IN 47907. Offers French (MA, MAT, PhD), including French (MA, PhD), French education (MAT); German (MA, MAT, PhD), including German (MA, PhD), German education (MAT); Japanese pedagogy (MA); Spanish (MA, MAT, PhD), including Spanish (MA, PhD), Spanish education (MAT). *Faculty:* 44 full-time (22 women), 1 (woman) part-time/adjunct. *Students:* 37 full-time (18 women), 41 part-time (30 women); includes 9 minority (1 Asian, non-Hispanic/Latino; 8 Hispanic/Latino), 52 international. Average age 32. 49 applicants, 39% accepted, 14 enrolled. In 2017, 11 master's, 5 doctorates awarded. Terminal master's awarded for partial completion of doctoral program. *Degree requirements:* For master's, one foreign language; for doctorate, 2 foreign languages, thesis/dissertation. *Entrance requirements:* For master's, GRE General Test (minimum score 600, 160 for new scoring), two writing samples, one in English, one in language (French, German, Japanese, or Spanish); sample recording of English and language of study; for doctorate, GRE General Test (minimum score 600, 160 for new scoring), master's degree with minimum GPA of 3.5 or equivalent; two writing samples, one in English, one in language (French, German, Japanese, or Spanish); sample recording of English and language of study. Additional exam requirements/recommendations for international students: Required—TOEFL (minimum score 550 paper-based; 77 iBT); Recommended—TWE. *Application deadline:* For fall admission, 12/12 for domestic and international students; for spring admission, 10/1 for domestic and international students. Applications are processed on a rolling basis. Application fee: $60 ($75 for international students). Electronic

applications accepted. *Financial support:* In 2017–18, fellowships with tuition reimbursements (averaging $15,750 per year), teaching assistantships with tuition reimbursements (averaging $13,463 per year) were awarded. Support available to part-time students. Financial award applicants required to submit FAFSA. *Faculty research:* Linguistics, semiotics, literary criticism, pedagogy. *Unit head:* Jennifer M. William, Head, 765-494-3834, E-mail: jmwilliam@purdue.edu. *Application contact:* Joni L. Hipsher, Graduate Contact, 765-494-3841, E-mail: jlhipshe@purdue.edu.
Website: http://www.cla.purdue.edu/slc/main/

Queen's University at Kingston, School of Graduate Studies, Faculty of Arts and Sciences, Program in German, Kingston, ON K7L 3N6, Canada. Offers MA, PhD. *Program availability:* Part-time. *Degree requirements:* For master's, thesis optional; for doctorate, one foreign language, comprehensive exam, thesis/dissertation. *Entrance requirements:* For master's, 7 German courses, honors bachelor's degree in German; for doctorate, MA or equivalent in German. Additional exam requirements/recommendations for international students: Required—TOEFL. Electronic applications accepted. *Faculty research:* Goethe and Weimar classicism, Romanticism, nineteenth- and twentieth-century German literature.

Rider University, College of Education and Human Services, Teacher Certification Program, Lawrenceville, NJ 08648-3001. Offers bilingual education (Certificate); business education (Certificate); early childhood education (Certificate); elementary education (Certificate); English as a second language (Certificate); English education (Certificate); mathematics education (Certificate); science education (Certificate); secondary education (Certificate); social studies education (Certificate); world languages (Certificate), including French, German, Spanish. *Program availability:* Part-time, online learning. *Degree requirements:* For Certificate, internship, professional portfolio. *Entrance requirements:* For degree, PRAXIS, resume. Additional exam requirements/recommendations for international students: Required—TOEFL (minimum score 550 paper-based). Electronic applications accepted. *Faculty research:* Conceptual foundations for optimal development of creativity; creative theory, cognitive processes in mathematics learning, teacher collaboration.

Rutgers University–New Brunswick, Graduate School-New Brunswick, Program in German, Piscataway, NJ 08854-8097. Offers German (MAT, PhD); German literature (MA, PhD). *Program availability:* Part-time, evening/weekend. Terminal master's awarded for partial completion of doctoral program. *Degree requirements:* For master's, one foreign language, comprehensive exam, thesis or alternative; for doctorate, 2 foreign languages, comprehensive exam, thesis/dissertation. *Entrance requirements:* For master's and doctorate, GRE General Test. Additional exam requirements/recommendations for international students: Required—TOEFL. Electronic applications accepted. *Faculty research:* Literature and ideology; early German novella; narrative structures, mythology, psychology, and realist literature; German-American cultural history; literary theory and aesthetics; German film.

San Francisco State University, Division of Graduate Studies, College of Liberal and Creative Arts, Department of Modern Languages and Literatures, Program in German, San Francisco, CA 94132-1722. Offers MA. *Application deadline:* Applications are processed on a rolling basis. *Unit head:* Volker Langbehn, Program Coordinator, 415-338-7422, Fax: 415-338-6159, E-mail: langbehn@sfsu.edu. *Application contact:* Dr. Llona Vandergriff, Graduate Advisor, 415-338-1106, Fax: 415-338-6159, E-mail: vdgriff@sfsu.edu.
Website: http://german.sfsu.edu/

Stanford University, School of Humanities and Sciences, Department of German Studies, Stanford, CA 94305-2004. Offers MA, PhD. *Degree requirements:* For master's, one foreign language, oral exam; for doctorate, 2 foreign languages, thesis/dissertation, oral exam, qualifying paper and exam. *Entrance requirements:* For master's and doctorate, GRE General Test. Additional exam requirements/recommendations for international students: Required—TOEFL. Electronic applications accepted. *Expenses: Tuition:* Full-time $48,987; part-time $10,620 per quarter. One-time fee: $400. Tuition and fees vary according to program.

Tufts University, Graduate School of Arts and Sciences, Department of International Literary and Cultural Studies, Medford, MA 02155. Offers German (MA); German with teaching licensure (MA). *Program availability:* Part-time. *Students:* 2 applicants, 50% accepted. *Degree requirements:* For master's, one foreign language, oral and written exam. *Entrance requirements:* For master's, GRE General Test. Additional exam requirements/recommendations for international students: Required—TOEFL (minimum score 550 paper-based; 80 iBT), IELTS (minimum score 6.5). *Application deadline:* For fall admission, 3/1 for domestic and international students; for spring admission, 10/15 for domestic and international students. Applications are processed on a rolling basis. Application fee: $85. Electronic applications accepted. *Expenses:* Contact institution. *Financial support:* Federal Work-Study, scholarships/grants, and tuition waivers (full and partial) available. Support available to part-time students. Financial award application deadline: 1/15. *Unit head:* Dr. Markus Wilczek, Graduate Program Director, 617-627-2576. *Application contact:* Office of Graduate Admissions, 617-627-3395, E-mail: gradadmissions@tufts.edu.
Website: http://ase.tufts.edu/ilcs/

Université de Montréal, Faculty of Arts and Sciences, Department of Literatures and Modern Languages, Program in German Studies, Montréal, QC H3C 3J7, Canada. Offers MA. *Degree requirements:* For master's, 2 foreign languages, thesis. Electronic applications accepted.

University at Buffalo, the State University of New York, Graduate School, Graduate School of Education, Department of Learning and Instruction, Buffalo, NY 14260. Offers biology education (Ed M, Certificate); chemistry education (Ed M, Certificate); childhood education (Ed M); childhood education with bilingual extension (Ed M); college teaching (Advanced Certificate); curriculum, instruction and the science of learning (PhD); early childhood education (Ed M); early childhood education with bilingual extension (Ed M); earth science education (Ed M, Certificate); education and technology (Ed M); education studies (Ed M); educational technology and new literacies (Certificate); educational technology and new literacies (Advanced Certificate); elementary education (Ed D); English education (Ed M, Certificate); English education studies (Ed M); English for speakers of other languages (Ed M); foreign and second language education (PhD); French education (Ed M, Certificate); German education (Ed M, Certificate); gifted education (Certificate); Latin education (Ed M, Certificate); literacy education studies (Ed M); literacy specialist (Ed M); literacy teaching and learning (Certificate); mathematics education (Ed M, Certificate); music education (Ed M, Certificate); music education studies (Ed M); music learning theory (Advanced Certificate); online education (Advanced Certificate); physics education (Ed M, Certificate); science and the public (Ed M); social studies education (Ed M, Certificate); Spanish education (Ed M, Certificate); special education (PhD); teaching English to speakers of other languages (Ed M). *Program availability:* Part-time, evening/weekend, 100% online. *Faculty:* 26 full-time (19 women), 74 part-time/adjunct (52 women). *Students:* 172 full-time (122 women), 325 part-time (226 women); includes 44 minority (25 Black or African American, non-Hispanic/Latino; 5 American Indian or Alaska Native, non-Hispanic/Latino; 14 Asian, non-Hispanic/Latino), 57 international. Average age 33. 316 applicants, 78% accepted, 174 enrolled. In 2017, 109 master's, 34 doctorates, 15 other advanced degrees awarded. *Degree requirements:* For master's, comprehensive exam; for doctorate, thesis/dissertation, research analysis exam, research experience. *Entrance requirements:* For master's, letters of reference; for doctorate, GRE General Test or MAT, interview, writing sample, letters of recommendation. Additional exam requirements/recommendations for international students: Required—TOEFL (minimum score 600 paper-based; 96 iBT). *Application deadline:* For fall admission, 2/1 priority date for domestic and international students; for spring admission, 11/15 priority date for domestic students, 10/1 for international students. Applications are processed on a rolling basis. Application fee: $50. Electronic applications accepted. *Financial support:* In 2017–18, 42 fellowships (averaging $5,181 per year), 44 research assistantships with tuition reimbursements (averaging $10,908 per year) were awarded; teaching assistantships, career-related internships or fieldwork, Federal Work-Study, institutionally sponsored loans, scholarships/grants, tuition waivers (full and partial), and unspecified assistantships also available. Financial award application deadline: 2/28; financial award applicants required to submit FAFSA. *Faculty research:* Science assessment, foreign language teaching and learning, early learning, new literacies, gender and education. *Total annual research expenditures:* $413,233. *Unit head:* Dr. David Bruce, Chair, 716-645-4069, Fax: 716-645-3161, E-mail: gse-info@buffalo.edu. *Application contact:* Luann Zak, Admissions Assistant, 716-645-2110, Fax: 716-645-7937, E-mail: luannzak@buffalo.edu.
Website: http://gse.buffalo.edu/lai

The University of Alabama, Graduate School, College of Arts and Sciences, Department of Modern Languages and Classics, Tuscaloosa, AL 35487. Offers French (MA, PhD); French and Spanish (PhD); German (MA); Romance languages (MA, PhD); Spanish (MA, PhD). *Program availability:* Part-time. *Faculty:* 30 full-time (18 women). *Students:* 45 full-time (27 women), 4 part-time (1 woman); includes 11 minority (5 Black or African American, non-Hispanic/Latino; 1 Asian, non-Hispanic/Latino; 3 Hispanic/Latino; 2 Two or more races, non-Hispanic/Latino), 14 international. Average age 32. 26 applicants, 88% accepted, 11 enrolled. In 2017, 18 master's awarded. *Degree requirements:* For master's, comprehensive exam, thesis optional; for doctorate, one foreign language, thesis/dissertation, preliminary exam. *Entrance requirements:* For master's and doctorate, minimum GPA of 3.0, writing sample. *Application deadline:* For fall admission, 7/6 priority date for domestic students, 1/15 priority date for international students; for spring admission, 12/5 priority date for domestic students, 6/1 priority date for international students. Applications are processed on a rolling basis. Application fee: $50 ($60 for international students). Electronic applications accepted. *Financial support:* In 2017–18, 40 students received support, including research assistantships with full tuition reimbursements available (averaging $10,291 per year), teaching assistantships with full tuition reimbursements available (averaging $10,291 per year); fellowships, career-related internships or fieldwork, Federal Work-Study, institutionally sponsored loans, and scholarships/grants also available. Financial award application deadline: 7/14. *Faculty research:* Non-English literature, linguistics, culture, film. *Unit head:* Dr. Douglas Lightfoot, Department Chair, 205-348-5059, E-mail: lightfoot@ua.edu. *Application contact:* Michael Picone, Graduate Director, 205-348-8473, E-mail: picone@ua.edu.
Website: http://bama.ua.edu/~mlc

University of Alberta, Faculty of Graduate Studies and Research, Department of Modern Languages and Cultural Studies, Edmonton, AB T6G 2E1, Canada. Offers applied linguistics (Germanic, Romance, Slavic) (MA); French language, literatures and linguistics (PhD); French language, literatures, and linguistics (MA); Germanic languages, literatures and linguistics (PhD); Germanic languages, literatures, and linguistics (MA); Italian studies (MA); Slavic languages and literatures (Russian, Ukrainian) (MA, PhD); Slavic linguistics (Russian, Ukrainian) (MA, PhD); Spanish and Latin American studies (MA, PhD); Ukrainian folklore (MA, PhD). *Program availability:* Part-time. *Degree requirements:* For master's, one foreign language, thesis; for doctorate, 2 foreign languages, comprehensive exam, thesis/dissertation. *Entrance requirements:* For master's and doctorate, 1 language other than English. Additional exam requirements/recommendations for international students: Required—Michigan English Language Assessment Battery or TOEFL (minimum score 550 paper-based). Electronic applications accepted. *Faculty research:* Russian/Ukrainian studies; German studies; contemporary Latin American, French and Francophone studies; Italian studies.

The University of Arizona, College of Humanities, Department of German Studies, Tucson, AZ 85721. Offers German (MA); transcultural German (PhD). *Degree requirements:* For master's, one foreign language, comprehensive exam, oral exam; for doctorate, 2 foreign languages, comprehensive exam, thesis/dissertation, oral exam, oral defense. *Entrance requirements:* For master's, minimum major GPA of 3.3, 3 letters of recommendation, audio sample, curriculum vitae. Additional exam requirements/recommendations for international students: Required—TOEFL (minimum score 550 paper-based; 79 iBT). Electronic applications accepted. *Faculty research:* Literature, language, and foreign language pedagogy; computer-assisted text analysis.

University of Arkansas, Graduate School, J. William Fulbright College of Arts and Sciences, Department of World Languages, Literatures and Cultures, Program in German, Fayetteville, AR 72701. Offers MA. In 2017, 12 master's awarded. *Degree requirements:* For master's, variable foreign language requirement. *Application deadline:* For fall admission, 8/1 for domestic students, 4/1 for international students; for spring admission, 12/1 for domestic students, 10/1 for international students; for summer admission, 4/15 for domestic students, 3/1 for international students. Applications are processed on a rolling basis. Application fee: $60. Electronic applications accepted. *Expenses:* Tuition, state resident: full-time $3782. Tuition, nonresident: full-time $10,238. *Financial support:* In 2017–18, 5 teaching assistantships were awarded; fellowships, research assistantships, career-related internships or fieldwork, and Federal Work-Study also available. Support available to part-time students. Financial award application deadline: 4/1; financial award applicants required to submit FAFSA. *Unit head:* Dr. Steven Bell, Department Chair, 479-575-2951, Fax: 479-575-6795, E-mail: sbell@uark.edu.
Website: https://fulbright.uark.edu/departments/world-languages/

The University of British Columbia, Faculty of Arts and Faculty of Graduate Studies, Department of Central, Eastern and Northern European Studies, Vancouver, BC V6T 1Z1, Canada. Offers Germanic studies (MA, PhD). *Program availability:* Part-time. *Degree requirements:* For master's, one foreign language, thesis optional, exam; for doctorate, one foreign language, comprehensive exam, thesis/dissertation. *Entrance requirements:* For master's, BA in German; for doctorate, MA in German. Additional exam requirements/recommendations for international students: Required—TOEFL. Electronic applications accepted. *Expenses:* Contact institution. *Faculty research:* Second language acquisition, media theory, performance theory, gender studies, cultural studies.

University of Calgary, Faculty of Graduate Studies, Faculty of Arts, Department of Linguistics, Languages and Culture, Calgary, AB T2N 1N4, Canada. Offers German (MA); linguistics (MA, PhD). *Degree requirements:* For master's, one foreign language, thesis; for doctorate, one foreign language, comprehensive exam, thesis/dissertation. *Entrance requirements:* For doctorate, MA. Additional exam requirements/recommendations for international students: Required—TOEFL (minimum score 560 paper-based). Electronic applications accepted. *Faculty research:* Theoretical linguistics, historical linguistics, language acquisition, Amerindian.

University of California, Berkeley, Graduate Division, College of Letters and Science, Department of German, Berkeley, CA 94720-1500. Offers PhD. *Degree requirements:* For doctorate, 2 foreign languages, thesis/dissertation, qualifying exam. *Entrance requirements:* For doctorate, GRE General Test, minimum GPA of 3.0, writing sample, 3 letters of recommendation. Electronic applications accepted. *Faculty research:* German literature/culture, film, Germanic linguistics, second-language acquisition.

University of California, Davis, Graduate Studies, Program in German, Davis, CA 95616. Offers MA, PhD. Terminal master's awarded for partial completion of doctoral program. *Degree requirements:* For master's, comprehensive exam (for some programs), thesis (for some programs); for doctorate, thesis/dissertation. *Entrance requirements:* For master's, GRE; for doctorate, GRE, master's degree or equivalent. Additional exam requirements/recommendations for international students: Required—TOEFL (minimum score 550 paper-based). Electronic applications accepted. *Faculty research:* Sixteenth to twentieth century medieval literature, critical theory, women's studies.

University of California, Irvine, School of Humanities, Department of European Languages and Studies, Irvine, CA 92697. Offers French (MA, PhD); German (MA, PhD). *Students:* 8 full-time (4 women); includes 1 minority (Hispanic/Latino), 3 international. Average age 29. 12 applicants, 42% accepted, 2 enrolled. In 2017, 2 master's awarded. *Entrance requirements:* For master's and doctorate, GRE General Test, minimum GPA of 3.0. Additional exam requirements/recommendations for international students: Required—TOEFL (minimum score 550 paper-based). *Application deadline:* For fall admission, 1/15 for domestic and international students. Applications are processed on a rolling basis. Application fee: $105 ($125 for international students). Electronic applications accepted. *Financial support:* Fellowships, research assistantships with full tuition reimbursements, teaching assistantships, institutionally sponsored loans, traineeships, health care benefits, and unspecified assistantships available. Financial award application deadline: 3/1; financial award applicants required to submit FAFSA. *Faculty research:* Montaigne, psychoanalysis, feminism and the problem of repression, aesthetics of nationalism and the limits of culture. *Unit head:* Prof. David Pan, Chair, 949-824-6406, Fax: 949-824-6416, E-mail: dtpan@uci.edu. *Application contact:* Bindya Baliga, Graduate Program Coordinator, 949-824-7968, Fax: 949-824-6416, E-mail: bbaliga@uci.edu.
Website: http://www.humanities.uci.edu/els/

University of California, Los Angeles, Graduate Division, College of Letters and Science, Department of Germanic Languages, Program in Germanic Languages, Los Angeles, CA 90095. Offers MA, PhD. Terminal master's awarded for partial completion of doctoral program. *Degree requirements:* For master's, one foreign language, comprehensive exam or thesis; for doctorate, 2 foreign languages, thesis/dissertation, oral and written qualifying exams. *Entrance requirements:* For master's, GRE General Test, bachelor's degree; minimum undergraduate GPA of 3.0 (or its equivalent if letter grade system not used); for doctorate, GRE General Test, master's degree; minimum undergraduate GPA of 3.0 (or its equivalent if letter grade system not used) Additional exam requirements/recommendations for international students: Required—TOEFL. Electronic applications accepted.

University of Chicago, Division of the Humanities, Department of Germanic Studies, Chicago, IL 60637. Offers PhD. *Students:* 21 full-time (9 women). 19 applicants, 32% accepted, 3 enrolled. Terminal master's awarded for partial completion of doctoral program. *Degree requirements:* For doctorate, 2 foreign languages, comprehensive exam, thesis/dissertation. *Entrance requirements:* For doctorate, GRE General Test, 15-20 page writing sample, statement of purpose, 3 letters of recommendation, transcripts for all previous degrees and institutions attended. Additional exam requirements/recommendations for international students: Required—TOEFL (minimum score 104 iBT), IELTS (minimum score 7). *Application deadline:* For fall admission, 12/15 for domestic and international students. Application fee: $90. Electronic applications accepted. *Financial support:* In 2017–18, fellowships with full tuition reimbursements (averaging $27,000 per year) were awarded; teaching assistantships with full tuition reimbursements, Federal Work-Study, institutionally sponsored loans, scholarships/grants, traineeships, and health care benefits also available. Financial award application deadline: 12/15. *Unit head:* Dr. Eric Santner, Chair, 773-834-8494, E-mail: german-department@uchicago.edu. *Application contact:* Michael Beetley, Assistant Dean of Students, Admissions and Fellowships, 773-702-1552, Fax: 773-834-9148, E-mail: humanitiesadmissions@uchicago.edu.
Website: http://german.uchicago.edu/

University of Chicago, Division of the Humanities, Master of Arts Program in the Humanities, Chicago, IL 60637. Offers art history (MA); cinema and media studies (MA); classic languages (MA); comparative literature (MA); creative writing (MA); cultural policy studies (MA); digital humanities (MA); East Asian languages and civilizations (MA); English language and literature (MA); gender and sexuality studies (MA); Germanic studies (MA); linguistics (MA); music (MA); near Eastern languages and civilizations (MA); philosophy (MA); poetics (MA); race, politics and culture (MA); Romance languages and literatures (MA); Slavic languages and literatures (MA); South Asian languages and civilizations (MA); theater and performance studies (MA). *Students:* 95 full-time (50 women), 6 part-time (4 women); includes 22 minority (1 Black or African American, non-Hispanic/Latino; 10 Asian, non-Hispanic/Latino; 11 Hispanic/Latino), 19 international. Average age 26. 708 applicants, 75% accepted, 101 enrolled. In 2017, 91 master's awarded. *Degree requirements:* For master's, thesis. *Entrance requirements:* For master's, GRE General Test, 10-15 page writing sample, statement of purpose, 3 letters of recommendation, transcripts for all previous degrees and institutions attended. Additional exam requirements/recommendations for international students: Required—TOEFL (minimum score 104 iBT), IELTS (minimum score 7). *Application deadline:* For fall admission, 1/3 priority date for domestic and international students. Application fee: $90. Electronic applications accepted. *Expenses:* Contact institution. *Financial support:* In 2017–18, fellowships with partial tuition reimbursements (averaging $12,000 per year) were awarded; Federal Work-Study, institutionally sponsored loans, scholarships/grants, and tuition waivers (partial) also available. Financial award application deadline: 4/30. *Unit head:* Thomas Christensen, Director, 773-834-1201, Fax: 773-834-7526, E-mail: ma-humanities@uchicago.edu. *Application contact:* Michael Beetley, Assistant Dean of Students for Admissions, 773-834-1552, E-mail: humanitiesadmissions@uchicago.edu.
Website: http://maph.uchicago.edu/

University of Cincinnati, Graduate School, McMicken College of Arts and Sciences, Department of German Studies, Cincinnati, OH 45221. Offers MA, PhD. *Program availability:* Part-time. Terminal master's awarded for partial completion of doctoral program. *Degree requirements:* For master's, one foreign language, thesis or alternative; for doctorate, 3 foreign languages, thesis/dissertation. *Entrance requirements:* For master's, GRE General Test; for doctorate, GRE General Test, MA in German or equivalent. Additional exam requirements/recommendations for international students: Required—TOEFL (minimum score 560 paper-based). Electronic applications accepted. *Expenses:* Tuition, area resident: Full-time $14,468. Tuition, state resident: full-time $14,968; part-time $754 per credit hour. Tuition, nonresident: full-time $24,210; part-time $1311 per credit hour. *International tuition:* $26,460 full-time. *Required fees:* $3958; $84 per credit hour. One-time fee: $85 full-time. Tuition and fees vary according to course load, degree level and program. *Faculty research:* German literary culture, language and linguistics, medieval and early modern, German-Jewish literature, 20th and 21st century German literature and film.

University of Colorado Boulder, Graduate School, College of Arts and Sciences, Department of Germanic and Slavic Languages and Literatures, Boulder, CO 80309. Offers MA. *Faculty:* 11 full-time (5 women). *Students:* 18 full-time (11 women); includes 2 minority (1 Asian, non-Hispanic/Latino; 1 Hispanic/Latino), 7 international. Average age 30. 10 applicants, 40% accepted, 3 enrolled. In 2017, 5 master's awarded. Terminal master's awarded for partial completion of doctoral program. *Degree requirements:* For master's, 2 foreign languages, comprehensive exam, thesis or alternative. *Entrance requirements:* For master's, minimum undergraduate GPA of 2.75. *Application deadline:* For fall admission, 1/10 for domestic students; for spring admission, 1/10 for domestic students. Application fee: $60 ($80 for international students). Electronic applications accepted. Application fee is waived when completed online. *Financial support:* In 2017–18, 70 students received support, including 24 fellowships (averaging $2,447 per year), 17 teaching assistantships with full and partial tuition reimbursements available (averaging $34,919 per year); institutionally sponsored loans, scholarships/grants, health care benefits, and unspecified assistantships also available. Financial award application deadline: 2/15; financial award applicants required to submit FAFSA. *Faculty research:* German language/literature, literary criticism, comparative literature, cultural history, culture. *Total annual research expenditures:* $3.6 million. *Application contact:* E-mail: gsll@colorado.edu.
Website: http://gsll.colorado.edu/

University of Delaware, College of Arts and Sciences, Department of Foreign Languages and Literatures, Newark, DE 19716. Offers foreign languages and literatures (MA), including French, German, Spanish; foreign languages pedagogy (MA), including French, German, Spanish; technical Chinese translation (MA). *Degree requirements:* For master's, one foreign language, comprehensive exam, thesis optional. *Entrance requirements:* For master's, GRE General Test, letters of recommendation, writing sample. Additional exam requirements/recommendations for international students: Required—TOEFL. Electronic applications accepted. *Faculty research:* Medieval to Modern French and Spanish literature, twentieth-century German, French, Spanish literature by women, computer-assisted instruction.

University of Florida, Graduate School, College of Liberal Arts and Sciences, Department of Languages, Literatures and Cultures, Gainesville, FL 32611. Offers French and Francophone studies (MA, PhD); German (MA, PhD), including women's and gender studies (PhD). *Degree requirements:* For master's, comprehensive exam, thesis optional; for doctorate, one foreign language, comprehensive exam, thesis/dissertation. *Entrance requirements:* For master's and doctorate, GRE General Test, minimum GPA of 3.0. Additional exam requirements/recommendations for international students: Required—TOEFL (minimum score 550 paper-based; 80 iBT), IELTS (minimum score 6). Electronic applications accepted. *Faculty research:* Medieval epic, romance, and allegory; Renaissance and Baroque poetry; the eighteenth-century novel; nineteenth-century prose, poetry, and poetics; the twentieth-century novel, theater, and poetry; the literatures of the Francophone world; French and Francophone film; the literatures in Breton and Occitan; criticism and critical theory; applied linguistics; the history of French; phonology; sociolinguistics; the structure of French; French and Haitian Creole linguistics.

University of Georgia, Franklin College of Arts and Sciences, Department of Germanic and Slavic Studies, Athens, GA 30602. Offers German (MA). *Degree requirements:* For master's, one foreign language, thesis. *Entrance requirements:* For master's, GRE General Test. Electronic applications accepted.

University of Illinois at Chicago, College of Liberal Arts and Sciences, School of Literatures, Cultural Studies and Linguistics, Department of Germanic Studies, Chicago, IL 60607-7128. Offers MA, PhD. PhD offered jointly with University of Illinois at Urbana–Champaign. *Program availability:* Part-time. Terminal master's awarded for partial completion of doctoral program. *Degree requirements:* For master's, thesis optional, exam; for doctorate, 2 foreign languages, thesis/dissertation. *Entrance requirements:* For master's and doctorate, GRE General Test, minimum GPA of 2.75. Additional exam requirements/recommendations for international students: Required—TOEFL. Electronic applications accepted. *Faculty research:* German literature.

University of Illinois at Urbana–Champaign, Graduate College, College of Liberal Arts and Sciences, School of Literatures, Cultures and Linguistics, Department of Germanic Languages and Literatures, Champaign, IL 61820. Offers German (MA, PhD).

University of Kentucky, Graduate School, College of Arts and Sciences, Program in German, Lexington, KY 40506-0032. Offers MA. *Degree requirements:* For master's, one foreign language, comprehensive exam, thesis optional. *Entrance requirements:* For master's, GRE General Test, minimum undergraduate GPA of 2.75. Additional exam requirements/recommendations for international students: Required—TOEFL (minimum score 550 paper-based). Electronic applications accepted. *Faculty research:* Medieval studies, literature from Enlightenment to present, literary theory, intellectual history, gender studies.

University of Lethbridge, School of Graduate Studies, Lethbridge, AB T1K 3M4, Canada. Offers addictions counseling (M Sc); agricultural biotechnology (M Sc); agricultural studies (M Sc, MA); anthropology (MA); archaeology (M Sc, MA); art (MA, MFA); biochemistry (M Sc); biological sciences (M Sc); biomolecular science (PhD); biosystems and biodiversity (PhD); Canadian studies (MA); chemistry (M Sc); computer science (M Sc); computer science and geographical information science (M Sc); counseling (MC); counseling psychology (M Ed); dramatic arts (MA); earth, space, and physical science (PhD); economics (MA); education (MA, PhD); educational leadership (M Ed); English (MA); environmental science (M Sc); evolution and behavior (PhD); exercise science (M Sc); French (MA); French/German (MA); French/Spanish (MA); general education (M Ed); geography (M Sc, MA); German (MA); health sciences (M Sc); individualized multidisciplinary (M Sc, MA); kinesiology (M Sc, MA); management (M Sc), including accounting, finance, human resource management and labor relations, information systems, international management, marketing, policy and strategy; mathematics (M Sc); music (M Mus, MA); Native American studies (MA); neuroscience (M Sc, PhD); new media (MA, MFA); nursing (M Sc, MN); philosophy (MA); physics (M Sc); political science (MA); psychology (M Sc, MA); religious studies (MA); sociology (MA); theatre and dramatic arts (MFA); theoretical and computational science (PhD); urban and regional studies (MA); women and gender studies (MA). *Program availability:* Part-time, evening/weekend. *Degree requirements:* For master's, thesis (for some programs); for doctorate, comprehensive exam, thesis/dissertation. *Entrance requirements:* For master's, GMAT (for M Sc in management), bachelor's degree in related field, minimum GPA of 3.0 during previous 20 graded semester courses, 2 years' teaching or related experience (M Ed); for doctorate, master's degree, minimum graduate GPA of 3.5. Additional exam requirements/recommendations for international students: Required—TOEFL (minimum score 580 paper-based; 93 iBT). Electronic applications accepted. *Faculty research:* Movement and brain plasticity, gibberellin physiology, photosynthesis, carbon cycling, molecular properties of main-group ring components.

German

The University of Manchester, School of Languages, Linguistics and Cultures, Manchester, United Kingdom. Offers Arab world studies (PhD); Chinese studies (M Phil, PhD); East Asian studies (M Phil, PhD); English language (PhD); French studies (M Phil, PhD); German studies (M Phil, PhD); interpreting studies (PhD); Italian studies (M Phil, PhD); Japanese studies (M Phil, PhD); Latin American cultural studies (M Phil, PhD); linguistics (M Phil, PhD); Middle Eastern studies (M Phil, PhD); Polish studies (M Phil, PhD); Portuguese studies (M Phil, PhD); Russian studies (M Phil, PhD); Spanish studies (M Phil, PhD); translation and intercultural studies (M Phil, PhD).

University of Manitoba, Faculty of Graduate Studies, Faculty of Arts, Department of German and Slavic Studies, Winnipeg, MB R3T 2N2, Canada. Offers German language and literature (MA); Slavic languages and literatures (MA). *Degree requirements:* For master's, one foreign language, thesis or alternative.

University of Maryland, College Park, Academic Affairs, College of Arts and Humanities, School of Languages, Literatures, and Cultures, Department of Germanic Studies, College Park, MD 20742. Offers Germanic language and literature (MA, PhD). *Degree requirements:* For master's, one foreign language, thesis optional, exams; for doctorate, 2 foreign languages, comprehensive exam, thesis/dissertation, reading exam, oral defense. *Entrance requirements:* For master's, writing sample, 3 letters of recommendation, interview; for doctorate, MA in German or related discipline. Additional exam requirements/recommendations for international students: Required—TOEFL. Electronic applications accepted. *Faculty research:* Language pedagogy, Germanic philology, medieval culture.

University of Massachusetts Amherst, Graduate School, College of Humanities and Fine Arts, Department of Languages, Literatures, and Cultures, Programs in German and Scandinavian Studies, Amherst, MA 01003. Offers MA, PhD. *Program availability:* Part-time. Terminal master's awarded for partial completion of doctoral program. *Degree requirements:* For master's, thesis or alternative; for doctorate, one foreign language, comprehensive exam, thesis/dissertation. *Entrance requirements:* For master's and doctorate, writing sample in English and German. Additional exam requirements/recommendations for international students: Required—TOEFL (minimum score 550 paper-based; 80 iBT), IELTS (minimum score 6.5). Electronic applications accepted.

University of Michigan, Rackham Graduate School, College of Literature, Science, and the Arts, Department of Germanic Languages and Literatures, Ann Arbor, MI 48109. Offers German (AM, PhD); German studies (Certificate). *Faculty:* 13 full-time (5 women), 3 part-time/adjunct (2 women). *Students:* 19 full-time (14 women); includes 2 minority (1 Black or African American, non-Hispanic/Latino; 1 Two or more races, non-Hispanic/Latino), 7 international. Average age 30. 21 applicants, 38% accepted, 3 enrolled. In 2017, 4 doctorates awarded. *Degree requirements:* For doctorate, one foreign language, comprehensive exam, thesis/dissertation, oral defense of dissertation, preliminary exam. *Entrance requirements:* For doctorate, GRE General Test. Additional exam requirements/recommendations for international students: Required—TOEFL (minimum score 560 paper-based). *Application deadline:* For fall and winter admission, 1/10 priority date for domestic and international students. Application fee: $75 ($90 for international students). Electronic applications accepted. *Expenses:* Tuition, state resident: full-time $22,368; part-time $1201 per credit hour. Tuition, nonresident: full-time $45,156; part-time $2467 per credit hour. *Required fees:* $376 per term. Tuition and fees vary according to course load, degree level and program. *Financial support:* In 2017–18, 16 students received support, including 12 fellowships with full tuition reimbursements available (averaging $21,500 per year), 19 teaching assistantships with full tuition reimbursements available (averaging $20,400 per year); scholarships/grants, health care benefits, and tuition waivers (full) also available. *Faculty research:* German history, German literature, literary theory, film, political and social theory. *Unit head:* Prof. Andreas Gailus, Chair, 734-764-8018, Fax: 734-763-6557, E-mail: gailus@umich.edu. *Application contact:* Jennifer Lucas, Student Services Coordinator, 734-936-0150, Fax: 734-763-6557, E-mail: jenpatri@umich.edu.
Website: http://www.lsa.umich.edu/german

University of Minnesota, Twin Cities Campus, Graduate School, College of Liberal Arts, Department of German, Scandinavian, and Dutch, Minneapolis, MN 55455. Offers Germanic studies (MA, PhD), including German, Germanic medieval studies, Scandinavian studies (MA). *Program availability:* Part-time. Terminal master's awarded for partial completion of doctoral program. *Degree requirements:* For doctorate, 2 foreign languages, thesis/dissertation. *Entrance requirements:* For master's, GRE General Test, BA in German, Scandinavian, or equivalent; for doctorate, MA in German, Scandinavian, or equivalent. Additional exam requirements/recommendations for international students: Required—TOEFL (minimum score 550 paper-based; 79 iBT). Electronic applications accepted. *Faculty research:* Cultural studies, literary theory, feminist criticism, film, Germanic medieval studies.

University of Missouri, Office of Research and Graduate Studies, College of Arts and Science, Department of German and Russian Studies, Columbia, MO 65211. Offers MA. *Entrance requirements:* For master's, GRE General Test, minimum GPA of 3.0. Additional exam requirements/recommendations for international students: Required—TOEFL (minimum score 500 paper-based; 61 iBT). Electronic applications accepted. *Faculty research:* German and Russian cultural studies including literature, film, media studies, philosophy, and the history of science.

University of Montana, Graduate School, College of Humanities and Sciences, Department of Modern and Classical Languages and Literatures, Missoula, MT 59812. Offers French (MA); German (MA); Spanish (MA). *Degree requirements:* For master's, one foreign language. *Entrance requirements:* For master's, GRE General Test. Additional exam requirements/recommendations for international students: Required—TOEFL.

University of Nebraska–Lincoln, Graduate College, College of Arts and Sciences, Department of Modern Languages and Literatures, Lincoln, NE 68588. Offers French (MA, PhD); German (MA, PhD); Spanish (MA, PhD). *Degree requirements:* For master's, thesis optional; for doctorate, comprehensive exam, thesis/dissertation. *Entrance requirements:* For master's and doctorate, writing sample in target language. Additional exam requirements/recommendations for international students: Required—TOEFL (minimum score 550 paper-based). Electronic applications accepted. *Faculty research:* French, German, and Spanish language, literature, and culture.

University of Nevada, Reno, Graduate School, College of Liberal Arts, Department of Foreign Languages and Literatures, Reno, NV 89557. Offers French (MA); German (MA); Spanish (MA). *Degree requirements:* For master's, one foreign language, thesis optional. *Entrance requirements:* For master's, GRE General Test, minimum GPA of 2.75. Additional exam requirements/recommendations for international students: Required—TOEFL (minimum score 500 paper-based; 61 iBT), IELTS (minimum score 6). *Faculty research:* Thirteenth century mysticism, contemporary Spanish and Latin American poetry and theater, French interrelation between narration and photography, exile literature and Holocaust.

University of New Mexico, Graduate Studies, College of Arts and Sciences, Program in Foreign Languages and Literatures, Albuquerque, NM 87131-2039. Offers comparative literature and cultural studies (MA); French (MA); French studies (PhD); German studies (MA). *Program availability:* Part-time. *Faculty:* 10 full-time (6 women), 1 (woman) part-time/adjunct. *Students:* 19 full-time (11 women), 10 part-time (6 women); includes 6 minority (4 Hispanic/Latino; 2 Two or more races, non-Hispanic/Latino), 7 international. Average age 29. 22 applicants, 59% accepted, 12 enrolled. In 2017, 9 master's awarded. *Degree requirements:* For master's, one foreign language, thesis optional; for doctorate, 2 foreign languages, thesis/dissertation. *Entrance requirements:* For master's and doctorate, transcript, writing sample, 3 letters of recommendation. Additional exam requirements/recommendations for international students: Required—TOEFL. *Application deadline:* For fall admission, 2/1 priority date for domestic students; for spring admission, 10/1 priority date for domestic students. Application fee: $50. Electronic applications accepted. *Financial support:* Research assistantships, teaching assistantships with tuition reimbursements, Federal Work-Study, health care benefits, and unspecified assistantships available. Financial award application deadline: 3/1; financial award applicants required to submit FAFSA. *Faculty research:* German, Russian, Italian, Japanese, French, comparative literature, culture studies, classics. *Unit head:* Dr. Walter Putnam, Chair, 505-277-4771, Fax: 505-277-3599, E-mail: wputnam@unm.edu. *Application contact:* Jacqueline Ochoa, Application and Graduation Advisor, 505-277-4471, Fax: 505-277-3599, E-mail: jochoa@unm.edu.
Website: http://www.unm.edu/~fll/

The University of North Carolina at Chapel Hill, Graduate School, College of Arts and Sciences, Department of Germanic and Slavic Languages and Literatures, Chapel Hill, NC 27599. Offers German studies (PhD). Program offered in collaboration with Duke University. *Program availability:* Part-time. Terminal master's awarded for partial completion of doctoral program. *Degree requirements:* For doctorate, one foreign language, comprehensive exam, thesis/dissertation. *Entrance requirements:* For doctorate, GRE General Test, minimum GPA of 3.0. *Faculty research:* Gender and sexuality, literature and politics, German and Jewish culture, medieval through modern literature, Germanic linguistics.

University of Oklahoma, College of Arts and Sciences, Department of Modern Languages, Literatures, and Linguistics, Program in German, Norman, OK 73019. Offers MA, MBA/MA. *Program availability:* Part-time. *Students:* 4 full-time (3 women); includes 2 minority (1 American Indian or Alaska Native, non-Hispanic/Latino; 1 Two or more races, non-Hispanic/Latino). Average age 30. 1 applicant, 100% accepted, 1 enrolled. In 2017, 2 master's awarded. Terminal master's awarded for partial completion of doctoral program. *Degree requirements:* For master's, comprehensive exam, two languages (one must be German); thesis or research papers. *Entrance requirements:* For master's, BA and major or minor in German. Additional exam requirements/recommendations for international students: Required—TOEFL (minimum score 79 iBT) or IELTS (minimum score 6.5). *Application deadline:* For fall admission, 2/1 for domestic and international students; for spring admission, 10/1 for domestic and international students. Application fee: $50 ($100 for international students). Electronic applications accepted. *Expenses:* Tuition, state resident: full-time $5119; part-time $213.30 per credit hour. Tuition, nonresident: full-time $19,778; part-time $824.10 per credit hour. *Required fees:* $3458; $133.55 per credit hour. $126.50 per semester. *Financial support:* In 2017–18, 4 students received support. Fellowships, teaching assistantships with full tuition reimbursements available, scholarships/grants, health care benefits, and unspecified assistantships available. Support available to part-time students. Financial award application deadline: 6/1; financial award applicants required to submit FAFSA. *Faculty research:* Goethe and German-Jewish studies, Arthurian romance, Kafka and turn-of-the-century Austria. *Unit head:* Dr. Karin Schutjer, Professor of German, 405-325-1907, Fax: 405-325-0103, E-mail: kschutjer@ou.edu. *Application contact:* Robert Lemon, Associate Professor of German/German Graduate Section Liaison, 405-325-1551, Fax: 405-325-0103, E-mail: rlemon@ou.edu.
Website: http://mlll.publishpath.com/german-ma

University of Oregon, Graduate School, College of Arts and Sciences, Department of Germanic Languages and Literatures, Eugene, OR 97403. Offers MA, PhD. *Degree requirements:* For master's, 2 foreign languages, thesis or alternative; for doctorate, 3 foreign languages, thesis/dissertation. *Entrance requirements:* For master's and doctorate, minimum GPA of 3.0. Additional exam requirements/recommendations for international students: Required—TOEFL. *Faculty research:* Medieval language and literature, eighteenth to twentieth century literature and philosophy, literary theory, feminist literature and theory, psychoanalysis and literature.

University of Pennsylvania, School of Arts and Sciences, Graduate Group in Germanic Languages, Philadelphia, PA 19104. Offers AM, PhD. *Faculty:* 11 full-time (4 women), 9 part-time/adjunct (1 woman). *Students:* 10 full-time (6 women); includes 1 minority (Hispanic/Latino), 2 international. Average age 30. 12 applicants, 50% accepted, 2 enrolled. In 2017, 1 master's, 1 doctorate awarded. Terminal master's awarded for partial completion of doctoral program.
Website: http://www.sas.upenn.edu/graduate-division

University of Saskatchewan, College of Graduate Studies and Research, College of Arts and Science, Department of Languages and Linguistics, Saskatoon, SK S7N 5A2, Canada. Offers MA. *Degree requirements:* For master's, 2 foreign languages, thesis. *Entrance requirements:* Additional exam requirements/recommendations for international students: Required—TOEFL (minimum score 80 iBT); Recommended—IELTS (minimum score 6.5). Electronic applications accepted.

University of South Africa, College of Human Sciences, Pretoria, South Africa. Offers adult education (M Ed); African languages (MA, PhD); African politics (MA, PhD); Afrikaans (MA, PhD); ancient history (MA, PhD); ancient Near Eastern studies (MA, PhD); anthropology (MA, PhD); applied linguistics (MA); Arabic (MA, PhD); archaeology (MA); art history (MA); Biblical archaeology (MA); Biblical studies (M Th, D Th, PhD); Christian spirituality (M Th, D Th); church history (M Th, D Th); classical studies (MA, PhD); clinical psychology (MA); communication (MA, PhD); comparative education (M Ed, Ed D); consulting psychology (D Admin, D Com, PhD); curriculum studies (M Ed, Ed D); development studies (M Admin, MA, D Admin, PhD); didactics (M Ed, Ed D); education (M Tech); education management (M Ed, Ed D); educational psychology (M Ed); English (MA); environmental education (M Ed); French (MA, PhD); German (MA, PhD); Greek (MA); guidance and counseling (M Ed); health studies (MA, PhD), including health sciences education (MA), health services management (MA), medical and surgical nursing science (critical care general) (MA), midwifery and neonatal nursing science (MA), trauma and emergency care (MA); history (MA, PhD); history of education (Ed D); inclusive education (M Ed, Ed D); information and communications technology policy and regulation (MA); information science (MA, MIS, PhD); international politics (MA, PhD); Islamic studies (MA, PhD); Italian (MA, PhD); Judaica (MA, PhD); linguistics (MA, PhD); mathematical education (M Ed); mathematics education (MA); missiology (M Th, D Th); modern Hebrew (MA, PhD); musicology (MA, MMus, D Mus, PhD); natural science education (M Ed); New Testament (M Th, D Th); Old Testament (D Th); pastoral therapy (M Th, D Th); philosophy (MA); philosophy of education (M Ed, Ed D); politics (MA, PhD); Portuguese (MA, PhD); practical theology (M Th, D Th); psychology (MA, MS, PhD); psychology of education (M Ed, Ed D); public health (MA); religious studies (MA, D Th, PhD); Romance languages (MA); Russian (MA, PhD); Semitic languages (MA, PhD); social behavior studies in HIV/AIDS (MA); social science (mental health) (MA); social science in development studies (MA); social science in psychology (MA); social science in social work (MA); social science in sociology (MA); social work (MSW, DSW, PhD); socio-education (M Ed, Ed D); sociolinguistics (MA); sociology (MA, PhD); Spanish (MA, PhD); systematic theology (M Th, D Th); TESOL (teaching English

to speakers of other languages) (MA); theological ethics (M Th, D Th); theory of literature (MA, PhD); urban ministries (D Th); urban ministry (M Th).

University of South Carolina, The Graduate School, College of Arts and Sciences, Department of Languages, Literatures, and Cultures, Columbia, SC 29208. Offers comparative literature (MA, PhD); foreign languages (MAT), including French, German, Spanish; French (MA); German (MA); Spanish (MA). MAT offered in cooperation with the College of Education. *Program availability:* Part-time. *Degree requirements:* For master's, one foreign language, comprehensive exam, thesis optional; for doctorate, 2 foreign languages, comprehensive exam, thesis/dissertation. *Entrance requirements:* For master's and doctorate, GRE General Test, writing sample. Additional exam requirements/recommendations for international students: Required—TOEFL (minimum score 75 iBT). Electronic applications accepted. *Faculty research:* Modern literature, linguistics, literature and culture, medieval literature, literary theory.

The University of Tennessee, Graduate School, College of Arts and Sciences, Department of Modern Foreign Languages and Literatures, Program in German, Knoxville, TN 37996. Offers MA. *Program availability:* Part-time. *Degree requirements:* For master's, one foreign language, thesis or alternative. *Entrance requirements:* For master's, minimum GPA of 2.7. Additional exam requirements/recommendations for international students: Required—TOEFL. Electronic applications accepted.

The University of Tennessee, Graduate School, College of Arts and Sciences, Department of Modern Foreign Languages and Literatures, Program in Modern Foreign Languages, Knoxville, TN 37996. Offers applied linguistics (PhD); French (PhD); German (PhD); Italian (PhD); Portuguese (PhD); Russian (PhD); Spanish (PhD). *Degree requirements:* For doctorate, 2 foreign languages, thesis/dissertation. *Entrance requirements:* For doctorate, minimum GPA of 2.7. Additional exam requirements/recommendations for international students: Required—TOEFL. Electronic applications accepted.

The University of Texas at Austin, Graduate School, College of Liberal Arts, Department of Germanic Studies, Austin, TX 78712-1111. Offers MA, PhD. *Degree requirements:* For master's, one foreign language, thesis or alternative; for doctorate, 2 foreign languages, thesis/dissertation. *Entrance requirements:* For master's and doctorate, GRE General Test. *Faculty research:* Germanic languages and culture (German, Austrian, Swiss, Dutch, Danish, Norwegian, Swedish, Yiddish), language pedagogy and linguistics.

The University of Toledo, College of Graduate Studies, College of Languages, Literature and Social Sciences, Department of Foreign Languages, Toledo, OH 43606-3390. Offers French (MA); German (MA); Spanish (MA). *Program availability:* Part-time. *Degree requirements:* For master's, one foreign language, comprehensive exam, comprehensive reading exam in 1 additional foreign language. *Entrance requirements:* For master's, minimum cumulative point-hour ratio of 2.7 for all previous academic work. Additional exam requirements/recommendations for international students: Required—TOEFL (minimum score 550 paper-based; 80 iBT). Electronic applications accepted.

University of Toronto, School of Graduate Studies, Faculty of Arts and Science, Department of Germanic Languages and Literatures, Toronto, ON M5S 1A1, Canada. Offers MA, PhD. *Program availability:* Part-time. *Degree requirements:* For master's, thesis optional, German language competence exam; for doctorate, thesis/dissertation, qualifying exam, thesis defense. *Entrance requirements:* For master's, 7 two-semester courses in German language and literature, 3 letters of recommendation; for doctorate, MA in German, minimum A- average, 3 letters of recommendation, writing sample, resume. Additional exam requirements/recommendations for international students: Required—TOEFL (minimum score 580 paper-based; 93 iBT), TWE (minimum score 5). Electronic applications accepted.

University of Vermont, Graduate College, College of Arts and Sciences, Program in German, Burlington, VT 05405. Offers MA. *Degree requirements:* For master's, one foreign language, thesis. *Entrance requirements:* For master's, GRE General Test. Additional exam requirements/recommendations for international students: Required—TOEFL (minimum score 550 paper-based; 90 iBT), IELTS (minimum score 6.5). *Application deadline:* For fall admission, 4/1 for domestic and international students. Applications are processed on a rolling basis. Application fee: $65. Electronic applications accepted. *Expenses:* Tuition, state resident: full-time $11,628; part-time $646 per credit. Tuition, nonresident: full-time $29,340; part-time $1630 per credit. *Required fees:* $1994; $10 per credit. Tuition and fees vary according to course load and program. *Financial support:* Fellowships and teaching assistantships available. Financial award application deadline: 3/1. *Faculty research:* Medieval, eighteenth-, and nineteenth-century literature; folklore. *Unit head:* Dr. Helga Schreckenberger, Chairperson, 802-656-3430, E-mail: schreckenberger@uvm.edu. *Website:* https://www.uvm.edu/cas/germanrussian/ma-german

University of Victoria, Faculty of Graduate Studies, Faculty of Humanities, Department of Germanic and Slavic Studies, Victoria, BC V8W 2Y2, Canada. Offers German studies (MA). *Program availability:* Part-time. *Degree requirements:* For master's, 2 foreign languages, oral defense of thesis. *Entrance requirements:* For master's, BA in German, minimum B+ average in undergraduate course work. Additional exam requirements/recommendations for international students: Required—TOEFL (minimum score 575 paper-based), IELTS (minimum score 7). Electronic applications accepted. *Faculty research:* Nineteenth and twentieth century German literature, literature and music, language acquisition, eighteenth and twentieth century drama and theater, military history.

University of Virginia, College and Graduate School of Arts and Sciences, Department of Germanic Languages and Literatures, Charlottesville, VA 22903. Offers German (MA). *Faculty:* 11 full-time (5 women), 3 part-time/adjunct (all women). *Students:* 1 full-time (0 women). Average age 33. 1 applicant, 100% accepted. In 2017, 2 master's awarded. *Degree requirements:* For master's, one foreign language, comprehensive exam, thesis. *Entrance requirements:* For master's, GRE General Test, 3 letters of recommendation, critical writing sample. Additional exam requirements/recommendations for international students: Required—TOEFL (minimum score 600 paper-based; 90 iBT), IELTS (minimum score 7). *Application deadline:* For fall admission, 1/15 for domestic and international students. Applications are processed on a rolling basis. Application fee: $60. Electronic applications accepted. *Financial support:* Applicants required to submit FAFSA. *Unit head:* Jeffrey Grossman, Chair, 434-924-3530, Fax: 434-924-6700, E-mail: jg2t@virginia.edu. *Application contact:* Benjamin Bennett, Graduate Admissions Contact, 434-924-3530, Fax: 434-924-6700, E-mail: bkb@virginia.edu.
Website: http://www.german.virginia.edu/

University of Washington, Graduate School, College of Arts and Sciences, Department of Germanics, Seattle, WA 98195. Offers MA, PhD. *Program availability:* Part-time. Terminal master's awarded for partial completion of doctoral program. *Degree requirements:* For master's, one foreign language, 2 research papers; for doctorate, 2 foreign languages, thesis/dissertation, 3 research papers. *Entrance requirements:* For master's and doctorate, GRE, minimum GPA of 3.0. Additional exam requirements/recommendations for international students: Required—TOEFL. Electronic applications accepted. *Faculty research:* Modern German literature, Germanic linguistics and philology, language pedagogy, literary theory, cinema studies.

University of Waterloo, Graduate Studies, Faculty of Arts, Department of Germanic and Slavic Studies, Waterloo, ON N2L 3G1, Canada. Offers German (MA, PhD); Russian (MA). *Program availability:* Part-time, evening/weekend. *Degree requirements:* For master's, one foreign language, thesis optional; for doctorate, 2 foreign languages, comprehensive exam, thesis/dissertation. *Entrance requirements:* For master's, honors degree, minimum B average; for doctorate, master's degree, minimum B average. Additional exam requirements/recommendations for international students: Required—TOEFL, IELTS, PTE. Electronic applications accepted. *Faculty research:* Medieval theatre; history and literature; German and Russian literary relations; seventeenth-, eighteenth-, nineteenth-, and twentieth-century German literature.

University of Wisconsin–Madison, Graduate School, College of Letters and Science, Department of German, Madison, WI 53706-1380. Offers MA, PhD. *Program availability:* Part-time. Terminal master's awarded for partial completion of doctoral program. *Degree requirements:* For master's, one foreign language, comprehensive exam, thesis optional; for doctorate, 2 foreign languages, comprehensive exam, thesis/dissertation. *Entrance requirements:* For master's and doctorate, GRE. Electronic applications accepted. *Faculty research:* Literature, culture/linguistics, film, Dutch.

University of Wisconsin–Milwaukee, Graduate School, College of Letters and Science, Department of Foreign Languages and Literature, Milwaukee, WI 53201-0413. Offers foreign languages and literature (MA), including classic Greek, classics, comparative literature, French/Francophone language, literature, and culture, German language, literature, and culture, interpreting, Latin, linguistics, Spanish language, literature, and culture, translation; interpreting (Graduate Certificate); language, literature, and translation (MA, MALLT); translation (Graduate Certificate). *Program availability:* Part-time. *Students:* 11 full-time (6 women), 40 part-time (29 women); includes 10 minority (2 Black or African American, non-Hispanic/Latino; 3 Hispanic/Latino; 5 Two or more races, non-Hispanic/Latino), 4 international. Average age 35. 37 applicants, 68% accepted, 20 enrolled. In 2017, 5 master's awarded. *Degree requirements:* For master's, 2 foreign languages, thesis or alternative. *Entrance requirements:* Additional exam requirements/recommendations for international students: Required—TOEFL (minimum score 550 paper-based; 79 iBT), IELTS (minimum score 6.5). *Application deadline:* For fall admission, 1/1 priority date for domestic students; for spring admission, 9/1 for domestic students. Application fee: $56 ($96 for international students). Electronic applications accepted. *Financial support:* Fellowships, research assistantships, teaching assistantships, career-related internships or fieldwork, health care benefits, unspecified assistantships, and project assistantships available. Support available to part-time students. Financial award application deadline: 4/15; financial award applicants required to submit FAFSA. *Unit head:* Kevin Muse, Department Chair, 414-229-5213, E-mail: kmuse@uwm.edu. *Application contact:* General Information Contact, 414-229-4982, Fax: 414-229-6967, E-mail: gradschool@uwm.edu.
Website: http://uwm.edu/foreign-languages-literature/

University of Wyoming, College of Arts and Sciences, Department of Modern and Classical Languages, Program in German, Laramie, WY 82071. Offers MA. *Program availability:* Part-time. *Degree requirements:* For master's, one foreign language, thesis or alternative. *Entrance requirements:* For master's, GRE General Test, minimum GPA of 3.0. *Faculty research:* East German literature, German literature, theatre, poetry.

Vanderbilt University, Department of Germanic and Slavic Languages, Nashville, TN 37240-1001. Offers German (MA, MAT, PhD). *Faculty:* 6 full-time (3 women). *Students:* 20 full-time (13 women); includes 4 minority (1 Black or African American, non-Hispanic/Latino; 1 Hispanic/Latino; 2 Two or more races, non-Hispanic/Latino), 3 international. Average age 30. 11 applicants, 36% accepted, 2 enrolled. In 2017, 1 master's, 2 doctorates awarded. Terminal master's awarded for partial completion of doctoral program. *Degree requirements:* For master's, one foreign language, comprehensive exam; for doctorate, 2 foreign languages, comprehensive exam, thesis/dissertation, qualifying and final exams. *Entrance requirements:* For master's and doctorate, GRE General Test, sample of written work. Additional exam requirements/recommendations for international students: Required—TOEFL (minimum score 570 paper-based; 88 iBT). *Application deadline:* For fall admission, 1/15 for domestic and international students. Electronic applications accepted. *Financial support:* Fellowships, teaching assistantships, career-related internships or fieldwork, Federal Work-Study, institutionally sponsored loans, scholarships/grants, and health care benefits available. Financial award application deadline: 1/15; financial award applicants required to submit CSS PROFILE or FAFSA. *Faculty research:* 1750 to present, Middle Ages, Baroque, language pedagogy, linguistics. *Unit head:* Dr. Lutz Koepnick, Chair, 615-322-2611, Fax: 615-343-7258, E-mail: lutz.koepnick@vanderbilt.edu. *Application contact:* Christoph Zeller, Director of Graduate Studies, 615-875-9065, Fax: 615-343-7258, E-mail: christoph.zeller@vanderbilt.edu.
Website: http://www.vanderbilt.edu/german/graduate/

Washington University in St. Louis, The Graduate School, Department of Germanic Languages and Literatures, St. Louis, MO 63130-4899. Offers PhD. Terminal master's awarded for partial completion of doctoral program. *Degree requirements:* For doctorate, thesis/dissertation. *Entrance requirements:* For doctorate, GRE General Test, sample of written work. Additional exam requirements/recommendations for international students: Required—TOEFL. Electronic applications accepted. *Faculty research:* German literature and culture from the Middle Ages through the 21st century; intellectual history; film and media studies; gender studies; Holocaust studies; history of the book; digital humanities.

Wayne State University, College of Liberal Arts and Sciences, Department of Classical and Modern Languages, Literatures, and Cultures, Detroit, MI 48202. Offers classics (MA), including ancient Greek and Latin, ancient studies, classics, Latin; German (MA); language learning (MALL), including Arabic (MA, MALL), French (MA, MALL, PhD), German (MALL, PhD), Italian (MA, MALL), Spanish (MA, MALL, PhD); modern languages (PhD), including French (MA, MALL, PhD), German (MALL, PhD), Spanish (MA, MALL, PhD); Near Eastern languages (MA), including Arabic (MA, MALL), Hebrew; Romance languages (MA), including French (MA, MALL, PhD), Italian (MA, MALL), Spanish (MA, MALL, PhD). *Faculty:* 22. *Students:* 24 full-time (18 women), 21 part-time (15 women); includes 11 minority (4 Black or African American, non-Hispanic/Latino; 1 American Indian or Alaska Native, non-Hispanic/Latino; 2 Asian, non-Hispanic/Latino; 2 Hispanic/Latino; 2 Two or more races, non-Hispanic/Latino), 3 international. Average age 37. 32 applicants, 63% accepted, 14 enrolled. In 2017, 10 master's awarded. *Degree requirements:* For master's, variable foreign language requirement, comprehensive exam (for some programs), thesis (for some programs); for doctorate, one foreign language, comprehensive exam, thesis/dissertation. *Entrance requirements:* Additional exam requirements/recommendations for international students: Required—TOEFL (minimum score 550 paper-based; 79 iBT), TWE (minimum score 5.5), Michigan English Language Assessment Battery (minimum score 85); Recommended—IELTS (minimum score 6.5). Application fee: $50. Electronic applications accepted. *Expenses:* Tuition, state resident: full-time $10,224; part-time $638.98 per credit hour. Tuition, nonresident: full-time $22,145; part-time $1384.04 per credit hour. Tuition and fees vary according to course load and program. *Financial support:* In 2017–18, 25 students received support, including 4 fellowships with tuition reimbursements available (averaging $13,500 per year), 17 teaching assistantships with tuition reimbursements

available (averaging $18,591 per year); research assistantships, scholarships/grants, health care benefits, and unspecified assistantships also available. Financial award applicants required to submit FAFSA. *Faculty research:* Classical and modern literature and culture (Greek, Latin, Arabic, Chinese, French, German, Russian, Spanish) including colonial studies and exile and Holocaust studies; critical theory (French, German, Slavic, Spanish); theoretical and applied linguistics (Arabic, Chinese, French, Spanish); area studies (Arabic, Near Eastern, classical, Islamic, and Judaic studies). *Unit head:* Dr. Anne Duggan, Department Chair, 313-577-6244, Fax: 313-577-6243, E-mail: a.duggan@wayne.edu.
Website: http://clas.wayne.edu/languages/

West Chester University of Pennsylvania, College of Arts and Humanities, Department of Languages and Cultures, West Chester, PA 19383. Offers French (Teaching Certificate); German (Teaching Certificate); languages and cultures (MA), including French, German, Spanish; Spanish (Teaching Certificate). *Program availability:* Part-time, evening/weekend, minimal on-campus study. *Students:* 8 full-time (all women), 24 part-time (19 women); includes 10 minority (all Hispanic/Latino), 1 international. Average age 30. 8 applicants, 88% accepted, 7 enrolled. In 2017, 10 master's awarded. *Degree requirements:* For master's, one foreign language, comprehensive exam, portfolio defended at oral exit exam, capstone project; for Teaching Certificate, one foreign language. *Entrance requirements:* For master's and Teaching Certificate, ACTFL OPI and WPT. Additional exam requirements/recommendations for international students: Required—TOEFL or IELTS. *Application deadline:* For fall admission, 5/15 for international students; for spring admission, 10/15 for international students. Applications are processed on a rolling basis. Application fee: $50. Electronic applications accepted. *Expenses:* Tuition, state resident: full-time $9000; part-time $500 per credit. Tuition, nonresident: full-time $13,500; part-time $750 per credit. *Required fees:* $2959; $149.79 per credit. *Financial support:* Scholarships/grants and unspecified assistantships available. Financial award application deadline: 2/15; financial award applicants required to submit FAFSA. *Faculty research:* Language structure, literature, film, culture, pedagogy, technology. *Unit head:* Dr. Mahmoud Amer, Chair, 610-430-5077, Fax: 610-436-3048, E-mail: mamer@wcupa.edu. *Application contact:* Dr. Maria Van Liew, Graduate Coordinator, 610-436-4746, Fax: 610-436-3048, E-mail: mvanliew@wcupa.edu.
Website: http://www.wcupa.edu/arts-humanities/languagesCultures/

Western Kentucky University, Graduate Studies, Potter College of Arts and Letters, Department of Modern Languages, Bowling Green, KY 42101. Offers French (MA Ed); German (MA Ed); Spanish (MA Ed).

Yale University, Graduate School of Arts and Sciences, Department of German, New Haven, CT 06520. Offers PhD. Terminal master's awarded for partial completion of doctoral program. *Degree requirements:* For doctorate, 3 foreign languages, thesis/dissertation. *Entrance requirements:* For doctorate, GRE General Test.

Hispanic and Latin American Languages

Boston University, Graduate School of Arts and Sciences, Department of Romance Studies, Boston, MA 02215. Offers Hispanic language and literature (MA, PhD). *Students:* 34 full-time (22 women), 2 part-time (1 woman); includes 9 minority (1 Black or African American, non-Hispanic/Latino; 8 Hispanic/Latino), 11 international. Average age 28. 46 applicants, 37% accepted, 7 enrolled. In 2017, 4 master's, 5 doctorates awarded. Terminal master's awarded for partial completion of doctoral program. *Degree requirements:* For master's, one foreign language, comprehensive exam; for doctorate, 2 foreign languages, comprehensive exam, thesis/dissertation. *Entrance requirements:* For master's and doctorate, GRE General Test, sample of written work, 3 letters of recommendation, transcripts, personal statement, summary of related coursework. Additional exam requirements/recommendations for international students: Required—TOEFL (minimum score 550 paper-based; 84 iBT). *Application deadline:* For fall admission, 1/15 for domestic and international students. Application fee: $95. Electronic applications accepted. *Financial support:* In 2017–18, 34 students received support, including 14 fellowships with full tuition reimbursements available (averaging $22,000 per year), 16 teaching assistantships with full tuition reimbursements available (averaging $22,000 per year); Federal Work-Study, scholarships/grants, and health care benefits also available. Financial award application deadline: 1/15. *Unit head:* Odile Cazenave, Chair, 617-353-6225, Fax: 617-353-6246, E-mail: cazenave@bu.edu. *Application contact:* Michael Williams, Administrative Assistant, 617-353-2641, Fax: 617-353-6246, E-mail: mawillia@bu.edu.
Website: http://www.bu.edu/rs/

Brigham Young University, Graduate Studies, College of Humanities, Department of Spanish and Portuguese, Provo, UT 84602. Offers Portuguese (MA), including Luso-Brazilian literatures, Portuguese linguistics, Portuguese pedagogy; Spanish (MA), including Hispanic linguistics, Hispanic literatures, Spanish pedagogy. *Faculty:* 30 full-time (6 women). *Students:* 32 full-time (17 women), 6 part-time (4 women); includes 16 minority (all Hispanic/Latino). Average age 31. 19 applicants, 68% accepted, 10 enrolled. In 2017, 6 master's awarded. *Degree requirements:* For master's, 2 foreign languages, comprehensive exam, thesis, 1 semester of teaching. *Entrance requirements:* For master's, minimum GPA of 3.5 in Spanish or Portuguese, 3.3 overall. Additional exam requirements/recommendations for international students: Required—TOEFL (minimum score 580 paper-based; 85 iBT), IELTS (minimum score 6.5), PTE (minimum score 53). *Application deadline:* For fall admission, 2/1 for domestic and international students. Application fee: $50. Electronic applications accepted. *Expenses:* Contact institution. *Financial support:* In 2017–18, 23 students received support, including 87 teaching assistantships (averaging $3,200 per year); research assistantships, institutionally sponsored loans, scholarships/grants, tuition waivers (partial), and unspecified assistantships also available. Support available to part-time students. *Faculty research:* Mexican prose; Latin American theater; literature; phonetics, and phonology; pedagogy; classical Portuguese literature. *Unit head:* Dr. Jeffrey S. Turley, Chair, 801-422-7019, Fax: 801-422-0628, E-mail: jeffrey_turley@byu.edu. *Application contact:* Patricia E. Wilson, Graduate Program Manager, 801-422-2838, Fax: 801-422-0628, E-mail: patricia_rubio@byu.edu.
Website: http://spanport.byu.edu/

California State University, San Marcos, College of Humanities, Arts, Behavioral and Social Sciences, Program in Spanish, San Marcos, CA 92096-0001. Offers Hispanic cultures and society (MA); Hispanic language and linguistics (MA); Hispanic literatures and literary theory (MA). *Program availability:* Part-time, evening/weekend. *Degree requirements:* For master's, 2 foreign languages, exam. *Entrance requirements:* For master's, GRE General Test, minimum GPA of 3.0 overall and in upper-division Spanish courses, official transcripts, three letters of recommendation, 750-word statement of purpose (in English), academic writing sample (in Spanish). Additional exam requirements/recommendations for international students: Required—TOEFL (minimum score 500 paper-based), TWE (minimum score 4.5). *Application deadline:* For fall admission, 3/15 priority date for domestic students. Applications are processed on a rolling basis. Application fee: $55. Electronic applications accepted. *Expenses:* Tuition, state resident: full-time $7176. Tuition, nonresident: full-time $9504. *Faculty research:* Applied linguistics, Golden Age Spanish literature, Latin American literature, poetry, Chicano studies. *Unit head:* Dr. Silvia Rolle-Rissetto, Graduate Coordinator, 760-750-4115, E-mail: srolle@csusm.edu.
Website: http://www.csusm.edu/modernlanguages/masters_degree/

Cornell University, Graduate School, Graduate Fields of Arts and Sciences, Field of Romance Studies, Ithaca, NY 14853. Offers French linguistics (PhD); French literature (PhD); Hispanic literature (PhD); Italian linguistics (PhD); Italian literature (PhD); Romance linguistics (PhD); Spanish linguistics (PhD). *Degree requirements:* For doctorate, 2 foreign languages, comprehensive exam, thesis/dissertation. *Entrance requirements:* For doctorate, GRE General Test, sample of written work, 3 letters of recommendation. Additional exam requirements/recommendations for international students: Required—TOEFL (minimum score 550 paper-based; 77 iBT). Electronic applications accepted. *Faculty research:* Literary theory, Hispanic studies, French studies, gender studies.

The Graduate Center, City University of New York, Graduate Studies, Program in Latin American, Iberian and Latino Cultures, New York, NY 10016-4039. Offers PhD. *Faculty:* 23 full-time (8 women). *Students:* 75 full-time (42 women); includes 28 minority (1 Asian, non-Hispanic/Latino; 27 Hispanic/Latino), 39 international. Average age 40. 58 applicants, 21% accepted, 9 enrolled. In 2017, 15 doctorates awarded. *Degree requirements:* For doctorate, 2 foreign languages, thesis/dissertation. *Entrance requirements:* For doctorate, GRE General Test. Additional exam requirements/recommendations for international students: Required—TOEFL. *Application deadline:* For fall admission, 1/15 priority date for domestic students; for spring admission, 11/15 for domestic students. Application fee: $125. Electronic applications accepted. *Financial support:* In 2017–18, 68 students received support, including 64 fellowships, 2 research assistantships, 9 teaching assistantships; career-related internships or fieldwork, Federal Work-Study, institutionally sponsored loans, and tuition waivers (full and partial) also available. Financial award application deadline: 2/1; financial award applicants required to submit FAFSA. *Unit head:* Prof. Fernando Degiovanni, Executive Officer, 212-817-8411, Fax: 212-817-1522, E-mail: fdegiovanni@gc.cuny.edu. *Application contact:* Les Gribben, Director of Admissions, 212-817-7470, Fax: 212-817-1624, E-mail: lgribben@gc.cuny.edu.
Website: https://www.gc.cuny.edu/Page-Elements/Academics-Research-Centers-Initiatives/Doctoral-Programs/Latin-American,-Iberian,-and-Latino-Cultures

Indiana University Bloomington, University Graduate School, College of Arts and Sciences, Department of Spanish and Portuguese, Bloomington, IN 47405. Offers Portuguese (MA, PhD); Spanish (MA, PhD), including Hispanic linguistics, Hispanic literatures. *Degree requirements:* For master's, one foreign language, comprehensive exam, thesis (for Spanish); for doctorate, 2 foreign languages, comprehensive exam, thesis/dissertation. *Entrance requirements:* For master's, GRE General Test, bachelor's degree in Portuguese or Spanish, minimum GPA of 3.0; for doctorate, GRE General Test, master's degree in Portuguese or Spanish, minimum GPA of 3.0. Additional exam requirements/recommendations for international students: Required—TOEFL (minimum score 79 iBT). Electronic applications accepted. *Faculty research:* Spanish American literature, Spanish peninsular literature, Hispanic linguistics, Luso-Brazilian studies, Catalan studies.

Indiana University of Pennsylvania, School of Graduate Studies and Research, College of Humanities and Social Sciences, Department of Foreign Languages, Program in Spanish/Hispanic Literatures and Cultures, Indiana, PA 15705. Offers MA. Application fee: $50. *Expenses:* Tuition, state resident: full-time $12,000; part-time $500 per credit. Tuition, nonresident: full-time $18,000; part-time $750 per credit. *Required fees:* $4073; $165.55 per credit. $64 per term. *Financial support:* Research assistantships with tuition reimbursements available. *Unit head:* Dr. Sean McDaniel, Chairperson, 724-357-7532, E-mail: mcdaniel@iup.edu.

Michigan State University, The Graduate School, College of Arts and Letters, Department of Spanish and Portuguese, East Lansing, MI 48824. Offers applied Spanish linguistics (MA); Hispanic cultural studies (PhD); Hispanic literatures (MA). *Entrance requirements:* Additional exam requirements/recommendations for international students: Required—TOEFL. Electronic applications accepted.

Queens College of the City University of New York, Arts and Humanities Division, Department of Hispanic Languages and Literatures, Queens, NY 11367-1597. Offers Spanish (MA). *Program availability:* Part-time. *Students:* 9 part-time (7 women); includes 8 minority (all Hispanic/Latino). Average age 47. *Degree requirements:* For master's, 3 foreign languages. *Entrance requirements:* For master's, minimum GPA of 3.0. Additional exam requirements/recommendations for international students: Required—TOEFL (minimum score 61 iBT), IELTS (minimum score 5). *Application deadline:* For fall admission, 4/1 for domestic students; for spring admission, 11/1 for domestic students. Applications are processed on a rolling basis. Application fee: $125. Electronic applications accepted. *Financial support:* Career-related internships or fieldwork available. Financial award application deadline: 4/1; financial award applicants required to submit FAFSA. *Unit head:* Dr. Jose Martinez-Torrejon, Chair, 718-997-5660, E-mail: jose.martinez-torrejon@qc.cuny.edu. *Application contact:* Elizabeth D'Amico-Ramirez, Assistant Director of Graduate Admissions, 718-997-5203, E-mail: elizabeth.damicoramirez@qc.cuny.edu.

Stony Brook University, State University of New York, Graduate School, College of Arts and Sciences, Department of Hispanic Languages and Literature, Stony Brook, NY 11794. Offers MA, PhD. *Program availability:* Evening/weekend. *Faculty:* 14 full-time (9 women), 3 part-time/adjunct (all women). *Students:* 28 full-time (16 women), 7 part-time (5 women); includes 16 minority (2 Black or African American, non-Hispanic/Latino; 14 Hispanic/Latino), 15 international. Average age 37. 29 applicants, 59% accepted, 7 enrolled. In 2017, 6 master's, 1 doctorate awarded. *Degree requirements:* For master's, one foreign language, thesis or alternative; for doctorate, 2 foreign languages, thesis/dissertation. *Entrance requirements:* For master's, GRE General Test, BA in Spanish; for doctorate, GRE General Test, MA in Spanish. Additional exam requirements/recommendations for international students: Required—TOEFL. *Application deadline:* For fall admission, 1/15 for domestic students; for spring admission, 10/1 for domestic

students. Application fee: $100. Electronic applications accepted. *Expenses:* Contact institution. *Financial support:* In 2017–18, 20 teaching assistantships were awarded; fellowships, research assistantships, tuition waivers, and unspecified assistantships also available. *Faculty research:* Latin American languages or literature, humanities, Latin American studies, Spanish, race. *Total annual research expenditures:* $26,060. *Unit head:* Dr. Kathleen M. Vernon, Chair, 631-632-9668, Fax: 631-632-9724, E-mail: kathleen.vernon@stonybrook.edu. *Application contact:* Mary Moran-Luba, Coordinator, 631-632-6935, Fax: 631-632-9724, E-mail: mary.moran-luba@stonybrook.edu. Website: https://www.stonybrook.edu/commcms/hispanic/

Université de Montréal, Faculty of Arts and Sciences, Department of Literatures and Modern Languages, Montréal, QC H3C 3J7, Canada. Offers German literature (PhD); German studies (MA); Hispanic literature (PhD); Hispanic studies (MA). Terminal master's awarded for partial completion of doctoral program. *Degree requirements:* For master's, 2 foreign languages, thesis; for doctorate, 2 foreign languages, thesis/dissertation, general exam. Electronic applications accepted.

University of California, Berkeley, Graduate Division, College of Letters and Science, Department of Spanish and Portuguese, Berkeley, CA 94720-1500. Offers Hispanic languages and literatures (PhD). *Degree requirements:* For doctorate, thesis/dissertation, qualifying exam. *Entrance requirements:* For doctorate, GRE General Test, minimum GPA of 3.0, 3 letters of recommendation. Additional exam requirements/recommendations for international students: Required—TOEFL (minimum score 570 paper-based; 90 iBT). Electronic applications accepted.

University of California, Los Angeles, Graduate Division, College of Letters and Science, Department of Spanish and Portuguese, Program in Hispanic Languages and Literature, Los Angeles, CA 90095. Offers PhD. *Degree requirements:* For doctorate, 2 foreign languages, thesis/dissertation, oral and written qualifying exams. *Entrance requirements:* For doctorate, GRE General Test, master's degree; minimum undergraduate GPA of 3.0 (or its equivalent if letter grade system not used); writing sample. Additional exam requirements/recommendations for international students: Required—TOEFL. Electronic applications accepted.

University of California, Santa Barbara, Graduate Division, College of Letters and Sciences, Division of Humanities and Fine Arts, Department of Spanish and Portuguese, Santa Barbara, CA 93106-4150. Offers Hispanic languages and literatures (PhD), including European medieval studies, feminist studies, Hispanic linguistics, Hispanic literature, Luso-Brazilian literature; Hispanic linguistics (MA); Luso-Brazilian literature (MA); Spanish or Spanish-American literature (MA); MA/PhD. Terminal master's awarded for partial completion of doctoral program. *Degree requirements:* For master's, 2 foreign languages, comprehensive exam (for some programs), thesis optional; for doctorate, 3 foreign languages, comprehensive exam, thesis/dissertation. *Entrance requirements:* For master's and doctorate, GRE. Additional exam requirements/recommendations for international students: Required—TOEFL (minimum score 550 paper-based; 80 iBT), IELTS (minimum score 7). Electronic applications accepted. *Faculty research:* Nineteenth-century Spanish and Portuguese literature, Spanish and Spanish-American literature, nineteenth- and twentieth-century Portuguese and Brazilian literatures, Hispanic linguistics, Catalan language and culture.

University of Colorado Boulder, Graduate School, College of Arts and Sciences, Department of Spanish and Portuguese, Boulder, CO 80309. Offers Hispanic linguistics (MA); medieval and early modern Hispanic literatures (PhD); peninsular and Latin American literature (MA). *Faculty:* 13 full-time (5 women). *Students:* 33 full-time (22 women), 3 part-time (all women); includes 7 minority (all Hispanic/Latino), 15 international. Average age 31. 31 applicants, 48% accepted, 8 enrolled. In 2017, 5 master's, 2 doctorates awarded. Terminal master's awarded for partial completion of doctoral program. *Degree requirements:* For master's, one foreign language, comprehensive exam, thesis or alternative; for doctorate, 2 foreign languages, thesis/dissertation. *Entrance requirements:* For master's, minimum undergraduate GPA of 2.75. *Application deadline:* For fall admission, 1/10 for domestic students; for spring admission, 1/10 for domestic students. Applications are processed on a rolling basis. Application fee: $60 ($80 for international students). Electronic applications accepted. Application fee is waived when completed online. *Financial support:* In 2017–18, 119 students received support, including 33 fellowships (averaging $583 per year), 31 teaching assistantships with full and partial tuition reimbursements available (averaging $33,436 per year); institutionally sponsored loans, scholarships/grants, health care benefits, and unspecified assistantships also available. Financial award application deadline: 2/15; financial award applicants required to submit FAFSA. *Faculty research:* Literary criticism, Spanish language/literature, Latin American languages/literature,

cultural history. *Total annual research expenditures:* $40,777. *Application contact:* E-mail: spanport@colorado.edu. Website: http://spanish.colorado.edu/

University of Illinois at Chicago, College of Liberal Arts and Sciences, School of Literatures, Cultural Studies and Linguistics, Chicago, IL 60607-7128. Offers French and Francophone studies (MA); Germanic studies (MA); Hispanic and Italian studies (MAT, PhD), including Hispanic linguistics (PhD), Hispanic literary and cultural studies (PhD), teaching of Spanish (MAT); linguistics (MA), including teaching English to speakers of other languages/applied linguistics; Slavic and Baltic languages and literatures (MA), including Slavic studies (MA, PhD); Slavic and Baltic languages and literatures (PhD), including Slavic studies (MA, PhD). *Program availability:* Part-time. Terminal master's awarded for partial completion of doctoral program. *Degree requirements:* For master's, one foreign language, exam. *Entrance requirements:* For master's, minimum GPA of 2.75. Additional exam requirements/recommendations for international students: Required—TOEFL. Electronic applications accepted. *Faculty research:* International studies, religious (Catholic, Jewish) studies, moving image arts.

University of Massachusetts Amherst, Graduate School, College of Humanities and Fine Arts, Department of Languages, Literatures, and Cultures, Program in Spanish and Portuguese Studies, Amherst, MA 01003. Offers Hispanic literatures, cultures and linguistics (MA, PhD); teaching Spanish (MAT). *Program availability:* Part-time. Terminal master's awarded for partial completion of doctoral program. *Degree requirements:* For master's, one foreign language, thesis or alternative; for doctorate, 2 foreign languages, comprehensive exam, thesis/dissertation. *Entrance requirements:* For master's and doctorate, GRE General Test, sample academic term paper. Additional exam requirements/recommendations for international students: Required—TOEFL (minimum score 550 paper-based; 80 iBT), IELTS (minimum score 6.5). Electronic applications accepted.

University of Minnesota, Twin Cities Campus, Graduate School, College of Liberal Arts, Department of Spanish and Portuguese Studies, Minneapolis, MN 55455-0213. Offers Hispanic and Lusophone literatures, cultures and linguistics (PhD); Hispanic linguistics (MA); Hispanic literature (MA); Lusophone literature (MA). *Degree requirements:* For master's, 2 foreign languages, comprehensive exam, thesis or alternative; for doctorate, 2 foreign languages, comprehensive exam, thesis/dissertation. *Entrance requirements:* For master's and doctorate, GRE General Test, samples of written work, 3 letters of recommendation, voice sample, statement of purpose. Additional exam requirements/recommendations for international students: Required—TOEFL (minimum score 550 paper-based; 79 iBT). Electronic applications accepted. *Faculty research:* Sociohistorical approaches to literature and culture, feminist studies, literary theory, ideologies and literature, pragmatics and sociolinguistics.

The University of North Carolina at Greensboro, Graduate School, College of Arts and Sciences, Department of Languages, Literatures, and Cultures, Program in Spanish, Greensboro, NC 27412-5001. Offers advanced Spanish language and Hispanic cultural studies (Certificate); Spanish (MA). *Degree requirements:* For master's, one foreign language, comprehensive exam, thesis or alternative. *Entrance requirements:* For master's, GRE General Test, 3-5 minute tape demonstrating foreign language proficiency, composition in Spanish, sample paper in English. Additional exam requirements/recommendations for international students: Required—TOEFL. Electronic applications accepted.

The University of Texas at Austin, Graduate School, College of Liberal Arts, Department of Spanish and Portuguese, Austin, TX 78712-1111. Offers Hispanic linguistics (MA, PhD); Hispanic literature (MA, PhD); Ibero-romance philology and linguistics (PhD); Luso-Brazilian literature (MA, PhD). *Degree requirements:* For master's, 2 foreign languages, thesis or alternative; for doctorate, 3 foreign languages, thesis/dissertation. *Entrance requirements:* For master's and doctorate, GRE General Test. Electronic applications accepted.

University of Washington, Graduate School, College of Arts and Sciences, Division of Spanish and Portuguese Studies, Seattle, WA 98195. Offers Hispanic literary and cultural studies (MA). *Degree requirements:* For master's, 2 foreign languages, thesis optional, exam. *Entrance requirements:* For master's, GRE General Test, minimum GPA of 3.0. Additional exam requirements/recommendations for international students: Required—TOEFL. Electronic applications accepted. *Faculty research:* Medieval through modern Spanish literature and film, Latin American literature, poetry and essay, pan-Hispanic ballad, Hispanic cultural studies, second language acquisition and applied linguistics.

Italian

Binghamton University, State University of New York, Graduate School, Harpur College of Arts and Sciences, Department of Romance Languages and Literatures, Program in Italian, Binghamton, NY 13902-6000. Offers MA. *Program availability:* Part-time. In 2017, 1 master's awarded. *Degree requirements:* For master's, one foreign language, comprehensive exam, thesis or alternative. *Entrance requirements:* For master's, GRE General Test. Additional exam requirements/recommendations for international students: Required—TOEFL (minimum score 550 paper-based; 80 iBT). *Application deadline:* For fall admission, 2/15 priority date for domestic and international students; for spring admission, 11/15 priority date for domestic and international students. Application fee: $75. Electronic applications accepted. *Financial support:* Career-related internships or fieldwork, Federal Work-Study, institutionally sponsored loans, scholarships/grants, health care benefits, and unspecified assistantships available. Financial award applicants required to submit FAFSA. *Unit head:* Dr. Dana Stewart, Chairperson, 607-777-2645, E-mail: stewart@binghamton.edu. *Application contact:* Ben Balkaya, Assistant Dean and Director, 607-777-2151, Fax: 607-777-2501, E-mail: balkaya@binghamton.edu.

Boston College, Graduate School of Arts and Sciences, Department of Romance Languages and Literatures, Chestnut Hill, MA 02467-3800. Offers French (MA); Italian (MA); Spanish (MA). *Program availability:* Part-time. Terminal master's awarded for partial completion of doctoral program. *Degree requirements:* For master's, one foreign language. *Entrance requirements:* Additional exam requirements/recommendations for international students: Required—TOEFL (minimum score 600 paper-based; 100 iBT), IELTS (minimum score 8). Electronic applications accepted. *Faculty research:* Spanish-American literature, philology, medieval French romance and troubadour lyrics, Golden Age Peninsular literature, secondary language acquisition and pedagogy, Hispanic studies, French language and literature, Italian language and literature.

Brown University, Graduate School, Department of Italian Studies, Providence, RI 02912. Offers PhD. Terminal master's awarded for partial completion of doctoral program. *Degree requirements:* For doctorate, 2 foreign languages, thesis/dissertation, preliminary exam.

Central Connecticut State University, School of Graduate Studies, College of Liberal Arts and Social Sciences, Department of Modern Languages, New Britain, CT 06050-4010. Offers modern language (MA, Certificate), including French, German (Certificate), Italian, Spanish (MA); Spanish (MS, Certificate). *Program availability:* Part-time, evening/weekend. *Faculty:* 7 full-time (6 women). *Students:* 6 full-time (5 women), 16 part-time (12 women); includes 9 minority (all Hispanic/Latino), 1 international. Average age 32. 8 applicants, 88% accepted, 5 enrolled. In 2017, 12 master's awarded. *Degree requirements:* For master's, one foreign language, comprehensive exam, thesis or alternative; for Certificate, qualifying exam. *Entrance requirements:* For master's, minimum undergraduate GPA of 2.7, 24 credits of undergraduate courses in each language in which graduate work will be undertaken. Additional exam requirements/recommendations for international students: Required—TOEFL (minimum score 550 paper-based; 79 iBT); Recommended—IELTS (minimum score 6.5). *Application deadline:* For fall admission, 8/1 for domestic students, 5/1 for international students; for spring admission, 11/1 for domestic and international students. Applications are processed on a rolling basis. Application fee: $50. Electronic applications accepted. *Expenses: Tuition, area resident:* Full-time $6757. *Tuition, state resident:* full-time $9750; part-time $374 per credit. *Tuition, nonresident:* full-time $18,102; part-time $374 per credit. *Required fees:* $4635; $255 per credit. *Financial support:* In 2017–18, 3 students received support. Career-related internships or fieldwork, Federal Work-Study, scholarships/grants, and unspecified assistantships available. Support available to part-time students. Financial award application deadline: 3/1; financial award applicants required to submit FAFSA. *Faculty research:* Quebecois literature, Caribbean literature, modern French/Spanish drama, Puerto Rican novel and drama. *Unit head:* Dr. Carmela

Italian

Pesca, Chair, 860-832-2875, E-mail: pescac@ccsu.edu. *Application contact:* Patricia Gardner, Associate Director of Graduate Studies, 860-832-2350, Fax: 860-832-2362. Website: http://www.ccsu.edu/modlang/

Columbia University, Graduate School of Arts and Sciences, New York, NY 10027. Offers African-American studies (MA); American studies (MA); anthropology (MA, PhD); art history and archaeology (MA, PhD); astronomy (PhD); biological sciences (PhD); biotechnology (MA); chemical physics (PhD); chemistry (PhD); classical studies (MA, PhD); classics (MA, PhD); climate and society (MA); conservation biology (MA); earth and environmental sciences (PhD); East Asia: regional studies (MA); East Asian languages and cultures (MA, PhD); ecology, evolution and environmental biology (MA), including conservation biology; ecology, evolution, and environmental biology (PhD), including ecology and evolutionary biology, evolutionary primatology; economics (MA, PhD); English and comparative literature (MA, PhD); French and Romance philology (MA, PhD); Germanic languages (MA, PhD); global French studies (MA); global thought (MA); Hispanic cultural studies (MA); history (PhD); history and literature (MA); human rights studies (MA); Islamic studies (MA); Italian (MA, PhD); Japanese pedagogy (MA); Jewish studies (MA); Latin America and the Caribbean: regional studies (MA); Latin American and Iberian cultures (PhD); mathematics (MA, PhD), including finance (MA); medieval and Renaissance studies (MA); Middle Eastern, South Asian, and African studies (MA, PhD); modern art: critical and curatorial studies (MA); modern European studies (MA); museum anthropology (MA); music (DMA, PhD); oral history (MA); philosophical foundations of physics (MA); philosophy (MA, PhD); physics (PhD); political science (MA, PhD); psychology (PhD); quantitative methods in the social sciences (MA); religion (MA, PhD); Russia, Eurasia and East Europe: regional studies (MA); Russian translation (MA); Slavic cultures (MA); Slavic languages (MA, PhD); sociology (MA, PhD); South Asian studies (MA); statistics (MA, PhD); theatre (PhD). Dual-degree programs require admission to both Graduate School of Arts and Sciences and another Columbia school. *Program availability:* Part-time. Terminal master's awarded for partial completion of doctoral program. *Degree requirements:* For master's, variable foreign language requirement, comprehensive exam (for some programs); thesis (for some programs); for doctorate, variable foreign language requirement, comprehensive exam (for some programs), thesis/dissertation. *Entrance requirements:* For master's and doctorate, GRE General Test, GRE Subject Test (for some programs). Additional exam requirements/recommendations for international students: Required—TOEFL, IELTS. Electronic applications accepted. *Expenses: Tuition:* Full-time $44,864; part-time $1704 per credit. *Required fees:* $2370 per semester. One-time fee: $105.

Cornell University, Graduate School, Graduate Fields of Arts and Sciences, Field of Romance Studies, Ithaca, NY 14853. Offers French linguistics (PhD); French literature (PhD); Hispanic literature (PhD); Italian linguistics (PhD); Italian literature (PhD); Romance linguistics (PhD); Spanish linguistics (PhD). *Degree requirements:* For doctorate, 2 foreign languages, comprehensive exam, thesis/dissertation. *Entrance requirements:* For doctorate, GRE General Test, sample of written work, 3 letters of recommendation. Additional exam requirements/recommendations for international students: Required—TOEFL (minimum score 550 paper-based; 77 iBT). Electronic applications accepted. *Faculty research:* Literary theory, Hispanic studies, French studies, gender studies.

DePaul University, College of Liberal Arts and Social Sciences, Chicago, IL 60614. Offers Arabic (MA); Chinese (MA); critical ethnic studies (MA); English (MA); French (MA); German (MA); history (MA); interdisciplinary studies (MA, MS); international public service (MS); international studies (MA); Italian (MA); Japanese (MA); liberal studies (MA); nonprofit management (MNM); public administration (MPA); public health (MPH); public policy (MPP); public service management (MS); refugee and forced migration studies (MS); social work (MSW); sociology (MA); Spanish (MA); sustainable urban development (MA); women's and gender studies (MA); writing and publishing (MA); writing, rhetoric and discourse (MA); MA/PhD. *Program availability:* Part-time, evening/weekend, online learning. Terminal master's awarded for partial completion of doctoral program. *Degree requirements:* For master's, variable foreign language requirement, comprehensive exam (for some programs), thesis (for some programs). *Application deadline:* Applications are processed on a rolling basis. Application fee: $40. Electronic applications accepted. *Financial support:* Applicants required to submit FAFSA. *Unit head:* Dr. Guillermo Vasquez de Velasco, Dean, 773-325-7305. *Application contact:* Ann Spittle, Director of Graduate Admission, 773-325-8369, Fax: 312-476-3244, E-mail: graddepaul@depaul.edu. Website: http://las.depaul.edu/

Drew University, Caspersen School of Graduate Studies, Madison, NJ 07940-1493. Offers conflict resolution and leadership (Certificate), including community leadership, moderation, peace building; education (M Ed); finance (MA); history and culture (MA, PhD), including American history, book history, British history, European history, Holocaust and genocide (M Litt, MA, D Litt, PhD), intellectual history, Irish history, print culture, public history; K-12 education (MAT), including art, biology, chemistry, elementary education, English, French, Italian, math, secondary education, special education, teacher of students with disabilities; liberal studies (M Litt, D Litt), including history, Holocaust and genocide (M Litt, MA, D Litt, PhD), Irish/Irish-American studies, literature (M Litt, MMH, D Litt, DMH, CMH), religion, spirituality, teaching in the two-year college, writing; medical humanities (MMH, DMH, CMH), including arts, health, healthcare, literature (M Litt, MMH, D Litt, DMH, CMH), scientific research; poetry (MFA). *Program availability:* Part-time, evening/weekend. *Faculty:* 4 full-time (2 women), 29 part-time/adjunct (15 women). *Students:* 77 full-time (42 women), 175 part-time (114 women); includes 39 minority (12 Black or African American, non-Hispanic/Latino; 6 Asian, non-Hispanic/Latino; 16 Hispanic/Latino; 5 Two or more races, non-Hispanic/Latino), 11 international. Average age 41. 126 applicants, 75% accepted, 52 enrolled. In 2017, 38 master's, 23 doctorates, 35 other advanced degrees awarded. Terminal master's awarded for partial completion of doctoral program. *Degree requirements:* For master's and other advanced degree, thesis (for some programs); for doctorate, one foreign language, comprehensive exam (for some programs), thesis/dissertation. *Entrance requirements:* For master's, PRAXIS Core and Subject Area tests (for MAT), GRE/GMAT (for M Fin), resume, transcripts, writing sample, personal statement, letters of recommendation; for doctorate, GRE (PhD in history and culture), resume, transcripts, writing sample, personal statement, letters of recommendation; for other advanced degree, resume, transcripts, personal statement. Additional exam requirements/recommendations for international students: Required—TOEFL (minimum score 587 paper-based; 80 iBT), IELTS (minimum score 6), TWE (minimum score 4). *Application deadline:* For fall admission, 8/1 for domestic students, 6/1 for international students; for spring admission, 12/1 for domestic students, 10/1 for international students. Applications are processed on a rolling basis. Application fee: $35. Electronic applications accepted. *Financial support:* Fellowships, research assistantships, teaching assistantships, career-related internships or fieldwork, Federal Work-Study, scholarships/grants, and unspecified assistantships available. Support available to part-time students. Financial award applicants required to submit FAFSA. *Faculty research:* Irish history and culture, conflict resolution and leadership. *Application contact:* Leanne Horinko, Director of Caspersen Admissions, 973-408-3280, E-mail: gradm@drew.edu. Website: http://www.drew.edu/caspersen

Duke University, Graduate School, Department of Romance Studies, Durham, NC 27708. Offers French (PhD); Italian (PhD); Spanish (PhD); JD/AM. *Degree requirements:* For doctorate, 2 foreign languages, thesis/dissertation. *Entrance requirements:* For doctorate, GRE General Test. Additional exam requirements/recommendations for international students: Required—TOEFL (minimum score 577 paper-based; 90 iBT) or IELTS (minimum score 7). Electronic applications accepted.

Florida State University, The Graduate School, College of Arts and Sciences, Department of Modern Languages and Linguistics, Program in Italian Studies, Tallahassee, FL 32306. Offers MA. *Faculty:* 6 full-time (4 women). *Students:* 8 full-time (5 women); includes 2 minority (both Two or more races, non-Hispanic/Latino). Average age 24. 5 applicants, 100% accepted, 4 enrolled. In 2017, 3 master's awarded. *Entrance requirements:* For master's, GRE General Test, minimum GPA of 3.0. Additional exam requirements/recommendations for international students: Required—TOEFL (minimum score 550 paper-based; 80 iBT). *Application deadline:* For fall admission, 2/15 for domestic and international students. Applications are processed on a rolling basis. Application fee: $30. Electronic applications accepted. *Financial support:* In 2017–18, 7 teaching assistantships with partial tuition reimbursements (averaging $14,000 per year) were awarded. Financial award application deadline: 2/15. *Unit head:* Dr. Mark Pietralunga, Coordinator, 850-644-8392, Fax: 850-644-0524, E-mail: mpietral@fsu.edu. *Application contact:* Wendy E. Pigott, Graduate Academic Coordinator, 850-644-8397, Fax: 850-644-0524, E-mail: wpigott@fsu.edu. Website: http://modlang.ez.fsu.edu/Language-divisions-programs/Italian-Division/Graduate-Program

The Graduate Center, City University of New York, Graduate Studies, Program in Comparative Literature, New York, NY 10016-4039. Offers comparative literature (MA, PhD), including Italian (PhD). *Faculty:* 16 full-time (3 women). *Students:* 97 full-time (51 women), 4 part-time (3 women); includes 8 minority (4 Asian, non-Hispanic/Latino; 4 Hispanic/Latino), 39 international. Average age 37. 74 applicants, 27% accepted, 14 enrolled. In 2017, 13 master's, 7 doctorates awarded. Terminal master's awarded for partial completion of doctoral program. *Degree requirements:* For master's, 2 foreign languages, comprehensive exam, thesis; for doctorate, 3 foreign languages, comprehensive exam, thesis/dissertation. *Entrance requirements:* For master's and doctorate, GRE General Test. Additional exam requirements/recommendations for international students: Required—TOEFL. *Application deadline:* For fall admission, 4/15 for domestic students; for spring admission, 11/15 for domestic students. Application fee: $125. Electronic applications accepted. *Financial support:* In 2017–18, 63 students received support, including 60 fellowships, 5 research assistantships, 14 teaching assistantships; career-related internships or fieldwork, Federal Work-Study, institutionally sponsored loans, and tuition waivers (full and partial) also available. Financial award application deadline: 2/1; financial award applicants required to submit FAFSA. *Unit head:* Dr. Giancarlo Lombardi, Executive Officer, 212-817-8170, Fax: 212-817-1509, E-mail: glombardi@gc.cuny.edu. *Application contact:* Les Gribben, Director of Admissions, 212-817-7470, Fax: 212-817-1624, E-mail: lgribben@gc.cuny.edu.

Harvard University, Graduate School of Arts and Sciences, Department of Romance Languages and Literatures, Cambridge, MA 02138. Offers French (AM, PhD); Italian (AM, PhD); Portuguese (AM, PhD); Spanish (AM, PhD). Terminal master's awarded for partial completion of doctoral program. *Degree requirements:* For master's, 2 foreign languages; for doctorate, 2 foreign languages, thesis/dissertation. *Entrance requirements:* For master's and doctorate, GRE General Test, sample of written work. Additional exam requirements/recommendations for international students: Required—TOEFL.

Hofstra University, School of Education, Programs in Teacher Education, Hempstead, NY 11549. Offers bilingual education (MA); bilingual extension (Advanced Certificate), including education/speech language pathology, intensive teacher institute; business education (MS Ed); curriculum studies (MS Ed); early childhood and childhood education (MS Ed); early childhood education (MA, MS Ed); educational technology (Advanced Certificate); elementary education (MA, MS Ed), including science, technology, engineering, and mathematics (STEM) (MA); English education (MS Ed); family and consumer science (MS Ed); fine arts and music education (Advanced Certificate); fine arts education (MS Ed); foreign language and TESOL (MS Ed); foreign language education (MA, MS Ed), including Arabic (MS Ed), biology, chemistry, Chinese (MS Ed), earth science, French, German, Italian (MS Ed), Mandarin (MS Ed), physics, Russian, Spanish; foundations of education (Advanced Certificate), including grades 5-6, grades 7-9; languages other than English and teaching English as a second language (MA); learning and teaching (Ed D), including applied linguistics, art education, arts and humanities, early childhood education, English education, human development, math education, math, science, and technology, multicultural education, physical education, science education, social studies education, special education; mathematics education (MA, MS Ed); music education (MA, MS Ed); science education (MA), including biology (MA, MS Ed), chemistry (MA, MS Ed), earth science (MA, MS Ed), physics (MA, MS Ed); secondary education (Advanced Certificate); social studies education (MA, MS Ed); teaching languages other than English and TESOL (MS Ed); technology for learning (MA); TESOL (MS Ed, Advanced Certificate); TESOL with specialization in STEM (MA); work based learning extension (Advanced Certificate). *Program availability:* Part-time, evening/weekend, blended/hybrid learning. *Students:* 119 full-time (83 women), 124 part-time (90 women); includes 54 minority (15 Black or African American, non-Hispanic/Latino; 9 Asian, non-Hispanic/Latino; 29 Hispanic/Latino; 1 Native Hawaiian or other Pacific Islander, non-Hispanic/Latino), 12 international. Average age 29. 205 applicants, 88% accepted, 93 enrolled. In 2017, 103 master's, 4 doctorates, 32 other advanced degrees awarded. *Degree requirements:* For master's, comprehensive exam, thesis (for some programs), exit project, student teaching, fieldwork, electronic portfolio, curriculum project, minimum GPA of 3.0; for doctorate, thesis/dissertation; for Advanced Certificate, 3 foreign languages, comprehensive exam (for some programs), thesis project. *Entrance requirements:* For master's, GRE, 2 letters of recommendation, portfolio, teacher certification (MA), interview, essay; for doctorate, GMAT, GRE, LSAT, or MAT; for Advanced Certificate, 2 letters of recommendation, essay, interview and/or portfolio, teaching certificate. Additional exam requirements/recommendations for international students: Required—TOEFL (minimum score 550 paper-based; 80 iBT). *Application deadline:* Applications are processed on a rolling basis. Application fee: $75. Electronic applications accepted. *Expenses: Tuition:* Full-time $1292. *Required fees:* $970. Tuition and fees vary according to program. *Financial support:* In 2017–18, 112 students received support, including 56 fellowships with full and partial tuition reimbursements available (averaging $4,998 per year), 2 research assistantships with full and partial tuition reimbursements available (averaging $8,753 per year); career-related internships or fieldwork, Federal Work-Study, institutionally sponsored loans, scholarships/grants, traineeships, tuition waivers (full and partial), and unspecified assistantships also available. Support available to part-time students. Financial award applicants required to submit FAFSA. *Faculty research:* Educational interventions that foster critical-thinking skills; teachers' attitudes about professional development; threats to teacher quality. *Unit head:* Dr. Eustace Thompson, Chairperson, 516-463-5749, Fax: 516-463-6275, E-mail: eustace.g.thompson@hofstra.edu. *Application contact:* Sunil Samuel, Assistant Vice President of Admissions, 516-463-4723, Fax: 516-463-4664, E-mail: graduateadmission@hofstra.edu. Website: http://www.hofstra.edu/education/

Hunter College of the City University of New York, Graduate School, School of Arts and Sciences, Department of Romance Languages, Program in Italian, New York, NY 10065-5085. Offers MA. *Degree requirements:* For master's, 2 foreign languages, comprehensive exam, thesis optional. *Entrance requirements:* For master's, GRE General Test, GRE Subject Test, ability to read, speak, and write Italian; interview. Additional exam requirements/recommendations for international students: Required—TOEFL. *Faculty research:* Dante, Middle Ages, Renaissance, contemporary Italian novel and poetry, late Renaissance and Baroque.

Indiana University Bloomington, University Graduate School, College of Arts and Sciences, Department of French and Italian, Bloomington, IN 47405. Offers French (MA, PhD), including French and Francophone studies (MA), French instruction (MA), French linguistics; Italian (MA, PhD). *Program availability:* Part-time. Terminal master's awarded for partial completion of doctoral program. *Degree requirements:* For master's, variable foreign language requirement, comprehensive exam (for some programs), thesis or alternative; for doctorate, variable foreign language requirement, comprehensive exam, thesis/dissertation. *Entrance requirements:* For master's, GRE General Test, BA or equivalent undergraduate preparation in French or Italian; for doctorate, GRE General Test, MA from degree program at IU; MA in the specific field. Additional exam requirements/recommendations for international students: Required—TOEFL (minimum score 550 paper-based; 79 iBT), GRE General Test (recommended). Electronic applications accepted. *Faculty research:* French and Italian literature, French linguistics, including the novel and political theory, literature and fine arts, literary theory, postcolonialism, French-Creole studies, French literature of Africa and its Diaspora, humanism, Medieval folklore and mythology, humor in Medieval and Renaissance literature, emigration, second language acquisition, syntax, sociolinguistics, phonology, lexicography, media and cultural studies, cinema, drama.

Johns Hopkins University, Zanvyl Krieger School of Arts and Sciences, Department of German and Romance Languages and Literatures, Baltimore, MD 21218. Offers German (MA, PhD); romance languages (PhD), including French, Italian, Spanish. *Faculty:* 49 full-time (30 women), 1 part-time/adjunct (0 women). *Students:* 55 full-time (31 women); includes 4 minority (3 Hispanic/Latino; 1 Two or more races, non-Hispanic/ Latino), 24 international. Average age 29. 39 applicants, 46% accepted, 8 enrolled. In 2017, 2 master's, 10 doctorates awarded. Terminal master's awarded for partial completion of doctoral program. *Degree requirements:* For master's, comprehensive exam; for doctorate, 2 foreign languages, comprehensive exam, thesis/dissertation. *Entrance requirements:* For doctorate, GRE General Test. Additional exam requirements/recommendations for international students: Required—TOEFL (minimum score 600 paper-based; 100 iBT), IELTS. *Application deadline:* For fall admission, 1/15 for domestic and international students. Application fee: $75. Electronic applications accepted. *Expenses:* Contact institution. *Financial support:* In 2017–18, 80 students received support, including 12 fellowships with full tuition reimbursements available (averaging $29,000 per year), 21 teaching assistantships with full tuition reimbursements available (averaging $29,000 per year); research assistantships, institutionally sponsored loans, and health care benefits also available. *Faculty research:* Nineteenth-century French prose and poetry, genetic theory and criticism; twentieth-century Latin American literature and film; medieval and Renaissance Italian literature; gender and queer theory in German literature; the ideology of Baroque and neo-Baroque aesthetics. *Unit head:* Dr. Derek Schilling, Chair, 410-516-4626, Fax: 410-516-5358, E-mail: dschill4@jhu.edu. *Application contact:* Kathy Loehmer, Senior Academic Coordinator, 410-516-7226, Fax: 410-516-5358, E-mail: kathy.grll@jhu.edu.
Website: http://grll.jhu.edu/

Manhattanville College, School of Education, Program in Teaching of Languages Other than English, Purchase, NY 10577-2132. Offers adolescence education (grades 7-12) foreign language (MAT, Advanced Certificate), including French, Italian, Latin (Advanced Certificate), Latin (MAT), Spanish. *Program availability:* Part-time, evening/ weekend. *Faculty:* 2 full-time (1 woman). *Students:* 3 part-time (2 women); includes 1 minority (Hispanic/Latino). Average age 31. In 2017, 4 master's, 1 other advanced degree awarded. *Degree requirements:* For master's, comprehensive exam (for some programs), thesis (for some programs), student teaching, research seminars, portfolios, internships, writing assessment; for Advanced Certificate, comprehensive exam (for some programs). *Entrance requirements:* For master's, GRE or MAT (for programs leading to certification), minimum GPA of 3.0, 2 letters of recommendation, interview, essay (2-3 page personal statement that describes reasons for choosing teaching or educational leadership as profession and philosophy of education), proof of immunization (for those born after 1957). Additional exam requirements/ recommendations for international students: Required—TOEFL (minimum score 600 paper-based; 110 iBT); Recommended—IELTS (minimum score 8). *Application deadline:* Applications are processed on a rolling basis. Application fee: $75. Electronic applications accepted. *Expenses:* $915 per credit. *Financial support:* Teaching assistantships, career-related internships or fieldwork, Federal Work-Study, institutionally sponsored loans, scholarships/grants, and unspecified assistantships available. Financial award application deadline: 3/15; financial award applicants required to submit FAFSA. *Faculty research:* Changing suburbs institute and community schools. *Unit head:* Dr. Shelly Wepner, Dean, 914-323-3153, Fax: 914-323-5493. *Application contact:* Alissa Wilson, Director, Graduate Admissions, 914-323-3150, Fax: 914-694-1732, E-mail: edschool@mville.edu.
Website: https://www.mville.edu/programs/teaching-languages-other-english

McGill University, Faculty of Graduate and Postdoctoral Studies, Faculty of Arts, Department of Italian Studies, Montréal, QC H3A 2T5, Canada. Offers MA, PhD.

Middlebury College, Language Schools, Italian School, Middlebury, VT 05753-6002. Offers MA, DML. *Degree requirements:* For master's, one foreign language; for doctorate, 2 foreign languages, comprehensive exam, thesis/dissertation, residence abroad, teaching experience. *Entrance requirements:* For master's, online placement exam, 3 letters of recommendation, writing sample in Italian, transcripts, 200-word essay; for doctorate, 1st and 2nd language online placement exams, 3 letters of recommendation, writing sample in Italian, transcripts, 200-word essay. *Application deadline:* Applications are processed on a rolling basis. Application fee: $75. Electronic applications accepted. *Expenses:* Contact institution. *Financial support:* Fellowships and scholarships/grants available. Financial award application deadline: 3/10; financial award applicants required to submit FAFSA. *Unit head:* Dr. Antonio Vitti, Director, 802-443-5727, Fax: 802-443-2075, E-mail: acvitti@middlebury.edu. *Application contact:* Joseph Tamagni, Coordinator, 802-443-5727, Fax: 802-443-2075, E-mail: italianschool@middlebury.edu.
Website: http://www.middlebury.edu/ls/grad_programs/italian

New York University, Graduate School of Arts and Science, Department of Italian Studies, New York, NY 10012-1019. Offers Italian (MA, PhD); Italian studies (MA). *Program availability:* Part-time. *Students:* Average age 35. 50 applicants, 60% accepted, 9 enrolled. In 2017, 7 master's, 3 doctorates awarded. Terminal master's awarded for partial completion of doctoral program. *Degree requirements:* For master's, one foreign language, thesis; for doctorate, 3 foreign languages, thesis/dissertation. *Entrance requirements:* For master's and doctorate, GRE General Test. Additional exam requirements/recommendations for international students: Required—TOEFL. *Application deadline:* For fall admission, 12/18 priority date for domestic students, 12/18 for international students. Application fee: $100. *Expenses: Tuition:* Full-time $41,352; part-time $19,968 per year. *Required fees:* $2496; $1628 per unit. $814 per term. Tuition and fees vary according to course load and program. *Financial support:* Fellowships, teaching assistantships, Federal Work-Study, institutionally sponsored loans, scholarships/grants, and unspecified assistantships available. Financial award application deadline: 12/18; financial award applicants required to submit FAFSA. *Faculty research:* Dante, early modern literature, fascism and culture, contemporary literature, feminist theory. *Unit head:* Virginia Cox, Chair, 212-998-8730, Fax: 212-995-4012, E-mail: italian.dept@nyu.edu. *Application contact:* Maria Luisa Ardizzone, Acting Director of Graduate Studies, 212-998-8730, Fax: 212-995-4012, E-mail: italian.dept@nyu.edu.
Website: http://www.nyu.edu/gsas/dept/italian/

New York University, Steinhardt School of Culture, Education, and Human Development, Department of Teaching and Learning, Program in Multilingual/ Multicultural Studies, New York, NY 10012. Offers bilingual education (MA, PhD, Advanced Certificate); foreign language education (MA); teaching English to speakers of other languages (MA, PhD); teaching foreign languages, 7-12 (MA), including Chinese, French, Italian, Japanese, Spanish; teaching French as a foreign language (MA), including teaching English to speakers of other languages; teaching Spanish as a foreign language (MA), including teaching English to speakers of other languages. MA in teaching English to speakers of other languages also offered in collaboration with NYU Shanghai. *Accreditation:* TEAC. *Program availability:* Part-time, evening/weekend. *Students:* Average age 29. 431 applicants, 61% accepted, 92 enrolled. In 2017, 121 master's, 1 doctorate, 2 other advanced degrees awarded. *Entrance requirements:* For doctorate, GRE General Test, interview; for Advanced Certificate, master's degree. Additional exam requirements/recommendations for international students: Required—TOEFL (minimum score 100 iBT). *Application deadline:* For fall admission, 12/1 priority date for domestic and international students; for spring admission, 10/1 for domestic and international students. Applications are processed on a rolling basis. Application fee: $75. Electronic applications accepted. *Expenses: Tuition:* Full-time $41,352; part-time $19,968 per year. *Required fees:* $2496; $1628 per unit. $814 per term. Tuition and fees vary according to course load and program. *Financial support:* Fellowships with full and partial tuition reimbursements, career-related internships or fieldwork, Federal Work-Study, institutionally sponsored loans, scholarships/grants, and tuition waivers (partial) available. Support available to part-time students. Financial award application deadline: 2/1; financial award applicants required to submit FAFSA. *Faculty research:* Second language acquisition, cross-cultural communication, technology-enhanced language learning, language variation, action learning. *Unit head:* Prof. Shondel Nero, Director, 212-998-5757, E-mail: shondel.nero@nyu.edu. *Application contact:* 212-998-5030, Fax: 212-995-4328, E-mail: steinhardt.gradadmissions@nyu.edu.
Website: http://steinhardt.nyu.edu/teachlearn/mms

Northwestern University, The Graduate School, Judd A. and Marjorie Weinberg College of Arts and Sciences, Department of French and Italian, Evanston, IL 60208. Offers French/Francophone studies (PhD); Italian studies (Graduate Certificate). Admissions and degrees offered through The Graduate School. *Degree requirements:* For doctorate, one foreign language, thesis/dissertation, written and oral exams. *Entrance requirements:* For doctorate, GRE, writing sample, cassette recording. Additional exam requirements/recommendations for international students: Required—TOEFL. *Faculty research:* Francophone studies, eighteenth century contemporary theory.

The Ohio State University, Graduate School, College of Arts and Sciences, Division of Arts and Humanities, Department of French and Italian, Columbus, OH 43210. Offers French (MA, PhD); Italian (MA); Italian studies (PhD). *Faculty:* 11. *Students:* 18 full-time (10 women), 7 international. Average age 30. In 2017, 5 master's, 4 doctorates awarded. Terminal master's awarded for partial completion of doctoral program. *Degree requirements:* For master's, variable foreign language requirement, thesis optional; for doctorate, variable foreign language requirement, thesis/dissertation. *Entrance requirements:* For master's and doctorate, GRE General Test. Additional exam requirements/recommendations for international students: Required—TOEFL (minimum score 550 paper-based; 79 iBT), IELTS (minimum score 7), Michigan English Language Assessment Battery (minimum score 82). *Application deadline:* For fall admission, 12/15 priority date for domestic students, 11/30 priority date for international students; for spring admission, 3/1 for domestic students, 2/1 for international students. Applications are processed on a rolling basis. Application fee: $60 ($70 for international students). Electronic applications accepted. *Financial support:* Fellowships, research assistantships, teaching assistantships, Federal Work-Study, institutionally sponsored loans, and unspecified assistantships available. Support available to part-time students. *Faculty research:* Italian and Romance linguistics. *Unit head:* Dr. Dana Renga, Chair, 614-292-4938, E-mail: renga.1@osu.edu. *Application contact:* Graduate and Professional Admissions, 614-292-9444, Fax: 614-292-3895, E-mail: gpadmissions@osu.edu.
Website: http://frit.osu.edu/

Queens College of the City University of New York, Arts and Humanities Division, Department of European Languages and Literatures, Queens, NY 11367-1597. Offers French (MA); Italian (MA). *Program availability:* Part-time-only, evening/weekend. *Faculty:* 10 full-time (5 women), 1 part-time/adjunct (0 women). *Students:* 1 full-time (0 women), 11 part-time (6 women); includes 6 minority (5 Black or African American, non-Hispanic/Latino; 1 Hispanic/Latino). Average age 42. 11 applicants, 82% accepted, 6 enrolled. In 2017, 4 master's awarded. *Degree requirements:* For master's, 2 foreign languages, thesis optional, oral exam. *Entrance requirements:* For master's, minimum GPA of 3.0. Additional exam requirements/recommendations for international students: Required—TOEFL (minimum score 61 iBT), IELTS (minimum score 5). *Application deadline:* For fall admission, 4/1 for domestic students; for spring admission, 11/1 for domestic students. Applications are processed on a rolling basis. Application fee: $125. Electronic applications accepted. *Financial support:* Career-related internships or fieldwork, Federal Work-Study, institutionally sponsored loans, and tuition waivers (partial) available. Financial award application deadline: 4/1; financial award applicants required to submit FAFSA. *Faculty research:* Italian literature and culture, French and Francophone literature and theory, Romance linguistics, French and Italian cinema. *Unit head:* Dr. David Andrew Jones, Chair, 718-997-5980, E-mail: david.jones@qc.cuny.edu. *Application contact:* Elizabeth D'Amico-Ramirez, Assistant Director of Graduate Admissions, 718-997-5203, E-mail: elizabeth.damicoramirez@qc.cuny.edu.

Rutgers University–New Brunswick, Graduate School-New Brunswick, Program in Italian, Piscataway, NJ 08854-8097. Offers Italian (MA, PhD); Italian literature and literary criticism (MA); language, literature and culture (MAT). *Program availability:* Part-time, evening/weekend. Terminal master's awarded for partial completion of doctoral program. *Degree requirements:* For master's, one foreign language, comprehensive exam (for some programs), thesis optional; for doctorate, 2 foreign languages, thesis/ dissertation, qualifying exam. *Entrance requirements:* For master's and doctorate, GRE General Test. Additional exam requirements/recommendations for international students: Required—TOEFL. *Faculty research:* Literature.

San Francisco State University, Division of Graduate Studies, College of Liberal and Creative Arts, Department of Modern Languages and Literatures, Program in Italian,

San Francisco, CA 94132-1722. Offers MA. *Application deadline:* Applications are processed on a rolling basis. *Unit head:* Olivia Albiero, Program Coordinator, 415-338-7452, Fax: 415-338-6159, E-mail: albiero@sfsu.edu. Website: http://mll.sfsu.edu/italian-program/

Stanford University, School of Humanities and Sciences, Department of French and Italian, Stanford, CA 94305-2004. Offers French (MA, PhD); French and Italian (PhD); Italian (MA, PhD). Terminal master's awarded for partial completion of doctoral program. *Degree requirements:* For master's, one foreign language, written exam; for doctorate, 2 foreign languages, thesis/dissertation, oral exam. *Entrance requirements:* For master's and doctorate, GRE General Test. Additional exam requirements/recommendations for international students: Required—TOEFL. Electronic applications accepted. *Expenses:* Tuition: Full-time $48,987; part-time $10,620 per quarter. One-time fee: $400. Tuition and fees vary according to program.

Stony Brook University, State University of New York, Graduate School, College of Arts and Sciences, Department of European Languages, Literatures, and Cultures, Program in Italian, Stony Brook, NY 11794. Offers MA. *Program availability:* Evening/weekend. *Students:* 5 part-time (4 women); includes 1 minority (Hispanic/Latino). 3 applicants, 100% accepted, 1 enrolled. In 2017, 1 master's awarded. *Degree requirements:* For master's, one foreign language. *Entrance requirements:* Additional exam requirements/recommendations for international students: Required—TOEFL. *Application deadline:* For fall admission, 1/15 for domestic students; for spring admission, 10/1 for domestic students. Application fee: $100. Electronic applications accepted. *Expenses:* Contact institution. *Unit head:* Prof. Giuseppe Gazzola, Coordinator, 631-632-7440, Fax: 631-632-9612, E-mail: giuseppe.gazzola@stonybrook.edu. *Application contact:* Elizabeth Tolson, Coordinator, 631-632-7440, Fax: 631-632-9612, E-mail: elizabeth-a.tolson@stonybrook.edu.

University of Alberta, Faculty of Graduate Studies and Research, Department of Modern Languages and Cultural Studies, Edmonton, AB T6G 2E1, Canada. Offers applied linguistics (Germanic, Romance, Slavic) (MA); French language, literatures and linguistics (PhD); French language, literatures, and linguistics (MA); Germanic languages, literatures and linguistics (PhD); Germanic languages, literatures, and linguistics (MA); Italian studies (MA); Slavic languages and literatures (Russian, Ukrainian) (MA, PhD); Slavic linguistics (Russian, Ukrainian) (MA, PhD); Spanish and Latin American studies (MA, PhD); Ukrainian folklore (MA, PhD). *Program availability:* Part-time. *Degree requirements:* For master's, one foreign language, thesis; for doctorate, 2 foreign languages, comprehensive exam, thesis/dissertation. *Entrance requirements:* For master's and doctorate, 1 language other than English. Additional exam requirements/recommendations for international students: Required—Michigan English Language Assessment Battery or TOEFL (minimum score 550 paper-based). Electronic applications accepted. *Faculty research:* Russian/Ukrainian studies; German studies; contemporary Latin American, French and Francophone studies; Italian studies.

University of California, Berkeley, Graduate Division, College of Letters and Science, Department of Italian Studies, Berkeley, CA 94720-1500. Offers PhD. *Degree requirements:* For doctorate, one foreign language, thesis/dissertation, oral and written qualifying exams. *Entrance requirements:* For doctorate, GRE General Test, minimum GPA of 3.0, 3 letters of recommendation. Additional exam requirements/recommendations for international students: Required—TOEFL (minimum score 570 paper-based; 90 iBT). Electronic applications accepted. *Faculty research:* Literature and culture of Italy in Middle Ages and the Renaissance, literature and culture of Italy in nineteenth and twentieth centuries, Italian film studies, interdisciplinary cultural studies.

University of California, Berkeley, Graduate Division, College of Letters and Science, Group in Romance Languages and Literatures, Berkeley, CA 94720-1500. Offers French (PhD); Italian (PhD); Spanish (PhD). *Degree requirements:* For doctorate, thesis/dissertation, qualifying exam. *Entrance requirements:* For doctorate, GRE General Test, minimum GPA of 3.0, 3 letters of recommendation. Additional exam requirements/recommendations for international students: Required—TOEFL (minimum score 570 paper-based; 90 iBT). Electronic applications accepted.

University of California, Los Angeles, Graduate Division, College of Letters and Science, Department of Italian, Los Angeles, CA 90095. Offers MA, PhD. Terminal master's awarded for partial completion of doctoral program. *Degree requirements:* For master's, one foreign language, comprehensive exam or thesis; for doctorate, 2 foreign languages, thesis/dissertation, oral and written qualifying exams. *Entrance requirements:* For master's, GRE General Test, bachelor's degree; minimum undergraduate GPA of 3.0 (or its equivalent if letter grade system not used); for doctorate, GRE General Test, master's degree; minimum undergraduate GPA of 3.0 (or its equivalent if letter grade system not used). Additional exam requirements/recommendations for international students: Required—TOEFL. Electronic applications accepted.

University of Chicago, Division of the Humanities, Department of Romance Languages and Literatures, Chicago, IL 60637. Offers French and Francophone studies (PhD); Hispanic and Luso-Brazilian studies (PhD); Italian studies (PhD); Renaissance and early modern studies (PhD). *Students:* 50 full-time (28 women); includes 12 minority (2 Asian, non-Hispanic/Latino; 9 Hispanic/Latino; 1 Two or more races, non-Hispanic/Latino), 25 international. Average age 30. 52 applicants, 31% accepted, 7 enrolled. In 2017, 4 doctorates awarded. Terminal master's awarded for partial completion of doctoral program. *Degree requirements:* For doctorate, 3 foreign languages, comprehensive exam, thesis/dissertation. *Entrance requirements:* For doctorate, GRE General Test, 15-20 page writing sample, statement of purpose, 3 letters of recommendation, transcripts for all previous degrees and institutions attended. Additional exam requirements/recommendations for international students: Required—TOEFL (minimum score 104 iBT), IELTS (minimum score 7). *Application deadline:* For fall admission, 12/15 for domestic and international students. Application fee: $90. Electronic applications accepted. *Financial support:* In 2017-18, fellowships with full tuition reimbursements (averaging $27,000 per year) were awarded; teaching assistantships with full tuition reimbursements, Federal Work-Study, institutionally sponsored loans, scholarships/grants, and health care benefits also available. Financial award application deadline: 12/15. *Unit head:* Daisy Delogu, Chair, 773-702-8481, E-mail: romance-languages@uchicago.edu. *Application contact:* Michael Beetley, Assistant Dean of Students, Admissions and Fellowships, 773-702-1552, Fax: 773-834-9148, E-mail: humanitiesadmissions@uchicago.edu. Website: http://rll.uchicago.edu

University of Georgia, Franklin College of Arts and Sciences, Department of Romance Languages, Athens, GA 30602. Offers French (PhD); Italian (MA, PhD); Portuguese (MA, PhD); romance linguistics (MA); Spanish (PhD). *Degree requirements:* For master's, one foreign language; for doctorate, 2 foreign languages, thesis/dissertation. *Entrance requirements:* For master's and doctorate, GRE General Test. Electronic applications accepted.

University of Illinois at Urbana–Champaign, Graduate College, College of Liberal Arts and Sciences, School of Literatures, Cultures and Linguistics, Department of Spanish, Italian and Portuguese, Champaign, IL 61820. Offers Italian (MA, PhD); Portuguese (MA, PhD); Spanish (MA, PhD).

The University of Manchester, School of Languages, Linguistics and Cultures, Manchester, United Kingdom. Offers Arab world studies (PhD); Chinese studies (M Phil, PhD); East Asian studies (M Phil, PhD); English language (PhD); French studies (M Phil, PhD); German studies (M Phil, PhD); interpreting studies (PhD); Italian studies (M Phil, PhD); Japanese studies (M Phil, PhD); Latin American cultural studies (M Phil, PhD); linguistics (M Phil, PhD); Middle Eastern studies (M Phil, PhD); Polish studies (M Phil, PhD); Portuguese studies (M Phil, PhD); Russian studies (M Phil, PhD); Spanish studies (M Phil, PhD); translation and intercultural studies (M Phil, PhD).

University of Massachusetts Amherst, Graduate School, College of Humanities and Fine Arts, Department of Languages, Literatures, and Cultures, Program in Italian Studies, Amherst, MA 01003. Offers MAT. *Program availability:* Part-time. *Degree requirements:* For master's, comprehensive exam, thesis or alternative. *Entrance requirements:* For master's, GRE General Test. Additional exam requirements/recommendations for international students: Required—TOEFL (minimum score 550 paper-based; 80 iBT), IELTS (minimum score 6.5). Electronic applications accepted.

University of Michigan, Rackham Graduate School, College of Literature, Science, and the Arts, Department of Romance Languages and Literatures, Program in Italian, Ann Arbor, MI 48109. Offers PhD. *Degree requirements:* For doctorate, 2 foreign languages, thesis/dissertation, oral defense of dissertation, preliminary exams in essay format. *Entrance requirements:* Additional exam requirements/recommendations for international students: Required—TOEFL or Michigan English Language Assessment Battery. Electronic applications accepted. *Expenses:* Tuition, state resident: full-time $22,368; part-time $1201 per credit hour. Tuition, nonresident: full-time $45,156; part-time $2467 per credit hour. *Required fees:* $376 per term. Tuition and fees vary according to course load, degree level and program. *Faculty research:* Cinema, transnational visual culture, nineteenth-twentieth century Italian literature, medieval and Renaissance literature, medieval Mediterranean literature.

The University of North Carolina at Chapel Hill, Graduate School, College of Arts and Sciences, Department of Romance Languages and Literatures, Chapel Hill, NC 27599. Offers French (MA, PhD); Italian (MA, PhD); Portuguese (MA, PhD); Romance languages (MA, PhD); Romance philology (MA, PhD); Spanish (MA, PhD). *Degree requirements:* For master's, one foreign language, comprehensive exam, thesis; for doctorate, 2 foreign languages, comprehensive exam, thesis/dissertation. *Entrance requirements:* For master's and doctorate, GRE General Test, minimum GPA of 3.0. Additional exam requirements/recommendations for international students: Required—TOEFL (minimum score 550 paper-based). Electronic applications accepted.

University of Notre Dame, Graduate School, College of Arts and Letters, Division of Humanities, Department of Romance Languages and Literatures, Notre Dame, IN 46556. Offers French and Francophone studies (MA); Iberian and Latin American studies (MA); Italian studies (MA); Romance literatures (MA). *Degree requirements:* For master's, 2 foreign languages, comprehensive exam, thesis optional. *Entrance requirements:* For master's, GRE General Test, BA in target language. Additional exam requirements/recommendations for international students: Required—TOEFL (minimum score 600 paper-based; 80 iBT). Electronic applications accepted. *Faculty research:* Literature of discovery and exploration, modern literature, literary criticism, medieval literature, feminist critical theory.

University of Oregon, Graduate School, College of Arts and Sciences, Department of Romance Languages, Program in Italian, Eugene, OR 97403. Offers MA. *Program availability:* Part-time. *Degree requirements:* For master's, variable foreign language requirement. *Entrance requirements:* For master's, GRE General Test, minimum GPA of 3.0. Additional exam requirements/recommendations for international students: Required—TOEFL.

University of Pennsylvania, School of Arts and Sciences, Graduate Group in Romance Languages, Philadelphia, PA 19104. Offers French (AM, PhD); Italian (AM, PhD); Spanish (AM, PhD). *Faculty:* 20 full-time (7 women), 6 part-time/adjunct (3 women). *Students:* 61 full-time (29 women); includes 7 minority (6 Hispanic/Latino; 1 Two or more races, non-Hispanic/Latino), 34 international. Average age 31. 82 applicants, 32% accepted, 13 enrolled. In 2017, 12 master's, 8 doctorates awarded. Terminal master's awarded for partial completion of doctoral program. Application fee: $70. Website: http://www.sas.upenn.edu/graduate-division

University of Pittsburgh, Kenneth P. Dietrich School of Arts and Sciences, Department of French and Italian Languages and Literatures, Pittsburgh, PA 15260. Offers French (MA, PhD), including film studies (PhD), French (MA), Romance languages and literatures (PhD); Italian (MA). *Program availability:* Part-time. *Faculty:* 12 full-time (6 women). *Students:* 26 full-time (15 women); includes 2 minority (1 Black or African American, non-Hispanic/Latino; 1 Hispanic/Latino), 9 international. Average age 31. 17 applicants, 53% accepted, 6 enrolled. In 2017, 3 master's, 5 doctorates awarded. Terminal master's awarded for partial completion of doctoral program. *Degree requirements:* For master's, one foreign language, comprehensive exam, thesis; for doctorate, variable foreign language requirement, comprehensive exam, thesis/dissertation. *Entrance requirements:* For master's, GRE General Test (for French), phone interview and writing samples in French and English (for French); minimum GPA of 3.0 and writing sample (for Italian); for doctorate, GRE General Test (for French), phone interview and writing samples in French and English (for French). Additional exam requirements/recommendations for international students: Required—TOEFL (minimum score 600 paper-based; 90 iBT), IELTS. *Application deadline:* For fall admission, 1/10 priority date for domestic and international students. Application fee: $50. Electronic applications accepted. *Expenses:* $22,290 in-state tuition, $36,980 out-of-state, $850 fees. *Financial support:* In 2017-18, 22 students received support, including 5 fellowships with full tuition reimbursements available (averaging $23,262 per year), 1 research assistantship with full tuition reimbursement available (averaging $18,815 per year), 16 teaching assistantships with full tuition reimbursements available (averaging $18,815 per year); traineeships, health care benefits, and unspecified assistantships also available. Financial award application deadline: 1/10. *Faculty research:* Literature and politics; gender and sexuality; Dante and his reception; seventeenth- and eighteenth-century Italian literature and culture; Italian theater; Renaissance studies; culture of the French Caribbean; West Africa and the Maghreb; environmental studies; post-coloniality; French culture from the Middle Ages to the 21st century; poetry and epistolarity; post-unification Italian culture, especially Fascism, World War II, the Holocaust, and Sicilian cultural production. *Total annual research expenditures:* $9,000. *Unit head:* Dr. Lina Insana, Chair, 412-624-6269, E-mail: insana@pitt.edu. *Application contact:* Keanna Cash, Graduate Administrator, 412-624-5227, Fax: 412-624-6263, E-mail: kec176@pitt.edu. Website: http://frenchanditalian.pitt.edu

University of South Africa, College of Human Sciences, Pretoria, South Africa. Offers adult education (M Ed); African languages (MA, PhD); African politics (MA, PhD); Afrikaans (MA, PhD); ancient history (MA, PhD); ancient Near Eastern studies (MA, PhD); anthropology (MA, PhD); applied linguistics (MA); Arabic (MA, PhD); archaeology (MA); art history (MA); Biblical archaeology (MA); Biblical studies (M Th, D Th, PhD); Christian spirituality (M Th, D Th); church history (M Th, D Th); classical studies (MA, PhD); clinical psychology (MA); communication (MA, PhD); comparative education

(M Ed, Ed D); consulting psychology (D Admin, D Com, PhD); curriculum studies (M Ed, Ed D); development studies (M Admin, MA, D Admin, PhD); didactics (M Ed, Ed D); education (M Tech); education management (M Ed, Ed D); educational psychology (M Ed); English (MA); environmental education (M Ed); French (MA, PhD); German (MA, PhD); Greek (MA); guidance and counseling (M Ed); health studies (MA, PhD), including health sciences education (MA), health services management (MA), medical and surgical nursing science (critical care general) (MA), midwifery and neonatal nursing science (MA), trauma and emergency care (MA); history (MA, PhD); history of education (Ed D); inclusive education (M Ed, Ed D); information and communications technology policy and regulation (MA); information science (MA, MIS, PhD); international politics (MA, PhD); Islamic studies (MA, PhD); Italian (MA, PhD); Judaica (MA, PhD); linguistics (MA, PhD); mathematical education (M Ed); mathematics education (MA); missiology (M Th, D Th); modern Hebrew (MA, PhD); musicology (MA, MMus, D Mus, PhD); natural science education (M Ed); New Testament (M Th, D Th); Old Testament (D Th); pastoral therapy (M Th, D Th); philosophy (MA); philosophy of education (M Ed, Ed D); politics (MA, PhD); Portuguese (MA, PhD); practical theology (M Th, D Th); psychology (MA, MS, PhD); psychology of education (M Ed, Ed D); public health (MA); religious studies (MA, D Th, PhD); Romance languages (MA); Russian (MA, PhD); Semitic languages (MA, PhD); social behavior studies in HIV/AIDS (MA); social science (mental health) (MA); social science in development studies (MA); social science in psychology (MA); social science in social work (MA); social science in sociology (MA); social work (MSW, DSW, PhD); socio-education (M Ed, Ed D); sociolinguistics (MA); sociology (MA, PhD); Spanish (MA, PhD); systematic theology (M Th, D Th); TESOL (teaching English to speakers of other languages) (MA); theological ethics (M Th, D Th); theory of literature (MA, PhD); urban ministries (D Th); urban ministry (M Th).

The University of Tennessee, Graduate School, College of Arts and Sciences, Department of Modern Foreign Languages and Literatures, Program in Modern Foreign Languages, Knoxville, TN 37996. Offers applied linguistics (PhD); French (PhD); German (PhD); Italian (PhD); Portuguese (PhD); Russian (PhD); Spanish (PhD). *Degree requirements:* For doctorate, 2 foreign languages, thesis/dissertation. *Entrance requirements:* For doctorate, minimum GPA of 2.7. Additional exam requirements/recommendations for international students: Required—TOEFL. Electronic applications accepted.

The University of Texas at Austin, Graduate School, College of Liberal Arts, Department of French and Italian, Austin, TX 78712-1111. Offers French linguistics (MA, PhD); French studies (MA, PhD); Italian studies (MA, PhD); Romance linguistics (PhD). *Program availability:* Part-time. *Degree requirements:* For master's, one foreign language, thesis; for doctorate, 2 foreign languages, thesis/dissertation. *Entrance requirements:* For master's, GRE General Test, minimum GPA of 3.0, bachelor's degree in French or equivalent; for doctorate, GRE General Test, minimum GPA of 3.0, master's degree in French. Additional exam requirements/recommendations for international students: Required—TOEFL. Electronic applications accepted. *Faculty research:* Nineteenth-century Italian literature, Italian Renaissance, twentieth-century French literature, Francophone literature, fifteenth-century literature and culture.

University of Toronto, School of Graduate Studies, Faculty of Arts and Science, Department of Italian Studies, Toronto, ON M5S 1A1, Canada. Offers MA, PhD. *Program availability:* Part-time. *Degree requirements:* For doctorate, 2 foreign languages, comprehensive exam, thesis/dissertation, oral defense, language exam(s). *Entrance requirements:* For master's, minimum B average in last 2 years in Italian and in final year overall; 2 letters of recommendation; for doctorate, MA in Italian, minimum A- average. Electronic applications accepted.

University of Victoria, Faculty of Graduate Studies, Faculty of Humanities, Department of Hispanic and Italian Studies, Victoria, BC V8W 2Y2, Canada. Offers Hispanic and Italian studies (MA); Hispanic studies (MA). *Degree requirements:* For master's, one foreign language, comprehensive exam, thesis (for some programs). *Entrance requirements:* For master's, undergraduate major in Hispanic studies, minimum B+ average. Additional exam requirements/recommendations for international students: Required—TOEFL (minimum score 575 paper-based), IELTS (minimum score 7). Electronic applications accepted. *Faculty research:* Medieval/Renaissance Spanish and Italian literature, Golden Age literature, Latin American literature.

University of Washington, Graduate School, College of Arts and Sciences, Division of French and Italian Studies, Seattle, WA 98195. Offers French (MA, PhD); Italian (MA). Terminal master's awarded for partial completion of doctoral program. *Degree requirements:* For master's, 2 foreign languages, exam; for doctorate, 3 foreign languages, thesis/dissertation, exam. *Entrance requirements:* For master's and doctorate, GRE General Test, minimum GPA of 3.0. Additional exam requirements/recommendations for international students: Required—TOEFL. Electronic applications accepted. *Faculty research:* Interdisciplinary studies, literary theory and criticism, film, major periods of French and Italian literature, Francophonie.

University of Wisconsin–Madison, Graduate School, College of Letters and Science, Department of French and Italian, Program in Italian, Madison, WI 53706-1380. Offers MA, PhD. *Program availability:* Part-time. *Degree requirements:* For master's, one foreign language; for doctorate, 2 foreign languages, thesis/dissertation. *Entrance requirements:* For master's and doctorate, GRE. Electronic applications accepted. *Faculty research:* Italian literature, culture, linguistics, cinema, and language.

Wayne State University, College of Liberal Arts and Sciences, Department of Classical and Modern Languages, Literatures, and Cultures, Detroit, MI 48202. Offers classics (MA), including ancient Greek and Latin, ancient studies, classics, Latin; German (MA); language learning (MALL), including Arabic (MA, MALL), French (MA, MALL, PhD), German (MALL, PhD), Italian (MA, MALL), Spanish (MA, MALL, PhD); modern languages (PhD), including French (MA, MALL, PhD), German (MALL, PhD), Spanish (MA, MALL, PhD); Near Eastern languages (MA), including Arabic (MA, MALL), Hebrew; Romance languages (MA), including French (MA, MALL, PhD), Italian (MA, MALL), Spanish (MA, MALL, PhD). *Faculty:* 22. *Students:* 24 full-time (18 women), 21 part-time (15 women); includes 11 minority (4 Black or African American, non-Hispanic/Latino; 1 American Indian or Alaska Native, non-Hispanic/Latino; 2 Asian, non-Hispanic/Latino; 2 Hispanic/Latino; 2 Two or more races, non-Hispanic/Latino), 3 international. Average age 37. 32 applicants, 63% accepted, 14 enrolled. In 2017, 10 master's awarded. *Degree requirements:* For master's, variable foreign language requirement, comprehensive exam (for some programs), thesis (for some programs); for doctorate, one foreign language, comprehensive exam, thesis/dissertation. *Entrance requirements:* Additional exam requirements/recommendations for international students: Required—TOEFL (minimum score 550 paper-based; 79 iBT), TWE (minimum score 5.5), Michigan English Language Assessment Battery (minimum score 85); Recommended—IELTS (minimum score 6.5). Application fee: $50. Electronic applications accepted. *Expenses:* Tuition, state resident: full-time $10,224; part-time $638.98 per credit hour. Tuition, nonresident: full-time $22,145; part-time $1384.04 per credit hour. Tuition and fees vary according to course load and program. *Financial support:* In 2017–18, 25 students received support, including 4 fellowships with tuition reimbursements available (averaging $13,500 per year), 17 teaching assistantships with tuition reimbursements available (averaging $18,591 per year); research assistantships, scholarships/grants, health care benefits, and unspecified assistantships also available. Financial award applicants required to submit FAFSA. *Faculty research:* Classical and modern literature and culture (Greek, Latin, Arabic, Chinese, French, German, Russian, Spanish) including colonial studies and exile and Holocaust studies; critical theory (French, German, Slavic, Spanish); theoretical and applied linguistics (Arabic, Chinese, French, Spanish); area studies (Arabic, Near Eastern, classical, Islamic, and Judaic studies). *Unit head:* Dr. Anne Duggan, Department Chair, 313-577-6244, Fax: 313-577-6243, E-mail: a.duggan@wayne.edu.
Website: http://clas.wayne.edu/languages/

Yale University, Graduate School of Arts and Sciences, Department of Italian Language and Literature, New Haven, CT 06520. Offers PhD. *Degree requirements:* For doctorate, 3 foreign languages, thesis/dissertation. *Entrance requirements:* For doctorate, GRE General Test.

Japanese

Arizona State University at the Tempe campus, College of Liberal Arts and Sciences, School of International Letters and Cultures, Program in Japanese, Tempe, AZ 85287-0202. Offers Asian languages and civilizations: Japanese (MA). *Program availability:* Part-time, evening/weekend. *Degree requirements:* For master's, thesis, oral defense, interactive Program of Study (iPOS) submitted no later than beginning of third semester of study. *Entrance requirements:* For master's, minimum GPA of 3.25 in the last two years of work leading to the bachelor's degree; BA in Japanese or at least 5 semesters of modern Japanese (preferred); personal statement; writing sample; 3 letters of recommendation. Additional exam requirements/recommendations for international students: Required—TOEFL (minimum score 550 paper-based; 83 iBT), IELTS (minimum score 6.5). Electronic applications accepted.

Columbia University, Graduate School of Arts and Sciences, New York, NY 10027. Offers African-American studies (MA); American studies (MA); anthropology (MA, PhD); art history and archaeology (MA, PhD); astronomy (PhD); biological sciences (PhD); biotechnology (MA); chemical physics (PhD); chemistry (PhD); classical studies (MA, PhD); classics (MA, PhD); climate and society (MA); conservation biology (MA); earth and environmental sciences (PhD); East Asia: regional studies (MA); East Asian languages and cultures (MA, PhD); ecology, evolution and environmental biology (MA), including conservation biology; ecology, evolution, and environmental biology (PhD), including ecology and evolutionary biology, evolutionary primatology; economics (MA, PhD); English and comparative literature (MA, PhD); French and Romance philology (MA, PhD); Germanic languages (MA, PhD); global French studies (MA); global thought (MA); Hispanic cultural studies (MA); history (PhD); history and literature (MA); human rights studies (MA); Islamic studies (MA); Italian (MA, PhD); Japanese pedagogy (MA); Jewish studies (MA); Latin America and the Caribbean: regional studies (MA); Latin American and Iberian cultures (PhD); mathematics (MA, PhD), including finance (MA); medieval and Renaissance studies (MA); Middle Eastern, South Asian, and African studies (MA, PhD); modern art: critical and curatorial studies (MA); modern European studies (MA); museum anthropology (MA); music (DMA, PhD); oral history (MA); philosophical foundations of physics (MA); philosophy (MA, PhD); physics (PhD); political science (MA, PhD); psychology (PhD); quantitative methods in the social sciences (MA); religion (MA, PhD); Russia, Eurasia and East Europe: regional studies (MA); Russian translation (MA); Slavic cultures (MA); Slavic languages (MA, PhD); sociology (MA, PhD); South Asian studies (MA); statistics (MA, PhD); theatre (PhD). Dual-degree programs require admission to both Graduate School of Arts and Sciences and another Columbia school. *Program availability:* Part-time. Terminal master's awarded for partial completion of doctoral program. *Degree requirements:* For master's, variable foreign language requirement, comprehensive exam (for some programs), thesis (for some programs); for doctorate, variable foreign language requirement, comprehensive exam (for some programs), thesis/dissertation. *Entrance requirements:* For master's and doctorate, GRE General Test, GRE Subject Test (for some programs). Additional exam requirements/recommendations for international students: Required—TOEFL, IELTS. Electronic applications accepted. *Expenses: Tuition:* Full-time $44,864; part-time $1704 per credit. *Required fees:* $2370 per semester. One-time fee: $105.

DePaul University, College of Liberal Arts and Social Sciences, Chicago, IL 60614. Offers Arabic (MA); Chinese (MA); critical ethnic studies (MA); English (MA); French (MA); German (MA); history (MA); interdisciplinary studies (MA, MS); international public service (MS); international studies (MA); Italian (MA); Japanese (MA); liberal studies (MA); nonprofit management (MNM); public administration (MPA); public health (MPH); public policy (MPP); public service management (MS); refugee and forced migration studies (MS); social work (MSW); sociology (MA); Spanish (MA); sustainable urban development (MA); women's and gender studies (MA); writing and publishing (MA); writing, rhetoric and discourse (MA); MA/PhD. *Program availability:* Part-time, evening/weekend, online learning. Terminal master's awarded for partial completion of doctoral program. *Degree requirements:* For master's, variable foreign language requirement, comprehensive exam (for some programs), thesis (for some programs). *Application deadline:* Applications are processed on a rolling basis. Application fee: $40. Electronic applications accepted. *Financial support:* Applicants required to submit FAFSA. *Unit head:* Dr. Guillermo Vasquez de Velasco, Dean, 773-325-7305. *Application contact:* Ann Spittle, Director of Graduate Admission, 773-325-8369, Fax: 312-476-3244, E-mail: graddepaul@depaul.edu.
Website: http://las.depaul.edu/

Harvard University, Graduate School of Arts and Sciences, Department of East Asian Languages and Civilizations, Cambridge, MA 02138. Offers Chinese (PhD); Japanese (PhD); Korean (PhD); Mongolian (PhD); Vietnamese (PhD). Terminal master's awarded for partial completion of doctoral program. *Degree requirements:* For doctorate, 3 foreign languages, thesis/dissertation, general exams. *Entrance requirements:* For doctorate, GRE General Test. Additional exam requirements/recommendations for international students: Required—TOEFL. *Faculty research:* Central Asian literature, religion, and premodern history.

Japanese

Indiana University Bloomington, University Graduate School, College of Arts and Sciences, School of Global and International Studies, Department of East Asian Languages and Cultures, Bloomington, IN 47408. Offers Chinese (MA, PhD); Chinese language pedagogy (MA); East Asian studies (MA); Japanese (MA, PhD); Japanese language pedagogy (MA). *Program availability:* Part-time. *Degree requirements:* For master's, one foreign language, thesis; for doctorate, 2 foreign languages, comprehensive exam, thesis/dissertation. *Entrance requirements:* Additional exam requirements/recommendations for international students: Required—TOEFL (minimum score 93 iBT). Electronic applications accepted. *Faculty research:* Modern East Asian history; politics and society; traditional Chinese thought and society; medieval and premodern Japanese history, literature and society; modern Chinese and Japanese film and literature; Chinese, Japanese, Korean language and linguistics.

Kent State University, College of Arts and Sciences, Department of Modern and Classical Language Studies, Kent, OH 44242-0001. Offers French (MA), including applied linguistics and pedagogy, literature; German (MA), including applied linguistics and pedagogy, literature; Latin (MA), including applied linguistics and pedagogy, literature; Spanish (MA), including applied linguistics and pedagogy, literature; translation (MA), including Arabic, French, German, Japanese, Russian, Spanish; translation studies (PhD); MA/MBA. *Program availability:* Part-time. *Faculty:* 21 full-time (13 women), 5 part-time/adjunct (3 women). *Students:* 78 full-time (50 women), 20 part-time (13 women); includes 18 minority (3 Black or African American, non-Hispanic/Latino; 1 Asian, non-Hispanic/Latino; 9 Hispanic/Latino; 5 Two or more races, non-Hispanic/Latino), 44 international. Average age 31. 95 applicants, 55% accepted, 27 enrolled. In 2017, 30 master's awarded. *Degree requirements:* For master's, variable foreign language requirement, comprehensive exam (for some programs), thesis (for some programs); for doctorate, variable foreign language requirement, comprehensive exam, thesis/dissertation. *Entrance requirements:* For master's, transcripts, goal statement, 3 letters of recommendation, CD/MP3 with oral sample of first and second languages, writing sample of second language; for doctorate, transcripts; MA in translation, a foreign language, or similar field; proficiency in a foreign language; minimum GPA of 3.5 from MA; goal statement; 3 letters of recommendation; essay or writing sample. Additional exam requirements/recommendations for international students: Required—TOEFL (minimum score 550 paper-based, 79 iBT), Michigan English Language Assessment Battery (minimum score 77), IELTS (minimum score 6.5) or PTE (minimum score 58). *Application deadline:* For fall admission, 2/1 for domestic and international students. Applications are processed on a rolling basis. Application fee: $45 ($70 for international students). Electronic applications accepted. *Expenses:* Tuition, state resident: full-time $11,310; part-time $515 per credit hour. Tuition, nonresident: full-time $20,396; part-time $928 per credit hour. *International tuition:* $18,544 full-time. *Financial support:* Fellowships with full tuition reimbursements, teaching assistantships with full tuition reimbursements, and unspecified assistantships available. Financial award application deadline: 2/1. *Unit head:* Dr. Keiran Dunne, Professor of French Translation/Chair, 330-672-2150, E-mail: kdunne@kent.edu. *Application contact:* Said Shiyab, Professor of Translation Studies/Graduate Coordinator, 330-672-1864, E-mail: sshiyab@kent.edu.
Website: http://www.kent.edu/mcls/

New York University, Steinhardt School of Culture, Education, and Human Development, Department of Teaching and Learning, Program in Multilingual/Multicultural Studies, New York, NY 10012. Offers bilingual education (MA, PhD, Advanced Certificate); foreign language education (MA); teaching English to speakers of other languages (MA, PhD); teaching foreign languages, 7-12 (MA), including Chinese, French, Italian, Japanese, Spanish; teaching French as a foreign language (MA), including teaching English to speakers of other languages; teaching Spanish as a foreign language (MA), including teaching English to speakers of other languages. MA in teaching English to speakers of other languages also offered in collaboration with NYU Shanghai. *Accreditation:* TEAC. *Program availability:* Part-time, evening/weekend. *Students:* Average age 29. 431 applicants, 61% accepted, 92 enrolled. In 2017, 121 master's, 1 doctorate, 2 other advanced degrees awarded. *Entrance requirements:* For doctorate, GRE General Test, interview; for Advanced Certificate, master's degree. Additional exam requirements/recommendations for international students: Required—TOEFL (minimum score 100 iBT). *Application deadline:* For fall admission, 12/1 priority date for domestic and international students; for spring admission, 10/1 for domestic and international students. Applications are processed on a rolling basis. Application fee: $75. Electronic applications accepted. *Expenses: Tuition:* Full-time $41,352; part-time $19,968 per year. *Required fees:* $2496; $1628 per unit. $814 per term. Tuition and fees vary according to course load and program. *Financial support:* Fellowships with full and partial tuition reimbursements, career-related internships or fieldwork, Federal Work-Study, institutionally sponsored loans, scholarships/grants, and tuition waivers (partial) available. Support available to part-time students. Financial award application deadline: 2/1; financial award applicants required to submit FAFSA. *Faculty research:* Second language acquisition, cross-cultural communication, technology-enhanced language learning, language variation, action learning. *Unit head:* Prof. Shondel Nero, Director, 212-998-5757, E-mail: shondel.nero@nyu.edu. *Application contact:* 212-998-5030, Fax: 212-995-4328, E-mail: steinhardt.gradadmissions@nyu.edu.
Website: http://steinhardt.nyu.edu/teachlearn/mms

The Ohio State University, Graduate School, College of Arts and Sciences, Division of Arts and Humanities, Department of East Asian Languages and Literatures, Columbus, OH 43210. Offers Chinese (MA, PhD); Japanese (MA, PhD). *Faculty:* 19. *Students:* 50 full-time (32 women), 4 part-time (2 women); includes 5 minority (all Asian, non-Hispanic/Latino), 24 international. Average age 30. In 2017, 9 master's, 6 doctorates awarded. Terminal master's awarded for partial completion of doctoral program. *Entrance requirements:* For master's and doctorate, GRE General Test (if applying for financial aid). Additional exam requirements/recommendations for international students: Required—TOEFL (minimum score 577 paper-based; 90 iBT); Recommended—IELTS (minimum score 7.5). *Application deadline:* For fall admission, 11/30 priority date for domestic and international students; for spring admission, 3/1 for domestic students, 2/1 for international students. Applications are processed on a rolling basis. Application fee: $60 ($70 for international students). Electronic applications accepted. *Financial support:* Fellowships, research assistantships, teaching assistantships, Federal Work-Study, institutionally sponsored loans, and unspecified assistantships available. Support available to part-time students. *Unit head:* Dr. Mark Bender, Chair and Professor, 614-688-5737, E-mail: bender.4@osu.edu. *Application contact:* Graduate and Professional Admissions, 614-292-9444, Fax: 614-292-3895, E-mail: gpadmissions@osu.edu.
Website: http://deall.osu.edu/

Portland State University, Graduate Studies, College of Liberal Arts and Sciences, Department of World Languages and Literatures, Portland, OR 97207-0751. Offers French (MA); German (MA); Japanese (MA); Spanish (MA); world literature and language (MA). *Program availability:* Part-time. *Faculty:* 61 full-time (37 women), 26 part-time/adjunct (20 women). *Students:* 22 full-time (13 women), 11 part-time (5 women); includes 7 minority (1 Asian, non-Hispanic/Latino; 6 Hispanic/Latino), 8 international. Average age 30. 26 applicants, 73% accepted, 16 enrolled. In 2017, 9 master's awarded. *Degree requirements:* For master's, variable foreign language requirement, thesis (for some programs). *Entrance requirements:* For master's, ACTFL, BA in the major language, minimum GPA of 3.0 in all coursework. Additional exam requirements/recommendations for international students: Required—TOEFL (minimum score 550 paper-based; 80 iBT), IELTS (minimum score 6.5). *Application deadline:* For fall admission, 4/1 for domestic students, 3/1 for international students; for winter admission, 9/1 for domestic students, 7/1 for international students; for spring admission, 11/1 for domestic and international students. Applications are processed on a rolling basis. Application fee: $65. *Expenses:* Tuition, state resident: full-time $14,436; part-time $401 per credit. Tuition, nonresident: full-time $21,780; part-time $605 per credit. *Required fees:* $1380; $22 per credit. $119 per quarter. One-time fee: $325. Tuition and fees vary according to program. *Financial support:* In 2017–18, 22 teaching assistantships with full and partial tuition reimbursements (averaging $11,431 per year) were awarded; research assistantships, Federal Work-Study, scholarships/grants, and unspecified assistantships also available. Support available to part-time students. Financial award application deadline: 3/1; financial award applicants required to submit FAFSA. *Faculty research:* Foreign language pedagogy, applied and social linguistics, literary history and criticism. *Total annual research expenditures:* $522,357. *Unit head:* Dr. Gina Greco, Chair, 503-725-5287, E-mail: grecog@pdx.edu. *Application contact:* Kelli Martin, Graduate Admissions Coordinator, 503-725-3243, E-mail: kmarti@pdx.edu.
Website: http://www.pdx.edu/wll/

Purdue University, Graduate School, College of Liberal Arts, School of Languages and Cultures, West Lafayette, IN 47907. Offers French (MA, MAT, PhD), including French (MA, PhD), French education (MAT); German (MA, MAT, PhD), including German (MA, PhD), German education (MAT); Japanese pedagogy (MA); Spanish (MA, MAT, PhD), including Spanish (MA, PhD), Spanish education (MAT). *Faculty:* 44 full-time (22 women), 1 (woman) part-time/adjunct. *Students:* 37 full-time (18 women), 41 part-time (30 women); includes 9 minority (1 Asian, non-Hispanic/Latino; 8 Hispanic/Latino), 52 international. Average age 32. 49 applicants, 39% accepted, 14 enrolled. In 2017, 11 master's, 5 doctorates awarded. Terminal master's awarded for partial completion of doctoral program. *Degree requirements:* For master's, one foreign language; for doctorate, 2 foreign languages, thesis/dissertation. *Entrance requirements:* For master's, GRE General Test (minimum score 600, 160 for new scoring), two writing samples, one in English, one in language (French, German, Japanese, or Spanish); sample recording of English and language of study; for doctorate, GRE General Test (minimum score 600, 160 for new scoring), master's degree with minimum GPA of 3.5 or equivalent; two writing samples, one in English, one in language (French, German, Japanese, or Spanish); sample recording of English and language of study. Additional exam requirements/recommendations for international students: Required—TOEFL (minimum score 550 paper-based; 77 iBT); Recommended—TWE. *Application deadline:* For fall admission, 12/12 for domestic and international students; for spring admission, 10/1 for domestic and international students. Applications are processed on a rolling basis. Application fee: $60 ($75 for international students). Electronic applications accepted. *Financial support:* In 2017–18, fellowships with tuition reimbursements (averaging $15,750 per year), teaching assistantships with tuition reimbursements (averaging $13,463 per year) were awarded. Support available to part-time students. Financial award applicants required to submit FAFSA. *Faculty research:* Linguistics, semiotics, literary criticism, pedagogy. *Unit head:* Jennifer M. William, Head, 765-494-3834, E-mail: jmwilliam@purdue.edu. *Application contact:* Joni L. Hipsher, Graduate Contact, 765-494-3841, E-mail: jlhipshe@purdue.edu.
Website: http://www.cla.purdue.edu/slc/main/

San Francisco State University, Division of Graduate Studies, College of Liberal and Creative Arts, Department of Modern Languages and Literatures, Program in Japanese, San Francisco, CA 94132-1722. Offers MA. *Program availability:* Part-time. *Application deadline:* Applications are processed on a rolling basis. *Unit head:* Dr. Makiko Asano, Program Coordinator, 415-338-1131, Fax: 415-338-6159, E-mail: masano@sfsu.edu. *Application contact:* Midori McKeon, Graduate Advisor, 415-338-1346, Fax: 415-338-6159, E-mail: mmckeon@sfsu.edu.
Website: http://mll.sfsu.edu/japanese-program/

Stanford University, School of Humanities and Sciences, Department of East Asian Languages and Cultures, Stanford, CA 94305-2004. Offers Chinese (MA, PhD); Japanese (MA, PhD). Terminal master's awarded for partial completion of doctoral program. *Degree requirements:* For master's, one foreign language, thesis or an annotated translation of a literary or historical text; for doctorate, 2 foreign languages, thesis/dissertation, field exams. *Entrance requirements:* For master's and doctorate, GRE General Test. Additional exam requirements/recommendations for international students: Required—TOEFL. Electronic applications accepted. *Expenses: Tuition:* Full-time $48,987; part-time $10,620 per quarter. One-time fee: $400. Tuition and fees vary according to program.

University of Alberta, Faculty of Graduate Studies and Research, Department of East Asian Studies, Edmonton, AB T6G 2E1, Canada. Offers Chinese literature (MA); East Asian interdisciplinary studies (MA); Japanese literature (MA). *Program availability:* Part-time. *Degree requirements:* For master's, one foreign language, thesis. *Entrance requirements:* Additional exam requirements/recommendations for international students: Required—TOEFL. Electronic applications accepted. *Faculty research:* Classical Chinese poetry and poetics, Chinese philosophy, modern/contemporary Chinese literature, modern Japanese literature and culture, Japanese women's writing.

University of California, Berkeley, Graduate Division, College of Letters and Science, Department of East Asian Languages and Cultures, Berkeley, CA 94720-1500. Offers Chinese language (PhD); Japanese language (PhD). *Degree requirements:* For doctorate, one foreign language, thesis/dissertation, oral qualifying exam. *Entrance requirements:* For doctorate, GRE General Test, minimum GPA of 3.0, MA thesis, 3 letters of recommendation. Electronic applications accepted. *Faculty research:* Chinese and Japanese modern and classical texts, prose, and poetry; Chinese and Japanese linguistics.

University of California, Irvine, School of Humanities, Department of East Asian Languages and Literatures, Irvine, CA 92697. Offers Chinese (MA, PhD); East Asian languages and literatures (MA, PhD); Japanese (MA, PhD). *Students:* 9 full-time (7 women), 3 part-time (2 women); includes 4 minority (all Asian, non-Hispanic/Latino), 4 international. Average age 31. 46 applicants, 9% accepted, 2 enrolled. In 2017, 2 doctorates awarded. *Entrance requirements:* For master's and doctorate, GRE General Test, minimum GPA of 3.0. Additional exam requirements/recommendations for international students: Required—TOEFL (minimum score 550 paper-based). *Application deadline:* For fall admission, 1/15 priority date for domestic students, 1/15 for international students. Application fee: $105 ($125 for international students). Electronic applications accepted. *Financial support:* Fellowships with tuition reimbursements, research assistantships with full tuition reimbursements, teaching assistantships with partial tuition reimbursements, institutionally sponsored loans, traineeships, health care benefits, and unspecified assistantships available. Financial award application deadline: 3/1; financial award applicants required to submit FAFSA. *Faculty research:* Chinese, Japanese, and Korean literature and culture; language and textual analysis; historical, social, and cultural dimensions of literary study. *Unit head:* Michael A. Fuller, Chair, 949-824-2802 Ext. 2227, Fax: 949-824-3248, E-mail: mafuller@uci.edu. *Application contact:* Hu Ying, Graduate Faculty Advisor, 949-824-6312, Fax: 949-824-3248, E-mail:

huying@uci.edu.
Website: http://www.hnet.uci.edu/eastasian/

University of Colorado Boulder, Graduate School, College of Arts and Sciences, Department of Asian Languages and Civilizations, Boulder, CO 80309. Offers MA, PhD. *Faculty:* 12 full-time (5 women). *Students:* 20 full-time (13 women), 1 (woman) part-time; includes 6 minority (3 Asian, non-Hispanic/Latino; 2 Hispanic/Latino; 1 Two or more races, non-Hispanic/Latino), 9 international. Average age 28. 53 applicants, 40% accepted, 6 enrolled. In 2017, 7 master's awarded. Terminal master's awarded for partial completion of doctoral program. *Degree requirements:* For master's, comprehensive exam. *Entrance requirements:* For master's, BA in Chinese or Japanese, minimum undergraduate GPA of 3.0. Additional exam requirements/recommendations for international students: Required—TOEFL. *Application deadline:* For fall admission, 12/1 for domestic and international students; for spring admission, 10/1 for domestic and international students. Applications are processed on a rolling basis. Application fee: $60 ($80 for international students). Electronic applications accepted. Application fee is waived when completed online. *Financial support:* In 2017–18, 90 students received support, including 41 fellowships (averaging $1,708 per year), 16 teaching assistantships with full and partial tuition reimbursements available (averaging $28,844 per year); institutionally sponsored loans, scholarships/grants, health care benefits, and unspecified assistantships also available. Financial award application deadline: 2/15; financial award applicants required to submit FAFSA. *Faculty research:* Asian languages/literature; Chinese language/literature; Asian religions; literary criticism; religious literature. *Application contact:* E-mail: dalc@colorado.edu. Website: http://alc.colorado.edu/

University of Hawaii at Manoa, Office of Graduate Education, College of Languages, Linguistics and Literature, Department of East Asian Languages and Literatures, Program in Japanese, Honolulu, HI 96822. Offers MA, PhD. *Program availability:* Part-time. *Degree requirements:* For master's, 2 foreign languages, thesis optional; for doctorate, 2 foreign languages, comprehensive exam, thesis/dissertation. *Entrance requirements:* For master's and doctorate, GRE General Test. Additional exam requirements/recommendations for international students: Required—TOEFL (minimum score 560 paper-based; 83 iBT), IELTS (minimum score 5).

University of Hawaii at Manoa, Office of Graduate Education, School of Pacific and Asian Studies, Program in Asian Studies, Concentration in Japanese Studies, Honolulu, HI 96822. Offers Graduate Certificate. *Program availability:* Part-time. *Degree requirements:* For Graduate Certificate, one foreign language. *Entrance requirements:* For degree, GRE. Additional exam requirements/recommendations for international students: Required—TOEFL (minimum score 560 paper-based; 83 iBT), IELTS (minimum score 5).

The University of Manchester, School of Languages, Linguistics and Cultures, Manchester, United Kingdom. Offers Arab world studies (PhD); Chinese studies (M Phil, PhD); East Asian studies (M Phil, PhD); English language (PhD); French studies (M Phil, PhD); German studies (M Phil, PhD); interpreting studies (PhD); Italian studies (M Phil, PhD); Japanese studies (M Phil, PhD); Latin American cultural studies (M Phil, PhD); linguistics (M Phil, PhD); Middle Eastern studies (M Phil, PhD); Polish studies (M Phil, PhD); Portuguese studies (M Phil, PhD); Russian studies (M Phil, PhD); Spanish studies (M Phil, PhD); translation and intercultural studies (M Phil, PhD).

University of Massachusetts Amherst, Graduate School, College of Humanities and Fine Arts, Department of Languages, Literatures, and Cultures, Programs in Asian Languages and Literatures, Amherst, MA 01003. Offers Chinese (MA); Japanese (MA). *Program availability:* Part-time. *Degree requirements:* For master's, thesis, general exam. *Entrance requirements:* For master's, GRE General Test. Additional exam requirements/recommendations for international students: Required—TOEFL (minimum score 550 paper-based; 80 iBT), IELTS (minimum score 6.5). Electronic applications accepted.

University of Oregon, Graduate School, College of Arts and Sciences, Department of East Asian Languages and Literature, Eugene, OR 97403. Offers Chinese (MA, PhD); Japanese (MA, PhD). *Entrance requirements:* Additional exam requirements/

recommendations for international students: Required—TOEFL. *Faculty research:* Linguistics, pedagogy.

University of Pittsburgh, Kenneth P. Dietrich School of Arts and Sciences, Department of East Asian Languages and Literatures, Pittsburgh, PA 15260. Offers Chinese (MA); Japanese (MA). *Program availability:* Part-time. *Faculty:* 18 full-time (11 women), 11 part-time/adjunct (all women). *Students:* 4 full-time (all women); includes 2 minority (both Asian, non-Hispanic/Latino). Average age 24. 13 applicants, 31% accepted, 3 enrolled. In 2017, 4 master's awarded. *Degree requirements:* For master's, one foreign language, thesis, oral comprehensive exam. *Entrance requirements:* For master's, GRE General Test, 2 years of college-level Chinese or Japanese, minimum QPA of 3.0, writing sample in English. Additional exam requirements/recommendations for international students: Required—TOEFL (minimum score 600 paper-based; 90 iBT), IELTS. *Application deadline:* For fall admission, 1/15 for domestic and international students. Application fee: $50. Electronic applications accepted. *Expenses:* $22,290 tuition, $850 fees. *Financial support:* In 2017–18, 5 students received support, including 1 fellowship with full tuition reimbursement available (averaging $23,262 per year); scholarships/grants and tuition waivers (full and partial) also available. Financial award application deadline: 1/15. *Faculty research:* Chinese literature, film, and poetry; Japanese literature, film, and theater; Chinese society and culture; East Asian foreign policy, security studies, and economic history; Japanese performing arts and fine arts translation studies; cultural studies; intellectual history; language and linguistics; second language acquisition; Japanese government; Japanese and Chinese history; ethnomusicology; religious studies. *Unit head:* Dr. Hiroshi Nara, Chair, 412-624-5579, Fax: 412-624-3458, E-mail: hnara@pitt.edu. *Application contact:* Keanna Cash, Graduate Administrator, 412-624-5227, E-mail: kec176@pitt.edu.
Website: http://deall.pitt.edu/

University of Washington, Graduate School, College of Arts and Sciences, Department of Asian Languages and Literature, Seattle, WA 98195. Offers Buddhist studies (MA, PhD); Chinese language and literature (MA, PhD); Japanese language and literature (MA, PhD); Korean language and literature (MA, PhD); South Asian language and literature (MA, PhD). *Degree requirements:* For master's, 2 foreign languages, general exam, thesis or 2 research papers; for doctorate, 3 foreign languages, thesis/dissertation, general exam. *Entrance requirements:* For master's, GRE, minimum GPA of 3.0; for doctorate, GRE, master's degree in related field, minimum GPA of 3.0. Additional exam requirements/recommendations for international students: Required—TOEFL. Electronic applications accepted. *Faculty research:* Textual, linguistic, philological, and literary study of languages and literatures of Asia.

University of Wisconsin–Madison, Graduate School, College of Letters and Science, Department of East Asian Languages and Literature, Program in Japanese Linguistics, Madison, WI 53706-1380. Offers MA, PhD. *Program availability:* Part-time. Terminal master's awarded for partial completion of doctoral program. *Degree requirements:* For master's, one foreign language, seminars, written exam; for doctorate, 3 foreign languages, thesis/dissertation, seminars, preliminary exams, oral exam. *Entrance requirements:* For master's, GRE General Test, bachelor's degree or equivalent in Japanese; for doctorate, GRE General Test, master's degree or equivalent in Japanese. Electronic applications accepted. *Faculty research:* Modern and historical Japanese linguistics, modern Japanese fiction and poetry, classical Japanese literature, language pedagogy.

Washington University in St. Louis, The Graduate School, Department of East Asian Languages and Cultures, St. Louis, MO 63130-4899. Offers Chinese (MA); Chinese and comparative literature (PhD); Chinese language and literature (PhD); East Asian studies (MA); Japanese (MA); Japanese and comparative literature (PhD); Japanese language and literature (PhD). Terminal master's awarded for partial completion of doctoral program. *Degree requirements:* For master's, thesis optional; for doctorate, thesis/dissertation. *Entrance requirements:* For master's and doctorate, GRE General Test. Additional exam requirements/recommendations for international students: Required—TOEFL. Electronic applications accepted. *Faculty research:* Chinese; Japanese; Chinese fiction, theater, poetry, modern literature; Japanese modern and classical fiction, translation theory.

Near and Middle Eastern Languages

The American University in Cairo, School of Humanities and Social Sciences, Cairo, Egypt. Offers Arab and Islamic civilizations (Graduate Diploma); Arabic studies (MA); comparative literary studies (Graduate Diploma); Egyptology and Coptology (MA); English and comparative literature (MA); humanities and social sciences (Graduate Diploma); philosophy (MA); psychology (MA); sociology and anthropology (MA); teaching Arabic as a foreign language (MA); teaching English to speakers of other languages (MA). *Program availability:* Part-time, evening/weekend. *Faculty:* 52 full-time (27 women), 7 part-time/adjunct (3 women). *Students:* 52 full-time (41 women), 159 part-time (119 women), 38 international. Average age 31. 209 applicants, 36% accepted, 39 enrolled. In 2017, 73 master's awarded. *Degree requirements:* For master's, comprehensive exam (for some programs), thesis (for some programs). *Entrance requirements:* Additional exam requirements/recommendations for international students: Required—TOEFL (minimum score 450 paper-based; 45 iBT), IELTS (minimum score 5). *Application deadline:* For fall admission, 2/1 priority date for domestic and international students; for spring admission, 10/15 priority date for domestic and international students. Applications are processed on a rolling basis. Application fee: $85. Electronic applications accepted. *Financial support:* Fellowships with partial tuition reimbursements, scholarships/grants, tuition waivers (partial), and unspecified assistantships available. Financial award application deadline: 3/10. *Faculty research:* English literature, political science, psychology, sociology, anthropology and Egyptology, philosophy, Arabic studies, history, teaching Arabic as a foreign language, teaching English to speakers of other languages. *Unit head:* Dr. Robert Switzer, Interim Dean, 20-2-2615-1068, E-mail: nbowditch@aucegypt.edu. *Application contact:* Maha Hegazi, Director for Graduate Admissions, 20-2-2615-1462, E-mail: mahahegazi@aucegypt.edu.
Website: http://www.aucegypt.edu/huss/Pages/default.aspx

American University of Beirut, Graduate Programs, Faculty of Arts and Sciences, 1107 2020, Lebanon. Offers anthropology (MA); Arab and Middle Eastern history (PhD); Arabic language and literature (MA, PhD); archaeology (MA); art history and curating (MA); biology (MS); cell and molecular biology (PhD); chemistry (MS); clinical psychology (MA); computational sciences (MS); computer science (MS); economics (MA); education (MA), including administration and policy studies, elementary education, mathematics education, psychology school guidance, psychology test and measurements, science education, teaching English as a foreign language; English

language (MA); English literature (MA); environmental policy planning (MS); financial economics (MAFE); general psychology (MA); geology (MS); history (MA); Islamic studies (MA); mathematics (MS); media studies (MA); Middle East studies (MA); philosophy (MA); physics (MS); political studies (MA); public administration (MA); public policy and international affairs (MA); sociology (MA); theoretical physics (PhD). *Program availability:* Part-time. *Faculty:* 108 full-time (36 women), 5 part-time/adjunct (4 women). *Students:* 251 full-time (180 women), 233 part-time (172 women). Average age 26. 425 applicants, 65% accepted, 121 enrolled. In 2017, 47 master's, 2 doctorates awarded. *Degree requirements:* For master's, one foreign language, comprehensive exam, thesis (for some programs), project; for doctorate, one foreign language, comprehensive exam, thesis/dissertation. *Entrance requirements:* For master's, GRE General Test (for some programs); for doctorate, GRE General Test (GRE Subject Test for theoretical physics). Additional exam requirements/recommendations for international students: Required—TOEFL (minimum score 583 paper-based; 97 iBT), IELTS (minimum score 7). *Application deadline:* For fall admission, 2/8 for domestic students; for spring admission, 11/3 for domestic students. Application fee: $50. Electronic applications accepted. *Expenses:* Contact institution. *Financial support:* In 2017–18, 29 fellowships, 40 research assistantships were awarded; teaching assistantships, scholarships/grants, tuition waivers (full and partial), and unspecified assistantships also available. Financial award application deadline: 4/4. *Unit head:* Dr. Nadia Maria El Cheikh, Dean, Faculty of Arts and Sciences, 961-1-374374 Ext. 3800, Fax: 961-1-744461, E-mail: nmcheikh@aub.edu.lb. *Application contact:* Rima Rassi, Graduate Studies Officer, 961-1-350000 Ext. 3833, Fax: 961-1-744461, E-mail: rr46@aub.edu.lb.
Website: http://www.aub.edu.lb/fas/pages/default.aspx

Bethel Seminary, Graduate and Professional Programs, St. Paul, MN 55112-6998. Offers Anglican studies (Certificate); children's and family ministry (MA); Christian studies (Certificate); Christian thought (MA); church planting (Certificate); Greek and Hebrew language (M Div); Greek language (M Div); Hebrew language (M Div); marriage and family therapy (MA, Certificate); mental health counseling (MA); ministry (MA, D Min); ministry practice (Certificate); theological studies (MA, Certificate); transformational leadership (MA); young life youth ministry (Certificate). *Accreditation:* ACIPE. *Program availability:* Part-time, evening/weekend, 100% online, blended/hybrid learning. *Faculty:* 16 full-time (4 women), 31 part-time/adjunct (15 women). *Students:* 380 full-time (170 women), 167 part-time (55 women); includes 161 minority (65 Black or

African American, non-Hispanic/Latino; 52 Asian, non-Hispanic/Latino; 31 Hispanic/Latino; 1 Native Hawaiian or other Pacific Islander, non-Hispanic/Latino; 12 Two or more races, non-Hispanic/Latino), 5 international. Average age 38. 356 applicants, 62% accepted, 156 enrolled. In 2017, 120 master's, 15 doctorates, 4 other advanced degrees awarded. *Degree requirements:* For master's, variable foreign language requirement, thesis (for some programs); for doctorate, thesis/dissertation. *Entrance requirements:* For master's, letters of reference, transcripts, personal statement; for doctorate, M Div, letters of reference, organizational support; for Certificate, letters of reference, family essay, personal statement, and family of origin paper (for marriage and family therapy). Additional exam requirements/recommendations for international students: Required—TOEFL (minimum score 550 paper-based; 87 iBT). *Application deadline:* For fall admission, 8/1 priority date for domestic students, 8/1 for international students; for winter admission, 12/1 priority date for domestic students; for spring admission, 1/1 priority date for domestic students. Applications are processed on a rolling basis. Application fee: $0. Electronic applications accepted. *Expenses:* Contact institution. *Financial support:* Teaching assistantships, career-related internships or fieldwork, Federal Work-Study, and scholarships/grants available. Financial award applicants required to submit FAFSA. *Faculty research:* Nature of theology, ethics, Biblical commentaries, nature of God, science and theology. *Unit head:* Dr. Randy Bergen, Associate Provost, 651-635-8000, E-mail: r-bergen@bethel.edu. *Application contact:* Director of Admissions, 651-638-8000, Fax: 651-638-6002, E-mail: seminary-admissions@bethel.edu.
Website: https://www.bethel.edu/seminary

Brandeis University, Graduate School of Arts and Sciences, Department of Near Eastern and Judaic Studies, Waltham, MA 02454-9110. Offers Near Eastern and Judaic studies (MA, PhD); near Eastern and Judaic studies/conflict resolution and coexistence (MA); near Eastern and Judaic studies/Jewish professional leadership (MA); near Eastern and Judaic studies/women's, gender, and sexuality studies (MA); teaching of Hebrew (MAT). Offered jointly with The Heller School of Social Policy and Management. *Program availability:* Part-time. *Faculty:* 24 full-time (10 women), 6 part-time/adjunct (3 women). *Students:* 41 full-time (17 women), 2 part-time (1 woman); includes 7 minority (2 Black or African American, non-Hispanic/Latino; 1 Asian, non-Hispanic/Latino; 4 Hispanic/Latino), 9 international. Average age 33. 47 applicants, 45% accepted, 4 enrolled. In 2017, 8 master's, 3 doctorates awarded. Terminal master's awarded for partial completion of doctoral program. *Degree requirements:* For master's, one foreign language, thesis or alternative, proseminar, capstone; for doctorate, variable foreign language requirement, comprehensive exam, thesis/dissertation. *Entrance requirements:* For master's and doctorate, GRE General Test (recommended), letters of recommendation, transcripts, statement of purpose, writing sample, resume. Additional exam requirements/recommendations for international students: Required—PTE (minimum score 68), TOEFL (minimum score 600 paper-based, 100 iBT) or IELTS (7). *Application deadline:* For fall admission, 1/15 priority date for domestic students. Applications are processed on a rolling basis. Application fee: $75. Electronic applications accepted. *Expenses: Tuition:* Full-time $48,720. *Required fees:* $88. Tuition and fees vary according to course load, degree level, program and student level. *Financial support:* In 2017–18, 29 students received support, including 20 fellowships with full tuition reimbursements available (averaging $24,480 per year), 1 teaching assistantship with partial tuition reimbursement available (averaging $2,500 per year); Federal Work-Study, scholarships/grants, health care benefits, and tuition waivers (partial) also available. Support available to part-time students. Financial award application deadline: 4/15; financial award applicants required to submit FAFSA. *Faculty research:* Bible and ancient Near East, Judaic Studies, Israel Studies, modern Middle East, Arabic and Islamic civilizations. *Unit head:* Dr. Eugene Sheppard, Department Chair, 781-736-2950, E-mail: sheppard@brandeis.edu. *Application contact:* Jean Mannion, Department Administrator, 781-736-2950, E-mail: mannion@brandeis.edu.
Website: http://www.brandeis.edu/gsas/programs/nejs.html

The Catholic University of America, School of Arts and Sciences, Department of Semitic and Egyptian Languages and Literatures, Washington, DC 20064. Offers ancient Near East (Biblical Hebrew/Aramaic) (MA, PhD); Arabic (PhD); Christian Near East (Biblical Hebrew/Aramaic) (MA); Coptic (MA, PhD); Syriac (MA, PhD). *Program availability:* Part-time. *Faculty:* 3 full-time (0 women), 2 part-time/adjunct (1 woman). *Students:* 16 full-time (1 woman), 17 part-time (6 women); includes 3 minority (1 Asian, non-Hispanic/Latino; 2 Two or more races, non-Hispanic/Latino), 4 international. Average age 35. 15 applicants, 87% accepted, 4 enrolled. In 2017, 6 master's, 3 doctorates awarded. Terminal master's awarded for partial completion of doctoral program. *Degree requirements:* For master's, one foreign language, comprehensive exam; for doctorate, 2 foreign languages, comprehensive exam, thesis/dissertation. *Entrance requirements:* For master's, GRE General Test, statement of purpose, official copies of academic transcripts, three letters of recommendation; for doctorate, GRE General Test, statement of purpose, official copies of academic transcripts, three letters of recommendation, successful completion of MA field. Additional exam requirements/recommendations for international students: Required—TOEFL (minimum score 550 paper-based; 80 iBT). *Application deadline:* For fall admission, 7/15 priority date for domestic students, 7/1 for international students; for spring admission, 11/15 priority date for domestic students, 11/1 for international students. Applications are processed on a rolling basis. Application fee: $55. Electronic applications accepted. *Expenses:* Contact institution. *Financial support:* Fellowships, research assistantships, teaching assistantships, Federal Work-Study, scholarships/grants, tuition waivers (full and partial), and unspecified assistantships available. Financial award application deadline: 2/1; financial award applicants required to submit FAFSA. *Faculty research:* Christian history and literature of the Near East, Biblical Hebrew, Arabic Christianity, Coptic, Syriac. *Unit head:* Dr. Andrew D. Gross, Chair, 202-319-5083, Fax: 202-319-4735, E-mail: grossa@cua.edu. *Application contact:* Dr. Steven Brown, Director of Graduate Admissions, 202-319-5057, Fax: 202-319-6533, E-mail: cua-admissions@cua.edu.
Website: http://semitics.cua.edu/

DePaul University, College of Liberal Arts and Social Sciences, Chicago, IL 60614. Offers Arabic (MA); Chinese (MA); critical ethnic studies (MA); English (MA); French (MA); German (MA); history (MA); interdisciplinary studies (MA, MS); international public service (MS); international studies (MA); Italian (MA); Japanese (MA); liberal studies (MA); nonprofit management (MNM); public administration (MPA); public health (MPH); public policy (MPP); public service management (MS); refugee and forced migration studies (MS); social work (MSW); sociology (MA); Spanish (MA); sustainable urban development (MA); women's and gender studies (MA); writing and publishing (MA); writing, rhetoric and discourse (MA); MA/PhD. *Program availability:* Part-time, evening/weekend, online learning. Terminal master's awarded for partial completion of doctoral program. *Degree requirements:* For master's, variable foreign language requirement, comprehensive exam (for some programs), thesis (for some programs). *Application deadline:* Applications are processed on a rolling basis. Application fee: $40. Electronic applications accepted. *Financial support:* Applicants required to submit FAFSA. *Unit head:* Dr. Guillermo Vasquez de Velasco, Dean, 773-325-7305. *Application contact:* Ann Spittle, Director of Graduate Admission, 773-325-8369, Fax: 312-476-3244, E-mail: graddepaul@depaul.edu.
Website: http://las.depaul.edu/

Georgetown University, Graduate School of Arts and Sciences, Walsh School of Foreign Service, The Center for Contemporary Arab Studies, Washington, DC 20057. Offers MA, Certificate, MA/JD, MA/PhD. *Degree requirements:* For master's, one foreign language, comprehensive exam, thesis or alternative, proficiency in Arabic. *Entrance requirements:* For master's, GRE, minimum GPA of 3.0. Additional exam requirements/recommendations for international students: Required—TOEFL (minimum score 600 paper-based; 100 iBT). Electronic applications accepted. *Faculty research:* Contemporary Arab world.

Harvard University, Graduate School of Arts and Sciences, Department of Near Eastern Languages and Civilizations, Cambridge, MA 02138. Offers Akkadian and Sumerian (AM, PhD); Arabic (AM, PhD); Armenian (AM, PhD); biblical history (AM, PhD); Hebrew (AM, PhD); Indo-Muslim culture (AM, PhD); Iranian (AM, PhD); Jewish history and literature (AM, PhD); Persian (AM, PhD); Semitic philology (AM, PhD); Syro-Palestinian archaeology (AM, PhD); Turkish (AM, PhD). *Degree requirements:* For doctorate, variable foreign language requirement, thesis/dissertation, general exams. *Entrance requirements:* For master's, GRE General Test; for doctorate, GRE General Test, proficiency in a Near Eastern language. Additional exam requirements/recommendations for international students: Required—TOEFL.

Hebrew Union College–Jewish Institute of Religion, School of Graduate Studies, Program in Hebrew Letters, New York, NY 10012-1186. Offers DHL. *Degree requirements:* For doctorate, one foreign language, thesis/dissertation. *Entrance requirements:* For doctorate, GRE. Additional exam requirements/recommendations for international students: Required—TOEFL. *Expenses:* Contact institution. *Faculty research:* Philosophy and theology, Bible, Hebrew, pastoral care, history and Rabbinics.

Hofstra University, School of Education, Programs in Teacher Education, Hempstead, NY 11549. Offers bilingual education (MA); bilingual extension (Advanced Certificate), including education/speech language pathology, intensive teacher institute; business education (MS Ed); curriculum studies (MS Ed); early childhood and childhood education (MS Ed); early childhood education (MA, MS Ed); educational technology (Advanced Certificate); elementary education (MA, MS Ed), including science, technology, engineering, and mathematics (STEM) (MA); English education (MS Ed); family and consumer science (MS Ed); fine arts and music education (Advanced Certificate); fine arts education (MS Ed); foreign language and TESOL (MS Ed); foreign language education (MA, MS Ed), including Arabic (MS Ed), biology, chemistry, Chinese (MS Ed), earth science, French, German, Italian (MS Ed), Mandarin (MS Ed), physics, Russian, Spanish; foundations of education (Advanced Certificate), including grades 5-6, grades 7-9; languages other than English and teaching English as a second language (MA); learning and teaching (Ed D), including applied linguistics, art education, arts and humanities, early childhood education, English education, human development, math education, math, science, and technology, multicultural education, physical education, science education, social studies education, special education; mathematics education (MA, MS Ed); music education (MA, MS Ed); science education (MA), including biology (MA, MS Ed), chemistry (MA, MS Ed), earth science (MA, MS Ed), physics (MA, MS Ed); secondary education (Advanced Certificate); social studies education (MA, MS Ed); teaching languages other than English and TESOL (MS Ed); technology for learning (MA); TESOL (MS Ed, Advanced Certificate); TESOL with specialization in STEM (MA); work based learning extension (Advanced Certificate). *Program availability:* Part-time, evening/weekend, blended/hybrid learning. *Students:* 119 full-time (83 women), 124 part-time (90 women); includes 54 minority (15 Black or African American, non-Hispanic/Latino; 9 Asian, non-Hispanic/Latino; 29 Hispanic/Latino; 1 Native Hawaiian or other Pacific Islander, non-Hispanic/Latino), 12 international. Average age 29. 205 applicants, 88% accepted, 93 enrolled. In 2017, 103 master's, 4 doctorates, 32 other advanced degrees awarded. *Degree requirements:* For master's, comprehensive exam, thesis (for some programs), exit project, student teaching, fieldwork, electronic portfolio, curriculum project, minimum GPA of 3.0; for doctorate, thesis/dissertation; for Advanced Certificate, 3 foreign languages, comprehensive exam (for some programs), thesis project. *Entrance requirements:* For master's, GRE, 2 letters of recommendation, portfolio, teacher certification (MA), interview, essay; for doctorate, GMAT, GRE, LSAT, or MAT; for Advanced Certificate, 2 letters of recommendation, essay, interview and/or portfolio, teaching certificate. Additional exam requirements/recommendations for international students: Required—TOEFL (minimum score 550 paper-based; 80 iBT). *Application deadline:* Applications are processed on a rolling basis. Application fee: $75. Electronic applications accepted. *Expenses: Tuition:* Full-time $1292. *Required fees:* $970. Tuition and fees vary according to program. *Financial support:* In 2017–18, 112 students received support, including 56 fellowships with full and partial tuition reimbursements available (averaging $4,998 per year), 2 research assistantships with full and partial tuition reimbursements available (averaging $8,753 per year); career-related internships or fieldwork, Federal Work-Study, institutionally sponsored loans, scholarships/grants, traineeships, tuition waivers (full and partial), and unspecified assistantships also available. Support available to part-time students. Financial award applicants required to submit FAFSA. *Faculty research:* Educational interventions that foster critical-thinking skills; teachers' attitudes about professional development; threats to teacher quality. *Unit head:* Dr. Eustace Thompson, Chairperson, 516-463-5749, Fax: 516-463-6275, E-mail: eustace.g.thompson@hofstra.edu. *Application contact:* Sunil Samuel, Assistant Vice President of Admissions, 516-463-4723, Fax: 516-463-4664, E-mail: graduateadmission@hofstra.edu.
Website: http://www.hofstra.edu/education/

Houston Baptist University, School of Christian Thought, Program in Biblical Languages, Houston, TX 77074-3298. Offers MA. *Students:* 2 full-time (1 woman), 6 part-time (2 women); includes 3 minority (all Black or African American, non-Hispanic/Latino). Average age 40. 9 applicants, 67% accepted, 2 enrolled. In 2017, 4 master's awarded. *Entrance requirements:* For master's, bachelor's degree conferred transcript, essay/personal statement, resume. Additional exam requirements/recommendations for international students: Required—TOEFL (minimum score 80 iBT), IELTS (minimum score 6.5). *Application deadline:* For fall admission, 8/1 for domestic students, 6/1 for international students; for spring admission, 1/1 for domestic students, 11/1 for international students. Applications are processed on a rolling basis. Application fee: $0 ($100 for international students). Electronic applications accepted. Application fee is waived when completed online. *Expenses:* $18,000 tuition; $4,500 fees (general, technology and parking). *Financial support:* In 2017–18, 1 student received support. Federal Work-Study and scholarships/grants available. Financial award application deadline: 4/1. *Unit head:* Dr. Steven Jones, Chair, 281-649-3635, Fax: 281-649-3012, E-mail: sljones@hbu.edu. *Application contact:* Celeste Risteski, Administrative Assistant to the Dean, 281-649-3383, Fax: 281-649-3012, E-mail: cristeski@hbu.edu.

Indiana University Bloomington, University Graduate School, College of Arts and Sciences, School of Global and International Studies, Department of Near Eastern Languages and Cultures, Bloomington, IN 47405-7000. Offers MA, PhD. *Program availability:* Part-time. Terminal master's awarded for partial completion of doctoral program. *Degree requirements:* For master's, 2 foreign languages, comprehensive exam, thesis or alternative; for doctorate, 3 foreign languages, comprehensive exam, thesis/dissertation. *Entrance requirements:* For master's and doctorate, GRE General Test. Additional exam requirements/recommendations for international students: Required—TOEFL. Electronic applications accepted. *Faculty research:* Classical and

modern Arabic literature and linguistics, Biblical and modern Hebrew studies, Persian language and literature, Islamic civilization, Iranian history and language.

Johns Hopkins University, Zanvyl Krieger School of Arts and Sciences, Department of Near Eastern Studies, Baltimore, MD 21218. Offers archaeology (PhD); Assyriology (PhD); Egyptology (PhD); Hebrew Bible/Northwest Semitics (PhD). *Faculty:* 8 full-time (2 women), 1 part-time/adjunct (0 women). *Students:* 22 full-time (13 women); includes 3 minority (1 Black or African American, non-Hispanic/Latino; 1 Asian, non-Hispanic/Latino; 1 Hispanic/Latino), 5 international. Average age 31. 54 applicants, 15% accepted, 4 enrolled. In 2017, 4 doctorates awarded. *Degree requirements:* For doctorate, 2 foreign languages, comprehensive exam, thesis/dissertation. *Entrance requirements:* For doctorate, GRE. Additional exam requirements/recommendations for international students: Required—TOEFL (minimum score 600 paper-based; 100 iBT); Recommended—IELTS. *Application deadline:* For fall admission, 12/15 for domestic and international students. Application fee: $75. Electronic applications accepted. *Expenses:* $10,434. *Financial support:* In 2017–18, 17 students received support, including 17 fellowships with full tuition reimbursements available (averaging $27,000 per year); teaching assistantships, career-related internships or fieldwork, Federal Work-Study, scholarships/grants, and health care benefits also available. Financial award application deadline: 4/15; financial award applicants required to submit FAFSA. *Faculty research:* Egyptology, Assyriology, Hebrew Bible/Northwest Semitic languages, Demotic Egyptian, archaeology. *Total annual research expenditures:* $64,479. *Unit head:* Dr. Glenn Schwartz, Chair, 410-516-8492, Fax: 410-516-5218, E-mail: schwartz@jhu.edu. *Application contact:* Glenda Hogan, Academic Program Coordinator, 410-516-7394, Fax: 410-516-5218, E-mail: ghogan@jhu.edu.
Website: http://neareast.jhu.edu/

Kent State University, College of Arts and Sciences, Department of Modern and Classical Language Studies, Kent, OH 44242-0001. Offers French (MA), including applied linguistics and pedagogy, literature; German (MA), including applied linguistics and pedagogy, literature; Latin (MA), including applied linguistics and pedagogy, literature; Spanish (MA), including applied linguistics and pedagogy, literature; translation (MA), including Arabic, French, German, Japanese, Russian, Spanish; translation studies (PhD); MA/MBA. *Program availability:* Part-time. *Faculty:* 21 full-time (13 women), 5 part-time/adjunct (3 women). *Students:* 78 full-time (50 women), 20 part-time (13 women); includes 18 minority (3 Black or African American, non-Hispanic/Latino; 1 Asian, non-Hispanic/Latino; 9 Hispanic/Latino; 5 Two or more races, non-Hispanic/Latino), 44 international. Average age 31. 95 applicants, 55% accepted, 27 enrolled. In 2017, 30 master's awarded. *Degree requirements:* For master's, variable foreign language requirement, comprehensive exam (for some programs), thesis (for some programs); for doctorate, variable foreign language requirement, comprehensive exam, thesis/dissertation. *Entrance requirements:* For master's, transcripts, goal statement, 3 letters of recommendation, CD/MP3 with oral sample of first and second languages, writing sample of second language; for doctorate, transcripts; MA in translation, a foreign language, or similar field; proficiency in a foreign language; minimum GPA of 3.5 from MA; goal statement; 3 letters of recommendation; essay or writing sample. Additional exam requirements/recommendations for international students: Required—TOEFL (minimum score 550 paper-based, 79 iBT), Michigan English Language Assessment Battery (minimum score 77), IELTS (minimum score 6.5) or PTE (minimum score 58). *Application deadline:* For fall admission, 2/1 for domestic and international students. Applications are processed on a rolling basis. Application fee: $45 ($70 for international students). Electronic applications accepted. *Expenses:* Tuition, state resident: full-time $11,310; part-time $515 per credit hour. Tuition, nonresident: full-time $20,396; part-time $928 per credit hour. *International tuition:* $18,544 full-time. *Financial support:* Fellowships with full tuition reimbursements, teaching assistantships with full tuition reimbursements, and unspecified assistantships available. Financial award application deadline: 2/1. *Unit head:* Dr. Keiran Dunne, Professor of French Translation/Chair, 330-672-2150, E-mail: kdunne@kent.edu. *Application contact:* Said Shiyab, Professor of Translation Studies/Graduate Coordinator, 330-672-1864, E-mail: sshiyab@kent.edu.
Website: http://www.kent.edu/mcls/

London Metropolitan University, Graduate Programs, London, United Kingdom. Offers applied psychology (M Sc); architecture (MA); biomedical science (M Sc); blood science (M Sc); cancer pharmacology (M Sc); computer networking and cyber security (M Sc); computing and information systems (M Sc); conference interpreting (MA); counter-terrorism studies (M Sc); creative, digital and professional writing (MA); crime, violence and prevention (M Sc); criminology (M Sc); curating contemporary art (MA); data analytics (M Sc); digital media (MA); early childhood studies (MA); education (MA, Ed D); financial services law, regulation and compliance (LL M); food science (M Sc); forensic psychology (M Sc); health and social care management and policy (M Sc); human nutrition (M Sc); human resource management (MA); human rights and international conflict (MA); information technology (M Sc); intelligence and security studies (M Sc); international oil, gas and energy law (LL M); international relations (MA); interpreting (MA); learning and teaching in higher education (MA); legal practice (LL M); media and entertainment law (LL M); organizational and consumer psychology (M Sc); psychological therapy (M Sc); psychology of mental health (M Sc); public health (M Sc); public policy and management (MPA); security studies (M Sc); social work (M Sc); spatial planning and urban design (MA); sports therapy (M Sc); supporting older children and young people with dyslexia (MA); teaching languages (MA), including Arabic, English; translation (MA); woman and child abuse (MA).

Middlebury College, Language Schools, Arabic School, Middlebury, VT 05753-6002. Offers Arabic language pedagogy (MA); Arabic studies (MA). *Degree requirements:* For master's, one foreign language. *Entrance requirements:* For master's, Arabic language oral and written proficiency tests, 3 letters of recommendation, personal statement, transcripts, writing sample in Arabic, Arabic course history, 4 years or equivalent of Arabic language study. Additional exam requirements/recommendations for international students: Required—TOEFL (minimum score 100 iBT). *Application deadline:* For summer admission, 5/1 for domestic and international students. Applications are processed on a rolling basis. Application fee: $75. Electronic applications accepted. *Expenses:* Contact institution. *Financial support:* Fellowships and scholarships/grants available. Financial award application deadline: 3/14; financial award applicants required to submit FAFSA. *Unit head:* Dr. Mahmoud Abdalla, Director, 802-443-5230, Fax: 802-443-2075, E-mail: mabdalla@miis.edu. *Application contact:* Barbara Walter, Coordinator, 802-443-5230, Fax: 802-443-2075, E-mail: bwalter@middlebury.edu.
Website: http://www.middlebury.edu/ls/grad_programs/arabic

Middlebury College, Language Schools, Hebrew School, Middlebury, VT 05753-6002. Offers MA. *Program availability:* Blended/hybrid learning. *Entrance requirements:* For master's, oral interview. *Application deadline:* Applications are processed on a rolling basis. Application fee: $75. Electronic applications accepted. *Expenses:* Contact institution. *Financial support:* Fellowships and scholarships/grants available. Financial award application deadline: 3/28; financial award applicants required to submit FAFSA. *Unit head:* Vardit Ringvald, Director, 802-443-3574, E-mail: vringval@middlebury.edu.
Website: http://www.middlebury.edu/ls/hebrew

The Ohio State University, Graduate School, College of Arts and Sciences, Division of Arts and Humanities, Department of Near Eastern Languages and Cultures, Columbus, OH 43210. Offers MA, PhD. *Faculty:* 11. *Students:* 11 full-time (6 women). Average age 33. In 2017, 3 doctorates awarded. Terminal master's awarded for partial completion of doctoral program. *Entrance requirements:* For master's and doctorate, GRE General Test, writing sample. Additional exam requirements/recommendations for international students: Required—TOEFL (minimum score 550 paper-based; 79 iBT), Michigan English Language Assessment Battery (minimum score 82); Recommended—IELTS (minimum score 7). *Application deadline:* For fall admission, 12/14 priority date for domestic students, 11/30 priority date for international students; for winter admission, 12/1 for domestic students, 11/1 for international students; for spring admission, 3/1 for domestic students, 2/1 for international students. Applications are processed on a rolling basis. Application fee: $60 ($70 for international students). Electronic applications accepted. *Financial support:* Fellowships, research assistantships, teaching assistantships, Federal Work-Study, and institutionally sponsored loans available. Support available to part-time students. *Unit head:* Dr. Morgan Liu, Interim Chair, 614-292-5619, E-mail: liu.737@osu.edu. *Application contact:* Graduate and Professional Admissions, 614-292-9444, Fax: 614-292-3895, E-mail: gpadmissions@osu.edu.
Website: http://nelc.osu.edu/

Oral Roberts University, School of Theology and Missions, Tulsa, OK 74171. Offers biblical literature (MA), including advanced languages, Judaic-Christian studies; church ministries and leadership (D Min); clinical pastoral education (M Div); missions (MA); pastoral care and chaplaincy (M Div, D Min); practical theology (MA), including teaching ministries, urban ministries; professional counseling (MA), including addiction studies, marriage and family therapy; theological/historical studies (MA). *Accreditation:* ATS. *Program availability:* Part-time, online learning. *Faculty:* 17 full-time (2 women). *Students:* 371 full-time (156 women), 110 part-time (65 women); includes 177 minority (127 Black or African American, non-Hispanic/Latino; 5 American Indian or Alaska Native, non-Hispanic/Latino; 20 Asian, non-Hispanic/Latino; 25 Hispanic/Latino), 82 international. Average age 36. 159 applicants, 95% accepted, 124 enrolled. In 2017, 52 master's, 10 doctorates awarded. *Degree requirements:* For master's, thesis (for some programs), practicum/internship; for doctorate, thesis/dissertation, applied research project. *Entrance requirements:* For master's, GRE General Test or MAT (waived for those with undergraduate degree from regionally accredited institution and 3.0 or higher GPA), minimum GPA of 2.5 (professional) or 3.0 (academic); for doctorate, M Div, minimum GPA of 3.0, 3 years of full-time ministry experience. Additional exam requirements/recommendations for international students: Recommended—TOEFL (minimum score 550 paper-based; 79 iBT), IELTS (minimum score 7). *Application deadline:* Applications are processed on a rolling basis. Application fee: $35. Electronic applications accepted. Application fee is waived when completed online. *Financial support:* Fellowships and scholarships/grants available. Financial award application deadline: 6/1. *Unit head:* Dr. Bill Buker, Chair, 918-495-6493, E-mail: bbuker@oru.edu. *Application contact:* Michael Thomas, Enrollment Counselor, 918-495-6618, E-mail: mthomas@oru.edu.
Website: http://www.gradtheology.oru.edu/

University of California, Los Angeles, Graduate Division, College of Letters and Science, Department of Near Eastern Languages and Cultures, Los Angeles, CA 90034. Offers MA, PhD. *Degree requirements:* For master's, one foreign language, comprehensive exam; for doctorate, 2 foreign languages, thesis/dissertation, oral and written qualifying exams. *Entrance requirements:* For master's, GRE General Test, bachelor's degree; minimum undergraduate GPA of 3.25 (or its equivalent if letter grade system not used); for doctorate, GRE General Test, master's degree; minimum undergraduate GPA of 3.25 (or its equivalent if letter grade system not used). Additional exam requirements/recommendations for international students: Required—TOEFL. Electronic applications accepted.

University of Chicago, Division of the Humanities, Department of Near Eastern Languages and Civilizations, Chicago, IL 60637. Offers PhD. *Students:* 103 full-time (37 women); includes 13 minority (1 Black or African American, non-Hispanic/Latino; 5 Asian, non-Hispanic/Latino; 4 Hispanic/Latino; 3 Two or more races, non-Hispanic/Latino), 24 international. Average age 31. 136 applicants, 11% accepted, 12 enrolled. In 2017, 16 doctorates awarded. Terminal master's awarded for partial completion of doctoral program. *Degree requirements:* For doctorate, 2 foreign languages, comprehensive exam, thesis/dissertation. *Entrance requirements:* For doctorate, GRE General Test, 15-20 page writing sample, statement of purpose, 3 letters of recommendation, transcripts for all previous degrees and institutions attended. Additional exam requirements/recommendations for international students: Required—TOEFL (minimum score 104 iBT), IELTS (minimum score 7). *Application deadline:* For fall admission, 12/15 for domestic and international students. Application fee: $90. Electronic applications accepted. *Financial support:* In 2017–18, fellowships with full tuition reimbursements (averaging $27,000 per year) were awarded; teaching assistantships with full tuition reimbursements, Federal Work-Study, institutionally sponsored loans, scholarships/grants, and health care benefits also available. Financial award application deadline: 12/15. *Faculty research:* Archaeology and history of the ancient near East, Middle Eastern history and civilization, Semitic language and literature, Middle Eastern languages and literatures. *Unit head:* Dr. Frank Lewis, Chair, E-mail: ne-lc@uchicago.edu. *Application contact:* Michael Beetley, Assistant Dean of Students, Admissions and Fellowships, 773-702-1552, Fax: 773-834-9148, E-mail: humanitiesadmissions@uchicago.edu.
Website: http://nelc.uchicago.edu/

The University of Manchester, School of Languages, Linguistics and Cultures, Manchester, United Kingdom. Offers Arab world studies (PhD); Chinese studies (M Phil, PhD); East Asian studies (M Phil, PhD); English language (PhD); French studies (M Phil, PhD); German studies (M Phil, PhD); interpreting studies (PhD); Italian studies (M Phil, PhD); Japanese studies (M Phil, PhD); Latin American cultural studies (M Phil, PhD); linguistics (M Phil, PhD); Middle Eastern studies (M Phil, PhD); Polish studies (M Phil, PhD); Portuguese studies (M Phil, PhD); Russian studies (M Phil, PhD); Spanish studies (M Phil, PhD); translation and intercultural studies (M Phil, PhD).

University of Michigan, Rackham Graduate School, College of Literature, Science, and the Arts, Department of Near Eastern Studies, Ann Arbor, MI 48109. Offers ancient Near Eastern studies (AM, PhD); Arabic for professional purposes (AM); Arabic language and literature (AM, PhD); Armenian studies (AM, PhD); Christianity in late antiquity (AM, PhD); Egyptology (AM, PhD); Hebrew Bible and ancient Israel (AM, PhD); Hebrew literature (AM, PhD); Islamic studies (AM, PhD); Jewish cultural studies (AM, PhD); Jewish mysticism (AM, PhD); Persian and Iranian studies (AM, PhD); Rabbinic literature (AM, PhD); Second Temple Judaism (AM, PhD); teaching Arabic as a foreign language (AM); Turkish studies (AM, PhD). *Faculty:* 27 full-time (8 women). *Students:* 31 full-time (12 women); includes 2 minority (1 Black or African American, non-Hispanic/Latino; 1 Asian, non-Hispanic/Latino), 13 international. Average age 33. 76 applicants, 11% accepted, 5 enrolled. In 2017, 4 master's, 4 doctorates awarded. Terminal master's awarded for partial completion of doctoral program. *Degree requirements:* For master's, 2 foreign languages; for doctorate, 4 foreign languages, comprehensive exam, thesis/dissertation, preliminary exams, oral defense of dissertation. *Entrance requirements:* For master's, ACTFL (for teaching Arabic as a foreign language MA program). Additional

exam requirements/recommendations for international students: Required—TOEFL (minimum score 560 paper-based; 84 iBT), IELTS (minimum score 6.5). *Application deadline:* For fall admission, 12/1 for domestic and international students. Application fee: $75 ($90 for international students). Electronic applications accepted. *Expenses:* Tuition, state resident: full-time $22,368; part-time $1201 per credit hour. Tuition, nonresident: full-time $45,156; part-time $2467 per credit hour. *Required fees:* $376 per term. Tuition and fees vary according to course load, degree level and program. *Financial support:* In 2017–18, 31 students received support. Fellowships with full tuition reimbursements available, teaching assistantships with full tuition reimbursements available, scholarships/grants, health care benefits, unspecified assistantships, and spring/summer stipends available. Financial award application deadline: 12/1. *Faculty research:* Middle and Near Eastern literatures, languages, cultures from ancient times to the present. *Unit head:* Prof. Gottfried Hagen, Chair, 734-764-0314, E-mail: nes-chair@umich.edu. *Application contact:* Student Services, 734-764-0315, E-mail: nes-gradservices@umich.edu.
Website: http://www.lsa.umich.edu/neareast/

University of South Africa, College of Human Sciences, Pretoria, South Africa. Offers adult education (M Ed); African languages (MA, PhD); African politics (MA, PhD); Afrikaans (MA, PhD); ancient history (MA, PhD); ancient Near Eastern studies (MA, PhD); anthropology (MA, PhD); applied linguistics (MA); Arabic (MA, PhD); archaeology (MA); art history (MA); Biblical archaeology (MA); Biblical studies (M Th, D Th, PhD); Christian spirituality (M Th, D Th); church history (M Th, D Th); classical studies (MA, PhD); clinical psychology (MA); communication (MA, PhD); comparative education (M Ed, Ed D); consulting psychology (D Admin, D Com, PhD); curriculum studies (M Ed, Ed D); development studies (M Admin, MA, D Admin, PhD); didactics (M Ed, Ed D); education (M Tech); education management (M Ed, Ed D); educational psychology (M Ed); English (MA); environmental education (M Ed); French (MA, PhD); German (MA, PhD); Greek (MA); guidance and counseling (M Ed); health studies (MA, PhD), including health sciences education (MA), health services management (MA), medical and surgical nursing science (critical care general) (MA), midwifery and neonatal nursing science (MA), trauma and emergency care (MA); history (MA, PhD); history of education (Ed D); inclusive education (M Ed, Ed D); information and communications technology policy and regulation (MA); information science (MA, MIS, PhD); international politics (MA, PhD); Islamic studies (MA, PhD); Italian (MA, PhD); Judaica (MA, PhD); linguistics (MA, PhD); mathematical education (M Ed); mathematics education (MA); missiology (M Th, D Th); modern Hebrew (MA, PhD); musicology (MA, MMus, D Mus, PhD); natural science education (M Ed); New Testament (M Th, D Th); Old Testament (D Th); pastoral therapy (M Th, D Th); philosophy (MA); philosophy of education (M Ed, Ed D); politics (MA, PhD); Portuguese (MA, PhD); practical theology (M Th, D Th); psychology (MA, MS, PhD); psychology of education (M Ed, Ed D); public health (MA); religious studies (MA, D Th, PhD); Romance languages (MA); Russian (MA, PhD); Semitic languages (MA, PhD); social behavior studies in HIV/AIDS (MA); social science (mental health) (MA); social science in development studies (MA); social science in psychology (MA); social science in social work (MA); social science in sociology (MA); social work (MSW, DSW, PhD); socio-education (M Ed, Ed D); sociolinguistics (MA); sociology (MA, PhD); Spanish (MA, PhD); systematic theology (M Th, D Th); TESOL (teaching English to speakers of other languages) (MA); theological ethics (M Th, D Th); theory of literature (MA, PhD); urban ministries (D Th); urban ministry (M Th).

The University of Texas at Austin, Graduate School, College of Liberal Arts, Department of Middle Eastern Studies, Austin, TX 78712-1111. Offers Middle Eastern languages and cultures (MA, PhD); Middle Eastern studies (MA); JD/MA; MA/M Sc; MA/MA; MBA/MA; MPA/MA. *Degree requirements:* For master's, one foreign language, comprehensive exam, thesis; for doctorate, 2 foreign languages, comprehensive exam, thesis/dissertation. *Entrance requirements:* For master's and doctorate, GRE General Test. Additional exam requirements/recommendations for international students: Required—TOEFL. Electronic applications accepted. *Faculty research:* Islamic studies, Persian language and literature, Hebrew language, Jewish studies, Arabic literature and language.

University of Utah, Graduate School, College of Humanities, Program in Middle East Studies, Salt Lake City, UT 84112. Offers Arabic (MA, PhD); Hebrew (MA); history (MA, PhD); Persian (MA, PhD); political science (MA, PhD). *Students:* 2 part-time (1 woman); includes 1 minority (Asian, non-Hispanic/Latino). In 2017, 1 doctorate awarded. *Entrance requirements:* For master's, GRE General Test, minimum GPA of 3.2; for doctorate, GRE General Test, MA in Middle East studies or equivalent, minimum GPA of 3.2. Additional exam requirements/recommendations for international students: Required—TOEFL (minimum score 580 paper-based; 92 iBT); Recommended—IELTS (minimum score 7). Application fee: $55 ($65 for international students). Electronic applications accepted. *Financial support:* In 2017–18, 5 students received support, including 2 teaching assistantships with full tuition reimbursements available (averaging $13,500 per year); fellowships and unspecified assistantships also available. Financial award application deadline: 1/15. *Faculty research:* Islamic studies; Middle Eastern history; political science; Judaic studies; anthropology; Arabic, Persian, Hebrew, and Turkish language and literature. *Unit head:* Johanna Watzinger-Tharp, Director, 801-581-7148, Fax: 801-581-6105, E-mail: j.tharp@utah.edu. *Application contact:* Kellie Hubbard, Academic Advisor, 801-581-5362, Fax: 801-581-6105, E-mail: kellie.hubbard@utah.edu.
Website: http://www.mec.utah.edu

University of Wisconsin–Madison, Graduate School, College of Letters and Science, Department of Hebrew and Semitic Studies, Madison, WI 53706-1380. Offers MA, PhD. Terminal master's awarded for partial completion of doctoral program. *Degree requirements:* For master's, 2 foreign languages; for doctorate, thesis/dissertation. *Entrance requirements:* For master's and doctorate, GRE. Electronic applications accepted. *Faculty research:* Biblical language and literature, Northwest Semitic languages.

Wayne State University, College of Liberal Arts and Sciences, Department of Classical and Modern Languages, Literatures, and Cultures, Detroit, MI 48202. Offers classics (MA), including ancient Greek and Latin, ancient studies, classics, Latin; German (MA); language learning (MALL), including Arabic (MA, MALL), French (MA, MALL, PhD), German (MALL, PhD), Italian (MA, MALL), Spanish (MA, MALL, PhD); modern languages (PhD), including French (MA, MALL, PhD), German (MALL, PhD), Spanish (MA, MALL, PhD); Near Eastern languages (MA), including Arabic (MA, MALL), Hebrew; Romance languages (MA), including French (MA, MALL, PhD), Italian (MA, MALL), Spanish (MA, MALL, PhD). *Faculty:* 22. *Students:* 24 full-time (18 women), 21 part-time (15 women); includes 11 minority (4 Black or African American, non-Hispanic/Latino; 1 American Indian or Alaska Native, non-Hispanic/Latino; 2 Asian, non-Hispanic/Latino; 2 Hispanic/Latino; 2 Two or more races, non-Hispanic/Latino), 3 international. Average age 37. 32 applicants, 63% accepted, 14 enrolled. In 2017, 10 master's awarded. *Degree requirements:* For master's, variable foreign language requirement, comprehensive exam (for some programs), thesis (for some programs); for doctorate, one foreign language, comprehensive exam, thesis/dissertation. *Entrance requirements:* Additional exam requirements/recommendations for international students: Required—TOEFL (minimum score 550 paper-based; 79 iBT), TWE (minimum score 5.5), Michigan English Language Assessment Battery (minimum score 85); Recommended—IELTS (minimum score 6.5). Application fee: $50. Electronic applications accepted. *Expenses:* Tuition, state resident: full-time $10,224; part-time $638.98 per credit hour. Tuition, nonresident: full-time $22,145; part-time $1384.04 per credit hour. Tuition and fees vary according to course load and program. *Financial support:* In 2017–18, 25 students received support, including 4 fellowships with tuition reimbursements available (averaging $13,500 per year), 17 teaching assistantships with tuition reimbursements available (averaging $18,591 per year); research assistantships, scholarships/grants, health care benefits, and unspecified assistantships also available. Financial award applicants required to submit FAFSA. *Faculty research:* Classical and modern literature and culture (Greek, Latin, Arabic, Chinese, French, German, Russian, Spanish) including colonial studies and exile and Holocaust studies; critical theory (French, German, Slavic, Spanish); theoretical and applied linguistics (Arabic, Chinese, French, Spanish); area studies (Arabic, Near Eastern, classical, Islamic, and Judaic studies). *Unit head:* Dr. Anne Duggan, Department Chair, 313-577-6244, Fax: 313-577-6243, E-mail: a.duggan@wayne.edu.
Website: http://clas.wayne.edu/languages/

Yale University, Graduate School of Arts and Sciences, Department of Near Eastern Languages and Civilizations, New Haven, CT 06520. Offers Arabic and Islamic studies (MA, PhD); archaeology of the ancient Near East (MA, PhD); Assyriology (MA, PhD); Egyptology (MA, PhD); Graeco-Arabic studies (MA, PhD); Northwest Semitic, Bible, comparative Semitics (MA, PhD). *Degree requirements:* For doctorate, 2 foreign languages, thesis/dissertation. *Entrance requirements:* For doctorate, GRE General Test.

Portuguese

Brigham Young University, Graduate Studies, College of Humanities, Department of Spanish and Portuguese, Provo, UT 84602. Offers Portuguese (MA), including Luso-Brazilian literatures, Portuguese linguistics, Portuguese pedagogy; Spanish (MA), including Hispanic linguistics, Hispanic literatures, Spanish pedagogy. *Faculty:* 30 full-time (6 women). *Students:* 32 full-time (17 women), 6 part-time (4 women); includes 16 minority (all Hispanic/Latino). Average age 31. 19 applicants, 68% accepted, 10 enrolled. In 2017, 6 master's awarded. *Degree requirements:* For master's, 2 foreign languages, comprehensive exam, thesis, 1 semester of teaching. *Entrance requirements:* For master's, minimum GPA of 3.5 in Spanish or Portuguese, 3.3 overall. Additional exam requirements/recommendations for international students: Required—TOEFL (minimum score 580 paper-based; 85 iBT), IELTS (minimum score 6.5), PTE (minimum score 53). *Application deadline:* For fall admission, 2/1 for domestic and international students. Application fee: $50. Electronic applications accepted. *Expenses:* Contact institution. *Financial support:* In 2017–18, 23 students received support, including 87 teaching assistantships (averaging $3,200 per year); research assistantships, institutionally sponsored loans, scholarships/grants, tuition waivers (partial), and unspecified assistantships also available. Support available to part-time students. *Faculty research:* Mexican prose; Latin American theater; literature; phonetics, and phonology; pedagogy; classical Portuguese literature. *Unit head:* Dr. Jeffrey S. Turley, Chair, 801-422-7019, Fax: 801-422-0628, E-mail: jeffrey_turley@byu.edu. *Application contact:* Patricia E. Wilson, Graduate Program Manager, 801-422-2838, Fax: 801-422-0628, E-mail: patricia_rubio@byu.edu.
Website: http://spanport.byu.edu/

Emory University, Laney Graduate School, Department of Spanish and Portuguese, Atlanta, GA 30322-1100. Offers comparative literature (Certificate); film studies (Certificate); Spanish (PhD); women's studies (Certificate). *Degree requirements:* For doctorate, 2 foreign languages, comprehensive exam, thesis/dissertation. *Entrance requirements:* For doctorate, GRE General Test. Additional exam requirements/recommendations for international students: Required—TOEFL. Electronic applications accepted. *Faculty research:* Spanish literature, Spanish American literature, literary theory, criticism, cultural studies.

Harvard University, Graduate School of Arts and Sciences, Department of Romance Languages and Literatures, Cambridge, MA 02138. Offers French (AM, PhD); Italian (AM, PhD); Portuguese (AM, PhD); Spanish (AM, PhD). Terminal master's awarded for partial completion of doctoral program. *Degree requirements:* For master's, 2 foreign languages; for doctorate, 2 foreign languages, thesis/dissertation. *Entrance requirements:* For master's and doctorate, GRE General Test, sample of written work. Additional exam requirements/recommendations for international students: Required—TOEFL.

Indiana University Bloomington, University Graduate School, College of Arts and Sciences, Department of Spanish and Portuguese, Bloomington, IN 47405. Offers Portuguese (MA, PhD); Spanish (MA, PhD), including Hispanic linguistics, Hispanic literatures. *Degree requirements:* For master's, one foreign language, comprehensive exam, thesis (for Spanish); for doctorate, 2 foreign languages, comprehensive exam, thesis/dissertation. *Entrance requirements:* For master's, GRE General Test, bachelor's degree in Portuguese or Spanish, minimum GPA of 3.0; for doctorate, GRE General Test, master's degree in Portuguese or Spanish, minimum GPA of 3.0. Additional exam requirements/recommendations for international students: Required—TOEFL (minimum score 79 iBT). Electronic applications accepted. *Faculty research:* Spanish American literature, Spanish peninsular literature, Hispanic linguistics, Luso-Brazilian studies, Catalan studies.

Michigan State University, The Graduate School, College of Arts and Letters, Department of Spanish and Portuguese, East Lansing, MI 48824. Offers applied Spanish linguistics (MA); Hispanic cultural studies (PhD); Hispanic literatures (MA). *Entrance requirements:* Additional exam requirements/recommendations for international students: Required—TOEFL. Electronic applications accepted.

New York University, Graduate School of Arts and Science, Department of Spanish and Portuguese Languages and Literatures, New York, NY 10012-1019. Offers

Portuguese (MA, PhD); Spanish (PhD); Spanish and Latin American literatures and cultures (MA); Spanish language and translation (MA). *Program availability:* Part-time. *Students:* Average age 32. 157 applicants, 43% accepted, 33 enrolled. In 2017, 29 master's, 5 doctorates awarded. *Degree requirements:* For master's, 2 foreign languages, thesis; for doctorate, 2 foreign languages, thesis/dissertation. *Entrance requirements:* For master's, GRE General Test; for doctorate, GRE General Test, master's degree. Additional exam requirements/recommendations for international students: Required—TOEFL. *Application deadline:* For fall admission, 1/4 priority date for domestic students, 1/4 for international students. Application fee: $100. *Expenses: Tuition:* Full-time $41,352; part-time $19,968 per year. *Required fees:* $2496; $1628 per unit. $814 per term. Tuition and fees vary according to course load and program. *Financial support:* Fellowships, teaching assistantships, career-related internships or fieldwork, Federal Work-Study, institutionally sponsored loans, scholarships/grants, health care benefits, and unspecified assistantships available. Financial award application deadline: 1/4; financial award applicants required to submit FAFSA. *Faculty research:* Gender and sexuality, transatlantic studies, literacy and cultural theories, Colonial and Post-Colonial studies, autobiography and modern subjectivities. *Unit head:* Gigi Dopico-Black, Chair, 212-998-8770, Fax: 212-995-4149, E-mail: spanish.portuguese.info@nyu.edu. *Application contact:* James Fernandez, Director of Graduate Studies, 212-998-8770, Fax: 212-995-4149, E-mail: spanish.portuguese.info@nyu.edu.
Website: http://spanish.as.nyu.edu/

Northwestern University, The Graduate School, Judd A. and Marjorie Weinberg College of Arts and Sciences, Department of Spanish and Portuguese, Evanston, IL 60208. Offers PhD.

The Ohio State University, Graduate School, College of Arts and Sciences, Division of Arts and Humanities, Department of Spanish and Portuguese, Columbus, OH 43210. Offers MA, PhD. *Faculty:* 26. *Students:* 60 (35 women); includes 10 minority (all Hispanic/Latino), 27 international. Average age 31. In 2017, 11 master's, 6 doctorates awarded. Terminal master's awarded for partial completion of doctoral program. *Entrance requirements:* For master's and doctorate, GRE General Test, sample of academic writing. Additional exam requirements/recommendations for international students: Required—TOEFL (minimum score 550 paper-based; 79 iBT), Michigan English Language Assessment Battery (minimum score 82); Recommended—IELTS (minimum score 7). *Application deadline:* For fall admission, 12/13 priority date for domestic students, 11/30 priority date for international students; for spring admission, 3/1 for domestic students, 2/1 for international students. Applications are processed on a rolling basis. Application fee: $60 ($70 for international students). Electronic applications accepted. *Financial support:* Fellowships, research assistantships, teaching assistantships, Federal Work-Study, institutionally sponsored loans, and unspecified assistantships available. Support available to part-time students. *Unit head:* Dr. Laura Podalsky, Chair, 614-688-3662, E-mail: spanport@osu.edu. *Application contact:* Graduate and Professional Admissions, 614-292-9444, Fax: 614-292-3895, E-mail: gpadmissions@osu.edu.
Website: http://sppo.osu.edu/

Princeton University, Graduate School, Department of Spanish and Portuguese, Princeton, NJ 08544-1019. Offers PhD. *Degree requirements:* For doctorate, variable foreign language requirement, thesis/dissertation. *Entrance requirements:* For doctorate, GRE General Test, sample of written work. Additional exam requirements/recommendations for international students: Required—TOEFL (minimum score 600 paper-based). Electronic applications accepted.

Tulane University, School of Liberal Arts, Department of Spanish and Portuguese, New Orleans, LA 70118-5669. Offers Portuguese (MA); Spanish and Portuguese (PhD). *Degree requirements:* For master's, 2 foreign languages; for doctorate, 2 foreign languages, thesis/dissertation. *Entrance requirements:* For master's, GRE General Test, minimum B average in undergraduate course work; for doctorate, GRE General Test. Additional exam requirements/recommendations for international students: Required—TOEFL. Electronic applications accepted. *Expenses: Tuition:* Full-time $50,920; part-time $2829 per credit hour. *Required fees:* $2040; $44.50 per credit hour. $580 per term. Tuition and fees vary according to course load, degree level and program.

University of California, Los Angeles, Graduate Division, College of Letters and Science, Department of Spanish and Portuguese, Program in Portuguese, Los Angeles, CA 90095. Offers MA. *Degree requirements:* For master's, one foreign language, comprehensive exam or thesis. *Entrance requirements:* For master's, GRE General Test, bachelor's degree; minimum undergraduate GPA of 3.0 (or its equivalent if letter grade system not used). Additional exam requirements/recommendations for international students: Required—TOEFL. Electronic applications accepted.

University of California, Santa Barbara, Graduate Division, College of Letters and Sciences, Division of Humanities and Fine Arts, Department of Spanish and Portuguese, Santa Barbara, CA 93106-4150. Offers Hispanic languages and literatures (PhD), including European medieval studies, feminist studies, Hispanic linguistics, Hispanic literature, Luso-Brazilian literature; Hispanic linguistics (MA); Luso-Brazilian literature (MA); Spanish or Spanish-American literature (MA); MA/PhD. Terminal master's awarded for partial completion of doctoral program. *Degree requirements:* For master's, 2 foreign languages, comprehensive exam (for some programs), thesis optional; for doctorate, 3 foreign languages, comprehensive exam, thesis/dissertation. *Entrance requirements:* For master's and doctorate, GRE. Additional exam requirements/recommendations for international students: Required—TOEFL (minimum score 550 paper-based; 80 iBT), IELTS (minimum score 7). Electronic applications accepted. *Faculty research:* Nineteenth-century Spanish and Portuguese literature, Spanish and Spanish-American literature, nineteenth- and twentieth-century Portuguese and Brazilian literatures, Hispanic linguistics, Catalan language and culture.

University of Georgia, Franklin College of Arts and Sciences, Department of Romance Languages, Athens, GA 30602. Offers French (PhD); Italian (MA, PhD); Portuguese (MA, PhD); romance linguistics (MA); Spanish (PhD). *Degree requirements:* For master's, one foreign language; for doctorate, 2 foreign languages, thesis/dissertation. *Entrance requirements:* For master's and doctorate, GRE General Test. Electronic applications accepted.

University of Illinois at Urbana–Champaign, Graduate College, College of Liberal Arts and Sciences, School of Literatures, Cultures and Linguistics, Department of Spanish, Italian and Portuguese, Champaign, IL 61820. Offers Italian (MA, PhD); Portuguese (MA, PhD); Spanish (MA, PhD).

University of Maryland, College Park, Academic Affairs, College of Arts and Humanities, School of Languages, Literatures, and Cultures, Spanish Language and Literatures Program, College Park, MD 20742. Offers MA, PhD. *Degree requirements:* For master's, comprehensive exam, thesis optional, scholarly paper; for doctorate, 2 foreign languages, thesis/dissertation. *Entrance requirements:* For master's, minimum GPA of 3.0, interview, sample research paper, minimum of 12 credits in upper-level literature, 3 letters of recommendation; for doctorate, minimum GPA of 3.0, interview, sample research paper, minimum of 12 credits in upper-level literature. Additional exam requirements/recommendations for international students: Required—TOEFL. Electronic applications accepted.

University of Massachusetts Amherst, Graduate School, College of Humanities and Fine Arts, Department of Languages, Literatures, and Cultures, Program in Spanish and Portuguese Studies, Amherst, MA 01003. Offers Hispanic literatures, cultures and linguistics (MA, PhD); teaching Spanish (MAT). *Program availability:* Part-time. Terminal master's awarded for partial completion of doctoral program. *Degree requirements:* For master's, one foreign language, thesis or alternative; for doctorate, 2 foreign languages, comprehensive exam, thesis/dissertation. *Entrance requirements:* For master's and doctorate, GRE General Test, sample academic term paper. Additional exam requirements/recommendations for international students: Required—TOEFL (minimum score 550 paper-based; 80 iBT), IELTS (minimum score 6.5). Electronic applications accepted.

University of Massachusetts Dartmouth, Graduate School, College of Arts and Sciences, Department of Portuguese, North Dartmouth, MA 02747-2300. Offers Luso-Afro Brazilian studies and theory (PhD); Portuguese studies (MA). *Program availability:* Part-time. *Faculty:* 5 full-time (2 women), 2 part-time/adjunct (0 women). *Students:* 6 full-time (5 women), 5 part-time (3 women); includes 4 minority (3 Hispanic/Latino; 1 Two or more races, non-Hispanic/Latino), 3 international. Average age 41. 4 applicants, 50% accepted. In 2017, 1 master's, 2 doctorates awarded. Terminal master's awarded for partial completion of doctoral program. *Degree requirements:* For master's, comprehensive exam, thesis, written exam or project; for doctorate, comprehensive exam, thesis/dissertation. *Entrance requirements:* For master's, GRE (recommended), statement of purpose (minimum of 300 words), resume, 3 letters of recommendation, official transcripts, writing samples in Portuguese (minimum of 10 pages of writing); for doctorate, GRE (recommended), statement of purpose (minimum of 300 words), resume, 3 letters of recommendation, official transcripts, scholarly writing sample (minimum of 10 pages). Additional exam requirements/recommendations for international students: Required—TOEFL (minimum score 500 paper-based; 61 iBT). *Application deadline:* For fall admission, 2/1 priority date for domestic students, 1/1 priority date for international students; for spring admission, 11/15 priority date for domestic students, 10/15 priority date for international students. Application fee: $60. Electronic applications accepted. *Expenses:* Tuition, state resident: full-time $15,449; part-time $643.71 per credit. Tuition, nonresident: full-time $27,880; part-time $1161.67 per credit. *Required fees:* $405; $25.88 per credit. Tuition and fees vary according to course load and reciprocity agreements. *Financial support:* In 2017–18, 8 fellowships (averaging $18,750 per year) were awarded; research assistantships, teaching assistantships, tuition waivers (full), and unspecified assistantships also available. Support available to part-time students. Financial award application deadline: 3/1; financial award applicants required to submit FAFSA. *Faculty research:* Teaching and learning Portuguese as a heritage language, literature in Luso-Afro-Brazilian studies, studies in ethnicity and migration, bi- and multi-linguicism, histories of translation and gender in romance literary traditions. *Total annual research expenditures:* $308,000. *Unit head:* Victor Mendes, Director of Graduate Studies, Department of Portuguese, 508-999-8338, Fax: 508-910-9272, E-mail: vmendes@umassd.edu. *Application contact:* Steven Briggs, Director of Marketing and Recruitment for Graduate Studies, 508-999-8604, Fax: 508-999-8183, E-mail: graduate@umassd.edu.
Website: http://www.umassd.edu/cas/departmentsanddegreeprograms/portguese

University of Minnesota, Twin Cities Campus, Graduate School, College of Liberal Arts, Department of Spanish and Portuguese Studies, Minneapolis, MN 55455-0213. Offers Hispanic and Lusophone literatures, cultures and linguistics (PhD); Hispanic linguistics (MA); Hispanic literature (MA); Lusophone literature (MA). *Degree requirements:* For master's, 2 foreign languages, comprehensive exam, thesis or alternative; for doctorate, 2 foreign languages, comprehensive exam, thesis/dissertation. *Entrance requirements:* For master's and doctorate, GRE General Test, samples of written work, 3 letters of recommendation, voice sample, statement of purpose. Additional exam requirements/recommendations for international students: Required—TOEFL (minimum score 550 paper-based; 79 iBT). Electronic applications accepted. *Faculty research:* Sociohistorical approaches to literature and culture, feminist studies, literary theory, ideologies and literature, pragmatics and sociolinguistics.

University of New Mexico, Graduate Studies, College of Arts and Sciences, Program in Spanish and Portuguese, Albuquerque, NM 87131. Offers Portuguese (MA); Spanish (MA); Spanish and Portuguese (PhD). *Program availability:* Part-time. *Faculty:* 11 full-time (5 women). *Students:* 41 full-time (29 women), 14 part-time (7 women); includes 32 minority (all Hispanic/Latino), 15 international. Average age 32. 53 applicants, 58% accepted, 21 enrolled. In 2017, 13 master's, 3 doctorates awarded. *Degree requirements:* For master's, one foreign language, comprehensive exam, thesis optional; for doctorate, one foreign language, comprehensive exam, thesis/dissertation. *Entrance requirements:* For master's, BA in Spanish or Portuguese, 3 letters of recommendation, letter of intent; for doctorate, GRE, 3 letters of recommendation, letter of intent, sample research paper. Additional exam requirements/recommendations for international students: Required—TOEFL (minimum score 550 paper-based). *Application deadline:* For fall admission, 1/15 priority date for domestic students; for spring admission, 11/15 for domestic students. Applications are processed on a rolling basis. Application fee: $50. Electronic applications accepted. *Financial support:* Research assistantships, teaching assistantships with tuition reimbursements, Federal Work-Study, institutionally sponsored loans, scholarships/grants, health care benefits, and unspecified assistantships available. Support available to part-time students. Financial award application deadline: 3/1; financial award applicants required to submit FAFSA. *Faculty research:* Languages and literatures from the Iberian Peninsula, Latin America and the American Southwest. *Unit head:* Dr. Anthony Cardenas, Chair, 505-277-5907, Fax: 505-277-3885, E-mail: ajcard@unm.edu. *Application contact:* Martha Hurd, Graduate Advisor, 505-277-2974, E-mail: marthah@unm.edu.
Website: http://spanport.unm.edu

The University of North Carolina at Chapel Hill, Graduate School, College of Arts and Sciences, Department of Romance Languages and Literatures, Chapel Hill, NC 27599. Offers French (MA, PhD); Italian (MA, PhD); Portuguese (MA, PhD); Romance languages (MA, PhD); Romance philology (MA, PhD); Spanish (MA, PhD). *Degree requirements:* For master's, one foreign language, comprehensive exam, thesis; for doctorate, 2 foreign languages, comprehensive exam, thesis/dissertation. *Entrance requirements:* For master's and doctorate, GRE General Test, minimum GPA of 3.0. Additional exam requirements/recommendations for international students: Required—TOEFL (minimum score 550 paper-based). Electronic applications accepted.

University of South Africa, College of Human Sciences, Pretoria, South Africa. Offers adult education (M Ed); African languages (MA, PhD); African politics (MA, PhD); Afrikaans (MA, PhD); ancient history (MA, PhD); ancient Near Eastern studies (MA, PhD); anthropology (MA, PhD); applied linguistics (MA); Arabic (MA, PhD); archaeology (MA); art history (MA); Biblical archaeology (MA); Biblical studies (M Th, D Th, PhD); Christian spirituality (M Th, D Th); church history (M Th, D Th); classical studies (MA, PhD); clinical psychology (MA); communication (MA, PhD); comparative education (M Ed, Ed D); consulting psychology (D Admin, D Com, PhD); curriculum studies (M Ed, Ed D); development studies (M Admin, MA, D Admin, PhD); didactics (M Ed, Ed D); education (M Tech); education management (M Ed, Ed D); educational psychology (M Ed); English (MA); environmental education (M Ed); French (MA, PhD); German (MA, PhD); Greek (MA); guidance and counseling (M Ed); health studies (MA, PhD),

including health sciences education (MA), health services management (MA), medical and surgical nursing science (critical care general) (MA), midwifery and neonatal nursing science (MA), trauma and emergency care (MA); history (MA, PhD); history of education (Ed D); inclusive education (M Ed, Ed D); information and communications technology policy and regulation (MA); information science (MA, MIS, PhD); international politics (MA, PhD); Islamic studies (MA, PhD); Italian (MA, PhD); Judaica (MA, PhD); linguistics (MA, PhD); mathematical education (M Ed); mathematics education (MA); missiology (M Th, D Th); modern Hebrew (MA, PhD); musicology (MA, MMus, D Mus, PhD); natural science education (M Ed); New Testament (M Th, D Th); Old Testament (D Th); pastoral therapy (M Th, D Th); philosophy (MA); philosophy of education (M Ed, Ed D); politics (MA, PhD); Portuguese (MA, PhD); practical theology (M Th, D Th); psychology (MA, MS, PhD); psychology of education (M Ed, Ed D); public health (MA); religious studies (MA, D Th, PhD); Romance languages (MA); Russian (MA, PhD); Semitic languages (MA, PhD); social behavior studies in HIV/AIDS (MA); social science (mental health) (MA); social science in development studies (MA); social science in psychology (MA); social science in social work (MA); social science in sociology (MA); social work (MSW, DSW, PhD); socio-education (M Ed, Ed D); sociolinguistics (MA); sociology (MA, PhD); Spanish (MA, PhD); systematic theology (M Th, D Th); TESOL (teaching English to speakers of other languages) (MA); theological ethics (M Th, D Th); theory of literature (MA, PhD); urban ministries (D Th); urban ministry (M Th).

The University of Tennessee, Graduate School, College of Arts and Sciences, Department of Modern Foreign Languages and Literatures, Program in Modern Foreign Languages, Knoxville, TN 37996. Offers applied linguistics (PhD); French (PhD); German (PhD); Italian (PhD); Portuguese (PhD); Russian (PhD); Spanish (PhD). *Degree requirements:* For doctorate, 2 foreign languages, thesis/dissertation. *Entrance requirements:* For doctorate, minimum GPA of 2.7. Additional exam requirements/recommendations for international students: Required—TOEFL. Electronic applications accepted.

The University of Texas at Austin, Graduate School, College of Liberal Arts, Department of Spanish and Portuguese, Austin, TX 78712-1111. Offers Hispanic linguistics (MA, PhD); Hispanic literature (MA, PhD); Ibero-romance philology and linguistics (PhD); Luso-Brazilian literature (MA, PhD). *Degree requirements:* For master's, 2 foreign languages, thesis or alternative; for doctorate, 3 foreign languages, thesis/dissertation. *Entrance requirements:* For master's and doctorate, GRE General Test. Electronic applications accepted.

University of Toronto, School of Graduate Studies, Faculty of Arts and Science, Department of Spanish and Portuguese, Toronto, ON M5S 1A1, Canada. Offers MA, PhD. *Program availability:* Part-time. *Degree requirements:* For doctorate, thesis/dissertation. *Entrance requirements:* For master's, minimum B average in final year, 2 letters of reference; for doctorate, minimum A- average, 2 letters of reference, writing sample. Additional exam requirements/recommendations for international students: Required—TWE (minimum score 5), TOEFL, Michigan English Language Assessment Battery, IELTS, or COPE. Electronic applications accepted.

University of Washington, Graduate School, College of Arts and Sciences, Division of Spanish and Portuguese Studies, Seattle, WA 98195. Offers Hispanic literary and cultural studies (MA). *Degree requirements:* For master's, 2 foreign languages, thesis optional, exam. *Entrance requirements:* For master's, GRE General Test, minimum GPA of 3.0. Additional exam requirements/recommendations for international students: Required—TOEFL. Electronic applications accepted. *Faculty research:* Medieval through modern Spanish literature and film, Latin American literature, poetry and essay, pan-Hispanic ballad, Hispanic cultural studies, second language acquisition and applied linguistics.

University of Wisconsin–Madison, Graduate School, College of Letters and Science, Department of Spanish and Portuguese, Program in Portuguese, Madison, WI 53706-1380. Offers MA, PhD. *Degree requirements:* For master's, one foreign language; for doctorate, 2 foreign languages, thesis/dissertation. *Entrance requirements:* For master's, GRE (recommended), minimum GPA of 3.25 in Spanish or Portuguese; for doctorate, GRE (recommended), minimum graduate GPA of 3.4. Additional exam requirements/recommendations for international students: Required—TOEFL. Electronic applications accepted. *Faculty research:* Portuguese and Brazilian literature.

University of Wisconsin–Milwaukee, Graduate School, College of Letters and Science, Department of Spanish and Portuguese, Milwaukee, WI 53201-0413. Offers MA. *Students:* 9 full-time (4 women), 6 part-time (3 women); includes 3 minority (1 Hispanic/Latino; 2 Two or more races, non-Hispanic/Latino), 7 international. Average age 28. 14 applicants, 64% accepted, 8 enrolled. In 2017, 3 master's awarded. *Entrance requirements:* For master's, bachelor's degree. Application fee: $56 ($96 for international students). Electronic applications accepted. *Financial support:* Fellowships, research assistantships, teaching assistantships, and unspecified assistantships available. Financial award applicants required to submit FAFSA. *Faculty research:* Sociolinguistics, Spanish-American literature, Spanish literature, Hispanic culture, Hispanic historiography. *Unit head:* John McCaw, Department Chair, 414-229-4257, E-mail: rjmccaw@uwm.edu. *Application contact:* General Information Contact, 414-229-4982, Fax: 414-229-6967, E-mail: gradschool@uwm.edu.
Website: https://uwm.edu/spanish-portuguese/

Vanderbilt University, Department of Spanish and Portuguese, Nashville, TN 37240-1001. Offers Portuguese (MA); Spanish (MA, MAT, PhD); Spanish and Portuguese (PhD). *Faculty:* 12 full-time (5 women). *Students:* 24 full-time (12 women); includes 7 minority (2 Black or African American, non-Hispanic/Latino; 5 Hispanic/Latino), 12 international. Average age 31. 39 applicants, 18% accepted, 6 enrolled. In 2017, 1 master's, 4 doctorates awarded. *Degree requirements:* For master's, one foreign language, thesis; for doctorate, 2 foreign languages, thesis/dissertation, final and qualifying exams. *Entrance requirements:* For master's, GRE General Test; for doctorate, GRE General Test, writing sample in Spanish. Additional exam requirements/recommendations for international students: Required—TOEFL (minimum score 570 paper-based; 88 iBT). *Application deadline:* For fall admission, 1/15 for domestic and international students. Electronic applications accepted. *Financial support:* Fellowships, teaching assistantships with full tuition reimbursements, Federal Work-Study, institutionally sponsored loans, and health care benefits available. Financial award application deadline: 1/15; financial award applicants required to submit CSS PROFILE or FAFSA. *Faculty research:* Spanish, Portuguese, and Latin American literatures; foreign language pedagogy; Renaissance and Baroque poetry; nineteenth-century Spanish novel. *Unit head:* Dr. Benigno Trigo, Chair, 615-322-6930, Fax: 615-343-7260, E-mail: benigno.trigo@vanderbilt.edu. *Application contact:* Andres Zamora, Director of Graduate Studies, 615-322-6930, Fax: 615-343-7260, E-mail: andres.zamora@vanderbilt.edu.
Website: http://as.vanderbilt.edu/spanish-portuguese/graduate/index.php

Yale University, Graduate School of Arts and Sciences, Department of Spanish and Portuguese, New Haven, CT 06520. Offers Latin American literature (PhD); Luso-Brazilian and Spanish/Spanish American literatures (PhD); Spanish peninsular literature (PhD). Terminal master's awarded for partial completion of doctoral program. *Degree requirements:* For doctorate, 3 foreign languages, thesis/dissertation. *Entrance requirements:* For doctorate, GRE General Test.

Romance Languages

Boston University, Graduate School of Arts and Sciences, Department of Romance Studies, Boston, MA 02215. Offers Hispanic language and literature (MA, PhD). *Students:* 34 full-time (22 women), 2 part-time (1 woman); includes 9 minority (1 Black or African American, non-Hispanic/Latino; 8 Hispanic/Latino), 11 international. Average age 28. 46 applicants, 37% accepted, 7 enrolled. In 2017, 4 master's, 5 doctorates awarded. Terminal master's awarded for partial completion of doctoral program. *Degree requirements:* For master's, one foreign language, comprehensive exam; for doctorate, 2 foreign languages, comprehensive exam, thesis/dissertation. *Entrance requirements:* For master's and doctorate, GRE General Test, sample of written work, 3 letters of recommendation, transcripts, personal statement, summary of related coursework. Additional exam requirements/recommendations for international students: Required—TOEFL (minimum score 550 paper-based; 84 iBT). *Application deadline:* For fall admission, 1/15 for domestic and international students. Application fee: $95. Electronic applications accepted. *Financial support:* In 2017–18, 34 students received support, including 14 fellowships with full tuition reimbursements available (averaging $22,000 per year), 16 teaching assistantships with full tuition reimbursements available (averaging $22,000 per year); Federal Work-Study, scholarships/grants, and health care benefits also available. Financial award application deadline: 1/15. *Unit head:* Odile Cazenave, Chair, 617-353-6225, Fax: 617-353-6246, E-mail: cazenave@bu.edu. *Application contact:* Michael Williams, Administrative Assistant, 617-353-2641, Fax: 617-353-6246, E-mail: mawillia@bu.edu.
Website: http://www.bu.edu/rs/

Columbia University, Graduate School of Arts and Sciences, New York, NY 10027. Offers African-American studies (MA); American studies (MA); anthropology (MA, PhD); art history and archaeology (MA, PhD); astronomy (PhD); biological sciences (PhD); biotechnology (MA); chemical physics (PhD); chemistry (PhD); classical studies (MA, PhD); classics (MA, PhD); climate and society (MA); conservation biology (MA); earth and environmental sciences (PhD); East Asia: regional studies (MA); East Asian languages and cultures (MA, PhD); ecology, evolution and environmental biology (MA), including conservation biology; ecology, evolution, and environmental biology (PhD), including ecology and evolutionary biology, evolutionary primatology; economics (MA, PhD); English and comparative literature (MA, PhD); French and Romance philology (MA, PhD); Germanic languages (MA, PhD); global French studies (MA); global thought (MA); Hispanic cultural studies (MA); history (PhD); history and literature (MA); human rights studies (MA); Islamic studies (MA); Italian (MA, PhD); Japanese pedagogy (MA); Jewish studies (MA); Latin America and the Caribbean: regional studies (MA); Latin American and Iberian cultures (PhD); mathematics (MA, PhD), including finance (MA); medieval and Renaissance studies (MA); Middle Eastern, South Asian, and African studies (MA, PhD); modern art: critical and curatorial studies (MA); modern European studies (MA); museum anthropology (MA); music (DMA, PhD); oral history (MA); philosophical foundations of physics (MA); philosophy (MA, PhD); physics (PhD); political science (MA, PhD); psychology (PhD); quantitative methods in the social sciences (MA); religion (MA, PhD); Russia, Eurasia and East Europe: regional studies (MA); Russian translation (MA); Slavic cultures (MA); Slavic languages (MA, PhD); sociology (MA, PhD); South Asian studies (MA); statistics (MA, PhD); theatre (PhD). Dual-degree programs require admission to both Graduate School of Arts and Sciences and another Columbia school. *Program availability:* Part-time. Terminal master's awarded for partial completion of doctoral program. *Degree requirements:* For master's, variable foreign language requirement, comprehensive exam (for some programs), thesis (for some programs); for doctorate, variable foreign language requirement, comprehensive exam (for some programs), thesis/dissertation. *Entrance requirements:* For master's and doctorate, GRE General Test, GRE Subject Test (for some programs). Additional exam requirements/recommendations for international students: Required—TOEFL, IELTS. Electronic applications accepted. *Expenses: Tuition:* Full-time $44,864; part-time $1704 per credit. *Required fees:* $2370 per semester. One-time fee: $105.

Cornell University, Graduate School, Graduate Fields of Arts and Sciences, Field of Linguistics, Ithaca, NY 14853. Offers applied linguistics (MA, PhD); East Asian linguistics (MA, PhD); English linguistics (MA, PhD); general linguistics (MA, PhD); Germanic linguistics (MA, PhD); Indo-European linguistics (MA, PhD); phonetics (MA, PhD); phonological theory (MA, PhD); Romance linguistics (MA, PhD); second language acquisition (MA, PhD); semantics (MA, PhD); Slavic linguistics (MA, PhD); sociolinguistics (MA, PhD); South Asian linguistics (MA, PhD); Southeast Asian linguistics (MA, PhD); syntactic theory (MA, PhD). Terminal master's awarded for partial completion of doctoral program. *Degree requirements:* For master's, one foreign language, thesis; for doctorate, one foreign language, comprehensive exam, thesis/dissertation. *Entrance requirements:* For master's and doctorate, GRE General Test, 2 letters of recommendation. Additional exam requirements/recommendations for international students: Required—TOEFL (minimum score 600 paper-based; 77 iBT). Electronic applications accepted. *Faculty research:* Phonology and phonetics, syntax and semantics, historical linguistics, philosophy of language, language acquisition.

Cornell University, Graduate School, Graduate Fields of Arts and Sciences, Field of Romance Studies, Ithaca, NY 14853. Offers French linguistics (PhD); French literature (PhD); Hispanic literature (PhD); Italian linguistics (PhD); Italian literature (PhD); Romance linguistics (PhD); Spanish linguistics (PhD). *Degree requirements:* For doctorate, 2 foreign languages, comprehensive exam, thesis/dissertation. *Entrance requirements:* For doctorate, GRE General Test, sample of written work, 3 letters of recommendation. Additional exam requirements/recommendations for international students: Required—TOEFL (minimum score 550 paper-based; 77 iBT). Electronic applications accepted. *Faculty research:* Literary theory, Hispanic studies, French studies, gender studies.

Hunter College of the City University of New York, Graduate School, School of Arts and Sciences, Department of Romance Languages, New York, NY 10065-5085. Offers French (MA); Italian (MA); Spanish (MA). *Program availability:* Part-time, evening/weekend. *Degree requirements:* For master's, 2 foreign languages, comprehensive exam, thesis optional. *Entrance requirements:* For master's, GRE General Test, GRE Subject Test, interview, proficiency in chosen language. Additional exam requirements/recommendations for international students: Required—TOEFL.

Johns Hopkins University, Zanvyl Krieger School of Arts and Sciences, Department of German and Romance Languages and Literatures, Baltimore, MD 21218. Offers German (MA, PhD); romance languages (PhD), including French, Italian, Spanish. *Faculty:* 49 full-time (30 women), 1 part-time/adjunct (0 women). *Students:* 55 full-time (31 women); includes 4 minority (3 Hispanic/Latino; 1 Two or more races, non-Hispanic/Latino), 24 international. Average age 29. 39 applicants, 46% accepted, 8 enrolled. In 2017, 2 master's, 10 doctorates awarded. Terminal master's awarded for partial completion of doctoral program. *Degree requirements:* For master's, comprehensive exam; for doctorate, 2 foreign languages, comprehensive exam, thesis/dissertation. *Entrance requirements:* For doctorate, GRE General Test. Additional exam requirements/recommendations for international students: Required—TOEFL (minimum score 600 paper-based; 100 iBT), IELTS. *Application deadline:* For fall admission, 1/15 for domestic and international students. Application fee: $75. Electronic applications accepted. *Expenses:* Contact institution. *Financial support:* In 2017–18, 80 students received support, including 12 fellowships with full tuition reimbursements available (averaging $29,000 per year), 21 teaching assistantships with full tuition reimbursements available (averaging $29,000 per year); research assistantships, institutionally sponsored loans, and health care benefits also available. *Faculty research:* Nineteenth-century French prose and poetry, genetic theory and criticism; twentieth-century Latin American literature and film; medieval and Renaissance Italian literature; gender and queer theory in German literature; the ideology of Baroque and neo-Baroque aesthetics. *Unit head:* Dr. Derek Schilling, Chair, 410-516-4626, Fax: 410-516-5358, E-mail: dschill4@jhu.edu. *Application contact:* Kathy Loehmer, Senior Academic Coordinator, 410-516-7226, Fax: 410-516-5358, E-mail: kathy.grll@jhu.edu.
Website: http://grll.jhu.edu/

Michigan State University, The Graduate School, College of Arts and Letters, Department of French, Classics, and Italian, East Lansing, MI 48824. Offers French (MA); French language and literature (PhD). *Entrance requirements:* Additional exam requirements/recommendations for international students: Required—TOEFL. Electronic applications accepted.

New York University, Graduate School of Arts and Science, Center for French Civilization and Culture, Department of French, New York, NY 10012-1019. Offers French (PhD); French language and civilization (MA); French literature (MA); Romance languages and literatures (MA). *Program availability:* Part-time. *Faculty:* 18 full-time (7 women), 2 part-time/adjunct (both women). *Students:* 52 full-time (36 women), 3 part-time (2 women); includes 10 minority (3 Black or African American, non-Hispanic/Latino; 2 Asian, non-Hispanic/Latino; 5 Hispanic/Latino), 12 international. Average age 29. 67 applicants, 58% accepted, 20 enrolled. In 2017, 15 master's, 15 doctorates awarded. Terminal master's awarded for partial completion of doctoral program. *Degree requirements:* For master's, one foreign language, thesis (for some programs); for doctorate, one foreign language, thesis/dissertation. *Entrance requirements:* For master's and doctorate, GRE General Test, proficiency in French. Additional exam requirements/recommendations for international students: Required—TOEFL. *Application deadline:* For fall admission, 1/4 for domestic and international students; for spring admission, 11/1 for domestic and international students. Application fee: $100. *Expenses: Tuition:* Full-time $41,352; part-time $19,968 per year. *Required fees:* $2496; $1628 per unit. $814 per term. Tuition and fees vary according to course load and program. *Financial support:* Fellowships, teaching assistantships, Federal Work-Study, institutionally sponsored loans, scholarships/grants, traineeships, health care benefits, unspecified assistantships, and instructorships available. Financial award application deadline: 1/4; financial award applicants required to submit FAFSA. *Faculty research:* French and Francophone literature, literary theory, and history; rhetoric and poetics; cultural history; theater and cinema. *Unit head:* Lucien Nouis, Director of Graduate Studies, 212-998-8700, Fax: 212-995-4187, E-mail: french.grad@nyu.edu. *Application contact:* Erin Brau, Graduate Administrator, 212-998-8700, Fax: 212-995-4187, E-mail: french.grad@nyu.edu.
Website: http://www.nyu.edu/gsas/dept/french/

New York University, Graduate School of Arts and Science, Department of Spanish and Portuguese Languages and Literatures, New York, NY 10012-1019. Offers Portuguese (MA, PhD); Spanish (PhD); Spanish and Latin American literatures and cultures (MA); Spanish language and translation (MA). *Program availability:* Part-time. *Students:* Average age 32. 157 applicants, 43% accepted, 33 enrolled. In 2017, 29 master's, 5 doctorates awarded. *Degree requirements:* For master's, 2 foreign languages, thesis; for doctorate, 2 foreign languages, thesis/dissertation. *Entrance requirements:* For master's, GRE General Test; for doctorate, GRE General Test, master's degree. Additional exam requirements/recommendations for international students: Required—TOEFL. *Application deadline:* For fall admission, 1/4 priority date for domestic students, 1/4 for international students. Application fee: $100. *Expenses: Tuition:* Full-time $41,352; part-time $19,968 per year. *Required fees:* $2496; $1628 per unit. $814 per term. Tuition and fees vary according to course load and program. *Financial support:* Fellowships, teaching assistantships, career-related internships or fieldwork, Federal Work-Study, institutionally sponsored loans, scholarships/grants, health care benefits, and unspecified assistantships available. Financial award application deadline: 1/4; financial award applicants required to submit FAFSA. *Faculty research:* Gender and sexuality, transatlantic studies, literacy and cultural theories, Colonial and Post-Colonial studies, autobiography and modern subjectivities. *Unit head:* Gigi Dopico-Black, Chair, 212-998-8770, Fax: 212-995-4149, E-mail: spanish.portuguese.info@nyu.edu. *Application contact:* James Fernandez, Director of Graduate Studies, 212-998-8770, Fax: 212-995-4149, E-mail: spanish.portuguese.info@nyu.edu.
Website: http://spanish.as.nyu.edu/

Northern Illinois University, Graduate School, College of Liberal Arts and Sciences, Department of Foreign Languages and Literatures, De Kalb, IL 60115-2854. Offers French (MA); Spanish (MA). *Program availability:* Part-time. *Faculty:* 25 full-time (11 women). *Students:* 5 full-time (2 women), 12 part-time (8 women); includes 11 minority (1 Black or African American, non-Hispanic/Latino; 10 Hispanic/Latino). Average age 32. 8 applicants, 88% accepted, 5 enrolled. In 2017, 2 master's awarded. *Degree requirements:* For master's, one foreign language, comprehensive exam, thesis or alternative, language proficiency exam. *Entrance requirements:* For master's, GRE General Test, interview, minimum GPA of 2.75, undergraduate major in French or Spanish. Additional exam requirements/recommendations for international students: Required—TOEFL (minimum score 550 paper-based). *Application deadline:* For fall admission, 6/1 for domestic students, 5/1 for international students; for spring admission, 11/1 for domestic students, 10/1 for international students. Applications are processed on a rolling basis. Application fee: $40. Electronic applications accepted. *Financial support:* In 2017–18, 7 teaching assistantships with full tuition reimbursements were awarded; fellowships with full tuition reimbursements, research assistantships with full tuition reimbursements, career-related internships or fieldwork, Federal Work-Study, scholarships/grants, tuition waivers (full), and unspecified assistantships also available. Support available to part-time students. Financial award applicants required to submit FAFSA. *Faculty research:* Francophone women writers, prosodies of French and Italian, early Spanish drama, business German, history of Burmese literature. *Unit head:* Dr. Katharina Barbe, Chair, 815-753-1559, Fax: 815-753-5989, E-mail: kbarbe@niu.edu. *Application contact:* Graduate School Office, 815-753-0395, E-mail: gradsch@niu.edu.
Website: http://www.forlangs.net/

Queens College of the City University of New York, Arts and Humanities Division, Department of European Languages and Literatures, Queens, NY 11367-1597. Offers French (MA); Italian (MA). *Program availability:* Part-time-only, evening/weekend. *Faculty:* 10 full-time (5 women), 1 part-time/adjunct (0 women). *Students:* 1 full-time (0 women), 11 part-time (6 women); includes 6 minority (5 Black or African American, non-Hispanic/Latino; 1 Hispanic/Latino). Average age 42. 11 applicants, 82% accepted, 6 enrolled. In 2017, 4 master's awarded. *Degree requirements:* For master's, 2 foreign languages, thesis optional, oral exam. *Entrance requirements:* For master's, minimum GPA of 3.0. Additional exam requirements/recommendations for international students: Required—TOEFL (minimum score 61 iBT), IELTS (minimum score 5). *Application deadline:* For fall admission, 4/1 for domestic students; for spring admission, 11/1 for domestic students. Applications are processed on a rolling basis. Application fee: $125. Electronic applications accepted. *Financial support:* Career-related internships or fieldwork, Federal Work-Study, institutionally sponsored loans, and tuition waivers (partial) available. Financial award application deadline: 4/1; financial award applicants required to submit FAFSA. *Faculty research:* Italian literature and culture, French and Francophone literature and theory, Romance linguistics, French and Italian cinema. *Unit head:* Dr. David Andrew Jones, Chair, 718-997-5980, E-mail: david.jones@qc.cuny.edu. *Application contact:* Elizabeth D'Amico-Ramirez, Assistant Director of Graduate Admissions, 718-997-5203, E-mail: elizabeth.damicoramirez@qc.cuny.edu.

San Diego State University, Graduate and Research Affairs, College of Arts and Letters, Department of European Studies, San Diego, CA 92182. Offers MA. *Degree requirements:* For master's, one foreign language. *Entrance requirements:* For master's, GRE General Test. Additional exam requirements/recommendations for international students: Required—TOEFL. Electronic applications accepted.

Stony Brook University, State University of New York, Graduate School, College of Arts and Sciences, Department of European Languages, Literatures, and Cultures, Program in French, Stony Brook, NY 11794. Offers Romance languages (MA). *Program availability:* Evening/weekend. *Students:* 2 part-time (both women). 1 applicant, 100% accepted. In 2017, 2 master's awarded. *Degree requirements:* For master's, one foreign language. *Entrance requirements:* For master's, GRE General Test. Additional exam requirements/recommendations for international students: Required—TOEFL. *Application deadline:* For fall admission, 1/15 for domestic students; for spring admission, 10/1 for domestic students. Application fee: $100. *Expenses:* Contact institution. *Unit head:* Dr. Prosper Sanou, Coordinator, 631-632-7440, Fax: 631-632-9612, E-mail: prosper.sanou@stonybrook.edu. *Application contact:* Elizabeth Tolson, Coordinator, 631-632-7440, Fax: 631-632-9612, E-mail: elizabeth-a.tolson@stonybrook.edu.

Texas Tech University, Graduate School, College of Arts and Sciences, Department of Biological Sciences, Lubbock, TX 79409-3131. Offers biology (MS, PhD); environmental sustainability and natural resource management (PSM); microbiology (MS); zoology (MS, PhD). *Program availability:* Part-time, blended/hybrid learning. *Faculty:* 44 full-time (16 women). *Students:* 103 full-time (56 women), 13 part-time (5 women); includes 12 minority (2 Black or African American, non-Hispanic/Latino; 2 Asian, non-Hispanic/Latino; 6 Hispanic/Latino; 2 Two or more races, non-Hispanic/Latino), 51 international. Average age 29. 77 applicants, 36% accepted, 17 enrolled. In 2017, 13 master's, 10 doctorates awarded. *Degree requirements:* For master's, comprehensive exam, thesis or alternative; for doctorate, comprehensive exam, thesis/dissertation. *Entrance requirements:* For master's and doctorate, GRE General Test. Additional exam requirements/recommendations for international students: Required—TOEFL (minimum score 550 paper-based; 79 iBT). *Application deadline:* For fall admission, 6/1 priority date for domestic students, 1/15 priority date for international students; for spring admission, 9/1 priority date for domestic students, 6/15 priority date for international students. Applications are processed on a rolling basis. Application fee: $60. Electronic applications accepted. *Expenses:* Contact institution. *Financial support:* In 2017–18, 110 students received support, including 85 fellowships (averaging $1,960 per year), 28 research assistantships (averaging $8,365 per year), 93 teaching assistantships (averaging $15,744 per year); Federal Work-Study and health care benefits also available. Financial award application deadline: 2/15; financial award applicants required to submit FAFSA. *Faculty research:* Biodiversity, genomics and evolution; climate change in arid ecosystems, plant biology and biotechnology; animal communication and behavior; microbiomes, zoonosis and emerging diseases. *Total annual research expenditures:* $1.7 million. *Unit head:* Dr. Ron Chesser, Chair, 806-834-0121, Fax: 806-742-2963, E-mail: ron.chesser@ttu.edu. *Application contact:* Dr. Lou Densmore, Graduate Adviser, 806-834-6479, Fax: 806-742-2963, E-mail: lou.densmore@ttu.edu.
Website: http://www.depts.ttu.edu/biology/

Texas Tech University, Graduate School, College of Arts and Sciences, Department of Classical and Modern Languages and Literatures, Lubbock, TX 79409. Offers languages and cultures (MA); Romance languages (MA); Spanish (PhD); MBA/MA. *Program availability:* Part-time. *Faculty:* 58 full-time (39 women), 1 (woman) part-time/adjunct. *Students:* 79 full-time (42 women), 15 part-time (11 women); includes 22 minority (1 Black or African American, non-Hispanic/Latino; 18 Hispanic/Latino; 3 Two or more races, non-Hispanic/Latino), 47 international. Average age 32. 51 applicants, 76% accepted, 27 enrolled. In 2017, 26 master's, 3 doctorates awarded. *Degree requirements:* For master's, comprehensive exam, thesis or alternative; for doctorate, comprehensive exam, thesis/dissertation. *Entrance requirements:* Additional exam requirements/recommendations for international students: Required—TOEFL (minimum score 550 paper-based; 79 iBT). *Application deadline:* For fall admission, 6/1 priority date for domestic students, 1/15 priority date for international students; for spring admission, 9/1 priority date for domestic students, 6/15 priority date for international students. Applications are processed on a rolling basis. Application fee: $60. Electronic applications accepted. *Expenses:* Contact institution. *Financial support:* In 2017–18, 80 students received support, including 52 fellowships (averaging $3,518 per year), 74 teaching assistantships (averaging $12,664 per year); research assistantships, Federal Work-Study, scholarships/grants, and unspecified assistantships also available. Financial award application deadline: 4/15; financial award applicants required to submit FAFSA. *Faculty research:* Literature, comparative literature, linguistics, culture, applied linguistics. *Total annual research expenditures:* $150,379. *Unit head:* Dr. Erin Collopy, Department Chair and Associate Professor, 806-834-8497, Fax: 806-742-3306, E-mail: erin.collopy@ttu.edu. *Application contact:* Carla Burrus, Senior Advisor, 806-834-3282, Fax: 806-742-3306, E-mail: carla.burrus@ttu.edu.
Website: http://www.depts.ttu.edu/classic_modern/

Romance Languages

University at Buffalo, the State University of New York, Graduate School, College of Arts and Sciences, Department of Romance Languages and Literatures, Buffalo, NY 14260-4620. Offers French (MA, PhD); Spanish (MA, PhD). *Program availability:* Part-time. Terminal master's awarded for partial completion of doctoral program. *Degree requirements:* For master's, one foreign language, comprehensive exam, thesis (for some programs); for doctorate, 2 foreign languages, comprehensive exam (for some programs), thesis/dissertation. *Entrance requirements:* For doctorate, GRE. Additional exam requirements/recommendations for international students: Required—TOEFL (minimum score 550 paper-based; 79 iBT), IELTS (minimum score 6.5), PTE (minimum score 55). Electronic applications accepted. *Faculty research:* Romance linguistics, cultural studies, literary studies, literature, philosophy and poetry.

The University of Alabama, Graduate School, College of Arts and Sciences, Department of Modern Languages and Classics, Tuscaloosa, AL 35487. Offers French (MA, PhD); French and Spanish (PhD); German (MA); Romance languages (MA, PhD); Spanish (MA, PhD). *Program availability:* Part-time. *Faculty:* 30 full-time (18 women). *Students:* 45 full-time (27 women), 4 part-time (1 woman); includes 11 minority (5 Black or African American, non-Hispanic/Latino; 1 Asian, non-Hispanic/Latino; 3 Hispanic/Latino; 2 Two or more races, non-Hispanic/Latino), 14 international. Average age 32. 26 applicants, 88% accepted, 11 enrolled. In 2017, 18 master's awarded. *Degree requirements:* For master's, comprehensive exam, thesis optional; for doctorate, one foreign language, thesis/dissertation, preliminary exam. *Entrance requirements:* For master's and doctorate, minimum GPA of 3.0, writing sample. *Application deadline:* For fall admission, 7/6 priority date for domestic students, 1/15 priority date for international students; for spring admission, 12/5 priority date for domestic students, 6/1 priority date for international students. Applications are processed on a rolling basis. Application fee: $50 ($60 for international students). Electronic applications accepted. *Financial support:* In 2017–18, 40 students received support, including research assistantships with full tuition reimbursements available (averaging $10,291 per year), teaching assistantships with full tuition reimbursements available (averaging $10,291 per year); fellowships, career-related internships or fieldwork, Federal Work-Study, institutionally sponsored loans, and scholarships/grants also available. Financial award application deadline: 7/14. *Faculty research:* Non-English literature, linguistics, culture, film. *Unit head:* Dr. Douglas Lightfoot, Department Chair, 205-348-5059, E-mail: lightfoot@ua.edu. *Application contact:* Michael Picone, Graduate Director, 205-348-8473, E-mail: picone@ua.edu.
Website: http://bama.ua.edu/~mlc

University of California, Berkeley, Graduate Division, College of Letters and Science, Group in Romance Languages and Literatures, Berkeley, CA 94720-1500. Offers French (PhD); Italian (PhD); Spanish (PhD). *Degree requirements:* For doctorate, thesis/dissertation, qualifying exam. *Entrance requirements:* For doctorate, GRE General Test, minimum GPA of 3.0, 3 letters of recommendation. Additional exam requirements/recommendations for international students: Required—TOEFL (minimum score 570 paper-based; 90 iBT). Electronic applications accepted.

University of Chicago, Division of the Humanities, Department of Romance Languages and Literatures, Chicago, IL 60637. Offers French and Francophone studies (PhD); Hispanic and Luso-Brazilian studies (PhD); Italian studies (PhD); Renaissance and early modern studies (PhD). *Students:* 50 full-time (28 women); includes 12 minority (2 Asian, non-Hispanic/Latino; 9 Hispanic/Latino; 1 Two or more races, non-Hispanic/Latino), 25 international. Average age 30. 52 applicants, 31% accepted, 7 enrolled. In 2017, 4 doctorates awarded. Terminal master's awarded for partial completion of doctoral program. *Degree requirements:* For doctorate, 3 foreign languages, comprehensive exam, thesis/dissertation. *Entrance requirements:* For doctorate, GRE General Test, 15-20 page writing sample, statement of purpose, 3 letters of recommendation, transcripts for all previous degrees and institutions attended. Additional exam requirements/recommendations for international students: Required—TOEFL (minimum score 104 iBT), IELTS (minimum score 7). *Application deadline:* For fall admission, 12/15 for domestic and international students. Application fee: $90. Electronic applications accepted. *Financial support:* In 2017–18, fellowships with full tuition reimbursements (averaging $27,000 per year) were awarded; teaching assistantships with full tuition reimbursements, Federal Work-Study, institutionally sponsored loans, scholarships/grants, and health care benefits also available. Financial award application deadline: 12/15. *Unit head:* Daisy Delogu, Chair, 773-702-8481, E-mail: romance-languages@uchicago.edu. *Application contact:* Michael Beetley, Assistant Dean of Students, Admissions and Fellowships, 773-702-1552, Fax: 773-834-9148, E-mail: humanitiesadmissions@uchicago.edu.
Website: http://rll.uchicago.edu

University of Chicago, Division of the Humanities, Master of Arts Program in the Humanities, Chicago, IL 60637. Offers art history (MA); cinema and media studies (MA); classic languages (MA); comparative literature (MA); creative writing (MA); cultural policy studies (MA); digital humanities (MA); East Asian languages and civilizations (MA); English language and literature (MA); gender and sexuality studies (MA); Germanic studies (MA); linguistics (MA); music (MA); near Eastern languages and civilizations (MA); philosophy (MA); poetics (MA); race, politics and culture (MA); Romance languages and literatures (MA); Slavic languages and literatures (MA); South Asian languages and civilizations (MA); theater and performance studies (MA). *Students:* 95 full-time (50 women), 6 part-time (4 women); includes 22 minority (1 Black or African American, non-Hispanic/Latino; 10 Asian, non-Hispanic/Latino; 11 Hispanic/Latino), 19 international. Average age 26. 708 applicants, 75% accepted, 101 enrolled. In 2017, 91 master's awarded. *Degree requirements:* For master's, thesis. *Entrance requirements:* For master's, GRE General Test, 10-15 page writing sample, statement of purpose, 3 letters of recommendation, transcripts for all previous degrees and institutions attended. Additional exam requirements/recommendations for international students: Required—TOEFL (minimum score 104 iBT), IELTS (minimum score 7). *Application deadline:* For fall admission, 1/3 priority date for domestic and international students. Application fee: $90. Electronic applications accepted. *Expenses:* Contact institution. *Financial support:* In 2017–18, fellowships with partial tuition reimbursements (averaging $12,000 per year) were awarded; Federal Work-Study, institutionally sponsored loans, scholarships/grants, and tuition waivers (partial) also available. Financial award application deadline: 4/30. *Unit head:* Thomas Christensen, Director, 773-834-1201, Fax: 773-834-7526, E-mail: ma-humanities@uchicago.edu. *Application contact:* Michael Beetley, Assistant Dean of Students for Admissions, 773-834-1552, E-mail: humanitiesadmissions@uchicago.edu.
Website: http://maph.uchicago.edu/

University of Cincinnati, Graduate School, McMicken College of Arts and Sciences, Department of Romance Languages and Literatures, Cincinnati, OH 45221. Offers French (MA, PhD); Romance languages and literatures (PhD); Spanish (MA, PhD). Terminal master's awarded for partial completion of doctoral program. *Degree requirements:* For master's, 2 foreign languages, comprehensive exam, thesis optional; for doctorate, 3 foreign languages, comprehensive exam, thesis/dissertation. *Entrance requirements:* For master's, minimum GPA of 3.0; for doctorate, MA or equivalent in French or Spanish language and literature. Additional exam requirements/recommendations for international students: Required—TOEFL (minimum score 520 paper-based). Electronic applications accepted. *Expenses: Tuition, area resident:* Full-time $14,468. Tuition, state resident: full-time $14,968; part-time $754 per credit hour. Tuition, nonresident: full-time $24,210; part-time $1311 per credit hour. *International tuition:* $26,460 full-time. *Required fees:* $3958; $84 per credit hour. One-time fee: $85 full-time. Tuition and fees vary according to course load, degree level and program. *Faculty research:* Teaching methods in Spanish, Spanish theater, Old French, Francophone studies, poetry.

University of Illinois at Urbana–Champaign, Graduate College, College of Liberal Arts and Sciences, School of Literatures, Cultures and Linguistics, Program in Romance Linguistics, Champaign, IL 61820. Offers PhD.

University of Miami, Graduate School, College of Arts and Sciences, Department of Modern Languages and Literatures, Coral Gables, FL 33124. Offers romance studies (PhD), including French, Spanish. *Degree requirements:* For doctorate, 2 foreign languages, thesis/dissertation, area exam, qualifying exam. *Entrance requirements:* For doctorate, 1 writing sample in English and 1 writing sample in French or Spanish, minimum GPA of 3.0, oral interview, letters of recommendation. Additional exam requirements/recommendations for international students: Required—TOEFL (minimum score 550 paper-based; 59 iBT). Electronic applications accepted. *Faculty research:* Transatlantic studies, Caribbean studies, comparative literature, gender theory, cultural studies.

University of Missouri, Office of Research and Graduate Studies, College of Arts and Science, Department of Romance Languages and Literatures, Columbia, MO 65211. Offers French (MA, PhD); literature (MA); Spanish (MA, PhD); teaching (MA). Terminal master's awarded for partial completion of doctoral program. *Degree requirements:* For master's, one foreign language; for doctorate, 4 foreign languages, comprehensive exam, thesis/dissertation. *Entrance requirements:* For master's, GRE General Test, minimum GPA of 3.0 in field of major; bachelor's degree; for doctorate, GRE General Test, minimum GPA of 3.0 in field of major; master's degree. Additional exam requirements/recommendations for international students: Required—TOEFL (minimum score 500 paper-based; 61 iBT). Electronic applications accepted.

University of Missouri–Kansas City, College of Arts and Sciences, Department of Foreign Languages and Literatures, Kansas City, MO 64110-2499. Offers romance languages and literatures (MA), including French, Spanish. *Program availability:* Part-time. *Degree requirements:* For master's, 2 foreign languages. *Entrance requirements:* For master's, GRE General Test, minimum GPA of 2.75, 2 letters of recommendation. Additional exam requirements/recommendations for international students: Required—TOEFL (minimum score 550 paper-based; 80 iBT). Electronic applications accepted. *Faculty research:* Literary analyses; psychology and literature; narrative techniques, poetic structure, and style; literature, politics, and society (especially in Latin America).

University of New Orleans, Graduate School, College of Liberal Arts, Department of Foreign Languages, New Orleans, LA 70148. Offers MA. *Program availability:* Part-time, evening/weekend. *Degree requirements:* For master's, one foreign language, thesis optional. *Entrance requirements:* For master's, GRE General Test, minimum B average. Additional exam requirements/recommendations for international students: Required—TOEFL (minimum score 550 paper-based; 79 iBT), IELTS (minimum score 6.5). Electronic applications accepted. *Faculty research:* Translation studies, Michelet, Scève, Spanish canzoniero, theories of representation.

The University of North Carolina at Chapel Hill, Graduate School, College of Arts and Sciences, Department of Romance Languages and Literatures, Chapel Hill, NC 27599. Offers French (MA, PhD); Italian (MA, PhD); Portuguese (MA, PhD); Romance languages (MA, PhD); Romance philology (MA, PhD); Spanish (MA, PhD). *Degree requirements:* For master's, one foreign language, comprehensive exam, thesis; for doctorate, 2 foreign languages, comprehensive exam, thesis/dissertation. *Entrance requirements:* For master's and doctorate, GRE General Test, minimum GPA of 3.0. Additional exam requirements/recommendations for international students: Required—TOEFL (minimum score 550 paper-based). Electronic applications accepted.

University of Notre Dame, Graduate School, College of Arts and Letters, Division of Humanities, Department of Romance Languages and Literatures, Notre Dame, IN 46556. Offers French and Francophone studies (MA); Iberian and Latin American studies (MA); Italian studies (MA); Romance literatures (MA). *Degree requirements:* For master's, 2 foreign languages, comprehensive exam, thesis optional. *Entrance requirements:* For master's, GRE General Test, BA in target language. Additional exam requirements/recommendations for international students: Required—TOEFL (minimum score 600 paper-based; 80 iBT). Electronic applications accepted. *Faculty research:* Literature of discovery and exploration, modern literature, literary criticism, medieval literature, feminist critical theory.

University of Oregon, Graduate School, College of Arts and Sciences, Department of Romance Languages, Program in Romance Languages, Eugene, OR 97403. Offers MA, PhD. *Program availability:* Part-time. *Degree requirements:* For master's, 2 foreign languages; for doctorate, 2 foreign languages, thesis/dissertation. *Entrance requirements:* For master's and doctorate, GRE General Test, minimum GPA of 3.0. Additional exam requirements/recommendations for international students: Required—TOEFL.

University of Pennsylvania, School of Arts and Sciences, Graduate Group in Romance Languages, Philadelphia, PA 19104. Offers French (AM, PhD); Italian (AM, PhD); Spanish (AM, PhD). *Faculty:* 20 full-time (7 women), 6 part-time/adjunct (3 women). *Students:* 61 full-time (29 women); includes 7 minority (6 Hispanic/Latino; 1 Two or more races, non-Hispanic/Latino), 34 international. Average age 31. 82 applicants, 32% accepted, 13 enrolled. In 2017, 12 master's, 8 doctorates awarded. Terminal master's awarded for partial completion of doctoral program. Application fee: $70.
Website: http://www.sas.upenn.edu/graduate-division

University of South Africa, College of Human Sciences, Pretoria, South Africa. Offers adult education (M Ed); African languages (MA, PhD); African politics (MA, PhD); Afrikaans (MA, PhD); ancient history (MA, PhD); ancient Near Eastern studies (MA, PhD); anthropology (MA, PhD); applied linguistics (MA); Arabic (MA, PhD); archaeology (MA); art history (MA); Biblical archaeology (MA); Biblical studies (M Th, D Th, PhD); Christian spirituality (M Th, D Th); church history (M Th, D Th); classical studies (MA, PhD); clinical psychology (MA); communication (MA, PhD); comparative education (M Ed, Ed D); consulting psychology (D Admin, D Com, PhD); curriculum studies (M Ed, Ed D); development studies (M Admin, MA, D Admin, PhD); didactics (M Ed, Ed D); education (M Tech); education management (M Ed, Ed D); educational psychology (M Ed); English (MA); environmental education (M Ed); French (MA, PhD); German (MA, PhD); Greek (MA); guidance and counseling (M Ed); health studies (MA, PhD), including health sciences education (MA), health services management (MA), medical and surgical nursing science (critical care general) (MA), midwifery and neonatal nursing science (MA), trauma and emergency care (MA); history (MA, PhD); history of education (Ed D); inclusive education (M Ed, Ed D); information and communications technology policy and regulation (MA); information science (MA, MIS, PhD); international politics (MA, PhD); Islamic studies (MA, PhD); Italian (MA, PhD); Judaica (MA, PhD); linguistics (MA, PhD); mathematical education (M Ed); mathematics education (MA); missiology (M Th, D Th); modern Hebrew (MA, PhD); musicology (MA, MMus, D Mus, PhD); natural science education (M Ed); New Testament (M Th, D Th); Old Testament (D Th);

pastoral therapy (M Th, D Th); philosophy (MA); philosophy of education (M Ed, Ed D); politics (MA, PhD); Portuguese (MA, PhD); practical theology (M Th, D Th); psychology (MA, MS, PhD); psychology of education (M Ed, Ed D); public health (MA); religious studies (MA, D Th, PhD); Romance languages (MA); Russian (MA, PhD); Semitic languages (MA, PhD); social behavior studies in HIV/AIDS (MA); social science (mental health) (MA); social science in development studies (MA); social science in psychology (MA); social science in social work (MA); social science in sociology (MA); social work (MSW, DSW, PhD); socio-education (M Ed, Ed D); sociolinguistics (MA); sociology (MA, PhD); Spanish (MA, PhD); systematic theology (M Th, D Th); TESOL (teaching English to speakers of other languages) (MA); theological ethics (M Th, D Th); theory of literature (MA, PhD); urban ministries (D Th); urban ministry (M Th).

The University of Texas at Austin, Graduate School, College of Liberal Arts, Department of French and Italian, Austin, TX 78712-1111. Offers French linguistics (MA, PhD); French studies (MA, PhD); Italian studies (MA, PhD); Romance linguistics (PhD). *Program availability:* Part-time. *Degree requirements:* For master's, one foreign language, thesis; for doctorate, 2 foreign languages, thesis/dissertation. *Entrance requirements:* For master's, GRE General Test, minimum GPA of 3.0, bachelor's degree in French or equivalent; for doctorate, GRE General Test, minimum GPA of 3.0, master's degree in French. Additional exam requirements/recommendations for international students: Required—TOEFL. Electronic applications accepted. *Faculty research:* Nineteenth-century Italian literature, Italian Renaissance, twentieth-century French literature, Francophone literature, fifteenth-century literature and culture.

Washington University in St. Louis, The Graduate School, Department of Romance Languages and Literatures, St. Louis, MO 63130-4899. Offers French (PhD), including French and comparative literature, French language and literature; Spanish (PhD), including Hispanic languages and literatures, Spanish and comparative literature. Terminal master's awarded for partial completion of doctoral program. *Degree requirements:* For doctorate, thesis/dissertation. *Entrance requirements:* For doctorate, GRE General Test. Additional exam requirements/recommendations for international students: Required—TOEFL. Electronic applications accepted. *Faculty research:* French language and literature; Latin American and Iberian literatures and languages, Spanish and comparative literature.

Wayne State University, College of Liberal Arts and Sciences, Department of Classical and Modern Languages, Literatures, and Cultures, Detroit, MI 48202. Offers classics (MA), including ancient Greek and Latin, ancient studies, classics, Latin; German (MA); language learning (MALL), including Arabic (MA, MALL), French (MA, MALL, PhD), German (MALL, PhD), Italian (MA, MALL), Spanish (MA, MALL, PhD); modern languages (PhD), including French (MA, MALL, PhD), German (MALL, PhD), Spanish (MA, MALL, PhD); Near Eastern languages (MA), including Arabic (MA, MALL), Hebrew; Romance languages (MA), including French (MA, MALL, PhD), Italian (MA, MALL), Spanish (MA, MALL, PhD). *Faculty:* 22. *Students:* 24 full-time (18 women), 21 part-time (15 women); includes 11 minority (4 Black or African American, non-Hispanic/Latino; 1 American Indian or Alaska Native, non-Hispanic/Latino; 2 Asian, non-Hispanic/Latino; 2 Hispanic/Latino; 2 Two or more races, non-Hispanic/Latino), 3 international. Average age 37. 32 applicants, 63% accepted, 14 enrolled. In 2017, 10 master's awarded. *Degree requirements:* For master's, variable foreign language requirement, comprehensive exam (for some programs), thesis (for some programs); for doctorate, one foreign language, comprehensive exam, thesis/dissertation. *Entrance requirements:* Additional exam requirements/recommendations for international students: Required—TOEFL (minimum score 550 paper-based; 79 iBT), TWE (minimum score 5.5), Michigan English Language Assessment Battery (minimum score 85); Recommended—IELTS (minimum score 6.5). Application fee: $50. Electronic applications accepted. *Expenses:* Tuition, state resident: full-time $10,224; part-time $638.98 per credit hour. Tuition, nonresident: full-time $22,145; part-time $1384.04 per credit hour. Tuition and fees vary according to course load and program. *Financial support:* In 2017–18, 25 students received support, including 4 fellowships with tuition reimbursements available (averaging $13,500 per year), 17 teaching assistantships with tuition reimbursements available (averaging $18,591 per year); research assistantships, scholarships/grants, health care benefits, and unspecified assistantships also available. Financial award applicants required to submit FAFSA. *Faculty research:* Classical and modern literature and culture (Greek, Latin, Arabic, Chinese, French, German, Russian, Spanish) including colonial studies and exile and Holocaust studies; critical theory (French, German, Slavic, Spanish); theoretical and applied linguistics (Arabic, Chinese, French, Spanish); area studies (Arabic, Near Eastern, classical, Islamic, and Judaic studies). *Unit head:* Dr. Anne Duggan, Department Chair, 313-577-6244, Fax: 313-577-6243, E-mail: a.duggan@wayne.edu.
Website: http://clas.wayne.edu/languages/

Russian

American University, College of Arts and Sciences, Department of World Languages and Cultures, Washington, DC 20016-8045. Offers Spanish: Latin American studies (MA); teaching English as a foreign language (MA); teaching English to speakers of other languages (MA, Certificate); translation: French (Certificate); translation: Russian (Certificate); translation: Spanish (Certificate). *Program availability:* Part-time, evening/weekend. *Faculty:* 43 full-time (33 women), 23 part-time/adjunct (17 women). *Students:* 17 full-time (14 women), 19 part-time (15 women); includes 10 minority (2 Black or African American, non-Hispanic/Latino; 6 Hispanic/Latino; 2 Two or more races, non-Hispanic/Latino), 5 international. Average age 32. 39 applicants, 97% accepted, 9 enrolled. In 2017, 16 master's, 11 other advanced degrees awarded. *Degree requirements:* For master's, one foreign language, comprehensive exam, thesis or alternative. *Entrance requirements:* For master's, GRE, writing sample, statement of purpose, transcripts, 2 letters of recommendation, resume; for Certificate, bachelor's degree, statement of purpose, transcripts, resume. Additional exam requirements/recommendations for international students: Required—TOEFL (minimum score 600 paper-based; 100 iBT). *Application deadline:* For fall admission, 2/1 priority date for domestic students; for spring admission, 11/1 priority date for domestic students. Application fee: $55. *Expenses:* Contact institution. *Financial support:* Institutionally sponsored loans, scholarships/grants, and unspecified assistantships available. Financial award application deadline: 2/1; financial award applicants required to submit FAFSA. *Unit head:* Henry Gerfen, Chair, 202-885-2385, Fax: 202-885-1076, E-mail: gerfen@american.edu. *Application contact:* Jonathan Harper, Director of Graduate Recruitment, 202-885-3622, E-mail: jharper@american.edu.
Website: http://www.american.edu/cas/wlc/

Boston College, Graduate School of Arts and Sciences, Department of Slavic and Eastern Languages and Literatures, Program in Russian, Chestnut Hill, MA 02467-3800. Offers MA, MA/JD, MBA/MA. *Degree requirements:* For master's, 3 foreign languages, comprehensive exam, thesis or alternative. *Entrance requirements:* Additional exam requirements/recommendations for international students: Required—TOEFL (minimum score 600 paper-based; 100 iBT), IELTS (minimum score 8). Electronic applications accepted. *Faculty research:* Structural analysis of language, poetry and semiotic systems.

Brown University, Graduate School, Department of Slavic Studies, Providence, RI 02912. Offers Russian language and literature (AM); Slavic linguistics (AM); Slavic studies (PhD). *Degree requirements:* For master's, one foreign language; for doctorate, 2 foreign languages, thesis/dissertation, preliminary exam.

Columbia University, Graduate School of Arts and Sciences, New York, NY 10027. Offers African-American studies (MA); American studies (MA); anthropology (MA, PhD); art history and archaeology (MA, PhD); astronomy (PhD); biological sciences (PhD); biotechnology (MA); chemical physics (PhD); chemistry (PhD); classical studies (MA, PhD); classics (MA, PhD); climate and society (MA); conservation biology (MA); earth and environmental sciences (PhD); East Asia: regional studies (MA); East Asian languages and cultures (MA, PhD); ecology, evolution and environmental biology (MA), including conservation biology; ecology, evolution, and environmental biology (PhD), including ecology and evolutionary biology, evolutionary primatology; economics (MA, PhD); English and comparative literature (MA, PhD); French and Romance philology (MA, PhD); Germanic languages (MA, PhD); global French studies (MA); global thought (MA); Hispanic cultural studies (MA); history (PhD); history and literature (MA); human rights studies (MA); Islamic studies (MA); Italian (MA, PhD); Japanese pedagogy (MA); Jewish studies (MA); Latin America and the Caribbean: regional studies (MA); Latin American and Iberian cultures (PhD); mathematics (MA, PhD), including finance (MA); medieval and Renaissance studies (MA); Middle Eastern, South Asian, and African studies (MA, PhD); modern art: critical and curatorial studies (MA); modern European studies (MA); museum anthropology (MA); music (DMA, PhD); oral history (MA); philosophical foundations of physics (MA); philosophy (MA, PhD); physics (PhD); political science (MA, PhD); psychology (PhD); quantitative methods in the social sciences (MA); religion (MA, PhD); Russia, Eurasia and East Europe: regional studies (MA); Russian translation (MA); Slavic cultures (MA); Slavic languages (MA, PhD); sociology (MA, PhD); South Asian studies (MA); statistics (MA, PhD); theatre (PhD).

Dual-degree programs require admission to both Graduate School of Arts and Sciences and another Columbia school. *Program availability:* Part-time. Terminal master's awarded for partial completion of doctoral program. *Degree requirements:* For master's, variable foreign language requirement, comprehensive exam (for some programs), thesis (for some programs); for doctorate, variable foreign language requirement, comprehensive exam (for some programs), thesis/dissertation. *Entrance requirements:* For master's and doctorate, GRE General Test, GRE Subject Test (for some programs). Additional exam requirements/recommendations for international students: Required—TOEFL, IELTS. Electronic applications accepted. *Expenses:* Tuition: Full-time $44,864; part-time $1704 per credit. *Required fees:* $2370 per semester. One-time fee: $105.

Harvard University, Graduate School of Arts and Sciences, Department of Slavic Languages and Literatures, Cambridge, MA 02138. Offers Polish (PhD); Russian (PhD); Serbo-Croatian (PhD); Slavic philology (PhD); Ukrainian (PhD). *Degree requirements:* For doctorate, 4 foreign languages, thesis/dissertation. *Entrance requirements:* For doctorate, GRE General Test, writing sample. Additional exam requirements/recommendations for international students: Required—TOEFL.

Hofstra University, School of Education, Programs in Teacher Education, Hempstead, NY 11549. Offers bilingual education (MA); bilingual extension (Advanced Certificate), including education/speech language pathology, intensive teacher institute; business education (MS Ed); curriculum studies (MS Ed); early childhood and childhood education (MS Ed); early childhood education (MA, MS Ed); educational technology (Advanced Certificate); elementary education (MA, MS Ed), including science, technology, engineering, and mathematics (STEM) (MA); English education (MS Ed); family and consumer science (MS Ed); fine arts and music education (Advanced Certificate); fine arts education (MS Ed); foreign language and TESOL (MS Ed); foreign language education (MA, MS Ed), including Arabic (MS Ed), biology, chemistry, Chinese (MS Ed), earth science, French, German, Italian (MS Ed), Mandarin (MS Ed), physics, Russian, Spanish; foundations of education (Advanced Certificate), including grades 5-6, grades 7-9; languages other than English and teaching English as a second language (MA); learning and teaching (Ed D), including applied linguistics, art education, arts and humanities, early childhood education, English education, human development, math education, math, science, and technology, multicultural education, physical education, science education, social studies education, special education; mathematics education (MA, MS Ed); music education (MA, MS Ed); science education (MA), including biology (MA, MS Ed), chemistry (MA, MS Ed), earth science (MA, MS Ed), physics (MA, MS Ed); secondary education (Advanced Certificate); social studies education (MA, MS Ed); teaching languages other than English and TESOL (MS Ed); technology for learning (MA); TESOL (MS Ed, Advanced Certificate); TESOL with specialization in STEM (MA); work based learning extension (Advanced Certificate). *Program availability:* Part-time, evening/weekend, blended/hybrid learning. *Students:* 119 full-time (83 women), 124 part-time (90 women); includes 54 minority (15 Black or African American, non-Hispanic/Latino; 9 Asian, non-Hispanic/Latino; 29 Hispanic/Latino; 1 Native Hawaiian or other Pacific Islander, non-Hispanic/Latino), 12 international. Average age 29. 205 applicants, 88% accepted, 93 enrolled. In 2017, 103 master's, 4 doctorates, 32 other advanced degrees awarded. *Degree requirements:* For master's, comprehensive exam, thesis (for some programs), exit project, student teaching, fieldwork, electronic portfolio, curriculum project, minimum GPA of 3.0; for doctorate, thesis/dissertation; for Advanced Certificate, 3 foreign languages, comprehensive exam (for some programs), thesis project. *Entrance requirements:* For master's, GRE, 2 letters of recommendation, portfolio, teacher certification (MA), interview, essay; for doctorate, GMAT, GRE, LSAT, or MAT; for Advanced Certificate, 2 letters of recommendation, essay, interview and/or portfolio, teaching certificate. Additional exam requirements/recommendations for international students: Required—TOEFL (minimum score 550 paper-based; 80 iBT). *Application deadline:* Applications are processed on a rolling basis. Application fee: $75. Electronic applications accepted. *Expenses:* Tuition: Full-time $1292. *Required fees:* $970. Tuition and fees vary according to program. *Financial support:* In 2017–18, 112 students received support, including 56 fellowships with full and partial tuition reimbursements available (averaging $4,998 per year), 2 research assistantships with full and partial tuition reimbursements available (averaging $8,753 per year); career-

related internships or fieldwork, Federal Work-Study, institutionally sponsored loans, scholarships/grants, traineeships, tuition waivers (full and partial), and unspecified assistantships also available. Support available to part-time students. Financial award applicants required to submit FAFSA. *Faculty research:* Educational interventions that foster critical-thinking skills; teachers' attitudes about professional development; threats to teacher quality. *Unit head:* Dr. Eustace Thompson, Chairperson, 516-463-5749, Fax: 516-463-6275, E-mail: eustace.g.thompson@hofstra.edu. *Application contact:* Sunil Samuel, Assistant Vice President of Admissions, 516-463-4723, Fax: 516-463-4664, E-mail: graduateadmission@hofstra.edu.
Website: http://www.hofstra.edu/education/

Kent State University, College of Arts and Sciences, Department of Modern and Classical Language Studies, Kent, OH 44242-0001. Offers French (MA), including applied linguistics and pedagogy, literature; German (MA), including applied linguistics and pedagogy, literature; Latin (MA), including applied linguistics and pedagogy, literature; Spanish (MA), including applied linguistics and pedagogy, literature; translation (MA), including Arabic, French, German, Japanese, Russian, Spanish; translation studies (PhD); MA/MBA. *Program availability:* Part-time. *Faculty:* 21 full-time (13 women), 5 part-time/adjunct (3 women). *Students:* 78 full-time (50 women), 20 part-time (13 women); includes 18 minority (3 Black or African American, non-Hispanic/Latino; 1 Asian, non-Hispanic/Latino; 9 Hispanic/Latino; 5 Two or more races, non-Hispanic/Latino), 44 international. Average age 31. 95 applicants, 55% accepted, 27 enrolled. In 2017, 30 master's awarded. *Degree requirements:* For master's, variable foreign language requirement, comprehensive exam (for some programs), thesis (for some programs); for doctorate, variable foreign language requirement, comprehensive exam, thesis/dissertation. *Entrance requirements:* For master's, transcripts, goal statement, 3 letters of recommendation, CD/MP3 with oral sample of first and second languages, writing sample of second language; for doctorate, transcripts; MA in translation, a foreign language, or similar field; proficiency in a foreign language; minimum GPA of 3.5 from MA; goal statement; 3 letters of recommendation; essay or writing sample. Additional exam requirements/recommendations for international students: Required—TOEFL (minimum score 550 paper-based, 79 iBT), Michigan English Language Assessment Battery (minimum score 77), IELTS (minimum score 6.5) or PTE (minimum score 58). *Application deadline:* For fall admission, 2/1 for domestic and international students. Applications are processed on a rolling basis. Application fee: $45 ($70 for international students). Electronic applications accepted. *Expenses:* Tuition, state resident: full-time $11,310; part-time $515 per credit hour. Tuition, nonresident: full-time $20,396; part-time $928 per credit hour. *International tuition:* $18,544 full-time. *Financial support:* Fellowships with full tuition reimbursements, teaching assistantships with full tuition reimbursements, and unspecified assistantships available. Financial award application deadline: 2/1. *Unit head:* Dr. Keiran Dunne, Professor of French Translation/Chair, 330-672-2150, E-mail: kdunne@kent.edu. *Application contact:* Said Shiyab, Professor of Translation Studies/Graduate Coordinator, 330-672-1864, E-mail: sshiyab@kent.edu.
Website: http://www.kent.edu/mcls/

McGill University, Faculty of Graduate and Postdoctoral Studies, Faculty of Arts, Department of Russian and Slavic Studies, Montréal, QC H3A 2T5, Canada. Offers Russian literature (MA, PhD).

Middlebury College, Language Schools, Russian School, Middlebury, VT 05753-6002. Offers MA, DML. *Degree requirements:* For master's, one foreign language; for doctorate, 2 foreign languages, comprehensive exam, thesis/dissertation. *Entrance requirements:* For master's, language proficiency exam, placement exam, 3 letters of recommendation, writing sample in Russian, personal statement, transcripts; for doctorate, 1st and 2nd language exams, 3 letters of recommendation, writing sample in Russian, personal statement, transcripts. *Application deadline:* Applications are processed on a rolling basis. Application fee: $75. Electronic applications accepted. *Expenses:* Contact institution. *Financial support:* Fellowships and scholarships/grants available. Financial award application deadline: 3/14; financial award applicants required to submit FAFSA. *Unit head:* Dr. Jason Merrill, Director, 802-443-5230, Fax: 802-443-2075, E-mail: jmerrill@middlebury.edu. *Application contact:* Oliver Carling, Coordinator, 802-443-2006, Fax: 802-443-2075, E-mail: ocarling@middlebury.edu.
Website: http://www.middlebury.edu/ls/grad_programs/russian

New York University, Graduate School of Arts and Science, Department of Russian and Slavic Studies, New York, NY 10012-1019. Offers Russian literature (MA); Slavic literature (MA). *Program availability:* Part-time. *Students:* Average age 29. 14 applicants, 86% accepted, 4 enrolled. In 2017, 5 master's awarded. *Degree requirements:* For master's, one foreign language, comprehensive exam, thesis. *Entrance requirements:* For master's, GRE General Test, minimum 3 years of undergraduate Russian or equivalent. Additional exam requirements/recommendations for international students: Required—TOEFL. *Application deadline:* For fall admission, 4/15 for domestic and international students; for spring admission, 11/1 for domestic and international students. Application fee: $100. *Expenses: Tuition:* Full-time $41,352; part-time $19,968 per year. *Required fees:* $2496; $1628 per unit. $814 per term. Tuition and fees vary according to course load and program. *Financial support:* Career-related internships or fieldwork, Federal Work-Study, and institutionally sponsored loans available. Financial award application deadline: 4/15; financial award applicants required to submit FAFSA. *Faculty research:* Modern Russian literature and art, contemporary Russian and East European literature, literary theory, Slavic linguistics, Russian journalism. *Unit head:* Anne Lounsbery, Chair, 212-998-8670, Fax: 212-995-4604, E-mail: gsas.russian.and.slavic@nyu.edu. *Application contact:* Michael Kunichika, Director of Graduate Studies, 212-998-8670, Fax: 212-995-4604, E-mail: gsas.russian.and.slavic@nyu.edu.
Website: http://russianslavic.as.nyu.edu/

Penn State University Park, Graduate School, College of the Liberal Arts, Department of Comparative Literature, University Park, PA 16802. Offers comparative literature (MA, PhD); Russian and comparative literature (MA). *Unit head:* Dr. Susan Welch, Dean, 814-865-7691, Fax: 814-863-2085. *Application contact:* Lori Hawn, Director, Graduate Student Services, 814-865-1795, Fax: 814-863-4627, E-mail: l-gswww@lists.psu.edu.
Website: http://complit.la.psu.edu/

Princeton University, Graduate School, Department of Slavic Languages and Literatures, Princeton, NJ 08544-1019. Offers Russian and Slavic linguistics (PhD); Russian literature (PhD). *Degree requirements:* For doctorate, variable foreign language requirement, thesis/dissertation. *Entrance requirements:* For doctorate, GRE General Test. Additional exam requirements/recommendations for international students: Required—TOEFL (minimum score 600 paper-based). Electronic applications accepted.

The University of Arizona, College of Humanities, Department of Russian and Slavic Studies, Tucson, AZ 85721. Offers Russian (MA). *Program availability:* Part-time. *Degree requirements:* For master's, one foreign language, comprehensive exam (for some programs), thesis (for some programs). *Entrance requirements:* For master's, 3 letters of recommendation, audio sample. Additional exam requirements/recommendations for international students: Required—TOEFL (minimum score 550 paper-based; 79 iBT). Electronic applications accepted. *Faculty research:* Russian literature, language/pedagogy, linguistics, Russian culture.

University of California, Berkeley, Graduate Division, College of Letters and Science, Department of Slavic Languages and Literatures, Berkeley, CA 94720-1500. Offers Czech (PhD), including Czech linguistics, Czech literature; Polish (PhD), including Polish linguistics, Polish literature; Russian (PhD), including Russian linguistics, Russian literature; Serbo-Croatian (PhD), including Serbo-Croatian linguistics, Serbo-Croatian literature. Terminal master's awarded for partial completion of doctoral program. *Degree requirements:* For doctorate, thesis/dissertation, oral and written exams. *Entrance requirements:* For doctorate, GRE General Test, minimum GPA of 3.0, 3 letters of recommendation. Additional exam requirements/recommendations for international students: Required—TOEFL (minimum score 570 paper-based). Electronic applications accepted.

The University of Manchester, School of Languages, Linguistics and Cultures, Manchester, United Kingdom. Offers Arab world studies (PhD); Chinese studies (M Phil, PhD); East Asian studies (M Phil, PhD); English language (PhD); French studies (M Phil, PhD); German studies (M Phil, PhD); interpreting studies (PhD); Italian studies (M Phil, PhD); Japanese studies (M Phil, PhD); Latin American cultural studies (M Phil, PhD); linguistics (M Phil, PhD); Middle Eastern studies (M Phil, PhD); Polish studies (M Phil, PhD); Portuguese studies (M Phil, PhD); Russian studies (M Phil, PhD); Spanish studies (M Phil, PhD); translation and intercultural studies (M Phil, PhD).

University of Missouri, Office of Research and Graduate Studies, College of Arts and Science, Department of German and Russian Studies, Columbia, MO 65211. Offers MA. *Entrance requirements:* For master's, GRE General Test, minimum GPA of 3.0. Additional exam requirements/recommendations for international students: Required—TOEFL (minimum score 500 paper-based; 61 iBT). Electronic applications accepted. *Faculty research:* German and Russian cultural studies including literature, film, media studies, philosophy, and the history of science.

University of Oregon, Graduate School, College of Arts and Sciences, Program in Russian and East European Studies, Eugene, OR 97403. Offers MA. *Program availability:* Part-time. *Degree requirements:* For master's, 2 foreign languages, thesis. *Entrance requirements:* For master's, GRE General Test (recommended), minimum GPA of 3.0. Additional exam requirements/recommendations for international students: Required—TOEFL. *Faculty research:* L. N. Tolstoy's middle years, Russian folklore in eighteenth-century contexts, Bulgarian syntax, medieval Bulgarian texts, contemporary Russian culture film.

University of South Africa, College of Human Sciences, Pretoria, South Africa. Offers adult education (M Ed); African languages (MA, PhD); African politics (MA, PhD); Afrikaans (MA, PhD); ancient history (MA, PhD); ancient Near Eastern studies (MA, PhD); anthropology (MA, PhD); applied linguistics (MA); Arabic (MA, PhD); archaeology (MA); art history (MA); Biblical archaeology (MA); Biblical studies (M Th, D Th, PhD); Christian spirituality (M Th, D Th); church history (M Th, D Th); classical studies (MA, PhD); clinical psychology (MA); communication (MA, PhD); comparative education (M Ed, Ed D); consulting psychology (D Admin, D Com, PhD); curriculum studies (M Ed, Ed D); development studies (M Admin, MA, D Admin, PhD); didactics (M Ed, Ed D); education (M Tech); education management (M Ed, Ed D); educational psychology (M Ed); English (MA); environmental education (M Ed); French (MA, PhD); German (MA, PhD); Greek (MA); guidance and counseling (M Ed); health studies (MA, PhD), including health sciences education (MA), health services management (MA), medical and surgical nursing science (critical care general) (MA), midwifery and neonatal nursing science (MA), trauma and emergency care (MA); history (MA, PhD); history of education (Ed D); inclusive education (M Ed, Ed D); information and communications technology policy and regulation (MA); information science (MA, MIS, PhD); international politics (MA, PhD); Islamic studies (MA, PhD); Italian (MA, PhD); Judaica (MA, PhD); linguistics (MA, PhD); mathematical education (M Ed); mathematics education (MA); missiology (M Th, D Th); modern Hebrew (MA, PhD); musicology (MA, MMus, D Mus, PhD); natural science education (M Ed); New Testament (M Th, D Th); Old Testament (D Th); pastoral therapy (M Th, D Th); philosophy (MA); philosophy of education (M Ed, Ed D); politics (MA, PhD); Portuguese (MA, PhD); practical theology (M Th, D Th); psychology (MA, MS, PhD); psychology of education (M Ed, Ed D); public health (MA); religious studies (MA, D Th, PhD); Romance languages (MA); Russian (MA, PhD); Semitic languages (MA, PhD); social behavior studies in HIV/AIDS (MA); social science (mental health) (MA); social science in development studies (MA); social science in psychology (MA); social science in social work (MA); social science in sociology (MA); social work (MSW, DSW, PhD); socio-education (M Ed, Ed D); sociolinguistics (MA); sociology (MA, PhD); Spanish (MA, PhD); systematic theology (M Th, D Th); TESOL (teaching English to speakers of other languages) (MA); theological ethics (M Th, D Th); theory of literature (MA, PhD); urban ministries (D Th); urban ministry (M Th).

The University of Tennessee, Graduate School, College of Arts and Sciences, Department of Modern Foreign Languages and Literatures, Program in Modern Foreign Languages, Knoxville, TN 37996. Offers applied linguistics (PhD); French (PhD); German (PhD); Italian (PhD); Portuguese (PhD); Russian (PhD); Spanish (PhD). *Degree requirements:* For doctorate, 2 foreign languages, thesis/dissertation. *Entrance requirements:* For doctorate, minimum GPA of 2.7. Additional exam requirements/recommendations for international students: Required—TOEFL. Electronic applications accepted.

University of Washington, Graduate School, College of Arts and Sciences, Department of Slavic Languages and Literatures, Seattle, WA 98195. Offers Russian literature (MA, PhD); Slavic linguistics (MA, PhD). *Degree requirements:* For master's, 2 foreign languages, thesis optional; for doctorate, 3 foreign languages, thesis/dissertation. *Entrance requirements:* For master's and doctorate, GRE General Test, minimum GPA of 3.0. Additional exam requirements/recommendations for international students: Required—TOEFL. Electronic applications accepted. *Faculty research:* Modern and medieval East European languages and literatures, comparative literature, Russian folk literature, Slavic literary theory and criticism, computerized morphology of Russian.

University of Waterloo, Graduate Studies, Faculty of Arts, Department of Germanic and Slavic Studies, Waterloo, ON N2L 3G1, Canada. Offers German (MA, PhD); Russian (MA). *Program availability:* Part-time, evening/weekend. *Degree requirements:* For master's, one foreign language, thesis optional; for doctorate, 2 foreign languages, comprehensive exam, thesis/dissertation. *Entrance requirements:* For master's, honors degree, minimum B average; for doctorate, master's degree, minimum B average. Additional exam requirements/recommendations for international students: Required—TOEFL, IELTS, PTE. Electronic applications accepted. *Faculty research:* Medieval theatre; history and literature; German and Russian literary relations; seventeenth-, eighteenth-, nineteenth-, and twentieth-century German literature.

Yale University, Graduate School of Arts and Sciences, Department of Slavic Languages and Literatures, New Haven, CT 06520. Offers medieval Slavic literature and philology (PhD); Polish literature (PhD); Russian literature (PhD); Slavic languages and literatures and film studies (PhD). *Degree requirements:* For doctorate, 3 foreign languages, thesis/dissertation. *Entrance requirements:* For doctorate, GRE General Test.

Scandinavian Languages

Cornell University, Graduate School, Graduate Fields of Arts and Sciences, Field of Germanic Studies, Ithaca, NY 14853. Offers German area studies (MA, PhD); German intellectual history (MA, PhD); Germanic linguistics (MA, PhD); Germanic literature (MA, PhD); old Norse (MA, PhD). Terminal master's awarded for partial completion of doctoral program. *Degree requirements:* For master's, one foreign language, thesis; for doctorate, 2 foreign languages, comprehensive exam, thesis/dissertation. *Entrance requirements:* For master's and doctorate, GRE General Test, fluency in German, writing sample, 2 letters of recommendation. Additional exam requirements/recommendations for international students: Required—TOEFL (minimum score 550 paper-based; 77 iBT). Electronic applications accepted. *Faculty research:* Women's studies, minority literature, literature and intellectual history, theater and film studies, Continental philosophy.

Harvard University, Graduate School of Arts and Sciences, Department of Germanic Languages and Literatures, Cambridge, MA 02138. Offers German (PhD); Scandinavian (PhD). Terminal master's awarded for partial completion of doctoral program. *Degree requirements:* For doctorate, 2 foreign languages, thesis/dissertation, exams. *Entrance requirements:* For doctorate, GRE General Test, German writing sample. Additional exam requirements/recommendations for international students: Required—TOEFL.

University of California, Berkeley, Graduate Division, College of Letters and Science, Department of Scandinavian Languages and Literatures, Berkeley, CA 94720-1500. Offers PhD. *Degree requirements:* For doctorate, 2 foreign languages, thesis/dissertation, 3 field papers, qualifying exam. *Entrance requirements:* For doctorate, GRE General Test, minimum GPA of 3.0, MA in Scandinavian language or equivalent, 3 letters of recommendation. Additional exam requirements/recommendations for international students: Required—TOEFL (minimum score 570 paper-based; 90 iBT). Electronic applications accepted. *Faculty research:* Modern literatures, old Norse language and literatures, folklore, film.

University of California, Los Angeles, Graduate Division, College of Letters and Science, Department of Germanic Languages, Program in Scandinavian, Los Angeles, CA 90095. Offers MA. *Degree requirements:* For master's, 3 foreign languages, comprehensive exam. *Entrance requirements:* For master's, GRE General Test, bachelor's degree; minimum undergraduate GPA of 3.0 (or its equivalent if letter grade system not used); writing sample. Additional exam requirements/recommendations for international students: Required—TOEFL. Electronic applications accepted.

University of Massachusetts Amherst, Graduate School, College of Humanities and Fine Arts, Department of Languages, Literatures, and Cultures, Programs in German and Scandinavian Studies, Amherst, MA 01003. Offers MA, PhD. *Program availability:* Part-time. Terminal master's awarded for partial completion of doctoral program. *Degree requirements:* For master's, thesis or alternative; for doctorate, one foreign language, comprehensive exam, thesis/dissertation. *Entrance requirements:* For master's and doctorate, writing sample in English and German. Additional exam requirements/recommendations for international students: Required—TOEFL (minimum score 550 paper-based; 80 iBT), IELTS (minimum score 6.5). Electronic applications accepted.

University of Minnesota, Twin Cities Campus, Graduate School, College of Liberal Arts, Department of German, Scandinavian, and Dutch, Minneapolis, MN 55455. Offers Germanic studies (MA, PhD), including German, Germanic medieval studies, Scandinavian studies (MA). *Program availability:* Part-time. Terminal master's awarded for partial completion of doctoral program. *Degree requirements:* For doctorate, 2 foreign languages, thesis/dissertation. *Entrance requirements:* For master's, GRE General Test, BA in German, Scandinavian, or equivalent; for doctorate, MA in German, Scandinavian, or equivalent. Additional exam requirements/recommendations for international students: Required—TOEFL (minimum score 550 paper-based; 79 iBT). Electronic applications accepted. *Faculty research:* Cultural studies, literary theory, feminist criticism, film, Germanic medieval studies.

University of Washington, Graduate School, College of Arts and Sciences, Department of Scandinavian Studies, Seattle, WA 98195. Offers MA, PhD. *Degree requirements:* For master's, one foreign language, comprehensive exam, thesis optional; for doctorate, 2 foreign languages, comprehensive exam, thesis/dissertation. *Entrance requirements:* For master's, GRE, BA in Scandinavian or equivalent, minimum GPA of 3.0; for doctorate, GRE, master's degree, minimum GPA of 3.0. Additional exam requirements/recommendations for international students: Required—TOEFL. *Faculty research:* Scandinavian folklore, history, and politics; medieval to modern Scandinavian literature; Scandinavian fiction, poetry, drama, literary history, and theory.

University of Wisconsin–Madison, Graduate School, College of Letters and Science, Department of Scandinavian Studies, Madison, WI 53706-1380. Offers area studies (MA); folklore (PhD); literature (MA, PhD); philology (PhD). *Program availability:* Part-time. *Degree requirements:* For master's, 2 foreign languages, exam; for doctorate, thesis/dissertation, exam. *Entrance requirements:* For master's, minimum GPA of 3.25; for doctorate, minimum GPA of 3.5. Electronic applications accepted. *Faculty research:* Historical fiction, Icelandic poetry, nineteenth-century literature, theater, gender studies, folklore.

Slavic Languages

Brown University, Graduate School, Department of Slavic Studies, Providence, RI 02912. Offers Russian language and literature (AM); Slavic linguistics (AM); Slavic studies (PhD). *Degree requirements:* For master's, one foreign language; for doctorate, 2 foreign languages, thesis/dissertation, preliminary exam.

Columbia University, Graduate School of Arts and Sciences, New York, NY 10027. Offers African-American studies (MA); American studies (MA); anthropology (MA, PhD); art history and archaeology (MA, PhD); astronomy (PhD); biological sciences (PhD); biotechnology (MA); chemical physics (PhD); chemistry (PhD); classical studies (MA, PhD); classics (MA, PhD); climate and society (MA); conservation biology (MA); earth and environmental sciences (PhD); East Asia: regional studies (MA); East Asian languages and cultures (MA, PhD); ecology, evolution and environmental biology (MA), including conservation biology; ecology, evolution, and environmental biology (PhD), including ecology and evolutionary biology, evolutionary primatology; economics (MA, PhD); English and comparative literature (MA, PhD); French and Romance philology (MA, PhD); Germanic languages (MA, PhD); global French studies (MA); global thought (MA); Hispanic cultural studies (MA); history (PhD); history and literature (MA); human rights studies (MA); Islamic studies (MA); Italian (MA, PhD); Japanese pedagogy (MA); Jewish studies (MA); Latin America and the Caribbean: regional studies (MA); Latin American and Iberian cultures (PhD); mathematics (MA, PhD), including finance (MA); medieval and Renaissance studies (MA); Middle Eastern, South Asian, and African studies (MA, PhD); modern art: critical and curatorial studies (MA); modern European studies (MA); museum anthropology (MA); music (DMA, PhD); oral history (MA); philosophical foundations of physics (MA); philosophy (MA, PhD); physics (PhD); political science (MA, PhD); psychology (PhD); quantitative methods in the social sciences (MA); religion (MA, PhD); Russia, Eurasia and East Europe: regional studies (MA); Russian translation (MA); Slavic cultures (MA); Slavic languages (MA, PhD); sociology (MA, PhD); South Asian studies (MA); statistics (MA, PhD); theatre (PhD). Dual-degree programs require admission to both Graduate School of Arts and Sciences and another Columbia school. *Program availability:* Part-time. Terminal master's awarded for partial completion of doctoral program. *Degree requirements:* For master's, variable foreign language requirement, comprehensive exam (for some programs), thesis (for some programs); for doctorate, variable foreign language requirement, comprehensive exam (for some programs), thesis/dissertation. *Entrance requirements:* For master's and doctorate, GRE General Test, GRE Subject Test (for some programs). Additional exam requirements/recommendations for international students: Required—TOEFL, IELTS. Electronic applications accepted. *Expenses: Tuition:* Full-time $44,864; part-time $1704 per credit. *Required fees:* $2370 per semester. One-time fee: $105.

Cornell University, Graduate School, Graduate Fields of Arts and Sciences, Field of Linguistics, Ithaca, NY 14853. Offers applied linguistics (MA, PhD); East Asian linguistics (MA, PhD); English linguistics (MA, PhD); general linguistics (MA, PhD); Germanic linguistics (MA, PhD); Indo-European linguistics (MA, PhD); phonetics (MA, PhD); phonological theory (MA, PhD); Romance linguistics (MA, PhD); second language acquisition (MA, PhD); semantics (MA, PhD); Slavic linguistics (MA, PhD); sociolinguistics (MA, PhD); South Asian linguistics (MA, PhD); Southeast Asian linguistics (MA, PhD); syntactic theory (MA, PhD). Terminal master's awarded for partial completion of doctoral program. *Degree requirements:* For master's, one foreign language, thesis; for doctorate, one foreign language, comprehensive exam, thesis/dissertation. *Entrance requirements:* For master's and doctorate, GRE General Test, 2 letters of recommendation. Additional exam requirements/recommendations for international students: Required—TOEFL (minimum score 600 paper-based; 77 iBT). Electronic applications accepted. *Faculty research:* Phonology and phonetics, syntax and semantics, historical linguistics, philosophy of language, language acquisition.

Duke University, Graduate School, Department of Slavic and Eurasian Studies, Durham, NC 27708. Offers AM, Certificate. *Program availability:* Part-time. *Entrance requirements:* For master's, GRE General Test, writing sample. Additional exam requirements/recommendations for international students: Required—TOEFL (minimum score 577 paper-based; 90 iBT) or IELTS (minimum score 7). Electronic applications accepted.

Florida State University, The Graduate School, College of Arts and Sciences, Department of Modern Languages and Linguistics, Program in Slavic Languages/Russian, Tallahassee, FL 32306. Offers Slavic languages and literatures (MA). *Faculty:* 3 full-time (2 women). *Students:* 6 full-time (3 women); includes 3 minority (1 Black or African American, non-Hispanic/Latino; 2 Two or more races, non-Hispanic/Latino). Average age 24. 3 applicants, 100% accepted, 2 enrolled. In 2017, 5 master's awarded. *Degree requirements:* For master's, thesis optional. *Entrance requirements:* For master's, GRE General Test, minimum GPA of 3.0. Additional exam requirements/recommendations for international students: Required—TOEFL (minimum score 550 paper-based; 80 iBT). *Application deadline:* For fall admission, 2/15 for domestic and international students. Applications are processed on a rolling basis. Application fee: $30. Electronic applications accepted. *Financial support:* In 2017–18, 3 students received support, including 4 teaching assistantships with partial tuition reimbursements available (averaging $14,000 per year); fellowships and institutionally sponsored loans also available. Financial award application deadline: 2/1; financial award applicants required to submit FAFSA. *Faculty research:* Contemporary literature, emigre literature, Old Russian word formation, political rhetoric, structure of modern Russian. *Total annual research expenditures:* $4,500. *Unit head:* Dr. Robert Romanchuk, Divisional Coordinator, 850-644-8198, Fax: 850-644-0524, E-mail: rromanch@fsu.edu. *Application contact:* Wendy E. Pigott, Graduate Academic Coordinator, 850-644-8397, Fax: 850-644-0524, E-mail: wpigott@fsu.edu.

Harvard University, Graduate School of Arts and Sciences, Department of Slavic Languages and Literatures, Cambridge, MA 02138. Offers Polish (PhD); Russian (PhD); Serbo-Croatian (PhD); Slavic philology (PhD); Ukrainian (PhD). *Degree requirements:* For doctorate, 4 foreign languages, thesis/dissertation. *Entrance requirements:* For doctorate, GRE General Test, writing sample. Additional exam requirements/recommendations for international students: Required—TOEFL.

Indiana University Bloomington, University Graduate School, College of Arts and Sciences, Department of Slavic Languages and Literatures, Bloomington, IN 47405. Offers MA, MAT, PhD. *Program availability:* Part-time. Terminal master's awarded for partial completion of doctoral program. *Degree requirements:* For master's, variable foreign language requirement; for doctorate, variable foreign language requirement, comprehensive exam, thesis/dissertation. *Entrance requirements:* For master's, GRE General Test. Additional exam requirements/recommendations for international students: Required—TOEFL. Electronic applications accepted. *Faculty research:* Russian stress, Slavic accentology and morphophonemics, Eastern European literature, Bible translation.

New York University, Graduate School of Arts and Science, Department of Russian and Slavic Studies, New York, NY 10012-1019. Offers Russian literature (MA); Slavic literature (MA). *Program availability:* Part-time. *Students:* Average age 29. 14 applicants, 86% accepted, 4 enrolled. In 2017, 5 master's awarded. *Degree requirements:* For

master's, one foreign language, comprehensive exam, thesis. *Entrance requirements:* For master's, GRE General Test, minimum 3 years of undergraduate Russian or equivalent. Additional exam requirements/recommendations for international students: Required—TOEFL. *Application deadline:* For fall admission, 4/15 for domestic and international students; for spring admission, 11/1 for domestic and international students. Application fee: $100. *Expenses: Tuition:* Full-time $41,352; part-time $19,968 per year. *Required fees:* $2496; $1628 per unit. $814 per term. Tuition and fees vary according to course load and program. *Financial support:* Career-related internships or fieldwork, Federal Work-Study, and institutionally sponsored loans available. Financial award application deadline: 4/15; financial award applicants required to submit FAFSA. *Faculty research:* Modern Russian literature and art, contemporary Russian and East European literature, literary theory, Slavic linguistics, Russian journalism. *Unit head:* Anne Lounsbery, Chair, 212-998-8670, Fax: 212-995-4604, E-mail: gsas.russian.and.slavic@nyu.edu. *Application contact:* Michael Kunichika, Director of Graduate Studies, 212-998-8670, Fax: 212-995-4604, E-mail: gsas.russian.and.slavic@nyu.edu.
Website: http://russianslavic.as.nyu.edu/

Northwestern University, The Graduate School, Judd A. and Marjorie Weinberg College of Arts and Sciences, Department of Slavic Languages and Literature, Evanston, IL 60208. Offers PhD. Admissions and degrees offered through The Graduate School. *Program availability:* Part-time. *Degree requirements:* For doctorate, 3 foreign languages, thesis/dissertation. *Entrance requirements:* For doctorate, GRE General Test. Additional exam requirements/recommendations for international students: Required—TOEFL. *Faculty research:* Russian poetry and prose, nineteenth through twentieth centuries, translation and Russian culture, Russian intellectual history, Slavic literature and nationalism, Polish poetry.

The Ohio State University, Graduate School, College of Arts and Sciences, Division of Arts and Humanities, Department of Slavic and East European Languages and Cultures, Columbus, OH 43210. Offers Slavic linguistics (MA, PhD); Slavic literature, film, and cultural studies (MA, PhD). *Faculty:* 10. *Students:* 16 full-time (11 women). Average age 31. In 2017, 1 master's, 4 doctorates awarded. Terminal master's awarded for partial completion of doctoral program. *Degree requirements:* For master's, variable foreign language requirement, thesis optional; for doctorate, variable foreign language requirement, thesis/dissertation. *Entrance requirements:* For master's and doctorate, GRE General Test, at least 3 years of Russian language study or equivalent. Additional exam requirements/recommendations for international students: Required—TOEFL (minimum score 550 paper-based; 79 iBT), Michigan English Language Assessment Battery (minimum score 82); Recommended—IELTS (minimum score 7). *Application deadline:* For fall admission, 12/12 priority date for domestic students, 11/30 priority date for international students; for spring admission, 3/1 for domestic students, 2/1 for international students. Applications are processed on a rolling basis. Application fee: $60 ($70 for international students). Electronic applications accepted. *Financial support:* Fellowships, teaching assistantships, Federal Work-Study, and institutionally sponsored loans available. Support available to part-time students. *Faculty research:* Polish literature. *Unit head:* Dr. Yana Hashamova, Chair and Professor, 614-292-6733, E-mail: hashamova.1@osu.edu. *Application contact:* Graduate and Professional Admissions, 614-292-9444, Fax: 614-292-3895, E-mail: gpadmissions@osu.edu.
Website: http://slavic.osu.edu/

Princeton University, Graduate School, Department of Slavic Languages and Literatures, Princeton, NJ 08544-1019. Offers Russian and Slavic linguistics (PhD); Russian literature (PhD). *Degree requirements:* For doctorate, variable foreign language requirement, thesis/dissertation. *Entrance requirements:* For doctorate, GRE General Test. Additional exam requirements/recommendations for international students: Required—TOEFL (minimum score 600 paper-based). Electronic applications accepted.

Stanford University, School of Humanities and Sciences, Department of Slavic Languages and Literatures, Stanford, CA 94305-2004. Offers PhD. Terminal master's awarded for partial completion of doctoral program. *Degree requirements:* For doctorate, 3 foreign languages, thesis/dissertation. *Entrance requirements:* For doctorate, GRE General Test. Additional exam requirements/recommendations for international students: Required—TOEFL. Electronic applications accepted. *Expenses: Tuition:* Full-time $48,987; part-time $10,620 per quarter. One-time fee: $400. Tuition and fees vary according to program.

University of Alberta, Faculty of Graduate Studies and Research, Department of Modern Languages and Cultural Studies, Edmonton, AB T6G 2E1, Canada. Offers applied linguistics (Germanic, Romance, Slavic) (MA); French language, literatures and linguistics (PhD); French language, literatures, and linguistics (MA); Germanic languages, literatures and linguistics (PhD); Germanic languages, literatures, and linguistics (MA); Italian studies (MA); Slavic languages and literatures (Russian, Ukrainian) (MA, PhD); Slavic linguistics (Russian, Ukrainian) (MA, PhD); Spanish and Latin American studies (MA, PhD); Ukrainian folklore (MA, PhD). *Program availability:* Part-time. *Degree requirements:* For master's, one foreign language, thesis; for doctorate, 2 foreign languages, comprehensive exam, thesis/dissertation. *Entrance requirements:* For master's and doctorate, 1 language other than English. Additional exam requirements/recommendations for international students: Required—Michigan English Language Assessment Battery or TOEFL (minimum score 550 paper-based). Electronic applications accepted. *Faculty research:* Russian/Ukrainian studies; German studies; contemporary Latin American, French and Francophone studies; Italian studies.

University of California, Berkeley, Graduate Division, College of Letters and Science, Department of Slavic Languages and Literatures, Berkeley, CA 94720-1500. Offers Czech (PhD), including Czech linguistics, Czech literature; Polish (PhD), including Polish linguistics, Polish literature; Russian (PhD), including Russian linguistics, Russian literature; Serbo-Croatian (PhD), including Serbo-Croatian linguistics, Serbo-Croatian literature. Terminal master's awarded for partial completion of doctoral program. *Degree requirements:* For doctorate, thesis/dissertation, oral and written exams. *Entrance requirements:* For doctorate, GRE General Test, minimum GPA of 3.0, 3 letters of recommendation. Additional exam requirements/recommendations for international students: Required—TOEFL (minimum score 570 paper-based). Electronic applications accepted.

University of California, Los Angeles, Graduate Division, College of Letters and Science, Department of Slavic Languages and Literatures, Los Angeles, CA 90095. Offers MA, PhD. Terminal master's awarded for partial completion of doctoral program. *Degree requirements:* For master's, 2 foreign languages, comprehensive exam; for doctorate, 2 foreign languages, thesis/dissertation, oral and written qualifying exams. *Entrance requirements:* For master's and doctorate, GRE General Test (not required for applicants whose native language not English), bachelor's degree; minimum undergraduate GPA of 3.0 (or its equivalent if letter grade system not used); writing sample. Additional exam requirements/recommendations for international students: Required—TOEFL. Electronic applications accepted.

University of Chicago, Division of the Humanities, Master of Arts Program in the Humanities, Chicago, IL 60637. Offers art history (MA); cinema and media studies (MA); classic languages (MA); comparative literature (MA); creative writing (MA); cultural policy studies (MA); digital humanities (MA); East Asian languages and civilizations (MA); English language and literature (MA); gender and sexuality studies (MA); Germanic studies (MA); linguistics (MA); music (MA); near Eastern languages and civilizations (MA); philosophy (MA); poetics (MA); race, politics and culture (MA); Romance languages and literatures (MA); Slavic languages and literatures (MA); South Asian languages and civilizations (MA); theater and performance studies (MA). *Students:* 95 full-time (50 women), 6 part-time (4 women); includes 22 minority (1 Black or African American, non-Hispanic/Latino; 10 Asian, non-Hispanic/Latino; 11 Hispanic/Latino), 19 international. Average age 26. 708 applicants, 75% accepted, 101 enrolled. In 2017, 91 master's awarded. *Degree requirements:* For master's, thesis. *Entrance requirements:* For master's, GRE General Test, 10-15 page writing sample, statement of purpose, 3 letters of recommendation, transcripts for all previous degrees and institutions attended. Additional exam requirements/recommendations for international students: Required—TOEFL (minimum score 104 iBT), IELTS (minimum score 7). *Application deadline:* For fall admission, 1/3 priority date for domestic and international students. Application fee: $90. Electronic applications accepted. *Expenses:* Contact institution. *Financial support:* In 2017–18, fellowships with partial tuition reimbursements (averaging $12,000 per year) were awarded; Federal Work-Study, institutionally sponsored loans, scholarships/grants, and tuition waivers (partial) also available. Financial award application deadline: 4/30. *Unit head:* Thomas Christensen, Director, 773-834-1201, Fax: 773-834-7526, E-mail: ma-humanities@uchicago.edu. *Application contact:* Michael Beetley, Assistant Dean of Students for Admissions, 773-834-1552, E-mail: humanitiesadmissions@uchicago.edu.
Website: http://maph.uchicago.edu/

University of Illinois at Chicago, College of Liberal Arts and Sciences, School of Literatures, Cultural Studies and Linguistics, Department of Slavic and Baltic Languages and Literatures, Chicago, IL 60607-7128. Offers Slavic studies (MA, PhD). *Program availability:* Evening/weekend. Terminal master's awarded for partial completion of doctoral program. *Degree requirements:* For doctorate, one foreign language, thesis/dissertation. *Entrance requirements:* For master's and doctorate, GRE General Test, minimum GPA of 3.0. Additional exam requirements/recommendations for international students: Required—TOEFL. Electronic applications accepted. *Faculty research:* Twentieth-century Polish literature and culture, Russian and Polish modernisms, nineteenth- and twentieth-century Russian literature, Lithuanian language, Polish-Jewish culture and history, Yiddish literature and language.

University of Illinois at Urbana–Champaign, Graduate College, College of Liberal Arts and Sciences, School of Literatures, Cultures and Linguistics, Department of Slavic Languages and Literatures, Champaign, IL 61820. Offers MA, PhD.

The University of Kansas, Graduate Studies, College of Liberal Arts and Sciences, Department of Slavic Languages and Literatures, Lawrence, KS 66160. Offers MA, PhD. *Students:* 13 full-time (8 women), 6 international. Average age 30. 12 applicants, 50% accepted, 3 enrolled. In 2017, 2 master's, 1 doctorate awarded. Terminal master's awarded for partial completion of doctoral program. *Entrance requirements:* For master's and doctorate, GRE, curriculum vitae, statement of academic objectives (500 words), Russian language essay (1-2 pages), writing sample (5000-7000 words), official transcripts. Additional exam requirements/recommendations for international students: Required—TOEFL (minimum score 80 iBT). *Application deadline:* For fall admission, 1/31 priority date for domestic and international students. Application fee: $65 ($85 for international students). Electronic applications accepted. *Financial support:* Fellowships, teaching assistantships, Federal Work-Study, institutionally sponsored loans, scholarships/grants, and unspecified assistantships available. Financial award application deadline: 1/31. *Faculty research:* Russian and south Slavic linguistics, Polish and Russian literature, folklore, Russian intellectual history, Slavic culture. *Unit head:* Stephen M. Dickey, Chair, 785-864-2357, E-mail: smd@ku.edu. *Application contact:* Cari Ann Kreienhop, Senior Academic Advisor, Graduate Programs, 785-864-3665, E-mail: ckreienhop@ku.edu.
Website: https://slavic.ku.edu/

The University of Manchester, School of Languages, Linguistics and Cultures, Manchester, United Kingdom. Offers Arab world studies (PhD); Chinese studies (M Phil, PhD); East Asian studies (M Phil, PhD); English language (PhD); French studies (M Phil, PhD); German studies (M Phil, PhD); interpreting studies (PhD); Italian studies (M Phil, PhD); Japanese studies (M Phil, PhD); Latin American cultural studies (M Phil, PhD); linguistics (M Phil, PhD); Middle Eastern studies (M Phil, PhD); Polish studies (M Phil, PhD); Portuguese studies (M Phil, PhD); Russian studies (M Phil, PhD); Spanish studies (M Phil, PhD); translation and intercultural studies (M Phil, PhD).

University of Manitoba, Faculty of Graduate Studies, Faculty of Arts, Department of German and Slavic Studies, Winnipeg, MB R3T 2N2, Canada. Offers German language and literature (MA); Slavic languages and literatures (MA). *Degree requirements:* For master's, one foreign language, thesis or alternative.

University of Michigan, Rackham Graduate School, College of Literature, Science, and the Arts, Department of Slavic Languages and Literatures, Ann Arbor, MI 48109-1275. Offers AM, PhD. *Faculty:* 9 full-time (3 women). *Students:* 12 full-time (8 women), 1 international. Average age 29. 12 applicants, 33% accepted. In 2017, 4 doctorates awarded. Terminal master's awarded for partial completion of doctoral program. *Degree requirements:* For doctorate, 3 foreign languages, comprehensive exam, thesis/dissertation, oral defense of dissertation, preliminary exam. *Entrance requirements:* For doctorate, GRE General Test. Additional exam requirements/recommendations for international students: Required—TOEFL (minimum score 560 paper-based). *Application deadline:* For fall admission, 1/15 priority date for domestic and international students. Application fee: $75 ($90 for international students). Electronic applications accepted. *Expenses:* Tuition, state resident: full-time $22,368; part-time $1201 per credit hour. Tuition, nonresident: full-time $45,156; part-time $2467 per credit hour. *Required fees:* $376 per term. Tuition and fees vary according to course load, degree level and program. *Financial support:* In 2017–18, 12 students received support, including 11 fellowships with full tuition reimbursements available (averaging $19,740 per year), 6 teaching assistantships with full tuition reimbursements available (averaging $19,737 per year); institutionally sponsored loans, scholarships/grants, health care benefits, and unspecified assistantships also available. Financial award application deadline: 1/15; financial award applicants required to submit FAFSA. *Faculty research:* Russian literature (all periods), Polish literature, South Slavic literatures, Czech literature, Ukrainian literature. *Unit head:* Dr. Mikhail Krutikov, Chair, 734-764-5355, Fax: 734-647-2127, E-mail: krutikov@umich.edu. *Application contact:* Zaineb Al-Kalby, Student Services Coordinator, 734-764-5355, Fax: 734-647-2127, E-mail: slavic@umich.edu.
Website: http://lsa.umich.edu/slavic

The University of North Carolina at Chapel Hill, Graduate School, College of Arts and Sciences, Department of Germanic and Slavic Languages and Literatures, Chapel Hill, NC 27599. Offers German studies (PhD). Program offered in collaboration with Duke University. *Program availability:* Part-time. Terminal master's awarded for partial completion of doctoral program. *Degree requirements:* For doctorate, one foreign language, comprehensive exam, thesis/dissertation. *Entrance requirements:* For doctorate, GRE General Test, minimum GPA of 3.0. *Faculty research:* Gender and sexuality, literature and politics, German and Jewish culture, medieval through modern literature, Germanic linguistics.

University of Pittsburgh, Kenneth P. Dietrich School of Arts and Sciences, Department of Slavic Languages and Literatures, Pittsburgh, PA 15260. Offers film studies (PhD), including Russian literature and culture; Russian literature and culture (MA, PhD). *Program availability:* Part-time. *Faculty:* 9 full-time (2 women), 1 (woman) part-time/adjunct. *Students:* 8 full-time (7 women); includes 2 minority (both Asian, non-Hispanic/Latino), 4 international. Average age 35. 9 applicants, 44% accepted, 1 enrolled. In 2017, 1 master's, 4 doctorates awarded. Terminal master's awarded for partial completion of doctoral program. *Degree requirements:* For master's, 2 foreign languages, comprehensive exam; for doctorate, 2 foreign languages, comprehensive exam, thesis/dissertation. *Entrance requirements:* For master's and doctorate, GRE General Test, writing sample in English or Russian. Additional exam requirements/recommendations for international students: Required—TOEFL (minimum score 600 paper-based; 90 iBT), IELTS. *Application deadline:* For fall admission, 1/15 priority date for domestic and international students. Application fee: $50. Electronic applications accepted. *Expenses:* $22,290 in-state tuition, $36,980 out-of-state, $850 fees. *Financial support:* In 2017–18, 7 students received support, including 4 fellowships with full tuition reimbursements available (averaging $23,262 per year), 3 teaching assistantships with full tuition reimbursements available (averaging $21,412 per year); scholarships/grants, health care benefits, tuition waivers (full), and unspecified assistantships also available. Financial award application deadline: 1/15. *Faculty research:* Russian cinema and media, twentieth-century and contemporary Russian culture, digital humanities, applied linguistics and language pedagogy. *Total annual research expenditures:* $266,000. *Unit head:* Dr. David J. Birnbaum, Co-Chair, 412-624-5712, Fax: 412-624-9714, E-mail: djbpitt@pitt.edu. *Application contact:* Keanna Cash, Graduate Administrator, 412-624-5227, E-mail: kec176@pitt.edu.
Website: http://www.slavic.pitt.edu

University of Southern California, Graduate School, Dana and David Dornsife College of Letters, Arts and Sciences, Department of Linguistics, Los Angeles, CA 90089. Offers East Asian linguistics (PhD); Hispanic linguistics (PhD); linguistics (PhD); Slavic linguistics (PhD). *Degree requirements:* For doctorate, comprehensive exam, thesis/dissertation. *Entrance requirements:* For doctorate, GRE. Additional exam requirements/recommendations for international students: Required—TOEFL (minimum score 100 iBT). Electronic applications accepted. *Faculty research:* Syntax, phonology, phonetics, semantics, sociolinguistics, psycholinguistics.

University of Southern California, Graduate School, Dana and David Dornsife College of Letters, Arts and Sciences, Department of Slavic Languages and Literatures, Los Angeles, CA 90089. Offers MA, PhD. *Degree requirements:* For master's, one foreign language, comprehensive exam, thesis or alternative, 30 units; for doctorate, 3 foreign languages, comprehensive exam, thesis/dissertation, 60 units. *Entrance requirements:* For doctorate, GRE, BA in Russian literature or equivalent. Additional exam requirements/recommendations for international students: Required—TOEFL. Electronic applications accepted. *Faculty research:* Russian avant-garde art, intertextuality in Russian literature, eighteenth-century Russian culture, Russian poetry, Russian music history, twentieth-century Russian literature.

The University of Texas at Austin, Graduate School, College of Liberal Arts, Department of Slavic and Eurasian Studies, Austin, TX 78712-1111. Offers applied linguistics/pedagogy (PhD); literature and culture (PhD); Slavic languages (MA); Slavic linguistics (PhD). *Degree requirements:* For master's, 2 foreign languages, thesis; for doctorate, 3 foreign languages, thesis/dissertation. *Entrance requirements:* For master's and doctorate, GRE General Test. Electronic applications accepted. *Faculty research:* Slavic linguistics; applied linguistics; Russian, Czech, and Slavic literature and culture.

University of Toronto, School of Graduate Studies, Faculty of Arts and Science, Department of Slavic Languages and Literatures, Toronto, ON M5S 1A1, Canada. Offers MA, PhD. *Program availability:* Part-time. *Degree requirements:* For doctorate, comprehensive exam, thesis/dissertation. *Entrance requirements:* For master's, BA in related area; minimum A- average in Slavic courses taken in final year, writing sample, 2 letters of recommendation; for doctorate, MA in Slavic languages and literatures, minimum A- average, writing sample, 2 letters of recommendation. Additional exam requirements/recommendations for international students: Required—TOEFL (minimum score 580 paper-based; 93 iBT), TWE (minimum score 5). Electronic applications accepted.

University of Virginia, College and Graduate School of Arts and Sciences, Department of Slavic Languages and Literatures, Charlottesville, VA 22903. Offers MA, PhD. *Faculty:* 7 full-time (2 women). *Students:* 13 full-time (10 women); includes 1 minority (Two or more races, non-Hispanic/Latino). Average age 28. 16 applicants, 69% accepted, 4 enrolled. In 2017, 7 master's, 1 doctorate awarded. *Degree requirements:* For master's, one foreign language, comprehensive exam, thesis (for some programs); for doctorate, one foreign language, comprehensive exam, thesis/dissertation. *Entrance requirements:* For master's, GRE General Test, 2 letters of recommendation, writing sample in English; for doctorate, GRE General Test, 2 letters of recommendation; writing sample in English. Additional exam requirements/recommendations for international students: Required—TOEFL (minimum score 600 paper-based; 90 iBT), IELTS (minimum score 7). *Application deadline:* Applications are processed on a rolling basis. Application fee: $60. Electronic applications accepted. *Financial support:* Teaching assistantships available. Financial award application deadline: 1/15; financial award applicants required to submit FAFSA. *Unit head:* David Herman, Chair, 434-924-3548, Fax: 434-982-2744, E-mail: herman@virginia.edu. *Application contact:* Edith Clowes, Director of Graduate Studies, 434-924-3548, Fax: 434-982-2744, E-mail: eec3c@virginia.edu.
Website: http://artsandsciences.virginia.edu/slavic/index.html

University of Washington, Graduate School, College of Arts and Sciences, Department of Slavic Languages and Literatures, Seattle, WA 98195. Offers Russian literature (MA, PhD); Slavic linguistics (MA, PhD). *Degree requirements:* For master's, 2 foreign languages, thesis optional; for doctorate, 3 foreign languages, thesis/dissertation. *Entrance requirements:* For master's and doctorate, GRE General Test, minimum GPA of 3.0. Additional exam requirements/recommendations for international students: Required—TOEFL. Electronic applications accepted. *Faculty research:* Modern and medieval East European languages and literatures, comparative literature, Russian folk literature, Slavic literary theory and criticism, computerized morphology of Russian.

University of Wisconsin–Madison, Graduate School, College of Letters and Science, Department of Slavic Languages and Literature, Madison, WI 53706-1380. Offers MA, PhD. *Program availability:* Part-time. Terminal master's awarded for partial completion of doctoral program. *Degree requirements:* For doctorate, thesis/dissertation. *Entrance requirements:* For master's and doctorate, GRE General Test. Additional exam requirements/recommendations for international students: Required—TOEFL. Electronic applications accepted. *Faculty research:* Polish literature, linguistics, South Slavic literature, second language acquisition, nineteenth- and twentieth-century Russian literature.

Yale University, Graduate School of Arts and Sciences, Department of Slavic Languages and Literatures, New Haven, CT 06520. Offers medieval Slavic literature and philology (PhD); Polish literature (PhD); Russian literature (PhD); Slavic languages and literatures and film studies (PhD). *Degree requirements:* For doctorate, 3 foreign languages, thesis/dissertation. *Entrance requirements:* For doctorate, GRE General Test.

Spanish

American University, College of Arts and Sciences, Department of World Languages and Cultures, Washington, DC 20016-8045. Offers Spanish: Latin American studies (MA); teaching English as a foreign language (MA); teaching English to speakers of other languages (MA, Certificate); translation: French (Certificate); translation: Russian (Certificate); translation: Spanish (Certificate). *Program availability:* Part-time, evening/weekend. *Faculty:* 43 full-time (33 women), 23 part-time/adjunct (17 women). *Students:* 17 full-time (14 women), 19 part-time (15 women); includes 10 minority (2 Black or African American, non-Hispanic/Latino; 6 Hispanic/Latino; 2 Two or more races, non-Hispanic/Latino), 5 international. Average age 32. 39 applicants, 97% accepted, 9 enrolled. In 2017, 16 master's, 11 other advanced degrees awarded. *Degree requirements:* For master's, one foreign language, comprehensive exam, thesis or alternative. *Entrance requirements:* For master's, GRE, writing sample, statement of purpose, transcripts, 2 letters of recommendation, resume; for Certificate, bachelor's degree, statement of purpose, transcripts, resume. Additional exam requirements/recommendations for international students: Required—TOEFL (minimum score 600 paper-based; 100 iBT). *Application deadline:* For fall admission, 2/1 priority date for domestic students; for spring admission, 11/1 priority date for domestic students. Application fee: $55. *Expenses:* Contact institution. *Financial support:* Institutionally sponsored loans, scholarships/grants, and unspecified assistantships available. Financial award application deadline: 2/1; financial award applicants required to submit FAFSA. *Unit head:* Henry Gerfen, Chair, 202-885-2385, Fax: 202-885-1076, E-mail: gerfen@american.edu. *Application contact:* Jonathan Harper, Director of Graduate Recruitment, 202-885-3622, E-mail: jharper@american.edu.
Website: http://www.american.edu/cas/wlc/

Arizona State University at the Tempe campus, College of Liberal Arts and Sciences, School of International Letters and Cultures, Program in Spanish, Tempe, AZ 85287-0202. Offers cultural studies (PhD); linguistics (MA), including second language acquisition/applied linguistics, sociolinguistics; literature (PhD); literature and culture (MA). *Program availability:* Part-time. Terminal master's awarded for partial completion of doctoral program. *Degree requirements:* For master's, thesis, oral defense; written comprehensive exam (literature and culture); portfolio review (linguistics); interactive Program of Study (iPOS) submitted before completing 50 percent of required credit hours; for doctorate, comprehensive exam, thesis/dissertation, interactive Program of Study (iPOS) submitted before completing 50 percent of required credit hours. *Entrance requirements:* For master's, GRE (recommended), BA in Spanish or close equivalent from accredited institution with minimum GPA of 3.5, 3 letters of recommendation, personal statement, academic writing sample; for doctorate, GRE (recommended), MA in Spanish or equivalent from accredited institution with minimum GPA of 3.75, 3 letters of recommendation, personal statement, academic writing sample. Additional exam requirements/recommendations for international students: Required—TOEFL (minimum

score 550 paper-based; 83 iBT), IELTS (minimum score 6.5). Electronic applications accepted.

Asbury University, School of Graduate and Professional Studies, Wilmore, KY 40390-1198. Offers biology: alternative certificate (MA Ed); chemistry: alternative certificate (MA Ed); English (MA Ed); English as a second language (MA Ed); ESL (MA Ed); French (MA Ed); Latin: alternative certificate (MA Ed); mathematics: alternative certificate (MA Ed); reading/writing endorsement (MA Ed); social studies (MA Ed); social work (MSW), including child and family services; Spanish (MA Ed); special education (MA Ed); special education: alternative certificate (MA Ed); teacher as leader endorsement (MA Ed). *Accreditation:* NCATE. *Program availability:* Part-time. *Degree requirements:* For master's, action research project, portfolio. *Entrance requirements:* For master's, PRAXIS/NTE, minimum GPA of 2.75, letters of recommendation. Additional exam requirements/recommendations for international students: Required—TOEFL (minimum score 550 paper-based). Electronic applications accepted.

Auburn University, Graduate School, College of Liberal Arts, Department of Foreign Languages and Literatures, Auburn University, AL 36849. Offers MA, MHS. *Program availability:* Part-time. *Faculty:* 30 full-time (19 women), 6 part-time/adjunct (4 women). *Students:* 16 full-time (10 women), 1 (woman) part-time; includes 3 minority (all Hispanic/Latino), 11 international. Average age 30. 12 applicants, 50% accepted, 6 enrolled. In 2017, 6 master's awarded. *Degree requirements:* For master's, one foreign language, comprehensive exam, thesis (for some programs). *Entrance requirements:* For master's, GRE General Test. *Application deadline:* Applications are processed on a rolling basis. Application fee: $50 ($60 for international students). Electronic applications accepted. *Expenses:* Tuition, state resident: full-time $10,974; part-time $519 per credit hour. Tuition, nonresident: full-time $29,658; part-time $1557 per credit hour. *Required fees:* $816 per semester. Tuition and fees vary according to degree level and program. *Financial support:* Fellowships, teaching assistantships, and Federal Work-Study available. Support available to part-time students. Financial award application deadline: 3/15; financial award applicants required to submit FAFSA. *Unit head:* Dr. Lourdes Betanzos, Chair, 334-844-6350, Fax: 334-844-6378. *Application contact:* Dr. George Flowers, Dean of the Graduate School, 334-844-2125.
Website: http://www.cla.auburn.edu/forlang/

Bard College, Master of Arts in Teaching Program, Annandale-on-Hudson, NY 12504. Offers secondary education (MAT), including biology, history, literature, mathematics, Spanish; MS/MAT. *Program availability:* Part-time. *Degree requirements:* For master's, year-long teaching residencies in area middle and high schools. *Entrance requirements:* For master's, GRE General Test, resume, 3 letters of recommendation, personal statement, official transcripts. Additional exam requirements/recommendations for international students: Required—TOEFL. Electronic applications accepted. Application fee is waived when completed online.

Spanish

Baylor University, Graduate School, College of Arts and Sciences, Department of Modern Languages and Cultures, Waco, TX 76798. Offers Spanish (MA). *Students:* 11 full-time (9 women); includes 3 minority (all Two or more races, non-Hispanic/Latino). Average age 30. 12 applicants, 58% accepted, 2 enrolled. In 2017, 4 master's awarded. *Entrance requirements:* For master's, GRE General Test. Additional exam requirements/recommendations for international students: Required—TOEFL. Application fee: $50. Electronic applications accepted. *Financial support:* In 2017–18, 6 students received support. Teaching assistantships, scholarships/grants, and unspecified assistantships available. Financial award application deadline: 2/1. *Faculty research:* Spanish post-civil war novel, Latin American detective fiction, Nineteenth- and Twentieth-Century Hispanic women writers, semantics and pragmatics, Miguel de Unamuno. *Unit head:* Dr. Jan E. Evans, Graduate Program Director, 254-710-7361, Fax: 254-710-3799, E-mail: jan_evans@baylor.edu. *Application contact:* Ann Westbrook, Administrative Assistant, 254-710-6027, Fax: 254-710-3870, E-mail: ann_westbrook@baylor.edu.
Website: http://www.baylor.edu/mfl/

Binghamton University, State University of New York, Graduate School, Harpur College of Arts and Sciences, Department of Romance Languages and Literatures, Program in Spanish, Binghamton, NY 13902-6000. Offers MA. *Program availability:* Part-time. *Students:* 2 full-time (both women), 4 part-time (3 women); includes 2 minority (both Hispanic/Latino). Average age 36. 3 applicants, 100% accepted, 3 enrolled. *Degree requirements:* For master's, one foreign language, comprehensive exam, thesis or alternative. *Entrance requirements:* For master's, GRE General Test. Additional exam requirements/recommendations for international students: Required—TOEFL (minimum score 550 paper-based; 80 iBT). *Application deadline:* For fall admission, 2/15 priority date for domestic and international students; for spring admission, 11/15 priority date for domestic and international students. Application fee: $75. Electronic applications accepted. *Financial support:* In 2017–18, 3 students received support. Career-related internships or fieldwork, Federal Work-Study, institutionally sponsored loans, scholarships/grants, health care benefits, and unspecified assistantships available. Financial award applicants required to submit FAFSA. *Unit head:* Dr. Dana Stewart, Chairperson, 607-777-2645, E-mail: stewart@binghamton.edu. *Application contact:* Ben Balkaya, Assistant Dean and Director, 607-777-2151, Fax: 607-777-2501, E-mail: balkaya@binghamton.edu.

Boston College, Graduate School of Arts and Sciences, Department of Romance Languages and Literatures, Chestnut Hill, MA 02467-3800. Offers French (MA); Italian (MA); Spanish (MA). *Program availability:* Part-time. Terminal master's awarded for partial completion of doctoral program. *Degree requirements:* For master's, one foreign language. *Entrance requirements:* Additional exam requirements/recommendations for international students: Required—TOEFL (minimum score 600 paper-based; 100 iBT), IELTS (minimum score 8). Electronic applications accepted. *Faculty research:* Spanish-American literature, philology, medieval French romance and troubadour lyrics, Golden Age Peninsular literature, secondary language acquisition and pedagogy, Hispanic studies, French language and literature, Italian language and literature.

Bowling Green State University, Graduate College, College of Arts and Sciences, Department of Romance and Classical Studies, Program in Spanish, Bowling Green, OH 43403. Offers Spanish (MA). *Program availability:* Part-time. *Degree requirements:* For master's, one foreign language, thesis or alternative. *Entrance requirements:* For master's, GRE General Test. Additional exam requirements/recommendations for international students: Required—TOEFL. Electronic applications accepted. *Faculty research:* U.S. Latino literature and culture, Latin American film and popular culture, applied linguistics, Spanish popular culture.

Brigham Young University, Graduate Studies, College of Humanities, Department of Spanish and Portuguese, Provo, UT 84602. Offers Portuguese (MA), including Luso-Brazilian literatures, Portuguese linguistics, Portuguese pedagogy; Spanish (MA), including Hispanic linguistics, Hispanic literatures, Spanish pedagogy; *Faculty:* 30 full-time (6 women). *Students:* 32 full-time (17 women), 6 part-time (4 women); includes 16 minority (all Hispanic/Latino). Average age 31. 19 applicants, 68% accepted, 10 enrolled. In 2017, 6 master's awarded. *Degree requirements:* For master's, 2 foreign languages, comprehensive exam, thesis, 1 semester of teaching. *Entrance requirements:* For master's, minimum GPA of 3.5 in Spanish or Portuguese, 3.3 overall. Additional exam requirements/recommendations for international students: Required—TOEFL (minimum score 580 paper-based; 85 iBT), IELTS (minimum score 6.5), PTE (minimum score 53). *Application deadline:* For fall admission, 2/1 for domestic and international students. Application fee: $50. Electronic applications accepted. *Expenses:* Contact institution. *Financial support:* In 2017–18, 23 students received support, including 87 teaching assistantships (averaging $3,200 per year); research assistantships, institutionally sponsored loans, scholarships/grants, tuition waivers (partial), and unspecified assistantships also available. Support available to part-time students. *Faculty research:* Mexican prose; Latin American theater; literature; phonetics, and phonology; pedagogy; classical Portuguese literature. *Unit head:* Dr. Jeffrey S. Turley, Chair, 801-422-7019, Fax: 801-422-0628, E-mail: jeffrey_turley@byu.edu. *Application contact:* Patricia E. Wilson, Graduate Program Manager, 801-422-2838, Fax: 801-422-0628, E-mail: patricia_rubio@byu.edu.
Website: http://spanport.byu.edu/

Brooklyn College of the City University of New York, School of Humanities and Social Sciences, Department of Modern Languages and Literatures, Brooklyn, NY 11210-2889. Offers French (MA); Spanish (MA). *Degree requirements:* For master's, comprehensive exam or research paper. *Entrance requirements:* For master's, 18 credits in advanced courses in Spanish, 2 letters of recommendation. Additional exam requirements/recommendations for international students: Required—TOEFL (minimum score 500 paper-based; 61 iBT). Electronic applications accepted. *Faculty research:* Latin American contemporary novel, Caribbean female contemporary literature, nineteenth- and twentieth-century Spanish novel, twentieth-century Mexican poetry.

California State University, Bakersfield, Division of Graduate Studies, School of Arts and Humanities, Program in Spanish, Bakersfield, CA 93311. Offers MA. *Faculty:* 3 full-time (2 women). *Students:* 6 full-time (5 women), 3 part-time (2 women); includes 8 minority (all Hispanic/Latino). Average age 30. 4 applicants, 50% accepted, 1 enrolled. *Degree requirements:* For master's, capstone course. *Expenses:* Tuition, state resident: full-time $7176; part-time $4164 per year. *Financial support:* In 2017–18, fellowships (averaging $1,850 per year) were awarded; Federal Work-Study, scholarships/grants, and tuition waivers (full and partial) also available. Financial award application deadline: 3/2; financial award applicants required to submit FAFSA. *Unit head:* Dr. Maryann Parada, Graduate Coordinator, 661-654-2377, Fax: 661-654-2017, E-mail: mparada1@csub.edu. *Application contact:* Debbie Blowers, Assistant Director of Admissions and Evaluations, 661-654-3381, E-mail: dblowers@csub.edu.
Website: https://www.csub.edu/modlang/department/Spanish%20M.A.%20index.html

California State University, Fresno, Division of Research and Graduate Studies, College of Arts and Humanities, Department of Modern and Classical Languages and Literatures, Fresno, CA 93740-8027. Offers Spanish (MA). *Program availability:* Part-time. *Degree requirements:* For master's, one foreign language, thesis or alternative. *Entrance requirements:* For master's, GRE General Test, BA in Spanish, minimum GPA of 3.0. Additional exam requirements/recommendations for international students: Required—TOEFL. Electronic applications accepted.

California State University, Fullerton, Graduate Studies, College of Humanities and Social Sciences, Department of Modern Languages and Literatures, Fullerton, CA 92831-3599. Offers Spanish (MA). *Program availability:* Part-time. *Faculty:* 4 full-time (0 women), 3 part-time/adjunct (2 women). *Students:* 39 full-time (27 women), 38 part-time (30 women); includes 45 minority (5 Asian, non-Hispanic/Latino; 38 Hispanic/Latino; 2 Two or more races, non-Hispanic/Latino), 19 international. Average age 31. 50 applicants, 78% accepted, 24 enrolled. *Degree requirements:* For master's, comprehensive exam, thesis or alternative. *Entrance requirements:* For master's, minimum GPA of 2.5 in last 60 hours of course work, undergraduate major in a language. Application fee: $55. *Financial support:* Career-related internships or fieldwork, Federal Work-Study, institutionally sponsored loans, and scholarships/grants available. Support available to part-time students. Financial award application deadline: 3/1; financial award applicants required to submit FAFSA. *Unit head:* Dr. Reyes Fidalgo, Chair, 657-278-4563. *Application contact:* Admissions/Applications, 657-278-2371.

California State University, Long Beach, Graduate Studies, College of Liberal Arts, Department of Romance, German, Russian Languages and Literatures, Program in Spanish, Long Beach, CA 90840. Offers MA. *Program availability:* Part-time. *Degree requirements:* For master's, one foreign language, thesis or alternative, research paper. *Entrance requirements:* For master's, BA in Spanish. Electronic applications accepted. *Faculty research:* Literary translation, literature and politics, women writers, Latin American poetry, Latin American theatre.

California State University, Los Angeles, Graduate Studies, College of Arts and Letters, Department of Modern Languages and Literatures, Los Angeles, CA 90032-8530. Offers French (MA); Spanish (MA). *Program availability:* Part-time, evening/weekend. *Degree requirements:* For master's, comprehensive exam. *Entrance requirements:* Additional exam requirements/recommendations for international students: Required—TOEFL (minimum score 500 paper-based). Electronic applications accepted. *Faculty research:* French literature, language teaching and methodology, Spanish poetry, Spanish American fiction and poetry.

California State University, Northridge, Graduate Studies, College of Humanities, Department of Modern and Classical Languages and Literatures, Northridge, CA 91330. Offers Spanish (MA). *Program availability:* Part-time, evening/weekend. *Students:* 40 full-time (22 women), 24 part-time (22 women); includes 33 minority (5 Asian, non-Hispanic/Latino; 28 Hispanic/Latino), 5 international. Average age 35. 46 applicants, 63% accepted, 21 enrolled. In 2017, 23 master's awarded. *Degree requirements:* For master's, one foreign language. *Entrance requirements:* For master's, GRE General Test or minimum GPA of 3.0. Additional exam requirements/recommendations for international students: Required—TOEFL. *Application deadline:* For fall admission, 11/30 for domestic students. Application fee: $55. *Financial support:* Application deadline: 3/1. *Unit head:* Dr. Adrain Perez-Boluda, Chair, 818-677-3467, E-mail: brian.castronovo@csun.edu.
Website: http://www.csun.edu/mcll

California State University, San Bernardino, Graduate Studies, College of Arts and Letters, Program in Spanish, San Bernardino, CA 92407. Offers MA. *Program availability:* Part-time, evening/weekend. *Faculty:* 3 full-time (1 woman). *Students:* 2 full-time (1 woman), 20 part-time (16 women); includes 19 minority (all Hispanic/Latino), 2 international. Average age 31. 10 applicants, 90% accepted, 5 enrolled. In 2017, 1 master's awarded. *Degree requirements:* For master's, comprehensive exam, advancement to candidacy. *Entrance requirements:* Additional exam requirements/recommendations for international students: Required—TOEFL. *Application deadline:* For fall admission, 7/16 for domestic students. Application fee: $55. *Financial support:* Institutionally sponsored loans available. *Unit head:* Thomas McGovern, Chair, 909-537-5849, Fax: 909-537-7091, E-mail: mcgovern@csusb.edu. *Application contact:* Dr. Dorota Huizinga, Dean of Graduate Studies, 909-537-3064, E-mail: dorota.huizinga@csusb.edu.

California State University, San Marcos, College of Humanities, Arts, Behavioral and Social Sciences, Program in Spanish, San Marcos, CA 92096-0001. Offers Hispanic cultures and society (MA); Hispanic language and linguistics (MA); Hispanic literatures and literary theory (MA). *Program availability:* Part-time, evening/weekend. *Degree requirements:* For master's, 2 foreign languages, exam. *Entrance requirements:* For master's, GRE General Test, minimum GPA of 3.0 overall and in upper-division Spanish courses, official transcripts, three letters of recommendation, 750-word statement of purpose (in English), academic writing sample (in Spanish). Additional exam requirements/recommendations for international students: Required—TOEFL (minimum score 500 paper-based), TWE (minimum score 4.5). *Application deadline:* For fall admission, 3/15 priority date for domestic students. Applications are processed on a rolling basis. Application fee: $55. Electronic applications accepted. *Expenses:* Tuition, state resident: full-time $7176. Tuition, nonresident: full-time $9504. *Faculty research:* Applied linguistics, Golden Age Spanish literature, Latin American literature, poetry, Chicano studies. *Unit head:* Dr. Silvia Rolle-Rissetto, Graduate Coordinator, 760-750-4115, E-mail: srolle@csusm.edu.
Website: http://www.csusm.edu/modernlanguages/masters_degree/

The Catholic University of America, School of Arts and Sciences, Department of Modern Languages and Literatures, Washington, DC 20064. Offers Hispanic studies (MA, PhD). *Program availability:* Part-time. *Faculty:* 22 full-time (17 women), 3 part-time/adjunct (2 women). *Students:* 3 full-time (1 woman), 4 part-time (3 women), 6 international. Average age 34. 7 applicants, 43% accepted, 3 enrolled. In 2017, 4 master's, 1 doctorate awarded. *Degree requirements:* For master's, comprehensive exam; for doctorate, one foreign language, comprehensive exam, thesis/dissertation, annotated bibliography; oral defense of the proposal; oral defense of the dissertation. *Entrance requirements:* For master's, GRE General Test, statement of purpose, official copies of academic transcripts, two letters of recommendation, sample of academic writing; for doctorate, GRE General Test, statement of purpose, official copies of academic transcripts, three letters of recommendation, sample of academic writing (20-25-pages long). Additional exam requirements/recommendations for international students: Required—TOEFL (minimum score 550 paper-based; 80 iBT). *Application deadline:* For fall admission, 7/15 priority date for domestic students, 7/1 for international students; for spring admission, 11/15 priority date for domestic students, 11/1 for international students. Applications are processed on a rolling basis. Application fee: $55. Electronic applications accepted. *Expenses:* Contact institution. *Financial support:* Fellowships, research assistantships, teaching assistantships, Federal Work-Study, scholarships/grants, tuition waivers (full and partial), and unspecified assistantships available. Financial award application deadline: 2/1; financial award applicants required to submit FAFSA. *Faculty research:* Golden age Spain; 18th-21st-century Spain; colonial/postcolonial Latin American and transatlantic studies; modern and contemporary Latin America; theory, criticism, and language teaching methodology. Total annual research expenditures: $32,340. *Unit head:* Dr. Claudia Bornholdt, Chair, 202-319-5240, Fax: 202-319-6077, E-mail: kassen@cua.edu. *Application contact:* Dr. Steven Brown, Director of Graduate Admissions, 202-319-5057, Fax: 202-319-6533, E-mail: cua-admissions@cua.edu.
Website: http://modernlanguages.cua.edu/

Central Connecticut State University, School of Graduate Studies, College of Liberal Arts and Social Sciences, Department of Modern Languages, New Britain, CT 06050-

4010. Offers modern language (MA, Certificate), including French, German (Certificate), Italian, Spanish (MA); Spanish (MS, Certificate). *Program availability:* Part-time, evening/weekend. *Faculty:* 7 full-time (6 women). *Students:* 6 full-time (5 women), 16 part-time (12 women); includes 9 minority (all Hispanic/Latino), 1 international. Average age 32. 8 applicants, 88% accepted, 5 enrolled. In 2017, 12 master's awarded. *Degree requirements:* For master's, one foreign language, comprehensive exam, thesis or alternative; for Certificate, qualifying exam. *Entrance requirements:* For master's, minimum undergraduate GPA of 2.7, 24 credits of undergraduate courses in each language in which graduate work will be undertaken. Additional exam requirements/recommendations for international students: Required—TOEFL (minimum score 550 paper-based; 79 iBT); Recommended—IELTS (minimum score 6.5). *Application deadline:* For fall admission, 8/1 for domestic students, 5/1 for international students; for spring admission, 11/1 for domestic and international students. Applications are processed on a rolling basis. Application fee: $50. Electronic applications accepted. *Expenses: Tuition, area resident:* Full-time $6757. Tuition, state resident: full-time $9750; part-time $374 per credit. Tuition, nonresident: full-time $18,102; part-time $374 per credit. *Required fees:* $4635; $255 per credit. *Financial support:* In 2017–18, 3 students received support. Career-related internships or fieldwork, Federal Work-Study, scholarships/grants, and unspecified assistantships available. Support available to part-time students. Financial award application deadline: 3/1; financial award applicants required to submit FAFSA. *Faculty research:* Quebecois literature, Caribbean literature, modern French/Spanish drama, Puerto Rican novel and drama. *Unit head:* Dr. Carmela Pesca, Chair, 860-832-2875, E-mail: pescac@ccsu.edu. *Application contact:* Patricia Gardner, Associate Director of Graduate Studies, 860-832-2350, Fax: 860-832-2362.
Website: http://www.ccsu.edu/modlang/

Central Michigan University, College of Graduate Studies, College of Humanities and Social and Behavioral Sciences, Department of Foreign Languages, Literatures, and Cultures, Mount Pleasant, MI 48859. Offers Spanish (MA). *Program availability:* Part-time. *Degree requirements:* For master's, thesis or alternative. Electronic applications accepted.

City College of the City University of New York, Graduate School, Division of Humanities and the Arts, Department of Classical and Modern Languages and Literatures, New York, NY 10031-9198. Offers Spanish (MA). *Degree requirements:* For master's, one foreign language, comprehensive exam, thesis or alternative. *Entrance requirements:* For master's, minimum GPA of 3.0. Additional exam requirements/recommendations for international students: Required—TOEFL (minimum score 500 paper-based; 61 iBT). Electronic applications accepted.

Cleveland State University, College of Graduate Studies, College of Liberal Arts and Social Sciences, Department of World Languages, Literatures, and Cultures, Cleveland, OH 44115. Offers Spanish (MA). *Program availability:* Part-time, evening/weekend. *Faculty:* 6 full-time (3 women), 1 (woman) part-time/adjunct. *Students:* 4 full-time (2 women), 6 part-time (4 women); includes 5 minority (all Hispanic/Latino). Average age 35. 3 applicants, 100% accepted, 1 enrolled. In 2017, 8 master's awarded. *Entrance requirements:* For master's, ACTFL oral proficiency rating, undergraduate major in Spanish or equivalent, essay in Spanish, writing sample, 2 letters of reference. Additional exam requirements/recommendations for international students: Required—TOEFL (minimum score 550 paper-based; 78 iBT). *Application deadline:* Applications are processed on a rolling basis. Application fee: $40. Electronic applications accepted. *Financial support:* In 2017–18, 5 students received support. Teaching assistantships, Federal Work-Study, and unspecified assistantships available. Financial award application deadline: 4/1. *Faculty research:* Peninsular poetry and prose, sociolinguistics, Latin American and Caribbean literature, Arabic diaspora in Latin America, border literature. *Unit head:* Dr. Antonio Medina-Rivera, Chairperson, 216-523-7175, Fax: 216-687-4650, E-mail: a.medinarivera@csuohio.edu. *Application contact:* Dr. Stephen Gingerich, Graduate Director, 216-687-4677, Fax: 216-687-4650, E-mail: s.gingerich@csuohio.edu.
Website: http://www.csuohio.edu/class/world-languages/world-languages

Columbia University, Graduate School of Arts and Sciences, New York, NY 10027. Offers African-American studies (MA); American studies (MA); anthropology (MA, PhD); art history and archaeology (MA, PhD); astronomy (PhD); biological sciences (PhD); biotechnology (MA); chemical physics (PhD); chemistry (PhD); classical studies (MA, PhD); classics (MA, PhD); climate and society (MA); conservation biology (MA); earth and environmental sciences (PhD); East Asia: regional studies (MA); East Asian languages and cultures (MA, PhD); ecology, evolution and environmental biology (MA), including conservation biology; ecology, evolution, and environmental biology (PhD), including ecology and evolutionary biology, evolutionary primatology; economics (MA, PhD); English and comparative literature (MA, PhD); French and Romance philology (MA, PhD); Germanic languages (MA, PhD); global French studies (MA); global thought (MA); Hispanic cultural studies (MA); history (PhD); history and literature (MA); human rights studies (MA); Islamic studies (MA); Italian (MA, PhD); Japanese pedagogy (MA); Jewish studies (MA); Latin America and the Caribbean: regional studies (MA); Latin American and Iberian cultures (PhD); mathematics (MA, PhD), including finance (MA); medieval and Renaissance studies (MA); Middle Eastern, South Asian, and African studies (MA, PhD); modern art: critical and curatorial studies (MA); modern European studies (MA); museum anthropology (MA); music (DMA, PhD); oral history (MA); philosophical foundations of physics (MA); philosophy (MA, PhD); physics (PhD); political science (MA, PhD); psychology (PhD); quantitative methods in the social sciences (MA); religion (MA, PhD); Russia, Eurasia and East Europe: regional studies (MA); Russian translation (MA); Slavic cultures (MA); Slavic languages (MA, PhD); sociology (MA, PhD); South Asian studies (MA); statistics (MA, PhD); theatre (PhD). Dual-degree programs require admission to both Graduate School of Arts and Sciences and another Columbia school. *Program availability:* Part-time. Terminal master's awarded for partial completion of doctoral program. *Degree requirements:* For master's, variable foreign language requirement, comprehensive exam (for some programs), thesis (for some programs); for doctorate, variable foreign language requirement, comprehensive exam (for some programs), thesis/dissertation. *Entrance requirements:* For master's and doctorate, GRE General Test, GRE Subject Test (for some programs). Additional exam requirements/recommendations for international students: Required—TOEFL, IELTS. Electronic applications accepted. *Expenses: Tuition:* Full-time $44,864; part-time $1704 per credit. *Required fees:* $2370 per semester. One-time fee: $105.

Cornell University, Graduate School, Graduate Fields of Arts and Sciences, Field of Romance Studies, Ithaca, NY 14853. Offers French linguistics (PhD); French literature (PhD); Hispanic literature (PhD); Italian linguistics (PhD); Italian literature (PhD); Romance linguistics (PhD); Spanish linguistics (PhD). *Degree requirements:* For doctorate, 2 foreign languages, comprehensive exam, thesis/dissertation. *Entrance requirements:* For doctorate, GRE General Test, sample of written work, 3 letters of recommendation. Additional exam requirements/recommendations for international students: Required—TOEFL (minimum score 550 paper-based; 77 iBT). Electronic applications accepted. *Faculty research:* Literary theory, Hispanic studies, French studies, gender studies.

DePaul University, College of Liberal Arts and Social Sciences, Chicago, IL 60614. Offers Arabic (MA); Chinese (MA); critical ethnic studies (MA); English (MA); French (MA); German (MA); history (MA); interdisciplinary studies (MA, MS); international public service (MS); international studies (MA); Italian (MA); Japanese (MA); liberal studies (MA); nonprofit management (MNM); public administration (MPA); public health (MPH); public policy (MPP); public service management (MS); refugee and forced migration studies (MS); social work (MSW); sociology (MA); Spanish (MA); sustainable urban development (MA); women's and gender studies (MA); writing and publishing (MA); writing, rhetoric and discourse (MA); MA/PhD. *Program availability:* Part-time, evening/weekend, online learning. Terminal master's awarded for partial completion of doctoral program. *Degree requirements:* For master's, variable foreign language requirement, comprehensive exam (for some programs), thesis (for some programs). *Application deadline:* Applications are processed on a rolling basis. Application fee: $40. Electronic applications accepted. *Financial support:* Applicants required to submit FAFSA. *Unit head:* Dr. Guillermo Vasquez de Velasco, Dean, 773-325-7305. *Application contact:* Ann Spittle, Director of Graduate Admission, 773-325-8369, Fax: 312-476-3244, E-mail: graddepaul@depaul.edu.
Website: http://las.depaul.edu/

Duke University, Graduate School, Department of Romance Studies, Durham, NC 27708. Offers French (PhD); Italian (PhD); Spanish (PhD); JD/AM. *Degree requirements:* For doctorate, 2 foreign languages, thesis/dissertation. *Entrance requirements:* For doctorate, GRE General Test. Additional exam requirements/recommendations for international students: Required—TOEFL (minimum score 577 paper-based; 90 iBT) or IELTS (minimum score 7). Electronic applications accepted.

Eastern University, Graduate Education Programs, St. Davids, PA 19087-3696. Offers ESL program specialist (K-12) (Certificate); general supervisor (PreK-12) (Certificate); health and physical education (K-12) (Certificate); middle level (4-8) (Certificate); multicultural education (M Ed); music (K-12) (Certificate); Pre K-4 (Certificate); Pre K-4 with special education (Certificate); reading (M Ed); reading specialist (K-12) (Certificate); reading supervisor (K-12) (Certificate); school counseling (MA, CAGS); school principalship (preK-12) (Certificate); school psychology (MS, CAGS); secondary biology education (7-12) (Certificate); secondary chemistry education (7-12) (Certificate); secondary communication education (7-12) (Certificate); secondary English education (7-12) (Certificate); secondary math education (7-12) (Certificate); secondary social studies education (7-12) (Certificate); special education (M Ed); special education (7-12) (Certificate); special education (Pre K-8) (Certificate); special education supervisor (K-12) (Certificate); TESOL (M Ed); world language (Certificate), including Spanish. *Program availability:* Part-time, evening/weekend, online learning. *Students:* 46 full-time (40 women), 115 part-time (93 women); includes 65 minority (42 Black or African American, non-Hispanic/Latino; 3 Asian, non-Hispanic/Latino; 14 Hispanic/Latino; 6 Two or more races, non-Hispanic/Latino), 1 international. Average age 32. In 2017, 72 master's awarded. *Entrance requirements:* Additional exam requirements/recommendations for international students: Required—TOEFL. *Application deadline:* Applications are processed on a rolling basis. Application fee: $35. Electronic applications accepted. Application fee is waived when completed online. *Expenses:* Contact institution. *Unit head:* Michael Dziedziak, Executive Director of Enrollment, 800-452-0996, E-mail: gpsadmissions@eastern.edu.
Website: https://www.eastern.edu/academics/programs/education-department-graduate-programs/graduate-programs

Emory University, Laney Graduate School, Department of Spanish and Portuguese, Atlanta, GA 30322-1100. Offers comparative literature (Certificate); film studies (Certificate); Spanish (PhD); women's studies (Certificate). *Degree requirements:* For doctorate, 2 foreign languages, comprehensive exam, thesis/dissertation. *Entrance requirements:* For doctorate, GRE General Test. Additional exam requirements/recommendations for international students: Required—TOEFL. Electronic applications accepted. *Faculty research:* Spanish literature, Spanish American literature, literary theory, criticism, cultural studies.

Florida Atlantic University, College of Education, Department of Teaching and Learning, Boca Raton, FL 33431-0991. Offers curriculum and instruction (M Ed), including art, biology, chemistry, English, French, German, mathematics, music, physics, Pre-K and primary education, reading, social sciences, Spanish; elementary education (M Ed); environmental education (M Ed); reading education (M Ed); social foundations of education (M Ed), including educational psychology, educational technology, multilingual education. *Accreditation:* NCATE. *Program availability:* Part-time, evening/weekend. *Faculty:* 13 full-time (10 women), 1 part-time/adjunct (0 women). *Students:* 26 full-time (22 women), 43 part-time (39 women); includes 19 minority (9 Black or African American, non-Hispanic/Latino; 1 Asian, non-Hispanic/Latino; 8 Hispanic/Latino; 1 Two or more races, non-Hispanic/Latino), 3 international. Average age 30. 91 applicants, 57% accepted, 33 enrolled. In 2017, 25 master's awarded. *Entrance requirements:* For master's, GRE General Test, minimum GPA of 3.0 in last 2 years of undergraduate course work. Additional exam requirements/recommendations for international students: Required—TOEFL (minimum score 500 paper-based; 61 iBT), IELTS (minimum score 6). *Application deadline:* For fall admission, 7/1 for domestic students, 2/15 for international students; for spring admission, 11/1 for domestic students, 7/15 for international students. Applications are processed on a rolling basis. Application fee: $30. *Expenses:* Tuition, state resident: full-time $7400; part-time $369.82 per credit. Tuition, nonresident: full-time $20,496; part-time $1042.81 per credit. *Financial support:* Fellowships with partial tuition reimbursements, research assistantships with partial tuition reimbursements, teaching assistantships with partial tuition reimbursements, career-related internships or fieldwork, scholarships/grants, and unspecified assistantships available. *Faculty research:* Technology, teaching English to speakers of other languages, math teaching, electronic portfolio assessment, global perspectives through social studies. *Unit head:* Dr. Barbara Ridener, Chairperson, 561-297-3588, E-mail: bridener@fau.edu. *Application contact:* Dr. Eliah Watlington, Associate Dean, 561-296-8520, Fax: 261-297-2991, E-mail: ewatling@fau.edu.
Website: http://www.coe.fau.edu/academicdepartments/tl/

Florida Atlantic University, Dorothy F. Schmidt College of Arts and Letters, Department of Languages, Linguistics, and Comparative Literature, Boca Raton, FL 33431-0991. Offers comparative literature (MA); French (MA); linguistics (MA); Spanish (MA). *Program availability:* Part-time. *Faculty:* 21 full-time (13 women). *Students:* 25 full-time (19 women), 16 part-time (12 women); includes 16 minority (5 Black or African American, non-Hispanic/Latino; 1 Asian, non-Hispanic/Latino; 10 Hispanic/Latino), 12 international. Average age 36. 42 applicants, 60% accepted, 18 enrolled. In 2017, 19 master's awarded. *Degree requirements:* For master's, one foreign language, comprehensive exam, thesis optional. *Entrance requirements:* For master's, GRE General Test, minimum GPA of 3.0. Additional exam requirements/recommendations for international students: Required—TOEFL (minimum score 500 paper-based; 61 iBT), IELTS (minimum score 6). *Application deadline:* For fall admission, 7/1 priority date for domestic students, 2/15 for international students; for spring admission, 11/1 for domestic students, 7/15 for international students. Applications are processed on a rolling basis. Application fee: $30. *Expenses:* Tuition, state resident: full-time $7400; part-time $369.82 per credit. Tuition, nonresident: full-time $20,496; part-time $1042.81 per credit. *Financial support:* Fellowships, research assistantships, teaching assistantships with partial tuition reimbursements, Federal Work-Study, and tuition waivers (partial) available. Support available to part-time students. Financial award

application deadline: 4/1. *Faculty research:* Modern European studies, modern Latin America, medieval Europe. *Unit head:* Dr. Marcella Munson, Chair, 561-297-2118, Fax: 561-297-2756, E-mail: mmunson@fau.edu. *Application contact:* Dr. Linda Johnson, Associate Dean, 561-297-0928, Fax: 561-297-2744.
Website: http://www.fau.edu/LLCL/

Florida International University, Steven J. Green School of International and Public Affairs, Department of Modern Languages, Miami, FL 33199. Offers Spanish (MA, PhD). PhD program has fall admissions only. *Program availability:* Part-time, evening/weekend. *Faculty:* 25 full-time (16 women), 23 part-time/adjunct (15 women). *Students:* 16 full-time (10 women), 14 part-time (7 women); includes 20 minority (1 Black or African American, non-Hispanic/Latino; 19 Hispanic/Latino), 9 international. Average age 38. 18 applicants, 50% accepted, 6 enrolled. In 2017, 14 master's, 2 doctorates awarded. *Degree requirements:* For master's, 2 foreign languages, comprehensive exam, thesis or 6 elective credits; for doctorate, 3 foreign languages, comprehensive exam, thesis/dissertation. *Entrance requirements:* For master's, minimum GPA of 3.0, resume, writing sample in Spanish (6-7 pages minimum), 2 letters of recommendation; for doctorate, GRE General Test (minimum score of 1120) or EXADEP (minimum score of 500), minimum GPA of 3.0, letter of intent, resume, writing sample in Spanish (15 pages minimum), 2 letters of recommendation. Additional exam requirements/recommendations for international students: Required—TOEFL (minimum score 550 paper-based; 80 iBT). *Application deadline:* For fall admission, 3/15 for domestic and international students. Application fee: $30. Electronic applications accepted. *Expenses:* Tuition, state resident: full-time $8912; part-time $446 per credit hour. Tuition, nonresident: full-time $21,393; part-time $992 per credit hour. *Required fees:* $390; $195 per semester. *Financial support:* Institutionally sponsored loans, scholarships/grants, and health care benefits available. Financial award application deadline: 3/1; financial award applicants required to submit FAFSA. *Faculty research:* Peninsular Spanish literature, Spanish-American literature, cultural studies, film studies, bilingualism. *Unit head:* Dr. Pascale Becel, Chair, 305-348-2851, Fax: 305-348-1085, E-mail: modlang@fiu.edu. *Application contact:* Nanett Rojas, Manager, Admissions Operations, 305-348-7464, Fax: 305-348-7441, E-mail: gradadm@fiu.edu.

Florida State University, The Graduate School, College of Arts and Sciences, Department of Modern Languages and Linguistics, Program in Spanish, Tallahassee, FL 32306. Offers MA, PhD. *Faculty:* 15 full-time (8 women), 1 (woman) part-time/adjunct. *Students:* 38 full-time (28 women), 1 (woman) part-time; includes 19 minority (2 Black or African American, non-Hispanic/Latino; 1 Asian, non-Hispanic/Latino; 3 Hispanic/Latino; 13 Two or more races, non-Hispanic/Latino). Average age 25. In 2017, 6 master's, 2 doctorates awarded. Terminal master's awarded for partial completion of doctoral program. *Degree requirements:* For master's, thesis optional; for doctorate, 2 foreign languages, thesis/dissertation. *Entrance requirements:* For master's and doctorate, GRE General Test, minimum GPA of 3.0. Additional exam requirements/recommendations for international students: Required—TOEFL (minimum score 550 paper-based; 80 iBT). *Application deadline:* For fall admission, 1/15 for domestic and international students. Applications are processed on a rolling basis. Application fee: $30. Electronic applications accepted. *Financial support:* In 2017–18, fellowships with partial tuition reimbursements (averaging $14,000 per year), research assistantships with partial tuition reimbursements (averaging $12,000 per year), 32 teaching assistantships with partial tuition reimbursements (averaging $17,000 per year) were awarded. Financial award application deadline: 1/15; financial award applicants required to submit FAFSA. *Faculty research:* Latin American theater, Hispanic literature of the United States, twentieth-century Latin American poetry, Spanish-American colonial. *Unit head:* Dr. Carolina Gonzalez, Divisional Coordinator/Professor, 850-644-3728, Fax: 850-644-0524, E-mail: cgonzalez3@fsu.edu. *Application contact:* Wendy E. Pigott, Graduate Academic Coordinator, 850-644-8397, Fax: 850-644-0524, E-mail: wpigott@fsu.edu.
Website: http://modlang.fsu.edu/Programs2/Spanish/Graduate-program-in-Spanish

George Mason University, College of Humanities and Social Sciences, Department of Modern and Classical Languages, Fairfax, VA 22030. Offers foreign languages (MA), including French, Spanish, Spanish and French, Spanish/bilingual-multicultural education. *Faculty:* 33 full-time (23 women), 38 part-time/adjunct (26 women). *Students:* 7 full-time (5 women), 17 part-time (11 women); includes 17 minority (3 Black or African American, non-Hispanic/Latino; 13 Hispanic/Latino; 1 Two or more races, non-Hispanic/Latino), 1 international. Average age 35. 12 applicants, 92% accepted, 6 enrolled. In 2017, 8 master's awarded. *Degree requirements:* For master's, one foreign language, thesis optional, take-home exit exam. *Entrance requirements:* For master's, goals statement, language proficiency statement. Additional exam requirements/recommendations for international students: Required—TOEFL (minimum score 575 paper-based; 88 iBT), IELTS (minimum score 6.5), PTE (minimum score 59). *Application deadline:* For fall admission, 4/15 for domestic students. Application fee: $75 ($80 for international students). Electronic applications accepted. *Expenses:* Tuition, state resident: full-time $11,228; part-time $459.50 per credit. Tuition, nonresident: full-time $30,932; part-time $1280.50 per credit. *Required fees:* $3252; $135.50 per credit. Part-time tuition and fees vary according to course load and program. *Financial support:* In 2017–18, 6 students received support, including 6 teaching assistantships with tuition reimbursements available (averaging $8,415 per year); career-related internships or fieldwork, Federal Work-Study, scholarships/grants, unspecified assistantships, and health care benefits (for full-time research or teaching assistantship recipients) also available. Support available to part-time students. Financial award application deadline: 3/1; financial award applicants required to submit FAFSA. *Faculty research:* Film and media studies; literary analysis, criticism, and theory; applied linguistics and pedagogy, sociolinguistics, interdisciplinary approaches. *Unit head:* Rei Berroa, Chair, 703-993-1220, Fax: 703-993-1245, E-mail: rberroa@gmu.edu. *Application contact:* Jen Barnard, Office Manager, 703-993-1230, Fax: 703-993-1245, E-mail: jbarnard@gmu.edu.
Website: http://mcl.gmu.edu/

Georgetown University, Graduate School of Arts and Sciences, Department of Spanish and Portuguese, Washington, DC 20057. Offers Spanish (MS, PhD), including Hispanic literature and cultural studies, Spanish linguistics, Spanish literature; MS/PhD. *Degree requirements:* For master's, one foreign language, research project; for doctorate, 3 foreign languages, thesis/dissertation. *Entrance requirements:* Additional exam requirements/recommendations for international students: Required—TOEFL.

Georgia Southern University, Jack N. Averitt College of Graduate Studies, College of Liberal Arts and Social Sciences, Program in Spanish, Statesboro, GA 30460. Offers MA. *Program availability:* Part-time, evening/weekend. *Faculty:* 14 full-time (6 women). *Students:* 12 full-time (10 women), 5 part-time (all women); includes 6 minority (4 Hispanic/Latino; 2 Two or more races, non-Hispanic/Latino), 2 international. Average age 29. 13 applicants, 85% accepted, 11 enrolled. In 2017, 8 master's awarded. *Degree requirements:* For master's, one foreign language, thesis optional. *Entrance requirements:* For master's, GRE, minimum GPA of 3.0, letters of reference. Additional exam requirements/recommendations for international students: Required—TOEFL (minimum score 550 paper-based; 80 iBT), IELTS (minimum score 6). *Application deadline:* For fall admission, 3/1 priority date for domestic and international students; for spring admission, 10/1 priority date for domestic students, 10/1 for international students. Applications are processed on a rolling basis. Application fee: $50. Electronic applications accepted. *Expenses:* Tuition, state resident: full-time $4986; part-time $3324 per year. Tuition, nonresident: full-time $21,982; part-time $15,352 per year. *Required fees:* $2092; $1802 per credit hour. $901 per semester. Tuition and fees vary according to course load, campus/location and program. *Financial support:* In 2017–18, 9 students received support, including 7 fellowships with full tuition reimbursements available (averaging $7,750 per year), 3 teaching assistantships with full tuition reimbursements available (averaging $7,750 per year); career-related internships or fieldwork, Federal Work-Study, scholarships/grants, tuition waivers (full), and unspecified assistantships also available. Support available to part-time students. Financial award application deadline: 4/15; financial award applicants required to submit FAFSA. *Faculty research:* Lettrism, twentieth-century France, Spanish medieval studies, Spanish Renaissance studies, Spanish-American colonial period, Mexican studies, Spanish linguistics, foreign language acquisition and education, drama and cinema of Spain and Latin America. *Unit head:* Dr. Eric Kartchner, Department Chair, 912-478-1381, Fax: 912-478-0652, E-mail: ekartchner@georgiasouthern.edu.
Website: http://class.georgiasouthern.edu/fl

Georgia State University, College of Arts and Sciences, Department of World Languages and Cultures, Program in Spanish, Atlanta, GA 30302-3083. Offers MA. *Entrance requirements:* For master's, GRE, statement of purpose, writing sample in the target language, 2 letters of recommendation, official transcripts. Additional exam requirements/recommendations for international students: Required—TOEFL (minimum score 79 iBT). Application fee: $50. Electronic applications accepted. *Expenses:* Tuition, state resident: full-time $7020. Tuition, nonresident: full-time $22,518. *Required fees:* $2128. Tuition and fees vary according to degree level and program. *Financial support:* Institutionally sponsored loans available. *Faculty research:* History and literature of colonial Latin America and the early modern Atlantic; contemporary Latin American poetry; interartistic and literary theory and culture; history of ideas in the Spanish Golden Age; interrelation between politics, cultural production in contemporary peninsular literature and film; second language acquisition; receptive skills as means to enhance language acquisition; acquisition of grammatical gender in Spanish as a foreign language. *Unit head:* Dr. Fernando Reati, Department Chair, 404-413-5984, Fax: 404-413-5982, E-mail: freati@gsu.edu. *Application contact:* Lita Malveaux, Administrative Academic Specialist, 404-413-5046, Fax: 404-413-5036, E-mail: lmalveaux@gsu.edu.
Website: http://www.gsu.edu/~wwwmcl/

Georgia State University, College of Arts and Sciences, Department of World Languages and Cultures, Program in Translation and Interpretation, Atlanta, GA 30302-3083. Offers interpretation (Certificate), including Spanish; translation (Certificate), including French, German, Spanish. *Program availability:* Part-time. *Entrance requirements:* For degree, entrance examination involving translating one passage from English to the target language and one passage from the target language to English, 3 letters of recommendation, resume/curriculum vitae, official transcripts. Additional exam requirements/recommendations for international students: Required—TOEFL (minimum score 79 iBT). Application fee: $50. Electronic applications accepted. *Expenses:* Tuition, state resident: full-time $7020. Tuition, nonresident: full-time $22,518. *Required fees:* $2128. Tuition and fees vary according to degree level and program. *Faculty research:* Romance linguistics and translation; theory and practice of translation; medical and legal interpretation. *Unit head:* Dr. Fernando Reati, Chair, 404-413-5984, Fax: 404-413-5982, E-mail: freati@gsu.edu. *Application contact:* Lita Malveaux, Administrative Academic Specialist, 404-413-5046, Fax: 404-413-5036, E-mail: lmalveaux@gsu.edu.
Website: http://wlc.gsu.edu/home/graduate/graduate-certificate/

Harvard University, Graduate School of Arts and Sciences, Department of Romance Languages and Literatures, Cambridge, MA 02138. Offers French (AM, PhD); Italian (AM, PhD); Portuguese (AM, PhD); Spanish (AM, PhD). Terminal master's awarded for partial completion of doctoral program. *Degree requirements:* For master's, 2 foreign languages; for doctorate, 2 foreign languages, thesis/dissertation. *Entrance requirements:* For master's and doctorate, GRE General Test, sample of written work. Additional exam requirements/recommendations for international students: Required—TOEFL.

Hofstra University, College of Liberal Arts and Sciences, Programs in Creative Writing and English Literature, Hempstead, NY 11549. Offers creative writing (MFA), including Spanish. *Program availability:* Part-time. *Students:* 8 full-time (4 women), 10 part-time (6 women); includes 3 minority (1 Asian, non-Hispanic/Latino; 2 Hispanic/Latino), 1 international. Average age 33. 14 applicants, 100% accepted, 4 enrolled. In 2017, 12 master's awarded. *Degree requirements:* For master's, thesis optional, minimum GPA of 3.0. *Entrance requirements:* For master's, writing sample, essay, minimum GPA of 3.0 in literature courses. Additional exam requirements/recommendations for international students: Required—TOEFL (minimum score 550 paper-based; 80 iBT). *Application deadline:* Applications are processed on a rolling basis. Application fee: $75. Electronic applications accepted. *Expenses: Tuition:* Full-time $1292. *Required fees:* $970. Tuition and fees vary according to program. *Financial support:* In 2017–18, 10 students received support, including 10 fellowships with full and partial tuition reimbursements available (averaging $4,338 per year); research assistantships with full and partial tuition reimbursements available, career-related internships or fieldwork, Federal Work-Study, institutionally sponsored loans, scholarships/grants, tuition waivers (full and partial), and unspecified assistantships also available. Support available to part-time students. Financial award applicants required to submit FAFSA. *Faculty research:* "The Penguin of Sonnets", Phillis Levin; "Lady Byron and Her Daughters", Julia Markus; "Gorgeous Lies", Martha McPhee; "This is the Place", Kelly McMasters; "Faces in the Crowd", Valeria Luiselli. *Unit head:* Dr. Craig Rustici, Chairperson, 516-463-5455, E-mail: craig.m.rustici@hofstra.edu. *Application contact:* Sunil Samuel, Assistant Vice President of Admissions, 516-463-4723, Fax: 516-463-4664, E-mail: graduateadmission@hofstra.edu.
Website: http://www.hofstra.edu/hclas

Hofstra University, School of Education, Programs in Teacher Education, Hempstead, NY 11549. Offers bilingual education (MA); bilingual extension (Advanced Certificate), including education/speech language pathology, intensive teacher institute; business education (MS Ed); curriculum studies (MS Ed); early childhood and childhood education (MS Ed); early childhood education (MA, MS Ed); educational technology (Advanced Certificate); elementary education (MA, MS Ed), including science, technology, engineering, and mathematics (STEM) (MA); English education (MS Ed); family and consumer science (MS Ed); fine arts and music education (Advanced Certificate); fine arts education (MS Ed); foreign language and TESOL (MS Ed); foreign language education (MA, MS Ed), including Arabic (MS Ed), biology, chemistry, Chinese (MS Ed), earth science, French, German, Italian (MS Ed), Mandarin (MS Ed), physics, Russian, Spanish; foundations of education (Advanced Certificate), including grades 5-6, grades 7-9; languages other than English and teaching English as a second language (MA); learning and teaching (Ed D), including applied linguistics, art education, arts and humanities, early childhood education, English education, human development, math education, math, science, and technology, multicultural education, physical education, science education, social studies education, special education; mathematics education (MA, MS Ed); music education (MA, MS Ed); science education (MA), including biology

(MA, MS Ed), chemistry (MA, MS Ed), earth science (MA, MS Ed), physics (MA, MS Ed); secondary education (Advanced Certificate); social studies education (MA, MS Ed); teaching languages other than English and TESOL (MS Ed); technology for learning (MA); TESOL (MS Ed, Advanced Certificate); TESOL with specialization in STEM (MA); work based learning extension (Advanced Certificate). *Program availability:* Part-time, evening/weekend, blended/hybrid learning. *Students:* 119 full-time (83 women), 124 part-time (90 women); includes 54 minority (15 Black or African American, non-Hispanic/Latino; 9 Asian, non-Hispanic/Latino; 29 Hispanic/Latino; 1 Native Hawaiian or other Pacific Islander, non-Hispanic/Latino), 12 international. Average age 29. 205 applicants, 88% accepted, 93 enrolled. In 2017, 103 master's, 4 doctorates, 32 other advanced degrees awarded. *Degree requirements:* For master's, comprehensive exam, thesis (for some programs), exit project, student teaching, fieldwork, electronic portfolio, curriculum project, minimum GPA of 3.0; for doctorate, thesis/dissertation; for Advanced Certificate, 3 foreign languages, comprehensive exam (for some programs), thesis project. *Entrance requirements:* For master's, GRE, 2 letters of recommendation, portfolio, teacher certification (MA), interview, essay; for doctorate, GMAT, GRE, LSAT, or MAT; for Advanced Certificate, 2 letters of recommendation, essay, interview and/or portfolio, teaching certificate. Additional exam requirements/recommendations for international students: Required—TOEFL (minimum score 550 paper-based; 80 iBT). *Application deadline:* Applications are processed on a rolling basis. Application fee: $75. Electronic applications accepted. *Expenses: Tuition:* Full-time $1292. *Required fees:* $970. Tuition and fees vary according to program. *Financial support:* In 2017–18, 112 students received support, including 56 fellowships with full and partial tuition reimbursements available (averaging $4,998 per year), 2 research assistantships with full and partial tuition reimbursements available (averaging $8,753 per year); career-related internships or fieldwork, Federal Work-Study, institutionally sponsored loans, scholarships/grants, traineeships, tuition waivers (full and partial), and unspecified assistantships also available. Support available to part-time students. Financial award applicants required to submit FAFSA. *Faculty research:* Educational interventions that foster critical-thinking skills; teachers' attitudes about professional development; threats to teacher quality. *Unit head:* Dr. Eustace Thompson, Chairperson, 516-463-5749, Fax: 516-463-6275, E-mail: eustace.g.thompson@hofstra.edu. *Application contact:* Sunil Samuel, Assistant Vice President of Admissions, 516-463-4723, Fax: 516-463-4664, E-mail: graduateadmission@hofstra.edu.
Website: http://www.hofstra.edu/education/

Houston Baptist University, School of Humanities, Program in Liberal Arts, Houston, TX 77074-3298. Offers education (EC-12 art, music, physical education, or Spanish) (MLA); education (EC-6 generalist) (MLA); general liberal arts (MLA); specialization in education (4-8 or 7-12) (MLA). *Program availability:* Part-time, evening/weekend. *Students:* 11 full-time (7 women), 13 part-time (9 women); includes 12 minority (5 Black or African American, non-Hispanic/Latino; 2 Asian, non-Hispanic/Latino; 5 Hispanic/Latino). Average age 31. 26 applicants, 73% accepted, 12 enrolled. In 2017, 15 master's awarded. *Entrance requirements:* For master's, minimum GPA of 2.5, essay/personal statement, resume, bachelor's degree transcript. Additional exam requirements/recommendations for international students: Required—TOEFL (minimum score 80 iBT), IELTS (minimum score 6.5). *Application deadline:* For fall admission, 8/1 for domestic students, 6/1 for international students; for spring admission, 1/1 for domestic students, 11/1 for international students; for summer admission, 5/1 for domestic students, 3/1 for international students. Applications are processed on a rolling basis. Application fee: $0 ($100 for international students). Electronic applications accepted. Application fee is waived when completed online. *Expenses:* $18,000 tuition; $4,500 fees (general, technology and parking). *Financial support:* In 2017–18, 12 students received support. Federal Work-Study and scholarships/grants available. Support available to part-time students. Financial award application deadline: 4/1; financial award applicants required to submit FAFSA. *Unit head:* Dr. Collin Garbarino, Graduate Programs Director, 281-649-3679, E-mail: cgarbarino@hbu.edu. *Application contact:* Kathy Holston, Administrative Assistant to the Dean, 281-649-3404, E-mail: kholston@hbu.edu.
Website: http://www.hbu.edu/mla

Howard University, Graduate School, Department of Modern Languages and Literatures, Washington, DC 20059-0002. Offers French (MA); Spanish (MA). *Program availability:* Part-time. *Degree requirements:* For master's, one foreign language, comprehensive exam, thesis. *Entrance requirements:* For master's, GRE General Test, writing samples in English and French or Spanish. *Faculty research:* African literature in French, Spanish linguistics, Spanish Peninsular literature, Spanish sociolinguistics.

Hunter College of the City University of New York, Graduate School, School of Arts and Sciences, Department of Romance Languages, Program in Spanish, New York, NY 10065-5085. Offers MA. *Program availability:* Part-time, evening/weekend. *Degree requirements:* For master's, 2 foreign languages, comprehensive exam, thesis optional. *Entrance requirements:* For master's, GRE General Test, GRE Subject Test, ability to read, speak, and write Spanish; interview. Additional exam requirements/recommendations for international students: Required—TOEFL. *Faculty research:* Galician studies, contemporary Spanish poetry, Lope de Vega, comparative Hispanic literatures, contemporary Hispanic poetry.

Illinois State University, Graduate School, College of Arts and Sciences, Department of Foreign Languages, Literatures and Cultures, Normal, IL 61790. Offers French (MA); French and German (MA); French and Spanish (MA); German (MA); German and Spanish (MA); Spanish (MA). *Degree requirements:* For master's, variable foreign language requirement, comprehensive exam, 1 term of residency. *Entrance requirements:* For master's, GRE General Test, minimum GPA of 2.8 in last 60 hours of course work.

Indiana State University, College of Graduate and Professional Studies, College of Arts and Sciences, Department of Languages, Literatures, and Linguistics, Terre Haute, IN 47809. Offers applied linguistics/teaching English as a second language (MA); language education (PhD); Spanish/teaching english as a second language (MA); TESL/TEFL (CAS). *Degree requirements:* For master's, comprehensive exam. Electronic applications accepted.

Indiana University Bloomington, University Graduate School, College of Arts and Sciences, Department of Spanish and Portuguese, Bloomington, IN 47405. Offers Portuguese (MA, PhD); Spanish (MA, PhD), including Hispanic linguistics, Hispanic literatures. *Degree requirements:* For master's, one foreign language, comprehensive exam, thesis (for Spanish); for doctorate, 2 foreign languages, comprehensive exam, thesis/dissertation. *Entrance requirements:* For master's, GRE General Test, bachelor's degree in Portuguese or Spanish, minimum GPA of 3.0; for doctorate, GRE General Test, master's degree in Portuguese or Spanish, minimum GPA of 3.0. Additional exam requirements/recommendations for international students: Required—TOEFL (minimum score 79 iBT). Electronic applications accepted. *Faculty research:* Spanish American literature, Spanish peninsular literature, Hispanic linguistics, Luso-Brazilian studies, Catalan studies.

Inter American University of Puerto Rico, Metropolitan Campus, Graduate Programs, Program in Spanish, San Juan, PR 00919-1293. Offers MA. *Program availability:* Part-time, evening/weekend. *Degree requirements:* For master's, one foreign language, comprehensive exam. *Entrance requirements:* For master's, GRE or

EXADEP, interview, minimum GPA of 2.5, 6 credits each of Spanish literature and Hispanic-American literature. Electronic applications accepted.

Inter American University of Puerto Rico, Metropolitan Campus, Graduate Programs, Program in Spanish Education, San Juan, PR 00919-1293. Offers MA.

Inter American University of Puerto Rico, Ponce Campus, Graduate School, Mercedita, PR 00715-1602. Offers accounting (MBA); biology (M Ed); chemistry (M Ed); criminal justice (MA); elementary education (M Ed); English as a Second Language (M Ed); finance (MBA); history (M Ed); human resources (MBA); marketing (MBA); mathematics (M Ed); Spanish (M Ed). *Entrance requirements:* For master's, minimum GPA of 2.5.

Iona College, School of Arts and Science, Department of Education, New Rochelle, NY 10801-1890. Offers adolescence education: biology (MS Ed, MST); adolescence education: English (MS Ed); adolescence education: mathematics (MST); adolescence education: social studies (MS Ed, MST); adolescence education: Spanish (MS Ed); adolescence special education 5-12 (MST); childhood and special education (MST); early childhood and childhood (MST); educational leadership (MS Ed). *Accreditation:* NCATE. *Program availability:* Part-time, evening/weekend. *Faculty:* 7 full-time (5 women), 2 part-time/adjunct (1 woman). *Students:* 23 full-time (18 women), 26 part-time (19 women); includes 12 minority (4 Black or African American, non-Hispanic/Latino; 8 Hispanic/Latino). Average age 26. 33 applicants, 97% accepted, 20 enrolled. In 2017, 31 master's awarded. *Degree requirements:* For master's, thesis or alternative. *Entrance requirements:* For master's, minimum GPA of 3.0, NY State teaching certificate and bachelor's degree (for MS Ed). Additional exam requirements/recommendations for international students: Required—TOEFL (minimum score 550 paper-based; 80 iBT), IELTS (minimum score 6.5). *Application deadline:* For fall admission, 8/1 priority date for domestic students, 5/1 priority date for international students; for spring admission, 1/1 priority date for domestic students, 9/1 priority date for international students. Applications are processed on a rolling basis. Electronic applications accepted. Tuition and fees vary according to program. *Financial support:* In 2017–18, 16 students received support. Unspecified assistantships available. Support available to part-time students. Financial award application deadline: 4/15; financial award applicants required to submit FAFSA. *Faculty research:* Engaging teacher educators in scientific process, cross-national comparisons of mathematics teaching, questioning strategies in the classroom, research methods, literacy development. *Unit head:* Margaret Smith, PhD, Chair, 914-633-2210, Fax: 914-633-2608, E-mail: msmith@iona.edu. *Application contact:* Richard McMahon, Coordinator, Graduate School of Education, 914-633-2552, E-mail: rmcmahon@iona.edu.
Website: http://www.iona.edu/Academics/School-of-Arts-Science/Departments/Education/Graduate-Programs.aspx

Johns Hopkins University, Zanvyl Krieger School of Arts and Sciences, Department of German and Romance Languages and Literatures, Baltimore, MD 21218. Offers German (MA, PhD); romance languages (PhD), including French, Italian, Spanish. *Faculty:* 49 full-time (30 women), 1 part-time/adjunct (0 women). *Students:* 55 full-time (31 women); includes 4 minority (3 Hispanic/Latino; 1 Two or more races, non-Hispanic/Latino), 24 international. Average age 29. 39 applicants, 46% accepted, 8 enrolled. In 2017, 2 master's, 10 doctorates awarded. Terminal master's awarded for partial completion of doctoral program. *Degree requirements:* For master's, comprehensive exam; for doctorate, 2 foreign languages, comprehensive exam, thesis/dissertation. *Entrance requirements:* For doctorate, GRE General Test. Additional exam requirements/recommendations for international students: Required—TOEFL (minimum score 600 paper-based; 100 iBT), IELTS. *Application deadline:* For fall admission, 1/15 for domestic and international students. Application fee: $75. Electronic applications accepted. *Expenses:* Contact institution. *Financial support:* In 2017–18, 80 students received support, including 12 fellowships with full tuition reimbursements available (averaging $29,000 per year), 21 teaching assistantships with full tuition reimbursements available (averaging $29,000 per year); research assistantships, institutionally sponsored loans, and health care benefits also available. *Faculty research:* Nineteenth-century French prose and poetry, genetic theory and criticism; twentieth-century Latin American literature and film; medieval and Renaissance Italian literature; gender and queer theory in German literature; the ideology of Baroque and neo-Baroque aesthetics. *Unit head:* Dr. Derek Schilling, Chair, 410-516-4626, Fax: 410-516-5358, E-mail: dschill4@jhu.edu. *Application contact:* Kathy Loehmer, Senior Academic Coordinator, 410-516-7226, Fax: 410-516-5358, E-mail: kathy.grll@jhu.edu.
Website: http://grll.jhu.edu/

Kansas State University, Graduate School, College of Arts and Sciences, Department of Modern Languages, Manhattan, KS 66506. Offers literature (MA), including French, German, Spanish; second language acquisition (MA), including French, German, Spanish, teaching English as a foreign language. *Program availability:* Part-time, evening/weekend, blended/hybrid learning. *Degree requirements:* For master's, thesis optional. *Entrance requirements:* For master's, teaching certificate. Additional exam requirements/recommendations for international students: Required—TOEFL (minimum score 550 paper-based; 83 iBT), TOEFL (minimum speaking-portion score of 26). Electronic applications accepted. *Faculty research:* Second language acquisitions; U.S. Latino literature; Francophone literature; German, French, Spanish, and Spanish-American literature from the Middle Ages to the modern era; teaching English as a foreign language; linguistics.

Kent State University, College of Arts and Sciences, Department of Modern and Classical Language Studies, Kent, OH 44242-0001. Offers French (MA), including applied linguistics and pedagogy, literature; German (MA), including applied linguistics and pedagogy, literature; Latin (MA), including applied linguistics and pedagogy, literature; Spanish (MA), including applied linguistics and pedagogy, literature; translation (MA), including Arabic, French, German, Japanese, Russian, Spanish; translation studies (PhD); MA/MBA. *Program availability:* Part-time. *Faculty:* 21 full-time (13 women), 5 part-time/adjunct (3 women). *Students:* 78 full-time (50 women), 20 part-time (13 women); includes 18 minority (3 Black or African American, non-Hispanic/Latino; 1 Asian, non-Hispanic/Latino; 9 Hispanic/Latino; 5 Two or more races, non-Hispanic/Latino), 44 international. Average age 31. 95 applicants, 55% accepted, 27 enrolled. In 2017, 30 master's awarded. *Degree requirements:* For master's, variable foreign language requirement, comprehensive exam (for some programs), thesis (for some programs); for doctorate, variable foreign language requirement, comprehensive exam, thesis/dissertation. *Entrance requirements:* For master's, transcripts, goal statement, 3 letters of recommendation, CD/MP3 with oral sample of first and second languages, writing sample of second language; for doctorate, transcripts; MA in translation, a foreign language, or similar field; proficiency in a foreign language; minimum GPA of 3.5 from MA; goal statement; 3 letters of recommendation; essay or writing sample. Additional exam requirements/recommendations for international students: Required—TOEFL (minimum score 550 paper-based, 79 iBT), Michigan English Language Assessment Battery (minimum score 77), IELTS (minimum score 6.5) or PTE (minimum score 58). *Application deadline:* For fall admission, 2/1 for domestic and international students. Applications are processed on a rolling basis. Application fee: $45 ($70 for international students). Electronic applications accepted. *Expenses:* Tuition, state resident: full-time $11,310; part-time $515 per credit hour. Tuition, nonresident: full-time $20,396; part-time $928 per credit hour. *International tuition:*

$18,544 full-time. *Financial support:* Fellowships with full tuition reimbursements, teaching assistantships with full tuition reimbursements, and unspecified assistantships available. Financial award application deadline: 2/1. *Unit head:* Dr. Keiran Dunne, Professor of French Translation/Chair, 330-672-2150, E-mail: kdunne@kent.edu. *Application contact:* Said Shiyab, Professor of Translation Studies/Graduate Coordinator, 330-672-1864, E-mail: sshiyab@kent.edu.
Website: http://www.kent.edu/mcls/

Lake Forest College, Graduate Program in Liberal Studies, Lake Forest, IL 60045. Offers American studies (MLS); cinema in East Asia (MLS); environmental studies (MLS); history (MLS); Medieval and Renaissance art (MLS); philosophy (MLS); Spanish (MLS); writing (MLS). *Program availability:* Part-time, evening/weekend. *Faculty:* 11 full-time (3 women). *Students:* 34 part-time (19 women); includes 3 minority (1 Asian, non-Hispanic/Latino; 2 Hispanic/Latino). Average age 36. 20 applicants, 55% accepted, 8 enrolled. In 2017, 5 master's awarded. *Degree requirements:* For master's, thesis optional, 8 courses, including at least 3 interdisciplinary seminars. *Entrance requirements:* For master's, transcript, essay, interview. Additional exam requirements/recommendations for international students: Required—TOEFL (minimum score 550 paper-based; 83 iBT); Recommended—IELTS (minimum score 6.5). *Application deadline:* For fall admission, 7/15 priority date for domestic students, 6/1 priority date for international students; for spring admission, 12/1 priority date for domestic students, 10/1 priority date for international students. Applications are processed on a rolling basis. Application fee: $30. Electronic applications accepted. *Expenses:* $2,650 per course. *Financial support:* In 2017–18, 2 students received support. Partial tuition grants (for full-time teachers) available. *Faculty research:* Religion in America, Asian philosophy, cinema studies, theater studies, sociology of religion. *Unit head:* Prof. D. L. LeMahieu, Director, 847-735-5133, Fax: 847-735-6291, E-mail: lemahieu@lakeforest.edu. *Application contact:* Prof. Carol Gayle, Associate Director, 847-735-5083, Fax: 847-735-6291, E-mail: gayle@lakeforest.edu.
Website: http://www.lakeforest.edu/academics/programs/mls/

Lake Forest College, Master of Arts in Teaching Program, Lake Forest, IL 60045. Offers elementary education (MAT); K-12 French (MAT); K-12 music (MAT); K-12 Spanish (MAT); K-12 visual art (MAT); secondary biology (MAT); secondary chemistry (MAT); secondary English (MAT); secondary history (MAT); secondary mathematics (MAT). *Degree requirements:* For master's, comprehensive exam, portfolio. *Entrance requirements:* For master's, GRE.

Lamar University, College of Graduate Studies, College of Arts and Sciences, Department of English and Modern Languages, Beaumont, TX 77701. Offers English (MA); teaching Spanish (MA). *Program availability:* Part-time, evening/weekend. *Faculty:* 30 full-time (18 women), 4 part-time/adjunct (3 women). *Students:* 9 full-time (7 women), 21 part-time (18 women); includes 17 minority (2 Black or African American, non-Hispanic/Latino; 15 Hispanic/Latino), 1 international. Average age 40. 18 applicants, 100% accepted, 10 enrolled. In 2017, 12 master's awarded. *Degree requirements:* For master's, one foreign language, thesis optional, practicum. *Entrance requirements:* For master's, GRE General Test, minimum GPA of 2.5 in last 60 hours of undergraduate course work. Additional exam requirements/recommendations for international students: Required—TOEFL (minimum score 550 paper-based; 79 iBT), IELTS (minimum score 6.5). *Application deadline:* For fall admission, 8/10 for domestic students, 7/1 for international students; for spring admission, 1/5 for domestic students, 12/1 for international students. Applications are processed on a rolling basis. Application fee: $25 ($50 for international students). Electronic applications accepted. *Expenses:* Contact institution. *Financial support:* In 2017–18, 4 teaching assistantships (averaging $8,000 per year) were awarded; career-related internships or fieldwork, Federal Work-Study, and institutionally sponsored loans also available. Support available to part-time students. Financial award application deadline: 4/1; financial award applicants required to submit FAFSA. *Faculty research:* British, Renaissance, nineteenth-century, and American literature; creative writing; modern literature; African-American literature. *Unit head:* Dr. Jim Sanderson, Chair, 409-880-8558, Fax: 409-880-8591. *Application contact:* Deidre Mayer, Interim Director, Admissions and Academic Services, 409-880-8888, Fax: 409-880-7419, E-mail: gradmissions@lamar.edu.
Website: http://artssciences.lamar.edu/english-and-modern-languages

Lee University, Program in Education, Cleveland, TN 37320-3450. Offers art (MAT); curriculum and instruction (M Ed, Ed S); early childhood (MAT); educational leadership (M Ed, Ed S); elementary education (MAT); English and math (MAT); English and science (MAT); English and social studies (MAT); higher education administration (MS); history (MAT); history and economics (MAT); math and science (MAT); math and social studies (MAT); middle grades (MAT); science and social studies (MASW); secondary education (MAT); Spanish (MAT); special education (M Ed, MAT); TESOL (MAT). *Accreditation:* NCATE. *Program availability:* Part-time. *Faculty:* 15 full-time (7 women), 8 part-time/adjunct (3 women). *Students:* 28 full-time (21 women), 77 part-time (48 women); includes 12 minority (7 Black or African American, non-Hispanic/Latino; 2 Hispanic/Latino; 3 Two or more races, non-Hispanic/Latino), 1 international. Average age 31. 35 applicants, 83% accepted, 22 enrolled. In 2017, 54 master's, 4 other advanced degrees awarded. *Degree requirements:* For master's, variable foreign language requirement, thesis optional, internship. *Entrance requirements:* For master's, MAT or GRE General Test, minimum undergraduate GPA of 2.75, 3 letters of recommendation, interview, writing sample, official transcripts, background check; for Ed S, minimum undergraduate and master's GPA of 2.75, official transcripts for undergraduate and master's degrees. Additional exam requirements/recommendations for international students: Required—TOEFL (minimum score 61 iBT). *Application deadline:* For fall admission, 6/1 priority date for domestic and international students; for spring admission, 11/1 priority date for domestic and international students; for summer admission, 4/1 priority date for domestic and international students. Applications are processed on a rolling basis. Application fee: $25. Electronic applications accepted. *Expenses: Tuition:* Full-time $12,780; part-time $710 per credit hour. *Required fees:* $60; $60 per term. Tuition and fees vary according to program. *Financial support:* In 2017–18, 32 students received support. Career-related internships or fieldwork, Federal Work-Study, institutionally sponsored loans, scholarships/grants, and unspecified assistantships available. Financial award application deadline: 3/1; financial award applicants required to submit FAFSA. *Unit head:* Dr. William Kamm, Director, 423-614-8544, E-mail: wkamm@leeuniversity.edu. *Application contact:* Crystal Keeter, Graduate Education Secretary, 423-614-8544, E-mail: ckeeter@leeuniversity.edu.
Website: http://www.leeuniversity.edu/academics/graduate/education

Lehman College of the City University of New York, School of Arts and Humanities, Department of Languages and Literatures, Bronx, NY 10468-1589. Offers Spanish (MA). *Program availability:* Part-time, evening/weekend. *Degree requirements:* For master's, one foreign language.

Loyola University Chicago, Graduate School, Department of Modern Languages and Literatures, Chicago, IL 60660. Offers Spanish (MA). *Program availability:* Part-time, evening/weekend. *Faculty:* 9 full-time (6 women). *Students:* 10 full-time (6 women), 3 part-time (all women); includes 6 minority (1 Asian, non-Hispanic/Latino; 5 Hispanic/Latino), 1 international. Average age 26. 12 applicants, 83% accepted, 4 enrolled. In 2017, 4 master's awarded. *Degree requirements:* For master's, one foreign language, comprehensive exam, thesis or alternative. *Entrance requirements:* Additional exam requirements/recommendations for international students: Required—TOEFL (minimum score 67 iBT), Oral Proficiency Interview in Spanish (for non-native speakers of Spanish). *Application deadline:* For fall admission, 2/10 for domestic students; for spring admission, 12/1 for domestic students. Application fee: $50. Tuition and fees vary according to course load, degree level and program. *Financial support:* In 2017–18, 6 students received support, including 3 teaching assistantships with full tuition reimbursements available (averaging $16,000 per year). Financial award application deadline: 2/1; financial award applicants required to submit FAFSA. *Faculty research:* Linguistics, Latin American contemporary narrative, Latin American culture and civilization, Hispanic women's studies, Twentieth Century peninsular writing, Golden Age, Don Quixote. *Unit head:* Dr. Susan Cavallo, Chair, 773-508-2870, E-mail: scavall@luc.edu.
Website: http://www.luc.edu/modernlang/

Manhattanville College, School of Education, Jump Start Program, Purchase, NY 10577-2132. Offers childhood education and special education (grades 1-6) (MPS); early childhood education (birth-grade 2) (MAT); education (Advanced Certificate); English and special education (grades 5-12) (MPS); mathematics and special education (grades 5-12) (MPS); science and special education (grades 5-12) (MPS); social studies and special education (grades 5-12) (MPS); Spanish (grades 7-12) (MAT); TESOL (all grades) (MPS). *Program availability:* Part-time, evening/weekend. *Faculty:* 10 full-time (7 women), 39 part-time/adjunct (27 women). *Students:* 3 full-time (2 women), 40 part-time (24 women); includes 11 minority (3 Black or African American, non-Hispanic/Latino; 6 Hispanic/Latino; 1 Native Hawaiian or other Pacific Islander, non-Hispanic/Latino; 1 Two or more races, non-Hispanic/Latino). Average age 33. 25 applicants, 60% accepted, 7 enrolled. In 2017, 17 master's, 2 other advanced degrees awarded. *Degree requirements:* For master's, comprehensive exam (for some programs), thesis (for some programs), student teaching, research seminars, portfolios, internships, writing assessment; for Advanced Certificate, comprehensive exam (for some programs). *Entrance requirements:* For master's, GRE or MAT (for programs leading to certification), minimum GPA of 3.0, 2 letters of recommendation, interview, essay (2-3 page personal statement that describes reasons for choosing teaching or educational leadership as profession and philosophy of education), proof of immunization (for those born after 1957). Additional exam requirements/recommendations for international students: Required—TOEFL (minimum score 600 paper-based; 110 iBT); Recommended—IELTS (minimum score 8). *Application deadline:* Applications are processed on a rolling basis. Application fee: $75. Electronic applications accepted. *Expenses:* $915 per credit. *Financial support:* Teaching assistantships, career-related internships or fieldwork, Federal Work-Study, institutionally sponsored loans, scholarships/grants, and unspecified assistantships available. Financial award application deadline: 3/15; financial award applicants required to submit FAFSA. *Faculty research:* Early childhood and technology, professional development schools and community schools, students with emotional difficulties, literacy and adolescents, mindfulness, changing suburbs institute, and community schools, studying the effects of the environment on special populations, the most difficult cases, students who are presented with multiple challenges: learning, behavioral and ACE experiences who see criminal behavior as a way to cope; working on giving them the tools they need to succeed. *Unit head:* Dr. Shelly Wepner, Dean, 914-323-3153, E-mail: shelly.wepner@mville.edu. *Application contact:* Alissa Wilson, Director, Graduate Admissions, 914-323-3150, Fax: 914-694-1732, E-mail: edschool@mville.edu.
Website: http://www.mville.edu/programs/jump-start

Manhattanville College, School of Education, Program in Teaching English to Speakers of Other Languages, Purchase, NY 10577-2132. Offers adult and international settings (MPS); bilingual education (childhood/Spanish) (Advanced Certificate); teaching English as a second language (all grades) (MPS, Certificate). *Program availability:* Part-time, evening/weekend. *Faculty:* 2 full-time (1 woman), 6 part-time/adjunct (4 women). *Students:* 5 full-time (all women), 22 part-time (17 women); includes 8 minority (1 Black or African American, non-Hispanic/Latino; 7 Hispanic/Latino). Average age 31. 9 applicants, 100% accepted, 8 enrolled. In 2017, 13 master's, 3 Advanced Certificates awarded. *Degree requirements:* For master's, comprehensive exam (for some programs), thesis (for some programs), student teaching, research seminars, portfolios, internships, writing assessment; for other advanced degree, comprehensive exam (for some programs). *Entrance requirements:* For master's, GRE or MAT (for programs leading to certification), minimum GPA of 3.0, 2 letters of recommendation, interview, essay (2-3 page personal statement that describes reasons for choosing teaching or educational leadership as profession and philosophy of education), proof of immunization (for those born after 1957). Additional exam requirements/recommendations for international students: Required—TOEFL (minimum score 600 paper-based; 110 iBT); Recommended—IELTS (minimum score 8). *Application deadline:* Applications are processed on a rolling basis. Application fee: $75. Electronic applications accepted. *Expenses:* $915 per credit. *Financial support:* Teaching assistantships, career-related internships or fieldwork, Federal Work-Study, institutionally sponsored loans, scholarships/grants, and unspecified assistantships available. Financial award application deadline: 3/15; financial award applicants required to submit FAFSA. *Faculty research:* Changing suburbs institute and community schools. *Unit head:* Dr. Shelly Wepner, Dean, 914-323-3153, Fax: 914-323-5493, E-mail: shelly.wepner@mville.edu. *Application contact:* Alissa Wilson, Director, Graduate Admissions, 914-323-3150, Fax: 914-694-1732, E-mail: edschool@mville.edu.
Website: http://www.mville.edu/programs/tesol-teaching-english-speakers-other-languages

Manhattanville College, School of Education, Program in Teaching of Languages Other than English, Purchase, NY 10577-2132. Offers adolescence education (grades 7-12) foreign language (MAT, Advanced Certificate), including French, Italian, Latin (Advanced Certificate), Latin (MAT), Spanish. *Program availability:* Part-time, evening/weekend. *Faculty:* 2 full-time (1 woman). *Students:* 3 part-time (2 women); includes 1 minority (Hispanic/Latino). Average age 31. In 2017, 4 master's, 1 other advanced degree awarded. *Degree requirements:* For master's, comprehensive exam (for some programs), thesis (for some programs), student teaching, research seminars, portfolios, internships, writing assessment; for Advanced Certificate, comprehensive exam (for some programs). *Entrance requirements:* For master's, GRE or MAT (for programs leading to certification), minimum GPA of 3.0, 2 letters of recommendation, interview, essay (2-3 page personal statement that describes reasons for choosing teaching or educational leadership as profession and philosophy of education), proof of immunization (for those born after 1957). Additional exam requirements/recommendations for international students: Required—TOEFL (minimum score 600 paper-based; 110 iBT); Recommended—IELTS (minimum score 8). *Application deadline:* Applications are processed on a rolling basis. Application fee: $75. Electronic applications accepted. *Expenses:* $915 per credit. *Financial support:* Teaching assistantships, career-related internships or fieldwork, Federal Work-Study, institutionally sponsored loans, scholarships/grants, and unspecified assistantships available. Financial award application deadline: 3/15; financial award applicants required to submit FAFSA. *Faculty research:* Changing suburbs institute and community schools. *Unit head:* Dr. Shelly Wepner, Dean, 914-323-3153, Fax: 914-323-5493. *Application contact:* Alissa Wilson, Director, Graduate Admissions, 914-323-3150, Fax: 914-694-

1732, E-mail: edschool@mville.edu.
Website: https://www.mville.edu/programs/teaching-languages-other-english

Marquette University, Graduate School, College of Arts and Sciences, Department of Foreign Languages and Literatures, Milwaukee, WI 53201-1881. Offers Spanish (MA). *Program availability:* Part-time, evening/weekend. *Degree requirements:* For master's, one foreign language, comprehensive exam. *Entrance requirements:* For master's, official transcripts from all current and previous colleges/universities except Marquette, three letters of recommendation, tape recording of foreign speaking voice. Additional exam requirements/recommendations for international students: Required—TOEFL. Electronic applications accepted. *Faculty research:* Latin American literature, Afro-Hispanic literature, descriptive Spanish linguistics, inter-American studies, foreign language education.

Michigan State University, The Graduate School, College of Arts and Letters, Department of Spanish and Portuguese, East Lansing, MI 48824. Offers applied Spanish linguistics (MA); Hispanic cultural studies (PhD); Hispanic literatures (MA). *Entrance requirements:* Additional exam requirements/recommendations for international students: Required—TOEFL. Electronic applications accepted.

Middlebury College, Language Schools, Spanish School, Middlebury, VT 05753-6002. Offers MA, DML. *Degree requirements:* For master's, one foreign language; for doctorate, 2 foreign languages, comprehensive exam, thesis/dissertation, residence abroad, teaching experience. *Entrance requirements:* For master's, online placement exam, 3 letters of recommendation, personal statement, transcripts, Spanish essay; for doctorate, 1st and 2nd language placement exams, 3 letters of recommendation, personal statement, transcripts, MA in Spanish. *Application deadline:* Applications are processed on a rolling basis. Application fee: $75. Electronic applications accepted. *Expenses:* Contact institution. *Financial support:* Fellowships and scholarships/grants available. Financial award application deadline: 3/8; financial award applicants required to submit FAFSA. *Unit head:* Dr. Jacobo Sefami, Director, 802-443-5539, Fax: 802-443-2075, E-mail: jsefami@middlebury.edu. *Application contact:* Audrey LaRock, Coordinator, 802-443-5539, Fax: 802-443-2075, E-mail: larock@middlebury.edu.
Website: http://www.middlebury.edu/ls/grad_programs/spanish

Middle Tennessee State University, College of Graduate Studies, College of Liberal Arts, Department of Foreign Languages and Literatures, Murfreesboro, TN 37132. Offers foreign languages (MAT), including French, German, Spanish. *Program availability:* Part-time, evening/weekend, online learning. *Degree requirements:* For master's, one foreign language, comprehensive exam, thesis optional. *Entrance requirements:* For master's, GRE. Additional exam requirements/recommendations for international students: Required—TOEFL (minimum score 525 paper-based; 71 iBT) or IELTS (minimum score 6). Electronic applications accepted.

Millersville University of Pennsylvania, College of Graduate Studies and Adult Learning, College of Arts, Humanities and Social Sciences, Department of Foreign Languages, Program in Languages and Cultures: Spanish Option, Millersville, PA 17551-0302. Offers MA. *Program availability:* Part-time. *Faculty:* 3 full-time (1 woman). *Students:* 9 part-time (6 women); includes 3 minority (all Hispanic/Latino). Average age 33. 2 applicants, 100% accepted, 1 enrolled. *Degree requirements:* For master's, one foreign language, comprehensive exam (for some programs), thesis optional, exam, portfolio, or research project and presentation. *Entrance requirements:* For master's, ACTFL, OPI, OPIc and WPT, baccalaureate degree from regionally-accredited four-year college or university, 24 undergraduate credits in selected language. Additional exam requirements/recommendations for international students: Required—TOEFL (minimum score 80 iBT), IELTS (minimum score 6.5), PTE (minimum score 60). *Application deadline:* Applications are processed on a rolling basis. Application fee: $40. Electronic applications accepted. *Expenses:* $500 per credit resident tuition and fees; $750 per credit non-resident tuition and fees; $114.75 per credit general fee (maximum of 12 credits); technology fee $27 per credit (resident), $39 per credit (non-resident). *Financial support:* Unspecified assistantships available. Financial award application deadline: 3/15; financial award applicants required to submit FAFSA. *Faculty research:* 20th century Spanish and Latin American poetry, comparative poetry (Spanish and American), contemporary Spanish literature, Spanish medieval literature, Spanish sociolinguistics and phonological variation. *Unit head:* Dr. Marco A. Antolin, Associate Professor/Program Contact, 717-871-7150, Fax: 717-871-7935, E-mail: marco.antolin@millersville.edu. *Application contact:* Dr. Victor S. DeSantis, Dean of College of Graduate Studies and Adult Learning/Associate Provost for Civic and Community Engagement, 717-871-7619, Fax: 717-871-7954, E-mail: victor.desantis@millersville.edu.
Website: http://www.millersville.edu/forlang/

Minnesota State University Mankato, College of Graduate Studies and Research, College of Arts and Humanities, Department of World Languages and Cultures, Program in Spanish, Mankato, MN 56001. Offers Spanish (MS); Spanish education (MS); Spanish for the professions (MS). *Degree requirements:* For master's, one foreign language, comprehensive exam, thesis. *Entrance requirements:* For master's, minimum GPA of 3.0 during previous 2 years. Electronic applications accepted.

Montclair State University, The Graduate School, College of Education and Human Services, MAT Program in Teaching, Montclair, NJ 07043-1624. Offers art (MAT); biology (MAT); chemistry (MAT); earth science (MAT); English (MAT); French (MAT); health and physical education (MAT); health education (MAT); mathematics (MAT); music (MAT); physical education (MAT); physical science (MAT); social studies (MAT); Spanish (MAT); teacher of English as a second language (MAT). *Degree requirements:* For master's, comprehensive exam, thesis or alternative. *Entrance requirements:* For master's, interview, 2 letters of recommendation. Additional exam requirements/recommendations for international students: Required—TOEFL (minimum score 83 iBT), IELTS (minimum score 6.5). Electronic applications accepted.

Montclair State University, The Graduate School, College of Humanities and Social Sciences, Program in Spanish, Montclair, NJ 07043-1624. Offers MA. *Program availability:* Part-time, evening/weekend. *Degree requirements:* For master's, comprehensive exam, thesis or alternative. *Entrance requirements:* For master's, GRE General Test, 2 letters of recommendation, essay. Additional exam requirements/recommendations for international students: Required—TOEFL (minimum score 83 iBT), IELTS (minimum score 6.5). Electronic applications accepted. *Faculty research:* Contemporary Spanish novel, Spanish poetry of the twentieth century, Golden Age drama, contemporary Spanish film, contemporary Latin American novel, nineteenth-century Latin American literature.

New Mexico State University, College of Arts and Sciences, Department of Languages and Linguistics, Las Cruces, NM 88003. Offers Spanish (MA). *Program availability:* Part-time, 100% online. *Faculty:* 11 full-time (5 women). *Students:* 11 full-time (4 women), 62 part-time (47 women); includes 40 minority (39 Hispanic/Latino; 1 Two or more races, non-Hispanic/Latino), 7 international. Average age 38. 27 applicants, 81% accepted, 14 enrolled. In 2017, 25 master's awarded. *Entrance requirements:* For master's, sample of written work in Spanish, 3 letters of reference, language evaluation form (or OPI score), letter of intent. Additional exam requirements/recommendations for international students: Required—TOEFL (minimum score 550 paper-based; 79 iBT), IELTS (minimum score 6.5). *Application deadline:* For fall admission, 1/15 for domestic students; for spring admission, 9/15 for domestic students. Applications are processed on a rolling basis. Application fee: $40 ($50 for international students). Electronic applications accepted. *Expenses:* Tuition, state resident: full-time $4390. Tuition, nonresident: full-time $15,309. *Required fees:* $853. *Financial support:* In 2017–18, 14 students received support, including 10 teaching assistantships (averaging $16,964 per year); career-related internships or fieldwork, Federal Work-Study, institutionally sponsored loans, scholarships/grants, traineeships, health care benefits, and unspecified assistantships also available. Support available to part-time students. Financial award application deadline: 3/1. *Faculty research:* Spanish-American literature, U.S. Hispanic and Chicano literature and border culture, Hispanic linguistics, bilingualism, language contact, sociolinguistics, Mexican literature. *Total annual research expenditures:* $3,439. *Unit head:* Dr. Glenn Fetzer, Department Head, 575-646-3408, E-mail: gwfetzer@nmsu.edu. *Application contact:* Dr. Jeff Longwell, Graduate Program Director, 575-646-2726, E-mail: jelongwe@nmsu.edu.
Website: http://www.nmsu.edu/~langling/

New Mexico State University, College of Education, Department of Curriculum and Instruction, Las Cruces, NM 88003. Offers bilingual education (MA); curriculum and instruction (MA, Ed D, PhD); early childhood education (MA); educational diagnostics (Ed S); language, literacy and culture (MA); learning design and technologies (MA); teaching (MAT), including dance, Spanish; teaching English to speakers of other languages (MA). *Accreditation:* NCATE. *Program availability:* Part-time, evening/weekend, 100% online. *Faculty:* 22 full-time (17 women), 7 part-time/adjunct (2 women). *Students:* 113 full-time (79 women), 194 part-time (138 women); includes 171 minority (15 Black or African American, non-Hispanic/Latino; 3 American Indian or Alaska Native, non-Hispanic/Latino; 4 Asian, non-Hispanic/Latino; 142 Hispanic/Latino; 7 Two or more races, non-Hispanic/Latino), 37 international. Average age 36. 106 applicants, 80% accepted, 56 enrolled. In 2017, 82 master's, 15 doctorates, 1 other advanced degree awarded. *Entrance requirements:* For master's, minimum cumulative GPA of 3.0; for doctorate, portfolio, minimum cumulative GPA of 3.0. Additional exam requirements/recommendations for international students: Required—TOEFL (minimum score 550 paper-based; 79 iBT), IELTS (minimum score 6.5). *Application deadline:* For fall admission, 12/15 priority date for domestic and international students; for spring admission, 11/1 for domestic students. Applications are processed on a rolling basis. Application fee: $40 ($50 for international students). Electronic applications accepted. *Expenses:* Tuition, state resident: full-time $4390. Tuition, nonresident: full-time $15,309. *Required fees:* $853. *Financial support:* In 2017–18, 97 students received support, including 2 fellowships (averaging $4,390 per year), 1 research assistantship (averaging $17,368 per year), 10 teaching assistantships (averaging $17,489 per year); career-related internships or fieldwork, Federal Work-Study, scholarships/grants, traineeships, health care benefits, and unspecified assistantships also available. Support available to part-time students. Financial award application deadline: 3/1. *Faculty research:* STEM education, bilingual and English as a second language education, critical pedagogy/multicultural education, learning design and technology, early childhood education. *Total annual research expenditures:* $13,518. *Unit head:* Dr. David Rutledge, Department Head, 575-646-5411, Fax: 575-646-5436, E-mail: rutledge@nmsu.edu. *Application contact:* Dr. David Rutledge, Associate Department Head for Graduate Programs, 575-646-5411, Fax: 575-646-5436, E-mail: rutledge@nmsu.edu.
Website: http://tpal.nmsu.edu/

New York University, Graduate School of Arts and Science, Department of Spanish and Portuguese Languages and Literatures, New York, NY 10012-1019. Offers Portuguese (MA, PhD); Spanish (PhD); Spanish and Latin American literatures and cultures (MA); Spanish language and translation (MA). *Program availability:* Part-time. *Students:* Average age 32. 157 applicants, 43% accepted, 33 enrolled. In 2017, 29 master's, 5 doctorates awarded. *Degree requirements:* For master's, 2 foreign languages, thesis; for doctorate, 2 foreign languages, thesis/dissertation. *Entrance requirements:* For master's, GRE General Test; for doctorate, GRE General Test, master's degree. Additional exam requirements/recommendations for international students: Required—TOEFL. *Application deadline:* For fall admission, 1/4 priority date for domestic students, 1/4 for international students. Application fee: $100. *Expenses: Tuition:* Full-time $41,352; part-time $19,968 per year. *Required fees:* $2496; $1628 per unit. $814 per term. Tuition and fees vary according to course load and program. *Financial support:* Fellowships, teaching assistantships, career-related internships or fieldwork, Federal Work-Study, institutionally sponsored loans, scholarships/grants, health care benefits, and unspecified assistantships available. Financial award application deadline: 1/4; financial award applicants required to submit FAFSA. *Faculty research:* Gender and sexuality, transatlantic studies, literacy and cultural theories, Colonial and Post-Colonial studies, autobiography and modern subjectivities. *Unit head:* Gigi Dopico-Black, Chair, 212-998-8770, Fax: 212-995-4149, E-mail: spanish.portuguese.info@nyu.edu. *Application contact:* James Fernandez, Director of Graduate Studies, 212-998-8770, Fax: 212-995-4149, E-mail: spanish.portuguese.info@nyu.edu.
Website: http://spanish.as.nyu.edu/

New York University, Steinhardt School of Culture, Education, and Human Development, Department of Teaching and Learning, Program in Multilingual/Multicultural Studies, New York, NY 10012. Offers bilingual education (MA, PhD, Advanced Certificate); foreign language education (MA); teaching English to speakers of other languages (MA, PhD); teaching foreign languages, 7-12 (MA), including Chinese, French, Italian, Japanese, Spanish; teaching French as a foreign language (MA), including teaching English to speakers of other languages; teaching Spanish as a foreign language (MA), including teaching English to speakers of other languages. MA in teaching English to speakers of other languages also offered in collaboration with NYU Shanghai. *Accreditation:* TEAC. *Program availability:* Part-time, evening/weekend. *Students:* Average age 29. 431 applicants, 61% accepted, 92 enrolled. In 2017, 121 master's, 1 doctorate, 2 other advanced degrees awarded. *Entrance requirements:* For doctorate, GRE General Test, interview; for Advanced Certificate, master's degree. Additional exam requirements/recommendations for international students: Required—TOEFL (minimum score 100 iBT). *Application deadline:* For fall admission, 12/1 priority date for domestic and international students; for spring admission, 10/1 for domestic and international students. Applications are processed on a rolling basis. Application fee: $75. Electronic applications accepted. *Expenses: Tuition:* Full-time $41,352; part-time $19,968 per year. *Required fees:* $2496; $1628 per unit. $814 per term. Tuition and fees vary according to course load and program. *Financial support:* Fellowships with full and partial tuition reimbursements, career-related internships or fieldwork, Federal Work-Study, institutionally sponsored loans, scholarships/grants, and tuition waivers (partial) available. Support available to part-time students. Financial award application deadline: 2/1; financial award applicants required to submit FAFSA. *Faculty research:* Second language acquisition, cross-cultural communication, technology-enhanced language learning, language variation, action learning. *Unit head:* Prof. Shondel Nero, Director, 212-998-5757, E-mail: shondel.nero@nyu.edu. *Application contact:* 212-998-5030, Fax: 212-995-4328, E-mail: steinhardt.gradadmissions@nyu.edu.
Website: http://steinhardt.nyu.edu/teachlearn/mms

North Carolina State University, Graduate School, College of Humanities and Social Sciences, Department of Foreign Languages and Literatures, Program in Spanish

Language and Literature, Raleigh, NC 27695. Offers MA. *Degree requirements:* For master's, thesis optional. *Entrance requirements:* For master's, fluency in Spanish. Electronic applications accepted. *Faculty research:* Applied linguistics, technology-assisted language instruction, Latin-American literature and culture, 20th and 21st Century Spanish narrative and film, children's literature.

Northern Arizona University, College of Arts and Letters, Department of Global Languages and Cultures, Flagstaff, AZ 86011. Offers Spanish (MAT); Spanish education (MAT). *Program availability:* Part-time. *Faculty:* 33 full-time (21 women), 2 part-time/adjunct (both women). *Students:* 20 full-time (11 women), 2 part-time (1 woman); includes 10 minority (9 Hispanic/Latino; 1 Two or more races, non-Hispanic/Latino), 4 international. Average age 30. 15 applicants, 73% accepted, 11 enrolled. In 2017, 7 master's awarded. *Degree requirements:* For master's, variable foreign language requirement, comprehensive exam (for some programs), thesis (for some programs). *Entrance requirements:* Additional exam requirements/recommendations for international students: Required—TOEFL (minimum score 80 iBT), IELTS (minimum score 7). *Application deadline:* For fall admission, 3/1 for domestic and international students; for spring admission, 10/1 for domestic and international students. Applications are processed on a rolling basis. Application fee: $65. Electronic applications accepted. *Expenses:* Tuition, state resident: full-time $9240; part-time $458 per credit hour. Tuition, nonresident: full-time $21,588; part-time $1199 per credit hour. *Required fees:* $1021; $14 per credit hour. $646 per semester. Tuition and fees vary according to course load, campus/location and program. *Financial support:* In 2017–18, 21 students received support, including 21 teaching assistantships with full and partial tuition reimbursements available (averaging $13,500 per year); institutionally sponsored loans, health care benefits, tuition waivers (full and partial), and unspecified assistantships also available. Financial award application deadline: 2/1; financial award applicants required to submit FAFSA. *Unit head:* Dr. Patricia Frederick, Chair, 928-523-9437, E-mail: patricia.frederick@nau.edu. *Application contact:* Alexandria McConocha, Administrative Associate, 928-523-6237, Fax: 928-523-0963, E-mail: alexandria.mcconocha@nau.edu.
Website: https://nau.edu/cal/modern-languages/

Northern Illinois University, Graduate School, College of Liberal Arts and Sciences, Department of Foreign Languages and Literatures, De Kalb, IL 60115-2854. Offers French (MA); Spanish (MA). *Program availability:* Part-time. *Faculty:* 25 full-time (11 women). *Students:* 5 full-time (2 women), 12 part-time (8 women); includes 11 minority (1 Black or African American, non-Hispanic/Latino; 10 Hispanic/Latino). Average age 32. 8 applicants, 88% accepted, 5 enrolled. In 2017, 2 master's awarded. *Degree requirements:* For master's, one foreign language, comprehensive exam, thesis or alternative, language proficiency exam. *Entrance requirements:* For master's, GRE General Test, interview, minimum GPA of 2.75, undergraduate major in French or Spanish. Additional exam requirements/recommendations for international students: Required—TOEFL (minimum score 550 paper-based). *Application deadline:* For fall admission, 6/1 for domestic students, 5/1 for international students; for spring admission, 11/1 for domestic students, 10/1 for international students. Applications are processed on a rolling basis. Application fee: $40. Electronic applications accepted. *Financial support:* In 2017–18, 7 teaching assistantships with full tuition reimbursements were awarded; fellowships with full tuition reimbursements, research assistantships with full tuition reimbursements, career-related internships or fieldwork, Federal Work-Study, scholarships/grants, tuition waivers (full), and unspecified assistantships also available. Support available to part-time students. Financial award applicants required to submit FAFSA. *Faculty research:* Francophone women writers, prosodies of French and Italian, early Spanish drama, business German, history of Burmese literature. *Unit head:* Dr. Katharina Barbe, Chair, 815-753-1559, Fax: 815-753-5989, E-mail: kbarbe@niu.edu. *Application contact:* Graduate School Office, 815-753-0395, E-mail: gradsch@niu.edu.
Website: http://www.forlangs.net/

Northwestern University, The Graduate School, Judd A. and Marjorie Weinberg College of Arts and Sciences, Department of Spanish and Portuguese, Evanston, IL 60208. Offers PhD.

The Ohio State University, Graduate School, College of Arts and Sciences, Division of Arts and Humanities, Department of Spanish and Portuguese, Columbus, OH 43210. Offers MA, PhD. *Faculty:* 26. *Students:* 60 (35 women); includes 10 minority (all Hispanic/Latino), 27 international. Average age 31. In 2017, 11 master's, 6 doctorates awarded. Terminal master's awarded for partial completion of doctoral program. *Entrance requirements:* For master's and doctorate, GRE General Test, sample of academic writing. Additional exam requirements/recommendations for international students: Required—TOEFL (minimum score 550 paper-based; 79 iBT), Michigan English Language Assessment Battery (minimum score 82); Recommended—IELTS (minimum score 7). *Application deadline:* For fall admission, 12/13 priority date for domestic students, 11/30 priority date for international students; for spring admission, 3/1 for domestic students, 2/1 for international students. Applications are processed on a rolling basis. Application fee: $60 ($70 for international students). Electronic applications accepted. *Financial support:* Fellowships, research assistantships, teaching assistantships, Federal Work-Study, institutionally sponsored loans, and unspecified assistantships available. Support available to part-time students. *Unit head:* Dr. Laura Podalsky, Chair, 614-688-3662, E-mail: spanport@osu.edu. *Application contact:* Graduate and Professional Admissions, 614-292-9444, Fax: 614-292-3895, E-mail: gpadmissions@osu.edu.
Website: http://sppo.osu.edu/

Ohio University, Graduate College, College of Arts and Sciences, Department of Modern Languages, Athens, OH 45701-2979. Offers French (MA); Spanish (MA). *Program availability:* Part-time. *Degree requirements:* For master's, 2 foreign languages, comprehensive exam, thesis optional. *Entrance requirements:* For master's, oral and written samples. Additional exam requirements/recommendations for international students: Required—TOEFL (minimum score 550 paper-based; 80 iBT) or IELTS (minimum score 6.5). Electronic applications accepted. *Faculty research:* French and Spanish language and literature.

Penn State University Park, Graduate School, College of the Liberal Arts, Department of Spanish, Italian, and Portuguese, University Park, PA 16802. Offers Spanish (MA, PhD). *Unit head:* Dr. Susan Welch, Dean, 814-865-7691, Fax: 814-863-2085. *Application contact:* Lori Hawn, Director, Graduate Student Services, 814-865-1795, Fax: 814-863-4627, E-mail: l-gswww@lists.psu.edu.
Website: http://sip.la.psu.edu/

Pontifical Catholic University of Puerto Rico, College of Arts and Humanities, Department of Hispanic Studies, Ponce, PR 00717-0777. Offers grammar and writing (Professional Certificate); Hispanic studies (MA). *Program availability:* Part-time, evening/weekend. *Degree requirements:* For master's, variable foreign language requirement, comprehensive exam, thesis or alternative. *Entrance requirements:* For master's, GRE General Test, 2 letters of recommendation, interview, minimum GPA of 2.75. Electronic applications accepted.

Portland State University, Graduate Studies, College of Liberal Arts and Sciences, Department of World Languages and Literatures, Portland, OR 97207-0751. Offers French (MA); German (MA); Japanese (MA); Spanish (MA); world literature and language (MA). *Program availability:* Part-time. *Faculty:* 61 full-time (37 women), 26 part-time/adjunct (20 women). *Students:* 22 full-time (13 women), 11 part-time (5 women); includes 7 minority (1 Asian, non-Hispanic/Latino; 6 Hispanic/Latino), 8 international. Average age 30. 26 applicants, 73% accepted, 16 enrolled. In 2017, 9 master's awarded. *Degree requirements:* For master's, variable foreign language requirement, thesis (for some programs). *Entrance requirements:* For master's, ACTFL, BA in the major language, minimum GPA of 3.0 in all coursework. Additional exam requirements/recommendations for international students: Required—TOEFL (minimum score 550 paper-based; 80 iBT), IELTS (minimum score 6.5). *Application deadline:* For fall admission, 4/1 for domestic students, 3/1 for international students; for winter admission, 9/1 for domestic students, 7/1 for international students; for spring admission, 11/1 for domestic and international students. Applications are processed on a rolling basis. Application fee: $65. *Expenses:* Tuition, state resident: full-time $14,436; part-time $401 per credit. Tuition, nonresident: full-time $21,780; part-time $605 per credit. *Required fees:* $1380; $22 per credit. $119 per quarter. One-time fee: $325. Tuition and fees vary according to program. *Financial support:* In 2017–18, 22 teaching assistantships with full and partial tuition reimbursements (averaging $11,431 per year) were awarded; research assistantships, Federal Work-Study, scholarships/grants, and unspecified assistantships also available. Support available to part-time students. Financial award application deadline: 3/1; financial award applicants required to submit FAFSA. *Faculty research:* Foreign language pedagogy, applied and social linguistics, literary history and criticism. *Total annual research expenditures:* $522,357. *Unit head:* Dr. Gina Greco, Chair, 503-725-5287, E-mail: grecog@pdx.edu. *Application contact:* Kelli Martin, Graduate Admissions Coordinator, 503-725-3243, E-mail: kmarti@pdx.edu.
Website: http://www.pdx.edu/wll/

Princeton University, Graduate School, Department of Spanish and Portuguese, Princeton, NJ 08544-1019. Offers PhD. *Degree requirements:* For doctorate, variable foreign language requirement, thesis/dissertation. *Entrance requirements:* For doctorate, GRE General Test, sample of written work. Additional exam requirements/recommendations for international students: Required—TOEFL (minimum score 600 paper-based). Electronic applications accepted.

Purdue University, Graduate School, College of Liberal Arts, School of Languages and Cultures, West Lafayette, IN 47907. Offers French (MA, MAT, PhD), including French (MA, PhD), French education (MAT); German (MA, MAT, PhD), including German (MA, PhD), German education (MAT); Japanese pedagogy (MA); Spanish (MA, MAT, PhD), including Spanish (MA, PhD), Spanish education (MAT). *Faculty:* 44 full-time (22 women), 1 (woman) part-time/adjunct. *Students:* 37 full-time (18 women), 41 part-time (30 women); includes 9 minority (1 Asian, non-Hispanic/Latino; 8 Hispanic/Latino), 52 international. Average age 32. 49 applicants, 39% accepted, 14 enrolled. In 2017, 11 master's, 5 doctorates awarded. Terminal master's awarded for partial completion of doctoral program. *Degree requirements:* For master's, one foreign language; for doctorate, 2 foreign languages, thesis/dissertation. *Entrance requirements:* For master's, GRE General Test (minimum score 600, 160 for new scoring), two writing samples, one in English, one in language (French, German, Japanese, or Spanish); sample recording of English and language of study; for doctorate, GRE General Test (minimum score 600, 160 for new scoring), master's degree with minimum GPA of 3.5 or equivalent; two writing samples, one in English, one in language (French, German, Japanese, or Spanish); sample recording of English and language of study. Additional exam requirements/recommendations for international students: Required—TOEFL (minimum score 550 paper-based; 77 iBT); Recommended—TWE. *Application deadline:* For fall admission, 12/12 for domestic and international students; for spring admission, 10/1 for domestic and international students. Applications are processed on a rolling basis. Application fee: $60 ($75 for international students). Electronic applications accepted. *Financial support:* In 2017–18, fellowships with tuition reimbursements (averaging $15,750 per year), teaching assistantships with tuition reimbursements (averaging $13,463 per year) were awarded. Support available to part-time students. Financial award applicants required to submit FAFSA. *Faculty research:* Linguistics, semiotics, literary criticism, pedagogy. *Unit head:* Jennifer M. William, Head, 765-494-3834, E-mail: jmwilliam@purdue.edu. *Application contact:* Joni L. Hipsher, Graduate Contact, 765-494-3841, E-mail: jlhipshe@purdue.edu.
Website: http://www.cla.purdue.edu/slc/main/

Queens College of the City University of New York, Arts and Humanities Division, Department of Hispanic Languages and Literatures, Queens, NY 11367-1597. Offers Spanish (MA). *Program availability:* Part-time. *Students:* 9 part-time (7 women); includes 8 minority (all Hispanic/Latino). Average age 47. *Degree requirements:* For master's, 3 foreign languages. *Entrance requirements:* For master's, minimum GPA of 3.0. Additional exam requirements/recommendations for international students: Required—TOEFL (minimum score 61 iBT), IELTS (minimum score 5). *Application deadline:* For fall admission, 4/1 for domestic students; for spring admission, 11/1 for domestic students. Applications are processed on a rolling basis. Application fee: $125. Electronic applications accepted. *Financial support:* Career-related internships or fieldwork available. Financial award application deadline: 4/1; financial award applicants required to submit FAFSA. *Unit head:* Dr. Jose Martinez-Torrejon, Chair, 718-997-5660, E-mail: jose.martinez-torrejon@qc.cuny.edu. *Application contact:* Elizabeth D'Amico-Ramirez, Assistant Director of Graduate Admissions, 718-997-5203, E-mail: elizabeth.damicoramirez@qc.cuny.edu.

Queen's University at Kingston, School of Graduate Studies, Faculty of Arts and Sciences, Department of Spanish and Italian, Kingston, ON K7L 3N6, Canada. Offers Spanish language and literature (MA). *Program availability:* Part-time. *Degree requirements:* For master's, one foreign language, thesis. *Entrance requirements:* Additional exam requirements/recommendations for international students: Required—TOEFL. Electronic applications accepted. *Faculty research:* Golden Age, nineteenth- and twentieth-century Peninsular novel, literary theory, colonial Latin America, nineteenth-and-twentieth century Latin America.

Rider University, College of Education and Human Services, Teacher Certification Program, Lawrenceville, NJ 08648-3001. Offers bilingual education (Certificate); business education (Certificate); early childhood education (Certificate); elementary education (Certificate); English as a second language (Certificate); English education (Certificate); mathematics education (Certificate); science education (Certificate); secondary education (Certificate); social studies education (Certificate); world languages (Certificate), including French, German, Spanish. *Program availability:* Part-time, online learning. *Degree requirements:* For Certificate, internship, professional portfolio. *Entrance requirements:* For degree, PRAXIS, resume. Additional exam requirements/recommendations for international students: Required—TOEFL (minimum score 550 paper-based). Electronic applications accepted. *Faculty research:* Conceptual foundations for optimal development of creativity; creative theory, cognitive processes in mathematics learning, teacher collaboration.

Rutgers University–New Brunswick, Graduate School-New Brunswick, Program in Spanish, Piscataway, NJ 08854-8097. Offers bilingualism and second language acquisition (MA, PhD); Spanish (MA, MAT, PhD); Spanish literature (MA, PhD); translation (MA). *Program availability:* Part-time. *Degree requirements:* For master's, comprehensive exam (for some programs), thesis (for some programs); for doctorate, 2

foreign languages, comprehensive exam, thesis/dissertation. *Entrance requirements:* For master's and doctorate, GRE General Test. Additional exam requirements/recommendations for international students: Required—TOEFL. Electronic applications accepted. *Faculty research:* Hispanic literature, Luso-Brazilian literature, Spanish linguistics, Spanish translation.

St. John's University, St. John's College of Liberal Arts and Sciences, Department of Languages and Literatures, Queens, NY 11439. Offers Spanish (MA). *Program availability:* Part-time, evening/weekend. *Faculty:* 15 full-time (10 women), 33 part-time/adjunct (13 women). *Students:* 9 full-time (7 women), 6 part-time (all women); includes 9 minority (1 Black or African American, non-Hispanic/Latino; 8 Hispanic/Latino). Average age 33. 7 applicants, 86% accepted, 5 enrolled. In 2017, 6 master's awarded. *Degree requirements:* For master's, comprehensive exam, thesis optional. *Entrance requirements:* For master's, letters of recommendation, transcripts, resume, personal statement, 24 prerequisite credits in history. Additional exam requirements/recommendations for international students: Required—TOEFL (minimum score 80 iBT), IELTS (minimum score 6.5). *Application deadline:* For fall admission, 5/1 for domestic students; for spring admission, 11/1 for domestic students. Applications are processed on a rolling basis. Application fee: $70. Electronic applications accepted. *Expenses: Tuition:* Full-time $44,280; part-time $1230 per credit. *Required fees:* $340; $340 per credit. Tuition and fees vary according to course load, degree level and program. *Financial support:* Research assistantships, teaching assistantships, scholarships/grants, tuition waivers, and unspecified assistantships available. Support available to part-time students. Financial award application deadline: 2/1; financial award applicants required to submit FAFSA. *Faculty research:* North American Spanish literature; medieval, Renaissance and Golden Century Spanish literature; Contemporary Latin American literature. *Unit head:* Dr. Alina Camacho-Gingerich, Chair, 718-990-1932, E-mail: camachoa@stjohns.edu. *Application contact:* Robert Medrano, Director of Graduate Admission, 718-990-1601, Fax: 718-990-5686, E-mail: gradhelp@stjohns.edu.
Website: https://www.stjohns.edu/academics/schools-and-colleges/st-johns-college-liberal-arts-and-sciences/languages-and-literatures

Saint Louis University, Graduate Programs, College of Arts and Sciences, Department of Languages, Literatures, and Cultures, St. Louis, MO 63103. Offers French (MA); Spanish (MA). *Program availability:* Part-time. *Degree requirements:* For master's, one foreign language, comprehensive exam, thesis/dissertation (Spanish). *Entrance requirements:* For master's, GRE General Test or MAT, letters of recommendation, resume, interview. Additional exam requirements/recommendations for international students: Required—TOEFL (minimum score 525 paper-based). Electronic applications accepted. *Faculty research:* Culture studies, literature studies, foreign language acquisition.

Saint Louis University–Madrid Campus, Graduate Programs, Master of Arts in Spanish Program, Madrid, Spain. Offers MA. *Program availability:* Part-time. *Degree requirements:* For master's, one foreign language, comprehensive exam, thesis optional. *Entrance requirements:* For master's, GRE General Test or MAT, 3 letters of recommendation, curriculum vitae, writing sample, interview. Additional exam requirements/recommendations for international students: Required—TOEFL. Electronic applications accepted. *Faculty research:* Spanish and Latin American literature, linguistics, cultural studies, gender studies.

Saint Xavier University, Graduate Studies, School of Education, Chicago, IL 60655-3105. Offers counseling (MA); curriculum and instruction (MA); early childhood education (MA); educational administration (MA); elementary education (MA); individualized studies (MA), including educational technology, English as a second language (ESL), ISTEM (integrative science, technology, engineering, and math), science education; music education (MA); reading (MA); secondary education (MA); Spanish education (MA); special education (MA); teaching and leadership (MA). *Accreditation:* NCATE. *Program availability:* Part-time, evening/weekend. *Degree requirements:* For master's, thesis or project. *Entrance requirements:* For master's, minimum GPA of 3.0. *Expenses:* Contact institution.

Salem State University, School of Graduate Studies, Program in Spanish, Salem, MA 01970-5353. Offers MAT. *Program availability:* Part-time, evening/weekend. *Entrance requirements:* For master's, GRE or MAT. Additional exam requirements/recommendations for international students: Required—TOEFL (minimum score 550 paper-based; 80 iBT) or IELTS (minimum score 5.5).

Sam Houston State University, College of Humanities and Social Sciences, Department of Foreign Languages, Huntsville, TX 77341. Offers Spanish (MA). *Program availability:* Part-time. *Degree requirements:* For master's, comprehensive exam, thesis (for some programs). *Entrance requirements:* For master's, GRE General Test, writing sample, letters of recommendation. Additional exam requirements/recommendations for international students: Required—TOEFL (minimum score 550 paper-based; 79 iBT), IELTS (minimum score 6.5). Electronic applications accepted. *Faculty research:* Pablo Picasso studies, Muslim women, Hispanic literature and art, sociolinguistics, language and the law, medical art and literature (Hispanic emphasis).

San Diego State University, Graduate and Research Affairs, College of Arts and Letters, Department of Spanish and Portuguese, San Diego, CA 92182. Offers Spanish (MA). *Degree requirements:* For master's, one foreign language. *Entrance requirements:* For master's, GRE General Test, 3 letters of reference. Additional exam requirements/recommendations for international students: Required—TOEFL. Electronic applications accepted. *Faculty research:* New strategies for teaching foreign languages.

San Francisco State University, Division of Graduate Studies, College of Liberal and Creative Arts, Department of Modern Languages and Literatures, Program in Spanish, San Francisco, CA 94132-1722. Offers MA. *Program availability:* Part-time. *Application deadline:* Applications are processed on a rolling basis. Electronic applications accepted. *Financial support:* Unspecified assistantships available. *Unit head:* Prof. Michael Hammer, Program Coordinator, 415-338-1658, Fax: 415-338-6159, E-mail: mhammer@sfsu.edu. *Application contact:* Prof. Gustavo Calderón, Graduate Advisor, 415-338-7426, Fax: 415-338-6159, E-mail: gusto@sfsu.edu.
Website: http://mll.sfsu.edu/spanish-program/

San Jose State University, Graduate Studies and Research, College of Humanities and the Arts, San Jose, CA 95192-0088. Offers art (MA, MFA), including digital media art (MFA), history and visual culture (MA), photography (MFA), pictorial art (MFA), spatial art (MFA); English (MA, MFA), including creative writing (MFA); linguistics (MA); music (MM); music education (MA); philosophy (MA); Spanish (MA); teaching English to speakers of other languages (MA). *Program availability:* Part-time. *Faculty:* 35 full-time (17 women), 19 part-time/adjunct (11 women). *Students:* 129 full-time (79 women), 106 part-time (71 women); includes 117 minority (5 Black or African American, non-Hispanic/Latino; 29 Asian, non-Hispanic/Latino; 44 Hispanic/Latino; 39 Two or more races, non-Hispanic/Latino), 28 international. Average age 35. 204 applicants, 65% accepted, 79 enrolled. In 2017, 85 master's awarded. *Degree requirements:* For master's, one foreign language, comprehensive exam (for some programs), thesis (for some programs), graduate writing assessment, special study/project, recital. *Entrance requirements:* Additional exam requirements/recommendations for international students: Required—

TOEFL (minimum score 550 paper-based; 80 iBT), IELTS (minimum score 6.5), PTE (minimum score 53). *Application deadline:* For fall admission, 2/1 for domestic and international students. Applications are processed on a rolling basis. Application fee: $55. Electronic applications accepted. *Expenses:* Tuition, state resident: full-time $7176. Tuition, nonresident: full-time $16,680. Tuition and fees vary according to course load and program. *Financial support:* Fellowships, research assistantships, Federal Work-Study, scholarships/grants, traineeships, tuition waivers (full and partial), and unspecified assistantships available. Support available to part-time students. Financial award application deadline: 4/28; financial award applicants required to submit FAFSA. *Unit head:* Dr. Shannon Miller, Dean, 408-924-4300, Fax: 408-924-4365, E-mail: shannon.miller@sjsu.edu.
Website: http://www.sjsu.edu/humanitiesandarts/

Southern Oregon University, Graduate Studies, Department of Foreign Languages and Literatures, Ashland, OR 97520. Offers French language teaching (MA); Spanish language teaching (MA). *Program availability:* Part-time, online learning. *Degree requirements:* For master's, thesis (for some programs). *Entrance requirements:* For master's, GRE General Test, minimum cumulative GPA of 3.0 in the last 90 quarter credits (60 semester credits) of undergraduate coursework. Additional exam requirements/recommendations for international students: Required—TOEFL (minimum score 540 paper-based; 76 iBT), IELTS (minimum score 6), ELPT (minimum score 964) or ELS (minimum score 112). Electronic applications accepted.

Stanford University, School of Humanities and Sciences, Department of Iberian and Latin American Cultures, Stanford, CA 94305-2004. Offers Spanish (MA, PhD). Terminal master's awarded for partial completion of doctoral program. *Degree requirements:* For master's, 2 foreign languages; for doctorate, 3 foreign languages, thesis/dissertation, oral exam. *Entrance requirements:* For master's and doctorate, GRE General Test. Additional exam requirements/recommendations for international students: Required—TOEFL. Electronic applications accepted. *Expenses: Tuition:* Full-time $48,987; part-time $10,620 per quarter. One-time fee: $400. Tuition and fees vary according to program.

State University of New York at New Paltz, Graduate and Extended Learning School, School of Education, Department of Teaching and Learning, New Paltz, NY 12561. Offers adolescence education: biology (MAT, MS Ed); adolescence education: chemistry (MAT, MS Ed); adolescence education: earth science (MAT, MS Ed); adolescence education: English (MAT, MS Ed); adolescence education: French (MAT, MS Ed); adolescence education: social studies (MAT, MS Ed); adolescence education: Spanish (MAT, MS Ed); second language education (MS Ed, AC), including second language education (MS Ed), teaching English language learners (AC). *Accreditation:* NCATE. *Program availability:* Part-time, evening/weekend. *Faculty:* 6 full-time (5 women), 10 part-time/adjunct (6 women). *Students:* 48 full-time (27 women), 54 part-time (41 women); includes 24 minority (2 Black or African American, non-Hispanic/Latino; 4 Asian, non-Hispanic/Latino; 15 Hispanic/Latino; 3 Two or more races, non-Hispanic/Latino). 33 applicants, 64% accepted, 12 enrolled. In 2017, 49 master's awarded. *Degree requirements:* For master's, comprehensive exam (for some programs), portfolio. *Entrance requirements:* For master's, minimum GPA of 3.0, New York state teaching certificate (MS Ed). Additional exam requirements/recommendations for international students: Required—TOEFL (minimum score 550 paper-based; 80 iBT), IELTS (minimum score 6.5). *Application deadline:* For fall admission, 3/1 priority date for domestic students, 3/1 for international students; for spring admission, 10/1 priority date for domestic students, 10/1 for international students. Application fee: $50. Electronic applications accepted. *Financial support:* Application deadline: 8/1. *Unit head:* Dr. Laura Dull, Chair, 845-257-2849, E-mail: dullj@newpaltz.edu. *Application contact:* Vika Shock, Director of Graduate Admissions, 845-257-3285, Fax: 845-257-3284, E-mail: gradschool@newpaltz.edu.
Website: http://www.newpaltz.edu/secondaryed/

State University of New York College at Geneseo, Graduate Studies, School of Education, Program in Adolescence Education, Geneseo, NY 14454-1401. Offers English 7-12 (MS Ed); French 7-12 (MS Ed); social studies 7-12 (MS Ed); Spanish 7-12 (MS Ed). *Program availability:* Part-time, evening/weekend. *Faculty:* 8 full-time (6 women), 1 (woman) part-time/adjunct. *Students:* 3 full-time (2 women), 2 part-time (1 woman). Average age 27. 9 applicants, 56% accepted, 3 enrolled. In 2017, 6 master's awarded. *Degree requirements:* For master's, 2 foreign languages, comprehensive examination, thesis or research project. *Entrance requirements:* For master's, GRE, MAT, EAS, edTPA, PRAXIS, or another substantially equivalent test, proof of New York State initial certification or equivalent certification from another state. Additional exam requirements/recommendations for international students: Required—TOEFL (minimum score 525 paper-based; 71 iBT), IELTS (minimum score 6.5), PTE, iTEP. *Application deadline:* For fall admission, 4/1 priority date for domestic students; for spring admission, 11/1 priority date for domestic students; for summer admission, 4/1 priority date for domestic students. Applications are processed on a rolling basis. Application fee: $50. Electronic applications accepted. *Expenses:* Contact institution. *Financial support:* In 2017–18, 3 students received support. Fellowships, research assistantships, scholarships/grants, health care benefits, tuition waivers (full and partial), and unspecified assistantships available. Support available to part-time students. Financial award application deadline: 4/1; financial award applicants required to submit FAFSA. *Unit head:* Dr. Anjoo Sikka, Dean of School of Education, 585-245-5151, Fax: 585-245-5220, E-mail: sikka@geneseo.edu. *Application contact:* Michael R. George, Director of Graduate Admissions, 585-245-5148, Fax: 585-245-5550, E-mail: georgem@geneseo.edu.

Syracuse University, College of Arts and Sciences, MA Program in Spanish Literature and Culture, Syracuse, NY 13207. Offers MA. *Program availability:* Part-time. *Students:* Average age 26. In 2017, 6 master's awarded. *Degree requirements:* For master's, comprehensive exam, thesis (for some programs). *Entrance requirements:* For master's, GRE General Test, official transcripts, resume, three letters of recommendation. Additional exam requirements/recommendations for international students: Required—TOEFL (minimum score 100 iBT). *Application deadline:* For fall admission, 2/1 priority date for domestic and international students. Application fee: $75. Electronic applications accepted. *Financial support:* Fellowships with full tuition reimbursements, teaching assistantships with tuition reimbursements, scholarships/grants, and tuition waivers available. Financial award application deadline: 1/1. *Faculty research:* Literature and culture of the Hispanic world, Hispanic linguistics, literatures and cultures of contemporary Spain, methodological approaches and to the orientations of contemporary theory. *Unit head:* M. Emma Ticio Quesada, Associate Professor/Program Director, 315-443-5488, E-mail: mticioqu@syr.edu.
Website: http://lll.syr.edu/spanish/graduate.html

Temple University, College of Liberal Arts, Department of Spanish and Portuguese, Philadelphia, PA 19122-6096. Offers Spanish (MA, PhD). *Program availability:* Part-time, evening/weekend. *Faculty:* 16 full-time (5 women), 7 part-time/adjunct (3 women). *Students:* 28 full-time (16 women), 5 part-time (2 women); includes 12 minority (1 Black or African American, non-Hispanic/Latino; 2 Asian, non-Hispanic/Latino; 9 Hispanic/Latino), 7 international. 9 applicants, 33% accepted, 1 enrolled. In 2017, 2 doctorates awarded. Terminal master's awarded for partial completion of doctoral program. *Degree requirements:* For master's, one foreign language; for doctorate, 2 foreign languages,

thesis/dissertation. *Entrance requirements:* For master's and doctorate, GRE General Test, minimum GPA of 3.0, 3 letters of recommendation. Additional exam requirements/recommendations for international students: Required—TOEFL. *Application deadline:* For fall admission, 1/15 for domestic students, 12/15 for international students; for spring admission, 9/30 for domestic students, 8/1 for international students. Applications are processed on a rolling basis. Application fee: $60. Electronic applications accepted. *Expenses:* Tuition, state resident: full-time $16,164; part-time $898 per credit hour. Tuition, nonresident: full-time $22,158; part-time $1231 per credit hour. *Required fees:* $890; $445 per semester. Full-time tuition and fees vary according to course load, degree level, campus/location and program. *Financial support:* Fellowships, teaching assistantships with full tuition reimbursements, and scholarships/grants available. Financial award application deadline: 1/15; financial award applicants required to submit FAFSA. *Faculty research:* Spanish literatures and cultures, Latin American literatures and cultures, Lusophone literatures and cultures, Spanish linguistics, literary and linguistic theory. *Unit head:* Victor Pueyo Zoco, Associate Chair for Graduate Studies, 215-204-5129, E-mail: vpueyozo@temple.edu. *Application contact:* Annette Vega, Coordinator, 215-204-2877, Fax: 215-204-3731, E-mail: avega1@temple.edu.
Website: http://www.cla.temple.edu/spanpor/

Texas A&M University, College of Liberal Arts, Department of Hispanic Studies, College Station, TX 77843. Offers Hispanic studies (MA, PhD). *Faculty:* 15. *Students:* 21 full-time (11 women), 15 part-time (11 women); includes 19 minority (all Hispanic/Latino), 8 international. Average age 41. 11 applicants, 82% accepted, 4 enrolled. In 2017, 10 doctorates awarded. *Entrance requirements:* Additional exam requirements/recommendations for international students: Required—TOEFL (minimum score 550 paper-based; 80 iBT), IELTS (minimum score 6), PTE (minimum score 53). *Application deadline:* For fall admission, 12/15 priority date for domestic and international students. Application fee: $50 ($90 for international students). *Expenses:* Contact institution. *Financial support:* In 2017–18, 22 students received support, including 6 fellowships with tuition reimbursements available (averaging $29,106 per year), 19 teaching assistantships with tuition reimbursements available (averaging $11,688 per year); career-related internships or fieldwork, institutionally sponsored loans, scholarships/grants, traineeships, health care benefits, tuition waivers (full and partial), and unspecified assistantships also available. Support available to part-time students. Financial award application deadline: 3/15; financial award applicants required to submit FAFSA. *Unit head:* Dr. Irene Moyna, Department Head, 979-845-2124, E-mail: moyna@tamu.edu. *Application contact:* Dr. Hilaire Kallendorf, Director of Graduate Studies, 979-458-0621, E-mail: h-kallendorf@tamu.edu.
Website: http://hispanicstudies.tamu.edu/

Texas A&M University–Commerce, College of Humanities, Social Sciences and Arts, Commerce, TX 75429. Offers applied criminology (MS); applied linguistics (MA, MS); art (MA, MFA); computational linguistics (Graduate Certificate); creative writing (Graduate Certificate); criminal justice management (Graduate Certificate); criminal justice studies (Graduate Certificate); English (MA, MS, PhD); film studies (Graduate Certificate); history (MA, MS); history of Christianity (Graduate Certificate); Holocaust studies (Graduate Certificate); homeland security (Graduate Certificate); music education (MM); music performance (MM); political science (MA, MS); public history (Graduate Certificate); sociology (MS); Spanish (MA); studies in children's and adolescent literature and culture (Graduate Certificate); teaching English to speakers of other languages (Graduate Certificate); theater (MA, MS); world history (Graduate Certificate). *Program availability:* Part-time. *Faculty:* 56 full-time (26 women), 10 part-time/adjunct (5 women). *Students:* 133 full-time (85 women), 439 part-time (311 women); includes 204 minority (79 Black or African American, non-Hispanic/Latino; 4 American Indian or Alaska Native, non-Hispanic/Latino; 9 Asian, non-Hispanic/Latino; 98 Hispanic/Latino; 14 Two or more races, non-Hispanic/Latino), 26 international. Average age 36. 261 applicants, 50% accepted, 113 enrolled. In 2017, 105 master's, 5 doctorates awarded. *Degree requirements:* For master's, one foreign language, comprehensive exam, thesis (for some programs); for doctorate, one foreign language, comprehensive exam, thesis/dissertation, departmental qualifying exam. *Entrance requirements:* For master's and doctorate, GRE General Test. Additional exam requirements/recommendations for international students: Required—TOEFL (minimum score 550 paper-based; 79 iBT), IELTS (minimum score 6). *Application deadline:* Applications are processed on a rolling basis. Application fee: $50. Electronic applications accepted. *Expenses:* Contact institution. *Financial support:* In 2017–18, 43 students received support, including 9 research assistantships with partial tuition reimbursements available (averaging $9,000 per year), 68 teaching assistantships with partial tuition reimbursements available (averaging $9,000 per year); Federal Work-Study, institutionally sponsored loans, scholarships/grants, health care benefits, and unspecified assistantships also available. Financial award application deadline: 5/1; financial award applicants required to submit FAFSA. *Unit head:* Dr. William F. Kuracina, Interim Dean, 903-886-5166, Fax: 903-886-5774, E-mail: william.kuracina@tamuc.edu. *Application contact:* Vicky Turner, Doctoral Degree and Special Programs Coordinator, 903-886-5167, E-mail: vicky.turner@tamuc.edu.
Website: http://www.tamuc.edu/academics/graduateSchool/programs/humanitiesSocialScienceArts/default.aspx

Texas A&M University–Kingsville, College of Graduate Studies, College of Arts and Sciences, Department of Language and Literature, Kingsville, TX 78363. Offers cultural studies (MA); English (MA, MS); Spanish (MA). *Entrance requirements:* Additional exam requirements/recommendations for international students: Required—TOEFL (minimum score 550 paper-based; 79 iBT); Recommended—IELTS. Electronic applications accepted.

Texas State University, The Graduate College, College of Liberal Arts, Program in Spanish, San Marcos, TX 78666. Offers MA. *Program availability:* Part-time, evening/weekend. *Faculty:* 16 full-time (8 women). *Students:* 9 full-time (4 women), 10 part-time (7 women); includes 13 minority (1 Asian, non-Hispanic/Latino; 12 Hispanic/Latino). Average age 35. 18 applicants, 67% accepted, 7 enrolled. In 2017, 2 master's awarded. *Degree requirements:* For master's, one foreign language, comprehensive exam, thesis optional. *Entrance requirements:* For master's, baccalaureate degree from regionally-accredited university with minimum GPA of 2.75 on last 60 undergraduate semester hours, 3.0 in 12 hours in Spanish; statement of purpose written in Spanish; resume including contact information for 3 references, 2 of which should be professors familiar with academic work. Additional exam requirements/recommendations for international students: Required—TOEFL (minimum score 550 paper-based; 78 iBT), IELTS (minimum score 6.5). *Application deadline:* For fall admission, 1/15 priority date for domestic and international students; for spring admission, 10/15 for domestic students, 10/1 for international students. Applications are processed on a rolling basis. Application fee: $40 ($90 for international students). Electronic applications accepted. *Expenses:* Tuition, state resident: full-time $7868; part-time $3934 per semester. Tuition, nonresident: full-time $17,828; part-time $8914 per semester. *Required fees:* $2092; $1435 per semester. Tuition and fees vary according to course load. *Financial support:* In 2017–18, 10 students received support, including 9 teaching assistantships (averaging $12,452 per year); research assistantships, career-related internships or fieldwork, Federal Work-Study, institutionally sponsored loans, scholarships/grants, and unspecified assistantships also available. Support available to part-time students. Financial award application deadline: 3/1; financial award applicants required to submit FAFSA. *Unit head:* Dr. George Y. Porras, Graduate Advisor, 512-245-2360, Fax: 512-245-8298, E-mail: gradspanish@txstate.edu. *Application contact:* Dr. Andrea Golato, Dean of Graduate School, 512-245-2581, Fax: 512-245-8365, E-mail: gradcollege@txstate.edu.
Website: http://www.modlang.txstate.edu/spanishma/

Texas Tech University, Graduate School, College of Arts and Sciences, Department of Classical and Modern Languages and Literatures, Lubbock, TX 79409. Offers languages and cultures (MA); Romance languages (MA); Spanish (PhD); MBA/MA. *Program availability:* Part-time. *Faculty:* 58 full-time (39 women), 1 (woman) part-time/adjunct. *Students:* 79 full-time (42 women), 15 part-time (11 women); includes 22 minority (1 Black or African American, non-Hispanic/Latino; 18 Hispanic/Latino; 3 Two or more races, non-Hispanic/Latino), 47 international. Average age 32. 51 applicants, 76% accepted, 27 enrolled. In 2017, 26 master's, 3 doctorates awarded. *Degree requirements:* For master's, comprehensive exam, thesis or alternative; for doctorate, comprehensive exam, thesis/dissertation. *Entrance requirements:* Additional exam requirements/recommendations for international students: Required—TOEFL (minimum score 550 paper-based; 79 iBT). *Application deadline:* For fall admission, 6/1 priority date for domestic students, 1/15 priority date for international students; for spring admission, 9/1 priority date for domestic students, 6/15 priority date for international students. Applications are processed on a rolling basis. Application fee: $60. Electronic applications accepted. *Expenses:* Contact institution. *Financial support:* In 2017–18, 80 students received support, including 52 fellowships (averaging $3,518 per year), 74 teaching assistantships (averaging $12,664 per year); research assistantships, Federal Work-Study, scholarships/grants, and unspecified assistantships also available. Financial award application deadline: 4/15; financial award applicants required to submit FAFSA. *Faculty research:* Literature, comparative literature, linguistics, culture, applied linguistics. *Total annual research expenditures:* $150,379. *Unit head:* Dr. Erin Collopy, Department Chair and Associate Professor, 806-834-8497, Fax: 806-742-3306, E-mail: erin.collopy@ttu.edu. *Application contact:* Carla Burrus, Senior Advisor, 806-834-3282, Fax: 806-742-3306, E-mail: carla.burrus@ttu.edu.
Website: http://www.depts.ttu.edu/classic_modern/

Tulane University, School of Liberal Arts, Department of Spanish and Portuguese, New Orleans, LA 70118-5669. Offers Portuguese (MA); Spanish and Portuguese (PhD). *Degree requirements:* For master's, 2 foreign languages; for doctorate, 2 foreign languages, thesis/dissertation. *Entrance requirements:* For master's, GRE General Test, minimum B average in undergraduate course work; for doctorate, GRE General Test. Additional exam requirements/recommendations for international students: Required—TOEFL. Electronic applications accepted. *Expenses: Tuition:* Full-time $50,920; part-time $2829 per credit hour. *Required fees:* $2040; $44.50 per credit hour. $580 per term. Tuition and fees vary according to course load, degree level and program.

Universidad Autonoma de Guadalajara, Graduate Programs, Guadalajara, Mexico. Offers administrative law and justice (LL M); advertising and corporate communications (MA); architecture (M Arch); business (MBA); computational science (MCC); education (Ed M, Ed D); English-Spanish translation (MA); entrepreneurship and management (MBA); integrated management of digital animation (MA); international business (MIB); international corporate law (LL M); internet technologies (MS); manufacturing systems (MMS); occupational health (MS); philosophy (MA, PhD); power electronics (MS); quality systems (MQS); renewable energy (MS); social evaluation of projects (MBA); strategic market research (MBA); tax law (MA); teaching mathematics (MA).

Université de Montréal, Faculty of Arts and Sciences, Department of Literatures and Modern Languages, Program in Hispanic Studies, Montréal, QC H3C 3J7, Canada. Offers MA. *Degree requirements:* For master's, 2 foreign languages, thesis. Electronic applications accepted. *Faculty research:* Spanish literature and culture, Latin American literature and culture.

Université Laval, Faculty of Letters, Department of Literature, Programs in Spanish Literatures, Québec, QC G1K 7P4, Canada. Offers MA, PhD. *Program availability:* Part-time. Terminal master's awarded for partial completion of doctoral program. *Degree requirements:* For master's, thesis; for doctorate, comprehensive exam, thesis/dissertation. *Entrance requirements:* For master's and doctorate, linguistics exams, knowledge of French and Spanish. Electronic applications accepted.

University at Albany, State University of New York, College of Arts and Sciences, Department of Languages, Literatures, and Cultures, Albany, NY 12222-0001. Offers Spanish (MA, PhD). *Faculty:* 4 full-time (2 women). *Students:* 9 full-time (5 women), 20 part-time (11 women); includes 12 minority (2 Black or African American, non-Hispanic/Latino; 10 Hispanic/Latino), 1 international. 15 applicants, 60% accepted, 5 enrolled. In 2017, 4 master's, 1 doctorate awarded. *Degree requirements:* For doctorate, thesis/dissertation. *Entrance requirements:* Additional exam requirements/recommendations for international students: Required—TOEFL (minimum score 550 paper-based). *Application deadline:* For fall admission, 8/1 for domestic students, 5/1 for international students. Application fee: $75. *Expenses:* Tuition, state resident: full-time $10,870; part-time $453 per credit hour. Tuition, nonresident: full-time $22,210; part-time $925 per credit hour. *Required fees:* $84.68 per credit hour. $508.06 per semester. Part-time tuition and fees vary according to course load and program. *Unit head:* Maurice Westmoreland, Chair, 518-442-4222, Fax: 518-442-4111, E-mail: mwestmoreland@albany.edu. *Application contact:* Michael DeRensis, Director, Graduate Admissions, 518-442-3980, Fax: 518-442-3922, E-mail: graduate@albany.edu.
Website: http://www.albany.edu/llc/

University at Buffalo, the State University of New York, Graduate School, College of Arts and Sciences, Department of Romance Languages and Literatures, Buffalo, NY 14260-4620. Offers French (MA, PhD); Spanish (MA, PhD). *Program availability:* Part-time. Terminal master's awarded for partial completion of doctoral program. *Degree requirements:* For master's, one foreign language, comprehensive exam, thesis (for some programs); for doctorate, 2 foreign languages, comprehensive exam (for some programs), thesis/dissertation. *Entrance requirements:* For doctorate, GRE. Additional exam requirements/recommendations for international students: Required—TOEFL (minimum score 550 paper-based; 79 iBT), IELTS (minimum score 6.5), PTE (minimum score 55). Electronic applications accepted. *Faculty research:* Romance linguistics, cultural studies, literary studies, literature, philosophy and poetry.

University at Buffalo, the State University of New York, Graduate School, Graduate School of Education, Department of Learning and Instruction, Buffalo, NY 14260. Offers biology education (Ed M, Certificate); chemistry education (Ed M, Certificate); childhood education (Ed M); childhood education with bilingual extension (Ed M); college teaching (Advanced Certificate); curriculum, instruction and the science of learning (PhD); early childhood education (Ed M); early childhood education with bilingual extension (Ed M); earth science education (Ed M, Certificate); education and technology (Ed M); education studies (Ed M); educational technology and new literacies (Certificate); educational technology and new literacies (Advanced Certificate); elementary education (Ed D); English education (Ed M, Certificate); English education studies (Ed M); English for speakers of other languages (Ed M); foreign and second language education (PhD); French education (Ed M, Certificate); German education (Ed M, Certificate); gifted education (Certificate); Latin education (Ed M, Certificate); literacy education studies

(Ed M); literacy specialist (Ed M); literacy teaching and learning (Certificate); mathematics education (Ed M, Certificate); music education (Ed M, Certificate); music education studies (Ed M); music learning theory (Advanced Certificate); online education (Advanced Certificate); physics education (Ed M, Certificate); science and the public (Ed M); social studies education (Ed M, Certificate); Spanish education (Ed M, Certificate); special education (PhD); teaching English to speakers of other languages (Ed M). *Program availability:* Part-time, evening/weekend, 100% online. *Faculty:* 26 full-time (19 women), 74 part-time/adjunct (52 women). *Students:* 172 full-time (122 women), 325 part-time (226 women); includes 44 minority (25 Black or African American, non-Hispanic/Latino; 5 American Indian or Alaska Native, non-Hispanic/Latino; 14 Asian, non-Hispanic/Latino), 57 international. Average age 33. 316 applicants, 78% accepted, 174 enrolled. In 2017, 109 master's, 34 doctorates, 15 other advanced degrees awarded. *Degree requirements:* For master's, comprehensive exam; for doctorate, thesis/dissertation, research analysis exam, research experience. *Entrance requirements:* For master's, letters of reference; for doctorate, GRE General Test or MAT, interview, writing sample, letters of recommendation. Additional exam requirements/recommendations for international students: Required—TOEFL (minimum score 600 paper-based; 96 iBT). *Application deadline:* For fall admission, 2/1 priority date for domestic and international students; for spring admission, 11/15 priority date for domestic students, 10/1 for international students. Applications are processed on a rolling basis. Application fee: $50. Electronic applications accepted. *Financial support:* In 2017–18, 42 fellowships (averaging $5,181 per year), 44 research assistantships with tuition reimbursements (averaging $10,908 per year) were awarded; teaching assistantships, career-related internships or fieldwork, Federal Work-Study, institutionally sponsored loans, scholarships/grants, tuition waivers (full and partial), and unspecified assistantships also available. Financial award application deadline: 2/28; financial award applicants required to submit FAFSA. *Faculty research:* Science assessment, foreign language teaching and learning, early learning, new literacies, gender and education. *Total annual research expenditures:* $413,233. *Unit head:* Dr. David Bruce, Chair, 716-645-4069, Fax: 716-645-3161, E-mail: gse-info@buffalo.edu. *Application contact:* Luann Zak, Admissions Assistant, 716-645-2110, Fax: 716-645-7937, E-mail: luannzak@buffalo.edu.
Website: http://gse.buffalo.edu/lai

The University of Akron, Graduate School, Buchtel College of Arts and Sciences, Department of Modern Languages, Akron, OH 44325. Offers Spanish (MA). *Program availability:* Part-time, evening/weekend. *Faculty:* 5 full-time (3 women). *Degree requirements:* For master's, one foreign language, comprehensive exam, essay, oral exam, research paper. *Entrance requirements:* For master's, baccalaureate degree in Spanish, minimum GPA of 2.75, interview, proficiency in Spanish, three letters of recommendation, statement of purpose. Additional exam requirements/recommendations for international students: Required—TOEFL (minimum score 79 iBT), IELTS (minimum score 6.5). *Application deadline:* Applications are processed on a rolling basis. Application fee: $45 ($70 for international students). Electronic applications accepted. *Financial support:* In 2017–18, 1 teaching assistantship with full tuition reimbursement was awarded. *Faculty research:* Spanish literature and culture from the Golden Age to the present, contemporary Spanish cinema and the plastic arts, contemporary Latin America narrative and poetry, Spanish applied linguistics and pedagogy. *Unit head:* Dr. Sheldon Wrice, Interim Department Chair, 330-972-6023, E-mail: swrice1@uakron.edu. *Application contact:* Dr. Parizad Dejbord-Sawan, Director of Graduate Studies, 330-972-7824, E-mail: parizad@uakron.edu.
Website: http://www.uakron.edu/modlang/

The University of Alabama, Graduate School, College of Arts and Sciences, Department of Modern Languages and Classics, Tuscaloosa, AL 35487. Offers French (MA, PhD); French and Spanish (PhD); German (MA); Romance languages (MA, PhD); Spanish (MA, PhD). *Program availability:* Part-time. *Faculty:* 30 full-time (18 women). *Students:* 45 full-time (27 women), 4 part-time (1 woman); includes 11 minority (5 Black or African American, non-Hispanic/Latino; 1 Asian, non-Hispanic/Latino; 3 Hispanic/Latino; 2 Two or more races, non-Hispanic/Latino), 14 international. Average age 32. 26 applicants, 88% accepted, 11 enrolled. In 2017, 18 master's awarded. *Degree requirements:* For master's, comprehensive exam, thesis optional; for doctorate, one foreign language, thesis/dissertation, preliminary exam. *Entrance requirements:* For master's and doctorate, minimum GPA of 3.0, writing sample. *Application deadline:* For fall admission, 7/6 priority date for domestic students, 1/15 priority date for international students; for spring admission, 12/5 priority date for domestic students, 6/1 priority date for international students. Applications are processed on a rolling basis. Application fee: $50 ($60 for international students). Electronic applications accepted. *Financial support:* In 2017–18, 40 students received support, including research assistantships with full tuition reimbursements available (averaging $10,291 per year), teaching assistantships with full tuition reimbursements available (averaging $10,291 per year); fellowships, career-related internships or fieldwork, Federal Work-Study, institutionally sponsored loans, and scholarships/grants also available. Financial award application deadline: 7/14. *Faculty research:* Non-English literature, linguistics, culture, film. *Unit head:* Dr. Douglas Lightfoot, Department Chair, 205-348-5059, E-mail: lightfoot@ua.edu. *Application contact:* Michael Picone, Graduate Director, 205-348-8473, E-mail: picone@ua.edu.
Website: http://bama.ua.edu/~mlc

The University of Arizona, College of Humanities, Department of Spanish and Portuguese, Tucson, AZ 85721. Offers Spanish (MA, PhD). Terminal master's awarded for partial completion of doctoral program. *Degree requirements:* For master's, one foreign language, comprehensive exam, thesis optional; for doctorate, 3 foreign languages, comprehensive exam, thesis/dissertation. *Entrance requirements:* For master's, GRE General Test, minimum GPA of 3.3, writing sample, 3 letters of recommendation, audio sample; for doctorate, GRE General Test, minimum GPA of 3.4, 3 letters of recommendation, statement of purpose, writing sample, audio sample. Additional exam requirements/recommendations for international students: Required—TOEFL (minimum score 550 paper-based; 79 iBT). Electronic applications accepted. *Faculty research:* Spanish and Latin American literature and linguistics, literary theory.

University of Arkansas, Graduate School, J. William Fulbright College of Arts and Sciences, Department of World Languages, Literatures and Cultures, Program in Spanish, Fayetteville, AR 72701. Offers MA. In 2017, 6 master's awarded. *Degree requirements:* For master's, one foreign language, comprehensive exam, thesis optional. *Entrance requirements:* Additional exam requirements/recommendations for international students: Required—TOEFL (minimum score 550 paper-based), IELTS (minimum score 6.5). *Application deadline:* For fall admission, 8/1 priority date for domestic students, 4/1 for international students; for spring admission, 12/1 priority date for domestic students, 10/1 for international students; for summer admission, 4/15 for domestic students, 3/1 for international students. Applications are processed on a rolling basis. Application fee: $60. Electronic applications accepted. *Expenses:* Tuition, state resident: full-time $3782. Tuition, nonresident: full-time $10,238. *Financial support:* In 2017–18, 1 research assistantship, 14 teaching assistantships (averaging $8,200 per year) were awarded; fellowships with tuition reimbursements, career-related internships or fieldwork, and Federal Work-Study also available. Support available to part-time students. Financial award application deadline: 1/15; financial award applicants required to submit FAFSA. *Faculty research:* Medieval and Golden Age poetry, colonial Latin

America, contemporary Latin America. *Unit head:* Dr. Steven Bell, Department Chair, 479-575-2951, Fax: 479-575-6795, E-mail: sbell@uark.edu. *Application contact:* Dr. Reina Ruiz, Graduate Coordinator, 479-575-2951, E-mail: rruiz@uark.edu.
Website: https://fulbright.uark.edu/departments/world-languages/

University of Calgary, Faculty of Graduate Studies, Faculty of Arts, Department of French, Italian and Spanish, Calgary, AB T2N 1N4, Canada. Offers French (MA, PhD); Spanish (MA, PhD). PhD offered in special cases only. *Program availability:* Part-time. *Degree requirements:* For master's, one foreign language, thesis, exam; for doctorate, 2 foreign languages, comprehensive exam, thesis/dissertation, candidacy exam. *Entrance requirements:* Additional exam requirements/recommendations for international students: Required—TOEFL (minimum score 550 paper-based; 80 iBT) or IELTS (minimum score 7). Electronic applications accepted. *Faculty research:* French and French-Canadian language and literature, Hispanic language and literature, comparative literature, language instruction, literary theory.

University of California, Berkeley, Graduate Division, College of Letters and Science, Group in Romance Languages and Literatures, Berkeley, CA 94720-1500. Offers French (PhD); Italian (PhD); Spanish (PhD). *Degree requirements:* For doctorate, thesis/dissertation, qualifying exam. *Entrance requirements:* For doctorate, GRE General Test, minimum GPA of 3.0, 3 letters of recommendation. Additional exam requirements/recommendations for international students: Required—TOEFL (minimum score 570 paper-based; 90 iBT). Electronic applications accepted.

University of California, Davis, Graduate Studies, Program in Spanish, Davis, CA 95616. Offers MA, PhD. Terminal master's awarded for partial completion of doctoral program. *Degree requirements:* For master's, comprehensive exam (for some programs), thesis (for some programs); for doctorate, 2 foreign languages, thesis/dissertation. *Entrance requirements:* For master's, GRE General Test, minimum GPA of 3.0; for doctorate, GRE General Test, master's degree, minimum GPA of 3.0. Additional exam requirements/recommendations for international students: Required—TOEFL (minimum score 550 paper-based). *Faculty research:* Medieval Spanish language and literature, Spanish linguistics, Latin American literature, nineteenth century Peninsular literature.

University of California, Irvine, School of Humanities, Department of Spanish and Portuguese, Irvine, CA 92697. Offers Spanish (MA, MAT, PhD). *Students:* 28 full-time (21 women), 2 part-time (0 women); includes 21 minority (20 Hispanic/Latino; 1 Two or more races, non-Hispanic/Latino), 4 international. Average age 36. 16 applicants, 44% accepted, 4 enrolled. In 2017, 3 master's, 4 doctorates awarded. *Entrance requirements:* For master's and doctorate, GRE General Test, minimum GPA of 3.0. Additional exam requirements/recommendations for international students: Required—TOEFL (minimum score 550 paper-based). *Application deadline:* For fall admission, 1/2 priority date for domestic students, 1/2 for international students. Applications are processed on a rolling basis. Application fee: $105 ($125 for international students). Electronic applications accepted. *Financial support:* Fellowships, teaching assistantships, institutionally sponsored loans, traineeships, health care benefits, and unspecified assistantships available. Financial award application deadline: 3/1; financial award applicants required to submit FAFSA. *Faculty research:* Latin American literature, Spanish literature, Spanish linguistics in Creole studies, Hispanic literature in the U.S., Luso-Brazilian literature. *Unit head:* Luis Aviles, Department Chair, 949-824-7268, Fax: 949-824-2803, E-mail: laviles@uci.edu. *Application contact:* Evelyn Flores, Graduate Program Coordinator, 949-824-8793, Fax: 949-824-2803, E-mail: evelynf@uci.edu.
Website: http://www.hnet.uci.edu/spanishandportuguese/

University of California, Los Angeles, Graduate Division, College of Letters and Science, Department of Spanish and Portuguese, Program in Spanish, Los Angeles, CA 90095. Offers MA. *Degree requirements:* For master's, one foreign language, comprehensive exam or thesis. *Entrance requirements:* For master's, GRE General Test, bachelor's degree; minimum undergraduate GPA of 3.0 (or its equivalent if letter grade system not used). Additional exam requirements/recommendations for international students: Required—TOEFL. Electronic applications accepted.

University of California, Riverside, Graduate Division, Department of Hispanic Studies, Riverside, CA 92521-0102. Offers Spanish (MA, PhD). Terminal master's awarded for partial completion of doctoral program. *Degree requirements:* For master's, one foreign language, comprehensive exam; for doctorate, one foreign language, thesis/dissertation, qualifying exams, 1 quarter of teaching experience. *Entrance requirements:* For master's and doctorate, GRE General Test, minimum GPA of 3.0. Additional exam requirements/recommendations for international students: Required—TOEFL (minimum score 550 paper-based; 80 iBT). Electronic applications accepted. *Expenses:* Tuition, state resident: full-time $5746. Tuition, nonresident: full-time $10,780. Tuition and fees vary according to campus/location and program. *Faculty research:* Spanish literature of the sixteenth-, seventeenth- and twentieth-century; pre-Columbian and colonial Latin American literature; nineteenth- and twentieth-century Latin American literature.

University of California, Santa Barbara, Graduate Division, College of Letters and Sciences, Division of Humanities and Fine Arts, Department of Spanish and Portuguese, Santa Barbara, CA 93106-4150. Offers Hispanic languages and literatures (PhD), including European medieval studies, feminist studies, Hispanic linguistics, Hispanic literature, Luso-Brazilian literature; Hispanic linguistics (MA); Luso-Brazilian literature (MA); Spanish or Spanish-American literature (MA); MA/PhD. Terminal master's awarded for partial completion of doctoral program. *Degree requirements:* For master's, 2 foreign languages, comprehensive exam (for some programs), thesis optional; for doctorate, 3 foreign languages, comprehensive exam, thesis/dissertation. *Entrance requirements:* For master's and doctorate, GRE. Additional exam requirements/recommendations for international students: Required—TOEFL (minimum score 550 paper-based; 80 iBT), IELTS (minimum score 7). Electronic applications accepted. *Faculty research:* Nineteenth-century Spanish and Portuguese literature, Spanish and Spanish-American literature, nineteenth- and twentieth-century Portuguese and Brazilian literatures, Hispanic linguistics, Catalan language and culture.

University of Central Florida, College of Arts and Humanities, Department of Modern Languages and Literatures, Program in Spanish, Orlando, FL 32816. Offers MA. *Program availability:* Part-time, evening/weekend. *Students:* 7 full-time (6 women), 11 part-time (10 women); includes 13 minority (all Hispanic/Latino), 1 international. Average age 39. 9 applicants, 78% accepted, 5 enrolled. In 2017, 5 master's awarded. *Degree requirements:* For master's, one foreign language, comprehensive exam, thesis or alternative. *Entrance requirements:* For master's, minimum GPA of 3.0 in last 60 hours, letters of recommendation, writing sample. Additional exam requirements/recommendations for international students: Required—TOEFL. *Application deadline:* For fall admission, 7/15 for domestic students; for spring admission, 12/1 for domestic students; for summer admission, 4/15 for domestic students. Application fee: $30. Electronic applications accepted. *Expenses:* Tuition, state resident: part-time $288.16 per credit hour. Tuition, nonresident: part-time $1073.31 per credit hour. Tuition and fees vary according to program. *Financial support:* In 2017–18, 5 students received support, including 5 teaching assistantships with partial tuition reimbursements available (averaging $9,632 per year); fellowships, career-related internships or fieldwork, Federal Work-Study, institutionally sponsored loans, health care benefits, tuition waivers (partial), and unspecified assistantships also available. Financial award application

deadline: 3/1; financial award applicants required to submit FAFSA. *Unit head:* Dr. Lisa Nalbone, Director, 407-823-2472, E-mail: lisa.nalbone@ucf.edu. *Application contact:* Associate Director, Graduate Admissions, 407-823-2766, Fax: 407-823-6442, E-mail: gradadmissions@ucf.edu.
Website: http://mll.cah.ucf.edu/graduate/index.php#SpanishMA

University of Chicago, Division of the Humanities, Department of Romance Languages and Literatures, Chicago, IL 60637. Offers French and Francophone studies (PhD); Hispanic and Luso-Brazilian studies (PhD); Italian studies (PhD); Renaissance and early modern studies (PhD). *Students:* 50 full-time (28 women); includes 12 minority (2 Asian, non-Hispanic/Latino; 9 Hispanic/Latino; 1 Two or more races, non-Hispanic/Latino), 25 international. Average age 30. 52 applicants, 31% accepted, 7 enrolled. In 2017, 4 doctorates awarded. Terminal master's awarded for partial completion of doctoral program. *Degree requirements:* For doctorate, 3 foreign languages, comprehensive exam, thesis/dissertation. *Entrance requirements:* For doctorate, GRE General Test, 15-20 page writing sample, statement of purpose, 3 letters of recommendation, transcripts for all previous degrees and institutions attended. Additional exam requirements/recommendations for international students: Required—TOEFL (minimum score 104 iBT), IELTS (minimum score 7). *Application deadline:* For fall admission, 12/15 for domestic and international students. Application fee: $90. Electronic applications accepted. *Financial support:* In 2017–18, fellowships with full tuition reimbursements (averaging $27,000 per year) were awarded; teaching assistantships with full tuition reimbursements, Federal Work-Study, institutionally sponsored loans, scholarships/grants, and health care benefits also available. Financial award application deadline: 12/15. *Unit head:* Daisy Delogu, Chair, 773-702-8481, E-mail: romance-languages@uchicago.edu. *Application contact:* Michael Beetley, Assistant Dean of Students, Admissions and Fellowships, 773-702-1552, Fax: 773-834-9148, E-mail: humanitiesadmissions@uchicago.edu.
Website: http://rll.uchicago.edu

University of Cincinnati, Graduate School, McMicken College of Arts and Sciences, Department of Romance Languages and Literatures, Program in Spanish, Cincinnati, OH 45221. Offers MA, PhD. Terminal master's awarded for partial completion of doctoral program. *Degree requirements:* For master's, thesis optional; for doctorate, 2 foreign languages, thesis/dissertation. *Entrance requirements:* For master's, minimum GPA of 3.0. Electronic applications accepted. *Expenses: Tuition, area resident:* Full-time $14,468. Tuition, state resident: full-time $14,968; part-time $754 per credit hour. Tuition, nonresident: full-time $24,210; part-time $1311 per credit hour. *International tuition:* $26,460 full-time. *Required fees:* $3958; $84 per credit hour. One-time fee: $85 full-time. Tuition and fees vary according to course load, degree level and program. *Faculty research:* Applied linguistics, Spanish essay, Latin American culture, women's studies, poetry.

University of Colorado Boulder, Graduate School, College of Arts and Sciences, Department of Spanish and Portuguese, Boulder, CO 80309. Offers Hispanic linguistics (MA); medieval and early modern Hispanic literatures (PhD); peninsular and Latin American literature (MA). *Faculty:* 13 full-time (5 women). *Students:* 33 full-time (22 women), 3 part-time (all women); includes 7 minority (all Hispanic/Latino), 15 international. Average age 31. 31 applicants, 48% accepted, 8 enrolled. In 2017, 5 master's, 2 doctorates awarded. Terminal master's awarded for partial completion of doctoral program. *Degree requirements:* For master's, one foreign language, comprehensive exam, thesis or alternative; for doctorate, 2 foreign languages, thesis/dissertation. *Entrance requirements:* For master's, minimum undergraduate GPA of 2.75. *Application deadline:* For fall admission, 1/10 for domestic students; for spring admission, 1/10 for domestic students. Applications are processed on a rolling basis. Application fee: $60 ($80 for international students). Electronic applications accepted. Application fee is waived when completed online. *Financial support:* In 2017–18, 119 students received support, including 33 fellowships (averaging $583 per year), 31 teaching assistantships with full and partial tuition reimbursements available (averaging $33,436 per year); institutionally sponsored loans, scholarships/grants, health care benefits, and unspecified assistantships also available. Financial award application deadline: 2/15; financial award applicants required to submit FAFSA. *Faculty research:* Literary criticism, Spanish language/literature, Latin American languages/literature, cultural history. *Total annual research expenditures:* $40,777. *Application contact:* E-mail: spanport@colorado.edu.
Website: http://spanish.colorado.edu/

University of Colorado Denver, College of Liberal Arts and Sciences, Department of Modern Languages, Denver, CO 80217. Offers Spanish (MA). *Program availability:* Part-time. *Degree requirements:* For master's, comprehensive exam, thesis or alternative, 33 credit hours of course work. *Entrance requirements:* For master's, BA in Spanish from accredited institution, or BA in another discipline plus language skills that meet department's standards; minimum GPA of 2.5, 3.0 in all Spanish courses; written statement in Spanish; oral interview after the application has been submitted; three letters of recommendation. Additional exam requirements/recommendations for international students: Required—TOEFL (minimum score 550 paper-based; 80 iBT). Electronic applications accepted. *Faculty research:* Spanish American literature; sociolinguistics, bilingualism, phonology and historical linguistics; Spanish peninsular literature; applied linguistics, pragmatics and second language acquisition.

University of Delaware, College of Arts and Sciences, Department of Foreign Languages and Literatures, Newark, DE 19716. Offers foreign languages and literatures (MA), including French, German, Spanish; foreign languages pedagogy (MA), including French, German, Spanish; technical Chinese translation (MA). *Degree requirements:* For master's, one foreign language, comprehensive exam, thesis optional. *Entrance requirements:* For master's, GRE General Test, letters of recommendation, writing sample. Additional exam requirements/recommendations for international students: Required—TOEFL. Electronic applications accepted. *Faculty research:* Medieval to Modern French and Spanish literature, twentieth-century German, French, Spanish literature by women, computer-assisted instruction.

University of Florida, Graduate School, College of Liberal Arts and Sciences, Department of Spanish and Portuguese Studies, Gainesville, FL 32611. Offers Spanish (MA, MAT, PhD). *Program availability:* Part-time. Terminal master's awarded for partial completion of doctoral program. *Degree requirements:* For master's, one foreign language, comprehensive exam, thesis or extended research paper; for doctorate, 2 foreign languages, comprehensive exam, thesis/dissertation, qualifying exam. *Entrance requirements:* For master's and doctorate, GRE General Test, minimum GPA of 3.0. Additional exam requirements/recommendations for international students: Required—TOEFL (minimum score 550 paper-based; 80 iBT), IELTS (minimum score 6). Electronic applications accepted. *Faculty research:* Spanish linguistics; second language acquisition and teaching; Spanish literature, film and culture; Latin American literature, film and culture; Portuguese literature, film and culture.

University of Georgia, Franklin College of Arts and Sciences, Department of Romance Languages, Athens, GA 30602. Offers French (PhD); Italian (MA, PhD); Portuguese (MA, PhD); romance linguistics (MA); Spanish (PhD). *Degree requirements:* For master's, one foreign language; for doctorate, 2 foreign languages, thesis/dissertation. *Entrance requirements:* For master's and doctorate, GRE General Test. Electronic applications accepted.

University of Hawaii at Manoa, Office of Graduate Education, College of Languages, Linguistics and Literature, Department of Languages and Literatures of Europe and the Americas, Program in Spanish, Honolulu, HI 96822. Offers MA. *Program availability:* Part-time. *Degree requirements:* For master's, one foreign language, thesis optional. *Entrance requirements:* For master's, GRE General Test. Additional exam requirements/recommendations for international students: Required—TOEFL (minimum score 580 paper-based; 92 iBT), IELTS (minimum score 5).

University of Houston, College of Liberal Arts and Social Sciences, Department of Hispanic Studies, Houston, TX 77204. Offers Hispanic literature and linguistics (PhD); Spanish (MA, PhD), including creative writing (PhD). *Program availability:* Part-time. *Degree requirements:* For master's, comprehensive exam, thesis optional; for doctorate, 2 foreign languages, comprehensive exam, thesis/dissertation. *Entrance requirements:* For master's and doctorate, GRE. Additional exam requirements/recommendations for international students: Required—TOEFL (minimum score 550 paper-based; 79 iBT); Recommended—IELTS (minimum score 6.5). Electronic applications accepted.

University of Houston, College of Liberal Arts and Social Sciences, Department of Modern and Classical Languages, Houston, TX 77204. Offers world cultures and literatures (MA). *Degree requirements:* For master's, one foreign language, thesis optional. *Entrance requirements:* For master's, GRE General Test, minimum GPA of 3.0 in last 60 hours of course work. Additional exam requirements/recommendations for international students: Required—TOEFL (minimum score 500 paper-based). Electronic applications accepted.

University of Illinois at Chicago, College of Liberal Arts and Sciences, School of Literatures, Cultural Studies and Linguistics, Department of Hispanic and Italian Studies, Chicago, IL 60607-7128. Offers Hispanic linguistics (PhD). *Program availability:* Part-time. Terminal master's awarded for partial completion of doctoral program. *Degree requirements:* For master's, one foreign language, departmental qualifying exam. *Entrance requirements:* For master's, GRE General Test, minimum GPA of 2.75, undergraduate major in Spanish. Additional exam requirements/recommendations for international students: Required—TOEFL. Electronic applications accepted. *Faculty research:* Linguistic competence of bilingual speakers as a window to understanding the human faculty of language, neurocognitive processing of language among different speakers and learners, how languages are used within their social contexts.

University of Illinois at Urbana–Champaign, Graduate College, College of Liberal Arts and Sciences, School of Literatures, Cultures and Linguistics, Department of Spanish, Italian and Portuguese, Champaign, IL 61820. Offers Italian (MA, PhD); Portuguese (MA, PhD); Spanish (MA, PhD).

The University of Iowa, Graduate College, College of Liberal Arts and Sciences, Department of Spanish and Portuguese, Iowa City, IA 52242-1316. Offers Spanish (MA, PhD); Spanish creative writing (MFA). *Degree requirements:* For master's, thesis optional, exam; for doctorate, comprehensive exam, thesis/dissertation. *Entrance requirements:* For master's and doctorate, GRE General Test, minimum GPA of 3.0. Additional exam requirements/recommendations for international students: Required—TOEFL (minimum score 600 paper-based; 100 iBT). Electronic applications accepted.

The University of Kansas, Graduate Studies, College of Liberal Arts and Sciences, Department of Spanish and Portuguese, Lawrence, KS 66045. Offers MA, PhD. *Students:* 28 full-time (17 women); includes 3 minority (all Hispanic/Latino), 12 international. Average age 32. 18 applicants, 61% accepted, 7 enrolled. In 2017, 6 master's, 3 doctorates awarded. *Entrance requirements:* For master's and doctorate, curriculum vitae, three letters of recommendation, writing sample, personal statement (500-750 words), official transcripts. Additional exam requirements/recommendations for international students: Required—TOEFL. *Application deadline:* For fall admission, 5/15 priority date for domestic students, 12/15 priority date for international students; for spring admission, 10/15 priority date for domestic students, 5/15 priority date for international students. Application fee: $65 ($85 for international students). Electronic applications accepted. *Financial support:* Fellowships, research assistantships, teaching assistantships, and unspecified assistantships available. Financial award application deadline: 1/15. *Faculty research:* Spanish and Latin American cultural studies, Spanish literature, Latin American literature, Hispanic linguistics. *Unit head:* Dr. Santa Arias, Chair, 785-864-3851, E-mail: sarias@ku.edu. *Application contact:* Jill Marietta Mignacca, Graduate Coordinator, 785-864-0279, E-mail: jmig@ku.edu.
Website: http://spanport.ku.edu/

University of Lethbridge, School of Graduate Studies, Lethbridge, AB T1K 3M4, Canada. Offers addictions counseling (M Sc); agricultural biotechnology (M Sc); agricultural studies (M Sc, MA); anthropology (MA); archaeology (M Sc, MA); art (MA, MFA); biochemistry (M Sc); biological sciences (M Sc); biomolecular science (PhD); biosystems and biodiversity (PhD); Canadian studies (MA); chemistry (M Sc); computer science (M Sc); computer science and geographical information science (M Sc); counseling (MC); counseling psychology (M Ed); dramatic arts (MA); earth, space, and physical science (PhD); economics (MA); education (MA, PhD); educational leadership (M Ed); English (MA); environmental science (M Sc); evolution and behavior (PhD); exercise science (M Sc); French (MA); French/German (MA); French/Spanish (MA); general education (M Ed); geography (M Sc, MA); German (MA); health sciences (M Sc); individualized multidisciplinary (M Sc, MA); kinesiology (M Sc, MA); management (M Sc), including accounting, finance, human resource management and labor relations, information systems, international management, marketing, policy and strategy; mathematics (M Sc); music (M Mus, MA); Native American studies (MA); neuroscience (M Sc, PhD); new media (MA, MFA); nursing (M Sc, MN); philosophy (MA); physics (M Sc); political science (MA); psychology (M Sc, MA); religious studies (MA); sociology (MA); theatre and dramatic arts (MFA); theoretical and computational science (PhD); urban and regional studies (MA); women and gender studies (MA). *Program availability:* Part-time, evening/weekend. *Degree requirements:* For master's, thesis (for some programs); for doctorate, comprehensive exam, thesis/dissertation. *Entrance requirements:* For master's, GMAT (for M Sc in management), bachelor's degree in related field, minimum GPA of 3.0 during previous 20 graded semester courses, 2 years' teaching or related experience (M Ed); for doctorate, master's degree, minimum graduate GPA of 3.5. Additional exam requirements/recommendations for international students: Required—TOEFL (minimum score 580 paper-based; 93 iBT). Electronic applications accepted. *Faculty research:* Movement and brain plasticity, gibberellin physiology, photosynthesis, carbon cycling, molecular properties of main-group ring components.

University of Louisville, Graduate School, College of Arts and Sciences, Department of Classical and Modern Languages, Louisville, KY 40292-0001. Offers French (MA); Spanish (MA); translation and interpretation (Certificate). *Program availability:* Part-time, evening/weekend. *Faculty:* 31 full-time (15 women), 14 part-time/adjunct (13 women). *Students:* 13 full-time (10 women), 14 part-time (10 women); includes 13 minority (2 Black or African American, non-Hispanic/Latino; 10 Hispanic/Latino; 1 Two or more races, non-Hispanic/Latino), 1 international. Average age 33. 17 applicants, 76% accepted, 11 enrolled. In 2017, 8 master's, 1 other advanced degree awarded. *Degree requirements:* For master's, one foreign language, thesis (for some programs). *Entrance requirements:* For master's, GRE General Test (recommended), letters of recommendation, transcripts, curriculum vitae, personal statement; for Certificate, GRE,

letters of recommendation, transcripts, curriculum vitae, personal statement. Additional exam requirements/recommendations for international students: Required—TOEFL (minimum score 550 paper-based; 79 iBT); Recommended—IELTS (minimum score 6.5). *Application deadline:* Applications are processed on a rolling basis. Application fee: $65. *Expenses:* Tuition, state resident: full-time $12,246; part-time $681 per credit hour. Tuition, nonresident: full-time $25,486; part-time $1417 per credit hour. *Required fees:* $196. Tuition and fees vary according to course load, program and reciprocity agreements. *Financial support:* In 2017–18, 12 teaching assistantships with full tuition reimbursements (averaging $14,000 per year) were awarded; scholarships/grants, health care benefits, and unspecified assistantships also available. Financial award applicants required to submit FAFSA. *Faculty research:* Medieval Spanish literature and culture, Modern Spanish literature and culture, translation and interpreting, film studies, Medieval French literature and culture, Modern, French literature and culture, American Sign Language studies. *Unit head:* Dr. Alan Leidner, Chair, 502-852-0483, Fax: 502-852-8885, E-mail: alan.leidner@louisville.edu. *Application contact:* Travis Henretty, Administrative Assistant, 502-852-6686, Fax: 502-852-8885, E-mail: travis.henretty@louisville.edu.
Website: http://louisville.edu/modernlanguages/

The University of Manchester, School of Languages, Linguistics and Cultures, Manchester, United Kingdom. Offers Arab world studies (PhD); Chinese studies (M Phil, PhD); East Asian studies (M Phil, PhD); English language (PhD); French studies (M Phil, PhD); German studies (M Phil, PhD); interpreting studies (PhD); Italian studies (M Phil, PhD); Japanese studies (M Phil, PhD); Latin American cultural studies (M Phil, PhD); linguistics (M Phil, PhD); Middle Eastern studies (M Phil, PhD); Polish studies (M Phil, PhD); Portuguese studies (M Phil, PhD); Russian studies (M Phil, PhD); Spanish studies (M Phil, PhD); translation and intercultural studies (M Phil, PhD).

University of Maryland, College Park, Academic Affairs, College of Arts and Humanities, School of Languages, Literatures, and Cultures, Spanish Language and Literatures Program, College Park, MD 20742. Offers MA, PhD. *Degree requirements:* For master's, comprehensive exam, thesis optional, scholarly paper; for doctorate, 2 foreign languages, thesis/dissertation. *Entrance requirements:* For master's, minimum GPA of 3.0, interview, sample research paper, minimum of 12 credits in upper-level literature, 3 letters of recommendation; for doctorate, minimum GPA of 3.0, interview, sample research paper, minimum of 12 credits in upper-level literature. Additional exam requirements/recommendations for international students: Required—TOEFL. Electronic applications accepted.

University of Massachusetts Amherst, Graduate School, College of Humanities and Fine Arts, Department of Languages, Literatures, and Cultures, Program in Spanish and Portuguese Studies, Amherst, MA 01003. Offers Hispanic literatures, cultures and linguistics (MA, PhD); teaching Spanish (MAT). *Program availability:* Part-time. Terminal master's awarded for partial completion of doctoral program. *Degree requirements:* For master's, one foreign language, thesis or alternative; for doctorate, 2 foreign languages, comprehensive exam, thesis/dissertation. *Entrance requirements:* For master's and doctorate, GRE General Test, sample academic term paper. Additional exam requirements/recommendations for international students: Required—TOEFL (minimum score 550 paper-based; 80 iBT), IELTS (minimum score 6.5). Electronic applications accepted.

University of Memphis, Graduate School, College of Arts and Sciences, Department of Foreign Languages and Literatures, Memphis, TN 38152. Offers romance languages (MA), including French, Spanish. *Program availability:* Part-time. *Faculty:* 6 full-time (2 women). *Students:* 15 full-time (13 women), 4 part-time (3 women); includes 11 minority (3 Black or African American, non-Hispanic/Latino; 8 Hispanic/Latino), 1 international. Average age 32. 13 applicants, 92% accepted, 9 enrolled. In 2017, 5 master's awarded. *Degree requirements:* For master's, 2 foreign languages, comprehensive exam. *Entrance requirements:* For master's, GRE, interview in language of concentration, writing sample, letter of intent, two letters of recommendation. Additional exam requirements/recommendations for international students: Required—TOEFL (minimum score 94 iBT). *Application deadline:* For fall admission, 5/15 for domestic students, 4/5 for international students; for spring admission, 11/30 for domestic students, 10/5 for international students. Applications are processed on a rolling basis. Application fee: $35 ($60 for international students). Electronic applications accepted. *Expenses:* Contact institution. *Financial support:* In 2017–18, 11 students received support, including 13 teaching assistantships with full tuition reimbursements available (averaging $12,846 per year); research assistantships with full tuition reimbursements available, Federal Work-Study, scholarships/grants, and unspecified assistantships also available. Financial award application deadline: 2/1; financial award applicants required to submit FAFSA. *Faculty research:* Latin American studies, Brazilian culture and literature, modernity and postmodernity, Hispanic studies, French studies, French and Hispanic culture and literature, Hispanic linguistics, applied linguistics. *Unit head:* Dr. William Thompson, Chair, 901-678-2507, E-mail: wjthmpsn@memphis.edu. *Application contact:* Dr. Fernando Burgos, Coordinator of Graduate Studies, 901-678-3158, E-mail: fburgos@memphis.edu.
Website: http://www.memphis.edu/fl/

University of Miami, Graduate School, College of Arts and Sciences, Department of Modern Languages and Literatures, Coral Gables, FL 33124. Offers romance studies (PhD), including French, Spanish. *Degree requirements:* For doctorate, 2 foreign languages, thesis/dissertation, area exam, qualifying exam. *Entrance requirements:* For doctorate, 1 writing sample in English and 1 writing sample in French or Spanish, minimum GPA of 3.0, oral interview, letters of recommendation. Additional exam requirements/recommendations for international students: Required—TOEFL (minimum score 550 paper-based; 59 iBT). Electronic applications accepted. *Faculty research:* Transatlantic studies, Caribbean studies, comparative literature, gender theory, cultural studies.

University of Miami, Graduate School, School of Communication, Coral Gables, FL 33124. Offers communication (PhD); communication studies (MA); film studies (MA, PhD); motion pictures (MFA), including production, producing, and screenwriting; print journalism (MA); public relations (MA); Spanish language journalism (MA); television broadcast journalism (MA). *Program availability:* Part-time. *Degree requirements:* For master's, comprehensive exam (for some programs), thesis (for some programs); for doctorate, comprehensive exam, thesis/dissertation. *Entrance requirements:* For master's, GRE General Test; for doctorate, GRE General Test, master's thesis or scholarly research. Additional exam requirements/recommendations for international students: Required—TOEFL (minimum score 600 paper-based; 100 iBT). Electronic applications accepted. *Faculty research:* Communication studies, mass communication, international/interpersonal communication, film studies, journalism.

University of Michigan, Rackham Graduate School, College of Literature, Science, and the Arts, Department of Romance Languages and Literatures, Program in Spanish, Ann Arbor, MI 48109-1275. Offers PhD. *Degree requirements:* For doctorate, 2 foreign languages, thesis/dissertation, oral defense of dissertation, preliminary exams in essay format. *Entrance requirements:* Additional exam requirements/recommendations for international students: Required—TOEFL or Michigan English Language Assessment Battery. Electronic applications accepted. *Expenses:* Tuition, state resident: full-time $22,368; part-time $1201 per credit hour. Tuition, nonresident: full-time $45,156; part-time $2467 per credit hour. *Required fees:* $376 per term. Tuition and fees vary according to course load, degree level and program. *Faculty research:* Comparative Romance studies, medieval and early modern studies, postcolonial and minority literatures, culture and materiality, reflection on the nature and function of scholarship.

University of Minnesota, Twin Cities Campus, Graduate School, College of Liberal Arts, Department of Spanish and Portuguese Studies, Minneapolis, MN 55455-0213. Offers Hispanic and Lusophone literatures, cultures and linguistics (PhD); Hispanic linguistics (MA); Hispanic literature (MA); Lusophone literature (MA). *Degree requirements:* For master's, 2 foreign languages, comprehensive exam, thesis or alternative; for doctorate, 2 foreign languages, comprehensive exam, thesis/dissertation. *Entrance requirements:* For master's and doctorate, GRE General Test, samples of written work, 3 letters of recommendation, voice sample, statement of purpose. Additional exam requirements/recommendations for international students: Required—TOEFL (minimum score 550 paper-based; 79 iBT). Electronic applications accepted. *Faculty research:* Sociohistorical approaches to literature and culture, feminist studies, literary theory, ideologies and literature, pragmatics and sociolinguistics.

University of Missouri, Office of Research and Graduate Studies, College of Arts and Science, Department of Romance Languages and Literatures, Columbia, MO 65211. Offers French (MA, PhD); literature (MA); Spanish (MA, PhD); teaching (MA). Terminal master's awarded for partial completion of doctoral program. *Degree requirements:* For master's, one foreign language; for doctorate, 4 foreign languages, comprehensive exam, thesis/dissertation. *Entrance requirements:* For master's, GRE General Test, minimum GPA of 3.0 in field of major; bachelor's degree; for doctorate, GRE General Test, minimum GPA of 3.0 in field of major; master's degree. Additional exam requirements/recommendations for international students: Required—TOEFL (minimum score 500 paper-based; 61 iBT). Electronic applications accepted.

University of Missouri–Kansas City, College of Arts and Sciences, Department of Foreign Languages and Literatures, Kansas City, MO 64110-2499. Offers romance languages and literatures (MA), including French, Spanish. *Program availability:* Part-time. *Degree requirements:* For master's, 2 foreign languages. *Entrance requirements:* For master's, GRE General Test, minimum GPA of 2.75, 2 letters of recommendation. Additional exam requirements/recommendations for international students: Required—TOEFL (minimum score 550 paper-based; 80 iBT). Electronic applications accepted. *Faculty research:* Literary analyses; psychology and literature; narrative techniques, poetic structure, and style; literature, politics, and society (especially in Latin America).

University of Montana, Graduate School, College of Humanities and Sciences, Department of Modern and Classical Languages and Literatures, Missoula, MT 59812. Offers French (MA); German (MA); Spanish (MA). *Degree requirements:* For master's, one foreign language. *Entrance requirements:* For master's, GRE General Test. Additional exam requirements/recommendations for international students: Required—TOEFL.

University of Nebraska–Lincoln, Graduate College, College of Arts and Sciences, Department of Modern Languages and Literatures, Lincoln, NE 68588. Offers French (MA, PhD); German (MA, PhD); Spanish (MA, PhD). *Degree requirements:* For master's, thesis optional; for doctorate, comprehensive exam, thesis/dissertation. *Entrance requirements:* For master's and doctorate, writing sample in target language. Additional exam requirements/recommendations for international students: Required—TOEFL (minimum score 550 paper-based). Electronic applications accepted. *Faculty research:* French, German, and Spanish language, literature, and culture.

University of Nevada, Reno, Graduate School, College of Liberal Arts, Department of Foreign Languages and Literatures, Reno, NV 89557. Offers French (MA); German (MA); Spanish (MA). *Degree requirements:* For master's, one foreign language, thesis optional. *Entrance requirements:* For master's, GRE General Test, minimum GPA of 2.75. Additional exam requirements/recommendations for international students: Required—TOEFL (minimum score 500 paper-based; 61 iBT), IELTS (minimum score 6). *Faculty research:* Thirteenth century mysticism, contemporary Spanish and Latin American poetry and theater, French interrelation between narration and photography, exile literature and Holocaust.

University of New Hampshire, Graduate School, College of Liberal Arts, Department of Spanish, Durham, NH 03824. Offers MA, Postbaccalaureate Certificate. *Students:* 4 full-time (1 woman), 1 part-time (0 women); includes 1 minority (Black or African American, non-Hispanic/Latino). Average age 26. 5 applicants, 100% accepted, 3 enrolled. In 2017, 2 master's awarded. *Entrance requirements:* Additional exam requirements/recommendations for international students: Required—TOEFL (minimum score 550 paper-based; 80 iBT). *Application deadline:* For fall admission, 4/1 for domestic and international students; for spring admission, 12/1 for domestic students; for summer admission, 4/1 for domestic students. Application fee: $65. Electronic applications accepted. *Financial support:* In 2017–18, 1 student received support, including 1 teaching assistantship; fellowships, research assistantships, career-related internships or fieldwork, Federal Work-Study, scholarships/grants, and tuition waivers (full and partial) also available. Support available to part-time students. Financial award application deadline: 2/15. *Unit head:* Holly Cashman, Chair, 603-862-3120. *Application contact:* Avary Thorne, Administrative Assistant, 603-862-4005, E-mail: spanish.master@unh.edu.
Website: http://cola.unh.edu/llc/program/spanish-ma

University of New Mexico, Graduate Studies, College of Arts and Sciences, Program in Spanish and Portuguese, Albuquerque, NM 87131. Offers Portuguese (MA); Spanish (MA); Spanish and Portuguese (PhD). *Program availability:* Part-time. *Faculty:* 11 full-time (5 women). *Students:* 41 full-time (29 women), 14 part-time (7 women); includes 32 minority (all Hispanic/Latino), 15 international. Average age 32. 53 applicants, 58% accepted, 21 enrolled. In 2017, 13 master's, 3 doctorates awarded. *Degree requirements:* For master's, one foreign language, comprehensive exam, thesis optional; for doctorate, one foreign language, comprehensive exam, thesis/dissertation. *Entrance requirements:* For master's, BA in Spanish or Portuguese, 3 letters of recommendation, letter of intent; for doctorate, GRE, 3 letters of recommendation, letter of intent, sample research paper. Additional exam requirements/recommendations for international students: Required—TOEFL (minimum score 550 paper-based). *Application deadline:* For fall admission, 1/15 priority date for domestic students; for spring admission, 11/15 for domestic students. Applications are processed on a rolling basis. Application fee: $50. Electronic applications accepted. *Financial support:* Research assistantships, teaching assistantships with tuition reimbursements, Federal Work-Study, institutionally sponsored loans, scholarships/grants, health care benefits, and unspecified assistantships available. Support available to part-time students. Financial award application deadline: 3/1; financial award applicants required to submit FAFSA. *Faculty research:* Languages and literatures from the Iberian Peninsula, Latin America and the American Southwest. *Unit head:* Dr. Anthony Cardenas, Chair, 505-277-5907, Fax: 505-277-3885, E-mail: ajcard@unm.edu. *Application contact:* Martha Hurd, Graduate Advisor, 505-277-2974, E-mail: marthah@unm.edu.
Website: http://spanport.unm.edu

The University of North Carolina at Chapel Hill, Graduate School, College of Arts and Sciences, Department of Romance Languages and Literatures, Chapel Hill, NC 27599. Offers French (MA, PhD); Italian (MA, PhD); Portuguese (MA, PhD); Romance

languages (MA, PhD); Romance philology (MA, PhD); Spanish (MA, PhD). *Degree requirements:* For master's, one foreign language, comprehensive exam, thesis; for doctorate, 2 foreign languages, comprehensive exam, thesis/dissertation. *Entrance requirements:* For master's and doctorate, GRE General Test, minimum GPA of 3.0. Additional exam requirements/recommendations for international students: Required—TOEFL (minimum score 550 paper-based). Electronic applications accepted.

The University of North Carolina at Charlotte, College of Liberal Arts and Sciences, Department of Languages and Culture Studies, Charlotte, NC 28223-0001. Offers languages and culture studies: translating (Graduate Certificate); Spanish (MA). *Program availability:* Part-time, evening/weekend. *Faculty:* 23 full-time (13 women). *Students:* 6 full-time (4 women), 7 part-time (5 women); includes 6 minority (1 Black or African American, non-Hispanic/Latino; 5 Hispanic/Latino). Average age 32. 11 applicants, 73% accepted, 7 enrolled. In 2017, 6 master's, 5 other advanced degrees awarded. *Degree requirements:* For master's, comprehensive exam, thesis, internship; for Graduate Certificate, internship. *Entrance requirements:* For master's, GRE, baccalaureate degree in Spanish or related field with minimum overall GPA of 2.75; essay that addresses the applicant's motivation for enrolling in program, to include particular areas of research interests and career or professional goals; three letters of reference; oral interview; for Graduate Certificate, GRE or MAT, essay in English that addresses applicant's motivation for seeking enrollment in program; three letters of recommendation; portfolio of best writing samples in both English and Spanish or of translations into each language; oral interview. Additional exam requirements/recommendations for international students: Required—TOEFL (minimum score 523 paper-based, 70 iBT) or IELTS (6.5). *Application deadline:* For fall admission, 3/1 priority date for domestic and international students; for spring admission, 10/1 priority date for domestic and international students. Applications are processed on a rolling basis. Application fee: $75. Electronic applications accepted. *Expenses:* Tuition, state resident: full-time $4337. Tuition, nonresident: full-time $17,771. *Required fees:* $3211. Tuition and fees vary according to course load and program. *Financial support:* In 2017–18, 7 students received support, including 4 research assistantships (averaging $7,000 per year), 3 teaching assistantships (averaging $8,667 per year); career-related internships or fieldwork, institutionally sponsored loans, scholarships/grants, and unspecified assistantships also available. Support available to part-time students. Financial award application deadline: 3/1; financial award applicants required to submit FAFSA. *Total annual research expenditures:* $13,367. *Unit head:* Ann Gonzalez, Chair, 704-687-8761, E-mail: abgonzal@uncc.edu. *Application contact:* Kathy B. Giddings, Director of Graduate Admissions, 704-687-5503, Fax: 704-687-1668, E-mail: gradadm@uncc.edu.
Website: https://languages.uncc.edu/

The University of North Carolina at Greensboro, Graduate School, College of Arts and Sciences, Department of Languages, Literatures, and Cultures, Program in Spanish, Greensboro, NC 27412-5001. Offers advanced Spanish language and Hispanic cultural studies (Certificate); Spanish (MA). *Degree requirements:* For master's, one foreign language, comprehensive exam, thesis or alternative. *Entrance requirements:* For master's, GRE General Test, 3-5 minute tape demonstrating foreign language proficiency, composition in Spanish, sample paper in English. Additional exam requirements/recommendations for international students: Required—TOEFL. Electronic applications accepted.

The University of North Carolina Wilmington, College of Arts and Sciences, Department of World Languages and Cultures, Wilmington, NC 28403-3297. Offers Hispanic studies (Postbaccalaureate Certificate); Spanish (MA). *Program availability:* Part-time. *Faculty:* 15 full-time (7 women). *Students:* 6 full-time (5 women), 10 part-time (7 women); includes 5 minority (all Hispanic/Latino), 2 international. Average age 28. 12 applicants, 75% accepted, 7 enrolled. In 2017, 6 master's awarded. *Degree requirements:* For master's, one foreign language, comprehensive exam, thesis (for some programs). *Entrance requirements:* For master's, 3 letters of recommendation, 2 three- to five-minute recorded speaking samples (both in English and Spanish), writing sample (both in English and Spanish). Additional exam requirements/recommendations for international students: Required—TOEFL (minimum score 550 paper-based; 79 iBT), IELTS (minimum score 6.5). *Application deadline:* For fall admission, 5/15 for domestic students; for spring admission, 11/1 for domestic students; for summer admission, 3/1 for domestic students. Applications are processed on a rolling basis. Application fee: $75. Electronic applications accepted. *Expenses:* Tuition, state resident: full-time $4626; part-time $226.76 per credit hour. Tuition, nonresident: full-time $17,834; part-time $874.22 per credit hour. *Required fees:* $2124. Tuition and fees vary according to program. *Financial support:* Teaching assistantships and scholarships/grants available. Financial award application deadline: 1/1; financial award applicants required to submit FAFSA. *Unit head:* Dr. Derrick Miller, Interim Chair, 910-962-2538, Fax: 910-962-7712, E-mail: millerd@uncw.edu. *Application contact:* Dr. Brian Chandler, Graduate Coordinator, 910-962-2299, Fax: 910-962-7712, E-mail: chandlerb@uncw.edu.
Website: http://www.uncw.edu/fll/spanish/spngraduate.html

University of Northern Iowa, Graduate College, College of Humanities, Arts and Sciences, Department of Languages and Literatures, MA Program in Spanish, Cedar Falls, IA 50614. Offers Spanish (MA); Spanish teaching (MA). *Program availability:* Part-time, evening/weekend. *Degree requirements:* For master's, one foreign language, comprehensive exam, thesis or alternative. *Entrance requirements:* For master's, minimum GPA of 3.0, valid teaching license, documentation of successful teaching experience. Additional exam requirements/recommendations for international students: Required—TOEFL (minimum score 600 paper-based; 100 iBT). Electronic applications accepted.

University of Northern Iowa, Graduate College, College of Humanities, Arts and Sciences, Department of Languages and Literatures, MA Program in TESOL/Spanish, Cedar Falls, IA 50614. Offers MA.

University of North Texas, Robert B. Toulouse School of Graduate Studies, Denton, TX 76203-5459. Offers accounting (MS); applied anthropology (MA, MS); applied behavior analysis (Certificate); applied geography (MA); applied technology and performance improvement (M Ed, MS); art education (MA); art history (MA); art museum education (Certificate); arts leadership (Certificate); audiology (Au D); behavior analysis (MS); behavioral science (PhD); biochemistry and molecular biology (MS); biology (MA, MS); biomedical engineering (MS); business analysis (MS); chemistry (MS); clinical health psychology (PhD); communication studies (MA, MS); computer engineering (MS); computer science (MS); counseling (M Ed, MS), including clinical mental health counseling (MS), college and university counseling, elementary school counseling, secondary school counseling; creative writing (MA); criminal justice (MS); curriculum and instruction (M Ed); decision sciences (MBA); design (MA, MFA), including fashion design (MFA), innovation studies, interior design (MFA); early childhood studies (MS); economics (MS); educational leadership (M Ed, Ed D); educational psychology (MS, PhD), including family studies (MS), gifted and talented (MS), human development (MS), learning and cognition (MS), research, measurement and evaluation (MS); electrical engineering (MS); emergency management (MPA); engineering technology (MS); English (MA); English as a second language (MA); environmental science (MS); finance (MBA, MS); financial management (MPA); French (MA); health services management (MBA); higher education (M Ed, Ed D); history (MA, MS); hospitality management (MS); human resources management (MPA); information science (MS); information systems (PhD); information technologies (MBA); interdisciplinary studies (MA, MS); international studies (MA); international sustainable tourism (MS); jazz studies (MM); journalism (MA, MJ, Graduate Certificate), including interactive and virtual digital communication (Graduate Certificate), narrative journalism (Graduate Certificate), public relations (Graduate Certificate); kinesiology (MS); linguistics (MA); local government management (MPA); logistics (PhD); logistics and supply chain management (MBA); long-term care, senior housing, and aging services (MA); management (PhD); marketing (MBA); mathematics (MA, MS); mechanical and energy engineering (MS, PhD); music (MA), including ethnomusicology, music theory, musicology, performance; music composition (PhD); music education (MM Ed, PhD); nonprofit management (MPA); operations and supply chain management (MBA); performance (MM, DMA); philosophy (MA); political science (MA); professional and technical communication (MA); radio, television and film (MA, MFA); rehabilitation counseling (Certificate); sociology (MA); Spanish (MA); special education (M Ed); speech-language pathology (MA); strategic management (MBA); studio art (MFA); teaching (M Ed); MBA/MS. *Program availability:* Part-time, evening/weekend, online learning. Terminal master's awarded for partial completion of doctoral program. *Degree requirements:* For master's, variable foreign language requirement, comprehensive exam (for some programs), thesis (for some programs); for doctorate, variable foreign language requirement, comprehensive exam (for some programs), thesis/dissertation; for other advanced degree, variable foreign language requirement, comprehensive exam (for some programs). *Entrance requirements:* For master's and doctorate, GRE, GMAT. Additional exam requirements/recommendations for international students: Required—TOEFL (minimum score 550 paper-based; 79 iBT). Electronic applications accepted.

University of Notre Dame, Graduate School, College of Arts and Letters, Division of Humanities, Department of Romance Languages and Literatures, Notre Dame, IN 46556. Offers French and Francophone studies (MA); Iberian and Latin American studies (MA); Italian studies (MA); Romance literatures (MA). *Degree requirements:* For master's, 2 foreign languages, comprehensive exam, thesis optional. *Entrance requirements:* For master's, GRE General Test, BA in target language. Additional exam requirements/recommendations for international students: Required—TOEFL (minimum score 600 paper-based; 80 iBT). Electronic applications accepted. *Faculty research:* Literature of discovery and exploration, modern literature, literary criticism, medieval literature, feminist critical theory.

University of Oklahoma, College of Arts and Sciences, Department of Modern Languages, Literatures, and Linguistics, Program in Spanish, Norman, OK 73019. Offers MA, PhD, MBA/MA. *Program availability:* Part-time. *Students:* 17 full-time (10 women), 10 part-time (5 women); includes 12 minority (all Hispanic/Latino), 7 international. Average age 36. 11 applicants, 55% accepted, 6 enrolled. In 2017, 3 master's, 3 doctorates awarded. Terminal master's awarded for partial completion of doctoral program. *Degree requirements:* For master's, comprehensive exam, thesis optional, 2 languages (Spanish plus one other language); for doctorate, comprehensive exam, thesis/dissertation, 2 languages (Spanish plus one other language). *Entrance requirements:* For master's, BA with at least 6 hours in Spanish literature; for doctorate, MA in any Spanish language-related literatures. Additional exam requirements/recommendations for international students: Required—TOEFL (minimum score 79 iBT) or IELTS (minimum score 6.5). *Application deadline:* For fall admission, 2/1 for domestic and international students; for spring admission, 10/1 for domestic and international students. Application fee: $50 ($100 for international students). Electronic applications accepted. *Expenses:* Tuition, state resident: full-time $5119; part-time $213.30 per credit hour. Tuition, nonresident: full-time $19,778; part-time $824.10 per credit hour. *Required fees:* $3458; $133.55 per credit hour. $126.50 per semester. *Financial support:* In 2017–18, 24 students received support. Fellowships, teaching assistantships with full tuition reimbursements available, scholarships/grants, health care benefits, and unspecified assistantships available. Support available to part-time students. Financial award application deadline: 6/1; financial award applicants required to submit FAFSA. *Faculty research:* 20th- and 21st-century Latin American literatures, colonial literature, 19th century literature, peninsular golden age literature, medieval literature, modern peninsular literature. *Unit head:* Dr. Robert Lauer, Professor of Spanish, 405-325-1409, Fax: 405-325-5845, E-mail: arlauer@ou.edu. *Application contact:* Julie Ann Ward, Assistant Professor of Spanish/Spanish Graduate Section Liaison, 405-325-6181, E-mail: wardjulie@ou.edu.
Website: http://mlll.publishpath.com/spanish-ma

University of Oregon, Graduate School, College of Arts and Sciences, Department of Romance Languages, Program in Spanish, Eugene, OR 97403. Offers MA. *Program availability:* Part-time. *Degree requirements:* For master's, one foreign language. *Entrance requirements:* For master's, GRE General Test, minimum GPA of 3.0. Additional exam requirements/recommendations for international students: Required—TOEFL.

University of Ottawa, Faculty of Graduate and Postdoctoral Studies, Faculty of Arts, Department of Modern Languages and Literatures, Ottawa, ON K1N 6N5, Canada. Offers Spanish (MA, PhD). *Program availability:* Part-time, evening/weekend. *Degree requirements:* For master's, one foreign language, thesis or alternative; for doctorate, one foreign language, comprehensive exam, thesis/dissertation. *Entrance requirements:* For master's, BA with honors in Spanish, minimum B average; for doctorate, MA in Spanish or equivalent, minimum B average. Electronic applications accepted. *Faculty research:* Spanish American literature, Mexican literature and film studies, Spanish golden age literature, twentieth-century Spanish literature, Hispanic linguistics with special emphasis on linguistic theory.

University of Pennsylvania, School of Arts and Sciences, Graduate Group in Romance Languages, Philadelphia, PA 19104. Offers French (AM, PhD); Italian (AM, PhD); Spanish (AM, PhD). *Faculty:* 20 full-time (7 women), 6 part-time/adjunct (3 women). *Students:* 61 full-time (29 women); includes 7 minority (6 Hispanic/Latino; 1 Two or more races, non-Hispanic/Latino), 34 international. Average age 31. 82 applicants, 32% accepted, 13 enrolled. In 2017, 12 master's, 8 doctorates awarded. Terminal master's awarded for partial completion of doctoral program. Application fee: $70.
Website: http://www.sas.upenn.edu/graduate-division

University of Pittsburgh, Kenneth P. Dietrich School of Arts and Sciences, Program in Hispanic Linguistics, Pittsburgh, PA 15260. Offers TESOL (PhD). *Faculty:* 2 full-time (1 woman). *Students:* 4 full-time (all women); includes 3 minority (all Hispanic/Latino). Average age 32. In 2017, 2 doctorates awarded. Terminal master's awarded for partial completion of doctoral program. *Degree requirements:* For doctorate, 2 foreign languages, comprehensive exam, thesis/dissertation. *Entrance requirements:* For doctorate, GRE General Test, proficiency in Spanish. Additional exam requirements/recommendations for international students: Required—TOEFL (minimum score 600 paper-based; 100 iBT). *Application deadline:* For fall admission, 12/15 priority date for domestic and international students. Application fee: $50. Electronic applications accepted. *Financial support:* In 2017–18, 6 students received support, including 2 fellowships with full tuition reimbursements available (averaging $18,620 per year), 3 teaching assistantships with full tuition reimbursements available (averaging $17,190 per year). Financial award application deadline: 12/15; financial award applicants

required to submit FAFSA. *Faculty research:* Hispanic linguistics, second language acquisition, phonetics, prosody, language variation and change. *Unit head:* Dr. Shelome Gooden, Chair, 412-624-5922, Fax: 412-624-5520, E-mail: sgooden@pitt.edu. *Application contact:* Margaret Bupp, Graduate Student Services Administrator, 412-624-6568, Fax: 412-624-5520, E-mail: maggiebupp@pitt.edu.
Website: http://www.linguistics.pitt.edu

University of Rhode Island, Graduate School, College of Arts and Sciences, Department of Modern and Classical Languages and Literatures, Kingston, RI 02881. Offers Spanish (MA). *Program availability:* Part-time. *Faculty:* 29 full-time (19 women). *Students:* 4 full-time (2 women), 7 part-time (2 women); includes 2 minority (both Hispanic/Latino), 2 international. 3 applicants, 100% accepted, 3 enrolled. In 2017, 6 master's awarded. *Entrance requirements:* For master's, 2 letters of recommendation. Additional exam requirements/recommendations for international students: Required—TOEFL. *Application deadline:* For fall admission, 7/15 for domestic students, 2/1 for international students; for spring admission, 11/15 for domestic students, 7/15 for international students. Application fee: $65. Electronic applications accepted. *Expenses:* Tuition, state resident: full-time $12,706; part-time $786 per credit. Tuition, nonresident: full-time $25,216; part-time $1401 per credit. *Required fees:* $1598; $45 per credit. One-time fee: $30 part-time. *Financial support:* In 2017–18, 3 teaching assistantships with tuition reimbursements (averaging $17,724 per year) were awarded. Financial award application deadline: 2/1; financial award applicants required to submit FAFSA. *Unit head:* Dr. Karen de Bruin, Department Chair, 401-874-4697, E-mail: debruin@uri.edu. *Application contact:* Dr. Clement White, Spanish Graduate Admission, 401-874-5742, E-mail: cwhite@uri.edu.
Website: http://web.uri.edu/languages/

University of South Africa, College of Human Sciences, Pretoria, South Africa. Offers adult education (M Ed); African languages (MA, PhD); African politics (MA, PhD); Afrikaans (MA, PhD); ancient history (MA, PhD); ancient Near Eastern studies (MA, PhD); anthropology (MA, PhD); applied linguistics (MA); Arabic (MA, PhD); archaeology (MA); art history (MA); Biblical archaeology (MA); Biblical studies (M Th, D Th, PhD); Christian spirituality (M Th, D Th); church history (M Th, D Th); classical studies (MA, PhD); clinical psychology (MA); communication (MA, PhD); comparative education (M Ed, Ed D); consulting psychology (D Admin, D Com, PhD); curriculum studies (M Ed, Ed D); development studies (M Admin, MA, D Admin, PhD); didactics (M Ed, Ed D); education (M Tech); education management (M Ed, Ed D); educational psychology (M Ed); English (MA); environmental education (M Ed); French (MA, PhD); German (MA, PhD); Greek (MA); guidance and counseling (M Ed); health studies (MA, PhD), including health sciences education (MA), health services management (MA), medical and surgical nursing science (critical care general) (MA), midwifery and neonatal nursing science (MA), trauma and emergency care (MA); history (MA, PhD); history of education (Ed D); inclusive education (M Ed, Ed D); information and communications technology policy and regulation (MA); information science (MA, MIS, PhD); international politics (MA, PhD); Islamic studies (MA, PhD); Italian (MA, PhD); Judaica (MA, PhD); linguistics (MA, PhD); mathematical education (M Ed); mathematics education (MA); missiology (M Th, D Th); modern Hebrew (MA, PhD); musicology (MA, MMus, D Mus, PhD); natural science education (M Ed); New Testament (M Th, D Th); Old Testament (D Th); pastoral therapy (M Th, D Th); philosophy (MA); philosophy of education (M Ed, Ed D); politics (MA, PhD); Portuguese (MA, PhD); practical theology (M Th, D Th); psychology (MA, MS, PhD); psychology of education (M Ed, Ed D); public health (MA); religious studies (MA, D Th, PhD); Romance languages (MA); Russian (MA, PhD); Semitic languages (MA, PhD); social behavior studies in HIV/AIDS (MA); social science (mental health) (MA); social science in development studies (MA); social science in psychology (MA); social science in social work (MA); social science in sociology (MA); social work (MSW, DSW, PhD); socio-education (M Ed, Ed D); sociolinguistics (MA); sociology (MA, PhD); Spanish (MA, PhD); systematic theology (M Th, D Th); TESOL (teaching English to speakers of other languages) (MA); theological ethics (M Th, D Th); theory of literature (MA, PhD); urban ministries (D Th); urban ministry (M Th).

University of South Carolina, The Graduate School, College of Arts and Sciences, Department of Languages, Literatures, and Cultures, Columbia, SC 29208. Offers comparative literature (MA, PhD); foreign languages (MAT), including French, German, Spanish; French (MA); German (MA); Spanish (MA). MAT offered in cooperation with the College of Education. *Program availability:* Part-time. *Degree requirements:* For master's, one foreign language, comprehensive exam, thesis optional; for doctorate, 2 foreign languages, comprehensive exam, thesis/dissertation. *Entrance requirements:* For master's and doctorate, GRE General Test, writing sample. Additional exam requirements/recommendations for international students: Required—TOEFL (minimum score 75 iBT). Electronic applications accepted. *Faculty research:* Modern literature, linguistics, literature and culture, medieval literature, literary theory.

University of Southern California, Graduate School, Dana and David Dornsife College of Letters, Arts and Sciences, Comparative Studies in Literature and Culture Doctoral Program, Los Angeles, CA 90089. Offers comparative literature (PhD); comparative media and culture (PhD); Spanish and Latin American studies (PhD). *Degree requirements:* For doctorate, 2 foreign languages, comprehensive exam, thesis/dissertation. *Entrance requirements:* For doctorate, GRE, competence in language other than English (highly recommended). Additional exam requirements/recommendations for international students: Required—TOEFL. Electronic applications accepted. *Faculty research:* Literary theory, Japanese film and contemporary fiction, Francophone literature and cinema, Latin American and Caribbean literature, Spanish literature and film, nineteenth and twentieth century British and American literature.

University of Southern Mississippi, College of Arts and Letters, Department of Foreign Languages and Literatures, Hattiesburg, MS 39406-0001. Offers Spanish (MATL). *Program availability:* 100% online. *Students:* 13 applicants, 77% accepted, 8 enrolled. In 2017, 41 master's awarded. *Degree requirements:* For master's, comprehensive exam. *Entrance requirements:* For master's, GRE General Test, minimum GPA of 3.0 in field of study, 2.75 in last 2 years. Additional exam requirements/recommendations for international students: Required—TOEFL, IELTS. *Application deadline:* For fall admission, 3/1 for domestic and international students. Applications are processed on a rolling basis. Application fee: $60. Electronic applications accepted. *Expenses:* Tuition, state resident: full-time $3830. *Financial support:* Teaching assistantships with full tuition reimbursements, Federal Work-Study, institutionally sponsored loans, scholarships/grants, health care benefits, and unspecified assistantships available. Financial award application deadline: 3/15; financial award applicants required to submit FAFSA. *Unit head:* Christopher Miles, Chair, 601-266-4964, Fax: 601-266-4583. *Application contact:* Laurel Abreau, Graduate Director, 601-266-4964.
Website: https://www.usm.edu/foreign-languages-literatures

University of South Florida, College of Arts and Sciences, Department of World Languages, Tampa, FL 33620-9951. Offers French (MA); linguistics (MA); linguistics and applied linguistics studies (PhD); linguistics: English as a second language (MA); Spanish (MA). *Program availability:* Part-time, evening/weekend. *Faculty:* 18 full-time (14 women). *Students:* 40 full-time (34 women), 9 part-time (7 women); includes 20 minority (1 Black or African American, non-Hispanic/Latino; 1 Asian, non-Hispanic/Latino; 16 Hispanic/Latino; 2 Two or more races, non-Hispanic/Latino), 16 international. Average age 33. 65 applicants, 62% accepted, 18 enrolled. In 2017, 30 master's awarded. *Degree requirements:* For master's, one foreign language, comprehensive exam, thesis optional; for doctorate, one foreign language, comprehensive exam, thesis/dissertation. *Entrance requirements:* For master's, GRE General Test, minimum undergraduate GPA of 3.0 and 2-3 letters of recommendation; two-page statement of purpose written in Spanish (for Spanish program); oral interview (for Spanish and French programs); writing sample (for French program); for doctorate, GRE General Test, minimum GPA of 3.5 or international equivalent; master's degree or equivalent academic level; statement of purpose; current curriculum vitae; three letters of recommendation; personal interview with faculty; evidence of research experience or scholarly promise. Additional exam requirements/recommendations for international students: Required—TOEFL minimum score 600 paper-based; 80 iBT or IELTS minimum score 6.5 (for MA); TOEFL minimum score 550 paper-based; 80 iBT or IELTS minimum score 6.5 (for PhD). *Application deadline:* For fall admission, 1/15 for domestic and international students; for spring admission, 10/15 for domestic students, 9/15 for international students. Application fee: $30. Electronic applications accepted. *Financial support:* In 2017–18, 10 students received support, including 43 teaching assistantships with tuition reimbursements available (averaging $10,152 per year); tuition waivers (partial) and unspecified assistantships also available. Financial award application deadline: 6/30. *Faculty research:* Second language acquisition, instructional technology, foreign language education, English for speakers of other languages, distance learning. *Total annual research expenditures:* $7,706. *Unit head:* Dr. Stephan Schindler, Chair and Professor, 813-974-2548, Fax: 813-905-9937, E-mail: skschindler@usf.edu. *Application contact:* Patricia Garcia, Academic Program Specialist, 813-974-2548, Fax: 813-905-9937, E-mail: pgarcia@usf.edu.
Website: http://languages.usf.edu/

The University of Tennessee, Graduate School, College of Arts and Sciences, Department of Modern Foreign Languages and Literatures, Program in Modern Foreign Languages, Knoxville, TN 37996. Offers applied linguistics (PhD); French (PhD); German (PhD); Italian (PhD); Portuguese (PhD); Russian (PhD); Spanish (PhD). *Degree requirements:* For doctorate, 2 foreign languages, thesis/dissertation. *Entrance requirements:* For doctorate, minimum GPA of 2.7. Additional exam requirements/recommendations for international students: Required—TOEFL. Electronic applications accepted.

The University of Tennessee, Graduate School, College of Arts and Sciences, Department of Modern Foreign Languages and Literatures, Program in Spanish, Knoxville, TN 37996. Offers MA. *Degree requirements:* For master's, one foreign language, thesis or alternative. *Entrance requirements:* For master's, minimum GPA of 2.7. Additional exam requirements/recommendations for international students: Required—TOEFL. Electronic applications accepted.

The University of Texas at Arlington, Graduate School, College of Liberal Arts, Department of Modern Languages, Arlington, TX 76019. Offers French (MA); Spanish (MA). *Program availability:* Part-time, evening/weekend. *Degree requirements:* For master's, 2 foreign languages, comprehensive exam, thesis optional. *Entrance requirements:* For master's, GRE General Test, minimum GPA of 3.0, 3 letters of recommendation. Additional exam requirements/recommendations for international students: Required—TOEFL (minimum score 550 paper-based).

The University of Texas at Austin, Graduate School, College of Liberal Arts, Department of Spanish and Portuguese, Austin, TX 78712-1111. Offers Hispanic linguistics (MA, PhD); Hispanic literature (MA, PhD); Ibero-romance philology and linguistics (PhD); Luso-Brazilian literature (MA, PhD). *Degree requirements:* For master's, 2 foreign languages, thesis or alternative; for doctorate, 3 foreign languages, thesis/dissertation. *Entrance requirements:* For master's and doctorate, GRE General Test. Electronic applications accepted.

The University of Texas at El Paso, Graduate School, College of Liberal Arts, Department of Creative Writing, El Paso, TX 79968-0001. Offers creative writing (MFA); creative writing of the Americas (MFA). *Program availability:* Part-time, evening/weekend, online learning. *Degree requirements:* For master's, thesis. *Entrance requirements:* For master's, minimum GPA of 3.0, letters of recommendation, writing sample. Additional exam requirements/recommendations for international students: Recommended—TOEFL, IELTS. Electronic applications accepted.

The University of Texas at El Paso, Graduate School, College of Liberal Arts, Department of Languages and Linguistics, El Paso, TX 79968-0001. Offers linguistics (MA); Spanish (MA); teaching English to speakers of other languages (Certificate). *Program availability:* Part-time, evening/weekend. *Degree requirements:* For master's, thesis optional. *Entrance requirements:* For master's, GRE General Test, departmental exam, minimum GPA of 3.0, letters of recommendation. Additional exam requirements/recommendations for international students: Required—TOEFL; Recommended—IELTS. Electronic applications accepted.

The University of Texas at San Antonio, College of Liberal and Fine Arts, Department of Modern Languages and Literatures, San Antonio, TX 78249-0617. Offers Spanish (MA). *Program availability:* Part-time. *Faculty:* 5 full-time (2 women). *Students:* 1 (woman) full-time, 16 part-time (12 women); includes 14 minority (1 Black or African American, non-Hispanic/Latino; 13 Hispanic/Latino). Average age 39. 11 applicants, 73% accepted, 6 enrolled. In 2017, 2 master's awarded. *Degree requirements:* For master's, one foreign language, comprehensive exam, thesis optional. *Entrance requirements:* For master's, minimum GPA of 3.0, sample of written and spoken work, letter of recommendation, statement of purpose. Additional exam requirements/recommendations for international students: Required—TOEFL (minimum score 550 paper-based; 79 iBT), IELTS (minimum score 6.5). *Application deadline:* For fall admission, 6/15 for domestic students, 3/1 for international students; for spring admission, 10/15 for domestic students, 9/15 for international students. Applications are processed on a rolling basis. Application fee: $50 ($90 for international students). Electronic applications accepted. *Expenses:* Tuition, state resident: full-time $5495. Tuition, nonresident: full-time $21,938. *Required fees:* $1915. Tuition and fees vary according to program. *Financial support:* Scholarships/grants available. *Faculty research:* Film studies, religious studies, Spanish literature, Spanish culture, Spanish linguistics. *Unit head:* Dr. Marita Nummikoski, Department Chair, 210-458-4377, E-mail: marita.nummikoski@utsa.edu.
Website: http://colfa.utsa.edu/modern-languages/

The University of Texas of the Permian Basin, Office of Graduate Studies, College of Arts and Sciences, Department of Literature and Languages, Odessa, TX 79762-0001. Offers English (MA); Spanish (MA). *Degree requirements:* For master's, comprehensive exam (for some programs), thesis (for some programs). *Entrance requirements:* For master's, GRE General Test. Additional exam requirements/recommendations for international students: Required—TOEFL (minimum score 550 paper-based).

The University of Texas Rio Grande Valley, College of Liberal Arts, Department of Literatures and Cultural Studies, Edinburg, TX 78539. Offers English (MA); Spanish (MA). MA in Spanish conducted in conjunction with Department of Writing and Language Studies. *Program availability:* Part-time, evening/weekend. *Faculty:* 11 full-time (6 women). *Students:* 14 full-time (9 women), 78 part-time (60 women); includes 85 minority (all Hispanic/Latino), 2 international. Average age 33. 26 applicants, 100%

accepted, 22 enrolled. In 2017, 32 master's awarded. *Degree requirements:* For master's, comprehensive exam, thesis optional. *Entrance requirements:* For master's, GRE General Test, minimum GPA of 3.0. Additional exam requirements/ recommendations for international students: Required—TOEFL or IELTS. *Application deadline:* For fall admission, 2/1 priority date for domestic students; for spring admission, 9/1 priority date for domestic students. Applications are processed on a rolling basis. Application fee: $50 ($100 for international students). *Expenses:* Tuition, state resident: full-time $5550; part-time $417 per credit hour. Tuition, nonresident: full-time $13,020; part-time $832 per credit hour. *Required fees:* $1169. *Financial support:* Application deadline: 4/15. *Faculty research:* Oral vs. literary culture, Borderland literature, Mexican-American literature, topics in British and American literature, discourse analysis. *Unit head:* Steve Wilson, Interim Chair, E-mail: steve.wilson@utrgv.edu.

The University of Texas Rio Grande Valley, College of Liberal Arts, Program in Interdisciplinary Studies, Edinburg, TX 78539. Offers interdisciplinary studies (MAIS, MSIS); Spanish translation and interpreting (MA). *Program availability:* Part-time, evening/weekend. *Faculty:* 3 full-time (2 women). *Students:* 17 full-time (13 women), 41 part-time (28 women); includes 47 minority (1 Asian, non-Hispanic/Latino; 46 Hispanic/ Latino), 2 international. Average age 36. 23 applicants, 100% accepted, 15 enrolled. In 2017, 25 master's awarded. *Degree requirements:* For master's, comprehensive exam, thesis or alternative. *Entrance requirements:* For master's, GRE General Test, minimum GPA of 3.0. Additional exam requirements/recommendations for international students: Required—TOEFL or IELTS. Application fee: $50 ($100 for international students). *Expenses:* Tuition, state resident: full-time $5550; part-time $417 per credit hour. Tuition, nonresident: full-time $13,020; part-time $832 per credit hour. *Required fees:* $1169. *Financial support:* Application deadline: 6/1. *Unit head:* Russel Skowronek, Associate Dean, E-mail: russell.skowronek@utrgv.edu.

The University of Toledo, College of Graduate Studies, College of Languages, Literature and Social Sciences, Department of Foreign Languages, Toledo, OH 43606-3390. Offers French (MA); German (MA); Spanish (MA). *Program availability:* Part-time. *Degree requirements:* For master's, one foreign language, comprehensive exam, comprehensive reading exam in 1 additional foreign language. *Entrance requirements:* For master's, minimum cumulative point-hour ratio of 2.7 for all previous academic work. Additional exam requirements/recommendations for international students: Required—TOEFL (minimum score 550 paper-based; 80 iBT). Electronic applications accepted.

University of Toronto, School of Graduate Studies, Faculty of Arts and Science, Department of Spanish and Portuguese, Toronto, ON M5S 1A1, Canada. Offers MA, PhD. *Program availability:* Part-time. *Degree requirements:* For doctorate, thesis/ dissertation. *Entrance requirements:* For master's, minimum B average in final year, 2 letters of reference; for doctorate, minimum A- average, 2 letters of reference, writing sample. Additional exam requirements/recommendations for international students: Required—TWE (minimum score 5), TOEFL, Michigan English Language Assessment Battery, IELTS, or COPE. Electronic applications accepted.

University of Utah, Graduate School, College of Humanities, Department of World Languages and Cultures, Salt Lake City, UT 84112. Offers comparative literary and cultural studies (MA, PhD); French (MA); Spanish (MA, MALP); world languages (MA). *Program availability:* Part-time. *Faculty:* 36 full-time (22 women). *Students:* 27 full-time (19 women), 8 part-time (6 women); includes 5 minority (4 Hispanic/Latino; 1 Two or more races, non-Hispanic/Latino), 10 international. Average age 27. 17 applicants, 76% accepted, 9 enrolled. In 2017, 13 master's, 2 doctorates awarded. Terminal master's awarded for partial completion of doctoral program. *Degree requirements:* For master's, variable foreign language requirement, comprehensive exam (for some programs), thesis (for some programs); for doctorate, 2 foreign languages, comprehensive exam, thesis/dissertation. *Entrance requirements:* For master's, bachelor's degree from regionally-accredited college or university with minimum undergraduate overall GPA of 3.0; for doctorate, MA from regionally-accredited college or university, advanced proficiency in target language. Additional exam requirements/recommendations for international students: Required—TOEFL (minimum score 550 paper-based; 80 iBT), IELTS (minimum score 6.5). *Application deadline:* For fall admission, 1/15 priority date for domestic students, 12/15 priority date for international students. Application fee: $55 ($65 for international students). Electronic applications accepted. *Financial support:* In 2017–18, 24 students received support, including 24 teaching assistantships with full and partial tuition reimbursements available (averaging $17,200 per year); unspecified assistantships also available. Financial award application deadline: 1/15. *Faculty research:* Literary study, literary theory, linguistics, cultural studies, comparative studies. *Unit head:* Dr. Katharina Gerstenberger, Chair, 801-585-7908, Fax: 801-581-7581, E-mail: katharina.gerstenberger@utah.edu. *Application contact:* Mackenzie Buie, Academic Coordinator, 801-581-7748, Fax: 801-581-7581, E-mail: mackenzie.buie@utah.edu.
Website: http://languages.utah.edu/

University of Virginia, College and Graduate School of Arts and Sciences, Department of Spanish, Italian and Portuguese, Charlottesville, VA 22903. Offers Spanish (MA, PhD). *Faculty:* 37 full-time (24 women), 1 part-time/adjunct (0 women). *Students:* 29 full-time (21 women); includes 5 minority (1 Black or African American, non-Hispanic/Latino; 4 Hispanic/Latino), 7 international. Average age 26. 26 applicants, 69% accepted, 5 enrolled. In 2017, 6 master's, 8 doctorates awarded. *Degree requirements:* For master's, comprehensive exam, thesis; for doctorate, one foreign language, comprehensive exam, thesis/dissertation. *Entrance requirements:* For master's and doctorate, GRE General Test, GRE Subject Test, 2 letters of recommendation. Additional exam requirements/recommendations for international students: Required—TOEFL (minimum score 600 paper-based; 90 iBT), IELTS (minimum score 7). *Application deadline:* For fall admission, 12/1 for domestic and international students. Applications are processed on a rolling basis. Application fee: $60. Electronic applications accepted. *Financial support:* Fellowships and teaching assistantships available. Financial award applicants required to submit FAFSA. *Unit head:* Joel Rini, Chair, 434-924-7159, Fax: 434-924-7160, E-mail: sipinfo@virginia.edu. *Application contact:* E. Michael Gerli, Director of Graduate Admissions, 434-924-7503, Fax: 434-924-7160, E-mail: sipinfo@virginia.edu.
Website: http://spanitalport.virginia.edu/

University of Washington, Graduate School, College of Arts and Sciences, Division of Spanish and Portuguese Studies, Seattle, WA 98195. Offers Hispanic literary and cultural studies (MA). *Degree requirements:* For master's, 2 foreign languages, thesis optional, exam. *Entrance requirements:* For master's, GRE General Test, minimum GPA of 3.0. Additional exam requirements/recommendations for international students: Required—TOEFL. Electronic applications accepted. *Faculty research:* Medieval through modern Spanish literature and film, Latin American literature, poetry and essay, pan-Hispanic ballad, Hispanic cultural studies, second language acquisition and applied linguistics.

The University of Western Ontario, Faculty of Graduate Studies, Faculty of Arts and Humanities, Department of Modern Languages and Literatures, London, ON N6A 5B8, Canada. Offers comparative literature (MA, PhD); Hispanic studies (MA, PhD). *Program availability:* Part-time. *Degree requirements:* For master's, 2 foreign languages, thesis (for some programs). *Entrance requirements:* For master's, honors degree in Spanish or equivalent, minimum B average. Additional exam requirements/recommendations for international students: Required—TOEFL (comparative literature). *Faculty research:* Spanish golden age, Latin-American, romance, medieval, film.

University of Wisconsin–Madison, Graduate School, College of Letters and Science, Department of Spanish and Portuguese, Program in Spanish, Madison, WI 53706-1380. Offers MA, PhD. *Degree requirements:* For master's, one foreign language; for doctorate, 2 foreign languages, thesis/dissertation. *Entrance requirements:* For master's, GRE (recommended), minimum GPA of 3.25 in Spanish or Portuguese; for doctorate, GRE (recommended), minimum graduate GPA of 3.4, writing sample. Additional exam requirements/recommendations for international students: Required—TOEFL. Electronic applications accepted. *Faculty research:* Hispanic linguistics, Spanish and Spanish-American literature.

University of Wisconsin–Milwaukee, Graduate School, College of Letters and Science, Department of Foreign Languages and Literature, Milwaukee, WI 53201-0413. Offers foreign languages and literature (MA), including classic Greek, classics, comparative literature, French/Francophone language, literature, and culture, German language, literature, and culture, interpreting, Latin, linguistics, Spanish language, literature, and culture, translation; interpreting (Graduate Certificate); language, literature, and translation (MA, MALLT); translation (Graduate Certificate). *Program availability:* Part-time. *Students:* 11 full-time (6 women), 40 part-time (29 women); includes 10 minority (2 Black or African American, non-Hispanic/Latino; 3 Hispanic/ Latino; 5 Two or more races, non-Hispanic/Latino), 4 international. Average age 35. 37 applicants, 68% accepted, 20 enrolled. In 2017, 5 master's awarded. *Degree requirements:* For master's, 2 foreign languages, thesis or alternative. *Entrance requirements:* Additional exam requirements/recommendations for international students: Required—TOEFL (minimum score 550 paper-based; 79 iBT), IELTS (minimum score 6.5). *Application deadline:* For fall admission, 1/1 priority date for domestic students; for spring admission, 9/1 for domestic students. Application fee: $56 ($96 for international students). Electronic applications accepted. *Financial support:* Fellowships, research assistantships, teaching assistantships, career-related internships or fieldwork, health care benefits, unspecified assistantships, and project assistantships available. Support available to part-time students. Financial award application deadline: 4/15; financial award applicants required to submit FAFSA. *Unit head:* Kevin Muse, Department Chair, 414-229-5213, E-mail: kmuse@uwm.edu. *Application contact:* General Information Contact, 414-229-4982, Fax: 414-229-6967, E-mail: gradschool@uwm.edu.
Website: http://uwm.edu/foreign-languages-literature/

University of Wisconsin–Milwaukee, Graduate School, College of Letters and Science, Department of Spanish and Portuguese, Milwaukee, WI 53201-0413. Offers MA. *Students:* 9 full-time (4 women), 6 part-time (3 women); includes 3 minority (1 Hispanic/Latino; 2 Two or more races, non-Hispanic/Latino), 7 international. Average age 28. 14 applicants, 64% accepted, 8 enrolled. In 2017, 3 master's awarded. *Entrance requirements:* For master's, bachelor's degree. Application fee: $56 ($96 for international students). Electronic applications accepted. *Financial support:* Fellowships, research assistantships, teaching assistantships, and unspecified assistantships available. Financial award applicants required to submit FAFSA. *Faculty research:* Sociolinguistics, Spanish-American literature, Spanish literature, Hispanic culture, Hispanic historiography. *Unit head:* John McCaw, Department Chair, 414-229-4257, E-mail: rjmccaw@uwm.edu. *Application contact:* General Information Contact, 414-229-4982, Fax: 414-229-6967, E-mail: gradschool@uwm.edu.
Website: https://uwm.edu/spanish-portuguese/

University of Wyoming, College of Arts and Sciences, Department of Modern and Classical Languages, Program in Spanish, Laramie, WY 82071. Offers MA. *Program availability:* Part-time. *Degree requirements:* For master's, one foreign language, thesis or alternative. *Entrance requirements:* For master's, GRE General Test, minimum GPA of 3.0. *Faculty research:* Peninsular literature, Latin American literature, theatre, science and literature, linguistics.

Vanderbilt University, Department of Spanish and Portuguese, Nashville, TN 37240-1001. Offers Portuguese (MA); Spanish (MA, MAT, PhD); Spanish and Portuguese (PhD). *Faculty:* 12 full-time (5 women). *Students:* 24 full-time (12 women); includes 7 minority (2 Black or African American, non-Hispanic/Latino; 5 Hispanic/Latino), 12 international. Average age 31. 39 applicants, 18% accepted, 6 enrolled. In 2017, 1 master's, 4 doctorates awarded. *Degree requirements:* For master's, one foreign language, thesis; for doctorate, 2 foreign languages, thesis/dissertation, final and qualifying exams. *Entrance requirements:* For master's, GRE General Test; for doctorate, GRE General Test, writing sample in Spanish. Additional exam requirements/ recommendations for international students: Required—TOEFL (minimum score 570 paper-based; 88 iBT). *Application deadline:* For fall admission, 1/15 for domestic and international students. Electronic applications accepted. *Financial support:* Fellowships, teaching assistantships with full tuition reimbursements, Federal Work-Study, institutionally sponsored loans, and health care benefits available. Financial award application deadline: 1/15; financial award applicants required to submit CSS PROFILE or FAFSA. *Faculty research:* Spanish, Portuguese, and Latin American literatures; foreign language pedagogy; Renaissance and Baroque poetry; nineteenth-century Spanish novel. *Unit head:* Dr. Benigno Trigo, Chair, 615-322-6930, Fax: 615-343-7260, E-mail: benigno.trigo@vanderbilt.edu. *Application contact:* Andres Zamora, Director of Graduate Studies, 615-322-6930, Fax: 615-343-7260, E-mail: andres.zamora@vanderbilt.edu.
Website: http://as.vanderbilt.edu/spanish-portuguese/graduate/index.php

Washington University in St. Louis, The Graduate School, Department of Romance Languages and Literatures, Program in Spanish, St. Louis, MO 63130-4899. Offers Hispanic languages and literatures (PhD); Spanish and comparative literature (PhD). Terminal master's awarded for partial completion of doctoral program. *Degree requirements:* For doctorate, thesis/dissertation. *Entrance requirements:* For doctorate, GRE General Test. Additional exam requirements/recommendations for international students: Required—TOEFL. Electronic applications accepted. *Faculty research:* Latin American and Iberian literatures and languages, Spanish and comparative literature.

Wayne State University, College of Liberal Arts and Sciences, Department of Classical and Modern Languages, Literatures, and Cultures, Detroit, MI 48202. Offers classics (MA), including ancient Greek and Latin, ancient studies, classics, Latin; German (MA); language learning (MALL), including Arabic (MA, MALL), French (MA, MALL, PhD), German (MALL, PhD), Italian (MA, MALL), Spanish (MA, MALL, PhD); modern languages (PhD), including French (MA, MALL, PhD), German (MALL, PhD), Spanish (MA, MALL, PhD); Near Eastern languages (MA), including Arabic (MA, MALL), Hebrew; Romance languages (MA), including French (MA, MALL, PhD), Italian (MA, MALL), Spanish (MA, MALL, PhD). *Faculty:* 22. *Students:* 24 full-time (18 women), 21 part-time (15 women); includes 11 minority (4 Black or African American, non-Hispanic/Latino; 1 American Indian or Alaska Native, non-Hispanic/Latino; 2 Asian, non-Hispanic/Latino; 2 Hispanic/Latino; 2 Two or more races, non-Hispanic/Latino), 3 international. Average age 37. 32 applicants, 63% accepted, 14 enrolled. In 2017, 10 master's awarded. *Degree requirements:* For master's, variable foreign language requirement, comprehensive exam (for some programs), thesis (for some programs); for doctorate, one foreign language, comprehensive exam, thesis/dissertation. *Entrance requirements:* Additional exam requirements/recommendations for international students: Required—

TOEFL (minimum score 550 paper-based; 79 iBT), TWE (minimum score 5.5), Michigan English Language Assessment Battery (minimum score 85); Recommended—IELTS (minimum score 6.5). Application fee: $50. Electronic applications accepted. *Expenses:* Tuition, state resident: full-time $10,224; part-time $638.98 per credit hour. Tuition, nonresident: full-time $22,145; part-time $1384.04 per credit hour. Tuition and fees vary according to course load and program. *Financial support:* In 2017–18, 25 students received support, including 4 fellowships with tuition reimbursements available (averaging $13,500 per year), 17 teaching assistantships with tuition reimbursements available (averaging $18,591 per year); research assistantships, scholarships/grants, health care benefits, and unspecified assistantships also available. Financial award applicants required to submit FAFSA. *Faculty research:* Classical and modern literature and culture (Greek, Latin, Arabic, Chinese, French, German, Russian, Spanish) including colonial studies and exile and Holocaust studies; critical theory (French, German, Slavic, Spanish); theoretical and applied linguistics (Arabic, Chinese, French, Spanish); area studies (Arabic, Near Eastern, classical, Islamic, and Judaic studies). *Unit head:* Dr. Anne Duggan, Department Chair, 313-577-6244, Fax: 313-577-6243, E-mail: a.duggan@wayne.edu.
Website: http://clas.wayne.edu/languages/

West Chester University of Pennsylvania, College of Arts and Humanities, Department of Languages and Cultures, West Chester, PA 19383. Offers French (Teaching Certificate); German (Teaching Certificate); languages and cultures (MA), including French, German, Spanish; Spanish (Teaching Certificate). *Program availability:* Part-time, evening/weekend, minimal on-campus study. *Students:* 8 full-time (all women), 24 part-time (19 women); includes 10 minority (all Hispanic/Latino), 1 international. Average age 30. 8 applicants, 88% accepted. In 2017, 10 master's awarded. *Degree requirements:* For master's, one foreign language, comprehensive exam, portfolio defended at oral exit exam, capstone project; for Teaching Certificate, one foreign language. *Entrance requirements:* For master's and Teaching Certificate, ACTFL OPI and WPT. Additional exam requirements/recommendations for international students: Required—TOEFL or IELTS. *Application deadline:* For fall admission, 5/15 for international students; for spring admission, 10/15 for international students. Applications are processed on a rolling basis. Application fee: $50. Electronic applications accepted. *Expenses:* Tuition, state resident: full-time $9000; part-time $500 per credit. Tuition, nonresident: full-time $13,500; part-time $750 per credit. *Required fees:* $2959; $149.79 per credit. *Financial support:* Scholarships/grants and unspecified assistantships available. Financial award application deadline: 2/15; financial award applicants required to submit FAFSA. *Faculty research:* Language structure, literature, film, culture, pedagogy, technology. *Unit head:* Dr. Mahmoud Amer, Chair, 610-430-5077, Fax: 610-436-3048, E-mail: mamer@wcupa.edu. *Application contact:* Dr. Maria Van Liew, Graduate Coordinator, 610-436-4746, Fax: 610-436-3048, E-mail: mvanliew@wcupa.edu.
Website: http://www.wcupa.edu/arts-humanities/languagesCultures/

Western Kentucky University, Graduate Studies, Potter College of Arts and Letters, Department of Modern Languages, Bowling Green, KY 42101. Offers French (MA Ed); German (MA Ed); Spanish (MA Ed).

Western Michigan University, Graduate College, College of Arts and Sciences, Department of Spanish, Kalamazoo, MI 49008. Offers MA, PhD.

Wichita State University, Graduate School, Fairmount College of Liberal Arts and Sciences, Department of Modern and Classical Languages and Literatures, Wichita, KS 67260. Offers Spanish (MA). *Program availability:* Part-time. *Unit head:* Dr. Wilson Baldridge, Chair, 316-978-3180, Fax: 316-978-3293, E-mail: wilson.baldridge@wichita.edu. *Application contact:* Jordan Oleson, Admissions Coordinator, 316-978-3095, Fax: 316-978-3253, E-mail: jordan.oleson@wichita.edu.
Website: http://www.wichita.edu/mcll

Worcester State University, Graduate School, Program in Spanish, Worcester, MA 01602-2597. Offers MA. *Program availability:* Part-time. *Faculty:* 3 full-time. *Students:* 10 part-time (8 women); includes 4 minority (all Hispanic/Latino), 1 international. Average age 35. 5 applicants, 80% accepted. In 2017, 8 master's awarded. *Degree requirements:* For master's, one foreign language, thesis or comprehensive exam. *Entrance requirements:* For master's, GRE, MAT, BA in Spanish or related field and/or interview with faculty member. Additional exam requirements/recommendations for international students: Required—TOEFL (minimum score 550 paper-based; 79 iBT). *Application deadline:* For fall admission, 6/15 for domestic and international students; for spring admission, 11/1 for domestic and international students; for summer admission, 3/1 for domestic students, 4/1 for international students. Applications are processed on a rolling basis. Application fee: $50. Electronic applications accepted. *Expenses:* Tuition, state resident: full-time $3042; part-time $169 per credit hour. Tuition, nonresident: full-time $3042; part-time $169 per credit hour. *Required fees:* $2754; $153 per credit hour. *Financial support:* Career-related internships or fieldwork, scholarships/grants, and unspecified assistantships available. Financial award application deadline: 3/1; financial award applicants required to submit FAFSA. *Unit head:* Dr. Antonio Guijarro-Donadios, Program Coordinator, 508-929-8619, E-mail: aguijarrodonadios@worcester.edu. *Application contact:* Sara Grady, Graduate Studies and Professional Development, 508-929-8130, E-mail: sara.grady@worcester.edu.

Yale University, Graduate School of Arts and Sciences, Department of Spanish and Portuguese, New Haven, CT 06520. Offers Latin American literature (PhD); Luso-Brazilian and Spanish/Spanish American literatures (PhD); Spanish peninsular literature (PhD). Terminal master's awarded for partial completion of doctoral program. *Degree requirements:* For doctorate, 3 foreign languages, thesis/dissertation. *Entrance requirements:* For doctorate, GRE General Test.

AUBURN UNIVERSITY
Graduate English Studies

 For more information, visit http://petersons.to/auburneng

Programs of Study

The Department of English at Auburn University makes it possible for students to engage in the most essential and valued skills in the liberal arts and humanities traditions. As a unified department of English Studies, it provides the following academic programs:

- Master of Arts in English, with concentrations in creative writing, literature, or rhetoric and composition
- Master of Technical and Professional Communication
- Doctor of Philosophy in English, with concentrations in literature or rhetoric and composition

Whether through analytic, professional, or creative writing, students and faculty engage continuously in the skills of careful reading, critical thinking, and communication.

Master of Arts (M.A.) in English: This program helps students develop their skills and professional experience within a sub-discipline in English Studies. The program emphasizes writing and research skills; it also gives students university-level experience as writing and literature teachers. Its curriculum has 30 hours of coursework including a concentration, foreign language requirement, and portfolio with oral defense.

The department offers concentrations in creative writing, literature, and rhetoric and composition. The literature concentration offers an array of critical perspectives on literary and cultural studies with a focus on American and British literature and theory. The creative writing concentration focuses on fiction and poetry. Students participate in intensive workshops and work toward producing a longer piece of work, usually a collection of short stories or poetry. The rhetoric and composition concentration offers an in-depth study of key theoretical and methodological approaches with a focus on writing pedagogy and rhetorical theory.

Master of Technical and Professional Communication (M.T.P.C.): This program emphasizes the theory and practice of technical communication. It prepares students for jobs as editors, information analysts, proposal specialists, web developers, technical writers/communicators, and other interesting and rewarding positions.

Its 30-hour curriculum consists of four required courses, three elective courses in English, and a coordinated minor in another field or three additional English courses. It also includes an academic portfolio and presentation of the portfolio. Courses frequently include client-based projects offering practice in website and print-document design, usability testing, and editing of technical documents. Recent elective courses have focused on topics of science communication, environmental rhetoric, and online learning development.

The academic portfolio includes a portfolio website, an introductory memo, a curriculum vita or resume, five documents from coursework, and short analyses contextualizing each document.

Doctor of Philosophy (Ph.D.) in English: The Ph.D. in English provides rigorous pedagogical and scholarly training for aspiring intellectual leaders and stewards of English Studies. Ph.D. students develop critical analysis of American and English literature—from the traditional canons to African-American, Anglophone, Irish, Southern, and trans-Atlantic literatures and cultures. Similarly, the Ph.D. includes rhetoric and composition specialties in community and public writing, compostion pedagogy, methodologies, and rhetorical theory.

The program's curriculum has a minimum of 60 hours beyond the bachelor's degree including 10 hours in the Research and Dissertation course. Students may transfer a maximum of 30 hours from a master's degree with approval from the dean of the Graduate School and the advisory committee.

The curriculum also includes proficiency in two foreign languages or advanced proficiency in one. A general examination, dissertation prospectus, dissertation, and final examination/dissertation defense are required as well.

Research Opportunities

Research at Auburn University provides a gateway for advancing scholarship, discovering new knowledge, and fueling economic development. It influences and enhances the lives of citizens of the state of Alabama, the country, and the world.

The Department of English embraces these activities through faculty research in an extensive range of topics including the following:

- Cultural studies
- Early women writers
- Feminist criticism
- Gender studies
- Green cultural studies
- Poetry
- Archival studies
- Community and public writing
- Composition pedagogy
- African-American literature
- Twentieth-century British literature

Financial Aid

Graduate students in English may qualify for a variety of financial resources including graduate assistantships with competitive stipends, master's and doctoral fellowships, employment at the Office of University Writing and Miller Writing Center, funding for professional travel and research projects, Federal loans, and alternative loans.

Cost of Study

For the 2018–19 academic year, tuition and fees per semester (for 9–15 credit hours) for graduate programs in English are $5,641 for Alabama students and $15,271 for nonresident students. Students who accept a teaching assistantship also receive tuition remission, so their cost of study only includes health insurance and student fees.

Location

Auburn University is located in Auburn, Alabama, which is situated in the southeastern region of the United States.

Auburn is a small, friendly university town located on the beautiful plains of eastern Alabama, about 50 miles east of Montgomery, Alabama's capital, and 115 miles southwest of Atlanta, Georgia. Other nearby cities are Birmingham (110 miles northwest) and Columbus, Georgia (35 miles east). The Gulf Coast of Florida is about four hours away by car. Auburn enjoys a warm and sunny climate with mild winters. It has excellent health and recreational facilities and a low crime rate.

Auburn has a population just over 40,000 and has the feel of a small town with big-city amenities. Auburn is a bike-friendly town with bike lanes around the University.

Auburn University

Concerts, clubs, and professional sporting events are a short drive away in Birmingham and Atlanta. Auburn boasts an impressively ranked public school system and a robust housing market to meet every need.

The University

Established in 1856, Auburn University is a land, sea, and space grant institution and one of the largest universities in the south. It is committed to providing high-quality graduate, professional, and undergraduate education for traditional and nontraditional students. To achieve this goal, it offers nearly 30,000 students 140 majors and 160 graduate programs through 15 schools and colleges.

Applying

Applications to the M.A. and Ph.D. programs are accepted for fall term only. To be considered for admission, the completed application must be received by the first business day after January 15. If positions remain available after the first round of admissions review, applications submitted later will also be considered. All applicants are automatically considered for financial aid in the form of a Graduate Teaching Assistantship (GTA); there is no separate application or deadline for the GTA.

Materials submitted for the M.A. and Ph.D. applications are the same: transcripts for all prior degrees; GRE General Test scores (the GRE Subject Test in English is no longer required for Ph.D. applications, effective fall 2011); a statement of purpose; a writing sample; and three confidential letters of recommendation.

Admission to the M.A. and Ph.D. programs is competitive. In considering applicants, the Graduate Studies Committee looks for students who will benefit from and succeed in the university's programs, and who will add vitality and diversity to the intellectual community of the English department through their contributions as graduate students and teachers. The Graduate Studies Committee takes care to look at the whole application, basing its decisions on several kinds of information: grades, letters of recommendation, GRE scores, a statement of purpose or professional goals, and a writing sample.

When considering qualified applicants, the Graduate Studies Committee pays careful attention to the variety and quality of the applicant's earlier course work and to the intellectual promise of the writing sample and Statement of Purpose. The writing sample is generally a 10–25 page term paper or critical essay, typically one which demonstrates the candidate's ability to work with scholarship and interpretation. The Statement of Purpose is a 1–2 page statement of goals for graduate study at Auburn. The application should also include three confidential letters of recommendation from current or former professors who can comment in detail on the applicant's academic work and potential for success as a graduate student and GTA. The graduate school application form will automatically email them to request a letter.

Applicants must complete the online application form and pay the application fee at www.grad.auburn.edu; request that official transcripts for all prior degrees be sent to the Graduate School; and take the GRE General Test and request that scores be sent to the Graduate School (ETS Institution Code 1005). Do not send scores to the English Department.

Applicants are notified of admissions decisions in the middle of March.

Correspondence and Information

Sunny Stalter-Pace
Director of Graduate Studies
Department of English
9096 Haley Center
Auburn University, Alabama 36849-9027
Phone: 334-844-4620
          334-844-9081
Fax: 334-844-9027
E-mail: sls0009@auburn.edu
Website: http://www.cla.auburn.edu/english/graduate-studies/

Section 10
Linguistic Studies

This section contains a directory of institutions offering graduate work in linguistic studies. Additional information about programs listed in the directory may be obtained by writing directly to the dean of a graduate school or chair of a department at the address given in the directory.

For programs offering related work, see also in this book *Area and Cultural Studies, Language and Literature,* and *Sociology, Anthropology, and Archaeology.*

CONTENTS

Program Directories

Linguistics

Arizona State University at the Tempe campus, College of Liberal Arts and Sciences, Department of English, Tempe, AZ 85287-0302. Offers applied linguistics (PhD); creative writing (MFA); English (MA, PhD), including comparative literature (MA), linguistics (MA), literature, rhetoric and composition (MA), rhetoric, composition, and linguistics (PhD); film and media studies (MAS), including American media and popular culture; linguistics (Graduate Certificate); teaching English to speakers of other languages (MTESOL); translation studies (Graduate Certificate). Terminal master's awarded for partial completion of doctoral program. *Degree requirements:* For master's, variable foreign language requirement, comprehensive exam (for some programs), thesis (for some programs), interactive Program of Study (iPOS) submitted before completing 50 percent of required credit hours; for doctorate, variable foreign language requirement, comprehensive exam, thesis/dissertation, interactive Program of Study (iPOS) submitted before completing 50 percent of required credit hours. *Entrance requirements:* For master's and doctorate, GRE, minimum GPA of 3.0 or equivalent in last 2 years of work leading to bachelor's degree. Additional exam requirements/ recommendations for international students: Required—TOEFL, IELTS, or PTE. Electronic applications accepted.

Ball State University, Graduate School, College of Sciences and Humanities, Department of English, Program in Linguistics, Muncie, IN 47306. Offers linguistics (MA); teaching English to speakers of other languages (TESOL) and linguistics (MA). *Program availability:* Part-time. *Students:* 8 full-time (3 women), 1 (woman) part-time; includes 1 minority (Asian, non-Hispanic/Latino), 7 international. Average age 28. 6 applicants, 67% accepted, 2 enrolled. In 2017, 2 master's awarded. *Entrance requirements:* For master's, GRE General Test, minimum baccalaureate GPA of 2.75 or 3.0 in latter half of baccalaureate, statement of purpose, writing sample, three letters of recommendation. Additional exam requirements/recommendations for international students: Required—TOEFL (minimum score 550 paper-based; 79 iBT), IELTS (minimum score 6.5). *Application deadline:* Applications are processed on a rolling basis. Application fee: $60. Electronic applications accepted. *Financial support:* Research assistantships with partial tuition reimbursements and teaching assistantships with partial tuition reimbursements available. Financial award application deadline: 3/1; financial award applicants required to submit FAFSA. *Faculty research:* Descriptive and theoretical linguistics. *Unit head:* Dr. Deborah Mix, Assistant Chair of Programs, 765-285-8401, Fax: 765-285-3765, E-mail: dmmix@bsu.edu. *Application contact:* Dr. Deborah Mix, Assistant Chair of Programs, 765-285-8401, Fax: 765-285-3765, E-mail: dmmix@bsu.edu.
Website: http://www.bsu.edu/english/

Biola University, Cook School of Intercultural Studies, La Mirada, CA 90639-0001. Offers anthropology (MA); applied linguistics (MA); intercultural education (PhD); intercultural studies (MA, PhD); linguistics (Certificate); linguistics and Biblical languages (MA); missiology (D Miss); missions (MA); teaching English to speakers of other languages (MA, Certificate). *Program availability:* Part-time, 100% online. *Faculty:* 19. *Students:* 127 full-time (64 women), 123 part-time (70 women); includes 72 minority (9 Black or African American, non-Hispanic/Latino; 2 American Indian or Alaska Native, non-Hispanic/Latino; 41 Asian, non-Hispanic/Latino; 17 Hispanic/Latino; 3 Two or more races, non-Hispanic/Latino), 26 international. In 2017, 28 master's, 16 doctorates awarded. *Entrance requirements:* For master's, minimum undergraduate GPA of 3.0; for doctorate, master's degree or equivalent, 3 years of cross-cultural experience, minimum graduate GPA of 3.3. Additional exam requirements/recommendations for international students: Required—TOEFL. *Application deadline:* For fall admission, 7/1 for domestic students, 6/1 for international students; for spring admission, 12/1 for domestic students; for summer admission, 5/1 for domestic students. Applications are processed on a rolling basis. Application fee: $65. Electronic applications accepted. *Financial support:* Scholarships/grants available. Support available to part-time students. Financial award applicants required to submit FAFSA. *Faculty research:* Linguistics, anthropology, intercultural studies, teaching English to speakers of other languages, missions, missiology. *Unit head:* Dr. Bulus Y. Galadima, Dean, 562-903-4844. *Application contact:* Graduate Admissions Office, 562-903-4752, E-mail: graduate.admissions@biola.edu.
Website: http://cook.biola.edu

Boston College, Graduate School of Arts and Sciences, Department of Slavic and Eastern Languages and Literatures, Program in Linguistics, Chestnut Hill, MA 02467-3800. Offers MA, MA/JD, MBA/MA. *Degree requirements:* For master's, 3 foreign languages, comprehensive exam, thesis or alternative. *Entrance requirements:* Additional exam requirements/recommendations for international students: Required—TOEFL (minimum score 600 paper-based; 100 iBT), IELTS (minimum score 8). Electronic applications accepted.

Boston University, Graduate School of Arts and Sciences, Program in Linguistics, Boston, MA 02215. Offers MA, PhD. *Program availability:* Part-time. *Students:* 17 full-time (11 women), 2 part-time (0 women); includes 2 minority (both Asian, non-Hispanic/ Latino), 3 international. Average age 26. 35 applicants, 54% accepted, 6 enrolled. In 2017, 4 master's, 1 doctorate awarded. Terminal master's awarded for partial completion of doctoral program. *Degree requirements:* For master's, one foreign language; for doctorate, 2 foreign languages, comprehensive exam, thesis/dissertation. *Entrance requirements:* For master's and doctorate, GRE General Test, 3 letters of recommendation, transcripts, personal statement, curriculum vitae, writing sample. Additional exam requirements/recommendations for international students: Required—TOEFL (minimum score 550 paper-based; 84 iBT). *Application deadline:* For fall admission, 1/5 for domestic and international students. Application fee: $95. Electronic applications accepted. *Financial support:* In 2017–18, 3 students received support, including 3 teaching assistantships with full tuition reimbursements available (averaging $22,000 per year); Federal Work-Study, scholarships/grants, and unspecified assistantships also available. Financial award application deadline: 1/5. *Faculty research:* Linguistic theory, experimental phonetics and phonology, morphology, syntax, semantics, pragmatics and information status, prosody sociolinguistics, language acquisition, language documentation and field linguistics, language change and variation, Romance linguistics, sign language linguistics. *Unit head:* Carol Neidle, Director, 617-353-6218, E-mail: carol@bu.edu. *Application contact:* Cameron Samuelson, Administrator, 617-358-4640, Fax: 617-358-4641, E-mail: linggrad@bu.edu.
Website: http://ling.bu.edu

Brandeis University, Graduate School of Arts and Sciences, Program in Computational Linguistics, Waltham, MA 02454-9110. Offers MS. *Faculty:* 15 full-time (5 women), 2 part-time/adjunct (0 women). *Students:* 27 full-time (15 women); includes 4 minority (1 Black or African American, non-Hispanic/Latino; 1 Hispanic/Latino; 2 Two or more races, non-Hispanic/Latino), 7 international. Average age 25. 55 applicants, 69% accepted, 14 enrolled. In 2017, 14 master's awarded. *Degree requirements:* For master's, internship in computational linguistics or thesis. *Entrance requirements:* For master's, GRE General Test, statement of purpose, letters of recommendation, transcripts, resume. Additional exam requirements/recommendations for international students: Required—PTE (minimum score 68), TOEFL (minimum score 600 paper-based, 100 iBT) or IELTS (7). *Application deadline:* For fall admission, 2/1 priority date for domestic students. Application fee: $75. Electronic applications accepted. *Expenses: Tuition:* Full-time $48,720. *Required fees:* $88. Tuition and fees vary according to course load, degree level, program and student level. *Financial support:* In 2017–18, 30 students received support, including 2 teaching assistantships (averaging $3,200 per year); Federal Work-Study, scholarships/grants, and tuition waivers (partial) also available. Financial award application deadline: 4/15; financial award applicants required to submit FAFSA. *Faculty research:* Computational linguistics, statistical natural language processing, machine learning, computer science, speech recognition, automated text analysis. *Unit head:* Dr. James Pustejovsky, Program Chair, 781-736-2709, E-mail: jamesp@brandeis.edu. *Application contact:* Anne Gudaitis, Department Administrator, 781-736-2723, E-mail: gudaitis@brandeis.edu.
Website: http://www.brandeis.edu/gsas/programs/comp_ling.html

Brigham Young University, Graduate Studies, College of Humanities, Department of Linguistics, Provo, UT 84602. Offers linguistics (MA); teaching English as a second language (MA). *Program availability:* Part-time. *Faculty:* 23 full-time (4 women), 8 part-time/adjunct (6 women). *Students:* 38 full-time (29 women), 24 part-time (18 women); includes 11 minority (1 American Indian or Alaska Native, non-Hispanic/Latino; 5 Asian, non-Hispanic/Latino; 4 Hispanic/Latino; 1 Native Hawaiian or other Pacific Islander, non-Hispanic/Latino), 12 international. Average age 31. 31 applicants, 87% accepted, 24 enrolled. In 2017, 18 master's awarded. *Degree requirements:* For master's, 2 foreign languages, thesis. *Entrance requirements:* For master's, GRE General Test, minimum GPA of 3.0 in last 60 hours of course work. Additional exam requirements/ recommendations for international students: Required—TOEFL (minimum score 580 paper-based; 90 iBT), TWE. *Application deadline:* 1/15 for domestic and international students. Application fee: $50. Electronic applications accepted. *Expenses:* Contact institution. *Financial support:* In 2017–18, 62 students received support, including 8 research assistantships with partial tuition reimbursements available (averaging $7,200 per year), 8 teaching assistantships with partial tuition reimbursements available (averaging $2,079 per year); fellowships with partial tuition reimbursements available, career-related internships or fieldwork, scholarships/grants, unspecified assistantships, and travel to conference presentations also available. Financial award application deadline: 7/1. *Faculty research:* Teaching English to speakers of other languages, second language acquisition, computational linguistics, semiotics and semantics, computer-assisted language instruction, forensic linguistics, endangered language documentation. *Unit head:* Dr. Norman Evans, Chair, 801-422-8472, E-mail: norm_evans@byu.edu. *Application contact:* Mary Beth Wald, Graduate Program Manager, 801-422-9010, Fax: 801-422-9010, E-mail: marybeth_wald@byu.edu.
Website: http://linguistics.byu.edu/

Brigham Young University, Graduate Studies, College of Humanities, Department of Spanish and Portuguese, Provo, UT 84602. Offers Portuguese (MA), including Luso-Brazilian literatures, Portuguese linguistics, Portuguese pedagogy; Spanish (MA), including Hispanic linguistics, Hispanic literatures, Spanish pedagogy. *Faculty:* 30 full-time (6 women). *Students:* 32 full-time (17 women), 6 part-time (4 women); includes 16 minority (all Hispanic/Latino). Average age 31. 19 applicants, 68% accepted, 10 enrolled. In 2017, 6 master's awarded. *Degree requirements:* For master's, 2 foreign languages, comprehensive exam, thesis, 1 semester of teaching. *Entrance requirements:* For master's, minimum GPA of 3.5 in Spanish or Portuguese, 3.3 overall. Additional exam requirements/recommendations for international students: Required—TOEFL (minimum score 580 paper-based; 85 iBT), IELTS (minimum score 6.5), PTE (minimum score 53). *Application deadline:* For fall admission, 2/1 for domestic and international students. Application fee: $50. Electronic applications accepted. *Expenses:* Contact institution. *Financial support:* In 2017–18, 23 students received support, including 87 teaching assistantships (averaging $3,200 per year); research assistantships, institutionally sponsored loans, scholarships/grants, tuition waivers (partial), and unspecified assistantships also available. Support available to part-time students. *Faculty research:* Mexican prose; Latin American theater; literature; phonetics, and phonology; pedagogy; classical Portuguese literature. *Unit head:* Dr. Jeffrey S. Turley, Chair, 801-422-7019, Fax: 801-422-0628, E-mail: jeffrey_turley@byu.edu. *Application contact:* Patricia E. Wilson, Graduate Program Manager, 801-422-2838, Fax: 801-422-0628, E-mail: patricia_rubio@byu.edu.
Website: http://spanport.byu.edu/

Brown University, Graduate School, Department of Cognitive, Linguistic and Psychological Sciences, Providence, RI 02912. Offers cognitive science (Sc M, PhD); linguistics (AM, PhD); psychology (PhD). *Degree requirements:* For master's, one foreign language, thesis or alternative; for doctorate, 2 foreign languages, thesis/ dissertation.

California State University, Fresno, Division of Research and Graduate Studies, College of Arts and Humanities, Department of Linguistics, Fresno, CA 93740-8027. Offers linguistics (MA), including teaching English as a second language. *Program availability:* Part-time, evening/weekend. *Degree requirements:* For master's, comprehensive exam. *Entrance requirements:* For master's, GRE General Test, minimum GPA of 3.0. Additional exam requirements/recommendations for international students: Required—TOEFL. Electronic applications accepted. *Faculty research:* Communication systems, bilingual education, animal communication, conflict resolution, literacy programs.

California State University, Fullerton, Graduate Studies, College of Humanities and Social Sciences, Department of English, Comparative Literature, and Linguistics, Fullerton, CA 92831-3599. Offers English (MA); linguistics (MA). *Program availability:* Part-time. *Faculty:* 9 full-time (4 women), 1 (woman) part-time/adjunct. *Students:* 44 full-time (30 women), 40 part-time (22 women); includes 38 minority (10 Asian, non-Hispanic/Latino; 24 Hispanic/Latino; 4 Two or more races, non-Hispanic/Latino), 14 international. Average age 29. 76 applicants, 58% accepted, 24 enrolled. *Degree requirements:* For master's, one foreign language, thesis or alternative, project. *Entrance requirements:* For master's, minimum GPA of 3.0, undergraduate major in linguistics or related field. Application fee: $55. *Financial support:* Career-related internships or fieldwork, Federal Work-Study, institutionally sponsored loans, and scholarships/grants available. Support available to part-time students. Financial award application deadline: 3/1; financial award applicants required to submit FAFSA. *Unit head:* Dr. Stephen J. Mexal, Chair, 657-278-3163.

California State University, Long Beach, Graduate Studies, College of Liberal Arts, Department of Linguistics, Long Beach, CA 90840. Offers general linguistics (MA); language and culture (MA); special concentration (MA); teaching English to speakers of

other languages (MA, Graduate Certificate). *Program availability:* Part-time, evening/weekend. *Degree requirements:* For master's, one foreign language, comprehensive exam, thesis optional. Electronic applications accepted. *Faculty research:* Pedagogy of language instruction, role of language in society, Khmer language instruction.

California State University, Northridge, Graduate Studies, College of Humanities, Linguistics Program, Northridge, CA 91330. Offers MA. *Program availability:* Part-time, evening/weekend. *Students:* 12 full-time (4 women), 8 part-time (3 women); includes 5 minority (1 Asian, non-Hispanic/Latino; 2 Hispanic/Latino; 2 Two or more races, non-Hispanic/Latino), 5 international. Average age 32. 24 applicants, 75% accepted, 9 enrolled. In 2017, 10 master's awarded. *Degree requirements:* For master's, one foreign language, comprehensive exam, thesis, or project. *Entrance requirements:* For master's, GRE General Test or minimum GPA of 3.0. Additional exam requirements/recommendations for international students: Required—TOEFL (minimum score 563 paper-based; 85 iBT). *Application deadline:* For fall admission, 11/30 for domestic students. Application fee: $55. *Financial support:* Application deadline: 3/1. *Faculty research:* Ethnography of communication, stylistics, natural language processing, linguistics and humor, Otomanguean phonology and reconstruction. *Unit head:* Dr. Kenneth Luna, Chair, 818-677-3453.
Website: http://www.csun.edu/linguistics/

Carleton University, Faculty of Graduate Studies, Faculty of Arts and Social Sciences, School of Linguistics and Applied Language Studies, Ottawa, ON K1S 5B6, Canada. Offers applied language studies (MA). *Degree requirements:* For master's, thesis optional. *Entrance requirements:* For master's, honors degree. Additional exam requirements/recommendations for international students: Required—TOEFL or CAEL. *Faculty research:* Language learning, acquisition and use of first and/or second languages in a variety of professional and academic contexts.

Carnegie Mellon University, Dietrich College of Humanities and Social Sciences, Department of Modern Languages, Pittsburgh, PA 15213-3891. Offers second language acquisition (MA, PhD). *Degree requirements:* For doctorate, one foreign language, comprehensive exam, thesis/dissertation. *Entrance requirements:* For doctorate, GRE General Test. Additional exam requirements/recommendations for international students: Required—TOEFL.

Case Western Reserve University, School of Graduate Studies, Department of Cognitive Science, Cleveland, OH 44106. Offers cognitive linguistics (MA). *Program availability:* Part-time. *Faculty:* 4 full-time (2 women), 4 part-time/adjunct (0 women). *Students:* 7 full-time (2 women), 1 part-time (0 women), 1 international. Average age 29. 5 applicants, 60% accepted, 2 enrolled. In 2017, 1 master's awarded. *Degree requirements:* For master's, thesis. *Entrance requirements:* For master's, GRE, statement of purpose, three letters of recommendation, writing sample. Additional exam requirements/recommendations for international students: Required—TOEFL (minimum score 577 paper-based; 90 iBT); Recommended—IELTS (minimum score 7). *Application deadline:* For fall admission, 5/1 priority date for domestic students. Application fee: $50. Electronic applications accepted. *Expenses:* Tuition: Full-time $43,854; part-time $1827 per credit hour. *Required fees:* $50; $50 per credit hour. Tuition and fees vary according to course load and program. *Faculty research:* Workings of the human mind in design, art, and technology; interaction of brain and culture in development and evolution; origins of human higher-order cognition; the role of the body and social interaction in shaping human cognition; operation of systems that human beings have invented to guide their thought and action individually and culturally. *Unit head:* Dr. William Deal, Chair, 216-368-2205, E-mail: william.deal@case.edu.
Website: http://cognitivescience.case.edu/

Concordia University, School of Graduate Studies, Faculty of Arts and Science, Department of Education, Program in Applied Linguistics, Montréal, QC H3G 1M8, Canada. Offers applied linguistics (MA); teaching English as a second language (Certificate).

Cornell University, Graduate School, Graduate Fields of Arts and Sciences, Field of Asian Studies, Ithaca, NY 14853. Offers East Asian linguistics (MA); East Asian studies (MA); South Asian linguistics (MA); South Asian studies (MA); Southeast Asian linguistics (MA); Southeast Asian studies (MA). *Degree requirements:* For master's, one foreign language, thesis. *Entrance requirements:* For master's, GRE General Test, 3 letters of recommendation. Additional exam requirements/recommendations for international students: Required—TOEFL (minimum score 550 paper-based; 77 iBT). Electronic applications accepted. *Faculty research:* East Asian studies, South Asian studies, Southeast Asian studies.

Cornell University, Graduate School, Graduate Fields of Arts and Sciences, Field of Linguistics, Ithaca, NY 14853. Offers applied linguistics (MA, PhD); East Asian linguistics (MA, PhD); English linguistics (MA, PhD); general linguistics (MA, PhD); Germanic linguistics (MA, PhD); Indo-European linguistics (MA, PhD); phonetics (MA, PhD); phonological theory (MA, PhD); Romance linguistics (MA, PhD); second language acquisition (MA, PhD); semantics (MA, PhD); Slavic linguistics (MA, PhD); sociolinguistics (MA, PhD); South Asian linguistics (MA, PhD); Southeast Asian linguistics (MA, PhD); syntactic theory (MA, PhD). Terminal master's awarded for partial completion of doctoral program. *Degree requirements:* For master's, one foreign language, thesis; for doctorate, one foreign language, comprehensive exam, thesis/dissertation. *Entrance requirements:* For master's and doctorate, GRE General Test, 2 letters of recommendation. Additional exam requirements/recommendations for international students: Required—TOEFL (minimum score 600 paper-based; 77 iBT). Electronic applications accepted. *Faculty research:* Phonology and phonetics, syntax and semantics, historical linguistics, philosophy of language, language acquisition.

East Carolina University, Graduate School, Thomas Harriot College of Arts and Sciences, Department of English, Greenville, NC 27858-4353. Offers creative writing (MA); English studies (MA); linguistics (MA); literature (MA); multicultural and transnational literatures (MA, Certificate); professional communication (Certificate); rhetoric and composition (MA); rhetoric, writing, and professional communication (PhD); teaching English in the two-year college (Certificate); teaching English to speakers of other languages (MA, Certificate); technical and professional communication (MA). *Program availability:* Part-time, evening/weekend, online learning. *Students:* 40 full-time (27 women), 74 part-time (57 women); includes 33 minority (23 Black or African American, non-Hispanic/Latino; 2 Asian, non-Hispanic/Latino; 4 Hispanic/Latino; 4 Two or more races, non-Hispanic/Latino). Average age 35. 36 applicants, 94% accepted, 25 enrolled. In 2017, 23 master's, 4 doctorates, 24 other advanced degrees awarded. *Degree requirements:* For master's, comprehensive exam, thesis optional; for doctorate, comprehensive exam, thesis/dissertation. *Entrance requirements:* For master's, GRE General Test or MAT; for doctorate, GRE General Test or MAT, writing samples. Additional exam requirements/recommendations for international students: Recommended—TOEFL (minimum score 78 iBT), IELTS (minimum score 6.5), TWE. *Application deadline:* For fall admission, 7/31 priority date for domestic students, 2/1 priority date for international students; for spring admission, 11/30 priority date for domestic students, 10/1 priority date for international students. Applications are processed on a rolling basis. Application fee: $75. Electronic applications accepted. *Expenses:* Tuition, state resident: full-time $4749; part-time $297 per credit hour. Tuition, nonresident: full-time $17,898; part-time $1119 per credit hour. *Required fees:*

$2691; $224 per credit hour. Part-time tuition and fees vary according to course load and program. *Financial support:* Research assistantships with partial tuition reimbursements, teaching assistantships with partial tuition reimbursements, and Federal Work-Study available. Support available to part-time students. Financial award application deadline: 3/1. *Faculty research:* Technical and professional communication, rhetoric/composition, multicultural and transnational literature, creative writing, film studies. *Unit head:* Dr. Marianne Montgomery, Chair, 252-328-6687, E-mail: montgomerym@ecu.edu. *Application contact:* Dean of Graduate School, 252-328-6012, Fax: 252-328-6071, E-mail: gradschool@ecu.edu.
Website: http://www.ecu.edu/cs-cas/engl/

Eastern Michigan University, Graduate School, College of Arts and Sciences, Department of English Language and Literature, Program in English Linguistics, Ypsilanti, MI 48197. Offers MA. *Program availability:* Part-time, evening/weekend, online learning. *Students:* 6 full-time (4 women), 5 part-time (3 women), 3 international. Average age 36. 13 applicants, 62% accepted, 2 enrolled. In 2017, 9 master's awarded. *Degree requirements:* For master's, thesis (for some programs). *Entrance requirements:* Additional exam requirements/recommendations for international students: Required—TOEFL. *Application deadline:* Applications are processed on a rolling basis. Application fee: $45. *Financial support:* Fellowships with tuition reimbursements, research assistantships with full tuition reimbursements, teaching assistantships with full tuition reimbursements, career-related internships or fieldwork, Federal Work-Study, institutionally sponsored loans, scholarships/grants, tuition waivers (partial), and unspecified assistantships available. Support available to part-time students. Financial award applicants required to submit FAFSA. *Application contact:* Dr. Veronica Grondona, Program Advisor, 734-487-4220, Fax: 734-483-9744, E-mail: vgrondona@emich.edu.

Florida Atlantic University, Dorothy F. Schmidt College of Arts and Letters, Department of Languages, Linguistics, and Comparative Literature, Boca Raton, FL 33431-0991. Offers comparative literature (MA); French (MA); linguistics (MA); Spanish (MA). *Program availability:* Part-time. *Faculty:* 21 full-time (13 women). *Students:* 25 full-time (19 women), 16 part-time (12 women); includes 16 minority (5 Black or African American, non-Hispanic/Latino; 1 Asian, non-Hispanic/Latino; 10 Hispanic/Latino), 12 international. Average age 36. 42 applicants, 60% accepted, 18 enrolled. In 2017, 19 master's awarded. *Degree requirements:* For master's, one foreign language, comprehensive exam, thesis optional. *Entrance requirements:* For master's, GRE General Test, minimum GPA of 3.0. Additional exam requirements/recommendations for international students: Required—TOEFL (minimum score 500 paper-based; 61 iBT), IELTS (minimum score 6). *Application deadline:* For fall admission, 7/1 priority date for domestic students, 2/15 for international students; for spring admission, 11/1 for domestic students, 7/15 for international students. Applications are processed on a rolling basis. Application fee: $30. *Expenses:* Tuition, state resident: full-time $7400; part-time $369.82 per credit. Tuition, nonresident: full-time $20,496; part-time $1042.81 per credit. *Financial support:* Fellowships, research assistantships, teaching assistantships with partial tuition reimbursements, Federal Work-Study, and tuition waivers (partial) available. Support available to part-time students. Financial award application deadline: 4/1. *Faculty research:* Modern European studies, modern Latin America, medieval Europe. *Unit head:* Dr. Marcella Munson, Chair, 561-297-2118, Fax: 561-297-2756, E-mail: mmunson@fau.edu. *Application contact:* Dr. Linda Johnson, Associate Dean, 561-297-0928, Fax: 561-297-2744.
Website: http://www.fau.edu/LLCL/

Florida International University, College of Arts, Sciences, and Education, Department of English, Miami, FL 33199. Offers creative writing (MFA); English (MA), including literature; linguistics (MA). *Program availability:* Part-time, evening/weekend. *Faculty:* 53 full-time (26 women), 38 part-time/adjunct (24 women). *Students:* 40 full-time (24 women), 33 part-time (19 women); includes 40 minority (6 Black or African American, non-Hispanic/Latino; 33 Hispanic/Latino; 1 Two or more races, non-Hispanic/Latino), 4 international. Average age 31. 50 applicants, 50% accepted, 20 enrolled. In 2017, 31 master's awarded. *Degree requirements:* For master's, thesis. *Entrance requirements:* For master's, GRE General Test, minimum undergraduate GPA of 3.0 (upper-level coursework), letter of intent, two letters of recommendation. Additional exam requirements/recommendations for international students: Required—TOEFL (minimum score 550 paper-based; 80 iBT). *Application deadline:* For fall admission, 2/1 for domestic and international students; for spring admission, 10/1 for domestic students, 9/1 for international students. Applications are processed on a rolling basis. Application fee: $30. Electronic applications accepted. *Expenses:* Tuition, state resident: full-time $8912; part-time $446 per credit hour. Tuition, nonresident: full-time $21,393; part-time $992 per credit hour. *Required fees:* $390; $195 per semester. *Financial support:* Institutionally sponsored loans and scholarships/grants available. Financial award application deadline: 3/1; financial award applicants required to submit FAFSA. *Unit head:* Dr. Heather Russell, Chair, 305-348-3369, Fax: 305-348-3878, E-mail: heather.russell@fiu.edu. *Application contact:* Nanett Rojas, Assistant Director, Graduate Admissions, 305-348-7464, Fax: 305-348-7441, E-mail: gradadm@fiu.edu.

Gallaudet University, The Graduate School, Washington, DC 20002-3625. Offers American Sign Language/English bilingual early childhood deaf education: birth to 5 (Certificate); audiology (Au D); clinical psychology (PhD); deaf and hard of hearing infants, toddlers, and their families (Certificate); deaf education (MA, Ed S); deaf history (Certificate); deaf studies (Certificate); educating deaf students with disabilities (Certificate); education: teacher preparation (MA), including deaf education, early childhood education and deaf education, elementary education and deaf education, secondary education and deaf education; educational neuroscience (PhD); hearing, speech and language sciences (MS, PhD); international development (MA); interpretation (MA, PhD), including combined interpreting practice and research (MA), interpreting research (MA); linguistics (MA, PhD); mental health counseling (MA); peer mentoring (Certificate); public administration (MPA); school counseling (MA); school psychology (Psy S); sign language teaching (MA); social work (MSW); speech-language pathology (MS). *Program availability:* Part-time. Terminal master's awarded for partial completion of doctoral program. *Degree requirements:* For master's, comprehensive exam (for some programs), thesis optional; for doctorate, comprehensive exam, thesis/dissertation. *Entrance requirements:* For master's and doctorate, GRE General Test or MAT, letters of recommendation, interviews, goals statement, American Sign Language proficiency interview, written English competency. Additional exam requirements/recommendations for international students: Required—TOEFL. Electronic applications accepted. *Faculty research:* Signing math dictionaries, telecommunications access, cancer genetics, linguistics, visual language and visual learning, integrated quantum materials, deaf legal discourse, advance recruitment and retention in geosciences.

George Mason University, College of Humanities and Social Sciences, Department of English, Fairfax, VA 22030. Offers college teaching (Certificate), including higher education pedagogy; creative writing (MFA), including fiction, nonfiction writing, poetry; English (MA), including cultural studies, linguistics, literature, professional writing and rhetoric, teaching of writing and literature; English pedagogy (Certificate); folklore studies (Certificate); linguistics (PhD); writing and rhetoric (PhD). *Program availability:* Part-time. *Faculty:* 78 full-time (40 women), 45 part-time/adjunct (30 women). *Students:* 120 full-time (84 women), 116 part-time (94 women); includes 43 minority (13 Black or

African American, non-Hispanic/Latino; 8 Asian, non-Hispanic/Latino; 14 Hispanic/Latino; 1 Native Hawaiian or other Pacific Islander, non-Hispanic/Latino; 7 Two or more races, non-Hispanic/Latino), 19 international. Average age 32. 224 applicants, 61% accepted, 68 enrolled. In 2017, 60 master's, 1 doctorate, 17 other advanced degrees awarded. *Degree requirements:* For master's, thesis (for some programs), proficiency in a foreign language by course work or translation test; for doctorate, comprehensive exam, thesis/dissertation, 2 papers. *Entrance requirements:* For master's, official transcripts; expanded goals statement; writing sample; portfolio; 2 letters of recommendation; resume; for doctorate, GRE (for linguistics), expanded goals statement; 2 letters of recommendation (writing and rhetoric); 3 letters of recommendation (linguistics); writing sample; introductory course in linguistics; official transcripts; master's degree in relevant field; for Certificate, official transcripts; expanded goals statement; 2 letters of recommendation; writing sample; resume. Additional exam requirements/recommendations for international students: Required—TOEFL (minimum score 575 paper-based; 88 iBT), IELTS (minimum score 6.5), PTE (minimum score 59). *Application deadline:* For fall admission, 3/15 for domestic and international students; for spring admission, 10/15 for domestic and international students. Application fee: $75 ($80 for international students). Electronic applications accepted. *Expenses:* Tuition, state resident: full-time $11,228; part-time $459.50 per credit. Tuition, nonresident: full-time $30,932; part-time $1280.50 per credit. *Required fees:* $3252; $135.50 per credit. Part-time tuition and fees vary according to course load and program. *Financial support:* In 2017–18, 84 students received support, including 9 research assistantships with tuition reimbursements available (averaging $17,199 per year), 76 teaching assistantships with tuition reimbursements available (averaging $11,917 per year); career-related internships or fieldwork, Federal Work-Study, scholarships/grants, unspecified assistantships, and health care benefits (for full-time research or teaching assistantship recipients) also available. Support available to part-time students. Financial award application deadline: 3/1; financial award applicants required to submit FAFSA. *Faculty research:* Literature, professional writing and editing, writing of fiction or poetry. *Total annual research expenditures:* $68,592. *Unit head:* Debra Lattanzi-Shutika, Chair, 703-993-1170, Fax: 703-993-1161, E-mail: dshutika@gmu.edu. *Application contact:* Alex Walsh, Graduate Admissions Coordinator, 703-993-1185, Fax: 703-993-1161, E-mail: awalsh7@gmu.edu.
Website: http://english.gmu.edu

Georgetown University, Graduate School of Arts and Sciences, Department of Linguistics, Washington, DC 20057. Offers language and communication (MA); linguistics (MS, PhD), including applied linguistics, computational linguistics, sociolinguistics, theoretical linguistics. Terminal master's awarded for partial completion of doctoral program. *Degree requirements:* For master's, one foreign language, comprehensive exam; for doctorate, 2 foreign languages, comprehensive exam, thesis/dissertation. *Entrance requirements:* For master's and doctorate, 18 undergraduate credits in a foreign language. Additional exam requirements/recommendations for international students: Required—TOEFL.

Georgia State University, College of Arts and Sciences, Department of Applied Linguistics and English as a Second Language, Atlanta, GA 30302. Offers applied linguistics (MA, PhD). *Program availability:* Part-time. *Faculty:* 13 full-time (8 women). *Students:* 47 full-time (30 women), 20 part-time (16 women); includes 18 minority (5 Black or African American, non-Hispanic/Latino; 6 Asian, non-Hispanic/Latino; 3 Hispanic/Latino; 1 Native Hawaiian or other Pacific Islander, non-Hispanic/Latino; 3 Two or more races, non-Hispanic/Latino), 16 international. Average age 35. 109 applicants, 38% accepted, 25 enrolled. In 2017, 21 master's, 6 doctorates awarded. *Degree requirements:* For master's, one foreign language, portfolio; for doctorate, one foreign language, comprehensive exam, thesis/dissertation, qualifying exam. *Entrance requirements:* For master's and doctorate, GRE. Additional exam requirements/recommendations for international students: Required—TWE (minimum score 4). *Application deadline:* For fall admission, 1/15 for domestic and international students; for spring admission, 11/15 for domestic and international students. Applications are processed on a rolling basis. Application fee: $50. Electronic applications accepted. *Expenses:* Tuition, state resident: full-time $7020. Tuition, nonresident: full-time $22,518. *Required fees:* $2128. Tuition and fees vary according to degree level and program. *Financial support:* In 2017–18, fellowships with full tuition reimbursements (averaging $23,500 per year), research assistantships with full tuition reimbursements (averaging $5,000 per year), teaching assistantships with full tuition reimbursements (averaging $8,500 per year) were awarded; scholarships/grants and unspecified assistantships also available. Financial award application deadline: 6/1. *Faculty research:* Corpus linguistics, second language acquisition, second language literacy, assessment, teacher education. *Unit head:* Dr. Diane C. Belcher, Chair, Fax: 404-413-5201, E-mail: dbelcher1@gsu.edu.
Website: http://www2.gsu.edu/~wwwesl/

Georgia State University, College of Arts and Sciences, Department of World Languages and Cultures, Program in French, Atlanta, GA 30302-3083. Offers applied linguistics and pedagogy (MA); French studies (MA); literature and culture (MA). *Program availability:* Part-time. *Entrance requirements:* For master's, GRE, statement of purpose, writing sample in the target language, 2 letters of recommendation, official transcripts. Additional exam requirements/recommendations for international students: Required—TOEFL (minimum score 79 iBT). Application fee: $50. Electronic applications accepted. *Expenses:* Tuition, state resident: full-time $7020. Tuition, nonresident: full-time $22,518. *Required fees:* $2128. Tuition and fees vary according to degree level and program. *Financial support:* Institutionally sponsored loans available. Financial award applicants required to submit FAFSA. *Faculty research:* The nineteenth-century novel, narratology, genetic criticism, poetics, semiotics, and intertextuality; Francophone and transnational studies; early modern travel literature; post/colonial and Diaspora studies; film studies; social and gender studies; eighteenth century French literature and history of ideas; history of civilization; Enlightenment, encyclopedism. *Unit head:* Dr. Fernando Reati, Department Chair, 404-413-5984, Fax: 404-413-5982, E-mail: freati@gsu.edu. *Application contact:* Lita Malveaux, Administrative Academic Specialist, 404-413-5046, Fax: 404-413-5036, E-mail: lmalveaux@gsu.edu.
Website: http://www.gsu.edu/~wwwmcl/

The Graduate Center, City University of New York, Graduate Studies, Program in Anthropology, New York, NY 10016-4039. Offers anthropological linguistics (PhD); archaeology (PhD); cultural anthropology (PhD); physical anthropology (PhD). *Faculty:* 39 full-time (14 women). *Students:* 166 full-time (103 women), 2 part-time (both women); includes 34 minority (5 Black or African American, non-Hispanic/Latino; 5 Asian, non-Hispanic/Latino; 21 Hispanic/Latino; 3 Two or more races, non-Hispanic/Latino), 39 international. Average age 33. 145 applicants, 14% accepted, 19 enrolled. In 2017, 14 doctorates awarded. *Degree requirements:* For doctorate, one foreign language, thesis/dissertation. *Entrance requirements:* For doctorate, GRE General Test. Additional exam requirements/recommendations for international students: Required—TOEFL. *Application deadline:* For fall admission, 1/8 priority date for domestic students. Application fee: $125. Electronic applications accepted. *Financial support:* In 2017–18, 111 students received support, including 88 fellowships, 16 research assistantships, 10 teaching assistantships; career-related internships or fieldwork, Federal Work-Study, institutionally sponsored loans, and tuition waivers (full and partial) also available. Financial award application deadline: 2/1; financial award applicants required to submit FAFSA. *Unit head:* Prof. Jeff Maskovsky, Acting Executive Officer, 212-817-8006, Fax: 212-817-1501, E-mail: jmaskovsky@gc.cuny.edu. *Application contact:* Information Contact, 212-817-8005, Fax: 212-817-1501, E-mail: anthro@gc.cuny.edu.

The Graduate Center, City University of New York, Graduate Studies, Program in Linguistics, New York, NY 10016-4039. Offers MA, PhD. *Faculty:* 20 full-time (5 women). *Students:* 68 full-time (41 women), 22 part-time (16 women); includes 12 minority (5 Asian, non-Hispanic/Latino; 6 Hispanic/Latino; 1 Two or more races, non-Hispanic/Latino), 24 international. Average age 34. 47 applicants, 89% accepted, 19 enrolled. In 2017, 21 master's, 4 doctorates awarded. Terminal master's awarded for partial completion of doctoral program. *Degree requirements:* For master's, one foreign language, thesis; for doctorate, 2 foreign languages, thesis/dissertation. *Entrance requirements:* For master's and doctorate, GRE General Test. Additional exam requirements/recommendations for international students: Required—TOEFL. *Application deadline:* For fall admission, 1/15 for domestic students. Application fee: $125. Electronic applications accepted. *Financial support:* In 2017–18, 43 students received support, including 49 fellowships, 2 research assistantships; teaching assistantships, career-related internships or fieldwork, Federal Work-Study, institutionally sponsored loans, and tuition waivers (full and partial) also available. Financial award application deadline: 2/1; financial award applicants required to submit FAFSA. *Unit head:* Dr. Gita Martohardjono, Executive Officer, 212-817-8501, Fax: 212-817-1526. *Application contact:* Les Gribben, Director of Admissions, 212-817-7470, Fax: 212-817-1624, E-mail: lgribben@gc.cuny.edu.

Graduate Institute of Applied Linguistics, Graduate Programs, Dallas, TX 75236. Offers applied linguistics (MA, Certificate); language development (MA). *Program availability:* Part-time. *Degree requirements:* For master's, one foreign language, comprehensive exam (for some programs), thesis (for some programs). *Entrance requirements:* For master's, GRE. Additional exam requirements/recommendations for international students: Required—TOEFL (minimum score 577 paper-based; 90 iBT). Electronic applications accepted. *Faculty research:* Minority languages, endangered languages, language documentation.

Grand Valley State University, College of Liberal Arts and Sciences, Program in Applied Linguistics, Allendale, MI 49401-9403. Offers MA. *Program availability:* Part-time. *Students:* 12 full-time (9 women), 5 part-time (3 women), 11 international. Average age 28. 13 applicants, 85% accepted, 7 enrolled. *Degree requirements:* For master's, thesis, project, or capstone. *Entrance requirements:* For master's, minimum GPA of 3.0 or GRE; personal statement; writing sample; 2 letters of recommendation. Additional exam requirements/recommendations for international students: Required—TOEFL (minimum iBT score of 79), IELTS (6.5), or Michigan English Language Assessment Battery (77). *Application deadline:* Applications are processed on a rolling basis. Application fee: $30. Electronic applications accepted. *Expenses:* $627 per credit hour. *Financial support:* In 2017–18, 3 students received support, including 1 fellowship with full and partial tuition reimbursement available (averaging $8,000 per year), 1 research assistantship with full and partial tuition reimbursement available (averaging $8,000 per year). *Unit head:* Dr. Ashley Shannon, Department Director, 616-331-3405, Fax: 616-331-3430, E-mail: shannoas@gvsu.edu. *Application contact:* Dr. Shinian Wu, Graduate Program Director, 616-331-3690, Fax: 616-331-3430, E-mail: wus@gvsu.edu.
Website: http://www.gvsu.edu/linguistics/

Harvard University, Graduate School of Arts and Sciences, Department of Linguistics, Cambridge, MA 02138. Offers descriptive linguistics (PhD); historical linguistics (PhD); theoretical linguistics (PhD). *Degree requirements:* For doctorate, 4 foreign languages, thesis/dissertation, field exam, Indo-European language exam, research paper. *Entrance requirements:* For doctorate, GRE General Test. Additional exam requirements/recommendations for international students: Required—TOEFL.

Hofstra University, College of Liberal Arts and Sciences, Programs in Forensic Linguistics and Applied Linguistics, Hempstead, NY 11549. Offers applied linguistics (TESOL) (MA); linguistics (MA), including forensic linguistics. *Program availability:* Part-time. *Students:* 28 full-time (21 women), 7 part-time (5 women); includes 15 minority (4 Black or African American, non-Hispanic/Latino; 3 Asian, non-Hispanic/Latino; 8 Hispanic/Latino), 2 international. Average age 27. 41 applicants, 90% accepted, 23 enrolled. In 2017, 22 master's awarded. *Degree requirements:* For master's, thesis, 36 credits, capstone, minimum GPA of 3.0. *Entrance requirements:* For master's, bachelor's degree in related area, interview, 2 letters of recommendation. Additional exam requirements/recommendations for international students: Required—TOEFL (minimum score 550 paper-based; 80 iBT). *Application deadline:* Applications are processed on a rolling basis. Application fee: $75. Electronic applications accepted. *Expenses: Tuition:* Full-time $1292. *Required fees:* $970. Tuition and fees vary according to program. *Financial support:* In 2017–18, 31 students received support, including 9 fellowships with full and partial tuition reimbursements available (averaging $4,731 per year), 1 research assistantship with full and partial tuition reimbursement available (averaging $1,698 per year); career-related internships or fieldwork, Federal Work-Study, institutionally sponsored loans, scholarships/grants, tuition waivers (full and partial), and unspecified assistantships also available. Support available to part-time students. Financial award applicants required to submit FAFSA. *Faculty research:* Threatening language, legal interpretation, cross-examination strategies in assault trials. *Unit head:* Dr. Patricia Welch, Chairperson, 516-463-6453, E-mail: patricia.m.welch@hofstra.edu. *Application contact:* Sunil Samuel, Assistant Vice President of Admissions, 516-463-4723, Fax: 516-463-4664, E-mail: graduateadmission@hofstra.edu.
Website: http://www.hofstra.edu/hclas

Hofstra University, School of Education, Programs in Teacher Education, Hempstead, NY 11549. Offers bilingual education (MA); bilingual extension (Advanced Certificate), including education/speech language pathology, intensive teacher institute; business education (MS Ed); curriculum studies (MS Ed); early childhood and childhood education (MS Ed); early childhood education (MA, MS Ed); educational technology (Advanced Certificate); elementary education (MA, MS Ed), including science, technology, engineering, and mathematics (STEM) (MA); English education (MS Ed); family and consumer science (MS Ed); fine arts and music education (Advanced Certificate); fine arts education (MS Ed); foreign language and TESOL (MS Ed); foreign language education (MA, MS Ed), including Arabic (MS Ed), biology, chemistry, Chinese (MS Ed), earth science, French, German, Italian (MS Ed), Mandarin (MS Ed), physics, Russian, Spanish; foundations of education (Advanced Certificate), including grades 5-6, grades 7-9; languages other than English and teaching English as a second language (MA); learning and teaching (Ed D), including applied linguistics, art education, arts and humanities, early childhood education, English education, human development, math education, math, science, and technology, multicultural education, physical education, science education, social studies education, special education; mathematics education (MA, MS Ed); music education (MA, MS Ed); science education (MA), including biology (MA, MS Ed), chemistry (MA, MS Ed), earth science (MA, MS Ed), physics (MA, MS Ed); secondary education (Advanced Certificate); social studies education (MA, MS Ed); teaching languages other than English and TESOL (MS Ed); technology for learning (MA); TESOL (MS Ed, Advanced Certificate); TESOL with specialization in STEM (MA); work based learning extension (Advanced Certificate). *Program availability:* Part-time, evening/weekend, blended/hybrid learning. *Students:* 119 full-time (83

women), 124 part-time (90 women); includes 54 minority (15 Black or African American, non-Hispanic/Latino; 9 Asian, non-Hispanic/Latino; 29 Hispanic/Latino; 1 Native Hawaiian or other Pacific Islander, non-Hispanic/Latino, 12 international. Average age 29. 205 applicants, 88% accepted, 93 enrolled. In 2017, 103 master's, 4 doctorates, 32 other advanced degrees awarded. *Degree requirements:* For master's, comprehensive exam, thesis (for some programs), exit project, student teaching, fieldwork, electronic portfolio, curriculum project, minimum GPA of 3.0; for doctorate, thesis/dissertation; for Advanced Certificate, 3 foreign languages, comprehensive exam (for some programs), thesis project. *Entrance requirements:* For master's, GRE, 2 letters of recommendation, portfolio, teacher certification (MA), interview, essay; for doctorate, GMAT, GRE, LSAT, or MAT; for Advanced Certificate, 2 letters of recommendation, essay, interview and/or portfolio, teaching certificate. Additional exam requirements/recommendations for international students: Required—TOEFL (minimum score 550 paper-based; 80 iBT). *Application deadline:* Applications are processed on a rolling basis. Application fee: $75. Electronic applications accepted. *Expenses: Tuition:* Full-time $1292. *Required fees:* $970. Tuition and fees vary according to program. *Financial support:* In 2017–18, 112 students received support, including 56 fellowships with full and partial tuition reimbursements available (averaging $4,998 per year), 2 research assistantships with full and partial tuition reimbursements available (averaging $8,753 per year); career-related internships or fieldwork, Federal Work-Study, institutionally sponsored loans, scholarships/grants, traineeships, tuition waivers (full and partial), and unspecified assistantships also available. Support available to part-time students. Financial award applicants required to submit FAFSA. *Faculty research:* Educational interventions that foster critical-thinking skills; teachers' attitudes about professional development; threats to teacher quality. *Unit head:* Dr. Eustace Thompson, Chairperson, 516-463-5749, Fax: 516-463-6275, E-mail: eustace.g.thompson@hofstra.edu. *Application contact:* Sunil Samuel, Assistant Vice President of Admissions, 516-463-4723, Fax: 516-463-4664, E-mail: graduateadmission@hofstra.edu.
Website: http://www.hofstra.edu/education/

Indiana State University, College of Graduate and Professional Studies, College of Arts and Sciences, Department of Languages, Literatures, and Linguistics, Terre Haute, IN 47809. Offers applied linguistics/teaching English as a second language (MA); language education (PhD); Spanish/teaching english as a second language (MA); TESL/TEFL (CAS). *Degree requirements:* For master's, comprehensive exam. Electronic applications accepted.

Indiana University Bloomington, University Graduate School, College of Arts and Sciences, Department of Anthropology, Bloomington, IN 47405. Offers anthropology (MA, PhD), including archaeology (PhD), bioanthropology (PhD), linguistic anthropology (PhD), social-cultural anthropology (PhD). *Degree requirements:* For master's, comprehensive exam (for some programs), thesis or alternative; for doctorate, 2 foreign languages, comprehensive exam, thesis/dissertation. *Entrance requirements:* For master's and doctorate, GRE General Test, minimum GPA of 3.0. Additional exam requirements/recommendations for international students: Required—TOEFL (minimum score 550 paper-based, 79 iBT) or IELTS. Electronic applications accepted. *Expenses:* Contact institution. *Faculty research:* Archaeology in social context; bioanthropology; anthropology of food and ecology; gender studies; communication, media and performance.

Indiana University Bloomington, University Graduate School, College of Arts and Sciences, Department of French and Italian, Bloomington, IN 47405. Offers French (MA, PhD), including French and Francophone studies (MA), French instruction (MA), French linguistics; Italian (MA, PhD). *Program availability:* Part-time. Terminal master's awarded for partial completion of doctoral program. *Degree requirements:* For master's, variable foreign language requirement, comprehensive exam (for some programs), thesis or alternative; for doctorate, variable foreign language requirement, comprehensive exam, thesis/dissertation. *Entrance requirements:* For master's, GRE General Test, BA or equivalent undergraduate preparation in French or Italian; for doctorate, GRE General Test, MA from degree program at IU; MA in the specific field. Additional exam requirements/recommendations for international students: Required—TOEFL (minimum score 550 paper-based; 79 iBT), GRE General Test (recommended). Electronic applications accepted. *Faculty research:* French and Italian literature, French linguistics, including the novel and political theory, literature and fine arts, literary theory, postcolonialism, French-Creole studies, French literature of Africa and its Diaspora, humanism, Medieval folklore and mythology, humor in Medieval and Renaissance literature, emigration, second language acquisition, syntax, sociolinguistics, phonology, lexicography, media and cultural studies, cinema, drama.

Indiana University Bloomington, University Graduate School, College of Arts and Sciences, Department of Germanic Studies, Bloomington, IN 47405-7000. Offers German philology and linguistics (PhD); German studies (MA, PhD), including German (MA), German literature and culture (MA), German literature and linguistics (MA); medieval German studies (PhD); teaching German (MAT). *Degree requirements:* For master's, one foreign language, project; for doctorate, one foreign language, comprehensive exam, thesis/dissertation. *Entrance requirements:* For master's, GRE General Test, BA in German or equivalent; for doctorate, GRE General Test, MA in German or equivalent. Additional exam requirements/recommendations for international students: Required—TOEFL. Electronic applications accepted. *Faculty research:* German and other European literature: medieval to modern/postmodern, German and culture studies, Germanic philology, literary theory, literature and the other arts.

Indiana University Bloomington, University Graduate School, College of Arts and Sciences, Department of Linguistics, Bloomington, IN 47405. Offers African languages and linguistics (PhD); computational linguistics (MA, MS, PhD); linguistics (MA, PhD). Terminal master's awarded for partial completion of doctoral program. *Degree requirements:* For master's, one foreign language, thesis optional; for doctorate, one foreign language, comprehensive exam, thesis/dissertation, proficiency in research tool appropriate to research area. *Entrance requirements:* For master's and doctorate, GRE General Test. Additional exam requirements/recommendations for international students: Required—TOEFL (minimum score 580 paper-based; 92 iBT). Electronic applications accepted. *Faculty research:* African linguistics and language, semantics, phonology, syntactic theory, historical linguistics, phonetics-phonology, syntax, sociolinguistics, computational linguistics.

Instituto Tecnologico de Santo Domingo, Graduate School, Area of Humanities and Social Sciences, Santo Domingo, Dominican Republic. Offers accounting (Certificate); adult education (Certificate); applied linguistics (MA); economics (MA); education (M Ed); educational psychology (MA, Certificate); gender and development (MA, Certificate); humanistic studies (MA); international marketing management (Certificate); international relations in the Caribbean basin (Certificate); intervention systems in family therapy (MA); linguistic and literary communication (Certificate); pedagogical support (MA); social science education (M Ed); sustainable human development (MA); terminal illness and death psychology (Certificate); youth and adult education (M Ed).

Iowa State University of Science and Technology, Program in Applied Linguistics and Technology, Ames, IA 50011. Offers PhD. *Entrance requirements:* For doctorate, GRE, official academic transcripts, resume, three letters of recommendation, writing sample. Additional exam requirements/recommendations for international students:

Required—TOEFL (minimum score 640 paper-based; 111 iBT), IELTS (minimum score 7.5). Electronic applications accepted.

Iowa State University of Science and Technology, Program in Teaching English as a Second Language/Applied Linguistics, Ames, IA 50011. Offers MA. *Entrance requirements:* For master's, GRE, official academic transcripts, resume, three letters of recommendation, statement of personal goals, writing sample. Additional exam requirements/recommendations for international students: Required—TOEFL (minimum score 600 paper-based; 100 iBT), IELTS (minimum score 7). Electronic applications accepted.

Kent State University, College of Arts and Sciences, Department of Modern and Classical Language Studies, Kent, OH 44242-0001. Offers French (MA), including applied linguistics and pedagogy, literature; German (MA), including applied linguistics and pedagogy, literature; Latin (MA), including applied linguistics and pedagogy, literature; Spanish (MA), including applied linguistics and pedagogy, literature; translation (MA), including Arabic, French, German, Japanese, Russian, Spanish; translation studies (PhD); MA/MBA. *Program availability:* Part-time. *Faculty:* 21 full-time (13 women), 5 part-time/adjunct (3 women). *Students:* 78 full-time (50 women), 20 part-time (13 women); includes 18 minority (3 Black or African American, non-Hispanic/Latino; 1 Asian, non-Hispanic/Latino; 9 Hispanic/Latino; 5 Two or more races, non-Hispanic/Latino), 44 international. Average age 31. 95 applicants, 55% accepted, 27 enrolled. In 2017, 30 master's awarded. *Degree requirements:* For master's, variable foreign language requirement, comprehensive exam (for some programs), thesis (for some programs); for doctorate, variable foreign language requirement, comprehensive exam, thesis/dissertation. *Entrance requirements:* For master's, transcripts, goal statement, 3 letters of recommendation, CD/MP3 with oral sample of first and second languages, writing sample of second language; for doctorate, transcripts; MA in translation, a foreign language, or similar field; proficiency in a foreign language; minimum GPA of 3.5 from MA; goal statement; 3 letters of recommendation; essay or writing sample. Additional exam requirements/recommendations for international students: Required—TOEFL (minimum score 550 paper-based, 79 iBT), Michigan English Language Assessment Battery (minimum score 77), IELTS (minimum score 6.5) or PTE (minimum score 58). *Application deadline:* For fall admission, 2/1 for domestic and international students. Applications are processed on a rolling basis. Application fee: $45 ($70 for international students). Electronic applications accepted. *Expenses:* Tuition, state resident: full-time $11,310; part-time $515 per credit hour. Tuition, nonresident: full-time $20,396; part-time $928 per credit hour. *International tuition:* $18,544 full-time. *Financial support:* Fellowships with full tuition reimbursements, teaching assistantships with full tuition reimbursements, and unspecified assistantships available. Financial award application deadline: 2/1. *Unit head:* Dr. Keiran Dunne, Professor of French Translation/Chair, 330-672-2150, E-mail: kdunne@kent.edu. *Application contact:* Said Shiyab, Professor of Translation Studies/Graduate Coordinator, 330-672-1864, E-mail: sshiyab@kent.edu.
Website: http://www.kent.edu/mcls

Massachusetts Institute of Technology, School of Humanities, Arts, and Social Sciences, Department of Linguistics and Philosophy, Linguistics Section, Cambridge, MA 02139. Offers PhD. *Degree requirements:* For doctorate, comprehensive exam, thesis/dissertation, teaching assistantship during two semesters. *Entrance requirements:* Additional exam requirements/recommendations for international students: Required—TOEFL, IELTS. Electronic applications accepted. *Faculty research:* Phonology and phonetics, syntax and semantics, morphology, psycholinguistics, language acquisition.

McGill University, Faculty of Graduate and Postdoctoral Studies, Faculty of Arts, Department of Linguistics, Montréal, QC H3A 2T5, Canada. Offers language acquisition (PhD); linguistics (MA, PhD).

Memorial University of Newfoundland, School of Graduate Studies, Department of Linguistics, St. John's, NL A1C 5S7, Canada. Offers MA, PhD. *Program availability:* Part-time. *Degree requirements:* For master's, one foreign language, thesis or comprehensive exam; for doctorate, 2 foreign languages, comprehensive exam, thesis/dissertation, oral defense of thesis. *Entrance requirements:* For master's, bachelor's degree in linguistics; for doctorate, master's degree in linguistics. Electronic applications accepted. *Faculty research:* Aboriginal languages of eastern North America, historical/comparative linguistics, languages and dialects of Newfoundland and Labrador.

Michigan State University, The Graduate School, College of Arts and Letters, Department of Linguistics and Germanic, Slavic, Asian, and African Languages, East Lansing, MI 48824. Offers German studies (MA, PhD); linguistics (MA, PhD); teaching English to speakers of other languages (MA). *Program availability:* Part-time, evening/weekend. *Entrance requirements:* For master's, GRE General Test, minimum GPA of 3.2 in last 2 undergraduate years, 2 years of college-level foreign language, 3 letters of recommendation, portfolio (German studies); for doctorate, GRE General Test, minimum graduate GPA of 3.5, 3 letters of recommendation, master's degree or sufficient graduate course work in linguistics or language of study, master's thesis or major research paper. Additional exam requirements/recommendations for international students: Required—TOEFL. Electronic applications accepted.

Michigan State University, The Graduate School, College of Arts and Letters, Department of Spanish and Portuguese, East Lansing, MI 48824. Offers applied Spanish linguistics (MA); Hispanic cultural studies (PhD); Hispanic literatures (MA). *Entrance requirements:* Additional exam requirements/recommendations for international students: Required—TOEFL. Electronic applications accepted.

Montclair State University, The Graduate School, College of Humanities and Social Sciences, Program in Applied Linguistics, Montclair, NJ 07043-1624. Offers MA. *Program availability:* Part-time, evening/weekend. *Degree requirements:* For master's, comprehensive exam. *Entrance requirements:* For master's, GRE General Test, 2 letters of recommendation, essay. Additional exam requirements/recommendations for international students: Required—TOEFL (minimum score 83 iBT), IELTS (minimum score 6.5). Electronic applications accepted. *Faculty research:* Research on short message service (SMS) text messaging; corpus building and research; research on online, hybrid, and mobile language learning; linguistic code switching and bilingual mental lexical, sentence comprehension; second language acquisition of American Sign Language; cognitive linguistics; phonetics.

Montclair State University, The Graduate School, College of Humanities and Social Sciences, Program in Computational Linguistics, Montclair, NJ 07043-1624. Offers Certificate. *Program availability:* Part-time, evening/weekend. *Entrance requirements:* For degree, 2 letters of recommendation, essay. Additional exam requirements/recommendations for international students: Required—TOEFL (minimum score 83 iBT), IELTS (minimum score 6.5). Electronic applications accepted. *Faculty research:* Resource light morphology, creativity, idiomatic sentence detection; computational approaches to deception detection; computational approaches to fusional morphology; computational approaches to figurative language.

New York University, Graduate School of Arts and Science, Department of Linguistics, New York, NY 10012-1019. Offers MA, PhD. *Program availability:* Part-time. *Students:* Average age 30. 124 applicants, 9% accepted, 4 enrolled. In 2017, 2 master's, 9 doctorates awarded. Terminal master's awarded for partial completion of doctoral

program. *Degree requirements:* For master's, one foreign language, comprehensive exam, thesis optional; for doctorate, one foreign language, thesis/dissertation, 2 publishable papers. *Entrance requirements:* For master's and doctorate, GRE General Test. Additional exam requirements/recommendations for international students: Required—TOEFL. *Application deadline:* For fall admission, 1/4 priority date for domestic students, 1/4 for international students. Application fee: $100. *Expenses: Tuition:* Full-time $41,352; part-time $19,968 per year. *Required fees:* $2496; $1628 per unit. $814 per term. Tuition and fees vary according to course load and program. *Financial support:* Fellowships, teaching assistantships, Federal Work-Study, institutionally sponsored loans, scholarships/grants, health care benefits, and unspecified assistantships available. Financial award application deadline: 1/4; financial award applicants required to submit FAFSA. *Faculty research:* Phonology, syntax, sociolinguistics, cognitive science. *Unit head:* Chris Barker, Chair, 212-998-7950, Fax: 212-995-4707, E-mail: linguistics@nyu.edu. *Application contact:* Lisa Davidson, Acting Director of Graduate Studies, 212-998-7950, Fax: 212-995-4707, E-mail: linguistics@nyu.edu.
Website: http://www.nyu.edu/gsas/dept/lingu/

Northeastern Illinois University, College of Graduate Studies and Research, College of Arts and Sciences, Program in Linguistics, Chicago, IL 60625. Offers linguistics (MA). *Program availability:* Part-time, evening/weekend. *Degree requirements:* For master's, one foreign language, comprehensive exam, thesis optional. *Entrance requirements:* For master's, 9 undergraduate hours in a foreign language or equivalent, minimum GPA of 2.75. Additional exam requirements/recommendations for international students: Required—TOEFL (minimum score 550 paper-based; 79 iBT). *Application deadline:* Applications are processed on a rolling basis. Application fee: $30. Electronic applications accepted. *Expenses:* Tuition, state resident: full-time $7274; part-time $404.11 per credit hour. Tuition, nonresident: full-time $14,548; part-time $808.23 per credit hour. *Required fees:* $1284. *Financial support:* Applicants required to submit FAFSA. *Faculty research:* Acquisition of literacy, Mayan language, Rotuman language, English as a second language methodology, Farsi language. *Unit head:* Dr. Richard Hallett, Coordinator, 773-442-5879, E-mail: r-hallett@neiu.edu. *Application contact:* Martha Narvaez, Graduate Admission Representative, 773-442-6006, E-mail: m-narvaez@neiu.edu.

Northern Arizona University, College of Arts and Letters, Department of English, Flagstaff, AZ 86011. Offers applied linguistics (PhD); creative writing (MFA), including creative writing; English (MA), including literature, professional writing, rhetoric, writing, and digital media studies, secondary education; professional writing (Graduate Certificate); rhetoric, writing and digital media studies (Graduate Certificate); teaching English as a second language (MA, Graduate Certificate). *Program availability:* Part-time, 100% online, blended/hybrid learning. *Faculty:* 62 full-time (43 women), 3 part-time/adjunct (2 women). *Students:* 115 full-time (78 women), 115 part-time (89 women); includes 57 minority (11 Black or African American, non-Hispanic/Latino; 3 American Indian or Alaska Native, non-Hispanic/Latino; 4 Asian, non-Hispanic/Latino; 26 Hispanic/Latino; 13 Two or more races, non-Hispanic/Latino), 19 international. Average age 35. 189 applicants, 56% accepted, 92 enrolled. In 2017, 82 master's, 5 doctorates, 15 other advanced degrees awarded. *Degree requirements:* For master's, variable foreign language requirement, comprehensive exam (for some programs), thesis (for some programs); for doctorate, variable foreign language requirement, comprehensive exam (for some programs), thesis/dissertation (for some programs); for Graduate Certificate, comprehensive exam (for some programs). *Entrance requirements:* Additional exam requirements/recommendations for international students: Required—TOEFL (minimum score 80 iBT), IELTS (minimum score 6.5). *Application deadline:* For fall admission, 1/30 for domestic and international students; for spring admission, 10/1 for domestic and international students. Application fee: $65. Electronic applications accepted. *Expenses:* Tuition, state resident: full-time $9240; part-time $458 per credit hour. Tuition, nonresident: full-time $21,588; part-time $1199 per credit hour. *Required fees:* $1021; $14 per credit hour. $646 per semester. Tuition and fees vary according to course load, campus/location and program. *Financial support:* In 2017–18, 69 students received support, including 4 fellowships with full and partial tuition reimbursements available (averaging $16,250 per year), 2 research assistantships with full and partial tuition reimbursements available (averaging $16,250 per year), 65 teaching assistantships with full and partial tuition reimbursements available (averaging $16,250 per year); institutionally sponsored loans, health care benefits, tuition waivers (full and partial), and unspecified assistantships also available. Financial award application deadline: 2/1; financial award applicants required to submit FAFSA. *Unit head:* Dr. Steven Rosendale, Chair, 928-523-4911, Fax: 928-523-7074, E-mail: steven.rosendale@nau.edu. *Application contact:* Tina Sutton, Coordinator, Graduate College, 928-523-4348, Fax: 928-523-8950, E-mail: graduate@nau.edu.
Website: https://nau.edu/cal/english/

Northwestern University, The Graduate School, Judd A. and Marjorie Weinberg College of Arts and Sciences, Department of Linguistics, Evanston, IL 60208. Offers PhD, JD/PhD. Admissions and degrees offered through The Graduate School. *Program availability:* Part-time. Terminal master's awarded for partial completion of doctoral program. *Degree requirements:* For doctorate, 2 foreign languages, thesis/dissertation, 2 qualifying papers. *Entrance requirements:* For doctorate, GRE General Test. Additional exam requirements/recommendations for international students: Required—TOEFL. Electronic applications accepted. *Faculty research:* Theoretical linguistics, empirical approaches to the study of language, language and cognition.

Oakland University, Graduate Study and Lifelong Learning, College of Arts and Sciences, Department of Linguistics, Rochester, MI 48309-4401. Offers linguistics (MA); teaching English as a second language (Certificate). *Program availability:* Part-time, evening/weekend. *Entrance requirements:* For master's, minimum GPA of 3.0. Additional exam requirements/recommendations for international students: Required—TOEFL (minimum score 550 paper-based). *Expenses:* Tuition, state resident: full-time $16,950; part-time $706.25 per credit. Tuition, nonresident: full-time $24,648; part-time $1027 per credit.

The Ohio State University, Graduate School, College of Arts and Sciences, Division of Arts and Humanities, Department of Linguistics, Columbus, OH 43210. Offers MA, PhD. *Faculty:* 17. *Students:* 32 (13 women), 8 international. Average age 30. In 2017, 4 master's, 3 doctorates awarded. Terminal master's awarded for partial completion of doctoral program. *Degree requirements:* For master's, one foreign language, exam or thesis; for doctorate, 2 foreign languages, thesis/dissertation, exam. *Entrance requirements:* For master's and doctorate, GRE General Test. Additional exam requirements/recommendations for international students: Required—TOEFL (minimum score 600 paper-based; 100 iBT), Michigan English Language Assessment Battery (minimum score 86); Recommended—IELTS (minimum score 8). *Application deadline:* For fall admission, 12/1 priority date for domestic students, 11/30 priority date for international students; for spring admission, 3/1 for domestic students, 2/1 for international students. Applications are processed on a rolling basis. Application fee: $60 ($70 for international students). Electronic applications accepted. *Financial support:* Fellowships, research assistantships, teaching assistantships, Federal Work-Study, and institutionally sponsored loans available. Support available to part-time students. *Faculty research:* Experimental phonetics, nonlinear phonology, process morphology (synchronically and diachronically), syntactic theory, Montague semantics. *Unit head:* Dr. Shari R. Speer, Chair, 617-292-5389, E-mail: speer.21@osu.edu. *Application contact:* Graduate and Professional Admissions, 614-292-9444, Fax: 614-292-3895, E-mail: gpadmissions@osu.edu.
Website: http://linguistics.osu.edu/

The Ohio State University, Graduate School, College of Arts and Sciences, Division of Arts and Humanities, Department of Slavic and East European Languages and Cultures, Columbus, OH 43210. Offers Slavic linguistics (MA, PhD); Slavic literature, film, and cultural studies (MA, PhD). *Faculty:* 10. *Students:* 16 full-time (11 women). Average age 31. In 2017, 1 master's, 4 doctorates awarded. Terminal master's awarded for partial completion of doctoral program. *Degree requirements:* For master's, variable foreign language requirement, thesis optional; for doctorate, variable foreign language requirement, thesis/dissertation. *Entrance requirements:* For master's and doctorate, GRE General Test, at least 3 years of Russian language study or equivalent. Additional exam requirements/recommendations for international students: Required—TOEFL (minimum score 550 paper-based; 79 iBT), Michigan English Language Assessment Battery (minimum score 82); Recommended—IELTS (minimum score 7). *Application deadline:* For fall admission, 12/12 priority date for domestic students, 11/30 priority date for international students; for spring admission, 3/1 for domestic students, 2/1 for international students. Applications are processed on a rolling basis. Application fee: $60 ($70 for international students). Electronic applications accepted. *Financial support:* Fellowships, teaching assistantships, Federal Work-Study, and institutionally sponsored loans available. Support available to part-time students. *Faculty research:* Polish literature. *Unit head:* Dr. Yana Hashamova, Chair and Professor, 614-292-6733, E-mail: hashamova.1@osu.edu. *Application contact:* Graduate and Professional Admissions, 614-292-9444, Fax: 614-292-3895, E-mail: gpadmissions@osu.edu.
Website: http://slavic.osu.edu/

Ohio University, Graduate College, College of Arts and Sciences, Department of Linguistics, Athens, OH 45701-2979. Offers applied linguistics (MA). *Program availability:* Part-time. *Degree requirements:* For master's, one foreign language, thesis or alternative. *Entrance requirements:* For master's, minimum GPA of 3.0. Additional exam requirements/recommendations for international students: Required—TOEFL (minimum score 600 paper-based; 100 iBT) or IELTS (minimum score 7). Electronic applications accepted. *Faculty research:* Syntax, language learning, language teaching, computers for teaching, sociolinguistics.

Old Dominion University, College of Arts and Letters, Program in Applied Linguistics, Norfolk, VA 23529. Offers sociolinguistics (MA); TESOL (MA). *Program availability:* Part-time. *Faculty:* 4 full-time (all women). *Students:* 7 full-time (4 women), 7 part-time (5 women); includes 6 minority (1 Black or African American, non-Hispanic/Latino; 1 Asian, non-Hispanic/Latino; 1 Hispanic/Latino; 3 Two or more races, non-Hispanic/Latino), 3 international. Average age 32. 23 applicants, 91% accepted, 11 enrolled. In 2017, 9 master's awarded. *Degree requirements:* For master's, one foreign language, comprehensive exam, thesis optional, program portfolio. *Entrance requirements:* For master's, GRE General Test, sample of written work; 12 hours in English, 9 on the upper-level; minimum B average; letters of recommendation; resume; essay. Additional exam requirements/recommendations for international students: Required—TOEFL (minimum score 570 paper-based; 88 iBT). *Application deadline:* For fall admission, 3/15 priority date for domestic and international students; for spring admission, 10/1 priority date for domestic and international students. Applications are processed on a rolling basis. Application fee: $50. Electronic applications accepted. *Expenses:* Tuition, state resident: full-time $8928; part-time $496 per credit. Tuition, nonresident: full-time $22,482; part-time $1249 per credit. *Required fees:* $66 per semester. *Financial support:* In 2017–18, 6 students received support. Career-related internships or fieldwork, institutionally sponsored loans, and unspecified assistantships available. Financial award application deadline: 2/15. *Faculty research:* Discourse analysis, phonology, syntax, second language acquisition, gender, sociolinguistics. *Unit head:* Dr. Bridget Anderson, Graduate Program Director, 757-683-4020, Fax: 757-683-3241, E-mail: linggpd@odu.edu. *Application contact:* Dr. David C. Earnest, Associate Dean, 757-683-6077, Fax: 757-683-5746, E-mail: dearnest@odu.edu.
Website: https://www.odu.edu/academics/programs/masters/applied-linguistics

Penn State University Park, Graduate School, College of the Liberal Arts, Department of Applied Linguistics, University Park, PA 16802. Offers applied linguistics (PhD); teaching English as a second language (MA). *Unit head:* Dr. Susan Welch, Dean, 814-865-7691, Fax: 814-863-2085. *Application contact:* Lori Hawn, Director, Graduate Student Services, 814-865-1795, Fax: 814-863-4627, E-mail: l-gswww@lists.psu.edu.
Website: http://aplng.la.psu.edu/

Purdue University, Graduate School, College of Health and Human Sciences, Department of Speech, Language, and Hearing Sciences, West Lafayette, IN 47907. Offers audiology clinic (MS, Au D, PhD); linguistics (MS, PhD); speech and hearing science (MS, PhD); speech-language pathology (MS, PhD). *Accreditation:* ASHA. *Faculty:* 32 full-time (21 women), 9 part-time/adjunct (8 women). *Students:* 106 full-time (98 women), 7 part-time (6 women); includes 10 minority (1 Black or African American, non-Hispanic/Latino; 4 Asian, non-Hispanic/Latino; 1 Hispanic/Latino; 4 Two or more races, non-Hispanic/Latino), 7 international. Average age 25. 301 applicants, 35% accepted, 48 enrolled. In 2017, 31 master's, 5 doctorates awarded. *Degree requirements:* For master's, comprehensive exam (for some programs), thesis optional; for doctorate, comprehensive exam, thesis/dissertation. *Entrance requirements:* For master's and doctorate, GRE General Test, minimum undergraduate GPA of 3.0 or equivalent. Additional exam requirements/recommendations for international students: Required—TOEFL (minimum score 77 iBT). *Application deadline:* For fall admission, 1/1 priority date for domestic and international students; for spring admission, 8/1 priority date for domestic and international students. Applications are processed on a rolling basis. Application fee: $60 ($75 for international students). Electronic applications accepted. *Financial support:* Fellowships with full tuition reimbursements, research assistantships with full tuition reimbursements, teaching assistantships with full tuition reimbursements, career-related internships or fieldwork, and scholarships/grants available. Support available to part-time students. Financial award application deadline: 2/1; financial award applicants required to submit FAFSA. *Faculty research:* Psychoacoustics, speech perception, speech physiology, stuttering, child language. *Unit head:* Dr. Keith R. Kluender, Head, 765-494-3788, E-mail: kkluender@purdue.edu. *Application contact:* Vickie L. Parker-Black, Graduate Contact, 765-494-3786, E-mail: vpblack@purdue.edu.
Website: http://www.purdue.edu/hhs/slhs/

Purdue University, Graduate School, College of Liberal Arts, Department of English, West Lafayette, IN 47907. Offers creative writing (MFA); literature (MA, PhD), including linguistics, literature and philosophy (PhD), rhetoric and composition, theory and cultural studies (PhD). *Program availability:* Part-time. *Faculty:* 57 full-time (26 women), 3 part-time/adjunct (all women). *Students:* 130 full-time (82 women), 50 part-time (28 women); includes 21 minority (6 Black or African American, non-Hispanic/Latino; 5 Asian, non-Hispanic/Latino; 7 Hispanic/Latino; 3 Two or more races, non-Hispanic/Latino), 31 international. Average age 31. 299 applicants, 14% accepted, 29 enrolled. In 2017, 19 master's, 26 doctorates awarded. *Degree requirements:* For master's, one foreign language, comprehensive exam (for some programs), thesis (for some programs); for

doctorate, one foreign language, comprehensive exam, thesis/dissertation. *Entrance requirements:* For master's, GRE General Test; GRE Subject Test in English literature (recommended for students applying to literary studies), minimum undergraduate GPA of 3.0 or equivalent; for doctorate, GRE General Test; GRE Subject Test in English literature (recommended for students applying to literary studies), master's degree. Additional exam requirements/recommendations for international students: Required—TOEFL (minimum score 620 paper-based; 77 iBT). *Application deadline:* For fall admission, 1/15 for domestic and international students. Applications are processed on a rolling basis. Application fee: $60 ($75 for international students). Electronic applications accepted. *Financial support:* Fellowships with tuition reimbursements and teaching assistantships with tuition reimbursements available. Support available to part-time students. Financial award application deadline: 1/15; financial award applicants required to submit FAFSA. *Faculty research:* Cultural studies, postmodern narrative, contemporary women writers, composition theory, slave narratives. *Unit head:* Dorsey Armstrong, Head, 765-494-6478, E-mail: darmstrong@purdue.edu. *Application contact:* Jill M. Quirk, Graduate Contact, 765-494-3748, Fax: 765-494-1700, E-mail: griff@purdue.edu.
Website: https://www.cla.purdue.edu/english/

Purdue University, Graduate School, College of Liberal Arts, Program in Linguistics, West Lafayette, IN 47907. Offers MS, PhD. *Students:* 12 full-time (9 women), 10 part-time (6 women); includes 3 minority (2 Asian, non-Hispanic/Latino; 1 Two or more races, non-Hispanic/Latino), 5 international. Average age 28. 41 applicants, 17% accepted, 6 enrolled. In 2017, 1 master's, 5 doctorates awarded. *Degree requirements:* For master's, one foreign language, thesis; for doctorate, 3 foreign languages, comprehensive exam, thesis/dissertation. *Entrance requirements:* For master's and doctorate, GRE General Test (minimum score of 500 for verbal and quantitative respectively), minimum undergraduate GPA of 3.4. Additional exam requirements/recommendations for international students: Required—TOEFL (minimum score 620 paper-based; 77 iBT), TWE. *Application deadline:* For fall admission, 1/1 for domestic and international students. Applications are processed on a rolling basis. Application fee: $60 ($75 for international students). Electronic applications accepted. *Financial support:* Fellowships, research assistantships, and teaching assistantships available. Support available to part-time students. Financial award applicants required to submit FAFSA. *Faculty research:* Sign languages, sociolinguistics and African American English, computational linguistics, indigenous languages, theoretical linguistics. *Unit head:* Alejandro Cuza-Blanco, Head, 765-496-1685, E-mail: acuza@purdue.edu. *Application contact:* Elsa Schirmer, Graduate Contact, 765-496-9629, E-mail: eschirme@purdue.edu.
Website: http://www.cla.purdue.edu/linguistics/

Queens College of the City University of New York, Arts and Humanities Division, Department of Linguistics and Communication Disorders, Queens, NY 11367-1597. Offers applied linguistics (MA); speech-language pathology (MA); TESOL (MS Ed, Post-Master's Certificate); TESOL and bilingual education (Post-Master's Certificate). *Accreditation:* ASHA. *Program availability:* Part-time. *Faculty:* 22 full-time (16 women), 19 part-time/adjunct (13 women). *Students:* 37 full-time (34 women), 123 part-time (112 women); includes 62 minority (10 Black or African American, non-Hispanic/Latino; 17 Asian, non-Hispanic/Latino; 32 Hispanic/Latino; 3 Two or more races, non-Hispanic/Latino), 3 international. Average age 27. 390 applicants, 25% accepted, 81 enrolled. In 2017, 59 master's, 24 other advanced degrees awarded. *Degree requirements:* For master's, 400 hours of supervised clinical teaching (for MA in speech-language pathology); 50-100 hours of student teaching (for MS Ed). *Entrance requirements:* For master's, minimum GPA of 3.0. Additional exam requirements/recommendations for international students: Required—TOEFL, IELTS. *Application deadline:* For fall admission, 4/1 for domestic students. Applications are processed on a rolling basis. Application fee: $125. Electronic applications accepted. *Expenses:* Contact institution. *Financial support:* Career-related internships or fieldwork available. Financial award application deadline: 4/1; financial award applicants required to submit FAFSA. *Unit head:* Arlene Kraat, Chair, 718-997-2940, E-mail: arlene.kraat@qc.cuny.edu. *Application contact:* Elizabeth D'Amico-Ramirez, Assistant Director of Graduate Admissions, 718-997-5203, E-mail: elizabeth.damicoramirez@qc.cuny.edu.

Rice University, Graduate Programs, School of Humanities, Department of Linguistics, Houston, TX 77251-1892. Offers MA, PhD. Terminal master's awarded for partial completion of doctoral program. *Degree requirements:* For master's, one foreign language, thesis; for doctorate, 2 foreign languages, thesis/dissertation, 3 research papers. *Entrance requirements:* For master's and doctorate, GRE General Test, minimum GPA of 3.0. Additional exam requirements/recommendations for international students: Required—TOEFL (minimum score 600 paper-based; 90 iBT). Electronic applications accepted. *Faculty research:* Typology, fieldwork and language description, cognitive grammar, historical linguistics, corpus linguistics.

Rutgers University–New Brunswick, Graduate School-New Brunswick, Department of Linguistics, Piscataway, NJ 08854-8097. Offers PhD. *Degree requirements:* For doctorate, thesis/dissertation, 2 qualifying papers. *Entrance requirements:* For doctorate, GRE General Test, 3 letters of recommendation, writing sample. Additional exam requirements/recommendations for international students: Recommended—TOEFL. Electronic applications accepted. *Faculty research:* Theoretical linguistics, syntax, semantics, phonology, computational linguistics, phoenetics.

San Diego State University, Graduate and Research Affairs, College of Arts and Letters, Department of Linguistics and Oriental Languages, San Diego, CA 92182. Offers applied linguistics and English as a second language (CAL); computational linguistics (MA); English as a second language/applied linguistics (MA); general linguistics (MA). *Degree requirements:* For master's, one foreign language, comprehensive exam, thesis optional. *Entrance requirements:* For master's, GRE General Test, 2 letters of recommendation. Additional exam requirements/recommendations for international students: Required—TOEFL (minimum score 570 paper-based). Electronic applications accepted. *Faculty research:* Cross-cultural linguistic studies of semantics.

San Francisco State University, Division of Graduate Studies, College of Liberal and Creative Arts, Department of English Language and Literature, Program in Linguistics, San Francisco, CA 94132-1722. Offers MA. *Program availability:* Part-time. *Degree requirements:* For master's, 2 foreign languages, thesis (for some programs). *Application deadline:* Applications are processed on a rolling basis. *Faculty research:* Mental lexicon, endangered languages, language and gender, linguistics, discourse analysis. *Unit head:* Dr. Sugie Goen-Salter, Chair, 415-338-7582, Fax: 415-338-6159, E-mail: sgoen@sfsu.edu. *Application contact:* Dr. Jenny Lederer, Coordinator, 415-388-7406, Fax: 415-338-6159, E-mail: lederer@sfsu.edu.
Website: http://english.sfsu.edu/graduate-linguistics

San Jose State University, Graduate Studies and Research, College of Humanities and the Arts, San Jose, CA 95192-0088. Offers art (MA, MFA), including digital media art (MFA), history and visual culture (MA), photography (MFA), pictorial art (MFA), spatial art (MFA); English (MA, MFA), including creative writing (MFA); linguistics (MA); music (MM); music education (MA); philosophy (MA); Spanish (MA); teaching English to speakers of other languages (MA). *Program availability:* Part-time. *Faculty:* 35 full-time (17 women), 19 part-time/adjunct (11 women). *Students:* 129 full-time (79 women), 106 part-time (71 women); includes 117 minority (5 Black or African American, non-Hispanic/Latino; 29 Asian, non-Hispanic/Latino; 44 Hispanic/Latino; 39 Two or more races, non-Hispanic/Latino), 28 international. Average age 35. 204 applicants, 65% accepted, 79 enrolled. In 2017, 85 master's awarded. *Degree requirements:* For master's, one foreign language, comprehensive exam (for some programs), thesis (for some programs), graduate writing assessment, special study/project, recital. *Entrance requirements:* Additional exam requirements/recommendations for international students: Required—TOEFL (minimum score 550 paper-based; 80 iBT), IELTS (minimum score 6.5), PTE (minimum score 53). *Application deadline:* For fall admission, 2/1 for domestic and international students. Applications are processed on a rolling basis. Application fee: $55. Electronic applications accepted. *Expenses:* Tuition, state resident: full-time $7176. Tuition, nonresident: full-time $16,680. Tuition and fees vary according to course load and program. *Financial support:* Fellowships, research assistantships, Federal Work-Study, scholarships/grants, traineeships, tuition waivers (full and partial), and unspecified assistantships available. Support available to part-time students. Financial award application deadline: 4/28; financial award applicants required to submit FAFSA. *Unit head:* Dr. Shannon Miller, Dean, 408-924-4300, Fax: 408-924-4365, E-mail: shannon.miller@sjsu.edu.
Website: http://www.sjsu.edu/humanitiesandarts/

Simon Fraser University, Office of Graduate Studies and Postdoctoral Fellows, Faculty of Arts and Social Sciences, Department of Linguistics, Burnaby, BC V5A 1S6, Canada. Offers MA, PhD. *Degree requirements:* For master's, one foreign language, thesis; for doctorate, 2 foreign languages, thesis/dissertation, qualifying papers. *Entrance requirements:* For master's, minimum GPA of 3.0 (on scale of 4.33) or 3.33 based on last 60 credits of undergraduate courses; for doctorate, minimum GPA of 3.5 (on scale of 4.33). Additional exam requirements/recommendations for international students: Recommended—TOEFL (minimum score 580 paper-based; 93 iBT), IELTS (minimum score 7), TWE (minimum score 5). Electronic applications accepted. *Faculty research:* History of linguistics, syntactic theory, relational grammar, experimental phonetics, pragmatics.

Southern Illinois University Carbondale, Graduate School, College of Liberal Arts, Department of Linguistics, Carbondale, IL 62901. Offers linguistics (MA); teaching English to speakers of other languages (MA). *Degree requirements:* For master's, one foreign language. *Entrance requirements:* For master's, minimum GPA of 3.0. Additional exam requirements/recommendations for international students: Required—TOEFL (minimum score 90 iBT). *Faculty research:* Theory and methods, second language acquisition, pidgin and Creole languages, cognitive grammar.

Stanford University, School of Humanities and Sciences, Department of Linguistics, Stanford, CA 94305-2004. Offers MA, PhD. *Degree requirements:* For master's, one foreign language, thesis; for doctorate, 2 foreign languages, thesis/dissertation, oral exam, qualifying papers. *Entrance requirements:* For master's and doctorate, GRE General Test. Additional exam requirements/recommendations for international students: Required—TOEFL. Electronic applications accepted. *Expenses: Tuition:* Full-time $48,987; part-time $10,620 per quarter. One-time fee: $400. Tuition and fees vary according to program.

Stony Brook University, State University of New York, Graduate School, College of Arts and Sciences, Department of Linguistics, Program in Linguistics, Stony Brook, NY 11794. Offers MA, PhD. *Faculty:* 25 full-time (13 women), 10 part-time/adjunct (8 women). *Students:* 37 full-time (21 women); includes 1 minority (American Indian or Alaska Native, non-Hispanic/Latino), 27 international. Average age 31. 36 applicants, 50% accepted, 7 enrolled. In 2017, 6 master's, 1 doctorate awarded. *Degree requirements:* For doctorate, thesis/dissertation. *Entrance requirements:* For doctorate, GRE. Additional exam requirements/recommendations for international students: Required—TOEFL (minimum score 90 iBT). *Application deadline:* For fall admission, 1/15 for domestic students; for spring admission, 10/1 for domestic students. Application fee: $100. Electronic applications accepted. *Expenses:* Contact institution. *Financial support:* In 2017–18, 1 fellowship, 1 research assistantship, 18 teaching assistantships were awarded. *Unit head:* Dr. Richard Larson, Chair, 631-632-7776, E-mail: richard.larson@stonybrook.edu. *Application contact:* Michelle Carbone, Coordinator, 631-632-7774, Fax: 631-632-9789, E-mail: michelle.carbone@stonybrook.edu.

Syracuse University, College of Arts and Sciences, MA Program in Linguistic Studies, Syracuse, NY 13244. Offers linguistic studies (MA), including information representation and retrieval, language acquisition, language, culture, and society, linguistic theory, logic and language, teaching language (TESOL/TLOTE). *Program availability:* Part-time. *Students:* Average age 25. *Degree requirements:* For master's, comprehensive exam, thesis or alternative. *Entrance requirements:* For master's, GRE General Test, personal statement detailing interest in field of linguistics and possible concentration areas, transcripts, three recommendation letters. Additional exam requirements/recommendations for international students: Required—TOEFL (minimum score 100 iBT). *Application deadline:* For fall admission, 1/15 priority date for domestic and international students. Application fee: $75. Electronic applications accepted. *Financial support:* Teaching assistantships with tuition reimbursements available. Financial award application deadline: 1/15. *Faculty research:* Information representation and retrieval, language acquisition, linguistic theory, logic and language, teaching languages. *Unit head:* Dr. Gerald R. Greenberg, Director, 315-443-1414, E-mail: ggreenbe@syr.edu. *Application contact:* Jaklin Kornfilt, Professor of Linguistics and Director of the Linguistic Studies Program, 315-443-5375, E-mail: kornfilt@syr.edu.
Website: http://lll.syr.edu/linguistics/graduate.html

Syracuse University, College of Arts and Sciences, MS Program in Computational Linguistics, Syracuse, NY 13244. Offers MS. Program held jointly with School of Information Studies and the College of Engineering and Computer Science. *Program availability:* Part-time. *Students:* Average age 27. *Degree requirements:* For master's, thesis or alternative, internship. *Entrance requirements:* For master's, GRE, resume, personal statement, transcripts, three letters of recommendation. Additional exam requirements/recommendations for international students: Required—TOEFL (minimum score 100 iBT). *Application deadline:* For fall admission, 2/1 for domestic students, 2/1 priority date for international students; for summer admission, 2/1 for domestic students, 2/1 priority date for international students. Application fee: $75. Electronic applications accepted. *Financial support:* Fellowships with full tuition reimbursements, research assistantships with tuition reimbursements, teaching assistantships with tuition reimbursements, and scholarships/grants available. Financial award application deadline: 1/1; financial award applicants required to submit FAFSA. *Faculty research:* Human interaction with computers, logic and language, artificial intelligence, theory of classification and subject representation, structured programming and formal methods. *Unit head:* Dr. Jaklin Kornfilt, Professor of Linguistics, 315-443-5375, E-mail: kornfilt@syr.edu.
Website: http://lll.syr.edu/graduate.html

Teachers College, Columbia University, Department of Arts and Humanities, New York, NY 10027. Offers applied linguistics (MA, Ed D); art and art education (Ed M, MA, Ed D, Ed DCT); arts administration (MA); bilingual and bicultural education (MA); global competence (Certificate); history and education (Ed D, PhD); music and music education (Ed DCT); philosophy and education (MA, Ed D, PhD); social studies education (Ed M, PhD); teaching English to speakers of other languages (Ed M);

teaching of English and English education (Ed M, MA, Ed D, PhD), including English education (Ed M, Ed D, PhD), teaching of English (MA); teaching of social studies (MA); TESOL (MA, Ed D). *Program availability:* Part-time, evening/weekend. *Students:* 391 full-time (305 women), 418 part-time (283 women); includes 246 minority (62 Black or African American, non-Hispanic/Latino; 3 American Indian or Alaska Native, non-Hispanic/Latino; 94 Asian, non-Hispanic/Latino; 75 Hispanic/Latino; 12 Two or more races, non-Hispanic/Latino), 209 international. Average age 30. 1,053 applicants, 60% accepted, 334 enrolled. Terminal master's awarded for partial completion of doctoral program. *Financial support:* Fellowships, research assistantships, teaching assistantships, career-related internships or fieldwork, Federal Work-Study, institutionally sponsored loans, tuition waivers (full and partial), and unspecified assistantships available. Support available to part-time students. *Unit head:* Prof. William Gaudelli, Department Chair, E-mail: gaudelli@tc.columbia.edu. *Application contact:* David Estrella, Director of Admissions, 212-678-3305, Fax: 212-678-4171, E-mail: estrella@tc.columbia.edu.

Texas A&M University–Commerce, College of Humanities, Social Sciences and Arts, Commerce, TX 75429. Offers applied criminology (MS); applied linguistics (MA, MS); art (MA, MFA); computational linguistics (Graduate Certificate); creative writing (Graduate Certificate); criminal justice management (Graduate Certificate); criminal justice studies (Graduate Certificate); English (MA, MS, PhD); film studies (Graduate Certificate); history (MA, MS); history of Christianity (Graduate Certificate); Holocaust studies (Graduate Certificate); homeland security (Graduate Certificate); music education (MM); music performance (MM); political science (MA, MS); public history (Graduate Certificate); sociology (MS); Spanish (MA); studies in children's and adolescent literature and culture (Graduate Certificate); teaching English to speakers of other languages (Graduate Certificate); theater (MA, MS); world history (Graduate Certificate). *Program availability:* Part-time. *Faculty:* 56 full-time (26 women), 10 part-time/adjunct (5 women). *Students:* 133 full-time (85 women), 439 part-time (311 women); includes 204 minority (79 Black or African American, non-Hispanic/Latino; 4 American Indian or Alaska Native, non-Hispanic/Latino; 9 Asian, non-Hispanic/Latino; 98 Hispanic/Latino; 14 Two or more races, non-Hispanic/Latino), 26 international. Average age 36. 261 applicants, 50% accepted, 113 enrolled. In 2017, 105 master's, 5 doctorates awarded. *Degree requirements:* For master's, one foreign language, comprehensive exam, thesis (for some programs); for doctorate, one foreign language, comprehensive exam, thesis/dissertation, departmental qualifying exam. *Entrance requirements:* For master's and doctorate, GRE General Test. Additional exam requirements/recommendations for international students: Required—TOEFL (minimum score 550 paper-based; 79 iBT), IELTS (minimum score 6). *Application deadline:* Applications are processed on a rolling basis. Application fee: $50. Electronic applications accepted. *Expenses:* Contact institution. *Financial support:* In 2017–18, 43 students received support, including 9 research assistantships with partial tuition reimbursements available (averaging $9,000 per year), 68 teaching assistantships with partial tuition reimbursements available (averaging $9,000 per year); Federal Work-Study, institutionally sponsored loans, scholarships/grants, health care benefits, and unspecified assistantships also available. Financial award application deadline: 5/1; financial award applicants required to submit FAFSA. *Unit head:* Dr. William F. Kuracina, Interim Dean, 903-886-5166, Fax: 903-886-5774, E-mail: william.kuracina@tamuc.edu. *Application contact:* Vicky Turner, Doctoral Degree and Special Programs Coordinator, 903-886-5167, E-mail: vicky.turner@tamuc.edu.
Website: http://www.tamuc.edu/academics/graduateSchool/programs/humanitiesSocialScienceArts/default.aspx

Trinity Western University, School of Graduate Studies, Program in Linguistics, Langley, BC V2Y 1Y1, Canada. Offers MA. *Degree requirements:* For master's, essay (for non-thesis students). *Entrance requirements:* For master's, minimum GPA of 2.7, 3.0 in last two years; 12 seminar hours; linguistic prerequisites; 1 foreign language. Additional exam requirements/recommendations for international students: Required—TOEFL (minimum score 600 paper-based). Electronic applications accepted. *Expenses:* Contact institution. *Faculty research:* Syntax, phonology, tone, historical and comparative, discourse analysis.

Universidad de las Américas Puebla, Division of Graduate Studies, School of Humanities, Program in Applied Linguistics, Puebla, Mexico. Offers linguistics (MA). *Program availability:* Part-time, evening/weekend. *Degree requirements:* For master's, one foreign language, thesis. *Entrance requirements:* Additional exam requirements/recommendations for international students: Required—TOEFL. *Faculty research:* English linguistics, teaching English to speakers of other languages.

Université de Montréal, Faculty of Arts and Sciences, Department of Linguistics and Translation, Montréal, QC H3C 3J7, Canada. Offers linguistics (MA, PhD); translation (MA, PhD, DESS). *Degree requirements:* For master's, thesis, general exam; for doctorate, thesis/dissertation, general exam. Electronic applications accepted.

Université de Sherbrooke, Faculty of Letters and Human Sciences, Department of Letters and Communications, Sherbrooke, QC J1K 2R1, Canada. Offers comparative Canadian literature (MA, PhD); French literature (MA, PhD); linguistics (MA); theatre (MA). *Degree requirements:* For master's, thesis or alternative; for doctorate, thesis/dissertation. *Entrance requirements:* For master's, minimum GPA of 2.8; for doctorate, minimum GPA of 3.0.

Université du Québec à Chicoutimi, Graduate Programs, Program in Linguistics, Chicoutimi, QC G7H 2B1, Canada. Offers MA. *Program availability:* Part-time. *Degree requirements:* For master's, thesis. *Entrance requirements:* For master's, appropriate bachelor's degree, proficiency in French.

Université du Québec à Montréal, Graduate Programs, Program in Linguistics, Montréal, QC H3C 3P8, Canada. Offers MA, PhD. *Program availability:* Part-time. *Degree requirements:* For master's, thesis optional; for doctorate, thesis/dissertation. *Entrance requirements:* For master's, appropriate bachelor's degree or equivalent, proficiency in French; for doctorate, appropriate master's degree or equivalent, proficiency in French.

Université Laval, Faculty of Letters, Department of Languages, Linguistics and Translations, Programs in Linguistics, Québec, QC G1K 7P4, Canada. Offers MA, PhD. Terminal master's awarded for partial completion of doctoral program. *Degree requirements:* For master's, thesis (for some programs); for doctorate, comprehensive exam, thesis/dissertation. *Entrance requirements:* For master's, English test (comprehension of written English), knowledge of French; for doctorate, English exam (comprehension of written English), knowledge of French. Electronic applications accepted.

University at Buffalo, the State University of New York, Graduate School, College of Arts and Sciences, Department of Linguistics, Buffalo, NY 14260. Offers interdisciplinary computational linguistics (MS); linguistics (MA, PhD). *Faculty:* 12 full-time (2 women). *Students:* 51 full-time (25 women), 4 part-time (3 women); includes 3 minority (1 American Indian or Alaska Native, non-Hispanic/Latino; 2 Hispanic/Latino), 17 international. Average age 30. 44 applicants, 77% accepted, 12 enrolled. In 2017, 7 master's, 3 doctorates awarded. Terminal master's awarded for partial completion of doctoral program. *Degree requirements:* For master's, exam, project, or thesis; for doctorate, thesis/dissertation, qualifying paper. *Entrance requirements:* For master's and doctorate, GRE General Test. Additional exam requirements/recommendations for international students: Required—TOEFL (minimum score 600 paper-based; 100 iBT). *Application deadline:* For fall admission, 4/1 for domestic students, 3/1 for international students. Application fee: $75. Electronic applications accepted. *Expenses:* $13,384 resident full-time per year, $24,724 non-resident full-time per year. *Financial support:* In 2017–18, 22 students received support, including 13 fellowships with full tuition reimbursements available (averaging $6,885 per year), 2 research assistantships with full tuition reimbursements available (averaging $14,627 per year), 18 teaching assistantships with full tuition reimbursements available (averaging $14,123 per year); scholarships/grants also available. Financial award application deadline: 12/15; financial award applicants required to submit FAFSA. *Faculty research:* Typology, psycholinguistics/experimental linguistics, syntax, semantics, language documentation. *Total annual research expenditures:* $417,386. *Unit head:* Dr. Jeff Good, Associate Professor/Chair, 716-645-2177, Fax: 716-645-3825, E-mail: jcgood@buffalo.edu. *Application contact:* Jodi L. Reiner, Department Secretary, 716-645-3794, Fax: 716-645-3825, E-mail: jlreiner@buffalo.edu.
Website: http://www.linguistics.buffalo.edu

University of Alaska Fairbanks, College of Liberal Arts, Program in Linguistics, Fairbanks, AK 99775-6280. Offers applied linguistics (MA), including language documentation, second language acquisition teacher education. *Program availability:* Part-time. *Degree requirements:* For master's, one foreign language, comprehensive exam, oral defense of project or thesis. *Entrance requirements:* For master's, bachelor's degree from accredited institution with minimum cumulative undergraduate and major GPA of 3.0. Additional exam requirements/recommendations for international students: Required—TOEFL (minimum score 550 paper-based; 79 iBT), IELTS (minimum score 6.5). Electronic applications accepted. *Faculty research:* Second language acquisition/teaching, Inupiaq, Athabaskan languages, language maintenance and shift, phonology, morphology.

University of Alberta, Faculty of Graduate Studies and Research, Department of Linguistics, Edmonton, AB T6G 2E1, Canada. Offers experimental linguistics (M Sc, PhD). *Degree requirements:* For master's, thesis (for some programs); for doctorate, thesis/dissertation. *Entrance requirements:* For master's, BA in linguistics; for doctorate, M Sc or MA in linguistics. Additional exam requirements/recommendations for international students: Required—TOEFL. *Faculty research:* Experimental phonetics, psycholinguistics, phonology, endangered languages, language acquisition.

University of Alberta, Faculty of Graduate Studies and Research, Department of Modern Languages and Cultural Studies, Edmonton, AB T6G 2E1, Canada. Offers applied linguistics (Germanic, Romance, Slavic) (MA); French language, literatures and linguistics (PhD); French language, literatures, and linguistics (MA); Germanic languages, literatures and linguistics (PhD); Germanic languages, literatures, and linguistics (MA); Italian studies (MA); Slavic languages and literatures (Russian, Ukrainian) (MA, PhD); Slavic linguistics (Russian, Ukrainian) (MA, PhD); Spanish and Latin American studies (MA, PhD); Ukrainian folklore (MA, PhD). *Program availability:* Part-time. *Degree requirements:* For master's, one foreign language, thesis; for doctorate, 2 foreign languages, comprehensive exam, thesis/dissertation. *Entrance requirements:* For master's and doctorate, 1 language other than English. Additional exam requirements/recommendations for international students: Required—Michigan English Language Assessment Battery or TOEFL (minimum score 550 paper-based). Electronic applications accepted. *Faculty research:* Russian/Ukrainian studies; German studies; contemporary Latin American, French and Francophone studies; Italian studies.

The University of Arizona, College of Social and Behavioral Sciences, Department of Linguistics, Tucson, AZ 85721. Offers human language technology (MS); linguistics and anthropology (PhD); Native American linguistics (MA). PhD in linguistics and anthropology offered jointly with Department of Anthropology. Terminal master's awarded for partial completion of doctoral program. *Degree requirements:* For master's, one foreign language, thesis; for doctorate, one foreign language, comprehensive exam, thesis/dissertation. *Entrance requirements:* For master's, GRE General Test, 3 letters of recommendation, writing sample, resume; for doctorate, GRE General Test, 3 letters of recommendation, statement of purpose, writing sample, resume. Additional exam requirements/recommendations for international students: Required—TOEFL (minimum score 550 paper-based; 79 iBT). Electronic applications accepted. *Faculty research:* Semantic, syntactic, morphological, and phonological theories of natural languages; native languages of the American Southwest, psycholinguistics and computational linguistics.

The University of Arizona, College of Social and Behavioral Sciences, Program in Human Language Technology, Tucson, AZ 85721. Offers MS. *Entrance requirements:* Additional exam requirements/recommendations for international students: Required—TOEFL (minimum score 550 paper-based; 79 iBT), GRE.

The University of British Columbia, Faculty of Arts and Faculty of Graduate Studies, Department of Linguistics, Vancouver, BC V6T 1Z4, Canada. Offers MA, PhD. *Program availability:* Part-time. *Degree requirements:* For master's, one foreign language, thesis optional; for doctorate, 2 foreign languages, thesis/dissertation, 2 qualifying papers. *Entrance requirements:* Additional exam requirements/recommendations for international students: Required—TOEFL. Electronic applications accepted. *Expenses:* Contact institution. *Faculty research:* Linguistic theory (phonology, syntax, semantics), Native American languages, African languages, first language acquisition, experimental phonetics.

University of Calgary, Faculty of Graduate Studies, Faculty of Arts, Department of Linguistics, Languages and Culture, Calgary, AB T2N 1N4, Canada. Offers German (MA); linguistics (MA, PhD). *Degree requirements:* For master's, one foreign language, thesis; for doctorate, one foreign language, comprehensive exam, thesis/dissertation. *Entrance requirements:* For doctorate, MA. Additional exam requirements/recommendations for international students: Required—TOEFL (minimum score 560 paper-based). Electronic applications accepted. *Faculty research:* Theoretical linguistics, historical linguistics, language acquisition, Amerindian.

University of California, Berkeley, Graduate Division, College of Letters and Science, Department of Linguistics, Berkeley, CA 94720-1500. Offers PhD. *Degree requirements:* For doctorate, thesis/dissertation, qualifying exam. *Entrance requirements:* For doctorate, GRE General Test, minimum GPA of 3.0, 3 letters of recommendation. Additional exam requirements/recommendations for international students: Required—TOEFL (minimum score 570 paper-based; 90 iBT). Electronic applications accepted.

University of California, Davis, Graduate Studies, Graduate Group in Linguistics, Davis, CA 95616. Offers applied linguistics (MA, PhD); linguistics (MA). *Degree requirements:* For master's, one foreign language, comprehensive exam (for some programs), thesis (for some programs); for doctorate, thesis/dissertation. *Entrance requirements:* For master's and doctorate, GRE General Test, minimum GPA of 3.0. Additional exam requirements/recommendations for international students: Required—TOEFL (minimum score 550 paper-based). Electronic applications accepted. *Faculty research:* Grammatical analysis and theory, sociolinguistics, historical linguistics, Romance linguistics, neurolinguistics.

University of California, Los Angeles, Graduate Division, College of Letters and Science, Department of Applied Linguistics and Teaching English as a Second

Language, Program in Applied Linguistics, Los Angeles, CA 90095. Offers MA, PhD. *Degree requirements:* For master's, one foreign language, thesis; for doctorate, one foreign language, thesis/dissertation, oral and written qualifying exams. *Entrance requirements:* For master's and doctorate, bachelor's degree; minimum undergraduate GPA of 3.0 (or its equivalent if letter grade system not used); research paper. Additional exam requirements/recommendations for international students: Required—TOEFL. Electronic applications accepted.

University of California, Los Angeles, Graduate Division, College of Letters and Science, Department of Linguistics, Los Angeles, CA 90095. Offers MA, PhD. Terminal master's awarded for partial completion of doctoral program. *Degree requirements:* For master's, one foreign language, comprehensive exam or thesis; for doctorate, thesis/dissertation, oral and written qualifying exams. *Entrance requirements:* For doctorate, bachelor's degree; minimum undergraduate GPA of 3.0 (or its equivalent if letter grade system not used); writing sample. Additional exam requirements/recommendations for international students: Required—TOEFL. Electronic applications accepted.

University of California, San Diego, Graduate Division, Department of Linguistics, La Jolla, CA 92093. Offers PhD. *Students:* 26 full-time (16 women). 64 applicants, 25% accepted, 9 enrolled. In 2017, 1 doctorate awarded. *Degree requirements:* For doctorate, one foreign language, comprehensive exam, thesis/dissertation, apprentice teaching. *Entrance requirements:* For doctorate, GRE General Test, writing samples, letters of recommendation. Additional exam requirements/recommendations for international students: Required—TOEFL (minimum score 550 paper-based; 80 iBT), IELTS (minimum score 7). *Application deadline:* For fall admission, 12/5 for domestic students. Application fee: $105 ($125 for international students). Electronic applications accepted. *Financial support:* Fellowships and teaching assistantships available. Financial award applicants required to submit FAFSA. *Faculty research:* Computational linguistics, computational psycholinguistics, experimental syntax, language acquisition and sign languages, language and the brain, speech production and perception. *Unit head:* Sharon Rose, Chair, 858-534-1159, E-mail: sxrose@ucsd.edu. *Application contact:* Alycia Randol, Graduate Coordinator, 858-534-1145, E-mail: arandol@ucsd.edu.
Website: http://ling.ucsd.edu

University of California, Santa Barbara, Graduate Division, College of Letters and Sciences, Division of Humanities and Fine Arts, Department of East Asian Languages and Cultural Studies, Santa Barbara, CA 93106-7075. Offers applied linguistics (PhD); East Asian languages and cultural studies (MA); translation studies (PhD). *Degree requirements:* For master's, one foreign language, comprehensive exam (for some programs), thesis (for some programs); for doctorate, 2 foreign languages, thesis/dissertation, methodology. *Entrance requirements:* For master's and doctorate, GRE General Test. Additional exam requirements/recommendations for international students: Required—TOEFL (minimum score 550 paper-based; 80 iBT), IELTS (minimum score 7). Electronic applications accepted. *Faculty research:* Chinese literature, Chinese film, Japanese society, Japanese literature, East Asian cultural studies.

University of California, Santa Barbara, Graduate Division, College of Letters and Sciences, Division of Humanities and Fine Arts, Department of Linguistics, Santa Barbara, CA 93106-9580. Offers PhD, MA/PhD. Terminal master's awarded for partial completion of doctoral program. *Degree requirements:* For doctorate, one foreign language, comprehensive exam, thesis/dissertation, qualifying paper. *Entrance requirements:* For doctorate, GRE. Additional exam requirements/recommendations for international students: Required—TOEFL (minimum score 550 paper-based; 80 iBT), IELTS (minimum score 7). Electronic applications accepted. *Faculty research:* Language documentation, discourse, typology, language and cognition, sociocultural linguistics.

University of California, Santa Barbara, Graduate Division, College of Letters and Sciences, Division of Humanities and Fine Arts, Department of Spanish and Portuguese, Santa Barbara, CA 93106-4150. Offers Hispanic languages and literatures (PhD), including European medieval studies, feminist studies, Hispanic linguistics, Hispanic literature, Luso-Brazilian literature; Hispanic linguistics (MA); Luso-Brazilian literature (MA); Spanish or Spanish-American literature (MA); MA/PhD. Terminal master's awarded for partial completion of doctoral program. *Degree requirements:* For master's, 2 foreign languages, comprehensive exam (for some programs), thesis optional; for doctorate, 3 foreign languages, comprehensive exam, thesis/dissertation. *Entrance requirements:* For master's and doctorate, GRE. Additional exam requirements/recommendations for international students: Required—TOEFL (minimum score 550 paper-based; 80 iBT), IELTS (minimum score 7). Electronic applications accepted. *Faculty research:* Nineteenth-century Spanish and Portuguese literature, Spanish and Spanish-American literature, nineteenth- and twentieth-century Portuguese and Brazilian literatures, Hispanic linguistics, Catalan language and culture.

University of California, Santa Cruz, Division of Graduate Studies, Division of Humanities, Department of Linguistics, Santa Cruz, CA 95064. Offers MA, PhD. Terminal master's awarded for partial completion of doctoral program. *Degree requirements:* For master's, one foreign language, research paper; for doctorate, one foreign language, thesis/dissertation, qualifying exam. *Entrance requirements:* For master's and doctorate, GRE General Test. Additional exam requirements/recommendations for international students: Required—TOEFL (minimum score 550 paper-based; 83 iBT); Recommended—IELTS (minimum score 8). Electronic applications accepted. *Faculty research:* Theoretical and descriptive linguistics: syntax, semantics and phonology.

University of Chicago, Division of the Humanities, Department of Linguistics, Chicago, IL 60637. Offers anthropology and linguistics (PhD); linguistics (PhD). *Students:* 42 full-time (22 women); includes 10 minority (1 American Indian or Alaska Native, non-Hispanic/Latino; 2 Asian, non-Hispanic/Latino; 5 Hispanic/Latino; 2 Two or more races, non-Hispanic/Latino), 15 international. Average age 28. 100 applicants, 12% accepted, 6 enrolled. In 2017, 2 doctorates awarded. Terminal master's awarded for partial completion of doctoral program. *Degree requirements:* For doctorate, 2 foreign languages, thesis/dissertation. *Entrance requirements:* For doctorate, GRE General Test, 15-20 page writing sample, statement of purpose, 3 letters of recommendation, transcripts for all previous degrees and institutions attended. Additional exam requirements/recommendations for international students: Required—TOEFL (minimum score 104 iBT), IELTS (minimum score 7). *Application deadline:* For fall admission, 12/15 for domestic and international students. Application fee: $90. Electronic applications accepted. *Financial support:* In 2017–18, fellowships with full tuition reimbursements (averaging $27,000 per year) were awarded; teaching assistantships with full tuition reimbursements, Federal Work-Study, institutionally sponsored loans, scholarships/grants, and health care benefits also available. Financial award application deadline: 12/15. *Unit head:* Dr. Lenore Grenoble, Chair, 773-702-8522, E-mail: linguistics@uchicago.edu. *Application contact:* Michael Beetley, Assistant Dean of Students, Admissions and Fellowships, 773-702-1552, Fax: 773-834-9148, E-mail: humanitiesadmissions@uchicago.edu.
Website: http://linguistics.uchicago.edu/

University of Chicago, Division of the Humanities, Master of Arts Program in the Humanities, Chicago, IL 60637. Offers art history (MA); cinema and media studies (MA); classic languages (MA); comparative literature (MA); creative writing (MA); cultural policy studies (MA); digital humanities (MA); East Asian languages and civilizations (MA); English language and literature (MA); gender and sexuality studies (MA); Germanic studies (MA); linguistics (MA); music (MA); near Eastern languages and civilizations (MA); philosophy (MA); poetics (MA); race, politics and culture (MA); Romance languages and literatures (MA); Slavic languages and literatures (MA); South Asian languages and civilizations (MA); theater and performance studies (MA). *Students:* 95 full-time (50 women), 6 part-time (4 women); includes 22 minority (1 Black or African American, non-Hispanic/Latino; 10 Asian, non-Hispanic/Latino; 11 Hispanic/Latino), 19 international. Average age 26. 708 applicants, 75% accepted, 101 enrolled. In 2017, 91 master's awarded. *Degree requirements:* For master's, thesis. *Entrance requirements:* For master's, GRE General Test, 10-15 page writing sample, statement of purpose, 3 letters of recommendation, transcripts for all previous degrees and institutions attended. Additional exam requirements/recommendations for international students: Required—TOEFL (minimum score 104 iBT), IELTS (minimum score 7). *Application deadline:* For fall admission, 1/3 priority date for domestic and international students. Application fee: $90. Electronic applications accepted. Expenses: Contact institution. *Financial support:* In 2017–18, fellowships with partial tuition reimbursements (averaging $12,000 per year) were awarded; Federal Work-Study, institutionally sponsored loans, scholarships/grants, and tuition waivers (partial) also available. Financial award application deadline: 4/30. *Unit head:* Thomas Christensen, Director, 773-834-1201, Fax: 773-834-7526, E-mail: ma-humanities@uchicago.edu. *Application contact:* Michael Beetley, Assistant Dean of Students for Admissions, 773-834-1552, E-mail: humanitiesadmissions@uchicago.edu.
Website: http://maph.uchicago.edu/

University of Colorado Boulder, Graduate School, College of Arts and Sciences, Department of Linguistics, Boulder, CO 80309. Offers MA, PhD. *Faculty:* 9 full-time (6 women). *Students:* 68 full-time (43 women), 2 part-time (both women); includes 13 minority (1 Black or African American, non-Hispanic/Latino; 8 Asian, non-Hispanic/Latino; 2 Hispanic/Latino; 2 Two or more races, non-Hispanic/Latino), 13 international. Average age 29. 95 applicants, 55% accepted, 27 enrolled. In 2017, 16 master's, 6 doctorates awarded. Terminal master's awarded for partial completion of doctoral program. *Degree requirements:* For master's, comprehensive exam, thesis optional; for doctorate, one foreign language, thesis/dissertation. *Entrance requirements:* For master's, GRE General Test, minimum undergraduate GPA of 2.75; for doctorate, GRE General Test. *Application deadline:* For fall admission, 1/10 for domestic students; for spring admission, 12/1 for domestic students. Applications are processed on a rolling basis. Application fee: $60 ($80 for international students). Electronic applications accepted. Application fee is waived when completed online. *Financial support:* In 2017–18, 111 students received support, including 26 fellowships (averaging $2,139 per year), 4 research assistantships with full and partial tuition reimbursements available (averaging $30,037 per year), 28 teaching assistantships with full and partial tuition reimbursements available (averaging $19,337 per year); institutionally sponsored loans, scholarships/grants, health care benefits, and unspecified assistantships also available. Financial award application deadline: 2/15; financial award applicants required to submit FAFSA. *Faculty research:* Linguistics/philology; phonology; semantics; artificial intelligence/cybernetics; cultural/social anthropology. *Total annual research expenditures:* $1.1 million. *Application contact:* E-mail: linguist@colorado.edu.
Website: http://www.colorado.edu/linguistics/

University of Colorado Denver, College of Liberal Arts and Sciences, Department of English, Denver, CO 80217. Offers applied linguistics (MA); literature (MA); rhetoric and teaching of writing (MA). *Program availability:* Part-time, evening/weekend. *Degree requirements:* For master's, variable foreign language requirement, comprehensive exam (for some programs), thesis (for some programs), minimum of 33 credit hours (for literature program), 30 (for rhetoric and teaching of writing and applied linguistics programs). *Entrance requirements:* For master's, GRE General Test, minimum GPA of 3.0 in undergraduate courses, critical writing sample, letters of recommendation, completion of 24 semester hours in English courses (at least 16 at the upper-division level), statement of purpose. Additional exam requirements/recommendations for international students: Required—TOEFL (minimum score 537 paper-based; 75 iBT); Recommended—IELTS (minimum score 6.5). Electronic applications accepted. *Faculty research:* Literature, rhetoric, teaching of writing, applied linguistics.

University of Connecticut, Graduate School, College of Liberal Arts and Sciences, Department of Linguistics, Storrs, CT 06269. Offers MA, PhD. *Degree requirements:* For doctorate, thesis/dissertation. *Entrance requirements:* For doctorate, GRE General Test. Additional exam requirements/recommendations for international students: Required—TOEFL (minimum score 550 paper-based). Electronic applications accepted.

University of Delaware, College of Arts and Sciences, Department of Linguistics and Cognitive Science, Newark, DE 19716. Offers linguistics (PhD); linguistics and cognitive science (MA). *Degree requirements:* For doctorate, one foreign language, comprehensive exam, thesis/dissertation, publishable research papers. *Entrance requirements:* For master's, GRE General Test; for doctorate, GRE General Test, writing sample. Additional exam requirements/recommendations for international students: Required—TOEFL (minimum score 600 paper-based). Electronic applications accepted. *Faculty research:* East Asian, Austronesian and Romance languages, phonology, phonetics, syntax, cognitive science, semantics, psycholinguistics, language acquisition, endangered languages.

The University of Findlay, Office of Graduate Admissions, Findlay, OH 45840. Offers applied security and analytics (MSAS); athletic training (MAT); business (MBA), including certified management accountant, certified public accountant, health care management, hospitality management; education (MA Ed, Ed D), including children's literature (MA Ed), curriculum and teaching (MA Ed), education (MA Ed), educational administration (MA Ed), human resource development (MA Ed), mathematics (MA Ed), reading (MA Ed), science education (MA Ed), superintendent (Ed D), teaching (Ed D), technology (MA Ed); environmental, safety, and health management (MSEM); health informatics (MS); occupational therapy (MOT); pharmacy (Pharm D); physical therapy (DPT); physician assistant (MPA); rhetoric and writing (MA); teaching English to speakers of other languages (TESOL) and applied linguistics (MA). *Program availability:* Part-time, evening/weekend, 100% online, blended/hybrid learning. *Students:* 688 full-time (430 women), 553 part-time (308 women), 170 international. Average age 28. In 2017, 366 master's, 137 doctorates awarded. *Degree requirements:* For master's, comprehensive exam (for some programs), thesis (for some programs), cumulative project, capstone project; for doctorate, thesis/dissertation (for some programs). *Entrance requirements:* For master's, GRE/GMAT, bachelor's degree from accredited institution, minimum undergraduate GPA of 2.5 in last 64 hours of course work; for doctorate, GRE, MAT, minimum cumulative GPA of 3.0. Additional exam requirements/recommendations for international students: Required—TOEFL (minimum score 79 iBT), IELTS (minimum score 7), PTE (minimum score 61). *Application deadline:* Applications are processed on a rolling basis. Electronic applications accepted. *Financial support:* In 2017–18, 10 research assistantships with partial tuition reimbursements (averaging $7,200 per year), 35 teaching assistantships with partial

tuition reimbursements (averaging $7,200 per year) were awarded; Federal Work-Study, institutionally sponsored loans, and unspecified assistantships also available. Financial award applicants required to submit FAFSA. *Unit head:* Christopher M. Harris, Director of Admissions, 419-434-4347, E-mail: harrisc1@findlay.edu. *Application contact:* Madeline Fauser Brennan, Graduate Admissions Counselor, 419-434-4636, Fax: 419-434-4898, E-mail: fauserbrennan@findlay.edu.
Website: http://www.findlay.edu/admissions/graduate/Pages/default.aspx

University of Florida, Graduate School, College of Liberal Arts and Sciences, Department of Linguistics, Gainesville, FL 32611. Offers linguistics (MA, PhD); teaching English as a second language (Certificate). *Program availability:* Part-time. Terminal master's awarded for partial completion of doctoral program. *Degree requirements:* For master's, one foreign language, comprehensive exam, thesis (for some programs); for doctorate, 2 foreign languages, comprehensive exam, thesis/dissertation. *Entrance requirements:* For master's and doctorate, GRE General Test, minimum GPA of 3.0. Additional exam requirements/recommendations for international students: Required—TOEFL (minimum score 550 paper-based; 80 iBT), IELTS (minimum score 6). Electronic applications accepted. *Faculty research:* Language documentation, psycholinguistics and neuro-linguistics, theoretical linguistics, sociolinguistics second language acquisition.

University of Georgia, Franklin College of Arts and Sciences, Program in Linguistics, Athens, GA 30602. Offers MA, PhD. *Degree requirements:* For master's, one foreign language, thesis; for doctorate, 2 foreign languages, comprehensive exam, thesis/dissertation. *Entrance requirements:* For master's and doctorate, GRE General Test. Electronic applications accepted. *Expenses:* Contact institution. *Faculty research:* Applied linguistics, English linguistics, dialectology, lexicography, discourse analysis.

University of Hawaii at Manoa, Office of Graduate Education, College of Languages, Linguistics and Literature, Department of Linguistics, Honolulu, HI 96822. Offers MA, PhD. *Program availability:* Part-time. Terminal master's awarded for partial completion of doctoral program. *Degree requirements:* For master's, 2 foreign languages, thesis optional; for doctorate, 2 foreign languages, comprehensive exam, thesis/dissertation. *Entrance requirements:* For master's and doctorate, GRE General Test. Additional exam requirements/recommendations for international students: Required—TOEFL (minimum score 600 paper-based; 100 iBT), IELTS (minimum score 7). *Faculty research:* Languages of the Pacific and Asia.

University of Houston, College of Liberal Arts and Social Sciences, Department of English, Houston, TX 77204. Offers applied English linguistics (MA); creative writing (MFA); creative writing and literature (MA, PhD); English (MA, PhD). *Degree requirements:* For master's, one foreign language, comprehensive exam (for some programs), thesis (MFA); for doctorate, 2 foreign languages, comprehensive exam, thesis/dissertation. *Entrance requirements:* For master's, GRE General Test, minimum GPA of 3.0 in last 60 hours of course work; for doctorate, GRE General Test, GRE Subject Test (literature), writing sample. Additional exam requirements/recommendations for international students: Required—TOEFL (minimum score 550 paper-based; 79 iBT). Electronic applications accepted.

University of Illinois at Chicago, College of Liberal Arts and Sciences, School of Literatures, Cultural Studies and Linguistics, Department of Linguistics, Chicago, IL 60607-7128. Offers MA. *Program availability:* Part-time. *Degree requirements:* For master's, one foreign language, comprehensive exam, thesis (for some programs). *Entrance requirements:* For master's, minimum GPA of 3.0. Additional exam requirements/recommendations for international students: Required—TOEFL. Electronic applications accepted. *Faculty research:* Second language acquisition, methodology of second language teaching, lexicography, language, sex and gender.

University of Illinois at Urbana–Champaign, Graduate College, College of Liberal Arts and Sciences, School of Literatures, Cultures and Linguistics, Department of Linguistics, Champaign, IL 61820. Offers linguistics (MA, PhD); teaching of English as a second language (MA).

University of Illinois at Urbana–Champaign, Graduate College, College of Liberal Arts and Sciences, School of Literatures, Cultures and Linguistics, Program in Romance Linguistics, Champaign, IL 61820. Offers PhD.

The University of Iowa, Graduate College, College of Liberal Arts and Sciences, Department of Linguistics, Iowa City, IA 52242-1316. Offers MA, PhD. *Degree requirements:* For master's, thesis optional, exam; for doctorate, comprehensive exam, thesis/dissertation. *Entrance requirements:* For master's and doctorate, GRE General Test, minimum GPA of 3.0. Additional exam requirements/recommendations for international students: Required—TOEFL (minimum score 550 paper-based; 81 iBT). Electronic applications accepted.

The University of Kansas, Graduate Studies, College of Liberal Arts and Sciences, Department of Linguistics, Lawrence, KS 66045. Offers MA, PhD. *Students:* 25 full-time (17 women); includes 1 minority (Hispanic/Latino), 15 international. Average age 26. 53 applicants, 23% accepted, 6 enrolled. In 2017, 6 master's, 6 doctorates awarded. Terminal master's awarded for partial completion of doctoral program. *Entrance requirements:* For master's and doctorate, GRE General Test, curriculum vitae, statement of purpose, 3 letters of recommendation. Additional exam requirements/recommendations for international students: Required—TOEFL. *Application deadline:* For fall admission, 1/1 for domestic and international students. Application fee: $65 ($85 for international students). Electronic applications accepted. *Financial support:* Fellowships, research assistantships, teaching assistantships, scholarships/grants, and unspecified assistantships available. Financial award application deadline: 1/1. *Faculty research:* Phonetics and phonology, syntax and semantics, psycholinguistics, neurolinguistics, first and second language acquisition. *Unit head:* Joan A. Sereno, Chair, 785-864-2619, E-mail: sereno@ku.edu. *Application contact:* Corinna Johnson, Office Manager, 785-864-3450, E-mail: cljohns@ku.edu.
Website: http://www.linguistics.ku.edu/

University of Louisville, Graduate School, College of Arts and Sciences, Department of Comparative Humanities, Louisville, KY 40292-0001. Offers civic leadership (MA); culture, criticism, and contemporary thought (PhD); linguistics (MA); public arts and letters (PhD); traditional humanities (MA); MA/JD; MA/MBA. *Program availability:* Part-time. *Faculty:* 14 full-time (6 women), 8 part-time/adjunct (4 women). *Students:* 33 full-time (21 women), 22 part-time (9 women); includes 7 minority (1 Black or African American, non-Hispanic/Latino; 1 Hispanic/Latino; 5 Two or more races, non-Hispanic/Latino), 4 international. Average age 39. 14 applicants, 79% accepted, 9 enrolled. In 2017, 3 master's, 10 doctorates awarded. *Degree requirements:* For master's, one foreign language, thesis or alternative, directed study culminating project; for doctorate, 2 foreign languages, comprehensive exam, thesis/dissertation, internship. *Entrance requirements:* For master's, GRE General Test, two letters of recommendation, transcripts from all institutions attended; for doctorate, GRE General Test, three letters of recommendation, statement of intent, scholarly writing sample, transcripts from all institutions attended. Additional exam requirements/recommendations for international students: Recommended—TOEFL. *Application deadline:* For fall admission, 1/15 for domestic and international students. Application fee: $65. Electronic applications accepted. *Expenses:* Contact institution. *Financial support:* In 2017–18, 1 fellowship with full tuition reimbursement (averaging $18,000 per year), 10 teaching assistantships with full tuition reimbursements (averaging $18,000 per year) were awarded. Financial award application deadline: 1/15. *Faculty research:* Literary studies, medieval studies;, religious studies, linguistics, translation studies. *Total annual research expenditures:* $7,733. *Unit head:* Dr. Ann Hall, Chair, 502-852-6805, Fax: 502-852-0078, E-mail: ann.hall@louisville.edu. *Application contact:* Latonia Craig, Director of Graduate Recruitment and Diversity Retention, 502-852-5207, Fax: 502-852-6536, E-mail: gradadm@louisville.edu.
Website: http://louisville.edu/humanities/

The University of Manchester, School of Languages, Linguistics and Cultures, Manchester, United Kingdom. Offers Arab world studies (PhD); Chinese studies (M Phil, PhD); East Asian studies (M Phil, PhD); English language (PhD); French studies (M Phil, PhD); German studies (M Phil, PhD); interpreting studies (PhD); Italian studies (M Phil, PhD); Japanese studies (M Phil, PhD); Latin American cultural studies (M Phil, PhD); linguistics (M Phil, PhD); Middle Eastern studies (M Phil, PhD); Polish studies (M Phil, PhD); Portuguese studies (M Phil, PhD); Russian studies (M Phil, PhD); Spanish studies (M Phil, PhD); translation and intercultural studies (M Phil, PhD).

University of Manitoba, Faculty of Graduate Studies, Faculty of Arts, Department of Linguistics, Winnipeg, MB R3T 2N2, Canada. Offers MA, PhD.

University of Maryland, Baltimore County, The Graduate School, College of Arts, Humanities and Social Sciences, Department of Modern Languages and Linguistics, Program in Intercultural Communication, Baltimore, MD 21250. Offers MA. *Program availability:* Part-time, evening/weekend. *Faculty:* 16 full-time (9 women). *Students:* 10 full-time (6 women), 2 part-time (1 woman); includes 2 minority (both Hispanic/Latino), 3 international. Average age 29. 10 applicants, 70% accepted, 4 enrolled. In 2017, 4 master's awarded. *Degree requirements:* For master's, one foreign language, comprehensive exam (for some programs), thesis (for some programs). *Entrance requirements:* For master's, GRE General Test, minimum GPA of 3.0, 3 letters of recommendation, self-evaluation and statement of support, resume, writing sample in modern language. Additional exam requirements/recommendations for international students: Required—TOEFL (minimum score 550 paper-based, 80 iBT) or IELTS. *Application deadline:* For fall admission, 1/31 for domestic and international students. Application fee: $50. Electronic applications accepted. *Expenses:* Contact institution. *Financial support:* In 2017–18, 7 students received support, including 5 teaching assistantships with full tuition reimbursements available (averaging $12,874 per year); Federal Work-Study, scholarships/grants, health care benefits, and tuition waivers (full) also available. Financial award application deadline: 1/31; financial award applicants required to submit FAFSA. *Faculty research:* Comparative television research-cross-cultural; cultural studies; social developments in Latin America; intercultural communication; French civilization and cultural studies; language, gender and sexuality; sociolinguistics; African linguistics; immigrants in U.S. and Latin American societies. *Unit head:* Dr. Edward Larkey, Interim Director, 410-455-2104, Fax: 410-455-1025, E-mail: larkey@umbc.edu.
Website: http://www.umbc.edu/mll/incc/

University of Maryland, College Park, Academic Affairs, College of Arts and Humanities, Department of Linguistics, College Park, MD 20742. Offers MA, PhD. *Degree requirements:* For master's, thesis or alternative; for doctorate, thesis/dissertation. *Entrance requirements:* For master's, GRE General Test, minimum GPA of 3.0, sample of work, 3 letters of recommendation; for doctorate, GRE General Test, minimum GPA of 3.0, sample of work. Additional exam requirements/recommendations for international students: Required—TOEFL. Electronic applications accepted. *Faculty research:* Psycholinguistics, computational linguistics.

University of Massachusetts Amherst, Graduate School, College of Humanities and Fine Arts, Department of Linguistics, Amherst, MA 01003. Offers MA, PhD. *Program availability:* Part-time. *Degree requirements:* For master's, thesis or alternative; for doctorate, comprehensive exam, thesis/dissertation. *Entrance requirements:* For doctorate, GRE General Test, writing sample. Additional exam requirements/recommendations for international students: Required—TOEFL (minimum score 550 paper-based; 80 iBT), IELTS (minimum score 6.5). Electronic applications accepted.

University of Massachusetts Boston, College of Liberal Arts, Program in Applied Linguistics, Boston, MA 02125-3393. Offers applied linguistics (PhD). *Program availability:* Part-time, evening/weekend. *Faculty:* 9 full-time (6 women), 4 part-time/adjunct (3 women). *Students:* 16 full-time (14 women), 139 part-time (91 women); includes 37 minority (9 Black or African American, non-Hispanic/Latino; 1 American Indian or Alaska Native, non-Hispanic/Latino; 4 Asian, non-Hispanic/Latino; 15 Hispanic/Latino; 8 Two or more races, non-Hispanic/Latino), 7 international. Average age 35. 89 applicants, 65% accepted, 32 enrolled. In 2017, 48 master's awarded. *Entrance requirements:* For master's, minimum GPA of 2.75. *Application deadline:* For fall admission, 2/1 for domestic students; for spring admission, 10/15 for domestic students. *Expenses:* Tuition, state resident: full-time $17,375. Tuition, nonresident: full-time $33,915. *Required fees:* $355. *Financial support:* Research assistantships, teaching assistantships, career-related internships or fieldwork, Federal Work-Study, and unspecified assistantships available. Support available to part-time students. Financial award application deadline: 3/1; financial award applicants required to submit FAFSA. *Faculty research:* Multicultural theory and curriculum development, foreign language pedagogy, language and culture, applied psycholinguistics, bilingual education. *Unit head:* Dr. Donaldo Macedo, Director, 617-287-5760, E-mail: donalde.macedo@umb.edu. *Application contact:* Graduate Admissions Coordinator, 617-287-6400, Fax: 617-287-6236, E-mail: bos.gadm@dpc.umassp.edu.

University of Memphis, Graduate School, College of Arts and Sciences, Department of English, Memphis, TN 38152. Offers African-American literature (Graduate Certificate); applied linguistics (PhD); composition studies (PhD); creative writing (MFA); English as a second language (MA); linguistics (MA); literary and cultural studies (PhD), including African-American literature; literature (MA); professional writing (MA, PhD); teaching English as a second/foreign language (Graduate Certificate). *Program availability:* Part-time, evening/weekend, 100% online. *Faculty:* 30 full-time (15 women). *Students:* 73 full-time (34 women), 80 part-time (52 women); includes 35 minority (20 Black or African American, non-Hispanic/Latino; 3 Asian, non-Hispanic/Latino; 9 Hispanic/Latino; 3 Two or more races, non-Hispanic/Latino), 36 international. Average age 35. 78 applicants, 88% accepted, 35 enrolled. In 2017, 27 master's, 15 doctorates, 10 other advanced degrees awarded. Terminal master's awarded for partial completion of doctoral program. *Degree requirements:* For master's, one foreign language, comprehensive exam, thesis optional; for doctorate, 2 foreign languages, comprehensive exam, thesis/dissertation, qualifying exam. *Entrance requirements:* For master's, GRE, minimum undergraduate GPA of 3.0, statement of purpose, two letters of recommendation; for doctorate, GRE, minimum undergraduate and graduate GPA of 3.25, statement of purpose, writing sample, three letters of recommendation. Additional exam requirements/recommendations for international students: Required—TOEFL. *Application deadline:* For fall admission, 1/15 for domestic students; for spring admission, 10/15 for domestic students. Applications are processed on a rolling basis. Application fee: $35 ($60 for international students). Electronic applications accepted. *Expenses:* Contact institution. *Financial support:* In 2017–18, 123 students received support, including 16 research assistantships with full tuition reimbursements available (averaging $15,704 per year), 23 teaching assistantships with full tuition

reimbursements available (averaging $22,076 per year); Federal Work-Study, scholarships/grants, and unspecified assistantships also available. Financial award application deadline: 2/1; financial award applicants required to submit FAFSA. *Faculty research:* Applied linguistics, British and American literature, professional writing, composition studies. *Unit head:* Dr. Joshua Phillips, Chair, 901-678-2651, Fax: 901-678-2226, E-mail: jsphllps@memphis.edu. *Application contact:* Dr. Jeffrey Scraba, Coordinator of Graduate Studies, 901-678-4768, Fax: 901-678-2226, E-mail: jscraba@memphis.edu.
Website: http://www.memphis.edu/english

University of Michigan, Rackham Graduate School, College of Literature, Science, and the Arts, Department of Anthropology, Ann Arbor, MI 48109. Offers anthropological archaeology (PhD); biological anthropology (PhD); linguistic anthropology (PhD); sociocultural anthropology (PhD). *Faculty:* 42 full-time (18 women), 3 part-time/adjunct (1 woman). *Students:* 99 full-time (62 women); includes 23 minority (1 Black or African American, non-Hispanic/Latino; 2 American Indian or Alaska Native, non-Hispanic/Latino; 7 Asian, non-Hispanic/Latino; 10 Hispanic/Latino; 3 Two or more races, non-Hispanic/Latino), 17 international. Average age 30. 181 applicants, 12% accepted, 12 enrolled. In 2017, 9 doctorates awarded. *Degree requirements:* For doctorate, one foreign language, comprehensive exam, thesis/dissertation, preliminary examination, oral defense of dissertation. *Entrance requirements:* For doctorate, GRE General Test. Additional exam requirements/recommendations for international students: Required—TOEFL (minimum score 560 paper-based; 84 iBT). *Application deadline:* For fall admission, 12/15 for domestic and international students. Application fee: $75 ($90 for international students). Electronic applications accepted. *Expenses:* Tuition, state resident: full-time $22,368; part-time $1201 per credit hour. Tuition, nonresident: full-time $45,156; part-time $2467 per credit hour. *Required fees:* $376 per term. Tuition and fees vary according to course load, degree level and program. *Financial support:* In 2017–18, 72 students received support, including 36 fellowships with full tuition reimbursements available (averaging $19,000 per year), 7 research assistantships with full tuition reimbursements available (averaging $20,398 per year), 31 teaching assistantships with full tuition reimbursements available (averaging $20,398 per year); scholarships/grants, traineeships, health care benefits, tuition waivers (full), and unspecified assistantships also available. Financial award application deadline: 3/1; financial award applicants required to submit FAFSA. *Faculty research:* Sociocultural, linguistic, biological and archaeological anthropology. *Unit head:* Dr. Andrew Shryock, Chair, 734-764-7274, Fax: 734-763-6077. *Application contact:* Katia Kitchen, Graduate Program Assistant, 734-936-7933, Fax: 734-763-6077, E-mail: kitchenk@umich.edu.
Website: http://www.lsa.umich.edu/anthro/

University of Michigan, Rackham Graduate School, College of Literature, Science, and the Arts, Department of Linguistics, Ann Arbor, MI 48109. Offers PhD. *Faculty:* 17 full-time (7 women). *Students:* 32 full-time (20 women); includes 6 minority (3 Black or African American, non-Hispanic/Latino; 3 Two or more races, non-Hispanic/Latino), 9 international. Average age 29. 115 applicants, 7% accepted, 6 enrolled. In 2017, 1 doctorate awarded. *Degree requirements:* For doctorate, 2 foreign languages, thesis/dissertation, oral defense of dissertation. *Entrance requirements:* Additional exam requirements/recommendations for international students: Required—TOEFL (minimum score 600 paper-based; 100 iBT), IELTS (minimum score 7.5), Michigan English Language Assessment Battery. *Application deadline:* For fall admission, 12/1 for domestic and international students. Application fee: $75 ($90 for international students). Electronic applications accepted. *Expenses:* Tuition, state resident: full-time $22,368; part-time $1201 per credit hour. Tuition, nonresident: full-time $45,156; part-time $2467 per credit hour. *Required fees:* $376 per term. Tuition and fees vary according to course load, degree level and program. *Financial support:* In 2017–18, 28 students received support, including 9 fellowships with full tuition reimbursements available (averaging $19,737 per year), 2 research assistantships with full tuition reimbursements available (averaging $19,737 per year), 16 teaching assistantships with full tuition reimbursements available (averaging $19,737 per year); health care benefits and tuition waivers (full) also available. Financial award application deadline: 12/1. *Faculty research:* Broad-based approach to linguistics as a cognitive and social science including theoretical, experimental and computational approaches. *Unit head:* Prof. Robin Queen, Professor/Chair, 734-764-0353, Fax: 734-936-3406, E-mail: linguistics@umich.edu. *Application contact:* Dr. Jennifer Nguyen, Senior Student Services Assistant, 734-936-3403, Fax: 734-936-3406, E-mail: linggradadmissions@umich.edu.
Website: http://www.lsa.umich.edu/linguistics/

University of Minnesota, Twin Cities Campus, Graduate School, College of Liberal Arts, Institute of Linguistics, English as a Second Language, and Slavic Languages and Literatures (ILES), Program in Linguistics, Minneapolis, MN 55455-0213. Offers MA, PhD. Terminal master's awarded for partial completion of doctoral program. *Degree requirements:* For master's, one foreign language, comprehensive exam, thesis; for doctorate, 2 foreign languages, comprehensive exam, thesis/dissertation. *Entrance requirements:* For master's and doctorate, GRE General Test, 3 letters of recommendation, unit questionnaire. Additional exam requirements/recommendations for international students: Required—TOEFL (minimum score 550 paper-based; 79 iBT). Electronic applications accepted. *Faculty research:* Pragmatics and language processing, syntactic theory, language policy and planning, contact linguistics, language and cognition.

University of Montana, Graduate School, College of Humanities and Sciences, Department of Anthropology, Missoula, MT 59812. Offers anthropology (MA, PhD); applied anthropology (PhD); applied medical anthropology (MA); cultural heritage (MA, PhD); forensic anthropology (MA); linguistic anthropology (MA). *Degree requirements:* For master's, thesis (for some programs). *Entrance requirements:* For master's, GRE General Test. Additional exam requirements/recommendations for international students: Required—TOEFL. *Faculty research:* Historical preservation, plateau-plains archaeology and ethnohistory.

University of Montana, Graduate School, College of Humanities and Sciences, Program in Linguistics, Missoula, MT 59812. Offers MA. *Entrance requirements:* For master's, GRE General Test. Additional exam requirements/recommendations for international students: Required—TOEFL.

University of New Hampshire, Graduate School, College of Liberal Arts, Department of English, Durham, NH 03824. Offers English (MST, PhD); language and linguistics (MA); literature (MA); writing (MFA). *Program availability:* Part-time. *Students:* 57 full-time (39 women), 39 part-time (28 women); includes 9 minority (4 Black or African American, non-Hispanic/Latino; 4 Hispanic/Latino; 1 Two or more races, non-Hispanic/Latino), 4 international. Average age 31. 117 applicants, 60% accepted, 27 enrolled. In 2017, 29 master's, 3 doctorates awarded. *Entrance requirements:* For master's, GRE General Test, sample of written work; for doctorate, GRE General Test, GRE Subject Test, sample of written work. Additional exam requirements/recommendations for international students: Required—TOEFL (minimum score 550 paper-based; 80 iBT). *Application deadline:* For fall admission, 1/15 for domestic and international students; for spring admission, 12/1 for domestic students. Application fee: $65. Electronic applications accepted. *Financial support:* In 2017–18, 64 students received support, including 2 fellowships, 37 teaching assistantships; research assistantships, career-

related internships or fieldwork, Federal Work-Study, scholarships/grants, and tuition waivers (full and partial) also available. Support available to part-time students. Financial award application deadline: 2/15. *Unit head:* Dr. Rachel Trubowitz, Chair, 603-862-0254. *Application contact:* Janine Wilks, Administrative Assistant, 603-862-3963, E-mail: engl.grad@unh.edu.
Website: http://cola.unh.edu/english

University of New Mexico, Graduate Studies, College of Arts and Sciences, Program in Linguistics, Albuquerque, NM 87131-2039. Offers MA, PhD. *Program availability:* Part-time. *Faculty:* 10 full-time (7 women). *Students:* 16 full-time (7 women), 38 part-time (22 women); includes 11 minority (3 American Indian or Alaska Native, non-Hispanic/Latino; 5 Hispanic/Latino; 3 Two or more races, non-Hispanic/Latino), 17 international. Average age 36. 35 applicants, 34% accepted, 8 enrolled. In 2017, 8 master's, 3 doctorates awarded. *Degree requirements:* For master's, comprehensive exam, thesis optional; for doctorate, one foreign language, comprehensive exam, thesis/dissertation, statistics through analysis of variance; knowledge of structure of a non-Indo European language. *Entrance requirements:* For master's, minimum GPA of 3.0, 3 letters of recommendation, letter of intent; for doctorate, MA in linguistics or equivalent, paper of publishable quality, 3 letters of recommendation, letter of intent. Additional exam requirements/recommendations for international students: Required—TOEFL (minimum score 550 paper-based; 79 iBT), IELTS (minimum score 7). *Application deadline:* For fall admission, 12/15 priority date for domestic and international students. Applications are processed on a rolling basis. Application fee: $50. Electronic applications accepted. *Financial support:* Fellowships with full tuition reimbursements, research assistantships, teaching assistantships with tuition reimbursements, Federal Work-Study, health care benefits, and tuition waivers (full and partial) available. Financial award application deadline: 1/15; financial award applicants required to submit FAFSA. *Faculty research:* Cognitive-functional linguistics, signed language linguistics, Native American languages of the Southwest, language acquisition, language in interaction (discourse, prosody). *Total annual research expenditures:* $121,296. *Unit head:* Dr. Caroline Smith, Chair, 505-277-6353, Fax: 505-277-6355, E-mail: caroline@unm.edu. *Application contact:* Jessica Slocum, Administrative Assistant III, 505-277-6353, Fax: 505-277-6355, E-mail: jslocum@unm.edu.
Website: http://www.unm.edu/~linguist/

University of New Mexico, Graduate Studies, College of Education, Program in Educational Linguistics, Albuquerque, NM 87131-2039. Offers PhD. *Program availability:* Part-time. *Students:* Average age 41. 13 applicants, 8% accepted, 1 enrolled. In 2017, 2 doctorates awarded. *Degree requirements:* For doctorate, comprehensive exam, thesis/dissertation. *Entrance requirements:* For doctorate, master's degree in linguistics or complementary field (recommended). Additional exam requirements/recommendations for international students: Required—TOEFL (minimum score 550 paper-based; 79 iBT). *Application deadline:* For fall admission, 12/1 for domestic and international students. Application fee: $50. Electronic applications accepted. *Financial support:* Teaching assistantships, career-related internships or fieldwork, institutionally sponsored loans, scholarships/grants, and unspecified assistantships available. Support available to part-time students. Financial award application deadline: 1/15; financial award applicants required to submit FAFSA. *Faculty research:* Bilingualism, language maintenance and loss, bilingual deaf education, Spanish dialectical studies, English as a second language, writing/composition, Native American language issues, language and thought, language policy studies, global English issues, assessment. *Unit head:* Dr. Holbrook Mahn, Graduate Director, 505-277-5887, Fax: 505-277-8362, E-mail: hmahn@unm.edu. *Application contact:* Mary Gurule Vernon, Administrator, 505-277-5282, Fax: 505-277-8362, E-mail: mgurule2@unm.edu.
Website: https://coe.unm.edu/departments-programs/llss/educational-linguistics/index.html

The University of North Carolina at Chapel Hill, Graduate School, College of Arts and Sciences, Department of Linguistics, Chapel Hill, NC 27599. Offers MA. *Degree requirements:* For master's, one foreign language, comprehensive exam, thesis. *Entrance requirements:* For master's, GRE General Test, minimum GPA of 3.0. Additional exam requirements/recommendations for international students: Required—TOEFL (minimum score 79 iBT). Electronic applications accepted. *Faculty research:* Phonetics, phonology, morphology, syntax, semantics, historical linguistics, language acquisition, Mayan linguistics.

The University of North Carolina at Charlotte, College of Liberal Arts and Sciences, Department of English, Charlotte, NC 28223-0001. Offers applied linguistics (Graduate Certificate); English (MA); technical and professional writing (Graduate Certificate). *Program availability:* Part-time, evening/weekend. *Faculty:* 33 full-time (19 women), 2 part-time/adjunct (1 woman). *Students:* 33 full-time (25 women), 20 part-time (14 women); includes 9 minority (1 Black or African American, non-Hispanic/Latino; 2 Asian, non-Hispanic/Latino; 5 Hispanic/Latino; 1 Two or more races, non-Hispanic/Latino), 2 international. Average age 30. 38 applicants, 87% accepted, 18 enrolled. In 2017, 19 master's, 2 other advanced degrees awarded. *Degree requirements:* For master's, comprehensive exam (for some programs), thesis, comprehensive exam, or project. *Entrance requirements:* For master's, GRE, MAT, minimum undergraduate GPA of 3.0, statement of purpose, recommendation letters; for Graduate Certificate, statement of purpose, three letters of recommendation, writing sample, minimum GPA of 2.75. Additional exam requirements/recommendations for international students: Required—TOEFL (minimum score 523 paper-based, 70 iBT) or IELTS (6.5). *Application deadline:* For fall admission, 3/1 priority date for domestic and international students; for spring admission, 10/1 priority date for domestic and international students; for summer admission, 4/1 priority date for domestic and international students. Applications are processed on a rolling basis. Application fee: $75. Electronic applications accepted. *Expenses:* Tuition, state resident: full-time $4337. Tuition, nonresident: full-time $17,771. *Required fees:* $3211. Tuition and fees vary according to course load and program. *Financial support:* In 2017–18, 17 students received support, including 17 teaching assistantships (averaging $8,118 per year); career-related internships or fieldwork, institutionally sponsored loans, scholarships/grants, and unspecified assistantships also available. Support available to part-time students. Financial award application deadline: 3/1; financial award applicants required to submit FAFSA. *Total annual research expenditures:* $30,460. *Unit head:* Dr. Mark West, Chair, 704-687-0618, E-mail: miwest@uncc.edu. *Application contact:* Kathy B. Giddings, Director of Graduate Admissions, 704-687-5503, Fax: 704-687-1668, E-mail: gradadm@uncc.edu.
Website: http://english.uncc.edu/

University of North Dakota, Graduate School, College of Arts and Sciences, Program in Linguistics, Grand Forks, ND 58202. Offers MA. *Degree requirements:* For master's, one foreign language, thesis, final examination. *Entrance requirements:* For master's, minimum GPA of 3.0. Additional exam requirements/recommendations for international students: Required—TOEFL (minimum score 550 paper-based; 79 iBT), IELTS (minimum score 6.5). Electronic applications accepted. *Faculty research:* Practice-based field studies.

University of North Texas, Robert B. Toulouse School of Graduate Studies, Denton, TX 76203-5459. Offers accounting (MS); applied anthropology (MA, MS); applied behavior analysis (Certificate); applied geography (MA); applied technology and

performance improvement (M Ed, MS); art education (MA); art history (MA); art museum education (Certificate); arts leadership (Certificate); audiology (Au D); behavior analysis (MS); behavioral science (PhD); biochemistry and molecular biology (MS); biology (MA, MS); biomedical engineering (MS); business analysis (MS); chemistry (MS); clinical health psychology (PhD); communication studies (MA, MS); computer engineering (MS); computer science (MS); counseling (M Ed, MS), including clinical mental health counseling (MS), college and university counseling, elementary school counseling, secondary school counseling; creative writing (MA); criminal justice (MS); curriculum and instruction (M Ed); decision sciences (MBA); design (MA, MFA), including fashion design (MFA), innovation studies, interior design (MFA); early childhood studies (MS); economics (MS); educational leadership (M Ed, Ed D); educational psychology (MS, PhD), including family studies (MS), gifted and talented (MS), human development (MS), learning and cognition (MS), research, measurement and evaluation (MS); electrical engineering (MS); emergency management (MPA); engineering technology (MS); English (MA); English as a second language (MA); environmental science (MS); finance (MBA, MS); financial management (MPA); French (MA); health services management (MBA); higher education (M Ed, Ed D); history (MA, MS); hospitality management (MS); human resources management (MPA); information science (MS); information systems (PhD); information technologies (MBA); interdisciplinary studies (MA, MS); international studies (MA); international sustainable tourism (MS); jazz studies (MM); journalism (MA, MJ, Graduate Certificate), including interactive and virtual digital communication (Graduate Certificate), narrative journalism (Graduate Certificate), public relations (Graduate Certificate); kinesiology (MS); linguistics (MA); local government management (MPA); logistics (PhD); logistics and supply chain management (MBA); long-term care, senior housing, and aging services (MA); management (PhD); marketing (MBA); mathematics (MA, MS); mechanical and energy engineering (MS, PhD); music (MA), including ethnomusicology, music theory, musicology, performance; music composition (PhD); music education (MM Ed, PhD); nonprofit management (MPA); operations and supply chain management (MBA); performance (MM, DMA); philosophy (MA); political science (MA); professional and technical communication (MA); radio, television and film (MA, MFA); rehabilitation counseling (Certificate); sociology (MA); Spanish (MA); special education (M Ed); speech-language pathology (MA); strategic management (MBA); studio art (MFA); teaching (M Ed); MBA/MS. *Program availability:* Part-time, evening/weekend, online learning. Terminal master's awarded for partial completion of doctoral program. *Degree requirements:* For master's, variable foreign language requirement, comprehensive exam (for some programs), thesis (for some programs); for doctorate, variable foreign language requirement, comprehensive exam (for some programs), thesis/dissertation; for other advanced degree, variable foreign language requirement, comprehensive exam (for some programs). *Entrance requirements:* For master's and doctorate, GRE, GMAT. Additional exam requirements/ recommendations for international students: Required—TOEFL (minimum score 550 paper-based; 79 iBT). Electronic applications accepted.

University of Oregon, Graduate School, College of Arts and Sciences, Department of Linguistics, Eugene, OR 97403. Offers language teaching studies (MA); linguistics (MA, PhD). Terminal master's awarded for partial completion of doctoral program. *Degree requirements:* For master's, 2 foreign languages; for doctorate, thesis/dissertation. *Entrance requirements:* For master's and doctorate, GRE General Test, minimum GPA of 3.0. Additional exam requirements/recommendations for international students: Required—TOEFL. *Faculty research:* Functional syntax, discourse, empirical methods.

University of Ottawa, Faculty of Graduate and Postdoctoral Studies, Faculty of Arts, Department of Linguistics, Ottawa, ON K1N 6N5, Canada. Offers MA, PhD. *Degree requirements:* For master's, one foreign language, thesis or alternative; for doctorate, 2 foreign languages, comprehensive exam, thesis/dissertation. *Entrance requirements:* For master's, honors degree or equivalent, minimum B average; for doctorate, master's degree, minimum B+ average. Electronic applications accepted. *Faculty research:* Empirical linguistics, formal linguistics.

University of Pennsylvania, Graduate School of Education, Division of Educational Linguistics, Program in Educational Linguistics, Philadelphia, PA 19104. Offers PhD. *Program availability:* Part-time-only. *Students:* 15 full-time (12 women), 2 part-time (0 women); includes 5 minority (3 Asian, non-Hispanic/Latino; 2 Hispanic/Latino), 4 international. Average age 30. 96 applicants, 2% accepted, 2 enrolled. *Financial support:* In 2017–18, 55 students received support.

University of Pennsylvania, School of Arts and Sciences, Graduate Group in Linguistics, Philadelphia, PA 19104. Offers AM, PhD. *Faculty:* 23 full-time (5 women), 1 part-time/adjunct (0 women). *Students:* 34 full-time (20 women); includes 3 minority (1 Black or African American, non-Hispanic/Latino; 2 Asian, non-Hispanic/Latino), 18 international. Average age 28. 125 applicants, 4% accepted, 1 enrolled. In 2017, 1 master's, 5 doctorates awarded. Terminal master's awarded for partial completion of doctoral program. *Entrance requirements:* For master's, GRE General Test.
Website: http://www.ling.upenn.edu/graduate/

University of Pittsburgh, Kenneth P. Dietrich School of Arts and Sciences, Department of Linguistics, Pittsburgh, PA 15260. Offers applied linguistics (MA); applied linguistics with TESOL (MA); sociolinguistics (PhD). *Faculty:* 7 full-time (4 women). *Students:* 14 full-time (7 women); includes 6 minority (3 Black or African American, non-Hispanic/Latino; 3 Asian, non-Hispanic/Latino). Average age 32. In 2017, 2 master's, 4 doctorates awarded. Terminal master's awarded for partial completion of doctoral program. *Degree requirements:* For master's, one foreign language, thesis optional; for doctorate, 2 foreign languages, comprehensive exam, thesis/dissertation. *Entrance requirements:* For master's, GRE General Test; for doctorate, GRE General Test, MA in linguistics. Additional exam requirements/recommendations for international students: Required—TOEFL (minimum score 600 paper-based; 100 iBT). *Application deadline:* For fall admission, 12/15 priority date for domestic and international students. Application fee: $50. Electronic applications accepted. *Financial support:* In 2017–18, 6 students received support, including 1 fellowship with full tuition reimbursement available (averaging $18,620 per year), 5 teaching assistantships with full tuition reimbursements available (averaging $17,910 per year); scholarships/grants, health care benefits, and employee tuition benefits also available. Financial award application deadline: 12/15; financial award applicants required to submit FAFSA. *Faculty research:* Second language acquisition, phonetics, intonation, sociolinguistics, language contact. *Unit head:* Dr. Shelome Gooden, Chair, 412-624-5922, Fax: 412-624-5520, E-mail: sgooden@pitt.edu. *Application contact:* Margaret Bupp, Graduate Student Services Administrator, 412-624-6568, Fax: 412-624-5520, E-mail: maggiebupp@pitt.edu.
Website: http://www.linguistics.pitt.edu/

University of Puerto Rico–Río Piedras, College of Humanities, Department of Hispanic Studies, San Juan, PR 00931-3300. Offers Hispanic linguistics (PhD); Hispanic studies (MA); Latin American literature (PhD); Puerto Rican literature (PhD); Spanish literature (PhD). *Program availability:* Part-time. *Degree requirements:* For master's, one foreign language, comprehensive exam, thesis; for doctorate, one foreign language, comprehensive exam, thesis/dissertation. *Entrance requirements:* For master's, PAEG or GRE, interview, minimum GPA of 3.0, letter of recommendation (2); for doctorate, PAEG or GRE, interview, master's degree, minimum GPA of 3.0, letter of recommendation (2). *Faculty research:* Poetry of Luis Palés Matos, short stories in Puerto Rico, language in the social process, "Decima Popular", Anglicism.

University of Puerto Rico–Río Piedras, College of Humanities, Department of Linguistics, San Juan, PR 00931-3300. Offers MA. *Program availability:* Part-time. *Degree requirements:* For master's, one foreign language, comprehensive exam, thesis. *Entrance requirements:* For master's, PAEG or GRE, interview, minimum GPA of 3.0, letter of recommendation (2).

University of Regina, Faculty of Graduate Studies and Research, Faculty of Arts, Program in Linguistics, Regina, SK S4S 0A2, Canada. Offers MA. Offered as a special case program. *Program availability:* Part-time. *Faculty:* 9 full-time (2 women), 4 part-time/adjunct (0 women). *Degree requirements:* For master's, thesis. *Entrance requirements:* Additional exam requirements/recommendations for international students: Required—TOEFL (minimum score 580 paper-based), IELTS (minimum score 6.5), PTE (minimum score 59). *Application deadline:* Applications are processed on a rolling basis. Application fee: $100. Electronic applications accepted. *Expenses:* Tuition, nonresident: full-time $21,330 Canadian dollars; part-time $18,165 Canadian dollars per year. *International tuition:* $24,713 Canadian dollars full-time. *Required fees:* $5136 Canadian dollars; $3118 Canadian dollars per credit hour. $1008 Canadian dollars per semester. Tuition and fees vary according to program. *Financial support:* Fellowships, research assistantships, teaching assistantships, and scholarships/grants available. Financial award application deadline: 6/15. *Faculty research:* Advanced phonology, advanced morphology, advanced syntax, advanced semantics, diachronic linguistics. *Unit head:* Dr. Arok Wolvengrey, Graduate Studies Advisor/Coordinator, 306-790-5950 Ext. 3310, Fax: 306-790-5994, E-mail: awolvengrey@fnuniv.ca.

University of Rochester, School of Arts and Sciences, Department of Linguistics, Rochester, NY 14627. Offers computational linguistics (MS); language documentation and description (MA); linguistics (MA). *Program availability:* Part-time. *Faculty:* 5 full-time (1 woman). *Students:* 9 full-time (6 women), 1 (woman) part-time, 6 international. Average age 25. 70 applicants, 27% accepted, 8 enrolled. In 2017, 1 master's awarded. Terminal master's awarded for partial completion of doctoral program. *Degree requirements:* For master's, final essay/presentation. *Entrance requirements:* For master's, GRE, statement of purpose, three letters of recommendation, official transcripts, writing sample. Additional exam requirements/recommendations for international students: Required—TOEFL. *Application deadline:* For fall admission, 1/15 for domestic and international students. Application fee: $60. Electronic applications accepted. *Expenses:* $1,596 per credit hour. *Financial support:* In 2017–18, 9 students received support, including 1 research assistantship (averaging $27,198 per year); scholarships/grants also available. Financial award application deadline: 1/15. *Faculty research:* Computational and experimental semantics and pragmatics, phonetics and phonology, language documentation and description, language and music, experimental syntax. *Total annual research expenditures:* $92,307. *Unit head:* Joyce McDonough, Professor and Chair, 585-275-3944, E-mail: joyce.mcdonough@rochester.edu. *Application contact:* Erica Dayton, Administrative Assistant, 585-275-8053, E-mail: erica.dayton@rochester.edu.
Website: http://www.sas.rochester.edu/lin/graduate/index.html

University of South Africa, College of Human Sciences, Pretoria, South Africa. Offers adult education (M Ed); African languages (MA, PhD); African politics (MA, PhD); Afrikaans (MA, PhD); ancient history (MA, PhD); ancient Near Eastern studies (MA, PhD); anthropology (MA, PhD); applied linguistics (MA); Arabic (MA, PhD); archaeology (MA); art history (MA); Biblical archaeology (MA); Biblical studies (M Th, D Th, PhD); Christian spirituality (M Th, D Th); church history (M Th, D Th); classical studies (MA, PhD); clinical psychology (MA); communication (MA, PhD); comparative education (M Ed, Ed D); consulting psychology (D Admin, D Com, PhD); curriculum studies (M Ed, Ed D); development studies (M Admin, MA, D Admin, PhD); didactics (M Ed, Ed D); education (M Tech); education management (M Ed, Ed D); educational psychology (M Ed); English (MA); environmental education (M Ed); French (MA, PhD); German (MA, PhD); Greek (MA); guidance and counseling (M Ed); health studies (MA, PhD), including health sciences education (MA), health services management (MA), medical and surgical nursing science (critical care general) (MA), midwifery and neonatal nursing science (MA), trauma and emergency care (MA); history (MA, PhD); history of education (Ed D); inclusive education (M Ed, Ed D); information and communications technology policy and regulation (MA); information science (MA, MIS, PhD); international politics (MA, PhD); Islamic studies (MA, PhD); Italian (MA, PhD); Judaica (MA, PhD); linguistics (MA, PhD); mathematical education (M Ed); mathematics education (MA); missiology (M Th, D Th); modern Hebrew (MA, PhD); musicology (MA, MMus, D Mus, PhD); natural science education (M Ed); New Testament (M Th, D Th); Old Testament (D Th); pastoral therapy (M Th, D Th); philosophy (MA); philosophy of education (M Ed, Ed D); politics (MA, PhD); Portuguese (MA, PhD); practical theology (M Th, D Th); psychology (MA, MS, PhD); psychology of education (M Ed, Ed D); public health (MA); religious studies (MA, D Th, PhD); Romance languages (MA); Russian (MA, PhD); Semitic languages (MA, PhD); social behavior studies in HIV/AIDS (MA); social science (mental health) (MA); social science in development studies (MA); social science in psychology (MA); social science in social work (MA); social science in sociology (MA); social work (MSW, DSW, PhD); socio-education (M Ed, Ed D); sociolinguistics (MA); sociology (MA, PhD); Spanish (MA, PhD); systematic theology (M Th, D Th); TESOL (teaching English to speakers of other languages) (MA); theological ethics (M Th, D Th); theory of literature (MA, PhD); urban ministries (D Th); urban ministry (M Th).

University of South Carolina, The Graduate School, College of Arts and Sciences, Linguistics Program, Columbia, SC 29208. Offers linguistics (MA, PhD); teaching English to speakers of other languages (Certificate). *Program availability:* Part-time. Terminal master's awarded for partial completion of doctoral program. *Degree requirements:* For master's, one foreign language, comprehensive exam, thesis optional; for doctorate, 3 foreign languages, comprehensive exam, thesis/dissertation. *Entrance requirements:* For master's and Certificate, GRE General Test, minimum GPA of 3.0; for doctorate, GRE General Test, minimum GPA of 3.5. Additional exam requirements/recommendations for international students: Required—TOEFL. Electronic applications accepted. *Faculty research:* Second language acquisition, sociolinguistics, syntax, historical linguistics and phonology.

University of Southern California, Graduate School, Dana and David Dornsife College of Letters, Arts and Sciences, Department of East Asian Languages and Cultures, Los Angeles, CA 90089. Offers classical Chinese literature (MA, PhD); classical Japanese literature (MA, PhD); linguistics (MA, PhD); modern Chinese literature (MA, PhD); modern Japanese literature (MA, PhD); modern Korean literature (MA, PhD). *Degree requirements:* For master's, thesis; for doctorate, 2 foreign languages, comprehensive exam, thesis/dissertation. *Entrance requirements:* For master's and doctorate, GRE, BA in relevant field. Additional exam requirements/recommendations for international students: Required—TOEFL. Electronic applications accepted. *Faculty research:* Gender, visual studies, multimedia, ecocriticism, second language acquisition.

University of Southern California, Graduate School, Dana and David Dornsife College of Letters, Arts and Sciences, Department of Linguistics, Los Angeles, CA 90089. Offers East Asian linguistics (PhD); Hispanic linguistics (PhD); linguistics (PhD); Slavic linguistics (PhD). *Degree requirements:* For doctorate, comprehensive exam, thesis/ dissertation. *Entrance requirements:* For doctorate, GRE. Additional exam requirements/recommendations for international students: Required—TOEFL (minimum

score 100 iBT). Electronic applications accepted. *Faculty research:* Syntax, phonology, phonetics, semantics, sociolinguistics, psycholinguistics.

University of South Florida, College of Arts and Sciences, Department of World Languages, Tampa, FL 33620-9951. Offers French (MA); linguistics (MA); linguistics and applied linguistics studies (PhD); linguistics: English as a second language (MA); Spanish (MA). *Program availability:* Part-time, evening/weekend. *Faculty:* 18 full-time (14 women). *Students:* 40 full-time (34 women), 9 part-time (7 women); includes 20 minority (1 Black or African American, non-Hispanic/Latino; 1 Asian, non-Hispanic/Latino; 16 Hispanic/Latino; 2 Two or more races, non-Hispanic/Latino), 16 international. Average age 33. 65 applicants, 62% accepted, 18 enrolled. In 2017, 30 master's awarded. *Degree requirements:* For master's, one foreign language, comprehensive exam, thesis optional; for doctorate, one foreign language, comprehensive exam, thesis/dissertation. *Entrance requirements:* For master's, GRE General Test, minimum undergraduate GPA of 3.0 and 2-3 letters of recommendation; two-page statement of purpose written in Spanish (for Spanish program); oral interview (for Spanish and French programs); writing sample (for French program); for doctorate, GRE General Test, minimum GPA of 3.5 or international equivalent; master's degree or equivalent academic level; statement of purpose; current curriculum vitae; three letters of recommendation; personal interview with faculty; evidence of research experience or scholarly promise. Additional exam requirements/recommendations for international students: Required—TOEFL minimum score 600 paper-based; 80 iBT or IELTS minimum score 6.5 (for MA); TOEFL minimum score 550 paper-based; 80 iBT or IELTS minimum score 6.5 (for PhD). *Application deadline:* For fall admission, 1/15 for domestic and international students; for spring admission, 10/15 for domestic students, 9/15 for international students. Application fee: $30. Electronic applications accepted. *Financial support:* In 2017–18, 10 students received support, including 43 teaching assistantships with tuition reimbursements available (averaging $10,152 per year); tuition waivers (partial) and unspecified assistantships also available. Financial award application deadline: 6/30. *Faculty research:* Second language acquisition, instructional technology, foreign language education, English for speakers of other languages, distance learning. *Total annual research expenditures:* $7,706. *Unit head:* Dr. Stephan Schindler, Chair and Professor, 813-974-2548, Fax: 813-905-9937, E-mail: skschindler@usf.edu. *Application contact:* Patricia Garcia, Academic Program Specialist, 813-974-2548, Fax: 813-905-9937, E-mail: pgarcia@usf.edu.
Website: http://languages.usf.edu/

The University of Tennessee, Graduate School, College of Arts and Sciences, Department of Modern Foreign Languages and Literatures, Program in Modern Foreign Languages, Knoxville, TN 37996. Offers applied linguistics (PhD); French (PhD); German (PhD); Italian (PhD); Portuguese (PhD); Russian (PhD); Spanish (PhD). *Degree requirements:* For doctorate, 2 foreign languages, thesis/dissertation. *Entrance requirements:* For doctorate, minimum GPA of 2.7. Additional exam requirements/recommendations for international students: Required—TOEFL. Electronic applications accepted.

The University of Texas at Arlington, Graduate School, College of Liberal Arts, Department of Linguistics and TESOL, Program in Linguistics, Arlington, TX 76019. Offers MA, PhD. *Program availability:* Part-time, evening/weekend. Terminal master's awarded for partial completion of doctoral program. *Degree requirements:* For master's, one foreign language, comprehensive exam (for some programs), thesis optional; for doctorate, 2 foreign languages, comprehensive exam, thesis/dissertation, qualifying exam, dissertation proposal defense, professional development. *Entrance requirements:* For master's, GRE General Test, minimum undergraduate GPA of 3.0, 9 credits of undergraduate foundation courses; for doctorate, GRE General Test, 30 hours of graduate work in linguistics or a related discipline, minimum GPA of 3.5. Additional exam requirements/recommendations for international students: Required—TOEFL (minimum score 550 paper-based). Electronic applications accepted. *Faculty research:* Field linguistics, discourse analysis, text linguistics, phonology, teaching English as a second language.

The University of Texas at Austin, Graduate School, College of Liberal Arts, Department of French and Italian, Austin, TX 78712-1111. Offers French linguistics (MA, PhD); French studies (MA, PhD); Italian studies (MA, PhD); Romance linguistics (PhD). *Program availability:* Part-time. *Degree requirements:* For master's, one foreign language, thesis; for doctorate, 2 foreign languages, thesis/dissertation. *Entrance requirements:* For master's, GRE General Test, minimum GPA of 3.0, bachelor's degree in French or equivalent; for doctorate, GRE General Test, minimum GPA of 3.0, master's degree in French. Additional exam requirements/recommendations for international students: Required—TOEFL. Electronic applications accepted. *Faculty research:* Nineteenth-century Italian literature, Italian Renaissance, twentieth-century French literature, Francophone literature, fifteenth-century literature and culture.

The University of Texas at Austin, Graduate School, College of Liberal Arts, Department of Linguistics, Austin, TX 78712-1111. Offers MA, PhD. *Degree requirements:* For master's, one foreign language, thesis; for doctorate, 2 foreign languages, thesis/dissertation. *Entrance requirements:* For master's and doctorate, GRE General Test. Electronic applications accepted. *Faculty research:* Theoretical linguistics, sociolinguistics, documentary and descriptive linguistics, computational linguistics.

The University of Texas at Austin, Graduate School, College of Liberal Arts, Department of Slavic and Eurasian Studies, Austin, TX 78712-1111. Offers applied linguistics/pedagogy (PhD); literature and culture (PhD); Slavic languages (MA); Slavic linguistics (PhD). *Degree requirements:* For master's, 2 foreign languages, thesis; for doctorate, 3 foreign languages, thesis/dissertation. *Entrance requirements:* For master's and doctorate, GRE General Test. Electronic applications accepted. *Faculty research:* Slavic linguistics; applied linguistics; Russian, Czech, and Slavic literature and culture.

The University of Texas at Austin, Graduate School, College of Liberal Arts, Department of Spanish and Portuguese, Austin, TX 78712-1111. Offers Hispanic linguistics (MA, PhD); Hispanic literature (MA, PhD); Ibero-romance philology and linguistics (PhD); Luso-Brazilian literature (MA, PhD). *Degree requirements:* For master's, 2 foreign languages, thesis or alternative; for doctorate, 3 foreign languages, thesis/dissertation. *Entrance requirements:* For master's and doctorate, GRE General Test. Electronic applications accepted.

The University of Texas at El Paso, Graduate School, College of Liberal Arts, Department of Languages and Linguistics, El Paso, TX 79968-0001. Offers linguistics (MA); Spanish (MA); teaching English to speakers of other languages (Certificate). *Program availability:* Part-time, evening/weekend. *Degree requirements:* For master's, thesis optional. *Entrance requirements:* For master's, GRE General Test, departmental exam, minimum GPA of 3.0, letters of recommendation. Additional exam requirements/recommendations for international students: Required—TOEFL; Recommended—IELTS. Electronic applications accepted.

University of Toronto, School of Graduate Studies, Faculty of Arts and Science, Department of Linguistics, Toronto, ON M5S 1A1, Canada. Offers MA, PhD. *Program availability:* Part-time. *Degree requirements:* For master's, 2 foreign languages; for doctorate, thesis/dissertation, oral thesis proposal. *Entrance requirements:* For master's, BA in linguistics; for doctorate, MA in linguistics. Electronic applications accepted.

University of Utah, Graduate School, College of Humanities, Department of Linguistics, Salt Lake City, UT 84112-0492. Offers MA, PhD. *Faculty:* 9 full-time (4 women), 1 part-time/adjunct (0 women). *Students:* 2 full-time (both women), 1 part-time (0 women); includes 1 minority (Hispanic/Latino). Average age 25. 43 applicants, 19% accepted, 3 enrolled. In 2017, 6 master's, 4 doctorates awarded. Terminal master's awarded for partial completion of doctoral program. *Entrance requirements:* For master's and doctorate, GRE General Test, minimum undergraduate GPA of 3.0. Additional exam requirements/recommendations for international students: Required—TOEFL (minimum score 600 paper-based; 100 iBT). Application fee: $55 ($65 for international students). Electronic applications accepted. *Expenses:* $3,627.74 per semester. *Financial support:* In 2017–18, 2 students received support, including 2 fellowships with full tuition reimbursements available (averaging $9,700 per year), 4 teaching assistantships with full tuition reimbursements available (averaging $18,300 per year); health care benefits also available. Financial award application deadline: 2/1. *Faculty research:* Phonology, second language acquisition, semantics, syntax, second language pedagogy. *Unit head:* Dr. Edward Rubin, Chair, 801-581-8047, Fax: 801-585-7351, E-mail: e.rubin@utah.edu. *Application contact:* Kacey Campbell, Academic Advisor, 801-581-3929, Fax: 801-585-7351, E-mail: kacey.campbell@utah.edu.
Website: http://www.linguistics.utah.edu

University of Victoria, Faculty of Graduate Studies, Faculty of Humanities, Department of Linguistics, Victoria, BC V8W 2Y2, Canada. Offers applied linguistics (MA); linguistics (MA, PhD). *Program availability:* Part-time. *Degree requirements:* For master's, one foreign language, thesis, colloquium; for doctorate, 2 foreign languages, comprehensive exam, thesis/dissertation, candidacy exam. *Entrance requirements:* For master's, GRE; for doctorate, GRE, sample of written work. Additional exam requirements/recommendations for international students: Required—TOEFL. Electronic applications accepted. *Faculty research:* Grammatical theory, syntactic analysis, morphology, Western Amerindian languages, Salishan, applied linguistics.

University of Virginia, College and Graduate School of Arts and Sciences, Program in Linguistics, Charlottesville, VA 22903. Offers MA. *Students:* 16 full-time (11 women); includes 2 minority (both Hispanic/Latino), 6 international. Average age 25. 21 applicants, 86% accepted, 10 enrolled. In 2017, 1 master's awarded. *Degree requirements:* For master's, one foreign language, comprehensive exam, thesis optional, reading knowledge of French or German. *Entrance requirements:* For master's, GRE General Test. Additional exam requirements/recommendations for international students: Required—TOEFL (minimum score 600 paper-based; 90 iBT), IELTS (minimum score 7). *Application deadline:* For fall admission, 2/15 for domestic and international students. Applications are processed on a rolling basis. Application fee: $60. Electronic applications accepted. *Financial support:* Teaching assistantships available. Financial award applicants required to submit FAFSA. *Unit head:* Lise Dobrin, Program Director, 434-924-7048, E-mail: ld4n@virginia.edu.
Website: http://artsandsciences.virginia.edu/linguistics/

University of Washington, Graduate School, College of Arts and Sciences, Department of Linguistics, Seattle, WA 98195. Offers computational linguistics (MA); linguistics (MA, PhD); Romance linguistics (MA, PhD). *Program availability:* Part-time. Terminal master's awarded for partial completion of doctoral program. *Degree requirements:* For master's, one foreign language, thesis; for doctorate, 2 foreign languages, thesis/dissertation. *Entrance requirements:* For master's, GRE General Test, minimum GPA of 3.0; for doctorate, GRE, minimum GPA of 3.0. Additional exam requirements/recommendations for international students: Required—TOEFL. Electronic applications accepted. *Faculty research:* Syntax, phonology, semantics, phonetics, sociolinguistics.

University of Washington, Graduate School, College of Arts and Sciences, Department of Slavic Languages and Literatures, Seattle, WA 98195. Offers Russian literature (MA, PhD); Slavic linguistics (MA, PhD). *Degree requirements:* For master's, 2 foreign languages, thesis optional; for doctorate, 3 foreign languages, thesis/dissertation. *Entrance requirements:* For master's and doctorate, GRE General Test, minimum GPA of 3.0. Additional exam requirements/recommendations for international students: Required—TOEFL. Electronic applications accepted. *Faculty research:* Modern and medieval East European languages and literatures, comparative literature, Russian folk literature, Slavic literary theory and criticism, computerized morphology of Russian.

University of Wisconsin–Madison, Graduate School, College of Letters and Science, Department of East Asian Languages and Literature, Program in Japanese Linguistics, Madison, WI 53706-1380. Offers MA, PhD. *Program availability:* Part-time. Terminal master's awarded for partial completion of doctoral program. *Degree requirements:* For master's, one foreign language, seminars, written exam; for doctorate, 3 foreign languages, thesis/dissertation, seminars, preliminary exams, oral exam. *Entrance requirements:* For master's, GRE General Test, bachelor's degree or equivalent in Japanese; for doctorate, GRE General Test, master's degree or equivalent in Japanese. Electronic applications accepted. *Faculty research:* Modern and historical Japanese linguistics, modern Japanese fiction and poetry, classical Japanese literature, language pedagogy.

University of Wisconsin–Madison, Graduate School, College of Letters and Science, Department of English, Madison, WI 53706-1380. Offers applied English linguistics (MA); composition and rhetoric (PhD); creative writing (MFA); English language and linguistics (PhD); literary studies (MA, PhD). *Degree requirements:* For doctorate, thesis/dissertation.

University of Wisconsin–Madison, Graduate School, College of Letters and Science, Department of Linguistics, Madison, WI 53706-1380. Offers MA, PhD. *Program availability:* Part-time. Terminal master's awarded for partial completion of doctoral program. *Degree requirements:* For master's, 2 foreign languages; for doctorate, 3 foreign languages, thesis/dissertation. Electronic applications accepted. *Faculty research:* Formal linguistics, acoustic phonetics, American studies, Indo-European linguistics.

University of Wisconsin–Milwaukee, Graduate School, College of Letters and Science, Department of Foreign Languages and Literature, Milwaukee, WI 53201-0413. Offers foreign languages and literature (MA), including classic Greek, classics, comparative literature, French/Francophone language, literature, and culture, German language, literature, and culture, interpreting, Latin, linguistics, Spanish language, literature, and culture, translation; interpreting (Graduate Certificate); language, literature, and translation (MA, MALLT); translation (Graduate Certificate). *Program availability:* Part-time. *Students:* 11 full-time (6 women), 40 part-time (29 women); includes 10 minority (2 Black or African American, non-Hispanic/Latino; 3 Hispanic/Latino; 5 Two or more races, non-Hispanic/Latino), 4 international. Average age 35. 37 applicants, 68% accepted, 20 enrolled. In 2017, 5 master's awarded. *Degree requirements:* For master's, 2 foreign languages, thesis or alternative. *Entrance requirements:* Additional exam requirements/recommendations for international students: Required—TOEFL (minimum score 550 paper-based; 79 iBT), IELTS (minimum score 6.5). *Application deadline:* For fall admission, 1/1 priority date for domestic students; for spring admission, 9/1 for domestic students. Application fee: $56 ($96 for international students). Electronic applications accepted. *Financial support:*

Fellowships, research assistantships, teaching assistantships, career-related internships or fieldwork, health care benefits, unspecified assistantships, and project assistantships available. Support available to part-time students. Financial award application deadline: 4/15; financial award applicants required to submit FAFSA. *Unit head:* Kevin Muse, Department Chair, 414-229-5213, E-mail: kmuse@uwm.edu. *Application contact:* General Information Contact, 414-229-4982, Fax: 414-229-6967, E-mail: gradschool@uwm.edu.
Website: http://uwm.edu/foreign-languages-literature/

University of Wisconsin–Milwaukee, Graduate School, College of Letters and Science, Department of Linguistics, Milwaukee, WI 53201-0413. Offers linguistics (MA, PhD), including teaching English to speakers of other languages (MA); teaching English to speakers of other languages, adult- and university-level (Graduate Certificate). *Students:* 19 full-time (5 women), 12 part-time (11 women); includes 1 minority (Two or more races, non-Hispanic/Latino), 18 international. Average age 33. 47 applicants, 34% accepted, 12 enrolled. In 2017, 4 master's, 2 other advanced degrees awarded. Electronic applications accepted. *Unit head:* Hamid Ouali, Department Chair, 414-229-1113, E-mail: ouali@uwm.edu. *Application contact:* General Information Contact, 414-229-4982, Fax: 414-229-6967, E-mail: gradschool@uwm.edu.
Website: http://www4.uwm.edu/letsci/linguistics/

Virginia International University, School of Education, Fairfax, VA 22030. Offers applied linguistics (MS); education (M Ed); teaching English to speakers of other languages (MA). *Program availability:* Part-time, online learning. *Entrance requirements:* For master's, bachelor's degree. Additional exam requirements/recommendations for international students: Required—TOEFL (minimum score 550 paper-based; 80 iBT), IELTS (minimum score 6). Electronic applications accepted.

Wayne State University, College of Liberal Arts and Sciences, Interdisciplinary Program in Linguistics, Detroit, MI 48202. Offers MA. *Students:* 11 full-time (4 women), 6 part-time (3 women); includes 3 minority (1 Asian, non-Hispanic/Latino; 1 Hispanic/Latino; 1 Two or more races, non-Hispanic/Latino), 10 international. Average age 29. 21 applicants, 43% accepted, 4 enrolled. In 2017, 9 master's awarded. *Degree requirements:* For master's, one foreign language, essay. *Entrance requirements:* For master's, minimum one year of foreign language; at least one course in linguistics; statement of purpose. Additional exam requirements/recommendations for international students: Required—TOEFL (minimum score 550 paper-based; 79 iBT), TWE (minimum score 5.5), Michigan English Language Assessment Battery (minimum score 85); Recommended—IELTS (minimum score 6.5). *Application deadline:* For fall admission, 6/1 priority date for domestic students, 5/1 priority date for international students; for winter admission, 10/1 priority date for domestic students, 9/1 priority date for international students; for spring admission, 2/1 priority date for domestic students, 1/1 priority date for international students. Applications are processed on a rolling basis. Application fee: $50. Electronic applications accepted. *Expenses:* Tuition, state resident: full-time $10,224; part-time $638.98 per credit hour. Tuition, nonresident: full-time $22,145; part-time $1384.04 per credit hour. Tuition and fees vary according to course load and program. *Financial support:* Scholarships/grants available. Financial award applicants required to submit FAFSA. *Faculty research:* Discourse/pragmatics, first language acquisition, historical linguistics, morphology, phonetics/phonology, psycholinguistics, second language acquisition, semantics, sociolinguistics, syntax. *Unit head:* Dr. Haiyong Liu, Associate Professor and Director of the Linguistics Program, 313-577-9937, E-mail: an1884@wayne.edu. *Application contact:* Dr. Peter Staroverov, Graduate Student Advisor, 313-577-7646, E-mail: staroverov@wayne.edu.
Website: http://clas.wayne.edu/linguistics/

Wesley Biblical Seminary, Graduate Programs, Jackson, MS 39206. Offers apologetics (MA); Biblical languages (M Div); Biblical literature (MA); Christian studies (MA); context and mission (M Div); honors research (M Div); interpretation (M Div); ministry (M Div); spiritual formation (M Div); teaching (M Div); theology (MA). *Accreditation:* ATS. *Program availability:* Part-time. *Degree requirements:* For master's, thesis. *Entrance requirements:* Additional exam requirements/recommendations for international students: Required—TOEFL. Electronic applications accepted. *Faculty research:* Patristics, missiology, culture, hermeneutics.

Yale University, Graduate School of Arts and Sciences, Department of Linguistics, New Haven, CT 06520. Offers PhD. *Degree requirements:* For doctorate, 2 foreign languages, thesis/dissertation. *Entrance requirements:* For doctorate, GRE General Test.

York University, Faculty of Graduate Studies, Faculty of Liberal Arts and Professional Studies, Program in Linguistics and Applied Linguistics, Toronto, ON M3J 1P3, Canada. Offers MA, PhD. *Degree requirements:* For master's, thesis.

Translation and Interpretation

American University of Sharjah, Graduate Programs, 26666, United Arab Emirates. Offers accounting (MS); biomedical engineering (MSBME); business administration (MBA); chemical engineering (MS Ch E); civil engineering (MSCE); computer engineering (MS); electrical engineering (MSEE); engineering systems management (MS, PhD); mathematics (MS); mechanical engineering (MSME); mechatronics engineering (MS); teaching English to speakers of other languages (MA); translation and interpreting (MA); urban planning (MUP). *Program availability:* Part-time, evening/weekend. *Students:* 108 full-time (73 women), 287 part-time (207 women). Average age 27. 203 applicants, 83% accepted, 121 enrolled. In 2017, 114 master's awarded. *Degree requirements:* For master's, thesis (for some programs). *Entrance requirements:* For master's, GMAT (for MBA). Additional exam requirements/recommendations for international students: Required—TOEFL (minimum score 550 paper-based; 80 iBT), TWE (minimum score 5); Recommended—IELTS (minimum score 6.5). *Application deadline:* For fall admission, 8/5 priority date for domestic students, 7/1 priority date for international students; for spring admission, 12/30 priority date for domestic students, 12/9 for international students; for summer admission, 5/21 for domestic and international students. Applications are processed on a rolling basis. Application fee: $110. Electronic applications accepted. *Expenses: Tuition:* Full-time $20,000; part-time $1350 per credit. Tuition and fees vary according to degree level and program. *Financial support:* In 2017–18, 82 students received support, including 54 research assistantships, 54 teaching assistantships; scholarships/grants also available. Financial award application deadline: 6/3. *Faculty research:* Water pollution, management and waste water treatment, energy and sustainability, air pollution, Islamic finance, family business and small and medium enterprises. *Unit head:* Salwa Mohammed, Office of Graduate Studies, 971-6515-2934, E-mail: ogs@aus.edu. *Application contact:* Salwa H. Mohammed, Office of Graduate Studies, 971-65152934, E-mail: ogs@aus.edu.
Website: https://www.aus.edu/masters-degrees

Arizona State University at the Tempe campus, College of Liberal Arts and Sciences, Department of English, Tempe, AZ 85287-0302. Offers applied linguistics (PhD); creative writing (MFA); English (MA, PhD), including comparative literature (MA), linguistics (MA), literature, rhetoric and composition (MA), rhetoric, composition, and linguistics (PhD); film and media studies (MAS), including American media and popular culture; linguistics (Graduate Certificate); teaching English to speakers of other languages (MTESOL); translation studies (Graduate Certificate). Terminal master's awarded for partial completion of doctoral program. *Degree requirements:* For master's, variable foreign language requirement, comprehensive exam (for some programs), thesis (for some programs), interactive Program of Study (iPOS) submitted before completing 50 percent of required credit hours; for doctorate, variable foreign language requirement, comprehensive exam, thesis/dissertation, interactive Program of Study (iPOS) submitted before completing 50 percent of required credit hours. *Entrance requirements:* For master's and doctorate, GRE, minimum GPA of 3.0 or equivalent in last 2 years of work leading to bachelor's degree. Additional exam requirements/recommendations for international students: Required—TOEFL, IELTS, or PTE. Electronic applications accepted.

Babel University Professional School of Translation, Program in Translation, Honolulu, HI 96815. Offers MS. *Program availability:* Part-time, evening/weekend, online learning. *Degree requirements:* For master's, comprehensive exam, thesis. *Entrance requirements:* For master's, translation exam. Additional exam requirements/recommendations for international students: Recommended—TOEFL (minimum score 550 paper-based).

Binghamton University, State University of New York, Graduate School, Harpur College of Arts and Sciences, Translation Research and Instruction Program, Binghamton, NY 13902-6000. Offers translation (Certificate); translation studies (PhD). *Program availability:* Part-time. *Students:* 20 full-time (16 women), 34 part-time (21 women); includes 3 minority (1 Asian, non-Hispanic/Latino; 2 Hispanic/Latino), 44 international. Average age 34. 32 applicants, 44% accepted, 8 enrolled. In 2017, 3 doctorates, 1 other advanced degree awarded. *Degree requirements:* For doctorate, one foreign language, comprehensive exam, thesis/dissertation; for Certificate, one foreign language, comprehensive exam. *Entrance requirements:* For doctorate and Certificate, GRE General Test, writing sample. Additional exam requirements/recommendations for international students: Required—TOEFL (minimum score 550 paper-based; 80 iBT). *Application deadline:* Applications are processed on a rolling basis. Application fee: $75. Electronic applications accepted. *Financial support:* In 2017–18, 10 students received support, including 4 teaching assistantships with full tuition reimbursements available (averaging $14,500 per year); career-related internships or fieldwork, Federal Work-Study, institutionally sponsored loans, scholarships/grants, health care benefits, and unspecified assistantships also available. Financial award applicants required to submit FAFSA. *Unit head:* Dr. Michael Pettid, Director, 607-777-3862, E-mail: mpettid@binghamton.edu. *Application contact:* Ben Balkaya, Assistant Dean and Director, 607-777-2151, Fax: 607-777-2501, E-mail: balkaya@binghamton.edu.
Website: https://www.binghamton.edu/comparative-literature/graduate/trip/

Columbia University, Graduate School of Arts and Sciences, New York, NY 10027. Offers African-American studies (MA); American studies (MA); anthropology (MA, PhD); art history and archaeology (MA, PhD); astronomy (PhD); biological sciences (PhD); biotechnology (MA); chemical physics (PhD); chemistry (PhD); classical studies (MA, PhD); classics (MA, PhD); climate and society (MA); conservation biology (MA); earth and environmental sciences (PhD); East Asia: regional studies (MA); East Asian languages and cultures (MA, PhD); ecology, evolution and environmental biology (MA), including conservation biology; ecology, evolution, and environmental biology (PhD), including ecology and evolutionary biology, evolutionary primatology; economics (MA, PhD); English and comparative literature (MA, PhD); French and Romance philology (MA, PhD); Germanic languages (MA, PhD); global French studies (MA); global thought (MA); Hispanic cultural studies (MA); history (PhD); history and literature (MA); human rights studies (MA); Islamic studies (MA); Italian (MA, PhD); Japanese pedagogy (MA); Jewish studies (MA); Latin America and the Caribbean: regional studies (MA); Latin American and Iberian cultures (PhD); mathematics (MA, PhD), including finance (MA); medieval and Renaissance studies (MA); Middle Eastern, South Asian, and African studies (MA, PhD); modern art: critical and curatorial studies (MA); modern European studies (MA); museum anthropology (MA); music (DMA, PhD); oral history (MA); philosophical foundations of physics (MA); philosophy (MA, PhD); physics (PhD); political science (MA, PhD); psychology (PhD); quantitative methods in the social sciences (MA); religion (MA, PhD); Russia, Eurasia and East Europe: regional studies (MA); Russian translation (MA); Slavic cultures (MA); Slavic languages (MA, PhD); sociology (MA, PhD); South Asian studies (MA); statistics (MA, PhD); theatre (PhD). Dual-degree programs require admission to both Graduate School of Arts and Sciences and another Columbia school. *Program availability:* Part-time. Terminal master's awarded for partial completion of doctoral program. *Degree requirements:* For master's, variable foreign language requirement, comprehensive exam (for some programs), thesis (for some programs); for doctorate, variable foreign language requirement, comprehensive exam (for some programs), thesis/dissertation. *Entrance requirements:* For master's and doctorate, GRE General Test, GRE Subject Test (for some programs). Additional exam requirements/recommendations for international students: Required—TOEFL, IELTS. Electronic applications accepted. *Expenses: Tuition:* Full-time $44,864; part-time $1704 per credit. *Required fees:* $2370 per semester. One-time fee: $105.

Concordia University, School of Graduate Studies, Faculty of Arts and Science, Department of Études Françaises, Montréal, QC H3G 1M8, Canada. Offers Anglais-Français en langue et techniques de localization (Certificate); littératures Francophones et résonances médiatiques (MA); translation (Diploma); translation studies (MA). *Degree requirements:* For other advanced degree, one foreign language.

East Tennessee State University, School of Graduate Studies, College of Arts and Sciences, Department of Literature and Language, Johnson City, TN 37614. Offers healthcare translation and interpreting (Postbaccalaureate Certificate); literature (MA); teaching English to speakers of other languages (Postbaccalaureate Certificate). *Program availability:* Part-time, evening/weekend. *Degree requirements:* For master's, comprehensive exam, thesis optional; for Postbaccalaureate Certificate, one foreign language. *Entrance requirements:* For master's, GRE General Test, minimum undergraduate GPA of 3.0 in English, writing sample, three letters of recommendation; for Postbaccalaureate Certificate, GRE General Test, speaking and listening assessment, resume, three letters of recommendation, two years of coursework or basic

proficiency in a foreign language. Additional exam requirements/recommendations for international students: Required—TOEFL (minimum score 550 paper-based; 79 iBT). *Application deadline:* For fall admission, 6/1 for domestic students, 4/29 for international students; for spring admission, 11/1 for domestic students, 9/29 for international students. Application fee: $55 ($65 for international students). Electronic applications accepted. *Financial support:* Research assistantships with full tuition reimbursements, teaching assistantships with full tuition reimbursements, career-related internships or fieldwork, institutionally sponsored loans, scholarships/grants, and unspecified assistantships available. Financial award application deadline: 7/1; financial award applicants required to submit FAFSA. *Faculty research:* Linguistics and dialectology, English education, critical literary theory, literary biography, environmental literature, modern and ancient languages. *Unit head:* Dr. Katherine Weiss, Chair, 423-439-4347, Fax: 423-439-7193, E-mail: weisk01@etsu.edu. *Application contact:* Dr. Michael A. Cody, Assistant Chair for Graduate Studies, 423-439-6676, Fax: 423-439-5624, E-mail: codym@etsu.edu.
Website: http://www.etsu.edu/cas/litlang/

Gallaudet University, The Graduate School, Washington, DC 20002-3625. Offers American Sign Language/English bilingual early childhood deaf education: birth to 5 (Certificate); audiology (Au D); clinical psychology (PhD); deaf and hard of hearing infants, toddlers, and their families (Certificate); deaf education (MA, Ed S); deaf history (Certificate); deaf studies (Certificate); educating deaf students with disabilities (Certificate); education: teacher preparation (MA), including deaf education, early childhood education and deaf education, elementary education and deaf education, secondary education and deaf education; educational neuroscience (PhD); hearing, speech and language sciences (MS, PhD); international development (MA); interpretation (MA, PhD), including combined interpreting practice and research (MA), interpreting research (MA); linguistics (MA, PhD); mental health counseling (MA); peer mentoring (Certificate); public administration (MPA); school counseling (MA); school psychology (Psy S); sign language teaching (MA); social work (MSW); speech-language pathology (MS). *Program availability:* Part-time. Terminal master's awarded for partial completion of doctoral program. *Degree requirements:* For master's, comprehensive exam (for some programs), thesis optional; for doctorate, comprehensive exam, thesis/dissertation. *Entrance requirements:* For master's and doctorate, GRE General Test or MAT, letters of recommendation, interviews, goals statement, American Sign Language proficiency interview, written English competency. Additional exam requirements/recommendations for international students: Required—TOEFL. Electronic applications accepted. *Faculty research:* Signing math dictionaries, telecommunications access, cancer genetics, linguistics, visual language and visual learning, integrated quantum materials, deaf legal discourse, advance recruitment and retention in geosciences.

Georgia State University, College of Arts and Sciences, Department of World Languages and Cultures, Program in Translation and Interpretation, Atlanta, GA 30302-3083. Offers interpretation (Certificate), including Spanish; translation (Certificate), including French, German, Spanish. *Program availability:* Part-time. *Entrance requirements:* For degree, entrance examination involving translating one passage from English to the target language and one passage from the target language to English, 3 letters of recommendation, resume/curriculum vitae, official transcripts. Additional exam requirements/recommendations for international students: Required—TOEFL (minimum score 79 iBT). Application fee: $50. Electronic applications accepted. *Expenses:* Tuition, state resident: full-time $7020. Tuition, nonresident: full-time $22,518. *Required fees:* $2128. Tuition and fees vary according to degree level and program. *Faculty research:* Romance linguistics and translation; theory and practice of translation; medical and legal interpretation. *Unit head:* Dr. Fernando Reati, Chair, 404-413-5984, Fax: 404-413-5982, E-mail: freati@gsu.edu. *Application contact:* Lita Malveaux, Administrative Academic Specialist, 404-413-5046, Fax: 404-413-5036, E-mail: lmalveaux@gsu.edu.
Website: http://wlc.gsu.edu/home/graduate/graduate-certificate/

Kent State University, College of Arts and Sciences, Department of Modern and Classical Language Studies, Kent, OH 44242-0001. Offers French (MA), including applied linguistics and pedagogy, literature; German (MA), including applied linguistics and pedagogy, literature; Latin (MA), including applied linguistics and pedagogy, literature; Spanish (MA), including applied linguistics and pedagogy, literature; translation (MA), including Arabic, French, German, Japanese, Russian, Spanish; translation studies (PhD); MA/MBA. *Program availability:* Part-time. *Faculty:* 21 full-time (13 women), 5 part-time/adjunct (3 women). *Students:* 78 full-time (50 women), 20 part-time (13 women); includes 18 minority (3 Black or African American, non-Hispanic/Latino; 1 Asian, non-Hispanic/Latino; 9 Hispanic/Latino; 5 Two or more races, non-Hispanic/Latino), 44 international. Average age 31. 95 applicants, 55% accepted, 27 enrolled. In 2017, 30 master's awarded. *Degree requirements:* For master's, variable foreign language requirement, comprehensive exam (for some programs), thesis (for some programs); for doctorate, variable foreign language requirement, comprehensive exam, thesis/dissertation. *Entrance requirements:* For master's, transcripts, goal statement, 3 letters of recommendation, CD/MP3 with oral sample of first and second languages, writing sample of second language; for doctorate, transcripts; MA in translation, a foreign language, or similar field; proficiency in a foreign language; minimum GPA of 3.5 from MA; goal statement; 3 letters of recommendation; essay or writing sample. Additional exam requirements/recommendations for international students: Required—TOEFL (minimum score 550 paper-based, 79 iBT), Michigan English Language Assessment Battery (minimum score 77), IELTS (minimum score 6.5) or PTE (minimum score 58). *Application deadline:* For fall admission, 2/1 for domestic and international students. Applications are processed on a rolling basis. Application fee: $45 ($70 for international students). Electronic applications accepted. *Expenses:* Tuition, state resident: full-time $11,310; part-time $515 per credit hour. Tuition, nonresident: full-time $20,396; part-time $928 per credit hour. International tuition: $18,544 full-time. *Financial support:* Fellowships with full tuition reimbursements, teaching assistantships with full tuition reimbursements, and unspecified assistantships available. Financial award application deadline: 2/1. *Unit head:* Dr. Keiran Dunne, Professor of French Translation/Chair, 330-672-2150, E-mail: kdunne@kent.edu. *Application contact:* Said Shiyab, Professor of Translation Studies/Graduate Coordinator, 330-672-1864, E-mail: sshiyab@kent.edu.
Website: http://www.kent.edu/mcls/

La Salle University, School of Arts and Sciences, Hispanic Institute, Philadelphia, PA 19141-1199. Offers bilingual/bicultural studies (MA); ESL program specialist (Certificate); interpretation: English/Spanish-Spanish/English (Certificate); teaching English to speakers of other languages (MA); translation and interpretation (MA); translation: English/Spanish-Spanish/English (Certificate). *Program availability:* Part-time, evening/weekend. *Faculty:* 2 full-time (1 woman), 5 part-time/adjunct (1 woman). *Students:* 1 (woman) full-time, 37 part-time (26 women); includes 21 minority (7 Black or African American, non-Hispanic/Latino; 1 American Indian or Alaska Native, non-Hispanic/Latino; 1 Asian, non-Hispanic/Latino; 10 Hispanic/Latino; 2 Two or more races, non-Hispanic/Latino), 2 international. Average age 33. 24 applicants, 79% accepted, 11 enrolled. In 2017, 4 master's, 1 other advanced degree awarded. *Degree requirements:* For master's, one foreign language, project or thesis. *Entrance requirements:* For master's, GRE, MAT, or GMAT, professional resume; two letters of recommendation; for Certificate, GRE, MAT, or GMAT, professional resume; two letters of recommendation;

evidence of an advanced level in Spanish. Additional exam requirements/recommendations for international students: Required—TOEFL. *Application deadline:* For fall admission, 8/15 priority date for domestic students, 7/15 for international students; for spring admission, 12/15 priority date for domestic students, 11/15 for international students; for summer admission, 4/15 priority date for domestic students, 3/15 for international students. Applications are processed on a rolling basis. Application fee: $35. Electronic applications accepted. Application fee is waived when completed online. *Expenses:* Contact institution. *Financial support:* In 2017–18, 10 students received support. Scholarships/grants available. Support available to part-time students. Financial award application deadline: 8/31; financial award applicants required to submit FAFSA. *Faculty research:* Puerto Rican literature, cross-cultural communication, English as a second language methodology, Spanish language. *Unit head:* Guadalupe Da Costa Montesinos, Director, 215-951-1209, Fax: 215-991-3506, E-mail: montesin@lasalle.edu. *Application contact:* Elizabeth Heenan, Director, Graduate and Adult Enrollment, 215-951-1100, Fax: 215-951-1462, E-mail: heenan@lasalle.edu.
Website: http://www.lasalle.edu/hispanic-institute/

London Metropolitan University, Graduate Programs, London, United Kingdom. Offers applied psychology (M Sc); architecture (MA); biomedical science (M Sc); blood science (M Sc); cancer pharmacology (M Sc); computer networking and cyber security (M Sc); computing and information systems (M Sc); conference interpreting (MA); counter-terrorism studies (M Sc); creative, digital and professional writing (MA); crime, violence and prevention (M Sc); criminology (M Sc); curating contemporary art (MA); data analytics (M Sc); digital media (MA); early childhood studies (MA); education (MA, Ed D); financial services law, regulation and compliance (LL M); food science (M Sc); forensic psychology (M Sc); health and social care management and policy (M Sc); human nutrition (M Sc); human resource management (MA); human rights and international conflict (MA); information technology (M Sc); intelligence and security studies (M Sc); international oil, gas and energy law (LL M); international relations (MA); interpreting (MA); learning and teaching in higher education (MA); legal practice (LL M); media and entertainment law (LL M); organizational and consumer psychology (M Sc); psychological therapy (M Sc); psychology of mental health (M Sc); public health (M Sc); public policy and management (MPA); security studies (M Sc); social work (M Sc); spatial planning and urban design (MA); sports therapy (M Sc); supporting older children and young people with dyslexia (MA); teaching languages (MA), including Arabic, English; translation (MA); woman and child abuse (MA).

Middlebury Institute of International Studies at Monterey, Graduate School of Translation, Interpretation and Language Education, Program in Translation and Interpretation, Monterey, CA 93940-2691. Offers conference interpretation (MA); translation (MA); translation and interpretation (MA); translation and localization management (MA). *Degree requirements:* For master's, one foreign language, thesis or alternative, exams. *Entrance requirements:* For master's, minimum GPA of 3.0, proficiency in a foreign language. Additional exam requirements/recommendations for international students: Required—TOEFL (minimum score 600 paper-based; 100 iBT). Electronic applications accepted. *Faculty research:* Assessment and testing in translation and interpretation, translation and interpretation pedagogy and curricula, integration of translation technology, language policy and planning.

Mills College, Graduate Studies, Department of English, Oakland, CA 94613-1000. Offers book art and creative writing (MFA); literature (MA); poetry (MFA); prose (MFA); Spanish creative writing (Certificate); translation (MFA). *Program availability:* Part-time. *Faculty:* 6 full-time (5 women), 4 part-time/adjunct (all women). *Students:* 36 full-time (29 women), 21 part-time (14 women); includes 26 minority (9 Black or African American, non-Hispanic/Latino; 3 Asian, non-Hispanic/Latino; 9 Hispanic/Latino; 5 Two or more races, non-Hispanic/Latino). Average age 32. 100 applicants, 95% accepted, 27 enrolled. In 2017, 18 master's awarded. *Degree requirements:* For master's, comprehensive exam, thesis. *Entrance requirements:* For master's, 15-20 page writing sample. Additional exam requirements/recommendations for international students: Required—TOEFL (minimum score 600 paper-based; 100 iBT), IELTS (minimum score 7). *Application deadline:* For fall admission, 12/15 priority date for domestic students, 12/15 for international students. Applications are processed on a rolling basis. Application fee: $50. Electronic applications accepted. *Expenses:* Contact institution. *Financial support:* In 2017–18, 23 students received support, including 23 fellowships with partial tuition reimbursements available (averaging $6,327 per year), 21 teaching assistantships with tuition reimbursements available; research assistantships and scholarships/grants also available. Support available to part-time students. Financial award application deadline: 2/1; financial award applicants required to submit FAFSA. *Faculty research:* Creative writing, African-American literature, Victorian women writers, theories of sexuality, Shakespeare. *Unit head:* Dr. Thomas Strychacz, Chair of the English Department, 510-430-2208, E-mail: toms@mills.edu. *Application contact:* Robynne Lofton, Director of Admissions, 510-430-3295, Fax: 510-430-2159, E-mail: grad-admission@mills.edu.
Website: http://www.mills.edu/english/

Montclair State University, The Graduate School, College of Humanities and Social Sciences, Translation and Interpreting in Spanish Certificate Program, Montclair, NJ 07043-1624. Offers Certificate.

New York University, School of Professional Studies, Center for Applied Liberal Arts, Division of Foreign Languages, Translation, and Interpreting, New York, NY 10012-1019. Offers translation (MS), including Chinese to English, English to Spanish, French to English, Spanish to English. *Program availability:* Part-time, evening/weekend, blended/hybrid learning. *Students:* 31 full-time (29 women), 38 part-time (29 women); includes 26 minority (4 Black or African American, non-Hispanic/Latino; 5 Asian, non-Hispanic/Latino; 16 Hispanic/Latino; 1 Two or more races, non-Hispanic/Latino), 20 international. Average age 31. 42 applicants, 71% accepted, 16 enrolled. In 2017, 40 master's awarded. *Degree requirements:* For master's, thesis. *Entrance requirements:* For master's, GRE or GMAT (only upon request), bachelor's degree, resume with relevant professional work, internship or volunteer experience, two letters of recommendation, statement of purpose. Additional exam requirements/recommendations for international students: Required—TOEFL (minimum score 600 paper-based; 100 iBT), IELTS (minimum score 7). *Application deadline:* For fall admission, 2/1 priority date for domestic and international students; for spring admission, 10/15 priority date for domestic students, 8/15 priority date for international students. Applications are processed on a rolling basis. Application fee: $150. Electronic applications accepted. *Expenses:* $20,244 per term. *Financial support:* Fellowships, career-related internships or fieldwork, Federal Work-Study, scholarships/grants, and health care benefits available. Support available to part-time students. Financial award application deadline: 6/30; financial award applicants required to submit FAFSA. *Unit head:* Billie Gastic, Associate Dean, 212-998-7272. *Application contact:* Office of Admissions, 212-998-7100, E-mail: sps.gradadmissions@nyu.edu.
Website: http://www.sps.nyu.edu/content/scps/academics/departments/foreign-languages.html

Rochester Institute of Technology, Graduate Enrollment Services, National Technical Institute for the Deaf, American Sign Language and Interpreting Education Department, MS Program in Health Care Interpretation, Rochester, NY 14623-5603. Offers MS. Program offered in collaboration with College of Health Sciences and Technology.

Translation and Interpretation

Program availability: Part-time, blended/hybrid learning. *Students:* 5 full-time (4 women), 10 part-time (all women); includes 3 minority (2 Hispanic/Latino; 1 Two or more races, non-Hispanic/Latino). Average age 40. *Entrance requirements:* For master's, ASL interpretation video sample, ASL/English certification or state licensure, two recommendation letters, audio gram (for deaf or hard-of-hearing applicants), personal statement, transcript with minimum GPA of 3.0. *Application deadline:* For summer admission, 1/15 priority date for domestic and international students. Applications are processed on a rolling basis. Application fee: $65. Electronic applications accepted. *Expenses:* $1,815 per credit hour. *Financial support:* Research assistantships with partial tuition reimbursements, teaching assistantships with partial tuition reimbursements, career-related internships or fieldwork, scholarships/grants, and unspecified assistantships available. Support available to part-time students. Financial award applicants required to submit FAFSA. *Faculty research:* Interpreter's ethics, decision-making in community interpreting, healthcare interpreting, ethical reasoning skills of interpreters, reflective practice of supervision with interpreters. *Unit head:* Kathleen Miraglia, Program Director, 585-475-5441, E-mail: kamnss@rit.edu. *Application contact:* Diane Ellison, Senior Associate Vice President, Graduate Enrollment Services, 585-475-2229, Fax: 585-475-7164, E-mail: gradinfo@rit.edu.
Website: http://www.ntid.rit.edu/aslie/mshci/overview

Rutgers University–New Brunswick, Graduate School-New Brunswick, Program in Spanish, Piscataway, NJ 08854-8097. Offers bilingualism and second language acquisition (MA, PhD); Spanish (MA, MAT, PhD); Spanish literature (MA, PhD); translation (MA). *Program availability:* Part-time. *Degree requirements:* For master's, comprehensive exam (for some programs), thesis (for some programs); for doctorate, 2 foreign languages, comprehensive exam, thesis/dissertation. *Entrance requirements:* For master's and doctorate, GRE General Test. Additional exam requirements/recommendations for international students: Required—TOEFL. Electronic applications accepted. *Faculty research:* Hispanic literature, Luso-Brazilian literature, Spanish linguistics, Spanish translation.

Texas A&M International University, Office of Graduate Studies and Research, College of Arts and Sciences, Department of Humanities, Laredo, TX 78041. Offers English (MA); Hispanic studies (PhD); history and political thought (MA); language, literature and translation (MA). *Degree requirements:* For master's, comprehensive exam (for some programs), thesis (for some programs). *Entrance requirements:* For master's, GRE General Test. Additional exam requirements/recommendations for international students: Required—TOEFL (minimum score 550 paper-based; 79 iBT).

Universidad Autonoma de Guadalajara, Graduate Programs, Guadalajara, Mexico. Offers administrative law and justice (LL M); advertising and corporate communications (MA); architecture (M Arch); business (MBA); computational science (MCC); education (Ed M, Ed D); English-Spanish translation (MA); entrepreneurship and management (MBA); integrated management of digital animation (MA); international business (MIB); international corporate law (LL M); internet technologies (MS); manufacturing systems (MMS); occupational health (MS); philosophy (MA, PhD); power electronics (MS); quality systems (MQS); renewable energy (MS); social evaluation of projects (MBA); strategic market research (MBA); tax law (MA); teaching mathematics (MA).

Université de Montréal, Faculty of Arts and Sciences, Department of Linguistics and Translation, Montréal, QC H3C 3J7, Canada. Offers linguistics (MA, PhD); translation (MA, PhD, DESS). *Degree requirements:* For master's, thesis, general exam; for doctorate, thesis/dissertation, general exam. Electronic applications accepted.

Université Laval, Faculty of Letters, Department of Languages, Linguistics and Translations, Programs in Terminology and Translation, Québec, QC G1K 7P4, Canada. Offers MA, Diploma. *Program availability:* Part-time. *Degree requirements:* For master's, thesis (for some programs). *Entrance requirements:* For master's and Diploma, knowledge of French and English. Electronic applications accepted.

University of California, Santa Barbara, Graduate Division, College of Letters and Sciences, Division of Humanities and Fine Arts, Department of East Asian Languages and Cultural Studies, Santa Barbara, CA 93106-7075. Offers applied linguistics (PhD); East Asian languages and cultural studies (MA); translation studies (PhD). *Degree requirements:* For master's, one foreign language, comprehensive exam (for some programs), thesis (for some programs); for doctorate, 2 foreign languages, thesis/dissertation, methodology. *Entrance requirements:* For master's and doctorate, GRE General Test. Additional exam requirements/recommendations for international students: Required—TOEFL (minimum score 550 paper-based; 80 iBT), IELTS (minimum score 7). Electronic applications accepted. *Faculty research:* Chinese literature, Chinese film, Japanese society, Japanese literature, East Asian cultural studies.

University of California, Santa Barbara, Graduate Division, College of Letters and Sciences, Division of Humanities and Fine Arts, Department of English, Santa Barbara, CA 93106-3170. Offers English (PhD), including environment and society, European medieval studies, feminist studies, global studies, technology and society, translation studies, writing studies; MA/PhD. Terminal master's awarded for partial completion of doctoral program. *Degree requirements:* For doctorate, one foreign language, comprehensive exam, thesis/dissertation. *Entrance requirements:* For doctorate, GRE General Test, GRE Subject Test (English literature). Additional exam requirements/recommendations for international students: Required—TOEFL (minimum score 550 paper-based; 80 iBT), IELTS (minimum score 7). Electronic applications accepted. *Faculty research:* Medieval, Romantic and Victorian studies; gender studies and feminist theory; literature and the mind; American literature; literature and new media/information culture.

University of California, Santa Barbara, Graduate Division, College of Letters and Sciences, Division of Humanities and Fine Arts, Department of Religious Studies, Santa Barbara, CA 93106-3130. Offers ancient Mediterranean studies (PhD); cognitive science (PhD); European medieval studies (PhD); feminist studies (PhD); global studies (PhD); religious studies (MA, PhD); translation studies (PhD); MA/PhD. Terminal master's awarded for partial completion of doctoral program. *Degree requirements:* For master's, one foreign language, comprehensive exam (for some programs), thesis (for some programs); for doctorate, 2 foreign languages, thesis/dissertation, methodology. *Entrance requirements:* For master's and doctorate, GRE General Test. Additional exam requirements/recommendations for international students: Required—TOEFL (minimum score 550 paper-based; 80 iBT), IELTS (minimum score 7). Electronic applications accepted. *Faculty research:* Area studies; religious traditions; theory and method in the study of religion; religion, culture, and politics; spirituality and religious experience.

University of California, Santa Barbara, Graduate Division, College of Letters and Sciences, Division of Humanities and Fine Arts, Program in Comparative Literature, Santa Barbara, CA 93106-4130. Offers comparative literature (PhD); East Asian literatures (PhD); feminist studies (PhD); French (PhD); global studies (PhD); translation studies (PhD); MA/PhD. *Degree requirements:* For doctorate, 2 foreign languages, comprehensive exam, thesis/dissertation. *Entrance requirements:* For doctorate, GRE. Additional exam requirements/recommendations for international students: Required—TOEFL (minimum score 550 paper-based; 80 iBT), IELTS (minimum score 7). Electronic applications accepted. *Faculty research:* Comparative literary studies in global context, critical theory, translation studies, media technological studies, trauma studies.

University of Delaware, College of Arts and Sciences, Department of Foreign Languages and Literatures, Newark, DE 19716. Offers foreign languages and literatures (MA), including French, German, Spanish; foreign languages pedagogy (MA), including French, German, Spanish; technical Chinese translation (MA). *Degree requirements:* For master's, one foreign language, comprehensive exam, thesis optional. *Entrance requirements:* For master's, GRE General Test, letters of recommendation, writing sample. Additional exam requirements/recommendations for international students: Required—TOEFL. Electronic applications accepted. *Faculty research:* Medieval to Modern French and Spanish literature, twentieth-century German, French, Spanish literature by women, computer-assisted instruction.

University of Denver, University College, Denver, CO 80208. Offers arts and culture (MA, Certificate); communication management (MS, Certificate), including translation studies (Certificate), world history and culture (Certificate); environmental policy and management (MS); geographic information systems (MS); global affairs (MA, Certificate), including human capital in organizations (Certificate), philanthropic leadership (Certificate), project management (Certificate), strategic innovation and change (Certificate); healthcare leadership (MS); information communications and technology (MS); leadership and organizations (MS); professional creative writing (MA, Certificate), including emergency planning and response (Certificate), organizational security (Certificate); security management (MS, Certificate); strategic human resources (Certificate). *Program availability:* Part-time, evening/weekend, online learning. *Faculty:* 118 part-time/adjunct (62 women). *Students:* 56 full-time (32 women), 1,287 part-time (707 women); includes 330 minority (99 Black or African American, non-Hispanic/Latino; 7 American Indian or Alaska Native, non-Hispanic/Latino; 43 Asian, non-Hispanic/Latino; 141 Hispanic/Latino; 3 Native Hawaiian or other Pacific Islander, non-Hispanic/Latino; 37 Two or more races, non-Hispanic/Latino), 84 international. Average age 34. 783 applicants, 86% accepted, 420 enrolled. In 2017, 461 master's, 173 other advanced degrees awarded. *Degree requirements:* For master's, capstone project. *Entrance requirements:* For master's, transcripts, two letters of recommendation, personal statement, resume. Additional exam requirements/recommendations for international students: Required—TOEFL (minimum score 550 paper-based; 80 iBT). *Application deadline:* For fall admission, 6/21 priority date for domestic students, 5/1 priority date for international students; for winter admission, 9/14 priority date for domestic students, 9/19 priority date for international students; for spring admission, 1/11 priority date for domestic students, 12/12 priority date for international students; for summer admission, 3/29 priority date for domestic students, 3/6 priority date for international students. Applications are processed on a rolling basis. Application fee: $75. Electronic applications accepted. *Expenses:* $7,968 per year half-time. *Financial support:* In 2017–18, 29 students received support. Teaching assistantships available. Financial award applicants required to submit FAFSA. *Unit head:* Dr. Michael McGuire, Dean, 303-871-3518, Fax: 303-871-3303, E-mail: mmcguire@du.edu. *Application contact:* Information Contact, 303-871-2291, E-mail: ucoladm@du.edu.
Website: http://universitycollege.du.edu/

University of Illinois at Urbana–Champaign, Graduate College, College of Liberal Arts and Sciences, School of Literatures, Cultures and Linguistics, Center for Translation Studies, Champaign, IL 61820. Offers translation and interpreting (MA). *Program availability:* Part-time, online learning. *Entrance requirements:* For master's, BA or BS in languages, linguistics, international studies, area studies, or a related field; three letters of recommendation; resume or curriculum vitae; official transcripts.

The University of Manchester, School of Languages, Linguistics and Cultures, Manchester, United Kingdom. Offers Arab world studies (PhD); Chinese studies (M Phil, PhD); East Asian studies (M Phil, PhD); English language (PhD); French studies (M Phil, PhD); German studies (M Phil, PhD); interpreting studies (PhD); Italian studies (M Phil, PhD); Japanese studies (M Phil, PhD); Latin American cultural studies (M Phil, PhD); linguistics (M Phil, PhD); Middle Eastern studies (M Phil, PhD); Polish studies (M Phil, PhD); Portuguese studies (M Phil, PhD); Russian studies (M Phil, PhD); Spanish studies (M Phil, PhD); translation and intercultural studies (M Phil, PhD).

University of Nevada, Las Vegas, Graduate College, College of Liberal Arts, Department of World Languages and Cultures, Las Vegas, NV 89154-5047. Offers Hispanic studies (MA); Spanish translation (Certificate). *Program availability:* Part-time. *Faculty:* 3 full-time (2 women), 1 (woman) part-time/adjunct. *Students:* 4 full-time (3 women), 8 part-time (5 women); includes 9 minority (all Hispanic/Latino), 1 international. Average age 35. 6 applicants, 50% accepted, 3 enrolled. In 2017, 1 master's awarded. *Degree requirements:* For master's, one foreign language, comprehensive exam, final research project. *Entrance requirements:* For master's, minimum GPA of 3.0; 2 letters of recommendation. Additional exam requirements/recommendations for international students: Required—TOEFL (minimum score 550 paper-based; 80 iBT), IELTS (minimum score 7). *Application deadline:* For fall admission, 5/1 for domestic students; for spring admission, 11/15 for domestic students. Application fee: $60 ($95 for international students). Electronic applications accepted. *Expenses:* Contact institution. *Financial support:* In 2017–18, 4 students received support, including 4 teaching assistantships with full and partial tuition reimbursements available (averaging $11,250 per year); institutionally sponsored loans, scholarships/grants, health care benefits, and unspecified assistantships also available. Financial award application deadline: 3/15; financial award applicants required to submit FAFSA. *Faculty research:* Spanish Golden Age poetry, prose and theater; Miguel de Cervantes; history of ideas in creative letters, historical linguistics (French/Spanish), Spanish sociolinguistics, second language acquisition, women narrators of Mexico and Spain, translation studies, Mexican film and culture. *Unit head:* Dr. Susan Byrne, Chair, 702-895-3464, Fax: 702-895-1226, E-mail: susan.byrne@unlv.edu. *Application contact:* Dr. Margarita Jara, Graduate Coordinator, 702-895-1690, Fax: 702-895-1226, E-mail: margarita.jara@unlv.edu.
Website: http://liberalarts.unlv.edu/Foreign_Languages/graduates.html

University of Northern Colorado, Graduate School, College of Education and Behavioral Sciences, Department of American Sign Language and Interpreting Studies, Greeley, CO 80639. Offers teaching American Sign Language (MA).

University of North Florida, College of Education and Human Services, Department of Exceptional, Deaf, and Interpreter Education, Jacksonville, FL 32224. Offers American Sign Language (MS); American Sign Language/English interpreting (M Ed); applied behavior analysis (M Ed); autism (M Ed); deaf education (M Ed); disability services (M Ed); exceptional student education (M Ed). *Accreditation:* NCATE. *Program availability:* Part-time, evening/weekend. *Entrance requirements:* For master's, GRE General Test, minimum GPA of 3.0 in last 60 hours, interview, 3 letters of recommendation. Additional exam requirements/recommendations for international students: Required—TOEFL (minimum score 500 paper-based). Electronic applications accepted. *Faculty research:* Transportation, energy, communications, healthcare, nano-science and engineering, unmanned aircraft systems, biomedical applications.

University of Ottawa, Faculty of Graduate and Postdoctoral Studies, Faculty of Arts, Institute of Canadian Studies, Ottawa, ON K1N 6N5, Canada. Offers economics (PhD); English (PhD); geography (PhD); history (PhD); lettres Françaises (PhD); linguistics (PhD); philosophy (PhD); political science (PhD); psychology (PhD); religious studies (PhD); translation studies (PhD). *Degree requirements:* For doctorate, comprehensive exam, thesis/dissertation.

University of Ottawa, Faculty of Graduate and Postdoctoral Studies, Faculty of Arts, School of Translation and Interpretation, Ottawa, ON K1N 6N5, Canada. Offers interpreting (MA); Spanish translation (MA); translation (MA); translation studies (PhD). *Degree requirements:* For master's, one foreign language, thesis or alternative, research paper; for doctorate, thesis/dissertation, doctoral exam. *Entrance requirements:* For master's, school-administered exam, honors degree or equivalent, minimum B average; for doctorate, master's degree, minimum B+ average. Electronic applications accepted. *Faculty research:* Theory of translation, Spanish translation, conference interpreting, legal translation, translation-oriented lexicology and terminology.

University of Puerto Rico–Río Piedras, College of Humanities, Program in Translation, San Juan, PR 00931-3300. Offers MA, Certificate. *Program availability:* Part-time, evening/weekend. *Degree requirements:* For master's, 2 foreign languages, comprehensive exam, thesis. *Entrance requirements:* For master's, PAEG, minimum GPA of 3.0, graduate-level knowledge of 2 languages (English, French, or Spanish), letter of recommendation.

University of Rochester, School of Arts and Sciences, Interdisciplinary Program in Literary Translation Studies, Rochester, NY 14627. Offers MA, AC. *Students:* 2 full-time (1 woman). Average age 23. 11 applicants, 82% accepted, 2 enrolled. In 2017, 4 master's awarded. Terminal master's awarded for partial completion of doctoral program. *Degree requirements:* For master's, essay. *Entrance requirements:* For master's, official transcripts, three letters of recommendation, personal statement, translation sample and copies of corresponding pages from source text. *Application deadline:* For fall admission, 2/1 for domestic and international students. Application fee: $60. Electronic applications accepted. *Expenses:* $1,596 per credit hour. *Financial support:* Tuition awards available. *Unit head:* Joanna Scott, Program Director/Professor of English, 585-275-2784, E-mail: joanna.scott@rochester.edu. *Application contact:* Jennifer Sherwood, Assistant Director of Multidisciplinary Studies Center, 585-276-5305, E-mail: jennifer.sherwood@rochester.edu.
Website: http://www.sas.rochester.edu/lts/graduate/index.html

The University of Texas Rio Grande Valley, College of Liberal Arts, Program in Interdisciplinary Studies, Edinburg, TX 78539. Offers interdisciplinary studies (MAIS, MSIS); Spanish translation and interpreting (MA). *Program availability:* Part-time, evening/weekend. *Faculty:* 3 full-time (2 women). *Students:* 17 full-time (13 women), 41 part-time (28 women); includes 47 minority (1 Asian, non-Hispanic/Latino; 46 Hispanic/Latino), 2 international. Average age 36. 23 applicants, 100% accepted, 15 enrolled. In 2017, 25 master's awarded. *Degree requirements:* For master's, comprehensive exam, thesis or alternative. *Entrance requirements:* For master's, GRE General Test, minimum GPA of 3.0. Additional exam requirements/recommendations for international students: Required—TOEFL or IELTS. Application fee: $50 ($100 for international students). *Expenses:* Tuition, state resident: full-time $5550; part-time $417 per credit hour.

Tuition, nonresident: full-time $13,020; part-time $832 per credit hour. *Required fees:* $1169. *Financial support:* Application deadline: 6/1. *Unit head:* Russel Skowronek, Associate Dean, E-mail: russell.skowronek@utrgv.edu.

University of Wisconsin–Milwaukee, Graduate School, College of Letters and Science, Department of Foreign Languages and Literature, Milwaukee, WI 53201-0413. Offers foreign languages and literature (MA), including classic Greek, classics, comparative literature, French/Francophone language, literature, and culture, German language, literature, and culture, interpreting, Latin, linguistics, Spanish language, literature, and culture, translation; interpreting (Graduate Certificate); language, literature, and translation (MA, MALLT); translation (Graduate Certificate). *Program availability:* Part-time. *Students:* 11 full-time (6 women), 40 part-time (29 women); includes 10 minority (2 Black or African American, non-Hispanic/Latino; 3 Hispanic/Latino; 5 Two or more races, non-Hispanic/Latino), 4 international. Average age 35. 37 applicants, 68% accepted, 20 enrolled. In 2017, 5 master's awarded. *Degree requirements:* For master's, 2 foreign languages, thesis or alternative. *Entrance requirements:* Additional exam requirements/recommendations for international students: Required—TOEFL (minimum score 550 paper-based; 79 iBT), IELTS (minimum score 6.5). *Application deadline:* For fall admission, 1/1 priority date for domestic students; for spring admission, 9/1 for domestic students. Application fee: $56 ($96 for international students). Electronic applications accepted. *Financial support:* Fellowships, research assistantships, teaching assistantships, career-related internships or fieldwork, health care benefits, unspecified assistantships, and project assistantships available. Support available to part-time students. Financial award application deadline: 4/15; financial award applicants required to submit FAFSA. *Unit head:* Kevin Muse, Department Chair, 414-229-5213, E-mail: kmuse@uwm.edu. *Application contact:* General Information Contact, 414-229-4982, Fax: 414-229-6967, E-mail: gradschool@uwm.edu.
Website: http://uwm.edu/foreign-languages-literature/

Wesley Biblical Seminary, Graduate Programs, Jackson, MS 39206. Offers apologetics (MA); Biblical languages (M Div); Biblical literature (MA); Christian studies (MA); context and mission (M Div); honors research (M Div); interpretation (M Div); ministry (M Div); spiritual formation (M Div); teaching (M Div); theology (MA). *Accreditation:* ATS. *Program availability:* Part-time. *Degree requirements:* For master's, thesis. *Entrance requirements:* Additional exam requirements/recommendations for international students: Required—TOEFL. Electronic applications accepted. *Faculty research:* Patristics, missiology, culture, hermeneutics.

York University, Faculty of Graduate Studies, Glendon Campus, Program in Translation, Toronto, ON M3J 1P3, Canada. Offers MA. *Degree requirements:* For master's, thesis or alternative. *Entrance requirements:* For master's, professional translating experience. Electronic applications accepted.

Section 11
Philosophy and Ethics

This section contains a directory of institutions offering graduate work in philosophy and ethics. Additional information about programs listed in the directory may be obtained by writing directly to the dean of a graduate school or chair of a department at the address given in the directory.

For programs offering related work, see also in this book *Area and Cultural Studies, History, Humanities, Religious Studies,* and *Social Sciences.*

CONTENTS

Ethics

American University, College of Arts and Sciences, Department of Philosophy and Religion, Washington, DC 22016-8056. Offers ethics, peace, and global affairs (MA); philosophy (MA). *Program availability:* Part-time, evening/weekend. *Faculty:* 14 full-time (8 women), 9 part-time/adjunct (5 women). *Students:* 9 full-time (2 women), 2 part-time (0 women). Average age 30. 31 applicants, 84% accepted, 10 enrolled. In 2017, 13 master's awarded. *Degree requirements:* For master's, comprehensive exam, thesis (for some programs). *Entrance requirements:* For master's, GRE, writing sample, statement of purpose, transcripts, 2 letters of recommendation, resume. Additional exam requirements/recommendations for international students: Required—TOEFL (minimum score 600 paper-based; 100 iBT). *Application deadline:* For fall admission, 2/1 priority date for domestic students; for spring admission, 11/1 priority date for domestic students. Application fee: $55. *Expenses:* Contact institution. *Financial support:* Research assistantships, teaching assistantships, scholarships/grants, and unspecified assistantships available. Financial award application deadline: 2/1; financial award applicants required to submit FAFSA. *Unit head:* Dr. Ellen Feder, Department Chair, 202-885-2931, Fax: 202-885-1094, E-mail: efeder@american.edu. *Application contact:* Jonathan Harper, Associate Director, Graduate Recruitment, 202-885-3622, E-mail: jharper@american.edu.
Website: http://www.american.edu/cas/philrel/

American University, School of International Service, Washington, DC 20016-8071. Offers comparative and regional studies (Certificate); cross-cultural communication (Certificate); development management (MS); ethics, peace, and global affairs (MA); European studies (Certificate); global environmental policy (MA, Certificate); global information technology (Certificate); global media (MA); international affairs (MA), including comparative and regional studies, global governance, politics, and security, international economic relations, natural resources and sustainable development, U.S. foreign policy and national security; international arts management (Certificate); international communication (MA, Certificate); international development (MA); international economic policy (Certificate); international economic relations (Certificate); international economics (MA); international peace and conflict resolution (MA, Certificate); international politics (Certificate); international relations (MA, PhD); international service (MIS); peacebuilding (Certificate); social enterprise (MA); the Americas (Certificate); United States foreign policy (Certificate); JD/MA. *Program availability:* Part-time, evening/weekend, 100% online. *Faculty:* 112 full-time (50 women), 46 part-time/adjunct (19 women). *Students:* 495 full-time (333 women), 518 part-time (276 women); includes 360 minority (95 Black or African American, non-Hispanic/Latino; 2 American Indian or Alaska Native, non-Hispanic/Latino; 60 Asian, non-Hispanic/Latino; 164 Hispanic/Latino; 39 Two or more races, non-Hispanic/Latino), 98 international. Average age 30. 1,559 applicants, 81% accepted, 356 enrolled. In 2017, 427 master's, 9 doctorates, 5 other advanced degrees awarded. Terminal master's awarded for partial completion of doctoral program. *Degree requirements:* For master's, one foreign language, comprehensive exam, thesis or alternative; for doctorate, one foreign language, comprehensive exam, thesis/dissertation. *Entrance requirements:* For master's, GRE; GMAT or GRE (for MA in social enterprise), transcripts, resume, 2 letters of recommendation, statement of purpose; for doctorate, GRE, transcripts, resume, 3 letters of recommendation, statement of purpose. Additional exam requirements/recommendations for international students: Required—TOEFL (minimum score 600 paper-based; 100 iBT). *Application deadline:* For fall admission, 1/15 for domestic students, 1/1 for international students; for spring admission, 10/1 for domestic students, 9/15 for international students. Application fee: $55. Electronic applications accepted. *Expenses:* Contact institution. *Financial support:* Research assistantships, teaching assistantships, institutionally sponsored loans, scholarships/grants, and unspecified assistantships available. Financial award application deadline: 1/15; financial award applicants required to submit FAFSA. *Application contact:* 202-885-1646, Fax: 202-885-1109, E-mail: sisgrad@american.edu.
Website: http://www.american.edu/sis/

Anabaptist Mennonite Biblical Seminary, Graduate and Professional Programs, Elkhart, IN 46517-1999. Offers chaplaincy (M Div); Christian faith formation (M Div); Christian formation (MA); Christian spiritual formation (Certificate); divinity (M Div); pastoral ministry (M Div); pastoral theology for financial professionals (Certificate); peace studies (M Div), including environmental sustainability leadership (M Div, MA); theological studies (M Div, Certificate), including peace studies (M Div), theology and ethics (M Div); theology and peace studies (MA), including conflict transformation, environmental sustainability leadership (M Div, MA), international development administration; United Methodist leadership (M Div). Conflict transformation and environmental sustainability leadership concentrations offered in cooperation with Goshen College; international development administration offered in cooperation with Andrews University. *Accreditation:* ACIPE; ATS. *Program availability:* Part-time, 100% online, blended/hybrid learning. *Degree requirements:* For master's, variable foreign language requirement, comprehensive exam (for some programs), thesis optional, senior interview. *Entrance requirements:* For master's, undergraduate degree transcripts, 3 letters of reference, essay. Additional exam requirements/recommendations for international students: Required—TOEFL (minimum score 90 iBT); Recommended—IELTS (minimum score 7). Electronic applications accepted. *Faculty research:* Biblical studies, peace studies, theology, ethics, creation care or environmental ethics, church history, church leadership, mission, ministry, preaching, pastoral leadership, social justice, peacemaking, Jesus Christ, Christianity, Anabaptism, Mennonite, Scripture, Bible, Old Testament, New Testament, spirituality, clinical pastoral education, teaching, faith formation, pastoral care, Koine Greek, Hebrew, Aramaic, Syriac, Ugaritic.

Arizona State University at the Tempe campus, College of Liberal Arts and Sciences, School of Life Sciences, Tempe, AZ 85287-4601. Offers animal behavior (PhD); applied ethics (biomedical and health ethics) (MA); biology (MS, PhD), including biology, biology and society, complex adaptive systems science (PhD), plant biology and conservation (MS); environmental life sciences (PhD); evolutionary biology (PhD); history and philosophy of science (PhD); human and social dimensions of science and technology (PhD); microbiology (PhD); molecular and cellular biology (PhD); neuroscience (PhD). Terminal master's awarded for partial completion of doctoral program. *Degree requirements:* For master's, thesis (for some programs), interactive Program of Study (iPOS) submitted before completing 50 percent of required credit hours; for doctorate, variable foreign language requirement, comprehensive exam, thesis/dissertation, interactive Program of Study (iPOS) submitted before completing 50 percent of required credit hours. *Entrance requirements:* For master's and doctorate, GRE, minimum GPA of 3.0 or equivalent in last 2 years of work leading to bachelor's degree. Additional exam requirements/recommendations for international students: Required—TOEFL (minimum score 600 paper-based; 100 iBT). Electronic applications accepted.

Arizona State University at the Tempe campus, New College of Interdisciplinary Arts and Sciences, Phoenix, AZ 85069-7100. Offers applied ethics and the professions (MA); communication studies (MA); interdisciplinary studies (MA); psychology (MS); social justice and human rights (MA). *Program availability:* Part-time, evening/weekend. *Degree requirements:* For master's, thesis (for some programs), interactive Program of Study (iPOS) submitted before completing 50 percent of required credit hours. *Entrance requirements:* For master's, GRE, minimum GPA of 3.0 or equivalent in last 2 years of work leading to bachelor's degree. Additional exam requirements/recommendations for international students: Required—TOEFL, IELTS, or PTE. Electronic applications accepted.

Arizona State University at the Tempe campus, School of Letters and Sciences, Program in Applied Ethics, Tempe, AZ 85287-4503. Offers biomedical and health ethics (MA); ethics and emerging technologies (MA); public administration, policy and ethics (MA); science, technology and ethics (MA). *Program availability:* Part-time, evening/weekend. *Degree requirements:* For master's, thesis or alternative, applied project, interactive Program of Study (iPOS) submitted before completing 50 percent of required credit hours. *Entrance requirements:* For master's, GRE (for ethics and emerging technologies concentration), minimum GPA of 3.0 or equivalent in last 2 years of work leading to bachelor's degree, 2 letters of recommendation, resume, personal statement of interest and qualifications. Additional exam requirements/recommendations for international students: Required—TOEFL (minimum score 550 paper-based; 80 iBT). Electronic applications accepted.

Azusa Pacific University, Azusa Pacific Seminary, Program in Theological Studies, Concentration in Theology and Ethics, Azusa, CA 91702-7000. Offers MA. *Accreditation:* ATS.

Boston University, School of Theology, Boston, MA 02215. Offers chaplaincy (M Div); choral conducting (MSM); church and the arts (M Div); community and global engagement (M Div); constructive theology and ethics (PhD), including constructive theology, theological ethics; history and hermeneutics (PhD), including biblical studies, church history and world Christianity, liturgical studies, mission studies; organ (MSM); pastoral ministry (M Div); practical theology (PhD), including church and society, congregation and community, evangelism and missiology, homiletics, leadership and administration, pastoral theology and psychology, religious education, spirtuality studies, worship; religion and the academy (M Div); transformational leadership (D Min); M Div/MSM; M Div/MSW; MTS/MSW. PhD in mission studies offered in collaboration with Gordon-Conwell Theological Seminary. *Accreditation:* ACIPE; ATS. *Program availability:* Part-time, blended/hybrid learning. *Faculty:* 39 full-time (17 women), 11 part-time/adjunct (5 women). *Students:* 256 full-time (135 women), 87 part-time (40 women); includes 82 minority (38 Black or African American, non-Hispanic/Latino; 10 Asian, non-Hispanic/Latino; 23 Hispanic/Latino; 1 Native Hawaiian or other Pacific Islander, non-Hispanic/Latino; 10 Two or more races, non-Hispanic/Latino), 66 international. Average age 34. 334 applicants, 69% accepted, 106 enrolled. In 2017, 62 master's, 9 doctorates awarded. *Degree requirements:* For master's, comprehensive exam (for some programs), thesis optional, contextual education; for doctorate, 2 languages, dissertation, and comprehensive exam (for PhD). *Entrance requirements:* For master's, minimum GPA of 3.0; for doctorate, GRE General Test, minimum GPA of 3.3. Additional exam requirements/recommendations for international students: Required—TOEFL (minimum score 570 paper-based; 89 iBT). *Application deadline:* For fall admission, 1/15 priority date for domestic and international students; for spring admission, 10/15 priority date for domestic and international students. Applications are processed on a rolling basis. Application fee: $95. Electronic applications accepted. *Expenses:* $20,100 tuition. *Financial support:* In 2017–18, 236 students received support, including 102 fellowships with full tuition reimbursements available (averaging $7,500 per year), 11 research assistantships with full tuition reimbursements available (averaging $22,000 per year), 12 teaching assistantships with full tuition reimbursements available (averaging $22,000 per year); career-related internships or fieldwork, Federal Work-Study, scholarships/grants, and health care benefits also available. Support available to part-time students. Financial award application deadline: 7/15. *Faculty research:* Practical theology, ethics, environmental theology, religion and conflict transformation, chaplaincy. *Total annual research expenditures:* $2.5 million. *Unit head:* Rev. Dr. Mary Elizabeth Moore, Dean, 617-353-3050, Fax: 617-353-3061, E-mail: memoore@bu.edu. *Application contact:* Rev. Dr. Anastasia Kidd, Director of Enrollment, 617-353-3036, Fax: 617-358-0140, E-mail: sthadmis@bu.edu.
Website: http://www.bu.edu/sth

Chicago Theological Seminary, Graduate and Professional Programs, Chicago, IL 60637-1507. Offers Bible, culture and hermeneutics (PhD); preaching (D Min); religion and health (D Min); religious studies (MA); spirituality and spiritual direction (D Min); theology (M Div); theology, ethics and the human sciences (PhD); M Div/MSW. *Accreditation:* ACIPE; ATS. *Program availability:* Part-time. *Degree requirements:* For master's, thesis; for doctorate, 2 foreign languages, comprehensive exam, thesis/dissertation. *Entrance requirements:* For doctorate, GRE General Test. Additional exam requirements/recommendations for international students: Required—TOEFL. *Faculty research:* Bible, culture and hermeneutics, theology, gender and sexuality, black faith and life, spirituality and psychology, practical theology.

Claremont Graduate University, Graduate Programs, School of Arts and Humanities, Department of Religion, Claremont, CA 91711-6160. Offers Hebrew Bible (MA, PhD); history of Christianity and religions of North America (MA, PhD); New Testament (MA, PhD); philosophy of religion and theology (MA, PhD); theology, ethics and culture (MA, PhD); women's studies in religion (MA, PhD); MA/PhD; MBA/PhD. *Program availability:* Part-time. Terminal master's awarded for partial completion of doctoral program. *Entrance requirements:* For master's and doctorate, GRE General Test. Additional exam requirements/recommendations for international students: Required—TOEFL (minimum score 75 iBT). Electronic applications accepted.

Claremont Lincoln University, Graduate Programs, Claremont, CA 91711. Offers ethical leadership (MA); interfaith action (MA); social impact (MA).

Claremont School of Theology, Graduate and Professional Programs, Program in Religion, Claremont, CA 91711-3199. Offers practical theology (PhD), including religious education and formation, spiritual care and counseling; religion (MA, PhD), including comparative theology and philosophy (PhD), Hebrew Bible and Jewish studies (PhD), New Testament and Christian origins (PhD), process studies (PhD), religion, ethics, and society (PhD). *Accreditation:* ACIPE; ATS. Terminal master's awarded for partial completion of doctoral program. *Degree requirements:* For master's, thesis; for doctorate, 2 foreign languages, thesis/dissertation. *Entrance requirements:* For doctorate, GRE General Test. Additional exam requirements/recommendations for international students: Required—TOEFL. Electronic applications accepted.

Columbia University, Graduate School of Business, MBA Program, New York, NY 10027. Offers accounting (MBA); decision, risk, and operations (MBA); entrepreneurship (MBA); finance and economics (MBA); healthcare and pharmaceutical management (MBA); human resource management (MBA); international business (MBA); leadership and ethics (MBA); management (MBA); marketing (MBA); media (MBA); private equity (MBA); real estate (MBA); social enterprise (MBA); value investing (MBA); DDS/MBA; JD/MBA; MBA/MIA; MBA/MPH; MBA/MS; MD/MBA. *Entrance requirements:* For master's, GMAT, 2 letters of recommendation. Additional exam requirements/recommendations for international students: Required—TOEFL. Electronic applications accepted. *Expenses:* Contact institution. *Faculty research:* Human decision making and behavioral research; real estate market and mortgage defaults; financial crisis and corporate governance; international business; security analysis and accounting.

Duke University, The Fuqua School of Business, The Duke MBA-Daytime Program, Durham, NC 27708-0586. Offers academic excellence in finance (Certificate); business administration (MBA); decision sciences (MBA); energy and environment (MBA); energy finance (MBA); entrepreneurship and innovation (MBA); finance (MBA); financial analysis (MBA); health sector management (Certificate); leadership and ethics (MBA); management (MBA); management science and technology management (Certificate); marketing (MBA); operations management (MBA); social entrepreneurship (MBA); strategy (MBA). *Faculty:* 96 full-time (19 women), 48 part-time/adjunct (15 women). *Students:* 876 full-time (297 women); includes 180 minority (39 Black or African American, non-Hispanic/Latino; 2 American Indian or Alaska Native, non-Hispanic/Latino; 83 Asian, non-Hispanic/Latino; 50 Hispanic/Latino; 6 Two or more races, non-Hispanic/Latino), 321 international. Average age 29. In 2017, 445 master's awarded. *Entrance requirements:* For master's, GMAT or GRE, transcripts, essays, resume, recommendation letters, interview. *Application deadline:* For fall admission, 9/12 for domestic and international students; for winter admission, 10/10 for domestic and international students; for spring admission, 1/3 for domestic and international students; for summer admission, 3/20 for domestic and international students. Application fee: $225. Electronic applications accepted. *Expenses:* $69,342 first-year tuition and fees. *Financial support:* In 2017–18, 423 students received support. Scholarships/grants available. Financial award applicants required to submit FAFSA. *Unit head:* Steve Misuraca, Assistant Dean, Daytime MBA Program. *Application contact:* Shari Hubert, Associate Dean, Office of Admissions, 919-660-7705, Fax: 919-681-8026, E-mail: admissions-info@fuqua.duke.edu.
Website: https://www.fuqua.duke.edu/programs/daytime-mba

Emory University, Candler School of Theology, Atlanta, GA 30322. Offers formation and witness (M Div); history, scripture and tradition (MTS); leadership in church and community (M Div); modern religious thought and experience (MTS); pastoral counseling (Th D); religion and race (M Div); religion, health and science (M Div); scripture and interpretation (M Div); society and personality (M Div); theology (Th M); theology and ethics (M Div); theology and the arts (M Div); traditions of the church (M Div); women and religion (M Div); JD/M Div; JD/MTS; M Div/MBA; M Div/MPH; MBA/MTS; MTS/MPH. *Accreditation:* ACIPE. *Program availability:* Part-time. *Degree requirements:* For master's, thesis optional; for doctorate, comprehensive exam, thesis/dissertation. *Entrance requirements:* For master's, minimum undergraduate GPA of 3.0; for doctorate, GRE, M Div, 8 units of course work in clinical pastoral education. Additional exam requirements/recommendations for international students: Required—TOEFL (minimum score 600 paper-based; 95 iBT). Electronic applications accepted. *Expenses:* Contact institution. *Faculty research:* Biblical studies, church history, ethics, ministry practice, pastoral care.

Fordham University, Graduate School of Arts and Sciences, Program in Ethics and Society, New York, NY 10458. Offers ethics and society (MA); health care ethics (Certificate). *Program availability:* Part-time. *Students:* 13 full-time (8 women), 7 part-time (2 women); includes 8 minority (3 Asian, non-Hispanic/Latino; 5 Hispanic/Latino), 1 international. Average age 34. 37 applicants, 59% accepted, 8 enrolled. In 2017, 8 master's awarded. *Entrance requirements:* Additional exam requirements/recommendations for international students: Required—TOEFL. *Application deadline:* For fall admission, 1/4 priority date for domestic students; for spring admission, 10/31 for domestic students. Applications are processed on a rolling basis. Application fee: $70. Electronic applications accepted. *Financial support:* In 2017–18, 1 student received support. Teaching assistantships, Federal Work-Study, institutionally sponsored loans, scholarships/grants, tuition waivers (partial), and unspecified assistantships available. Financial award application deadline: 1/4. *Unit head:* Dr. Bryan Pilkington, Director of Academic Programs, Fordham University Center for Ethics Education, 718-817-3775, Fax: 212-759-2009, E-mail: afried@fordham.edu. *Application contact:* Bernadette Valentino-Morrison, Director of Graduate Admissions, 718-817-4419, Fax: 718-817-3566, E-mail: valentinomor@fordham.edu.

Freed-Hardeman University, Program in Business Administration, Henderson, TN 38340-2399. Offers accounting (MBA); corporate responsibility (MBA); leadership (MBA). *Accreditation:* ACBSP. *Program availability:* Part-time, evening/weekend, online learning. *Entrance requirements:* For master's, GMAT. Additional exam requirements/recommendations for international students: Required—TOEFL (minimum score 500 paper-based).

George Mason University, College of Humanities and Social Sciences, Department of Philosophy, Fairfax, VA 22030. Offers ethics and public affairs (MA); philosophy and cultural theory (MA). *Faculty:* 11 full-time (3 women), 8 part-time/adjunct (0 women). *Students:* 10 part-time (3 women); includes 1 minority (Hispanic/Latino). Average age 39. 9 applicants, 67% accepted, 1 enrolled. In 2017, 4 master's awarded. *Degree requirements:* For master's, thesis optional. *Entrance requirements:* For master's, college transcripts, goals statement, 2 letters of recommendation, resume, writing sample; completion of certain undergraduate preparation coursework with grades of B or higher in each course (for philosophy and cultural theory). Additional exam requirements/recommendations for international students: Required—TOEFL (minimum score 575 paper-based, 88 iBT), IELTS (6.5), or PTE (59). *Application deadline:* For fall admission, 3/1 for domestic and international students; for spring admission, 11/1 for domestic and international students. Application fee: $75 ($80 for international students). Electronic applications accepted. *Expenses:* Tuition, state resident: full-time $11,228; part-time $459.50 per credit. Tuition, nonresident: full-time $30,932; part-time $1280.50 per credit. *Required fees:* $3252; $135.50 per credit. Part-time tuition and fees vary according to course load and program. *Financial support:* In 2017–18, 1 student received support, including 1 research assistantship with tuition reimbursement available; career-related internships or fieldwork, Federal Work-Study, scholarships/grants, unspecified assistantships, and health care benefits (for full-time research or teaching assistantship recipients) also available. Financial award application deadline: 3/1; financial award applicants required to submit FAFSA. *Faculty research:* History of philosophy (particularly Asian and modern); Anglo-American and analytic philosophy; continental philosophy; ethics (including bioethics and feminist ethics); philosophy and public policy. *Total annual research expenditures:* $131,560. *Unit head:* Ted Kinnaman, Chair/Associate Professor, 703-993-4328, Fax: 703-993-1297, E-mail: tkinnama@gmu.edu. *Application contact:* Rose Cherubin, Associate Professor and Graduate Coordinator, 703-993-1332, Fax: 703-993-1297, E-mail: rcherubi@gmu.edu.
Website: http://philosophy.gmu.edu/

Georgetown University, Graduate School of Arts and Sciences, School of Continuing Studies, Washington, DC 20057. Offers American studies (MALS); applied intelligence (MPS); Catholic studies (MALS); classical civilizations (MALS); emergency and disaster management (MPS); ethics and the professions (MALS); global strategic communications (MPS); hospitality management (MPS); human resources management (MPS); humanities (MALS); individualized study (MALS); integrated marketing communications (MPS); international affairs (MALS); Islam and Muslim-Christian relations (MALS); journalism (MPS); liberal studies (DLS); literature and society (MALS); medieval and early modern European studies (MALS); public relations and corporate communications (MPS); real estate (MPS); religious studies (MALS); social and public policy (MALS); sports industry management (MPS); systems engineering management (MPS); technology management (MPS); the theory and practice of American democracy (MALS); urban and regional planning (MPS); visual culture (MALS). MPS in systems engineering management offered jointly with Stevens Institute of Technology. *Entrance requirements:* Additional exam requirements/recommendations for international students: Required—TOEFL.

Graduate Theological Union, Graduate Programs, Berkeley, CA 94709-1212. Offers art and religion (MA, PhD, Th D); biblical languages (MA); biblical studies (MA); Biblical studies (PhD, Th D); Buddhist studies (MA); Christian spirituality (MA, PhD, Th D); cultural and historical studies of religions (MA, PhD, Th D); ethics and social theory (PhD, Th D); history (MA, PhD, Th D); homiletics (MA, PhD, Th D); interdisciplinary studies (PhD, Th D); Jewish studies (MA, PhD, Th D, Certificate); liturgical studies (MA, PhD, Th D); Near Eastern religions (PhD, Th D); Orthodox Christian studies (MA); religion and psychology (MA, PhD, Th D); religion and society/ethics and social theory (MA); systematic and philosophical theology (MA, PhD, Th D). PhD programs in Jewish studies and Near Eastern religions offered jointly with University of California, Berkeley. *Accreditation:* ATS. Terminal master's awarded for partial completion of doctoral program. *Degree requirements:* For master's, one foreign language, thesis; for doctorate, one foreign language, comprehensive exam, thesis/dissertation. *Entrance requirements:* For master's, GRE General Test; for doctorate, GRE General Test, MA or M Div. Additional exam requirements/recommendations for international students: Required—TOEFL. Electronic applications accepted.

John Brown University, Soderquist College of Business, Siloam Springs, AR 72761-2121. Offers international business (MBA); leadership and ethics (MBA, MS). *Accreditation:* ACBSP. *Program availability:* Part-time, evening/weekend, online only, 100% online, blended/hybrid learning. *Entrance requirements:* For master's, MAT, GMAT or GRE if undergraduate GPA is less than 3.0, recommendation forms from three people, 200-word essay describing professional plans and reason for seeking acceptance. Additional exam requirements/recommendations for international students: Required—TOEFL (minimum score 550 paper-based; 79 iBT). Electronic applications accepted. *Faculty research:* Ethical leadership.

Kennesaw State University, Siegel Institute for Leadership, Ethics and Character, Kennesaw, GA 30144. Offers leadership and ethics (Graduate Certificate). *Program availability:* Part-time, evening/weekend, online learning. *Entrance requirements:* Additional exam requirements/recommendations for international students: Required—TOEFL (minimum score 550 paper-based; 80 iBT), IELTS (minimum score 6.5). Electronic applications accepted.

Lancaster Theological Seminary, Graduate and Professional Programs, Lancaster, PA 17603-2812. Offers biblical studies (MAR); Christian education (MAR); Christianity and the arts (MAR); church history (MAR); congregational life (MAR); lay leadership (Certificate); theological studies (M Div); theology (D Min); theology and ethics (MAR). *Accreditation:* ACIPE; ATS. *Degree requirements:* For doctorate, thesis/dissertation.

Lebanon Valley College, Program in Business Administration, Annville, PA 17003-1400. Offers business administration (MBA); healthcare management (MBA); human resources (MBA); leadership and ethics (MBA); project management (MBA). *Program availability:* Part-time, evening/weekend. *Faculty:* 7 full-time (1 woman), 8 part-time/adjunct (1 woman). *Students:* 11 full-time (5 women), 66 part-time (28 women); includes 11 minority (3 Black or African American, non-Hispanic/Latino; 4 Asian, non-Hispanic/Latino; 4 Hispanic/Latino), 3 international. Average age 34. 21 applicants, 81% accepted, 16 enrolled. In 2017, 32 master's awarded. *Degree requirements:* For master's, capstone course. *Entrance requirements:* For master's, GMAT, 3 years of work experience, resume, professional statement (application form, resume, personal statement, transcripts). Additional exam requirements/recommendations for international students: Required—TOEFL (minimum score 80 iBT), IELTS (minimum score 6.5) or STEP Eiken (grade 1). *Application deadline:* Applications are processed on a rolling basis. Application fee: $0. Electronic applications accepted. *Expenses:* $660 per credit hour. *Financial support:* Career-related internships or fieldwork and scholarships/grants available. Financial award application deadline: 3/1; financial award applicants required to submit FAFSA. *Faculty research:* Leadership, motivation, BI, information systems strategies, emerging market development, the role of informational business education, economic growth. *Unit head:* Dr. David Setley, Associate Professor/Chair of Business Administration/Director of the MBA Program, 717-867-6104, Fax: 717-867-6018, E-mail: setley@lvc.edu. *Application contact:* Christine M. Martin, Enrollment and Operations Specialist, 717-867-6486, Fax: 717-867-6013, E-mail: cmartin@lvc.edu.
Website: http://www.lvc.edu/mba

Lee University, Programs in Religion, Cleveland, TN 37320-3450. Offers biblical studies (MA); ministry studies/leadership (MA); ministry studies/worship (MA); ministry studies/youth and family (MA); theological studies (MA), including ethics, religion. *Program availability:* Part-time, 100% online. *Faculty:* 9 full-time (3 women), 3 part-time/adjunct (0 women). *Students:* 62 full-time (16 women), 99 part-time (36 women); includes 68 minority (9 Black or African American, non-Hispanic/Latino; 1 Asian, non-Hispanic/Latino; 57 Hispanic/Latino; 1 Two or more races, non-Hispanic/Latino), 6 international. Average age 37. 21 applicants, 86% accepted, 8 enrolled. In 2017, 13 master's awarded. *Degree requirements:* For master's, variable foreign language requirement, comprehensive exam (for some programs), thesis (for some programs). *Entrance requirements:* For master's, GRE or MAT (for biblical/theological studies only), minimum GPA of 3.0, 3 letters of recommendation, interview, official transcripts, essay. Additional exam requirements/recommendations for international students: Required—TOEFL (minimum score 61 iBT). *Application deadline:* For fall admission, 4/1 priority date for domestic and international students; for spring admission, 10/1 priority date for domestic and international students. Applications are processed on a rolling basis. Application fee: $25. Electronic applications accepted. *Expenses:* Contact institution. *Financial support:* In 2017–18, 34 students received support, including 12 teaching assistantships (averaging $1,886 per year); career-related internships or fieldwork, Federal Work-Study, institutionally sponsored loans, scholarships/grants, and unspecified assistantships also available. Financial award application deadline: 3/1; financial award applicants required to submit FAFSA. *Faculty research:* Spiritual and discipleship formation, leadership, Biblical studies, theological studies, ethics. *Unit head:* Dr. Lisa Long, Director, 423-303-5100, E-mail: llong@leeuniversity.edu.
Website: http://www.leeuniversity.edu/academics/graduate/

Loyola University Chicago, Quinlan School of Business, MBA Programs, Chicago, IL 60611. Offers accounting (MBA); business ethics (MBA); derivative markets (MBA);

economics (MBA); entrepreneurship (MBA); finance (MBA); healthcare management (MBA); human resources management (MBA); information systems management (MBA); international business (MBA); management (MBA); marketing (MBA); risk management (MBA); supply chain management (MBA). *Program availability:* Part-time, evening/weekend. *Faculty:* 84 full-time (28 women), 12 part-time/adjunct (3 women). *Students:* 253 full-time (118 women), 76 part-time (35 women); includes 83 minority (21 Black or African American, non-Hispanic/Latino; 1 American Indian or Alaska Native, non-Hispanic/Latino; 33 Asian, non-Hispanic/Latino; 24 Hispanic/Latino; 4 Two or more races, non-Hispanic/Latino), 37 international. Average age 30. 334 applicants, 52% accepted, 80 enrolled. In 2017, 220 master's awarded. *Entrance requirements:* For master's, GMAT or GRE, official transcripts, two letters of recommendation, statement of purpose, resume. Additional exam requirements/recommendations for international students: Required—TOEFL (minimum score 90 iBT) or IELTS (minimum score 6.5). *Application deadline:* For fall admission, 7/15 for domestic and international students; for winter admission, 10/1 for domestic and international students; for spring admission, 1/15 for domestic and international students; for summer admission, 4/1 for domestic and international students. Applications are processed on a rolling basis. Application fee: $50. Electronic applications accepted. Application fee is waived when completed online. *Expenses:* $4,488 per course. *Financial support:* In 2017–18, 11 students received support. Research assistantships, career-related internships or fieldwork, Federal Work-Study, scholarships/grants, and health care benefits available. *Faculty research:* Social enterprise and responsibility, emerging markets, supply chain management, risk management. *Unit head:* Katherine Acles, Assistant Dean for Graduate Programs, 312-915-6124, Fax: 312-915-7207, E-mail: kacles@luc.edu.

Lutheran Theological Seminary Saskatoon, Graduate and Professional Programs, Saskatoon, SK S7N 0X3, Canada. Offers Biblical studies (MTS); church history (MTS); ethics/church and society (MTS); history of Christianity (STM); New Testament (STM); Old Testament (STM); pastoral studies (STM); pastoral theology (MTS); systematic theology (MTS); systematic theology and philosophy of religion (STM); theology (M Div, D Div). STM programs offered jointly with College of Emmanuel and St. Chad and St. Andrew's College. *Accreditation:* ATS. *Program availability:* Part-time. *Degree requirements:* For master's, thesis.

Marquette University, Graduate School, College of Arts and Sciences, Department of Philosophy, Milwaukee, WI 53201-1881. Offers ancient philosophy (PhD); British empiricism and analytic philosophy (PhD); Christian philosophy (PhD); early modern European philosophy (PhD); ethics (PhD); German philosophy (PhD); history of philosophy (MA); medieval philosophy (PhD); phenomenology and existentialism (PhD); philosophy of religion (PhD); social and applied philosophy (MA); JD/MA. *Program availability:* Part-time. Terminal master's awarded for partial completion of doctoral program. *Degree requirements:* For master's, variable foreign language requirement, comprehensive exam, thesis or alternative; for doctorate, 2 foreign languages, thesis/dissertation, written and oral qualifying exams. *Entrance requirements:* For master's and doctorate, GRE General Test, official transcripts from all current and previous colleges/universities except Marquette, statement of purpose, at least three letters of recommendation, sample of philosophical writing. Additional exam requirements/recommendations for international students: Required—TOEFL (minimum score 530 paper-based). Electronic applications accepted. *Faculty research:* Aristotle, Augustine, Descartes, Hegel, Heidegger.

New England College of Business and Finance, Program in Business Ethics and Compliance, Boston, MA 02111-2645. Offers MS. *Program availability:* Online learning.

Northwestern University, School of Professional Studies, Program in Liberal Studies, Evanston, IL 60208. Offers American studies (MA); history (MA); religious and ethical studies (MA). *Program availability:* Part-time, evening/weekend.
Website: https://sps.northwestern.edu/masters/liberal-studies/index.php

Oregon State University, College of Liberal Arts, Program in Applied Ethics, Corvallis, OR 97331. Offers biomedical ethics (MA). *Program availability:* Part-time. *Entrance requirements:* For master's, writing sample of 5-7 pages. Additional exam requirements/recommendations for international students: Required—TOEFL (minimum score 80 iBT), IELTS (minimum score 6.5). *Application deadline:* For fall admission, 1/15 priority date for domestic and international students. Application fee: $75 ($85 for international students). *Unit head:* Allen Thompson, Director of Graduate Studies, 541-737-5654, E-mail: thompsan@oregonstate.edu. *Application contact:* Dr. Allen Thompson, Director of Graduate Studies, 541-737-5654, E-mail: allen.thompson@oregonstate.edu.
Website: http://liberalarts.oregonstate.edu/shpr/philosophy

Phillips Theological Seminary, Programs in Theology, Tulsa, OK 74116. Offers administration of church agencies (M Div); campus ministry (M Div); church-related social work (M Div); college and seminary teaching (M Div); global mission work (M Div); institutional chaplaincy (M Div); ministerial vocations in Christian education (M Div); ministry (D Min), including parish ministry, pastoral counseling, practices of ministry; ministry and culture (MAMC), including Christian education, congregational leadership, history and practice of Christian spirituality, theology, ethics, and culture; ministry of music (M Div); pastoral care and counseling (M Div); pastoral ministry (M Div); theological studies (MTS). *Accreditation:* ATS. *Program availability:* Part-time, online learning. *Degree requirements:* For master's, thesis (for some programs); for doctorate, thesis/dissertation. *Entrance requirements:* For master's, minimum GPA of 2.5; for doctorate, M Div, minimum GPA of 3.0. *Faculty research:* Biblical studies, historical studies, theology and culture, practical theology, theology and film.

Pontifical John Paul II Institute for Studies on Marriage and Family, Graduate Programs, Washington, DC 20064. Offers biotechnology and ethics (MTS); marriage and family (MTS, STD, STL); theology (PhD).

Santa Clara University, Jesuit School of Theology, Berkeley, CA 94709. Offers Biblical studies (MTS); Christian spirituality (MTS); church history (MTS); cultural and historical studies of Catholicism (MTS); ethics and social theory/religion and society (MTS); history of art and religion (MTS); liturgical studies (MTS); systematic and philosophical theology (MTS); theology (M Div, Th M, STD, STB, STL); M Div/MA. MA programs offered jointly with Graduate Theological Union. *Program availability:* Part-time, evening/weekend, 100% online. *Faculty:* 19 full-time (5 women), 9 part-time/adjunct (5 women). *Students:* 120 full-time (26 women), 15 part-time (6 women); includes 78 minority (24 Black or African American, non-Hispanic/Latino; 2 American Indian or Alaska Native, non-Hispanic/Latino; 25 Asian, non-Hispanic/Latino; 20 Hispanic/Latino; 3 Native Hawaiian or other Pacific Islander, non-Hispanic/Latino; 4 Two or more races, non-Hispanic/Latino). Average age 38. 99 applicants, 96% accepted, 54 enrolled. In 2017, 52 master's, 9 doctorates awarded. *Entrance requirements:* For master's, GRE (except Th M), 2 letters of recommendation, resume or curriculum vitae, official transcripts, statement of purpose; for doctorate, master's degree or equivalent, resume or curriculum vitae, statement of purpose, official transcripts, 2 letters of recommendation, research paper. Additional exam requirements/recommendations for international students: Required—TOEFL (minimum score 90 iBT). *Application deadline:* For fall admission, 3/1 priority date for domestic students; for spring admission, 10/1 priority date for domestic students. Applications are processed on a rolling basis. Application fee: $50 ($0 for international students). Electronic applications accepted. *Expenses:* Contact institution. *Financial support:* Scholarships/grants and unspecified assistantships available. Support available to part-time students. Financial award application deadline: 3/1; financial award applicants required to submit FAFSA. *Faculty research:* Religion and culture, interreligious dialogue, social ethics and restorative justice, Ignatian spirituality. *Unit head:* Rev. Kevin O'Brien, Dean, 510-549-5040, E-mail: kfobrien@scu.edu. *Application contact:* Drew Roborts, Assistant Dean of Enrollment Management and Marketing, 510-549-5016, E-mail: ajroberts@scu.edu.
Website: http://www.scu.edu/jst/

Schreiner University, MBA Program, Kerrville, TX 78028-5697. Offers ethical leadership (MBA). *Program availability:* Part-time, online learning. *Entrance requirements:* For master's, 3 recommendations; personal essay; transcripts; resume. Additional exam requirements/recommendations for international students: Required—TOEFL. Electronic applications accepted. *Expenses:* Contact institution.

Southeastern Baptist Theological Seminary, Graduate and Professional Programs, Wake Forest, NC 27587. Offers advanced biblical studies (M Div); Christian education (M Div, MACE); Christian ethics (PhD); Christian ministry (M Div); Christian planting (M Div); church music (MACM); counseling (MACO); evangelism (PhD); language (M Div); ministry (D Min); New Testament (PhD); Old Testament (PhD); philosophy (PhD); theology (Th M, PhD); women's studies (M Div). *Accreditation:* ACIPE; ATS (one or more programs are accredited). *Degree requirements:* For master's, thesis (for some programs), oral exam; for doctorate, thesis/dissertation, fieldwork. *Entrance requirements:* For master's, Cooperative English Test, minimum GPA of 2.0, M Div or equivalent (Th M); for doctorate, GRE General Test or MAT, Cooperative English Test, M Div or equivalent, 3 years of professional experience.

Southern Methodist University, Dedman College of Humanities and Sciences, Graduate Program in Religious Studies, Dallas, TX 75275-0133. Offers Hebrew Bible/Old Testament (PhD); history of the Christian tradition (PhD); New Testament (PhD); religion and culture (PhD); religious ethics (PhD); religious studies (MA); systematics theology (PhD). Terminal master's awarded for partial completion of doctoral program. *Degree requirements:* For master's, one foreign language, thesis, oral and written exams; for doctorate, variable foreign language requirement, thesis/dissertation, oral and written exams. *Entrance requirements:* For master's and doctorate, GRE General Test, minimum GPA of 3.0, course work in religion. Additional exam requirements/recommendations for international students: Required—TOEFL (minimum score 550 paper-based; 79 iBT). Electronic applications accepted. *Faculty research:* Theology, religious ethics, Biblical studies, history of Christianity, religion and culture.

Spring Hill College, Graduate Programs, Program in Liberal Arts, Mobile, AL 36608-1791. Offers fine arts (MLA); leadership and ethics (MLA, Postbaccalaureate Certificate); literature (MLA). *Program availability:* Part-time, evening/weekend. *Faculty:* 11 full-time (1 woman). *Students:* 1 (woman) full-time, 21 part-time (7 women); includes 5 minority (4 Black or African American, non-Hispanic/Latino; 1 Hispanic/Latino), 6 international. Average age 31. In 2017, 12 master's awarded. *Degree requirements:* For master's, capstone course, completion of program within 6 years of initial admittance. *Entrance requirements:* For master's, bachelor's degree with minimum undergraduate GPA of 3.0 or graduate/professional degree. Additional exam requirements/recommendations for international students: Required—TOEFL (minimum score 550 paper-based; 80 iBT), IELTS (minimum score 6.5), CPE or CAE (minimum score C), Michigan English Language Assessment Battery (minimum score 90). *Application deadline:* For fall admission, 8/1 priority date for domestic and international students; for spring admission, 12/1 priority date for domestic and international students. Applications are processed on a rolling basis. Application fee: $25 ($35 for international students). Electronic applications accepted. *Expenses:* Contact institution. *Financial support:* Applicants required to submit FAFSA. *Unit head:* Dr. Thomas J. Hoffman, Director, 251-380-4184, Fax: 251-460-2115, E-mail: thoffman@shc.edu. *Application contact:* Robert Stewart, Vice President of Enrollment, 251-380-3030, Fax: 251-460-2186, E-mail: rstewart@shc.edu.
Website: http://ug.shc.edu/graduate-degrees/master-liberal-arts/

Stevens Institute of Technology, Graduate School, College of Arts and Letters, Program in Policy and Innovation, Hoboken, NJ 07030. Offers MA, Graduate Certificate. *Program availability:* Part-time, evening/weekend. *Students:* 1 full-time (0 women), 2 part-time (both women). Average age 28. 10 applicants, 40% accepted, 3 enrolled. In 2017, 1 master's awarded. *Degree requirements:* For master's, thesis optional, minimum B average in major field and overall; for Graduate Certificate, minimum B average. *Entrance requirements:* Additional exam requirements/recommendations for international students: Required—TOEFL (minimum score 74 iBT), IELTS (minimum score 6). *Application deadline:* For fall admission, 7/1 for domestic students, 4/15 for international students; for spring admission, 12/1 for domestic and international students. Applications are processed on a rolling basis. Application fee: $60. Electronic applications accepted. *Expenses: Tuition:* Full-time $34,494; part-time $1554 per credit. *Required fees:* $291 per semester. *Financial support:* Fellowships, research assistantships, teaching assistantships, career-related internships or fieldwork, Federal Work-Study, scholarships/grants, and unspecified assistantships available. Financial award application deadline: 2/15; financial award applicants required to submit FAFSA. *Unit head:* Andrew Russell, Director, 201-216-5400, Fax: 201-216-8245, E-mail: arussell@stevens.edu. *Application contact:* Graduate Admission, 888-783-8367, Fax: 888-511-1306, E-mail: graduate@stevens.edu.
Website: https://www.stevens.edu/college-arts-and-letters/graduate-programs

Suffolk University, College of Arts and Sciences, Department of Philosophy, Boston, MA 02108-2770. Offers administration of higher education (M Ed, CAGS); disability services (Certificate); ethics and public policy (MS). *Program availability:* Part-time, evening/weekend. *Faculty:* 4 full-time (0 women), 2 part-time/adjunct (0 women). *Students:* 23 full-time (11 women), 37 part-time (27 women); includes 17 minority (6 Black or African American, non-Hispanic/Latino; 2 Asian, non-Hispanic/Latino; 7 Hispanic/Latino; 2 Two or more races, non-Hispanic/Latino), 2 international. Average age 31. 24 applicants, 75% accepted, 3 enrolled. In 2017, 21 master's awarded. *Degree requirements:* For master's, internship or thesis; practicum (for M Ed). *Entrance requirements:* For master's, GRE General Test, MAT, GMAT, statement of professional goals, official transcripts, 2 letters of recommendation, resume. Additional exam requirements/recommendations for international students: Required—TOEFL (minimum score 550 paper-based; 80 iBT). *Application deadline:* For fall admission, 3/15 priority date for domestic and international students; for spring admission, 10/15 priority date for domestic and international students. Applications are processed on a rolling basis. Application fee: $50. Electronic applications accepted. *Expenses:* $29,520 per year full-time tuition; $1,230 per credit part-time. *Financial support:* In 2017–18, 50 students received support, including 13 fellowships (averaging $5,915 per year); career-related internships or fieldwork, Federal Work-Study, institutionally sponsored loans, and unspecified assistantships also available. Support available to part-time students. Financial award application deadline: 4/1; financial award applicants required to submit FAFSA. *Faculty research:* Predicting competent Head Start preschoolers, cultural differences, school counseling technology, sibling attachment in divorce cases, consequences of ethical breaches by human resource professionals. *Unit head:* Dr. Greg Fried, Chair of Philosophy Department, 617-573-8109, E-mail: gfried@suffolk.edu. *Application contact:* Mara Marzocchi, Associate Director of Graduate Admissions, 617-

573-8302, Fax: 617-305-1733, E-mail: grad.admission@suffolk.edu.
Website: http://www.suffolk.edu/college/graduate/69296.php

Texas State University, The Graduate College, College of Liberal Arts, Applied Philosophy and Ethics Program, San Marcos, TX 78666. Offers MA. *Program availability:* Part-time. *Faculty:* 24 full-time (8 women), 2 part-time/adjunct (both women). *Students:* 14 full-time (6 women), 7 part-time (1 woman); includes 9 minority (2 Black or African American, non-Hispanic/Latino; 7 Hispanic/Latino). Average age 31. 11 applicants, 82% accepted, 3 enrolled. In 2017, 13 master's awarded. *Degree requirements:* For master's, comprehensive exam, thesis optional. *Entrance requirements:* For master's, baccalaureate degree from regionally-accredited university with minimum GPA of 3.0 on last 60 undergraduate semester hours, statement of purpose, 2 letters of recommendation, writing sample. Additional exam requirements/recommendations for international students: Required—TOEFL (minimum score 550 paper-based; 78 iBT), IELTS (minimum score 6). *Application deadline:* For fall admission, 3/1 priority date for domestic and international students; for spring admission, 10/15 for domestic students, 10/1 for international students; for summer admission, 4/15 for domestic students, 3/15 for international students. Applications are processed on a rolling basis. Application fee: $40 ($90 for international students). Electronic applications accepted. *Expenses:* Tuition, state resident: full-time $7868; part-time $3934 per semester. Tuition, nonresident: full-time $17,828; part-time $8914 per semester. *Required fees:* $2092; $1435 per semester. Tuition and fees vary according to course load. *Financial support:* In 2017–18, 13 students received support, including 1 research assistantship (averaging $12,892 per year), 13 teaching assistantships (averaging $12,272 per year); scholarships/grants and unspecified assistantships also available. Support available to part-time students. Financial award application deadline: 3/1; financial award applicants required to submit FAFSA. *Faculty research:* Engagement: philosophy, practice and performance, climate corps. *Total annual research expenditures:* $8,567. *Unit head:* Dr. Audrey Mckinney, Graduate Advisor, 512-245-2047, Fax: 512-245-8336, E-mail: am04@txstate.edu. *Application contact:* Dr. Andrea Golato, Dean of Graduate School, 512-245-2581, Fax: 512-245-8365, E-mail: gradcollege@txstate.edu.
Website: http://www.txstate.edu/philosophy/courses-programs/graduate/graduate-MA-Requirements.html

Université de Sherbrooke, Faculty of Theology and Religious Studies, Sherbrooke, QC J1K 2R1, Canada. Offers applied ethics (Diploma); human science of religions (MA); intercultural training (Diploma); philosophy (MA, PhD); spiritual anthropology (Diploma); theology (MA, PhD, Diploma). *Program availability:* Part-time, evening/weekend, online learning. Terminal master's awarded for partial completion of doctoral program. *Entrance requirements:* For master's, bachelor's degree in related discipline; for doctorate, master's degree in related discipline. *Faculty research:* Faith and culture interrelation.

Université du Québec à Chicoutimi, Graduate Programs, Program in Ethics, Chicoutimi, QC G7H 2B1, Canada. Offers Diploma. *Entrance requirements:* For degree, appropriate bachelor's degree, proficiency in French.

Université du Québec à Rimouski, Graduate Programs, Program in Ethics, Rimouski, QC G5L 3A1, Canada. Offers MA, Diploma. *Program availability:* Part-time. *Degree requirements:* For master's, thesis. *Entrance requirements:* For master's, appropriate bachelor's degree, proficiency in French.

Université Laval, Faculty of Theology and Religious Sciences, Program in Applied Ethics, Québec, QC G1K 7P4, Canada. Offers DESS. *Program availability:* Part-time. *Entrance requirements:* For degree, knowledge of French. Electronic applications accepted.

University of Baltimore, Graduate School, Yale Gordon College of Arts and Sciences, Program in Legal and Ethical Studies, Baltimore, MD 21201-5779. Offers MA. *Program availability:* Part-time, evening/weekend. *Degree requirements:* For master's, thesis optional. *Entrance requirements:* For master's, minimum GPA of 3.0. Additional exam requirements/recommendations for international students: Required—TOEFL (minimum score 550 paper-based). Electronic applications accepted. *Faculty research:* Morality in law and economics, religion in lawmaking, comparative legal history, law and social change, critical issues in Constitutional law, theories of justice.

University of Chicago, Divinity School, PhD Program, Chicago, IL 60637. Offers anthropology and sociology of religions (PhD); Bible (PhD); history of Christianity (PhD); history of Judaism (PhD); history of religions (PhD); Islamic studies (PhD); philosophy of religions (PhD); religion, literature, and visual culture (PhD); religions in America (PhD); religious ethics (PhD); theology (PhD). *Students:* 157 full-time (59 women); includes 23 minority (6 Black or African American, non-Hispanic/Latino; 11 Asian, non-Hispanic/Latino; 3 Hispanic/Latino; 3 Two or more races, non-Hispanic/Latino), 24 international. Average age 33. 184 applicants, 11% accepted, 17 enrolled. In 2017, 12 doctorates awarded. *Degree requirements:* For doctorate, 2 foreign languages, comprehensive exam, thesis/dissertation. *Entrance requirements:* For doctorate, GRE General Test, 3 letters of recommendation; transcripts; curriculum vitae or resume; writing sample. Additional exam requirements/recommendations for international students: Required—TOEFL (minimum score 600 paper-based; 104 iBT), IELTS (minimum score 7). *Application deadline:* For fall admission, 12/15 for domestic and international students. Application fee: $75. Electronic applications accepted. *Financial support:* In 2017–18, fellowships with full tuition reimbursements (averaging $27,000 per year), teaching assistantships with full tuition reimbursements (averaging $27,000 per year) were awarded; Federal Work-Study, institutionally sponsored loans, scholarships/grants, and health care benefits also available. Financial award application deadline: 12/15. *Faculty research:* Constructive studies (philosophy of religion, religious ethics, and theology); historical studies (Bible, history of Christianity, and history of Judaism); religion and the human sciences (anthropology and sociology of religion, history of religions, and religion, literature, and visual culture); Islamic studies; religions in America. *Unit head:* Dr. David Nirenberg, Interim Dean/Executive Vice Provost, 773-702-8200, E-mail: divinityadmissions@uchicago.edu. *Application contact:* Anita Lumpkin, Associate Dean of Students, 773-702-8249, E-mail: divinityadmissions@uchicago.edu.
Website: http://divinity.uchicago.edu/doctoral-program-phd

University of Detroit Mercy, College of Business Administration, Detroit, MI 48221. Offers business administration (MBA); business fundamentals (Certificate); business turnaround management (Certificate); ethical leadership and change management (Certificate); finance (Certificate); forensic accounting (Certificate); JD/MBA; MBA/MHSA. *Program availability:* Part-time, evening/weekend, 100% online, blended/hybrid learning. *Entrance requirements:* For master's, GMAT, resume, letter of recommendation, transcripts; for Certificate, resume, letter of recommendation, transcripts. Electronic applications accepted. Application fee is waived when completed online. *Expenses:* Contact institution. *Faculty research:* Ethics, international finance, trade policy, leadership, information technology.

University of Maryland, Baltimore, Graduate School, Program in Research Ethics, Baltimore, MD 21201. Offers Certificate. *Program availability:* Part-time, online learning. *Students:* 12 part-time (10 women); includes 2 minority (1 Black or African American, non-Hispanic/Latino; 1 Hispanic/Latino), 7 international. Average age 37. 13 applicants, 85% accepted, 10 enrolled. In 2017, 4 Certificates awarded. *Entrance requirements:* For degree, minimum GPA of 3.0, curriculum vitae, essay. Additional exam requirements/recommendations for international students: Required—TOEFL (minimum score 80 iBT); Recommended—IELTS (minimum score 7). *Application deadline:* For fall admission, 7/31 priority date for domestic students, 1/15 for international students; for spring admission, 12/15 for domestic students; for summer admission, 4/15 for domestic students. Applications are processed on a rolling basis. Application fee: $75. Electronic applications accepted. *Expenses:* Contact institution. *Financial support:* Application deadline: 3/1; applicants required to submit FAFSA. *Unit head:* Dr. Bruce E. Jarrell, Graduate School Dean, 410-706-2304, Fax: 410-706-0500, E-mail: bjarrell@som.umaryland.edu. *Application contact:* Dr. Henry Silverman, Program Director, 410-328-4881, E-mail: hsilverm@medicine.umaryland.edu.
Website: http://www.graduate.umaryland.edu/research-ethics/

The University of North Carolina at Charlotte, College of Liberal Arts and Sciences, Department of Philosophy, Charlotte, NC 28223-0001. Offers ethics and applied philosophy (MA, Graduate Certificate). *Program availability:* Part-time. *Faculty:* 12 full-time (6 women). *Students:* 7 full-time (3 women), 9 part-time (3 women); includes 4 minority (all Black or African American, non-Hispanic/Latino). Average age 30. 14 applicants, 79% accepted, 9 enrolled. In 2017, 7 master's awarded. *Degree requirements:* For master's, thesis or internship. *Entrance requirements:* For master's, GRE or MAT, statement of purpose outlining why applicant seeks admission to program; three recommendations; one official transcript from all colleges or universities attended; philosophical writing sample; for Graduate Certificate, personal statement outlining why the applicant seeks admission to the program; two academic letters of recommendation, in addition to the recommendation forms required by the graduate school, which address the student's philosophical skills and/or ethical reasoning. Additional exam requirements/recommendations for international students: Required—TOEFL (minimum score 523 paper-based, 70 iBT) or IELTS (6.5). *Application deadline:* For fall admission, 3/1 priority date for domestic and international students; for spring admission, 10/1 priority date for domestic and international students; for summer admission, 4/1 priority date for domestic and international students. Applications are processed on a rolling basis. Application fee: $75. Electronic applications accepted. *Expenses:* Tuition, state resident: full-time $4337. Tuition, nonresident: full-time $17,771. *Required fees:* $3211. Tuition and fees vary according to course load and program. *Financial support:* In 2017–18, 6 students received support, including 3 teaching assistantships (averaging $3,500 per year); career-related internships or fieldwork, institutionally sponsored loans, scholarships/grants, unspecified assistantships, and administrative assistantships also available. Support available to part-time students. Financial award application deadline: 3/1; financial award applicants required to submit FAFSA. *Total annual research expenditures:* $85,549. *Unit head:* Dr. Shannon Sullivan, Chair, 704-687-5418. *Application contact:* Kathy B. Giddings, Director of Graduate Admissions, 704-687-5503, Fax: 704-687-1668, E-mail: gradadm@uncc.edu.
Website: http://philosophy.uncc.edu/

University of North Florida, College of Arts and Sciences, Department of Philosophy, Jacksonville, FL 32224. Offers applied ethics (Graduate Certificate); practical philosophy and applied ethics (MA). *Program availability:* Part-time, evening/weekend. *Entrance requirements:* For master's, GRE General Test, minimum GPA of 3.0 in last 60 hours, 3 letters of recommendation, writing sample. Additional exam requirements/recommendations for international students: Required—TOEFL (minimum score 500 paper-based; 61 iBT). Electronic applications accepted. *Faculty research:* Late modern philosophy, pragmatism, religion and American culture, hermeneutics, philosophy of mind.

University of Pennsylvania, Wharton School, Legal Studies and Business Ethics Department, Philadelphia, PA 19104. Offers MBA, PhD.

University of St. Thomas, School of Law, Minneapolis, MN 55403-2015. Offers law (JD); organizational ethics and compliance (LL M, MSL); U.S. law (LL M); JD/LL M; JD/MA; JD/MBA; JD/MSW. *Accreditation:* ABA. *Program availability:* 100% online. *Faculty:* 29 full-time (8 women), 68 part-time/adjunct (26 women). *Students:* 387 full-time (207 women); includes 65 minority (21 Black or African American, non-Hispanic/Latino; 1 American Indian or Alaska Native, non-Hispanic/Latino; 13 Asian, non-Hispanic/Latino; 20 Hispanic/Latino; 10 Two or more races, non-Hispanic/Latino), 9 international. Average age 25. 545 applicants, 64% accepted, 145 enrolled. In 2017, 5 master's, 122 doctorates awarded. *Degree requirements:* For doctorate, mentor externship, public service. *Entrance requirements:* For doctorate, LSAT, 2 letters of recommendation, personal statement. Additional exam requirements/recommendations for international students: Recommended—TOEFL (minimum score 80 iBT). *Application deadline:* For fall admission, 8/1 priority date for domestic and international students. Applications are processed on a rolling basis. Application fee: $0. Electronic applications accepted. *Expenses:* $40,247 per academic year. *Financial support:* In 2017–18, 364 students received support. Scholarships/grants available. Financial award application deadline: 7/1; financial award applicants required to submit FAFSA. *Faculty research:* Constitutional law (executive powers and First Amendment); banking, securities, and financial markets; law, religion, and jurisprudence; international law, development and dispute resolution; formation of professional identity, values, and skills. *Unit head:* Robert K. Vischer, Dean, 651-962-4838, Fax: 651-962-4881, E-mail: rkvischer@stthomas.edu. *Application contact:* Cari Haaland, Assistant Dean for Admissions, 651-962-4872, Fax: 651-962-4876, E-mail: lawschool@stthomas.edu.
Website: http://www.stthomas.edu/law/

University of South Africa, College of Human Sciences, Pretoria, South Africa. Offers adult education (M Ed); African languages (MA, PhD); African politics (MA, PhD); Afrikaans (MA, PhD); ancient history (MA, PhD); ancient Near Eastern studies (MA, PhD); anthropology (MA, PhD); applied linguistics (MA); Arabic (MA, PhD); archaeology (MA); art history (MA); Biblical archaeology (MA); Biblical studies (M Th, D Th, PhD); Christian spirituality (M Th, D Th); church history (M Th, D Th); classical studies (MA, PhD); clinical psychology (MA); communication (MA, PhD); comparative education (M Ed, Ed D); consulting psychology (D Admin, D Com, PhD); curriculum studies (M Ed, Ed D); development studies (M Admin, MA, D Admin, PhD); didactics (M Ed, Ed D); education (M Tech); education management (M Ed, Ed D); educational psychology (M Ed); English (MA); environmental education (M Ed); French (MA, PhD); German (MA, PhD); Greek (MA); guidance and counseling (M Ed); health studies (MA, PhD), including health sciences education (MA), health services management (MA), medical and surgical nursing science (critical care general) (MA), midwifery and neonatal nursing science (MA), trauma and emergency care (MA); history (MA, PhD); history of education (Ed D); inclusive education (M Ed, Ed D); information and communications technology policy and regulation (MA); information science (MA, MIS, PhD); international politics (MA, PhD); Islamic studies (MA, PhD); Italian (MA, PhD); Judaica (MA, PhD); linguistics (MA, PhD); mathematical education (M Ed); mathematics education (MA); missiology (M Th, D Th); modern Hebrew (MA, PhD); musicology (MA, MMus, D Mus, PhD); natural science education (M Ed); New Testament (M Th, D Th); Old Testament (D Th); pastoral therapy (M Th, D Th); philosophy (MA); philosophy of education (M Ed, Ed D); politics (MA, PhD); Portuguese (MA, PhD); practical theology (M Th, D Th); psychology (MA, MS, PhD); psychology of education (M Ed, Ed D); public health (MA); religious studies (MA, D Th, PhD); Romance languages (MA); Russian (MA, PhD); Semitic languages (MA, PhD); social behavior studies in HIV/AIDS (MA); social science (mental

health) (MA); social science in development studies (MA); social science in psychology (MA); social science in social work (MA); social science in sociology (MA); social work (MSW, DSW, PhD); socio-education (M Ed, Ed D); sociolinguistics (MA); sociology (MA, PhD); Spanish (MA, PhD); systematic theology (M Th, D Th); TESOL (teaching English to speakers of other languages) (MA); theological ethics (M Th, D Th); theory of literature (MA, PhD); urban ministries (D Th); urban ministry (M Th).

The University of Tennessee at Chattanooga, Engineering Management and Technology Program, Chattanooga, TN 37403. Offers construction management (Graduate Certificate); engineering management (MS); fundamentals of engineering management (Graduate Certificate); leadership and ethics (Graduate Certificate); logistics and supply chain management (Graduate Certificate); power systems management (Graduate Certificate); project and technology management (Graduate Certificate); quality management (Graduate Certificate). *Program availability:* 100% online, blended/hybrid learning. *Students:* 14 full-time (3 women), 50 part-time (11 women); includes 17 minority (10 Black or African American, non-Hispanic/Latino; 1 Asian, non-Hispanic/Latino; 6 Hispanic/Latino), 5 international. Average age 33. 34 applicants, 94% accepted, 20 enrolled. In 2017, 18 master's, 6 other advanced degrees awarded. *Degree requirements:* For master's, thesis. *Entrance requirements:* For master's, GRE General Test, letters of recommendation; minimum undergraduate GPA of 2.7 overall or 3.0 in final two years; for Graduate Certificate, baccalaureate degree and professional experience or have already been admitted to engineering/engineering management graduate program. Additional exam requirements/recommendations for international students: Required—TOEFL (minimum score 550 paper-based; 79 iBT), IELTS (minimum score 6). *Application deadline:* For fall admission, 6/15 priority date for domestic students, 7/1 for international students; for spring admission, 11/1 priority date for domestic students, 11/1 for international students. Applications are processed on a rolling basis. Application fee: $35 ($40 for international students). Electronic applications accepted. *Expenses:* Contact institution. *Financial support:* Research assistantships, teaching assistantships, career-related internships or fieldwork, scholarships/grants, and unspecified assistantships available. Support available to part-time students. Financial award application deadline: 7/1; financial award applicants required to submit FAFSA. *Faculty research:* Plant layout design, lean manufacturing, Six Sigma, value management, product development. *Total annual research expenditures:* $108,577. *Unit head:* Dr. Neslihan Alp, Department Head, 423-425-4032, Fax: 423-425-5818, E-mail: neslihan-alp@utc.edu. *Application contact:* Dr. Joanne Romagni, Dean of the Graduate School, 423-425-4478, Fax: 423-425-5223, E-mail: joanne-romagni@utc.edu.
Website: https://www.utc.edu/college-engineering-computer-science/programs/engineering-management-and-technology/index.php

Valparaiso University, Graduate School and Continuing Education, Programs in Humane Education, Valparaiso, IN 46383. Offers M Ed, MA, Graduate Certificate. Program offered in collaboration with Institute for Humane Education. *Program availability:* Part-time, evening/weekend. *Degree requirements:* For master's, thesis, project. *Entrance requirements:* For master's, minimum GPA of 3.0, two letters of reference, official transcripts, personal statement, interview. Additional exam requirements/recommendations for international students: Required—TOEFL (minimum score 550 paper-based; 80 iBT), IELTS (minimum score 6). Electronic applications accepted. *Expenses: Tuition:* Full-time $11,340; part-time $630 per credit hour. *Required fees:* $520; $250 per year. $125 per semester. Tuition and fees vary according to program and reciprocity agreements.

Viterbo University, Master of Arts in Servant Leadership Program, La Crosse, WI 54601-4797. Offers ethical leadership in organizations (Certificate); servant leadership (MA). *Program availability:* Part-time, evening/weekend. *Degree requirements:* For master's, 30 credits (15 credits of Servant Leadership core courses and any combination of 15 elective credits). *Entrance requirements:* For master's, letter of reference, statement of goals, baccalaureate degree, transcript, interview. Additional exam requirements/recommendations for international students: Required—TOEFL (minimum score 525 paper-based). Electronic applications accepted. *Expenses:* Contact institution. *Faculty research:* Organizational culture, community building, ethical decision-making, leadership theory and practice.

West Chester University of Pennsylvania, College of Arts and Humanities, Department of Philosophy, West Chester, PA 19383. Offers business ethics (Certificate); health care ethics (Certificate); philosophy (MA); philosophy: applied ethics (MA). *Program availability:* Part-time, evening/weekend. *Students:* 1 full-time (0 women), 13 part-time (1 woman). Average age 44. 4 applicants, 75% accepted, 2 enrolled. In 2017, 3 master's awarded. *Degree requirements:* For master's, comprehensive exam, thesis optional, 30 credits. *Entrance requirements:* For master's, GRE or writing sample, three letters of reference, minimum undergraduate GPA of 2.8; for Certificate, undergraduate transcripts, minimum undergraduate GPA of 2.8. Additional exam requirements/recommendations for international students: Required—TOEFL or IELTS. *Application deadline:* For fall admission, 5/15 for international students; for spring admission, 10/15 for international students. Applications are processed on a rolling basis. Application fee: $50. Electronic applications accepted. *Expenses:* Tuition, state resident: full-time $9000; part-time $500 per credit. Tuition, nonresident: full-time $13,500; part-time $750 per credit. *Required fees:* $2959; $149.79 per credit. *Financial support:* Scholarships/grants and unspecified assistantships available. Financial award application deadline: 2/15; financial award applicants required to submit FAFSA. *Faculty research:* Ethics: theory and application; social and political, feminist, continental, Asian, post-colonial, American pragmatism, analytic philosophy. *Unit head:* Dr. Helen Daley Schroepfer, Chair, 610-436-2841, E-mail: hschroepfer@wcupa.edu. *Application contact:* Dr. Joan Woolfrey, Graduate Coordinator, 610-436-0731, E-mail: jwoolfrey@wcupa.edu.
Website: http://www.wcupa.edu/arts-humanities/philosophy/

Xavier University, Williams College of Business, Master of Business Administration Program, Cincinnati, OH 45207. Offers business administration (Exec MBA, MBA); business intelligence (MBA); finance (MBA); health industry (MBA); international business (MBA); marketing (MBA); values-based leadership (MBA); MBA/MHSA; MSN/MBA. *Accreditation:* AACSB. *Program availability:* Part-time, evening/weekend. *Degree requirements:* For master's, capstone course. *Entrance requirements:* For master's, GMAT or GRE, official transcript; resume. Additional exam requirements/recommendations for international students: Required—TOEFL (minimum score 550 paper-based; 79 iBT). Electronic applications accepted. Application fee is waived when completed online. *Expenses:* Contact institution.

Philosophy

Acadia University, Faculty of Arts, Program in Social and Political Thought, Wolfville, NS B4P 2R6, Canada. Offers MA. *Entrance requirements:* Additional exam requirements/recommendations for international students: Required—TOEFL (minimum score 580 paper-based; 93 iBT), IELTS (minimum score 6.5). *Application deadline:* For fall admission, 2/1 priority date for domestic students, 2/1 for international students. Applications are processed on a rolling basis. Application fee: $50. *Unit head:* Geoffrey Whitehall, Graduate Advisor, 902-585-1288, E-mail: geoffrey.whitehall@acadiau.ca. *Application contact:* Theresa Starratt, Graduate Studies Officer, 902-585-1914, Fax: 902-585-1096, E-mail: gradadmissions@acadiau.ca.
Website: http://spt.acadiau.ca/

American University, College of Arts and Sciences, Department of Philosophy and Religion, Washington, DC 22016-8056. Offers ethics, peace, and global affairs (MA); philosophy (MA). *Program availability:* Part-time, evening/weekend. *Faculty:* 14 full-time (8 women), 9 part-time/adjunct (5 women). *Students:* 9 full-time (2 women), 2 part-time (0 women). Average age 30. 31 applicants, 84% accepted, 10 enrolled. In 2017, 13 master's awarded. *Degree requirements:* For master's, comprehensive exam, thesis (for some programs). *Entrance requirements:* For master's, GRE, writing sample, statement of purpose, transcripts, 2 letters of recommendation, resume. Additional exam requirements/recommendations for international students: Required—TOEFL (minimum score 600 paper-based; 100 iBT). *Application deadline:* For fall admission, 2/1 priority date for domestic students; for spring admission, 11/1 priority date for domestic students. Application fee: $55. *Expenses:* Contact institution. *Financial support:* Research assistantships, teaching assistantships, scholarships/grants, and unspecified assistantships available. Financial award application deadline: 2/1; financial award applicants required to submit FAFSA. *Unit head:* Dr. Ellen Feder, Department Chair, 202-885-2931, Fax: 202-885-1094, E-mail: efeder@american.edu. *Application contact:* Jonathan Harper, Associate Director, Graduate Recruitment, 202-885-3622, E-mail: jharper@american.edu.
Website: http://www.american.edu/cas/philrel/

The American University in Cairo, School of Humanities and Social Sciences, Cairo, Egypt. Offers Arab and Islamic civilizations (Graduate Diploma); Arabic studies (MA); comparative literary studies (Graduate Diploma); Egyptology and Coptology (MA); English and comparative literature (MA); humanities and social sciences (Graduate Diploma); philosophy (MA); psychology (MA); sociology and anthropology (MA); teaching Arabic as a foreign language (MA); teaching English to speakers of other languages (MA). *Program availability:* Part-time, evening/weekend. *Faculty:* 52 full-time (27 women), 7 part-time/adjunct (3 women). *Students:* 52 full-time (41 women), 159 part-time (119 women), 38 international. Average age 31. 209 applicants, 36% accepted, 39 enrolled. In 2017, 73 master's awarded. *Degree requirements:* For master's, comprehensive exam (for some programs), thesis (for some programs). *Entrance requirements:* Additional exam requirements/recommendations for international students: Required—TOEFL (minimum score 450 paper-based; 45 iBT), IELTS (minimum score 5). *Application deadline:* For fall admission, 2/1 priority date for domestic and international students; for spring admission, 10/15 priority date for domestic and international students. Applications are processed on a rolling basis. Application fee: $85. Electronic applications accepted. *Financial support:* Fellowships with partial tuition reimbursements, scholarships/grants, tuition waivers (partial), and unspecified assistantships available. Financial award application deadline: 3/10. *Faculty research:* English literature, political science, psychology, sociology, anthropology and Egyptology, philosophy, Arabic studies, history, teaching Arabic as a foreign language, teaching English to speakers of other languages. *Unit head:* Dr. Robert Switzer, Interim Dean, 20-2-2615-1068, E-mail: nbowditch@aucegypt.edu. *Application contact:* Maha Hegazi, Director for Graduate Admissions, 20-2-2615-1462, E-mail: mahahegazi@aucegypt.edu.
Website: http://www.aucegypt.edu/huss/Pages/default.aspx

American University of Beirut, Graduate Programs, Faculty of Arts and Sciences, 1107 2020, Lebanon. Offers anthropology (MA); Arab and Middle Eastern history (PhD); Arabic language and literature (MA, PhD); archaeology (MA); art history and curating (MA); biology (MS); cell and molecular biology (PhD); chemistry (MS); clinical psychology (MA); computational sciences (MS); computer science (MS); economics (MA); education (MA), including administration and policy studies, elementary education, mathematics education, psychology school guidance, psychology test and measurements, science education, teaching English as a foreign language; English language (MA); English literature (MA); environmental policy planning (MS); financial economics (MAFE); general psychology (MA); geology (MS); history (MA); Islamic studies (MA); mathematics (MS); media studies (MA); Middle East studies (MA); philosophy (MA); physics (MS); political studies (MA); public administration (MA); public policy and international affairs (MA); sociology (MA); theoretical physics (PhD). *Program availability:* Part-time. *Faculty:* 108 full-time (36 women), 5 part-time/adjunct (4 women). *Students:* 251 full-time (180 women), 233 part-time (172 women). Average age 26. 425 applicants, 65% accepted, 121 enrolled. In 2017, 47 master's, 2 doctorates awarded. *Degree requirements:* For master's, one foreign language, comprehensive exam, thesis (for some programs), project; for doctorate, one foreign language, comprehensive exam, thesis/dissertation. *Entrance requirements:* For master's, GRE General Test (for some programs); for doctorate, GRE General Test (GRE Subject Test for theoretical physics). Additional exam requirements/recommendations for international students: Required—TOEFL (minimum score 583 paper-based; 97 iBT), IELTS (minimum score 7). *Application deadline:* For fall admission, 2/8 for domestic students; for spring admission, 11/3 for domestic students. Application fee: $50. Electronic applications accepted. *Expenses:* Contact institution. *Financial support:* In 2017–18, 29 fellowships, 40 research assistantships were awarded; teaching assistantships, scholarships/grants, tuition waivers (full and partial), and unspecified assistantships also available. Financial award application deadline: 4/4. *Unit head:* Dr. Nadia Maria El Cheikh, Dean, Faculty of Arts and Sciences, 961-1-374374 Ext. 3800, Fax: 961-1-744461, E-mail: nmcheikh@aub.edu.lb. *Application contact:* Rima Rassi, Graduate Studies Officer, 961-1-350000 Ext. 3833, Fax: 961-1-744461, E-mail: rr46@aub.edu.lb.
Website: http://www.aub.edu.lb/fas/pages/default.aspx

Arizona State University at the Tempe campus, College of Liberal Arts and Sciences, School of Historical, Philosophical and Religious Studies, Tempe, AZ 85287-4301. Offers European history (MA, PhD); medieval studies (Graduate Certificate); North American history (MA, PhD); philosophy (MA, PhD); public history (MA); religious studies (MA, PhD); Renaissance studies (Graduate Certificate); scholarly publishing (Graduate Certificate). *Program availability:* Part-time. Terminal master's awarded for partial completion of doctoral program. *Degree requirements:* For master's, thesis or

alternative, interactive Program of Study (iPOS) submitted before completing 50 percent of required credit hours; for doctorate, variable foreign language requirement, comprehensive exam, thesis/dissertation, interactive Program of Study (iPOS) submitted before completing 50 percent of required credit hours. *Entrance requirements:* For master's and doctorate, GRE, minimum GPA of 3.0 or equivalent in last 2 years of work leading to bachelor's degree. Additional exam requirements/recommendations for international students: Required—TOEFL, IELTS, or PTE. Electronic applications accepted.

Baylor University, Graduate School, College of Arts and Sciences, Department of Philosophy, Waco, TX 76798. Offers MA, PhD. *Faculty:* 14 full-time (2 women). *Students:* 31 full-time (9 women); includes 3 minority (1 Asian, non-Hispanic/Latino; 2 Hispanic/Latino), 3 international. 57 applicants, 9% accepted, 4 enrolled. In 2017, 3 master's, 4 doctorates awarded. Terminal master's awarded for partial completion of doctoral program. *Degree requirements:* For master's, comprehensive exam; for doctorate, comprehensive exam, thesis/dissertation. *Entrance requirements:* For master's and doctorate, GRE General Test. Additional exam requirements/recommendations for international students: Required—TOEFL. *Application deadline:* For fall admission, 1/2 for domestic and international students. Application fee: $50. Electronic applications accepted. *Financial support:* In 2017–18, 31 students received support, including 22 fellowships with full tuition reimbursements available (averaging $5,000 per year), 30 teaching assistantships with full tuition reimbursements available (averaging $17,500 per year); scholarships/grants, health care benefits, tuition waivers (full), and unspecified assistantships also available. Financial award application deadline: 1/2. *Faculty research:* Epistemology, metaphysics, philosophy of religion, moral psychology, Kierkegaard. *Unit head:* Dr. Alexander Robert Pruss, Graduate Program Director, 254-710-3458, Fax: 254-710-3838, E-mail: alexander_pruss@baylor.edu. *Application contact:* Nancy Kallus, Office Administrator, 254-710-4237, Fax: 254-710-3838, E-mail: nancy_kallus@baylor.edu.
Website: http://www.baylor.edu/philosophy/

Binghamton University, State University of New York, Graduate School, Harpur College of Arts and Sciences, Department of Philosophy, Binghamton, NY 13902-6000. Offers MA, PhD. *Program availability:* Part-time. *Faculty:* 14 full-time (6 women). *Students:* 1 full-time (0 women), 8 part-time (6 women); includes 4 minority (1 Black or African American, non-Hispanic/Latino; 1 Asian, non-Hispanic/Latino; 2 Hispanic/Latino), 3 international. Average age 42. 1 applicant, 100% accepted, 1 enrolled. In 2017, 2 doctorates awarded. Terminal master's awarded for partial completion of doctoral program. *Degree requirements:* For master's, 2 foreign languages, comprehensive exam (for some programs), thesis or alternative; for doctorate, one foreign language, thesis/dissertation. *Entrance requirements:* For master's and doctorate, GRE General Test, writing sample. Additional exam requirements/recommendations for international students: Required—TOEFL (minimum score 550 paper-based; 80 iBT). *Application deadline:* For fall admission, 2/1 for domestic and international students; for spring admission, 10/15 for domestic and international students. Application fee: $75. Electronic applications accepted. *Financial support:* In 2017–18, 24 students received support. Career-related internships or fieldwork, Federal Work-Study, institutionally sponsored loans, scholarships/grants, health care benefits, tuition waivers (full and partial), and unspecified assistantships also available. Financial award applicants required to submit FAFSA. *Unit head:* Anja Karnein, Graduate Director, 607-777-2778, E-mail: akarnein@binghamton.edu. *Application contact:* Ben Balkaya, Assistant Dean and Director, 607-777-2151, Fax: 607-777-2501, E-mail: balkaya@binghamton.edu.
Website: http://www2.binghamton.edu/philosophy/

Binghamton University, State University of New York, Graduate School, Harpur College of Arts and Sciences, Program in Social, Political, Ethical and Legal Philosophy, Binghamton, NY 13902-6000. Offers MA, PhD. *Program availability:* Part-time. *Faculty:* 14 full-time (6 women), 2 part-time/adjunct (0 women). *Students:* 13 full-time (4 women), 23 part-time (9 women); includes 5 minority (1 Black or African American, non-Hispanic/Latino; 1 Asian, non-Hispanic/Latino; 3 Hispanic/Latino), 6 international. Average age 32. 38 applicants, 47% accepted, 4 enrolled. In 2017, 2 master's, 4 doctorates awarded. Terminal master's awarded for partial completion of doctoral program. *Degree requirements:* For master's, comprehensive exam, thesis or alternative; for doctorate, one foreign language, thesis/dissertation. *Entrance requirements:* For master's and doctorate, GRE General Test, writing sample. Additional exam requirements/recommendations for international students: Required—TOEFL (minimum score 550 paper-based; 80 iBT). *Application deadline:* For fall admission, 2/1 for domestic and international students; for spring admission, 10/15 for domestic and international students. Application fee: $75. Electronic applications accepted. *Financial support:* In 2017–18, 23 students received support, including 23 teaching assistantships with full tuition reimbursements available (averaging $15,000 per year); career-related internships or fieldwork, Federal Work-Study, institutionally sponsored loans, scholarships/grants, health care benefits, tuition waivers (full and partial), and unspecified assistantships also available. Financial award applicants required to submit FAFSA. *Unit head:* Dr. Christopher M. Knapp, Chairperson, 607-777-4163, E-mail: c.morgan-knapp@binghamton.edu. *Application contact:* Ben Balkaya, Assistant Dean and Director, 607-777-2151, Fax: 607-777-2501, E-mail: balkaya@binghamton.edu.
Website: http://philosophy.binghamton.edu

Boston College, Graduate School of Arts and Sciences, Department of Philosophy, Chestnut Hill, MA 02467-3800. Offers MA, PhD. Terminal master's awarded for partial completion of doctoral program. *Degree requirements:* For master's, one foreign language, thesis optional; for doctorate, 2 foreign languages, thesis/dissertation. *Entrance requirements:* For master's and doctorate, GRE General Test. Additional exam requirements/recommendations for international students: Required—TOEFL (minimum score 600 paper-based; 100 iBT), IELTS (minimum score 8). *Faculty research:* History of philosophy, metaphysics, ethics, Continental philosophy, ancient philosophy, philosophy of science, social theory.

Boston College, Graduate School of Arts and Sciences, Department of Theology, Chestnut Hill, MA 02467-3800. Offers philosophy and theology (MA); theology (PhD). *Accreditation:* ATS. Terminal master's awarded for partial completion of doctoral program. *Degree requirements:* For master's, one foreign language, thesis optional; for doctorate, thesis/dissertation. *Entrance requirements:* For master's and doctorate, GRE General Test. Additional exam requirements/recommendations for international students: Required—TOEFL (minimum score 600 paper-based; 100 iBT), IELTS (minimum score 8). Electronic applications accepted. *Faculty research:* Historical theology, history of Christianity, systematic theology, Biblical studies, theological ethics, comparative theology.

Boston University, Graduate School of Arts and Sciences, Department of Philosophy, Boston, MA 02215. Offers MA, PhD, JD/MA. *Students:* 48 full-time (13 women), 2 part-time (0 women); includes 3 minority (1 Asian, non-Hispanic/Latino; 1 Hispanic/Latino; 1 Two or more races, non-Hispanic/Latino), 10 international. Average age 26. 169 applicants, 17% accepted, 10 enrolled. In 2017, 4 master's, 4 doctorates awarded. Terminal master's awarded for partial completion of doctoral program. *Degree requirements:* For master's, one foreign language, thesis; for doctorate, one foreign language, comprehensive exam, thesis/dissertation. *Entrance requirements:* For master's and doctorate, GRE General Test, 3 letters of recommendation, transcripts, personal statement, scholarly writing sample. Additional exam requirements/recommendations for international students: Required—TOEFL (minimum score 550 paper-based; 84 iBT). *Application deadline:* For fall admission, 2/1 for domestic and international students. Application fee: $95. Electronic applications accepted. *Financial support:* In 2017–18, 44 students received support, including 12 fellowships with full tuition reimbursements available (averaging $22,000 per year), 26 teaching assistantships with full tuition reimbursements available (averaging $22,000 per year); Federal Work-Study, scholarships/grants, and health care benefits also available. Financial award application deadline: 2/1. *Unit head:* C. Allen Speight, Chair, 617-353-3067, Fax: 617-353-6805, E-mail: casp8@bu.edu. *Application contact:* Laura Hubbard, Senior Program Coordinator, 617-353-2571, Fax: 617-353-6805, E-mail: casphilo@bu.edu.
Website: http://www.bu.edu/philo/

Bowling Green State University, Graduate College, College of Arts and Sciences, Department of Philosophy, Bowling Green, OH 43403. Offers applied philosophy (PhD); institutional theory and history (PhD); philosophy (MA). *Program availability:* Part-time. Terminal master's awarded for partial completion of doctoral program. *Degree requirements:* For master's, thesis or alternative; for doctorate, comprehensive exam, thesis/dissertation, foreign language or research tool. *Entrance requirements:* For master's and doctorate, GRE General Test. Additional exam requirements/recommendations for international students: Required—TOEFL. Electronic applications accepted. *Faculty research:* Moral philosophy and ethics, political and social philosophy, decision theory, applied ethics, public policy.

Brandeis University, Graduate School of Arts and Sciences, Department of Philosophy, Waltham, MA 02454-9110. Offers MA. *Program availability:* Part-time. *Faculty:* 11 full-time (3 women). *Students:* 20 full-time (5 women); includes 2 minority (1 Black or African American, non-Hispanic/Latino; 1 Hispanic/Latino), 1 international. Average age 25. 94 applicants, 37% accepted, 12 enrolled. In 2017, 9 master's awarded. *Degree requirements:* For master's, thesis or alternative, proseminar; symbolic logic; paper. *Entrance requirements:* For master's, GRE General Test, transcripts, recommendation letters, resume, statement of purpose, critical writing sample. Additional exam requirements/recommendations for international students: Required—PTE (minimum score 68), TOEFL (minimum score 600 paper-based, 100 iBT) or IELTS (7). *Application deadline:* For fall admission, 2/15 priority date for domestic students. Applications are processed on a rolling basis. Application fee: $75. Electronic applications accepted. *Expenses: Tuition:* Full-time $48,720. *Required fees:* $88. Tuition and fees vary according to course load, degree level, program and student level. *Financial support:* In 2017–18, 18 students received support, including 31 teaching assistantships with partial tuition reimbursements available (averaging $3,200 per year); Federal Work-Study, scholarships/grants, and tuition waivers (partial) also available. Support available to part-time students. Financial award application deadline: 4/15; financial award applicants required to submit FAFSA. *Faculty research:* Metaphysics and epistemology, ethics, social and political philosophy, philosophy of language, logic, philosophy of mind and cognitive science, early modern philosophy, aesthetics, philosophy of law. *Unit head:* Dr. Kate Moran, Department Chair, 781-736-2789, E-mail: kmoran@brandeis.edu. *Application contact:* Julie Seeger, Department Administrator, 781-736-2789, E-mail: jseeger@brandeis.edu.
Website: http://www.brandeis.edu/gsas/programs/philosophy.html

Brock University, Faculty of Graduate Studies, Faculty of Humanities, Program in Philosophy, St. Catharines, ON L2S 3A1, Canada. Offers MA. *Program availability:* Part-time. *Degree requirements:* For master's, thesis optional. *Entrance requirements:* For master's, honors BA in philosophy. Additional exam requirements/recommendations for international students: Required—TOEFL (minimum score 550 paper-based; 80 iBT), IELTS (minimum score 6.5), TWE (minimum score 4). Electronic applications accepted. *Faculty research:* Contemporary continental philosophy, Chinese and comparative philosophy, Indian philosophy, ethics.

Brown University, Graduate School, Department of Philosophy, Providence, RI 02912. Offers PhD. *Faculty:* 14 full-time (3 women), 1 (woman) part-time/adjunct. *Students:* 27 full-time (6 women); includes 4 minority (3 Asian, non-Hispanic/Latino; 1 Hispanic/Latino). Average age 26. 240 applicants, 6% accepted, 6 enrolled. In 2017, 3 doctorates awarded. Terminal master's awarded for partial completion of doctoral program. *Degree requirements:* For doctorate, variable foreign language requirement, thesis/dissertation. *Entrance requirements:* For doctorate, GRE General Test. Additional exam requirements/recommendations for international students: Required—TOEFL, GRE. *Application deadline:* For fall admission, 1/2 priority date for domestic students. Application fee: $75. Electronic applications accepted. *Financial support:* In 2017–18, 27 students received support, including 5 fellowships with full tuition reimbursements available (averaging $30,000 per year), 10 teaching assistantships with full tuition reimbursements available (averaging $30,000 per year); health care benefits, tuition waivers (full), unspecified assistantships, and proctorships also available. Financial award application deadline: 1/2. *Faculty research:* Metaphysics, epistemology, ethics, political philosophy, history of philosophy. *Unit head:* Prof. Paul Guyer, Chair, 401-863-2718, Fax: 401-863-2719, E-mail: paul_guyer@brown.edu. *Application contact:* Admission Office, 401-863-2600.
Website: http://www.brown.edu/philosophy

California Institute of Integral Studies, School of Consciousness and Transformation, San Francisco, CA 94103. Offers anthropology and social change (MA, PhD); Asian philosophies and cultures (MA); creative inquiry/interdisciplinary arts (MFA); East-West psychology (MA, PhD); integral and transpersonal psychology (PhD); philosophy and religion (PhD), including ecology, spirituality, and religion, philosophy, cosmology, and consciousness, women's spirituality; philosophy, cosmology, and consciousness (Certificate); transformative leadership (MA); transformative studies (PhD); women, gender, spirituality and social justice (MA); writing and consciousness (MFA). *Program availability:* Part-time, evening/weekend, 100% online, blended/hybrid learning. *Students:* 392 full-time (265 women), 141 part-time (98 women); includes 145 minority (40 Black or African American, non-Hispanic/Latino; 1 American Indian or Alaska Native, non-Hispanic/Latino; 19 Asian, non-Hispanic/Latino; 54 Hispanic/Latino; 31 Two or more races, non-Hispanic/Latino), 61 international. Average age 43. 212 applicants, 96% accepted, 153 enrolled. In 2017, 49 master's, 36 doctorates awarded. Terminal master's awarded for partial completion of doctoral program. *Degree requirements:* For master's, thesis optional; for doctorate, comprehensive exam, thesis/dissertation, 1 foreign language (for Asian philosophies and cultures). *Entrance requirements:* For master's, minimum GPA of 3.0, letters of recommendation, writing sample; for doctorate, master's degree, minimum GPA of 3.0, letters of recommendation, writing sample. Additional exam requirements/recommendations for international students: Required—TOEFL. *Application deadline:* For fall admission, 2/1 priority date for domestic and international students; for spring admission, 10/15 priority date for domestic and international students. Applications are processed on a rolling basis. Application fee: $65. Electronic applications accepted. *Expenses:* $21,400 tuition and fees (for MA); $28,390 (for MFA); $24,658 (for PhD). *Financial support:* Fellowships, research assistantships, teaching assistantships, career-related internships or fieldwork, Federal Work-Study, and scholarships/grants available. Support available to part-time students. Financial award

application deadline: 4/15; financial award applicants required to submit FAFSA. *Faculty research:* Ecology and sustainability, philosophy and religion, East-West psychology, integrative health, social and cultural anthropology, transformative leadership. *Unit head:* Kathy Littles, Academic Dean, 415-575-6100, E-mail: klittles@ciis.edu. *Application contact:* Ellen Durst, Director of Admissions, 415-575-6100, Fax: 415-575-1268, E-mail: admissions@ciis.edu.
Website: http://www.ciis.edu/

California State University, Long Beach, Graduate Studies, College of Liberal Arts, Department of Philosophy, Long Beach, CA 90840. Offers MA. *Program availability:* Part-time. *Degree requirements:* For master's, comprehensive exam or thesis. Electronic applications accepted. *Faculty research:* Philosophy of science, ethics.

California State University, Los Angeles, Graduate Studies, College of Arts and Letters, Department of Philosophy, Los Angeles, CA 90032-8530. Offers MA, Graduate Certificate. *Program availability:* Part-time, evening/weekend. *Degree requirements:* For master's, comprehensive exam. *Entrance requirements:* Additional exam requirements/recommendations for international students: Required—TOEFL (minimum score 500 paper-based). Electronic applications accepted. *Faculty research:* Aesthetics, philosophy of language, ethics, philosophy of science, history of philosophy.

Carleton University, Faculty of Graduate Studies, Faculty of Arts and Social Sciences, Department of Philosophy, Ottawa, ON K1S 5B6, Canada. Offers MA. *Degree requirements:* For master's, thesis optional. *Entrance requirements:* For master's, honors degree. Additional exam requirements/recommendations for international students: Required—TOEFL. *Faculty research:* Application of philosophical theory to issues of current concern, history of philosophy, contemporary philosophy in North America and Europe.

Carnegie Mellon University, Dietrich College of Humanities and Social Sciences, Department of Philosophy, Pittsburgh, PA 15213-3891. Offers logic, computation and methodology (MS, PhD); philosophy (MA, PhD); pure and applied logic (PhD). *Program availability:* Part-time. *Degree requirements:* For master's, thesis; for doctorate, comprehensive exam, thesis/dissertation. *Entrance requirements:* For master's and doctorate, GRE General Test. Additional exam requirements/recommendations for international students: Required—TOEFL. Electronic applications accepted. *Faculty research:* Philosophy of science, artificial intelligence.

The Catholic University of America, School of Philosophy, Washington, DC 20064. Offers MA, PhD, Ph L, MA/JD. MA/JD offered in combination with Columbus School of Law. *Program availability:* Part-time. *Faculty:* 23 full-time (5 women), 5 part-time/adjunct (2 women). *Students:* 51 full-time (6 women), 58 part-time (12 women); includes 12 minority (2 Asian, non-Hispanic/Latino; 5 Hispanic/Latino; 5 Two or more races, non-Hispanic/Latino), 6 international. Average age 31. 92 applicants, 47% accepted, 30 enrolled. In 2017, 18 master's, 11 doctorates awarded. *Degree requirements:* For master's, one foreign language, thesis, oral exam; for doctorate, 2 foreign languages, comprehensive exam, thesis/dissertation, oral exam. *Entrance requirements:* For master's, GRE General Test, statement of purpose, official copies of academic transcripts, three letters of recommendation, writing sample; for doctorate, GRE General Test, statement of purpose, official copies of academic transcripts, three letters of recommendation. Additional exam requirements/recommendations for international students: Required—TOEFL (minimum score 550 paper-based; 80 iBT). *Application deadline:* For fall admission, 7/15 priority date for domestic students, 7/1 for international students; for spring admission, 11/15 priority date for domestic students, 11/1 for international students. Applications are processed on a rolling basis. Application fee: $55. Electronic applications accepted. *Expenses:* Contact institution. *Financial support:* Fellowships, research assistantships, teaching assistantships, Federal Work-Study, scholarships/grants, tuition waivers (full and partial), and unspecified assistantships available. Financial award application deadline: 2/1; financial award applicants required to submit FAFSA. *Faculty research:* Ancient philosophy (Plato, Aristotle, Neo-Platonism), medieval philosophy (Aquinas, Scotus, Ockham, medieval Islamic), 19th- and 20th-century German philosophy (especially Kant, Hegel, Husserl and Heidegger), metaphysics, ethics, political philosophy. *Unit head:* Dr. John McCarthy, Dean, 202-319-6649, Fax: 202-319-4731, E-mail: mccartjc@cua.edu. *Application contact:* Dr. Steven Brown, Director of Graduate Admissions, 202-319-5057, Fax: 202-319-6533, E-mail: cua-admissions@cua.edu.
Website: http://philosophy.cua.edu/

Central European University, Department of Philosophy, 1051, Hungary. Offers MA, PhD. *Faculty:* 9 full-time (2 women), 4 part-time/adjunct (1 woman). *Students:* 49 full-time (10 women). Average age 28. 177 applicants, 26% accepted, 25 enrolled. In 2017, 20 master's awarded. *Degree requirements:* For master's, one foreign language, thesis; for doctorate, one foreign language, comprehensive exam, thesis/dissertation. *Entrance requirements:* For master's and doctorate, interview. Additional exam requirements/recommendations for international students: Required—TOEFL (minimum score 570 paper-based); Recommended—IELTS (minimum score 6.5). *Application deadline:* For fall admission, 2/4 for domestic and international students. Application fee: $30. Electronic applications accepted. *Expenses: Tuition:* Full-time 12,000 euros. *Required fees:* 230 euros. One-time fee: 30 euros full-time. Tuition and fees vary according to course level, course load, degree level and program. *Financial support:* In 2017–18, 45 students received support. Fellowships, teaching assistantships, scholarships/grants, health care benefits, and tuition waivers (full and partial) available. *Faculty research:* Questions of metaphysics, both in a contemporary and historical perspective issues about the freedom of the will; ancient metaphysics and philosophy of nature modality in early modern philosophy; the philosophy of mind; perception; political philosophy; cognitive science; ethics and met ethics. *Unit head:* Dr. Hanoch Ben-Yami, Head of Department, 36 1 327-3806, Fax: 36-1-327-3072, E-mail: philosophy@ceu.edu. *Application contact:* Zsuzsanna Jaszberenyi, Admissions Officer, 361-324-3009, Fax: 367-327-3211, E-mail: admissions@ceu.edu.
Website: http://philosophy.ceu.edu

Claremont Graduate University, Graduate Programs, School of Arts and Humanities, Department of Philosophy, Claremont, CA 91711-6160. Offers MA, PhD, MA/PhD, MBA/MA, MBA/PhD. *Program availability:* Part-time. *Degree requirements:* For doctorate, research folio. *Entrance requirements:* For master's and doctorate, GRE General Test. Additional exam requirements/recommendations for international students: Required—TOEFL (minimum score 75 iBT). Electronic applications accepted. *Faculty research:* Ancient philosophy, philosophy of science, probability theory, philosophical logic, philosophy of logic.

Cleveland State University, College of Graduate Studies, College of Liberal Arts and Social Sciences, Department of Philosophy and Comparative Religion, Cleveland, OH 44115. Offers bioethics (MA, Certificate), including bioethics (MA); philosophy (MA), including philosophy. *Program availability:* Part-time, evening/weekend. *Faculty:* 4 full-time (all women), 2 part-time/adjunct (1 woman). *Students:* 3 full-time (0 women), 2 part-time (1 woman); includes 1 minority (Asian, non-Hispanic/Latino). Average age 35. 11 applicants, 100% accepted, 4 enrolled. In 2017, 2 master's, 1 other advanced degree awarded. *Degree requirements:* For master's, comprehensive exam, thesis optional, 32 credit hours of coursework; for Certificate, 12 credit hours of coursework. *Entrance requirements:* For master's and Certificate, BA, BS, or equivalent degree with minimum

GPA of 2.75. Additional exam requirements/recommendations for international students: Required—TOEFL (minimum score 550 paper-based; 78 iBT). *Application deadline:* For fall admission, 7/1 priority date for domestic students, 5/15 priority date for international students; for spring admission, 11/15 for domestic students, 11/1 for international students; for summer admission, 4/1 for domestic students, 3/15 for international students. Applications are processed on a rolling basis. Application fee: $40. Electronic applications accepted. *Financial support:* In 2017–18, 5 students received support, including 5 teaching assistantships with full tuition reimbursements available (averaging $4,000 per year); health care benefits, tuition waivers (full), and unspecified assistantships also available. Support available to part-time students. *Faculty research:* Ethics, early modern philosophy, bioethics, social and political philosophy, history of women philosophers. *Unit head:* Dr. Mary Ellen Waithe, Chairperson, 216-687-3900, Fax: 216-523-7482, E-mail: m.waithe@csuohio.edu. *Application contact:* Deborah L. Brown, Interim Assistant Director, Graduate Admissions, 216-523-7572, Fax: 216-687-5400, E-mail: d.l.brown@csuohio.edu.
Website: http://www.csuohio.edu/class/philosophy-religion/philosophy-religion

Collège Dominicain de Philosophie et de Théologie, Graduate Programs, Faculty of Philosophy, Ottawa, ON K1R 7G3, Canada. Offers MA Ph, PhD. *Degree requirements:* For master's, thesis; for doctorate, 2 foreign languages, thesis/dissertation, candidacy exam. *Entrance requirements:* For master's, honors degree in philosophy, minimum B average in undergraduate course work; for doctorate, master's degree in philosophy, minimum A average in graduate course work. *Faculty research:* Ethics, philosophy of Kant.

Colorado State University, College of Liberal Arts, Department of Philosophy, Fort Collins, CO 80523-1781. Offers MA. *Program availability:* Part-time. *Faculty:* 7 full-time (2 women). *Students:* 11 full-time (5 women), 15 part-time (3 women); includes 3 minority (all Hispanic/Latino). Average age 27. 57 applicants, 28% accepted, 8 enrolled. In 2017, 3 master's awarded. *Degree requirements:* For master's, comprehensive exam (for some programs), thesis or alternative, 30-33 credit hours of coursework. *Entrance requirements:* For master's, bachelor's degree; minimum undergraduate GPA of 3.25; statement of purpose; writing sample; letters of recommendation. Additional exam requirements/recommendations for international students: Required—TOEFL (minimum score 550 paper-based; 80 iBT), IELTS (minimum score 6.5), PTE (minimum score 58). *Application deadline:* For fall admission, 2/15 for domestic and international students. Application fee: $60 ($70 for international students). Electronic applications accepted. *Expenses:* Tuition, state resident: full-time $9917. Tuition, nonresident: full-time $24,312. *Required fees:* $2284. Tuition and fees vary according to course load and program. *Financial support:* In 2017–18, 13 students received support, including 13 teaching assistantships with full tuition reimbursements available (averaging $14,256 per year); fellowships with full tuition reimbursements available, scholarships/grants, and health care benefits also available. Financial award application deadline: 2/15. *Faculty research:* Environmental ethics, animal ethics, non-Western philosophy, metaethics, epistemology. *Total annual research expenditures:* $15,000. *Unit head:* Dr. John Didier, Department Chair, 970-491-6315, Fax: 970-491-4900, E-mail: john.didier@colostate.edu. *Application contact:* Gaylene Wolfe, Graduate Coordinator, 970-491-6315, Fax: 970-491-4900, E-mail: gaylene.wolfe@colostate.edu.
Website: http://philosophy.colostate.edu/

Columbia University, Graduate School of Arts and Sciences, New York, NY 10027. Offers African-American studies (MA); American studies (MA); anthropology (MA, PhD); art history and archaeology (MA, PhD); astronomy (PhD); biological sciences (PhD); biotechnology (MA); chemical physics (PhD); chemistry (PhD); classical studies (MA, PhD); classics (MA, PhD); climate and society (MA); conservation biology (MA); earth and environmental sciences (PhD); East Asia: regional studies (MA); East Asian languages and cultures (MA, PhD); ecology, evolution and environmental biology (MA), including conservation biology; ecology, evolution, and environmental biology (PhD), including ecology and evolutionary biology, evolutionary primatology; economics (MA, PhD); English and comparative literature (MA, PhD); French and Romance philology (MA, PhD); Germanic languages (MA, PhD); global French studies (MA); global thought (MA); Hispanic cultural studies (MA); history (PhD); history and literature (MA); human rights studies (MA); Islamic studies (MA); Italian (MA, PhD); Japanese pedagogy (MA); Jewish studies (MA); Latin America and the Caribbean: regional studies (MA); Latin American and Iberian cultures (PhD); mathematics (MA, PhD), including finance (MA); medieval and Renaissance studies (MA); Middle Eastern, South Asian, and African studies (MA, PhD); modern art: critical and curatorial studies (MA); modern European studies (MA); museum anthropology (MA); music (DMA, PhD); oral history (MA); philosophical foundations of physics (MA); philosophy (MA, PhD); physics (PhD); political science (MA, PhD); psychology (PhD); quantitative methods in the social sciences (MA); religion (MA, PhD); Russia, Eurasia and East Europe: regional studies (MA); Russian translation (MA); Slavic cultures (MA); Slavic languages (MA, PhD); sociology (MA, PhD); South Asian studies (MA); statistics (MA, PhD); theatre (PhD). Dual-degree programs require admission to both Graduate School of Arts and Sciences and another Columbia school. *Program availability:* Part-time. Terminal master's awarded for partial completion of doctoral program. *Degree requirements:* For master's, variable foreign language requirement, comprehensive exam (for some programs), thesis (for some programs); for doctorate, variable foreign language requirement, comprehensive exam (for some programs), thesis/dissertation. *Entrance requirements:* For master's and doctorate, GRE General Test, GRE Subject Test (for some programs). Additional exam requirements/recommendations for international students: Required—TOEFL, IELTS. Electronic applications accepted. *Expenses: Tuition:* Full-time $44,864; part-time $1704 per credit. *Required fees:* $2370 per semester. One-time fee: $105.

Concordia University, School of Graduate Studies, Faculty of Arts and Science, Department of Philosophy, Montréal, QC H3G 1M8, Canada. Offers MA. *Degree requirements:* For master's, comprehensive exam, thesis or alternative. *Entrance requirements:* For master's, honors degree in philosophy or equivalent. *Faculty research:* Anglo-American analytic thought, Continental thought, pragmatic thought.

Cornell University, Graduate School, Graduate Fields of Arts and Sciences, Field of Philosophy, Ithaca, NY 14853. Offers PhD. *Degree requirements:* For doctorate, comprehensive exam, thesis/dissertation, teaching experience. *Entrance requirements:* For doctorate, sample of written work in philosophy, 2 letters of recommendation. Additional exam requirements/recommendations for international students: Required—TOEFL (minimum score 550 paper-based; 77 iBT). Electronic applications accepted.

Dalhousie University, Faculty of Arts and Social Science, Department of Philosophy, Halifax, NS B3H 4R2, Canada. Offers MA, PhD. *Entrance requirements:* For doctorate, MA in philosophy. Additional exam requirements/recommendations for international students: Required—TOEFL, IELTS, CANTEST, CAEL, or Michigan English Language Assessment Battery. Electronic applications accepted. *Faculty research:* Ethical and political philosophy; epistemology; philosophy of language, history, and logic; bioethics; feminist theory.

Dallas Theological Seminary, Graduate Programs, Dallas, TX 75204-6499. Offers adult education (Th M); apologetics (Th M); Bible backgrounds (Th M); Bible translation (Th M); Biblical and theological studies (Certificate); biblical counseling (MA); biblical exegesis and linguistics (MA); biblical exposition (PhD); biblical studies (MA); Biblical theology (Th M); children's education (Th M); Christian education (MA, D Min); Christian

leadership (MA); cross-cultural ministries (MA); educational administration (Th M); educational leadership (Th M); evangelism and discipleship (Th M); exposition of Biblical books (Th M); family life education (Th M); general studies (Th M); Hebrew and cognate studies (Th M); hermeneutics (Th M); historical theology (Th M); homiletics (Th M); intercultural ministries (Th M); Jesus studies (Th M); leadership studies (Th M); media and communication (MA); media arts (Th M); ministry (D Min); ministry with women (Th M); New Testament studies (Th M, PhD); Old Testament studies (Th M, PhD); parachurch ministries (Th M); pastoral care and counseling (Th M); pastoral theology and practice (Th M); philosophy (Th M); sacred theology (STM); spiritual formation (Th M); systematic theology (Th M); teaching in Christian institutions (Th M); theological studies (PhD); urban ministries (Th M); worship studies (Th M); youth education (Th M). *Program availability:* Part-time, online learning. *Degree requirements:* For master's, variable foreign language requirement, thesis (for some programs); for doctorate, 2 foreign languages, thesis/dissertation. *Entrance requirements:* For master's, GRE or MAT (if minimum undergraduate cumulative GPA is below 2.5 or undergraduate degree is unaccredited). Additional exam requirements/recommendations for international students: Required—TOEFL (minimum score 575 paper-based; 85 iBT), TWE. Electronic applications accepted.

Delta State University, Graduate Programs, College of Arts and Sciences, Program in Liberal Studies, Cleveland, MS 38733-0001. Offers evolving human voices (MALS); gender and diversity studies (MALS); globalization studies (MALS); Mississippi Delta studies (MALS); philosophy (MALS); religious studies (MALS). *Degree requirements:* For master's, oral and/or written comprehensive exam.

Dominican School of Philosophy and Theology, Graduate Programs, Berkeley, CA 94708. Offers philosophy (MA); theology (M Div, MA, MTS, Certificate); M Div/MA; MA/MA. *Accreditation:* ATS. *Program availability:* Part-time. *Degree requirements:* For master's, one foreign language, thesis. *Entrance requirements:* For master's, GRE General Test (for MA), minimum GPA of 3.0 (for MA), 2.3 (for M Div); academic writing sample (for MA); statement of purpose, official transcripts, letters of recommendation. Additional exam requirements/recommendations for international students: Required—TOEFL (minimum score 570 paper-based; 80 iBT), IELTS. Electronic applications accepted.

Dominican University of California, School of Liberal Arts and Education, Humanities Program, San Rafael, CA 94901-2298. Offers applied music (MA); art history (MA); creative writing (MA); gender studies (MA); history (MA); philosophy (MA); political theory (MA); religion (MA). *Program availability:* Part-time. *Faculty:* 7 full-time (4 women), 1 (woman) part-time/adjunct. *Students:* 6 full-time (5 women), 16 part-time (12 women); includes 8 minority (3 Black or African American, non-Hispanic/Latino; 4 Hispanic/Latino; 1 Two or more races, non-Hispanic/Latino), 2 international. Average age 45. 7 applicants, 100% accepted, 5 enrolled. In 2017, 14 master's awarded. *Degree requirements:* For master's, thesis or alternative. *Entrance requirements:* For master's, minimum GPA of 3.0, interview. Additional exam requirements/recommendations for international students: Required—TOEFL (minimum score 550 paper-based; 80 iBT), IELTS (minimum score 6.5). *Application deadline:* For fall admission, 5/15 priority date for domestic and international students; for spring admission, 11/15 priority date for domestic and international students. Applications are processed on a rolling basis. Application fee: $0. Electronic applications accepted. *Expenses: Tuition:* Full-time $17,370; part-time $965 per credit. *Required fees:* $150 per semester. Tuition and fees vary according to course load and program. *Financial support:* In 2017–18, 4 students received support. Scholarships/grants available. Support available to part-time students. Financial award application deadline: 3/2; financial award applicants required to submit FAFSA. *Unit head:* Joan Baranow, Program Director, 415-485-3264, E-mail: joan.baranow@dominican.edu. *Application contact:* Michael Lavigna, Assistant Director of Graduate Admissions, 415-485-3253, Fax: 415-485-3214, E-mail: gradmissions@dominican.edu.
Website: https://www.dominican.edu/academics/lae/graduate-programs/ma-in-humanities/index_html

Duke University, Graduate School, Department of Philosophy, Durham, NC 27708. Offers PhD, JD/AM, JD/PhD. *Degree requirements:* For doctorate, one foreign language, thesis/dissertation. *Entrance requirements:* For doctorate, GRE General Test. Additional exam requirements/recommendations for international students: Required—TOEFL (minimum score 577 paper-based; 90 iBT) or IELTS (minimum score 7). Electronic applications accepted.

Duquesne University, Graduate School of Liberal Arts, Department of Philosophy, Pittsburgh, PA 15282-0001. Offers MA, PhD. *Program availability:* Part-time, evening/weekend. *Faculty:* 18 full-time (5 women), 4 part-time/adjunct (2 women). *Students:* 51 full-time (12 women), 1 part-time (0 women); includes 2 minority (1 Hispanic/Latino; 1 Two or more races, non-Hispanic/Latino), 16 international. Average age 29. 94 applicants, 41% accepted, 15 enrolled. In 2017, 6 master's, 4 doctorates awarded. Terminal master's awarded for partial completion of doctoral program. *Degree requirements:* For master's, one foreign language; for doctorate, 2 foreign languages, comprehensive exam, thesis/dissertation. *Entrance requirements:* For master's, GRE General Test, bachelor's degree in philosophy, minimum GPA of 3.5; for doctorate, GRE General Test, master's degree in philosophy, minimum GPA of 3.75. Additional exam requirements/recommendations for international students: Required—TOEFL. *Application deadline:* For fall admission, 2/15 for domestic and international students. Application fee: $0. Electronic applications accepted. *Expenses:* $1,259 per credit. *Financial support:* In 2017–18, 28 students received support, including 18 teaching assistantships with full tuition reimbursements available (averaging $18,000 per year); Federal Work-Study, scholarships/grants, tuition waivers (partial), and unspecified assistantships also available. Financial award application deadline: 5/1. *Faculty research:* Phenomenology, Twentieth-Century Continental philosophy, history of philosophy. *Unit head:* Dr. Ronald Polansky, Chair, 412-396-6500, E-mail: polansky@duq.edu. *Application contact:* Linda Rendulic, Assistant to the Dean, 412-396-6400, Fax: 412-396-5265, E-mail: rendulic@duq.edu.
Website: http://www.duq.edu/academics/schools/liberal-arts/graduate-school/programs/philosophy

Eastern Michigan University, Graduate School, College of Arts and Sciences, Department of History and Philosophy, Program in Philosophy, Ypsilanti, MI 48197. Offers MA. *Program availability:* Part-time, evening/weekend, online learning. *Students:* 8 full-time (5 women), 11 part-time (2 women); includes 3 minority (1 Black or African American, non-Hispanic/Latino; 2 Hispanic/Latino). Average age 33. 18 applicants, 83% accepted, 8 enrolled. *Degree requirements:* For master's, thesis optional. *Entrance requirements:* Additional exam requirements/recommendations for international students: Required—TOEFL. *Application deadline:* Applications are processed on a rolling basis. Application fee: $45. *Financial support:* Fellowships, research assistantships with full tuition reimbursements, teaching assistantships with full tuition reimbursements, career-related internships or fieldwork, Federal Work-Study, institutionally sponsored loans, traineeships, and unspecified assistantships available. Support available to part-time students. Financial award applicants required to submit FAFSA. *Application contact:* Dr. Laura McMahon, Advisor, 734-487-1018, Fax: 734-487-6835, E-mail: lmcmaho1@emich.edu.

Emory University, Laney Graduate School, Department of Comparative Literature, Atlanta, GA 30322-1100. Offers comparative literature (PhD); philosophy (Certificate); psychoanalytic studies (PhD); women's studies (Certificate). *Degree requirements:* For doctorate, 2 foreign languages, comprehensive exam, thesis/dissertation. *Entrance requirements:* For doctorate, GRE General Test, minimum GPA of 3.0. Additional exam requirements/recommendations for international students: Required—TOEFL. Electronic applications accepted. *Faculty research:* Literary theory, psychoanalysis trauma and testimony, literature and religion, literature and technology, literature and philosophy, politics and global culture, literature and aesthetics.

Emory University, Laney Graduate School, Department of Philosophy, Atlanta, GA 30322-1100. Offers PhD. *Degree requirements:* For doctorate, 2 foreign languages, comprehensive exam, thesis/dissertation. *Entrance requirements:* For doctorate, GRE General Test, minimum GPA of 3.0. Additional exam requirements/recommendations for international students: Required—TOEFL. Electronic applications accepted. *Faculty research:* History of philosophy, German idealism, twentieth century Continental philosophy, ethics, social theory.

Florida State University, The Graduate School, College of Arts and Sciences, Department of Philosophy, Tallahassee, FL 32306-1500. Offers history and philosophy of science (MA); philosophy (MA, PhD). *Faculty:* 14 full-time (3 women), 2 part-time/adjunct (1 woman). *Students:* 58 full-time (14 women), 2 part-time (both women); includes 13 minority (2 Black or African American, non-Hispanic/Latino; 3 Asian, non-Hispanic/Latino; 3 Hispanic/Latino; 5 Two or more races, non-Hispanic/Latino). Average age 25. 67 applicants, 30% accepted, 9 enrolled. In 2017, 5 master's, 4 doctorates awarded. Terminal master's awarded for partial completion of doctoral program. *Degree requirements:* For master's, one foreign language, comprehensive exam, thesis or alternative; for doctorate, one foreign language, comprehensive exam, thesis/dissertation. *Entrance requirements:* For master's and doctorate, GRE General Test. Additional exam requirements/recommendations for international students: Required—TOEFL (minimum score 550 paper-based; 80 iBT). *Application deadline:* For fall admission, 3/31 priority date for domestic and international students; for winter admission, 10/19 for domestic and international students; for spring admission, 11/1 priority date for domestic and international students; for summer admission, 3/1 priority date for domestic and international students. Applications are processed on a rolling basis. Application fee: $30. Electronic applications accepted. *Financial support:* In 2017–18, 59 students received support, including 2 fellowships with full tuition reimbursements available (averaging $30,000 per year), 57 teaching assistantships with full tuition reimbursements available (averaging $16,392 per year); Federal Work-Study, scholarships/grants, health care benefits, and tuition waivers (full and partial) also available. Financial award application deadline: 3/31; financial award applicants required to submit FAFSA. *Faculty research:* Philosophy of biology, Greek philosophy, ethics, action theory, philosophy of mind, metaphysics. *Unit head:* Dr. John Piers Rawling, Chairman, 850-644-1483, Fax: 850-644-3832, E-mail: prawling@fsu.edu. *Application contact:* 850-644-1483, Fax: 850-644-3832, E-mail: philosophy@admin.fsu.edu.
Website: http://philosophy.fsu.edu/

Fordham University, Graduate School of Arts and Sciences, Department of Philosophy, New York, NY 10458. Offers MA, PhD. *Program availability:* Part-time, evening/weekend. *Faculty:* 31 full-time (10 women). *Students:* 58 full-time (17 women), 8 part-time (0 women); includes 7 minority (2 Asian, non-Hispanic/Latino; 5 Hispanic/Latino), 5 international. Average age 30. 144 applicants, 22% accepted, 16 enrolled. In 2017, 10 master's, 8 doctorates awarded. Terminal master's awarded for partial completion of doctoral program. *Degree requirements:* For master's, one foreign language, comprehensive exam; for doctorate, 2 foreign languages, comprehensive exam, thesis/dissertation. *Entrance requirements:* For master's and doctorate, GRE General Test. Additional exam requirements/recommendations for international students: Required—TOEFL (minimum score 650 paper-based). *Application deadline:* For fall admission, 1/4 priority date for domestic students; for spring admission, 11/1 for domestic students. Application fee: $70. Electronic applications accepted. *Financial support:* In 2017–18, 45 students received support, including 3 fellowships with tuition reimbursements available (averaging $21,605 per year), 1 research assistantship with tuition reimbursement available (averaging $25,390 per year), 26 teaching assistantships with tuition reimbursements available (averaging $23,644 per year); institutionally sponsored loans, tuition waivers (full and partial), and unspecified assistantships also available. Support available to part-time students. Financial award application deadline: 1/4. *Faculty research:* Contemporary Continental philosophy (including German idealism), philosophy of religion, medieval philosophy, ethics, epistemology. *Unit head:* Dr. Giorgio Pini, Department Chair, 718-817-2779, Fax: 718-817-3300, E-mail: pini@fordham.edu. *Application contact:* Travis Strattion, Interim Director of Graduate Admissions, 718-817-4417, Fax: 718-817-3566, E-mail: tstrattion@fordham.edu.

Franciscan University of Steubenville, Graduate Programs, Department of Philosophy, Steubenville, OH 43952-1763. Offers MA. *Program availability:* Part-time. *Degree requirements:* For master's, one foreign language, thesis. *Entrance requirements:* For master's, minimum undergraduate GPA of 3.0. Additional exam requirements/recommendations for international students: Required—TOEFL. Electronic applications accepted. Application fee is waived when completed online. *Expenses: Tuition:* Full-time $9000; part-time $500 per semester hour. *Required fees:* $16 per semester hour. Tuition and fees vary according to program.

George Mason University, College of Humanities and Social Sciences, Department of Philosophy, Fairfax, VA 22030. Offers ethics and public affairs (MA); philosophy and cultural theory (MA). *Faculty:* 11 full-time (3 women), 8 part-time/adjunct (0 women). *Students:* 10 part-time (3 women); includes 1 minority (Hispanic/Latino). Average age 39. 9 applicants, 67% accepted, 1 enrolled. In 2017, 4 master's awarded. *Degree requirements:* For master's, thesis optional. *Entrance requirements:* For master's, college transcripts, goals statement, 2 letters of recommendation, resume, writing sample; completion of certain undergraduate preparation coursework with grades of B or higher in each course (for philosophy and cultural theory). Additional exam requirements/recommendations for international students: Required—TOEFL (minimum score 575 paper-based, 88 iBT), IELTS (6.5), or PTE (59). *Application deadline:* For fall admission, 3/1 for domestic and international students; for spring admission, 11/1 for domestic and international students. Application fee: $75 ($80 for international students). Electronic applications accepted. *Expenses:* Tuition, state resident: full-time $11,228; part-time $459.50 per credit. Tuition, nonresident: full-time $30,932; part-time $1280.50 per credit. *Required fees:* $3252; $135.50 per credit. Part-time tuition and fees vary according to course load and program. *Financial support:* In 2017–18, 1 student received support, including 1 research assistantship with tuition reimbursement available; career-related internships or fieldwork, Federal Work-Study, scholarships/grants, unspecified assistantships, and health care benefits (for full-time research or teaching assistantship recipients) also available. Financial award application deadline: 3/1; financial award applicants required to submit FAFSA. *Faculty research:* History of philosophy (particularly Asian and modern); Anglo-American and analytic philosophy; continental philosophy; ethics (including bioethics and feminist ethics); philosophy and public policy. *Total annual research expenditures:* $131,560. *Unit head:* Ted Kinnaman, Chair/Associate Professor, 703-993-4328, Fax: 703-993-1297, E-mail: tkinnama@gmu.edu. *Application contact:* Rose Cherubin, Associate Professor and Graduate Coordinator, 703-993-1332, Fax: 703-993-1297, E-mail: rcherubi@gmu.edu.
Website: http://philosophy.gmu.edu/

Philosophy

Georgetown University, Graduate School of Arts and Sciences, Department of Philosophy, Washington, DC 20057. Offers bioethics (MA); philosophy (PhD); JD/MA; JD/PhD; MD/PhD. *Degree requirements:* For master's, thesis or alternative; for doctorate, 2 foreign languages, comprehensive exam, thesis/dissertation. *Entrance requirements:* For master's and doctorate, GRE General Test. Additional exam requirements/recommendations for international students: Required—TOEFL.

The George Washington University, Columbian College of Arts and Sciences, Department of Philosophy, Washington, DC 20052. Offers philosophy and social policy (MA). *Faculty:* 10 full-time (4 women), 9 part-time/adjunct (1 woman). *Students:* 3 full-time (2 women), 5 part-time (2 women); includes 2 minority (1 Asian, non-Hispanic/Latino; 1 Hispanic/Latino). Average age 26. 26 applicants, 92% accepted, 4 enrolled. *Degree requirements:* For master's, comprehensive exam, thesis or alternative. *Entrance requirements:* For master's, GRE General Test, interview, minimum GPA of 3.0. Additional exam requirements/recommendations for international students: Required—TOEFL (minimum score 600 paper-based; 100 iBT). *Application deadline:* For fall admission, 4/1 priority date for domestic and international students; for spring admission, 10/1 priority date for domestic students, 9/1 priority date for international students. Applications are processed on a rolling basis. Application fee: $60. Electronic applications accepted. *Expenses: Tuition:* Full-time $28,800; part-time $1655 per credit hour. *Required fees:* $45; $2.75 per credit hour. *Financial support:* Fellowships with tuition reimbursements, Federal Work-Study, and institutionally sponsored loans available. Financial award application deadline: 1/15. *Unit head:* Tad Zawidzki, Chair, 202-994-6444, E-mail: zawidzki@gwu.edu. *Application contact:* Amanda McLaughlin, Executive Aide, 202-994-6265, Fax: 202-994-8683, E-mail: philosop@gwu.edu.
Website: https://philosophy.columbian.gwu.edu/

Georgia State University, College of Arts and Sciences, Department of Philosophy, Atlanta, GA 30302-4089. Offers MA, MA/JD. *Program availability:* Part-time. *Faculty:* 17 full-time (4 women). *Students:* 55 full-time (12 women); includes 7 minority (2 Asian, non-Hispanic/Latino; 3 Hispanic/Latino; 2 Two or more races, non-Hispanic/Latino), 9 international. Average age 25. 153 applicants, 42% accepted, 22 enrolled. In 2017, 22 master's awarded. *Entrance requirements:* For master's, GRE, writing sample, 3 letters of recommendation. Additional exam requirements/recommendations for international students: Required—TOEFL (minimum score 550 paper-based; 80 iBT). *Application deadline:* For fall admission, 2/1 priority date for domestic and international students. Applications are processed on a rolling basis. Application fee: $50. Electronic applications accepted. *Expenses:* Tuition, state resident: full-time $7020. Tuition, nonresident: full-time $22,518. *Required fees:* $2128. Tuition and fees vary according to degree level and program. *Financial support:* In 2017–18, fellowships with full tuition reimbursements (averaging $15,000 per year), research assistantships with full tuition reimbursements (averaging $6,000 per year), teaching assistantships with full tuition reimbursements (averaging $10,000 per year) were awarded; health care benefits also available. Financial award application deadline: 8/1; financial award applicants required to submit FAFSA. *Faculty research:* Social and political philosophy, neurophilosophy (empirical philosophy of mind), Kant and post-Kantian German philosophy. *Unit head:* Dr. George Rainbolt, Chair, 404-413-6109, Fax: 404-413-6124, E-mail: grainbolt@gsu.edu. *Application contact:* Dr. Tim O'Keefe, Director of Graduate Studies, 404-413-6108, Fax: 404-413-6124, E-mail: tokeefe@gsu.edu.
Website: http://www2.gsu.edu/~wwwphi/

Gonzaga University, College of Arts and Sciences, Spokane, WA 99258. Offers philosophy (MA); theology and leadership (MA). *Program availability:* Part-time, blended/hybrid learning. *Faculty:* 9 full-time (3 women). *Students:* 1 full-time (0 women), 43 part-time (21 women); includes 9 minority (4 Black or African American, non-Hispanic/Latino; 1 American Indian or Alaska Native, non-Hispanic/Latino; 3 Asian, non-Hispanic/Latino; 1 Hispanic/Latino), 2 international. Average age 37. 47 applicants, 79% accepted, 22 enrolled. In 2017, 4 master's awarded. *Degree requirements:* For master's, comprehensive exam. *Entrance requirements:* For master's, GRE or MAT, minimum GPA of 3.0, official transcripts, two to three letters of recommendation, personal statement, writing sample, resume/curriculum vitae. Additional exam requirements/recommendations for international students: Required—TOEFL (minimum score 88 iBT) or IELTS (minimum score 6.5). *Application deadline:* For fall admission, 7/15 for domestic students; for spring admission, 11/1 for domestic students; for summer admission, 4/9 for domestic students. Applications are processed on a rolling basis. Application fee: $50. Electronic applications accepted. *Expenses:* $700 per credit (theology and leadership); $830 per credit (philosophy). *Financial support:* In 2017–18, 38 students received support. Scholarships/grants and unspecified assistantships available. Support available to part-time students. Financial award applicants required to submit FAFSA. *Faculty research:* Environmental ethics, phenomenology and religion, healthcare ethics, ancient philosophy. *Unit head:* Dr. Patricia Terry, Interim Dean of the College of Arts and Sciences, 509-313-5522, Fax: 509-313-6684, E-mail: terry@gonzaga.edu. *Application contact:* Carolyn Von Muller, Assistant to the Dean, 509-313-5522, E-mail: vonmuller@gonzaga.edu.
Website: https://www.gonzaga.edu/college-of-arts-sciences

The Graduate Center, City University of New York, Graduate Studies, Program in Philosophy, New York, NY 10016-4039. Offers MA, PhD. *Faculty:* 30 full-time (8 women). *Students:* 102 full-time (35 women), 2 part-time (1 woman); includes 12 minority (10 Hispanic/Latino; 2 Two or more races, non-Hispanic/Latino), 27 international. Average age 34. 251 applicants, 12% accepted, 18 enrolled. In 2017, 9 master's, 11 doctorates awarded. Terminal master's awarded for partial completion of doctoral program. *Degree requirements:* For master's, thesis; for doctorate, one foreign language, comprehensive exam, thesis/dissertation. *Entrance requirements:* For master's, GRE General Test; for doctorate, GRE General Test, 3 letters of recommendation, writing sample. Additional exam requirements/recommendations for international students: Required—TOEFL. *Application deadline:* For fall admission, 1/15 for domestic students. Application fee: $125. Electronic applications accepted. *Financial support:* In 2017–18, 81 students received support, including 60 fellowships, 5 research assistantships, 9 teaching assistantships; career-related internships or fieldwork, Federal Work-Study, institutionally sponsored loans, and tuition waivers (full and partial) also available. Financial award application deadline: 2/1. *Unit head:* Prof. Nickolas Pappas, Executive Officer, 212-817-8616, Fax: 212-817-1530. *Application contact:* Les Gribben, Director of Admissions, 212-817-7470, Fax: 212-817-1624, E-mail: lgribben@gc.cuny.edu.

Harrison Middleton University, Graduate Program, Tempe, AZ 85282. Offers education (MA, Ed D); humanities (MA); imaginative literature (MA); interdisciplinary studies (DA); jurisprudence (MA); natural science (MA); philosophy and religion (MA); social science (MA). *Program availability:* Part-time, evening/weekend, online learning. *Degree requirements:* For master's and doctorate, capstone project. *Entrance requirements:* For master's, interview; for doctorate, 2 academic letters of reference, interview, essay. Additional exam requirements/recommendations for international students: Required—TOEFL (minimum score 550 paper-based; 80 iBT). Electronic applications accepted. *Faculty research:* Japanese animation, educational leadership, war art, John Muir's wilderness.

Harvard University, Graduate School of Arts and Sciences, Department of Philosophy, Cambridge, MA 02138. Offers classical philosophy (PhD); philosophy (PhD). *Degree requirements:* For doctorate, 2 foreign languages, thesis/dissertation, final exams. *Entrance requirements:* For doctorate, GRE General Test. Additional exam requirements/recommendations for international students: Required—TOEFL.

Harvard University, Graduate School of Arts and Sciences, Department of Sanskrit and Indian Studies, Cambridge, MA 02138. Offers Indian philosophy (AM, PhD); Pali (AM, PhD); Sanskrit (AM, PhD); Tibetan (AM, PhD); Urdu (AM, PhD). Terminal master's awarded for partial completion of doctoral program. *Degree requirements:* For master's, 3 foreign languages; for doctorate, 3 foreign languages, thesis/dissertation. *Entrance requirements:* For master's, GRE General Test; for doctorate, GRE General Test, proficiency in French and German. Additional exam requirements/recommendations for international students: Required—TOEFL.

Harvard University, Graduate School of Arts and Sciences, Department of the Classics, Cambridge, MA 02138. Offers Byzantine Greek (PhD); classical archaeology (PhD); classical philology (PhD); classical philosophy (PhD); medieval Latin (PhD). *Degree requirements:* For doctorate, 4 foreign languages, thesis/dissertation, preliminary and special exams. *Entrance requirements:* For doctorate, GRE General Test. Additional exam requirements/recommendations for international students: Required—TOEFL.

Houston Baptist University, School of Humanities, Program in Philosophy, Houston, TX 77074-3298. Offers MA. *Students:* 7 full-time (2 women), 13 part-time (2 women); includes 10 minority (3 Black or African American, non-Hispanic/Latino; 1 American Indian or Alaska Native, non-Hispanic/Latino; 2 Asian, non-Hispanic/Latino; 2 Hispanic/Latino; 2 Two or more races, non-Hispanic/Latino). Average age 33. 26 applicants, 69% accepted, 9 enrolled. In 2017, 5 master's awarded. *Entrance requirements:* For master's, bachelor's degree conferred transcript, resume, essay/personal statement. Additional exam requirements/recommendations for international students: Required—TOEFL (minimum score 80 iBT), IELTS (minimum score 6.5). *Application deadline:* For fall admission, 8/1 for domestic students, 6/1 for international students; for spring admission, 1/1 for domestic students, 11/1 for international students; for summer admission, 5/1 for domestic students, 3/1 for international students. Applications are processed on a rolling basis. Application fee: $0 ($100 for international students). Electronic applications accepted. Application fee is waived when completed online. *Expenses:* $18,000 tuition; $4,500 fees (general, technology and parking). *Financial support:* In 2017–18, 7 students received support. Federal Work-Study and scholarships/grants available. Financial award application deadline: 4/1. *Unit head:* Dr. Russell Hemati, Chair, 281-649-3083, E-mail: rhemati@hbu.edu. *Application contact:* Allyson Cates, Director of Admissions, Graduate School, 281-649-3099, Fax: 281-649-3390, E-mail: acates@hbu.edu.

Howard University, Graduate School, Department of Philosophy, Washington, DC 20059-0002. Offers MA. *Program availability:* Part-time. *Degree requirements:* For master's, one foreign language, comprehensive exam, thesis. *Entrance requirements:* For master's, GRE General Test. Additional exam requirements/recommendations for international students: Required—TOEFL. *Faculty research:* African and African-American philosophy, social and political philosophy, ethics, philosophy of culture, applied philosophy.

Indiana University Bloomington, School of Education, Department of Educational Leadership and Policy Studies, Bloomington, IN 47405. Offers educational leadership (MS, Ed D, Ed S); higher education (Ed D, PhD); higher education and student affairs (MS); history and philosophy of education (MS); history, philosophy, and policy in education (PhD), including education policy studies, history of education, philosophy of education; international and comparative education (MS). *Accreditation:* NCATE. *Degree requirements:* For master's, thesis optional; for doctorate, comprehensive exam, thesis/dissertation; for Ed S, comprehensive exam or project. *Entrance requirements:* For master's, doctorate, and Ed S, GRE General Test. Additional exam requirements/recommendations for international students: Required—TOEFL (minimum score 79 iBT). Electronic applications accepted. *Faculty research:* Culturally engaging campus environments, school choice policy analysis, democracy and education in the national and international context, and principal leadership.

Indiana University Bloomington, University Graduate School, College of Arts and Sciences, Department of Philosophy, Bloomington, IN 47405. Offers MA, PhD. Terminal master's awarded for partial completion of doctoral program. *Degree requirements:* For master's, variable foreign language requirement, thesis optional; for doctorate, comprehensive exam, thesis/dissertation, qualifying paper. *Entrance requirements:* For master's and doctorate, GRE General Test, writing sample. Additional exam requirements/recommendations for international students: Required—TOEFL. Electronic applications accepted. *Faculty research:* Algebraic logic, cognitive science, history of modern philosophy, ancient and Jewish philosophy, medieval logic and semantics, epistemology, ethics, history, philosophy of mind, philosophy of language.

Indiana University–Purdue University Indianapolis, School of Liberal Arts, Department of Philosophy, Indianapolis, IN 46202. Offers American philosophy (Certificate); bioethics (Certificate); philosophy (MA); philosophy/bioethics (MA); JD/MA; MD/MA. *Program availability:* Part-time. *Degree requirements:* For master's, thesis optional. *Entrance requirements:* For master's, GRE, writing sample, transcripts, three letters of recommendation, personal statement; for Certificate, letter of recommendation, transcripts, statement of purpose. Additional exam requirements/recommendations for international students: Required—TOEFL, PTE, IUPUI ESL Exam. Electronic applications accepted. *Expenses:* Contact institution. *Faculty research:* American philosophy, pierce bioethics, metaphysics, ethical theory, philosophy of science, early modern philosophy (esp. Kant).

Institute for Christian Studies, Graduate Programs, Toronto, ON M5T 1R4, Canada. Offers education (M Phil F, PhD); history of philosophy (M Phil F, PhD); philosophical aesthetics (M Phil F, PhD); philosophy of religion (M Phil F, PhD); political theory (M Phil F, PhD); systematic philosophy (M Phil F, PhD); theology (M Phil F, PhD); worldview studies (MWS). *Program availability:* Part-time, online learning. *Degree requirements:* For master's, one foreign language, thesis; for doctorate, 2 foreign languages, thesis/dissertation. *Entrance requirements:* For master's and doctorate, philosophy background. Additional exam requirements/recommendations for international students: Required—TOEFL (minimum score 600 paper-based). *Faculty research:* Human rights, anthropology of self, medieval discourse, gender and body, post-modern thought; biblical hermeneutics, creational aesthetics, ecumenism, epistemology, political theory and public policy, relational psychotherapy.

Institute for Doctoral Studies in the Visual Arts, PhD Program in Visual Art: Philosophy, Aesthetics, and Art Theory, Portland, ME 04102. Offers aesthetics (PhD); art theory (PhD); philosophy (PhD). *Program availability:* Online learning. *Faculty:* 3 full-time, 7 part-time/adjunct. *Students:* 60 full-time. *Degree requirements:* For doctorate, comprehensive exam, thesis/dissertation, dissertation defense. *Entrance requirements:* For doctorate, curriculum vitae, writing sample, portfolio, interview. *Application deadline:* Applications are processed on a rolling basis. Application fee: $60. Electronic applications accepted. Application fee is waived when completed online. *Financial support:* Fellowships, teaching assistantships, and scholarships/grants available. Financial award applicants required to submit FAFSA. *Faculty research:* Visual culture, cultural studies, feminism, contemporary art. *Application contact:* Molly M. Davis,

Director of Administration/Co-Director of Admissions, 207-771-8887, E-mail: info@idsva.edu.
Website: https://www.idsva.edu

Johns Hopkins University, Zanvyl Krieger School of Arts and Sciences, Department of Philosophy, Baltimore, MD 21218. Offers MA, PhD. *Faculty:* 13 full-time (3 women). *Students:* 34 full-time (8 women); includes 7 minority (1 Black or African American, non-Hispanic/Latino; 3 Asian, non-Hispanic/Latino; 1 Hispanic/Latino; 2 Two or more races, non-Hispanic/Latino). Average age 28. 82 applicants, 12% accepted, 5 enrolled. In 2017, 3 master's, 6 doctorates awarded. *Degree requirements:* For doctorate, comprehensive exam, thesis/dissertation. *Entrance requirements:* For master's and doctorate, GRE General Test. Additional exam requirements/recommendations for international students: Required—TOEFL (minimum score 100 iBT), IELTS (minimum score 7). *Application deadline:* For fall admission, 1/15 for domestic and international students. Application fee: $65. Electronic applications accepted. *Expenses:* Contact institution. *Financial support:* In 2017–18, 28 students received support, including 15 fellowships with full tuition reimbursements available (averaging $17,400 per year), 13 teaching assistantships with full tuition reimbursements available (averaging $24,884 per year); health care benefits and unspecified assistantships also available. Financial award application deadline: 1/15. *Faculty research:* Historical and analytical research on range of philosophical topics. *Unit head:* Dr. Richard Bett, Acting Chair/Professor, 410-516-6863, Fax: 410-516-6848, E-mail: rbett1@jhu.edu. *Application contact:* Veronica Feldkircher-Reed, Academic Program Coordinator, 410-516-7524, Fax: 410-516-6848, E-mail: vfeldki1@jhu.edu.
Website: http://philosophy.jhu.edu/

Kent State University, College of Arts and Sciences, Department of Philosophy, Kent, OH 44242-0001. Offers MA. *Program availability:* Part-time. *Faculty:* 6 full-time (2 women), 1 (woman) part-time/adjunct. *Students:* 8 full-time (1 woman), 2 part-time (0 women). Average age 31. 8 applicants, 100% accepted, 6 enrolled. In 2017, 6 master's awarded. *Degree requirements:* For master's, thesis optional, 2 seminars, first-year paper. *Entrance requirements:* For master's, GRE, 3 letters of recommendation, goal statement, transcripts. Additional exam requirements/recommendations for international students: Required—TOEFL (minimum score 587 paper-based, 94 iBT), Michigan English Language Assessment Battery (minimum score 82), IELTS (minimum score 7.0) or PTE (minimum score 65). *Application deadline:* For fall admission, 2/1 for domestic and international students. Applications are processed on a rolling basis. Application fee: $45 ($70 for international students). Electronic applications accepted. *Expenses:* Tuition, state resident: full-time $11,310; part-time $515 per credit hour. Tuition, nonresident: full-time $20,396; part-time $928 per credit hour. *International tuition:* $18,544 full-time. *Financial support:* Research assistantships, teaching assistantships with full tuition reimbursements, and unspecified assistantships available. Financial award application deadline: 2/1. *Unit head:* Dr. Deborah R. Barnbaum, Professor and Chair, 330-672-4363, E-mail: dbarnbau@kent.edu. *Application contact:* Dr. Michael Byron, Professor and Graduate Coordinator, 330-672-0273, E-mail: mbyron@kent.edu.
Website: http://www.kent.edu/philosophy

Lake Forest College, Graduate Program in Liberal Studies, Lake Forest, IL 60045. Offers American studies (MLS); cinema in East Asia (MLS); environmental studies (MLS); history (MLS); Medieval and Renaissance art (MLS); philosophy (MLS); Spanish (MLS); writing (MLS). *Program availability:* Part-time, evening/weekend. *Faculty:* 11 full-time (3 women). *Students:* 34 part-time (19 women); includes 3 minority (1 Asian, non-Hispanic/Latino; 2 Hispanic/Latino). Average age 36. 20 applicants, 55% accepted, 8 enrolled. In 2017, 5 master's awarded. *Degree requirements:* For master's, thesis optional, 8 courses, including at least 3 interdisciplinary seminars. *Entrance requirements:* For master's, transcript, essay, interview. Additional exam requirements/recommendations for international students: Required—TOEFL (minimum score 550 paper-based; 83 iBT); Recommended—IELTS (minimum score 6.5). *Application deadline:* For fall admission, 7/15 priority date for domestic students, 6/1 priority date for international students; for spring admission, 12/1 priority date for domestic students, 10/1 priority date for international students. Applications are processed on a rolling basis. Application fee: $30. Electronic applications accepted. *Expenses:* $2,650 per course. *Financial support:* In 2017–18, 2 students received support. Partial tuition grants (for full-time teachers) available. *Faculty research:* Religion in America, Asian philosophy, cinema studies, theater studies, sociology of religion. *Unit head:* Prof. D. L. LeMahieu, Director, 847-735-5133, Fax: 847-735-6291, E-mail: lemahieu@lakeforest.edu. *Application contact:* Prof. Carol Gayle, Associate Director, 847-735-5083, Fax: 847-735-6291, E-mail: gayle@lakeforest.edu.
Website: http://www.lakeforest.edu/academics/programs/mls/

Lincoln Christian University, Graduate Programs, Lincoln, IL 62656-2167. Offers Bible and theology (MA); Biblical studies (MA); church history/historical theology (MA); counseling (MA); formative worship (MA); intercultural studies (MA); ministry (MA); organizational leadership (MA); philosophy and apologetics (MA); spiritual formation (MA); theology (MA). MA in spiritual formation offered in Normal, IL. *Program availability:* Online learning. *Faculty:* 21 full-time (3 women), 29 part-time/adjunct (7 women). *Students:* 97 full-time (42 women), 226 part-time (81 women). Average age 39. *Entrance requirements:* For master's, minimum cumulative GPA of 2.5 in undergraduate degree studies. Additional exam requirements/recommendations for international students: Required—TOEFL (minimum score 550 paper-based); Recommended—IELTS (minimum score 6). *Application deadline:* For fall admission, 8/1 for domestic students, 3/1 for international students; for spring admission, 11/15 for domestic students, 11/1 for international students. Application fee: $25 ($50 for international students). Application fee is waived when completed online. *Expenses: Tuition:* Full-time $7920; part-time $5280 per credit hour. *Required fees:* $150; $150 per course. *Financial support:* Applicants required to submit FAFSA. *Application contact:* Lindsey Clark, Associate Director of Graduate Enrollment, 217-732-3168 Ext. 2398, E-mail: lclark@lincolnchristian.edu.
Website: https://lincolnchristian.edu/academics/programs/masters/

Louisiana State University and Agricultural & Mechanical College, Graduate School, College of Humanities and Social Sciences, Department of Philosophy and Religious Studies, Baton Rouge, LA 70803. Offers philosophy (MA). *Faculty:* 18 full-time (5 women). *Students:* 10 full-time (1 woman), 2 part-time (1 woman); includes 4 minority (2 Black or African American, non-Hispanic/Latino; 2 Hispanic/Latino), 1 international. Average age 30. 17 applicants, 100% accepted, 6 enrolled. In 2017, 3 master's awarded. *Financial support:* In 2017–18, 1 research assistantship (averaging $17,000 per year), 7 teaching assistantships (averaging $17,000 per year) were awarded. *Total annual research expenditures:* $5,970.

Loyola Marymount University, Bellarmine College of Liberal Arts, Program in Philosophy, Los Angeles, CA 90045-2659. Offers MA. *Unit head:* Dr. Brad Stone, Graduate Program Director, Philosophy, 310-338-5807, E-mail: bstone@lmu.edu. *Application contact:* Chake H. Kouyoumjian, Associate Dean of Graduate Studies, 310-338-2721, Fax: 310-338-6086, E-mail: graduateinfo@lmu.edu.
Website: http://bellarmine.lmu.edu/philosophy/graduateprogram

Loyola University Chicago, Graduate School, Department of Philosophy, Chicago, IL 60611. Offers applied philosophy and philosophy (MA); philosophy (PhD). *Program availability:* Part-time, evening/weekend. *Faculty:* 22 full-time (7 women). *Students:* 60 full-time (11 women), 3 part-time (0 women); includes 17 minority (1 Black or African American, non-Hispanic/Latino; 6 Asian, non-Hispanic/Latino; 8 Hispanic/Latino; 2 Two or more races, non-Hispanic/Latino), 6 international. Average age 33. 131 applicants, 27% accepted, 16 enrolled. In 2017, 6 master's, 3 doctorates awarded. Terminal master's awarded for partial completion of doctoral program. *Degree requirements:* For master's, oral exam paper/thesis; for doctorate, one foreign language, thesis/dissertation, oral exam. *Entrance requirements:* For master's and doctorate, GRE General Test. Additional exam requirements/recommendations for international students: Required—TOEFL (minimum score 79 iBT). *Application deadline:* For fall admission, 1/15 priority date for domestic and international students. Applications are processed on a rolling basis. Application fee: $50. Electronic applications accepted. Application fee is waived when completed online. *Expenses:* $1,033 per credit hour. *Financial support:* In 2017–18, 18 students received support, including 1 fellowship with full tuition reimbursement available (averaging $21,000 per year), 17 teaching assistantships with full tuition reimbursements available (averaging $19,029 per year); institutionally sponsored loans, health care benefits, unspecified assistantships, and McNair Scholar Merit Funding also available. Financial award application deadline: 1/15; financial award applicants required to submit FAFSA. *Faculty research:* Social-political philosophy, ethics, continental philosophy, history of philosophy, analytic philosophy. *Unit head:* Dr. Mark Waymack, Chair, 773-508-2738, Fax: 773-508-2292, E-mail: mwaymac@luc.edu. *Application contact:* Miguel Diaz, Graduate Program Assistant, 773-508-2453, Fax: 773-508-2292, E-mail: mdiaz1@luc.edu.
Website: http://www.luc.edu/philosophy/

Marquette University, Graduate School, College of Arts and Sciences, Department of Philosophy, Milwaukee, WI 53201-1881. Offers ancient philosophy (PhD); British empiricism and analytic philosophy (PhD); Christian philosophy (PhD); early modern European philosophy (PhD); ethics (PhD); German philosophy (PhD); history of philosophy (MA); medieval philosophy (PhD); phenomenology and existentialism (PhD); philosophy of religion (PhD); social and applied philosophy (MA); JD/MA. *Program availability:* Part-time. Terminal master's awarded for partial completion of doctoral program. *Degree requirements:* For master's, variable foreign language requirement, comprehensive exam, thesis or alternative; for doctorate, 2 foreign languages, thesis/dissertation, written and oral qualifying exams. *Entrance requirements:* For master's and doctorate, GRE General Test, official transcripts from all current and previous colleges/universities except Marquette, statement of purpose, at least three letters of recommendation, sample of philosophical writing. Additional exam requirements/recommendations for international students: Required—TOEFL (minimum score 530 paper-based). Electronic applications accepted. *Faculty research:* Aristotle, Augustine, Descartes, Hegel, Heidegger.

Massachusetts Institute of Technology, School of Humanities, Arts, and Social Sciences, Department of Linguistics and Philosophy, Philosophy Section, Cambridge, MA 02139. Offers PhD. *Degree requirements:* For doctorate, comprehensive exam, thesis/dissertation, teaching requirement. *Entrance requirements:* For doctorate, GRE General Test. Additional exam requirements/recommendations for international students: Required—TOEFL, IELTS. Electronic applications accepted. *Faculty research:* Metaphysics, philosophy of mind, philosophy of language, ethics, feminist philosophy.

McGill University, Faculty of Graduate and Postdoctoral Studies, Faculty of Arts, Department of Philosophy, Montréal, QC H3A 2T5, Canada. Offers bioethics (MA); philosophy (PhD).

McMaster University, School of Graduate Studies, Faculty of Humanities, Department of Philosophy, Hamilton, ON L8S 4M2, Canada. Offers MA, PhD. *Program availability:* Part-time. *Degree requirements:* For master's, thesis; for doctorate, one foreign language, thesis/dissertation. *Entrance requirements:* For master's, honors degree in philosophy; minimum average B+; for doctorate, master's degree in philosophy. Additional exam requirements/recommendations for international students: Required—TOEFL (minimum score 580 paper-based). *Faculty research:* Twentieth-century European philosophy, twentieth-century Anglo-American philosophy, political philosophy, ethics, argumentation.

Memorial University of Newfoundland, School of Graduate Studies, Department of Philosophy, St. John's, NL A1C 5S7, Canada. Offers MA, PhD. *Program availability:* Part-time. *Degree requirements:* For master's, thesis; for doctorate, comprehensive exam, thesis/dissertation. *Entrance requirements:* For master's, first-class undergraduate degree in philosophy; for doctorate, MA in philosophy or equivalent. Electronic applications accepted. *Faculty research:* History of philosophy, philosophy of science, phenomenology and existentialism, contemporary metaphysics.

Miami University, College of Arts and Science, Department of Philosophy, Oxford, OH 45056. Offers MA. In 2017, 3 master's awarded. *Expenses:* Tuition, state resident: full-time $13,812; part-time $575 per credit hour. Tuition, nonresident: full-time $30,860; part-time $1286 per credit hour. *Unit head:* Dr. Emily Zakin, Chair, 513-529-2428, E-mail: zakinea@miamioh.edu. *Application contact:* Dr. Pascal Massie, Associate Professor and Director of the Graduate Program, 513-529-2458, E-mail: massiep@miamioh.edu.
Website: http://www.MiamiOH.edu/philosophy/

Michigan State University, The Graduate School, College of Arts and Letters, Department of Philosophy, East Lansing, MI 48824. Offers MA, PhD. *Entrance requirements:* Additional exam requirements/recommendations for international students: Required—TOEFL. Electronic applications accepted.

Midwestern State University, Billie Doris McAda Graduate School, Prothro-Yeager College of Humanities and Social Sciences, Department of English, Humanities, and Philosophy, Wichita Falls, TX 76308. Offers English (MA); philosophy (PhD). *Program availability:* Part-time, evening/weekend. *Degree requirements:* For master's, one foreign language, thesis optional. *Entrance requirements:* For master's, GRE General Test, MAT or GMAT. Additional exam requirements/recommendations for international students: Required—TOEFL (minimum score 550 paper-based). Electronic applications accepted. *Faculty research:* Mythology, Shakespeare, Oscar Hahn, origins of language, modern American literature.

Mount St. Mary's University, Program in Philosophical Studies, Emmitsburg, MD 21727-7799. Offers MA. *Program availability:* Part-time. *Degree requirements:* For master's, one foreign language, thesis. *Entrance requirements:* For master's, undergraduate degree, minimum cumulative undergraduate GPA of 3.0. Additional exam requirements/recommendations for international students: Required—TOEFL (minimum score 550 paper-based; 83 iBT). *Expenses:* Contact institution.

The New School, The New School for Social Research, Department of Philosophy, New York, NY 10003. Offers philosophy (MA); psychoanalysis (PhD). *Program availability:* Part-time. *Faculty:* 10 full-time (4 women), 6 part-time/adjunct (0 women). *Students:* 129 full-time (39 women), 18 part-time (4 women); includes 21 minority (2 Black or African American, non-Hispanic/Latino; 1 Asian, non-Hispanic/Latino; 11 Hispanic/Latino; 7 Two or more races, non-Hispanic/Latino), 37 international. Average age 33. 154 applicants, 65% accepted, 20 enrolled. In 2017, 20 master's, 13 doctorates awarded. Terminal master's awarded for partial completion of doctoral program. *Degree requirements:* For master's, one foreign language, comprehensive exam, thesis; for doctorate, one foreign language, comprehensive exam, thesis/dissertation. *Entrance*

requirements: For master's, GRE, letters of recommendation, writing sample, essays, transcript; for doctorate, letters of recommendation, writing sample, essays, transcript. Additional exam requirements/recommendations for international students: Required—TOEFL (minimum score 100 iBT), IELTS (minimum score 7), PTE (minimum score 68). *Application deadline:* For fall admission, 1/5 priority date for domestic and international students; for spring admission, 10/15 priority date for domestic and international students. Applications are processed on a rolling basis. Application fee: $50. Electronic applications accepted. *Expenses:* $2,180 per credit. *Financial support:* In 2017–18, 90 students received support, including 13 fellowships (averaging $23,707 per year), 2 research assistantships (averaging $17,240 per year), 22 teaching assistantships with full and partial tuition reimbursements available (averaging $9,841 per year); Federal Work-Study and scholarships/grants also available. Support available to part-time students. Financial award application deadline: 2/1; financial award applicants required to submit FAFSA. *Unit head:* Dr. William Milberg, Dean, The New School for Social Research, 212-229-5777, E-mail: milbergw@newschool.edu. *Application contact:* Dana Messinger, Director of Graduate Admission, 212-229-5150 Ext. 2300, E-mail: socialresearchadmit@newschool.edu.
Website: http://www.newschool.edu/nssr/philosophy/

New York University, Graduate School of Arts and Science, Department of Philosophy, New York, NY 10012-1019. Offers MA, PhD, JD/MA, JD/PhD, MD/MA. *Program availability:* Part-time. *Students:* Average age 28. 320 applicants, 6% accepted, 11 enrolled. In 2017, 3 master's, 16 doctorates awarded. *Degree requirements:* For master's, thesis or alternative; for doctorate, one foreign language, thesis/dissertation. *Entrance requirements:* For master's and doctorate, GRE General Test, sample of written work. Additional exam requirements/recommendations for international students: Required—TOEFL. *Application deadline:* For fall admission, 1/4 for domestic and international students. Application fee: $100. *Expenses: Tuition:* Full-time $41,352; part-time $19,968 per year. *Required fees:* $2496; $1628 per unit. $814 per term. Tuition and fees vary according to course load and program. *Financial support:* Fellowships, teaching assistantships, Federal Work-Study, institutionally sponsored loans, scholarships/grants, health care benefits, and unspecified assistantships available. Financial award application deadline: 1/4; financial award applicants required to submit FAFSA. *Faculty research:* Philosophy of mind and language, metaphysics, ethics and political philosophy. *Unit head:* Don Garrett, Chair, 212-998-8320, Fax: 212-995-4179, E-mail: philosophy.admissions@nyu.edu. *Application contact:* David Chalmers, Director of Admissions, 212-998-8320, Fax: 212-995-4179, E-mail: philosophy.admissions@nyu.edu.
Website: http://www.nyu.edu/gsas/dept/philo/

Northern Illinois University, Graduate School, College of Liberal Arts and Sciences, Department of Philosophy, De Kalb, IL 60115-2854. Offers MA. *Program availability:* Part-time. *Faculty:* 12 full-time (2 women), 1 part-time/adjunct (0 women). *Students:* 23 full-time (5 women), 4 part-time (1 woman); includes 6 minority (1 Black or African American, non-Hispanic/Latino; 1 Asian, non-Hispanic/Latino; 1 Hispanic/Latino; 3 Two or more races, non-Hispanic/Latino), 3 international. Average age 25. 91 applicants, 65% accepted, 12 enrolled. In 2017, 14 master's awarded. *Degree requirements:* For master's, comprehensive exam, thesis optional. *Entrance requirements:* For master's, GRE General Test, minimum GPA of 2.75, writing sample, major or minor in philosophy. Additional exam requirements/recommendations for international students: Required—TOEFL (minimum score 550 paper-based). *Application deadline:* For fall admission, 3/1 priority date for domestic students, 5/1 for international students; for spring admission, 11/1 for domestic students, 10/1 for international students. Applications are processed on a rolling basis. Application fee: $40. Electronic applications accepted. *Financial support:* In 2017–18, 15 teaching assistantships with full tuition reimbursements were awarded; fellowships with full tuition reimbursements, research assistantships with full tuition reimbursements, Federal Work-Study, scholarships/grants, tuition waivers (full), and unspecified assistantships also available. Support available to part-time students. Financial award applicants required to submit FAFSA. *Faculty research:* Epistemology, philosophy of biology, animal rights, philosophy of war, international ethics. *Unit head:* Dr. David J. Buller, Chair, 815-753-6299, Fax: 815-753-6302, E-mail: buller@niu.edu. *Application contact:* Dr. Geoff Pynn, Graduate Advisor, 815-753-6414, E-mail: askphilosophy@niu.edu.
Website: http://www.niu.edu/phil/

Northwestern University, The Graduate School, Judd A. and Marjorie Weinberg College of Arts and Sciences, Department of Philosophy, Evanston, IL 60208. Offers ancient philosophy (PhD); philosophy (PhD). Admissions and degrees offered through The Graduate School. *Degree requirements:* For doctorate, 2 foreign languages, thesis/dissertation. *Entrance requirements:* For doctorate, GRE General Test, sample of written work. Additional exam requirements/recommendations for international students: Required—TOEFL. Electronic applications accepted. *Faculty research:* Phenomenology, philosophy of science, history of philosophy, ethics, social and political philosophy, epistemology.

The Ohio State University, Graduate School, College of Arts and Sciences, Division of Arts and Humanities, Department of Philosophy, Columbus, OH 43210. Offers MA, PhD. *Faculty:* 17. *Students:* 32 full-time (11 women). Average age 28. In 2017, 5 doctorates awarded. Terminal master's awarded for partial completion of doctoral program. *Entrance requirements:* For doctorate, GRE General Test, writing sample. Additional exam requirements/recommendations for international students: Required—TOEFL (minimum score 600 paper-based; 100 iBT); Recommended—IELTS (minimum score 8). *Application deadline:* For fall admission, 12/15 priority date for domestic students, 12/1 priority date for international students; for spring admission, 3/1 for domestic students, 2/1 for international students. Applications are processed on a rolling basis. Application fee: $60 ($70 for international students). Electronic applications accepted. *Financial support:* Fellowships, research assistantships, teaching assistantships, Federal Work-Study, institutionally sponsored loans, and unspecified assistantships available. Support available to part-time students. *Unit head:* Dr. Justin D'Arms, Chair and Professor, 614-292-7914, E-mail: philosophy@osu.edu. *Application contact:* Graduate and Professional Admissions, 614-292-9444, Fax: 614-292-3895, E-mail: gpadmissions@osu.edu.
Website: http://philosophy.osu.edu/

Ohio University, Graduate College, College of Arts and Sciences, Department of Philosophy, Athens, OH 45701-2979. Offers MA. *Program availability:* Part-time. *Degree requirements:* For master's, thesis. *Entrance requirements:* For master's, 28 hours in philosophy including logic, ancient and modern philosophy; minimum GPA of 3.0; sample of philosophical writing. Additional exam requirements/recommendations for international students: Required—TOEFL (minimum score 550 paper-based; 80 iBT) or IELTS (minimum score 6.5). Electronic applications accepted. *Faculty research:* Ethics, phenomenology, applied ethics, Aristotle, Kant, epistemology.

Oklahoma State University, College of Arts and Sciences, Department of Philosophy, Stillwater, OK 74078. Offers MA. *Faculty:* 19 full-time (5 women), 3 part-time/adjunct (0 women). *Students:* 4 full-time (0 women), 6 part-time (1 woman); includes 1 minority (American Indian or Alaska Native, non-Hispanic/Latino). Average age 30. 14 applicants, 50% accepted, 5 enrolled. In 2017, 4 master's awarded. *Entrance requirements:* For master's, GRE, 2 letters of recommendation. Additional exam requirements/recommendations for international students: Required—TOEFL (minimum score 550 paper-based; 79 iBT). *Application deadline:* For fall admission, 3/1 priority date for international students; for spring admission, 8/1 priority date for international students. Applications are processed on a rolling basis. Application fee: $40 ($75 for international students). Electronic applications accepted. *Expenses:* Tuition, state resident: full-time $4019; part-time $2679.60 per year. Tuition, nonresident: full-time $15,286; part-time $10,190.40 per year. *Required fees:* $2129; $1419 per unit. Tuition and fees vary according to program. *Financial support:* Teaching assistantships, career-related internships or fieldwork, Federal Work-Study, scholarships/grants, health care benefits, tuition waivers (partial), and unspecified assistantships available. Support available to part-time students. Financial award application deadline: 3/1; financial award applicants required to submit FAFSA. *Faculty research:* Theoretical and applied ethics, history and philosophy of science, east/west comparative philosophy, social/political/legal philosophy, truth and theory of knowledge. *Unit head:* Dr. Scott Gelfand, Department Head, 405-744-9238, Fax: 405-744-4635, E-mail: scott.gelfand@okstate.edu. *Application contact:* Dr. Eric Reitan, Professor and Graduate Advisor, 405-744-7753, E-mail: eric.reitan@okstate.edu.
Website: http://philosophy.okstate.edu

Old Dominion University, College of Arts and Letters, Institute for the Humanities, Norfolk, VA 23529. Offers arts and entrepreneurship (Certificate); cultural and human geography (MA); cultural studies (MA); gender and sexuality studies (MA); health, communication and culture (Certificate); media and popular culture studies (MA); philosophy and religious studies (MA); social justice and entrepreneurship (Certificate); visual studies (MA); world cultures (MA). *Program availability:* Part-time, evening/weekend. *Faculty:* 1 full-time (0 women), 1 part-time/adjunct (0 women). *Students:* 20 full-time (16 women), 13 part-time (8 women); includes 15 minority (8 Black or African American, non-Hispanic/Latino; 2 Asian, non-Hispanic/Latino; 2 Hispanic/Latino; 3 Two or more races, non-Hispanic/Latino), 2 international. Average age 35. 27 applicants, 96% accepted, 22 enrolled. In 2017, 3 master's awarded. *Degree requirements:* For master's, thesis optional, project. *Entrance requirements:* For master's, GRE General Test, minimum GPA of 3.25. *Application deadline:* For fall admission, 6/15 for domestic students; for spring admission, 11/15 for domestic students; for summer admission, 4/15 for domestic students. Applications are processed on a rolling basis. Application fee: $50. Electronic applications accepted. *Expenses:* Tuition, state resident: full-time $8928; part-time $496 per credit. Tuition, nonresident: full-time $22,482; part-time $1249 per credit. *Required fees:* $66 per semester. *Financial support:* In 2017–18, 3 students received support, including 5 research assistantships (averaging $10,000 per year); career-related internships or fieldwork, scholarships/grants, and unspecified assistantships also available. Financial award application deadline: 3/15; financial award applicants required to submit FAFSA. *Faculty research:* Media studies, cultural studies, gender studies, American literature, philosophy, art history, cultural geography. *Unit head:* Dr. Avi D. Santo, Graduate Program Director, 757-683-3719, Fax: 757-683-6191, E-mail: humgpd@odu.edu. *Application contact:* Dr. David C. Earnest, Associate Dean, 757-683-6077, Fax: 757-683-5746, E-mail: dearnest@odu.edu.
Website: http://al.odu.edu/hum/

Open University, Graduate Programs, Milton Keynes, United Kingdom. Offers business (MBA); education (M Ed); engineering (M Eng); history (MA); music (MA); philosophy (MA).

Penn State University Park, Graduate School, College of the Liberal Arts, Department of Philosophy, University Park, PA 16802. Offers MA, PhD. *Unit head:* Dr. Susan Welch, Dean, 814-865-7691, Fax: 814-863-2085. *Application contact:* Lori Hawn, Director, Graduate Student Services, 814-865-1795, Fax: 814-863-4627, E-mail: l-gswww@lists.psu.edu.
Website: http://philosophy.la.psu.edu/

Princeton University, Graduate School, Department of Classics, Princeton, NJ 08544-1019. Offers classical and hellenic studies (PhD); classical philosophy (PhD); history (the ancient world) (PhD); literature and philology (PhD). *Degree requirements:* For doctorate, thesis/dissertation. *Entrance requirements:* For doctorate, GRE General Test, sample of written work. Additional exam requirements/recommendations for international students: Required—TOEFL (minimum score 600 paper-based). Electronic applications accepted.

Princeton University, Graduate School, Department of Philosophy, Princeton, NJ 08544-1019. Offers classical philosophy (PhD); philosophy (PhD); philosophy of science (PhD). *Degree requirements:* For doctorate, variable foreign language requirement, thesis/dissertation. *Entrance requirements:* For doctorate, GRE General Test, sample of written work. Additional exam requirements/recommendations for international students: Required—TOEFL (minimum score 600 paper-based). Electronic applications accepted.

Princeton University, Graduate School, Department of Politics, Princeton, NJ 08544-1019. Offers political philosophy (PhD); politics (PhD). *Degree requirements:* For doctorate, comprehensive exam, thesis/dissertation, teaching experience. *Entrance requirements:* For doctorate, GRE General Test, sample of written work, letters of recommendation. Additional exam requirements/recommendations for international students: Required—TOEFL (minimum score 600 paper-based). Electronic applications accepted. *Faculty research:* American politics, comparative politics, formal and quantitative methods, international relations, public law, political theory.

Purdue University, Graduate School, College of Liberal Arts, Department of Philosophy, West Lafayette, IN 47907. Offers MA, PhD. *Program availability:* Part-time. *Faculty:* 19 full-time (4 women), 1 part-time/adjunct (0 women). *Students:* 36 full-time (5 women), 9 part-time (5 women); includes 4 minority (1 American Indian or Alaska Native, non-Hispanic/Latino; 2 Hispanic/Latino; 1 Two or more races, non-Hispanic/Latino), 6 international. Average age 29. 66 applicants, 14% accepted, 4 enrolled. In 2017, 2 master's, 5 doctorates awarded. Terminal master's awarded for partial completion of doctoral program. *Degree requirements:* For master's, thesis optional; for doctorate, comprehensive exam, thesis/dissertation. *Entrance requirements:* For master's and doctorate, GRE General Test, minimum undergraduate GPA of 3.4 or equivalent. Additional exam requirements/recommendations for international students: Required—TOEFL (minimum score 550 paper-based; 100 iBT). *Application deadline:* For fall admission, 1/2 for domestic and international students; for spring admission, 12/1 for domestic and international students. Applications are processed on a rolling basis. Application fee: $60 ($75 for international students). Electronic applications accepted. *Financial support:* Fellowships with tuition reimbursements, research assistantships with tuition reimbursements, and teaching assistantships with tuition reimbursements available. Support available to part-time students. Financial award application deadline: 1/15; financial award applicants required to submit FAFSA. *Faculty research:* Continental philosophy, ethics and social philosophy, analytic philosophy, history of philosophy, logic. *Unit head:* Christopher L. Yeomans, Head, 765-494-4275, E-mail: cyeomans@purdue.edu. *Application contact:* Vickie Sanders, Graduate Contact, 765-494-4275, E-mail: sanders@purdue.edu.
Website: http://www.cla.purdue.edu/philosophy/

Purdue University, Graduate School, Program in Philosophy and Literature, West Lafayette, IN 47907. Offers PhD. Program offered jointly with Department of English, School of Languages and Cultures, and Department of Philosophy. *Faculty:* 19 full-time (4 women), 1 part-time/adjunct (0 women). *Students:* 36 full-time (5 women), 9 part-time

(5 women); includes 4 minority (1 American Indian or Alaska Native, non-Hispanic/Latino; 2 Hispanic/Latino; 1 Two or more races, non-Hispanic/Latino), 6 international. Average age 29. 66 applicants, 14% accepted, 4 enrolled. In 2017, 5 doctorates awarded. *Degree requirements:* For doctorate, one foreign language, comprehensive exam, thesis/dissertation. *Entrance requirements:* For doctorate, GRE, master's degree in either English, philosophy or foreign languages. Additional exam requirements/recommendations for international students: Required—TOEFL. *Application deadline:* For fall admission, 1/10 priority date for domestic students, 1/10 for international students. Application fee: $60 ($75 for international students). Electronic applications accepted. *Financial support:* In 2017–18, teaching assistantships (averaging $1,415 per year) were awarded; fellowships and research assistantships also available. *Unit head:* Venetria K. Patton, Head of the Graduate Program, 765-496-1848, E-mail: vpatton@purdue.edu. *Application contact:* Elsa Schirmer, Graduate Contact, 765-496-9629, E-mail: eschirme@purdue.edu.
Website: http://www.cla.purdue.edu/phil-lit/graduate/

Queen's University at Kingston, School of Graduate Studies, Faculty of Arts and Sciences, Department of Philosophy, Kingston, ON K7L 3N6, Canada. Offers MA, PhD. *Program availability:* Part-time. *Degree requirements:* For master's, thesis; for doctorate, comprehensive exam, thesis/dissertation. *Entrance requirements:* Additional exam requirements/recommendations for international students: Required—TOEFL. Electronic applications accepted. *Faculty research:* Ethics, social and political philosophy, philosophy of language, epistemology, metaphysics.

Regis College, Graduate and Professional Programs, Toronto, ON M5S 2Z5, Canada. Offers eastern Christian studies (Certificate); Ignatian spirituality (Diploma); ministry (D Min); ministry and spirituality (MAMS); philosophical studies (Diploma); retreat direction (Certificate); sacred theology (STM, STD, STB, STL); spiritual direction (Diploma); theological studies (MTS, Diploma); theology (M Div, MA, Th M, PhD, Th D); M Div/MA. *Accreditation:* ATS (one or more programs are accredited). Terminal master's awarded for partial completion of doctoral program. *Degree requirements:* For master's, 2 foreign languages, thesis; for doctorate, 3 foreign languages, comprehensive exam, thesis/dissertation. *Entrance requirements:* For doctorate, minimum GPA of 3.7. Additional exam requirements/recommendations for international students: Required—TOEFL (minimum score 580 paper-based; 93 iBT), TWE (minimum score 5).

Rice University, Graduate Programs, School of Humanities, Department of Philosophy, Houston, TX 77251-1892. Offers MA, PhD. Terminal master's awarded for partial completion of doctoral program. *Degree requirements:* For master's, one foreign language; for doctorate, one foreign language, comprehensive exam, thesis/dissertation. *Entrance requirements:* For master's and doctorate, GRE General Test, minimum GPA of 3.0. Additional exam requirements/recommendations for international students: Required—TOEFL (minimum score 600 paper-based; 90 iBT). Electronic applications accepted. *Faculty research:* Metaphysics, philosophy of law, philosophy of science, medical ethics, philosophy of language.

Roosevelt University, Graduate Division, College of Arts and Sciences, Department of History and Philosophy, Chicago, IL 60605. Offers history (MA). *Program availability:* Part-time, evening/weekend. *Students:* 1 full-time (0 women), 10 part-time (7 women); includes 4 minority (all Black or African American, non-Hispanic/Latino). Average age 36. 5 applicants, 100% accepted, 3 enrolled. In 2017, 3 master's awarded. *Application deadline:* Applications are processed on a rolling basis. Application fee: $40. Electronic applications accepted. *Financial support:* Scholarships/grants and unspecified assistantships available. *Application contact:* Sivling Lam, Graduate Admission Counselor, 312-281-3252, E-mail: slam02@roosevelt.edu.

Rutgers University–New Brunswick, Graduate School-New Brunswick, Program in Philosophy, Piscataway, NJ 08854-8097. Offers PhD. *Degree requirements:* For doctorate, comprehensive exam, thesis/dissertation. *Entrance requirements:* For doctorate, GRE General Test, writing sample. Electronic applications accepted. *Faculty research:* Philosophy of mind, epistemology, philosophy of language, philosophy of science, metaphysics.

Saint Louis University, Graduate Programs, College of Arts and Sciences and Graduate Programs, Department of Philosophy, St. Louis, MO 63103. Offers MA, MA-R, PhD. *Program availability:* Part-time. *Degree requirements:* For master's, one foreign language, thesis, comprehensive oral and written exams; for doctorate, 2 foreign languages, thesis/dissertation, preliminary exams, comprehensive oral and written exams. *Entrance requirements:* For master's, GRE General Test, letters of recommendation, resume, writing sample, interview; for doctorate, GRE General Test, letters of recommendation, resumé, writing sample, interview, goal statement, transcripts. Additional exam requirements/recommendations for international students: Required—TOEFL (minimum score 550 paper-based). Electronic applications accepted. *Faculty research:* Medieval philosophy, philosophy of religion, political philosophy, ethics, epistemology.

Saint Mary's University, Faculty of Arts, Department of Philosophy, Halifax, NS B3H 3C3, Canada. Offers MA. *Degree requirements:* For master's, thesis. *Entrance requirements:* For master's, 3 letters of recommendation, 2 samples of written work. Additional exam requirements/recommendations for international students: Required—TOEFL. *Faculty research:* History of philosophy, analytic philosophy, ethics, social philosophy, logic.

San Diego State University, Graduate and Research Affairs, College of Arts and Letters, Department of Philosophy, San Diego, CA 92182. Offers MA. *Program availability:* Part-time. *Entrance requirements:* For master's, GRE General Test. Additional exam requirements/recommendations for international students: Required—TOEFL. Electronic applications accepted. *Faculty research:* Ancient philosophy, modern philosophy, philosophy of technology, logic, philosophy of mind.

San Francisco State University, Division of Graduate Studies, College of Liberal and Creative Arts, Department of Philosophy, San Francisco, CA 94132-1722. Offers MA. *Program availability:* Part-time. *Application deadline:* Applications are processed on a rolling basis. *Unit head:* Dr. Justin Tiwald, Chair, 415-338-1598, Fax: 415-338-6159, E-mail: jtiwald@sfsu.edu. *Application contact:* Dr. Alice Sowaal, Graduate Coordinator, 415-338-3136, Fax: 415-338-6159, E-mail: asowaal@sfsu.edu.
Website: http://philosophy.sfsu.edu/

San Jose State University, Graduate Studies and Research, College of Humanities and the Arts, San Jose, CA 95192-0088. Offers art (MA, MFA), including digital media art (MFA), history and visual culture (MA), photography (MFA), pictorial art (MFA), spatial art (MFA); English (MA, MFA), including creative writing (MFA); linguistics (MA); music (MM); music education (MA); philosophy (MA); Spanish (MA); teaching English to speakers of other languages (MA). *Program availability:* Part-time. *Faculty:* 35 full-time (17 women), 19 part-time/adjunct (11 women). *Students:* 129 full-time (79 women), 106 part-time (71 women); includes 117 minority (5 Black or African American, non-Hispanic/Latino; 29 Asian, non-Hispanic/Latino; 44 Hispanic/Latino; 39 Two or more races, non-Hispanic/Latino), 28 international. Average age 35. 204 applicants, 65% accepted, 79 enrolled. In 2017, 85 master's awarded. *Degree requirements:* For master's, one foreign language, comprehensive exam (for some programs), thesis (for some programs), graduate writing assessment, special study/project, recital. *Entrance requirements:* Additional exam requirements/recommendations for international students: Required—TOEFL (minimum score 550 paper-based; 80 iBT), IELTS (minimum score 6.5), PTE (minimum score 53). *Application deadline:* For fall admission, 2/1 for domestic and international students. Applications are processed on a rolling basis. Application fee: $55. Electronic applications accepted. *Expenses:* Tuition, state resident: full-time $7176. Tuition, nonresident: full-time $16,680. Tuition and fees vary according to course load and program. *Financial support:* Fellowships, research assistantships, Federal Work-Study, scholarships/grants, traineeships, tuition waivers (full and partial), and unspecified assistantships available. Support available to part-time students. Financial award application deadline: 4/28; financial award applicants required to submit FAFSA. *Unit head:* Dr. Shannon Miller, Dean, 408-924-4300, Fax: 408-924-4365, E-mail: shannon.miller@sjsu.edu.
Website: http://www.sjsu.edu/humanitiesandarts/

Simon Fraser University, Office of Graduate Studies and Postdoctoral Fellows, Faculty of Arts and Social Sciences, Department of Philosophy, Burnaby, BC V5A 1S6, Canada. Offers MA, PhD. *Degree requirements:* For master's, thesis or alternative; for doctorate, comprehensive exam, thesis/dissertation. *Entrance requirements:* For master's, minimum GPA of 3.0 (on scale of 4.33) or 3.33 based on last 60 credits of undergraduate courses; for doctorate, minimum GPA of 3.5 (on scale of 4.33). Additional exam requirements/recommendations for international students: Recommended—TOEFL (minimum score 580 paper-based; 93 iBT), IELTS (minimum score 7), TWE (minimum score 5). Electronic applications accepted. *Faculty research:* Ethics; philosophy of mind; philosophy of science; epistemology and metaphysics; history of early modern, ancient, and analytic philosophy and logic.

Southeastern Baptist Theological Seminary, Graduate and Professional Programs, Wake Forest, NC 27587. Offers advanced biblical studies (M Div); Christian education (M Div, MACE); Christian ethics (PhD); Christian ministry (M Div); Christian planting (M Div); church music (MACM); counseling (MACO); evangelism (PhD); language (M Div); ministry (D Min); New Testament (PhD); Old Testament (PhD); philosophy (PhD); theology (Th M, PhD); women's studies (M Div). *Accreditation:* ACIPE; ATS (one or more programs are accredited). *Degree requirements:* For master's, thesis (for some programs), oral exam; for doctorate, thesis/dissertation, fieldwork. *Entrance requirements:* For master's, Cooperative English Test, minimum GPA of 2.0, M Div or equivalent (Th M); for doctorate, GRE General Test or MAT, Cooperative English Test, M Div or equivalent, 3 years of professional experience.

The Southern Baptist Theological Seminary, School of Theology, Louisville, KY 40280-0004. Offers applied theology (D Min); biblical and theological studies (M Div); biblical counseling (M Div, MA, D Min); biblical spirituality (D Min); Christian ministry (M Div); expository preaching (D Min); pastoral studies (M Div); theological studies (MA); theology (Th M, PhD); worldview and apologetics (M Div). *Program availability:* Part-time, evening/weekend, online learning. *Degree requirements:* For master's, 2 foreign languages, thesis; for doctorate, 4 foreign languages, thesis/dissertation. *Entrance requirements:* For master's, GRE General Test, MAT, M Div; for doctorate, GRE General Test, MAT, interview, M Div, field essay. Additional exam requirements/recommendations for international students: Required—TOEFL, TWE. *Faculty research:* Biblical studies, contemporary theology, church history, pastoral care, ministry/missions studies.

Southern Evangelical Seminary, Graduate Programs, Matthews, NC 28105. Offers apologetics (MA, D Min, Certificate); Christian education (MA); church ministry (MA, Certificate); divinity (Certificate), including apologetics (M Div, Certificate); Islamic studies (MA, Certificate); Jewish studies (MA); philosophy (MA); philosophy of religion (PhD); religion (MA); theology (M Div), including apologetics (M Div, Certificate), Biblical studies; youth ministry (MA). *Program availability:* Part-time, evening/weekend, online learning. *Degree requirements:* For master's, thesis (for some programs); for doctorate, 2 foreign languages, comprehensive exam (for some programs), thesis/dissertation. *Entrance requirements:* Additional exam requirements/recommendations for international students: Required—TOEFL (minimum score 600 paper-based).

Southern Illinois University Carbondale, Graduate School, College of Liberal Arts, Department of Philosophy, Carbondale, IL 62901-4701. Offers MA, PhD. *Degree requirements:* For master's, one foreign language, thesis; for doctorate, 2 foreign languages, thesis/dissertation. *Entrance requirements:* For master's, GRE General Test, minimum GPA of 2.7; for doctorate, GRE General Test, minimum GPA of 3.25. Additional exam requirements/recommendations for international students: Required—TOEFL. *Faculty research:* Continental philosophy, American philosophy, philosophy of mind, Asian philosophy.

Stanford University, School of Humanities and Sciences, Department of Philosophy, Stanford, CA 94305-2004. Offers MA, PhD. Terminal master's awarded for partial completion of doctoral program. *Degree requirements:* For master's, oral exam; for doctorate, thesis/dissertation, oral exam. *Entrance requirements:* For master's and doctorate, GRE General Test. Additional exam requirements/recommendations for international students: Required—TOEFL. Electronic applications accepted. *Expenses: Tuition:* Full-time $48,987; part-time $10,620 per quarter. One-time fee: $400. Tuition and fees vary according to program.

Stony Brook University, State University of New York, Graduate School, College of Arts and Sciences, Department of Philosophy, Stony Brook, NY 11794. Offers MA, PhD, Advanced Certificate. *Program availability:* Evening/weekend. *Faculty:* 16 full-time (5 women), 1 (woman) part-time/adjunct. *Students:* 48 full-time (13 women), 4 part-time (1 woman); includes 7 minority (1 Black or African American, non-Hispanic/Latino; 1 American Indian or Alaska Native, non-Hispanic/Latino; 4 Hispanic/Latino; 1 Two or more races, non-Hispanic/Latino), 12 international. Average age 32. 141 applicants, 38% accepted, 8 enrolled. In 2017, 4 master's, 9 doctorates awarded. *Degree requirements:* For doctorate, one foreign language, thesis/dissertation. *Entrance requirements:* For master's and doctorate, GRE General Test. Additional exam requirements/recommendations for international students: Required—TOEFL (minimum score 90 iBT). *Application deadline:* For fall admission, 1/15 for domestic students; for spring admission, 10/1 for domestic students. Application fee: $100. Electronic applications accepted. *Expenses:* Contact institution. *Financial support:* In 2017–18, 19 teaching assistantships were awarded; fellowships and research assistantships also available. *Faculty research:* Humanities, philosophy, philosophy of religion, race, Asian-Americans. *Unit head:* Dr. Robert Cresae, Chair, 631-632-7570, Fax: 631-632-7522, E-mail: robert.crease@stonybrook.edu. *Application contact:* 631-632-7590, Fax: 631-632-7522, E-mail: alissa.betz@stonybrook.edu.
Website: http://www.sunysb.edu/philosophy/

Syracuse University, College of Arts and Sciences, Department of Philosophy, Syracuse, NY 13244. Offers MA, PhD. *Degree requirements:* For master's, thesis; for doctorate, thesis/dissertation. *Entrance requirements:* For master's and doctorate, GRE, transcripts from previous institutions, three letters of recommendation, personal statement, writing sample. Additional exam requirements/recommendations for international students: Required—TOEFL (minimum score 100 iBT). *Application deadline:* For fall admission, 1/1 priority date for domestic and international students. Application fee: $75. Electronic applications accepted. *Financial support:* Fellowships with full tuition reimbursements, teaching assistantships with tuition reimbursements,

and scholarships/grants available. Financial award application deadline: 1/1. *Faculty research:* Ethics, metaphysics, epistemology, philosophy of language. *Unit head:* Dr. Mark Heller, Department Chair and Professor of Philosophy, 315-443-5813, E-mail: heller@syr.edu. *Application contact:* Lisa Farnsworth, Secretary/Office Coordinator, 315-443-2245, E-mail: lfarmswo@syr.edu.
Website: http://philosophy.syr.edu/graduate/overview.html

Teachers College, Columbia University, Department of Arts and Humanities, New York, NY 10027. Offers applied linguistics (MA, Ed D); art and art education (Ed M, MA, Ed D, Ed DCT); arts administration (MA); bilingual and bicultural education (MA); global competence (Certificate); history and education (Ed D, PhD); music and music education (Ed DCT); philosophy and education (MA, Ed D, PhD); social studies education (Ed M, PhD); teaching English to speakers of other languages (Ed M); teaching of English and English education (Ed M, MA, Ed D, PhD), including English education (Ed M, Ed D, PhD), teaching of English (MA); teaching of social studies (MA); TESOL (MA, Ed D). *Program availability:* Part-time, evening/weekend. *Students:* 391 full-time (305 women), 418 part-time (283 women); includes 246 minority (62 Black or African American, non-Hispanic/Latino; 3 American Indian or Alaska Native, non-Hispanic/Latino; 94 Asian, non-Hispanic/Latino; 75 Hispanic/Latino; 12 Two or more races, non-Hispanic/Latino), 209 international. Average age 30. 1,053 applicants, 60% accepted, 334 enrolled. Terminal master's awarded for partial completion of doctoral program. *Financial support:* Fellowships, research assistantships, teaching assistantships, career-related internships or fieldwork, Federal Work-Study, institutionally sponsored loans, tuition waivers (full and partial), and unspecified assistantships available. Support available to part-time students. *Unit head:* Prof. William Gaudelli, Department Chair, E-mail: gaudelli@tc.columbia.edu. *Application contact:* David Estrella, Director of Admissions, 212-678-3305, Fax: 212-678-4171, E-mail: estrella@tc.columbia.edu.

Temple University, College of Liberal Arts, Department of Philosophy, Philadelphia, PA 19122-6096. Offers MA, PhD. *Program availability:* Part-time. *Faculty:* 13 full-time (4 women), 2 part-time/adjunct (1 woman). *Students:* 29 full-time (10 women), 4 part-time (2 women); includes 6 minority (1 Asian, non-Hispanic/Latino; 3 Hispanic/Latino; 2 Two or more races, non-Hispanic/Latino), 2 international. 25 applicants, 48% accepted, 3 enrolled. In 2017, 3 master's, 1 doctorate awarded. Terminal master's awarded for partial completion of doctoral program. *Degree requirements:* For master's, thesis or alternative; for doctorate, one foreign language, thesis/dissertation. *Entrance requirements:* For master's and doctorate, GRE General Test, minimum GPA of 3.0, 3 letters of recommendation. Additional exam requirements/recommendations for international students: Required—TOEFL (minimum score 550 paper-based; 79 iBT). *Application deadline:* For fall admission, 1/1 for domestic students, 12/15 for international students; for spring admission, 10/1 for domestic students, 8/1 for international students. Applications are processed on a rolling basis. Application fee: $60. Electronic applications accepted. *Expenses:* Tuition, state resident: full-time $16,164; part-time $898 per credit hour. Tuition, nonresident: full-time $22,158; part-time $1231 per credit hour. *Required fees:* $890; $445 per semester. Full-time tuition and fees vary according to course load, degree level, campus/location and program. *Financial support:* Fellowships with full tuition reimbursements, teaching assistantships with full tuition reimbursements, institutionally sponsored loans, and tuition waivers (partial) available. Financial award application deadline: 1/15; financial award applicants required to submit FAFSA. *Faculty research:* History of philosophy, European philosophy, aesthetics, analytic philosophy, pragmatism. *Unit head:* Dr. Kristen Gjesdal, Director, 215-715-7519, E-mail: kgjesdal@temple.edu. *Application contact:* Sonia Lawson, Coordinator, 215-204-1742, Fax: 215-204-0200, E-mail: slawson@temple.edu.
Website: http://www.cla.temple.edu/philosophy/

Texas A&M University, College of Liberal Arts, Department of Philosophy, College Station, TX 77843. Offers MA, PhD. *Program availability:* Part-time. *Faculty:* 19. *Students:* 21 full-time (5 women), 5 part-time (0 women); includes 8 minority (1 Black or African American, non-Hispanic/Latino; 1 Asian, non-Hispanic/Latino; 6 Hispanic/Latino), 3 international. Average age 27. 6 applicants, 100% accepted, 5 enrolled. In 2017, 4 doctorates awarded. Terminal master's awarded for partial completion of doctoral program. *Degree requirements:* For master's, thesis optional; for doctorate, comprehensive exam, thesis/dissertation. *Entrance requirements:* For master's, GRE General Test, letter of recommendation, resume, writing sample; for doctorate, GRE General Test, letters of recommendation, resume, writing sample. Additional exam requirements/recommendations for international students: Required—TOEFL (minimum score 550 paper-based; 80 iBT), IELTS (minimum score 6), PTE (minimum score 53). *Application deadline:* For fall admission, 1/15 for domestic and international students. Application fee: $50 ($90 for international students). Electronic applications accepted. *Expenses:* Contact institution. *Financial support:* In 2017–18, 25 students received support, including 2 fellowships with tuition reimbursements available (averaging $18,000 per year), 5 research assistantships with tuition reimbursements available (averaging $8,238 per year), 23 teaching assistantships with tuition reimbursements available (averaging $10,791 per year); career-related internships or fieldwork, institutionally sponsored loans, scholarships/grants, traineeships, health care benefits, tuition waivers (full and partial), and unspecified assistantships also available. Support available to part-time students. Financial award application deadline: 3/15; financial award applicants required to submit FAFSA. *Faculty research:* American philosophy, applied ethics, philosophy of mind, philosophy of religion, history and philosophy of logic. *Unit head:* Dr. Theodore George, Interim Head, 979-845-5605, E-mail: t-george@tamu.edu. *Application contact:* Dr. Clare Palmer, Director of Graduate Program, 979-862-1435, E-mail: c.palmer@tamu.edu.
Website: http://philosophy.tamu.edu

Texas State University, The Graduate College, College of Liberal Arts, Applied Philosophy and Ethics Program, San Marcos, TX 78666. Offers MA. *Program availability:* Part-time. *Faculty:* 24 full-time (8 women), 2 part-time/adjunct (both women). *Students:* 14 full-time (6 women), 7 part-time (1 woman); includes 9 minority (2 Black or African American, non-Hispanic/Latino; 7 Hispanic/Latino). Average age 31. 11 applicants, 82% accepted, 3 enrolled. In 2017, 13 master's awarded. *Degree requirements:* For master's, comprehensive exam, thesis optional. *Entrance requirements:* For master's, baccalaureate degree from regionally-accredited university with minimum GPA of 3.0 on last 60 undergraduate semester hours, statement of purpose, 2 letters of recommendation, writing sample. Additional exam requirements/recommendations for international students: Required—TOEFL (minimum score 550 paper-based; 78 iBT), IELTS (minimum score 6). *Application deadline:* For fall admission, 3/1 priority date for domestic and international students; for spring admission, 10/15 for domestic students, 10/1 for international students; for summer admission, 4/15 for domestic students, 3/15 for international students. Applications are processed on a rolling basis. Application fee: $40 ($90 for international students). Electronic applications accepted. *Expenses:* Tuition, state resident: full-time $7868; part-time $3934 per semester. Tuition, nonresident: full-time $17,828; part-time $8914 per semester. *Required fees:* $2092; $1435 per semester. Tuition and fees vary according to course load. *Financial support:* In 2017–18, 13 students received support, including 1 research assistantship (averaging $12,892 per year), 13 teaching assistantships (averaging $12,272 per year); scholarships/grants and unspecified assistantships also available. Support available to part-time students. Financial award application deadline: 3/1; financial award applicants required to submit FAFSA. *Faculty research:* Engagement: philosophy, practice and performance, climate corps. *Total annual research expenditures:* $8,567. *Unit head:* Dr. Audrey Mckinney, Graduate Advisor, 512-245-2047, Fax: 512-245-8336, E-mail: am04@txstate.edu. *Application contact:* Dr. Andrea Golato, Dean of Graduate School, 512-245-2581, Fax: 512-245-8365, E-mail: gradcollege@txstate.edu.
Website: http://www.txstate.edu/philosophy/courses-programs/graduate/graduate-MA-Requirements.html

Texas Tech University, Graduate School, College of Arts and Sciences, Department of Philosophy, Lubbock, TX 79409-3092. Offers MA. *Program availability:* Part-time. *Faculty:* 13 full-time (2 women), 1 part-time/adjunct (0 women). *Students:* 14 full-time (2 women); includes 1 minority (Hispanic/Latino), 2 international. Average age 26. 28 applicants, 61% accepted, 8 enrolled. In 2017, 7 master's awarded. *Degree requirements:* For master's, thesis or alternative. *Entrance requirements:* For master's, GRE General Test. Additional exam requirements/recommendations for international students: Required—TOEFL (minimum score 550 paper-based; 79 iBT). *Application deadline:* For fall admission, 6/1 priority date for domestic students, 1/15 priority date for international students; for spring admission, 9/1 priority date for domestic students, 6/15 priority date for international students. Applications are processed on a rolling basis. Application fee: $60. Electronic applications accepted. *Expenses:* Contact institution. *Financial support:* In 2017–18, 15 students received support, including 6 fellowships (averaging $4,182 per year), 15 teaching assistantships (averaging $12,567 per year); research assistantships, Federal Work-Study, and scholarships/grants also available. Financial award application deadline: 4/15; financial award applicants required to submit FAFSA. *Faculty research:* Aesthetics, ethics, history of philosophy, philosophy of mind, philosophy of science. *Unit head:* Dr. Mark O. Webb, Professor and Chair, 806-742-3275, Fax: 806-742-0730, E-mail: mark.webb@ttu.edu. *Application contact:* Dr. Daniel O. Nathan, Director of Graduate Studies, 806-742-0373 Ext. 340, Fax: 806-742-0730, E-mail: daniel.nathan@ttu.edu.
Website: http://www.philosophy.ttu.edu/

Trinity Western University, School of Graduate Studies, Program in Interdisciplinary Humanities, Langley, BC V2Y 1Y1, Canada. Offers general humanities (MAIH); specialized (MAIH), including English, history, philosophy. *Program availability:* Part-time. *Degree requirements:* For master's, thesis or alternative, 36 semester hours. *Entrance requirements:* For master's, strong undergraduate degree in humanities or English, history or philosophy. Additional exam requirements/recommendations for international students: Recommended—TOEFL. Electronic applications accepted. *Faculty research:* Literary theory, gender, medieval and early modern literature, philosophy of religion, Thomas Merton's poetics.

Tufts University, Graduate School of Arts and Sciences, Department of Philosophy, Medford, MA 02155. Offers MA. *Students:* 19 full-time (4 women); includes 1 minority (Black or African American, non-Hispanic/Latino), 4 international. Average age 25. 119 applicants, 21% accepted, 9 enrolled. In 2017, 14 master's awarded. *Degree requirements:* For master's, comprehensive exam, departmental qualifying exam. *Entrance requirements:* For master's, GRE General Test, writing sample. Additional exam requirements/recommendations for international students: Required—TOEFL (minimum score 550 paper-based; 80 iBT), IELTS (minimum score 6.5). *Application deadline:* For fall admission, 1/15 for domestic and international students. Applications are processed on a rolling basis. Application fee: $85. Electronic applications accepted. *Expenses:* Contact institution. *Financial support:* Teaching assistantships, Federal Work-Study, scholarships/grants, tuition waivers (full and partial), and unspecified assistantships available. Financial award application deadline: 1/15. *Unit head:* Dr. Lionel McPherson, Graduate Program Director, 617-627-2346. *Application contact:* Office of Graduate Admissions, 617-627-3395, E-mail: gradadmissions@tufts.edu.
Website: http://ase.tufts.edu/philosophy/

Tulane University, School of Liberal Arts, Department of Philosophy, New Orleans, LA 70118-5669. Offers MA, PhD. *Degree requirements:* For master's, thesis or alternative; for doctorate, one foreign language, thesis/dissertation. *Entrance requirements:* For master's, GRE General Test, minimum B average in undergraduate course work; for doctorate, GRE General Test. Additional exam requirements/recommendations for international students: Required—TOEFL. Electronic applications accepted. *Expenses:* *Tuition:* Full-time $50,920; part-time $2829 per credit hour. *Required fees:* $2040; $44.50 per credit hour. $580 per term. Tuition and fees vary according to course load, degree level and program.

Universidad Autonoma de Guadalajara, Graduate Programs, Guadalajara, Mexico. Offers administrative law and justice (LL M); advertising and corporate communications (MA); architecture (M Arch); business (MBA); computational science (MCC); education (Ed M, Ed D); English-Spanish translation (MA); entrepreneurship and management (MBA); integrated management of digital animation (MA); international business (MIB); international corporate law (LL M); internet technologies (MS); manufacturing systems (MMS); occupational health (MS); philosophy (MA, PhD); power electronics (MS); quality systems (MQS); renewable energy (MS); social evaluation of projects (MBA); strategic market research (MBA); tax law (MA); teaching mathematics (MA).

Université de Montréal, Faculty of Arts and Sciences, Department of Philosophy, Montréal, QC H3C 3J7, Canada. Offers MA, PhD. *Degree requirements:* For master's, 2 foreign languages, thesis; for doctorate, thesis/dissertation, general exam. Electronic applications accepted. *Faculty research:* Ancient and modern philosophy; logic and philosophy of language, ethics, and politics; contemporary Continental philosophy.

Université de Sherbrooke, Faculty of Letters and Human Sciences, Department of Human Sciences, Sherbrooke, QC J1K 2R1, Canada. Offers history (MA); philosophy (MA). *Degree requirements:* For master's, thesis. *Entrance requirements:* For master's, minimum GPA of 2.75. *Faculty research:* Political, social, and urban history; history of women.

Université de Sherbrooke, Faculty of Theology and Religious Studies, Sherbrooke, QC J1K 2R1, Canada. Offers applied ethics (Diploma); human science of religions (MA); intercultural training (Diploma); philosophy (MA, PhD); spiritual anthropology (Diploma); theology (MA, PhD, Diploma). *Program availability:* Part-time, evening/weekend, online learning. Terminal master's awarded for partial completion of doctoral program. *Entrance requirements:* For master's, bachelor's degree in related discipline; for doctorate, master's degree in related discipline. *Faculty research:* Faith and culture interrelation.

Université du Québec à Montréal, Graduate Programs, Program in Philosophy, Montréal, QC H3C 3P8, Canada. Offers MA, PhD. PhD offered jointly with Université du Québec à Trois-Rivières. *Program availability:* Part-time. *Degree requirements:* For master's, thesis; for doctorate, thesis/dissertation. *Entrance requirements:* For master's, appropriate bachelor's degree or equivalent, proficiency in French; for doctorate, appropriate master's degree or equivalent, proficiency in French.

Université du Québec à Trois-Rivières, Graduate Programs, Program in Philosophy, Trois-Rivières, QC G9A 5H7, Canada. Offers MA, PhD. PhD offered jointly with Université du Québec à Montréal. *Program availability:* Part-time. *Degree requirements:* For master's, thesis; for doctorate, thesis/dissertation. *Entrance requirements:* For master's, appropriate bachelor's degree, proficiency in French; for doctorate, appropriate master's degree, proficiency in French.

Université Laval, Faculty of Philosophy, Programs in Philosophy, Québec, QC G1K 7P4, Canada. Offers MA, PhD. Terminal master's awarded for partial completion of doctoral program. *Degree requirements:* For master's, thesis; for doctorate, comprehensive exam, thesis/dissertation. *Entrance requirements:* For master's and doctorate, French exam. Electronic applications accepted.

University at Albany, State University of New York, College of Arts and Sciences, Department of Philosophy, Albany, NY 12222-0001. Offers MA, PhD. *Faculty:* 10 full-time (3 women). *Students:* 10 full-time (2 women), 17 part-time (6 women); includes 2 minority (1 Black or African American, non-Hispanic/Latino; 1 Asian, non-Hispanic/Latino), 2 international. 20 applicants, 60% accepted, 6 enrolled. In 2017, 1 master's awarded. *Degree requirements:* For master's, one foreign language, thesis; for doctorate, thesis/dissertation. *Entrance requirements:* For master's and doctorate, GRE General Test. Additional exam requirements/recommendations for international students: Required—TOEFL (minimum score 550 paper-based). *Application deadline:* For fall admission, 2/15 for domestic students, 5/1 for international students; for spring admission, 11/1 for international students. Applications are processed on a rolling basis. Application fee: $75. Electronic applications accepted. *Expenses:* Tuition, state resident: full-time $10,870; part-time $453 per credit hour. Tuition, nonresident: full-time $22,210; part-time $925 per credit hour. *Required fees:* $84.68 per credit hour. $508.06 per semester. Part-time tuition and fees vary according to course load and program. *Financial support:* Fellowships available. Financial award application deadline: 3/15. *Faculty research:* Philosophical logic, ethics, ancient philosophy/metaphysics, aesthetics, biomedical ethics. *Unit head:* P. D. Magnus, Chair, 518-442-4250, Fax: 518-442-4259, E-mail: pmagnus@albany.edu. *Application contact:* Michael DeRensis, Director, Graduate Admissions, 518-442-3980, Fax: 518-442-3922, E-mail: graduate@albany.edu.
Website: http://www.albany.edu/philosophy/

University at Buffalo, the State University of New York, Graduate School, College of Arts and Sciences, Department of Philosophy, Buffalo, NY 14260. Offers MA, PhD. *Faculty:* 18 full-time (3 women), 2 part-time/adjunct (1 woman). *Students:* 30 full-time (2 women), 18 part-time (3 women); includes 5 minority (4 Asian, non-Hispanic/Latino; 1 Hispanic/Latino), 9 international. Average age 28. 26 applicants, 77% accepted, 14 enrolled. In 2017, 3 master's, 9 doctorates awarded. Terminal master's awarded for partial completion of doctoral program. *Degree requirements:* For master's, variable foreign language requirement, thesis or alternative; for doctorate, variable foreign language requirement, comprehensive exam, thesis/dissertation. *Entrance requirements:* For master's and doctorate, GRE General Test, minimum GPA of 3.0. Additional exam requirements/recommendations for international students: Required—TOEFL (minimum score 550 paper-based; 79 iBT). *Application deadline:* For fall admission, 1/2 for domestic and international students. Applications are processed on a rolling basis. Application fee: $75. Electronic applications accepted. *Financial support:* In 2017–18, 19 students received support, including 1 fellowship with full tuition reimbursement available (averaging $7,500 per year), 19 teaching assistantships with full tuition reimbursements available (averaging $13,500 per year); institutionally sponsored loans, tuition waivers (full), and unspecified assistantships also available. Financial award application deadline: 1/20; financial award applicants required to submit FAFSA. *Faculty research:* Logic, metaphysics (historical and contemporary), aesthetics, epistemology, ethics (historical and contemporary), ontology, social and political. *Total annual research expenditures:* $3.7 million. *Unit head:* Dr. Neil Williams, Chair, 716-645-0161, Fax: 716-645-6139, E-mail: new@buffalo.edu. *Application contact:* Dr. David Braun, Director of Graduate Studies, 716-645-0162, Fax: 716-645-6139, E-mail: dbraun2@buffalo.edu.
Website: http://wings.buffalo.edu/philosophy/

University of Alberta, Faculty of Graduate Studies and Research, Department of Philosophy, Edmonton, AB T6G 2E1, Canada. Offers MA, PhD. *Program availability:* Part-time. *Degree requirements:* For master's, thesis; for doctorate, thesis/dissertation. *Entrance requirements:* Additional exam requirements/recommendations for international students: Required—TOEFL (minimum score 550 paper-based). Electronic applications accepted. *Faculty research:* Philosophy of science, cognitive science, social and political philosophy, philosophy of language and logic, environmental aesthetics.

The University of Arizona, College of Social and Behavioral Sciences, Department of Philosophy, Tucson, AZ 85721. Offers MA, PhD. *Program availability:* Part-time. Terminal master's awarded for partial completion of doctoral program. *Degree requirements:* For master's, exams, qualifying paper; for doctorate, thesis/dissertation, preliminary exams. *Entrance requirements:* For doctorate, GRE General Test, 3 letters of recommendation, writing sample. Additional exam requirements/recommendations for international students: Required—TOEFL (minimum score 550 paper-based; 79 iBT). Electronic applications accepted. *Faculty research:* Law, social, and political philosophy; epistemology; philosophy of mind; cognitive science.

University of Arkansas, Graduate School, J. William Fulbright College of Arts and Sciences, Department of Philosophy, Fayetteville, AR 72701. Offers MA, PhD. *Program availability:* Part-time. In 2017, 2 master's, 3 doctorates awarded. *Degree requirements:* For master's, thesis; for doctorate, 2 foreign languages, thesis/dissertation. *Application deadline:* For fall admission, 8/1 for domestic students, 4/1 for international students; for spring admission, 12/1 for domestic students, 10/1 for international students; for summer admission, 4/15 for domestic students, 3/1 for international students. Applications are processed on a rolling basis. Application fee: $60. Electronic applications accepted. *Expenses:* Tuition, state resident: full-time $3782. Tuition, nonresident: full-time $10,238. *Financial support:* In 2017–18, 1 research assistantship, 10 teaching assistantships were awarded; fellowships with tuition reimbursements, career-related internships or fieldwork, and Federal Work-Study also available. Support available to part-time students. Financial award application deadline: 4/1; financial award applicants required to submit FAFSA. *Unit head:* Dr. Edward H. Minar, Department Chair, 479-575-8712, Fax: 479-575-2642, E-mail: eminar@uark.edu. *Application contact:* Dr. Erick Funkhouser, Graduate Coordinator, 479-575-7441, E-mail: efunkho@uark.edu.
Website: https://fulbright.uark.edu/departments/philosophy/

The University of British Columbia, Faculty of Arts and Faculty of Graduate Studies, Department of Philosophy, Vancouver, BC V6T 1Z1, Canada. Offers MA, PhD. *Accreditation:* NCATE. *Program availability:* Part-time. *Degree requirements:* For master's, thesis (for some programs); for doctorate, comprehensive exam, thesis/dissertation. *Entrance requirements:* For master's, bachelor's degree with minimum GPA of 3.0 in 3rd- and 4th-year coursework; 3 credits in formal logic; 6 credits at the upper-level in the history of philosophy and in metaphysics, epistemology, or philosophy; 3 credits at the upper-level in ethics or value theory; for doctorate, MA, honors BA with first class standing, or BA with first class standing in philosophy. Additional exam requirements/recommendations for international students: Required—TOEFL, IELTS, Michigan English Language Assessment Battery (minimum score 81). Electronic applications accepted. *Expenses:* Contact institution. *Faculty research:* Ethics and applied ethics, metaphysics and epistemology, history of philosophy, philosophy of science, philosophy of biology, philosophy of mind, philosophy of cognitive science.

University of Calgary, Faculty of Graduate Studies, Faculty of Arts, Department of Philosophy, Calgary, AB T2N 1N4, Canada. Offers MA, PhD. *Program availability:* Part-time. *Degree requirements:* For master's, comprehensive exam (for some programs), thesis (for some programs); for doctorate, thesis/dissertation, candidacy exam. *Entrance requirements:* Additional exam requirements/recommendations for international students: Required—TOEFL (minimum score 550 paper-based). Electronic applications accepted. *Faculty research:* Ethics and political philosophy, metaphysics, philosophy of mind, philosophy of language.

University of California, Berkeley, Graduate Division, College of Letters and Science, Department of Philosophy, Berkeley, CA 94720-1500. Offers PhD. *Degree requirements:* For doctorate, thesis/dissertation, qualifying exam. *Entrance requirements:* For doctorate, GRE General Test, minimum GPA of 3.0, writing sample, 3 letters of recommendation. Electronic applications accepted.

University of California, Davis, Graduate Studies, Program in Philosophy, Davis, CA 95616. Offers MA, PhD. Terminal master's awarded for partial completion of doctoral program. *Degree requirements:* For doctorate, thesis/dissertation. *Entrance requirements:* For master's and doctorate, GRE General Test, minimum GPA of 3.0. Additional exam requirements/recommendations for international students: Required—TOEFL (minimum score 550 paper-based). Electronic applications accepted. *Faculty research:* Moral and political philosophy, philosophy of language, metaphysics, philosophy of science, history of philosophy.

University of California, Irvine, School of Humanities, Department of Philosophy, Irvine, CA 92697. Offers MA, PhD. *Students:* 21 full-time (5 women); includes 7 minority (1 Black or African American, non-Hispanic/Latino; 3 Hispanic/Latino; 3 Two or more races, non-Hispanic/Latino), 1 international. Average age 30. 52 applicants, 31% accepted, 5 enrolled. In 2017, 5 master's, 6 doctorates awarded. *Entrance requirements:* For master's and doctorate, GRE General Test, minimum GPA of 3.0. Additional exam requirements/recommendations for international students: Required—TOEFL (minimum score 550 paper-based). *Application deadline:* For fall admission, 1/15 priority date for domestic students, 1/15 for international students. Applications are processed on a rolling basis. Application fee: $105 ($125 for international students). Electronic applications accepted. *Financial support:* Fellowships with tuition reimbursements, teaching assistantships with partial tuition reimbursements, institutionally sponsored loans, traineeships, health care benefits, and unspecified assistantships available. Financial award application deadline: 3/1; financial award applicants required to submit FAFSA. *Faculty research:* Philosophy of action and decision theory, philosophy of language, philosophy of mathematics, virtue ethics, modern and contemporary Continental philosophy. *Unit head:* Aaron James, Department Chair, E-mail: aaron.james@uci.edu. *Application contact:* Kirsten S. Alonso, Department Coordinator, 949-824-6525, Fax: 949-824-6520, E-mail: kalonso@uci.edu.
Website: http://www.hnet.uci.edu/philosophy/

University of California, Irvine, School of Social Sciences, Department of Logic and Philosophy of Science, Irvine, CA 92697. Offers philosophy (PhD). *Students:* 39 full-time (14 women); includes 5 minority (1 Asian, non-Hispanic/Latino; 1 Hispanic/Latino; 3 Two or more races, non-Hispanic/Latino), 13 international. Average age 27. 64 applicants, 33% accepted, 15 enrolled. In 2017, 2 doctorates awarded. *Entrance requirements:* For doctorate, GRE, minimum GPA of 3.0. Additional exam requirements/recommendations for international students: Required—TOEFL (minimum score 550 paper-based). *Application deadline:* For fall admission, 1/15 for domestic and international students. Application fee: $105 ($125 for international students). *Financial support:* Fellowships, research assistantships with full tuition reimbursements, teaching assistantships, institutionally sponsored loans, traineeships, health care benefits, and unspecified assistantships available. Financial award application deadline: 3/1. *Unit head:* P. Kyle Stanford, Chair, 949-824-6398, Fax: 949-824-8388, E-mail: stanford@uci.edu. *Application contact:* John Manchak, Graduate Program Director, 949-824-7374, E-mail: jmanchak@uci.edu.
Website: http://www.lps.uci.edu/

University of California, Los Angeles, Graduate Division, College of Letters and Science, Department of Philosophy, Los Angeles, CA 90095. Offers MA, PhD. Terminal master's awarded for partial completion of doctoral program. *Degree requirements:* For master's, one foreign language, comprehensive exam; for doctorate, one foreign language, thesis/dissertation, oral and written qualifying exams, 3 quarters of teaching experience. *Entrance requirements:* For doctorate, GRE General Test, bachelor's degree; minimum undergraduate GPA of 3.0 (or its equivalent if letter grade system not used); writing sample. Additional exam requirements/recommendations for international students: Required—TOEFL. Electronic applications accepted.

University of California, Riverside, Graduate Division, Department of Philosophy, Riverside, CA 92521-0102. Offers MA, PhD. Terminal master's awarded for partial completion of doctoral program. *Degree requirements:* For master's, logic exam, professional paper; for doctorate, one foreign language, thesis/dissertation, logic exam, proposition papers, qualifying exams. *Entrance requirements:* For master's, GRE General Test, minimum GPA of 3.2; for doctorate, GRE General Test, master's degree in philosophy, minimum GPA of 3.2. Additional exam requirements/recommendations for international students: Required—TOEFL (minimum score 550 paper-based; 80 iBT). Electronic applications accepted. *Expenses:* Tuition, state resident: full-time $5746. Tuition, nonresident: full-time $10,780. Tuition and fees vary according to campus/location and program. *Faculty research:* Moral philosophy, philosophy of science, history of philosophy, philosophy of language, Continental philosophy.

University of California, San Diego, Graduate Division, Department of Philosophy, La Jolla, CA 92093. Offers PhD. *Students:* 41 full-time (10 women), 1 part-time (0 women). 224 applicants, 13% accepted, 7 enrolled. In 2017, 3 doctorates awarded. *Degree requirements:* For doctorate, thesis/dissertation, 3 quarters of teaching assistantship; original essay. *Entrance requirements:* For doctorate, GRE General Test, writing sample. Additional exam requirements/recommendations for international students: Required—TOEFL (minimum score 550 paper-based; 80 iBT), IELTS (minimum score 7). *Application deadline:* For fall admission, 1/20 for domestic students. Application fee: $105 ($125 for international students). Electronic applications accepted. *Financial support:* Fellowships, teaching assistantships, and scholarships/grants available. Financial award applicants required to submit FAFSA. *Faculty research:* Philosophy of science, ethics and social-political philosophy, history of philosophy, epistemology and metaphysics, philosophy of mind and language. *Unit head:* Jonathan Cohen, Chair, 858-534-6812, E-mail: joncohen@aardvark.ucsd.edu. *Application contact:* Anna Shonle, Graduate Coordinator, 858-534-3076, E-mail: ashonle@ucsd.edu.
Website: http://philosophy.ucsd.edu/

University of California, Santa Barbara, Graduate Division, College of Letters and Sciences, Division of Humanities and Fine Arts, Department of Philosophy, Santa Barbara, CA 93106-9580. Offers PhD, MA/PhD. Terminal master's awarded for partial completion of doctoral program. *Degree requirements:* For doctorate, thesis/dissertation. *Entrance requirements:* For doctorate, GRE. Additional exam requirements/recommendations for international students: Required—TOEFL (minimum score 550 paper-based; 80 iBT), IELTS (minimum score 7). Electronic applications accepted. *Faculty research:* Epistemology, philosophy of language, philosophy of mind, history of philosophy, logic.

University of California, Santa Cruz, Division of Graduate Studies, Division of Humanities, Department of Philosophy, Santa Cruz, CA 95064. Offers MA, PhD. *Degree*

requirements: For doctorate, thesis/dissertation, qualifying exam. *Entrance requirements:* For master's, GRE, 3 letters of recommendation; for doctorate, GRE, official transcripts, 3 letters of recommendation. Additional exam requirements/recommendations for international students: Required—TOEFL (minimum score 550 paper-based; 83 iBT); Recommended—IELTS (minimum score 8). Electronic applications accepted. *Faculty research:* Philosophy of science.

University of Chicago, Division of the Humanities, Department of Philosophy, Chicago, IL 60637. Offers ancient philosophy (PhD); philosophy (PhD). *Students:* 44 full-time (12 women); includes 3 minority (2 Asian, non-Hispanic/Latino; 1 Hispanic/Latino), 19 international. Average age 30. 236 applicants, 6% accepted, 7 enrolled. In 2017, 3 doctorates awarded. Terminal master's awarded for partial completion of doctoral program. *Degree requirements:* For doctorate, variable foreign language requirement, thesis/dissertation. *Entrance requirements:* For doctorate, GRE General Test, 15-20 page writing sample, statement of purpose, 3 letters of recommendation, transcripts for all previous degrees and institutions attended. Additional exam requirements/recommendations for international students: Required—TOEFL (minimum score 104 iBT), IELTS (minimum score 7). *Application deadline:* For fall admission, 12/15 for domestic and international students. Application fee: $90. Electronic applications accepted. *Financial support:* In 2017–18, fellowships with full tuition reimbursements (averaging $27,000 per year) were awarded; teaching assistantships with full tuition reimbursements, Federal Work-Study, institutionally sponsored loans, scholarships/grants, and health care benefits also available. Financial award application deadline: 12/15. *Faculty research:* Kant, history of analytic philosophy, ancient philosophy, philosophy of mind, philosophy of action. *Unit head:* Dr. Gabriel Lear, Chair, 773-702-5078, E-mail: wweaver@uchicago.edu. *Application contact:* Michael Beetley, Assistant Dean of Students, Admissions and Fellowships, 773-702-1552, Fax: 773-834-9148, E-mail: humanitiesadmissions@uchicago.edu.
Website: http://philosophy.uchicago.edu/

University of Chicago, Division of the Humanities, Master of Arts Program in the Humanities, Chicago, IL 60637. Offers art history (MA); cinema and media studies (MA); classic languages (MA); comparative literature (MA); creative writing (MA); cultural policy studies (MA); digital humanities (MA); East Asian languages and civilizations (MA); English language and literature (MA); gender and sexuality studies (MA); Germanic studies (MA); linguistics (MA); music (MA); near Eastern languages and civilizations (MA); philosophy (MA); poetics (MA); race, politics and culture (MA); Romance languages and literatures (MA); Slavic languages and literatures (MA); South Asian languages and civilizations (MA); theater and performance studies (MA). *Students:* 95 full-time (50 women), 6 part-time (4 women); includes 22 minority (1 Black or African American, non-Hispanic/Latino; 10 Asian, non-Hispanic/Latino; 11 Hispanic/Latino), 19 international. Average age 26. 708 applicants, 75% accepted, 101 enrolled. In 2017, 91 master's awarded. *Degree requirements:* For master's, thesis. *Entrance requirements:* For master's, GRE General Test, 10-15 page writing sample, statement of purpose, 3 letters of recommendation, transcripts for all previous degrees and institutions attended. Additional exam requirements/recommendations for international students: Required—TOEFL (minimum score 104 iBT), IELTS (minimum score 7). *Application deadline:* For fall admission, 1/3 priority date for domestic and international students. Application fee: $90. Electronic applications accepted. *Expenses:* Contact institution. *Financial support:* In 2017–18, fellowships with partial tuition reimbursements (averaging $12,000 per year) were awarded; Federal Work-Study, institutionally sponsored loans, scholarships/grants, and tuition waivers (partial) also available. Financial award application deadline: 4/30. *Unit head:* Thomas Christensen, Director, 773-834-1201, Fax: 773-834-7526, E-mail: ma-humanities@uchicago.edu. *Application contact:* Michael Beetley, Assistant Dean of Students for Admissions, 773-834-1552, E-mail: humanitiesadmissions@uchicago.edu.
Website: http://maph.uchicago.edu/

University of Cincinnati, Graduate School, McMicken College of Arts and Sciences, Department of Philosophy, Cincinnati, OH 45221. Offers MA, PhD. Terminal master's awarded for partial completion of doctoral program. *Degree requirements:* For master's, thesis; for doctorate, one foreign language, comprehensive exam, thesis/dissertation. *Entrance requirements:* For master's and doctorate, GRE General Test, BA in philosophy or equivalent experience. Additional exam requirements/recommendations for international students: Required—TOEFL. Electronic applications accepted. *Expenses: Tuition, area resident:* Full-time $14,468. Tuition, state resident: full-time $14,968; part-time $754 per credit hour. Tuition, nonresident: full-time $24,210; part-time $1311 per credit hour. *International tuition:* $26,460 full-time. *Required fees:* $3958; $84 per credit hour. One-time fee: $85 full-time. Tuition and fees vary according to course load, degree level and program.

University of Colorado Boulder, Graduate School, College of Arts and Sciences, Department of Philosophy, Boulder, CO 80309. Offers MA, PhD. *Faculty:* 18 full-time (5 women). *Students:* 44 full-time (11 women), 1 part-time (0 women); includes 7 minority (3 Black or African American, non-Hispanic/Latino; 3 Hispanic/Latino; 1 Two or more races, non-Hispanic/Latino), 5 international. Average age 31. 169 applicants, 26% accepted, 10 enrolled. In 2017, 3 master's, 4 doctorates awarded. Terminal master's awarded for partial completion of doctoral program. *Degree requirements:* For master's, comprehensive exam, thesis; for doctorate, one foreign language, thesis/dissertation, logic and qualifying papers, oral exam. *Entrance requirements:* For master's, GRE General Test, writing sample, minimum undergraduate GPA of 2.75; for doctorate, GRE General Test. *Application deadline:* For fall admission, 1/10 for domestic students; for spring admission, 12/1 for domestic students. Applications are processed on a rolling basis. Application fee: $60 ($80 for international students). Electronic applications accepted. Application fee is waived when completed online. *Financial support:* In 2017–18, 96 students received support, including 20 fellowships (averaging $7,297 per year), 5 research assistantships with full and partial tuition reimbursements available (averaging $25,191 per year), 27 teaching assistantships with full and partial tuition reimbursements available (averaging $21,281 per year); institutionally sponsored loans, scholarships/grants, health care benefits, and unspecified assistantships also available. Financial award application deadline: 2/15; financial award applicants required to submit FAFSA. *Faculty research:* Philosophy; ethics; history of philosophy; political philosophy; history of science and technology. *Total annual research expenditures:* $42,749. *Application contact:* E-mail: phildept@colorado.edu.
Website: http://www.colorado.edu/philosophy/

University of Connecticut, Graduate School, College of Liberal Arts and Sciences, Department of Philosophy, Storrs, CT 06269. Offers MA, PhD. Terminal master's awarded for partial completion of doctoral program. *Degree requirements:* For master's, comprehensive exam; for doctorate, 2 foreign languages, thesis/dissertation. *Entrance requirements:* For master's and doctorate, GRE General Test. Additional exam requirements/recommendations for international students: Required—TOEFL (minimum score 550 paper-based). Electronic applications accepted.

University of Dallas, Braniff Graduate School of Liberal Arts, Institute of Philosophic Studies, Doctoral Program in Philosophy, Irving, TX 75062-4736. Offers PhD. *Degree requirements:* For doctorate, 2 foreign languages, comprehensive exam, thesis/dissertation, qualifying exams. *Entrance requirements:* For doctorate, GRE General Test. *Application deadline:* For fall admission, 2/15 priority date for domestic students. Application fee: $50. *Expenses: Tuition:* Full-time $33,750; part-time $22,500 per year. Tuition and fees vary according to program. *Financial support:* Application deadline: 2/15. *Faculty research:* Aesthetics, postmodernism, Hegel, ethics, Aristotle. *Unit head:* Dr. Joshua Parens, Dean, 972-721-5231, Fax: 972-721-4005, E-mail: parens@udallas.edu.

University of Dallas, Braniff Graduate School of Liberal Arts, Master's Program in Philosophy, Irving, TX 75062-4736. Offers MA. *Degree requirements:* For master's, one foreign language, comprehensive exam, thesis. *Entrance requirements:* For master's, GRE General Test. Additional exam requirements/recommendations for international students: Required—TOEFL. *Application deadline:* For fall admission, 2/15 priority date for domestic students; for spring admission, 11/15 for domestic students. Applications are processed on a rolling basis. Application fee: $50. *Expenses: Tuition:* Full-time $33,750; part-time $22,500 per year. Tuition and fees vary according to program. *Financial support:* Application deadline: 2/15. *Faculty research:* Aesthetics, postmodernism, Hegel, ethics, Aristotle. *Unit head:* Dr. Chad Engelland, Program Director, 972-721-5231, Fax: 972-721-4005, E-mail: cengelland@udallas.edu.

University of Florida, Graduate School, College of Liberal Arts and Sciences, Department of Philosophy, Gainesville, FL 32611. Offers MA, PhD. *Program availability:* Part-time. *Degree requirements:* For doctorate, one foreign language, comprehensive exam, thesis/dissertation. *Entrance requirements:* For master's and doctorate, GRE General Test, minimum GPA of 3.0. Additional exam requirements/recommendations for international students: Required—TOEFL (minimum score 550 paper-based; 80 iBT), IELTS (minimum score 6). Electronic applications accepted. *Faculty research:* Philosophy of mind, metaphysics, philosophy of science, ancient philosophy, philosophical logic.

University of Georgia, Franklin College of Arts and Sciences, Department of Philosophy, Athens, GA 30602. Offers MA, PhD. *Program availability:* Part-time. *Degree requirements:* For master's, one foreign language, thesis; for doctorate, one foreign language, thesis/dissertation. *Entrance requirements:* For master's and doctorate, GRE General Test. Additional exam requirements/recommendations for international students: Required—TOEFL. Electronic applications accepted.

University of Guelph, Graduate Studies, College of Arts, Department of Philosophy, Guelph, ON N1G 2W1, Canada. Offers MA, PhD. PhD offered jointly with McMaster University, Wilfrid Laurier University. *Program availability:* Part-time. *Degree requirements:* For master's, thesis (for some programs); for doctorate, one foreign language, thesis/dissertation. *Entrance requirements:* For master's, minimum B-average during previous 2 years of course work; for doctorate, minimum B average. Additional exam requirements/recommendations for international students: Required—TOEFL (minimum score 550 paper-based). Electronic applications accepted. *Faculty research:* Philosophy of science, ethics, modern philosophy, social philosophy, Continental philosophy.

University of Hawaii at Manoa, Office of Graduate Education, College of Arts and Humanities, Department of Philosophy, Honolulu, HI 96822. Offers MA, PhD. *Program availability:* Part-time. *Degree requirements:* For master's, variable foreign language requirement, thesis optional, culminating exam; for doctorate, variable foreign language requirement, comprehensive exam, thesis/dissertation, final oral presentation. *Entrance requirements:* For master's and doctorate, GRE General Test. Additional exam requirements/recommendations for international students: Required—TOEFL (minimum score 600 paper-based; 100 iBT), IELTS (minimum score 7). *Faculty research:* Renaissance philosophy, Indian philosophy, logic, ethics, philosophy of science, philosophy of mathematics, Chinese philosophy.

University of Houston, College of Liberal Arts and Social Sciences, Department of Philosophy, Houston, TX 77204. Offers MA. *Degree requirements:* For master's, thesis (for some programs), thesis or additional course requirements. *Entrance requirements:* For master's, GRE General Test, minimum of 18 hours of course work in philosophy; minimum GPA of 3.3 in last 60 hours. Additional exam requirements/recommendations for international students: Required—TOEFL (minimum score 550 paper-based; 79 iBT). Electronic applications accepted. *Faculty research:* Skepticism, nominalism, history of philosophy, cognitive science.

University of Idaho, College of Graduate Studies, College of Letters, Arts and Social Sciences, Department of Politics and Philosophy, Moscow, ID 83844. Offers political science (MA, PhD); public administration (MPA). *Faculty:* 5 full-time. *Students:* 7 full-time, 10 part-time. Average age 31. In 2017, 7 master's, 1 doctorate awarded. *Entrance requirements:* For master's, GRE, minimum GPA of 3.0. Additional exam requirements/recommendations for international students: Required—TOEFL (minimum score 96 iBT). *Expenses:* Tuition, state resident: full-time $6722; part-time $430 per credit hour. Tuition, nonresident: full-time $23,046; part-time $1337 per credit hour. *Required fees:* $2142; $63 per credit hour. *Faculty research:* Political socialization, international and domestic conflict processes, constitutional law. *Unit head:* Dr. Brian Ellison, Chair, 208-885-6328, E-mail: politicsphilosophy@uidaho.edu. *Application contact:* Sean Scoggin, Graduate Recruitment Coordinator, 208-885-4723, E-mail: graduateadmissions@uidaho.edu.
Website: https://www.uidaho.edu/class/politics-and-philosophy

University of Illinois at Chicago, College of Liberal Arts and Sciences, Department of Philosophy, Chicago, IL 60607-7128. Offers MA, PhD. Terminal master's awarded for partial completion of doctoral program. *Degree requirements:* For doctorate, thesis/dissertation, preliminary exams. *Entrance requirements:* For master's and doctorate, minimum GPA of 2.75. Additional exam requirements/recommendations for international students: Required—TOEFL. Electronic applications accepted. *Faculty research:* Philosophy of science, philosophy of language, epistemology and metaphysics, ethics, aesthetics.

University of Illinois at Urbana–Champaign, Graduate College, College of Liberal Arts and Sciences, Department of Philosophy, Champaign, IL 61820. Offers MA, PhD, PhD/JD.

The University of Iowa, Graduate College, College of Liberal Arts and Sciences, Department of Philosophy, Iowa City, IA 52242-1316. Offers PhD. *Degree requirements:* For doctorate, comprehensive exam, thesis/dissertation. *Entrance requirements:* For doctorate, GRE General Test, minimum GPA of 3.0. Additional exam requirements/recommendations for international students: Required—TOEFL (minimum score 550 paper-based; 81 iBT). Electronic applications accepted.

The University of Kansas, Graduate Studies, College of Liberal Arts and Sciences, Department of Philosophy, Lawrence, KS 66045. Offers MA, PhD. *Program availability:* Part-time. *Students:* 28 full-time (9 women); includes 2 minority (1 Hispanic/Latino; 1 Two or more races, non-Hispanic/Latino), 7 international. Average age 30. 14 applicants, 71% accepted, 2 enrolled. In 2017, 3 master's, 2 doctorates awarded. Terminal master's awarded for partial completion of doctoral program. *Entrance requirements:* For master's and doctorate, GRE, curriculum vitae or resume, statement of purpose, writing sample, three letters of recommendation, official academic transcripts. Additional exam requirements/recommendations for international students: Required—TOEFL. *Application deadline:* For fall admission, 5/1 for domestic and international students. Application fee: $65 ($85 for international students). Electronic applications accepted. *Financial support:* Fellowships, teaching assistantships, Federal

Work-Study, scholarships/grants, and unspecified assistantships available. Financial award application deadline: 2/1. *Faculty research:* Theoretical and applied ethics, social and political philosophy, history of philosophy, analytic philosophy, philosophy of mind and language. *Unit head:* John Symons, Chair, 785-864-1948, E-mail: johnsymons@ku.edu. *Application contact:* Cari Ann Kreienhop, Graduate Program Coordinator, 785-864-3665, E-mail: ckreienhop@ku.edu.
Website: http://www.philosophy.ku.edu

University of Kentucky, Graduate School, College of Arts and Sciences, Program in Philosophy, Lexington, KY 40506-0032. Offers MA, PhD. *Degree requirements:* For master's, one foreign language, comprehensive exam, thesis; for doctorate, one foreign language, comprehensive exam, thesis/dissertation. *Entrance requirements:* For master's, GRE General Test, minimum undergraduate GPA of 2.75; for doctorate, GRE General Test, minimum graduate GPA of 3.0. Additional exam requirements/recommendations for international students: Required—TOEFL (minimum score 550 paper-based). Electronic applications accepted. *Faculty research:* History of philosophy, history and philosophy of science, ethics, social and political philosophy.

University of Lethbridge, School of Graduate Studies, Lethbridge, AB T1K 3M4, Canada. Offers addictions counseling (M Sc); agricultural biotechnology (M Sc); agricultural studies (M Sc, MA); anthropology (MA); archaeology (M Sc, MA); art (MA, MFA); biochemistry (M Sc); biological sciences (M Sc); biomolecular science (PhD); biosystems and biodiversity (PhD); Canadian studies (MA); chemistry (M Sc); computer science (M Sc); computer science and geographical information science (M Sc); counseling (MC); counseling psychology (M Ed); dramatic arts (MA); earth, space, and physical science (PhD); economics (MA); education (MA, PhD); educational leadership (M Ed); English (MA); environmental science (M Sc); evolution and behavior (PhD); exercise science (M Sc); French (MA); French/German (MA); French/Spanish (MA); general education (M Ed); geography (M Sc, MA); German (MA); health sciences (M Sc); individualized multidisciplinary (M Sc, MA); kinesiology (M Sc, MA); management (M Sc), including accounting, finance, human resource management and labor relations, information systems, international management, marketing, policy and strategy; mathematics (M Sc); music (M Mus, MA); Native American studies (MA); neuroscience (M Sc, PhD); new media (MA, MFA); nursing (M Sc, MN); philosophy (MA); physics (M Sc); political science (MA); psychology (M Sc, MA); religious studies (MA); sociology (MA); theatre and dramatic arts (MFA); theoretical and computational science (PhD); urban and regional studies (MA); women and gender studies (MA). *Program availability:* Part-time, evening/weekend. *Degree requirements:* For master's, thesis (for some programs); for doctorate, comprehensive exam, thesis/dissertation. *Entrance requirements:* For master's, GMAT (for M Sc in management), bachelor's degree in related field, minimum GPA of 3.0 during previous 20 graded semester courses, 2 years' teaching or related experience (M Ed); for doctorate, master's degree, minimum graduate GPA of 3.5. Additional exam requirements/recommendations for international students: Required—TOEFL (minimum score 580 paper-based; 93 iBT). Electronic applications accepted. *Faculty research:* Movement and brain plasticity, gibberellin physiology, photosynthesis, carbon cycling, molecular properties of main-group ring components.

University of Louisville, Graduate School, College of Arts and Sciences, Department of Philosophy, Louisville, KY 40292-0001. Offers humanities (MA, PhD). *Faculty:* 11 full-time (3 women), 5 part-time/adjunct (2 women). *Students:* 7 part-time (6 women); includes 6 minority (all Black or African American, non-Hispanic/Latino). Average age 37. *Degree requirements:* For master's, one foreign language, thesis or alternative. *Entrance requirements:* For master's, GRE General Test. Additional exam requirements/recommendations for international students: Required—TOEFL (minimum score 550 paper-based; 79 iBT), IELTS (minimum score 6.5). *Application deadline:* Applications are processed on a rolling basis. Application fee: $65. Electronic applications accepted. *Expenses:* Tuition, state resident: full-time $12,246; part-time $681 per credit hour. Tuition, nonresident: full-time $25,486; part-time $1417 per credit hour. *Required fees:* $196. Tuition and fees vary according to course load, program and reciprocity agreements. *Faculty research:* Philosophy of race; feminist philosophy; political philosophy, bioethics, ethics. *Unit head:* Dr. David S. Owen, Chair and Professor, 502-852-0488, Fax: 502-852-0459, E-mail: david.owen@louisville.edu. *Application contact:* Latonia Craig, Director of Graduate Recruitment and Diversity Retention, 502-852-5207, Fax: 502-852-6536, E-mail: gradadm@louisville.edu.
Website: http://louisville.edu/philosophy

The University of Manchester, School of Social Sciences, Manchester, United Kingdom. Offers ethnographic documentary (M Phil); interdisciplinary study of culture (PhD); philosophy (PhD); politics (PhD); social anthropology (PhD); social anthropology with visual media (PhD); social change (PhD); social statistics (PhD); sociology (PhD); visual anthropology (M Phil).

University of Manitoba, Faculty of Graduate Studies, Faculty of Arts, Department of Philosophy, Winnipeg, MB R3T 2N2, Canada. Offers MA. *Degree requirements:* For master's, variable foreign language requirement, thesis or alternative.

University of Maryland, College Park, Academic Affairs, College of Arts and Humanities, Department of Philosophy, College Park, MD 20742. Offers MA, PhD. *Degree requirements:* For master's, thesis optional; for doctorate, thesis/dissertation, 2 semesters of undergraduate teaching, qualification in symbolic logic. *Entrance requirements:* For master's, GRE General Test, minimum GPA of 3.0, philosophy paper, writing sample, 3 letters of recommendation; for doctorate, GRE General Test, minimum GPA of 3.0, philosophy paper, writing sample. Electronic applications accepted. *Faculty research:* Contemporary British and American philosophy, the relationship between philosophy and other disciplines, ethical and conceptual issues in public policy.

University of Massachusetts Amherst, Graduate School, College of Humanities and Fine Arts, Department of Philosophy, Amherst, MA 01003. Offers MA, PhD. *Program availability:* Part-time. Terminal master's awarded for partial completion of doctoral program. *Degree requirements:* For master's, thesis optional; for doctorate, comprehensive exam, thesis/dissertation. *Entrance requirements:* For master's and doctorate, GRE General Test, writing sample, 3 letters of recommendation. Additional exam requirements/recommendations for international students: Required—TOEFL (minimum score 550 paper-based; 80 iBT), IELTS (minimum score 6.5). Electronic applications accepted.

University of Memphis, Graduate School, College of Arts and Sciences, Department of Philosophy, Memphis, TN 38152. Offers MA, PhD. *Program availability:* Part-time, evening/weekend. *Faculty:* 7 full-time (2 women), 2 part-time/adjunct (1 woman). *Students:* 19 full-time (4 women), 12 part-time (6 women); includes 6 minority (5 Black or African American, non-Hispanic/Latino; 1 Two or more races, non-Hispanic/Latino), 2 international. Average age 32. 42 applicants, 19% accepted, 8 enrolled. In 2017, 3 master's, 4 doctorates awarded. Terminal master's awarded for partial completion of doctoral program. *Degree requirements:* For master's, comprehensive exam, thesis optional, 33 hours of class work; for doctorate, 2 foreign languages, comprehensive exam, thesis/dissertation, 72 hours of class work. *Entrance requirements:* For master's, GRE General Test, minimum GPA of 2.5, 18 hours of undergraduate course work in philosophy, 3 letters of recommendation, writing sample; for doctorate, GRE General Test, minimum GPA of 3.0, bachelor's degree in philosophy, 3 letters of recommendation, writing sample. Additional exam requirements/recommendations for international students: Required—TOEFL (minimum score 550 paper-based; 79 iBT). *Application deadline:* For fall admission, 1/5 priority date for domestic students. Applications are processed on a rolling basis. Application fee: $35 ($60 for international students). Electronic applications accepted. *Expenses:* Contact institution. *Financial support:* In 2017–18, 9 students received support, including 2 research assistantships with full tuition reimbursements available (averaging $16,120 per year), 21 teaching assistantships with full tuition reimbursements available (averaging $31,158 per year); fellowships with full tuition reimbursements available, Federal Work-Study, scholarships/grants, tuition waivers (full), and unspecified assistantships also available. Financial award application deadline: 2/1; financial award applicants required to submit FAFSA. *Faculty research:* Continental philosophy, ethics, analytic philosophy, feminist theory, Africana philosophy. *Unit head:* Dr. Mary Beth Mader, Chair, 901-678-2535, Fax: 901-678-4365, E-mail: mmader@memphis.edu. *Application contact:* Dr. Timothy Roche, Director of Graduate Studies, 901-678-4365, E-mail: troche@memphis.edu.
Website: http://www.memphis.edu/philosophy/

University of Miami, Graduate School, College of Arts and Sciences, Department of Philosophy, Coral Gables, FL 33124. Offers MA, PhD. *Program availability:* Part-time. Terminal master's awarded for partial completion of doctoral program. *Degree requirements:* For master's, thesis or alternative; for doctorate, comprehensive exam, thesis/dissertation. *Entrance requirements:* For master's, GRE General Test; for doctorate, GRE General Test, minimum GPA of 3.0, 3 letters of recommendation, writing sample. Additional exam requirements/recommendations for international students: Required—TOEFL. Electronic applications accepted. *Faculty research:* Ethics, epistemology, pragmatism, philosophy of science, metaphysics.

University of Michigan, Rackham Graduate School, College of Literature, Science, and the Arts, Department of Philosophy, Ann Arbor, MI 48109-1003. Offers AM, PhD. *Faculty:* 23 full-time (8 women). *Students:* 43 full-time (17 women); includes 11 minority (6 Asian, non-Hispanic/Latino; 4 Hispanic/Latino; 1 Two or more races, non-Hispanic/Latino). Average age 28. 263 applicants, 7% accepted, 7 enrolled. In 2017, 3 doctorates awarded. Terminal master's awarded for partial completion of doctoral program. *Degree requirements:* For doctorate, thesis/dissertation, oral defense of dissertation. *Entrance requirements:* For master's and doctorate, 3 letters of recommendation, writing sample. Additional exam requirements/recommendations for international students: Required—TOEFL (minimum score 560 paper-based; 84 iBT), IELTS (minimum score 6.5). *Application deadline:* For fall admission, 12/13 for domestic and international students. Application fee: $75 ($90 for international students). Electronic applications accepted. *Expenses:* $47,252 pre-candidate tuition and fees. *Financial support:* In 2017–18, 41 students received support, including 39 fellowships with full tuition reimbursements available (averaging $26,432 per year), 27 teaching assistantships with full tuition reimbursements available (averaging $42,055 per year); health care benefits also available. Financial award application deadline: 12/13. *Faculty research:* Ethics, metaphysics, philosophy of language and mind, political and social philosophy, philosophy of science. *Total annual research expenditures:* $42,504. *Unit head:* Prof. Elizabeth S. Anderson, Chair, 734-764-6285, Fax: 734-763-8071, E-mail: phil-chair@umich.edu. *Application contact:* Carson Maynard, Graduate Program Coordinator, 734-764-3260, Fax: 734-763-8071, E-mail: phil-admissions@umich.edu.
Website: http://www.lsa.umich.edu/philosophy/

University of Minnesota, Twin Cities Campus, Graduate School, College of Liberal Arts, Department of Philosophy, Minneapolis, MN 55455-0213. Offers MA, PhD. *Program availability:* Part-time. Terminal master's awarded for partial completion of doctoral program. *Degree requirements:* For master's, comprehensive exam, thesis or 3 papers; oral exam; for doctorate, comprehensive exam, thesis/dissertation. *Entrance requirements:* For master's and doctorate, GRE. Additional exam requirements/recommendations for international students: Required—TOEFL (minimum score 550 paper-based), IELTS (minimum score 6.5), or Michigan English Language Assessment Battery (minimum score 80). Electronic applications accepted. *Faculty research:* Philosophy of science; ethics and social/political philosophy; logic, language, and mind.

University of Mississippi, Graduate School, College of Liberal Arts, University, MS 38677. Offers anthropology (MA); biology (MS, PhD); chemistry (MS, DA, PhD); creative writing (MFA); documentary expression (MFA); economics (MA, PhD); English (MA, PhD); experimental psychology (PhD); history (MA, PhD); mathematics (MS, PhD); modern languages (MA); music (MM); philosophy (MA); physics (MA, MS, PhD); political science (MA, PhD); Southern studies (MA); studio art (MFA). *Program availability:* Part-time. *Faculty:* 465 full-time (207 women), 82 part-time/adjunct (46 women). *Students:* 466 full-time (229 women), 72 part-time (34 women); includes 87 minority (38 Black or African American, non-Hispanic/Latino; 18 Asian, non-Hispanic/Latino; 24 Hispanic/Latino; 7 Two or more races, non-Hispanic/Latino), 121 international. Average age 29. *Degree requirements:* For doctorate, thesis/dissertation. *Entrance requirements:* For master's, GRE General Test, minimum GPA of 3.0; for doctorate, GRE General Test. Additional exam requirements/recommendations for international students: Required—TOEFL. *Application deadline:* For fall admission, 2/1 priority date for domestic students; for spring admission, 10/1 for domestic students. Applications are processed on a rolling basis. Application fee: $50. Electronic applications accepted. *Financial support:* Fellowships, research assistantships, teaching assistantships, career-related internships or fieldwork, Federal Work-Study, institutionally sponsored loans, scholarships/grants, and unspecified assistantships available. Financial award application deadline: 3/1; financial award applicants required to submit FAFSA. *Unit head:* Dr. Lee Michael Cohen, Dean, 662-915-7177, Fax: 662-915-5792, E-mail: libarts@olemiss.edu. *Application contact:* Dr. Christy M. Wyandt, Associate Dean of Graduate School, 662-915-7474, Fax: 662-915-7577, E-mail: cwyandt@olemiss.edu.

University of Missouri, Office of Research and Graduate Studies, College of Arts and Science, Department of Philosophy, Columbia, MO 65211. Offers PhD. Terminal master's awarded for partial completion of doctoral program. *Degree requirements:* For doctorate, one foreign language, comprehensive exam, thesis/dissertation. *Entrance requirements:* For doctorate, GRE General Test (minimum score 650 verbal, 700 quantitative), minimum GPA of 3.0, 3.9 in major. Additional exam requirements/recommendations for international students: Required—TOEFL (minimum score 500 paper-based; 61 iBT). Electronic applications accepted. *Faculty research:* Epistemology, political philosophy, philosophy of biology, decision/game/rational choice theory, ethics, philosophy of mind and psychology, Indian philosophy, metaphysics, action theory.

University of Missouri–St. Louis, College of Arts and Sciences, Department of Philosophy, St. Louis, MO 63121. Offers MA. *Program availability:* Part-time, evening/weekend. *Faculty:* 10 full-time (2 women), 1 (woman) part-time/adjunct. *Students:* 8 full-time (3 women), 8 part-time (1 woman); includes 2 minority (1 Black or African American, non-Hispanic/Latino; 1 Hispanic/Latino). 27 applicants, 78% accepted, 6 enrolled. *Entrance requirements:* For master's, writing sample, 3 letters of recommendation, personal statement. Additional exam requirements/recommendations for international students: Required—TOEFL (minimum score 550 paper-based; 79 iBT), IELTS (minimum score 6.5). *Application deadline:* For fall admission, 7/1 priority date for domestic and international students; for spring admission, 12/1 priority date for domestic and international students. Applications are processed on a rolling basis. Application fee: $50 ($40 for international students). Electronic applications accepted. *Expenses:*

Tuition, state resident: part-time $476.50 per credit hour. Tuition, nonresident: part-time $1169.70 per credit hour. *Financial support:* Research assistantships with tuition reimbursements and teaching assistantships with tuition reimbursements available. Financial award application deadline: 2/15; financial award applicants required to submit FAFSA. *Faculty research:* Ethics, philosophy and history of science, philosophical social science, aesthetics. *Unit head:* Dr. Eric Wiland, Graduate Program Director, 314-516-5495, Fax: 314-516-5816, E-mail: wiland@umsl.edu. *Application contact:* 314-516-5458, Fax: 314-516-6996, E-mail: gradadm@umsl.edu.
Website: http://www.umsl.edu/~philo/

University of Montana, Graduate School, College of Humanities and Sciences, Department of Philosophy, Missoula, MT 59812. Offers MA. *Degree requirements:* For master's, thesis or additional course work/professional paper. *Entrance requirements:* For master's, GRE General Test. Additional exam requirements/recommendations for international students: Required—TOEFL (minimum score 525 paper-based). *Faculty research:* Philosophy of law, natural science, feminism, and technology; environmental, business, and medical ethics.

University of Nebraska–Lincoln, Graduate College, College of Arts and Sciences, Department of Philosophy, Lincoln, NE 68588. Offers MA, PhD. *Degree requirements:* For master's, thesis optional; for doctorate, comprehensive exam, thesis/dissertation. *Entrance requirements:* For master's and doctorate, GRE General Test, writing sample. Additional exam requirements/recommendations for international students: Required—TOEFL (minimum score 600 paper-based). Electronic applications accepted. *Faculty research:* Ethics, epistemology, metaphysics, cognitive science, history of philosophy.

University of Nevada, Reno, Graduate School, College of Liberal Arts, Department of Philosophy, Reno, NV 89557. Offers MA. *Degree requirements:* For master's, thesis optional. *Entrance requirements:* For master's, GRE General Test, minimum GPA of 2.75. Additional exam requirements/recommendations for international students: Required—TOEFL (minimum score 500 paper-based; 61 iBT), IELTS (minimum score 6). Electronic applications accepted. *Faculty research:* Ancient philosophy (Aristotle), ethics, political theory, violence, Continental philosophy.

University of New Mexico, Graduate Studies, College of Arts and Sciences, Program in Philosophy, Albuquerque, NM 87131-2039. Offers MA, PhD. *Program availability:* Part-time. *Students:* Average age 34. 57 applicants, 32% accepted, 10 enrolled. In 2017, 5 master's, 5 doctorates awarded. Terminal master's awarded for partial completion of doctoral program. *Degree requirements:* For master's, thesis (for some programs); for doctorate, one foreign language, comprehensive exam, thesis/dissertation. *Entrance requirements:* For master's and doctorate, GRE. Additional exam requirements/recommendations for international students: Required—TOEFL. *Application deadline:* For fall admission, 3/1 for domestic and international students; for spring admission, 11/1 for domestic and international students. Application fee: $50. Electronic applications accepted. *Financial support:* Fellowships, research assistantships, and teaching assistantships available. Financial award application deadline: 3/1; financial award applicants required to submit FAFSA. *Faculty research:* Continental philosophy, Indian philosophy, history of philosophy, ethics, phenomenology and existentialism, philosophy of art and literature. *Unit head:* Dr. Richard Hayes, Chair, 505-277-2405, Fax: 505-277-6362, E-mail: rhayes@unm.edu. *Application contact:* Mercedes Nysus, Administrative Assistant II, 505-277-2405, Fax: 505-277-6362, E-mail: thinker@unm.edu.
Website: http://philosophy.unm.edu/

The University of North Carolina at Chapel Hill, Graduate School, College of Arts and Sciences, Department of Philosophy, Chapel Hill, NC 27599. Offers MA, PhD. *Degree requirements:* For master's, comprehensive exam, thesis; for doctorate, comprehensive exam, thesis/dissertation. *Entrance requirements:* For master's and doctorate, GRE General Test, minimum GPA of 3.0.

The University of North Carolina at Charlotte, College of Liberal Arts and Sciences, Department of Philosophy, Charlotte, NC 28223-0001. Offers ethics and applied philosophy (MA, Graduate Certificate). *Program availability:* Part-time. *Faculty:* 12 full-time (6 women). *Students:* 7 full-time (3 women), 9 part-time (3 women); includes 4 minority (all Black or African American, non-Hispanic/Latino). Average age 30. 14 applicants, 79% accepted, 9 enrolled. In 2017, 7 master's awarded. *Degree requirements:* For master's, thesis or internship. *Entrance requirements:* For master's, GRE or MAT, statement of purpose outlining why applicant seeks admission to program; three recommendations; one official transcript from all colleges or universities attended; philosophical writing sample; for Graduate Certificate, personal statement outlining why the applicant seeks admission to the program; two academic letters of recommendation, in addition to the recommendation forms required by the graduate school, which address the student's philosophical skills and/or ethical reasoning. Additional exam requirements/recommendations for international students: Required—TOEFL (minimum score 523 paper-based, 70 iBT) or IELTS (6.5). *Application deadline:* For fall admission, 3/1 priority date for domestic and international students; for spring admission, 10/1 priority date for domestic and international students; for summer admission, 4/1 priority date for domestic and international students. Applications are processed on a rolling basis. Application fee: $75. Electronic applications accepted. *Expenses:* Tuition, state resident: full-time $4337. Tuition, nonresident: full-time $17,771. *Required fees:* $3211. Tuition and fees vary according to course load and program. *Financial support:* In 2017–18, 6 students received support, including 3 teaching assistantships (averaging $3,500 per year); career-related internships or fieldwork, institutionally sponsored loans, scholarships/grants, unspecified assistantships, and administrative assistantships also available. Support available to part-time students. Financial award application deadline: 3/1; financial award applicants required to submit FAFSA. *Total annual research expenditures:* $85,549. *Unit head:* Dr. Shannon Sullivan, Chair, 704-687-5418. *Application contact:* Kathy B. Giddings, Director of Graduate Admissions, 704-687-5503, Fax: 704-687-1668, E-mail: gradadm@uncc.edu.
Website: http://philosophy.uncc.edu/

University of North Florida, College of Arts and Sciences, Department of Philosophy, Jacksonville, FL 32224. Offers applied ethics (Graduate Certificate); practical philosophy and applied ethics (MA). *Program availability:* Part-time, evening/weekend. *Entrance requirements:* For master's, GRE General Test, minimum GPA of 3.0 in last 60 hours, 3 letters of recommendation, writing sample. Additional exam requirements/recommendations for international students: Required—TOEFL (minimum score 500 paper-based; 61 iBT). Electronic applications accepted. *Faculty research:* Late modern philosophy, pragmatism, religion and American culture, hermeneutics, philosophy of mind.

University of North Georgia, Department of History, Anthropology and Philosophy, Dahlonega, GA 30597. Offers history (MA), including American history, military history, world history. *Program availability:* Part-time, evening/weekend. *Faculty:* 10 full-time (5 women), 1 part-time/adjunct (0 women). *Students:* 2 full-time (0 women), 13 part-time (4 women); includes 1 minority (Hispanic/Latino). Average age 34. 9 applicants, 78% accepted, 3 enrolled. In 2017, 2 master's awarded. *Degree requirements:* For master's, thesis optional. *Entrance requirements:* For master's, GRE, 3 recommendations, writing sample, letter of intent, minimum GPA of 3.0. Additional exam requirements/recommendations for international students: Required—TOEFL (minimum score 550 paper-based; 79 iBT), IELTS (minimum score 6.5). *Application deadline:* For fall admission, 4/1 priority date for domestic students. Applications are processed on a rolling basis. Application fee: $40. Electronic applications accepted. *Expenses:* Contact institution. *Financial support:* Unspecified assistantships available. Financial award application deadline: 3/17; financial award applicants required to submit FAFSA. *Unit head:* Dr. Jeff Pardue, Department Head, 678-717-3867. *Application contact:* Melinda Maxwell, Director of Graduate Admissions, 706-864-1543, E-mail: melinda.maxwell@ung.edu.
Website: http://ung.edu/history-anthropology-philosophy/

University of North Texas, Robert B. Toulouse School of Graduate Studies, Denton, TX 76203-5459. Offers accounting (MS); applied anthropology (MA, MS); applied behavior analysis (Certificate); applied geography (MA); applied technology and performance improvement (M Ed, MS); art education (MA); art history (MA); art museum education (Certificate); arts leadership (Certificate); audiology (Au D); behavior analysis (MS); behavioral science (PhD); biochemistry and molecular biology (MS); biology (MA, MS); biomedical engineering (MS); business analysis (MS); chemistry (MS); clinical health psychology (PhD); communication studies (MA, MS); computer engineering (MS); computer science (MS); counseling (M Ed, MS), including clinical mental health counseling (MS), college and university counseling, elementary school counseling, secondary school counseling; creative writing (MA); criminal justice (MS); curriculum and instruction (M Ed); decision sciences (MBA); design (MA, MFA), including fashion design (MFA), innovation studies, interior design (MFA); early childhood studies (MS); economics (MS); educational leadership (M Ed, Ed D); educational psychology (MS, PhD), including family studies (MS), gifted and talented (MS), human development (MS), learning and cognition (MS), research, measurement and evaluation (MS); electrical engineering (MS); emergency management (MPA); engineering technology (MS); English (MA); English as a second language (MA); environmental science (MS); finance (MBA, MS); financial management (MPA); French (MA); health services management (MBA); higher education (M Ed, Ed D); history (MA, MS); hospitality management (MS); human resources management (MPA); information science (MS); information systems (PhD); information technologies (MBA); interdisciplinary studies (MA, MS); international studies (MA); international sustainable tourism (MS); jazz studies (MM); journalism (MA, MJ, Graduate Certificate), including interactive and virtual digital communication (Graduate Certificate), narrative journalism (Graduate Certificate), public relations (Graduate Certificate); kinesiology (MS); linguistics (MA); local government management (MPA); logistics (PhD); logistics and supply chain management (MBA); long-term care, senior housing, and aging services (MA); management (PhD); marketing (MBA); mathematics (MA, MS); mechanical and energy engineering (MS, PhD); music (MA), including ethnomusicology, music theory, musicology, performance; music composition (PhD); music education (MM Ed, PhD); nonprofit management (MPA); operations and supply chain management (MBA); performance (MM, DMA); philosophy (MA); political science (MA); professional and technical communication (MA); radio, television and film (MA, MFA); rehabilitation counseling (Certificate); sociology (MA); Spanish (MA); special education (M Ed); speech-language pathology (MA); strategic management (MBA); studio art (MFA); teaching (M Ed); MBA/MS. *Program availability:* Part-time, evening/weekend, online learning. Terminal master's awarded for partial completion of doctoral program. *Degree requirements:* For master's, variable foreign language requirement, comprehensive exam (for some programs), thesis (for some programs); for doctorate, variable foreign language requirement, comprehensive exam (for some programs), thesis/dissertation; for other advanced degree, variable foreign language requirement, comprehensive exam (for some programs). *Entrance requirements:* For master's and doctorate, GRE, GMAT. Additional exam requirements/recommendations for international students: Required—TOEFL (minimum score 550 paper-based; 79 iBT). Electronic applications accepted.

University of Notre Dame, Graduate School, College of Arts and Letters, Division of Humanities, Department of Philosophy, Notre Dame, IN 46556. Offers PhD. *Degree requirements:* For doctorate, 2 foreign languages, thesis/dissertation, candidacy exam. *Entrance requirements:* For doctorate, GRE General Test. Additional exam requirements/recommendations for international students: Required—TOEFL (minimum score 600 paper-based; 80 iBT). Electronic applications accepted. *Faculty research:* History of philosophy, ethics, philosophy of science and logic, philosophy of religion, Continental philosophy, metaphysics.

University of Oklahoma, College of Arts and Sciences, Department of Philosophy, Norman, OK 73019-2006. Offers MA, PhD. *Program availability:* Part-time. *Faculty:* 12 full-time (3 women). *Students:* 23 full-time (6 women), 5 part-time (1 woman); includes 5 minority (1 Asian, non-Hispanic/Latino; 3 Hispanic/Latino; 1 Two or more races, non-Hispanic/Latino), 4 international. Average age 29. 39 applicants, 38% accepted, 7 enrolled. In 2017, 6 master's, 6 doctorates awarded. Terminal master's awarded for partial completion of doctoral program. *Degree requirements:* For doctorate, comprehensive exam, thesis/dissertation. *Entrance requirements:* Additional exam requirements/recommendations for international students: Required—TOEFL (minimum score 79 iBT) or IELTS (minimum score 6.5). *Application deadline:* For fall admission, 1/15 for domestic and international students; for spring admission, 8/31 for domestic and international students. Application fee: $50 ($100 for international students). Electronic applications accepted. *Expenses:* Tuition, state resident: full-time $5119; part-time $213.30 per credit hour. Tuition, nonresident: full-time $19,778; part-time $824.10 per credit hour. *Required fees:* $3458; $133.55 per credit hour. $126.50 per semester. *Financial support:* In 2017–18, 26 students received support, including 3 fellowships with full tuition reimbursements available (averaging $2,833 per year), 2 research assistantships with full tuition reimbursements available (averaging $16,000 per year), 20 teaching assistantships with full tuition reimbursements available (averaging $17,125 per year); scholarships/grants, health care benefits, and unspecified assistantships also available. Financial award application deadline: 6/1; financial award applicants required to submit FAFSA. *Faculty research:* Epistemology, ethics, philosophy of religion, Chinese philosophy. *Unit head:* Dr. Wayne Riggs, Professor, 405-325-5950, E-mail: wriggs@ou.edu. *Application contact:* Martin Montminy, Professor, 405-325-6324, E-mail: montminy@ou.edu.
Website: http://philosophy.ou.edu/

University of Oregon, Graduate School, College of Arts and Sciences, Department of Philosophy, Eugene, OR 97403. Offers MA, PhD. Terminal master's awarded for partial completion of doctoral program. *Degree requirements:* For master's, one foreign language, thesis or alternative; for doctorate, one foreign language, thesis/dissertation. *Entrance requirements:* For master's and doctorate, GRE General Test. Additional exam requirements/recommendations for international students: Required—TOEFL. *Faculty research:* Social and political philosophy, feminist philosophy, American philosophy, aesthetics, philosophy of mind.

University of Ottawa, Faculty of Graduate and Postdoctoral Studies, Faculty of Arts, Department of Philosophy, Ottawa, ON K1N 6N5, Canada. Offers MA, PhD. *Degree requirements:* For master's, thesis or alternative; for doctorate, comprehensive exam, thesis/dissertation. *Entrance requirements:* For master's, honors degree or equivalent, minimum B average; for doctorate, master's degree, minimum B+ average. Electronic applications accepted. *Faculty research:* History of philosophy (ancient, medieval,

modern and contemporary); metaphysics/epistemology; value theory: political philosophy, ethics.

University of Pennsylvania, School of Arts and Sciences, Graduate Group in Philosophy, Philadelphia, PA 19104. Offers AM, PhD, JD/PhD. *Faculty:* 16 full-time (5 women), 3 part-time/adjunct (0 women). *Students:* 33 full-time (10 women), 2 part-time (1 woman); includes 6 minority (1 Black or African American, non-Hispanic/Latino; 1 Asian, non-Hispanic/Latino; 2 Hispanic/Latino; 2 Two or more races, non-Hispanic/Latino), 15 international. Average age 31. 91 applicants, 16% accepted, 7 enrolled. In 2017, 1 master's, 4 doctorates awarded. Terminal master's awarded for partial completion of doctoral program. *Financial support:* Application deadline: 12/1.
Website: http://www.sas.upenn.edu/graduate-division

University of Pittsburgh, Kenneth P. Dietrich School of Arts and Sciences, Department of History and Philosophy of Science, Pittsburgh, PA 15260. Offers PhD. *Faculty:* 8 full-time (2 women). *Students:* 32 full-time (14 women); includes 3 minority (1 American Indian or Alaska Native, non-Hispanic/Latino; 1 Native Hawaiian or other Pacific Islander, non-Hispanic/Latino; 1 Two or more races, non-Hispanic/Latino), 10 international. Average age 28. 52 applicants, 13% accepted, 6 enrolled. In 2017, 1 doctorate awarded. Terminal master's awarded for partial completion of doctoral program. *Degree requirements:* For doctorate, one foreign language, comprehensive exam, thesis/dissertation, minimum of 72 credit hours, proficiency in logic. *Entrance requirements:* For doctorate, GRE General Test, curriculum vitae, statement of career objective, 3 letters of recommendation, sample of written work. Additional exam requirements/recommendations for international students: Required—TOEFL (minimum score 577 paper-based; 90 iBT), IELTS (minimum score 7). *Application deadline:* For fall admission, 1/10 for domestic and international students. Application fee: $50. Electronic applications accepted. *Financial support:* In 2017–18, 26 students received support, including 14 fellowships with full tuition reimbursements available (averaging $24,710 per year), 11 teaching assistantships with full tuition reimbursements available (averaging $24,710 per year); health care benefits and tuition waivers (full) also available. Financial award application deadline: 1/10. *Faculty research:* History and philosophy of biology, psychology, and neuroscience; history and philosophy of physics; early modern science; cognitive science; philosophy of social science; philosophy of mind and perception. *Unit head:* Dr. John D. Norton, Chair, 412-624-1051, E-mail: jdnorton@pitt.edu. *Application contact:* Kathleen U. Labuda, Graduate Administrator, 412-624-5774, Fax: 412-624-5377, E-mail: kathleenlabuda@pitt.edu.
Website: http://www.hps.pitt.edu/

University of Pittsburgh, Kenneth P. Dietrich School of Arts and Sciences, Department of Philosophy, Pittsburgh, PA 15260. Offers PhD. *Faculty:* 17 full-time (4 women). *Students:* 50 full-time (17 women); includes 6 minority (2 Asian, non-Hispanic/Latino; 3 Hispanic/Latino; 1 Two or more races, non-Hispanic/Latino), 20 international. 169 applicants, 11% accepted, 8 enrolled. In 2017, 2 doctorates awarded. Terminal master's awarded for partial completion of doctoral program. *Degree requirements:* For doctorate, one foreign language, comprehensive exam, thesis/dissertation, minimum of 72 credit hours, proficiency in logic. *Entrance requirements:* For doctorate, GRE General Test, curriculum vitae, statement of purpose, 3 letters of recommendation, sample of written work. Additional exam requirements/recommendations for international students: Required—TOEFL (minimum score 577 paper-based; 90 iBT), IELTS (minimum score 7). *Application deadline:* For fall admission, 1/10 for domestic and international students. Application fee: $50. Electronic applications accepted. *Financial support:* In 2017–18, 44 students received support, including 18 fellowships with full tuition reimbursements available (averaging $24,710 per year), 2 research assistantships with full tuition reimbursements available (averaging $24,402 per year), 24 teaching assistantships with full tuition reimbursements available (averaging $24,710 per year); scholarships/grants, health care benefits, and tuition waivers (full) also available. Financial award application deadline: 1/10. *Faculty research:* Metaphysics and epistemology, logic and philosophy of science, history of Western philosophy, moral and political philosophy, philosophy of mind and language. *Unit head:* Dr. Robert Batterman, Chair, 412-624-5775. *Application contact:* Kathleen U. Labuda, Graduate Administrator, 412-624-5774.
Website: http://www.philosophy.pitt.edu/

University of Puerto Rico–Río Piedras, College of Humanities, Department of Philosophy, San Juan, PR 00931-3300. Offers MA. *Program availability:* Part-time. *Degree requirements:* For master's, one foreign language, comprehensive exam, thesis. *Entrance requirements:* For master's, PAEG or GRE, interview, minimum GPA of 3.0, letter of recommendation (2).

University of Regina, Faculty of Graduate Studies and Research, Faculty of Arts, Department of Philosophy, Regina, SK S4S 0A2, Canada. Offers MA. Offered as a special case program. *Program availability:* Part-time. *Faculty:* 8 full-time (2 women), 2 part-time/adjunct (0 women). *Degree requirements:* For master's, thesis. *Entrance requirements:* Additional exam requirements/recommendations for international students: Required—TOEFL (minimum score 580 paper-based; 80 iBT), IELTS (minimum score 6.5), PTE (minimum score 59). *Application deadline:* Applications are processed on a rolling basis. Application fee: $100. Electronic applications accepted. *Expenses:* $10,362. *Financial support:* Fellowships, research assistantships, teaching assistantships, and scholarships/grants available. Financial award application deadline: 6/15. *Faculty research:* Ethics, politics, religion, history, critical thinking. *Unit head:* Dr. David Elliott, Department Head, 306-585-4324, Fax: 306-585-4827, E-mail: david.elliott@uregina.ca.
Website: http://www.uregina.ca/arts/philosophy-classics

University of Regina, Faculty of Graduate Studies and Research, Faculty of Arts, Program in Social and Political Thought, Regina, SK S4S 0A2, Canada. Offers MA. *Program availability:* Part-time. *Faculty:* 11 full-time (4 women). *Students:* 7 full-time (3 women), 5 part-time (1 woman). 9 applicants, 11% accepted. In 2017, 2 master's awarded. *Degree requirements:* For master's, thesis. *Entrance requirements:* Additional exam requirements/recommendations for international students: Required—TOEFL (minimum score 580 paper-based; 80 iBT), IELTS (minimum score 6.5), PTE (minimum score 59). *Application deadline:* For fall admission, 3/30 for domestic and international students. Application fee: $100. Electronic applications accepted. *Expenses:* $10,681. *Financial support:* In 2017–18, fellowships (averaging $6,000 per year), 2 teaching assistantships (averaging $2,562 per year) were awarded; research assistantships and scholarships/grants also available. Financial award application deadline: 6/15. *Faculty research:* Liberalism and freedom, neo-conservatism, Aristotle's ethics, Kant's ethical theory and political philosophy, Hegel's philosophy of right. *Unit head:* Dr. Lee Ward, Graduate Coordinator, 306-359-1259, E-mail: lee.ward@uregina.ca. *Application contact:* Doreen Thompson, Administrative Assistant, 306-585-4332, E-mail: doreen.thompson@uregina.ca.

University of Rochester, School of Arts and Sciences, Department of Philosophy, Rochester, NY 14627-0078. Offers epistemology (PhD); ethics (PhD); history of ancient philosophy (PhD); history of modern philosophy (PhD); metaphysics (PhD); philosophy of language (PhD); philosophy of mind (PhD). *Faculty:* 9 full-time (3 women). *Students:* 19 full-time (1 woman), 2 part-time (0 women); includes 4 minority (all Hispanic/Latino), 1 international. Average age 30. 40 applicants, 20% accepted, 2 enrolled. In 2017, 1 doctorate awarded. Terminal master's awarded for partial completion of doctoral program. *Degree requirements:* For doctorate, comprehensive exam (for some programs), thesis/dissertation, qualifying exam. *Entrance requirements:* For doctorate, GRE General Test, personal statement, transcript, three (or more) confidential letters of recommendation, writing sample in philosophy, list of prior philosophy courses as cover sheet for work sample. Additional exam requirements/recommendations for international students: Required—TOEFL. *Application deadline:* For fall admission, 1/15 for domestic and international students. Applications are processed on a rolling basis. Application fee: $60. Electronic applications accepted. *Expenses:* $1,596 per credit hour. *Financial support:* In 2017–18, 13 students received support, including 3 fellowships with full tuition reimbursements available (averaging $18,000 per year); tuition waivers (full) also available. Financial award application deadline: 1/15. *Faculty research:* Ancient Greek philosophy and moral education, clinical bioethics, ethical realism, baruch spinoza and physical science, philosophy of religion. *Total annual research expenditures:* $602. *Unit head:* Randall Curren, Department Chair, 585-275-8112, E-mail: randall.curren@rochester.edu. *Application contact:* Cheryl Kingston, Administrative Assistant, 585-275-4105, E-mail: cheryl.kingston@rochester.edu.
Website: https://www.sas.rochester.edu/phl/graduate/index.html

University of St. Thomas, Center for Thomistic Studies, Houston, TX 77006-4696. Offers philosophy (MA, PhD). *Program availability:* Part-time. *Faculty:* 5 full-time (1 woman). *Students:* 9 full-time (2 women), 22 part-time (2 women); includes 6 minority (1 Asian, non-Hispanic/Latino; 3 Hispanic/Latino; 2 Two or more races, non-Hispanic/Latino), 1 international. Average age 33. 11 applicants, 64% accepted, 7 enrolled. In 2017, 4 master's, 4 doctorates awarded. Terminal master's awarded for partial completion of doctoral program. *Degree requirements:* For master's, one foreign language, comprehensive exam, thesis (for some programs); for doctorate, 2 foreign languages, comprehensive exam, thesis/dissertation. *Entrance requirements:* For master's, GRE, bachelor's degree with minimum GPA of 3.0 and at least 18 hours of undergraduate philosophy coursework, 3 letters of recommendation from professional educators, writing sample; for doctorate, GRE, MA in philosophy, 3 letters of recommendation from professional educators, writing sample, fulfillment of Latin language requirement (if not available at time of admission, must be completed no later than the third semester of doctoral study). Additional exam requirements/recommendations for international students: Required—TOEFL (minimum score 550 paper-based; 79 iBT), IELTS (minimum score 6.5), PTE (minimum score 53). *Application deadline:* For fall admission, 2/1 priority date for domestic and international students. Applications are processed on a rolling basis. Application fee: $35. Electronic applications accepted. *Expenses: Tuition:* Full-time $20,934; part-time $1163 per credit hour. *Required fees:* $250; $210 per semester. *Financial support:* In 2017–18, 18 students received support. Fellowships with tuition reimbursements available, teaching assistantships, Federal Work-Study, scholarships/grants, unspecified assistantships, and state work-study, institutional employment available. Support available to part-time students. Financial award application deadline: 2/1; financial award applicants required to submit FAFSA. *Faculty research:* Biomedical ethics, Islamic philosophy, metaphysics, virtue ethics, semiotics. *Unit head:* Dr. Thomas Osborne, Director, 713-942-3483, Fax: 713-942-3464, E-mail: osborntm@stthom.edu. *Application contact:* Valerie Hall, Administrative Assistant II, 713-525-3591, Fax: 713-942-3464, E-mail: hallvl@stthom.edu.
Website: http://www.stthom.edu/Academics/School_of_Arts_and_Sciences/Graduate/Philosophy/Philosophy_MA_PhD.aqf

University of Saskatchewan, College of Graduate Studies and Research, College of Arts and Science, Department of Philosophy, Saskatoon, SK S7N 5A2, Canada. Offers MA. *Degree requirements:* For master's, thesis. *Entrance requirements:* Additional exam requirements/recommendations for international students: Required—TOEFL (minimum score 80 iBT); Recommended—IELTS (minimum score 6.5). Electronic applications accepted.

University of South Africa, College of Human Sciences, Pretoria, South Africa. Offers adult education (M Ed); African languages (MA, PhD); African politics (MA, PhD); Afrikaans (MA, PhD); ancient history (MA, PhD); ancient Near Eastern studies (MA, PhD); anthropology (MA, PhD); applied linguistics (MA); Arabic (MA, PhD); archaeology (MA); art history (MA); Biblical archaeology (MA); Biblical studies (M Th, D Th, PhD); Christian spirituality (M Th, D Th); church history (M Th, D Th); classical studies (MA, PhD); clinical psychology (MA); communication (MA, PhD); comparative education (M Ed, Ed D); consulting psychology (D Admin, D Com, PhD); curriculum studies (M Ed, Ed D); development studies (M Admin, MA, D Admin, PhD); didactics (M Ed, Ed D); education (M Tech); education management (M Ed, Ed D); educational psychology (M Ed); English (MA); environmental education (M Ed); French (MA, PhD); German (MA, PhD); Greek (MA); guidance and counseling (M Ed); health studies (MA, PhD), including health sciences education (MA), health services management (MA), medical and surgical nursing science (critical care general) (MA), midwifery and neonatal nursing science (MA), trauma and emergency care (MA); history (MA, PhD); history of education (Ed D); inclusive education (M Ed, Ed D); information and communications technology policy and regulation (MA); information science (MA, MIS, PhD); international politics (MA, PhD); Islamic studies (MA, PhD); Italian (MA, PhD); Judaica (MA, PhD); linguistics (MA, PhD); mathematical education (M Ed); mathematics education (MA); missiology (M Th, D Th); modern Hebrew (MA, PhD); musicology (MA, MMus, D Mus, PhD); natural science education (M Ed); New Testament (M Th, D Th); Old Testament (D Th); pastoral therapy (M Th, D Th); philosophy (MA); philosophy of education (M Ed, Ed D); politics (MA, PhD); Portuguese (MA, PhD); practical theology (M Th, D Th); psychology (MA, MS, PhD); psychology of education (M Ed, Ed D); public health (MA); religious studies (MA, D Th, PhD); Romance languages (MA); Russian (MA, PhD); Semitic languages (MA, PhD); social behavior studies in HIV/AIDS (MA); social science (mental health) (MA); social science in development studies (MA); social science in psychology (MA); social science in social work (MA); social science in sociology (MA); social work (MSW, DSW, PhD); socio-education (M Ed, Ed D); sociolinguistics (MA); sociology (MA, PhD); Spanish (MA, PhD); systematic theology (M Th, D Th); TESOL (teaching English to speakers of other languages) (MA); theological ethics (M Th, D Th); theory of literature (MA, PhD); urban ministries (D Th); urban ministry (M Th).

University of South Carolina, The Graduate School, College of Arts and Sciences, Department of Philosophy, Columbia, SC 29208. Offers MA, PhD. *Program availability:* Part-time. *Degree requirements:* For master's, one foreign language, comprehensive exam, thesis optional; for doctorate, one foreign language, comprehensive exam, thesis/dissertation, candidacy exam. *Entrance requirements:* For master's and doctorate, GRE General Test, 18 hours in philosophy, 3 letters of recommendation, writing sample. Additional exam requirements/recommendations for international students: Required—TOEFL (minimum score 590 paper-based). Electronic applications accepted. *Faculty research:* History of philosophy, ethics, philosophy of science, social philosophy.

University of Southern California, Graduate School, Dana and David Dornsife College of Letters, Arts and Sciences, School of Philosophy, Los Angeles, CA 90089. Offers MA, PhD, MA/JD. *Degree requirements:* For doctorate, one foreign language, thesis/dissertation, area exam, qualifying exam. *Entrance requirements:* For doctorate, GRE General Test. Additional exam requirements/recommendations for international students: Required—TOEFL. Electronic applications accepted. *Faculty research:* Logic, epistemology, ethics/metaethics, philosophy of language, philosophy of law.

Philosophy

University of South Florida, College of Arts and Sciences, Department of Philosophy, Tampa, FL 33620-9951. Offers liberal arts (MA), including social and political thought; philosophy (MA, PhD), including philosophy and religion. *Program availability:* Part-time, evening/weekend. *Faculty:* 14 full-time (2 women). *Students:* 41 full-time (7 women), 15 part-time (3 women); includes 10 minority (2 Black or African American, non-Hispanic/Latino; 3 Asian, non-Hispanic/Latino; 4 Hispanic/Latino; 1 Two or more races, non-Hispanic/Latino), 1 international. Average age 35. 29 applicants, 76% accepted, 9 enrolled. In 2017, 7 master's, 7 doctorates awarded. Terminal master's awarded for partial completion of doctoral program. *Degree requirements:* For master's, comprehensive exam, thesis optional; for doctorate, comprehensive exam, thesis/dissertation. *Entrance requirements:* For master's and doctorate, GRE General Test, minimum GPA of 3.0, three letters of recommendation, 10-page philosophy writing sample, statement of philosophical interests. Additional exam requirements/recommendations for international students: Required—TOEFL (minimum score 550 paper-based; 79 iBT) or IELTS (minimum score 6.5). *Application deadline:* For fall admission, 1/2 priority date for domestic students, 2/15 for international students; for spring admission, 10/15 priority date for domestic students, 8/1 for international students. Application fee: $30. Electronic applications accepted. *Financial support:* In 2017–18, 5 students received support, including 32 teaching assistantships with tuition reimbursements available (averaging $11,025 per year); unspecified assistantships also available. Financial award application deadline: 1/1. *Faculty research:* Medieval philosophy, early modern philosophy (seventeenth-, eighteenth-, and twentieth-century Continental philosophy), feminist philosophy, social philosophy, ethics, philosophy of science. *Total annual research expenditures:* $10,921. *Unit head:* Dr. Alex Levine, Professor and Chairperson, 813-974-5508, E-mail: levineat@usf.edu. *Application contact:* Dr. William Goodwin, Associate Professor, 813-974-5670, E-mail: wgoodwin@usf.edu.
Website: http://philosophy.usf.edu/

The University of Tennessee, Graduate School, College of Arts and Sciences, Department of Philosophy, Knoxville, TN 37996. Offers medical ethics (MA, PhD); philosophy (MA, PhD); religious studies (MA). *Program availability:* Part-time. *Degree requirements:* For master's, thesis or alternative; for doctorate, one foreign language, thesis/dissertation. *Entrance requirements:* For master's and doctorate, GRE General Test, minimum GPA of 2.7. Additional exam requirements/recommendations for international students: Required—TOEFL. Electronic applications accepted.

The University of Texas at Austin, Graduate School, College of Liberal Arts, Department of Philosophy, Austin, TX 78712-1111. Offers PhD. *Program availability:* Part-time. Terminal master's awarded for partial completion of doctoral program. *Degree requirements:* For doctorate, one foreign language, thesis/dissertation. *Entrance requirements:* For doctorate, GRE General Test. Electronic applications accepted. *Faculty research:* Ancient philosophy, cognitive science, Continental philosophy, history and philosophy of science.

The University of Texas at El Paso, Graduate School, College of Liberal Arts, Department of Philosophy, El Paso, TX 79968-0001. Offers MA. *Degree requirements:* For master's, thesis, oral examination. *Entrance requirements:* For master's, GRE, 2 letters of recommendation.

The University of Texas at San Antonio, College of Liberal and Fine Arts, Department of Philosophy and Classics, San Antonio, TX 78249-0617. Offers MA. *Program availability:* Part-time. *Faculty:* 6 full-time (2 women). *Students:* 4 full-time (1 woman), 16 part-time (3 women); includes 8 minority (7 Hispanic/Latino; 1 Two or more races, non-Hispanic/Latino). Average age 33. 4 applicants, 100% accepted, 4 enrolled. In 2017, 2 master's awarded. *Degree requirements:* For master's, comprehensive exam, thesis. *Entrance requirements:* For master's, GRE. Additional exam requirements/recommendations for international students: Required—TOEFL (minimum score 550 paper-based; 79 iBT), IELTS (minimum score 6.5). *Application deadline:* For fall admission, 6/15 for domestic students, 3/1 for international students; for spring admission, 10/15 for domestic students, 9/15 for international students. Application fee: $50 ($90 for international students). Electronic applications accepted. *Expenses:* Contact institution. *Financial support:* Career-related internships or fieldwork, scholarships/grants, and unspecified assistantships available. Financial award applicants required to submit FAFSA. *Faculty research:* Metaphysics, epistemology, ethics. *Unit head:* Dr. Eve Browning, Department Chair, 210-458-6031, E-mail: eve.browning@utsa.edu.
Website: http://colfa.utsa.edu/philosophy-classics/

The University of Toledo, College of Graduate Studies, College of Languages, Literature and Social Sciences, Department of Philosophy, Toledo, OH 43606-3390. Offers MA. *Program availability:* Part-time. *Degree requirements:* For master's, comprehensive exam, thesis, exam. *Entrance requirements:* For master's, minimum cumulative point-hour ratio of 2.7 for all previous academic work, three letters of recommendation. Additional exam requirements/recommendations for international students: Required—TOEFL (minimum score 550 paper-based; 80 iBT). Electronic applications accepted. *Faculty research:* History of philosophy, ethics, social/political philosophy, philosophy of science, European philosophy.

University of Toronto, School of Graduate Studies, Faculty of Arts and Science, Department of Philosophy, Toronto, ON M5S 1A1, Canada. Offers MA, PhD. *Program availability:* Part-time. *Degree requirements:* For doctorate, one foreign language, thesis/dissertation. *Entrance requirements:* For master's, GRE, 6 courses in philosophy; minimum A- average in philosophy courses, B overall; 2 letters of reference; writing sample; for doctorate, GRE, MA in philosophy, minimum A- average, 2 letters of reference, writing sample. Additional exam requirements/recommendations for international students: Required—TOEFL (minimum score 600 paper-based), TWE (minimum score 5). Electronic applications accepted.

University of Utah, Graduate School, College of Humanities, Department of Philosophy, Salt Lake City, UT 84112. Offers MA, MS, PhD. *Program availability:* Part-time. *Faculty:* 18 full-time (9 women), 4 part-time/adjunct (0 women). *Students:* 17 full-time (5 women), 4 part-time (0 women); includes 2 minority (1 Asian, non-Hispanic/Latino; 1 Hispanic/Latino), 3 international. Average age 26. 38 applicants, 11% accepted, 4 enrolled. In 2017, 1 master's, 4 doctorates awarded. *Entrance requirements:* For master's, GRE General Test, minimum undergraduate GPA of 3.0; for doctorate, GRE General Test. Additional exam requirements/recommendations for international students: Required—TOEFL (minimum score 650 paper-based). Application fee: $55 ($65 for international students). Electronic applications accepted. *Financial support:* In 2017–18, 19 students received support, including 3 fellowships with full and partial tuition reimbursements available (averaging $17,700 per year), 1 research assistantship with full tuition reimbursement available (averaging $19,000 per year), 15 teaching assistantships with full tuition reimbursements available (averaging $17,700 per year); Federal Work-Study, institutionally sponsored loans, scholarships/grants, health care benefits, and unspecified assistantships also available. Financial award application deadline: 2/15; financial award applicants required to submit FAFSA. *Faculty research:* Philosophy of biology, philosophy of science, applied ethics, practical reasoning, political philosophy, philosophy of cognitive science. *Total annual research expenditures:* $15,000. *Unit head:* Dr. Eric Hutton, Chair, 801-585-3765, Fax: 801-585-5195, E-mail: matt.haber@utah.edu. *Application contact:* Connie Gladden Corbett, Academic Advisor, 801-581-8162, Fax: 801-585-5195, E-mail: c.corbett@utah.edu. Website: http://www.hum.utah.edu/philosophy/

University of Victoria, Faculty of Graduate Studies, Faculty of Humanities, Department of Philosophy, Victoria, BC V8W 2Y2, Canada. Offers MA. *Program availability:* Part-time, evening/weekend. *Degree requirements:* For master's, thesis. *Entrance requirements:* For master's, writing sample. Additional exam requirements/recommendations for international students: Required—TOEFL (minimum score 575 paper-based), IELTS (minimum score 7). *Faculty research:* Ethics, metaphysics, philosophy of mind, history of philosophy, political philosophy.

University of Virginia, College and Graduate School of Arts and Sciences, Department of Philosophy, Charlottesville, VA 22903. Offers MA, PhD, JD/MA. *Faculty:* 14 full-time (5 women), 1 part-time/adjunct (0 women). *Students:* 26 full-time (10 women); includes 2 minority (both Asian, non-Hispanic/Latino), 7 international. Average age 28. 130 applicants, 10% accepted, 7 enrolled. In 2017, 4 master's, 6 doctorates awarded. *Degree requirements:* For master's, 2 papers; for doctorate, thesis/dissertation, 2 papers. *Entrance requirements:* For master's, GRE General Test, GRE Subject Test, 3 letters of recommendation, writing sample; for doctorate, GRE General Test, GRE Subject Test, 3 letters of recommendation; writing sample. Additional exam requirements/recommendations for international students: Required—TOEFL (minimum score 600 paper-based; 90 iBT), IELTS. *Application deadline:* For fall admission, 1/1 for domestic students, 1/5 for international students. Applications are processed on a rolling basis. Application fee: $60. Electronic applications accepted. *Financial support:* Fellowships and teaching assistantships available. Financial award applicants required to submit FAFSA. *Unit head:* Brie Gertler, Chair, 434-982-4544, Fax: 434-924-6927, E-mail: gertler@virginia.edu. *Application contact:* Antonia LoLordo, Director of Graduate Admissions, 434-924-7701, Fax: 434-924-6927, E-mail: lolordo@virginia.edu. Website: http://philosophy.virginia.edu/

University of Washington, Graduate School, College of Arts and Sciences, Department of Classics, Seattle, WA 98195-3110. Offers classics (MA, PhD), including ancient philosophy (PhD), classics (PhD), textual studies (PhD), theory and criticism (PhD). *Program availability:* Part-time. *Faculty:* 11 full-time (7 women). *Students:* 15 full-time (9 women), 2 part-time (both women); includes 3 minority (1 Black or African American, non-Hispanic/Latino; 1 American Indian or Alaska Native, non-Hispanic/Latino; 1 Hispanic/Latino), 4 international. Average age 29. 45 applicants, 42% accepted. In 2017, 3 doctorates awarded. Terminal master's awarded for partial completion of doctoral program. *Degree requirements:* For master's, one foreign language, thesis or alternative; for doctorate, 2 foreign languages, comprehensive exam, thesis/dissertation. *Entrance requirements:* For master's, GRE, bachelor's degree in classics, Greek, or Latin; minimum GPA of 3.0; for doctorate, GRE, minimum GPA of 3.0. Additional exam requirements/recommendations for international students: Required—TOEFL (minimum score 82 iBT). *Application deadline:* For fall admission, 1/5 for domestic students. Application fee: $75. Electronic applications accepted. *Financial support:* In 2017–18, 12 students received support, including 3 fellowships with full tuition reimbursements available (averaging $23,850 per year), research assistantships with full tuition reimbursements available (averaging $23,850 per year), 10 teaching assistantships with full tuition reimbursements available (averaging $23,148 per year); Federal Work-Study, institutionally sponsored loans, health care benefits, and tuition waivers (partial) also available. Financial award application deadline: 1/5; financial award applicants required to submit FAFSA. *Faculty research:* Greek and Latin poetry, Greek and Roman cultural institutions, Greek and Latin historiography, Greek tragedy. *Unit head:* Prof. Catherine M. Connors, Chair, 206-543-2266, Fax: 206-543-2267, E-mail: cconnors@uw.edu. *Application contact:* Prof. Deborah Kamen, Graduate Program Coordinator, 206-543-2526, Fax: 206-543-2267, E-mail: dkamen@uw.edu. Website: http://classics.washington.edu

University of Washington, Graduate School, College of Arts and Sciences, Department of Philosophy, Seattle, WA 98195. Offers classics and philosophy (PhD); philosophy (MA, PhD). Terminal master's awarded for partial completion of doctoral program. *Degree requirements:* For master's, 3 papers; for doctorate, thesis/dissertation, general exam. *Entrance requirements:* For master's and doctorate, GRE, minimum GPA of 3.0. Additional exam requirements/recommendations for international students: Required—TOEFL. *Faculty research:* History and philosophy of science, epistemology, Aristotle's metaphysics, ethics and politics, causation in modern philosophy.

University of Waterloo, Graduate Studies, Faculty of Arts, Department of Philosophy, Waterloo, ON N2L 3G1, Canada. Offers MA, PhD. *Degree requirements:* For master's, thesis or alternative; for doctorate, one foreign language, thesis/dissertation. *Entrance requirements:* For master's, honors degree, minimum B+ average, writing sample, resume; for doctorate, master's degree, minimum A- average, resume. Additional exam requirements/recommendations for international students: Required—TOEFL, IELTS, PTE. Electronic applications accepted. *Faculty research:* Logic, ethics, social/political, cognitive science, philosophy of science.

The University of Western Ontario, Faculty of Graduate Studies, Faculty of Arts and Humanities, Department of Philosophy, London, ON N6A 5B8, Canada. Offers MA, PhD. *Degree requirements:* For master's, 1 competency exam; for doctorate, comprehensive exam, thesis/dissertation, 2 competency exams. *Entrance requirements:* For master's, honors degree. Additional exam requirements/recommendations for international students: Required—TOEFL (minimum score 600 paper-based). Electronic applications accepted. *Faculty research:* Philosophy of science, history of philosophy, philosophy of law, ethics, epistemology.

University of Windsor, Faculty of Graduate Studies, Faculty of Arts and Social Sciences, Department of Philosophy, Windsor, ON N9B 3P4, Canada. Offers MA. *Program availability:* Part-time. *Degree requirements:* For master's, thesis. *Entrance requirements:* For master's, minimum B average. Additional exam requirements/recommendations for international students: Required—TOEFL (minimum score 600 paper-based). Electronic applications accepted. *Faculty research:* Informal logic, contemporary Continental philosophy, epistemology.

University of Wisconsin–Madison, Graduate School, College of Letters and Science, Department of Philosophy, Madison, WI 53706-1380. Offers MA, PhD. *Program availability:* Part-time. Terminal master's awarded for partial completion of doctoral program. *Degree requirements:* For master's, thesis, preliminary exams; for doctorate, thesis/dissertation, preliminary exams. *Entrance requirements:* For doctorate, GRE, BA in philosophy or related area. Additional exam requirements/recommendations for international students: Required—TOEFL. Electronic applications accepted. *Faculty research:* History of philosophy, logic, philosophy of science, philosophy of mind, metaphysics.

University of Wisconsin–Milwaukee, Graduate School, College of Letters and Science, Department of Philosophy, Milwaukee, WI 53201-0413. Offers MA. *Program availability:* Part-time. *Students:* 20 full-time (3 women); includes 4 minority (1 Hispanic/Latino; 3 Two or more races, non-Hispanic/Latino), 2 international. Average age 26. 88 applicants, 14% accepted, 12 enrolled. In 2017, 8 master's awarded. *Entrance requirements:* For master's, GRE General Test. Additional exam requirements/recommendations for international students: Required—TOEFL (minimum score 550

paper-based; 79 iBT), IELTS (minimum score 6.5). *Application deadline:* For fall admission, 1/1 priority date for domestic students; for spring admission, 9/1 for domestic students. Application fee: $56 ($96 for international students). Electronic applications accepted. *Financial support:* Fellowships, teaching assistantships, career-related internships or fieldwork, unspecified assistantships, and project assistantships available. Support available to part-time students. Financial award application deadline: 4/15; financial award applicants required to submit FAFSA. *Unit head:* Richard J. Tierney, Chair, 414-229-5217, E-mail: rtierney@uwm.edu. *Application contact:* Carla Bagnoli, General Information Contact, 414-229-5215, Fax: 414-229-6967, E-mail: cbagnoli@uwm.edu.
Website: http://www.uwm.edu/dept/philosophy/

University of Wyoming, College of Arts and Sciences, Department of Philosophy, Laramie, WY 82071. Offers MA. *Program availability:* Part-time. *Degree requirements:* For master's, thesis, logic proficiency, first-year paper. *Entrance requirements:* For master's, GRE General Test, minimum GPA of 3.0. Additional exam requirements/recommendations for international students: Required—TOEFL (minimum score 525 paper-based). Electronic applications accepted. *Faculty research:* Philosophy of science, political and ethical theory, philosophy of language, epistemology, philosophy of mind, early modern philosophy.

Vanderbilt University, Department of Philosophy, Nashville, TN 37240-1001. Offers MA, PhD. *Faculty:* 13 full-time (3 women). *Students:* 28 full-time (17 women); includes 9 minority (1 Black or African American, non-Hispanic/Latino; 2 Asian, non-Hispanic/Latino; 3 Hispanic/Latino; 3 Two or more races, non-Hispanic/Latino), 1 international. Average age 28. 153 applicants, 6% accepted, 6 enrolled. In 2017, 1 master's, 5 doctorates awarded. Terminal master's awarded for partial completion of doctoral program. *Degree requirements:* For doctorate, one foreign language, comprehensive exam, thesis/dissertation, final and qualifying exams. *Entrance requirements:* For doctorate, GRE General Test, writing sample. Additional exam requirements/recommendations for international students: Required—TOEFL (minimum score 570 paper-based; 88 iBT). *Application deadline:* For fall admission, 1/15 for domestic and international students. Electronic applications accepted. *Financial support:* Fellowships with full tuition reimbursements, teaching assistantships with full tuition reimbursements, Federal Work-Study, institutionally sponsored loans, scholarships/grants, and health care benefits available. Financial award application deadline: 1/15; financial award applicants required to submit CSS PROFILE or FAFSA. *Faculty research:* Ancient, medieval, and modern philosophy; philosophy of science; ethics; philosophy of language; philosophy of religion. *Unit head:* Dr. Robert Talisse, Chair, 615-343-5349, Fax: 615-343-7259, E-mail: robert.talisse@vanderbilt.edu. *Application contact:* Julian Wuerth, Director of Graduate Studies, 615-322-2637, Fax: 615-343-7259, E-mail: julian.wuerth@vanderbilt.edu.
Website: http://www.vanderbilt.edu/AnS/philosophy/

Villanova University, Graduate School of Liberal Arts and Sciences, Department of Philosophy, Villanova, PA 19085-1699. Offers PhD. *Program availability:* Part-time, evening/weekend. *Faculty:* 4. *Students:* 48 full-time (21 women); includes 12 minority (2 Black or African American, non-Hispanic/Latino; 4 Asian, non-Hispanic/Latino; 5 Hispanic/Latino; 1 Two or more races, non-Hispanic/Latino), 5 international. Average age 31. 102 applicants, 6% accepted, 9 enrolled. In 2017, 9 doctorates awarded. *Degree requirements:* For doctorate, 2 foreign languages, comprehensive exam, thesis/dissertation. *Entrance requirements:* For doctorate, GRE, 3 recommendation letters, writing sample, curriculum vitae. Additional exam requirements/recommendations for international students: Required—TOEFL. *Application deadline:* For fall admission, 1/10 priority date for domestic and international students. Application fee: $50. *Financial support:* Research assistantships, teaching assistantships, scholarships/grants, and unspecified assistantships available. Financial award applicants required to submit FAFSA. *Unit head:* Dr. Yannik Thiem, Program Director, 610-519-5313.
Website: http://www1.villanova.edu/villanova/artsci/philosophy/academic-programs/doctorate.html

Washington University in St. Louis, The Graduate School, Department of Philosophy, St. Louis, MO 63130-4899. Offers philosophy (PhD); philosophy-neuroscience-psychology (PhD). *Degree requirements:* For doctorate, thesis/dissertation. *Entrance requirements:* For doctorate, GRE General Test, sample of written work. Additional exam requirements/recommendations for international students: Required—TOEFL. Electronic applications accepted. *Faculty research:* Ethics; social, political philosophy; history of philosophy; philosophy of law; philosophy of science, of mind and of language; theory of knowledge; aesthetics.

Wayne State University, College of Liberal Arts and Sciences, Department of Philosophy, Detroit, MI 48202. Offers MA, PhD. *Faculty:* 9. *Students:* 8 full-time (0 women), 5 part-time (1 woman); includes 2 minority (both Hispanic/Latino). Average age 30. 35 applicants, 17% accepted, 3 enrolled. In 2017, 3 master's awarded. Terminal master's awarded for partial completion of doctoral program. *Degree requirements:* For

master's, comprehensive exam, thesis (for some programs), essay or thesis; for doctorate, comprehensive exam, thesis/dissertation, oral exam, classroom lectures under supervision of Philosophy Department. *Entrance requirements:* For master's, GRE if upper-division GPA is below 2.75 (or 3.0 if from unaccredited college), writing sample; personal statement; three letters of recommendation; prerequisite courses in logic, value theory, and the history of philosophy; for doctorate, minimum undergraduate upper-division GPA of 3.0, undergraduate major or substantial work in philosophy, writing sample, personal statement, three letters of recommendation. Additional exam requirements/recommendations for international students: Required—TOEFL (minimum score 550 paper-based), TWE (minimum score 5.5), Michigan English Language Assessment Battery (minimum score 85); Recommended—IELTS (minimum score 6.5). *Application deadline:* For fall admission, 2/1 priority date for domestic and international students; for winter admission, 10/1 priority date for domestic students, 9/1 priority date for international students. Applications are processed on a rolling basis. Application fee: $50. Electronic applications accepted. *Expenses:* Tuition, state resident: full-time $10,224; part-time $638.98 per credit hour. Tuition, nonresident: full-time $22,145; part-time $1384.04 per credit hour. Tuition and fees vary according to course load and program. *Financial support:* In 2017–18, 10 students received support, including 2 fellowships with tuition reimbursements available (averaging $13,500 per year), 1 research assistantship with tuition reimbursement available (averaging $22,241 per year), 6 teaching assistantships with tuition reimbursements available (averaging $18,534 per year); scholarships/grants, health care benefits, and unspecified assistantships also available. Financial award applicants required to submit FAFSA. *Faculty research:* Epistemology, ethics and value theory, history and philosophy, metaphysics, philosophy of logic, language, and mathematics. *Unit head:* Dr. Eric Hiddleston, Associate Professor and interim Chair, 313-577-2475, E-mail: eric.hiddleston@wayne.edu. *Application contact:* Dr. Josh Wilburn, Director of Graduate Admissions/Graduate Advisor, 313-577-6103, E-mail: jwilburn@wayne.edu.
Website: http://clas.wayne.edu/Philosophy

West Chester University of Pennsylvania, College of Arts and Humanities, Department of Philosophy, West Chester, PA 19383. Offers business ethics (Certificate); health care ethics (Certificate); philosophy (MA); philosophy: applied ethics (MA). *Program availability:* Part-time, evening/weekend. *Students:* 1 full-time (0 women), 13 part-time (1 woman). Average age 44. 4 applicants, 75% accepted, 2 enrolled. In 2017, 3 master's awarded. *Degree requirements:* For master's, comprehensive exam, thesis optional, 30 credits. *Entrance requirements:* For master's, GRE or writing sample, three letters of reference, minimum undergraduate GPA of 2.8; for Certificate, undergraduate transcripts, minimum undergraduate GPA of 2.8. Additional exam requirements/recommendations for international students: Required—TOEFL or IELTS. *Application deadline:* For fall admission, 5/15 for international students; for spring admission, 10/15 for international students. Applications are processed on a rolling basis. Application fee: $50. Electronic applications accepted. *Expenses:* Tuition, state resident: full-time $9000; part-time $500 per credit. Tuition, nonresident: full-time $13,500; part-time $750 per credit. Required fees: $2959; $149.79 per credit. *Financial support:* Scholarships/grants and unspecified assistantships available. Financial award application deadline: 2/15; financial award applicants required to submit FAFSA. *Faculty research:* Ethics: theory and application; social and political, feminist, continental, Asian, post-colonial, American pragmatism, analytic philosophy. *Unit head:* Dr. Helen Daley Schroepfer, Chair, 610-436-2841, E-mail: hschroepfer@wcupa.edu. *Application contact:* Dr. Joan Woolfrey, Graduate Coordinator, 610-436-0731, E-mail: jwoolfrey@wcupa.edu.
Website: http://www.wcupa.edu/arts-humanities/philosophy/

Western Michigan University, Graduate College, College of Arts and Sciences, Department of Philosophy, Kalamazoo, MI 49008. Offers MA. *Degree requirements:* For master's, thesis optional.

Wilfrid Laurier University, Faculty of Graduate and Postdoctoral Studies, Faculty of Arts, Department of Philosophy, Waterloo, ON N2L 3C5, Canada. Offers agency (MA); community (MA); self (MA). *Entrance requirements:* For master's, honours BA in philosophy or equivalent with minimum B+ average in philosophy and in final year. Additional exam requirements/recommendations for international students: Required—TOEFL (minimum score 89 iBT). Electronic applications accepted. *Faculty research:* Self, agency, community.

Yale University, Graduate School of Arts and Sciences, Department of Philosophy, New Haven, CT 06520. Offers PhD. *Degree requirements:* For doctorate, 2 foreign languages, thesis/dissertation. *Entrance requirements:* For doctorate, GRE General Test.

York University, Faculty of Graduate Studies, Faculty of Liberal Arts and Professional Studies, Program in Philosophy, Toronto, ON M3J 1P3, Canada. Offers MA, PhD. *Program availability:* Part-time. *Degree requirements:* For master's, thesis or alternative; for doctorate, one foreign language, thesis/dissertation. Electronic applications accepted.

Section 12
Religious Studies

This section contains a directory of institutions offering graduate work in religious studies. Additional information about programs listed in the directory may be obtained by writing directly to the dean of a graduate school or chair of a department at the address given in the directory.

For programs offering related work, see also in this book *Area and Cultural Studies, History, Humanities,* and *Philosophy.* In another guide in this series:

Graduate Programs in Business, Education, Information Studies, Law & Social Work
See *Subject Areas (Religious Education)*

CONTENTS

Program Directories

Missions and Missiology

Abilene Christian University, Graduate Programs, College of Biblical Studies, Graduate School of Theology, Program in Divinity, Abilene, TX 79699. Offers ministry (M Div); missions (M Div). *Accreditation:* ATS. *Program availability:* Part-time, evening/weekend, blended/hybrid learning. *Students:* 22 full-time (4 women), 45 part-time (9 women); includes 8 minority (all Black or African American, non-Hispanic/Latino), 6 international. 26 applicants, 54% accepted, 9 enrolled. In 2017, 3 master's awarded. *Degree requirements:* For master's, comprehensive exam, e-portfolio review. *Entrance requirements:* Additional exam requirements/recommendations for international students: Required—TOEFL (minimum score 80 iBT), IELTS (minimum score 6), PTE. *Application deadline:* For fall admission, 8/11 for domestic students; for spring admission, 11/1 for domestic students. Applications are processed on a rolling basis. Application fee: $50. Electronic applications accepted. *Expenses:* $618 per hour. *Financial support:* In 2017–18, 14 students received support. Scholarships/grants available. Financial award application deadline: 4/1; financial award applicants required to submit FAFSA. *Unit head:* Dr. Kelli Gibson, Graduate Advisor, 325-674-3709, Fax: 325-674-6716, E-mail: kelli.gibson@acu.edu. *Application contact:* Graduate Admissions, 325-674-6911, Fax: 325-674-6717, E-mail: gradinfo@acu.edu.
Website: http://www.acu.edu/graduate/academics/divinity.html

Abilene Christian University, Graduate Programs, College of Biblical Studies, Graduate School of Theology, Program in Global Service, Abilene, TX 79699. Offers MA. *Program availability:* Part-time. *Students:* 7 part-time (3 women). 4 applicants, 100% accepted, 1 enrolled. *Degree requirements:* For master's, comprehensive exam, thesis. *Entrance requirements:* Additional exam requirements/recommendations for international students: Required—TOEFL (minimum score 80 iBT), IELTS (minimum score 6), PTE. *Application deadline:* For fall admission, 4/1 priority date for domestic students; for spring admission, 11/1 for domestic students. Applications are processed on a rolling basis. Application fee: $50. Electronic applications accepted. *Expenses:* $637 per hour. *Financial support:* In 2017–18, 1 student received support. Teaching assistantships, career-related internships or fieldwork, and scholarships/grants available. Financial award application deadline: 4/1; financial award applicants required to submit FAFSA. *Faculty research:* Animism, contextualization, missions education. *Unit head:* Dr. Chris Flanders, Graduate Adviser, 325-674-3742, Fax: 325-674-6180, E-mail: chris.flanders@acu.edu. *Application contact:* Graduate Admissions, 325-674-6911, Fax: 325-674-6717, E-mail: gradinfo@acu.edu.
Website: http://www.acu.edu/online/academics/global-service.html

Acadia University, Divinity College, Wolfville, NS B4P 2R6, Canada. Offers divinity (M Div); ministry (D Min); theology (MA), including chaplaincy and spiritual care, Christian history, discipleship, evangelism and mission, indigenous community development, leadership and spiritual formation, New Testament, next generation ministry, Old Testament, pastoral care and counseling, prison chaplaincy, Second Temple Judaism, theology. *Accreditation:* ATS. *Program availability:* Part-time. *Degree requirements:* For master's, variable foreign language requirement, thesis (for some programs); for doctorate, one foreign language, comprehensive exam, thesis/dissertation. *Entrance requirements:* For doctorate, minimum GPA of 3.0, 3 years' ministry experience. Additional exam requirements/recommendations for international students: Required—TOEFL. *Application deadline:* For fall admission, 6/30 priority date for domestic students, 4/1 priority date for international students; for spring admission, 4/30 priority date for domestic students. Applications are processed on a rolling basis. Application fee: $50. *Expenses:* Contact institution. *Financial support:* Application deadline: 8/12. *Faculty research:* Biblical canon, Jesus, Dead Sea Scrolls, Baptist studies, Old Testament-Septuagint. *Unit head:* Dr. Harry Gardner, President/Dean of Theology, 902-585-2213, Fax: 902-585-2233, E-mail: harry.gardner@acadiau.ca. *Application contact:* Shawna Peverill, Registrar, 902-585-2215, Fax: 902-585-2233, E-mail: shawna.peverill@acadiau.ca.
Website: http://divinity.acadiau.ca/

Anderson University, School of Theology, Anderson, IN 46012-3495. Offers missions (MA); theology (M Div, MTS, D Min). *Accreditation:* ACIPE; ATS. *Program availability:* Part-time. *Degree requirements:* For master's, variable foreign language requirement, thesis (for some programs); for doctorate, thesis/dissertation. *Faculty research:* Small-church/bivocational ministry, women in ministry.

Asbury Theological Seminary, Graduate and Professional Programs, Wilmore, KY 40390-1199. Offers M Div, MA, MAAS, MACE, MACL, MACM, MACP, MAMFC, MAMHC, MAPC, MASF, MAYM, Th M, D Min, PhD, Certificate. *Accreditation:* ATS. *Program availability:* Part-time, online learning. Terminal master's awarded for partial completion of doctoral program. *Degree requirements:* For master's, thesis (for some programs); for doctorate, thesis/dissertation, qualifying exam. *Entrance requirements:* For master's, minimum GPA of 2.75; for doctorate, minimum GPA of 3.0. Additional exam requirements/recommendations for international students: Required—TOEFL, IELTS. Electronic applications accepted.

Assemblies of God Theological Seminary, Graduate and Professional Programs, Springfield, MO 65802. Offers Biblical interpretation and theology (PhD); Christian ministries (MA); divinity (M Div); intercultural studies (MA, PhD); leadership and ministry (MLM); ministry (D Min); missiology (DAIS); pastoral studies (MPL); theological studies (MA, Th M). *Accreditation:* ATS. *Program availability:* Part-time, evening/weekend, 100% online. *Faculty:* 12 full-time (3 women), 15 part-time/adjunct (4 women). *Students:* 153 full-time (48 women), 159 part-time (41 women); includes 62 minority (20 Black or African American, non-Hispanic/Latino; 4 American Indian or Alaska Native, non-Hispanic/Latino; 14 Asian, non-Hispanic/Latino; 18 Hispanic/Latino; 6 Two or more races, non-Hispanic/Latino), 12 international. Average age 46. 69 applicants, 88% accepted, 48 enrolled. In 2017, 35 master's, 22 doctorates awarded. *Degree requirements:* For master's, variable foreign language requirement, thesis; for doctorate, variable foreign language requirement, comprehensive exam, thesis/dissertation. *Entrance requirements:* For master's, minimum GPA of 2.5; for doctorate, GRE (for PhD in Bible theology), minimum GPA of 3.0. Additional exam requirements/recommendations for international students: Required—TOEFL (minimum score 550 paper-based; 80 iBT). *Application deadline:* For fall admission, 7/1 priority date for domestic students, 6/1 priority date for international students; for spring admission, 12/1 priority date for domestic students, 11/1 priority date for international students. Applications are processed on a rolling basis. Application fee: $75. Electronic applications accepted. *Financial support:* Career-related internships or fieldwork and scholarships/grants available. Support available to part-time students. Financial award application deadline: 7/15; financial award applicants required to submit FAFSA. *Unit head:* Dr. Timothy A. Hager, Dean, 417-268-1000, Fax: 417-268-1001. *Application contact:* Erin Leonard, Seminary Enrollment Coordinator, 417-268-1000, Fax: 417-268-1001, E-mail: info@agts.edu.
Website: http://www.agts.edu

Bethel Seminary, Graduate and Professional Programs, St. Paul, MN 55112-6998. Offers Anglican studies (Certificate); children's and family ministry (MA); Christian studies (Certificate); Christian thought (MA); church planting (Certificate); Greek and Hebrew language (M Div); Greek language (M Div); Hebrew language (M Div); marriage and family therapy (MA, Certificate); mental health counseling (MA); ministry (MA, D Min); ministry practice (Certificate); theological studies (MA, Certificate); transformational leadership (MA); young life youth ministry (Certificate). *Accreditation:* ACIPE. *Program availability:* Part-time, evening/weekend, 100% online, blended/hybrid learning. *Faculty:* 16 full-time (4 women), 31 part-time/adjunct (15 women). *Students:* 380 full-time (170 women), 167 part-time (55 women); includes 161 minority (65 Black or African American, non-Hispanic/Latino; 52 Asian, non-Hispanic/Latino; 31 Hispanic/Latino; 1 Native Hawaiian or other Pacific Islander, non-Hispanic/Latino; 12 Two or more races, non-Hispanic/Latino), 5 international. Average age 38. 356 applicants, 62% accepted, 156 enrolled. In 2017, 120 master's, 15 doctorates, 4 other advanced degrees awarded. *Degree requirements:* For master's, variable foreign language requirement, thesis (for some programs); for doctorate, thesis/dissertation. *Entrance requirements:* For master's, letters of reference, transcripts, personal statement; for doctorate, M Div, letters of reference, organizational support; for Certificate, letters of reference, family essay, personal statement, and family of origin paper (for marriage and family therapy). Additional exam requirements/recommendations for international students: Required—TOEFL (minimum score 550 paper-based; 87 iBT). *Application deadline:* For fall admission, 8/1 priority date for domestic students, 8/1 for international students; for winter admission, 12/1 priority date for domestic students; for spring admission, 1/1 priority date for domestic students. Applications are processed on a rolling basis. Application fee: $0. Electronic applications accepted. *Expenses:* Contact institution. *Financial support:* Teaching assistantships, career-related internships or fieldwork, Federal Work-Study, and scholarships/grants available. Financial award applicants required to submit FAFSA. *Faculty research:* Nature of theology, ethics, Biblical commentaries, nature of God, science and theology. *Unit head:* Dr. Randy Bergen, Associate Provost, 651-635-8000, E-mail: r-bergen@bethel.edu. *Application contact:* Director of Admissions, 651-638-8000, Fax: 651-638-6002, E-mail: seminary-admissions@bethel.edu.
Website: https://www.bethel.edu/seminary

Biblical Theological Seminary, Graduate and Professional Programs, Hatfield, PA 19440-2499. Offers advanced missional leadership (D Min); advanced pastoral studies (Certificate); biblical counseling (Certificate); biblical studies (MA, Certificate); counseling (MA); ministry (M Div, MA); missional theology (MA). *Accreditation:* ATS. *Program availability:* Part-time, evening/weekend. *Faculty:* 9 full-time (1 woman), 20 part-time/adjunct (5 women). *Students:* 138 full-time (41 women), 78 part-time (31 women); includes 83 minority (51 Black or African American, non-Hispanic/Latino; 1 American Indian or Alaska Native, non-Hispanic/Latino; 26 Asian, non-Hispanic/Latino; 3 Hispanic/Latino; 2 Two or more races, non-Hispanic/Latino), 65 international. Average age 41. 83 applicants, 64% accepted, 49 enrolled. In 2017, 50 master's, 12 doctorates awarded. *Degree requirements:* For master's, variable foreign language requirement, thesis optional; for doctorate, thesis/dissertation. *Entrance requirements:* Additional exam requirements/recommendations for international students: Required—TOEFL (minimum score 550 paper-based; 80 iBT). *Application deadline:* Applications are processed on a rolling basis. Application fee: $30. Electronic applications accepted. *Expenses: Tuition:* Full-time $12,360; part-time $6180 per credit. *Required fees:* $50 per semester. One-time fee: $30. *Financial support:* In 2017–18, 194 students received support. Career-related internships or fieldwork, institutionally sponsored loans, and scholarships/grants available. Support available to part-time students. Financial award application deadline: 8/30; financial award applicants required to submit FAFSA. *Faculty research:* Theology, culture, Biblical interpretation. *Application contact:* Rev. Michael Heath, Student Advancement Counselor, 215-368-5000 Ext. 152, Fax: 215-368-7002, E-mail: mheath@biblical.edu.
Website: http://www.biblical.edu/

Biola University, Cook School of Intercultural Studies, La Mirada, CA 90639-0001. Offers anthropology (MA); applied linguistics (MA); intercultural education (PhD); intercultural studies (MA, PhD); linguistics (Certificate); linguistics and Biblical languages (MA); missiology (D Miss); missions (MA); teaching English to speakers of other languages (MA, Certificate). *Program availability:* Part-time, 100% online. *Faculty:* 19. *Students:* 127 full-time (64 women), 123 part-time (70 women); includes 72 minority (9 Black or African American, non-Hispanic/Latino; 2 American Indian or Alaska Native, non-Hispanic/Latino; 41 Asian, non-Hispanic/Latino; 17 Hispanic/Latino; 3 Two or more races, non-Hispanic/Latino), 26 international. In 2017, 28 master's, 16 doctorates awarded. *Entrance requirements:* For master's, minimum undergraduate GPA of 3.0; for doctorate, master's degree or equivalent, 3 years of cross-cultural experience, minimum graduate GPA of 3.3. Additional exam requirements/recommendations for international students: Required—TOEFL. *Application deadline:* For fall admission, 7/1 for domestic students, 6/1 for international students; for spring admission, 12/1 for domestic students; for summer admission, 5/1 for domestic students. Applications are processed on a rolling basis. Application fee: $65. Electronic applications accepted. *Financial support:* Scholarships/grants available. Support available to part-time students. Financial award applicants required to submit FAFSA. *Faculty research:* Linguistics, anthropology, intercultural studies, teaching English to speakers of other languages, missions, missiology. *Unit head:* Dr. Bulus Y. Galadima, Dean, 562-903-4844. *Application contact:* Graduate Admissions Office, 562-903-4752, E-mail: graduate.admissions@biola.edu.
Website: http://cook.biola.edu

Biola University, Talbot School of Theology, La Mirada, CA 90639-0001. Offers adult/family ministry (MACE); Bible exposition (MA, Th M); Biblical and theological studies (Certificate); children's ministry (MACE); Christian education (M Div); cross-cultural education ministry (MACE); educational studies (Ed D, PhD); evangelism and discipleship (M Div); general Christian education (MACE); Messianic Jewish studies (M Div, Certificate); missions and intercultural studies (M Div); New Testament (MA, Th M); Old Testament (MA); Old Testament and Semitics (Th M); pastoral and general ministry (M Div); pastoral care and counseling (M Div, MACML); philosophy (MA); preaching and pastoral ministry (MACML); spiritual formation (M Div, Certificate); spiritual formation and soul care (MA); sports ministry (MACML); theology (MA, Th M, D Min, Certificate); youth ministry (MACE). *Program availability:* Part-time, evening/weekend. *Students:* 475 full-time (113 women), 603 part-time (176 women); includes 541 minority (39 Black or African American, non-Hispanic/Latino; 2 American Indian or Alaska Native, non-Hispanic/Latino; 378 Asian, non-Hispanic/Latino; 84 Hispanic/Latino; 1 Native Hawaiian or other Pacific Islander, non-Hispanic/Latino; 37 Two or more races, non-Hispanic/Latino), 105 international. 437 applicants, 78% accepted, 241 enrolled. In 2017, 177 master's, 24 doctorates awarded. *Entrance requirements:* For master's, bachelor's degree from accredited college or university; minimum GPA of 2.6 (for M

Div), 3.0 (for MA); for doctorate, M Div or MA. Additional exam requirements/recommendations for international students: Required—TOEFL (minimum score 600 paper-based; 88 iBT). *Application deadline:* For fall admission, 7/1 for domestic students, 6/1 for international students; for spring admission, 12/1 priority date for domestic students. Applications are processed on a rolling basis. Application fee: $65. Electronic applications accepted. *Financial support:* Scholarships/grants and unspecified assistantships available. Support available to part-time students. Financial award applicants required to submit FAFSA. *Faculty research:* New Testament, Old Testament, spiritual formation, Christian education, theological studies, Christian ministry, preaching and pastoral ministry, language and literature, bible exposition, Christian leadership. *Unit head:* Dr. Clint Arnold, Dean, 562-903-4816, Fax: 562-903-4748. *Application contact:* Graduate Admissions Office, 562-903-4752, E-mail: graduate.admissions@biola.edu.
Website: http://www.talbot.edu/

Boston University, School of Theology, Boston, MA 02215. Offers chaplaincy (M Div); choral conducting (MSM); church and the arts (M Div); community and global engagement (M Div); constructive theology and ethics (PhD), including constructive theology, theological ethics; history and hermeneutics (PhD), including biblical studies, church history and world Christianity, liturgical studies, mission studies; organ (MSM); pastoral ministry (M Div); practical theology (PhD), including church and society, congregation and community, evangelism and missiology, homiletics, leadership and administration, pastoral theology and psychology, religious education, spirituality studies, worship; religion and the academy (M Div); transformational leadership (D Min); M Div/MSM; M Div/MSW; MTS/MSW. PhD in mission studies offered in collaboration with Gordon-Conwell Theological Seminary. *Accreditation:* ACIPE; ATS. *Program availability:* Part-time, blended/hybrid learning. *Faculty:* 39 full-time (17 women), 11 part-time/adjunct (5 women). *Students:* 256 full-time (135 women), 87 part-time (40 women); includes 82 minority (38 Black or African American, non-Hispanic/Latino; 10 Asian, non-Hispanic/Latino; 23 Hispanic/Latino; 1 Native Hawaiian or other Pacific Islander, non-Hispanic/Latino; 10 Two or more races, non-Hispanic/Latino), 66 international. Average age 34. 334 applicants, 69% accepted, 106 enrolled. In 2017, 62 master's, 9 doctorates awarded. *Degree requirements:* For master's, comprehensive exam (for some programs), thesis optional, contextual education; for doctorate, 2 languages, dissertation, and comprehensive exam (for PhD). *Entrance requirements:* For master's, minimum GPA of 3.0; for doctorate, GRE General Test, minimum GPA of 3.3. Additional exam requirements/recommendations for international students: Required—TOEFL (minimum score 570 paper-based; 89 iBT). *Application deadline:* For fall admission, 1/15 priority date for domestic and international students; for spring admission, 10/15 priority date for domestic and international students. Applications are processed on a rolling basis. Application fee: $95. Electronic applications accepted. *Expenses:* $20,100 tuition. *Financial support:* In 2017–18, 236 students received support, including 102 fellowships with full tuition reimbursements available (averaging $7,500 per year), 11 research assistantships with full tuition reimbursements available (averaging $22,000 per year), 12 teaching assistantships with full tuition reimbursements available (averaging $22,000 per year); career-related internships or fieldwork, Federal Work-Study, scholarships/grants, and health care benefits also available. Support available to part-time students. Financial award application deadline: 7/15. *Faculty research:* Practical theology, ethics, environmental theology, religion and conflict transformation, chaplaincy. *Total annual research expenditures:* $2.5 million. *Unit head:* Rev. Dr. Mary Elizabeth Moore, Dean, 617-353-3050, Fax: 617-353-3061, E-mail: memoore@bu.edu. *Application contact:* Rev. Dr. Anastasia Kidd, Director of Enrollment, 617-353-3036, Fax: 617-358-0140, E-mail: sthadmis@bu.edu.
Website: http://www.bu.edu/sth

Briercrest Seminary, Graduate Programs, Program in Christian Ministries, Caronport, SK S0H 0S0, Canada. Offers leadership (MA); marriage and family counseling (MA); missions (MA); pastoral counseling (MA); worship (MA); youth and family ministry (MA). *Program availability:* Part-time. *Degree requirements:* For master's, comprehensive exam, thesis optional. *Entrance requirements:* Additional exam requirements/recommendations for international students: Required—TOEFL (minimum score 550 paper-based).

Calvin Theological Seminary, Graduate and Professional Programs, Grand Rapids, MI 49546-4387. Offers Bible and theology (MA); divinity (M Div), including ancient near eastern languages and literature, contextual ministry, evangelism and teaching, history of Christianity, new church development, New Testament, Old Testament, pastoral care and leadership, preaching and worship, theological studies, youth and family ministries; educational ministry (MA); historical theology (PhD); missions and evangelism (MA); pastoral care (MA); philosophical and moral theology (PhD); systematic theology (PhD); theological studies (MTS); theology (Th M); worship (MA); youth and family ministries (MA). *Accreditation:* ACIPE; ATS. *Program availability:* Part-time. *Degree requirements:* For master's, variable foreign language requirement, thesis (for some programs); for doctorate, 4 foreign languages, comprehensive exam, thesis/dissertation. *Entrance requirements:* For doctorate, GRE General Test, Hebrew, Greek, and a modern foreign language. Additional exam requirements/recommendations for international students: Required—TOEFL (minimum score 550 paper-based), TWE (minimum score 4). Electronic applications accepted. *Faculty research:* Recent Trinity theory, Christian anthropology, Proverbs, reformed confessions, Paul's view of law.

Catholic Theological Union, Graduate and Professional Programs, Chicago, IL 60615-5698. Offers biblical spirituality (Certificate); cross-cultural ministries (D Min); cross-cultural missions (Certificate); divinity (M Div); liturgical studies (Certificate); liturgy (D Min); pastoral studies (MAPS, Certificate); spiritual formation (Certificate); spirituality (D Min); theology (MA); M Div/MA; M Div/MSW; M Div/PhD. M Div/PhD offered jointly with University of Chicago; M Div/MSW with Loyola University Chicago and University of Chicago. *Accreditation:* ACIPE; ATS. *Program availability:* Part-time, evening/weekend. *Degree requirements:* For master's, one foreign language, comprehensive exam (for some programs), thesis (for some programs); for doctorate, thesis/dissertation. *Entrance requirements:* For doctorate, master's degree, 5 years of active ministry. *Faculty research:* Doctrine, sacraments, ethics, Bible.

Cedarville University, Graduate Programs, Cedarville, OH 45314. Offers business administration (MBA); family nurse practitioner (MSN); global ministry (M Div); global public health nursing (MSN); healthcare administration (MBA); ministry (M Min); nurse educator (MSN); operations management (MBA); pharmacy (Pharm D). *Program availability:* Part-time, evening/weekend, 100% online, blended/hybrid learning. *Faculty:* 23 full-time (9 women), 48 part-time/adjunct (21 women). *Students:* 202 full-time (123 women), 146 part-time (96 women); includes 63 minority (39 Black or African American, non-Hispanic/Latino; 3 American Indian or Alaska Native, non-Hispanic/Latino; 15 Asian, non-Hispanic/Latino; 2 Hispanic/Latino; 1 Native Hawaiian or other Pacific Islander, non-Hispanic/Latino; 3 Two or more races, non-Hispanic/Latino), 3 international. Average age 24. 345 applicants, 37% accepted, 91 enrolled. In 2017, 53 master's, 47 doctorates awarded. *Degree requirements:* For master's, portfolio; for doctorate, comprehensive exam. *Entrance requirements:* For master's, GRE, 2 professional recommendations; for doctorate, PCAT, professional recommendation from a practicing pharmacist or current employer/supervisor, resume, essay, interview. Additional exam requirements/recommendations for international students: Required—TOEFL (minimum score 550 paper-based; 80 iBT). *Application deadline:* For fall admission, 5/1 priority date for domestic and international students; for spring admission, 11/1 priority date for domestic and international students. Applications are processed on a rolling basis. Application fee: $0. Electronic applications accepted. *Expenses: Tuition:* Full-time $12,594; part-time $566 per credit. One-time fee: $100 full-time. Tuition and fees vary according to degree level and program. *Financial support:* Scholarships/grants and unspecified assistantships available. Support available to part-time students. Financial award application deadline: 1/30; financial award applicants required to submit FAFSA. *Faculty research:* Establishing competencies of clinical reasoning for nursing students in Taiwan, social determinants of health in pediatric primary care, meeting needs of palliative care populations, natural product utility in cancer, monoclonal antibodies directed at angiogenesis regulation. *Total annual research expenditures:* $3,800. *Unit head:* Dr. Janice Supplee, Dean of Graduate Studies, 937-766-7700, E-mail: suppleej@cedarville.edu. *Application contact:* Jim Amstutz, Director of Graduate Admissions, 937-766-7878, Fax: 937-766-7575, E-mail: amstutzj@cedarville.edu.
Website: https://www.cedarville.edu/Admissions/Graduate/Graduate-Programs.aspx

Central Baptist Theological Seminary, Graduate and Professional Programs, Shawnee, KS 66226. Offers missional church studies (MA); theological studies (MA); theology (M Div, Diploma). *Accreditation:* ACIPE; ATS (one or more programs are accredited). *Program availability:* Part-time. *Degree requirements:* For master's, thesis optional. *Entrance requirements:* Additional exam requirements/recommendations for international students: Required—TOEFL (minimum score 547 paper-based; 77 iBT). Electronic applications accepted.

Clarks Summit University, Baptist Bible Seminary, South Abington Township, PA 18411. Offers Biblical apologetics (MA); Biblical studies (MA); church education (M Min); church planting (M Div, M Min); communication (D Min); counseling and spiritual development (D Min); global ministry (M Min, D Min); ministry (PhD); missions (M Min); organizational leadership (M Min); outreach pastor (M Min); pastoral counseling (M Min); pastoral leadership (M Div, M Min); pastoral ministry (D Min); theological studies (D Min); theology (Th M); youth pastor (M Min). M Min in missions available only for Association of Baptists for World Evangelism missionary personnel. *Program availability:* Part-time, evening/weekend, online learning. Terminal master's awarded for partial completion of doctoral program. *Degree requirements:* For master's, 2 foreign languages, thesis, oral exam (for M Div); for doctorate, 2 foreign languages, comprehensive exam (for some programs), thesis/dissertation, oral exam. *Entrance requirements:* For doctorate, Greek and Hebrew entrance exams (for PhD). *Application deadline:* Applications are processed on a rolling basis. Application fee: $30. Electronic applications accepted. *Financial support:* Career-related internships or fieldwork and scholarships/grants available. Support available to part-time students. *Unit head:* Dr. Wayne Slusser, Dean, 570-585-9348, Fax: 570-585-4057, E-mail: wslusser@clarkssummitu.edu. *Application contact:* Dr. Wayne Slusser, Dean, 570-585-9348, Fax: 570-585-4057, E-mail: wslusser@clarkssummitu.edu.
Website: https://www.clarkssummitu.edu/seminary/

Columbia International University, Seminary and School of Ministry, Columbia, SC 29203. Offers academic ministries (M Div); Bible and theology (Certificate); bible exposition (M Div, MABE); Biblical ministry (Certificate); chaplaincy (M Div); intercultural studies (MAIS); leadership (D Min); member care (D Min); missions (D Min); preaching (D Min); theological studies (MA). *Program availability:* Part-time, evening/weekend. *Degree requirements:* For doctorate, comprehensive exam, thesis/dissertation. *Entrance requirements:* For doctorate, 3 years of ministerial experience, M Div. Additional exam requirements/recommendations for international students: Required—TOEFL. Electronic applications accepted.

Dallas Baptist University, Graduate School of Ministry, Program in Global Leadership, Dallas, TX 75211-9299. Offers church planting (MA); East Asian Studies (MA); English as a second language (MA); general studies (MA); global communication (MA); global studies (MA); international business (MA); leading the nonprofit organization (MA); missions (MA); small group ministry (MA); urban ministry (MA). *Program availability:* Part-time, evening/weekend. *Application deadline:* Applications are processed on a rolling basis. Application fee: $25. Electronic applications accepted. Application fee is waived when completed online. *Expenses: Tuition:* Full-time $16,308; part-time $906 per credit hour. *Required fees:* $900; $450 per semester. Tuition and fees vary according to course load and degree level. *Unit head:* Dr. Robert R. Brooks, Dean, 214-333-5494, Fax: 214-333-5673, E-mail: bobb@dbu.edu. *Application contact:* Dr. Brent Thomason, Program Director, 214-333-5236, E-mail: brentt@dbu.edu.
Website: http://www.dbu.edu/ministry/degree-programs/m-a-in-global-leadership

Dallas Baptist University, Liberal Arts Program, Dallas, TX 75211-9299. Offers art (MLA); Christian studies (MLA); commercial art (MLA); East Asian studies (MLA); English (MLA); English as a second language (MLA); fine arts (MLA); history (MLA); missions (MLA); political science (MLA). *Program availability:* Part-time, evening/weekend. *Application deadline:* Applications are processed on a rolling basis. Application fee: $25. Electronic applications accepted. Application fee is waived when completed online. *Expenses: Tuition:* Full-time $16,308; part-time $906 per credit hour. *Required fees:* $900; $450 per semester. Tuition and fees vary according to course load and degree level. *Unit head:* Jared Ingram, Director, 214-333-5584, E-mail: jaredi@dbu.edu. *Application contact:* Bobby Soto, Director of Admissions, 214-333-5242, E-mail: bobby@dbu.edu.
Website: http://www3.dbu.edu/graduate/mla.asp

Dallas Theological Seminary, Graduate Programs, Dallas, TX 75204-6499. Offers adult education (Th M); apologetics (Th M); Bible backgrounds (Th M); Bible translation (Th M); Biblical and theological studies (Certificate); biblical counseling (MA); biblical exegesis and linguistics (MA); biblical exposition (PhD); biblical studies (MA); Biblical theology (Th M); children's education (Th M); Christian education (MA, D Min); Christian leadership (MA); cross-cultural ministries (MA); educational administration (Th M); educational leadership (Th M); evangelism and discipleship (Th M); exposition of Biblical books (Th M); family life education (Th M); general studies (Th M); Hebrew and cognate studies (Th M); hermeneutics (Th M); historical theology (Th M); homiletics (Th M); intercultural ministries (Th M); Jesus studies (Th M); leadership studies (Th M); media and communication (MA); media arts (Th M); ministry (D Min); ministry with women (Th M); New Testament studies (Th M, PhD); Old Testament studies (Th M, PhD); parachurch ministries (Th M); pastoral care and counseling (Th M); pastoral theology and practice (Th M); philosophy (Th M); sacred theology (STM); spiritual formation (Th M); systematic theology (Th M); teaching in Christian institutions (Th M); theological studies (PhD); urban ministries (Th M); worship studies (Th M); youth education (Th M). *Program availability:* Part-time, online learning. *Degree requirements:* For master's, variable foreign language requirement, thesis (for some programs); for doctorate, 2 foreign languages, thesis/dissertation. *Entrance requirements:* For master's, GRE or MAT (if minimum undergraduate cumulative GPA is below 2.5 or undergraduate degree is unaccredited). Additional exam requirements/recommendations for international students: Required—TOEFL (minimum score 575 paper-based; 85 iBT), TWE. Electronic applications accepted.

Eastern University, Department of Global Studies and Mission, St. Davids, PA 19087-3696. Offers international development (MA); theological and cultural anthropology

(MA). *Students:* 23 full-time (11 women), 26 part-time (15 women); includes 11 minority (8 Black or African American, non-Hispanic/Latino; 1 Asian, non-Hispanic/Latino; 2 Hispanic/Latino), 1 international. Average age 35. In 2017, 19 master's awarded. *Application deadline:* Applications are processed on a rolling basis. Application fee: $35. Electronic applications accepted. Application fee is waived when completed online. *Expenses:* Contact institution. *Unit head:* Michael Dziedziak, Executive Director of Enrollment, 800-452-0996, E-mail: gpsadmissions@eastern.edu.
Website: https://www.eastern.edu/academics/global-studies-mission

Ecclesia College, Graduate School, Springdale, AR 72762. Offers Christian leadership (MCL). *Program availability:* Online learning.

Evangelical Seminary, Graduate and Professional Programs, Myerstown, PA 17067-1212. Offers Biblical studies (MAR); congregational ministry (M Div); global and contextual studies (M Div, MAR); historical and theological studies (MAR); interdisciplinary studies (MAR); marriage and family counseling (M Div); marriage and family therapy (MA); New Testament (MAR); Old Testament (MAR); spiritual formation (MAR); teaching ministry (M Div); youth ministry (M Div). *Accreditation:* ATS (one or more programs are accredited). *Program availability:* Part-time, online learning. *Degree requirements:* For master's, 2 foreign languages. *Entrance requirements:* For master's, minimum GPA of 2.5. Additional exam requirements/recommendations for international students: Required—TOEFL (minimum score 550 paper-based). *Faculty research:* Literary form and structure within the Hebrew and Greek scriptures, Wesley studies, esoteric biblical languages, the Mosaic law and the Christian, ethics.

Fresno Pacific University, Biblical Seminary, Program in Urban Mission, Fresno, CA 93702-4709. Offers MA. *Entrance requirements:* For master's, minimum GPA of 2.5.

Fuller Theological Seminary, Graduate Programs, Pasadena, CA 91182. Offers Christian leadership (MACL); clinical psychology (PhD, Psy D); family studies (MA); global leadership (MA); global ministries (D Min); global ministries (Korean language) (D Min); intercultural studies (MA, Th M, PhD); intercultural studies (Korean language) (MA); marital and family therapy (MS); marriage and family enrichment (Certificate); ministry (M Div, D Min); missiology (D Miss); missiology (Korean language) (Th M); theology (MA, Th M, PhD), including evangelism (MA), family life education (MA), pastoral ministry (MA), recovery ministry (MA), worship music ministry (MA), worship, theology, and the arts (MA), youth, family, and culture (MA); theology and ministry (MA).

Gardner-Webb University, School of Divinity, Boiling Springs, NC 28017. Offers biblical studies (M Div); Christian education and formation (M Div); intercultural studies (M Div); ministry (D Min); missiology (M Div); pastoral care and counseling (M Div); pastoral care and counseling/member care for missionaries (D Min); pastoral studies (M Div); M Div/MA; M Div/MBA. *Accreditation:* ACIPE. *Program availability:* Part-time. *Faculty:* 10 full-time (1 woman), 4 part-time/adjunct (2 women). *Students:* 102 full-time (47 women), 56 part-time (15 women); includes 67 minority (63 Black or African American, non-Hispanic/Latino; 3 Asian, non-Hispanic/Latino; 1 Hispanic/Latino). Average age 38. *Entrance requirements:* For master's, minimum GPA of 2.6; for doctorate, minimum GPA of 2.75. Additional exam requirements/recommendations for international students: Required—TOEFL (minimum score 500 paper-based; 61 iBT). *Application deadline:* Applications are processed on a rolling basis. Electronic applications accepted. *Expenses:* Contact institution. *Financial support:* Fellowships, institutionally sponsored loans, and unspecified assistantships available. Support available to part-time students. Financial award application deadline: 5/15. *Faculty research:* Jewish-Christian dialogue, Islam. *Unit head:* Dr. Robert W. Canoy, Sr., Dean, 704-406-4400, Fax: 704-406-3935, E-mail: rcanoy@gardner-webb.edu. *Application contact:* Kheresa Harmon, Director of Admissions, 704-406-3205, Fax: 704-406-3895, E-mail: kharmon@gardner-webb.edu.
Website: http://gardner-webb.edu/academic-programs-and-resources/colleges-and-schools/divinity/index

Global University, Graduate School of Theology, Springfield, MO 65804. Offers bible and theology (D Min); biblical language (M Div); biblical studies (MA); Christian ministry (M Div, D Min); ministerial studies (MA), including education, leadership, missions, New Testament, Old Testament. *Program availability:* Part-time, evening/weekend, online learning. *Degree requirements:* For master's, thesis (for some programs). *Entrance requirements:* For master's, minimum undergraduate GPA of 3.0. Electronic applications accepted. *Faculty research:* Higher education, cross-cultural missions.

Gordon-Conwell Theological Seminary, Graduate and Professional Programs, South Hamilton, MA 01982. Offers Biblical languages (MABL); church history (MACH); counseling (MACO); ministry (D Min); missions/evangelism (MAME); New Testament (MANT); Old Testament (MAOT); religion (MAR); theology (M Div, MATH, Th M, Th D). *Accreditation:* ACIPE; ATS (one or more programs are accredited). *Program availability:* Part-time, evening/weekend. *Degree requirements:* For master's, one foreign language, thesis optional; for doctorate, 2 foreign languages, thesis/dissertation. *Entrance requirements:* For master's, minimum GPA of 2.5; for doctorate, minimum GPA of 3.0.

Grace Mission University, Graduate School, Fullerton, CA 92833. Offers M Div, MACE, MAICS, D Miss.

Grace Theological Seminary, Graduate and Professional Programs, Winona Lake, IN 46590-9907. Offers biblical studies (Certificate); chaplaincy (M Div); exegetical studies (M Div); intercultural studies (M Div, MA, D Min); local church ministry (MA), including camp administration, women's leadership; pastoral counseling (M Div); pastoral studies (M Div, D Min); theology (Diploma). *Accreditation:* ATS. *Program availability:* Part-time, online learning. *Degree requirements:* For master's, thesis optional; for doctorate, 2 foreign languages, thesis/dissertation. *Entrance requirements:* For master's, MAT, minimum GPA of 2.5. Electronic applications accepted. *Faculty research:* Biblical theology, language, and church ministries.

Hope International University, School of Graduate and Professional Studies, Programs in Ministry, Fullerton, CA 92831-3138. Offers Christian leadership (MCM); church music (MA); church music (Korean track) (MCM); church planting (MCM); intercultural studies (MCM); worship (MCM). *Program availability:* Part-time, evening/weekend, online learning. *Degree requirements:* For master's, thesis (for some programs), project. *Entrance requirements:* For master's, minimum GPA of 3.0, MCM program requires an undergraduate degree in music, 2 references. Additional exam requirements/recommendations for international students: Required—TOEFL (minimum score 550 paper-based; 86 iBT); Recommended—IELTS (minimum score 6.5). Electronic applications accepted. *Expenses:* Contact institution. *Faculty research:* Church dynamics, growth methodologies.

Liberty University, School of Divinity, Lynchburg, VA 24515. Offers Biblical exposition (MA); Biblical languages (M Div); Biblical studies (M Div, MA, MAR, Th M, D Min); chaplaincy (M Div, D Min); Christian apologetics (M Div, MA, MAR, Th M); Christian leadership and church ministries (M Div); Christian ministries (M Div); Christian ministry (MA); Christian thought (M Div); church history (M Div, MAR, Th M); community chaplaincy (M Div, MAR); discipleship (D Min); discipleship and church ministry (M Div, MAR, MCM); evangelism and church planting (MAR, MCM, D Min); expository preaching (D Min); global ministry (MA); global studies (M Div, MAR, MCM, MGS, Th M); healthcare chaplaincy (M Div); homiletics (M Div, MAR, Th M); leadership (M Div, MAR); marketplace chaplaincy (M Div, MCM); ministry leadership (Ed D); pastoral counseling (M Div, MA, MAR, D Min), including addictions and recovery (MA), crisis response and trauma (MA), discipleship and church ministries (MA), leadership (MA), life coaching (MA), marketplace chaplaincy (MA), marriage and family (MA), military resilience (MA), pastoral counseling (MA); pastoral leadership (D Min); pastoral ministries (M Div, M Serv Soc, MCM); religious education (MRE); sports chaplaincy (MA); theology (M Div, MAR, MTS, Th M); theology and apologetics (D Min, PhD); worship (M Div, MAR, MCM, D Min); youth and family ministries (M Div). *Program availability:* Part-time, online learning. *Students:* 2,140 full-time (615 women), 3,020 part-time (906 women); includes 1,312 minority (1,016 Black or African American, non-Hispanic/Latino; 9 American Indian or Alaska Native, non-Hispanic/Latino; 100 Asian, non-Hispanic/Latino; 90 Hispanic/Latino; 7 Native Hawaiian or other Pacific Islander, non-Hispanic/Latino; 90 Two or more races, non-Hispanic/Latino), 158 international. Average age 42. 4,673 applicants, 33% accepted, 977 enrolled. In 2017, 904 master's, 54 doctorates awarded. *Degree requirements:* For master's, 2 foreign languages, thesis (for some programs); for doctorate, 2 foreign languages, thesis/dissertation. *Entrance requirements:* For master's, minimum undergraduate GPA of 2.0; for doctorate, GRE General Test or MAT, minimum graduate GPA of 3.0. Additional exam requirements/recommendations for international students: Required—TOEFL (minimum score 600 paper-based; 100 iBT). *Application deadline:* For fall admission, 6/1 for domestic students; for spring admission, 11/1 for domestic students. Applications are processed on a rolling basis. Application fee: $50. Electronic applications accepted. *Expenses:* Contact institution. *Financial support:* Teaching assistantships with tuition reimbursements, career-related internships or fieldwork, and Federal Work-Study available. Financial award applicants required to submit FAFSA. *Unit head:* Dr. Ed Hindson, Dean, 434-592-4140, Fax: 434-522-0415, E-mail: ehindson@liberty.edu. *Application contact:* Jay Bridge, Director of Graduate Admissions, 800-424-9595, Fax: 800-628-7977, E-mail: gradadmissions@liberty.edu.
Website: https://www.liberty.edu/divinity/

Luther Seminary, Graduate and Professional Programs, St. Paul, MN 55108-1445. Offers aging and health (MA); Biblical preaching (D Min); children, youth and family (M Div, MA); congregational mission and leadership (M Th, MA, D Min); history of Christianity (M Th, MA); missions and world religions (M Th); New Testament (M Th, MA); Old Testament (M Th, MA); pastoral care: clinical pastoral theology (M Th); pastoral theology and ministry (M Th); systematic theology (M Th, MA). *Accreditation:* ACIPE; ATS. *Program availability:* Part-time, online learning. *Degree requirements:* For master's, thesis or alternative; for doctorate, 2 foreign languages, thesis/dissertation. *Entrance requirements:* For master's, minimum GPA of 3.0; for doctorate, GRE General Test. Additional exam requirements/recommendations for international students: Required—TOEFL, IELTS. Electronic applications accepted. *Faculty research:* Theology, psychology (pastoral care), church history, Bible.

Mid-America Baptist Theological Seminary, Graduate and Professional Programs, Cordova, TN 38016. Offers biblical counseling (M Div); Christian education (M Div, MACE); ministry (D Min); missiology and intercultural studies (M Div); pastoral ministry (M Div); theology (MA, PhD); worship (MA). *Degree requirements:* For doctorate, 4 foreign languages, thesis/dissertation. *Entrance requirements:* For doctorate, MAT. Additional exam requirements/recommendations for international students: Required—TOEFL (minimum score 600 paper-based). *Application deadline:* For fall admission, 7/20 priority date for domestic students. Applications are processed on a rolling basis. Application fee: $35. Electronic applications accepted. *Expenses: Tuition:* Part-time $250 per credit hour. One-time fee: $500 part-time. *Unit head:* Dr. Michael R. Spradlin, President, 901-751-3048. *Application contact:* Tanner Hickman, Director of Admissions, 901-751-3015, Fax: 901-751-8454, E-mail: tannerh@mabts.edu.

Milligan College, Emmanuel Christian Seminary at Milligan College, Milligan College, TN 37682. Offers Christian care and counseling (M Div); Christian education (M Div); Christian ministries (MACM, Graduate Certificate); Christian ministry (M Div); Christian theology (M Div, MAR); church history (MAR); church history/historical theology (M Div); general studies (M Div); ministry (D Min); New Testament (M Div, MAR); Old Testament (M Div, MAR); urban ministry (M Div); world missions (M Div). *Accreditation:* ACIPE; ATS. *Program availability:* Part-time, blended/hybrid learning. *Faculty:* 10 full-time (1 woman), 8 part-time/adjunct (0 women). *Students:* 52 full-time (23 women), 57 part-time (18 women); includes 11 minority (7 Black or African American, non-Hispanic/Latino; 1 Asian, non-Hispanic/Latino; 3 Hispanic/Latino), 7 international. Average age 35. 62 applicants, 89% accepted, 39 enrolled. In 2017, 19 master's, 3 doctorates awarded. *Degree requirements:* For master's, 2 foreign languages, thesis or alternative, portfolio; for doctorate, thesis/dissertation. *Entrance requirements:* For master's, undergraduate degree and supporting transcripts, essay/personal statement, professional recommendations, interview; for doctorate, M Div or equivalent, essay/personal statement, professional recommendations. Additional exam requirements/recommendations for international students: Required—TOEFL (minimum score 550 paper-based, 79 iBT) or IELTS (6.5). *Application deadline:* For fall admission, 8/1 for domestic students, 6/1 for international students; for spring admission, 12/15 for domestic students, 8/1 for international students. Applications are processed on a rolling basis. Application fee: $30 ($0 for international students). Electronic applications accepted. *Expenses:* Contact institution. *Financial support:* In 2017–18, 124 students received support. Scholarships/grants and unspecified assistantships available. Financial award application deadline: 12/1; financial award applicants required to submit FAFSA. *Faculty research:* Theology of Old Testament prophets; performance criticism of New Testament texts; practical theology and spiritual formation for Christian leaders; church history and missions; constructive theology, art and imagination. *Unit head:* Dr. Rollin Ramsaran, Academic Dean, Emmanuel Christian Seminary, 423-461-1524, Fax: 423-926-6198, E-mail: raramsaran@milligan.edu. *Application contact:* Lauren Gullett, Director of Admissions and Recruitment for Emmanuel Christian Seminary, 423-461-1535, Fax: 423-926-6198, E-mail: lwgullett@milligan.edu.
Website: http://ecs.milligan.edu/

Northern Seminary, Graduate and Professional Programs, Lombard, IL 60148-5698. Offers Biblical studies (M Div); Christian community development (MA, D Min); Christian ministry (MACM); contextual theology (D Min); missional church ministry (M Div); New Testament (M Div, MANT); New Testament context (D Min); Old Testament (M Div); preaching (D Min); theology (M Div); theology and mission (MA); urban leadership (MA); worship (M Div, MAW). *Program availability:* Part-time, evening/weekend. *Faculty:* 6 full-time (1 woman), 33 part-time/adjunct (8 women). *Students:* 208 full-time (62 women); includes 89 minority (73 Black or African American, non-Hispanic/Latino; 6 Asian, non-Hispanic/Latino; 8 Hispanic/Latino; 2 Two or more races, non-Hispanic/Latino), 3 international. Average age 44. *Degree requirements:* For master's, thesis (for some programs); for doctorate, thesis/dissertation. *Entrance requirements:* For master's, writing test, all official transcripts, letter of reference from church, 3 letters of reference, autobiographical statement (400 words or more); for doctorate, M Div, 3 years in the ministry post-M Div, 3 letters of reference. Additional exam requirements/recommendations for international students: Required—TOEFL (minimum score 550 paper-based). *Application deadline:* Applications are processed on a rolling basis. Application fee: $35. Electronic applications accepted. *Expenses: Tuition:* Full-time $14,253; part-time $9627 per credit. *Required fees:* $125 per quarter. *Financial support:* Teaching assistantships with partial tuition reimbursements, Federal Work-Study, and scholarships/grants available. Support available to part-time students. Financial award

application deadline: 9/1; financial award applicants required to submit FAFSA. *Faculty research:* Theology and mission, worship studies, church history, evangelism, Christian ministry, urban leadership, New Testament. *Unit head:* Dr. William Shiell, President, 630-620-2101, Fax: 630-620-2190. *Application contact:* Greg Armstrong, Director of Admissions, 630-620-2175, Fax: 630-620-2190, E-mail: admissions@seminary.edu.

Northwest Nazarene University, Program in Religion, Nampa, ID 83686-5897. Offers missional leadership (M Div, MA); pastoral ministry (MA); spiritual formation (M Div, MA); youth, children, and family ministry (M Div, MA). *Program availability:* Part-time, online only, 100% online. *Students:* Average age 39. 37 applicants, 76% accepted, 24 enrolled. In 2017, 40 master's awarded. *Entrance requirements:* For master's, minimum GPA of 2.5; 8 semester or 12 quarter credits of Bible, theology and/or Western philosophy. Additional exam requirements/recommendations for international students: Required—TOEFL (minimum score 85 iBT). *Application deadline:* For fall admission, 7/31 for domestic students, 7/1 for international students; for spring admission, 2/1 for domestic students, 1/5 for international students. Applications are processed on a rolling basis. Application fee: $50. Electronic applications accepted. *Expenses:* Contact institution. *Financial support:* In 2017–18, 3 students received support. Scholarships/grants available. *Unit head:* Dr. Jay Akkerman, Director, Graduate Studies, 208-467-8437, Fax: 208-467-8252. *Application contact:* Vicki Funk, Program Coordinator, 208-467-8432, Fax: 208-467-8252, E-mail: vlfunk@nnu.edu.
Website: http://www.nnu.edu/ministry/

Northwest University, College of Ministry, Kirkland, WA 98033. Offers ministry (MIM); missional leadership (MA); theology and culture (MA). *Program availability:* Part-time, evening/weekend, online learning. *Degree requirements:* For master's, comprehensive exam (for some programs), thesis (for some programs). *Entrance requirements:* Additional exam requirements/recommendations for international students: Required—TOEFL (minimum score 550 paper-based; 75 iBT). Electronic applications accepted.

Nyack College, Alliance Theological Seminary, Nyack, NY 10960. Offers Biblical literature (MA), including New Testament, Old Testament; Biblical studies (MA); Christian ministry (MPS); intercultural studies (MA); ministry (D Min), including Christian leadership in the global context; theology and missions (M Div); urban ministry (MPS). *Program availability:* Part-time, evening/weekend, 100% online, blended/hybrid learning. *Students:* 265 full-time (107 women), 356 part-time (162 women); includes 490 minority (161 Black or African American, non-Hispanic/Latino; 2 American Indian or Alaska Native, non-Hispanic/Latino; 123 Asian, non-Hispanic/Latino; 198 Hispanic/Latino; 6 Two or more races, non-Hispanic/Latino), 37 international. Average age 42. In 2017, 100 master's, 23 doctorates awarded. *Degree requirements:* For master's, comprehensive exam (for some programs), thesis optional, internship; for doctorate, thesis/dissertation. *Entrance requirements:* For master's, transcripts, Christian experience statement, recommendations; for doctorate, transcripts, documented three years of ministry experience subsequent to 1st graduate theological degree, reference letters, formal academic paper. Additional exam requirements/recommendations for international students: Required—TOEFL (minimum score 550 paper-based; 80 iBT). *Application deadline:* Applications are processed on a rolling basis. Application fee: $30. Electronic applications accepted. *Expenses:* $585 per credit (master's-level); $22,060 for total program (for D Min). *Financial support:* Career-related internships or fieldwork, Federal Work-Study, and scholarships/grants available. Financial award applicants required to submit FAFSA. *Unit head:* Dr. Ronald Walborn, Dean, 845-770-5715, Fax: 845-358-1663. *Application contact:* Jennifer Reimer, Associate Director of Admissions, 845-770-5709, E-mail: admissions.grad@nyack.edu.
Website: http://www.nyack.edu/ats

Oral Roberts University, School of Theology and Missions, Tulsa, OK 74171. Offers biblical literature (MA), including advanced languages, Judaic-Christian studies; church ministries and leadership (D Min); clinical pastoral education (M Div); missions (MA); pastoral care and chaplaincy (M Div, D Min); practical theology (MA), including teaching ministries, urban ministries; professional counseling (MA), including addiction studies, marriage and family therapy; theological/historical studies (MA). *Accreditation:* ATS. *Program availability:* Part-time, online learning. *Faculty:* 17 full-time (2 women). *Students:* 371 full-time (156 women), 110 part-time (65 women); includes 177 minority (127 Black or African American, non-Hispanic/Latino; 5 American Indian or Alaska Native, non-Hispanic/Latino; 20 Asian, non-Hispanic/Latino; 25 Hispanic/Latino), 82 international. Average age 36. 159 applicants, 95% accepted, 124 enrolled. In 2017, 52 master's, 10 doctorates awarded. *Degree requirements:* For master's, thesis (for some programs), practicum/internship; for doctorate, thesis/dissertation, applied research project. *Entrance requirements:* For master's, GRE General Test or MAT (waived for those with undergraduate degree from regionally accredited institution and 3.0 or higher GPA), minimum GPA of 2.5 (professional) or 3.0 (academic); for doctorate, M Div, minimum GPA of 3.0, 3 years of full-time ministry experience. Additional exam requirements/recommendations for international students: Recommended—TOEFL (minimum score 550 paper-based; 79 iBT), IELTS (minimum score 7). *Application deadline:* Applications are processed on a rolling basis. Application fee: $35. Electronic applications accepted. Application fee is waived when completed online. *Financial support:* Fellowships and scholarships/grants available. Financial award application deadline: 6/1. *Unit head:* Dr. Bill Buker, Chair, 918-495-6493, E-mail: bbuker@oru.edu. *Application contact:* Michael Thomas, Enrollment Counselor, 918-495-6618, E-mail: mthomas@oru.edu.
Website: http://www.gradtheology.oru.edu/

Phillips Theological Seminary, Programs in Theology, Tulsa, OK 74116. Offers administration of church agencies (M Div); campus ministry (M Div); church-related social work (M Div); college and seminary teaching (M Div); global mission work (M Div); institutional chaplaincy (M Div); ministerial vocations in Christian education (M Div); ministry (D Min), including parish ministry, pastoral counseling, practices of ministry; ministry and culture (MAMC), including Christian education, congregational leadership, history and practice of Christian spirituality, theology, ethics, and culture; ministry of music (M Div); pastoral care and counseling (M Div); pastoral ministry (M Div); theological studies (MTS). *Accreditation:* ATS. *Program availability:* Part-time, online learning. *Degree requirements:* For master's, thesis (for some programs); for doctorate, thesis/dissertation. *Entrance requirements:* For master's, minimum GPA of 2.5; for doctorate, M Div, minimum GPA of 3.0. *Faculty research:* Biblical studies, historical studies, theology and culture, practical theology, theology and film.

Providence University College & Theological Seminary, Theological Seminary, Otterburne, MB R0A 1G0, Canada. Offers children's ministry (Certificate); Christian studies (MA, Certificate); counseling (MA); cross-cultural discipleship (Certificate); divinity (M Div); educational studies (MA), including counseling psychology, educational ministries, student development, teaching English to speakers of other languages, training teachers of English to speakers of other languages; global studies (MA); lay counseling (Diploma); ministry (D Min); teaching English to speakers of other languages (Certificate); theological studies (MA); training teacher of English to speakers of other languages (Certificate); youth ministry (Certificate). *Accreditation:* ATS. *Program availability:* Part-time. *Degree requirements:* For master's, variable foreign language requirement, thesis (for some programs); for doctorate, thesis/dissertation. *Entrance requirements:* Additional exam requirements/recommendations for international students: Recommended—TOEFL (minimum score 550 paper-based). *Faculty research:* Studies in Isaiah, theology of sin.

Reformed Theological Seminary–Jackson Campus, Graduate and Professional Programs, Jackson, MS 39209-3004. Offers Bible, theology, and missions (Certificate); Biblical exegesis (M Div); biblical studies (MA); Christian education (MA); counseling (M Div); marriage and family therapy (MA); ministry (D Min); missions (M Div, MA, D Min); theological studies (MA). *Accreditation:* AAMFT/COAMFTE (one or more programs are accredited); ATS (one or more programs are accredited). *Degree requirements:* For master's, thesis (for some programs), fieldwork; for doctorate, 2 foreign languages, thesis/dissertation. *Entrance requirements:* For master's, minimum GPA of 2.6; for doctorate, minimum GPA of 3.0. Additional exam requirements/recommendations for international students: Required—TOEFL.

Regent University, Graduate School, School of Divinity, Virginia Beach, VA 23464-9800. Offers Christian spirituality and formation (MA); divinity (M Div), including Biblical studies (M Div, MTS, Th M, PhD), chaplain ministry, Christian theology (M Div, MTS, Th M, PhD), church and ministry (M Div, MA), history of Christianity (M Div, MTS, Th M, PhD), inter-cultural studies (M Div, MA), interdisciplinary studies (M Div, MA, MTS), marketplace ministry (M Div, MA), missional discipleship, practical healing ministry (M Div, MA), worship and media (M Div, MA); leadership and renewal (D Min), including Christian leadership and renewal, clinical pastoral education, community transformation, military ministry, ministry leadership coaching; practical theology (MA), including church and ministry (M Div, MA), cosmogony, inter-cultural studies (M Div, MA), interdisciplinary studies (M Div, MA, MTS), marketplace ministry (M Div, MA), practical healing ministry (M Div, MA), worship and media (M Div, MA); renewal theology (PhD), including Biblical studies (M Div, MTS, Th M, PhD), Christian theology (M Div, MTS, Th M, PhD), history of Christianity (M Div, MTS, Th M, PhD), practical theology; theological studies (MTS), including Biblical studies (M Div, MTS, Th M, PhD), Christian theology (M Div, MTS, Th M, PhD), history of Christianity (M Div, MTS, Th M, PhD), interdisciplinary studies (M Div, MA, MTS); theology (Th M), including Biblical studies (M Div, MTS, Th M, PhD), Christian theology (M Div, MTS, Th M, PhD), history of Christianity (M Div, MTS, Th M, PhD). *Accreditation:* ACIPE; ATS. *Program availability:* Part-time, evening/weekend, 100% online, blended/hybrid learning. *Faculty:* 17 full-time (3 women), 66 part-time/adjunct (9 women). *Students:* 146 full-time (54 women), 917 part-time (404 women); includes 563 minority (470 Black or African American, non-Hispanic/Latino; 1 American Indian or Alaska Native, non-Hispanic/Latino; 17 Asian, non-Hispanic/Latino; 56 Hispanic/Latino; 1 Native Hawaiian or other Pacific Islander, non-Hispanic/Latino; 18 Two or more races, non-Hispanic/Latino), 27 international. Average age 44. 1,321 applicants, 39% accepted, 295 enrolled. In 2017, 146 master's, 25 doctorates awarded. *Degree requirements:* For master's, comprehensive exam, thesis or alternative, internship; for doctorate, thesis/dissertation or alternative. *Entrance requirements:* For master's, minimum undergraduate GPA of 2.75, writing sample, personal goal statement, college transcripts; for doctorate, GRE, minimum graduate GPA of 3.5 (PhD), 3.0 (D Min); clergy recommendations; writing sample; transcripts; resume; interview. Additional exam requirements/recommendations for international students: Required—TOEFL (minimum score 577 paper-based). *Application deadline:* For fall admission, 5/1 priority date for domestic students. Applications are processed on a rolling basis. Application fee: $50. Electronic applications accepted. *Expenses:* $495 per credit (master's); $595 per credit (D Min); $650 per credit (PhD); $300 per semester technology fee. *Financial support:* In 2017–18, 721 students received support. Career-related internships or fieldwork, scholarships/grants, and unspecified assistantships available. Support available to part-time students. *Faculty research:* Greek and Hebrew, theology, spiritual formation, global missions and world Christianity, women in ministry leadership. *Unit head:* Dr. Cornelius Bekker, Dean, 757-352-4401, Fax: 757-352-4597, E-mail: clbekker@regent.edu. *Application contact:* Heidi Cece, Assistant Vice President of Enrollment Management, 800-373-5504, Fax: 757-352-4381, E-mail: admissions@regent.edu.
Website: https://www.regent.edu/school-of-divinity/

Rochester College, Center for Missional Leadership, Rochester Hills, MI 48307-2764. Offers MRE.

Saint Paul University, Faculty of Human Sciences, Program in Mission and Interreligious Studies, Ottawa, ON K1S 1C4, Canada. Offers MA. *Degree requirements:* For master's, one foreign language, thesis. *Entrance requirements:* For master's, honors BA in mission, minimum B average. *Faculty research:* Theology of mission; mission and sociology; history of mission; faith, religion, and culture; world religions; practice of mission; religious anthropology; sociocultural anthropology.

Simpson University, A.W. Tozer Theological Seminary, Redding, CA 96003-8606. Offers ministry leadership (MA). *Program availability:* Part-time, evening/weekend, 100% online, blended/hybrid learning. *Entrance requirements:* For master's, GRE General Test (if undergraduate GPA less than 2.5), Christian statement, one spiritual recommendation, one academic recommendation. Additional exam requirements/recommendations for international students: Required—TOEFL (minimum score 583 paper-based; 94 iBT). Electronic applications accepted. *Expenses:* Contact institution.

Southeastern Baptist Theological Seminary, Graduate and Professional Programs, Wake Forest, NC 27587. Offers advanced biblical studies (M Div); Christian education (M Div, MACE); Christian ethics (PhD); Christian ministry (M Div); Christian planting (M Div); church music (MACM); counseling (MACO); evangelism (PhD); language (M Div); ministry (D Min); New Testament (PhD); Old Testament (PhD); philosophy (PhD); theology (Th M, PhD); women's studies (M Div). *Accreditation:* ACIPE; ATS (one or more programs are accredited). *Degree requirements:* For master's, thesis (for some programs), oral exam; for doctorate, thesis/dissertation, fieldwork. *Entrance requirements:* For master's, Cooperative English Test, minimum GPA of 2.0, M Div or equivalent (Th M); for doctorate, GRE General Test or MAT, Cooperative English Test, M Div or equivalent, 3 years of professional experience.

Southern Adventist University, School of Religion, Collegedale, TN 37315-0370. Offers Biblical and theological studies (MA); church leadership and management (M Min); church ministry and homiletics (M Min); evangelism and world mission (M Min); religious studies (MA). *Program availability:* Part-time. *Degree requirements:* For master's, comprehensive exam, thesis (for some programs). *Entrance requirements:* For master's, GRE. Additional exam requirements/recommendations for international students: Required—TOEFL (minimum score 600 paper-based). *Application deadline:* For spring admission, 5/1 priority date for domestic students, 4/30 for international students. Applications are processed on a rolling basis. Application fee: $40. *Expenses: Tuition:* Full-time $11,430; part-time $635 per credit hour. Tuition and fees vary according to degree level and program. *Financial support:* Tuition waivers (full) available. Support available to part-time students. Financial award application deadline: 4/1; financial award applicants required to submit FAFSA. *Faculty research:* Biblical archaeology. *Unit head:* Dr. Greg A. King, Dean, 423-236-2975, Fax: 423-236-1976, E-mail: gking@southern.edu. *Application contact:* Susan L. Brown, Administrative Assistant, 423-236-2033, Fax: 423-236-1977, E-mail: sbrown@southern.edu.
Website: https://www.southern.edu/academics/academic-sites/religion/

The Southern Baptist Theological Seminary, Billy Graham School of Missions, Evangelism and Ministry, Louisville, KY 40280-0004. Offers ministry (D Min); missiology

(MA, D Miss); missions and evangelism (M Div, Th M, PhD); theological studies (MA). *Accreditation:* ATS. *Program availability:* Part-time, evening/weekend, online learning. *Degree requirements:* For master's, 2 foreign languages; for doctorate, 4 foreign languages, thesis/dissertation. *Entrance requirements:* For doctorate, GRE General Test, MAT, M Div. Additional exam requirements/recommendations for international students: Required—TOEFL, TWE. *Faculty research:* Assimilation of church congregants, effective methodologies of evangelism, expectations of church members, spiritual warfare literature, formative church discipline.

Southern Evangelical Seminary, Graduate Programs, Matthews, NC 28105. Offers apologetics (MA, D Min, Certificate); Christian education (MA); church ministry (MA, Certificate); divinity (Certificate), including apologetics (M Div, Certificate); Islamic studies (MA, Certificate); Jewish studies (MA); philosophy (MA); philosophy of religion (PhD); religion (MA); theology (M Div), including apologetics (M Div, Certificate), Biblical studies; youth ministry (MA). *Program availability:* Part-time, evening/weekend, online learning. *Degree requirements:* For master's, thesis (for some programs); for doctorate, 2 foreign languages, comprehensive exam (for some programs), thesis/dissertation. *Entrance requirements:* Additional exam requirements/recommendations for international students: Required—TOEFL (minimum score 600 paper-based).

Southwestern Assemblies of God University, Thomas F. Harrison School of Graduate Studies, Program in Theological Studies, Waxahachie, TX 75165-5735. Offers Bible and theology (MS); Biblical studies (M Div); counseling (M Div); cross cultural missions (M Div); practical theology (M Div); theological studies (M Div). *Program availability:* Online learning. *Degree requirements:* For master's, comprehensive written and oral exams. *Entrance requirements:* For master's, GRE General Test, minimum GPA of 2.5. Electronic applications accepted.

Southwestern Baptist Theological Seminary, Roy Fish School of Evangelism and Missions, Fort Worth, TX 76122-0000. Offers cross-cultural missions (MTS); evangelism (M Div); evangelism and missions (D Min); international church planting (M Div); Islamic studies (M Div, MA Islamic); missiology (MA Miss); missions (M Div); North American church planting (M Div); North American evangelism and international missions (D Min); theology (Th M); world Christian studies (PhD).

Southwestern Christian University, Program in Ministry, Bethany, OK 73008-0340. Offers church planting (M Min); church revitalization and renewal (M Min); intercultural studies (M Min); leadership (M Min); life coaching (M Min); pastoral ministries (M Min); work place ministries (M Min). *Program availability:* Part-time. *Degree requirements:* For master's, thesis. *Entrance requirements:* For master's, minimum GPA of 2.5. Additional exam requirements/recommendations for international students: Required—TOEFL (minimum score 500 paper-based). Electronic applications accepted.

Taylor College and Seminary, Graduate and Professional Programs, Edmonton, AB T6J 4T3, Canada. Offers Christian studies (Diploma); intercultural studies (MA, Diploma), including intercultural studies (Diploma), TESOL; theology (M Div, MTS). *Accreditation:* ATS. *Program availability:* Part-time, online learning. *Degree requirements:* For master's, thesis optional. *Entrance requirements:* Additional exam requirements/recommendations for international students: Required—TOEFL (minimum score 550 paper-based; 80 iBT), IELTS (minimum score 6.5). *Faculty research:* Biblical studies, administration and organization, world religions, ethics, missiology.

Theological University of the Caribbean, Graduate Programs, Saint Just, PR 00978-0901. Offers childhood and adolescent education (MA); counseling and pastoral care (MA); ministry (D Min); missions (MA).

Trinity Bible College and Graduate School, Graduate School, Ellendale, ND 58436. Offers global theology (MA); missional leadership (MA); rural ministries (MA).

Trinity International University, Trinity Evangelical Divinity School, Deerfield, IL 60015-1284. Offers academic ministry (M Div); Biblical and Near Eastern archaeology and languages (MA); chaplaincy and ministry care (MA); Christian studies (Certificate); church and parachurch ministry (M Div); church history (MA, Th M); counseling (Th M); educational ministries (MA); educational ministry (Th M); educational studies (PhD); intercultural studies (MA, PhD); leadership and management (D Min); mental health counseling (MA); military chaplaincy (D Min); ministry (MA); missions (Th M); missions and evangelism (D Min); New Testament (MA, Th M); Old Testament (Th M); Old Testament and Semitic languages (MA); pastoral ministry and care (D Min); pastoral theology (Th M); preaching and teaching (D Min); spiritual formation and education (D Min); systematic theology (MA, Th M); theological studies (MA, PhD); urban ministry (MA). *Program availability:* Part-time, online learning. *Degree requirements:* For master's, comprehensive exam, thesis, fieldwork; for doctorate, comprehensive exam (for some programs), thesis/dissertation; for Certificate, comprehensive exam, integrative papers. *Entrance requirements:* For master's, GRE, MAT, minimum cumulative undergraduate GPA of 3.0; for doctorate, GRE, minimum cumulative graduate GPA of 3.2; for Certificate, GRE, MAT, minimum undergraduate GPA of 2.5. Additional exam requirements/recommendations for international students: Required—TOEFL (minimum score 580 paper-based), TWE (minimum score 4). Electronic applications accepted.

Trinity Lutheran Seminary, Graduate and Professional Programs, Columbus, OH 43209-2334. Offers African American studies (MTS); Biblical studies (MTS, STM); Christian education (MA); Christian spirituality (STM); church in the world (MTS); church music (MA); divinity (M Div); general theological studies (MTS); mission and evangelism (STM); pastoral leadership and practice (STM); youth and family ministry (MA); MSN/MTS; MTS/JD. *Accreditation:* ACIPE; ATS. *Program availability:* Part-time. *Degree requirements:* For master's, variable foreign language requirement, comprehensive exam (for some programs), thesis (for some programs), field experience (for some programs). *Entrance requirements:* For master's, BA or equivalent (for MA, M Div, MTS); M Div, MTS, or equivalent (for STM); audition (for MACM). Additional exam requirements/recommendations for international students: Required—TOEFL. Electronic applications accepted. *Expenses:* Contact institution.

Trinity School for Ministry, Graduate Programs, Ambridge, PA 15003-2397. Offers Anglican studies (Diploma); basic Christian studies (Diploma); divinity (M Div); ministry (D Min); mission and evangelism (MAME, Diploma); religion (MAR); youth ministry (Diploma). *Program availability:* Part-time. *Degree requirements:* For master's, thesis optional; for doctorate, thesis/dissertation. *Entrance requirements:* Additional exam requirements/recommendations for international students: Required—TOEFL. *Faculty research:* Pauline Epistles, contemporary theology, history of Anglican liturgy, book of Ruth, biblical theology.

Tyndale University College & Seminary, Graduate Programs, Toronto, ON M2M 3S4, Canada. Offers Biblical studies (M Div); Christian foundations (MTS); Christian studies (Diploma); counseling (M Div); educational ministry (M Div); missions (M Div, Diploma); pastoral and Chinese ministry (M Div); pastoral ministry (M Div); Pentecostal studies (MTS); spiritual formation (M Div, Diploma); theological studies (M Div); theology (Th M); worship and liturgy (M Div, MTS); youth and family ministry (M Div). *Accreditation:* ATS. *Program availability:* Part-time, online learning. *Entrance requirements:* For master's and Diploma, minimum C+ average in undergraduate course work. Additional exam requirements/recommendations for international students: Required—TOEFL (minimum score 570 paper-based), TWE (minimum score 5). Electronic applications accepted. *Faculty research:* Canadian church history, Chinese church history, Old Testament, counseling ministries (narrative therapy), world religions.

University of South Africa, College of Human Sciences, Pretoria, South Africa. Offers adult education (M Ed); African languages (MA, PhD); African politics (MA, PhD); Afrikaans (MA, PhD); ancient history (MA, PhD); ancient Near Eastern studies (MA, PhD); anthropology (MA, PhD); applied linguistics (MA); Arabic (MA, PhD); archaeology (MA); art history (MA); Biblical archaeology (MA); Biblical studies (M Th, D Th, PhD); Christian spirituality (M Th, D Th); church history (M Th, D Th); classical studies (MA, PhD); clinical psychology (MA); communication (MA, PhD); comparative education (M Ed, Ed D); consulting psychology (D Admin, D Com, PhD); curriculum studies (M Ed, Ed D); development studies (M Admin, MA, D Admin, PhD); didactics (M Ed, Ed D); education (M Tech); education management (M Ed, Ed D); educational psychology (M Ed); English (MA); environmental education (M Ed); French (MA, PhD); German (MA, PhD); Greek (MA); guidance and counseling (M Ed); health studies (MA, PhD), including health sciences education (MA), health services management (MA), medical and surgical nursing science (critical care general) (MA), midwifery and neonatal nursing science (MA), trauma and emergency care (MA); history (MA, PhD); history of education (Ed D); inclusive education (M Ed, Ed D); information and communications technology policy and regulation (MA); information science (MA, MIS, PhD); international politics (MA, PhD); Islamic studies (MA, PhD); Italian (MA, PhD); Judaica (MA, PhD); linguistics (MA, PhD); mathematical education (M Ed); mathematics education (MA); missiology (M Th, D Th); modern Hebrew (MA, PhD); musicology (MA, MMus, D Mus, PhD); natural science education (M Ed); New Testament (M Th, D Th); Old Testament (D Th); pastoral therapy (M Th, D Th); philosophy (MA); philosophy of education (M Ed, Ed D); politics (MA, PhD); Portuguese (MA, PhD); practical theology (M Th, D Th); psychology (MA, MS, PhD); psychology of education (M Ed, Ed D); public health (MA); religious studies (MA, D Th, PhD); Romance languages (MA); Russian (MA, PhD); Semitic languages (MA, PhD); social behavior studies in HIV/AIDS (MA); social science (mental health) (MA); social science in development studies (MA); social science in psychology (MA); social science in social work (MA); social science in sociology (MA); social work (MSW, DSW, PhD); socio-education (M Ed, Ed D); sociolinguistics (MA); sociology (MA, PhD); Spanish (MA, PhD); systematic theology (M Th, D Th); TESOL (teaching English to speakers of other languages) (MA); theological ethics (M Th, D Th); theory of literature (MA, PhD); urban ministries (D Th); urban ministry (M Th).

Villanova University, Villanova School of Business, Master of Science in Church Management Program, Villanova, PA 19085. Offers MSCM. *Program availability:* Part-time-only, online only, 100% online, residence week at beginning of program. *Faculty:* 68 full-time (22 women), 65 part-time/adjunct (11 women). In 2017, 38 master's awarded. *Degree requirements:* For master's, minimum GPA of 3.0. *Entrance requirements:* For master's, current resume, official academic transcripts, two letters of recommendation, personal essay. Additional exam requirements/recommendations for international students: Required—TOEFL (minimum score 550 paper-based; 100 iBT). *Application deadline:* For fall admission, 5/10 for domestic and international students. Applications are processed on a rolling basis. Application fee: $50. Electronic applications accepted. *Expenses:* Contact institution. *Financial support:* Scholarships/grants available. Support available to part-time students. Financial award application deadline: 6/30; financial award applicants required to submit FAFSA. *Faculty research:* Business analytics; creativity, innovation and entrepreneurship; global leadership; real estate; church management; business ethics; marketing and consumer insights. *Unit head:* Dr. Matt Manion, Faculty Director, 610-519-6430, E-mail: matthew.manion@villanova.edu. *Application contact:* James Gallo, Staff Director, 610-519-6015, E-mail: james.gallo@villanova.edu.
Website: http://www.villanova.edu/business/graduate/church/

Wesley Biblical Seminary, Graduate Programs, Jackson, MS 39206. Offers apologetics (MA); Biblical languages (M Div); Biblical literature (MA); Christian studies (MA); context and mission (M Div); honors research (M Div); interpretation (M Div); ministry (M Div); spiritual formation (M Div); teaching (M Div); theology (MA). *Accreditation:* ATS. *Program availability:* Part-time. *Degree requirements:* For master's, thesis. *Entrance requirements:* Additional exam requirements/recommendations for international students: Required—TOEFL. Electronic applications accepted. *Faculty research:* Patristics, missiology, culture, hermeneutics.

Westminster Theological Seminary, Graduate and Professional Programs, Philadelphia, PA 19118. Offers apologetics (Th M); Biblical and urban studies (Certificate); Biblical counseling (MA); biblical studies (MAR); Christian studies (Certificate); church history (Th M); counseling (M Div); general studies (M Div, MAR); hermeneutics and Bible interpretations (PhD); historical and theological studies (PhD); historical theology (Th M); New Testament (Th M); Old Testament (Th M); pastoral counseling (D Min); pastoral ministry (M Div, D Min); systematic theology (Th M); theological studies (MAR); urban missions (M Div, MA, MAR, D Min). *Accreditation:* ATS. *Program availability:* Part-time. Terminal master's awarded for partial completion of doctoral program. *Degree requirements:* For master's, thesis (for some programs); for doctorate, 4 foreign languages, comprehensive exam (for some programs), thesis/dissertation. *Entrance requirements:* For doctorate, GRE General Test. Additional exam requirements/recommendations for international students: Required—TOEFL, TWE.

Wheaton College, Graduate School, Department of Evangelism, Wheaton, IL 60187-5593. Offers evangelism and leadership (MA); missional church movements (MA). *Program availability:* Part-time. *Faculty:* 1 full-time (0 women). *Students:* 2 full-time (0 women), 45 part-time (10 women); includes 7 minority (3 Black or African American, non-Hispanic/Latino; 1 American Indian or Alaska Native, non-Hispanic/Latino; 2 Asian, non-Hispanic/Latino; 1 Hispanic/Latino), 22 international. Average age 40. 12 applicants, 75% accepted, 6 enrolled. In 2017, 8 master's awarded. *Degree requirements:* For master's, thesis or alternative. *Entrance requirements:* For master's, GRE or MAT. Additional exam requirements/recommendations for international students: Required—TOEFL (minimum score 550 paper-based; 80 iBT), IELTS (minimum score 6.5). *Application deadline:* For fall admission, 3/1 priority date for domestic students, 1/1 for international students; for spring admission, 11/1 for domestic students. Applications are processed on a rolling basis. Application fee: $30. Electronic applications accepted. *Expenses: Tuition:* Full-time $19,800; part-time $825 per credit hour. Tuition and fees vary according to degree level and program. *Financial support:* Career-related internships or fieldwork, Federal Work-Study, scholarships/grants, and unspecified assistantships available. Financial award application deadline: 3/1; financial award applicants required to submit FAFSA. *Unit head:* Dr. Ed Stetzer, Chair, 630-752-5806, E-mail: evangelism.leadership@wheaton.edu. *Application contact:* Director of Graduate Admissions, 630-752-5195, Fax: 630-752-7047, E-mail: graduate.admissions@wheaton.edu.
Website: https://www.wheaton.edu/graduate-school/degrees/ma-in-evangelism-and-leadership/

Wheaton College, Graduate School, Department of Intercultural Studies, Wheaton, IL 60187-5593. Offers global engagement (Certificate); intercultural studies (MA); intercultural studies/teaching English as a second language (MA); teaching English as a second language (Certificate). *Program availability:* Part-time. *Faculty:* 1 full-time (0 women), 6 part-time/adjunct (all women). *Students:* 18 full-time (13 women), 32 part-time (23 women); includes 8 minority (2 Black or African American, non-Hispanic/Latino;

3 Asian, non-Hispanic/Latino; 2 Hispanic/Latino; 1 Two or more races, non-Hispanic/Latino), 11 international. Average age 33. 32 applicants, 97% accepted, 12 enrolled. In 2017, 20 master's awarded. *Degree requirements:* For master's, comprehensive exam, thesis or alternative. *Entrance requirements:* For master's, GRE General Test, MAT. Additional exam requirements/recommendations for international students: Required—TOEFL (minimum score 550 paper-based; 80 iBT), IELTS (minimum score 6.5). *Application deadline:* For fall admission, 5/1 for domestic students, 1/1 for international students; for spring admission, 11/1 for domestic students. Applications are processed on a rolling basis. Application fee: $30. Electronic applications accepted. *Expenses: Tuition:* Full-time $19,800; part-time $825 per credit hour. Tuition and fees vary according to degree level and program. *Financial support:* Career-related internships or fieldwork, scholarships/grants, and unspecified assistantships available. Financial award application deadline: 3/1; financial award applicants required to submit FAFSA. *Unit head:* Dr. Robert Gallagher, Chair, 630-752-5948, E-mail: intercultural.studies@wheaton.edu. *Application contact:* Director of Graduate Admissions, 630-752-5195, Fax: 630-752-5047, E-mail: graduate.admissions@wheaton.edu.
Website: https://www.wheaton.edu/graduate-school/degrees/ma-in-intercultural-studies/

Whitworth University, Graduate Studies in Theology, Spokane, WA 99251-0001. Offers Christian ministry (MA); mission and culture (MA); theology (MA). *Program availability:* Part-time, evening/weekend. *Faculty:* 19. *Students:* 47 part-time (21 women); includes 6 minority (2 Black or African American, non-Hispanic/Latino; 1 American Indian or Alaska Native, non-Hispanic/Latino; 3 Hispanic/Latino). Average age 35. *Application deadline:* For fall admission, 8/7 for domestic students; for spring admission, 1/1 for domestic students; for summer admission, 4/15 for domestic students. Applications are processed on a rolling basis. Electronic applications accepted. *Financial support:* In 2017–18, 17 students received support. Research assistantships, career-related internships or fieldwork, scholarships/grants, and unspecified assistantships available. Financial award application deadline: 8/7; financial award applicants required to submit FAFSA. *Unit head:* Dr. Jeremy Wynne, Director, 509-777-3222, E-mail: graduateandcsadmissions@whitworth.edu. *Application contact:* Hannah Fischer, Graduate Admissions, 509-777-3222, E-mail: graduateandcsadmissions@whitworth.edu.
Website: http://www.whitworth.edu/cms/academics/graduate-studies-in-theology/

Pastoral Ministry and Counseling

Abilene Christian University, Graduate Programs, College of Biblical Studies, Graduate School of Theology, Program in Divinity, Abilene, TX 79699. Offers ministry (M Div); missions (M Div). *Accreditation:* ATS. *Program availability:* Part-time, evening/weekend, blended/hybrid learning. *Students:* 22 full-time (4 women), 45 part-time (9 women); includes 8 minority (all Black or African American, non-Hispanic/Latino), 6 international. 26 applicants, 54% accepted, 9 enrolled. In 2017, 3 master's awarded. *Degree requirements:* For master's, comprehensive exam, e-portfolio review. *Entrance requirements:* Additional exam requirements/recommendations for international students: Required—TOEFL (minimum score 80 iBT), IELTS (minimum score 6), PTE. *Application deadline:* For fall admission, 8/11 for domestic students; for spring admission, 11/1 for domestic students. Applications are processed on a rolling basis. Application fee: $50. Electronic applications accepted. *Expenses:* $618 per hour. *Financial support:* In 2017–18, 14 students received support. Scholarships/grants available. Financial award application deadline: 4/1; financial award applicants required to submit FAFSA. *Unit head:* Dr. Kelli Gibson, Graduate Advisor, 325-674-3709, Fax: 325-674-6716, E-mail: kelli.gibson@acu.edu. *Application contact:* Graduate Admissions, 325-674-6911, Fax: 325-674-6717, E-mail: gradinfo@acu.edu.
Website: http://www.acu.edu/graduate/academics/divinity.html

Abilene Christian University, Graduate Programs, College of Biblical Studies, Graduate School of Theology, Program in Ministry, Abilene, TX 79699. Offers Christian spiritual formation (D Min); leadership for missional renewal (D Min); preaching for community transformation (D Min). *Program availability:* Part-time. *Students:* 21 part-time (3 women); includes 3 minority (1 Black or African American, non-Hispanic/Latino; 1 Asian, non-Hispanic/Latino; 1 Hispanic/Latino). 11 applicants, 91% accepted, 7 enrolled. In 2017, 3 doctorates awarded. *Degree requirements:* For doctorate, one foreign language, comprehensive exam, thesis/dissertation. *Entrance requirements:* Additional exam requirements/recommendations for international students: Required—TOEFL (minimum score 80 iBT), IELTS (minimum score 6), PTE. *Application deadline:* For summer admission, 1/31 for domestic students. Applications are processed on a rolling basis. Application fee: $50. *Expenses:* $363 per hour. *Financial support:* In 2017–18, 15 students received support. Scholarships/grants available. Financial award application deadline: 4/1; financial award applicants required to submit FAFSA. *Faculty research:* Church growth, ministry evaluation, leadership. *Unit head:* Dr. Carson Reed, Graduate Director, 325-674-3732, Fax: 325-674-6716, E-mail: carson.reed@acu.edu. *Application contact:* Graduate Admissions, 325-674-6911, Fax: 325-674-6717, E-mail: gradinfo@acu.edu.
Website: http://www.acu.edu/graduate/academics/doctor-of-ministry.html

Abilene Christian University, Graduate Programs, College of Biblical Studies, Graduate School of Theology, Programs in Christian Ministry, Abilene, TX 79699. Offers MACM. *Program availability:* Part-time, online learning. *Students:* 6 full-time (1 woman), 39 part-time (8 women); includes 11 minority (8 Black or African American, non-Hispanic/Latino; 1 American Indian or Alaska Native, non-Hispanic/Latino; 2 Hispanic/Latino). 36 applicants, 31% accepted, 5 enrolled. In 2017, 14 master's awarded. *Degree requirements:* For master's, comprehensive exam, thesis. *Entrance requirements:* Additional exam requirements/recommendations for international students: Required—TOEFL (minimum score 80 iBT), IELTS (minimum score 6), PTE. *Application deadline:* For fall admission, 8/11 for domestic students; for spring admission, 11/1 for domestic students. Applications are processed on a rolling basis. Application fee: $50. Electronic applications accepted. *Expenses:* $637 per hour. *Financial support:* In 2017–18, 1 student received support. Scholarships/grants available. Financial award application deadline: 4/1; financial award applicants required to submit FAFSA. *Faculty research:* Program innovation, instruments for educational evaluation. *Unit head:* Dr. Melinda Thompson, Graduate Advisor, 325-674-3706, Fax: 325-674-6180, E-mail: melinda.thompson@acu.edu. *Application contact:* Graduate Admissions, 325-674-6911, Fax: 325-674-6717, E-mail: gradinfo@acu.edu.
Website: http://www.acu.edu/graduate/academics/christian-ministry.html

Acadia University, Divinity College, Wolfville, NS B4P 2R6, Canada. Offers divinity (M Div); ministry (D Min); theology (MA), including chaplaincy and spiritual care, Christian history, discipleship, evangelism and mission, indigenous community development, leadership and spiritual formation, New Testament, next generation ministry, Old Testament, pastoral care and counseling, prison chaplaincy, Second Temple Judaism, theology. *Accreditation:* ATS. *Program availability:* Part-time. *Degree requirements:* For master's, variable foreign language requirement, thesis (for some programs); for doctorate, one foreign language, comprehensive exam, thesis/dissertation. *Entrance requirements:* For doctorate, minimum GPA of 3.0, 3 years' ministry experience. Additional exam requirements/recommendations for international students: Required—TOEFL. *Application deadline:* For fall admission, 6/30 priority date for domestic students, 4/1 priority date for international students; for spring admission, 4/30 priority date for domestic students. Applications are processed on a rolling basis. Application fee: $50. *Expenses:* Contact institution. *Financial support:* Application deadline: 8/12. *Faculty research:* Biblical canon, Jesus, Dead Sea Scrolls, Baptist studies, Old Testament-Septuagint. *Unit head:* Dr. Harry Gardner, President/Dean of Theology, 902-585-2213, Fax: 902-585-2233, E-mail: harry.gardner@acadiau.ca. *Application contact:* Shawna Peverill, Registrar, 902-585-2215, Fax: 902-585-2233, E-mail: shawna.peverill@acadiau.ca.
Website: http://divinity.acadiau.ca/

Ambrose University, Ambrose Seminary, Calgary, AB T3H 0L5, Canada. Offers Biblical/theological studies (MA), including New Testament, Old Testament, theology; Christian studies (MCS, Diploma); intercultural ministries (M Div, MA); leadership (Certificate); leadership and ministry (MA), including chaplaincy, leadership; pastoral ministry (M Div). *Accreditation:* ATS (one or more programs are accredited). *Program availability:* Part-time, blended/hybrid learning. *Degree requirements:* For master's, variable foreign language requirement, thesis (for some programs), internship (for M Div, MA in leadership and ministry, MA in intercultural ministries); thesis (for MA in Biblical/theological studies). *Entrance requirements:* For master's, undergraduate degree from other accredited university or bible college, minimum GPA of 2.0. Additional exam requirements/recommendations for international students: Required—PTE (minimum score 58), TOEFL (minimum score 560 paper-based, 83 iBT) or IELTS (minimum score 6.5). Electronic applications accepted. *Faculty research:* Evangelicalism and sociology, missiological trends, chaplaincy, intertestamental studies, postmodernism.

American Baptist Seminary of the West, Graduate and Professional Programs, Berkeley, CA 94704-3029. Offers community leadership (MA); theology (M Div, MA). MA program in theology offered jointly with Graduate Theological Union. *Accreditation:* ACIPE; ATS (one or more programs are accredited). *Program availability:* Part-time, evening/weekend, online learning. *Entrance requirements:* Additional exam requirements/recommendations for international students: Required—TOEFL (minimum score 550 paper-based). Electronic applications accepted.

Amridge University, Graduate and Professional Programs, Montgomery, AL 36117. Offers Biblical studies (MA, PhD); Christian ministry (MS); family therapy (D Min); human services (MS); leadership and management (MS); marriage and family therapy (M Div, MA, PhD); ministerial leadership (M Div, MS); New Testament studies (MA); Old Testament studies (MA); professional counseling (M Div, MA, PhD); theology (M Div, D Min). *Program availability:* Part-time, evening/weekend, online learning. *Faculty:* 23 full-time (3 women), 9 part-time/adjunct (5 women). *Students:* 105 full-time (55 women), 250 part-time (152 women); includes 217 minority (167 Black or African American, non-Hispanic/Latino; 4 Asian, non-Hispanic/Latino; 42 Hispanic/Latino; 4 Native Hawaiian or other Pacific Islander, non-Hispanic/Latino). Average age 42. 160 applicants, 100% accepted, 110 enrolled. *Degree requirements:* For master's, one foreign language, comprehensive exam (for some programs), thesis (for some programs); for doctorate, one foreign language, comprehensive exam (for some programs), thesis/dissertation (for some programs). *Entrance requirements:* For master's, official transcript showing an earned 4-year BA or BS from regionally- or nationally-accredited institution; for doctorate, official transcript showing earned graduate degree from regionally- or nationally-accredited institution; writing sample (e.g. career monograph, published journal article, term paper from master's degree or doctoral dissertation); interview. Additional exam requirements/recommendations for international students: Required—TOEFL (minimum score 79 iBT). *Application deadline:* Applications are processed on a rolling basis. Application fee: $50. Electronic applications accepted. *Financial support:* In 2017–18, 33 students received support. Federal Work-Study and scholarships/grants available. Support available to part-time students. Financial award applicants required to submit FAFSA. *Faculty research:* Technology and mental healthcare, resilience in black families, theology and congregational ministry. *Unit head:* Laina Costanza, Vice President, Student Affairs, 888-790-8080 Ext. 1, Fax: 334-387-3878, E-mail: cc@amridgeuniversity.edu. *Application contact:* Brooks Housley, Student Affairs Coordinator, 888-790-8080 Ext. 1, Fax: 334-387-3878, E-mail: admissions@amridgeuniversity.edu.

Anabaptist Mennonite Biblical Seminary, Graduate and Professional Programs, Elkhart, IN 46517-1999. Offers chaplaincy (M Div); Christian faith formation (M Div); Christian formation (MA); Christian spiritual formation (Certificate); divinity (M Div); pastoral ministry (M Div); pastoral theology for financial professionals (Certificate); peace studies (M Div), including environmental sustainability leadership (M Div, MA); theological studies (M Div, Certificate), including peace studies (M Div), theology and ethics (M Div); theology and peace studies (MA), including conflict transformation, environmental sustainability leadership (M Div, MA), international development administration; United Methodist leadership (M Div). Conflict transformation and environmental sustainability leadership concentrations offered in cooperation with Goshen College; international development administration offered in cooperation with Andrews University. *Accreditation:* ACIPE; ATS. *Program availability:* Part-time, 100% online, blended/hybrid learning. *Degree requirements:* For master's, variable foreign language requirement, comprehensive exam (for some programs), thesis optional, senior interview. *Entrance requirements:* For master's, undergraduate degree transcripts, 3 letters of reference, essay. Additional exam requirements/recommendations for international students: Required—TOEFL (minimum score 90 iBT); Recommended—IELTS (minimum score 7). Electronic applications accepted. *Faculty research:* Biblical studies, peace studies, theology, ethics, creation care or environmental ethics, church history, church leadership, mission, ministry, preaching, pastoral leadership, social justice, peacemaking, Jesus Christ, Christianity, Anabaptism, Mennonite, Scripture, Bible, Old Testament, New Testament, spirituality, clinical pastoral education, teaching, faith formation, pastoral care, Koine Greek, Hebrew, Aramaic, Syriac, Ugaritic.

Pastoral Ministry and Counseling

Anderson University, Clamp Divinity School, Anderson, SC 29621-4035. Offers 21st-century ministry (D Min); Christian studies (M Div); ministry (M Min). *Program availability:* Online learning. *Degree requirements:* For master's, capstone course, ministry project. *Entrance requirements:* For master's, 3 references. *Expenses: Tuition:* Full-time $24,290; part-time $650 per credit hour. Full-time tuition and fees vary according to degree level and program. *Financial support:* Tuition waivers available. Financial award application deadline: 3/1; financial award applicants required to submit FAFSA. *Unit head:* Dr. Michael Duduit, Dean, 864-328-1809, E-mail: ministry@andersonuniversity.edu. *Application contact:* Mallory Knight, Graduate Admission Counselor, 864-231-2182, Fax: 864-231-2115, E-mail: malloryknight@andersonuniversity.edu.
Website: https://www.andersonuniversity.edu/christian-studies/david-t-clamp-graduate-school-christian-ministry

Andrews University, School of Graduate Studies, Seventh-day Adventist Theological Seminary, Berrien Springs, MI 49104. Offers ministry (M Div, D Min); pastoral ministry (MA); religious education (MA, Ed D, PhD, Ed S); theology (M Th, Th D); youth ministry (MA). *Faculty:* 40 full-time (5 women), 12 part-time/adjunct (2 women). *Students:* 529 full-time (70 women), 419 part-time (69 women); includes 480 minority (217 Black or African American, non-Hispanic/Latino; 7 American Indian or Alaska Native, non-Hispanic/Latino; 53 Asian, non-Hispanic/Latino; 190 Hispanic/Latino; 5 Native Hawaiian or other Pacific Islander, non-Hispanic/Latino; 8 Two or more races, non-Hispanic/Latino), 242 international. Average age 40. 497 applicants, 46% accepted, 216 enrolled. In 2017, 147 master's, 46 doctorates awarded. *Degree requirements:* For master's, thesis optional; for doctorate, variable foreign language requirement, thesis/dissertation. *Entrance requirements:* For master's, GRE Subject Test, minimum GPA of 2.0. Additional exam requirements/recommendations for international students: Required—TOEFL (minimum score 550 paper-based). *Application deadline:* Applications are processed on a rolling basis. Application fee: $40. *Financial support:* Fellowships, research assistantships, teaching assistantships, career-related internships or fieldwork, Federal Work-Study, and institutionally sponsored loans available. *Faculty research:* Biblical archaeology, biblical studies, biblical language learning methods, church growth. *Unit head:* Dr. Jiri Moskala, Dean, 269-471-3537. *Application contact:* Justina Clayburn, Director, 800-253-2874, Fax: 269-471-6321.

Appalachian Bible College, Graduate Program, Mount Hope, WV 25880. Offers ministry (MA). *Program availability:* Part-time, online learning. *Entrance requirements:* For master's, ABHE Bible Content Exam, bachelor's degree, 3 references, minimum undergraduate cumulative GPA of 2.5. Additional exam requirements/recommendations for international students: Required—TOEFL (minimum score 550 paper-based). Application fee: $35. Electronic applications accepted. *Unit head:* Dr. John Rinehart, Dean of Graduate Studies, 304-877-6428, E-mail: john.rinehart@abc.edu. *Application contact:* Benjamin Cale, Director of Admissions, 304-877-6428, Fax: 304-877-5082, E-mail: admissions@abc.edu.
Website: http://abc.edu/graduate

Aquinas Institute of Theology, Graduate and Professional Programs, St. Louis, MO 63108. Offers biblical studies (Certificate); church music (MM); health care mission (MAHCM); ministry (M Div); pastoral care (Certificate); pastoral ministry (MAPM); pastoral studies (MAPS); preaching (D Min); spiritual direction (Certificate); theology (M Div, MA); Thomistic studies (Certificate); M Div/MA; MA/PhD; MAPS/MSW. *Accreditation:* ATS (one or more programs are accredited). *Program availability:* Part-time, evening/weekend, online learning. *Degree requirements:* For master's, variable foreign language requirement, comprehensive exam (for some programs), thesis (for some programs); for doctorate, thesis/dissertation. *Entrance requirements:* For master's and Certificate, MAT; for doctorate, 3 years of ministerial experience, 6 hours of graduate course work in homiletics, M Div or the equivalent, minimum GPA of 3.0. Additional exam requirements/recommendations for international students: Required—TOEFL. *Expenses:* Contact institution. *Faculty research:* Theology of preaching, hermeneutics, lay ecclesial ministry, pastoral and practical theology.

Asbury Theological Seminary, Graduate and Professional Programs, Wilmore, KY 40390-1199. Offers M Div, MA, MAAS, MACE, MACL, MACM, MACP, MAMFC, MAMHC, MAPC, MASF, MAYM, Th M, D Min, PhD, Certificate. *Accreditation:* ATS. *Program availability:* Part-time, online learning. Terminal master's awarded for partial completion of doctoral program. *Degree requirements:* For master's, thesis (for some programs); for doctorate, thesis/dissertation, qualifying exam. *Entrance requirements:* For master's, minimum GPA of 2.75; for doctorate, minimum GPA of 3.0. Additional exam requirements/recommendations for international students: Required—TOEFL, IELTS. Electronic applications accepted.

Ashland Theological Seminary, Graduate Programs, Ashland, OH 44805. Offers Biblical studies (MA); Christian ministries (MACM), including Black church studies (MACM, D Min), general Christian ministries, leadership, spiritual formation (MACM, D Min); clinical mental health counseling (MA); counseling (MAC); historical and theological studies (MA), including Anabaptism and Pietism, Christian theology, church history, New Testament, Old Testament; ministry (D Min), including Black church studies (MACM, D Min), chaplaincy (M Div, D Min), independent design, spiritual formation (MACM, D Min), transformational leadership; pastoral ministry (M Div), including chaplaincy (M Div, D Min), general ministry. MAC program offered in Detroit, MI. *Accreditation:* ATS. *Program availability:* Part-time. *Degree requirements:* For master's, 2 foreign languages, comprehensive exam (for some programs), thesis (for some programs); for doctorate, thesis/dissertation. *Entrance requirements:* For master's, bachelor's degree from accredited institution with minimum undergraduate GPA of 2.75; for doctorate, M Div, minimum undergraduate GPA of 3.0. Additional exam requirements/recommendations for international students: Required—TOEFL (minimum score 500 paper-based; 65 iBT). Electronic applications accepted. *Faculty research:* Semitic languages and linguistics, rhetorical and social-scientific criticism, Anabaptist studies, inner spiritual healing, African-American clergy in film and literature.

Assemblies of God Theological Seminary, Graduate and Professional Programs, Springfield, MO 65802. Offers Biblical interpretation and theology (PhD); Christian ministries (MA); divinity (M Div); intercultural studies (MA, PhD); leadership and ministry (MLM); ministry (D Min); missiology (DAIS); pastoral studies (MPL); theological studies (MA, Th M). *Accreditation:* ATS. *Program availability:* Part-time, evening/weekend, 100% online. *Faculty:* 12 full-time (3 women), 15 part-time/adjunct (4 women). *Students:* 153 full-time (48 women), 159 part-time (41 women); includes 62 minority (20 Black or African American, non-Hispanic/Latino; 4 American Indian or Alaska Native, non-Hispanic/Latino; 14 Asian, non-Hispanic/Latino; 18 Hispanic/Latino; 6 Two or more races, non-Hispanic/Latino), 12 international. Average age 46. 69 applicants, 88% accepted, 48 enrolled. In 2017, 35 master's, 22 doctorates awarded. *Degree requirements:* For master's, variable foreign language requirement, thesis; for doctorate, variable foreign language requirement, comprehensive exam, thesis/dissertation. *Entrance requirements:* For master's, minimum GPA of 2.5; for doctorate, GRE (for PhD in Bible theology), minimum GPA of 3.0. Additional exam requirements/recommendations for international students: Required—TOEFL (minimum score 550 paper-based; 80 iBT). *Application deadline:* For fall admission, 7/1 priority date for domestic students, 6/1 priority date for international students; for spring admission, 12/1 priority date for domestic students, 11/1 priority date for international students. Applications are processed on a rolling basis. Application fee: $75. Electronic applications accepted. *Financial support:* Career-related internships or fieldwork and scholarships/grants available. Support available to part-time students. Financial award application deadline: 7/15; financial award applicants required to submit FAFSA. *Unit head:* Dr. Timothy A. Hager, Dean, 417-268-1000, Fax: 417-268-1001. *Application contact:* Erin Leonard, Seminary Enrollment Coordinator, 417-268-1000, Fax: 417-268-1001, E-mail: info@agts.edu.
Website: http://www.agts.edu

Atlantic School of Theology, Graduate and Professional Programs, Halifax, NS B3H 3B5, Canada. Offers ministry (M Div); theological studies (Graduate Certificate). *Accreditation:* ATS. *Program availability:* Part-time, online learning. *Degree requirements:* For master's, thesis (for some programs). *Entrance requirements:* For master's and Graduate Certificate, minimum B average in undergraduate course work. *Faculty research:* Ethics and biology; death, dying and pastoral care; theology and the economy; adult education; John and anti-Judaism.

Atlantic University, Spiritual Guidance Mentor Program, Virginia Beach, VA 23451-2061. Offers Certificate. *Program availability:* Online learning. *Degree requirements:* For Certificate, final essay. *Entrance requirements:* For degree, 500-word essay. *Application deadline:* For fall admission, 9/17 for domestic students; for winter admission, 3/26 for domestic students; for spring admission, 12/18 for domestic students; for summer admission, 6/25 for domestic students. Applications are processed on a rolling basis. Application fee: $35. Electronic applications accepted. *Expenses:* $750 per course. *Application contact:* Rachel Alvidrez, Educational Services Manager, 757-631-8101, Fax: 757-631-8096, E-mail: info@atlanticuniv.edu.
Website: https://www.atlanticuniv.edu/academics/programs/spiritual-mentor-certificate/

Austin Presbyterian Theological Seminary, Graduate and Professional Programs, Austin, TX 78705-5797. Offers divinity (M Div); ministry (D Min); ministry practice (MA); theological studies (MA); youth ministry (MA); M Div/MSSW. M Div/MSSW offered in collaboration with The University of Texas at Austin School of Social Work. *Accreditation:* ACIPE; ATS. *Faculty:* 21 full-time (6 women), 4 part-time/adjunct (0 women). *Students:* 80 full-time (50 women), 77 part-time (45 women). *Degree requirements:* For master's, Greek, Hebrew (for M Div); for doctorate, thesis/dissertation. *Entrance requirements:* For master's, references (for M Div). Additional exam requirements/recommendations for international students: Required—TOEFL (minimum score 550 paper-based; 79 iBT). *Application deadline:* For fall admission, 5/1 for domestic students, 1/1 for international students; for winter admission, 9/6 for domestic students; for summer admission, 2/2 for domestic students. Applications are processed on a rolling basis. Application fee: $50. Electronic applications accepted. *Expenses: Tuition:* Full-time $13,500; part-time $6750 per credit. *Required fees:* $120; $120 per credit. One-time fee: $150. Tuition and fees vary according to program. *Financial support:* Fellowships, career-related internships or fieldwork, institutionally sponsored loans, and scholarships/grants available. Support available to part-time students. Financial award application deadline: 2/1; financial award applicants required to submit FAFSA. *Faculty research:* Mystical theology, religious pluralism, narrative preaching, social ethics, pastoral care and healing. *Unit head:* Dr. David Jensen, Academic Dean, 512-404-4821, Fax: 512-479-0738, E-mail: dean@austinseminary.edu. *Application contact:* Dr. Jack Barden, Vice President for Enrollment Management, 512-404-4827, Fax: 512-472-7089, E-mail: admissions@austinseminary.edu.

Ave Maria University, Graduate Programs, Ave Maria, FL 34142. Offers pastoral theology (MTS); theology (MA, PhD). Terminal master's awarded for partial completion of doctoral program. *Degree requirements:* For master's, one foreign language, thesis; for doctorate, 3 foreign languages, comprehensive exam, thesis/dissertation. *Entrance requirements:* For master's, GRE; for doctorate, GRE, M Div or equivalent; MA or MTS in religion, theology, or philosophy; bachelor's degree with strong background in religion, theology, and/or philosophy.

Azusa Pacific University, Azusa Pacific Seminary, Program in Divinity, Azusa, CA 91702-7000. Offers Biblical studies (M Div). Program also offered in Korean at Los Angeles campus, and in Spanish. *Expenses:* Contact institution.

Azusa Pacific University, Azusa Pacific Seminary, Program in Pastoral Studies, Concentration in Church Leadership and Development, Azusa, CA 91702-7000. Offers MAPS. *Degree requirements:* For master's, project.

Bakke Graduate University, Programs in Pastoral Ministry and Business, Dallas, TX 75243-7039. Offers business administration (MBA); church and ministry multiplication (D Min); global urban leadership (MA); leadership (D Min); ministry in complex contexts (D Min); social and civic entrepreneurship (MA); theology of work (D Min); theology reflection (D Min); transformational leadership (DTL); urban youth ministry (D Min). *Program availability:* Part-time, online learning. *Faculty:* 5 full-time (3 women), 27 part-time/adjunct (12 women). *Students:* 120 full-time (48 women), 54 part-time (24 women). *Degree requirements:* For master's, thesis; for doctorate, thesis/dissertation. *Entrance requirements:* For master's, 2 years of ministry experience, BA in Biblical studies or theology; for doctorate, 3 years of ministry experience, M Div. Additional exam requirements/recommendations for international students: Required—TOEFL. *Application deadline:* For fall admission, 7/1 priority date for domestic students; for winter admission, 12/1 for domestic students; for spring admission, 3/15 for domestic students. Applications are processed on a rolling basis. Application fee: $50. Electronic applications accepted. *Expenses: Tuition:* Full-time $6120; part-time $3000 per credit. *Required fees:* $50 per course. $50 per quarter. *Financial support:* Scholarships/grants and tuition waivers (partial) available. Financial award applicants required to submit FAFSA. *Faculty research:* Theological systems, church management, worship. *Unit head:* Dr. Gwen Dewey, Senior Vice President of International Partnerships, 214-329-4447 Ext. 119, E-mail: gwen.dewey@bgu.edu. *Application contact:* Traci Tucker, Director of Admissions, 214-329-4447 Ext. 122, Fax: 214-347-9367, E-mail: traci.tucker@bgu.edu.
Website: http://www.bgu.edu/

Baptist Bible College, Graduate and Professional Programs, Springfield, MO 65803-3498. Offers biblical counseling (MA); church ministry (MA); theology (M Div). *Program availability:* Part-time. *Faculty:* 1 full-time (0 women), 6 part-time/adjunct (0 women). *Students:* 2 full-time (0 women), 27 part-time (4 women); includes 5 minority (2 Black or African American, non-Hispanic/Latino; 1 Asian, non-Hispanic/Latino; 2 Hispanic/Latino), 3 international. *Entrance requirements:* Additional exam requirements/recommendations for international students: Required—TOEFL. *Application deadline:* For fall admission, 8/1 priority date for domestic students; for spring admission, 1/14 for domestic students. Applications are processed on a rolling basis. Application fee: $40. Electronic applications accepted. *Expenses:* $450 per credit hour tuition, $200 student fee per semester. *Financial support:* Application deadline: 3/6; applicants required to submit FAFSA. *Unit head:* Mark Milioni, President, 417-268-6008, Fax: 800-819-8330. *Application contact:* Mark Milioni, President, 417-268-6008, Fax: 800-819-8330.
Website: http://gobbc.edu/academics-2/seminary-degrees/

The Baptist College of Florida, Graduate Programs, Graceville, FL 32440. Offers Christian ministry (MA); Christian studies (MA), including Biblical studies; music and worship leadership (MA). *Program availability:* Part-time, 100% online, blended/hybrid learning. *Faculty:* 12 full-time (0 women). *Students:* 33 full-time (6 women); includes 2

minority (1 Black or African American, non-Hispanic/Latino; 1 Hispanic/Latino). Average age 28. 10 applicants, 100% accepted, 10 enrolled. In 2017, 3 master's awarded. *Degree requirements:* For master's, variable foreign language requirement, comprehensive exam (for some programs), thesis (for some programs). *Entrance requirements:* For master's, regionally-accredited undergraduate degree, undergraduate courses in field, minimum GPA of 2.5. Additional exam requirements/recommendations for international students: Required—TOEFL. *Application deadline:* For fall admission, 8/15 for domestic students; for spring admission, 1/15 for domestic students. Applications are processed on a rolling basis. Application fee: $25. Electronic applications accepted. *Expenses:* Contact institution. *Financial support:* In 2017–18, 2 students received support. *Faculty research:* Biblical studies, ministry studies. *Unit head:* Dr. Ed Scott, Chair of the Graduate Division, 850-263-3261 Ext. 488, E-mail: eescott@baptistcollege.edu. *Application contact:* Sandra Richards, Director of Student Life and Marketing, 850-263-3261 Ext. 415.
Website: http://www.baptistcollege.edu

Baptist Theological Seminary at Richmond, Graduate and Professional Programs, Richmond, VA 23228. Offers Biblical interpretation (M Div); Christian education formation (M Div); Christian ministry (MCM); justice and peacebuilding (M Div); ministry (D Min); religious freedom (M Div); theological studies (MTS, Graduate Certificate); theology (M Div); youth and student ministries (M Div); M Div/MBA; M Div/MS; M Div/MSW. *Accreditation:* ATS. *Program availability:* Part-time, 100% online, blended/hybrid learning. *Faculty:* 2 full-time (1 woman), 8 part-time/adjunct (2 women). *Students:* 38 full-time (14 women), 31 part-time (22 women); includes 15 minority (11 Black or African American, non-Hispanic/Latino; 4 Asian, non-Hispanic/Latino). Average age 46. In 2017, 15 master's, 2 doctorates awarded. *Degree requirements:* For master's and Graduate Certificate, thesis optional; for doctorate, comprehensive exam, thesis/dissertation, field study, independent study. *Entrance requirements:* For master's, BA/BS, minimum GPA of 2.2, 2 references, resume, official transcripts, writing sample; for doctorate, MAT (minimum score of 400), M Div with minimum GPA of 2.75, 3 years of full-time ministry experience, 3 references, resume, official transcripts, writing sample, personal statement. Additional exam requirements/recommendations for international students: Required—TOEFL (minimum score 550 paper-based), IELTS (minimum score 5.5). *Application deadline:* For fall admission, 7/1 for domestic students, 5/1 for international students; for winter admission, 12/15 for domestic students, 9/1 for international students; for spring admission, 1/15 for domestic students, 10/1 for international students. Applications are processed on a rolling basis. Application fee: $35. Electronic applications accepted. *Financial support:* In 2017–18, 46 students received support, including 9 teaching assistantships (averaging $3,300 per year); scholarships/grants also available. Financial award application deadline: 2/1. *Faculty research:* Biblical studies, pastoral care, church history, theology, ministry. *Unit head:* Dr. Linda M. Bridges, President, 804-204-1201, Fax: 804-355-8182, E-mail: lmbridges@btsr.edu. *Application contact:* Melissa Fallen, Director of Admissions and Recruitment, 804-204-1208, E-mail: admissions@btsr.edu.
Website: http://www.btsr.edu/programs/degree-programs/

Barry University, College of Arts and Sciences, Department of Theology and Philosophy, Miami Shores, FL 33161-6695. Offers ministry (D Min); pastoral ministry for Hispanics (MA); pastoral theology (MA); practical theology (MA). *Accreditation:* ATS. *Program availability:* Part-time, evening/weekend. *Degree requirements:* For master's, comprehensive exam, thesis optional; for doctorate, thesis/dissertation. *Entrance requirements:* For master's, GRE General Test or MAT, minimum GPA of 3.0. Electronic applications accepted. *Faculty research:* Fundamental morals, bioethics, social ethics, liturgical and sacramental theology, biblical studies.

Bethany Global University, Graduate Programs, Bloomington, MN 55438. Offers intercultural ministry education (MA); intercultural ministry leadership (MA); intercultural ministry studies (MA). *Program availability:* Part-time, evening/weekend, online only, 100% online. *Degree requirements:* For master's, thesis (for some programs). *Entrance requirements:* For master's, bachelor's degree, Christian testimony. Additional exam requirements/recommendations for international students: Required—TOEFL. Electronic applications accepted. *Expenses:* Contact institution. *Faculty research:* Cross cultural training.

Bethany Theological Seminary, Graduate and Professional Programs, Richmond, IN 47374-4019. Offers biblical studies (MA Th); ministry studies (M Div); peace studies (M Div, MA Th); theological studies (MA Th, CATS); youth ministry (M Div). *Accreditation:* ACIPE; ATS. *Program availability:* Part-time, online learning. *Degree requirements:* For master's, thesis (for some programs). *Entrance requirements:* For master's, letters of reference. Additional exam requirements/recommendations for international students: Required—TOEFL (minimum score 550 paper-based).

Bethel College, Adult and Graduate Programs, Program in Ministries, Mishawaka, IN 46545-5591. Offers M Min. *Program availability:* Part-time, evening/weekend, 100% online, blended/hybrid learning. *Faculty:* 4 full-time (0 women), 2 part-time/adjunct (0 women). *Students:* 5 full-time (2 women), 26 part-time (9 women); includes 9 minority (4 Black or African American, non-Hispanic/Latino; 2 Hispanic/Latino; 3 Two or more races, non-Hispanic/Latino). Average age 37. 25 applicants, 68% accepted, 17 enrolled. In 2017, 16 master's awarded. *Degree requirements:* For master's, thesis or alternative. *Entrance requirements:* Additional exam requirements/recommendations for international students: Required—TOEFL (minimum score 540 paper-based). *Application deadline:* For fall admission, 5/1 for international students; for spring admission, 10/1 for international students. Applications are processed on a rolling basis. Application fee: $0. Electronic applications accepted. Tuition and fees vary according to program. *Financial support:* Career-related internships or fieldwork available. Financial award applicants required to submit FAFSA. *Unit head:* Dr. Terence Linhart, Dean of Adult and Graduate Studies, 574-807-7394, E-mail: linhart@bethelcollege.edu.

Bethel Seminary, Graduate and Professional Programs, St. Paul, MN 55112-6998. Offers Anglican studies (Certificate); children's and family ministry (MA); Christian studies (Certificate); Christian thought (MA); church planting (Certificate); Greek and Hebrew language (M Div); Greek language (M Div); Hebrew language (M Div); marriage and family therapy (MA, Certificate); mental health counseling (MA); ministry (MA, D Min); ministry practice (Certificate); theological studies (MA, Certificate); transformational leadership (MA); young life youth ministry (Certificate). *Accreditation:* ACIPE. *Program availability:* Part-time, evening/weekend, 100% online, blended/hybrid learning. *Faculty:* 16 full-time (4 women), 31 part-time/adjunct (15 women). *Students:* 380 full-time (170 women), 167 part-time (55 women); includes 161 minority (65 Black or African American, non-Hispanic/Latino; 52 Asian, non-Hispanic/Latino; 31 Hispanic/Latino; 1 Native Hawaiian or other Pacific Islander, non-Hispanic/Latino; 12 Two or more races, non-Hispanic/Latino), 5 international. Average age 38. 356 applicants, 62% accepted, 156 enrolled. In 2017, 120 master's, 15 doctorates, 4 other advanced degrees awarded. *Degree requirements:* For master's, variable foreign language requirement, thesis (for some programs); for doctorate, thesis/dissertation. *Entrance requirements:* For master's, letters of reference, transcripts, personal statement; for doctorate, M Div, letters of reference, organizational support; for Certificate, letters of reference, family essay, personal statement, and family of origin paper (for marriage and family therapy). Additional exam requirements/recommendations for international students: Required—TOEFL (minimum score 550 paper-based; 87 iBT). *Application deadline:* For fall

admission, 8/1 priority date for domestic students, 8/1 for international students; for winter admission, 12/1 priority date for domestic students; for spring admission, 1/1 priority date for domestic students. Applications are processed on a rolling basis. Application fee: $0. Electronic applications accepted. *Expenses:* Contact institution. *Financial support:* Teaching assistantships, career-related internships or fieldwork, Federal Work-Study, and scholarships/grants available. Financial award applicants required to submit FAFSA. *Faculty research:* Nature of theology, ethics, Biblical commentaries, nature of God, science and theology. *Unit head:* Dr. Randy Bergen, Associate Provost, 651-635-8000, E-mail: r-bergen@bethel.edu. *Application contact:* Director of Admissions, 651-638-8000, Fax: 651-638-6002, E-mail: seminary-admissions@bethel.edu.
Website: https://www.bethel.edu/seminary

Biblical Theological Seminary, Graduate and Professional Programs, Hatfield, PA 19440-2499. Offers advanced missional leadership (D Min); advanced pastoral studies (Certificate); biblical counseling (Certificate); biblical studies (MA, Certificate); counseling (MA); ministry (M Div, MA); missional theology (MA). *Accreditation:* ATS. *Program availability:* Part-time, evening/weekend. *Faculty:* 9 full-time (1 woman), 20 part-time/adjunct (5 women). *Students:* 138 full-time (41 women), 78 part-time (31 women); includes 83 minority (51 Black or African American, non-Hispanic/Latino; 1 American Indian or Alaska Native, non-Hispanic/Latino; 26 Asian, non-Hispanic/Latino; 3 Hispanic/Latino; 2 Two or more races, non-Hispanic/Latino), 65 international. Average age 41. 83 applicants, 64% accepted, 49 enrolled. In 2017, 50 master's, 12 doctorates awarded. *Degree requirements:* For master's, variable foreign language requirement, thesis optional; for doctorate, thesis/dissertation. *Entrance requirements:* Additional exam requirements/recommendations for international students: Required—TOEFL (minimum score 550 paper-based; 80 iBT). *Application deadline:* Applications are processed on a rolling basis. Application fee: $30. Electronic applications accepted. *Expenses:* Tuition: Full-time $12,360; part-time $6180 per credit. *Required fees:* $50 per semester. One-time fee: $30. *Financial support:* In 2017–18, 194 students received support. Career-related internships or fieldwork, institutionally sponsored loans, and scholarships/grants available. Support available to part-time students. Financial award application deadline: 8/30; financial award applicants required to submit FAFSA. *Faculty research:* Theology, culture, Biblical interpretation. *Application contact:* Rev. Michael Heath, Student Advancement Counselor, 215-368-5000 Ext. 152, Fax: 215-368-7002, E-mail: mheath@biblical.edu.
Website: http://www.biblical.edu/

Biola University, Talbot School of Theology, La Mirada, CA 90639-0001. Offers adult/family ministry (MACE); Bible exposition (MA, Th M); Biblical and theological studies (Certificate); children's ministry (MACE); Christian education (M Div); cross-cultural education ministry (MACE); educational studies (Ed D, PhD); evangelism and discipleship (M Div); general Christian education (MACE); Messianic Jewish studies (M Div, Certificate); missions and intercultural studies (M Div); New Testament (MA, Th M); Old Testament (MA); Old Testament and Semitics (Th M); pastoral and general ministry (M Div); pastoral care and counseling (M Div, MACML); philosophy (MA); preaching and pastoral ministry (MACML); spiritual formation (M Div, Certificate); spiritual formation and soul care (MA); sports ministry (MACML); theology (MA, Th M, D Min, Certificate); youth ministry (MACE). *Program availability:* Part-time, evening/weekend. *Students:* 475 full-time (113 women), 603 part-time (176 women); includes 541 minority (39 Black or African American, non-Hispanic/Latino; 2 American Indian or Alaska Native, non-Hispanic/Latino; 378 Asian, non-Hispanic/Latino; 84 Hispanic/Latino; 1 Native Hawaiian or other Pacific Islander, non-Hispanic/Latino; 37 Two or more races, non-Hispanic/Latino), 105 international. 437 applicants, 78% accepted, 241 enrolled. In 2017, 177 master's, 24 doctorates awarded. *Entrance requirements:* For master's, bachelor's degree from accredited college or university; minimum GPA of 2.6 (for M Div), 3.0 (for MA); for doctorate, M Div or MA. Additional exam requirements/recommendations for international students: Required—TOEFL (minimum score 600 paper-based; 88 iBT). *Application deadline:* For fall admission, 7/1 for domestic students, 6/1 for international students; for spring admission, 12/1 priority date for domestic students. Applications are processed on a rolling basis. Application fee: $65. Electronic applications accepted. *Financial support:* Scholarships/grants and unspecified assistantships available. Support available to part-time students. Financial award applicants required to submit FAFSA. *Faculty research:* New Testament, Old Testament, spiritual formation, Christian education, theological studies, Christian ministry, preaching and pastoral ministry, language and literature, bible exposition, Christian leadership. *Unit head:* Dr. Clint Arnold, Dean, 562-903-4816, Fax: 562-903-4748. *Application contact:* Graduate Admissions Office, 562-903-4752, E-mail: graduate.admissions@biola.edu.
Website: http://www.talbot.edu/

Bob Jones University, Graduate Programs, Greenville, SC 29614. Offers accountancy (MS); Bible (MA); Bible translation (MA); Biblical studies (Certificate); broadcast management (MS); business administration (MBA); church history (MA, PhD); church ministries (MA); church music (MM); cinema and video production (MA); counseling (MS); curriculum and instruction (Ed D); divinity (M Div); dramatic production (MA); educational leadership (MS, Ed D, Ed S); elementary education (M Ed, MAT); English (M Ed, MA, MAT); fine arts (MA); graphic design (MA); history (M Ed, MA); illustration (MA); interpretative speech (MA); mathematics (M Ed, MAT); medical missions (Certificate); ministry (MM, D Min); multi-categorical special education (M Ed, MAT); music (M Ed); New Testament interpretation (PhD); Old Testament interpretation (PhD); orchestral instrument performance (MM); organ performance (MM); pastoral studies (MA); personnel services (MS, Ed S); piano pedagogy (MM); piano performance (MM); platform arts (MA); radio and television broadcasting (MS); rhetoric and public address (MA); secondary education (M Ed); studio art (MA); teaching Bible (MA); theology (MA, PhD); voice performance (MM); youth ministries (MA); M Div/MM.

Boston College, School of Theology and Ministry, Chestnut Hill, MA 02467-3800. Offers church leadership (MA); divinity (M Div); pastoral ministry (MA), including Hispanic ministry, liturgy and worship, pastoral care and counseling, spirituality; religious education (MA, PhD); sacred theology (STD, STL); social justice/social ministry (MA); spiritual direction (MA); theological studies (MTS); theology (Th M, PhD); youth ministry (MA); MA/MA; MS/MA; MSW/MA. *Accreditation:* TEAC. *Program availability:* Part-time. *Degree requirements:* For doctorate, one foreign language, thesis/dissertation. *Entrance requirements:* For doctorate, GRE. Additional exam requirements/recommendations for international students: Required—TOEFL (minimum score 550 paper-based). Electronic applications accepted. *Faculty research:* Philosophy and practice of religious education, pastoral psychology, liturgical and spiritual theology, spiritual formation for the practice of ministry.

Boston University, School of Theology, Boston, MA 02215. Offers chaplaincy (M Div); choral conducting (MSM); church and the arts (M Div); community and global engagement (M Div); constructive theology and ethics (PhD), including constructive theology, theological ethics; history and hermeneutics (PhD), including biblical studies, church history and world Christianity, liturgical studies, mission studies; organ (MSM); pastoral ministry (M Div); practical theology (PhD), including church and society, congregation and community, evangelism and missiology, homiletics, leadership and administration, pastoral theology and psychology, religious education, spirituality studies,

worship; religion and the academy (M Div); transformational leadership (D Min); M Div/MSM; M Div/MSW; MTS/MSW. PhD in mission studies offered in collaboration with Gordon-Conwell Theological Seminary. *Accreditation:* ACIPE; ATS. *Program availability:* Part-time, blended/hybrid learning. *Faculty:* 39 full-time (17 women), 11 part-time/adjunct (5 women). *Students:* 256 full-time (135 women), 87 part-time (40 women); includes 82 minority (38 Black or African American, non-Hispanic/Latino; 10 Asian, non-Hispanic/Latino; 23 Hispanic/Latino; 1 Native Hawaiian or other Pacific Islander, non-Hispanic/Latino; 10 Two or more races, non-Hispanic/Latino), 66 international. Average age 34. 334 applicants, 69% accepted, 106 enrolled. In 2017, 62 master's, 9 doctorates awarded. *Degree requirements:* For master's, comprehensive exam (for some programs), thesis optional, contextual education; for doctorate, 2 languages, dissertation, and comprehensive exam (for PhD). *Entrance requirements:* For master's, minimum GPA of 3.0; for doctorate, GRE General Test, minimum GPA of 3.3. Additional exam requirements/recommendations for international students: Required—TOEFL (minimum score 570 paper-based; 89 iBT). *Application deadline:* For fall admission, 1/15 priority date for domestic and international students; for spring admission, 10/15 priority date for domestic and international students. Applications are processed on a rolling basis. Application fee: $95. Electronic applications accepted. *Expenses:* $20,100 tuition. *Financial support:* In 2017–18, 236 students received support, including 102 fellowships with full tuition reimbursements available (averaging $7,500 per year), 11 research assistantships with full tuition reimbursements available (averaging $22,000 per year), 12 teaching assistantships with full tuition reimbursements available (averaging $22,000 per year); career-related internships or fieldwork, Federal Work-Study, scholarships/grants, and health care benefits also available. Support available to part-time students. Financial award application deadline: 7/15. *Faculty research:* Practical theology, ethics, environmental theology, religion and conflict transformation, chaplaincy. *Total annual research expenditures:* $2.5 million. *Unit head:* Rev. Dr. Mary Elizabeth Moore, Dean, 617-353-3050, Fax: 617-353-3061, E-mail: memoore@bu.edu. *Application contact:* Rev. Dr. Anastasia Kidd, Director of Enrollment, 617-353-3036, Fax: 617-358-0140, E-mail: sthadmis@bu.edu.
Website: http://www.bu.edu/sth

Briercrest Seminary, Graduate Programs, Program in Christian Ministries, Caronport, SK S0H 0S0, Canada. Offers leadership (MA); marriage and family counseling (MA); missions (MA); pastoral counseling (MA); worship (MA); youth and family ministry (MA). *Program availability:* Part-time. *Degree requirements:* For master's, comprehensive exam, thesis optional. *Entrance requirements:* Additional exam requirements/recommendations for international students: Required—TOEFL (minimum score 550 paper-based).

Briercrest Seminary, Graduate Programs, Program in Theology, Caronport, SK S0H 0S0, Canada. Offers Biblical studies (M Div); leadership and management (M Div); New Testament (MATS); Old Testament (MATS); pastoral counseling (M Div); pastoral ministry (M Div); theological studies (M Div); theology (MATS); worship (M Div); youth and family ministry (M Div). *Accreditation:* ATS. *Program availability:* Part-time. *Degree requirements:* For master's, comprehensive exam, thesis optional. *Entrance requirements:* Additional exam requirements/recommendations for international students: Required—TOEFL (minimum score 550 paper-based).

Brite Divinity School, Graduate and Professional Programs, Fort Worth, TX 76109. Offers Biblical interpretation (PhD); divinity (M Div); ministry (D Min); pastoral theology (PhD); theological studies (MTS, CTS); theology (Th M); theology and ministry (MA). *Accreditation:* ACIPE; ATS (one or more programs are accredited); SACS/CC. *Program availability:* Part-time, evening/weekend. *Entrance requirements:* For master's, minimum GPA of 2.5. Additional exam requirements/recommendations for international students: Required—TOEFL.

Bryan College, MBA Program, Dayton, TN 37321. Offers business administration (MBA); healthcare administration (MBA); human resources (MBA); marketing (MBA); ministry (MBA); sports management (MBA). *Program availability:* Online only, 100% online. *Entrance requirements:* For master's, resume, 2 letters of recommendation. Additional exam requirements/recommendations for international students: Required—TOEFL. *Application deadline:* For fall admission, 7/1 for domestic and international students; for winter admission, 11/15 for domestic and international students; for spring admission, 12/1 for domestic and international students; for summer admission, 5/1 for domestic and international students. Applications are processed on a rolling basis. Application fee: $50. Electronic applications accepted. *Expenses:* Contact institution. *Financial support:* Scholarships/grants available. Financial award applicants required to submit FAFSA. *Unit head:* Dr. Adina Scruggs, Dean of Adult and Graduate Studies, 423-634-2057, E-mail: adina.scruggs@bryan.edu. *Application contact:* Mandi K Sullivan, Director of Academic Programs, 423-634-9880, E-mail: mandi.sullivan@bryan.edu.
Website: http://www.bryan.edu/academics/adult-education/graduate/online-mba/

Cairn University, Department of Counseling, Langhorne, PA 19047-2990. Offers MS. *Program availability:* Part-time, evening/weekend. *Entrance requirements:* Additional exam requirements/recommendations for international students: Required—TOEFL (minimum score 550 paper-based). Electronic applications accepted. Application fee is waived when completed online. *Expenses:* Contact institution.

California Baptist University, Program in Counseling Ministry, Riverside, CA 92504-3206. Offers professional ministry (MA); research in counseling ministry (MA). *Program availability:* Part-time, evening/weekend. *Faculty:* 2 full-time (0 women), 1 part-time/adjunct (0 women). *Students:* 6 full-time (5 women), 3 part-time (1 woman); includes 3 minority (all Hispanic/Latino). Average age 35. 2 applicants, 50% accepted, 1 enrolled. In 2017, 5 master's awarded. *Degree requirements:* For master's, comprehensive exam, additional professional ministry practicum or research thesis. *Entrance requirements:* For master's, GRE (minimum score of 300 for applicants with a GPA below 2.75), minimum undergraduate GPA of 2.75; official transcripts; three recommendations; comprehensive essay; interview; three prerequisite classes completed with minimum C grade. Additional exam requirements/recommendations for international students: Required—TOEFL (minimum score 80 iBT). *Application deadline:* For fall admission, 8/1 priority date for domestic students, 7/1 for international students; for spring admission, 12/1 priority date for domestic students, 11/1 for international students. Applications are processed on a rolling basis. Application fee: $45. Electronic applications accepted. *Expenses:* Contact institution. *Financial support:* In 2017–18, 2 students received support. Federal Work-Study and scholarships/grants available. Financial award applicants required to submit CSS PROFILE or FAFSA. *Faculty research:* Social psychology, clinical psychology, psychology of religion, child development, marriage and family therapy. *Unit head:* Dr. Jacqueline Gustafson, Dean, School of Behavioral Sciences, 951-343-4487, E-mail: jcraig@calbaptist.edu. *Application contact:* Deanna Meyer, Graduate Admissions Counselor, 951-343-4463, E-mail: dmeyer@calbaptist.edu.
Website: http://www.calbaptist.edu/macounseling/

California Baptist University, Program in Counseling Ministry and Counseling Psychology (Dual Master's), Riverside, CA 92504-3206. Offers MA/MS. *Program availability:* Part-time, evening/weekend. *Faculty:* 18 full-time (11 women), 10 part-time/adjunct (7 women). *Students:* 12 full-time (9 women), 1 part-time (0 women); includes 8 minority (2 Black or African American, non-Hispanic/Latino; 1 Asian, non-Hispanic/Latino; 5 Hispanic/Latino). Average age 29. 7 applicants, 57% accepted, 3 enrolled. *Entrance requirements:* Additional exam requirements/recommendations for international students: Required—TOEFL (minimum score 80 iBT). *Application deadline:* For fall admission, 8/1 priority date for domestic students, 7/1 for international students; for spring admission, 12/1 priority date for domestic students, 11/1 for international students. Applications are processed on a rolling basis. Application fee: $45. Electronic applications accepted. *Expenses:* Contact institution. *Financial support:* In 2017–18, 2 students received support. Federal Work-Study and scholarships/grants available. Financial award applicants required to submit CSS PROFILE or FAFSA. *Faculty research:* Law enforcement psychology, neuroethology, organizational neuroscience, integration of theology and behavioral science, cognitive development/cross-cultural psychology. *Unit head:* Dr. Jacqueline Gustafson, Dean, School of Behavioral Sciences, 951-343-4487, E-mail: jcraig@calbaptist.edu. *Application contact:* Mischa Routon, Director of Counseling Psychology Program, 951-343-4206, Fax: 877-228-8877, E-mail: mrouton@calbaptist.edu.
Website: http://www.calbaptist.edu/mft

Calvary University, Graduate School and Seminary, Kansas City, MO 64147. Offers Bible and theology (MS); Biblical counseling (MA); education (MS), including administration and leadership, Christian education, curriculum and instruction, elementary education; organizational development (MS); pastoral studies (M Div); worship arts (MS). *Program availability:* Part-time, evening/weekend. *Faculty:* 6 full-time (2 women), 2 part-time/adjunct (1 woman). *Students:* 11 full-time (3 women), 29 part-time (15 women); includes 12 minority (4 Black or African American, non-Hispanic/Latino; 1 American Indian or Alaska Native, non-Hispanic/Latino; 6 Asian, non-Hispanic/Latino; 1 Native Hawaiian or other Pacific Islander, non-Hispanic/Latino). Average age 39. *Degree requirements:* For master's, variable foreign language requirement, comprehensive exam, thesis or alternative. *Entrance requirements:* For master's, minimum GPA of 2.5, BA or BS, doctrine agreement. Additional exam requirements/recommendations for international students: Required—TOEFL (minimum score 550 paper-based). *Application deadline:* Applications are processed on a rolling basis. Application fee: $0. Electronic applications accepted. *Expenses:* Contact institution. *Financial support:* Scholarships/grants available. Financial award application deadline: 11/5; financial award applicants required to submit FAFSA. *Unit head:* Dr. Thomas Baurain, Director of Seminary, 816-322-0110 Ext. 1502, Fax: 816-331-4474, E-mail: thomas.baurain@calvary.edu. *Application contact:* Ann Rogers, Admissions Office Assistant, 800-326-3960 Ext. 1321, Fax: 816-331-4474, E-mail: admissions@calvary.edu.
Website: http://www.calvary.edu

Calvin Theological Seminary, Graduate and Professional Programs, Grand Rapids, MI 49546-4387. Offers Bible and theology (MA); divinity (M Div), including ancient near eastern languages and literature, contextual ministry, evangelism and teaching, history of Christianity, new church development, New Testament, Old Testament, pastoral care and leadership, preaching and worship, theological studies, youth and family ministries; educational ministry (MA); historical theology (PhD); missions and evangelism (MA); pastoral care (MA); philosophical and moral theology (PhD); systematic theology (PhD); theological studies (MTS); theology (Th M); worship (MA); youth and family ministries (MA). *Accreditation:* ACIPE; ATS. *Program availability:* Part-time. *Degree requirements:* For master's, variable foreign language requirement, thesis (for some programs); for doctorate, 4 foreign languages, comprehensive exam, thesis/dissertation. *Entrance requirements:* For doctorate, GRE General Test, Hebrew, Greek, and a modern foreign language. Additional exam requirements/recommendations for international students: Required—TOEFL (minimum score 550 paper-based), TWE (minimum score 4). Electronic applications accepted. *Faculty research:* Recent Trinity theory, Christian anthropology, Proverbs, reformed confessions, Paul's view of law.

Campbell University, Graduate and Professional Programs, Divinity School, Buies Creek, NC 27506. Offers Christian ministry (MA); divinity (M Div); ministry (D Min); JD/M Div; M Div/MA; M Div/MBA. *Accreditation:* ATS. *Degree requirements:* For doctorate, final project. *Entrance requirements:* For master's, minimum GPA of 2.5; for doctorate, MAT, M Div, minimum graduate GPA of 3.0. Additional exam requirements/recommendations for international students: Required—TOEFL (minimum score 580 paper-based). *Expenses:* Contact institution. *Faculty research:* New Testament, theology, spiritual formation, Old Testament, Christian leadership.

Canadian Southern Baptist Seminary, Graduate Programs, Cochrane, AB T4C 2G1, Canada. Offers Biblical studies (MBS); Christian ministry (MCMin); Christian studies (MCS); ministry (M Div). *Accreditation:* ATS. *Program availability:* Part-time, 100% online, blended/hybrid learning. *Faculty:* 5 full-time (0 women), 5 part-time/adjunct (1 woman). *Students:* 20 full-time (6 women), 19 part-time (3 women); includes 7 minority (2 Black or African American, non-Hispanic/Latino; 5 Asian, non-Hispanic/Latino), 9 international. Average age 29. 16 applicants, 63% accepted, 10 enrolled. In 2017, 7 master's awarded. *Entrance requirements:* Additional exam requirements/recommendations for international students: Required—TOEFL (minimum score 560 paper-based; 83 iBT); Recommended—IELTS (minimum score 6.5). *Application deadline:* For fall admission, 7/1 priority date for domestic students, 3/1 priority date for international students; for winter admission, 11/15 priority date for domestic students. Applications are processed on a rolling basis. Application fee: $50 ($150 for international students). *Expenses: Tuition:* Full-time $7500 Canadian dollars; part-time $375 Canadian dollars per credit hour. *Required fees:* $450 Canadian dollars; $20 Canadian dollars per credit hour. *Financial support:* Scholarships/grants available. Financial award application deadline: 7/1. *Unit head:* Dr. Steve Booth, Academic Dean, 403-932-6622 Ext. 232, E-mail: steve.booth@csbs.ca. *Application contact:* David Ong, Director of Admissions, 403-932-6622 Ext. 251, E-mail: admissions@csbs.ca.

Cardinal Stritch University, College of Arts and Sciences, Department of Religious Studies, Milwaukee, WI 53217-3985. Offers ministry (MA); religious studies (MA). *Program availability:* Part-time, evening/weekend. *Students:* 14 part-time (7 women); includes 2 minority (1 Black or African American, non-Hispanic/Latino; 1 Native Hawaiian or other Pacific Islander, non-Hispanic/Latino), 1 international. Average age 46. In 2017, 2 master's awarded. *Degree requirements:* For master's, comprehensive exam, thesis, research project. *Entrance requirements:* For master's, interview, minimum GPA of 2.75. Additional exam requirements/recommendations for international students: Required—TOEFL (minimum score 79 iBT), IELTS (minimum score 6.5). *Application deadline:* For fall admission, 7/15 priority date for domestic students; for spring admission, 12/15 priority date for domestic students. Applications are processed on a rolling basis. Electronic applications accepted. *Expenses:* $782 per credit. *Financial support:* Research assistantships with partial tuition reimbursements, career-related internships or fieldwork, Federal Work-Study, and scholarships/grants available. Financial award applicants required to submit FAFSA. *Unit head:* Dr. Michelle Gilgannon, Chair, 414-410-4047, E-mail: mlgilgannon@stritch.edu. *Application contact:* Graduate Admissions, 800-347-8822 Ext. 4042, E-mail: admissions@stritch.edu.

Carolina Christian College, Program in Religious Education, Winston-Salem, NC 27102-0777. Offers Christian education (MRE); pastoral care (MRE). *Entrance requirements:* For master's, bachelor's degree from accredited institution, minimum undergraduate "B" average.

Catholic Theological Union, Graduate and Professional Programs, Chicago, IL 60615-5698. Offers biblical spirituality (Certificate); cross-cultural ministries (D Min); cross-

cultural missions (Certificate); divinity (M Div); liturgical studies (Certificate); liturgy (D Min); pastoral studies (MAPS, Certificate); spiritual formation (Certificate); spirituality (D Min); theology (MA); M Div/MA; M Div/MSW; M Div/PhD. M Div/PhD offered jointly with University of Chicago; M Div/MSW with Loyola University Chicago and University of Chicago. *Accreditation:* ACIPE; ATS. *Program availability:* Part-time, evening/weekend. *Degree requirements:* For master's, one foreign language, comprehensive exam (for some programs), thesis (for some programs); for doctorate, thesis/dissertation. *Entrance requirements:* For doctorate, master's degree, 5 years of active ministry. *Faculty research:* Doctrine, sacraments, ethics, Bible.

The Catholic University of America, School of Theology and Religious Studies, Washington, DC 20064. Offers M Cat, M Div, MA, D Min, PhD, STD, Certificate, STB, STL, MSLS/MA, STB/M Div. MSLA/MA offered in conjunction with Department of Library and Information Science. *Program availability:* Part-time. *Faculty:* 42 full-time (3 women), 11 part-time/adjunct (1 woman). *Students:* 146 full-time (11 women), 201 part-time (44 women); includes 70 minority (9 Black or African American, non-Hispanic/Latino; 1 American Indian or Alaska Native, non-Hispanic/Latino; 9 Asian, non-Hispanic/Latino; 25 Hispanic/Latino; 26 Two or more races, non-Hispanic/Latino), 53 international. Average age 36. 180 applicants, 67% accepted, 66 enrolled. In 2017, 59 master's, 25 doctorates awarded. Terminal master's awarded for partial completion of doctoral program. *Degree requirements:* For master's, variable foreign language requirement, comprehensive exam (for some programs), thesis (for some programs); for doctorate, variable foreign language requirement, comprehensive exam, thesis/dissertation. *Entrance requirements:* For master's and doctorate, GRE General Test, statement of purpose, official copies of academic transcripts, three letters of recommendation. Additional exam requirements/recommendations for international students: Required—TOEFL (minimum score 550 paper-based; 80 iBT). *Application deadline:* For fall admission, 7/15 priority date for domestic students, 7/1 for international students; for spring admission, 11/15 priority date for domestic students, 11/1 for international students. Applications are processed on a rolling basis. Application fee: $55. Electronic applications accepted. *Expenses:* Contact institution. *Financial support:* Fellowships, research assistantships, teaching assistantships, Federal Work-Study, scholarships/grants, tuition waivers (full and partial), and unspecified assistantships available. Financial award application deadline: 2/1; financial award applicants required to submit FAFSA. *Faculty research:* Historical and systematic theology, religious education and Catechetics, moral theology and ethics, Biblical studies, liturgical studies and sacramental theology, religion and culture. *Total annual research expenditures:* $389,160. *Unit head:* Very Rev. Mark Morozowich, Dean, 202-319-5684, Fax: 202-319-4967, E-mail: morozowich@cua.edu. *Application contact:* Dr. Steven Brown, Director of Graduate Admissions, 202-319-5057, Fax: 202-319-6533, E-mail: cua-admissions@cua.edu.
Website: https://trs.catholic.edu/

Cedarville University, Graduate Programs, Cedarville, OH 45314. Offers business administration (MBA); family nurse practitioner (MSN); global ministry (M Div); global public health nursing (MSN); healthcare administration (MBA); ministry (M Min); nurse educator (MSN); operations management (MBA); pharmacy (Pharm D). *Program availability:* Part-time, evening/weekend, 100% online, blended/hybrid learning. *Faculty:* 23 full-time (9 women), 48 part-time/adjunct (21 women). *Students:* 202 full-time (123 women), 146 part-time (96 women); includes 63 minority (39 Black or African American, non-Hispanic/Latino; 3 American Indian or Alaska Native, non-Hispanic/Latino; 15 Asian, non-Hispanic/Latino; 2 Hispanic/Latino; 1 Native Hawaiian or other Pacific Islander, non-Hispanic/Latino; 3 Two or more races, non-Hispanic/Latino), 3 international. Average age 24. 345 applicants, 37% accepted, 91 enrolled. In 2017, 53 master's, 47 doctorates awarded. *Degree requirements:* For master's, portfolio; for doctorate, comprehensive exam. *Entrance requirements:* For master's, GRE, 2 professional recommendations; for doctorate, PCAT, professional recommendation from a practicing pharmacist or current employer/supervisor, resume, essay, interview. Additional exam requirements/recommendations for international students: Required—TOEFL (minimum score 550 paper-based; 80 iBT). *Application deadline:* For fall admission, 5/1 priority date for domestic and international students; for spring admission, 11/1 priority date for domestic and international students. Applications are processed on a rolling basis. Application fee: $0. Electronic applications accepted. *Expenses: Tuition:* Full-time $12,594; part-time $566 per credit. One-time fee: $100 full-time. Tuition and fees vary according to degree level and program. *Financial support:* Scholarships/grants and unspecified assistantships available. Support available to part-time students. Financial award application deadline: 1/30; financial award applicants required to submit FAFSA. *Faculty research:* Establishing competencies of clinical reasoning for nursing students in Taiwan, social determinants of health in pediatric primary care, meeting needs of palliative care populations, natural product utility in cancer, monoclonal antibodies directed at angiogenesis regulation. *Total annual research expenditures:* $3,800. *Unit head:* Dr. Janice Supplee, Dean of Graduate Studies, 937-766-7700, E-mail: suppleej@cedarville.edu. *Application contact:* Jim Amstutz, Director of Graduate Admissions, 937-766-7878, Fax: 937-766-7575, E-mail: amstutzj@cedarville.edu.
Website: https://www.cedarville.edu/Admissions/Graduate/Graduate-Programs.aspx

Chaminade University of Honolulu, Office of Professional and Continuing Education, Program in Pastoral Theology, Honolulu, HI 96816-1578. Offers diaconate education (MPT); pastoral counseling and spiritual direction (MPT). *Program availability:* Part-time, evening/weekend, blended/hybrid learning. *Faculty:* 1 full-time (0 women), 1 part-time/adjunct (0 women). *Students:* 9 full-time (2 women), 5 part-time (2 women); includes 10 minority (5 Asian, non-Hispanic/Latino; 2 Hispanic/Latino; 3 Native Hawaiian or other Pacific Islander, non-Hispanic/Latino). Average age 51. 2 applicants, 100% accepted, 2 enrolled. In 2017, 6 master's awarded. *Degree requirements:* For master's, capstone course. *Entrance requirements:* For master's, minimum GPA of 2.5, resume, 2 letters of recommendation, letter of intent, article reflection essay. Additional exam requirements/recommendations for international students: Required—TOEFL (minimum score 550 paper-based; 79 iBT). *Application deadline:* Applications are processed on a rolling basis. Application fee: $40. Electronic applications accepted. *Expenses:* Contact institution. *Financial support:* Applicants required to submit FAFSA. *Unit head:* Dr. David Coleman, Director, 808-739-8341, E-mail: paul.fitzpatrick@chaminade.edu. *Application contact:* 808-735-4755, E-mail: gradserv@chaminade.edu.
Website: https://pace.chaminade.edu/graduate-programs/mpt-program/

Charlotte Christian College and Theological Seminary, Graduate Program, Charlotte, NC 28206. Offers Biblical studies (MA), including New Testament, Old Testament, theology; chaplaincy (M Div); general pastoral studies (M Div); ministry (D Min); pastoral counseling (M Div); urban Christian ministry (MA), including multi-cultural studies, youth ministry. *Program availability:* Part-time, evening/weekend. *Faculty:* 5 full-time (0 women), 6 part-time/adjunct (0 women). *Students:* 17 full-time (8 women), 21 part-time (11 women); includes 31 minority (29 Black or African American, non-Hispanic/Latino; 1 Asian, non-Hispanic/Latino; 1 Two or more races, non-Hispanic/Latino), 2 international. Average age 48. 13 applicants, 100% accepted, 9 enrolled. In 2017, 2 master's awarded. *Degree requirements:* For master's, variable foreign language requirement, thesis; for doctorate, thesis/dissertation. *Entrance requirements:* For master's, 1000-2000 word essay. Additional exam requirements/recommendations for international students: Required—TOEFL, IELTS. *Application deadline:* For fall

admission, 8/3 for domestic and international students; for spring admission, 12/8 for domestic and international students; for summer admission, 4/7 for domestic and international students. Application fee: $50. Electronic applications accepted. *Expenses:* Contact institution. *Financial support:* In 2017–18, 2 students received support. Teaching assistantships, Federal Work-Study, and scholarships/grants available. Financial award application deadline: 4/1; financial award applicants required to submit FAFSA. *Faculty research:* Pastoral topics, urban ministry topics, Biblical topics. *Unit head:* Dr. Eddie G. Grigg, President, 704-344-6882 Ext. 101, Fax: 704-334-6885, E-mail: egrigg@charlottechristian.edu. *Application contact:* George Shears, Director of Admissions, 704-334-6882 Ext. 115, Fax: 704-334-6885, E-mail: gshears@charlottechristian.edu.
Website: http://www.charlottechristian.edu

Chicago Theological Seminary, Graduate and Professional Programs, Chicago, IL 60637-1507. Offers Bible, culture and hermeneutics (PhD); preaching (D Min); religion and health (D Min); religious studies (MA); spirituality and spiritual direction (D Min); theology (M Div); theology, ethics and the human sciences (PhD); M Div/MSW. *Accreditation:* ACIPE; ATS. *Program availability:* Part-time. *Degree requirements:* For master's, thesis; for doctorate, 2 foreign languages, comprehensive exam, thesis/dissertation. *Entrance requirements:* For doctorate, GRE General Test. Additional exam requirements/recommendations for international students: Required—TOEFL. *Faculty research:* Bible, culture and hermeneutics, theology, gender and sexuality, black faith and life, spirituality and psychology, practical theology.

Christian Theological Seminary, Graduate and Professional Programs, Indianapolis, IN 46208-3301. Offers educational and arts ministries (MA); marriage and family therapy (MA); pastoral care and counseling (D Min); psychotherapy and faith (MA); theological studies (MTS); theology (M Div). *Accreditation:* AAMFT/COAMFTE (one or more programs are accredited); ACIPE; ATS. *Program availability:* Part-time. Terminal master's awarded for partial completion of doctoral program. *Degree requirements:* For master's, comprehensive exam (for some programs), thesis (for some programs), missionary and cross-cultural experience (for M Div); for doctorate, comprehensive exam, thesis/dissertation. *Entrance requirements:* For doctorate, M Div. Additional exam requirements/recommendations for international students: Recommended—TOEFL. Electronic applications accepted. *Faculty research:* Faith formation, peer learning post graduation.

Christ the King Seminary, Graduate and Professional Programs, East Aurora, NY 14052. Offers divinity (M Div); pastoral ministry (MA); theology (MA). *Accreditation:* ATS. *Program availability:* Part-time, evening/weekend. *Degree requirements:* For master's, comprehensive exam, thesis. *Entrance requirements:* For master's, previous course work in philosophy and religious studies.

Cincinnati Christian University, Graduate School, Program in Counseling, Cincinnati, OH 45204-3200. Offers MAC. *Degree requirements:* For master's, thesis or alternative, integration paper. *Entrance requirements:* For master's, GRE General Test, interview, minimum undergraduate GPA of 3.0. Additional exam requirements/recommendations for international students: Required—TOEFL. Electronic applications accepted. *Expenses:* Contact institution.

City Vision University, Program in Technology and Ministry, Kansas City, MO 64109-1845. Offers MS. *Program availability:* Online learning. *Degree requirements:* For master's, capstone project.

Claremont Lincoln University, Graduate Programs, Claremont, CA 91711. Offers ethical leadership (MA); interfaith action (MA); social impact (MA).

Claremont School of Theology, Graduate and Professional Programs, Master of Divinity Program, Claremont, CA 91711-3199. Offers interfaith chaplaincy (M Div); Islamic chaplaincy (M Div); ministerial leadership (M Div). *Accreditation:* ACIPE; ATS. *Program availability:* Part-time, 100% online, blended/hybrid learning. *Entrance requirements:* Additional exam requirements/recommendations for international students: Required—TOEFL. Electronic applications accepted.

Claremont School of Theology, Graduate and Professional Programs, Program in Ministry, Claremont, CA 91711-3199. Offers practical theology of conflict, healing and transformation in Korean contexts (D Min); spiritual renewal, contemplative practice, and strategic leadership (D Min). *Accreditation:* ACIPE. *Program availability:* 100% online, blended/hybrid learning. *Degree requirements:* For doctorate, thesis/dissertation. *Entrance requirements:* For doctorate, GRE General Test. Additional exam requirements/recommendations for international students: Required—TOEFL. Electronic applications accepted.

Claremont School of Theology, Graduate and Professional Programs, Program in Religion, Claremont, CA 91711-3199. Offers practical theology (PhD), including religious education and formation, spiritual care and counseling; religion (MA, PhD), including comparative theology and philosophy (PhD), Hebrew Bible and Jewish studies (PhD), New Testament and Christian origins (PhD), process studies (PhD), religion, ethics, and society (PhD). *Accreditation:* ACIPE; ATS. Terminal master's awarded for partial completion of doctoral program. *Degree requirements:* For master's, thesis; for doctorate, 2 foreign languages, thesis/dissertation. *Entrance requirements:* For doctorate, GRE General Test. Additional exam requirements/recommendations for international students: Required—TOEFL. Electronic applications accepted.

Clarks Summit University, Baptist Bible Seminary, South Abington Township, PA 18411. Offers Biblical apologetics (MA); Biblical studies (MA); church education (M Min); church planting (M Div, M Min); communication (D Min); counseling and spiritual development (D Min); global ministry (M Min, D Min); ministry (PhD); missions (M Min); organizational leadership (M Min); outreach pastor (M Min); pastoral counseling (M Min); pastoral leadership (M Div, M Min); pastoral ministry (D Min); theological studies (D Min); theology (Th M); youth pastor (M Min). M Min in missions available only for Association of Baptists for World Evangelism missionary personnel. *Program availability:* Part-time, evening/weekend, online learning. Terminal master's awarded for partial completion of doctoral program. *Degree requirements:* For master's, 2 foreign languages, thesis, oral exam (for M Div); for doctorate, 2 foreign languages, comprehensive exam (for some programs), thesis/dissertation, oral exam. *Entrance requirements:* For doctorate, Greek and Hebrew entrance exams (for PhD). *Application deadline:* Applications are processed on a rolling basis. Application fee: $30. Electronic applications accepted. *Financial support:* Career-related internships or fieldwork and scholarships/grants available. Support available to part-time students. *Unit head:* Dr. Wayne Slusser, Dean, 570-585-9348, Fax: 570-585-4057, E-mail: wslusser@clarkssummitu.edu. *Application contact:* Dr. Wayne Slusser, Dean, 570-585-9348, Fax: 570-585-4057, E-mail: wslusser@clarkssummitu.edu.
Website: https://www.clarkssummitu.edu/seminary/

College of Saint Elizabeth, Department of Theology and Philosophy, Morristown, NJ 07960-6989. Offers Catholic studies (Certificate); pastoral care (Certificate); spirituality (Certificate); theology (MA), including Catholic studies, pastoral care, spirituality, theological studies. *Program availability:* Part-time. *Faculty:* 1 (woman) full-time, 2 part-time/adjunct (0 women). *Students:* 10 part-time (8 women); includes 2 minority (1 Black or African American, non-Hispanic/Latino; 1 Asian, non-Hispanic/Latino). Average age 56. 4 applicants, 100% accepted, 3 enrolled. In 2017, 1 master's awarded. *Degree*

requirements: For master's, thesis. *Entrance requirements:* For master's, baccalaureate degree from accredited institution, personal interview with coordinator and another faculty member, minimum cumulative GPA of 3.0. Additional exam requirements/recommendations for international students: Required—TOEFL (minimum score 550 paper-based; 79 iBT), IELTS (minimum score 6.5). *Application deadline:* For fall admission, 5/1 for international students. Applications are processed on a rolling basis. Application fee: $35. Electronic applications accepted. Application fee is waived when completed online. *Financial support:* Career-related internships or fieldwork, scholarships/grants, tuition waivers (partial), and unspecified assistantships available. Financial award applicants required to submit FAFSA. *Unit head:* Dr. Anthony Santamaria, Chairperson, 973-290-4338, Fax: 973-290-4312, E-mail: asantamaria@cse.edu. *Application contact:* Lori J. Fragoso, Director of Graduate and Continuing Studies Admissions, 973-290-4413, Fax: 973-290-4710, E-mail: apply@cse.edu.
Website: http://www.cse.edu/academics/aas/theology/

Columbia International University, Seminary and School of Ministry, Columbia, SC 29203. Offers academic ministries (M Div); Bible and theology (Certificate); bible exposition (M Div, MABE); Biblical ministry (Certificate); chaplaincy (M Div); intercultural studies (MAIS); leadership (D Min); member care (D Min); missions (D Min); preaching (D Min); theological studies (MA). *Program availability:* Part-time, evening/weekend. *Degree requirements:* For doctorate, comprehensive exam, thesis/dissertation. *Entrance requirements:* For doctorate, 3 years of ministerial experience, M Div. Additional exam requirements/recommendations for international students: Required—TOEFL. Electronic applications accepted.

Concordia University, Nebraska, Graduate Programs in Education, Program in Family Life Ministry, Seward, NE 68434. Offers MS. *Program availability:* Part-time, evening/weekend. *Degree requirements:* For master's, thesis or alternative. *Entrance requirements:* For master's, GRE, MAT, or NTE, minimum GPA of 3.0, BS in education or equivalent.

Corban University, Graduate School, Program in Counseling, Salem, OR 97301-9392. Offers MA. *Degree requirements:* For master's, internship, practicum.

Corban University, Graduate School, School of Ministry, Salem, OR 97301-9392. Offers Biblical languages (M Div); Biblical leadership (Certificate); Christian leadership (MA); Church ministry (M Div); ministry (D Min). *Program availability:* Part-time, evening/weekend. *Degree requirements:* For master's, thesis. *Entrance requirements:* Additional exam requirements/recommendations for international students: Required—TOEFL (minimum score 550 paper-based), IELTS (minimum score 6).

Covenant Theological Seminary, Graduate and Professional Programs, St. Louis, MO 63141-8697. Offers M Div, MA, MAC, MAEM, Th M, D Min, Certificate. *Accreditation:* ATS (one or more programs are accredited). *Program availability:* Part-time, evening/weekend, online learning. *Degree requirements:* For master's, 2 foreign languages, thesis (for some programs); for doctorate, 2 foreign languages, thesis/dissertation; for Certificate, 2 foreign languages. *Entrance requirements:* For doctorate and Certificate, M Div. Additional exam requirements/recommendations for international students: Required—TOEFL (minimum score 550 paper-based). Electronic applications accepted.

Criswell College, Graduate School of the Bible, Dallas, TX 75246-1537. Offers biblical studies (M Div); Christian leadership (MA); counseling (MA); Jewish studies (MA); ministry (MA); theological and biblical studies (MA). *Program availability:* Part-time. *Degree requirements:* For master's, 2 foreign languages, thesis optional. *Entrance requirements:* For master's, GRE General Test, minimum GPA of 2.5. Electronic applications accepted. *Faculty research:* Emphasis on biblical languages (Hebrew and Greek), expository preaching and evangelism in the local church.

Dallas Baptist University, Gary Cook School of Leadership, Program in Leadership Studies, Dallas, TX 75211-9299. Offers leadership studies (PhD), including business, general leadership, higher education, ministry. *Program availability:* Part-time. *Degree requirements:* For doctorate, thesis/dissertation. *Application deadline:* Applications are processed on a rolling basis. Application fee: $25. Electronic applications accepted. Application fee is waived when completed online. *Expenses: Tuition:* Full-time $16,308; part-time $906 per credit hour. *Required fees:* $900; $450 per semester. Tuition and fees vary according to course load and degree level. *Unit head:* Dr. Jack Goodyear, Director, 214-333-5595, Fax: 214-333-6809, E-mail: jackg@dbu.edu. *Application contact:* Dr. Mary Nelson, Program Director, 214-333-5396, E-mail: maryn@dbu.edu.
Website: http://www4.dbu.edu/leadership/phdleadership

Dallas Baptist University, Graduate School of Ministry, Program in Children's Ministry, Dallas, TX 75211-9299. Offers general (MA); special needs children ministry (MA). *Program availability:* Part-time, evening/weekend. *Application deadline:* Applications are processed on a rolling basis. Application fee: $25. Electronic applications accepted. Application fee is waived when completed online. *Expenses: Tuition:* Full-time $16,308; part-time $906 per credit hour. *Required fees:* $900; $450 per semester. Tuition and fees vary according to course load and degree level. *Unit head:* Dr. Robert R. Brooks, Dean, 214-333-5494, Fax: 214-333-5673, E-mail: bobb@dbu.edu. *Application contact:* Shelly Melia, Program Director, 214-333-5943, E-mail: shelly@dbu.edu.
Website: http://www.dbu.edu/ministry/degree-programs/ma-in-childrens-ministry

Dallas Baptist University, Graduate School of Ministry, Program in Christian Counseling, Dallas, TX 75211-9299. Offers MA. *Program availability:* Part-time, evening/weekend. *Application deadline:* Applications are processed on a rolling basis. Application fee: $25. Electronic applications accepted. Application fee is waived when completed online. *Expenses: Tuition:* Full-time $16,308; part-time $906 per credit hour. *Required fees:* $900; $450 per semester. Tuition and fees vary according to course load and degree level. *Unit head:* Dr. Robert R. Brooks, Dean, 214-333-5494, Fax: 214-333-5673, E-mail: bobb@dbu.edu. *Application contact:* Dr. Dana Wicker, Program Director, 214-333-5883, Fax: 214-333-5689, E-mail: dana@dbu.edu.
Website: http://www.dbu.edu/ministry/degree-programs/ma-christian-counseling

Dallas Baptist University, Graduate School of Ministry, Program in Christian Ministry, Dallas, TX 75211-9299. Offers chaplaincy (MA); counseling ministry (MA); family ministry (MA); general ministry (MA); leading the nonprofit organization (MA); ministry leadership (MA); professional life coaching (MA); urban ministry (MA). *Program availability:* Part-time, evening/weekend. *Application deadline:* Applications are processed on a rolling basis. Application fee: $25. Electronic applications accepted. Application fee is waived when completed online. *Expenses: Tuition:* Full-time $16,308; part-time $906 per credit hour. *Required fees:* $900; $450 per semester. Tuition and fees vary according to course load and degree level. *Unit head:* Dr. Robert R. Brooks, Dean, 214-333-5494, Fax: 214-333-5673, E-mail: bobb@dbu.edu. *Application contact:* Dr. Jon Choi, Program Director, 214-333-5375, Fax: 214-333-5689, E-mail: jon@dbu.edu.
Website: http://www.dbu.edu/ministry/degree-programs/m-a-in-christian-ministry

Dallas Baptist University, Graduate School of Ministry, Program in Discipleship, Dallas, TX 75211-9299. Offers discipleship for the family (MA); discipleship through communications (MA); local church discipleship (MA). *Program availability:* Part-time. *Application deadline:* Applications are processed on a rolling basis. Application fee: $25. Electronic applications accepted. Application fee is waived when completed online. *Expenses: Tuition:* Full-time $16,308; part-time $906 per credit hour. *Required fees:* $900; $450 per semester. Tuition and fees vary according to course load and degree level. *Unit head:* Dr. Robert R. Brooks, Dean, 214-333-5494, Fax: 214-333-5673, E-mail: bobb@dbu.edu. *Application contact:* Dr. Chris Shirley, Program Director, 214-333-5256, Fax: 214-333-5689, E-mail: chrissh@dbu.edu.
Website: http://www.dbu.edu/ministry/degree-programs/m-a-in-discipleship

Dallas Baptist University, Graduate School of Ministry, Program in Family Ministry, Dallas, TX 75211-9299. Offers Christian counseling (MA); general (MA); leadership (MA); special needs family ministry (MA). *Program availability:* Part-time, evening/weekend. *Application deadline:* Applications are processed on a rolling basis. Application fee: $25. Electronic applications accepted. Application fee is waived when completed online. *Expenses: Tuition:* Full-time $16,308; part-time $906 per credit hour. *Required fees:* $900; $450 per semester. Tuition and fees vary according to course load and degree level. *Unit head:* Dr. Robert R. Brooks, Dean, 214-333-5494, Fax: 214-333-5673, E-mail: bobb@dbu.edu. *Application contact:* Shelly Melia, Program Director, 214-333-5943, E-mail: shelly@dbu.edu.
Website: http://www.dbu.edu/ministry/degree-programs/m-a-in-family-ministry

Dallas Baptist University, Graduate School of Ministry, Program in Global Leadership, Dallas, TX 75211-9299. Offers church planting (MA); East Asian Studies (MA); English as a second language (MA); general studies (MA); global communication (MA); global studies (MA); international business (MA); leading the nonprofit organization (MA); missions (MA); small group ministry (MA); urban ministry (MA). *Program availability:* Part-time, evening/weekend. *Application deadline:* Applications are processed on a rolling basis. Application fee: $25. Electronic applications accepted. Application fee is waived when completed online. *Expenses: Tuition:* Full-time $16,308; part-time $906 per credit hour. *Required fees:* $900; $450 per semester. Tuition and fees vary according to course load and degree level. *Unit head:* Dr. Robert R. Brooks, Dean, 214-333-5494, Fax: 214-333-5673, E-mail: bobb@dbu.edu. *Application contact:* Dr. Brent Thomason, Program Director, 214-333-5236, E-mail: brentt@dbu.edu.
Website: http://www.dbu.edu/ministry/degree-programs/m-a-in-global-leadership

Dallas Baptist University, Graduate School of Ministry, Program in Student Ministry, Dallas, TX 75211-9299. Offers MA. *Program availability:* Part-time, evening/weekend. *Application deadline:* Applications are processed on a rolling basis. Application fee: $25. Electronic applications accepted. Application fee is waived when completed online. *Expenses: Tuition:* Full-time $16,308; part-time $906 per credit hour. *Required fees:* $900; $450 per semester. Tuition and fees vary according to course load and degree level. *Unit head:* Dr. Robert R. Brooks, Dean, 214-333-5494, Fax: 214-333-5673, E-mail: bobb@dbu.edu. *Application contact:* Dr. Chris Shirley, Program Director, 214-333-5256, Fax: 214-333-5689, E-mail: chrissh@dbu.edu.
Website: http://www.dbu.edu/ministry/degree-programs/m-a-in-student-ministry

Dallas Baptist University, Graduate School of Ministry, Program in Theological Studies, Dallas, TX 75211-9299. Offers Christian heritage (MA); Christian ministry (MA); Christian scriptures (MA). *Program availability:* Part-time, evening/weekend. *Application deadline:* Applications are processed on a rolling basis. Application fee: $25. Electronic applications accepted. Application fee is waived when completed online. *Expenses: Tuition:* Full-time $16,308; part-time $906 per credit hour. *Required fees:* $900; $450 per semester. Tuition and fees vary according to course load and degree level. *Unit head:* Dr. Robert R. Brooks, Dean, 214-333-5494, Fax: 214-333-5673, E-mail: bobb@dbu.edu. *Application contact:* Dr. Jim Lemons, Program Director, 214-333-5366, Fax: 214-333-5689, E-mail: jiml@dbu.edu.
Website: http://www.dbu.edu/ministry/degree-programs/m-a-in-theological-studies

Dallas Baptist University, Graduate School of Ministry, Worship Studies Program, Dallas, TX 75211-9299. Offers worship leadership (MA); worship theology (MA). *Program availability:* Part-time, evening/weekend. *Application deadline:* Applications are processed on a rolling basis. Application fee: $25. Electronic applications accepted. Application fee is waived when completed online. *Expenses: Tuition:* Full-time $16,308; part-time $906 per credit hour. *Required fees:* $900; $450 per semester. Tuition and fees vary according to course load and degree level. *Unit head:* Dr. Robert R. Brooks, Dean, 214-333-5494, Fax: 214-333-5673, E-mail: bobb@dbu.edu. *Application contact:* Dr. Jon Choi, Program Director, 214-333-5375, Fax: 214-333-5689, E-mail: jon@dbu.edu.
Website: http://www.dbu.edu/ministry/degree-programs/m-a-in-worship-studies

Dallas Baptist University, Professional Development Program, Dallas, TX 75211-9299. Offers accounting (MA); church leadership (MA); communication (MA); counseling (MA); criminal justice (MA); English as a second language (MA); finance (MA); higher education (MA); leadership studies (MA); management (MA). *Program availability:* Part-time, evening/weekend. *Application deadline:* Applications are processed on a rolling basis. Application fee: $25. Electronic applications accepted. Application fee is waived when completed online. *Expenses: Tuition:* Full-time $16,308; part-time $906 per credit hour. *Required fees:* $900; $450 per semester. Tuition and fees vary according to course load and degree level. *Unit head:* Jared Ingram, Program Director, 214-333-5584, E-mail: jaredi@dbu.edu. *Application contact:* Bobby Soto, Director of Admissions, 214-333-5242, E-mail: bobby@dbu.edu.
Website: http://www3.dbu.edu/graduate/mapd.asp

Dallas Theological Seminary, Graduate Programs, Dallas, TX 75204-6499. Offers adult education (Th M); apologetics (Th M); Bible backgrounds (Th M); Bible translation (Th M); Biblical and theological studies (Certificate); biblical counseling (MA); biblical exegesis and linguistics (MA); biblical exposition (PhD); biblical studies (MA); Biblical theology (Th M); children's education (Th M); Christian education (MA, D Min); Christian leadership (MA); cross-cultural ministries (MA); educational administration (Th M); educational leadership (Th M); evangelism and discipleship (Th M); exposition of Biblical books (Th M); family life education (Th M); general studies (Th M); Hebrew and cognate studies (Th M); hermeneutics (Th M); historical theology (Th M); homiletics (Th M); intercultural ministries (Th M); Jesus studies (Th M); leadership studies (Th M); media and communication (MA); media arts (Th M); ministry (D Min); ministry with women (Th M); New Testament studies (Th M, PhD); Old Testament studies (Th M, PhD); parachurch ministries (Th M); pastoral care and counseling (Th M); pastoral theology and practice (Th M); philosophy (Th M); sacred theology (STM); spiritual formation (Th M); systematic theology (Th M); teaching in Christian institutions (Th M); theological studies (PhD); urban ministries (Th M); worship studies (Th M); youth education (Th M). *Program availability:* Part-time, online learning. *Degree requirements:* For master's, variable foreign language requirement, thesis (for some programs); for doctorate, 2 foreign languages, thesis/dissertation. *Entrance requirements:* For master's, GRE or MAT (if minimum undergraduate cumulative GPA is below 2.5 or undergraduate degree is unaccredited). Additional exam requirements/recommendations for international students: Required—TOEFL (minimum score 575 paper-based; 85 iBT), TWE. Electronic applications accepted.

Denver Seminary, Graduate and Professional Programs, Littleton, CO 80120. Offers apologetics (Certificate); biblical studies (MA); Christian formation and soul care (MA, Certificate); Christian studies (MA, Certificate); church and parachurch leadership (D Min); counseling licensure (MA); counseling ministry (MA); intercultural ministry (Certificate); leadership (MA, Certificate); marriage and family counseling (D Min);

pastoral ministry (D Min); philosophy of religion (MA); spiritual guidance (Certificate); theology (M Div, Certificate); worship (Certificate); youth and family ministry (MA). *Accreditation:* ACA; ACIPE; ATS (one or more programs are accredited). *Program availability:* Part-time, evening/weekend, online learning. *Degree requirements:* For master's, 2 foreign languages, thesis (for some programs); for doctorate, 2 foreign languages, thesis/dissertation. *Entrance requirements:* For doctorate, M Div, 3 years of ministry experience. Additional exam requirements/recommendations for international students: Required—TOEFL (minimum score 575 paper-based; 90 iBT). Electronic applications accepted.

Earlham School of Religion, Graduate Programs, Richmond, IN 47374-5360. Offers ministry (M Min); religion (MA); theology (M Div). *Accreditation:* ACIPE; ATS. *Program availability:* Part-time, online learning. *Faculty:* 8 full-time (2 women), 2 part-time/adjunct (1 woman). *Students:* 26 full-time (15 women), 32 part-time (21 women). *Degree requirements:* For master's, variable foreign language requirement, comprehensive exam (for some programs), thesis (for some programs), internship (M Div). *Entrance requirements:* For master's, 3 references, academic writing sample, official college transcripts. Additional exam requirements/recommendations for international students: Required—TOEFL (minimum score 550 paper-based; 82 iBT), IELTS (minimum score 7). *Application deadline:* For fall admission, 7/15 priority date for domestic students; for winter admission, 12/15 priority date for domestic students. Applications are processed on a rolling basis. Application fee: $35. Electronic applications accepted. *Expenses: Tuition:* Full-time $15,741; part-time $1741 per course. *Required fees:* $450. *Financial support:* Scholarships/grants and tuition waivers (full and partial) available. Financial award application deadline: 4/15; financial award applicants required to submit FAFSA. *Faculty research:* Digitizing Quaker texts, vital Quaker ministry, research in Quaker studies and other seminary areas. *Unit head:* Jay W. Marshall, Dean, 800-432-1377, Fax: 765-983-1688, E-mail: marshja@earlham.edu. *Application contact:* Matthew Hisrich, Director of Recruitment and Admissions, 765-983-1523, Fax: 765-983-1688, E-mail: hisrima@earlham.edu.
Website: http://esr.earlham.edu/academic-programs

Eastern Mennonite University, Eastern Mennonite Seminary, Harrisonburg, VA 22802-2462. Offers Christian leadership (MA); divinity (M Div); ministry studies (Certificate); religion (MA); theological studies (Certificate). *Accreditation:* ATS. *Program availability:* Part-time. *Degree requirements:* For master's, thesis (for some programs), supervised field education (for M Div). *Entrance requirements:* For master's, minimum GPA of 2.5. Additional exam requirements/recommendations for international students: Required—TOEFL (minimum score 550 paper-based). *Application deadline:* For fall admission, 6/15 priority date for domestic and international students; for winter admission, 11/15 priority date for domestic and international students; for spring admission, 3/15 priority date for domestic and international students. Applications are processed on a rolling basis. Application fee: $25. *Expenses:* Contact institution. *Financial support:* Application deadline: 6/30; applicants required to submit FAFSA. *Faculty research:* Spiritual direction and culture of call, leadership coaching: an approach to leadership in a culture of call, clarity of call in the probationary process for United Methodist clergy in Virginia, EMS women's experiences of culture of call efforts, practices of excellent and fruitful Mennonite pastoral ministry. *Unit head:* Sue Cockley, Dean, 540-432-4984, Fax: 540-432-4444, E-mail: cockleys@emu.edu. *Application contact:* Laura Lehman, Director of Seminary Admissions, 540-432-4268, Fax: 540-432-4598, E-mail: semadmiss@emu.edu.
Website: http://www.emu.edu/seminary/

Eastern Mennonite University, Master of Arts in Counseling Program, Harrisonburg, VA 22802-2462. Offers MA, M Div/MA. *Accreditation:* ACA (one or more programs are accredited); ACIPE. *Program availability:* Part-time. *Degree requirements:* For master's, practicum, internship. *Entrance requirements:* For master's, minimum GPA of 3.0. Additional exam requirements/recommendations for international students: Required—TOEFL (minimum score 550 paper-based; 79 iBT). *Application deadline:* For fall admission, 3/1 for domestic and international students. Application fee: $50. Electronic applications accepted. *Expenses:* Contact institution. *Financial support:* Scholarships/grants available. Financial award application deadline: 6/30; financial award applicants required to submit FAFSA. *Faculty research:* Career and gender, empathy and consciousness, emotion theory, education models. *Unit head:* Dr. Teresa J. Haase, Director, 540-432-4248, Fax: 540-432-4444, E-mail: teresa.haase@emu.edu. *Application contact:* Amanda Williams, Administrative Assistant, 540-432-4243, Fax: 540-432-4444, E-mail: amanda.k.williams@emu.edu.
Website: http://www.emu.edu/graduate-counseling/

Ecumenical Theological Seminary, Program in Ministry, Detroit, MI 48201. Offers D Min. *Accreditation:* ACIPE.

Emory University, Candler School of Theology, Atlanta, GA 30322. Offers formation and witness (M Div); history, scripture and tradition (MTS); leadership in church and community (M Div); modern religious thought and experience (MTS); pastoral counseling (Th D); religion and race (M Div); religion, health and science (M Div); scripture and interpretation (M Div); society and personality (M Div); theology (Th M); theology and ethics (M Div); theology and the arts (M Div); traditions of the church (M Div); women and religion (M Div); JD/M Div; JD/MTS; M Div/MBA; M Div/MPH; MBA/MTS; MTS/MPH. *Accreditation:* ACIPE. *Program availability:* Part-time. *Degree requirements:* For master's, thesis optional; for doctorate, comprehensive exam, thesis/dissertation. *Entrance requirements:* For master's, minimum undergraduate GPA of 3.0; for doctorate, GRE, M Div, 8 units of course work in clinical pastoral education. Additional exam requirements/recommendations for international students: Required—TOEFL (minimum score 600 paper-based; 95 iBT). Electronic applications accepted. *Expenses:* Contact institution. *Faculty research:* Biblical studies, church history, ethics, ministry practice, pastoral care.

Evangelical Seminary, Graduate and Professional Programs, Myerstown, PA 17067-1212. Offers Biblical studies (MAR); congregational ministry (M Div); global and contextual studies (M Div, MAR); historical and theological studies (MAR); interdisciplinary studies (MAR); marriage and family counseling (M Div); marriage and family therapy (MA); New Testament (MAR); Old Testament (MAR); spiritual formation (MAR); teaching ministry (M Div); youth ministry (M Div). *Accreditation:* ATS (one or more programs are accredited). *Program availability:* Part-time, online learning. *Degree requirements:* For master's, 2 foreign languages. *Entrance requirements:* For master's, minimum GPA of 2.5. Additional exam requirements/recommendations for international students: Required—TOEFL (minimum score 550 paper-based). *Faculty research:* Literary form and structure within the Hebrew and Greek scriptures, Wesley studies, esoteric biblical languages, the Mosaic law and the Christian, ethics.

Fairfield University, Graduate School of Education and Allied Professions, Fairfield, CT 06824. Offers applied behavior analysis (ATC); applied psychology (MA); clinical mental health counseling (MA, CAS); educational technology (MA); elementary education (MA, CAS); family studies (MA); integration of spirituality and religion in counseling (ATC); marriage and family therapy (MA); reading and language development (Sixth Year Certificate); school counseling (MA, CAS); school psychology (MA, CAS); school-based marriage and family therapy (ATC); secondary education (MA); special education (MA, CAS); substance abuse counseling (ATC); teaching (Certificate); teaching and foundations (MA, CAS); TESOL, world languages, and bilingual education (MA, CAS).

Accreditation: NCATE. *Program availability:* Part-time, evening/weekend. *Faculty:* 23 full-time (17 women), 39 part-time/adjunct (28 women). *Students:* 199 full-time (168 women), 251 part-time (206 women); includes 85 minority (21 Black or African American, non-Hispanic/Latino; 9 Asian, non-Hispanic/Latino; 49 Hispanic/Latino; 6 Two or more races, non-Hispanic/Latino), 4 international. Average age 32. 370 applicants, 56% accepted, 125 enrolled. In 2017, 136 master's, 28 other advanced degrees awarded. *Degree requirements:* For master's, comprehensive exam. *Entrance requirements:* For master's, minimum GPA of 3.0, 2 recommendations, resume. Additional exam requirements/recommendations for international students: Required—TOEFL (minimum score 550 paper-based; 84 iBT) or IELTS (minimum score 7.5). *Application deadline:* For fall admission, 2/15 for international students; for spring admission, 10/1 for international students. Application fee: $60. Electronic applications accepted. *Expenses:* $750 per credit hour. *Financial support:* In 2017–18, 34 students received support. Career-related internships or fieldwork and unspecified assistantships available. Support available to part-time students. Financial award applicants required to submit FAFSA. *Faculty research:* Reading and literacy, writing, social justice and inequality in education, addictions and mental health issues, therapeutic relationships and clinical supervision. *Unit head:* Dr. Robert D. Hannafin, Dean, 203-254-4250, Fax: 203-254-4241, E-mail: rhannafin@fairfield.edu. *Application contact:* Marianne Gumpper, Director of Graduate Admission, 203-254-4184, Fax: 203-254-4073, E-mail: gradadmis@fairfield.edu.
Website: http://www.fairfield.edu/gseap

Faith Baptist Bible College and Theological Seminary, Graduate Program, Ankeny, IA 50023. Offers Biblical studies (MA); pastoral studies (M Div); pastoral training (MA); religion (MA); theological studies (MA). *Program availability:* Part-time. *Degree requirements:* For master's, thesis or alternative. *Entrance requirements:* Additional exam requirements/recommendations for international students: Required—TOEFL (minimum score 550 paper-based; 79 iBT), IELTS (minimum score 6.5). Electronic applications accepted. *Faculty research:* Baptist theology, American church history.

Faulkner University, College of Biblical Studies, Montgomery, AL 36109-3398. Offers Biblical studies (MA, PhD); Christian counseling and family ministry (MA); Christian ministry (MA). *Program availability:* Part-time, evening/weekend, 100% online, blended/hybrid learning, synchronous online/on-ground. *Faculty:* 7 full-time (1 woman). *Students:* 28 full-time (9 women), 16 part-time (2 women); includes 21 minority (18 Black or African American, non-Hispanic/Latino; 2 Hispanic/Latino; 1 Two or more races, non-Hispanic/Latino), 1 international. Average age 39. 42 applicants, 45% accepted, 15 enrolled. In 2017, 5 master's awarded. Terminal master's awarded for partial completion of doctoral program. *Degree requirements:* For master's, comprehensive exam, thesis (for some programs); for doctorate, 3 foreign languages, thesis/dissertation. *Entrance requirements:* Additional exam requirements/recommendations for international students: Required—TOEFL (minimum score 500 paper-based). *Application deadline:* For fall admission, 6/1 for domestic students; for spring admission, 11/1 for domestic students; for summer admission, 4/1 for domestic students. Application fee: $35. Electronic applications accepted. *Expenses:* $540 per hour tuition (for MA); $550 per hour tuition (for PhD); $220 per semester fees. *Financial support:* Applicants required to submit FAFSA. *Unit head:* Dr. G. Scott Gleaves, Dean/Vice President, Black College of Biblical Studies, 334-386-7660, Fax: 334-386-7203, E-mail: sgleaves@faulkner.edu. *Application contact:* Dr. Randall C. Bailey, Director, Kearly Graduate School of Theology, 334-386-7663, Fax: 334-386-7203, E-mail: rbailey@faulkner.edu.
Website: https://www.faulkner.edu/graduate/graduate_academics/kearley-graduate-school-of-theology/

Fordham University, Graduate School of Religion and Religious Education, New York, NY 10458. Offers pastoral counseling and spiritual care (MA); pastoral ministry/spirituality/pastoral counseling (D Min); religion and religious education (MA); religious education (MS, PhD, PD); spiritual direction (Certificate). *Program availability:* Part-time. Terminal master's awarded for partial completion of doctoral program. *Degree requirements:* For master's, research paper; for doctorate, comprehensive exam, thesis/dissertation. *Entrance requirements:* For doctorate, MAT. Electronic applications accepted. *Expenses:* Contact institution. *Faculty research:* Spirituality and spiritual direction, pastoral care and counseling, adult family and community, growth and young adult.

Freed-Hardeman University, School of Biblical Studies, Program in Ministry, Henderson, TN 38340-2399. Offers M Min. *Program availability:* Part-time. *Degree requirements:* For master's, comprehensive exam, internship. *Entrance requirements:* For master's, GRE General Test or MAT. Additional exam requirements/recommendations for international students: Required—TOEFL (minimum score 500 paper-based).

Fresno Pacific University, Biblical Seminary, Program in Christian Ministry, Fresno, CA 93702-4709. Offers MA. *Program availability:* Part-time. *Entrance requirements:* For master's, minimum GPA of 2.5. Additional exam requirements/recommendations for international students: Required—TOEFL (minimum score 550 paper-based). *Expenses:* Contact institution.

Fuller Theological Seminary, Graduate Programs, Pasadena, CA 91182. Offers Christian leadership (MACL); clinical psychology (PhD, Psy D); family studies (MA); global leadership (MA); global ministries (D Min); global ministries (Korean language) (D Min); intercultural studies (MA, Th M, PhD); intercultural studies (Korean language) (MA); marital and family therapy (MS); marriage and family enrichment (Certificate); ministry (M Div, D Min); missiology (D Miss); missiology (Korean language) (Th M); theology (MA, Th M, PhD), including evangelism (MA), family life education (MA), pastoral ministry (MA), recovery ministry (MA), worship music ministry (MA), worship, theology, and the arts (MA), youth, family, and culture (MA); theology and ministry (MA).

Gannon University, School of Graduate Studies, College of Humanities, Education, and Social Sciences, School of Humanities, Program in Pastoral Studies, Erie, PA 16541-0001. Offers pastoral studies (MA); theological studies (Certificate). *Program availability:* Part-time, evening/weekend. *Degree requirements:* For master's, comprehensive exam, thesis or alternative, research project, internship, written evaluation. *Entrance requirements:* Additional exam requirements/recommendations for international students: Required—TOEFL (minimum score 79 iBT). Electronic applications accepted. Application fee is waived when completed online.

Gardner-Webb University, School of Divinity, Boiling Springs, NC 28017. Offers biblical studies (M Div); Christian education and formation (M Div); intercultural studies (M Div); ministry (D Min); missiology (M Div); pastoral care and counseling (M Div); pastoral care and counseling/member care for missionaries (D Min); pastoral studies (M Div); M Div/MA; M Div/MBA. *Accreditation:* ACIPE. *Program availability:* Part-time. *Faculty:* 10 full-time (1 woman), 4 part-time/adjunct (2 women). *Students:* 102 full-time (47 women), 56 part-time (15 women); includes 67 minority (63 Black or African American, non-Hispanic/Latino; 3 Asian, non-Hispanic/Latino; 1 Hispanic/Latino). Average age 38. *Entrance requirements:* For master's, minimum GPA of 2.6; for doctorate, minimum GPA of 2.75. Additional exam requirements/recommendations for international students: Required—TOEFL (minimum score 500 paper-based; 61 iBT). *Application deadline:* Applications are processed on a rolling basis. Electronic applications accepted. *Expenses:* Contact institution. *Financial support:* Fellowships,

institutionally sponsored loans, and unspecified assistantships available. Support available to part-time students. Financial award application deadline: 5/15. *Faculty research:* Jewish-Christian dialogue, Islam. *Unit head:* Dr. Robert W. Canoy, Sr., Dean, 704-406-4400, Fax: 704-406-3935, E-mail: rcanoy@gardner-webb.edu. *Application contact:* Kheresa Harmon, Director of Admissions, 704-406-3205, Fax: 704-406-3895, E-mail: kharmon@gardner-webb.edu.
Website: http://gardner-webb.edu/academic-programs-and-resources/colleges-and-schools/divinity/index

Garrett-Evangelical Theological Seminary, Graduate and Professional Programs, Evanston, IL 60201-3298. Offers Bible and culture (PhD); Christian education (MA); Christian education and congregational studies (PhD); contemporary theology and culture (PhD); divinity (M Div); ethics, church, and society (MA); liturgical studies (PhD); ministry (D Min); music ministry (MA); pastoral care and counseling (MA); pastoral theology, personality, and culture (PhD); spiritual formation and evangelism (MA); theological studies (MTS); M Div/MSW. M Div/MSW offered jointly with Loyola University Chicago. *Accreditation:* ACIPE; ATS (one or more programs are accredited). *Program availability:* Part-time. *Degree requirements:* For master's, thesis (for some programs); for doctorate, thesis/dissertation. *Entrance requirements:* For doctorate, GRE (PhD). Additional exam requirements/recommendations for international students: Required—TOEFL (minimum score 560 paper-based). Electronic applications accepted.

Gateway Seminary, Graduate and Professional Programs, Ontario, CA 91761-8642. Offers divinity (M Div); early childhood education (Certificate); education leadership (MAEL, Diploma); ministry (D Min); theological studies (MTS); theology (Th M); youth ministry (Certificate). *Accreditation:* ACIPE; ATS. *Program availability:* Part-time, evening/weekend. *Degree requirements:* For master's, thesis (for some programs); for doctorate, 2 foreign languages, thesis/dissertation. *Entrance requirements:* For doctorate, MAT. Additional exam requirements/recommendations for international students: Required—TOEFL (minimum score 550 paper-based). Electronic applications accepted.

General Theological Seminary, Graduate and Professional Programs, New York, NY 10011-4977. Offers Anglican studies (STM, Th D, Certificate); ascetical theology (Certificate); biblical studies (Certificate); congregational development (Certificate); divinity (M Div); historical and theological studies (Certificate); spiritual direction (MASD, STM, Certificate); theology (MA). *Accreditation:* ACIPE; ATS. *Program availability:* Part-time, evening/weekend. Terminal master's awarded for partial completion of doctoral program. *Degree requirements:* For master's, thesis; for doctorate, 2 foreign languages, thesis/dissertation. *Entrance requirements:* For master's, GRE General Test; for doctorate, GRE, M Div or MA. Additional exam requirements/recommendations for international students: Required—TOEFL. *Faculty research:* Liturgy, New Testament, ethics, history, ecumenical relations.

Geneva College, Program in Leadership Studies, Beaver Falls, PA 15010-3599. Offers business management (MS); ministry leadership (MS); non-profit leadership (MS); organizational management (MS); project management (MS). *Program availability:* Online only, 100% online. *Faculty:* 4 part-time/adjunct (1 woman). *Students:* 32 full-time (22 women); includes 10 minority (8 Black or African American, non-Hispanic/Latino; 1 Asian, non-Hispanic/Latino; 1 Hispanic/Latino). Average age 43. 25 applicants, 60% accepted, 11 enrolled. In 2017, 35 master's awarded. *Degree requirements:* For master's, thesis or alternative, capstone leadership studies project. *Entrance requirements:* For master's, undergraduate degree from regionally-accredited college or university, one to three years of experience in the workplace, minimum GPA of 3.0 (preferred), resume, essay, two recommendations. Additional exam requirements/recommendations for international students: Required—TOEFL. *Application deadline:* For fall admission, 9/21 for domestic students; for spring admission, 2/23 for domestic students; for summer admission, 7/22 for domestic students. Applications are processed on a rolling basis. Electronic applications accepted. *Expenses:* $640 per credit. *Financial support:* Scholarships/grants available. Financial award application deadline: 8/1; financial award applicants required to submit FAFSA. *Faculty research:* Servant leadership, leadership essentials. *Unit head:* John D. Gallo, Dean of Graduate, Adult and Online Programs, 800-576-3111, Fax: 724-847-6839, E-mail: msls@geneva.edu. *Application contact:* Graduate Enrollment Representative, 800-576-3111, Fax: 724-847-6839, E-mail: msls@geneva.edu.
Website: http://www.geneva.edu/graduate/leadership-studies/

George Fox University, Portland Seminary, Portland, OR 97223. Offers Biblical studies (M Div, MA); chaplaincy (M Div); Christian history and theology (M Div, MA); creation care (M Div, MA); intercultural studies (M Div, MA); leadership (M Div, MA); leadership and global perspectives (D Min); leadership and spiritual formation (D Min); semiotics and future studies (D Min); spiritual direction (MA, Certificate); spiritual direction supervision (M Div, MA, Certificate); spiritual formation and discipleship (M Div, MA, Certificate). *Accreditation:* ACIPE. *Program availability:* Part-time, evening/weekend, online learning. *Entrance requirements:* For master's, resume, three references (one pastoral, one academic or professional, one personal), one official transcript from each college or university attended; for doctorate, resume, 3 references (1 professional, 1 academic, 1 personal), one official transcript from each college or university attended. Additional exam requirements/recommendations for international students: Required—TOEFL (minimum score 577 paper-based; 90 iBT). Electronic applications accepted. *Expenses:* Contact institution.

Global University, Graduate School of Theology, Springfield, MO 65804. Offers bible and theology (D Min); biblical language (M Div); biblical studies (MA); Christian ministry (M Div, D Min); ministerial studies (MA), including education, leadership, missions, New Testament, Old Testament. *Program availability:* Part-time, evening/weekend, online learning. *Degree requirements:* For master's, thesis (for some programs). *Entrance requirements:* For master's, minimum undergraduate GPA of 3.0. Electronic applications accepted. *Faculty research:* Higher education, cross-cultural missions.

Gordon-Conwell Theological Seminary, Graduate and Professional Programs, South Hamilton, MA 01982. Offers Biblical languages (MABL); church history (MACH); counseling (MACO); ministry (D Min); missions/evangelism (MAME); New Testament (MANT); Old Testament (MAOT); religion (MAR); theology (M Div, MATH, Th M, Th D). *Accreditation:* ACIPE; ATS (one or more programs are accredited). *Program availability:* Part-time, evening/weekend. *Degree requirements:* For master's, one foreign language, thesis optional; for doctorate, 2 foreign languages, thesis/dissertation. *Entrance requirements:* For master's, minimum GPA of 2.5; for doctorate, minimum GPA of 3.0.

Grace Theological Seminary, Graduate and Professional Programs, Winona Lake, IN 46590-9907. Offers biblical studies (Certificate); chaplaincy (M Div); exegetical studies (M Div); intercultural studies (M Div, MA, D Min); local church ministry (MA), including camp administration, women's leadership; pastoral counseling (M Div); pastoral studies (M Div, D Min); theology (Diploma). *Accreditation:* ATS. *Program availability:* Part-time, online learning. *Degree requirements:* For master's, thesis optional; for doctorate, 2 foreign languages, thesis/dissertation. *Entrance requirements:* For master's, MAT, minimum GPA of 2.5. Electronic applications accepted. *Faculty research:* Biblical theology, language, and church ministries.

Grand Canyon University, College of Doctoral Studies, Phoenix, AZ 85017-1097. Offers data analytics (DBA); general psychology (PhD), including cognition and instruction, industrial and organizational psychology, integrating technology, learning, and psychology, performance psychology; management (DBA); marketing (DBA); organizational leadership (Ed D), including behavioral health, Christian ministry, health care administration, organizational development. *Degree requirements:* For doctorate, comprehensive exam, thesis/dissertation. *Entrance requirements:* For doctorate, minimum GPA of 3.4 on earned advanced degree from regionally-accredited institution; transcripts; goals statement.

Grand Rapids Theological Seminary of Cornerstone University, Graduate Programs, Grand Rapids, MI 49525-5897. Offers academic (M Div); chaplaincy ministries (M Div); Christian formation (MA); counseling (MA); formation and soul care ministries (M Div); intercultural ministries (M Div); interdisciplinary studies (MA); New Testament (Th M); Old Testament (Th M); pastoral ministries (M Div); small group and discipleship ministries (M Div); student and family ministries (M Div). *Accreditation:* ATS. *Program availability:* Part-time, evening/weekend, 100% online, blended/hybrid learning. *Faculty:* 9 full-time (2 women), 14 part-time/adjunct (5 women). *Students:* 100 full-time (53 women), 211 part-time (102 women); includes 71 minority (54 Black or African American, non-Hispanic/Latino; 1 American Indian or Alaska Native, non-Hispanic/Latino; 3 Asian, non-Hispanic/Latino; 12 Hispanic/Latino; 1 Two or more races, non-Hispanic/Latino), 3 international. Average age 36. 165 applicants, 76% accepted, 99 enrolled. In 2017, 75 master's awarded. *Entrance requirements:* Additional exam requirements/recommendations for international students: Required—TOEFL (minimum score 577 paper-based; 90 iBT), IELTS (minimum score 7). *Application deadline:* For fall admission, 8/15 for domestic students, 6/15 for international students; for spring admission, 1/10 for domestic students, 11/10 for international students; for summer admission, 4/30 for domestic students. Applications are processed on a rolling basis. Electronic applications accepted. *Expenses: Tuition:* Full-time $9720; part-time $540 per credit hour. *Required fees:* $832; $374 per semester. Tuition and fees vary according to course load and program. *Financial support:* In 2017–18, 96 students received support, including 8 fellowships with partial tuition reimbursements available; career-related internships or fieldwork and scholarships/grants also available. Support available to part-time students. Financial award application deadline: 8/15; financial award applicants required to submit FAFSA. *Unit head:* Dr. John F. VerBerkmoes, Executive Vice President and Academic Dean, 616-222-1422, E-mail: john.verberkmoes@cornerstone.edu. *Application contact:* Ashley VanBemmelen, Director of Admissions, 800-697-1133, E-mail: ashley.vanbemmelen@cornerstone.edu.

Greenville University, Program in Leadership and Ministry, Greenville, IL 62246-0159. Offers MA. *Program availability:* Part-time. *Degree requirements:* For master's, 6 hours of research/practicum in applied ministry. *Entrance requirements:* For master's, 1 year of work experience in Christian ministry, interview. Additional exam requirements/recommendations for international students: Required—TOEFL (minimum score 525 paper-based). Electronic applications accepted.

Hampton University, School of Liberal Arts and Education, Program in Counseling, Hampton, VA 23668. Offers college student development (MA); community agency counseling (MA); counseling (Ed S); counselor education and supervision (PhD); pastoral counseling (MA); school counseling (MA). *Accreditation:* ACA; NCATE. *Program availability:* Part-time, evening/weekend, online learning. *Students:* 30 full-time (28 women), 15 part-time (13 women); includes 39 minority (all Black or African American, non-Hispanic/Latino), 1 international. Average age 33. 28 applicants, 25% accepted, 3 enrolled. In 2017, 16 master's awarded. *Degree requirements:* For master's, comprehensive exam; for doctorate, comprehensive exam, thesis/dissertation. *Entrance requirements:* For master's, GRE General Test, personal statement, two letters of recommendation; for doctorate, GRE General Test, personal statement, writing sample, three letters of recommendation; for Ed S, personal statement, two letters of recommendation. Additional exam requirements/recommendations for international students: Required—TOEFL (minimum score 525 paper-based) or IELTS (6.5). *Application deadline:* For fall admission, 6/1 priority date for domestic students, 4/1 priority date for international students; for winter admission, 9/1 priority date for international students; for spring admission, 11/1 priority date for domestic students, 9/1 for international students; for summer admission, 4/1 priority date for domestic students, 2/1 priority date for international students. Applications are processed on a rolling basis. Application fee: $35. Electronic applications accepted. *Expenses: Tuition:* Full-time $22,630; part-time $575 per semester hour. *Required fees:* $70. Tuition and fees vary according to program. *Financial support:* Fellowships, research assistantships, teaching assistantships, career-related internships or fieldwork, Federal Work-Study, institutionally sponsored loans, and scholarships/grants available. Support available to part-time students. Financial award application deadline: 6/30; financial award applicants required to submit FAFSA. *Faculty research:* Personality development, temperament, post-traumatic stress disorder, continuum of normal to abnormal personality. *Unit head:* Dr. Richard Mason, Chairperson, 757-728-6160, E-mail: richard.mason@hamptonu.edu.
Website: http://edhd.hamptonu.edu/counseling/

Harding School of Theology, Graduate Programs, Memphis, TN 38117-5499. Offers Christian ministry (MA); historical theology (MA); ministry (M Div); New Testament (MA); Old Testament (MA); systematic theology (MA); transforming leadership (D Min). *Accreditation:* ATS. *Program availability:* Part-time, online learning. *Faculty:* 6 full-time (0 women), 2 part-time/adjunct (1 woman). *Students:* 28 full-time (7 women), 99 part-time (7 women); includes 26 minority (23 Black or African American, non-Hispanic/Latino; 2 Asian, non-Hispanic/Latino; 1 Hispanic/Latino), 2 international. *Degree requirements:* For master's, variable foreign language requirement, thesis (for some programs); for doctorate, one foreign language, thesis/dissertation. *Entrance requirements:* For master's, minimum GPA of 2.7; for doctorate, minimum GPA of 3.0. Additional exam requirements/recommendations for international students: Required—TOEFL (minimum score 550 paper-based; 79 iBT). *Application deadline:* For fall admission, 12/7 priority date for domestic students; for spring admission, 5/3 priority date for domestic students. Applications are processed on a rolling basis. Application fee: $40. Electronic applications accepted. *Expenses: Tuition:* Full-time $14,000. *Required fees:* $525. One-time fee: $40 full-time. *Financial support:* Research assistantships with partial tuition reimbursements, career-related internships or fieldwork, institutionally sponsored loans, scholarships/grants, tuition waivers (partial), and unspecified assistantships available. Support available to part-time students. Financial award application deadline: 3/1; financial award applicants required to submit FAFSA. *Unit head:* Dr. Allen Black, Dean, 901-761-1352, Fax: 901-761-1358, E-mail: ablack@hst.edu. *Application contact:* Dr. Matt R. Carter, Director of Admissions, 901-761-1356, Fax: 901-761-1358, E-mail: mrcarter@harding.edu.
Website: https://hst.edu/academics/degrees/

Harding University, College of Bible and Ministry, Searcy, AR 72149-0001. Offers M Min. *Program availability:* Part-time, online learning. *Faculty:* 3 full-time (1 woman). *Students:* 13 part-time (1 woman); includes 1 minority (Black or African American, non-Hispanic/Latino). Average age 48. In 2017, 6 master's awarded. *Entrance requirements:* Additional exam requirements/recommendations for international students: Required—TOEFL (minimum score 550 paper-based; 79 iBT). Tuition and fees vary according to course load, degree level, campus/location and program. *Financial support:* In 2017–18, 12 students received support. Scholarships/grants and unspecified assistantships

available. Financial award applicants required to submit FAFSA. *Faculty research:* Forgiveness, substance abuse, post-traumatic stress disorder. *Unit head:* Dr. Monte Cox, Dean, 501-279-4448, Fax: 501-279-4042, E-mail: mcox@harding.edu. *Application contact:* 501-279-4448, Fax: 501-279-5192, E-mail: bible@harding.edu.
Website: http://www.harding.edu/bible

Hardin-Simmons University, Graduate School, Logsdon School of Theology, Logsdon Seminary, Program in Family Ministry, Abilene, TX 79698-0001. Offers MA. *Program availability:* Part-time. *Faculty:* 2 full-time (0 women). *Students:* 9 full-time (5 women), 11 part-time (all women); includes 2 minority (both Hispanic/Latino), 1 international. Average age 30. In 2017, 4 master's awarded. *Degree requirements:* For master's, comprehensive exam, minimum cumulative GPA of 3.0, clinical experience, project. *Entrance requirements:* For master's, letters of recommendation; interview; church endorsement. Additional exam requirements/recommendations for international students: Required—TOEFL (minimum score 550 paper-based; 75 iBT). *Application deadline:* For fall admission, 8/15 priority date for domestic students, 4/1 for international students; for spring admission, 1/5 priority date for domestic students, 9/1 for international students. Applications are processed on a rolling basis. Application fee: $50 ($150 for international students). Electronic applications accepted. *Expenses: Tuition:* Full-time $13,500; part-time $750 per semester hour. *Required fees:* $220 per term. One-time fee: $50. Tuition and fees vary according to course load, campus/location and program. *Financial support:* In 2017–18, 15 students received support. Fellowships, career-related internships or fieldwork, and scholarships/grants available. Support available to part-time students. Financial award application deadline: 6/30; financial award applicants required to submit FAFSA. *Unit head:* Dr. Randall Maurer, Program Director, 325-670-1599, Fax: 325-670-1406, E-mail: rmaurer@hsutx.edu. *Application contact:* Dr. Nancy Kucinski, Dean of Graduate Studies, 325-670-1298, Fax: 325-670-1564, E-mail: gradoff@hsutx.edu.
Website: http://www.logsdonseminary.org/index.php/academics/mafm

Hardin-Simmons University, Graduate School, Logsdon School of Theology, Logsdon Seminary, Program in Ministry, Abilene, TX 79698-0001. Offers D Min. *Program availability:* Part-time. *Faculty:* 2 full-time (0 women), 1 part-time/adjunct (0 women). *Students:* 31 part-time (1 woman); includes 6 minority (4 Black or African American, non-Hispanic/Latino; 1 Asian, non-Hispanic/Latino; 1 Hispanic/Latino), 1 international. Average age 43. In 2017, 3 doctorates awarded. *Degree requirements:* For doctorate, ministry project. *Entrance requirements:* For doctorate, GRE or MAT, M Div or equivalent, minimum graduate GPA of 3.0, minimum 3 years' ministry experience, active current ministry involvement, interview, 4 letters of recommendation, church endorsement. *Application deadline:* For fall admission, 4/30 for domestic students. Application fee: $50 ($150 for international students). *Expenses: Tuition:* Full-time $13,500; part-time $750 per semester hour. *Required fees:* $220 per term. One-time fee: $50. Tuition and fees vary according to course load, campus/location and program. *Financial support:* In 2017–18, 23 students received support. Fellowships and scholarships/grants available. Financial award application deadline: 6/30; financial award applicants required to submit FAFSA. *Unit head:* Dr. Larry Baker, Program Director, 325-671-2110, Fax: 325-670-1406, E-mail: lbaker@hsutx.edu. *Application contact:* Dr. Nancy Kucinski, Dean of Graduate Studies, 325-670-1298, Fax: 325-670-1564, E-mail: gradoff@hsutx.edu.
Website: http://www.logsdonseminary.org/index.php/academics/doctor-of-ministry

Hartford Seminary, Graduate Programs, Hartford, CT 06105-2279. Offers Islamic studies (MA); ministry (D Min); religious studies (MA); spirituality (Certificate). *Accreditation:* ATS (one or more programs are accredited). *Program availability:* Part-time, evening/weekend, online learning. *Degree requirements:* For master's, thesis optional, oral exam; for doctorate, thesis/dissertation, oral exam. *Entrance requirements:* For doctorate, experience in ministry, M Div. Additional exam requirements/recommendations for international students: Required—TOEFL (minimum score 550 paper-based; 80 iBT). *Faculty research:* Liturgy and social justice, professional leadership in ministry, congregational studies, Christian-Muslim relations, American religion.

Heritage Christian University, Graduate Programs, Florence, AL 35630. Offers counseling (MM); Greek (MA); ministry (MM); New Testament (MA). *Degree requirements:* For master's, practicum (MM), major research paper (MA). *Entrance requirements:* For master's, MAT or GRE, bachelor's degree in Bible from an accredited college or university, minimum GPA of 2.75, 3 letters of recommendation.

Holmes Institute, Graduate Program, Golden, CO 80401. Offers consciousness studies (MS). *Program availability:* Online learning. *Degree requirements:* For master's, comprehensive exam, 2 spiritual retreats per year, internship (1 per term), 2 spiritual conferences. *Entrance requirements:* For master's, 2 letters of recommendation, interview, official transcripts of an accredited bachelor's degree. Additional exam requirements/recommendations for international students: Required—TOEFL (minimum score 530 paper-based).

Holy Names University, Graduate Division, Department of Counseling Psychology, Oakland, CA 94619-1699. Offers counseling and forensic counseling (MA); counseling psychology (MA); forensic psychology (MA). *Program availability:* Part-time, evening/weekend. *Degree requirements:* For master's, comprehensive paper, seminars. *Entrance requirements:* For master's, minimum undergraduate GPA of 2.6 overall, 3.0 in major. Additional exam requirements/recommendations for international students: Required—TOEFL (minimum score 550 paper-based; 79 iBT). Electronic applications accepted. Application fee is waived when completed online. *Expenses:* Contact institution. *Faculty research:* Cognitive psychology, anger management, grief and grief counseling, post-modernism and psychotherapy, spirituality and psychology.

Houston Baptist University, College of Education and Behavioral Sciences, Program in Counseling, Houston, TX 77074-3298. Offers Christian counseling (MACC); counseling (MAC); marriage and family therapy (MA); pastoral counseling (MA), including addiction and recovery, crisis response, human sexuality, marriage and family therapy, military and veteran care and counseling, professional life coaching. *Program availability:* Part-time, evening/weekend, 100% online. *Students:* 42 full-time (35 women), 103 part-time (91 women); includes 80 minority (31 Black or African American, non-Hispanic/Latino; 10 Asian, non-Hispanic/Latino; 36 Hispanic/Latino; 3 Two or more races, non-Hispanic/Latino), 4 international. Average age 29. 178 applicants, 16% accepted, 16 enrolled. In 2017, 22 master's awarded. *Degree requirements:* For master's, comprehensive exam, practicum. *Entrance requirements:* For master's, GRE (waived if GPA is 3.0 or higher), two academic or professional recommendations, bachelor's degree conferred transcript, resume, interview. Additional exam requirements/recommendations for international students: Required—TOEFL (minimum score 80 iBT), IELTS (minimum score 6.5). *Application deadline:* For fall admission, 8/1 for domestic students, 6/1 for international students; for spring admission, 1/1 for domestic students, 11/1 for international students; for summer admission, 5/1 for domestic students, 3/1 for international students. Applications are processed on a rolling basis. Application fee: $0 ($100 for international students). Electronic applications accepted. Application fee is waived when completed online. *Expenses:* $33,000 tuition; $4,500 fees (general, technology and parking). *Financial support:* In 2017–18, 9 students received support. Career-related internships or fieldwork, Federal Work-Study, and scholarships/grants available. Support available to part-time students. Financial award application deadline: 4/1; financial award applicants required to submit FAFSA. *Faculty research:* Multicultural psychology, counseling: technology integration. *Unit head:* Dr. Maria Soto-Leggett, Program Coordinator, 281-649-3310, E-mail: msotoleggett@hbu.edu. *Application contact:* Victoria Humphreys, Administrative Assistant to the Dean, 281-649-3131, E-mail: vhumphreys@hbu.edu.
Website: http://www.hbu.edu/mac

Houston Baptist University, School of Christian Thought, Program in Christian Leadership, Houston, TX 77074-3298. Offers MA. *Program availability:* Evening/weekend, 100% online. *Students:* 4 full-time (all women), 6 part-time (4 women); includes 6 minority (3 Black or African American, non-Hispanic/Latino; 2 Hispanic/Latino; 1 Two or more races, non-Hispanic/Latino), 3 international. Average age 34. 17 applicants, 59% accepted, 8 enrolled. *Entrance requirements:* For master's, bachelor's degree conferred transcript, resume, essay/personal statement. Additional exam requirements/recommendations for international students: Required—TOEFL (minimum score 80 iBT), IELTS (minimum score 6.5). *Application deadline:* For fall admission, 8/1 for domestic students, 6/1 for international students; for spring admission, 1/1 for domestic students, 11/1 for international students; for summer admission, 5/1 for domestic students, 3/1 for international students. Applications are processed on a rolling basis. Application fee: $0 ($100 for international students). Electronic applications accepted. Application fee is waived when completed online. *Expenses:* $18,000 tuition; $4,500 fees (general, technology and parking). *Financial support:* In 2017–18, 6 students received support. Federal Work-Study and scholarships/grants available. Financial award application deadline: 4/1; financial award applicants required to submit FAFSA. *Unit head:* Dr. Timothy Brookins, Graduate Programs Director, 281-649-3632, E-mail: tbrookins@hbu.edu. *Application contact:* Celeste Risteski, Administrative Assistant to the Dean, 281-649-3383, Fax: 281-649-3012, E-mail: cristeski@hbu.edu.

Houston Graduate School of Theology, Graduate Programs, Houston, TX 77092. Offers counseling (MA); pastoral ministry (M Div, D Min); theology (MA). *Accreditation:* ATS (one or more programs are accredited). *Program availability:* Part-time, evening/weekend. *Degree requirements:* For master's, thesis (for some programs); for doctorate, thesis/dissertation. *Entrance requirements:* For doctorate, GRE General Test or MAT, M Div or equivalent. Additional exam requirements/recommendations for international students: Required—TOEFL (minimum score 550 paper-based). *Faculty research:* Hermeneutics, spirituality, religion of Eastern Europe.

Howard Payne University, Program in Youth Ministry, Brownwood, TX 76801-2715. Offers MA. *Program availability:* Part-time. *Degree requirements:* For master's, three 2-hour internships/mentorships. *Entrance requirements:* For master's, undergraduate degree from accredited university; leveling courses (for students who do not have undergraduate coursework in Old Testament, New Testament, and youth ministry). Additional exam requirements/recommendations for international students: Required—TOEFL (minimum score 79 iBT). Electronic applications accepted.

Huntington University, Graduate School, Huntington, IN 46750-1299. Offers adolescent and young adult education (M Ed); business administration (MBA); counseling (MA), including licensed mental health counselor; early adolescent education (M Ed); elementary education (M Ed); global youth ministry (MA); occupational therapy (OTD); organizational leadership (MA); pastoral leadership (MA); TESOL education (M Ed). *Program availability:* Part-time, online learning. *Faculty:* 17 full-time (10 women), 14 part-time/adjunct (4 women). *Students:* 221 full-time (163 women), 22 part-time (13 women). *Degree requirements:* For master's, comprehensive exam (for some programs), thesis (for some programs). *Entrance requirements:* For master's, GRE (for counseling and education students only); for doctorate, GRE (for occupational therapy students). Additional exam requirements/recommendations for international students: Required—TOEFL (minimum score 85 iBT), IELTS (minimum score 6.5). *Application deadline:* For fall admission, 7/1 for domestic students, 5/1 for international students; for winter admission, 10/1 for domestic students, 9/1 for international students; for spring admission, 11/30 for domestic students, 10/30 for international students. Applications are processed on a rolling basis. Application fee: $30. Electronic applications accepted. *Expenses:* Contact institution. *Financial support:* Scholarships/grants and unspecified assistantships available. Support available to part-time students. Financial award application deadline: 8/1; financial award applicants required to submit FAFSA. *Faculty research:* Leadership, educational technology trends, evangelism, youth ministry, mental health. *Unit head:* Michael Wanous, Vice President for Academic Affairs, 260-359-4008, Fax: 260-359-4126, E-mail: mwanous@huntington.edu. *Application contact:* Evan Bennett, Assistant Director of Graduate Admissions, 260-359-4111, Fax: 260-359-4126, E-mail: graduate@huntington.edu.
Website: http://www.huntington.edu/graduate

Huntsville Bible College, Program in Ministry, Huntsville, AL 35811-1632. Offers biblical leadership (MM); pastoral studies (MM).

Iliff School of Theology, Graduate and Professional Programs, Denver, CO 80210-4798. Offers biblical studies (MA); church history (MA); religion (MA); religion and social change (MA); specialized ministry (MASM), including justice and peace, pastoral theology and care, religions leadership; theology (M Div, MTS, D Min, PhD), including Biblical studies (PhD), religion and psychological studies (PhD), religion and social change (PhD), theology, philosophy and culture (PhD); theology/ethics (MA). PhD offered jointly with University of Denver. *Accreditation:* ACIPE; ATS. *Program availability:* Part-time, evening/weekend. *Degree requirements:* For master's, one foreign language, thesis (for some programs); for doctorate, 2 foreign languages, comprehensive exam, thesis/dissertation. *Entrance requirements:* For master's, minimum GPA of 3.0, writing sample, references; for doctorate, GRE General Test, minimum GPA of 3.0, writing sample, letters of recommendation. Additional exam requirements/recommendations for international students: Required—TOEFL (minimum score 550 paper-based). Electronic applications accepted. *Faculty research:* Pastoral care, history, church music, contemporary church, biblical studies.

Indiana Wesleyan University, Graduate School, Wesley Seminary, Program in Ministry, Marion, IN 46953-4974. Offers children, youth and family ministry (MA); ministerial leadership (MA). *Accreditation:* ATS. *Program availability:* Part-time, online learning. *Degree requirements:* For master's, one foreign language, capstone practicum and/or project. *Entrance requirements:* Additional exam requirements/recommendations for international students: Required—TOEFL. Electronic applications accepted. *Expenses:* Contact institution. *Faculty research:* History of worship innovation, history of New Testament afterlife traditions, second century mantanism, cross-cultural ministry, church health and growth, leadership in Christian organizations, managing change in the church, effective youth ministry, women in ministry, Biblical hermeneutics.

Inter American University of Puerto Rico, Metropolitan Campus, Graduate Programs, Program in Pastoral Theology, San Juan, PR 00919-1293. Offers PhD.

Interdenominational Theological Center, Graduate and Professional Programs, Atlanta, GA 30314-4112. Offers Christian education (MACE); ministry (D Min); pastoral counseling (Th D); theology (M Div); M Div/MACE. D Min and Th D programs offered in collaboration with the Atlanta Theological Association. *Accreditation:* ACIPE; ATS (one or more programs are accredited). *Program availability:* Part-time, evening/weekend, blended/hybrid learning. *Degree requirements:* For doctorate, thesis/dissertation. *Entrance requirements:* For doctorate, master's degree. Electronic applications accepted.

Pastoral Ministry and Counseling

International Baptist College and Seminary, Program in Ministry, Chandler, AZ 85286. Offers M Min, D Min.

Johnson University, Graduate and Professional Programs, Knoxville, TN 37998-1001. Offers biblical interpretation (Graduate Certificate); business administration (MBA); Christian ministries (Graduate Certificate); clinical mental health counseling (MA); educational technology (MA); intercultural studies (MA); leadership (MBA); leadership studies (PhD); New Testament (MA); nonprofit management (MBA); school counseling (MA); spiritual formation and leadership (Graduate Certificate); strategic ministry (MA); teacher education (MA). *Program availability:* Part-time, evening/weekend, 100% online, blended/hybrid learning. *Degree requirements:* For master's, variable foreign language requirement, comprehensive exam, thesis (for some programs), internships; for doctorate, variable foreign language requirement, comprehensive exam, thesis/dissertation, internships. *Entrance requirements:* For master's, PRAXIS (for MA in teacher education); MAT (for counseling); GRE or GMAT (for MBA), interview, 3 references, transcripts, essay, minimum GPA of 2.5 or 3.0 (depending on program); for doctorate, GRE or MAT (taken not less than 5 years prior), interview, 3 references, transcripts, essay, minimum GPA of 3.0; for Graduate Certificate, interview, 3 references, transcripts, essay, minimum GPA of 3.0. Additional exam requirements/recommendations for international students: Required—TOEFL (minimum score 527 paper-based; 71 iBT). Electronic applications accepted. *Expenses:* Contact institution.

Johnson University Florida, Program in Strategic Ministry, Kissimmee, FL 34744-5301. Offers children and family (MSM); church administration (MSM); church planting (MSM); intercultural studies (MSM); pastoral ministry (MSM); special needs (MSM); sports ministry (MSM); worship (MSM); youth ministry (MSM). *Program availability:* Online learning. *Degree requirements:* For master's, research trip to Israel, 9-month ministry apprenticeship.

Judson University, Master of Leadership in Ministry Program, Elgin, IL 60123-1498. Offers MLM. *Program availability:* Evening/weekend, online only, blended/hybrid learning. *Faculty:* 4 full-time (2 women), 5 part-time/adjunct (1 woman). *Students:* 7 part-time (4 women); includes 3 minority (all Black or African American, non-Hispanic/Latino). Average age 39. 14 applicants, 93% accepted, 11 enrolled. In 2017, 1 master's awarded. *Degree requirements:* For master's, thesis or alternative. *Entrance requirements:* For master's, prior ministry experience (professional or volunteer); undergraduate degree in a ministry-related field (preferred). *Application deadline:* Applications are processed on a rolling basis. Application fee: $35. Electronic applications accepted. *Expenses:* Contact institution. *Financial support:* In 2017–18, 5 students received support. Scholarships/grants and tuition waivers available. Financial award application deadline: 8/15; financial award applicants required to submit FAFSA. *Faculty research:* Volunteer development, ministry team development, ministry with military teams, intergenerational leadership, intercultural preaching and teaching, social justice through non-governmental organizations, Jewish context of the New Testament. *Unit head:* Dr. David Sanders, Director, 847-628-1052, E-mail: dsanders@judsonu.edu. *Application contact:* Debbie Sanders, Assistant, Department of Christian Ministries, 847-628-1124, E-mail: deborah.sanders@judsonu.edu.
Website: http://www.judsonu.edu/Graduate/Master_of_Leadership_in_Ministry/Overview/

The King's University, Graduate and Professional Programs, Southlake, TX 76092. Offers Biblical studies (Graduate Certificate); Christian ministry (Graduate Certificate); ministry (M Div, MPT, D Min).

Kingswood University, Program in Pastoral Theology, Sussex, NB E4E 5L2, Canada. Offers MA. *Faculty:* 1 full-time (0 women), 1 part-time/adjunct (0 women). *Students:* 8 full-time (4 women), 1 part-time (0 women). Average age 34. *Entrance requirements:* For master's, official transcripts, 3 references, statement of purpose. *Expenses: Tuition:* Part-time $355 Canadian dollars per credit hour. One-time fee: $150 Canadian dollars part-time. *Application contact:* Enrolment Office, 506-432-4422, Fax: 506-432-4442, E-mail: enrolment@kingswood.edu.
Website: http://kingswood.edu/academics/programs/master-of-arts-in-pastoral-theology/

Knox Theological Seminary, Graduate Programs, Program in Ministry, Fort Lauderdale, FL 33308. Offers D Min. *Program availability:* Part-time. *Degree requirements:* For doctorate, thesis/dissertation. *Entrance requirements:* For doctorate, M Div or equivalent. Additional exam requirements/recommendations for international students: Required—TOEFL, TWE (minimum score 5).

Lancaster Bible College, Capital Bible Seminary, Lancaster, PA 17601. Offers biblical studies (MA, Certificate); Christian counseling and discipleship (MA, Certificate); ministry (MA); theology (M Div). *Program availability:* Part-time, evening/weekend. *Degree requirements:* For master's, 2 foreign languages, comprehensive exam, thesis (for some programs). *Entrance requirements:* For master's, GRE General Test, Greek exam for those with 2 years of Greek, proficiency exam in theology, previous course work in Biblical studies. Additional exam requirements/recommendations for international students: Required—TOEFL (minimum score 550 paper-based). *Faculty research:* Dead Sea Scrolls, spiritual gifts, hermeneutics.

Lancaster Bible College, Graduate School, Lancaster, PA 17601-5036. Offers adult ministries (MA); Bible (MA); children and family ministry (MA); church planting (MA); consulting resource teacher (M Ed); elementary school counseling (M Ed); leadership (PhD); leadership studies (MA); marriage and family counseling (MA); mental health counseling (MA); pastoral studies (MA); secondary school counseling (M Ed); sports ministry (MA); student ministry (MA); town and country ministry (MA). *Program availability:* Part-time, evening/weekend. *Degree requirements:* For master's, comprehensive exam (for some programs), thesis (for some programs). *Entrance requirements:* For master's, bachelor's degree with a minimum of 30 credits of course work in Bible, minimum undergraduate GPA of 3.0, interview. Additional exam requirements/recommendations for international students: Required—TOEFL.

La Sierra University, School of Religion, Riverside, CA 92505. Offers pastoral ministry (M Div); religion (MA); religious education (MA); religious studies (MA). *Program availability:* Part-time. *Degree requirements:* For master's, one foreign language, thesis or alternative. *Entrance requirements:* For master's, GRE General Test, minimum GPA of 3.0.

Lee University, Programs in Religion, Cleveland, TN 37320-3450. Offers biblical studies (MA); ministry studies/leadership (MA); ministry studies/worship (MA); ministry studies/youth and family (MA); theological studies (MA), including ethics, religion. *Program availability:* Part-time, 100% online. *Faculty:* 9 full-time (3 women), 3 part-time/adjunct (0 women). *Students:* 62 full-time (16 women), 99 part-time (36 women); includes 68 minority (9 Black or African American, non-Hispanic/Latino; 1 Asian, non-Hispanic/Latino; 57 Hispanic/Latino; 1 Two or more races, non-Hispanic/Latino), 6 international. Average age 37. 21 applicants, 86% accepted, 8 enrolled. In 2017, 13 master's awarded. *Degree requirements:* For master's, variable foreign language requirement, comprehensive exam (for some programs), thesis (for some programs). *Entrance requirements:* For master's, GRE or MAT (for biblical/theological studies only), minimum GPA of 3.0, 3 letters of recommendation, interview, official transcripts, essay. Additional exam requirements/recommendations for international students: Required—TOEFL (minimum score 61 iBT). *Application deadline:* For fall admission, 4/1 priority date for domestic and international students; for spring admission, 10/1 priority date for domestic and international students. Applications are processed on a rolling basis. Application fee: $25. Electronic applications accepted. *Expenses:* Contact institution. *Financial support:* In 2017–18, 34 students received support, including 12 teaching assistantships (averaging $1,886 per year); career-related internships or fieldwork, Federal Work-Study, institutionally sponsored loans, scholarships/grants, and unspecified assistantships also available. Financial award application deadline: 3/1; financial award applicants required to submit FAFSA. *Faculty research:* Spiritual and discipleship formation, leadership, Biblical studies, theological studies, ethics. *Unit head:* Dr. Lisa Long, Director, 423-303-5100, E-mail: llong@leeuniversity.edu.
Website: http://www.leeuniversity.edu/academics/graduate/

Liberty University, School of Behavioral Sciences, Lynchburg, VA 24515. Offers applied psychology (MA), including developmental psychology (MA, MS), industrial/organizational psychology (MA, MS); clinical mental health counseling (MA); community care and counseling (Ed D), including marriage and family counseling, pastoral care and counseling, traumatology; counselor education and supervision (PhD); human services counseling (MA), including addictions and recovery, business, child and family law, Christian ministries, criminal justice, crisis response and trauma, executive leadership, health and wellness, life coaching, marriage and family, military resilience; marriage and family counseling (MA); marriage and family therapy (MA); military resilience (Certificate); pastoral counseling (MA), including addictions and recovery, community chaplaincy, crisis response and trauma, discipleship and church ministry, leadership, life coaching, marriage and family, marriage and family studies, military resilience, parenting and child/adolescent, pastoral counseling, theology; professional counseling (MA); psychology (MS), including developmental psychology (MA, MS), industrial/organizational psychology (MA, MS); school counseling (M Ed). *Program availability:* Part-time, online learning. *Students:* 2,649 full-time (2,085 women), 5,086 part-time (4,015 women); includes 2,275 minority (1,784 Black or African American, non-Hispanic/Latino; 44 American Indian or Alaska Native, non-Hispanic/Latino; 67 Asian, non-Hispanic/Latino; 200 Hispanic/Latino; 11 Native Hawaiian or other Pacific Islander, non-Hispanic/Latino; 169 Two or more races, non-Hispanic/Latino), 145 international. Average age 39. 5,839 applicants, 51% accepted, 1710 enrolled. In 2017, 1,626 master's, 7 doctorates, 61 other advanced degrees awarded. *Application deadline:* Applications are processed on a rolling basis. Application fee: $50. Electronic applications accepted. *Financial support:* Applicants required to submit FAFSA. *Unit head:* Dr. Ronald Hawkins, Founding Dean, School of Behavioral Sciences. *Application contact:* Jay Bridge, Director of Admissions, 800-424-9595, Fax: 800-628-7977, E-mail: gradadmissions@liberty.edu.

Liberty University, School of Divinity, Lynchburg, VA 24515. Offers Biblical exposition (MA); Biblical languages (M Div); Biblical studies (M Div, MA, MAR, Th M, D Min); chaplaincy (M Div, D Min); Christian apologetics (M Div, MA, MAR, Th M); Christian leadership and church ministries (M Div); Christian ministries (M Div); Christian ministry (MA); Christian thought (M Div); church history (M Div, MAR, Th M); community chaplaincy (M Div, MAR); discipleship (D Min); discipleship and church ministry (M Div, MAR, MCM); evangelism and church planting (MAR, MCM, D Min); expository preaching (D Min); global ministry (MA); global studies (M Div, MAR, MCM, MGS, Th M); healthcare chaplaincy (M Div); homiletics (M Div, MAR, Th M); leadership (M Div, MAR); marketplace chaplaincy (M Div, MCM); ministry leadership (Ed D); pastoral counseling (M Div, MA, MAR, D Min), including addictions and recovery (MA), crisis response and trauma (MA), discipleship and church ministries (MA), leadership (MA), life coaching (MA), marketplace chaplaincy (MA), marriage and family (MA), military resilience (MA), pastoral counseling (MA); pastoral leadership (D Min); pastoral ministries (M Div, M Serv Soc, MCM); religious education (MRE); sports chaplaincy (MA); theology (M Div, MAR, MTS, Th M); theology and apologetics (D Min, PhD); worship (M Div, MAR, MCM, D Min); youth and family ministries (M Div). *Program availability:* Part-time, online learning. *Students:* 2,140 full-time (615 women), 3,020 part-time (906 women); includes 1,312 minority (1,016 Black or African American, non-Hispanic/Latino; 9 American Indian or Alaska Native, non-Hispanic/Latino; 100 Asian, non-Hispanic/Latino; 90 Hispanic/Latino; 7 Native Hawaiian or other Pacific Islander, non-Hispanic/Latino; 90 Two or more races, non-Hispanic/Latino), 158 international. Average age 42. 4,673 applicants, 33% accepted, 977 enrolled. In 2017, 904 master's, 54 doctorates awarded. *Degree requirements:* For master's, 2 foreign languages, thesis (for some programs); for doctorate, 2 foreign languages, thesis/dissertation. *Entrance requirements:* For master's, minimum undergraduate GPA of 2.0; for doctorate, GRE General Test or MAT, minimum graduate GPA of 3.0. Additional exam requirements/recommendations for international students: Required—TOEFL (minimum score 600 paper-based; 100 iBT). *Application deadline:* For fall admission, 6/1 for domestic students; for spring admission, 11/1 for domestic students. Applications are processed on a rolling basis. Application fee: $50. Electronic applications accepted. *Expenses:* Contact institution. *Financial support:* Teaching assistantships with tuition reimbursements, career-related internships or fieldwork, and Federal Work-Study available. Financial award applicants required to submit FAFSA. *Unit head:* Dr. Ed Hindson, Dean, 434-592-4140, Fax: 434-522-0415, E-mail: ehindson@liberty.edu. *Application contact:* Jay Bridge, Director of Graduate Admissions, 800-424-9595, Fax: 800-628-7977, E-mail: gradadmissions@liberty.edu.
Website: https://www.liberty.edu/divinity/

Liberty University, School of Music, Lynchburg, VA 24515. Offers ethnomusicology (MA); music and worship (MA); music education (MA); worship studies (MA, DWS), including ethnomusicology (MA), leadership (MA), pastoral counseling (MA), worship techniques (MA). *Accreditation:* NASM. *Program availability:* Part-time, online learning. *Students:* 93 full-time (43 women), 181 part-time (89 women); includes 69 minority (44 Black or African American, non-Hispanic/Latino; 1 American Indian or Alaska Native, non-Hispanic/Latino; 6 Asian, non-Hispanic/Latino; 12 Hispanic/Latino; 6 Two or more races, non-Hispanic/Latino), 9 international. Average age 37. 307 applicants, 43% accepted, 69 enrolled. In 2017, 26 master's, 2 doctorates awarded. *Entrance requirements:* For master's, minimum GPA of 3.0; interview; letter of recommendation; statement of purpose; bachelor's/master's degree in music, worship, or related field, or 5 years of experience. Additional exam requirements/recommendations for international students: Required—TOEFL (minimum score 600 paper-based; 100 iBT). *Application deadline:* Applications are processed on a rolling basis. Application fee: $50. Electronic applications accepted. *Financial support:* Applicants required to submit FAFSA. *Unit head:* Dr. Vernon Whaley, Dean, 434-592-3463, E-mail: vwhaley@liberty.edu. *Application contact:* Jay Bridge, Director of Admissions, 800-424-9595, Fax: 800-628-7977, E-mail: gradadmissions@liberty.edu.
Website: http://www.liberty.edu/academics/music/

Lincoln Christian Seminary, Graduate and Professional Programs, Lincoln, IL 62656-2167. Offers Bible and theology (MA); Christian ministries (MA); counseling (MA); divinity (M Div); leadership ministry (D Min); religious education (MRE). *Accreditation:* ACIPE; ATS. *Program availability:* Part-time. *Degree requirements:* For master's, 2 foreign languages, thesis; for doctorate, thesis/dissertation. *Entrance requirements:* For master's, minimum GPA of 2.5; for doctorate, M Div or equivalent. Additional exam requirements/recommendations for international students: Required—TOEFL (minimum score 550 paper-based). Electronic applications accepted.

Lincoln Christian University, Graduate Programs, Lincoln, IL 62656-2167. Offers Bible and theology (MA); Biblical studies (MA); church history/historical theology (MA); counseling (MA); formative worship (MA); intercultural studies (MA); ministry (MA); organizational leadership (MA); philosophy and apologetics (MA); spiritual formation (MA); theology (MA). MA in spiritual formation offered in Normal, IL. *Program availability:* Online learning. *Faculty:* 21 full-time (3 women), 29 part-time/adjunct (7 women). *Students:* 97 full-time (42 women), 226 part-time (81 women). Average age 39. *Entrance requirements:* For master's, minimum cumulative GPA of 2.5 in undergraduate degree studies. Additional exam requirements/recommendations for international students: Required—TOEFL (minimum score 550 paper-based); Recommended—IELTS (minimum score 6). *Application deadline:* For fall admission, 8/1 for domestic students, 3/1 for international students; for spring admission, 11/15 for domestic students, 11/1 for international students. Application fee: $25 ($50 for international students). Application fee is waived when completed online. *Expenses: Tuition:* Full-time $7920; part-time $5280 per credit hour. *Required fees:* $150; $150 per course. *Financial support:* Applicants required to submit FAFSA. *Application contact:* Lindsey Clark, Associate Director of Graduate Enrollment, 217-732-3168 Ext. 2398, E-mail: lclark@lincolnchristian.edu.
Website: https://lincolnchristian.edu/academics/programs/masters/

Lipscomb University, Hazelip School of Theology, Nashville, TN 37204-3951. Offers missional and spiritual formation (D Min); theology (M Div). *Program availability:* Part-time, evening/weekend, online learning. *Faculty:* 13 full-time (0 women), 4 part-time/adjunct (2 women). *Students:* 89 full-time (24 women), 38 part-time (10 women); includes 20 minority (12 Black or African American, non-Hispanic/Latino; 2 Asian, non-Hispanic/Latino; 3 Hispanic/Latino; 3 Two or more races, non-Hispanic/Latino), 2 international. Average age 36. 89 applicants, 51% accepted, 33 enrolled. In 2017, 24 master's, 10 doctorates awarded. *Degree requirements:* For master's, 2 foreign languages, comprehensive exam (for some programs), thesis optional; for doctorate, comprehensive exam, thesis/dissertation. *Entrance requirements:* For master's, 3 references, transcripts, goals statement; for doctorate, 3 references, transcripts, documentation of full-time participation in ministry, writing sample, interview. Additional exam requirements/recommendations for international students: Required—TOEFL (minimum score 570 paper-based; 80 iBT). *Application deadline:* For fall admission, 8/1 priority date for domestic students; for spring admission, 12/15 for domestic students. Applications are processed on a rolling basis. Application fee: $50 ($75 for international students). Electronic applications accepted. *Expenses:* Contact institution. *Financial support:* Scholarships/grants and unspecified assistantships available. Financial award application deadline: 3/1; financial award applicants required to submit FAFSA. *Faculty research:* Status of Churches of Christ in foreign nations, Hebrew grammar, marriage and family. *Unit head:* Frank Guertin, Director, 615-966-5709, Fax: 615-966-5352, E-mail: frank.guertin@lipscomb.edu. *Application contact:* Kellye McCool, Coordinator of Student Services, 615-966-5458, Fax: 615-966-6052, E-mail: kellye.mccool@lipscomb.edu.
Website: http://www.lipscomb.edu/hst

Loras College, Graduate Division, Program in Theology and Ministry, Dubuque, IA 52004-0178. Offers ministry (MA); theology (MA). *Program availability:* Part-time, evening/weekend. *Degree requirements:* For master's, comprehensive exam (for some programs), thesis (for some programs). *Entrance requirements:* For master's, bachelor's degree or undergraduate minor in religious studies or equivalent, minimum undergraduate GPA of 2.75.

Louisiana College, Caskey School of Divinity, Pineville, LA 71359-0001. Offers biblical and theological studies (MA); pastoral ministry (MA).

Loyola Marymount University, Bellarmine College of Liberal Arts, Program in Pastoral Theology, Los Angeles, CA 90045-2659. Offers MA. *Unit head:* Dr. Brett Hoover, Director, Pastoral Theology Program, 310-338-1664, E-mail: bhoover@lmu.edu. *Application contact:* Chake H. Kouyoumjian, Associate Dean of Graduate Studies, 310-338-2721, Fax: 310-338-6086, E-mail: graduateinfo@lmu.edu.
Website: http://bellarmine.lmu.edu/theologicalstudies/graduateprograms/academics/mainpastoraltheology

Loyola University Chicago, Institute of Pastoral Studies, Chicago, IL 60611. Offers Christian spirituality (MA), including spiritual direction; church management (Certificate); counseling for ministry (MA); divinity (M Div); health care ministry leadership (Certificate); health care mission leadership (MA); pastoral counseling (MA, Certificate); pastoral studies (MA); religious education (Certificate); social justice (MA, Certificate); spiritual direction (Certificate); M Div/MA; M Div/MSW; MSW/MA. MSW/MA offered with School of Social Work. *Accreditation:* ACIPE. *Program availability:* Part-time, evening/weekend, 100% online, blended/hybrid learning. *Faculty:* 11 full-time (5 women), 20 part-time/adjunct (9 women). *Students:* 80 full-time (51 women), 150 part-time (107 women); includes 58 minority (24 Black or African American, non-Hispanic/Latino; 7 Asian, non-Hispanic/Latino; 27 Hispanic/Latino), 29 international. Average age 45. 128 applicants, 79% accepted, 72 enrolled. In 2017, 53 master's, 5 other advanced degrees awarded. *Degree requirements:* For master's, thesis optional, project. *Entrance requirements:* Additional exam requirements/recommendations for international students: Required—TOEFL (minimum score 550 paper-based; 79 iBT), IELTS (minimum score 6.5). *Application deadline:* Applications are processed on a rolling basis. Application fee: $50. Electronic applications accepted. Application fee is waived when completed online. *Expenses:* Contact institution. *Financial support:* In 2017–18, 111 students received support. Career-related internships or fieldwork, Federal Work-Study, scholarships/grants, and unspecified assistantships available. Support available to part-time students. Financial award application deadline: 3/15. *Faculty research:* Catholic theology, skills of religious ministry, family ministries, spirituality and divorced men. *Unit head:* Dr. Brian J. Schmisek, Dean, 312-915-7400, Fax: 312-915-7410, E-mail: bschmisek@luc.edu. *Application contact:* Dr. M. Therese Lysaught, Associate Dean, 312-915-7485, Fax: 312-915-7410, E-mail: mlysaught@luc.edu.
Website: http://www.luc.edu/ips/

Lutheran School of Theology at Chicago, Graduate and Professional Programs, Chicago, IL 60615-5199. Offers ministry (MAM, D Min); theological studies (MATS, PhD); theology (M Div). *Accreditation:* ACIPE; ATS (one or more programs are accredited). *Program availability:* Part-time. Terminal master's awarded for partial completion of doctoral program. *Degree requirements:* For master's, variable foreign language requirement; for doctorate, variable foreign language requirement, comprehensive exam, thesis/dissertation. *Entrance requirements:* For doctorate, GRE, M Div or equivalent, 3 years of professional experience (D Min).

Lutheran Theological Seminary Saskatoon, Graduate and Professional Programs, Saskatoon, SK S7N 0X3, Canada. Offers Biblical studies (MTS); church history (MTS); ethics/church and society (MTS); history of Christianity (STM); New Testament (STM); Old Testament (STM); pastoral studies (STM); pastoral theology (MTS); systematic theology (MTS); systematic theology and philosophy of religion (STM); theology (M Div, D Div). STM programs offered jointly with College of Emmanuel and St. Chad and St. Andrew's College. *Accreditation:* ATS. *Program availability:* Part-time. *Degree requirements:* For master's, thesis.

Luther Rice College & Seminary, Graduate Programs, Lithonia, GA 30038-2454. Offers apologetics (MA); Bible languages (M Div); Biblical counseling (MA); Christian ministry (M Div, D Min); Christian studies (MA); leadership (MA). *Program availability:* Part-time, evening/weekend, online learning. *Degree requirements:* For doctorate, thesis/dissertation. *Entrance requirements:* For master's, bachelor's degree or equivalent; for doctorate, M Div. Additional exam requirements/recommendations for international students: Required—TOEFL (minimum score 550 paper-based). Electronic applications accepted.

Luther Seminary, Graduate and Professional Programs, St. Paul, MN 55108-1445. Offers aging and health (MA); Biblical preaching (D Min); children, youth and family (M Div, MA); congregational mission and leadership (M Th, MA, D Min); history of Christianity (M Th, MA); missions and world religions (M Th); New Testament (M Th, MA); Old Testament (M Th, MA); pastoral care: clinical pastoral theology (M Th); pastoral theology and ministry (M Th); systematic theology (M Th, MA). *Accreditation:* ACIPE; ATS. *Program availability:* Part-time, online learning. *Degree requirements:* For master's, thesis or alternative; for doctorate, 2 foreign languages, thesis/dissertation. *Entrance requirements:* For master's, minimum GPA of 3.0; for doctorate, GRE General Test. Additional exam requirements/recommendations for international students: Required—TOEFL, IELTS. Electronic applications accepted. *Faculty research:* Theology, psychology (pastoral care), church history, Bible.

Madonna University, Program in Religious Studies, Livonia, MI 48150-1173. Offers pastoral ministry (MA).

Maple Springs Baptist Bible College and Seminary, Graduate and Professional Programs, Capitol Heights, MD 20743. Offers biblical studies (MA, Certificate); Christian counseling (MA); church administration (MA); divinity (M Div); ministry (D Min); religious education (MRE).

Maranatha Baptist University, Chaplaincy Program, Watertown, WI 53094. Offers M Div.

Maranatha Baptist University, Doctor of Ministry Program, Watertown, WI 53094. Offers D Min. *Degree requirements:* For doctorate, project. *Entrance requirements:* For doctorate, M Div or MA plus sufficient course work to total 60 hours.

Maranatha Baptist University, Program in Biblical Counseling, Watertown, WI 53094. Offers MA. *Program availability:* Part-time. *Entrance requirements:* For master's, BA or BS. Additional exam requirements/recommendations for international students: Recommended—TOEFL.

Martin University, Graduate School of Urban Ministry, Indianapolis, IN 46218-3867. Offers urban ministry studies (MA). *Program availability:* Part-time, evening/weekend. *Degree requirements:* For master's, Greek, oral and written comprehensive exam or thesis. *Faculty research:* How to bridge the gap between black theology and the black church.

Marymount University, School of Education and Human Services, Program in Counseling, Arlington, VA 22207-4299. Offers clinical mental health counseling (MA); pastoral counseling (MA); school counseling (MA); MA/MA. *Accreditation:* ACA (one or more programs are accredited). *Program availability:* Part-time, evening/weekend. *Faculty:* 9 full-time (7 women), 5 part-time/adjunct (all women). *Students:* 108 full-time (97 women), 38 part-time (32 women); includes 61 minority (28 Black or African American, non-Hispanic/Latino; 1 American Indian or Alaska Native, non-Hispanic/Latino; 5 Asian, non-Hispanic/Latino; 20 Hispanic/Latino; 7 Two or more races, non-Hispanic/Latino). Average age 29. 74 applicants, 92% accepted, 59 enrolled. In 2017, 40 master's awarded. *Degree requirements:* For master's, thesis or alternative, capstone/internship. *Entrance requirements:* For master's, GRE, 2 letters of recommendation, interview, resume, personal statement. Additional exam requirements/recommendations for international students: Required—TOEFL (minimum score 600 paper-based; 96 iBT), IELTS (minimum score 6.5). *Application deadline:* For fall admission, 1/15 priority date for domestic and international students. Applications are processed on a rolling basis. Application fee: $40. Electronic applications accepted. *Expenses: Tuition:* Full-time $17,550; part-time $975 per credit hour. *Required fees:* $198; $11 per credit hour. One-time fee: $250. Tuition and fees vary according to program. *Financial support:* In 2017–18, 19 students received support, including 4 research assistantships with full and partial tuition reimbursements available (averaging $8,325 per year), 8 teaching assistantships with full and partial tuition reimbursements available (averaging $8,016 per year); career-related internships or fieldwork, Federal Work-Study, scholarships/grants, and unspecified assistantships also available. Support available to part-time students. Financial award application deadline: 3/1; financial award applicants required to submit FAFSA. *Unit head:* Dr. Lisa Jackson-Cherry, Chair, Counseling, 703-284-1633, Fax: 703-284-5708, E-mail: lisa.jackson-cherry@marymount.edu. *Application contact:* Francesca Reed, Director, Graduate Admissions, 703-284-5901, Fax: 703-527-3815, E-mail: grad.admissions@marymount.edu.
Website: http://www.marymount.edu/Academics/School-of-Education-Human-Services/Graduate-Programs/Counseling-(M-A-)

The Master's University, The Master's Seminary, Santa Clarita, CA 91321-1200. Offers biblical counseling (MABC); New Testament (Th D); Old Testament (Th D); preaching (D Min); theology (M Div, M Th, Th D). *Program availability:* Part-time. *Degree requirements:* For master's, 2 foreign languages, thesis; for doctorate, 4 foreign languages, thesis/dissertation. *Entrance requirements:* For master's, minimum GPA of 2.75; for doctorate, Th M, minimum GPA of 3.5. Additional exam requirements/recommendations for international students: Required—TOEFL (minimum score 550 paper-based).

McCormick Theological Seminary, Graduate and Professional Programs, Chicago, IL 60615. Offers ministry (D Min); theological studies (MATS, Certificate); theology (M Div); M Div/MSW. M Div/MSW offered jointly with Loyola University Chicago, University of Chicago, and University of Illinois at Chicago. *Accreditation:* ACIPE; ATS (one or more programs are accredited). *Program availability:* Part-time, evening/weekend. *Degree requirements:* For master's, thesis (for some programs); for doctorate, thesis/dissertation. *Entrance requirements:* For master's, minimum GPA of 3.0; for doctorate, M Div, minimum 3 years in pastorate. *Faculty research:* Faith formation, families, biblical literature, Dead Sea scrolls, women in antiquity.

McMaster University, McMaster Divinity College, Hamilton, ON L8S 4M2, Canada. Offers biblical studies (M Div); Biblical studies (MA, MTS, Diploma); Christian interpretation/history (M Div, MA, MTS, Diploma); Christian ministry (M Div, MA, MTS, Diploma); Christian Studies (Certificate); Christian theology (PhD). Affiliated with the Toronto School of Theology. *Accreditation:* ATS. *Program availability:* Part-time. *Degree requirements:* For master's, one foreign language, thesis optional; for doctorate, 3 foreign languages, comprehensive exam, thesis/dissertation; for other advanced degree, 2 foreign languages, thesis. *Entrance requirements:* For master's, minimum B average in undergraduate course work, 3 letters of reference; for doctorate, minimum B+ average in bachelor's and master's, appropriate modern/ancient language, interview; for other advanced degree, 6 units of related Biblical language, minimum B+ average in undergraduate course work, minimum 15 units of course work in related area of study, 3 letters of recommendation. Additional exam requirements/recommendations for international students: Required—TOEFL (minimum score 550 paper-based). *Faculty research:* Ethics, Biblical studies, language studies, church history, Christian ministry.

Pastoral Ministry and Counseling

Meadville Lombard Theological School, Graduate and Professional Programs, Chicago, IL 60637-1602. Offers divinity (M Div); ministry (D Min); religion (MA); M Div/MSW. M Div/MSW offered jointly with University of Chicago. *Accreditation:* ACIPE; ATS. *Program availability:* Part-time, online learning. *Entrance requirements:* For master's, bachelor's degree; for doctorate, bachelor's and masters degrees, 3 years of ministry.

Mercer University, Graduate Studies, Cecil B. Day Campus, James and Carolyn McAfee School of Theology, Atlanta, GA 30341. Offers Christian ministry (MACM); Christian spirituality (D Min); divinity (M Div); preaching (D Min); M Div/MBA; M Div/MS. *Program availability:* Part-time, 100% online. *Faculty:* 14 full-time (7 women), 5 part-time/adjunct (0 women). *Students:* 93 full-time (60 women), 63 part-time (29 women); includes 88 minority (80 Black or African American, non-Hispanic/Latino; 1 American Indian or Alaska Native, non-Hispanic/Latino; 1 Asian, non-Hispanic/Latino; 4 Hispanic/Latino; 1 Native Hawaiian or other Pacific Islander, non-Hispanic/Latino; 1 Two or more races, non-Hispanic/Latino), 1 international. Average age 37. 36 applicants, 58% accepted, 14 enrolled. In 2017, 40 master's, 9 doctorates awarded. *Degree requirements:* For master's, variable foreign language requirement, thesis (for some programs), minimum GPA of 2.5, portfolio; for doctorate, thesis/dissertation, fieldwork, seminars. *Entrance requirements:* For master's and doctorate, regionally-accredited bachelor's degree with liberal arts core or proof of equivalent degree from foreign university; transcripts; letters of recommendation; resume; essays; writing sample; interview; background check. Additional exam requirements/recommendations for international students: Required—TOEFL (minimum score 550 paper-based; 79 iBT). *Application deadline:* For fall admission, 7/1 for domestic and international students; for spring admission, 11/15 for domestic and international students. Applications are processed on a rolling basis. Application fee: $50. Electronic applications accepted. *Expenses:* $425 per credit hour tuition, $17 per credit hour fee up to a maximum of $150. *Financial support:* In 2017–18, 70 students received support. Career-related internships or fieldwork, Federal Work-Study, institutionally sponsored loans, and scholarships/grants available. Support available to part-time students. Financial award application deadline: 10/1; financial award applicants required to submit FAFSA. *Faculty research:* Biblical studies, Baptist heritage, Christian heritage, theology, pastoral care, ethics, global missions, academic research. *Unit head:* Dr. Jeffrey Willetts, Dean, 678-547-6470, Fax: 678-547-6478, E-mail: willetts_jg@mercer.edu. *Application contact:* Nathan Cost, Director of Admissions, 678-547-6451, Fax: 678-547-6478, E-mail: cost_na@mercer.edu.
Website: http://www.mercer.edu/theology

Mesivta Torah Vodaath Rabbinical Seminary, Graduate Programs, Brooklyn, NY 11218-5299. Offers rabbinical studies (Certificate); theological and ministerial studies (Certificate). *Accreditation:* AARTS.

Mid-America Baptist Theological Seminary, Graduate and Professional Programs, Cordova, TN 38016. Offers biblical counseling (M Div); Christian education (M Div, MACE); ministry (D Min); missiology and intercultural studies (M Div); pastoral ministry (M Div); theology (MA, PhD); worship (MA). *Degree requirements:* For doctorate, 4 foreign languages, thesis/dissertation. *Entrance requirements:* For doctorate, MAT. Additional exam requirements/recommendations for international students: Required—TOEFL (minimum score 600 paper-based). *Application deadline:* For fall admission, 7/20 priority date for domestic students. Applications are processed on a rolling basis. Application fee: $35. Electronic applications accepted. *Expenses: Tuition:* Part-time $250 per credit hour. One-time fee: $500 part-time. *Unit head:* Dr. Michael R. Spradlin, President, 901-751-3048. *Application contact:* Tanner Hickman, Director of Admissions, 901-751-3015, Fax: 901-751-8454, E-mail: tannerh@mabts.edu.

Mid-America Christian University, Program in Counseling, Oklahoma City, OK 73170-4504. Offers marital and family therapy (MS); pastoral/spiritual direction (MS); professional counselor (MS). *Entrance requirements:* For master's, MAT, bachelor's degree from a regionally accredited college or university, minimum overall cumulative GPA of 2.75 of bachelor course work. Additional exam requirements/recommendations for international students: Required—TOEFL (minimum score 550 paper-based).

Midwestern Baptist Theological Seminary, Graduate and Professional Programs, Kansas City, MO 64118-4697. Offers Christian education (MACE); Christian foundations (Graduate Certificate); church music (MCM); counseling (MA); ministry (D Ed Min, D Min); Old or New Testament studies (PhD); theology (M Div). *Accreditation:* ATS. *Program availability:* Part-time, online learning. *Degree requirements:* For doctorate, thesis/dissertation. *Entrance requirements:* For doctorate, MAT. Electronic applications accepted. *Faculty research:* Ministerial studies, Biblical and theological studies, missions, counseling.

Milligan College, Area of Counselor Education Programs, Milligan College, TN 37682. Offers clinical mental health counseling (MSC); counseling ministry (Graduate Certificate); school counseling (MSC). *Program availability:* Part-time. *Faculty:* 4 full-time (all women), 2 part-time/adjunct (0 women). *Students:* 24 full-time (17 women), 7 part-time (6 women); includes 4 minority (3 Black or African American, non-Hispanic/Latino; 1 Two or more races, non-Hispanic/Latino), 1 international. Average age 32. 30 applicants, 70% accepted, 13 enrolled. In 2017, 9 master's awarded. *Degree requirements:* For master's, thesis or alternative. *Entrance requirements:* For master's, GRE General Test if undergraduate GPA is less than 3.0, undergraduate degree and supporting transcripts, essay/personal statement, professional recommendations, interview. Additional exam requirements/recommendations for international students: Required—TOEFL (minimum score 550 paper-based, 79 iBT) or IELTS (6.5). *Application deadline:* For fall admission, 8/1 for domestic students, 6/1 for international students. Applications are processed on a rolling basis. Application fee: $30. Electronic applications accepted. *Expenses:* $440 per hour tuition; $325 per semester tech/activity fees. *Financial support:* Scholarships/grants available. Financial award application deadline: 12/1; financial award applicants required to submit FAFSA. *Faculty research:* Parent-child interaction therapy/autism; childhood developmental trauma/childhood sexual abuse; poverty and homelessness; social justice advocacy and multicultural competencies; school based mental health. *Unit head:* Dr. Christine Browning, Director of Master of Science in Counseling Program, 423-461-3513, Fax: 423-461-8777, E-mail: cmbrowning@milligan.edu. *Application contact:* Jenni Duran, Graduate Admissions Recruiter, Healthcare Programs, 423-461-8424, Fax: 423-461-8789, E-mail: jduran@milligan.edu.

Milligan College, Emmanuel Christian Seminary at Milligan College, Milligan College, TN 37682. Offers Christian care and counseling (M Div); Christian education (M Div); Christian ministries (MACM, Graduate Certificate); Christian ministry (M Div); Christian theology (M Div, MAR); church history (MAR); church history/historical theology (M Div); general studies (M Div); ministry (D Min); New Testament (M Div, MAR); Old Testament (M Div, MAR); urban ministry (M Div); world missions (M Div). *Accreditation:* ACIPE; ATS. *Program availability:* Part-time, blended/hybrid learning. *Faculty:* 10 full-time (1 woman), 8 part-time/adjunct (0 women). *Students:* 52 full-time (23 women), 57 part-time (18 women); includes 11 minority (7 Black or African American, non-Hispanic/Latino; 1 Asian, non-Hispanic/Latino; 3 Hispanic/Latino), 7 international. Average age 35. 62 applicants, 89% accepted, 39 enrolled. In 2017, 19 master's, 3 doctorates awarded. *Degree requirements:* For master's, 2 foreign languages, thesis or alternative, portfolio; for doctorate, thesis/dissertation. *Entrance requirements:* For master's, undergraduate degree and supporting transcripts, essay/personal statement, professional recommendations, interview; for doctorate, M Div or equivalent, essay/personal statement, professional recommendations. Additional exam requirements/recommendations for international students: Required—TOEFL (minimum score 550 paper-based, 79 iBT) or IELTS (6.5). *Application deadline:* For fall admission, 8/1 for domestic students, 6/1 for international students; for spring admission, 12/15 for domestic students, 8/1 for international students. Applications are processed on a rolling basis. Application fee: $30 ($0 for international students). Electronic applications accepted. *Expenses:* Contact institution. *Financial support:* In 2017–18, 124 students received support. Scholarships/grants and unspecified assistantships available. Financial award application deadline: 12/1; financial award applicants required to submit FAFSA. *Faculty research:* Theology of Old Testament prophets; performance criticism of New Testament texts; practical theology and spiritual formation for Christian leaders; church history and missions; constructive theology, art and imagination. *Unit head:* Dr. Rollin Ramsaran, Academic Dean, Emmanuel Christian Seminary, 423-461-1524, Fax: 423-926-6198, E-mail: raramsaran@milligan.edu. *Application contact:* Lauren Gullett, Director of Admissions and Recruitment for Emmanuel Christian Seminary, 423-461-1535, Fax: 423-926-6198, E-mail: lwgullett@milligan.edu.
Website: http://ecs.milligan.edu/

Missouri Baptist University, Graduate Programs, St. Louis, MO 63141-8660. Offers business administration (MBA); Christian ministries (MACM); counseling (MAC); education (MSE); education administration (MEA); educational leadership (MSE, Ed S); teaching (MAT).

Moody Bible Institute, Graduate School, Chicago, IL 60610-3284. Offers biblical studies (MABS, Graduate Certificate); intercultural studies (MAIS, Graduate Certificate); ministry (M Div, M Min); spiritual formation and discipleship (MASF, Graduate Certificate); urban studies (MA, Graduate Certificate). *Program availability:* Part-time. *Degree requirements:* For master's, 2 foreign languages, fieldwork (MABS); colloquium, field research project (MA Min). *Entrance requirements:* For master's, 30 hours in Bible/theology, 2 years of ministry experience (MA Min).

Mount Marty College, Graduate Studies Division, Yankton, SD 57078-3724. Offers business administration (MBA); nurse anesthesia (MS); nursing (MSN); pastoral ministries (MPM). *Accreditation:* AANA/CANAEP (one or more programs are accredited). *Degree requirements:* For master's, thesis or alternative. *Entrance requirements:* For master's, GRE General Test, minimum GPA of 3.0. Electronic applications accepted. *Faculty research:* Clinical anesthesia, professional characteristics, motivations of applicants.

Mount St. Joseph University, Graduate Program in Religious Studies, Cincinnati, OH 45233-1670. Offers religious studies (MA); spirituality and wellness (Certificate). *Program availability:* Part-time, evening/weekend. *Faculty:* 1 (woman) full-time. *Students:* 1 (woman) full-time, 8 part-time (7 women); includes 4 minority (3 Black or African American, non-Hispanic/Latino; 1 Hispanic/Latino). Average age 45. In 2017, 1 master's awarded. *Degree requirements:* For master's, comprehensive exam, 36 hours of credit, pastoral PRAXIS component (3 credit hours), integrating project (3 credit hours). *Entrance requirements:* For master's, undergraduate transcript with minimum overall GPA of 3.0, 3 letters of recommendation from professional colleagues, 3-page essay, interview with the Graduate Admissions Committee, current work resume. Additional exam requirements/recommendations for international students: Required—TOEFL (minimum score 560 paper-based; 83 iBT). *Application deadline:* Applications are processed on a rolling basis. Application fee: $50. Electronic applications accepted. *Expenses:* $600 per credit hour. *Financial support:* In 2017–18, 7 students received support. Scholarships/grants available. Financial award applicants required to submit FAFSA. *Faculty research:* Contextual/cultural/systematic theology, historical/spiritual theology, business/economics ethics, social justice, Biblical/cultural/pastoral theology. *Unit head:* Dr. John Trokan, Associate Professor of Religious and Pastoral Studies/Director of Graduate Program, 513-244-4272, Fax: 513-244-4222, E-mail: john.trokan@msj.edu. *Application contact:* Mary Brigham, Assistant Director of Graduate Recruitment, 513-244-4233, Fax: 513-244-4629, E-mail: mary.brigham@msj.edu.
Website: http://www.msj.edu/academics/graduate-programs/religious-studies-programs/

Nashotah House Theological Seminary, Graduate Programs, Nashotah, WI 53058-9793. Offers Anglican studies (Certificate); Biblical studies (STM); Christian spirituality (STM); church history (STM); liturgy (STM); ministry (M Div, MM); pastoral ministry (MPM); theological studies (MTS); theology (STM, D Min). *Accreditation:* ACIPE; ATS (one or more programs are accredited). *Program availability:* Part-time. *Degree requirements:* For master's, thesis optional. *Entrance requirements:* For master's and Certificate, GRE General Test or MAT, interview, 3 recommendations. Additional exam requirements/recommendations for international students: Required—TOEFL. Electronic applications accepted. *Expenses:* Contact institution. *Faculty research:* Formation for parochial ministry, ancient Semitic epigraphy.

Neumann University, Program in Pastoral Clinical Mental Health Counseling, Aston, PA 19014-1298. Offers pastoral care specialist (Certificate); pastoral clinical mental health counseling (MS); pastoral clinical mental health counseling certificate of advanced study (Certificate); pastoral counseling (PhD); spiritual formation and direction (CSD); spiritual formation and direction supervision certificate of advanced study (Certificate). *Program availability:* Part-time, evening/weekend. *Faculty:* 8 full-time (5 women), 1 (woman) part-time/adjunct. *Students:* 9 full-time (all women), 58 part-time (40 women); includes 17 minority (13 Black or African American, non-Hispanic/Latino; 1 Hispanic/Latino; 3 Two or more races, non-Hispanic/Latino), 1 international. Average age 47. 35 applicants, 40% accepted, 14 enrolled. In 2017, 22 master's, 2 doctorates awarded. *Degree requirements:* For doctorate, comprehensive exam, thesis/dissertation. *Entrance requirements:* For master's and other advanced degree, official transcripts from all institutions attended, letter of intent, three letters of recommendation; for doctorate, MAT, master's degree, official transcripts from all institutions attended, resume or curriculum vitae, letter of intent, two official letters of recommendation. Additional exam requirements/recommendations for international students: Required—TOEFL (minimum score 70 iBT). *Application deadline:* For fall admission, 8/1 for domestic students; for spring admission, 12/1 for domestic students. Applications are processed on a rolling basis. Application fee: $0. Electronic applications accepted. *Expenses:* $670 per credit hour (for master's degree); $830 per credit hour (for PhD). *Financial support:* Scholarships/grants and health care benefits available. Support available to part-time students. Financial award application deadline: 3/15; financial award applicants required to submit FAFSA. *Unit head:* Sr. Suzanne Mayer, Director of Pastoral Clinical Mental Health Counseling Program, 610-361-2292, Fax: 610-358-4525, E-mail: mayers@neumann.edu. *Application contact:* Dr. Erika K. Davis, Director of Adult and Graduate Admissions, 800-9-NEUMANN Ext. 5208, Fax: 610-361-2548, E-mail: gradadultadmiss@neumann.edu.

New Brunswick Theological Seminary, Graduate and Professional Programs, New Brunswick, NJ 08901-1196. Offers pastoral care and counseling (D Min). *Accreditation:* ACIPE; ATS. *Program availability:* Part-time, evening/weekend. *Degree requirements:* For master's, variable foreign language requirement, thesis (for some programs); for doctorate, thesis/dissertation. *Entrance requirements:* For master's, BA/BS with minimum GPA of 3.0 (for MA), 2.5 (for M Div); for doctorate, M Div. Additional exam requirements/recommendations for international students: Required—TOEFL (minimum

score 550 paper-based; 79 iBT); Recommended—IELTS (minimum score 6). Electronic applications accepted.

New Orleans Baptist Theological Seminary, Graduate and Professional Programs, Division of Pastoral Ministries, New Orleans, LA 70126-4858. Offers M Div, MAMFC, D Min, PhD. *Accreditation:* ACIPE. *Program availability:* Online learning. *Degree requirements:* For master's, 2 foreign languages, thesis (for some programs); for doctorate, 3 foreign languages, comprehensive exam, thesis/dissertation. *Entrance requirements:* For master's and doctorate, GRE General Test. Additional exam requirements/recommendations for international students: Required—TOEFL.

Northern Seminary, Graduate and Professional Programs, Lombard, IL 60148-5698. Offers Biblical studies (M Div); Christian community development (MA, D Min); Christian ministry (MACM); contextual theology (D Min); missional church ministry (M Div); New Testament (M Div, MANT); New Testament context (D Min); Old Testament (M Div); preaching (D Min); theology (M Div); theology and mission (MA); urban leadership (MA); worship (M Div, MAW). *Program availability:* Part-time, evening/weekend. *Faculty:* 6 full-time (1 woman), 33 part-time/adjunct (8 women). *Students:* 208 full-time (62 women); includes 89 minority (73 Black or African American, non-Hispanic/Latino; 6 Asian, non-Hispanic/Latino; 8 Hispanic/Latino; 2 Two or more races, non-Hispanic/Latino), 3 international. Average age 44. *Degree requirements:* For master's, thesis (for some programs); for doctorate, thesis/dissertation. *Entrance requirements:* For master's, writing test, all official transcripts, letter of reference from church, 3 letters of reference, autobiographical statement (400 words or more); for doctorate, M Div, 3 years in the ministry post-M Div, 3 letters of reference. Additional exam requirements/recommendations for international students: Required—TOEFL (minimum score 550 paper-based). *Application deadline:* Applications are processed on a rolling basis. Application fee: $35. Electronic applications accepted. *Expenses: Tuition:* Full-time $14,253; part-time $9627 per credit. *Required fees:* $125 per quarter. *Financial support:* Teaching assistantships with partial tuition reimbursements, Federal Work-Study, and scholarships/grants available. Support available to part-time students. Financial award application deadline: 9/1; financial award applicants required to submit FAFSA. *Faculty research:* Theology and mission, worship studies, church history, evangelism, Christian ministry, urban leadership, New Testament. *Unit head:* Dr. William Shiell, President, 630-620-2101, Fax: 630-620-2190. *Application contact:* Greg Armstrong, Director of Admissions, 630-620-2175, Fax: 630-620-2190, E-mail: admissions@seminary.edu.

North Greenville University, T. Walter Brashier Graduate School, Greer, SC 29651. Offers Christian ministry (MCM, D Min); education (M Ed, MAT); financial planning (MBA); human resources (MBA). *Program availability:* Part-time, evening/weekend, online learning. *Degree requirements:* For master's, comprehensive exam (for some programs), thesis or alternative, capstone course. *Entrance requirements:* For master's, minimum GPA of 2.25 overall, 2.5 in major; for doctorate, MAT. Additional exam requirements/recommendations for international students: Required—TOEFL (minimum score 550 paper-based). Electronic applications accepted. *Faculty research:* Organizational behavior, church growth, homiletics, human resources, business strategy.

North Park Theological Seminary, Graduate and Professional Programs, Program in Christian Ministry, Chicago, IL 60625-4895. Offers MACM, MA/MBA, MA/MM.

North Park Theological Seminary, Graduate and Professional Programs, Program in Christian Studies, Chicago, IL 60625-4895. Offers adult ministry (Certificate); camping and retreat ministry (Certificate); children and family ministry (Certificate); Christian formation (Certificate); faith and health (Certificate); intercultural studies (Certificate); justice ministry (Certificate); leadership and administration (Certificate); spiritual direction (Certificate); youth ministry (Certificate). *Accreditation:* ACIPE. *Program availability:* Part-time. *Entrance requirements:* For degree, minimum GPA of 2.5. Additional exam requirements/recommendations for international students: Required—TOEFL.

Northwest Nazarene University, Program in Religion, Nampa, ID 83686-5897. Offers missional leadership (M Div, MA); pastoral ministry (MA); spiritual formation (M Div, MA); youth, children, and family ministry (M Div, MA). *Program availability:* Part-time, online only, 100% online. *Students:* Average age 39. 37 applicants, 76% accepted, 24 enrolled. In 2017, 40 master's awarded. *Entrance requirements:* For master's, minimum GPA of 2.5; 8 semester or 12 quarter credits of Bible, theology and/or Western philosophy. Additional exam requirements/recommendations for international students: Required—TOEFL (minimum score 85 iBT). *Application deadline:* For fall admission, 7/31 for domestic students, 7/1 for international students; for spring admission, 2/1 for domestic students, 1/5 for international students. Applications are processed on a rolling basis. Application fee: $50. Electronic applications accepted. *Expenses:* Contact institution. *Financial support:* In 2017–18, 3 students received support. Scholarships/grants available. *Unit head:* Dr. Jay Akkerman, Director, Graduate Studies, 208-467-8437, Fax: 208-467-8252. *Application contact:* Vicki Funk, Program Coordinator, 208-467-8432, Fax: 208-467-8252, E-mail: vlfunk@nnu.edu.
Website: http://www.nnu.edu/ministry/

Northwest University, College of Ministry, Kirkland, WA 98033. Offers ministry (MIM); missional leadership (MA); theology and culture (MA). *Program availability:* Part-time, evening/weekend, online learning. *Degree requirements:* For master's, comprehensive exam (for some programs), thesis (for some programs). *Entrance requirements:* Additional exam requirements/recommendations for international students: Required—TOEFL (minimum score 550 paper-based; 75 iBT). Electronic applications accepted.

Nyack College, Alliance Theological Seminary, Nyack, NY 10960. Offers Biblical literature (MA), including New Testament, Old Testament; Biblical studies (MA); Christian ministry (MPS); intercultural studies (MA); ministry (D Min), including Christian leadership in the global context; theology and missions (M Div); urban ministry (MPS). *Program availability:* Part-time, evening/weekend, 100% online, blended/hybrid learning. *Students:* 265 full-time (107 women), 356 part-time (162 women); includes 490 minority (161 Black or African American, non-Hispanic/Latino; 2 American Indian or Alaska Native, non-Hispanic/Latino; 123 Asian, non-Hispanic/Latino; 198 Hispanic/Latino; 6 Two or more races, non-Hispanic/Latino), 37 international. Average age 42. In 2017, 100 master's, 23 doctorates awarded. *Degree requirements:* For master's, comprehensive exam (for some programs), thesis optional, internship; for doctorate, thesis/dissertation. *Entrance requirements:* For master's, transcripts, Christian experience statement, recommendations; for doctorate, transcripts, documented three years of ministry experience subsequent to 1st graduate theological degree, reference letters, formal academic paper. Additional exam requirements/recommendations for international students: Required—TOEFL (minimum score 550 paper-based; 80 iBT). *Application deadline:* Applications are processed on a rolling basis. Application fee: $30. Electronic applications accepted. *Expenses:* $585 per credit (master's-level); $22,060 for total program (for D Min). *Financial support:* Career-related internships or fieldwork, Federal Work-Study, and scholarships/grants available. Financial award applicants required to submit FAFSA. *Unit head:* Dr. Ronald Walborn, Dean, 845-770-5715, Fax: 845-358-1663. *Application contact:* Jennifer Reimer, Associate Director of Admissions, 845-770-5709, E-mail: admissions.grad@nyack.edu.
Website: http://www.nyack.edu/ats

Oakwood University, Program in Pastoral Studies, Huntsville, AL 35896. Offers MA. *Entrance requirements:* For master's, Biblical Literacy Entrance Test (BLET), minimum cumulative GPA of 2.5, 2 letters of recommendation, current resume, 3 years of pastoral or local church leadership experience. Additional exam requirements/recommendations for international students: Required—TOEFL (minimum score 500 paper-based).

Oblate School of Theology, Graduate and Professional Programs, San Antonio, TX 78216-6693. Offers African-American pastoral leadership (D Min); divinity (M Div); pastoral leadership (D Min); pastoral ministry (MAP Min); pastoral studies (Certificate); spiritual formation in the local community (D Min); spirituality (MA Sp, PhD); spirituality and ministry (D Min); theology (MA Th); U.S. Hispanic/Latino ministry (D Min); M Div/MA Th. *Accreditation:* ACIPE; ATS (one or more programs are accredited). *Program availability:* Part-time, 100% online, blended/hybrid learning. *Faculty:* 21 full-time (5 women), 4 part-time/adjunct (0 women). *Students:* 89 full-time (9 women), 54 part-time (31 women); includes 77 minority (11 Black or African American, non-Hispanic/Latino; 8 Asian, non-Hispanic/Latino; 57 Hispanic/Latino; 1 Two or more races, non-Hispanic/Latino), 24 international. Average age 39. In 2017, 24 master's, 1 doctorate awarded. *Degree requirements:* For master's, comprehensive exam (for some programs), thesis (for some programs), practicum; for doctorate, one foreign language, comprehensive exam, thesis/dissertation, paper, practicum. *Entrance requirements:* For master's, MAT, interview, prerequisite course work in theology or religious studies and philosophy, minimum GPA of 2.5; for doctorate, D Min, M Div, MA Th, MA Sp, MA PM. Additional exam requirements/recommendations for international students: Required—TOEFL (minimum score 71 iBT). *Application deadline:* For fall admission, 6/30 priority date for domestic and international students; for winter admission, 11/30 for domestic and international students; for spring admission, 11/30 for domestic and international students; for summer admission, 4/30 for domestic and international students. Applications are processed on a rolling basis. Application fee: $65. Electronic applications accepted. *Expenses:* $605.00 per credit hour (for master's degrees); $680 per credit hour (for doctoral degrees); $55 registration fee. *Financial support:* In 2017–18, 25 students received support. Scholarships/grants available. Support available to part-time students. Financial award application deadline: 8/15; financial award applicants required to submit FAFSA. *Unit head:* Dr. R. Scott Woodward, Academic Dean, 210-341-1366, Fax: 210-341-4519, E-mail: rsw@ost.edu. *Application contact:* Brenda Reyna, Registrar, 210-341-1366 Ext. 226, Fax: 210-341-4519, E-mail: registrar@ost.edu.

Ohio Christian University, Graduate Programs, Circleville, OH 43113. Offers accounting (MBA); business administration (MBA); digital marketing (MBA); finance (MBA); healthcare management (MBA); human resources (MBA); management (MM); organizational leadership (MBA); pastoral care and counseling (MAM); practical theology (MAM).

Oral Roberts University, School of Theology and Missions, Tulsa, OK 74171. Offers biblical literature (MA), including advanced languages, Judaic-Christian studies; church ministries and leadership (D Min); clinical pastoral education (M Div); missions (MA); pastoral care and chaplaincy (M Div, D Min); practical theology (MA), including teaching ministries, urban ministries; professional counseling (MA), including addiction studies, marriage and family therapy; theological/historical studies (MA). *Accreditation:* ATS. *Program availability:* Part-time, online learning. *Faculty:* 17 full-time (2 women). *Students:* 371 full-time (156 women), 110 part-time (65 women); includes 177 minority (127 Black or African American, non-Hispanic/Latino; 5 American Indian or Alaska Native, non-Hispanic/Latino; 20 Asian, non-Hispanic/Latino; 25 Hispanic/Latino), 82 international. Average age 36. 159 applicants, 95% accepted, 124 enrolled. In 2017, 52 master's, 10 doctorates awarded. *Degree requirements:* For master's, thesis (for some programs), practicum/internship; for doctorate, thesis/dissertation, applied research project. *Entrance requirements:* For master's, GRE General Test or MAT (waived for those with undergraduate degree from regionally accredited institution and 3.0 or higher GPA), minimum GPA of 2.5 (professional) or 3.0 (academic); for doctorate, M Div, minimum GPA of 3.0, 3 years of full-time ministry experience. Additional exam requirements/recommendations for international students: Recommended—TOEFL (minimum score 550 paper-based; 79 iBT), IELTS (minimum score 7). *Application deadline:* Applications are processed on a rolling basis. Application fee: $35. Electronic applications accepted. Application fee is waived when completed online. *Financial support:* Fellowships and scholarships/grants available. Financial award application deadline: 6/1. *Unit head:* Dr. Bill Buker, Chair, 918-495-6493, E-mail: bbuker@oru.edu. *Application contact:* Michael Thomas, Enrollment Counselor, 918-495-6618, E-mail: mthomas@oru.edu.
Website: http://www.gradtheology.oru.edu/

Ottawa University, Graduate Studies-Arizona, Program in Professional Counseling, Ottawa, KS 66067-3399. Offers Christian counseling (MA); expressive arts therapy (MA); marriage and family therapy (MA); treatment of trauma, abuse and deprivation (MA). Programs offered in Mesa, Phoenix, Tempe and West Valley, AZ. *Program availability:* Part-time, evening/weekend, online learning. *Degree requirements:* For master's, comprehensive exam, thesis or alternative, field experience, practicum. *Entrance requirements:* For master's, minimum undergraduate GPA of 3.0; course work in theories of personality, abnormal psychology, and human growth and development. Additional exam requirements/recommendations for international students: Required—TOEFL (minimum score 550 paper-based).

Pacific Rim Christian University, Program in Christian Ministry, Honolulu, HI 96819. Offers MA.

Pentecostal Theological Seminary, Graduate and Professional Programs, Cleveland, TN 37320-3330. Offers biblical studies (MTS); church ministries (MA); counseling (MA); discipleship and Christian formation (MA); ministry (D Min); Pentecostal theology (MTS); theology (M Div). *Accreditation:* ACIPE; ATS. *Program availability:* Part-time. *Degree requirements:* For master's, variable foreign language requirement, thesis (for some programs), internship. *Faculty research:* Biblical exegesis.

Pepperdine University, Seaver College, Division of Religion, Malibu, CA 90263. Offers ministry (MS); religion (M Div, MA). *Program availability:* Part-time, evening/weekend. *Students:* 3 full-time (1 woman), 12 part-time (3 women); includes 5 minority (2 Black or African American, non-Hispanic/Latino; 1 Asian, non-Hispanic/Latino; 2 Hispanic/Latino). Average age 33. In 2017, 7 master's awarded. *Entrance requirements:* For master's, GRE General Test, letters of recommendation, writing sample. Additional exam requirements/recommendations for international students: Required—TOEFL. *Application deadline:* For fall admission, 2/1 priority date for domestic students. Applications are processed on a rolling basis. Application fee: $65. Electronic applications accepted. *Financial support:* Applicants required to submit FAFSA. *Unit head:* Dr. Timothy Willis, Chair/Professor, 310-506-4352, Fax: 310-506-7271, E-mail: timothy.willis@pepperdine.edu. *Application contact:* Hayley Wolf, Director of Admission, 310-506-4392, E-mail: hayley.wolf@pepperdine.edu.
Website: http://seaver.pepperdine.edu/religion/graduate/mareligion/

Phillips Theological Seminary, Programs in Theology, Doctor of Ministry Program, Tulsa, OK 74116. Offers parish ministry (D Min); pastoral counseling (D Min); practices of ministry (D Min). *Accreditation:* ATS. *Program availability:* Part-time. *Degree requirements:* For doctorate, thesis/dissertation. *Entrance requirements:* For doctorate, M Div, minimum GPA of 3.0, 3 years of post-M Div pastoral experience. *Expenses:* Contact institution. *Faculty research:* Politics and theology, media and theology, ecology and theology.

Pastoral Ministry and Counseling

Phoenix Seminary, Graduate Programs, Phoenix, AZ 85018. Offers Biblical and theological studies (Graduate Diploma); Biblical communication (M Div); Biblical leadership (MA); Christian counseling (Graduate Diploma); counseling and family (M Div); leadership development (M Div); ministry (D Min); professional counseling (MA). *Accreditation:* ATS (one or more programs are accredited). *Program availability:* Part-time, evening/weekend. *Degree requirements:* For master's, 2 foreign languages, comprehensive exam; for doctorate, 2 foreign languages, thesis/dissertation. *Entrance requirements:* For master's, undergraduate degree with minimum GPA of 2.5; for doctorate, M Div (94 hours) with minimum GPA of 3.0. Additional exam requirements/recommendations for international students: Required—TOEFL (minimum score 587 paper-based; 92 iBT), TWE (minimum score 4.5).

Piedmont International University, Graduate School, Winston-Salem, NC 27101-5197. Offers Biblical studies (PhD); curriculum and instruction (M Ed); divinity (M Div); educational leadership (M Ed); leadership (MA, PhD); ministry (MA Min, D Min); non-language track (MABS); PhD preparation track (MABS). *Program availability:* Part-time, online learning. Terminal master's awarded for partial completion of doctoral program. *Degree requirements:* For master's, 2 foreign languages, comprehensive exam, thesis or alternative; for doctorate, 2 foreign languages, comprehensive exam. *Entrance requirements:* For master's, GRE General Test; for doctorate, Hebrew and Greek proficiency, MA. Additional exam requirements/recommendations for international students: Required—TOEFL (minimum score 500 paper-based; 60 iBT). Electronic applications accepted. *Faculty research:* Theological and biblical studies.

Pittsburgh Theological Seminary, Graduate and Professional Programs, Pittsburgh, PA 15206. Offers divinity (M Div); theological studies (MA); theology (Th M); theology and ministry (MA, D Min); JD/M Div; M Div/MS; M Div/MSW. M Div/MSW offered jointly with University of Pittsburgh; JD/M Div with Duquesne University; M Div/MSPPM with Carnegie Mellon University. *Accreditation:* ATS (one or more programs are accredited). *Program availability:* Part-time, evening/weekend. *Faculty:* 16 full-time (5 women), 6 part-time/adjunct (2 women). *Students:* 170 full-time (70 women), 43 part-time (25 women); includes 56 minority (45 Black or African American, non-Hispanic/Latino; 5 Asian, non-Hispanic/Latino; 3 Hispanic/Latino; 1 Native Hawaiian or other Pacific Islander, non-Hispanic/Latino; 2 Two or more races, non-Hispanic/Latino), 13 international. Average age 35. 57 applicants, 93% accepted, 44 enrolled. In 2017, 26 master's, 9 doctorates awarded. *Degree requirements:* For master's, one foreign language, comprehensive exam (for some programs), thesis (for some programs); for doctorate, thesis/dissertation. *Entrance requirements:* For master's, bachelor's degree with minimum GPA of 2.7, interview, references; for doctorate, M Div or equivalent, interview, references. Additional exam requirements/recommendations for international students: Required—TOEFL (minimum score 570 paper-based; 89 iBT). *Application deadline:* For fall admission, 6/30 priority date for domestic students, 12/1 for international students; for winter admission, 10/15 priority date for domestic students; for spring admission, 1/15 priority date for domestic students. Applications are processed on a rolling basis. Application fee: $50. Electronic applications accepted. *Expenses: Tuition:* Full-time $11,988; part-time $358 per credit hour. *Required fees:* $100 per term. Tuition and fees vary according to degree level. *Financial support:* In 2017–18, 104 students received support. Career-related internships or fieldwork, scholarships/grants, and institutional work-study available. Financial award application deadline: 5/1; financial award applicants required to submit FAFSA. *Unit head:* Dr. Heather H. Vacek, Dean of Faculty and Vice President for Academic Affairs, 412-924-1374, Fax: 412-924-1774, E-mail: hvacek@pts.edu. *Application contact:* Tracy Riggle Young, Director of Enrollment and Retention, 412-924-1423, Fax: 412-924-1723, E-mail: triggleyoung@pts.edu.
Website: http://www.pts.edu/

Point Loma Nazarene University, School of Theology and Christian Ministry, San Diego, CA 92106-2899. Offers M Min. *Program availability:* Part-time, online only, nine-week quads with eight weeks of online coursework and a one-week intensive. *Faculty:* 1 full-time (0 women), 1 part-time/adjunct (0 women). *Students:* 15 part-time (6 women); includes 7 minority (all Hispanic/Latino). Average age 40. 4 applicants, 100% accepted, 3 enrolled. In 2017, 2 master's awarded. *Degree requirements:* For master's, thesis optional. *Entrance requirements:* For master's, letters of recommendation, essay, transcripts, interview. Additional exam requirements/recommendations for international students: Recommended—TOEFL. *Application deadline:* For fall admission, 8/30 priority date for domestic students; for spring admission, 4/4 priority date for domestic students; for summer admission, 6/20 priority date for domestic students. Applications are processed on a rolling basis. Application fee: $0. Electronic applications accepted. *Expenses:* Contact institution. *Financial support:* Scholarships/grants available. Financial award application deadline: 6/5; financial award applicants required to submit FAFSA. *Faculty research:* Theology, Christian education, church administration. *Unit head:* Dr. Mark Maddix, Dean, 619-849-2234, E-mail: markmaddix@pointloma.edu. *Application contact:* Joanie Joy, Senior Director of Enrollment Management, 619-329-6785, E-mail: gradinfo@pointloma.edu.
Website: https://www.pointloma.edu/graduate-studies/programs/master-ministry

Point University, Graduate Programs, West Point, GA 31833. Offers business transformation (MBA); transformative ministry (MTM). *Program availability:* Part-time, 100% online, blended/hybrid learning. *Students:* 24 full-time (9 women), 2 part-time (both women); includes 7 minority (6 Black or African American, non-Hispanic/Latino; 1 Hispanic/Latino). Average age 36. *Application deadline:* Applications are processed on a rolling basis. Electronic applications accepted. *Expenses:* $515 per credit hour (for MBA); $450 per credit hour (for MTM).

Providence University College & Theological Seminary, Theological Seminary, Otterburne, MB R0A 1G0, Canada. Offers children's ministry (Certificate); Christian studies (MA, Certificate); counseling (MA); cross-cultural discipleship (Certificate); divinity (M Div); educational studies (MA), including counseling psychology, educational ministries, student development, teaching English to speakers of other languages, training teachers of English to speakers of other languages; global studies (MA); lay counseling (Diploma); ministry (D Min); teaching English to speakers of other languages (Certificate); theological studies (MA); training teacher of English to speakers of other languages (Certificate); youth ministry (Certificate). *Accreditation:* ATS. *Program availability:* Part-time. *Degree requirements:* For master's, variable foreign language requirement, thesis (for some programs); for doctorate, thesis/dissertation. *Entrance requirements:* Additional exam requirements/recommendations for international students: Recommended—TOEFL (minimum score 550 paper-based). *Faculty research:* Studies in Isaiah, theology of sin.

Randall University, Department of Bible Studies, Moore, OK 73160-1208. Offers ministry (MA). *Program availability:* Part-time, evening/weekend. *Degree requirements:* For master's, thesis optional. *Entrance requirements:* Additional exam requirements/recommendations for international students: Recommended—TOEFL (minimum score 500 paper-based).

Reformed Theological Seminary–Charlotte Campus, Graduate and Professional Programs, Charlotte, NC 28226-6318. Offers biblical studies (MA); ministry (D Min); pastoral ministry (M Div); theological studies (MA). *Program availability:* Part-time. *Degree requirements:* For master's, comprehensive exam; for doctorate, thesis/dissertation. *Entrance requirements:* For master's, minimum GPA of 2.6; for doctorate, minimum GPA of 3.0. Additional exam requirements/recommendations for international students: Required—TOEFL (minimum score 550 paper-based). Electronic applications accepted.

Reformed Theological Seminary–Jackson Campus, Graduate and Professional Programs, Jackson, MS 39209-3004. Offers Bible, theology, and missions (Certificate); Biblical exegesis (M Div); biblical studies (MA); Christian education (MA); counseling (M Div); marriage and family therapy (MA); ministry (D Min); missions (M Div, MA, D Min); theological studies (MA). *Accreditation:* AAMFT/COAMFTE (one or more programs are accredited); ATS (one or more programs are accredited). *Degree requirements:* For master's, thesis (for some programs); fieldwork; for doctorate, 2 foreign languages, thesis/dissertation. *Entrance requirements:* For master's, minimum GPA of 2.6; for doctorate, minimum GPA of 3.0. Additional exam requirements/ recommendations for international students: Required—TOEFL.

Reformed Theological Seminary–Orlando Campus, Graduate Programs, Oviedo, FL 32765. Offers Bible (Certificate); biblical studies (MA); counseling (MA); missions (Certificate); reformed expository preaching (D Min); reformed theology and ministry (D Min); theological studies (MA); theology (M Div, Certificate). *Program availability:* Part-time, online learning. *Faculty:* 12 full-time (0 women), 11 part-time/adjunct (2 women). *Students:* 340. *Application deadline:* Applications are processed on a rolling basis. Application fee: $75. Electronic applications accepted. *Expenses: Tuition:* Full-time $18,025; part-time $8755 per semester hour. *Required fees:* $160; $160 per semester hour. $80 per semester. *Unit head:* Dr. Scott R. Swain, President, 407-278-4406, Fax: 407-366-9425. *Application contact:* Winston J. Miller, Director of Admissions, 800-752-4382, Fax: 407-366-9425, E-mail: applications.orlando@rts.edu.

Regent University, Graduate School, School of Divinity, Virginia Beach, VA 23464-9800. Offers Christian spirituality and formation (MA); divinity (M Div), including Biblical studies (M Div, MTS, Th M, PhD), chaplain ministry, Christian theology (M Div, MTS, Th M, PhD), church and ministry (M Div, MA), history of Christianity (M Div, MTS, Th M, PhD), inter-cultural studies (M Div, MA), interdisciplinary studies (M Div, MA, MTS), marketplace ministry (M Div, MA), missional discipleship, practical healing ministry (M Div, MA), worship and media (M Div, MA); leadership and renewal (D Min), including Christian leadership and renewal, clinical pastoral education, community transformation, military ministry, ministry leadership coaching; practical theology (MA), including church and ministry (M Div, MA), cosmogony, inter-cultural studies (M Div, MA), interdisciplinary studies (M Div, MA, MTS), marketplace ministry (M Div, MA), practical healing ministry (M Div, MA), worship and media (M Div, MA); renewal theology (PhD), including Biblical studies (M Div, MTS, Th M, PhD), Christian theology (M Div, MTS, Th M, PhD), history of Christianity (M Div, MTS, Th M, PhD), practical theology; theological studies (MTS), including Biblical studies (M Div, MTS, Th M, PhD), Christian theology (M Div, MTS, Th M, PhD), history of Christianity (M Div, MTS, Th M, PhD), interdisciplinary studies (M Div, MA, MTS); theology (Th M), including Biblical studies (M Div, MTS, Th M, PhD), Christian theology (M Div, MTS, Th M, PhD), history of Christianity (M Div, MTS, Th M, PhD). *Accreditation:* ACIPE; ATS. *Program availability:* Part-time, evening/weekend, 100% online, blended/hybrid learning. *Faculty:* 17 full-time (3 women), 66 part-time/adjunct (9 women). *Students:* 146 full-time (54 women), 917 part-time (404 women); includes 563 minority (470 Black or African American, non-Hispanic/Latino; 1 American Indian or Alaska Native, non-Hispanic/Latino; 17 Asian, non-Hispanic/Latino; 56 Hispanic/Latino; 1 Native Hawaiian or other Pacific Islander, non-Hispanic/Latino; 18 Two or more races, non-Hispanic/Latino), 27 international. Average age 44. 1,321 applicants, 39% accepted, 295 enrolled. In 2017, 146 master's, 25 doctorates awarded. *Degree requirements:* For master's, comprehensive exam, thesis or alternative, internship; for doctorate, thesis/dissertation or alternative. *Entrance requirements:* For master's, minimum undergraduate GPA of 2.75, writing sample, personal goal statement, college transcripts; for doctorate, GRE, minimum graduate GPA of 3.5 (PhD), 3.0 (D Min); clergy recommendations; writing sample; transcripts; resume; interview. Additional exam requirements/recommendations for international students: Required—TOEFL (minimum score 577 paper-based). *Application deadline:* For fall admission, 5/1 priority date for domestic students. Applications are processed on a rolling basis. Application fee: $50. Electronic applications accepted. *Expenses:* $495 per credit (master's); $595 per credit (D Min); $650 per credit (PhD); $300 per semester technology fee. *Financial support:* In 2017–18, 721 students received support. Career-related internships or fieldwork, scholarships/grants, and unspecified assistantships available. Support available to part-time students. *Faculty research:* Greek and Hebrew, theology, spiritual formation, global missions and world Christianity, women in ministry leadership. *Unit head:* Dr. Cornelius Bekker, Dean, 757-352-4401, Fax: 757-352-4597, E-mail: clbekker@regent.edu. *Application contact:* Heidi Cece, Assistant Vice President of Enrollment Management, 800-373-5504, Fax: 757-352-4381, E-mail: admissions@regent.edu.
Website: https://www.regent.edu/school-of-divinity/

Regent University, Graduate School, School of Psychology and Counseling, Virginia Beach, VA 23464-9800. Offers clinical mental health counseling (MA); clinical psychology (Psy D); counseling and psychological studies - clinical (PhD); counseling and psychological studies - research (PhD); counseling studies (CAGS); counselor education and supervision (PhD); general psychology (MS); human services (MA), including addictions counseling, Biblical counseling, Christian counseling, conflict and mediation ministry, criminal justice and ministry, grief counseling, human services counseling, human services for student affairs, life coaching, marriage and family ministry, trauma and crisis counseling; marriage, couple, and family counseling (MA); pastoral counseling (MA); school counseling (MA); M Div/MA; M Ed/MA; MBA/MA. *Accreditation:* ACA; APA (one or more programs are accredited). *Program availability:* Part-time, evening/weekend, 100% online, blended/hybrid learning. *Faculty:* 28 full-time (16 women), 51 part-time/adjunct (30 women). *Students:* 294 full-time (236 women), 404 part-time (317 women); includes 286 minority (218 Black or African American, non-Hispanic/Latino; 4 American Indian or Alaska Native, non-Hispanic/Latino; 17 Asian, non-Hispanic/Latino; 30 Hispanic/Latino; 17 Two or more races, non-Hispanic/Latino), 13 international. Average age 37. 2,109 applicants, 18% accepted, 233 enrolled. In 2017, 158 master's, 28 doctorates awarded. *Degree requirements:* For master's, thesis or alternative, internship, practicum, written competency exam; for doctorate, thesis/ dissertation or alternative. *Entrance requirements:* For master's, GRE General Test (including writing exam) or MAT, minimum undergraduate GPA of 3.0, resume, transcripts, writing sample, personal goals statement; for doctorate, GRE General Test (including writing exam), minimum undergraduate GPA of 3.0, graduate 3.5; writing sample; 3 recommendations; resume; college transcripts; personal goals statement. Additional exam requirements/recommendations for international students: Required— TOEFL (minimum score 577 paper-based). *Application deadline:* For fall admission, 4/1 priority date for domestic students; for spring admission, 11/1 priority date for domestic students. Applications are processed on a rolling basis. Application fee: $50. Electronic applications accepted. *Expenses:* Contact institution. *Financial support:* In 2017–18, 557 students received support, including 5 fellowships (averaging $10,000 per year), 11 research assistantships (averaging $3,200 per year); career-related internships or fieldwork, scholarships/grants, and unspecified assistantships also available. Support available to part-time students. *Faculty research:* Marriage enrichment, clinical psychology, troubled youth, faith and learning, trauma. *Unit head:* Dr. William Hathaway, Dean, 757-352-4294, Fax: 757-352-4282, E-mail: willhat@regent.edu. *Application*

contact: Heidi Cece, Assistant Vice President of Enrollment Management, 800-373-5504, Fax: 757-352-4381, E-mail: admissions@regent.edu.
Website: https://www.regent.edu/school-of-psychology-and-counseling/

Regis College, Graduate and Professional Programs, Toronto, ON M5S 2Z5, Canada. Offers eastern Christian studies (Certificate); Ignatian spirituality (Diploma); ministry (D Min); ministry and spirituality (MAMS); philosophical studies (Diploma); retreat direction (Certificate); sacred theology (STM, STD, STB, STL); spiritual direction (Diploma); theological studies (MTS, Diploma); theology (M Div, MA, Th M, PhD, Th D); M Div/MA. *Accreditation:* ATS (one or more programs are accredited). Terminal master's awarded for partial completion of doctoral program. *Degree requirements:* For master's, 2 foreign languages, thesis; for doctorate, 3 foreign languages, comprehensive exam, thesis/dissertation. *Entrance requirements:* For doctorate, minimum GPA of 3.7. Additional exam requirements/recommendations for international students: Required—TOEFL (minimum score 580 paper-based; 93 iBT), TWE (minimum score 5).

Richmont Graduate University, School of Ministry, Atlanta, GA 30339. Offers ministry (MA); spiritual direction (Graduate Certificate); spiritual formation and direction (MA). *Program availability:* Part-time, evening/weekend, 100% online, blended/hybrid learning. *Degree requirements:* For master's, thesis optional. *Entrance requirements:* For master's, transcripts, recommendation, personal statement, resume. Electronic applications accepted. *Expenses:* Contact institution. *Faculty research:* Integration of Biblical/theological studies; personal and spiritual formation, leadership enrichment; Biblical interpretation; leadership; spiritual formation.

Sacred Heart Major Seminary, School of Theology, Detroit, MI 48206-1799. Offers pastoral studies (MAPS); theology (M Div, MA). *Accreditation:* ACIPE; ATS. *Program availability:* Part-time, evening/weekend. *Degree requirements:* For master's, one foreign language, thesis optional, integrating project. *Entrance requirements:* For master's, GRE, previous course work in philosophy and theology. *Faculty research:* Local church history, patristics, spirituality, religious education.

St. Ambrose University, College of Arts and Sciences, Program in Pastoral Theology, Davenport, IA 52803-2898. Offers MP Th. *Program availability:* Part-time. *Degree requirements:* For master's, integration project. *Entrance requirements:* For master's, minimum GPA of 2.6, prior pastoral experience, 9 credits of course work in theology. Additional exam requirements/recommendations for international students: Required—TOEFL. Electronic applications accepted. *Expenses:* Contact institution. *Faculty research:* Theological education, ecclesiology, spirituality and liturgy, medical ethics.

St. Augustine's Seminary of Toronto, Graduate and Professional Programs, Scarborough, ON M1M 1M3, Canada. Offers divinity (M Div); lay ministry (Diploma); religious education (MRE); theological studies (MTS, Diploma). *Accreditation:* ATS. *Program availability:* Part-time, evening/weekend. *Entrance requirements:* Additional exam requirements/recommendations for international students: Required—TOEFL (minimum score 580 paper-based), TWE (minimum score 5).

St. Bernard's School of Theology and Ministry, Graduate and Professional Programs, Rochester, NY 14618. Offers pastoral studies (MA, Certificate); theological studies (MA); theology (M Div). *Accreditation:* ATS (one or more programs are accredited). *Program availability:* Part-time, evening/weekend. *Degree requirements:* For master's, variable foreign language requirement, thesis (for some programs). *Entrance requirements:* For master's, minimum GPA of 2.5.

St. Catherine University, Graduate Programs, Program in Theology, St. Paul, MN 55105. Offers pastoral ministry (Certificate); spiritual direction (Certificate); theology (MA). *Program availability:* Part-time. *Degree requirements:* For master's, comprehensive exam, thesis (for some programs). *Entrance requirements:* For master's, MAT, minimum GPA of 3.0. Additional exam requirements/recommendations for international students: Required—Michigan English Language Assessment Battery or TOEFL (minimum score 600 paper-based; 100 iBT). *Application deadline:* For fall admission, 8/1 priority date for domestic students. Applications are processed on a rolling basis. Application fee: $35. *Expenses:* $678 per credit. *Financial support:* Research assistantships, career-related internships or fieldwork, and institutionally sponsored loans available. Support available to part-time students. Financial award application deadline: 4/1; financial award applicants required to submit FAFSA. *Faculty research:* Feminist scholarship, historical theology, symbols, rites of purification, spirituality. *Unit head:* Dr. William McDonough, Coordinator, 651-690-6072, Fax: 651-690-6024.

St. John's Seminary, Graduate and Professional Programs, Camarillo, CA 93012-2598. Offers divinity (M Div); pastoral ministry (MAPM); theology (MA). *Accreditation:* ATS. *Program availability:* Part-time. *Degree requirements:* For master's, comprehensive exam (for some programs), thesis optional, comprehensive integration paper (MAPM). *Entrance requirements:* For master's, GRE General Test, minimum GPA of 3.5 (MA), 2.5 (MAPM). Additional exam requirements/recommendations for international students: Required—TOEFL (minimum score 550 paper-based; 79 iBT). Electronic applications accepted. *Faculty research:* Biblical studies, moral theology, church history, systematic theology, spiritual theology.

Saint John's University, Saint John's School of Theology and Seminary, Collegeville, MN 56321. Offers divinity (M Div); liturgical music (MA); liturgical studies (MA); pastoral ministry (MA); theology (MA), including church history, liturgy, monastic studies, scripture, spirituality, systematics; M Div/MA. *Program availability:* Part-time, online learning. *Degree requirements:* For master's, one foreign language, comprehensive exam (for some programs), thesis (for some programs). *Entrance requirements:* For master's, GRE General Test or MAT. Electronic applications accepted. *Faculty research:* Religious education, biblical literature.

Saint Joseph's College of Maine, Master of Arts in Pastoral Theology Program, Standish, ME 04084. Offers MA. *Program availability:* Part-time, online learning. *Entrance requirements:* For master's, baccalaureate degree with minimum cumulative GPA of 2.5.

St. Joseph's Seminary, Graduate and Professional Programs, Yonkers, NY 10704. Offers Catholic philosophical studies (MA); divinity (M Div); pastoral studies (MAPS); theology (MA). *Accreditation:* ATS. *Degree requirements:* For master's, one foreign language, thesis. *Entrance requirements:* For master's, 27 credits in philosophy and 9 in theology.

Saint Paul University, Faculty of Canon Law, Ottawa, ON K1S 1C4, Canada. Offers canon law (MCL, JCD, PhD, Graduate Certificate, JCL); canonical practice (Graduate Certificate); ecclesiastical administration (Graduate Certificate). *Program availability:* Part-time. *Degree requirements:* For master's, one foreign language; for doctorate, one foreign language, comprehensive exam, thesis/dissertation; for other advanced degree, one foreign language, comprehensive exam and seminar paper (JCL). *Entrance requirements:* For master's, appropriate bachelor's degree, 18 credits in theology; for doctorate, JCL or MCL; for other advanced degree, B Th or equivalent (JCL), appropriate bachelor's degree, 18 credits in theology. *Faculty research:* Questions related to Church law.

Saint Paul University, Faculty of Human Sciences, Program in Counseling and Spirituality, Ottawa, ON K1S 1C4, Canada. Offers individual or marital/couple counseling (MA); spiritual care (MA). *Program availability:* Part-time. *Degree requirements:* For master's, research project or thesis. *Entrance requirements:* For master's, honors BA in human sciences, minimum B average, 12 theology credits.

Saints Cyril and Methodius Seminary, Graduate and Professional Programs, Orchard Lake, MI 48324. Offers pastoral ministry (MAPM); religious education (MARE); theology (M Div, MA). *Program availability:* Part-time.

St. Stephen's College, Programs in Theology, Edmonton, AB T6G 2J6, Canada. Offers ministry (D Min); pastoral counseling (MA); social transformation ministry (MA); spirituality and liturgy (MA); theological studies (MTS); theology (M Th). *Program availability:* Part-time, evening/weekend, online learning. Terminal master's awarded for partial completion of doctoral program. *Degree requirements:* For master's, thesis; for doctorate, thesis/dissertation. *Entrance requirements:* Additional exam requirements/recommendations for international students: Required—TOEFL. Electronic applications accepted. *Faculty research:* Methodology for theological education, practice and supervision for ministry.

St. Thomas University, School of Theology and Ministry, Institute for Pastoral Ministries, Miami Gardens, FL 33054-6459. Offers pastoral ministries (MA, Certificate); practical theology (PhD). *Program availability:* Part-time, evening/weekend. *Degree requirements:* For master's, comprehensive exam; for doctorate, comprehensive exam, thesis/dissertation. *Entrance requirements:* For master's, interview, minimum GPA of 3.0 or GRE; for doctorate, GRE, MA in theology. Additional exam requirements/recommendations for international students: Required—TOEFL (minimum score 550 paper-based; 79 iBT). Electronic applications accepted.

Saint Vincent Seminary, School of Theology, Latrobe, PA 15650-2690. Offers Catholic philosophical studies (MA); ecclesial ministry (MA); ministry (M Div); monastic studies (MA); sacred scripture (MA); systematic theology (MA). Saint Vincent College provides philosophy courses for the MA in Catholic Philosophical Studies degree program only. *Accreditation:* ATS. *Program availability:* Part-time, evening/weekend. *Faculty:* 8 full-time (2 women), 12 part-time/adjunct (1 woman). *Students:* 38 full-time (0 women), 9 part-time (0 women); includes 2 minority (both Asian, non-Hispanic/Latino), 12 international. Average age 34. 11 applicants, 100% accepted, 10 enrolled. In 2017, 12 master's awarded. *Degree requirements:* For master's, one foreign language, comprehensive exam, thesis optional, public presentation. *Entrance requirements:* For master's, minimum GPA of 2.5. Additional exam requirements/recommendations for international students: Required—TOEFL (minimum score 550 paper-based; 79 iBT). *Application deadline:* For fall admission, 8/15 for domestic and international students. Applications are processed on a rolling basis. Application fee: $34. *Expenses:* $27,636 per year full-time, $918 per credit part-time. *Financial support:* In 2017–18, 47 students received support. Scholarships/grants available. Support available to part-time students. Financial award application deadline: 8/15. *Faculty research:* Church history, preaching, psychology of religion, Biblical studies, moral theology. *Unit head:* Very Rev. Edward M. Mazich, OSB, President/Rector, 724-805-2845, Fax: 724-532-5052, E-mail: edward.mazich@stvincent.edu. *Application contact:* Rev. Patrick T. Cronauer, OSB, Academic Dean, 724-805-2324, Fax: 724-805-2880, E-mail: patrick.cronauer@stvincent.edu.
Website: http://www.saintvincentseminary.edu

Santa Clara University, College of Arts and Sciences, Santa Clara, CA 95053. Offers pastoral ministries (MA). *Program availability:* Part-time. *Faculty:* 2 full-time (0 women), 5 part-time/adjunct (2 women). *Students:* 7 full-time (6 women), 67 part-time (44 women); includes 44 minority (3 Black or African American, non-Hispanic/Latino; 1 American Indian or Alaska Native, non-Hispanic/Latino; 8 Asian, non-Hispanic/Latino; 28 Hispanic/Latino; 1 Native Hawaiian or other Pacific Islander, non-Hispanic/Latino; 3 Two or more races, non-Hispanic/Latino). Average age 48. 31 applicants, 97% accepted, 25 enrolled. In 2017, 11 master's awarded. *Degree requirements:* For master's, comprehensive exam, thesis optional. *Entrance requirements:* For master's, 2 letters of recommendation, statement of purpose, 2 official transcripts. Additional exam requirements/recommendations for international students: Required—TOEFL (minimum score 90 iBT) or IELTS (6.5). *Application deadline:* For fall admission, 7/1 for domestic students; for winter admission, 10/1 for domestic students; for spring admission, 2/14 for domestic students. Applications are processed on a rolling basis. Application fee: $50. Electronic applications accepted. *Expenses:* $570 per unit. *Financial support:* In 2017–18, 93 students received support. Fellowships, research assistantships, teaching assistantships, Federal Work-Study, scholarships/grants, tuition waivers, and unspecified assistantships available. Financial award applicants required to submit FAFSA. *Unit head:* Joseph Morris, Director, Graduate Program in Pastoral Ministries, 408-554-2357, E-mail: jamorris@scu.edu. *Application contact:* Lynne Lukenbill, Senior Administrative Assistant, 408-554-4831, E-mail: llukenbill@scu.edu.
Website: https://www.scu.edu/cas/academics/graduate-program-in-pastoral-ministries/

Seattle University, School of Theology and Ministry, Program in Pastoral Studies, Seattle, WA 98122-1090. Offers MAPS. *Program availability:* Part-time, evening/weekend. *Faculty:* 15 full-time (7 women), 18 part-time/adjunct (11 women). *Students:* 4 full-time (2 women), 18 part-time (12 women); includes 4 minority (1 Black or African American, non-Hispanic/Latino; 3 Two or more races, non-Hispanic/Latino), 1 international. Average age 46. 10 applicants, 50% accepted, 5 enrolled. In 2017, 10 master's awarded. *Degree requirements:* For master's, project. *Entrance requirements:* For master's, minimum GPA of 2.75 (3.0 for international students); two years of experience in some form of education, ministry, or service as a profession or volunteer; recommendations; interview with admissions committee. *Application deadline:* For fall admission, 7/1 priority date for domestic students. Application fee: $55. *Expenses: Tuition:* Full-time $12,960. *Required fees:* $570. Tuition and fees vary according to program. *Financial support:* In 2017–18, 13 students received support. Application deadline: 4/1; applicants required to submit FAFSA. *Unit head:* Dr. Mark Markuly, Director, 206-296-5330, Fax: 206-296-5329, E-mail: markulym@seattleu.edu. *Application contact:* Catherine Kehoe Fallon, Admissions Coordinator, 206-296-5333, Fax: 206-296-5329, E-mail: fallon@seattleu.edu.
Website: https://www.seattleu.edu/stm/degrees/maps/

Seattle University, School of Theology and Ministry, Program in Transformational Leadership, Seattle, WA 98122-1090. Offers MATL. *Faculty:* 15 full-time (7 women), 18 part-time/adjunct (11 women). *Students:* 1 (woman) full-time, 19 part-time (11 women); includes 1 minority (Black or African American, non-Hispanic/Latino). Average age 40. 3 applicants, 100% accepted, 3 enrolled. In 2017, 16 master's awarded. *Degree requirements:* For master's, project. *Entrance requirements:* For master's, minimum GPA of 2.75 (3.0 for international students); two years of experience in some form of education, ministry, or service as a profession or volunteer; recommendations; interview with admissions committee. *Application deadline:* For fall admission, 7/1 priority date for domestic students. Application fee: $55. *Expenses: Tuition:* Full-time $12,960. *Required fees:* $570. Tuition and fees vary according to program. *Financial support:* In 2017–18, 10 students received support. Application deadline: 4/1; applicants required to submit FAFSA. *Unit head:* Dr. Mark Markuly, Dean, 206-296-5330, Fax: 206-296-5329, E-mail: stm@seattleu.edu. *Application contact:* Jean Adler Stean, Assistant Director of Admissions and Student Services, 206-296-5333, Fax: 206-296-5329, E-mail: fallon@seattleu.edu.
Website: http://www.seattleu.edu/stm/degrees/matl/

Pastoral Ministry and Counseling

Selma University, Graduate Programs, Selma, AL 36701-5299. Offers Bible and Christian education (MA); Bible and pastoral ministry (MA).

Seminary of the Southwest, Graduate and Professional Programs, Austin, TX 78768-2247. Offers Anglican studies (Advanced Diploma); chaplaincy and pastoral care (MA); clinical mental health counseling (MA); Latino/Hispanic studies (M Div); ministry (M Div); religion (MAR); spiritual formation (MA). *Accreditation:* ACIPE; ATS (one or more programs are accredited). *Program availability:* Part-time, evening/weekend. *Faculty:* 10 full-time (5 women), 12 part-time/adjunct (5 women). *Students:* 60 full-time (31 women), 56 part-time (42 women); includes 22 minority (10 Black or African American, non-Hispanic/Latino; 1 American Indian or Alaska Native, non-Hispanic/Latino; 2 Asian, non-Hispanic/Latino; 6 Hispanic/Latino; 3 Two or more races, non-Hispanic/Latino). Average age 38. 49 applicants, 98% accepted, 31 enrolled. In 2017, 27 master's, 3 other advanced degrees awarded. *Degree requirements:* For master's, comprehensive exam (for some programs), thesis (for some programs). *Entrance requirements:* For master's, GRE, MAT, interview; for Advanced Diploma, interview. Additional exam requirements/recommendations for international students: Recommended—TOEFL. *Application deadline:* For fall admission, 6/30 priority date for domestic and international students; for spring admission, 12/1 for domestic and international students. Applications are processed on a rolling basis. Application fee: $50. Electronic applications accepted. *Expenses:* Contact institution. *Financial support:* In 2017–18, 92 students received support. Career-related internships or fieldwork and scholarships/grants available. Support available to part-time students. Financial award application deadline: 6/15; financial award applicants required to submit FAFSA. *Unit head:* Rev. Dr. Cynthia Briggs Kittredge, Dean and President, 512-472-4133 Ext. 332, Fax: 512-472-3098, E-mail: cynthia.kittredge@ssw.edu. *Application contact:* Hope Benko, Director of Enrollment Management, 512-472-4133 Ext. 375, Fax: 512-472-3098, E-mail: hope.benko@ssw.edu.

Seton Hall University, Immaculate Conception Seminary School of Theology, South Orange, NJ 07079-2697. Offers Christian spirituality (Certificate); great spiritual books (Certificate); pastoral ministry (M Div, MA, Certificate); scripture studies (Certificate); Seminary's Theological Education for Parish Services (STEPS) (Certificate); theology (MA). *Program availability:* Part-time, evening/weekend. *Degree requirements:* For master's, comprehensive exam (for some programs), thesis (for some programs), final project (for some programs); 1 foreign language (for MA in theology research option). *Entrance requirements:* For master's, GRE General Test or MAT. Additional exam requirements/recommendations for international students: Required—TOEFL (minimum score 600 paper-based; 100 iBT). Electronic applications accepted. *Expenses:* Contact institution. *Faculty research:* Pauline literature, history of Biblical interpretation and theological exegesis, spirituality of St. Edith Stein, Thomism, history of Catholicism in America.

Shasta Bible College, Program in Biblical Counseling, Redding, CA 96002. Offers biblical counseling and Christian family life education (MA). *Program availability:* Part-time. *Degree requirements:* For master's, comprehensive exam (for some programs), thesis or alternative. *Entrance requirements:* For master's, minimum GPA of 2.5. Additional exam requirements/recommendations for international students: Required—TOEFL (minimum score 550 paper-based).

Shasta Bible College, Program in Christian Ministry, Redding, CA 96002. Offers MA. *Program availability:* Part-time, online learning. *Entrance requirements:* Additional exam requirements/recommendations for international students: Required—TOEFL (minimum score 550 paper-based).

Shepherds Theological Seminary, Graduate Programs, Cary, NC 27518. Offers Biblical literature and languages (MA); church ministry (MA); ministry (MTS); New Testament (M Div); Old Testament (M Div); theology (M Div). *Accreditation:* ATS. *Degree requirements:* For master's, thesis.

Shiloh University, Graduate Programs, Kalona, IA 52247. Offers Christian ministries (M Div); leadership of church and spiritual formation (D Min); theological studies (MA). *Program availability:* Part-time, evening/weekend, online only, 100% online. *Faculty:* 5 full-time (1 woman), 11 part-time/adjunct (2 women). *Students:* 10 full-time (3 women), 24 part-time (12 women); includes 10 minority (9 Black or African American, non-Hispanic/Latino; 1 Asian, non-Hispanic/Latino). Average age 51. 11 applicants, 91% accepted, 8 enrolled. In 2017, 3 master's awarded. *Degree requirements:* For master's, variable foreign language requirement, thesis optional; for doctorate, comprehensive exam, thesis/dissertation. *Entrance requirements:* For master's, bachelor's degree or educational equivalent from accredited school with minimum GPA of 2.5 on undergraduate work; for doctorate, M Div or equivalent with minimum GPA of 2.5 on graduate work; three years of ministry experience. Additional exam requirements/recommendations for international students: Recommended—TOEFL (minimum score 540 paper-based; 76 iBT), IELTS (minimum score 6.5). *Application deadline:* For fall admission, 6/18 priority date for domestic and international students; for spring admission, 10/22 priority date for domestic and international students; for summer admission, 2/15 priority date for domestic and international students. Applications are processed on a rolling basis. Application fee: $0. Electronic applications accepted. *Expenses:* $175 per credit hour, estimated $100 per course for books and supplies. *Financial support:* In 2017–18, 2 students received support. Scholarships/grants available. Financial award application deadline: 8/1; financial award applicants required to submit FAFSA. *Faculty research:* New Testament theology, Pauline literature, relational theology, Jewish foundations of Christianity, Judeo-Christian relations. *Unit head:* Dr. Ana Wood, Dean of Graduate Studies, 319-656-2447, Fax: 319-656-2448, E-mail: chiqui.wood@shilohuniversity.edu. *Application contact:* Katie Nisly, Admissions Coordinator, 319-656-2447, Fax: 319-656-2448, E-mail: admissions@shilohuniversity.edu.
Website: http://www.shilohuniversity.edu/academics/

Simpson University, A.W. Tozer Theological Seminary, Redding, CA 96003-8606. Offers ministry leadership (MA). *Program availability:* Part-time, evening/weekend, 100% online, blended/hybrid learning. *Entrance requirements:* For master's, GRE General Test (if undergraduate GPA less than 2.5), Christian statement, one spiritual recommendation, one academic recommendation. Additional exam requirements/recommendations for international students: Required—TOEFL (minimum score 583 paper-based; 94 iBT). Electronic applications accepted. *Expenses:* Contact institution.

Sioux Falls Seminary, Graduate and Professional Programs, Master of Divinity Program, Sioux Falls, SD 57105-1599. Offers marriage and family therapy (M Div); pastoral care and counseling (M Div). Program also offered in Omaha, NE. *Accreditation:* ACIPE. *Program availability:* Part-time, online learning.

Sioux Falls Seminary, Graduate and Professional Programs, Program in Counseling, Sioux Falls, SD 57105-1599. Offers MA. *Program availability:* Part-time. *Entrance requirements:* For master's, minimum GPA of 2.5.

Southeastern University, Barnett College of Ministry and Theology, Lakeland, FL 33801-6099. Offers family ministry (MA); ministerial leadership (MA, D Min); theological studies (MA); theology (M Div). *Program availability:* Evening/weekend, online learning. *Faculty:* 22 full-time (5 women), 10 part-time/adjunct (9 women). *Students:* 81 full-time (28 women), 131 part-time (49 women); includes 63 minority (31 Black or African American, non-Hispanic/Latino; 7 Asian, non-Hispanic/Latino; 24 Hispanic/Latino; 1 Two or more races, non-Hispanic/Latino), 4 international. Average age 38. *Degree requirements:* For master's, thesis/project. Application fee: $50. Electronic applications accepted. *Unit head:* Dean, 863-667-5000.
Website: http://www.seu.edu/ministry/

The Southern Baptist Theological Seminary, Billy Graham School of Missions, Evangelism and Ministry, Louisville, KY 40280-0004. Offers ministry (D Min); missiology (MA, D Miss); missions and evangelism (M Div, Th M, PhD); theological studies (MA). *Accreditation:* ATS. *Program availability:* Part-time, evening/weekend, online learning. *Degree requirements:* For master's, 2 foreign languages; for doctorate, 4 foreign languages, thesis/dissertation. *Entrance requirements:* For doctorate, GRE General Test, MAT, M Div. Additional exam requirements/recommendations for international students: Required—TOEFL, TWE. *Faculty research:* Assimilation of church congregants, effective methodologies of evangelism, expectations of church members, spiritual warfare literature, formative church discipline.

The Southern Baptist Theological Seminary, School of Theology, Louisville, KY 40280-0004. Offers applied theology (D Min); biblical and theological studies (M Div); biblical counseling (M Div, MA, D Min); biblical spirituality (D Min); Christian ministry (M Div); expository preaching (D Min); pastoral studies (M Div); theological studies (MA); theology (Th M, PhD); worldview and apologetics (M Div). *Program availability:* Part-time, evening/weekend, online learning. *Degree requirements:* For master's, 2 foreign languages, thesis; for doctorate, 4 foreign languages, thesis/dissertation. *Entrance requirements:* For master's, GRE General Test, MAT, M Div; for doctorate, GRE General Test, MAT, interview, M Div, field essay. Additional exam requirements/recommendations for international students: Required—TOEFL, TWE. *Faculty research:* Biblical studies, contemporary theology, church history, pastoral care, ministry/missions studies.

Southern Evangelical Seminary, Graduate Programs, Matthews, NC 28105. Offers apologetics (MA, D Min, Certificate); Christian education (MA); church ministry (MA, Certificate); divinity (Certificate), including apologetics (M Div, Certificate); Islamic studies (MA, Certificate); Jewish studies (MA); philosophy (MA); philosophy of religion (PhD); religion (MA); theology (M Div), including apologetics (M Div, Certificate), Biblical studies; youth ministry (MA). *Program availability:* Part-time, evening/weekend, online learning. *Degree requirements:* For master's, thesis (for some programs); for doctorate, 2 foreign languages, comprehensive exam (for some programs), thesis/dissertation. *Entrance requirements:* Additional exam requirements/recommendations for international students: Required—TOEFL (minimum score 600 paper-based).

Southern Wesleyan University, Program in Christian Ministries, Central, SC 29630-1020. Offers M Min. *Program availability:* Part-time, evening/weekend. *Entrance requirements:* For master's, GRE General Test or MAT, biographical paper; 12 semester credit hours of undergraduate work in religion, Bible, or ethics; 2 years of full-time Christian ministry experience. Additional exam requirements/recommendations for international students: Required—TOEFL (minimum score 500 paper-based).

South University, Graduate Programs, Doctor of Ministry Program, Savannah, GA 31406. Offers D Min.

Southwestern Assemblies of God University, Thomas F. Harrison School of Graduate Studies, Program in Theological Studies, Waxahachie, TX 75165-5735. Offers Bible and theology (MS); Biblical studies (M Div); counseling (M Div); cross cultural missions (M Div); practical theology (M Div); theological studies (M Div). *Program availability:* Online learning. *Degree requirements:* For master's, comprehensive written and oral exams. *Entrance requirements:* For master's, GRE General Test, minimum GPA of 2.5. Electronic applications accepted.

Southwestern Baptist Theological Seminary, School of Preaching, Fort Worth, TX 76122-0000. Offers Th M, D Min, PhD, Certificate.

Southwestern Baptist Theological Seminary, School of Theology, Fort Worth, TX 76122-0000. Offers ministry (D Min); theology (PhD). *Accreditation:* ACIPE; ATS (one or more programs are accredited). *Program availability:* Part-time, evening/weekend. Terminal master's awarded for partial completion of doctoral program. *Degree requirements:* For master's, 2 foreign languages, thesis (for some programs); for doctorate, 2 foreign languages, comprehensive exam, thesis/dissertation, oral exams. *Entrance requirements:* For doctorate, GRE, M Div or equivalent. Additional exam requirements/recommendations for international students: Required—TOEFL. Electronic applications accepted.

Southwestern Christian University, Program in Ministry, Bethany, OK 73008-0340. Offers church planting (M Min); church revitalization and renewal (M Min); intercultural studies (M Min); leadership (M Min); life coaching (M Min); pastoral ministries (M Min); work place ministries (M Min). *Program availability:* Part-time. *Degree requirements:* For master's, thesis. *Entrance requirements:* For master's, minimum GPA of 2.5. Additional exam requirements/recommendations for international students: Required—TOEFL (minimum score 500 paper-based). Electronic applications accepted.

Spring Arbor University, School of Arts and Sciences, Spring Arbor, MI 49283-9799. Offers communication (MA); spiritual formation and leadership (MA). *Program availability:* Part-time, online learning. *Degree requirements:* For master's, thesis (for some programs). *Entrance requirements:* For master's, GRE (minimum score of 40th percentile and taken within last 5 years), bachelor's degree from regionally-accredited college or university, minimum GPA of 3.0 for at least the last two years of the bachelor's degree, at least two recommendations from professional/academic individuals. Additional exam requirements/recommendations for international students: Required—TOEFL (minimum score 600 paper-based). *Expenses:* Contact institution.

Spring Hill College, Graduate Programs, Program in Theology, Mobile, AL 36608-1791. Offers faith companioning (Postbaccalaureate Certificate); pastoral ministry (Postbaccalaureate Certificate); pastoral studies (MPS); spiritual direction (Postbaccalaureate Certificate); theological studies (MTS); theology (MA). *Program availability:* Part-time, evening/weekend. *Faculty:* 6 full-time (1 woman), 2 part-time/adjunct (0 women). *Students:* 31 part-time (16 women); includes 5 minority (1 Black or African American, non-Hispanic/Latino; 1 American Indian or Alaska Native, non-Hispanic/Latino; 1 Asian, non-Hispanic/Latino; 1 Hispanic/Latino; 1 Two or more races, non-Hispanic/Latino), 2 international. Average age 42. In 2017, 11 master's, 2 other advanced degrees awarded. *Degree requirements:* For master's, variable foreign language requirement, comprehensive exam, thesis (for some programs), completion of program within 6 calendar years of initial enrollment (MTS, MPS); completion of program within 4 1/2 calendar years of formal acceptance (MA). *Entrance requirements:* For master's, bachelor's degree with minimum undergraduate GPA of 3.0; six hours of undergraduate theology, religious studies, or unquestioned equivalency. Additional exam requirements/recommendations for international students: Required—TOEFL (minimum score 550 paper-based; 80 iBT), IELTS (minimum score 6.5), CPE or CAE (minimum score C), Michigan English Language Assessment Battery (minimum score 90). *Application deadline:* For fall admission, 8/1 priority date for domestic and international students; for spring admission, 12/1 priority date for domestic and international students. Applications are processed on a rolling basis. Application fee: $25 ($35 for international students). Electronic applications accepted. *Expenses:* *Tuition:* Full-time $9270; part-time $515 per credit hour. Tuition and fees vary according

to program. *Financial support:* Applicants required to submit FAFSA. *Unit head:* Dr. Timothy R. Carmody, Director, 251-380-4665, Fax: 251-460-2194, E-mail: carmody@shc.edu. *Application contact:* Robert Stewart, Vice President of Enrollment, 251-380-3030, Fax: 251-460-2186, E-mail: rstewart@shc.edu. Website: http://ug.shc.edu/graduate-degrees/master-arts-theological-studies/

SUM Bible College & Theological Seminary, Graduate Programs, Oakland, CA 94603. Offers biblical studies (MA); Christian leadership (MA); theology (M Div). *Entrance requirements:* For master's, minimum GPA of 2.5, currently active in ministry.

Theological University of the Caribbean, Graduate Programs, Saint Just, PR 00978-0901. Offers childhood and adolescent education (MA); counseling and pastoral care (MA); ministry (D Min); missions (MA).

Trevecca Nazarene University, Graduate Religion Programs, Nashville, TN 37210-2877. Offers biblical and theological studies (MA); Christian ministry (MA); pastoral counseling (MA). *Program availability:* Part-time, online learning. *Faculty:* 10 full-time (2 women), 7 part-time/adjunct (0 women). *Students:* 74 full-time (40 women), 22 part-time (13 women); includes 38 minority (26 Black or African American, non-Hispanic/Latino; 1 American Indian or Alaska Native, non-Hispanic/Latino; 1 Asian, non-Hispanic/Latino; 7 Hispanic/Latino; 3 Two or more races, non-Hispanic/Latino), 1 international. Average age 41. In 2017, 22 master's awarded. *Degree requirements:* For master's, research project. *Entrance requirements:* For master's, minimum GPA of 2.7, official transcript from regionally accredited institution, letter of recommendation. Additional exam requirements/recommendations for international students: Required—TOEFL (minimum score 550 paper-based; 80 iBT). *Application deadline:* Applications are processed on a rolling basis. Application fee: $0. Electronic applications accepted. *Expenses:* $350 per credit hour. *Financial support:* Applicants required to submit FAFSA. *Unit head:* Dr. Tim Green, Dean, School of Theology and Christian Ministry/Director, Graduate Religion Program, 615-248-1378, Fax: 615-248-7417. *Application contact:* 844-TNU-GRAD, E-mail: sgcsadmissions@trevecca.edu. Website: http://www.trevecca.edu/gradreligion

Trinity Bible College and Graduate School, Graduate School, Ellendale, ND 58436. Offers global theology (MA); missional leadership (MA); rural ministries (MA).

Trinity College, Faculty of Divinity, Toronto, ON M5S 1H8, Canada. Offers ministry (Diploma); ministry for church musicians (Diploma); theology (M Div, MA, MTS, Th M, D Min, PhD, Th D, Diploma, L Th); M Div/MA. *Accreditation:* ATS. *Program availability:* Part-time. *Degree requirements:* For master's, 2 foreign languages, thesis (for some programs); for doctorate, 3 foreign languages, comprehensive exam, thesis/dissertation; for other advanced degree, thesis (for some programs). *Entrance requirements:* For master's, 1 language (modern or ancient), interview; for doctorate, 2 languages (modern and ancient). Additional exam requirements/recommendations for international students: Required—TOEFL, TWE. *Faculty research:* Interreligious dialogue, feminist theology, systematic theology, philosophy of religion, pastoral theology.

Trinity International University, Trinity Evangelical Divinity School, Deerfield, IL 60015-1284. Offers academic ministry (M Div); Biblical and Near Eastern archaeology and languages (MA); chaplaincy and ministry care (MA); Christian studies (Certificate); church and parachurch ministry (M Div); church history (MA, Th M); counseling (Th M); educational ministries (MA); educational ministry (Th M); educational studies (PhD); intercultural studies (MA, PhD); leadership and management (D Min); mental health counseling (MA); military chaplaincy (D Min); ministry (MA); missions (Th M); missions and evangelism (D Min); New Testament (MA, Th M); Old Testament (Th M); Old Testament and Semitic languages (MA); pastoral ministry and care (D Min); pastoral theology (Th M); preaching and teaching (D Min); spiritual formation and education (D Min); systematic theology (MA, Th M); theological studies (MA, PhD); urban ministry (MA). *Program availability:* Part-time, online learning. *Degree requirements:* For master's, comprehensive exam, thesis, fieldwork; for doctorate, comprehensive exam (for some programs), thesis/dissertation; for Certificate, comprehensive exam, integrative papers. *Entrance requirements:* For master's, GRE, MAT, minimum cumulative undergraduate GPA of 3.0; for doctorate, GRE, minimum cumulative graduate GPA of 3.2; for Certificate, GRE, MAT, minimum undergraduate GPA of 2.5. Additional exam requirements/recommendations for international students: Required—TOEFL (minimum score 580 paper-based), TWE (minimum score 4). Electronic applications accepted.

Trinity Lutheran Seminary, Graduate and Professional Programs, Columbus, OH 43209-2334. Offers African American studies (MTS); Biblical studies (MTS, STM); Christian education (MA); Christian spirituality (STM); church in the world (MTS); church music (MA); divinity (M Div); general theological studies (MTS); mission and evangelism (STM); pastoral leadership and practice (STM); youth and family ministry (MA); MSN/MTS; MTS/JD. *Accreditation:* ACIPE; ATS. *Program availability:* Part-time. *Degree requirements:* For master's, variable foreign language requirement, comprehensive exam (for some programs), thesis (for some programs), field experience (for some programs). *Entrance requirements:* For master's, BA or equivalent (for MA, M Div, MTS); M Div, MTS, or equivalent (for STM); audition (for MACM). Additional exam requirements/recommendations for international students: Required—TOEFL. Electronic applications accepted. *Expenses:* Contact institution.

Trinity School for Ministry, Graduate Programs, Ambridge, PA 15003-2397. Offers Anglican studies (Diploma); basic Christian studies (Diploma); divinity (M Div); ministry (D Min); mission and evangelism (MAME, Diploma); religion (MAR); youth ministry (Diploma). *Program availability:* Part-time. *Degree requirements:* For master's, thesis optional; for doctorate, thesis/dissertation. *Entrance requirements:* Additional exam requirements/recommendations for international students: Required—TOEFL. *Faculty research:* Pauline Epistles, contemporary theology, history of Anglican liturgy, book of Ruth, biblical theology.

Trinity Western University, ACTS Seminaries, Langley, BC V2Y 1Y1, Canada. Offers Christian studies (MA); cross cultural ministry (MA); theology (M Div, M Th, MAMFT, MLE, MTS, D Min). *Program availability:* Part-time. *Degree requirements:* For master's, thesis (for some programs), internship. *Entrance requirements:* For doctorate, M Div or equivalent. Additional exam requirements/recommendations for international students: Required—TOEFL. *Expenses:* Contact institution. *Faculty research:* Theology of leadership.

Tyndale University College & Seminary, Graduate Programs, Toronto, ON M2M 3S4, Canada. Offers Biblical studies (M Div); Christian foundations (MTS); Christian studies (Diploma); counseling (M Div); educational ministry (M Div); missions (M Div, Diploma); pastoral and Chinese ministry (M Div); pastoral ministry (M Div); Pentecostal studies (MTS); spiritual formation (M Div, Diploma); theological studies (M Div); theology (Th M); worship and liturgy (M Div, MTS); youth and family ministry (M Div). *Accreditation:* ATS. *Program availability:* Part-time, online learning. *Entrance requirements:* For master's and Diploma, minimum C+ average in undergraduate course work. Additional exam requirements/recommendations for international students: Required—TOEFL (minimum score 570 paper-based), TWE (minimum score 5). Electronic applications accepted. *Faculty research:* Canadian church history, Chinese church history, Old Testament, counseling ministries (narrative therapy), world religions.

Union University, School of Theology and Missions, Jackson, TN 38305-3697. Offers Christian studies (MCS); expository preaching (D Min). *Program availability:* Part-time, evening/weekend, online learning. Electronic applications accepted.

United Lutheran Seminary, Graduate and Professional Programs, Gettysburg, PA 17325-1795. Offers divinity (M Div); ministerial studies (MAMS); outdoor ministry (MAR); parish ministry (D Min); theology (STM). *Accreditation:* ACIPE; ATS (one or more programs are accredited). *Program availability:* Part-time, online learning. *Degree requirements:* For master's, thesis (for some programs). Electronic applications accepted.

United Lutheran Seminary, Graduate School, Philadelphia, PA 19119-1794. Offers divinity (M Div); ministry (D Min); public leadership (MA); religion (MAR); social ministry and church (Certificate); theology (STM, PhD). *Accreditation:* ACIPE. *Program availability:* Part-time, evening/weekend. *Degree requirements:* For master's, one foreign language, comprehensive exam (for some programs), thesis (for some programs); for doctorate, thesis/dissertation. *Entrance requirements:* For master's, minimum undergraduate GPA of 2.8; for doctorate, minimum GPA of 3.0. Additional exam requirements/recommendations for international students: Required—TOEFL (minimum score 550 paper-based; 89 iBT), TWE. Electronic applications accepted.

United Theological Seminary, Graduate and Professional Programs, Dayton, OH 45426. Offers Christian ministries (MA); ministry (M Div, D Min); theological studies (MTS). *Accreditation:* ATS. *Program availability:* Part-time, evening/weekend, online learning. *Degree requirements:* For master's, thesis (for some programs); for doctorate, thesis/dissertation, final exam. *Entrance requirements:* For master's, minimum GPA of 2.5, interview, 5 letters of recommendation; for doctorate, minimum GPA of 3.0, 2 letters of recommendation, interview. Additional exam requirements/recommendations for international students: Required—TOEFL (minimum score 550 paper-based). Electronic applications accepted.

United Theological Seminary of the Twin Cities, Graduate Programs, New Brighton, MN 55112-2598. Offers advanced theological studies (Diploma); justice and peace studies (M Div, MA); leadership toward racial justice (M Div, MA, Certificate); Methodist studies (M Div, MA, Certificate); ministry (D Min); ministry renewal and professional development (Certificate); pastoral care and counseling (M Div, MA, MARL); religion and theology (MA); theological and religious studies (Certificate); theology and the arts (M Div, MA); urban ministry (M Div, MA, MARL); women's studies: religion, theology and ministry (M Div, MA). *Accreditation:* ACIPE; ATS. *Program availability:* Part-time, evening/weekend. *Degree requirements:* For master's, thesis; for doctorate, comprehensive exam, thesis/dissertation. *Entrance requirements:* For master's, minimum GPA of 2.75; strong analytical, reflective thinking and writing skills; vocational and academic goals compatible with those of Seminary; for doctorate, M Div or equivalent, minimum GPA of 3.0, 3 years experience in professional ministry; for other advanced degree, BA or equivalent life experience; strong analytical, reflective thinking and writing skills (Certificate); proficiency in English language, previous study of theology at a theological school, recommendation of student's denomination (Diploma). Additional exam requirements/recommendations for international students: Required—TOEFL (minimum score 550 paper-based).

University of Chicago, Divinity School, Program in Ministry, Chicago, IL 60637. Offers M Div. *Students:* 39 full-time (16 women), 4 part-time (1 woman); includes 12 minority (4 Black or African American, non-Hispanic/Latino; 4 Asian, non-Hispanic/Latino; 2 Hispanic/Latino; 2 Two or more races, non-Hispanic/Latino), 3 international. Average age 28. 49 applicants, 78% accepted, 18 enrolled. In 2017, 17 master's awarded. *Degree requirements:* For master's, one foreign language, thesis, field education. *Entrance requirements:* For master's, GRE General Test, 3 letters of recommendation; transcripts; curriculum vitae or resume. Additional exam requirements/recommendations for international students: Required—TOEFL (minimum score 600 paper-based; 104 iBT), IELTS (minimum score 7). *Application deadline:* For fall admission, 1/15 priority date for domestic and international students. Application fee: $75. Electronic applications accepted. *Expenses:* Contact institution. *Financial support:* Career-related internships or fieldwork, Federal Work-Study, institutionally sponsored loans, scholarships/grants, and tuition waivers (partial) available. Support available to part-time students. Financial award application deadline: 1/15. *Faculty research:* Constructive studies (philosophy of religion, religious ethics, and theology); historical studies (Bible, history of Christianity, and history of Judaism); religion and the human sciences (anthropology and sociology of religion, history of religions, and religion, literature, and visual culture); Islamic studies; religions in America. *Unit head:* Dr. Cynthia G. Lindner, Director of Ministry Studies/Clinical Professor of Preaching and Pastoral Care, 773-702-8280, E-mail: clindner@uchicago.edu. *Application contact:* Anita Lumpkin, Associate Dean of Students, 773-702-8249, E-mail: divinityadmissions@uchicago.edu. Website: http://divinity.uchicago.edu/ministry-program-mdiv

University of Dallas, Ann and Joe O. Neuhoff School of Ministry, Irving, TX 75062-4736. Offers MCSL. *Accreditation:* ACIPE. *Program availability:* Part-time, evening/weekend, online learning. *Application deadline:* For fall admission, 7/15 for domestic students; for spring admission, 11/15 for domestic students. Application fee: $50. *Expenses: Tuition:* Full-time $33,750; part-time $22,500 per year. Tuition and fees vary according to program. *Financial support:* Application deadline: 2/15. *Faculty research:* Scripture, pastoral theology, ecclesiology, systematic theology, theological anthropology. *Unit head:* Sheri Collier, Coordinator of Graduate Enrollment and Student Services, 972-721-5814, Fax: 972-721-4076, E-mail: scollier@udallas.edu. Website: https://udallas.edu/ministry/

University of Dayton, Department of Religious Studies, Dayton, OH 45469. Offers pastoral ministry (MA); theological studies (MA); theology (PhD). *Program availability:* Part-time. *Faculty:* 23 full-time (7 women), 2 part-time/adjunct (1 woman). *Students:* 48 full-time (24 women), 10 part-time (4 women); includes 7 minority (2 Black or African American, non-Hispanic/Latino; 2 Asian, non-Hispanic/Latino; 3 Hispanic/Latino), 1 international. Average age 34. 53 applicants, 57% accepted. In 2017, 10 master's, 5 doctorates awarded. *Degree requirements:* For master's, thesis or alternative; for doctorate, 2 foreign languages, comprehensive exam, thesis/dissertation. *Entrance requirements:* For master's, 3 letters of recommendation, personal statement, all previous official transcript(s); for doctorate, GRE General Test (minimum score 600 verbal previous scale, 160 current scale), academic writing sample, 3 letters of recommendation, official transcript(s). Additional exam requirements/recommendations for international students: Required—TOEFL (minimum score 550 paper-based; 80 iBT). *Application deadline:* For fall admission, 2/1 priority date for domestic students, 2/1 for international students. Applications are processed on a rolling basis. Application fee: $0 ($50 for international students). Electronic applications accepted. *Expenses:* Contact institution. *Financial support:* In 2017–18, 21 research assistantships with full tuition reimbursements (averaging $11,250 per year), 20 teaching assistantships with full tuition reimbursements (averaging $18,130 per year) were awarded; fellowships and institutionally sponsored loans also available. Financial award application deadline: 3/1; financial award applicants required to submit FAFSA. *Faculty research:* Practical/constructive theology, theological ethics, U.S. Catholic/Christian life and thought, methodologies in Biblical studies, religion and science. *Unit head:* Dr. Daniel Thompson, Chair, 937-229-4321, Fax: 937-229-4330. *Application contact:* Amy Doorley, Coordinator of Graduate Studies, 937-229-4321, Fax: 937-229-4330, E-mail: adoorley1@udayton.edu. Website: http://www.udayton.edu/artssciences/academics/religiousstudies/welcome/index.php

Pastoral Ministry and Counseling

University of Fort Lauderdale, Graduate Program, Lauderhill, FL 33313. Offers MS. *Degree requirements:* For master's, thesis.

University of Northwestern–St. Paul, Master of Divinity Program, St. Paul, MN 55113-1598. Offers M Div. *Program availability:* Part-time, evening/weekend, online learning. *Application deadline:* Applications are processed on a rolling basis. Electronic applications accepted. *Application contact:* Graduate Studies Admissions, 651-631-5200, E-mail: gradstudies@unwsp.edu.
Website: https://www.unwsp.edu/web/graduate-studies/master-of-divinity

University of Portland, Department of Theology, Portland, OR 97203-5798. Offers pastoral ministry (MA). *Program availability:* Part-time. *Entrance requirements:* For master's, GRE or MAT, 3 letters of recommendation, minimum GPA of 3.0. Additional exam requirements/recommendations for international students: Required—TOEFL (minimum score 550 paper-based; 80 iBT), IELTS (minimum score 7).

University of Saint Mary of the Lake–Mundelein Seminary, Graduate and Professional Programs, Mundelein, IL 60060. Offers liturgical studies (MA); ministry (D Min); pastoral studies (MA); theology (M Div). *Accreditation:* ATS (one or more programs are accredited). *Degree requirements:* For doctorate, 2 foreign languages, comprehensive exam, thesis/dissertation. *Entrance requirements:* For master's and doctorate, bachelor's degree. Additional exam requirements/recommendations for international students: Required—TOEFL (minimum score 550 paper-based). Electronic applications accepted.

University of St. Michael's College, Faculty of Theology, Toronto, ON M5S 1J4, Canada. Offers Catholic leadership (MA); eastern Christian studies (Diploma); religious education (Diploma); theological studies (Diploma); theology (M Div, MA, MRE, MTS, D Min, PhD, Th D); theology and Jewish studies (MA). Th D offered jointly with University of Toronto. *Accreditation:* ATS (one or more programs are accredited). *Program availability:* Part-time. *Degree requirements:* For master's, thesis (for some programs), 1 foreign language (MA), 2 foreign languages (Th M); for doctorate, 3 foreign languages, comprehensive exam, thesis/dissertation; for other advanced degree, thesis optional. *Entrance requirements:* For master's, M Div or BA, course work in an ancient or modern language, minimum GPA of 3.3; for doctorate, MA in theology, Th M, or M Div with thesis, minimum GPA of 3.7; for other advanced degree, minimum GPA of 2.7. Additional exam requirements/recommendations for international students: Required—TOEFL (minimum score 600 paper-based). Electronic applications accepted. *Expenses:* Contact institution. *Faculty research:* Patristics, eastern Christianity, ecology and theology, ecumenism, Jewish Christian studies.

University of St. Thomas, The Saint Paul Seminary School of Divinity, St. Paul, MN 55105. Offers pastoral ministry (MAPM); religious education (MARE); theology (MA). *Accreditation:* ACIPE; ATS. *Program availability:* Part-time, evening/weekend. *Degree requirements:* For master's, one foreign language, comprehensive exam (for some programs), thesis (for some programs). *Entrance requirements:* For master's, GRE, 3 letters of recommendation, interview. Additional exam requirements/recommendations for international students: Required—TOEFL (minimum score 550 paper-based). *Application deadline:* For fall admission, 6/1 priority date for domestic students. Applications are processed on a rolling basis. Application fee: $40. Electronic applications accepted. *Expenses:* Contact institution. *Financial support:* Fellowships, research assistantships, institutionally sponsored loans, and scholarships/grants available. Support available to part-time students. Financial award application deadline: 4/1; financial award applicants required to submit FAFSA. *Faculty research:* Theological education. *Unit head:* Rev. Msgr. Aloysius R. Callaghan, Rector/Vice President, 651-962-5052, Fax: 651-962-5790, E-mail: arcallaghan@stthomas.edu. *Application contact:* Ana Theisen, Recruiter/Admissions Counselor, 651-962-5069, Fax: 651-962-5790, E-mail: aztheisen@stthomas.edu.
Website: http://www.stthomas.edu/spssod/

University of St. Thomas, School of Theology, Houston, TX 77006-4696. Offers divinity (M Div); pastoral studies (MAPS); theological studies (MA). *Accreditation:* ATS. *Program availability:* Part-time. *Faculty:* 10 full-time (2 women), 7 part-time/adjunct (1 woman). *Students:* 80 full-time (3 women), 78 part-time (29 women); includes 64 minority (5 Black or African American, non-Hispanic/Latino; 24 Asian, non-Hispanic/Latino; 34 Hispanic/Latino; 1 Two or more races, non-Hispanic/Latino), 25 international. Average age 38. 56 applicants, 100% accepted, 18 enrolled. In 2017, 38 master's awarded. *Degree requirements:* For master's, variable foreign language requirement, comprehensive exam. *Entrance requirements:* For master's, BA, BS or equivalent; personal essay (for some programs); undergraduate philosophy or theology courses; 2 letters of recommendation. Additional exam requirements/recommendations for international students: Required—TOEFL (minimum score 550 paper-based; 79 iBT), IELTS (minimum score 6.5), PTE (minimum score 53). *Application deadline:* Applications are processed on a rolling basis. Application fee: $10. Electronic applications accepted. *Expenses:* Contact institution. *Financial support:* In 2017–18, 9 students received support. Scholarships/grants available. Support available to part-time students. Financial award application deadline: 4/15; financial award applicants required to submit FAFSA. *Unit head:* Dr. Sandra C. Magie, Dean, 713-686-4345 Ext. 242, Fax: 713-683-8673, E-mail: smagie@stthom.edu. *Application contact:* E-mail: sms@stthom.edu.
Website: http://www.stthom.edu/Academics/School_of_Theology_at_St_Marys_Seminary/Index.aqf

University of South Africa, College of Human Sciences, Pretoria, South Africa. Offers adult education (M Ed); African languages (MA, PhD); African politics (MA, PhD); Afrikaans (MA, PhD); ancient history (MA, PhD); ancient Near Eastern studies (MA, PhD); anthropology (MA, PhD); applied linguistics (MA); Arabic (MA, PhD); archaeology (MA); art history (MA); Biblical archaeology (MA); Biblical studies (M Th, D Th, PhD); Christian spirituality (M Th, D Th); church history (M Th, D Th); classical studies (MA, PhD); clinical psychology (MA); communication (MA, PhD); comparative education (M Ed, Ed D); consulting psychology (D Admin, D Com, PhD); curriculum studies (M Ed, Ed D); development studies (M Admin, MA, D Admin, PhD); didactics (M Ed, Ed D); education (M Tech); education management (M Ed, Ed D); educational psychology (M Ed); English (MA); environmental education (M Ed); French (MA, PhD); German (MA, PhD); Greek (MA); guidance and counseling (M Ed); health studies (MA, PhD), including health sciences education (MA), health services management (MA), medical and surgical nursing science (critical care general) (MA), midwifery and neonatal nursing science (MA), trauma and emergency care (MA); history (MA, PhD); history of education (Ed D); inclusive education (M Ed, Ed D); information and communications technology policy and regulation (MA); information science (MA, MIS, PhD); international politics (MA, PhD); Islamic studies (MA, PhD); Italian (MA, PhD); Judaica (MA, PhD); linguistics (MA, PhD); mathematical education (M Ed); mathematics education (MA); missiology (M Th, D Th); modern Hebrew (MA, PhD); musicology (MA, MMus, D Mus, PhD); natural science education (M Ed); New Testament (M Th, D Th); Old Testament (D Th); pastoral therapy (M Th, D Th); philosophy (MA); philosophy of education (M Ed, Ed D); politics (MA, PhD); Portuguese (MA, PhD); practical theology (M Th, D Th); psychology (MA, MS, PhD); psychology of education (M Ed, Ed D); public health (MA); religious studies (MA, D Th, PhD); Romance languages (MA); Russian (MA, PhD); Semitic languages (MA, PhD); social behavior studies in HIV/AIDS (MA); social science (mental health) (MA); social science in development studies (MA); social science in psychology (MA); social science in social work (MA); social science in sociology (MA); social work (MSW, DSW, PhD); socio-education (M Ed, Ed D); sociolinguistics (MA); sociology (MA, PhD); Spanish (MA, PhD); systematic theology (M Th, D Th); TESOL (teaching English to speakers of other languages) (MA); theological ethics (M Th, D Th); theory of literature (MA, PhD); urban ministries (D Th); urban ministry (M Th).

University of the Incarnate Word, College of Humanities, Arts, and Social Sciences, San Antonio, TX 78209-6397. Offers multidisciplinary studies (MA); pastoral ministry (MA). *Program availability:* Part-time, evening/weekend. *Faculty:* 4 full-time (2 women). *Students:* 2 full-time (1 woman), 1 (woman) part-time; includes 2 minority (both Hispanic/Latino). In 2017, 3 master's awarded. *Degree requirements:* For master's, thesis or alternative. *Entrance requirements:* For master's, GRE/MAT or three letters of recommendation and personal statement of ministerial and educational goals. Additional exam requirements/recommendations for international students: Required—TOEFL (minimum score 560 paper-based; 83 iBT). *Application deadline:* Applications are processed on a rolling basis. Application fee: $20. Electronic applications accepted. *Expenses: Tuition:* Full-time $16,470; part-time $915 per credit hour. Tuition and fees vary according to degree level, program and student level. *Financial support:* Research assistantships, scholarships/grants, tuition waivers, and unspecified assistantships available. Financial award applicants required to submit FAFSA. *Faculty research:* Migration patterns in southeast Asia; women in the criminal justice system; cultural, racial and ethnic diversity; Hispanic religion and theology; substance use disorders. *Unit head:* Dr. Kevin Vichcales, Dean, 210-829-2759, Fax: 210-829-3830, E-mail: vichcale@uiwtx.edu. *Application contact:* Johnny Garcia, Graduate Admissions Counselor, 210-829-6005, Fax: 210-829-3921, E-mail: admis@uiwtx.edu.
Website: http://www.uiw.edu/hass/index.htm

Ursuline College, School of Graduate and Professional Studies, Theological and Pastoral Studies Program, Pepper Pike, OH 44124-4398. Offers MA. *Program availability:* Part-time. *Faculty:* 3 full-time (all women). *Students:* 7 part-time (4 women); includes 6 minority (all Black or African American, non-Hispanic/Latino). Average age 56. 4 applicants, 100% accepted, 4 enrolled. In 2017, 2 master's awarded. *Degree requirements:* For master's, thesis. *Entrance requirements:* For master's, GRE when GPA under 3.0, minimum undergraduate GPA of 3.0, interview. Additional exam requirements/recommendations for international students: Required—TOEFL (minimum score 550 paper-based; 80 iBT). *Application deadline:* For fall admission, 8/1 priority date for domestic students. Applications are processed on a rolling basis. Application fee: $25. Electronic applications accepted. *Expenses:* Contact institution. *Financial support:* Scholarships/grants available. Financial award application deadline: 3/1; financial award applicants required to submit FAFSA. *Faculty research:* Household codes of Ephesians, cosmology of Ephesians, early Christian families, the use of theological reflection in integrative education for ministry, premillennial dispensationalism and the politics of the religious right in the United States. *Unit head:* Dr. Linda Martin, Director, 440-646-8191, Fax: 440-684-6088, E-mail: lmartin@ursuline.edu. *Application contact:* Melanie Steele, Director, Graduate Admissions, 440-646-8146, Fax: 440-684-6138, E-mail: graduateadmissions@ursuline.edu.

Virginia Beach Theological Seminary, Graduate Programs, Virginia Beach, VA 23464. Offers Biblical studies (MBS, Th M); chaplaincy (MBS); ministry (M Div). *Program availability:* Online learning. *Entrance requirements:* For master's, GRE, interview, minimum cumulative GPA of 2.4, church endorsement, 3 recommendations. Electronic applications accepted.

Virginia University of Lynchburg, Graduate Programs, Lynchburg, VA 24501-6417. Offers Christian ministry (M Div); ministry (D Min). *Program availability:* Online learning.

Viterbo University, Master of Arts in Servant Leadership Program, La Crosse, WI 54601-4797. Offers ethical leadership in organizations (Certificate); servant leadership (MA). *Program availability:* Part-time, evening/weekend. *Degree requirements:* For master's, 30 credits (15 credits of Servant Leadership core courses and any combination of 15 elective credits). *Entrance requirements:* For master's, letter of reference, statement of goals, baccalaureate degree, transcript, interview. Additional exam requirements/recommendations for international students: Required—TOEFL (minimum score 525 paper-based). Electronic applications accepted. *Expenses:* Contact institution. *Faculty research:* Organizational culture, community building, ethical decision-making, leadership theory and practice.

Walla Walla University, Graduate Studies, Center for Cinema, Religion, and Worldview, College Place, WA 99324. Offers Web and interactive media (MA). *Entrance requirements:* For master's, three professional references, transcripts, personal statement. *Application deadline:* For fall admission, 8/15 for domestic students. Application fee: $50. *Unit head:* Lynelle Ellis, Director, 509-527-2843, Fax: 509-527-2237, E-mail: lynelle.ellis@wallawalla.edu. *Application contact:* Rachel Scribner, Coordinator, 509-527-2832, Fax: 509-527-2237, E-mail: rachel.scribner@wallawalla.edu.
Website: https://www.wallawalla.edu/academics/grad-studies/cinema-religion-worldview/

Walsh University, Graduate Programs, Master of Arts in Theology Program, North Canton, OH 44720-3396. Offers parish administration (MA); pastoral ministry (MA); religious education (MA). *Program availability:* Part-time, evening/weekend. *Degree requirements:* For master's, thesis or alternative, culminating assignment. *Entrance requirements:* For master's, MAT or GRE (minimum scores: Verbal 145, Quantitative 146, Combined 291, Writing 3.0), minimum GPA of 3.0. Additional exam requirements/recommendations for international students: Required—TOEFL. Electronic applications accepted. Application fee is waived when completed online. *Expenses:* Contact institution. *Faculty research:* Cardinal Newman, phenomenological method, Flavius Josephus, post-conciliar moral teaching.

Wayland Baptist University, Graduate Programs, Programs in Religion, Plainview, TX 79072-6998. Offers Christian ministry (MCM); divinity (M Div); religion (MA). *Program availability:* Part-time, evening/weekend, online learning. *Faculty:* 15 full-time (1 woman), 12 part-time/adjunct (0 women). *Students:* 3 full-time (0 women), 97 part-time (27 women); includes 61 minority (36 Black or African American, non-Hispanic/Latino; 1 American Indian or Alaska Native, non-Hispanic/Latino; 6 Asian, non-Hispanic/Latino; 9 Hispanic/Latino; 2 Native Hawaiian or other Pacific Islander, non-Hispanic/Latino; 7 Two or more races, non-Hispanic/Latino). Average age 45. 22 applicants, 95% accepted, 16 enrolled. In 2017, 26 master's awarded. *Degree requirements:* For master's, comprehensive exam. *Entrance requirements:* For master's, GRE or MAT, minimum GPA of 3.0; letter of endorsement from Christian congregation, one academic and one personal letter of recommendation (for M Div). Additional exam requirements/recommendations for international students: Required—TOEFL (minimum score 500 paper-based; 61 iBT). *Application deadline:* Applications are processed on a rolling basis. Application fee: $50. Electronic applications accepted. *Expenses: Tuition:* Full-time $11,250; part-time $625 per credit hour. *Required fees:* $1200. *Financial support:* Federal Work-Study, institutionally sponsored loans, and scholarships/grants available. Support available to part-time students. Financial award application deadline: 5/1; financial award applicants required to submit FAFSA. *Unit head:* Dr. Clinton Lowin, Chairman, 806-291-1165, Fax: 806-291-1969, E-mail: lowinc@wbu.edu. *Application*

contact: Amanda Stanton, Coordinator of Graduate Studies, 806-291-3423, Fax: 806-291-1950, E-mail: stanton@wbu.edu.

Welch College, Program in Theology and Ministry, Gallatin, TN 37066. Offers MA. *Program availability:* Online learning.

Wesley Biblical Seminary, Graduate Programs, Jackson, MS 39206. Offers apologetics (MA); Biblical languages (M Div); Biblical literature (MA); Christian studies (MA); context and mission (M Div); honors research (M Div); interpretation (M Div); ministry (M Div); spiritual formation (M Div); teaching (M Div); theology (MA). *Accreditation:* ATS. *Program availability:* Part-time. *Degree requirements:* For master's, thesis. *Entrance requirements:* Additional exam requirements/recommendations for international students: Required—TOEFL. Electronic applications accepted. *Faculty research:* Patristics, missiology, culture, hermeneutics.

Western Seminary, Graduate Programs, Program in Counseling, Portland, OR 97215-3367. Offers counseling (MA, Certificate); pastoral counseling (M Div); M Div/MA. *Program availability:* Part-time, evening/weekend. *Degree requirements:* For master's, practicum. *Entrance requirements:* Additional exam requirements/recommendations for international students: Required—TOEFL. *Expenses:* Contact institution.

Western Seminary, Graduate Programs, Program in Intercultural Studies, Portland, OR 97215-3367. Offers MA, D Miss, Certificate, G Dip. *Program availability:* Part-time, evening/weekend. *Degree requirements:* For master's, practicum; for doctorate, 2 foreign languages, thesis/dissertation. *Entrance requirements:* Additional exam requirements/recommendations for international students: Required—TOEFL.

Western Seminary, Graduate Programs, Program in Ministry and Leadership, Portland, OR 97215-3367. Offers chaplaincy (MA); coaching (MA); Jewish ministry (MA); pastoral care to women (MA); youth ministry (MA). *Degree requirements:* For master's, practicum. *Entrance requirements:* Additional exam requirements/recommendations for international students: Required—TOEFL.

Western Seminary–Sacramento Campus, Graduate Certificate Programs, Rocklin, CA 95765. Offers Bible (Graduate Certificate); coaching (Graduate Certificate); pastoral care to women (Graduate Certificate); theology (Graduate Certificate); youth and family (Graduate Certificate). *Program availability:* Online learning. *Entrance requirements:* For degree, essays, undergraduate transcripts, 4 recommendations. Additional exam requirements/recommendations for international students: Required—TOEFL.

Western Seminary–Sacramento Campus, Graduate Diploma Programs, Rocklin, CA 95765. Offers Bible and theology (Graduate Diploma); ministry (Graduate Diploma); pastoral care to women (Graduate Diploma). *Entrance requirements:* For degree, essays, undergraduate transcripts, 4 recommendations. Additional exam requirements/recommendations for international students: Required—TOEFL.

Western Seminary–Sacramento Campus, Program in Ministry and Leadership, Rocklin, CA 95765. Offers MA. *Entrance requirements:* For master's, essays, undergraduate transcripts, 4 recommendations. Additional exam requirements/recommendations for international students: Required—TOEFL.

Western Seminary–San Jose Campus, Graduate Programs, Milpitas, CA 95035. Offers Bible and theology (Graduate Diploma); Bible, camp and conference ministry (CGS); Biblical and theological studies (MA), including exegetical track, theological track; coaching (CGS); expositional ministry (M Div); marital and family therapy (MA); ministry (Graduate Diploma); ministry and leadership (MA), including camp and conference ministry, coaching, pastoral care to women, youth ministry; pastoral care to women (CGS, Graduate Diploma); pastoral ministry (M Div); theology (CGS); youth and family (CGS). *Program availability:* Part-time, evening/weekend, online learning. *Entrance requirements:* For master's, minimum GPA of 3.0. Electronic applications accepted.

Western Theological Seminary, Graduate and Professional Programs, Holland, MI 49423-3622. Offers divinity (M Div); ministry (D Min); theology (M Th, MA); urban pastoral ministry (Graduate Certificate); M Div/MSW. *Accreditation:* ACIPE; ATS. *Program availability:* Part-time, 100% online, blended/hybrid learning. *Degree requirements:* For doctorate, thesis/dissertation. *Entrance requirements:* Additional exam requirements/recommendations for international students: Required—TOEFL. Electronic applications accepted.

Westminster Theological Seminary, Graduate and Professional Programs, Philadelphia, PA 19118. Offers apologetics (Th M); Biblical and urban studies (Certificate); Biblical counseling (MA); biblical studies (MAR); Christian studies (Certificate); church history (Th M); counseling (M Div); general studies (M Div, MAR); hermeneutics and Bible interpretations (PhD); historical and theological studies (PhD); historical theology (Th M); New Testament (Th M); Old Testament (Th M); pastoral counseling (D Min); pastoral ministry (M Div, D Min); systematic theology (Th M); theological studies (MAR); urban missions (M Div, MA, MAR, D Min). *Accreditation:* ATS. *Program availability:* Part-time. Terminal master's awarded for partial completion of doctoral program. *Degree requirements:* For master's, thesis (for some programs); for doctorate, 4 foreign languages, comprehensive exam (for some programs), thesis/dissertation. *Entrance requirements:* For doctorate, GRE General Test. Additional exam requirements/recommendations for international students: Required—TOEFL, TWE.

Whitworth University, Graduate Studies in Theology, Spokane, WA 99251-0001. Offers Christian ministry (MA); mission and culture (MA); theology (MA). *Program availability:* Part-time, evening/weekend. *Faculty:* 19. *Students:* 47 part-time (21 women); includes 6 minority (2 Black or African American, non-Hispanic/Latino; 1 American Indian or Alaska Native, non-Hispanic/Latino; 3 Hispanic/Latino). Average age 35. *Application deadline:* For fall admission, 8/7 for domestic students; for spring admission, 1/1 for domestic students; for summer admission, 4/15 for domestic students. Applications are processed on a rolling basis. Electronic applications accepted. *Financial support:* In 2017–18, 17 students received support. Research assistantships, career-related internships or fieldwork, scholarships/grants, and unspecified assistantships available. Financial award application deadline: 8/7; financial award applicants required to submit FAFSA. *Unit head:* Dr. Jeremy Wynne, Director, 509-777-3222, E-mail: graduateandcsadmissions@whitworth.edu. *Application contact:* Hannah Fischer, Graduate Admissions, 509-777-3222, E-mail: graduateandcsadmissions@whitworth.edu.
Website: http://www.whitworth.edu/cms/academics/graduate-studies-in-theology/

Wilfrid Laurier University, Waterloo Lutheran Seminary, Waterloo, ON N2L 3C5, Canada. Offers divinity (M Div); multifaith spiritual care and counseling (Diploma); pastoral leadership (D Min); spiritual care and counseling (D Min); theology (M Th, MTS); M Div/MTS/MSW. *Accreditation:* ATS. *Program availability:* Part-time. *Degree requirements:* For master's, one foreign language, thesis (for some programs); for doctorate, thesis/dissertation. *Entrance requirements:* For master's, two letters of reference; for doctorate, M Div, two letters of reference. Additional exam requirements/recommendations for international students: Required—TOEFL (minimum score 573 paper-based; 89 iBT), IELTS (minimum score 7). Electronic applications accepted. *Expenses:* Contact institution. *Faculty research:* Biblical study, church history, systematic theology.

World Mission University, Graduate Programs, Los Angeles, CA 90020. Offers biblical preaching (M Div); Christian counseling (M Div, MACC); church ministry (M Div); church music (M Div, DCM); ministry (D Min); music (MA); theology (MAT). *Program availability:* Online learning.

Xavier University, College of Arts and Sciences, Department of Theology, Cincinnati, OH 45207. Offers health care mission integration (MA); theology (MA), including religious education, social and pastoral ministry, theology. *Program availability:* Part-time, evening/weekend. *Degree requirements:* For master's, final paper (or thesis) and defense or comprehension exam. *Entrance requirements:* For master's, MAT or GRE, 2 letters of recommendation; statement of reasons and goals for enrolling in program (1,000-2,000 words); resume; transcript. Additional exam requirements/recommendations for international students: Required—TOEFL (minimum score 550 paper-based; 79 iBT). Electronic applications accepted. Application fee is waived when completed online. *Expenses:* Contact institution. *Faculty research:* Scripture, ethics, constructive theology, historical theology.

Xavier University of Louisiana, Graduate School, Institute for Black Catholic Studies, New Orleans, LA 70125. Offers pastoral theology (Th M). *Program availability:* Part-time. *Degree requirements:* For master's, comprehensive exam, practicum. *Entrance requirements:* For master's, GRE General Test, MAT, minimum GPA of 2.5. Additional exam requirements/recommendations for international students: Required—TOEFL.

Religion

Abilene Christian University, Graduate Programs, College of Biblical Studies, Graduate School of Theology, Program in Ancient and Oriental Christianity, Abilene, TX 79699. Offers MA. *Program availability:* Part-time. *Students:* 2 part-time (0 women). 1 applicant, 100% accepted, 1 enrolled. In 2017, 2 master's awarded. *Degree requirements:* For master's, comprehensive exam, thesis. *Entrance requirements:* Additional exam requirements/recommendations for international students: Required—TOEFL (minimum score 80 iBT), IELTS (minimum score 6). *Application deadline:* For fall admission, 8/11 for domestic students; for spring admission, 11/1 for domestic students. Application fee: $50. *Expenses:* $618 per hour. *Financial support:* Application deadline: 4/1; applicants required to submit FAFSA. *Unit head:* Dr. Jeff Childers, Graduate Advisor, 325-674-3797, Fax: 325-674-6180, E-mail: jeff.childers@acu.edu. *Application contact:* Graduate Admissions, 325-674-6911, Fax: 325-674-6717, E-mail: gradinfo@acu.edu.
Website: http://www.acu.edu/graduate/academics/ancient-and-oriental-christianity.html

Abilene Christian University, Graduate Programs, College of Biblical Studies, Graduate School of Theology, Program in Modern and American Christianity, Abilene, TX 79699. Offers MA. *Program availability:* Part-time. *Students:* 2 part-time (0 women). In 2017, 1 master's awarded. *Degree requirements:* For master's, comprehensive exam, thesis. *Entrance requirements:* Additional exam requirements/recommendations for international students: Required—TOEFL (minimum score 80 iBT), IELTS (minimum score 6), PTE. *Application deadline:* For fall admission, 8/11 for domestic students; for spring admission, 11/1 for domestic students. Applications are processed on a rolling basis. Application fee: $50. Electronic applications accepted. *Expenses:* $637 per hour. *Financial support:* Scholarships/grants available. Financial award application deadline: 4/1; financial award applicants required to submit FAFSA. *Unit head:* Dr. Douglas Foster, Graduate Advisor, 325-674-3795, Fax: 325-674-6180, E-mail: doug.foster@acu.edu. *Application contact:* Graduate Admissions, 325-674-6911, Fax: 325-674-6717, E-mail: gradinfo@acu.edu.
Website: http://www.acu.edu/graduate/academics/modern-and-american-christianity.html

Ambrose University, Ambrose Seminary, Calgary, AB T3H 0L5, Canada. Offers Biblical/theological studies (MA), including New Testament, Old Testament, theology; Christian studies (MCS, Diploma); intercultural ministries (M Div, MA); leadership (Certificate); leadership and ministry (MA), including chaplaincy, leadership; pastoral ministry (M Div). *Accreditation:* ATS (one or more programs are accredited). *Program availability:* Part-time, blended/hybrid learning. *Degree requirements:* For master's, variable foreign language requirement, thesis (for some programs), internship (for M Div, MA in leadership and ministry, MA in intercultural ministries); thesis (for MA in Biblical/theological studies). *Entrance requirements:* For master's, undergraduate degree from other accredited university or bible college, minimum GPA of 2.0. Additional exam requirements/recommendations for international students: Required—PTE (minimum score 58), TOEFL (minimum score 560 paper-based, 83 iBT) or IELTS (minimum score 6.5). Electronic applications accepted. *Faculty research:* Evangelicalism and sociology, missiological trends, chaplaincy, intertestamental studies, postmodernism.

The American University of Rome, Graduate School, Rome, Italy. Offers religious studies (MA); sustainable cultural heritage (MA). *Degree requirements:* For master's, thesis, internship. *Entrance requirements:* For master's, bachelor's degree in the liberal arts, humanities or social sciences; minimum GPA of 2.75. Additional exam requirements/recommendations for international students: Required—TOEFL (minimum score 550 paper-based; 80 iBT), IELTS (minimum score 6.5). Electronic applications accepted. *Faculty research:* Sustainable cultural heritage, archaeology in Europe and Italy.

Amridge University, Graduate and Professional Programs, Montgomery, AL 36117. Offers Biblical studies (MA, PhD); Christian ministry (MS); family therapy (D Min); human services (MS); leadership and management (MS); marriage and family therapy (M Div, MA, PhD); ministerial leadership (M Div, MS); New Testament studies (MA); Old Testament studies (MA); professional counseling (M Div, MA, PhD); theology (M Div, D Min). *Program availability:* Part-time, evening/weekend, online learning. *Faculty:* 23 full-time (3 women), 9 part-time/adjunct (5 women). *Students:* 105 full-time (55 women), 250 part-time (152 women); includes 217 minority (167 Black or African American, non-Hispanic/Latino; 4 Asian, non-Hispanic/Latino; 42 Hispanic/Latino; 4 Native Hawaiian or other Pacific Islander, non-Hispanic/Latino). Average age 42. 160 applicants, 100% accepted, 110 enrolled. *Degree requirements:* For master's, one foreign language,

comprehensive exam (for some programs), thesis (for some programs); for doctorate, one foreign language, comprehensive exam (for some programs), thesis/dissertation (for some programs). *Entrance requirements:* For master's, official transcript showing an earned 4-year BA or BS from regionally- or nationally-accredited institution; for doctorate, official transcript showing earned graduate degree from regionally- or nationally-accredited institution; writing sample (e.g. career monograph, published journal article, term paper from master's degree or doctoral dissertation); interview. Additional exam requirements/recommendations for international students: Required—TOEFL (minimum score 79 iBT). *Application deadline:* Applications are processed on a rolling basis. Application fee: $50. Electronic applications accepted. *Financial support:* In 2017–18, 33 students received support. Federal Work-Study and scholarships/grants available. Support available to part-time students. Financial award applicants required to submit FAFSA. *Faculty research:* Technology and mental healthcare, resilience in black families, theology and congregational ministry. *Unit head:* Laina Costanza, Vice President, Student Affairs, 888-790-8080 Ext. 1, Fax: 334-387-3878, E-mail: cc@amridgeuniversity.edu. *Application contact:* Brooks Housley, Student Affairs Coordinator, 888-790-8080 Ext. 1, Fax: 334-387-3878, E-mail: admissions@amridgeuniversity.edu.

Arizona State University at the Tempe campus, College of Liberal Arts and Sciences, School of Historical, Philosophical and Religious Studies, Tempe, AZ 85287-4301. Offers European history (MA, PhD); medieval studies (Graduate Certificate); North American history (MA, PhD); philosophy (MA, PhD); public history (MA); religious studies (MA, PhD); Renaissance studies (Graduate Certificate); scholarly publishing (Graduate Certificate). *Program availability:* Part-time. Terminal master's awarded for partial completion of doctoral program. *Degree requirements:* For master's, thesis or alternative, interactive Program of Study (iPOS) submitted before completing 50 percent of required credit hours; for doctorate, variable foreign language requirement, comprehensive exam, thesis/dissertation, interactive Program of Study (iPOS) submitted before completing 50 percent of required credit hours. *Entrance requirements:* For master's and doctorate, GRE, minimum GPA of 3.0 or equivalent in last 2 years of work leading to bachelor's degree. Additional exam requirements/recommendations for international students: Required—TOEFL, IELTS, or PTE. Electronic applications accepted.

Athens State University, Graduate Programs, Athens, AL 35611. Offers career and technical education (M Ed); global logistics and supply chain management (MS); religious studies (MA). *Students:* 28 full-time (19 women), 119 part-time (55 women). *Expenses:* Tuition, state resident: full-time $3900; part-time $325 per credit hour. Tuition, nonresident: full-time $3900; part-time $325 per credit hour.
Website: http://www.athens.edu/masters/

The Baptist College of Florida, Graduate Programs, Graceville, FL 32440. Offers Christian ministry (MA); Christian studies (MA), including Biblical studies; music and worship leadership (MA). *Program availability:* Part-time, 100% online, blended/hybrid learning. *Faculty:* 12 full-time (0 women). *Students:* 33 full-time (6 women); includes 2 minority (1 Black or African American, non-Hispanic/Latino; 1 Hispanic/Latino). Average age 28. 10 applicants, 100% accepted, 10 enrolled. In 2017, 3 master's awarded. *Degree requirements:* For master's, variable foreign language requirement, comprehensive exam (for some programs), thesis (for some programs). *Entrance requirements:* For master's, regionally-accredited undergraduate degree, undergraduate courses in field, minimum GPA of 2.5. Additional exam requirements/recommendations for international students: Required—TOEFL. *Application deadline:* For fall admission, 8/15 for domestic students; for spring admission, 1/15 for domestic students. Applications are processed on a rolling basis. Application fee: $25. Electronic applications accepted. *Expenses:* Contact institution. *Financial support:* In 2017–18, 2 students received support. *Faculty research:* Biblical studies, ministry studies. *Unit head:* Dr. Ed Scott, Chair of the Graduate Division, 850-263-3261 Ext. 488, E-mail: eescott@baptistcollege.edu. *Application contact:* Sandra Richards, Director of Student Life and Marketing, 850-263-3261 Ext. 415.
Website: http://www.baptistcollege.edu

Baptist Theological Seminary at Richmond, Graduate and Professional Programs, Richmond, VA 23228. Offers Biblical interpretation (M Div); Christian education formation (M Div); Christian ministry (MCM); justice and peacebuilding (M Div); ministry (D Min); religious freedom (M Div); theological studies (MTS, Graduate Certificate); theology (M Div); youth and student ministries (M Div); M Div/MBA; M Div/MS; M Div/MSW. *Accreditation:* ATS. *Program availability:* Part-time, 100% online, blended/hybrid learning. *Faculty:* 2 full-time (1 woman), 8 part-time/adjunct (2 women). *Students:* 38 full-time (14 women), 31 part-time (22 women); includes 15 minority (11 Black or African American, non-Hispanic/Latino; 4 Asian, non-Hispanic/Latino). Average age 46. In 2017, 15 master's, 2 doctorates awarded. *Degree requirements:* For master's and Graduate Certificate, thesis optional; for doctorate, comprehensive exam, thesis/dissertation, field study, independent study. *Entrance requirements:* For master's, BA/BS, minimum GPA of 2.2, 2 references, resume, official transcripts, writing sample; for doctorate, MAT (minimum score of 400), M Div with minimum GPA of 2.75, 3 years of full-time ministry experience, 3 references, resume, official transcripts, writing sample, personal statement. Additional exam requirements/recommendations for international students: Required—TOEFL (minimum score 550 paper-based), IELTS (minimum score 5.5). *Application deadline:* For fall admission, 7/1 for domestic students, 5/1 for international students; for winter admission, 12/15 for domestic students, 9/1 for international students; for spring admission, 1/15 for domestic students, 10/1 for international students. Applications are processed on a rolling basis. Application fee: $35. Electronic applications accepted. *Financial support:* In 2017–18, 46 students received support, including 9 teaching assistantships (averaging $3,300 per year); scholarships/grants also available. Financial award application deadline: 2/1. *Faculty research:* Biblical studies, pastoral care, church history, theology, ministry. *Unit head:* Dr. Linda M. Bridges, President, 804-204-1201, Fax: 804-355-8182, E-mail: lmbridges@btsr.edu. *Application contact:* Melissa Fallen, Director of Admissions and Recruitment, 804-204-1208, E-mail: admissions@btsr.edu.
Website: http://www.btsr.edu/programs/degree-programs/

Baylor University, Graduate School, College of Arts and Sciences, Department of Religion, Waco, TX 76798. Offers MA, PhD. *Faculty:* 18 full-time (4 women). *Students:* 55 full-time (16 women); includes 11 minority (2 Black or African American, non-Hispanic/Latino; 6 Asian, non-Hispanic/Latino; 2 Hispanic/Latino; 1 Two or more races, non-Hispanic/Latino). 53 applicants, 19% accepted, 10 enrolled. In 2017, 2 master's, 8 doctorates awarded. Terminal master's awarded for partial completion of doctoral program. *Degree requirements:* For master's, one foreign language, thesis; for doctorate, 2 foreign languages, thesis/dissertation. *Entrance requirements:* For master's and doctorate, GRE General Test. Additional exam requirements/recommendations for international students: Required—TOEFL. *Application deadline:* For fall admission, 12/1 for domestic and international students. Application fee: $50. Electronic applications accepted. *Financial support:* In 2017–18, 40 students received support. Fellowships with full tuition reimbursements available, research assistantships with full tuition reimbursements available, teaching assistantships with full tuition reimbursements available, Federal Work-Study, institutionally sponsored loans, scholarships/grants, and unspecified assistantships available. *Unit head:* Dr. James D. Nogalski, Graduate Program Director, 254-710-1592, Fax: 254-710-3740, E-mail: james_nogalski@baylor.edu. *Application contact:* Coco DiMauro, Academic and Student Support Associate, 254-710-3742, Fax: 254-710-3740, E-mail: coco_dimauro@baylor.edu.
Website: http://www.baylor.edu/religion/

Bethany Theological Seminary, Graduate and Professional Programs, Richmond, IN 47374-4019. Offers biblical studies (MA Th); ministry studies (M Div); peace studies (M Div, MA Th); theological studies (MA Th, CATS); youth ministry (M Div). *Accreditation:* ACIPE; ATS. *Program availability:* Part-time, online learning. *Degree requirements:* For master's, thesis (for some programs). *Entrance requirements:* For master's, letters of reference. Additional exam requirements/recommendations for international students: Required—TOEFL (minimum score 550 paper-based).

Bethel Seminary, Graduate and Professional Programs, St. Paul, MN 55112-6998. Offers Anglican studies (Certificate); children's and family ministry (MA); Christian studies (Certificate); Christian thought (MA); church planting (Certificate); Greek and Hebrew language (M Div); Greek language (M Div); Hebrew language (M Div); marriage and family therapy (MA, Certificate); mental health counseling (MA); ministry (MA, D Min); ministry practice (Certificate); theological studies (MA, Certificate); transformational leadership (MA); young life youth ministry (Certificate). *Accreditation:* ACIPE. *Program availability:* Part-time, evening/weekend, 100% online, blended/hybrid learning. *Faculty:* 16 full-time (4 women), 31 part-time/adjunct (15 women). *Students:* 380 full-time (170 women), 167 part-time (55 women); includes 161 minority (65 Black or African American, non-Hispanic/Latino; 52 Asian, non-Hispanic/Latino; 31 Hispanic/Latino; 1 Native Hawaiian or other Pacific Islander, non-Hispanic/Latino; 12 Two or more races, non-Hispanic/Latino), 5 international. Average age 38. 356 applicants, 62% accepted, 156 enrolled. In 2017, 120 master's, 15 doctorates, 4 other advanced degrees awarded. *Degree requirements:* For master's, variable foreign language requirement, thesis (for some programs); for doctorate, thesis/dissertation. *Entrance requirements:* For master's, letters of reference, transcripts, personal statement; for doctorate, M Div, letters of reference, organizational support; for Certificate, letters of reference, family essay, personal statement, and family of origin paper (for marriage and family therapy). Additional exam requirements/recommendations for international students: Required—TOEFL (minimum score 550 paper-based; 87 iBT). *Application deadline:* For fall admission, 8/1 priority date for domestic students, 8/1 for international students; for winter admission, 12/1 priority date for domestic students; for spring admission, 1/1 priority date for domestic students. Applications are processed on a rolling basis. Application fee: $0. Electronic applications accepted. *Expenses:* Contact institution. *Financial support:* Teaching assistantships, career-related internships or fieldwork, Federal Work-Study, and scholarships/grants available. Financial award applicants required to submit FAFSA. *Faculty research:* Nature of theology, ethics, Biblical commentaries, nature of God, science and theology. *Unit head:* Dr. Randy Bergen, Associate Provost, 651-635-8000, E-mail: r-bergen@bethel.edu. *Application contact:* Director of Admissions, 651-638-8000, Fax: 651-638-6002, E-mail: seminary-admissions@bethel.edu.
Website: https://www.bethel.edu/seminary

Bethesda University, Graduate and Professional Programs, Anaheim, CA 92801. Offers biblical studies (MA); music (MA); theology (M Div). *Entrance requirements:* For master's, interview. Additional exam requirements/recommendations for international students: Recommended—TOEFL.

Beulah Heights University, Graduate School, Atlanta, GA 30316. Offers biblical studies (MA); leadership studies (MA). *Entrance requirements:* Additional exam requirements/recommendations for international students: Required—TOEFL (minimum score 500 paper-based). Electronic applications accepted.

Biola University, School of Arts and Sciences, La Mirada, CA 90639-0001. Offers Christian apologetics (MA, Certificate); science and religion (MA); speech language pathology (MA). *Program availability:* Part-time, evening/weekend, online learning. *Faculty:* 20. *Students:* 24 full-time (7 women), 251 part-time (49 women); includes 80 minority (21 Black or African American, non-Hispanic/Latino; 1 American Indian or Alaska Native, non-Hispanic/Latino; 31 Asian, non-Hispanic/Latino; 19 Hispanic/Latino; 8 Two or more races, non-Hispanic/Latino), 15 international. 168 applicants, 70% accepted, 77 enrolled. In 2017, 64 master's awarded. *Entrance requirements:* For master's, minimum GPA of 3.0, bachelor's degree from accredited college or university (in science-related field for science and religion program). Additional exam requirements/recommendations for international students: Required—TOEFL (minimum score 600 paper-based; 100 iBT). *Application deadline:* For fall admission, 7/1 for domestic students, 6/1 for international students; for spring admission, 12/1 for domestic students. Applications are processed on a rolling basis. Application fee: $65. Electronic applications accepted. *Financial support:* Scholarships/grants and unspecified assistantships available. Support available to part-time students. Financial award applicants required to submit FAFSA. *Faculty research:* Apologetics, science and religion, intelligent design. *Application contact:* Graduate Admissions Office, 562-903-4752, E-mail: graduate.admissions@biola.edu.
Website: http://www.biola.edu/academics/sas/

Biola University, Talbot School of Theology, La Mirada, CA 90639-0001. Offers adult/family ministry (MACE); Bible exposition (MA, Th M); Biblical and theological studies (Certificate); children's ministry (MACE); Christian education (M Div); cross-cultural education ministry (MACE); educational studies (Ed D, PhD); evangelism and discipleship (M Div); general Christian education (MACE); Messianic Jewish studies (M Div, Certificate); missions and intercultural studies (M Div); New Testament (MA, Th M); Old Testament (MA); Old Testament and Semitics (Th M); pastoral and general ministry (M Div); pastoral care and counseling (M Div, MACML); philosophy (MA); preaching and pastoral ministry (MACML); spiritual formation (M Div, Certificate); spiritual formation and soul care (MA); sports ministry (MACML); theology (MA, Th M, D Min, Certificate); youth ministry (MACE). *Program availability:* Part-time, evening/weekend. *Students:* 475 full-time (113 women), 603 part-time (176 women); includes 541 minority (39 Black or African American, non-Hispanic/Latino; 2 American Indian or Alaska Native, non-Hispanic/Latino; 378 Asian, non-Hispanic/Latino; 84 Hispanic/Latino; 1 Native Hawaiian or other Pacific Islander, non-Hispanic/Latino; 37 Two or more races, non-Hispanic/Latino), 105 international. 437 applicants, 78% accepted, 241 enrolled. In 2017, 177 master's, 24 doctorates awarded. *Entrance requirements:* For master's, bachelor's degree from accredited college or university; minimum GPA of 2.6 (for M Div), 3.0 (for MA); for doctorate, M Div or MA. Additional exam requirements/recommendations for international students: Required—TOEFL (minimum score 600 paper-based; 88 iBT). *Application deadline:* For fall admission, 7/1 for domestic students, 6/1 for international students; for spring admission, 12/1 priority date for domestic students. Applications are processed on a rolling basis. Application fee: $65. Electronic applications accepted. *Financial support:* Scholarships/grants and unspecified assistantships available. Support available to part-time students. Financial award applicants required to submit FAFSA. *Faculty research:* New Testament, Old Testament, spiritual formation, Christian education, theological studies, Christian ministry, preaching and pastoral ministry, language and literature, bible exposition, Christian leadership. *Unit head:* Dr. Clint Arnold, Dean, 562-903-4816, Fax: 562-903-4748. *Application contact:* Graduate Admissions Office, 562-903-4752, E-mail: graduate.admissions@biola.edu.
Website: http://www.talbot.edu/

Bob Jones University, Graduate Programs, Greenville, SC 29614. Offers accountancy (MS); Bible (MA); Bible translation (MA); Biblical studies (Certificate); broadcast management (MS); business administration (MBA); church history (MA, PhD); church ministries (MA); church music (MM); cinema and video production (MA); counseling (MS); curriculum and instruction (Ed D); divinity (M Div); dramatic production (MA); educational leadership (MS, Ed D, Ed S); elementary education (M Ed, MAT); English (M Ed, MA, MAT); fine arts (MA); graphic design (MA); history (M Ed, MA); illustration (MA); interpretative speech (MA); mathematics (M Ed, MAT); medical missions (Certificate); ministry (MM, D Min); multi-categorical special education (M Ed, MAT); music (M Ed); New Testament interpretation (PhD); Old Testament interpretation (PhD); orchestral instrument performance (MM); organ performance (MM); pastoral studies (MA); personnel services (MS, Ed S); piano pedagogy (MM); piano performance (MM); platform arts (MA); radio and television broadcasting (MS); rhetoric and public address (MA); secondary education (M Ed); studio art (MA); teaching Bible (MA); theology (MA, PhD); voice performance (MM); youth ministries (MA); M Div/MM.

Boston University, Graduate School of Arts and Sciences, Graduate Program in Religion, Boston, MA 02215. Offers MA, PhD. *Students:* 43 full-time (20 women), 4 part-time (2 women); includes 8 minority (2 Black or African American, non-Hispanic/Latino; 2 Asian, non-Hispanic/Latino; 3 Hispanic/Latino; 1 Two or more races, non-Hispanic/Latino), 4 international. Average age 28. In 2017, 2 master's, 6 doctorates awarded. Terminal master's awarded for partial completion of doctoral program. *Degree requirements:* For master's, one foreign language, comprehensive exam, thesis; for doctorate, 2 foreign languages, comprehensive exam, thesis/dissertation. *Entrance requirements:* For doctorate, GRE General Test, 3 letters of recommendation, transcripts, personal statement, academic writing sample. Additional exam requirements/recommendations for international students: Required—TOEFL (minimum score 550 paper-based; 84 iBT). *Application deadline:* For fall admission, 1/15 for domestic and international students. Application fee: $95. Electronic applications accepted. *Financial support:* In 2017–18, 46 students received support, including 15 fellowships with full tuition reimbursements available (averaging $22,000 per year), 1 research assistantship with full tuition reimbursement available (averaging $22,000 per year), 14 teaching assistantships with full tuition reimbursements available (averaging $22,000 per year); career-related internships or fieldwork, Federal Work-Study, scholarships/grants, health care benefits, and unspecified assistantships also available. Financial award application deadline: 1/15. *Unit head:* Adam Seligman, Director, 617-358-0262, Fax: 617-358-3087, E-mail: seligman@bu.edu. *Application contact:* Karen Nardella, Department Administrator, 617-353-2636, Fax: 617-358-3087, E-mail: kcn@bu.edu.
Website: http://www.bu.edu/gpr/

Boston University, School of Theology, Boston, MA 02215. Offers chaplaincy (M Div); choral conducting (MSM); church and the arts (M Div); community and global engagement (M Div); constructive theology and ethics (PhD), including constructive theology, theological ethics; history and hermeneutics (PhD), including biblical studies, church history and world Christianity, liturgical studies, mission studies; organ (MSM); pastoral ministry (M Div); practical theology (PhD), including church and society, congregation and community, evangelism and missiology, homiletics, leadership and administration, pastoral theology and psychology, religious education, spirituality studies, worship; religion and the academy (M Div); transformational leadership (D Min); M Div/MSM; M Div/MSW; MTS/MSW. PhD in mission studies offered in collaboration with Gordon-Conwell Theological Seminary. *Accreditation:* ACIPE; ATS. *Program availability:* Part-time, blended/hybrid learning. *Faculty:* 39 full-time (17 women), 11 part-time/adjunct (5 women). *Students:* 256 full-time (135 women), 87 part-time (40 women); includes 82 minority (38 Black or African American, non-Hispanic/Latino; 10 Asian, non-Hispanic/Latino; 23 Hispanic/Latino; 1 Native Hawaiian or other Pacific Islander, non-Hispanic/Latino; 10 Two or more races, non-Hispanic/Latino), 66 international. Average age 34. 334 applicants, 69% accepted, 106 enrolled. In 2017, 62 master's, 9 doctorates awarded. *Degree requirements:* For master's, comprehensive exam (for some programs), thesis optional, contextual education; for doctorate, 2 languages, dissertation, and comprehensive exam (for PhD). *Entrance requirements:* For master's, minimum GPA of 3.0; for doctorate, GRE General Test, minimum GPA of 3.3. Additional exam requirements/recommendations for international students: Required—TOEFL (minimum score 570 paper-based; 89 iBT). *Application deadline:* For fall admission, 1/15 priority date for domestic and international students; for spring admission, 10/15 priority date for domestic and international students. Applications are processed on a rolling basis. Application fee: $95. Electronic applications accepted. *Expenses:* $20,100 tuition. *Financial support:* In 2017–18, 236 students received support, including 102 fellowships with full tuition reimbursements available (averaging $7,500 per year), 11 research assistantships with full tuition reimbursements available (averaging $22,000 per year), 12 teaching assistantships with full tuition reimbursements available (averaging $22,000 per year); career-related internships or fieldwork, Federal Work-Study, scholarships/grants, and health care benefits also available. Support available to part-time students. Financial award application deadline: 7/15. *Faculty research:* Practical theology, ethics, environmental theology, religion and conflict transformation, chaplaincy. *Total annual research expenditures:* $2.5 million. *Unit head:* Rev. Dr. Mary Elizabeth Moore, Dean, 617-353-3050, Fax: 617-353-3061, E-mail: memoore@bu.edu. *Application contact:* Rev. Dr. Anastasia Kidd, Director of Enrollment, 617-353-3036, Fax: 617-358-0140, E-mail: sthadmis@bu.edu.
Website: http://www.bu.edu/sth

Briercrest Seminary, Graduate Programs, Program in Christian Ministries, Caronport, SK S0H 0S0, Canada. Offers leadership (MA); marriage and family counseling (MA); missions (MA); pastoral counseling (MA); worship (MA); youth and family ministry (MA). *Program availability:* Part-time. *Degree requirements:* For master's, comprehensive exam, thesis optional. *Entrance requirements:* Additional exam requirements/recommendations for international students: Required—TOEFL (minimum score 550 paper-based).

Briercrest Seminary, Graduate Programs, Program in Theology, Caronport, SK S0H 0S0, Canada. Offers Biblical studies (M Div); leadership and management (M Div); New Testament (MATS); Old Testament (MATS); pastoral counseling (M Div); pastoral ministry (M Div); theological studies (M Div); theology (MATS); worship (M Div); youth and family ministry (M Div). *Accreditation:* ATS. *Program availability:* Part-time. *Degree requirements:* For master's, comprehensive exam, thesis optional. *Entrance requirements:* Additional exam requirements/recommendations for international students: Required—TOEFL (minimum score 550 paper-based).

Brown University, Graduate School, Department of Religious Studies, Providence, RI 02912. Offers Asian religious traditions (PhD); Islam, society and culture (PhD); religion and critical thought (PhD); religions of the ancient Mediterranean (PhD). *Faculty:* 14 full-time (3 women), 2 part-time/adjunct (1 woman). *Students:* 27 full-time (11 women). 82 applicants, 13% accepted. In 2017, 4 doctorates awarded. *Degree requirements:* For doctorate, variable foreign language requirement, thesis/dissertation. *Entrance requirements:* For doctorate, GRE General Test. Additional exam requirements/recommendations for international students: Required—TOEFL. *Application deadline:* For fall admission, 1/5 priority date for domestic and international students. Application fee: $75. Electronic applications accepted. *Financial support:* In 2017–18, 27 students received support, including 13 fellowships, 11 teaching assistantships; institutionally sponsored loans, health care benefits, tuition waivers (full and partial), and proctorships also available. Financial award application deadline: 1/5. *Faculty research:* Asian religious traditions; Islam, society, and culture; religions of the ancient Mediterranean; and religion and critical thought. *Unit head:* Mark S. Cladis, Chair, 401-863-3104. *Application contact:* Nicole L. Vadnais, Academic Department and Graduate Program Manager, 401-863-3104, E-mail: religious_studies@brown.edu.
Website: http://www.brown.edu/academics/religious-studies

Bryn Athyn College of the New Church, Academy of the New Church Theological School, Bryn Athyn, PA 19009-0717. Offers divinity (M Div); religious studies (MA). *Program availability:* Part-time, online learning. *Degree requirements:* For master's, variable foreign language requirement, thesis. *Entrance requirements:* Additional exam requirements/recommendations for international students: Required—TOEFL.

Cairn University, School of Divinity, Langhorne, PA 19047-2990. Offers divinity (M Div); religion (MA); theology (Th M). *Program availability:* Part-time, evening/weekend, 100% online, blended/hybrid learning. *Entrance requirements:* Additional exam requirements/recommendations for international students: Required—TOEFL (minimum score 550 paper-based). Electronic applications accepted. Application fee is waived when completed online. *Expenses:* Contact institution.

California Institute of Integral Studies, School of Consciousness and Transformation, San Francisco, CA 94103. Offers anthropology and social change (MA, PhD); Asian philosophies and cultures (MA); creative inquiry/interdisciplinary arts (MFA); East-West psychology (MA, PhD); integral and transpersonal psychology (PhD); philosophy and religion (PhD), including ecology, spirituality, and religion, philosophy, cosmology, and consciousness, women's spirituality; philosophy, cosmology, and consciousness (Certificate); transformative leadership (MA); transformative studies (PhD); women, gender, spirituality and social justice (MA); writing and consciousness (MFA). *Program availability:* Part-time, evening/weekend, 100% online, blended/hybrid learning. *Students:* 392 full-time (265 women), 141 part-time (98 women); includes 145 minority (40 Black or African American, non-Hispanic/Latino; 1 American Indian or Alaska Native, non-Hispanic/Latino; 19 Asian, non-Hispanic/Latino; 54 Hispanic/Latino; 31 Two or more races, non-Hispanic/Latino), 61 international. Average age 43. 212 applicants, 96% accepted, 153 enrolled. In 2017, 49 master's, 36 doctorates awarded. Terminal master's awarded for partial completion of doctoral program. *Degree requirements:* For master's, thesis optional; for doctorate, comprehensive exam, thesis/dissertation, 1 foreign language (for Asian philosophies and cultures). *Entrance requirements:* For master's, minimum GPA of 3.0, letters of recommendation, writing sample; for doctorate, master's degree, minimum GPA of 3.0, letters of recommendation, writing sample. Additional exam requirements/recommendations for international students: Required—TOEFL. *Application deadline:* For fall admission, 2/1 priority date for domestic and international students; for spring admission, 10/15 priority date for domestic and international students. Applications are processed on a rolling basis. Application fee: $65. Electronic applications accepted. *Expenses:* $21,400 tuition and fees (for MA); $28,390 (for MFA); $24,658 (for PhD). *Financial support:* Fellowships, research assistantships, teaching assistantships, career-related internships or fieldwork, Federal Work-Study, and scholarships/grants available. Support available to part-time students. Financial award application deadline: 4/15; financial award applicants required to submit FAFSA. *Faculty research:* Ecology and sustainability, philosophy and religion, East-West psychology, integrative health, social and cultural anthropology, transformative leadership. *Unit head:* Kathy Littles, Academic Dean, 415-575-6100, E-mail: klittles@ciis.edu. *Application contact:* Ellen Durst, Director of Admissions, 415-575-6100, Fax: 415-575-1268, E-mail: admissions@ciis.edu.
Website: http://www.ciis.edu/

California State University, Long Beach, Graduate Studies, College of Liberal Arts, Department of Religious Studies, Long Beach, CA 90840. Offers MA. *Program availability:* Part-time, evening/weekend. *Entrance requirements:* Additional exam requirements/recommendations for international students: Required—TOEFL. Electronic applications accepted.

Calvin Theological Seminary, Graduate and Professional Programs, Grand Rapids, MI 49546-4387. Offers Bible and theology (MA); divinity (M Div), including ancient near eastern languages and literature, contextual ministry, evangelism and teaching, history of Christianity, new church development, New Testament, Old Testament, pastoral care and leadership, preaching and worship, theological studies, youth and family ministries; educational ministry (MA); historical theology (PhD); missions and evangelism (MA); pastoral care (MA); philosophical and moral theology (PhD); systematic theology (PhD); theological studies (MTS); theology (Th M); worship (MA); youth and family ministries (MA). *Accreditation:* ACIPE; ATS. *Program availability:* Part-time. *Degree requirements:* For master's, variable foreign language requirement, thesis (for some programs); for doctorate, 4 foreign languages, comprehensive exam, thesis/dissertation. *Entrance requirements:* For doctorate, GRE General Test, Hebrew, Greek, and a modern foreign language. Additional exam requirements/recommendations for international students: Required—TOEFL (minimum score 550 paper-based), TWE (minimum score 4). Electronic applications accepted. *Faculty research:* Recent Trinity theory, Christian anthropology, Proverbs, reformed confessions, Paul's view of law.

Canadian Southern Baptist Seminary, Graduate Programs, Cochrane, AB T4C 2G1, Canada. Offers Biblical studies (MBS); Christian ministry (MCMin); Christian studies (MCS); ministry (M Div). *Accreditation:* ATS. *Program availability:* Part-time, 100% online, blended/hybrid learning. *Faculty:* 5 full-time (0 women), 5 part-time/adjunct (1 woman). *Students:* 20 full-time (6 women), 19 part-time (3 women); includes 7 minority (2 Black or African American, non-Hispanic/Latino; 5 Asian, non-Hispanic/Latino), 9 international. Average age 29. 16 applicants, 63% accepted, 10 enrolled. In 2017, 7 master's awarded. *Entrance requirements:* Additional exam requirements/recommendations for international students: Required—TOEFL (minimum score 560 paper-based; 83 iBT); Recommended—IELTS (minimum score 6.5). *Application deadline:* For fall admission, 7/1 priority date for domestic students, 3/1 priority date for international students; for winter admission, 11/15 priority date for domestic students. Applications are processed on a rolling basis. Application fee: $50 ($150 for international students). *Expenses: Tuition:* Full-time $7500 Canadian dollars; part-time $375 Canadian dollars per credit hour. *Required fees:* $450 Canadian dollars; $20 Canadian dollars per credit hour. *Financial support:* Scholarships/grants available. Financial award application deadline: 7/1. *Unit head:* Dr. Steve Booth, Academic Dean, 403-932-6622 Ext. 232, E-mail: steve.booth@csbs.ca. *Application contact:* David Ong, Director of Admissions, 403-932-6622 Ext. 251, E-mail: admissions@csbs.ca.

Cardinal Stritch University, College of Arts and Sciences, Department of Religious Studies, Milwaukee, WI 53217-3985. Offers ministry (MA); religious studies (MA). *Program availability:* Part-time, evening/weekend. *Students:* 14 part-time (7 women); includes 2 minority (1 Black or African American, non-Hispanic/Latino; 1 Native Hawaiian or other Pacific Islander, non-Hispanic/Latino), 1 international. Average age 46. In 2017, 2 master's awarded. *Degree requirements:* For master's, comprehensive exam, thesis, research project. *Entrance requirements:* For master's, interview, minimum GPA of 2.75. Additional exam requirements/recommendations for international students: Required—TOEFL (minimum score 79 iBT), IELTS (minimum score 6.5). *Application deadline:* For fall admission, 7/15 priority date for domestic students; for

spring admission, 12/15 priority date for domestic students. Applications are processed on a rolling basis. Electronic applications accepted. *Expenses:* $782 per credit. *Financial support:* Research assistantships with partial tuition reimbursements, career-related internships or fieldwork, Federal Work-Study, and scholarships/grants available. Financial award applicants required to submit FAFSA. *Unit head:* Dr. Michelle Gilgannon, Chair, 414-410-4047, E-mail: mlgilgannon@stritch.edu. *Application contact:* Graduate Admissions, 800-347-8822 Ext. 4042, E-mail: admissions@stritch.edu.

The Catholic University of America, School of Arts and Sciences, Program in Early Christian Studies, Washington, DC 20064. Offers MA, PhD. *Program availability:* Part-time. *Faculty:* 1 full-time (0 women). *Students:* 1 full-time (0 women), 2 part-time (1 woman). Average age 29. 1 applicant, 100% accepted, 1 enrolled. In 2017, 1 doctorate awarded. *Degree requirements:* For master's, one foreign language, comprehensive exam; for doctorate, 2 foreign languages, comprehensive exam, thesis/dissertation. *Entrance requirements:* For master's and doctorate, GRE General Test, statement of purpose, official copies of academic transcripts, three letters of recommendation, writing sample. Additional exam requirements/recommendations for international students: Required—TOEFL (minimum score 550 paper-based; 80 iBT). *Application deadline:* For fall admission, 7/15 priority date for domestic students, 7/1 for international students; for spring admission, 11/15 priority date for domestic students, 11/1 for international students. Applications are processed on a rolling basis. Application fee: $55. Electronic applications accepted. *Expenses:* Contact institution. *Financial support:* Fellowships, research assistantships, teaching assistantships, Federal Work-Study, scholarships/grants, tuition waivers (full and partial), and unspecified assistantships available. Financial award application deadline: 2/1; financial award applicants required to submit FAFSA. *Faculty research:* Asceticism and Christian culture, languages and literatures of the Christian Near East, early Christian spirituality, Greek and Latin patristics, late ancient philosophy. *Unit head:* Dr. William E. Klingshirn, Director, 202-319-5795, Fax: 202-319-6609, E-mail: klingshirn@cua.edu. *Application contact:* Dr. Steven Brown, Director of Graduate Admissions, 202-319-5057, Fax: 202-319-6533, E-mail: cua-admissions@cua.edu.
Website: http://earlychristianity.cua.edu/

The Catholic University of America, School of Theology and Religious Studies, Washington, DC 20064. Offers M Cat, M Div, MA, D Min, PhD, STD, Certificate, STB, STL, MSLS/MA, STB/M Div. MSLA/MA offered in conjunction with Department of Library and Information Science. *Program availability:* Part-time. *Faculty:* 42 full-time (3 women), 11 part-time/adjunct (1 woman). *Students:* 146 full-time (11 women), 201 part-time (44 women); includes 70 minority (9 Black or African American, non-Hispanic/Latino; 1 American Indian or Alaska Native, non-Hispanic/Latino; 9 Asian, non-Hispanic/Latino; 25 Hispanic/Latino; 26 Two or more races, non-Hispanic/Latino), 53 international. Average age 36. 180 applicants, 67% accepted, 66 enrolled. In 2017, 59 master's, 25 doctorates awarded. Terminal master's awarded for partial completion of doctoral program. *Degree requirements:* For master's, variable foreign language requirement, comprehensive exam (for some programs), thesis (for some programs); for doctorate, variable foreign language requirement, comprehensive exam, thesis/dissertation. *Entrance requirements:* For master's and doctorate, GRE General Test, statement of purpose, official copies of academic transcripts, three letters of recommendation. Additional exam requirements/recommendations for international students: Required—TOEFL (minimum score 550 paper-based; 80 iBT). *Application deadline:* For fall admission, 7/15 priority date for domestic students, 7/1 for international students; for spring admission, 11/15 priority date for domestic students, 11/1 for international students. Applications are processed on a rolling basis. Application fee: $55. Electronic applications accepted. *Expenses:* Contact institution. *Financial support:* Fellowships, research assistantships, teaching assistantships, Federal Work-Study, scholarships/grants, tuition waivers (full and partial), and unspecified assistantships available. Financial award application deadline: 2/1; financial award applicants required to submit FAFSA. *Faculty research:* Historical and systematic theology, religious education and Catechetics, moral theology and ethics, Biblical studies, liturgical studies and sacramental theology, religion and culture. *Total annual research expenditures:* $389,160. *Unit head:* Very Rev. Mark Morozowich, Dean, 202-319-5684, Fax: 202-319-4967, E-mail: morozowich@cua.edu. *Application contact:* Dr. Steven Brown, Director of Graduate Admissions, 202-319-5057, Fax: 202-319-6533, E-mail: cua-admissions@cua.edu.
Website: https://trs.catholic.edu/

Charlotte Christian College and Theological Seminary, Graduate Program, Charlotte, NC 28206. Offers Biblical studies (MA), including New Testament, Old Testament, theology; chaplaincy (M Div); general pastoral studies (M Div); ministry (D Min); pastoral counseling (M Div); urban Christian ministry (MA), including multi-cultural studies, youth ministry. *Program availability:* Part-time, evening/weekend. *Faculty:* 5 full-time (0 women), 6 part-time/adjunct (0 women). *Students:* 17 full-time (8 women), 21 part-time (11 women); includes 31 minority (29 Black or African American, non-Hispanic/Latino; 1 Asian, non-Hispanic/Latino; 1 Two or more races, non-Hispanic/Latino), 2 international. Average age 48. 13 applicants, 100% accepted, 9 enrolled. In 2017, 2 master's awarded. *Degree requirements:* For master's, variable foreign language requirement, thesis; for doctorate, thesis/dissertation. *Entrance requirements:* For master's, 1000-2000 word essay. Additional exam requirements/recommendations for international students: Required—TOEFL, IELTS. *Application deadline:* For fall admission, 8/3 for domestic and international students; for spring admission, 12/8 for domestic and international students; for summer admission, 4/7 for domestic and international students. Application fee: $50. Electronic applications accepted. *Expenses:* Contact institution. *Financial support:* In 2017–18, 2 students received support. Teaching assistantships, Federal Work-Study, and scholarships/grants available. Financial award application deadline: 4/1; financial award applicants required to submit FAFSA. *Faculty research:* Pastoral topics, urban ministry topics, Biblical topics. *Unit head:* Dr. Eddie G. Grigg, President, 704-344-6882 Ext. 101, Fax: 704-334-6885, E-mail: egrigg@charlottechristian.edu. *Application contact:* George Shears, Director of Admissions, 704-334-6882 Ext. 115, Fax: 704-334-6885, E-mail: gshears@charlottechristian.edu.
Website: http://www.charlottechristian.edu

Chicago Theological Seminary, Graduate and Professional Programs, Chicago, IL 60637-1507. Offers Bible, culture and hermeneutics (PhD); preaching (D Min); religion and health (D Min); religious studies (MA); spirituality and spiritual direction (D Min); theology (M Div); theology, ethics and the human sciences (PhD); M Div/MSW. *Accreditation:* ACIPE; ATS. *Program availability:* Part-time. *Degree requirements:* For master's, thesis; for doctorate, 2 foreign languages, comprehensive exam, thesis/dissertation. *Entrance requirements:* For doctorate, GRE General Test. Additional exam requirements/recommendations for international students: Required—TOEFL. *Faculty research:* Bible, culture and hermeneutics, theology, gender and sexuality, black faith and life, spirituality and psychology, practical theology.

Christian Brothers University, School of Arts, Memphis, TN 38104-5581. Offers Catholic studies (MACS); educational leadership (MSEL); teacher-leadership (M Ed); teaching (MAT). *Program availability:* Part-time, evening/weekend. *Entrance requirements:* For master's, GRE, GMAT, PRAXIS II. *Expenses:* Contact institution.

Christian Theological Seminary, Graduate and Professional Programs, Indianapolis, IN 46208-3301. Offers educational and arts ministries (MA); marriage and family therapy (MA); pastoral care and counseling (D Min); psychotherapy and faith (MA); theological studies (MTS); theology (M Div). *Accreditation:* AAMFT/COAMFTE (one or more programs are accredited); ACIPE; ATS. *Program availability:* Part-time. Terminal master's awarded for partial completion of doctoral program. *Degree requirements:* For master's, comprehensive exam (for some programs), thesis (for some programs), missionary and cross-cultural experience (for M Div); for doctorate, comprehensive exam, thesis/dissertation. *Entrance requirements:* For doctorate, M Div. Additional exam requirements/recommendations for international students: Recommended—TOEFL. Electronic applications accepted. *Faculty research:* Faith formation, peer learning post graduation.

Cincinnati Christian University, Graduate School, Cincinnati, OH 45204-3200. Offers biblical studies (MA); church history (MA); counseling (MAC); divinity (M Div); ministry (M Min); practical ministries (MA); theological studies (MA). *Program availability:* Part-time. *Degree requirements:* For master's, variable foreign language requirement, thesis (for some programs), oral exam (for M Div). *Entrance requirements:* Additional exam requirements/recommendations for international students: Required—TOEFL. Electronic applications accepted.

Claremont Graduate University, Graduate Programs, School of Arts and Humanities, Department of Religion, Claremont, CA 91711-6160. Offers Hebrew Bible (MA, PhD); history of Christianity and religions of North America (MA, PhD); New Testament (MA, PhD); philosophy of religion and theology (MA, PhD); theology, ethics and culture (MA, PhD); women's studies in religion (MA, PhD); MA/PhD; MBA/PhD. *Program availability:* Part-time. Terminal master's awarded for partial completion of doctoral program. *Entrance requirements:* For master's and doctorate, GRE General Test. Additional exam requirements/recommendations for international students: Required—TOEFL (minimum score 75 iBT). Electronic applications accepted.

Claremont Lincoln University, Graduate Programs, Claremont, CA 91711. Offers ethical leadership (MA); interfaith action (MA); social impact (MA).

Claremont School of Theology, Graduate and Professional Programs, Program in Religion, Claremont, CA 91711-3199. Offers practical theology (PhD), including religious education and formation, spiritual care and counseling; religion (MA, PhD), including comparative theology and philosophy (PhD), Hebrew Bible and Jewish studies (PhD), New Testament and Christian origins (PhD), process studies (PhD), religion, ethics, and society (PhD). *Accreditation:* ACIPE; ATS. Terminal master's awarded for partial completion of doctoral program. *Degree requirements:* For master's, thesis; for doctorate, 2 foreign languages, thesis/dissertation. *Entrance requirements:* For doctorate, GRE General Test. Additional exam requirements/recommendations for international students: Required—TOEFL. Electronic applications accepted.

Clarks Summit University, Baptist Bible Seminary, South Abington Township, PA 18411. Offers Biblical apologetics (MA); Biblical studies (MA); church education (M Min); church planting (M Div, M Min); communication (D Min); counseling and spiritual development (D Min); global ministry (M Min, D Min); ministry (PhD); missions (M Min); organizational leadership (M Min); outreach pastor (M Min); pastoral counseling (M Min); pastoral leadership (M Div, M Min); pastoral ministry (D Min); theological studies (D Min); theology (Th M); youth pastor (M Min). M Min in missions available only for Association of Baptists for World Evangelism missionary personnel. *Program availability:* Part-time, evening/weekend, online learning. Terminal master's awarded for partial completion of doctoral program. *Degree requirements:* For master's, 2 foreign languages, thesis, oral exam (for M Div); for doctorate, 2 foreign languages, comprehensive exam (for some programs), thesis/dissertation, oral exam. *Entrance requirements:* For doctorate, Greek and Hebrew entrance exams (for PhD). *Application deadline:* Applications are processed on a rolling basis. Application fee: $30. Electronic applications accepted. *Financial support:* Career-related internships or fieldwork and scholarships/grants available. Support available to part-time students. *Unit head:* Dr. Wayne Slusser, Dean, 570-585-9348, Fax: 570-585-4057, E-mail: wslusser@clarkssummitu.edu. *Application contact:* Dr. Wayne Slusser, Dean, 570-585-9348, Fax: 570-585-4057, E-mail: wslusser@clarkssummitu.edu.
Website: https://www.clarkssummitu.edu/seminary/

Columbia University, Graduate School of Arts and Sciences, New York, NY 10027. Offers African-American studies (MA); American studies (MA); anthropology (MA, PhD); art history and archaeology (MA, PhD); astronomy (PhD); biological sciences (PhD); biotechnology (MA); chemical physics (PhD); chemistry (PhD); classical studies (MA, PhD); classics (MA, PhD); climate and society (MA); conservation biology (MA); earth and environmental sciences (PhD); East Asia: regional studies (MA); East Asian languages and cultures (MA, PhD); ecology, evolution and environmental biology (MA), including conservation biology; ecology, evolution, and environmental biology (PhD), including ecology and evolutionary biology, evolutionary primatology; economics (MA, PhD); English and comparative literature (MA, PhD); French and Romance philology (MA, PhD); Germanic languages (MA, PhD); global French studies (MA); global thought (MA); Hispanic cultural studies (MA); history (PhD); history and literature (MA); human rights studies (MA); Islamic studies (MA); Italian (MA, PhD); Japanese pedagogy (MA); Jewish studies (MA); Latin America and the Caribbean: regional studies (MA); Latin American and Iberian cultures (PhD); mathematics (MA, PhD), including finance (MA); medieval and Renaissance studies (MA); Middle Eastern, South Asian, and African studies (MA, PhD); modern art: critical and curatorial studies (MA); modern European studies (MA); museum anthropology (MA); music (DMA, PhD); oral history (MA); philosophical foundations of physics (MA); philosophy (MA, PhD); physics (PhD); political science (MA, PhD); psychology (PhD); quantitative methods in the social sciences (MA); religion (MA, PhD); Russia, Eurasia and East Europe: regional studies (MA); Russian translation (MA); Slavic cultures (MA); Slavic languages (MA, PhD); sociology (MA, PhD); South Asian studies (MA); statistics (MA, PhD); theatre (PhD). Dual-degree programs require admission to both Graduate School of Arts and Sciences and another Columbia school. *Program availability:* Part-time. Terminal master's awarded for partial completion of doctoral program. *Degree requirements:* For master's, variable foreign language requirement, comprehensive exam (for some programs), thesis (for some programs); for doctorate, variable foreign language requirement, comprehensive exam (for some programs), thesis/dissertation. *Entrance requirements:* For master's and doctorate, GRE General Test, GRE Subject Test (for some programs). Additional exam requirements/recommendations for international students: Required—TOEFL, IELTS. Electronic applications accepted. *Expenses: Tuition:* Full-time $44,864; part-time $1704 per credit. *Required fees:* $2370 per semester. One-time fee: $105.

Concordia University, School of Graduate Studies, Faculty of Arts and Science, Department of Religion, MA Program in Religion, Montréal, QC H3G 1M8, Canada. Offers MA. *Degree requirements:* For master's, comprehensive exam, thesis optional.

Concordia University, School of Graduate Studies, Faculty of Arts and Science, Department of Religion, Program in Religion, Montréal, QC H3G 1M8, Canada. Offers PhD. Program offered jointly with Universityé du Quebec à Montréal. *Degree requirements:* For doctorate, one foreign language, comprehensive exam, thesis/dissertation.

Concordia University Chicago, College of Graduate and Innovative Programs, Program in Religion, River Forest, IL 60305-1499. Offers MA. *Program availability:* Part-time, evening/weekend. *Degree requirements:* For master's, comprehensive exam, thesis. *Entrance requirements:* For master's, minimum GPA of 2.9. Additional exam requirements/recommendations for international students: Required—TOEFL (minimum score 550 paper-based). Electronic applications accepted. *Faculty research:* Dead Sea Scrolls, cultural construction of gender in early modern Europe, Luther, Luther's theology of the cross, gospels of Mark and John.

Concordia University Irvine, School of Theology, Irvine, CA 92612-3299. Offers Christian leadership (MA); research in theology (MA); theology and culture (MA). *Program availability:* Part-time, evening/weekend. *Degree requirements:* For master's, project/thesis or vicarage. *Entrance requirements:* For master's, official college transcript(s), statement of intent, 2 references, interview. Additional exam requirements/recommendations for international students: Required—TOEFL. Electronic applications accepted. *Expenses:* Contact institution.

Concordia University of Edmonton, Program in Biblical and Christian Studies, Edmonton, AB T5B 4E4, Canada. Offers MA.

Cornell University, Graduate School, Graduate Fields of Arts and Sciences, Field of Asian Literature, Religion and Culture, Ithaca, NY 14853. Offers Asian religions (MA, PhD); Chinese philosophy (PhD); classical Chinese literature (PhD); classical Japanese literature (PhD); East Asian literature and culture (PhD); Korean literature (PhD); modern Chinese literature (PhD); modern Japanese literature (PhD); South Asian literature and culture (PhD); Southeast Asian literature and culture (PhD). *Degree requirements:* For doctorate, comprehensive exam, thesis/dissertation. *Entrance requirements:* For doctorate, GRE General Test, academic writing sample, 3 letters of recommendation. Additional exam requirements/recommendations for international students: Required—TOEFL (minimum score 600 paper-based; 77 iBT). Electronic applications accepted.

Dallas Baptist University, Liberal Arts Program, Dallas, TX 75211-9299. Offers art (MLA); Christian studies (MLA); commercial art (MLA); East Asian studies (MLA); English (MLA); English as a second language (MLA); fine arts (MLA); history (MLA); missions (MLA); political science (MLA). *Program availability:* Part-time, evening/weekend. *Application deadline:* Applications are processed on a rolling basis. Application fee: $25. Electronic applications accepted. Application fee is waived when completed online. *Expenses: Tuition:* Full-time $16,308; part-time $906 per credit hour. *Required fees:* $900; $450 per semester. Tuition and fees vary according to course load and degree level. *Unit head:* Jared Ingram, Director, 214-333-5584, E-mail: jaredi@dbu.edu. *Application contact:* Bobby Soto, Director of Admissions, 214-333-5242, E-mail: bobby@dbu.edu.
Website: http://www3.dbu.edu/graduate/mla.asp

Dallas Theological Seminary, Graduate Programs, Dallas, TX 75204-6499. Offers adult education (Th M); apologetics (Th M); Bible backgrounds (Th M); Bible translation (Th M); Biblical and theological studies (Certificate); biblical counseling (MA); biblical exegesis and linguistics (MA); biblical exposition (PhD); biblical studies (MA); Biblical theology (Th M); children's education (Th M); Christian education (MA, D Min); Christian leadership (MA); cross-cultural ministries (MA); educational administration (Th M); educational leadership (Th M); evangelism and discipleship (Th M); exposition of Biblical books (Th M); family life education (Th M); general studies (Th M); Hebrew and cognate studies (Th M); hermeneutics (Th M); historical theology (Th M); homiletics (Th M); intercultural ministries (Th M); Jesus studies (Th M); leadership studies (Th M); media and communication (MA); media arts (Th M); ministry (D Min); ministry with women (Th M); New Testament studies (Th M, PhD); Old Testament studies (Th M, PhD); parachurch ministries (Th M); pastoral care and counseling (Th M); pastoral theology and practice (Th M); philosophy (Th M); sacred theology (STM); spiritual formation (Th M); systematic theology (Th M); teaching in Christian institutions (Th M); theological studies (PhD); urban ministries (Th M); worship studies (Th M); youth education (Th M). *Program availability:* Part-time, online learning. *Degree requirements:* For master's, variable foreign language requirement, thesis (for some programs); for doctorate, 2 foreign languages, thesis/dissertation. *Entrance requirements:* For master's, GRE or MAT (if minimum undergraduate cumulative GPA is below 2.5 or undergraduate degree is unaccredited). Additional exam requirements/recommendations for international students: Required—TOEFL (minimum score 575 paper-based; 85 iBT), TWE. Electronic applications accepted.

Delta State University, Graduate Programs, College of Arts and Sciences, Program in Liberal Studies, Cleveland, MS 38733-0001. Offers evolving human voices (MALS); gender and diversity studies (MALS); globalization studies (MALS); Mississippi Delta studies (MALS); philosophy (MALS); religious studies (MALS). *Degree requirements:* For master's, oral and/or written comprehensive exam.

Denver Seminary, Graduate and Professional Programs, Littleton, CO 80120. Offers apologetics (Certificate); biblical studies (MA); Christian formation and soul care (MA, Certificate); Christian studies (MA, Certificate); church and parachurch leadership (D Min); counseling licensure (MA); counseling ministry (MA); intercultural ministry (Certificate); leadership (MA, Certificate); marriage and family counseling (D Min); pastoral ministry (D Min); philosophy of religion (MA); spiritual guidance (Certificate); theology (M Div, Certificate); worship (Certificate); youth and family ministry (MA). *Accreditation:* ACA; ACIPE; ATS (one or more programs are accredited). *Program availability:* Part-time, evening/weekend, online learning. *Degree requirements:* For master's, 2 foreign languages, thesis (for some programs); for doctorate, 2 foreign languages, thesis/dissertation. *Entrance requirements:* For doctorate, M Div, 3 years of ministry experience. Additional exam requirements/recommendations for international students: Required—TOEFL (minimum score 575 paper-based; 90 iBT). Electronic applications accepted.

Dominican University of California, School of Liberal Arts and Education, Humanities Program, San Rafael, CA 94901-2298. Offers applied music (MA); art history (MA); creative writing (MA); gender studies (MA); history (MA); philosophy (MA); political theory (MA); religion (MA). *Program availability:* Part-time. *Faculty:* 7 full-time (4 women), 1 (woman) part-time/adjunct. *Students:* 6 full-time (5 women), 16 part-time (12 women); includes 8 minority (3 Black or African American, non-Hispanic/Latino; 4 Hispanic/Latino; 1 Two or more races, non-Hispanic/Latino), 2 international. Average age 45. 7 applicants, 100% accepted, 5 enrolled. In 2017, 14 master's awarded. *Degree requirements:* For master's, thesis or alternative. *Entrance requirements:* For master's, minimum GPA of 3.0, interview. Additional exam requirements/recommendations for international students: Required—TOEFL (minimum score 550 paper-based; 80 iBT), IELTS (minimum score 6.5). *Application deadline:* For fall admission, 5/15 priority date for domestic and international students; for spring admission, 11/15 priority date for domestic and international students. Applications are processed on a rolling basis. Application fee: $0. Electronic applications accepted. *Expenses: Tuition:* Full-time $17,370; part-time $965 per credit. *Required fees:* $150 per semester. Tuition and fees vary according to course load and program. *Financial support:* In 2017–18, 4 students received support. Scholarships/grants available. Support available to part-time students. Financial award application deadline: 3/2; financial award applicants required to submit FAFSA. *Unit head:* Joan Baranow, Program Director, 415-485-3264, E-mail: joan.baranow@dominican.edu. *Application contact:* Michael Lavigna, Assistant Director of Graduate Admissions, 415-485-3253, Fax: 415-485-3214, E-mail: gradmissions@dominican.edu.
Website: https://www.dominican.edu/academics/lae/graduate-programs/ma-in-humanities/index_html

Drew University, Caspersen School of Graduate Studies, Madison, NJ 07940-1493. Offers conflict resolution and leadership (Certificate), including community leadership, moderation, peace building; education (M Ed); finance (MA); history and culture (MA, PhD), including American history, book history, British history, European history, Holocaust and genocide (M Litt, MA, D Litt, PhD), intellectual history, Irish history, print culture, public history; K-12 education (MAT), including art, biology, chemistry, elementary education, English, French, Italian, math, secondary education, special education, teacher of students with disabilities; liberal studies (M Litt, D Litt), including history, Holocaust and genocide (M Litt, MA, D Litt, PhD), Irish/Irish-American studies, literature (M Litt, MMH, D Litt, DMH, CMH); religion, spirituality, teaching in the two-year college, writing; medical humanities (MMH, DMH, CMH), including arts, health, healthcare, literature (M Litt, MMH, D Litt, DMH, CMH); scientific research; poetry (MFA). *Program availability:* Part-time, evening/weekend. *Faculty:* 4 full-time (2 women), 29 part-time/adjunct (15 women). *Students:* 77 full-time (42 women), 175 part-time (114 women); includes 39 minority (12 Black or African American, non-Hispanic/Latino; 6 Asian, non-Hispanic/Latino; 16 Hispanic/Latino; 5 Two or more races, non-Hispanic/Latino), 11 international. Average age 41. 126 applicants, 75% accepted, 52 enrolled. In 2017, 38 master's, 23 doctorates, 35 other advanced degrees awarded. Terminal master's awarded for partial completion of doctoral program. *Degree requirements:* For master's and other advanced degree, thesis (for some programs); for doctorate, one foreign language, comprehensive exam (for some programs), thesis/dissertation. *Entrance requirements:* For master's, PRAXIS Core and Subject Area tests (for MAT), GRE/GMAT (for M Fin), resume, transcripts, writing sample, personal statement, letters of recommendation; for doctorate, GRE (PhD in history and culture), resume, transcripts, writing sample, personal statement, letters of recommendation; for other advanced degree, resume, transcripts, personal statement. Additional exam requirements/recommendations for international students: Required—TOEFL (minimum score 587 paper-based; 80 iBT), IELTS (minimum score 6), TWE (minimum score 4). *Application deadline:* For fall admission, 8/1 for domestic students, 6/1 for international students; for spring admission, 12/1 for domestic students, 10/1 for international students. Applications are processed on a rolling basis. Application fee: $35. Electronic applications accepted. *Financial support:* Fellowships, research assistantships, teaching assistantships, career-related internships or fieldwork, Federal Work-Study, scholarships/grants, and unspecified assistantships available. Support available to part-time students. Financial award applicants required to submit FAFSA. *Faculty research:* Irish history and culture, conflict resolution and leadership. *Application contact:* Leanne Horinko, Director of Caspersen Admissions, 973-408-3280, E-mail: gradm@drew.edu.
Website: http://www.drew.edu/caspersen

Duke University, Graduate School, Department of Religion, Durham, NC 27708. Offers MA, PhD, JD/MA. *Program availability:* Part-time. Terminal master's awarded for partial completion of doctoral program. *Degree requirements:* For master's, one foreign language, thesis or alternative; for doctorate, 2 foreign languages, thesis/dissertation. *Entrance requirements:* For master's and doctorate, GRE General Test. Additional exam requirements/recommendations for international students: Required—TOEFL (minimum score 577 paper-based; 90 iBT) or IELTS (minimum score 7). Electronic applications accepted.

Earlham School of Religion, Graduate Programs, Richmond, IN 47374-5360. Offers ministry (M Min); religion (MA); theology (M Div). *Accreditation:* ACIPE; ATS. *Program availability:* Part-time, online learning. *Faculty:* 8 full-time (2 women), 2 part-time/adjunct (1 woman). *Students:* 26 full-time (15 women), 32 part-time (21 women). *Degree requirements:* For master's, variable foreign language requirement, comprehensive exam (for some programs), thesis (for some programs), internship (M Div). *Entrance requirements:* For master's, 3 references, academic writing sample, official college transcripts. Additional exam requirements/recommendations for international students: Required—TOEFL (minimum score 550 paper-based; 82 iBT), IELTS (minimum score 7). *Application deadline:* For fall admission, 7/15 priority date for domestic students; for winter admission, 12/15 priority date for domestic students. Applications are processed on a rolling basis. Application fee: $35. Electronic applications accepted. *Expenses: Tuition:* Full-time $15,741; part-time $1741 per course. *Required fees:* $450. *Financial support:* Scholarships/grants and tuition waivers (full and partial) available. Financial award application deadline: 4/15; financial award applicants required to submit FAFSA. *Faculty research:* Digitizing Quaker texts, vital Quaker ministry, research in Quaker studies and other seminary areas. *Unit head:* Jay W. Marshall, Dean, 800-432-1377, Fax: 765-983-1688, E-mail: marshja@earlham.edu. *Application contact:* Matthew Hisrich, Director of Recruitment and Admissions, 765-983-1523, Fax: 765-983-1688, E-mail: hisrima@earlham.edu.
Website: http://esr.earlham.edu/academic-programs

Eastern Mennonite University, Eastern Mennonite Seminary, Harrisonburg, VA 22802-2462. Offers Christian leadership (MA); divinity (M Div); ministry studies (Certificate); religion (MA); theological studies (Certificate). *Accreditation:* ATS. *Program availability:* Part-time. *Degree requirements:* For master's, thesis (for some programs), supervised field education (for M Div). *Entrance requirements:* For master's, minimum GPA of 2.5. Additional exam requirements/recommendations for international students: Required—TOEFL (minimum score 550 paper-based). *Application deadline:* For fall admission, 6/15 priority date for domestic and international students; for winter admission, 11/15 priority date for domestic and international students; for spring admission, 3/15 priority date for domestic and international students. Applications are processed on a rolling basis. Application fee: $25. *Expenses:* Contact institution. *Financial support:* Application deadline: 6/30; applicants required to submit FAFSA. *Faculty research:* Spiritual direction and culture of call, leadership coaching: an approach to leadership in a culture of call, clarity of call in the probationary process for United Methodist clergy in Virginia, EMS women's experiences of culture of call efforts, practices of excellent and fruitful Mennonite pastoral ministry. *Unit head:* Sue Cockley, Dean, 540-432-4984, Fax: 540-432-4444, E-mail: cockleys@emu.edu. *Application contact:* Laura Lehman, Director of Seminary Admissions, 540-432-4268, Fax: 540-432-4598, E-mail: semadmiss@emu.edu.
Website: http://www.emu.edu/seminary/

East Texas Baptist University, School of Christian Studies, Marshall, TX 75670-1498. Offers MA, MACM. *Program availability:* Part-time, evening/weekend, blended/hybrid learning. *Faculty:* 4 full-time (0 women), 1 part-time/adjunct (0 women). *Students:* 9 full-time (4 women), 5 part-time (1 woman); includes 4 minority (2 Black or African American, non-Hispanic/Latino; 1 Hispanic/Latino; 1 Two or more races, non-Hispanic/Latino). Average age 26. 13 applicants, 62% accepted, 7 enrolled. In 2017, 3 master's awarded. *Degree requirements:* For master's, thesis optional. *Entrance requirements:* Additional exam requirements/recommendations for international students: Recommended—TOEFL (minimum score 550 paper-based; 79 iBT). *Application deadline:* For fall admission, 8/13 for domestic students; for spring admission, 1/7 for domestic students; for summer admission, 5/10 for domestic students. Applications are

processed on a rolling basis. Application fee: $50. Electronic applications accepted. *Expenses:* $735 per credit hour tuition, $150 per semester fees ($75 per semester if less than 6 hours). *Financial support:* In 2017–18, 6 students received support. Federal Work-Study, scholarships/grants, unspecified assistantships, and staff grants available. Financial award applicants required to submit FAFSA. *Unit head:* Dr. Warren Johnson, Director, 903-923-2182, Fax: 903-923-2077, E-mail: christianstudiesma@etbu.edu. *Application contact:* Den Murley, Director of Graduate Admissions, 903-923-2079, Fax: 903-934-8115, E-mail: gradadmissions@etbu.edu.
Website: https://www.etbu.edu/christian-studies/masters-degrees/

Elms College, Religious Studies Department, Chicopee, MA 01013-2839. Offers MAAT. *Program availability:* Part-time, evening/weekend. *Faculty:* 1 full-time (0 women), 3 part-time/adjunct (1 woman). *Students:* 1 full-time (0 women), 3 part-time (2 women). Average age 55. 2 applicants, 100% accepted, 2 enrolled. In 2017, 32 master's awarded. *Degree requirements:* For master's, thesis. *Entrance requirements:* For master's, minimum GPA of 3.0. Additional exam requirements/recommendations for international students: Required—TOEFL. *Application deadline:* For fall admission, 7/1 priority date for domestic students; for spring admission, 11/1 priority date for domestic students. Applications are processed on a rolling basis. Application fee: $30. *Expenses: Tuition:* Full-time $13,860; part-time $770 per credit hour. *Required fees:* $200. Tuition and fees vary according to degree level and program. *Financial support:* Applicants required to submit FAFSA. *Unit head:* Dr. Martin Pion, Director of Religious Studies, 413-265-3581, Fax: 413-594-3951, E-mail: pionm@elms.edu. *Application contact:* School of Graduate and Professional Studies, 413-265-2445, E-mail: graduateeducation@elms.edu.

Emory University, Laney Graduate School, Division of Religion, Atlanta, GA 30322-1100. Offers PhD. *Degree requirements:* For doctorate, 2 foreign languages, comprehensive exam, thesis/dissertation. *Entrance requirements:* For doctorate, GRE General Test, minimum GPA of 3.0. Additional exam requirements/recommendations for international students: Required—TOEFL. Electronic applications accepted. *Faculty research:* Systematic and historical theology, Biblical studies.

Faith Baptist Bible College and Theological Seminary, Graduate Program, Ankeny, IA 50023. Offers Biblical studies (MA); pastoral studies (M Div); pastoral training (MA); religion (MA); theological studies (MA). *Program availability:* Part-time. *Degree requirements:* For master's, thesis or alternative. *Entrance requirements:* Additional exam requirements/recommendations for international students: Required—TOEFL (minimum score 550 paper-based; 79 iBT), IELTS (minimum score 6.5). Electronic applications accepted. *Faculty research:* Baptist theology, American church history.

Florida International University, Steven J. Green School of International and Public Affairs, Department of Religious Studies, Miami, FL 33199. Offers MA, MA/PhD. *Program availability:* Part-time, evening/weekend. *Faculty:* 11 full-time (2 women), 21 part-time/adjunct (9 women). *Students:* 10 full-time (4 women), 6 part-time (4 women); includes 7 minority (1 Black or African American, non-Hispanic/Latino; 1 Asian, non-Hispanic/Latino; 5 Hispanic/Latino), 6 international. Average age 34. 15 applicants, 53% accepted, 4 enrolled. In 2017, 8 master's awarded. *Degree requirements:* For master's, thesis or alternative. *Entrance requirements:* For master's, minimum GPA of 3.0, 2 letters of recommendation. Additional exam requirements/recommendations for international students: Required—TOEFL (minimum score 550 paper-based; 80 iBT). *Application deadline:* For fall admission, 2/15 for domestic and international students; for spring admission, 10/1 for domestic students, 9/1 for international students. Application fee: $30. Electronic applications accepted. *Expenses:* Tuition, state resident: full-time $8912; part-time $446 per credit hour. Tuition, nonresident: full-time $21,393; part-time $992 per credit hour. *Required fees:* $390; $195 per semester. *Financial support:* Institutionally sponsored loans and scholarships/grants available. Financial award application deadline: 3/1; financial award applicants required to submit FAFSA. *Unit head:* Dr. Erik Larson, Chair, 305-348-3518, Fax: 305-348-1879, E-mail: larsone@fiu.edu. *Application contact:* Nanett Rojas, Manager, Admissions Operations, 305-348-7464, Fax: 305-348-7441, E-mail: nanett.rojas@fiu.edu.

Florida State University, The Graduate School, College of Arts and Sciences, Department of Religion, Tallahassee, FL 32306-1520. Offers humanities (PhD), including religion; religion (MA, PhD). *Faculty:* 18 full-time (4 women), 4 part-time/adjunct (2 women). *Students:* 76 full-time (22 women), 5 part-time (1 woman); includes 10 minority (2 Black or African American, non-Hispanic/Latino; 2 Asian, non-Hispanic/Latino; 6 Two or more races, non-Hispanic/Latino). Average age 26. 45 applicants, 49% accepted, 16 enrolled. In 2017, 9 master's, 12 doctorates awarded. Terminal master's awarded for partial completion of doctoral program. *Degree requirements:* For master's, one foreign language, comprehensive exam (for some programs), thesis (for some programs); for doctorate, 2 foreign languages, thesis/dissertation. *Entrance requirements:* For master's, GRE General Test, minimum GPA of 3.0; for doctorate, GRE General Test, MA in religion. Additional exam requirements/recommendations for international students: Required—TOEFL (minimum score 550 paper-based; 80 iBT). *Application deadline:* For fall admission, 12/15 for domestic and international students. Application fee: $30. Electronic applications accepted. *Financial support:* In 2017–18, 63 students received support, including 5 fellowships with partial tuition reimbursements available (averaging $15,000 per year), 26 research assistantships with partial tuition reimbursements available (averaging $10,500 per year), 32 teaching assistantships with partial tuition reimbursements available (averaging $12,000 per year); institutionally sponsored loans, tuition waivers (partial), and unspecified assistantships also available. Financial award application deadline: 1/15; financial award applicants required to submit FAFSA. *Faculty research:* American religious history, comparative religious ethics, religions of Western antiquity, Asian religions and culture, history and ethnography of religion. *Unit head:* Dr. Aline Kalbian, Chair, 850-644-1020, Fax: 850-644-7225, E-mail: akalbian@fsu.edu. *Application contact:* Dr. Matthew Goff, Director of Graduate Studies, 850-644-1020, Fax: 850-644-7225, E-mail: mgoff@fsu.edu.
Website: http://www.religion.fsu.edu

Fordham University, Graduate School of Religion and Religious Education, New York, NY 10458. Offers pastoral counseling and spiritual care (MA); pastoral ministry/spirituality/pastoral counseling (D Min); religion and religious education (MA); religious education (MS, PhD, PD); spiritual direction (Certificate). *Program availability:* Part-time. Terminal master's awarded for partial completion of doctoral program. *Degree requirements:* For master's, research paper; for doctorate, comprehensive exam, thesis/dissertation. *Entrance requirements:* For doctorate, MAT. Electronic applications accepted. *Expenses:* Contact institution. *Faculty research:* Spirituality and spiritual direction, pastoral care and counseling, adult family and community, growth and young adult.

General Theological Seminary, Graduate and Professional Programs, New York, NY 10011-4977. Offers Anglican studies (STM, Th D, Certificate); ascetical theology (Certificate); biblical studies (Certificate); congregational development (Certificate); divinity (M Div); historical and theological studies (Certificate); spiritual direction (MASD, STM, Certificate); theology (MA). *Accreditation:* ACIPE; ATS. *Program availability:* Part-time, evening/weekend. Terminal master's awarded for partial completion of doctoral program. *Degree requirements:* For master's, thesis; for doctorate, 2 foreign languages, thesis/dissertation. *Entrance requirements:* For master's, GRE General Test; for doctorate, GRE, M Div or MA. Additional exam requirements/recommendations for international students: Required—TOEFL. *Faculty research:* Liturgy, New Testament, ethics, history, ecumenical relations.

George Mason University, College of Humanities and Social Sciences, Interdisciplinary Studies Program, Fairfax, VA 22030. Offers computational social science (MAIS); energy and sustainability (MAIS); folklore studies (MAIS); higher education (MAIS); individualized studies (MAIS); religion, culture, and values (MAIS); social entrepreneurship (MAIS); social justice and human rights (MAIS); war and the military in society (MAIS); women and gender studies (MAIS). *Faculty:* 10 full-time (3 women), 15 part-time/adjunct (7 women). *Students:* 29 full-time (23 women), 76 part-time (50 women); includes 39 minority (18 Black or African American, non-Hispanic/Latino; 6 Asian, non-Hispanic/Latino; 11 Hispanic/Latino; 4 Two or more races, non-Hispanic/Latino), 7 international. Average age 32. 71 applicants, 90% accepted, 29 enrolled. In 2017, 23 master's awarded. *Degree requirements:* For master's, thesis or alternative, experiential learning (for some programs). *Entrance requirements:* Additional exam requirements/recommendations for international students: Required—TOEFL (minimum score 575 paper-based; 88 iBT), IELTS (minimum score 6.5), PTE (minimum score 59). *Application deadline:* For fall admission, 3/1 for domestic and international students; for spring admission, 10/15 for domestic and international students. Application fee: $75 ($80 for international students). Electronic applications accepted. *Expenses:* Tuition, state resident: full-time $11,228; part-time $459.50 per credit. Tuition, nonresident: full-time $30,932; part-time $1280.50 per credit. *Required fees:* $3252; $135.50 per credit. Part-time tuition and fees vary according to course load and program. *Financial support:* In 2017–18, 9 students received support, including 2 research assistantships with tuition reimbursements available, 7 teaching assistantships with tuition reimbursements available (averaging $8,599 per year); career-related internships or fieldwork, Federal Work-Study, scholarships/grants, unspecified assistantships, and health care benefits (for full-time research or teaching assistantship recipients) also available. Support available to part-time students. Financial award application deadline: 3/1; financial award applicants required to submit FAFSA. *Faculty research:* Combined English and folklore, religious and cultural studies (Christianity and Muslim society). *Unit head:* Meredith H. Lair, Director, 703-993-2159, Fax: 703-993-1251, E-mail: mlair@gmu.edu. *Application contact:* Morgan Fisher, Graduate Coordinator, 703-993-8762, E-mail: mfisherb@gmu.edu.
Website: http://mais.gmu.edu

Georgetown University, Graduate School of Arts and Sciences, School of Continuing Studies, Washington, DC 20057. Offers American studies (MALS); applied intelligence (MPS); Catholic studies (MALS); classical civilizations (MALS); emergency and disaster management (MPS); ethics and the professions (MALS); global strategic communications (MPS); hospitality management (MPS); human resources management (MPS); humanities (MALS); individualized study (MALS); integrated marketing communications (MPS); international affairs (MALS); Islam and Muslim-Christian relations (MALS); journalism (MPS); liberal studies (DLS); literature and society (MALS); medieval and early modern European studies (MALS); public relations and corporate communications (MPS); real estate (MPS); religious studies (MALS); social and public policy (MALS); sports industry management (MPS); systems engineering management (MPS); technology management (MPS); the theory and practice of American democracy (MALS); urban and regional planning (MPS); visual culture (MALS). MPS in systems engineering management offered jointly with Stevens Institute of Technology. *Entrance requirements:* Additional exam requirements/recommendations for international students: Required—TOEFL.

The George Washington University, Columbian College of Arts and Sciences, Department of Religion, Washington, DC 20052. Offers Islam (MA), including Hinduism and Islam. *Program availability:* Part-time, evening/weekend. *Faculty:* 7 full-time (3 women), 7 part-time/adjunct (2 women). *Students:* 10 full-time (7 women), 4 part-time (3 women); includes 2 minority (1 Black or African American, non-Hispanic/Latino; 1 Asian, non-Hispanic/Latino), 6 international. Average age 31. 26 applicants, 73% accepted, 6 enrolled. In 2017, 4 master's awarded. *Degree requirements:* For master's, one foreign language, comprehensive exam, thesis. *Entrance requirements:* For master's, GRE General Test, interview, minimum GPA of 3.0. Additional exam requirements/recommendations for international students: Required—TOEFL (minimum score 550 paper-based; 80 iBT). *Application deadline:* For fall admission, 4/1 priority date for domestic students, 1/15 priority date for international students; for spring admission, 10/1 priority date for domestic students, 9/1 priority date for international students. Applications are processed on a rolling basis. Application fee: $75. Electronic applications accepted. *Expenses: Tuition:* Full-time $28,800; part-time $1655 per credit hour. *Required fees:* $45; $2.75 per credit hour. *Financial support:* In 2017–18, 1 student received support. Federal Work-Study and tuition waivers available. *Unit head:* Dr. Robert Eisen, Chair, 202-994-6327, Fax: 202-994-9379, E-mail: eisen@gwu.edu. *Application contact:* Information Contact, 202-994-6325, Fax: 202-994-9379, E-mail: religion@gwu.edu.
Website: http://religion.columbian.gwu.edu/

Georgia State University, College of Arts and Sciences, Department of Religious Studies, Atlanta, GA 30302-4089. Offers MA. *Program availability:* Part-time. *Faculty:* 9 full-time (4 women). *Students:* 18 full-time (8 women), 4 part-time (2 women); includes 6 minority (4 Black or African American, non-Hispanic/Latino; 1 Hispanic/Latino; 1 Two or more races, non-Hispanic/Latino). Average age 38. 16 applicants, 94% accepted, 9 enrolled. In 2017, 12 master's awarded. *Entrance requirements:* For master's, GRE. Additional exam requirements/recommendations for international students: Required—TOEFL (minimum score 79 iBT). *Application deadline:* For fall admission, 2/1 priority date for domestic and international students. Application fee: $50. Electronic applications accepted. *Expenses:* Tuition, state resident: full-time $7020. Tuition, nonresident: full-time $22,518. *Required fees:* $2128. Tuition and fees vary according to degree level and program. *Financial support:* In 2017–18, research assistantships with full tuition reimbursements (averaging $5,000 per year), teaching assistantships with full tuition reimbursements (averaging $6,000 per year) were awarded; career-related internships or fieldwork, health care benefits, and unspecified assistantships also available. Financial award application deadline: 2/1; financial award applicants required to submit FAFSA. *Faculty research:* Comparative/world religions; religion in the Americas; religion, gender and sexuality; religion and public policy/non-profit management; religion, ethics and politics. *Unit head:* Dr. Kathryn McClymond, Chairperson, 404-413-6119, Fax: 404-413-6124, E-mail: kmcclymond@gsu.edu. *Application contact:* Dr. Molly Bassett, Director of Graduate Studies, 404-413-6134, E-mail: mbassett@gsu.edu.
Website: http://religiousstudies.gsu.edu/graduate/

Gordon-Conwell Theological Seminary, Graduate and Professional Programs, South Hamilton, MA 01982. Offers Biblical languages (MABL); church history (MACH); counseling (MACO); ministry (D Min); missions/evangelism (MAME); New Testament (MANT); Old Testament (MAOT); religion (MAR); theology (M Div, MATH, Th M, Th D). *Accreditation:* ACIPE; ATS (one or more programs are accredited). *Program availability:* Part-time, evening/weekend. *Degree requirements:* For master's, one foreign language, thesis optional; for doctorate, 2 foreign languages, thesis/dissertation. *Entrance requirements:* For master's, minimum GPA of 2.5; for doctorate, minimum GPA of 3.0.

Grace College of Divinity, Graduate Program, Fayetteville, NC 28314. Offers MCL.

Graceland University, Community of Christ Seminary, Independence, MO 64050. Offers MAR. *Program availability:* Part-time. *Faculty:* 1 full-time (0 women), 1 part-time/adjunct (0 women). *Students:* 14 full-time (10 women), 17 part-time (9 women); includes 2 minority (1 Asian, non-Hispanic/Latino; 1 Native Hawaiian or other Pacific Islander, non-Hispanic/Latino), 2 international. Average age 41. 16 applicants, 100% accepted, 11 enrolled. In 2017, 12 master's awarded. *Degree requirements:* For master's, portfolio. *Entrance requirements:* For master's, minimum cumulative GPA of 3.0. Additional exam requirements/recommendations for international students: Required—TOEFL (minimum score 550 paper-based; 79 iBT). *Application deadline:* For fall admission, 8/15 priority date for domestic students. Applications are processed on a rolling basis. Application fee: $50. Electronic applications accepted. *Expenses:* Contact institution. *Financial support:* In 2017–18, 1 student received support. Scholarships/grants available. Financial award application deadline: 12/15; financial award applicants required to submit FAFSA. *Faculty research:* Theology, scripture. *Unit head:* Dr. Matthew Frizzell, Dean, 641-784-5276, E-mail: mfrizzel@graceland.edu. *Application contact:* Sharon Ward, Administrative Assistant, 816-423-4676, Fax: 816-423-4753, E-mail: ward@graceland.edu. Website: http://www.graceland.edu/seminary

Graduate Theological Union, Graduate Programs, Berkeley, CA 94709-1212. Offers art and religion (MA, PhD, Th D); biblical languages (MA); biblical studies (MA); Biblical studies (PhD, Th D); Buddhist studies (MA); Christian spirituality (MA, PhD, Th D); cultural and historical studies of religions (MA, PhD, Th D); ethics and social theory (PhD, Th D); history (MA, PhD, Th D); homiletics (MA, PhD, Th D); interdisciplinary studies (PhD, Th D); Jewish studies (MA, PhD, Th D, Certificate); liturgical studies (MA, PhD, Th D); Near Eastern religions (PhD, Th D); Orthodox Christian studies (MA); religion and psychology (MA, PhD, Th D); religion and society/ethics and social theory (MA); systematic and philosophical theology (MA, PhD, Th D). PhD programs in Jewish studies and Near Eastern religions offered jointly with University of California, Berkeley. *Accreditation:* ATS. Terminal master's awarded for partial completion of doctoral program. *Degree requirements:* For master's, one foreign language, thesis; for doctorate, one foreign language, comprehensive exam, thesis/dissertation. *Entrance requirements:* For master's, GRE General Test; for doctorate, GRE General Test, MA or M Div. Additional exam requirements/recommendations for international students: Required—TOEFL. Electronic applications accepted.

Grand Rapids Theological Seminary of Cornerstone University, Graduate Programs, Grand Rapids, MI 49525-5897. Offers academic (M Div); chaplaincy ministries (M Div); Christian formation (MA); counseling (MA); formation and soul care ministries (M Div); intercultural ministries (M Div); interdisciplinary studies (MA); New Testament (Th M); Old Testament (Th M); pastoral ministries (M Div); small group and discipleship ministries (M Div); student and family ministries (M Div). *Accreditation:* ATS. *Program availability:* Part-time, evening/weekend, 100% online, blended/hybrid learning. *Faculty:* 9 full-time (2 women), 14 part-time/adjunct (5 women). *Students:* 100 full-time (53 women), 211 part-time (102 women); includes 71 minority (54 Black or African American, non-Hispanic/Latino; 1 American Indian or Alaska Native, non-Hispanic/Latino; 3 Asian, non-Hispanic/Latino; 12 Hispanic/Latino; 1 Two or more races, non-Hispanic/Latino), 3 international. Average age 36. 165 applicants, 76% accepted, 99 enrolled. In 2017, 75 master's awarded. *Entrance requirements:* Additional exam requirements/recommendations for international students: Required—TOEFL (minimum score 577 paper-based; 90 iBT), IELTS (minimum score 7). *Application deadline:* For fall admission, 8/15 for domestic students, 6/15 for international students; for spring admission, 1/10 for domestic students, 11/10 for international students; for summer admission, 4/30 for domestic students. Applications are processed on a rolling basis. Electronic applications accepted. *Expenses: Tuition:* Full-time $9720; part-time $540 per credit hour. *Required fees:* $832; $374 per semester. Tuition and fees vary according to course load and program. *Financial support:* In 2017–18, 96 students received support, including 8 fellowships with partial tuition reimbursements available; career-related internships or fieldwork and scholarships/grants also available. Support available to part-time students. Financial award application deadline: 8/15; financial award applicants required to submit FAFSA. *Unit head:* Dr. John F. VerBerkmoes, Executive Vice President and Academic Dean, 616-222-1422, E-mail: john.verberkmoes@cornerstone.edu. *Application contact:* Ashley VanBemmelen, Director of Admissions, 800-697-1133, E-mail: ashley.vanbemmelen@cornerstone.edu.

Hardin-Simmons University, Graduate School, Logsdon School of Theology, Program in Religion, Abilene, TX 79698-0001. Offers MA. *Program availability:* Part-time. *Faculty:* 8 full-time (1 woman), 12 part-time/adjunct (1 woman). *Students:* 7 part-time (1 woman); includes 1 minority (Hispanic/Latino). Average age 42. In 2017, 1 master's awarded. *Degree requirements:* For master's, one foreign language, comprehensive exam, thesis or alternative. *Entrance requirements:* For master's, minimum undergraduate GPA of 3.0 in major, 2.7 overall; 18 hours of course work in religious studies; interview. Additional exam requirements/recommendations for international students: Required—TOEFL (minimum score 550 paper-based; 75 iBT). *Application deadline:* For fall admission, 8/15 priority date for domestic students, 4/1 for international students; for spring admission, 1/5 priority date for domestic students, 9/1 for international students. Applications are processed on a rolling basis. Application fee: $50 ($150 for international students). Electronic applications accepted. *Expenses:* Contact institution. *Financial support:* In 2017–18, 5 students received support. Fellowships and scholarships/grants available. Support available to part-time students. Financial award application deadline: 6/30; financial award applicants required to submit FAFSA. *Faculty research:* Archaeology research in Christian origins, Hebrew grammar, history of Christian education, training of ministers into the twenty-first century, role of women in the Old Testament, contemporary ethical issues. *Unit head:* Dr. Dan Stiver, Program Director, 325-670-1398, Fax: 325-670-1406, E-mail: dstiver@hsutx.edu. *Application contact:* Dr. Nancy Kucinski, Dean of Graduate Studies, 325-670-1298, Fax: 325-670-1564, E-mail: gradoff@hsutx.edu. Website: http://www.logsdonseminary.org/academics/religion/

Harrison Middleton University, Graduate Program, Tempe, AZ 85282. Offers education (MA, Ed D); humanities (MA); imaginative literature (MA); interdisciplinary studies (DA); jurisprudence (MA); natural science (MA); philosophy and religion (MA); social science (MA). *Program availability:* Part-time, evening/weekend, online learning. *Degree requirements:* For master's and doctorate, capstone project. *Entrance requirements:* For master's, interview; for doctorate, 2 academic letters of reference, interview, essay. Additional exam requirements/recommendations for international students: Required—TOEFL (minimum score 550 paper-based; 80 iBT). Electronic applications accepted. *Faculty research:* Japanese animation, educational leadership, war art, John Muir's wilderness.

Hartford Seminary, Graduate Programs, Hartford, CT 06105-2279. Offers Islamic studies (MA); ministry (D Min); religious studies (MA); spirituality (Certificate). *Accreditation:* ATS (one or more programs are accredited). *Program availability:* Part-time, evening/weekend, online learning. *Degree requirements:* For master's, thesis optional, oral exam; for doctorate, thesis/dissertation, oral exam. *Entrance requirements:* For doctorate, experience in ministry, M Div. Additional exam requirements/recommendations for international students: Required—TOEFL (minimum score 550 paper-based; 80 iBT). *Faculty research:* Liturgy and social justice, professional leadership in ministry, congregational studies, Christian-Muslim relations, American religion.

Harvard University, Graduate School of Arts and Sciences, Committee on the Study of Religion, Cambridge, MA 02138. Offers PhD. Program offered jointly with Harvard Divinity School. *Degree requirements:* For doctorate, 2 foreign languages, thesis/dissertation. *Entrance requirements:* For doctorate, GRE General Test. Additional exam requirements/recommendations for international students: Required—TOEFL.

Heritage Christian University, Graduate Programs, Florence, AL 35630. Offers counseling (MM); Greek (MA); ministry (MM); New Testament (MA). *Degree requirements:* For master's, practicum (MM), major research paper (MA). *Entrance requirements:* For master's, MAT or GRE, bachelor's degree in Bible from an accredited college or university, minimum GPA of 2.75, 3 letters of recommendation.

Hope International University, School of Graduate and Professional Studies, Programs in Ministry, Fullerton, CA 92831-3138. Offers Christian leadership (MCM); church music (MA); church music (Korean track) (MCM); church planting (MCM); intercultural studies (MCM); worship (MCM). *Program availability:* Part-time, evening/weekend, online learning. *Degree requirements:* For master's, thesis (for some programs), project. *Entrance requirements:* For master's, minimum GPA of 3.0, MCM program requires an undergraduate degree in music, 2 references. Additional exam requirements/recommendations for international students: Required—TOEFL (minimum score 550 paper-based; 86 iBT); Recommended—IELTS (minimum score 6.5). Electronic applications accepted. *Expenses:* Contact institution. *Faculty research:* Church dynamics, growth methodologies.

Iliff School of Theology, Graduate and Professional Programs, Denver, CO 80210-4798. Offers biblical studies (MA); church history (MA); religion (MA); religion and social change (MA); specialized ministry (MASM), including justice and peace, pastoral theology and care, religions leadership; theology (M Div, MTS, D Min, PhD), including Biblical studies (PhD), religion and psychological studies (PhD), religion and social change (PhD), theology, philosophy and culture (PhD); theology/ethics (MA). PhD offered jointly with University of Denver. *Accreditation:* ACIPE; ATS. *Program availability:* Part-time, evening/weekend. *Degree requirements:* For master's, one foreign language, thesis (for some programs); for doctorate, 2 foreign languages, comprehensive exam, thesis/dissertation. *Entrance requirements:* For master's, minimum GPA of 3.0, writing sample, references; for doctorate, GRE General Test, minimum GPA of 3.0, writing sample, letters of recommendation. Additional exam requirements/recommendations for international students: Required—TOEFL (minimum score 550 paper-based). Electronic applications accepted. *Faculty research:* Pastoral care, history, church music, contemporary church, biblical studies.

Indiana University Bloomington, University Graduate School, College of Arts and Sciences, Department of Religious Studies, Bloomington, IN 47405-7005. Offers MA, PhD. *Program availability:* Part-time. Terminal master's awarded for partial completion of doctoral program. *Degree requirements:* For master's, one foreign language, thesis or alternative; for doctorate, 2 foreign languages, thesis/dissertation. *Entrance requirements:* For master's, GRE General Test; for doctorate, GRE, MA, writing sample. Additional exam requirements/recommendations for international students: Required—TOEFL. Electronic applications accepted. *Faculty research:* Ancient Mediterranean and near eastern religions; religions of Americas; Islamic studies; Buddhist studies; religion, literature, and cultural imagination.

The Jewish Theological Seminary, The Graduate School, New York, NY 10027-4649. Offers ancient Judaism (MA, DHL, PhD); Bible and ancient Semitic languages (MA, DHL, PhD); interdepartmental studies (MA); Jewish art and visual culture (MA); Jewish gender and women's studies (MA); Jewish history (MA, DHL, PhD); Jewish literature (MA, DHL, PhD); Jewish philosophy (DHL); Jewish thought (MA, PhD); liturgy (MA, DHL, PhD); medieval Jewish studies (MA, DHL, PhD); Midrash (DHL); Midrash and scriptural interpretation (MA, PhD); modern Jewish studies (MA, DHL, PhD); Talmud and rabbinics (MA, DHL, PhD); MA/MSW. MA/MSW offered jointly with Columbia University. *Accreditation:* ACIPE. *Program availability:* Part-time. Terminal master's awarded for partial completion of doctoral program. *Degree requirements:* For master's, one foreign language, comprehensive exam (for some programs), thesis (for some programs); for doctorate, 3 foreign languages, comprehensive exam (for some programs), thesis/dissertation. *Entrance requirements:* For master's, GRE or MAT, 3 letters of recommendation, writing sample; for doctorate, GRE or MAT, 3 letters of recommendation, writing research sample. Additional exam requirements/recommendations for international students: Required—TOEFL.

John Carroll University, Graduate Studies, Department of Theology and Religious Studies, University Heights, OH 44118. Offers MA. *Program availability:* Part-time, evening/weekend. *Faculty:* 3 full-time (2 women). *Students:* 1 full-time (0 women), 8 part-time (4 women); includes 2 minority (1 Black or African American, non-Hispanic/Latino; 1 Hispanic/Latino). Average age 35. In 2017, 2 master's awarded. *Degree requirements:* For master's, comprehensive exam, research essay or thesis, foreign language proficiency. *Entrance requirements:* For master's, GRE General Test or MAT, minimum GPA of 2.5. Additional exam requirements/recommendations for international students: Required—TOEFL. *Application deadline:* For fall admission, 8/30 priority date for domestic students; for spring admission, 1/11 priority date for domestic students. Applications are processed on a rolling basis. Application fee: $25 ($35 for international students). Electronic applications accepted. *Expenses: Tuition:* Full-time $16,238; part-time $788 per credit hour. One-time fee: $200. Part-time tuition and fees vary according to course load and program. *Financial support:* Teaching assistantships with full tuition reimbursements, scholarships/grants, tuition waivers (partial), and unspecified assistantships available. Support available to part-time students. Financial award application deadline: 3/1; financial award applicants required to submit FAFSA. *Faculty research:* Ethics, women's studies, contemporary theology, Bible studies, Latin American theology. *Unit head:* Dr. Sheila E. McGinn, Chair, 216-397-4700, Fax: 216-397-4518, E-mail: trs@jcu.edu. *Application contact:* Jennifer L. Tucker, Records Management Assistant, 216-397-1925, Fax: 216-397-1835, E-mail: jtucker@jcu.edu. Website: http://www.jcu.edu/religion/Gr_prog.htm

Kentucky Christian University, Graduate School, Grayson, KY 41143-2205. Offers Biblical studies (MA); Christian leadership (MA). *Program availability:* Part-time. *Degree requirements:* For master's, comprehensive exam (for some programs), thesis optional. *Entrance requirements:* For master's, minimum cumulative GPA of 2.75 in major or 2.5 overall; 6 additional hours in Bible (for non-Biblical undergraduate majors). Additional exam requirements/recommendations for international students: Required—TOEFL (minimum score 550 paper-based). Electronic applications accepted.

Knox Theological Seminary, Graduate Programs, Master of Arts Programs, Fort Lauderdale, FL 33308. Offers Biblical and theological studies (MA); Christian and classical studies (MA). *Accreditation:* ATS. *Program availability:* Part-time, evening/weekend. *Entrance requirements:* Additional exam requirements/recommendations for international students: Required—TOEFL (minimum score 520 paper-based; 83 iBT), TWE (minimum score 5).

Lancaster Theological Seminary, Graduate and Professional Programs, Lancaster, PA 17603-2812. Offers biblical studies (MAR); Christian education (MAR); Christianity and the arts (MAR); church history (MAR); congregational life (MAR); lay leadership (Certificate); theological studies (M Div); theology (D Min); theology and ethics (MAR). *Accreditation:* ACIPE; ATS. *Degree requirements:* For doctorate, thesis/dissertation.

Religion

La Sierra University, School of Religion, Riverside, CA 92505. Offers pastoral ministry (M Div); religion (MA); religious education (MA); religious studies (MA). *Program availability:* Part-time. *Degree requirements:* For master's, one foreign language, thesis or alternative. *Entrance requirements:* For master's, GRE General Test, minimum GPA of 3.0.

Lee University, Programs in Religion, Cleveland, TN 37320-3450. Offers biblical studies (MA); ministry studies/leadership (MA); ministry studies/worship (MA); ministry studies/youth and family (MA); theological studies (MA), including ethics, religion. *Program availability:* Part-time, 100% online. *Faculty:* 9 full-time (3 women), 3 part-time/adjunct (0 women). *Students:* 62 full-time (16 women), 99 part-time (36 women); includes 68 minority (9 Black or African American, non-Hispanic/Latino; 1 Asian, non-Hispanic/Latino; 57 Hispanic/Latino; 1 Two or more races, non-Hispanic/Latino), 6 international. Average age 37. 21 applicants, 86% accepted, 8 enrolled. In 2017, 13 master's awarded. *Degree requirements:* For master's, variable foreign language requirement, comprehensive exam (for some programs), thesis (for some programs). *Entrance requirements:* For master's, GRE or MAT (for biblical/theological studies only), minimum GPA of 3.0, 3 letters of recommendation, interview, official transcripts, essay. Additional exam requirements/recommendations for international students: Required—TOEFL (minimum score 61 iBT). *Application deadline:* For fall admission, 4/1 priority date for domestic and international students; for spring admission, 10/1 priority date for domestic and international students. Applications are processed on a rolling basis. Application fee: $25. Electronic applications accepted. *Expenses:* Contact institution. *Financial support:* In 2017–18, 34 students received support, including 12 teaching assistantships (averaging $1,886 per year); career-related internships or fieldwork, Federal Work-Study, institutionally sponsored loans, scholarships/grants, and unspecified assistantships also available. Financial award application deadline: 3/1; financial award applicants required to submit FAFSA. *Faculty research:* Spiritual and discipleship formation, leadership, Biblical studies, theological studies, ethics. *Unit head:* Dr. Lisa Long, Director, 423-303-5100, E-mail: llong@leeuniversity.edu. Website: http://www.leeuniversity.edu/academics/graduate/

Liberty University, School of Divinity, Lynchburg, VA 24515. Offers Biblical exposition (MA); Biblical languages (M Div); Biblical studies (M Div, MA, MAR, Th M, D Min); chaplaincy (M Div, D Min); Christian apologetics (M Div, MA, MAR, Th M); Christian leadership and church ministries (M Div); Christian ministries (M Div); Christian ministry (MA); Christian thought (M Div); church history (M Div, MAR, Th M); community chaplaincy (M Div, MAR); discipleship (D Min); discipleship and church ministry (M Div, MAR, MCM); evangelism and church planting (MAR, MCM, D Min); expository preaching (D Min); global ministry (MA); global studies (M Div, MAR, MCM, MGS, Th M); healthcare chaplaincy (M Div); homiletics (M Div, MAR, Th M); leadership (M Div, MAR); marketplace chaplaincy (M Div, MCM); ministry leadership (Ed D); pastoral counseling (M Div, MA, MAR, D Min), including addictions and recovery (MA), crisis response and trauma (MA), discipleship and church ministries (MA), leadership (MA), life coaching (MA), marketplace chaplaincy (MA), marriage and family (MA), military resilience (MA), pastoral counseling (MA); pastoral leadership (D Min); pastoral ministries (M Div, M Serv Soc, MCM); religious education (MRE); sports chaplaincy (MA); theology (M Div, MAR, MTS, Th M); theology and apologetics (D Min, PhD); worship (M Div, MAR, MCM, D Min); youth and family ministries (M Div). *Program availability:* Part-time, online learning. *Students:* 2,140 full-time (615 women), 3,020 part-time (906 women); includes 1,312 minority (1,016 Black or African American, non-Hispanic/Latino; 9 American Indian or Alaska Native, non-Hispanic/Latino; 100 Asian, non-Hispanic/Latino; 90 Hispanic/Latino; 7 Native Hawaiian or other Pacific Islander, non-Hispanic/Latino; 90 Two or more races, non-Hispanic/Latino), 158 international. Average age 42. 4,673 applicants, 33% accepted, 977 enrolled. In 2017, 904 master's, 54 doctorates awarded. *Degree requirements:* For master's, 2 foreign languages, thesis (for some programs); for doctorate, 2 foreign languages, thesis/dissertation. *Entrance requirements:* For master's, minimum undergraduate GPA of 2.0; for doctorate, GRE General Test or MAT, minimum graduate GPA of 3.0. Additional exam requirements/recommendations for international students: Required—TOEFL (minimum score 600 paper-based; 100 iBT). *Application deadline:* For fall admission, 6/1 for domestic students; for spring admission, 11/1 for domestic students. Applications are processed on a rolling basis. Application fee: $50. Electronic applications accepted. *Expenses:* Contact institution. *Financial support:* Teaching assistantships with tuition reimbursements, career-related internships or fieldwork, and Federal Work-Study available. Financial award applicants required to submit FAFSA. *Unit head:* Dr. Ed Hindson, Dean, 434-592-4140, Fax: 434-522-0415, E-mail: ehindson@liberty.edu. *Application contact:* Jay Bridge, Director of Graduate Admissions, 800-424-9595, Fax: 800-628-7977, E-mail: gradadmissions@liberty.edu. Website: https://www.liberty.edu/divinity/

Lincoln Christian University, Graduate Programs, Lincoln, IL 62656-2167. Offers Bible and theology (MA); Biblical studies (MA); church history/historical theology (MA); counseling (MA); formative worship (MA); intercultural studies (MA); ministry (MA); organizational leadership (MA); philosophy and apologetics (MA); spiritual formation (MA); theology (MA). MA in spiritual formation offered in Normal, IL. *Program availability:* Online learning. *Faculty:* 21 full-time (3 women), 29 part-time/adjunct (7 women). *Students:* 97 full-time (42 women), 226 part-time (81 women). Average age 39. *Entrance requirements:* For master's, minimum cumulative GPA of 2.5 in undergraduate degree studies. Additional exam requirements/recommendations for international students: Required—TOEFL (minimum score 550 paper-based); Recommended—IELTS (minimum score 6). *Application deadline:* For fall admission, 8/1 for domestic students, 3/1 for international students; for spring admission, 11/15 for domestic students, 11/1 for international students. Application fee: $25 ($50 for international students). Application fee is waived when completed online. *Expenses:* Tuition: Full-time $7920; part-time $5280 per credit hour. *Required fees:* $150; $150 per course. *Financial support:* Applicants required to submit FAFSA. *Application contact:* Lindsey Clark, Associate Director of Graduate Enrollment, 217-732-3168 Ext. 2398, E-mail: lclark@lincolnchristian.edu. Website: https://lincolnchristian.edu/academics/programs/masters/

Loma Linda University, School of Religion, Program in Religion and Society, Loma Linda, CA 92350. Offers MA. *Degree requirements:* For master's, comprehensive exam, thesis optional. *Entrance requirements:* Additional exam requirements/recommendations for international students: Required—TOEFL. Electronic applications accepted.

Louisville Presbyterian Theological Seminary, Graduate and Professional Programs, Louisville, KY 40205-1798. Offers Bible (MAR); divinity (M Div); ministry (D Min); religious thought (MAR); JD/M Div; M Div/MBA; M Div/MSSW. JD/M Div, M Div/MBA, and M Div/MSSW offered jointly with University of Louisville. *Accreditation:* AAMFT/COAMFTE (one or more programs are accredited); ACIPE; ATS (one or more programs are accredited). *Program availability:* Part-time. *Faculty:* 16 full-time (6 women), 14 part-time/adjunct (5 women). *Students:* 115 full-time (74 women), 37 part-time (20 women); includes 51 minority (41 Black or African American, non-Hispanic/Latino; 2 Asian, non-Hispanic/Latino; 7 Hispanic/Latino; 1 Native Hawaiian or other Pacific Islander, non-Hispanic/Latino), 1 international. Average age 41. In 2017, 32 master's, 6 doctorates awarded. *Degree requirements:* For master's, 2 foreign languages, thesis (for some

programs); for doctorate, thesis/dissertation. *Entrance requirements:* For doctorate, M Div. Additional exam requirements/recommendations for international students: Required—TOEFL (minimum score 550 paper-based). *Application deadline:* For fall admission, 6/1 priority date for domestic students, 2/1 priority date for international students; for spring admission, 11/1 priority date for domestic students. Applications are processed on a rolling basis. Application fee: $50. Electronic applications accepted. *Financial support:* Career-related internships or fieldwork, Federal Work-Study, institutionally sponsored loans, and scholarships/grants available. Financial award application deadline: 2/1. *Unit head:* Dr. Susan R. Garrett, Dean, 502-895-3411, Fax: 502-895-1096, E-mail: sgarrett@lpts.edu. *Application contact:* Rev. Emily Miller, Director of Admissions, 502-895-3411, Fax: 502-895-1096, E-mail: emiller@lpts.edu. Website: http://www.lpts.edu/

Lutheran Theological Seminary Saskatoon, Graduate and Professional Programs, Saskatoon, SK S7N 0X3, Canada. Offers Biblical studies (MTS); church history (MTS); ethics/church and society (MTS); history of Christianity (STM); New Testament (STM); Old Testament (STM); pastoral studies (STM); pastoral theology (MTS); systematic theology (MTS); systematic theology and philosophy of religion (STM); theology (M Div, D Div). STM programs offered jointly with College of Emmanuel and St. Chad and St. Andrew's College. *Accreditation:* ATS. *Program availability:* Part-time. *Degree requirements:* For master's, thesis.

Luther Rice College & Seminary, Graduate Programs, Lithonia, GA 30038-2454. Offers apologetics (MA); Bible languages (M Div); Biblical counseling (MA); Christian ministry (M Div, D Min); Christian studies (MA); leadership (MA). *Program availability:* Part-time, evening/weekend, online learning. *Degree requirements:* For doctorate, thesis/dissertation. *Entrance requirements:* For master's, bachelor's degree or equivalent; for doctorate, M Div. Additional exam requirements/recommendations for international students: Required—TOEFL (minimum score 550 paper-based). Electronic applications accepted.

Maranatha Baptist University, Master of Arts in English Bible Program, Watertown, WI 53094. Offers MA. *Program availability:* Part-time, 100% online. *Entrance requirements:* For master's, BA or BS.

McGill University, Faculty of Graduate and Postdoctoral Studies, Faculty of Religious Studies, Montréal, QC H3A 2T5, Canada. Offers MA, STM, PhD. *Accreditation:* ATS.

McMaster University, School of Graduate Studies, Faculty of Social Sciences, Department of Religious Studies, Hamilton, ON L8S 4M2, Canada. Offers MA, PhD. *Program availability:* Part-time. *Degree requirements:* For master's, one foreign language, thesis; for doctorate, 2 foreign languages, comprehensive exam, thesis/dissertation. *Entrance requirements:* For master's, minimum B+ average. Additional exam requirements/recommendations for international students: Required—TOEFL (minimum score 580 paper-based). *Faculty research:* Hellenistic Judaism, religious biographies in Asia, medieval India, synoptic gospels, ritual and belief systems.

Memorial University of Newfoundland, School of Graduate Studies, Department of Religious Studies, St. John's, NL A1C 5S7, Canada. Offers MA. *Program availability:* Part-time. *Degree requirements:* For master's, one foreign language, thesis. *Entrance requirements:* For master's, honors degree in religious studies or equivalent. Electronic applications accepted. *Faculty research:* Biblical studies, Christian thought and history, world religions, ethics, contemporary spirituality.

Milligan College, Emmanuel Christian Seminary at Milligan College, Milligan College, TN 37682. Offers Christian care and counseling (M Div); Christian education (M Div); Christian ministries (MACM, Graduate Certificate); Christian ministry (M Div); Christian theology (M Div, MAR); church history (MAR); church history/historical theology (M Div); general studies (M Div); ministry (D Min); New Testament (M Div, MAR); Old Testament (M Div, MAR); urban ministry (M Div); world missions (M Div). *Accreditation:* ACIPE; ATS. *Program availability:* Part-time, blended/hybrid learning. *Faculty:* 10 full-time (1 woman), 8 part-time/adjunct (0 women). *Students:* 52 full-time (23 women), 57 part-time (18 women); includes 11 minority (7 Black or African American, non-Hispanic/Latino; 1 Asian, non-Hispanic/Latino; 3 Hispanic/Latino), 7 international. Average age 35. 62 applicants, 89% accepted, 39 enrolled. In 2017, 19 master's, 3 doctorates awarded. *Degree requirements:* For master's, 2 foreign languages, thesis or alternative, portfolio; for doctorate, thesis/dissertation. *Entrance requirements:* For master's, undergraduate degree and supporting transcripts, essay/personal statement, professional recommendations, interview; for doctorate, M Div or equivalent, essay/personal statement, professional recommendations. Additional exam requirements/recommendations for international students: Required—TOEFL (minimum score 550 paper-based, 79 iBT) or IELTS (6.5). *Application deadline:* For fall admission, 8/1 for domestic students, 6/1 for international students; for spring admission, 12/15 for domestic students, 8/1 for international students. Applications are processed on a rolling basis. Application fee: $30 ($0 for international students). Electronic applications accepted. *Expenses:* Contact institution. *Financial support:* In 2017–18, 124 students received support. Scholarships/grants and unspecified assistantships available. Financial award application deadline: 12/1; financial award applicants required to submit FAFSA. *Faculty research:* Theology of Old Testament prophets; performance criticism of New Testament texts; practical theology and spiritual formation for Christian leaders; church history and missions; constructive theology, art and imagination. *Unit head:* Dr. Rollin Ramsaran, Academic Dean, Emmanuel Christian Seminary, 423-461-1524, Fax: 423-926-6198, E-mail: raramsaran@milligan.edu. *Application contact:* Lauren Gullett, Director of Admissions and Recruitment for Emmanuel Christian Seminary, 423-461-1535, Fax: 423-926-6198, E-mail: lwgullett@milligan.edu. Website: http://ecs.milligan.edu/

Missouri State University, Graduate College, College of Humanities and Public Affairs, Department of Religious Studies, Springfield, MO 65897. Offers MA, Certificate. *Program availability:* Part-time. *Faculty:* 11 full-time (3 women). *Students:* 7 full-time (2 women), 9 part-time (3 women); includes 1 minority (Hispanic/Latino). Average age 24. 7 applicants, 57% accepted, 4 enrolled. In 2017, 4 master's awarded. *Degree requirements:* For master's, one foreign language, comprehensive exam, thesis or alternative. *Entrance requirements:* For master's, GRE, minimum GPA of 3.2. Additional exam requirements/recommendations for international students: Required—TOEFL (minimum score 550 paper-based; 79 iBT), IELTS (minimum score 6). *Application deadline:* For fall admission, 7/20 priority date for domestic students, 5/1 for international students; for spring admission, 12/20 priority date for domestic students, 9/1 for international students. Applications are processed on a rolling basis. Application fee: $35 ($50 for international students). Electronic applications accepted. *Expenses:* Tuition, state resident: full-time $2915; part-time $2021 per credit hour. Tuition, nonresident: full-time $5354; part-time $3647 per credit hour. *International tuition:* $11,992 full-time. *Required fees:* $173; $173 per credit hour. Tuition and fees vary according to class time, course level, course load, degree level, campus/location and program. *Financial support:* Federal Work-Study, institutionally sponsored loans, scholarships/grants, and unspecified assistantships available. Financial award application deadline: 3/31; financial award applicants required to submit FAFSA. *Faculty research:* Apocalyptic literature, Protestantism in American society, contemporary Hinduism, Christian history. *Unit head:* Dr. Stephen Berkwitz, Department Head, 417-836-4147, Fax: 417-836-4757, E-mail: religiousstudies@missouristate.edu. *Application*

contact: Stephanie Praschan, Director, Graduate Enrollment Management, 417-836-5330, Fax: 417-836-6200, E-mail: stephaniepraschan@missouristate.edu.
Website: http://www.missouristate.edu/relst/

Moody Theological Seminary–Michigan, Graduate Programs, Plymouth, MI 48170. Offers Bible (Graduate Certificate); Christian education (MA); counseling psychology (MA); divinity (M Div); theological studies (MA). *Accreditation:* ATS. *Program availability:* Part-time, evening/weekend. *Degree requirements:* For master's, one foreign language, thesis. *Faculty research:* Judaism, cults, world religions.

Mount St. Joseph University, Graduate Program in Religious Studies, Cincinnati, OH 45233-1670. Offers religious studies (MA); spirituality and wellness (Certificate). *Program availability:* Part-time, evening/weekend. *Faculty:* 1 (woman) full-time. *Students:* 1 (woman) full-time, 8 part-time (7 women); includes 4 minority (3 Black or African American, non-Hispanic/Latino; 1 Hispanic/Latino). Average age 45. In 2017, 1 master's awarded. *Degree requirements:* For master's, comprehensive exam, 36 hours of credit, pastoral PRAXIS component (3 credit hours), integrating project (3 credit hours). *Entrance requirements:* For master's, undergraduate transcript with minimum overall GPA of 3.0, 3 letters of recommendation from professional colleagues, 3-page essay, interview with the Graduate Admissions Committee, current work resume. Additional exam requirements/recommendations for international students: Required—TOEFL (minimum score 560 paper-based; 83 iBT). *Application deadline:* Applications are processed on a rolling basis. Application fee: $50. Electronic applications accepted. *Expenses:* $600 per credit hour. *Financial support:* In 2017–18, 7 students received support. Scholarships/grants available. Financial award applicants required to submit FAFSA. *Faculty research:* Contextual/cultural/systematic theology, historical/spiritual theology, business/economics ethics, social justice, Biblical/cultural/pastoral theology. *Unit head:* Dr. John Trokan, Associate Professor of Religious and Pastoral Studies/ Director of Graduate Program, 513-244-4272, Fax: 513-244-4222, E-mail: john.trokan@msj.edu. *Application contact:* Mary Brigham, Assistant Director of Graduate Recruitment, 513-244-4233, Fax: 513-244-4629, E-mail: mary.brigham@msj.edu.
Website: http://www.msj.edu/academics/graduate-programs/religious-studies-programs/

Mount Saint Mary's University, Graduate Division, Los Angeles, CA 90049. Offers business administration (MBA); counseling psychology (MS); creative writing (MFA); education (MS, Certificate); film and television (MFA); health policy and management (MS); humanities (MA); nursing (MSN, Certificate); physical therapy (DPT); religious studies (MA). *Program availability:* Part-time, evening/weekend. *Faculty:* 50 full-time (35 women), 116 part-time/adjunct (81 women). *Students:* 670 full-time (518 women), 147 part-time (116 women); includes 414 minority (73 Black or African American, non-Hispanic/Latino; 4 American Indian or Alaska Native, non-Hispanic/Latino; 60 Asian, non-Hispanic/Latino; 259 Hispanic/Latino; 7 Native Hawaiian or other Pacific Islander, non-Hispanic/Latino; 11 Two or more races, non-Hispanic/Latino), 4 international. Average age 32. 1,398 applicants, 21% accepted, 242 enrolled. In 2017, 170 master's, 28 doctorates, 35 other advanced degrees awarded. *Entrance requirements:* Additional exam requirements/recommendations for international students: Required—TOEFL. *Application deadline:* For fall admission, 6/30 priority date for domestic and international students; for spring admission, 10/30 priority date for domestic and international students; for summer admission, 3/30 priority date for domestic and international students. Applications are processed on a rolling basis. Application fee: $50. Electronic applications accepted. *Expenses: Tuition:* Part-time $905 per unit. One-time fee: $155 part-time. Tuition and fees vary according to degree level and program. *Financial support:* Career-related internships or fieldwork, Federal Work-Study, institutionally sponsored loans, and tuition waivers (full and partial) available. Support available to part-time students. Financial award application deadline: 3/15; financial award applicants required to submit FAFSA. *Unit head:* Albert Ramos, Director of Graduate Admissions, 213-477-2800, E-mail: gradprograms@msmu.edu. *Application contact:* Shawn Peters, Graduate Admission Counselor, 213-477-2676, E-mail: gradprograms@msmu.edu.
Website: http://www.msmu.edu/graduate-programs/

Naropa University, Graduate Programs, Program in Religious Studies, Boulder, CO 80302-6697. Offers MA. *Faculty:* 8 full-time (4 women), 3 part-time/adjunct (1 woman). *Students:* 10 full-time (3 women), 4 part-time (3 women); includes 3 minority (1 American Indian or Alaska Native, non-Hispanic/Latino; 1 Hispanic/Latino; 1 Two or more races, non-Hispanic/Latino), 2 international. Average age 35. 3 applicants, 100% accepted, 1 enrolled. In 2017, 3 master's awarded. *Degree requirements:* For master's, comprehensive exam, thesis. *Entrance requirements:* For master's, interview; transcripts; letter of interest; resume/curriculum vitae with pertinent academic, employment and volunteer activity; 2 letters of recommendation. Additional exam requirements/recommendations for international students: Required—TOEFL (minimum score 550 paper-based; 80 iBT). *Application deadline:* For fall admission, 1/15 priority date for domestic and international students. Applications are processed on a rolling basis. Application fee: $60. Electronic applications accepted. *Expenses:* $995 per credit. *Financial support:* In 2017–18, 4 students received support. Research assistantships with partial tuition reimbursements available, teaching assistantships with partial tuition reimbursements available, career-related internships or fieldwork, Federal Work-Study, scholarships/grants, tuition waivers (partial), and unspecified assistantships available. Support available to part-time students. Financial award application deadline: 3/1; financial award applicants required to submit FAFSA. *Unit head:* Dr. Elaine Yuen, Chair, Department of Wisdom Traditions, 303-245-4718, E-mail: eyuen@naropa.edu. *Application contact:* Office of Admissions, 303-546-3572, Fax: 303-546-3583, E-mail: admissions@naropa.edu.
Website: http://www.naropa.edu/academics/masters/religious-studies/index.php

Naropa University, Graduate Programs, Program in Religious Studies with Language, Boulder, CO 80302-6697. Offers MA. Program allows for addition of two years of Sanskrit and/or Tibetan language. *Faculty:* 8 full-time (4 women), 3 part-time/adjunct (1 woman). *Students:* 13 full-time (2 women), 2 part-time (both women); includes 3 minority (all Hispanic/Latino), 1 international. Average age 30. 14 applicants, 93% accepted, 9 enrolled. In 2017, 5 master's awarded. *Degree requirements:* For master's, comprehensive exam, thesis. *Entrance requirements:* For master's, interview; transcripts; resume/curriculum vitae with pertinent academic, employment and volunteer activity; 2 letters of recommendation; letter of interest. Additional exam requirements/ recommendations for international students: Required—TOEFL (minimum score 550 paper-based; 80 iBT). *Application deadline:* For fall admission, 1/15 priority date for domestic and international students. Applications are processed on a rolling basis. Application fee: $60. Electronic applications accepted. *Expenses:* $995 per credit. *Financial support:* In 2017–18, 9 students received support, including 1 research assistantship with partial tuition reimbursement available (averaging $1,500 per year); teaching assistantships with partial tuition reimbursements available, career-related internships or fieldwork, Federal Work-Study, scholarships/grants, tuition waivers (partial), and unspecified assistantships also available. Support available to part-time students. Financial award application deadline: 3/1; financial award applicants required to submit FAFSA. *Unit head:* Dr. Elaine Yuen, Chair, Department of Wisdom Traditions, 303-245-4718, E-mail: eyuen@naropa.edu. *Application contact:* Office of Admissions, 303-546-3572, Fax: 303-546-3583, E-mail: admissions@naropa.edu.
Website: http://www.naropa.edu/academics/masters/religious-studies/index.php

Nashotah House Theological Seminary, Graduate Programs, Nashotah, WI 53058-9793. Offers Anglican studies (Certificate); Biblical studies (STM); Christian spirituality (STM); church history (STM); liturgy (STM); ministry (M Div, MM); pastoral ministry (MPM); theological studies (MTS); theology (STM, D Min). *Accreditation:* ACIPE; ATS (one or more programs are accredited). *Program availability:* Part-time. *Degree requirements:* For master's, thesis optional. *Entrance requirements:* For master's and Certificate, GRE General Test or MAT, interview, 3 recommendations. Additional exam requirements/recommendations for international students: Required—TOEFL. Electronic applications accepted. *Expenses:* Contact institution. *Faculty research:* Formation for parochial ministry, ancient Semitic epigraphy.

New Saint Andrews College, Graduate School, Moscow, ID 83843. Offers classical Christian studies (Graduate Certificate); creative writing (MFA); theology and letters (MA). *Program availability:* Part-time, blended/hybrid learning. *Faculty:* 12 part-time/ adjunct (0 women). *Students:* 12 full-time (3 women), 8 part-time (5 women), 1 international. Average age 25. 15 applicants, 53% accepted, 7 enrolled. In 2017, 3 master's awarded. *Degree requirements:* For master's, comprehensive exam (for some programs), thesis (for some programs), final oral exam. *Entrance requirements:* For master's, GRE, 2 letters of recommendation; for Graduate Certificate, GRE, bachelor's degree, essays, 2 letters of recommendation. *Application deadline:* For fall admission, 12/1 for domestic students. Applications are processed on a rolling basis. Application fee: $50. Electronic applications accepted. *Expenses: Tuition:* Full-time $7600; part-time $475 per credit. *Faculty research:* Hebrew, theology, literature. *Unit head:* Benjamin Merkle, President, 208-882-1566 Ext. 104, E-mail: bmerkle@nsa.edu. *Application contact:* Brenda Schlect, Director of Admissions, 208-882-1566 Ext. 113, Fax: 208-882-4293, E-mail: admissions@nsa.edu.
Website: http://www.nsa.edu/academics/graduate-school/

New York University, Graduate School of Arts and Science, Draper Interdisciplinary Program in Humanities and Social Thought, New York, NY 10012-1019. Offers humanities and social thought (MA); religion (Advanced Certificate); social theory (Advanced Certificate). *Program availability:* Part-time. *Students:* Average age 29. 118 applicants, 67% accepted, 38 enrolled. In 2017, 50 master's awarded. *Degree requirements:* For master's, thesis, comprehensive exam or essay. *Entrance requirements:* For master's, GRE General Test; for Advanced Certificate, master's degree. Additional exam requirements/recommendations for international students: Required—TOEFL. *Application deadline:* For fall admission, 7/1 for domestic and international students; for spring admission, 12/1 for domestic and international students. Applications are processed on a rolling basis. Application fee: $100. *Expenses: Tuition:* Full-time $41,352; part-time $19,968 per year. *Required fees:* $2496; $1628 per unit. $814 per term. Tuition and fees vary according to course load and program. *Financial support:* Teaching assistantships, Federal Work-Study, institutionally sponsored loans, and tuition waivers (partial) available. Financial award application deadline: 7/1; financial award applicants required to submit FAFSA. *Faculty research:* Art world, gender politics, global histories, literary cultures, the city. *Unit head:* Robin Nagle, Director, 212-998-8070, Fax: 212-995-4691, E-mail: draper.program@nyu.edu. *Application contact:* Robert Dimit, Director of Graduate Studies, 212-998-8070, Fax: 212-995-4691, E-mail: draper.program@nyu.edu.
Website: http://www.nyu.edu/gsas/dept/draper/

New York University, Graduate School of Arts and Science, Program in Religious Studies, New York, NY 10012-1019. Offers MA. *Program availability:* Part-time. *Students:* Average age 25. 14 applicants, 57% accepted, 2 enrolled. In 2017, 3 master's awarded. *Degree requirements:* For master's, one foreign language, thesis. *Entrance requirements:* For master's, GRE General Test. Additional exam requirements/ recommendations for international students: Required—TOEFL. *Application deadline:* For fall admission, 1/4 priority date for domestic students, 1/4 for international students. Application fee: $100. *Expenses: Tuition:* Full-time $41,352; part-time $19,968 per year. *Required fees:* $2496; $1628 per unit. $814 per term. Tuition and fees vary according to course load and program. *Financial support:* Teaching assistantships, Federal Work-Study, and institutionally sponsored loans available. Financial award application deadline: 1/4; financial award applicants required to submit FAFSA. *Faculty research:* Biblical and rabbinic Judaism, New Testament and early Christianity, comparative mysticism, gender and embodiment, East Asian religions. *Unit head:* Adam Becker, Director of Graduate Studies, 212-998-3756, Fax: 212-995-4827, E-mail: religious.studies@nyu.edu. *Application contact:* Janine Paolucci, Program Administrator, 212-998-3756, Fax: 212-995-4827, E-mail: religious.studies@nyu.edu.
Website: http://religiousstudies.as.nyu.edu/page/home

Northern Seminary, Graduate and Professional Programs, Lombard, IL 60148-5698. Offers Biblical studies (M Div); Christian community development (MA, D Min); Christian ministry (MACM); contextual theology (D Min); missional church ministry (M Div); New Testament (M Div, MANT); New Testament context (D Min); Old Testament (M Div); preaching (D Min); theology (M Div); theology and mission (MA); urban leadership (MA); worship (M Div, MAW). *Program availability:* Part-time, evening/weekend. *Faculty:* 6 full-time (1 woman), 33 part-time/adjunct (8 women). *Students:* 208 full-time (62 women); includes 89 minority (73 Black or African American, non-Hispanic/Latino; 6 Asian, non-Hispanic/Latino; 8 Hispanic/Latino; 2 Two or more races, non-Hispanic/Latino), 3 international. Average age 44. *Degree requirements:* For master's, thesis (for some programs); for doctorate, thesis/dissertation. *Entrance requirements:* For master's, writing test, all official transcripts, letter of reference from church, 3 letters of reference, autobiographical statement (400 words or more); for doctorate, M Div, 3 years in the ministry post-M Div, 3 letters of reference. Additional exam requirements/ recommendations for international students: Required—TOEFL (minimum score 550 paper-based). *Application deadline:* Applications are processed on a rolling basis. Application fee: $35. Electronic applications accepted. *Expenses: Tuition:* Full-time $14,253; part-time $9627 per credit. *Required fees:* $125 per quarter. *Financial support:* Teaching assistantships with partial tuition reimbursements, Federal Work-Study, and scholarships/grants available. Support available to part-time students. Financial award application deadline: 9/1; financial award applicants required to submit FAFSA. *Faculty research:* Theology and mission, worship studies, church history, evangelism, Christian ministry, urban leadership, New Testament. *Unit head:* Dr. William Shiell, President, 630-620-2101, Fax: 630-620-2190. *Application contact:* Greg Armstrong, Director of Admissions, 630-620-2175, Fax: 630-620-2190, E-mail: admissions@seminary.edu.

Northwestern University, The Graduate School, Judd A. and Marjorie Weinberg College of Arts and Sciences, Department of Religious Studies, Evanston, IL 60208. Offers PhD.

Northwestern University, School of Professional Studies, Program in Liberal Studies, Evanston, IL 60208. Offers American studies (MA); history (MA); religious and ethical studies (MA). *Program availability:* Part-time, evening/weekend.
Website: https://sps.northwestern.edu/masters/liberal-studies/index.php

Northwest Nazarene University, Program in Religion, Nampa, ID 83686-5897. Offers missional leadership (M Div, MA); pastoral ministry (MA); spiritual formation (M Div, MA); youth, children, and family ministry (M Div, MA). *Program availability:* Part-time,

online only, 100% online. *Students:* Average age 39. 37 applicants, 76% accepted, 24 enrolled. In 2017, 40 master's awarded. *Entrance requirements:* For master's, minimum GPA of 2.5; 8 semester or 12 quarter credits of Bible, theology and/or Western philosophy. Additional exam requirements/recommendations for international students: Required—TOEFL (minimum score 85 iBT). *Application deadline:* For fall admission, 7/31 for domestic students, 7/1 for international students; for spring admission, 2/1 for domestic students, 1/5 for international students. Applications are processed on a rolling basis. Application fee: $50. Electronic applications accepted. *Expenses:* Contact institution. *Financial support:* In 2017–18, 3 students received support. Scholarships/grants available. *Unit head:* Dr. Jay Akkerman, Director, Graduate Studies, 208-467-8437, Fax: 208-467-8252. *Application contact:* Vicki Funk, Program Coordinator, 208-467-8432, Fax: 208-467-8252, E-mail: vlfunk@nnu.edu. Website: http://www.nnu.edu/ministry/

Nyack College, College of Bible and Christian Ministry, Nyack, NY 10960. Offers ancient Judaism and Christian origins (MA). *Program availability:* Part-time, evening/weekend, 100% online, blended/hybrid learning. *Students:* 1 (woman) full-time, 7 part-time (1 woman); includes 5 minority (2 Black or African American, non-Hispanic/Latino; 1 American Indian or Alaska Native, non-Hispanic/Latino; 2 Hispanic/Latino). Average age 46. In 2017, 2 master's awarded. *Degree requirements:* For master's, 2 foreign languages, comprehensive exam. *Entrance requirements:* For master's, GRE, proficiency exam in Biblical Hebrew, essay, Christian experience statement, pastoral reference, academic references, writing sample. Additional exam requirements/recommendations for international students: Required—TOEFL (minimum score 550 paper-based; 80 iBT). *Application deadline:* Applications are processed on a rolling basis. Application fee: $30. Electronic applications accepted. *Expenses:* $585 per credit. *Financial support:* Applicants required to submit FAFSA. *Unit head:* Dr. Steven Notley, Director, 646-378-6148, E-mail: steven.notley@nyack.edu. *Application contact:* 646-378-6113, E-mail: admissions.grad@nyack.edu.

Oblate School of Theology, Graduate and Professional Programs, San Antonio, TX 78216-6693. Offers African-American pastoral leadership (D Min); divinity (M Div); pastoral leadership (D Min); pastoral ministry (MAP Min); pastoral studies (Certificate); spiritual formation in the local community (D Min); spirituality (MA Sp, PhD); spirituality and ministry (D Min); theology (MA Th); U.S. Hispanic/Latino ministry (D Min); M Div/MA Th. *Accreditation:* ACIPE; ATS (one or more programs are accredited). *Program availability:* Part-time, 100% online, blended/hybrid learning. *Faculty:* 21 full-time (5 women), 4 part-time/adjunct (0 women). *Students:* 89 full-time (9 women), 54 part-time (31 women); includes 77 minority (11 Black or African American, non-Hispanic/Latino; 8 Asian, non-Hispanic/Latino; 57 Hispanic/Latino; 1 Two or more races, non-Hispanic/Latino), 24 international. Average age 39. In 2017, 24 master's, 1 doctorate awarded. *Degree requirements:* For master's, comprehensive exam (for some programs), thesis (for some programs), practicum; for doctorate, one foreign language, comprehensive exam, thesis/dissertation, paper, practicum. *Entrance requirements:* For master's, MAT, interview, prerequisite course work in theology or religious studies and philosophy, minimum GPA of 2.5; for doctorate, D Min, M Div, MA Th, MA Sp, MA PM. Additional exam requirements/recommendations for international students: Required—TOEFL (minimum score 71 iBT). *Application deadline:* For fall admission, 6/30 priority date for domestic and international students; for winter admission, 11/30 for domestic and international students; for spring admission, 11/30 for domestic and international students; for summer admission, 4/30 for domestic and international students. Applications are processed on a rolling basis. Application fee: $65. Electronic applications accepted. *Expenses:* $605.00 per credit hour (for master's degrees); $680 per credit hour (for doctoral degrees); $55 registration fee. *Financial support:* In 2017–18, 25 students received support. Scholarships/grants available. Support available to part-time students. Financial award application deadline: 8/15; financial award applicants required to submit FAFSA. *Unit head:* Dr. R. Scott Woodward, Academic Dean, 210-341-1366, Fax: 210-341-4519, E-mail: rsw@ost.edu. *Application contact:* Brenda Reyna, Registrar, 210-341-1366 Ext. 226, Fax: 210-341-4519, E-mail: registrar@ost.edu.

Olivet Nazarene University, Graduate School, Division of Religion, Bourbonnais, IL 60914. Offers biblical literature (MA); religion (MA); theology (MA). *Program availability:* Part-time. *Degree requirements:* For master's, thesis or alternative.

Oxford Graduate School, Graduate Programs, Dayton, TN 37321-6736. Offers family life education (M Litt); integration of religion and society (D Phil); organizational leadership (M Litt). *Entrance requirements:* For master's, official transcripts, three letters of recommendation, bachelor's degree or its equivalent, minimum undergraduate GPA of 3.0, minimum of 3 years of professional experience; for doctorate, official transcripts, three letters of recommendation, master's degree with minimum GPA of 3.0, minimum of 5 years of professional experience. *Expenses:* Contact institution.

Pacific School of Religion, Graduate and Professional Programs, Berkeley, CA 94709-1323. Offers M Div, MA, MTS, D Min, PhD, Th D, CAPS, CMS, CSS, CTS. MA, PhD, Th D offered jointly with Graduate Theological Union; D Min with Church Divinity School of the Pacific. *Accreditation:* ACIPE; ATS (one or more programs are accredited). *Program availability:* Part-time. *Degree requirements:* For master's, one foreign language, thesis (for some programs); for doctorate, thesis/dissertation. *Entrance requirements:* For master's, minimum GPA of 3.0; for doctorate, M Div, minimum GPA of 3.0 (D Min); for other advanced degree, M Div, minimum GPA of 3.0 (CAPS). Additional exam requirements/recommendations for international students: Required—TOEFL (minimum score 550 paper-based). Electronic applications accepted. *Faculty research:* Medical ethics, gay/lesbian studies in religion, Asian-American religion, race, culture and theology, theology in context.

Pepperdine University, Seaver College, Division of Religion, Malibu, CA 90263. Offers ministry (MS); religion (M Div, MA). *Program availability:* Part-time, evening/weekend. *Students:* 3 full-time (1 woman), 12 part-time (3 women); includes 5 minority (2 Black or African American, non-Hispanic/Latino; 1 Asian, non-Hispanic/Latino; 2 Hispanic/Latino). Average age 33. In 2017, 7 master's awarded. *Entrance requirements:* For master's, GRE General Test, letters of recommendation, writing sample. Additional exam requirements/recommendations for international students: Required—TOEFL. *Application deadline:* For fall admission, 2/1 priority date for domestic students. Applications are processed on a rolling basis. Application fee: $65. Electronic applications accepted. *Financial support:* Applicants required to submit FAFSA. *Unit head:* Dr. Timothy Willis, Chair/Professor, 310-506-4352, Fax: 310-506-7271, E-mail: timothy.willis@pepperdine.edu. *Application contact:* Hayley Wolf, Director of Admission, 310-506-4392, E-mail: hayley.wolf@pepperdine.edu. Website: http://seaver.pepperdine.edu/religion/graduate/mareligion/

Princeton Theological Seminary, Graduate and Professional Programs, Princeton, NJ 08542-0803. Offers M Div, MA, Th M, D Min, PhD. *Accreditation:* ACIPE; ATS. *Program availability:* Part-time. Terminal master's awarded for partial completion of doctoral program. *Degree requirements:* For doctorate, 2 foreign languages, thesis/dissertation, comprehensive exam (PhD), French and German. *Entrance requirements:* For doctorate, GRE General Test. Additional exam requirements/recommendations for international students: Required—TOEFL. Electronic applications accepted.

Princeton University, Graduate School, Department of Religion, Princeton, NJ 08544-1019. Offers PhD. *Degree requirements:* For doctorate, variable foreign language requirement, comprehensive exam, thesis/dissertation. *Entrance requirements:* For doctorate, GRE General Test. Additional exam requirements/recommendations for international students: Required—TOEFL (minimum score 600 paper-based). Electronic applications accepted.

Queen's University at Kingston, School of Graduate Studies, Faculty of Arts and Sciences, Department of Religious Studies, Kingston, ON K7L 3N6, Canada. Offers MA. *Degree requirements:* For master's, one foreign language, essay. *Entrance requirements:* For master's, honors BA in religious studies or equivalent. Additional exam requirements/recommendations for international students: Required—TOEFL (minimum score 600 paper-based). *Faculty research:* Modernity, culture, feminism, world religions, traditions.

Reformed Theological Seminary–Charlotte Campus, Graduate and Professional Programs, Charlotte, NC 28226-6318. Offers biblical studies (MA); ministry (D Min); pastoral ministry (M Div); theological studies (MA). *Program availability:* Part-time. *Degree requirements:* For master's, comprehensive exam; for doctorate, thesis/dissertation. *Entrance requirements:* For master's, minimum GPA of 2.6; for doctorate, minimum GPA of 3.0. Additional exam requirements/recommendations for international students: Required—TOEFL (minimum score 550 paper-based). Electronic applications accepted.

Reformed Theological Seminary–Houston Campus, Graduate Program, Houston, TX 77024. Offers MA. Electronic applications accepted.

Reformed Theological Seminary–Jackson Campus, Graduate and Professional Programs, Jackson, MS 39209-3004. Offers Bible, theology, and missions (Certificate); Biblical exegesis (M Div); biblical studies (MA); Christian education (MA); counseling (M Div); marriage and family therapy (MA); ministry (D Min); missions (M Div, MA, D Min); theological studies (MA). *Accreditation:* AAMFT/COAMFTE (one or more programs are accredited); ATS (one or more programs are accredited). *Degree requirements:* For master's, thesis (for some programs), fieldwork; for doctorate, 2 foreign languages, thesis/dissertation. *Entrance requirements:* For master's, minimum GPA of 2.6; for doctorate, minimum GPA of 3.0. Additional exam requirements/recommendations for international students: Required—TOEFL.

Reformed Theological Seminary–Washington D.C., Graduate and Professional Programs, McLean, VA 22102. Offers Bible (M Div); biblical studies (MA); practical theology (M Div); religion (MA); theology (M Div). *Program availability:* Part-time, evening/weekend. *Faculty:* 4 full-time (0 women), 8 part-time/adjunct (2 women). *Students:* 6 full-time (0 women), 124 part-time (17 women); includes 21 minority (5 Black or African American, non-Hispanic/Latino; 14 Asian, non-Hispanic/Latino; 2 Hispanic/Latino). Average age 35. 66 applicants, 95% accepted, 48 enrolled. In 2017, 15 master's awarded. *Degree requirements:* For master's, variable foreign language requirement, comprehensive exam (for some programs), integrative paper. *Entrance requirements:* For master's, minimum undergraduate GPA of 2.6. Additional exam requirements/recommendations for international students: Required—TOEFL (minimum score 550 paper-based), TWE. *Application deadline:* Applications are processed on a rolling basis. Application fee: $75. Electronic applications accepted. *Expenses:* $515 per credit hour. *Financial support:* In 2017–18, 128 students received support. Scholarships/grants and tuition waivers (partial) available. Support available to part-time students. Financial award application deadline: 7/15. *Faculty research:* Theology, Biblical studies, cultural studies. *Unit head:* Dr. John S. Redd, Jr., President, 703-448-3393 Ext. 5107, E-mail: sredd@rts.edu. *Application contact:* Timo Sazo, Director of Admissions, 703-448-3393 Ext. 5104, Fax: 571-297-8010, E-mail: tsazo@rts.edu. Website: http://www.rts.edu/

Regent University, Graduate School, Robertson School of Government, Virginia Beach, VA 23464. Offers government (MA), including American government, healthcare policy and ethics (MA, MPA), international relations, law and public policy, national security studies, political communication, political theory, religion and politics; national security studies (MA), including cybersecurity, homeland security, international security, Middle East politics; public administration (MPA), including emergency management and homeland security, federal government, general public administration, healthcare policy and ethics (MA, MPA), law, nonprofit administration and faith-based organizations, public leadership and management, servant leadership. *Program availability:* Part-time, evening/weekend, 100% online, blended/hybrid learning. *Faculty:* 8 full-time (1 woman), 20 part-time/adjunct (3 women). *Students:* 39 full-time (23 women), 137 part-time (78 women); includes 83 minority (49 Black or African American, non-Hispanic/Latino; 1 American Indian or Alaska Native, non-Hispanic/Latino; 7 Asian, non-Hispanic/Latino; 15 Hispanic/Latino; 11 Two or more races, non-Hispanic/Latino). Average age 35. 345 applicants, 31% accepted, 57 enrolled. In 2017, 38 master's awarded. *Degree requirements:* For master's, thesis optional, internship. *Entrance requirements:* For master's, GRE General Test or LSAT, personal essay, writing sample, resume, college transcripts. Additional exam requirements/recommendations for international students: Required—TOEFL (minimum score 577 paper-based). *Application deadline:* For fall admission, 5/1 priority date for domestic students; for spring admission, 11/1 priority date for domestic students. Applications are processed on a rolling basis. Application fee: $50. Electronic applications accepted. *Expenses:* $650 per credit; $300 technology fee per semester. *Financial support:* In 2017–18, 116 students received support. Career-related internships or fieldwork, scholarships/grants, and unspecified assistantships available. Support available to part-time students. *Faculty research:* International relations and politics, public administration, leadership and ethics, Biblical law, Constitutional law and Supreme Court. *Unit head:* Dr. Eric Patterson, Dean, 757-352-4616, Fax: 757-352-4735, E-mail: epatterson@regent.edu. *Application contact:* Heidi Cece, Assistant Vice President of Enrollment Management, 800-373-5504, Fax: 757-352-4381, E-mail: admissions@regent.edu. Website: https://www.regent.edu/robertson-school-of-government/

Regent University, Graduate School, School of Divinity, Virginia Beach, VA 23464-9800. Offers Christian spirituality and formation (MA); divinity (M Div), including Biblical studies (M Div, MTS, Th M, PhD), chaplain ministry, Christian theology (M Div, MTS, Th M, PhD), church and ministry (M Div, MA), history of Christianity (M Div, MTS, Th M, PhD), inter-cultural studies (M Div, MA), interdisciplinary studies (M Div, MA, MTS), marketplace ministry (M Div, MA), missional discipleship, practical healing ministry (M Div, MA), worship and media (M Div, MA); leadership and renewal (D Min), including Christian leadership and renewal, clinical pastoral education, community transformation, military ministry, ministry leadership coaching; practical theology (MA), including church and ministry (M Div, MA), cosmogony, inter-cultural studies (M Div, MA), interdisciplinary studies (M Div, MA, MTS), marketplace ministry (M Div, MA), practical healing ministry (M Div, MA), worship and media (M Div, MA); renewal theology (PhD), including Biblical studies (M Div, MTS, Th M, PhD), Christian theology (M Div, MTS, Th M, PhD), history of Christianity (M Div, MTS, Th M, PhD), practical theology; theological studies (MTS), including Biblical studies (M Div, MTS, Th M, PhD), Christian theology (M Div, MTS, Th M, PhD), history of Christianity (M Div, MTS, Th M, PhD), interdisciplinary studies (M Div, MA, MTS); theology (Th M), including Biblical studies (M Div, MTS, Th M, PhD), Christian theology (M Div, MTS, Th M, PhD), history of Christianity (M Div, MTS, Th M, PhD). *Accreditation:* ACIPE; ATS. *Program availability:*

Part-time, evening/weekend, 100% online, blended/hybrid learning. *Faculty:* 17 full-time (3 women), 66 part-time/adjunct (9 women). *Students:* 146 full-time (54 women), 917 part-time (404 women); includes 563 minority (470 Black or African American, non-Hispanic/Latino; 1 American Indian or Alaska Native, non-Hispanic/Latino; 17 Asian, non-Hispanic/Latino; 56 Hispanic/Latino; 1 Native Hawaiian or other Pacific Islander, non-Hispanic/Latino; 18 Two or more races, non-Hispanic/Latino), 27 international. Average age 44. 1,321 applicants, 39% accepted, 295 enrolled. In 2017, 146 master's, 25 doctorates awarded. *Degree requirements:* For master's, comprehensive exam, thesis or alternative, internship; for doctorate, thesis/dissertation or alternative. *Entrance requirements:* For master's, minimum undergraduate GPA of 2.75, writing sample, personal goal statement, college transcripts; for doctorate, GRE, minimum graduate GPA of 3.5 (PhD), 3.0 (D Min); clergy recommendations; writing sample; transcripts; resume; interview. Additional exam requirements/recommendations for international students: Required—TOEFL (minimum score 577 paper-based). *Application deadline:* For fall admission, 5/1 priority date for domestic students. Applications are processed on a rolling basis. Application fee: $50. Electronic applications accepted. *Expenses:* $495 per credit (master's); $595 per credit (D Min); $650 per credit (PhD); $300 per semester technology fee. *Financial support:* In 2017–18, 721 students received support. Career-related internships or fieldwork, scholarships/grants, and unspecified assistantships available. Support available to part-time students. *Faculty research:* Greek and Hebrew, theology, spiritual formation, global missions and world Christianity, women in ministry leadership. *Unit head:* Dr. Cornelius Bekker, Dean, 757-352-4401, Fax: 757-352-4597, E-mail: clbekker@regent.edu. *Application contact:* Heidi Cece, Assistant Vice President of Enrollment Management, 800-373-5504, Fax: 757-352-4381, E-mail: admissions@regent.edu.
Website: https://www.regent.edu/school-of-divinity/

Rice University, Graduate Programs, School of Humanities, Department of Religious Studies, Houston, TX 77251-1892. Offers African religions (PhD); African-American religions (PhD); contemplative studies (PhD); ghosticism, esotericism, mysticism (PhD); Islam (PhD); Jewish thought and philosophy (PhD); modern Christianity in thought and popular culture (PhD); psychology of religion (PhD); the Bible and beyond (PhD). *Degree requirements:* For doctorate, 2 foreign languages, comprehensive exam, thesis/dissertation. *Entrance requirements:* For doctorate, GRE, letters of recommendation, writing sample. Additional exam requirements/recommendations for international students: Required—TOEFL (minimum score 600 paper-based; 90 iBT). Electronic applications accepted. *Faculty research:* Origins and historical development of Islam, history of Christianity, the study of comparative religion, African-American religion, religion and culture.

The Robert E. Webber Institute for Worship Studies, Doctor of Worship Studies Program, Jacksonville, FL 32207. Offers DWS. *Degree requirements:* For doctorate, thesis/dissertation, practicum.

The Robert E. Webber Institute for Worship Studies, Master of Worship Studies Program, Jacksonville, FL 32207. Offers MWS. *Degree requirements:* For master's, internship.

Rutgers University–New Brunswick, Graduate School-New Brunswick, Department of Religion, Piscataway, NJ 08854-8097. Offers religious studies (MA, Graduate Certificate). *Entrance requirements:* For master's and Graduate Certificate, GRE, personal statement, two letters of recommendation, official transcripts. Electronic applications accepted.

Saint Charles Borromeo Seminary, Overbrook, Graduate and Professional Programs, Program of Catholic Studies, Wynnewood, PA 19096. Offers MA. *Program availability:* Part-time, evening/weekend. *Degree requirements:* For master's, comprehensive exam. *Entrance requirements:* For master's, 18 undergraduate credits in theology and/or philosophy or the equivalent. Additional exam requirements/recommendations for international students: Required—TOEFL.

Saint John's Seminary, Graduate Programs, Brighton, MA 02135. Offers M Div, MA Th, MAM.

St. Joseph's Seminary, Graduate and Professional Programs, Yonkers, NY 10704. Offers Catholic philosophical studies (MA); divinity (M Div); pastoral studies (MAPS); theology (MA). *Accreditation:* ATS. *Degree requirements:* For master's, one foreign language, thesis. *Entrance requirements:* For master's, 27 credits in philosophy and 9 in theology.

Saint Mary's University, Faculty of Arts, Department of Religious Studies, Halifax, NS B3H 3C3, Canada. Offers theology and religious studies (MA).

Salve Regina University, Program in Humanities, Newport, RI 02840-4192. Offers humanitarian assistance (MA); humanities (PhD); public humanities (MA); religion, peace and justice (MA). *Program availability:* Part-time, evening/weekend, online learning. *Degree requirements:* For master's, thesis optional; for doctorate, one foreign language, comprehensive exam, thesis/dissertation. *Entrance requirements:* For master's, GMAT, GRE General Test, or MAT; for doctorate, GRE General Test. Additional exam requirements/recommendations for international students: Required—TOEFL (minimum score 600 paper-based; 100 iBT) or IELTS. Electronic applications accepted.

Santa Clara University, Jesuit School of Theology, Berkeley, CA 94709. Offers Biblical studies (MTS); Christian spirituality (MTS); church history (MTS); cultural and historical studies of Catholicism (MTS); ethics and social theory/religion and society (MTS); history of art and religion (MTS); liturgical studies (MTS); systematic and philosophical theology (MTS); theology (M Div, Th M, STD, STB, STL); M Div/MA. MA programs offered jointly with Graduate Theological Union. *Program availability:* Part-time, evening/weekend, 100% online. *Faculty:* 19 full-time (5 women), 9 part-time/adjunct (5 women). *Students:* 120 full-time (26 women), 15 part-time (6 women); includes 78 minority (24 Black or African American, non-Hispanic/Latino; 2 American Indian or Alaska Native, non-Hispanic/Latino; 25 Asian, non-Hispanic/Latino; 20 Hispanic/Latino; 3 Native Hawaiian or other Pacific Islander, non-Hispanic/Latino; 4 Two or more races, non-Hispanic/Latino). Average age 38. 99 applicants, 96% accepted, 54 enrolled. In 2017, 52 master's, 9 doctorates awarded. *Entrance requirements:* For master's, GRE (except Th M), 2 letters of recommendation, resume or curriculum vitae, official transcripts, statement of purpose; for doctorate, master's degree or equivalent, resume or curriculum vitae, statement of purpose, official transcripts, 2 letters of recommendation, research paper. Additional exam requirements/recommendations for international students: Required—TOEFL (minimum score 90 iBT). *Application deadline:* For fall admission, 3/1 priority date for domestic students; for spring admission, 10/1 priority date for domestic students. Applications are processed on a rolling basis. Application fee: $50 ($0 for international students). Electronic applications accepted. *Expenses:* Contact institution. *Financial support:* Scholarships/grants and unspecified assistantships available. Support available to part-time students. Financial award application deadline: 3/1; financial award applicants required to submit FAFSA. *Faculty research:* Religion and culture, interreligious dialogue, social ethics and restorative justice, Ignatian spirituality. *Unit head:* Rev. Kevin O'Brien, Dean, 510-549-5040, E-mail: kfobrien@scu.edu. *Application contact:* Drew Roborts, Assistant Dean of Enrollment Management and Marketing, 510-549-5016, E-mail: ajroberts@scu.edu.
Website: http://www.scu.edu/jst/

Seattle Pacific University, Master of Arts in Theology Program, Seattle, WA 98119-1997. Offers Asian American ministry (MA); business and applied theology (MA); Christian leadership (MA); Christian scripture (MA); Christian studies (Graduate Certificate); reconciliation and intercultural studies (MA); theology (MA). *Students:* 25 full-time (13 women), 42 part-time (20 women); includes 11 minority (4 Black or African American, non-Hispanic/Latino; 4 Asian, non-Hispanic/Latino; 3 Two or more races, non-Hispanic/Latino), 2 international. Average age 34. 19 applicants, 79% accepted, 11 enrolled. In 2017, 4 master's awarded. *Degree requirements:* For master's, internship or thesis. *Entrance requirements:* For master's, two letters of recommendation; personal statement; bachelor's degree from regionally-accredited college or university or its equivalent; official copy of transcripts from college or university that granted the bachelor's degree and any institution attended since that time; minimum GPA of 3.0. Additional exam requirements/recommendations for international students: Required—TOEFL (minimum score 600 paper-based; 100 iBT). *Application deadline:* For fall admission, 7/31 for domestic students, 6/15 for international students; for winter admission, 11/15 for domestic students; for spring admission, 2/15 for domestic students; for summer admission, 5/1 for domestic students. Applications are processed on a rolling basis. Application fee: $50. Electronic applications accepted. *Financial support:* Application deadline: 4/1; applicants required to submit FAFSA. *Unit head:* Dr. Doug Strong, Dean, 206-281-2473, E-mail: dstrong@spu.edu.
Website: http://spu.edu/academics/school-of-theology/seattle-pacific-seminary/seminary-degrees/ma-theology

The Seattle School of Theology and Psychology, Graduate Programs, Seattle, WA 98121. Offers Christian studies (MA); counseling psychology (MA); divinity (M Div). *Program availability:* Part-time. *Entrance requirements:* For master's, MAT.

Selma University, Graduate Programs, Selma, AL 36701-5299. Offers Bible and Christian education (MA); Bible and pastoral ministry (MA).

Seminary of the Southwest, Graduate and Professional Programs, Austin, TX 78768-2247. Offers Anglican studies (Advanced Diploma); chaplaincy and pastoral care (MA); clinical mental health counseling (MA); Latino/Hispanic studies (M Div); ministry (M Div); religion (MAR); spiritual formation (MA). *Accreditation:* ACIPE; ATS (one or more programs are accredited). *Program availability:* Part-time, evening/weekend. *Faculty:* 10 full-time (5 women), 12 part-time/adjunct (5 women). *Students:* 60 full-time (31 women), 56 part-time (42 women); includes 22 minority (10 Black or African American, non-Hispanic/Latino; 1 American Indian or Alaska Native, non-Hispanic/Latino; 2 Asian, non-Hispanic/Latino; 6 Hispanic/Latino; 3 Two or more races, non-Hispanic/Latino). Average age 38. 49 applicants, 98% accepted, 31 enrolled. In 2017, 27 master's, 3 other advanced degrees awarded. *Degree requirements:* For master's, comprehensive exam (for some programs), thesis (for some programs). *Entrance requirements:* For master's, GRE, MAT, interview; for Advanced Diploma, interview. Additional exam requirements/recommendations for international students: Recommended—TOEFL. *Application deadline:* For fall admission, 6/30 priority date for domestic and international students; for spring admission, 12/1 for domestic and international students. Applications are processed on a rolling basis. Application fee: $50. Electronic applications accepted. *Expenses:* Contact institution. *Financial support:* In 2017–18, 92 students received support. Career-related internships or fieldwork and scholarships/grants available. Support available to part-time students. Financial award application deadline: 6/15; financial award applicants required to submit FAFSA. *Unit head:* Rev. Dr. Cynthia Briggs Kittredge, Dean and President, 512-472-4133 Ext. 332, Fax: 512-472-3098, E-mail: cynthia.kittredge@ssw.edu. *Application contact:* Hope Benko, Director of Enrollment Management, 512-472-4133 Ext. 375, Fax: 512-472-3098, E-mail: hope.benko@ssw.edu.

Seton Hall University, College of Arts and Sciences, Department of Religion, South Orange, NJ 07079-2697. Offers Jewish-Christian studies (MA). *Program availability:* Part-time, evening/weekend. *Degree requirements:* For master's, thesis optional. *Entrance requirements:* For master's, interview or suitable correspondence with department chair. Additional exam requirements/recommendations for international students: Required—TOEFL. Electronic applications accepted. *Faculty research:* Jewish-Christian issues, Biblical studies, Holocaust studies.

Seton Hall University, Immaculate Conception Seminary School of Theology, South Orange, NJ 07079-2697. Offers Christian spirituality (Certificate); great spiritual books (Certificate); pastoral ministry (M Div, MA, Certificate); scripture studies (Certificate); Seminary's Theological Education for Parish Services (STEPS) (Certificate); theology (MA). *Program availability:* Part-time, evening/weekend. *Degree requirements:* For master's, comprehensive exam (for some programs), thesis (for some programs), final project (for some programs); 1 foreign language (for MA in theology research option). *Entrance requirements:* For master's, GRE General Test or MAT. Additional exam requirements/recommendations for international students: Required—TOEFL (minimum score 600 paper-based; 100 iBT). Electronic applications accepted. *Expenses:* Contact institution. *Faculty research:* Pauline literature, history of Biblical interpretation and theological exegesis, spirituality of St. Edith Stein, Thomism, history of Catholicism in America.

Sioux Falls Seminary, Graduate and Professional Programs, Program in Christian Leadership, Sioux Falls, SD 57105-1599. Offers MA. *Program availability:* Online learning.

Southern Adventist University, School of Religion, Collegedale, TN 37315-0370. Offers Biblical and theological studies (MA); church leadership and management (M Min); church ministry and homiletics (M Min); evangelism and world mission (M Min); religious studies (MA). *Program availability:* Part-time. *Degree requirements:* For master's, comprehensive exam, thesis (for some programs). *Entrance requirements:* For master's, GRE. Additional exam requirements/recommendations for international students: Required—TOEFL (minimum score 600 paper-based). *Application deadline:* For spring admission, 5/1 priority date for domestic students, 4/30 for international students. Applications are processed on a rolling basis. Application fee: $40. *Expenses:* *Tuition:* Full-time $11,430; part-time $635 per credit hour. Tuition and fees vary according to degree level and program. *Financial support:* Tuition waivers (full) available. Support available to part-time students. Financial award application deadline: 4/1; financial award applicants required to submit FAFSA. *Faculty research:* Biblical archaeology. *Unit head:* Dr. Greg A. King, Dean, 423-236-2975, Fax: 423-236-1976, E-mail: gking@southern.edu. *Application contact:* Susan L. Brown, Administrative Assistant, 423-236-2033, Fax: 423-236-1977, E-mail: sbrown@southern.edu.
Website: https://www.southern.edu/academics/academic-sites/religion/

The Southern Baptist Theological Seminary, School of Theology, Louisville, KY 40280-0004. Offers applied theology (D Min); biblical and theological studies (M Div); biblical counseling (M Div, MA, D Min); biblical spirituality (D Min); Christian ministry (M Div); expository preaching (D Min); pastoral studies (M Div); theological studies (MA); theology (Th M, PhD); worldview and apologetics (M Div). *Program availability:* Part-time, evening/weekend, online learning. *Degree requirements:* For master's, 2 foreign languages, thesis; for doctorate, 4 foreign languages, thesis/dissertation. *Entrance requirements:* For master's, GRE General Test, MAT, M Div; for doctorate, GRE General Test, MAT, interview, M Div, field essay. Additional exam requirements/recommendations for international students: Required—TOEFL, TWE. *Faculty research:* Biblical studies, contemporary theology, church history, pastoral care, ministry/missions studies.

Religion

Southern California Seminary, Graduate and Professional Programs, El Cajon, CA 92019. Offers Biblical studies (MABS); counseling psychology (MACP); marriage and family therapy (MAMFT); psychology (Psy D); religious studies (MRS); theology (M Div). *Program availability:* Part-time, evening/weekend, online learning. *Degree requirements:* For master's, thesis (for some programs); for doctorate, thesis/dissertation. *Entrance requirements:* For doctorate, master's degree in psychology. Additional exam requirements/recommendations for international students: Required—TOEFL (minimum score 550 paper-based). Electronic applications accepted.

Southern Evangelical Seminary, Graduate Programs, Matthews, NC 28105. Offers apologetics (MA, D Min, Certificate); Christian education (MA); church ministry (MA, Certificate); divinity (Certificate), including apologetics (M Div, Certificate); Islamic studies (MA, Certificate); Jewish studies (MA); philosophy (MA); philosophy of religion (PhD); religion (MA); theology (M Div), including apologetics (M Div, Certificate), Biblical studies; youth ministry (MA). *Program availability:* Part-time, evening/weekend, online learning. *Degree requirements:* For master's, thesis (for some programs); for doctorate, 2 foreign languages, comprehensive exam (for some programs), thesis/dissertation. *Entrance requirements:* Additional exam requirements/recommendations for international students: Required—TOEFL (minimum score 600 paper-based).

Southern Methodist University, Dedman College of Humanities and Sciences, Graduate Program in Religious Studies, Dallas, TX 75275-0133. Offers Hebrew Bible/Old Testament (PhD); history of the Christian tradition (PhD); New Testament (PhD); religion and culture (PhD); religious ethics (PhD); religious studies (MA); systematics theology (PhD). Terminal master's awarded for partial completion of doctoral program. *Degree requirements:* For master's, one foreign language, thesis, oral and written exams; for doctorate, variable foreign language requirement, thesis/dissertation, oral and written exams. *Entrance requirements:* For master's and doctorate, GRE General Test, minimum GPA of 3.0, course work in religion. Additional exam requirements/recommendations for international students: Required—TOEFL (minimum score 550 paper-based; 79 iBT). Electronic applications accepted. *Faculty research:* Theology, religious ethics, Biblical studies, history of Christianity, religion and culture.

Southwestern Assemblies of God University, Thomas F. Harrison School of Graduate Studies, Program in Theological Studies, Waxahachie, TX 75165-5735. Offers Bible and theology (MS); Biblical studies (M Div); counseling (M Div); cross cultural missions (M Div); practical theology (M Div); theological studies (M Div). *Program availability:* Online learning. *Degree requirements:* For master's, comprehensive written and oral exams. *Entrance requirements:* For master's, GRE General Test, minimum GPA of 2.5. Electronic applications accepted.

Stanford University, School of Humanities and Sciences, Department of Religious Studies, Stanford, CA 94305-2004. Offers PhD. Terminal master's awarded for partial completion of doctoral program. *Degree requirements:* For doctorate, 2 foreign languages, thesis/dissertation, qualifying exam. *Entrance requirements:* For doctorate, GRE General Test. Additional exam requirements/recommendations for international students: Required—TOEFL. Electronic applications accepted. *Expenses: Tuition:* Full-time $48,987; part-time $10,620 per quarter. One-time fee: $400. Tuition and fees vary according to program.

SUM Bible College & Theological Seminary, Graduate Programs, Oakland, CA 94603. Offers biblical studies (MA); Christian leadership (MA); theology (M Div). *Entrance requirements:* For master's, minimum GPA of 2.5, currently active in ministry.

Syracuse University, College of Arts and Sciences, Department of Religion, Syracuse, NY 13207. Offers MA, PhD. *Students:* Average age 33. Terminal master's awarded for partial completion of doctoral program. *Degree requirements:* For master's, one foreign language, comprehensive exam, thesis optional; for doctorate, 2 foreign languages, comprehensive exam, thesis/dissertation. *Entrance requirements:* For master's and doctorate, GRE General Test, transcripts from all previous institutions; three letters of recommendation; personal statement of not more than 1000 words, including choice of concentration and religious culture to study at SU. Additional exam requirements/recommendations for international students: Required—TOEFL (minimum score 100 iBT). *Application deadline:* For fall admission, 1/10 for domestic and international students. Application fee: $75. Electronic applications accepted. *Financial support:* Fellowships with full tuition reimbursements, teaching assistantships with tuition reimbursements, scholarships/grants, and tuition waivers available. Financial award application deadline: 1/10; financial award applicants required to submit FAFSA. *Faculty research:* Modern theology, religion and aesthetics, gender politics in Islam, global Hinduism, research and writing in religion and society. *Unit head:* Dr. Virginia Burrus, Professor/Director of Graduate Studies in Religion, 315-443-3861, E-mail: mvburrus@syr.edu. *Application contact:* Deborah Pratt, Recruiting Contact, 315-443-3863, E-mail: dpratt@syr.edu.
Website: http://religion.syr.edu/graduate-overview.html

Temple University, College of Liberal Arts, Department of Religion, Philadelphia, PA 19122-6096. Offers MA, PhD. *Program availability:* Part-time. *Faculty:* 13 full-time (5 women), 2 part-time/adjunct (1 woman). *Students:* 34 full-time (14 women), 7 part-time (2 women); includes 13 minority (6 Black or African American, non-Hispanic/Latino; 4 Asian, non-Hispanic/Latino; 3 Hispanic/Latino), 6 international. 19 applicants, 47% accepted, 5 enrolled. In 2017, 4 master's, 5 doctorates awarded. *Degree requirements:* For doctorate, variable foreign language requirement, thesis/dissertation. *Entrance requirements:* For master's and doctorate, GRE General Test, minimum GPA of 3.0, 3 letters of recommendation. Additional exam requirements/recommendations for international students: Required—TOEFL (minimum score 600 paper-based; 100 iBT). *Application deadline:* For fall admission, 1/15 for domestic students, 12/15 for international students. Application fee: $60. Electronic applications accepted. *Expenses:* Tuition, state resident: full-time $16,164; part-time $898 per credit hour. Tuition, nonresident: full-time $22,158; part-time $1231 per credit hour. *Required fees:* $890; $445 per semester. Full-time tuition and fees vary according to course load, degree level, campus/location and program. *Financial support:* Fellowships, teaching assistantships, Federal Work-Study, institutionally sponsored loans, and tuition waivers (full and partial) available. Financial award application deadline: 1/15; financial award applicants required to submit FAFSA. *Faculty research:* Buddhism, gender/sexuality, Hebrew Bible, Islam, world religions. *Unit head:* Dr. Jeremy Schipper, Graduate Director, 215-204-7252, E-mail: jeremy.schipper@temple.edu. *Application contact:* Linda Jenkins, Coordinator, 215-204-7973, Fax: 215-204-2535, E-mail: jenkinsl@temple.edu.
Website: http://www.cla.temple.edu/religion/

Trevecca Nazarene University, Graduate Religion Programs, Nashville, TN 37210-2877. Offers biblical and theological studies (MA); Christian ministry (MA); pastoral counseling (MA). *Program availability:* Part-time, online learning. *Faculty:* 10 full-time (2 women), 7 part-time/adjunct (0 women). *Students:* 74 full-time (40 women), 22 part-time (13 women); includes 38 minority (26 Black or African American, non-Hispanic/Latino; 1 American Indian or Alaska Native, non-Hispanic/Latino; 1 Asian, non-Hispanic/Latino; 7 Hispanic/Latino; 3 Two or more races, non-Hispanic/Latino), 1 international. Average age 41. In 2017, 22 master's awarded. *Degree requirements:* For master's, research project. *Entrance requirements:* For master's, minimum GPA of 2.7, official transcript from regionally accredited institution, letter of recommendation. Additional exam requirements/recommendations for international students: Required—TOEFL (minimum

score 550 paper-based; 80 iBT). *Application deadline:* Applications are processed on a rolling basis. Application fee: $0. Electronic applications accepted. *Expenses:* $350 per credit hour. *Financial support:* Applicants required to submit FAFSA. *Unit head:* Dr. Tim Green, Dean, School of Theology and Christian Ministry/Director, Graduate Religion Program, 615-248-1378, Fax: 615-248-7417. *Application contact:* 844-TNU-GRAD, E-mail: sgcsadmissions@trevecca.edu.
Website: http://www.trevecca.edu/gradreligion

Trinity Baptist College, Graduate Programs, Jacksonville, FL 32221. Offers Bible (MA); curriculum and instruction (M Ed); educational leadership (M Ed); special education (M Ed). *Program availability:* Online learning. *Faculty:* 6 full-time (1 woman), 5 part-time/adjunct (1 woman). *Students:* 13 part-time (5 women). *Entrance requirements:* For master's, GRE (for M Ed), 2 letters of recommendation; minimum GPA of 2.5 (for M Min), 3.0 (for M Ed); goals essay; official transcripts. Application fee: $45. *Expenses: Tuition:* Part-time $295 per hour. *Required fees:* $50 per term. One-time fee: $45 part-time. *Unit head:* Dr. Matthew Beemer, Senior Vice President, 904-596-2400, Fax: 904-596-2531, E-mail: mbeemer@tbc.edu.

Trinity International University Florida, Divinity School, Davie, FL 33324. Offers MA, Certificate.

Trinity School for Ministry, Graduate Programs, Ambridge, PA 15003-2397. Offers Anglican studies (Diploma); basic Christian studies (Diploma); divinity (M Div); ministry (D Min); mission and evangelism (MAME, Diploma); religion (MAR); youth ministry (Diploma). *Program availability:* Part-time. *Degree requirements:* For master's, thesis optional; for doctorate, thesis/dissertation. *Entrance requirements:* Additional exam requirements/recommendations for international students: Required—TOEFL. *Faculty research:* Pauline Epistles, contemporary theology, history of Anglican liturgy, book of Ruth, biblical theology.

Union University, School of Theology and Missions, Jackson, TN 38305-3697. Offers Christian studies (MCS); expository preaching (D Min). *Program availability:* Part-time, evening/weekend, online learning. Electronic applications accepted.

United Lutheran Seminary, Graduate and Professional Programs, Gettysburg, PA 17325-1795. Offers divinity (M Div); ministerial studies (MAMS); outdoor ministry (MAR); parish ministry (D Min); theology (STM). *Accreditation:* ACIPE; ATS (one or more programs are accredited). *Program availability:* Part-time, online learning. *Degree requirements:* For master's, thesis (for some programs). Electronic applications accepted.

United Lutheran Seminary, Graduate School, Philadelphia, PA 19119-1794. Offers divinity (M Div); ministry (D Min); public leadership (MA); religion (MAR); social ministry and church (Certificate); theology (STM, PhD). *Accreditation:* ACIPE. *Program availability:* Part-time, evening/weekend. *Degree requirements:* For master's, one foreign language, comprehensive exam (for some programs), thesis (for some programs); for doctorate, thesis/dissertation. *Entrance requirements:* For master's, minimum undergraduate GPA of 2.8; for doctorate, minimum GPA of 3.0. Additional exam requirements/recommendations for international students: Required—TOEFL (minimum score 550 paper-based; 89 iBT), TWE. Electronic applications accepted.

United Theological Seminary of the Twin Cities, Graduate Programs, New Brighton, MN 55112-2598. Offers advanced theological studies (Diploma); justice and peace studies (M Div, MA); leadership toward racial justice (M Div, MA, Certificate); Methodist studies (M Div, MA, Certificate); ministry (D Min); ministry renewal and professional development (Certificate); pastoral care and counseling (M Div, MA, MARL); religion and theology (MA); theological and religious studies (Certificate); theology and the arts (M Div, MA); urban ministry (M Div, MA, MARL); women's studies: religion, theology and ministry (M Div, MA). *Accreditation:* ACIPE; ATS. *Program availability:* Part-time, evening/weekend. *Degree requirements:* For master's, thesis; for doctorate, comprehensive exam, thesis/dissertation. *Entrance requirements:* For master's, minimum GPA of 2.75; strong analytical, reflective thinking and writing skills; vocational and academic goals compatible with those of Seminary; for doctorate, M Div or equivalent, minimum GPA of 3.0, 3 years experience in professional ministry; for other advanced degree, BA or equivalent life experience; strong analytical, reflective thinking and writing skills (Certificate); proficiency in English language, previous study of theology at a theological school, recommendation of student's denomination (Diploma). Additional exam requirements/recommendations for international students: Required—TOEFL (minimum score 550 paper-based).

Université de Montréal, Faculty of Theology and Sciences of Religions, Montréal, QC H3C 3J7, Canada. Offers health, spirituality and bioethics (DESS); practical theology (MA, PhD); religious sciences (MA, PhD); theology (MA, D Th, PhD, L Th); theology-Biblical studies (PhD). *Degree requirements:* For master's, one foreign language; for doctorate, 2 foreign languages, thesis/dissertation, general exam. Electronic applications accepted.

Université de Sherbrooke, Faculty of Theology and Religious Studies, Sherbrooke, QC J1K 2R1, Canada. Offers applied ethics (Diploma); human science of religions (MA); intercultural training (Diploma); philosophy (MA, PhD); spiritual anthropology (Diploma); theology (MA, PhD, Diploma). *Program availability:* Part-time, evening/weekend, online learning. Terminal master's awarded for partial completion of doctoral program. *Entrance requirements:* For master's, bachelor's degree in related discipline; for doctorate, master's degree in related discipline. *Faculty research:* Faith and culture interrelation.

Université du Québec à Montréal, Graduate Programs, Program in Religious Sciences, Montréal, QC H3C 3P8, Canada. Offers MA, PhD. MA offered jointly with Concordia University. *Program availability:* Part-time. *Degree requirements:* For master's, thesis; for doctorate, thesis/dissertation. *Entrance requirements:* For master's, appropriate bachelor's degree or equivalent, proficiency in French; for doctorate, appropriate master's degree or equivalent, proficiency in French.

Université Laval, Faculty of Theology and Religious Sciences, Programs in Human Sciences of Religion, Québec, QC G1K 7P4, Canada. Offers MA, PhD. Terminal master's awarded for partial completion of doctoral program. *Degree requirements:* For master's, thesis (for some programs); for doctorate, comprehensive exam, thesis/dissertation. *Entrance requirements:* For master's, knowledge of French, comprehension of a second language; for doctorate, knowledge of French and English. Electronic applications accepted.

The University of British Columbia, Faculty of Arts, Department of Classical, Near Eastern and Religious Studies, Program in Ancient Culture, Religion and Ethnicity, Vancouver, BC V6T 1Z1, Canada. Offers MA. *Degree requirements:* For master's, thesis.

The University of British Columbia, Faculty of Arts, Department of Classical, Near Eastern and Religious Studies, Program in Religious Studies, Vancouver, BC V6T 1Z1, Canada. Offers MA, PhD. *Program availability:* Part-time. *Degree requirements:* For master's, 2 foreign languages, comprehensive exam, thesis optional; for doctorate, 2 foreign languages, comprehensive exam, thesis/dissertation. *Entrance requirements:* For doctorate, MA. Additional exam requirements/recommendations for international students: Required—TOEFL, IELTS. Electronic applications accepted. *Expenses:* Contact institution. *Faculty research:* Hebrew Bible in ancient Near Eastern context,

Christian scriptures in Greco-Roman context, mystical aspects of religion, the feminine in western traditions, modern Jewish experience.

University of Calgary, Faculty of Graduate Studies, Faculty of Arts, Department of Religious Studies, Calgary, AB T2N 1N4, Canada. Offers MA, PhD. *Program availability:* Part-time. *Degree requirements:* For master's, one foreign language, thesis; for doctorate, 2 foreign languages, thesis/dissertation, candidacy exam. *Entrance requirements:* For master's, minimum GPA of 3.3; for doctorate, minimum GPA of 3.5. Additional exam requirements/recommendations for international students: Required—TOEFL (minimum score 550 paper-based). *Faculty research:* Eastern religions, Western religions, nature of religion.

University of California, Berkeley, Graduate Division, College of Letters and Science, Group in Buddhist Studies, Berkeley, CA 94720-1500. Offers PhD. *Degree requirements:* For doctorate, 4 foreign languages, thesis/dissertation, dissertation defense, qualifying exam. *Entrance requirements:* For doctorate, GRE General Test, MA in Japanese, Chinese, or Sanskrit; minimum GPA of 3.0; 3 letters of recommendation. Electronic applications accepted.

University of California, Riverside, Graduate Division, Department of Religious Studies, Riverside, CA 92521. Offers MA, PhD. Terminal master's awarded for partial completion of doctoral program. *Degree requirements:* For master's, one foreign language, comprehensive exam; for doctorate, 2 foreign languages, comprehensive exam. *Entrance requirements:* For master's, GRE, 3 letters of recommendation from academic references, statement of purpose, personal history, scholarly acuity and interest in the critical questions of the discipline of religious studies; for doctorate, GRE General Test, 3 letters of recommendation from academic references; statement of purpose; personal history; basic and advanced courses in religious studies, beginning work in foreign language and ability to work across methods, traditions, and disciplines. Additional exam requirements/recommendations for international students: Required—TOEFL (minimum score 550 paper-based; 80 iBT); Recommended—IELTS (minimum score 7). Electronic applications accepted. *Expenses:* Tuition, state resident: full-time $5746. Tuition, nonresident: full-time $10,780. Tuition and fees vary according to campus/location and program. *Faculty research:* American religions, southeast Asian religions, transnational Buddhism, modern Hinduism, gender theory, Sikh studies.

University of California, Santa Barbara, Graduate Division, College of Letters and Sciences, Division of Humanities and Fine Arts, Department of Religious Studies, Santa Barbara, CA 93106-3130. Offers ancient Mediterranean studies (PhD); cognitive science (PhD); European medieval studies (PhD); feminist studies (PhD); global studies (PhD); religious studies (MA, PhD); translation studies (PhD); MA/PhD. Terminal master's awarded for partial completion of doctoral program. *Degree requirements:* For master's, one foreign language, comprehensive exam (for some programs), thesis (for some programs); for doctorate, 2 foreign languages, thesis/dissertation, methodology. *Entrance requirements:* For master's and doctorate, GRE General Test. Additional exam requirements/recommendations for international students: Required—TOEFL (minimum score 550 paper-based; 80 iBT), IELTS (minimum score 7). Electronic applications accepted. *Faculty research:* Area studies; religious traditions; theory and method in the study of religion; religion, culture, and politics; spirituality and religious experience.

University of California, Santa Barbara, Graduate Division, College of Letters and Sciences, Division of Social Sciences, Department of Global Studies, Santa Barbara, CA 93106-7065. Offers global culture, ideology, and religion (MA, PhD); global government, human rights, and civil society (MA, PhD); political economy, sustainable development, and the environment (MA, PhD). *Degree requirements:* For master's, one foreign language, thesis, 2 years of a second language; for doctorate, one foreign language, thesis/dissertation, reading proficiency in at least one language other than English. *Entrance requirements:* For master's, GRE, 2 years of a second language with minimum B grade in the final term, statement of purpose, resume or curriculum vitae, 3 letters of recommendation, transcripts (from all post-secondary institutions attended), writing sample (15-20 pages); for doctorate, GRE, statement of purpose, personal achievements/contributions statement, resume or curriculum vitae, 3 letters of recommendation, transcripts from all post-secondary institutions attended, writing sample (15-20 pages). Additional exam requirements/recommendations for international students: Required—TOEFL (minimum score 600 paper-based; 94 iBT), IELTS (minimum score 7). Electronic applications accepted.

University of Chicago, Divinity School, Master of Arts in Religious Studies Program, Chicago, IL 60637. Offers MA. *Program availability:* Part-time. *Students:* 1 (woman) full-time, 2 part-time (0 women). 9 applicants, 44% accepted, 3 enrolled. In 2017, 3 master's awarded. *Degree requirements:* For master's, oral examination. *Entrance requirements:* For master's, GRE General Test, 3 letters of recommendation; transcripts; curriculum vitae or resume. Additional exam requirements/recommendations for international students: Required—TOEFL (minimum score 600 paper-based; 104 iBT), IELTS (minimum score 7). *Application deadline:* For fall admission, 4/15 for domestic students, 1/15 for international students; for winter admission, 10/13 for domestic students, 4/15 for international students; for spring admission, 1/15 for domestic students, 10/13 for international students. Applications are processed on a rolling basis. Application fee: $75. Electronic applications accepted. *Expenses:* Contact institution. *Financial support:* Federal Work-Study, institutionally sponsored loans, scholarships/grants, and tuition waivers (partial) available. Support available to part-time students. *Faculty research:* Constructive studies (philosophy of religion, religious ethics, and theology); historical studies (Bible, history of Christianity, and history of Judaism); religion and the human sciences (anthropology and sociology of religion, history of religions, and religion, literature, and visual culture); Islamic studies; religions in America. *Unit head:* Joshua Feigelson, Dean of Students, 773-702-8217, E-mail: divinityadmissions@uchicago.edu. *Application contact:* Anita Lumpkin, Associate Dean of Students, 773-702-8249, E-mail: divinityadmissions@uchicago.edu.
Website: http://divinity.uchicago.edu/master-arts-religious-studies-amrs

University of Chicago, Divinity School, Master of Arts Program, Chicago, IL 60637. Offers MA. *Students:* 66 full-time (24 women), 8 part-time (4 women); includes 4 minority (2 Black or African American, non-Hispanic/Latino; 1 Hispanic/Latino; 1 Two or more races, non-Hispanic/Latino), 7 international. Average age 27. 144 applicants, 76% accepted, 37 enrolled. *Degree requirements:* For master's, one foreign language, 15 courses with minimum B- grade. *Entrance requirements:* For master's, GRE General Test, 3 letters of recommendation; transcripts; curriculum vitae or resume. Additional exam requirements/recommendations for international students: Required—TOEFL (minimum score 600 paper-based; 104 iBT), IELTS (minimum score 7). *Application deadline:* For fall admission, 1/8 priority date for domestic and international students. Application fee: $75. Electronic applications accepted. *Financial support:* Federal Work-Study, institutionally sponsored loans, scholarships/grants, and tuition waivers (full and partial) available. Support available to part-time students. Financial award application deadline: 1/8. *Faculty research:* Constructive studies (philosophy of religion, religious ethics, and theology); historical studies (Bible, history of Christianity, and history of Judaism); religion and the human sciences (anthropology and sociology of religion, history of religions, and religion, literature, and visual culture); Islamic studies; religions in America. *Unit head:* Dr. Sarah E. Hammerschlag, Director/Assistant Professor of Religion and Literature, 773-702-8200. *Application contact:* Anita Lumpkin, Associate Dean of Students, 773-702-8249, E-mail: divinityadmissions@uchicago.edu.
Website: http://divinity.uchicago.edu/master-arts-ma

University of Chicago, Divinity School, PhD Program, Chicago, IL 60637. Offers anthropology and sociology of religions (PhD); Bible (PhD); history of Christianity (PhD); history of Judaism (PhD); history of religions (PhD); Islamic studies (PhD); philosophy of religions (PhD); religion, literature, and visual culture (PhD); religions in America (PhD); religious ethics (PhD); theology (PhD). *Students:* 157 full-time (59 women); includes 23 minority (6 Black or African American, non-Hispanic/Latino; 11 Asian, non-Hispanic/Latino; 3 Hispanic/Latino; 3 Two or more races, non-Hispanic/Latino), 24 international. Average age 33. 184 applicants, 11% accepted, 17 enrolled. In 2017, 12 doctorates awarded. *Degree requirements:* For doctorate, 2 foreign languages, comprehensive exam, thesis/dissertation. *Entrance requirements:* For doctorate, GRE General Test, 3 letters of recommendation; transcripts; curriculum vitae or resume; writing sample. Additional exam requirements/recommendations for international students: Required—TOEFL (minimum score 600 paper-based; 104 iBT), IELTS (minimum score 7). *Application deadline:* For fall admission, 12/15 for domestic and international students. Application fee: $75. Electronic applications accepted. *Financial support:* In 2017–18, fellowships with full tuition reimbursements (averaging $27,000 per year), teaching assistantships with full tuition reimbursements (averaging $27,000 per year) were awarded; Federal Work-Study, institutionally sponsored loans, scholarships/grants, and health care benefits also available. Financial award application deadline: 12/15. *Faculty research:* Constructive studies (philosophy of religion, religious ethics, and theology); historical studies (Bible, history of Christianity, and history of Judaism); religion and the human sciences (anthropology and sociology of religion, history of religions, and religion, literature, and visual culture); Islamic studies; religions in America. *Unit head:* Dr. David Nirenberg, Interim Dean/Executive Vice Provost, 773-702-8200, E-mail: divinityadmissions@uchicago.edu. *Application contact:* Anita Lumpkin, Associate Dean of Students, 773-702-8249, E-mail: divinityadmissions@uchicago.edu.
Website: http://divinity.uchicago.edu/doctoral-program-phd

University of Colorado Boulder, Graduate School, College of Arts and Sciences, Department of Religious Studies, Boulder, CO 80309. Offers MA. *Faculty:* 9 full-time (3 women). *Students:* 18 full-time (6 women); includes 1 minority (Asian, non-Hispanic/Latino), 5 international. Average age 29. 18 applicants, 83% accepted, 5 enrolled. In 2017, 6 master's awarded. Terminal master's awarded for partial completion of doctoral program. *Degree requirements:* For master's, one foreign language, comprehensive exam, thesis. *Entrance requirements:* For master's, minimum undergraduate GPA of 2.75. *Application deadline:* For fall admission, 1/10 for domestic students; for spring admission, 1/10 for domestic students. Applications are processed on a rolling basis. Application fee: $60 ($80 for international students). Electronic applications accepted. Application fee is waived when completed online. *Financial support:* In 2017–18, 5 fellowships (averaging $2,220 per year), 15 teaching assistantships with full and partial tuition reimbursements (averaging $9,842 per year) were awarded; institutionally sponsored loans, scholarships/grants, health care benefits, and unspecified assistantships also available. Financial award application deadline: 2/15; financial award applicants required to submit FAFSA. *Faculty research:* Religious studies; comparative religion; religious history; area studies (arts/humanities); arts/humanities/cultural activities. *Total annual research expenditures:* $10,191. *Application contact:* E-mail: rlst@colorado.edu.
Website: http://www.colorado.edu/ReligiousStudies

University of Denver, Division of Arts, Humanities and Social Sciences, Department of Religious Studies, Denver, CO 80208. Offers critical theory and religion (MA); lived religions (MA); philosophy of religion (MA); religion and international studies (MA); sacred texts (MA). *Students:* Average age 30. 14 applicants, 64% accepted, 6 enrolled. In 2017, 3 master's awarded. *Degree requirements:* For master's, variable foreign language requirement, comprehensive exam, thesis. *Entrance requirements:* For master's, GRE General Test, bachelor's degree, transcripts, personal statement, writing sample, three letters of recommendation. Additional exam requirements/recommendations for international students: Required—TOEFL (minimum score 550 paper-based; 80 iBT). *Application deadline:* For fall admission, 2/15 priority date for domestic and international students. Applications are processed on a rolling basis. Application fee: $65. Electronic applications accepted. *Expenses:* Contact institution. *Financial support:* In 2017–18, 13 students received support. Federal Work-Study, scholarships/grants, and unspecified assistantships available. Financial award application deadline: 2/15; financial award applicants required to submit FAFSA. *Unit head:* Dr. Ginni Ishimatsu, Interim Chair, 303-871-2751, Fax: 303-871-2750, E-mail: gishimat@du.edu. *Application contact:* Dr. Carl Raschke, Professor and Graduate Advisor, 303-871-3117, Fax: 303-871-2750, E-mail: rlgs@du.edu.
Website: http://www.du.edu/ahss/religiousstudies

University of Denver, DU/Iliff Joint PhD Program in the Study of Religion, Denver, CO 80208. Offers future faculty in religion (Certificate); Latinx studies (Certificate); study of religion (PhD). Program jointly offered with Iliff School of Theology. *Program availability:* Part-time. *Faculty:* 10 part-time/adjunct (4 women). *Students:* 29 full-time (7 women), 19 part-time (6 women); includes 10 minority (1 Black or African American, non-Hispanic/Latino; 1 Asian, non-Hispanic/Latino; 6 Hispanic/Latino; 2 Two or more races, non-Hispanic/Latino), 2 international. Average age 39. 26 applicants, 54% accepted, 7 enrolled. In 2017, 9 doctorates awarded. *Degree requirements:* For doctorate, one foreign language, comprehensive exam, thesis/dissertation. *Entrance requirements:* For doctorate, GRE General Test, transcripts, three letters of recommendation, personal statement, writing sample, research paper. Additional exam requirements/recommendations for international students: Required—TOEFL (minimum score 600 paper-based; 100 iBT). *Application deadline:* For fall admission, 1/15 priority date for domestic and international students. Applications are processed on a rolling basis. Application fee: $65. Electronic applications accepted. *Expenses:* $31,935 per year full-time. *Financial support:* In 2017–18, 30 students received support, including 11 teaching assistantships with tuition reimbursements available (averaging $2,788 per year); scholarships/grants and unspecified assistantships also available. Financial award application deadline: 1/15. *Faculty research:* Religion and social change, theology, philosophy and cultural theory (including comparative religious study), Biblical interpretation. *Unit head:* Annette Stott, Director, 303-871-3278. *Application contact:* Information Contact, 303-765-3136, Fax: 303-871-4942, E-mail: jointphd@iliff.edu.
Website: http://www.du.edu/duiliffjoint

University of Denver, Josef Korbel School of International Studies, Denver, CO 80208. Offers conflict resolution (MA); global business and corporate social responsibility (Certificate); global finance, trade and economic integration (MA); global health affairs (Certificate); homeland security (Certificate); humanitarian assistance (Certificate); international administration (MA); international development (MA); international human rights (MA); international security (MA); international studies (MA, PhD); public policy studies (MPP); religion and international affairs (Certificate). *Program availability:* Part-time. *Faculty:* 46 full-time (16 women), 28 part-time/adjunct (8 women). *Students:* 245 full-time (132 women), 40 part-time (21 women); includes 58 minority (8 Black or African American, non-Hispanic/Latino; 2 American Indian or Alaska Native, non-Hispanic/Latino; 11 Asian, non-Hispanic/Latino; 27 Hispanic/Latino; 10 Two or more races, non-Hispanic/Latino), 22 international. Average age 27. 627 applicants, 74% accepted, 106

enrolled. In 2017, 218 master's, 6 doctorates, 25 other advanced degrees awarded. *Degree requirements:* For master's, one foreign language, thesis (for some programs); for doctorate, one foreign language, comprehensive exam, thesis/dissertation, two extended research papers. *Entrance requirements:* For master's, GRE General Test, bachelor's degree, transcripts, two letters of recommendation, statement of purpose, resume or curriculum vitae; for doctorate, GRE General Test, master's degree, transcripts, three letters of recommendation, statement of purpose, resume or curriculum vitae, writing sample; for Certificate, bachelor's degree, transcripts, two letters of recommendation, statement of purpose, resume or curriculum vitae. Additional exam requirements/recommendations for international students: Required—TOEFL (minimum score 587 paper-based; 95 iBT). *Application deadline:* For fall admission, 1/15 priority date for domestic and international students; for winter admission, 11/1 for domestic and international students. Applications are processed on a rolling basis. Application fee: $65. Electronic applications accepted. *Expenses:* $47,823 per year full-time. *Financial support:* In 2017–18, 225 students received support, including 1 teaching assistantship with tuition reimbursement available (averaging $2,236 per year); research assistantships with tuition reimbursements available, career-related internships or fieldwork, Federal Work-Study, institutionally sponsored loans, scholarships/grants, and unspecified assistantships also available. Support available to part-time students. Financial award application deadline: 2/15; financial award applicants required to submit FAFSA. *Faculty research:* Human rights and international security, international politics and economics, economic-social and political development, international technology analysis and management. *Unit head:* Dr. Pardis Mahdavi, Dean, 303-871-6338, E-mail: pardis.mahdavi@du.edu. *Application contact:* Admissions Contact, E-mail: korbeladm@du.edu.
Website: http://www.du.edu/korbel

University of Florida, Graduate School, College of Liberal Arts and Sciences, Department of Religion, Gainesville, FL 32611. Offers Jewish studies (MA); religion (MA, PhD); tropical conservation and development (MA, PhD); women's and gender studies (MA, PhD). *Program availability:* Part-time. *Degree requirements:* For master's, one foreign language, thesis optional; for doctorate, one foreign language, comprehensive exam, thesis/dissertation. *Entrance requirements:* For master's, GRE General Test, minimum GPA of 3.0. Additional exam requirements/recommendations for international students: Required—TOEFL (minimum score 550 paper-based; 80 iBT), IELTS (minimum score 6). Electronic applications accepted. *Faculty research:* Religion in America, Christian thought, Islam, religions of India, comparative religion.

University of Georgia, Franklin College of Arts and Sciences, Department of Religion, Athens, GA 30602. Offers MA. *Degree requirements:* For master's, one foreign language, thesis. *Entrance requirements:* For master's, GRE General Test. Electronic applications accepted.

University of Hawaii at Manoa, Office of Graduate Education, College of Arts and Humanities, Department of Religion, Honolulu, HI 96822. Offers MA. *Program availability:* Part-time. *Degree requirements:* For master's, one foreign language, thesis optional. *Entrance requirements:* For master's, GRE General Test. Additional exam requirements/recommendations for international students: Required—TOEFL (minimum score 600 paper-based; 100 iBT), IELTS (minimum score 7). *Faculty research:* Buddhism, East Asian religion, South Asian religion, Polynesian religion, Western religions.

University of Illinois at Urbana–Champaign, Graduate College, College of Liberal Arts and Sciences, School of Literatures, Cultures and Linguistics, Department of Religion, Champaign, IL 61820. Offers religious studies (MA). *Degree requirements:* For master's, one foreign language, comprehensive exam, thesis optional.

The University of Iowa, Graduate College, College of Liberal Arts and Sciences, Department of Religious Studies, Iowa City, IA 52242-1316. Offers MA, PhD. Terminal master's awarded for partial completion of doctoral program. *Degree requirements:* For master's, thesis optional, exam; for doctorate, comprehensive exam, thesis/dissertation. *Entrance requirements:* For master's and doctorate, GRE General Test, minimum GPA of 3.0. Additional exam requirements/recommendations for international students: Required—TOEFL (minimum score 550 paper-based; 81 iBT). Electronic applications accepted. *Faculty research:* Eastern and Western religion.

The University of Kansas, Graduate Studies, College of Liberal Arts and Sciences, Department of Religious Studies, Lawrence, KS 66045. Offers MA, Graduate Certificate. *Program availability:* Part-time. *Students:* 8 full-time (3 women); includes 1 minority (Black or African American, non-Hispanic/Latino), 2 international. Average age 27. 9 applicants, 67% accepted, 3 enrolled. In 2017, 4 master's awarded. *Entrance requirements:* For master's, official transcripts, three letters of recommendation, essay of interest and purpose, resume. Additional exam requirements/recommendations for international students: Required—TOEFL. *Application deadline:* For fall admission, 2/1 for domestic and international students. Application fee: $65 ($85 for international students). Electronic applications accepted. *Financial support:* Fellowships, teaching assistantships, scholarships/grants, and unspecified assistantships available. Financial award application deadline: 1/1. *Faculty research:* Hinduism, Chinese Buddhism, Islam, Biblical literatures, American and indigenous people's religion. *Unit head:* Daniel B. Stevenson, Chair, 785-864-7258, E-mail: dbsteve@ku.edu. *Application contact:* Graduate Admission Contact, 785-864-4341, E-mail: rstudies@ku.edu.
Website: https://religiousstudies.ku.edu/

University of Lethbridge, School of Graduate Studies, Lethbridge, AB T1K 3M4, Canada. Offers addictions counseling (M Sc); agricultural biotechnology (M Sc); agricultural studies (M Sc, MA); anthropology (MA); archaeology (M Sc, MA); art (MA, MFA); biochemistry (M Sc); biological sciences (M Sc); biomolecular science (PhD); biosystems and biodiversity (PhD); Canadian studies (MA); chemistry (M Sc); computer science (M Sc); computer science and geographical information science (M Sc); counseling (MC); counseling psychology (M Ed); dramatic arts (MA); earth, space, and physical science (PhD); economics (MA); education (MA, PhD); educational leadership (M Ed); English (MA); environmental science (M Sc); evolution and behavior (PhD); exercise science (M Sc); French (MA); French/German (MA); French/Spanish (MA); general education (M Ed); geography (M Sc, MA); German (MA); health sciences (M Sc); individualized multidisciplinary (M Sc, MA); kinesiology (M Sc, MA); management (M Sc), including accounting, finance, human resource management and labor relations, information systems, international management, marketing, policy and strategy; mathematics (M Sc); music (M Mus, MA); Native American studies (MA); neuroscience (M Sc, PhD); new media (MA, MFA); nursing (M Sc, MN); philosophy (MA); physics (M Sc); political science (MA); psychology (M Sc, MA); religious studies (MA); sociology (MA); theatre and dramatic arts (MFA); theoretical and computational science (PhD); urban and regional studies (MA); women and gender studies (MA). *Program availability:* Part-time, evening/weekend. *Degree requirements:* For master's, thesis (for some programs); for doctorate, comprehensive exam, thesis/dissertation. *Entrance requirements:* For master's, GMAT (for M Sc in management), bachelor's degree in related field, minimum GPA of 3.0 during previous 20 graded semester courses, 2 years' teaching or related experience (M Ed); for doctorate, master's degree, minimum graduate GPA of 3.5. Additional exam requirements/recommendations for international students: Required—TOEFL (minimum score 580 paper-based; 93 iBT). Electronic applications accepted. *Faculty research:* Movement and brain plasticity, gibberellin physiology, photosynthesis, carbon cycling, molecular properties of main-group ring components.

The University of Manchester, School of Arts, Histories and Cultures, Manchester, United Kingdom. Offers anthropology, media and performance (PhD); applied theatre professional (PhD); archaeology (PhD); art history and visual studies (PhD); arts management and cultural policy (PhD); classics and ancient history (PhD); composition (PhD); creative writing (PhD); drama (PhD); economic and social history (PhD); electroacoustic composition (PhD); English and American studies (PhD); history (PhD); humanitarianism and conflict response (PhD); museology (PhD); music (PhD); musicology (PhD); religions and theology (PhD).

University of Manitoba, Faculty of Graduate Studies, Faculty of Arts, Department of Religion, Winnipeg, MB R3T 2N2, Canada. Offers MA, PhD. MA offered jointly with The University of Winnipeg. *Degree requirements:* For master's, one foreign language, thesis or alternative.

University of Michigan, Rackham Graduate School, College of Literature, Science, and the Arts, Department of Near Eastern Studies, Ann Arbor, MI 48109. Offers ancient Near Eastern studies (AM, PhD); Arabic for professional purposes (AM); Arabic language and literature (AM, PhD); Armenian studies (AM, PhD); Christianity in late antiquity (AM, PhD); Egyptology (AM, PhD); Hebrew Bible and ancient Israel (AM, PhD); Hebrew literature (AM, PhD); Islamic studies (AM, PhD); Jewish cultural studies (AM, PhD); Jewish mysticism (AM, PhD); Persian and Iranian studies (AM, PhD); Rabbinic literature (AM, PhD); Second Temple Judaism (AM, PhD); teaching Arabic as a foreign language (AM); Turkish studies (AM, PhD). *Faculty:* 27 full-time (8 women). *Students:* 31 full-time (12 women); includes 2 minority (1 Black or African American, non-Hispanic/Latino; 1 Asian, non-Hispanic/Latino), 13 international. Average age 33. 76 applicants, 11% accepted, 5 enrolled. In 2017, 4 master's, 4 doctorates awarded. Terminal master's awarded for partial completion of doctoral program. *Degree requirements:* For master's, 2 foreign languages; for doctorate, 4 foreign languages, comprehensive exam, thesis/dissertation, preliminary exams, oral defense of dissertation. *Entrance requirements:* For master's, ACTFL (for teaching Arabic as a foreign language MA program). Additional exam requirements/recommendations for international students: Required—TOEFL (minimum score 560 paper-based; 84 iBT), IELTS (minimum score 6.5). *Application deadline:* For fall admission, 12/1 for domestic and international students. Application fee: $75 ($90 for international students). Electronic applications accepted. *Expenses:* Tuition, state resident: full-time $22,368; part-time $1201 per credit hour. Tuition, nonresident: full-time $45,156; part-time $2467 per credit hour. *Required fees:* $376 per term. Tuition and fees vary according to course load, degree level and program. *Financial support:* In 2017–18, 31 students received support. Fellowships with full tuition reimbursements available, teaching assistantships with full tuition reimbursements available, scholarships/grants, health care benefits, unspecified assistantships, and spring/summer stipends available. Financial award application deadline: 12/1. *Faculty research:* Middle and Near Eastern literatures, languages, cultures from ancient times to the present. *Unit head:* Prof. Gottfried Hagen, Chair, 734-764-0314, E-mail: nes-chair@umich.edu. *Application contact:* Student Services, 734-764-0315, E-mail: nes-gradservices@umich.edu.
Website: http://www.lsa.umich.edu/neareast/

University of Minnesota, Twin Cities Campus, Graduate School, College of Liberal Arts, Department of Classical and Near Eastern Studies, Minneapolis, MN 55455-0213. Offers ancient and medieval art and archaeology (MA, PhD); classics (MA, PhD); Greek (MA, PhD); Latin (MA, PhD); religions in antiquity (MA). *Program availability:* Part-time. Terminal master's awarded for partial completion of doctoral program. *Degree requirements:* For master's, 2 foreign languages, comprehensive exam, thesis or alternative; for doctorate, variable foreign language requirement, comprehensive exam, thesis/dissertation. *Entrance requirements:* For master's and doctorate, GRE, 3 letters of recommendation, writing sample, copies of transcripts, personal statement. Additional exam requirements/recommendations for international students: Required—TOEFL. Electronic applications accepted. *Faculty research:* Greek and Latin literature, religions in antiquity, ancient Near East.

University of Missouri, Office of Research and Graduate Studies, College of Arts and Science, Department of Religious Studies, Columbia, MO 65211. Offers MA. *Entrance requirements:* For master's, GRE General Test, minimum GPA of 3.0. Additional exam requirements/recommendations for international students: Required—TOEFL (minimum score 550 paper-based; 80 iBT). Electronic applications accepted. *Faculty research:* American religious history, Biblical studies, history of Christianity, religion and society, religions of East Asia, religions of indigenous peoples, religions of South Asia, women and religion.

The University of North Carolina at Chapel Hill, Graduate School, College of Arts and Sciences, Department of Religious Studies, Chapel Hill, NC 27599. Offers MA, PhD. Terminal master's awarded for partial completion of doctoral program. *Degree requirements:* For master's, one foreign language, comprehensive exam, thesis; for doctorate, 2 foreign languages, comprehensive exam, thesis/dissertation. *Entrance requirements:* For master's and doctorate, GRE General Test, minimum GPA of 3.0. Additional exam requirements/recommendations for international students: Required—TOEFL. Electronic applications accepted. *Faculty research:* Religion.

The University of North Carolina at Charlotte, College of Liberal Arts and Sciences, Department of Religious Studies, Charlotte, NC 28223-0001. Offers MA. *Program availability:* Part-time. *Faculty:* 11 full-time (4 women). *Students:* 5 full-time (3 women), 9 part-time (3 women); includes 2 minority (1 Black or African American, non-Hispanic/Latino; 1 Hispanic/Latino). Average age 33. 8 applicants, 100% accepted, 6 enrolled. In 2017, 5 master's awarded. *Degree requirements:* For master's, thesis or comprehensive exam. *Entrance requirements:* For master's, GRE or MAT, official transcripts of all previous academic work attempted beyond high school; at least three letters of reference from persons familiar with the applicant's academic prowess and qualifications; essay (statement of purpose). Additional exam requirements/recommendations for international students: Required—TOEFL (minimum score 523 paper-based, 70 iBT) or IELTS (6.5). *Application deadline:* For fall admission, 5/1 for domestic and international students; for spring admission, 10/1 for domestic and international students. Applications are processed on a rolling basis. Application fee: $75. Electronic applications accepted. *Expenses:* Tuition, state resident: full-time $4337. Tuition, nonresident: full-time $17,771. *Required fees:* $3211. Tuition and fees vary according to course load and program. *Financial support:* In 2017–18, 4 students received support, including 4 teaching assistantships (averaging $8,125 per year); career-related internships or fieldwork, institutionally sponsored loans, scholarships/grants, and unspecified assistantships also available. Support available to part-time students. Financial award application deadline: 3/1; financial award applicants required to submit FAFSA. *Total annual research expenditures:* $12,901. *Unit head:* Dr. Joanne Robinson, Chair, 704-687-5187, E-mail: joanne.robinson@uncc.edu. *Application contact:* Kathy B. Giddings, Director of Graduate Admissions, 704-687-5503, Fax: 704-687-1668, E-mail: gradadm@uncc.edu.
Website: http://religiousstudies.uncc.edu/

University of Notre Dame, Graduate School, College of Arts and Letters, Division of Humanities, Program in Early Christian Studies, Notre Dame, IN 46556. Offers MA.

Degree requirements: For master's, 3 foreign languages, comprehensive exam. *Entrance requirements:* For master's, GRE General Test. Additional exam requirements/recommendations for international students: Required—TOEFL (minimum score 600 paper-based; 80 iBT). Electronic applications accepted. *Faculty research:* Early Christian theology, worship and scriptural interpretation; late antique and Byzantine history; art and culture; Greek and Latin literature.

University of Ottawa, Faculty of Graduate and Postdoctoral Studies, Faculty of Arts, Department of Classics and Religious Studies, Ottawa, ON K1N 6N5, Canada. Offers classical studies (MA); religious studies (PhD). *Degree requirements:* For master's, comprehensive exam, thesis or alternative; for doctorate, comprehensive exam, thesis/dissertation. *Entrance requirements:* For master's, honors degree or equivalent, minimum B average; for doctorate, master's degree, minimum B+ average. Electronic applications accepted. *Faculty research:* Religions in Canada, including Amerindian and Inuit religions; religion and culture; late antiquity.

University of Pennsylvania, School of Arts and Sciences, Graduate Group in Religious Studies, Philadelphia, PA 19104. Offers PhD. *Faculty:* 20 full-time (8 women), 10 part-time/adjunct (3 women). *Students:* 13 full-time (2 women), 2 part-time (1 woman); includes 3 minority (2 Asian, non-Hispanic/Latino; 1 Hispanic/Latino), 4 international. Average age 31. 38 applicants, 13% accepted, 4 enrolled. In 2017, 4 doctorates awarded. *Financial support:* In 2017–18, 10 students received support. Website: http://www.sas.upenn.edu/religious_studies/graduate

University of Regina, Faculty of Graduate Studies and Research, Faculty of Arts, Department of Religious Studies, Regina, SK S4S 0A2, Canada. Offers MA. *Program availability:* Part-time. *Faculty:* 7 full-time (2 women), 2 part-time/adjunct (both women). *Students:* 4 full-time (2 women), 3 part-time (2 women). 7 applicants, 86% accepted. In 2017, 1 master's awarded. *Degree requirements:* For master's, thesis. *Entrance requirements:* Additional exam requirements/recommendations for international students: Required—TOEFL (minimum score 580 paper-based; 80 iBT), IELTS (minimum score 6.5), PTE (minimum score 59). *Application deadline:* Applications are processed on a rolling basis. Application fee: $100. Electronic applications accepted. *Expenses:* $10,681. *Financial support:* In 2017–18, 2 teaching assistantships (averaging $2,562 per year) were awarded; fellowships, research assistantships, and scholarships/grants also available. Financial award application deadline: 6/15. *Faculty research:* Comparative religion; religious traditions; thematic and methodological studies; advanced studies in Christianity, Islam, and ancient religions. *Unit head:* Dr. William Arnal, Department Head, 306-585.5680, Fax: 306-585-4815, E-mail: william.arnal@uregina.ca.
Website: http://www.uregina.ca/arts/religious-studies

University of St. Thomas, Center for Faith and Culture, Houston, TX 77006-4696. Offers MA. *Program availability:* Part-time. *Faculty:* 1 full-time (0 women), 1 part-time/adjunct (0 women). *Students:* 1 full-time (0 women), 10 part-time (8 women); includes 3 minority (1 Black or African American, non-Hispanic/Latino; 1 Asian, non-Hispanic/Latino; 1 Hispanic/Latino). Average age 51. 1 applicant, 100% accepted. In 2017, 10 master's awarded. *Degree requirements:* For master's, service learning and leadership practicum, integrating presentation. *Entrance requirements:* For master's, bachelor's degree with minimum GPA of 2.75 or advanced degree; 3 letters of recommendation (professional or academic only); essay on student goals and expectations; interview with CFC admissions committee; writing sample; favorable review by admissions committee. Additional exam requirements/recommendations for international students: Required—TOEFL (minimum score 550 paper-based; 100 iBT), IELTS (minimum score 6.5), PTE (minimum score 53). *Application deadline:* For fall admission, 7/1 for domestic students, 6/1 for international students; for spring admission, 11/1 for domestic students, 10/1 for international students. Applications are processed on a rolling basis. Application fee: $35. Electronic applications accepted. *Expenses:* Tuition: Full-time $20,934; part-time $1163 per credit hour. *Required fees:* $250; $210 per semester. *Financial support:* In 2017–18, 6 students received support. Federal Work-Study, scholarships/grants, and state work-study, institutional employment available. Support available to part-time students. Financial award application deadline: 4/15; financial award applicants required to submit FAFSA. *Unit head:* Fr. Donald S. Nesti, Director, 713-942-5066, E-mail: cfc@stthom.edu. *Application contact:* Dr. Adam Martinez, Program Director, 713-942-5066, E-mail: cfc@stthom.edu.
Website: http://www.stthom.edu/Academics/Centers_of_Excellence/Center_for_Faith_Culture/Index.aqf

University of St. Thomas, College of Arts and Sciences, Master of Arts Program in Catholic Studies, St. Paul, MN 55105-1096. Offers MA. *Program availability:* Part-time, evening/weekend. *Degree requirements:* For master's, thesis. *Entrance requirements:* For master's, bachelor's degree with minimum GPA of 3.0, writing sample, personal essay, 3 letters of recommendation. Additional exam requirements/recommendations for international students: Required—TOEFL (minimum score 550 paper-based). *Application deadline:* For fall admission, 3/1 for domestic and international students; for spring admission, 11/1 for domestic and international students. Applications are processed on a rolling basis. Electronic applications accepted. Tuition and fees vary according to course load, degree level, campus/location and program. *Financial support:* Fellowships with full tuition reimbursements, research assistantships, and tuition waivers (partial) available. *Unit head:* Dr. Erika Kidd, Director, 651-962-5788, Fax: 651-962-5710, E-mail: kidd3020@stthomas.edu. *Application contact:* Maureen Huss, Coordinator, Center for Catholic Studies, 651-962-5704, Fax: 651-962-5710, E-mail: huss1887@stthomas.edu.
Website: http://www.stthomas.edu/catholicstudies/masters/

University of Saskatchewan, College of Graduate Studies and Research, College of Arts and Science, Department of Religion and Culture, Saskatoon, SK S7N 5A2, Canada. Offers MA. *Degree requirements:* For master's, thesis. *Entrance requirements:* Additional exam requirements/recommendations for international students: Required—TOEFL (minimum score 80 iBT); Recommended—IELTS (minimum score 6.5). Electronic applications accepted.

University of South Africa, College of Human Sciences, Pretoria, South Africa. Offers adult education (M Ed); African languages (MA, PhD); African politics (MA, PhD); Afrikaans (MA, PhD); ancient history (MA, PhD); ancient Near Eastern studies (MA, PhD); anthropology (MA, PhD); applied linguistics (MA); Arabic (MA, PhD); archaeology (MA); art history (MA); Biblical archaeology (MA); Biblical studies (M Th, D Th, PhD); Christian spirituality (M Th, D Th); church history (M Th, D Th); classical studies (MA, PhD); clinical psychology (MA); communication (MA, PhD); comparative education (M Ed, Ed D); consulting psychology (D Admin, D Com, PhD); curriculum studies (M Ed, Ed D); development studies (M Admin, MA, D Admin, PhD); didactics (M Ed, Ed D); education (M Tech); education management (M Ed, Ed D); educational psychology (M Ed); English (MA); environmental education (M Ed); French (MA, PhD); German (MA, PhD); Greek (MA); guidance and counseling (M Ed); health studies (MA, PhD), including health sciences education (MA), health services management (MA), medical and surgical nursing science (critical care general) (MA), midwifery and neonatal nursing science (MA), trauma and emergency care (MA); history (MA, PhD); history of education (Ed D); inclusive education (M Ed, Ed D); information and communications technology policy and regulation (MA); information science (MA, MIS, PhD); international politics

(MA, PhD); Islamic studies (MA, PhD); Italian (MA, PhD); Judaica (MA, PhD); linguistics (MA, PhD); mathematical education (M Ed); mathematics education (MA); missiology (M Th, D Th); modern Hebrew (MA, PhD); musicology (MA, MMus, D Mus, PhD); natural science education (M Ed); New Testament (M Th, D Th); Old Testament (D Th); pastoral therapy (M Th, D Th); philosophy (MA); philosophy of education (M Ed, Ed D); politics (MA, PhD); Portuguese (MA, PhD); practical theology (M Th, D Th); psychology (MA, MS, PhD); psychology of education (M Ed, Ed D); public health (MA); religious studies (MA, D Th, PhD); Romance languages (MA); Russian (MA, PhD); Semitic languages (MA, PhD); social behavior studies in HIV/AIDS (MA); social science (mental health) (MA); social science in development studies (MA); social science in psychology (MA); social science in social work (MA); social science in sociology (MA); social work (MSW, DSW, PhD); socio-education (M Ed, Ed D); sociolinguistics (MA); sociology (MA, PhD); Spanish (MA, PhD); systematic theology (M Th, D Th); TESOL (teaching English to speakers of other languages) (MA); theological ethics (M Th, D Th); theory of literature (MA, PhD); urban ministries (D Th); urban ministry (M Th).

University of South Carolina, The Graduate School, College of Arts and Sciences, Department of Religious Studies, Columbia, SC 29208. Offers MA. *Program availability:* Part-time. *Degree requirements:* For master's, one foreign language, comprehensive exam, thesis. *Entrance requirements:* For master's, GRE General Test or MAT. Additional exam requirements/recommendations for international students: Required—TOEFL. Electronic applications accepted. *Faculty research:* Biblical and Near Eastern studies, theology and religious thought, religion and culture, South Asian religions, Islamic studies.

University of South Florida, College of Arts and Sciences, Department of Philosophy, Tampa, FL 33620-9951. Offers liberal arts (MA), including social and political thought; philosophy (MA, PhD), including philosophy and religion. *Program availability:* Part-time, evening/weekend. *Faculty:* 14 full-time (2 women). *Students:* 41 full-time (7 women), 15 part-time (3 women); includes 10 minority (2 Black or African American, non-Hispanic/Latino; 3 Asian, non-Hispanic/Latino; 4 Hispanic/Latino; 1 Two or more races, non-Hispanic/Latino), 1 international. Average age 35. 29 applicants, 76% accepted, 9 enrolled. In 2017, 7 master's, 7 doctorates awarded. Terminal master's awarded for partial completion of doctoral program. *Degree requirements:* For master's, comprehensive exam, thesis optional; for doctorate, comprehensive exam, thesis/dissertation. *Entrance requirements:* For master's and doctorate, GRE General Test, minimum GPA of 3.0, three letters of recommendation, 10-page philosophy writing sample, statement of philosophical interests. Additional exam requirements/recommendations for international students: Required—TOEFL (minimum score 550 paper-based; 79 iBT) or IELTS (minimum score 6.5). *Application deadline:* For fall admission, 1/2 priority date for domestic students, 2/15 for international students; for spring admission, 10/15 priority date for domestic students, 8/1 for international students. Application fee: $30. Electronic applications accepted. *Financial support:* In 2017–18, 5 students received support, including 32 teaching assistantships with tuition reimbursements available (averaging $11,025 per year); unspecified assistantships also available. Financial award application deadline: 1/1. *Faculty research:* Medieval philosophy, early modern philosophy (seventeenth-, eighteenth-, and twentieth-century Continental philosophy, feminist philosophy, social philosophy, ethics, philosophy of science. Total annual research expenditures: $10,921. *Unit head:* Dr. Alex Levine, Professor and Chairperson, 813-974-5508, E-mail: levineat@usf.edu. *Application contact:* Dr. William Goodwin, Associate Professor, 813-974-5670, E-mail: wgoodwin@usf.edu.
Website: http://philosophy.usf.edu/

University of South Florida, College of Arts and Sciences, Department of Religious Studies, Tampa, FL 33620-9951. Offers MA. *Program availability:* Part-time, evening/weekend. *Faculty:* 3 full-time (0 women). *Students:* 10 full-time (4 women), 4 part-time (1 woman); includes 3 minority (all Hispanic/Latino), 1 international. Average age 34. 10 applicants, 100% accepted, 10 enrolled. In 2017, 2 master's awarded. *Degree requirements:* For master's, comprehensive exam, thesis optional. *Entrance requirements:* For master's, GRE General Test (recommended), minimum GPA of 3.0, three letters of recommendation, 1-3 page personal statement of intellectual interest, writing sample. Additional exam requirements/recommendations for international students: Required—TOEFL (minimum score 550 paper-based; 79 iBT) or IELTS (minimum score 6.5). *Application deadline:* For fall admission, 2/15 priority date for domestic and international students; for spring admission, 10/15 priority date for domestic students, 9/15 priority date for international students. Applications are processed on a rolling basis. Application fee: $30. Electronic applications accepted. *Financial support:* In 2017–18, 3 students received support, including 7 teaching assistantships with tuition reimbursements available (averaging $9,751 per year); unspecified assistantships also available. Financial award applicants required to submit FAFSA. *Faculty research:* Biblical studies, Biblical archaeology, Christianity, Judaism, Mysticism, philosophy of religion, Buddhism, Daoism, Confucianism, Hinduism, Chinese medicine, Vedic religion, Hinduism, religion in culture and society, African religion, African-American religion, Afro-Caribbean religion. *Unit head:* Dr. Michael DeJonge, Professor and Chair, 813-974-1848, E-mail: mdejonge@usf.edu. *Application contact:* Dr. Gil Ben-Herut, Associate Professor and Graduate Program Director, 813-974-1852, E-mail: gilb@usf.edu.
Website: http://religious-studies.usf.edu/

The University of Tennessee, Graduate School, College of Arts and Sciences, Department of Philosophy, Knoxville, TN 37996. Offers medical ethics (MA, PhD); philosophy (MA, PhD); religious studies (MA). *Program availability:* Part-time. *Degree requirements:* For master's, thesis or alternative; for doctorate, one foreign language, thesis/dissertation. *Entrance requirements:* For master's and doctorate, GRE General Test, minimum GPA of 2.7. Additional exam requirements/recommendations for international students: Required—TOEFL. Electronic applications accepted.

University of the Cumberlands, Program in Christian Studies, Williamsburg, KY 40769-1372. Offers MA. *Program availability:* Part-time, evening/weekend, online learning. *Entrance requirements:* For master's, GRE or MAT. Additional exam requirements/recommendations for international students: Required—TOEFL. Electronic applications accepted.

University of the West, Department of Psychology, Rosemead, CA 91770. Offers Buddhist psychology (MA); multicultural counseling (MA). *Program availability:* Part-time, evening/weekend. *Degree requirements:* For master's, fieldwork; comprehensive exam or thesis.

University of the West, Department of Religious Studies, Rosemead, CA 91770. Offers religious studies (MA, PhD), including Buddhism (PhD), Buddhist studies (MA), comparative religions (PhD), comparative religious studies (MA). *Program availability:* Part-time, evening/weekend. *Degree requirements:* For master's, thesis or comprehensive exam, competency in language associated with Buddhist Canon literature; for doctorate, 2 foreign languages, comprehensive exam, thesis/dissertation. *Entrance requirements:* For master's and doctorate, BA in religious studies, theology, philosophy or equivalent from an accredited university; official transcript; three letters of recommendation; essay. Additional exam requirements/recommendations for international students: Required—TOEFL, IELTS.

Religion

University of Toronto, School of Graduate Studies, Faculty of Arts and Science, Centre for the Study of Religion, Toronto, ON M5S 1A1, Canada. Offers MA, PhD. *Program availability:* Part-time. *Degree requirements:* For master's, one foreign language, research paper, language examination; for doctorate, 2 foreign languages, thesis/dissertation, language examinations, general examinations, oral examination. *Entrance requirements:* For master's, BA in religion or a related field; minimum A-average in final year, 3 letters of recommendation, resume; for doctorate, MA in religion, minimum average of A- in MA courses with no individual grade below a B, 3 letters of recommendation, resume, brief writing sample. Additional exam requirements/recommendations for international students: Required—TOEFL (minimum score 580 paper-based; 93 iBT), TWE (minimum score 5). Electronic applications accepted.

University of Valley Forge, Program in Christian Leadership, Phoenixville, PA 19460. Offers MA. *Degree requirements:* For master's, project.

University of Valley Forge, Program in Worship Studies, Phoenixville, PA 19460. Offers MA.

University of Virginia, College and Graduate School of Arts and Sciences, Department of Religious Studies, Charlottesville, VA 22903. Offers religion, politics and global society (MA); religious studies (MA, PhD). *Faculty:* 36 full-time (15 women). *Students:* 75 full-time (32 women); includes 12 minority (4 Asian, non-Hispanic/Latino; 4 Hispanic/Latino; 4 Two or more races, non-Hispanic/Latino), 12 international. Average age 30. 149 applicants, 30% accepted, 26 enrolled. In 2017, 8 master's, 16 doctorates awarded. *Degree requirements:* For master's, one foreign language, thesis optional; for doctorate, 2 foreign languages, comprehensive exam, thesis/dissertation. *Entrance requirements:* For master's and doctorate, GRE General Test, 3 letters of recommendation. Additional exam requirements/recommendations for international students: Required—TOEFL (minimum score 600 paper-based; 90 iBT), IELTS (minimum score 7). *Application deadline:* For fall admission, 12/1 for domestic students, 12/3 for international students. Applications are processed on a rolling basis. Application fee: $60. Electronic applications accepted. *Financial support:* Fellowships and teaching assistantships available. Financial award applicants required to submit FAFSA. *Unit head:* Kurtis Schaeffer, Chair, 434-924-6705, Fax: 434-924-1467, E-mail: ks6bb@virginia.edu. *Application contact:* Matthew Hedstrom, Director of Graduate Studies, 434-924-6705, Fax: 434-924-1467, E-mail: msh6q@virginia.edu.
Website: http://religiousstudies.virginia.edu/

University of Washington, Graduate School, College of Arts and Sciences, Department of Asian Languages and Literature, Seattle, WA 98195. Offers Buddhist studies (MA, PhD); Chinese language and literature (MA, PhD); Japanese language and literature (MA, PhD); Korean language and literature (MA, PhD); South Asian language and literature (MA, PhD). *Degree requirements:* For master's, 2 foreign languages, general exam, thesis or 2 research papers; for doctorate, 3 foreign languages, thesis/dissertation, general exam. *Entrance requirements:* For master's, GRE, minimum GPA of 3.0; for doctorate, GRE, master's degree in related field, minimum GPA of 3.0. Additional exam requirements/recommendations for international students: Required—TOEFL. Electronic applications accepted. *Faculty research:* Textual, linguistic, philological, and literary study of languages and literatures of Asia.

University of Washington, Graduate School, College of Arts and Sciences, Henry M. Jackson School of International Studies, Comparative Religion Program, Seattle, WA 98195. Offers MAIS. *Degree requirements:* For master's, 2 foreign languages. *Entrance requirements:* For master's, GRE General Test, minimum GPA of 3.0 in last two years. Additional exam requirements/recommendations for international students: Required—TOEFL (minimum score 500 paper-based; 92 iBT), IELTS (minimum score 7). Electronic applications accepted.

University of Waterloo, Graduate Studies, Faculty of Arts, Department of Religious Studies, Waterloo, ON N2L 3G1, Canada. Offers religious diversity in North America (PhD). *Degree requirements:* For doctorate, thesis/dissertation. *Entrance requirements:* Additional exam requirements/recommendations for international students: Required—TOEFL, IELTS, PTE. Electronic applications accepted. *Faculty research:* Religious diversity in North America.

The University of Winnipeg, Graduate Studies, Department of Religious Studies, Winnipeg, MB R3B 2E9, Canada. Offers MA. Program offered jointly with University of Manitoba. *Program availability:* Part-time. *Faculty research:* Religion and culture, social ethics, religious liberalism, history of Canaanite and Israelite religion, literary criticism of the Hebrew Bible.

Vancouver School of Theology, Graduate and Professional Programs, Vancouver, BC V6T 1Z1, Canada. Offers denominational studies (Diploma); indigenous and inter-religious studies (MA, Diploma); public and pastoral leadership (MA); public and pastoral leadership in spiritual care (MA); theological studies (MATS, Diploma, Graduate Diploma); theology (M Div, Th M). *Accreditation:* ATS. *Program availability:* Part-time, online learning. *Degree requirements:* For master's, comprehensive exam (for some programs), thesis (for some programs); for other advanced degree, one foreign language, thesis. *Entrance requirements:* Additional exam requirements/recommendations for international students: Required—TOEFL (minimum score 80 iBT); Recommended—IELTS (minimum score 6.5). *Application deadline:* For fall admission, 10/15 for domestic and international students; for spring admission, 3/15 for domestic and international students. Application fee: $75 Canadian dollars. Electronic applications accepted. One-time fee: $426 Canadian dollars full-time. *Financial support:* Research assistantships with partial tuition reimbursements, teaching assistantships with partial tuition reimbursements, career-related internships or fieldwork, scholarships/grants, and tuition waivers (partial) available. Support available to part-time students. Financial award application deadline: 3/15. *Faculty research:* Old Testament studies, pastoral theology, New Testament studies, field education, church history, systematic theology, spirituality. *Unit head:* Rev. Dr. Richard Topping, Principal, 604-822-9808, Fax: 604-822-9212. *Application contact:* Anita Fast, Registrar, 604-822-9563, Fax: 604-822-9212, E-mail: afast@vst.edu.
Website: https://vst.edu/students/prospective/degree-programs/graduate-degrees

Vanderbilt University, Department of Religion, Nashville, TN 37240-1001. Offers MA, PhD. *Faculty:* 30 full-time (10 women). *Students:* 65 full-time (37 women); includes 20 minority (15 Black or African American, non-Hispanic/Latino; 2 Asian, non-Hispanic/Latino; 2 Hispanic/Latino; 1 Two or more races, non-Hispanic/Latino), 4 international. Average age 33. 128 applicants, 13% accepted, 12 enrolled. In 2017, 7 master's, 12 doctorates awarded. *Degree requirements:* For master's, one foreign language, thesis; for doctorate, 2 foreign languages, thesis/dissertation, final and qualifying exams. *Entrance requirements:* For master's and doctorate, GRE General Test. Additional exam requirements/recommendations for international students: Required—TOEFL (minimum score 570 paper-based; 88 iBT). *Application deadline:* For fall admission, 12/15 for domestic and international students. Electronic applications accepted. *Financial support:* Fellowships, teaching assistantships, Federal Work-Study, institutionally sponsored loans, health care benefits, and tuition waivers (full and partial) available. Support available to part-time students. Financial award application deadline: 1/15; financial award applicants required to submit CSS PROFILE or FAFSA. *Faculty research:* Hebrew Bible, New Testament, church history, theology, ethics. *Unit head:* Dr. James Byrd, Jr., Chair and Director of Graduate Studies, 615-343-9977, Fax: 615-343-9957,

E-mail: james.p.byrd@vanderbilt.edu. *Application contact:* Karen Eardley, Administrative Assistant, 615-343-3977, Fax: 615-343-9957, E-mail: karen.eardley@vanderbilt.edu.
Website: http://divinity.vanderbilt.edu/degrees/graduate/index.php

Vanguard University of Southern California, Graduate Programs in Religion, Costa Mesa, CA 92626. Offers leadership studies (MA); theological studies (MTS). *Program availability:* Part-time, evening/weekend. *Degree requirements:* For master's, comprehensive exam (for some programs), thesis (for some programs). *Entrance requirements:* For master's, minimum GPA of 3.0 (MA), 2.5 (MTS). Additional exam requirements/recommendations for international students: Required—TOEFL (minimum score 550 paper-based; 79 iBT). Electronic applications accepted. *Expenses:* Contact institution. *Faculty research:* Narrative theology, ecumenism and Pentecost, leadership studies.

Virginia University of Lynchburg, Graduate Programs, Lynchburg, VA 24501-6417. Offers Christian ministry (M Div); ministry (D Min). *Program availability:* Online learning.

Wake Forest University, Graduate School of Arts and Sciences, Department of Religion, Winston-Salem, NC 27109. Offers MA. *Accreditation:* ACIPE. *Program availability:* Part-time. *Degree requirements:* For master's, one foreign language, thesis. *Entrance requirements:* For master's, GRE General Test. Additional exam requirements/recommendations for international students: Required—TOEFL (minimum score 79 iBT). Electronic applications accepted. *Faculty research:* Christian origins, biblical archaeology, psychology and religion, religion and literature.

Walla Walla University, Graduate Studies, Center for Cinema, Religion, and Worldview, College Place, WA 99324. Offers Web and interactive media (MA). *Entrance requirements:* For master's, three professional references, transcripts, personal statement. *Application deadline:* For fall admission, 8/15 for domestic students. Application fee: $50. *Unit head:* Lynelle Ellis, Director, 509-527-2843, Fax: 509-527-2237, E-mail: lynelle.ellis@wallawalla.edu. *Application contact:* Rachel Scribner, Coordinator, 509-527-2832, Fax: 509-527-2237, E-mail: rachel.scribner@wallawalla.edu.
Website: https://www.wallawalla.edu/academics/grad-studies/cinema-religion-worldview/

Washington Adventist University, Program in Religion, Takoma Park, MD 20912. Offers MAR. *Program availability:* Part-time. *Students:* 16 part-time (4 women); includes 12 minority (9 Black or African American, non-Hispanic/Latino; 2 Asian, non-Hispanic/Latino; 1 Hispanic/Latino). Average age 46. In 2017, 1 master's awarded. *Entrance requirements:* Additional exam requirements/recommendations for international students: Required—TOEFL (minimum score 550 paper-based), IELTS (minimum score 5). *Application deadline:* Applications are processed on a rolling basis. *Expenses: Tuition:* Part-time $625 per credit. *Financial support:* Available to part-time students. Applicants required to submit FAFSA. *Unit head:* Dr. Patrick Williams, Associate Provost, 301-891-4116, E-mail: pawillia@wau.edu. *Application contact:* Jessica Ritchie, Program Coordinator, 301-891-4086, Fax: 301-891-4023, E-mail: jritchie@wau.edu.
Website: http://www.wau.edu/index.php?option-com_content&view-article&id-411temid-968

Washington University in St. Louis, The Graduate School, Department of Jewish, Islamic, and Near Eastern Languages and Cultures, St. Louis, MO 63130-4899. Offers Islamic and Near Eastern studies (MA); Jewish studies (MA). *Degree requirements:* For master's, one foreign language, thesis (for some programs). *Entrance requirements:* For master's, GRE General Test. Additional exam requirements/recommendations for international students: Required—TOEFL. Electronic applications accepted. *Faculty research:* Islamic and Near Eastern studies (Islamic history; Arabic language and literature, modern Middle East history); Jewish studies (Hebrew Bible, Rabbinic literature, Jewish history, modern Hebrew literature).

Wayland Baptist University, Graduate Programs, Programs in Religion, Plainview, TX 79072-6998. Offers Christian ministry (MCM); divinity (M Div); religion (MA). *Program availability:* Part-time, evening/weekend, online learning. *Faculty:* 15 full-time (1 woman), 12 part-time/adjunct (0 women). *Students:* 3 full-time (0 women), 97 part-time (27 women); includes 61 minority (36 Black or African American, non-Hispanic/Latino; 1 American Indian or Alaska Native, non-Hispanic/Latino; 6 Asian, non-Hispanic/Latino; 9 Hispanic/Latino; 2 Native Hawaiian or other Pacific Islander, non-Hispanic/Latino; 7 Two or more races, non-Hispanic/Latino). Average age 45. 22 applicants, 95% accepted, 16 enrolled. In 2017, 26 master's awarded. *Degree requirements:* For master's, comprehensive exam. *Entrance requirements:* For master's, GRE or MAT, minimum GPA of 3.0; letter of endorsement from Christian congregation, one academic and one personal letter of recommendation (for M Div). Additional exam requirements/recommendations for international students: Required—TOEFL (minimum score 500 paper-based; 61 iBT). *Application deadline:* Applications are processed on a rolling basis. Application fee: $50. Electronic applications accepted. *Expenses: Tuition:* Full-time $11,250; part-time $625 per credit hour. *Required fees:* $1200. *Financial support:* Federal Work-Study, institutionally sponsored loans, and scholarships/grants available. Support available to part-time students. Financial award application deadline: 5/1; financial award applicants required to submit FAFSA. *Unit head:* Dr. Clinton Lowin, Chairman, 806-291-1165, Fax: 806-291-1969, E-mail: lowinc@wbu.edu. *Application contact:* Amanda Stanton, Coordinator of Graduate Studies, 806-291-3423, Fax: 806-291-1950, E-mail: stanton@wbu.edu.

Wesley Biblical Seminary, Graduate Programs, Jackson, MS 39206. Offers apologetics (MA); Biblical languages (M Div); Biblical literature (MA); Christian studies (MA); context and mission (M Div); honors research (M Div); interpretation (M Div); ministry (M Div); spiritual formation (M Div); teaching (M Div); theology (MA). *Accreditation:* ATS. *Program availability:* Part-time. *Degree requirements:* For master's, thesis. *Entrance requirements:* Additional exam requirements/recommendations for international students: Required—TOEFL. Electronic applications accepted. *Faculty research:* Patristics, missiology, culture, hermeneutics.

Western Michigan University, Graduate College, College of Arts and Sciences, Department of Comparative Religion, Kalamazoo, MI 49008. Offers MA, Graduate Certificate. *Degree requirements:* For master's, one foreign language, thesis optional.

Western Seminary, Graduate Programs, Program in Biblical and Theological Studies, Portland, OR 97215-3367. Offers biblical and theological studies (MA, G Dip); biblical studies (Certificate); theology (Th M). *Accreditation:* ATS. *Program availability:* Part-time, evening/weekend. *Degree requirements:* For master's, thesis or alternative, practicum. *Entrance requirements:* Additional exam requirements/recommendations for international students: Required—TOEFL.

Westminster Seminary California, Programs in Theology, Escondido, CA 92027-4128. Offers Biblical studies (MA); historical theology (MA); theological studies (M Div, MA). *Program availability:* Part-time, evening/weekend. *Degree requirements:* For master's, 2 foreign languages, thesis (for some programs). *Entrance requirements:* For master's, 2 letters of reference. Additional exam requirements/recommendations for international students: Required—TOEFL (minimum score 570 paper-based; 89 iBT), TWE (minimum score 4.5). *Faculty research:* Neo-paganism, New Testament background, eschatology, Protestant scholasticism, Ezekiel.

Westminster Theological Seminary, Graduate and Professional Programs, Philadelphia, PA 19118. Offers apologetics (Th M); Biblical and urban studies (Certificate); Biblical counseling (MA); biblical studies (MAR); Christian studies (Certificate); church history (Th M); counseling (M Div); general studies (M Div, MAR); hermeneutics and Bible interpretations (PhD); historical and theological studies (PhD); historical theology (Th M); New Testament (Th M); Old Testament (Th M); pastoral counseling (D Min); pastoral ministry (M Div, D Min); systematic theology (Th M); theological studies (MAR); urban missions (M Div, MA, MAR, D Min). *Accreditation:* ATS. *Program availability:* Part-time. Terminal master's awarded for partial completion of doctoral program. *Degree requirements:* For master's, thesis (for some programs); for doctorate, 4 foreign languages, comprehensive exam (for some programs), thesis/dissertation. *Entrance requirements:* For doctorate, GRE General Test. Additional exam requirements/recommendations for international students: Required—TOEFL, TWE.

Wilfrid Laurier University, Faculty of Graduate and Postdoctoral Studies, Faculty of Arts, Department of Religion and Culture, Waterloo, ON N2L 3C5, Canada. Offers religion and culture (MA); religious diversity of North America (PhD). *Program availability:* Part-time. *Degree requirements:* For master's, thesis optional; for doctorate, thesis/dissertation. *Entrance requirements:* For master's, honors BA or the equivalent in religious studies or other interdisciplinary social science or humanities program, minimum B average in overall undergraduate course work, B+ average in the undergraduate major; for doctorate, MA in religious studies, minimum A- average. Additional exam requirements/recommendations for international students: Required—TOEFL (minimum score 89 iBT). Electronic applications accepted. *Faculty research:* Religious diversity in North America.

WON Institute of Graduate Studies, Won Buddhist Studies Program, Glenside, PA 19038. Offers MWBS. *Program availability:* Part-time. *Students:* 4 full-time (2 women), 3 part-time (1 woman); includes 4 minority (all Asian, non-Hispanic/Latino). Average age 34. *Degree requirements:* For master's, comprehensive exam, comprehensive ordination exam or thesis. *Entrance requirements:* For master's, bachelor's degree or one-year preparatory course in Won Buddhist studies. Additional exam requirements/recommendations for international students: Required—TOEFL (minimum score 550 paper-based; 79 iBT). *Application deadline:* For fall admission, 8/1 for domestic students; for spring admission, 12/1 for domestic students. Applications are processed on a rolling basis. Application fee: $75. *Financial support:* Application deadline: 8/1. *Faculty research:* Environmental ethics, the concept of religion. *Unit head:* Rev. Dr. Sanghyeon Cheon, Chair, 215-884-8942, E-mail: wbschair@woninstitute.edu. *Application contact:* Jennifer Cake, Enrollment Management Counselor, 215-884-8942 Ext. 219, E-mail: jennifer.cake@woninstitute.edu.
Website: https://www.woninstitute.edu/academics/master-of-won-buddhism-degree/

Wycliffe College, Division of Advanced Degree Studies, Toronto, ON M5S 1H7, Canada. Offers MA, Th M, D Min, PhD, Th D. PhD, D Min, MA offered jointly with Toronto School of Theology; Th D, Th M with University of Toronto. *Accreditation:* ATS (one or more programs are accredited). *Program availability:* Part-time. Terminal master's awarded for partial completion of doctoral program. *Degree requirements:* For master's, 2 foreign languages, thesis (for some programs); for doctorate, 3 foreign languages, thesis/dissertation. *Entrance requirements:* Additional exam requirements/recommendations for international students: Required—TOEFL (minimum score 600 paper-based). *Expenses:* Contact institution. *Faculty research:* Old and New Testament, doctrine, ethics, philosophy, history.

Wycliffe College, Division of Basic Degree Studies, Toronto, ON M5S 1H7, Canada. Offers Christian Studies (Diploma); theology (M Div, M Rel, MTS). M Div, M Rel, MTS offered jointly with University of Toronto. *Accreditation:* ATS. *Program availability:* Part-time. *Degree requirements:* For master's, one foreign language, thesis. *Entrance requirements:* Additional exam requirements/recommendations for international students: Required—TOEFL (minimum score 580 paper-based).

Yale University, Graduate School of Arts and Sciences, Department of Religious Studies, New Haven, CT 06520. Offers PhD. *Degree requirements:* For doctorate, 2 foreign languages, thesis/dissertation. *Entrance requirements:* For doctorate, GRE General Test.

Yeshiva Derech Chaim, Graduate Program, Brooklyn, NY 11218. Offers PhD. *Accreditation:* AARTS.

Theology

Abilene Christian University, Graduate Programs, College of Biblical Studies, Graduate School of Theology, Program in Divinity, Abilene, TX 79699. Offers ministry (M Div); missions (M Div). *Accreditation:* ATS. *Program availability:* Part-time, evening/weekend, blended/hybrid learning. *Students:* 22 full-time (4 women), 45 part-time (9 women); includes 8 minority (all Black or African American, non-Hispanic/Latino), 6 international. 26 applicants, 54% accepted, 9 enrolled. In 2017, 3 master's awarded. *Degree requirements:* For master's, comprehensive exam, e-portfolio review. *Entrance requirements:* Additional exam requirements/recommendations for international students: Required—TOEFL (minimum score 80 iBT), IELTS (minimum score 6), PTE. *Application deadline:* For fall admission, 8/11 for domestic students; for spring admission, 11/1 for domestic students. Applications are processed on a rolling basis. Application fee: $50. Electronic applications accepted. *Expenses:* $618 per hour. *Financial support:* In 2017–18, 14 students received support. Scholarships/grants available. Financial award application deadline: 4/1; financial award applicants required to submit FAFSA. *Unit head:* Dr. Kelli Gibson, Graduate Advisor, 325-674-3709, Fax: 325-674-6716, E-mail: kelli.gibson@acu.edu. *Application contact:* Graduate Admissions, 325-674-6911, Fax: 325-674-6717, E-mail: gradinfo@acu.edu.
Website: http://www.acu.edu/graduate/academics/divinity.html

Abilene Christian University, Graduate Programs, College of Biblical Studies, Graduate School of Theology, Program in New Testament, Abilene, TX 79699. Offers MA. *Accreditation:* ATS. *Program availability:* Part-time. *Students:* 3 full-time (1 woman), 1 part-time (0 women). 3 applicants. *Degree requirements:* For master's, comprehensive exam, thesis. *Entrance requirements:* Additional exam requirements/recommendations for international students: Required—TOEFL (minimum score 80 iBT), IELTS (minimum score 6), PTE. *Application deadline:* For fall admission, 8/11 for domestic students; for spring admission, 11/1 for domestic students. Applications are processed on a rolling basis. Application fee: $50. Electronic applications accepted. *Expenses:* $637 per hour. *Financial support:* Scholarships/grants available. Financial award application deadline: 4/1; financial award applicants required to submit FAFSA. *Unit head:* Dr. Richard Wright, Graduate Advisor, 325-674-3708, Fax: 325-674-6180, E-mail: richard.wright@acu.edu. *Application contact:* Graduate Admissions, 325-674-6911, Fax: 325-674-6717, E-mail: gradinfo@acu.edu.
Website: http://www.acu.edu/graduate/academics/new-testament.html

Abilene Christian University, Graduate Programs, College of Biblical Studies, Graduate School of Theology, Program in Old Testament, Abilene, TX 79699. Offers MA. *Accreditation:* ATS. *Program availability:* Part-time. *Students:* 1 part-time (0 women). In 2017, 2 master's awarded. *Degree requirements:* For master's, comprehensive exam, thesis. *Entrance requirements:* Additional exam requirements/recommendations for international students: Required—TOEFL (minimum score 80 iBT), IELTS (minimum score 6), PTE. *Application deadline:* For fall admission, 8/11 for domestic students; for spring admission, 11/1 for domestic students. Applications are processed on a rolling basis. Application fee: $50. Electronic applications accepted. *Expenses:* $637 per hour. *Financial support:* Scholarships/grants available. Financial award application deadline: 4/1; financial award applicants required to submit FAFSA. *Unit head:* Dr. Mark Hamilton, Graduate Advisor, 325-674-3765, Fax: 325-674-6180, E-mail: mark.hamilton@acu.edu. *Application contact:* Graduate Admissions, 325-674-6911, Fax: 325-674-6717, E-mail: gradinfo@acu.edu.
Website: http://www.acu.edu/graduate/academics/old-testament.html

Abilene Christian University, Graduate Programs, College of Biblical Studies, Graduate School of Theology, Program in Theology, Abilene, TX 79699. Offers MA. *Accreditation:* ATS. *Program availability:* Part-time. *Students:* 2 full-time (0 women), 7 part-time (3 women); includes 1 minority (Hispanic/Latino). 8 applicants, 25% accepted, 1 enrolled. In 2017, 1 master's awarded. *Degree requirements:* For master's, comprehensive exam, thesis. *Entrance requirements:* Additional exam requirements/recommendations for international students: Required—TOEFL (minimum score 80 iBT), IELTS (minimum score 6), PTE. *Application deadline:* For fall admission, 8/11 for domestic students; for spring admission, 11/1 for domestic students. Applications are processed on a rolling basis. Application fee: $50. Electronic applications accepted. *Expenses:* $637 per hour. *Financial support:* Application deadline: 4/1; applicants required to submit FAFSA. *Unit head:* Dr. Frederick Aquino, Graduate Advisor, 325-674-3789, Fax: 325-674-6180, E-mail: frederick.aquino@acu.edu. *Application contact:* Graduate Admissions, 325-674-6911, Fax: 325-674-6717, E-mail: gradinfo@acu.edu.
Website: http://www.acu.edu/graduate/academics/theology.html

Acadia University, Divinity College, Wolfville, NS B4P 2R6, Canada. Offers divinity (M Div); ministry (D Min); theology (MA), including chaplaincy and spiritual care, Christian history, discipleship, evangelism and mission, indigenous community development, leadership and spiritual formation, New Testament, next generation ministry, Old Testament, pastoral care and counseling, prison chaplaincy, Second Temple Judaism, theology. *Accreditation:* ATS. *Program availability:* Part-time. *Degree requirements:* For master's, variable foreign language requirement, thesis (for some programs); for doctorate, one foreign language, comprehensive exam, thesis/dissertation. *Entrance requirements:* For doctorate, minimum GPA of 3.0, 3 years' ministry experience. Additional exam requirements/recommendations for international students: Required—TOEFL. *Application deadline:* For fall admission, 6/30 priority date for domestic students, 4/1 priority date for international students; for spring admission, 4/30 priority date for domestic students. Applications are processed on a rolling basis. Application fee: $50. *Expenses:* Contact institution. *Financial support:* Application deadline: 8/12. *Faculty research:* Biblical canon, Jesus, Dead Sea Scrolls, Baptist studies, Old Testament-Septuagint. *Unit head:* Dr. Harry Gardner, President/Dean of Theology, 902-585-2213, Fax: 902-585-2233, E-mail: harry.gardner@acadiau.ca. *Application contact:* Shawna Peverill, Registrar, 902-585-2215, Fax: 902-585-2233, E-mail: shawna.peverill@acadiau.ca.
Website: http://divinity.acadiau.ca/

Ambrose University, Ambrose Seminary, Calgary, AB T3H 0L5, Canada. Offers Biblical/theological studies (MA), including New Testament, Old Testament, theology; Christian studies (MCS, Diploma); intercultural ministries (M Div, MA); leadership (Certificate); leadership and ministry (MA), including chaplaincy, leadership; pastoral ministry (M Div). *Accreditation:* ATS (one or more programs are accredited). *Program availability:* Part-time, blended/hybrid learning. *Degree requirements:* For master's, variable foreign language requirement, thesis (for some programs), internship (for M Div, MA in leadership and ministry, MA in intercultural ministries); thesis (for MA in Biblical/theological studies). *Entrance requirements:* For master's, undergraduate degree from other accredited university or bible college, minimum GPA of 2.0. Additional exam requirements/recommendations for international students: Required—PTE (minimum score 58), TOEFL (minimum score 560 paper-based, 83 iBT) or IELTS (minimum score 6.5). Electronic applications accepted. *Faculty research:* Evangelicalism and sociology, missiological trends, chaplaincy, intertestamental studies, postmodernism.

American Baptist Seminary of the West, Graduate and Professional Programs, Berkeley, CA 94704-3029. Offers community leadership (MA); theology (M Div, MA). MA program in theology offered jointly with Graduate Theological Union. *Accreditation:* ACIPE; ATS (one or more programs are accredited). *Program availability:* Part-time, evening/weekend, online learning. *Entrance requirements:* Additional exam requirements/recommendations for international students: Required—TOEFL (minimum score 550 paper-based). Electronic applications accepted.

American Jewish University, Ziegler School of Rabbinic Studies, Bel Air, CA 90077-1599. Offers MARS. *Degree requirements:* For master's, one foreign language. *Entrance requirements:* For master's, GRE General Test, interview. Additional exam requirements/recommendations for international students: Required—TOEFL.

Amridge University, Graduate and Professional Programs, Montgomery, AL 36117. Offers Biblical studies (MA, PhD); Christian ministry (MS); family therapy (D Min); human services (MS); leadership and management (MS); marriage and family therapy (M Div, MA, PhD); ministerial leadership (M Div, MS); New Testament studies (MA); Old Testament studies (MA); professional counseling (M Div, MA, PhD); theology (M Div, D Min). *Program availability:* Part-time, evening/weekend, online learning. *Faculty:* 23 full-time (3 women), 9 part-time/adjunct (5 women). *Students:* 105 full-time (55 women), 250 part-time (152 women); includes 217 minority (167 Black or African American, non-Hispanic/Latino; 4 Asian, non-Hispanic/Latino; 42 Hispanic/Latino; 4 Native Hawaiian or other Pacific Islander, non-Hispanic/Latino). Average age 42. 160 applicants, 100% accepted, 110 enrolled. *Degree requirements:* For master's, one foreign language, comprehensive exam (for some programs), thesis (for some programs); for doctorate, one foreign language, comprehensive exam (for some programs), thesis/dissertation

(for some programs). *Entrance requirements:* For master's, official transcript showing an earned 4-year BA or BS from regionally- or nationally-accredited institution; for doctorate, official transcript showing earned graduate degree from regionally- or nationally-accredited institution; writing sample (e.g. career monograph, published journal article, term paper from master's degree or doctoral dissertation); interview. Additional exam requirements/recommendations for international students: Required—TOEFL (minimum score 79 iBT). *Application deadline:* Applications are processed on a rolling basis. Application fee: $50. Electronic applications accepted. *Financial support:* In 2017–18, 33 students received support. Federal Work-Study and scholarships/grants available. Support available to part-time students. Financial award applicants required to submit FAFSA. *Faculty research:* Technology and mental healthcare, resilience in black families, theology and congregational ministry. *Unit head:* Laina Costanza, Vice President, Student Affairs, 888-790-8080 Ext. 1, Fax: 334-387-3878, E-mail: cc@amridgeuniversity.edu. *Application contact:* Brooks Housley, Student Affairs Coordinator, 888-790-8080 Ext. 1, Fax: 334-387-3878, E-mail: admissions@amridgeuniversity.edu.

Anabaptist Mennonite Biblical Seminary, Graduate and Professional Programs, Elkhart, IN 46517-1999. Offers chaplaincy (M Div); Christian faith formation (M Div); Christian formation (MA); Christian spiritual formation (Certificate); divinity (M Div); pastoral ministry (M Div); pastoral theology for financial professionals (Certificate); peace studies (M Div), including environmental sustainability leadership (M Div, MA); theological studies (M Div, Certificate), including peace studies (M Div), theology and ethics (M Div); theology and peace studies (MA), including conflict transformation, environmental sustainability leadership (M Div, MA), international development administration; United Methodist leadership (M Div). Conflict transformation and environmental sustainability leadership concentrations offered in cooperation with Goshen College; international development administration offered in cooperation with Andrews University. *Accreditation:* ACIPE; ATS. *Program availability:* Part-time, 100% online, blended/hybrid learning. *Degree requirements:* For master's, variable foreign language requirement, comprehensive exam (for some programs), thesis optional, senior interview. *Entrance requirements:* For master's, undergraduate degree transcripts, 3 letters of reference, essay. Additional exam requirements/recommendations for international students: Required—TOEFL (minimum score 90 iBT); Recommended—IELTS (minimum score 7). Electronic applications accepted. *Faculty research:* Biblical studies, peace studies, theology, ethics, creation care or environmental ethics, church history, church leadership, mission, ministry, preaching, pastoral leadership, social justice, peacemaking, Jesus Christ, Christianity, Anabaptism, Mennonite, Scripture, Bible, Old Testament, New Testament, spirituality, clinical pastoral education, teaching, faith formation, pastoral care, Koine Greek, Hebrew, Aramaic, Syriac, Ugaritic.

Anderson University, School of Theology, Anderson, IN 46012-3495. Offers missions (MA); theology (M Div, MTS, D Min). *Accreditation:* ACIPE; ATS. *Program availability:* Part-time. *Degree requirements:* For master's, variable foreign language requirement, thesis (for some programs); for doctorate, thesis/dissertation. *Faculty research:* Small-church/bivocational ministry, women in ministry.

Andrews University, School of Graduate Studies, Seventh-day Adventist Theological Seminary, Berrien Springs, MI 49104. Offers ministry (M Div, D Min); pastoral ministry (MA); religious education (MA, Ed D, PhD, Ed S); theology (M Th, Th D); youth ministry (MA). *Faculty:* 40 full-time (5 women), 12 part-time/adjunct (2 women). *Students:* 529 full-time (70 women), 419 part-time (69 women); includes 480 minority (217 Black or African American, non-Hispanic/Latino; 7 American Indian or Alaska Native, non-Hispanic/Latino; 53 Asian, non-Hispanic/Latino; 190 Hispanic/Latino; 5 Native Hawaiian or other Pacific Islander, non-Hispanic/Latino; 8 Two or more races, non-Hispanic/Latino), 242 international. Average age 40. 497 applicants, 46% accepted, 216 enrolled. In 2017, 147 master's, 46 doctorates awarded. *Degree requirements:* For master's, thesis optional; for doctorate, variable foreign language requirement, thesis/dissertation. *Entrance requirements:* For master's, GRE Subject Test, minimum GPA of 2.0. Additional exam requirements/recommendations for international students: Required—TOEFL (minimum score 550 paper-based). *Application deadline:* Applications are processed on a rolling basis. Application fee: $40. *Financial support:* Fellowships, research assistantships, teaching assistantships, career-related internships or fieldwork, Federal Work-Study, and institutionally sponsored loans available. *Faculty research:* Biblical archaeology, biblical studies, biblical language learning methods, church growth. *Unit head:* Dr. Jiri Moskala, Dean, 269-471-3537. *Application contact:* Justina Clayburn, Director, 800-253-2874, Fax: 269-471-6321.

Apex School of Theology, Graduate Programs, Durham, NC 27703. Offers M Div, MACC, MCE, D Min. *Faculty research:* Sociology, educational sciences, economics.

Aquinas Institute of Theology, Graduate and Professional Programs, St. Louis, MO 63108. Offers biblical studies (Certificate); church music (MM); health care mission (MAHCM); ministry (M Div); pastoral care (Certificate); pastoral ministry (MAPM); pastoral studies (MAPS); preaching (D Min); spiritual direction (Certificate); theology (M Div, MA); Thomistic studies (Certificate); M Div/MA; MA/PhD; MAPS/MSW. *Accreditation:* ATS (one or more programs are accredited). *Program availability:* Part-time, evening/weekend, online learning. *Degree requirements:* For master's, variable foreign language requirement, comprehensive exam (for some programs), thesis (for some programs); for doctorate, thesis/dissertation. *Entrance requirements:* For master's and Certificate, MAT; for doctorate, 3 years of ministerial experience, 6 hours of graduate course work in homiletics, M Div or the equivalent, minimum GPA of 3.0. Additional exam requirements/recommendations for international students: Required—TOEFL. *Expenses:* Contact institution. *Faculty research:* Theology of preaching, hermeneutics, lay ecclesial ministry, pastoral and practical theology.

Arlington Baptist University, Program in Biblical and Theological Studies, Arlington, TX 76012-3425. Offers MA. *Entrance requirements:* For master's, official transcript, letter of reference from pastor, two letters of recommendation, essay. Additional exam requirements/recommendations for international students: Required—TOEFL. Electronic applications accepted.

Asbury Theological Seminary, Graduate and Professional Programs, Wilmore, KY 40390-1199. Offers M Div, MA, MAAS, MACE, MACL, MACM, MACP, MAMFC, MAMHC, MAPC, MASF, MAYM, Th M, D Min, PhD, Certificate. *Accreditation:* ATS. *Program availability:* Part-time, online learning. Terminal master's awarded for partial completion of doctoral program. *Degree requirements:* For master's, thesis (for some programs); for doctorate, thesis/dissertation, qualifying exam. *Entrance requirements:* For master's, minimum GPA of 2.75; for doctorate, minimum GPA of 3.0. Additional exam requirements/recommendations for international students: Required—TOEFL, IELTS. Electronic applications accepted.

Ashland Theological Seminary, Graduate Programs, Ashland, OH 44805. Offers Biblical studies (MA); Christian ministries (MACM), including Black church studies (MACM, D Min), general Christian ministries, leadership, spiritual formation (MACM, D Min); clinical mental health counseling (MA); counseling (MAC); historical and theological studies (MA), including Anabaptism and Pietism, Christian theology, church history, New Testament, Old Testament; ministry (D Min), including Black church studies (MACM, D Min), chaplaincy (M Div, D Min), independent design, spiritual

formation (MACM, D Min), transformational leadership; pastoral ministry (M Div), including chaplaincy (M Div, D Min), general ministry. MAC program offered in Detroit, MI. *Accreditation:* ATS. *Program availability:* Part-time. *Degree requirements:* For master's, 2 foreign languages, comprehensive exam (for some programs), thesis (for some programs); for doctorate, thesis/dissertation. *Entrance requirements:* For master's, bachelor's degree from accredited institution with minimum undergraduate GPA of 2.75; for doctorate, M Div, minimum undergraduate GPA of 3.0. Additional exam requirements/recommendations for international students: Required—TOEFL (minimum score 500 paper-based; 65 iBT). Electronic applications accepted. *Faculty research:* Semitic languages and linguistics, rhetorical and social-scientific criticism, Anabaptist studies, inner spiritual healing, African-American clergy in film and literature.

Assemblies of God Theological Seminary, Graduate and Professional Programs, Springfield, MO 65802. Offers Biblical interpretation and theology (PhD); Christian ministries (MA); divinity (M Div); intercultural studies (MA, PhD); leadership and ministry (MLM); ministry (D Min); missiology (DAIS); pastoral studies (MPL); theological studies (MA, Th M). *Accreditation:* ATS. *Program availability:* Part-time, evening/weekend, 100% online. *Faculty:* 12 full-time (3 women), 15 part-time/adjunct (4 women). *Students:* 153 full-time (48 women), 159 part-time (41 women); includes 62 minority (20 Black or African American, non-Hispanic/Latino; 4 American Indian or Alaska Native, non-Hispanic/Latino; 14 Asian, non-Hispanic/Latino; 18 Hispanic/Latino; 6 Two or more races, non-Hispanic/Latino), 12 international. Average age 46. 69 applicants, 88% accepted, 48 enrolled. In 2017, 35 master's, 22 doctorates awarded. *Degree requirements:* For master's, variable foreign language requirement, thesis; for doctorate, variable foreign language requirement, comprehensive exam, thesis/dissertation. *Entrance requirements:* For master's, minimum GPA of 2.5; for doctorate, GRE (for PhD in Bible theology), minimum GPA of 3.0. Additional exam requirements/recommendations for international students: Required—TOEFL (minimum score 550 paper-based; 80 iBT). *Application deadline:* For fall admission, 7/1 priority date for domestic students, 6/1 priority date for international students; for spring admission, 12/1 priority date for domestic students, 11/1 priority date for international students. Applications are processed on a rolling basis. Application fee: $75. Electronic applications accepted. *Financial support:* Career-related internships or fieldwork and scholarships/grants available. Support available to part-time students. Financial award application deadline: 7/15; financial award applicants required to submit FAFSA. *Unit head:* Dr. Timothy A. Hager, Dean, 417-268-1000, Fax: 417-268-1001. *Application contact:* Erin Leonard, Seminary Enrollment Coordinator, 417-268-1000, Fax: 417-268-1001, E-mail: info@agts.edu.
Website: http://www.agts.edu

The Athenaeum of Ohio, Graduate Programs, Cincinnati, OH 45230-5900. Offers M Div, MA, MA Th, MABS, Certificate, M Div/MA Th, M Div/MABS. *Program availability:* Part-time, evening/weekend. *Students:* 80 full-time (1 woman), 62 part-time (31 women); includes 12 minority (1 Black or African American, non-Hispanic/Latino; 3 Asian, non-Hispanic/Latino; 6 Hispanic/Latino; 2 Two or more races, non-Hispanic/Latino), 10 international. In 2017, 16 master's awarded. *Degree requirements:* For master's, variable foreign language requirement, comprehensive exam (for some programs), thesis or alternative. *Entrance requirements:* For master's, bachelor's degree, minimum GPA of 3.0. *Application deadline:* For fall admission, 4/15 priority date for domestic students; for spring admission, 11/1 priority date for domestic students. Applications are processed on a rolling basis. Application fee: $30. *Financial support:* Scholarships/grants available. Support available to part-time students. Financial award application deadline: 8/1. *Unit head:* Fr. David J. Endres, Dean, 513-231-2223, Fax: 513-231-3254, E-mail: dendres@athenaeum.edu. *Application contact:* Nicholas Jobe, Registrar, 513-231-2223, Fax: 513-231-3254, E-mail: njobe@athenaeum.edu.
Website: http://www.athenaeum.edu/

Atlantic School of Theology, Graduate and Professional Programs, Halifax, NS B3H 3B5, Canada. Offers ministry (M Div); theological studies (Graduate Certificate). *Accreditation:* ATS. *Program availability:* Part-time, online learning. *Degree requirements:* For master's, thesis (for some programs). *Entrance requirements:* For master's and Graduate Certificate, minimum B average in undergraduate course work. *Faculty research:* Ethics and biology; death, dying and pastoral care; theology and the economy; adult education; John and anti-Judaism.

Austin Graduate School of Theology, Program in Theological Studies, Austin, TX 78752. Offers MATS. *Program availability:* Part-time. *Faculty:* 4 full-time (0 women), 4 part-time/adjunct (0 women). *Students:* 6 full-time (1 woman), 8 part-time (4 women). *Degree requirements:* For master's, 2 foreign languages, comprehensive exam, faculty forums. *Entrance requirements:* For master's, 3 letters of reference, essay, minimum cumulative GPA of 2.5, bachelor's degree, official transcripts. Additional exam requirements/recommendations for international students: Required—TOEFL (minimum score 550 paper-based; 80 iBT). *Application deadline:* For fall admission, 7/1 priority date for domestic and international students; for spring admission, 10/1 priority date for domestic and international students. Applications are processed on a rolling basis. Application fee: $25. Electronic applications accepted. Application fee is waived when completed online. *Financial support:* Federal Work-Study and scholarships/grants available. Support available to part-time students. Financial award application deadline: 7/1. *Faculty research:* Revelation, synoptic problem, Acadian, Biblical archaeology, worship. *Unit head:* Dr. Keith Stanglin, Graduate Student Advisor, 512-476-2772, Fax: 512-476-3919, E-mail: stanglin@austingrad.edu. *Application contact:* Dawn Bond, Director of Admissions/Registrar, 512-476-2772 Ext. 103, Fax: 512-476-3919, E-mail: dbond@austingrad.edu.
Website: http://www.austingrad.edu/academics_mats.html

Austin Presbyterian Theological Seminary, Graduate and Professional Programs, Austin, TX 78705-5797. Offers divinity (M Div); ministry (D Min); ministry practice (MA); theological studies (MA); youth ministry (MA); M Div/MSSW. M Div/MSSW offered in collaboration with The University of Texas at Austin School of Social Work. *Accreditation:* ACIPE; ATS. *Faculty:* 21 full-time (6 women), 4 part-time/adjunct (0 women). *Students:* 80 full-time (50 women), 77 part-time (45 women). *Degree requirements:* For master's, Greek, Hebrew (for M Div); for doctorate, thesis/dissertation. *Entrance requirements:* For master's, references (for M Div). Additional exam requirements/recommendations for international students: Required—TOEFL (minimum score 550 paper-based; 79 iBT). *Application deadline:* For fall admission, 5/1 for domestic students, 1/1 for international students; for winter admission, 9/6 for domestic students; for summer admission, 2/2 for domestic students. Applications are processed on a rolling basis. Application fee: $50. Electronic applications accepted. *Expenses:* Tuition: Full-time $13,500; part-time $6750 per credit. *Required fees:* $120; $120 per credit. One-time fee: $150. Tuition and fees vary according to program. *Financial support:* Fellowships, career-related internships or fieldwork, institutionally sponsored loans, and scholarships/grants available. Support available to part-time students. Financial award application deadline: 2/1; financial award applicants required to submit FAFSA. *Faculty research:* Mystical theology, religious pluralism, narrative preaching, social ethics, pastoral care and healing. *Unit head:* Dr. David Jensen, Academic Dean, 512-404-4821, Fax: 512-479-0738, E-mail: dean@austinseminary.edu. *Application contact:* Dr. Jack Barden, Vice President for Enrollment Management, 512-404-4827, Fax: 512-472-7089, E-mail: admissions@austinseminary.edu.

Ave Maria University, Graduate Programs, Ave Maria, FL 34142. Offers pastoral theology (MTS); theology (MA, PhD). Terminal master's awarded for partial completion of doctoral program. *Degree requirements:* For master's, one foreign language, thesis; for doctorate, 3 foreign languages, comprehensive exam, thesis/dissertation. *Entrance requirements:* For master's, GRE; for doctorate, GRE, M Div or equivalent; MA or MTS in religion, theology, or philosophy; bachelor's degree with strong background in religion, theology, and/or philosophy.

Azusa Pacific University, Azusa Pacific Seminary, Program in Divinity, Azusa, CA 91702-7000. Offers Biblical studies (M Div). Program also offered in Korean at Los Angeles campus, and in Spanish. *Expenses:* Contact institution.

Azusa Pacific University, Azusa Pacific Seminary, Program in Ministry, Azusa, CA 91702-7000. Offers D Min. Program also offered in Korean at Los Angeles campus. *Accreditation:* ATS. *Expenses:* Contact institution.

Azusa Pacific University, Azusa Pacific Seminary, Program in Theological Studies, Concentration in Biblical Studies, Azusa, CA 91702-7000. Offers MA. *Accreditation:* ATS.

Azusa Pacific University, Azusa Pacific Seminary, Program in Theological Studies, Concentration in Theology and Ethics, Azusa, CA 91702-7000. Offers MA. *Accreditation:* ATS.

Azusa Pacific University, College of Liberal Arts and Sciences, Haggard Graduate School of Theology, Azusa, CA 91702-7000. Offers MA. *Expenses:* Contact institution.

Bakke Graduate University, Programs in Pastoral Ministry and Business, Dallas, TX 75243-7039. Offers business administration (MBA); church and ministry multiplication (D Min); global urban leadership (MA); leadership (D Min); ministry in complex contexts (D Min); social and civic entrepreneurship (MA); theology of work (D Min); theology reflection (D Min); transformational leadership (DTL); urban youth ministry (D Min). *Program availability:* Part-time, online learning. *Faculty:* 5 full-time (3 women), 27 part-time/adjunct (12 women). *Students:* 120 full-time (48 women), 54 part-time (24 women). *Degree requirements:* For master's, thesis; for doctorate, thesis/dissertation. *Entrance requirements:* For master's, 2 years of ministry experience, BA in Biblical studies or theology; for doctorate, 3 years of ministry experience, M Div. Additional exam requirements/recommendations for international students: Required—TOEFL. *Application deadline:* For fall admission, 7/1 priority date for domestic students; for winter admission, 12/1 for domestic students; for spring admission, 3/15 for domestic students. Applications are processed on a rolling basis. Application fee: $50. Electronic applications accepted. *Expenses: Tuition:* Full-time $6120; part-time $3000 per credit. *Required fees:* $50 per course. $50 per quarter. *Financial support:* Scholarships/grants and tuition waivers (partial) available. Financial award applicants required to submit FAFSA. *Faculty research:* Theological systems, church management, worship. *Unit head:* Dr. Gwen Dewey, Senior Vice President of International Partnerships, 214-329-4447 Ext. 119, E-mail: gwen.dewey@bgu.edu. *Application contact:* Traci Tucker, Director of Admissions, 214-329-4447 Ext. 122, Fax: 214-347-9367, E-mail: traci.tucker@bgu.edu.
Website: http://www.bgu.edu/

Baptist Bible College, Graduate and Professional Programs, Springfield, MO 65803-3498. Offers biblical counseling (MA); church ministry (MA); theology (M Div). *Program availability:* Part-time. *Faculty:* 1 full-time (0 women), 6 part-time/adjunct (0 women). *Students:* 2 full-time (0 women), 27 part-time (4 women); includes 5 minority (2 Black or African American, non-Hispanic/Latino; 1 Asian, non-Hispanic/Latino; 2 Hispanic/Latino), 3 international. *Entrance requirements:* Additional exam requirements/recommendations for international students: Required—TOEFL. *Application deadline:* For fall admission, 8/1 priority date for domestic students; for spring admission, 1/14 for domestic students. Applications are processed on a rolling basis. Application fee: $40. Electronic applications accepted. *Expenses:* $450 per credit hour tuition, $200 student fee per semester. *Financial support:* Application deadline: 3/6; applicants required to submit FAFSA. *Unit head:* Mark Milioni, President, 417-268-6008, Fax: 800-819-8330. *Application contact:* Mark Milioni, President, 417-268-6008, Fax: 800-819-8330.
Website: http://gobbc.edu/academics-2/seminary-degrees/

The Baptist College of Florida, Graduate Programs, Graceville, FL 32440. Offers Christian ministry (MA); Christian studies (MA), including Biblical studies; music and worship leadership (MA). *Program availability:* Part-time, 100% online, blended/hybrid learning. *Faculty:* 12 full-time (0 women). *Students:* 33 full-time (6 women); includes 2 minority (1 Black or African American, non-Hispanic/Latino; 1 Hispanic/Latino). Average age 28. 10 applicants, 100% accepted, 10 enrolled. In 2017, 3 master's awarded. *Degree requirements:* For master's, variable foreign language requirement, comprehensive exam (for some programs), thesis (for some programs). *Entrance requirements:* For master's, regionally-accredited undergraduate degree, undergraduate courses in field, minimum GPA of 2.5. Additional exam requirements/recommendations for international students: Required—TOEFL. *Application deadline:* For fall admission, 8/15 for domestic students; for spring admission, 1/15 for domestic students. Applications are processed on a rolling basis. Application fee: $25. Electronic applications accepted. *Expenses:* Contact institution. *Financial support:* In 2017–18, 2 students received support. *Faculty research:* Biblical studies, ministry studies. *Unit head:* Dr. Ed Scott, Chair of the Graduate Division, 850-263-3261 Ext. 488, E-mail: eescott@baptistcollege.edu. *Application contact:* Sandra Richards, Director of Student Life and Marketing, 850-263-3261 Ext. 415.
Website: http://www.baptistcollege.edu

Baptist Missionary Association Theological Seminary, Graduate and Professional Programs, Jacksonville, TX 75766-5407. Offers M Div, MAR. *Accreditation:* ATS. *Program availability:* Part-time. *Degree requirements:* For master's, variable foreign language requirement, thesis optional. *Entrance requirements:* Additional exam requirements/recommendations for international students: Required—TOEFL (minimum score 550 paper-based). Electronic applications accepted. *Faculty research:* Education, Biblical studies.

Baptist Theological Seminary at Richmond, Graduate and Professional Programs, Richmond, VA 23228. Offers Biblical interpretation (M Div); Christian education formation (M Div); Christian ministry (MCM); justice and peacebuilding (M Div); ministry (D Min); religious freedom (M Div); theological studies (MTS, Graduate Certificate); theology (M Div); youth and student ministries (M Div); M Div/MBA; M Div/MS; M Div/MSW. *Accreditation:* ATS. *Program availability:* Part-time, 100% online, blended/hybrid learning. *Faculty:* 2 full-time (1 woman), 8 part-time/adjunct (2 women). *Students:* 38 full-time (14 women), 31 part-time (22 women); includes 15 minority (11 Black or African American, non-Hispanic/Latino; 4 Asian, non-Hispanic/Latino). Average age 46. In 2017, 15 master's, 2 doctorates awarded. *Degree requirements:* For master's and Graduate Certificate, thesis optional; for doctorate, comprehensive exam, thesis/dissertation, field study, independent study. *Entrance requirements:* For master's, BA/BS, minimum GPA of 2.2, 2 references, resume, official transcripts, writing sample; for doctorate, MAT (minimum score of 400), M Div with minimum GPA of 2.75, 3 years of full-time ministry experience, 3 references, resume, official transcripts, writing sample, personal statement. Additional exam requirements/recommendations for international students: Required—TOEFL (minimum score 550 paper-based), IELTS (minimum score 5.5). *Application deadline:* For fall admission, 7/1 for domestic students, 5/1 for international students; for winter admission, 12/15 for domestic students, 9/1 for international students; for spring admission, 1/15 for domestic students, 10/1 for international students. Applications are processed on a rolling basis. Application fee: $35. Electronic applications accepted. *Financial support:* In 2017–18, 46 students received support, including 9 teaching assistantships (averaging $3,300 per year); scholarships/grants also available. Financial award application deadline: 2/1. *Faculty research:* Biblical studies, pastoral care, church history, theology, ministry. *Unit head:* Dr. Linda M. Bridges, President, 804-204-1201, Fax: 804-355-8182, E-mail: lmbridges@btsr.edu. *Application contact:* Melissa Fallen, Director of Admissions and Recruitment, 804-204-1208, E-mail: admissions@btsr.edu.
Website: http://www.btsr.edu/programs/degree-programs/

Barclay College, Master of Arts Program, Haviland, KS 67059-0288. Offers MA. *Program availability:* Online learning. *Degree requirements:* For master's, comprehensive exam, capstone project. *Entrance requirements:* Additional exam requirements/recommendations for international students: Required—TOEFL. Electronic applications accepted.

Barry University, College of Arts and Sciences, Department of Theology and Philosophy, Miami Shores, FL 33161-6695. Offers ministry (D Min); pastoral ministry for Hispanics (MA); pastoral theology (MA); practical theology (MA). *Accreditation:* ATS. *Program availability:* Part-time, evening/weekend. *Degree requirements:* For master's, comprehensive exam, thesis optional; for doctorate, thesis/dissertation. *Entrance requirements:* For master's, GRE General Test or MAT, minimum GPA of 3.0. Electronic applications accepted. *Faculty research:* Fundamental morals, bioethics, social ethics, liturgical and sacramental theology, biblical studies.

Baylor University, George W. Truett Theological Seminary, Waco, TX 76798. Offers M Div, MACM, MTS, D Min, JD/M Div, M Div/MBA, M Div/MM, M Div/MS Ed, M Div/MSW, MTS/MSW. *Program availability:* Part-time. *Faculty:* 21 full-time (2 women), 14 part-time/adjunct (4 women). *Students:* 267 full-time (94 women), 75 part-time (22 women); includes 102 minority (55 Black or African American, non-Hispanic/Latino; 1 American Indian or Alaska Native, non-Hispanic/Latino; 6 Asian, non-Hispanic/Latino; 24 Hispanic/Latino; 16 Two or more races, non-Hispanic/Latino), 18 international. Average age 30. 129 applicants, 95% accepted, 91 enrolled. In 2017, 67 master's, 7 doctorates awarded. *Degree requirements:* For master's, 2 foreign languages, thesis or alternative; for doctorate, comprehensive exam, thesis/dissertation, 12 hours of seminars, 12 hours of directed study (including 2 annotated bibliographies reflecting at least 4800 pages of reading, 10 meetings with a field supervisor, 20 meetings with a faculty supervisor, and 3 major learning events). *Entrance requirements:* For master's, 4 recommendations, 2 essays, transcripts from all colleges/universities attended to include conferred undergraduate degree or equivalent, minimum GPA of 2.7, evidence of Christian commitment and leadership; for doctorate, 4 recommendations, 3 essays, writing sample, church recommendation, interview, transcripts from all colleges/universities attended to include conferred M Div or equivalent, minimum GPA of 3.0, 3 years of ministry experience subsequent to M Div. Additional exam requirements/recommendations for international students: Required—TOEFL (minimum score 550 paper-based; 80 iBT), IELTS (minimum score 6.5). *Application deadline:* For fall admission, 5/1 priority date for domestic students, 6/10 for international students; for spring admission, 11/15 for domestic students, 10/10 for international students; for summer admission, 4/1 for domestic students, 3/10 for international students. Applications are processed on a rolling basis. Application fee: $35. Electronic applications accepted. Application fee is waived when completed online. *Expenses:* Contact institution. *Financial support:* In 2017–18, 342 students received support, including 38 research assistantships with partial tuition reimbursements available (averaging $5,130 per year); career-related internships or fieldwork, Federal Work-Study, scholarships/grants, and unspecified assistantships also available. Support available to part-time students. Financial award application deadline: 8/1; financial award applicants required to submit FAFSA. *Faculty research:* Spiritual companioning in protestant theology and practice; emerging divide in evangelical theology; sports and violence; ancient African church; church world encounter. *Total annual research expenditures:* $257,821. *Unit head:* Dr. Todd D. Still, Dean, 254-710-6080, Fax: 254-710-7234, E-mail: todd_still@baylor.edu. *Application contact:* Carley Lund, Administrative Associate, Admission Services, 254-710-7334, Fax: 254-710-7233, E-mail: carley_lund@baylor.edu.
Website: http://www.baylor.edu/truett/

Bethany Theological Seminary, Graduate and Professional Programs, Richmond, IN 47374-4019. Offers biblical studies (MA Th); ministry studies (M Div); peace studies (M Div, MA Th); theological studies (MA Th, CATS); youth ministry (M Div). *Accreditation:* ACIPE; ATS. *Program availability:* Part-time, online learning. *Degree requirements:* For master's, thesis (for some programs). *Entrance requirements:* For master's, letters of reference. Additional exam requirements/recommendations for international students: Required—TOEFL (minimum score 550 paper-based).

Bethel College, Adult and Graduate Programs, Program in Theological Studies, Mishawaka, IN 46545-5591. Offers MATS. *Program availability:* Part-time, evening/weekend, 100% online, blended/hybrid learning. *Faculty:* 4 full-time (0 women), 2 part-time/adjunct (0 women). *Students:* 8 part-time (4 women); includes 2 minority (1 Black or African American, non-Hispanic/Latino; 1 Two or more races, non-Hispanic/Latino). Average age 35. 2 applicants, 50% accepted, 1 enrolled. In 2017, 1 master's awarded. *Entrance requirements:* Additional exam requirements/recommendations for international students: Required—TOEFL (minimum score 540 paper-based). *Application deadline:* For fall admission, 5/1 for international students; for spring admission, 10/1 for international students. Applications are processed on a rolling basis. Application fee: $0. Electronic applications accepted. Tuition and fees vary according to program. *Financial support:* Career-related internships or fieldwork available. Financial award applicants required to submit FAFSA. *Unit head:* Dr. Terence Linhart, Dean of Adult and Graduate Studies, 574-807-7394, E-mail: linhart@bethelcollege.edu.

Bethel Seminary, Graduate and Professional Programs, St. Paul, MN 55112-6998. Offers Anglican studies (Certificate); children's and family ministry (MA); Christian studies (Certificate); Christian thought (MA); church planting (Certificate); Greek and Hebrew language (M Div); Greek language (M Div); Hebrew language (M Div); marriage and family therapy (MA, Certificate); mental health counseling (MA); ministry (MA, D Min); ministry practice (Certificate); theological studies (MA, Certificate); transformational leadership (MA); young life youth ministry (Certificate). *Accreditation:* ACIPE. *Program availability:* Part-time, evening/weekend, 100% online, blended/hybrid learning. *Faculty:* 16 full-time (4 women), 31 part-time/adjunct (15 women). *Students:* 380 full-time (170 women), 167 part-time (55 women); includes 161 minority (65 Black or African American, non-Hispanic/Latino; 52 Asian, non-Hispanic/Latino; 31 Hispanic/Latino; 1 Native Hawaiian or other Pacific Islander, non-Hispanic/Latino; 12 Two or more races, non-Hispanic/Latino), 5 international. Average age 38. 356 applicants, 62% accepted, 156 enrolled. In 2017, 120 master's, 15 doctorates, 4 other advanced degrees awarded. *Degree requirements:* For master's, variable foreign language requirement, thesis (for some programs); for doctorate, thesis/dissertation. *Entrance requirements:* For master's, letters of reference, transcripts, personal statement; for doctorate, M Div, letters of reference, organizational support; for Certificate, letters of reference, family essay, personal statement, and family of origin paper (for marriage and family therapy).

Additional exam requirements/recommendations for international students: Required—TOEFL (minimum score 550 paper-based; 87 iBT). *Application deadline:* For fall admission, 8/1 priority date for domestic students, 8/1 for international students; for winter admission, 12/1 priority date for domestic students; for spring admission, 1/1 priority date for domestic students. Applications are processed on a rolling basis. Application fee: $0. Electronic applications accepted. *Expenses:* Contact institution. *Financial support:* Teaching assistantships, career-related internships or fieldwork, Federal Work-Study, and scholarships/grants available. Financial award applicants required to submit FAFSA. *Faculty research:* Nature of theology, ethics, Biblical commentaries, nature of God, science and theology. *Unit head:* Dr. Randy Bergen, Associate Provost, 651-635-8000, E-mail: r-bergen@bethel.edu. *Application contact:* Director of Admissions, 651-638-8000, Fax: 651-638-6002, E-mail: seminary-admissions@bethel.edu.
Website: https://www.bethel.edu/seminary

Bethesda University, Graduate and Professional Programs, Anaheim, CA 92801. Offers biblical studies (MA); music (MA); theology (M Div). *Entrance requirements:* For master's, interview. Additional exam requirements/recommendations for international students: Recommended—TOEFL.

Beth HaMedrash Shaarei Yosher Institute, Graduate Programs, Brooklyn, NY 11204. *Accreditation:* AARTS.

Beth Hatalmud Rabbinical College, Graduate Programs, Brooklyn, NY 11214. *Accreditation:* AARTS.

Bethlehem College & Seminary, Graduate and Professional Programs, Minneapolis, MN 55415. Offers church planting and revitalization (M Div); exegesis and theology (MA); theology (Th M); worship pastor (M Div). *Faculty:* 16 full-time (0 women), 26 part-time/adjunct (4 women). *Students:* 56 full-time (0 women), 14 part-time (0 women). *Degree requirements:* For master's, thesis (for some programs). *Expenses: Tuition:* Full-time $6000. One-time fee: $275 full-time. Tuition and fees vary according to class time and program. *Application contact:* Daniel Kleven, Director of Admissions, 612-455-3420 Ext. 418, E-mail: admissions@bcsmn.edu.

Beth Medrash Govoha, Graduate Programs, Lakewood, NJ 08701-2797. *Accreditation:* AARTS.

Bethune-Cookman University, School of Graduate Studies, Daytona Beach, FL 32114-3099. Offers transformative leadership (MS). *Program availability:* Online learning. *Degree requirements:* For master's, thesis. *Entrance requirements:* For master's, GRE or MAT, minimum GPA of 2.75 in the last 60 semester hours; 3 letters of recommendation. Additional exam requirements/recommendations for international students: Required—TOEFL (minimum score 550 paper-based). Electronic applications accepted. *Faculty research:* Civic engagement, communication ethics, service learning in higher education women in leadership.

Bexley Seabury Seminary, Graduate Programs, Chicago, IL 60637. Offers Anglican studies (Diploma); congregational development (D Min); preaching (D Min); theology (M Div). *Accreditation:* ACIPE. *Program availability:* Part-time. *Faculty:* 2 full-time (1 woman), 10 part-time/adjunct (3 women). *Students:* 45 part-time (20 women); includes 6 minority (2 Black or African American, non-Hispanic/Latino; 2 American Indian or Alaska Native, non-Hispanic/Latino; 2 Hispanic/Latino), 2 international. In 2017, 3 master's, 2 doctorates, 3 other advanced degrees awarded. *Degree requirements:* For master's, thesis; for doctorate, thesis/dissertation; for Diploma, thesis (for some programs). *Entrance requirements:* For master's, interview, sample of written work. *Application deadline:* Applications are processed on a rolling basis. Application fee: $25. *Financial support:* Career-related internships or fieldwork, institutionally sponsored loans, and scholarships/grants available. Financial award application deadline: 5/1; financial award applicants required to submit FAFSA. *Faculty research:* Liturgical interpretations of baptism, Trinitarian theology, congregational development, post modern Biblical criticism of Matthew. *Unit head:* Therese DeLisio, Acting President, 773-380-6787, E-mail: tdelisio@bexleyseabury.edu. *Application contact:* Jaime Briceno, Recruiter and Digital Missioner, 773-380-7045, Fax: 773-380-5788, E-mail: jbriceno@bexleyseabury.edu.
Website: https://www.bexleyseabury.edu/academic-programs/

Biblical Theological Seminary, Graduate and Professional Programs, Hatfield, PA 19440-2499. Offers advanced missional leadership (D Min); advanced pastoral studies (Certificate); biblical counseling (Certificate); biblical studies (MA, Certificate); counseling (MA); ministry (M Div, MA); missional theology (MA). *Accreditation:* ATS. *Program availability:* Part-time, evening/weekend. *Faculty:* 9 full-time (1 woman), 20 part-time/adjunct (5 women). *Students:* 138 full-time (41 women), 78 part-time (31 women); includes 83 minority (51 Black or African American, non-Hispanic/Latino; 1 American Indian or Alaska Native, non-Hispanic/Latino; 26 Asian, non-Hispanic/Latino; 3 Hispanic/Latino; 2 Two or more races, non-Hispanic/Latino), 65 international. Average age 41. 83 applicants, 64% accepted, 49 enrolled. In 2017, 50 master's, 12 doctorates awarded. *Degree requirements:* For master's, variable foreign language requirement, thesis optional; for doctorate, thesis/dissertation. *Entrance requirements:* Additional exam requirements/recommendations for international students: Required—TOEFL (minimum score 550 paper-based; 80 iBT). *Application deadline:* Applications are processed on a rolling basis. Application fee: $30. Electronic applications accepted. *Expenses: Tuition:* Full-time $12,360; part-time $6180 per credit. *Required fees:* $50 per semester. One-time fee: $30. *Financial support:* In 2017–18, 194 students received support. Career-related internships or fieldwork, institutionally sponsored loans, and scholarships/grants available. Support available to part-time students. Financial award application deadline: 8/30; financial award applicants required to submit FAFSA. *Faculty research:* Theology, culture, Biblical interpretation. *Application contact:* Rev. Michael Heath, Student Advancement Counselor, 215-368-5000 Ext. 152, Fax: 215-368-7002, E-mail: mheath@biblical.edu.
Website: http://www.biblical.edu/

Biola University, Talbot School of Theology, La Mirada, CA 90639-0001. Offers adult/family ministry (MACE); Bible exposition (MA, Th M); Biblical and theological studies (Certificate); children's ministry (MACE); Christian education (M Div); cross-cultural education ministry (MACE); educational studies (Ed D, PhD); evangelism and discipleship (M Div); general Christian education (MACE); Messianic Jewish studies (M Div, Certificate); missions and intercultural studies (M Div); New Testament (MA, Th M); Old Testament (MA); Old Testament and Semitics (Th M); pastoral and general ministry (M Div); pastoral care and counseling (M Div, MACML); philosophy (MA); preaching and pastoral ministry (MACML); spiritual formation (M Div, Certificate); spiritual formation and soul care (MA); sports ministry (MACML); theology (MA, Th M, D Min, Certificate); youth ministry (MACE). *Program availability:* Part-time, evening/weekend. *Students:* 475 full-time (113 women), 603 part-time (176 women); includes 541 minority (39 Black or African American, non-Hispanic/Latino; 2 American Indian or Alaska Native, non-Hispanic/Latino; 378 Asian, non-Hispanic/Latino; 84 Hispanic/Latino; 1 Native Hawaiian or other Pacific Islander, non-Hispanic/Latino; 37 Two or more races, non-Hispanic/Latino), 105 international. 437 applicants, 78% accepted, 241 enrolled. In 2017, 177 master's, 24 doctorates awarded. *Entrance requirements:* For master's, bachelor's degree from accredited college or university; minimum GPA of 2.6 (for M Div), 3.0 (for MA); for doctorate, M Div or MA. Additional exam requirements/recommendations for international students: Required—TOEFL (minimum score 600 paper-based; 88 iBT). *Application deadline:* For fall admission, 7/1 for domestic students, 6/1 for international students; for spring admission, 12/1 priority date for domestic students. Applications are processed on a rolling basis. Application fee: $65. Electronic applications accepted. *Financial support:* Scholarships/grants and unspecified assistantships available. Support available to part-time students. Financial award applicants required to submit FAFSA. *Faculty research:* New Testament, Old Testament, spiritual formation, Christian education, theological studies, Christian ministry, preaching and pastoral ministry, language and literature, bible exposition, Christian leadership. *Unit head:* Dr. Clint Arnold, Dean, 562-903-4816, Fax: 562-903-4748. *Application contact:* Graduate Admissions Office, 562-903-4752, E-mail: graduate.admissions@biola.edu.
Website: http://www.talbot.edu/

Bob Jones University, Graduate Programs, Greenville, SC 29614. Offers accountancy (MS); Bible (MA); Bible translation (MA); Biblical studies (Certificate); broadcast management (MS); business administration (MBA); church history (MA, PhD); church ministries (MA); church music (MM); cinema and video production (MA); counseling (MS); curriculum and instruction (Ed D); divinity (M Div); dramatic production (MA); educational leadership (MS, Ed D, Ed S); elementary education (M Ed, MAT); English (M Ed, MA, MAT); fine arts (MA); graphic design (MA); history (M Ed, MA); illustration (MA); interpretative speech (MA); mathematics (M Ed, MAT); medical missions (Certificate); ministry (MM, D Min); multi-categorical special education (M Ed, MAT); music (M Ed); New Testament interpretation (PhD); Old Testament interpretation (PhD); orchestral instrument performance (MM); organ performance (MM); pastoral studies (MA); personnel services (MS, Ed S); piano pedagogy (MM); piano performance (MM); platform arts (MA); radio and television broadcasting (MS); rhetoric and public address (MA); secondary education (M Ed); studio art (MA); teaching Bible (MA); theology (MA, PhD); voice performance (MM); youth ministries (MA); M Div/MM.

Boston College, Graduate School of Arts and Sciences, Department of Theology, Chestnut Hill, MA 02467-3800. Offers philosophy and theology (MA); theology (PhD). *Accreditation:* ATS. Terminal master's awarded for partial completion of doctoral program. *Degree requirements:* For master's, one foreign language, thesis optional; for doctorate, thesis/dissertation. *Entrance requirements:* For master's and doctorate, GRE General Test. Additional exam requirements/recommendations for international students: Required—TOEFL (minimum score 600 paper-based; 100 iBT), IELTS (minimum score 8). Electronic applications accepted. *Faculty research:* Historical theology, history of Christianity, systematic theology, Biblical studies, theological ethics, comparative theology.

Boston College, School of Theology and Ministry, Chestnut Hill, MA 02467-3800. Offers church leadership (MA); divinity (M Div); pastoral ministry (MA), including Hispanic ministry, liturgy and worship, pastoral care and counseling, spirituality; religious education (MA, PhD); sacred theology (STD, STL); social justice/social ministry (MA); spiritual direction (MA); theological studies (MTS); theology (Th M, PhD); youth ministry (MA); MA/MA; MS/MA; MSW/MA. *Accreditation:* TEAC. *Program availability:* Part-time. *Degree requirements:* For doctorate, one foreign language, thesis/dissertation. *Entrance requirements:* For doctorate, GRE. Additional exam requirements/recommendations for international students: Required—TOEFL (minimum score 550 paper-based). Electronic applications accepted. *Faculty research:* Philosophy and practice of religious education, pastoral psychology, liturgical and spiritual theology, spiritual formation for the practice of ministry.

Boston University, School of Theology, Boston, MA 02215. Offers chaplaincy (M Div); choral conducting (MSM); church and the arts (M Div); community and global engagement (M Div); constructive theology and ethics (PhD), including constructive theology, theological ethics; history and hermeneutics (PhD), including biblical studies, church history and world Christianity, liturgical studies, mission studies; organ (MSM); pastoral ministry (M Div); practical theology (PhD), including church and society, congregation and community, evangelism and missiology, homiletics, leadership and administration, pastoral theology and psychology, religious education, spirituality studies, worship; religion and the academy (M Div); transformational leadership (D Min); M Div/MSM; M Div/MSW; MTS/MSW. PhD in mission studies offered in collaboration with Gordon-Conwell Theological Seminary. *Accreditation:* ACIPE; ATS. *Program availability:* Part-time, blended/hybrid learning. *Faculty:* 39 full-time (17 women), 11 part-time/adjunct (5 women). *Students:* 256 full-time (135 women), 87 part-time (40 women); includes 82 minority (38 Black or African American, non-Hispanic/Latino; 10 Asian, non-Hispanic/Latino; 23 Hispanic/Latino; 1 Native Hawaiian or other Pacific Islander, non-Hispanic/Latino; 10 Two or more races, non-Hispanic/Latino), 66 international. Average age 34. 334 applicants, 69% accepted, 106 enrolled. In 2017, 62 master's, 9 doctorates awarded. *Degree requirements:* For master's, comprehensive exam (for some programs), thesis optional, contextual education; for doctorate, 2 languages, dissertation, and comprehensive exam (for PhD). *Entrance requirements:* For master's, minimum GPA of 3.0; for doctorate, GRE General Test, minimum GPA of 3.3. Additional exam requirements/recommendations for international students: Required—TOEFL (minimum score 570 paper-based; 89 iBT). *Application deadline:* For fall admission, 1/15 priority date for domestic and international students; for spring admission, 10/15 priority date for domestic and international students. Applications are processed on a rolling basis. Application fee: $95. Electronic applications accepted. *Expenses:* $20,100 tuition. *Financial support:* In 2017–18, 236 students received support, including 102 fellowships with full tuition reimbursements available (averaging $7,500 per year), 11 research assistantships with full tuition reimbursements available (averaging $22,000 per year), 12 teaching assistantships with full tuition reimbursements available (averaging $22,000 per year); career-related internships or fieldwork, Federal Work-Study, scholarships/grants, and health care benefits also available. Support available to part-time students. Financial award application deadline: 7/15. *Faculty research:* Practical theology, ethics, environmental theology, religion and conflict transformation, chaplaincy. *Total annual research expenditures:* $2.5 million. *Unit head:* Rev. Dr. Mary Elizabeth Moore, Dean, 617-353-3050, Fax: 617-353-3061, E-mail: memoore@bu.edu. *Application contact:* Rev. Dr. Anastasia Kidd, Director of Enrollment, 617-353-3036, Fax: 617-358-0140, E-mail: sthadmis@bu.edu.
Website: http://www.bu.edu/sth

Briercrest Seminary, Graduate Programs, Program in Theology, Caronport, SK S0H 0S0, Canada. Offers Biblical studies (M Div); leadership and management (M Div); New Testament (MATS); Old Testament (MATS); pastoral counseling (M Div); pastoral ministry (M Div); theological studies (M Div); theology (MATS); worship (M Div); youth and family ministry (M Div). *Accreditation:* ATS. *Program availability:* Part-time. *Degree requirements:* For master's, comprehensive exam, thesis optional. *Entrance requirements:* Additional exam requirements/recommendations for international students: Required—TOEFL (minimum score 550 paper-based).

Brite Divinity School, Graduate and Professional Programs, Fort Worth, TX 76109. Offers Biblical interpretation (PhD); divinity (M Div); ministry (D Min); pastoral theology (PhD); theological studies (MTS, CTS); theology (Th M); theology and ministry (MA). *Accreditation:* ACIPE; ATS (one or more programs are accredited); SACS/CC. *Program availability:* Part-time, evening/weekend. *Entrance requirements:* For master's, minimum

GPA of 2.5. Additional exam requirements/recommendations for international students: Required—TOEFL.

Bryn Athyn College of the New Church, Academy of the New Church Theological School, Bryn Athyn, PA 19009-0717. Offers divinity (M Div); religious studies (MA). *Program availability:* Part-time, online learning. *Degree requirements:* For master's, variable foreign language requirement, thesis. *Entrance requirements:* Additional exam requirements/recommendations for international students: Required—TOEFL.

Byzantine Catholic Seminary of Saints Cyril and Methodius, Graduate and Professional Programs, Pittsburgh, PA 15214. Offers M Div, MAT. *Accreditation:* ATS.

Cairn University, School of Divinity, Langhorne, PA 19047-2990. Offers divinity (M Div); religion (MA); theology (Th M). *Program availability:* Part-time, evening/weekend, 100% online, blended/hybrid learning. *Entrance requirements:* Additional exam requirements/recommendations for international students: Required—TOEFL (minimum score 550 paper-based). Electronic applications accepted. Application fee is waived when completed online. *Expenses:* Contact institution.

California Institute of Integral Studies, School of Consciousness and Transformation, San Francisco, CA 94103. Offers anthropology and social change (MA, PhD); Asian philosophies and cultures (MA); creative inquiry/interdisciplinary arts (MFA); East-West psychology (MA, PhD); integral and transpersonal psychology (PhD); philosophy and religion (PhD), including ecology, spirituality, and religion, philosophy, cosmology, and consciousness, women's spirituality; philosophy, cosmology, and consciousness (Certificate); transformative leadership (MA); transformative studies (PhD); women, gender, spirituality and social justice (MA); writing and consciousness (MFA). *Program availability:* Part-time, evening/weekend, 100% online, blended/hybrid learning. *Students:* 392 full-time (265 women), 141 part-time (98 women); includes 145 minority (40 Black or African American, non-Hispanic/Latino; 1 American Indian or Alaska Native, non-Hispanic/Latino; 19 Asian, non-Hispanic/Latino; 54 Hispanic/Latino; 31 Two or more races, non-Hispanic/Latino), 61 international. Average age 43. 212 applicants, 96% accepted, 153 enrolled. In 2017, 49 master's, 36 doctorates awarded. Terminal master's awarded for partial completion of doctoral program. *Degree requirements:* For master's, thesis optional; for doctorate, comprehensive exam, thesis/dissertation, 1 foreign language (for Asian philosophies and cultures). *Entrance requirements:* For master's, minimum GPA of 3.0, letters of recommendation, writing sample; for doctorate, master's degree, minimum GPA of 3.0, letters of recommendation, writing sample. Additional exam requirements/recommendations for international students: Required—TOEFL. *Application deadline:* For fall admission, 2/1 priority date for domestic and international students; for spring admission, 10/15 priority date for domestic and international students. Applications are processed on a rolling basis. Application fee: $65. Electronic applications accepted. *Expenses:* $21,400 tuition and fees (for MA); $28,390 (for MFA); $24,658 (for PhD). *Financial support:* Fellowships, research assistantships, teaching assistantships, career-related internships or fieldwork, Federal Work-Study, and scholarships/grants available. Support available to part-time students. Financial award application deadline: 4/15; financial award applicants required to submit FAFSA. *Faculty research:* Ecology and sustainability, philosophy and religion, East-West psychology, integrative health, social and cultural anthropology, transformative leadership. *Unit head:* Kathy Littles, Academic Dean, 415-575-6100, E-mail: klittles@ciis.edu. *Application contact:* Ellen Durst, Director of Admissions, 415-575-6100, Fax: 415-575-1268, E-mail: admissions@ciis.edu.
Website: http://www.ciis.edu/

California Lutheran University, Graduate Studies, Pacific Lutheran Theological Seminary, Thousand Oaks, CA 91360-2787. Offers M Div, MA, MCM, MTS, PhD, Th D, Certificate, M Div/MA. MA, Th D, PhD offered jointly with Graduate Theological Union; PhD with University of California, Berkeley. *Accreditation:* ACIPE. *Program availability:* Part-time. *Faculty:* 8 full-time (6 women), 3 part-time/adjunct (1 woman). *Students:* 41 full-time (26 women), 8 part-time (3 women); includes 9 minority (1 Black or African American, non-Hispanic/Latino; 1 Asian, non-Hispanic/Latino; 3 Hispanic/Latino; 4 Two or more races, non-Hispanic/Latino), 2 international. Average age 34. 23 applicants, 74% accepted, 14 enrolled. In 2017, 7 master's awarded. *Degree requirements:* For master's, variable foreign language requirement, thesis or alternative. *Application deadline:* For fall admission, 8/1 priority date for domestic students; for spring admission, 1/1 priority date for domestic students. Applications are processed on a rolling basis. Application fee: $25. Electronic applications accepted. *Expenses: Tuition:* Full-time $15,000. Full-time tuition and fees vary according to degree level and program. *Financial support:* In 2017–18, 104 students received support. Teaching assistantships, career-related internships or fieldwork, Federal Work-Study, institutionally sponsored loans, and scholarships/grants available. Support available to part-time students. Financial award application deadline: 3/15; financial award applicants required to submit FAFSA. *Faculty research:* Theology and genetics, power and prayer, liturgy and ethics, Christianity and Confucianism, religion and abuse. *Unit head:* Alica Vargas, Dean, 510-559-2732, E-mail: avargas@plts.edu. *Application contact:* 805-493-3325, Fax: 805-493-3861, E-mail: clugrad@callutheran.edu.

Calvary University, Graduate School and Seminary, Kansas City, MO 64147. Offers Bible and theology (MS); Biblical counseling (MA); education (MS), including administration and leadership, Christian education, curriculum and instruction, elementary education; organizational development (MS); pastoral studies (M Div); worship arts (MS). *Program availability:* Part-time, evening/weekend. *Faculty:* 6 full-time (2 women), 2 part-time/adjunct (1 woman). *Students:* 11 full-time (3 women), 29 part-time (15 women); includes 12 minority (4 Black or African American, non-Hispanic/Latino; 1 American Indian or Alaska Native, non-Hispanic/Latino; 6 Asian, non-Hispanic/Latino; 1 Native Hawaiian or other Pacific Islander, non-Hispanic/Latino). Average age 39. *Degree requirements:* For master's, variable foreign language requirement, comprehensive exam, thesis or alternative. *Entrance requirements:* For master's, minimum GPA of 2.5, BA or BS, doctrine agreement. Additional exam requirements/recommendations for international students: Required—TOEFL (minimum score 550 paper-based). *Application deadline:* Applications are processed on a rolling basis. Application fee: $0. Electronic applications accepted. *Expenses:* Contact institution. *Financial support:* Scholarships/grants available. Financial award application deadline: 11/5; financial award applicants required to submit FAFSA. *Unit head:* Dr. Thomas Baurain, Director of Seminary, 816-322-0110 Ext. 1502, Fax: 816-331-4474, E-mail: thomas.baurain@calvary.edu. *Application contact:* Ann Rogers, Admissions Office Assistant, 800-326-3960 Ext. 1321, Fax: 816-331-4474, E-mail: admissions@calvary.edu.
Website: http://www.calvary.edu

Calvin Theological Seminary, Graduate and Professional Programs, Grand Rapids, MI 49546-4387. Offers Bible and theology (MA); divinity (M Div), including ancient near eastern languages and literature, contextual ministry, evangelism and teaching, history of Christianity, new church development, New Testament, Old Testament, pastoral care and leadership, preaching and worship, theological studies, youth and family ministries; educational ministry (MA); historical theology (PhD); missions and evangelism (MA); pastoral care (MA); philosophical and moral theology (PhD); systematic theology (PhD); theological studies (MTS); theology (Th M); worship (MA); youth and family ministries (MA). *Accreditation:* ACIPE; ATS. *Program availability:* Part-time. *Degree requirements:* For master's, variable foreign language requirement, thesis (for some programs); for doctorate, 4 foreign languages, comprehensive exam, thesis/dissertation. *Entrance requirements:* For doctorate, GRE General Test, Hebrew, Greek, and a modern foreign language. Additional exam requirements/recommendations for international students: Required—TOEFL (minimum score 550 paper-based), TWE (minimum score 4). Electronic applications accepted. *Faculty research:* Recent Trinity theory, Christian anthropology, Proverbs, reformed confessions, Paul's view of law.

Campbellsville University, School of Theology, Campbellsville, KY 42718-2799. Offers marriage and family therapy (MMFT); theology (M Th). *Program availability:* Part-time, evening/weekend, 100% online, blended/hybrid learning. *Faculty:* 14 full-time (3 women), 2 part-time/adjunct (0 women). *Students:* 7 full-time (6 women), 83 part-time (44 women); includes 32 minority (30 Black or African American, non-Hispanic/Latino; 2 Hispanic/Latino). Average age 43. 58 applicants, 64% accepted, 29 enrolled. In 2017, 32 master's awarded. *Degree requirements:* For master's, comprehensive exam, thesis optional. *Entrance requirements:* For master's, GRE General Test, minimum GPA of 3.0 in major, 2.75 overall; 18 hours of undergraduate coursework in Christian studies; college transcripts; letters of recommendation. Additional exam requirements/recommendations for international students: Recommended—TOEFL (minimum score 550 paper-based; 79 iBT), IELTS (minimum score 6). *Application deadline:* Applications are processed on a rolling basis. Application fee: $25. Electronic applications accepted. Application fee is waived when completed online. *Expenses:* $299 per credit hour (Th M), $399 per credit hour (MMFT). *Financial support:* In 2017–18, 22 students received support. Unspecified assistantships and employee tuition waivers available. Financial award application deadline: 6/1; financial award applicants required to submit FAFSA. *Faculty research:* Clergy needing graduate theology education, trinity and Christian faith, Old Testament David narratives, leadership principles on Christian university integration of Christian principles in counseling process, church history; Women in Church History. *Unit head:* Dr. John E. Hurtgen, Dean, 270-789-5077, Fax: 270-789-5050, E-mail: jehurtgen@campbellsville.edu. *Application contact:* Monica Bamwine, Assistant Director of Graduate Admissions, 270-789-5221, Fax: 270-789-5071, E-mail: mkbamwine@campbellsville.edu.
Website: http://www.campbellsville.edu/

Campbell University, Graduate and Professional Programs, Divinity School, Buies Creek, NC 27506. Offers Christian ministry (MA); divinity (M Div); ministry (D Min); JD/M Div; M Div/MA; M Div/MBA. *Accreditation:* ATS. *Degree requirements:* For doctorate, final project. *Entrance requirements:* For master's, minimum GPA of 2.5; for doctorate, MAT, M Div, minimum graduate GPA of 3.0. Additional exam requirements/recommendations for international students: Required—TOEFL (minimum score 580 paper-based). *Expenses:* Contact institution. *Faculty research:* New Testament, theology, spiritual formation, Old Testament, Christian leadership.

Canadian Southern Baptist Seminary, Graduate Programs, Cochrane, AB T4C 2G1, Canada. Offers Biblical studies (MBS); Christian ministry (MCMin); Christian studies (MCS); ministry (M Div). *Accreditation:* ATS. *Program availability:* Part-time, 100% online, blended/hybrid learning. *Faculty:* 5 full-time (0 women), 5 part-time/adjunct (1 woman). *Students:* 20 full-time (6 women), 19 part-time (3 women); includes 7 minority (2 Black or African American, non-Hispanic/Latino; 5 Asian, non-Hispanic/Latino), 9 international. Average age 29. 16 applicants, 63% accepted, 10 enrolled. In 2017, 7 master's awarded. *Entrance requirements:* Additional exam requirements/recommendations for international students: Required—TOEFL (minimum score 560 paper-based; 83 iBT); Recommended—IELTS (minimum score 6.5). *Application deadline:* For fall admission, 7/1 priority date for domestic students, 3/1 priority date for international students; for winter admission, 11/15 priority date for domestic students. Applications are processed on a rolling basis. Application fee: $50 ($150 for international students). *Expenses: Tuition:* Full-time $7500 Canadian dollars; part-time $375 Canadian dollars per credit hour. *Required fees:* $450 Canadian dollars; $20 Canadian dollars per credit hour. *Financial support:* Scholarships/grants available. Financial award application deadline: 7/1. *Unit head:* Dr. Steve Booth, Academic Dean, 403-932-6622 Ext. 232, E-mail: steve.booth@csbs.ca. *Application contact:* David Ong, Director of Admissions, 403-932-6622 Ext. 251, E-mail: admissions@csbs.ca.

Carey Theological College, Graduate Programs, Vancouver, BC V6T 1J6, Canada. Offers M Div, MASF, D Min. *Accreditation:* ATS. *Program availability:* Part-time. *Degree requirements:* For doctorate, thesis/dissertation. *Entrance requirements:* For master's, undergraduate degree with minimum GPA of 2.7; for doctorate, M Div with minimum GPA of 3.5. Additional exam requirements/recommendations for international students: Required—TOEFL (minimum score 577 paper-based; 90 iBT). Electronic applications accepted. *Faculty research:* Missional church, new monasticism, women in leadership, spiritual formation, applied theology.

Carson-Newman University, Program in Applied Theology, Jefferson City, TN 37760. Offers MAAT. *Program availability:* Part-time, evening/weekend. *Faculty:* 2 full-time (0 women). *Students:* 6 part-time (3 women); includes 2 minority (1 Black or African American, non-Hispanic/Latino; 1 Hispanic/Latino). Average age 49. 3 applicants, 100% accepted, 2 enrolled. In 2017, 1 master's awarded. *Degree requirements:* For master's, thesis optional, completetion of degree within five years of admission into program. *Entrance requirements:* For master's, GRE (minimum score of 290), minimum GPA of 3.0. Additional exam requirements/recommendations for international students: Recommended—TOEFL (minimum score 79 iBT), IELTS (minimum score 6.5), TSE (minimum score 53). *Application deadline:* For fall admission, 7/15 priority date for domestic students. Applications are processed on a rolling basis. Application fee: $50. *Expenses: Tuition:* Full-time $10,516; part-time $478 per credit hour. *Required fees:* $240; $120 per semester. One-time fee: $150. *Financial support:* Federal Work-Study and tuition waivers (full and partial) available. Financial award applicants required to submit FAFSA. *Unit head:* Dr. David E. Crutchley, Dean, School of Religion, 865-471-3277, E-mail: dcruthley@cn.edu. *Application contact:* Nilma Stewart, Graduate Admissions and Services Adviser, 865-473-3468, Fax: 865-471-3875, E-mail: adults@cn.edu.
Website: http://www.cn.edu/graduate-adult-studies/programs/religion-graduate

Catholic Distance University, Graduate Programs, Charles Town, WV 25414. Offers religious studies (MRS); theology (MA). *Program availability:* Part-time, evening/weekend, online learning. *Degree requirements:* For master's, comprehensive exam, capstone paper or project.

Catholic Theological Union, Graduate and Professional Programs, Chicago, IL 60615-5698. Offers biblical spirituality (Certificate); cross-cultural ministries (D Min); cross-cultural missions (Certificate); divinity (M Div); liturgical studies (Certificate); liturgy (D Min); pastoral studies (MAPS, Certificate); spiritual formation (Certificate); spirituality (D Min); theology (MA); M Div/MA; M Div/MSW; M Div/PhD. M Div/PhD offered jointly with University of Chicago; M Div/MSW with Loyola University Chicago and University of Chicago. *Accreditation:* ACIPE; ATS. *Program availability:* Part-time, evening/weekend. *Degree requirements:* For master's, one foreign language, comprehensive exam (for some programs), thesis (for some programs); for doctorate, thesis/dissertation. *Entrance requirements:* For doctorate, master's degree, 5 years of active ministry. *Faculty research:* Doctrine, sacraments, ethics, Bible.

The Catholic University of America, School of Canon Law, Washington, DC 20064. Offers Canon law (JCD, JCL); church administration (MCA); JD/JCL. JD/JCL offered

jointly with Columbus School of Law. *Program availability:* Part-time. *Faculty:* 7 full-time (1 woman), 2 part-time/adjunct (0 women). *Students:* 32 full-time (6 women), 49 part-time (6 women); includes 9 minority (2 Black or African American, non-Hispanic/Latino; 3 Asian, non-Hispanic/Latino; 2 Hispanic/Latino; 2 Two or more races, non-Hispanic/Latino), 13 international. Average age 38. 36 applicants, 89% accepted, 27 enrolled. In 2017, 10 master's, 3 doctorates awarded. *Degree requirements:* For master's, one foreign language, comprehensive exam, thesis, fluency in canonical Latin; for doctorate, 2 foreign languages, thesis/dissertation, fluency in canonical Latin. *Entrance requirements:* For master's, GRE General Test, statement of purpose, official copies of academic transcripts, two letters of recommendation; for doctorate, GRE General Test, minimum A- average, JCL. Additional exam requirements/recommendations for international students: Required—TOEFL (minimum score 550 paper-based; 80 iBT). *Application deadline:* For fall admission, 7/15 priority date for domestic students, 7/1 for international students; for spring admission, 11/15 priority date for domestic students, 11/1 for international students. Applications are processed on a rolling basis. Application fee: $55. Electronic applications accepted. *Expenses:* Contact institution. *Financial support:* Fellowships, research assistantships, teaching assistantships, Federal Work-Study, scholarships/grants, tuition waivers (full and partial), and unspecified assistantships available. Financial award application deadline: 2/1; financial award applicants required to submit FAFSA. *Faculty research:* Ecclesiology and the Sacrament of Orders, procedural law, temporal goods, matrimonial jurisprudence, sacramental and liturgical law. *Unit head:* Msgr. Ronny Jenkins, Dean, 202-319-5492, Fax: 202-319-4187, E-mail: cua-canonlaw@cua.edu. *Application contact:* Dr. Steven Brown, Director of Graduate Admissions, 202-319-5057, Fax: 202-319-6533, E-mail: cua-admissions@cua.edu.
Website: https://canonlaw.catholic.edu/

The Catholic University of America, School of Theology and Religious Studies, Washington, DC 20064. Offers M Cat, M Div, MA, D Min, PhD, STD, Certificate, STB, STL, MSLS/MA, STB/M Div. MSLA/MA offered in conjunction with Department of Library and Information Science. *Program availability:* Part-time. *Faculty:* 42 full-time (3 women), 11 part-time/adjunct (1 woman). *Students:* 146 full-time (11 women), 201 part-time (44 women); includes 70 minority (9 Black or African American, non-Hispanic/Latino; 1 American Indian or Alaska Native, non-Hispanic/Latino; 9 Asian, non-Hispanic/Latino; 25 Hispanic/Latino; 26 Two or more races, non-Hispanic/Latino), 53 international. Average age 36. 180 applicants, 67% accepted, 66 enrolled. In 2017, 59 master's, 25 doctorates awarded. Terminal master's awarded for partial completion of doctoral program. *Degree requirements:* For master's, variable foreign language requirement, comprehensive exam (for some programs), thesis (for some programs); for doctorate, variable foreign language requirement, comprehensive exam, thesis/dissertation. *Entrance requirements:* For master's and doctorate, GRE General Test, statement of purpose, official copies of academic transcripts, three letters of recommendation. Additional exam requirements/recommendations for international students: Required—TOEFL (minimum score 550 paper-based; 80 iBT). *Application deadline:* For fall admission, 7/15 priority date for domestic students, 7/1 for international students; for spring admission, 11/15 priority date for domestic students, 11/1 for international students. Applications are processed on a rolling basis. Application fee: $55. Electronic applications accepted. *Expenses:* Contact institution. *Financial support:* Fellowships, research assistantships, teaching assistantships, Federal Work-Study, scholarships/grants, tuition waivers (full and partial), and unspecified assistantships available. Financial award application deadline: 2/1; financial award applicants required to submit FAFSA. *Faculty research:* Historical and systematic theology, religious education and Catechetics, moral theology and ethics, Biblical studies, liturgical studies and sacramental theology, religion and culture. *Total annual research expenditures:* $389,160. *Unit head:* Very Rev. Mark Morozowich, Dean, 202-319-5684, Fax: 202-319-4967, E-mail: morozowich@cua.edu. *Application contact:* Dr. Steven Brown, Director of Graduate Admissions, 202-319-5057, Fax: 202-319-6533, E-mail: cua-admissions@cua.edu.
Website: https://trs.catholic.edu/

Central Baptist Theological Seminary, Graduate and Professional Programs, Shawnee, KS 66226. Offers missional church studies (MA); theological studies (MA); theology (M Div, Diploma). *Accreditation:* ACIPE; ATS (one or more programs are accredited). *Program availability:* Part-time. *Degree requirements:* For master's, thesis optional. *Entrance requirements:* Additional exam requirements/recommendations for international students: Required—TOEFL (minimum score 547 paper-based; 77 iBT). Electronic applications accepted.

Central Yeshiva Tomchei Tmimim-Lubavitch, Graduate Programs, Brooklyn, NY 11230. Offers Jewish/Judaic studies (MA); Talmudic studies (MA). *Accreditation:* AARTS.

Chaminade University of Honolulu, Office of Professional and Continuing Education, Program in Pastoral Theology, Honolulu, HI 96816-1578. Offers diaconate education (MPT); pastoral counseling and spiritual direction (MPT). *Program availability:* Part-time, evening/weekend, blended/hybrid learning. *Faculty:* 1 full-time (0 women), 1 part-time/adjunct (0 women). *Students:* 9 full-time (2 women), 5 part-time (2 women); includes 10 minority (5 Asian, non-Hispanic/Latino; 2 Hispanic/Latino; 3 Native Hawaiian or other Pacific Islander, non-Hispanic/Latino). Average age 51. 2 applicants, 100% accepted, 2 enrolled. In 2017, 6 master's awarded. *Degree requirements:* For master's, capstone course. *Entrance requirements:* For master's, minimum GPA of 2.5, resume, 2 letters of recommendation, letter of intent, article reflection essay. Additional exam requirements/recommendations for international students: Required—TOEFL (minimum score 550 paper-based; 79 iBT). *Application deadline:* Applications are processed on a rolling basis. Application fee: $40. Electronic applications accepted. *Expenses:* Contact institution. *Financial support:* Applicants required to submit FAFSA. *Unit head:* Dr. David Coleman, Director, 808-739-8341, E-mail: paul.fitzpatrick@chaminade.edu. *Application contact:* 808-735-4755, E-mail: gradserv@chaminade.edu.
Website: https://pace.chaminade.edu/graduate-programs/mpt-program/

Charlotte Christian College and Theological Seminary, Graduate Program, Charlotte, NC 28206. Offers Biblical studies (MA), including New Testament, Old Testament, theology; chaplaincy (M Div); general pastoral studies (M Div); ministry (D Min); pastoral counseling (M Div); urban Christian ministry (MA), including multi-cultural studies, youth ministry. *Program availability:* Part-time, evening/weekend. *Faculty:* 5 full-time (0 women), 6 part-time/adjunct (0 women). *Students:* 17 full-time (8 women), 21 part-time (11 women); includes 31 minority (29 Black or African American, non-Hispanic/Latino; 1 Asian, non-Hispanic/Latino; 1 Two or more races, non-Hispanic/Latino), 2 international. Average age 48. 13 applicants, 100% accepted, 9 enrolled. In 2017, 2 master's awarded. *Degree requirements:* For master's, variable foreign language requirement, thesis; for doctorate, thesis/dissertation. *Entrance requirements:* For master's, 1000-2000 word essay. Additional exam requirements/recommendations for international students: Required—TOEFL, IELTS. *Application deadline:* For fall admission, 8/3 for domestic and international students; for spring admission, 12/8 for domestic and international students; for summer admission, 4/7 for domestic and international students. Application fee: $50. Electronic applications accepted. *Expenses:* Contact institution. *Financial support:* In 2017–18, 2 students received support. Teaching assistantships, Federal Work-Study, and scholarships/grants available. Financial award application deadline: 4/1; financial award applicants required to submit FAFSA. *Faculty research:* Pastoral topics, urban ministry topics, Biblical topics. *Unit head:* Dr. Eddie G. Grigg, President, 704-344-6882 Ext. 101, Fax: 704-334-6885, E-mail: egrigg@charlottechristian.edu. *Application contact:* George Shears, Director of Admissions, 704-334-6882 Ext. 115, Fax: 704-334-6885, E-mail: gshears@charlottechristian.edu.
Website: http://www.charlottechristian.edu

Chicago Theological Seminary, Graduate and Professional Programs, Chicago, IL 60637-1507. Offers Bible, culture and hermeneutics (PhD); preaching (D Min); religion and health (D Min); religious studies (MA); spirituality and spiritual direction (D Min); theology (M Div); theology, ethics and the human sciences (PhD); M Div/MSW. *Accreditation:* ACIPE; ATS. *Program availability:* Part-time. *Degree requirements:* For master's, thesis; for doctorate, 2 foreign languages, comprehensive exam, thesis/dissertation. *Entrance requirements:* For doctorate, GRE General Test. Additional exam requirements/recommendations for international students: Required—TOEFL. *Faculty research:* Bible, culture and hermeneutics, theology, gender and sexuality, black faith and life, spirituality and psychology, practical theology.

Christendom College, Graduate School of Theology, Alexandria, VA 22312. Offers theological studies (MA), including consecrated life, evangelization and catechesis, moral theology, spirituality, systematic theology. *Program availability:* Part-time, evening/weekend, 100% online, blended/hybrid learning. *Degree requirements:* For master's, one foreign language, comprehensive exam, thesis or alternative. *Application deadline:* For fall admission, 6/1 priority date for domestic students; for spring admission, 11/1 priority date for domestic students. Applications are processed on a rolling basis. Application fee: $100. Electronic applications accepted. *Expenses: Tuition:* Part-time $390 per credit. Part-time tuition and fees vary according to program. *Unit head:* Dr. Robert J. Matava, Dean, 703-658-4304. *Application contact:* Sam Phillips, Director of Admissions, 703-658-4304, E-mail: graduate.school@christendom.edu.
Website: http://graduate.christendom.edu/

Christian Theological Seminary, Graduate and Professional Programs, Indianapolis, IN 46208-3301. Offers educational and arts ministries (MA); marriage and family therapy (MA); pastoral care and counseling (D Min); psychotherapy and faith (MA); theological studies (MTS); theology (M Div). *Accreditation:* AAMFT/COAMFTE (one or more programs are accredited); ACIPE; ATS. *Program availability:* Part-time. Terminal master's awarded for partial completion of doctoral program. *Degree requirements:* For master's, comprehensive exam (for some programs), thesis (for some programs), missionary and cross-cultural experience (for M Div); for doctorate, comprehensive exam, thesis/dissertation. *Entrance requirements:* For doctorate, M Div. Additional exam requirements/recommendations for international students: Recommended—TOEFL. Electronic applications accepted. *Faculty research:* Faith formation, peer learning post graduation.

Christ the King Seminary, Graduate and Professional Programs, East Aurora, NY 14052. Offers divinity (M Div); pastoral ministry (MA); theology (MA). *Accreditation:* ATS. *Program availability:* Part-time, evening/weekend. *Degree requirements:* For master's, comprehensive exam, thesis. *Entrance requirements:* For master's, previous course work in philosophy and religious studies.

Church Divinity School of the Pacific, Graduate and Professional Programs, Berkeley, CA 94709-1217. Offers M Div, MA, MTS, D Min, Certificate. MA program offered jointly with Graduate Theological Union. *Accreditation:* ACIPE; ATS (one or more programs are accredited). *Program availability:* Part-time. *Degree requirements:* For master's, one foreign language, thesis (for some programs); for doctorate, thesis/dissertation. *Entrance requirements:* For master's and Certificate, GRE General Test, letters of reference; for doctorate, letters of reference. Additional exam requirements/recommendations for international students: Required—TOEFL. Electronic applications accepted.

Cincinnati Christian University, Graduate School, Cincinnati, OH 45204-3200. Offers biblical studies (MA); church history (MA); counseling (MAC); divinity (M Div); ministry (M Min); practical ministries (MA); theological studies (MA). *Program availability:* Part-time. *Degree requirements:* For master's, variable foreign language requirement, thesis (for some programs), oral exam (for M Div). *Entrance requirements:* Additional exam requirements/recommendations for international students: Required—TOEFL. Electronic applications accepted.

Claremont Graduate University, Graduate Programs, School of Arts and Humanities, Department of Religion, Claremont, CA 91711-6160. Offers Hebrew Bible (MA, PhD); history of Christianity and religions of North America (MA, PhD); New Testament (MA, PhD); philosophy of religion and theology (MA, PhD); theology, ethics and culture (MA, PhD); women's studies in religion (MA, PhD); MA/PhD; MBA/PhD. *Program availability:* Part-time. Terminal master's awarded for partial completion of doctoral program. *Entrance requirements:* For master's and doctorate, GRE General Test. Additional exam requirements/recommendations for international students: Required—TOEFL (minimum score 75 iBT). Electronic applications accepted.

Claremont School of Theology, Graduate and Professional Programs, Master of Divinity Program, Claremont, CA 91711-3199. Offers interfaith chaplaincy (M Div); Islamic chaplaincy (M Div); ministerial leadership (M Div). *Accreditation:* ACIPE; ATS. *Program availability:* Part-time, 100% online, blended/hybrid learning. *Entrance requirements:* Additional exam requirements/recommendations for international students: Required—TOEFL. Electronic applications accepted.

Claremont School of Theology, Graduate and Professional Programs, Program in Religion, Claremont, CA 91711-3199. Offers practical theology (PhD), including religious education and formation, spiritual care and counseling; religion (MA, PhD), including comparative theology and philosophy (PhD), Hebrew Bible and Jewish studies (PhD), New Testament and Christian origins (PhD), process studies (PhD), religion, ethics, and society (PhD). *Accreditation:* ACIPE; ATS. Terminal master's awarded for partial completion of doctoral program. *Degree requirements:* For master's, thesis; for doctorate, 2 foreign languages, thesis/dissertation. *Entrance requirements:* For doctorate, GRE General Test. Additional exam requirements/recommendations for international students: Required—TOEFL. Electronic applications accepted.

Clarks Summit University, Baptist Bible Seminary, South Abington Township, PA 18411. Offers Biblical apologetics (MA); Biblical studies (MA); church education (M Min); church planting (M Div, M Min); communication (D Min); counseling and spiritual development (D Min); global ministry (M Min, D Min); ministry (PhD); missions (M Min); organizational leadership (M Min); outreach pastor (M Min); pastoral counseling (M Min); pastoral leadership (M Div, M Min); pastoral ministry (D Min); theological studies (D Min); theology (Th M); youth pastor (M Min). M Min in missions available only for Association of Baptists for World Evangelism missionary personnel. *Program availability:* Part-time, evening/weekend, online learning. Terminal master's awarded for partial completion of doctoral program. *Degree requirements:* For master's, 2 foreign languages, thesis, oral exam (for M Div); for doctorate, 2 foreign languages, comprehensive exam (for some programs), thesis/dissertation, oral exam. *Entrance requirements:* For doctorate, Greek and Hebrew entrance exams (for PhD). *Application deadline:* Applications are processed on a rolling basis. Application fee: $30. Electronic applications accepted. *Financial support:* Career-related internships or fieldwork and scholarships/grants available. Support available to part-time students. *Unit head:* Dr. Wayne Slusser, Dean, 570-585-9348, Fax: 570-585-4057, E-mail:

wslusser@clarkssummitu.edu. *Application contact:* Dr. Wayne Slusser, Dean, 570-585-9348, Fax: 570-585-4057, E-mail: wslusser@clarkssummitu.edu. Website: https://www.clarkssummitu.edu/seminary/

Clarks Summit University, Online Master's Programs, South Abington Township, PA 18411. Offers Bible (MA); counseling (MA, MS); curriculum and instruction (M Ed); educational administration (M Ed); literature (MA); organizational leadership (MA). *Program availability:* Part-time, evening/weekend, online learning. *Entrance requirements:* Additional exam requirements/recommendations for international students: Required—TOEFL (minimum score 500 paper-based). *Application deadline:* Applications are processed on a rolling basis. Application fee: $30. *Financial support:* Institutionally sponsored loans and scholarships/grants available. Financial award application deadline: 8/20; financial award applicants required to submit FAFSA. *Unit head:* Dr. James Lytle, President, 570-586-2400 Ext. 9222, Fax: 570-586-1753. *Application contact:* Drew Whipple, Vice President for Enrollment Management, 570-585-9370, Fax: 570-585-9299, E-mail: awhipple@clarkssummitu.edu. Website: https://www.clarkssummitu.edu/online-masters-degrees/

Colgate Rochester Crozer Divinity School, Graduate and Professional Programs, Rochester, NY 14620-2530. Offers divinity (M Div, MA, Certificate); peace building and interfaith dialogue (D Min); prophetic preaching (D Min); transformative leadership (D Min). *Accreditation:* ACIPE; ATS (one or more programs are accredited). *Program availability:* Part-time, evening/weekend. *Faculty:* 7 full-time (3 women), 15 part-time/adjunct (7 women). *Students:* 70 full-time, 24 part-time; includes 58 minority (48 Black or African American, non-Hispanic/Latino; 3 Asian, non-Hispanic/Latino; 3 Hispanic/Latino; 4 Two or more races, non-Hispanic/Latino). Average age 43. 23 applicants, 96% accepted, 21 enrolled. In 2017, 21 master's, 3 doctorates awarded. *Degree requirements:* For master's, thesis (for some programs), supervised ministry year (for M Div); for doctorate, thesis/dissertation. *Entrance requirements:* For master's, BA/BS, personal statement, 4 recommendations; for doctorate, M Div, 3 years' professional experience, writing sample, personal statement, curriculum vitae, 4 recommendations. Additional exam requirements/recommendations for international students: Required—TOEFL (minimum score 600 paper-based; 93 iBT). *Application deadline:* For fall admission, 7/1 priority date for domestic students, 3/1 for international students; for spring admission, 12/1 priority date for domestic students, 9/1 for international students. Applications are processed on a rolling basis. Application fee: $35. Electronic applications accepted. *Expenses:* $11,030. *Financial support:* In 2017–18, 26 students received support. Scholarships/grants available. Financial award application deadline: 9/1; financial award applicants required to submit FAFSA. *Faculty research:* Book of Jeremiah, postcolonial Asian feminist biblical interpretation, Charles Wesley, Christian ethics, black church studies. *Unit head:* Rev. Marvin A. McMickle, PhD, President, 585-271-1320 Ext. 680, Fax: 585-271-8013. *Application contact:* Rev. Melissa M. Morral, Vice President for Enrollment Services, 585-340-9633, Fax: 585-340-9644, E-mail: mmorral@crcds.edu. Website: http://www.crcds.edu

Collège Dominicain de Philosophie et de Théologie, Graduate Programs, Faculty of Theology, Ottawa, ON K1R 7G3, Canada. Offers M Th, MA Th, PhD, Th D, L Th. *Program availability:* Part-time, evening/weekend. *Degree requirements:* For master's, 2 foreign languages, research paper; for doctorate, 2 foreign languages, thesis/dissertation, candidacy exam. *Entrance requirements:* For master's, B Th or equivalent, minimum A- average in undergraduate course work; for doctorate, MA Th or equivalent, minimum A- average in graduate course work. *Faculty research:* Exegese, bioethics, history of church, New Testament.

College of Emmanuel and St. Chad, Bachelor of Theology Program, Saskatoon, SK S7N 0W6, Canada. Offers B Th. *Program availability:* Part-time, online learning. *Degree requirements:* For B Th, internship. *Entrance requirements:* For degree, 1 year of university-level work or equivalent. Additional exam requirements/recommendations for international students: Required—TOEFL. *Faculty research:* Pauline studies, New Testament, ethics, congregational development, trauma and spirituality.

College of Emmanuel and St. Chad, Graduate Programs, Saskatoon, SK S7N 0W6, Canada. Offers M Div, MTS, STM, D Min, L Th. STM and D Min programs offered jointly with Lutheran Theological Seminary and St. Andrew's College. *Program availability:* Part-time. *Degree requirements:* For master's, thesis optional. *Entrance requirements:* For master's, M Div or MTS (for STM). Additional exam requirements/recommendations for international students: Required—TOEFL. *Faculty research:* New Testament, systematics, Christian education, theology, ethics.

College of Saint Elizabeth, Department of Theology and Philosophy, Morristown, NJ 07960-6989. Offers Catholic studies (Certificate); pastoral care (Certificate); spirituality (Certificate); theology (MA), including Catholic studies, pastoral care, spirituality, theological studies. *Program availability:* Part-time. *Faculty:* 1 (woman) full-time, 2 part-time/adjunct (0 women). *Students:* 10 part-time (8 women); includes 2 minority (1 Black or African American, non-Hispanic/Latino; 1 Asian, non-Hispanic/Latino). Average age 56. 4 applicants, 100% accepted, 3 enrolled. In 2017, 1 master's awarded. *Degree requirements:* For master's, thesis. *Entrance requirements:* For master's, baccalaureate degree from accredited institution, personal interview with coordinator and another faculty member, minimum cumulative GPA of 3.0. Additional exam requirements/recommendations for international students: Required—TOEFL (minimum score 550 paper-based; 79 iBT), IELTS (minimum score 6.5). *Application deadline:* For fall admission, 5/1 for international students. Applications are processed on a rolling basis. Application fee: $35. Electronic applications accepted. Application fee is waived when completed online. *Financial support:* Career-related internships or fieldwork, scholarships/grants, tuition waivers (partial), and unspecified assistantships available. Financial award applicants required to submit FAFSA. *Unit head:* Dr. Anthony Santamaria, Chairperson, 973-290-4338, Fax: 973-290-4312, E-mail: asantamaria@cse.edu. *Application contact:* Lori J. Fragoso, Director of Graduate and Continuing Studies Admissions, 973-290-4413, Fax: 973-290-4710, E-mail: apply@cse.edu. Website: http://www.cse.edu/academics/aas/theology/

Columbia International University, Seminary and School of Ministry, Columbia, SC 29203. Offers academic ministries (M Div); Bible and theology (Certificate); bible exposition (M Div, MABE); Biblical ministry (Certificate); chaplaincy (M Div); intercultural studies (MAIS); leadership (D Min); member care (D Min); missions (D Min); preaching (D Min); theological studies (MA). *Program availability:* Part-time, evening/weekend. *Degree requirements:* For doctorate, comprehensive exam, thesis/dissertation. *Entrance requirements:* For doctorate, 3 years of ministerial experience, M Div. Additional exam requirements/recommendations for international students: Required—TOEFL. Electronic applications accepted.

Columbia Theological Seminary, Graduate and Professional Programs, Decatur, GA 30031-0520. Offers M Div, MATS, Th M, D Min, Th D. Th D program offered jointly with Emory University; D Min with Interdenominational Theological Center. *Accreditation:* ACIPE; ATS (one or more programs are accredited). Terminal master's awarded for partial completion of doctoral program. *Degree requirements:* For master's, variable foreign language requirement, thesis (for some programs); for doctorate, one foreign language, thesis/dissertation. *Entrance requirements:* For doctorate, M Div or equivalent, 3 years practice of ministry. Additional exam requirements/recommendations for international students: Required—TOEFL.

Concordia Lutheran Seminary, Graduate and Professional Programs, Edmonton, AB T5B 4E3, Canada. Offers M Div, Graduate Certificate. *Accreditation:* ATS (one or more programs are accredited). *Program availability:* Part-time. *Degree requirements:* For master's, thesis or alternative. *Entrance requirements:* For master's, GRE General Test. Additional exam requirements/recommendations for international students: Required—TOEFL. *Faculty research:* Lutheran Pietism, Christianity and culture, missiology, Christian worship, homiletics.

Concordia Seminary, Graduate Programs, St. Louis, MO 63105-3199. Offers M Div, MA, STM, D Min, PhD, Certificate. *Accreditation:* ACIPE; ATS (one or more programs are accredited). Terminal master's awarded for partial completion of doctoral program. *Degree requirements:* For master's, variable foreign language requirement, comprehensive exam (for some programs), thesis (for some programs); for doctorate, 4 foreign languages, thesis/dissertation. *Entrance requirements:* For master's, GRE General Test, previous course work in public speaking, Greek, Hebrew, Old Testament, New Testament, and Christian Doctrine (for M Div); for doctorate, GRE General Test, theological essay in English (foreign students only). Additional exam requirements/recommendations for international students: Required—TOEFL. *Faculty research:* Family counseling, educational administration, contemporary theology, pastoral office, humanism and education.

Concordia Theological Seminary, Graduate and Professional Programs, Fort Wayne, IN 46825-4996. Offers M Div, MA, STM, D Min, PhD. *Accreditation:* ATS. *Program availability:* Part-time. *Degree requirements:* For master's, variable foreign language requirement, thesis (for some programs); for doctorate, comprehensive exam, thesis/dissertation, oral exam. *Entrance requirements:* For master's, GRE General Test (for M Div), minimum GPA of 2.25 (for M Div).

Concordia University, School of Graduate Studies, Faculty of Arts and Science, Department of Theological Studies, Montréal, QC H3G 1M8, Canada. Offers MA. *Degree requirements:* For master's, one foreign language, research papers or thesis. *Entrance requirements:* For master's, minimum B average in theology. *Faculty research:* Interpretation theory, theological methodology.

Concordia University Irvine, School of Theology, Irvine, CA 92612-3299. Offers Christian leadership (MA); research in theology (MA); theology and culture (MA). *Program availability:* Part-time, evening/weekend. *Degree requirements:* For master's, project/thesis or vicarage. *Entrance requirements:* For master's, official college transcript(s), statement of intent, 2 references, interview. Additional exam requirements/recommendations for international students: Required—TOEFL. Electronic applications accepted. *Expenses:* Contact institution.

Concordia University of Edmonton, Program in Biblical and Christian Studies, Edmonton, AB T5B 4E4, Canada. Offers MA.

Corban University, Graduate School, School of Ministry, Salem, OR 97301-9392. Offers Biblical languages (M Div); Biblical leadership (Certificate); Christian leadership (MA); Church ministry (M Div); ministry (D Min). *Program availability:* Part-time, evening/weekend. *Degree requirements:* For master's, thesis. *Entrance requirements:* Additional exam requirements/recommendations for international students: Required—TOEFL (minimum score 550 paper-based), IELTS (minimum score 6).

Covenant Theological Seminary, Graduate and Professional Programs, St. Louis, MO 63141-8697. Offers M Div, MA, MAC, MAEM, Th M, D Min, Certificate. *Accreditation:* ATS (one or more programs are accredited). *Program availability:* Part-time, evening/weekend, online learning. *Degree requirements:* For master's, 2 foreign languages, thesis (for some programs); for doctorate, 2 foreign languages, thesis/dissertation; for Certificate, 2 foreign languages. *Entrance requirements:* For doctorate and Certificate, M Div. Additional exam requirements/recommendations for international students: Required—TOEFL (minimum score 550 paper-based). Electronic applications accepted.

Creighton University, Graduate School, College of Arts and Sciences, Department of Theology, Omaha, NE 68178-0001. Offers MA. *Program availability:* Part-time, evening/weekend, blended/hybrid learning. *Faculty:* 18 full-time (6 women), 2 part-time/adjunct (1 woman). *Students:* 1 (woman) full-time, 15 part-time (9 women); includes 1 minority (Asian, non-Hispanic/Latino), 3 international. Average age 40. 3 applicants, 67% accepted, 1 enrolled. In 2017, 15 master's awarded. *Degree requirements:* For master's, thesis (for some programs). *Entrance requirements:* For master's, GRE General Test, 9 hours of theology course work, 3 letters of recommendation. Additional exam requirements/recommendations for international students: Required—TOEFL (minimum score 90 iBT). *Application deadline:* For fall admission, 3/1 for domestic and international students; for winter admission, 10/1 for domestic students, 5/1 for international students; for spring admission, 4/1 for domestic students, 10/1 for international students; for summer admission, 3/1 for domestic and international students. Applications are processed on a rolling basis. Application fee: $50. Electronic applications accepted. Part-time tuition and fees vary according to course load, degree level, campus/location and program. *Financial support:* Scholarships/grants and tuition waivers (partial) available. Support available to part-time students. Financial award applicants required to submit FAFSA. *Unit head:* Dr. Richard Miller, Director, 402-280-3618, E-mail: richardmiller@creighton.edu. *Application contact:* Lindsay Johnson, Director of Graduate and Adult Recruitment, 402-280-2703, Fax: 402-280-2423, E-mail: gradschool@creighton.edu.

Criswell College, Graduate School of the Bible, Dallas, TX 75246-1537. Offers biblical studies (M Div); Christian leadership (MA); counseling (MA); Jewish studies (MA); ministry (MA); theological and biblical studies (MA). *Program availability:* Part-time. *Degree requirements:* For master's, 2 foreign languages, thesis optional. *Entrance requirements:* For master's, GRE General Test, minimum GPA of 2.5. Electronic applications accepted. *Faculty research:* Emphasis on biblical languages (Hebrew and Greek), expository preaching and evangelism in the local church.

Crown College, Adult and Graduate Studies, St. Bonifacius, MN 55375-9001. Offers Christian studies (MA); instructional leadership (MA); international leadership (MA); ministry leadership (MA); organizational leadership (MA). *Program availability:* Part-time, evening/weekend, online learning. *Degree requirements:* For master's, thesis optional. *Entrance requirements:* For master's, 12 credits in foundational studies, minimum GPA of 2.5 and bachelor's degree from regionally-accredited college. Additional exam requirements/recommendations for international students: Required—TOEFL (minimum score 550 paper-based; 80 iBT). Electronic applications accepted.

Dallas Baptist University, Graduate School of Ministry, Program in Theological Studies, Dallas, TX 75211-9299. Offers Christian heritage (MA); Christian ministry (MA); Christian scriptures (MA). *Program availability:* Part-time, evening/weekend. *Application deadline:* Applications are processed on a rolling basis. Application fee: $25. Electronic applications accepted. Application fee is waived when completed online. *Expenses:* Tuition: Full-time $16,308; part-time $906 per credit hour. *Required fees:* $900; $450 per semester. Tuition and fees vary according to course load and degree level. *Unit head:* Dr. Robert R. Brooks, Dean, 214-333-5494, Fax: 214-333-5673, E-mail: bobb@dbu.edu. *Application contact:* Dr. Jim Lemons, Program Director, 214-333-5366, Fax: 214-333-5689, E-mail: jiml@dbu.edu. Website: http://www.dbu.edu/ministry/degree-programs/m-a-in-theological-studies

Theology

Dallas Theological Seminary, Graduate Programs, Dallas, TX 75204-6499. Offers adult education (Th M); apologetics (Th M); Bible backgrounds (Th M); Bible translation (Th M); Biblical and theological studies (Certificate); biblical counseling (MA); biblical exegesis and linguistics (MA); biblical exposition (PhD); biblical studies (MA); Biblical theology (Th M); children's education (Th M); Christian education (MA, D Min); Christian leadership (MA); cross-cultural ministries (MA); educational administration (Th M); educational leadership (Th M); evangelism and discipleship (Th M); exposition of Biblical books (Th M); family life education (Th M); general studies (Th M); Hebrew and cognate studies (Th M); hermeneutics (Th M); historical theology (Th M); homiletics (Th M); intercultural ministries (Th M); Jesus studies (Th M); leadership studies (Th M); media and communication (MA); media arts (Th M); ministry (D Min); ministry with women (Th M); New Testament studies (Th M, PhD); Old Testament studies (Th M, PhD); parachurch ministries (Th M); pastoral care and counseling (Th M); pastoral theology and practice (Th M); philosophy (Th M); sacred theology (STM); spiritual formation (Th M); systematic theology (Th M); teaching in Christian institutions (Th M); theological studies (PhD); urban ministries (Th M); worship studies (Th M); youth education (Th M). *Program availability:* Part-time, online learning. *Degree requirements:* For master's, variable foreign language requirement, thesis (for some programs); for doctorate, 2 foreign languages, thesis/dissertation. *Entrance requirements:* For master's, GRE or MAT (if minimum undergraduate cumulative GPA is below 2.5 or undergraduate degree is unaccredited). Additional exam requirements/recommendations for international students: Required—TOEFL (minimum score 575 paper-based; 85 iBT), TWE. Electronic applications accepted.

Denver Seminary, Graduate and Professional Programs, Littleton, CO 80120. Offers apologetics (Certificate); biblical studies (MA); Christian formation and soul care (MA, Certificate); Christian studies (MA, Certificate); church and parachurch leadership (D Min); counseling licensure (MA); counseling ministry (MA); intercultural ministry (Certificate); leadership (MA, Certificate); marriage and family counseling (D Min); pastoral ministry (D Min); philosophy of religion (MA); spiritual guidance (Certificate); theology (M Div, Certificate); worship (Certificate); youth and family ministry (MA). *Accreditation:* ACA; ACIPE; ATS (one or more programs are accredited). *Program availability:* Part-time, evening/weekend, online learning. *Degree requirements:* For master's, 2 foreign languages, thesis (for some programs); for doctorate, 2 foreign languages, thesis/dissertation. *Entrance requirements:* For doctorate, M Div, 3 years of ministry experience. Additional exam requirements/recommendations for international students: Required—TOEFL (minimum score 575 paper-based; 90 iBT). Electronic applications accepted.

Dominican House of Studies, Pontifical Faculty of the Immaculate Conception, Graduate and Professional Programs in Theology, Washington, DC 20017-1585. Offers moral theology (STL); sacred scripture (STL); systematic theology (STL); theology (M Div, MA, STB); Thomistic studies (MA, STD, STL). *Accreditation:* ATS (one or more programs are accredited). *Program availability:* Part-time. *Faculty:* 18 full-time (1 woman), 6 part-time/adjunct (3 women). *Students:* 75 full-time (7 women), 9 part-time (3 women); includes 2 minority (both Asian, non-Hispanic/Latino), 13 international. Average age 33. 36 applicants, 100% accepted, 33 enrolled. In 2017, 32 master's awarded. *Degree requirements:* For master's, one foreign language, comprehensive exam, thesis, thesis defense; for other advanced degree, 3 foreign languages, comprehensive exam (for some programs), thesis (for some programs), lecture. *Entrance requirements:* For master's, 18 credits of philosophy, reading knowledge of Latin, BA with minimum GPA of 3.0; for other advanced degree, 36 credits of philosophy, BA with minimum GPA of 3.25 (for STB). Additional exam requirements/recommendations for international students: Required—TOEFL (minimum score 550 paper-based; 96 iBT). *Application deadline:* For fall admission, 7/1 for domestic and international students; for spring admission, 12/1 for domestic and international students. Applications are processed on a rolling basis. Application fee: $150. Electronic applications accepted. *Expenses: Tuition:* Full-time $16,080; part-time $670 per credit hour. *Required fees:* $280; $140 per semester. Part-time tuition and fees vary according to course load. *Financial support:* In 2017–18, 3 students received support. Career-related internships or fieldwork and Federal Work-Study available. Support available to part-time students. Financial award application deadline: 6/30; financial award applicants required to submit FAFSA. *Faculty research:* Sacred scripture, moral theology, systematic theology, philosophy, languages. *Unit head:* Rev. Thomas Petri, OP, Vice-President/Academic Dean, 202-495-3832, Fax: 202-495-3873, E-mail: dean@dhs.edu. *Application contact:* Rev. Albert Trudel, Registrar, 202-495-3836, Fax: 202-495-3873, E-mail: registrar@dhs.edu.

Dominican School of Philosophy and Theology, Graduate Programs, Berkeley, CA 94708. Offers philosophy (MA); theology (M Div, MA, MTS, Certificate); M Div/MA; MA/MA. *Accreditation:* ATS. *Program availability:* Part-time. *Degree requirements:* For master's, one foreign language, thesis. *Entrance requirements:* For master's, GRE General Test (for MA), minimum GPA of 3.0 (for MA), 2.3 (for M Div); academic writing sample (for MA); statement of purpose, official transcripts, letters of recommendation. Additional exam requirements/recommendations for international students: Required—TOEFL (minimum score 570 paper-based; 80 iBT), IELTS. Electronic applications accepted.

Drew University, Caspersen School of Graduate Studies, Madison, NJ 07940-1493. Offers conflict resolution and leadership (Certificate), including community leadership, moderation, peace building; education (M Ed); finance (MA); history and culture (MA, PhD), including American history, book history, British history, European history, Holocaust and genocide (M Litt, MA, D Litt, PhD), intellectual history, Irish history, print culture, public history; K-12 education (MAT), including art, biology, chemistry, elementary education, English, French, Italian, math, secondary education, special education, teacher of students with disabilities; liberal studies (M Litt, D Litt), including history, Holocaust and genocide (M Litt, MA, D Litt, PhD), Irish/Irish-American studies, literature (M Litt, MMH, D Litt, DMH, CMH), religion, spirituality, teaching in the two-year college, writing; medical humanities (MMH, DMH, CMH), including arts, health, healthcare, literature (M Litt, MMH, D Litt, DMH, CMH), scientific research; poetry (MFA). *Program availability:* Part-time, evening/weekend. *Faculty:* 4 full-time (2 women), 29 part-time/adjunct (15 women). *Students:* 77 full-time (42 women), 175 part-time (114 women); includes 39 minority (12 Black or African American, non-Hispanic/Latino; 6 Asian, non-Hispanic/Latino; 16 Hispanic/Latino; 5 Two or more races, non-Hispanic/Latino), 11 international. Average age 41. 126 applicants, 75% accepted, 52 enrolled. In 2017, 38 master's, 23 doctorates, 35 other advanced degrees awarded. Terminal master's awarded for partial completion of doctoral program. *Degree requirements:* For master's and other advanced degree, thesis (for some programs); for doctorate, one foreign language, comprehensive exam (for some programs), thesis/dissertation. *Entrance requirements:* For master's, PRAXIS Core and Subject Area tests (for MAT), GRE/GMAT (for M Fin), resume, transcripts, writing sample, personal statement, letters of recommendation; for doctorate, GRE (PhD in history and culture), resume, transcripts, writing sample, personal statement, letters of recommendation; for other advanced degree, resume, transcripts, personal statement. Additional exam requirements/recommendations for international students: Required—TOEFL (minimum score 587 paper-based; 80 iBT), IELTS (minimum score 6), TWE (minimum score 4). *Application deadline:* For fall admission, 8/1 for domestic students, 6/1 for international students; for spring admission, 12/1 for domestic students, 10/1 for international students. Applications are processed on a rolling basis. Application fee: $35. Electronic applications accepted. *Financial support:* Fellowships, research assistantships, teaching assistantships, career-related internships or fieldwork, Federal Work-Study, scholarships/grants, and unspecified assistantships available. Support available to part-time students. Financial award applicants required to submit FAFSA. *Faculty research:* Irish history and culture, conflict resolution and leadership. *Application contact:* Leanne Horinko, Director of Caspersen Admissions, 973-408-3280, E-mail: gradm@drew.edu.
Website: http://www.drew.edu/caspersen

Drew University, Theological School, Madison, NJ 07940-1493. Offers M Div, MA, MA Min, STM, D Min, PhD, Certificate. *Accreditation:* ACIPE; ATS. *Program availability:* Part-time, blended/hybrid learning. *Faculty:* 21 full-time (9 women), 20 part-time/adjunct (9 women). *Students:* 186 full-time (97 women), 134 part-time (59 women); includes 128 minority (85 Black or African American, non-Hispanic/Latino; 1 American Indian or Alaska Native, non-Hispanic/Latino; 17 Asian, non-Hispanic/Latino; 19 Hispanic/Latino; 6 Two or more races, non-Hispanic/Latino), 84 international. Average age 41. 201 applicants, 78% accepted, 94 enrolled. In 2017, 58 master's, 33 doctorates awarded. *Degree requirements:* For doctorate, thesis/dissertation. *Entrance requirements:* For master's, resume, transcripts, writing sample, personal statement, letters of recommendation. Additional exam requirements/recommendations for international students: Required—TOEFL (minimum score 580 paper-based; 70 iBT), IELTS (minimum score 6), TWE. *Application deadline:* For fall admission, 8/1 for domestic students, 4/1 for international students; for spring admission, 12/1 for domestic students, 10/1 for international students. Applications are processed on a rolling basis. Application fee: $35. Electronic applications accepted. *Expenses:* Contact institution. *Financial support:* Fellowships, career-related internships or fieldwork, Federal Work-Study, institutionally sponsored loans, and scholarships/grants available. Support available to part-time students. Financial award application deadline: 2/15; financial award applicants required to submit FAFSA. *Faculty research:* Biblical studies, constructive theology, ecology and religion, gender and religion, race/ethnicity and religion. *Unit head:* Dr. Javier Viera, Dean of the Theological School, 973-408-3418, E-mail: jviera@drew.edu. *Application contact:* Rev. Dr. Kevin D. Miller, Director of Theological Admissions, 973-408-3111, E-mail: kmiller@drew.edu.
Website: http://www.drew.edu/theological/

Duke University, Divinity School, Durham, NC 27708-0586. Offers M Div, MACP, MACS, MTS, Th M, D Min, Th D, JD/MTS, M Div/MSW. *Accreditation:* ACIPE; ATS. *Program availability:* Part-time, online learning. Terminal master's awarded for partial completion of doctoral program. *Degree requirements:* For master's, thesis (for some programs); for doctorate, 2 foreign languages, comprehensive exam (for some programs), thesis/dissertation. *Entrance requirements:* For master's, 5 letters of reference, bachelor's degree from regionally-accredited college or university prior to intended date of enrollment, minimum GPA of 2.75, commitment to some form of ordained or lay ministry; for doctorate, GRE, M Div, MTS or comparable master's degree from institution accredited by ATS; bachelor's degree from regionally-accredited college or university prior to intended date of enrollment; 4 letters of reference; 2-page statement of purpose; one sample of academic writing. Additional exam requirements/recommendations for international students: Required—TOEFL (minimum score 580 paper-based; 93 iBT). Electronic applications accepted. *Expenses:* Contact institution. *Faculty research:* Biblical studies, historical church studies, theological studies, church ministry studies.

Duquesne University, Graduate School of Liberal Arts, Department of Theology, Pittsburgh, PA 15282-0001. Offers pastoral ministry (MA); religious education (MA); systematic theology (PhD); theology (MA). *Program availability:* Part-time, evening/weekend, blended/hybrid learning. *Faculty:* 17 full-time (6 women). *Students:* 50 full-time (12 women), 7 part-time (6 women); includes 8 minority (3 Black or African American, non-Hispanic/Latino; 2 Hispanic/Latino; 3 Two or more races, non-Hispanic/Latino), 20 international. Average age 40. 25 applicants, 52% accepted, 11 enrolled. In 2017, 69 master's, 5 doctorates awarded. Terminal master's awarded for partial completion of doctoral program. *Degree requirements:* For master's, comprehensive exam; for doctorate, 2 foreign languages, comprehensive exam, thesis/dissertation. *Entrance requirements:* For master's and doctorate, GRE General Test. Additional exam requirements/recommendations for international students: Required—TOEFL. *Application deadline:* For fall admission, 2/1 for domestic and international students. Application fee: $0. Electronic applications accepted. *Expenses:* $1,259 per credit. *Financial support:* In 2017–18, 36 students received support, including 17 teaching assistantships with full tuition reimbursements available (averaging $17,000 per year); career-related internships or fieldwork, scholarships/grants, tuition waivers (partial), and unspecified assistantships also available. Support available to part-time students. Financial award application deadline: 5/1. *Unit head:* Dr. Marinus Iwuchukwu, Chair, 412-396-1014, E-mail: iwuchukwum@duq.edu. *Application contact:* Linda Rendulic, Assistant to the Dean, 412-396-6400, Fax: 412-396-5265, E-mail: rendulic@duq.edu.

Earlham School of Religion, Graduate Programs, Richmond, IN 47374-5360. Offers ministry (M Min); religion (MA); theology (M Div). *Accreditation:* ACIPE; ATS. *Program availability:* Part-time, online learning. *Faculty:* 8 full-time (2 women), 2 part-time/adjunct (1 woman). *Students:* 26 full-time (15 women), 32 part-time (21 women). *Degree requirements:* For master's, variable foreign language requirement, comprehensive exam (for some programs), thesis (for some programs), internship (M Div). *Entrance requirements:* For master's, 3 references, academic writing sample, official college transcripts. Additional exam requirements/recommendations for international students: Required—TOEFL (minimum score 550 paper-based; 82 iBT), IELTS (minimum score 7). *Application deadline:* For fall admission, 7/15 priority date for domestic students; for winter admission, 12/15 priority date for domestic students. Applications are processed on a rolling basis. Application fee: $35. Electronic applications accepted. *Expenses: Tuition:* Full-time $15,741; part-time $1741 per course. *Required fees:* $450. *Financial support:* Scholarships/grants and tuition waivers (full and partial) available. Financial award application deadline: 4/15; financial award applicants required to submit FAFSA. *Faculty research:* Digitizing Quaker texts, vital Quaker ministry, research in Quaker studies and other seminary areas. *Unit head:* Jay W. Marshall, Dean, 800-432-1377, Fax: 765-983-1688, E-mail: marshja@earlham.edu. *Application contact:* Matthew Hisrich, Director of Recruitment and Admissions, 765-983-1523, Fax: 765-983-1688, E-mail: hisrima@earlham.edu.
Website: http://esr.earlham.edu/academic-programs

Eastern Mennonite University, Eastern Mennonite Seminary, Harrisonburg, VA 22802-2462. Offers Christian leadership (MA); divinity (M Div); ministry studies (Certificate); religion (MA); theological studies (Certificate). *Accreditation:* ATS. *Program availability:* Part-time. *Degree requirements:* For master's, thesis (for some programs), supervised field education (for M Div). *Entrance requirements:* For master's, minimum GPA of 2.5. Additional exam requirements/recommendations for international students: Required—TOEFL (minimum score 550 paper-based). *Application deadline:* For fall admission, 6/15 priority date for domestic and international students; for winter admission, 11/15 priority date for domestic and international students; for spring admission, 3/15 priority date for domestic and international students. Applications are processed on a rolling basis. Application fee: $25. *Expenses:* Contact institution. *Financial support:* Application deadline: 6/30; applicants required to submit FAFSA.

Faculty research: Spiritual direction and culture of call, leadership coaching: an approach to leadership in a culture of call, clarity of call in the probationary process for United Methodist clergy in Virginia, EMS women's experiences of culture of call efforts, practices of excellent and fruitful Mennonite pastoral ministry. *Unit head:* Sue Cockley, Dean, 540-432-4984, Fax: 540-432-4444, E-mail: cockleys@emu.edu. *Application contact:* Laura Lehman, Director of Seminary Admissions, 540-432-4268, Fax: 540-432-4598, E-mail: semadmiss@emu.edu.
Website: http://www.emu.edu/seminary/

Eastern University, Palmer Theological Seminary, St. Davids, PA 19096-3430. Offers divinity (M Div); theological studies (MTS); M Div/MA; M Div/MBA. *Accreditation:* ACIPE; MSA/CIHE. *Program availability:* Part-time, online learning. *Students:* 77 full-time (35 women), 161 part-time (61 women); includes 95 minority (82 Black or African American, non-Hispanic/Latino; 4 Asian, non-Hispanic/Latino; 9 Hispanic/Latino), 9 international. Average age 45. In 2017, 41 master's awarded. *Application deadline:* Applications are processed on a rolling basis. Application fee: $30. Electronic applications accepted. Application fee is waived when completed online. *Expenses:* Contact institution. *Unit head:* Michael Dziedziak, Executive Director of Enrollment, 800-452-0996, E-mail: semadmis@eastern.edu.
Website: https://www.palmerseminary.edu/

Ecumenical Theological Seminary, Professional Program, Detroit, MI 48201. Offers M Div. *Accreditation:* ACIPE; ATS.

Eden Theological Seminary, Graduate and Professional Programs, St. Louis, MO 63119-3192. Offers M Div, MAPS, MTS, D Min. *Accreditation:* ACIPE; ATS. *Degree requirements:* For master's, comprehensive exam (for some programs), thesis (for some programs), 2 oral exams; for doctorate, professional essay, supervised in-service projects. *Entrance requirements:* For master's, interview, minimum GPA of 2.7; for doctorate, interview, minimum GPA of 3.0. Additional exam requirements/recommendations for international students: Required—TOEFL (minimum score 550 paper-based). Electronic applications accepted. *Faculty research:* Psalms, pastoral ethics, historical Jesus, leadership roles, congregational life.

Emory University, Candler School of Theology, Atlanta, GA 30322. Offers formation and witness (M Div); history, scripture and tradition (MTS); leadership in church and community (M Div); modern religious thought and experience (MTS); pastoral counseling (Th D); religion and race (M Div); religion, health and science (M Div); scripture and interpretation (M Div); society and personality (M Div); theology (Th M); theology and ethics (M Div); theology and the arts (M Div); traditions of the church (M Div); women and religion (M Div); JD/M Div; JD/MTS; M Div/MBA; M Div/MPH; MBA/MTS; MTS/MPH. *Accreditation:* ACIPE. *Program availability:* Part-time. *Degree requirements:* For master's, thesis optional; for doctorate, comprehensive exam, thesis/dissertation. *Entrance requirements:* For master's, minimum undergraduate GPA of 3.0; for doctorate, GRE, M Div, 8 units of course work in clinical pastoral education. Additional exam requirements/recommendations for international students: Required—TOEFL (minimum score 600 paper-based; 95 iBT). Electronic applications accepted. *Expenses:* Contact institution. *Faculty research:* Biblical studies, church history, ethics, ministry practice, pastoral care.

Erskine Theological Seminary, Graduate and Professional Programs, Due West, SC 29639-0668. Offers M Div, MAPM, MATS, Th M, D Min. *Accreditation:* ATS. *Program availability:* Part-time, evening/weekend. *Degree requirements:* For doctorate, thesis/dissertation. *Entrance requirements:* For master's, Myers-Briggs Type Indicator, Taylor Johnson Temperament Analysis, Ministry Specialties Test (MACM), minimum GPA of 3.0, interview with committee (MACM); for doctorate, minimum GPA of 3.0 during M Div. Additional exam requirements/recommendations for international students: Required—TOEFL (minimum score 550 paper-based). Electronic applications accepted. *Faculty research:* Church administration, biblical studies.

Evangelical Seminary, Graduate and Professional Programs, Myerstown, PA 17067-1212. Offers Biblical studies (MAR); congregational ministry (M Div); global and contextual studies (M Div, MAR); historical and theological studies (MAR); interdisciplinary studies (MAR); marriage and family counseling (M Div); marriage and family therapy (MA); New Testament (MAR); Old Testament (MAR); spiritual formation (MAR); teaching ministry (M Div); youth ministry (M Div). *Accreditation:* ATS (one or more programs are accredited). *Program availability:* Part-time, online learning. *Degree requirements:* For master's, 2 foreign languages. *Entrance requirements:* For master's, minimum GPA of 2.5. Additional exam requirements/recommendations for international students: Required—TOEFL (minimum score 550 paper-based). *Faculty research:* Literary form and structure within the Hebrew and Greek scriptures, Wesley studies, esoteric biblical languages, the Mosaic law and the Christian, ethics.

Evangelical Seminary of Puerto Rico, Graduate and Professional Programs, San Juan, PR 00925-2207. Offers M Div, MAR, D Min. *Accreditation:* ATS. *Program availability:* Part-time. *Degree requirements:* For master's, comprehensive exam. *Entrance requirements:* For doctorate, 3 years experience in ministry service. Additional exam requirements/recommendations for international students: Required—TOEFL. *Faculty research:* Protestantism in Puerto Rico.

Faith Baptist Bible College and Theological Seminary, Graduate Program, Ankeny, IA 50023. Offers Biblical studies (MA); pastoral studies (M Div); pastoral training (MA); religion (MA); theological studies (MA). *Program availability:* Part-time. *Degree requirements:* For master's, thesis or alternative. *Entrance requirements:* Additional exam requirements/recommendations for international students: Required—TOEFL (minimum score 550 paper-based; 79 iBT), IELTS (minimum score 6.5). Electronic applications accepted. *Faculty research:* Baptist theology, American church history.

Faith International University, Graduate and Professional Programs, Tacoma, WA 98407. Offers M Div, MACM, MTS, D Min. *Program availability:* Part-time, evening/weekend, online learning. *Degree requirements:* For master's, thesis optional; for doctorate, thesis/dissertation. *Entrance requirements:* For master's, minimum undergraduate GPA of 2.7; for doctorate, minimum graduate GPA of 3.0. Additional exam requirements/recommendations for international students: Required—TOEFL (minimum score 550 paper-based).

Faith Theological Seminary, Graduate Programs, Baltimore, MD 21212. Offers M Div, D Min, Th D.

Faulkner University, College of Biblical Studies, Montgomery, AL 36109-3398. Offers Biblical studies (MA, PhD); Christian counseling and family ministry (MA); Christian ministry (MA). *Program availability:* Part-time, evening/weekend, 100% online, blended/hybrid learning, synchronous online/on-ground. *Faculty:* 7 full-time (1 woman). *Students:* 28 full-time (9 women), 16 part-time (2 women); includes 21 minority (18 Black or African American, non-Hispanic/Latino; 2 Hispanic/Latino; 1 Two or more races, non-Hispanic/Latino), 1 international. Average age 39. 42 applicants, 45% accepted, 15 enrolled. In 2017, 5 master's awarded. Terminal master's awarded for partial completion of doctoral program. *Degree requirements:* For master's, comprehensive exam, thesis (for some programs); for doctorate, 3 foreign languages, thesis/dissertation. *Entrance requirements:* Additional exam requirements/recommendations for international students: Required—TOEFL (minimum score 500 paper-based). *Application deadline:* For fall admission, 6/1 for domestic students; for spring admission, 11/1 for domestic students; for summer admission, 4/1 for domestic students. Application fee: $35. Electronic applications accepted. *Expenses:* $540 per hour tuition (for MA); $550 per hour tuition (for PhD); $220 per semester fees. *Financial support:* Applicants required to submit FAFSA. *Unit head:* Dr. G. Scott Gleaves, Dean/Vice President, Black College of Biblical Studies, 334-386-7660, Fax: 334-386-7203, E-mail: sgleaves@faulkner.edu. *Application contact:* Dr. Randall C. Bailey, Director, Kearly Graduate School of Theology, 334-386-7663, Fax: 334-386-7203, E-mail: rbailey@faulkner.edu.
Website: https://www.faulkner.edu/graduate/graduate_academics/kearley-graduate-school-of-theology/

Fordham University, Graduate School of Arts and Sciences, Department of Theology, New York, NY 10458. Offers MA, PhD. *Program availability:* Part-time, evening/weekend. *Faculty:* 22 full-time (7 women). *Students:* 52 full-time (18 women), 5 part-time (1 woman); includes 15 minority (3 Black or African American, non-Hispanic/Latino; 1 American Indian or Alaska Native, non-Hispanic/Latino; 5 Asian, non-Hispanic/Latino; 6 Hispanic/Latino), 4 international. Average age 37. 51 applicants, 47% accepted, 9 enrolled. In 2017, 2 master's, 5 doctorates awarded. Terminal master's awarded for partial completion of doctoral program. *Degree requirements:* For master's, one foreign language, comprehensive exam; for doctorate, 2 foreign languages, comprehensive exam, thesis/dissertation. *Entrance requirements:* For master's and doctorate, GRE General Test. Additional exam requirements/recommendations for international students: Required—TOEFL (minimum score 650 paper-based). *Application deadline:* For fall admission, 1/4 priority date for domestic students; for spring admission, 11/1 for domestic students. Application fee: $70. Electronic applications accepted. *Financial support:* In 2017–18, 45 students received support, including 2 fellowships with tuition reimbursements available (averaging $25,960 per year), 33 teaching assistantships with tuition reimbursements available (averaging $21,887 per year); institutionally sponsored loans, tuition waivers (full and partial), and unspecified assistantships also available. Support available to part-time students. Financial award application deadline: 1/4. *Faculty research:* History of Christian tradition, contemporary systematic theology, theological/feminist ethics, American Catholicism, Biblical exegesis and theology. *Unit head:* Dr. Kathryn Reklis, Chair, 718-817-3258, E-mail: kreklis@fordham.edu. *Application contact:* Travis Strattion, Interim Director of Graduate Admissions, 718-817-4417, Fax: 718-817-3566, E-mail: tstrattion@fordham.edu.

Franciscan School of Theology, Graduate and Professional Programs, Oceanside, CA 92057. Offers M Div, MA, MAMC, MTS. *Accreditation:* ATS (one or more programs are accredited). *Program availability:* Part-time. *Degree requirements:* For master's, one foreign language, thesis. *Entrance requirements:* For master's, GRE General Test (MA). Additional exam requirements/recommendations for international students: Required—TOEFL (minimum score 550 paper-based). *Faculty research:* Church history, multicultural ministries, ethics and morality, catechesis, biblical studies.

Franciscan University of Steubenville, Graduate Programs, Department of Theology, Steubenville, OH 43952-1763. Offers theology and Christian ministry (MA). *Program availability:* Part-time, online learning. *Degree requirements:* For master's, comprehensive exam. *Entrance requirements:* For master's, minimum undergraduate GPA of 3.0. Additional exam requirements/recommendations for international students: Required—TOEFL. Electronic applications accepted. Application fee is waived when completed online. *Expenses: Tuition:* Full-time $9000; part-time $500 per semester hour. *Required fees:* $16 per semester hour. Tuition and fees vary according to program.

Freed-Hardeman University, School of Biblical Studies, Program in Divinity, Henderson, TN 38340-2399. Offers M Div. *Accreditation:* ATS. *Program availability:* Part-time. *Degree requirements:* For master's, comprehensive exam. *Entrance requirements:* For master's, GRE General Test or MAT. Additional exam requirements/recommendations for international students: Required—TOEFL (minimum score 500 paper-based).

Freed-Hardeman University, School of Biblical Studies, Program in New Testament, Henderson, TN 38340-2399. Offers MA. *Program availability:* Part-time. *Degree requirements:* For master's, one foreign language, comprehensive exam, thesis. *Entrance requirements:* For master's, GRE General Test or MAT. Additional exam requirements/recommendations for international students: Required—TOEFL (minimum score 500 paper-based).

Fresno Pacific University, Biblical Seminary, Program in Divinity, Fresno, CA 93702-4709. Offers M Div. *Accreditation:* ATS. *Entrance requirements:* For master's, minimum GPA of 2.5. *Expenses:* Contact institution.

Fresno Pacific University, Biblical Seminary, Programs in New Testament, Old Testament, and Theology, Fresno, CA 93702-4709. Offers New Testament (MA); Old Testament (MA); theology (MA). *Accreditation:* ATS. *Program availability:* Part-time. *Entrance requirements:* Additional exam requirements/recommendations for international students: Required—TOEFL (minimum score 550 paper-based).

Fuller Theological Seminary, Graduate Programs, Pasadena, CA 91182. Offers Christian leadership (MACL); clinical psychology (PhD, Psy D); family studies (MA); global leadership (MA); global ministries (D Min); global ministries (Korean language) (D Min); intercultural studies (MA, Th M, PhD); intercultural studies (Korean language) (MA); marital and family therapy (MS); marriage and family enrichment (Certificate); ministry (M Div, D Min); missiology (D Miss); missiology (Korean language) (Th M); theology (MA, Th M, PhD), including evangelism (MA), family life education (MA), pastoral ministry (MA), recovery ministry (MA), worship music ministry (MA), worship, theology, and the arts (MA), youth, family, and culture (MA); theology and ministry (MA).

Gannon University, School of Graduate Studies, College of Humanities, Education, and Social Sciences, School of Humanities, Program in Pastoral Studies, Erie, PA 16541-0001. Offers pastoral studies (MA); theological studies (Certificate). *Program availability:* Part-time, evening/weekend. *Degree requirements:* For master's, comprehensive exam, thesis or alternative, research project, internship, written evaluation. *Entrance requirements:* Additional exam requirements/recommendations for international students: Required—TOEFL (minimum score 79 iBT). Electronic applications accepted. Application fee is waived when completed online.

Gardner-Webb University, School of Divinity, Boiling Springs, NC 28017. Offers biblical studies (M Div); Christian education and formation (M Div); intercultural studies (M Div); ministry (D Min); missiology (M Div); pastoral care and counseling (M Div); pastoral care and counseling/member care for missionaries (D Min); pastoral studies (M Div); M Div/MA; M Div/MBA. *Accreditation:* ACIPE. *Program availability:* Part-time. *Faculty:* 10 full-time (1 woman), 4 part-time/adjunct (2 women). *Students:* 102 full-time (47 women), 56 part-time (15 women); includes 67 minority (63 Black or African American, non-Hispanic/Latino; 3 Asian, non-Hispanic/Latino; 1 Hispanic/Latino). Average age 38. *Entrance requirements:* For master's, minimum GPA of 2.6; for doctorate, minimum GPA of 2.75. Additional exam requirements/recommendations for international students: Required—TOEFL (minimum score 500 paper-based; 61 iBT). *Application deadline:* Applications are processed on a rolling basis. Electronic applications accepted. *Expenses:* Contact institution. *Financial support:* Fellowships, institutionally sponsored loans, and unspecified assistantships available. Support available to part-time students. Financial award application deadline: 5/15. *Faculty research:* Jewish-Christian dialogue, Islam. *Unit head:* Dr. Robert W. Canoy, Sr., Dean,

704-406-4400, Fax: 704-406-3935, E-mail: rcanoy@gardner-webb.edu. *Application contact:* Kheresa Harmon, Director of Admissions, 704-406-3205, Fax: 704-406-3895, E-mail: kharmon@gardner-webb.edu.
Website: http://gardner-webb.edu/academic-programs-and-resources/colleges-and-schools/divinity/index

Garrett-Evangelical Theological Seminary, Graduate and Professional Programs, Evanston, IL 60201-3298. Offers Bible and culture (PhD); Christian education (MA); Christian education and congregational studies (PhD); contemporary theology and culture (PhD); divinity (M Div); ethics, church, and society (MA); liturgical studies (PhD); ministry (D Min); music ministry (MA); pastoral care and counseling (MA); pastoral theology, personality, and culture (PhD); spiritual formation and evangelism (MA); theological studies (MTS); M Div/MSW. M Div/MSW offered jointly with Loyola University Chicago. *Accreditation:* ACIPE; ATS (one or more programs are accredited). *Program availability:* Part-time. *Degree requirements:* For master's, thesis (for some programs); for doctorate, thesis/dissertation. *Entrance requirements:* For doctorate, GRE (PhD). Additional exam requirements/recommendations for international students: Required—TOEFL (minimum score 560 paper-based). Electronic applications accepted.

Gateway Seminary, Graduate and Professional Programs, Ontario, CA 91761-8642. Offers divinity (M Div); early childhood education (Certificate); education leadership (MAEL, Diploma); ministry (D Min); theological studies (MTS); theology (Th M); youth ministry (Certificate). *Accreditation:* ACIPE; ATS. *Program availability:* Part-time, evening/weekend. *Degree requirements:* For master's, thesis (for some programs); for doctorate, 2 foreign languages, thesis/dissertation. *Entrance requirements:* For doctorate, MAT. Additional exam requirements/recommendations for international students: Required—TOEFL (minimum score 550 paper-based). Electronic applications accepted.

General Theological Seminary, Graduate and Professional Programs, New York, NY 10011-4977. Offers Anglican studies (STM, Th D, Certificate); ascetical theology (Certificate); biblical studies (Certificate); congregational development (Certificate); divinity (M Div); historical and theological studies (Certificate); spiritual direction (MASD, STM, Certificate); theology (MA). *Accreditation:* ACIPE; ATS. *Program availability:* Part-time, evening/weekend. Terminal master's awarded for partial completion of doctoral program. *Degree requirements:* For master's, thesis; for doctorate, 2 foreign languages, thesis/dissertation. *Entrance requirements:* For master's, GRE General Test; for doctorate, GRE, M Div or MA. Additional exam requirements/recommendations for international students: Required—TOEFL. *Faculty research:* Liturgy, New Testament, ethics, history, ecumenical relations.

George Fox University, Portland Seminary, Portland, OR 97223. Offers Biblical studies (M Div, MA); chaplaincy (M Div); Christian history and theology (M Div, MA); creation care (M Div, MA); intercultural studies (M Div, MA); leadership (M Div, MA); leadership and global perspectives (D Min); leadership and spiritual formation (D Min); semiotics and future studies (D Min); spiritual direction (MA, Certificate); spiritual direction supervision (M Div, MA, Certificate); spiritual formation and discipleship (M Div, MA, Certificate). *Accreditation:* ACIPE. *Program availability:* Part-time, evening/weekend, online learning. *Entrance requirements:* For master's, resume, three references (one pastoral, one academic or professional, one personal), one official transcript from each college or university attended; for doctorate, resume, 3 references (1 professional, 1 academic, 1 personal), one official transcript from each college or university attended. Additional exam requirements/recommendations for international students: Required—TOEFL (minimum score 577 paper-based; 90 iBT). Electronic applications accepted. *Expenses:* Contact institution.

Georgetown University, Graduate School of Arts and Sciences, Department of Theology, Washington, DC 20057. Offers PhD.

Georgian Court University, School of Arts and Sciences, Lakewood, NJ 08701-2697. Offers applied behavior analysis (MA); autism spectrum disorders (Certificate); clinical mental health counseling (MA); criminal justice and human rights (MS); holistic health studies (MA, Certificate); homeland security (Certificate); instructional technology (CPC); mercy spirituality (Certificate); parish business management (Certificate); professional counselor (Certificate); school psychology (MA, Certificate); theology (MA, Certificate). *Program availability:* Part-time, evening/weekend. *Faculty:* 18 full-time (11 women), 8 part-time/adjunct (4 women). *Students:* 100 full-time (86 women), 92 part-time (67 women); includes 34 minority (9 Black or African American, non-Hispanic/Latino; 1 Asian, non-Hispanic/Latino; 20 Hispanic/Latino; 4 Two or more races, non-Hispanic/Latino), 2 international. Average age 34. 187 applicants, 56% accepted, 78 enrolled. In 2017, 58 master's, 20 other advanced degrees awarded. *Degree requirements:* For master's, comprehensive exam (for some programs), thesis (for some programs). *Entrance requirements:* For master's, GRE, GMAT, or NTE/PRAXIS, 3 letters of recommendation. Additional exam requirements/recommendations for international students: Required—TOEFL (minimum score 550 paper-based). *Application deadline:* For fall admission, 8/15 for domestic students, 5/1 for international students; for spring admission, 1/15 for domestic students, 10/1 for international students. Applications are processed on a rolling basis. Application fee: $40. Electronic applications accepted. *Expenses: Tuition:* Part-time $839 per credit. *Required fees:* $248 per semester. Tuition and fees vary according to campus/location and program. *Financial support:* Scholarships/grants, health care benefits, and unspecified assistantships available. Financial award application deadline: 4/15; financial award applicants required to submit FAFSA. *Unit head:* Dr. Mary Chinery, Dean, 732-987-2493, Fax: 732-987-2007, E-mail: mchinery@georgian.edu. *Application contact:* Patrick Givens, Director of Graduate and Professional Studies Admissions, 732-987-2736, Fax: 732-987-2000, E-mail: gps@georgian.edu.
Website: https://georgian.edu/academics/school-of-arts-sciences/

Global University, Graduate School of Theology, Springfield, MO 65804. Offers bible and theology (D Min); biblical language (M Div); biblical studies (MA); Christian ministry (M Div, D Min); ministerial studies (MA), including education, leadership, missions, New Testament, Old Testament. *Program availability:* Part-time, evening/weekend, online learning. *Degree requirements:* For master's, thesis (for some programs). *Entrance requirements:* For master's, minimum undergraduate GPA of 3.0. Electronic applications accepted. *Faculty research:* Higher education, cross-cultural missions.

Gonzaga University, College of Arts and Sciences, Spokane, WA 99258. Offers philosophy (MA); theology and leadership (MA). *Program availability:* Part-time, blended/hybrid learning. *Faculty:* 9 full-time (3 women). *Students:* 1 full-time (0 women), 43 part-time (21 women); includes 9 minority (4 Black or African American, non-Hispanic/Latino; 1 American Indian or Alaska Native, non-Hispanic/Latino; 3 Asian, non-Hispanic/Latino; 1 Hispanic/Latino), 2 international. Average age 37. 47 applicants, 79% accepted, 22 enrolled. In 2017, 4 master's awarded. *Degree requirements:* For master's, comprehensive exam. *Entrance requirements:* For master's, GRE or MAT, minimum GPA of 3.0, official transcripts, two to three letters of recommendation, personal statement, writing sample, resume/curriculum vitae. Additional exam requirements/recommendations for international students: Required—TOEFL (minimum score 88 iBT) or IELTS (minimum score 6.5). *Application deadline:* For fall admission, 7/15 for domestic students; for spring admission, 11/1 for domestic students; for summer admission, 4/9 for domestic students. Applications are processed on a rolling basis. Application fee: $50. Electronic applications accepted. *Expenses:* $700 per credit (theology and leadership); $830 per credit (philosophy). *Financial support:* In 2017–18, 38 students received support. Scholarships/grants and unspecified assistantships available. Support available to part-time students. Financial award applicants required to submit FAFSA. *Faculty research:* Environmental ethics, phenomenology and religion, healthcare ethics, ancient philosophy. *Unit head:* Dr. Patricia Terry, Interim Dean of the College of Arts and Sciences, 509-313-5522, Fax: 509-313-6684, E-mail: terry@gonzaga.edu. *Application contact:* Carolyn Von Muller, Assistant to the Dean, 509-313-5522, E-mail: vonmuller@gonzaga.edu.
Website: https://www.gonzaga.edu/college-of-arts-sciences

Gordon-Conwell Theological Seminary, Graduate and Professional Programs, South Hamilton, MA 01982. Offers Biblical languages (MABL); church history (MACH); counseling (MACO); ministry (D Min); missions/evangelism (MAME); New Testament (MANT); Old Testament (MAOT); religion (MAR); theology (M Div, MATH, Th M, Th D). *Accreditation:* ACIPE; ATS (one or more programs are accredited). *Program availability:* Part-time, evening/weekend. *Degree requirements:* For master's, one foreign language, thesis optional; for doctorate, 2 foreign languages, thesis/dissertation. *Entrance requirements:* For master's, minimum GPA of 2.5; for doctorate, minimum GPA of 3.0.

Graceland University, Community of Christ Seminary, Independence, MO 64050. Offers MAR. *Program availability:* Part-time. *Faculty:* 1 full-time (0 women), 1 part-time/adjunct (0 women). *Students:* 14 full-time (10 women), 17 part-time (9 women); includes 2 minority (1 Asian, non-Hispanic/Latino; 1 Native Hawaiian or other Pacific Islander, non-Hispanic/Latino), 2 international. Average age 41. 16 applicants, 100% accepted, 11 enrolled. In 2017, 12 master's awarded. *Degree requirements:* For master's, portfolio. *Entrance requirements:* For master's, minimum cumulative GPA of 3.0. Additional exam requirements/recommendations for international students: Required—TOEFL (minimum score 550 paper-based; 79 iBT). *Application deadline:* For fall admission, 8/15 priority date for domestic students. Applications are processed on a rolling basis. Application fee: $50. Electronic applications accepted. *Expenses:* Contact institution. *Financial support:* In 2017–18, 1 student received support. Scholarships/grants available. Financial award application deadline: 12/15; financial award applicants required to submit FAFSA. *Faculty research:* Theology, scripture. *Unit head:* Dr. Matthew Frizzell, Dean, 641-784-5276, E-mail: mfrizzel@graceland.edu. *Application contact:* Sharon Ward, Administrative Assistant, 816-423-4676, Fax: 816-423-4753, E-mail: ward@graceland.edu.
Website: http://www.graceland.edu/seminary

Grace School of Theology, Graduate Programs, Conroe, TX 77384-4894. Offers M Div, MABS, MM, Th M.

Grace Theological Seminary, Graduate and Professional Programs, Winona Lake, IN 46590-9907. Offers biblical studies (Certificate); chaplaincy (M Div); exegetical studies (M Div); intercultural studies (M Div, MA, D Min); local church ministry (MA), including camp administration, women's leadership; pastoral counseling (M Div); pastoral studies (M Div, D Min); theology (Diploma). *Accreditation:* ATS. *Program availability:* Part-time, online learning. *Degree requirements:* For master's, thesis optional; for doctorate, 2 foreign languages, thesis/dissertation. *Entrance requirements:* For master's, MAT, minimum GPA of 2.5. Electronic applications accepted. *Faculty research:* Biblical theology, language, and church ministries.

Graduate Theological Union, Graduate Programs, Berkeley, CA 94709-1212. Offers art and religion (MA, PhD, Th D); biblical languages (MA); biblical studies (MA); Biblical studies (PhD, Th D); Buddhist studies (MA); Christian spirituality (MA, PhD, Th D); cultural and historical studies of religions (MA, PhD, Th D); ethics and social theory (PhD, Th D); history (MA, PhD, Th D); homiletics (MA, PhD, Th D); interdisciplinary studies (PhD, Th D); Jewish studies (MA, PhD, Th D, Certificate); liturgical studies (MA, PhD, Th D); Near Eastern religions (PhD, Th D); Orthodox Christian studies (MA); religion and psychology (MA, PhD, Th D); religion and society/ethics and social theory (MA); systematic and philosophical theology (MA, PhD, Th D). PhD programs in Jewish studies and Near Eastern religions offered jointly with University of California, Berkeley. *Accreditation:* ATS. Terminal master's awarded for partial completion of doctoral program. *Degree requirements:* For master's, one foreign language, thesis; for doctorate, one foreign language, comprehensive exam, thesis/dissertation. *Entrance requirements:* For master's, GRE General Test; for doctorate, GRE General Test, MA or M Div. Additional exam requirements/recommendations for international students: Required—TOEFL. Electronic applications accepted.

Grand Rapids Theological Seminary of Cornerstone University, Graduate Programs, Grand Rapids, MI 49525-5897. Offers academic (M Div); chaplaincy ministries (M Div); Christian formation (MA); counseling (MA); formation and soul care ministries (M Div); intercultural ministries (M Div); interdisciplinary studies (MA); New Testament (Th M); Old Testament (Th M); pastoral ministries (M Div); small group and discipleship ministries (M Div); student and family ministries (M Div). *Accreditation:* ATS. *Program availability:* Part-time, evening/weekend, 100% online, blended/hybrid learning. *Faculty:* 9 full-time (2 women), 14 part-time/adjunct (5 women). *Students:* 100 full-time (53 women), 211 part-time (102 women); includes 71 minority (54 Black or African American, non-Hispanic/Latino; 1 American Indian or Alaska Native, non-Hispanic/Latino; 3 Asian, non-Hispanic/Latino; 12 Hispanic/Latino; 1 Two or more races, non-Hispanic/Latino), 3 international. Average age 36. 165 applicants, 76% accepted, 99 enrolled. In 2017, 75 master's awarded. *Entrance requirements:* Additional exam requirements/recommendations for international students: Required—TOEFL (minimum score 577 paper-based; 90 iBT), IELTS (minimum score 7). *Application deadline:* For fall admission, 8/15 for domestic students, 6/15 for international students; for spring admission, 1/10 for domestic students, 11/10 for international students; for summer admission, 4/30 for domestic students. Applications are processed on a rolling basis. Electronic applications accepted. *Expenses: Tuition:* Full-time $9720; part-time $540 per credit hour. *Required fees:* $832; $374 per semester. Tuition and fees vary according to course load and program. *Financial support:* In 2017–18, 96 students received support, including 8 fellowships with partial tuition reimbursements available; career-related internships or fieldwork and scholarships/grants also available. Support available to part-time students. Financial award application deadline: 8/15; financial award applicants required to submit FAFSA. *Unit head:* Dr. John F. VerBerkmoes, Executive Vice President and Academic Dean, 616-222-1422, E-mail: john.verberkmoes@cornerstone.edu. *Application contact:* Ashley VanBemmelen, Director of Admissions, 800-697-1133, E-mail: ashley.vanbemmelen@cornerstone.edu.

Harding School of Theology, Graduate Programs, Memphis, TN 38117-5499. Offers Christian ministry (MA); historical theology (MA); ministry (M Div); New Testament (MA); Old Testament (MA); systematic theology (MA); transforming leadership (D Min). *Accreditation:* ATS. *Program availability:* Part-time, online learning. *Faculty:* 6 full-time (0 women), 2 part-time/adjunct (1 woman). *Students:* 28 full-time (7 women), 99 part-time (7 women); includes 26 minority (23 Black or African American, non-Hispanic/Latino; 2 Asian, non-Hispanic/Latino; 1 Hispanic/Latino), 2 international. *Degree requirements:* For master's, variable foreign language requirement, thesis (for some programs); for doctorate, one foreign language, thesis/dissertation. *Entrance requirements:* For master's, minimum GPA of 2.7; for doctorate, minimum GPA of 3.0. Additional exam requirements/recommendations for international students: Required—TOEFL (minimum score 550 paper-based; 79 iBT). *Application deadline:* For fall admission, 12/7 priority

date for domestic students; for spring admission, 5/3 priority date for domestic students. Applications are processed on a rolling basis. Application fee: $40. Electronic applications accepted. *Expenses: Tuition:* Full-time $14,000. *Required fees:* $525. One-time fee: $40 full-time. *Financial support:* Research assistantships with partial tuition reimbursements, career-related internships or fieldwork, institutionally sponsored loans, scholarships/grants, tuition waivers (partial), and unspecified assistantships available. Support available to part-time students. Financial award application deadline: 3/1; financial award applicants required to submit FAFSA. *Unit head:* Dr. Allen Black, Dean, 901-761-1352, Fax: 901-761-1358, E-mail: ablack@hst.edu. *Application contact:* Dr. Matt R. Carter, Director of Admissions, 901-761-1356, Fax: 901-761-1358, E-mail: mrcarter@harding.edu.
Website: https://hst.edu/academics/degrees/

Hardin-Simmons University, Graduate School, Logsdon School of Theology, Abilene, TX 79698-0001. Offers M Div, MA, D Min. *Program availability:* Part-time, evening/weekend. *Faculty:* 13 full-time (3 women), 17 part-time/adjunct (2 women). *Students:* 52 full-time (13 women), 105 part-time (31 women); includes 42 minority (14 Black or African American, non-Hispanic/Latino; 5 Asian, non-Hispanic/Latino; 23 Hispanic/Latino), 1 international. Average age 41. 31 applicants, 87% accepted, 12 enrolled. In 2017, 4 master's, 3 doctorates awarded. *Entrance requirements:* For master's, bachelor's degree; personal statement; three letters of recommendation; interview. Additional exam requirements/recommendations for international students: Required—TOEFL (minimum score 550 paper-based; 79 iBT). *Application deadline:* For fall admission, 8/15 priority date for domestic students, 4/1 for international students; for spring admission, 1/5 priority date for domestic students, 9/1 for international students. Applications are processed on a rolling basis. Application fee: $50. Electronic applications accepted. *Expenses: Tuition:* Full-time $13,500; part-time $750 per semester hour. *Required fees:* $220 per term. One-time fee: $50. Tuition and fees vary according to course load, campus/location and program. *Financial support:* In 2017–18, 127 students received support. Fellowships and scholarships/grants available. Support available to part-time students. Financial award application deadline: 6/30; financial award applicants required to submit FAFSA. *Unit head:* Dr. Don Williford, Dean, 325-670-1491, Fax: 325-671-2157, E-mail: willifrd@hsutx.edu. *Application contact:* Dr. Nancy Kucinski, Dean of Graduate Studies, 325-670-1298, Fax: 325-670-1564, E-mail: gradoff@hsutx.edu.
Website: http://www.hsutx.edu/academics/logsdon

Hardin-Simmons University, Graduate School, Logsdon School of Theology, Logsdon Seminary, Program in Theology, Abilene, TX 79698-0001. Offers M Div. *Program availability:* Part-time. *Faculty:* 12 full-time (3 women), 17 part-time/adjunct (2 women). *Students:* 43 full-time (8 women), 56 part-time (18 women); includes 34 minority (11 Black or African American, non-Hispanic/Latino; 3 Asian, non-Hispanic/Latino; 20 Hispanic/Latino), 5 international. Average age 37. In 2017, 14 master's awarded. *Degree requirements:* For master's, ministry formation. *Entrance requirements:* Additional exam requirements/recommendations for international students: Required—TOEFL (minimum score 550 paper-based; 75 iBT). *Application deadline:* For fall admission, 8/15 priority date for domestic students, 4/1 for international students; for spring admission, 1/5 priority date for domestic students, 9/1 for international students. Applications are processed on a rolling basis. Application fee: $50 ($150 for international students). Electronic applications accepted. *Expenses:* Contact institution. *Financial support:* In 2017–18, 100 students received support. Fellowships, career-related internships or fieldwork, and scholarships/grants available. Support available to part-time students. Financial award application deadline: 6/30; financial award applicants required to submit FAFSA. *Faculty research:* Hebrew grammar, history of Christian education, training of ministers into the twenty-first century, role of women in the Old Testament, contemporary ethical issues, Ricouer in contemporary theology. *Unit head:* Dr. Kenneth Lyle, Program Director, 325-670-5858, Fax: 325-670-5895, E-mail: klyle@hsutx.edu. *Application contact:* Dr. Nancy Kucinski, Dean of Graduate Studies, 325-670-1298, Fax: 325-670-1564, E-mail: gradoff@hsutx.edu.
Website: http://www.logsdonseminary.org/index.php/academics/mdiv

Hartford Seminary, Graduate Programs, Hartford, CT 06105-2279. Offers Islamic studies (MA); ministry (D Min); religious studies (MA); spirituality (Certificate). *Accreditation:* ATS (one or more programs are accredited). *Program availability:* Part-time, evening/weekend, online learning. *Degree requirements:* For master's, thesis optional, oral exam; for doctorate, thesis/dissertation, oral exam. *Entrance requirements:* For doctorate, experience in ministry, M Div. Additional exam requirements/recommendations for international students: Required—TOEFL (minimum score 550 paper-based; 80 iBT). *Faculty research:* Liturgy and social justice, professional leadership in ministry, congregational studies, Christian-Muslim relations, American religion.

Harvard University, Harvard Divinity School, Cambridge, MA 02138. Offers M Div, MTS, Th M. *Accreditation:* ACIPE; ATS. *Degree requirements:* For master's, one foreign language, thesis (for some programs). *Entrance requirements:* For master's, GRE General Test. Additional exam requirements/recommendations for international students: Required—TOEFL. Electronic applications accepted. *Expenses:* Contact institution. *Faculty research:* Theology, women's studies, history, comparative religion, ministry studies.

Hebrew College, Rabbinical School, Newton Centre, MA 02459. Offers MA. *Entrance requirements:* For master's, interview. Additional exam requirements/recommendations for international students: Required—TOEFL.

Hebrew Union College–Jewish Institute of Religion, Rabbinical School, New York, NY 10012-1186. Offers MAHL. *Degree requirements:* For master's, one foreign language. *Entrance requirements:* For master's, GRE, language exam, minimum GPA of 3.0, minimum 2 years of college-level Hebrew. Additional exam requirements/recommendations for international students: Required—TOEFL. *Faculty research:* Philosophy and theology, Bible, Hebrew, pastoral care, history and Rabbinics.

Hebrew Union College–Jewish Institute of Religion, School of Graduate Studies, Program in Pastoral Counseling, New York, NY 10012-1186. Offers D Min. *Accreditation:* ACIPE. *Degree requirements:* For doctorate, thesis/dissertation. *Entrance requirements:* For doctorate, M Div (or higher), ordination/certification for ministry. Additional exam requirements/recommendations for international students: Required—TOEFL. *Expenses:* Contact institution. *Faculty research:* Philosophy and theology, Bible, Hebrew, pastoral care, history and Rabbinics.

Heritage College and Seminary, Graduate and Professional Programs, Cambridge, ON N3C 3T2, Canada. Offers general (M Div); intercultural studies (M Div); pastoral (M Div); research (M Div); theological studies (MTS, CTS).

Holy Apostles College and Seminary, Department of Theology, Cromwell, CT 06416-2005. Offers bioethics (MA, Certificate, Post Master's Certificate); church history (MA, Certificate, Post Master's Certificate); dogmatic theology (MA, Certificate, Post Master's Certificate); liturgical music (MA, Certificate, Post Master's Certificate); liturgy (MA, Certificate, Post Master's Certificate); moral theology (MA, Certificate, Post Master's Certificate); philosophical theology (MA, Certificate, Post Master's Certificate); religious education (MA, Certificate, Post Master's Certificate); sacred scripture (MA, Post Master's Certificate); sacred scriptures (Certificate); theology (M Div). *Accreditation:* ATS. *Program availability:* Part-time, evening/weekend, online learning. *Degree requirements:* For master's, one foreign language, comprehensive exam, thesis optional; for other advanced degree, culminating paper. *Entrance requirements:* For master's, minimum undergraduate GPA of 3.0; for other advanced degree, minimum graduate GPA of 3.0. Electronic applications accepted. *Faculty research:* Roman Catholic theology, philosophy.

Holy Cross Greek Orthodox School of Theology, Theological Programs, Brookline, MA 02445-7496. Offers M Div, MTS, Th M. *Accreditation:* ATS. *Program availability:* Part-time. *Degree requirements:* For master's, 2 foreign languages, thesis (for some programs). *Entrance requirements:* For master's, GRE General Test, interview, official transcripts, letters of recommendation, health report and immunization verification. Additional exam requirements/recommendations for international students: Required—TOEFL (minimum score 550 paper-based; 80 iBT). *Faculty research:* Spirituality, liturgies, ecumenism, church history.

Hood Theological Seminary, Graduate and Professional Programs, Salisbury, NC 28144. Offers M Div, MTS, D Min. *Accreditation:* ATS. *Program availability:* Part-time, evening/weekend, online learning. *Degree requirements:* For master's, thesis optional; for doctorate, thesis/dissertation. *Faculty research:* Old Testament human sexuality, preaching and the vulnerable, socio-historical issues, Pauline studies, multiculturalism/African-American studies.

Houston Baptist University, School of Christian Thought, Program in Apologetics, Houston, TX 77074-3298. Offers cultural apologetics (MA); philosophical apologetics (MA). *Program availability:* 100% online. *Students:* 6 full-time (3 women), 59 part-time (24 women); includes 7 minority (3 Black or African American, non-Hispanic/Latino; 3 Hispanic/Latino; 1 Two or more races, non-Hispanic/Latino). Average age 39. 62 applicants, 58% accepted, 17 enrolled. In 2017, 16 master's awarded. *Entrance requirements:* For master's, bachelor's degree conferred transcript, essay/personal statement, resume. Additional exam requirements/recommendations for international students: Required—TOEFL (minimum score 80 iBT), IELTS (minimum score 6.5). *Application deadline:* For fall admission, 8/1 for domestic students, 6/1 for international students; for spring admission, 1/1 for domestic students, 11/1 for international students; for summer admission, 5/1 for domestic students, 3/1 for international students. Applications are processed on a rolling basis. Application fee: $0 ($100 for international students). Electronic applications accepted. Application fee is waived when completed online. *Expenses:* $18,000 tuition; $4,500 fees (general, technology and parking). *Financial support:* Federal Work-Study and scholarships/grants available. Financial award application deadline: 4/1; financial award applicants required to submit FAFSA. *Unit head:* Dr. Philip Tallon, Director, 281-649-3403, E-mail: ptallon@hbu.edu. *Application contact:* Celeste Risteski, Administrative Assistant to the Dean, 281-649-3383, Fax: 281-649-3012, E-mail: cristeski@hbu.edu.

Houston Baptist University, School of Christian Thought, Program in Divinity, Houston, TX 77074-3298. Offers Biblical languages (M Div); English languages (M Div). *Program availability:* Part-time, evening/weekend. *Students:* 10 full-time (3 women), 17 part-time (8 women); includes 12 minority (9 Black or African American, non-Hispanic/Latino; 3 Hispanic/Latino), 1 international. Average age 40. 22 applicants, 55% accepted, 9 enrolled. *Entrance requirements:* For master's, bachelor's degree conferred transcript, resume, essay/personal statement. Additional exam requirements/recommendations for international students: Required—TOEFL (minimum score 80 iBT), IELTS (minimum score 6.5). *Application deadline:* For fall admission, 8/1 for domestic students, 6/1 for international students; for spring admission, 1/1 for domestic students, 11/1 for international students; for summer admission, 5/1 for domestic students, 3/1 for international students. Applications are processed on a rolling basis. Application fee: $0 ($100 for international students). Electronic applications accepted. Application fee is waived when completed online. *Expenses:* $36,000 tuition; $6,750 fees (general, technology and parking). *Financial support:* In 2017–18, 7 students received support. Federal Work-Study and scholarships/grants available. Financial award application deadline: 4/1; financial award applicants required to submit FAFSA. *Unit head:* Dr. Jeffrey Green, Interim Dean, 281-649-3197, Fax: 281-649-3012, E-mail: jgreen@hbu.edu. *Application contact:* Celeste Risteski, Administrative Assistant to the Dean, 281-649-3383, Fax: 281-649-3012, E-mail: cristeski@hbu.edu.

Houston Baptist University, School of Christian Thought, Program in Theological Studies, Houston, TX 77074-3298. Offers MA. *Program availability:* Part-time, evening/weekend, 100% online. *Students:* 9 full-time (2 women), 31 part-time (11 women); includes 15 minority (8 Black or African American, non-Hispanic/Latino; 2 Asian, non-Hispanic/Latino; 4 Hispanic/Latino; 1 Two or more races, non-Hispanic/Latino), 4 international. Average age 37. 43 applicants, 37% accepted, 10 enrolled. In 2017, 12 master's awarded. *Degree requirements:* For master's, thesis optional. *Entrance requirements:* For master's, bachelor's degree conferred transcript, resume, essay/personal statement. Additional exam requirements/recommendations for international students: Required—TOEFL (minimum score 80 iBT), IELTS (minimum score 6.5). *Application deadline:* For fall admission, 8/1 for domestic students, 6/1 for international students; for spring admission, 1/1 for domestic students, 11/1 for international students; for summer admission, 5/1 for domestic students, 3/1 for international students. Applications are processed on a rolling basis. Application fee: $0 ($100 for international students). Electronic applications accepted. Application fee is waived when completed online. *Expenses:* $18,000 tuition; $4,500 fees (general, technology and parking). *Financial support:* In 2017–18, 19 students received support. Federal Work-Study and scholarships/grants available. Financial award application deadline: 4/1; financial award applicants required to submit FAFSA. *Unit head:* Dr. Jeffrey Green, Interim Dean, 281-649-3197, Fax: 281-649-3012, E-mail: jgreen@hbu.edu. *Application contact:* Celeste Risteski, Administrative Assistant to the Dean, 281-649-3383, Fax: 281-649-3012, E-mail: cristeski@hbu.edu.

Houston Graduate School of Theology, Graduate Programs, Houston, TX 77092. Offers counseling (MA); pastoral ministry (M Div, D Min); theology (MA). *Accreditation:* ATS (one or more programs are accredited). *Program availability:* Part-time, evening/weekend. *Degree requirements:* For master's, thesis (for some programs); for doctorate, thesis/dissertation. *Entrance requirements:* For doctorate, GRE General Test or MAT, M Div or equivalent. Additional exam requirements/recommendations for international students: Required—TOEFL (minimum score 550 paper-based). *Faculty research:* Hermeneutics, spirituality, religion of Eastern Europe.

Howard Payne University, Program in Theology and Ministry, Brownwood, TX 76801-2715. Offers MA. *Program availability:* Part-time. *Degree requirements:* For master's, three 2-hour internships/mentorships. *Entrance requirements:* For master's, undergraduate degree from accredited university; leveling courses (for students without undergraduate coursework in Old Testament, New Testament, and theology). Additional exam requirements/recommendations for international students: Required—TOEFL (minimum score 79 iBT). Electronic applications accepted.

Howard University, School of Divinity, Washington, DC 20017. Offers M Div, MARS, D Min. *Accreditation:* ACIPE; ATS. *Program availability:* Part-time, evening/weekend. *Degree requirements:* For master's, thesis; for doctorate, thesis/dissertation. *Entrance requirements:* For master's and doctorate, minimum GPA of 3.0. Electronic applications accepted. *Faculty research:* African-American religious experience, women in ministry, ecumenics, biblical studies.

Iliff School of Theology, Graduate and Professional Programs, Denver, CO 80210-4798. Offers biblical studies (MA); church history (MA); religion (MA); religion and social change (MA); specialized ministry (MASM), including justice and peace, pastoral theology and care, religions leadership; theology (M Div, MTS, D Min, PhD), including Biblical studies (PhD), religion and psychological studies (PhD), religion and social change (PhD), theology, philosophy and culture (PhD); theology/ethics (MA). PhD offered jointly with University of Denver. *Accreditation:* ACIPE; ATS. *Program availability:* Part-time, evening/weekend. *Degree requirements:* For master's, one foreign language, thesis (for some programs); for doctorate, 2 foreign languages, comprehensive exam, thesis/dissertation. *Entrance requirements:* For master's, minimum GPA of 3.0, writing sample, references; for doctorate, GRE General Test, minimum GPA of 3.0, writing sample, letters of recommendation. Additional exam requirements/recommendations for international students: Required—TOEFL (minimum score 550 paper-based). Electronic applications accepted. *Faculty research:* Pastoral care, history, church music, contemporary church, biblical studies.

Indiana Wesleyan University, Graduate School, Wesley Seminary, Master of Divinity Program, Marion, IN 46953-4974. Offers M Div. *Program availability:* Online learning.

Institute for Christian Studies, Graduate Programs, Toronto, ON M5T 1R4, Canada. Offers education (M Phil F, PhD); history of philosophy (M Phil F, PhD); philosophical aesthetics (M Phil F, PhD); philosophy of religion (M Phil F, PhD); political theory (M Phil F, PhD); systematic philosophy (M Phil F, PhD); theology (M Phil F, PhD); worldview studies (MWS). *Program availability:* Part-time, online learning. *Degree requirements:* For master's, one foreign language, thesis; for doctorate, 2 foreign languages, thesis/dissertation. *Entrance requirements:* For master's and doctorate, philosophy background. Additional exam requirements/recommendations for international students: Required—TOEFL (minimum score 600 paper-based). *Faculty research:* Human rights, anthropology of self, medieval discourse, gender and body, post-modern thought; biblical hermeneutics, creational aesthetics, ecumenism, epistemology, political theory and public policy, relational psychotherapy.

Inter American University of Puerto Rico, Metropolitan Campus, Graduate Programs, Program in Theological Studies, San Juan, PR 00919-1293. Offers PhD.

Interdenominational Theological Center, Graduate and Professional Programs, Atlanta, GA 30314-4112. Offers Christian education (MACE); ministry (D Min); pastoral counseling (Th D); theology (M Div); M Div/MACE. D Min and Th D programs offered in collaboration with the Atlanta Theological Association. *Accreditation:* ACIPE; ATS (one or more programs are accredited). *Program availability:* Part-time, evening/weekend, blended/hybrid learning. *Degree requirements:* For doctorate, thesis/dissertation. *Entrance requirements:* For doctorate, master's degree. Electronic applications accepted.

International Baptist College and Seminary, Program in Biblical Studies, Chandler, AZ 85286. Offers MA.

The Jewish Theological Seminary, The Graduate School, New York, NY 10027-4649. Offers ancient Judaism (MA, DHL, PhD); Bible and ancient Semitic languages (MA, DHL, PhD); interdepartmental studies (MA); Jewish art and visual culture (MA); Jewish gender and women's studies (MA); Jewish history (MA, DHL, PhD); Jewish literature (MA, DHL, PhD); Jewish philosophy (DHL); Jewish thought (MA, PhD); liturgy (MA, DHL, PhD); medieval Jewish studies (MA, DHL, PhD); Midrash (DHL); Midrash and scriptural interpretation (MA, PhD); modern Jewish studies (MA, DHL, PhD); Talmud and rabbinics (MA, DHL, PhD); MA/MSW. MA/MSW offered jointly with Columbia University. *Accreditation:* ACIPE. *Program availability:* Part-time. Terminal master's awarded for partial completion of doctoral program. *Degree requirements:* For master's, one foreign language, comprehensive exam (for some programs), thesis (for some programs); for doctorate, 3 foreign languages, comprehensive exam (for some programs), thesis/dissertation. *Entrance requirements:* For master's, GRE or MAT, 3 letters of recommendation, writing sample; for doctorate, GRE or MAT, 3 letters of recommendation, writing research sample. Additional exam requirements/recommendations for international students: Required—TOEFL.

The Jewish Theological Seminary, The Rabbinical School, New York, NY 10027-4649. Offers MA, Rabbi. *Accreditation:* ACIPE. *Degree requirements:* For master's and Rabbi, one foreign language, competency exams. *Entrance requirements:* For master's and Rabbi, GRE, interview, writing sample. Additional exam requirements/recommendations for international students: Required—TOEFL. *Expenses:* Contact institution.

John Carroll University, Graduate Studies, Department of Theology and Religious Studies, University Heights, OH 44118. Offers MA. *Program availability:* Part-time, evening/weekend. *Faculty:* 3 full-time (2 women). *Students:* 1 full-time (0 women), 8 part-time (4 women); includes 2 minority (1 Black or African American, non-Hispanic/Latino; 1 Hispanic/Latino). Average age 35. In 2017, 2 master's awarded. *Degree requirements:* For master's, comprehensive exam, research essay or thesis, foreign language proficiency. *Entrance requirements:* For master's, GRE General Test or MAT, minimum GPA of 2.5. Additional exam requirements/recommendations for international students: Required—TOEFL. *Application deadline:* For fall admission, 8/30 priority date for domestic students; for spring admission, 1/11 priority date for domestic students. Applications are processed on a rolling basis. Application fee: $25 ($35 for international students). Electronic applications accepted. *Expenses:* Tuition: Full-time $16,238; part-time $788 per credit hour. One-time fee: $200. Part-time tuition and fees vary according to course load and program. *Financial support:* Teaching assistantships with full tuition reimbursements, scholarships/grants, tuition waivers (partial), and unspecified assistantships available. Support available to part-time students. Financial award application deadline: 3/1; financial award applicants required to submit FAFSA. *Faculty research:* Ethics, women's studies, contemporary theology, Bible studies, Latin American theology. *Unit head:* Dr. Sheila E. McGinn, Chair, 216-397-4700, Fax: 216-397-4518, E-mail: trs@jcu.edu. *Application contact:* Jennifer L. Tucker, Records Management Assistant, 216-397-1925, Fax: 216-397-1835, E-mail: jtucker@jcu.edu. Website: http://www.jcu.edu/religion/Gr_prog.htm

John Paul the Great Catholic University, School of Theology, Escondido, CA 92025. Offers biblical theology (MA).

Johnson University, Graduate and Professional Programs, Knoxville, TN 37998-1001. Offers biblical interpretation (Graduate Certificate); business administration (MBA); Christian ministries (Graduate Certificate); clinical mental health counseling (MA); educational technology (MA); intercultural studies (MA); leadership (MBA); leadership studies (PhD); New Testament (MA); nonprofit management (MBA); school counseling (MA); spiritual formation and leadership (Graduate Certificate); strategic ministry (MA); teacher education (MA). *Program availability:* Part-time, evening/weekend, 100% online, blended/hybrid learning. *Degree requirements:* For master's, variable foreign language requirement, comprehensive exam, thesis (for some programs), internships; for doctorate, variable foreign language requirement, comprehensive exam, thesis/dissertation, internships. *Entrance requirements:* For master's, PRAXIS (for MA in teacher education); MAT (for counseling); GRE or GMAT (for MBA), interview, 3 references, transcripts, essay, minimum GPA of 2.5 or 3.0 (depending on program); for doctorate, GRE or MAT (taken not less than 5 years prior), interview, 3 references, transcripts, essay, minimum GPA of 3.0; for Graduate Certificate, interview, 3

references, transcripts, essay, minimum GPA of 3.0. Additional exam requirements/recommendations for international students: Required—TOEFL (minimum score 527 paper-based; 71 iBT). Electronic applications accepted. *Expenses:* Contact institution.

Kehilath Yakov Rabbinical Seminary, Graduate Programs, Ossining, NY 10562. *Accreditation:* AARTS.

Kenrick-Glennon Seminary, Graduate and Professional Programs, St. Louis, MO 63119-4330. Offers M Div, MA. *Accreditation:* ATS. *Degree requirements:* For master's, thesis optional.

Kentucky Christian University, Graduate School, Grayson, KY 41143-2205. Offers Biblical studies (MA); Christian leadership (MA). *Program availability:* Part-time. *Degree requirements:* For master's, comprehensive exam (for some programs), thesis optional. *Entrance requirements:* For master's, minimum cumulative GPA of 2.75 in major or 2.5 overall; 6 additional hours in Bible (for non-Biblical undergraduate majors). Additional exam requirements/recommendations for international students: Required—TOEFL (minimum score 550 paper-based). Electronic applications accepted.

The King's University, Graduate and Professional Programs, Southlake, TX 76092. Offers Biblical studies (Graduate Certificate); Christian ministry (Graduate Certificate); ministry (M Div, MPT, D Min).

Kingswood University, Program in Pastoral Theology, Sussex, NB E4E 5L2, Canada. Offers MA. *Faculty:* 1 full-time (0 women), 1 part-time/adjunct (0 women). *Students:* 8 full-time (4 women), 1 part-time (0 women). Average age 34. *Entrance requirements:* For master's, official transcripts, 3 references, statement of purpose. *Expenses:* Tuition: Part-time $355 Canadian dollars per credit hour. One-time fee: $150 Canadian dollars part-time. *Application contact:* Enrolment Office, 506-432-4422, Fax: 506-432-4442, E-mail: enrolment@kingswood.edu. Website: http://kingswood.edu/academics/programs/master-of-arts-in-pastoral-theology/

Knox College, College of Theology, Toronto, ON M5S 2E6, Canada. Offers M Div, MRE, MTS, Th M, D Min, Th D. Applicants for D Min, Th M, and Th D must apply to Toronto School of Theology; MRE, M Div, MTS, Th D, and Th M programs offered jointly with University of Toronto. *Accreditation:* ATS. *Program availability:* Part-time. *Degree requirements:* For master's, one foreign language, thesis (for some programs); for doctorate, 2 foreign languages, thesis/dissertation. *Entrance requirements:* For doctorate, M Div. Additional exam requirements/recommendations for international students: Required—TOEFL (minimum score 580 paper-based), TWE (minimum score 5). *Faculty research:* Nineteenth century theologians.

Knox Theological Seminary, Graduate Programs, Master of Arts Programs, Fort Lauderdale, FL 33308. Offers Biblical and theological studies (MA); Christian and classical studies (MA). *Accreditation:* ATS. *Program availability:* Part-time, evening/weekend. *Entrance requirements:* Additional exam requirements/recommendations for international students: Required—TOEFL (minimum score 520 paper-based; 83 iBT), TWE (minimum score 5).

Knox Theological Seminary, Graduate Programs, Program in Divinity, Fort Lauderdale, FL 33308. Offers M Div. *Accreditation:* ATS. *Program availability:* Part-time, evening/weekend, online only, blended/hybrid learning. *Entrance requirements:* Additional exam requirements/recommendations for international students: Required—TOEFL (minimum score 520 paper-based; 83 iBT), TWE (minimum score 5).

Lakeland University, Graduate Studies Division, Program in Theology, Plymouth, WI 53073. Offers MAT.

Lancaster Bible College, Capital Bible Seminary, Lancaster, PA 17601. Offers biblical studies (MA, Certificate); Christian counseling and discipleship (MA, Certificate); ministry (MA); theology (M Div). *Program availability:* Part-time, evening/weekend. *Degree requirements:* For master's, 2 foreign languages, comprehensive exam, thesis (for some programs). *Entrance requirements:* For master's, GRE General Test, Greek exam for those with 2 years of Greek, proficiency exam in theology, previous course work in Biblical studies. Additional exam requirements/recommendations for international students: Required—TOEFL (minimum score 550 paper-based). *Faculty research:* Dead Sea Scrolls, spiritual gifts, hermeneutics.

Lancaster Bible College, Graduate School, Lancaster, PA 17601-5036. Offers adult ministries (MA); Bible (MA); children and family ministry (MA); church planting (MA); consulting resource teacher (M Ed); elementary school counseling (M Ed); leadership (PhD); leadership studies (MA); marriage and family counseling (MA); mental health counseling (MA); pastoral studies (MA); secondary school counseling (M Ed); sports ministry (MA); student ministry (MA); town and country ministry (MA). *Program availability:* Part-time, evening/weekend. *Degree requirements:* For master's, comprehensive exam (for some programs), thesis (for some programs). *Entrance requirements:* For master's, bachelor's degree with a minimum of 30 credits of course work in Bible, minimum undergraduate GPA of 3.0, interview. Additional exam requirements/recommendations for international students: Required—TOEFL.

Lancaster Theological Seminary, Graduate and Professional Programs, Lancaster, PA 17603-2812. Offers biblical studies (MAR); Christian education (MAR); Christianity and the arts (MAR); church history (MAR); congregational life (MAR); lay leadership (Certificate); theological studies (M Div); theology (D Min); theology and ethics (MAR). *Accreditation:* ACIPE; ATS. *Degree requirements:* For doctorate, thesis/dissertation.

Lee University, Programs in Religion, Cleveland, TN 37320-3450. Offers biblical studies (MA); ministry studies/leadership (MA); ministry studies/worship (MA); ministry studies/youth and family (MA); theological studies (MA), including ethics, religion. *Program availability:* Part-time, 100% online. *Faculty:* 9 full-time (3 women), 3 part-time/adjunct (0 women). *Students:* 62 full-time (16 women), 99 part-time (36 women); includes 68 minority (9 Black or African American, non-Hispanic/Latino; 1 Asian, non-Hispanic/Latino; 57 Hispanic/Latino; 1 Two or more races, non-Hispanic/Latino), 6 international. Average age 37. 21 applicants, 86% accepted, 8 enrolled. In 2017, 13 master's awarded. *Degree requirements:* For master's, variable foreign language requirement, comprehensive exam (for some programs), thesis (for some programs). *Entrance requirements:* For master's, GRE or MAT (for biblical/theological studies only), minimum GPA of 3.0, 3 letters of recommendation, interview, official transcripts, essay. Additional exam requirements/recommendations for international students: Required—TOEFL (minimum score 61 iBT). *Application deadline:* For fall admission, 4/1 priority date for domestic and international students; for spring admission, 10/1 priority date for domestic and international students. Applications are processed on a rolling basis. Application fee: $25. Electronic applications accepted. *Expenses:* Contact institution. *Financial support:* In 2017–18, 34 students received support, including 12 teaching assistantships (averaging $1,886 per year); career-related internships or fieldwork, Federal Work-Study, institutionally sponsored loans, scholarships/grants, and unspecified assistantships also available. Financial award application deadline: 3/1; financial award applicants required to submit FAFSA. *Faculty research:* Spiritual and discipleship formation, leadership, Biblical studies, theological studies, ethics. *Unit head:* Dr. Lisa Long, Director, 423-303-5100, E-mail: llong@leeuniversity.edu. Website: http://www.leeuniversity.edu/academics/graduate/

Lenoir-Rhyne University, Graduate Programs, Lutheran Theological Southern Seminary, Hickory, NC 28601. Offers M Div, MACM, MAR, STM. *Accreditation:* ACIPE.

Program availability: Part-time. *Degree requirements:* For master's, comprehensive exam (for some programs), thesis (for some programs). *Entrance requirements:* Additional exam requirements/recommendations for international students: Recommended—TOEFL. *Expenses:* Contact institution. *Faculty research:* Theology in the twenty-first century, Biblical interpretation.

Lexington Theological Seminary, Graduate and Professional Programs, Lexington, KY 40508-3218. Offers M Div, MA, MAPS, D Min, M Div/MSW. M Div/MSW offered jointly with University of Kentucky. *Accreditation:* ACIPE; ATS. *Program availability:* Part-time, evening/weekend. *Degree requirements:* For master's, thesis; for doctorate, thesis/dissertation. *Entrance requirements:* Additional exam requirements/recommendations for international students: Required—TOEFL (minimum score 600 paper-based). *Faculty research:* History of biblical interpretation, biblical apocalyptic, psalms, history of Stone-Campbell traditions.

Liberty University, School of Behavioral Sciences, Lynchburg, VA 24515. Offers applied psychology (MA), including developmental psychology (MA, MS), industrial/organizational psychology (MA, MS); clinical mental health counseling (MA); community care and counseling (Ed D), including marriage and family counseling, pastoral care and counseling, traumatology; counselor education and supervision (PhD); human services counseling (MA), including addictions and recovery, business, child and family law, Christian ministries, criminal justice, crisis response and trauma, executive leadership, health and wellness, life coaching, marriage and family, military resilience; marriage and family counseling (MA); marriage and family therapy (MA); military resilience (Certificate); pastoral counseling (MA), including addictions and recovery, community chaplaincy, crisis response and trauma, discipleship and church ministry, leadership, life coaching, marriage and family, marriage and family studies, military resilience, parenting and child/adolescent, pastoral counseling, theology; professional counseling (MA); psychology (MS), including developmental psychology (MA, MS), industrial/organizational psychology (MA, MS); school counseling (M Ed). *Program availability:* Part-time, online learning. *Students:* 2,649 full-time (2,085 women), 5,086 part-time (4,015 women); includes 2,275 minority (1,784 Black or African American, non-Hispanic/Latino; 44 American Indian or Alaska Native, non-Hispanic/Latino; 67 Asian, non-Hispanic/Latino; 200 Hispanic/Latino; 11 Native Hawaiian or other Pacific Islander, non-Hispanic/Latino; 169 Two or more races, non-Hispanic/Latino), 145 international. Average age 39. 5,839 applicants, 51% accepted, 1710 enrolled. In 2017, 1,626 master's, 7 doctorates, 61 other advanced degrees awarded. *Application deadline:* Applications are processed on a rolling basis. Application fee: $50. Electronic applications accepted. *Financial support:* Applicants required to submit FAFSA. *Unit head:* Dr. Ronald Hawkins, Founding Dean, School of Behavioral Sciences. *Application contact:* Jay Bridge, Director of Admissions, 800-424-9595, Fax: 800-628-7977, E-mail: gradadmissions@liberty.edu.

Liberty University, School of Divinity, Lynchburg, VA 24515. Offers Biblical exposition (MA); Biblical languages (M Div); Biblical studies (M Div, MA, MAR, Th M, D Min); chaplaincy (M Div, D Min); Christian apologetics (M Div, MA, MAR, Th M); Christian leadership and church ministries (M Div); Christian ministries (M Div); Christian ministry (MA); Christian thought (M Div); church history (M Div, MAR, Th M); community chaplaincy (M Div, MAR); discipleship (D Min); discipleship and church ministry (M Div, MAR, MCM); evangelism and church planting (MAR, MCM, D Min); expository preaching (D Min); global ministry (MA); global studies (M Div, MAR, MCM, MGS, Th M); healthcare chaplaincy (M Div); homiletics (M Div, MAR, Th M); leadership (M Div, MAR); marketplace chaplaincy (M Div, MCM); ministry leadership (Ed D); pastoral counseling (M Div, MA, MAR, D Min), including addictions and recovery (MA), crisis response and trauma (MA), discipleship and church ministries (MA), leadership (MA), life coaching (MA), marketplace chaplaincy (MA), marriage and family (MA), military resilience (MA), pastoral counseling (MA); pastoral leadership (D Min); pastoral ministries (M Div, M Serv Soc, MCM); religious education (MRE); sports chaplaincy (MA); theology (M Div, MAR, MTS, Th M); theology and apologetics (D Min, PhD); worship (M Div, MAR, MCM, D Min); youth and family ministries (M Div). *Program availability:* Part-time, online learning. *Students:* 2,140 full-time (615 women), 3,020 part-time (906 women); includes 1,312 minority (1,016 Black or African American, non-Hispanic/Latino; 9 American Indian or Alaska Native, non-Hispanic/Latino; 100 Asian, non-Hispanic/Latino; 90 Hispanic/Latino; 7 Native Hawaiian or other Pacific Islander, non-Hispanic/Latino; 90 Two or more races, non-Hispanic/Latino), 158 international. Average age 42. 4,673 applicants, 33% accepted, 977 enrolled. In 2017, 904 master's, 54 doctorates awarded. *Degree requirements:* For master's, 2 foreign languages, thesis (for some programs); for doctorate, 2 foreign languages, thesis/dissertation. *Entrance requirements:* For master's, minimum undergraduate GPA of 2.0; for doctorate, GRE General Test or MAT, minimum graduate GPA of 3.0. Additional exam requirements/recommendations for international students: Required—TOEFL (minimum score 600 paper-based; 100 iBT). *Application deadline:* For fall admission, 6/1 for domestic students; for spring admission, 11/1 for domestic students. Applications are processed on a rolling basis. Application fee: $50. Electronic applications accepted. *Expenses:* Contact institution. *Financial support:* Teaching assistantships with tuition reimbursements, career-related internships or fieldwork, and Federal Work-Study available. Financial award applicants required to submit FAFSA. *Unit head:* Dr. Ed Hindson, Dean, 434-592-4140, Fax: 434-522-0415, E-mail: ehindson@liberty.edu. *Application contact:* Jay Bridge, Director of Graduate Admissions, 800-424-9595, Fax: 800-628-7977, E-mail: gradadmissions@liberty.edu.
Website: https://www.liberty.edu/divinity/

Lincoln Christian Seminary, Graduate and Professional Programs, Lincoln, IL 62656-2167. Offers Bible and theology (MA); Christian ministries (MA); counseling (MA); divinity (M Div); leadership ministry (D Min); religious education (MRE). *Accreditation:* ACIPE; ATS. *Program availability:* Part-time. *Degree requirements:* For master's, 2 foreign languages, thesis; for doctorate, thesis/dissertation. *Entrance requirements:* For master's, minimum GPA of 2.5; for doctorate, M Div or equivalent. Additional exam requirements/recommendations for international students: Required—TOEFL (minimum score 550 paper-based). Electronic applications accepted.

Lincoln Christian University, Graduate Programs, Lincoln, IL 62656-2167. Offers Bible and theology (MA); Biblical studies (MA); church history/historical theology (MA); counseling (MA); formative worship (MA); intercultural studies (MA); ministry (MA); organizational leadership (MA); philosophy and apologetics (MA); spiritual formation (MA); theology (MA). MA in spiritual formation offered in Normal, IL. *Program availability:* Online learning. *Faculty:* 21 full-time (3 women), 29 part-time/adjunct (7 women). *Students:* 97 full-time (42 women), 226 part-time (81 women). Average age 39. *Entrance requirements:* For master's, minimum cumulative GPA of 2.5 in undergraduate degree studies. Additional exam requirements/recommendations for international students: Required—TOEFL (minimum score 550 paper-based); Recommended—IELTS (minimum score 6). *Application deadline:* For fall admission, 8/1 for domestic students, 3/1 for international students; for spring admission, 11/15 for domestic students, 11/1 for international students. Application fee: $25 ($50 for international students). Application fee is waived when completed online. *Expenses: Tuition:* Full-time $7920; part-time $5280 per credit hour. *Required fees:* $150; $150 per course. *Financial support:* Applicants required to submit FAFSA. *Application contact:* Lindsey Clark, Associate Director of Graduate Enrollment, 217-732-3168 Ext. 2398, E-mail: lclark@lincolnchristian.edu.
Website: https://lincolnchristian.edu/academics/programs/masters/

Lipscomb University, Hazelip School of Theology, Nashville, TN 37204-3951. Offers missional and spiritual formation (D Min); theology (M Div). *Program availability:* Part-time, evening/weekend, online learning. *Faculty:* 13 full-time (0 women), 4 part-time/adjunct (2 women). *Students:* 89 full-time (24 women), 38 part-time (10 women); includes 20 minority (12 Black or African American, non-Hispanic/Latino; 2 Asian, non-Hispanic/Latino; 3 Hispanic/Latino; 3 Two or more races, non-Hispanic/Latino), 2 international. Average age 36. 89 applicants, 51% accepted, 33 enrolled. In 2017, 24 master's, 10 doctorates awarded. *Degree requirements:* For master's, 2 foreign languages, comprehensive exam (for some programs), thesis optional; for doctorate, comprehensive exam, thesis/dissertation. *Entrance requirements:* For master's, 3 references, transcripts, goals statement; for doctorate, 3 references, transcripts, documentation of full-time participation in ministry, writing sample, interview. Additional exam requirements/recommendations for international students: Required—TOEFL (minimum score 570 paper-based; 80 iBT). *Application deadline:* For fall admission, 8/1 priority date for domestic students; for spring admission, 12/15 for domestic students. Applications are processed on a rolling basis. Application fee: $50 ($75 for international students). Electronic applications accepted. *Expenses:* Contact institution. *Financial support:* Scholarships/grants and unspecified assistantships available. Financial award application deadline: 3/1; financial award applicants required to submit FAFSA. *Faculty research:* Status of Churches of Christ in foreign nations, Hebrew grammar, marriage and family. *Unit head:* Frank Guertin, Director, 615-966-5709, Fax: 615-966-5352, E-mail: frank.guertin@lipscomb.edu. *Application contact:* Kellye McCool, Coordinator of Student Services, 615-966-5458, Fax: 615-966-6052, E-mail: kellye.mccool@lipscomb.edu.
Website: http://www.lipscomb.edu/hst

Logos Evangelical Seminary, Graduate Programs, El Monte, CA 91731. Offers M Div, MA, MAFM, MAICS, Th M, D Min, PhD, Diploma. *Accreditation:* ATS (one or more programs are accredited). *Program availability:* Part-time, 100% online, blended/hybrid learning. *Faculty:* 15 full-time (6 women), 10 part-time/adjunct (3 women). *Students:* 64 full-time (31 women), 131 part-time (62 women); includes 99 minority (all Asian, non-Hispanic/Latino), 96 international. Average age 48. 55 applicants, 93% accepted, 48 enrolled. In 2017, 27 master's, 11 doctorates awarded. *Degree requirements:* For master's, variable foreign language requirement, comprehensive exam (for some programs), thesis (for some programs); for doctorate, variable foreign language requirement, comprehensive exam (for some programs), thesis/dissertation. *Entrance requirements:* For master's, Biblical Language proficiency exam (for Th M), MA in Biblical studies with minimum GPA of 3.33, 1.5 years of Biblical language studies, 2 recommendations, and 1 research paper (for Th M); for doctorate, Biblical Language proficiency exam and research language exam (for PhD), M Div or its equivalent with minimum GPA of 3.0, at least three years of experience in full-time ministry after receiving M Div, and recommendations by two church leaders (for D Min). Additional exam requirements/recommendations for international students: Required—TOEFL (minimum score 470 paper-based; 52 iBT); Recommended—IELTS. *Application deadline:* For fall admission, 6/15 for domestic students, 5/15 for international students; for spring admission, 11/15 for domestic students, 10/15 for international students. Applications are processed on a rolling basis. Application fee: $75. Electronic applications accepted. *Expenses: Tuition:* Full-time $10,110; part-time $5055 per year. *Required fees:* $250; $150 per unit. *Faculty research:* Biblical hermeneutics, historical theology, Biblical studies, parenting of teens and young adults, marriage and family. *Unit head:* Rev. Ekron Chen, PhD, Academic Dean, 626-571-5110 Ext. 120, Fax: 626-571-5119, E-mail: ekron@les.edu. *Application contact:* Becky Perng, Admission Specialist, 626-571-5110 Ext. 112, Fax: 626-571-5119, E-mail: admission@les.edu.
Website: https://www.les.edu/language/en/

Loras College, Graduate Division, Program in Theology and Ministry, Dubuque, IA 52004-0178. Offers ministry (MA); theology (MA). *Program availability:* Part-time, evening/weekend. *Degree requirements:* For master's, comprehensive exam (for some programs), thesis (for some programs). *Entrance requirements:* For master's, bachelor's degree or undergraduate minor in religious studies or equivalent, minimum undergraduate GPA of 2.75.

Louisiana College, Caskey School of Divinity, Pineville, LA 71359-0001. Offers biblical and theological studies (MA); pastoral ministry (MA).

Louisville Presbyterian Theological Seminary, Graduate and Professional Programs, Louisville, KY 40205-1798. Offers Bible (MAR); divinity (M Div); ministry (D Min); religious thought (MAR); JD/M Div; M Div/MBA; M Div/MSSW. JD/M Div, M Div/MBA, and M Div/MSSW offered jointly with University of Louisville. *Accreditation:* AAMFT/COAMFTE (one or more programs are accredited); ACIPE; ATS (one or more programs are accredited). *Program availability:* Part-time. *Faculty:* 16 full-time (6 women), 14 part-time/adjunct (5 women). *Students:* 115 full-time (74 women), 37 part-time (20 women); includes 51 minority (41 Black or African American, non-Hispanic/Latino; 2 Asian, non-Hispanic/Latino; 7 Hispanic/Latino; 1 Native Hawaiian or other Pacific Islander, non-Hispanic/Latino), 1 international. Average age 41. In 2017, 32 master's, 6 doctorates awarded. *Degree requirements:* For master's, 2 foreign languages, thesis (for some programs); for doctorate, thesis/dissertation. *Entrance requirements:* For doctorate, M Div. Additional exam requirements/recommendations for international students: Required—TOEFL (minimum score 550 paper-based). *Application deadline:* For fall admission, 6/1 priority date for domestic students, 2/1 priority date for international students; for spring admission, 11/1 priority date for domestic students. Applications are processed on a rolling basis. Application fee: $50. Electronic applications accepted. *Financial support:* Career-related internships or fieldwork, Federal Work-Study, institutionally sponsored loans, and scholarships/grants available. Financial award application deadline: 2/1. *Unit head:* Dr. Susan R. Garrett, Dean, 502-895-3411, Fax: 502-895-1096, E-mail: sgarrett@lpts.edu. *Application contact:* Rev. Emily Miller, Director of Admissions, 502-895-3411, Fax: 502-895-1096, E-mail: emiller@lpts.edu.
Website: http://www.lpts.edu/

Lourdes University, Graduate School, Sylvania, OH 43560-2898. Offers business (MBA); leadership (M Ed); nurse anesthesia (MSN); nurse educator (MSN); nurse leader (MSN); organizational leadership (MOL); reading (M Ed); teaching and curriculum (M Ed); theology (MA). *Program availability:* Evening/weekend. *Entrance requirements:* Additional exam requirements/recommendations for international students: Required—TOEFL.

Loyola Marymount University, Bellarmine College of Liberal Arts, Program in Theology, Los Angeles, CA 90045-2659. Offers MA. *Accreditation:* ATS. *Unit head:* Dr. Brett Hoover, Director, Theology Program, 310-338-1664, E-mail: bhoover@lmu.edu. *Application contact:* Chake H. Kouyoumjian, Associate Dean of Graduate Studies, 310-338-2721, Fax: 310-338-6086, E-mail: graduateinfo@lmu.edu.
Website: http://bellarmine.lmu.edu/theologicalstudies/graduateprograms/academics/maintheologyprogram

Loyola University Chicago, Graduate School, Department of Theology, Chicago, IL 60660. Offers MA, PhD. *Program availability:* Part-time, evening/weekend. *Faculty:* 23 full-time (9 women). *Students:* 43 full-time (12 women), 6 part-time (3 women); includes

5 minority (2 Black or African American, non-Hispanic/Latino; 2 Hispanic/Latino; 1 Native Hawaiian or other Pacific Islander, non-Hispanic/Latino), 7 international. Average age 33. 43 applicants, 44% accepted, 7 enrolled. In 2017, 1 master's, 8 doctorates awarded. Terminal master's awarded for partial completion of doctoral program. *Degree requirements:* For master's, comprehensive exam; for doctorate, 2 foreign languages, comprehensive exam, thesis/dissertation. *Entrance requirements:* For master's, GRE General Test, minimum GPA of 3.0, 9 hours of course work in theology; for doctorate, GRE General Test, minimum GPA of 3.0, master's degree or equivalent. Additional exam requirements/recommendations for international students: Required—TOEFL (minimum score 550 paper-based), IELTS. *Application deadline:* For fall admission, 1/15 for domestic and international students; for spring admission, 12/1 for domestic and international students. Application fee: $50. Electronic applications accepted. Application fee is waived when completed online. *Expenses:* $1,033 per credit hour tuition, $432 pere semester mandatory fees. *Financial support:* In 2017–18, 12 students received support, including 12 research assistantships (averaging $18,000 per year); fellowships, teaching assistantships, and institutionally sponsored loans also available. Financial award application deadline: 1/15; financial award applicants required to submit FAFSA. *Faculty research:* Systematics, historical theology, constructive theology, scripture, theological ethics. *Unit head:* Dr. Robert Di Vito, Chair, 773-508-8453, Fax: 773-508-2386, E-mail: rdivito@luc.edu. *Application contact:* Dr. Sandra Sullivan-Dunbar, Graduate Program Director, 773-508-2481, Fax: 312-915-8905, E-mail: ssull1@luc.edu.
Website: http://luc.edu/theology/

Loyola University Chicago, Institute of Pastoral Studies, Chicago, IL 60611. Offers Christian spirituality (MA), including spiritual direction; church management (Certificate); counseling for ministry (MA); divinity (M Div); health care ministry leadership (Certificate); health care mission leadership (MA); pastoral counseling (MA, Certificate); pastoral studies (MA); religious education (Certificate); social justice (MA, Certificate); spiritual direction (Certificate); M Div/MA; M Div/MSW; MSW/MA. MSW/MA offered with School of Social Work. *Accreditation:* ACIPE. *Program availability:* Part-time, evening/weekend, 100% online, blended/hybrid learning. *Faculty:* 11 full-time (5 women), 20 part-time/adjunct (9 women). *Students:* 80 full-time (51 women), 150 part-time (107 women); includes 58 minority (24 Black or African American, non-Hispanic/Latino; 7 Asian, non-Hispanic/Latino; 27 Hispanic/Latino), 29 international. Average age 45. 128 applicants, 79% accepted, 72 enrolled. In 2017, 53 master's, 5 other advanced degrees awarded. *Degree requirements:* For master's, thesis optional, project. *Entrance requirements:* Additional exam requirements/recommendations for international students: Required—TOEFL (minimum score 550 paper-based; 79 iBT), IELTS (minimum score 6.5). *Application deadline:* Applications are processed on a rolling basis. Application fee: $50. Electronic applications accepted. Application fee is waived when completed online. *Expenses:* Contact institution. *Financial support:* In 2017–18, 111 students received support. Career-related internships or fieldwork, Federal Work-Study, scholarships/grants, and unspecified assistantships available. Support available to part-time students. Financial award application deadline: 3/15. *Faculty research:* Catholic theology, skills of religious ministry, family ministries, spirituality and divorced men. *Unit head:* Dr. Brian J. Schmisek, Dean, 312-915-7400, Fax: 312-915-7410, E-mail: bschmisek@luc.edu. *Application contact:* Dr. M. Therese Lysaught, Associate Dean, 312-915-7485, Fax: 312-915-7410, E-mail: mlysaught@luc.edu.
Website: http://www.luc.edu/ips/

Loyola University Maryland, Graduate Programs, Loyola College of Arts and Sciences, Department of Theology, Baltimore, MD 21210-2699. Offers MTS. *Faculty:* 64 full-time (37 women), 31 part-time/adjunct (20 women). *Students:* 7 full-time (4 women), 8 part-time (3 women); includes 6 minority (3 Black or African American, non-Hispanic/Latino; 1 Asian, non-Hispanic/Latino; 2 Hispanic/Latino), 1 international. Average age 39. In 2017, 4 master's awarded. *Entrance requirements:* Additional exam requirements/recommendations for international students: Required—TOEFL, IELTS. *Application deadline:* For fall admission, 5/1 for domestic students. Application fee: $60. Electronic applications accepted. *Expenses:* Contact institution. *Financial support:* Scholarships/grants available. Financial award application deadline: 4/15; financial award applicants required to submit FAFSA. *Unit head:* Dr. Claire R. Mathews McGinnis, Chair, 410-617-2356, E-mail: cmathews@loyola.edu. *Application contact:* Office of Graduate Admission, 410-617-5020, E-mail: graduate@loyola.edu.
Website: http://www.loyola.edu/academic/theology/graduate.aspx

Loyola University New Orleans, College of Nursing and Health, Loyola Institute for Ministry, New Orleans, LA 70118-6195. Offers pastoral studies (MPS); religious education (MRE); theology and ministry (Certificate). *Program availability:* Part-time, evening/weekend, online learning. *Faculty:* 3 full-time (1 woman), 4 part-time/adjunct (2 women). *Students:* 2 full-time (both women), 133 part-time (96 women); includes 28 minority (12 Black or African American, non-Hispanic/Latino; 1 American Indian or Alaska Native, non-Hispanic/Latino; 2 Asian, non-Hispanic/Latino; 13 Hispanic/Latino), 2 international. Average age 47. 36 applicants, 94% accepted, 26 enrolled. In 2017, 41 master's awarded. *Entrance requirements:* For master's, minimum GPA of 2.5, resume, 2 letters of recommendation, work experience, 3-page statement of purpose. Additional exam requirements/recommendations for international students: Required—TOEFL (minimum score 550 paper-based; 79 iBT). *Application deadline:* For fall admission, 8/15 for domestic and international students; for spring admission, 1/1 for domestic and international students. Applications are processed on a rolling basis. Application fee: $20. Electronic applications accepted. Application fee is waived when completed online. *Expenses:* $818 per hour tuition; $738 per semester full-time fees, $376.50 part-time. *Financial support:* Career-related internships or fieldwork, scholarships/grants, health care benefits, and tuition waivers (partial) available. Support available to part-time students. Financial award application deadline: 5/1; financial award applicants required to submit FAFSA. *Faculty research:* Practical theology, ministry education, small Christian communities, religion and ecology, Christian spirituality. *Unit head:* Dr. Tom Ryan, Director, 504-865-2069, Fax: 504-865-2066, E-mail: tfryan@loyno.edu. *Application contact:* Diane Blair, Manager of Admissions, 504-865-3728, Fax: 504-865-2066, E-mail: lim@loyno.edu.
Website: http://lim.loyno.edu/

Lubbock Christian University, Graduate Biblical Studies, Lubbock, TX 79407-2099. Offers Bible and ministry (MS); biblical interpretation (MA). *Program availability:* Part-time. *Degree requirements:* For master's, one foreign language, thesis (for some programs). *Entrance requirements:* For master's, GRE General Test or MAT. *Faculty research:* Commentary on John, commentary on First and Second Thessalonians, mission teams, church leadership, family systems.

Lutheran School of Theology at Chicago, Graduate and Professional Programs, Chicago, IL 60615-5199. Offers ministry (MAM, D Min); theological studies (MATS, PhD); theology (M Div). *Accreditation:* ACIPE; ATS (one or more programs are accredited). *Program availability:* Part-time. Terminal master's awarded for partial completion of doctoral program. *Degree requirements:* For master's, variable foreign language requirement; for doctorate, variable foreign language requirement, comprehensive exam, thesis/dissertation. *Entrance requirements:* For doctorate, GRE, M Div or equivalent, 3 years of professional experience (D Min).

Lutheran Theological Seminary Saskatoon, Graduate and Professional Programs, Saskatoon, SK S7N 0X3, Canada. Offers Biblical studies (MTS); church history (MTS); ethics/church and society (MTS); history of Christianity (STM); New Testament (STM); Old Testament (STM); pastoral studies (STM); pastoral theology (MTS); systematic theology (MTS); systematic theology and philosophy of religion (STM); theology (M Div, D Div). STM programs offered jointly with College of Emmanuel and St. Chad and St. Andrew's College. *Accreditation:* ATS. *Program availability:* Part-time. *Degree requirements:* For master's, thesis.

Luther Rice College & Seminary, Graduate Programs, Lithonia, GA 30038-2454. Offers apologetics (MA); Bible languages (M Div); Biblical counseling (MA); Christian ministry (M Div, D Min); Christian studies (MA); leadership (MA). *Program availability:* Part-time, evening/weekend, online learning. *Degree requirements:* For doctorate, thesis/dissertation. *Entrance requirements:* For master's, bachelor's degree or equivalent; for doctorate, M Div. Additional exam requirements/recommendations for international students: Required—TOEFL (minimum score 550 paper-based). Electronic applications accepted.

Luther Seminary, Graduate and Professional Programs, St. Paul, MN 55108-1445. Offers aging and health (MA); Biblical preaching (D Min); children, youth and family (M Div, MA); congregational mission and leadership (M Th, MA, D Min); history of Christianity (M Th, MA); missions and world religions (M Th); New Testament (M Th, MA); Old Testament (M Th, MA); pastoral care: clinical pastoral theology (M Th); pastoral theology and ministry (M Th); systematic theology (M Th, MA). *Accreditation:* ACIPE; ATS. *Program availability:* Part-time, online learning. *Degree requirements:* For master's, thesis or alternative; for doctorate, 2 foreign languages, thesis/dissertation. *Entrance requirements:* For master's, minimum GPA of 3.0; for doctorate, GRE General Test. Additional exam requirements/recommendations for international students: Required—TOEFL, IELTS. Electronic applications accepted. *Faculty research:* Theology, psychology (pastoral care), church history, Bible.

Machzikei Hadath Rabbinical College, Graduate Programs, Brooklyn, NY 11204-1805. Offers First Talmudic Degree. *Accreditation:* AARTS.

Madonna University, Program in Religious Studies, Livonia, MI 48150-1173. Offers pastoral ministry (MA).

Malone University, Graduate Program in Theological Studies, Canton, OH 44709. Offers MA. *Program availability:* Part-time, evening/weekend. *Entrance requirements:* For master's, minimum GPA of 3.0. Additional exam requirements/recommendations for international students: Required—TOEFL (minimum score 550 paper-based; 79 iBT). *Expenses:* Contact institution. *Faculty research:* Sacramental nature of the Biblical canon, theological anthropology, narrative criticism of the New Testament, Old Testament prophets, rhetorical criticism of the New Testament.

Maple Springs Baptist Bible College and Seminary, Graduate and Professional Programs, Capitol Heights, MD 20743. Offers biblical studies (MA, Certificate); Christian counseling (MA); church administration (MA); divinity (M Div); ministry (D Min); religious education (MRE).

Maranatha Baptist University, Master of Divinity Program, Watertown, WI 53094. Offers M Div. *Program availability:* Part-time. *Degree requirements:* For master's, 2 foreign languages. *Entrance requirements:* Additional exam requirements/recommendations for international students: Required—TOEFL. *Faculty research:* Church history, counseling techniques, Bible structure, ancient language.

Maranatha Baptist University, Program in Biblical Studies, Watertown, WI 53094. Offers MA. *Program availability:* Part-time. *Degree requirements:* For master's, one foreign language. *Entrance requirements:* For master's, BA or BS. *Faculty research:* Bible structure, counseling techniques, church history.

Marquette University, Graduate School, College of Arts and Sciences, Department of Theology, Milwaukee, WI 53201-1881. Offers MA, PhD. *Program availability:* Part-time, evening/weekend. Terminal master's awarded for partial completion of doctoral program. *Degree requirements:* For master's, one foreign language, comprehensive exam, thesis or alternative; for doctorate, 2 foreign languages, comprehensive exam, thesis/dissertation. *Entrance requirements:* For master's, GRE General Test, official transcripts from all current and previous colleges/universities except Marquette, three letters of recommendation, short personal statement; for doctorate, GRE General Test, official transcripts from all current and previous colleges/universities except Marquette, three letters of recommendation, short personal statement, academic writing sample. Additional exam requirements/recommendations for international students: Required—TOEFL (minimum score 530 paper-based). Electronic applications accepted. *Faculty research:* Old Testament theology, New Testament theology, church history, Christian ethics.

The Master's University, The Master's Seminary, Santa Clarita, CA 91321-1200. Offers biblical counseling (MABC); New Testament (Th D); Old Testament (Th D); preaching (D Min); theology (M Div, M Th, Th D). *Program availability:* Part-time. *Degree requirements:* For master's, 2 foreign languages, thesis; for doctorate, 4 foreign languages, thesis/dissertation. *Entrance requirements:* For master's, minimum GPA of 2.75; for doctorate, Th M, minimum GPA of 3.5. Additional exam requirements/recommendations for international students: Required—TOEFL (minimum score 550 paper-based).

McCormick Theological Seminary, Graduate and Professional Programs, Chicago, IL 60615. Offers ministry (D Min); theological studies (MATS, Certificate); theology (M Div); M Div/MSW. M Div/MSW offered jointly with Loyola University Chicago, University of Chicago, and University of Illinois at Chicago. *Accreditation:* ACIPE; ATS (one or more programs are accredited). *Program availability:* Part-time, evening/weekend. *Degree requirements:* For master's, thesis (for some programs); for doctorate, thesis/dissertation. *Entrance requirements:* For master's, minimum GPA of 3.0; for doctorate, M Div, minimum 3 years in pastorate. *Faculty research:* Faith formation, families, biblical literature, Dead Sea scrolls, women in antiquity.

McGill University, Faculty of Graduate and Postdoctoral Studies, Faculty of Religious Studies, Montréal, QC H3A 2T5, Canada. Offers MA, STM, PhD. *Accreditation:* ATS.

McMaster University, McMaster Divinity College, Hamilton, ON L8S 4M2, Canada. Offers biblical studies (M Div); Biblical studies (MA, MTS, Diploma); Christian interpretation/history (M Div, MA, MTS, Diploma); Christian ministry (M Div, MA, MTS, Diploma); Christian Studies (Certificate); Christian theology (PhD). Affiliated with the Toronto School of Theology. *Accreditation:* ATS. *Program availability:* Part-time. *Degree requirements:* For master's, one foreign language, thesis optional; for doctorate, 3 foreign languages, comprehensive exam, thesis/dissertation; for other advanced degree, 2 foreign languages, thesis. *Entrance requirements:* For master's, minimum B average in undergraduate course work, 3 letters of reference; for doctorate, minimum B+ average in bachelor's and master's, appropriate modern/ancient language, interview; for other advanced degree, 6 units of related Biblical language, minimum B+ average in undergraduate course work, minimum 15 units of course work in related area of study, 3 letters of recommendation. Additional exam requirements/recommendations for international students: Required—TOEFL (minimum score 550 paper-based). *Faculty research:* Ethics, Biblical studies, language studies, church history, Christian ministry.

Meadville Lombard Theological School, Graduate and Professional Programs, Chicago, IL 60637-1602. Offers divinity (M Div); ministry (D Min); religion (MA); M Div/MSW. M Div/MSW offered jointly with University of Chicago. *Accreditation:* ACIPE; ATS. *Program availability:* Part-time, online learning. *Entrance requirements:* For master's, bachelor's degree; for doctorate, bachelor's and masters degrees, 3 years of ministry.

Memphis Theological Seminary, Graduate and Professional Programs, Memphis, TN 38104-4395. Offers M Div, MAR, D Min. *Accreditation:* ATS. *Program availability:* Part-time. *Degree requirements:* For doctorate, thesis/dissertation. *Entrance requirements:* For doctorate, M Div, 3 years in ministry.

Mercer University, Graduate Studies, Cecil B. Day Campus, James and Carolyn McAfee School of Theology, Atlanta, GA 30341. Offers Christian ministry (MACM); Christian spirituality (D Min); divinity (M Div); preaching (D Min); M Div/MBA; M Div/MS. *Program availability:* Part-time, 100% online. *Faculty:* 14 full-time (7 women), 5 part-time/adjunct (0 women). *Students:* 93 full-time (60 women), 63 part-time (29 women); includes 88 minority (80 Black or African American, non-Hispanic/Latino; 1 American Indian or Alaska Native, non-Hispanic/Latino; 1 Asian, non-Hispanic/Latino; 4 Hispanic/Latino; 1 Native Hawaiian or other Pacific Islander, non-Hispanic/Latino; 1 Two or more races, non-Hispanic/Latino), 1 international. Average age 37. 36 applicants, 58% accepted, 14 enrolled. In 2017, 40 master's, 9 doctorates awarded. *Degree requirements:* For master's, variable foreign language requirement, thesis (for some programs), minimum GPA of 2.5, portfolio; for doctorate, thesis/dissertation, fieldwork, seminars. *Entrance requirements:* For master's and doctorate, regionally-accredited bachelor's degree with liberal arts core or proof of equivalent degree from foreign university; transcripts; letters of recommendation; resume; essays; writing sample; interview; background check. Additional exam requirements/recommendations for international students: Required—TOEFL (minimum score 550 paper-based; 79 iBT). *Application deadline:* For fall admission, 7/1 for domestic and international students; for spring admission, 11/15 for domestic and international students. Applications are processed on a rolling basis. Application fee: $50. Electronic applications accepted. *Expenses:* $425 per credit hour tuition, $17 per credit hour fee up to a maximum of $150. *Financial support:* In 2017–18, 70 students received support. Career-related internships or fieldwork, Federal Work-Study, institutionally sponsored loans, and scholarships/grants available. Support available to part-time students. Financial award application deadline: 10/1; financial award applicants required to submit FAFSA. *Faculty research:* Biblical studies, Baptist heritage, Christian heritage, theology, pastoral care, ethics, global missions, academic research. *Unit head:* Dr. Jeffrey Willetts, Dean, 678-547-6470, Fax: 678-547-6478, E-mail: willetts_jg@mercer.edu. *Application contact:* Nathan Cost, Director of Admissions, 678-547-6451, Fax: 678-547-6478, E-mail: cost_na@mercer.edu.
Website: http://www.mercer.edu/theology

Merrimack College, School of Liberal Arts, North Andover, MA 01845-5800. Offers clinical mental health counseling (MS); interfaith spirituality (Certificate); public affairs (MPA); spiritual direction (MA, Certificate); spirituality (MA). *Program availability:* Part-time, evening/weekend. *Faculty:* 7 full-time, 4 part-time/adjunct. *Students:* 30 full-time (23 women), 3 part-time (2 women); includes 3 minority (2 Black or African American, non-Hispanic/Latino; 1 Hispanic/Latino), 1 international. Average age 30. 40 applicants, 88% accepted, 20 enrolled. In 2017, 9 master's awarded. *Degree requirements:* For master's, internship/strategic capstone (for MPA); 700-hour fieldwork placement (for MS); practicum (for MA in spiritual direction); for Certificate, practicum (for spiritual direction). *Entrance requirements:* For master's, official college transcripts, resume, personal statement, 2 recommendations (3 for MS in clinical mental health counseling); interview (for MA in spirituality). Additional exam requirements/recommendations for international students: Required—TOEFL (minimum score 84 iBT), IELTS (minimum score 6.5), PTE (minimum score 56). *Application deadline:* For fall admission, 8/24 for domestic students, 7/30 for international students; for spring admission, 1/10 for domestic students, 12/10 for international students; for summer admission, 5/10 for domestic students, 4/10 for international students. Applications are processed on a rolling basis. Electronic applications accepted. *Expenses:* $865 per credit hour tuition; comprehensive fees are $165 for 1-8 credit hours per semester, $320 for 9+ credit hours per semester. *Financial support:* Career-related internships or fieldwork, scholarships/grants, and health care benefits available. Support available to part-time students. Financial award application deadline: 5/1; financial award applicants required to submit FAFSA. *Application contact:* Jennifer Greenwood, Graduate Admissions Counselor, 978-837-3563, E-mail: greenwoodjl@merrimack.edu.

Mesivta of Eastern Parkway–Yeshiva Zichron Meilech, Graduate Programs, Brooklyn, NY 11218-5559. *Accreditation:* AARTS.

Mesivta Torah Vodaath Rabbinical Seminary, Graduate Programs, Brooklyn, NY 11218-5299. Offers rabbinical studies (Certificate); theological and ministerial studies (Certificate). *Accreditation:* AARTS.

Mesivtha Tifereth Jerusalem of America, Graduate Programs, New York, NY 10002-6301. *Accreditation:* AARTS.

Methodist Theological School in Ohio, Graduate and Professional Programs, Delaware, OH 43015-8004. Offers M Div, MACE, MACM, MTS, D Min. *Accreditation:* ACIPE; ATS. *Program availability:* Part-time. *Entrance requirements:* For master's, 3 letters of recommendation. Additional exam requirements/recommendations for international students: Required—TOEFL (minimum score 577 paper-based; 90 iBT).

Mid-America Baptist Theological Seminary, Graduate and Professional Programs, Cordova, TN 38016. Offers biblical counseling (M Div); Christian education (M Div, MACE); ministry (D Min); missiology and intercultural studies (M Div); pastoral ministry (M Div); theology (MA, PhD); worship (MA). *Degree requirements:* For doctorate, 4 foreign languages, thesis/dissertation. *Entrance requirements:* For doctorate, MAT. Additional exam requirements/recommendations for international students: Required—TOEFL (minimum score 600 paper-based). *Application deadline:* For fall admission, 7/20 priority date for domestic students. Applications are processed on a rolling basis. Application fee: $35. Electronic applications accepted. *Expenses: Tuition:* Part-time $250 per credit hour. One-time fee: $500 part-time. *Unit head:* Dr. Michael R. Spradlin, President, 901-751-3048. *Application contact:* Tanner Hickman, Director of Admissions, 901-751-3015, Fax: 901-751-8454, E-mail: tannerh@mabts.edu.

Mid-America Baptist Theological Seminary Northeast Branch, Program in Theology, Schenectady, NY 12303-3463. Offers M Div. *Program availability:* Part-time, evening/weekend. *Entrance requirements:* Additional exam requirements/recommendations for international students: Required—TOEFL. Electronic applications accepted.

Mid-America Reformed Seminary, Graduate Programs, Dyer, IN 46311. Offers M Div, MTS. *Accreditation:* ATS. *Entrance requirements:* Additional exam requirements/recommendations for international students: Required—TOEFL (minimum score 550 paper-based).

Midwestern Baptist Theological Seminary, Graduate and Professional Programs, Kansas City, MO 64118-4697. Offers Christian education (MACE); Christian foundations (Graduate Certificate); church music (MCM); counseling (MA); ministry (D Ed Min, D Min); Old or New Testament studies (PhD); theology (M Div). *Accreditation:* ATS. *Program availability:* Part-time, online learning. *Degree requirements:* For doctorate, thesis/dissertation. *Entrance requirements:* For doctorate, MAT. Electronic applications accepted. *Faculty research:* Ministerial studies, Biblical and theological studies, missions, counseling.

Milligan College, Emmanuel Christian Seminary at Milligan College, Milligan College, TN 37682. Offers Christian care and counseling (M Div); Christian education (M Div); Christian ministries (MACM, Graduate Certificate); Christian ministry (M Div); Christian theology (M Div, MAR); church history (MAR); church history/historical theology (M Div); general studies (M Div); ministry (D Min); New Testament (M Div, MAR); Old Testament (M Div, MAR); urban ministry (M Div); world missions (M Div). *Accreditation:* ACIPE; ATS. *Program availability:* Part-time, blended/hybrid learning. *Faculty:* 10 full-time (1 woman), 8 part-time/adjunct (0 women). *Students:* 52 full-time (23 women), 57 part-time (18 women); includes 11 minority (7 Black or African American, non-Hispanic/Latino; 1 Asian, non-Hispanic/Latino; 3 Hispanic/Latino), 7 international. Average age 35. 62 applicants, 89% accepted, 39 enrolled. In 2017, 19 master's, 3 doctorates awarded. *Degree requirements:* For master's, 2 foreign languages, thesis or alternative, portfolio; for doctorate, thesis/dissertation. *Entrance requirements:* For master's, undergraduate degree and supporting transcripts, essay/personal statement, professional recommendations, interview; for doctorate, M Div or equivalent, essay/personal statement, professional recommendations. Additional exam requirements/recommendations for international students: Required—TOEFL (minimum score 550 paper-based, 79 iBT) or IELTS (6.5). *Application deadline:* For fall admission, 8/1 for domestic students, 6/1 for international students; for spring admission, 12/15 for domestic students, 8/1 for international students. Applications are processed on a rolling basis. Application fee: $30 ($0 for international students). Electronic applications accepted. *Expenses:* Contact institution. *Financial support:* In 2017–18, 124 students received support. Scholarships/grants and unspecified assistantships available. Financial award application deadline: 12/1; financial award applicants required to submit FAFSA. *Faculty research:* Theology of Old Testament prophets; performance criticism of New Testament texts; practical theology and spiritual formation for Christian leaders; church history and missions; constructive theology, art and imagination. *Unit head:* Dr. Rollin Ramsaran, Academic Dean, Emmanuel Christian Seminary, 423-461-1524, Fax: 423-926-6198, E-mail: raramsaran@milligan.edu. *Application contact:* Lauren Gullett, Director of Admissions and Recruitment for Emmanuel Christian Seminary, 423-461-1535, Fax: 423-926-6198, E-mail: lwgullett@milligan.edu.
Website: http://ecs.milligan.edu/

Mirrer Yeshiva Central Institute, Graduate Programs, Brooklyn, NY 11223-2010. *Accreditation:* AARTS.

Moody Bible Institute, Graduate School, Chicago, IL 60610-3284. Offers biblical studies (MABS, Graduate Certificate); intercultural studies (MAIS, Graduate Certificate); ministry (M Div, M Min); spiritual formation and discipleship (MASF, Graduate Certificate); urban studies (MA, Graduate Certificate). *Program availability:* Part-time. *Degree requirements:* For master's, 2 foreign languages, fieldwork (MABS); colloquium, field research project (MA Min). *Entrance requirements:* For master's, 30 hours in Bible/theology, 2 years of ministry experience (MA Min).

Moody Theological Seminary–Michigan, Graduate Programs, Plymouth, MI 48170. Offers Bible (Graduate Certificate); Christian education (MA); counseling psychology (MA); divinity (M Div); theological studies (MA). *Accreditation:* ATS. *Program availability:* Part-time, evening/weekend. *Degree requirements:* For master's, one foreign language, thesis. *Faculty research:* Judaism, cults, world religions.

Moravian Theological Seminary, Graduate and Certificate Programs, Bethlehem, PA 18018-6614. Offers Biblical studies (Graduate Certificate); formative spirituality (M Div, Graduate Certificate); spiritual direction (MATS, Graduate Certificate); M Div/MACC; M Div/MATS. *Accreditation:* ACIPE; ATS (one or more programs are accredited). *Program availability:* Part-time. *Faculty:* 8 full-time (3 women), 10 part-time/adjunct (6 women). *Students:* 26 full-time (12 women), 68 part-time (51 women); includes 17 minority (11 Black or African American, non-Hispanic/Latino; 5 Hispanic/Latino; 1 Two or more races, non-Hispanic/Latino), 1 international. Average age 48. 37 applicants, 65% accepted, 22 enrolled. In 2017, 20 master's, 6 other advanced degrees awarded. *Degree requirements:* For master's, thesis (for some programs). *Entrance requirements:* For master's, reference forms, essay, denominational endorsement (M Div); for Graduate Certificate, reference forms, essay, Spiritual Direction experience (for spiritual direction). Additional exam requirements/recommendations for international students: Required—TOEFL (minimum score 550 paper-based; 79 iBT), IELTS (minimum score 6.5). *Application deadline:* For fall admission, 7/15 for domestic students, 4/1 priority date for international students; for spring admission, 11/15 for domestic students, 9/1 priority date for international students. Applications are processed on a rolling basis. Application fee: $50. Electronic applications accepted. *Expenses:* $570 per credit full-time; $634 per credit part-time. *Financial support:* In 2017–18, 52 students received support. Career-related internships or fieldwork, Federal Work-Study, and scholarships/grants available. Support available to part-time students. Financial award application deadline: 7/15; financial award applicants required to submit FAFSA. *Faculty research:* Intercultural pedagogy, wisdom school spiritual direction, gender and sexuality, Moravian history and theology, holistic clinical counseling. *Unit head:* Rev. Dr. Frank L. Crouch, Dean and Vice President, 610-861-1516, E-mail: crouchf@moravian.edu. *Application contact:* Dr. David H. DeRemer, Director of Enrollment, 610-861-1512, Fax: 610-861-1569, E-mail: deremerd@moravian.edu.
Website: http://moravianseminary.edu

Mount Angel Seminary, Program in Theology, Saint Benedict, OR 97373. Offers M Div, MA. *Accreditation:* ACIPE; ATS. *Program availability:* Part-time. *Degree requirements:* For master's, thesis optional.

Mount St. Joseph University, Graduate Program in Religious Studies, Cincinnati, OH 45233-1670. Offers religious studies (MA); spirituality and wellness (Certificate). *Program availability:* Part-time, evening/weekend. *Faculty:* 1 (woman) full-time. *Students:* 1 (woman) full-time, 8 part-time (7 women); includes 4 minority (3 Black or African American, non-Hispanic/Latino; 1 Hispanic/Latino). Average age 45. In 2017, 1 master's awarded. *Degree requirements:* For master's, comprehensive exam, 36 hours of credit, pastoral PRAXIS component (3 credit hours), integrating project (3 credit hours). *Entrance requirements:* For master's, undergraduate transcript with minimum overall GPA of 3.0, 3 letters of recommendation from professional colleagues, 3-page essay, interview with the Graduate Admissions Committee, current work resume. Additional exam requirements/recommendations for international students: Required—TOEFL (minimum score 560 paper-based; 83 iBT). *Application deadline:* Applications are processed on a rolling basis. Application fee: $50. Electronic applications accepted. *Expenses:* $600 per credit hour. *Financial support:* In 2017–18, 7 students received support. Scholarships/grants available. Financial award applicants required to submit FAFSA. *Faculty research:* Contextual/cultural/systematic theology, historical/spiritual theology, business/economics ethics, social justice, Biblical/cultural/pastoral theology. *Unit head:* Dr. John Trokan, Associate Professor of Religious and Pastoral Studies/Director of Graduate Program, 513-244-4272, Fax: 513-244-4222, E-mail: john.trokan@msj.edu. *Application contact:* Mary Brigham, Assistant Director of Graduate Recruitment, 513-244-4233, Fax: 513-244-4629, E-mail: mary.brigham@msj.edu.
Website: http://www.msj.edu/academics/graduate-programs/religious-studies-programs/

Theology

Mount St. Mary's University, Graduate Seminary, Emmitsburg, MD 21727-7799. Offers M Div, MA. *Accreditation:* ATS. *Degree requirements:* For master's, one foreign language, comprehensive exam, thesis, language proficiency exams. *Entrance requirements:* For master's, 18 credits of course work in philosophy. Additional exam requirements/recommendations for international students: Required—TOEFL (minimum score 550 paper-based; 83 iBT). *Expenses:* Contact institution.

Mount Vernon Nazarene University, Program in Ministry, Mount Vernon, OH 43050-9500. Offers M Min. *Program availability:* Part-time, evening/weekend. *Degree requirements:* For master's, project. *Faculty research:* Pastoral effectiveness and professional development.

Multnomah University, Multnomah Biblical Seminary, Portland, OR 97220-5898. Offers M Div, MABS, MACL, MATS, Th M, D Min. *Accreditation:* ATS. *Program availability:* Part-time. *Faculty:* 4 full-time (1 woman), 14 part-time/adjunct (1 woman). *Students:* 80 full-time (23 women), 83 part-time (29 women); includes 32 minority (8 Black or African American, non-Hispanic/Latino; 10 Asian, non-Hispanic/Latino; 8 Hispanic/Latino; 6 Two or more races, non-Hispanic/Latino). Average age 35. 71 applicants, 69% accepted, 38 enrolled. In 2017, 35 master's, 6 doctorates awarded. *Degree requirements:* For master's, variable foreign language requirement, thesis (for some programs). *Entrance requirements:* For master's, interview; for doctorate, interview, M Div equivalency. Additional exam requirements/recommendations for international students: Required—TOEFL (minimum score 550 paper-based). *Application deadline:* For fall and spring admission, 12/1 priority date for domestic and international students. Applications are processed on a rolling basis. Application fee: $40. *Expenses: Tuition:* Full-time $8720; part-time $5450 per credit hour. *Required fees:* $110; $55 per credit hour. Tuition and fees vary according to course load, degree level and program. *Financial support:* Career-related internships or fieldwork and scholarships/grants available. Support available to part-time students. Financial award application deadline: 7/1; financial award applicants required to submit FAFSA. *Faculty research:* Grief theology, intercultural studies, New Testament, theology and culture, historical theology, Biblical theology. *Unit head:* Dr. Derek Chinn, Dean, 503-252-6731, Fax: 503-251-6444, E-mail: dchinn@multnomah.edu. *Application contact:* Mindy Kate Hasenkamp, Director of Admissions, 503-251-6483, Fax: 503-254-1268, E-mail: admiss@multnomah.edu.

Naropa University, Graduate Programs, Program in Divinity, Boulder, CO 80302-6697. Offers M Div. *Faculty:* 8 full-time (4 women), 3 part-time/adjunct (1 woman). *Students:* 15 full-time (8 women), 9 part-time (5 women); includes 5 minority (1 Black or African American, non-Hispanic/Latino; 1 Asian, non-Hispanic/Latino; 2 Hispanic/Latino; 1 Two or more races, non-Hispanic/Latino), 2 international. Average age 39. 18 applicants, 89% accepted, 8 enrolled. In 2017, 8 master's awarded. *Degree requirements:* For master's, comprehensive exam, thesis, clinical pastoral education or fieldwork placement. *Entrance requirements:* For master's, resume/curriculum vitae with pertinent academic, employment and volunteer activity; 2 letters of recommendation; letter of interest; transcripts; phone interview. Additional exam requirements/recommendations for international students: Required—TOEFL (minimum score 550 paper-based; 80 iBT). *Application deadline:* For fall admission, 1/15 priority date for domestic and international students. Applications are processed on a rolling basis. Application fee: $60. Electronic applications accepted. *Expenses:* $995 per credit. *Financial support:* In 2017–18, 15 students received support. Research assistantships with partial tuition reimbursements available, teaching assistantships with partial tuition reimbursements available, career-related internships or fieldwork, Federal Work-Study, scholarships/grants, and unspecified assistantships available. Support available to part-time students. Financial award application deadline: 3/1; financial award applicants required to submit FAFSA. *Unit head:* Dr. Elaine Yuen, Chair, Department of Wisdom Traditions, 303-245-4718, E-mail: eyuen@naropa.edu. *Application contact:* Office of Admissions, 303-546-3572, Fax: 303-546-3583, E-mail: admissions@naropa.edu. Website: http://www.naropa.edu/academics/masters/divinity/index.php

Nashotah House Theological Seminary, Graduate Programs, Nashotah, WI 53058-9793. Offers Anglican studies (Certificate); Biblical studies (STM); Christian spirituality (STM); church history (STM); liturgy (STM); ministry (M Div, MM); pastoral ministry (MPM); theological studies (MTS); theology (STM, D Min). *Accreditation:* ACIPE; ATS (one or more programs are accredited). *Program availability:* Part-time. *Degree requirements:* For master's, thesis optional. *Entrance requirements:* For master's and Certificate, GRE General Test or MAT, interview, 3 recommendations. Additional exam requirements/recommendations for international students: Required—TOEFL. Electronic applications accepted. *Expenses:* Contact institution. *Faculty research:* Formation for parochial ministry, ancient Semitic epigraphy.

Nazarene Theological Seminary, Graduate and Professional Programs, Kansas City, MO 64131-1263. Offers Christian formation and discipleship (MA); intercultural studies (MA); pastoral theology (Graduate Certificate); theological studies (MA); theology (M Div, D Min). *Accreditation:* ACIPE; ATS. *Program availability:* Part-time. *Faculty:* 12 full-time (2 women), 16 part-time/adjunct (3 women). *Students:* 54 full-time (25 women), 156 part-time (55 women); includes 22 minority (7 Black or African American, non-Hispanic/Latino; 1 American Indian or Alaska Native, non-Hispanic/Latino; 1 Asian, non-Hispanic/Latino; 9 Hispanic/Latino; 4 Two or more races, non-Hispanic/Latino), 29 international. *Degree requirements:* For master's, comprehensive exam (for some programs), thesis (for some programs); for doctorate, thesis/dissertation. *Entrance requirements:* For master's and Graduate Certificate, three references; for doctorate, three references, interview. Additional exam requirements/recommendations for international students: Required—TOEFL (minimum score 550 paper-based; 80 iBT). *Application deadline:* For fall admission, 2/15 for domestic and international students; for spring admission, 11/1 for domestic and international students. Applications are processed on a rolling basis. Application fee: $50. Electronic applications accepted. *Expenses: Tuition:* Full-time $11,445; part-time $8175 per credit hour. *Required fees:* $200 per semester. *Financial support:* Teaching assistantships, institutionally sponsored loans, and scholarships/grants available. Support available to part-time students. Financial award application deadline: 3/1; financial award applicants required to submit FAFSA. *Unit head:* Dr. Josh Sweeden, Dean of the Faculty, 816-268-5402, Fax: 816-268-5500, E-mail: jsweeden@nts.edu. *Application contact:* Pamala J. Asher, Registrar/Director of Enrollment Services, 816-268-5442, Fax: 816-268-5500, E-mail: pjasher@nts.edu.

Ner Israel Rabbinical College, Graduate Programs, Baltimore, MD 21208. Offers MTL, DTL, Professional Certificate. *Accreditation:* AARTS.

Ner Israel Yeshiva College of Toronto, Graduate Programs, Thornhill, ON L4J 8A7, Canada. *Accreditation:* AARTS.

New Brunswick Theological Seminary, Graduate and Professional Programs, New Brunswick, NJ 08901-1196. Offers pastoral care and counseling (D Min). *Accreditation:* ACIPE; ATS. *Program availability:* Part-time, evening/weekend. *Degree requirements:* For master's, variable foreign language requirement, thesis (for some programs); for doctorate, thesis/dissertation. *Entrance requirements:* For master's, BA/BS with minimum GPA of 3.0 (for MA), 2.5 (for M Div); for doctorate, M Div. Additional exam requirements/recommendations for international students: Required—TOEFL (minimum score 550 paper-based; 79 iBT); Recommended—IELTS (minimum score 6). Electronic applications accepted.

Newman Theological College, Theology Programs, Edmonton, AB T6V 1H3, Canada. Offers M Div, M Th, MTS. *Accreditation:* ATS. *Program availability:* Part-time. *Faculty:* 10 full-time (1 woman), 8 part-time/adjunct (1 woman). *Students:* 26 full-time (4 women), 10 part-time (5 women). 10 applicants, 100% accepted, 8 enrolled. In 2017, 14 master's awarded. *Degree requirements:* For master's, comprehensive exam, thesis. *Entrance requirements:* For master's, bachelor's degree. Additional exam requirements/recommendations for international students: Required—TOEFL (minimum score 560 paper-based; 86 iBT), IELTS (minimum score 6.5). *Application deadline:* For fall admission, 8/21 priority date for domestic students; for winter admission, 11/22 priority date for domestic students; for spring admission, 4/21 priority date for domestic students. Applications are processed on a rolling basis. Application fee: $45 ($250 for international students). *Expenses:* $639 per course; $426 lay formation fee; $35 administrative fee per semester; $10 library fee per course; $40 full-time/$25 part-time student association fee. *Financial support:* In 2017–18, 6 students received support. Tuition bursaries available. Support available to part-time students. Financial award application deadline: 5/31. *Faculty research:* New Testament and inter-testament period, philosophy of Jacques Maritain, philosophy of Catholic education, trinity and immutability, medical ethics. *Unit head:* Dr. Ryan Topping, Academic Dean/Vice President, 780-392-2450 Ext. 2444, Fax: 780-462-4013, E-mail: ryan.topping@newman.edu. *Application contact:* Maria Saulnier, Registrar, 780-392-2451, Fax: 780-462-4013, E-mail: registrar@newman.edu. Website: http://www.newman.edu/

Newman University, Graduate Theology Program, Wichita, KS 67213-2097. Offers theological studies (MTS); theology (MA). *Program availability:* Part-time, online learning. *Degree requirements:* For master's, 2 foreign languages, comprehensive exam (for some programs), thesis (for some programs). *Entrance requirements:* For master's, letter of recommendation from pastor; bachelor's degree in theology or related field (MA), in any field (MTS). Additional exam requirements/recommendations for international students: Required—TOEFL (minimum score 600 paper-based; 100 iBT). *Expenses:* Contact institution.

New Orleans Baptist Theological Seminary, Graduate and Professional Programs, Division of Biblical Studies, New Orleans, LA 70126-4858. Offers M Div, MA, PhD. *Accreditation:* ACIPE; ATS (one or more programs are accredited). *Degree requirements:* For master's, 2 foreign languages, comprehensive exam (for some programs), thesis (for some programs); for doctorate, 4 foreign languages, comprehensive exam, thesis/dissertation. *Entrance requirements:* For doctorate, GRE General Test.

New Orleans Baptist Theological Seminary, Graduate and Professional Programs, Division of Theological and Historical Studies, New Orleans, LA 70126-4858. Offers M Div, MA, D Min, PhD. *Accreditation:* ACIPE; ATS (one or more programs are accredited). *Program availability:* Online learning. *Degree requirements:* For master's, 2 foreign languages, comprehensive exam (for some programs), thesis (for some programs); for doctorate, 3 foreign languages, comprehensive exam, thesis/dissertation. *Entrance requirements:* For doctorate, GRE General Test. Additional exam requirements/recommendations for international students: Required—TOEFL.

New Saint Andrews College, Graduate School, Moscow, ID 83843. Offers classical Christian studies (Graduate Certificate); creative writing (MFA); theology and letters (MA). *Program availability:* Part-time, blended/hybrid learning. *Faculty:* 12 part-time/adjunct (0 women). *Students:* 12 full-time (3 women), 8 part-time (5 women), 1 international. Average age 25. 15 applicants, 53% accepted, 7 enrolled. In 2017, 3 master's awarded. *Degree requirements:* For master's, comprehensive exam (for some programs), thesis (for some programs), final oral exam. *Entrance requirements:* For master's, GRE, 2 letters of recommendation; for Graduate Certificate, GRE, bachelor's degree, essays, 2 letters of recommendation. *Application deadline:* For fall admission, 12/1 for domestic students. Applications are processed on a rolling basis. Application fee: $50. Electronic applications accepted. *Expenses: Tuition:* Full-time $7600; part-time $475 per credit. *Faculty research:* Hebrew, theology, literature. *Unit head:* Benjamin Merkle, President, 208-882-1566 Ext. 104, E-mail: bmerkle@nsa.edu. *Application contact:* Brenda Schlect, Director of Admissions, 208-882-1566 Ext. 113, Fax: 208-882-4293, E-mail: admissions@nsa.edu. Website: http://www.nsa.edu/academics/graduate-school/

New York Theological Seminary, Graduate and Professional Programs, New York, NY 10115. Offers M Div, MPS, MSW, D Min. MSW offered jointly with Fordham University. *Accreditation:* ACIPE; ATS (one or more programs are accredited). *Program availability:* Part-time. *Degree requirements:* For doctorate, thesis/dissertation. *Entrance requirements:* For doctorate, M Div, 3 years of ministry experience, interview. Additional exam requirements/recommendations for international students: Required—TOEFL. *Faculty research:* Women in leadership; crime and punishment; church history; culture, politics and theology.

Northeastern Seminary at Roberts Wesleyan College, Graduate and Professional Programs, Rochester, NY 14624. Offers ministry (D Min); theological studies (MA); theology (M Div); theology and social justice (MA); transformational leadership (MA); M Div/MSW. M Div/MSW offered jointly with Roberts Wesleyan College. *Accreditation:* ATS. *Program availability:* Evening/weekend. *Faculty:* 7 full-time (2 women), 17 part-time/adjunct (2 women). *Students:* 87 full-time (42 women), 30 part-time (12 women); includes 42 minority (33 Black or African American, non-Hispanic/Latino; 9 Hispanic/Latino), 4 international. Average age 47. *Degree requirements:* For master's, thesis (for some programs); for doctorate, one foreign language, thesis/dissertation. *Entrance requirements:* For doctorate, M Div, 3 years of full-time ministry experience. Additional exam requirements/recommendations for international students: Required—TOEFL (minimum score 550 paper-based). *Application deadline:* For fall admission, 8/1 priority date for domestic and international students; for spring admission, 12/15 priority date for domestic and international students. Applications are processed on a rolling basis. Application fee: $35. Electronic applications accepted. *Expenses: Tuition:* Full-time $9234; part-time $4617 per credit. *Required fees:* $500; $250 per credit. Tuition and fees vary according to course load, degree level and program. *Financial support:* Teaching assistantships with partial tuition reimbursements, career-related internships or fieldwork, institutionally sponsored loans, scholarships/grants, and tuition waivers (partial) available. Financial award applicants required to submit FAFSA. *Faculty research:* Historical theology, spiritual formation, biblical theology, counseling education. *Unit head:* Dr. Douglas Cullum, Vice President and Dean, 585-594-6331, Fax: 585-594-6801, E-mail: cullumd@roberts.edu. *Application contact:* Cheryl Murray, Admission Assistant, 585-594-6802, Fax: 585-594-6801, E-mail: nesadmissions@roberts.edu.

Northern Seminary, Graduate and Professional Programs, Lombard, IL 60148-5698. Offers Biblical studies (M Div); Christian community development (MA, D Min); Christian ministry (MACM); contextual theology (D Min); missional church ministry (M Div); New Testament (M Div, MANT); New Testament context (D Min); Old Testament (M Div); preaching (D Min); theology (M Div); theology and mission (MA); urban leadership (MA); worship (M Div, MAW). *Program availability:* Part-time, evening/weekend. *Faculty:* 6 full-time (1 woman), 33 part-time/adjunct (8 women). *Students:* 208 full-time (62 women);

includes 89 minority (73 Black or African American, non-Hispanic/Latino; 6 Asian, non-Hispanic/Latino; 8 Hispanic/Latino; 2 Two or more races, non-Hispanic/Latino), 3 international. Average age 44. *Degree requirements:* For master's, thesis (for some programs); for doctorate, thesis/dissertation. *Entrance requirements:* For master's, writing test, all official transcripts, letter of reference from church, 3 letters of reference, autobiographical statement (400 words or more); for doctorate, M Div, 3 years in the ministry post-M Div, 3 letters of reference. Additional exam requirements/recommendations for international students: Required—TOEFL (minimum score 550 paper-based). *Application deadline:* Applications are processed on a rolling basis. Application fee: $35. Electronic applications accepted. *Expenses: Tuition:* Full-time $14,253; part-time $9627 per credit. *Required fees:* $125 per quarter. *Financial support:* Teaching assistantships with partial tuition reimbursements, Federal Work-Study, and scholarships/grants available. Support available to part-time students. Financial award application deadline: 9/1; financial award applicants required to submit FAFSA. *Faculty research:* Theology and mission, worship studies, church history, evangelism, Christian ministry, urban leadership, New Testament. *Unit head:* Dr. William Shiell, President, 630-620-2101, Fax: 630-620-2190. *Application contact:* Greg Armstrong, Director of Admissions, 630-620-2175, Fax: 630-620-2190, E-mail: admissions@seminary.edu.

North Park Theological Seminary, Graduate and Professional Programs, Professional Program, Chicago, IL 60625-4895. Offers M Div, M Div/MBA, M Div/MM. M Div/MBA offered jointly with North Park University. *Accreditation:* ACIPE; ATS. *Program availability:* Part-time. *Entrance requirements:* Additional exam requirements/recommendations for international students: Required—TOEFL.

North Park Theological Seminary, Graduate and Professional Programs, Program in Christian Formation, Chicago, IL 60625-4895. Offers MA, MA/MM. *Accreditation:* ATS.

North Park Theological Seminary, Graduate and Professional Programs, Program in Preaching, Chicago, IL 60625-4895. Offers D Min. Program offered jointly with Chicago Theological Seminary, Lutheran School of Theology at Chicago, McCormick Theological Seminary, Seabury-Western Theological Seminary. *Accreditation:* ACIPE; ATS. *Degree requirements:* For doctorate, thesis/dissertation. *Entrance requirements:* For doctorate, 3 years of preaching experience.

North Park Theological Seminary, Graduate and Professional Programs, Program in Theological Studies, Chicago, IL 60625-4895. Offers MATS, MATS/MBA, MATS/MM. MATS/MBA offered jointly with North Park University. *Accreditation:* ACIPE; ATS. *Program availability:* Part-time. *Degree requirements:* For master's, comprehensive exam or thesis. *Entrance requirements:* For master's, minimum GPA of 2.5. Additional exam requirements/recommendations for international students: Required—TOEFL.

Northwest Nazarene University, Program in Religion, Nampa, ID 83686-5897. Offers missional leadership (M Div, MA); pastoral ministry (MA); spiritual formation (M Div, MA); youth, children, and family ministry (M Div, MA). *Program availability:* Part-time, online only, 100% online. *Students:* Average age 39. 37 applicants, 76% accepted, 24 enrolled. In 2017, 40 master's awarded. *Entrance requirements:* For master's, minimum GPA of 2.5; 8 semester or 12 quarter credits of Bible, theology and/or Western philosophy. Additional exam requirements/recommendations for international students: Required—TOEFL (minimum score 85 iBT). *Application deadline:* For fall admission, 7/31 for domestic students, 7/1 for international students; for spring admission, 2/1 for domestic students, 1/5 for international students. Applications are processed on a rolling basis. Application fee: $50. Electronic applications accepted. *Expenses:* Contact institution. *Financial support:* In 2017–18, 3 students received support. Scholarships/grants available. *Unit head:* Dr. Jay Akkerman, Director, Graduate Studies, 208-467-8437, Fax: 208-467-8252. *Application contact:* Vicki Funk, Program Coordinator, 208-467-8432, Fax: 208-467-8252, E-mail: vlfunk@nnu.edu.
Website: http://www.nnu.edu/ministry/

Northwest University, College of Ministry, Kirkland, WA 98033. Offers ministry (MIM); missional leadership (MA); theology and culture (MA). *Program availability:* Part-time, evening/weekend, online learning. *Degree requirements:* For master's, comprehensive exam (for some programs), thesis (for some programs). *Entrance requirements:* Additional exam requirements/recommendations for international students: Required—TOEFL (minimum score 550 paper-based; 75 iBT). Electronic applications accepted.

Notre Dame Seminary, Graduate School of Theology, New Orleans, LA 70118-4391. Offers M Div, MA. *Accreditation:* ACIPE; ATS. *Program availability:* Part-time. *Degree requirements:* For master's, one foreign language, comprehensive exam, thesis. *Entrance requirements:* For master's, GRE. Additional exam requirements/recommendations for international students: Required—TOEFL.

Nyack College, Alliance Theological Seminary, Nyack, NY 10960. Offers Biblical literature (MA), including New Testament, Old Testament; Biblical studies (MA); Christian ministry (MPS); intercultural studies (MA); ministry (D Min), including Christian leadership in the global context; theology and missions (M Div); urban ministry (MPS). *Program availability:* Part-time, evening/weekend, 100% online, blended/hybrid learning. *Students:* 265 full-time (107 women), 356 part-time (162 women); includes 490 minority (161 Black or African American, non-Hispanic/Latino; 2 American Indian or Alaska Native, non-Hispanic/Latino; 123 Asian, non-Hispanic/Latino; 198 Hispanic/Latino; 6 Two or more races, non-Hispanic/Latino), 37 international. Average age 42. In 2017, 100 master's, 23 doctorates awarded. *Degree requirements:* For master's, comprehensive exam (for some programs), thesis optional, internship; for doctorate, thesis/dissertation. *Entrance requirements:* For master's, transcripts, Christian experience statement, recommendations; for doctorate, transcripts, documented three years of ministry experience subsequent to 1st graduate theological degree, reference letters, formal academic paper. Additional exam requirements/recommendations for international students: Required—TOEFL (minimum score 550 paper-based; 80 iBT). *Application deadline:* Applications are processed on a rolling basis. Application fee: $30. Electronic applications accepted. *Expenses:* $585 per credit (master's-level); $22,060 for total program (for D Min). *Financial support:* Career-related internships or fieldwork, Federal Work-Study, and scholarships/grants available. Financial award applicants required to submit FAFSA. *Unit head:* Dr. Ronald Walborn, Dean, 845-770-5715, Fax: 845-358-1663. *Application contact:* Jennifer Reimer, Associate Director of Admissions, 845-770-5709, E-mail: admissions.grad@nyack.edu.
Website: http://www.nyack.edu/ats

Oakland City University, Chapman Seminary, Oakland City, IN 47660-1099. Offers M Div, D Min. *Program availability:* Part-time. *Degree requirements:* For doctorate, thesis/dissertation. *Entrance requirements:* For doctorate, GRE, MAT, letters of recommendation. Additional exam requirements/recommendations for international students: Required—TOEFL. *Expenses:* Contact institution. *Faculty research:* Pastoral ministry, Christian education, missions.

Oblate School of Theology, Graduate and Professional Programs, San Antonio, TX 78216-6693. Offers African-American pastoral leadership (D Min); divinity (M Div); pastoral leadership (D Min); pastoral ministry (MAP Min); pastoral studies (Certificate); spiritual formation in the local community (D Min); spirituality (MA Sp, PhD); spirituality and ministry (D Min); theology (MA Th); U.S. Hispanic/Latino ministry (D Min); M Div/MA Th. *Accreditation:* ACIPE; ATS (one or more programs are accredited). *Program availability:* Part-time, 100% online, blended/hybrid learning. *Faculty:* 21 full-time (5 women), 4 part-time/adjunct (0 women). *Students:* 89 full-time (9 women), 54 part-time

(31 women); includes 77 minority (11 Black or African American, non-Hispanic/Latino; 8 Asian, non-Hispanic/Latino; 57 Hispanic/Latino; 1 Two or more races, non-Hispanic/Latino), 24 international. Average age 39. In 2017, 24 master's, 1 doctorate awarded. *Degree requirements:* For master's, comprehensive exam (for some programs), thesis (for some programs), practicum; for doctorate, one foreign language, comprehensive exam, thesis/dissertation, paper, practicum. *Entrance requirements:* For master's, MAT, interview, prerequisite course work in theology or religious studies and philosophy, minimum GPA of 2.5; for doctorate, D Min, M Div, MA Th, MA Sp, MA PM. Additional exam requirements/recommendations for international students: Required—TOEFL (minimum score 71 iBT). *Application deadline:* For fall admission, 6/30 priority date for domestic and international students; for winter admission, 11/30 for domestic and international students; for spring admission, 11/30 for domestic and international students; for summer admission, 4/30 for domestic and international students. Applications are processed on a rolling basis. Application fee: $65. Electronic applications accepted. *Expenses:* $605.00 per credit hour (for master's degrees); $680 per credit hour (for doctoral degrees); $55 registration fee. *Financial support:* In 2017–18, 25 students received support. Scholarships/grants available. Support available to part-time students. Financial award application deadline: 8/15; financial award applicants required to submit FAFSA. *Unit head:* Dr. R. Scott Woodward, Academic Dean, 210-341-1366, Fax: 210-341-4519, E-mail: rsw@ost.edu. *Application contact:* Brenda Reyna, Registrar, 210-341-1366 Ext. 226, Fax: 210-341-4519, E-mail: registrar@ost.edu.

Ohio Christian University, Graduate Programs, Circleville, OH 43113. Offers accounting (MBA); business administration (MBA); digital marketing (MBA); finance (MBA); healthcare management (MBA); human resources (MBA); management (MM); organizational leadership (MBA); pastoral care and counseling (MAM); practical theology (MAM).

Ohio Dominican University, Division of Arts and Letters, Program in Theology, Columbus, OH 43219-2099. Offers MA. *Program availability:* Part-time, evening/weekend. *Faculty:* 1 full-time (0 women), 2 part-time/adjunct (1 woman). *Students:* 16 part-time (8 women); includes 1 minority (Hispanic/Latino). Average age 46. 6 applicants, 67% accepted, 3 enrolled. In 2017, 5 master's awarded. *Degree requirements:* For master's, thesis or alternative. *Entrance requirements:* For master's, 3 letters of recommendation, interview, essay. Additional exam requirements/recommendations for international students: Required—TOEFL (minimum score 550 paper-based), IELTS (minimum score 6.5). *Application deadline:* For fall admission, 8/15 for domestic students, 6/10 for international students; for spring admission, 1/4 for domestic students, 11/2 for international students; for summer admission, 5/30 for domestic students. Applications are processed on a rolling basis. Application fee: $25. Electronic applications accepted. *Expenses:* $600 per credit hour, $175 per semester technology fee, $50 per semester activity fee. *Financial support:* Applicants required to submit FAFSA. *Unit head:* Dr. Barbara Finan, Program Director, 614-251-4578, E-mail: finanb@ohiodominican.edu. *Application contact:* John W. Naughton, Associate Vice President for Enrollment Management, 614-251-4615, Fax: 614-251-6654, E-mail: grad@ohiodominican.edu.
Website: http://www.ohiodominican.edu/academics/graduate/ma-theology

Ohr Hameir Theological Seminary, Graduate Programs, Cortlandt Manor, NY 10567. *Accreditation:* AARTS.

Oklahoma Christian University, Graduate School of Theology, Oklahoma City, OK 73136-1100. Offers scripture (MTS); theology (M Div, MACM, MTS). *Program availability:* Part-time. *Degree requirements:* For master's, variable foreign language requirement, comprehensive exam, thesis (for some programs). *Entrance requirements:* For master's, bachelor's degree, minimum GPA of 3.0. Additional exam requirements/recommendations for international students: Recommended—TOEFL (minimum score 550 paper-based; 79 iBT), IELTS (minimum score 6.5). Electronic applications accepted. *Expenses:* Contact institution. *Faculty research:* Old Testament studies, New Testament studies, church history, Hellenistic Greek and Linguistics, Semitic Languages.

Oklahoma Wesleyan University, Professional Studies Division, Bartlesville, OK 74006-6299. Offers nursing administration (MSN); nursing education (MSN); strategic leadership (MS); theology and apologetics (MA).

Olivet Nazarene University, Graduate School, Department of Practical Ministries, Bourbonnais, IL 60914. Offers MPM. *Program availability:* Part-time. *Degree requirements:* For master's, thesis or alternative.

Olivet Nazarene University, Graduate School, Division of Religion, Bourbonnais, IL 60914. Offers biblical literature (MA); religion (MA); theology (MA). *Program availability:* Part-time. *Degree requirements:* For master's, thesis or alternative.

Oral Roberts University, School of Theology and Missions, Tulsa, OK 74171. Offers biblical literature (MA), including advanced languages, Judaic-Christian studies; church ministries and leadership (D Min); clinical pastoral education (M Div); missions (MA); pastoral care and chaplaincy (M Div, D Min); practical theology (MA), including teaching ministries, urban ministries; professional counseling (MA), including addiction studies, marriage and family therapy; theological/historical studies (MA). *Accreditation:* ATS. *Program availability:* Part-time, online learning. *Faculty:* 17 full-time (2 women). *Students:* 371 full-time (156 women), 110 part-time (65 women); includes 177 minority (127 Black or African American, non-Hispanic/Latino; 5 American Indian or Alaska Native, non-Hispanic/Latino; 20 Asian, non-Hispanic/Latino; 25 Hispanic/Latino), 82 international. Average age 36. 159 applicants, 95% accepted, 124 enrolled. In 2017, 52 master's, 10 doctorates awarded. *Degree requirements:* For master's, thesis (for some programs), practicum/internship; for doctorate, thesis/dissertation, applied research project. *Entrance requirements:* For master's, GRE General Test or MAT (waived for those with undergraduate degree from regionally accredited institution and 3.0 or higher GPA), minimum GPA of 2.5 (professional) or 3.0 (academic); for doctorate, M Div, minimum GPA of 3.0, 3 years of full-time ministry experience. Additional exam requirements/recommendations for international students: Recommended—TOEFL (minimum score 550 paper-based; 79 iBT), IELTS (minimum score 7). *Application deadline:* Applications are processed on a rolling basis. Application fee: $35. Electronic applications accepted. Application fee is waived when completed online. *Financial support:* Fellowships and scholarships/grants available. Financial award application deadline: 6/1. *Unit head:* Dr. Bill Buker, Chair, 918-495-6493, E-mail: bbuker@oru.edu. *Application contact:* Michael Thomas, Enrollment Counselor, 918-495-6618, E-mail: mthomas@oru.edu.
Website: http://www.gradtheology.oru.edu/

Pacific School of Religion, Graduate and Professional Programs, Berkeley, CA 94709-1323. Offers M Div, MA, MTS, D Min, PhD, Th D, CAPS, CMS, CSS, CTS. MA, PhD, Th D offered jointly with Graduate Theological Union; D Min with Church Divinity School of the Pacific. *Accreditation:* ACIPE; ATS (one or more programs are accredited). *Program availability:* Part-time. *Degree requirements:* For master's, one foreign language, thesis (for some programs); for doctorate, thesis/dissertation. *Entrance requirements:* For master's, minimum GPA of 3.0; for doctorate, M Div, minimum GPA of 3.0 (D Min); for other advanced degree, M Div, minimum GPA of 3.0 (CAPS). Additional exam requirements/recommendations for international students: Required—TOEFL (minimum score 550 paper-based). Electronic applications accepted. *Faculty research:* Medical ethics, gay/lesbian studies in religion, Asian-American religion, race, culture and theology, theology in context.

Theology

Palm Beach Atlantic University, School of Ministry, West Palm Beach, FL 33416-4708. Offers Christian studies (MA); ministry (M Div). *Program availability:* Part-time. *Degree requirements:* For master's, one foreign language, comprehensive exam (for some programs), thesis optional, 8 credits of biblical language (for M Div). *Entrance requirements:* For master's, minimum GPA of 2.75; writing samples. Additional exam requirements/recommendations for international students: Required—TOEFL (minimum score 550 paper-based; 79 iBT). Electronic applications accepted. *Faculty research:* Ethics, apologetics, spiritual formation, theology.

Payne Theological Seminary, Program in Theology, Wilberforce, OH 45384-3474. Offers M Div. *Accreditation:* ACIPE; ATS. *Program availability:* Part-time, evening/weekend, online learning.

Pentecostal Theological Seminary, Graduate and Professional Programs, Cleveland, TN 37320-3330. Offers biblical studies (MTS); church ministries (MA); counseling (MA); discipleship and Christian formation (MA); ministry (D Min); Pentecostal theology (MTS); theology (M Div). *Accreditation:* ACIPE; ATS. *Program availability:* Part-time. *Degree requirements:* For master's, variable foreign language requirement, thesis (for some programs), internship. *Faculty research:* Biblical exegesis.

Pfeiffer University, Program in Practical Theology, Misenheimer, NC 28109-0960. Offers MA. *Program availability:* Part-time, evening/weekend. *Entrance requirements:* For master's, minimum GPA of 2.75.

Phillips Theological Seminary, Programs in Theology, Tulsa, OK 74116. Offers administration of church agencies (M Div); campus ministry (M Div); church-related social work (M Div); college and seminary teaching (M Div); global mission work (M Div); institutional chaplaincy (M Div); ministerial vocations in Christian education (M Div); ministry (D Min), including parish ministry, pastoral counseling, practices of ministry; ministry and culture (MAMC), including Christian education, congregational leadership, history and practice of Christian spirituality, theology, ethics, and culture; ministry of music (M Div); pastoral care and counseling (M Div); pastoral ministry (M Div); theological studies (MTS). *Accreditation:* ATS. *Program availability:* Part-time, online learning. *Degree requirements:* For master's, thesis (for some programs); for doctorate, thesis/dissertation. *Entrance requirements:* For master's, minimum GPA of 2.5; for doctorate, M Div, minimum GPA of 3.0. *Faculty research:* Biblical studies, historical studies, theology and culture, practical theology, theology and film.

Phoenix Seminary, Graduate Programs, Phoenix, AZ 85018. Offers Biblical and theological studies (Graduate Diploma); Biblical communication (M Div); Biblical leadership (MA); Christian counseling (Graduate Diploma); counseling and family (M Div); leadership development (M Div); ministry (D Min); professional counseling (MA). *Accreditation:* ATS (one or more programs are accredited). *Program availability:* Part-time, evening/weekend. *Degree requirements:* For master's, 2 foreign languages, comprehensive exam; for doctorate, 2 foreign languages, thesis/dissertation. *Entrance requirements:* For master's, undergraduate degree with minimum GPA of 2.5; for doctorate, M Div (94 hours) with minimum GPA of 3.0. Additional exam requirements/recommendations for international students: Required—TOEFL (minimum score 587 paper-based; 92 iBT), TWE (minimum score 4.5).

Piedmont International University, Graduate School, Winston-Salem, NC 27101-5197. Offers Biblical studies (PhD); curriculum and instruction (M Ed); divinity (M Div); educational leadership (M Ed); leadership (MA, PhD); ministry (MA Min, D Min); non-language track (MABS); PhD preparation track (MABS). *Program availability:* Part-time, online learning. Terminal master's awarded for partial completion of doctoral program. *Degree requirements:* For master's, 2 foreign languages, comprehensive exam, thesis or alternative; for doctorate, 2 foreign languages, comprehensive exam. *Entrance requirements:* For master's, GRE General Test; for doctorate, Hebrew and Greek proficiency, MA. Additional exam requirements/recommendations for international students: Required—TOEFL (minimum score 500 paper-based; 60 iBT). Electronic applications accepted. *Faculty research:* Theological and biblical studies.

Piedmont International University, Temple Baptist Seminary, Winston-Salem, NC 27101-5197. Offers M Div, D Min. *Program availability:* Part-time, evening/weekend, online learning. *Degree requirements:* For master's, comprehensive exam; for doctorate, comprehensive exam, thesis/dissertation. *Entrance requirements:* For master's, bachelor's degree or equivalent from accredited or recognized college or university with minimum GPA of 2.75 and one of the following: aptitude for graduate studies evidenced by the transcript record, the GRE, or ministry achievement; for doctorate, appropriate master's degree with minimum GPA of 3.0 including 6 semester hours each of Greek, Hebrew, and Biblical introduction (Old Testament and New Testament) and 12 semester hours of systematic theology. Additional exam requirements/recommendations for international students: Required—TOEFL (minimum score 500 paper-based; 60 iBT).

Pittsburgh Theological Seminary, Graduate and Professional Programs, Pittsburgh, PA 15206. Offers divinity (M Div); theological studies (MA); theology (Th M); theology and ministry (MA, D Min); JD/M Div; M Div/MS; M Div/MSW. M Div/MSW offered jointly with University of Pittsburgh; JD/M Div with Duquesne University; M Div/MSPPM with Carnegie Mellon University. *Accreditation:* ATS (one or more programs are accredited). *Program availability:* Part-time, evening/weekend. *Faculty:* 16 full-time (5 women), 6 part-time/adjunct (2 women). *Students:* 170 full-time (70 women), 43 part-time (25 women); includes 56 minority (45 Black or African American, non-Hispanic/Latino; 5 Asian, non-Hispanic/Latino; 3 Hispanic/Latino; 1 Native Hawaiian or other Pacific Islander, non-Hispanic/Latino; 2 Two or more races, non-Hispanic/Latino), 13 international. Average age 35. 57 applicants, 93% accepted, 44 enrolled. In 2017, 26 master's, 9 doctorates awarded. *Degree requirements:* For master's, one foreign language, comprehensive exam (for some programs), thesis (for some programs); for doctorate, thesis/dissertation. *Entrance requirements:* For master's, bachelor's degree with minimum GPA of 2.7, interview, references; for doctorate, M Div or equivalent, interview, references. Additional exam requirements/recommendations for international students: Required—TOEFL (minimum score 570 paper-based; 89 iBT). *Application deadline:* For fall admission, 6/30 priority date for domestic students, 12/1 for international students; for winter admission, 10/15 priority date for domestic students; for spring admission, 1/15 priority date for domestic students. Applications are processed on a rolling basis. Application fee: $50. Electronic applications accepted. *Expenses: Tuition:* Full-time $11,988; part-time $358 per credit hour. *Required fees:* $100 per term. Tuition and fees vary according to degree level. *Financial support:* In 2017–18, 104 students received support. Career-related internships or fieldwork, scholarships/grants, and institutional work-study available. Financial award application deadline: 5/1; financial award applicants required to submit FAFSA. *Unit head:* Dr. Heather H. Vacek, Dean of Faculty and Vice President for Academic Affairs, 412-924-1374, Fax: 412-924-1774, E-mail: hvacek@pts.edu. *Application contact:* Tracy Riggle Young, Director of Enrollment and Retention, 412-924-1423, Fax: 412-924-1723, E-mail: triggleyoung@pts.edu.
Website: http://www.pts.edu/

Point Loma Nazarene University, School of Theology and Christian Ministry, San Diego, CA 92106-2899. Offers M Min. *Program availability:* Part-time, online only, nine-week quads with eight weeks of online coursework and a one-week intensive. *Faculty:* 1 full-time (0 women), 1 part-time/adjunct (0 women). *Students:* 15 part-time (6 women); includes 7 minority (all Hispanic/Latino). Average age 40. 4 applicants, 100% accepted, 3 enrolled. In 2017, 2 master's awarded. *Degree requirements:* For master's, thesis optional. *Entrance requirements:* For master's, letters of recommendation, essay, transcripts, interview. Additional exam requirements/recommendations for international students: Recommended—TOEFL. *Application deadline:* For fall admission, 8/30 priority date for domestic students; for spring admission, 4/4 priority date for domestic students; for summer admission, 6/20 priority date for domestic students. Applications are processed on a rolling basis. Application fee: $0. Electronic applications accepted. *Expenses:* Contact institution. *Financial support:* Scholarships/grants available. Financial award application deadline: 6/5; financial award applicants required to submit FAFSA. *Faculty research:* Theology, Christian education, church administration. *Unit head:* Dr. Mark Maddix, Dean, 619-849-2234, E-mail: markmaddix@pointloma.edu. *Application contact:* Joanie Joy, Senior Director of Enrollment Management, 619-329-6785, E-mail: gradinfo@pointloma.edu.
Website: https://www.pointloma.edu/graduate-studies/programs/master-ministry

Pontifical Catholic University of Puerto Rico, College of Arts and Humanities, Department of Theology and Philosophy, Ponce, PR 00717-0777. Offers M Div.

Pontifical College Josephinum, School of Theology, Columbus, OH 43235. Offers M Div, MA. All students are sponsored/selected by their diocese. *Accreditation:* ATS. *Program availability:* Part-time. *Degree requirements:* For master's, 3 foreign languages, comprehensive exam, thesis. *Entrance requirements:* For master's, GRE General Test, 15 credit hours of course work in philosophy, 6 credit hours of course work in scripture. Additional exam requirements/recommendations for international students: Required—TOEFL (minimum score 600 paper-based).

Pontifical John Paul II Institute for Studies on Marriage and Family, Graduate Programs, Washington, DC 20064. Offers biotechnology and ethics (MTS); marriage and family (MTS, STD, STL); theology (PhD).

Pope St. John XXIII National Seminary, Graduate Program, Weston, MA 02493-2618. Offers M Div. *Accreditation:* ATS.

Princeton Theological Seminary, Graduate and Professional Programs, Princeton, NJ 08542-0803. Offers M Div, MA, Th M, D Min, PhD. *Accreditation:* ACIPE; ATS. *Program availability:* Part-time. Terminal master's awarded for partial completion of doctoral program. *Degree requirements:* For doctorate, 2 foreign languages, thesis/dissertation, comprehensive exam (PhD), French and German. *Entrance requirements:* For doctorate, GRE General Test. Additional exam requirements/recommendations for international students: Required—TOEFL. Electronic applications accepted.

Providence College, Department of Theology, Providence, RI 02918. Offers Biblical studies (MA); theology (MA, MTS). *Program availability:* Part-time, evening/weekend. *Degree requirements:* For master's, comprehensive exam, thesis. *Entrance requirements:* For master's, GRE (for MA). Additional exam requirements/recommendations for international students: Required—TOEFL (minimum score 577 paper-based; 90 iBT). *Expenses:* Contact institution.

Providence University College & Theological Seminary, Theological Seminary, Otterburne, MB R0A 1G0, Canada. Offers children's ministry (Certificate); Christian studies (MA, Certificate); counseling (MA); cross-cultural discipleship (Certificate); divinity (M Div); educational studies (MA), including counseling psychology, educational ministries, student development, teaching English to speakers of other languages, training teachers of English to speakers of other languages; global studies (MA); lay counseling (Diploma); ministry (D Min); teaching English to speakers of other languages (Certificate); theological studies (MA); training teacher of English to speakers of other languages (Certificate); youth ministry (Certificate). *Accreditation:* ATS. *Program availability:* Part-time. *Degree requirements:* For master's, variable foreign language requirement, thesis (for some programs); for doctorate, thesis/dissertation. *Entrance requirements:* Additional exam requirements/recommendations for international students: Recommended—TOEFL (minimum score 550 paper-based). *Faculty research:* Studies in Isaiah, theology of sin.

Queen's University at Kingston, Queen's School of Religion, Kingston, ON K7L 3N6, Canada. Offers M Div, MTS, Certificate. *Program availability:* Part-time. *Degree requirements:* For master's, thesis (for some programs). *Entrance requirements:* For master's, minimum undergraduate B average. Additional exam requirements/recommendations for international students: Required—TOEFL (minimum score 580 paper-based). *Faculty research:* Early Christian group formations, pastoral care and spiritual direction, feminist theology, public religion, interpretation of Biblical texts using psychologies of shame and trauma.

Rabbinical Academy Mesivta Rabbi Chaim Berlin, Graduate Program, Brooklyn, NY 11230-4715. Offers Advanced Talmudic Degree, Second Talmudic Degree. *Accreditation:* AARTS. *Degree requirements:* For other advanced degree, 2 foreign languages. *Entrance requirements:* For degree, must be a graduate of a rabbinical school.

Rabbinical College Beth Shraga, Graduate Programs, Monsey, NY 10952-3035. *Accreditation:* AARTS.

Rabbinical College Bobover Yeshiva B'nei Zion, Graduate Programs, Brooklyn, NY 11219. Offers First Talmudic Degree, Rabbi. *Accreditation:* AARTS.

Rabbinical College of Long Island, Graduate Programs, Long Beach, NY 11561-3305. *Accreditation:* AARTS.

Rabbinical Seminary of America, Graduate Programs, Flushing, NY 11367. School offers a master's and first professional degree. *Accreditation:* AARTS.

Reconstructionist Rabbinical College, Graduate Programs, Wyncote, PA 19095-1898. Offers Jewish studies (MAJS); rabbinics (MAHL, DHL); women's studies (Certificate). Certificate offered jointly with Temple University. *Program availability:* Part-time. *Degree requirements:* For master's, one foreign language, thesis (MAJS), completion of rabbinical program (MAHL); for doctorate, one foreign language. *Entrance requirements:* For master's, GRE General Test; placement examinations in Hebrew and Judaism (MAHL); for doctorate, GRE General Test, placement examinations in Hebrew and Judaism. *Faculty research:* Bible, Hebrew Semitic texts, contemporary Judaism.

Reformed Episcopal Seminary, Graduate Program, Blue Bell, PA 19422. Offers M Div. *Accreditation:* ATS. *Entrance requirements:* For master's, personal reference letter, pastor's reference letter, transcript.

Reformed Presbyterian Theological Seminary, Graduate and Professional Programs, Pittsburgh, PA 15208-2594. Offers M Div, MTS, D Min. *Accreditation:* ATS. *Program availability:* Part-time, evening/weekend. Electronic applications accepted. *Faculty research:* Prayer.

Reformed Theological Seminary–Atlanta Campus, Graduate Programs, Marietta, GA 30067. Offers M Div, MABS, MAR, D Min, Certificate.

Reformed Theological Seminary–Charlotte Campus, Graduate and Professional Programs, Charlotte, NC 28226-6318. Offers biblical studies (MA); ministry (D Min); pastoral ministry (M Div); theological studies (MA). *Program availability:* Part-time. *Degree requirements:* For master's, comprehensive exam; for doctorate, thesis/dissertation. *Entrance requirements:* For master's, minimum GPA of 2.6; for doctorate, minimum GPA of 3.0. Additional exam requirements/recommendations for international

students: Required—TOEFL (minimum score 550 paper-based). Electronic applications accepted.

Reformed Theological Seminary–Dallas Campus, Graduate and Professional Programs, Dallas, TX 75207. Offers theological studies (MA); theology (M Div).

Reformed Theological Seminary–Jackson Campus, Graduate and Professional Programs, Jackson, MS 39209-3004. Offers Bible, theology, and missions (Certificate); Biblical exegesis (M Div); biblical studies (MA); Christian education (MA); counseling (M Div); marriage and family therapy (MA); ministry (D Min); missions (M Div, MA, D Min); theological studies (MA). *Accreditation:* AAMFT/COAMFTE (one or more programs are accredited); ATS (one or more programs are accredited). *Degree requirements:* For master's, thesis (for some programs), fieldwork; for doctorate, 2 foreign languages, thesis/dissertation. *Entrance requirements:* For master's, minimum GPA of 2.6; for doctorate, minimum GPA of 3.0. Additional exam requirements/recommendations for international students: Required—TOEFL.

Reformed Theological Seminary–Orlando Campus, Graduate Programs, Oviedo, FL 32765. Offers Bible (Certificate); biblical studies (MA); counseling (MA); missions (Certificate); reformed expository preaching (D Min); reformed theology and ministry (D Min); theological studies (MA); theology (M Div, Certificate). *Program availability:* Part-time, online learning. *Faculty:* 12 full-time (0 women), 11 part-time/adjunct (2 women). *Students:* 340. *Application deadline:* Applications are processed on a rolling basis. Application fee: $75. Electronic applications accepted. *Expenses: Tuition:* Full-time $18,025; part-time $8755 per semester hour. *Required fees:* $160; $160 per semester hour. $80 per semester. *Unit head:* Dr. Scott R. Swain, President, 407-278-4406, Fax: 407-366-9425. *Application contact:* Winston J. Miller, Director of Admissions, 800-752-4382, Fax: 407-366-9425, E-mail: applications.orlando@rts.edu.

Reformed Theological Seminary–Washington D.C., Graduate and Professional Programs, McLean, VA 22102. Offers Bible (M Div); biblical studies (MA); practical theology (M Div); religion (MA); theology (M Div). *Program availability:* Part-time, evening/weekend. *Faculty:* 4 full-time (0 women), 8 part-time/adjunct (2 women). *Students:* 6 full-time (0 women), 124 part-time (17 women); includes 21 minority (5 Black or African American, non-Hispanic/Latino; 14 Asian, non-Hispanic/Latino; 2 Hispanic/Latino). Average age 35. 66 applicants, 95% accepted, 48 enrolled. In 2017, 15 master's awarded. *Degree requirements:* For master's, variable foreign language requirement, comprehensive exam (for some programs), integrative paper. *Entrance requirements:* For master's, minimum undergraduate GPA of 2.6. Additional exam requirements/recommendations for international students: Required—TOEFL (minimum score 550 paper-based), TWE. *Application deadline:* Applications are processed on a rolling basis. Application fee: $75. Electronic applications accepted. *Expenses:* $515 per credit hour. *Financial support:* In 2017–18, 128 students received support. Scholarships/grants and tuition waivers (partial) available. Support available to part-time students. Financial award application deadline: 7/15. *Faculty research:* Theology, Biblical studies, cultural studies. *Unit head:* Dr. John S. Redd, Jr., President, 703-448-3393 Ext. 5107, E-mail: sredd@rts.edu. *Application contact:* Timo Sazo, Director of Admissions, 703-448-3393 Ext. 5104, Fax: 571-297-8010, E-mail: tsazo@rts.edu.
Website: http://www.rts.edu/

Regent College, Program in Theology, Vancouver, BC V6T 2E4, Canada. Offers Christian history and theology (M Div, MATS); Christian studies (MATS, G Dip); Christianity, church and culture (M Div, MATS); scripture (M Div, MATS); theology (Th M). *Accreditation:* ATS (one or more programs are accredited). *Program availability:* Part-time. *Degree requirements:* For master's, one foreign language, comprehensive exam (for some programs), thesis (for some programs). *Entrance requirements:* For master's, minimum GPA of 2.8 (MATS, M Div), 3.3 (Th M); for G Dip, minimum GPA of 2.8. Additional exam requirements/recommendations for international students: Required—TOEFL (minimum score 575 paper-based; 90 iBT), IELTS (minimum score 6.5). Electronic applications accepted. *Expenses:* Contact institution. *Faculty research:* Integration of theology with culture, Biblical studies.

Regent University, Graduate School, School of Divinity, Virginia Beach, VA 23464-9800. Offers Christian spirituality and formation (MA); divinity (M Div), including Biblical studies (M Div, MTS, Th M, PhD), chaplain ministry, Christian theology (M Div, MTS, Th M, PhD), church and ministry (M Div, MA), history of Christianity (M Div, MTS, Th M, PhD), inter-cultural studies (M Div, MA), interdisciplinary studies (M Div, MA, MTS), marketplace ministry (M Div, MA), missional discipleship, practical healing ministry (M Div, MA), worship and media (M Div, MA); leadership and renewal (D Min), including Christian leadership and renewal, clinical pastoral education, community transformation, military ministry, ministry leadership coaching; practical theology (MA), including church and ministry (M Div, MA), cosmogony, inter-cultural studies (M Div, MA), interdisciplinary studies (M Div, MA, MTS), marketplace ministry (M Div, MA), practical healing ministry (M Div, MA), worship and media (M Div, MA); renewal theology (PhD), including Biblical studies (M Div, MTS, Th M, PhD), Christian theology (M Div, MTS, Th M, PhD), history of Christianity (M Div, MTS, Th M, PhD), practical theology; theological studies (MTS), including Biblical studies (M Div, MTS, Th M, PhD), Christian theology (M Div, MTS, Th M, PhD), history of Christianity (M Div, MTS, Th M, PhD), interdisciplinary studies (M Div, MA, MTS); theology (Th M), including Biblical studies (M Div, MTS, Th M, PhD), Christian theology (M Div, MTS, Th M, PhD), history of Christianity (M Div, MTS, Th M, PhD). *Accreditation:* ACIPE; ATS. *Program availability:* Part-time, evening/weekend, 100% online, blended/hybrid learning. *Faculty:* 17 full-time (3 women), 66 part-time/adjunct (9 women). *Students:* 146 full-time (54 women), 917 part-time (404 women); includes 563 minority (470 Black or African American, non-Hispanic/Latino; 1 American Indian or Alaska Native, non-Hispanic/Latino; 17 Asian, non-Hispanic/Latino; 56 Hispanic/Latino; 1 Native Hawaiian or other Pacific Islander, non-Hispanic/Latino; 18 Two or more races, non-Hispanic/Latino), 27 international. Average age 44. 1,321 applicants, 39% accepted, 295 enrolled. In 2017, 146 master's, 25 doctorates awarded. *Degree requirements:* For master's, comprehensive exam, thesis or alternative, internship; for doctorate, thesis/dissertation or alternative. *Entrance requirements:* For master's, minimum undergraduate GPA of 2.75, writing sample, personal goal statement, college transcripts; for doctorate, GRE, minimum graduate GPA of 3.5 (PhD), 3.0 (D Min); clergy recommendations; writing sample; transcripts; resume; interview. Additional exam requirements/recommendations for international students: Required—TOEFL (minimum score 577 paper-based). *Application deadline:* For fall admission, 5/1 priority date for domestic students. Applications are processed on a rolling basis. Application fee: $50. Electronic applications accepted. *Expenses:* $495 per credit (master's); $595 per credit (D Min); $650 per credit (PhD); $300 per semester technology fee. *Financial support:* In 2017–18, 721 students received support. Career-related internships or fieldwork, scholarships/grants, and unspecified assistantships available. Support available to part-time students. *Faculty research:* Greek and Hebrew, theology, spiritual formation, global missions and world Christianity, women in ministry leadership. *Unit head:* Dr. Cornelius Bekker, Dean, 757-352-4401, Fax: 757-352-4597, E-mail: clbekker@regent.edu. *Application contact:* Heidi Cece, Assistant Vice President of Enrollment Management, 800-373-5504, Fax: 757-352-4381, E-mail: admissions@regent.edu.
Website: https://www.regent.edu/school-of-divinity/

Regis College, Graduate and Professional Programs, Toronto, ON M5S 2Z5, Canada. Offers eastern Christian studies (Certificate); Ignatian spirituality (Diploma); ministry (D Min); ministry and spirituality (MAMS); philosophical studies (Diploma); retreat direction (Certificate); sacred theology (STM, STD, STB, STL); spiritual direction (Diploma); theological studies (MTS, Diploma); theology (M Div, MA, Th M, PhD, Th D); M Div/MA. *Accreditation:* ATS (one or more programs are accredited). Terminal master's awarded for partial completion of doctoral program. *Degree requirements:* For master's, 2 foreign languages, thesis; for doctorate, 3 foreign languages, comprehensive exam, thesis/dissertation. *Entrance requirements:* For doctorate, minimum GPA of 3.7. Additional exam requirements/recommendations for international students: Required—TOEFL (minimum score 580 paper-based; 93 iBT), TWE (minimum score 5).

Sacred Heart Major Seminary, School of Theology, Detroit, MI 48206-1799. Offers pastoral studies (MAPS); theology (M Div, MA). *Accreditation:* ACIPE; ATS. *Program availability:* Part-time, evening/weekend. *Degree requirements:* For master's, one foreign language, thesis optional, integrating project. *Entrance requirements:* For master's, GRE, previous course work in philosophy and theology. *Faculty research:* Local church history, patristics, spirituality, religious education.

Sacred Heart Seminary and School of Theology, Graduate and Professional Programs, Hales Corners, WI 53130-0429. Offers priestly formation (Certificate); theology (M Div, MA). *Accreditation:* ACIPE; ATS. *Program availability:* Part-time. *Degree requirements:* For master's, essay or comprehensive exam. *Entrance requirements:* For master's, MAT, 6 hours of course work each in philosophy and theology, letter of recommendation. Additional exam requirements/recommendations for international students: Required—TOEFL.

St. Andrew's College, Graduate Programs in Theology, Saskatoon, SK S7N 0W3, Canada. Offers M Div, MTS, STM, D Min, Diploma. *Accreditation:* ATS. *Entrance requirements:* Additional exam requirements/recommendations for international students: Required—TOEFL.

St. Andrew's College in Winnipeg, Graduate Programs, Winnipeg, MB R3T 2M7, Canada. Offers M Div. *Faculty research:* Church history, doctrine, liturgical theology.

St. Augustine's Seminary of Toronto, Graduate and Professional Programs, Scarborough, ON M1M 1M3, Canada. Offers divinity (M Div); lay ministry (Diploma); religious education (MRE); theological studies (MTS, Diploma). *Accreditation:* ATS. *Program availability:* Part-time, evening/weekend. *Entrance requirements:* Additional exam requirements/recommendations for international students: Required—TOEFL (minimum score 580 paper-based), TWE (minimum score 5).

St. Bernard's School of Theology and Ministry, Graduate and Professional Programs, Rochester, NY 14618. Offers pastoral studies (MA, Certificate); theological studies (MA); theology (M Div). *Accreditation:* ATS (one or more programs are accredited). *Program availability:* Part-time, evening/weekend. *Degree requirements:* For master's, variable foreign language requirement, thesis (for some programs). *Entrance requirements:* For master's, minimum GPA of 2.5.

St. Catherine University, Graduate Programs, Program in Theology, St. Paul, MN 55105. Offers pastoral ministry (Certificate); spiritual direction (Certificate); theology (MA). *Program availability:* Part-time. *Degree requirements:* For master's, comprehensive exam, thesis (for some programs). *Entrance requirements:* For master's, MAT, minimum GPA of 3.0. Additional exam requirements/recommendations for international students: Required—Michigan English Language Assessment Battery or TOEFL (minimum score 600 paper-based; 100 iBT). *Application deadline:* For fall admission, 8/1 priority date for domestic students. Applications are processed on a rolling basis. Application fee: $35. *Expenses:* $678 per credit. *Financial support:* Research assistantships, career-related internships or fieldwork, and institutionally sponsored loans available. Support available to part-time students. Financial award application deadline: 4/1; financial award applicants required to submit FAFSA. *Faculty research:* Feminist scholarship, historical theology, symbols, rites of purification, spirituality. *Unit head:* Dr. William McDonough, Coordinator, 651-690-6072, Fax: 651-690-6024.

Saint Charles Borromeo Seminary, Overbrook, Graduate and Professional Programs, Division of Theology, Wynnewood, PA 19096. Offers M Div, MA. *Degree requirements:* For master's, comprehensive exam, research papers. *Entrance requirements:* For master's, M Div. Additional exam requirements/recommendations for international students: Required—TOEFL.

St. John's Seminary, Graduate and Professional Programs, Camarillo, CA 93012-2598. Offers divinity (M Div); pastoral ministry (MAPM); theology (MA). *Accreditation:* ATS. *Program availability:* Part-time. *Degree requirements:* For master's, comprehensive exam (for some programs), thesis optional, comprehensive integration paper (MAPM). *Entrance requirements:* For master's, GRE General Test, minimum GPA of 3.5 (MA), 2.5 (MAPM). Additional exam requirements/recommendations for international students: Required—TOEFL (minimum score 550 paper-based; 79 iBT). Electronic applications accepted. *Faculty research:* Biblical studies, moral theology, church history, systematic theology, spiritual theology.

Saint John's Seminary, Graduate Programs, Brighton, MA 02135. Offers M Div, MA Th, MAM.

St. John's University, St. John's College of Liberal Arts and Sciences, Department of Theology and Religious Studies, Queens, NY 11439. Offers theology (MA). *Accreditation:* ACIPE. *Program availability:* Part-time, evening/weekend, 100% online, blended/hybrid learning. *Faculty:* 21 full-time (6 women), 39 part-time/adjunct (21 women). *Students:* 8 full-time (4 women), 18 part-time (11 women); includes 8 minority (5 Black or African American, non-Hispanic/Latino; 1 Asian, non-Hispanic/Latino; 2 Hispanic/Latino), 6 international. Average age 40. 25 applicants, 68% accepted, 7 enrolled. In 2017, 8 master's awarded. *Degree requirements:* For master's, comprehensive exam, thesis optional, portfolio. *Entrance requirements:* For master's, letters of recommendation, transcripts, resume, personal statement. Additional exam requirements/recommendations for international students: Required—TOEFL (minimum score 80 iBT), IELTS (minimum score 6.5). *Application deadline:* For fall admission, 5/1 for domestic students; for spring admission, 11/1 for domestic students. Applications are processed on a rolling basis. Application fee: $70. Electronic applications accepted. *Expenses: Tuition:* Full-time $44,280; part-time $1230 per credit. *Required fees:* $340; $340 per credit. Tuition and fees vary according to course load, degree level and program. *Financial support:* Fellowships, research assistantships, teaching assistantships, scholarships/grants, tuition waivers, and unspecified assistantships available. Support available to part-time students. Financial award application deadline: 2/1; financial award applicants required to submit FAFSA. *Faculty research:* Systematic theology, moral theory, Biblical studies, pastoral theology, church history. *Total annual research expenditures:* $248. *Unit head:* Dr. Christopher Vogt, Chair, 718-990-1556, E-mail: vogtc@stjohns.edu. *Application contact:* Robert Medrano, Director of Graduate Admission, 718-990-1601, Fax: 718-990-5686, E-mail: gradhelp@stjohns.edu.
Website: https://www.stjohns.edu/academics/schools-and-colleges/st-johns-college-liberal-arts-and-sciences/theology-and-religious-studies

Saint John's University, Saint John's School of Theology and Seminary, Collegeville, MN 56321. Offers divinity (M Div); liturgical music (MA); liturgical studies (MA); pastoral ministry (MA); theology (MA), including church history, liturgy, monastic studies,

scripture, spirituality, systematics; M Div/MA. *Program availability:* Part-time, online learning. *Degree requirements:* For master's, one foreign language, comprehensive exam (for some programs), thesis (for some programs). *Entrance requirements:* For master's, GRE General Test or MAT. Electronic applications accepted. *Faculty research:* Religious education, biblical literature.

St. Joseph's Seminary, Graduate and Professional Programs, Yonkers, NY 10704. Offers Catholic philosophical studies (MA); divinity (M Div); pastoral studies (MAPS); theology (MA). *Accreditation:* ATS. *Degree requirements:* For master's, one foreign language, thesis. *Entrance requirements:* For master's, 27 credits in philosophy and 9 in theology.

Saint Leo University, Graduate Studies in Theology, Saint Leo, FL 33574-6665. Offers MA, Certificate. *Program availability:* Part-time, evening/weekend, 100% online, blended/hybrid learning. *Faculty:* 10 full-time (0 women), 10 part-time/adjunct (3 women). *Students:* 228 part-time (73 women); includes 35 minority (18 Black or African American, non-Hispanic/Latino; 1 Asian, non-Hispanic/Latino; 13 Hispanic/Latino; 1 Native Hawaiian or other Pacific Islander, non-Hispanic/Latino; 2 Two or more races, non-Hispanic/Latino), 4 international. Average age 50. 139 applicants, 76% accepted, 89 enrolled. In 2017, 52 master's, 2 other advanced degrees awarded. *Entrance requirements:* For master's, official transcripts, letter of recommendation, bachelor's degree from regionally-accredited university with minimum GPA of 3.0. Additional exam requirements/recommendations for international students: Required—TOEFL (minimum score 550 paper-based; 78 iBT). *Application deadline:* For fall admission, 7/1 priority date for domestic and international students; for spring admission, 11/1 priority date for domestic and international students. Applications are processed on a rolling basis. Application fee: $80. Electronic applications accepted. *Expenses:* $480 per credit hour. *Financial support:* In 2017–18, 4 students received support. Scholarships/grants, health care benefits, and tuition remission for Saint Leo employees and their dependents available. Financial award application deadline: 3/1; financial award applicants required to submit FAFSA. *Faculty research:* Patristic theology, Catholic education, Christian anthropology, ecclesiology, Catholic-Jewish relations. *Unit head:* Dr. Randall Woodard, Director, Graduate Theology, 352-588-8239, Fax: 352-588-8404, E-mail: randall.woodard@saintleo.edu. *Application contact:* Mark Russum, Assistant Vice President, Enrollment, 800-707-8846, Fax: 352-588-7873, E-mail: grad.admissions@saintleo.edu.
Website: https://www.saintleo.edu/theology-master-degree

Saint Louis University, Graduate Programs, College of Arts and Sciences, Department of Theological Studies, St. Louis, MO 63103. Offers historical theology (MA, PhD); theology (MA). *Program availability:* Part-time. *Degree requirements:* For master's, comprehensive exam; for doctorate, 4 foreign languages, comprehensive exam, thesis/dissertation, preliminary exams. *Entrance requirements:* For master's, GRE General Test, letters of recommendation, resume; for doctorate, GRE General Test, letters of recommendation, resumé, interview, transcripts, goal statement. Additional exam requirements/recommendations for international students: Required—TOEFL (minimum score 550 paper-based). Electronic applications accepted. *Faculty research:* Biblical and early church studies, medieval and renaissance studies, modern and American Christianity, comparative and interreligious studies, moral and ethical theology.

Saint Mary Seminary and Graduate School of Theology, Graduate and Professional Programs, Wickliffe, OH 44092-2527. Offers M Div, MA, D Min. *Accreditation:* ATS. *Program availability:* Part-time. *Degree requirements:* For master's, comprehensive exam, symposium; for doctorate, thesis/dissertation, final project, symposium. *Entrance requirements:* For master's, GRE General Test, previous course work in religion; for doctorate, M Div or equivalent, 3 years in full-time ministry, interviews, ministry profile report. *Faculty research:* Pastoral ministry, theology of ministry, ecclesiology, American Catholics.

St. Mary's Seminary and University, Ecumenical Institute of Theology, Baltimore, MD 21210-1994. Offers church ministries (MA); theology (MA Th, Certificate). *Accreditation:* ATS. *Program availability:* Part-time, evening/weekend. *Degree requirements:* For master's, thesis or alternative, comprehensive exam or colloquium. *Expenses:* Contact institution. *Faculty research:* Scripture and ethics, theology and literature, early Christianity and Judaism, medical and social ethics.

St. Mary's Seminary and University, School of Theology, Baltimore, MD 21210-1994. Offers M Div, MA Th, STD, STB, STL. *Accreditation:* ATS (one or more programs are accredited). *Program availability:* Part-time. Terminal master's awarded for partial completion of doctoral program. *Degree requirements:* For master's, comprehensive exam; for other advanced degree, one foreign language, thesis. *Entrance requirements:* For master's, Computerized Adaptive Placement Assessment and Support System.

Saint Mary's University, Faculty of Arts, Department of Religious Studies, Halifax, NS B3H 3C3, Canada. Offers theology and religious studies (MA).

St. Mary's University, Graduate Studies, Program in Theology, San Antonio, TX 78228. Offers MA. *Program availability:* Part-time, evening/weekend. *Students:* 6 full-time (3 women), 20 part-time (15 women); includes 16 minority (1 Asian, non-Hispanic/Latino; 14 Hispanic/Latino; 1 Two or more races, non-Hispanic/Latino). Average age 36. 21 applicants, 57% accepted, 8 enrolled. In 2017, 4 master's awarded. *Degree requirements:* For master's, comprehensive exam, thesis optional, 10 clock hours (Graduate Learning Community Experience). *Entrance requirements:* For master's, undergraduate transcripts, writing sample. Additional exam requirements/recommendations for international students: Required—TOEFL (minimum score 550 paper-based; 80 iBT), IELTS (minimum score 6). *Application deadline:* For fall admission, 7/1 for domestic students; for spring admission, 11/15 for domestic students; for summer admission, 4/1 for domestic students. Applications are processed on a rolling basis. Application fee: $0. Electronic applications accepted. *Expenses: Tuition:* Full-time $16,200; part-time $900 per credit hour. *Required fees:* $810; $405 per semester. *Financial support:* Research assistantships, career-related internships or fieldwork, Federal Work-Study, institutionally sponsored loans, scholarships/grants, health care benefits, and unspecified assistantships available. Financial award application deadline: 3/31; financial award applicants required to submit FAFSA. *Faculty research:* Catholic social teaching, recovery of the Jewishness of Jesus and of Christian beginnings, pneumatology of Old and New Testament, ethics of war and nonviolence, inter-religious dialogue. *Unit head:* Dr. Allison Gray, Graduate Theology Program Director, 210-436-3310, E-mail: agray7@stmarytx.edu.
Website: https://www.stmarytx.edu/academics/programs/master-theology/

Saint Meinrad School of Theology, Master of Arts (Catholic Philosophical Studies) Program, Saint Meinrad, IN 47577. Offers MA. *Accreditation:* ATS. *Faculty:* 6 full-time (1 woman), 4 part-time/adjunct (1 woman). *Students:* 25 full-time (0 women), 3 international. Average age 31. In 2017, 8 master's awarded. *Degree requirements:* For master's, thesis. *Entrance requirements:* Additional exam requirements/recommendations for international students: Required—TOEFL (minimum score 550 paper-based; 80 iBT). *Application deadline:* For fall admission, 7/31 for domestic and international students; for winter admission, 11/15 for domestic and international students. Applications are processed on a rolling basis. Electronic applications accepted. *Expenses: Tuition:* Part-time $475 per credit hour. *Required fees:* $34 per course. *Financial support:* Federal Work-Study and scholarships/grants available. Financial award applicants required to submit FAFSA. *Unit head:* Dr. Robert Alvis, Academic Dean, 812-357-6543, Fax: 812-357-6816, E-mail: ralvis@saintmeinrad.edu. *Application contact:* Dr. John Schlachter, Director of Admissions, 812-357-6142, Fax: 812-357-6816, E-mail: jschlachter@saintmeinrad.edu.
Website: http://www.saintmeinrad.edu/priesthood-formation/academic-formation/pre-theologyma/

Saint Meinrad School of Theology, Master of Arts (Theology) Program, Saint Meinrad, IN 47577. Offers MA. *Accreditation:* ATS. *Program availability:* Part-time, evening/weekend. *Faculty:* 20 full-time (2 women), 6 part-time/adjunct (1 woman). *Students:* 2 full-time (both women), 56 part-time (24 women); includes 5 minority (all Hispanic/Latino), 1 international. Average age 49. In 2017, 23 master's awarded. *Degree requirements:* For master's, comprehensive exam, three capstone essays or one research paper. *Entrance requirements:* Additional exam requirements/recommendations for international students: Required—TOEFL (minimum score 550 paper-based; 80 iBT). *Application deadline:* For fall admission, 7/31 for domestic and international students; for winter admission, 11/15 for domestic and international students. Applications are processed on a rolling basis. Application fee: $30. Electronic applications accepted. *Expenses: Tuition:* Part-time $475 per credit hour. *Required fees:* $34 per course. *Financial support:* Federal Work-Study, institutionally sponsored loans, and scholarships/grants available. Support available to part-time students. Financial award application deadline: 7/31; financial award applicants required to submit FAFSA. *Unit head:* Sr. Jeana Visel, OSB, Director of Graduate Theology Programs, 812-357-6721, Fax: 812-357-6816. *Application contact:* Dr. John Schlachter, Director of Admissions, 812-357-6142, Fax: 812-357-6816, E-mail: apply@saintmeinrad.edu.

Saint Meinrad School of Theology, Master of Divinity Program, Saint Meinrad, IN 47577. Offers M Div. *Accreditation:* ATS. *Faculty:* 21 full-time (2 women), 6 part-time/adjunct (1 woman). *Students:* 85 full-time (0 women); includes 4 minority (1 Asian, non-Hispanic/Latino; 3 Hispanic/Latino), 26 international. Average age 30. In 2017, 28 master's awarded. *Entrance requirements:* Additional exam requirements/recommendations for international students: Required—TOEFL (minimum score 550 paper-based; 80 iBT). *Application deadline:* For fall admission, 7/31 for domestic and international students; for winter admission, 11/15 for domestic and international students. Applications are processed on a rolling basis. Application fee: $0. Electronic applications accepted. *Expenses: Tuition:* Part-time $475 per credit hour. *Required fees:* $34 per course. *Financial support:* Federal Work-Study, institutionally sponsored loans, and scholarships/grants available. Support available to part-time students. Financial award application deadline: 7/31; financial award applicants required to submit FAFSA. *Unit head:* Dr. Robert Alvis, Academic Dean, 812-357-6543, Fax: 812-357-6816, E-mail: ralvis@saintmeinrad.edu. *Application contact:* Dr. John Schlachter, Director of Admissions, 812-357-6142, Fax: 812-357-6816, E-mail: apply@saintmeinrad.edu.
Website: http://www.saintmeinrad.edu/priesthood-formation/academic-formation/master-of-divinity/

St. Norbert College, Master of Theological Studies Program, De Pere, WI 54115-2099. Offers MTS. *Program availability:* Part-time-only, evening/weekend, students from New Mexico site video conference in to a live class in DePere. *Faculty:* 8 part-time/adjunct (4 women). *Students:* 34 part-time (20 women); includes 9 minority (8 Hispanic/Latino; 1 Two or more races, non-Hispanic/Latino). Average age 50. 2 applicants, 100% accepted, 2 enrolled. In 2017, 4 master's awarded. *Degree requirements:* For master's, comprehensive exam, thesis. *Entrance requirements:* For master's, minimum of 6 credits of course work in theology/religious studies, BA from accredited institution. *Application deadline:* Applications are processed on a rolling basis. Application fee: $50. Electronic applications accepted. *Expenses: Tuition:* Part-time $675 per credit. Tuition and fees vary according to program. *Financial support:* In 2017–18, 16 students received support. Scholarships/grants available. Support available to part-time students. *Faculty research:* Practical theology, Karl Rahner, women in the Bible and Christian ethics. *Unit head:* Dr. Howard Ebert, Director, 920-403-3956, E-mail: howard.ebert@snc.edu. *Application contact:* Dinah Grassel, Program Coordinator, 920-403-3957, E-mail: dinah.grassel@snc.edu.
Website: http://www.snc.edu/mts/

St. Patrick's Seminary & University, School of Theology, Menlo Park, CA 94025-3596. Offers M Div, MA, STB. STB offered jointly with St. Mary's Seminary and University. *Accreditation:* ATS (one or more programs are accredited). *Program availability:* Part-time. *Degree requirements:* For master's, comprehensive exam, thesis or alternative. *Entrance requirements:* For master's, GRE General Test, minimum GPA of 3.0, interview. Additional exam requirements/recommendations for international students: Required—TOEFL (minimum score 550 paper-based; 80 iBT), TWE. *Faculty research:* Systematic theology, sacred scripture, moral theology, liturgy.

Saint Paul School of Theology, Graduate and Professional Programs, Overland Park, KS 66211. Offers M Div, MA, MTS, D Min. *Accreditation:* ACIPE; ATS. *Program availability:* Part-time. *Degree requirements:* For doctorate, thesis/dissertation. *Entrance requirements:* For master's, minimum GPA of 2.75; for doctorate, minimum GPA of 3.0. Additional exam requirements/recommendations for international students: Required—TOEFL. *Faculty research:* Religion and aging; leadership development; feminist, African-American, and liberation theology; rural ministry; worship and the arts.

Saint Paul University, Faculty of Canon Law, Ottawa, ON K1S 1C4, Canada. Offers canon law (MCL, JCD, PhD, Graduate Certificate, JCL); canonical practice (Graduate Certificate); ecclesiastical administration (Graduate Certificate). *Program availability:* Part-time. *Degree requirements:* For master's, one foreign language; for doctorate, one foreign language, comprehensive exam, thesis/dissertation; for other advanced degree, one foreign language, comprehensive exam and seminar paper (JCL). *Entrance requirements:* For master's, appropriate bachelor's degree, 18 credits in theology; for doctorate, JCL or MCL; for other advanced degree, B Th or equivalent (JCL), appropriate bachelor's degree, 18 credits in theology. *Faculty research:* Questions related to Church law.

Saint Paul University, Faculty of Human Sciences, Program in Counseling and Spirituality, Ottawa, ON K1S 1C4, Canada. Offers individual or marital/couple counseling (MA); spiritual care (MA). *Program availability:* Part-time. *Degree requirements:* For master's, research project or thesis. *Entrance requirements:* For master's, honors BA in human sciences, minimum B average, 12 theology credits.

Saint Paul University, Faculty of Theology, Ottawa, ON K1S 1C4, Canada. Offers MA Th, MP Th, MRE, D Min, D Th, PhD, L Th. *Accreditation:* ATS. *Degree requirements:* For master's and L Th, one foreign language; for doctorate, one foreign language, comprehensive exam, thesis/dissertation. *Entrance requirements:* For master's, B Th; for doctorate, MA Th, L Th, MP Th, M Div. *Faculty research:* Biblical studies, systematic and historical theology, ethics, spirituality, Eastern Christian studies, applied theology.

St. Peter's Seminary, Department of Theology, London, ON N6A 3Y1, Canada. Offers M Div, MTS. *Accreditation:* ATS.

Saints Cyril and Methodius Seminary, Graduate and Professional Programs, Orchard Lake, MI 48324. Offers pastoral ministry (MAPM); religious education (MARE); theology (M Div, MA). *Program availability:* Part-time.

St. Stephen's College, Programs in Theology, Edmonton, AB T6G 2J6, Canada. Offers ministry (D Min); pastoral counseling (MA); social transformation ministry (MA); spirituality and liturgy (MA); theological studies (MTS); theology (M Th). *Program availability:* Part-time, evening/weekend, online learning. Terminal master's awarded for partial completion of doctoral program. *Degree requirements:* For master's, thesis; for doctorate, thesis/dissertation. *Entrance requirements:* Additional exam requirements/recommendations for international students: Required—TOEFL. Electronic applications accepted. *Faculty research:* Methodology for theological education, practice and supervision for ministry.

St. Thomas University, School of Theology and Ministry, Institute for Pastoral Ministries, Miami Gardens, FL 33054-6459. Offers pastoral ministries (MA, Certificate); practical theology (PhD). *Program availability:* Part-time, evening/weekend. *Degree requirements:* For master's, comprehensive exam; for doctorate, comprehensive exam, thesis/dissertation. *Entrance requirements:* For master's, interview, minimum GPA of 3.0 or GRE; for doctorate, GRE, MA in theology. Additional exam requirements/recommendations for international students: Required—TOEFL (minimum score 550 paper-based; 79 iBT). Electronic applications accepted.

St. Tikhon's Orthodox Theological Seminary, Divinity Program, South Canaan, PA 18459. Offers M Div. *Accreditation:* ATS. *Program availability:* Part-time. *Degree requirements:* For master's, thesis optional. *Entrance requirements:* For master's, reference letters, official transcripts. Additional exam requirements/recommendations for international students: Required—TOEFL (minimum score 560 paper-based; 87 iBT), IELTS (minimum score 5.5). *Expenses:* Contact institution. *Faculty research:* Church history, patristics, scripture, spirituality.

St. Vincent de Paul Regional Seminary, Graduate and Professional Programs, Boynton Beach, FL 33436-4899. Offers theology (M Div, MA Th). *Accreditation:* ATS. *Program availability:* Part-time. *Degree requirements:* For master's, comprehensive exam (for some programs), thesis optional. *Entrance requirements:* For master's, GRE General Test, MAT. Additional exam requirements/recommendations for international students: Required—TOEFL.

Saint Vincent Seminary, School of Theology, Latrobe, PA 15650-2690. Offers Catholic philosophical studies (MA); ecclesial ministry (MA); ministry (M Div); monastic studies (MA); sacred scripture (MA); systematic theology (MA). Saint Vincent College provides philosophy courses for the MA in Catholic Philosophical Studies degree program only. *Accreditation:* ATS. *Program availability:* Part-time, evening/weekend. *Faculty:* 8 full-time (2 women), 12 part-time/adjunct (1 woman). *Students:* 38 full-time (0 women), 9 part-time (0 women); includes 2 minority (both Asian, non-Hispanic/Latino), 12 international. Average age 34. 11 applicants, 100% accepted, 10 enrolled. In 2017, 12 master's awarded. *Degree requirements:* For master's, one foreign language, comprehensive exam, thesis optional, public presentation. *Entrance requirements:* For master's, minimum GPA of 2.5. Additional exam requirements/recommendations for international students: Required—TOEFL (minimum score 550 paper-based; 79 iBT). *Application deadline:* For fall admission, 8/15 for domestic and international students. Applications are processed on a rolling basis. Application fee: $34. *Expenses:* $27,636 per year full-time, $918 per credit part-time. *Financial support:* In 2017–18, 47 students received support. Scholarships/grants available. Support available to part-time students. Financial award application deadline: 8/15. *Faculty research:* Church history, preaching, psychology of religion, Biblical studies, moral theology. *Unit head:* Very Rev. Edward M. Mazich, OSB, President/Rector, 724-805-2845, Fax: 724-532-5052, E-mail: edward.mazich@stvincent.edu. *Application contact:* Rev. Patrick T. Cronauer, OSB, Academic Dean, 724-805-2324, Fax: 724-805-2880, E-mail: patrick.cronauer@stvincent.edu.
Website: http://www.saintvincentseminary.edu

St. Vladimir's Orthodox Theological Seminary, Graduate School of Theology, Crestwood, NY 10707-1699. Offers general theological studies (MA); theology (M Div, M Th, D Min). MA and M Div offered jointly with St. Nersess Armenian Seminary. *Accreditation:* ATS. *Program availability:* Part-time. *Faculty:* 8 full-time (1 woman), 21 part-time/adjunct (2 women). *Students:* 71 full-time (6 women), 4 part-time (0 women); includes 8 minority (2 Black or African American, non-Hispanic/Latino; 6 Asian, non-Hispanic/Latino), 15 international. Average age 29. 41 applicants, 95% accepted, 37 enrolled. In 2017, 26 master's awarded. *Degree requirements:* For master's, one foreign language, thesis (for some programs), fieldwork; for doctorate, thesis/dissertation, fieldwork. *Entrance requirements:* For doctorate, M Div, minimum GPA of 3.0. Additional exam requirements/recommendations for international students: Required—TOEFL (minimum score 96 iBT). *Application deadline:* For fall admission, 5/1 priority date for domestic and international students. Applications are processed on a rolling basis. Application fee: $75. Electronic applications accepted. *Expenses:* Tuition: Full-time $12,000; part-time $500 per credit. *Required fees:* $150; $150 per semester. Tuition and fees vary according to course load and reciprocity agreements. *Financial support:* In 2017–18, 75 students received support. Fellowships, research assistantships, teaching assistantships, and scholarships/grants available. Financial award application deadline: 4/1; financial award applicants required to submit FAFSA. *Faculty research:* Patristics, New Testament, homiletics, hospital ministry. *Unit head:* Rev. Dr. Chad Hatfield, President, 914-961-8313 Ext. 323, Fax: 914-961-4507, E-mail: hatfield@svots.edu. *Application contact:* Gabrielle Russin, Student Affairs Administrator, 914-961-8313 Ext. 348, Fax: 914-961-4507, E-mail: grussin@svots.edu.

Samford University, Beeson School of Divinity, Birmingham, AL 35229. Offers M Div, MATS, D Min, JD/M Div, JD/MATS, M Div/M Ed, M Div/MBA, M Div/MM, M Div/MSW, MATS/MSW. *Program availability:* Part-time. *Faculty:* 13 full-time (1 woman), 2 part-time/adjunct (0 women). *Students:* 146 full-time (30 women), 8 part-time (4 women); includes 24 minority (22 Black or African American, non-Hispanic/Latino; 1 Asian, non-Hispanic/Latino; 1 Two or more races, non-Hispanic/Latino), 7 international. Average age 30. 61 applicants, 93% accepted, 31 enrolled. In 2017, 40 master's, 10 doctorates awarded. *Degree requirements:* For master's, 2 foreign languages, thesis optional; for doctorate, thesis/dissertation. *Entrance requirements:* For master's, minimum GPA of 2.5; for doctorate, minimum GPA of 3.0. Additional exam requirements/recommendations for international students: Required—TOEFL (minimum score 550 paper-based; 80 iBT). *Application deadline:* For fall admission, 2/15 for domestic and international students; for spring admission, 10/1 for domestic and international students. Application fee: $35. Electronic applications accepted. *Expenses:* $14,374 per year. *Financial support:* In 2017–18, 135 students received support, including 6 teaching assistantships (averaging $1,200 per year); Federal Work-Study, scholarships/grants, and tuition waivers (full and partial) also available. Financial award application deadline: 2/15; financial award applicants required to submit FAFSA. *Faculty research:* Pastoral epistles, Jewish Christian theology, The Reformation and preaching, Romans, theology of Deuteronomy. *Total annual research expenditures:* $45,000. *Unit head:* Dr. Timothy George, Dean, 205-726-2632, E-mail: tfgeorge@samford.edu. *Application contact:* Sherri S. Brown, Director of Admission, 205-726-2066, E-mail: sbrown5@samford.edu.
Website: http://www.beesondivinity.com/

San Francisco Theological Seminary, Graduate and Professional Programs, San Anselmo, CA 94960. Offers M Div, MA, MATS, D Min, PhD, Th D, M Div/MA. MA, Th D, PhD, M Div/MA offered jointly with Graduate Theological Union. *Accreditation:* ACIPE;

ATS (one or more programs are accredited). *Program availability:* Part-time. *Degree requirements:* For master's, one foreign language, thesis (for some programs); for doctorate, thesis/dissertation. *Entrance requirements:* For master's, minimum GPA of 3.0; for doctorate, M Div. Additional exam requirements/recommendations for international students: Required—TOEFL.

Santa Clara University, Jesuit School of Theology, Berkeley, CA 94709. Offers Biblical studies (MTS); Christian spirituality (MTS); church history (MTS); cultural and historical studies of Catholicism (MTS); ethics and social theory/religion and society (MTS); history of art and religion (MTS); liturgical studies (MTS); systematic and philosophical theology (MTS); theology (M Div, Th M, STD, STB, STL); M Div/MA. MA programs offered jointly with Graduate Theological Union. *Program availability:* Part-time, evening/weekend, 100% online. *Faculty:* 19 full-time (5 women), 9 part-time/adjunct (5 women). *Students:* 120 full-time (26 women), 15 part-time (6 women); includes 78 minority (24 Black or African American, non-Hispanic/Latino; 2 American Indian or Alaska Native, non-Hispanic/Latino; 25 Asian, non-Hispanic/Latino; 20 Hispanic/Latino; 3 Native Hawaiian or other Pacific Islander, non-Hispanic/Latino; 4 Two or more races, non-Hispanic/Latino). Average age 38. 99 applicants, 96% accepted, 54 enrolled. In 2017, 52 master's, 9 doctorates awarded. *Entrance requirements:* For master's, GRE (except Th M), 2 letters of recommendation, resume or curriculum vitae, official transcripts, statement of purpose; for doctorate, master's degree or equivalent, resume or curriculum vitae, statement of purpose, official transcripts, 2 letters of recommendation, research paper. Additional exam requirements/recommendations for international students: Required—TOEFL (minimum score 90 iBT). *Application deadline:* For fall admission, 3/1 priority date for domestic students; for spring admission, 10/1 priority date for domestic students. Applications are processed on a rolling basis. Application fee: $50 ($0 for international students). Electronic applications accepted. *Expenses:* Contact institution. *Financial support:* Scholarships/grants and unspecified assistantships available. Support available to part-time students. Financial award application deadline: 3/1; financial award applicants required to submit FAFSA. *Faculty research:* Religion and culture, interreligious dialogue, social ethics and restorative justice, Ignatian spirituality. *Unit head:* Rev. Kevin O'Brien, Dean, 510-549-5040, E-mail: kfobrien@scu.edu. *Application contact:* Drew Roberts, Assistant Dean of Enrollment Management and Marketing, 510-549-5016, E-mail: ajroberts@scu.edu.
Website: http://www.scu.edu/jst/

Seattle Pacific University, Master of Arts in Theology Program, Seattle, WA 98119-1997. Offers Asian American ministry (MA); business and applied theology (MA); Christian leadership (MA); Christian scripture (MA); Christian studies (Graduate Certificate); reconciliation and intercultural studies (MA); theology (MA). *Students:* 25 full-time (13 women), 42 part-time (20 women); includes 11 minority (4 Black or African American, non-Hispanic/Latino; 4 Asian, non-Hispanic/Latino; 3 Two or more races, non-Hispanic/Latino), 2 international. Average age 34. 19 applicants, 79% accepted, 11 enrolled. In 2017, 4 master's awarded. *Degree requirements:* For master's, internship or thesis. *Entrance requirements:* For master's, two letters of recommendation; personal statement; bachelor's degree from regionally-accredited college or university or its equivalent; official copy of transcripts from college or university that granted the bachelor's degree and any institution attended since that time; minimum GPA of 3.0. Additional exam requirements/recommendations for international students: Required—TOEFL (minimum score 600 paper-based; 100 iBT). *Application deadline:* For fall admission, 7/31 for domestic students; 6/15 for international students; for winter admission, 11/15 for domestic students; for spring admission, 2/15 for domestic students; for summer admission, 5/1 for domestic students. Applications are processed on a rolling basis. Application fee: $50. Electronic applications accepted. *Financial support:* Application deadline: 4/1; applicants required to submit FAFSA. *Unit head:* Dr. Doug Strong, Dean, 206-281-2473, E-mail: dstrong@spu.edu.
Website: http://spu.edu/academics/school-of-theology/seattle-pacific-seminary/seminary-degrees/ma-theology

Seattle Pacific University, Master of Divinity Program, Seattle, WA 98119-1997. Offers M Div. *Students:* 2 full-time (1 woman), 3 part-time (0 women). Average age 32. 24 applicants, 75% accepted, 13 enrolled. In 2017, 2 master's awarded. *Entrance requirements:* For master's, two letters of recommendation; personal statement; BA; official transcript; minimum GPA of 3.0. Additional exam requirements/recommendations for international students: Required—TOEFL (minimum score 600 paper-based; 100 iBT). *Application deadline:* For fall admission, 7/31 for domestic students; for winter admission, 11/15 for domestic students; for spring admission, 2/15 for domestic students; for summer admission, 5/1 for domestic students. Application fee: $50. *Financial support:* Scholarships/grants available. Financial award applicants required to submit FAFSA. *Unit head:* Dr. Doug Strong, Dean, 206-281-2473, E-mail: dstrong@spu.edu.
Website: http://spu.edu/academics/seattle-pacific-seminary/programs/ma-divinity

The Seattle School of Theology and Psychology, Graduate Programs, Seattle, WA 98121. Offers Christian studies (MA); counseling psychology (MA); divinity (M Div). *Program availability:* Part-time. *Entrance requirements:* For master's, MAT.

Seattle University, School of Theology and Ministry, Program in Divinity, Seattle, WA 98122-1090. Offers M Div, D Min. *Accreditation:* ATS. *Program availability:* Part-time, evening/weekend. *Faculty:* 15 full-time (7 women), 18 part-time/adjunct (11 women). *Students:* 6 full-time (4 women), 43 part-time (30 women); includes 17 minority (8 Black or African American, non-Hispanic/Latino; 1 American Indian or Alaska Native, non-Hispanic/Latino; 3 Asian, non-Hispanic/Latino; 4 Hispanic/Latino; 1 Native Hawaiian or other Pacific Islander, non-Hispanic/Latino), 2 international. Average age 46. 10 applicants, 50% accepted, 4 enrolled. In 2017, 11 master's, 3 doctorates awarded. *Entrance requirements:* For master's, minimum GPA of 2.75 (3.0 for international students); two years of experience in some form of education, ministry, or service as a profession or volunteer; recommendations; interview with admissions committee. *Application deadline:* For fall admission, 7/1 priority date for domestic students. *Expenses:* Tuition: Full-time $12,960. *Required fees:* $570. Tuition and fees vary according to program. *Financial support:* In 2017–18, 31 students received support. Career-related internships or fieldwork and Federal Work-Study available. Support available to part-time students. Financial award applicants required to submit FAFSA. *Unit head:* Dr. Mark Markuly, Dean, 206-296-5330, Fax: 206-296-5329, E-mail: markulym@seattleu.edu. *Application contact:* Catherine Kehoe Fallon, Admissions Coordinator, 206-296-5333, Fax: 206-296-5329, E-mail: fallon@seattleu.edu.
Website: https://www.seattleu.edu/stm/degrees/mdiv/

Seattle University, School of Theology and Ministry, Program in Transforming Spirituality, Seattle, WA 98122-1090. Offers MATS, Certificate. *Accreditation:* ATS. *Program availability:* Part-time, evening/weekend. *Faculty:* 15 full-time (7 women), 18 part-time/adjunct (11 women). *Students:* 3 full-time (all women), 10 part-time (7 women); includes 2 minority (1 American Indian or Alaska Native, non-Hispanic/Latino; 1 Hispanic/Latino), 1 international. Average age 48. 7 applicants, 71% accepted, 4 enrolled. In 2017, 3 master's, 1 Certificate awarded. *Degree requirements:* For master's, project. *Entrance requirements:* For master's, minimum GPA of 2.75 (3.0 for international students); two years of experience in some form of education, ministry, or service as a profession or volunteer; recommendations; interview with admissions committee. *Application deadline:* For fall admission, 7/1 for domestic students.

Application fee: $55. *Expenses: Tuition:* Full-time $12,960. *Required fees:* $570. Tuition and fees vary according to program. *Financial support:* In 2017–18, 8 students received support. Career-related internships or fieldwork and Federal Work-Study available. Support available to part-time students. Financial award application deadline: 4/1; financial award applicants required to submit FAFSA. *Unit head:* Dr. Mark Markuly, Director, 206-296-5330, Fax: 206-296-5329, E-mail: markulym@seattleu.edu. *Application contact:* Jean Adler Stean, Assistant Director of Admissions and Student Services, 206-296-5333, Fax: 206-296-5329, E-mail: steanj@seattleu.edu.
Website: http://www.seattleu.edu/stm/degrees/mats/

Seminary of the Southwest, Graduate and Professional Programs, Austin, TX 78768-2247. Offers Anglican studies (Advanced Diploma); chaplaincy and pastoral care (MA); clinical mental health counseling (MA); Latino/Hispanic studies (M Div); ministry (M Div); religion (MAR); spiritual formation (MA). *Accreditation:* ACIPE; ATS (one or more programs are accredited). *Program availability:* Part-time, evening/weekend. *Faculty:* 10 full-time (5 women), 12 part-time/adjunct (5 women). *Students:* 60 full-time (31 women), 56 part-time (42 women); includes 22 minority (10 Black or African American, non-Hispanic/Latino; 1 American Indian or Alaska Native, non-Hispanic/Latino; 2 Asian, non-Hispanic/Latino; 6 Hispanic/Latino; 3 Two or more races, non-Hispanic/Latino). Average age 38. 49 applicants, 98% accepted, 31 enrolled. In 2017, 27 master's, 3 other advanced degrees awarded. *Degree requirements:* For master's, comprehensive exam (for some programs), thesis (for some programs). *Entrance requirements:* For master's, GRE, MAT, interview; for Advanced Diploma, interview. Additional exam requirements/recommendations for international students: Recommended—TOEFL. *Application deadline:* For fall admission, 6/30 priority date for domestic and international students; for spring admission, 12/1 for domestic and international students. Applications are processed on a rolling basis. Application fee: $50. Electronic applications accepted. *Expenses:* Contact institution. *Financial support:* In 2017–18, 92 students received support. Career-related internships or fieldwork and scholarships/grants available. Support available to part-time students. Financial award application deadline: 6/15; financial award applicants required to submit FAFSA. *Unit head:* Rev. Dr. Cynthia Briggs Kittredge, Dean and President, 512-472-4133 Ext. 332, Fax: 512-472-3098, E-mail: cynthia.kittredge@ssw.edu. *Application contact:* Hope Benko, Director of Enrollment Management, 512-472-4133 Ext. 375, Fax: 512-472-3098, E-mail: hope.benko@ssw.edu.

Seton Hall University, Immaculate Conception Seminary School of Theology, South Orange, NJ 07079-2697. Offers Christian spirituality (Certificate); great spiritual books (Certificate); pastoral ministry (M Div, MA, Certificate); scripture studies (Certificate); Seminary's Theological Education for Parish Services (STEPS) (Certificate); theology (MA). *Program availability:* Part-time, evening/weekend. *Degree requirements:* For master's, comprehensive exam (for some programs), thesis (for some programs), final project (for some programs); 1 foreign language (for MA in theology research option). *Entrance requirements:* For master's, GRE General Test or MAT. Additional exam requirements/recommendations for international students: Required—TOEFL (minimum score 600 paper-based; 100 iBT). Electronic applications accepted. *Expenses:* Contact institution. *Faculty research:* Pauline literature, history of Biblical interpretation and theological exegesis, spirituality of St. Edith Stein, Thomism, history of Catholicism in America.

Shaw University, Divinity School, Raleigh, NC 27601-2399. Offers M Div, MACE. *Accreditation:* ATS. *Program availability:* Part-time, evening/weekend. *Degree requirements:* For master's, thesis. *Entrance requirements:* For master's, official undergraduate transcripts, letters of reference, essay, interview. Electronic applications accepted. *Faculty research:* Health disparities and the African-American Church, Christian community development, teaching for social change, technology and theological education, best practices in historically black theological schools.

Shepherds Theological Seminary, Graduate Programs, Cary, NC 27518. Offers Biblical literature and languages (MA); church ministry (MA); ministry (MTS); New Testament (M Div); Old Testament (M Div); theology (M Div). *Accreditation:* ATS. *Degree requirements:* For master's, thesis.

Shiloh University, Graduate Programs, Kalona, IA 52247. Offers Christian ministries (M Div); leadership of church and spiritual formation (D Min); theological studies (MA). *Program availability:* Part-time, evening/weekend, online only, 100% online. *Faculty:* 5 full-time (1 woman), 11 part-time/adjunct (2 women). *Students:* 10 full-time (3 women), 24 part-time (12 women); includes 10 minority (9 Black or African American, non-Hispanic/Latino; 1 Asian, non-Hispanic/Latino). Average age 51. 11 applicants, 91% accepted, 8 enrolled. In 2017, 3 master's awarded. *Degree requirements:* For master's, variable foreign language requirement, thesis optional; for doctorate, comprehensive exam, thesis/dissertation. *Entrance requirements:* For master's, bachelor's degree or educational equivalent from accredited school with minimum GPA of 2.5 on undergraduate work; for doctorate, M Div or equivalent with minimum GPA of 2.5 on graduate work; three years of ministry experience. Additional exam requirements/recommendations for international students: Recommended—TOEFL (minimum score 540 paper-based; 76 iBT), IELTS (minimum score 6.5). *Application deadline:* For fall admission, 6/18 priority date for domestic and international students; for spring admission, 10/22 priority date for domestic and international students; for summer admission, 2/15 priority date for domestic and international students. Applications are processed on a rolling basis. Application fee: $0. Electronic applications accepted. *Expenses:* $175 per credit hour, estimated $100 per course for books and supplies. *Financial support:* In 2017–18, 2 students received support. Scholarships/grants available. Financial award application deadline: 8/1; financial award applicants required to submit FAFSA. *Faculty research:* New Testament theology, Pauline literature, relational theology, Jewish foundations of Christianity, Judeo-Christian relations. *Unit head:* Dr. Ana Wood, Dean of Graduate Studies, 319-656-2447, Fax: 319-656-2448, E-mail: chiqui.wood@shilohuniversity.edu. *Application contact:* Katie Nisly, Admissions Coordinator, 319-656-2447, Fax: 319-656-2448, E-mail: admissions@shilohuniversity.edu.
Website: http://www.shilohuniversity.edu/academics/

Sh'or Yoshuv Rabbinical College, Graduate Programs, Far Rockaway, NY 11691-4002. *Accreditation:* AARTS.

Sioux Falls Seminary, Graduate and Professional Programs, Master of Divinity Program, Sioux Falls, SD 57105-1599. Offers marriage and family therapy (M Div); pastoral care and counseling (M Div). Program also offered in Omaha, NE. *Accreditation:* ACIPE. *Program availability:* Part-time, online learning.

Sioux Falls Seminary, Graduate and Professional Programs, Program in Bible and Theology, Sioux Falls, SD 57105-1599. Offers MA. *Accreditation:* ACIPE; ATS. *Program availability:* Part-time, online learning. *Degree requirements:* For master's, 2 foreign languages, thesis or alternative. *Entrance requirements:* For master's, minimum GPA of 2.5.

Sioux Falls Seminary, Graduate and Professional Programs, Program in Ministry, Sioux Falls, SD 57105-1599. Offers D Min. *Accreditation:* ACIPE. *Program availability:* Part-time. *Degree requirements:* For doctorate, thesis/dissertation. *Entrance requirements:* For doctorate, M Div, 3 years of ministry.

Sioux Falls Seminary, Graduate and Professional Programs, Program in Theological Studies, Sioux Falls, SD 57105-1599. Offers Certificate.

Southeastern Baptist Theological Seminary, Graduate and Professional Programs, Wake Forest, NC 27587. Offers advanced biblical studies (M Div); Christian education (M Div, MACE); Christian ethics (PhD); Christian ministry (M Div); Christian planting (M Div); church music (MACM); counseling (MACO); evangelism (PhD); language (M Div); ministry (D Min); New Testament (PhD); Old Testament (PhD); philosophy (PhD); theology (Th M, PhD); women's studies (M Div). *Accreditation:* ACIPE; ATS (one or more programs are accredited). *Degree requirements:* For master's, thesis (for some programs), oral exam; for doctorate, thesis/dissertation, fieldwork. *Entrance requirements:* For master's, Cooperative English Test, minimum GPA of 2.0, M Div or equivalent (Th M); for doctorate, GRE General Test or MAT, Cooperative English Test, M Div or equivalent, 3 years of professional experience.

Southeastern University, Barnett College of Ministry and Theology, Lakeland, FL 33801-6099. Offers family ministry (MA); ministerial leadership (MA, D Min); theological studies (MA); theology (M Div). *Program availability:* Evening/weekend, online learning. *Faculty:* 22 full-time (5 women), 10 part-time/adjunct (9 women). *Students:* 81 full-time (28 women), 131 part-time (49 women); includes 63 minority (31 Black or African American, non-Hispanic/Latino; 7 Asian, non-Hispanic/Latino; 24 Hispanic/Latino; 1 Two or more races, non-Hispanic/Latino), 4 international. Average age 38. *Degree requirements:* For master's, thesis/project. Application fee: $50. Electronic applications accepted. *Unit head:* Dean, 863-667-5000.
Website: http://www.seu.edu/ministry/

Southern Adventist University, School of Religion, Collegedale, TN 37315-0370. Offers Biblical and theological studies (MA); church leadership and management (M Min); church ministry and homiletics (M Min); evangelism and world mission (M Min); religious studies (MA). *Program availability:* Part-time. *Degree requirements:* For master's, comprehensive exam, thesis (for some programs). *Entrance requirements:* For master's, GRE. Additional exam requirements/recommendations for international students: Required—TOEFL (minimum score 600 paper-based). *Application deadline:* For spring admission, 5/1 priority date for domestic students, 4/30 for international students. Applications are processed on a rolling basis. Application fee: $40. *Expenses: Tuition:* Full-time $11,430; part-time $635 per credit hour. Tuition and fees vary according to degree level and program. *Financial support:* Tuition waivers (full) available. Support available to part-time students. Financial award application deadline: 4/1; financial award applicants required to submit FAFSA. *Faculty research:* Biblical archaeology. *Unit head:* Dr. Greg A. King, Dean, 423-236-2975, Fax: 423-236-1976, E-mail: gking@southern.edu. *Application contact:* Susan L. Brown, Administrative Assistant, 423-236-2033, Fax: 423-236-1977, E-mail: sbrown@southern.edu.
Website: https://www.southern.edu/academics/academic-sites/religion/

The Southern Baptist Theological Seminary, Billy Graham School of Missions, Evangelism and Ministry, Louisville, KY 40280-0004. Offers ministry (D Min); missiology (MA, D Miss); missions and evangelism (M Div, Th M, PhD); theological studies (MA). *Accreditation:* ATS. *Program availability:* Part-time, evening/weekend, online learning. *Degree requirements:* For master's, 2 foreign languages; for doctorate, 4 foreign languages, thesis/dissertation. *Entrance requirements:* For doctorate, GRE General Test, MAT, M Div. Additional exam requirements/recommendations for international students: Required—TOEFL, TWE. *Faculty research:* Assimilation of church congregants, effective methodologies of evangelism, expectations of church members, spiritual warfare literature, formative church discipline.

The Southern Baptist Theological Seminary, School of Theology, Louisville, KY 40280-0004. Offers applied theology (D Min); biblical and theological studies (M Div); biblical counseling (M Div, MA, D Min); biblical spirituality (D Min); Christian ministry (M Div); expository preaching (D Min); pastoral studies (M Div); theological studies (MA); theology (Th M, PhD); worldview and apologetics (M Div). *Program availability:* Part-time, evening/weekend, online learning. *Degree requirements:* For master's, 2 foreign languages, thesis; for doctorate, 4 foreign languages, thesis/dissertation. *Entrance requirements:* For master's, GRE General Test, MAT, M Div; for doctorate, GRE General Test, MAT, interview, M Div, field essay. Additional exam requirements/recommendations for international students: Required—TOEFL, TWE. *Faculty research:* Biblical studies, contemporary theology, church history, pastoral care, ministry/missions studies.

Southern California Seminary, Graduate and Professional Programs, El Cajon, CA 92019. Offers Biblical studies (MABS); counseling psychology (MACP); marriage and family therapy (MAMFT); psychology (Psy D); religious studies (MRS); theology (M Div). *Program availability:* Part-time, evening/weekend, online learning. *Degree requirements:* For master's, thesis (for some programs); for doctorate, thesis/dissertation. *Entrance requirements:* For doctorate, master's degree in psychology. Additional exam requirements/recommendations for international students: Required—TOEFL (minimum score 550 paper-based). Electronic applications accepted.

Southern Evangelical Seminary, Graduate Programs, Matthews, NC 28105. Offers apologetics (MA, D Min, Certificate); Christian education (MA); church ministry (MA, Certificate); divinity (Certificate), including apologetics (M Div, Certificate); Islamic studies (MA, Certificate); Jewish studies (MA); philosophy (MA); philosophy of religion (PhD); religion (MA); theology (M Div), including apologetics (M Div, Certificate), Biblical studies; youth ministry (MA). *Program availability:* Part-time, evening/weekend, online learning. *Degree requirements:* For master's, thesis (for some programs); for doctorate, 2 foreign languages, comprehensive exam (for some programs), thesis/dissertation. *Entrance requirements:* Additional exam requirements/recommendations for international students: Required—TOEFL (minimum score 600 paper-based).

Southern Methodist University, Dedman College of Humanities and Sciences, Graduate Program in Religious Studies, Dallas, TX 75275-0133. Offers Hebrew Bible/Old Testament (PhD); history of the Christian tradition (PhD); New Testament (PhD); religion and culture (PhD); religious ethics (PhD); religious studies (MA); systematics theology (PhD). Terminal master's awarded for partial completion of doctoral program. *Degree requirements:* For master's, one foreign language, thesis, oral and written exams; for doctorate, variable foreign language requirement, thesis/dissertation, oral and written exams. *Entrance requirements:* For master's and doctorate, GRE General Test, minimum GPA of 3.0, course work in religion. Additional exam requirements/recommendations for international students: Required—TOEFL (minimum score 550 paper-based; 79 iBT). Electronic applications accepted. *Faculty research:* Theology, religious ethics, Biblical studies, history of Christianity, religion and culture.

Southern Methodist University, Perkins School of Theology, Dallas, TX 75275. Offers CMM, M Div, MSM, MTS, D Min. *Accreditation:* ACIPE. *Program availability:* Part-time. *Degree requirements:* For master's, thesis (for some programs), internship; for doctorate, internship, oral exam, professional project. *Entrance requirements:* For master's, minimum GPA of 2.75; for doctorate, minimum graduate GPA of 3.0, M Div or equivalent, 3 years of ministry experience. Additional exam requirements/recommendations for international students: Required—TOEFL (minimum score 600 paper-based; 100 iBT), TWE. *Expenses:* Contact institution.

South Florida Bible College and Theological Seminary, Graduate Programs, Deerfield Beach, FL 33442. Offers biblical studies (MA); theology (M Div). *Degree requirements:* For master's, thesis.

Southwestern Assemblies of God University, Thomas F. Harrison School of Graduate Studies, Program in Theological Studies, Waxahachie, TX 75165-5735. Offers Bible and theology (MS); Biblical studies (M Div); counseling (M Div); cross cultural missions (M Div); practical theology (M Div); theological studies (M Div). *Program availability:* Online learning. *Degree requirements:* For master's, comprehensive written and oral exams. *Entrance requirements:* For master's, GRE General Test, minimum GPA of 2.5. Electronic applications accepted.

Southwestern Baptist Theological Seminary, Roy Fish School of Evangelism and Missions, Fort Worth, TX 76122-0000. Offers cross-cultural missions (MTS); evangelism (M Div); evangelism and missions (D Min); international church planting (M Div); Islamic studies (M Div, MA Islamic); missiology (MA Miss); missions (M Div); North American church planting (M Div); North American evangelism and international missions (D Min); theology (Th M); world Christian studies (PhD).

Southwestern Baptist Theological Seminary, School of Theology, Fort Worth, TX 76122-0000. Offers ministry (D Min); theology (PhD). *Accreditation:* ACIPE; ATS (one or more programs are accredited). *Program availability:* Part-time, evening/weekend. Terminal master's awarded for partial completion of doctoral program. *Degree requirements:* For master's, 2 foreign languages, thesis (for some programs); for doctorate, 2 foreign languages, comprehensive exam, thesis/dissertation, oral exams. *Entrance requirements:* For doctorate, GRE, M Div or equivalent. Additional exam requirements/recommendations for international students: Required—TOEFL. Electronic applications accepted.

Spring Arbor University, School of Arts and Sciences, Spring Arbor, MI 49283-9799. Offers communication (MA); spiritual formation and leadership (MA). *Program availability:* Part-time, online learning. *Degree requirements:* For master's, thesis (for some programs). *Entrance requirements:* For master's, GRE (minimum score of 40th percentile and taken within last 5 years), bachelor's degree from regionally-accredited college or university, minimum GPA of 3.0 for at least the last two years of the bachelor's degree, at least two recommendations from professional/academic individuals. Additional exam requirements/recommendations for international students: Required—TOEFL (minimum score 600 paper-based). *Expenses:* Contact institution.

Spring Hill College, Graduate Programs, Program in Theology, Mobile, AL 36608-1791. Offers faith companioning (Postbaccalaureate Certificate); pastoral ministry (Postbaccalaureate Certificate); pastoral studies (MPS); spiritual direction (Postbaccalaureate Certificate); theological studies (MTS); theology (MA). *Program availability:* Part-time, evening/weekend. *Faculty:* 6 full-time (1 woman), 2 part-time/adjunct (0 women). *Students:* 31 part-time (16 women); includes 5 minority (1 Black or African American, non-Hispanic/Latino; 1 American Indian or Alaska Native, non-Hispanic/Latino; 1 Asian, non-Hispanic/Latino; 1 Hispanic/Latino; 1 Two or more races, non-Hispanic/Latino), 2 international. Average age 42. In 2017, 11 master's, 2 other advanced degrees awarded. *Degree requirements:* For master's, variable foreign language requirement, comprehensive exam, thesis (for some programs), completion of program within 6 calendar years of initial enrollment (MTS, MPS); completion of program within 4 1/2 calendar years of formal acceptance (MA). *Entrance requirements:* For master's, bachelor's degree with minimum undergraduate GPA of 3.0; six hours of undergraduate theology, religious studies, or unquestioned equivalency. Additional exam requirements/recommendations for international students: Required—TOEFL (minimum score 550 paper-based; 80 iBT), IELTS (minimum score 6.5), CPE or CAE (minimum score C), Michigan English Language Assessment Battery (minimum score 90). *Application deadline:* For fall admission, 8/1 priority date for domestic and international students; for spring admission, 12/1 priority date for domestic and international students. Applications are processed on a rolling basis. Application fee: $25 ($35 for international students). Electronic applications accepted. *Expenses: Tuition:* Full-time $9270; part-time $515 per credit hour. Tuition and fees vary according to program. *Financial support:* Applicants required to submit FAFSA. *Unit head:* Dr. Timothy R. Carmody, Director, 251-380-4665, Fax: 251-460-2194, E-mail: carmody@shc.edu. *Application contact:* Robert Stewart, Vice President of Enrollment, 251-380-3030, Fax: 251-460-2186, E-mail: rstewart@shc.edu.
Website: http://ug.shc.edu/graduate-degrees/master-arts-theological-studies/

Starr King School for the Ministry, Professional Program, Berkeley, CA 94709-1209. Offers M Div. *Accreditation:* ACIPE; ATS.

SUM Bible College & Theological Seminary, Graduate Programs, Oakland, CA 94603. Offers biblical studies (MA); Christian leadership (MA); theology (M Div). *Entrance requirements:* For master's, minimum GPA of 2.5, currently active in ministry.

Talmudic University, Program in Talmudic Law, Miami Beach, FL 33140. Offers MRE. *Accreditation:* AARTS. *Degree requirements:* For master's, 2 foreign languages. *Entrance requirements:* For master's, oral exam, undergraduate Judaic studies degree.

Taylor College and Seminary, Graduate and Professional Programs, Edmonton, AB T6J 4T3, Canada. Offers Christian studies (Diploma); intercultural studies (MA, Diploma), including intercultural studies (Diploma), TESOL; theology (M Div, MTS). *Accreditation:* ATS. *Program availability:* Part-time, online learning. *Degree requirements:* For master's, thesis optional. *Entrance requirements:* Additional exam requirements/recommendations for international students: Required—TOEFL (minimum score 550 paper-based; 80 iBT), IELTS (minimum score 6.5). *Faculty research:* Biblical studies, administration and organization, world religions, ethics, missiology.

Toronto School of Theology, Graduate Programs, Toronto, ON M5S 2C3, Canada. Offers M Div, MA, MAMS, MPS, MRE, MSM, MTS, Th M, D Min, PhD, Th D. *Program availability:* Online learning. Terminal master's awarded for partial completion of doctoral program. *Degree requirements:* For master's, 2 foreign languages, thesis; for doctorate, 3 foreign languages, comprehensive exam, thesis/dissertation. *Entrance requirements:* For master's, language exams, minimum B+ average in undergraduate course work; for doctorate, language exams, first-class standing in master's program. Additional exam requirements/recommendations for international students: Required—TOEFL, IELTS. Electronic applications accepted.

Trinity Bible College and Graduate School, Graduate School, Ellendale, ND 58436. Offers global theology (MA); missional leadership (MA); rural ministries (MA).

Trinity College, Faculty of Divinity, Toronto, ON M5S 1H8, Canada. Offers ministry (Diploma); ministry for church musicians (Diploma); theology (M Div, MA, MTS, Th M, D Min, PhD, Th D, Diploma, L Th); M Div/MA. *Accreditation:* ATS. *Program availability:* Part-time. *Degree requirements:* For master's, 2 foreign languages, thesis (for some programs); for doctorate, 3 foreign languages, comprehensive exam, thesis/dissertation; for other advanced degree, thesis (for some programs). *Entrance requirements:* For master's, 1 language (modern or ancient), interview; for doctorate, 2 languages (modern and ancient). Additional exam requirements/recommendations for international students: Required—TOEFL, TWE. *Faculty research:* Interreligious dialogue, feminist theology, systematic theology, philosophy of religion, pastoral theology.

Trinity International University, Trinity Evangelical Divinity School, Deerfield, IL 60015-1284. Offers academic ministry (M Div); Biblical and Near Eastern archaeology and languages (MA); chaplaincy and ministry care (MA); Christian studies (Certificate); church and parachurch ministry (M Div); church history (MA, Th M); counseling (Th M); educational ministries (MA); educational ministry (Th M); educational studies (PhD); intercultural studies (MA, PhD); leadership and management (D Min); mental health counseling (MA); military chaplaincy (D Min); ministry (MA); missions (Th M); missions and evangelism (D Min); New Testament (MA, Th M); Old Testament (Th M); Old Testament and Semitic languages (MA); pastoral ministry and care (D Min); pastoral theology (Th M); preaching and teaching (D Min); spiritual formation and education (D Min); systematic theology (MA, Th M); theological studies (MA, PhD); urban ministry (MA). *Program availability:* Part-time, online learning. *Degree requirements:* For master's, comprehensive exam, thesis, fieldwork; for doctorate, comprehensive exam (for some programs), thesis/dissertation; for Certificate, comprehensive exam, integrative papers. *Entrance requirements:* For master's, GRE, MAT, minimum cumulative undergraduate GPA of 3.0; for doctorate, GRE, minimum cumulative graduate GPA of 3.2; for Certificate, GRE, MAT, minimum undergraduate GPA of 2.5. Additional exam requirements/recommendations for international students: Required—TOEFL (minimum score 580 paper-based), TWE (minimum score 4). Electronic applications accepted.

Trinity Lutheran Seminary, Graduate and Professional Programs, Columbus, OH 43209-2334. Offers African American studies (MTS); Biblical studies (MTS, STM); Christian education (MA); Christian spirituality (STM); church in the world (MTS); church music (MA); divinity (M Div); general theological studies (MTS); mission and evangelism (STM); pastoral leadership and practice (STM); youth and family ministry (MA); MSN/MTS; MTS/JD. *Accreditation:* ACIPE; ATS. *Program availability:* Part-time. *Degree requirements:* For master's, variable foreign language requirement, comprehensive exam (for some programs), thesis (for some programs), field experience (for some programs). *Entrance requirements:* For master's, BA or equivalent (for MA, M Div, MTS); M Div, MTS, or equivalent (for STM); audition (for MACM). Additional exam requirements/recommendations for international students: Required—TOEFL. Electronic applications accepted. *Expenses:* Contact institution.

Trinity School for Ministry, Graduate Programs, Ambridge, PA 15003-2397. Offers Anglican studies (Diploma); basic Christian studies (Diploma); divinity (M Div); ministry (D Min); mission and evangelism (MAME, Diploma); religion (MAR); youth ministry (Diploma). *Program availability:* Part-time. *Degree requirements:* For master's, thesis optional; for doctorate, thesis/dissertation. *Entrance requirements:* Additional exam requirements/recommendations for international students: Required—TOEFL. *Faculty research:* Pauline Epistles, contemporary theology, history of Anglican liturgy, book of Ruth, biblical theology.

Trinity Western University, ACTS Seminaries, Langley, BC V2Y 1Y1, Canada. Offers Christian studies (MA); cross cultural ministry (MA); theology (M Div, M Th, MAMFT, MLE, MTS, D Min). *Program availability:* Part-time. *Degree requirements:* For master's, thesis (for some programs), internship. *Entrance requirements:* For doctorate, M Div or equivalent. Additional exam requirements/recommendations for international students: Required—TOEFL. *Expenses:* Contact institution. *Faculty research:* Theology of leadership.

Trinity Western University, School of Graduate Studies, Program in Biblical Studies, Langley, BC V2Y 1Y1, Canada. Offers MA. *Accreditation:* ATS. *Program availability:* Part-time. *Degree requirements:* For master's, 2 foreign languages, thesis, 2 years Greek, 2 years Hebrew. *Entrance requirements:* For master's, minimum GPA of 3.0, degree in biblical studies, master of divinity or 42 hours Biblical Study credit. Additional exam requirements/recommendations for international students: Required—TOEFL (minimum score 600 paper-based). Electronic applications accepted. *Faculty research:* Intertestamental literature, Dead Sea Scrolls, Biblical literature, history of Jesus, ancient languages.

Tri-State Bible College, Graduate Program, South Point, OH 45680-8402. Offers MA. *Entrance requirements:* For master's, bachelor's degree, minimum undergraduate GPA of 2.75, autobiographical statement, two letters of recommendation. Electronic applications accepted.

Truett McConnell University, Balthasar Hubmaier School of Theology and Missions, Cleveland, GA 30528. Offers theology (MA). *Program availability:* Part-time, 100% online. *Students:* 18 full-time (1 woman), 10 part-time (2 women). In 2017, 4 master's awarded. *Entrance requirements:* For master's, bachelor's degree from accredited institution, minimum cumulative GPA of 2.5. *Application deadline:* Applications are processed on a rolling basis. Electronic applications accepted. *Expenses: Tuition:* Part-time $325 per credit hour. *Required fees:* $910 per year. $455 per semester. *Financial support:* Application deadline: 8/1; applicants required to submit FAFSA. *Unit head:* Dr. Jason Graffagnino, Dean, 706-865-2134 Ext. 3002, E-mail: jgraffagnino@truett.edu. *Application contact:* Jim Dunnington, Coordinator of Online and Graduate Admissions, 706-865-2134 Ext. 2131, E-mail: jdunnington@truett.edu.

Tyndale University College & Seminary, Graduate Programs, Toronto, ON M2M 3S4, Canada. Offers Biblical studies (M Div); Christian foundations (MTS); Christian studies (Diploma); counseling (M Div); educational ministry (M Div); missions (M Div, Diploma); pastoral and Chinese ministry (M Div); pastoral ministry (M Div); Pentecostal studies (MTS); spiritual formation (M Div, Diploma); theological studies (M Div); theology (Th M); worship and liturgy (M Div, MTS); youth and family ministry (M Div). *Accreditation:* ATS. *Program availability:* Part-time, online learning. *Entrance requirements:* For master's and Diploma, minimum C+ average in undergraduate course work. Additional exam requirements/recommendations for international students: Required—TOEFL (minimum score 570 paper-based), TWE (minimum score 5). Electronic applications accepted. *Faculty research:* Canadian church history, Chinese church history, Old Testament, counseling ministries (narrative therapy), world religions.

Unification Theological Seminary, Graduate Programs, Barrytown, NY 12507. Offers family and educational ministry (D Min); interfaith peacebuilding (MRE); peace and justice ministry (D Min); religious education (MRE), including interfaith peacebuilding; religious studies (MA); theology (M Div). *Program availability:* Part-time, evening/weekend, online learning. *Degree requirements:* For master's, variable foreign language requirement, thesis (for some programs); for doctorate, thesis/dissertation. *Entrance requirements:* For master's, bachelor's degree; for doctorate, M Div or equivalency. Additional exam requirements/recommendations for international students: Required—TOEFL (minimum score 550 paper-based). *Application deadline:* For fall admission, 3/15 priority date for domestic and international students; for spring admission, 9/15 priority date for domestic and international students. Applications are processed on a rolling basis. Application fee: $30. Electronic applications accepted. *Expenses: Tuition:* Full-time $12,000; part-time $500 per credit. *Required fees:* $260; $210 per year. $105 per semester. Tuition and fees vary according to campus/location. *Financial support:* Scholarships/grants available. Financial award application deadline: 6/15; financial award applicants required to submit FAFSA. *Faculty research:* Church leadership, church history, world religions, ecumenism, interfaith peace building, service-learning. *Unit head:* Michael Mickler, Vice-President for Administration, 845-752-3235, Fax: 845-752-3014, E-mail: mm@uts.edu. *Application contact:* Henry Christopher, Director of Admissions and Financial Aid, 212-563-6647 Ext. 105, Fax: 845-752-3014, E-mail: admissions@uts.edu.
Website: http://www.uts.edu/academics/academic-programs

Theology

Union Theological Seminary in the City of New York, Graduate and Professional Programs, New York, NY 10027-5710. Offers M Div, MA, STM, D Min, PhD, M Div/MSSW. M Div/MSSW with Columbia University. *Accreditation:* ACIPE; ATS (one or more programs are accredited). *Program availability:* Part-time. *Degree requirements:* For master's, one foreign language, thesis; for doctorate, 2 foreign languages, thesis/dissertation. *Entrance requirements:* For doctorate, GRE General Test, sample of written work. *Faculty research:* American religious history, psychiatry and religion, Christian ethics, New Testament.

United Lutheran Seminary, Graduate and Professional Programs, Gettysburg, PA 17325-1795. Offers divinity (M Div); ministerial studies (MAMS); outdoor ministry (MAR); parish ministry (D Min); theology (STM). *Accreditation:* ACIPE; ATS (one or more programs are accredited). *Program availability:* Part-time, online learning. *Degree requirements:* For master's, thesis (for some programs). Electronic applications accepted.

United Lutheran Seminary, Graduate School, Philadelphia, PA 19119-1794. Offers divinity (M Div); ministry (D Min); public leadership (MA); religion (MAR); social ministry and church (Certificate); theology (STM, PhD). *Accreditation:* ACIPE. *Program availability:* Part-time, evening/weekend. *Degree requirements:* For master's, one foreign language, comprehensive exam (for some programs), thesis (for some programs); for doctorate, thesis/dissertation. *Entrance requirements:* For master's, minimum undergraduate GPA of 2.8; for doctorate, minimum GPA of 3.0. Additional exam requirements/recommendations for international students: Required—TOEFL (minimum score 550 paper-based; 89 iBT), TWE. Electronic applications accepted.

United Talmudical Seminary, Graduate Programs, Brooklyn, NY 11211. *Accreditation:* AARTS.

United Theological Seminary, Graduate and Professional Programs, Dayton, OH 45426. Offers Christian ministries (MA); ministry (M Div, D Min); theological studies (MTS). *Accreditation:* ATS. *Program availability:* Part-time, evening/weekend, online learning. *Degree requirements:* For master's, thesis (for some programs); for doctorate, thesis/dissertation, final exam. *Entrance requirements:* For master's, minimum GPA of 2.5, interview, 5 letters of recommendation; for doctorate, minimum GPA of 3.0, 2 letters of recommendation, interview. Additional exam requirements/recommendations for international students: Required—TOEFL (minimum score 550 paper-based). Electronic applications accepted.

United Theological Seminary of the Twin Cities, Graduate Programs, New Brighton, MN 55112-2598. Offers advanced theological studies (Diploma); justice and peace studies (M Div, MA); leadership toward racial justice (M Div, MA, Certificate); Methodist studies (M Div, MA, Certificate); ministry (D Min); ministry renewal and professional development (Certificate); pastoral care and counseling (M Div, MA, MARL); religion and theology (MA); theological and religious studies (Certificate); theology and the arts (M Div, MA); urban ministry (M Div, MA, MARL); women's studies: religion, theology and ministry (M Div, MA). *Accreditation:* ACIPE; ATS. *Program availability:* Part-time, evening/weekend. *Degree requirements:* For master's, thesis; for doctorate, comprehensive exam, thesis/dissertation. *Entrance requirements:* For master's, minimum GPA of 2.75; strong analytical, reflective thinking and writing skills; vocational and academic goals compatible with those of Seminary; for doctorate, M Div or equivalent, minimum GPA of 3.0, 3 years experience in professional ministry; for other advanced degree, BA or equivalent life experience; strong analytical, reflective thinking and writing skills (Certificate); proficiency in English language, previous study of theology at a theological school, recommendation of student's denomination (Diploma). Additional exam requirements/recommendations for international students: Required—TOEFL (minimum score 550 paper-based).

Université de Montréal, Faculty of Theology and Sciences of Religions, Montréal, QC H3C 3J7, Canada. Offers health, spirituality and bioethics (DESS); practical theology (MA, PhD); religious sciences (MA, PhD); theology (MA, D Th, PhD, L Th); theology-Biblical studies (PhD). *Degree requirements:* For master's, one foreign language; for doctorate, 2 foreign languages, thesis/dissertation, general exam. Electronic applications accepted.

Université de Sherbrooke, Faculty of Theology and Religious Studies, Sherbrooke, QC J1K 2R1, Canada. Offers applied ethics (Diploma); human science of religions (MA); intercultural training (Diploma); philosophy (MA, PhD); spiritual anthropology (Diploma); theology (MA, PhD, Diploma). *Program availability:* Part-time, evening/weekend, online learning. Terminal master's awarded for partial completion of doctoral program. *Entrance requirements:* For master's, bachelor's degree in related discipline; for doctorate, master's degree in related discipline. *Faculty research:* Faith and culture interrelation.

Université du Québec à Chicoutimi, Graduate Programs, Program in Theology (Pastoral Studies), Chicoutimi, QC G7H 2B1, Canada. Offers MA, PhD. Programs offered jointly with Université de Montréal. *Program availability:* Part-time. *Degree requirements:* For doctorate, thesis/dissertation. *Entrance requirements:* For master's, appropriate bachelor's degree, proficiency in French; for doctorate, appropriate master's degree, proficiency in French.

Université Laval, Faculty of Theology and Religious Sciences, Program in Practical Theology, Québec, QC G1K 7P4, Canada. Offers D Th P. *Program availability:* Part-time. *Degree requirements:* For doctorate, comprehensive exam, thesis/dissertation. *Entrance requirements:* For doctorate, knowledge of French and English. Electronic applications accepted.

Université Laval, Faculty of Theology and Religious Sciences, Programs in Theology, Québec, QC G1K 7P4, Canada. Offers MA, PhD. Terminal master's awarded for partial completion of doctoral program. *Degree requirements:* For master's, thesis (for some programs); for doctorate, comprehensive exam, thesis/dissertation. *Entrance requirements:* For master's and doctorate, knowledge of French, comprehension of written English. Electronic applications accepted.

University of Chicago, Divinity School, PhD Program, Chicago, IL 60637. Offers anthropology and sociology of religions (PhD); Bible (PhD); history of Christianity (PhD); history of Judaism (PhD); history of religions (PhD); Islamic studies (PhD); philosophy of religions (PhD); religion, literature, and visual culture (PhD); religions in America (PhD); religious ethics (PhD); theology (PhD). *Students:* 157 full-time (59 women); includes 23 minority (6 Black or African American, non-Hispanic/Latino; 11 Asian, non-Hispanic/Latino; 3 Hispanic/Latino; 3 Two or more races, non-Hispanic/Latino), 24 international. Average age 33. 184 applicants, 11% accepted, 17 enrolled. In 2017, 12 doctorates awarded. *Degree requirements:* For doctorate, 2 foreign languages, comprehensive exam, thesis/dissertation. *Entrance requirements:* For doctorate, GRE General Test, 3 letters of recommendation; transcripts; curriculum vitae or resume; writing sample. Additional exam requirements/recommendations for international students: Required—TOEFL (minimum score 600 paper-based; 104 iBT), IELTS (minimum score 7). *Application deadline:* For fall admission, 12/15 for domestic and international students. Application fee: $75. Electronic applications accepted. *Financial support:* In 2017–18, fellowships with full tuition reimbursements (averaging $27,000 per year), teaching assistantships with full tuition reimbursements (averaging $27,000 per year) were awarded; Federal Work-Study, institutionally sponsored loans, scholarships/grants, and health care benefits also available. Financial award application deadline: 12/15. *Faculty research:* Constructive studies (philosophy of religion, religious ethics, and theology); historical studies (Bible, history of Christianity, and history of Judaism); religion and the human sciences (anthropology and sociology of religion, history of religions, and religion, literature, and visual culture); Islamic studies; religions in America. *Unit head:* Dr. David Nirenberg, Interim Dean/Executive Vice Provost, 773-702-8200, E-mail: divinityadmissions@uchicago.edu. *Application contact:* Anita Lumpkin, Associate Dean of Students, 773-702-8249, E-mail: divinityadmissions@uchicago.edu.
Website: http://divinity.uchicago.edu/doctoral-program-phd

University of Dallas, Braniff Graduate School of Liberal Arts, Department of Theology, Irving, TX 75062-4736. Offers M Th, MA. *Program availability:* Part-time. *Degree requirements:* For master's, one foreign language, comprehensive exam, thesis (for some programs). *Entrance requirements:* For master's, GRE General Test. *Application deadline:* For fall admission, 2/15 priority date for domestic students; for spring admission, 11/15 for domestic students. Applications are processed on a rolling basis. Application fee: $50. *Expenses: Tuition:* Full-time $33,750; part-time $22,500 per year. Tuition and fees vary according to program. *Financial support:* Application deadline: 2/15. *Faculty research:* Patristics, justice in the Old and New Testament, Pauline literature, Christology, theology of the Trinity. *Unit head:* Dr. Ron Rombs, Department Chair, 972-721-5237, Fax: 972-721-4007, E-mail: rrombs@udallas.edu.

University of Dayton, Department of Religious Studies, Dayton, OH 45469. Offers pastoral ministry (MA); theological studies (MA); theology (PhD). *Program availability:* Part-time. *Faculty:* 23 full-time (7 women), 2 part-time/adjunct (1 woman). *Students:* 48 full-time (24 women), 10 part-time (4 women); includes 7 minority (2 Black or African American, non-Hispanic/Latino; 2 Asian, non-Hispanic/Latino; 3 Hispanic/Latino), 1 international. Average age 34. 53 applicants, 57% accepted. In 2017, 10 master's, 5 doctorates awarded. *Degree requirements:* For master's, thesis or alternative; for doctorate, 2 foreign languages, comprehensive exam, thesis/dissertation. *Entrance requirements:* For master's, 3 letters of recommendation, personal statement, all previous official transcript(s); for doctorate, GRE General Test (minimum score 600 verbal previous scale, 160 current scale), academic writing sample, 3 letters of recommendation, official transcript(s). Additional exam requirements/recommendations for international students: Required—TOEFL (minimum score 550 paper-based; 80 iBT). *Application deadline:* For fall admission, 2/1 priority date for domestic students, 2/1 for international students. Applications are processed on a rolling basis. Application fee: $0 ($50 for international students). Electronic applications accepted. *Expenses:* Contact institution. *Financial support:* In 2017–18, 21 research assistantships with full tuition reimbursements (averaging $11,250 per year), 20 teaching assistantships with full tuition reimbursements (averaging $18,130 per year) were awarded; fellowships and institutionally sponsored loans also available. Financial award application deadline: 3/1; financial award applicants required to submit FAFSA. *Faculty research:* Practical/constructive theology, theological ethics, U.S. Catholic/Christian life and thought, methodologies in Biblical studies, religion and science. *Unit head:* Dr. Daniel Thompson, Chair, 937-229-4321, Fax: 937-229-4330. *Application contact:* Amy Doorley, Coordinator of Graduate Studies, 937-229-4321, Fax: 937-229-4330, E-mail: adoorley1@udayton.edu.
Website: http://www.udayton.edu/artssciences/academics/religiousstudies/welcome/index.php

University of Denver, DU/Iliff Joint PhD Program in the Study of Religion, Denver, CO 80208. Offers future faculty in religion (Certificate); Latinx studies (Certificate); study of religion (PhD). Program jointly offered with Iliff School of Theology. *Program availability:* Part-time. *Faculty:* 10 part-time/adjunct (4 women). *Students:* 29 full-time (7 women), 19 part-time (6 women); includes 10 minority (1 Black or African American, non-Hispanic/Latino; 1 Asian, non-Hispanic/Latino; 6 Hispanic/Latino; 2 Two or more races, non-Hispanic/Latino), 2 international. Average age 39. 26 applicants, 54% accepted, 7 enrolled. In 2017, 9 doctorates awarded. *Degree requirements:* For doctorate, one foreign language, comprehensive exam, thesis/dissertation. *Entrance requirements:* For doctorate, GRE General Test, transcripts, three letters of recommendation, personal statement, writing sample, research paper. Additional exam requirements/recommendations for international students: Required—TOEFL (minimum score 600 paper-based; 100 iBT). *Application deadline:* For fall admission, 1/15 priority date for domestic and international students. Applications are processed on a rolling basis. Application fee: $65. Electronic applications accepted. *Expenses:* $31,935 per year full-time. *Financial support:* In 2017–18, 30 students received support, including 11 teaching assistantships with tuition reimbursements available (averaging $2,788 per year); scholarships/grants and unspecified assistantships also available. Financial award application deadline: 1/15. *Faculty research:* Religion and social change, theology, philosophy and cultural theory (including comparative religious study), Biblical interpretation. *Unit head:* Annette Stott, Director, 303-871-3278. *Application contact:* Information Contact, 303-765-3136, Fax: 303-871-4942, E-mail: jointphd@iliff.edu.
Website: http://www.du.edu/duiliffjoint

University of Dubuque, University of Dubuque Theological Seminary, Dubuque, IA 52001. Offers M Div, D Min. *Accreditation:* ACIPE; ATS. *Program availability:* Part-time, 100% online, blended/hybrid learning. *Degree requirements:* For doctorate, thesis/dissertation. *Entrance requirements:* Additional exam requirements/recommendations for international students: Recommended—TOEFL (minimum score 550 paper-based; 80 iBT). Electronic applications accepted. *Faculty research:* Biblical theology, reformed history and theology, pastoral theology, homiletics.

University of Holy Cross, Graduate Programs, New Orleans, LA 70131-7399. Offers biomedical sciences (MS); Catholic theology (MA); counseling (MA, PhD), including community counseling (MA), marriage and family counseling (MA), school counseling (MA); educational leadership (M Ed); executive leadership (Ed D); management (MS), including healthcare management, operations management; teaching and learning (M Ed). *Accreditation:* ACA; NCATE. *Program availability:* Part-time, evening/weekend, online learning. *Faculty:* 7 full-time (4 women), 8 part-time/adjunct (3 women). *Students:* 67 full-time (55 women), 69 part-time (55 women); includes 51 minority (46 Black or African American, non-Hispanic/Latino; 2 American Indian or Alaska Native, non-Hispanic/Latino; 1 Asian, non-Hispanic/Latino; 2 Hispanic/Latino). Average age 30. 20 applicants, 50% accepted. In 2017, 28 degrees awarded. *Degree requirements:* For master's, thesis. *Entrance requirements:* For master's, GRE General Test, minimum GPA of 2.7. *Application deadline:* For fall admission, 9/1 for domestic students. Application fee: $15. *Expenses: Tuition:* Full-time $10,890; part-time $605 per credit hour. *Required fees:* $1624; $812 per semester. One-time fee: $50. *Financial support:* Federal Work-Study and tuition waivers (partial) available. Support available to part-time students. Financial award application deadline: 6/1. *Unit head:* Dr. Myles Seghers, Dean of Humanities, Education, and Counseling, 504-394-7744 Ext. 214, Fax: 504-391-2421, E-mail: mseghers@olhcc.edu. *Application contact:* Anne-Katherine Lene, Director of Student Enrollment, 504-394-7744 Ext. 110, Fax: 504-391-2421, E-mail: aklene@olhcc.edu.

The University of Manchester, School of Arts, Histories and Cultures, Manchester, United Kingdom. Offers anthropology, media and performance (PhD); applied theatre professional (PhD); archaeology (PhD); art history and visual studies (PhD); arts management and cultural policy (PhD); classics and ancient history (PhD); composition

(PhD); creative writing (PhD); drama (PhD); economic and social history (PhD); electroacoustic composition (PhD); English and American studies (PhD); history (PhD); humanitarianism and conflict response (PhD); museology (PhD); music (PhD); musicology (PhD); religions and theology (PhD).

University of Northwestern–St. Paul, Master of Arts in Theological Studies Program, St. Paul, MN 55113-1598. Offers MATS. *Program availability:* Part-time, evening/weekend, online learning. *Application deadline:* Applications are processed on a rolling basis. Electronic applications accepted. *Application contact:* Graduate Studies Admissions, 651-631-5200, E-mail: gradstudies@unwsp.edu.
Website: https://www.unwsp.edu/web/graduate-studies/master-of-arts-in-theological-studies

University of Northwestern–St. Paul, Master of Divinity Program, St. Paul, MN 55113-1598. Offers M Div. *Program availability:* Part-time, evening/weekend, online learning. *Application deadline:* Applications are processed on a rolling basis. Electronic applications accepted. *Application contact:* Graduate Studies Admissions, 651-631-5200, E-mail: gradstudies@unwsp.edu.
Website: https://www.unwsp.edu/web/graduate-studies/master-of-divinity

University of Notre Dame, Graduate School, College of Arts and Letters, Division of Humanities, Department of Theology, Notre Dame, IN 46556. Offers M Div, MA, MSM, MTS, PhD. *Accreditation:* ACIPE; ATS. Terminal master's awarded for partial completion of doctoral program. *Degree requirements:* For master's, one foreign language, comprehensive exam, thesis or alternative; for doctorate, 3 foreign languages, comprehensive exam, thesis/dissertation, candidacy exam. *Entrance requirements:* For master's and doctorate, GRE General Test. Additional exam requirements/recommendations for international students: Required—TOEFL (minimum score 600 paper-based; 80 iBT). Electronic applications accepted. *Faculty research:* Liturgy, ethics, historical studies, Biblical studies, systematic theology.

University of Notre Dame, Graduate School, College of Arts and Letters, Division of Humanities, Program in History and Philosophy of Science, Notre Dame, IN 46556. Offers history and philosophy of science (MA, PhD); theology and science (PhD). *Degree requirements:* For doctorate, 2 foreign languages, comprehensive exam, thesis/dissertation, candidacy exam. *Entrance requirements:* For doctorate, GRE General Test. Additional exam requirements/recommendations for international students: Required—TOEFL (minimum score 600 paper-based; 80 iBT). Electronic applications accepted. *Faculty research:* Philosophy of physics, science and ethics, history and philosophy of biology, history of medicine and technology, history and philosophy of economics.

University of Philosophical Research, Master's in Consciousness Studies Program, Los Angeles, CA 90027. Offers MA. *Degree requirements:* For master's, thesis. Electronic applications accepted.

University of Philosophical Research, Master's in Transformational Psychology Program, Los Angeles, CA 90027. Offers MA. *Degree requirements:* For master's, thesis. Electronic applications accepted.

University of Saint Mary of the Lake–Mundelein Seminary, Graduate and Professional Programs, Mundelein, IL 60060. Offers liturgical studies (MA); ministry (D Min); pastoral studies (MA); theology (M Div). *Accreditation:* ATS (one or more programs are accredited). *Degree requirements:* For doctorate, 2 foreign languages, comprehensive exam, thesis/dissertation. *Entrance requirements:* For master's and doctorate, bachelor's degree. Additional exam requirements/recommendations for international students: Required—TOEFL (minimum score 550 paper-based). Electronic applications accepted.

University of St. Michael's College, Faculty of Theology, Toronto, ON M5S 1J4, Canada. Offers Catholic leadership (MA); eastern Christian studies (Diploma); religious education (Diploma); theological studies (Diploma); theology (M Div, MA, MRE, MTS, D Min, PhD, Th D); theology and Jewish studies (MA). Th D offered jointly with University of Toronto. *Accreditation:* ATS (one or more programs are accredited). *Program availability:* Part-time. *Degree requirements:* For master's, thesis (for some programs), 1 foreign language (MA), 2 foreign languages (Th M); for doctorate, 3 foreign languages, comprehensive exam, thesis/dissertation; for other advanced degree, thesis optional. *Entrance requirements:* For master's, M Div or BA, course work in an ancient or modern language, minimum GPA of 3.3; for doctorate, MA in theology, Th M, or M Div with thesis, minimum GPA of 3.7; for other advanced degree, minimum GPA of 2.7. Additional exam requirements/recommendations for international students: Required—TOEFL (minimum score 600 paper-based). Electronic applications accepted. *Expenses:* Contact institution. *Faculty research:* Patristics, eastern Christianity, ecology and theology, ecumenism, Jewish Christian studies.

University of St. Thomas, The Saint Paul Seminary School of Divinity, St. Paul, MN 55105. Offers pastoral ministry (MAPM); religious education (MARE); theology (MA). *Accreditation:* ACIPE; ATS. *Program availability:* Part-time, evening/weekend. *Degree requirements:* For master's, one foreign language, comprehensive exam (for some programs), thesis (for some programs). *Entrance requirements:* For master's, GRE, 3 letters of recommendation, interview. Additional exam requirements/recommendations for international students: Required—TOEFL (minimum score 550 paper-based). *Application deadline:* For fall admission, 6/1 priority date for domestic students. Applications are processed on a rolling basis. Application fee: $40. Electronic applications accepted. *Expenses:* Contact institution. *Financial support:* Fellowships, research assistantships, institutionally sponsored loans, and scholarships/grants available. Support available to part-time students. Financial award application deadline: 4/1; financial award applicants required to submit FAFSA. *Faculty research:* Theological education. *Unit head:* Rev. Msgr. Aloysius R. Callaghan, Rector/Vice President, 651-962-5052, Fax: 651-962-5790, E-mail: arcallaghan@stthomas.edu. *Application contact:* Ana Theisen, Recruiter/Admissions Counselor, 651-962-5069, Fax: 651-962-5790, E-mail: aztheisen@stthomas.edu.
Website: http://www.stthomas.edu/spssod/

University of St. Thomas, School of Theology, Houston, TX 77006-4696. Offers divinity (M Div); pastoral studies (MAPS); theological studies (MA). *Accreditation:* ATS. *Program availability:* Part-time. *Faculty:* 10 full-time (2 women), 7 part-time/adjunct (1 woman). *Students:* 80 full-time (3 women), 78 part-time (29 women); includes 64 minority (5 Black or African American, non-Hispanic/Latino; 24 Asian, non-Hispanic/Latino; 34 Hispanic/Latino; 1 Two or more races, non-Hispanic/Latino), 25 international. Average age 38. 56 applicants, 100% accepted, 18 enrolled. In 2017, 38 master's awarded. *Degree requirements:* For master's, variable foreign language requirement, comprehensive exam. *Entrance requirements:* For master's, BA, BS or equivalent; personal essay (for some programs); undergraduate philosophy or theology courses; 2 letters of recommendation. Additional exam requirements/recommendations for international students: Required—TOEFL (minimum score 550 paper-based; 79 iBT), IELTS (minimum score 6.5), PTE (minimum score 53). *Application deadline:* Applications are processed on a rolling basis. Application fee: $10. Electronic applications accepted. *Expenses:* Contact institution. *Financial support:* In 2017–18, 9 students received support. Scholarships/grants available. Support available to part-time students. Financial award application deadline: 4/15; financial award applicants required to submit FAFSA. *Unit head:* Dr. Sandra C. Magie, Dean, 713-686-4345 Ext. 242, Fax: 713-683-8673, E-mail: smagie@stthom.edu. *Application contact:* E-mail: sms@stthom.edu.
Website: http://www.stthom.edu/Academics/School_of_Theology_at_St_Marys_Seminary/Index.aqf

The University of Scranton, College of Arts and Sciences, Program in Theology, Scranton, PA 18510. Offers MA. *Program availability:* Part-time, evening/weekend. *Degree requirements:* For master's, comprehensive exam (for some programs), thesis (for some programs), capstone experience. *Entrance requirements:* For master's, minimum GPA of 3.0, three letters of reference. Additional exam requirements/recommendations for international students: Required—TOEFL (minimum score 500 paper-based; 80 iBT), IELTS (minimum score 6.5). Electronic applications accepted.

University of South Africa, College of Human Sciences, Pretoria, South Africa. Offers adult education (M Ed); African languages (MA, PhD); African politics (MA, PhD); Afrikaans (MA, PhD); ancient history (MA, PhD); ancient Near Eastern studies (MA, PhD); anthropology (MA, PhD); applied linguistics (MA); Arabic (MA, PhD); archaeology (MA); art history (MA); Biblical archaeology (MA); Biblical studies (M Th, D Th, PhD); Christian spirituality (M Th, D Th); church history (M Th, D Th); classical studies (MA, PhD); clinical psychology (MA); communication (MA, PhD); comparative education (M Ed, Ed D); consulting psychology (D Admin, D Com, PhD); curriculum studies (M Ed, Ed D); development studies (M Admin, MA, D Admin, PhD); didactics (M Ed, Ed D); education (M Tech); education management (M Ed, Ed D); educational psychology (M Ed); English (MA); environmental education (M Ed); French (MA, PhD); German (MA, PhD); Greek (MA); guidance and counseling (M Ed); health studies (MA, PhD), including health sciences education (MA), health services management (MA), medical and surgical nursing science (critical care general) (MA), midwifery and neonatal nursing science (MA), trauma and emergency care (MA); history (MA, PhD); history of education (Ed D); inclusive education (M Ed, Ed D); information and communications technology policy and regulation (MA); information science (MA, MIS, PhD); international politics (MA, PhD); Islamic studies (MA, PhD); Italian (MA, PhD); Judaica (MA, PhD); linguistics (MA, PhD); mathematical education (M Ed); mathematics education (MA); missiology (M Th, D Th); modern Hebrew (MA, PhD); musicology (MA, MMus, D Mus, PhD); natural science education (M Ed); New Testament (M Th, D Th); Old Testament (D Th); pastoral therapy (M Th, D Th); philosophy (MA); philosophy of education (M Ed, Ed D); politics (MA, PhD); Portuguese (MA, PhD); practical theology (M Th, D Th); psychology (MA, MS, PhD); psychology of education (M Ed, Ed D); public health (MA); religious studies (MA, D Th, PhD); Romance languages (MA); Russian (MA, PhD); Semitic languages (MA, PhD); social behavior studies in HIV/AIDS (MA); social science (mental health) (MA); social science in development studies (MA); social science in psychology (MA); social science in social work (MA); social science in sociology (MA); social work (MSW, DSW, PhD); socio-education (M Ed, Ed D); sociolinguistics (MA); sociology (MA, PhD); Spanish (MA, PhD); systematic theology (M Th, D Th); TESOL (teaching English to speakers of other languages) (MA); theological ethics (M Th, D Th); theory of literature (MA, PhD); urban ministries (D Th); urban ministry (M Th).

The University of the South, School of Theology, Sewanee, TN 37383. Offers M Div, MA, STM, D Min. *Accreditation:* ACIPE. *Program availability:* Part-time. *Faculty:* 8 full-time (3 women), 10 part-time/adjunct (4 women). *Students:* 61 full-time (23 women), 7 part-time (3 women); includes 6 minority (3 Black or African American, non-Hispanic/Latino; 1 American Indian or Alaska Native, non-Hispanic/Latino; 2 Two or more races, non-Hispanic/Latino), 5 international. Average age 39. In 2017, 31 master's, 10 doctorates awarded. *Degree requirements:* For master's, thesis (for some programs); for doctorate, thesis/dissertation. *Entrance requirements:* For master's, M Div (for STM); for doctorate, M Div. Additional exam requirements/recommendations for international students: Required—TOEFL. *Application deadline:* For fall admission, 7/1 for domestic students, 1/15 for international students. Applications are processed on a rolling basis. Application fee: $0. Electronic applications accepted. *Expenses:* Contact institution. *Financial support:* Institutionally sponsored loans and scholarships/grants available. Support available to part-time students. *Unit head:* Very Rev. Dr. J. Neil Alexander, Dean, 931-598-1288, Fax: 931-598-1412, E-mail: deansot@sewanee.edu. *Application contact:* Stephanie Borne, Administrative Assistant for Recruitment and Admission, 931-598-1283, E-mail: theologyadmissions@sewanee.edu.
Website: http://theology.sewanee.edu/

University of the West, Program in Buddhist Chaplaincy, Rosemead, CA 91770. Offers M Div. *Entrance requirements:* Additional exam requirements/recommendations for international students: Required—TOEFL (minimum score 550 paper-based; 79 iBT); Recommended—IELTS.

University of Valley Forge, Program in Theology, Phoenixville, PA 19460. Offers MA. *Degree requirements:* For master's, project.

The University of Winnipeg, Faculty of Theology, Winnipeg, MB R3B 2E9, Canada. Offers marriage and family therapy (MMFT, Certificate); sacred theology (STM); theology (M Div). *Accreditation:* AAMFT/COAMFTE. *Program availability:* Part-time.

Urshan Graduate School of Theology, Graduate Programs, Florissant, MO 63031. Offers M Div, MACM, MTS. *Accreditation:* ATS. *Program availability:* Online learning. *Degree requirements:* For master's, capstone project (for MACM and MTS); portfolio (for M Div).

Ursuline College, School of Graduate and Professional Studies, Theological and Pastoral Studies Program, Pepper Pike, OH 44124-4398. Offers MA. *Program availability:* Part-time. *Faculty:* 3 full-time (all women). *Students:* 7 part-time (4 women); includes 6 minority (all Black or African American, non-Hispanic/Latino). Average age 56. 4 applicants, 100% accepted, 4 enrolled. In 2017, 2 master's awarded. *Degree requirements:* For master's, thesis. *Entrance requirements:* For master's, GRE when GPA under 3.0, minimum undergraduate GPA of 3.0, interview. Additional exam requirements/recommendations for international students: Required—TOEFL (minimum score 550 paper-based; 80 iBT). *Application deadline:* For fall admission, 8/1 priority date for domestic students. Applications are processed on a rolling basis. Application fee: $25. Electronic applications accepted. *Expenses:* Contact institution. *Financial support:* Scholarships/grants available. Financial award application deadline: 3/1; financial award applicants required to submit FAFSA. *Faculty research:* Household codes of Ephesians, cosmology of Ephesians, early Christian families, the use of theological reflection in integrative education for ministry, premillennial dispensationalism and the politics of the religious right in the United States. *Unit head:* Dr. Linda Martin, Director, 440-646-8191, Fax: 440-684-6088, E-mail: lmartin@ursuline.edu. *Application contact:* Melanie Steele, Director, Graduate Admissions, 440-646-8146, Fax: 440-684-6138, E-mail: graduateadmissions@ursuline.edu.

Vancouver School of Theology, Graduate and Professional Programs, Vancouver, BC V6T 1Z1, Canada. Offers denominational studies (Diploma); indigenous and inter-religious studies (MA, Diploma); public and pastoral leadership (MA); public and pastoral leadership in spiritual care (MA); theological studies (MATS, Diploma, Graduate Diploma); theology (M Div, Th M). *Accreditation:* ATS. *Program availability:* Part-time, online learning. *Degree requirements:* For master's, comprehensive exam (for some programs), thesis (for some programs); for other advanced degree, one foreign language, thesis. *Entrance requirements:* Additional exam requirements/

recommendations for international students: Required—TOEFL (minimum score 80 iBT); Recommended—IELTS (minimum score 6.5). *Application deadline:* For fall admission, 10/15 for domestic and international students; for spring admission, 3/15 for domestic and international students. Application fee: $75 Canadian dollars. Electronic applications accepted. One-time fee: $426 Canadian dollars full-time. *Financial support:* Research assistantships with partial tuition reimbursements, teaching assistantships with partial tuition reimbursements, career-related internships or fieldwork, scholarships/grants, and tuition waivers (partial) available. Support available to part-time students. Financial award application deadline: 3/15. *Faculty research:* Old Testament studies, pastoral theology, New Testament studies, field education, church history, systematic theology, spirituality. *Unit head:* Rev. Dr. Richard Topping, Principal, 604-822-9808, Fax: 604-822-9212. *Application contact:* Anita Fast, Registrar, 604-822-9563, Fax: 604-822-9212, E-mail: afast@vst.edu.
Website: https://vst.edu/students/prospective/degree-programs/graduate-degrees

Vanderbilt University, Divinity School, Nashville, TN 37240. Offers M Div, MTS, JD/M Div, JD/MTS, M Div/M Ed, MBA/M Div, MBA/MTS, MD/M Div, MD/MTS, MSN/M Div, MSN/MTS. *Accreditation:* ACIPE; ATS. *Program availability:* Part-time. *Entrance requirements:* Additional exam requirements/recommendations for international students: Required—TOEFL (minimum score 600 paper-based; 95 iBT), IELTS (minimum score 7). Electronic applications accepted.

Vanguard University of Southern California, Graduate Programs in Religion, Costa Mesa, CA 92626. Offers leadership studies (MA); theological studies (MTS). *Program availability:* Part-time, evening/weekend. *Degree requirements:* For master's, comprehensive exam (for some programs), thesis (for some programs). *Entrance requirements:* For master's, minimum GPA of 3.0 (MA), 2.5 (MTS). Additional exam requirements/recommendations for international students: Required—TOEFL (minimum score 550 paper-based; 79 iBT). Electronic applications accepted. *Expenses:* Contact institution. *Faculty research:* Narrative theology, ecumenism and Pentecost, leadership studies.

Victoria University, Emmanuel College, Toronto, ON M5S 1K7, Canada. Offers M Div, MA, MPS, MRE, MSMus, MTS, Th M, D Min, PhD, Th D, Certificate, Diploma, L Th, M Div/MA, M Div/MPS, M Div/MRE, M Div, MRE, Th M, Th D, M Div/MA, M Div/MRE, M Div/MPS offered jointly with University of Toronto; MA, PhD with University of St. Michael's College. Terminal master's awarded for partial completion of doctoral program. *Degree requirements:* For master's, variable foreign language requirement, thesis (for some programs); for doctorate, 2 foreign languages, thesis/dissertation. *Entrance requirements:* For master's and other advanced degree, BA, BSc; for doctorate, M Div, MA, MTS, Th M. Additional exam requirements/recommendations for international students: Required—TOEFL (minimum score 600 paper-based; 100 iBT), IELTS (minimum score 7), TWE (minimum score 5). Electronic applications accepted. *Faculty research:* New Testament and Old Testament hermeneutics, religious symbolism, Reformation, liberation theology, Canadian church history.

Villanova University, Graduate School of Liberal Arts and Sciences, Department of Theology, Villanova, PA 19085-1699. Offers MA, PhD. *Program availability:* Part-time, evening/weekend. *Faculty:* 18. *Students:* 37 full-time (18 women), 10 part-time (4 women); includes 5 minority (2 Black or African American, non-Hispanic/Latino; 2 Hispanic/Latino; 1 Two or more races, non-Hispanic/Latino), 7 international. Average age 34. 45 applicants, 62% accepted, 22 enrolled. In 2017, 9 master's awarded. *Degree requirements:* For master's, variable foreign language requirement, comprehensive exam (for some programs), thesis optional; for doctorate, variable foreign language requirement, comprehensive exam (for some programs), thesis/dissertation. *Entrance requirements:* For master's, minimum GPA of 3.0, statement of goals, 3 recommendation letters; for doctorate, transcripts, 3 recommendation letters, essay, curriculum vitae or resume. Additional exam requirements/recommendations for international students: Required—TOEFL. *Application deadline:* For fall admission, 3/1 for domestic students, 5/1 priority date for international students; for spring admission, 11/15 for domestic students, 10/15 for international students; for summer admission, 5/1 for domestic students. Applications are processed on a rolling basis. Application fee: $50. Electronic applications accepted. *Financial support:* Research assistantships, teaching assistantships, scholarships/grants, and unspecified assistantships available. Financial award applicants required to submit FAFSA. *Unit head:* Dr. Edward Hastings, Program Director, 610-519-6476.
Website: http://www1.villanova.edu/villanova/artsci/theology/graduate.html

Virginia Baptist College, Graduate Programs, Fredericksburg, VA 22407. Offers MBS, MCE, MM.

Virginia Beach Theological Seminary, Graduate Programs, Virginia Beach, VA 23464. Offers Biblical studies (MBS, Th M); chaplaincy (MBS); ministry (M Div). *Program availability:* Online learning. *Entrance requirements:* For master's, GRE, interview, minimum cumulative GPA of 2.4, church endorsement, 3 recommendations. Electronic applications accepted.

Virginia Theological Seminary, Graduate and Professional Programs, Alexandria, VA 22304. Offers Christian spirituality (D Min); educational leadership (D Ed Min, D Min); ministry development (D Min); theology (M Div, MA). *Accreditation:* ATS. *Program availability:* Part-time. *Degree requirements:* For master's, 2 foreign languages, thesis; for doctorate, thesis/dissertation. *Entrance requirements:* For master's and doctorate, GRE General Test.

Virginia Union University, Samuel DeWitt Proctor School of Theology, Richmond, VA 23220-1170. Offers M Div, D Min. *Accreditation:* ACIPE. *Program availability:* Part-time, evening/weekend. *Entrance requirements:* Additional exam requirements/recommendations for international students: Required—TOEFL.

Walsh University, Graduate Programs, Master of Arts in Theology Program, North Canton, OH 44720-3396. Offers parish administration (MA); pastoral ministry (MA); religious education (MA). *Program availability:* Part-time, evening/weekend. *Degree requirements:* For master's, thesis or alternative, culminating assignment. *Entrance requirements:* For master's, MAT or GRE (minimum scores: Verbal 145, Quantitative 146, Combined 291, Writing 3.0), minimum GPA of 3.0. Additional exam requirements/recommendations for international students: Required—TOEFL. Electronic applications accepted. Application fee is waived when completed online. *Expenses:* Contact institution. *Faculty research:* Cardinal Newman, phenomenological method, Flavius Josephus, post-conciliar moral teaching.

Wartburg Theological Seminary, Graduate and Professional Programs, Dubuque, IA 52004-5004. Offers diaconal ministry (MA); ministry (M Div); theology (MA). *Accreditation:* ACIPE; ATS. *Program availability:* Online learning. *Degree requirements:* For master's, thesis (for some programs). *Entrance requirements:* For master's, minimum GPA of 3.0 (STM). Additional exam requirements/recommendations for international students: Required—TOEFL (minimum score 500 paper-based; 80 iBT). Electronic applications accepted.

Wayland Baptist University, Graduate Programs, Programs in Religion, Plainview, TX 79072-6998. Offers Christian ministry (MCM); divinity (M Div); religion (MA). *Program availability:* Part-time, evening/weekend, online learning. *Faculty:* 15 full-time (1 woman), 12 part-time/adjunct (0 women). *Students:* 3 full-time (0 women), 97 part-time

(27 women); includes 61 minority (36 Black or African American, non-Hispanic/Latino; 1 American Indian or Alaska Native, non-Hispanic/Latino; 6 Asian, non-Hispanic/Latino; 9 Hispanic/Latino; 2 Native Hawaiian or other Pacific Islander, non-Hispanic/Latino; 7 Two or more races, non-Hispanic/Latino). Average age 45. 22 applicants, 95% accepted, 16 enrolled. In 2017, 26 master's awarded. *Degree requirements:* For master's, comprehensive exam. *Entrance requirements:* For master's, GRE or MAT, minimum GPA of 3.0; letter of endorsement from Christian congregation, one academic and one personal letter of recommendation (for M Div). Additional exam requirements/recommendations for international students: Required—TOEFL (minimum score 500 paper-based; 61 iBT). *Application deadline:* Applications are processed on a rolling basis. Application fee: $50. Electronic applications accepted. *Expenses: Tuition:* Full-time $11,250; part-time $625 per credit hour. *Required fees:* $1200. *Financial support:* Federal Work-Study, institutionally sponsored loans, and scholarships/grants available. Support available to part-time students. Financial award application deadline: 5/1; financial award applicants required to submit FAFSA. *Unit head:* Dr. Clinton Lowin, Chairman, 806-291-1165, Fax: 806-291-1969, E-mail: lowinc@wbu.edu. *Application contact:* Amanda Stanton, Coordinator of Graduate Studies, 806-291-3423, Fax: 806-291-1950, E-mail: stanton@wbu.edu.

Welch College, Program in Theology and Ministry, Gallatin, TN 37066. Offers MA. *Program availability:* Online learning.

Wesley Biblical Seminary, Graduate Programs, Jackson, MS 39206. Offers apologetics (MA); Biblical languages (M Div); Biblical literature (MA); Christian studies (MA); context and mission (M Div); honors research (M Div); interpretation (M Div); ministry (M Div); spiritual formation (M Div); teaching (M Div); theology (MA). *Accreditation:* ATS. *Program availability:* Part-time. *Degree requirements:* For master's, thesis. *Entrance requirements:* Additional exam requirements/recommendations for international students: Required—TOEFL. Electronic applications accepted. *Faculty research:* Patristics, missiology, culture, hermeneutics.

Wesley Theological Seminary, Graduate and Professional Programs, Washington, DC 20016-5690. Offers M Div, MA, MTS, D Min, M Div/MA, M Div/MTS. *Accreditation:* ACIPE; ATS. *Program availability:* Part-time. *Degree requirements:* For master's, thesis; for doctorate, thesis/dissertation. *Entrance requirements:* For master's, minimum GPA of 2.7; for doctorate, minimum GPA of 3.0.

Western Seminary, Graduate Programs, Master of Divinity Program, Portland, OR 97215-3367. Offers M Div. *Entrance requirements:* Additional exam requirements/recommendations for international students: Required—TOEFL.

Western Seminary, Graduate Programs, Program in Biblical and Theological Studies, Portland, OR 97215-3367. Offers biblical and theological studies (MA, G Dip); biblical studies (Certificate); theology (Th M). *Accreditation:* ATS. *Program availability:* Part-time, evening/weekend. *Degree requirements:* For master's, thesis or alternative, practicum. *Entrance requirements:* Additional exam requirements/recommendations for international students: Required—TOEFL.

Western Seminary–Sacramento Campus, Graduate Certificate Programs, Rocklin, CA 95765. Offers Bible (Graduate Certificate); coaching (Graduate Certificate); pastoral care to women (Graduate Certificate); theology (Graduate Certificate); youth and family (Graduate Certificate). *Program availability:* Online learning. *Entrance requirements:* For degree, essays, undergraduate transcripts, 4 recommendations. Additional exam requirements/recommendations for international students: Required—TOEFL.

Western Seminary–Sacramento Campus, Graduate Diploma Programs, Rocklin, CA 95765. Offers Bible and theology (Graduate Diploma); ministry (Graduate Diploma); pastoral care to women (Graduate Diploma). *Entrance requirements:* For degree, essays, undergraduate transcripts, 4 recommendations. Additional exam requirements/recommendations for international students: Required—TOEFL.

Western Seminary–Sacramento Campus, Master of Divinity Program, Rocklin, CA 95765. Offers M Div. *Entrance requirements:* Additional exam requirements/recommendations for international students: Required—TOEFL.

Western Seminary–Sacramento Campus, Program in Biblical and Theological Studies, Rocklin, CA 95765. Offers MA. *Entrance requirements:* For master's, essays, undergraduate transcripts, 4 recommendations. Additional exam requirements/recommendations for international students: Required—TOEFL.

Western Seminary–San Jose Campus, Graduate Programs, Milpitas, CA 95035. Offers Bible and theology (Graduate Diploma); Bible, camp and conference ministry (CGS); Biblical and theological studies (MA), including exegetical track, theological track; coaching (CGS); expositional ministry (M Div); marital and family therapy (MA); ministry (Graduate Diploma); ministry and leadership (MA), including camp and conference ministry, coaching, pastoral care to women, youth ministry; pastoral care to women (CGS, Graduate Diploma); pastoral ministry (M Div); theology (CGS); youth and family (CGS). *Program availability:* Part-time, evening/weekend, online learning. *Entrance requirements:* For master's, minimum GPA of 3.0. Electronic applications accepted.

Western Theological Seminary, Graduate and Professional Programs, Holland, MI 49423-3622. Offers divinity (M Div); ministry (D Min); theology (M Th, MA); urban pastoral ministry (Graduate Certificate); M Div/MSW. *Accreditation:* ACIPE; ATS. *Program availability:* Part-time, 100% online, blended/hybrid learning. *Degree requirements:* For doctorate, thesis/dissertation. *Entrance requirements:* Additional exam requirements/recommendations for international students: Required—TOEFL. Electronic applications accepted.

Westminster Seminary California, Programs in Theology, Escondido, CA 92027-4128. Offers Biblical studies (MA); historical theology (MA); theological studies (M Div, MA). *Program availability:* Part-time, evening/weekend. *Degree requirements:* For master's, 2 foreign languages, thesis (for some programs). *Entrance requirements:* For master's, 2 letters of reference. Additional exam requirements/recommendations for international students: Required—TOEFL (minimum score 570 paper-based; 89 iBT), TWE (minimum score 4.5). *Faculty research:* Neo-paganism, New Testament background, eschatology, Protestant scholasticism, Ezekiel.

Westminster Theological Seminary, Graduate and Professional Programs, Philadelphia, PA 19118. Offers apologetics (Th M); Biblical and urban studies (Certificate); Biblical counseling (MA); biblical studies (MAR); Christian studies (Certificate); church history (Th M); counseling (M Div); general studies (M Div, MAR); hermeneutics and Bible interpretations (PhD); historical and theological studies (PhD); historical theology (Th M); New Testament (Th M); Old Testament (Th M); pastoral counseling (D Min); pastoral ministry (M Div, D Min); systematic theology (Th M); theological studies (MAR); urban missions (M Div, MA, MAR, D Min). *Accreditation:* ATS. *Program availability:* Part-time. Terminal master's awarded for partial completion of doctoral program. *Degree requirements:* For master's, thesis (for some programs); for doctorate, 4 foreign languages, comprehensive exam (for some programs), thesis/dissertation. *Entrance requirements:* For doctorate, GRE General Test. Additional exam requirements/recommendations for international students: Required—TOEFL, TWE.

Wheaton College, Graduate School, Department of Biblical and Theological Studies, Wheaton, IL 60187-5593. Offers Biblical and theological studies (PhD); Biblical

archaeology (MA); Biblical exegesis (MA); Biblical studies (MA); general theological studies (MA); historical and systematic theology (MA), including Biblical and theological studies; history of Christianity (MA), including Biblical and theological studies. *Program availability:* Part-time. *Faculty:* 7 full-time (1 woman), 2 part-time/adjunct (both women). *Students:* 50 full-time (14 women), 44 part-time (22 women); includes 16 minority (5 Black or African American, non-Hispanic/Latino; 7 Asian, non-Hispanic/Latino; 2 Hispanic/Latino; 2 Two or more races, non-Hispanic/Latino), 23 international. Average age 34. 103 applicants, 67% accepted, 34 enrolled. In 2017, 44 master's, 6 doctorates awarded. *Degree requirements:* For doctorate, thesis/dissertation. *Entrance requirements:* For master's, GRE General Test. Additional exam requirements/recommendations for international students: Required—TOEFL (minimum score 550 paper-based; 80 iBT), IELTS (minimum score 6.5). *Application deadline:* For fall admission, 1/1 priority date for domestic students, 1/1 for international students; for spring admission, 11/1 for domestic students. Applications are processed on a rolling basis. Application fee: $30. Electronic applications accepted. *Expenses: Tuition:* Full-time $19,800; part-time $825 per credit hour. Tuition and fees vary according to degree level and program. *Financial support:* Fellowships, scholarships/grants, and unspecified assistantships available. Financial award application deadline: 3/1; financial award applicants required to submit FAFSA. *Unit head:* Dr. David Capes, Associate Dean, 630-752-5054. *Application contact:* Director of Graduate Admissions, 630-752-5195, Fax: 630-752-7047, E-mail: graduate.admissions@wheaton.edu.
Website: https://www.wheaton.edu/academics/programs/theology/biblical-and-theological-graduate-studies/

Wheaton College, Graduate School, Department of Evangelism, Wheaton, IL 60187-5593. Offers evangelism and leadership (MA); missional church movements (MA). *Program availability:* Part-time. *Faculty:* 1 full-time (0 women). *Students:* 2 full-time (0 women), 45 part-time (10 women); includes 7 minority (3 Black or African American, non-Hispanic/Latino; 1 American Indian or Alaska Native, non-Hispanic/Latino; 2 Asian, non-Hispanic/Latino; 1 Hispanic/Latino), 22 international. Average age 40. 12 applicants, 75% accepted, 6 enrolled. In 2017, 8 master's awarded. *Degree requirements:* For master's, thesis or alternative. *Entrance requirements:* For master's, GRE or MAT. Additional exam requirements/recommendations for international students: Required—TOEFL (minimum score 550 paper-based; 80 iBT), IELTS (minimum score 6.5). *Application deadline:* For fall admission, 3/1 priority date for domestic students, 1/1 for international students; for spring admission, 11/1 for domestic students. Applications are processed on a rolling basis. Application fee: $30. Electronic applications accepted. *Expenses: Tuition:* Full-time $19,800; part-time $825 per credit hour. Tuition and fees vary according to degree level and program. *Financial support:* Career-related internships or fieldwork, Federal Work-Study, scholarships/grants, and unspecified assistantships available. Financial award application deadline: 3/1; financial award applicants required to submit FAFSA. *Unit head:* Dr. Ed Stetzer, Chair, 630-752-5806, E-mail: evangelism.leadership@wheaton.edu. *Application contact:* Director of Graduate Admissions, 630-752-5195, Fax: 630-752-7047, E-mail: graduate.admissions@wheaton.edu.
Website: https://www.wheaton.edu/graduate-school/degrees/ma-in-evangelism-and-leadership/

Whitworth University, Graduate Studies in Theology, Spokane, WA 99251-0001. Offers Christian ministry (MA); mission and culture (MA); theology (MA). *Program availability:* Part-time, evening/weekend. *Faculty:* 19. *Students:* 47 part-time (21 women); includes 6 minority (2 Black or African American, non-Hispanic/Latino; 1 American Indian or Alaska Native, non-Hispanic/Latino; 3 Hispanic/Latino). Average age 35. *Application deadline:* For fall admission, 8/7 for domestic students; for spring admission, 1/1 for domestic students; for summer admission, 4/15 for domestic students. Applications are processed on a rolling basis. Electronic applications accepted. *Financial support:* In 2017–18, 17 students received support. Research assistantships, career-related internships or fieldwork, scholarships/grants, and unspecified assistantships available. Financial award application deadline: 8/7; financial award applicants required to submit FAFSA. *Unit head:* Dr. Jeremy Wynne, Director, 509-777-3222, E-mail: graduateandcsadmissions@whitworth.edu. *Application contact:* Hannah Fischer, Graduate Admissions, 509-777-3222, E-mail: graduateandcsadmissions@whitworth.edu.
Website: http://www.whitworth.edu/cms/academics/graduate-studies-in-theology/

Wilfrid Laurier University, Waterloo Lutheran Seminary, Waterloo, ON N2L 3C5, Canada. Offers divinity (M Div); multifaith spiritual care and counseling (Diploma); pastoral leadership (D Min); spiritual care and counseling (D Min); theology (M Th, MTS); M Div/MTS/MSW. *Accreditation:* ATS. *Program availability:* Part-time. *Degree requirements:* For master's, one foreign language, thesis (for some programs); for doctorate, thesis/dissertation. *Entrance requirements:* For master's, two letters of reference; for doctorate, M Div, two letters of reference. Additional exam requirements/recommendations for international students: Required—TOEFL (minimum score 573

paper-based; 89 iBT), IELTS (minimum score 7). Electronic applications accepted. *Expenses:* Contact institution. *Faculty research:* Biblical study, church history, systematic theology.

Winebrenner Theological Seminary, Graduate Programs, Findlay, OH 45840. Offers clinical counseling (MA); family ministry (MA); practical theology (MA); theological and ministerial studies (M Div, D Min); theological studies (MA). *Accreditation:* ATS (one or more programs are accredited). *Program availability:* Part-time, 100% online, blended/hybrid learning. *Degree requirements:* For master's, variable foreign language requirement, thesis (for some programs); for doctorate, thesis/dissertation. *Entrance requirements:* For doctorate, 3 years of post-M Div full-time ministry. Additional exam requirements/recommendations for international students: Required—TOEFL (minimum score 550 paper-based; 80 iBT). Electronic applications accepted. *Faculty research:* Inductive biblical language grammar; review of Tobias Hagerland's "Jesus and the Scriptures"; Teleios profile of student wholeness; Puritanism; theological aesthetics.

World Mission University, Graduate Programs, Los Angeles, CA 90020. Offers biblical preaching (M Div); Christian counseling (M Div, MACC); church ministry (M Div); church music (M Div, DCM); ministry (D Min); music (MA); theology (MAT). *Program availability:* Online learning.

Wycliffe College, Division of Advanced Degree Studies, Toronto, ON M5S 1H7, Canada. Offers MA, Th M, D Min, PhD, Th D. PhD, D Min, MA offered jointly with Toronto School of Theology; Th D, Th M with University of Toronto. *Accreditation:* ATS (one or more programs are accredited). *Program availability:* Part-time. Terminal master's awarded for partial completion of doctoral program. *Degree requirements:* For master's, 2 foreign languages, thesis (for some programs); for doctorate, 3 foreign languages, thesis/dissertation. *Entrance requirements:* Additional exam requirements/recommendations for international students: Required—TOEFL (minimum score 600 paper-based). *Expenses:* Contact institution. *Faculty research:* Old and New Testament, doctrine, ethics, philosophy, history.

Wycliffe College, Division of Basic Degree Studies, Toronto, ON M5S 1H7, Canada. Offers Christian Studies (Diploma); theology (M Div, M Rel, MTS). M Div, M Rel, MTS offered jointly with University of Toronto. *Accreditation:* ATS. *Program availability:* Part-time. *Degree requirements:* For master's, one foreign language, thesis. *Entrance requirements:* Additional exam requirements/recommendations for international students: Required—TOEFL (minimum score 580 paper-based).

Xavier University, College of Arts and Sciences, Department of Theology, Cincinnati, OH 45207. Offers health care mission integration (MA); theology (MA), including religious education, social and pastoral ministry, theology. *Program availability:* Part-time, evening/weekend. *Degree requirements:* For master's, final paper (or thesis) and defense or comprehension exam. *Entrance requirements:* For master's, MAT or GRE, 2 letters of recommendation; statement of reasons and goals for enrolling in program (1,000-2,000 words); resume; transcript. Additional exam requirements/recommendations for international students: Required—TOEFL (minimum score 550 paper-based; 79 iBT). Electronic applications accepted. Application fee is waived when completed online. *Expenses:* Contact institution. *Faculty research:* Scripture, ethics, constructive theology, historical theology.

Xavier University of Louisiana, Graduate School, Institute for Black Catholic Studies, New Orleans, LA 70125. Offers pastoral theology (Th M). *Program availability:* Part-time. *Degree requirements:* For master's, comprehensive exam, practicum. *Entrance requirements:* For master's, GRE General Test, MAT, minimum GPA of 2.5. Additional exam requirements/recommendations for international students: Required—TOEFL.

Yale University, Yale Divinity School, New Haven, CT 06511. Offers M Div, MAR, STM, JD/M Div, JD/MAR, M Div/MBA, M Div/MF, M Div/MSN, M Div/MSW, MAR/MSN, MAR/MSW, MD/M Div, MD/MAR. *Accreditation:* ACIPE; ATS. *Program availability:* Part-time. *Entrance requirements:* Additional exam requirements/recommendations for international students: Required—IELTS (minimum score 7). Electronic applications accepted. *Expenses:* Contact institution.

Yeshiva Beth Moshe, Graduate Programs, Scranton, PA 18505-2124. Offers Second Talmudical Degree, Talmudic Fellow Degree. *Accreditation:* AARTS.

Yeshiva Karlin Stolin, Graduate Programs, Brooklyn, NY 11204. Offers Advanced Rabbinical Degree. *Accreditation:* AARTS.

Yeshiva of Nitra Rabbinical College, Graduate Programs, Mount Kisco, NY 10549. Offers First Talmudic Degree, Second Talmudic Degree. *Accreditation:* AARTS.

Yeshiva Shaar Hatorah Talmudic Research Institute, Graduate Programs, Kew Gardens, NY 11418-1469. *Accreditation:* AARTS.

Yeshivath Zichron Moshe, Graduate Programs, South Fallsburg, NY 12779. Offers Advanced Talmudic Degree, Talmudic Scholar Degree. *Accreditation:* AARTS. *Program availability:* Part-time.

Section 13
Writing

This section contains a directory of institutions offering graduate work in writing, followed by an in-depth entry submitted by an institution that chose to prepare a detailed program description. Additional information about programs listed in the directory but not augmented by an in-depth entry may be obtained by writing directly to the dean of a graduate school or chair of a department at the address given in the directory.

For programs offering related work, see also in this book *Communication and Media* and *Language and Literature.*

CONTENTS

Program Directories

Featured Schools: Displays and Close-Ups

See:

Technical Writing

Carnegie Mellon University, Dietrich College of Humanities and Social Sciences, Department of English, Program in Professional Writing, Pittsburgh, PA 15213-3891. Offers editing and publishing (MAPW); policy and non-profit communication (MAPW); public and media relations/corporate communications (MAPW); science or healthcare communication (MAPW); technical writing (MAPW); writing for new media (MAPW); writing for print media (MAPW). *Program availability:* Part-time. *Entrance requirements:* For master's, GRE General Test. Additional exam requirements/recommendations for international students: Required—TOEFL, TWE.

Drexel University, College of Arts and Sciences, Department of Communication, Culture and Media, Philadelphia, PA 19104-2875. Offers communication (MS), including public communication, science communication, technical communication. *Program availability:* Part-time, evening/weekend. *Degree requirements:* For master's, internship, professional portfolio. *Entrance requirements:* Additional exam requirements/ recommendations for international students: Required—TOEFL. Electronic applications accepted. *Faculty research:* Science information and attitudes, science influence on literature, process of technical writing, document design, software documentation.

Illinois Institute of Technology, Graduate College, Lewis College of Human Sciences, Department of Humanities, Chicago, IL 60616. Offers information architecture (MS); technical communication (PhD); technical communication and information design (MS). *Program availability:* Part-time. *Degree requirements:* For master's, comprehensive exam, thesis or alternative; for doctorate, comprehensive exam, thesis/dissertation. *Entrance requirements:* For master's, GRE General Test (minimum score 144 Quantitative, 153 Verbal, and 4.0 Analytical Writing), minimum undergraduate GPA of 3.0; 2 letters of recommendation from faculty or supervisors; professional statement discussing academic goals; for doctorate, GRE General Test (minimum score 144 Quantitative, 153 Verbal, and 4.0 Analytical Writing), bachelor's or master's degree in a field that, in combination with the 27-credit hour technical core, would provide a solid basis for advanced academic work leading to original research in the field; 3 letters of recommendation from faculty or supervisors; professional statement discussing academic goals. Additional exam requirements/recommendations for international students: Required—TOEFL (minimum score 95 iBT); Recommended—IELTS (minimum score 7). Electronic applications accepted. *Faculty research:* Linguistics, punishment theory, political communication, gender and technology, philosophical and ethical issues in neuroscience.

James Madison University, The Graduate School, College of Arts and Letters, Program in Writing, Rhetoric, and Technical Communication, Harrisonburg, VA 22801. Offers MA, MS. *Program availability:* Part-time. *Students:* 9 full-time (8 women), 3 part-time (all women); includes 1 minority (Asian, non-Hispanic/Latino), 1 international. Average age 30. In 2017, 13 master's awarded. Application fee: $55. Electronic applications accepted. *Expenses:* Tuition, state resident: full-time $10,512; part-time $438 per credit hour. Tuition, nonresident: full-time $28,358; part-time $1162 per credit hour. *Required fees:* $1128. *Financial support:* In 2017–18, 8 students received support, including 5 fellowships, 3 teaching assistantships with full tuition reimbursements available (averaging $9,284 per year); career-related internships or fieldwork, Federal Work-Study, and assistantships (averaging $7911) also available. Financial award application deadline: 3/1; financial award applicants required to submit FAFSA. *Unit head:* Dr. Traci A. Zimmerman, Director of the School of Writing, Rhetoric and Technical Communication, 540-568-2334, E-mail: zimmerta@jmu.edu. *Application contact:* Lynette D. Michael, Director of Graduate Admissions, 540-568-6131 Ext. 6395, Fax: 540-568-7860, E-mail: michaeld@jmu.edu.
Website: http://www.jmu.edu/wrtc/

Johns Hopkins University, Zanvyl Krieger School of Arts and Sciences, Advanced Academic Programs, Program in Writing, Washington, DC 20036. Offers science writing (MA, Certificate); writing (MA). *Program availability:* Part-time, evening/weekend. *Degree requirements:* For master's, thesis. *Entrance requirements:* For master's, minimum GPA of 3.0, writing samples. Additional exam requirements/recommendations for international students: Required—TOEFL (minimum score 600 paper-based; 100 iBT). Electronic applications accepted.

Laurentian University, School of Graduate Studies and Research, Programme in Science Communication, Sudbury, ON P3E 2C6, Canada. Offers G Dip.

Louisiana Tech University, Graduate School, College of Liberal Arts, Ruston, LA 71272. Offers architecture (M Arch); art (MFA), including graphic design, photography, studio; audiology (Au D); communication (MA), including speech communication, theatre; English (MA), including literature, technical writing; history (MA); speech pathology (MA); technical writing and communication (Graduate Certificate). *Program availability:* Part-time. *Faculty:* 63 full-time (25 women), 5 part-time/adjunct (3 women). *Students:* 114 full-time (29 women), 31 part-time (19 women); includes 12 minority (4 Black or African American, non-Hispanic/Latino; 1 Asian, non-Hispanic/Latino; 3 Hispanic/Latino; 4 Two or more races, non-Hispanic/Latino), 5 international. Average age 30. 146 applicants, 59% accepted, 37 enrolled. In 2017, 49 master's, 3 doctorates awarded. *Degree requirements:* For master's, thesis (for some programs); for doctorate, thesis/dissertation. *Entrance requirements:* For master's, GRE General Test; for doctorate, GRE General Test, bachelor's degree, minimum GPA of 3.0 or 3.2 on last 60 hours attempted. Additional exam requirements/recommendations for international students: Required—TOEFL (minimum score 550 paper-based; 80 iBT), IELTS (minimum score 6.5). *Application deadline:* For fall admission, 8/1 priority date for domestic students, 6/1 for international students; for winter admission, 11/1 priority date for domestic students, 9/1 for international students; for spring admission, 2/1 priority date for domestic students, 12/1 for international students; for summer admission, 5/1 priority date for domestic students, 3/1 for international students. Application fee: $40 ($50 for international students). Electronic applications accepted. *Expenses:* Tuition, state resident: full-time $5146. Tuition, nonresident: full-time $10,147. *International tuition:* $10,267 full-time. *Required fees:* $2273. *Financial support:* In 2017–18, 63 students received support, including 46 research assistantships (averaging $5,229 per year), 7 teaching assistantships (averaging $5,543 per year); fellowships, career-related internships or fieldwork, Federal Work-Study, institutionally sponsored loans, tuition waivers (partial), and unspecified assistantships also available. Financial award application deadline: 2/1. *Faculty research:* Contributing to the expansion of historical and social scientific knowledge and understanding through original research and publication; diverse language, ethnic, cultural, and socioeconomic backgrounds with disorders of speech, language, swallowing, hearing, and cognitive aspects of communication; prevention of communication, swallowing, and hearing disorders. *Unit head:* Dr. Donald P. Kaczvinsky, Dean, 318-257-4805, Fax: 318-257-3935, E-mail: dkaczv@latech.edu. *Application contact:* Mary Green, Administrative Assistant, 318-257-2924, Fax: 318-257-4487, E-mail: meg@latech.edu.
Website: http://liberalarts.latech.edu/

Massachusetts Institute of Technology, School of Humanities, Arts, and Social Sciences, Program in Comparative Media Studies/Writing, Graduate Program in Science Writing, Cambridge, MA 02139. Offers SM. *Degree requirements:* For master's, thesis. *Entrance requirements:* For master's, GRE General Test. Additional exam requirements/recommendations for international students: Required—TOEFL, IELTS. Electronic applications accepted. *Faculty research:* Communicating science to the public; digital media; investigative journalism; documentary film.

Metropolitan State University, College of Liberal Arts, St. Paul, MN 55106-5000. Offers liberal studies (MA); technical communication (MS). *Program availability:* Part-time, evening/weekend. *Entrance requirements:* For master's, minimum GPA of 2.75, resume. Additional exam requirements/recommendations for international students: Required—TOEFL (minimum score 550 paper-based). *Application deadline:* For fall admission, 8/1 priority date for domestic students, 3/15 for international students; for winter admission, 10/15 for international students; for spring admission, 12/1 priority date for domestic students, 3/15 for international students. Applications are processed on a rolling basis. Application fee: $20. Electronic applications accepted. *Expenses:* Tuition, state resident: part-time $388.55 per credit. Tuition, nonresident: part-time $777.11 per credit. *Required fees:* $35.11 per credit. Part-time tuition and fees vary according to campus/location and program. *Financial support:* Research assistantships available. Financial award applicants required to submit FAFSA. *Application contact:* Susan Honsvall, Office and Administrative Specialist, 651-793-1445, E-mail: susan.honsvall@metrostate.edu.
Website: https://www.metrostate.edu/academics/liberal-arts

Texas Tech University, Graduate School, College of Arts and Sciences, Department of English, Lubbock, TX 79409-3091. Offers English (MA, PhD); technical communication (MA); technical communication and rhetoric (PhD). *Program availability:* Part-time, 100% online, blended/hybrid learning. *Faculty:* 79 full-time (46 women), 9 part-time/adjunct (4 women). *Students:* 80 full-time (46 women), 88 part-time (60 women); includes 32 minority (9 Black or African American, non-Hispanic/Latino; 1 American Indian or Alaska Native, non-Hispanic/Latino; 3 Asian, non-Hispanic/Latino; 13 Hispanic/Latino; 6 Two or more races, non-Hispanic/Latino), 8 international. Average age 35. 136 applicants, 32% accepted, 32 enrolled. In 2017, 28 master's, 16 doctorates awarded. Terminal master's awarded for partial completion of doctoral program. *Degree requirements:* For master's, variable foreign language requirement, comprehensive exam, thesis optional; for doctorate, variable foreign language requirement, comprehensive exam, thesis/dissertation. *Entrance requirements:* For master's and doctorate, GRE General Test. Additional exam requirements/recommendations for international students: Required—TOEFL (minimum score 550 paper-based; 79 iBT), IELTS (minimum score 6.5). *Application deadline:* For fall admission, 6/1 priority date for domestic students, 1/15 priority date for international students; for spring admission, 9/1 priority date for domestic students, 6/15 priority date for international students. Applications are processed on a rolling basis. Application fee: $60. Electronic applications accepted. *Expenses:* Contact institution. *Financial support:* In 2017–18, 101 students received support, including 84 fellowships (averaging $2,712 per year), 6 research assistantships (averaging $17,139 per year), 76 teaching assistantships (averaging $15,638 per year); career-related internships or fieldwork, Federal Work-Study, scholarships/grants, and unspecified assistantships also available. Financial award application deadline: 1/8; financial award applicants required to submit FAFSA. *Faculty research:* American, British, and comparative literature; creative writing; linguistics; film; technical communication and rhetoric. *Total annual research expenditures:* $21,274. *Unit head:* Dr. Brian Still, Department Chair, 806-834-6439, Fax: 806-742-0989, E-mail: brian.still@ttu.edu. *Application contact:* Dr. Julie Nelson Couch, Director of Graduate Studies, 806-834-1742, Fax: 806-742-0989, E-mail: english.gradadvisor@ttu.edu.
Website: http://www.english.ttu.edu/

The University of Alabama in Huntsville, School of Graduate Studies, College of Arts, Humanities, and Social Sciences, Department of English, Huntsville, AL 35899. Offers education (MA); English (MA); technical writing (Certificate); TESOL (Certificate). *Program availability:* Part-time, evening/weekend. *Degree requirements:* For master's, one foreign language, comprehensive exam, thesis or alternative, oral and written exams. *Entrance requirements:* For master's and Certificate, GRE General Test, minimum GPA of 3.0. Additional exam requirements/recommendations for international students: Required—TOEFL (minimum score 500 paper-based; 80 iBT), IELTS (minimum score 6.5). Electronic applications accepted. *Faculty research:* Fiction and identity, Shakespeare, science fiction, eighteenth-century literature, technical writing.

University of Arkansas at Little Rock, Graduate School, College of Social Sciences and Communication, Department of Rhetoric and Writing, Little Rock, AR 72204-1099. Offers professional and technical writing (MA). *Program availability:* Part-time, evening/weekend. *Degree requirements:* For master's, thesis or alternative, oral defense of final project. *Entrance requirements:* For master's, GRE, minimum GPA of 3.0, writing portfolio. *Faculty research:* Writing for industry, science, business, and government; composition and rhetorical theory; writing nonfiction; teaching of writing.

University of North Alabama, College of Arts and Sciences, Department of English, Program in Writing, Florence, AL 35632-0001. Offers creative writing (MA); rhetoric and composition (MA); technical writing (MA). *Program availability:* Part-time, 100% online. *Faculty:* 12 full-time (8 women). *Students:* 5 part-time (4 women). Average age 31. 5 applicants, 60% accepted, 3 enrolled. *Degree requirements:* For master's, comprehensive exam (for some programs), thesis (for some programs). *Entrance requirements:* For master's, GRE, MAT, three letters of recommendation; writing sample. Additional exam requirements/recommendations for international students: Required—TOEFL (minimum score 79 iBT), IELTS (minimum score 6), PTE (minimum score 54). *Application deadline:* Applications are processed on a rolling basis. Application fee: $50 ($100 for international students). Electronic applications accepted. *Expenses:* Tuition, state resident: full-time $7824; part-time $5943 per year. Tuition, nonresident: full-time $15,648; part-time $11,736 per year. *Required fees:* $3064; $2298 per unit. Tuition and fees vary according to course load and reciprocity agreements. *Financial support:* In 2017–18, 2 students received support. Federal Work-Study, scholarships/grants, and unspecified assistantships available. Financial award application deadline: 2/1; financial award applicants required to submit FAFSA. *Unit head:* Dr. Tammy Winner, Coordinator, 256-660-9026, E-mail: twinner@una.edu. *Application contact:* Hillary N. Coats, Graduate Admissions Coordinator, 256-765-4447, E-mail: graduate@una.edu.
Website: https://www.una.edu/english/master-of-arts-in-writing.html

The University of North Carolina at Charlotte, College of Liberal Arts and Sciences, Department of English, Charlotte, NC 28223-0001. Offers applied linguistics (Graduate Certificate); English (MA); technical and professional writing (Graduate Certificate).

Program availability: Part-time, evening/weekend. *Faculty:* 33 full-time (19 women), 2 part-time/adjunct (1 woman). *Students:* 33 full-time (25 women), 20 part-time (14 women); includes 9 minority (1 Black or African American, non-Hispanic/Latino; 2 Asian, non-Hispanic/Latino; 5 Hispanic/Latino; 1 Two or more races, non-Hispanic/Latino), 2 international. Average age 30. 38 applicants, 87% accepted, 18 enrolled. In 2017, 19 master's, 2 other advanced degrees awarded. *Degree requirements:* For master's, comprehensive exam (for some programs), thesis, comprehensive exam, or project. *Entrance requirements:* For master's, GRE, MAT, minimum undergraduate GPA of 3.0, statement of purpose, recommendation letters; for Graduate Certificate, statement of purpose, three letters of recommendation, writing sample, minimum GPA of 2.75. Additional exam requirements/recommendations for international students: Required—TOEFL (minimum score 523 paper-based, 70 iBT) or IELTS (6.5). *Application deadline:* For fall admission, 3/1 priority date for domestic and international students; for spring admission, 10/1 priority date for domestic and international students; for summer admission, 4/1 priority date for domestic and international students. Applications are processed on a rolling basis. Application fee: $75. Electronic applications accepted. *Expenses:* Tuition, state resident: full-time $4337. Tuition, nonresident: full-time $17,771. *Required fees:* $3211. Tuition and fees vary according to course load and program. *Financial support:* In 2017–18, 17 students received support, including 17 teaching assistantships (averaging $8,118 per year); career-related internships or fieldwork, institutionally sponsored loans, scholarships/grants, and unspecified assistantships also available. Support available to part-time students. Financial award application deadline: 3/1; financial award applicants required to submit FAFSA. *Total annual research expenditures:* $30,460. *Unit head:* Dr. Mark West, Chair, 704-687-0618, E-mail: miwest@uncc.edu. *Application contact:* Kathy B. Giddings, Director of Graduate Admissions, 704-687-5503, Fax: 704-687-1668, E-mail: gradadm@uncc.edu. Website: http://english.uncc.edu/

The University of North Carolina at Greensboro, Graduate School, College of Arts and Sciences, Department of English, Greensboro, NC 27412-5001. Offers creative writing (MFA); English (M Ed, MA, PhD, Certificate), including American literature (PhD), English (M Ed, MA), English literature (PhD), rhetoric and composition (PhD), technical writing (Certificate), women's studies (Certificate). *Degree requirements:* For master's, comprehensive exam; for doctorate, variable foreign language requirement, thesis/dissertation, preliminary exam. *Entrance requirements:* For master's, GRE General Test, minimum GPA of 3.0; for doctorate, GRE General Test, GRE Subject Test, critical writing sample, minimum GPA of 3.0. Additional exam requirements/recommendations for international students: Required—TOEFL. Electronic applications accepted.

University of the Sciences, Program in Biomedical Writing, Philadelphia, PA 19104-4495. Offers biomedical writing (MS); medical marketing writing (Certificate); regulatory affairs writing (Certificate). *Program availability:* Part-time, evening/weekend, online

learning. *Entrance requirements:* For master's, GRE General Test. Additional exam requirements/recommendations for international students: Required—TOEFL, TWE. *Expenses:* Contact institution.

University of Waterloo, Graduate Studies, Faculty of Arts, Department of English Language and Literature, Waterloo, ON N2L 3G1, Canada. Offers English language and literature (PhD); literary studies (MA); rhetoric and communication design (MA). *Program availability:* Part-time. *Degree requirements:* For master's, one foreign language, thesis optional; for doctorate, 2 foreign languages, thesis/dissertation. *Entrance requirements:* For master's, honors degree, minimum B+ average; for doctorate, master's degree, minimum A- average. Additional exam requirements/recommendations for international students: Required—TOEFL, IELTS, PTE. Electronic applications accepted. *Faculty research:* Shakespeare, American literature, rhetoric, Romantics, moderns.

Western Carolina University, Graduate School, College of Arts and Sciences, Department of English, Cullowhee, NC 28723. Offers literature (MA); professional writing (MA); rhetoric and composition (MA); teaching English to speakers of other languages (Certificate); technical and professional writing (Certificate). *Program availability:* Part-time, evening/weekend. *Students:* 31. *Degree requirements:* For master's, one foreign language, comprehensive exam, thesis (for some programs). *Entrance requirements:* For master's, appropriate undergraduate degree, writing sample, 3 letters of recommendation. Additional exam requirements/recommendations for international students: Required—TOEFL (minimum score 550 paper-based, 79 iBT) or IELTS (6.5). *Application deadline:* For fall admission, 2/15 priority date for domestic and international students; for spring admission, 11/15 priority date for domestic students, 10/15 priority date for international students. Applications are processed on a rolling basis. Application fee: $65. Electronic applications accepted. *Expenses:* $10,000 per year in-state full-time; $20,308 per year out-of-state full-time. *Financial support:* In 2017–18, 1 research assistantship with full and partial tuition reimbursement (averaging $9,000 per year), 16 teaching assistantships with full and partial tuition reimbursements (averaging $9,500 per year) were awarded; career-related internships or fieldwork, institutionally sponsored loans, scholarships/grants, and unspecified assistantships also available. Financial award application deadline: 2/15; financial award applicants required to submit FAFSA. *Faculty research:* Teaching English to speakers of other languages (TESOL), language assessment, applied linguistics, poetry, folk and fairy tales, post World War II British literature, Appalachian and Southern literature. *Unit head:* Dr. Brent Kinser, Department Head, E-mail: bkinser@wcu.edu. *Application contact:* Bobbi Smith, Graduate Admissions Coordinator, E-mail: bobbismith@email.wcu.edu. Website: https://www.wcu.edu/learn/departments-schools-colleges/cas/humanities/english/enggrad/index.aspx

Writing

Abilene Christian University, Graduate Programs, College of Arts and Sciences, Department of English, Abilene, TX 79699. Offers composition/rhetoric (MA); literature (MA); writing (MA). *Program availability:* Part-time. *Faculty:* 16 part-time/adjunct (6 women). *Students:* 4 full-time (3 women), 1 (woman) part-time. 8 applicants, 50% accepted, 1 enrolled. In 2017, 8 master's awarded. *Degree requirements:* For master's, one foreign language, comprehensive exam (for some programs), thesis (for some programs). *Entrance requirements:* For master's, GRE General Test. Additional exam requirements/recommendations for international students: Required—TOEFL (minimum score 80 iBT), IELTS (minimum score 6), PTE. *Application deadline:* For fall admission, 8/11 for domestic students; for spring admission, 11/1 for domestic students. Applications are processed on a rolling basis. Application fee: $50. Electronic applications accepted. *Expenses:* $1,148 per hour. *Financial support:* In 2017–18, 4 students received support, including 4 teaching assistantships with partial tuition reimbursements available (averaging $5,800 per year); Federal Work-Study and scholarships/grants also available. Support available to part-time students. Financial award application deadline: 4/1; financial award applicants required to submit FAFSA. *Faculty research:* Feminism, Shakespearean dimensions of new literature, poetic consciousness, deconstruction myths. *Unit head:* Dr. William Carroll, Graduate Director, 325-674-2556, Fax: 325-674-2408, E-mail: william.carroll@acu.edu. *Application contact:* Graduate Admissions, 325-674-6911, Fax: 325-674-6717, E-mail: gradinfo@acu.edu. Website: http://www.acu.edu/graduate/academics/english.html

Academy of Art University, Graduate Programs, School of Motion Pictures and Television, San Francisco, CA 94105-3410. Offers motion pictures and television (MFA); writing and directing for film (MA). *Program availability:* Part-time, 100% online. *Faculty:* 8 full-time (2 women), 37 part-time/adjunct (10 women). *Students:* 147 full-time (73 women), 69 part-time (27 women); includes 24 minority (10 Black or African American, non-Hispanic/Latino; 1 American Indian or Alaska Native, non-Hispanic/Latino; 4 Asian, non-Hispanic/Latino; 5 Hispanic/Latino; 4 Two or more races, non-Hispanic/Latino), 148 international. Average age 29. 69 applicants, 100% accepted, 44 enrolled. In 2017, 75 master's awarded. *Degree requirements:* For master's, final review. *Entrance requirements:* For master's, statement of intent; resume; portfolio/reel; official college transcripts. *Application deadline:* Applications are processed on a rolling basis. Application fee: $50. Electronic applications accepted. *Expenses: Tuition:* Part-time $982 per unit. *Financial support:* Career-related internships or fieldwork, Federal Work-Study, and scholarships/grants available. Financial award application deadline: 8/10; financial award applicants required to submit FAFSA. *Unit head:* 800-544-ARTS, E-mail: info@academyart.edu. *Application contact:* 800-544-ARTS, E-mail: info@academyart.edu. Website: http://www.academyart.edu/film-school/index.html

Academy of Art University, Graduate Programs, School of Writing for Film, Television and Digital Media, San Francisco, CA 94105-3410. Offers MFA. *Program availability:* Part-time, 100% online. *Faculty:* 13 part-time/adjunct (4 women). *Students:* 14 full-time (9 women), 23 part-time (19 women); includes 13 minority (5 Black or African American, non-Hispanic/Latino; 1 American Indian or Alaska Native, non-Hispanic/Latino; 4 Hispanic/Latino; 3 Two or more races, non-Hispanic/Latino), 7 international. Average age 36. 15 applicants, 100% accepted, 9 enrolled. In 2017, 3 master's awarded. *Degree requirements:* For master's, final review. *Entrance requirements:* For master's, statement of intent; resume; portfolio/reel; official college transcripts. *Application deadline:* Applications are processed on a rolling basis. Application fee: $50. Electronic applications accepted. *Expenses: Tuition:* Part-time $982 per unit. *Financial support:* Career-related internships or fieldwork, Federal Work-Study, and scholarships/grants available. Financial award application deadline: 8/10; financial award applicants required to submit FAFSA. *Unit head:* 800-544-ARTS, E-mail: info@academyart.edu. *Application*

contact: 800-544-ARTS, E-mail: info@academyart.edu. Website: http://www.academyart.edu/academics/writing-film-television-digital-media

Adelphi University, College of Arts and Sciences, Program in Creative Writing, Garden City, NY 11530-0701. Offers MFA. *Program availability:* Part-time, evening/weekend. *Students:* 5 full-time (all women), 10 part-time (7 women); includes 10 minority (1 Black or African American, non-Hispanic/Latino; 3 Asian, non-Hispanic/Latino; 5 Hispanic/Latino; 1 Two or more races, non-Hispanic/Latino), 1 international. Average age 30. 52 applicants, 50% accepted, 6 enrolled. In 2017, 5 master's awarded. *Degree requirements:* For master's, thesis. *Entrance requirements:* For master's, 2 letters of reference, manuscript in chosen genre (poetry, fiction, playwriting), personal statement essay, college transcript. Additional exam requirements/recommendations for international students: Required—TOEFL (minimum score 550 paper-based; 80 iBT), IELTS (minimum score 6.5). *Application deadline:* For fall admission, 5/1 priority date for international students; for spring admission, 11/1 priority date for international students. Applications are processed on a rolling basis. Application fee: $50. Electronic applications accepted. *Expenses:* Contact institution. *Financial support:* Research assistantships, teaching assistantships, career-related internships or fieldwork, institutionally sponsored loans, scholarships/grants, traineeships, and unspecified assistantships available. Support available to part-time students. *Unit head:* Judith Baumel, Director, 516-877-4031, E-mail: baumel@adelphi.edu. *Application contact:* E-mail: graduateadmissions@adelphi.edu. Website: http://academics.adelphi.edu/artsci/creativewriting/

Albertus Magnus College, Master of Fine Arts in Writing Program, New Haven, CT 06511-1189. Offers MFA. *Program availability:* Part-time, evening/weekend, 100% online, blended/hybrid learning. *Degree requirements:* For master's, thesis, project, minimum cumulative GPA of 3.0, completion of all requirements within seven years of matriculation. *Entrance requirements:* Additional exam requirements/recommendations for international students: Recommended—TOEFL (minimum score 550 paper-based; 80 iBT). *Application deadline:* For fall admission, 8/15 for domestic students; for spring admission, 1/15 for domestic students. Applications are processed on a rolling basis. Application fee: $50. Electronic applications accepted. *Expenses:* Contact institution. *Financial support:* Federal Work-Study and unspecified assistantships available. Support available to part-time students. Financial award applicants required to submit FAFSA. *Unit head:* Charles Rafferty, Director, 203-773-6901, Fax: 203-777-3701, E-mail: crafferty@albertus.edu. *Application contact:* Prof. Sarah Wallman, Co-Director, 203-777-4473, Fax: 203-777-3701, E-mail: swallman@albertus.edu. Website: http://www.albertus.edu/fine-arts/mfa/

American College Dublin, Graduate Programs, Dublin, Ireland. Offers business administration (MBA); creative writing (MFA); international business (MBA); oil and gas management (MBA); performance (MFA).

American University, College of Arts and Sciences, Department of Literature, Washington, DC 20016-8047. Offers creative writing (MFA); literature (MA). *Program availability:* Part-time, evening/weekend. *Faculty:* 53 full-time (36 women), 14 part-time/adjunct (9 women). *Students:* 39 full-time (22 women), 22 part-time (13 women); includes 22 minority (10 Black or African American, non-Hispanic/Latino; 5 Asian, non-Hispanic/Latino; 6 Hispanic/Latino; 1 Two or more races, non-Hispanic/Latino), 3 international. Average age 34. 136 applicants, 77% accepted, 21 enrolled. In 2017, 17 master's awarded. *Degree requirements:* For master's, comprehensive exam. *Entrance requirements:* For master's, GRE, writing sample, statement of purpose, transcripts, 2 letters of recommendation, resume. Additional exam requirements/recommendations for international students: Required—TOEFL (minimum score 600 paper-based; 100 iBT). *Application deadline:* For fall admission, 2/1 priority date for domestic students; for spring admission, 11/1 priority date for domestic students. Application fee: $55.

Expenses: Contact institution. *Financial support:* Institutionally sponsored loans and unspecified assistantships available. Financial award application deadline: 2/1; financial award applicants required to submit FAFSA. *Unit head:* Dr. David Pike, Department Chair, 202-885-2996, E-mail: dpike@american.edu. *Application contact:* Jonathan Harper, Assistant Director, Graduate Recruitment, 202-855-3622, E-mail: jharper@american.edu.
Website: http://www.american.edu/cas/literature/

Antioch University Santa Barbara, Program in Writing and Contemporary Media, Santa Barbara, CA 93101-1581. Offers MFA. *Program availability:* Part-time. *Degree requirements:* For master's, thesis project.

Arcadia University, College of Arts and Sciences, Department of English, Program in Creative Writing, Glenside, PA 19038-3295. Offers MFA. *Expenses:* Contact institution.

Arizona State University at the Tempe campus, College of Liberal Arts and Sciences, Department of English, Interdisciplinary Program in Creative Writing, Tempe, AZ 85287-0302. Offers MFA. *Degree requirements:* For master's, thesis, practicum (9 hours). *Entrance requirements:* For master's, undergraduate major in English or creative writing (preferred), minimum GPA of 3.0, 3 letters of recommendation, resume or curriculum vitae, personal statement, official transcripts, 3 copies of manuscript sample (20 pages of poetry, 30 pages of prose, or both). Additional exam requirements/recommendations for international students: Required—TOEFL, IELTS, or PTE. Electronic applications accepted.

Arizona State University at the Tempe campus, Herberger Institute for Design and the Arts, School of Film, Dance and Theatre, Tempe, AZ 85287-2002. Offers dance (MFA), including dance, interdisciplinary digital media and performance; theatre (MA, MFA, PhD), including arts entrepreneurship and management (MFA), directing (MFA), dramatic writing (MFA), interdisciplinary digital media and performance (MFA), performance (MFA), performance design (MFA), theatre (MFA), theatre and performance of the Americas (PhD), theatre for youth (MFA, PhD). Terminal master's awarded for partial completion of doctoral program. *Degree requirements:* For master's, comprehensive exam (for some programs), thesis (for some programs), applied project (for some programs); interactive Program of Study (iPOS) submitted before completing 50 percent of required credit hours; for doctorate, comprehensive exam, thesis/dissertation, interactive Program of Study (iPOS) submitted before completing 50 percent of required credit hours. *Entrance requirements:* For master's, GRE or MAT, minimum GPA of 3.0 in last 2 years of work leading to bachelor's degree (depending on program); for doctorate, GRE, minimum GPA of 3.0 or equivalent in last 2 years of work leading to bachelor's degree, 3 letters of recommendation, resume, scholarly writing sample, statement of purpose. Additional exam requirements/recommendations for international students: Required—TOEFL, IELTS, or PTE. Electronic applications accepted.

Asbury University, School of Graduate and Professional Studies, Wilmore, KY 40390-1198. Offers biology: alternative certificate (MA Ed); chemistry: alternative certificate (MA Ed); English (MA Ed); English as a second language (MA Ed); ESL (MA Ed); French (MA Ed); Latin: alternative certificate (MA Ed); mathematics: alternative certificate (MA Ed); reading/writing endorsement (MA Ed); social studies (MA Ed); social work (MSW), including child and family services; Spanish (MA Ed); special education (MA Ed); special education: alternative certificate (MA Ed); teacher as leader endorsement (MA Ed). *Accreditation:* NCATE. *Program availability:* Part-time. *Degree requirements:* For master's, action research project, portfolio. *Entrance requirements:* For master's, PRAXIS/NTE, minimum GPA of 2.75, letters of recommendation. Additional exam requirements/recommendations for international students: Required—TOEFL (minimum score 550 paper-based). Electronic applications accepted.

Ashland University, College of Arts and Sciences, Program in Creative Writing, Ashland, OH 44805-3702. Offers MFA. *Program availability:* Online learning. *Degree requirements:* For master's, thesis. *Entrance requirements:* For master's, writing sample, minimum GPA of 2.75. *Application deadline:* For fall admission, 2/1 priority date for domestic students; for winter admission, 9/1 priority date for domestic students. Applications are processed on a rolling basis. Application fee: $30. Electronic applications accepted. *Expenses:* Contact institution. *Financial support:* Career-related internships or fieldwork, Federal Work-Study, and institutionally sponsored loans available. Financial award application deadline: 4/15; financial award applicants required to submit FAFSA. *Unit head:* Dr. Christian Kiefer, Director, MFA Program, 419-289-5979, Fax: 419-289-5255, E-mail: mfa@ashland.edu. *Application contact:* Bernie Bannin, Director, Graduate, Online, and Adult Admissions, 419-289-5291, E-mail: grad-admissions@ashland.edu.

Auburn University at Montgomery, College of Arts and Sciences, Department of English and Philosophy, Montgomery, AL 36124-4023. Offers teaching writing (MTW). In 2017, 16 master's awarded. *Degree requirements:* For master's, thesis. *Entrance requirements:* For master's, GRE General Test or MAT. Additional exam requirements/recommendations for international students: Required—TOEFL (minimum score 500 paper-based; 61 iBT), IELTS (minimum score 5.5), PTE (minimum score 44). *Application deadline:* For fall admission, 7/15 for international students; for spring admission, 11/15 for international students; for summer admission, 4/15 for international students. Applications are processed on a rolling basis. Electronic applications accepted. *Expenses:* Tuition, state resident: full-time $6930; part-time $385 per credit hour. Tuition, nonresident: full-time $15,588; part-time $866 per credit hour. *Required fees:* $640. *Financial support:* Application deadline: 3/1; applicants required to submit FAFSA. *Unit head:* Dr. John Havard, Chair, 334-244-3228, E-mail: jhavard@aum.edu.
Website: http://www.cas.aum.edu/departments/english-and-philosophy

Ball State University, Graduate School, College of Sciences and Humanities, Department of English, Muncie, IN 47306. Offers English (MA, PhD), including composition (MA), creative writing (MA), literature, rhetoric and composition; linguistics (MA), including linguistics, teaching English to speakers of other languages (TESOL) and linguistics. *Program availability:* Part-time. *Faculty:* 20 full-time (15 women), 2 part-time/adjunct (both women). *Students:* 45 full-time (30 women), 30 part-time (17 women); includes 5 minority (2 Asian, non-Hispanic/Latino; 3 Hispanic/Latino), 17 international. Average age 29. 93 applicants, 61% accepted, 32 enrolled. In 2017, 20 master's, 7 doctorates awarded. *Degree requirements:* For doctorate, variable foreign language requirement, thesis/dissertation. *Entrance requirements:* For master's, GRE General Test, minimum baccalaureate GPA of 2.75 or 3.0 in latter half of baccalaureate, statement of purpose, writing sample, three letters of recommendation; for doctorate, GRE General Test, GRE Subject Test, minimum graduate GPA of 3.2, statement of purpose, writing sample, three letters of recommendation. Additional exam requirements/recommendations for international students: Required—TOEFL (minimum score 550 paper-based; 79 iBT), IELTS (minimum score 6.5). *Application deadline:* Applications are processed on a rolling basis. Application fee: $60. Electronic applications accepted. *Financial support:* In 2017–18, 46 students received support, including 5 research assistantships with partial tuition reimbursements available (averaging $15,132 per year), 28 teaching assistantships with partial tuition reimbursements available (averaging $13,595 per year); unspecified assistantships also available. Financial award application deadline: 3/1; financial award applicants required to submit FAFSA. *Faculty research:* American literature; literary editing; medieval, Renaissance, and eighteenth-century British literature; rhetoric. *Unit head:* Dr. Deborah Mix, Assistant Chair of Programs, 765-285-8401, Fax: 765-285-3765, E-mail: dmmix@bsu.edu. *Application contact:* Dr. Deborah Mix, Assistant Chair of Programs, 765-285-8401, Fax: 765-285-3765, E-mail: dmmix@bsu.edu.
Website: http://www.bsu.edu/english/

Bard College, Milton Avery Graduate School of the Arts, Annandale-on-Hudson, NY 12504. Offers film/video (MFA); music/sound (MFA); painting (MFA); photography (MFA); sculpture (MFA); writing (MFA). *Degree requirements:* For master's, thesis, project, 8-week summer residency, independent study. *Entrance requirements:* For master's, interview, portfolio, 2 letters of recommendation, history of work in the arts. Additional exam requirements/recommendations for international students: Required—TOEFL (minimum score 550 paper-based). Electronic applications accepted. *Expenses:* Contact institution. *Faculty research:* Original work in painting, writing, sculpture, photography, video/film, sound/music.

Bay Path University, Program in Creative Nonfiction, Longmeadow, MA 01106-2292. Offers MFA. *Program availability:* Part-time, evening/weekend, online only, 100% online. *Students:* 3 full-time (all women), 34 part-time (29 women); includes 6 minority (2 Black or African American, non-Hispanic/Latino; 2 Hispanic/Latino; 2 Two or more races, non-Hispanic/Latino). Average age 48. In 2017, 7 master's awarded. *Entrance requirements:* For master's, minimum GPA of 3.0 or minimum B grades in English and/or writing classes. *Application deadline:* Applications are processed on a rolling basis. Application fee: $45. Electronic applications accepted. Application fee is waived when completed online. *Expenses:* $730 per credit. *Financial support:* Applicants required to submit FAFSA. *Unit head:* Leanne James Blackwell, Director, 413-565-1232, E-mail: ljblackwell@baypath.edu. *Application contact:* Diane Ranaldi, Dean of Graduate Admissions, 413-565-1332, Fax: 413-565-1250, E-mail: dranaldi@baypath.edu.
Website: http://graduate.baypath.edu/graduate-programs/programs-online/mfa-program/creative-nonfiction

Bennington College, Graduate Programs, MFA Program in Writing, Bennington, VT 05201. Offers MFA. *Program availability:* Online learning. *Degree requirements:* For master's, thesis, collection of essays or poems, or collection of short stories and/or a novel. *Entrance requirements:* For master's, manuscript. *Expenses:* Contact institution.

Binghamton University, State University of New York, Graduate School, Harpur College of Arts and Sciences, Department of English, Binghamton, NY 13902-6000. Offers creative writing (MA); English (PhD); English/American literature (MA). *Program availability:* Part-time. *Faculty:* 33 full-time (20 women). *Students:* 36 full-time (25 women), 47 part-time (26 women); includes 12 minority (3 Black or African American, non-Hispanic/Latino; 1 American Indian or Alaska Native, non-Hispanic/Latino; 4 Asian, non-Hispanic/Latino; 3 Hispanic/Latino; 1 Two or more races, non-Hispanic/Latino), 21 international. Average age 32. 74 applicants, 57% accepted, 16 enrolled. In 2017, 12 master's, 10 doctorates awarded. Terminal master's awarded for partial completion of doctoral program. *Degree requirements:* For master's, one foreign language, thesis; for doctorate, one foreign language, comprehensive exam, thesis/dissertation. *Entrance requirements:* For master's and doctorate, GRE General Test, writing sample. Additional exam requirements/recommendations for international students: Required—TOEFL (minimum score 550 paper-based; 80 iBT). *Application deadline:* For fall admission, 2/15 priority date for domestic and international students; for spring admission, 11/15 priority date for domestic and international students. Application fee: $75. Electronic applications accepted. *Financial support:* In 2017–18, 38 students received support, including 1 fellowship with full tuition reimbursement available (averaging $15,000 per year), 1 research assistantship (averaging $9,000 per year), 30 teaching assistantships with full tuition reimbursements available (averaging $15,000 per year); career-related internships or fieldwork, Federal Work-Study, institutionally sponsored loans, scholarships/grants, health care benefits, tuition waivers (full and partial), and unspecified assistantships also available. Financial award applicants required to submit FAFSA. *Unit head:* Praseeda Gopinath, Graduate Director, 607-777-2033, Fax: 607-777-2408, E-mail: gopinath@binghamton.edu. *Application contact:* Ben Balkaya, Assistant Dean and Director, 607-777-2151, Fax: 607-777-2501, E-mail: balkaya@binghamton.edu.
Website: http://www2.binghamton.edu/english/

Boston University, Graduate School of Arts and Sciences, Creative Writing Program, Boston, MA 02215. Offers MFA. *Students:* 20 full-time (11 women), 8 part-time (6 women); includes 8 minority (7 Asian, non-Hispanic/Latino; 1 Hispanic/Latino), 5 international. Average age 30. 725 applicants, 2% accepted, 18 enrolled. In 2017, 21 master's awarded. *Degree requirements:* For master's, one foreign language, thesis. *Entrance requirements:* Additional exam requirements/recommendations for international students: Required—TOEFL (minimum score 550 paper-based; 84 iBT). *Application deadline:* For fall admission, 2/1 for domestic and international students. Application fee: $95. Electronic applications accepted. *Financial support:* In 2017–18, 18 students received support, including teaching assistantships with full tuition reimbursements available (averaging $14,000 per year); Federal Work-Study, scholarships/grants, health care benefits, and unspecified assistantships also available. Financial award application deadline: 2/1. *Unit head:* Ha Jin, Director, 617-353-2510, Fax: 617-353-3653, E-mail: xjin@bu.edu. *Application contact:* Catherine Con, Administrative Coordinator, 617-353-2510, Fax: 617-353-3653, E-mail: crwr@bu.edu.
Website: http://www.bu.edu/creativewriting/

Boston University, Graduate School of Arts and Sciences, Editorial Institute, Boston, MA 02215. Offers MA. *Students:* 13 full-time (8 women), 4 part-time (2 women); includes 3 minority (2 Hispanic/Latino; 1 Two or more races, non-Hispanic/Latino), 1 international. Average age 31. 3 applicants. In 2017, 1 master's awarded. *Degree requirements:* For master's, thesis. *Entrance requirements:* For master's, GRE General Test, thesis proposal, 3 letters of recommendation, transcripts, personal statement. Additional exam requirements/recommendations for international students: Required—TOEFL (minimum score 550 paper-based; 84 iBT). *Application deadline:* For fall admission, 4/15 for domestic and international students. Application fee: $95. Electronic applications accepted. *Financial support:* In 2017–18, 16 students received support, including fellowships with full tuition reimbursements available (averaging $22,000 per year), 5 research assistantships with full tuition reimbursements available (averaging $22,000 per year), 5 teaching assistantships with full tuition reimbursements available (averaging $22,000 per year); Federal Work-Study, scholarships/grants, and health care benefits also available. Financial award application deadline: 1/15. *Unit head:* Archie Burnett, Director, 617-353-6631, E-mail: burnetta@bu.edu. *Application contact:* Ellen Wrigley, Administrative Assistant, 617-353-6631, Fax: 617-353-6917, E-mail: ellen@bu.edu.
Website: http://www.bu.edu/editinst/

Boston University, Graduate School of Arts and Sciences, Playwriting Program, Boston, MA 02215. Offers MFA. Program admits students in even-numbered years. *Students:* 5 full-time (4 women), 1 part-time (0 women); includes 1 minority (Hispanic/Latino), 2 international. Average age 27. In 2017, 4 master's awarded. *Degree requirements:* For master's, one foreign language. *Entrance requirements:* For master's, GRE, 3 letters of recommendation, one original full-length play or two one-act plays, transcripts, personal statement, curriculum vitae, ability to read or speak a foreign language. Additional exam requirements/recommendations for international students:

Required—TOEFL (minimum score 550 paper-based; 84 iBT). *Application deadline:* For fall admission, 2/15 for domestic and international students. Application fee: $95. Electronic applications accepted. *Financial support:* In 2017–18, 5 students received support, including 2 teaching assistantships with full tuition reimbursements available (averaging $11,000 per year); Federal Work-Study, scholarships/grants, health care benefits, and unspecified assistantships also available. Financial award application deadline: 2/15. *Unit head:* Katherine Snodgrass, Artistic Director, 617-353-5104, Fax: 617-353-6196, E-mail: ksnodgra@bu.edu. *Application contact:* Martin Gastmann, Assistant Director of Admissions and Financial Aid, 617-353-2696, Fax: 617-358-5492, E-mail: grs@bu.edu.
Website: http://www.bu.edu/playwriting

Bowling Green State University, Graduate College, College of Arts and Sciences, Department of English, Program in Creative Writing, Bowling Green, OH 43403. Offers fiction (MFA); poetry (MFA). *Program availability:* Part-time. *Degree requirements:* For master's, thesis or alternative. *Entrance requirements:* For master's, GRE General Test. Additional exam requirements/recommendations for international students: Required—TOEFL. Electronic applications accepted. *Faculty research:* Poetry, criticism, novels, translation, travel writing.

Bowling Green State University, Graduate College, College of Arts and Sciences, Department of English, Program in English, Bowling Green, OH 43403. Offers English (MA, PhD); literature (MA); rhetoric and writing (PhD); scientific and technical communication (MA). *Program availability:* Part-time. *Degree requirements:* For master's, thesis or alternative; for doctorate, comprehensive exam, thesis/dissertation, foreign language or proficiency in Old English. *Entrance requirements:* For master's and doctorate, GRE General Test. Additional exam requirements/recommendations for international students: Required—TOEFL. Electronic applications accepted. *Faculty research:* Postmodern literary theory, rhetorical theory, ethnic American literature, literature and culture, composition pedagogy.

Brigham Young University, Graduate Studies, College of Humanities, Department of English, Provo, UT 84602. Offers creative writing (MFA); literature (MA); rhetoric/composition (MA). *Faculty:* 53 full-time (15 women). *Students:* 68 full-time (44 women), 1 part-time (0 women); includes 3 minority (1 Asian, non-Hispanic/Latino; 2 Hispanic/Latino). Average age 28. 44 applicants, 64% accepted, 24 enrolled. In 2017, 31 master's awarded. *Degree requirements:* For master's, variable foreign language requirement, comprehensive exam, thesis. *Entrance requirements:* For master's, GRE General Test, creative portfolio (for MFA). *Application deadline:* For fall admission, 1/15 for domestic and international students. Application fee: $50. Electronic applications accepted. *Expenses: Tuition:* Full-time $6880; part-time $405 per credit hour. Tuition and fees vary according to course load, program and student's religious affiliation. *Financial support:* In 2017–18, 67 students received support, including 10 research assistantships (averaging $4,000 per year), 62 teaching assistantships (averaging $6,700 per year); career-related internships or fieldwork, institutionally sponsored loans, and scholarships/grants also available. Support available to part-time students. Financial award application deadline: 3/15. *Faculty research:* English literature, American literature, rhetoric, creative writing. *Unit head:* Prof. Phillip Snyder, Head, 801-422-2487, Fax: 801-422-0221, E-mail: phillip_snyder@byu.edu. *Application contact:* Danielle N. Steed, Graduate Secretary and English Program Manager, 801-422-8673, Fax: 801-422-0221, E-mail: danielle-steed@byu.edu.
Website: http://english.byu.edu/

Brooklyn College of the City University of New York, School of Humanities and Social Sciences, Department of English, Brooklyn, NY 11210-2889. Offers creative writing (MFA), including fiction, playwriting, poetry; English (MA). *Program availability:* Part-time, evening/weekend. *Degree requirements:* For master's, one foreign language, comprehensive exam (for some programs), thesis (for some programs). *Entrance requirements:* For master's, advanced undergraduate courses in English, 2 letters of recommendation, writing sample, statement of purpose. Additional exam requirements/recommendations for international students: Required—TOEFL. Electronic applications accepted. *Faculty research:* Cultural studies, medieval literature, Virginia Woolf.

Brown University, Graduate School, Department of English, Providence, RI 02912. Offers English (PhD); literary arts (MFA). *Degree requirements:* For doctorate, thesis/dissertation. *Entrance requirements:* For master's and doctorate, GRE General Test, GRE Subject Test.

Butler University, College of Liberal Arts and Sciences, Department of English, Indianapolis, IN 46208-3485. Offers creative writing (MFA); English (MA). *Program availability:* Part-time, evening/weekend. *Faculty:* 7 full-time (3 women), 5 part-time/adjunct (2 women). *Students:* 6 full-time (2 women), 44 part-time (26 women); includes 7 minority (3 Black or African American, non-Hispanic/Latino; 1 Hispanic/Latino; 3 Two or more races, non-Hispanic/Latino). Average age 33. 48 applicants, 79% accepted, 14 enrolled. In 2017, 20 master's awarded. *Degree requirements:* For master's, thesis (for some programs). *Entrance requirements:* For master's, minimum GPA of 3.0, 350-word statement of purpose, and 7-12 page sample essay (for MA); writing sample in intended genre (12 pages of poetry or 30 pages of prose), statement of interest (1-2 pages), two letters of recommendation, and transcripts from all undergraduate and graduate institutions attended (for MFA). Additional exam requirements/recommendations for international students: Required—TOEFL (minimum score 550 paper-based; 79 iBT), IELTS (minimum score 6). *Application deadline:* For fall admission, 2/15 for domestic and international students; for spring admission, 9/15 for domestic and international students. Applications are processed on a rolling basis. Application fee: $0. Electronic applications accepted. *Expenses:* $560 per credit (for MA); $820 per credit (for MFA). *Financial support:* In 2017–18, 19 students received support. Scholarships/grants, tuition waivers (full and partial), and unspecified assistantships available. Financial award application deadline: 7/15; financial award applicants required to submit FAFSA. *Faculty research:* Novel, poetry, screenplay and creative nonfiction writing; literary and cultural theory; American literature and culture; British and Postcolonial literature. *Unit head:* Dr. Dan Barden, Director of MFA Program, Department of English Language and Literature, 317-940-9688, E-mail: dbarden@butler.edu. *Application contact:* Diane Dubord, Graduate Student Services Specialist, 317-940-8107, Fax: 317-940-8250, E-mail: ddubord@butler.edu.
Website: https://www.butler.edu/english/graduate-studies/ma-english

California College of the Arts, Graduate Programs, MFA in Writing Program, San Francisco, CA 94107. Offers creative non-fiction (MFA); fiction (MFA); poetry (MFA). *Program availability:* Part-time. *Faculty:* 7 full-time (5 women), 3 part-time/adjunct (1 woman). *Students:* 22 full-time (16 women); includes 13 minority (5 Black or African American, non-Hispanic/Latino; 1 Asian, non-Hispanic/Latino; 7 Hispanic/Latino). Average age 36. In 2017, 16 master's awarded. *Degree requirements:* For master's, thesis. *Entrance requirements:* For master's, appropriate bachelor's degree, portfolio, transcripts, letters of recommendation. Additional exam requirements/recommendations for international students: Required—TOEFL, IELTS, or PTE. *Application deadline:* For fall admission, 1/31 priority date for domestic and international students. Applications are processed on a rolling basis. Application fee: $70. Electronic applications accepted. *Expenses:* $39,384 per year full-time tuition, $490 per year fees; $1,641 per unit part-time tuition. *Financial support:* In 2017–18, fellowships (averaging $22,000 per year), teaching assistantships (averaging $2,000 per year) were awarded; career-related internships or fieldwork, Federal Work-Study, scholarships/grants, health care benefits, and unspecified assistantships also available. Financial award application deadline: 7/31; financial award applicants required to submit FAFSA. *Unit head:* Leslie Roberts, Chair, E-mail: lroberts2@cca.edu. *Application contact:* Wes Fanelli, Assistant Director of Graduate Admissions, 415-703-9533, Fax: 415-703-9539, E-mail: wfanelli@cca.edu.

California Institute of Integral Studies, School of Consciousness and Transformation, San Francisco, CA 94103. Offers anthropology and social change (MA, PhD); Asian philosophies and cultures (MA); creative inquiry/interdisciplinary arts (MFA); East-West psychology (MA, PhD); integral and transpersonal psychology (PhD); philosophy and religion (PhD), including ecology, spirituality, and religion, philosophy, cosmology, and consciousness, women's spirituality; philosophy, cosmology, and consciousness (Certificate); transformative leadership (MA); transformative studies (PhD); women, gender, spirituality and social justice (MA); writing and consciousness (MFA). *Program availability:* Part-time, evening/weekend, 100% online, blended/hybrid learning. *Students:* 392 full-time (265 women), 141 part-time (98 women); includes 145 minority (40 Black or African American, non-Hispanic/Latino; 1 American Indian or Alaska Native, non-Hispanic/Latino; 19 Asian, non-Hispanic/Latino; 54 Hispanic/Latino; 31 Two or more races, non-Hispanic/Latino), 61 international. Average age 43. 212 applicants, 96% accepted, 153 enrolled. In 2017, 49 master's, 36 doctorates awarded. Terminal master's awarded for partial completion of doctoral program. *Degree requirements:* For master's, thesis optional; for doctorate, comprehensive exam, thesis/dissertation, 1 foreign language (for Asian philosophies and cultures). *Entrance requirements:* For master's, minimum GPA of 3.0, letters of recommendation, writing sample; for doctorate, master's degree, minimum GPA of 3.0, letters of recommendation, writing sample. Additional exam requirements/recommendations for international students: Required—TOEFL. *Application deadline:* For fall admission, 2/1 priority date for domestic and international students; for spring admission, 10/15 priority date for domestic and international students. Applications are processed on a rolling basis. Application fee: $65. Electronic applications accepted. *Expenses:* $21,400 tuition and fees (for MA); $28,390 (for MFA); $24,658 (for PhD). *Financial support:* Fellowships, research assistantships, teaching assistantships, career-related internships or fieldwork, Federal Work-Study, and scholarships/grants available. Support available to part-time students. Financial award application deadline: 4/15; financial award applicants required to submit FAFSA. *Faculty research:* Ecology and sustainability, philosophy and religion, East-West psychology, integrative health, social and cultural anthropology, transformative leadership. *Unit head:* Kathy Littles, Academic Dean, 415-575-6100, E-mail: klittles@ciis.edu. *Application contact:* Ellen Durst, Director of Admissions, 415-575-6100, Fax: 415-575-1268, E-mail: admissions@ciis.edu.
Website: http://www.ciis.edu/

California Institute of the Arts, School of Critical Studies, Valencia, CA 91355-2340. Offers writing (MFA, Adv C). *Entrance requirements:* For master's, portfolio. Additional exam requirements/recommendations for international students: Required—TOEFL.

California State University, Fresno, Division of Research and Graduate Studies, College of Arts and Humanities, Department of English, Fresno, CA 93740-8027. Offers creative writing (MFA); literature (MA); rhetoric and writing studies (MA). *Program availability:* Part-time, evening/weekend. *Degree requirements:* For master's, one foreign language, thesis. *Entrance requirements:* For master's, GRE General Test, minimum GPA of 3.0, writing sample. Additional exam requirements/recommendations for international students: Required—TOEFL. Electronic applications accepted. *Faculty research:* American literature, Renaissance literature, foreign literature.

California State University, Long Beach, Graduate Studies, College of Liberal Arts, Department of English, Long Beach, CA 90840. Offers creative writing (MFA); English (MA). *Program availability:* Part-time. *Degree requirements:* For master's, one foreign language, comprehensive exam or thesis. *Entrance requirements:* For master's, GRE Subject Test, minimum GPA of 3.0 in English. Electronic applications accepted. *Faculty research:* English and American literature, literary theory, linguistics, rhetoric and composition.

California State University, Northridge, Graduate Studies, College of Humanities, Department of English, Northridge, CA 91330. Offers creative writing (MA); literature (MA); rhetoric and composition theory (MA). *Program availability:* Part-time, evening/weekend. *Students:* 24 full-time (19 women), 66 part-time (40 women); includes 39 minority (4 Black or African American, non-Hispanic/Latino; 5 Asian, non-Hispanic/Latino; 23 Hispanic/Latino; 1 Native Hawaiian or other Pacific Islander, non-Hispanic/Latino; 6 Two or more races, non-Hispanic/Latino), 1 international. Average age 34. 74 applicants, 77% accepted, 33 enrolled. In 2017, 42 master's awarded. *Degree requirements:* For master's, thesis or alternative. *Entrance requirements:* For master's, writing proficiency test, GRE General Test or minimum GPA of 3.0. Additional exam requirements/recommendations for international students: Required—TOEFL. *Application deadline:* For fall admission, 11/30 for domestic students. Application fee: $55. *Financial support:* Teaching assistantships available. Financial award application deadline: 3/1. *Faculty research:* Reading improvement, professional writing, Dickens, Shaw, English as a second language. *Unit head:* Kent Baxter, Chair, 818-677-3431.
Website: http://www.csun.edu/english/index.php

California State University, Sacramento, College of Arts and Letters, Department of English, Sacramento, CA 95819. Offers composition (MA); creative writing (MA); literature (MA); teaching English to speakers of other languages (MA). *Program availability:* Part-time. *Students:* 25 full-time (15 women), 36 part-time (27 women); includes 18 minority (4 Black or African American, non-Hispanic/Latino; 3 Asian, non-Hispanic/Latino; 11 Hispanic/Latino). Average age 30. 47 applicants, 81% accepted, 31 enrolled. In 2017, 19 master's awarded. *Degree requirements:* For master's, thesis, project, or comprehensive exam; TESOL exam; writing proficiency exam. *Entrance requirements:* For master's, portfolio (creative writing); minimum GPA of 3.0 in English and overall during previous 2 years. Additional exam requirements/recommendations for international students: Required—TOEFL (minimum score 600 paper-based; 100 iBT). *Application deadline:* For fall admission, 2/15 for domestic students, 3/1 for international students; for spring admission, 9/30 for international students. Applications are processed on a rolling basis. Application fee: $55. Electronic applications accepted. *Expenses:* Contact institution. *Financial support:* Teaching assistantships, career-related internships or fieldwork, Federal Work-Study, and scholarships/grants available. Support available to part-time students. Financial award application deadline: 3/1; financial award applicants required to submit FAFSA. *Faculty research:* Teaching composition, remedial writing. *Unit head:* Dr. David Toise, Chair, 916-278-6586, E-mail: dwtoise@csus.edu. *Application contact:* Jose Martinez, Graduate Admissions Supervisor, 916-278-7871, E-mail: martinj@skymail.csus.edu.
Website: http://www.csus.edu/engl

California State University, San Bernardino, Graduate Studies, College of Arts and Letters, Program in English, San Bernardino, CA 92407. Offers creative writing (MFA), including fiction; English composition (MA), including composition. *Program availability:* Part-time, evening/weekend. *Faculty:* 6 full-time (all women), 1 (woman) part-time/adjunct. *Students:* 2 full-time (both women), 59 part-time (44 women); includes 38 minority (6 Black or African American, non-Hispanic/Latino; 1 Asian, non-Hispanic/Latino; 29 Hispanic/Latino; 2 Two or more races, non-Hispanic/Latino). Average age 31. 18 applicants, 72% accepted, 11 enrolled. In 2017, 16 master's awarded. *Degree*

requirements: For master's, one foreign language, thesis. *Entrance requirements:* Additional exam requirements/recommendations for international students: Required—TOEFL. *Application deadline:* For fall admission, 7/16 for domestic students. Application fee: $55. *Financial support:* Application deadline: 3/1. *Unit head:* Dr. David Carlson, Chair, 909-537-5834, Fax: 909-537-7086, E-mail: dajcarls@csusb.edu. *Application contact:* Dr. Dorota Huizinga, Dean of Graduate Studies, 909-537-3064, Fax: 909-537-5078, E-mail: dorota.huizinga@csusb.edu.

California State University, San Marcos, College of Humanities, Arts, Behavioral and Social Sciences, Program in Literature and Writing Studies, San Marcos, CA 92096-0001. Offers MA. *Program availability:* Part-time, evening/weekend. *Degree requirements:* For master's, one foreign language, thesis. *Entrance requirements:* For master's, GRE General Test, minimum GPA of 3.0, writing sample. *Application deadline:* For fall admission, 3/15 priority date for domestic students; for spring admission, 11/15 for domestic students. Applications are processed on a rolling basis. Application fee: $55. *Expenses:* Tuition, state resident: full-time $7176. Tuition, nonresident: full-time $9504. *Faculty research:* Postcolonialism, feminism rhetoric, cultural studies, creative writing, critical theory. *Unit head:* Salah Moukhlis, Department Chair, 760-750-8081, E-mail: smoukhli@csusm.edu.

California State University, Stanislaus, College of the Arts, Humanities and Social Sciences, MA Program in English, Turlock, CA 95382. Offers literature (Certificate); rhetoric and teaching writing (MA); teaching English to speakers of other languages (MA). *Program availability:* Part-time. *Degree requirements:* For master's, comprehensive exam, thesis or alternative. *Entrance requirements:* For master's, GRE, minimum GPA of 3.0, 2 letters of reference, personal statement. Additional exam requirements/recommendations for international students: Required—TOEFL (minimum score 575 paper-based), TWE (minimum score 4). Electronic applications accepted. *Faculty research:* Transnational literacies, Renaissance and medieval literature, abolition writings and slave narratives, qualitative writing.

Carlow University, College of Learning and Innovation, Program in Creative Writing, Pittsburgh, PA 15213-3165. Offers fiction (MFA); non-fiction (MFA); poetry (MFA). *Program availability:* Part-time, evening/weekend, low-residency. *Students:* 22 part-time (19 women); includes 1 minority (American Indian or Alaska Native, non-Hispanic/Latino), 1 international. Average age 37. 1 applicant, 100% accepted, 1 enrolled. In 2017, 7 master's awarded. *Degree requirements:* For master's, thesis, manuscript. *Entrance requirements:* For master's, two essays, sample of writing, two letters of recommendation, resume/curriculum vitae. Additional exam requirements/recommendations for international students: Required—TOEFL (minimum score 550 paper-based). *Application deadline:* Applications are processed on a rolling basis. Electronic applications accepted. *Expenses:* Contact institution. *Financial support:* Application deadline: 4/1; applicants required to submit FAFSA. *Unit head:* Janet Beatty, Program Director, MFA in Creative Writing, 412-578-6081, Fax: 412-578-8722, E-mail: jpbeatty@carlow.edu. *Application contact:* 412-578-6059, E-mail: gradstudies@carlow.edu.
Website: http://www.carlow.edu/Master_of_Fine_Arts_in_Creative_Writing.aspx

Carnegie Mellon University, Dietrich College of Humanities and Social Sciences, Department of English, Program in Professional Writing, Pittsburgh, PA 15213-3891. Offers editing and publishing (MAPW); policy and non-profit communication (MAPW); public and media relations/corporate communications (MAPW); science or healthcare communication (MAPW); technical writing (MAPW); writing for new media (MAPW); writing for print media (MAPW). *Program availability:* Part-time. *Entrance requirements:* For master's, GRE General Test. Additional exam requirements/recommendations for international students: Required—TOEFL, TWE.

Cedar Crest College, Program in Creative Writing, Allentown, PA 18104-6196. Offers MFA. *Program availability:* Part-time, evening/weekend, blended/hybrid learning. *Faculty:* 3 part-time/adjunct (1 woman). *Students:* 8 part-time (7 women). Average age 33. In 2017, 6 master's awarded. *Degree requirements:* For master's, final book-length creative thesis. *Application deadline:* Applications are processed on a rolling basis. Electronic applications accepted. *Expenses:* Contact institution. *Unit head:* Allison Wellford, Director of Writing Program, 610-606-4666 Ext. 3474, E-mail: acwellfo@cedarcrest.edu. *Application contact:* Nancy Wunderly, Director of School of Adult and Graduate Education, 610-437-4471, E-mail: sage@cedarcrest.edu.
Website: http://sage.cedarcrest.edu/graduate/mfa/

Central Michigan University, College of Graduate Studies, College of Humanities and Social and Behavioral Sciences, Department of English Language and Literature, Mount Pleasant, MI 48859. Offers English composition and communication (MA); English language and literature (MA), including children's and young adult literature, creative writing, English language and literature; TESOL: teaching English to speakers of other languages (MA). *Program availability:* Part-time, evening/weekend. *Degree requirements:* For master's, thesis or alternative. Electronic applications accepted. *Faculty research:* Composition theory, science fiction history and bibliography, children's and young adult literature, nineteenth century American literature, applied linguistics.

Central Washington University, School of Graduate Studies and Research, College of Arts and Humanities, Department of English, Ellensburg, WA 98926. Offers literature (MA); professional and creative writing (MA); teaching English to speakers of other languages (MA). *Program availability:* Part-time. *Entrance requirements:* For master's, GRE General Test, minimum GPA of 3.0, writing sample. Additional exam requirements/recommendations for international students: Required—TOEFL (minimum score 550 paper-based; 79 iBT) or IELTS (minimum score 6.5). *Application deadline:* For fall admission, 2/1 priority date for domestic students; for winter admission, 10/1 for domestic students; for spring admission, 1/1 for domestic students. Applications are processed on a rolling basis. Application fee: $50. Electronic applications accepted. *Financial support:* Application deadline: 3/1; applicants required to submit FAFSA. *Unit head:* Dr. Bobby Cummings, Graduate Coordinator, 509-963-1075, E-mail: bobby.cummings@cwu.edu. *Application contact:* Justine Eason, Admissions Program Coordinator, 509-963-3103, Fax: 509-963-1799, E-mail: masters@cwu.edu.
Website: http://www.cwu.edu/~english/

Chapman University, Wilkinson College of Arts, Humanities, and Social Sciences, Department of English, Orange, CA 92866. Offers creative writing (MFA); English (MA). *Program availability:* Part-time, evening/weekend. *Faculty:* 23 full-time (11 women), 43 part-time/adjunct (28 women). *Students:* 48 full-time (29 women), 17 part-time (12 women); includes 17 minority (1 Black or African American, non-Hispanic/Latino; 5 Asian, non-Hispanic/Latino; 9 Hispanic/Latino; 2 Two or more races, non-Hispanic/Latino), 5 international. Average age 30. 88 applicants, 90% accepted, 23 enrolled. In 2017, 24 master's awarded. *Degree requirements:* For master's, thesis. *Entrance requirements:* For master's, GRE (if undergraduate GPA less than 3.0), minimum undergraduate GPA of 2.5. *Application deadline:* For fall admission, 2/1 priority date for domestic students. Applications are processed on a rolling basis. Application fee: $60. Electronic applications accepted. *Expenses:* Contact institution. *Financial support:* Fellowships, teaching assistantships, Federal Work-Study, and scholarships/grants available. Financial award applicants required to submit FAFSA. *Unit head:* Dr. Joanna Levin, Director, 714-997-6534, E-mail: jlevin@chapman.edu. *Application contact:* Sharnique Dow, Graduate Admission Counselor, 714-997-6770, E-mail: sdow@chapman.edu.
Website: https://www.chapman.edu/wilkinson/english/index.aspx

Chatham University, Program in Writing, Pittsburgh, PA 15232-2826. Offers children's writing (MFA); fiction (MFA); non-fiction (MFA); poetry (MFA); professional writing (MPW); screenwriting (MFA). *Program availability:* Part-time, evening/weekend, online learning. *Faculty:* 14 part-time/adjunct (11 women). *Students:* 36 full-time (26 women), 36 part-time (28 women); includes 12 minority (7 Black or African American, non-Hispanic/Latino; 4 Hispanic/Latino; 1 Two or more races, non-Hispanic/Latino). Average age 32. 90 applicants, 80% accepted, 30 enrolled. In 2017, 36 master's awarded. *Entrance requirements:* For master's, minimum GPA of 3.0, writing sample, recommendation letters. Additional exam requirements/recommendations for international students: Required—TOEFL (minimum score 600 paper-based; 100 iBT), IELTS (minimum score 7), TWE. *Application deadline:* For fall admission, 1/15 priority date for domestic and international students; for spring admission, 11/1 priority date for domestic students, 10/1 priority date for international students. Applications are processed on a rolling basis. Application fee: $45. Electronic applications accepted. Application fee is waived when completed online. *Expenses: Tuition:* Full-time $16,740; part-time $930 per credit. *Required fees:* $486; $27 per credit. $243 per semester. *Financial support:* Career-related internships or fieldwork available. Financial award applicants required to submit FAFSA. *Faculty research:* Ecopoetics; environment and culture; wilderness and literature; literature of exploration, exile, and home. *Unit head:* Dr. Sheryl St. Germain, Director, 412-365-1190, Fax: 412-365-1505, E-mail: sstgermain@chatham.edu. *Application contact:* Katie Noel, Assistant Director of Graduate Admission, 412-365-2758, Fax: 412-365-1609, E-mail: gradadmissions@chatham.edu.
Website: http://www.chatham.edu/mfa

Chicago State University, School of Graduate and Professional Studies, College of Arts and Sciences, Department of English, Foreign Languages and Literatures, Chicago, IL 60628. Offers creative writing (MFA); English (MA). *Degree requirements:* For master's, comprehensive exam (for some programs), thesis (for some programs). *Entrance requirements:* For master's, minimum GPA of 3.0. *Application deadline:* For fall admission, 7/1 for domestic students; for spring admission, 11/10 for domestic students. Application fee: $25. *Unit head:* Dr. Brenda Aghahowa, Graduate Advisor, 773-995-2203, E-mail: baghahow@csu.edu. *Application contact:* Anika Miller, Graduate Studies Office, 773-995-2404, E-mail: g-studies1@csu.edu.
Website: http://www.csu.edu/cas/englishforeignlanguageliterature/

City College of the City University of New York, Graduate School, Division of Humanities and the Arts, Department of English, Program in Creative Writing, New York, NY 10031-9198. Offers MFA. *Degree requirements:* For master's, one foreign language, comprehensive exam, thesis. *Entrance requirements:* For master's, minimum GPA of 3.0, 10-15 poems or 30-50 pages of fiction (short stories or novel excerpt). Additional exam requirements/recommendations for international students: Required—TOEFL (minimum score 600 paper-based; 100 iBT). Electronic applications accepted.

Claremont Graduate University, Graduate Programs, School of Arts and Humanities, Department of English, Claremont, CA 91711-6160. Offers American studies (MA, PhD); critical theory (MA, PhD); early modern studies (MA, PhD); English (M Phil, MA, PhD); literary theory (PhD); literature (MA, PhD); literature and creative writing (MA); literature and film (MA); MBA/MA; MBA/PhD. *Program availability:* Part-time. *Entrance requirements:* For master's and doctorate, GRE General Test. Additional exam requirements/recommendations for international students: Required—TOEFL (minimum score 75 iBT). Electronic applications accepted. *Faculty research:* American, comparative, and English Renaissance literature; modernism; feminist literature and theory.

Clemson University, Graduate School, College of Architecture, Arts, and Humanities, Department of English, Clemson, SC 29634. Offers English (MA); rhetoric, communication and information design (PhD); writing, rhetoric and media (MA). *Program availability:* Part-time. *Faculty:* 66 full-time (32 women), 7 part-time/adjunct (5 women). *Students:* 51 full-time (34 women), 16 part-time (9 women); includes 4 minority (1 Asian, non-Hispanic/Latino; 2 Hispanic/Latino; 1 Two or more races, non-Hispanic/Latino), 5 international. Average age 32. 30 applicants, 67% accepted, 9 enrolled. In 2017, 8 master's, 8 doctorates awarded. *Degree requirements:* For master's, variable foreign language requirement, thesis (for some programs). *Entrance requirements:* For master's, GRE General Test, unofficial transcripts, personal statement, writing sample, letters of recommendation. Additional exam requirements/recommendations for international students: Required—TOEFL (minimum score 80 iBT), IELTS (minimum score 6.5), PTE (minimum score 54). *Application deadline:* For fall admission, 2/1 priority date for domestic and international students. Application fee: $80 ($90 for international students). Electronic applications accepted. *Expenses:* $5,174 per semester full-time resident, $9,714 per semester full-time non-resident, $511 per credit hour part-time resident, $1,017 per credit hour part-time non-resident; $741 per credit hour online; other fees may apply per session. *Financial support:* In 2017–18, 13 students received support, including 8 teaching assistantships with partial tuition reimbursements available (averaging $12,843 per year); unspecified assistantships also available. Financial award application deadline: 2/1. *Faculty research:* English literature, British literature, American literature, literary theory. *Total annual research expenditures:* $20,544. *Unit head:* Dr. Susanna Ashton, Department Chair, 864-656-3151, E-mail: sashton@clemson.edu. *Application contact:* Dr. William Stockton, Graduate Program Coordinator, 864-656-3151, E-mail: wstockt@clemson.edu.
Website: https://www.clemson.edu/caah/departments/english/

Cleveland State University, College of Graduate Studies, College of Liberal Arts and Social Sciences, Department of English, Cleveland, OH 44115. Offers creative writing (MFA), including fiction, non-fiction, playwriting, poetry. *Program availability:* Part-time, evening/weekend. *Faculty:* 14 full-time (8 women), 14 part-time/adjunct (4 women). *Students:* 22 full-time (17 women), 26 part-time (17 women); includes 8 minority (6 Black or African American, non-Hispanic/Latino; 1 Asian, non-Hispanic/Latino; 1 Two or more races, non-Hispanic/Latino). Average age 34. 38 applicants, 68% accepted, 9 enrolled. In 2017, 21 master's awarded. *Entrance requirements:* For master's, minimum GPA of 2.75, undergraduate concentration in English, writing sample, portfolio. Additional exam requirements/recommendations for international students: Required—TOEFL (minimum score 550 paper-based; 78 iBT). *Application deadline:* Applications are processed on a rolling basis. Application fee: $40. Electronic applications accepted. *Financial support:* In 2017–18, 20 students received support. Teaching assistantships, tuition waivers (full and partial), and unspecified assistantships available. Financial award application deadline: 2/1; financial award applicants required to submit FAFSA. *Faculty research:* Literary history and criticism, literature, creative writing. *Total annual research expenditures:* $5,000. *Application contact:* Dr. James J. Marino, Associate Professor/Director of Graduate Studies, 216-687-6874, Fax: 216-687-6943, E-mail: j.marino22@csuohio.edu.
Website: http://www.csuohio.edu/class/english/english

Coastal Carolina University, Thomas W. and Robin W. Edwards College of Humanities and Fine Arts, Conway, SC 29528-6054. Offers liberal studies (MA); writing (MA). *Program availability:* Part-time, evening/weekend. *Faculty:* 20 full-time (12 women), 1 (woman) part-time/adjunct. *Students:* 29 full-time (17 women), 13 part-time (8

women); includes 7 minority (6 Black or African American, non-Hispanic/Latino; 1 Two or more races, non-Hispanic/Latino), 2 international. Average age 32. 32 applicants, 72% accepted, 19 enrolled. In 2017, 18 master's awarded. *Entrance requirements:* For master's, GRE, official transcripts, 2 letters of recommendation, writing sample; 2-page statement of interest, minimum GPA of 3.3 in 18 hours of undergraduate and graduate coursework in English or related discipline. Additional exam requirements/recommendations for international students: Required—TOEFL (minimum score 550 paper-based; 79 iBT), IELTS (minimum score 6.5). *Application deadline:* For fall admission, 5/15 priority date for domestic and international students; for spring admission, 11/15 priority date for domestic and international students. Applications are processed on a rolling basis. Application fee: $45. Electronic applications accepted. *Expenses:* Tuition, state resident: full-time $5184; part-time $576 per credit hour. Tuition, nonresident: full-time $9369; part-time $1041 per credit hour. *Required fees:* $90; $5 per credit hour. *Financial support:* Fellowships, research assistantships, teaching assistantships, and tuition waivers available. Financial award application deadline: 3/1; financial award applicants required to submit FAFSA. *Unit head:* Dr. Daniel J. Ennis, Dean/Vice President for Academic Outreach, 843-349-2746, E-mail: dennis@coastal.edu. *Application contact:* Dr. James O. Luken, Associate Provost for Graduate Program/Vice-Dean of the Coastal Environment, 843-349-2235, Fax: 843-349-6444, E-mail: joluken@coastal.edu.
Website: https://www.coastal.edu/humanities/

The College at Brockport, State University of New York, School of Arts and Sciences, Department of English, Brockport, NY 14420-2997. Offers creative writing (AGC); English (MA), including creative writing, literature. *Program availability:* Part-time. *Faculty:* 8 full-time (3 women). *Students:* 17 full-time (13 women), 13 part-time (7 women); includes 2 minority (1 Hispanic/Latino; 1 Two or more races, non-Hispanic/Latino), 1 international. 13 applicants, 92% accepted, 5 enrolled. In 2017, 10 master's, 1 other advanced degree awarded. *Degree requirements:* For master's, thesis. *Entrance requirements:* For master's, minimum GPA of 3.0, letters of recommendation, writing sample. Additional exam requirements/recommendations for international students: Required—TOEFL (minimum score 550 paper-based; 79 iBT), IELTS (minimum score 6.5). *Application deadline:* For fall admission, 4/15 priority date for domestic and international students; for spring admission, 11/15 priority date for domestic and international students; for summer admission, 4/15 priority date for domestic and international students. Application fee: $50. Electronic applications accepted. *Expenses:* Tuition, state resident: full-time $10,870; part-time $453 per credit hour. Tuition, nonresident: full-time $22,210. *Required fees:* $988; $246 per semester. *Financial support:* In 2017–18, 3 teaching assistantships with full tuition reimbursements (averaging $6,000 per year) were awarded; Federal Work-Study, scholarships/grants, and unspecified assistantships also available. Support available to part-time students. Financial award application deadline: 3/15; financial award applicants required to submit FAFSA. *Faculty research:* British and American literature, creative writing, film studies, children's literature, ancient and modern world literature. *Unit head:* Dr. Jennifer Haytock, Chairperson, 585-395-5832, Fax: 585-395-2391, E-mail: jhaytock@brockport.edu. *Application contact:* Dr. Gregory Garvey, Graduate Program Director, 585-395-5712, Fax: 585-395-5487, E-mail: tgarvey@brockport.edu.
Website: https://www.brockport.edu/academics/english/

College of Charleston, Graduate School, School of Humanities and Social Sciences, Program in Creative Writing, Charleston, SC 29424-0001. Offers MFA.

Colorado State University, College of Liberal Arts, Department of English, Fort Collins, CO 80523-1773. Offers creative writing (MFA); rhetoric and composition (MA). *Faculty:* 17 full-time (7 women), 10 part-time/adjunct (9 women). *Students:* 64 full-time (44 women), 33 part-time (28 women); includes 6 minority (2 Black or African American, non-Hispanic/Latino; 1 Asian, non-Hispanic/Latino; 3 Hispanic/Latino), 12 international. Average age 30. 207 applicants, 38% accepted, 23 enrolled. In 2017, 33 master's awarded. *Degree requirements:* For master's, thesis (for some programs), portfolio, project or thesis. *Entrance requirements:* For master's, BA/BS or equivalent with minimum cumulative undergraduate GPA of 3.0, transcripts, writing sample, statement of purpose, 3 letters of recommendation. Additional exam requirements/recommendations for international students: Recommended—TOEFL (minimum score 550 paper-based; 80 iBT), IELTS (minimum score 6.5). Application fee: $60 ($70 for international students). Electronic applications accepted. *Expenses:* Tuition, state resident: full-time $9917. Tuition, nonresident: full-time $24,312. *Required fees:* $2284. Tuition and fees vary according to course load and program. *Financial support:* In 2017–18, 1 fellowship with full and partial tuition reimbursement (averaging $14,256 per year), 40 teaching assistantships with full and partial tuition reimbursements (averaging $14,678 per year) were awarded; scholarships/grants and unspecified assistantships also available. *Faculty research:* Narratives written in new media; racial, gender, and sexual identity in the United States; the rhetoric of social change; pedagogical potential of graphic narratives. *Total annual research expenditures:* $134,319. *Unit head:* Louann Reid, Professor, 970-491-6428, E-mail: louann.reid@colostate.edu. *Application contact:* Marnie Leonard, Administrative Assistant, 970-491-2403, E-mail: marnie.leonard@colostate.edu.
Website: http://english.colostate.edu/

Columbia College Chicago, School of Graduate Studies, English and Creative Writing Department, Chicago, IL 60605-1996. Offers fiction (MFA); nonfiction (MFA); poetry (MFA). *Program availability:* Part-time, evening/weekend. *Students:* 45 full-time (24 women), 21 part-time (12 women); includes 18 minority (11 Black or African American, non-Hispanic/Latino; 3 Asian, non-Hispanic/Latino; 3 Hispanic/Latino; 1 Two or more races, non-Hispanic/Latino). 118 applicants, 88% accepted, 28 enrolled. *Degree requirements:* For master's, thesis. *Entrance requirements:* For master's, self-assessment essay, work samples, letters of recommendation, transcripts. Additional exam requirements/recommendations for international students: Required—TOEFL, IELTS. *Application deadline:* For fall admission, 1/15 priority date for domestic and international students. Applications are processed on a rolling basis. Application fee: $55 ($100 for international students). Electronic applications accepted. *Expenses:* Tuition: Full-time $26,808; part-time $1117 per credit. *Required fees:* $572; $155 per credit. *Financial support:* In 2017–18, 18 students received support. Teaching assistantships, career-related internships or fieldwork, Federal Work-Study, scholarships/grants, and unspecified assistantships available. Financial award application deadline: 1/15. *Unit head:* Kenneth Daley, Chair, 312-369-8121, E-mail: kdaley@colum.edu. *Application contact:* Emily Schmidt, Graduate Admissions, 312-369-7298, E-mail: eschmidt@colum.edu.
Website: https://www.colum.edu/academics/liberal-arts-and-sciences/english-and-creative-writing/index.html

Columbia University, School of the Arts, Writing Program, New York, NY 10027. Offers writing (MFA), including fiction, nonfiction, poetry. *Faculty:* 29 full-time (12 women), 73 part-time/adjunct (41 women). *Students:* 345 full-time (218 women); includes 84 minority (21 Black or African American, non-Hispanic/Latino; 2 American Indian or Alaska Native, non-Hispanic/Latino; 14 Asian, non-Hispanic/Latino; 27 Hispanic/Latino; 20 Two or more races, non-Hispanic/Latino), 48 international. Average age 29. 495 applicants, 53% accepted, 136 enrolled. In 2017, 101 master's awarded. *Degree requirements:* For master's, thesis. *Entrance requirements:* For master's, 3 letters of recommendation,

writing sample. Additional exam requirements/recommendations for international students: Required—TOEFL (minimum score 600 paper-based; 100 iBT). *Application deadline:* For fall admission, 1/5 for domestic and international students. Application fee: $110. Electronic applications accepted. *Expenses:* Contact institution. *Financial support:* In 2017–18, 165 students received support, including 16 teaching assistantships with full and partial tuition reimbursements available; fellowships, research assistantships, career-related internships or fieldwork, Federal Work-Study, scholarships/grants, and unspecified assistantships also available. Financial award application deadline: 2/1; financial award applicants required to submit FAFSA. *Unit head:* Sam Lipsyte, Chair, 212-854-4391, E-mail: writing@columbia.edu. *Application contact:* Kenny Wong, Director of Admissions and Financial Aid, 212-854-2134, E-mail: admissions-arts@columbia.edu.
Website: http://arts.columbia.edu/writing

See Display on page 133 and Close-Up on page 185.

Concordia University, School of Graduate Studies, Faculty of Arts and Science, Department of English, Program in Creative Writing, Montréal, QC H3G 1M8, Canada. Offers MA. *Degree requirements:* For master's, one foreign language, thesis. *Entrance requirements:* For master's, honors degree in English, minimum GPA of 3.3 in English literature, portfolio. *Faculty research:* Fiction, poetry, prose, drama.

Converse College, Program in Creative Writing, Spartanburg, SC 29302. Offers MFA. *Unit head:* Rick Mulkey, Director, 864-596-9685, E-mail: rick.mulkey@converse.edu.

Cornell University, Graduate School, Graduate Fields of Arts and Sciences, Field of English Language and Literature, Ithaca, NY 14853. Offers African-American literature (PhD); American literature after 1865 (PhD); American literature to 1865 (PhD); American studies (PhD); colonial and postcolonial literatures (PhD); creative writing (MFA); cultural studies (PhD); dramatic literature (PhD); English poetry (PhD); English Renaissance to 1660 (PhD); lesbian, bisexual, and gay literary studies (PhD); literary criticism and theory (PhD); Old and Middle English (PhD); prose fiction (PhD); Restoration and the eighteenth-century (PhD); the nineteenth century (PhD); the twentieth century (PhD); women's literature (PhD); MFA/PhD. Terminal master's awarded for partial completion of doctoral program. *Degree requirements:* For master's, one foreign language, thesis; for doctorate, one foreign language, comprehensive exam, thesis/dissertation, teaching experience. *Entrance requirements:* For master's, GRE General Test, 3 letters of recommendation, creative writing sample; for doctorate, GRE General Test, GRE Subject Test (English), 3 letters of recommendation, writing sample. Additional exam requirements/recommendations for international students: Required—TOEFL (minimum score 600 paper-based; 77 iBT). Electronic applications accepted. *Faculty research:* English and American literature, women's writing, ethnic and postcolonial literature, critical theory, medievalism.

Creighton University, Graduate School, College of Arts and Sciences, Department of English, Omaha, NE 68178-0001. Offers creative writing (MA, MFA). *Program availability:* Part-time. *Faculty:* 15 full-time (8 women), 1 part-time/adjunct (0 women). *Students:* 6 full-time (4 women), 1 (woman) part-time, 1 international. Average age 27. 31 applicants, 87% accepted, 6 enrolled. In 2017, 1 master's awarded. *Degree requirements:* For master's, thesis optional. *Entrance requirements:* For master's, 10-15 page writing sample, 3 letters of recommendation. Additional exam requirements/recommendations for international students: Required—TOEFL (minimum score 90 iBT). *Application deadline:* For fall admission, 3/15 priority date for domestic and international students. Application fee: $50. Electronic applications accepted. Part-time tuition and fees vary according to course load, degree level, campus/location and program. *Financial support:* In 2017–18, 5 fellowships with tuition reimbursements (averaging $11,465 per year) were awarded; scholarships/grants, tuition waivers (full and partial), and unspecified assistantships also available. Financial award applicants required to submit FAFSA. *Faculty research:* Henry James letters. *Unit head:* Dr. Robert Whipple, Director, 402-280-2520, E-mail: whippl@creighton.edu. *Application contact:* Lindsay Johnson, Director of Graduate and Adult Recruitment, 402-280-2703, Fax: 402-280-2423, E-mail: gradschool@creighton.edu.

DePaul University, College of Liberal Arts and Social Sciences, Chicago, IL 60614. Offers Arabic (MA); Chinese (MA); critical ethnic studies (MA); English (MA); French (MA); German (MA); history (MA); interdisciplinary studies (MA, MS); international public service (MS); international studies (MA); Italian (MA); Japanese (MA); liberal studies (MA); nonprofit management (MNM); public administration (MPA); public health (MPH); public policy (MPP); public service management (MS); refugee and forced migration studies (MS); social work (MSW); sociology (MA); Spanish (MA); sustainable urban development (MA); women's and gender studies (MA); writing and publishing (MA); writing, rhetoric and discourse (MA); MA/PhD. *Program availability:* Part-time, evening/weekend, online learning. Terminal master's awarded for partial completion of doctoral program. *Degree requirements:* For master's, variable foreign language requirement, comprehensive exam (for some programs), thesis (for some programs). *Application deadline:* Applications are processed on a rolling basis. Application fee: $40. Electronic applications accepted. *Financial support:* Applicants required to submit FAFSA. *Unit head:* Dr. Guillermo Vasquez de Velasco, Dean, 773-325-7305. *Application contact:* Ann Spittle, Director of Graduate Admission, 773-325-8369, Fax: 312-476-3244, E-mail: graddepaul@depaul.edu.
Website: http://las.depaul.edu/

Dominican University of California, School of Liberal Arts and Education, Humanities Program, San Rafael, CA 94901-2298. Offers applied music (MA); art history (MA); creative writing (MA); gender studies (MA); history (MA); philosophy (MA); political theory (MA); religion (MA). *Program availability:* Part-time. *Faculty:* 7 full-time (4 women), 1 (woman) part-time/adjunct. *Students:* 6 full-time (5 women), 16 part-time (12 women); includes 8 minority (3 Black or African American, non-Hispanic/Latino; 4 Hispanic/Latino; 1 Two or more races, non-Hispanic/Latino), 2 international. Average age 45. 7 applicants, 100% accepted, 5 enrolled. In 2017, 14 master's awarded. *Degree requirements:* For master's, thesis or alternative. *Entrance requirements:* For master's, minimum GPA of 3.0, interview. Additional exam requirements/recommendations for international students: Required—TOEFL (minimum score 550 paper-based; 80 iBT), IELTS (minimum score 6.5). *Application deadline:* For fall admission, 5/15 priority date for domestic and international students; for spring admission, 11/15 priority date for domestic and international students. Applications are processed on a rolling basis. Application fee: $0. Electronic applications accepted. *Expenses:* Tuition: Full-time $17,370; part-time $965 per credit. *Required fees:* $150 per semester. Tuition and fees vary according to course load and program. *Financial support:* In 2017–18, 4 students received support. Scholarships/grants available. Support available to part-time students. Financial award application deadline: 3/2; financial award applicants required to submit FAFSA. *Unit head:* Joan Baranow, Program Director, 415-485-3264, E-mail: joan.baranow@dominican.edu. *Application contact:* Michael Lavigna, Assistant Director of Graduate Admissions, 415-485-3253, Fax: 415-485-3214, E-mail: gradmissions@dominican.edu.
Website: https://www.dominican.edu/academics/lae/graduate-programs/ma-in-humanities/index_html

Drew University, Caspersen School of Graduate Studies, Madison, NJ 07940-1493. Offers conflict resolution and leadership (Certificate), including community leadership,

moderation, peace building; education (M Ed); finance (MA); history and culture (MA, PhD), including American history, book history, British history, European history, Holocaust and genocide (M Litt, MA, D Litt, PhD), intellectual history, Irish history, print culture, public history; K-12 education (MAT), including art, biology, chemistry, elementary education, English, French, Italian, math, secondary education, special education, teacher of students with disabilities; liberal studies (M Litt, D Litt), including history, Holocaust and genocide (M Litt, MA, D Litt, PhD), Irish/Irish-American studies, literature (M Litt, MMH, D Litt, DMH, CMH), religion, spirituality, teaching in the two-year college, writing; medical humanities (MMH, DMH, CMH), including arts, health, healthcare, literature (M Litt, MMH, D Litt, DMH, CMH), scientific research; poetry (MFA). *Program availability:* Part-time, evening/weekend. *Faculty:* 4 full-time (2 women), 29 part-time/adjunct (15 women). *Students:* 77 full-time (42 women), 175 part-time (114 women); includes 39 minority (12 Black or African American, non-Hispanic/Latino; 6 Asian, non-Hispanic/Latino; 16 Hispanic/Latino; 5 Two or more races, non-Hispanic/Latino), 11 international. Average age 41. 126 applicants, 75% accepted, 52 enrolled. In 2017, 38 master's, 23 doctorates, 35 other advanced degrees awarded. Terminal master's awarded for partial completion of doctoral program. *Degree requirements:* For master's and other advanced degree, thesis (for some programs); for doctorate, one foreign language, comprehensive exam (for some programs), thesis/dissertation. *Entrance requirements:* For master's, PRAXIS Core and Subject Area tests (for MAT), GRE/GMAT (for M Fin), resume, transcripts, writing sample, personal statement, letters of recommendation; for doctorate, GRE (PhD in history and culture), resume, transcripts, writing sample, personal statement, letters of recommendation; for other advanced degree, resume, transcripts, personal statement. Additional exam requirements/recommendations for international students: Required—TOEFL (minimum score 587 paper-based; 80 iBT), IELTS (minimum score 6), TWE (minimum score 4). *Application deadline:* For fall admission, 8/1 for domestic students, 6/1 for international students; for spring admission, 12/1 for domestic students, 10/1 for international students. Applications are processed on a rolling basis. Application fee: $35. Electronic applications accepted. *Financial support:* Fellowships, research assistantships, teaching assistantships, career-related internships or fieldwork, Federal Work-Study, scholarships/grants, and unspecified assistantships available. Support available to part-time students. Financial award applicants required to submit FAFSA. *Faculty research:* Irish history and culture, conflict resolution and leadership. *Application contact:* Leanne Horinko, Director of Caspersen Admissions, 973-408-3280, E-mail: gradm@drew.edu. Website: http://www.drew.edu/caspersen

East Carolina University, Graduate School, Thomas Harriot College of Arts and Sciences, Department of English, Greenville, NC 27858-4353. Offers creative writing (MA); English studies (MA); linguistics (MA); literature (MA); multicultural and transnational literatures (MA, Certificate); professional communication (Certificate); rhetoric and composition (MA); rhetoric, writing, and professional communication (PhD); teaching English in the two-year college (Certificate); teaching English to speakers of other languages (MA, Certificate); technical and professional communication (MA). *Program availability:* Part-time, evening/weekend, online learning. *Students:* 40 full-time (27 women), 74 part-time (57 women); includes 33 minority (23 Black or African American, non-Hispanic/Latino; 2 Asian, non-Hispanic/Latino; 4 Hispanic/Latino; 4 Two or more races, non-Hispanic/Latino). Average age 35. 36 applicants, 94% accepted, 25 enrolled. In 2017, 23 master's, 4 doctorates, 24 other advanced degrees awarded. *Degree requirements:* For master's, comprehensive exam, thesis optional; for doctorate, comprehensive exam, thesis/dissertation. *Entrance requirements:* For master's, GRE General Test or MAT; for doctorate, GRE General Test or MAT, writing samples. Additional exam requirements/recommendations for international students: Recommended—TOEFL (minimum score 78 iBT), IELTS (minimum score 6.5), TWE. *Application deadline:* For fall admission, 7/31 priority date for domestic students, 2/1 priority date for international students; for spring admission, 11/30 priority date for domestic students, 10/1 priority date for international students. Applications are processed on a rolling basis. Application fee: $75. Electronic applications accepted. *Expenses:* Tuition, state resident: full-time $4749; part-time $297 per credit hour. Tuition, nonresident: full-time $17,898; part-time $1119 per credit hour. *Required fees:* $2691; $224 per credit hour. Part-time tuition and fees vary according to course load and program. *Financial support:* Research assistantships with partial tuition reimbursements, teaching assistantships with partial tuition reimbursements, and Federal Work-Study available. Support available to part-time students. Financial award application deadline: 3/1. *Faculty research:* Technical and professional communication, rhetoric/composition, multicultural and transnational literature, creative writing, film studies. *Unit head:* Dr. Marianne Montgomery, Chair, 252-328-6687, E-mail: montgomerym@ecu.edu. *Application contact:* Dean of Graduate School, 252-328-6012, Fax: 252-328-6071, E-mail: gradschool@ecu.edu.
Website: http://www.ecu.edu/cs-cas/engl/

Eastern Kentucky University, The Graduate School, College of Arts and Sciences, Department of English and Theatre, Richmond, KY 40475-3102. Offers creative writing (MFA); English (MA). *Program availability:* Part-time, evening/weekend. *Degree requirements:* For master's, thesis optional. *Entrance requirements:* For master's, GRE General Test, minimum GPA of 2.5, minor in English with 3.0 GPA. *Faculty research:* Old English, Victorian studies, women's studies, rhetoric, popular culture, novel studies.

Eastern Michigan University, Graduate School, College of Arts and Sciences, Department of English Language and Literature, Program in Creative Writing, Ypsilanti, MI 48197. Offers MA. *Program availability:* Part-time, evening/weekend, online learning. *Students:* 3 full-time (1 woman), 11 part-time (8 women); includes 1 minority (Black or African American, non-Hispanic/Latino). Average age 28. 12 applicants, 67% accepted, 6 enrolled. In 2017, 4 master's awarded. *Entrance requirements:* Additional exam requirements/recommendations for international students: Required—TOEFL. *Application deadline:* Applications are processed on a rolling basis. Application fee: $45. *Financial support:* Fellowships, research assistantships with full tuition reimbursements, teaching assistantships with full tuition reimbursements, career-related internships or fieldwork, Federal Work-Study, institutionally sponsored loans, scholarships/grants, tuition waivers (partial), and unspecified assistantships available. Support available to part-time students. Financial award applicants required to submit FAFSA. *Application contact:* Dr. Carla Harryman, Graduate Coordinator, 734-487-3173, Fax: 734-483-9744, E-mail: charryma@emich.edu.

Eastern Michigan University, Graduate School, College of Arts and Sciences, Department of English Language and Literature, Programs in Written Communication, Ypsilanti, MI 48197. Offers technical communication (Graduate Certificate); written communication (MA). *Program availability:* Part-time, evening/weekend, online learning. *Students:* 1 full-time (0 women), 18 part-time (14 women); includes 5 minority (3 Black or African American, non-Hispanic/Latino; 1 Asian, non-Hispanic/Latino; 1 Hispanic/Latino). Average age 36. 8 applicants, 88% accepted, 6 enrolled. In 2017, 8 master's awarded. *Entrance requirements:* Additional exam requirements/recommendations for international students: Required—TOEFL. *Application deadline:* Applications are processed on a rolling basis. Application fee: $45. *Financial support:* Fellowships, research assistantships with full tuition reimbursements, teaching assistantships with full tuition reimbursements, career-related internships or fieldwork, Federal Work-Study, institutionally sponsored loans, scholarships/grants, tuition waivers (partial), and unspecified assistantships available. Support available to part-time students. Financial award applicants required to submit FAFSA. *Application contact:* Dr. Steve Benninghoff, Program Coordinator, 734-487-2075, Fax: 734-483-9744, E-mail: steve.benninghoff@emich.edu.

Emerson College, Graduate Studies, Boston, MA 02116-4624. Offers civic media (MA), including art and practice; communication disorders (MS); creative writing (MFA); digital marketing (MA), including data analytics; film and media art (MFA); journalism (MA); popular fiction writing and publishing (MFA); public relations (MA); publishing and writing (MA); strategic communication for marketing (MA); theatre education (MA); writing for film and television (MFA). *Program availability:* Part-time, evening/weekend. *Faculty:* 202 full-time (86 women), 252 part-time/adjunct (125 women). *Students:* 571 full-time (423 women), 82 part-time (60 women); includes 102 minority (24 Black or African American, non-Hispanic/Latino; 19 Asian, non-Hispanic/Latino; 38 Hispanic/Latino; 1 Native Hawaiian or other Pacific Islander, non-Hispanic/Latino; 20 Two or more races, non-Hispanic/Latino), 170 international. Average age 27. 1,578 applicants, 57% accepted, 297 enrolled. In 2017, 271 master's awarded. *Entrance requirements:* For master's, GRE or GMAT (for certain programs). Additional exam requirements/recommendations for international students: Required—TOEFL (minimum score 550 paper-based; 80 iBT), IELTS (minimum score 6.5). *Application deadline:* Applications are processed on a rolling basis. Application fee: $60 ($75 for international students). Electronic applications accepted. *Expenses: Tuition:* Full-time $20,016; part-time $1251 per credit. *Required fees:* $624; $232 per credit. $116 per semester. *Financial support:* In 2017–18, 382 students received support, including 382 fellowships with partial tuition reimbursements available (averaging $7,551 per year); research assistantships with partial tuition reimbursements available, Federal Work-Study, scholarships/grants, and unspecified assistantships also available. Financial award application deadline: 3/1; financial award applicants required to submit FAFSA. *Application contact:* Leanda Ferland, Director of Graduate Admission, 617-824-8610, Fax: 617-824-8614, E-mail: gradadmission@emerson.edu.
Website: http://www.emerson.edu/academics/graduate-degrees

Fairfield University, College of Arts and Sciences, Fairfield, CT 06824. Offers American studies (MA); communication (MA); creative writing (MFA); mathematics (MS); public administration (MPA). *Program availability:* Part-time, evening/weekend, online learning. *Faculty:* 16 full-time (8 women), 12 part-time/adjunct (8 women). *Students:* 67 full-time (46 women), 64 part-time (35 women); includes 27 minority (8 Black or African American, non-Hispanic/Latino; 1 Asian, non-Hispanic/Latino; 14 Hispanic/Latino; 4 Two or more races, non-Hispanic/Latino), 10 international. Average age 32. 80 applicants, 81% accepted, 43 enrolled. In 2017, 38 master's awarded. *Degree requirements:* For master's, capstone research course. *Entrance requirements:* For master's, minimum GPA of 3.0, 2 letters of recommendation, resume, personal statement. Additional exam requirements/recommendations for international students: Required—TOEFL (minimum score 550 paper-based; 80 iBT) or IELTS (minimum score 6.5). *Application deadline:* For fall admission, 5/15 for international students; for spring admission, 10/15 for international students. Applications are processed on a rolling basis. Application fee: $60. Electronic applications accepted. *Expenses:* $725 per credit hour (for American studies, communication and math programs); $575 per credit hour (for MFA); $775 per credit hour (for MPA). *Financial support:* In 2017–18, 11 students received support. Scholarships/grants and unspecified assistantships available. Financial award applicants required to submit FAFSA. *Faculty research:* Nutrition and physiology, media industries, community-based teaching and learning, non commutative algebra and partial differential equations, cancer research in biology and physics. *Unit head:* Dr. Richard Greenwald, Dean, 203-254-4000 Ext. 2221, Fax: 203-254-4119, E-mail: rgreenwald@fairfield.edu. *Application contact:* Marianne Gumpper, Director of Graduate Admission, 203-254-4184, Fax: 203-254-4073, E-mail: gradadmis@fairfield.edu.
Website: http://www.fairfield.edu/cas

Fairleigh Dickinson University, Florham Campus, Maxwell Becton College of Arts and Sciences, Department of English, Communication and Philosophy, Program in Creative Writing, Madison, NJ 07940-1099. Offers creative nonfiction (MFA); fiction (MFA); literary translation (MFA); poetry (MFA); writing for young adults (MFA).

Fairleigh Dickinson University, Florham Campus, Maxwell Becton College of Arts and Sciences, Department of English, Communication and Philosophy, Program in Creative Writing and Literature for Educators, Madison, NJ 07940-1099. Offers MA.

Fitchburg State University, Division of Graduate and Continuing Education, Program in Applied Communications, Fitchburg, MA 01420-2697. Offers applied communication studies (MS); technical and professional writing (MS). *Program availability:* Part-time, evening/weekend. *Faculty:* 6 full-time (4 women). *Students:* 1 (woman) full-time, 18 part-time (11 women); includes 3 minority (1 Hispanic/Latino; 2 Two or more races, non-Hispanic/Latino). Average age 36. 6 applicants, 100% accepted, 4 enrolled. In 2017, 6 master's awarded. *Entrance requirements:* Additional exam requirements/recommendations for international students: Required—TOEFL (minimum score 550 paper-based; 79 iBT). *Application deadline:* For fall admission, 7/15 for international students; for spring admission, 12/1 for international students. Applications are processed on a rolling basis. Application fee: $50. Electronic applications accepted. *Expenses:* Contact institution. *Financial support:* In 2017–18, research assistantships with partial tuition reimbursements (averaging $5,500 per year) were awarded; Federal Work-Study, scholarships/grants, and unspecified assistantships also available. Support available to part-time students. Financial award application deadline: 3/1; financial award applicants required to submit FAFSA. *Unit head:* Dr. Viera Lorencova, Chair, 978-665-4856, Fax: 978-665-3658, E-mail: gce@fitchburgstate.edu. *Application contact:* Jinawa McNeil, Director of Admissions, 978-665-3140, Fax: 978-665-4540, E-mail: admissions@fitchburgstate.edu.

Florida International University, College of Arts, Sciences, and Education, Department of English, Miami, FL 33199. Offers creative writing (MFA); English (MA), including literature; linguistics (MA). *Program availability:* Part-time, evening/weekend. *Faculty:* 53 full-time (26 women), 38 part-time/adjunct (24 women). *Students:* 40 full-time (24 women), 33 part-time (19 women); includes 40 minority (6 Black or African American, non-Hispanic/Latino; 33 Hispanic/Latino; 1 Two or more races, non-Hispanic/Latino), 4 international. Average age 31. 50 applicants, 50% accepted, 20 enrolled. In 2017, 31 master's awarded. *Degree requirements:* For master's, thesis. *Entrance requirements:* For master's, GRE General Test, minimum undergraduate GPA of 3.0 (upper-level coursework), letter of intent, two letters of recommendation. Additional exam requirements/recommendations for international students: Required—TOEFL (minimum score 550 paper-based; 80 iBT). *Application deadline:* For fall admission, 2/1 for domestic and international students; for spring admission, 10/1 for domestic students, 9/1 for international students. Applications are processed on a rolling basis. Application fee: $30. Electronic applications accepted. *Expenses:* Tuition, state resident: full-time $8912; part-time $446 per credit hour. Tuition, nonresident: full-time $21,393; part-time $992 per credit hour. *Required fees:* $390; $195 per semester. *Financial support:* Institutionally sponsored loans and scholarships/grants available. Financial award application deadline: 3/1; financial award applicants required to submit FAFSA. *Unit head:* Dr. Heather Russell, Chair, 305-348-3369, Fax: 305-348-3878, E-mail: heather.russell@fiu.edu. *Application contact:* Nanett Rojas, Assistant Director, Graduate Admissions, 305-348-7464, Fax: 305-348-7441, E-mail: gradadm@fiu.edu.

Florida State University, The Graduate School, College of Arts and Sciences, Department of English, Tallahassee, FL 32312. Offers English (MA, MFA, PhD), including creative writing (MFA, PhD), literature (MA, PhD), rhetoric and composition (MA, PhD). *Program availability:* Part-time. *Faculty:* 47 full-time (24 women), 2 part-time/adjunct (1 woman). *Students:* 142 full-time (80 women), 31 part-time (23 women); includes 44 minority (17 Black or African American, non-Hispanic/Latino; 1 American Indian or Alaska Native, non-Hispanic/Latino; 12 Asian, non-Hispanic/Latino; 5 Hispanic/Latino; 9 Two or more races, non-Hispanic/Latino), 9 international. Average age 30. 307 applicants, 22% accepted, 47 enrolled. In 2017, 21 master's, 24 doctorates awarded. *Degree requirements:* For master's, one foreign language, 33 hours of coursework including capstone essay, thesis or portfolio (MA); 45 hours of coursework including 9-12 thesis hours (MFA); for doctorate, one foreign language, comprehensive exam, thesis/dissertation, 27 hours of coursework, 24 hours of dissertation work. *Entrance requirements:* For master's and doctorate, GRE General Test, sample of written work, 3 letters of recommendation, resume. Additional exam requirements/recommendations for international students: Required—TOEFL. *Application deadline:* For fall admission, 12/17 priority date for domestic and international students. Application fee: $30. Electronic applications accepted. *Financial support:* In 2017–18, 132 students received support, including 5 fellowships with tuition reimbursements available, teaching assistantships with tuition reimbursements available (averaging $13,500 per year); career-related internships or fieldwork, Federal Work-Study, and institutionally sponsored loans also available. Financial award application deadline: 8/1; financial award applicants required to submit FAFSA. *Faculty research:* British and Irish literature, American literature, creative writing, rhetoric and composition, multiethnic transnational literature, history of text technologies. *Unit head:* Dr. Gary Taylor, Chair, 850-644-4230, Fax: 850-644-0811, E-mail: gtaylor@fsu.edu. *Application contact:* Ginger Martin, Senior Graduate Academic Coordinator, 850-644-1081, Fax: 850-644-9656, E-mail: vmartin@fsu.edu.
Website: http://english.fsu.edu/

Florida State University, The Graduate School, College of Motion Picture Arts, Tallahassee, FL 32306-2350. Offers film production (MFA); screenwriting (MFA). *Faculty:* 28 full-time (8 women), 3 part-time/adjunct (1 woman). *Students:* 62 full-time (26 women); includes 20 minority (10 Black or African American, non-Hispanic/Latino; 1 American Indian or Alaska Native, non-Hispanic/Latino; 4 Asian, non-Hispanic/Latino; 3 Hispanic/Latino; 2 Two or more races, non-Hispanic/Latino), 14 international. Average age 25. 217 applicants, 15% accepted, 32 enrolled. In 2017, 28 master's awarded. *Degree requirements:* For master's, thesis, thesis film project. *Entrance requirements:* For master's, GRE (for MFA in writing), minimum GPA of 3.0, resume, statement of purpose, writing sample, 3 letters of recommendation, creative portfolio. Additional exam requirements/recommendations for international students: Required—TOEFL (minimum score 550 paper-based; 80 iBT). *Application deadline:* For fall admission, 12/1 for domestic and international students. Application fee: $30. Electronic applications accepted. *Expenses:* Contact institution. *Financial support:* In 2017–18, 20 students received support, including 20 teaching assistantships with partial tuition reimbursements available (averaging $5,500 per year); institutionally sponsored loans and unspecified assistantships also available. Financial award application deadline: 12/1; financial award applicants required to submit FAFSA. *Faculty research:* Producing, screenwriting, directing, cinematography, editing. *Unit head:* Reb Braddock, Dean, 850-644-8712, Fax: 850-644-2626. *Application contact:* Gloria McElroy, Staff Director of Admissions and Recruitment, 850-644-8524, Fax: 850-644-2626, E-mail: gmcelroy@fsu.edu.
Website: http://film.fsu.edu/

Full Sail University, Creative Writing Master of Fine Arts Program - Online, Winter Park, FL 32792-7437. Offers MFA. *Program availability:* Online learning.

George Mason University, College of Humanities and Social Sciences, Department of English, Program in Creative Writing, Fairfax, VA 22030. Offers fiction (MFA); nonfiction writing (MFA); poetry (MFA). *Faculty:* 13 full-time (7 women), 1 (woman) part-time/adjunct. *Students:* 57 full-time (35 women), 31 part-time (23 women); includes 12 minority (5 Asian, non-Hispanic/Latino; 4 Hispanic/Latino; 3 Two or more races, non-Hispanic/Latino), 1 international. Average age 30. 94 applicants, 62% accepted, 29 enrolled. In 2017, 25 master's awarded. *Degree requirements:* For master's, one foreign language, comprehensive exam (for some programs), thesis, written exam (for poetry); written exam or project (for fiction). *Entrance requirements:* For master's, expanded goals statement; 2 letters of recommendation; portfolio; official transcripts; resume; writing sample. Additional exam requirements/recommendations for international students: Required—TOEFL (minimum score 575 paper-based; 88 iBT), IELTS (minimum score 6.5), PTE (minimum score 59). *Application deadline:* For fall admission, 1/10 priority date for domestic and international students. Application fee: $75 ($80 for international students). Electronic applications accepted. *Expenses:* Tuition, state resident: full-time $11,228; part-time $459.50 per credit. Tuition, nonresident: full-time $30,932; part-time $1280.50 per credit. *Required fees:* $3252; $135.50 per credit. Part-time tuition and fees vary according to course load and program. *Financial support:* In 2017–18, 55 students received support, including 3 research assistantships with tuition reimbursements available (averaging $13,800 per year), 52 teaching assistantships with tuition reimbursements available (averaging $11,941 per year); career-related internships or fieldwork, Federal Work-Study, scholarships/grants, unspecified assistantships, and health care benefits (for full-time research or teaching assistantship recipients) also available. Support available to part-time students. Financial award application deadline: 3/1; financial award applicants required to submit FAFSA. *Faculty research:* British romantic poetry and literary celebrity, Arab feminist novelists in the west, masculinity and African-American culture, public rhetoric and the South African truth commission, the origins of children's literature in Eighteenth and Nineteenth century Britain. *Unit head:* William Miller, Director, 703-993-2763, Fax: 703-993-1161, E-mail: wmiller@gmu.edu. *Application contact:* Jay Patel, Graduate Coordinator, 703-993-1180, Fax: 703-993-1161, E-mail: jpatel2@gmu.edu.
Website: http://creativewriting.gmu.edu/

Georgia College & State University, Graduate School, College of Arts and Sciences, Department of English, Program in Creative Writing, Milledgeville, GA 31061. Offers MFA. *Program availability:* Part-time, evening/weekend. *Students:* 12 full-time (9 women), 18 part-time (9 women); includes 9 minority (3 Black or African American, non-Hispanic/Latino; 1 Asian, non-Hispanic/Latino; 5 Hispanic/Latino). Average age 30. 32 applicants, 56% accepted, 11 enrolled. In 2017, 10 master's awarded. Terminal master's awarded for partial completion of doctoral program. *Degree requirements:* For master's, thesis, complete program in no more than 4 years. *Entrance requirements:* For master's, writing portfolio, 3 letters of recommendation, statement of purpose, official transcript. *Application deadline:* For fall admission, 2/1 priority date for domestic students. Applications are processed on a rolling basis. Application fee: $40. Electronic applications accepted. *Expenses:* $288 per credit hour full-time in-state, $2,592 per semester; $1,027 per credit hour full-time out-of-state, $9,243 per semester; $343 per semester fees. *Financial support:* In 2017–18, 10 students received support. Unspecified assistantships available. Support available to part-time students. Financial award application deadline: 2/1; financial award applicants required to submit FAFSA. *Unit head:* Dr. Allen Gee, Coordinator, 478-445-3509, E-mail: mfa@gcsu.edu. *Application contact:* Kate Marshall, Graduate Admissions Coordinator, 478-445-1184, Fax: 478-445-1336, E-mail: grad-admit@gcsu.edu.
Website: http://www.gcsu.edu/artsandsciences/english/mfa

Georgia Southern University–Armstrong Campus, College of Graduate Studies, Program in Professional Communication and Leadership, Savannah, GA 31419-1997. Offers MA, Certificate. *Program availability:* Part-time, evening/weekend. *Faculty:* 2 full-time (1 woman), 1 (woman) part-time/adjunct. *Students:* 26 full-time (16 women), 48 part-time (37 women); includes 46 minority (39 Black or African American, non-Hispanic/Latino; 7 Hispanic/Latino). Average age 35. 53 applicants, 53% accepted, 21 enrolled. In 2017, 29 master's awarded. *Degree requirements:* For master's, comprehensive exam, project. *Entrance requirements:* For master's, minimum GPA of 2.5, letters of recommendation, letter of intent, resume. Additional exam requirements/recommendations for international students: Required—TOEFL (minimum score 523 paper-based; 70 iBT). *Application deadline:* For fall admission, 6/1 priority date for domestic students, 5/1 priority date for international students; for spring admission, 11/15 priority date for domestic students, 9/15 priority date for international students; for summer admission, 4/15 for domestic students, 9/15 priority date for international students. Applications are processed on a rolling basis. Application fee: $30. Electronic applications accepted. *Expenses:* Tuition, state resident: part-time $211 per credit hour. Tuition, nonresident: part-time $782 per credit hour. *Required fees:* $737 per semester. Tuition and fees vary according to course load, degree level, campus/location and program. *Financial support:* In 2017–18, research assistantships with full tuition reimbursements (averaging $5,000 per year) were awarded; scholarships/grants and unspecified assistantships also available. Financial award application deadline: 3/15; financial award applicants required to submit FAFSA. *Faculty research:* Organizational communication, conflict resolution and mediation, rhetoric and language identity, brand identity and marketing, communication theory. *Unit head:* Dr. Kimberly Martin, Program Coordinator, 912-344-2698, E-mail: kimberly.martin@armstrong.edu. *Application contact:* McKenzie Peterman, Graduate Admissions Specialist, 912-478-5678, Fax: 912-478-0740, E-mail: mpeterman@georgiasouthern.edu.
Website: http://www.armstrong.edu/Majors/degree/master_professional_communication_leadership

Georgia State University, College of Arts and Sciences, Department of English, Program in Creative Writing, Atlanta, GA 30302-3083. Offers creative writing (PhD); fiction (MA, MFA); poetry (MA, MFA). *Program availability:* Part-time. *Entrance requirements:* For master's and doctorate, GRE. Additional exam requirements/recommendations for international students: Required—TOEFL (minimum score 550 paper-based; 80 iBT). Application fee: $50. Electronic applications accepted. *Expenses:* Tuition, state resident: full-time $7020. Tuition, nonresident: full-time $22,518. *Required fees:* $2128. Tuition and fees vary according to degree level and program. *Financial support:* Research assistantships, teaching assistantships, and unspecified assistantships available. *Faculty research:* Poetry writing, fiction writing, contemporary poetry, contemporary fiction, form and theory of fiction and poetry. *Unit head:* Dr. Josh Russell, Co-Director of the Creative Writing Program, 404-413-5800, Fax: 404-413-5830, E-mail: josh@gsu.edu.
Website: http://www.english.gsu.edu

Goddard College, Graduate Division, Master of Fine Arts in Creative Writing Program, Plainfield, VT 05667-9432. Offers MFA. Program residency available in Plainfield, VT or Port Townsend, WA. *Program availability:* Online learning. *Degree requirements:* For master's, thesis, completed full-length manuscript, teaching practicum, 3 critical papers, annotations of 45 to 60 literary works. *Entrance requirements:* For master's, statement of purpose, preliminary bibliography, creative portfolio, three letters of recommendation. Electronic applications accepted. *Expenses:* Contact institution.

Goucher College, MA and MFA Programs, Baltimore, MD 21204-2794. Offers art and technology (MFA); arts administration (MA); cultural sustainability (MA); digital arts (MA); historic preservation (MA); nonfiction (MFA). *Program availability:* Part-time, evening/weekend, blended/hybrid learning. *Degree requirements:* For master's, thesis, e-portfolio. *Entrance requirements:* For master's, digital portfolio (for MA, MFA in digital arts); writing sample (for MFA in creative nonfiction). Additional exam requirements/recommendations for international students: Required—TOEFL (minimum score 550 paper-based; 80 iBT). *Application deadline:* Applications are processed on a rolling basis. Application fee: $75. Electronic applications accepted. *Expenses:* Contact institution. *Financial support:* Scholarships/grants and unspecified assistantships available. Financial award application deadline: 4/15; financial award applicants required to submit FAFSA. *Unit head:* Leslie Rubinkowski, Acting Assistant Provost for Limited Residency Graduate Programs, 410-337-6200, E-mail: leslie.rubinkowski@goucher.edu. *Application contact:* Carlton E. Surbeck, III, Director of Admissions, 410-337-6100, Fax: 410-337-6200, E-mail: admissions@goucher.edu.
Website: http://www.goucher.edu/grad

Hamline University, College of Liberal Arts, St. Paul, MN 55104-1284. Offers creative writing (MFA); creative writing for children and young adults (MFA); law (MSL). *Program availability:* Part-time, evening/weekend. *Faculty:* 6 full-time (5 women), 6 part-time/adjunct (3 women). *Students:* 7 full-time (5 women), 157 part-time (112 women); includes 29 minority (6 Black or African American, non-Hispanic/Latino; 1 American Indian or Alaska Native, non-Hispanic/Latino; 9 Asian, non-Hispanic/Latino; 7 Hispanic/Latino; 6 Two or more races, non-Hispanic/Latino), 1 international. Average age 38. 46 applicants, 65% accepted, 16 enrolled. In 2017, 44 master's awarded. *Degree requirements:* For master's, thesis. *Entrance requirements:* For master's, letters of recommendation, official transcripts, personal statement, resume. Additional exam requirements/recommendations for international students: Required—TOEFL (minimum score 550 paper-based; 80 iBT), IELTS (minimum score 6.5). *Application deadline:* For fall admission, 6/1 priority date for domestic and international students; for spring admission, 11/1 priority date for domestic students, 10/1 priority date for international students; for summer admission, 3/1 priority date for domestic students, 2/1 priority date for international students. Applications are processed on a rolling basis. Application fee: $0 ($100 for international students). Electronic applications accepted. Application fee is waived when completed online. *Expenses:* Contact institution. *Financial support:* Federal Work-Study and scholarships/grants available. Support available to part-time students. Financial award application deadline: 4/20; financial award applicants required to submit FAFSA. *Unit head:* Dr. Marcela Kostihova, Dean, 651-523-2206, Fax: 651-523-3055, E-mail: cladean@hamline.edu. *Application contact:* Shawn Skoog, Director of Graduate Recruitment and Admission, 651-523-2900, Fax: 651-523-3058, E-mail: gradprog@hamline.edu.
Website: http://www.hamline.edu/cla/

Hofstra University, College of Liberal Arts and Sciences, Programs in Creative Writing and English Literature, Hempstead, NY 11549. Offers creative writing (MFA), including Spanish. *Program availability:* Part-time. *Students:* 8 full-time (4 women), 10 part-time (6 women); includes 3 minority (1 Asian, non-Hispanic/Latino; 2 Hispanic/Latino), 1 international. Average age 33. 14 applicants, 100% accepted, 4 enrolled. In 2017, 12 master's awarded. *Degree requirements:* For master's, thesis optional, minimum GPA of 3.0. *Entrance requirements:* For master's, writing sample, essay, minimum GPA of 3.0 in literature courses. Additional exam requirements/recommendations for international students: Required—TOEFL (minimum score 550 paper-based; 80 iBT). *Application deadline:* Applications are processed on a rolling basis. Application fee: $75. Electronic

applications accepted. *Expenses: Tuition:* Full-time $1292. *Required fees:* $970. Tuition and fees vary according to program. *Financial support:* In 2017–18, 10 students received support, including 10 fellowships with full and partial tuition reimbursements available (averaging $4,338 per year); research assistantships with full and partial tuition reimbursements available, career-related internships or fieldwork, Federal Work-Study, institutionally sponsored loans, scholarships/grants, tuition waivers (full and partial), and unspecified assistantships also available. Support available to part-time students. Financial award applicants required to submit FAFSA. *Faculty research:* "The Penguin of Sonnets", Phillis Levin; "Lady Byron and Her Daughters", Julia Markus; "Gorgeous Lies", Martha McPhee; "This is the Place", Kelly McMasters; "Faces in the Crowd", Valeria Luiselli. *Unit head:* Dr. Craig Rustici, Chairperson, 516-463-5455, E-mail: craig.m.rustici@hofstra.edu. *Application contact:* Sunil Samuel, Assistant Vice President of Admissions, 516-463-4723, Fax: 516-463-4664, E-mail: graduateadmission@hofstra.edu.
Website: http://www.hofstra.edu/hclas

Hollins University, Graduate Programs, Program in Children's Literature, Roanoke, VA 24020. Offers children's book illustration (Certificate); children's book writing and illustrating (MFA); children's literature (MA, MFA). Program offered during summer only. *Program availability:* Part-time. *Faculty:* 2 full-time (both women), 8 part-time/adjunct (7 women). *Students:* 40 full-time (38 women), 6 part-time (5 women); includes 6 minority (1 Black or African American, non-Hispanic/Latino; 1 Asian, non-Hispanic/Latino; 3 Hispanic/Latino; 1 Two or more races, non-Hispanic/Latino). Average age 35. 24 applicants, 96% accepted, 10 enrolled. In 2017, 11 master's awarded. *Degree requirements:* For master's, one foreign language, comprehensive exam, thesis. *Entrance requirements:* For master's, transcripts, letters of recommendation, portfolio, personal statement of educational objectives. Additional exam requirements/recommendations for international students: Required—TOEFL (minimum score 550 paper-based; 79 iBT), IELTS (minimum score 6.5). *Application deadline:* For summer admission, 2/15 priority date for domestic and international students. Application fee: $40. Electronic applications accepted. *Expenses:* Contact institution. *Financial support:* Federal Work-Study and scholarships/grants available. Support available to part-time students. Financial award application deadline: 2/15; financial award applicants required to submit FAFSA. *Faculty research:* Fantasy, children's film, young adult fiction, picture books, mythology and folk tales. *Unit head:* Amanda Cockrell, Director, 540-362-6024, Fax: 540-362-6642, E-mail: acockrell@hollins.edu. *Application contact:* Cathy S. Koon, Manager of Graduate Services, 540-362-6326, Fax: 540-362-6288, E-mail: ckoon@hollins.edu.

Hollins University, Graduate Programs, Program in Creative Writing, Roanoke, VA 24020. Offers MFA. *Faculty:* 7 full-time (4 women). *Students:* 21 full-time (19 women); includes 2 minority (both Hispanic/Latino). Average age 26. 140 applicants, 18% accepted, 13 enrolled. In 2017, 12 master's awarded. *Degree requirements:* For master's, comprehensive exam, thesis. *Entrance requirements:* For master's, portfolio of original work, 3 letters of recommendation, undergraduate transcript, statement of educational objectives. Additional exam requirements/recommendations for international students: Required—TOEFL (minimum score 550 paper-based; 80 iBT), IELTS (minimum score 6.5). *Application deadline:* For fall admission, 1/6 priority date for domestic and international students. Application fee: $40. Electronic applications accepted. *Expenses:* Contact institution. *Financial support:* In 2017–18, 21 students received support, including 6 teaching assistantships with tuition reimbursements available; fellowships with tuition reimbursements available, scholarships/grants, tuition waivers (full), and unspecified assistantships also available. Financial award application deadline: 1/6; financial award applicants required to submit FAFSA. *Faculty research:* Poetry, fiction, creative nonfiction, literary criticism, literary theory. *Unit head:* Thorpe Moeckel, Director, 540-362-6427, Fax: 540-362-6097, E-mail: tmoeckel@hollins.edu. *Application contact:* Cathy S. Koon, Manager of Graduate Programs, 540-362-6326, Fax: 540-362-6288, E-mail: ckoon@hollins.edu.
Website: http://www.hollins.edu/academics/graduate-degrees/creative-writing-mfa/

Hollins University, Graduate Programs, Program in Playwriting, Roanoke, VA 24020. Offers new play directing (Certificate); new play performance (Certificate); playwriting (MFA). *Program availability:* Part-time. *Faculty:* 7 full-time (3 women). *Students:* 30 full-time (18 women), 1 (woman) part-time; includes 2 minority (both Black or African American, non-Hispanic/Latino). Average age 35. 18 applicants, 83% accepted, 7 enrolled. In 2017, 4 master's awarded. *Degree requirements:* For master's, comprehensive exam, thesis. *Entrance requirements:* For master's, letters of recommendation, bachelor's degree, undergraduate transcripts, manuscript. Additional exam requirements/recommendations for international students: Required—TOEFL (minimum score 550 paper-based; 80 iBT), IELTS (minimum score 6.5). *Application deadline:* For summer admission, 2/15 priority date for domestic and international students. Application fee: $40. Electronic applications accepted. *Expenses:* Contact institution. *Financial support:* Scholarships/grants available. Support available to part-time students. Financial award application deadline: 2/15; financial award applicants required to submit FAFSA. *Unit head:* Todd Ristau, Director, 540-362-6386, E-mail: tristau@hollins.edu. *Application contact:* Cathy S. Koon, Manager of Graduate Programs, 540-362-6326, Fax: 540-362-6288, E-mail: ckoon@hollins.edu.
Website: http://www.hollins.edu/academics/graduate-degrees/playwriting/

Hollins University, Graduate Programs, Program in Screenwriting and Film Studies, Roanoke, VA 24020. Offers screenwriting (MFA); screenwriting and film studies (MA). Program offered during summer only. *Program availability:* Part-time. *Faculty:* 5 full-time (2 women). *Students:* 23 full-time (14 women), 5 part-time (3 women); includes 5 minority (1 Black or African American, non-Hispanic/Latino; 1 Asian, non-Hispanic/Latino; 2 Hispanic/Latino; 1 Two or more races, non-Hispanic/Latino). Average age 40. 15 applicants, 100% accepted, 7 enrolled. In 2017, 5 master's awarded. *Degree requirements:* For master's, one foreign language, comprehensive exam, thesis. *Entrance requirements:* For master's, letters of recommendation, portfolio, transcript review. Additional exam requirements/recommendations for international students: Required—TOEFL (minimum score 550 paper-based; 80 iBT), IELTS (minimum score 6.5). *Application deadline:* For summer admission, 2/15 priority date for domestic and international students. Application fee: $40. Electronic applications accepted. *Expenses:* Contact institution. *Financial support:* Federal Work-Study and scholarships/grants available. Support available to part-time students. Financial award application deadline: 2/15; financial award applicants required to submit FAFSA. *Faculty research:* Censorship, minorities in film, writing for television, new media. *Unit head:* Dr. Tim Albaugh, Director, 540-362-6575, E-mail: hugrad@hollins.edu. *Application contact:* Cathy S. Koon, Manager of Graduate Programs, 540-362-6326, Fax: 540-362-6288, E-mail: ckoon@hollins.edu.
Website: https://www.hollins.edu/academics/graduate-degrees/mfa-screenwriting-film-studies/

Holy Names University, Graduate Division, Master of Arts in English: The Writer's Craft Program, Oakland, CA 94619-1699. Offers MA. *Entrance requirements:* For master's, two recommendations, writing sample. Additional exam requirements/recommendations for international students: Required—TOEFL (minimum score 550 paper-based; 79 iBT). Electronic applications accepted. Application fee is waived when completed online.

Hunter College of the City University of New York, Graduate School, School of Arts and Sciences, Department of English, Program in Creative Writing, New York, NY 10065-5085. Offers fiction (MFA); memoir (MFA); poetry (MFA). *Program availability:* Part-time, evening/weekend. *Degree requirements:* For master's, thesis. *Entrance requirements:* For master's, creative writing manuscript (up to 10 pages of poetry or 25-30 pages of fiction or nonfiction), nonfiction proposal (for nonfiction applicants only), statement of purpose. Electronic applications accepted.

Hunter College of the City University of New York, Graduate School, School of Arts and Sciences, Department of Theatre, Program in Playwriting, New York, NY 10065-5085. Offers MFA. *Entrance requirements:* For master's, GRE, bachelor's degree, two letters of recommendation, full-length or one-act play of at least 40 pages (both hard copy and PDF attachment). Additional exam requirements/recommendations for international students: Required—TOEFL (minimum score 550 paper-based; 60 iBT).

Illinois State University, Graduate School, College of Arts and Sciences, Department of English, Program in Writing, Normal, IL 61790. Offers Postbaccalaureate Certificate.

Indiana State University, College of Graduate and Professional Studies, College of Arts and Sciences, Department of English, Terre Haute, IN 47809. Offers British and American literature (MA); English (MA); writing (MA). *Program availability:* Part-time, evening/weekend. *Degree requirements:* For master's, one foreign language, thesis optional. *Entrance requirements:* For master's, minimum GPA of 2.75 in all English courses above freshman level. Additional exam requirements/recommendations for international students: Required—TOEFL (minimum score 550 paper-based). Electronic applications accepted.

Indiana University Bloomington, University Graduate School, College of Arts and Sciences, Department of English, Bloomington, IN 47405. Offers creative writing (MA, MFA), including fiction (MFA), poetry (MFA); literature (PhD); rhetoric (PhD). *Degree requirements:* For master's, 30-36 credit hours plus one language proficiency (for MA); 60 credit hours plus thesis (for MFA); for doctorate, thesis/dissertation, qualifying exam; 90 credit hours; 2nd language proficiency or one language only if acquired at in-depth level. *Entrance requirements:* For master's, GRE General Test, GRE Subject Test (for all but MFA and MA in creative writing), minimum GPA of 3.5; for doctorate, GRE General Test, GRE Subject Test, minimum GPA of 3.7. Additional exam requirements/recommendations for international students: Required—TOEFL (minimum score 550 paper-based; 79 iBT), IELTS (minimum score 6.5). Electronic applications accepted.

Indiana University–Purdue University Indianapolis, School of Liberal Arts, Department of English, Indianapolis, IN 46202. Offers English (MA); teaching English to speakers of other languages (TESOL) (MA, Certificate); teaching literature (Certificate); teaching writing (Certificate). *Entrance requirements:* For master's, GRE. Additional exam requirements/recommendations for international students: Required—TOEFL.

Indiana University South Bend, College of Liberal Arts and Sciences, South Bend, IN 46615. Offers advanced computer programming (Graduate Certificate); applied informatics (Graduate Certificate); applied mathematics and computer science (MS); behavior modification (Graduate Certificate); computer applications (Graduate Certificate); computer programming (Graduate Certificate); correctional management and supervision (Graduate Certificate); English (MA); health systems management (Graduate Certificate); international studies (Graduate Certificate); liberal studies (MLS); nonprofit management (Graduate Certificate); paralegal studies (Graduate Certificate); professional writing (Graduate Certificate); public affairs (MPA); public management (Graduate Certificate); social and cultural diversity (Graduate Certificate); strategic sustainability leadership (Graduate Certificate); technology for administration (Graduate Certificate). *Program availability:* Part-time, evening/weekend. *Degree requirements:* For master's, variable foreign language requirement, thesis (for some programs). *Entrance requirements:* For master's, minimum GPA of 3.0. Additional exam requirements/recommendations for international students: Required—TOEFL (minimum score 550 paper-based; 80 iBT). *Expenses:* Contact institution. *Faculty research:* Artificial intelligence, bioinformatics, English language and literature, creative writing, computer networks.

Institute of American Indian Arts, Low Residency MFA in Creative Writing Program, Santa Fe, NM 87508. Offers creative writing (MFA), including poetry. *Program availability:* Low-residency. *Students:* 46 full-time (25 women), 4 part-time (all women); includes 34 minority (24 American Indian or Alaska Native, non-Hispanic/Latino; 7 Hispanic/Latino; 1 Native Hawaiian or other Pacific Islander, non-Hispanic/Latino; 2 Two or more races, non-Hispanic/Latino). In 2017, 25 master's awarded. *Degree requirements:* For master's, thesis. *Entrance requirements:* For master's, sample of creative work, essay, sample of craft or scholarly essay, two letters of recommendation, all official college transcripts. *Application deadline:* For fall admission, 2/15 priority date for domestic and international students. Applications are processed on a rolling basis. Application fee: $25. Electronic applications accepted. Application fee is waived when completed online. *Expenses:* Tuition, state resident: full-time $12,000; part-time $500 per credit. Tuition, nonresident: full-time $12,000; part-time $500 per credit. *Required fees:* $680. *Financial support:* Scholarships/grants available. Financial award application deadline: 2/15; financial award applicants required to submit FAFSA. *Unit head:* Jon Davis, Director, Low Residency MFA in Creative Writing, 505-424-2365, Fax: 505-424-3030, E-mail: mfa@iaia.edu. *Application contact:* Jon Davis, Director, Low Residency MFA in Creative Writing, 505-424-2365, Fax: 505-424-3030, E-mail: mfa@iaia.edu.
Website: https://iaia.edu/academics/degree-programs/creative-writing-mfa/

Iowa State University of Science and Technology, Department of English, Ames, IA 50011. Offers creative writing (MFA); English (MA); rhetoric and professional communication (PhD). *Degree requirements:* For master's, thesis or alternative; for doctorate, thesis/dissertation. *Entrance requirements:* For master's, GRE General Test, sample of written work, resume, portfolio in creative writing; for doctorate, GRE General Test, sample of written work, resume. Additional exam requirements/recommendations for international students: Required—TOEFL (minimum score 600 paper-based; 100 iBT), IELTS (minimum score 7). Electronic applications accepted. *Faculty research:* Creative writing, literature, rhetoric, composition and professional communication, teaching English as a second language, applied linguistics.

Iowa State University of Science and Technology, Program in Creative Writing and Environment, Ames, IA 50011. Offers MFA. *Entrance requirements:* For master's, GRE, official academic transcripts, resume, three letters of recommendation, statement of personal goals, writing samples. Additional exam requirements/recommendations for international students: Required—TOEFL (minimum score 600 paper-based; 100 iBT), IELTS (minimum score 7). Electronic applications accepted.

Ithaca College, Roy H. Park School of Communications, Program in Image Text, Ithaca, NY 14850. Offers MFA. *Program availability:* Part-time-only. *Faculty:* 9 full-time (2 women). *Students:* 18 part-time (9 women); includes 5 minority (3 Hispanic/Latino; 2 Two or more races, non-Hispanic/Latino). Average age 28. 20 applicants, 70% accepted, 10 enrolled. *Degree requirements:* For master's, thesis, field practicum. *Entrance requirements:* Additional exam requirements/recommendations for international students: Required—TOEFL (minimum score 550 paper-based; 80 iBT). *Application deadline:* For fall admission, 3/15 for domestic and international students; for spring admission, 12/1 for domestic and international students. Applications are processed on a rolling basis. Application fee: $40. Electronic applications accepted. *Expenses:* Contact

institution. *Financial support:* In 2017–18, 18 students received support, including 18 fellowships (averaging $4,868 per year); career-related internships or fieldwork, Federal Work-Study, and scholarships/grants also available. Support available to part-time students. Financial award application deadline: 3/1; financial award applicants required to submit FAFSA. *Unit head:* Nicholas Muellner, Co-Director, 607-274-1984, E-mail: nmuellner@ithaca.edu. *Application contact:* Nicole Eversley Bradwell, Director, Office of Admission, 607-274-3124, Fax: 607-274-1263, E-mail: admission@ithaca.edu.
Website: http://www.ithaca.edu/gradprograms/image-text

James Madison University, The Graduate School, College of Arts and Letters, Program in Writing, Rhetoric, and Technical Communication, Harrisonburg, VA 22801. Offers MA, MS. *Program availability:* Part-time. *Students:* 9 full-time (8 women), 3 part-time (all women); includes 1 minority (Asian, non-Hispanic/Latino), 1 international. Average age 30. In 2017, 13 master's awarded. Application fee: $55. Electronic applications accepted. *Expenses:* Tuition, state resident: full-time $10,512; part-time $438 per credit hour. Tuition, nonresident: full-time $28,358; part-time $1162 per credit hour. *Required fees:* $1128. *Financial support:* In 2017–18, 8 students received support, including 5 fellowships, 3 teaching assistantships with full tuition reimbursements available (averaging $9,284 per year); career-related internships or fieldwork, Federal Work-Study, and assistantships (averaging $7911) also available. Financial award application deadline: 3/1; financial award applicants required to submit FAFSA. *Unit head:* Dr. Traci A. Zimmerman, Director of the School of Writing, Rhetoric and Technical Communication, 540-568-2334, E-mail: zimmerta@jmu.edu. *Application contact:* Lynette D. Michael, Director of Graduate Admissions, 540-568-6131 Ext. 6395, Fax: 540-568-7860, E-mail: michaeld@jmu.edu.
Website: http://www.jmu.edu/wrtc/

Johns Hopkins University, Zanvyl Krieger School of Arts and Sciences, Advanced Academic Programs, Program in Writing, Washington, DC 20036. Offers science writing (MA, Certificate); writing (MA). *Program availability:* Part-time, evening/weekend. *Degree requirements:* For master's, thesis. *Entrance requirements:* For master's, minimum GPA of 3.0, writing samples. Additional exam requirements/recommendations for international students: Required—TOEFL (minimum score 600 paper-based; 100 iBT). Electronic applications accepted.

Johns Hopkins University, Zanvyl Krieger School of Arts and Sciences, The Writing Seminars, Baltimore, MD 21218. Offers fiction writing (MFA); poetry (MFA). *Faculty:* 7 full-time (3 women), 1 (woman) part-time/adjunct. *Students:* 20 full-time (8 women); includes 5 minority (1 Black or African American, non-Hispanic/Latino; 2 Asian, non-Hispanic/Latino; 1 Hispanic/Latino; 1 Two or more races, non-Hispanic/Latino), 1 international. Average age 26. 198 applicants, 8% accepted, 8 enrolled. In 2017, 13 master's awarded. *Degree requirements:* For master's, one foreign language, thesis, foreign language exam (MFA). *Entrance requirements:* For master's, GRE General Test (recommended), GRE Subject Test (recommended), foreign language exam, sample of written work, 3 letters of recommendation, transcripts of all college/university course work. Additional exam requirements/recommendations for international students: Required—TOEFL (minimum score 600 paper-based; 100 iBT). *Application deadline:* For fall admission, 12/15 for domestic and international students. Application fee: $75. Electronic applications accepted. *Expenses:* $52,170 tuition; $1,880 health insurance. *Financial support:* In 2017–18, 24 students received support, including 2 teaching assistantships with full tuition reimbursements available (averaging $5,000 per year); fellowships, research assistantships with full tuition reimbursements available, Federal Work-Study, institutionally sponsored loans, scholarships/grants, health care benefits, and tuition waivers (partial) also available. Financial award application deadline: 3/1; financial award applicants required to submit FAFSA. *Faculty research:* Contemporary fiction and poetry, film history, literary criticism, psychoanalysis. *Unit head:* David Yezzi, Associate Professor and Chair, 410-516-3409, Fax: 410-516-6828, E-mail: dyezzi@jhu.edu. *Application contact:* Yvonne Gobble, Admissions Coordinator, 410-516-6286, Fax: 410-516-6828, E-mail: ygobble1@jhu.edu.
Website: http://web.jhu.edu/writingseminars/

Kean University, College of Liberal Arts, Program in English Writing Studies, Union, NJ 07083. Offers MA. *Program availability:* Part-time. *Faculty:* 10 full-time (6 women). *Students:* 6 full-time (5 women), 5 part-time (all women); includes 4 minority (3 Black or African American, non-Hispanic/Latino; 1 Two or more races, non-Hispanic/Latino). Average age 30. 5 applicants, 100% accepted, 3 enrolled. In 2017, 10 master's awarded. *Degree requirements:* For master's, thesis. *Entrance requirements:* For master's, GRE General Test, minimum GPA of 3.0, official transcripts from all institutions attended, two letters of recommendation, personal statement, professional resume/curriculum vitae. Additional exam requirements/recommendations for international students: Required—TOEFL (minimum score 550 paper-based; 79 iBT), IELTS (minimum score 6.5). *Application deadline:* For fall admission, 6/30 for domestic and international students; for spring admission, 12/8 for domestic and international students. Applications are processed on a rolling basis. Application fee: $75. Electronic applications accepted. *Expenses:* Tuition, state resident: full-time $13,419; part-time $653 per credit. Tuition, nonresident: full-time $18,188; part-time $801 per credit. *Required fees:* $3382; $154 per credit. Tuition and fees vary according to course level, course load, degree level and program. *Financial support:* Scholarships/grants and unspecified assistantships available. Financial award applicants required to submit FAFSA. *Unit head:* Dr. Mia Zamora, Program Coordinator, 908-737-0385, E-mail: schandler@kean.edu. *Application contact:* Amy Clark, Program Assistant, 908-737-7100, E-mail: grad-adm@kean.edu.
Website: http://grad.kean.edu/masters-programs/english-writing-studies

Kennesaw State University, College of Humanities and Social Sciences, Program in Professional Writing, Kennesaw, GA 30144. Offers MAPW. *Program availability:* Part-time, evening/weekend. *Degree requirements:* For master's, thesis optional. *Entrance requirements:* For master's, GRE General Test, minimum GPA of 2.5, writing sample. Additional exam requirements/recommendations for international students: Required—TOEFL (minimum score 550 paper-based; 80 iBT), IELTS (minimum score 6.5). Electronic applications accepted.

Kent State University, College of Arts and Sciences, Department of English, Kent, OH 44242-0001. Offers creative writing (MFA); English (MA, PhD); English for teachers (MA); literature and writing (MA); rhetoric and composition (PhD); teaching English as a second language (MA). MFA program offered jointly with Cleveland State University, The University of Akron, and Youngstown State University. *Program availability:* Part-time. *Faculty:* 25 full-time (13 women), 2 part-time/adjunct (1 woman). *Students:* 101 full-time (69 women), 19 part-time (11 women); includes 10 minority (4 Black or African American, non-Hispanic/Latino; 1 Asian, non-Hispanic/Latino; 2 Hispanic/Latino; 3 Two or more races, non-Hispanic/Latino), 20 international. Average age 34. 63 applicants, 76% accepted, 18 enrolled. In 2017, 37 master's, 6 doctorates awarded. *Degree requirements:* For master's, one foreign language, thesis (for some programs), final portfolio, final exam, or thesis (for MA in teaching English as a second language); for doctorate, one foreign language, comprehensive exam, thesis/dissertation. *Entrance requirements:* For master's, GRE General Test, goal statement, 3 letters of recommendation, 8-15 page writing sample relevant to the field of study (waived for MA in English for teachers concentration), transcripts; for doctorate, GRE General Test, statement of purpose, 3 letters of recommendation, 8-15 page writing sample relevant to field of study, transcripts. Additional exam requirements/recommendations for international students: Required—TOEFL (minimum score 587 paper-based, 94 iBT), Michigan English Language Assessment Battery (minimum score 82), IELTS (minimum score 7.0) or PTE (minimum score 65). *Application deadline:* For fall admission, 1/15 for domestic and international students. Applications are processed on a rolling basis. Application fee: $45 ($70 for international students). Electronic applications accepted. *Expenses:* Tuition, state resident: full-time $11,310; part-time $515 per credit hour. Tuition, nonresident: full-time $20,396; part-time $928 per credit hour. *International tuition:* $18,544 full-time. *Financial support:* Fellowships with full tuition reimbursements, teaching assistantships with full tuition reimbursements, and unspecified assistantships available. Financial award application deadline: 1/15. *Unit head:* Dr. Robert Trogdon, Chair, 330-672-2676, E-mail: rtrogdon@kent.edu. *Application contact:* Wesley Raabe, Graduate Studies Coordinator, E-mail: wraabe@kent.edu.
Website: http://www.kent.edu/english/

Lake Forest College, Graduate Program in Liberal Studies, Lake Forest, IL 60045. Offers American studies (MLS); cinema in East Asia (MLS); environmental studies (MLS); history (MLS); Medieval and Renaissance art (MLS); philosophy (MLS); Spanish (MLS); writing (MLS). *Program availability:* Part-time, evening/weekend. *Faculty:* 11 full-time (3 women). *Students:* 34 part-time (19 women); includes 3 minority (1 Asian, non-Hispanic/Latino; 2 Hispanic/Latino). Average age 36. 20 applicants, 55% accepted, 8 enrolled. In 2017, 5 master's awarded. *Degree requirements:* For master's, thesis optional, 8 courses, including at least 3 interdisciplinary seminars. *Entrance requirements:* For master's, transcript, essay, interview. Additional exam requirements/recommendations for international students: Required—TOEFL (minimum score 550 paper-based; 83 iBT); Recommended—IELTS (minimum score 6.5). *Application deadline:* For fall admission, 7/15 priority date for domestic students, 6/1 priority date for international students; for spring admission, 12/1 priority date for domestic students, 10/1 priority date for international students. Applications are processed on a rolling basis. Application fee: $30. Electronic applications accepted. *Expenses:* $2,650 per course. *Financial support:* In 2017–18, 2 students received support. Partial tuition grants (for full-time teachers) available. *Faculty research:* Religion in America, Asian philosophy, cinema studies, theater studies, sociology of religion. *Unit head:* Prof. D. L. LeMahieu, Director, 847-735-5133, Fax: 847-735-6291, E-mail: lemahieu@lakeforest.edu. *Application contact:* Prof. Carol Gayle, Associate Director, 847-735-5083, Fax: 847-735-6291, E-mail: gayle@lakeforest.edu.
Website: http://www.lakeforest.edu/academics/programs/mls/

La Sierra University, College of Arts and Sciences, Department of English and Communication, Riverside, CA 92505. Offers communication (MA), including public relations/advertising, theory emphasis; English (MA), including literary emphasis, writing emphasis. *Program availability:* Part-time. *Degree requirements:* For master's, one foreign language. *Entrance requirements:* For master's, GRE General Test.

Lenoir-Rhyne University, Graduate Programs, School of Arts and Letters, Program in Writing, Hickory, NC 28601. Offers MA. *Entrance requirements:* For master's, GRE General Test or MAT, essay; resume; minimum GPA of 2.7 undergraduate, 3.0 graduate. Additional exam requirements/recommendations for international students: Required—TOEFL (minimum score 600 paper-based). Electronic applications accepted. *Expenses:* Contact institution.

Lesley University, Graduate School of Arts and Social Sciences, Cambridge, MA 02138-2790. Offers clinical mental health counseling (MA), including holistic counseling, school and community counseling, trauma studies; counseling psychology (MA, CAGS), including professional counseling (MA), school counseling (MA); creative writing (MFA); expressive therapies (MA, PhD, CAGS), including art (MA), clinical mental health counseling (MA), dance (MA), expressive therapies (MA), music (MA); independent studies (CAGS); independent study (MA); intercultural relations (MA, CAGS); interdisciplinary studies (MA), including individualized studies, integrative holistic health, mindfulness studies, peace and conflict transformation, trauma sensitive assessment, intervention, and consultation, women's studies; urban environmental leadership (MA). *Program availability:* Part-time, online learning. *Degree requirements:* For master's, internship, practicum, thesis (for expressive therapies); for doctorate, thesis/dissertation, arts apprenticeship, field placement; for CAGS, thesis, internship (for counseling psychology, expressive therapies). *Entrance requirements:* For master's, MAT (counseling psychology), interview, writing samples, art portfolio; for doctorate, GRE or MAT, interview, master's degree; for CAGS, interview, master's degree. Additional exam requirements/recommendations for international students: Required—TOEFL (minimum score 550 paper-based; 80 iBT). Electronic applications accepted. *Faculty research:* Psychotherapy and culture; psychotherapy and psychological trauma; women's issues in art, teaching and psychotherapy; community-based art, psycho-spiritual inquiry.

Lindenwood University, Graduate Programs, School of Accelerated Degree Programs, St. Charles, MO 63301-1695. Offers administration (MSA), including management, marketing, project management; business administration (MBA); communications (MA), including digital and multimedia, media management, promotions, training and development; criminal justice and administration (MS); healthcare administration (MS); human resource management (MS); information technology (Certificate); managing information security (MS); managing information technology (MS); managing virtualization and cloud computing (MS); writing (MFA). *Program availability:* Part-time, evening/weekend, 100% online. *Faculty:* 12 full-time (5 women), 90 part-time/adjunct (37 women). *Students:* 597 full-time (383 women), 202 part-time (138 women); includes 248 minority (206 Black or African American, non-Hispanic/Latino; 3 American Indian or Alaska Native, non-Hispanic/Latino; 6 Asian, non-Hispanic/Latino; 21 Hispanic/Latino; 1 Native Hawaiian or other Pacific Islander, non-Hispanic/Latino; 11 Two or more races, non-Hispanic/Latino), 69 international. Average age 36. 526 applicants, 46% accepted, 204 enrolled. In 2017, 537 master's awarded. *Degree requirements:* For master's, thesis (for some programs), minimum cumulative GPA of 3.0; for Certificate, minimum cumulative GPA of 3.0. *Entrance requirements:* For master's, resume, personal statement, official undergraduate transcript, minimum undergraduate cumulative GPA of 3.0. Additional exam requirements/recommendations for international students: Required—TOEFL (minimum score 550 paper-based; 80 iBT); Recommended—IELTS (minimum score 6.5). *Application deadline:* For fall admission, 9/24 priority date for domestic and international students; for winter admission, 1/7 priority date for domestic and international students; for spring admission, 4/8 priority date for domestic and international students; for summer admission, 7/8 priority date for domestic and international students. Applications are processed on a rolling basis. Application fee: $30 ($100 for international students). Electronic applications accepted. *Expenses: Tuition:* Full-time $16,300; part-time $460 per credit. *Required fees:* $660; $330 per credit. Tuition and fees vary according to degree level and program. *Financial support:* In 2017–18, 738 students received support. Career-related internships or fieldwork, institutionally sponsored loans, scholarships/grants, tuition waivers (partial), and unspecified assistantships available. Financial award application deadline: 6/30; financial award applicants required to submit FAFSA. *Unit head:* Dr. Gina Ganahl, Dean, Accelerated Degree Programs, 636-949-4501, Fax: 636-949-4505, E-mail: gganahl@lindenwood.edu. *Application contact:* Kara Schilli, Director, Evening and Graduate Admissions, 636-949-4349, Fax: 636-949-4109, E-mail: adultadmissions@lindenwood.edu.
Website: http://www.lindenwood.edu/academics/academic-schools/school-of-accelerated-degree-programs/

Writing

Lipscomb University, Program in Film and Creative Media, Nashville, TN 37204-3951. Offers writer/director (MFA); MFA/MBA. *Program availability:* Part-time, evening/weekend. *Faculty:* 7 full-time (1 woman), 1 part-time/adjunct (0 women). *Students:* 23 full-time (12 women); includes 10 minority (all Black or African American, non-Hispanic/Latino). Average age 32. 26 applicants, 46% accepted, 9 enrolled. In 2017, 12 master's awarded. *Degree requirements:* For master's, professional practicum, portfolio. *Entrance requirements:* For master's, GRE or MAT, 2 references, resume, video portfolio. Additional exam requirements/recommendations for international students: Required—TOEFL (minimum score 570 paper-based; 80 iBT). *Application deadline:* Applications are processed on a rolling basis. Application fee: $50 ($75 for international students). Electronic applications accepted. *Expenses:* $1,013. *Financial support:* Unspecified assistantships available. Financial award applicants required to submit FAFSA. *Unit head:* David DeBorde, Director, 615-966-7111, E-mail: david.deborde@lipscomb.edu. *Application contact:* Josh Link, Recruiting and Marketing Coordinator, 615-966-6005, E-mail: josh.link@lipscomb.edu.
Website: http://www.lipscomb.edu/cinematicarts/graduate-programs

London Metropolitan University, Graduate Programs, London, United Kingdom. Offers applied psychology (M Sc); architecture (MA); biomedical science (M Sc); blood science (M Sc); cancer pharmacology (M Sc); computer networking and cyber security (M Sc); computing and information systems (M Sc); conference interpreting (MA); counter-terrorism studies (M Sc); creative, digital and professional writing (MA); crime, violence and prevention (M Sc); criminology (M Sc); curating contemporary art (MA); data analytics (M Sc); digital media (MA); early childhood studies (MA); education (MA, Ed D); financial services law, regulation and compliance (LL M); food science (M Sc); forensic psychology (M Sc); health and social care management and policy (M Sc); human nutrition (M Sc); human resource management (MA); human rights and international conflict (MA); information technology (M Sc); intelligence and security studies (M Sc); international oil, gas and energy law (LL M); international relations (MA); interpreting (MA); learning and teaching in higher education (MA); legal practice (LL M); media and entertainment law (LL M); organizational and consumer psychology (M Sc); psychological therapy (M Sc); psychology of mental health (M Sc); public health (M Sc); public policy and management (MPA); security studies (M Sc); social work (M Sc); spatial planning and urban design (MA); sports therapy (M Sc); supporting older children and young people with dyslexia (MA); teaching languages (MA), including Arabic, English; translation (MA); woman and child abuse (MA).

Long Island University–LIU Brooklyn, Richard L. Conolly College of Liberal Arts and Sciences, Brooklyn, NY 11201-8423. Offers biology (MS); chemistry (MS); clinical psychology (PhD); creative writing (MFA); English (MA); media arts (MA, MFA); political science (MA); psychology (MA); social science (MS); United Nations (Advanced Certificate); urban studies (MA); writing and production for television (MFA). *Program availability:* Part-time. *Faculty:* 32 full-time (13 women), 17 part-time/adjunct (6 women). *Students:* 178 full-time (123 women), 143 part-time (96 women); includes 128 minority (65 Black or African American, non-Hispanic/Latino; 22 Asian, non-Hispanic/Latino; 31 Hispanic/Latino; 10 Two or more races, non-Hispanic/Latino), 54 international. Average age 30. 629 applicants, 38% accepted, 74 enrolled. In 2017, 147 master's, 9 doctorates, 8 other advanced degrees awarded. Terminal master's awarded for partial completion of doctoral program. *Degree requirements:* For master's, comprehensive exam (for some programs), thesis (for some programs); for doctorate, thesis/dissertation. *Entrance requirements:* For doctorate, GRE. Additional exam requirements/recommendations for international students: Required—TOEFL (minimum score 550 paper-based, 79 iBT) or IELTS. *Application deadline:* Applications are processed on a rolling basis. Application fee: $50. Electronic applications accepted. *Expenses: Tuition:* Full-time $21,618; part-time $1201 per credit. *Required fees:* $1840; $920 per term. Tuition and fees vary according to course load. *Financial support:* In 2017–18, 214 students received support, including 120 fellowships with full and partial tuition reimbursements available (averaging $915 per year), 5 research assistantships with full and partial tuition reimbursements available (averaging $2,300 per year), 136 teaching assistantships with full and partial tuition reimbursements available (averaging $2,300 per year); career-related internships or fieldwork, Federal Work-Study, institutionally sponsored loans, scholarships/grants, and unspecified assistantships also available. Support available to part-time students. Financial award application deadline: 2/15; financial award applicants required to submit FAFSA. *Faculty research:* Quantum gravity and astrophysics; string theory; pharmaceutical biotechnology with a focus on molecular details of drug susceptibility/resistance mechanisms; entomology, population and community ecology, agroecology, and biodiversity; psychotherapy process-outcome, particularly therapeutic alliance development, the role of common factors, and the study of treatment failures; personality pathology, borderline personality disorder and pathological narcissism. *Unit head:* Dr. Scott Krawczyk, Dean, 718-488-1003, E-mail: scott.krawczyk@liu.edu. *Application contact:* Bayu Sutrisno, Graduate Admissions Counselor, 718-488-1564, Fax: 718-780-6110, E-mail: bayu.sutrisno@liu.edu.

Louisiana State University and Agricultural & Mechanical College, Graduate School, College of Humanities and Social Sciences, Department of English, Baton Rouge, LA 70803. Offers creative writing (MFA); English (MA, PhD). *Faculty:* 43 full-time (23 women). *Students:* 77 full-time (48 women), 12 part-time (8 women); includes 16 minority (8 Black or African American, non-Hispanic/Latino; 2 Asian, non-Hispanic/Latino; 5 Hispanic/Latino; 1 Two or more races, non-Hispanic/Latino), 10 international. Average age 30. 191 applicants, 13% accepted, 2 enrolled. In 2017, 11 master's, 9 doctorates awarded. *Financial support:* In 2017–18, 3 fellowships (averaging $28,784 per year), 1 research assistantship (averaging $25,000 per year), 65 teaching assistantships (averaging $23,755 per year) were awarded. *Total annual research expenditures:* $80,469.

Loyola Marymount University, School of Film and Television, Writing for the Screen Program, Los Angeles, CA 90045-2659. Offers MFA. *Unit head:* Karol Hoeffner, Director, Writing for the Screen, 310-338-3033, E-mail: khoeffne@lmu.edu. *Application contact:* Chake H. Kouyoumjian, Associate Dean of Graduate Studies, 310-338-2721, Fax: 310-338-6086, E-mail: graduateinfo@lmu.edu.
Website: http://sftv.lmu.edu/academics/graduateprograms/writingforthescreen

Maharishi University of Management, Graduate Studies, Program in Screenwriting, Fairfield, IA 52557. Offers MFA.

Manhattanville College, Master of Fine Arts in Creative Writing Program, Purchase, NY 10577-2132. Offers MFA. *Program availability:* Part-time, evening/weekend. *Faculty:* 5 part-time/adjunct (3 women). *Students:* 5 full-time (4 women), 10 part-time (7 women). Average age 35. In 2017, 11 master's awarded. *Degree requirements:* For master's, thesis. *Entrance requirements:* For master's, 2 letters of recommendation, 2-3 page autobiographical essay, 10-12 page writing sample, official transcripts of all undergraduate work. *Application deadline:* Applications are processed on a rolling basis. Application fee: $75. Electronic applications accepted. *Expenses:* $770 per credit. *Financial support:* Fellowships, Federal Work-Study, scholarships/grants, tuition waivers (partial), and unspecified assistantships available. Financial award application deadline: 3/15; financial award applicants required to submit FAFSA. *Faculty research:* Fiction, labor/social justice issues, literary nonfiction, memoir, poetry, screenwriting. *Unit head:* Lori Soderlind, Program Director, 914-323-5239, E-mail: lori.soderlind@mville.edu. *Application contact:* Alissa Wilson, Director, Graduate Admissions, 914-323-3150, E-mail: mfa@mville.edu.
Website: http://mvillemfa.com

Massachusetts Institute of Technology, School of Humanities, Arts, and Social Sciences, Program in Comparative Media Studies/Writing, Graduate Program in Science Writing, Cambridge, MA 02139. Offers SM. *Degree requirements:* For master's, thesis. *Entrance requirements:* For master's, GRE General Test. Additional exam requirements/recommendations for international students: Required—TOEFL, IELTS. Electronic applications accepted. *Faculty research:* Communicating science to the public; digital media; investigative journalism; documentary film.

McDaniel College, Graduate and Professional Studies, Program in Liberal Arts, Westminster, MD 21157-4390. Offers liberal arts (MLA); writing for children and young adults (Postbaccalaureate Certificate). *Program availability:* Part-time, evening/weekend, 100% online. *Faculty:* 2 full-time (both women), 6 part-time/adjunct (4 women). *Students:* 2 full-time (both women), 10 part-time (all women). Average age 35. 4 applicants, 50% accepted. In 2017, 6 master's awarded. *Degree requirements:* For master's, final project. *Entrance requirements:* For master's, 3 recommendations. Additional exam requirements/recommendations for international students: Required—TOEFL (minimum score 79 iBT), IELTS (minimum score 6). *Application deadline:* For fall admission, 6/1 priority date for domestic students; for spring admission, 11/1 priority date for domestic students; for summer admission, 3/1 priority date for domestic students. Applications are processed on a rolling basis. Application fee: $75. Electronic applications accepted. *Expenses: Tuition:* Full-time $11,760; part-time $490 per credit hour. Tuition and fees vary according to course load and program. *Financial support:* Application deadline: 3/1; applicants required to submit FAFSA. *Unit head:* E-mail: gradadms@mcdaniel.edu. *Application contact:* Crystal L. Perry, Assistant Director, Graduate Enrollment Management, 410-857-2516, Fax: 410-857-2515, E-mail: cperry@mcdaniel.edu.

McNeese State University, Doré School of Graduate Studies, College of Liberal Arts, Department of English and Foreign Languages, Program in Creative Writing, Lake Charles, LA 70609. Offers MFA. *Program availability:* Evening/weekend. *Degree requirements:* For master's, thesis, public reading. *Entrance requirements:* For master's, GRE, writing sample. *Application deadline:* For fall admission, 5/15 priority date for domestic and international students; for spring admission, 10/15 priority date for domestic and international students. Applications are processed on a rolling basis. Application fee: $20 ($30 for international students). *Financial support:* Application deadline: 5/1. *Unit head:* Dr. Scott E. Goins, Head, 337-475-5456, Fax: 337-475-5327, E-mail: sgoins@mcneese.edu. *Application contact:* Dr. Dustin M. Hebert, Director of Dore' School of Graduate Studies, 337-475-5396, Fax: 337-475-5397, E-mail: admissions@mcneese.edu.

Michigan State University, The Graduate School, College of Arts and Letters, Program in Rhetoric and Writing, East Lansing, MI 48824. Offers critical studies in literacy and pedagogy (MA); digital rhetoric and professional writing (MA); rhetoric and writing (PhD). *Entrance requirements:* Additional exam requirements/recommendations for international students: Required—TOEFL. Electronic applications accepted. *Faculty research:* Rhetoric, writing and communication studies; media studies; technical communication, writing for digital environments.

Millersville University of Pennsylvania, College of Graduate Studies and Adult Learning, College of Arts, Humanities and Social Sciences, Department of English, Millersville, PA 17551-0302. Offers English (M Ed, MA); writing (Postbaccalaureate Certificate). *Program availability:* Part-time, evening/weekend. *Faculty:* 7 full-time (3 women). *Students:* 5 full-time (2 women), 20 part-time (15 women); includes 2 minority (1 Black or African American, non-Hispanic/Latino; 1 Asian, non-Hispanic/Latino), 6 international. Average age 32. 16 applicants, 94% accepted, 8 enrolled. In 2017, 9 master's awarded. *Degree requirements:* For master's, one foreign language, thesis optional. *Entrance requirements:* For master's, GRE or MAT. Additional exam requirements/recommendations for international students: Required—TOEFL (minimum score 80 iBT), IELTS (minimum score 6.5), PTE (minimum score 60). *Application deadline:* Applications are processed on a rolling basis. Application fee: $40. Electronic applications accepted. *Expenses:* $500 per credit resident tuition and fees; $750 per credit non-resident tuition and fees; $114.75 per credit general fee (maximum of 12 credits); technology fee $27 per credit (resident), $39 per credit (non-resident). *Financial support:* In 2017–18, 4 students received support. Unspecified assistantships available. Financial award application deadline: 3/15; financial award applicants required to submit FAFSA. *Faculty research:* Film studies; critical theory; narrative studies; literacy narratives; multicultural issues surrounding literacy; African American literature and rhetorical traditions; writing pedagogy; public and civic discourse; civic engagement; academic, workplace, and community literacy; grounded theory; critical discourse analysis; rhetorical theory; composition theory; science writing; technical writing; environmental rhetoric; rhetoric of place; public sphere theory. *Unit head:* Dr. Jill R. Craven, Chair, 717-871-7385, Fax: 717-871-7933, E-mail: jill.craven@millersville.edu. *Application contact:* Dr. Victor S. DeSantis, Dean of College of Graduate Studies and Adult Learning/Associate Provost for Civic and Community Engagement, 717-871-7619, Fax: 717-871-7954, E-mail: victor.desantis@millersville.edu.
Website: http://www.millersville.edu/english/graduate/index.php

Mills College, Graduate Studies, Department of English, Oakland, CA 94613-1000. Offers book art and creative writing (MFA); literature (MA); poetry (MFA); prose (MFA); Spanish creative writing (Certificate); translation (MFA). *Program availability:* Part-time. *Faculty:* 6 full-time (5 women), 4 part-time/adjunct (all women). *Students:* 36 full-time (29 women), 21 part-time (14 women); includes 26 minority (9 Black or African American, non-Hispanic/Latino; 3 Asian, non-Hispanic/Latino; 9 Hispanic/Latino; 5 Two or more races, non-Hispanic/Latino). Average age 32. 100 applicants, 95% accepted, 27 enrolled. In 2017, 18 master's awarded. *Degree requirements:* For master's, comprehensive exam, thesis. *Entrance requirements:* For master's, 15-20 page writing sample. Additional exam requirements/recommendations for international students: Required—TOEFL (minimum score 600 paper-based; 100 iBT), IELTS (minimum score 7). *Application deadline:* For fall admission, 12/15 priority date for domestic students, 12/15 for international students. Applications are processed on a rolling basis. Application fee: $50. Electronic applications accepted. *Expenses:* Contact institution. *Financial support:* In 2017–18, 23 students received support, including 23 fellowships with partial tuition reimbursements available (averaging $6,327 per year), 21 teaching assistantships with tuition reimbursements available; research assistantships and scholarships/grants also available. Support available to part-time students. Financial award application deadline: 2/1; financial award applicants required to submit FAFSA. *Faculty research:* Creative writing, African-American literature, Victorian women writers, theories of sexuality, Shakespeare. *Unit head:* Dr. Thomas Strychacz, Chair of the English Department, 510-430-2208, E-mail: toms@mills.edu. *Application contact:* Robynne Lofton, Director of Admissions, 510-430-3295, Fax: 510-430-2159, E-mail: grad-admission@mills.edu.
Website: http://www.mills.edu/english/

Mills College, Graduate Studies, Program in Book Art and Creative Writing, Oakland, CA 94613-1000. Offers MFA. *Program availability:* Part-time. *Faculty:* 3 full-time (all women), 6 part-time/adjunct (5 women). *Students:* 2 full-time (both women), 2 part-time (both women). Average age 31. 16 applicants, 81% accepted, 1 enrolled. In 2017, 3

master's awarded. *Degree requirements:* For master's, thesis project. *Entrance requirements:* For master's, visual portfolio of 15-25 images, written portfolio sample (for creative writing program). Additional exam requirements/recommendations for international students: Required—TOEFL (minimum score 600 paper-based; 100 iBT), IELTS (minimum score 7). *Application deadline:* For fall admission, 12/15 priority date for domestic students, 12/15 for international students. Application fee: $50. Electronic applications accepted. *Expenses: Tuition:* Full-time $33,480; part-time $1000 per credit. *Required fees:* $1479. Tuition and fees vary according to program. *Financial support:* In 2017–18, 4 students received support, including 4 fellowships with tuition reimbursements available (averaging $5,323 per year), 3 teaching assistantships with tuition reimbursements available. Financial award application deadline: 2/1; financial award applicants required to submit FAFSA. *Unit head:* Kathleen Walkup, Professor of Book Arts, 510-430-2001, Fax: 510-430-2159, E-mail: kwalk@mills.edu. *Application contact:* Robynne Lofton, Director of Admissions, 510-430-3295, Fax: 510-430-2159, E-mail: grad-admission@mills.edu.
Website: http://www.mills.edu/academics/graduate/eng/programs/MFA_in_bookart.php

Minnesota State University Mankato, College of Graduate Studies and Research, College of Arts and Humanities, Department of English, Mankato, MN 56001. Offers communication and composition (MA); creative writing (MFA); English studies (MA); teaching English as a second language (MA, Certificate); technical communication (MA, Certificate). *Program availability:* Part-time. *Degree requirements:* For master's, one foreign language, comprehensive exam, thesis or alternative. *Entrance requirements:* For master's, minimum GPA of 3.0 during previous 2 years, writing sample (MFA). Additional exam requirements/recommendations for international students: Required—TOEFL (minimum score 500 paper-based; 61 iBT). Electronic applications accepted.

Missouri State University, Graduate College, College of Arts and Letters, Department of English, Springfield, MO 65897. Offers applied second language acquisition (MASLA); English (MA); English education (MS Ed); teaching English to speakers of other languages (Certificate); writing (MA). MASLA offered with the Department of Modern and Classical Languages. *Program availability:* Part-time, evening/weekend. *Faculty:* 25 full-time (18 women), 5 part-time/adjunct (2 women). *Students:* 34 full-time (26 women), 85 part-time (73 women); includes 9 minority (1 Black or African American, non-Hispanic/Latino; 1 Asian, non-Hispanic/Latino; 3 Hispanic/Latino; 1 Native Hawaiian or other Pacific Islander, non-Hispanic/Latino; 3 Two or more races, non-Hispanic/Latino), 14 international. Average age 26. 97 applicants, 65% accepted, 56 enrolled. In 2017, 57 master's awarded. *Degree requirements:* For master's, one foreign language, comprehensive exam, thesis or alternative. *Entrance requirements:* For master's, GRE (for MA), 9-12 teacher certification (MS Ed); minimum GPA of 3.0 (MA); personal statement (200- to 250-word description of reasons and goals behind interest in English graduate studies); at least two letters of recommendation from individuals able to speak of the applicant's academic achievements and potential; writing sample. Additional exam requirements/recommendations for international students: Required—TOEFL (minimum score 550 paper-based; 79 iBT), IELTS (minimum score 6). *Application deadline:* For fall admission, 3/1 priority date for domestic students, 3/1 for international students; for spring admission, 10/1 priority date for domestic students, 10/1 for international students. Applications are processed on a rolling basis. Application fee: $35 ($50 for international students). Electronic applications accepted. *Expenses:* Tuition, state resident: full-time $2915; part-time $2021 per credit hour. Tuition, nonresident: full-time $5354; part-time $3647 per credit hour. *International tuition:* $11,992 full-time. *Required fees:* $173; $173 per credit hour. Tuition and fees vary according to class time, course level, course load, degree level, campus/location and program. *Financial support:* In 2017–18, 23 teaching assistantships with full tuition reimbursements (averaging $8,772 per year) were awarded; Federal Work-Study, institutionally sponsored loans, scholarships/grants, and unspecified assistantships also available. Financial award application deadline: 3/31; financial award applicants required to submit FAFSA. *Faculty research:* History of rhetoric, modern poetry, African-American literature, digital writing, teaching English to speakers of other languages. *Unit head:* Dr. W. D. Blackmon, Department Head, 417-836-5107, Fax: 417-836-6940, E-mail: english@missouristate.edu. *Application contact:* Stephanie Praschan, Director, Graduate Enrollment Management, 417-836-5330, Fax: 417-836-6200, E-mail: stephaniepraschan@missouristate.edu.
Website: http://english.missouristate.edu/

Missouri Western State University, Program in Written Communication, St. Joseph, MO 64507-2294. Offers teaching of writing (Graduate Certificate); technical communication (MAA); writing studies (MAA). *Program availability:* Part-time. *Students:* 6 full-time (5 women), 6 part-time (4 women), 6 international. Average age 31. 4 applicants, 100% accepted, 4 enrolled. In 2017, 2 master's, 2 other advanced degrees awarded. *Entrance requirements:* For master's, minimum undergraduate GPA of 3.0, portfolio, 3 letters of reference. Additional exam requirements/recommendations for international students: Recommended—TOEFL (minimum score 79 iBT), IELTS (minimum score 6). *Application deadline:* For fall admission, 7/15 for domestic and international students; for spring admission, 10/1 for domestic and international students; for summer admission, 3/15 for domestic students. Applications are processed on a rolling basis. Application fee: $45 ($50 for international students). Electronic applications accepted. *Expenses:* Tuition, state resident: full-time $6391; part-time $336 per credit hour. Tuition, nonresident: full-time $11,483; part-time $604 per credit hour. *Required fees:* $542; $99 per credit hour. $176 per semester. One-time fee: $45. Tuition and fees vary according to course load and program. *Financial support:* Scholarships/grants and unspecified assistantships available. Support available to part-time students. *Unit head:* Dr. Michael Charlton, Associate Professor, 816-271-4310, E-mail: mcharlton@missouriwestern.edu. *Application contact:* Dr. Benjamin D. Caldwell, Dean of the Graduate School, 816-271-4394, Fax: 816-271-4525, E-mail: graduate@missouriwestern.edu.
Website: https://www.missouriwestern.edu/eml/maawc/

Monmouth University, Graduate Studies, Department of English, West Long Branch, NJ 07764-1898. Offers creative writing (MA); literature (MA); rhetoric and writing (MA). *Program availability:* Part-time, evening/weekend. *Faculty:* 5 full-time (3 women). *Students:* 1 full-time (0 women), 28 part-time (21 women); includes 2 minority (1 Hispanic/Latino; 1 Two or more races, non-Hispanic/Latino). Average age 30. In 2017, 9 master's awarded. *Degree requirements:* For master's, comprehensive exam (for some programs), thesis. *Entrance requirements:* For master's, minimum overall GPA of 2.75, fifteen or more credits in literature or related field, essay of 1000 words describing interest and goals, two letters of recommendation, creative writing sample. Additional exam requirements/recommendations for international students: Required—TOEFL (minimum score 550 paper-based; 79 iBT), IELTS (minimum score 6), Michigan English Language Assessment Battery (minimum score 77) or Certificate of Advanced English (minimum score of 160). *Application deadline:* For fall admission, 7/15 for domestic students, 6/1 for international students; for spring admission, 12/1 for domestic students, 11/1 for international students; for summer admission, 5/1 for domestic students. Applications are processed on a rolling basis. Application fee: $50. Electronic applications accepted. *Expenses: Tuition:* Full-time $21,366; part-time $7122 per credit. *Required fees:* $700; $175 per term. *Financial support:* In 2017–18, 7 students received support. Institutionally sponsored loans, scholarships/grants, and unspecified assistantships available. Support available to part-time students. Financial award

applicants required to submit FAFSA. *Faculty research:* Renaissance and medieval literature, nineteenth-century American literature, eighteenth-century British literature and women's studies, Old and Middle English, African diaspora and African post-colonial literature. *Unit head:* Dr. Kristin Bluemel, Program Director, 732-571-3622, Fax: 732-263-5242, E-mail: kbluemel@monmouth.edu. *Application contact:* Andrea Thompson, Graduate Admission Counselor, 732-571-3452, Fax: 732-263-5123, E-mail: gradadm@monmouth.edu.
Website: https://www.monmouth.edu/graduate/ma-english/

Montclair State University, The Graduate School, College of Humanities and Social Sciences, Teaching Writing Certificate Program, Montclair, NJ 07043-1624. Offers Certificate. *Program availability:* Part-time, evening/weekend. *Entrance requirements:* For degree, 2 letters of recommendation, essay. Additional exam requirements/recommendations for international students: Required—TOEFL (minimum score 83 iBT), IELTS (minimum score 6.5). Electronic applications accepted. *Faculty research:* Pedagogy in writing.

Mount Mary University, Graduate Programs, Program in English, Milwaukee, WI 53222-4597. Offers creative writing (MA); professional and new media writing (MA). *Program availability:* Part-time, evening/weekend. *Degree requirements:* For master's, comprehensive exam, thesis or alternative. *Entrance requirements:* For master's, minimum GPA of 2.75. Additional exam requirements/recommendations for international students: Required—TOEFL (minimum score 550 paper-based; 80 iBT); Recommended—IELTS (minimum score 6.5). Electronic applications accepted. *Expenses:* Contact institution.

Mount Saint Mary's University, Graduate Division, Los Angeles, CA 90049. Offers business administration (MBA); counseling psychology (MS); creative writing (MFA); education (MS, Certificate); film and television (MFA); health policy and management (MS); humanities (MA); nursing (MSN, Certificate); physical therapy (DPT); religious studies (MA). *Program availability:* Part-time, evening/weekend. *Faculty:* 50 full-time (35 women), 116 part-time/adjunct (81 women). *Students:* 670 full-time (518 women), 147 part-time (116 women); includes 414 minority (73 Black or African American, non-Hispanic/Latino; 4 American Indian or Alaska Native, non-Hispanic/Latino; 60 Asian, non-Hispanic/Latino; 259 Hispanic/Latino; 7 Native Hawaiian or other Pacific Islander, non-Hispanic/Latino; 11 Two or more races, non-Hispanic/Latino), 4 international. Average age 32. 1,398 applicants, 21% accepted, 242 enrolled. In 2017, 170 master's, 28 doctorates, 35 other advanced degrees awarded. *Entrance requirements:* Additional exam requirements/recommendations for international students: Required—TOEFL. *Application deadline:* For fall admission, 6/30 priority date for domestic and international students; for spring admission, 10/30 priority date for domestic and international students; for summer admission, 3/30 priority date for domestic and international students. Applications are processed on a rolling basis. Application fee: $50. Electronic applications accepted. *Expenses: Tuition:* Part-time $905 per unit. One-time fee: $155 part-time. Tuition and fees vary according to degree level and program. *Financial support:* Career-related internships or fieldwork, Federal Work-Study, institutionally sponsored loans, and tuition waivers (full and partial) available. Support available to part-time students. Financial award application deadline: 3/15; financial award applicants required to submit FAFSA. *Unit head:* Albert Ramos, Director of Graduate Admissions, 213-477-2800, E-mail: gradprograms@msmu.edu. *Application contact:* Shawn Peters, Graduate Admission Counselor, 213-477-2676, E-mail: gradprograms@msmu.edu.
Website: http://www.msmu.edu/graduate-programs/

Murray State University, College of Humanities and Fine Arts, Department of English and Philosophy, Murray, KY 42071. Offers creative writing (MFA); English (MA); English pedagogy and technology (DA); gender studies (Certificate); teaching English to speakers of other languages (TESOL) (MA). *Program availability:* Part-time, 100% online, blended/hybrid learning. *Faculty:* 26 full-time (14 women), 1 part-time/adjunct (0 women). *Students:* 31 full-time (12 women), 91 part-time (61 women); includes 11 minority (5 Black or African American, non-Hispanic/Latino; 2 American Indian or Alaska Native, non-Hispanic/Latino; 2 Asian, non-Hispanic/Latino; 2 Two or more races, non-Hispanic/Latino), 23 international. Average age 36. 55 applicants, 95% accepted, 30 enrolled. In 2017, 21 master's awarded. *Entrance requirements:* For master's, doctorate, and Certificate, GRE or GMAT, minimum university GPA of 2.75. Additional exam requirements/recommendations for international students: Required—TOEFL (minimum score 527 paper-based; 71 iBT). *Application deadline:* Applications are processed on a rolling basis. Application fee: $40 ($50 for international students). Electronic applications accepted. *Expenses:* Tuition, state resident: full-time $9504. Tuition, nonresident: full-time $26,811. *International tuition:* $14,400 full-time. Tuition and fees vary according to course load, degree level and reciprocity agreements. *Financial support:* In 2017–18, 3 teaching assistantships were awarded; Federal Work-Study and unspecified assistantships also available. Financial award applicants required to submit FAFSA. *Unit head:* Dr. Sue Sroda, Chair, Department of English and Philosophy, 270-809-4715, Fax: 270-809-4545, E-mail: msroda@murraystate.edu. *Application contact:* Kaitlyn Burzynski, Interim Assistant Director for Graduate Admission and Records, 270-809-5732, Fax: 270-809-3780, E-mail: msu.graduateadmissions@murraystate.edu.
Website: https://www.murraystate.edu/academics/CollegesDepartments/CollegeOfHumanitiesAndFineArts/EnglishAndPhilosophy/index.aspx

Naropa University, Graduate Programs, Program in Creative Writing, Boulder, CO 80302-6697. Offers MFA. *Program availability:* Part-time, blended/hybrid learning. *Faculty:* 7 full-time (5 women), 1 (woman) part-time/adjunct. *Students:* 13 part-time (10 women); includes 1 minority (Asian, non-Hispanic/Latino). Average age 41. 8 applicants, 63% accepted, 5 enrolled. In 2017, 1 master's awarded. *Degree requirements:* For master's, thesis. *Entrance requirements:* For master's, creative writing sample; resume/curriculum vitae with pertinent academic, employment and volunteer activities; transcripts; 2 letters of recommendation; letter of interest. Additional exam requirements/recommendations for international students: Required—TOEFL (minimum score 550 paper-based; 80 iBT). *Application deadline:* For fall admission, 1/13 priority date for domestic students, 1/15 priority date for international students; for spring admission, 10/15 for domestic students, 10/15 priority date for international students. Applications are processed on a rolling basis. Application fee: $60. Electronic applications accepted. *Expenses:* $995 per credit. *Financial support:* In 2017–18, 2 students received support. Career-related internships or fieldwork, Federal Work-Study, scholarships/grants, tuition waivers (partial), and unspecified assistantships available. Support available to part-time students. Financial award application deadline: 3/1; financial award applicants required to submit FAFSA. *Unit head:* Jeffrey Pethybridge, Chair, School of the Arts and Jack Kerouac School, 303-546-5296, E-mail: jpethybridge@naropa.edu. *Application contact:* Office of Admissions, 303-546-3572, Fax: 303-546-3583, E-mail: admissions@naropa.edu.
Website: http://www.naropa.edu/academics/masters/creative-writing-low-residency/index.php

Naropa University, Graduate Programs, Program in Creative Writing and Poetics, Boulder, CO 80302-6697. Offers MFA. *Program availability:* Part-time. *Faculty:* 3 full-time (1 woman), 5 part-time/adjunct (all women). *Students:* 19 full-time (12 women), 2 part-time (0 women); includes 8 minority (2 Black or African American, non-Hispanic/Latino; 1 American Indian or Alaska Native, non-Hispanic/Latino; 4 Hispanic/Latino; 1

Two or more races, non-Hispanic/Latino). Average age 29. 33 applicants, 91% accepted, 8 enrolled. In 2017, 11 master's awarded. *Degree requirements:* For master's, thesis. *Entrance requirements:* For master's, resume/curriculum vitae with pertinent academic, employment and volunteer activity; 2 letters of recommendation; transcripts; statement of interest; 10-15 page creative writing sample; phone interview. Additional exam requirements/recommendations for international students: Required—TOEFL (minimum score 550 paper-based; 80 iBT). *Application deadline:* For fall admission, 1/15 priority date for domestic and international students; for spring admission, 10/15 priority date for domestic and international students. Applications are processed on a rolling basis. Application fee: $60. Electronic applications accepted. *Expenses:* $995 per credit. *Financial support:* In 2017–18, 14 students received support, including 5 fellowships with full tuition reimbursements available (averaging $3,000 per year), 2 teaching assistantships with partial tuition reimbursements available (averaging $1,500 per year); research assistantships, career-related internships or fieldwork, scholarships/grants, tuition waivers (partial), and unspecified assistantships also available. Support available to part-time students. Financial award application deadline: 3/1; financial award applicants required to submit FAFSA. *Unit head:* Jeffrey Pethybridge, Chair, School of the Arts and Jack Kerouac School, 303-546-5296, E-mail: jpethybridge@naropa.edu. *Application contact:* Office of Admissions, 303-546-3572, Fax: 303-546-3583, E-mail: admissions@naropa.edu.
Website: http://www.naropa.edu/academics/masters/creative-writing-poetics/index.php

National Louis University, College of Arts and Sciences, Chicago, IL 60603. Offers adult education (Ed D); counseling and human services (MS); language and academic development (M Ed, Certificate); psychology (MA, PhD, Certificate); public policy (MA); written communication (MS, Certificate). *Program availability:* Part-time, evening/weekend, online learning. *Degree requirements:* For master's and Certificate, comprehensive exam (for some programs), thesis (for some programs); for doctorate, thesis/dissertation. *Entrance requirements:* For master's, MAT or GRE, 3 professional or academic references, interview, minimum GPA of 3.0; for doctorate, GRE General Test, MAT, or Watson-Glaser Critical Thinking Appraisal, three professional or academic references, statement of academic and professional goals, 3 years of experience in field, interview, master's degree, resume, writing sample; for Certificate, GRE, MAT, or Watson-Glaser Critical Thinking Appraisal, three professional or academic references, statement of academic and professional goals, interview, minimum GPA of 3.0. Additional exam requirements/recommendations for international students: Required—Department of Language Studies Assessment or TOEFL (minimum score 550 paper-based; 79 iBT). Electronic applications accepted.

National University, Academic Affairs, College of Letters and Sciences, La Jolla, CA 92037-1011. Offers biology (MS); counseling psychology (MA), including licensed professional clinical counseling, marriage and family therapy; creative writing (MFA); english (MA); film studies (MA); forensic and crime scene investigations (Certificate); forensic sciences (MFS); human behavior (MA); mathematics for educators (MS); performance psychology (MA); strategic communications (MA). *Program availability:* Part-time, evening/weekend, 100% online, blended/hybrid learning. *Degree requirements:* For master's, thesis (for some programs). *Entrance requirements:* For master's, interview, minimum GPA of 2.5. Additional exam requirements/recommendations for international students: Required—TOEFL (minimum score 550 paper-based; 79 iBT), IELTS (minimum score 6). *Application deadline:* Applications are processed on a rolling basis. Application fee: $60 ($65 for international students). Electronic applications accepted. *Expenses: Tuition:* Part-time $430 per quarter hour. *Financial support:* Career-related internships or fieldwork, institutionally sponsored loans, scholarships/grants, and tuition waivers (partial) available. Support available to part-time students. Financial award application deadline: 6/30; financial award applicants required to submit FAFSA. *Unit head:* Dr. Carol Richardson, Dean, 858-642-8450, E-mail: cols@nu.edu. *Application contact:* Brandon Jouganatos, Interim Vice President for Enrollment Services, 800-628-8648, E-mail: advisor@nu.edu.
Website: http://www.nu.edu/OurPrograms/CollegeOfLettersAndSciences.html

National University, Academic Affairs, School of Professional Studies, La Jolla, CA 92037-1011. Offers criminal justice (MCJ); digital cinema production (MFA); digital journalism (MA); homeland security and emergency management (MS); juvenile justice (MS); professional screenwriting (MFA); public administration (MPA), including human resource management, organizational leadership. *Program availability:* Part-time, evening/weekend, 100% online, blended/hybrid learning. *Degree requirements:* For master's, thesis (for some programs). *Entrance requirements:* For master's, interview, minimum GPA of 2.5. Additional exam requirements/recommendations for international students: Required—TOEFL (minimum score 550 paper-based; 79 iBT), IELTS (minimum score 6). *Application deadline:* Applications are processed on a rolling basis. Application fee: $60 ($65 for international students). Electronic applications accepted. *Expenses: Tuition:* Part-time $430 per quarter hour. *Financial support:* Career-related internships or fieldwork, institutionally sponsored loans, scholarships/grants, and tuition waivers (partial) available. Support available to part-time students. Financial award application deadline: 6/30; financial award applicants required to submit FAFSA. *Unit head:* Dr. Daniel Donaldson, Dean, 858-642-8480, E-mail: sops@nu.edu. *Application contact:* Brandon Jouganatos, Vice President for Enrollment Services, 800-628-8648, E-mail: advisor@nu.edu.
Website: http://www.nu.edu/OurPrograms/School-of-Professional-Studies.html

New England College, Programs in Writing, Henniker, NH 03242-3293. Offers poetry (MFA); professional writing (MA). *Program availability:* Part-time, evening/weekend. Electronic applications accepted. *Faculty research:* Poetry collections.

New Hampshire Institute of Art, Graduate Studies, Manchester, NH 03104. Offers art education (MA); creative writing (MFA); photography (MFA); teaching visual arts (MAT); visual arts (MFA). *Accreditation:* NASAD. *Faculty:* 31 part-time/adjunct (14 women). *Students:* 59 full-time (42 women), 6 part-time (3 women); includes 2 minority (1 Asian, non-Hispanic/Latino; 1 Hispanic/Latino). Average age 43. 33 applicants, 36% accepted, 5 enrolled. In 2017, 2 master's awarded. *Degree requirements:* For master's, thesis, corresponding exhibition and artist talk. *Entrance requirements:* For master's, writing sample or visual art portfolio; curriculum vitae; transcripts; letters of recommendation. Additional exam requirements/recommendations for international students: Required—TOEFL (minimum score 550 paper-based; 80 iBT), IELTS (minimum score 6.5). *Application deadline:* For fall admission, 5/1 priority date for domestic students; for spring admission, 11/1 priority date for domestic students. Applications are processed on a rolling basis. Application fee: $75. Electronic applications accepted. *Expenses:* Contact institution. *Financial support:* In 2017–18, 2 teaching assistantships (averaging $1,200 per year) were awarded; scholarships/grants and unspecified assistantships also available. Support available to part-time students. Financial award application deadline: 6/1; financial award applicants required to submit FAFSA. *Faculty research:* Fine arts - visual arts, photography, creative writing; art education. *Unit head:* Lucinda Bliss, Dean of Graduate Studies, 603-836-2522, E-mail: lucindabliss@nhia.edu. *Application contact:* Moriah Billups, Graduate Admissions Coordinator, 603-836 2588, E-mail: gradadmissions@nhia.edu.
Website: http://www.nhia.edu/graduate-studies

New Mexico Highlands University, Graduate Studies, College of Arts and Sciences, Department of English, Las Vegas, NM 87701. Offers English (MA), including creative writing, language, rhetoric and composition, literature. *Degree requirements:* For master's, comprehensive exam, thesis. *Entrance requirements:* For master's, minimum undergraduate GPA of 3.0. Additional exam requirements/recommendations for international students: Required—TOEFL (minimum score 540 paper-based). *Faculty research:* Twentieth-century literature, life path writing in homeless shelters, native American philosophy, medieval intellectual and cultural history, creating pedagogical tools for teaching law.

New Mexico State University, College of Arts and Sciences, Department of English, Las Cruces, NM 88003. Offers creative writing (MFA); English (MA), including creative writing, English studies for teachers, literature, rhetoric and professional communication; rhetoric and professional communication (PhD). *Program availability:* Part-time. *Faculty:* 17 full-time (9 women), 3 part-time/adjunct (1 woman). *Students:* 50 full-time (32 women), 21 part-time (14 women); includes 19 minority (2 Black or African American, non-Hispanic/Latino; 2 Asian, non-Hispanic/Latino; 14 Hispanic/Latino; 1 Two or more races, non-Hispanic/Latino), 8 international. Average age 35. 68 applicants, 50% accepted, 12 enrolled. In 2017, 13 master's, 1 doctorate awarded. *Entrance requirements:* For master's and doctorate, sample of written work. Additional exam requirements/recommendations for international students: Required—TOEFL (minimum score 550 paper-based; 79 iBT), IELTS (minimum score 6.5). *Application deadline:* For fall admission, 2/1 for domestic and international students. Application fee: $40 ($50 for international students). Electronic applications accepted. *Expenses:* Tuition, state resident: full-time $4390. Tuition, nonresident: full-time $15,309. *Required fees:* $853. *Financial support:* In 2017–18, 49 students received support, including 6 fellowships (averaging $4,390 per year), 41 teaching assistantships (averaging $17,317 per year); career-related internships or fieldwork, Federal Work-Study, scholarships/grants, traineeships, health care benefits, and unspecified assistantships also available. Support available to part-time students. Financial award application deadline: 3/1. *Faculty research:* Composition research, history and theory of rhetoric, technical/professional communication, creative writing, English and American literature. *Total annual research expenditures:* $10,666. *Unit head:* Dr. Elizabeth Schirmer, Interim Department Head, 575-646-3931, Fax: 575-646-7725, E-mail: eschirme@nmsu.edu. *Application contact:* Dr. Tracey Eileen Miller-Tomlinson, Director of Graduate Studies, 575-646-2213, Fax: 575-646-7725, E-mail: tomlin@nmsu.edu.
Website: http://english.nmsu.edu

New Saint Andrews College, Graduate School, Moscow, ID 83843. Offers classical Christian studies (Graduate Certificate); creative writing (MFA); theology and letters (MA). *Program availability:* Part-time, blended/hybrid learning. *Faculty:* 12 part-time/adjunct (0 women). *Students:* 12 full-time (3 women), 8 part-time (5 women), 1 international. Average age 25. 15 applicants, 53% accepted, 7 enrolled. In 2017, 3 master's awarded. *Degree requirements:* For master's, comprehensive exam (for some programs), thesis (for some programs), final oral exam. *Entrance requirements:* For master's, GRE, 2 letters of recommendation; for Graduate Certificate, GRE, bachelor's degree, essays, 2 letters of recommendation. *Application deadline:* For fall admission, 12/1 for domestic students. Applications are processed on a rolling basis. Application fee: $50. Electronic applications accepted. *Expenses: Tuition:* Full-time $7600; part-time $475 per credit. *Faculty research:* Hebrew, theology, literature. *Unit head:* Benjamin Merkle, President, 208-882-1566 Ext. 104, E-mail: bmerkle@nsa.edu. *Application contact:* Brenda Schlect, Director of Admissions, 208-882-1566 Ext. 113, Fax: 208-882-4293, E-mail: admissions@nsa.edu.
Website: http://www.nsa.edu/academics/graduate-school/

The New School, Schools of Public Engagement, Creative Writing Program, New York, NY 10011. Offers MFA. *Program availability:* Part-time. *Faculty:* 7 full-time (3 women), 25 part-time/adjunct (16 women). *Students:* 185 full-time (129 women), 5 part-time (2 women); includes 62 minority (22 Black or African American, non-Hispanic/Latino; 9 Asian, non-Hispanic/Latino; 25 Hispanic/Latino; 6 Two or more races, non-Hispanic/Latino), 24 international. Average age 29. 403 applicants, 78% accepted, 111 enrolled. In 2017, 83 master's awarded. *Degree requirements:* For master's, thesis. *Entrance requirements:* For master's, transcripts, recommendation letters, statement of purpose, writing portfolio, resume. Additional exam requirements/recommendations for international students: Required—TOEFL (minimum score 92 iBT), IELTS (minimum score 7), PTE (minimum score 68). *Application deadline:* For fall admission, 1/15 priority date for domestic and international students. Applications are processed on a rolling basis. Application fee: $50. Electronic applications accepted. *Expenses:* $15,871 per term full-time, $1,744 per credit part-time. *Financial support:* In 2017–18, 176 students received support, including 6 teaching assistantships (averaging $5,110 per year); career-related internships or fieldwork, scholarships/grants, and unspecified assistantships also available. Financial award application deadline: 2/1; financial award applicants required to submit FAFSA. *Unit head:* Chair, 212-229-5611 Ext. 2346, E-mail: jaramillo@newschool.edu. *Application contact:* Karl Ramos, Assistant Director, Graduate Admission, 212-229-5630 Ext. 2330, E-mail: ramosk@newschool.edu.
Website: https://www.newschool.edu/public-engagement/mfa-creative-writing/

New York University, Graduate School of Arts and Science, Program in Creative Writing, New York, NY 10012-1019. Offers MA, MFA. *Program availability:* Part-time, evening/weekend. *Students:* Average age 31. 553 applicants, 21% accepted, 68 enrolled. In 2017, 60 master's awarded. *Degree requirements:* For master's, one foreign language, thesis or alternative. *Entrance requirements:* For master's, GRE General Test, sample of written work. Additional exam requirements/recommendations for international students: Required—TOEFL. *Application deadline:* For fall admission, 12/18 for domestic and international students. Application fee: $100. *Expenses: Tuition:* Full-time $41,352; part-time $19,968 per year. *Required fees:* $2496; $1628 per unit. $814 per term. Tuition and fees vary according to course load and program. *Financial support:* Fellowships, teaching assistantships, Federal Work-Study, institutionally sponsored loans, scholarships/grants, health care benefits, tuition waivers (full and partial), and unspecified assistantships available. Financial award application deadline: 12/18; financial award applicants required to submit FAFSA. *Faculty research:* Fiction, poetry. *Unit head:* Deborah Landau, Director, 212-998-8816, Fax: 212-995-4864, E-mail: creative.writing@nyu.edu. *Application contact:* Zachary Sussman, Graduate Program Manager, 212-998-8816, Fax: 212-995-4864, E-mail: creative.writing@nyu.edu.
Website: http://www.nyu.edu/gsas/program/cwp/

New York University, School of Professional Studies, Center for Applied Liberal Arts, Division of Humanities, Arts, and Writing, New York, NY 10012-1019. Offers professional writing (MS). *Program availability:* Part-time, evening/weekend, 100% online, blended/hybrid learning. *Students:* 35 full-time (31 women), 72 part-time (59 women); includes 37 minority (10 Black or African American, non-Hispanic/Latino; 1 American Indian or Alaska Native, non-Hispanic/Latino; 5 Asian, non-Hispanic/Latino; 19 Hispanic/Latino; 2 Two or more races, non-Hispanic/Latino), 23 international. Average age 32. 66 applicants, 74% accepted, 29 enrolled. In 2017, 50 master's awarded. *Degree requirements:* For master's, thesis. *Entrance requirements:* For master's, GRE or GMAT (only upon request), bachelor's degree, resume with relevant professional work, internship or volunteer experience, two letters of recommendation, statement of purpose. Additional exam requirements/recommendations for international students: Required—TOEFL (minimum score 600 paper-based; 100 iBT), IELTS

(minimum score 7). *Application deadline:* For fall admission, 2/1 priority date for domestic and international students; for spring admission, 10/15 priority date for domestic students, 8/15 priority date for international students. Applications are processed on a rolling basis. Application fee: $150. Electronic applications accepted. *Expenses:* $20,244 per term. *Financial support:* Fellowships, career-related internships or fieldwork, Federal Work-Study, scholarships/grants, and health care benefits available. Support available to part-time students. Financial award application deadline: 6/30; financial award applicants required to submit FAFSA. *Unit head:* Billie Gastic, Associate Dean, 212-998-7272. *Application contact:* Office of Admissions, 212-998-7100, E-mail: sps.gradadmissions@nyu.edu.
Website: http://www.sps.nyu.edu/content/scps/academics/departments/humanities-arts-and-writing.html

New York University, Tisch School of the Arts, Rita and Burton Goldberg Department of Dramatic Writing, New York, NY 10012-1019. Offers MFA. *Faculty:* 15 full-time, 16 part-time/adjunct. *Students:* 47 full-time (25 women); includes 20 minority (8 Black or African American, non-Hispanic/Latino; 1 Asian, non-Hispanic/Latino; 6 Hispanic/Latino; 5 Two or more races, non-Hispanic/Latino), 5 international. Average age 30. 223 applicants, 21% accepted, 29 enrolled. In 2017, 21 master's awarded. *Entrance requirements:* For master's, writing sample. Application fee: $60. Electronic applications accepted. *Expenses: Tuition:* Full-time $41,352; part-time $19,968 per year. *Required fees:* $2496; $1628 per unit. $814 per term. Tuition and fees vary according to course load and program. *Financial support:* In 2017–18, 19 students received support. Fellowships, career-related internships or fieldwork, Federal Work-Study, institutionally sponsored loans, and scholarships/grants available. Financial award application deadline: 2/15; financial award applicants required to submit FAFSA. *Faculty research:* Craft of screenwriting film story analysis, production elements in film and theatre. *Unit head:* Dr. Sheril D. Antonio, Chair, 212-998-1940, Fax: 212-995-4069. *Application contact:* Dan Sandford, Director of Graduate Admissions, 212-998-1918, Fax: 212-995-4060, E-mail: tisch.gradadmissions@nyu.edu.
Website: http://www.ddw.tisch.nyu.edu/

North Carolina State University, Graduate School, College of Humanities and Social Sciences, Department of English, Program in Creative Writing, Raleigh, NC 27695. Offers MFA. *Degree requirements:* For master's, thesis optional. *Entrance requirements:* For master's, GRE. Electronic applications accepted. *Faculty research:* Science fiction, Asian poetry, translation, Southern writers, satiric fiction.

North Dakota State University, College of Graduate and Interdisciplinary Studies, College of Arts, Humanities and Social Sciences, Department of English, Fargo, ND 58102. Offers composition (MA); literature (MA); rhetoric, writing and culture (PhD). *Program availability:* Part-time. *Degree requirements:* For master's, one foreign language, thesis. *Entrance requirements:* Additional exam requirements/recommendations for international students: Required—TOEFL (minimum score 600 paper-based; 100 iBT), IELTS (minimum score 7). Electronic applications accepted. *Faculty research:* American and English literature, women's studies, language attitudes, composition practices, computers and composition.

See Display on page 736 and Close-Up on page 747.

Northern Arizona University, College of Arts and Letters, Department of English, Flagstaff, AZ 86011. Offers applied linguistics (PhD); creative writing (MFA), including creative writing; English (MA), including literature, professional writing, rhetoric, writing, and digital media studies, secondary education; professional writing (Graduate Certificate); rhetoric, writing and digital media studies (Graduate Certificate); teaching English as a second language (MA, Graduate Certificate). *Program availability:* Part-time, 100% online, blended/hybrid learning. *Faculty:* 62 full-time (43 women), 3 part-time/adjunct (2 women). *Students:* 115 full-time (78 women), 115 part-time (89 women); includes 57 minority (11 Black or African American, non-Hispanic/Latino; 3 American Indian or Alaska Native, non-Hispanic/Latino; 4 Asian, non-Hispanic/Latino; 26 Hispanic/Latino; 13 Two or more races, non-Hispanic/Latino), 19 international. Average age 35. 189 applicants, 56% accepted, 92 enrolled. In 2017, 82 master's, 5 doctorates, 15 other advanced degrees awarded. *Degree requirements:* For master's, variable foreign language requirement, comprehensive exam (for some programs), thesis (for some programs); for doctorate, variable foreign language requirement, comprehensive exam (for some programs), thesis/dissertation (for some programs); for Graduate Certificate, comprehensive exam (for some programs). *Entrance requirements:* Additional exam requirements/recommendations for international students: Required—TOEFL (minimum score 80 iBT), IELTS (minimum score 6.5). *Application deadline:* For fall admission, 1/30 for domestic and international students; for spring admission, 10/1 for domestic and international students. Application fee: $65. Electronic applications accepted. *Expenses:* Tuition, state resident: full-time $9240; part-time $458 per credit hour. Tuition, nonresident: full-time $21,588; part-time $1199 per credit hour. *Required fees:* $1021; $14 per credit hour. $646 per semester. Tuition and fees vary according to course load, campus/location and program. *Financial support:* In 2017–18, 69 students received support, including 4 fellowships with full and partial tuition reimbursements available (averaging $16,250 per year), 2 research assistantships with full and partial tuition reimbursements available (averaging $16,250 per year), 65 teaching assistantships with full and partial tuition reimbursements available (averaging $16,250 per year); institutionally sponsored loans, health care benefits, tuition waivers (full and partial), and unspecified assistantships also available. Financial award application deadline: 2/1; financial award applicants required to submit FAFSA. *Unit head:* Dr. Steven Rosendale, Chair, 928-523-4911, Fax: 928-523-7074, E-mail: steven.rosendale@nau.edu. *Application contact:* Tina Sutton, Coordinator, Graduate College, 928-523-4348, Fax: 928-523-8950, E-mail: graduate@nau.edu.
Website: https://nau.edu/cal/english/

Northern Kentucky University, Office of Graduate Programs, College of Arts and Sciences, Program in English, Highland Heights, KY 41099. Offers composition and rhetoric (Certificate); creative writing (Certificate); cultural studies and discourses (Certificate); English (MA); professional writing (Certificate). *Program availability:* Part-time, evening/weekend. *Degree requirements:* For master's, comprehensive exam (for some programs), capstone (thesis, portfolio, project, or exams); 30 hours of credit; for Certificate, 18 hours of credit. *Entrance requirements:* For master's, bachelor's degree in English or related field from regionally-accredited institution with minimum GPA of 3.0 in major or cognate area coursework; official transcripts for all undergraduate and graduate work; two letters of reference; for Certificate, official transcripts for all undergraduate and graduate work; bachelor's degree from regionally-accredited institution; minimum undergraduate GPA of 2.5. Additional exam requirements/recommendations for international students: Required—TOEFL (minimum score 79 iBT); Recommended—IELTS (minimum score 6.5). Electronic applications accepted.

Northern Michigan University, Office of Graduate Education and Research, College of Arts and Sciences, Department of English, Marquette, MI 49855-5301. Offers creative writing (MFA); literature (MA); pedagogy (MA); teaching English to speakers of other languages (Graduate Certificate); theater (MA); writing (MA). *Program availability:* Part-time, evening/weekend. Terminal master's awarded for partial completion of doctoral program. *Degree requirements:* For master's, capstone project: thesis, practicum or portfolio (for MA); thesis (for MFA); for Graduate Certificate, one foreign language.

Entrance requirements: For master's, minimum GPA of 3.0; bachelor's degree in English or minimum of 30 credit hours in undergraduate English; statement of purpose; resume; critical essay; 3 letters of recommendation; for Graduate Certificate, bachelor's degree. Additional exam requirements/recommendations for international students: Required—TOEFL (minimum score 550 paper-based; 79 iBT), IELTS (minimum score 6.5). *Application deadline:* For fall admission, 2/1 for domestic students; for winter admission, 2/1 for domestic students; for spring admission, 3/17 for domestic students. Applications are processed on a rolling basis. Application fee: $50. Electronic applications accepted. *Expenses:* Tuition, state resident: full-time $9417; part-time $542 per credit hour. Tuition, nonresident: full-time $12,873; part-time $758 per credit hour. Tuition and fees vary according to course load, degree level and program. *Financial support:* Research assistantships with full tuition reimbursements, teaching assistantships with full tuition reimbursements, Federal Work-Study, institutionally sponsored loans, and unspecified assistantships available. Support available to part-time students. Financial award application deadline: 3/1; financial award applicants required to submit FAFSA. *Faculty research:* Modern Arabic literature, British literature (medieval to contemporary), postcolonial literature, Native and African-American literature, creative writing, critical theory, pedagogy. *Unit head:* Lynn Domina, Head, 906-227-2711, E-mail: ldomina@nmu.edu. *Application contact:* Dr. Russell Prather, Director of MA Program/Professor, 906-227-2857, E-mail: rprather@nmu.edu.
Website: http://www.nmu.edu/english/

Northwestern University, Medill School of Journalism, Media, and Integrated Marketing Communications, Evanston, IL 60208. Offers integrated marketing communications (MSIMC), including brand strategy, content marketing, direct and interactive marketing, marketing analytics, strategic communications; interactive publishing (MSJ); magazine writing/editing (MSJ); reporting (MSJ); video/broadcast (MSJ). *Entrance requirements:* For master's, GRE General Test, GMAT or LSAT (for MSJ). Additional exam requirements/recommendations for international students: Required—TOEFL. Electronic applications accepted. *Expenses:* Contact institution. *Faculty research:* Web business journalism, cultural stereotypes, voter apathy, digital television.

Northwestern University, School of Professional Studies, Program in Creative Writing, Evanston, IL 60208. Offers MA, MFA.
Website: https://sps.northwestern.edu/masters/creative-writing/index.php

Oklahoma City University, Petree College of Arts and Sciences, Oklahoma City, OK 73106-1402. Offers applied behavioral studies (M Ed); applied sociology: nonprofit leadership (MA); creative writing (MFA); criminology (MS); early childhood education (M Ed); elementary education (M Ed); general studies (MLA); leadership/management (MLA); moving image arts (MFA); professional counseling (M Ed); teaching (MA); teaching English to speakers of other languages (MA). *Program availability:* Part-time, evening/weekend. *Faculty:* 6 full-time (2 women), 16 part-time/adjunct (10 women). *Students:* 84 full-time (61 women), 32 part-time (23 women); includes 31 minority (13 Black or African American, non-Hispanic/Latino; 3 American Indian or Alaska Native, non-Hispanic/Latino; 1 Asian, non-Hispanic/Latino; 9 Hispanic/Latino; 5 Two or more races, non-Hispanic/Latino), 30 international. Average age 34. 192 applicants, 67% accepted, 57 enrolled. In 2017, 65 master's awarded. *Degree requirements:* For master's, capstone/practicum. *Entrance requirements:* For master's, bachelor's degree from accredited institution with minimum GPA of 3.0, essay, recommendation letters. Additional exam requirements/recommendations for international students: Required—TOEFL (minimum score 550 paper-based; 80 iBT). *Application deadline:* Applications are processed on a rolling basis. Application fee: $50. Electronic applications accepted. *Expenses:* $8,580. *Financial support:* In 2017–18, 19 students received support. Federal Work-Study, institutionally sponsored loans, scholarships/grants, and tuition waivers (full and partial) available. Support available to part-time students. Financial award application deadline: 6/1; financial award applicants required to submit FAFSA. *Unit head:* Dr. Amy Cataldi, Dean, 405-208-5446, Fax: 405-208-5447, E-mail: acataldi@okcu.edu. *Application contact:* Michael Harrington, Director of Graduate Admissions, 800-633-7242, Fax: 405-208-5356, E-mail: gadmissions@okcu.edu.
Website: https://www.okcu.edu/artsci/home

Oklahoma State University, College of Arts and Sciences, Department of English, Stillwater, OK 74078. Offers creative writing (MFA); English (MA, PhD). *Faculty:* 60 full-time (33 women), 7 part-time/adjunct (3 women). *Students:* 7 full-time (4 women), 106 part-time (59 women); includes 18 minority (6 Black or African American, non-Hispanic/Latino; 4 American Indian or Alaska Native, non-Hispanic/Latino; 2 Asian, non-Hispanic/Latino; 4 Hispanic/Latino; 2 Two or more races, non-Hispanic/Latino), 21 international. Average age 32. 99 applicants, 34% accepted, 21 enrolled. In 2017, 21 master's, 12 doctorates awarded. *Entrance requirements:* For master's, GRE General Test, minimum GPA of 3.0, writing sample; for doctorate, GRE General Test, minimum GPA of 3.5, writing sample. Additional exam requirements/recommendations for international students: Required—TOEFL (minimum score 550 paper-based; 79 iBT). *Application deadline:* For fall admission, 3/1 priority date for international students; for spring admission, 8/1 priority date for international students. Applications are processed on a rolling basis. Application fee: $40 ($75 for international students). Electronic applications accepted. *Expenses:* Tuition, state resident: full-time $4019; part-time $2679.60 per year. Tuition, nonresident: full-time $15,286; part-time $10,190.40 per year. *Required fees:* $2129; $1419 per unit. Tuition and fees vary according to program. *Financial support:* Research assistantships, teaching assistantships, career-related internships or fieldwork, Federal Work-Study, scholarships/grants, health care benefits, tuition waivers (partial), and unspecified assistantships available. Support available to part-time students. Financial award application deadline: 3/1; financial award applicants required to submit FAFSA. *Faculty research:* American and British novels, poetry, and autobiography; Native American languages and literature; institutional history of American film, history, and adaptations; rhetoric and theories of human communication; learning strategies of second language learners. *Unit head:* Dr. Richard Frohock, Department Head, 405-744-9474, Fax: 405-744-6326, E-mail: richard.frohock@okstate.edu.
Website: http://english.okstate.edu/

Old Dominion University, College of Arts and Letters, Master of Arts in English Program, Norfolk, VA 23529. Offers literature (MA); professional writing (MA); rhetoric and composition (MA). *Program availability:* Part-time, evening/weekend. *Faculty:* 15 full-time (7 women). *Students:* 7 full-time (4 women), 16 part-time (13 women); includes 9 minority (2 Black or African American, non-Hispanic/Latino; 1 American Indian or Alaska Native, non-Hispanic/Latino; 3 Hispanic/Latino; 3 Two or more races, non-Hispanic/Latino). Average age 34. 12 applicants, 67% accepted, 7 enrolled. In 2017, 11 master's awarded. Terminal master's awarded for partial completion of doctoral program. *Degree requirements:* For master's, comprehensive exam, thesis optional. *Entrance requirements:* For master's, GRE General Test, 24 hours in English, sample of written work, BA. Additional exam requirements/recommendations for international students: Required—TOEFL. *Application deadline:* For fall admission, 3/15 priority date for domestic and international students; for winter admission, 11/1 for domestic students, 10/1 for international students; for spring admission, 11/1 priority date for domestic students, 11/1 for international students. Applications are processed on a rolling basis. Application fee: $50. Electronic applications accepted. *Expenses:* Tuition,

state resident: full-time $8928; part-time $496 per credit. Tuition, nonresident: full-time $22,482; part-time $1249 per credit. *Required fees:* $66 per semester. *Financial support:* In 2017–18, 9 students received support, including 4 research assistantships (averaging $10,000 per year), 6 teaching assistantships (averaging $10,000 per year); career-related internships or fieldwork and unspecified assistantships also available. Financial award application deadline: 2/15; financial award applicants required to submit FAFSA. *Faculty research:* Literary theory, composition theory, professional writing, rhetoric, British and American literature. *Total annual research expenditures:* $3,451. *Unit head:* Dr. Drew Lopenzina, Graduate Program Director, 757-683-4033, E-mail: alopenzi@odu.edu. *Application contact:* Dr. Dale Miller, Associate Dean, 757-683-6077, Fax: 757-683-5746, E-mail: demiller@odu.edu.

Old Dominion University, College of Arts and Letters, MFA Program in Creative Writing, Norfolk, VA 23529. Offers MFA. *Program availability:* Part-time. *Faculty:* 6 full-time (3 women), 5 part-time/adjunct (all women). *Students:* 23 full-time (12 women), 9 part-time (6 women); includes 5 minority (2 Black or African American, non-Hispanic/Latino; 1 Asian, non-Hispanic/Latino; 2 Hispanic/Latino), 2 international. Average age 31. 60 applicants, 30% accepted, 12 enrolled. In 2017, 10 master's awarded. *Degree requirements:* For master's, comprehensive exam, thesis. *Entrance requirements:* For master's, sample of written work. Additional exam requirements/recommendations for international students: Required—TOEFL. *Application deadline:* For fall admission, 3/1 for domestic students. Application fee: $50. Electronic applications accepted. *Expenses:* Tuition, state resident: full-time $8928; part-time $496 per credit. Tuition, nonresident: full-time $22,482; part-time $1249 per credit. *Required fees:* $66 per semester. *Financial support:* In 2017–18, 17 students received support, including 2 fellowships with full tuition reimbursements available (averaging $12,000 per year), 3 research assistantships with full tuition reimbursements available (averaging $10,000 per year), 6 teaching assistantships with full tuition reimbursements available (averaging $10,000 per year); scholarships/grants and unspecified assistantships also available. Financial award application deadline: 3/1. *Faculty research:* Literary fiction, nonfiction, poetry. *Total annual research expenditures:* $35,000. *Unit head:* Prof. John McManus, Graduate Program Director, 757-683-4010, Fax: 757-683-3241, E-mail: cwgpd@odu.edu.
Website: http://al.odu.edu/english/mfacw/

Oregon State University, College of Liberal Arts, Program in Creative Writing, Corvallis, OR 97331. Offers fiction (MFA). *Program availability:* Part-time. *Entrance requirements:* Additional exam requirements/recommendations for international students: Required—TOEFL (minimum score 80 iBT), IELTS (minimum score 6.5). *Application deadline:* For fall admission, 1/3 for domestic and international students. Application fee: $75 ($85 for international students). *Financial support:* Application deadline: 1/4. *Unit head:* Molly McFerran, Office Specialist, 541-737-1635, E-mail: molly.mcferran@oregonstate.edu. *Application contact:* Molly McFerran, Office Specialist, 541-737-1635, E-mail: molly.mcferran@oregonstate.edu.
Website: http://liberalarts.oregonstate.edu/wlf/mfa

Oregon State University, College of Liberal Arts, Program in English, Corvallis, OR 97331. Offers film and visual studies (MA); literature and culture (MA); rhetoric, writing and composition (MA). *Program availability:* Part-time. *Entrance requirements:* For master's, GRE (recommended). Additional exam requirements/recommendations for international students: Required—TOEFL (minimum score 80 iBT), IELTS (minimum score 6.5). *Application deadline:* For fall admission, 1/3 for domestic and international students. Application fee: $75 ($85 for international students). *Financial support:* Application deadline: 1/3. *Unit head:* Molly McFerran, Office Specialist, 541-737-1635, E-mail: molly.mcferran@oregonstate.edu. *Application contact:* Dr. Raymond Malewitz, Assistant Professor and Director, 541-737-1656, E-mail: raymond.malewitz@oregonstate.edu.
Website: http://liberalarts.oregonstate.edu/wlf/ma

Otis College of Art and Design, Program in Writing, Los Angeles, CA 90045-9785. Offers MFA. *Degree requirements:* For master's, thesis. *Entrance requirements:* For master's, writing sample. Electronic applications accepted.

Our Lady of the Lake University, College of Arts and Sciences, Programs in English, San Antonio, TX 78207-4689. Offers literature, creative writing, and social justice (MA); MA/MFA. Program offered jointly with University of the Incarnate Word and St. Mary's University. *Program availability:* Part-time, evening/weekend. *Faculty:* 2 part-time/adjunct (1 woman). *Students:* 15 full-time (12 women), 7 part-time (all women); includes 17 minority (1 Black or African American, non-Hispanic/Latino; 16 Hispanic/Latino). Average age 33. 7 applicants, 100% accepted, 5 enrolled. In 2017, 2 master's awarded. *Degree requirements:* For master's, comprehensive exam, thesis optional. *Entrance requirements:* For master's, GRE General Test or MAT taken within the last 5 years, bachelor's degree with at least 18 hours of advanced course work in English and/or communication arts with minimum cumulative GPA of 2.5; 2 letters of recommendation; samples of creative and scholarly writing (25 pages total); personal statement. Additional exam requirements/recommendations for international students: Required—TOEFL. *Application deadline:* For fall admission, 6/15 for domestic and international students; for spring admission, 11/15 for domestic and international students; for summer admission, 4/15 for domestic and international students. Applications are processed on a rolling basis. Application fee: $40 ($50 for international students). Electronic applications accepted. Application fee is waived when completed online. *Expenses: Tuition:* Full-time $10,668; part-time $5334 per year. *Required fees:* $816; $816 per year. $408 per semester. *Financial support:* In 2017–18, 8 students received support. Federal Work-Study, scholarships/grants, unspecified assistantships, and tuition discounts available. Support available to part-time students. Financial award application deadline: 5/1; financial award applicants required to submit FAFSA. *Unit head:* Dr. Candance Zepeda, Chair of the English, Mass Communications and Drama Department, 210-431-4166, E-mail: llarson@ollusa.edu. *Application contact:* Office of Graduate Admissions, 210-431-3995, Fax: 210-431-3945, E-mail: gradadm@ollusa.edu.
Website: http://www.ollusa.edu/s/1190/hybrid/default-hybrid-ollu.aspx?sid-1190&gid-1&pgid-7884

Pacific Lutheran University, Division of Humanities, Tacoma, WA 98447. Offers creative writing (MFA). *Program availability:* Part-time, blended/hybrid learning. *Degree requirements:* For master's, thesis, final residency including teaching class. *Entrance requirements:* For master's, portfolio, book review. Additional exam requirements/recommendations for international students: Required—TOEFL. Electronic applications accepted. *Expenses:* Contact institution.

Pacific University, Program in Writing, Forest Grove, OR 97116-1797. Offers MFA. *Program availability:* Part-time.

Park University, School of Graduate and Professional Studies, Kansas City, MO 54105. Offers adult education (M Ed); business and government leadership (Graduate Certificate); business, government, and global society (MPA); communication and leadership (MA); creative and life writing (Graduate Certificate); disaster and emergency management (MPA, Graduate Certificate); educational leadership (M Ed); finance (MBA, Graduate Certificate); general business (MBA); global business (Graduate Certificate); healthcare administration (MHA); healthcare services management and leadership (Graduate Certificate); international business (MBA); language and literacy (M Ed), including English for speakers of other languages, special reading teacher/literacy coach; leadership of international healthcare organizations (Graduate Certificate); management information systems (MBA, Graduate Certificate); music performance (ADP, Graduate Certificate), including cello (MM, ADP), piano (MM, ADP), viola (MM, ADP), violin (MM, ADP); nonprofit and community services management (MPA); nonprofit leadership (Graduate Certificate); performance (MM), including cello (MM, ADP), piano (MM, ADP), viola (MM, ADP), violin (MM, ADP); public management (MPA); social work (MSW); teacher leadership (M Ed), including curriculum and assessment, instructional leader. *Program availability:* Part-time, evening/weekend, online learning. *Degree requirements:* For master's, comprehensive exam (for some programs), thesis (for some programs), internship (for some programs); exam (for some programs). *Entrance requirements:* For master's, GRE or GMAT (for some programs), teacher certification (for some M Ed programs), letters of recommendation, essay, resume (for some programs). Additional exam requirements/recommendations for international students: Required—TOEFL (minimum score 550 paper-based; 79 iBT), IELTS (minimum score 6). Electronic applications accepted.

Pepperdine University, Seaver College, Division of Humanities, Malibu, CA 90263. Offers American studies (MA); writing for screen and television (MFA). *Program availability:* Part-time. *Students:* 9 full-time (7 women), 41 part-time (23 women); includes 10 minority (4 Black or African American, non-Hispanic/Latino; 1 Asian, non-Hispanic/Latino; 3 Hispanic/Latino; 2 Two or more races, non-Hispanic/Latino), 2 international. Average age 31. In 2017, 13 master's awarded. *Degree requirements:* For master's, oral and written exams. *Entrance requirements:* For master's, GRE General Test, writing sample, letters of recommendation. Additional exam requirements/recommendations for international students: Required—TOEFL. *Application deadline:* For fall admission, 2/1 priority date for domestic students. Applications are processed on a rolling basis. Application fee: $65. *Financial support:* Applicants required to submit FAFSA. *Unit head:* Dr. Michael G. Ditmore, Chair/Professor of English, 310-506-4182, Fax: 310-506-7307, E-mail: michael.ditmore@pepperdine.edu. *Application contact:* Hayley Wolf, Director of Admission, 310-506-4392, E-mail: hayley.wolf@pepperdine.edu.
Website: http://seaver.pepperdine.edu/humanities/default.htm

Pittsburg State University, Graduate School, College of Arts and Sciences, Department of English and Modern Languages, Pittsburg, KS 66762. Offers English (MA), including creative writing, literature, professional writing. *Program availability:* Part-time. *Students:* 16 (12 women). In 2017, 9 master's awarded. *Degree requirements:* For master's, thesis or alternative. *Entrance requirements:* Additional exam requirements/recommendations for international students: Required—TOEFL (minimum score 550 paper-based; 79 iBT), IELTS (minimum score 6.5), PTE (minimum score 53). *Application deadline:* For fall admission, 7/15 for domestic students, 6/1 for international students; for spring admission, 12/15 for domestic students, 10/15 for international students; for summer admission, 5/15 for domestic students, 4/1 for international students. Applications are processed on a rolling basis. Application fee: $35 ($60 for international students). Electronic applications accepted. *Expenses:* Contact institution. *Financial support:* In 2017–18, 10 teaching assistantships with full tuition reimbursements (averaging $8,000 per year) were awarded; career-related internships or fieldwork, Federal Work-Study, and unspecified assistantships also available. Financial award application deadline: 2/1; financial award applicants required to submit FAFSA. *Faculty research:* American fiction, American poetry, British fiction, British poetry, composition theory, creative writing. *Unit head:* Dr. Celia Patterson, Chairperson, 620-235-4689, E-mail: cpatterson@pittstate.edu. *Application contact:* Lisa Allen, Assistant Director of Graduate and Continuing Studies, 620-235-4223, Fax: 620-235-4219, E-mail: lallen@pittstate.edu.

Portland State University, Graduate Studies, College of Liberal Arts and Sciences, Department of English, Portland, OR 97207-0751. Offers creative writing (MFA); English (MA); MA/MS. *Program availability:* Part-time, evening/weekend. *Faculty:* 37 full-time (22 women), 35 part-time/adjunct (20 women). *Students:* 88 full-time (61 women), 47 part-time (25 women); includes 20 minority (2 Black or African American, non-Hispanic/Latino; 1 American Indian or Alaska Native, non-Hispanic/Latino; 2 Asian, non-Hispanic/Latino; 7 Hispanic/Latino; 1 Native Hawaiian or other Pacific Islander, non-Hispanic/Latino; 7 Two or more races, non-Hispanic/Latino), 2 international. Average age 32. 181 applicants, 43% accepted, 45 enrolled. In 2017, 67 master's awarded. *Degree requirements:* For master's, one foreign language, comprehensive exam (for some programs), thesis (for some programs), oral and written exams. *Entrance requirements:* For master's, GRE (for some programs), statement of purpose, 2 letters of recommendation, transcripts, critical writing sample. Additional exam requirements/recommendations for international students: Required—TOEFL (minimum score 600 paper-based; 100 iBT). *Application deadline:* For fall admission, 1/3 for domestic and international students; for winter admission, 9/1 for domestic and international students; for spring admission, 11/1 for domestic and international students. Application fee: $65. *Expenses:* Tuition, state resident: full-time $14,436; part-time $401 per credit. Tuition, nonresident: full-time $21,780; part-time $605 per credit. *Required fees:* $1380; $22 per credit. $119 per quarter. One-time fee: $325. Tuition and fees vary according to program. *Financial support:* In 2017–18, 40 students received support, including 18 teaching assistantships with full and partial tuition reimbursements available (averaging $8,289 per year); career-related internships or fieldwork, Federal Work-Study, scholarships/grants, tuition waivers (full and partial), and unspecified assistantships also available. Support available to part-time students. Financial award application deadline: 3/1; financial award applicants required to submit FAFSA. *Faculty research:* American literature and cultural studies, medieval and British literature, writing prose fiction and poetry, rhetoric and composition, women's literature. *Total annual research expenditures:* $28,767. *Unit head:* Dr. Paul Collins, Chair, 503-725-9777, Fax: 503-725-3561, E-mail: pcollins@pdx.edu. *Application contact:* Matt Swetnam, Academic and Program Coordinator, 503-725-3623, Fax: 503-725-3561, E-mail: grdstudy@pdx.edu.
Website: http://www.pdx.edu/english/

Pratt Institute, School of Liberal Arts and Sciences, Program in Writing, Brooklyn, NY 11205-3899. Offers MFA. *Students:* 23 full-time (15 women); includes 16 minority (7 Black or African American, non-Hispanic/Latino; 3 Asian, non-Hispanic/Latino; 4 Hispanic/Latino; 2 Two or more races, non-Hispanic/Latino), 2 international. Average age 28. 96 applicants, 52% accepted, 12 enrolled. In 2017, 11 master's awarded. *Degree requirements:* For master's, thesis. *Entrance requirements:* For master's, writing sample. Additional exam requirements/recommendations for international students: Required—TOEFL (minimum score 600 paper-based; 100 iBT). *Application deadline:* For fall admission, 1/5 for domestic and international students; for spring admission, 10/1 for domestic and international students. Application fee: $50 ($90 for international students). Electronic applications accepted. *Expenses: Tuition:* Full-time $30,834. *Required fees:* $1974. *Financial support:* Career-related internships or fieldwork, Federal Work-Study, institutionally sponsored loans, scholarships/grants, health care benefits, and unspecified assistantships available. Support available to part-time students. Financial award application deadline: 2/1; financial award applicants required to submit FAFSA. *Unit head:* Arlene Keizer, Chairperson, 718-636-3421, E-mail: akeizer@pratt.edu. *Application contact:* Natalie Capannelli, Director of Graduate

Admissions, 718-636-3551, Fax: 718-399-4242, E-mail: ncapanne@pratt.edu.
Website: https://www.pratt.edu/academics/liberal-arts-and-sciences/graduate-writing/

See Display on page 725 and Close-Up on page 749.

Purdue University, Graduate School, College of Liberal Arts, Department of English, West Lafayette, IN 47907. Offers creative writing (MFA); literature (MA, PhD), including linguistics, literature and philosophy (PhD), rhetoric and composition, theory and cultural studies (PhD). *Program availability:* Part-time. *Faculty:* 57 full-time (26 women), 3 part-time/adjunct (all women). *Students:* 130 full-time (82 women), 50 part-time (28 women); includes 21 minority (6 Black or African American, non-Hispanic/Latino; 5 Asian, non-Hispanic/Latino; 7 Hispanic/Latino; 3 Two or more races, non-Hispanic/Latino), 31 international. Average age 31. 299 applicants, 14% accepted, 29 enrolled. In 2017, 19 master's, 26 doctorates awarded. *Degree requirements:* For master's, one foreign language, comprehensive exam (for some programs), thesis (for some programs); for doctorate, one foreign language, comprehensive exam, thesis/dissertation. *Entrance requirements:* For master's, GRE General Test; GRE Subject Test in English literature (recommended for students applying to literary studies), minimum undergraduate GPA of 3.0 or equivalent; for doctorate, GRE General Test; GRE Subject Test in English literature (recommended for students applying to literary studies), master's degree. Additional exam requirements/recommendations for international students: Required—TOEFL (minimum score 620 paper-based; 77 iBT). *Application deadline:* For fall admission, 1/15 for domestic and international students. Applications are processed on a rolling basis. Application fee: $60 ($75 for international students). Electronic applications accepted. *Financial support:* Fellowships with tuition reimbursements and teaching assistantships with tuition reimbursements available. Support available to part-time students. Financial award application deadline: 1/15; financial award applicants required to submit FAFSA. *Faculty research:* Cultural studies, postmodern narrative, contemporary women writers, composition theory, slave narratives. *Unit head:* Dorsey Armstrong, Head, 765-494-6478, E-mail: darmstrong@purdue.edu. *Application contact:* Jill M. Quirk, Graduate Contact, 765-494-3748, Fax: 765-494-1700, E-mail: griff@purdue.edu.
Website: https://www.cla.purdue.edu/english/

Queens College of the City University of New York, Arts and Humanities Division, Department of English, Queens, NY 11367-1597. Offers creative writing and literary translation (MFA); English (MA). *Program availability:* Part-time, evening/weekend. *Faculty:* 36 full-time (17 women), 1 (woman) part-time/adjunct. *Students:* 1 (woman) full-time, 99 part-time (57 women); includes 31 minority (10 Black or African American, non-Hispanic/Latino; 4 Asian, non-Hispanic/Latino; 14 Hispanic/Latino; 3 Two or more races, non-Hispanic/Latino), 3 international. Average age 31. 188 applicants, 35% accepted, 32 enrolled. In 2017, 41 master's awarded. *Degree requirements:* For master's, thesis, oral exam/thesis defense. *Entrance requirements:* For master's, minimum GPA of 3.0; minimum 24 undergraduate credits in English or related field and 10-15 page writing sample (for MA); manuscript (for MFA). Additional exam requirements/recommendations for international students: Required—TOEFL (minimum score 100 iBT), IELTS (minimum score 7). *Application deadline:* For fall admission, 4/1 for domestic students; for spring admission, 11/1 for domestic students. Applications are processed on a rolling basis. Application fee: $125. Electronic applications accepted. *Expenses:* $2,640 to $10,450 range (depending on number of credits). *Financial support:* In 2017–18, 6 students received support, including 2 fellowships (averaging $20,801 per year), 1 research assistantship (averaging $988 per year); career-related internships or fieldwork and scholarships/grants also available. Financial award application deadline: 4/1; financial award applicants required to submit FAFSA. *Faculty research:* Global Anglophone literature; race and ethnic studies; gender and sexuality studies; creative writing; literary translation. *Unit head:* Glenn Burger, Chair, 718-997-4658, E-mail: glenn.burger@qc.cuny.edu. *Application contact:* Elizabeth D'Amico-Ramirez, Assistant Director of Graduate Admissions, 718-997-5203, E-mail: elizabeth.damicoramirez@qc.cuny.edu.

Queens University of Charlotte, College of Arts and Sciences, Charlotte, NC 28274-0002. Offers creative writing (MFA); interior design (MA). *Program availability:* Part-time, online learning. Electronic applications accepted.

Randolph College, Program in Creative Writing, Lynchburg, VA 24503. Offers MFA.

Regent University, Graduate School, School of Communication and the Arts, Virginia Beach, VA 23464-9800. Offers acting (MFA); communication (MA, PhD), including media and arts management and promotion (MA), political communication (MA), strategic communication (MA), technical communication (MA); film and TV (MA), including producing (MA, MFA), production, script writing; film-television (MFA), including directing, producing (MA, MFA), script and screenwriting; journalism (MA); theatre (MA). *Program availability:* Part-time, evening/weekend, 100% online, blended/hybrid learning. *Faculty:* 15 full-time (2 women), 66 part-time/adjunct (23 women). *Students:* 101 full-time (65 women), 342 part-time (237 women); includes 177 minority (127 Black or African American, non-Hispanic/Latino; 4 American Indian or Alaska Native, non-Hispanic/Latino; 9 Asian, non-Hispanic/Latino; 25 Hispanic/Latino; 12 Two or more races, non-Hispanic/Latino), 11 international. Average age 37. 498 applicants, 36% accepted, 124 enrolled. In 2017, 93 master's, 22 doctorates awarded. *Degree requirements:* For master's, thesis or alternative; for doctorate, thesis/dissertation. *Entrance requirements:* For master's, transcripts, writing sample, resume, audition (for MFA programs); for doctorate, GRE General Test, resume, writing sample, recommendations, interview, transcripts, personal goals statement. Additional exam requirements/recommendations for international students: Required—TOEFL (minimum score 577 paper-based). *Application deadline:* For fall admission, 3/1 priority date for domestic students; for spring admission, 10/1 priority date for domestic students. Applications are processed on a rolling basis. Application fee: $50. Electronic applications accepted. *Expenses:* $650 per credit (MA, MFA); $885 per credit (PhD); $300 per semester technology fee. *Financial support:* In 2017–18, 234 students received support, including 2 fellowships (averaging $10,000 per year); career-related internships or fieldwork, scholarships/grants, and unspecified assistantships also available. Support available to part-time students. *Faculty research:* Screenwriting, digital media production, communication, acting, directing. *Unit head:* Dr. Robert Herron, Dean, 757-352-4500, E-mail: rherron@regent.edu. *Application contact:* Heidi Cece, Assistant Vice President of Enrollment Management, 800-373-5504, Fax: 757-352-4381, E-mail: admissions@regent.edu.
Website: https://www.regent.edu/school-of-communication-and-the-arts/

Regis University, College of Contemporary Liberal Studies, Denver, CO 80221-1099. Offers creative writing (MFA); criminology (M Sc); curriculum, instruction and assessment (M Ed); education - teacher leadership (M Ed); educational leadership (M Ed); elementary education (M Ed); literacy (Certificate); reading (M Ed); secondary education (M Ed); special education (M Ed); teacher academic leadership (Certificate); teacher leadership (MA); teacher/educational leadership (M Ed); teaching the linguistically diverse (M Ed). *Program availability:* Part-time, evening/weekend, 100% online, blended/hybrid learning. *Degree requirements:* For master's, thesis (for some programs). *Entrance requirements:* For master's, official transcript reflecting baccalaureate degree awarded from regionally-accredited college or university, work experience, resume, letters of recommendation. Additional exam requirements/recommendations for international students: Required—TOEFL (minimum score 550 paper-based; 82 iBT). Electronic applications accepted. *Expenses:* Contact institution.

Reinhardt University, Program in Creative Writing, Waleska, GA 30183-2981. Offers MFA.

Rhode Island College, School of Graduate Studies, Faculty of Arts and Sciences, Department of English, Providence, RI 02908-1991. Offers creative writing (MA, CGS); English (MA); literature (CGS). *Program availability:* Part-time, evening/weekend. *Faculty:* 6 full-time (2 women). *Students:* 3 full-time (1 woman), 5 part-time (1 woman); includes 1 minority (Hispanic/Latino). Average age 31. In 2017, 5 master's awarded. *Degree requirements:* For master's, thesis (for some programs). *Entrance requirements:* For master's, GRE General Test, 3 letters of recommendation, interview. Additional exam requirements/recommendations for international students: Recommended—TOEFL (minimum score 550 paper-based; 79 iBT). *Application deadline:* For fall admission, 3/1 for domestic students; for spring admission, 11/1 for domestic students. Applications are processed on a rolling basis. Application fee: $50. *Expenses:* Tuition, state resident: full-time $9768; part-time $407 per credit. Tuition, nonresident: full-time $19,008; part-time $792 per credit. *Required fees:* $696; $29 per credit. One-time fee: $200 full-time; $100 part-time. Tuition and fees vary according to course load. *Financial support:* In 2017–18, 1 teaching assistantship with full tuition reimbursement (averaging $3,000 per year) was awarded; career-related internships or fieldwork, Federal Work-Study, scholarships/grants, health care benefits, and unspecified assistantships also available. Support available to part-time students. Financial award application deadline: 5/15; financial award applicants required to submit FAFSA. *Unit head:* Dr. Stephen Brown, Co-Chair, 401-456-8028.
Website: http://www.ric.edu/english/index.php

Rivier University, School of Graduate Studies, Department of English, Nashua, NH 03060. Offers English (MAT); writing and literature (MA). *Program availability:* Part-time, evening/weekend. *Degree requirements:* For master's, comprehensive exam (for some programs). *Entrance requirements:* For master's, GRE Subject Test.

Roosevelt University, Graduate Division, College of Arts and Sciences, Department of Humanities, Chicago, IL 60605. Offers creative writing (MFA). *Students:* 19 full-time (13 women), 5 part-time (3 women); includes 12 minority (5 Black or African American, non-Hispanic/Latino; 1 Asian, non-Hispanic/Latino; 3 Hispanic/Latino; 3 Two or more races, non-Hispanic/Latino). Average age 28. 11 applicants, 100% accepted, 9 enrolled. In 2017, 11 master's awarded. *Application deadline:* Applications are processed on a rolling basis. Application fee: $40. Electronic applications accepted. *Expenses:* Contact institution. *Financial support:* Scholarships/grants and unspecified assistantships available. *Application contact:* Sivling Lam, Graduate Admission Counselor, 312-281-3252, E-mail: slam02@roosevelt.edu.

Rosemont College, Schools of Graduate and Professional Studies, Creative Writing Program, Rosemont, PA 19010-1699. Offers MFA. *Program availability:* Part-time, evening/weekend. *Degree requirements:* For master's, comprehensive exam, thesis. *Entrance requirements:* For master's, 3 letters of recommendation, baccalaureate degree with minimum GPA of 3.0, writing sample. Additional exam requirements/recommendations for international students: Required—TOEFL. Electronic applications accepted. Application fee is waived when completed online.

Rowan University, Graduate School, College of Communication and Creative Arts, Program in Writing, Glassboro, NJ 08028-1701. Offers MA. *Program availability:* Part-time, evening/weekend. *Degree requirements:* For master's, thesis. *Entrance requirements:* For master's, GRE General Test. Additional exam requirements/recommendations for international students: Required—TOEFL. Electronic applications accepted. *Expenses:* Tuition, state resident: full-time $15,020; part-time $751 per semester hour. Tuition, nonresident: full-time $15,020; part-time $751 per semester hour. *Required fees:* $3158; $157.90 per semester hour. Tuition and fees vary according to course load, campus/location and program.

Rowan University, Graduate School, College of Communication and Creative Arts, Writing, Composition, and Rhetoric Certificate of Graduate Study Program, Glassboro, NJ 08028-1701. Offers CGS. *Expenses:* Tuition, state resident: full-time $15,020; part-time $751 per semester hour. Tuition, nonresident: full-time $15,020; part-time $751 per semester hour. *Required fees:* $3158; $157.90 per semester hour. Tuition and fees vary according to course load, campus/location and program.

Rutgers University–Camden, Graduate School of Arts and Sciences, Program in Creative Writing, Camden, NJ 08102. Offers MFA. *Program availability:* Part-time, evening/weekend. *Degree requirements:* For master's, thesis, 42 credits. *Entrance requirements:* For master's, GRE (for assistantships), 2 letters of recommendation, writing sample, statement of personal, professional, and academic goals. Additional exam requirements/recommendations for international students: Required—TOEFL, IELTS. Electronic applications accepted. *Faculty research:* Poetry, fiction, nonfiction.

Rutgers University–Newark, Graduate School, Program in Creative Writing, Newark, NJ 07102. Offers MFA. *Entrance requirements:* For master's, GRE, minimum undergraduate B average.

Rutgers University–New Brunswick, Mason Gross School of the Arts, Theater Department, New Brunswick, NJ 08901. Offers acting (MFA); design (MFA); playwriting (MFA); stage management (MFA); technical direction (MFA). *Degree requirements:* For master's, thesis (for some programs), performance project. *Entrance requirements:* For master's, audition, interview, portfolio. Additional exam requirements/recommendations for international students: Required—TOEFL (minimum score 550 paper-based), IELTS (minimum score 7). Electronic applications accepted. *Faculty research:* Faculty of working professional.

St. Joseph's College, New York, Program in Creative Writing, Brooklyn, NY 11205-3688. Offers MFA. *Program availability:* Part-time, evening/weekend. *Faculty:* 1 (woman) full-time, 3 part-time/adjunct (2 women). *Students:* 14 full-time (10 women); includes 7 minority (2 Black or African American, non-Hispanic/Latino; 1 Asian, non-Hispanic/Latino; 3 Hispanic/Latino; 1 Two or more races, non-Hispanic/Latino). Average age 31. 31 applicants, 77% accepted, 3 enrolled. In 2017, 11 master's awarded. *Entrance requirements:* For master's, official transcripts, manuscript, resume, personal statement, 2 recommendation letters. Additional exam requirements/recommendations for international students: Required—TOEFL (minimum score 80 iBT). *Application deadline:* Applications are processed on a rolling basis. Electronic applications accepted. *Expenses:* $26,520 per year. *Financial support:* In 2017–18, 14 students received support. *Unit head:* Theodore Hamm, Associate Professor/Chair, 718-940-5307, E-mail: thamm@sjcny.edu.

Saint Joseph's University, College of Arts and Sciences, Program in Writing Studies, Philadelphia, PA 19131-1395. Offers MA. *Program availability:* Part-time, evening/weekend. *Faculty:* 7 full-time (4 women), 2 part-time/adjunct (both women). *Students:* 4 full-time (3 women), 21 part-time (12 women); includes 3 minority (1 Black or African American, non-Hispanic/Latino; 1 Hispanic/Latino; 1 Two or more races, non-Hispanic/Latino). Average age 33. 14 applicants, 79% accepted, 6 enrolled. In 2017, 12 master's awarded. *Entrance requirements:* For master's, 2 letters of recommendation, resume, 2 writing samples. Additional exam requirements/recommendations for international students: Required—TOEFL (minimum score 550 paper-based; 80 iBT). *Application*

deadline: For fall admission, 7/15 for international students; for spring admission, 11/1 for international students. Applications are processed on a rolling basis. Application fee: $35. Electronic applications accepted. *Expenses:* Contact institution. *Financial support:* In 2017–18, 4 students received support. Scholarships/grants and unspecified assistantships available. Financial award application deadline: 5/1; financial award applicants required to submit FAFSA. *Unit head:* Dr. Tenaya Darlington, Director, 610-660-3131, E-mail: gradcas@sju.edu. *Application contact:* Graduate Admissions, College of Arts and Sciences, 610-660-3131, E-mail: gradcas@sju.edu.
Website: https://www.sju.edu/majors-programs/graduate-arts-sciences/masters/writing-studies-ma

Saint Leo University, Graduate Studies in Creative Writing, Saint Leo, FL 33574-6665. Offers creative writing (MA); war literature and writing for veterans (MA). *Program availability:* Part-time. *Faculty:* 3 full-time (1 woman), 3 part-time/adjunct (1 woman). *Students:* 28 part-time (18 women); includes 5 minority (3 Black or African American, non-Hispanic/Latino; 2 Hispanic/Latino). Average age 40. 21 applicants, 57% accepted, 12 enrolled. *Degree requirements:* For master's, thesis. *Entrance requirements:* For master's, official transcripts, 2 professional recommendations, personal statement, bachelor's degree from regionally-accredited university with minimum GPA of 3.25, writing sample. *Application deadline:* For fall admission, 7/1 priority date for domestic and international students; for spring admission, 11/1 priority date for domestic and international students. Applications are processed on a rolling basis. Application fee: $80. Electronic applications accepted. Application fee is waived when completed online. *Expenses:* $615 per credit hour. *Financial support:* In 2017–18, 6 students received support. Scholarships/grants, health care benefits, and tuition remission for Saint Leo employees and their dependents available. Financial award application deadline: 3/1; financial award applicants required to submit FAFSA. *Faculty research:* Writing fiction, writing poetry, writing by veterans, war literature, writing creative nonfiction, best practices in teaching creative writing, creative writing pedagogy. *Unit head:* Dr. Steve Kistulentz, Director, 352-588-7218, Fax: 352-588-8300, E-mail: steven.kistulentz@saintleo.edu. *Application contact:* Mark Russum, Assistant Vice President, Enrollment, 800-707-8846, Fax: 352-588-7873, E-mail: grad.admissions@saintleo.edu.
Website: http://www.saintleo.edu/academics/graduate/creative-writing.aspx

Saint Mary's College of California, School of Liberal Arts, MFA Program in Creative Writing, Moraga, CA 94575. Offers MFA. *Degree requirements:* For master's, thesis. *Entrance requirements:* For master's, sample of written work. Electronic applications accepted. *Faculty research:* Poetry, fiction, nonfiction.

Salve Regina University, The Newport MFA in Creative Writing Program, Newport, RI 02840-4192. Offers MFA.

Sam Houston State University, College of Humanities and Social Sciences, Department of English, Huntsville, TX 77341. Offers creative writing, editing, and publishing (MFA); English (MA). *Program availability:* Part-time. *Degree requirements:* For master's, comprehensive exam, thesis optional. *Entrance requirements:* For master's, GRE General Test, creative writing sample, letters of recommendation. Additional exam requirements/recommendations for international students: Required—TOEFL (minimum score 550 paper-based; 79 iBT), IELTS (minimum score 6.5). Electronic applications accepted.

San Diego State University, Graduate and Research Affairs, College of Arts and Letters, Department of English and Comparative Literature, San Diego, CA 92182. Offers creative writing (MFA); English (MA). *Degree requirements:* For master's, one foreign language, comprehensive exam (for some programs), thesis (for some programs). *Entrance requirements:* For master's, GRE General Test, minimum GPA of 2.85, writing sample, 3 letters of recommendation. Additional exam requirements/recommendations for international students: Required—TOEFL. Electronic applications accepted.

San Diego State University, Graduate and Research Affairs, College of Arts and Letters, Department of Rhetoric and Writing Studies, San Diego, CA 92182. Offers MA. *Program availability:* Part-time. *Degree requirements:* For master's, thesis. *Entrance requirements:* For master's, GRE General Test, writing sample, 3 letters of reference. Additional exam requirements/recommendations for international students: Required—TOEFL. Electronic applications accepted.

San Francisco State University, Division of Graduate Studies, College of Liberal and Creative Arts, Department of Creative Writing, San Francisco, CA 94132-1722. Offers MA, MFA. *Program availability:* Part-time. *Degree requirements:* For master's, thesis. *Financial support:* Career-related internships or fieldwork and Federal Work-Study available. *Unit head:* Paul Hoover, Acting Chair, 415-338-1891, Fax: 415-338-6159, E-mail: viridian@sfsu.edu. *Application contact:* Maxine Chernoff, Graduate Coordinator, 415-338-2019, Fax: 415-338-6159, E-mail: chernoff@sfsu.edu.
Website: http://creativewriting.sfsu.edu/

San Jose State University, Graduate Studies and Research, College of Humanities and the Arts, San Jose, CA 95192-0088. Offers art (MA, MFA), including digital media art (MFA), history and visual culture (MA), photography (MFA), pictorial art (MFA), spatial art (MFA); English (MA, MFA), including creative writing (MFA); linguistics (MA); music (MM); music education (MA); philosophy (MA); Spanish (MA); teaching English to speakers of other languages (MA). *Program availability:* Part-time. *Faculty:* 35 full-time (17 women), 19 part-time/adjunct (11 women). *Students:* 129 full-time (79 women), 106 part-time (71 women); includes 117 minority (5 Black or African American, non-Hispanic/Latino; 29 Asian, non-Hispanic/Latino; 44 Hispanic/Latino; 39 Two or more races, non-Hispanic/Latino), 28 international. Average age 35. 204 applicants, 65% accepted, 79 enrolled. In 2017, 85 master's awarded. *Degree requirements:* For master's, one foreign language, comprehensive exam (for some programs), thesis (for some programs), graduate writing assessment, special study/project, recital. *Entrance requirements:* Additional exam requirements/recommendations for international students: Required—TOEFL (minimum score 550 paper-based; 80 iBT), IELTS (minimum score 6.5), PTE (minimum score 53). *Application deadline:* For fall admission, 2/1 for domestic and international students. Applications are processed on a rolling basis. Application fee: $55. Electronic applications accepted. *Expenses:* Tuition, state resident: full-time $7176. Tuition, nonresident: full-time $16,680. Tuition and fees vary according to course load and program. *Financial support:* Fellowships, research assistantships, Federal Work-Study, scholarships/grants, traineeships, tuition waivers (full and partial), and unspecified assistantships available. Support available to part-time students. Financial award application deadline: 4/28; financial award applicants required to submit FAFSA. *Unit head:* Dr. Shannon Miller, Dean, 408-924-4300, Fax: 408-924-4365, E-mail: shannon.miller@sjsu.edu.
Website: http://www.sjsu.edu/humanitiesandarts/

Sarah Lawrence College, Graduate Studies, Program in Writing, Bronxville, NY 10708-5999. Offers creative non-fiction (MFA); fiction (MFA); poetry (MFA). *Program availability:* Part-time. *Degree requirements:* For master's, thesis. *Entrance requirements:* For master's, sample of creative writing, minimum B average in undergraduate course work. Additional exam requirements/recommendations for international students: Required—TOEFL (minimum score 600 paper-based).

Savannah College of Art and Design, Program in Dramatic Writing, Savannah, GA 31402-3146. Offers MFA. *Program availability:* Part-time. *Faculty:* 5 full-time (2 women), 1 (woman) part-time/adjunct. *Students:* 18 full-time (11 women), 1 part-time (0 women); includes 7 minority (all Black or African American, non-Hispanic/Latino), 4 international. Average age 25. 28 applicants, 61% accepted, 10 enrolled. In 2017, 10 master's awarded. *Degree requirements:* For master's, thesis. *Entrance requirements:* For master's, GRE (recommended), portfolio (submitted in digital format), audition or writing submission, resume, statement of purpose, two letters of recommendation. Additional exam requirements/recommendations for international students: Recommended—TOEFL (minimum score 550 paper-based; 85 iBT), IELTS (minimum score 6.5). *Application deadline:* For fall admission, 4/1 for domestic and international students. Applications are processed on a rolling basis. Application fee: $40. Electronic applications accepted. *Expenses: Tuition:* Full-time $36,765; part-time $817 per credit hour. One-time fee: $500. *Financial support:* Career-related internships or fieldwork, Federal Work-Study, and scholarships/grants available. Financial award application deadline: 4/1; financial award applicants required to submit FAFSA. *Unit head:* Averie Storck, Academic Program Coordinator. *Application contact:* Jenny Jaquillard, Executive Director of Admissions, Recruitment and Events, 912-525-5100, Fax: 912-525-5985, E-mail: admission@scad.edu.
Website: http://www.scad.edu/academics/programs/dramatic-writing

Savannah College of Art and Design, Program in Writing, Savannah, GA 31402-3146. Offers MFA. *Program availability:* Part-time, 100% online. *Faculty:* 6 full-time (2 women), 1 (woman) part-time/adjunct. *Students:* 37 full-time (31 women), 22 part-time (17 women); includes 24 minority (19 Black or African American, non-Hispanic/Latino; 1 Asian, non-Hispanic/Latino; 4 Hispanic/Latino), 5 international. Average age 32. 47 applicants, 38% accepted, 10 enrolled. In 2017, 12 master's awarded. *Degree requirements:* For master's, thesis. *Entrance requirements:* For master's, GRE (recommended), portfolio (submitted in digital format), audition or writing submission, resume, statement of purpose, two letters of recommendation. Additional exam requirements/recommendations for international students: Recommended—TOEFL (minimum score 550 paper-based; 85 iBT), IELTS (minimum score 6.5). *Application deadline:* For fall admission, 4/1 for domestic and international students. Applications are processed on a rolling basis. Application fee: $40. Electronic applications accepted. *Expenses: Tuition:* Full-time $36,765; part-time $817 per credit hour. One-time fee: $500. *Financial support:* Career-related internships or fieldwork, Federal Work-Study, and scholarships/grants available. Financial award application deadline: 4/1; financial award applicants required to submit FAFSA. *Unit head:* Dr. Beth Concepcion, Dean, School of Liberal Arts. *Application contact:* Jenny Jaquillard, Executive Director of Admissions, Recruitment and Events, 912-525-5100, Fax: 912-525-5985, E-mail: admission@scad.edu.
Website: http://www.scad.edu/academics/programs/writing

School of the Art Institute of Chicago, Graduate Division, Program in Writing, Chicago, IL 60603-3103. Offers MFA, Certificate. *Entrance requirements:* Additional exam requirements/recommendations for international students: Required—TOEFL.

School of Visual Arts, Graduate Programs, Program in Visual Narrative, New York, NY 10010-3994. Offers MFA. Summer admission only. *Degree requirements:* For master's, thesis, 60 credits, including all required courses. *Entrance requirements:* For master's, portfolio, statement of purpose; unique and complete short story/visual narrative (minimum 2-5 pages/images, or 2-5 minutes for video or animation submissions). Additional exam requirements/recommendations for international students: Required—TOEFL (minimum score 550 paper-based; 79 iBT). Electronic applications accepted. *Faculty research:* Storytelling, animation, design, illustration, art history, painting, printmaking, writing, graphic novels.

Seattle Pacific University, Master of Fine Arts in Creative Writing Program, Seattle, WA 98119-1997. Offers MFA. *Program availability:* Part-time. *Students:* 30 part-time (22 women), 1 international. Average age 34. In 2017, 12 master's awarded. *Degree requirements:* For master's, thesis. *Entrance requirements:* For master's, 10 pages of poetry or 25 to 30 double-spaced pages of prose, whether of fiction or creative nonfiction, in the student's chosen genre; three- to four-page (double-spaced) personal essay describing development as writer and as person of faith; three recommendations; bachelor's degree; official transcripts from previous schools attended. *Application deadline:* For winter admission, 11/15 for domestic students; for summer admission, 5/15 for domestic students. Application fee: $50. Electronic applications accepted. *Financial support:* Applicants required to submit FAFSA. *Unit head:* Dr. Scott Cairns, Director, 206-281-2109, E-mail: gwolfe@spu.edu. *Application contact:* The Graduate Center, 206-281-2091.
Website: http://spu.edu/academics/college-of-arts-sciences/mfa

Seton Hill University, MFA Program in Writing Popular Fiction, Greensburg, PA 15601. Offers MFA. *Program availability:* Part-time. *Entrance requirements:* For master's, 10-page writing sample, 3 letters of recommendation, resume, letter of intent, official transcripts. Additional exam requirements/recommendations for international students: Required—TOEFL (minimum score 650 paper-based; 114 iBT), IELTS (minimum score 7). *Application deadline:* For fall admission, 10/1 priority date for domestic students; for spring admission, 3/1 priority date for domestic students. Applications are processed on a rolling basis. Electronic applications accepted. *Expenses: Tuition:* Part-time $734 per credit. Tuition and fees vary according to class time, course level, course load and program. *Financial support:* Scholarships/grants and tuition discounts available. Financial award application deadline: 8/15; financial award applicants required to submit FAFSA. *Unit head:* Dr. Nicole Peeler, Associate Professor, English/Program Director, Writing Popular Fiction, E-mail: peeler@setonhill.edu.
Website: http://www.setonhill.edu/academics/graduate_programs/fiction

Shenandoah University, School of Education and Leadership, Winchester, VA 22601. Offers administration and supervision (Certificate); administrative leadership (D Ed); early childhood literacy (MS); educational administration (MSE); elementary school teacher education (Certificate); emphasis in teaching (MSE); health and physical education (Certificate); individualized focus (MS, MSE); literacy education (MS); middle school teacher education (Certificate); organizational leadership (MS, D Prof); reading licensure (MS, Certificate); reading non-licensure (MS); secondary school teacher education (Certificate); special education (MSE); writing (MS). *Accreditation:* TEAC. *Program availability:* Part-time, evening/weekend. *Faculty:* 8 full-time (7 women), 22 part-time/adjunct (16 women). *Students:* 16 full-time (14 women), 221 part-time (167 women); includes 32 minority (17 Black or African American, non-Hispanic/Latino; 1 American Indian or Alaska Native, non-Hispanic/Latino; 6 Asian, non-Hispanic/Latino; 5 Hispanic/Latino; 1 Native Hawaiian or other Pacific Islander, non-Hispanic/Latino; 2 Two or more races, non-Hispanic/Latino), 3 international. Average age 38. 81 applicants, 99% accepted, 63 enrolled. In 2017, 53 master's, 11 doctorates, 49 other advanced degrees awarded. *Degree requirements:* For master's, comprehensive exam (for some programs), thesis (for some programs); for doctorate, comprehensive exam, thesis/dissertation. *Entrance requirements:* For degree, PRAXIS Academic Core, SAT/ACT, PRAXIS Academic Core Math, or VCLA, three letters of recommendation, writing sample, undergraduate degree. Additional exam requirements/recommendations for international students: Required—TOEFL (minimum score 550 paper-based, 79 iBT) or IELTS (6.5). *Application deadline:* For fall admission, 5/1 priority date for domestic

students, 5/1 for international students; for spring admission, 10/15 priority date for domestic students, 10/15 for international students; for summer admission, 3/15 priority date for domestic students, 3/15 for international students. Application fee: $30. Electronic applications accepted. *Expenses:* $15,600 tuition plus $1,296 fees (technology and student services). *Financial support:* In 2017–18, 26 students received support. Scholarships/grants and unspecified assistantships available. Financial award applicants required to submit FAFSA. *Faculty research:* Mentoring, behavior support for students, teacher change agency, educational technology in pedagogy, literacy education. *Unit head:* Jill Lindsey, PhD, Director, 540-535-7324, Fax: 540-665-4726, E-mail: jlindsey@su.edu. *Application contact:* Andrew Woodall, Executive Director of Recruitment and Admissions, 540-665-4581, Fax: 540-665-4627, E-mail: admit@su.edu.
Website: http://www.su.edu/education/

Simmons College, School of Library and Information Science, Boston, MA 02115. Offers children's literature (MA); library and information science (MS, PhD, Certificate), including archives management (MS), cultural heritage (MS), information science and technology (MS), school library teacher (MS); writing for children (MFA); MA/MA; MA/MAT; MA/MFA; MS/MA. *Accreditation:* ALA (one or more programs are accredited). *Program availability:* Part-time, evening/weekend, 100% online, blended/hybrid learning. *Faculty:* 28 full-time (21 women), 34 part-time/adjunct (25 women). *Students:* 339 full-time (287 women), 509 part-time (415 women); includes 91 minority (15 Black or African American, non-Hispanic/Latino; 18 Asian, non-Hispanic/Latino; 35 Hispanic/Latino; 23 Two or more races, non-Hispanic/Latino), 12 international. Average age 30. 533 applicants, 98% accepted, 268 enrolled. In 2017, 300 master's, 10 doctorates, 5 other advanced degrees awarded. *Degree requirements:* For master's, thesis optional, capstone project experience; for doctorate, comprehensive exam, thesis/dissertation, 36 credit hours. *Entrance requirements:* For master's, GRE when applicants' GPA is below 3.0 for all degrees, statement of purpose, current resume or curriculum vitae, college transcripts, three letters of recommendation; for doctorate, GRE or MTEL, transcripts, personal statement, resume, recommendations, master's degree. Additional exam requirements/recommendations for international students: Required—TOEFL (minimum score 550 paper-based; 79 iBT), IELTS (minimum score 7). *Application deadline:* For fall admission, 3/1 for domestic and international students; for spring admission, 9/1 for domestic and international students; for summer admission, 2/1 for domestic and international students. Applications are processed on a rolling basis. Application fee: $65. Electronic applications accepted. *Expenses:* $1,135 per credit, $3,405 per course, $55 activity fee per semester. *Financial support:* In 2017–18, 10 fellowships with partial tuition reimbursements were awarded; scholarships/grants and unspecified assistantships also available. Support available to part-time students. Financial award application deadline: 6/1; financial award applicants required to submit FAFSA. *Faculty research:* Archives and social justice, information-seeking behavior, information retrieval, organization of information, cultural heritage informatics. *Unit head:* Dr. Eileen G. Abels, Dean, 617-521-2869. *Application contact:* Kate Benson, Director, SLIS Admission, 617-521-2801, Fax: 617-521-3192, E-mail: slisadm@simmons.edu.
Website: http://www.simmons.edu/slis/

Sonoma State University, Department of English, Rohnert Park, CA 94928. Offers American literature (MA); creative writing (MA); English literature (MA); world literature (MA). *Program availability:* Part-time, evening/weekend. *Degree requirements:* For master's, one foreign language, thesis or alternative. *Entrance requirements:* For master's, minimum GPA of 2.5. Additional exam requirements/recommendations for international students: Required—TOEFL (minimum score 500 paper-based). *Application deadline:* For fall admission, 11/30 priority date for domestic students. Application fee: $55. *Financial support:* Fellowships, teaching assistantships, career-related internships or fieldwork, and Federal Work-Study available. Financial award application deadline: 3/2; financial award applicants required to submit FAFSA. *Unit head:* Brantley L. Bryant, Chair, 707-664-2164, E-mail: brantley.bryant@sonoma.edu. *Application contact:* Dr. Stefan Kiesbye, Chair of Graduate Studies, 707-664-2403, Fax: 707-664-6040, E-mail: kiesbye@sonoma.edu.
Website: http://www.sonoma.edu/english/programs/ma-program.html

Southeastern Louisiana University, College of Arts, Humanities and Social Sciences, Department of English, Hammond, LA 70402. Offers creative writing (MA); language and theory (MA); professional writing (MA); publishing studies (MA). *Program availability:* Part-time. *Faculty:* 10 full-time (2 women). *Students:* 11 full-time (9 women), 11 part-time (10 women); includes 5 minority (2 Black or African American, non-Hispanic/Latino; 2 Hispanic/Latino; 1 Two or more races, non-Hispanic/Latino). Average age 25. 8 applicants, 38% accepted, 3 enrolled. In 2017, 8 master's awarded. *Degree requirements:* For master's, comprehensive exam, thesis optional. *Entrance requirements:* For master's, GRE (minimum score of 290 combined verbal and quantitative). Additional exam requirements/recommendations for international students: Required—TOEFL (minimum score 500 paper-based; 61 iBT), IELTS (minimum score 5.5). *Application deadline:* For fall admission, 7/15 priority date for domestic students, 6/1 priority date for international students; for spring admission, 12/1 priority date for domestic students, 10/1 priority date for international students. Applications are processed on a rolling basis. Application fee: $20 ($30 for international students). Electronic applications accepted. *Expenses:* Tuition, state resident: full-time $6684. Tuition, nonresident: full-time $19,162. *Required fees:* $2088. *Financial support:* In 2017–18, 16 students received support, including 7 teaching assistantships (averaging $5,415 per year); research assistantships, institutionally sponsored loans, scholarships/grants, and unspecified assistantships also available. Support available to part-time students. Financial award application deadline: 5/1; financial award applicants required to submit FAFSA. *Faculty research:* John Ruskin, animal studies, linguistics, film studies. *Unit head:* Dr. David Hanson, Department Head, 985-549-2100, Fax: 985-549-5021, E-mail: dhanson@southeastern.edu. *Application contact:* Amanda Harper, Graduate Admissions Analyst, 985-549-5620, Fax: 985-549-5632, E-mail: admissions@southeastern.edu.
Website: http://www.southeastern.edu/acad_research/depts/engl

Southern Illinois University Carbondale, Graduate School, College of Liberal Arts, Department of English, Program in Creative Writing, Carbondale, IL 62901-4701. Offers MFA. *Degree requirements:* For master's, one foreign language, thesis. *Entrance requirements:* For master's, GRE General Test, GRE Subject Test, minimum GPA of 2.7. Additional exam requirements/recommendations for international students: Required—TOEFL.

Southern Illinois University Edwardsville, Graduate School, College of Arts and Sciences, Department of English Language and Literature, Program in Creative Writing, Edwardsville, IL 62026. Offers MA. *Program availability:* Part-time. *Degree requirements:* For master's, one foreign language, thesis. *Entrance requirements:* Additional exam requirements/recommendations for international students: Required—TOEFL (minimum score 550 paper-based, 79 iBT), IELTS (minimum score 6.5), Michigan Test of English Language Proficiency or PTE. Electronic applications accepted.

Southern New Hampshire University, School of Arts and Sciences, Manchester, NH 03106-1045. Offers clinical mental health counseling (MS); creative writing (MA); criminal justice (MS); cyber security (MS); English (MA); fiction and nonfiction (MFA);

history (MA); political science (MS); psychology (MS). *Program availability:* Part-time, evening/weekend. *Degree requirements:* For master's, one foreign language, thesis. *Entrance requirements:* For master's, minimum GPA of 2.75 (for MS in teaching English as a foreign language), 3.0 (for MFA). Additional exam requirements/recommendations for international students: Required—TOEFL (minimum score 550 paper-based; 79 iBT), IELTS (minimum score 6.5), TWE (minimum score 5). *Application deadline:* For fall admission, 7/1 priority date for domestic students; for winter admission, 11/1 priority date for domestic students; for spring admission, 6/1 priority date for domestic students. Applications are processed on a rolling basis. Application fee: $40. Electronic applications accepted. *Expenses:* Contact institution. *Financial support:* Research assistantships, career-related internships or fieldwork, and scholarships/grants available. Financial award applicants required to submit FAFSA. *Faculty research:* Action research, state of the art practice in behavioral health services, wraparound approaches to working with youth, learning styles. *Unit head:* Steven K. Johnson, Dean, 603-629-4626. *Application contact:* Office of Graduate Admission, 888-327-SNHU, Fax: 603-644-3144, E-mail: enroll@snhu.edu.

Spalding University, Graduate Studies, College of Social Sciences and Humanities, Master of Fine Arts in Writing Program, Louisville, KY 40203-2188. Offers MFA. *Program availability:* Online learning. *Degree requirements:* For master's, thesis. *Entrance requirements:* For master's, writing sample, letters of recommendation, personal essays. Additional exam requirements/recommendations for international students: Required—TOEFL (minimum score 535 paper-based). Electronic applications accepted. *Faculty research:* Fiction, creative nonfiction, poetry, writing for children, playwriting/screenwriting.

State University of New York at Fredonia, College of Liberal Arts and Sciences, Fredonia, NY 14063-1136. Offers biology (MS); English (MA); English education 7-12 (MA); interdisciplinary studies (MA, MS); math education (MS Ed); professional writing (CAS); speech pathology (MS); MA/MS. *Program availability:* Part-time, evening/weekend. *Students:* 73 full-time (62 women), 9 part-time (6 women); includes 7 minority (1 Black or African American, non-Hispanic/Latino; 1 Asian, non-Hispanic/Latino; 2 Hispanic/Latino; 1 Native Hawaiian or other Pacific Islander, non-Hispanic/Latino; 2 Two or more races, non-Hispanic/Latino). Average age 24. 200 applicants, 25% accepted, 43 enrolled. In 2017, 41 master's, 1 other advanced degree awarded. *Degree requirements:* For master's, comprehensive exam (for some programs), thesis (for some programs). *Entrance requirements:* For master's, GRE. Additional exam requirements/recommendations for international students: Required—TOEFL (minimum score 79 iBT), IELTS (minimum score 6.5). *Application deadline:* Applications are processed on a rolling basis. Application fee: $75. Electronic applications accepted. *Expenses:* Tuition, state resident: full-time $8154. Tuition, nonresident: full-time $16,650. *Required fees:* $1209. *Financial support:* In 2017–18, 5 students received support, including 14 teaching assistantships with full and partial tuition reimbursements available (averaging $5,957 per year); tuition waivers (full and partial) and unspecified assistantships also available. *Faculty research:* Immunology/microbiology, applied human physiology, ecology and evolution, invertebrate biology, molecular biology, biochemistry, physiology, animal behavior, science education, vertebrate physiology, cell biology, plant biology, developmental biology, aquatic ecology, bilingual language acquisition, bilingual language acquisition and disorders, augmentative and alternate communication with ALS, World War I, Zweig, environmental literature, editing, adolescent literature, pedagogy. *Unit head:* Dr. Andy Karafa, Dean, 716-673-3173, Fax: 716-673-3338, E-mail: andy.karafa@gmail.com. *Application contact:* Wendy S. Dunst, Interim Graduate Recruitment and Admissions Associate, 716-673-3808, Fax: 716-673-3712, E-mail: wendy.dunst@fredonia.edu.
Website: http://www.fredonia.edu/clas/

Stephens College, Division of Graduate and Continuing Studies, Columbia, MO 65215-0002. Offers counseling (M Ed), including addictions counseling, clinical mental health counseling, school counseling; health information administration (Postbaccalaureate Certificate); physician assistant studies (MPAS); TV and screenwriting (MFA). *Program availability:* Part-time, evening/weekend, online learning. *Entrance requirements:* For master's, minimum GPA of 3.0 in last 60 hours. Additional exam requirements/recommendations for international students: Required—TOEFL (minimum score 79 iBT). Electronic applications accepted. *Faculty research:* Educational psychology, outcomes assessment.

Stetson University, College of Arts and Sciences, Department of English, DeLand, FL 32723. Offers creative writing (MFA). *Program availability:* Blended/hybrid learning. *Faculty:* 1 (woman) full-time, 5 part-time/adjunct (4 women). *Students:* 17 full-time (13 women); includes 4 minority (3 Hispanic/Latino; 1 Two or more races, non-Hispanic/Latino), 1 international. Average age 38. 1 applicant, 100% accepted, 1 enrolled. *Degree requirements:* For master's, book-length project. *Entrance requirements:* For master's, GRE General Test, writing sample. Additional exam requirements/recommendations for international students: Required—TOEFL (minimum score 90 iBT), IELTS (minimum score 7). *Application deadline:* For fall admission, 8/1 priority date for domestic students; for spring admission, 1/1 priority date for domestic students; for summer admission, 5/1 priority date for domestic students. Applications are processed on a rolling basis. Application fee: $50. Electronic applications accepted. *Expenses:* $911 per credit hour. *Financial support:* In 2017–18, 1 student received support. Career-related internships or fieldwork, Federal Work-Study, scholarships/grants, unspecified assistantships, and tuition waivers (for staff and dependents) available. Support available to part-time students. Financial award applicants required to submit FAFSA. *Unit head:* Teresa Carmody, Director, MFA of the Americas Creative Writing Program, 386-822-7741, E-mail: tcarmody@stetson.edu. *Application contact:* Jamie Vanderlip, Director of Admissions for Graduate, Transfer and Adult Programs, 386-822-7100, Fax: 386-822-7112, E-mail: jlvander@stetson.edu.

Stony Brook University, State University of New York, Graduate School, College of Arts and Sciences, Program in Writing and Rhetoric, Stony Brook, NY 11794. Offers teaching writing (Graduate Certificate). *Faculty:* 26 full-time (12 women), 13 part-time/adjunct (8 women). *Students:* 1 (woman) part-time. 1 applicant. In 2017, 4 Graduate Certificates awarded. *Degree requirements:* For Graduate Certificate, practicum. *Entrance requirements:* For degree, two letters of recommendation, statement of purpose. Additional exam requirements/recommendations for international students: Required—TOEFL. *Application deadline:* For fall admission, 1/15 for domestic students; for spring admission, 10/1 for domestic students. *Expenses:* Contact institution. *Financial support:* Teaching assistantships available. *Faculty research:* Composition, creative writing, fiction, rhetoric, writing. *Unit head:* Dr. Eugene Hammond, Director, 631-632-9277, E-mail: eugene.hammond@stonybrook.edu. *Application contact:* Adam Schultheiss, Coordinator, 631-632-7390, E-mail: adam.schultheiss@stonybrook.edu.
Website: http://www.stonybrook.edu/commcms/writrhet//

Stony Brook University, State University of New York, Stony Brook Southampton, Program in Creative Writing and Literature, Stony Brook, NY 11794. Offers fiction (MFA); poetry (MFA); scientific writing (MFA), including environmental, medical, technological; scriptwriting (MFA). *Faculty:* 8 full-time (4 women), 37 part-time/adjunct (19 women). *Students:* 25 full-time (19 women), 49 part-time (37 women); includes 8 minority (4 Black or African American, non-Hispanic/Latino; 1 Asian, non-Hispanic/Latino; 3 Hispanic/Latino), 1 international. 49 applicants, 71% accepted, 10 enrolled. In

2017, 19 master's awarded. *Entrance requirements:* Additional exam requirements/recommendations for international students: Required—TOEFL (minimum score 85 iBT), IELTS (minimum score 6.5). *Application deadline:* For fall admission, 1/15 for domestic students; for spring admission, 10/1 for domestic students. Applications are processed on a rolling basis. Application fee: $100. *Expenses:* Contact institution. *Financial support:* In 2017–18, 9 teaching assistantships were awarded. *Unit head:* Lou Ann Walker, Director, 631-632-5031, Fax: 631-982-7318, E-mail: louann.walker@stonybrook.edu. *Application contact:* Margaret S. Grigonis, Coordinator, 631-632-5028, Fax: 631-982-7318, E-mail: margaret.grigonis@stonybrook.edu.
Website: http://www.stonybrook.edu/southampton/mfa/cwl/index.html

Syracuse University, College of Arts and Sciences, MFA Program in Creative Writing, Syracuse, NY 13244. Offers MFA. *Students:* Average age 29. *Degree requirements:* For master's, thesis. *Entrance requirements:* For master's, writing sample, statement of purpose, teaching statement, transcript(s) from undergraduate/graduate institution, three letters of recommendation. Additional exam requirements/recommendations for international students: Required—TOEFL (minimum score 100 iBT). *Application deadline:* For fall admission, 12/15 priority date for domestic and international students. Application fee: $75. Electronic applications accepted. *Financial support:* Fellowships with full tuition reimbursements, teaching assistantships with full tuition reimbursements, and scholarships/grants available. Financial award application deadline: 1/1. *Faculty research:* Literary process, the craft and quality of literary writing, creative writing. *Unit head:* Christopher Kennedy, Professor, English/Director, MFA Program in Creative Writing, 315-443-2174, E-mail: ckennedy@syr.edu. *Application contact:* Terri Zollo, Graduate Coordinator, 315-443-2174, E-mail: tazollo@syr.edu.
Website: http://english.syr.edu/cw/cw-program.html##

Syracuse University, College of Arts and Sciences, PhD Program in Composition and Cultural Rhetoric, Syracuse, NY 13244. Offers PhD. *Degree requirements:* For doctorate, comprehensive exam, thesis/dissertation. *Entrance requirements:* For doctorate, GRE, three letters of recommendation, essay on intellectual history and academic interests, statement about teaching interests and practical experience, resume, transcripts. Additional exam requirements/recommendations for international students: Required—TOEFL (minimum score 100 iBT). *Application deadline:* For fall admission, 1/15 for domestic and international students. Application fee: $75. Electronic applications accepted. *Financial support:* Fellowships with tuition reimbursements, teaching assistantships with tuition reimbursements, scholarships/grants, and unspecified assistantships available. Financial award application deadline: 1/15; financial award applicants required to submit FAFSA. *Faculty research:* American ethnic rhetorics, authorship studies, composition studies and pedagogies, studies of gender and sexuality, transnational rhetorics and globalization. *Unit head:* Prof. Eileen Schell, Associate Professor, Writing and Rhetoric/Director of Graduate Studies, 315-443-1067, E-mail: eeschell@syr.edu. *Application contact:* Kristen Krause, Graduate Program Coordinator, 315-443-5146, E-mail: ccr@syr.edu.
Website: http://wrt.syr.edu/graduate/welcome.html

Temple University, Center for the Performing and Cinematic Arts, School of Theater, Film and Media Arts, Department of Theater, Philadelphia, PA 19122. Offers acting (MFA); design (MFA); directing (MFA); musical theater collaboration (MFA); musical theater studies (MA); playwriting (MFA). *Accreditation:* NAST. *Program availability:* Part-time. *Faculty:* 15 full-time (7 women), 18 part-time/adjunct (13 women). *Students:* 28 full-time (16 women), 1 (woman) part-time; includes 7 minority (4 Black or African American, non-Hispanic/Latino; 3 Hispanic/Latino), 3 international. 22 applicants, 41% accepted, 8 enrolled. In 2017, 6 master's awarded. *Degree requirements:* For master's, thesis (for some programs). *Entrance requirements:* For master's, minimum GPA of 3.0; audition/interview, portfolio, or samples of written work. Additional exam requirements/recommendations for international students: Required—TOEFL (minimum score 550 paper-based; 79 iBT). *Application deadline:* For fall admission, 12/15 for international students. Application fee: $60. Electronic applications accepted. *Expenses:* Contact institution. *Financial support:* Teaching assistantships with full tuition reimbursements, Federal Work-Study, institutionally sponsored loans, and unspecified assistantships available. Financial award application deadline: 3/1; financial award applicants required to submit FAFSA. *Faculty research:* Acting/voice/speech/movement, theatrical design and production, musical theater, directing, playwriting. *Unit head:* Robert Hedley, Chair, 215-204-8413, E-mail: robert.hedley@temple.edu. *Application contact:* Leah Dempsey, Assistant Director for Administration, 215-204-8791, E-mail: leahdempsey@temple.edu.
Website: https://tfma.temple.edu/theater

Temple University, College of Liberal Arts, Department of English, Philadelphia, PA 19122-6096. Offers creative writing (MFA); English (MA, PhD). *Program availability:* Part-time. *Faculty:* 22 full-time (9 women), 14 part-time/adjunct (4 women). *Students:* 71 full-time (39 women), 8 part-time (7 women); includes 17 minority (4 Black or African American, non-Hispanic/Latino; 1 American Indian or Alaska Native, non-Hispanic/Latino; 7 Asian, non-Hispanic/Latino; 5 Hispanic/Latino), 5 international. 107 applicants, 67% accepted, 17 enrolled. In 2017, 9 master's, 8 doctorates awarded. *Degree requirements:* For doctorate, 2 foreign languages, thesis/dissertation. *Entrance requirements:* For master's and doctorate, GRE General Test, minimum GPA of 3.0; 3 letters of recommendation. Additional exam requirements/recommendations for international students: Required—TOEFL (minimum score 620 paper-based; 105 iBT). *Application deadline:* For fall admission, 12/15 for domestic and international students. Application fee: $60. Electronic applications accepted. *Expenses:* Tuition, state resident: full-time $16,164; part-time $898 per credit hour. Tuition, nonresident: full-time $22,158; part-time $1231 per credit hour. *Required fees:* $890; $445 per semester. Full-time tuition and fees vary according to course load, degree level, campus/location and program. *Financial support:* Fellowships, teaching assistantships, and Federal Work-Study available. Financial award application deadline: 1/15; financial award applicants required to submit FAFSA. *Faculty research:* Early modern British literature, American literature, modernism, critical theory, rhetoric, composition. *Unit head:* Don Lee, MFA Program Director, 215-204-1796, Fax: 215-204-9620, E-mail: don.lee@temple.edu. *Application contact:* Sharon Logan, Coordinator, 215-204-1796, Fax: 215-204-9620, E-mail: logansd@temple.edu.
Website: http://www.cla.temple.edu/english/

Texas A&M University–Commerce, College of Humanities, Social Sciences and Arts, Commerce, TX 75429. Offers applied criminology (MS); applied linguistics (MA, MS); art (MA, MFA); computational linguistics (Graduate Certificate); creative writing (Graduate Certificate); criminal justice management (Graduate Certificate); criminal justice studies (Graduate Certificate); English (MA, MS, PhD); film studies (Graduate Certificate); history (MA, MS); history of Christianity (Graduate Certificate); Holocaust studies (Graduate Certificate); homeland security (Graduate Certificate); music education (MM); music performance (MM); political science (MA, MS); public history (Graduate Certificate); sociology (MS); Spanish (MA); studies in children's and adolescent literature and culture (Graduate Certificate); teaching English to speakers of other languages (Graduate Certificate); theater (MA, MS); world history (Graduate Certificate). *Program availability:* Part-time. *Faculty:* 56 full-time (26 women), 10 part-time/adjunct (5 women). *Students:* 133 full-time (85 women), 439 part-time (311 women); includes 204 minority (79 Black or African American, non-Hispanic/Latino; 4 American Indian or Alaska Native, non-Hispanic/Latino; 9 Asian, non-Hispanic/Latino; 98 Hispanic/Latino; 14 Two or more races, non-Hispanic/Latino), 26 international. Average age 36. 261 applicants, 50% accepted, 113 enrolled. In 2017, 105 master's, 5 doctorates awarded. *Degree requirements:* For master's, one foreign language, comprehensive exam, thesis (for some programs); for doctorate, one foreign language, comprehensive exam, thesis/dissertation, departmental qualifying exam. *Entrance requirements:* For master's and doctorate, GRE General Test. Additional exam requirements/recommendations for international students: Required—TOEFL (minimum score 550 paper-based; 79 iBT), IELTS (minimum score 6). *Application deadline:* Applications are processed on a rolling basis. Application fee: $50. Electronic applications accepted. *Expenses:* Contact institution. *Financial support:* In 2017–18, 43 students received support, including 9 research assistantships with partial tuition reimbursements available (averaging $9,000 per year), 68 teaching assistantships with partial tuition reimbursements available (averaging $9,000 per year); Federal Work-Study, institutionally sponsored loans, scholarships/grants, health care benefits, and unspecified assistantships also available. Financial award application deadline: 5/1; financial award applicants required to submit FAFSA. *Unit head:* Dr. William F. Kuracina, Interim Dean, 903-886-5166, Fax: 903-886-5774, E-mail: william.kuracina@tamuc.edu. *Application contact:* Vicky Turner, Doctoral Degree and Special Programs Coordinator, 903-886-5167, E-mail: vicky.turner@tamuc.edu.
Website: http://www.tamuc.edu/academics/graduateSchool/programs/humanitiesSocialScienceArts/default.aspx

Texas State University, The Graduate College, College of Fine Arts and Communication, Program in Theatre Arts, San Marcos, TX 78666. Offers design (MFA); directing (MFA); dramatic writing (MFA); theatre history, dramatic criticism and dramaturgy (MA). *Program availability:* Part-time, evening/weekend. *Faculty:* 20 full-time (10 women), 5 part-time/adjunct (3 women). *Students:* 27 full-time (12 women), 1 (woman) part-time; includes 5 minority (2 Black or African American, non-Hispanic/Latino; 2 Hispanic/Latino; 1 Two or more races, non-Hispanic/Latino). Average age 31. 35 applicants, 40% accepted, 12 enrolled. In 2017, 3 master's awarded. *Degree requirements:* For master's, comprehensive exam, thesis (for some programs). *Entrance requirements:* For master's, GRE General Test with minimum preferred score of 300 verbal and quantitative combined (for MA), baccalaureate degree from regionally-accredited institution with minimum GPA of 2.75 in last 60 hours of undergraduate course work, 2 letters of recommendation, statement of purpose, curriculum vitae/resume; writing sample (for playwriting applicants only); interview (for directing applicants only). Additional exam requirements/recommendations for international students: Required—TOEFL (minimum score 550 paper-based; 78 iBT), IELTS (minimum score 6). *Application deadline:* For fall admission, 3/15 for domestic and international students. Applications are processed on a rolling basis. Application fee: $40 ($90 for international students). Electronic applications accepted. *Expenses:* Tuition, state resident: full-time $7868; part-time $3934 per semester. Tuition, nonresident: full-time $17,828; part-time $8914 per semester. *Required fees:* $2092; $1435 per semester. Tuition and fees vary according to course load. *Financial support:* In 2017–18, 25 teaching assistantships (averaging $12,453 per year) were awarded; research assistantships, Federal Work-Study, institutionally sponsored loans, scholarships/grants, and unspecified assistantships also available. Support available to part-time students. Financial award application deadline: 3/1; financial award applicants required to submit FAFSA. *Faculty research:* Black and Latino playwright conference, creation in motion. *Total annual research expenditures:* $2,900. *Unit head:* Dr. Sandra Mayo, Graduate Advisor, 512-245-7889, Fax: 512-245-8440, E-mail: th_gradadvisor@txstate.edu. *Application contact:* Dr. Andrea Golato, Dean of Graduate School, 512-245-2581, Fax: 512-245-8365, E-mail: gradcollege@txstate.edu.
Website: http://www.theatreanddance.txstate.edu/

Texas State University, The Graduate College, College of Liberal Arts, Program in Creative Writing, San Marcos, TX 78666. Offers MFA. *Program availability:* Part-time, evening/weekend. *Faculty:* 11 full-time (4 women). *Students:* 55 full-time (32 women), 11 part-time (4 women); includes 14 minority (1 Black or African American, non-Hispanic/Latino; 2 Asian, non-Hispanic/Latino; 9 Hispanic/Latino; 2 Two or more races, non-Hispanic/Latino), 1 international. Average age 29. 98 applicants, 63% accepted, 31 enrolled. In 2017, 21 master's awarded. *Degree requirements:* For master's, comprehensive exam, thesis. *Entrance requirements:* For master's, baccalaureate degree from regionally-accredited university with minimum GPA of 2.75 on last 60 undergraduate semester hours, portfolio; 2-3 short stories or up to 30 pages of novel (for fiction); 12 to 15 poems (for poetry). Additional exam requirements/recommendations for international students: Required—TOEFL (minimum score 550 paper-based; 78 iBT), IELTS (minimum score 6.5). *Application deadline:* For fall admission, 1/15 for domestic and international students; for spring admission, 11/1 for domestic students, 10/1 for international students. Applications are processed on a rolling basis. Application fee: $40 ($90 for international students). Electronic applications accepted. *Expenses:* Tuition, state resident: full-time $7868; part-time $3934 per semester. Tuition, nonresident: full-time $17,828; part-time $8914 per semester. *Required fees:* $2092; $1435 per semester. Tuition and fees vary according to course load. *Financial support:* In 2017–18, 46 students received support, including 2 research assistantships (averaging $15,457 per year), 30 teaching assistantships (averaging $14,656 per year); Federal Work-Study, institutionally sponsored loans, and scholarships/grants also available. Support available to part-time students. Financial award application deadline: 3/1; financial award applicants required to submit FAFSA. *Unit head:* Doug Dorst, Graduate Adviser, 512-245-7681, Fax: 512-245-8546, E-mail: dd35@txstate.edu. *Application contact:* Dr. Andrea Golato, Dean of Graduate School, 512-245-2581, Fax: 512-245-8365, E-mail: gradcollege@txstate.edu.
Website: http://www.english.txstate.edu/mfa/

Tiffin University, Program in Humanities, Tiffin, OH 44883-2161. Offers art and visual media (MH); communication (MH); creative writing (MH); English (MH); film studies (MH); humanities (MH); individualized studies (MH). *Program availability:* Part-time, evening/weekend, online only, 100% online, blended/hybrid learning. *Entrance requirements:* For master's, work experience. Additional exam requirements/recommendations for international students: Required—TOEFL (minimum score 550 paper-based; 79 iBT). Electronic applications accepted. Application fee is waived when completed online. *Expenses:* Contact institution.

Towson University, College of Liberal Arts, Program in Professional Writing, Towson, MD 21252-0001. Offers MS. *Program availability:* Part-time, evening/weekend. *Students:* 10 full-time (7 women), 35 part-time (24 women); includes 11 minority (7 Black or African American, non-Hispanic/Latino; 1 American Indian or Alaska Native, non-Hispanic/Latino; 1 Asian, non-Hispanic/Latino; 1 Hispanic/Latino; 1 Two or more races, non-Hispanic/Latino). *Degree requirements:* For master's, thesis optional. *Entrance requirements:* For master's, sample of written work, minimum GPA of 3.0, 2 letters of recommendation, essay. *Application deadline:* For fall admission, 1/17 for domestic students, 5/15 for international students; for spring admission, 10/15 for domestic students, 12/1 for international students. Applications are processed on a rolling basis. Application fee: $45. Electronic applications accepted. *Expenses:* Tuition, state resident: full-time $7960; part-time $398 per unit. Tuition, nonresident: full-time $16,480; part-time $824 per unit. *Required fees:* $2600; $130 per year. $390 per term. *Financial support:* Application deadline: 4/1. *Unit head:* Prof. Goeffrey Becker, Graduate Program Director, 410-704-5196, E-mail: gbecker@towson.edu. *Application contact:* Coverley

Beidleman, Assistant Director of Graduate Admissions, 410-704-2113, Fax: 410-704-3030, E-mail: grads@towson.edu.
Website: http://www.towson.edu/cla/departments/english/gradwriting/

Trinity College, Graduate Programs, Program in English, Hartford, CT 06106-3100. Offers literary studies (MA); writing, rhetoric, and media arts (MA). *Program availability:* Part-time, evening/weekend. *Degree requirements:* For master's, thesis (for some programs). *Entrance requirements:* For master's, minimum GPA of 3.0.

Union Institute & University, Master of Arts Program, Cincinnati, OH 45206-1925. Offers creativity studies (MA); health and wellness (MA); history and culture (MA); leadership, public policy, and social issues (MA); literature and writing (MA). *Program availability:* Part-time, online only, 100% online. *Students:* 9 full-time (7 women), 70 part-time (56 women); includes 33 minority (22 Black or African American, non-Hispanic/Latino; 1 American Indian or Alaska Native, non-Hispanic/Latino; 6 Hispanic/Latino; 4 Two or more races, non-Hispanic/Latino). Average age 40. *Degree requirements:* For master's, thesis. *Entrance requirements:* For master's, transcript, essay, 3 letters of recommendation, resume. Additional exam requirements/recommendations for international students: Recommended—TOEFL. *Application deadline:* For spring admission, 3/13 for domestic students. Applications are processed on a rolling basis. Application fee: $50. Electronic applications accepted. *Expenses:* Contact institution. *Financial support:* Career-related internships or fieldwork and tuition waivers available. Financial award applicants required to submit FAFSA. *Unit head:* Elden Golden, Director, 513-487-1153, E-mail: elden.golden@myunion.edu. *Application contact:* Director of Admissions, 800-861-6400.

The University of Akron, Graduate School, Buchtel College of Arts and Sciences, Department of English, Northeast Ohio MFA Program in Creative Writing, Akron, OH 44325. Offers MFA. Program offered jointly with Cleveland State University, Kent State University, and Youngstown State University. *Entrance requirements:* For master's, three letters of recommendation; writing portfolio. Additional exam requirements/recommendations for international students: Required—TOEFL (minimum score 92 iBT). *Financial support:* Unspecified assistantships available. *Unit head:* David Giffels, Campus Coordinator, 330-972-6604, E-mail: dg36@uakron.edu.
Website: http://www.uakron.edu/english/academics/graduate/neomfa.dot

The University of Akron, Graduate School, Buchtel College of Arts and Sciences, Department of English, Program in Composition, Akron, OH 44325. Offers MA. *Students:* 18 full-time (11 women), 12 part-time (9 women); includes 2 minority (1 Black or African American, non-Hispanic/Latino; 1 Asian, non-Hispanic/Latino), 3 international. Average age 33. 11 applicants, 100% accepted, 6 enrolled. In 2017, 16 master's awarded. *Degree requirements:* For master's, one foreign language, thesis optional. *Entrance requirements:* For master's, statement of purpose. Additional exam requirements/recommendations for international students: Required—TOEFL (minimum score 92 iBT). *Application deadline:* For fall admission, 8/28 for domestic students. Applications are processed on a rolling basis. Application fee: $25 ($50 for international students). *Financial support:* Application deadline: 3/1. *Unit head:* Dr. Sheldon Wrice, Interim Chair, 330-972-6023, E-mail: swrice1@uakron.edu. *Application contact:* David Giffels, Director of Graduate Studies, 330-972-6604, E-mail: dg36@uakron.edu.

The University of Alabama, Graduate School, College of Arts and Sciences, Department of English, Tuscaloosa, AL 35487. Offers composition and rhetoric (PhD); creative writing (MFA), including fiction, poetry; literature (MA, PhD); rhetoric and composition (MA); teaching English as a second language (MATESOL). *Faculty:* 37 full-time (21 women). *Students:* 123 full-time (71 women), 11 part-time (8 women); includes 22 minority (10 Black or African American, non-Hispanic/Latino; 1 Asian, non-Hispanic/Latino; 6 Hispanic/Latino; 5 Two or more races, non-Hispanic/Latino), 2 international. Average age 29. 378 applicants, 17% accepted, 44 enrolled. In 2017, 32 master's, 7 doctorates awarded. *Degree requirements:* For master's, one foreign language, comprehensive exam, thesis; for doctorate, 2 foreign languages, comprehensive exam, thesis/dissertation. *Entrance requirements:* For master's, GRE (minimum score of 300, except for MFA), minimum GPA of 3.0, critical writing sample; for doctorate, GRE (minimum score of 300), minimum GPA of 3.5 on master's or equivalent graduate work, critical writing sample. Additional exam requirements/recommendations for international students: Recommended—TOEFL (minimum score 550 paper-based; 79 iBT). *Application deadline:* For fall admission, 12/20 for domestic and international students. Application fee: $50 ($60 for international students). Electronic applications accepted. *Financial support:* In 2017–18, 113 students received support, including fellowships with full tuition reimbursements available (averaging $15,000 per year), research assistantships with full tuition reimbursements available (averaging $13,500 per year), teaching assistantships with full tuition reimbursements available (averaging $13,500 per year); career-related internships or fieldwork, scholarships/grants, health care benefits, and unspecified assistantships also available. Financial award application deadline: 12/20. *Faculty research:* American literature, British literature, composition/rhetoric, applied linguistics, creative writing. *Unit head:* Prof. Joel Brouwer, Department Chair, 205-348-5065, Fax: 205-348-1388, E-mail: joel.brouwer@ua.edu. *Application contact:* Jennifer Fuqua, Graduate Coordinator, 205-348-0766, Fax: 205-348-1388, E-mail: jfuqua@ua.edu.

The University of Alabama at Birmingham, College of Arts and Sciences, Program in English, Birmingham, AL 35294. Offers creative writing (MA); literature (MA); rhetoric and composition (MA). *Program availability:* Part-time. *Degree requirements:* For master's, one foreign language, comprehensive exam, thesis or alternative. *Entrance requirements:* For master's, GRE General Test or MAT, minimum GPA of 2.75. Electronic applications accepted.

University of Alaska Anchorage, College of Arts and Sciences, Program in Creative Writing and Literary Arts, Anchorage, AK 99508. Offers MFA. *Program availability:* Part-time. *Degree requirements:* For master's, comprehensive exam, thesis or alternative. *Entrance requirements:* For master's, portfolio, minimum GPA of 3.0. Additional exam requirements/recommendations for international students: Required—TOEFL (minimum score 550 paper-based). *Faculty research:* Alaska Quarterly Review publications, feminist studies, ecocriticism and native writing, poetry.

University of Alaska Fairbanks, College of Liberal Arts, Department of English, Fairbanks, AK 99775-5720. Offers creative writing (MFA); literature (MA); MA/MFA. *Program availability:* Part-time. *Degree requirements:* For master's, comprehensive exam, oral defense of project or thesis. *Entrance requirements:* For master's, GRE General Test, bachelor's degree from accredited institution with minimum cumulative undergraduate and major GPA of 3.0, academic writing sample. Additional exam requirements/recommendations for international students: Required—TOEFL (minimum score 550 paper-based; 79 iBT), IELTS (minimum score 6.5). Electronic applications accepted.

The University of Arizona, College of Humanities, Department of English, Program in Creative Writing, Tucson, AZ 85721. Offers MFA. *Entrance requirements:* Additional exam requirements/recommendations for international students: Required—TOEFL (minimum score 550 paper-based; 79 iBT). Electronic applications accepted.

University of Arkansas, Graduate School, J. William Fulbright College of Arts and Sciences, Department of English, Program in Creative Writing, Fayetteville, AR 72701. Offers MFA. In 2017, 8 master's awarded. *Degree requirements:* For master's, thesis. *Application deadline:* For fall admission, 8/1 for domestic students, 4/1 for international students; for spring admission, 12/1 for domestic students, 10/1 for international students; for summer admission, 4/15 for domestic students, 3/1 for international students. Applications are processed on a rolling basis. Application fee: $60. Electronic applications accepted. *Expenses:* Tuition, state resident: full-time $3782. Tuition, nonresident: full-time $10,238. *Financial support:* In 2017–18, 1 research assistantship, 29 teaching assistantships were awarded; fellowships with tuition reimbursements, career-related internships or fieldwork, and Federal Work-Study also available. Support available to part-time students. Financial award application deadline: 4/1; financial award applicants required to submit FAFSA. *Unit head:* Dr. Davis McCombs, Program Director, 479-575-4301, Fax: 479-575-5919, E-mail: dmccomb@uark.edu.
Website: https://fulbright.uark.edu/departments/english/

University of Arkansas at Little Rock, Graduate School, College of Social Sciences and Communication, Department of Rhetoric and Writing, Little Rock, AR 72204-1099. Offers professional and technical writing (MA). *Program availability:* Part-time, evening/weekend. *Degree requirements:* For master's, thesis or alternative, oral defense of final project. *Entrance requirements:* For master's, GRE, minimum GPA of 3.0, writing portfolio. *Faculty research:* Writing for industry, science, business, and government; composition and rhetorical theory; writing nonfiction; teaching of writing.

University of Baltimore, Graduate School, Yale Gordon College of Arts and Sciences, Program in Creative Writing and Publishing Arts, Baltimore, MD 21201-5779. Offers MFA. *Program availability:* Part-time, evening/weekend. *Entrance requirements:* Additional exam requirements/recommendations for international students: Required—TOEFL.

University of Baltimore, Graduate School, Yale Gordon College of Arts and Sciences, Program in Publications Design, Baltimore, MD 21201-5779. Offers MA. *Program availability:* Part-time, evening/weekend. *Degree requirements:* For master's, seminar project. *Entrance requirements:* For master's, minimum GPA of 3.0, portfolio, interview. Additional exam requirements/recommendations for international students: Required—TOEFL (minimum score 550 paper-based). Electronic applications accepted. *Faculty research:* Communication theory, graphic design, media technology.

The University of British Columbia, Faculty of Arts, Creative Writing Program, Vancouver, BC V6T 1Z1, Canada. Offers creative writing (MFA); creative writing and theatre (MFA); film production and creative writing (MFA). *Program availability:* Part-time, online learning. *Degree requirements:* For master's, thesis. *Entrance requirements:* For master's, sample of written work. Additional exam requirements/recommendations for international students: Required—TOEFL. Electronic applications accepted. *Expenses:* Contact institution. *Faculty research:* Writing of fiction; poetry, creative nonfiction, plays for stage, screen, television, radio, writing for children and translation, song lyrics and libretto, new media and graphic novel.

The University of British Columbia, Faculty of Arts and Faculty of Graduate Studies, Department of Theatre and Film, Vancouver, BC V6T 1Z2, Canada. Offers film (MA, MFA), including creative writing and film production (MFA), film production (MFA), film studies (MA); theatre (MA, MFA, PhD), including theatre (MA, PhD), theatre design (MFA), theatre directing (MFA). Terminal master's awarded for partial completion of doctoral program. *Degree requirements:* For master's, variable foreign language requirement, comprehensive exam, thesis; for doctorate, one foreign language, comprehensive exam, thesis/dissertation. *Entrance requirements:* For master's, BA or equivalent; portfolio (for MFA). Additional exam requirements/recommendations for international students: Required—TOEFL. *Expenses:* Contact institution. *Faculty research:* Dramatic literature, theatrical history, criticism, playwriting, directing, film studies and production, film theory and violence, American and European cinema, cult cinema, Irish cinema.

University of California, Berkeley, UC Berkeley Extension, Certificate Programs in Writing, Editing and Technical Communication, Berkeley, CA 94720-1500. Offers writing (Postbaccalaureate Certificate). *Program availability:* Online learning.

University of California, Davis, Graduate Studies, Program in English, Davis, CA 95616. Offers creative writing (MA); English (MA, PhD). Terminal master's awarded for partial completion of doctoral program. *Degree requirements:* For master's, one foreign language, thesis optional; for doctorate, 2 foreign languages, thesis/dissertation. *Entrance requirements:* For master's and doctorate, GRE General Test, GRE Subject Test, minimum GPA of 3.0, writing sample. Additional exam requirements/recommendations for international students: Required—TOEFL (minimum score 550 paper-based). Electronic applications accepted. *Faculty research:* Feminist theory, ethnic literature, literary theory, history of literature, literature of nature.

University of California, Irvine, School of Humanities, Department of English, Program in Writing, Irvine, CA 92697. Offers creative writing (MFA), including fiction, poetry. *Students:* 33 full-time (17 women); includes 6 minority (3 Asian, non-Hispanic/Latino; 3 Two or more races, non-Hispanic/Latino). Average age 29. 396 applicants, 3% accepted, 11 enrolled. In 2017, 11 master's awarded. *Entrance requirements:* For master's, minimum GPA of 3.0, sample of written work. *Application deadline:* For fall admission, 1/15 for domestic and international students. Application fee: $105 ($125 for international students). Electronic applications accepted. *Financial support:* Fellowships with tuition reimbursements, research assistantships, teaching assistantships with partial tuition reimbursements, institutionally sponsored loans, and tuition waivers (full and partial) available. Financial award application deadline: 3/1; financial award applicants required to submit FAFSA. *Unit head:* Michael Ryan, Director, 949-824-8773, Fax: 949-824-2916, E-mail: mryan@uci.edu. *Application contact:* Sandy Mueller, Graduate Administrator, 949-824-6718, Fax: 949-824-2916, E-mail: slmuelle@uci.edu.

University of California, Riverside, Graduate Division, Program in Creative Writing and Writing for the Performing Arts, Riverside, CA 92211. Offers MFA. Program also offered at Palm Desert Graduate Center. *Degree requirements:* For master's, thesis. *Entrance requirements:* For master's, writing sample. Additional exam requirements/recommendations for international students: Required—TOEFL (minimum score 550 paper-based; 80 iBT). Electronic applications accepted. *Expenses:* Tuition, state resident: full-time $5746. Tuition, nonresident: full-time $10,780. Tuition and fees vary according to campus/location and program. *Faculty research:* Non-fiction, playwriting, screenwriting, poetry, fiction.

University of California, San Diego, Graduate Division, Department of Literature, La Jolla, CA 92093. Offers literature (PhD); writing (MFA). *Students:* 73 full-time (50 women), 2 part-time (both women). 195 applicants, 28% accepted, 22 enrolled. In 2017, 10 master's, 9 doctorates awarded. *Degree requirements:* For master's, thesis; for doctorate, one foreign language, comprehensive exam, thesis/dissertation, 3 quarters of teaching assistantship. *Entrance requirements:* For master's, writing sample; for doctorate, GRE General Test, writing sample. Additional exam requirements/recommendations for international students: Required—TOEFL (minimum score 550 paper-based; 80 iBT), IELTS (minimum score 7); Recommended—TSE. *Application deadline:* For fall admission, 12/15 for domestic students. Application fee: $105 ($125 for international students). Electronic applications accepted. *Financial support:* Fellowships, research assistantships, teaching assistantships, scholarships/grants, and readerships available. Financial award applicants required to submit FAFSA. *Faculty research:* Chicano/a-Latino/a studies, European studies, film studies and visual culture,

Latin American literary and cultural studies, medieval/early modern studies, transnational Africa/African diaspora studies, transnational Asia/Asian diaspora studies. *Unit head:* Yingjin Zhang, Chair, 858-534-5991, E-mail: litchair@ucsd.edu. *Application contact:* Graduate Coordinator, 858-534-3217, E-mail: litgrad@ucsd.edu.
Website: http://literature.ucsd.edu

University of California, Santa Barbara, Graduate Division, College of Letters and Sciences, Division of Humanities and Fine Arts, Department of English, Santa Barbara, CA 93106-3170. Offers English (PhD), including environment and society, European medieval studies, feminist studies, global studies, technology and society, translation studies, writing studies; MA/PhD. Terminal master's awarded for partial completion of doctoral program. *Degree requirements:* For doctorate, one foreign language, comprehensive exam, thesis/dissertation. *Entrance requirements:* For doctorate, GRE General Test, GRE Subject Test (English literature). Additional exam requirements/recommendations for international students: Required—TOEFL (minimum score 550 paper-based; 80 iBT), IELTS (minimum score 7). Electronic applications accepted. *Faculty research:* Medieval, Romantic and Victorian studies; gender studies and feminist theory; literature and the mind; American literature; literature and new media/information culture.

University of California, Santa Cruz, Division of Graduate Studies, Division of Social Sciences, Program in Social Documentation, Santa Cruz, CA 95064. Offers MA. *Entrance requirements:* For master's, resume or curriculum vitae, sample of documentary production work. Additional exam requirements/recommendations for international students: Required—TOEFL (minimum score 550 paper-based; 83 iBT); Recommended—IELTS (minimum score 8). Electronic applications accepted. *Faculty research:* Documentation of underrepresented areas of community life.

University of Central Arkansas, Graduate School, College of Fine Arts and Communication, Program in Creative Writing, Conway, AR 72035-0001. Offers MFA. *Degree requirements:* For master's, thesis project. *Entrance requirements:* For master's, GRE. Electronic applications accepted.

University of Central Florida, College of Arts and Humanities, Department of English, Orlando, FL 32816. Offers creative writing (MFA); English (MA, Certificate); texts and technology (PhD). *Program availability:* Part-time, evening/weekend. *Students:* 72 full-time (53 women), 87 part-time (62 women); includes 36 minority (2 Black or African American, non-Hispanic/Latino; 3 Asian, non-Hispanic/Latino; 27 Hispanic/Latino; 4 Two or more races, non-Hispanic/Latino), 5 international. Average age 33. 117 applicants, 65% accepted, 53 enrolled. In 2017, 37 master's, 6 doctorates, 5 other advanced degrees awarded. *Degree requirements:* For master's, one foreign language, thesis or alternative; for doctorate, thesis/dissertation. *Entrance requirements:* For master's, GRE General Test, letters of recommendation, goal statement. Additional exam requirements/recommendations for international students: Required—TOEFL. *Application deadline:* For fall admission, 3/30 for domestic students; for spring admission, 11/1 for domestic students. Application fee: $30. Electronic applications accepted. *Expenses:* Tuition, state resident: part-time $288.16 per credit hour. Tuition, nonresident: part-time $1073.31 per credit hour. Tuition and fees vary according to program. *Financial support:* In 2017–18, 56 students received support, including 18 fellowships with partial tuition reimbursements available (averaging $6,500 per year), 18 research assistantships with partial tuition reimbursements available (averaging $8,328 per year), 35 teaching assistantships with partial tuition reimbursements available (averaging $10,144 per year); career-related internships or fieldwork, Federal Work-Study, institutionally sponsored loans, tuition waivers (partial), and unspecified assistantships also available. Financial award application deadline: 3/1; financial award applicants required to submit FAFSA. *Unit head:* Dr. Trey Philpotts, Chair, 407-823-1159, E-mail: trey.philpotts@ucf.edu. *Application contact:* Associate Director, Graduate Admissions, 407-823-2766, Fax: 407-823-6442, E-mail: gradadmissions@ucf.edu.
Website: http://www.english.cah.ucf.edu/

University of Central Oklahoma, The Jackson College of Graduate Studies, College of Liberal Arts, Department of English, Edmond, OK 73034-5209. Offers composition and rhetoric (MA); creative writing (MA); literature (MA); teaching English as a second language (MA). *Program availability:* Part-time. *Faculty:* 21 full-time (14 women). *Students:* 30 full-time (17 women), 45 part-time (23 women); includes 17 minority (3 Black or African American, non-Hispanic/Latino; 3 American Indian or Alaska Native, non-Hispanic/Latino; 2 Asian, non-Hispanic/Latino; 3 Hispanic/Latino; 2 Native Hawaiian or other Pacific Islander, non-Hispanic/Latino; 4 Two or more races, non-Hispanic/Latino), 13 international. Average age 32. 34 applicants, 76% accepted, 18 enrolled. In 2017, 30 master's awarded. *Degree requirements:* For master's, variable foreign language requirement, comprehensive exam (for some programs), thesis (for some programs), portfolio. *Entrance requirements:* For master's, 18-24 hours of course work in English language and literature; writing sample; essay. Additional exam requirements/recommendations for international students: Required—TOEFL (minimum score 550 paper-based; 79 iBT), IELTS (minimum score 6.5). *Application deadline:* For fall admission, 7/15 for international students; for spring admission, 11/15 for international students. Applications are processed on a rolling basis. Application fee: $60. Electronic applications accepted. *Expenses:* Tuition, state resident: full-time $5375; part-time $268.75 per credit hour. Tuition, nonresident: full-time $13,295; part-time $664.75 per credit hour. *Required fees:* $626; $31.30 per credit hour. One-time fee: $50. Tuition and fees vary according to program. *Financial support:* In 2017–18, 22 students received support, including 4 research assistantships with partial tuition reimbursements available (averaging $11,830 per year), 8 teaching assistantships with partial tuition reimbursements available (averaging $11,830 per year); career-related internships or fieldwork, Federal Work-Study, scholarships/grants, tuition waivers (partial), and unspecified assistantships also available. Financial award application deadline: 3/31; financial award applicants required to submit FAFSA. *Unit head:* Dr. Matt Hollrah, Chairperson, 405-974-5540, Fax: 405-974-3823, E-mail: gradcoll@uco.edu.
Website: http://www.uco.edu/la/english/

University of Chicago, Division of the Humanities, Master of Arts Program in the Humanities, Chicago, IL 60637. Offers art history (MA); cinema and media studies (MA); classic languages (MA); comparative literature (MA); creative writing (MA); cultural policy studies (MA); digital humanities (MA); East Asian languages and civilizations (MA); English language and literature (MA); gender and sexuality studies (MA); Germanic studies (MA); linguistics (MA); music (MA); near Eastern languages and civilizations (MA); philosophy (MA); poetics (MA); race, politics and culture (MA); Romance languages and literatures (MA); Slavic languages and literatures (MA); South Asian languages and civilizations (MA); theater and performance studies (MA). *Students:* 95 full-time (50 women), 6 part-time (4 women); includes 22 minority (1 Black or African American, non-Hispanic/Latino; 10 Asian, non-Hispanic/Latino; 11 Hispanic/Latino), 19 international. Average age 26. 708 applicants, 75% accepted, 101 enrolled. In 2017, 91 master's awarded. *Degree requirements:* For master's, thesis. *Entrance requirements:* For master's, GRE General Test, 10-15 page writing sample, statement of purpose, 3 letters of recommendation, transcripts for all previous degrees and institutions attended. Additional exam requirements/recommendations for international students: Required—TOEFL (minimum score 104 iBT), IELTS (minimum score 7). *Application deadline:* For fall admission, 1/3 priority date for domestic and international students. Application fee: $90. Electronic applications accepted. *Expenses:* Contact institution. *Financial support:* In 2017–18, fellowships with partial tuition reimbursements (averaging $12,000 per year) were awarded; Federal Work-Study, institutionally sponsored loans, scholarships/grants, and tuition waivers (partial) also available. Financial award application deadline: 4/30. *Unit head:* Thomas Christensen, Director, 773-834-1201, Fax: 773-834-7526, E-mail: ma-humanities@uchicago.edu. *Application contact:* Michael Beetley, Assistant Dean of Students for Admissions, 773-834-1552, E-mail: humanitiesadmissions@uchicago.edu.
Website: http://maph.uchicago.edu/

University of Colorado Boulder, Graduate School, College of Arts and Sciences, Department of English, Boulder, CO 80309. Offers literature (MA, PhD), including creative writing (MA). *Faculty:* 44 full-time (26 women). *Students:* 86 full-time (58 women), 3 part-time (1 woman); includes 20 minority (4 Black or African American, non-Hispanic/Latino; 3 American Indian or Alaska Native, non-Hispanic/Latino; 3 Asian, non-Hispanic/Latino; 9 Hispanic/Latino; 1 Two or more races, non-Hispanic/Latino), 2 international. Average age 29. 328 applicants, 28% accepted, 26 enrolled. In 2017, 26 master's, 11 doctorates awarded. Terminal master's awarded for partial completion of doctoral program. *Degree requirements:* For master's, one foreign language, comprehensive exam, thesis or alternative; for doctorate, 2 foreign languages, comprehensive exam, thesis/dissertation. *Entrance requirements:* For master's, GRE General Test, GRE Subject Test, minimum undergraduate GPA of 3.0; for doctorate, GRE General Test, GRE Subject Test. *Application deadline:* For fall admission, 1/10 for domestic students; for spring admission, 12/1 for domestic students. Application fee: $60 ($80 for international students). Electronic applications accepted. Application fee is waived when completed online. *Financial support:* In 2017–18, 195 students received support, including 36 fellowships (averaging $3,412 per year), 5 research assistantships with full and partial tuition reimbursements available (averaging $32,381 per year), 51 teaching assistantships with full and partial tuition reimbursements available (averaging $18,748 per year); institutionally sponsored loans, scholarships/grants, health care benefits, and unspecified assistantships also available. Financial award application deadline: 2/15; financial award applicants required to submit FAFSA. *Faculty research:* Literary criticism; English language/literature; literary history; fiction; fiction language/literature. *Total annual research expenditures:* $808,950. *Application contact:* E-mail: gsengl@colorado.edu.
Website: http://english.colorado.edu/

University of Colorado Denver, School of Education and Human Development, Teacher Education Programs, Denver, CO 80217. Offers elementary linguistically diverse education (MA); elementary math and science education (MA); elementary math education (MA); elementary reading and writing (MA); elementary science education (MA); secondary English education (MA); secondary linguistically diverse education (MA); secondary math education (MA); secondary reading and writing (MA); secondary science education (MA); special education (MA). *Accreditation:* NCATE. *Program availability:* Part-time, evening/weekend. *Degree requirements:* For master's, comprehensive exam. *Entrance requirements:* For master's, GRE or MAT (for those with GPA below 2.75), transcripts, resume, letters of recommendation. Additional exam requirements/recommendations for international students: Required—TOEFL (minimum score 537 paper-based; 75 iBT); Recommended—IELTS (minimum score 6.5). Electronic applications accepted. *Expenses:* Contact institution. *Faculty research:* Linguistically diverse education/ESL, elementary reading and writing, elementary teacher education, secondary teacher education, special education.

University of Dayton, Department of English, Dayton, OH 45469. Offers literary and cultural studies (MA); teaching English to speakers of other languages (TESOL) (MA); writing and rhetoric (MA). *Program availability:* Part-time. *Faculty:* 22 full-time (11 women). *Students:* 20 full-time (14 women), 1 (woman) part-time; includes 2 minority (both Black or African American, non-Hispanic/Latino), 7 international. Average age 26. 35 applicants, 34% accepted. In 2017, 9 master's awarded. *Degree requirements:* For master's, thesis optional. *Entrance requirements:* For master's, 24 undergraduate-level semester hours in literature and/or writing; minimum GPA of 3.0; transcripts; personal statement; 8-10 page writing sample; three professional letters of recommendation. Additional exam requirements/recommendations for international students: Required—TOEFL (minimum score 550 paper-based, 80 iBT) or IELTS. *Application deadline:* For fall admission, 6/15 priority date for domestic and international students; for spring admission, 12/15 priority date for domestic and international students. Applications are processed on a rolling basis. Application fee: $0 ($50 for international students). Electronic applications accepted. Tuition and fees vary according to degree level and program. *Financial support:* In 2017–18, 9 teaching assistantships with full tuition reimbursements (averaging $11,105 per year) were awarded; institutionally sponsored loans also available. Financial award application deadline: 3/1; financial award applicants required to submit FAFSA. *Faculty research:* Gender and Victorian periodicals; literature and human rights; Paul Lawrence Dunbar; the archetype of the Indian princess; Amish country. *Unit head:* Dr. Andrew Slade, Chair, 937-229-3434, Fax: 937-229-3563, E-mail: aslade1@udayton.edu. *Application contact:* Dr. Tereza Szeghi, Director of Graduate Studies, 937-229-3443, E-mail: tszeghi1@udayton.edu.
Website: https://www.udayton.edu/artssciences/academics/english/welcome/index.php

University of Denver, Division of Arts, Humanities and Social Sciences, Department of English, Denver, CO 80208. Offers creative writing (PhD); literary studies (MA, PhD). *Program availability:* Part-time. *Students:* Average age 33. 165 applicants, 13% accepted, 10 enrolled. In 2017, 3 master's, 9 doctorates awarded. *Degree requirements:* For master's, one foreign language, comprehensive exam, thesis; for doctorate, 2 foreign languages, comprehensive exam, thesis/dissertation. *Entrance requirements:* For master's, GRE General Test, GRE Subject Test (advanced literature), bachelor's degree, transcripts, academic essay, statement of intent, three letters of recommendation; for doctorate, GRE General Test, GRE Subject Test (advanced literature), master's degree, transcripts, academic essay, statement of intent, three letters of recommendation, and a writing sample (creative writing program only). Additional exam requirements/recommendations for international students: Required—TOEFL (minimum score 570 paper-based; 88 iBT). *Application deadline:* For fall admission, 1/1 priority date for domestic and international students. Applications are processed on a rolling basis. Application fee: $65. Electronic applications accepted. *Expenses:* Contact institution. *Financial support:* In 2017–18, 34 students received support, including 21 teaching assistantships with tuition reimbursements available (averaging $17,500 per year); Federal Work-Study, institutionally sponsored loans, scholarships/grants, and unspecified assistantships also available. Support available to part-time students. Financial award application deadline: 2/15; financial award applicants required to submit FAFSA. *Faculty research:* African diaspora semiotics, Susan Howe's poetics, Renaissance drama and emblematic culture, New England Colonial literature, postmodern literature. *Unit head:* Dr. Clark Davis, Professor and Chair, 303-871-2900, Fax: 303-871-2853, E-mail: cldavis@du.edu. *Application contact:* Dr. Adam Rovner, Associate Professor and Director of Graduate Studies, 303-871-2861, Fax: 303-871-2853, E-mail: adam.rovner@du.edu.
Website: http://www.du.edu/ahss/english

University of Denver, University College, Denver, CO 80208. Offers arts and culture (MA, Certificate); communication management (MS, Certificate), including translation studies (Certificate), world history and culture (Certificate); environmental policy and

management (MS); geographic information systems (MS); global affairs (MA, Certificate), including human capital in organizations (Certificate), philanthropic leadership (Certificate), project management (Certificate), strategic innovation and change (Certificate); healthcare leadership (MS); information communications and technology (MS); leadership and organizations (MS); professional creative writing (MA, Certificate), including emergency planning and response (Certificate), organizational security (Certificate); security management (MS, Certificate); strategic human resources (Certificate). *Program availability:* Part-time, evening/weekend, online learning. *Faculty:* 118 part-time/adjunct (62 women). *Students:* 56 full-time (32 women), 1,287 part-time (707 women); includes 330 minority (99 Black or African American, non-Hispanic/Latino; 7 American Indian or Alaska Native, non-Hispanic/Latino; 43 Asian, non-Hispanic/Latino; 141 Hispanic/Latino; 3 Native Hawaiian or other Pacific Islander, non-Hispanic/Latino; 37 Two or more races, non-Hispanic/Latino), 84 international. Average age 34. 783 applicants, 86% accepted, 420 enrolled. In 2017, 461 master's, 173 other advanced degrees awarded. *Degree requirements:* For master's, capstone project. *Entrance requirements:* For master's, transcripts, two letters of recommendation, personal statement, resume. Additional exam requirements/recommendations for international students: Required—TOEFL (minimum score 550 paper-based; 80 iBT). *Application deadline:* For fall admission, 6/21 priority date for domestic students, 5/1 priority date for international students; for winter admission, 9/14 priority date for domestic students, 9/19 priority date for international students; for spring admission, 1/11 priority date for domestic students, 12/12 priority date for international students; for summer admission, 3/29 priority date for domestic students, 3/6 priority date for international students. Applications are processed on a rolling basis. Application fee: $75. Electronic applications accepted. *Expenses:* $7,968 per year half-time. *Financial support:* In 2017–18, 29 students received support. Teaching assistantships available. Financial award applicants required to submit FAFSA. *Unit head:* Dr. Michael McGuire, Dean, 303-871-3518, Fax: 303-871-3303, E-mail: mmcguire@du.edu. *Application contact:* Information Contact, 303-871-2291, E-mail: ucoladm@du.edu.
Website: http://universitycollege.du.edu/

The University of Findlay, Office of Graduate Admissions, Findlay, OH 45840. Offers applied security and analytics (MSAS); athletic training (MAT); business (MBA), including certified management accountant, certified public accountant, health care management, hospitality management; education (MA Ed, Ed D), including children's literature (MA Ed), curriculum and teaching (MA Ed), education (MA Ed), educational administration (MA Ed), human resource development (MA Ed), mathematics (MA Ed), reading (MA Ed), science education (MA Ed), superintendent (Ed D), teaching (Ed D), technology (MA Ed); environmental, safety, and health management (MSEM); health informatics (MS); occupational therapy (MOT); pharmacy (Pharm D); physical therapy (DPT); physician assistant (MPA); rhetoric and writing (MA); teaching English to speakers of other languages (TESOL) and applied linguistics (MA). *Program availability:* Part-time, evening/weekend, 100% online, blended/hybrid learning. *Students:* 688 full-time (430 women), 553 part-time (308 women), 170 international. Average age 28. In 2017, 366 master's, 137 doctorates awarded. *Degree requirements:* For master's, comprehensive exam (for some programs), thesis (for some programs), cumulative project, capstone project; for doctorate, thesis/dissertation (for some programs). *Entrance requirements:* For master's, GRE/GMAT, bachelor's degree from accredited institution, minimum undergraduate GPA of 2.5 in last 64 hours of course work; for doctorate, GRE, MAT, minimum cumulative GPA of 3.0. Additional exam requirements/recommendations for international students: Required—TOEFL (minimum score 79 iBT), IELTS (minimum score 7), PTE (minimum score 61). *Application deadline:* Applications are processed on a rolling basis. Electronic applications accepted. *Financial support:* In 2017–18, 10 research assistantships with partial tuition reimbursements (averaging $7,200 per year), 35 teaching assistantships with partial tuition reimbursements (averaging $7,200 per year) were awarded; Federal Work-Study, institutionally sponsored loans, and unspecified assistantships also available. Financial award applicants required to submit FAFSA. *Unit head:* Christopher M. Harris, Director of Admissions, 419-434-4347, E-mail: harrisc1@findlay.edu. *Application contact:* Madeline Fauser Brennan, Graduate Admissions Counselor, 419-434-4636, Fax: 419-434-4898, E-mail: fauserbrennan@findlay.edu.
Website: http://www.findlay.edu/admissions/graduate/Pages/default.aspx

University of Florida, Graduate School, College of Liberal Arts and Sciences, Department of English, Gainesville, FL 32611. Offers creative writing (MFA); English (MA, PhD). *Degree requirements:* For master's, one foreign language, comprehensive exam, thesis or alternative; for doctorate, one foreign language, comprehensive exam, thesis/dissertation. *Entrance requirements:* For master's and doctorate, GRE General Test, minimum GPA of 3.0. Additional exam requirements/recommendations for international students: Required—TOEFL (minimum score 550 paper-based; 80 iBT), IELTS (minimum score 6). Electronic applications accepted. *Faculty research:* Modern global literatures in English, film and media studies, cultural studies and critical theory, American literature, English literature.

University of Houston, College of Liberal Arts and Social Sciences, Department of English, Houston, TX 77204. Offers applied English linguistics (MA); creative writing (MFA); creative writing and literature (MA, PhD); English (MA, PhD). *Degree requirements:* For master's, one foreign language, comprehensive exam (for some programs), thesis (MFA); for doctorate, 2 foreign languages, comprehensive exam, thesis/dissertation. *Entrance requirements:* For master's, GRE General Test, minimum GPA of 3.0 in last 60 hours of course work; for doctorate, GRE General Test, GRE Subject Test (literature), writing sample. Additional exam requirements/recommendations for international students: Required—TOEFL (minimum score 550 paper-based; 79 iBT). Electronic applications accepted.

University of Houston, College of Liberal Arts and Social Sciences, Department of Hispanic Studies, Houston, TX 77204. Offers Hispanic literature and linguistics (PhD); Spanish (MA, PhD), including creative writing (PhD). *Program availability:* Part-time. *Degree requirements:* For master's, comprehensive exam, thesis optional; for doctorate, 2 foreign languages, comprehensive exam, thesis/dissertation. *Entrance requirements:* For master's and doctorate, GRE. Additional exam requirements/recommendations for international students: Required—TOEFL (minimum score 550 paper-based; 79 iBT); Recommended—IELTS (minimum score 6.5). Electronic applications accepted.

University of Houston–Victoria, School of Arts and Sciences, Program in Creative Writing, Victoria, TX 77901-4450. Offers MFA. *Degree requirements:* For master's, thesis. *Entrance requirements:* For master's, GRE, two letters of recommendation, twenty- to thirty-page creative writing sample.

University of Idaho, College of Graduate Studies, College of Letters, Arts and Social Sciences, Department of English, Moscow, ID 83844. Offers creative writing (MFA); English (MA, MAT). *Faculty:* 15. *Students:* 38 full-time, 11 part-time. Average age 30. In 2017, 34 master's awarded. *Entrance requirements:* For master's, minimum GPA of 3.0. Additional exam requirements/recommendations for international students: Required—TOEFL. *Application deadline:* For fall admission, 8/1 for domestic students; for spring admission, 12/15 for domestic students. Applications are processed on a rolling basis. Application fee: $60. Electronic applications accepted. *Expenses:* Tuition, state resident: full-time $6722; part-time $430 per credit hour. Tuition, nonresident: full-time $23,046; part-time $1337 per credit hour. *Required fees:* $2142; $63 per credit hour.

Financial support: Research assistantships and teaching assistantships available. Financial award applicants required to submit FAFSA. *Unit head:* Dr. Scott Slovic, Chair, 208-885-6156, E-mail: englishdept@uidaho.edu. *Application contact:* Sean Scoggin, Graduate Recruitment Coordinator, 208-885-4723, Fax: 208-885-4406, E-mail: graduateadmissions@uidaho.edu.
Website: https://www.uidaho.edu/class/english

University of Illinois at Urbana–Champaign, Graduate College, College of Liberal Arts and Sciences, Department of English, Champaign, IL 61820. Offers creative writing (MFA); English (MA, PhD).

The University of Iowa, Graduate College, College of Liberal Arts and Sciences, Department of English, Iowa City, IA 52242-1316. Offers English (PhD); literary studies (MA); nonfiction writing (MFA). *Degree requirements:* For master's, thesis (for some programs), exam; for doctorate, comprehensive exam, thesis/dissertation. *Entrance requirements:* For master's and doctorate, GRE General Test, minimum GPA of 3.0. Additional exam requirements/recommendations for international students: Required—TOEFL (minimum score 640 paper-based; 111 iBT). Electronic applications accepted.

The University of Iowa, Graduate College, College of Liberal Arts and Sciences, Department of Spanish and Portuguese, Iowa City, IA 52242-1316. Offers Spanish (MA, PhD); Spanish creative writing (MFA). *Degree requirements:* For master's, thesis optional, exam; for doctorate, comprehensive exam, thesis/dissertation. *Entrance requirements:* For master's and doctorate, GRE General Test, minimum GPA of 3.0. Additional exam requirements/recommendations for international students: Required—TOEFL (minimum score 600 paper-based; 100 iBT). Electronic applications accepted.

The University of Kansas, Graduate Studies, College of Liberal Arts and Sciences, Department of English, Lawrence, KS 66045. Offers creative writing (MFA), including fine arts/creative writing; English (MA, PhD). *Program availability:* Part-time. *Students:* 86 full-time (49 women), 6 part-time (4 women); includes 16 minority (8 Black or African American, non-Hispanic/Latino; 1 Asian, non-Hispanic/Latino; 4 Hispanic/Latino; 3 Two or more races, non-Hispanic/Latino), 8 international. Average age 30. 165 applicants, 20% accepted, 16 enrolled. In 2017, 9 master's, 9 doctorates awarded. *Entrance requirements:* For master's and doctorate, GRE General Test, two examples of academic writing; resume; statement of approximately 500 words describing interests, training, experience (including teaching experience), academic ability, and goals; three letters of recommendation; official transcripts. Additional exam requirements/recommendations for international students: Required—TOEFL or IELTS. *Application deadline:* For fall admission, 12/31 for domestic and international students. Application fee: $65 ($85 for international students). Electronic applications accepted. *Financial support:* Fellowships, research assistantships, teaching assistantships, and unspecified assistantships available. *Faculty research:* Ecocriticism and science/science fiction writing; gender and sexuality studies; U.S. ethnic literatures, race, and diaspora studies; composition, rhetoric, and language studies; creative writing. *Unit head:* Anna Neill, Chair, 785-864-2521, E-mail: aneill@ku.edu. *Application contact:* Lydia Ash, Graduate Secretary, 785-864-2518, E-mail: lash@ku.edu.
Website: http://www.english.ku.edu

University of King's College, Graduate and Advanced Programs, Halifax, NS B3H 2A1, Canada. Offers creative nonfiction (MFA); journalism (MJ).

University of Louisiana at Lafayette, College of Liberal Arts, Department of English, Lafayette, LA 70504. Offers British and American literature (MA), including creative writing, folklore, rhetoric; creative writing (PhD); literature (PhD); rhetoric (PhD). *Program availability:* Part-time. Terminal master's awarded for partial completion of doctoral program. *Degree requirements:* For master's, one foreign language, thesis or alternative; for doctorate, 2 foreign languages, comprehensive exam, thesis/dissertation. *Entrance requirements:* For master's, GRE General Test, minimum GPA of 2.75; for doctorate, GRE General Test, minimum GPA of 3.0. Additional exam requirements/recommendations for international students: Required—TOEFL (minimum score 550 paper-based). Electronic applications accepted. *Faculty research:* Composition theory, Southern literature, medieval literature.

University of Louisville, Graduate School, College of Arts and Sciences, Department of English, Louisville, KY 40292. Offers English (MA), including creative writing, literature, rhetoric and composition (MA, PhD); rhetoric and composition (PhD), including rhetoric and composition (MA, PhD). *Program availability:* Part-time, evening/weekend. *Faculty:* 37 full-time (20 women), 3 part-time/adjunct (2 women). *Students:* 43 full-time (24 women), 12 part-time (9 women); includes 5 minority (2 Black or African American, non-Hispanic/Latino; 1 Asian, non-Hispanic/Latino; 1 Hispanic/Latino; 1 Two or more races, non-Hispanic/Latino). Average age 31. 47 applicants, 66% accepted, 15 enrolled. In 2017, 12 master's, 6 doctorates awarded. *Degree requirements:* For master's, one foreign language, thesis optional, culminating project of 25-30 pages; for doctorate, one foreign language, comprehensive exam, thesis/dissertation. *Entrance requirements:* For master's and doctorate, GRE General Test. Additional exam requirements/recommendations for international students: Required—TOEFL (minimum score 600 paper-based) or IELTS (6.5). *Application deadline:* Applications are processed on a rolling basis. Application fee: $65. Electronic applications accepted. *Expenses:* Contact institution. *Financial support:* In 2017–18, 3 fellowships with full tuition reimbursements (averaging $20,000 per year), 2 research assistantships (averaging $17,750 per year), 34 teaching assistantships with full tuition reimbursements (averaging $17,750 per year) were awarded; health care benefits and unspecified assistantships also available. Financial award application deadline: 1/5. *Faculty research:* Rhetoric and composition, creative writing, Eighteenth- and Nineteenth-Century British literature, Nineteenth-Century American literature, critical theory. *Total annual research expenditures:* $124,449. *Unit head:* Dr. Glynis Ridley, Chair, 502-852-6803, E-mail: glynis.ridley@louisville.edu. *Application contact:* Annelise Gray, Senior Program Assistant, 502-852-0505, E-mail: annelise.gray@louisville.edu.
Website: http://www.louisville.edu/english/graduate

The University of Manchester, School of Arts, Histories and Cultures, Manchester, United Kingdom. Offers anthropology, media and performance (PhD); applied theatre professional (PhD); archaeology (PhD); art history and visual studies (PhD); arts management and cultural policy (PhD); classics and ancient history (PhD); composition (PhD); creative writing (PhD); drama (PhD); economic and social history (PhD); electroacoustic composition (PhD); English and American studies (PhD); history (PhD); humanitarianism and conflict response (PhD); museology (PhD); music (PhD); musicology (PhD); religions and theology (PhD).

University of Maryland, College Park, Academic Affairs, College of Arts and Humanities, Department of English, Creative Writing Program, College Park, MD 20742. Offers MA, MFA, PhD. *Degree requirements:* For master's, thesis optional, written exam; for doctorate, one foreign language, oral and written exams. *Entrance requirements:* For master's, GRE General Test, writing sample, 3 letters of recommendation. Additional exam requirements/recommendations for international students: Required—TOEFL. Electronic applications accepted. *Faculty research:* Early British literature, American literature.

University of Massachusetts Amherst, Graduate School, College of Humanities and Fine Arts, Department of English, Amherst, MA 01003. Offers American studies (PhD); composition and rhetoric (PhD); creative writing (MFA); English and American literature

(MA, PhD). *Program availability:* Part-time. Terminal master's awarded for partial completion of doctoral program. *Degree requirements:* For master's, one foreign language, thesis optional; for doctorate, one foreign language, comprehensive exam, thesis/dissertation. *Entrance requirements:* For master's, manuscript; for doctorate, GRE General Test, manuscript. Additional exam requirements/recommendations for international students: Required—TOEFL (minimum score 550 paper-based; 80 iBT), IELTS (minimum score 6.5). Electronic applications accepted.

University of Massachusetts Boston, College of Liberal Arts, Program in Creative Writing, Boston, MA 02125-3393. Offers MFA. *Students:* 28 full-time (21 women), 4 part-time (2 women); includes 3 minority (1 Black or African American, non-Hispanic/Latino; 1 Asian, non-Hispanic/Latino; 1 Two or more races, non-Hispanic/Latino). Average age 27. 76 applicants, 39% accepted, 17 enrolled. In 2017, 5 master's awarded. *Application deadline:* For fall admission, 1/15 for domestic students. *Expenses:* Tuition, state resident: full-time $17,375. Tuition, nonresident: full-time $33,915. *Required fees:* $355. *Unit head:* Jill McDonough, Director, 617-287-6700, E-mail: jill.mcdonough@umb.edu. *Application contact:* Graduate Admissions Coordinator, 617-287-6400, Fax: 617-287-6236, E-mail: bos.gadm@dpc.umassp.edu.
Website: http://www.umb.edu/academics/cla/english/grad/mfa

University of Massachusetts Dartmouth, Graduate School, College of Arts and Sciences, Program in Professional Writing, North Dartmouth, MA 02747-2300. Offers MA, Postbaccalaureate Certificate. *Program availability:* Part-time. *Faculty:* 34 full-time (21 women), 19 part-time/adjunct (11 women). *Students:* 5 full-time (3 women), 13 part-time (8 women); includes 1 minority (Two or more races, non-Hispanic/Latino). Average age 31. 16 applicants, 88% accepted, 11 enrolled. In 2017, 6 master's awarded. *Degree requirements:* For master's, thesis. *Entrance requirements:* For master's, statement of purpose (minimum of 300 words), resume, 3 letters of recommendation, official transcripts, writing samples (minimum of 10 pages of writing); for Postbaccalaureate Certificate, statement of purpose (minimum of 300 words), resume, official transcripts. Additional exam requirements/recommendations for international students: Required—TOEFL (minimum score 533 paper-based; 72 iBT), IELTS (minimum score 6). *Application deadline:* Applications are processed on a rolling basis. Application fee: $60. Electronic applications accepted. *Expenses:* Tuition, state resident: full-time $15,449; part-time $643.71 per credit. Tuition, nonresident: full-time $27,880; part-time $1161.67 per credit. *Required fees:* $405; $25.88 per credit. Tuition and fees vary according to course load and reciprocity agreements. *Financial support:* In 2017–18, 11 fellowships (averaging $12,727 per year), 1 research assistantship (averaging $11,999 per year), 2 teaching assistantships (averaging $7,000 per year) were awarded; tuition waivers (full) and unspecified assistantships also available. Support available to part-time students. Financial award application deadline: 3/1; financial award applicants required to submit FAFSA. *Faculty research:* Digital literacies; rhetoric of popular culture; discourse analysis; technology transfer, movement of intellectual property from university or lab to industry, rhetoric of science and technology. *Total annual research expenditures:* $308,000. *Unit head:* Karen Gulbrandsen, Graduate Program Director, Professional Writing, 508-910-6932, E-mail: kgulbrandsen@umassd.edu. *Application contact:* Steven Briggs, Director of Marketing and Recruitment for Graduate Studies, 508-999-8604, Fax: 508-999-8183, E-mail: graduate@umassd.edu.
Website: http://www.umassd.edu/cas/english/graduateprograms

University of Memphis, Graduate School, College of Arts and Sciences, Department of English, Memphis, TN 38152. Offers African-American literature (Graduate Certificate); applied linguistics (PhD); composition studies (PhD); creative writing (MFA); English as a second language (MA); linguistics (MA); literary and cultural studies (PhD), including African-American literature; literature (MA); professional writing (MA, PhD); teaching English as a second/foreign language (Graduate Certificate). *Program availability:* Part-time, evening/weekend, 100% online. *Faculty:* 30 full-time (15 women). *Students:* 73 full-time (34 women), 80 part-time (52 women); includes 35 minority (20 Black or African American, non-Hispanic/Latino; 3 Asian, non-Hispanic/Latino; 9 Hispanic/Latino; 3 Two or more races, non-Hispanic/Latino), 36 international. Average age 35. 78 applicants, 88% accepted, 35 enrolled. In 2017, 27 master's, 15 doctorates, 10 other advanced degrees awarded. Terminal master's awarded for partial completion of doctoral program. *Degree requirements:* For master's, one foreign language, comprehensive exam, thesis optional; for doctorate, 2 foreign languages, comprehensive exam, thesis/dissertation, qualifying exam. *Entrance requirements:* For master's, GRE, minimum undergraduate GPA of 3.0, statement of purpose, two letters of recommendation; for doctorate, GRE, minimum undergraduate and graduate GPA of 3.25, statement of purpose, writing sample, three letters of recommendation. Additional exam requirements/recommendations for international students: Required—TOEFL. *Application deadline:* For fall admission, 1/15 for domestic students; for spring admission, 10/15 for domestic students. Applications are processed on a rolling basis. Application fee: $35 ($60 for international students). Electronic applications accepted. *Expenses:* Contact institution. *Financial support:* In 2017–18, 123 students received support, including 16 research assistantships with full tuition reimbursements available (averaging $15,704 per year), 23 teaching assistantships with full tuition reimbursements available (averaging $22,076 per year); Federal Work-Study, scholarships/grants, and unspecified assistantships also available. Financial award application deadline: 2/1; financial award applicants required to submit FAFSA. *Faculty research:* Applied linguistics, British and American literature, professional writing, composition studies. *Unit head:* Dr. Joshua Phillips, Chair, 901-678-2651, Fax: 901-678-2226, E-mail: jsphllps@memphis.edu. *Application contact:* Dr. Jeffrey Scraba, Coordinator of Graduate Studies, 901-678-4768, Fax: 901-678-2226, E-mail: jscraba@memphis.edu.
Website: http://www.memphis.edu/english

University of Miami, Graduate School, College of Arts and Sciences, Department of English, Coral Gables, FL 33124. Offers creative writing (MFA); English (MA, PhD). *Program availability:* Part-time. Terminal master's awarded for partial completion of doctoral program. *Degree requirements:* For master's, one foreign language, thesis optional; for doctorate, one foreign language, thesis/dissertation. *Entrance requirements:* For master's and doctorate, GRE General Test. Electronic applications accepted. *Faculty research:* Anglo-Irish literature, feminist criticism and theory, Caribbean literature, early modern literature and culture, postcolonial and ethnic studies.

University of Michigan, Rackham Graduate School, College of Literature, Science, and the Arts, Department of English Language and Literature, Helen Zell Writer's Program, Ann Arbor, MI 48109. Offers MFA. *Faculty:* 9 full-time (4 women). *Students:* 41 full-time (25 women); includes 6 minority (1 American Indian or Alaska Native, non-Hispanic/Latino; 2 Asian, non-Hispanic/Latino; 1 Hispanic/Latino; 2 Two or more races, non-Hispanic/Latino), 9 international. Average age 27. 925 applicants, 4% accepted, 22 enrolled. In 2017, 22 master's awarded. *Degree requirements:* For master's, comprehensive exam, thesis. *Entrance requirements:* For master's, writing sample. Additional exam requirements/recommendations for international students: Required—TOEFL (minimum score 620 paper-based; 106 iBT). *Application deadline:* For fall admission, 12/15 for domestic and international students. Application fee: $75 ($90 for international students). Electronic applications accepted. *Expenses:* Tuition, state resident: full-time $22,368; part-time $1201 per credit hour. Tuition, nonresident: full-time $45,156; part-time $2467 per credit hour. *Required fees:* $376 per term. Tuition and fees vary according to course load, degree level and program. *Financial support:* Fellowships with tuition reimbursements, teaching assistantships with tuition reimbursements, and health care benefits available. Financial award application deadline: 12/15. *Faculty research:* Prose, poetry. *Application contact:* Graduate Admissions Office, 734-763-4139, Fax: 734-763-3128, E-mail: graduate.english@umich.edu.
Website: http://www.lsa.umich.edu/writers

University of Michigan–Flint, College of Arts and Sciences, Program in English Language and Literature, Flint, MI 48502-1950. Offers literature (MA); writing and rhetoric (MA). *Program availability:* Part-time. *Faculty:* 26 full-time (17 women), 3 part-time/adjunct (2 women). *Students:* 7 full-time (6 women), 16 part-time (13 women); includes 6 minority (1 Black or African American, non-Hispanic/Latino; 3 Hispanic/Latino; 2 Two or more races, non-Hispanic/Latino), 1 international. Average age 37. 16 applicants, 69% accepted, 9 enrolled. In 2017, 4 master's awarded. *Degree requirements:* For master's, thesis optional. *Entrance requirements:* For master's, bachelor's degree with major or significant coursework in English or related fields from regionally-accredited institution; minimum overall undergraduate GPA of 3.0. Additional exam requirements/recommendations for international students: Required—TOEFL (minimum score 84 iBT), IELTS (minimum score 6.5). *Application deadline:* For fall admission, 8/1 for domestic students, 5/1 for international students; for winter admission, 11/15 for domestic students, 9/1 for international students; for spring admission, 3/15 for domestic students, 1/1 for international students; for summer admission, 5/15 for domestic students. Applications are processed on a rolling basis. Application fee: $55. Electronic applications accepted. *Expenses:* Contact institution. *Financial support:* Career-related internships or fieldwork, Federal Work-Study, scholarships/grants, and unspecified assistantships available. Support available to part-time students. Financial award application deadline: 3/1; financial award applicants required to submit FAFSA. *Unit head:* Dr. Suzanne Knight, Director, 810-762-0145, E-mail: suknight@umflint.edu. *Application contact:* Bradley T. Maki, Director of Graduate Admissions, 810-762-3171, Fax: 810-766-6789, E-mail: bmaki@umflint.edu.
Website: http://www.umflint.edu/graduateprograms/english-language-and-literature-ma

University of Mississippi, Graduate School, College of Liberal Arts, University, MS 38677. Offers anthropology (MA); biology (MS, PhD); chemistry (MS, DA, PhD); creative writing (MFA); documentary expression (MFA); economics (MA, PhD); English (MA, PhD); experimental psychology (PhD); history (MA, PhD); mathematics (MS, PhD); modern languages (MA); music (MM); philosophy (MA); physics (MA, MS, PhD); political science (MA, PhD); Southern studies (MA); studio art (MFA). *Program availability:* Part-time. *Faculty:* 465 full-time (207 women), 82 part-time/adjunct (46 women). *Students:* 466 full-time (229 women), 72 part-time (34 women); includes 87 minority (38 Black or African American, non-Hispanic/Latino; 18 Asian, non-Hispanic/Latino; 24 Hispanic/Latino; 7 Two or more races, non-Hispanic/Latino), 121 international. Average age 29. *Degree requirements:* For doctorate, thesis/dissertation. *Entrance requirements:* For master's, GRE General Test, minimum GPA of 3.0; for doctorate, GRE General Test. Additional exam requirements/recommendations for international students: Required—TOEFL. *Application deadline:* For fall admission, 2/1 priority date for domestic students; for spring admission, 10/1 for domestic students. Applications are processed on a rolling basis. Application fee: $50. Electronic applications accepted. *Financial support:* Fellowships, research assistantships, teaching assistantships, career-related internships or fieldwork, Federal Work-Study, institutionally sponsored loans, scholarships/grants, and unspecified assistantships available. Financial award application deadline: 3/1; financial award applicants required to submit FAFSA. *Unit head:* Dr. Lee Michael Cohen, Dean, 662-915-7177, Fax: 662-915-5792, E-mail: libarts@olemiss.edu. *Application contact:* Dr. Christy M. Wyandt, Associate Dean of Graduate School, 662-915-7474, Fax: 662-915-7577, E-mail: cwyandt@olemiss.edu.

University of Missouri–St. Louis, College of Arts and Sciences, Department of English, St. Louis, MO 63121. Offers creative writing (MFA); English (MA). *Program availability:* Part-time, evening/weekend. *Faculty:* 19 full-time (7 women), 4 part-time/adjunct (2 women). *Students:* 16 full-time (9 women), 48 part-time (33 women); includes 12 minority (6 Black or African American, non-Hispanic/Latino; 2 Asian, non-Hispanic/Latino; 1 Hispanic/Latino; 3 Two or more races, non-Hispanic/Latino), 1 international. 37 applicants, 84% accepted, 17 enrolled. *Degree requirements:* For master's, thesis optional. *Entrance requirements:* For master's, two letters of recommendation; writing sample (MFA). Additional exam requirements/recommendations for international students: Required—TOEFL (minimum score 550 paper-based; 79 iBT), IELTS (minimum score 6.5). *Application deadline:* For fall admission, 7/1 priority date for domestic and international students; for spring admission, 12/1 priority date for domestic and international students. Applications are processed on a rolling basis. Application fee: $50 ($40 for international students). Electronic applications accepted. *Expenses:* Tuition, state resident: part-time $476.50 per credit hour. Tuition, nonresident: part-time $1169.70 per credit hour. *Financial support:* Teaching assistantships with tuition reimbursements available. Financial award applicants required to submit FAFSA. *Faculty research:* Victorian literature, Shakespeare and Renaissance literature, eighteenth-century literature, composition theory. *Unit head:* Dr. Frank Grady, Chair, 314-516-5510, Fax: 314-516-5781, E-mail: fgrady@umsl.edu. *Application contact:* 314-516-5458, Fax: 314-516-5310, E-mail: gradadm@umsl.edu.
Website: http://www.umsl.edu/divisions/artscience/english/

University of Montana, Graduate School, College of Humanities and Sciences, Department of English, Program in Creative Writing, Missoula, MT 59812. Offers fiction (MFA); non-fiction (MFA); poetry (MFA). *Degree requirements:* For master's, final creative paper. *Entrance requirements:* For master's, GRE General Test, sample of written work. Additional exam requirements/recommendations for international students: Required—TOEFL. *Faculty research:* Fiction, poetry, nonfiction.

University of Nebraska at Kearney, College of Fine Arts and Humanities, Department of English, Kearney, NE 68849-0001. Offers creative writing (MA); literature (MA); writing (MA). *Program availability:* Part-time, evening/weekend, online learning. *Degree requirements:* For master's, comprehensive exam (for some programs), thesis optional, thesis or exam (for literature option). *Entrance requirements:* For master's, writing sample, three letters of recommendation, letter of interest. Additional exam requirements/recommendations for international students: Recommended—TOEFL (minimum score 550 paper-based; 79 iBT), IELTS (minimum score 6.5). Electronic applications accepted. *Faculty research:* Narrative theory, popular culture, western and plains literature, women's studies, media studies, children's literature, poetry, speculative fiction, creative writing, comics, composition and rhetoric, renaissance drama, film studies, ecocriticism.

University of Nebraska at Omaha, Graduate Studies, College of Arts and Sciences, Department of English, Omaha, NE 68182. Offers advanced writing (Certificate); English (MA); teaching English to speakers of other languages (Certificate); technical communication (Certificate). *Program availability:* Part-time, evening/weekend. *Degree requirements:* For master's, comprehensive exam, thesis (for some programs). *Entrance requirements:* For master's, GRE or MAT, minimum GPA of 3.0, transcripts, 3 letters of recommendation, statement of purpose, writing sample; for Certificate, minimum GPA of 3.0, transcripts, statement of purpose. Additional exam requirements/recommendations

for international students: Required—TOEFL, IELTS, PTE. Electronic applications accepted.

University of Nebraska at Omaha, Graduate Studies, College of Communication, Fine Arts and Media, Writer's Workshop, Omaha, NE 68182. Offers MFA. *Program availability:* Online learning. *Entrance requirements:* For master's, 3 letters of recommendation, statement of purpose, writing sample, minimum GPA of 3.0, official transcripts. Additional exam requirements/recommendations for international students: Required—TOEFL, IELTS, PTE. Electronic applications accepted.

University of Nebraska–Lincoln, Graduate College, College of Arts and Sciences, Department of English, Lincoln, NE 68588-0333. Offers composition and rhetoric (MA, PhD); creative writing (MA, PhD); literature studies (MA, PhD). *Degree requirements:* For master's, thesis optional; for doctorate, one foreign language, comprehensive exam, thesis/dissertation. *Entrance requirements:* For master's, writing sample; for doctorate, GRE General Test, writing sample. Additional exam requirements/recommendations for international students: Required—TOEFL (minimum score 600 paper-based). Electronic applications accepted. *Faculty research:* Creative writing, composition and rhetoric, women's studies, North American literature, medieval/Renaissance studies.

University of Nevada, Las Vegas, Graduate College, College of Fine Arts, Department of Film, Las Vegas, NV 89154-5015. Offers film/writing for dramatic media (MFA); writing for dramatic media (Certificate). *Program availability:* Part-time. *Faculty:* 2 full-time (0 women). *Students:* 8 full-time (6 women); includes 1 minority (Asian, non-Hispanic/Latino), 1 international. Average age 32. 5 applicants, 60% accepted, 3 enrolled. In 2017, 3 master's, 1 other advanced degree awarded. *Degree requirements:* For master's, thesis, creative project and defense; for Certificate, creative project and defense. *Entrance requirements:* For master's, writing sample. Additional exam requirements/recommendations for international students: Required—TOEFL (minimum score 550 paper-based; 80 iBT), IELTS (minimum score 7). *Application deadline:* For fall admission, 1/15 for domestic students. Application fee: $60 ($95 for international students). Electronic applications accepted. *Expenses:* $275 per credit, $850 per course, $7,969 per year resident, $22,157 per year non-resident, $7,094 non-resident fee (7 credits or more), $1,307 annual health insurance fee. *Financial support:* In 2017–18, 8 students received support, including 8 teaching assistantships with full tuition reimbursements available (averaging $15,250 per year); institutionally sponsored loans, scholarships/grants, health care benefits, and unspecified assistantships also available. Financial award application deadline: 3/15; financial award applicants required to submit FAFSA. *Faculty research:* Screenplay, stage play, television series, Web entertainment content, production. *Unit head:* Dr. Heather Addison, Chair/Professor, 702-895-3547, Fax: 702-895-4395, E-mail: heather.addison@unlv.edu. *Application contact:* Sean Clark, Graduate Coordinator, 702-895-2442, Fax: 702-895-4395, E-mail: sean.clark@unlv.edu.
Website: http://film.unlv.edu/

University of Nevada, Las Vegas, Graduate College, College of Liberal Arts, Department of English, Las Vegas, NV 89154-5011. Offers creative writing (MFA); English (MA, PhD). *Program availability:* Part-time. *Faculty:* 23 full-time (10 women), 1 (woman) part-time/adjunct. *Students:* 69 full-time (38 women), 16 part-time (7 women); includes 24 minority (1 Black or African American, non-Hispanic/Latino; 7 Asian, non-Hispanic/Latino; 9 Hispanic/Latino; 1 Native Hawaiian or other Pacific Islander, non-Hispanic/Latino; 6 Two or more races, non-Hispanic/Latino), 2 international. Average age 33. 141 applicants, 22% accepted, 24 enrolled. In 2017, 14 master's, 5 doctorates awarded. *Degree requirements:* For master's, one foreign language, comprehensive exam (for some programs), thesis, creative thesis; for doctorate, one foreign language, comprehensive exam, thesis/dissertation. *Entrance requirements:* For master's, GRE General Test, GRE Subject Test, writing sample; statement of purpose; 2 letters of recommendation; transcripts from all colleges; for doctorate, GRE General Test, GRE Subject Test, MA in English with minimum GPA of 3.5; writing sample; 3 letters of recommendation; statement of purpose. Additional exam requirements/recommendations for international students: Required—TOEFL (minimum score 550 paper-based; 80 iBT), IELTS (minimum score 7). *Application deadline:* For fall admission, 1/15 for domestic students; for spring admission, 11/1 for domestic students. Application fee: $60 ($95 for international students). Electronic applications accepted. *Expenses:* Contact institution. *Financial support:* In 2017–18, 63 students received support, including 2 research assistantships with full tuition reimbursements available (averaging $17,500 per year), 61 teaching assistantships with full tuition reimbursements available (averaging $15,512 per year); institutionally sponsored loans, scholarships/grants, health care benefits, and unspecified assistantships also available. Financial award application deadline: 3/15; financial award applicants required to submit FAFSA. *Faculty research:* Creative writing, poetry, fiction. *Total annual research expenditures:* $22,954. *Unit head:* Dr. Gary Totten, Chair/Professor, 702-895-1258, Fax: 702-895-4801, E-mail: gary.totten@unlv.edu. *Application contact:* Anne Stevens, Graduate Coordinator, 702-895-3500, E-mail: anne.stevens@unlv.edu.
Website: http://english.unlv.edu/

University of New Hampshire, Graduate School, College of Liberal Arts, Department of English, Durham, NH 03824. Offers English (MST, PhD); language and linguistics (MA); literature (MA); writing (MFA). *Program availability:* Part-time. *Students:* 57 full-time (39 women), 39 part-time (28 women); includes 9 minority (4 Black or African American, non-Hispanic/Latino; 4 Hispanic/Latino; 1 Two or more races, non-Hispanic/Latino), 4 international. Average age 31. 117 applicants, 60% accepted, 27 enrolled. In 2017, 29 master's, 3 doctorates awarded. *Entrance requirements:* For master's, GRE General Test, sample of written work; for doctorate, GRE General Test, GRE Subject Test, sample of written work. Additional exam requirements/recommendations for international students: Required—TOEFL (minimum score 550 paper-based; 80 iBT). *Application deadline:* For fall admission, 1/15 for domestic and international students; for spring admission, 12/1 for domestic students. Application fee: $65. Electronic applications accepted. *Financial support:* In 2017–18, 64 students received support, including 2 fellowships, 37 teaching assistantships; research assistantships, career-related internships or fieldwork, Federal Work-Study, scholarships/grants, and tuition waivers (full and partial) also available. Support available to part-time students. Financial award application deadline: 2/15. *Unit head:* Dr. Rachel Trubowitz, Chair, 603-862-0254. *Application contact:* Janine Wilks, Administrative Assistant, 603-862-3963, E-mail: engl.grad@unh.edu.
Website: http://cola.unh.edu/english

University of New Mexico, Graduate Studies, College of Arts and Sciences, Program in Creative Writing, Albuquerque, NM 87131. Offers MFA. *Faculty:* 8 full-time (4 women). *Students:* 15 full-time (7 women), 2 part-time (1 woman); includes 7 minority (1 Black or African American, non-Hispanic/Latino; 2 American Indian or Alaska Native, non-Hispanic/Latino; 3 Hispanic/Latino; 1 Two or more races, non-Hispanic/Latino), 2 international. Average age 33. 85 applicants, 7% accepted, 6 enrolled. In 2017, 3 master's awarded. *Degree requirements:* For master's, comprehensive exam, thesis. *Entrance requirements:* For master's, writing sample. *Application deadline:* For fall admission, 1/15 for domestic and international students. Application fee: $50. Electronic applications accepted. *Financial support:* Teaching assistantships with tuition reimbursements, health care benefits, and unspecified assistantships available. Financial award application deadline: 1/15. *Faculty research:* Creative writing, fiction, creative non-fiction, poetry. *Unit head:* Dr. Gail Turley Houston, Chair, 505-277-6347, Fax: 505-277-0021, E-mail: ghouston@unm.edu. *Application contact:* N. Ezra Meier, Graduate Advisor, 505-277-4437, Fax: 505-277-0021, E-mail: nezra@unm.edu.
Website: http://english.unm.edu/graduate/master-of-fine-arts/index.html

University of New Mexico, Graduate Studies, College of Fine Arts, Department of Theatre and Dance, Albuquerque, NM 87131-2039. Offers dance (MFA); dance history (MA); dramatic writing (MFA); theatre education and outreach (MA). *Accreditation:* NASD; NAST. *Students:* Average age 36. 15 applicants, 53% accepted, 7 enrolled. In 2017, 4 master's awarded. *Degree requirements:* For master's, comprehensive exam (for some programs), thesis (for some programs). *Entrance requirements:* For master's, minimum GPA of 3.0; undergraduate major in theatre, dance or closely-related field; 3 letters of recommendation; letter of intent; BA, BFA, BS, or MA in dance movement science or related field, or equivalent experience (for MFA in dance). *Application deadline:* For fall admission, 4/15 for domestic students; for spring admission, 11/10 for domestic students. Application fee: $50. Electronic applications accepted. *Financial support:* Fellowships, research assistantships with partial tuition reimbursements, teaching assistantships with partial tuition reimbursements, Federal Work-Study, health care benefits, tuition waivers (partial), and unspecified assistantships available. Financial award application deadline: 3/1; financial award applicants required to submit FAFSA. *Faculty research:* Theater education and outreach, choreography, dramatic writing, dance history/criticism. *Unit head:* Bill Liotta, Chair, 505-277-4332, Fax: 505-277-8921, E-mail: wliotta@unm.edu. *Application contact:* Christina Squire, Administrator II, 505-277-7362, Fax: 505-277-8921, E-mail: csquire@unm.edu.
Website: http://theatredance.unm.edu

University of North Alabama, College of Arts and Sciences, Department of English, Program in Writing, Florence, AL 35632-0001. Offers creative writing (MA); rhetoric and composition (MA); technical writing (MA). *Program availability:* Part-time, 100% online. *Faculty:* 12 full-time (8 women). *Students:* 5 part-time (4 women). Average age 31. 5 applicants, 60% accepted, 3 enrolled. *Degree requirements:* For master's, comprehensive exam (for some programs), thesis (for some programs). *Entrance requirements:* For master's, GRE, MAT, three letters of recommendation; writing sample. Additional exam requirements/recommendations for international students: Required—TOEFL (minimum score 79 iBT), IELTS (minimum score 6), PTE (minimum score 54). *Application deadline:* Applications are processed on a rolling basis. Application fee: $50 ($100 for international students). Electronic applications accepted. *Expenses:* Tuition, state resident: full-time $7824; part-time $5943 per year. Tuition, nonresident: full-time $15,648; part-time $11,736 per year. *Required fees:* $3064; $2298 per unit. Tuition and fees vary according to course load and reciprocity agreements. *Financial support:* In 2017–18, 2 students received support. Federal Work-Study, scholarships/grants, and unspecified assistantships available. Financial award application deadline: 2/1; financial award applicants required to submit FAFSA. *Unit head:* Dr. Tammy Winner, Coordinator, 256-660-9026, E-mail: twinner@una.edu. *Application contact:* Hillary N. Coats, Graduate Admissions Coordinator, 256-765-4447, E-mail: graduate@una.edu.
Website: https://www.una.edu/english/master-of-arts-in-writing.html

The University of North Carolina at Charlotte, College of Liberal Arts and Sciences, Department of English, Charlotte, NC 28223-0001. Offers applied linguistics (Graduate Certificate); English (MA); technical and professional writing (Graduate Certificate). *Program availability:* Part-time, evening/weekend. *Faculty:* 33 full-time (19 women), 2 part-time/adjunct (1 woman). *Students:* 33 full-time (25 women), 20 part-time (14 women); includes 9 minority (1 Black or African American, non-Hispanic/Latino; 2 Asian, non-Hispanic/Latino; 5 Hispanic/Latino; 1 Two or more races, non-Hispanic/Latino), 2 international. Average age 30. 38 applicants, 87% accepted, 18 enrolled. In 2017, 19 master's, 2 other advanced degrees awarded. *Degree requirements:* For master's, comprehensive exam (for some programs), thesis, comprehensive exam, or project. *Entrance requirements:* For master's, GRE, MAT, minimum undergraduate GPA of 3.0, statement of purpose, recommendation letters; for Graduate Certificate, statement of purpose, three letters of recommendation, writing sample, minimum GPA of 2.75. Additional exam requirements/recommendations for international students: Required—TOEFL (minimum score 523 paper-based, 70 iBT) or IELTS (6.5). *Application deadline:* For fall admission, 3/1 priority date for domestic and international students; for spring admission, 10/1 priority date for domestic and international students; for summer admission, 4/1 priority date for domestic and international students. Applications are processed on a rolling basis. Application fee: $75. Electronic applications accepted. *Expenses:* Tuition, state resident: full-time $4337. Tuition, nonresident: full-time $17,771. *Required fees:* $3211. Tuition and fees vary according to course load and program. *Financial support:* In 2017–18, 17 students received support, including 17 teaching assistantships (averaging $8,118 per year); career-related internships or fieldwork, institutionally sponsored loans, scholarships/grants, and unspecified assistantships also available. Support available to part-time students. Financial award application deadline: 3/1; financial award applicants required to submit FAFSA. *Total annual research expenditures:* $30,460. *Unit head:* Dr. Mark West, Chair, 704-687-0618, E-mail: miwest@uncc.edu. *Application contact:* Kathy B. Giddings, Director of Graduate Admissions, 704-687-5503, Fax: 704-687-1668, E-mail: gradadm@uncc.edu.
Website: http://english.uncc.edu/

The University of North Carolina at Greensboro, Graduate School, College of Arts and Sciences, Department of English, Program in Creative Writing, Greensboro, NC 27412-5001. Offers MFA. *Degree requirements:* For master's, comprehensive exam, thesis. *Entrance requirements:* For master's, GRE General Test, minimum GPA of 3.0, writing sample. Additional exam requirements/recommendations for international students: Required—TOEFL. Electronic applications accepted. *Faculty research:* Fiction, poetry, science fiction, film studies.

The University of North Carolina Wilmington, College of Arts and Sciences, Department of Creative Writing, Wilmington, NC 28403-3297. Offers MFA. *Faculty:* 12 full-time (7 women). *Students:* 41 full-time (25 women), 22 part-time (13 women); includes 7 minority (3 Black or African American, non-Hispanic/Latino; 2 Asian, non-Hispanic/Latino; 1 Hispanic/Latino; 1 Two or more races, non-Hispanic/Latino), 1 international. Average age 29. 131 applicants, 19% accepted, 21 enrolled. In 2017, 17 master's awarded. *Degree requirements:* For master's, comprehensive exam, thesis. *Entrance requirements:* For master's, writing sample, 3 letters of recommendation, statement of interest. Additional exam requirements/recommendations for international students: Required—TOEFL (minimum score 550 paper-based; 79 iBT), IELTS (minimum score 6.5). *Application deadline:* For fall admission, 1/5 for domestic students. Applications are processed on a rolling basis. Application fee: $75. Electronic applications accepted. *Expenses:* Tuition, state resident: full-time $4626; part-time $226.76 per credit hour. Tuition, nonresident: full-time $17,834; part-time $874.22 per credit hour. *Required fees:* $2124. Tuition and fees vary according to program. *Financial support:* Teaching assistantships, scholarships/grants, and unspecified assistantships available. Financial award application deadline: 1/1; financial award applicants required to submit FAFSA. *Unit head:* Dr. David Gessner, Chair, 910-962-7489, Fax: 910-962-7461, E-mail: gessnerdm@uncw.edu. *Application contact:* Melissa Crowe, MFA Coordinator, 910-962-3436, Fax: 910-962-7461, E-mail: crowem@uncw.edu.
Website: http://uncw.edu/writers/mfa/index.html

Writing

University of Northern Iowa, Graduate College, College of Humanities, Arts and Sciences, Department of Languages and Literatures, MA Program in English, Cedar Falls, IA 50614. Offers creative writing (MA); English (MA); literature (MA). *Program availability:* Part-time, evening/weekend. *Degree requirements:* For master's, one foreign language, comprehensive exam, thesis or alternative, portfolio. *Entrance requirements:* Additional exam requirements/recommendations for international students: Required—TOEFL (minimum score 600 paper-based; 100 iBT). Electronic applications accepted.

University of North Florida, College of Arts and Sciences, Department of English, Jacksonville, FL 32224. Offers MA. *Program availability:* Part-time, evening/weekend. *Degree requirements:* For master's, comprehensive exam, thesis optional. *Entrance requirements:* For master's, GRE General Test, minimum GPA of 3.0 in last 60 hours, writing sample. Additional exam requirements/recommendations for international students: Required—TOEFL (minimum score 500 paper-based; 61 iBT). Electronic applications accepted.

University of North Texas, Robert B. Toulouse School of Graduate Studies, Denton, TX 76203-5459. Offers accounting (MS); applied anthropology (MA, MS); applied behavior analysis (Certificate); applied geography (MA); applied technology and performance improvement (M Ed, MS); art education (MA); art history (MA); art museum education (Certificate); arts leadership (Certificate); audiology (Au D); behavior analysis (MS); behavioral science (PhD); biochemistry and molecular biology (MS); biology (MA, MS); biomedical engineering (MS); business analysis (MS); chemistry (MS); clinical health psychology (PhD); communication studies (MA, MS); computer engineering (MS); computer science (MS); counseling (M Ed, MS), including clinical mental health counseling (MS), college and university counseling, elementary school counseling, secondary school counseling; creative writing (MA); criminal justice (MS); curriculum and instruction (M Ed); decision sciences (MBA); design (MA, MFA), including fashion design (MFA), innovation studies, interior design (MFA); early childhood studies (MS); economics (MS); educational leadership (M Ed, Ed D); educational psychology (MS, PhD), including family studies (MS), gifted and talented (MS), human development (MS), learning and cognition (MS), research, measurement and evaluation (MS); electrical engineering (MS); emergency management (MPA); engineering technology (MS); English (MA); English as a second language (MA); environmental science (MS); finance (MBA, MS); financial management (MPA); French (MA); health services management (MBA); higher education (M Ed, Ed D); history (MA, MS); hospitality management (MS); human resources management (MPA); information science (MS); information systems (PhD); information technologies (MBA); interdisciplinary studies (MA, MS); international studies (MA); international sustainable tourism (MS); jazz studies (MM); journalism (MA, MJ, Graduate Certificate), including interactive and virtual digital communication (Graduate Certificate), narrative journalism (Graduate Certificate), public relations (Graduate Certificate); kinesiology (MS); linguistics (MA); local government management (MPA); logistics (PhD); logistics and supply chain management (MBA); long-term care, senior housing, and aging services (MA); management (PhD); marketing (MBA); mathematics (MA, MS); mechanical and energy engineering (MS, PhD); music (MA), including ethnomusicology, music theory, musicology, performance; music composition (PhD); music education (MM Ed, PhD); nonprofit management (MPA); operations and supply chain management (MBA); performance (MM, DMA); philosophy (MA); political science (MA); professional and technical communication (MA); radio, television and film (MA, MFA); rehabilitation counseling (Certificate); sociology (MA); Spanish (MA); special education (M Ed); speech-language pathology (MA); strategic management (MBA); studio art (MFA); teaching (M Ed); MBA/MS. *Program availability:* Part-time, evening/weekend, online learning. Terminal master's awarded for partial completion of doctoral program. *Degree requirements:* For master's, variable foreign language requirement, comprehensive exam (for some programs), thesis (for some programs); for doctorate, variable foreign language requirement, comprehensive exam (for some programs), thesis/dissertation; for other advanced degree, variable foreign language requirement, comprehensive exam (for some programs). *Entrance requirements:* For master's and doctorate, GRE, GMAT. Additional exam requirements/recommendations for international students: Required—TOEFL (minimum score 550 paper-based; 79 iBT). Electronic applications accepted.

University of Notre Dame, Graduate School, College of Arts and Letters, Division of Humanities, Department of English, Creative Writing Program, Notre Dame, IN 46556. Offers MFA. *Degree requirements:* For master's, thesis. *Entrance requirements:* For master's, GRE General Test, minimum GPA of 3.0. Additional exam requirements/recommendations for international students: Required—TOEFL (minimum score 600 paper-based; 80 iBT). Electronic applications accepted. *Faculty research:* Novels, stories, poetry.

University of Oklahoma, College of Arts and Sciences, Department of English, Norman, OK 73019. Offers literary and cultural studies (MA, PhD); writing and rhetoric studies (MA, PhD). *Program availability:* Part-time. *Faculty:* 25 full-time (13 women), 1 part-time/adjunct (0 women). *Students:* 29 full-time (21 women), 17 part-time (8 women); includes 9 minority (1 American Indian or Alaska Native, non-Hispanic/Latino; 2 Asian, non-Hispanic/Latino; 5 Hispanic/Latino; 1 Two or more races, non-Hispanic/Latino), 2 international. Average age 31. 34 applicants, 71% accepted, 18 enrolled. In 2017, 7 master's, 4 doctorates awarded. *Degree requirements:* For master's, one foreign language, comprehensive exam (for some programs), thesis (for some programs), exam or thesis; for doctorate, one foreign language, comprehensive exam, thesis/dissertation. *Entrance requirements:* For master's, GRE, BA in English or related field; for doctorate, GRE, MA in English or related field. Additional exam requirements/recommendations for international students: Required—TOEFL (minimum score 79 iBT) or IELTS (minimum score 6.5). *Application deadline:* For fall admission, 1/5 priority date for domestic and international students. Application fee: $50 ($100 for international students). Electronic applications accepted. *Expenses:* Tuition, state resident: full-time $5119; part-time $213.30 per credit hour. Tuition, nonresident: full-time $19,778; part-time $824.10 per credit hour. *Required fees:* $3458; $133.55 per credit hour. $126.50 per semester. *Financial support:* In 2017–18, 40 students received support, including 6 research assistantships with full tuition reimbursements available (averaging $14,515 per year), 31 teaching assistantships with full tuition reimbursements available (averaging $12,496 per year); fellowships with full tuition reimbursements available, scholarships/grants, health care benefits, and unspecified assistantships also available. Financial award application deadline: 6/1; financial award applicants required to submit FAFSA. *Faculty research:* American Indian literature and culture; composition and rhetoric; American literature; British literature; postcolonial literature and culture. *Total annual research expenditures:* $101. *Unit head:* Dr. Daniela Garofalo, Professor and Chair, 405-325-4661, Fax: 405-325-0831, E-mail: dg@ou.edu. *Application contact:* Sara Day, Graduate Assistant, 405-325-0489, Fax: 405-325-0831, E-mail: redpanda@ou.edu.
Website: http://cas.ou.edu/english

University of Oklahoma, Gaylord College of Journalism and Mass Communication, Program in Professional Writing, Norman, OK 73019. Offers MPW. *Program availability:* Part-time. *Students:* 7 full-time (3 women), 4 part-time (3 women); includes 3 minority (1 Black or African American, non-Hispanic/Latino; 1 Hispanic/Latino; 1 Two or more races, non-Hispanic/Latino). Average age 29. 2 applicants, 100% accepted, 1 enrolled. In 2017, 3 master's awarded. *Degree requirements:* For master's, professional project (e.g., novel, theater or film script). *Entrance requirements:* For master's, GRE, 50-page writing sample, 2 letters of recommendation, resume, personal statement, minimum GPA of 3.2. Additional exam requirements/recommendations for international students: Required—TOEFL (minimum score 79 iBT) or IELTS (minimum score 6.5). *Application deadline:* For fall admission, 5/1 for domestic students, 3/1 for international students; for spring admission, 11/1 for domestic students, 9/1 for international students. Application fee: $50 ($100 for international students). Electronic applications accepted. *Expenses:* Tuition, state resident: full-time $5119; part-time $213.30 per credit hour. Tuition, nonresident: full-time $19,778; part-time $824.10 per credit hour. *Required fees:* $3458; $133.55 per credit hour. $126.50 per semester. *Financial support:* In 2017–18, 10 students received support. Teaching assistantships, career-related internships or fieldwork, institutionally sponsored loans, scholarships/grants, health care benefits, unspecified assistantships, and McNair fellowships available. Support available to part-time students. Financial award application deadline: 6/1; financial award applicants required to submit FAFSA. *Faculty research:* General fiction, novel writing, non-fiction, screenwriting. *Unit head:* Dr. Peter Gade, Director of Graduate Studies/Professor of Journalism, 405-325-5528, Fax: 405-325-7565, E-mail: pgade@ou.edu. *Application contact:* Larry Laneer, Administrative Assistant to Director/Graduate Advisor, 405-325-2722, Fax: 405-325-7565, E-mail: llaneer@ou.edu.
Website: http://www.ou.edu/content/gaylord/graduate.html

University of Oregon, Graduate School, College of Arts and Sciences, Department of Creative Writing, Eugene, OR 97403. Offers MFA. *Degree requirements:* For master's, thesis, exam. *Entrance requirements:* For master's, minimum GPA of 3.0. Additional exam requirements/recommendations for international students: Required—TOEFL. *Faculty research:* Poetry, fiction, literary nonfiction.

University of Pittsburgh, Kenneth P. Dietrich School of Arts and Sciences, Department of English, Pittsburgh, PA 15260. Offers English (MA, PhD); writing (MFA). *Faculty:* 59 full-time (27 women). *Students:* 108 full-time (76 women); includes 43 minority (11 Black or African American, non-Hispanic/Latino; 1 American Indian or Alaska Native, non-Hispanic/Latino; 17 Asian, non-Hispanic/Latino; 12 Hispanic/Latino; 2 Two or more races, non-Hispanic/Latino). Average age 29. 285 applicants, 14% accepted, 24 enrolled. In 2017, 16 master's, 8 doctorates awarded. Terminal master's awarded for partial completion of doctoral program. *Degree requirements:* For master's, variable foreign language requirement, thesis; for doctorate, variable foreign language requirement, comprehensive exam, thesis/dissertation. *Entrance requirements:* For master's and doctorate, GRE General Test, writing sample. Additional exam requirements/recommendations for international students: Required—TOEFL (minimum score 550 paper-based, 90 iBT) or IELTS (7.0). *Application deadline:* For fall admission, 12/10 for domestic and international students. Application fee: $50. Electronic applications accepted. *Financial support:* In 2017–18, 22 fellowships with full tuition reimbursements (averaging $22,896 per year), 11 research assistantships with full and partial tuition reimbursements (averaging $15,060 per year), 56 teaching assistantships with full and partial tuition reimbursements (averaging $18,815 per year) were awarded; Federal Work-Study, institutionally sponsored loans, scholarships/grants, health care benefits, tuition waivers (full and partial), and unspecified assistantships also available. Support available to part-time students. Financial award application deadline: 12/10. *Faculty research:* Cultural studies, literary studies, film and media studies, composition and rhetoric. *Unit head:* Dr. Don Bialostosky, Chair, 412-624-6509, Fax: 412-624-6639, E-mail: dhb2@pitt.edu. *Application contact:* Jesse Daugherty, Graduate Administrator, 412-624-6549, Fax: 412-624-6639, E-mail: jed110@pitt.edu.
Website: http://www.english.pitt.edu

University of Regina, Faculty of Graduate Studies and Research, Faculty of Arts, Department of English, Regina, SK S4S 0A2, Canada. Offers creative writing (MA); English (MA, PhD). PhD program is a special case provision. *Program availability:* Part-time. *Faculty:* 21 full-time (9 women), 1 part-time/adjunct (0 women). *Students:* 11 full-time (8 women), 4 part-time (3 women). 19 applicants, 16% accepted. In 2017, 5 master's awarded. *Degree requirements:* For master's, thesis (for some programs); for doctorate, thesis/dissertation. *Entrance requirements:* For master's, writing sample and portfolio of creative material (for creative writing). Additional exam requirements/recommendations for international students: Required—TOEFL (minimum score 600 paper-based; 100 iBT), IELTS (minimum score 7.5), PTE (minimum score 59). *Application deadline:* For fall admission, 4/15 for domestic and international students; for winter admission, 10/15 for domestic and international students; for spring admission, 2/15 for domestic and international students. Application fee: $100. Electronic applications accepted. *Expenses:* $10,681. *Financial support:* In 2017–18, 2 fellowships (averaging $6,000 per year), 4 teaching assistantships (averaging $2,562 per year) were awarded; research assistantships and scholarships/grants also available. Financial award application deadline: 6/15. *Faculty research:* British, American, and Canadian literature; sixteenth-, eighteenth-, nineteenth-, and twentieth-century literature; literary theory. *Unit head:* Dr. Marcel DeCoste, Department Head, 306-585-4691, Fax: 306-585-5429, E-mail: marcel.decoste@uregina.ca. *Application contact:* Dr. Susan Johnston, Graduate Chair, 306-585-4672, Fax: 306-585-5429, E-mail: susan.johnston@uregina.ca.
Website: http://www.uregina.ca/arts/english

University of Rhode Island, Graduate School, College of Arts and Sciences, Department of English, Kingston, RI 02881. Offers American literature and culture (PhD); British literature and culture (PhD); creative writing (PhD); critical theories (PhD); English (MA); film (PhD); gender studies (PhD); MLIS/MA. *Program availability:* Part-time. *Faculty:* 17 full-time (10 women). *Students:* 36 full-time (27 women), 7 part-time (4 women); includes 2 minority (both Black or African American, non-Hispanic/Latino), 7 international. 34 applicants, 65% accepted, 10 enrolled. In 2017, 4 master's, 8 doctorates awarded. *Entrance requirements:* Additional exam requirements/recommendations for international students: Required—TOEFL (minimum score 91 iBT). *Application deadline:* For fall admission, 1/15 for domestic and international students. Application fee: $65. Electronic applications accepted. *Expenses:* Tuition, state resident: full-time $12,706; part-time $786 per credit. Tuition, nonresident: full-time $25,216; part-time $1401 per credit. *Required fees:* $1598; $45 per credit. One-time fee: $30 part-time. *Financial support:* In 2017–18, 28 teaching assistantships with tuition reimbursements (averaging $17,158 per year) were awarded. Financial award application deadline: 1/15; financial award applicants required to submit FAFSA. *Unit head:* Dr. Travis Williams, Chair, 401-874-9501, E-mail: tdwilliams@uri.edu. *Application contact:* Dr. David Faflik, Director of Graduate Studies, 401-874-4670, E-mail: faflik@uri.edu.
Website: http://www.uri.edu/artsci/eng/

University of St. Thomas, College of Arts and Sciences, Graduate Program in English, St. Paul, MN 55105. Offers creative writing and publishing (MA); English literature (MA); teaching college English (Certificate). *Program availability:* Part-time, evening/weekend. *Faculty:* 24 full-time (15 women). *Students:* 41 full-time (29 women); includes 4 minority (3 Black or African American, non-Hispanic/Latino; 1 Asian, non-Hispanic/Latino). Average age 30. 9 applicants, 89% accepted, 8 enrolled. In 2017, 16 master's awarded. *Degree requirements:* For master's, essay. *Entrance requirements:* For master's, minimum GPA of 3.0, minimum 5 upper-level undergraduate courses in literature, sample of written work, personal statement, BA from accredited university, transcripts. Additional exam requirements/recommendations for international students: Required—

TOEFL (minimum score 80 iBT), IELTS (minimum score 6.5). *Application deadline:* For fall admission, 3/1 priority date for domestic and international students; for spring admission, 10/1 priority date for domestic and international students; for summer admission, 3/1 priority date for domestic and international students. Applications are processed on a rolling basis. Application fee: $0. Electronic applications accepted. *Expenses:* $2,572.50 per course, $857.50 per credit; $55 technology fee per semester part-time, $111 full-time. *Financial support:* In 2017–18, 23 students received support, including 18 fellowships with partial tuition reimbursements available (averaging $5,145 per year), 3 research assistantships (averaging $2,000 per year), 4 teaching assistantships (averaging $750 per year); institutionally sponsored loans, scholarships/grants, traineeships, and unspecified assistantships also available. Support available to part-time students. Financial award application deadline: 3/1; financial award applicants required to submit FAFSA. *Faculty research:* Multicultural literature, literature and theory, regional writers, creative writing, 19th-century American literature. *Unit head:* Dr. Alexis Easley, Director, 651-962-5653, Fax: 651-962-5623, E-mail: maeasley@stthomas.edu. *Application contact:* Soren Hoeger-Lerdal, Coordinator, 651-962-5628, Fax: 651-962-5623, E-mail: gradenglish@stthomas.edu.
Website: http://www.stthomas.edu/english/graduate/

University of San Francisco, College of Arts and Sciences, Program in Writing, San Francisco, CA 94117-1080. Offers MFA. *Program availability:* Part-time, evening/weekend. *Degree requirements:* For master's, thesis. *Entrance requirements:* For master's, minimum overall GPA of 2.7, writing sample, 2 letters of recommendation, resume, interview. Additional exam requirements/recommendations for international students: Required—TOEFL (minimum score 550 paper-based; 79 iBT), IELTS, PTE. Electronic applications accepted. *Faculty research:* Techniques of teaching the novel to writers, oral history.

University of South Alabama, College of Arts and Sciences, Department of English, Mobile, AL 36688. Offers creative writing (MA); literature (MA). *Program availability:* Part-time, evening/weekend. *Faculty:* 9 full-time (3 women). *Students:* 15 full-time (8 women), 10 part-time (6 women); includes 4 minority (2 Black or African American, non-Hispanic/Latino; 2 Two or more races, non-Hispanic/Latino). Average age 31. 13 applicants, 54% accepted, 7 enrolled. In 2017, 5 master's awarded. *Degree requirements:* For master's, one foreign language, comprehensive exam, thesis optional. *Entrance requirements:* For master's, GRE General Test, BA in English or 30 hours of course work in English, minimum GPA of 3.0, personal statement. Additional exam requirements/recommendations for international students: Required—TOEFL (minimum score 535 paper-based; 79 iBT), IELTS (minimum score 6.5). *Application deadline:* For fall admission, 7/15 priority date for domestic students, 5/15 priority date for international students; for spring admission, 12/1 priority date for domestic students, 11/1 priority date for international students; for summer admission, 5/1 for domestic students, 4/1 for international students. Applications are processed on a rolling basis. Application fee: $35. Electronic applications accepted. *Expenses:* Tuition, state resident: full-time $10,104; part-time $421 per semester hour. Tuition, nonresident: full-time $20,208; part-time $842 per semester hour. *Financial support:* Fellowships, research assistantships, teaching assistantships, career-related internships or fieldwork, Federal Work-Study, institutionally sponsored loans, scholarships/grants, and unspecified assistantships available. Support available to part-time students. Financial award application deadline: 3/31; financial award applicants required to submit FAFSA. *Unit head:* Dr. Steven Trout, Chair, English, 251-460-6439, E-mail: strout@southalabama.edu. *Application contact:* Dr. Ellen B. Harrington, Graduate Coordinator, English, 251-460-7326, E-mail: eharrington@southalabama.edu.
Website: http://www.southalabama.edu/colleges/artsandsci/english/

University of South Carolina, The Graduate School, College of Arts and Sciences, Department of English Language and Literature, Columbia, SC 29208. Offers creative writing (MFA); English (MA, PhD); English education (MAT); MLIS/MA. MAT offered in cooperation with the College of Education. *Program availability:* Part-time. *Degree requirements:* For master's, one foreign language, comprehensive exam, thesis; for doctorate, 2 foreign languages, comprehensive exam, thesis/dissertation. *Entrance requirements:* For master's, GRE General Test (MFA), GRE Subject Test (MA, MAT), sample of written work; for doctorate, GRE General Test, GRE Subject Test, sample of written work. Additional exam requirements/recommendations for international students: Required—TOEFL. Electronic applications accepted. *Faculty research:* American literature, British literature, composition and rhetoric, linguistics, speech communication.

University of Southern California, Graduate School, Dana and David Dornsife College of Letters, Arts and Sciences, Department of English, Los Angeles, CA 90089. Offers English (MA, PhD); literature and creative writing (PhD). Terminal master's awarded for partial completion of doctoral program. *Degree requirements:* For doctorate, one foreign language, comprehensive exam, thesis/dissertation. *Entrance requirements:* For doctorate, GRE General Test, GRE Subject Test (English literature). Additional exam requirements/recommendations for international students: Required—TOEFL. Electronic applications accepted. *Faculty research:* Creative writing and literature; early modern studies; gender and sexuality; narrative studies; poetry and poetics; media, film, and popular culture; studies in race and minority literature.

University of Southern California, Graduate School, Dana and David Dornsife College of Letters, Arts and Sciences, Master of Professional Writing Program, Los Angeles, CA 90089. Offers MPW. *Program availability:* Part-time, evening/weekend. *Degree requirements:* For master's, thesis. *Entrance requirements:* For master's, GRE. Additional exam requirements/recommendations for international students: Required—TOEFL. Electronic applications accepted. *Faculty research:* Creative writing including fiction, creative nonfiction, screenwriting, television writing, playwriting, poetry, Internet writing; publishing in electronic media; book and film reviewing; teaching.

University of Southern Maine, College of Arts, Humanities, and Social Sciences, Program in Creative Writing, Portland, ME 04104. Offers MFA.

University of Southern Mississippi, College of Arts and Letters, Department of English, Hattiesburg, MS 39406-0001. Offers creative writing (MA, PhD); English education (MA); literature (MA, PhD). *Students:* 16 full-time (12 women), 2 part-time (both women). 48 applicants, 65% accepted, 18 enrolled. In 2017, 73 master's, 16 doctorates awarded. *Degree requirements:* For master's, one foreign language, comprehensive exam, thesis; for doctorate, 2 foreign languages, comprehensive exam, thesis/dissertation. *Entrance requirements:* For master's, GRE General Test, minimum GPA of 3.0 in field of study, 2.75 in last 2 years; for doctorate, GRE General Test, minimum GPA of 3.5. Additional exam requirements/recommendations for international students: Required—TOEFL, IELTS. *Application deadline:* For fall admission, 3/15 priority date for domestic students, 3/15 for international students. Application fee: $60. Electronic applications accepted. *Expenses:* Tuition, state resident: full-time $3830. *Financial support:* Fellowships, research assistantships with full tuition reimbursements, teaching assistantships with full tuition reimbursements, Federal Work-Study, institutionally sponsored loans, scholarships/grants, and unspecified assistantships available. Financial award application deadline: 3/15; financial award applicants required to submit FAFSA. *Faculty research:* English and American literature, critical theory and cultural studies, creative writing. *Unit head:* Dr. Luis Iglesias, Chair, 601-266-4060, Fax: 601-266-5757, E-mail: luis.iglesias@usm.edu. *Application contact:* Dr. Alexandra Valint,

Director, Graduate Studies, 601-266-4070.
Website: https://www.usm.edu/english

University of South Florida, College of Arts and Sciences, Department of English, Tampa, FL 33620-9951. Offers creative writing (MFA), including fiction, poetry; English (MA, PhD), including literature, rhetoric and composition. *Program availability:* Part-time, evening/weekend. *Faculty:* 24 full-time (13 women). *Students:* 70 full-time (51 women), 17 part-time (15 women); includes 14 minority (6 Black or African American, non-Hispanic/Latino; 3 Asian, non-Hispanic/Latino; 3 Hispanic/Latino; 2 Two or more races, non-Hispanic/Latino). Average age 32. 74 applicants, 54% accepted, 25 enrolled. In 2017, 22 master's, 10 doctorates awarded. *Degree requirements:* For master's, comprehensive exam, thesis (for MFA); thesis or portfolio (for MA); for doctorate, one foreign language, comprehensive exam, thesis/dissertation. *Entrance requirements:* For master's, GRE General Test, minimum undergraduate GPA of 3.5 (for MA), 3.2 (for MFA); three letters of recommendation; personal statement; writing sample from 10 to 20 pages (depending on genre); for doctorate, GRE General Test, minimum graduate GPA of 3.7; three letters of recommendation; 2-3 page personal statement; 2500-word writing sample from English coursework. Additional exam requirements/recommendations for international students: Required—TOEFL minimum score 550 paper-based; 79 iBT or IELTS minimum score 6.5 (for MA and PhD); TOEFL minimum score 600 paper-based (for MFA). *Application deadline:* For fall admission, 1/1 for domestic and international students. Applications are processed on a rolling basis. Application fee: $30. Electronic applications accepted. *Financial support:* In 2017–18, 20 students received support, including 2 research assistantships (averaging $17,221 per year), 79 teaching assistantships with tuition reimbursements available (averaging $11,576 per year); unspecified assistantships also available. Financial award application deadline: 6/30; financial award applicants required to submit FAFSA. *Faculty research:* British and American literature, rhetoric and composition, world and comparative literatures, creative writing, gender and sexuality studies, women's literature, film and genre studies, literary theory, popular and visual culture, textual and translation studies. *Total annual research expenditures:* $202,166. *Unit head:* Dr. Laura Runge, Professor and Chairperson, 813-974-9496, E-mail: runge@usf.edu. *Application contact:* Dr. John Lennon, Associate Professor and Graduate Director, 813-974-2663, Fax: 813-974-2270, E-mail: jflennon@usf.edu.
Website: http://english.usf.edu/

University of South Florida, Innovative Education, Tampa, FL 33620-9951. Offers adult, career and higher education (Graduate Certificate), including college teaching, leadership in developing human resources, leadership in higher education; Africana studies (Graduate Certificate), including diasporas and health disparities, genocide and human rights; aging studies (Graduate Certificate), including gerontology; art research (Graduate Certificate), including museum studies; business foundations (Graduate Certificate); chemical and biomedical engineering (Graduate Certificate), including materials science and engineering, water, health and sustainability; child and family studies (Graduate Certificate), including positive behavior support; civil and industrial engineering (Graduate Certificate), including transportation systems analysis; community and family health (Graduate Certificate), including maternal and child health, social marketing and public health, violence and injury: prevention and intervention, women's health; criminology (Graduate Certificate), including criminal justice administration; data science for public administration (Graduate Certificate); digital humanities (Graduate Certificate); educational measurement and research (Graduate Certificate), including evaluation; English (Graduate Certificate), including comparative literary studies, creative writing, professional and technical communication; entrepreneurship (Graduate Certificate); environmental health (Graduate Certificate), including safety management; epidemiology and biostatistics (Graduate Certificate), including applied biostatistics, biostatistics, concepts and tools of epidemiology, epidemiology, epidemiology of infectious diseases; geography, environment and planning (Graduate Certificate), including community development, environmental policy and management, geographical information systems; geology (Graduate Certificate), including hydrogeology; global health (Graduate Certificate), including disaster management, global health and Latin American and Caribbean studies, global health practice, humanitarian assistance, infection control; government and international affairs (Graduate Certificate), including Cuban studies, globalization studies; health policy and management (Graduate Certificate), including health management and leadership, public health policy and programs; hearing specialist: early intervention (Graduate Certificate); industrial and management systems engineering (Graduate Certificate), including systems engineering, technology management; information studies (Graduate Certificate), including school library media specialist; information systems/decision sciences (Graduate Certificate), including analytics and business intelligence; instructional technology (Graduate Certificate), including distance education, Florida digital/virtual educator, instructional design, multimedia design, Web design; internal medicine, bioethics and medical humanities (Graduate Certificate), including biomedical ethics; Latin American and Caribbean studies (Graduate Certificate); leadership for coastal resiliency planning (Graduate Certificate); mass communications (Graduate Certificate), including multimedia journalism; mathematics and statistics (Graduate Certificate), including mathematics; medicine (Graduate Certificate), including aging and neuroscience, bioinformatics, biotechnology, brain fitness and memory management, clinical investigation, hand and upper limb rehabilitation, health informatics, health sciences, integrative weight management, intellectual property, medicine and gender, metabolic and nutritional medicine, metabolic cardiology, pharmacy sciences; national and competitive intelligence (Graduate Certificate); nursing (Graduate Certificate), including simulation based academic fellowship in advanced pain management; psychological and social foundations (Graduate Certificate), including career counseling, college teaching, diversity in education, mental health counseling, school counseling; public affairs (Graduate Certificate), including nonprofit management, public management, research administration; public health (Graduate Certificate), including assessing chemical toxicity and public health risks, health equity, pharmacoepidemiology, public health generalist, toxicology, translational research in adolescent behavioral health; public health practices (Graduate Certificate), including planning for healthy communities; rehabilitation and mental health counseling (Graduate Certificate), including integrative mental health care, marriage and family therapy, rehabilitation technology; secondary education (Graduate Certificate), including ESOL, foreign language education: culture and content, foreign language education: professional; social work (Graduate Certificate), including geriatric social work/clinical gerontology; special education (Graduate Certificate), including autism spectrum disorder, disabilities education: severe/profound; world languages (Graduate Certificate), including teaching English as a second language (TESL) or foreign language. *Unit head:* Dr. Cynthia DeLuca, Associate Vice President and Assistant Vice Provost, 813-974-3077, Fax: 813-974-7061, E-mail: deluca@usf.edu. *Application contact:* Owen Hooper, Director, Summer and Alternative Calendar Programs, 813-974-6917, E-mail: hooper@usf.edu.
Website: http://www.usf.edu/innovative-education/

The University of Tampa, Program in Creative Writing, Tampa, FL 33606-1490. Offers MFA. *Program availability:* Part-time. *Faculty:* 3 full-time (1 woman), 11 part-time/adjunct (3 women). *Students:* 56 full-time (34 women); includes 13 minority (3 Black or African American, non-Hispanic/Latino; 1 Asian, non-Hispanic/Latino; 7 Hispanic/Latino; 2 Two

Writing

or more races, non-Hispanic/Latino). Average age 39. 51 applicants, 55% accepted, 14 enrolled. In 2017, 30 master's awarded. *Degree requirements:* For master's, capstone. *Entrance requirements:* For master's, official transcripts from all colleges and/or universities previously attended, resume, personal statement, letters of recommendation, creative writing sample in genre. Additional exam requirements/recommendations for international students: Required—TOEFL (minimum score 577 paper-based; 90 iBT), IELTS (minimum score 7.5). *Application deadline:* Applications are processed on a rolling basis. Application fee: $40. Electronic applications accepted. *Expenses:* Contact institution. *Financial support:* In 2017–18, 11 students received support. Career-related internships or fieldwork, scholarships/grants, and unspecified assistantships available. Financial award applicants required to submit FAFSA. *Unit head:* Dr. Erica Dawson, Director, 813-257-6311, E-mail: edawson@ut.edu. *Application contact:* Chanelle Cox, Staff Assistant, Graduate and Continuing Studies, 813-253-6249, E-mail: ccox@ut.edu.
Website: http://www.ut.edu/mfacw/

The University of Tennessee at Chattanooga, Program in English, Chattanooga, TN 37403. Offers creative writing (MA); literary study (MA); rhetoric and writing (MA). *Program availability:* Part-time. *Students:* 12 full-time (8 women), 14 part-time (11 women); includes 4 minority (1 Black or African American, non-Hispanic/Latino; 1 Asian, non-Hispanic/Latino; 1 Hispanic/Latino; 1 Two or more races, non-Hispanic/Latino). Average age 27. 10 applicants, 100% accepted, 7 enrolled. In 2017, 12 master's awarded. *Degree requirements:* For master's, comprehensive exam, thesis. *Entrance requirements:* For master's, minimum GPA of 3.0 in English, two letters of recommendation. Additional exam requirements/recommendations for international students: Required—TOEFL (minimum score 550 paper-based; 79 iBT), IELTS (minimum score 6). *Application deadline:* For fall admission, 6/15 priority date for domestic students, 7/1 for international students; for spring admission, 11/1 priority date for domestic students, 11/1 for international students. Applications are processed on a rolling basis. Application fee: $35 ($40 for international students). Electronic applications accepted. *Expenses:* Contact institution. *Financial support:* Research assistantships, teaching assistantships, career-related internships or fieldwork, scholarships/grants, health care benefits, and unspecified assistantships available. Support available to part-time students. Financial award application deadline: 7/1; financial award applicants required to submit FAFSA. *Faculty research:* Technical writing, African-American literature, Milton, creative writing and poetry, American modernism and gender theory. *Total annual research expenditures:* $6,000. *Unit head:* Dr. Christopher Stuart, Department Head, 423-425-2140, Fax: 423-425-2282, E-mail: chris-stuart@utc.edu. *Application contact:* Dr. Joanne Romagni, Dean of the Graduate School, 423-425-4478, Fax: 423-425-5223, E-mail: joanne-romagni@utc.edu.
Website: http://www.utc.edu/english/

The University of Texas at Austin, Graduate School, College of Liberal Arts, Department of English, Austin, TX 78712-1111. Offers creative writing (MFA); English (MA, PhD). *Program availability:* Part-time. Terminal master's awarded for partial completion of doctoral program. *Degree requirements:* For master's, 2 foreign languages; for doctorate, variable foreign language requirement. *Entrance requirements:* For master's and doctorate, GRE General Test. Electronic applications accepted.

The University of Texas at Austin, Graduate School, Michener Center for Writers, Austin, TX 78712-1111. Offers fiction (MFA); playwriting (MFA); poetry (MFA); screenwriting (MFA). Electronic applications accepted.

The University of Texas at El Paso, Graduate School, College of Liberal Arts, Department of Creative Writing, El Paso, TX 79968-0001. Offers creative writing (MFA); creative writing of the Americas (MFA). *Program availability:* Part-time, evening/weekend, online learning. *Degree requirements:* For master's, thesis. *Entrance requirements:* For master's, minimum GPA of 3.0, letters of recommendation, writing sample. Additional exam requirements/recommendations for international students: Recommended—TOEFL, IELTS. Electronic applications accepted.

The University of Texas at El Paso, Graduate School, College of Liberal Arts, Department of English, El Paso, TX 79968-0001. Offers bilingual professional writing (Certificate); English and American literature (MA); rhetoric and composition (PhD); rhetoric and writing studies (MA); teaching English (MAT). *Program availability:* Part-time, evening/weekend. *Degree requirements:* For master's, thesis optional. *Entrance requirements:* For master's, GRE General Test, minimum GPA of 3.0. Additional exam requirements/recommendations for international students: Required—TOEFL. Electronic applications accepted. *Faculty research:* Literature, creative writing, literary theory.

The University of Texas Rio Grande Valley, College of Fine Arts, Program in Creative Writing, Edinburg, TX 78539. Offers MFA. *Program availability:* Part-time. *Faculty:* 5 full-time (1 woman), 1 (woman) part-time/adjunct. *Students:* 13 full-time (9 women), 19 part-time (7 women); includes 28 minority (27 Hispanic/Latino; 1 Two or more races, non-Hispanic/Latino), 2 international. Average age 29. 9 applicants, 89% accepted, 3 enrolled. In 2017, 10 master's awarded. *Entrance requirements:* Additional exam requirements/recommendations for international students: Required—TOEFL or IELTS. *Expenses:* Tuition, state resident: full-time $5550; part-time $417 per credit hour. Tuition, nonresident: full-time $13,020; part-time $832 per credit hour. *Required fees:* $1169. *Unit head:* Dr. Dahlia Guerra, Interim Dean. *Application contact:* Stephanie Ozuna, Graduate Student Recruiter, 956-665-3558, E-mail: stephanie.ozuna@utrgv.edu.

University of the Sacred Heart, Graduate Programs, Department of Communication, San Juan, PR 00914-0383. Offers contemporary culture and media (MA); digital journalism (MA, Certificate); editing for media (MA, Certificate); public relations (MA, Certificate); publicity (MA, Certificate); scriptwriting (MA, Certificate). *Program availability:* Part-time, evening/weekend. *Degree requirements:* For master's, thesis.

University of the Sacred Heart, Graduate Programs, Program in Creative Writing, San Juan, PR 00914-0383. Offers MFA, Certificate.

The University of the South, Sewanee School of Letters, Sewanee, TN 37383-1000. Offers American and English literature (MA); creative writing (MFA). *Program availability:* Part-time. *Faculty:* 1 full-time (0 women), 10 part-time/adjunct (7 women). *Students:* 53 part-time (33 women); includes 4 minority (1 Black or African American, non-Hispanic/Latino; 3 Two or more races, non-Hispanic/Latino), 1 international. Average age 41. In 2017, 13 master's awarded. *Degree requirements:* For master's, thesis (for some programs). *Entrance requirements:* For master's, writing sample, two letters of recommendation, official transcripts. *Application deadline:* Applications are processed on a rolling basis. Application fee: $40. Electronic applications accepted. *Expenses:* Contact institution. *Financial support:* Institutionally sponsored loans and scholarships/grants available. *Unit head:* Dr. John Gatta, Interim Director, 931-598-1636, E-mail: sletters@sewanee.edu. *Application contact:* April R. Alvarez, Administrator, 931-598-1636, E-mail: sletters@sewanee.edu.
Website: http://letters.sewanee.edu/

The University of Toledo, College of Graduate Studies, College of Languages, Literature and Social Sciences, Department of English Language and Literature, Toledo, OH 43606-3390. Offers English as a second language (MA); teaching of writing (Certificate). *Program availability:* Part-time. *Degree requirements:* For master's, thesis. *Entrance requirements:* For master's, GRE if GPA is less than 3.0, minimum cumulative point-hour ratio of 2.7 for all previous academic work, three letters of recommendation, transcripts from all prior institutions attended, critical essay; for Certificate, statement of purpose, transcripts from all prior institutions attended, 2 letters of recommendation. Additional exam requirements/recommendations for international students: Required—TOEFL (minimum score 550 paper-based; 80 iBT). Electronic applications accepted. *Faculty research:* Literary criticism, linguistics, creative writing, folklore and cultural studies.

University of Toronto, School of Graduate Studies, Faculty of Arts and Science, Department of English, Toronto, ON M5S 1A1, Canada. Offers creative writing (MA); English (MA, PhD); JD/MA. *Program availability:* Part-time. *Degree requirements:* For master's, thesis optional; for doctorate, 2 foreign languages, thesis/dissertation. *Entrance requirements:* For master's, minimum B+ average, 2 letters of reference, portfolio (creative writing program); for doctorate, minimum A- average, 2 letters of reference, writing sample. Additional exam requirements/recommendations for international students: Required—TOEFL (minimum score 580 paper-based; 93 iBT), TWE (minimum score 5). Electronic applications accepted.

University of Utah, Graduate School, College of Humanities, Department of English, Salt Lake City, UT 84112. Offers English (MA, MFA, PhD), including creative writing (MFA, PhD), literary and cultural studies (MA, PhD), rhetoric and composition (MA, PhD). *Program availability:* Part-time. *Faculty:* 31 full-time (13 women), 5 part-time/adjunct (2 women). *Students:* 43 full-time (24 women), 25 part-time (15 women); includes 13 minority (5 Asian, non-Hispanic/Latino; 5 Hispanic/Latino; 3 Two or more races, non-Hispanic/Latino), 3 international. Average age 26. 225 applicants, 17% accepted, 14 enrolled. In 2017, 1 master's, 8 doctorates awarded. Terminal master's awarded for partial completion of doctoral program. *Entrance requirements:* For master's and doctorate, GRE General Test, minimum GPA of 3.2. Additional exam requirements/recommendations for international students: Required—TOEFL (minimum score 650 paper-based; 115 iBT); Recommended—IELTS (minimum score 9), TSE. *Application deadline:* For fall admission, 12/15 for domestic and international students. Application fee: $55 ($65 for international students). Electronic applications accepted. *Financial support:* In 2017–18, 39 students received support, including 10 fellowships (averaging $18,600 per year), 29 teaching assistantships with full tuition reimbursements available (averaging $18,600 per year); health care benefits also available. Financial award application deadline: 12/15; financial award applicants required to submit FAFSA. *Faculty research:* Creative writing including poetics and modern poetry, fiction, and experimental forms; nineteenth- and twentieth-century British and American literature; American Studies, the American West, and environmental studies; critical theory and practice; race and gender studies. *Total annual research expenditures:* $126,500. *Unit head:* Prof. Barry L. Weller, Department Chair, 801-581-6168, Fax: 801-585-5167, E-mail: barry.weller@utah.edu. *Application contact:* Prof. Andrew Franta, Director of Graduate Studies, 801-581-7850, Fax: 801-585-5167, E-mail: a.franta@utah.edu.
Website: http://english.utah.edu/

University of Victoria, Faculty of Graduate Studies, Faculty of Fine Arts, Department of Writing, Victoria, BC V8W 2Y2, Canada. Offers MFA. *Entrance requirements:* For master's, portfolio, 2 letters of reference.

University of Virginia, College and Graduate School of Arts and Sciences, Department of English Language and Literature, Program in Creative Writing, Charlottesville, VA 22903. Offers MFA. *Faculty:* 7 full-time (4 women). *Students:* 26 full-time (17 women); includes 3 minority (1 Black or African American, non-Hispanic/Latino; 1 Asian, non-Hispanic/Latino; 1 Two or more races, non-Hispanic/Latino), 4 international. Average age 28. 666 applicants, 2% accepted, 10 enrolled. In 2017, 8 master's awarded. *Degree requirements:* For master's, comprehensive exam, thesis. *Entrance requirements:* For master's, GRE General Test, writing sample. Additional exam requirements/recommendations for international students: Required—TOEFL (minimum score 600 paper-based; 90 iBT), IELTS (minimum score 7). *Application deadline:* For fall admission, 1/1 for domestic students, 1/4 for international students. Application fee: $60. Electronic applications accepted. *Financial support:* Fellowships and teaching assistantships available. Financial award application deadline: 1/4; financial award applicants required to submit FAFSA. *Unit head:* Jane Alison, Director, 434-924-8607, Fax: 434-924-1478, E-mail: ct2a@virginia.edu.
Website: http://www.engl.virginia.edu/creativewriting/

University of Washington, Graduate School, College of Arts and Sciences, Department of English, Program in Creative Writing, Seattle, WA 98195. Offers MFA. *Entrance requirements:* For master's, GRE, GMAT. Additional exam requirements/recommendations for international students: Required—TOEFL (minimum score 550 paper-based). Electronic applications accepted.

University of Washington, Bothell, Program in Creative Writing and Poetics, Bothell, WA 98011. Offers MFA.

University of West Florida, College of Arts, Social Sciences, and Humanities, Department of English, Pensacola, FL 32514-5750. Offers creative writing (MA); literature (MA). *Program availability:* Part-time, evening/weekend. *Degree requirements:* For master's, thesis. *Entrance requirements:* For master's, GRE (minimum score: verbal 500, writing 4.5) or MAT (minimum score 413), official transcripts; two-page statement of purpose; writing sample (2500 words of literary analysis for literature track, or 2500 words of fiction/non-fiction prose or 10 poems for creative writing track); three letters of recommendation from instructors; 20 hours' upper-division undergraduate coursework in English. Additional exam requirements/recommendations for international students: Required—TOEFL (minimum score 550 paper-based). *Faculty research:* Faulkner, Shakespeare, American humor, women's studies, poetry.

University of Windsor, Faculty of Graduate Studies, Faculty of Arts and Social Sciences, Department of English Language, Literature and Creative Writing, Windsor, ON N9B 3P4, Canada. Offers English: creative writing and language and literature (MA); English: language and literature (MA). *Program availability:* Part-time. *Degree requirements:* For master's, thesis. *Entrance requirements:* For master's, minimum B average, portfolio. Additional exam requirements/recommendations for international students: Required—TOEFL (minimum score 600 paper-based). Electronic applications accepted. *Faculty research:* Use of gender-related terms in popular culture; international and Aboriginal literatures: expression of cultural identity; critical analysis of authors: Pope, Munroe, Lady Morgan, Orwell, Thomas; the "feminine" voice in literature and contemporary culture.

University of Wisconsin–Eau Claire, College of Arts and Sciences, Program in English, Eau Claire, WI 54702-4004. Offers literature and textual interpretation (MA); writing (MA). *Program availability:* Part-time. *Degree requirements:* For master's, oral defense with thesis. *Entrance requirements:* For master's, minimum GPA of 3.25 in English, 3.0 overall; bachelor's degree with minimum of 24 credits in English. Additional exam requirements/recommendations for international students: Required—TOEFL (minimum score 79 iBT).

University of Wisconsin–Madison, Graduate School, College of Letters and Science, Department of English, Madison, WI 53706-1380. Offers applied English linguistics

(MA); composition and rhetoric (PhD); creative writing (MFA); English language and linguistics (PhD); literary studies (MA, PhD). *Degree requirements:* For doctorate, thesis/dissertation.

University of Wisconsin–Milwaukee, Graduate School, College of Letters and Science, Department of English, Milwaukee, WI 53201-0413. Offers English (MA, PhD), including creative writing, English language and linguistics, English secondary education, literary and critical studies, literature and cultural theory (PhD), literature and language studies, literature, culture, and media, media, cinema and digital studies, professional and technical communication (MA), professional and technical writing, professional writing (PhD), rhetoric and composition (PhD), rhetoric and writing. *Students:* 90 full-time (54 women), 42 part-time (17 women); includes 12 minority (2 Black or African American, non-Hispanic/Latino; 1 American Indian or Alaska Native, non-Hispanic/Latino; 4 Asian, non-Hispanic/Latino; 1 Hispanic/Latino; 4 Two or more races, non-Hispanic/Latino), 9 international. Average age 34. 166 applicants, 21% accepted, 27 enrolled. In 2017, 10 master's, 12 doctorates awarded. *Degree requirements:* For master's, thesis or alternative; for doctorate, one foreign language, thesis/dissertation. *Entrance requirements:* For master's, GRE General Test, GRE Subject Test; for doctorate, GRE. Additional exam requirements/recommendations for international students: Required—TOEFL (minimum score 550 paper-based; 79 iBT), IELTS (minimum score 6.5). *Application deadline:* For fall admission, 1/1 priority date for domestic students; for spring admission, 9/1 for domestic students. Application fee: $56 ($96 for international students). Electronic applications accepted. *Financial support:* Fellowships, research assistantships, teaching assistantships, career-related internships or fieldwork, unspecified assistantships, and project assistantships available. Support available to part-time students. Financial award application deadline: 4/15; financial award applicants required to submit FAFSA. *Unit head:* Mark Netzloff, Department Chair, 414-229-4511, E-mail: netzloff@uwm.edu. *Application contact:* General Information Contact, 414-229-4982, Fax: 414-229-6967, E-mail: gradschool@uwm.edu.
Website: https://uwm.edu/english/

University of Wyoming, College of Arts and Sciences, Department of English, Laramie, WY 82071. Offers creative writing (MFA); English (MA). *Program availability:* Part-time. *Degree requirements:* For master's, thesis or alternative, internship. *Entrance requirements:* For master's, GRE General Test, minimum GPA of 3.0. Electronic applications accepted. *Faculty research:* Literature and theory, creative writing, English as a second language, ethnic and women's studies, composition.

Utah State University, School of Graduate Studies, College of Humanities and Social Sciences, Department of English, Logan, UT 84322. Offers American studies (MA, MS), including folklore, western American literature and culture; English (MA, MS), including literature and writing, technical writing. *Program availability:* Part-time, evening/weekend. *Degree requirements:* For master's, thesis or alternative. *Entrance requirements:* For master's, GRE General Test or MAT, minimum GPA of 3.0, recommendation letters, writing samples. Additional exam requirements/recommendations for international students: Required—TOEFL. *Faculty research:* Scottish enlightenment, material culture, composition theory, creative nonfiction, literary criticism.

Vanderbilt University, Program in Creative Writing, Nashville, TN 37240-1001. Offers MFA. *Students:* Average age 27. 426 applicants, 2% accepted, 6 enrolled. In 2017, 6 master's awarded. *Degree requirements:* For master's, comprehensive exam, thesis. *Entrance requirements:* For master's, GRE General Test, sample of written work. Additional exam requirements/recommendations for international students: Required—TOEFL (minimum score 570 paper-based; 88 iBT). *Application deadline:* For fall admission, 1/15 for domestic and international students. Electronic applications accepted. *Financial support:* Fellowships, teaching assistantships, Federal Work-Study, institutionally sponsored loans, and health care benefits available. Financial award application deadline: 1/15; financial award applicants required to submit CSS PROFILE or FAFSA. *Unit head:* Dr. Dana Nelson, Chair, 615-322-2541, E-mail: dana.d.nelson@vanderbilt.edu. *Application contact:* Katherine Daniels, Director of Graduate Studies, 615-322-2541, E-mail: kate.daniels@vanderbilt.edu.
Website: http://www.vanderbilt.edu/creativewriting/

Vermont College of Fine Arts, MFA in Writing and Publishing Program, Montpelier, VT 05602. Offers MFA. *Faculty:* 5 full-time (3 women). *Students:* 25 full-time (17 women), 1 (woman) part-time; includes 6 minority (1 American Indian or Alaska Native, non-Hispanic/Latino; 2 Asian, non-Hispanic/Latino; 2 Hispanic/Latino; 1 Two or more races, non-Hispanic/Latino), 3 international. Average age 31. In 2017, 6 master's awarded. *Expenses:* Contact institution. *Financial support:* In 2017–18, 26 students received support, including 6 fellowships (averaging $3,000 per year); scholarships/grants also available. *Unit head:* Miciah Gault, Director, 802-828-8534. *Application contact:* David Markow, Director of Enrollment Management, 802-828-8535, E-mail: admissions@vcfa.edu.
Website: http://vcfa.edu/writing-publishing

Vermont College of Fine Arts, MFA in Writing for Children and Young Adults Program, Montpelier, VT 05602. Offers MFA. *Faculty:* 25 part-time/adjunct (18 women). *Students:* 91 full-time (82 women); includes 17 minority (1 Black or African American, non-Hispanic/Latino; 4 Asian, non-Hispanic/Latino; 6 Hispanic/Latino; 6 Two or more races, non-Hispanic/Latino), 3 international. Average age 41. 47 applicants, 68% accepted, 28 enrolled. In 2017, 47 master's awarded. *Entrance requirements:* For master's, original work, bachelor's degree. *Application deadline:* Applications are processed on a rolling basis. Application fee: $75. Electronic applications accepted. *Expenses:* Contact institution. *Financial support:* In 2017–18, 60 students received support. Scholarships/grants available. Financial award applicants required to submit FAFSA. *Unit head:* Melissa Fisher, Program Director, 802-828-8696, E-mail: melissa.fisher@vcfa.edu.
Website: http://vcfa.edu/wcya

Vermont College of Fine Arts, MFA in Writing Program, Montpelier, VT 05602. Offers MFA. *Faculty:* 36 part-time/adjunct (17 women). *Students:* 111 full-time (87 women); includes 11 minority (5 Black or African American, non-Hispanic/Latino; 2 Asian, non-Hispanic/Latino; 1 Hispanic/Latino; 3 Two or more races, non-Hispanic/Latino), 2 international. Average age 42. 123 applicants, 63% accepted, 36 enrolled. In 2017, 56 master's awarded. *Entrance requirements:* For master's, original work; bachelor's degree; evidence of exceptional academic, literary and/or publishing background. Application fee: $75. *Expenses:* Contact institution. *Financial support:* Scholarships/grants available. Financial award applicants required to submit FAFSA. *Unit head:* Melissa Hammerle, Program Director, 802-828-8840, E-mail: melissa.hammerle@vcfa.edu. *Application contact:* Ann Cardinal, Director of Student Recruitment, 802-828-8589, E-mail: ann.cardinal@vcfa.edu.
Website: http://www.vcfa.edu/writing

Virginia Commonwealth University, Graduate School, College of Humanities and Sciences, Department of English, Program in Creative Writing, Richmond, VA 23284-9005. Offers dual genre (MFA); fiction (MFA); poetry (MFA). *Program availability:* Part-time. *Entrance requirements:* For master's, GRE General Test, portfolio. Additional exam requirements/recommendations for international students: Required—TOEFL (minimum score 600 paper-based; 100 iBT) or IELTS (minimum score 6.5). Electronic applications accepted. *Faculty research:* Poetry, fiction.

Virginia Polytechnic Institute and State University, Graduate School, College of Liberal Arts and Human Sciences, Blacksburg, VA 24061. Offers career and technical education (MS Ed, Ed S); communication (MA); counselor education (MA); creative writing (MFA); curriculum and instruction (MA Ed, Ed S); educational leadership and policy studies (Ed S); educational research and evaluation (PhD); English (MA); social, political, ethical, and cultural thought (PhD); Ed D/PhD. *Faculty:* 411 full-time (213 women), 3 part-time/adjunct (all women). *Students:* 623 full-time (427 women), 431 part-time (278 women); includes 203 minority (115 Black or African American, non-Hispanic/Latino; 4 American Indian or Alaska Native, non-Hispanic/Latino; 29 Asian, non-Hispanic/Latino; 33 Hispanic/Latino; 2 Native Hawaiian or other Pacific Islander, non-Hispanic/Latino; 20 Two or more races, non-Hispanic/Latino), 87 international. Average age 34. 898 applicants, 50% accepted, 329 enrolled. In 2017, 314 master's, 102 doctorates awarded. *Degree requirements:* For master's, comprehensive exam (for some programs), thesis (for some programs); for doctorate, comprehensive exam (for some programs), thesis/dissertation (for some programs). *Entrance requirements:* For master's and doctorate, GRE/GMAT. Additional exam requirements/recommendations for international students: Required—TOEFL (minimum score 80 iBT). *Application deadline:* For fall admission, 8/1 for domestic students, 4/1 for international students; for spring admission, 1/1 for domestic students, 9/1 for international students. Applications are processed on a rolling basis. Application fee: $75. Electronic applications accepted. *Expenses:* Tuition, state resident: full-time $15,072; part-time $718.50 per credit hour. Tuition, nonresident: full-time $28,810; part-time $1448.25 per credit hour. *Required fees:* $2741; $502 per semester. Tuition and fees vary according to course load, campus/location and program. *Financial support:* In 2017–18, 19 research assistantships with full tuition reimbursements (averaging $19,611 per year), 226 teaching assistantships with full tuition reimbursements (averaging $16,220 per year) were awarded. Financial award application deadline: 3/1; financial award applicants required to submit FAFSA. *Total annual research expenditures:* $7.9 million. *Unit head:* Dr. Rosemary Blieszner, Dean, 540-231-6779, Fax: 540-231-7157, E-mail: rmb@vt.edu. *Application contact:* Chelsea Blanchet, Executive Assistant, 540-231-6779, Fax: 540-231-7157, E-mail: bchels1@vt.edu.
Website: http://www.liberalarts.vt.edu/

Warren Wilson College, MFA Program for Writers, Asheville, NC 28815-9000. Offers MFA. *Program availability:* Online learning. *Degree requirements:* For master's, thesis, public reading, critical essay in 3rd semester. *Entrance requirements:* For master's, manuscript of creative work; personal essay; critical essay. Electronic applications accepted. *Expenses:* Contact institution. *Faculty research:* Poetry and fiction writing, analytic writing, creative and analytic study of literature, literary craft instruction.

Washington & Jefferson College, Graduate and Continuing Studies, Washington, PA 15301. Offers applied health care economics and outcomes management (MS); professional accounting (MAC); professional writing (Graduate Certificate); thanatology (Graduate Certificate).

Washington University in St. Louis, The Graduate School, Department of English, Writing Program, St. Louis, MO 63130-4899. Offers MFA. *Degree requirements:* For master's, thesis or written exam. *Entrance requirements:* For master's, GRE General Test, sample of written work. Additional exam requirements/recommendations for international students: Required—TOEFL. Electronic applications accepted. *Faculty research:* Fiction, nonfiction, poetry writing.

Wayne State University, College of Liberal Arts and Sciences, Department of English, Detroit, MI 48202. Offers English (MA); film and media studies (PhD); literary and cultural studies (PhD); rhetoric and composition studies (PhD). *Faculty:* 23. *Students:* 68 full-time (34 women), 24 part-time (17 women); includes 22 minority (10 Black or African American, non-Hispanic/Latino; 2 Asian, non-Hispanic/Latino; 6 Hispanic/Latino; 4 Two or more races, non-Hispanic/Latino), 5 international. Average age 33. 110 applicants, 35% accepted, 17 enrolled. In 2017, 15 master's, 15 doctorates awarded. Terminal master's awarded for partial completion of doctoral program. *Degree requirements:* For master's, variable foreign language requirement, essay, thesis, or portfolio of work approved by Director of Graduate Studies; for doctorate, one foreign language, comprehensive exam, thesis/dissertation. *Entrance requirements:* For master's, statement of purpose; two academic letters of reference; sample essay from previous English course; for doctorate, GRE General Test, statement of purpose; two academic letters of reference; sample of scholarly or critical writing. Additional exam requirements/recommendations for international students: Required—TOEFL (minimum score 550 paper-based; 79 iBT), TWE (minimum score 5.5), Michigan English Language Assessment Battery (minimum score 85); Recommended—IELTS (minimum score 6.5). *Application deadline:* For fall admission, 1/15 for domestic students. Applications are processed on a rolling basis. Application fee: $50. Electronic applications accepted. *Expenses:* Tuition, state resident: full-time $10,224; part-time $638.98 per credit hour. Tuition, nonresident: full-time $22,145; part-time $1384.04 per credit hour. Tuition and fees vary according to course load and program. *Financial support:* In 2017–18, 61 students received support, including 6 fellowships with tuition reimbursements available (averaging $15,583 per year), 30 teaching assistantships with tuition reimbursements available (averaging $18,534 per year); research assistantships with tuition reimbursements available, scholarships/grants, health care benefits, and unspecified assistantships also available. Financial award applicants required to submit FAFSA. *Faculty research:* Literary and cultural studies, film and new media studies, rhetoric and composition studies, linguistics, and creative writing. *Unit head:* Dr. Kenneth Jackson, Chair and Professor, 313-577-7692, E-mail: ai4054@wayne.edu. *Application contact:* Dr. Carolin Maun, Director of Graduate Studies, 313-577-7694, E-mail: caroline.maun@wayne.edu.
Website: http://clas.wayne.edu/english/

Wesleyan University, Graduate Liberal Studies Program, Middletown, CT 06459. Offers liberal arts (M Phil); liberal studies (MALS); writing (Graduate Certificate). *Program availability:* Part-time, evening/weekend. *Degree requirements:* For master's, thesis optional; for Graduate Certificate, thesis. *Entrance requirements:* For master's, statement of intent, essay, undergraduate transcripts, two letters of recommendation. Additional exam requirements/recommendations for international students: Required—TOEFL (minimum score 100 iBT), IELTS (minimum score 7). *Application deadline:* For fall admission, 7/16 for domestic students; for spring admission, 11/14 for domestic students; for summer admission, 4/15 for domestic students. Applications are processed on a rolling basis. Application fee: $100. Electronic applications accepted. *Expenses:* Contact institution. *Financial support:* Scholarships/grants available. Support available to part-time students. *Faculty research:* Interdisciplinary studies. *Unit head:* Jennifer Curran, Director, 860-685-3338, Fax: 860-685-2901, E-mail: jcurran@wesleyan.edu. *Application contact:* Sarah-Jane Ripa, Associate Director, Student Services and Outreach, 860-685-3345, Fax: 860-685-2901, E-mail: sripa@wesleyan.edu.
Website: http://www.wesleyan.edu/masters/

West Chester University of Pennsylvania, College of Arts and Humanities, Department of English, West Chester, PA 19383. Offers English (MA), including creative writing, literature, writing, teaching, and criticism; publishing (Certificate); secondary English (Teaching Certificate). *Program availability:* Part-time, evening/weekend.

Students: 25 full-time (17 women), 47 part-time (27 women); includes 5 minority (1 Black or African American, non-Hispanic/Latino; 1 Asian, non-Hispanic/Latino; 3 Two or more races, non-Hispanic/Latino), 2 international. Average age 29. 43 applicants, 88% accepted, 25 enrolled. In 2017, 10 master's, 1 other advanced degree awarded. *Degree requirements:* For master's, thesis optional; for other advanced degree, capstone internship and e-portfolio (for Certificate in publishing). *Entrance requirements:* For master's, minimum GPA of 2.8, two letters of recommendation, writing sample, goals statement, official transcripts; for other advanced degree, two letters of recommendation, statement of goals, official transcripts; undergraduate degree (for Certificate); minimum GPA of 2.85 and writing sample (for Teaching Certificate). Additional exam requirements/recommendations for international students: Required—TOEFL or IELTS. *Application deadline:* For fall admission, 5/15 for international students; for spring admission, 10/15 for international students. Applications are processed on a rolling basis. Application fee: $50. Electronic applications accepted. *Expenses:* Tuition, state resident: full-time $9000; part-time $500 per credit. Tuition, nonresident: full-time $13,500; part-time $750 per credit. *Required fees:* $2959; $149.79 per credit. *Financial support:* Scholarships/grants and unspecified assistantships available. Financial award application deadline: 2/15; financial award applicants required to submit FAFSA. *Faculty research:* Critical theory, cultural studies, literature, rhetoric and composition, creative writing. *Unit head:* Dr. Rodney Mader, Chair, 610-436-2822, Fax: 610-738-0516, E-mail: rmader@wcupa.edu. *Application contact:* Dr. Eleanor Shevlin, Graduate Coordinator for English, 610-436-2745, Fax: 610-738-0516, E-mail: eshevlin@wcupa.edu.
Website: http://www.wcupa.edu/arts-humanities/english/

Western Carolina University, Graduate School, College of Arts and Sciences, Department of English, Cullowhee, NC 28723. Offers literature (MA); professional writing (MA); rhetoric and composition (MA); teaching English to speakers of other languages (Certificate); technical and professional writing (Certificate). *Program availability:* Part-time, evening/weekend. *Students:* 31. *Degree requirements:* For master's, one foreign language, comprehensive exam, thesis (for some programs). *Entrance requirements:* For master's, appropriate undergraduate degree, writing sample, 3 letters of recommendation. Additional exam requirements/recommendations for international students: Required—TOEFL (minimum score 550 paper-based, 79 iBT) or IELTS (6.5). *Application deadline:* For fall admission, 2/15 priority date for domestic and international students; for spring admission, 11/15 priority date for domestic students, 10/15 priority date for international students. Applications are processed on a rolling basis. Application fee: $65. Electronic applications accepted. *Expenses:* $10,000 per year in-state full-time; $20,308 per year out-of-state full-time. *Financial support:* In 2017–18, 1 research assistantship with full and partial tuition reimbursement (averaging $9,000 per year), 16 teaching assistantships with full and partial tuition reimbursements (averaging $9,500 per year) were awarded; career-related internships or fieldwork, institutionally sponsored loans, scholarships/grants, and unspecified assistantships also available. Financial award application deadline: 2/15; financial award applicants required to submit FAFSA. *Faculty research:* Teaching English to speakers of other languages (TESOL), language assessment, applied linguistics, poetry, folk and fairy tales, post World War II British literature, Appalachian and Southern literature. *Unit head:* Dr. Brent Kinser, Department Head, E-mail: bkinser@wcu.edu. *Application contact:* Bobbi Smith, Graduate Admissions Coordinator, E-mail: bobbismith@email.wcu.edu.
Website: https://www.wcu.edu/learn/departments-schools-colleges/cas/humanities/english/enggrad/index.aspx

Western Connecticut State University, Division of Graduate Studies, Maricostas School of Arts and Sciences, Department of Writing, Linguistics, and Creative Process, Danbury, CT 06810-6885. Offers creative and professional writing (MFA). *Program availability:* Part-time. *Degree requirements:* For master's, thesis, completion of program within 4 years, enrichment project that compliments course of study. *Entrance requirements:* For master's, 2 writing samples: a 20-50 page portfolio of previous writing and a brief essay. Additional exam requirements/recommendations for international students: Recommended—TOEFL (minimum score 550 paper-based; 79 iBT), IELTS (minimum score 6). *Expenses:* Contact institution. *Faculty research:* Creativity, chaos.

Western Kentucky University, Graduate Studies, Potter College of Arts and Letters, Department of English, Bowling Green, KY 42101. Offers education (MA); English (MA Ed); literature (MA), including American literature, British literature, literary theory, women writers, world literature; teaching English as a second language (MA); writing (MA). *Program availability:* Part-time, evening/weekend. *Degree requirements:* For master's, comprehensive exam, thesis optional, final exam. *Entrance requirements:* For master's, GRE General Test, minimum GPA of 2.75. Additional exam requirements/recommendations for international students: Required—TOEFL (minimum score 555 paper-based; 79 iBT). *Faculty research:* Improving writing, linking teacher knowledge and performance, Victorian women writers, Kentucky women writers, Kentucky poets.

Western Michigan University, Graduate College, College of Arts and Sciences, Department of English, Kalamazoo, MI 49008. Offers creative writing (MFA, PhD); English (MA, PhD); English teaching (MA). *Degree requirements:* For doctorate, one foreign language, thesis/dissertation.

Western New England University, College of Arts and Sciences, Program in Creative Writing, Springfield, MA 01119. Offers MFA. *Program availability:* Part-time, evening/weekend. *Faculty:* 15 full-time (9 women). *Students:* 8 part-time (6 women); includes 1 minority (Asian, non-Hispanic/Latino). Average age 36. 6 applicants, 100% accepted, 3 enrolled. In 2017, 7 master's awarded. *Entrance requirements:* For master's, official transcripts, two letters of recommendation, writing sample, personal narrative, resume. Additional exam requirements/recommendations for international students: Required—TOEFL (minimum score 79 iBT). *Application deadline:* Applications are processed on a rolling basis. Application fee: $30. Electronic applications accepted. *Expenses:* Contact institution. *Financial support:* Application deadline: 4/15; applicants required to submit FAFSA. *Unit head:* Pearl Abraham, Director, 413-782-1338, E-mail: pearl.abraham@wne.edu. *Application contact:* Matthew Fox, Director of Admissions for Graduate Students and Adult Learners, 413-782-1410, Fax: 413-782-1777, E-mail: study@wne.edu.
Website: http://www1.wne.edu/academics/graduate/mfa.cfm

Western State Colorado University, Program in Creative Writing, Gunnison, CO 81231. Offers mainstream genre fiction (MFA); poetry (MFA); screenwriting (MFA). *Program availability:* Online learning. *Degree requirements:* For master's, thesis.

Westminster College, Program in Professional Communication, Salt Lake City, UT 84105-3697. Offers MPC, MSC. *Faculty:* 3 full-time (2 women), 2 part-time/adjunct (both women). *Students:* 29 full-time (19 women), 6 part-time (all women); includes 11 minority (2 Asian, non-Hispanic/Latino; 5 Hispanic/Latino; 4 Two or more races, non-Hispanic/Latino), 1 international. Average age 34. 18 applicants, 89% accepted, 15 enrolled. In 2017, 22 master's awarded. *Degree requirements:* For master's, capstone project. *Entrance requirements:* For master's, GRE, resume, personal statement of intent, official transcripts, two letters of recommendation, writing sample. Additional exam requirements/recommendations for international students: Required—TOEFL (minimum score 84 iBT), IELTS (minimum score 7). *Application deadline:* Applications are processed on a rolling basis. Application fee: $50. Electronic applications accepted. Application fee is waived when completed online. *Expenses:* $850 per credit hour (for MSC); $1,010 per credit hour (for MPC); $13 student fee per credit hour. *Financial support:* In 2017–18, 13 students received support. Career-related internships or fieldwork, scholarships/grants, unspecified assistantships, and tuition remission available. Financial award applicants required to submit FAFSA. *Faculty research:* Diversity in higher education, communication pedagogy, mass media law and ethics, impact of new technologies on society, rhetorical theory, feminism and popular culture, critical communication pedagogy. *Unit head:* Dr. Curtis Newbold, Director, 801-832-2827, Fax: 801-832-3102, E-mail: cnewbold@westminstercollege.edu. *Application contact:* Lauren Erlacher, Associate Director, Graduate Admissions, 801-832-2208, Fax: 801-832-3101, E-mail: lerlacher@westminstercollege.edu.
Website: https://www.westminstercollege.edu/graduate/programs

West Virginia University, Eberly College of Arts and Sciences, Morgantown, WV 26506. Offers biology (MS, PhD); chemistry (MS, PhD); communication studies (MA, PhD); computational statistics (PhD); creative writing (MFA); English (MA, PhD); forensic and investigative science (MS); forensic science (PhD); geography (MA); geology (MA, PhD); history (MA, PhD); legal studies (MLS); math (MS); physics (MS, PhD); political science (MA, PhD); professional writing and editing (MA); psychology (MA); public administration (MPA); social work (MSW); sociology (MA, PhD); statistics (MS). *Program availability:* Part-time, evening/weekend, online learning. *Students:* 831 full-time (437 women), 236 part-time (142 women); includes 112 minority (35 Black or African American, non-Hispanic/Latino; 15 Asian, non-Hispanic/Latino; 29 Hispanic/Latino; 33 Two or more races, non-Hispanic/Latino), 235 international. Terminal master's awarded for partial completion of doctoral program. *Degree requirements:* For master's, thesis (for some programs); for doctorate, comprehensive exam, thesis/dissertation. *Entrance requirements:* For master's and doctorate, GRE. Additional exam requirements/recommendations for international students: Required—TOEFL (minimum score 600 paper-based); Recommended—TWE. *Application deadline:* For spring admission, 2/15 priority date for domestic and international students. Applications are processed on a rolling basis. Application fee: $45. Electronic applications accepted. *Expenses:* Tuition, state resident: full-time $9450. Tuition, nonresident: full-time $24,390. *Financial support:* Fellowships with full tuition reimbursements, research assistantships with full tuition reimbursements, teaching assistantships with full tuition reimbursements, career-related internships or fieldwork, Federal Work-Study, institutionally sponsored loans, scholarships/grants, health care benefits, tuition waivers (full and partial), unspecified assistantships, and administrative assistantships available. Financial award application deadline: 2/1; financial award applicants required to submit FAFSA. *Faculty research:* Humanities, social sciences, life science, physical sciences, mathematics. *Unit head:* Dr. Mary Ellen Mazey, Dean, 304-293-4611, Fax: 304-293-6858, E-mail: mary.mazey@mail.wvu.edu. *Application contact:* Dr. Fred L. King, Associate Dean for Graduate Studies, 304-293-4611 Ext. 5205, Fax: 304-293-6858, E-mail: fred.king@mail.wvu.edu.
Website: http://www.as.wvu.edu/

West Virginia Wesleyan College, Program in Creative Writing, Buckhannon, WV 26201. Offers MFA.

Wichita State University, Graduate School, Fairmount College of Liberal Arts and Sciences, Department of English, Wichita, KS 67260. Offers creative writing (MFA); English (MA). *Program availability:* Part-time, evening/weekend. *Entrance requirements:* For master's, writing sample (MFA). *Unit head:* Dr. Mary Waters, Chair, 316-978-3130, Fax: 316-978-3548, E-mail: mary.waters@wichita.edu. *Application contact:* Jordan Oleson, Admissions Coordinator, 316-978-3095, Fax: 316-978-3253, E-mail: jordan.oleson@wichita.edu.
Website: http://www.wichita.edu/english

Wilkes University, College of Graduate and Professional Studies, Program in Creative Writing, Wilkes-Barre, PA 18766-0002. Offers MA, MFA. *Program availability:* Part-time, blended/hybrid learning. *Students:* 44 full-time (31 women), 16 part-time (10 women); includes 10 minority (6 Black or African American, non-Hispanic/Latino; 2 Asian, non-Hispanic/Latino; 2 Two or more races, non-Hispanic/Latino). Average age 39. In 2017, 49 master's awarded. *Entrance requirements:* Additional exam requirements/recommendations for international students: Required—TOEFL (minimum score 550 paper-based; 79 iBT). *Application deadline:* Applications are processed on a rolling basis. Application fee: $35 ($65 for international students). Electronic applications accepted. *Expenses:* Contact institution. *Financial support:* Unspecified assistantships available. Financial award application deadline: 3/1; financial award applicants required to submit FAFSA. *Unit head:* Dr. Bonnie Culver, Director, 570-408-4527, Fax: 570-408-7846, E-mail: bonnie.culver@wilkes.edu.
Website: http://www.wilkes.edu/academics/graduate-programs/masters-programs/creative-writing-ma-mfa/index.aspx

William Paterson University of New Jersey, College of Humanities and Social Sciences, Wayne, NJ 07470-8420. Offers applied sociology (MA); assessment and evaluation research (Certificate); bilingual education (Certificate); clinical and counseling psychology (MA); clinical psychology (Psy D); creative and professional writing (MFA); English (MA); history (MA); public policy and international affairs (MA); teaching English as a second language (Certificate). *Program availability:* Part-time. *Faculty:* 36 full-time (21 women), 10 part-time/adjunct (5 women). *Students:* 62 full-time (44 women), 102 part-time (71 women); includes 76 minority (12 Black or African American, non-Hispanic/Latino; 8 Asian, non-Hispanic/Latino; 50 Hispanic/Latino; 6 Two or more races, non-Hispanic/Latino), 6 international. Average age 33. 156 applicants, 51% accepted, 52 enrolled. In 2017, 39 master's awarded. *Degree requirements:* For master's, thesis (for some programs), internship (for some programs). *Entrance requirements:* For master's, GRE/MAT, minimum GPA of 3.0; 2 letters of recommendation; writing sample/personal statement. Additional exam requirements/recommendations for international students: Required—TOEFL (minimum score 550 paper-based; 79 iBT), IELTS (minimum score 6). *Application deadline:* For fall admission, 6/1 for domestic students, 3/1 for international students; for spring admission, 11/1 for domestic students, 10/1 for international students. Applications are processed on a rolling basis. Application fee: $50. Electronic applications accepted. *Expenses:* Tuition, state resident: full-time $13,920; part-time $6264 per year. Tuition, nonresident: full-time $21,700; part-time $9765 per year. *Required fees:* $80; $36 per year. Tuition and fees vary according to course load, degree level and program. *Financial support:* In 2017–18, 3,480 students received support. Career-related internships or fieldwork, Federal Work-Study, scholarships/grants, and unspecified assistantships available. Support available to part-time students. Financial award application deadline: 3/15; financial award applicants required to submit FAFSA. *Faculty research:* Relationship violence, work-family balance, social development of Japan, theories justifying war, reactions to trauma. *Total annual research expenditures:* $32,300. *Unit head:* Dr. Kara Rabbitt, Dean, 973-720-2180, Fax: 973-720-2955, E-mail: rabbittk@wpunj.edu. *Application contact:* Tinu Adeniran, Associate Director, Graduate Admissions, 973-720-2764, Fax: 973-720-2035, E-mail: adenirant@wpunj.edu.
Website: http://www.wpunj.edu/cohss

Yale University, School of Drama, New Haven, CT 06520. Offers acting (MFA, Certificate); design (MFA, Certificate), including costume design, lighting design, projection design, set design; directing (MFA, Certificate); dramaturgy and dramatic criticism (MFA, DFA); playwriting (MFA, Certificate); sound design (MFA, Certificate);

stage management (MFA, Certificate); technical design and production (MFA, Certificate); theater management (MFA); MFA/MBA. *Degree requirements:* For master's, comprehensive exam (for some programs), thesis (for some programs); for doctorate, thesis/dissertation, oral and written comprehensive exams. *Entrance requirements:* For master's, GRE (verbal, quantitative, and analytical), in-person audition (for acting); portfolio review (for design). Additional exam requirements/recommendations for international students: Required—TOEFL. Electronic applications accepted.

ACADEMIC AND PROFESSIONAL PROGRAMS IN INTERDISCIPLINARY STUDIES

Section 14
Interdisciplinary Studies

This section contains a directory of institutions offering graduate work in interdisciplinary studies. Additional information about programs listed in the directory may be obtained by writing directly to the dean of a graduate school or chair of a department at the address given in the directory.

For programs offering related work, see also in this book *Comparative and Interdisciplinary Arts, Humanities,* and *Social Sciences.*

CONTENTS

Program Directory

Interdisciplinary Studies

Alaska Pacific University, Graduate Programs, Liberal Studies Department, Self-Designed Programs, Anchorage, AK 99508-4672. Offers MA. *Program availability:* Part-time, evening/weekend. *Degree requirements:* For master's, thesis or project. *Entrance requirements:* For master's, MAT (preferred), GRE General Test or GMAT. *Expenses:* Contact institution.

Amberton University, Graduate School, Program in Professional Development, Garland, TX 75041-5595. Offers MA. *Program availability:* Part-time, evening/weekend, online learning. *Entrance requirements:* For master's, minimum GPA of 3.0. *Application deadline:* Applications are processed on a rolling basis. Application fee: $0. *Expenses: Tuition:* Part-time $795 per course. *Unit head:* Dr. Don Hebbard, Academic Dean, 972-382-7113 Ext. 157, Fax: 972-279-9773, E-mail: dhebbard@amberton.edu. *Application contact:* Adviser, 972-279-6511 Ext. 180, Fax: 972-279-9773, E-mail: advisor@amberton.edu.
Website: http://www.amberton.edu/programs-and-courses/masters-degree-programs/professional-development/index.html

Antioch University New England, Graduate School, Department of Environmental Studies, Self-Designed Studies Program, Keene, NH 03431-3552. Offers MS. *Degree requirements:* For master's, practicum, seminar, thesis or project. *Entrance requirements:* For master's, detailed proposal. Additional exam requirements/recommendations for international students: Required—TOEFL (minimum score 550 paper-based).

Arizona State University at the Tempe campus, New College of Interdisciplinary Arts and Sciences, Program in Interdisciplinary Studies, Phoenix, AZ 85069-7100. Offers MA. *Program availability:* Part-time, evening/weekend. *Degree requirements:* For master's, thesis or alternative, research paper or applied project; interactive Program of Study (iPOS) submitted before completing 50 percent of required credit hours. *Entrance requirements:* For master's, GRE (if GPA less than 3.0 in last 60 hours of undergraduate study), minimum GPA of 3.0 or equivalent in last 2 years of work leading to bachelor's degree, 3 letters of recommendation, official transcripts, personal statement, writing sample of scholarly work or example of professional activities. Additional exam requirements/recommendations for international students: Required—TOEFL, IELTS, or PTE. Electronic applications accepted. *Faculty research:* Comparative politics, foreign policy, world religions, African and African-American folklore, British modernism, English Renaissance drama, physiological psychology, sociology of health and illness, gender/race/class/sexuality, applied ethics, borderland theories.

Athabasca University, Centre for Interdisciplinary Studies, Athabasca, AB T9S 3A3, Canada. Offers adult education (MA); community studies (MA); cultural studies (MA); educational studies (MA); global change (MA); heritage resource management (Postbaccalaureate Certificate); legislative drafting (Postbaccalaureate Certificate); work, organization, and leadership (MA). *Program availability:* Part-time, evening/weekend, online learning. *Degree requirements:* For master's, project. *Entrance requirements:* Additional exam requirements/recommendations for international students: Required—TOEFL (minimum score 560 paper-based). Electronic applications accepted. *Faculty research:* Women's history, literature and culture studies, sustainable development, labor and education.

Baylor University, Graduate School, College of Arts and Sciences, The Institute of Ecological, Earth and Environmental Sciences, Waco, TX 76798. Offers PhD. *Faculty:* 24 full-time (4 women). *Students:* 5 full-time (1 woman); includes 2 minority (1 Asian, non-Hispanic/Latino; 1 Hispanic/Latino), 2 international. Average age 25. 8 applicants, 25% accepted, 1 enrolled. In 2017, 1 doctorate awarded. *Degree requirements:* For doctorate, comprehensive exam, thesis/dissertation. *Entrance requirements:* For doctorate, GRE. Additional exam requirements/recommendations for international students: Required—TOEFL (minimum score 550 paper-based; 80 iBT); Recommended—IELTS (minimum score 6.5). *Application deadline:* For fall admission, 2/15 priority date for domestic and international students. Application fee: $40. Electronic applications accepted. *Expenses:* Contact institution. *Financial support:* In 2017–18, 5 students received support, including 5 research assistantships with full and partial tuition reimbursements available (averaging $22,000 per year), 5 teaching assistantships with full and partial tuition reimbursements available (averaging $22,000 per year); scholarships/grants, health care benefits, tuition waivers (partial), and unspecified assistantships also available. Financial award application deadline: 2/15. *Faculty research:* Ecosystem processes, environmental toxicology and risk assessment, biogeochemical cycling, chemical fate and transport, conservation management. *Unit head:* Dr. Joe C. Yelderman, Jr., Director, 254-710-2224, E-mail: joe_yelderman@baylor.edu. *Application contact:* Shannon Koehler, Office Manager, 254-710-2224, Fax: 254-710-2298, E-mail: shannon_koehler@baylor.edu.
Website: http://www.baylor.edu/TIEEES

Boise State University, College of Arts and Sciences, Program in Interdisciplinary Studies, Boise, ID 83725-0399. Offers MA, MS. *Program availability:* Part-time. *Students:* 4 full-time (3 women), 10 part-time (7 women); includes 1 minority (Hispanic/Latino). Average age 37. 7 applicants, 71% accepted, 3 enrolled. In 2017, 2 master's awarded. *Degree requirements:* For master's, thesis or alternative. *Entrance requirements:* For master's, minimum GPA of 3.0. Additional exam requirements/recommendations for international students: Required—TOEFL (minimum score 550 paper-based; 80 iBT), IELTS (minimum score 6). *Application deadline:* For fall admission, 3/1 for domestic students; for spring admission, 10/1 for domestic students. Application fee: $65 ($95 for international students). Electronic applications accepted. *Expenses:* Tuition, state resident: full-time $6471; part-time $390 per credit. Tuition, nonresident: full-time $21,787; part-time $685 per credit. *Required fees:* $2283; $100 per term. Part-time tuition and fees vary according to course load and program. *Financial support:* Scholarships/grants and unspecified assistantships available. Financial award applicants required to submit FAFSA. *Unit head:* Dr. Nicole Molumby, Director, 208-426-1414, Fax: 208-426-3006, E-mail: nicolemolumby@boisestate.edu.
Website: http://coas.boisestate.edu/interdisciplinary-studies-program/

Bowling Green State University, Graduate College, Interdisciplinary Studies, Bowling Green, OH 43403. Offers M Ed, MA, MS, PhD. *Program availability:* Part-time. *Degree requirements:* For master's, thesis or alternative; for doctorate, comprehensive exam, thesis/dissertation. *Entrance requirements:* For master's and doctorate, GRE General Test. Additional exam requirements/recommendations for international students: Required—TOEFL. Electronic applications accepted.

Buffalo State College, State University of New York, The Graduate School, Program in Multidisciplinary Studies, Buffalo, NY 14222-1095. Offers MA, MS. *Program availability:* Part-time, evening/weekend. *Degree requirements:* For master's, thesis or project. *Entrance requirements:* For master's, minimum GPA of 2.5. Additional exam requirements/recommendations for international students: Required—TOEFL (minimum score 550 paper-based).

California Institute of Integral Studies, School of Consciousness and Transformation, San Francisco, CA 94103. Offers anthropology and social change (MA, PhD); Asian philosophies and cultures (MA); creative inquiry/interdisciplinary arts (MFA); East-West psychology (MA, PhD); integral and transpersonal psychology (PhD); philosophy and religion (PhD), including ecology, spirituality, and religion, philosophy, cosmology, and consciousness, women's spirituality; philosophy, cosmology, and consciousness (Certificate); transformative leadership (MA); transformative studies (PhD); women, gender, spirituality and social justice (MA); writing and consciousness (MFA). *Program availability:* Part-time, evening/weekend, 100% online, blended/hybrid learning. *Students:* 392 full-time (265 women), 141 part-time (98 women); includes 145 minority (40 Black or African American, non-Hispanic/Latino; 1 American Indian or Alaska Native, non-Hispanic/Latino; 19 Asian, non-Hispanic/Latino; 54 Hispanic/Latino; 31 Two or more races, non-Hispanic/Latino), 61 international. Average age 43. 212 applicants, 96% accepted, 153 enrolled. In 2017, 49 master's, 36 doctorates awarded. Terminal master's awarded for partial completion of doctoral program. *Degree requirements:* For master's, thesis optional; for doctorate, comprehensive exam, thesis/dissertation, 1 foreign language (for Asian philosophies and cultures). *Entrance requirements:* For master's, minimum GPA of 3.0, letters of recommendation, writing sample; for doctorate, master's degree, minimum GPA of 3.0, letters of recommendation, writing sample. Additional exam requirements/recommendations for international students: Required—TOEFL. *Application deadline:* For fall admission, 2/1 priority date for domestic and international students; for spring admission, 10/15 priority date for domestic and international students. Applications are processed on a rolling basis. Application fee: $65. Electronic applications accepted. *Expenses:* $21,400 tuition and fees (for MA); $28,390 (for MFA); $24,658 (for PhD). *Financial support:* Fellowships, research assistantships, teaching assistantships, career-related internships or fieldwork, Federal Work-Study, and scholarships/grants available. Support available to part-time students. Financial award application deadline: 4/15; financial award applicants required to submit FAFSA. *Faculty research:* Ecology and sustainability, philosophy and religion, East-West psychology, integrative health, social and cultural anthropology, transformative leadership. *Unit head:* Kathy Littles, Academic Dean, 415-575-6100, E-mail: klittles@ciis.edu. *Application contact:* Ellen Durst, Director of Admissions, 415-575-6100, Fax: 415-575-1268, E-mail: admissions@ciis.edu.
Website: http://www.ciis.edu/

California State University, Bakersfield, Division of Graduate Studies, Program in Interdisciplinary Studies, Bakersfield, CA 93311. Offers MA. *Faculty:* 1 part-time/adjunct (0 women). *Students:* 1 full-time (0 women), 3 part-time (1 woman); includes 1 minority (Hispanic/Latino). Average age 44. *Degree requirements:* For master's, thesis or project. *Entrance requirements:* For master's, minimum GPA of 3.0 in last 90 quarter units, baccalaureate degree. Additional exam requirements/recommendations for international students: Required—TOEFL (minimum score 550 paper-based). Application fee: $55. Electronic applications accepted. *Expenses:* Tuition, state resident: full-time $7176; part-time $4164 per year. *Faculty research:* Ethics, physical education and health. *Unit head:* Dr. Vandana Kohli, Associate Dean of Undergraduate and Graduate Studies, 661-654-2786, Fax: 661-654-2791, E-mail: vkohli@csub.edu. *Application contact:* Martha Manriquez, Administrative Coordinator, Graduate Student Center, 661-664-2792, Fax: 661-654-2791, E-mail: mmanriquez5@csub.edu.
Website: http://www.csub.edu/interdisciplinary/index.html

California State University, East Bay, Office of Graduate Studies, Interdisciplinary Programs, Hayward, CA 94542-3000. Offers MA, MS. *Program availability:* Part-time. In 2017, 2 master's awarded. *Degree requirements:* For master's, comprehensive exam, project or thesis. *Entrance requirements:* Additional exam requirements/recommendations for international students: Required—TOEFL (minimum score 550 paper-based). *Application deadline:* For fall admission, 6/1 for domestic and international students. Applications are processed on a rolling basis. Application fee: $55. Electronic applications accepted. *Financial support:* Fellowships, teaching assistantships, Federal Work-Study, institutionally sponsored loans, and scholarships/grants available. Support available to part-time students. Financial award application deadline: 3/2; financial award applicants required to submit FAFSA. *Unit head:* Philip Cole-Regis, Administrative Support Coordinator, 510-885-3286, E-mail: philip.coleregis@csueastbay.edu. *Application contact:* Philip Cole-Regis, Administrative Support Coordinator, 510-885-3286, E-mail: philip.coleregis@csueastbay.edu.
Website: http://www.csueastbay.edu/gradprograms/

California State University, San Bernardino, Graduate Studies, Interdisciplinary Programs, San Bernardino, CA 92407. Offers integrative studies (MA). *Program availability:* Part-time, evening/weekend. *Students:* 6 part-time (3 women); includes 4 minority (2 Black or African American, non-Hispanic/Latino; 2 Hispanic/Latino). Average age 43. 3 applicants, 67% accepted, 2 enrolled. In 2017, 1 master's awarded. *Degree requirements:* For master's, thesis or alternative. *Entrance requirements:* Additional exam requirements/recommendations for international students: Required—TOEFL. *Application deadline:* For fall admission, 7/16 for domestic students; for winter admission, 10/16 for domestic students; for spring admission, 1/22 for domestic students. Application fee: $55. *Financial support:* Application deadline: 3/1. *Unit head:* Dr. Dorota Huizinga, Dean of Graduate Studies, 909-537-3064, Fax: 909-537-7034, E-mail: dorota.huizinga@csusb.edu. *Application contact:* Olivia Rosas, Associate Vice President for Enrollment Services, 909-537-7577, Fax: 909-537-7034, E-mail: orosas@csusb.edu.

California State University, Stanislaus, College of the Arts, Humanities and Social Sciences, Programs in Interdisciplinary Studies, Turlock, CA 95382. Offers MA, MS. *Program availability:* Part-time, evening/weekend. *Degree requirements:* For master's, thesis. *Entrance requirements:* For master's, GRE, minimum GPA of 3.0, personal statement. Additional exam requirements/recommendations for international students: Required—TOEFL (minimum score 550 paper-based). Electronic applications accepted.

Cambridge College, School of Education, Boston, MA 02129. Offers autism specialist (M Ed); autism/behavior analyst (M Ed); behavior analyst (Post-Master's Certificate); behavioral management (M Ed); early childhood teacher (M Ed); education specialist in curriculum and instruction (CAGS); educational leadership (Ed D); elementary teacher (M Ed); English as a second language (M Ed, Certificate); general science (M Ed); health education (Post-Master's Certificate); health/family and consumer sciences (M Ed); history (M Ed); individualized (M Ed); information technology literacy (M Ed); instructional technology (M Ed); interdisciplinary studies (M Ed); library teacher (M Ed); literacy education (M Ed); mathematics (M Ed); mathematics specialist (Certificate); middle school mathematics and science (M Ed); school administration (M Ed, CAGS); school guidance counselor (M Ed); school nurse education (M Ed); school social worker/school adjustment counselor (M Ed); special education administrator (CAGS); special education/moderate disabilities (M Ed); teaching skills and methodologies (M Ed). *Program availability:* Part-time, evening/weekend, online learning. *Degree requirements:*

For master's, thesis, internship/practicum (licensure program only); for doctorate, thesis/dissertation; for other advanced degree, thesis. *Entrance requirements:* For master's, interview, resume, documentation of licensure, 2 professional references; for doctorate, official transcripts, interview, resume, documentation of licensure (if any), written personal statement/essay, portfolio of scholarly and professional work, qualifying assessment, 2 professional references, health insurance, immunizations form; for other advanced degree, official transcripts, interview, resume, documentation of licensure (if any), written personal statement/essay, 2 professional references, health insurance, immunizations form. Additional exam requirements/recommendations for international students: Required—TOEFL (minimum score 550 paper-based; 79 iBT), Michigan English Language Assessment Battery (minimum score 85); Recommended—IELTS (minimum score 6). Electronic applications accepted. *Expenses:* Contact institution. *Faculty research:* Adult education, accelerated learning, mathematics education, brain compatible learning, special education and law.

Campbell University, Graduate and Professional Programs, School of Education, Buies Creek, NC 27506. Offers elementary education (M Ed); interdisciplinary studies (M Ed); middle grades education (M Ed); physical education (M Ed); school administration (MSA); school counseling (M Ed); secondary education (M Ed). *Accreditation:* NCATE. *Program availability:* Part-time, evening/weekend. *Degree requirements:* For master's, comprehensive exam. *Entrance requirements:* For master's, GRE General Test, minimum GPA of 2.7. *Faculty research:* Spiritual values and wellness issues in counseling, stress and professional burnout among counselors, thinking strategies, leadership, adaptive technology.

Central Washington University, School of Graduate Studies and Research, Individual Studies Program, Ellensburg, WA 98926. Offers M Ed, MA, MFA, MS. *Program availability:* Part-time. *Entrance requirements:* For master's, GRE General Test, minimum GPA of 3.0. Additional exam requirements/recommendations for international students: Required—TOEFL (minimum score 550 paper-based; 79 iBT). *Application deadline:* For fall admission, 2/1 priority date for domestic students; for winter admission, 10/1 for domestic students; for spring admission, 1/1 for domestic students. Applications are processed on a rolling basis. Application fee: $50. Electronic applications accepted. *Financial support:* Application deadline: 3/1; applicants required to submit FAFSA. *Unit head:* Kevin Archer, Program Director, 509-963-3101, E-mail: kevin.archer@cwu.edu. *Application contact:* Justine Eason, Admissions Program Coordinator, 509-963-3103, Fax: 509-963-1799, E-mail: masters@cwu.edu.

The Citadel, The Military College of South Carolina, Citadel Graduate College, Zucker Family School of Education, Charleston, SC 29409. Offers elementary/secondary school administration and supervision (M Ed); elementary/secondary school counseling (M Ed); interdisciplinary STEM education (M Ed); literacy education (M Ed, Graduate Certificate); middle grades (MAT), including English, mathematics, science, social studies; physical education (grades K-12) (MAT); school superintendency (Ed S); secondary education (MAT), including biology, English, mathematics, social studies; student affairs (Graduate Certificate); student affairs and college counseling (M Ed). *Accreditation:* NCATE. *Program availability:* Part-time, evening/weekend, 100% online, blended/hybrid learning. *Degree requirements:* For master's, comprehensive exam (for some programs). *Entrance requirements:* For master's, GRE (minimum combined verbal and quantitative score of 290) or MAT (minimum score 396). Additional exam requirements/recommendations for international students: Required—TOEFL (minimum score 550 paper-based; 79 iBT). Electronic applications accepted. *Expenses:* Tuition, state resident: part-time $587 per credit hour. Tuition, nonresident: part-time $988 per credit hour. *Required fees:* $90 per term.

Clarkson University, Wallace H. Coulter School of Engineering, Program in Interdisciplinary Engineering Science, Potsdam, NY 13699. Offers MS, PhD. *Students:* 4 full-time (1 woman), 3 part-time (0 women); includes 1 minority (Asian, non-Hispanic/Latino), 1 international. 1 applicant. *Degree requirements:* For master's, thesis; for doctorate, comprehensive exam, thesis/dissertation. *Entrance requirements:* For master's and doctorate, GRE. Additional exam requirements/recommendations for international students: Required—TOEFL (minimum score 550 paper-based, 80 iBT) or IELTS (6.5). *Application deadline:* Applications are processed on a rolling basis. Application fee: $50. Electronic applications accepted. *Expenses: Tuition:* Full-time $24,210; part-time $1345 per credit hour. Tuition and fees vary according to campus/location and program. *Financial support:* Scholarships/grants and unspecified assistantships available. *Unit head:* Dr. William Jemison, Dean of Engineering, 315-268-6446, E-mail: wjemison@clarkson.edu. *Application contact:* Dan Capogna, Director of Graduate Admissions, 518-631-9910, E-mail: graduate@clarkson.edu.
Website: https://www.clarkson.edu/academics/graduate

Colorado State University, Interdisciplinary College, Interdisciplinary Programs, Fort Collins, CO 80523-1617. Offers MS, PhD. *Students:* 66 full-time (46 women), 124 part-time (70 women); includes 27 minority (1 Black or African American, non-Hispanic/Latino; 10 Asian, non-Hispanic/Latino; 8 Hispanic/Latino; 8 Two or more races, non-Hispanic/Latino), 30 international. Average age 31. 181 applicants, 24% accepted, 32 enrolled. In 2017, 25 master's, 21 doctorates awarded. *Degree requirements:* For master's, comprehensive exam (for some programs), thesis (for some programs); for doctorate, comprehensive exam (for some programs), thesis/dissertation. *Entrance requirements:* For master's, GRE (for some programs), minimum GPA of 3.0; for doctorate, GRE, minimum GPA of 3.0. Additional exam requirements/recommendations for international students: Required—TOEFL, IELTS. Application fee: $60 ($70 for international students). Electronic applications accepted. *Expenses:* Tuition, state resident: full-time $9917. Tuition, nonresident: full-time $24,312. *Required fees:* $2284. Tuition and fees vary according to course load and program. *Financial support:* Fellowships with full and partial tuition reimbursements, research assistantships with full and partial tuition reimbursements, teaching assistantships with full and partial tuition reimbursements, scholarships/grants, traineeships, health care benefits, and unspecified assistantships available. *Faculty research:* Cancer biology; metabolic regulation; cognitive neuroscience; evolutionary ecology; molecular ecology.
Website: http://mcin.colostate.edu/

Concordia University, School of Graduate Studies, Special Individualized Programs, Montréal, QC H3G 1M8, Canada. Offers M Sc, MA, PhD. *Degree requirements:* For master's, comprehensive exam, thesis; for doctorate, one foreign language, comprehensive exam, thesis/dissertation.

Dalhousie University, Faculty of Graduate Studies, Interdisciplinary PhD Program, Halifax, NS B3H 4H6, Canada. Offers PhD. *Degree requirements:* For doctorate, thesis/dissertation. *Entrance requirements:* Additional exam requirements/recommendations for international students: Required—TOEFL, IELTS, CANTEST, CAEL, or Michigan English Language Assessment Battery. Electronic applications accepted. *Expenses:* Contact institution.

Dallas Baptist University, Gary Cook School of Leadership, Program in Higher Education, Dallas, TX 75211-9299. Offers leadership studies (M Ed); student affairs leadership (M Ed), including community college leadership, distance learning, interdisciplinary studies, student affairs leadership. *Program availability:* Part-time, evening/weekend. *Application deadline:* Applications are processed on a rolling basis. Application fee: $25. Electronic applications accepted. Application fee is waived when completed online. *Expenses: Tuition:* Full-time $16,308; part-time $906 per credit hour. *Required fees:* $900; $450 per semester. Tuition and fees vary according to course load and degree level. *Unit head:* Dr. Jack Goodyear, Dean, 214-333-5595, Fax: 214-333-6809, E-mail: jackg@dbu.edu. *Application contact:* Dr. Sena Baker, Program Director, 214-333-6850, E-mail: sena@dbu.edu.
Website: http://www4.dbu.edu/leadership/hied/

Dallas Baptist University, Professional Development Program, Dallas, TX 75211-9299. Offers accounting (MA); church leadership (MA); communication (MA); counseling (MA); criminal justice (MA); English as a second language (MA); finance (MA); higher education (MA); leadership studies (MA); management (MA). *Program availability:* Part-time, evening/weekend. *Application deadline:* Applications are processed on a rolling basis. Application fee: $25. Electronic applications accepted. Application fee is waived when completed online. *Expenses: Tuition:* Full-time $16,308; part-time $906 per credit hour. *Required fees:* $900; $450 per semester. Tuition and fees vary according to course load and degree level. *Unit head:* Jared Ingram, Program Director, 214-333-5584, E-mail: jaredi@dbu.edu. *Application contact:* Bobby Soto, Director of Admissions, 214-333-5242, E-mail: bobby@dbu.edu.
Website: http://www3.dbu.edu/graduate/mapd.asp

DePaul University, College of Liberal Arts and Social Sciences, Chicago, IL 60614. Offers Arabic (MA); Chinese (MA); critical ethnic studies (MA); English (MA); French (MA); German (MA); history (MA); interdisciplinary studies (MA, MS); international public service (MS); international studies (MA); Italian (MA); Japanese (MA); liberal studies (MA); nonprofit management (MNM); public administration (MPA); public health (MPH); public policy (MPP); public service management (MS); refugee and forced migration studies (MS); social work (MSW); sociology (MA); Spanish (MA); sustainable urban development (MA); women's and gender studies (MA); writing and publishing (MA); writing, rhetoric and discourse (MA); MA/PhD. *Program availability:* Part-time, evening/weekend, online learning. Terminal master's awarded for partial completion of doctoral program. *Degree requirements:* For master's, variable foreign language requirement, comprehensive exam (for some programs), thesis (for some programs). *Application deadline:* Applications are processed on a rolling basis. Application fee: $40. Electronic applications accepted. *Financial support:* Applicants required to submit FAFSA. *Unit head:* Dr. Guillermo Vasquez de Velasco, Dean, 773-325-7305. *Application contact:* Ann Spittle, Director of Graduate Admission, 773-325-8369, Fax: 312-476-3244, E-mail: graddepaul@depaul.edu.
Website: http://las.depaul.edu/

Eastern Washington University, Graduate Studies, Interdisciplinary Studies, Cheney, WA 99004-2431. Offers MA, MS. *Students:* 3 full-time (2 women), 4 part-time (2 women). Average age 31. 1 applicant, 100% accepted, 1 enrolled. *Degree requirements:* For master's, comprehensive exam, thesis or alternative. *Entrance requirements:* For master's, minimum GPA of 3.0. Additional exam requirements/recommendations for international students: Required—TOEFL (minimum score 580 paper-based; 90 iBT), IELTS (minimum score 7), PTE (minimum score 63). *Application deadline:* For fall admission, 4/1 priority date for domestic students; for spring admission, 1/15 for domestic students. Applications are processed on a rolling basis. Application fee: $75. Electronic applications accepted. *Expenses:* Tuition, state resident: full-time $11,191; part-time $373.06 per credit. Tuition, nonresident: full-time $25,995; part-time $866.52 per credit. *Financial support:* Teaching assistantships with partial tuition reimbursements, career-related internships or fieldwork, Federal Work-Study, institutionally sponsored loans, scholarships/grants, health care benefits, tuition waivers (partial), and unspecified assistantships available. Support available to part-time students. Financial award application deadline: 2/1; financial award applicants required to submit FAFSA. *Application contact:* Kathy White, Advisor/Recruiter for Graduate Studies, 509-359-6297, Fax: 509-359-6044, E-mail: gradprograms@ewu.edu.

Emory University, Laney Graduate School, Graduate Institute of the Liberal Arts, Atlanta, GA 30322-1100. Offers PhD. *Degree requirements:* For doctorate, one foreign language, comprehensive exam, thesis/dissertation. *Entrance requirements:* For doctorate, GRE General Test. Additional exam requirements/recommendations for international students: Recommended—TOEFL. Electronic applications accepted. *Faculty research:* American cultural criticism, intellectual history, psychoanalysis, history of science, popular culture.

Fitchburg State University, Division of Graduate and Continuing Education, Program in Interdisciplinary Studies, Fitchburg, MA 01420-2697. Offers applied communications (CAGS); counseling/psychology (CAGS); individualized track (CAGS); reading specialist (CAGS). *Program availability:* Part-time, evening/weekend. *Students:* 11 full-time (all women), 14 part-time (13 women); includes 3 minority (all Hispanic/Latino). Average age 36. 5 applicants, 100% accepted, 5 enrolled. In 2017, 14 CAGSs awarded. *Entrance requirements:* Additional exam requirements/recommendations for international students: Required—TOEFL (minimum score 550 paper-based; 79 iBT). *Application deadline:* For fall admission, 7/15 for international students; for spring admission, 12/1 for international students. Applications are processed on a rolling basis. Application fee: $50. Electronic applications accepted. *Expenses:* Contact institution. *Financial support:* In 2017–18, research assistantships with partial tuition reimbursements (averaging $5,500 per year) were awarded; Federal Work-Study, scholarships/grants, and unspecified assistantships also available. Support available to part-time students. Financial award application deadline: 3/1; financial award applicants required to submit FAFSA. *Unit head:* Dr. Jessica Robey, Chair, 978-665-3386, Fax: 978-665-3658, E-mail: gce@fitchburgstate.edu. *Application contact:* Jinawa McNeil, Director of Admissions, 978-665-3140, Fax: 978-665-4540, E-mail: admissions@fitchburgstate.edu.

Florida Gulf Coast University, Elaine Nicpon Marieb College of Health and Human Services, Program in Health Science, Fort Myers, FL 33965-6565. Offers MS. *Program availability:* Part-time, evening/weekend, online learning. *Faculty:* 71 full-time (49 women), 49 part-time/adjunct (32 women). *Students:* 9 full-time (7 women), 31 part-time (20 women); includes 7 minority (6 Black or African American, non-Hispanic/Latino; 1 Hispanic/Latino). Average age 32. 20 applicants, 85% accepted, 13 enrolled. In 2017, 17 master's awarded. *Degree requirements:* For master's, final project or thesis. *Entrance requirements:* For master's, GRE General Test or MAT, minimum GPA of 3.0. Additional exam requirements/recommendations for international students: Required—TOEFL (minimum score 550 paper-based). *Application deadline:* For fall admission, 7/1 priority date for domestic students; for spring admission, 11/15 priority date for domestic students. Applications are processed on a rolling basis. Application fee: $30. Electronic applications accepted. *Expenses:* Tuition, state resident: part-time $290 per credit hour. Tuition, nonresident: part-time $1173 per credit hour. *Required fees:* $127 per credit hour. Tuition and fees vary according to course load. *Financial support:* In 2017–18, 4 students received support. Career-related internships or fieldwork available. Financial award application deadline: 6/30; financial award applicants required to submit FAFSA. *Faculty research:* Health services administration, gerontology, therapeutic recreation, health professions education, exercise physiology. *Unit head:* Dr. Joan Glacken, Chair, 239-590-7498, Fax: 239-590-7474, E-mail: jglacken@fgcu.edu. *Application contact:* Susan Baurer, Administrative Assistant, 239-590-7451, E-mail: sbaurer@fgcu.edu.
Website: http://www.fgcu.edu/chpsw/hs/

Interdisciplinary Studies

Florida Institute of Technology, College of Science, Program in Interdisciplinary Science, Melbourne, FL 32901-6975. Offers MS. *Students:* Average age 26. 3 applicants, 67% accepted, 2 enrolled. *Degree requirements:* For master's, comprehensive exam (for some programs), thesis optional, minimum of 31 credit hours. *Entrance requirements:* For master's, undergraduate STEM degree, 2 letters of recommendations, resume, statement of objectives. Additional exam requirements/recommendations for international students: Required—TOEFL (minimum score 550 paper-based; 79 iBT). *Application deadline:* Applications are processed on a rolling basis. Electronic applications accepted. *Expenses: Tuition:* Part-time $1241 per credit hour. Part-time tuition and fees vary according to campus/location. *Financial support:* Applicants required to submit FAFSA. *Unit head:* Dr. Ken Lindeman, Professor, 321-674-7370, Fax: 321-674-7598, E-mail: lindeman@fit.edu. *Application contact:* Cheryl A. Brown, Associate Director of Graduate Admissions, 321-674-7581, Fax: 321-723-9468, E-mail: cbrown@fit.edu.
Website: http://cos.fit.edu/education/

Fresno Pacific University, Graduate Programs, Individualized Study Program, Fresno, CA 93702-4709. Offers MA. *Program availability:* Part-time, evening/weekend. *Degree requirements:* For master's, thesis. *Entrance requirements:* For master's, GMAT, GRE General Test, or MAT, interview. Additional exam requirements/recommendations for international students: Required—TOEFL (minimum score 550 paper-based). Electronic applications accepted. *Expenses:* Contact institution.

Frostburg State University, College of Education, Department of Educational Professions, Program in Interdisciplinary Education, Frostburg, MD 21532. Offers M Ed, Ed D. *Program availability:* Part-time, evening/weekend. *Students:* 20 full-time (12 women), 16 part-time (10 women); includes 4 minority (3 Black or African American, non-Hispanic/Latino; 1 Two or more races, non-Hispanic/Latino), 2 international. Average age 26. 20 applicants, 90% accepted, 13 enrolled. In 2017, 6 master's, 2 doctorates awarded. *Degree requirements:* For master's, thesis or alternative. *Entrance requirements:* Additional exam requirements/recommendations for international students: Required—TOEFL. *Application deadline:* For fall admission, 7/15 priority date for domestic students. Applications are processed on a rolling basis. Application fee: $45. Electronic applications accepted. *Expenses:* Tuition, state resident: part-time $433 per credit hour. Tuition, nonresident: part-time $557 per credit hour. *Required fees:* $121 per credit hour. $27 per term. *Financial support:* In 2017–18, 1 research assistantship with full tuition reimbursement (averaging $5,000 per year) was awarded; career-related internships or fieldwork also available. Financial award application deadline: 4/1; financial award applicants required to submit FAFSA. *Unit head:* Dr. William AuMiller, Coordinator, 301-687-4374, E-mail: wjaumiller@frostburg.edu. *Application contact:* Vickie Mazer, Director, Graduate Services, 301-687-7053, Fax: 301-687-4597, E-mail: vmmazer@frostburg.edu.

George Mason University, College of Humanities and Social Sciences, Interdisciplinary Studies Program, Fairfax, VA 22030. Offers computational social science (MAIS); energy and sustainability (MAIS); folklore studies (MAIS); higher education (MAIS); individualized studies (MAIS); religion, culture, and values (MAIS); social entrepreneurship (MAIS); social justice and human rights (MAIS); war and the military in society (MAIS); women and gender studies (MAIS). *Faculty:* 10 full-time (3 women), 15 part-time/adjunct (7 women). *Students:* 29 full-time (23 women), 76 part-time (50 women); includes 39 minority (18 Black or African American, non-Hispanic/Latino; 6 Asian, non-Hispanic/Latino; 11 Hispanic/Latino; 4 Two or more races, non-Hispanic/Latino), 7 international. Average age 32. 71 applicants, 90% accepted, 29 enrolled. In 2017, 23 master's awarded. *Degree requirements:* For master's, thesis or alternative, experiential learning (for some programs). *Entrance requirements:* Additional exam requirements/recommendations for international students: Required—TOEFL (minimum score 575 paper-based; 88 iBT), IELTS (minimum score 6.5), PTE (minimum score 59). *Application deadline:* For fall admission, 3/1 for domestic and international students; for spring admission, 10/15 for domestic and international students. Application fee: $75 ($80 for international students). Electronic applications accepted. *Expenses:* Tuition, state resident: full-time $11,228; part-time $459.50 per credit. Tuition, nonresident: full-time $30,932; part-time $1280.50 per credit. *Required fees:* $3252; $135.50 per credit. Part-time tuition and fees vary according to course load and program. *Financial support:* In 2017–18, 9 students received support, including 2 research assistantships with tuition reimbursements available, 7 teaching assistantships with tuition reimbursements available (averaging $8,599 per year); career-related internships or fieldwork, Federal Work-Study, scholarships/grants, unspecified assistantships, and health care benefits (for full-time research or teaching assistantship recipients) also available. Support available to part-time students. Financial award application deadline: 3/1; financial award applicants required to submit FAFSA. *Faculty research:* Combined English and folklore, religious and cultural studies (Christianity and Muslim society). *Unit head:* Meredith H. Lair, Director, 703-993-2159, Fax: 703-993-1251, E-mail: mlair@gmu.edu. *Application contact:* Morgan Fisher, Graduate Coordinator, 703-993-8762, E-mail: mfisherb@gmu.edu.
Website: http://mais.gmu.edu

Georgetown University, Graduate School of Arts and Sciences, School of Continuing Studies, Washington, DC 20057. Offers American studies (MALS); applied intelligence (MPS); Catholic studies (MALS); classical civilizations (MALS); emergency and disaster management (MPS); ethics and the professions (MALS); global strategic communications (MPS); hospitality management (MPS); human resources management (MPS); humanities (MALS); individualized study (MALS); integrated marketing communications (MPS); international affairs (MALS); Islam and Muslim-Christian relations (MALS); journalism (MPS); liberal studies (DLS); literature and society (MALS); medieval and early modern European studies (MALS); public relations and corporate communications (MPS); real estate (MPS); religious studies (MALS); social and public policy (MALS); sports industry management (MPS); systems engineering management (MPS); technology management (MPS); the theory and practice of American democracy (MALS); urban and regional planning (MPS); visual culture (MALS). MPS in systems engineering management offered jointly with Stevens Institute of Technology. *Entrance requirements:* Additional exam requirements/recommendations for international students: Required—TOEFL.

Goddard College, Graduate Division, Individualized Master of Arts Program, Plainfield, VT 05667-9432. Offers consciousness studies (MA); transformative language arts (MA). *Program availability:* Part-time. *Degree requirements:* For master's, thesis. *Entrance requirements:* For master's, 3 letters of recommendation, interview. Electronic applications accepted. *Expenses:* Contact institution.

Grand Rapids Theological Seminary of Cornerstone University, Graduate Programs, Grand Rapids, MI 49525-5897. Offers academic (M Div); chaplaincy ministries (M Div); Christian formation (MA); counseling (MA); formation and soul care ministries (M Div); intercultural ministries (M Div); interdisciplinary studies (MA); New Testament (Th M); Old Testament (Th M); pastoral ministries (M Div); small group and discipleship ministries (M Div); student and family ministries (M Div). *Accreditation:* ATS. *Program availability:* Part-time, evening/weekend, 100% online, blended/hybrid learning. *Faculty:* 9 full-time (2 women), 14 part-time/adjunct (5 women). *Students:* 100 full-time (53 women), 211 part-time (102 women); includes 71 minority (54 Black or African American, non-Hispanic/Latino; 1 American Indian or Alaska Native, non-Hispanic/Latino; 3 Asian, non-Hispanic/Latino; 12 Hispanic/Latino; 1 Two or more races, non-Hispanic/Latino), 3 international. Average age 36. 165 applicants, 76% accepted, 99 enrolled. In 2017, 75 master's awarded. *Entrance requirements:* Additional exam requirements/recommendations for international students: Required—TOEFL (minimum score 577 paper-based; 90 iBT), IELTS (minimum score 7). *Application deadline:* For fall admission, 8/15 for domestic students, 6/15 for international students; for spring admission, 1/10 for domestic students, 11/10 for international students; for summer admission, 4/30 for domestic students. Applications are processed on a rolling basis. Electronic applications accepted. *Expenses: Tuition:* Full-time $9720; part-time $540 per credit hour. *Required fees:* $832; $374 per semester. Tuition and fees vary according to course load and program. *Financial support:* In 2017–18, 96 students received support, including 8 fellowships with partial tuition reimbursements available; career-related internships or fieldwork and scholarships/grants also available. Support available to part-time students. Financial award application deadline: 8/15; financial award applicants required to submit FAFSA. *Unit head:* Dr. John F. VerBerkmoes, Executive Vice President and Academic Dean, 616-222-1422, E-mail: john.verberkmoes@cornerstone.edu. *Application contact:* Ashley VanBemmelen, Director of Admissions, 800-697-1133, E-mail: ashley.vanbemmelen@cornerstone.edu.

Harrison Middleton University, Graduate Program, Tempe, AZ 85282. Offers education (MA, Ed D); humanities (MA); imaginative literature (MA); interdisciplinary studies (DA); jurisprudence (MA); natural science (MA); philosophy and religion (MA); social science (MA). *Program availability:* Part-time, evening/weekend, online learning. *Degree requirements:* For master's and doctorate, capstone project. *Entrance requirements:* For master's, interview; for doctorate, 2 academic letters of reference, interview, essay. Additional exam requirements/recommendations for international students: Required—TOEFL (minimum score 550 paper-based; 80 iBT). Electronic applications accepted. *Faculty research:* Japanese animation, educational leadership, war art, John Muir's wilderness.

Hiram College, Graduate Studies, Hiram, OH 44234. Offers MAIS. *Program availability:* Part-time, evening/weekend. *Degree requirements:* For master's, two seminars, capstone research project. *Entrance requirements:* For master's, bachelor's degree from an accredited institution, 2 letters of recommendation, writing sample, interview.

Hollins University, Graduate Programs, Program in Liberal Studies, Roanoke, VA 24020. Offers humanities (MALS); interdisciplinary studies (MALS); leadership (MALS); social sciences (MALS); visual and performing arts (MALS). *Program availability:* Part-time, evening/weekend, 100% online, blended/hybrid learning. *Faculty:* 5 part-time/adjunct (2 women). *Students:* 5 full-time (4 women), 29 part-time (25 women); includes 9 minority (6 Black or African American, non-Hispanic/Latino; 1 Asian, non-Hispanic/Latino; 1 Hispanic/Latino; 1 Two or more races, non-Hispanic/Latino). Average age 40. 7 applicants, 86% accepted, 3 enrolled. In 2017, 11 master's awarded. *Degree requirements:* For master's, thesis. *Entrance requirements:* For master's, three letters of recommendation, interview, bachelor's degree, undergraduate transcripts, statement of educational objectives. Additional exam requirements/recommendations for international students: Required—TOEFL (minimum score 550 paper-based; 80 iBT), IELTS (minimum score 6.5). *Application deadline:* Applications are processed on a rolling basis. Application fee: $40. Electronic applications accepted. *Expenses:* Contact institution. *Financial support:* Scholarships/grants available. Financial award application deadline: 7/15; financial award applicants required to submit FAFSA. *Faculty research:* Diversity, gender and women's studies, political science, leadership. *Unit head:* Dr. Lorraine Lange, Director, 540-362-6576, Fax: 540-362-6288, E-mail: hugrad@hollins.edu. *Application contact:* Cathy S. Koon, Manager of Graduate Programs, 540-362-6326, Fax: 540-362-6288, E-mail: hugrad@hollins.edu.
Website: http://www.hollins.edu/academics/graduate-degrees/liberal-studies/

Hood College, Graduate School, Programs in Human Behavior, Frederick, MD 21701-8575. Offers interdisciplinary studies in human behavior (MA), including psychology; thanatology (Certificate). *Program availability:* Part-time, evening/weekend. *Faculty:* 1 (woman) full-time, 2 part-time/adjunct (0 women). *Students:* 9 full-time (6 women), 22 part-time (16 women); includes 4 minority (2 Black or African American, non-Hispanic/Latino; 2 Two or more races, non-Hispanic/Latino), 2 international. Average age 37. 7 applicants, 100% accepted, 2 enrolled. In 2017, 9 master's, 11 other advanced degrees awarded. *Degree requirements:* For master's, comprehensive exam, thesis optional, capstone/research project. *Entrance requirements:* For master's, minimum GPA of 2.75, essay; for Certificate, minimum GPA of 2.75, essay, resume. Additional exam requirements/recommendations for international students: Required—TOEFL (minimum score 575 paper-based; 89 iBT), IELTS (minimum score 6.5). *Application deadline:* For fall admission, 8/15 priority date for domestic students, 8/5 for international students; for spring admission, 12/1 priority date for domestic students, 12/1 for international students; for summer admission, 5/1 priority date for domestic students, 4/15 for international students. Applications are processed on a rolling basis. Application fee: $35. Electronic applications accepted. *Expenses:* $465 per credit hour plus $110 comprehensive fee per semester. *Financial support:* Research assistantships with full tuition reimbursements, tuition waivers (partial), and unspecified assistantships available. Financial award applicants required to submit FAFSA. *Faculty research:* Mind-body medicine and multicultural healing, the New Orleans jazz funeral, death practices in African-American culture, bereavement theories and gender differences, Piaget's theory of cognitive development as a formal mathematical model. *Unit head:* Dr. April M. Boulton, Dean of the Graduate School, 301-696-3600, E-mail: gofurther@hood.edu. *Application contact:* Jan Marcus, Assistant Director of Graduate Admissions, 301-696-3600, E-mail: gofurther@hood.edu.
Website: http://www.hood.edu/graduate

Indiana University Southeast, Master of Interdisciplinary Studies Program, New Albany, IN 47150-6405. Offers MIS, Graduate Certificate. *Program availability:* Part-time. *Degree requirements:* For master's, thesis or alternative. *Entrance requirements:* For master's, GRE, 3 letters of recommendation, interview. Electronic applications accepted. *Expenses:* Contact institution.

Iowa State University of Science and Technology, Program in Interdisciplinary Graduate Studies, Ames, IA 50011. Offers MA, MS. *Entrance requirements:* For master's, GRE. Additional exam requirements/recommendations for international students: Recommended—TOEFL (minimum score 550 paper-based; 79 iBT), IELTS (minimum score 6.5). Electronic applications accepted.

Kansas State University, Graduate School, School of Applied and Interdisciplinary Studies, Olathe, KS 66061. Offers applied science and technology (PSM); professional interdisciplinary sciences (Graduate Certificate); professional skills for STEM practitioners (Graduate Certificate). *Program availability:* Part-time, 100% online, blended/hybrid learning. *Degree requirements:* For master's, capstone experience and/or internship. *Entrance requirements:* Additional exam requirements/recommendations for international students: Required—TOEFL (minimum score 550 paper-based; 79 iBT), IELTS (minimum score 6.5), PTE (minimum score 58). Electronic applications accepted. *Faculty research:* Applied and interdisciplinary science, food science, diagnostic medicine and pathobiology, adult education and leadership dynamics, horticulture and urban food systems.

Lehigh University, P.C. Rossin College of Engineering and Applied Science and College of Arts and Sciences, Center for Polymer Science and Engineering, Bethlehem, PA 18015. Offers M Eng, MS, PhD. *Program availability:* Part-time, evening/weekend, 100% online, blended/hybrid learning. *Faculty:* 21 full-time (2 women), 1 part-time/adjunct (0 women). *Students:* 7 full-time (4 women), 26 part-time (8 women); includes 7 minority (1 Black or African American, non-Hispanic/Latino; 5 Asian, non-Hispanic/Latino; 1 Native Hawaiian or other Pacific Islander, non-Hispanic/Latino), 6 international. Average age 30. 50 applicants, 26% accepted, 12 enrolled. In 2017, 6 master's, 1 doctorate awarded. Terminal master's awarded for partial completion of doctoral program. *Degree requirements:* For master's, thesis (for some programs); for doctorate, thesis/dissertation. *Entrance requirements:* For master's and doctorate, GRE General Test. Additional exam requirements/recommendations for international students: Required—TOEFL (minimum score 487 paper-based, 85 iBT) or IELTS (6.5). *Application deadline:* For fall admission, 7/15 for domestic students, 1/15 for international students; for spring admission, 12/1 for domestic and international students; for summer admission, 4/30 for domestic and international students. Applications are processed on a rolling basis. Application fee: $75. Electronic applications accepted. *Expenses:* $1,460 per credit hour. *Financial support:* In 2017–18, research assistantships with full tuition reimbursements (averaging $28,707 per year), teaching assistantships with full tuition reimbursements (averaging $22,050 per year) were awarded; health care benefits also available. Financial award application deadline: 1/15. *Faculty research:* Polymer colloids, polymer coatings, blends and composites, polymer interfaces, emulsion polymer. *Unit head:* Dr. Raymond A. Pearson, Director, 610-758-3857, Fax: 610-758-3526, E-mail: rp02@lehigh.edu. *Application contact:* James E. Roberts, Chair, Polymer Education Committee, 610-758-4841, Fax: 610-758-6536, E-mail: jer1@lehigh.edu.
Website: http://www.lehigh.edu/~inpcreng/academics/graduate/polymerscieng.html

Lesley University, Graduate School of Arts and Social Sciences, Cambridge, MA 02138-2790. Offers clinical mental health counseling (MA), including holistic counseling, school and community counseling, trauma studies; counseling psychology (MA, CAGS), including professional counseling (MA), school counseling (MA); creative writing (MFA); expressive therapies (MA, PhD, CAGS), including art (MA), clinical mental health counseling (MA), dance (MA), expressive therapies (MA), music (MA); independent studies (CAGS); independent study (MA); intercultural relations (MA, CAGS); interdisciplinary studies (MA), including individualized studies, integrative holistic health, mindfulness studies, peace and conflict transformation, trauma sensitive assessment, intervention, and consultation, women's studies; urban environmental leadership (MA). *Program availability:* Part-time, online learning. *Degree requirements:* For master's, internship, practicum, thesis (for expressive therapies); for doctorate, thesis/dissertation, arts apprenticeship, field placement; for CAGS, thesis, internship (for counseling psychology, expressive therapies). *Entrance requirements:* For master's, MAT (counseling psychology), interview, writing samples, art portfolio; for doctorate, GRE or MAT, interview, master's degree; for CAGS, interview, master's degree. Additional exam requirements/recommendations for international students: Required—TOEFL (minimum score 550 paper-based; 80 iBT). Electronic applications accepted. *Faculty research:* Psychotherapy and culture; psychotherapy and psychological trauma; women's issues in art, teaching and psychotherapy; community-based art, psycho-spiritual inquiry.

Long Island University–LIU Post, College of Education, Information and Technology, Brookville, NY 11548-1300. Offers adolescence education (MS); adolescence education 7-12 (MS); archives and records management (AC); art education (MS); childhood education (MS); childhood education/literacy B-6 (MS); childhood education/special education (MS); clinical mental health counseling (MS, AC); early childhood education (MS); early childhood education/childhood education (MS); educational leadership (AC); educational technology (MS); information studies (PhD); interdisciplinary educational studies (Ed D); middle childhood education (MS); music education (MS); public library administration (AC); school counselor (MS); special education (MS Ed); speech-language pathology (MA); students with disabilities, 7-12 generalist (AC); TESOL (MA). *Accreditation:* TEAC. *Program availability:* Part-time, 100% online, blended/hybrid learning. *Faculty:* 40 full-time (26 women), 73 part-time/adjunct (38 women). *Students:* 472 full-time (400 women), 696 part-time (543 women); includes 254 minority (93 Black or African American, non-Hispanic/Latino; 46 Asian, non-Hispanic/Latino; 105 Hispanic/Latino; 10 Two or more races, non-Hispanic/Latino), 33 international. Average age 33. 917 applicants, 82% accepted, 357 enrolled. In 2017, 408 master's, 31 other advanced degrees awarded. Terminal master's awarded for partial completion of doctoral program. *Degree requirements:* For master's, variable foreign language requirement, comprehensive exam (for some programs), thesis optional; for doctorate, comprehensive exam, thesis/dissertation. *Entrance requirements:* For master's and AC, GRE (for some programs). Additional exam requirements/recommendations for international students: Required—TOEFL (minimum score 550 paper-based, 75 iBT), IELTS, or PTE. *Application deadline:* Applications are processed on a rolling basis. Application fee: $50. Electronic applications accepted. *Expenses: Tuition:* Full-time $21,618; part-time $1201 per credit. *Required fees:* $1840; $920 per term. Tuition and fees vary according to course load. *Financial support:* In 2017–18, 376 students received support. Career-related internships or fieldwork, Federal Work-Study, institutionally sponsored loans, scholarships/grants, tuition waivers (partial), and unspecified assistantships available. Support available to part-time students. Financial award application deadline: 2/15; financial award applicants required to submit FAFSA. *Faculty research:* Sleep; use of technology to develop executive function by students with disabilities; early childhood literacy development through play; social justice through education; using a structured protocol to discuss Bad News. *Unit head:* Dr. Albert Inserra, Dean, 516-299-2210, E-mail: albert.inserra@liu.edu. *Application contact:* Rita Langdon, Graduate Admissions, 516-299-2900, Fax: 516-299-2137, E-mail: post-enroll@liu.edu.
Website: http://liu.edu/CWPost/Academics/College-of-Education-Information-and-Technology

Long Island University–LIU Post, College of Liberal Arts and Sciences, Brookville, NY 11548-1300. Offers applied mathematics (MS); behavior analysis (MA); biology (MS); criminal justice (MS); earth science (MS); English (MA); environmental sustainability (MS); genetic counseling (MS); history (MA); interdisciplinary studies (MA, MS); political science (MA); psychology (MA). *Program availability:* Part-time, evening/weekend, blended/hybrid learning. *Faculty:* 41 full-time (21 women), 24 part-time/adjunct (13 women). *Students:* 173 full-time (124 women), 62 part-time (35 women); includes 54 minority (11 Black or African American, non-Hispanic/Latino; 13 Asian, non-Hispanic/Latino; 23 Hispanic/Latino; 7 Two or more races, non-Hispanic/Latino), 12 international. Average age 28. 368 applicants, 54% accepted, 74 enrolled. In 2017, 89 master's, 15 other advanced degrees awarded. Terminal master's awarded for partial completion of doctoral program. *Degree requirements:* For master's, comprehensive exam (for some programs), thesis (for some programs). *Entrance requirements:* Additional exam requirements/recommendations for international students: Required—TOEFL, IELTS, or PTE. *Application deadline:* Applications are processed on a rolling basis. Application fee: $50. Electronic applications accepted. *Expenses: Tuition:* Full-time $21,618; part-time $1201 per credit. *Required fees:* $1840; $920 per term. Tuition and fees vary according to course load. *Financial support:* In 2017–18, 165 students received support. Fellowships, research assistantships, teaching assistantships, career-related internships or fieldwork, Federal Work-Study, scholarships/grants, tuition waivers (partial), and unspecified assistantships available. Support available to part-time students. Financial award application deadline: 2/15; financial award applicants required to submit FAFSA. *Faculty research:* Biology, environmental sustainability, mathematics, psychology, genetic counseling. *Unit head:* Dr. Nathaniel Bowditch, Dean, 516-299-2234, Fax: 516-299-4140, E-mail: nathaniel.bowditch@liu.edu. *Application contact:* Rita Langdon, Graduate Admissions, 516-299-2900, Fax: 516-299-2137, E-mail: post-enroll@liu.edu.
Website: http://liu.edu/CWPost/Academics/Schools/CLAS

Marquette University, Graduate School, Interdisciplinary PhD Program, Milwaukee, WI 53201-1881. Offers PhD. *Program availability:* Part-time. *Degree requirements:* For doctorate, thesis/dissertation. *Entrance requirements:* For doctorate, GRE General Test. Additional exam requirements/recommendations for international students: Required—TOEFL (minimum score 630 paper-based). Electronic applications accepted.

Marywood University, Academic Affairs, Center for Interdisciplinary Studies, Scranton, PA 18509-1598. Offers human development (PhD), including educational administration, health promotion, higher education administration, instructional leadership, social work. *Program availability:* Part-time. Electronic applications accepted. *Expenses:* Contact institution.

Massachusetts College of Art and Design, Graduate Programs, MFA Program, Boston, MA 02115-5882. Offers 2D fine arts (MFA), including painting, printmaking; 3D fine arts (MFA), including ceramics, fibers, glass, jewelry and metalsmithing, sculpture; design (MFA, Postbaccalaureate Certificate), including dynamic media; fine arts (MFA), including interdisciplinary; media arts (MFA, Postbaccalaureate Certificate), including film/video (MFA), photography. *Accreditation:* NASAD. *Faculty:* 28 full-time (8 women), 28 part-time/adjunct (17 women). *Students:* 44 full-time (26 women), 28 part-time (17 women); includes 8 minority (5 Asian, non-Hispanic/Latino; 3 Hispanic/Latino), 18 international. 247 applicants, 52% accepted, 47 enrolled. In 2017, 42 master's, 5 other advanced degrees awarded. *Degree requirements:* For master's, thesis, thesis exhibition (for fine arts programs); thesis project and document (for design/dynamic media program). *Entrance requirements:* For master's, portfolio, college transcripts, resume, statement of purpose, letters of reference, interview, 6 credits of art history taken prior to or during MFA program; for Postbaccalaureate Certificate, portfolio, college transcripts, resume, statement of purpose, letters of reference, interview. Additional exam requirements/recommendations for international students: Required—TOEFL (minimum score 550 paper-based, 85 iBT) or IELTS (6). *Application deadline:* For fall admission, 1/4 priority date for domestic and international students; for summer admission, 1/4 priority date for domestic and international students. Applications are processed on a rolling basis. Application fee: $90. Electronic applications accepted. *Expenses:* $780 per credit. *Financial support:* In 2017–18, 51 students received support, including 1 research assistantship (averaging $2,160 per year), 33 teaching assistantships (averaging $2,160 per year); fellowships, career-related internships or fieldwork, scholarships/grants, tuition waivers (partial), unspecified assistantships, and adjunct co-teaching positions also available. Support available to part-time students. Financial award application deadline: 1/4; financial award applicants required to submit FAFSA. *Faculty research:* Painting and printmaking, sculpture, photography, film and video, dynamic media design. *Unit head:* Paul Paturzo, Dean of Graduate Studies, 617-879-7166, E-mail: pjpaturzo@massart.edu. *Application contact:* Lauren O'Neill, Assistant Director of Graduate Admissions, 617-879-7222, E-mail: gradadmissions@massart.edu.
Website: http://www.massart.edu/Admissions/Graduate_Programs.html

Michigan Technological University, Graduate School, Interdisciplinary Programs, Houghton, MI 49931. Offers atmospheric sciences (PhD); automotive systems and controls (Graduate Certificate); biochemistry and molecular biology (PhD); computational science and engineering (PhD); data science (MS, Graduate Certificate); engineering-environmental (PhD); international profile (Graduate Certificate); nanotechnology (Graduate Certificate); sustainability (Graduate Certificate); sustainable water resources systems (Graduate Certificate). *Program availability:* Part-time. *Faculty:* 115 full-time (26 women), 9 part-time/adjunct (2 women). *Students:* 58 full-time (18 women), 17 part-time (5 women). Average age 28. 508 applicants, 28% accepted, 27 enrolled. In 2017, 10 master's, 7 doctorates, 11 other advanced degrees awarded. Terminal master's awarded for partial completion of doctoral program. *Degree requirements:* For master's, comprehensive exam (for some programs), thesis (for some programs); for doctorate, comprehensive exam, thesis/dissertation. *Entrance requirements:* For master's, doctorate, and Graduate Certificate, GRE, statement of purpose, personal statement, official transcripts, 2-3 letters of recommendation. Additional exam requirements/recommendations for international students: Required—TOEFL or IELTS. *Application deadline:* Applications are processed on a rolling basis. Electronic applications accepted. *Expenses:* Tuition, state resident: full-time $17,100; part-time $950 per credit. Tuition, nonresident: full-time $17,100; part-time $950 per credit. *Required fees:* $248; $124 per term. Tuition and fees vary according to course load and program. *Financial support:* In 2017–18, 67 students received support, including 9 fellowships with tuition reimbursements available (averaging $15,790 per year), 17 research assistantships with tuition reimbursements available (averaging $15,790 per year), 7 teaching assistantships with tuition reimbursements available (averaging $15,790 per year); career-related internships or fieldwork, Federal Work-Study, scholarships/grants, health care benefits, unspecified assistantships, and cooperative program also available. Financial award applicants required to submit FAFSA. *Faculty research:* Big data, atmospheric sciences, bioinformatics and systems biology, molecular dynamics, environmental studies. *Unit head:* Dr. Pushpalatha Murthy, Dean of the Graduate School/Associate Provost for Graduate Education, 906-487-3007, Fax: 906-487-2284, E-mail: ppmurthy@mtu.edu. *Application contact:* Carol T. Wingerson, Administrative Aide, 906-487-2328, Fax: 906-487-2284, E-mail: gradadms@mtu.edu.

Mills College, Graduate Studies, Program in Computer Science, Oakland, CA 94613-1000. Offers computer science (Certificate); interdisciplinary computer science (MA). *Program availability:* Part-time. *Faculty:* 4 full-time (all women). *Students:* 9 full-time (7 women), 3 part-time (all women); includes 6 minority (2 Asian, non-Hispanic/Latino; 2 Hispanic/Latino; 2 Two or more races, non-Hispanic/Latino). Average age 23. 13 applicants, 62% accepted, 5 enrolled. In 2017, 8 master's awarded. *Degree requirements:* For master's, thesis. *Entrance requirements:* For master's, three letters of recommendation. Additional exam requirements/recommendations for international students: Required—TOEFL (minimum score 600 paper-based; 100 iBT) or IELTS (minimum score 7). *Application deadline:* For fall admission, 2/1 priority date for domestic students, 12/15 for international students; for spring admission, 11/1 priority date for domestic students, 10/1 for international students. Applications are processed on a rolling basis. Application fee: $50. Electronic applications accepted. *Expenses:* Contact institution. *Financial support:* In 2017–18, 19 students received support, including 19 fellowships with tuition reimbursements available (averaging $3,015 per year), 16 teaching assistantships with tuition reimbursements available; career-related internships or fieldwork, institutionally sponsored loans, and scholarships/grants also available. Support available to part-time students. Financial award application deadline: 2/1; financial award applicants required to submit FAFSA. *Faculty research:* Dynamical

systems, linear programming, theory of computer viruses, interface design, intelligent tutoring systems. *Total annual research expenditures:* $893. *Unit head:* Susan S. Wang, Department Head, 510-430-2138, E-mail: wang@mills.edu. *Application contact:* Robynne Lofton, Director of Admissions, 510-430-3295, Fax: 510-430-2159, E-mail: grad-admission@mills.edu.
Website: http://www.mills.edu/ics

Minnesota State University Mankato, College of Graduate Studies and Research, Program in Cross-disciplinary Studies, Mankato, MN 56001. Offers MS. *Program availability:* Part-time, evening/weekend. *Degree requirements:* For master's, comprehensive exam, thesis or alternative. *Entrance requirements:* For master's, GRE General Test, minimum GPA of 3.0 during previous 2 years. Additional exam requirements/recommendations for international students: Required—TOEFL. Electronic applications accepted.

Montana State University Billings, College of Education, Department of Educational Theory and Practice, Option in Interdisciplinary Studies, Billings, MT 59101. Offers M Ed. *Program availability:* Part-time, 100% online, blended/hybrid learning. *Degree requirements:* For master's, thesis or alternative. *Entrance requirements:* For master's, GRE General Test or MAT, minimum GPA of 3.0. Additional exam requirements/recommendations for international students: Required—TOEFL (minimum score 79 iBT), IELTS (minimum score 6.5). *Application deadline:* For fall admission, 7/15 for domestic students; for spring admission, 12/1 for domestic students. Applications are processed on a rolling basis. Application fee: $40. Electronic applications accepted. *Expenses:* Tuition, state resident: full-time $11,740; part-time $7880 per year. Tuition, nonresident: full-time $32,200; part-time $24,140 per year. *Financial support:* Teaching assistantships with partial tuition reimbursements, career-related internships or fieldwork, Federal Work-Study, institutionally sponsored loans, scholarships/grants, tuition waivers (partial), and unspecified assistantships available. Support available to part-time students. Financial award application deadline: 5/1; financial award applicants required to submit FAFSA. *Unit head:* Dr. Cindy Dell, Chair, Educational Theory and Practice, 406-657-1614, Fax: 406-657-2807, E-mail: cdell@msubillings.edu. *Application contact:* Dr. Cindy Dell, Chair, Educational Theory and Practice, 406-657-1614, Fax: 406-657-2807, E-mail: cdell@msubillings.edu.

Montana Tech of The University of Montana, Interdisciplinary Program, Butte, MT 59701-8997. Offers MS. *Program availability:* Part-time. *Degree requirements:* For master's, comprehensive exam (for some programs), thesis optional. *Entrance requirements:* For master's, GRE General Test, minimum GPA of 3.0. Additional exam requirements/recommendations for international students: Required—TOEFL (minimum score 545 paper-based; 78 iBT), IELTS (minimum score 6.5).

Murray State University, College of Education and Human Services, Department of Early Childhood and Elementary Education, Murray, KY 42071. Offers elementary teacher leader (MA Ed); interdisciplinary early childhood education (MA Ed), including elementary education (MA Ed, Ed S), reading and writing; teacher education and professional development (Ed S), including elementary education (MA Ed, Ed S). *Accreditation:* NCATE. *Program availability:* Part-time. *Faculty:* 17 full-time (16 women), 1 (woman) part-time/adjunct. *Students:* 10 full-time (all women), 91 part-time (87 women); includes 7 minority (4 Black or African American, non-Hispanic/Latino; 1 Hispanic/Latino; 2 Two or more races, non-Hispanic/Latino). Average age 33. 27 applicants, 89% accepted, 19 enrolled. In 2017, 35 master's awarded. *Entrance requirements:* For master's and Ed S, GRE or GMAT, minimum university GPA of 2.75. Additional exam requirements/recommendations for international students: Required—TOEFL (minimum score 527 paper-based; 71 iBT). *Application deadline:* Applications are processed on a rolling basis. Application fee: $40 ($50 for international students). Electronic applications accepted. *Expenses:* Tuition, state resident: full-time $9504. Tuition, nonresident: full-time $26,811. *International tuition:* $14,400 full-time. Tuition and fees vary according to course load, degree level and reciprocity agreements. *Financial support:* Federal Work-Study and unspecified assistantships available. Financial award applicants required to submit FAFSA. *Unit head:* Dr. Jacqueline Hansen, Chair, Department of Early Childhood and Elementary Education, 270-809-2500, Fax: 270-809-3799, E-mail: jhansen@murraystate.edu. *Application contact:* Kaitlyn Burzynski, Interim Assistant Director for Graduate Admission and Records, 270-809-5732, Fax: 270-809-3780, E-mail: msu.graduateadmissions@murraystate.edu.
Website: http://www.murraystate.edu/academics/CollegesDepartments/CollegeOfEducationandHumanServices/coehsacademicunits/EarlyChildhoodandElementaryEducation/in

New Mexico State University, Graduate School, Interdisciplinary Program, Las Cruces, NM 88003. Offers MA, MS, PhD. *Program availability:* Part-time, blended/hybrid learning. *Students:* 5 full-time (3 women), 7 part-time (3 women); includes 3 minority (all Hispanic/Latino), 4 international. Average age 42. 1 applicant, 100% accepted, 1 enrolled. In 2017, 2 master's, 3 doctorates awarded. *Entrance requirements:* For master's, GRE General Test, minimum GPA of 2.5; for doctorate, GRE General Test, minimum GPA of 3.0. Additional exam requirements/recommendations for international students: Required—TOEFL (minimum score 550 paper-based; 79 iBT), IELTS (minimum score 6.5). *Application deadline:* Applications are processed on a rolling basis. Application fee: $40 ($50 for international students). Electronic applications accepted. *Expenses:* Tuition, state resident: full-time $4390. Tuition, nonresident: full-time $15,309. *Required fees:* $853. *Financial support:* In 2017–18, 7 students received support, including 2 fellowships (averaging $4,390 per year); career-related internships or fieldwork, Federal Work-Study, scholarships/grants, traineeships, health care benefits, and unspecified assistantships also available. Support available to part-time students. Financial award application deadline: 3/1. *Total annual research expenditures:* $1,789. *Unit head:* Dr. Loui Reyes, Dean of Graduate School, 575-646-5746, Fax: 575-646-7758, E-mail: gradinfo@nmsu.edu. *Application contact:* Graduate Admissions, 575-646-3121, E-mail: admissions@nmsu.edu.
Website: http://idsas.nmsu.edu

New York Institute of Technology, School of Interdisciplinary Studies and Education, Old Westbury, NY 11568-8000. Offers MA, MAT, MS, Advanced Certificate, Advanced Diploma. *Accreditation:* NCATE. *Program availability:* Part-time, evening/weekend, 100% online, blended/hybrid learning. *Faculty:* 12 full-time (7 women), 23 part-time/adjunct (14 women). *Students:* 80 full-time (67 women), 203 part-time (142 women); includes 72 minority (25 Black or African American, non-Hispanic/Latino; 13 Asian, non-Hispanic/Latino; 30 Hispanic/Latino; 4 Two or more races, non-Hispanic/Latino), 6 international. Average age 32. 151 applicants, 66% accepted, 65 enrolled. In 2017, 83 master's, 38 other advanced degrees awarded. *Entrance requirements:* Additional exam requirements/recommendations for international students: Required—TOEFL (minimum score 79 iBT), IELTS (minimum score 6). *Application deadline:* Applications are processed on a rolling basis. Application fee: $50. Electronic applications accepted. *Expenses:* $1,285 per credit plus fees. *Financial support:* Career-related internships or fieldwork, Federal Work-Study, scholarships/grants, tuition waivers (full and partial), and unspecified assistantships available. Support available to part-time students. Financial award application deadline: 2/15; financial award applicants required to submit FAFSA. *Unit head:* Dr. Christian Pomgratz, Interim Dean, 516-686-1474, E-mail: soeinfo@nyit.edu. *Application contact:* Alice Dolitsky, Director, Graduate Admissions, 516-686-7520, Fax: 516-686-1116, E-mail: nyitgrad@nyit.edu.
Website: http://www.nyit.edu/interdisciplinary

New York University, Gallatin School of Individualized Study, New York, NY 10003. Offers MA. *Program availability:* Part-time, evening/weekend. *Faculty:* 59 full-time (33 women), 129 part-time/adjunct (66 women). *Students:* 47 full-time (38 women), 85 part-time (61 women); includes 39 minority (18 Black or African American, non-Hispanic/Latino; 6 Asian, non-Hispanic/Latino; 10 Hispanic/Latino; 1 Native Hawaiian or other Pacific Islander, non-Hispanic/Latino; 4 Two or more races, non-Hispanic/Latino), 26 international. Average age 32. 157 applicants, 59% accepted, 40 enrolled. In 2017, 57 master's awarded. *Degree requirements:* For master's, thesis. *Entrance requirements:* Additional exam requirements/recommendations for international students: Required—TOEFL. *Application deadline:* For fall admission, 1/15 priority date for domestic and international students; for spring admission, 10/1 for domestic and international students. Applications are processed on a rolling basis. Application fee: $50. Electronic applications accepted. *Expenses:* $2,231 per unit tuition and fees. *Financial support:* In 2017–18, 65 students received support. Federal Work-Study, institutionally sponsored loans, scholarships/grants, health care benefits, tuition waivers (full and partial), and unspecified assistantships available. Support available to part-time students. Financial award application deadline: 1/15; financial award applicants required to submit FAFSA. *Faculty research:* Visual and performing arts and writing, media studies, political and social thought and human rights, literary and cultural studies, environmental and global studies, gender studies. *Unit head:* Dr. Susanne L. Wofford, Dean, 212-998-7370. *Application contact:* Frances R. Levin, Director of Enrollment, 212-998-7349, E-mail: gallatin.gradadmissions@nyu.edu.
Website: https://gallatin.nyu.edu/

Niagara University, Graduate Division of Arts and Sciences, Program in Interdisciplinary Studies, Niagara University, NY 14109. Offers MA. *Program availability:* Part-time. *Students:* 11 full-time (5 women), 5 part-time (all women); includes 2 minority (both Black or African American, non-Hispanic/Latino), 7 international. Average age 34. In 2017, 2 master's awarded. *Entrance requirements:* Additional exam requirements/recommendations for international students: Required—TOEFL (minimum score 550 paper-based; 79 iBT), IELTS (minimum score 6). *Application deadline:* For fall admission, 8/1 for domestic students. Applications are processed on a rolling basis. Electronic applications accepted. *Expenses:* Contact institution. *Financial support:* Research assistantships with tuition reimbursements, teaching assistantships with tuition reimbursements, career-related internships or fieldwork, Federal Work-Study, scholarships/grants, and unspecified assistantships available. Financial award application deadline: 4/15; financial award applicants required to submit FAFSA. *Unit head:* Dr. Mustafa Gokcek, Director, 716-286-8195, E-mail: gokcek@niagara.edu. *Application contact:* Evan Pierce, Associate Director of Graduate Recruitment, 716-286-8769, Fax: 716-286-8710, E-mail: epierce@niagara.edu.
Website: http://www.niagara.edu/mais

Northeastern University, Bouvé College of Health Sciences, Boston, MA 02115-5096. Offers applied behavior analysis (MS); audiology (Au D); counseling psychology (MS, PhD, CAGS); exercise science (MS); nursing (MS, PhD, CAGS), including administration (MS), adult-gerontology acute care nurse practitioner (MS, CAGS), adult-gerontology primary care nurse practitioner (MS, CAGS), anesthesia (MS), family nurse practitioner (MS, CAGS), neonatal nurse practitioner (MS, CAGS), pediatric nurse practitioner (MS, CAGS), psychiatric mental health nurse practitioner (MS, CAGS); nursing practice (DNP); pharmaceutical sciences (MS, PhD), including interdisciplinary concentration, pharmaceutics and drug delivery systems; pharmacology (MS); pharmacy (Pharm D); school psychology (PhD); speech-language pathology (MS); urban health (MPH); MS/MBA. *Accreditation:* ACPE (one or more programs are accredited). *Program availability:* Part-time, evening/weekend, online learning. *Faculty:* 192 full-time. *Students:* 1,685. In 2017, 352 master's, 312 doctorates, 25 other advanced degrees awarded. *Degree requirements:* For doctorate, thesis/dissertation (for some programs); for CAGS, comprehensive exam. Application fee: $75. Electronic applications accepted. *Expenses:* Contact institution. *Financial support:* Fellowships, research assistantships, teaching assistantships, career-related internships or fieldwork, scholarships/grants, health care benefits, tuition waivers, and unspecified assistantships available. Support available to part-time students. Financial award applicants required to submit FAFSA. *Unit head:* Susan L. Parish, Dean, Bouve College of Health Sciences, 617-373-3321, Fax: 617-373-3030, E-mail: s.parish@northeastern.edu. *Application contact:* 617-373-2708, Fax: 617-373-4701, E-mail: bouvegrad@northeastern.edu.
Website: https://www.northeastern.edu/bouve/

Northeastern University, College of Engineering, Boston, MA 02115-5096. Offers bioengineering (MS, PhD); chemical engineering (MS, PhD); civil engineering (MS, PhD); computer engineering (PhD); computer systems engineering (MS); electrical and computer engineering (MS); electrical and computer engineering leadership (MS); electrical engineering (PhD); energy systems (MS); engineering and public policy (MS); engineering management (MS, Certificate); environmental engineering (MS); industrial engineering (MS, PhD); information assurance (PhD); information systems (MS); interdisciplinary engineering (PhD); mechanical engineering (PhD); operations research (MS); telecommunication systems management (MS). *Program availability:* Part-time, online learning. *Faculty:* 225 full-time. *Students:* 3,720. In 2017, 851 master's, 74 doctorates awarded. Application fee: $75. Electronic applications accepted. *Expenses:* Contact institution. *Financial support:* Fellowships, research assistantships, teaching assistantships, career-related internships or fieldwork, scholarships/grants, health care benefits, tuition waivers, and unspecified assistantships available. Support available to part-time students. Financial award applicants required to submit FAFSA. *Unit head:* Dr. Nadine Aubry, Dean, College of Engineering, 617-373-5847, E-mail: n.aubry@neu.edu. *Application contact:* Jeffery Hengel, Director of Graduate Admissions, 617-373-2711, E-mail: j.hengel@northeastern.edu.
Website: http://www.coe.neu.edu/

Nova Southeastern University, College of Arts, Humanities, and Social Sciences, Fort Lauderdale, FL 33314-7796. Offers advanced conflict resolution practice (Graduate Certificate); child protection (MHS); college student affairs (MS); conflict analysis and resolution (MS, PhD); criminal justice (MS, PhD); cross-disciplinary studies (MA); developmental disabilities (MS); family studies (Graduate Certificate); family systems health care (Graduate Certificate); family therapy (MS, PhD); marriage and family therapy (DMFT); peace studies (Graduate Certificate); qualitative research (Graduate Certificate); solution focused coaching (Graduate Certificate). *Accreditation:* AAMFT/COAMFTE (one or more programs are accredited). *Program availability:* Part-time, evening/weekend, 100% online, blended/hybrid learning. *Faculty:* 29 full-time (18 women), 27 part-time/adjunct (21 women). *Students:* 303 full-time (238 women), 903 part-time (677 women); includes 689 minority (385 Black or African American, non-Hispanic/Latino; 4 American Indian or Alaska Native, non-Hispanic/Latino; 31 Asian, non-Hispanic/Latino; 234 Hispanic/Latino; 1 Native Hawaiian or other Pacific Islander, non-Hispanic/Latino; 34 Two or more races, non-Hispanic/Latino), 60 international. Average age 37. 624 applicants, 61% accepted, 285 enrolled. In 2017, 277 master's, 62 doctorates, 25 other advanced degrees awarded. *Degree requirements:* For master's, thesis optional, comprehensive exams, portfolios (for some programs), table-top exams (for some programs); for doctorate, comprehensive exam, thesis/dissertation, qualifying

exams, portfolios (for some programs). *Entrance requirements:* For master's, interview, minimum GPA of 3.0, writing sample; for doctorate, interview, minimum GPA of 3.5, master's degree in related field, writing sample; for Graduate Certificate, minimum GPA of 3.0. Additional exam requirements/recommendations for international students: Required—TOEFL. *Application deadline:* For fall admission, 5/17 priority date for domestic and international students; for winter admission, 12/1 priority date for domestic and international students; for spring admission, 4/1 priority date for domestic and international students. Applications are processed on a rolling basis. Application fee: $50. Electronic applications accepted. *Expenses:* Contact institution. *Financial support:* In 2017–18, 170 students received support. Career-related internships or fieldwork, Federal Work-Study, scholarships/grants, and unspecified assistantships available. Financial award application deadline: 4/1; financial award applicants required to submit CSS PROFILE. *Faculty research:* Conflict resolution, family therapy, peace research, international conflict, multi-disciplinary studies, college student affairs, national security affairs, health care conflict resolution, family systems health care, advanced family systems, qualitative research, solution-focused coaching. *Unit head:* Dr. Honggang Yang, Dean, 954-262-3016, Fax: 954-262-3968, E-mail: yangh@nova.edu. *Application contact:* Marcia Arango, Student Recruitment Coordinator, 954-262-3006, Fax: 954-262-3968, E-mail: marango@nsu.nova.edu.
Website: http://cahss.nova.edu/

The Ohio State University, Graduate School, College of Arts and Sciences, Division of Arts and Humanities, Department of Comparative Studies, Columbus, OH 43210. Offers MA, PhD. *Faculty:* 16. *Students:* 25 (15 women). Average age 30. In 2017, 3 master's, 5 doctorates awarded. Terminal master's awarded for partial completion of doctoral program. *Degree requirements:* For doctorate, thesis/dissertation. *Entrance requirements:* For master's and doctorate, GRE General Test. Additional exam requirements/recommendations for international students: Required—TOEFL (minimum score 550 paper-based; 79 iBT), Michigan English Language Assessment Battery (minimum score 82); Recommended—IELTS (minimum score 7). *Application deadline:* For fall admission, 11/30 priority date for domestic and international students; for spring admission, 3/1 for domestic students, 2/1 for international students. Applications are processed on a rolling basis. Application fee: $60 ($70 for international students). Electronic applications accepted. *Financial support:* Fellowships with tuition reimbursements, research assistantships with tuition reimbursements, teaching assistantships with tuition reimbursements, Federal Work-Study, institutionally sponsored loans, and unspecified assistantships available. Support available to part-time students. *Unit head:* Dr. Barry Shank, Chair, 614-688-2559, E-mail: shank.46@osu.edu. *Application contact:* Graduate and Professional Admissions, 614-292-9444, Fax: 614-292-3895, E-mail: gpadmissions@osu.edu.
Website: http://comparativestudies.osu.edu/

Oregon State University, Interdisciplinary/Institutional Programs, Program in Interdisciplinary Studies, Corvallis, OR 97331. Offers MAIS. Program focuses on three areas of study and must include at least one area of study in liberal arts. *Program availability:* Part-time. *Entrance requirements:* Additional exam requirements/recommendations for international students: Required—TOEFL (minimum score 80 iBT), IELTS (minimum score 6.5). *Application deadline:* For fall admission, 3/1 for domestic and international students. Application fee: $75 ($85 for international students). *Unit head:* Dr. David Bernell, Program Director, 541-737-6281, E-mail: david.bernell@oregonstate.edu. *Application contact:* Dr. David Bernell, Program Director, 541-737-6281, E-mail: david.bernell@oregonstate.edu.
Website: http://oregonstate.edu/dept/grad_school/mais.html

Regent University, Graduate School, School of Business and Leadership, Virginia Beach, VA 23464-9800. Offers business administration (MBA), including accounting, economics, entrepreneurship, finance and investing, general management, healthcare management (MA, MBA), human resource management (MA, MBA), innovation management, leadership, marketing, not-for-profit management (MA, MBA); business analytics (MS); business and design management (MA); church leadership (MA); leadership (Certificate); organizational leadership (MA, PhD), including ecclesial leadership (DSL, PhD), entrepreneurial leadership (PhD), healthcare management (MA, MBA), human resource development (PhD), human resource management (MA, MBA), individualized studies (DSL, PhD), interdisciplinary studies (MA), leadership coaching and mentoring (MA), not-for-profit management (MA, MBA), organizational development consulting (MA), servant leadership (MA, DSL); strategic leadership (DSL), including ecclesial leadership (DSL, PhD), global consulting, healthcare leadership, individualized studies (DSL, PhD), leadership coaching, servant leadership (MA, DSL), strategic foresight. *Program availability:* Part-time, evening/weekend, 100% online, blended/hybrid learning. *Faculty:* 9 full-time (2 women), 38 part-time/adjunct (11 women). *Students:* 129 full-time (80 women), 1,152 part-time (598 women); includes 685 minority (546 Black or African American, non-Hispanic/Latino; 10 American Indian or Alaska Native, non-Hispanic/Latino; 29 Asian, non-Hispanic/Latino; 65 Hispanic/Latino; 6 Native Hawaiian or other Pacific Islander, non-Hispanic/Latino; 29 Two or more races, non-Hispanic/Latino), 62 international. Average age 41. 1,721 applicants, 48% accepted, 624 enrolled. In 2017, 125 master's, 69 doctorates awarded. *Degree requirements:* For master's, thesis or alternative, 3-credit hour culminating experience; for doctorate, thesis/dissertation. *Entrance requirements:* For master's, college transcripts, resume, essay; for doctorate, college transcripts, resume, essay, writing sample; for Certificate, writing sample, resume, transcripts. Additional exam requirements/recommendations for international students: Required—TOEFL (minimum score 577 paper-based). *Application deadline:* For fall admission, 5/1 priority date for domestic students; for spring admission, 10/1 priority date for domestic students. Applications are processed on a rolling basis. Application fee: $50. Electronic applications accepted. *Expenses:* $650 per credit (MA, MS, MBA); $995 per credit (PhD); $300 per semester technology fee. *Financial support:* In 2017–18, 829 students received support. Career-related internships or fieldwork, scholarships/grants, and unspecified assistantships available. Support available to part-time students. *Faculty research:* Servant leadership, global business, team effectiveness, technology utilization, leadership development. *Unit head:* Dr. Doris Gomez, Dean, 757-352-4686, Fax: 757-352-4634, E-mail: dorigom@regent.edu. *Application contact:* Heidi Cece, Assistant Vice President of Enrollment Management, 800-373-5504, Fax: 757-352-4381, E-mail: admissions@regent.edu.
Website: https://www.regent.edu/school-of-business-and-leadership/

Regent University, Graduate School, School of Divinity, Virginia Beach, VA 23464-9800. Offers Christian spirituality and formation (MA); divinity (M Div), including Biblical studies (M Div, MTS, Th M, PhD), chaplain ministry, Christian theology (M Div, MTS, Th M, PhD), church and ministry (M Div, MA), history of Christianity (M Div, MTS, Th M, PhD), inter-cultural studies (M Div, MA), interdisciplinary studies (M Div, MA, MTS), marketplace ministry (M Div, MA), missional discipleship, practical healing ministry (M Div, MA), worship and media (M Div, MA); leadership and renewal (D Min), including Christian leadership and renewal, clinical pastoral education, community transformation, military ministry, ministry leadership coaching; practical theology (MA), including church and ministry (M Div, MA), cosmogony, inter-cultural studies (M Div, MA), interdisciplinary studies (M Div, MA, MTS), marketplace ministry (M Div, MA), practical healing ministry (M Div, MA), worship and media (M Div, MA); renewal theology (PhD), including Biblical studies (M Div, MTS, Th M, PhD), Christian theology (M Div, MTS, Th M, PhD), history of Christianity (M Div, MTS, Th M, PhD), practical theology; theological studies (MTS), including Biblical studies (M Div, MTS, Th M, PhD), Christian theology (M Div, MTS, Th M, PhD), history of Christianity (M Div, MTS, Th M, PhD), interdisciplinary studies (M Div, MA, MTS); theology (Th M), including Biblical studies (M Div, MTS, Th M, PhD), Christian theology (M Div, MTS, Th M, PhD), history of Christianity (M Div, MTS, Th M, PhD). *Accreditation:* ACIPE; ATS. *Program availability:* Part-time, evening/weekend, 100% online, blended/hybrid learning. *Faculty:* 17 full-time (3 women), 66 part-time/adjunct (9 women). *Students:* 146 full-time (54 women), 917 part-time (404 women); includes 563 minority (470 Black or African American, non-Hispanic/Latino; 1 American Indian or Alaska Native, non-Hispanic/Latino; 17 Asian, non-Hispanic/Latino; 56 Hispanic/Latino; 1 Native Hawaiian or other Pacific Islander, non-Hispanic/Latino; 18 Two or more races, non-Hispanic/Latino), 27 international. Average age 44. 1,321 applicants, 39% accepted, 295 enrolled. In 2017, 146 master's, 25 doctorates awarded. *Degree requirements:* For master's, comprehensive exam, thesis or alternative, internship; for doctorate, thesis/dissertation or alternative. *Entrance requirements:* For master's, minimum undergraduate GPA of 2.75, writing sample, personal goal statement, college transcripts; for doctorate, GRE, minimum graduate GPA of 3.5 (PhD), 3.0 (D Min); clergy recommendations; writing sample; transcripts; resume; interview. Additional exam requirements/recommendations for international students: Required—TOEFL (minimum score 577 paper-based). *Application deadline:* For fall admission, 5/1 priority date for domestic students. Applications are processed on a rolling basis. Application fee: $50. Electronic applications accepted. *Expenses:* $495 per credit (master's); $595 per credit (D Min); $650 per credit (PhD); $300 per semester technology fee. *Financial support:* In 2017–18, 721 students received support. Career-related internships or fieldwork, scholarships/grants, and unspecified assistantships available. Support available to part-time students. *Faculty research:* Greek and Hebrew, theology, spiritual formation, global missions and world Christianity, women in ministry leadership. *Unit head:* Dr. Cornelius Bekker, Dean, 757-352-4401, Fax: 757-352-4597, E-mail: clbekker@regent.edu. *Application contact:* Heidi Cece, Assistant Vice President of Enrollment Management, 800-373-5504, Fax: 757-352-4381, E-mail: admissions@regent.edu.
Website: https://www.regent.edu/school-of-divinity/

Rensselaer Polytechnic Institute, Graduate School, School of Science, Program in Multi-Disciplinary Science, Troy, NY 12180-3590. Offers MS, PhD. *Faculty:* 127 full-time (33 women), 9 part-time/adjunct (4 women). *Students:* 5 full-time (2 women), 2 international. Average age 34. 5 applicants, 20% accepted, 1 enrolled. In 2017, 2 doctorates awarded. Terminal master's awarded for partial completion of doctoral program. *Degree requirements:* For master's, comprehensive exam (for some programs), thesis optional; for doctorate, comprehensive exam, thesis/dissertation. *Entrance requirements:* For master's and doctorate, GRE. Additional exam requirements/recommendations for international students: Required—TOEFL (minimum score 600 paper-based; 100 iBT), IELTS (minimum score 7), PTE (minimum score 68). *Application deadline:* For fall admission, 1/1 priority date for domestic and international students; for spring admission, 8/15 priority date for domestic and international students. Applications are processed on a rolling basis. Application fee: $75. Electronic applications accepted. *Expenses: Tuition:* Full-time $52,550; part-time $2125 per credit hour. *Required fees:* $2890. *Financial support:* In 2017–18, research assistantships (averaging $23,000 per year), teaching assistantships (averaging $23,000 per year) were awarded; fellowships also available. Financial award application deadline: 1/1. *Total annual research expenditures:* $1.9 million. *Unit head:* Dr. Sibel Adali, Graduate Program Director, 518-276-6455, E-mail: sibel@cs.rpi.edu.
Website: https://science.rpi.edu/itws/programs/graduate/ms/phd-multidisciplinary-science

Rochester Institute of Technology, Graduate Enrollment Services, School of Individualized Study, Graduate Programs Department, MS Program in Professional Studies, Rochester, NY 14623. Offers MS. *Program availability:* Part-time, evening/weekend, 100% online, blended/hybrid learning. *Students:* 17 full-time (8 women), 51 part-time (31 women); includes 8 minority (2 Black or African American, non-Hispanic/Latino; 4 Asian, non-Hispanic/Latino; 2 Hispanic/Latino), 12 international. Average age 34. 53 applicants, 62% accepted, 15 enrolled. In 2017, 34 master's awarded. *Entrance requirements:* For master's, minimum GPA of 3.0. Additional exam requirements/recommendations for international students: Required—TOEFL (minimum score 550 paper-based; 79 iBT), IELTS (minimum score 6.5), PTE (minimum score 58). *Application deadline:* Applications are processed on a rolling basis. Application fee: $65. Electronic applications accepted. *Expenses:* $1,815 per credit hour (classroom), $1,035 per credit hour (online study). *Financial support:* In 2017–18, 10 students received support. Career-related internships or fieldwork, scholarships/grants, and unspecified assistantships available. Support available to part-time students. Financial award applicants required to submit FAFSA. *Faculty research:* Interdisciplinary entrepreneurship; non-profit management; educational innovation; technology and work in the 21st century; professional development and leadership. *Unit head:* Peter Boyd, Graduate Program Director, 585-475-6320, Fax: 585-475-6292, E-mail: sois@rit.edu. *Application contact:* Diane Ellison, Senior Associate Vice President, Graduate Enrollment Services, 585-475-2229, Fax: 585-475-7164, E-mail: gradinfo@rit.edu.
Website: http://www.rit.edu/academicaffairs/sois/getting-started/graduate/graduate-degrees-programs

Rosalind Franklin University of Medicine and Science, College of Health Professions, Department of Interprofessional Healthcare Studies, Interprofessional Studies Program, North Chicago, IL 60064-3095. Offers interprofessional studies (D Sc). *Program availability:* Part-time, online learning. *Degree requirements:* For doctorate, comprehensive exam, thesis/dissertation. *Entrance requirements:* For doctorate, GRE. Additional exam requirements/recommendations for international students: Required—TOEFL. *Faculty research:* Interprofessional education.

Rutgers University–New Brunswick, Graduate School-New Brunswick, BioMaPS Institute for Quantitative Biology, Piscataway, NJ 08854-8097. Offers computational biology and molecular biophysics (PhD). *Degree requirements:* For doctorate, comprehensive exam, thesis/dissertation. *Entrance requirements:* For doctorate, GRE. Additional exam requirements/recommendations for international students: Required—TOEFL. Electronic applications accepted. *Faculty research:* Structural biology, systems biology, bioinformatics, translational medicine, genomics.

San Diego State University, Graduate and Research Affairs, Interdisciplinary Studies, San Diego, CA 92182. Offers MA, MS. *Program availability:* Part-time. *Degree requirements:* For master's, thesis. *Entrance requirements:* For master's, GRE General Test. Additional exam requirements/recommendations for international students: Required—TOEFL. Electronic applications accepted.

Sonoma State University, School of Science and Technology, Department of Kinesiology, Rohnert Park, CA 94928. Offers exercise science/pre-physical therapy (MA); interdisciplinary (MA); interdisciplinary pre-occupational therapy (MA); lifetime physical activity (MA), including coach education, fitness and wellness. *Program availability:* Part-time. *Degree requirements:* For master's, thesis, oral exam. *Entrance requirements:* For master's, minimum GPA of 2.8. Additional exam requirements/recommendations for international students: Required—TOEFL (minimum score 500 paper-based). *Application deadline:* For fall admission, 11/30 for domestic students; for

spring admission, 9/1 for domestic students. Applications are processed on a rolling basis. Application fee: $55. *Financial support:* Career-related internships or fieldwork available. Financial award application deadline: 3/2; financial award applicants required to submit FAFSA. *Unit head:* Dr. Steven Winter, Chair, 707-664-2188, E-mail: steven.winter@sonoma.edu. *Application contact:* Dr. Bulent Sokmen, Graduate Coordinator, 707-664-2789, E-mail: sokmen@sonoma.edu.
Website: http://www.sonoma.edu/kinesiology/

Southern Illinois University Edwardsville, Graduate School, Program in Integrative Studies, Edwardsville, IL 62026. Offers cultural heritage and resources management (MA, MS); diversity training (MA, MS); organizational design thinking (MS); sustainability (MS). *Program availability:* Part-time, evening/weekend. *Degree requirements:* For master's, variable foreign language requirement, comprehensive exam (for some programs), thesis (for some programs). *Entrance requirements:* Additional exam requirements/recommendations for international students: Required—TOEFL (minimum score 550 paper-based; 79 iBT), IELTS (minimum score 6.5). Electronic applications accepted.

Southern Oregon University, Graduate Studies, Program in Interdisciplinary Studies, Ashland, OR 97520. Offers MIS. *Program availability:* Part-time, online learning. *Degree requirements:* For master's, thesis (for some programs). *Entrance requirements:* For master's, GRE General Test, minimum cumulative GPA of 3.0 in the last 90 quarter credits (60 semester credits) of undergraduate coursework. Additional exam requirements/recommendations for international students: Required—TOEFL (minimum score 540 paper-based; 76 iBT), IELTS (minimum score 6), ELPT (minimum score 964) or ELS (minimum score 112). Electronic applications accepted.

Southern Utah University, Program in Interdisciplinary Studies, Cedar City, UT 84720-2498. Offers MIS. *Program availability:* 100% online. *Entrance requirements:* For master's, GRE. Additional exam requirements/recommendations for international students: Required—TOEFL (minimum score 550 paper-based; 79 iBT), IELTS (minimum score 6). Application fee: $60 ($65 for international students).
Website: https://www.suu.edu/graduatestudies/mis/

State University of New York at Fredonia, College of Liberal Arts and Sciences, Fredonia, NY 14063-1136. Offers biology (MS); English (MA); English education 7-12 (MA); interdisciplinary studies (MA, MS); math education (MS Ed); professional writing (CAS); speech pathology (MS); MA/MS. *Program availability:* Part-time, evening/weekend. *Students:* 73 full-time (62 women), 9 part-time (6 women); includes 7 minority (1 Black or African American, non-Hispanic/Latino; 1 Asian, non-Hispanic/Latino; 2 Hispanic/Latino; 1 Native Hawaiian or other Pacific Islander, non-Hispanic/Latino; 2 Two or more races, non-Hispanic/Latino). Average age 24. 200 applicants, 25% accepted, 43 enrolled. In 2017, 41 master's, 1 other advanced degree awarded. *Degree requirements:* For master's, comprehensive exam (for some programs), thesis (for some programs). *Entrance requirements:* For master's, GRE. Additional exam requirements/recommendations for international students: Required—TOEFL (minimum score 79 iBT), IELTS (minimum score 6.5). *Application deadline:* Applications are processed on a rolling basis. Application fee: $75. Electronic applications accepted. *Expenses:* Tuition, state resident: full-time $8154. Tuition, nonresident: full-time $16,650. *Required fees:* $1209. *Financial support:* In 2017–18, 5 students received support, including 14 teaching assistantships with full and partial tuition reimbursements available (averaging $5,957 per year); tuition waivers (full and partial) and unspecified assistantships also available. *Faculty research:* Immunology/microbiology, applied human physiology, ecology and evolution, invertebrate biology, molecular biology, biochemistry, physiology, animal behavior, science education, vertebrate physiology, cell biology, plant biology, developmental biology, aquatic ecology, bilingual language acquisition, bilingual language acquisition and disorders, augmentative and alternate communication with ALS, World War I, Zweig, environmental literature, editing, adolescent literature, pedagogy. *Unit head:* Dr. Andy Karafa, Dean, 716-673-3173, Fax: 716-673-3338, E-mail: andy.karafa@gmail.com. *Application contact:* Wendy S. Dunst, Interim Graduate Recruitment and Admissions Associate, 716-673-3808, Fax: 716-673-3712, E-mail: wendy.dunst@fredonia.edu.
Website: http://www.fredonia.edu/clas/

Stephen F. Austin State University, Graduate School, College of Applied Arts and Science, Program in Interdisciplinary Studies, Nacogdoches, TX 75962. Offers MIS. *Program availability:* Part-time. *Degree requirements:* For master's, comprehensive exam, thesis optional. *Entrance requirements:* For master's, GRE General Test. Additional exam requirements/recommendations for international students: Required—TOEFL (minimum score 550 paper-based).

Teachers College, Columbia University, Interdisciplinary Programs, New York, NY 10027-6696. Offers Ed M, MA, ME, Ed D. *Program availability:* Part-time. *Students:* 13 full-time (7 women), 23 part-time (14 women); includes 10 minority (6 Black or African American, non-Hispanic/Latino; 1 Asian, non-Hispanic/Latino; 1 Hispanic/Latino; 1 Native Hawaiian or other Pacific Islander, non-Hispanic/Latino; 1 Two or more races, non-Hispanic/Latino), 8 international. Average age 40. 5 applicants, 60% accepted, 2 enrolled. Terminal master's awarded for partial completion of doctoral program. *Degree requirements:* For doctorate, thesis/dissertation. *Application contact:* David Estrella, Director of Admissions, 212-678-3305, E-mail: estrella@tc.columbia.edu.

Texas A&M University–Texarkana, Graduate Studies and Research, College of Education and Liberal Arts, Texarkana, TX 75503. Offers adult education (MS); curriculum and instruction (M Ed); education (MS); educational administration (M Ed); English (MA); instructional technology (MS); interdisciplinary studies (MA, MS); special education (MS). *Program availability:* Part-time, evening/weekend. *Degree requirements:* For master's, comprehensive exam (for some programs), thesis optional. *Entrance requirements:* For master's, minimum GPA of 2.5 on last 60 hours of bachelor's degree. Additional exam requirements/recommendations for international students: Required—TOEFL. Electronic applications accepted.

Texas State University, The Graduate College, College of Applied Arts, Interdisciplinary Studies Program in Occupational Education, San Marcos, TX 78666. Offers MAIS, MSIS. *Program availability:* Part-time, evening/weekend, blended/hybrid learning. *Faculty:* 7 full-time (4 women), 6 part-time/adjunct (3 women). *Students:* 19 full-time (9 women), 43 part-time (29 women); includes 31 minority (14 Black or African American, non-Hispanic/Latino; 1 Asian, non-Hispanic/Latino; 15 Hispanic/Latino; 1 Two or more races, non-Hispanic/Latino), 1 international. Average age 36. 42 applicants, 67% accepted, 12 enrolled. In 2017, 23 master's awarded. *Degree requirements:* For master's, comprehensive exam, thesis optional. *Entrance requirements:* For master's, baccalaureate degree from regionally-accredited university; minimum GPA of 2.75 for last 60 hours of undergraduate work or GRE General Test; statement of personal goals. Additional exam requirements/recommendations for international students: Required—TOEFL (minimum score 550 paper-based; 78 iBT), IELTS (minimum score 6.5). *Application deadline:* For fall admission, 2/15 priority date for domestic and international students; for spring admission, 10/15 priority date for domestic students, 10/1 for international students; for summer admission, 4/15 for domestic students, 3/15 for international students. Applications are processed on a rolling basis. Application fee: $40 ($90 for international students). Electronic applications accepted. *Expenses:* Tuition, state resident: full-time $7868; part-time $3934 per semester. Tuition, nonresident: full-time $17,828; part-time $8914 per semester. *Required fees:* $2092; $1435 per semester. Tuition and fees vary according to course load. *Financial support:* In 2017–18, 48 students received support, including 5 research assistantships (averaging $13,059 per year); teaching assistantships, Federal Work-Study, institutionally sponsored loans, scholarships/grants, health care benefits, and unspecified assistantships also available. Support available to part-time students. Financial award application deadline: 3/1; financial award applicants required to submit FAFSA. *Faculty research:* Reaching under served rural agricultural Latinos and veterans; College Credit for Heroes;. *Total annual research expenditures:* $113,885. *Unit head:* Dr. Mary Jo Garcia Biggs, Chair of Occupational, Workforce, and Leadership Studies Department, 512-245-1680, E-mail: mb56@txstate.edu. *Application contact:* Dr. Andrea Golato, Dean of Graduate School, 512-245-2581, Fax: 512-245-8365, E-mail: gradcollege@txstate.edu.
Website: http://www.OCED.txstate.edu/

Texas Tech University, Graduate School, Interdisciplinary Programs, Lubbock, TX 79409. Offers arid land studies (MS); biotechnology (MS); heritage and museum sciences (MA); interdisciplinary studies (MA, MS); wind science and engineering (PhD); JD/MS. *Program availability:* Part-time, blended/hybrid learning. *Faculty:* 11 full-time (5 women). *Students:* 106 full-time (56 women), 85 part-time (52 women); includes 65 minority (23 Black or African American, non-Hispanic/Latino; 2 American Indian or Alaska Native, non-Hispanic/Latino; 3 Asian, non-Hispanic/Latino; 32 Hispanic/Latino; 5 Two or more races, non-Hispanic/Latino), 30 international. Average age 30. 116 applicants, 67% accepted, 55 enrolled. In 2017, 52 master's, 1 doctorate awarded. Terminal master's awarded for partial completion of doctoral program. *Degree requirements:* For master's, comprehensive exam (for some programs), thesis (for some programs); for doctorate, comprehensive exam, thesis/dissertation (for some programs). *Entrance requirements:* Additional exam requirements/recommendations for international students: Required—TOEFL (minimum score 550 paper-based; 79 iBT), IELTS (minimum score 6.5), PTE (minimum score 60), Cambridge advanced (B), Cambridge Proficiency (C), ELS English for Academic Purposes (Level 112). *Application deadline:* For fall admission, 6/1 priority date for domestic students, 1/15 priority date for international students; for spring admission, 9/1 priority date for domestic students, 6/15 priority date for international students. Applications are processed on a rolling basis. Application fee: $60. Electronic applications accepted. *Expenses:* Tuition, state resident: full-time $7632; part-time $318 per credit hour. Tuition, nonresident: full-time $17,424; part-time $726 per credit hour. *Required fees:* $2428; $50.50 per credit hour. $608 per semester. Tuition and fees vary according to program. *Financial support:* In 2017–18, 124 students received support, including 106 fellowships (averaging $4,660 per year), 25 research assistantships (averaging $16,239 per year), 16 teaching assistantships (averaging $10,391 per year); scholarships/grants and unspecified assistantships also available. Financial award application deadline: 4/15; financial award applicants required to submit FAFSA. *Total annual research expenditures:* $2.2 million. *Unit head:* Dr. Mark Sheridan, Vice Provost for Graduate and Postdoctoral Affairs/Dean of the Graduate School, 806-742-2787, Fax: 806-742-1746, E-mail: mark.sheridan@ttu.edu. *Application contact:* Claudia Simon, Senior Academic Advisor, 806-834-8290, Fax: 806-742-4038, E-mail: claudia.simon@ttu.edu.
Website: http://www.depts.ttu.edu/gradschool/

Trinity Western University, School of Graduate Studies, Program in Interdisciplinary Humanities, Langley, BC V2Y 1Y1, Canada. Offers general humanities (MAIH); specialized (MAIH), including English, history, philosophy. *Program availability:* Part-time. *Degree requirements:* For master's, thesis or alternative, 36 semester hours. *Entrance requirements:* For master's, strong undergraduate degree in humanities or English, history or philosophy. Additional exam requirements/recommendations for international students: Recommended—TOEFL. Electronic applications accepted. *Faculty research:* Literary theory, gender, medieval and early modern literature, philosophy of religion, Thomas Merton's poetics.

Tufts University, Graduate School of Arts and Sciences, Interdisciplinary Doctoral Program, Medford, MA 02155. Offers PhD. *Students:* 4 full-time (2 women), 3 international. Average age 41. 4 applicants. *Degree requirements:* For doctorate, thesis/dissertation. *Entrance requirements:* Additional exam requirements/recommendations for international students: Required—TOEFL (minimum score 550 paper-based; 80 iBT), IELTS (minimum score 6.5). *Application deadline:* For fall admission, 1/15 for domestic and international students. Application fee: $85. Electronic applications accepted. *Expenses:* Contact institution. *Financial support:* Research assistantships, teaching assistantships, Federal Work-Study, scholarships/grants, health care benefits, tuition waivers (full and partial), and unspecified assistantships available. Financial award application deadline: 1/15. *Unit head:* Dr. Sergio Fantini, Director, 617-627-4356. *Application contact:* Office of Graduate Admissions, 617-627-3395, E-mail: gradadmissions@tufts.edu.
Website: http://gsas.tufts.edu/academics/interdisciplinary.htm

Tulane University, School of Science and Engineering, Interdisciplinary PhD Program, New Orleans, LA 70118-5669. Offers PhD. *Expenses: Tuition:* Full-time $50,920; part-time $2829 per credit hour. *Required fees:* $2040; $44.50 per credit hour. $580 per term. Tuition and fees vary according to course load, degree level and program.

Union Institute & University, PhD Program in Interdisciplinary Studies, Cincinnati, OH 45206-1925. Offers educational studies (PhD), including Martin Luther King studies; ethical and creative leadership (PhD); humanities and culture (PhD); public policy and social change (PhD). Program requires participation in brief on-campus residencies twice each year (January and July). *Program availability:* Part-time, online only, blended/hybrid learning. *Degree requirements:* For doctorate, comprehensive exam, thesis/dissertation. *Entrance requirements:* For doctorate, master's degree, three letters of recommendation, statement of purpose. Additional exam requirements/recommendations for international students: Required—TOEFL. *Application deadline:* Applications are processed on a rolling basis. Application fee: $50. Electronic applications accepted. *Expenses:* Contact institution. *Financial support:* Federal Work-Study and scholarships/grants available. Financial award application deadline: 5/1; financial award applicants required to submit FAFSA. *Faculty research:* Social responsibility, ethical leadership, Martin Luther King studies. *Unit head:* Dr. Michael Raffanti, Dean of Graduate College, 800-641-6400 Ext. 1237, E-mail: michael.raffanti@myunion.edu. *Application contact:* Admissions Counselor, 800-486-3116.
Website: https://myunion.edu/academics/doctoral/

University at Buffalo, the State University of New York, Graduate School, College of Arts and Sciences, Program in Interdisciplinary Studies, Buffalo, NY 14260. Offers humanities (MA); natural sciences (MS); social sciences (MS). *Program availability:* Part-time. *Entrance requirements:* Additional exam requirements/recommendations for international students: Required—TOEFL (minimum score 550 paper-based; 79 iBT). *Application deadline:* For fall admission, 6/1 priority date for domestic students, 1/1 priority date for international students; for spring admission, 12/1 priority date for domestic students, 10/1 priority date for international students. Applications are processed on a rolling basis. Electronic applications accepted. *Financial support:* Fellowships, research assistantships, teaching assistantships, and unspecified assistantships available. *Unit head:* Danielle Lewis, Assistant Director, Strategic

Programs, 716-645-1457, E-mail: dvegas@buffalo.edu.
Website: http://gradidp.buffalo.edu/

The University of Alabama, Interdisciplinary Programs, Tuscaloosa, AL 35487. Offers PhD. *Program availability:* Part-time, evening/weekend. *Students:* 6 full-time (4 women), 8 part-time (5 women); includes 2 minority (both Black or African American, non-Hispanic/Latino). Average age 41. 2 applicants, 100% accepted, 2 enrolled. In 2017, 2 doctorates awarded. *Degree requirements:* For doctorate, comprehensive exam, thesis/dissertation. *Entrance requirements:* For doctorate, GRE (minimum score of 300), MAT (above 50th percentile), GMAT (minimum score 500). Additional exam requirements/recommendations for international students: Required—TOEFL (minimum score 79 iBT), IELTS (minimum score 6.5). *Application deadline:* For fall admission, 5/1 for international students; for winter admission, 9/15 for international students. Applications are processed on a rolling basis. Electronic applications accepted. *Unit head:* Dr. Andrew Mark Goodliffe, Assistant Dean of the Graduate School, 205-348-8283, Fax: 205-348-0400, E-mail: amg@ua.edu. *Application contact:* Patrick D. Fuller, Senior Graduate Admissions Counselor, 205-348-5923, Fax: 205-348-0400, E-mail: patrick.d.fuller@ua.edu.
Website: http://graduate.ua.edu

University of Alaska Anchorage, College of Arts and Sciences, Program in Interdisciplinary Studies, Anchorage, AK 99508. Offers MA, MS. *Program availability:* Part-time. *Entrance requirements:* For master's, GRE General Test, GRE Subject Test, minimum GPA of 3.0. Additional exam requirements/recommendations for international students: Required—TOEFL (minimum score 550 paper-based).

University of Alaska Fairbanks, Graduate School for Interdisciplinary Studies, Fairbanks, AK 99775-7560. Offers indigenous studies (PhD); interdisciplinary studies (MA, MS, PhD). *Program availability:* Part-time. *Degree requirements:* For master's, comprehensive exam (for some programs), oral defense of project or thesis; for doctorate, one foreign language, comprehensive exam, thesis/dissertation, oral defense of dissertation. *Entrance requirements:* For master's, GRE General Test, bachelor's degree from accredited institution with minimum cumulative undergraduate and major GPA of 3.0; for doctorate, GRE General Test, minimum cumulative GPA of 3.0. Additional exam requirements/recommendations for international students: Required—TOEFL (minimum score 550 paper-based; 80 iBT). Electronic applications accepted.

The University of Arizona, Graduate Interdisciplinary Programs, Tucson, AZ 85721. Offers American Indian studies (MA, PhD); applied mathematics (MS, PMS, PhD), including applied mathematics (MS, PhD), mathematical sciences (PMS); biomedical engineering (MS, PhD); cancer biology (PhD); entomology (MA); entomology and insect science (MS, PhD); genetics (MS, PhD); neuroscience (PhD); physiological sciences (MS, PhD); second language acquisition and teaching (PhD); statistics (MS, PhD). *Program availability:* Part-time. *Entrance requirements:* Additional exam requirements/recommendations for international students: Required—TOEFL (minimum score 550 paper-based; 79 iBT).

University of Arkansas at Little Rock, Graduate School, College of Arts, Letters, and Sciences, Department of Philosophy and Interdisciplinary Studies, Little Rock, AR 72204-1099. Offers MA. *Entrance requirements:* For master's, GRE.

University of California, Santa Barbara, Graduate Division, College of Letters and Sciences, Division of Social Sciences, Department of Sociology, Santa Barbara, CA 93106-9430. Offers interdisciplinary emphasis: Black studies (PhD); interdisciplinary emphasis: environment and society (PhD); interdisciplinary emphasis: feminist studies (PhD); interdisciplinary emphasis: global studies (PhD); interdisciplinary emphasis: language, interaction and social organization (PhD); interdisciplinary emphasis: quantitative methods in the social sciences (PhD); interdisciplinary emphasis: technology and society (PhD); sociology (PhD); MA/PhD. Terminal master's awarded for partial completion of doctoral program. *Degree requirements:* For doctorate, comprehensive exam, thesis/dissertation. *Entrance requirements:* For doctorate, GRE General Test. Additional exam requirements/recommendations for international students: Required—TOEFL (minimum score 550 paper-based; 80 iBT), IELTS (minimum score 7). Electronic applications accepted. *Faculty research:* Gender and sexualities, race/ethnicity, social movements, conversation analysis, global sociology.

University of California, Santa Cruz, Division of Graduate Studies, Division of the Arts, Department of Music, Santa Cruz, CA 95064. Offers ethnomusicology (MA); music (PhD), including cross-cultural and interdisciplinary studies; music composition (MA, DMA), including world music composition (DMA); music composition (DMA), including computer-assisted (algorithmic) composition; performance practice (MA). *Degree requirements:* For master's, one foreign language, thesis, recital; for doctorate, one foreign language, thesis/dissertation, qualifying and final examinations. *Entrance requirements:* For master's, GRE General Test, 3 letters of recommendation, writing or composition sample, 10-20 minute unedited recording; for doctorate, GRE General Test, 3 letters of recommendation, writing sample. Additional exam requirements/recommendations for international students: Required—TOEFL (minimum score 550 paper-based; 83 iBT); Recommended—IELTS (minimum score 8). Electronic applications accepted. *Faculty research:* Western music history, new music, composition, ethnomusicology, musicology.

University of Central Florida, College of Graduate Studies, Program in Interdisciplinary Studies, Orlando, FL 32816. Offers geographic information systems (Certificate); interdisciplinary studies (MA, MS). *Students:* 14 full-time (11 women), 36 part-time (24 women); includes 16 minority (5 Black or African American, non-Hispanic/Latino; 1 Asian, non-Hispanic/Latino; 9 Hispanic/Latino; 1 Two or more races, non-Hispanic/Latino), 2 international. Average age 30. 44 applicants, 84% accepted, 30 enrolled. In 2017, 3 master's, 1 other advanced degree awarded. *Degree requirements:* For master's, thesis or alternative. *Entrance requirements:* For master's, GRE, minimum GPA of 3.0 in last 60 hours, letters of recommendation, resume, personal statement. Additional exam requirements/recommendations for international students: Required—TOEFL. *Application deadline:* For fall admission, 7/15 for domestic students; for spring admission, 12/1 for domestic students. Application fee: $30. Electronic applications accepted. *Expenses:* Tuition, state resident: part-time $288.16 per credit hour. Tuition, nonresident: part-time $1073.31 per credit hour. Tuition and fees vary according to program. *Financial support:* Teaching assistantships available. Financial award application deadline: 3/1; financial award applicants required to submit FAFSA. *Unit head:* Dr. John Weishampel, Associate Dean, 407-823-6634, E-mail: john.weishampel@ucf.edu. *Application contact:* Associate Director, Graduate Admissions, 407-823-2766, Fax: 407-823-6442, E-mail: gradadmissions@ucf.edu.
Website: https://www.graduate.ucf.edu/IDS/

University of Central Oklahoma, The Jackson College of Graduate Studies, College of Education and Professional Studies, Department of Adult Education and Safety Science, Edmond, OK 73034-5209. Offers adult and higher education (M Ed), including interdisciplinary studies, student personnel, training. *Program availability:* Part-time. *Faculty:* 9 full-time (4 women), 8 part-time/adjunct (4 women). *Students:* 25 full-time (14 women), 85 part-time (61 women); includes 43 minority (25 Black or African American, non-Hispanic/Latino; 2 American Indian or Alaska Native, non-Hispanic/Latino; 1 Asian, non-Hispanic/Latino; 10 Hispanic/Latino; 5 Two or more races, non-Hispanic/Latino), 4 international. Average age 34. 49 applicants, 78% accepted, 23 enrolled. In 2017, 40

master's awarded. *Degree requirements:* For master's, comprehensive exam (for some programs), thesis (for some programs). *Entrance requirements:* Additional exam requirements/recommendations for international students: Required—TOEFL (minimum score 550 paper-based; 79 iBT), IELTS (minimum score 6.5). *Application deadline:* For fall admission, 7/15 for international students; for spring admission, 11/15 for international students. Applications are processed on a rolling basis. Application fee: $60. Electronic applications accepted. *Expenses:* Tuition, state resident: full-time $5375; part-time $268.75 per credit hour. Tuition, nonresident: full-time $13,295; part-time $664.75 per credit hour. *Required fees:* $626; $31.30 per credit hour. One-time fee: $50. Tuition and fees vary according to program. *Financial support:* In 2017–18, 38 students received support, including 1 research assistantship with partial tuition reimbursement available (averaging $2,958 per year); teaching assistantships, career-related internships or fieldwork, scholarships/grants, tuition waivers (partial), and unspecified assistantships also available. Financial award application deadline: 3/31; financial award applicants required to submit FAFSA. *Unit head:* Dr. Candy Sebert, Chair, 405-974-5741, Fax: 405-974-3809. *Application contact:* Carlie Wellington, Assistant Director, CEPS Graduate Enrollment, 405-974-5105, Fax: 405-974-3851, E-mail: gradcoll@uco.edu.
Website: http://sites.uco.edu/ceps/dept/Professional-Studies-Programs/aess/index.asp

University of Cincinnati, Graduate School, McMicken College of Arts and Sciences, Interdisciplinary Studies Program, Cincinnati, OH 45221. Offers PhD. *Entrance requirements:* For doctorate, GRE General Test. Electronic applications accepted. *Expenses:* Tuition, area resident: Full-time $14,468. Tuition, state resident: full-time $14,968; part-time $754 per credit hour. Tuition, nonresident: full-time $24,210; part-time $1311 per credit hour. *International tuition:* $26,460 full-time. *Required fees:* $3958; $84 per credit hour. One-time fee: $85 full-time. Tuition and fees vary according to course load, degree level and program.

University of Colorado Colorado Springs, College of Letters, Arts and Sciences, Master of Sciences Program, Colorado Springs, CO 80918. Offers interdisciplinary sciences (M Sc). *Program availability:* Part-time. *Students:* 51 full-time (39 women), 40 part-time (23 women); includes 20 minority (1 Black or African American, non-Hispanic/Latino; 1 American Indian or Alaska Native, non-Hispanic/Latino; 4 Asian, non-Hispanic/Latino; 10 Hispanic/Latino; 4 Two or more races, non-Hispanic/Latino), 5 international. Average age 27. 123 applicants, 52% accepted, 42 enrolled. In 2017, 40 master's awarded. *Degree requirements:* For master's, thesis or alternative. *Entrance requirements:* For master's, minimum GPA of 2.75. Additional exam requirements/recommendations for international students: Required—TOEFL (minimum score 525 paper-based; 80 iBT), Recommended—IELTS (minimum score 6.5). *Application deadline:* For fall admission, 3/1 priority date for domestic and international students; for spring admission, 6/1 priority date for domestic and international students. Applications are processed on a rolling basis. Application fee: $60 ($100 for international students). Electronic applications accepted. *Expenses:* $10,350 per year resident tuition, $20,935 nonresident, $11,961 nonresidential online; annual costs vary depending on program, course-load, and residency status. *Financial support:* In 2017–18, 36 students received support. Career-related internships or fieldwork, Federal Work-Study, scholarships/grants, and unspecified assistantships available. Support available to part-time students. Financial award application deadline: 3/1; financial award applicants required to submit FAFSA. *Faculty research:* Molecular and cellular biology, exercise science, ecology and evolution, analytical chemistry, biochemistry, inorganic chemistry, organic chemistry, physical chemistry, health promotion, athletic training and strength and conditioning, athlete development, sport nutrition. *Unit head:* Dr. Kelli Klebe, Dean, 719-255-3779, E-mail: kklebe@uccs.edu. *Application contact:* KrisAnn McBroom, Academic Services Specialist, 719-255-3567, E-mail: kmcbroom@uccs.edu.

University of Dayton, Department of Teacher Education, Dayton, OH 45469. Offers adolescence to young adult education (MS Ed); early childhood leadership and advocacy (MS Ed); interdisciplinary education (MS Ed), including visual arts; interdisciplinary education studies (MS Ed); leadership in educational systems (MS Ed); literacy (MS Ed); mathematics education (MS Ed); middle childhood education (MS Ed); multi-age education (MS Ed), including world languages; music education (MS Ed); teacher as leader (MS Ed); teacher education (MS Ed); technology-enhanced learning (MS Ed); trans-disciplinary early childhood education (MS Ed). *Program availability:* Part-time, 100% online. *Faculty:* 23 full-time (20 women), 41 part-time/adjunct (36 women). *Students:* 45 full-time (38 women), 68 part-time (57 women); includes 7 minority (3 Black or African American, non-Hispanic/Latino; 1 Hispanic/Latino; 3 Two or more races, non-Hispanic/Latino), 6 international. Average age 31. 106 applicants, 28% accepted. In 2017, 70 master's awarded. *Degree requirements:* For master's, variable foreign language requirement, thesis or alternative, internship (for teaching licensure or endorsement). *Entrance requirements:* For master's, GRE (minimum score of 149 verbal, 4 on writing) or MAT (minimum score of 396) if undergraduate GPA was under 2.75, minimum GPA of 2.75, 3 letters of recommendation, personal statement or resume, official transcripts. Additional exam requirements/recommendations for international students: Required—TOEFL (minimum score 550 paper-based; 80 iBT); Recommended—IELTS (minimum score 6.5). *Application deadline:* Applications are processed on a rolling basis. Application fee: $0 ($50 for international students). Electronic applications accepted. *Expenses:* Contact institution. *Financial support:* In 2017–18, 5 research assistantships with partial tuition reimbursements (averaging $9,640 per year) were awarded; teaching assistantships, career-related internships or fieldwork, institutionally sponsored loans, and unspecified assistantships also available. Financial award application deadline: 3/1; financial award applicants required to submit FAFSA. *Faculty research:* Social emotional learning, culturally responsive teaching, urban teaching, literacy, instructional strategies, pre-service teacher education preparation. *Unit head:* Dr. Connie L. Bowman, Chair, 937-229-3348, E-mail: cbowman1@udayton.edu. *Application contact:* Gina Seiter, Coordinator of Graduate Programs and Licensing, 937-229-3103, E-mail: gseiter1@udayton.edu.
Website: https://www.udayton.edu/education/departments_and_programs/edt

University of Florida, Graduate School, College of Public Health and Health Professions, Department of Environmental and Global Health, Gainesville, FL 32611. Offers environmental health (PhD); one health (MHS, PhD). *Entrance requirements:* For master's and doctorate, GRE, minimum GPA of 3.0. Additional exam requirements/recommendations for international students: Required—TOEFL (minimum score 550 paper-based; 80 iBT), IELTS (minimum score 6).

University of Houston–Victoria, School of Arts and Sciences, Program in Interdisciplinary Studies, Victoria, TX 77901-4450. Offers MAIS. *Program availability:* Part-time, evening/weekend, online learning. *Degree requirements:* For master's, comprehensive exam or thesis. *Entrance requirements:* For master's, GRE General Test, official transcript, essay. Additional exam requirements/recommendations for international students: Required—TOEFL (minimum score 550 paper-based). Electronic applications accepted.

University of Idaho, College of Graduate Studies, College of Art and Architecture, Program in Bioregional Planning and Community Design, Moscow, ID 83844. Offers MS. *Faculty:* 2. *Students:* 4. In 2017, 2 master's awarded. *Entrance requirements:* For master's, GRE or LSAT, minimum GPA of 3.0. Additional exam requirements/recommendations for international students: Required—TOEFL (minimum score 550

paper-based; 79 iBT), IELTS (minimum score 6.5), Michigan English Language Assessment Battery (minimum score of 77). *Application deadline:* Applications are processed on a rolling basis. Application fee: $60. Electronic applications accepted. *Expenses:* Tuition, state resident: full-time $6722; part-time $430 per credit hour. Tuition, nonresident: full-time $23,046; part-time $1337 per credit hour. *Required fees:* $2142; $63 per credit hour. *Financial support:* Applicants required to submit FAFSA. *Faculty research:* Environment and behavior interaction, geographic trade, design development, economic development, natural resource policy. *Unit head:* Dr. Shauna Corry, Interim Dean, 208-885-4409, E-mail: bioregionalplanning@uidaho.edu. *Application contact:* Sean Scoggin, Graduate Recruitment Coordinator, 208-885-4001, Fax: 208-805-4406, E-mail: graduateadmissions@uidaho.edu.
Website: http://www.uidaho.edu/caa/programs/biop

University of Idaho, College of Graduate Studies, Program in Interdisciplinary Studies, Moscow, ID 83844. Offers MA, MS. *Faculty:* 3. *Students:* 1. In 2017, 1 master's awarded. *Entrance requirements:* For master's, GRE, minimum GPA of 3.0. Additional exam requirements/recommendations for international students: Required—TOEFL (minimum score 79 iBT). *Application deadline:* For fall admission, 8/1 for domestic students; for spring admission, 12/15 for domestic students. Applications are processed on a rolling basis. Application fee: $60. Electronic applications accepted. *Expenses:* Tuition, state resident: full-time $6722; part-time $430 per credit hour. Tuition, nonresident: full-time $23,046; part-time $1337 per credit hour. *Required fees:* $2142; $63 per credit hour. *Financial support:* Applicants required to submit FAFSA. *Unit head:* Dr. Jerry McMurtry, Dean of Graduate Studies, 208-885-6243, E-mail: uigrad@uidaho.edu. *Application contact:* Sean Scoggin, Graduate Recruitment Coordinator, 208-885-4723, Fax: 208-885-4406, E-mail: gadms@uidaho.edu.
Website: https://www.uidaho.edu/cogs/programs-offered/interdisciplinary-studies

University of Illinois at Chicago, Program in Learning Sciences, Chicago, IL 60607-7128. Offers PhD.

University of Illinois at Springfield, Graduate Programs, College of Liberal Arts and Sciences, Department of Liberal and Integrative Studies, Springfield, IL 62703-5407. Offers MA. *Program availability:* Part-time, evening/weekend, 100% online, blended/hybrid learning. *Faculty:* 8 full-time (4 women). *Students:* 18 part-time (12 women); includes 8 minority (6 Black or African American, non-Hispanic/Latino; 1 Hispanic/Latino; 1 Two or more races, non-Hispanic/Latino). Average age 42. 10 applicants, 40% accepted, 2 enrolled. In 2017, 12 master's awarded. *Degree requirements:* For master's, project or thesis. *Entrance requirements:* For master's, 2 letters of reference; interview; two- to three-page statement of educational goals, background, and reasons for requesting admission to the program; minimum GPA of 2.5 (for campus-based students), 3.0 (for online students). Additional exam requirements/recommendations for international students: Required—TOEFL (minimum score 500 paper-based; 61 iBT). *Application deadline:* Applications are processed on a rolling basis. Application fee: $60 ($75 for international students). Electronic applications accepted. *Expenses:* Tuition, state resident: full-time $7896; part-time $329 per credit hour. Tuition, nonresident: full-time $16,200; part-time $675 per credit hour. Tuition and fees vary according to program. *Financial support:* In 2017–18, research assistantships with full tuition reimbursements (averaging $10,249 per year), teaching assistantships with full tuition reimbursements (averaging $10,303 per year) were awarded; fellowships, career-related internships or fieldwork, Federal Work-Study, scholarships/grants, health care benefits, and unspecified assistantships also available. Support available to part-time students. Financial award application deadline: 11/15; financial award applicants required to submit FAFSA. *Unit head:* Dr. Kamau Kemayo, Program Administrator, 217-206-6962, Fax: 217-206-6217, E-mail: lnt@uis.edu.
Website: http://www.uis.edu/ino/

University of Illinois at Urbana–Champaign, Graduate College, College of Liberal Arts and Sciences, School of Literatures, Cultures and Linguistics, Program in Romance Linguistics, Champaign, IL 61820. Offers PhD.

The University of Kansas, University of Kansas Medical Center, School of Medicine, Interdisciplinary Graduate Program in Biomedical Sciences (IGPBS), Kansas City, KS 66160. Offers PhD, MD/PhD. *Students:* 15 full-time (11 women); includes 2 minority (both Asian, non-Hispanic/Latino), 5 international. Average age 27. 120 applicants, 14% accepted, 15 enrolled. Terminal master's awarded for partial completion of doctoral program. *Degree requirements:* For doctorate, comprehensive exam, thesis/dissertation. *Entrance requirements:* For doctorate, GRE. Additional exam requirements/recommendations for international students: Required—TOEFL. *Application deadline:* For fall admission, 12/1 priority date for domestic and international students. Applications are processed on a rolling basis. Application fee: $60. Electronic applications accepted. *Financial support:* In 2017–18, 1 student received support, including 3 research assistantships with full tuition reimbursements available (averaging $24,000 per year), 18 teaching assistantships with full tuition reimbursements available (averaging $24,000 per year); scholarships/grants and unspecified assistantships also available. Financial award application deadline: 3/1; financial award applicants required to submit FAFSA. *Faculty research:* Cardiovascular biology, neurosciences, signal transduction and cancer biology, molecular biology and genetics, developmental biology. *Unit head:* Dr. Michael J. Werle, Director, 913-588-7491, Fax: 913-588-2710, E-mail: mwerle@kumc.edu. *Application contact:* Martin J. Graham, Coordinator, 913-588-2719, Fax: 913-588-5242, E-mail: mgraham4@kumc.edu.
Website: http://www.kumc.edu/igpbs.html

University of Louisville, School of Interdisciplinary and Graduate Studies, Louisville, KY 40292. Offers interdisciplinary studies (MA, MS, PhD), including bioethics and medical humanities (MA), bioinformatics (PhD), sustainability (MA, MS), translational bioengineering (PhD), translational neuroscience (PhD). *Program availability:* Part-time. *Students:* 26 full-time (17 women), 12 part-time (6 women); includes 5 minority (1 Black or African American, non-Hispanic/Latino; 2 Hispanic/Latino; 2 Two or more races, non-Hispanic/Latino), 9 international. Average age 31. 29 applicants, 38% accepted, 11 enrolled. *Degree requirements:* For master's, variable foreign language requirement, comprehensive exam (for some programs), thesis (for some programs); for doctorate, variable foreign language requirement, comprehensive exam, thesis/dissertation. *Entrance requirements:* For master's and doctorate, GRE General Test, 3 letters of recommendation, transcripts from previous post-secondary educational institutions. Additional exam requirements/recommendations for international students: Required—TOEFL (minimum score 550 paper-based; 79 iBT), IELTS (minimum score 6.5). *Application deadline:* For fall admission, 12/1 priority date for domestic and international students; for winter admission, 11/1 for domestic students, 6/1 for international students; for spring admission, 11/1 for domestic students, 6/1 for international students; for summer admission, 4/1 for domestic students, 1/1 for international students. Applications are processed on a rolling basis. Application fee: $65. Electronic applications accepted. *Expenses:* Tuition, state resident: full-time $12,246; part-time $681 per credit hour. Tuition, nonresident: full-time $25,486; part-time $1417 per credit hour. *Required fees:* $196. Tuition and fees vary according to course load, program and reciprocity agreements. *Financial support:* In 2017–18, 120 fellowships with full tuition reimbursements (averaging $20,000 per year) were awarded. Financial award application deadline: 1/15. *Unit head:* Dr. Beth A. Boehm, Dean and Vice Provost for Graduate Affairs, 502-852-6495, E-mail: beth.boehm@louisville.edu. *Application contact:* Dr. Paul DeMarco, Associate Dean, 502-852-6490, E-mail: gradadm@louisville.edu.
Website: http://www.graduate.louisville.edu

University of Maine, Graduate School, Interdisciplinary Doctoral Program, Orono, ME 04469. Offers PhD. *Program availability:* Part-time, evening/weekend. *Students:* 5 full-time (4 women), 17 part-time (10 women); includes 2 minority (both American Indian or Alaska Native, non-Hispanic/Latino), 1 international. Average age 47. 2 applicants, 100% accepted, 2 enrolled. In 2017, 2 doctorates awarded. *Degree requirements:* For doctorate, comprehensive exam, thesis/dissertation. *Entrance requirements:* For doctorate, GRE General Test, master's degree. Additional exam requirements/recommendations for international students: Required—TOEFL. *Application deadline:* For fall admission, 4/1 for domestic students; for spring admission, 11/1 for domestic students. Applications are processed on a rolling basis. Application fee: $65. Electronic applications accepted. *Expenses:* Tuition, state resident: full-time $7722; part-time $429 per credit hour. Tuition, nonresident: full-time $25,146; part-time $1397 per credit hour. *Required fees:* $1162; $581 per credit hour. *Financial support:* In 2017–18, 7 students received support, including 1 fellowship with full tuition reimbursement available (averaging $34,000 per year), 1 research assistantship with full tuition reimbursement available (averaging $15,600 per year); scholarships/grants and unspecified assistantships also available. Financial award application deadline: 3/1. *Unit head:* Scott G. Delcourt, Assistant Vice President for Graduate Studies/Senior Associate Dean, 207-581-3291, Fax: 207-581-3232, E-mail: graduate@maine.edu.
Website: http://umaine.edu/graduate/

University of Maine, Graduate School, Master of Arts in Interdisciplinary Studies Program, Orono, ME 04469. Offers MA. *Program availability:* Part-time, evening/weekend. *Faculty:* 3 full-time (1 woman), 6 part-time/adjunct (3 women). *Students:* 8 full-time (7 women), 15 part-time (10 women); includes 4 minority (1 American Indian or Alaska Native, non-Hispanic/Latino; 2 Hispanic/Latino; 1 Two or more races, non-Hispanic/Latino), 1 international. Average age 40. 9 applicants, 100% accepted, 7 enrolled. In 2017, 5 master's awarded. *Degree requirements:* For master's, thesis or alternative, project. *Entrance requirements:* Additional exam requirements/recommendations for international students: Required—TOEFL. *Application deadline:* For fall admission, 4/1 for domestic students; for spring admission, 11/1 for domestic students; for summer admission, 4/1 for domestic students. Applications are processed on a rolling basis. Application fee: $65. Electronic applications accepted. *Expenses:* Tuition, state resident: full-time $7722; part-time $429 per credit hour. Tuition, nonresident: full-time $25,146; part-time $1397 per credit hour. *Required fees:* $1162; $581 per credit hour. *Financial support:* In 2017–18, 1 student received support. Federal Work-Study, institutionally sponsored loans, and unspecified assistantships available. Financial award application deadline: 3/1. *Application contact:* Scott G. Delcourt, Assistant Vice President for Graduate Studies and Senior Associate Dean, 207-581-3291, Fax: 207-581-3232, E-mail: graduate@maine.edu.
Website: http://umaine.edu/graduate/

University of Manitoba, Faculty of Graduate Studies, Interdisciplinary Programs, Individual Interdisciplinary Programs, Winnipeg, MB R3T 2N2, Canada. Offers M Sc, MA, PhD.

University of Massachusetts Medical School, Graduate School of Biomedical Sciences, Worcester, MA 01655-0115. Offers biomedical sciences (PhD), including biochemistry and molecular pharmacology, bioinformatics and computational biology, cancer biology, immunology and microbiology, interdisciplinary, neuroscience, translational science; biomedical sciences (millennium program) (PhD); clinical and population health research (PhD); clinical investigation (MS). *Faculty:* 1,316 full-time (526 women), 357 part-time/adjunct (229 women). *Students:* 347 full-time (180 women); includes 61 minority (10 Black or African American, non-Hispanic/Latino; 1 American Indian or Alaska Native, non-Hispanic/Latino; 35 Asian, non-Hispanic/Latino; 15 Hispanic/Latino), 130 international. Average age 29. 608 applicants, 28% accepted, 54 enrolled. In 2017, 6 master's, 51 doctorates awarded. Terminal master's awarded for partial completion of doctoral program. *Degree requirements:* For master's, comprehensive exam, thesis; for doctorate, comprehensive exam, thesis/dissertation. *Entrance requirements:* For master's, MD, PhD, DVM, or PharmD; for doctorate, GRE General Test, bachelor's degree. Additional exam requirements/recommendations for international students: Required—TOEFL (minimum score 90 iBT) or IELTS (minimum score 7.0). *Application deadline:* For fall admission, 12/15 for domestic and international students. Applications are processed on a rolling basis. Application fee: $80. Electronic applications accepted. Application fee is waived when completed online. *Expenses:* $14,883 in-state tuition and mandatory fees; $31,486 out-of-state. *Financial support:* In 2017–18, 15 fellowships with partial tuition reimbursements (averaging $29,000 per year), 296 research assistantships with full tuition reimbursements (averaging $31,212 per year) were awarded; institutionally sponsored loans and scholarships/grants also available. Financial award application deadline: 5/15. *Faculty research:* RNA biology, molecular/cell/developmental/metabolic biology, bioinformatics and computational biology, clinical/translational research, infectious disease and immunology. *Total annual research expenditures:* $279 million. *Unit head:* Dr. Mary Ellen Lane, Dean, 508-856-4018, E-mail: maryellen.lane@umassmed.edu. *Application contact:* Dr. Kendall Knight, Assistant Vice Provost for Admissions, 508-856-5628, Fax: 508-856-3659, E-mail: kendall.knight@umassmed.edu.
Website: http://www.umassmed.edu/gsbs/

University of Memphis, Graduate School, College of Arts and Sciences, Department of Earth Sciences, Memphis, TN 38152. Offers earth sciences (MA, MS, PhD), including archaeology (MS), geography (MS), geology (MS), geophysics (MS), interdisciplinary studies (MS); geographic information systems (Graduate Certificate), including geographic information systems, GIS educator, GIS planning, GIS professional. *Program availability:* Part-time, evening/weekend. *Faculty:* 18 full-time (3 women), 4 part-time/adjunct (0 women). *Students:* 55 full-time (23 women), 24 part-time (4 women); includes 5 minority (1 Black or African American, non-Hispanic/Latino; 4 Asian, non-Hispanic/Latino), 19 international. Average age 31. 17 applicants, 82% accepted, 11 enrolled. In 2017, 7 master's, 5 doctorates, 3 other advanced degrees awarded. Terminal master's awarded for partial completion of doctoral program. *Degree requirements:* For master's, comprehensive exam, thesis, seminar presentation; for doctorate, comprehensive exam, thesis/dissertation, qualifying exam, submission of two manuscripts for publication in peer-reviewed journal or books. *Entrance requirements:* For master's, GRE General Test, 3 letters of recommendation, statement of research interests; for doctorate, GRE General Test, 2 letters of recommendation, resume, personal statement. Additional exam requirements/recommendations for international students: Required—TOEFL (minimum score 550 paper-based; 79 iBT). *Application deadline:* For fall admission, 1/15 for domestic students; for spring admission, 11/1 for domestic students. Applications are processed on a rolling basis. Application fee: $35 ($60 for international students). Electronic applications accepted. *Expenses:* Contact institution. *Financial support:* In 2017–18, 18 students received support, including 2 research assistantships with full tuition reimbursements available (averaging $17,000 per year), 13 teaching assistantships with full tuition reimbursements available (averaging $16,692 per year); fellowships with full tuition reimbursements available, Federal Work-Study, scholarships/grants, and unspecified assistantships also available.

Financial award application deadline: 2/1; financial award applicants required to submit FAFSA. *Faculty research:* Hazards, active tectonics, geophysics, hydrology and water resources, spatial analysis. *Unit head:* Dr. Daniel Larsen, Chair, 901-678-4538, Fax: 901-678-2178, E-mail: dlarsen@memphis.edu. *Application contact:* Dr. Randel T. Cox, Graduate Coordinator, 901-678-4361, Fax: 901-678-2178, E-mail: randycox@memphis.edu.
Website: http://www.memphis.edu/earthsciences/

University of Minnesota, Twin Cities Campus, Graduate School, College of Liberal Arts, Department of Cultural Studies and Comparative Literature, Program in Comparative Studies in Discourse and Society, Minneapolis, MN 55455-0213. Offers PhD. *Degree requirements:* For doctorate, 2 foreign languages, thesis/dissertation. *Entrance requirements:* For doctorate, GRE General Test, sample of written work. Additional exam requirements/recommendations for international students: Required—TOEFL. *Faculty research:* Cultural theory; music; architecture, space, and urbanism; body and gender; film and popular culture.

University of Missouri–Kansas City, School of Graduate Studies, Kansas City, MO 64110-2499. Offers interdisciplinary studies (PhD), including art history, cell biology and biophysics, chemistry, computer and electrical engineering, computer science and informatics, economics, education, engineering, English, entrepreneurship and innovation, geosciences, history, mathematics and statistics, molecular biology and biochemistry, music education, oral and craniofacial sciences, pharmaceutical sciences, pharmacology, physics, political science, public affairs and administration, religious studies, social science, telecommunications and computer networking; PMBA/MHA. *Degree requirements:* For doctorate, comprehensive exam, thesis/dissertation, residency. *Entrance requirements:* For doctorate, GRE General Test, minimum GPA of 2.75 (undergraduate), 3.0 (graduate). Additional exam requirements/recommendations for international students: Required—TOEFL (minimum score 550 paper-based; 80 iBT), TWE (minimum score 4). Electronic applications accepted.

University of Montana, Graduate School, College of Humanities and Sciences, Division of Biological Sciences, Interdisciplinary Program in Systems Ecology, Missoula, MT 59812. Offers MS, PhD.

University of Montana, Graduate School, Program in Interdisciplinary Studies, Missoula, MT 59812. Offers individualized interdisciplinary studies (PhD); interdisciplinary studies (MIS). *Degree requirements:* For doctorate, thesis/dissertation. *Entrance requirements:* For master's, GRE General Test. Additional exam requirements/recommendations for international students: Required—TOEFL.

University of New Brunswick Fredericton, School of Graduate Studies, Interdisciplinary Studies Program, Fredericton, NB E3B 5A3, Canada. Offers M IDST, PhD. *Degree requirements:* For master's, thesis; for doctorate, comprehensive exam, thesis/dissertation. *Entrance requirements:* For master's, BA honors degree, minimum GPA of 3.3; for doctorate, master's degree with thesis; minimum A- average. Additional exam requirements/recommendations for international students: Required—TOEFL (minimum score 600 paper-based; 100 iBT), IELTS (minimum score 7), TWE (minimum score 5.5). Electronic applications accepted.

University of North Alabama, College of Arts and Sciences, Department of Interdisciplinary and Professional Studies, Florence, AL 35632-0001. Offers professional studies (MPS), including community development, information technology, security and safety leadership. *Program availability:* Part-time, 100% online. *Faculty:* 4 full-time (1 woman), 1 part-time/adjunct (0 women). *Students:* 19 full-time (9 women), 24 part-time (12 women); includes 7 minority (5 Black or African American, non-Hispanic/Latino; 1 American Indian or Alaska Native, non-Hispanic/Latino; 1 Asian, non-Hispanic/Latino), 13 international. Average age 35. 34 applicants, 65% accepted, 17 enrolled. In 2017, 24 master's awarded. *Degree requirements:* For master's, thesis optional. *Entrance requirements:* For master's, ETS PPI, personal statement; three letters of recommendation. Additional exam requirements/recommendations for international students: Required—TOEFL (minimum score 79 iBT), IELTS (minimum score 6), PTE (minimum score 54). *Application deadline:* Applications are processed on a rolling basis. Application fee: $50 ($100 for international students). Electronic applications accepted. *Expenses:* Tuition, state resident: full-time $7824; part-time $5943 per year. Tuition, nonresident: full-time $15,648; part-time $11,736 per year. *Required fees:* $3064; $2298 per unit. Tuition and fees vary according to course load and reciprocity agreements. *Financial support:* In 2017–18, 17 students received support. Federal Work-Study, scholarships/grants, and unspecified assistantships available. Financial award application deadline: 2/1; financial award applicants required to submit FAFSA. *Unit head:* Dr. Craig T. Robertson, Director, 256-765-5003, E-mail: ctrobertson@una.edu. *Application contact:* Hillary N. Coats, Graduate Admissions Coordinator, 256-765-4447, E-mail: graduate@una.edu.
Website: https://www.una.edu/interdisciplinary-studies/

The University of North Carolina at Charlotte, College of Liberal Arts and Sciences, Interdisciplinary Liberal Arts and Sciences Programs, Charlotte, NC 28223-0001. Offers gender, sexuality, and women's studies (Graduate Certificate); gerontology (MA, Graduate Certificate); Latin American studies (MA); liberal studies (MA); organizational science (PhD); public policy (PhD). *Program availability:* Part-time, evening/weekend. *Faculty:* 1 full-time (0 women). *Students:* 66 full-time (48 women), 66 part-time (52 women); includes 41 minority (14 Black or African American, non-Hispanic/Latino; 2 Asian, non-Hispanic/Latino; 24 Hispanic/Latino; 1 Two or more races, non-Hispanic/Latino), 16 international. Average age 27. 129 applicants, 53% accepted, 43 enrolled. In 2017, 22 master's, 10 doctorates, 9 other advanced degrees awarded. *Degree requirements:* For master's, comprehensive exam (for some programs), thesis (for some programs), practicum, project; for doctorate, comprehensive exam, thesis/dissertation; for Graduate Certificate, practicum (for gerontology). *Entrance requirements:* For master's, GRE General Test or MAT, bachelor's degree from accredited college or university; official transcripts of all previous academic work attempted beyond high school with minimum overall GPA of 3.0; statement of purpose; recommendation letters; for doctorate, GRE or GMAT, statement of purpose discussing interest in program and objectives for pursuing degree, current resume or curriculum vitae, unofficial transcripts; for Graduate Certificate, bachelor's degree from accredited university and either enrolled and in good standing in a graduate degree program at UNC Charlotte or have a minimum undergraduate GPA of 3.0. Additional exam requirements/recommendations for international students: Required—TOEFL (minimum score 523 paper-based, 70 iBT) or IELTS (6.5). *Application deadline:* For fall admission, 2/15 for domestic and international students; for spring admission, 10/1 for domestic and international students; for summer admission, 4/1 for domestic and international students. Applications are processed on a rolling basis. Application fee: $75. Electronic applications accepted. *Expenses:* Tuition, state resident: full-time $4337. Tuition, nonresident: full-time $17,771. *Required fees:* $3211. Tuition and fees vary according to course load and program. *Financial support:* In 2017–18, 21 students received support, including 19 research assistantships (averaging $12,011 per year), 1 teaching assistantship (averaging $18,600 per year); career-related internships or fieldwork, institutionally sponsored loans, scholarships/grants, unspecified assistantships, and administrative assistantships also available. Support available to part-time students. Financial award application deadline: 3/1; financial award applicants required to submit FAFSA. *Unit head:* Dr. Nancy A. Gutierrez, Dean, 704-687-0081, E-mail: ngutierr@uncc.edu. *Application contact:* Kathy B. Giddings, Director of Graduate Admissions, 704-687-5503, Fax: 704-687-3279, E-mail: gradadm@uncc.edu.
Website: http://clas.uncc.edu/academics

University of Northern British Columbia, Office of Graduate Studies, Prince George, BC V2N 4Z9, Canada. Offers business administration (Diploma); community health science (M Sc); disability management (MA); education (M Ed); first nations studies (MA); gender studies (MA); history (MA); interdisciplinary studies (MA); international studies (MA); mathematical, computer and physical sciences (M Sc); natural resources and environmental studies (M Sc, MA, MNRES, PhD); political science (MA); psychology (M Sc, PhD); social work (MSW). *Program availability:* Part-time, evening/weekend, online learning. *Degree requirements:* For master's, thesis; for doctorate, thesis/dissertation. *Entrance requirements:* For master's, GRE, minimum B average in undergraduate course work; for doctorate, candidacy exam, minimum A average in graduate course work.

University of North Texas, Robert B. Toulouse School of Graduate Studies, Denton, TX 76203-5459. Offers accounting (MS); applied anthropology (MA, MS); applied behavior analysis (Certificate); applied geography (MA); applied technology and performance improvement (M Ed, MS); art education (MA); art history (MA); art museum education (Certificate); arts leadership (Certificate); audiology (Au D); behavior analysis (MS); behavioral science (PhD); biochemistry and molecular biology (MS); biology (MA, MS); biomedical engineering (MS); business analysis (MS); chemistry (MS); clinical health psychology (PhD); communication studies (MA, MS); computer engineering (MS); computer science (MS); counseling (M Ed, MS), including clinical mental health counseling (MS), college and university counseling, elementary school counseling, secondary school counseling; creative writing (MA); criminal justice (MS); curriculum and instruction (M Ed); decision sciences (MBA); design (MA, MFA), including fashion design (MFA), innovation studies, interior design (MFA); early childhood studies (MS); economics (MS); educational leadership (M Ed, Ed D); educational psychology (MS, PhD), including family studies (MS), gifted and talented (MS), human development (MS), learning and cognition (MS), research, measurement and evaluation (MS); electrical engineering (MS); emergency management (MPA); engineering technology (MS); English (MA); English as a second language (MA); environmental science (MS); finance (MBA, MS); financial management (MPA); French (MA); health services management (MBA); higher education (M Ed, Ed D); history (MA, MS); hospitality management (MS); human resources management (MPA); information science (MS); information systems (PhD); information technologies (MBA); interdisciplinary studies (MA, MS); international studies (MA); international sustainable tourism (MS); jazz studies (MM); journalism (MA, MJ, Graduate Certificate), including interactive and virtual digital communication (Graduate Certificate), narrative journalism (Graduate Certificate), public relations (Graduate Certificate); kinesiology (MS); linguistics (MA); local government management (MPA); logistics (PhD); logistics and supply chain management (MBA); long-term care, senior housing, and aging services (MA); management (PhD); marketing (MBA); mathematics (MA, MS); mechanical and energy engineering (MS, PhD); music (MA), including ethnomusicology, music theory, musicology, performance; music composition (PhD); music education (MM Ed, PhD); nonprofit management (MPA); operations and supply chain management (MBA); performance (MM, DMA); philosophy (MA); political science (MA); professional and technical communication (MA); radio, television and film (MA, MFA); rehabilitation counseling (Certificate); sociology (MA); Spanish (MA); special education (M Ed); speech-language pathology (MA); strategic management (MBA); studio art (MFA); teaching (M Ed); MBA/MS. *Program availability:* Part-time, evening/weekend, online learning. Terminal master's awarded for partial completion of doctoral program. *Degree requirements:* For master's, variable foreign language requirement, comprehensive exam (for some programs), thesis (for some programs); for doctorate, variable foreign language requirement, comprehensive exam (for some programs), thesis/dissertation; for other advanced degree, variable foreign language requirement, comprehensive exam (for some programs). *Entrance requirements:* For master's and doctorate, GRE, GMAT. Additional exam requirements/recommendations for international students: Required—TOEFL (minimum score 550 paper-based; 79 iBT). Electronic applications accepted.

University of Oklahoma, Graduate College, Program in Interdisciplinary Studies, Norman, OK 73019. Offers MA, MS, PhD. *Program availability:* Part-time, evening/weekend, blended/hybrid learning. *Students:* 13 full-time (3 women), 66 part-time (30 women); includes 25 minority (4 Black or African American, non-Hispanic/Latino; 3 American Indian or Alaska Native, non-Hispanic/Latino; 4 Asian, non-Hispanic/Latino; 9 Hispanic/Latino; 1 Native Hawaiian or other Pacific Islander, non-Hispanic/Latino; 4 Two or more races, non-Hispanic/Latino), 4 international. Average age 39. 22 applicants, 73% accepted, 2 enrolled. In 2017, 33 master's, 6 doctorates awarded. *Entrance requirements:* Additional exam requirements/recommendations for international students: Required—TOEFL (minimum score 79 iBT) or IELTS (minimum score 6.5). *Application deadline:* For fall admission, 4/1 for international students; for spring admission, 9/1 for international students; for summer admission, 2/1 for international students. Applications are processed on a rolling basis. Application fee: $50 ($100 for international students). Electronic applications accepted. *Expenses:* Tuition, state resident: full-time $5119; part-time $213.30 per credit hour. Tuition, nonresident: full-time $19,778; part-time $824.10 per credit hour. *Required fees:* $3458; $133.55 per credit hour. $126.50 per semester. *Financial support:* In 2017–18, 6 students received support. Research assistantships, teaching assistantships, and unspecified assistantships available. Financial award applicants required to submit FAFSA. *Unit head:* Dr. Randall S. Hewes, Dean and Professor, 405-325-3811, Fax: 405-325-5343, E-mail: hewes@ou.edu. *Application contact:* Amy Shaw, Director, Office of Graduate Admissions, 405-325-6765, Fax: 405-325-5345, E-mail: ashaw@ou.edu.

University of Oregon, Graduate School, Interdisciplinary Program in Applied Information Management, Eugene, OR 97403. Offers MS. *Program availability:* Part-time, online learning. *Degree requirements:* For master's, project. *Entrance requirements:* Additional exam requirements/recommendations for international students: Required—TOEFL. Electronic applications accepted. *Expenses:* Contact institution. *Faculty research:* Business management, information design.

University of Ottawa, Faculty of Graduate and Postdoctoral Studies, Interdisciplinary Programs, Ottawa, ON K1N 6N5, Canada. Offers e-business (Certificate); e-commerce (Certificate); finance (Certificate); health services and policies research (Diploma); population health (PhD); population health risk assessment and management (Certificate); public management and governance (Certificate); systems science (Certificate).

University of Pittsburgh, School of Medicine, Graduate Programs in Medicine, Interdisciplinary Biomedical Graduate Program, Pittsburgh, PA 15260. Offers PhD. *Faculty:* 221 full-time (52 women). *Students:* 16 full-time (9 women); includes 3 minority (1 Asian, non-Hispanic/Latino; 2 Hispanic/Latino), 4 international. Average age 24. 350 applicants, 21% accepted, 16 enrolled. *Degree requirements:* For doctorate, comprehensive exam, thesis/dissertation. *Entrance requirements:* For doctorate, GRE General Test, minimum GPA of 3.2, 3 letters of recommendation, official transcripts, baccalaureate degree. Additional exam requirements/recommendations for international students: Required—TOEFL (minimum score 600 paper-based; 100 iBT), IELTS (minimum score 7). *Application deadline:* For fall admission, 12/1 priority date for

domestic and international students. Application fee: $50. Electronic applications accepted. *Expenses:* $26,782 in-state, $42,006 out-of-state. *Financial support:* In 2017–18, 16 students received support. Traineeships available. *Faculty research:* Cell biology and molecular physiology, cellular and molecular pathology, molecular genetics and developmental biology, molecular pharmacology. *Unit head:* Dr. John Horn, Director, 412-648-8957, Fax: 412-648-1077, E-mail: gradstudies@medschool.pitt.edu. *Application contact:* Carol Williams, Admissions and Recruiting Manager, 412-648-8957, Fax: 412-648-1077, E-mail: gradstudies@medschool.pitt.edu.
Website: http://www.gradbiomed.pitt.edu/

University of Regina, Faculty of Graduate Studies and Research, Faculty of Media, Art, and Performance, Department of Visual Arts, Regina, SK S4S 0A2, Canada. Offers ceramics (MFA); drawing (MFA); interdisciplinary studies (MA, MFA); intermedia (MFA); painting (MFA); sculpture (MFA). *Faculty:* 10 full-time (5 women), 3 part-time/adjunct (1 woman). *Students:* 2 part-time (1 woman). 12 applicants, 17% accepted. In 2017, 3 master's awarded. *Degree requirements:* For master's, exhibition, support paper, oral defense. *Entrance requirements:* For master's, portfolio. Additional exam requirements/recommendations for international students: Required—TOEFL (minimum score 580 paper-based; 80 iBT), IELTS (minimum score 6.5), PTE (minimum score 59). *Application deadline:* For fall admission, 1/15 for domestic and international students. Applications are processed on a rolling basis. Application fee: $100. Electronic applications accepted. *Expenses:* CAD$10,681 per year. *Financial support:* In 2017–18, fellowships (averaging $6,000 per year), teaching assistantships (averaging $2,562 per year) were awarded; research assistantships and scholarships/grants also available. Financial award application deadline: 6/15. *Faculty research:* Contemporary visual art theory and practice; art history; curatorial practice; print media; drawing/painting, sculpture, and ceramics. *Unit head:* Dr. Robert Truszkowski, Department Head, 306-585-5574, Fax: 306-585-5526, E-mail: robert.truszkowski@uregina.ca. *Application contact:* Leesa Streifler, Graduate Coordinator, Visual Arts, 306-585-5529, Fax: 306-585-5526, E-mail: leesa.streifler@uregina.ca.

University of South Dakota, Graduate School, Interdisciplinary Studies Program, Vermillion, SD 57069. Offers MA. *Program availability:* Part-time, online learning. *Degree requirements:* For master's, thesis or alternative. *Entrance requirements:* For master's, minimum GPA of 2.7. Additional exam requirements/recommendations for international students: Required—TOEFL (minimum score 550 paper-based; 79 iBT). *Application deadline:* Applications are processed on a rolling basis. Application fee: $35. Electronic applications accepted. *Financial support:* Research assistantships with partial tuition reimbursements, Federal Work-Study, and unspecified assistantships available. Financial award applicants required to submit FAFSA. *Application contact:* Graduate School, 605-658-6140, Fax: 605-677-6118, E-mail: grad@usd.edu.
Website: http://www.usd.edu/onlinemais

University of South Florida, College of Arts and Sciences, School of Interdisciplinary Global Studies, Tampa, FL 33620-9951. Offers government (PhD); Latin American, Caribbean and Latino studies (MA); liberal arts (MA), including Africana studies; political science (MA), including comparative government and politics. *Accreditation:* NASPAA. *Program availability:* Part-time, evening/weekend. *Faculty:* 14 full-time (2 women). *Students:* 3 applicants. In 2017, 9 master's, 1 doctorate awarded. *Degree requirements:* For master's, comprehensive exam, thesis; for doctorate, comprehensive exam, thesis/dissertation. *Entrance requirements:* For master's, GRE General Test, minimum GPA of 3.0 in upper-division undergraduate course work; letters of recommendation (2 for MPA, 3 for MS); 500-word personal statement and undergraduate background in political science or related fields (for MS); one-page career statement (for MPA); for doctorate, GRE General Test, 500-word personal statement, three letters of recommendation, transcripts of MA/BA coursework, writing sample. Additional exam requirements/recommendations for international students: Required—TOEFL (minimum score 550 paper-based; 79 iBT) or IELTS (minimum score 6.5). *Application deadline:* For fall admission, 1/5 for domestic and international students; for spring admission, 10/15 for domestic students, 9/15 for international students. Applications are processed on a rolling basis. Application fee: $30. Electronic applications accepted. *Financial support:* In 2017–18, 3 students received support, including 18 teaching assistantships with tuition reimbursements available (averaging $12,390 per year); unspecified assistantships also available. Financial award application deadline: 4/1. *Faculty research:* Citizenship and identity, social movements, global governance, American politics, public policy. *Total annual research expenditures:* $195,426. *Unit head:* Dr. Steven Tauber, Associate Professor/Interim Chair, 813-974-2278, Fax: 813-974-0832, E-mail: stauber@usf.edu. *Application contact:* Dr. Bernd Reiter, Associate Professor and Director of Graduate Studies, 813-974-3583, Fax: 813-974-0832, E-mail: breiter@usf.edu.
Website: http://gia.usf.edu/

University of South Florida, Morsani College of Medicine and College of Graduate Studies, Graduate Programs in Medical Sciences, Tampa, FL 33620-9951. Offers advanced athletic training (MS); athletic training (MS); bioinformatics and computational biology (MSBCB); biotechnology (MSB); health informatics (MSHI); medical sciences (MSMS, PhD), including aging and neuroscience (MSMS), allergy, immunology and infectious disease (PhD), anatomy, biochemistry and molecular biology, clinical and translational research, health science (MSMS), interdisciplinary medical sciences (MSMS), medical microbiology and immunology (MSMS), metabolic and nutritional medicine (MSMS), microbiology and immunology (PhD), molecular medicine, molecular pharmacology and physiology (PhD), neuroscience (PhD), pathology and cell biology (PhD), women's health (MSMS). *Students:* 372 full-time (212 women), 216 part-time (142 women); includes 257 minority (78 Black or African American, non-Hispanic/Latino; 1 American Indian or Alaska Native, non-Hispanic/Latino; 79 Asian, non-Hispanic/Latino; 84 Hispanic/Latino; 15 Two or more races, non-Hispanic/Latino), 62 international. Average age 28. 1,048 applicants, 46% accepted, 309 enrolled. In 2017, 351 master's, 56 doctorates awarded. Terminal master's awarded for partial completion of doctoral program. *Degree requirements:* For master's, comprehensive exam, thesis; for doctorate, comprehensive exam, thesis/dissertation. *Entrance requirements:* For master's, GRE General Test or GMAT, bachelor's degree or equivalent from regionally-accredited university with minimum GPA of 3.0 in upper-division sciences coursework; prerequisites in general biology, general chemistry, general physics, organic chemistry, quantitative analysis, and integral and differential calculus; for doctorate, GRE General Test, bachelor's degree from regionally-accredited university with minimum GPA of 3.0 in upper-division sciences coursework; 3 letters of recommendation; personal interview; 1-2 page personal statement; prerequisites in biology, chemistry, physics, organic chemistry, quantitative analysis, and integral/differential calculus. Additional exam requirements/recommendations for international students: Required—TOEFL (minimum score 550 paper-based; 79 iBT) or IELTS (minimum score 6.5). *Application deadline:* For fall admission, 2/1 priority date for domestic students, 2/1 for international students. Application fee: $30. Electronic applications accepted. *Expenses:* Contact institution. *Financial support:* In 2017–18, 109 students received support. *Faculty research:* Anatomy, biochemistry, cancer biology, cardiovascular disease, cell biology, immunology, microbiology, molecular biology, neuroscience, pharmacology, physiology. *Total annual research expenditures:* $45.3 million. *Unit head:* Dr. Michael Barber, Professor/Associate Dean for Graduate and Postdoctoral Affairs, 813-974-9908, Fax: 813-974-4317, E-mail: mbarber@health.usf.edu. *Application contact:* Dr. Eric Bennett, Graduate Director, PhD Program in Medical Sciences, 813-974-1545, Fax: 813-974-4317, E-mail: esbennet@health.usf.edu.
Website: http://health.usf.edu/nocms/medicine/graduatestudies/

The University of Tennessee at Martin, Graduate Programs, College of Education, Health and Behavioral Sciences, Program in Teaching, Martin, TN 38238. Offers curriculum and instruction (MS Ed), including 7-12, K-6; initial licensure (MS Ed), including elementary education, secondary education; initial licensure K-12 (MS Ed), including physical education, special education; interdisciplinary (MS Ed). *Program availability:* Part-time, online only, 100% online. *Students:* 20 full-time (17 women), 92 part-time (66 women); includes 20 minority (14 Black or African American, non-Hispanic/Latino; 2 Hispanic/Latino; 4 Two or more races, non-Hispanic/Latino). Average age 32. 79 applicants, 70% accepted, 38 enrolled. In 2017, 14 master's awarded. *Entrance requirements:* Additional exam requirements/recommendations for international students: Required—TOEFL (minimum score 525 paper-based; 71 iBT). *Application deadline:* For fall admission, 7/27 for domestic and international students; for spring admission, 12/17 for domestic and international students; for summer admission, 5/10 for domestic and international students. Applications are processed on a rolling basis. Electronic applications accepted. *Expenses:* Tuition, state resident: full-time $8658; part-time $481 per credit hour. Tuition, nonresident: full-time $14,418; part-time $801 per credit hour. *International tuition:* $22,602 full-time. *Required fees:* $1404; $79 per credit hour. Part-time tuition and fees vary according to course load. *Financial support:* In 2017–18, 26 students received support, including 1 research assistantship with full tuition reimbursement available (averaging $6,283 per year), 5 teaching assistantships with full tuition reimbursements available (averaging $7,001 per year); scholarships/grants and tuition waivers also available. Financial award applicants required to submit FAFSA. *Faculty research:* Special education, science/math/technology, school reform, reading. *Unit head:* Cynthia West, Dean, 731-881-7125, Fax: 731-881-7975, E-mail: cwest@utm.edu. *Application contact:* Jolene L. Cunningham, Student Services Specialist, 731-881-7012, Fax: 731-881-7499, E-mail: jcunningham@utm.edu.

The University of Texas at Dallas, School of Interdisciplinary Studies, Richardson, TX 75080. Offers MA. *Program availability:* Part-time, evening/weekend. *Faculty:* 3 full-time (2 women), 1 (woman) part-time/adjunct. *Students:* 5 full-time (3 women), 8 part-time (5 women); includes 5 minority (1 Black or African American, non-Hispanic/Latino; 2 Asian, non-Hispanic/Latino; 2 Hispanic/Latino). Average age 36. 8 applicants, 63% accepted, 3 enrolled. In 2017, 6 master's awarded. *Degree requirements:* For master's, research project, seminar. *Entrance requirements:* For master's, GRE General Test, minimum GPA of 3.0. Additional exam requirements/recommendations for international students: Required—TOEFL (minimum score 550 paper-based). *Application deadline:* For fall admission, 7/15 for domestic students, 5/1 priority date for international students; for spring admission, 11/15 for domestic students, 9/1 priority date for international students. Applications are processed on a rolling basis. Application fee: $50 ($100 for international students). Electronic applications accepted. *Expenses:* Tuition, state resident: full-time $12,916; part-time $718 per credit hour. Tuition, nonresident: full-time $25,252; part-time $1403 per credit hour. *Financial support:* In 2017–18, 10 students received support. Research assistantships with partial tuition reimbursements available, teaching assistantships with partial tuition reimbursements available, career-related internships or fieldwork, Federal Work-Study, institutionally sponsored loans, and scholarships/grants available. Support available to part-time students. Financial award application deadline: 4/30; financial award applicants required to submit FAFSA. *Faculty research:* Education of homeless children and youths. *Unit head:* Dr. George Fair, Dean, 972-883-2350, Fax: 972-883-2440, E-mail: gwfair@utdallas.edu. *Application contact:* Becky Wiser, Academic Support Coordinator, 972-883-2354, Fax: 972-883-2440, E-mail: rwiser@utdallas.edu.
Website: http://www.utdallas.edu/is

The University of Texas at El Paso, Graduate School, College of Liberal Arts, Master of Arts in Interdisciplinary Studies Program, El Paso, TX 79968-0001. Offers MAIS. *Program availability:* Part-time, evening/weekend. *Entrance requirements:* For master's, GRE, minimum GPA of 3.0, letters of recommendation. Additional exam requirements/recommendations for international students: Required—TOEFL; Recommended—IELTS. Electronic applications accepted.

The University of Texas at San Antonio, College of Education and Human Development, Department of Interdisciplinary Learning and Teaching, San Antonio, TX 78249-0617. Offers education (MA), including curriculum and instruction, early childhood and elementary education, instructional technology, reading and literacy, special education; interdisciplinary learning and teaching (PhD). *Program availability:* Part-time, evening/weekend. *Faculty:* 24 full-time (16 women), 5 part-time/adjunct (3 women). *Students:* 73 full-time (57 women), 227 part-time (206 women); includes 179 minority (25 Black or African American, non-Hispanic/Latino; 10 Asian, non-Hispanic/Latino; 140 Hispanic/Latino; 1 Native Hawaiian or other Pacific Islander, non-Hispanic/Latino; 3 Two or more races, non-Hispanic/Latino), 7 international. Average age 34. 107 applicants, 88% accepted, 70 enrolled. In 2017, 103 master's, 5 doctorates awarded. *Degree requirements:* For master's, comprehensive exam, thesis optional, 36 hours of course work without thesis (33 with thesis); for doctorate, comprehensive exam, thesis/dissertation, minimum of 60 semester credit hours. *Entrance requirements:* For master's, bachelor's degree with minimum GPA of 3.0 in last 60 hours of coursework; 18 hours of undergraduate coursework in education or related field; for doctorate, GRE, transcripts from all colleges and universities attended, professional vitae demonstrating experience in work environment where education was primary professional emphasis, 3 letters of recommendation, statement of purpose, minimum GPA of 3.5. Additional exam requirements/recommendations for international students: Required—TOEFL (minimum score 550 paper-based; 79 iBT), IELTS (minimum score 6.5). *Application deadline:* For fall admission, 6/15 for domestic students, 3/1 for international students; for spring admission, 10/15 for domestic students, 9/15 for international students. Applications are processed on a rolling basis. Application fee: $50 ($90 for international students). Electronic applications accepted. *Expenses:* Tuition, state resident: full-time $5495. Tuition, nonresident: full-time $21,938. *Required fees:* $1915. Tuition and fees vary according to program. *Financial support:* Career-related internships or fieldwork, Federal Work-Study, and scholarships/grants available. Support available to part-time students. *Faculty research:* Explorations of science, learning and teaching, family involvement in early childhood, culturally-responsive literacy instruction in diverse settings, STEM education, autism spectrum disorder. *Total annual research expenditures:* $511,331. *Unit head:* Dr. Mari R. Cortez, Department Chair, 210-458-4414, Fax: 210-458-7281, E-mail: mari.cortez@utsa.edu. *Application contact:* Elizabeth Narvaez, Student Development Specialist, 210-458-7443, E-mail: elizabeth.narvaez@utsa.edu.
Website: http://education.utsa.edu/interdisciplinary_learning_and_teaching/

The University of Texas at Tyler, College of Arts and Sciences, Department of Art and Art History, Tyler, TX 75799-0001. Offers art history (MA); interdisciplinary (MAIS); studio art (MFA). *Degree requirements:* For master's, thesis, graduate committee review. *Entrance requirements:* For master's, minimum GPA of 3.0. Additional exam requirements/recommendations for international students: Required—TOEFL. *Faculty research:* Classical myths in contemporary art, social issues in contemporary art, casting methods, Renaissance art.

The University of Texas at Tyler, College of Arts and Sciences, Department of Biology, Tyler, TX 75799-0001. Offers biology (MS); interdisciplinary studies (MSIS). *Degree requirements:* For master's, comprehensive exam, thesis, oral qualifying exam, thesis defense. *Entrance requirements:* For master's, GRE General Test, GRE Subject Test, bachelor's degree in biology or equivalent. Additional exam requirements/ recommendations for international students: Required—TOEFL. Electronic applications accepted. *Faculty research:* Phenotypic plasticity and heritability of life history traits, invertebrate ecology and genetics, systematics and phylogenetics of reptiles, hibernation physiology in turtles, landscape ecology, host-microbe interaction, outer membrane proteins in bacteria.

The University of Texas at Tyler, College of Arts and Sciences, Department of Literature and Languages, Tyler, TX 75799-0001. Offers English (MA); interdisciplinary studies (MAIS). *Program availability:* Part-time, evening/weekend. *Degree requirements:* For master's, one foreign language, comprehensive exam, thesis optional. *Entrance requirements:* For master's, GRE General Test, minimum GPA of 3.0; four semesters or the equivalent of one foreign language. Additional exam requirements/recommendations for international students: Required—TOEFL. Electronic applications accepted. *Faculty research:* Medieval and Tudor drama, Shakespeare, British Romanticism, British and Irish modernism, American realism, Greek drama, nineteenth-century American literature.

The University of Texas at Tyler, College of Education and Psychology, Department of Psychology and Counseling, Tyler, TX 75799-0001. Offers clinical psychology (MS), including neuropsychology, school psychology; counseling psychology (MA), including general, marriage and family; interdisciplinary studies (MSIS); school counseling (MA). *Program availability:* Part-time, evening/weekend. *Degree requirements:* For master's, comprehensive exam, thesis optional. *Entrance requirements:* For master's, GRE General Test, minimum GPA of 3.0. Additional exam requirements/recommendations for international students: Required—TOEFL. Electronic applications accepted. *Faculty research:* Neuropsychology, child abuse, psychometric properties of psychological instruments, maternal behavior, clinical practice issues, victimization of women, post-traumatic stress disorder.

The University of Texas Health Science Center at San Antonio, Graduate School of Biomedical Sciences, Integrated Biomedical Sciences Program, San Antonio, TX 78229-3900. Offers PhD. *Degree requirements:* For doctorate, comprehensive exam, thesis/dissertation.

The University of Texas Rio Grande Valley, College of Liberal Arts, Program in Interdisciplinary Studies, Edinburg, TX 78539. Offers interdisciplinary studies (MAIS, MSIS); Spanish translation and interpreting (MA). *Program availability:* Part-time, evening/weekend. *Faculty:* 3 full-time (2 women). *Students:* 17 full-time (13 women), 41 part-time (28 women); includes 47 minority (1 Asian, non-Hispanic/Latino; 46 Hispanic/Latino), 2 international. Average age 36. 23 applicants, 100% accepted, 15 enrolled. In 2017, 25 master's awarded. *Degree requirements:* For master's, comprehensive exam, thesis or alternative. *Entrance requirements:* For master's, GRE General Test, minimum GPA of 3.0. Additional exam requirements/recommendations for international students: Required—TOEFL or IELTS. Application fee: $50 ($100 for international students). *Expenses:* Tuition, state resident: full-time $5550; part-time $417 per credit hour. Tuition, nonresident: full-time $13,020; part-time $832 per credit hour. *Required fees:* $1169. *Financial support:* Application deadline: 6/1. *Unit head:* Russel Skowronek, Associate Dean, E-mail: russell.skowronek@utrgv.edu.

University of Vermont, Graduate College, College of Education and Social Services, Program in Interdisciplinary Studies, Burlington, VT 05405. Offers M Ed. *Students:* 36 (28 women); includes 3 minority (1 Black or African American, non-Hispanic/Latino; 1 Asian, non-Hispanic/Latino; 1 Hispanic/Latino), 2 international. 19 applicants, 100% accepted, 18 enrolled. In 2017, 11 master's awarded. *Degree requirements:* For master's, thesis or alternative. *Entrance requirements:* For master's, resume, writing sample. Additional exam requirements/recommendations for international students: Required—TOEFL (minimum score 550 paper-based, 90 iBT) or IELTS (6.5). *Application deadline:* Applications are processed on a rolling basis. Application fee: $65. Electronic applications accepted. *Expenses:* Tuition, state resident: full-time $11,628; part-time $646 per credit. Tuition, nonresident: full-time $29,340; part-time $1630 per credit. *Required fees:* $1994; $10 per credit. Tuition and fees vary according to course load and program. *Financial support:* Research assistantships and teaching assistantships available. Financial award application deadline: 3/1. *Unit head:* Dr. Robert Nash, Director, 802-656-2030.
Website: https://www.uvm.edu/cess/dlds/interdisciplinary_studies

University of Virginia, College and Graduate School of Arts and Sciences, Program in Art and Architectural History, Charlottesville, VA 22903. Offers MA, PhD. *Faculty:* 21 full-time (10 women), 2 part-time/adjunct (both women). *Students:* 27 full-time (16 women); includes 6 minority (1 Black or African American, non-Hispanic/Latino; 2 Asian, non-Hispanic/Latino; 2 Hispanic/Latino; 1 Two or more races, non-Hispanic/Latino), 3 international. Average age 31. 56 applicants, 21% accepted, 5 enrolled. In 2017, 7 doctorates awarded. *Degree requirements:* For master's, one foreign language, comprehensive exam, thesis; for doctorate, 2 foreign languages, thesis/dissertation, oral exam. *Entrance requirements:* For master's and doctorate, GRE, 2 letters of recommendation. *Application deadline:* For fall admission, 12/7 for domestic and international students. Applications are processed on a rolling basis. Application fee: $60. Electronic applications accepted. *Financial support:* Application deadline: 12/7. *Unit head:* Larry Goedde, Chair, 434-924-3541, Fax: 434-924-3647, E-mail: artdept@virginia.edu. *Application contact:* Carmenita Higginbotham, Director of Graduate Studies, 434-243-2342, Fax: 434-924-3647, E-mail: artdept@virginia.edu. Website: http://www.virginia.edu/art/phd-program/

University of Washington, Tacoma, Graduate Programs, Interdisciplinary Studies Program, Tacoma, WA 98402-3100. Offers MA. *Program availability:* Part-time, evening/weekend. *Degree requirements:* For master's, thesis or project. *Entrance requirements:* For master's, GRE, statement of intended area of focus, two official transcripts from every college attended, copy of current resume, three recommendations. Additional exam requirements/recommendations for international students: Required—TOEFL. Electronic applications accepted. *Faculty research:* American history, political and social theory, political economy of labor, human rights; African-American, labor, and ethnic studies; South Asian art, aesthetics, semiotics, and modes of creative practice; social movements.

The University of Western Ontario, Faculty of Graduate Studies, Center for the Study of Theory and Criticism, London, ON N6A 5B8, Canada. Offers MA, PhD. *Degree requirements:* For master's, one foreign language, thesis; for doctorate, one foreign language, comprehensive exam, thesis/dissertation. *Entrance requirements:* For master's, honors degree or equivalent, minimum B+ average, 2 samples of written work; for doctorate, MA in humanities or social sciences.

Virginia Commonwealth University, Graduate School, Program in Interdisciplinary Studies, Richmond, VA 23284-9005. Offers MIS. *Program availability:* Part-time. *Degree requirements:* For master's, thesis optional. *Entrance requirements:* For master's, GRE General Test, minimum GPA of 3.0. Additional exam requirements/recommendations for

international students: Required—TOEFL (minimum score 600 paper-based; 100 iBT); Recommended—IELTS (minimum score 6.5). Electronic applications accepted.

Virginia Polytechnic Institute and State University, Graduate School, Intercollege, Blacksburg, VA 24061. Offers genetics, bioinformatics, and computational biology (PhD); information technology (MIT); macromolecular science and engineering (MS, PhD); translational biology, medicine, and health (PhD). *Students:* 167 full-time (86 women), 776 part-time (278 women); includes 252 minority (60 Black or African American, non-Hispanic/Latino; 113 Asian, non-Hispanic/Latino; 41 Hispanic/Latino; 1 Native Hawaiian or other Pacific Islander, non-Hispanic/Latino; 37 Two or more races, non-Hispanic/Latino), 81 international. Average age 33. 664 applicants, 65% accepted, 304 enrolled. In 2017, 93 master's, 13 doctorates awarded. *Degree requirements:* For master's, comprehensive exam (for some programs), thesis (for some programs); for doctorate, comprehensive exam (for some programs), thesis/dissertation (for some programs). *Entrance requirements:* For master's and doctorate, GRE/GMAT. Additional exam requirements/recommendations for international students: Required—TOEFL (minimum score 80 iBT). *Application deadline:* For fall admission, 8/1 for domestic students, 4/1 for international students; for spring admission, 1/1 for domestic students, 9/1 for international students. Applications are processed on a rolling basis. Application fee: $75. Electronic applications accepted. *Expenses:* Tuition, state resident: full-time $15,072; part-time $718.50 per credit hour. Tuition, nonresident: full-time $28,810; part-time $1448.25 per credit hour. *Required fees:* $2741; $502 per semester. Tuition and fees vary according to course load, campus/location and program. *Financial support:* In 2017–18, 39 fellowships with full and partial tuition reimbursements (averaging $17,696 per year), 119 research assistantships with full tuition reimbursements (averaging $24,500 per year), 20 teaching assistantships with full tuition reimbursements (averaging $24,663 per year) were awarded. Financial award application deadline: 3/1; financial award applicants required to submit FAFSA. *Unit head:* Dr. Karen P. DePauw, Vice President and Dean for Graduate Education, 540-231-7581, Fax: 540-231-1670, E-mail: kpdepauw@vt.edu.

Virginia State University, College of Graduate Studies, Program in Interdisciplinary Studies, Petersburg, VA 23806-0001. Offers MIS. Program offered jointly with Virginia Commonwealth University. *Degree requirements:* For master's, thesis optional.

Walden University, Graduate Programs, School of Nursing, Minneapolis, MN 55401. Offers adult-gerontology acute care nurse practitioner (MSN); adult-gerontology nurse practitioner (MSN); education (MSN); family nurse practitioner (MSN); informatics (MSN); leadership and management (MSN); nursing (PhD, Post-Master's Certificate), including education (PhD), healthcare administration (PhD), interdisciplinary health (PhD), leadership (PhD), nursing education (Post-Master's Certificate), nursing informatics (Post-Master's Certificate), nursing leadership and management (Post-Master's Certificate), public health policy (PhD); nursing practice (DNP); psychiatric mental health (MSN). *Accreditation:* AACN. *Program availability:* Part-time, evening/weekend, online only, 100% online. *Degree requirements:* For doctorate, thesis/dissertation (for some programs), residency (for some programs), field experience (for some programs). *Entrance requirements:* For master's, bachelor's degree or equivalent in related field or RN; minimum GPA of 2.5; official transcripts; goal statement (for some programs); access to computer and Internet; for doctorate, master's degree or higher; RN; three years of related professional or academic experience; goal statement; access to computer and Internet; for Post-Master's Certificate, relevant work experience; access to computer and Internet. Additional exam requirements/recommendations for international students: Required—TOEFL (minimum score 550 paper-based, 79 iBT), IELTS (minimum score 6.5), Michigan English Language Assessment Battery (minimum score 82), or PTE (minimum score 53). Electronic applications accepted.

Washington State University, College of Agricultural, Human, and Natural Resource Sciences, Department of Human Development, Pullman, WA 99164-4852. Offers prevention science (PhD). Program also offered at the Spokane campus. *Program availability:* Part-time. *Degree requirements:* For doctorate, comprehensive exam, thesis/dissertation. *Entrance requirements:* For doctorate, GRE General Test, bachelor's or master's degree in prevention science related field (e.g., communication, educational psychology, human development, nursing, psychology, sociology); written statement specifying qualifications, educational goals, and career objectives; official copies of all college transcripts; three letters of reference. Additional exam requirements/recommendations for international students: Required—TOEFL, IELTS. Electronic applications accepted. *Faculty research:* Prevention science, program implementation and dissemination, drug and alcohol prevention, health communication, equine assisted interventions, obesity prevention, health promotion in emerging adulthood, family processes, disenfranchised youth, rural poverty, adolescent sexuality, cultural competency, community collaborations, parent-child relationships, healthy aging.

Western Kentucky University, Graduate Studies, College of Education and Behavioral Sciences, School of Teacher Education, Bowling Green, KY 42101. Offers elementary education (MAE, Ed S); exceptional education: learning and behavioral disorders (MAE); exceptional education: moderate and severe disabilities (MAE); instructional design (MS); interdisciplinary early childhood education (MAE); library media education (MS); literacy education (MAE); middle grades education (MAE); secondary education (MAE, Ed S). *Program availability:* Part-time, evening/weekend, online learning. *Degree requirements:* For master's, comprehensive exam. *Entrance requirements:* For master's, GRE General Test. Additional exam requirements/recommendations for international students: Required—TOEFL (minimum score 555 paper-based; 79 iBT). *Faculty research:* Teacher preparation in moderate/severe disabilities.

Western New Mexico University, Graduate Division, Interdisciplinary Studies, Silver City, NM 88062-0680. Offers MA. *Program availability:* Part-time, online learning. *Degree requirements:* For master's, comprehensive exam (for some programs), thesis optional. *Entrance requirements:* For master's, GRE General Test, GRE Subject Test, minimum GPA of 3.2 in last 64 hours of undergraduate study. Additional exam requirements/recommendations for international students: Required—TOEFL (minimum score 550 paper-based).

West Texas A&M University, Program in Interdisciplinary Studies, Canyon, TX 79015. Offers MA, MS. *Program availability:* Part-time, evening/weekend. *Degree requirements:* For master's, comprehensive exam, thesis or alternative. *Entrance requirements:* Additional exam requirements/recommendations for international students: Required—TOEFL. Electronic applications accepted.

Worcester Polytechnic Institute, Graduate Admissions, Department of Social Science and Policy Studies, Worcester, MA 01609-2280. Offers interdisciplinary social science (PhD); system dynamics (MS, Graduate Certificate). *Program availability:* Part-time, evening/weekend, 100% online. *Faculty:* 4 full-time (2 women), 4 part-time/adjunct (1 woman). *Students:* 7 part-time (1 woman), 1 international. Average age 48. 5 applicants, 80% accepted, 2 enrolled. In 2017, 4 master's, 1 doctorate, 2 other advanced degrees awarded. *Entrance requirements:* For master's and doctorate, GRE General Test, 3 letters of recommendation, statement of purpose. Additional exam requirements/recommendations for international students: Required—TOEFL (minimum score 563 paper-based; 84 iBT), IELTS (minimum score 7). *Application deadline:* For fall admission, 1/1 priority date for domestic students, 1/1 for international students; for spring admission, 10/1 priority date for domestic students, 10/1 for international

Interdisciplinary Studies

students. Applications are processed on a rolling basis. Application fee: $70. Electronic applications accepted. *Expenses: Tuition:* Full-time $26,226; part-time $1457 per credit. *Required fees:* $60; $30 per credit. One-time fee: $15. Tuition and fees vary according to course load. *Financial support:* Research assistantships, teaching assistantships, career-related internships or fieldwork, institutionally sponsored loans, scholarships/grants, and unspecified assistantships available. Financial award application deadline: 1/1. *Unit head:* Dr. Emily Douglas, Head, 508-831-5296, Fax: 508-831-5896, E-mail: emdouglas@wpi.edu. *Application contact:* Dr. Khalid Saeed, Graduate Coordinator, 508-831-5296, Fax: 508-831-5896, E-mail: saeed@wpi.edu.
Website: https://www.wpi.edu/academics/departments/social-science-policy-studies

Worcester Polytechnic Institute, Graduate Admissions, Programs in Interdisciplinary Studies, Worcester, MA 01609-2280. Offers bioscience administration (MS); nuclear science and engineering (Graduate Certificate); power systems management (MS); social science (PhD); system dynamics and innovation management (MS, Graduate Certificate); systems modeling (MS). *Program availability:* Part-time, evening/weekend, 100% online. *Students:* 5 full-time (3 women), 50 part-time (11 women); includes 16 minority (7 Black or African American, non-Hispanic/Latino; 5 Asian, non-Hispanic/Latino; 3 Hispanic/Latino; 1 Two or more races, non-Hispanic/Latino), 3 international. Average age 34. 25 applicants, 96% accepted, 13 enrolled. In 2017, 10 master's, 1 doctorate, 7 other advanced degrees awarded. Terminal master's awarded for partial completion of doctoral program. *Degree requirements:* For master's, thesis; for doctorate, comprehensive exam, thesis/dissertation. *Entrance requirements:* For master's and doctorate, 3 letters of recommendation. Additional exam requirements/recommendations for international students: Required—TOEFL (minimum score 563 paper-based; 84 iBT), IELTS (minimum score 7). *Application deadline:* For fall admission, 1/1 priority date for domestic students, 1/1 for international students; for spring admission, 10/1 priority date for domestic students, 10/1 for international students. Applications are processed on a rolling basis. Application fee: $70. Electronic applications accepted. *Expenses: Tuition:* Full-time $26,226; part-time $1457 per credit. *Required fees:* $60; $30 per credit. One-time fee: $15. Tuition and fees vary according to course load. *Financial support:* Institutionally sponsored loans, scholarships/grants, and unspecified assistantships available. Financial award application deadline: 1/1. *Unit head:* Michale McGrade, Dean, 508-831-5301, Fax: 508-831-5717, E-mail: grad@wpi.edu. *Application contact:* Lynne Dougherty, Administrative Assistant, 508-831-5301, Fax: 508-831-5717, E-mail: grad@wpi.edu.

York University, Faculty of Graduate Studies, Program in Interdisciplinary Studies, Toronto, ON M3J 1P3, Canada. Offers MA. *Program availability:* Part-time. *Degree requirements:* For master's, thesis or alternative. Electronic applications accepted.

ACADEMIC AND PROFESSIONAL PROGRAMS IN THE SOCIAL SCIENCES

Section 15
Area and Cultural Studies

This section contains a directory of institutions offering graduate work in area and cultural studies. Additional information about programs listed in the directory may be obtained by writing directly to the dean of a graduate school or chair of a department at the address given in the directory.

For programs offering related work, see also in this book *Geography, History, Language and Literature, Political Science and International Affairs,* and *Sociology, Anthropology, and Archaeology.*

CONTENTS

Program Directories

Featured School: Display and Close-Up

See:

African-American Studies

Boston University, Graduate School of Arts and Sciences, Program in African American Studies, Boston, MA 02215. Offers MA. *Students:* 2 full-time (1 woman); both minorities (both Black or African American, non-Hispanic/Latino). Average age 24. 5 applicants, 100% accepted, 2 enrolled. *Degree requirements:* For master's, one foreign language, comprehensive exam, two major research papers. *Entrance requirements:* For master's, GRE General Test, 3 letters of recommendation, transcripts, personal statement, curriculum vitae, writing sample. Additional exam requirements/ recommendations for international students: Required—TOEFL (minimum score 550 paper-based; 84 iBT). *Application deadline:* For fall admission, 1/31 for domestic and international students. Application fee: $95. Electronic applications accepted. *Financial support:* In 2017–18, 1 student received support. Federal Work-Study and scholarships/ grants available. Financial award application deadline: 1/31. *Unit head:* John Thornton, Director, 617-358-1423, Fax: 617-353-0455, E-mail: jkthorn@bu.edu. *Application contact:* Deirdre James, Program Administrator, 617-358-1421, Fax: 617-353-0455, E-mail: dejames@bu.edu.
Website: http://www.bu.edu/afam/

Carnegie Mellon University, Dietrich College of Humanities and Social Sciences, Department of History, Pittsburgh, PA 15213-3891. Offers African and African-American diaspora (PhD); culture and power (PhD); labor, politics and social movements (PhD); technology, environment, science and health (PhD); women, gender and the family (PhD). *Program availability:* Part-time. *Degree requirements:* For doctorate, oral and written comprehensive exams, dissertation defense. *Entrance requirements:* For doctorate, GRE General Test. Additional exam requirements/recommendations for international students: Required—TOEFL. Electronic applications accepted. *Faculty research:* Anthropology and history, African-American history, technology/environment, cultural history analysis.

Clark Atlanta University, School of Arts and Sciences, Department of African American Studies, Africana Women's Studies, and History, Atlanta, GA 30314. Offers MA, PhD. *Program availability:* Part-time. *Faculty:* 7 full-time (4 women), 8 part-time/adjunct (4 women). *Students:* 17 full-time (10 women), 43 part-time (30 women); includes 55 minority (all Black or African American, non-Hispanic/Latino). Average age 37. 21 applicants, 100% accepted, 11 enrolled. In 2017, 3 master's, 1 doctorate awarded. *Degree requirements:* For master's, one foreign language, comprehensive exam, thesis optional; for doctorate, one foreign language, comprehensive exam, thesis/dissertation. *Entrance requirements:* For master's, GRE General Test, minimum GPA of 2.5. Additional exam requirements/recommendations for international students: Required—TOEFL (minimum score 500 paper-based; 61 iBT). *Application deadline:* For fall admission, 4/1 for domestic and international students; for spring admission, 11/1 for domestic and international students. Applications are processed on a rolling basis. Application fee: $40 ($55 for international students). Electronic applications accepted. *Financial support:* Scholarships/grants available. Financial award application deadline: 4/30; financial award applicants required to submit FAFSA. *Unit head:* Dr. Stephanie Evans, Chairperson, 404-880-6352, E-mail: sevans@cau.edu.
Website: http://www.cau.edu/department-of-africana-womens-history/index.html

Columbia University, Graduate School of Arts and Sciences, New York, NY 10027. Offers African-American studies (MA); American studies (MA); anthropology (MA, PhD); art history and archaeology (MA, PhD); astronomy (PhD); biological sciences (PhD); biotechnology (MA); chemical physics (PhD); chemistry (PhD); classical studies (MA, PhD); classics (MA, PhD); climate and society (MA); conservation biology (MA); earth and environmental sciences (PhD); East Asia: regional studies (MA); East Asian languages and cultures (MA, PhD); ecology, evolution and environmental biology (MA), including conservation biology; ecology, evolution, and environmental biology (PhD), including ecology and evolutionary biology, evolutionary primatology; economics (MA, PhD); English and comparative literature (MA, PhD); French and Romance philology (MA, PhD); Germanic languages (MA, PhD); global French studies (MA); global thought (MA); Hispanic cultural studies (MA); history (PhD); history and literature (MA); human rights studies (MA); Islamic studies (MA); Italian (MA, PhD); Japanese pedagogy (MA); Jewish studies (MA); Latin America and the Caribbean: regional studies (MA); Latin American and Iberian cultures (PhD); mathematics (MA, PhD), including finance (MA); medieval and Renaissance studies (MA); Middle Eastern, South Asian, and African studies (MA, PhD); modern art: critical and curatorial studies (MA); modern European studies (MA); museum anthropology (MA); music (DMA, PhD); oral history (MA); philosophical foundations of physics (MA); philosophy (MA, PhD); physics (PhD); political science (MA, PhD); psychology (PhD); quantitative methods in the social sciences (MA); religion (MA, PhD); Russia, Eurasia and East Europe: regional studies (MA); Russian translation (MA); Slavic cultures (MA); Slavic languages (MA, PhD); sociology (MA, PhD); South Asian studies (MA); statistics (MA, PhD); theatre (PhD). Dual-degree programs require admission to both Graduate School of Arts and Sciences and another Columbia school. *Program availability:* Part-time. Terminal master's awarded for partial completion of doctoral program. *Degree requirements:* For master's, variable foreign language requirement, comprehensive exam (for some programs), thesis (for some programs); for doctorate, variable foreign language requirement, comprehensive exam (for some programs), thesis/dissertation. *Entrance requirements:* For master's and doctorate, GRE General Test, GRE Subject Test (for some programs). Additional exam requirements/recommendations for international students: Required—TOEFL, IELTS. Electronic applications accepted. *Expenses: Tuition:* Full-time $44,864; part-time $1704 per credit. *Required fees:* $2370 per semester. One-time fee: $105.

Cornell University, Graduate School, Graduate Fields of Arts and Sciences, Field of African and African-American Studies, Ithaca, NY 14853. Offers African studies (MPS); African-American studies (MPS); Africana studies (PhD). *Degree requirements:* For master's, thesis. *Entrance requirements:* For master's, GRE General Test (recommended), 3 letters of recommendation; for doctorate, GRE General Test (recommended), 3 letters of recommendation, personal statement, writing sample. Additional exam requirements/recommendations for international students: Required—TOEFL (minimum score 550 paper-based; 77 iBT). Electronic applications accepted. *Faculty research:* African-American literature, art, cinema and theater; African-American politics and public policy; African history, politics and art; Caribbean politics and Africana diaspora.

Cornell University, Graduate School, Graduate Fields of Arts and Sciences, Field of English Language and Literature, Ithaca, NY 14853. Offers African-American literature (PhD); American literature after 1865 (PhD); American literature to 1865 (PhD); American studies (PhD); colonial and postcolonial literatures (PhD); creative writing (MFA); cultural studies (PhD); dramatic literature (PhD); English poetry (PhD); English Renaissance to 1660 (PhD); lesbian, bisexual, and gay literary studies (PhD); literary criticism and theory (PhD); Old and Middle English (PhD); prose fiction (PhD); Restoration and the eighteenth-century (PhD); the nineteenth century (PhD); the twentieth century (PhD); women's literature (PhD); MFA/PhD. Terminal master's awarded for partial completion of doctoral program. *Degree requirements:* For master's, one foreign language, thesis; for doctorate, one foreign language, comprehensive exam, thesis/dissertation, teaching experience. *Entrance requirements:* For master's, GRE General Test, 3 letters of recommendation, creative writing sample; for doctorate, GRE General Test, GRE Subject Test (English), 3 letters of recommendation, writing sample. Additional exam requirements/recommendations for international students: Required—TOEFL (minimum score 600 paper-based; 77 iBT). Electronic applications accepted. *Faculty research:* English and American literature, women's writing, ethnic and post-colonial literature, critical theory, medievalism.

Eastern Michigan University, Graduate School, College of Arts and Sciences, Department of Africology and African-American Studies, Ypsilanti, MI 48197. Offers Graduate Certificate. *Faculty:* 3 full-time (2 women). *Students:* 1 part-time (0 women); minority (Two or more races, non-Hispanic/Latino). Average age 65. 2 applicants, 100% accepted, 1 enrolled. In 2017, 3 Graduate Certificates awarded. *Entrance requirements:* For degree, bachelor's degree with minimum GPA of 2.7, two letters of reference. *Application deadline:* Applications are processed on a rolling basis. Application fee: $45. *Unit head:* Dr. Victor Okafor, Department Head, 734-487-3460, Fax: 734-487-6891, E-mail: victor.okafor@emich.edu.
Website: http://www.emich.edu/aas/

Georgia State University, College of Arts and Sciences, Department of African-American Studies, Atlanta, GA 30302-3083. Offers MA. *Program availability:* Part-time. *Faculty:* 7 full-time (4 women). *Students:* 19 full-time (13 women), 10 part-time (8 women); includes 26 minority (25 Black or African American, non-Hispanic/Latino; 1 Two or more races, non-Hispanic/Latino), 1 international. Average age 31. 25 applicants, 68% accepted, 11 enrolled. In 2017, 7 master's awarded. *Degree requirements:* For master's, thesis. *Entrance requirements:* For master's, GRE. Additional exam requirements/recommendations for international students: Required—TOEFL (minimum score 550 paper-based; 80 iBT). *Application deadline:* For fall admission, 4/15 for domestic and international students. Application fee: $50. Electronic applications accepted. *Expenses:* Tuition, state resident: full-time $7020. Tuition, nonresident: full-time $22,518. *Required fees:* $2128. Tuition and fees vary according to degree level and program. *Financial support:* In 2017–18, research assistantships with tuition reimbursements (averaging $4,200 per year), teaching assistantships with tuition reimbursements (averaging $4,000 per year) were awarded; health care benefits and unspecified assistantships also available. Financial award applicants required to submit FAFSA. *Faculty research:* HIV prevention education and culturally relevant praxis; African-American women's activism and social movements; narrative therapy and family counseling; African women's history; African-American social movements, civil rights, and Black power movements. *Unit head:* Dr. Akinyele Umoja, Chair, Department of African-American Studies, 404-413-5137, Fax: 404-413-5140, E-mail: aadaku@gsu.edu. *Application contact:* Dr. Sarita Kaya Davis, Graduate Program Director, 404-413-5134, Fax: 404-413-5140, E-mail: saritadavis@gsu.edu.
Website: http://www2.gsu.edu/~wwwaad/

Harvard University, Graduate School of Arts and Sciences, Department of African and African American Studies, Cambridge, MA 02138. Offers PhD.

Indiana University Bloomington, University Graduate School, College of Arts and Sciences, Department of African American and African Diaspora Studies, Bloomington, IN 47405-7000. Offers MA, PhD. *Entrance requirements:* For master's and doctorate, GRE, minimum GPA of 3.0. Additional exam requirements/recommendations for international students: Required—TOEFL. Electronic applications accepted. *Expenses:* Contact institution.

Michigan State University, The Graduate School, College of Arts and Letters, Program in African American and African Studies, East Lansing, MI 48824. Offers MA, PhD. *Entrance requirements:* Additional exam requirements/recommendations for international students: Required—TOEFL. Electronic applications accepted. *Faculty research:* Black American and diasporic studies, comparative communities of color.

Morgan State University, School of Graduate Studies, College of Liberal Arts, Department of History and Geography, Baltimore, MD 21251. Offers African-American studies (MA); history (MA, PhD); museum studies and historic preservation (MA). *Program availability:* Part-time, evening/weekend. *Degree requirements:* For master's, comprehensive exam, thesis; for doctorate, comprehensive exam, thesis/dissertation. *Entrance requirements:* For master's, minimum GPA of 2.5; for doctorate, GRE or MAT. Additional exam requirements/recommendations for international students: Required—TOEFL (minimum score 550 paper-based). *Application deadline:* For fall admission, 2/1 priority date for domestic students; for spring admission, 10/1 priority date for domestic students. Applications are processed on a rolling basis. Application fee: $0. *Expenses:* Tuition, state resident: part-time $433 per credit. Tuition, nonresident: part-time $851 per credit. *Required fees:* $81.50 per credit. *Financial support:* Application deadline: 2/1. *Faculty research:* Women's history, African diaspora history, urban history. *Unit head:* Dr. Jeremiah I. Dibua, Graduate Coordinator, 443-885-3400, Fax: 443-885-8227, E-mail: jeremiah.dibua@morgan.edu. *Application contact:* Dr. Dean Campbell, Graduate Recruitment Specialist, 443-885-3185, Fax: 443-885-8226, E-mail: dean.campbell@morgan.edu.

North Carolina Agricultural and Technical State University, School of Graduate Studies, College of Arts and Sciences, Department of English, Program in English and African-American Literature, Greensboro, NC 27411. Offers MA. *Program availability:* Part-time, evening/weekend. *Degree requirements:* For master's, comprehensive exam, qualifying exam. *Entrance requirements:* For master's, GRE General Test, minimum GPA of 3.0.

Northwestern University, The Graduate School, Judd A. and Marjorie Weinberg College of Arts and Sciences, Department of African American Studies, Evanston, IL 60208. Offers PhD.

Oblate School of Theology, Graduate and Professional Programs, San Antonio, TX 78216-6693. Offers African-American pastoral leadership (D Min); divinity (M Div); pastoral leadership (D Min); pastoral ministry (MAP Min); pastoral studies (Certificate); spiritual formation in the local community (D Min); spirituality (MA Sp, PhD); spirituality and ministry (D Min); theology (MA Th); U.S. Hispanic/Latino ministry (D Min); M Div/ MA Th. *Accreditation:* ACIPE; ATS (one or more programs are accredited). *Program availability:* Part-time, 100% online, blended/hybrid learning. *Faculty:* 21 full-time (5 women), 4 part-time/adjunct (0 women). *Students:* 89 full-time (9 women), 54 part-time (31 women); includes 77 minority (11 Black or African American, non-Hispanic/Latino; 8 Asian, non-Hispanic/Latino; 57 Hispanic/Latino; 1 Two or more races, non-Hispanic/ Latino), 24 international. Average age 39. In 2017, 24 master's, 1 doctorate awarded. *Degree requirements:* For master's, comprehensive exam (for some programs), thesis (for some programs), practicum; for doctorate, one foreign language, comprehensive

exam, thesis/dissertation, paper, practicum. *Entrance requirements:* For master's, MAT, interview, prerequisite course work in theology or religious studies and philosophy, minimum GPA of 2.5; for doctorate, D Min, M Div, MA Th, MA Sp, MA PM. Additional exam requirements/recommendations for international students: Required—TOEFL (minimum score 71 iBT). *Application deadline:* For fall admission, 6/30 priority date for domestic and international students; for winter admission, 11/30 for domestic and international students; for spring admission, 11/30 for domestic and international students; for summer admission, 4/30 for domestic and international students. Applications are processed on a rolling basis. Application fee: $65. Electronic applications accepted. *Expenses:* $605.00 per credit hour (for master's degrees); $680 per credit hour (for doctoral degrees); $55 registration fee. *Financial support:* In 2017–18, 25 students received support. Scholarships/grants available. Support available to part-time students. Financial award application deadline: 8/15; financial award applicants required to submit FAFSA. *Unit head:* Dr. R. Scott Woodward, Academic Dean, 210-341-1366, Fax: 210-341-4519, E-mail: rsw@ost.edu. *Application contact:* Brenda Reyna, Registrar, 210-341-1366 Ext. 226, Fax: 210-341-4519, E-mail: registrar@ost.edu.

The Ohio State University, Graduate School, College of Arts and Sciences, Division of Arts and Humanities, Department of African-American and African Studies, Columbus, OH 43210. Offers MA, PhD. *Faculty:* 12. *Students:* 16 (11 women). Average age 28. In 2017, 2 master's awarded. *Degree requirements:* For master's, comprehensive exam (for some programs), thesis (for some programs), thesis or comprehensive written examination; for doctorate, thesis/dissertation. *Entrance requirements:* For master's and doctorate, GRE General Test. Additional exam requirements/recommendations for international students: Required—TOEFL (minimum score 550 paper-based; 79 iBT), Michigan English Language Assessment Battery (minimum score 82); Recommended—IELTS (minimum score 7). *Application deadline:* For fall admission, 12/1 priority date for domestic students, 11/30 priority date for international students; for spring admission, 3/1 for domestic students, 2/1 for international students. Applications are processed on a rolling basis. Application fee: $60 ($70 for international students). Electronic applications accepted. *Financial support:* Fellowships with tuition reimbursements, research assistantships with tuition reimbursements, teaching assistantships with tuition reimbursements, Federal Work-Study, institutionally sponsored loans, and unspecified assistantships available. Support available to part-time students. *Unit head:* Valerie Lee, Interim Chair, 614-292-0116, E-mail: lee.89@osu.edu. *Application contact:* Graduate and Professional Admissions, 614-292-9444, Fax: 614-292-3895, E-mail: gpadmissions@osu.edu.
Website: http://aaas.osu.edu/

Rutgers University–New Brunswick, Graduate School-New Brunswick, Program in History, Piscataway, NJ 08854-8097. Offers African-American history (PhD); early American history (PhD); early modern European history (PhD); east Asian history (PhD); global and comparative history (PhD); history (PhD); history of diplomacy and foreign relations (PhD); history of technology, environment and health (PhD); history of the Atlantic cultures and African diaspora (PhD); Latin American history (PhD); medieval history (PhD); modern European history (PhD); nineteenth and twentieth century American history (PhD); women's and gender history (PhD). *Degree requirements:* For doctorate, thesis/dissertation. *Entrance requirements:* For doctorate, GRE General Test, sample of written work. Electronic applications accepted. *Faculty research:* American history, European history, Afro-American history, women's history, Latin American history.

Syracuse University, College of Arts and Sciences, MA Program in Pan-African Studies, Syracuse, NY 13244. Offers MA. *Students:* Average age 30. *Degree requirements:* For master's, thesis. *Entrance requirements:* For master's, GRE General Test (recommended), personal statement, resume, three letters of recommendation, writing sample (10-12 pages), transcripts. Additional exam requirements/recommendations for international students: Required—TOEFL (minimum score 600 paper-based; 100 iBT). *Application deadline:* For fall admission, 1/10 priority date for domestic and international students. Application fee: $75. Electronic applications accepted. *Financial support:* Fellowships with tuition reimbursements, teaching assistantships with tuition reimbursements, and scholarships/grants available. Financial award application deadline: 1/1. *Faculty research:* African American studies, African American history, Francophone African/Caribbean literatures, African archaeology. *Unit head:* Dr. Herbert G. Ruffin, II, Associate Professor, History/Chair of African American Studies, 315-443-3005, E-mail: hruffin@syr.edu. *Application contact:* Ajajielle Brown, Administrative Assistant, 315-443-5599, E-mail: aabrow02@syr.edu.
Website: http://aas.syr.edu/graduate/program-description.html

Temple University, College of Liberal Arts, Department of African American Studies, Philadelphia, PA 19122-6096. Offers MA, PhD. *Faculty:* 7 full-time (3 women), 5 part-time/adjunct (0 women). *Students:* 27 full-time (12 women), 7 part-time (5 women); includes 28 minority (26 Black or African American, non-Hispanic/Latino; 2 Two or more races, non-Hispanic/Latino), 3 international. 27 applicants, 41% accepted, 8 enrolled. In 2017, 4 master's, 2 doctorates awarded. Terminal master's awarded for partial completion of doctoral program. *Degree requirements:* For master's, comprehensive exam; for doctorate, one foreign language, thesis/dissertation, oral and written qualifying exams. *Entrance requirements:* For master's, GRE, 3 letters of recommendation; minimum GPA of 3.0; for doctorate, GRE, MA in African American studies; 3 letters of recommendation; minimum GPA of 3.0. Additional exam requirements/recommendations for international students: Required—TOEFL (minimum score 550 paper-based; 79 iBT). *Application deadline:* For fall admission, 1/15 for domestic students, 12/15 for international students. Applications are processed on a rolling basis. Application fee: $60. Electronic applications accepted. *Expenses:* Tuition, state resident: full-time $16,164; part-time $898 per credit hour. Tuition, nonresident: full-time $22,158; part-time $1231 per credit hour. *Required fees:* $890; $445 per semester. Full-time tuition and fees vary according to course load, degree level, campus/location and program. *Financial support:* Teaching assistantships and Federal Work-Study available. Financial award application deadline: 1/15; financial award applicants required to submit FAFSA. *Faculty research:* African history and civilization, contemporary political and cultural developments, identity, African diaspora history and culture. *Unit head:* Dr. Ama Mazama, Graduate Director, 215-204-1992, Fax: 215-204-5953, E-mail: afam@temple.edu. *Application contact:* Tammey Abner, Graduate Coordinator, 215-204-8491, Fax: 215-204-5953, E-mail: tammy.abner@temple.edu.
Website: http://www.cla.temple.edu/africanamericanstudies

Trinity Lutheran Seminary, Graduate and Professional Programs, Columbus, OH 43209-2334. Offers African American studies (MTS); Biblical studies (MTS, STM); Christian education (MA); Christian spirituality (STM); church in the world (MTS); church music (MA); divinity (M Div); general theological studies (MTS); mission and evangelism (STM); pastoral leadership and practice (STM); youth and family ministry (MA); MSN/MTS; MTS/JD. *Accreditation:* ACIPE; ATS. *Program availability:* Part-time. *Degree requirements:* For master's, variable foreign language requirement, comprehensive exam (for some programs), thesis (for some programs), field experience (for some programs). *Entrance requirements:* For master's, BA or equivalent (for MA, M Div, MTS); M Div, MTS, or equivalent (for STM); audition (for MACM). Additional exam

requirements/recommendations for international students: Required—TOEFL. Electronic applications accepted. *Expenses:* Contact institution.

University at Albany, State University of New York, College of Arts and Sciences, Department of Africana Studies, Albany, NY 12222-0001. Offers African studies (MA); Afro-American studies (MA). *Program availability:* Part-time, evening/weekend. *Faculty:* 5 full-time (2 women). *Students:* 13 full-time (9 women), 7 part-time (5 women); includes 13 minority (10 Black or African American, non-Hispanic/Latino; 1 Hispanic/Latino; 2 Two or more races, non-Hispanic/Latino). 13 applicants, 92% accepted, 8 enrolled. In 2017, 5 master's awarded. *Entrance requirements:* Additional exam requirements/recommendations for international students: Required—TOEFL (minimum score 550 paper-based). *Application deadline:* For fall admission, 5/15 for international students; for spring admission, 11/1 for international students. Applications are processed on a rolling basis. Application fee: $75. Electronic applications accepted. *Expenses:* Tuition, state resident: full-time $10,870; part-time $453 per credit hour. Tuition, nonresident: full-time $22,210; part-time $925 per credit hour. *Required fees:* $84.68 per credit hour. $508.06 per semester. Part-time tuition and fees vary according to course load and program. *Financial support:* Fellowships, teaching assistantships, and Federal Work-Study available. Financial award application deadline: 5/1. *Faculty research:* The Black family, Afro-centricity in poetry, black women in U.S. literature, African economic development, African American history. *Unit head:* Oscar Williams, Chair, 518-442-4730, Fax: 518-442-2569, E-mail: owilliams@albany.edu. *Application contact:* Michael DeRensis, Director, Graduate Admissions, 518-442-3980, Fax: 518-442-3922, E-mail: graduate@albany.edu.
Website: http://www.albany.edu/africana/

University of California, Berkeley, Graduate Division, College of Letters and Science, Department of African American Studies, Berkeley, CA 94720-1500. Offers PhD. *Degree requirements:* For doctorate, one foreign language, thesis/dissertation. *Entrance requirements:* For doctorate, minimum GPA of 3.0, 3 letters of recommendation. Additional exam requirements/recommendations for international students: Required—TOEFL (minimum score 570 paper-based, 90 iBT) or IELTS (minimum score 7). Electronic applications accepted. *Faculty research:* Black influence on U. S. foreign policy, black intellectuals, ethnic space in urban society, representation in museums of African-Americans and British Americans during slavery.

University of California, Los Angeles, Graduate Division, College of Letters and Science, Interdepartmental Program in Afro-American Studies, Los Angeles, CA 90095. Offers MA, MA/JD. *Degree requirements:* For master's, one foreign language, comprehensive exam or thesis. *Entrance requirements:* For master's, GRE General Test, bachelor's degree; minimum undergraduate GPA of 3.0 (or its equivalent if letter grade system not used); writing sample. Additional exam requirements/recommendations for international students: Required—TOEFL. Electronic applications accepted.

University of California, Santa Barbara, Graduate Division, College of Letters and Sciences, Division of Social Sciences, Department of Sociology, Santa Barbara, CA 93106-9430. Offers interdisciplinary emphasis: Black studies (PhD); interdisciplinary emphasis: environment and society (PhD); interdisciplinary emphasis: feminist studies (PhD); interdisciplinary emphasis: global studies (PhD); interdisciplinary emphasis: language, interaction and social organization (PhD); interdisciplinary emphasis: quantitative methods in the social sciences (PhD); interdisciplinary emphasis: technology and society (PhD); sociology (PhD); MA/PhD. Terminal master's awarded for partial completion of doctoral program. *Degree requirements:* For doctorate, comprehensive exam, thesis/dissertation. *Entrance requirements:* For doctorate, GRE General Test. Additional exam requirements/recommendations for international students: Required—TOEFL (minimum score 550 paper-based; 80 iBT), IELTS (minimum score 7). Electronic applications accepted. *Faculty research:* Gender and sexualities, race/ethnicity, social movements, conversation analysis, global sociology.

The University of Kansas, Graduate Studies, College of Liberal Arts and Sciences, Department of African and African-American Studies, Lawrence, KS 66045. Offers African and African-American studies (MA); African studies (Graduate Certificate). *Program availability:* Part-time. *Students:* 9 full-time (7 women), 1 part-time (0 women); includes 6 minority (3 Black or African American, non-Hispanic/Latino; 3 Two or more races, non-Hispanic/Latino). Average age 29. 7 applicants, 100% accepted, 5 enrolled. In 2017, 9 master's awarded. *Entrance requirements:* For master's, GRE, all academic transcripts, 3 letters of recommendation, personal statement of purpose, writing sample. Additional exam requirements/recommendations for international students: Required—TOEFL, IELTS. *Application deadline:* For fall admission, 5/1 for domestic and international students; for spring admission, 10/1 for domestic and international students. Application fee: $65 ($85 for international students). Electronic applications accepted. *Financial support:* Application deadline: 4/15. *Faculty research:* African theatre, YaKuur culture, interracial communication, African development and urban planning, African literature, Muslim women in West Africa, identity formation in African and Diasporan settings, African-American history, North African and Arab societies, civil rights, black urban communities. *Unit head:* Dr. Lang Clarence, Chairperson, 785-864-3054, E-mail: celang@ku.edu. *Application contact:* Shawn Alexander, Director of Graduate Studies, 785-864-3054, E-mail: slalexan@ku.edu.
Website: http://www.afs.ku.edu

University of Louisville, Graduate School, College of Arts and Sciences, Department of Pan-African Studies, Louisville, KY 40292. Offers African and Diaspora studies (MA); African-American studies (MA); MSSW/MA. *Program availability:* Part-time. *Faculty:* 11 full-time (6 women), 2 part-time/adjunct (1 woman). *Students:* 18 full-time (13 women), 7 part-time (5 women); includes 24 minority (20 Black or African American, non-Hispanic/Latino; 1 Hispanic/Latino; 3 Two or more races, non-Hispanic/Latino), 1 international. Average age 33. 18 applicants, 56% accepted, 6 enrolled. *Degree requirements:* For master's, comprehensive exam, thesis optional. *Entrance requirements:* For master's, GRE General Test. Additional exam requirements/recommendations for international students: Required—TOEFL (minimum score 550 paper-based; 79 iBT). *Application deadline:* For fall admission, 3/15 for domestic students, 5/1 priority date for international students; for spring admission, 10/15 for domestic students, 11/1 priority date for international students; for summer admission, 4/1 priority date for international students. Applications are processed on a rolling basis. Application fee: $65. Electronic applications accepted. *Expenses:* Tuition, state resident: full-time $12,246; part-time $681 per credit hour. Tuition, nonresident: full-time $25,486; part-time $1417 per credit hour. *Required fees:* $196. Tuition and fees vary according to course load, program and reciprocity agreements. *Financial support:* Teaching assistantships available. Financial award application deadline: 3/3; financial award applicants required to submit FAFSA. *Faculty research:* African popular culture, black male identity development, education and retention, contemporary politics in Nigeria, poverty in the Caribbean. *Total annual research expenditures:* $72,938. *Unit head:* Dr. Ricky L. Jones, Chair, 502-852-0027, E-mail: ricky.jones@louisville.edu. *Application contact:* Latonia Craig, Director of Graduate Recruitment and Diversity Retention, 502-852-5207, E-mail: gradadm@louisville.edu.
Website: http://www.louisville.edu/panafricanstudies

University of Massachusetts Amherst, Graduate School, College of Humanities and Fine Arts, Department of Afro-American Studies, Amherst, MA 01003. Offers MA, PhD.

Program availability: Part-time. Terminal master's awarded for partial completion of doctoral program. *Degree requirements:* For master's, thesis or alternative; for doctorate, comprehensive exam, thesis/dissertation. *Entrance requirements:* For master's and doctorate, writing sample, 3 letters of recommendation. Additional exam requirements/recommendations for international students: Required—TOEFL (minimum score 550 paper-based; 80 iBT), IELTS (minimum score 6.5). Electronic applications accepted.

University of Memphis, Graduate School, College of Arts and Sciences, Department of English, Memphis, TN 38152. Offers African-American literature (Graduate Certificate); applied linguistics (PhD); composition studies (PhD); creative writing (MFA); English as a second language (MA); linguistics (MA); literary and cultural studies (PhD), including African-American literature; literature (MA); professional writing (MA, PhD); teaching English as a second/foreign language (Graduate Certificate). *Program availability:* Part-time, evening/weekend, 100% online. *Faculty:* 30 full-time (15 women). *Students:* 73 full-time (34 women), 80 part-time (52 women); includes 35 minority (20 Black or African American, non-Hispanic/Latino; 3 Asian, non-Hispanic/Latino; 9 Hispanic/Latino; 3 Two or more races, non-Hispanic/Latino), 36 international. Average age 35. 78 applicants, 88% accepted, 35 enrolled. In 2017, 27 master's, 15 doctorates, 10 other advanced degrees awarded. Terminal master's awarded for partial completion of doctoral program. *Degree requirements:* For master's, one foreign language, comprehensive exam, thesis optional; for doctorate, 2 foreign languages, comprehensive exam, thesis/dissertation, qualifying exam. *Entrance requirements:* For master's, GRE, minimum undergraduate GPA of 3.0, statement of purpose, two letters of recommendation; for doctorate, GRE, minimum undergraduate and graduate GPA of 3.25, statement of purpose, writing sample, three letters of recommendation. Additional exam requirements/recommendations for international students: Required—TOEFL. *Application deadline:* For fall admission, 1/15 for domestic students; for spring admission, 10/15 for domestic students. Applications are processed on a rolling basis. Application fee: $35 ($60 for international students). Electronic applications accepted. *Expenses:* Contact institution. *Financial support:* In 2017–18, 123 students received support, including 16 research assistantships with full tuition reimbursements available (averaging $15,704 per year), 23 teaching assistantships with full tuition reimbursements available (averaging $22,076 per year); Federal Work-Study, scholarships/grants, and unspecified assistantships also available. Financial award application deadline: 2/1; financial award applicants required to submit FAFSA. *Faculty research:* Applied linguistics, British and American literature, professional writing, composition studies. *Unit head:* Dr. Joshua Phillips, Chair, 901-678-2651, Fax: 901-678-2226, E-mail: jsphllps@memphis.edu. *Application contact:* Dr. Jeffrey Scraba, Coordinator of Graduate Studies, 901-678-4768, Fax: 901-678-2226, E-mail: jscraba@memphis.edu.
Website: http://www.memphis.edu/english

University of Wisconsin–Madison, Graduate School, College of Letters and Science, Department of Afro-American Studies, Madison, WI 53706-1380. Offers MA. *Degree requirements:* For master's, thesis or alternative. *Entrance requirements:* For master's, bachelor's degree in related field, minimum GPA of 3.0. Additional exam requirements/recommendations for international students: Required—TOEFL. Electronic applications accepted. *Faculty research:* Afro American art, history, music, literature, and culture.

Wayne State University, College of Liberal Arts and Sciences, Department of History, Detroit, MI 48202. Offers history (MA, PhD); public history (MA), including African American history and culture, cultural resource management, gender, sexuality, and women's studies, labor and urban history, museum studies, public policy; world history (Graduate Certificate); JD/MA; M Ed/MA; MLIS/MA. Doctoral program admits for fall only. *Program availability:* Evening/weekend. *Faculty:* 17. *Students:* 21 full-time (7 women), 20 part-time (7 women); includes 9 minority (5 Black or African American, non-Hispanic/Latino; 1 Hispanic/Latino; 3 Two or more races, non-Hispanic/Latino). Average age 40. 50 applicants, 16% accepted, 5 enrolled. In 2017, 11 master's, 2 doctorates awarded. *Degree requirements:* For master's, comprehensive exam, thesis (for some programs), final oral exam on thesis or essay and seminar; internship and project (for public history); for doctorate, variable foreign language requirement, comprehensive exam, thesis/dissertation, qualifying exam in 4 fields of history. *Entrance requirements:* For master's, GRE General Test, minimum undergraduate GPA of 3.25 in history, 3.0 overall; at least 18 credits in history and related subjects at the advanced undergraduate level; foreign language; letter of intent; research paper; at least two letters of recommendation from former instructors; for doctorate, GRE General Test, minimum GPA of 3.0, 3.25 in minimum of 18 semester credits in history and related subjects; letter of intent; research paper; at least three letters of recommendation from former professors; for Graduate Certificate, baccalaureate degree from accredited college or university; minimum GPA of 3.0, 3.25 in a minimum of eighteen semester credits in history and related subjects at the advanced undergraduate level. Additional exam requirements/recommendations for international students: Required—TOEFL (minimum score 550 paper-based; 79 iBT), TWE (minimum score 5.5), Michigan English Language Assessment Battery (minimum score 85); Recommended—IELTS (minimum score 6.5). *Application deadline:* For fall admission, 2/1 priority date for domestic and international students; for winter admission, 11/1 for domestic students, 10/1 priority date for international students; for spring admission, 2/1 for domestic students, 1/1 priority date for international students. Application fee: $50. Electronic applications accepted. *Expenses:* Tuition, state resident: full-time $10,224; part-time $638.98 per credit hour. Tuition, nonresident: full-time $22,145; part-time $1384.04 per credit hour. Tuition and fees vary according to course load and program. *Financial support:* In 2017–18, 17 students received support, including 3 fellowships with tuition reimbursements available (averaging $17,198 per year), 1 research assistantship with tuition reimbursement available (averaging $22,241 per year), 6 teaching assistantships with tuition reimbursements available (averaging $18,534 per year); scholarships/grants, health care benefits, and unspecified assistantships also available. Financial award applicants required to submit FAFSA. *Faculty research:* Urban history, labor, political history, history of gender and women. *Unit head:* Dr. Elizabeth V. Faue, Professor/Chair, 313-577-2525, E-mail: evfaue@wayne.edu. *Application contact:* Dr. Eric Ash, Associate Professor and Director of Graduate Studies, 313-577-2525, E-mail: ericash@wayne.edu.
Website: http://clas.wayne.edu/history/

Yale University, Graduate School of Arts and Sciences, Interdisciplinary Program in African-American Studies, New Haven, CT 06520. Offers PhD. *Entrance requirements:* For doctorate, GRE General Test.

African Studies

Arizona State University at the Tempe campus, College of Liberal Arts and Sciences, School of Social Transformation, Tempe, AZ 85287-4902. Offers African studies (Graduate Certificate); gender studies (PhD, Graduate Certificate); justice studies (MS, PhD); social and cultural pedagogy (MA); socio-economic justice (Graduate Certificate); PhD/JD. *Program availability:* Part-time. Terminal master's awarded for partial completion of doctoral program. *Degree requirements:* For master's, thesis or alternative, interactive Program of Study (iPOS) submitted before completing 50 percent of required credit hours; for doctorate, comprehensive exam, thesis/dissertation, interactive Program of Study (iPOS) submitted before completing 50 percent of required credit hours. *Entrance requirements:* For master's, GRE or LSAT, minimum GPA of 3.0 or equivalent in last 2 years of work leading to bachelor's degree; for doctorate, GRE or LSAT (for justice studies program), minimum GPA of 3.0 or equivalent in last 2 years of work leading to bachelor's degree. Additional exam requirements/recommendations for international students: Required—TOEFL, IELTS, or PTE. Electronic applications accepted.

California State University, Long Beach, Graduate Studies, College of Liberal Arts, Department of History, Long Beach, CA 90840. Offers Africa and the Middle East (MA). *Program availability:* Part-time, evening/weekend. *Degree requirements:* For master's, one foreign language, comprehensive exam or thesis. Electronic applications accepted. *Faculty research:* All periods of European and American history, recent Asian and African history.

Carnegie Mellon University, Dietrich College of Humanities and Social Sciences, Department of History, Pittsburgh, PA 15213-3891. Offers African and African-American diaspora (PhD); culture and power (PhD); labor, politics and social movements (PhD); technology, environment, science and health (PhD); women, gender and the family (PhD). *Program availability:* Part-time. *Degree requirements:* For doctorate, oral and written comprehensive exams, dissertation defense. *Entrance requirements:* For doctorate, GRE General Test. Additional exam requirements/recommendations for international students: Required—TOEFL. Electronic applications accepted. *Faculty research:* Anthropology and history, African-American history, technology/environment, cultural history analysis.

Claremont Graduate University, Graduate Programs, School of Arts and Humanities, Department of History, Claremont, CA 91711-6160. Offers Africana history (Certificate); American studies and U.S. history (MA, PhD); archival studies (MA); early modern studies (MA, PhD); European studies (MA, PhD); oral history (MA, PhD); MBA/MA; MBA/PhD. Terminal master's awarded for partial completion of doctoral program. *Entrance requirements:* For master's and doctorate, GRE General Test. Additional exam requirements/recommendations for international students: Required—TOEFL (minimum score 75 iBT). Electronic applications accepted. *Faculty research:* Intellectual and social history, cultural studies, gender studies, Western history, Chicano history.

Claremont Graduate University, Graduate Programs, School of Educational Studies, Claremont, CA 91711-6160. Offers Africana education (Certificate); education and policy (MA, PhD); higher education/student affairs (MA, PhD); human development (MA, PhD); public school administration (MA, PhD); quantitative evaluation (MA, PhD); special education (MA, PhD); teacher education (MA); teaching and learning (MA, PhD); urban leadership (PhD); MBA/PhD. PhD program offered jointly with San Diego State University. *Program availability:* Part-time. Terminal master's awarded for partial completion of doctoral program. *Entrance requirements:* For master's and doctorate, GRE General Test. Additional exam requirements/recommendations for international students: Required—TOEFL (minimum score 75 iBT). Electronic applications accepted. *Faculty research:* Education administration, K-12 and higher education, multicultural education, education policy, diversity in higher education, faculty issues.

College of Staten Island of the City University of New York, Graduate Programs, Division of Humanities and Social Sciences, Program in History, Staten Island, NY 10314-6600. Offers history (MA), including Africa and the Middle East, Asia, Europe, Latin America and the Caribbean, United States. *Program availability:* Part-time, evening/weekend. *Faculty:* 2 full-time (1 woman). *Students:* 18. 19 applicants, 79% accepted, 11 enrolled. In 2017, 3 master's awarded. *Degree requirements:* For master's, comprehensive exam (for some programs), 32 credits (total of eight courses); thesis or portfolio. *Entrance requirements:* For master's, bachelor's degree with minimum GPA of 3.0 overall and in undergraduate history courses, two letters of recommendation, letter of interest, research-based writing sample. Additional exam requirements/recommendations for international students: Required—TOEFL (minimum score 550 paper-based; 79 iBT), IELTS (minimum score 6.5). *Application deadline:* For fall admission, 5/10 priority date for domestic and international students; for spring admission, 12/2 priority date for domestic and international students. Applications are processed on a rolling basis. Application fee: $125. Electronic applications accepted. *Expenses:* Tuition, state resident: full-time $10,450; part-time $440 per credit. Tuition, nonresident: full-time $19,320; part-time $440 per credit. *Required fees:* $181.10 per semester. Tuition and fees vary according to program. *Faculty research:* African and African diaspora history, South Asian history, Middle Eastern history, U.S. history, environmental history. *Unit head:* Dr. John Dixon, Graduate Program Coordinator, 718-982-3307, E-mail: john.dixon@csi.cuny.edu. *Application contact:* Sasha Spence, Associate Director for Graduate Admissions, 718-982-2019, Fax: 718-982-2500, E-mail: sasha.spence@csi.cuny.edu.
Website: https://www.csi.cuny.edu/sites/default/files/pdf/admissions/grad/pdf/History%20Fact%20Sheet.pdf

Columbia University, Graduate School of Arts and Sciences, New York, NY 10027. Offers African-American studies (MA); American studies (MA); anthropology (MA, PhD); art history and archaeology (MA, PhD); astronomy (PhD); biological sciences (PhD); biotechnology (MA); chemical physics (PhD); chemistry (PhD); classical studies (MA, PhD); classics (MA, PhD); climate and society (MA); conservation biology (MA); earth and environmental sciences (PhD); East Asia: regional studies (MA); East Asian languages and cultures (MA, PhD); ecology, evolution and environmental biology (MA), including conservation biology; ecology, evolution, and environmental biology (PhD), including ecology and evolutionary biology, evolutionary primatology; economics (MA, PhD); English and comparative literature (MA, PhD); French and Romance philology (MA, PhD); Germanic languages (MA, PhD); global French studies (MA); global thought (MA); Hispanic cultural studies (MA); history (PhD); history and literature (MA); human rights studies (MA); Islamic studies (MA); Italian (MA, PhD); Japanese pedagogy (MA); Jewish studies (MA); Latin America and the Caribbean: regional studies (MA); Latin American and Iberian cultures (PhD); mathematics (MA, PhD), including finance (MA);

medieval and Renaissance studies (MA); Middle Eastern, South Asian, and African studies (MA, PhD); modern art: critical and curatorial studies (MA); modern European studies (MA); museum anthropology (MA); music (DMA, PhD); oral history (MA); philosophical foundations of physics (MA); philosophy (MA, PhD); physics (PhD); political science (MA, PhD); psychology (PhD); quantitative methods in the social sciences (MA); religion (MA, PhD); Russia, Eurasia and East Europe: regional studies (MA); Russian translation (MA); Slavic cultures (MA); Slavic languages (MA, PhD); sociology (MA, PhD); South Asian studies (MA); statistics (MA, PhD); theatre (PhD). Dual-degree programs require admission to both Graduate School of Arts and Sciences and another Columbia school. *Program availability:* Part-time. Terminal master's awarded for partial completion of doctoral program. *Degree requirements:* For master's, variable foreign language requirement, comprehensive exam (for some programs), thesis (for some programs); for doctorate, variable foreign language requirement, comprehensive exam (for some programs), thesis/dissertation. *Entrance requirements:* For master's and doctorate, GRE General Test, GRE Subject Test (for some programs). Additional exam requirements/recommendations for international students: Required—TOEFL, IELTS. Electronic applications accepted. *Expenses: Tuition:* Full-time $44,864; part-time $1704 per credit. *Required fees:* $2370 per semester. One-time fee: $105.

Cornell University, Graduate School, Graduate Fields of Arts and Sciences, Field of African and African-American Studies, Ithaca, NY 14853. Offers African studies (MPS); African-American studies (MPS); Africana studies (PhD). *Degree requirements:* For master's, thesis. *Entrance requirements:* For master's, GRE General Test (recommended), 3 letters of recommendation; for doctorate, GRE General Test (recommended), 3 letters of recommendation, personal statement, writing sample. Additional exam requirements/recommendations for international students: Required—TOEFL (minimum score 550 paper-based; 77 iBT). Electronic applications accepted. *Faculty research:* African-American literature, art, cinema and theater; African-American politics and public policy; African history, politics and art; Caribbean politics and Africana diaspora.

Cornell University, Graduate School, Graduate Fields of Arts and Sciences, Field of History, Ithaca, NY 14853. Offers African history (MA, PhD); American history (MA, PhD); ancient Greek history (PhD); ancient history (MA, PhD); ancient Roman history (PhD); early modern European history (MA, PhD); English history (MA, PhD); French history (MA, PhD); German history (MA, PhD); history of science (MA, PhD); Korean history (PhD); Latin American history (MA, PhD); medieval Chinese history (MA, PhD); medieval history (MA, PhD); modern Chinese history (MA, PhD); modern European history (MA, PhD); modern Japanese history (MA, PhD); modern Middle Eastern history (PhD); premodern Islamic history (MA, PhD); premodern Japanese history (MA, PhD); Renaissance history (MA, PhD); Russian history (MA, PhD); South Asian history (PhD); Southeast Asian history (MA, PhD). Terminal master's awarded for partial completion of doctoral program. *Degree requirements:* For master's, thesis; for doctorate, 2 foreign languages, comprehensive exam, thesis/dissertation, 1 year of teaching experience. *Entrance requirements:* For master's and doctorate, GRE General Test, writing sample, 3 letters of recommendation. Additional exam requirements/recommendations for international students: Required—TOEFL (minimum score 550 paper-based; 77 iBT). Electronic applications accepted.

Florida International University, Steven J. Green School of International and Public Affairs, Program in African and African Diaspora Studies, Miami, FL 33199. Offers MA, MA/PhD. *Program availability:* Part-time, evening/weekend. *Faculty:* 2 part-time/adjunct (1 woman). *Students:* 4 full-time (3 women), 1 (woman) part-time; includes 4 minority (3 Black or African American, non-Hispanic/Latino; 1 Two or more races, non-Hispanic/Latino), 1 international. Average age 30. 10 applicants, 50% accepted, 4 enrolled. In 2017, 3 master's awarded. Terminal master's awarded for partial completion of doctoral program. *Degree requirements:* For master's, one foreign language, thesis optional, minimum GPA of 3.0. *Entrance requirements:* For master's, GRE General Test, BA with minimum GPA of 3.0, 2 letters of recommendation, examples of written work. Additional exam requirements/recommendations for international students: Required—TOEFL (minimum score 80 iBT). *Application deadline:* For fall admission, 2/1 for domestic and international students; for spring admission, 10/1 for domestic students, 9/1 for international students. Application fee: $30. Electronic applications accepted. *Expenses:* Tuition, state resident: full-time $8912; part-time $446 per credit hour. Tuition, nonresident: full-time $21,393; part-time $992 per credit hour. *Required fees:* $390; $195 per semester. *Financial support:* Institutionally sponsored loans, scholarships/grants, and unspecified assistantships available. Financial award application deadline: 3/1; financial award applicants required to submit FAFSA. *Faculty research:* African diaspora in Latin America, Haitian Creole phonology and culture, racial/ethnic minority sexual health, African-American labor and southern history, gendered perspective of the development of racial science. *Unit head:* Dr. Percy Hintzen, Director, 305-348-2247, Fax: 305-348-3270, E-mail: percy.hintzen@fiu.edu. *Application contact:* Nanett Rojas, Manager, Admissions Operations, 305-348-7464, Fax: 305-348-7441, E-mail: gradadm@fiu.edu.

Harvard University, Graduate School of Arts and Sciences, Department of African and African American Studies, Cambridge, MA 02138. Offers PhD.

Howard University, Graduate School, Department of African Studies, Washington, DC 20059-0002. Offers MA, PhD. *Program availability:* Part-time. *Degree requirements:* For master's, one foreign language, comprehensive exam, thesis, internship; for doctorate, 2 foreign languages, comprehensive exam, thesis/dissertation, field research for some. *Entrance requirements:* For master's, GRE General Test, minimum GPA of 3.0; for doctorate, GRE General Test, minimum GPA of 3.5. Electronic applications accepted. *Faculty research:* African literature and film, economics of Africa, international relations, public policy analysis, gender.

Indiana University Bloomington, University Graduate School, College of Arts and Sciences, School of Global and International Studies, African Studies Program, Bloomington, IN 47408. Offers MA. *Entrance requirements:* Additional exam requirements/recommendations for international students: Required—TOEFL. Electronic applications accepted.

Lehigh University, College of Arts and Sciences, Program in American Studies, Bethlehem, PA 18015. Offers Africana studies (Graduate Certificate); American studies (MA); documentary film (Graduate Certificate). *Faculty:* 3 full-time (2 women), 1 part-time/adjunct (0 women). *Students:* 3 full-time (all women), 3 part-time (2 women); includes 1 minority (Black or African American, non-Hispanic/Latino). Average age 26. 6 applicants, 100% accepted, 3 enrolled. In 2017, 3 master's awarded. *Degree requirements:* For master's, thesis. *Entrance requirements:* For master's, GRE, writing sample, essay, minimum GPA of 2.75, 2 letters of recommendation. Additional exam requirements/recommendations for international students: Required—TOEFL (minimum score 85 iBT), IELTS (minimum score 6.5). *Application deadline:* For fall admission, 1/1 for domestic students, 7/15 for international students; for spring admission, 12/1 for domestic and international students. Applications are processed on a rolling basis. Application fee: $75. *Expenses:* $1,460 per credit. *Financial support:* Fellowships and tuition remission available. Financial award application deadline: 1/1. *Faculty research:* War; media and video games; social movements; community identity and narrative; traditional eighteenth-, nineteenth-, and twentieth-century literature and history; gender and popular culture. *Unit head:* Prof. Jodi Eichler-Levine, Director, 610-758-3370, Fax: 610-758-2131, E-mail: amstdgrad@lehigh.edu. *Application contact:* Gary Burgess, Graduate Coordinator, 610-758-4281, Fax: 610-758-6554, E-mail: amstdgrad@lehigh.edu.
Website: http://american.cas2.lehigh.edu/

Michigan State University, The Graduate School, College of Arts and Letters, Program in African American and African Studies, East Lansing, MI 48824. Offers MA, PhD. *Entrance requirements:* Additional exam requirements/recommendations for international students: Required—TOEFL. Electronic applications accepted. *Faculty research:* Black American and diasporic studies, comparative communities of color.

New York University, Graduate School of Arts and Science, Department of History, New York, NY 10012-1019. Offers African diaspora (PhD); African history (PhD); archival management (Advanced Certificate); Atlantic history (PhD); French studies/history (PhD); Hebrew and Judaic studies/history (PhD); history (MA, PhD), including Europe (PhD), Latin America and the Caribbean (PhD), United States (PhD), women's history (MA); Middle Eastern history (MA); Middle Eastern studies/history (PhD); public history (Advanced Certificate); world history (MA); JD/MA; MA/Advanced Certificate. *Program availability:* Part-time. *Students:* Average age 29. 401 applicants, 31% accepted, 38 enrolled. In 2017, 24 master's, 16 doctorates awarded. Terminal master's awarded for partial completion of doctoral program. *Degree requirements:* For master's, seminar paper; for doctorate, one foreign language, thesis/dissertation, oral and written exams; for Advanced Certificate, internship. *Entrance requirements:* For master's, GRE General Test, minimum GPA of 3.0, writing sample; for doctorate, GRE. Additional exam requirements/recommendations for international students: Required—TOEFL. *Application deadline:* For fall admission, 12/18 for domestic and international students. Application fee: $100. *Expenses: Tuition:* Full-time $41,352; part-time $19,968 per year. *Required fees:* $2496; $1628 per unit. $814 per term. Tuition and fees vary according to course load and program. *Financial support:* Fellowships, research assistantships, teaching assistantships, career-related internships or fieldwork, Federal Work-Study, institutionally sponsored loans, scholarships/grants, health care benefits, and unspecified assistantships available. Financial award application deadline: 12/18; financial award applicants required to submit FAFSA. *Faculty research:* African, East Asian, medieval, early modern, and modern European history; U.S. history; African and African diaspora; Latin American history; Atlantic world. *Unit head:* Barbara Weinstein, Chair, 212-998-8600, Fax: 212-995-4017, E-mail: history.admissions@nyu.edu. *Application contact:* Stepfanos Geroulanos, Director of Graduate Studies, 212-998-8600, Fax: 212-995-4017, E-mail: history.admissions@nyu.edu.
Website: http://history.as.nyu.edu/

New York University, Graduate School of Arts and Science, Program in Africana Studies, New York, NY 10012-1019. Offers MA. *Students:* Average age 27. 20 applicants, 70% accepted, 3 enrolled. In 2017, 5 master's awarded. *Entrance requirements:* For master's, GRE, sample of written work. Additional exam requirements/recommendations for international students: Required—TOEFL. *Application deadline:* For fall admission, 1/4 for domestic and international students. Application fee: $95. *Expenses: Tuition:* Full-time $41,352; part-time $19,968 per year. *Required fees:* $2496; $1628 per unit. $814 per term. Tuition and fees vary according to course load and program. *Financial support:* Fellowships, Federal Work-Study, and institutionally sponsored loans available. Financial award application deadline: 1/4; financial award applicants required to submit FAFSA. *Faculty research:* Pan-Africanism, black urban studies, film and literature of black Diaspora, cultural politics and theory, politics of identity. *Unit head:* Renee Blake, Director, 212-992-9650, Fax: 212-995-4665, E-mail: africana@nyu.edu. *Application contact:* Raechel Bosch, Graduate Administrator, 212-998-9650, Fax: 212-995-4665, E-mail: africana@nyu.edu.
Website: http://www.nyu.edu/gsas/dept/africana/

New York University, Graduate School of Arts and Science, Program in Museum Studies, New York, NY 10012-1019. Offers museum studies (MA, Advanced Certificate), including Africana studies (MA), Hebrew and Judaic studies (MA), Latin American and Caribbean studies (MA), Near Eastern studies (MA). *Program availability:* Part-time, evening/weekend. *Students:* Average age 26. 123 applicants, 81% accepted, 29 enrolled. In 2017, 35 master's, 1 other advanced degree awarded. *Entrance requirements:* For master's, GRE General Test; for Advanced Certificate, master's degree or PhD. Additional exam requirements/recommendations for international students: Required—TOEFL. *Application deadline:* For fall admission, 2/15 for domestic and international students; for spring admission, 11/1 for domestic and international students. Application fee: $100. *Expenses: Tuition:* Full-time $41,352; part-time $19,968 per year. *Required fees:* $2496; $1628 per unit. $814 per term. Tuition and fees vary according to course load and program. *Financial support:* Application deadline: 2/15. *Faculty research:* Modern and contemporary art, history of museums and exhibitions, conservation of cultural materials, museum anthropology, ethnography. *Unit head:* Bruce Altshuler, Director, 212-998-8080, Fax: 212-995-4185, E-mail: museum.studies@nyu.edu. *Application contact:* Tatiana Kamorina, Department Administrator, 212-998-8080, Fax: 212-995-4185, E-mail: museum.studies@nyu.edu.
Website: http://www.nyu.edu/fas/program/museumstudies/

Northwestern University, The Graduate School, Judd A. and Marjorie Weinberg College of Arts and Sciences, Program of African Studies, Evanston, IL 60208. Offers Graduate Certificate. *Degree requirements:* For Graduate Certificate, one foreign language. *Faculty research:* Collapsing states in Africa, HIV/AIDS in Africa, Islam in Africa, African philosophy.

The Ohio State University, Graduate School, College of Arts and Sciences, Division of Arts and Humanities, Department of African-American and African Studies, Columbus, OH 43210. Offers MA, PhD. *Faculty:* 12. *Students:* 16 (11 women). Average age 28. In 2017, 2 master's awarded. *Degree requirements:* For master's, comprehensive exam (for some programs), thesis (for some programs), thesis or comprehensive written examination; for doctorate, thesis/dissertation. *Entrance requirements:* For master's and doctorate, GRE General Test. Additional exam requirements/recommendations for international students: Required—TOEFL (minimum score 550 paper-based; 79 iBT), Michigan English Language Assessment Battery (minimum score 82); Recommended—IELTS (minimum score 7). *Application deadline:* For fall admission, 12/1 priority date for domestic students, 11/30 priority date for international students; for spring admission, 3/1 for domestic students, 2/1 for international students. Applications are processed on a rolling basis. Application fee: $60 ($70 for international students). Electronic applications accepted. *Financial support:* Fellowships with tuition reimbursements, research assistantships with tuition reimbursements, teaching assistantships with tuition reimbursements, Federal Work-Study, institutionally sponsored loans, and unspecified assistantships available. Support available to part-time students. *Unit head:* Valerie Lee, Interim Chair, 614-292-0116, E-mail: lee.89@osu.edu. *Application contact:* Graduate and Professional Admissions, 614-292-9444, Fax: 614-292-3895, E-mail: gpadmissions@osu.edu.
Website: http://aaas.osu.edu/

Ohio University, Graduate College, Center for International Studies, Program in African Studies, Athens, OH 45701. Offers MA. *Program availability:* Part-time. *Degree requirements:* For master's, one foreign language, thesis optional. *Entrance requirements:* For master's, minimum GPA of 3.0. Additional exam requirements/recommendations for international students: Required—TOEFL (minimum score 550 paper-based; 80 iBT), IELTS (minimum score 6.5). *Faculty research:* African social sciences and the humanities.

African Studies

Rice University, Graduate Programs, School of Humanities, Department of Religious Studies, Houston, TX 77251-1892. Offers African religions (PhD); African-American religions (PhD); contemplative studies (PhD); ghosticism, esotericism, mysticism (PhD); Islam (PhD); Jewish thought and philosophy (PhD); modern Christianity in thought and popular culture (PhD); psychology of religion (PhD); the Bible and beyond (PhD). *Degree requirements:* For doctorate, 2 foreign languages, comprehensive exam, thesis/dissertation. *Entrance requirements:* For doctorate, GRE, letters of recommendation, writing sample. Additional exam requirements/recommendations for international students: Required—TOEFL (minimum score 600 paper-based; 90 iBT). Electronic applications accepted. *Faculty research:* Origins and historical development of Islam, history of Christianity, the study of comparative religion, African-American religion, religion and culture.

Rutgers University–New Brunswick, Graduate School-New Brunswick, Program in History, Piscataway, NJ 08854-8097. Offers African-American history (PhD); early American history (PhD); early modern European history (PhD); east Asian history (PhD); global and comparative history (PhD); history (PhD); history of diplomacy and foreign relations (PhD); history of technology, environment and health (PhD); history of the Atlantic cultures and African diaspora (PhD); Latin American history (PhD); medieval history (PhD); modern European history (PhD); nineteenth and twentieth century American history (PhD); women's and gender history (PhD). *Degree requirements:* For doctorate, thesis/dissertation. *Entrance requirements:* For doctorate, GRE General Test, sample of written work. Electronic applications accepted. *Faculty research:* American history, European history, Afro-American history, women's history, Latin American history.

Stony Brook University, State University of New York, Graduate School, College of Arts and Sciences, Department of Africana Studies, Stony Brook, NY 11794. Offers MA, Certificate. *Faculty:* 7 full-time (3 women), 1 (woman) part-time/adjunct. *Students:* 1 (woman) full-time, 1 (woman) part-time; includes 1 minority (Black or African American, non-Hispanic/Latino). Average age 35. *Degree requirements:* For master's, research thesis project, research seminar. *Entrance requirements:* For master's, GRE General Test, minimum GPA of 3.0, 3 letters of recommendation, bachelor's degree with minimum GPA of 3.0 in all social science and humanities courses. Additional exam requirements/recommendations for international students: Required—TOEFL (minimum score 85 iBT). *Application deadline:* For fall admission, 1/15 for domestic students; for spring admission, 10/1 for domestic students. Application fee: $100. *Expenses:* Contact institution. *Financial support:* Teaching assistantships available. *Faculty research:* Ethnic studies, humanities, African studies, African-American studies, African-Americans. *Unit head:* Dr. Tracey L. Walters, Chair, 631-632-7470, E-mail: tracey.walters@stonybrook.edu. *Application contact:* Ann Berrios, Coordinator, 631-632-7470, Fax: 631-632-7794, E-mail: ann.berrios@stonybrook.edu.
Website: http://www.stonybrook.edu/commcms/africana-studies//

Syracuse University, College of Arts and Sciences, MA Program in Pan-African Studies, Syracuse, NY 13244. Offers MA. *Students:* Average age 30. *Degree requirements:* For master's, thesis. *Entrance requirements:* For master's, GRE General Test (recommended), personal statement, resume, three letters of recommendation, writing sample (10-12 pages), transcripts. Additional exam requirements/recommendations for international students: Required—TOEFL (minimum score 600 paper-based; 100 iBT). *Application deadline:* For fall admission, 1/10 priority date for domestic and international students. Application fee: $75. Electronic applications accepted. *Financial support:* Fellowships with tuition reimbursements, teaching assistantships with tuition reimbursements, and scholarships/grants available. Financial award application deadline: 1/1. *Faculty research:* African American studies, African American history, Francophone African/Caribbean literatures, African archaeology. *Unit head:* Dr. Herbert G. Ruffin, II, Associate Professor, History/Chair of African American Studies, 315-443-3005, E-mail: hruffin@syr.edu. *Application contact:* Ajajielle Brown, Administrative Assistant, 315-443-5599, E-mail: aabrow02@syr.edu.
Website: http://aas.syr.edu/graduate/program-description.html

University at Albany, State University of New York, College of Arts and Sciences, Department of Africana Studies, Albany, NY 12222-0001. Offers African studies (MA); Afro-American studies (MA). *Program availability:* Part-time, evening/weekend. *Faculty:* 5 full-time (2 women). *Students:* 13 full-time (9 women), 7 part-time (5 women); includes 13 minority (10 Black or African American, non-Hispanic/Latino; 1 Hispanic/Latino; 2 Two or more races, non-Hispanic/Latino). 13 applicants, 92% accepted, 8 enrolled. In 2017, 5 master's awarded. *Entrance requirements:* Additional exam requirements/recommendations for international students: Required—TOEFL (minimum score 550 paper-based). *Application deadline:* For fall admission, 5/15 for international students; for spring admission, 11/1 for international students. Applications are processed on a rolling basis. Application fee: $75. Electronic applications accepted. *Expenses:* Tuition, state resident: full-time $10,870; part-time $453 per credit hour. Tuition, nonresident: full-time $22,210; part-time $925 per credit hour. *Required fees:* $84.68 per credit hour. $508.06 per semester. Part-time tuition and fees vary according to course load and program. *Financial support:* Fellowships, teaching assistantships, and Federal Work-Study available. Financial award application deadline: 5/1. *Faculty research:* The Black family, Afro-centricity in poetry, black women in U.S. literature, African economic development, African American history. *Unit head:* Oscar Williams, Chair, 518-442-4730, Fax: 518-442-2569, E-mail: owilliams@albany.edu. *Application contact:* Michael DeRensis, Director, Graduate Admissions, 518-442-3980, Fax: 518-442-3922, E-mail: graduate@albany.edu.
Website: http://www.albany.edu/africana/

The University of Arizona, College of Social and Behavioral Sciences, School of Middle Eastern and North African Studies, Tucson, AZ 85721. Offers MA, PhD, Graduate Certificate. *Program availability:* Part-time, evening/weekend. Terminal master's awarded for partial completion of doctoral program. *Degree requirements:* For master's, one foreign language; for doctorate, 3 foreign languages, thesis/dissertation. *Entrance requirements:* For master's, GRE General Test, 3 letters of recommendation, statement of purpose, curriculum vitae, writing sample; for doctorate, GRE General Test, 3 letters of recommendation, curriculum vitae, writing sample. Additional exam requirements/recommendations for international students: Required—TOEFL (minimum score 550 paper-based; 79 iBT). Electronic applications accepted.

University of California, Los Angeles, Graduate Division, International Institute, Interdepartmental Program in African Studies, Los Angeles, CA 90095. Offers MA, MPH/MA. *Degree requirements:* For master's, one foreign language, comprehensive exam or thesis. *Entrance requirements:* For master's, GRE General Test, bachelor's degree; minimum undergraduate GPA of 3.0 (or its equivalent if letter grade system not used); writing sample. Additional exam requirements/recommendations for international students: Required—TOEFL. Electronic applications accepted.

University of Illinois at Urbana–Champaign, Graduate College, College of Liberal Arts and Sciences, Center for African Studies, Champaign, IL 61820. Offers MA, MA/MS.

The University of Kansas, Graduate Studies, College of Liberal Arts and Sciences, Department of African and African-American Studies, Lawrence, KS 66045. Offers African and African-American studies (MA); African studies (Graduate Certificate). *Program availability:* Part-time. *Students:* 9 full-time (7 women), 1 part-time (0 women); includes 6 minority (3 Black or African American, non-Hispanic/Latino; 3 Two or more races, non-Hispanic/Latino). Average age 29. 7 applicants, 100% accepted, 5 enrolled. In 2017, 9 master's awarded. *Entrance requirements:* For master's, GRE, all academic transcripts, 3 letters of recommendation, personal statement of purpose, writing sample. Additional exam requirements/recommendations for international students: Required—TOEFL, IELTS. *Application deadline:* For fall admission, 5/1 for domestic and international students; for spring admission, 10/1 for domestic and international students. Application fee: $65 ($85 for international students). Electronic applications accepted. *Financial support:* Application deadline: 4/15. *Faculty research:* African theatre, YaKuur culture, interracial communication, African development and urban planning, African literature, Muslim women in West Africa, identity formation in African and Diasporan settings, African-American history, North African and Arab societies, civil rights, black urban communities. *Unit head:* Dr. Lang Clarence, Chairperson, 785-864-3054, E-mail: celang@ku.edu. *Application contact:* Shawn Alexander, Director of Graduate Studies, 785-864-3054, E-mail: slalexan@ku.edu.
Website: http://www.afs.ku.edu

University of Louisville, Graduate School, College of Arts and Sciences, Department of Pan-African Studies, Louisville, KY 40292. Offers African and Diaspora studies (MA); African-American studies (MA); MSSW/MA. *Program availability:* Part-time. *Faculty:* 11 full-time (6 women), 2 part-time/adjunct (1 woman). *Students:* 18 full-time (13 women), 7 part-time (5 women); includes 24 minority (20 Black or African American, non-Hispanic/Latino; 1 Hispanic/Latino; 3 Two or more races, non-Hispanic/Latino), 1 international. Average age 33. 18 applicants, 56% accepted, 6 enrolled. *Degree requirements:* For master's, comprehensive exam, thesis optional. *Entrance requirements:* For master's, GRE General Test. Additional exam requirements/recommendations for international students: Required—TOEFL (minimum score 550 paper-based; 79 iBT). *Application deadline:* For fall admission, 3/15 for domestic students, 5/1 priority date for international students; for spring admission, 10/15 for domestic students, 11/1 priority date for international students; for summer admission, 4/1 priority date for international students. Applications are processed on a rolling basis. Application fee: $65. Electronic applications accepted. *Expenses:* Tuition, state resident: full-time $12,246; part-time $681 per credit hour. Tuition, nonresident: full-time $25,486; part-time $1417 per credit hour. *Required fees:* $196. Tuition and fees vary according to course load, program and reciprocity agreements. *Financial support:* Teaching assistantships available. Financial award application deadline: 3/3; financial award applicants required to submit FAFSA. *Faculty research:* African popular culture, black male identity development, education and retention, contemporary politics in Nigeria, poverty in the Caribbean. *Total annual research expenditures:* $72,938. *Unit head:* Dr. Ricky L. Jones, Chair, 502-852-0027, E-mail: ricky.jones@louisville.edu. *Application contact:* Latonia Craig, Director of Graduate Recruitment and Diversity Retention, 502-852-5207, E-mail: gradadm@louisville.edu.
Website: http://www.louisville.edu/panafricanstudies

University of Michigan, Rackham Graduate School, College of Literature, Science, and the Arts, Center for Middle Eastern and North African Studies, Ann Arbor, MI 48109-1106. Offers AM, JD/AM, MBA/AM. *Program availability:* Part-time. *Faculty:* 78 full-time (24 women), 1 (woman) part-time/adjunct. *Students:* 11 full-time (7 women); includes 2 minority (1 Black or African American, non-Hispanic/Latino; 1 Asian, non-Hispanic/Latino). Average age 30. 20 applicants, 75% accepted, 5 enrolled. In 2017, 3 master's awarded. *Degree requirements:* For master's, one foreign language, thesis or alternative. *Entrance requirements:* For master's, GRE General Test. Additional exam requirements/recommendations for international students: Required—TOEFL (minimum score 560 paper-based; 84 iBT). *Application deadline:* For fall admission, 12/15 for domestic and international students. Application fee: $75 ($90 for international students). Electronic applications accepted. *Expenses:* Tuition, state resident: full-time $22,368; part-time $1201 per credit hour. Tuition, nonresident: full-time $45,156; part-time $2467 per credit hour. *Required fees:* $376 per term. Tuition and fees vary according to course load, degree level and program. *Financial support:* In 2017–18, 4 students received support, including 4 fellowships with tuition reimbursements available (averaging $15,000 per year); teaching assistantships, career-related internships or fieldwork, Federal Work-Study, scholarships/grants, health care benefits, and Richard P. Mitchell Memorial Prize also available. Support available to part-time students. Financial award application deadline: 1/15; financial award applicants required to submit FAFSA. *Faculty research:* Middle East and North Africa. *Unit head:* Dr. Samer Mahdy Ali, Director, 734-764-1401, E-mail: ii-gradadvising@umich.edu. *Application contact:* Julie E. Burnett, Graduate Academic Services Coordinator, 734-936-1842, Fax: 734-615-9158, E-mail: ii-gradadvising@umich.edu.
Website: https://www.ii.umich.edu/cmenas/

The University of North Carolina at Charlotte, College of Liberal Arts and Sciences, Department of Africana Studies, Charlotte, NC 28223-0001. Offers Graduate Certificate. *Program availability:* Part-time. *Faculty:* 6 full-time (3 women). *Students:* 2 part-time (both women); both minorities (both Black or African American, non-Hispanic/Latino). Average age 35. 1 applicant, 100% accepted. *Entrance requirements:* For degree, bachelor's degree from accredited university with minimum cumulative GPA of 3.0 or enrolled and in good standing in a graduate degree program at UNC Charlotte; official transcripts; two-page statement of purpose explaining applicant's educational and work background, interests, and plans. Additional exam requirements/recommendations for international students: Required—TOEFL (minimum score 523 paper-based, 70 iBT) or IELTS (6.5). *Application deadline:* For fall admission, 3/1 priority date for domestic and international students; for spring admission, 10/1 priority date for domestic and international students; for summer admission, 4/1 priority date for domestic and international students. Applications are processed on a rolling basis. Application fee: $75. Electronic applications accepted. *Expenses:* Tuition, state resident: full-time $4337. Tuition, nonresident: full-time $17,771. *Required fees:* $3211. Tuition and fees vary according to course load and program. *Financial support:* Institutionally sponsored loans, scholarships/grants, and unspecified assistantships available. Support available to part-time students. Financial award application deadline: 3/1; financial award applicants required to submit FAFSA. *Total annual research expenditures:* $366. *Unit head:* Dr. Akin Ogundiran, Chair, 704-687-5161, E-mail: ogundiran@uncc.edu. *Application contact:* Kathy B. Giddings, Director of Graduate Admissions, 704-687-5503, Fax: 704-687-1668, E-mail: gradadm@uncc.edu.
Website: http://africana.uncc.edu/

University of Pennsylvania, School of Arts and Sciences, Program in Africana Studies, Philadelphia, PA 19104. Offers MA, PhD. *Faculty:* 17 full-time (12 women), 3 part-time/adjunct (1 woman). *Students:* 17 full-time (13 women); includes 13 minority (9 Black or African American, non-Hispanic/Latino; 1 Asian, non-Hispanic/Latino; 1 Hispanic/Latino; 2 Two or more races, non-Hispanic/Latino), 3 international. Average age 30. 57 applicants, 7% accepted, 3 enrolled.
Website: https://africana.sas.upenn.edu/

University of Pittsburgh, University Center for International Studies, Pittsburgh, PA 15260. Offers African studies (Certificate); Asian studies (Certificate); European Union studies (Certificate); global studies (Certificate); Latin American studies (Certificate); Russian and East European studies (Certificate); West European studies (Certificate).

Program availability: Part-time, evening/weekend, online learning. *Students:* 183 full-time (108 women), 9 part-time (all women); includes 78 minority (6 Black or African American, non-Hispanic/Latino; 23 Asian, non-Hispanic/Latino; 47 Hispanic/Latino; 2 Two or more races, non-Hispanic/Latino). Average age 29. *Degree requirements:* For Certificate, one foreign language, comprehensive exam (for some programs). *Entrance requirements:* Additional exam requirements/recommendations for international students: Required—TOEFL. *Expenses:* No tuition and fees. *Financial support:* In 2017–18, 25 fellowships with full tuition reimbursements (averaging $26,117 per year) were awarded; scholarships/grants, traineeships, health care benefits, and unspecified assistantships also available. *Unit head:* Dr. Ariel Armony, Director, 412-648-7374, Fax: 412-624-4672, E-mail: armony@pitt.edu.
Website: http://www.ucis.pitt.edu

University of South Florida, College of Arts and Sciences, School of Interdisciplinary Global Studies, Tampa, FL 33620-9951. Offers government (PhD); Latin American, Caribbean and Latino studies (MA); liberal arts (MA), including Africana studies; political science (MA), including comparative government and politics. *Accreditation:* NASPAA. *Program availability:* Part-time, evening/weekend. *Faculty:* 14 full-time (2 women). *Students:* 3 applicants. In 2017, 9 master's, 1 doctorate awarded. *Degree requirements:* For master's, comprehensive exam, thesis; for doctorate, comprehensive exam, thesis/dissertation. *Entrance requirements:* For master's, GRE General Test, minimum GPA of 3.0 in upper-division undergraduate course work; letters of recommendation (2 for MPA, 3 for MS); 500-word personal statement and undergraduate background in political science or related fields (for MS); one-page career statement (for MPA); for doctorate, GRE General Test, 500-word personal statement, three letters of recommendation, transcripts of MA/BA coursework, writing sample. Additional exam requirements/recommendations for international students: Required—TOEFL (minimum score 550 paper-based; 79 iBT) or IELTS (minimum score 6.5). *Application deadline:* For fall admission, 1/5 for domestic and international students; for spring admission, 10/15 for domestic students, 9/15 for international students. Applications are processed on a rolling basis. Application fee: $30. Electronic applications accepted. *Financial support:* In 2017–18, 3 students received support, including 18 teaching assistantships with tuition reimbursements available (averaging $12,390 per year); unspecified assistantships also available. Financial award application deadline: 4/1. *Faculty research:* Citizenship and identity, social movements, global governance, American politics, public policy. *Total annual research expenditures:* $195,426. *Unit head:* Dr. Steven Tauber, Associate Professor/Interim Chair, 813-974-2278, Fax: 813-974-0832, E-mail: stauber@usf.edu. *Application contact:* Dr. Bernd Reiter, Associate Professor and Director of Graduate Studies, 813-974-3583, Fax: 813-974-0832, E-mail: breiter@usf.edu.
Website: http://gia.usf.edu/

University of South Florida, Innovative Education, Tampa, FL 33620-9951. Offers adult, career and higher education (Graduate Certificate), including college teaching, leadership in developing human resources, leadership in higher education; Africana studies (Graduate Certificate), including diasporas and health disparities, genocide and human rights; aging studies (Graduate Certificate), including gerontology; art research (Graduate Certificate), including museum studies; business foundations (Graduate Certificate); chemical and biomedical engineering (Graduate Certificate), including materials science and engineering, water, health and sustainability; child and family studies (Graduate Certificate), including positive behavior support; civil and industrial engineering (Graduate Certificate), including transportation systems analysis; community and family health (Graduate Certificate), including maternal and child health, social marketing and public health, violence and injury: prevention and intervention, women's health; criminology (Graduate Certificate), including criminal justice administration; data science for public administration (Graduate Certificate); digital humanities (Graduate Certificate); educational measurement and research (Graduate Certificate), including evaluation; English (Graduate Certificate), including comparative literary studies, creative writing, professional and technical communication; entrepreneurship (Graduate Certificate); environmental health (Graduate Certificate), including safety management; epidemiology and biostatistics (Graduate Certificate), including applied biostatistics, biostatistics, concepts and tools of epidemiology, epidemiology, epidemiology of infectious diseases; geography, environment and planning (Graduate Certificate), including community development, environmental policy and management, geographical information systems; geology (Graduate Certificate), including hydrogeology; global health (Graduate Certificate), including disaster management, global health and Latin American and Caribbean studies, global health practice, humanitarian assistance, infection control; government and international affairs (Graduate Certificate), including Cuban studies, globalization studies; health policy and management (Graduate Certificate), including health management and leadership, public health policy and programs; hearing specialist: early intervention (Graduate Certificate); industrial and management systems engineering (Graduate Certificate), including systems engineering, technology management; information studies (Graduate Certificate), including school library media specialist; information systems/decision sciences (Graduate Certificate), including analytics and business intelligence; instructional technology (Graduate Certificate), including distance education, Florida digital/virtual educator, instructional design, multimedia design, Web design; internal medicine, bioethics and medical humanities (Graduate Certificate), including biomedical ethics; Latin American and Caribbean studies (Graduate Certificate); leadership for coastal resiliency planning (Graduate Certificate); mass communications (Graduate Certificate), including multimedia journalism; mathematics and statistics (Graduate Certificate), including mathematics; medicine (Graduate Certificate), including aging and neuroscience, bioinformatics, biotechnology, brain fitness and memory management, clinical investigation, hand and upper limb rehabilitation, health informatics, health sciences, integrative weight management, intellectual property, medicine and gender, metabolic and nutritional medicine, metabolic cardiology, pharmacy sciences; national and competitive intelligence (Graduate Certificate); nursing (Graduate Certificate), including simulation based academic fellowship in advanced pain management; psychological and social foundations (Graduate Certificate), including career counseling, college teaching, diversity in education, mental health counseling, school counseling; public affairs (Graduate Certificate), including nonprofit management, public management, research administration; public health (Graduate Certificate), including assessing chemical toxicity and public health risks, health equity, pharmacoepidemiology, public health generalist, toxicology, translational research in adolescent behavioral health; public health practices (Graduate Certificate), including planning for healthy communities; rehabilitation and mental health counseling (Graduate Certificate), including integrative mental health care, marriage and family therapy, rehabilitation technology; secondary education (Graduate Certificate), including ESOL, foreign language education: culture and content, foreign language education: professional; social work (Graduate Certificate), including geriatric social work/clinical gerontology; special education (Graduate Certificate), including autism spectrum disorder, disabilities education: severe/profound; world languages (Graduate Certificate), including teaching English as a second language (TESL) or foreign language. *Unit head:* Dr. Cynthia DeLuca, Associate Vice President and Assistant Vice Provost, 813-974-3077, Fax: 813-974-7061, E-mail: deluca@usf.edu. *Application contact:* Owen Hooper, Director, Summer and Alternative Calendar Programs, 813-974-6917, E-mail: hooper@usf.edu.
Website: http://www.usf.edu/innovative-education/

The University of Texas at Austin, Graduate School, College of Liberal Arts, John L. Warfield Center for African and African American Studies, Austin, TX 78712-1111. Offers African Diaspora studies (MA, PhD). *Program availability:* Part-time. *Degree requirements:* For master's, one foreign language, thesis. *Entrance requirements:* For master's, GRE General Test. Electronic applications accepted.

University of Wisconsin–Madison, Graduate School, College of Letters and Science, Department of African Languages and Literature, Madison, WI 53706-1380. Offers MA, PhD. *Program availability:* Part-time. *Degree requirements:* For master's, one foreign language, thesis; for doctorate, 2 foreign languages, comprehensive exam, thesis/dissertation. *Entrance requirements:* For master's, BA in African language and literature; for doctorate, MA in African language and literature. Electronic applications accepted. *Faculty research:* Oral traditions, language pedagogy, stylistics, sociolinguistics, literary criticism.

University of Wisconsin–Madison, Graduate School, College of Letters and Science, Department of History, Madison, WI 53706-1380. Offers African history (MA, PhD); Central Asian history (MA, PhD); comparative world history (MA, PhD); East Asian history (MA, PhD); European history (MA, PhD); gender and women's history (MA, PhD); Latin American and Caribbean history (MA, PhD); Middle Eastern history (MA, PhD); South Asian history (MA, PhD); Southeast Asian history (MA, PhD); United States history (MA, PhD). Terminal master's awarded for partial completion of doctoral program. *Degree requirements:* For master's, thesis (for some programs); for doctorate, variable foreign language requirement, thesis/dissertation. *Entrance requirements:* For master's and doctorate, GRE General Test. Additional exam requirements/recommendations for international students: Required—Michigan English Language Assessment Battery or TOEFL. Electronic applications accepted. *Faculty research:* American, African, European, Asian, Latin American, and Middle Eastern history.

University of Wisconsin–Milwaukee, Graduate School, College of Letters and Science, Department of Africology, Milwaukee, WI 53201-0413. Offers Africology (PhD), including culture and society: Africa and the African diaspora, political economy and public policy. *Program availability:* Part-time. *Students:* 5 full-time (3 women), 3 part-time (2 women); includes 7 minority (all Black or African American, non-Hispanic/Latino), 1 international. Average age 39. 15 applicants, 33% accepted, 3 enrolled. *Degree requirements:* For doctorate, comprehensive exam. *Entrance requirements:* For doctorate, GRE General Test. Additional exam requirements/recommendations for international students: Required—TOEFL (minimum score 550 paper-based; 79 iBT), IELTS (minimum score 6.5). Application fee: $56 ($96 for international students). Electronic applications accepted. *Financial support:* Fellowships, research assistantships, teaching assistantships, and unspecified assistantships available. *Unit head:* Erin N. Winkler, Department Chair, 414-229-5080, E-mail: winklere@uwm.edu. *Application contact:* General Information Contact, 414-229-4982, Fax: 414-229-6967, E-mail: gradschool@uwm.edu.
Website: https://uwm.edu/letters-science/programs/?discipline-Africology

Yale University, Graduate School of Arts and Sciences, Interdisciplinary Program in African Studies, New Haven, CT 06520. Offers MA. *Degree requirements:* For master's, one foreign language, thesis. *Entrance requirements:* For master's, GRE General Test.

American Indian/Native American Studies

Central Michigan University, College of Graduate Studies, College of Humanities and Social and Behavioral Sciences, Program in Humanities, Mount Pleasant, MI 48859. Offers humanities (MA), including contemporary issues in the humanities: race, class, and gender, images and ideas of self, Native American issues in modern culture, popular culture studies, the rise of industrial society. *Program availability:* Part-time, evening/weekend. *Degree requirements:* For master's, thesis or alternative. Electronic applications accepted. *Faculty research:* Rise of industrial society; images and ideas of self; contemporary issues of race, class, and gender; popular culture; Native American issues in modern culture.

Montana State University, The Graduate School, College of Letters and Science, Department of Native American Studies, Bozeman, MT 59717. Offers MA. *Program availability:* Part-time, online learning. *Degree requirements:* For master's, comprehensive exam. *Entrance requirements:* For master's, minimum GPA of 3.0; 3 letters of recommendation; 2 academic writing samples; statement of purpose. Additional exam requirements/recommendations for international students: Required—TOEFL (minimum score 550 paper-based). Electronic applications accepted. *Faculty research:* Federal Indian law and policy, contemporary Native film and literature, tribal colleges and Native Americans in higher education, Native veterans, native land rights.

Navajo Technical University, Program in Dine Studies, Crownpoint, NM 87313. Offers MA. *Entrance requirements:* For master's, bachelor's degree, Certificate of Indian Blood (CIB) for tribal eligibility, three letters of recommendation, 500-word essay.

Northeastern State University, College of Liberal Arts, Department of Cherokee and Indigenous Studies, Tahlequah, OK 74464-2399. Offers American studies (MA). *Program availability:* Part-time, evening/weekend. *Faculty:* 9 full-time (4 women). *Students:* 5 full-time (4 women), 10 part-time (9 women); includes 8 minority (1 Black or African American, non-Hispanic/Latino; 2 American Indian or Alaska Native, non-Hispanic/Latino; 3 Hispanic/Latino; 2 Two or more races, non-Hispanic/Latino). Average age 35. In 2017, 2 master's awarded. *Degree requirements:* For master's, thesis, written and oral examinations. *Entrance requirements:* For master's, GRE, minimum GPA of 2.5. Additional exam requirements/recommendations for international students: Required—TOEFL. *Application deadline:* For fall admission, 6/1 priority date for domestic students. Applications are processed on a rolling basis. Application fee: $25. Electronic applications accepted. *Expenses:* Tuition, state resident: part-time $222 per credit hour. Tuition, nonresident: part-time $501.75 per credit hour. *Required fees:* $37.40 per credit hour. Tuition and fees vary according to degree level. *Financial support:* Teaching assistantships and Federal Work-Study available. Financial award

application deadline: 3/1. *Unit head:* Dr. Mike Chanslor, Coordinator, 918-444-3617, E-mail: chanslor@nsuok.edu. *Application contact:* Josh McCollum, Graduate Coordinator, 918-444-2093, E-mail: mccolluj@nsuok.edu.
Website: http://catalog.nsuok.edu/preview_program.php?catoid-12&poid-947&returnto-333

Northern Arizona University, College of Social and Behavioral Sciences, Department of Applied Indigenous Studies, Flagstaff, AZ 86011. Offers indigenous and tribal nation-building (Graduate Certificate). *Program availability:* Part-time, evening/weekend, online only, 100% online, blended/hybrid learning. *Faculty:* 8 full-time (3 women). *Students:* 2 applicants. *Degree requirements:* For Graduate Certificate, comprehensive exam (for some programs). *Entrance requirements:* For degree, undergraduate degree from regionally-accredited institution with minimum GPA of 3.0, or the equivalent. Additional exam requirements/recommendations for international students: Required—TOEFL (minimum score 80 iBT), IELTS (minimum score 6.5). *Application deadline:* For fall admission, 3/1 for domestic and international students; for spring admission, 10/1 for domestic and international students. Application fee: $65. Electronic applications accepted. *Expenses:* Tuition, state resident: full-time $9240; part-time $458 per credit hour. Tuition, nonresident: full-time $21,588; part-time $1199 per credit hour. *Required fees:* $1021; $14 per credit hour. $646 per semester. Tuition and fees vary according to course load, campus/location and program. *Financial support:* Institutionally sponsored loans available. Financial award application deadline: 2/1; financial award applicants required to submit FAFSA. *Unit head:* Karen Jarratt-Snider, Chair, 928-523-6219, Fax: 928-523-5560, E-mail: karen.jarratt-snider@nau.edu. *Application contact:* Tina Sutton, Coordinator, Graduate College, 928-523-4348, Fax: 928-523-8950, E-mail: graduate@nau.edu.
Website: https://nau.edu/sbs/ais/

Trent University, Graduate Studies, The Frost Centre for Canadian Studies and Indigenous Studies, Peterborough, ON K9J 7B8, Canada. Offers Canadian studies (PhD); Canadian studies and indigenous studies (MA). *Program availability:* Part-time. *Degree requirements:* For master's, thesis. *Entrance requirements:* For master's, honors degree. *Faculty research:* Native community-based socioeconomic development, environmental and social impact inventory, regional studies.

Trent University, Graduate Studies, Program in Indigenous Studies, Peterborough, ON K9J 7B8, Canada. Offers PhD. *Program availability:* Part-time. *Degree requirements:* For doctorate, thesis/dissertation. *Entrance requirements:* For doctorate, master's degree.

The University of Arizona, Graduate Interdisciplinary Programs, Graduate Interdisciplinary Program in American Indian Studies, Tucson, AZ 85721. Offers MA, PhD. *Program availability:* Part-time. *Degree requirements:* For master's, thesis; for doctorate, one foreign language, comprehensive exam, thesis/dissertation. *Entrance requirements:* For master's, 3 letters of recommendation, 2 writing samples, resume; for doctorate, statement of purpose, 3 letters of recommendation, 2 writing samples, resume. Additional exam requirements/recommendations for international students: Required—TOEFL (minimum score 550 paper-based; 79 iBT). Electronic applications accepted. *Faculty research:* Indian law and policy, Indian societies, Indian language and literature, Indian education.

University of California, Davis, Graduate Studies, Program in Native American Studies, Davis, CA 95616. Offers MA, PhD. Terminal master's awarded for partial completion of doctoral program. *Degree requirements:* For master's, comprehensive exam (for some programs), thesis (for some programs); for doctorate, thesis/dissertation. *Entrance requirements:* For doctorate, GRE. Additional exam requirements/recommendations for international students: Required—TOEFL (minimum score 550 paper-based).

University of California, Los Angeles, Graduate Division, College of Letters and Science, Interdepartmental Program in American Indian Studies, Los Angeles, CA 90095. Offers MA, JD/MA. *Degree requirements:* For master's, comprehensive exam or thesis. *Entrance requirements:* For master's, GRE General Test (recommended), bachelor's degree; minimum undergraduate GPA of 3.0 (or its equivalent if letter grade system not used). Additional exam requirements/recommendations for international students: Required—TOEFL. Electronic applications accepted.

The University of Kansas, Graduate Studies, College of Liberal Arts and Sciences, Indigenous Studies Program, Lawrence, KS 66045-7515. Offers MA, Graduate Certificate. *Program availability:* Part-time. *Students:* 9 full-time (4 women), 3 part-time (0 women); includes 7 minority (6 American Indian or Alaska Native, non-Hispanic/Latino; 1 Two or more races, non-Hispanic/Latino). Average age 33. 9 applicants, 100% accepted, 7 enrolled. In 2017, 1 master's, 1 other advanced degree awarded. *Entrance requirements:* For master's, GRE, resume, writing sample, minimum GPA of 3.0 (preferred), 3 recommendations, original transcript, 2-page personal statement. Additional exam requirements/recommendations for international students: Required—TOEFL or IELTS. *Application deadline:* For fall admission, 4/1 priority date for domestic and international students; for spring admission, 10/1 priority date for domestic and international students. Application fee: $65 ($85 for international students). Electronic applications accepted. *Financial support:* Fellowships, research assistantships, teaching assistantships, Federal Work-Study, institutionally sponsored loans, and scholarships/grants available. Support available to part-time students. Financial award application deadline: 4/1; financial award applicants required to submit FAFSA. *Unit head:* Dr. Stephanie Fitzgerald, Director, 785-864-2586, E-mail: sfitzger@ku.edu. *Application contact:* Graduate Admission Contact, 785-864-2660, E-mail: indigenous@ku.edu.
Website: http://www.indigenous.ku.edu

University of Lethbridge, School of Graduate Studies, Lethbridge, AB T1K 3M4, Canada. Offers addictions counseling (M Sc); agricultural biotechnology (M Sc); agricultural studies (M Sc, MA); anthropology (MA); archaeology (M Sc, MA); art (MA, MFA); biochemistry (M Sc); biological sciences (M Sc); biomolecular science (PhD); biosystems and biodiversity (PhD); Canadian studies (MA); chemistry (M Sc); computer science (M Sc); computer science and geographical information science (M Sc); counseling (MC); counseling psychology (M Ed); dramatic arts (MA); earth, space, and physical science (PhD); economics (MA); education (MA, PhD); educational leadership (M Ed); English (MA); environmental science (M Sc); evolution and behavior (PhD); exercise science (M Sc); French (MA); French/German (MA); French/Spanish (MA); general education (M Ed); geography (M Sc, MA); German (MA); health sciences (M Sc); individualized multidisciplinary (M Sc, MA); kinesiology (M Sc, MA); management (M Sc), including accounting, finance, human resource management and labor relations, information systems, international management, marketing, policy and strategy; mathematics (M Sc); music (M Mus, MA); Native American studies (MA); neuroscience (M Sc, PhD); new media (MA, MFA); nursing (M Sc, MN); philosophy (MA); physics (M Sc); political science (MA); psychology (M Sc, MA); religious studies (MA); sociology (MA); theatre and dramatic arts (MFA); theoretical and computational science (PhD); urban and regional studies (MA); women and gender studies (MA). *Program availability:* Part-time, evening/weekend. *Degree requirements:* For master's, thesis (for some programs); for doctorate, comprehensive exam, thesis/dissertation. *Entrance requirements:* For master's, GMAT (for M Sc in management), bachelor's degree in related field, minimum GPA of 3.0 during previous 20 graded semester courses, 2 years' teaching or related experience (M Ed); for doctorate, master's degree, minimum graduate GPA of 3.5. Additional exam requirements/recommendations for international students: Required—TOEFL (minimum score 580 paper-based; 93 iBT). Electronic applications accepted. *Faculty research:* Movement and brain plasticity, gibberellin physiology, photosynthesis, carbon cycling, molecular properties of main-group ring components.

University of Manitoba, Faculty of Graduate Studies, Faculty of Arts, Department of Native Studies, Winnipeg, MB R3T 2N2, Canada. Offers MA.

University of New Mexico, Graduate Studies, College of Education, Program in Language, Literacy and Sociocultural Studies, Albuquerque, NM 87131. Offers American Indian education (MA); bilingual education (MA, PhD); educational linguistics (PhD); educational thought and sociocultural studies (MA, PhD); literacy/language arts (MA, PhD); social studies (MA); TESOL (MA, PhD). *Faculty:* 16 full-time (10 women), 4 part-time/adjunct (all women). *Students:* 56 full-time (34 women), 129 part-time (97 women); includes 93 minority (7 Black or African American, non-Hispanic/Latino; 15 American Indian or Alaska Native, non-Hispanic/Latino; 9 Asian, non-Hispanic/Latino; 56 Hispanic/Latino; 6 Two or more races, non-Hispanic/Latino), 44 international. Average age 40. 61 applicants, 38% accepted, 23 enrolled. In 2017, 36 master's, 4 doctorates awarded. *Degree requirements:* For master's, comprehensive exam, thesis optional; for doctorate, comprehensive exam, thesis/dissertation, research skills. *Entrance requirements:* For master's, letter of intent, 3 letters of recommendation, resume, BA/BS, department demographic form, transcripts; for doctorate, writing sample, letter of intent, 3 letters of recommendation, resume, BA/BS, MA, department demographic form, transcripts. Additional exam requirements/recommendations for international students: Required—TOEFL. *Application deadline:* For fall admission, 12/1 for domestic and international students; for spring admission, 9/15 for domestic and international students. Application fee: $50. Electronic applications accepted. *Financial support:* Fellowships, research assistantships, teaching assistantships, career-related internships or fieldwork, institutionally sponsored loans, scholarships/grants, and unspecified assistantships available. Support available to part-time students. Financial award application deadline: 3/1; financial award applicants required to submit FAFSA. *Faculty research:* School reform, professional development, history of education, Native American education, politics of education, feminism and issues of sexual identity, critical race theory, bilingualism, literacy reading, adolescent literature, second language acquisition, critical theory and schooling, indigenous languages. *Unit head:* Dr. Lois M. Meyer, Chair, 505-277-7244, Fax: 505-277-8362, E-mail: lsmeyer@unm.edu. *Application contact:* Debra Schaffer, Administrative Assistant, 505-277-0437, Fax: 505-277-8362, E-mail: schaffer@unm.edu.
Website: http://coe.unm.edu/departments-programs/llss/index.html

University of Oklahoma, College of Arts and Sciences, Department of Native American Studies, Norman, OK 73019. Offers MA, JD/MA. *Program availability:* Part-time. *Faculty:* 15 full-time (7 women). *Students:* 12 full-time (5 women), 4 part-time (2 women); includes 14 minority (10 American Indian or Alaska Native, non-Hispanic/Latino; 1 Hispanic/Latino; 3 Two or more races, non-Hispanic/Latino). Average age 32. 6 applicants, 67% accepted, 3 enrolled. In 2017, 9 master's awarded. *Degree requirements:* For master's, one foreign language, thesis or exam. *Entrance requirements:* For master's, BA or BS in related area. Additional exam requirements/recommendations for international students: Required—TOEFL (minimum score 79 iBT) or IELTS (minimum score 6.5). *Application deadline:* Applications are processed on a rolling basis. Application fee: $50 ($100 for international students). Electronic applications accepted. *Expenses:* Tuition, state resident: full-time $5119; part-time $213.30 per credit hour. Tuition, nonresident: full-time $19,778; part-time $824.10 per credit hour. *Required fees:* $3458; $133.55 per credit hour. $126.50 per semester. *Financial support:* In 2017–18, 14 students received support, including 8 teaching assistantships (averaging $10,400 per year); research assistantships and health care benefits also available. Financial award application deadline: 6/1; financial award applicants required to submit FAFSA. *Faculty research:* Tribal governance and policy; indigenous media and arts; language, cultural knowledge, and history. *Total annual research expenditures:* $144,298. *Unit head:* Dr. Amanda Cobb-Greethan, Chair, 405-325-2312, Fax: 405-325-0842, E-mail: nas@ou.edu.
Website: http://nas.ou.edu

University of South Dakota, Graduate School, School of Education, Division of Curriculum and Instruction, Vermillion, SD 57069. Offers American Indian education (Certificate); curriculum and instruction (Ed D, Ed S); elementary education (MA), including elementary education; English language learners (Certificate); literacy leadership and coaching (Certificate); reading interventionist (Certificate); science, technology and math pedagogy (Certificate); secondary education (MA), including secondary education; special education (MA), including special education; technology for education and training (MS), including technology for education and training. *Accreditation:* NCATE. *Program availability:* Part-time, online learning. *Degree requirements:* For master's and other advanced degree, comprehensive exam, thesis or alternative; for doctorate, comprehensive exam, thesis/dissertation. *Entrance requirements:* For master's, doctorate, and other advanced degree, GRE General Test, MAT, minimum GPA of 2.7. Additional exam requirements/recommendations for international students: Required—TOEFL (minimum score 550 paper-based; 79 iBT). *Application deadline:* Applications are processed on a rolling basis. Application fee: $35. Electronic applications accepted. *Financial support:* Research assistantships with partial tuition reimbursements, teaching assistantships with partial tuition reimbursements, career-related internships or fieldwork, Federal Work-Study, and unspecified assistantships available. Financial award applicants required to submit FAFSA. *Application contact:* Graduate School, 605-658-6140, Fax: 605-677-6118, E-mail: grad@usd.edu.
Website: http://www.usd.edu/ci

The University of Tulsa, College of Law, Tulsa, OK 74104. Offers American Indian and indigenous law (LL M); American law for foreign lawyers (LL M); energy and natural resources law (LL M); energy law (MJ); health law (Certificate); Indian law (MJ); law (JD); Native American law (Certificate); sustainable energy and resources law (Certificate); JD/MA; JD/MBA; JD/MS. *Accreditation:* ABA. *Program availability:* Part-time, 100% online. *Faculty:* 24 full-time (13 women), 14 part-time/adjunct (7 women). *Students:* 243 full-time (105 women), 29 part-time (12 women); includes 75 minority (12 Black or African American, non-Hispanic/Latino; 17 American Indian or Alaska Native, non-Hispanic/Latino; 1 Asian, non-Hispanic/Latino; 11 Hispanic/Latino; 34 Two or more races, non-Hispanic/Latino), 4 international. Average age 28. 567 applicants, 45% accepted, 94 enrolled. In 2017, 3 master's, 86 doctorates, 26 Certificates awarded. *Degree requirements:* For master's, thesis optional. *Entrance requirements:* For master's, JD from an ABA-approved U.S. law school or a JD equivalent from non-U.S. university; for doctorate, LSAT, BS or BA from 4-year regionally-accredited college/university; for Certificate, BS or BA from 4-year regionally-accredited college/university. Additional exam requirements/recommendations for international students: Required—TOEFL (minimum score 570 paper-based; 90 iBT), IELTS (minimum score 6.5). *Application deadline:* For fall admission, 7/31 priority date for domestic and international students; for spring admission, 12/5 priority date for domestic students, 12/5 for

international students; for summer admission, 4/13 for domestic and international students. Applications are processed on a rolling basis. Application fee: $30. Electronic applications accepted. *Expenses:* $24,600 per year tuition; $564 fees. *Financial support:* In 2017–18, 261 students received support. Scholarships/grants available. Support available to part-time students. Financial award application deadline: 8/1; financial award applicants required to submit FAFSA. *Faculty research:* Native American law,

criminal law, commercial speech, copyright law, international law. *Unit head:* Prof. Lyn Suzanne Entzeroth, Dean, 918-631-2400, Fax: 918-631-3126, E-mail: lyn-entzeroth@utulsa.edu. *Application contact:* April M. Fox, Associate Dean of Admissions and Financial Aid, 918-631-2406, Fax: 918-631-3630, E-mail: april-fox@utulsa.edu. Website: http://www.utulsa.edu/law/

American Studies

American Public University System, AMU/APU Graduate Programs, Charles Town, WV 25414. Offers accounting (MS); applied business analytics (MS); business administration (MBA); criminal justice (MA); cybersecurity studies (MS); educational leadership (M Ed); environmental policy and management (MS); global security (DGS); health information management (MS); history (MA), including American military history, American Revolution, civil war, war since 1945, World War II; information technology (MS); international relations and conflict resolution (MA), including American politics and government, comparative government and development, general, international relations, public policy; national security studies (MA); nursing (MSN); political science (MA); public policy (MPP); reverse logistics management (MA), including comparative and security issues, conflict resolution, international and transnational security issues, peacekeeping; space studies (MS); sports management (MS); strategic intelligence (DSI); teaching (M Ed), including secondary social studies; transportation and logistics management (MA). *Program availability:* Part-time, evening/weekend, online only, 100% online. *Students:* 455 full-time (227 women), 7,939 part-time (3,353 women); includes 2,793 minority (1,429 Black or African American, non-Hispanic/Latino; 48 American Indian or Alaska Native, non-Hispanic/Latino; 205 Asian, non-Hispanic/Latino; 766 Hispanic/Latino; 62 Native Hawaiian or other Pacific Islander, non-Hispanic/Latino; 283 Two or more races, non-Hispanic/Latino), 101 international. Average age 37. In 2017, 2,977 master's awarded. *Degree requirements:* For master's, comprehensive exam or practicum. *Entrance requirements:* For master's, official transcript showing earned bachelor's degree from institution accredited by recognized accrediting body. Additional exam requirements/recommendations for international students: Required—TOEFL (minimum score 550 paper-based), IELTS (minimum score 6.5). *Application deadline:* Applications are processed on a rolling basis. Application fee: $0. Electronic applications accepted. *Expenses:* Tuition: Full-time $6300; part-time $350 per credit. *Required fees:* $300; $50 per course. *Financial support:* Scholarships/grants available. Financial award applicants required to submit FAFSA. *Unit head:* Dr. Wallace Boston, President, 877-468-6268, Fax: 304-728-2348, E-mail: president@apus.edu. *Application contact:* Yoci Deal, Associate Vice President, Graduate and International Admissions, 877-468-6268, Fax: 304-724-3764, E-mail: info@apus.edu.
Website: http://www.apus.edu

American University, School of International Service, Washington, DC 20016-8071. Offers comparative and regional studies (Certificate); cross-cultural communication (Certificate); development management (MS); ethics, peace, and global affairs (MA); European studies (Certificate); global environmental policy (MA, Certificate); global information technology (Certificate); global media (MA); international affairs (MA), including comparative and regional studies, global governance, politics, and security, international economic relations, natural resources and sustainable development, U.S. foreign policy and national security; international arts management (Certificate); international communication (MA, Certificate); international development (MA); international economic policy (Certificate); international economic relations (Certificate); international economics (MA); international peace and conflict resolution (MA, Certificate); international politics (Certificate); international relations (MA, PhD); international service (MIS); peacebuilding (Certificate); social enterprise (MA); the Americas (Certificate); United States foreign policy (Certificate); JD/MA. *Program availability:* Part-time, evening/weekend, 100% online. *Faculty:* 112 full-time (50 women), 46 part-time/adjunct (19 women). *Students:* 495 full-time (333 women), 518 part-time (276 women); includes 360 minority (95 Black or African American, non-Hispanic/Latino; 2 American Indian or Alaska Native, non-Hispanic/Latino; 60 Asian, non-Hispanic/Latino; 164 Hispanic/Latino; 39 Two or more races, non-Hispanic/Latino), 98 international. Average age 30. 1,559 applicants, 81% accepted, 356 enrolled. In 2017, 427 master's, 9 doctorates, 5 other advanced degrees awarded. Terminal master's awarded for partial completion of doctoral program. *Degree requirements:* For master's, one foreign language, comprehensive exam, thesis or alternative; for doctorate, one foreign language, comprehensive exam, thesis/dissertation. *Entrance requirements:* For master's, GRE; GMAT or GRE (for MA in social enterprise), transcripts, resume, 2 letters of recommendation, statement of purpose; for doctorate, GRE, transcripts, resume, 3 letters of recommendation, statement of purpose. Additional exam requirements/recommendations for international students: Required—TOEFL (minimum score 600 paper-based; 100 iBT). *Application deadline:* For fall admission, 1/15 for domestic students, 1/1 for international students; for spring admission, 10/1 for domestic students, 9/15 for international students. Application fee: $55. Electronic applications accepted. *Expenses:* Contact institution. *Financial support:* Research assistantships, teaching assistantships, institutionally sponsored loans, scholarships/grants, and unspecified assistantships available. Financial award application deadline: 1/15; financial award applicants required to submit FAFSA. *Application contact:* 202-885-1646, Fax: 202-885-1109, E-mail: sisgrad@american.edu.
Website: http://www.american.edu/sis/

Appalachian State University, Cratis D. Williams Graduate School, Center for Appalachian Studies, Boone, NC 28608. Offers culture (MA). *Program availability:* Part-time. *Degree requirements:* For master's, one foreign language, comprehensive exam, thesis optional. *Entrance requirements:* For master's, GRE General Test, 3 letters of recommendation. Additional exam requirements/recommendations for international students: Required—TOEFL (minimum score 570 paper-based; 79 iBT), IELTS (minimum score 6.5). Electronic applications accepted. *Faculty research:* Appalachian culture, sustainable development, Appalachian music.

Baylor University, Graduate School, College of Arts and Sciences, Program in American Studies, Waco, TX 76798. Offers MA. *Students:* 1 full-time (0 women); minority (Two or more races, non-Hispanic/Latino). *Entrance requirements:* For master's, GRE General Test, 24 semester hours of course work in subjects with American content. *Application deadline:* Applications are processed on a rolling basis. Application fee: $25. *Financial support:* Fellowships, Federal Work-Study, and institutionally sponsored loans available. Financial award application deadline: 4/15. *Unit head:* Dr. Mia N. Moody-Ramirez, Graduate Program Director, 254-710-7247, Fax: 254-710-7247, E-mail: mia_moody@baylor.edu. *Application contact:* Margaret Kramer, Administrative Assistant, 254-710-4350, Fax: 254-710-3870, E-mail:

margaret_kramer@baylor.edu.
Website: http://www.baylor.edu/American_Studies/

Boston University, Graduate School of Arts and Sciences, Program in American and New England Studies, Boston, MA 02215. Offers PhD. *Students:* 39 full-time (23 women), 6 part-time (5 women); includes 3 minority (2 Black or African American, non-Hispanic/Latino; 1 Hispanic/Latino), 1 international. Average age 28. 64 applicants, 17% accepted, 8 enrolled. In 2017, 5 doctorates awarded. *Degree requirements:* For doctorate, one foreign language, comprehensive exam, thesis/dissertation. *Entrance requirements:* For doctorate, GRE General Test, scholarly writing sample, 3 letters of recommendation, transcripts, personal statement, curriculum vitae. Additional exam requirements/recommendations for international students: Required—TOEFL (minimum score 550 paper-based; 84 iBT). *Application deadline:* For fall admission, 1/5 for domestic and international students. Application fee: $95. Electronic applications accepted. *Financial support:* In 2017–18, 45 students received support, including 19 fellowships with full tuition reimbursements available (averaging $22,000 per year), 1 research assistantship with full tuition reimbursement available (averaging $22,000 per year), 15 teaching assistantships with full tuition reimbursements available (averaging $22,000 per year); career-related internships or fieldwork, Federal Work-Study, scholarships/grants, health care benefits, and unspecified assistantships also available. Financial award application deadline: 1/5. *Unit head:* William Moore, Director, 617-353-9912, Fax: 617-353-2556, E-mail: moorewd@bu.edu. *Application contact:* Julia Kline, Senior Program Coordinator, 617-353-2948, Fax: 617-353-2556, E-mail: jgawle@bu.edu.
Website: http://www.bu.edu/AMNESP/

Bowling Green State University, Graduate College, College of Arts and Sciences, American Culture Studies Program, Bowling Green, OH 43403. Offers MA, PhD. *Program availability:* Part-time. *Degree requirements:* For master's, thesis or alternative; for doctorate, comprehensive exam, thesis/dissertation. *Entrance requirements:* For master's and doctorate, GRE General Test. Additional exam requirements/recommendations for international students: Required—TOEFL. Electronic applications accepted. *Faculty research:* Race and ethnicity, gender, popular culture.

Bowling Green State University, Graduate College, College of Arts and Sciences, Department of Popular Culture, Bowling Green, OH 43403. Offers MA. *Program availability:* Part-time. *Degree requirements:* For master's, thesis or alternative. *Entrance requirements:* For master's, GRE General Test. Additional exam requirements/recommendations for international students: Required—TOEFL. Electronic applications accepted. *Faculty research:* Mass media (popular film, TV, and music); folklore/folk life; ritual, festival, celebration, and holidays; global, international, and popular culture; nineteenth-century everyday life.

Brown University, Graduate School, Department of American Studies, Providence, RI 02912. Offers American studies (PhD); American studies for international students (MA); public humanities (MA). *Degree requirements:* For doctorate, thesis/dissertation, preliminary exam.

California State University, Fullerton, Graduate Studies, College of Humanities and Social Sciences, Department of American Studies, Fullerton, CA 92831-3599. Offers MA. *Program availability:* Part-time. *Faculty:* 6 full-time (4 women). *Students:* 9 full-time (5 women), 22 part-time (14 women); includes 19 minority (3 Black or African American, non-Hispanic/Latino; 14 Hispanic/Latino; 2 Two or more races, non-Hispanic/Latino), 2 international. Average age 28. 20 applicants, 95% accepted, 16 enrolled. *Entrance requirements:* For master's, minimum GPA of 3.0 in major, 2.5 in last 60 hours. Application fee: $55. *Financial support:* Federal Work-Study, institutionally sponsored loans, and scholarships/grants available. Support available to part-time students. Financial award application deadline: 3/1; financial award applicants required to submit FAFSA. *Unit head:* Leila Zenderland, Chair, 657-278-3800, E-mail: lzenderland@fullerton.edu. *Application contact:* Admissions/Applications, 657-278-2371.

The Catholic University of America, School of Arts and Sciences, Department of History, Washington, DC 20064. Offers history (MA, PhD), including early modern European history, medieval history, modern European history, U.S. history; religion and society in the late medieval and early modern world (MA); MA/JD; MSLS/MA. *Program availability:* Part-time. *Faculty:* 15 full-time (6 women), 1 part-time/adjunct (0 women). *Students:* 6 full-time (0 women), 19 part-time (7 women); includes 3 minority (all Two or more races, non-Hispanic/Latino), 2 international. Average age 31. 11 applicants, 82% accepted, 3 enrolled. In 2017, 4 master's, 2 doctorates awarded. Terminal master's awarded for partial completion of doctoral program. *Degree requirements:* For master's, one foreign language, comprehensive exam, thesis optional, 2 languages (for medievalists), one of which must be Latin; for doctorate, 2 foreign languages, comprehensive exam, thesis/dissertation, 3 languages (for medievalists), one of which must be Latin. *Entrance requirements:* For master's and doctorate, GRE General Test, statement of purpose, official copies of academic transcripts, three letters of recommendation, writing sample. Additional exam requirements/recommendations for international students: Required—TOEFL (minimum score 550 paper-based; 80 iBT). *Application deadline:* For fall admission, 7/15 priority date for domestic students, 7/1 for international students; for spring admission, 11/15 priority date for domestic students, 11/1 for international students. Applications are processed on a rolling basis. Application fee: $55. Electronic applications accepted. *Expenses:* Contact institution. *Financial support:* Fellowships, research assistantships, teaching assistantships, Federal Work-Study, scholarships/grants, tuition waivers (full and partial), and unspecified assistantships available. Financial award application deadline: 2/1; financial award applicants required to submit FAFSA. *Faculty research:* Medieval history, including the Islamic Middle East, with particular expertise in later medieval religious, social, and economic history and early medieval and late antique history; European and American intellectual history; renaissance, reformation, catholic reformation; U.S. Catholic history; history of immigration. *Unit head:* Dr. Katherine Jansen, Chair, 202-319-5484, Fax: 202-319-5569, E-mail: jansen@cua.edu. *Application contact:* Dr. Steven Brown, Director of Graduate Admissions, 202-319-5057, Fax: 202-319-6533, E-mail: cua-admissions@cua.edu.
Website: http://history.cua.edu/

American Studies

Central Michigan University, College of Graduate Studies, College of Humanities and Social and Behavioral Sciences, Department of History, Mount Pleasant, MI 48859. Offers European history (Graduate Certificate); history (MA); modern history (Graduate Certificate); United States history (Graduate Certificate); MA/PhD. *Program availability:* Part-time. *Degree requirements:* For master's, thesis or alternative. Electronic applications accepted. *Faculty research:* Colonial and revolutionary United States history, modern European history, Latin American and transatlantic history, transnational and comparative history, United States social history.

Claremont Graduate University, Graduate Programs, School of Arts and Humanities, Department of English, Claremont, CA 91711-6160. Offers American studies (MA, PhD); critical theory (MA, PhD); early modern studies (MA, PhD); English (M Phil, MA, PhD); literary theory (PhD); literature (MA, PhD); literature and creative writing (MA); literature and film (MA); MBA/MA; MBA/PhD. *Program availability:* Part-time. *Entrance requirements:* For master's and doctorate, GRE General Test. Additional exam requirements/recommendations for international students: Required—TOEFL (minimum score 75 iBT). Electronic applications accepted. *Faculty research:* American, comparative, and English Renaissance literature; modernism; feminist literature and theory.

Claremont Graduate University, Graduate Programs, School of Arts and Humanities, Department of History, Claremont, CA 91711-6160. Offers Africana history (Certificate); American studies and U.S. history (MA, PhD); archival studies (MA); early modern studies (MA, PhD); European studies (MA, PhD); oral history (MA, PhD); MBA/MA; MBA/PhD. Terminal master's awarded for partial completion of doctoral program. *Entrance requirements:* For master's and doctorate, GRE General Test. Additional exam requirements/recommendations for international students: Required—TOEFL (minimum score 75 iBT). Electronic applications accepted. *Faculty research:* Intellectual and social history, cultural studies, gender studies, Western history, Chicano history.

Clark University, Graduate School, Department of History, Program in United States and Atlantic History, Worcester, MA 01610-1477. Offers history of the Atlantic world (PhD); history of the United States (PhD). *Students:* 14 full-time (4 women), 1 international. Average age 36. 14 applicants, 43% accepted, 6 enrolled. In 2017, 1 doctorate awarded. *Application deadline:* For fall admission, 1/15 for domestic students. Application fee: $75. *Financial support:* Fellowships, research assistantships, and teaching assistantships available. *Faculty research:* American political history, comparative history, American family history. *Unit head:* Dr. Nina Kushner, Professor, 508-421-3797, E-mail: nkushner@clarku.edu. *Application contact:* Diane Fenner, Department Assistant, 508-793-7288, Fax: 508-793-8816, E-mail: dfenner@clarku.edu.

The College at Brockport, State University of New York, School of Arts and Sciences, Department of History, Brockport, NY 14420-2997. Offers history (MA), including American and world history, American history, American public history, world history. *Program availability:* Part-time, evening/weekend. *Faculty:* 9 full-time (5 women). *Students:* 15 full-time (5 women), 19 part-time (10 women); includes 1 minority (Black or African American, non-Hispanic/Latino). 20 applicants, 75% accepted, 10 enrolled. In 2017, 10 master's awarded. *Degree requirements:* For master's, thesis or alternative. *Entrance requirements:* For master's, minimum GPA of 3.0, writing sample, letters of recommendation, statement of objectives. Additional exam requirements/recommendations for international students: Required—TOEFL (minimum score 550 paper-based; 79 iBT), IELTS (minimum score 6.5). *Application deadline:* For fall admission, 7/1 priority date for domestic and international students; for spring admission, 11/15 priority date for domestic and international students; for summer admission, 4/15 for domestic and international students. Application fee: $50. Electronic applications accepted. *Expenses:* Tuition, state resident: full-time $10,870; part-time $453 per credit hour. Tuition, nonresident: full-time $22,210. *Required fees:* $988; $246 per semester. *Financial support:* In 2017–18, 1 fellowship with tuition reimbursement (averaging $3,750 per year), 2 teaching assistantships with full tuition reimbursements (averaging $6,000 per year) were awarded; Federal Work-Study, scholarships/grants, and unspecified assistantships also available. Support available to part-time students. Financial award application deadline: 3/15; financial award applicants required to submit FAFSA. *Faculty research:* American history, women's history, European history, world history, cultural history. *Unit head:* Dr. Owen Steve Ireland, Chairperson, 585-395-5627, Fax: 585-395-2620, E-mail: oireland@brockport.edu. *Application contact:* Dr. Morag Martin, Graduate Director, 585-395-5690, Fax: 585-395-2620, E-mail: mmartin@brockport.edu.
Website: https://www.brockport.edu/academics/history/graduate/masters.html

College of Staten Island of the City University of New York, Graduate Programs, Division of Humanities and Social Sciences, Program in History, Staten Island, NY 10314-6600. Offers history (MA), including Africa and the Middle East, Asia, Europe, Latin America and the Caribbean, United States. *Program availability:* Part-time, evening/weekend. *Faculty:* 2 full-time (1 woman). *Students:* 18. 19 applicants, 79% accepted, 11 enrolled. In 2017, 3 master's awarded. *Degree requirements:* For master's, comprehensive exam (for some programs), 32 credits (total of eight courses); thesis or portfolio. *Entrance requirements:* For master's, bachelor's degree with minimum GPA of 3.0 overall and in undergraduate history courses, two letters of recommendation, letter of interest, research-based writing sample. Additional exam requirements/recommendations for international students: Required—TOEFL (minimum score 550 paper-based; 79 iBT), IELTS (minimum score 6.5). *Application deadline:* For fall admission, 5/10 priority date for domestic and international students; for spring admission, 12/2 priority date for domestic and international students. Applications are processed on a rolling basis. Application fee: $125. Electronic applications accepted. *Expenses:* Tuition, state resident: full-time $10,450; part-time $440 per credit. Tuition, nonresident: full-time $19,320; part-time $440 per credit. *Required fees:* $181.10 per semester. Tuition and fees vary according to program. *Faculty research:* African and African diaspora history, South Asian history, Middle Eastern history, U.S. history, environmental history. *Unit head:* Dr. John Dixon, Graduate Program Coordinator, 718-982-3307, E-mail: john.dixon@csi.cuny.edu. *Application contact:* Sasha Spence, Associate Director for Graduate Admissions, 718-982-2019, Fax: 718-982-2500, E-mail: sasha.spence@csi.cuny.edu.
Website: https://www.csi.cuny.edu/sites/default/files/pdf/admissions/grad/pdf/History%20Fact%20Sheet.pdf

The College of William and Mary, Faculty of Arts and Sciences, American Studies Program, Williamsburg, VA 23187-8795. Offers MA, PhD, JD/MA. *Program availability:* Part-time. *Faculty:* 4 full-time (2 women). *Students:* 34 full-time (21 women), 1 (woman) part-time; includes 11 minority (5 Black or African American, non-Hispanic/Latino; 2 Asian, non-Hispanic/Latino; 2 Hispanic/Latino; 2 Two or more races, non-Hispanic/Latino), 2 international. Average age 30. 38 applicants, 53% accepted, 11 enrolled. In 2017, 3 master's, 11 doctorates awarded. Terminal master's awarded for partial completion of doctoral program. *Degree requirements:* For master's, thesis; for doctorate, one foreign language, comprehensive exam, thesis/dissertation. *Entrance requirements:* For master's, GRE; for doctorate, GRE, MA. Additional exam requirements/recommendations for international students: Required—TOEFL. *Application deadline:* For fall admission, 1/1 for domestic and international students. Application fee: $50. Electronic applications accepted. *Financial support:* In 2017–18, 22 students received support, including 20 fellowships with full tuition reimbursements available (averaging $22,800 per year); career-related internships or fieldwork and unspecified assistantships also available. Financial award application deadline: 1/1. *Faculty research:* American cultural history, literature, material culture, art history, visual culture, mass and popular culture since the eighteenth century; African American studies; Native American studies; LGBTQ studies; digital humanities; environmental humanities. *Unit head:* Dr. Leisa Meyer, Director, 757-221-3720, Fax: 757-221-1287, E-mail: ldmeye@wm.edu. *Application contact:* Jean Brown, Program Administrator, 757-221-1275, Fax: 757-221-1287, E-mail: jxbrow@wm.edu.
Website: http://www.wm.edu/americanstudies/

The Colorado College, Education Department, Experienced Teacher Program, Colorado Springs, CO 80903-3294. Offers arts and humanities (MAT); integrated natural sciences (MAT); liberal arts (MAT); Southwest studies (MAT). Programs offered during summer only. *Program availability:* Part-time. *Degree requirements:* For master's, thesis, oral exam, 50-page paper. *Expenses:* Contact institution.

Columbia University, Graduate School of Arts and Sciences, New York, NY 10027. Offers African-American studies (MA); American studies (MA); anthropology (MA, PhD); art history and archaeology (MA, PhD); astronomy (PhD); biological sciences (PhD); biotechnology (MA); chemical physics (PhD); chemistry (PhD); classical studies (MA, PhD); classics (MA, PhD); climate and society (MA); conservation biology (MA); earth and environmental sciences (PhD); East Asia: regional studies (MA); East Asian languages and cultures (MA, PhD); ecology, evolution and environmental biology (MA), including conservation biology; ecology, evolution, and environmental biology (PhD), including ecology and evolutionary biology, evolutionary primatology; economics (MA, PhD); English and comparative literature (MA, PhD); French and Romance philology (MA, PhD); Germanic languages (MA, PhD); global French studies (MA); global thought (MA); Hispanic cultural studies (MA); history (PhD); history and literature (MA); human rights studies (MA); Islamic studies (MA); Italian (MA, PhD); Japanese pedagogy (MA); Jewish studies (MA); Latin America and the Caribbean: regional studies (MA); Latin American and Iberian cultures (PhD); mathematics (MA, PhD), including finance (MA); medieval and Renaissance studies (MA); Middle Eastern, South Asian, and African studies (MA, PhD); modern art: critical and curatorial studies (MA); modern European studies (MA); museum anthropology (MA); music (DMA, PhD); oral history (MA); philosophical foundations of physics (MA); philosophy (MA, PhD); physics (PhD); political science (MA, PhD); psychology (PhD); quantitative methods in the social sciences (MA); religion (MA, PhD); Russia, Eurasia and East Europe: regional studies (MA); Russian translation (MA); Slavic cultures (MA); Slavic languages (MA, PhD); sociology (MA, PhD); South Asian studies (MA); statistics (MA, PhD); theatre (PhD). Dual-degree programs require admission to both Graduate School of Arts and Sciences and another Columbia school. *Program availability:* Part-time. Terminal master's awarded for partial completion of doctoral program. *Degree requirements:* For master's, variable foreign language requirement, comprehensive exam (for some programs), thesis (for some programs); for doctorate, variable foreign language requirement, comprehensive exam (for some programs), thesis/dissertation. *Entrance requirements:* For master's and doctorate, GRE General Test, GRE Subject Test (for some programs). Additional exam requirements/recommendations for international students: Required—TOEFL, IELTS. Electronic applications accepted. *Expenses: Tuition:* Full-time $44,864; part-time $1704 per credit. *Required fees:* $2370 per semester. One-time fee: $105.

Cornell University, Graduate School, Graduate Fields of Arts and Sciences, Field of English Language and Literature, Ithaca, NY 14853. Offers African-American literature (PhD); American literature after 1865 (PhD); American literature to 1865 (PhD); American studies (PhD); colonial and postcolonial literatures (PhD); creative writing (MFA); cultural studies (PhD); dramatic literature (PhD); English poetry (PhD); English Renaissance to 1660 (PhD); lesbian, bisexual, and gay literary studies (PhD); literary criticism and theory (PhD); Old and Middle English (PhD); prose fiction (PhD); Restoration and the eighteenth-century (PhD); the nineteenth century (PhD); the twentieth century (PhD); women's literature (PhD); MFA/PhD. Terminal master's awarded for partial completion of doctoral program. *Degree requirements:* For master's, one foreign language, thesis; for doctorate, one foreign language, comprehensive exam, thesis/dissertation, teaching experience. *Entrance requirements:* For master's, GRE General Test, 3 letters of recommendation, creative writing sample; for doctorate, GRE General Test, GRE Subject Test (English), 3 letters of recommendation, writing sample. Additional exam requirements/recommendations for international students: Required—TOEFL (minimum score 600 paper-based; 77 iBT). Electronic applications accepted. *Faculty research:* English and American literature, women's writing, ethnic and post-colonial literature, critical theory, medievalism.

Cornell University, Graduate School, Graduate Fields of Arts and Sciences, Field of History, Ithaca, NY 14853. Offers African history (MA, PhD); American history (MA, PhD); ancient Greek history (PhD); ancient history (MA, PhD); ancient Roman history (PhD); early modern European history (MA, PhD); English history (MA, PhD); French history (MA, PhD); German history (MA, PhD); history of science (MA, PhD); Korean history (PhD); Latin American history (MA, PhD); medieval Chinese history (MA, PhD); medieval history (MA, PhD); modern Chinese history (MA, PhD); modern European history (MA, PhD); modern Japanese history (MA, PhD); modern Middle Eastern history (PhD); premodern Islamic history (MA, PhD); premodern Japanese history (MA, PhD); Renaissance history (MA, PhD); Russian history (MA, PhD); South Asian history (PhD); Southeast Asian history (MA, PhD). Terminal master's awarded for partial completion of doctoral program. *Degree requirements:* For master's, thesis; for doctorate, 2 foreign languages, comprehensive exam, thesis/dissertation, 1 year of teaching experience. *Entrance requirements:* For master's and doctorate, GRE General Test, writing sample, 3 letters of recommendation. Additional exam requirements/recommendations for international students: Required—TOEFL (minimum score 550 paper-based; 77 iBT). Electronic applications accepted.

Cornell University, Graduate School, Graduate Fields of Arts and Sciences, Field of History of Art, Archaeology and Visual Studies, Ithaca, NY 14853. Offers 19th century art (PhD); African, African American and African diaspora (PhD); American art (PhD); ancient art and archaeology (PhD); Asian American art (PhD); Baroque art (PhD); comparative modernities (PhD); digital art (PhD); East Asian art (PhD); history of photography (PhD); Islamic art (PhD); Latin American art (PhD); medieval art (PhD); modern art (PhD); Renaissance art (PhD); Southeast Asian art (PhD); theory and criticism (PhD); visual studies (PhD). *Degree requirements:* For doctorate, one foreign language, comprehensive exam, thesis/dissertation, general exams in 3 areas. *Entrance requirements:* For doctorate, GRE General Test, sample of written work, 3 letters of recommendation. Additional exam requirements/recommendations for international students: Required—TOEFL (minimum score 550 paper-based; 77 iBT). Electronic applications accepted.

Drew University, Caspersen School of Graduate Studies, Madison, NJ 07940-1493. Offers conflict resolution and leadership (Certificate), including community leadership, moderation, peace building; education (M Ed); finance (MA); history and culture (MA, PhD), including American history, book history, British history, European history, Holocaust and genocide (M Litt, MA, D Litt, PhD), intellectual history, Irish history, print culture, public history; K-12 education (MAT), including art, biology, chemistry, elementary education, English, French, Italian, math, secondary education, special education, teacher of students with disabilities; liberal studies (M Litt, D Litt), including

history, Holocaust and genocide (M Litt, MA, D Litt, PhD), Irish/Irish-American studies, literature (M Litt, MMH, D Litt, DMH, CMH), religion, spirituality, teaching in the two-year college, writing; medical humanities (MMH, DMH, CMH), including arts, health, healthcare, literature (M Litt, MMH, D Litt, DMH, CMH), scientific research; poetry (MFA). *Program availability:* Part-time, evening/weekend. *Faculty:* 4 full-time (2 women), 29 part-time/adjunct (15 women). *Students:* 77 full-time (42 women), 175 part-time (114 women); includes 39 minority (12 Black or African American, non-Hispanic/Latino; 6 Asian, non-Hispanic/Latino; 16 Hispanic/Latino; 5 Two or more races, non-Hispanic/Latino), 11 international. Average age 41. 126 applicants, 75% accepted, 52 enrolled. In 2017, 38 master's, 23 doctorates, 35 other advanced degrees awarded. Terminal master's awarded for partial completion of doctoral program. *Degree requirements:* For master's and other advanced degree, thesis (for some programs); for doctorate, one foreign language, comprehensive exam (for some programs), thesis/dissertation. *Entrance requirements:* For master's, PRAXIS Core and Subject Area tests (for MAT), GRE/GMAT (for M Fin), resume, transcripts, writing sample, personal statement, letters of recommendation; for doctorate, GRE (PhD in history and culture), resume, transcripts, writing sample, personal statement, letters of recommendation; for other advanced degree, resume, transcripts, personal statement. Additional exam requirements/recommendations for international students: Required—TOEFL (minimum score 587 paper-based; 80 iBT), IELTS (minimum score 6), TWE (minimum score 4). *Application deadline:* For fall admission, 8/1 for domestic students, 6/1 for international students; for spring admission, 12/1 for domestic students, 10/1 for international students. Applications are processed on a rolling basis. Application fee: $35. Electronic applications accepted. *Financial support:* Fellowships, research assistantships, teaching assistantships, career-related internships or fieldwork, Federal Work-Study, scholarships/grants, and unspecified assistantships available. Support available to part-time students. Financial award applicants required to submit FAFSA. *Faculty research:* Irish history and culture, conflict resolution and leadership. *Application contact:* Leanne Horinko, Director of Caspersen Admissions, 973-408-3280, E-mail: gradm@drew.edu.
Website: http://www.drew.edu/caspersen

East Carolina University, Graduate School, Thomas Harriot College of Arts and Sciences, Department of History, Greenville, NC 27858-4353. Offers American history (MA); Atlantic world (MA); European history (MA); maritime studies (MA); military history (MA); public history (MA). *Program availability:* Part-time. *Students:* 39 full-time (16 women), 49 part-time (21 women); includes 11 minority (2 Black or African American, non-Hispanic/Latino; 1 Asian, non-Hispanic/Latino; 5 Hispanic/Latino; 3 Two or more races, non-Hispanic/Latino), 1 international. Average age 29. 35 applicants, 83% accepted, 19 enrolled. In 2017, 15 master's awarded. *Degree requirements:* For master's, one foreign language, comprehensive exam, thesis. *Entrance requirements:* For master's, GRE General Test. Additional exam requirements/recommendations for international students: Recommended—TOEFL (minimum score 78 iBT), IELTS (minimum score 6.5). *Application deadline:* For fall admission, 4/1 priority date for domestic and international students; for spring admission, 10/15 priority date for domestic and international students. Applications are processed on a rolling basis. Application fee: $75. Electronic applications accepted. *Expenses:* Tuition, state resident: full-time $4749; part-time $297 per credit hour. Tuition, nonresident: full-time $17,898; part-time $1119 per credit hour. *Required fees:* $2691; $224 per credit hour. Part-time tuition and fees vary according to course load and program. *Financial support:* Fellowships, research assistantships with partial tuition reimbursements, teaching assistantships with partial tuition reimbursements, and Federal Work-Study available. Support available to part-time students. Financial award application deadline: 1/15. *Unit head:* Dr. Christopher Oakley, Chair, 252-328-1025, E-mail: oakleyc@ecu.edu. *Application contact:* Dean of Graduate School, 252-328-6012, E-mail: gradschool@ecu.edu.
Website: http://www.ecu.edu/cs-cas/history/

Emory & Henry College, Graduate Programs, Emory, VA 24327. Offers American history (MA Ed); education professional studies (M Ed); occupational therapy (MOT); organizational leadership (MCOL); physical therapy (DPT); physician assistant studies (MPAS); reading specialist (MA Ed). *Program availability:* Part-time. *Faculty:* 7 full-time (3 women). *Students:* 194 full-time (128 women), 4 part-time (2 women); includes 6 minority (2 Black or African American, non-Hispanic/Latino; 1 American Indian or Alaska Native, non-Hispanic/Latino; 1 Asian, non-Hispanic/Latino; 2 Hispanic/Latino). Average age 25. 525 applicants, 21% accepted, 74 enrolled. In 2017, 24 master's awarded. *Degree requirements:* For master's, thesis optional; for doctorate, thesis/dissertation optional. *Entrance requirements:* For master's, GRE or PRAXIS I, official transcripts from all colleges previously attended, three professional recommendations, essay. Additional exam requirements/recommendations for international students: Recommended—TOEFL, IELTS (minimum score 6). *Application deadline:* Applications are processed on a rolling basis. Electronic applications accepted. *Expenses:* Contact institution. *Financial support:* Application deadline: 10/15; applicants required to submit FAFSA. *Unit head:* Dr. Michael Puglisi, Associate Dean for Academic Affairs, 276-944-6662, E-mail: mpuglisi@ehc.edu. *Application contact:* Mary Bolt, Director of Transfer and Graduate Admission, 276-944-6135, E-mail: mbolt@ehc.edu.

Fairfield University, College of Arts and Sciences, Fairfield, CT 06824. Offers American studies (MA); communication (MA); creative writing (MFA); mathematics (MS); public administration (MPA). *Program availability:* Part-time, evening/weekend, online learning. *Faculty:* 16 full-time (8 women), 12 part-time/adjunct (8 women). *Students:* 67 full-time (46 women), 64 part-time (35 women); includes 27 minority (8 Black or African American, non-Hispanic/Latino; 1 Asian, non-Hispanic/Latino; 14 Hispanic/Latino; 4 Two or more races, non-Hispanic/Latino), 10 international. Average age 32. 80 applicants, 81% accepted, 43 enrolled. In 2017, 38 master's awarded. *Degree requirements:* For master's, capstone research course. *Entrance requirements:* For master's, minimum GPA of 3.0, 2 letters of recommendation, resume, personal statement. Additional exam requirements/recommendations for international students: Required—TOEFL (minimum score 550 paper-based; 80 iBT) or IELTS (minimum score 6.5). *Application deadline:* For fall admission, 5/15 for international students; for spring admission, 10/15 for international students. Applications are processed on a rolling basis. Application fee: $60. Electronic applications accepted. *Expenses:* $725 per credit hour (for American studies, communication and math programs); $575 per credit hour (for MFA); $775 per credit hour (for MPA). *Financial support:* In 2017–18, 11 students received support. Scholarships/grants and unspecified assistantships available. Financial award applicants required to submit FAFSA. *Faculty research:* Nutrition and physiology, media industries, community-based teaching and learning, non commutative algebra and partial differential equations, cancer research in biology and physics. *Unit head:* Dr. Richard Greenwald, Dean, 203-254-4000 Ext. 2221, Fax: 203-254-4119, E-mail: rgreenwald@fairfield.edu. *Application contact:* Marianne Gumpper, Director of Graduate Admission, 203-254-4184, Fax: 203-254-4073, E-mail: gradadmis@fairfield.edu.
Website: http://www.fairfield.edu/cas

Florida State University, The Graduate School, College of Fine Arts, School of Dance, Tallahassee, FL 32306-2120. Offers American dance studies (MA); dance (MFA); studio and related studies (MA). *Accreditation:* NASD. *Faculty:* 20 full-time (13 women), 1 (woman) part-time/adjunct. *Students:* 25 full-time (19 women); includes 9 minority (6 Black or African American, non-Hispanic/Latino; 1 Asian, non-Hispanic/Latino; 2 Hispanic/Latino). Average age 28. 21 applicants, 67% accepted, 12 enrolled. In 2017, 12 master's awarded. *Degree requirements:* For master's, comprehensive exam (for some programs), thesis (for some programs), 1 foreign language (for MA in American dance studies). *Entrance requirements:* For master's, GRE General Test or minimum GPA of 3.0 (for MA in American dance studies), letters of recommendation; writing sample, audition and interview (for MFA, MA in studio and related studies); writing sample (for MA in American dance studies). Additional exam requirements/recommendations for international students: Required—TOEFL (minimum score 550 paper-based, 80 iBT), IELTS (minimum score 6.5) or Michigan English Language Assessment Battery (minimum score 77). *Application deadline:* For fall admission, 1/1 priority date for domestic and international students. Applications are processed on a rolling basis. Application fee: $30. Electronic applications accepted. *Expenses:* Contact institution. *Financial support:* In 2017–18, 44 students received support, including 3 fellowships with full tuition reimbursements available (averaging $15,000 per year), 30 research assistantships with full tuition reimbursements available (averaging $6,558 per year), 14 teaching assistantships with full tuition reimbursements available (averaging $6,558 per year); scholarships/grants, health care benefits, tuition waivers (full), and unspecified assistantships also available. Financial award application deadline: 1/1; financial award applicants required to submit FAFSA. *Faculty research:* Choreography, performance, dance and cultural significance, American dance history, dance technology, critical dance theory. *Unit head:* Prof. Josephine Garibaldi, Associate Professor and Chair, 850-644-1024, Fax: 850-644-1277, E-mail: jgaribaldi@fsu.edu. *Application contact:* Dr. Jeff Bray, Academic Program Manager, 850-644-1023, Fax: 850-644-1277, E-mail: jbray@fsu.edu.
Website: http://dance.fsu.edu/

Florida State University, The Graduate School, College of Social Sciences and Public Policy, Department of Political Science, Tallahassee, FL 32306-2230. Offers applied American politics and policy (MS); political science (MS, PhD). *Program availability:* Part-time. *Faculty:* 22 full-time (4 women), 1 part-time/adjunct (0 women). *Students:* 42 full-time (15 women), 33 part-time (12 women); includes 24 minority (5 Black or African American, non-Hispanic/Latino; 5 Asian, non-Hispanic/Latino; 12 Hispanic/Latino; 2 Two or more races, non-Hispanic/Latino). Average age 25. 73 applicants, 70% accepted, 34 enrolled. In 2017, 28 master's, 5 doctorates awarded. Terminal master's awarded for partial completion of doctoral program. *Degree requirements:* For master's, thesis optional; for doctorate, comprehensive exam, thesis/dissertation. *Entrance requirements:* For master's, GRE General Test, minimum undergraduate GPA of 3.0; for doctorate, GRE General Test, minimum graduate GPA of 3.5, undergraduate 3.0. Additional exam requirements/recommendations for international students: Required—TOEFL (minimum score 600 paper-based; 100 iBT). *Application deadline:* For fall admission, 1/15 priority date for domestic and international students. Applications are processed on a rolling basis. Application fee: $30. Electronic applications accepted. *Financial support:* In 2017–18, 34 students received support, including 25 research assistantships with full tuition reimbursements available (averaging $17,500 per year), 9 teaching assistantships with full tuition reimbursements available (averaging $17,500 per year); Federal Work-Study, institutionally sponsored loans, scholarships/grants, and unspecified assistantships also available. Financial award application deadline: 1/15; financial award applicants required to submit FAFSA. *Faculty research:* American government, international relations, comparative government, public policy. *Total annual research expenditures:* $130,000. *Unit head:* Dr. Mark Souva, Director of Graduate Studies, 850-644-7315, Fax: 850-644-1367, E-mail: msouva@fsu.edu. *Application contact:* Jeremiah J. Fisher, Academic Coordinator, 850-644-7305, Fax: 850-644-1367, E-mail: jeremiah.fisher@fsu.edu.
Website: http://coss.fsu.edu/polisci/

Georgetown University, Graduate School of Arts and Sciences, School of Continuing Studies, Washington, DC 20057. Offers American studies (MALS); applied intelligence (MPS); Catholic studies (MALS); classical civilizations (MALS); emergency and disaster management (MPS); ethics and the professions (MALS); global strategic communications (MPS); hospitality management (MPS); human resources management (MPS); humanities (MALS); individualized study (MALS); integrated marketing communications (MPS); international affairs (MALS); Islam and Muslim-Christian relations (MALS); journalism (MPS); liberal studies (DLS); literature and society (MALS); medieval and early modern European studies (MALS); public relations and corporate communications (MPS); real estate (MPS); religious studies (MALS); social and public policy (MALS); sports industry management (MPS); systems engineering management (MPS); technology management (MPS); the theory and practice of American democracy (MALS); urban and regional planning (MPS); visual culture (MALS). MPS in systems engineering management offered jointly with Stevens Institute of Technology. *Entrance requirements:* Additional exam requirements/recommendations for international students: Required—TOEFL.

The George Washington University, Columbian College of Arts and Sciences, Department of American Studies, Washington, DC 20052. Offers American studies (PhD); folk life (MA); historic preservation (MA); material culture (MA). *Program availability:* Part-time, evening/weekend. *Faculty:* 10 full-time (5 women), 1 part-time/adjunct (0 women). *Students:* 18 full-time (14 women), 17 part-time (13 women); includes 13 minority (6 Black or African American, non-Hispanic/Latino; 3 Asian, non-Hispanic/Latino; 2 Hispanic/Latino; 2 Two or more races, non-Hispanic/Latino). Average age 28. 103 applicants, 31% accepted, 12 enrolled. In 2017, 9 master's, 2 doctorates awarded. Terminal master's awarded for partial completion of doctoral program. *Degree requirements:* For master's, comprehensive exam; for doctorate, one foreign language, thesis/dissertation, general exam. *Entrance requirements:* For master's and doctorate, GRE General Test, minimum GPA of 3.0. Additional exam requirements/recommendations for international students: Required—TOEFL (minimum score 550 paper-based; 80 iBT). *Application deadline:* For fall admission, 1/15 priority date for domestic and international students; for spring admission, 10/1 for domestic students. Application fee: $75. *Expenses: Tuition:* Full-time $28,800; part-time $1655 per credit hour. *Required fees:* $45; $2.75 per credit hour. *Financial support:* In 2017–18, 22 students received support. Fellowships, research assistantships, teaching assistantships, career-related internships or fieldwork, Federal Work-Study, institutionally sponsored loans, and tuition waivers available. Financial award application deadline: 1/15. *Unit head:* Melanie McAlister, Chair, 202-994-7244, E-mail: jam@gwu.edu. *Application contact:* Information Contact, 202-994-6070, Fax: 202-994-8651, E-mail: amst@gwu.edu.
Website: http://departments.columbian.gwu.edu/americanstudies/

Georgia Southern University–Armstrong Campus, College of Graduate Studies, Program in History, Savannah, GA 31419-1997. Offers American and European history (MA); public history (MA). *Program availability:* Part-time, evening/weekend. *Faculty:* 11 full-time (3 women), 1 (woman) part-time/adjunct. *Students:* 7 full-time (3 women), 10 part-time (5 women); includes 3 minority (all Black or African American, non-Hispanic/Latino). Average age 43. 14 applicants, 43% accepted, 5 enrolled. In 2017, 5 master's awarded. *Degree requirements:* For master's, one foreign language, comprehensive exam (for some programs), thesis (for some programs), thesis, internship, or advanced fieldwork. *Entrance requirements:* For master's, GRE General Test, minimum GPA of 3.0, letters of recommendation, BA in history or equivalent. Additional exam requirements/recommendations for international students: Required—TOEFL (minimum score 523 paper-based; 70 iBT). *Application deadline:* For fall admission, 6/30 priority

date for domestic students, 5/1 priority date for international students; for spring admission, 11/15 priority date for domestic students, 9/15 priority date for international students; for summer admission, 4/15 priority date for domestic students, 9/15 for international students. Applications are processed on a rolling basis. Application fee: $30. Electronic applications accepted. *Expenses:* Tuition, state resident: part-time $211 per credit hour. Tuition, nonresident: part-time $782 per credit hour. *Required fees:* $737 per semester. Tuition and fees vary according to course load, degree level, campus/location and program. *Financial support:* In 2017–18, research assistantships with full tuition reimbursements (averaging $5,000 per year) were awarded; career-related internships or fieldwork, Federal Work-Study, and unspecified assistantships also available. Support available to part-time students. Financial award application deadline: 3/15; financial award applicants required to submit FAFSA. *Faculty research:* Public history; European, Latin American, African, and United States history. *Unit head:* Dr. Christopher Hendricks, Interim Department Head, 912-344-2725, Fax: 912-344-3451, E-mail: chris.hendricks@armstrong.edu. *Application contact:* McKenzie Peterman, Graduate Admissions Specialist, 912-478-5678, Fax: 912-478-0740, E-mail: mpeterman@georgiasouthern.edu.
Website: http://www.armstrong.edu/Liberal_Arts/history/history_graduate_program

Harvard University, Graduate School of Arts and Sciences, Committee on History of American Civilization, Cambridge, MA 02138. Offers PhD. *Degree requirements:* For doctorate, 2 foreign languages, thesis/dissertation. *Entrance requirements:* For doctorate, GRE General Test, GRE Subject Test (recommended). Additional exam requirements/recommendations for international students: Required—TOEFL. *Faculty research:* American history, literature, and religion in the Colonial era; twentieth-century American history, literature, and law; Southern literature, history, and sociology.

Indiana University–Purdue University Indianapolis, School of Liberal Arts, Department of History, Indianapolis, IN 46202. Offers European history (MA); public history (MA); United States history (MA); MA/MA; MA/MLS. *Program availability:* Part-time, evening/weekend. *Degree requirements:* For master's, one foreign language, thesis. *Entrance requirements:* For master's, GRE General Test, minimum GPA of 3.0. Electronic applications accepted.

Indiana University–Purdue University Indianapolis, School of Liberal Arts, Program in American Studies, Indianapolis, IN 46202. Offers PhD.

Inter American University of Puerto Rico, Metropolitan Campus, Graduate Programs, Program in History, San Juan, PR 00919-1293. Offers American history (PhD); history (MA, PhD).

James Madison University, The Graduate School, College of Arts and Letters, Program in History, Harrisonburg, VA 22801. Offers public history (MA); U.S. history (MA); world history (MA). *Program availability:* Part-time. *Students:* 16 full-time (6 women), 10 part-time (4 women). Average age 30. In 2017, 8 master's awarded. *Degree requirements:* For master's, one foreign language, comprehensive exam, thesis. Application fee: $55. Electronic applications accepted. *Expenses:* Tuition, state resident: full-time $10,512; part-time $438 per credit hour. Tuition, nonresident: full-time $28,358; part-time $1162 per credit hour. *Required fees:* $1128. *Financial support:* In 2017–18, 10 students received support, including 7 fellowships, 3 teaching assistantships with full tuition reimbursements available (averaging $9,284 per year); Federal Work-Study and assistantships (averaging $7911) also available. Financial award application deadline: 3/1; financial award applicants required to submit FAFSA. *Unit head:* Dr. Gabrielle Lanier, Department Head, 540-568-6132, E-mail: laniergm@jmu.edu. *Application contact:* Lynette D. Michael, Director of Graduate Admissions, 540-568-6131 Ext. 6395, Fax: 540-568-7860, E-mail: michaeld@jmu.edu.
Website: http://www.jmu.edu/history

Kennesaw State University, College of Humanities and Social Sciences, Master of Arts in American Studies Program, Kennesaw, GA 30144. Offers MA. *Program availability:* Part-time, evening/weekend. *Degree requirements:* For master's, one foreign language, thesis optional. *Entrance requirements:* For master's, GRE. Additional exam requirements/recommendations for international students: Required—TOEFL (minimum score 550 paper-based; 80 iBT), IELTS (minimum score 6.5). Electronic applications accepted.

Lake Forest College, Graduate Program in Liberal Studies, Lake Forest, IL 60045. Offers American studies (MLS); cinema in East Asia (MLS); environmental studies (MLS); history (MLS); Medieval and Renaissance art (MLS); philosophy (MLS); Spanish (MLS); writing (MLS). *Program availability:* Part-time, evening/weekend. *Faculty:* 11 full-time (3 women). *Students:* 34 part-time (19 women); includes 3 minority (1 Asian, non-Hispanic/Latino; 2 Hispanic/Latino). Average age 36. 20 applicants, 55% accepted, 8 enrolled. In 2017, 5 master's awarded. *Degree requirements:* For master's, thesis optional, 8 courses, including at least 3 interdisciplinary seminars. *Entrance requirements:* For master's, transcript, essay, interview. Additional exam requirements/recommendations for international students: Required—TOEFL (minimum score 550 paper-based; 83 iBT); Recommended—IELTS (minimum score 6.5). *Application deadline:* For fall admission, 7/15 priority date for domestic students, 6/1 priority date for international students; for spring admission, 12/1 priority date for domestic students, 10/1 priority date for international students. Applications are processed on a rolling basis. Application fee: $30. Electronic applications accepted. *Expenses:* $2,650 per course. *Financial support:* In 2017–18, 2 students received support. Partial tuition grants (for full-time teachers) available. *Faculty research:* Religion in America, Asian philosophy, cinema studies, theater studies, sociology of religion. *Unit head:* Prof. D. L. LeMahieu, Director, 847-735-5133, Fax: 847-735-6291, E-mail: lemahieu@lakeforest.edu. *Application contact:* Prof. Carol Gayle, Associate Director, 847-735-5083, Fax: 847-735-6291, E-mail: gayle@lakeforest.edu.
Website: http://www.lakeforest.edu/academics/programs/mls/

La Salle University, School of Arts and Sciences, Program in History, Philadelphia, PA 19141-1199. Offers American history (Certificate); European history (Certificate); history (MA); history for educators (MA); public history (MA); teaching advanced placement history (Certificate); world history (Certificate). *Program availability:* Part-time. *Faculty:* 4 full-time (1 woman), 2 part-time/adjunct (0 women). *Students:* 2 full-time (0 women), 10 part-time (5 women); includes 1 minority (Asian, non-Hispanic/Latino). Average age 37. 9 applicants, 78% accepted, 2 enrolled. In 2017, 7 master's awarded. *Degree requirements:* For master's, thesis or comprehensive exam. *Entrance requirements:* For master's, GRE or MAT, 18 hours of undergraduate coursework in history or a related discipline with minimum GPA of 3.0; two letters of recommendation; brief personal statement (250 to 500 words); writing sample (preferably from an undergraduate research paper). Additional exam requirements/recommendations for international students: Required—TOEFL. *Application deadline:* For fall admission, 8/15 priority date for domestic students, 7/15 for international students; for spring admission, 12/15 priority date for domestic students, 11/15 for international students; for summer admission, 4/15 priority date for domestic students, 3/15 for international students. Applications are processed on a rolling basis. Application fee: $35. Electronic applications accepted. Application fee is waived when completed online. *Expenses:* Contact institution. *Financial support:* In 2017–18, 1 student received support. Scholarships/grants available. Support available to part-time students. Financial award application deadline: 8/31; financial award applicants required to submit FAFSA. *Unit head:* Dr. George B.

Stow, Director, 215-951-1097, E-mail: grahis@lasalle.edu. *Application contact:* Elizabeth Heenan, Director, Graduate and Adult Enrollment, 215-951-1100, Fax: 215-951-1462, E-mail: heenan@lasalle.edu.
Website: http://www.lasalle.edu/master-history/

Lehigh University, College of Arts and Sciences, Department of History, Bethlehem, PA 18015. Offers Atlantic world (PhD); British history (PhD); history (MA); industrial and modern America (PhD); public history (MA). *Program availability:* Part-time. *Faculty:* 14 full-time (7 women). *Students:* 19 full-time (6 women), 15 part-time (2 women); includes 2 minority (1 Black or African American, non-Hispanic/Latino; 1 Two or more races, non-Hispanic/Latino), 2 international. Average age 35. 12 applicants, 58% accepted, 1 enrolled. In 2017, 3 master's, 2 doctorates awarded. Terminal master's awarded for partial completion of doctoral program. *Degree requirements:* For master's, comprehensive exam (for some programs), thesis (for some programs), comprehensive exam or thesis; for doctorate, comprehensive exam, thesis/dissertation. *Entrance requirements:* For master's, GRE General Test, recommendations, writing sample; for doctorate, GRE General Test, recommendations, writing samples. Additional exam requirements/recommendations for international students: Required—TOEFL. *Application deadline:* For fall admission, 2/15 for domestic and international students. Application fee: $75. *Financial support:* In 2017–18, 2 fellowships with full tuition reimbursements (averaging $22,500 per year), 10 teaching assistantships with full tuition reimbursements (averaging $10,000 per year) were awarded; research assistantships, institutionally sponsored loans, scholarships/grants, tuition waivers (full and partial), and unspecified assistantships also available. Financial award application deadline: 1/15. *Faculty research:* Colonial America, modern America, history of technology, Atlantic world, French Atlantic, Spanish Atlantic, British empire, gender, intellectual history, African diaspora history. *Unit head:* Prof. John Pettegrew, Chairman, 610-758-3360, Fax: 610-758-6554, E-mail: jcp5@lehigh.edu. *Application contact:* Dr. John Savage, Graduate Coordinator, 610-758-3363, Fax: 610-758-6554, E-mail: jms8@lehigh.edu.
Website: http://history.cas2.lehigh.edu/

Lehigh University, College of Arts and Sciences, Program in American Studies, Bethlehem, PA 18015. Offers Africana studies (Graduate Certificate); American studies (MA); documentary film (Graduate Certificate). *Faculty:* 3 full-time (2 women), 1 part-time/adjunct (0 women). *Students:* 3 full-time (all women), 3 part-time (2 women); includes 1 minority (Black or African American, non-Hispanic/Latino). Average age 26. 6 applicants, 100% accepted, 3 enrolled. In 2017, 3 master's awarded. *Degree requirements:* For master's, thesis. *Entrance requirements:* For master's, GRE, writing sample, essay, minimum GPA of 2.75, 2 letters of recommendation. Additional exam requirements/recommendations for international students: Required—TOEFL (minimum score 85 iBT), IELTS (minimum score 6.5). *Application deadline:* For fall admission, 1/1 for domestic students, 7/15 for international students; for spring admission, 12/1 for domestic and international students. Applications are processed on a rolling basis. Application fee: $75. *Expenses:* $1,460 per credit. *Financial support:* Fellowships and tuition remission available. Financial award application deadline: 1/1. *Faculty research:* War; media and video games; social movements; community identity and narrative; traditional eighteenth-, nineteenth-, and twentieth-century literature and history; gender and popular culture. *Unit head:* Prof. Jodi Eichler-Levine, Director, 610-758-3370, Fax: 610-758-2131, E-mail: amstdgrad@lehigh.edu. *Application contact:* Gary Burgess, Graduate Coordinator, 610-758-4281, Fax: 610-758-6554, E-mail: amstdgrad@lehigh.edu.
Website: http://american.cas2.lehigh.edu/

Michigan State University, The Graduate School, College of Arts and Letters, Program in American Studies, East Lansing, MI 48824. Offers MA, PhD. *Entrance requirements:* Additional exam requirements/recommendations for international students: Required—TOEFL. Electronic applications accepted.

Monmouth University, Graduate Studies, Program in History, West Long Branch, NJ 07764-1898. Offers European history (MA); United States history (MA); world history (MA). *Program availability:* Part-time, evening/weekend. *Faculty:* 4 full-time (2 women). *Students:* 3 full-time (2 women), 22 part-time (7 women); includes 4 minority (all Hispanic/Latino). Average age 33. In 2017, 14 master's awarded. *Degree requirements:* For master's, comprehensive exam (for some programs), thesis (for some programs). *Entrance requirements:* For master's, minimum GPA of 3.0 in major, 2.5 overall; two letters of recommendation; statement describing historical areas of interest and how graduate study will contribute to professional and academic goals. Additional exam requirements/recommendations for international students: Required—TOEFL (minimum score 550 paper-based; 79 iBT), IELTS (minimum score 6) or Michigan English Language Assessment Battery (minimum score 77). *Application deadline:* For fall admission, 7/15 priority date for domestic students, 6/1 for international students; for spring admission, 12/15 priority date for domestic students, 11/1 for international students. Applications are processed on a rolling basis. Application fee: $50. Electronic applications accepted. *Expenses:* Tuition: Full-time $21,366; part-time $7122 per credit. *Required fees:* $700; $175 per term. *Financial support:* In 2017–18, 4 students received support. Institutionally sponsored loans, scholarships/grants, and unspecified assistantships available. Support available to part-time students. Financial award applicants required to submit FAFSA. *Faculty research:* British, German, and French Revolutions; Soviet Union; Africa; English history; U.S. military; women's history. *Unit head:* Dr. Maryann Rhett, Director, 732-263-5768, Fax: 732-263-5112, E-mail: mrhett@monmouth.edu. *Application contact:* Andrea Thompson, Graduate Admission Counselor, 732-571-3452, Fax: 732-263-5123, E-mail: gradadm@monmouth.edu.
Website: https://www.monmouth.edu/graduate/ma-history/

New Mexico Highlands University, Graduate Studies, College of Arts and Sciences, Department of Social and Behavioral Sciences, Las Vegas, NM 87701. Offers psychology (MS), including clinical psychology/counseling, general psychology; public affairs (MA), including applied sociology; Southwest studies (MA), including anthropology. *Program availability:* Part-time. *Degree requirements:* For master's, comprehensive exam, thesis or alternative. *Entrance requirements:* For master's, minimum undergraduate GPA of 3.0. Additional exam requirements/recommendations for international students: Required—TOEFL (minimum score 540 paper-based). *Faculty research:* Southwest Native American resettlement development, community-level interventions, neurochemistry of personality, comparative criminal justice, social theory and activism.

New York University, Graduate School of Arts and Science, Program in American Studies, New York, NY 10012-1019. Offers MA, PhD. *Program availability:* Part-time. *Students:* Average age 33. 186 applicants, 10% accepted, 7 enrolled. In 2017, 4 master's, 5 doctorates awarded. *Degree requirements:* For master's, one foreign language, thesis; for doctorate, 2 foreign languages, thesis/dissertation. *Entrance requirements:* For master's and doctorate, GRE General Test, writing sample. Additional exam requirements/recommendations for international students: Required—TOEFL. *Application deadline:* For fall admission, 12/18 for domestic and international students. Application fee: $100. *Expenses:* Tuition: Full-time $41,352; part-time $19,968 per year. *Required fees:* $2496; $1628 per unit. $814 per term. Tuition and fees vary according to course load and program. *Financial support:* Fellowships, teaching assistantships, Federal Work-Study, institutionally sponsored loans, and unspecified assistantships

available. Financial award application deadline: 12/18; financial award applicants required to submit FAFSA. *Faculty research:* Cultural politics; race, gender, and sexuality studies; nationalism and transnationalism; science and technology; urban and suburban studies. *Unit head:* Andrew Ross, Director, 212-998-9650, Fax: 212-995-4665, E-mail: amstudies@nyu.edu. *Application contact:* Raechel Bosch, Graduate Administrator, 212-998-9650, Fax: 212-995-4665, E-mail: amstudies@nyu.edu.
Website: http://www.nyu.edu/gsas/dept/amerstu/

New York University, Graduate School of Arts and Science, Program in Irish and Irish American Studies, New York, NY 10012-1019. Offers MA. *Program availability:* Part-time. *Students:* Average age 41. 29 applicants, 100% accepted, 19 enrolled. In 2017, 5 master's awarded. *Entrance requirements:* For master's, GRE General Test. Additional exam requirements/recommendations for international students: Required—TOEFL. *Application deadline:* For fall admission, 3/1 priority date for domestic students, 3/1 for international students. Application fee: $100. *Expenses: Tuition:* Full-time $41,352; part-time $19,968 per year. *Required fees:* $2496; $1628 per unit. $814 per term. Tuition and fees vary according to course load and program. *Financial support:* Federal Work-Study, scholarships/grants, health care benefits, and unspecified assistantships available. Financial award application deadline: 3/1. *Unit head:* John Waters, Director of Graduate Studies, 212-998-3950, Fax: 212-995-4373, E-mail: gsas.irishstudies.ma@nyu.edu. *Application contact:* Miriam Nyhan, Graduate Program Administrator, 212-998-3950, Fax: 212-995-4373, E-mail: gsas.irishstudies.ma@nyu.edu.

Northwestern Oklahoma State University, Program in American Studies, Alva, OK 73717. Offers MA. *Program availability:* Part-time. *Degree requirements:* For master's, comprehensive exam, thesis optional. *Entrance requirements:* For master's, GRE or MAT, at least 12 upper-level undergraduate hours in history and/or literature. *Faculty research:* Literary history of Oklahoma, Oklahoma Poets Laureate, American naturalism, Lincoln studies, public service and policy studies.

Northwestern University, School of Professional Studies, Program in Liberal Studies, Evanston, IL 60208. Offers American studies (MA); history (MA); religious and ethical studies (MA). *Program availability:* Part-time, evening/weekend.
Website: https://sps.northwestern.edu/masters/liberal-studies/index.php

Penn State Harrisburg, Graduate School, School of Humanities, Middletown, PA 17057. Offers American studies (MA, PhD); communications (MA); folklore and ethnography (Certificate); heritage and museum practice (Certificate); humanities (MA). *Program availability:* Evening/weekend. *Unit head:* Dr. Mukund S. Kulkarni, Jr., Chancellor, 717-948-6105, Fax: 717-948-6452. *Application contact:* Robert W. Coffman, Jr., Director of Enrollment Management, Recruitment and Admissions, 717-948-6250, Fax: 717-948-6325, E-mail: hbgadmit@psu.edu.
Website: https://harrisburg.psu.edu/humanities

Pepperdine University, Seaver College, Division of Humanities, Malibu, CA 90263. Offers American studies (MA); writing for screen and television (MFA). *Program availability:* Part-time. *Students:* 9 full-time (7 women), 41 part-time (23 women); includes 10 minority (4 Black or African American, non-Hispanic/Latino; 1 Asian, non-Hispanic/Latino; 3 Hispanic/Latino; 2 Two or more races, non-Hispanic/Latino), 2 international. Average age 31. In 2017, 13 master's awarded. *Degree requirements:* For master's, oral and written exams. *Entrance requirements:* For master's, GRE General Test, writing sample, letters of recommendation. Additional exam requirements/recommendations for international students: Required—TOEFL. *Application deadline:* For fall admission, 2/1 priority date for domestic students. Applications are processed on a rolling basis. Application fee: $65. *Financial support:* Applicants required to submit FAFSA. *Unit head:* Dr. Michael G. Ditmore, Chair/Professor of English, 310-506-4182, Fax: 310-506-7307, E-mail: michael.ditmore@pepperdine.edu. *Application contact:* Hayley Wolf, Director of Admission, 310-506-4392, E-mail: hayley.wolf@pepperdine.edu.
Website: http://seaver.pepperdine.edu/humanities/default.htm

Portland State University, Graduate Studies, College of Urban and Public Affairs, Hatfield School of Government, Division of Political Science, Portland, OR 97207-0751. Offers political science (MA), including American politics, comparative politics, international relations, political theory. *Program availability:* Part-time. *Faculty:* 10 full-time (4 women), 8 part-time/adjunct (2 women). *Students:* 9 full-time (4 women), 11 part-time (3 women); includes 1 minority (Asian, non-Hispanic/Latino), 2 international. Average age 36. 13 applicants, 69% accepted, 8 enrolled. In 2017, 2 master's awarded. *Degree requirements:* For master's, variable foreign language requirement, comprehensive exam, thesis. *Entrance requirements:* For master's, GRE General Test, minimum undergraduate GPA of 3.0 or 3.1 in graduate-level coursework, 2 letters of recommendation, statement of intent. Additional exam requirements/recommendations for international students: Required—TOEFL (minimum score 550 paper-based; 90 iBT). *Application deadline:* For fall admission, 4/1 priority date for domestic students, 3/1 priority date for international students; for spring admission, 11/1 for domestic and international students. Application fee: $65. *Expenses:* Tuition, state resident: full-time $14,436; part-time $401 per credit. Tuition, nonresident: full-time $21,780; part-time $605 per credit. *Required fees:* $1380; $22 per credit. $119 per quarter. One-time fee: $325. Tuition and fees vary according to program. *Financial support:* In 2017–18, 6 students received support, including 8 research assistantships with full and partial tuition reimbursements available (averaging $3,572 per year), 2 teaching assistantships with full and partial tuition reimbursements available (averaging $7,443 per year); career-related internships or fieldwork, Federal Work-Study, and unspecified assistantships also available. Support available to part-time students. Financial award application deadline: 3/1; financial award applicants required to submit FAFSA. *Faculty research:* Congress, presidency, political reform, international environment, hate speech. *Unit head:* Christopher Shortell, Chair, 503-725-5139, Fax: 503-725-8444, E-mail: shortell@pdx.edu.
Website: https://www.pdx.edu/hatfieldschool/political-science

Providence College, Department of History, Providence, RI 02918. Offers American history (MA); modern European history (MA). *Program availability:* Part-time, evening/weekend. *Degree requirements:* For master's, comprehensive exam, thesis optional. *Entrance requirements:* Additional exam requirements/recommendations for international students: Required—TOEFL (minimum score 577 paper-based; 90 iBT). *Expenses:* Contact institution. *Faculty research:* American history, modern European history, Medieval history, Native American history, religion, slavery, western civilization, labor movements, Japanese and Asian history, early modern Europe.

Purdue University, Graduate School, College of Liberal Arts, Program in American Studies, West Lafayette, IN 47907. Offers MA, PhD. *Students:* 30 full-time (22 women), 9 part-time (5 women); includes 18 minority (11 Black or African American, non-Hispanic/Latino; 3 Asian, non-Hispanic/Latino; 3 Hispanic/Latino; 1 Two or more races, non-Hispanic/Latino), 7 international. Average age 33. 35 applicants, 29% accepted, 4 enrolled. In 2017, 3 master's, 2 doctorates awarded. *Degree requirements:* For master's, essay; for doctorate, one foreign language, thesis/dissertation. *Entrance requirements:* For master's, GRE General Test, minimum undergraduate GPA of 3.0 or equivalent; writing sample; for doctorate, GRE General Test, minimum undergraduate GPA of 3.0 or equivalent; writing sample; master's degree with minimum GPA of 3.0 or equivalent. Additional exam requirements/recommendations for international students: Required—TOEFL (minimum score 550 paper-based; 77 iBT), TWE. *Application deadline:* For fall admission, 1/15 priority date for domestic students, 1/15 for international students. Applications are processed on a rolling basis. Application fee: $60 ($75 for international students). Electronic applications accepted. *Financial support:* In 2017–18, 34 students received support, including teaching assistantships with tuition reimbursements available (averaging $14,150 per year); fellowships also available. Support available to part-time students. Financial award application deadline: 1/15; financial award applicants required to submit FAFSA. *Faculty research:* African American studies; critical race theory; women, gender and sexuality studies; popular culture; transnational studies; U.S. social movements; ecocriticism. *Unit head:* Dr. Rayvon D. Fouche, Director, 765-496-9629, E-mail: rfouche@purdue.edu. *Application contact:* Eisa Schirmer, Graduate Contact, 765-496-9629, E-mail: eschirme@purdue.edu.
Website: http://www.cla.purdue.edu/american-studies/

Regent University, Graduate School, Robertson School of Government, Virginia Beach, VA 23464. Offers government (MA), including American government, healthcare policy and ethics (MA, MPA), international relations, law and public policy, national security studies, political communication, political theory, religion and politics; national security studies (MA), including cybersecurity, homeland security, international security, Middle East politics; public administration (MPA), including emergency management and homeland security, federal government, general public administration, healthcare policy and ethics (MA, MPA), law, nonprofit administration and faith-based organizations, public leadership and management, servant leadership. *Program availability:* Part-time, evening/weekend, 100% online, blended/hybrid learning. *Faculty:* 8 full-time (1 woman), 20 part-time/adjunct (3 women). *Students:* 39 full-time (23 women), 137 part-time (78 women); includes 83 minority (49 Black or African American, non-Hispanic/Latino; 1 American Indian or Alaska Native, non-Hispanic/Latino; 7 Asian, non-Hispanic/Latino; 15 Hispanic/Latino; 11 Two or more races, non-Hispanic/Latino). Average age 35. 345 applicants, 31% accepted, 57 enrolled. In 2017, 38 master's awarded. *Degree requirements:* For master's, thesis optional, internship. *Entrance requirements:* For master's, GRE General Test or LSAT, personal essay, writing sample, resume, college transcripts. Additional exam requirements/recommendations for international students: Required—TOEFL (minimum score 577 paper-based). *Application deadline:* For fall admission, 5/1 priority date for domestic students; for spring admission, 11/1 priority date for domestic students. Applications are processed on a rolling basis. Application fee: $50. Electronic applications accepted. *Expenses:* $650 per credit; $300 technology fee per semester. *Financial support:* In 2017–18, 116 students received support. Career-related internships or fieldwork, scholarships/grants, and unspecified assistantships available. Support available to part-time students. *Faculty research:* International relations and politics, public administration, leadership and ethics, Biblical law, Constitutional law and Supreme Court. *Unit head:* Dr. Eric Patterson, Dean, 757-352-4616, Fax: 757-352-4735, E-mail: epatterson@regent.edu. *Application contact:* Heidi Cece, Assistant Vice President of Enrollment Management, 800-373-5504, Fax: 757-352-4381, E-mail: admissions@regent.edu.
Website: https://www.regent.edu/robertson-school-of-government/

Rice University, Graduate Programs, School of Humanities, Department of Religious Studies, Houston, TX 77251-1892. Offers African religions (PhD); African-American religions (PhD); contemplative studies (PhD); ghosticism, esotericism, mysticism (PhD); Islam (PhD); Jewish thought and philosophy (PhD); modern Christianity in thought and popular culture (PhD); psychology of religion (PhD); the Bible and beyond (PhD). *Degree requirements:* For doctorate, 2 foreign languages, comprehensive exam, thesis/dissertation. *Entrance requirements:* For doctorate, GRE, letters of recommendation, writing sample. Additional exam requirements/recommendations for international students: Required—TOEFL (minimum score 600 paper-based; 90 iBT). Electronic applications accepted. *Faculty research:* Origins and historical development of Islam, history of Christianity, the study of comparative religion, African-American religion, religion and culture.

Rutgers University–Newark, Graduate School, Program in American Studies, Newark, NJ 07102. Offers MA, PhD. *Entrance requirements:* For master's and doctorate, GRE, minimum undergraduate B average.

Saint Louis University, Graduate Programs, College of Arts and Sciences, Department of American Studies, St. Louis, MO 63103. Offers MA, MA-R, PhD. *Program availability:* Part-time. *Degree requirements:* For master's, thesis optional, comprehensive written and oral exams; for doctorate, one foreign language, comprehensive exam, thesis/dissertation, preliminary exams. *Entrance requirements:* For master's, GRE General Test, letters of recommendation, resume; for doctorate, GRE General Test, letters of recommendation, resumé, goal statement, transcripts. Additional exam requirements/recommendations for international students: Required—TOEFL (minimum score 525 paper-based). Electronic applications accepted. *Faculty research:* Urban studies, American religion, intellectual history, southern culture, African-American literature.

Salisbury University, Department of History, Salisbury, MD 21801-6837. Offers history (MA), including Colonial and Revolutionary American history, history of the Chesapeake Bay region, United States history in the 19th and 20th centuries, world history. *Program availability:* Part-time, evening/weekend. *Faculty:* 7 full-time (3 women). *Students:* 5 full-time (2 women), 6 part-time (1 woman); includes 1 minority (Two or more races, non-Hispanic/Latino). Average age 31. 7 applicants, 86% accepted, 6 enrolled. In 2017, 10 master's awarded. *Degree requirements:* For master's, comprehensive exam, thesis optional. *Entrance requirements:* For master's, three letters of recommendation; transcripts for colleges and universities attended; personal statement; writing sample; minimum GPA of 3.0. Additional exam requirements/recommendations for international students: Required—TOEFL (minimum score 587 paper-based, 94 iBT), Michigan English Language Assessment Battery (82), IELTS (7.0), or PTE (65). *Application deadline:* For fall admission, 4/15 priority date for domestic and international students; for spring admission, 10/15 priority date for domestic and international students. Applications are processed on a rolling basis. Application fee: $65. Electronic applications accepted. *Expenses:* $392 per credit hour resident; $703 per credit hour non-resident; $92 per credit hour fees. *Financial support:* In 2017–18, 5 students received support, including 1 teaching assistantship with full tuition reimbursement available (averaging $8,000 per year); career-related internships or fieldwork and scholarships/grants also available. Support available to part-time students. Financial award application deadline: 3/1; financial award applicants required to submit FAFSA. *Faculty research:* Chesapeake studies (regional focus 17th-20th century), African American history, Native American history (minorities/ethnic focus), Afro-Asia (transitional topic), 20th century U.S. history. *Unit head:* Dr. Celine Carayon, Graduate Program Director, 410-677-3251, E-mail: cxcarayon@salisbury.edu.
Website: http://www.salisbury.edu/gsr/gradstudies/HISTpage.html

Stockton University, Office of Graduate Studies, Program in American Studies, Galloway, NJ 08205-9441. Offers MA, Certificate. *Program availability:* Part-time. *Faculty:* 4 full-time (3 women), 1 part-time/adjunct (0 women). *Students:* 4 full-time (2 women), 9 part-time (6 women); includes 1 minority (Two or more races, non-Hispanic/Latino). Average age 32. 5 applicants, 60% accepted, 3 enrolled. In 2017, 7 master's awarded. *Application deadline:* For fall admission, 7/1 for domestic and international students; for winter admission, 11/1 for international students; for spring admission, 12/1

for domestic students. Applications are processed on a rolling basis. Application fee: $50. Electronic applications accepted. *Expenses:* Contact institution. *Financial support:* Fellowships, research assistantships, scholarships/grants, and unspecified assistantships available. *Unit head:* Dr. Kristin Jacobson, Program Director, 609-626-5581, E-mail: gradschool@stockton.edu. *Application contact:* Tara Williams, Assistant Director of Enrollment Management, 609-626-3640, Fax: 609-626-6050, E-mail: gradschool@stockton.edu.

Texas Christian University, AddRan College of Liberal Arts, Department of History, Fort Worth, TX 76129. Offers Latin America (MA, PhD); United States (MA, PhD). *Faculty:* 18 full-time (6 women). *Students:* 50 full-time (20 women); includes 6 minority (5 Hispanic/Latino; 1 Two or more races, non-Hispanic/Latino), 1 international. Average age 34. 21 applicants, 57% accepted, 9 enrolled. In 2017, 1 master's, 6 doctorates awarded. Terminal master's awarded for partial completion of doctoral program. *Degree requirements:* For master's, comprehensive exam, thesis or alternative; for doctorate, one foreign language, comprehensive exam, thesis/dissertation. *Entrance requirements:* For master's and doctorate, GRE General Test. Additional exam requirements/recommendations for international students: Recommended—TOEFL. *Application deadline:* 2/1 for domestic and international students; for summer admission, 2/1 for domestic and international students. Application fee: $60. Electronic applications accepted. *Financial support:* In 2017–18, 50 students received support, including 3 fellowships with full tuition reimbursements available (averaging $20,000 per year), 15 research assistantships with full tuition reimbursements available (averaging $17,500 per year), 5 teaching assistantships with full tuition reimbursements available (averaging $17,500 per year); tuition waivers (full) also available. Financial award application deadline: 2/1. *Faculty research:* U.S. South, Latin American history, Atlantic World history, American West. *Total annual research expenditures:* $140,000. *Unit head:* Dr. Jodi Campbell, Professor, 817-257-5882, Fax: 817-257-5650, E-mail: j.campbell@tcu.edu. *Application contact:* Heather Confessore, Administrative Assistant, 817-257-7288, Fax: 817-257-5650, E-mail: h.confessore@tcu.edu.
Website: http://www.his.tcu.edu/graduate.asp

Trinity College, Graduate Programs, Program in American Studies, Hartford, CT 06106-3100. Offers American culture studies (MA); museums and communities (MA). *Program availability:* Part-time, evening/weekend. *Degree requirements:* For master's, thesis or alternative. *Entrance requirements:* For master's, minimum GPA of 3.0.

Universidad de las Américas Puebla, Division of Graduate Studies, School of Social Sciences, Program in American Studies, Puebla, Mexico. Offers MA. *Program availability:* Part-time, evening/weekend. *Degree requirements:* For master's, one foreign language, thesis. *Faculty research:* NAFTA, technology, culture, politics and economics in NAFTA region.

University at Buffalo, the State University of New York, Graduate School, College of Arts and Sciences, Department of Transnational Studies, Buffalo, NY 14214. Offers American studies (MA, PhD); Canadian studies (MA); global gender studies (MA, PhD). *Program availability:* Part-time. *Faculty:* 16 full-time (8 women), 3 part-time/adjunct (1 woman). *Students:* 71 full-time (42 women); includes 26 minority (9 Black or African American, non-Hispanic/Latino; 6 American Indian or Alaska Native, non-Hispanic/Latino; 9 Asian, non-Hispanic/Latino; 2 Hispanic/Latino). Average age 33. 30 applicants, 70% accepted, 9 enrolled. In 2017, 7 master's, 15 doctorates awarded. Terminal master's awarded for partial completion of doctoral program. *Degree requirements:* For master's, comprehensive exam (for some programs), thesis optional; for doctorate, comprehensive exam, thesis/dissertation. *Entrance requirements:* For master's, minimum GPA of 3.0; for doctorate, GRE, minimum GPA of 3.0. Additional exam requirements/recommendations for international students: Required—TOEFL (minimum score 550 paper-based; 79 iBT), IELTS (minimum score 6.5). *Application deadline:* For fall admission, 8/28 priority date for domestic students, 6/15 priority date for international students; for winter admission, 2/1 for domestic and international students; for spring admission, 1/28 priority date for domestic students, 11/15 priority date for international students. Applications are processed on a rolling basis. Application fee: $75. Electronic applications accepted. *Financial support:* In 2017–18, 20 students received support, including 2 fellowships with full tuition reimbursements available (averaging $13,060 per year), 15 teaching assistantships with full tuition reimbursements available (averaging $13,060 per year); research assistantships, career-related internships or fieldwork, institutionally sponsored loans, scholarships/grants, health care benefits, and unspecified assistantships also available. Financial award application deadline: 1/1. *Faculty research:* Native American, intercultural and indigenous people's studies, border theory, cultural studies, American pop culture, feminist theory, construction of gender in society. *Unit head:* Dr. Cecil Foster, Chair, 716-645-0786, Fax: 716-645-5976, E-mail: cecilfos@buffalo.edu. *Application contact:* Karen M. Reinard, Graduate Coordinator, 716-645-0797, Fax: 716-645-5976, E-mail: kreinard@buffalo.edu.
Website: http://transnationalstudies.buffalo.edu/

The University of Alabama, Graduate School, College of Arts and Sciences, Department of American Studies, Tuscaloosa, AL 35487. Offers MA. *Program availability:* Part-time. *Faculty:* 12 full-time (5 women). *Students:* 9 full-time (5 women), 4 part-time (2 women); includes 4 minority (all Black or African American, non-Hispanic/Latino), 1 international. Average age 27. 18 applicants, 67% accepted, 9 enrolled. In 2017, 6 master's awarded. *Degree requirements:* For master's, comprehensive exam, thesis optional. *Entrance requirements:* For master's, GRE or MAT. Additional exam requirements/recommendations for international students: Required—TOEFL. *Application deadline:* For fall admission, 1/15 priority date for domestic and international students; for spring admission, 11/30 priority date for domestic and international students; for summer admission, 1/15 for domestic and international students. Applications are processed on a rolling basis. Application fee: $50 ($60 for international students). Electronic applications accepted. *Financial support:* Teaching assistantships with full tuition reimbursements, career-related internships or fieldwork, health care benefits, and unspecified assistantships available. Financial award application deadline: 1/10; financial award applicants required to submit FAFSA. *Faculty research:* Social and cultural history, popular music and popular culture, African-American arts and education, the culture and environment of the South, gender and sexuality, Asian-American studies, sports, Latino Studies. *Unit head:* Dr. Lynne M. Adrian, Chair and Associate Professor, 205-348-5940, Fax: 205-348-9766, E-mail: ladrian@ua.edu. *Application contact:* Patrick D. Fuller, Senior Graduate Admissions Counselor, 205-348-5923, Fax: 205-348-0400, E-mail: patrick.d.fuller@ua.edu.
Website: http://ams.ua.edu/

University of Colorado Denver, College of Liberal Arts and Sciences, Department of History, Denver, CO 80217. Offers European history (MA); global history (MA); public history (MA); U.S. history (MA). *Program availability:* Part-time, evening/weekend. *Degree requirements:* For master's, comprehensive exam, thesis optional, 36 semester hours (12 courses). *Entrance requirements:* For master's, GRE General Test, writing sample, minimum undergraduate GPA of 3.25, three letters of recommendation, statement of purpose addressing any weaknesses in academic record. Additional exam requirements/recommendations for international students: Required—TOEFL (minimum score 537 paper-based; 75 iBT); Recommended—IELTS (minimum score 6.5). Electronic applications accepted. *Faculty research:* Uses of pre-modern Islamic heritage in modern India; relationship between liberal understandings of democracy, crime, and police discretion; relationships between gender, class, health, and welfare in nineteenth and early twentieth century England; U.S. business cultures and their influences on marketing and personnel practices; intersection of business and political ideologies; social and environmental history of the Rocky Mountain West.

University of Dallas, Braniff Graduate School of Liberal Arts, Program in American Studies, Irving, TX 75062-4736. Offers MAS. *Program availability:* Part-time. *Entrance requirements:* For master's, GRE General Test. *Application deadline:* For fall admission, 2/15 priority date for domestic students; for spring admission, 11/15 for domestic students. Applications are processed on a rolling basis. Application fee: $50. *Expenses: Tuition:* Full-time $33,750; part-time $22,500 per year. Tuition and fees vary according to program. *Financial support:* Application deadline: 2/15. *Faculty research:* Shakespeare, Milton, Melville, Hawthorne, liberty and American literature. *Unit head:* Dr. Richard Dougherty, Graduate Director, 972-721-5043, Fax: 972-721-4007, E-mail: doughr@udallas.edu.

University of Delaware, College of Arts and Sciences, Winterthur Program in American Material Culture, Newark, DE 19716. Offers MA. *Degree requirements:* For master's, thesis. *Entrance requirements:* For master's, GRE General Test, minimum GPA of 3.0. Electronic applications accepted. *Faculty research:* American material culture, American studies, decorative arts.

University of Hawaii at Manoa, Office of Graduate Education, College of Arts and Humanities, Department of American Studies, Honolulu, HI 96822. Offers American studies (MA, PhD); historic preservation (Graduate Certificate); museum studies (Graduate Certificate). *Program availability:* Part-time. *Degree requirements:* For master's, comprehensive exam (for some programs), thesis (for some programs); for doctorate, comprehensive exam, thesis/dissertation. *Entrance requirements:* For master's and doctorate, GRE General Test. Additional exam requirements/recommendations for international students: Required—TOEFL (minimum score 600 paper-based; 100 iBT), IELTS (minimum score 7). *Faculty research:* Ethnicity and race, popular culture, historic preservation, arts and culture, international relations.

The University of Iowa, Graduate College, College of Liberal Arts and Sciences, Department of American Studies, Iowa City, IA 52242-1316. Offers MA, PhD. *Degree requirements:* For master's, thesis optional, exam; for doctorate, comprehensive exam, thesis/dissertation. *Entrance requirements:* For master's and doctorate, GRE General Test, minimum GPA of 3.0. Additional exam requirements/recommendations for international students: Required—TOEFL (minimum score 550 paper-based; 81 iBT). Electronic applications accepted.

The University of Kansas, Graduate Studies, College of Liberal Arts and Sciences, Department of American Studies, Lawrence, KS 66045. Offers MA, PhD, MUP/MA. *Program availability:* Part-time. *Students:* 33 full-time (22 women), 1 part-time (0 women); includes 10 minority (6 Black or African American, non-Hispanic/Latino; 3 Hispanic/Latino; 1 Two or more races, non-Hispanic/Latino), 3 international. Average age 33. 18 applicants, 39% accepted, 4 enrolled. In 2017, 2 master's awarded. Terminal master's awarded for partial completion of doctoral program. *Entrance requirements:* For master's and doctorate, GRE General Test, resume, statement of purpose, three letters of recommendation, official transcripts of all undergraduate and graduate study completed, writing sample. *Application deadline:* For fall admission, 12/1 priority date for domestic and international students. Applications are processed on a rolling basis. Application fee: $65 ($85 for international students). Electronic applications accepted. *Financial support:* Fellowships, research assistantships, teaching assistantships, Federal Work-Study, scholarships/grants, health care benefits, and unspecified assistantships available. Financial award application deadline: 12/1. *Unit head:* Margaret Kelley, Director of Graduate Studies, 785-864-6927, E-mail: mskelley@ku.edu. *Application contact:* Kay Isbell, Graduate Admissions Contact, 785-864-2957, E-mail: kisbell@ku.edu.
Website: http://americanstudies.ku.edu

University of Louisiana at Lafayette, College of Liberal Arts, Department of Modern Languages, Program in Francophone Studies, Lafayette, LA 70504. Offers PhD. *Degree requirements:* For doctorate, 2 foreign languages, comprehensive exam, thesis/dissertation. *Entrance requirements:* For doctorate, GRE General Test, minimum GPA of 2.75. Additional exam requirements/recommendations for international students: Required—TOEFL (minimum score 550 paper-based). Electronic applications accepted. *Faculty research:* Louisiana folklore, eighteenth-century French literature, contemporary criticism.

University of Maryland, College Park, Academic Affairs, College of Arts and Humanities, Department of American Studies, College Park, MD 20742. Offers MA, PhD. *Degree requirements:* For master's, thesis or scholarly paper and exam; for doctorate, thesis/dissertation, 3 comprehensive exams. *Entrance requirements:* For master's, GRE General Test, minimum GPA of 3.0, writing sample, 3 letters of recommendation; for doctorate, GRE General Test. Additional exam requirements/recommendations for international students: Required—TOEFL. Electronic applications accepted. *Faculty research:* Material culture, modes of culture, cultural movements, popular culture, ethnography.

University of Massachusetts Amherst, Graduate School, College of Humanities and Fine Arts, Department of English, Amherst, MA 01003. Offers American studies (PhD); composition and rhetoric (PhD); creative writing (MFA); English and American literature (MA, PhD). *Program availability:* Part-time. Terminal master's awarded for partial completion of doctoral program. *Degree requirements:* For master's, one foreign language, thesis optional; for doctorate, one foreign language, comprehensive exam, thesis/dissertation. *Entrance requirements:* For master's, manuscript; for doctorate, GRE General Test, manuscript. Additional exam requirements/recommendations for international students: Required—TOEFL (minimum score 550 paper-based; 80 iBT), IELTS (minimum score 6.5). Electronic applications accepted.

University of Massachusetts Boston, College of Liberal Arts, Program in American Studies, Boston, MA 02125-3393. Offers MA. *Program availability:* Part-time, evening/weekend. *Faculty:* 8 full-time (5 women), 6 part-time/adjunct (4 women). *Students:* 11 full-time (7 women), 7 part-time (6 women); includes 5 minority (2 Black or African American, non-Hispanic/Latino; 1 Asian, non-Hispanic/Latino; 2 Two or more races, non-Hispanic/Latino). Average age 31. 17 applicants, 100% accepted, 11 enrolled. In 2017, 4 master's awarded. *Entrance requirements:* For master's, minimum GPA of 2.75. *Application deadline:* For fall admission, 3/1 for domestic students; for spring admission, 11/1 for domestic students. *Expenses:* Tuition, state resident: full-time $17,375. Tuition, nonresident: full-time $33,915. *Required fees:* $355. *Financial support:* Research assistantships, teaching assistantships, career-related internships or fieldwork, Federal Work-Study, and unspecified assistantships available. Support available to part-time students. Financial award application deadline: 3/1; financial award applicants required to submit FAFSA. *Faculty research:* War in American culture, immigration history, Latin Americans, history of race and popular music, education and Asian Americans. *Unit head:* Dr. Aaron Lecklider, Department Chair of American Studies, 617-287-6771, E-mail: aaron.lecklider@umb.edu. *Application contact:* Graduate Admissions Coordinator, 617-287-6400, Fax: 617-287-6236, E-mail: bos.gadm@dpc.umassp.edu.

University of Michigan, Rackham Graduate School, College of Literature, Science, and the Arts, Department of American Culture, Ann Arbor, MI 48109-1045. Offers AM,

PhD. *Faculty:* 37 full-time (22 women), 4 part-time/adjunct (1 woman). *Students:* 37 full-time (25 women); includes 26 minority (8 Black or African American, non-Hispanic/Latino; 1 American Indian or Alaska Native, non-Hispanic/Latino; 8 Asian, non-Hispanic/Latino; 9 Hispanic/Latino), 1 international. Average age 30. 108 applicants, 9% accepted, 6 enrolled. In 2017, 12 doctorates awarded. Terminal master's awarded for partial completion of doctoral program. *Degree requirements:* For doctorate, comprehensive exam, thesis/dissertation, preliminary exams, field exams, oral defense of dissertation. *Entrance requirements:* For doctorate, sample of written work. Additional exam requirements/recommendations for international students: Required—TOEFL. *Application deadline:* For fall admission, 12/1 for domestic and international students. Application fee: $75 ($90 for international students). Electronic applications accepted. *Expenses:* Tuition, state resident: full-time $22,368; part-time $1201 per credit hour. Tuition, nonresident: full-time $45,156; part-time $2467 per credit hour. *Required fees:* $376 per term. Tuition and fees vary according to course load, degree level and program. *Financial support:* In 2017–18, 34 students received support, including 26 fellowships with full tuition reimbursements available (averaging $26,400 per year), 10 teaching assistantships with full tuition reimbursements available (averaging $26,400 per year); research assistantships and health care benefits also available. *Faculty research:* Cultural studies, ethnic studies, American culture methodology, literature, history. *Unit head:* Alexandra Stern, Chair, 734-763-1460, Fax: 734-936-1967, E-mail: ac.inq@umich.edu. *Application contact:* Marlene Moore, Graduate Student Coordinator, 734-647-9533, Fax: 734-936-1967, E-mail: ac.inq@umich.edu.
Website: http://www.lsa.umich.edu/ac/

University of Michigan–Flint, College of Arts and Sciences, Program in Social Sciences, Flint, MI 48502-1950. Offers gender studies (MA); global studies (MA); U.S. history and politics (MA). *Program availability:* Part-time. *Faculty:* 12 full-time (7 women), 6 part-time/adjunct (4 women). *Students:* 2 full-time (1 woman), 12 part-time (6 women); includes 4 minority (3 Black or African American, non-Hispanic/Latino; 1 Hispanic/Latino). Average age 43. 8 applicants, 88% accepted, 6 enrolled. In 2017, 11 master's awarded. *Entrance requirements:* For master's, bachelor's degree from regionally-accredited institution, minimum overall undergraduate GPA of 3.0. Additional exam requirements/recommendations for international students: Required—TOEFL (minimum score 84 iBT), IELTS (minimum score 6.5). *Application deadline:* For fall admission, 8/1 for domestic students, 5/1 for international students; for winter admission, 11/15 for domestic students, 9/1 for international students; for spring admission, 3/15 for domestic students, 1/1 for international students; for summer admission, 5/15 for domestic students. Applications are processed on a rolling basis. Application fee: $55. Electronic applications accepted. *Expenses:* Contact institution. *Financial support:* Federal Work-Study, scholarships/grants, and unspecified assistantships available. Financial award application deadline: 3/1; financial award applicants required to submit FAFSA. *Unit head:* Dr. Adam Lutzker, Director, 810-762-3470, Fax: 810-762-3281, E-mail: alutzker@umflint.edu. *Application contact:* Bradley T. Maki, Director of Graduate Admissions, 810-762-3171, Fax: 810-766-6789, E-mail: bmaki@umflint.edu.
Website: http://www.umflint.edu/graduateprograms/social-sciences-ma

University of Michigan–Flint, Graduate Programs, Program in Liberal Studies, Flint, MI 48502-1950. Offers MA, MLS. *Program availability:* Part-time, evening/weekend, 100% online. *Faculty:* 8 full-time (3 women), 1 part-time/adjunct (0 women). *Students:* 1 (woman) full-time, 19 part-time (8 women); includes 6 minority (1 Black or African American, non-Hispanic/Latino; 2 American Indian or Alaska Native, non-Hispanic/Latino; 1 Asian, non-Hispanic/Latino; 1 Hispanic/Latino; 1 Two or more races, non-Hispanic/Latino). Average age 47. 12 applicants, 58% accepted, 5 enrolled. In 2017, 3 master's awarded. *Entrance requirements:* For master's, bachelor's degree from accredited institution; minimum overall undergraduate GPA of 3.0; undergraduate course work totaling 24 credit hours, primarily in the humanities and social sciences. Additional exam requirements/recommendations for international students: Required—TOEFL (minimum score 84 iBT), IELTS (minimum score 6.5). *Application deadline:* For fall admission, 8/1 for domestic students, 5/1 for international students; for winter admission, 11/15 for domestic students, 9/1 for international students; for spring admission, 3/15 for domestic students, 1/1 for international students; for summer admission, 5/15 for domestic students. Applications are processed on a rolling basis. Application fee: $55. Electronic applications accepted. *Expenses:* Contact institution. *Financial support:* Federal Work-Study, scholarships/grants, and unspecified assistantships available. Support available to part-time students. Financial award application deadline: 3/1; financial award applicants required to submit FAFSA. *Unit head:* Dr. Jan Furman, Director, 810-762-3285, E-mail: jfurman@umflint.edu. *Application contact:* Bradley T. Maki, Director of Graduate Admissions, 810-762-3171, Fax: 810-766-6789, E-mail: bmaki@umflint.edu.
Website: https://www.umflint.edu/graduateprograms/liberal-studies-american-culture-ma

University of Minnesota, Twin Cities Campus, Graduate School, College of Liberal Arts, Department of American Studies, Minneapolis, MN 55455. Offers PhD. *Degree requirements:* For doctorate, one foreign language, comprehensive exam, thesis/dissertation. *Entrance requirements:* For doctorate, GRE General Test, sample of written work, 3 letters of recommendation. Additional exam requirements/recommendations for international students: Required—TOEFL (minimum score 550 paper-based). *Faculty research:* American Indian history, nationalism/transnationalism, gender and sexuality, race and ethnicity.

University of Missouri–St. Louis, College of Arts and Sciences, Department of Political Science, St. Louis, MO 63121. Offers American politics (MA); comparative politics (MA); international politics (MA); political process and behavior (MA); political science (PhD); public administration and public policy (MA); urban and regional politics (MA). *Program availability:* Part-time, evening/weekend. *Faculty:* 15 full-time (5 women), 9 part-time/adjunct (2 women). *Students:* 32 full-time (11 women), 21 part-time (9 women); includes 11 minority (10 Black or African American, non-Hispanic/Latino; 1 Hispanic/Latino), 4 international. 10 applicants, 80% accepted, 7 enrolled. Terminal master's awarded for partial completion of doctoral program. *Degree requirements:* For master's, thesis optional; for doctorate, thesis/dissertation. *Entrance requirements:* For master's, GRE General Test, 2 letters of recommendation, statement of purpose; for doctorate, GRE General Test, 3 letters of recommendation, statement of purpose. Additional exam requirements/recommendations for international students: Required—TOEFL (minimum score 550 paper-based; 79 iBT), IELTS (minimum score 6.5). *Application deadline:* For fall admission, 2/15 priority date for domestic and international students; for winter admission, 10/15 for domestic and international students; for spring admission, 10/15 priority date for domestic and international students. Applications are processed on a rolling basis. Application fee: $50 ($40 for international students). Electronic applications accepted. *Expenses:* Tuition, state resident: part-time $476.50 per credit hour. Tuition, nonresident: part-time $1169.70 per credit hour. *Financial support:* Fellowships, research assistantships with tuition reimbursements, teaching assistantships with tuition reimbursements, and career-related internships or fieldwork available. Support available to part-time students. Financial award application deadline: 3/15; financial award applicants required to submit FAFSA. *Faculty research:* Public policy, urban politics and administration, American government. *Unit head:* Dave Robertson, Chairperson, 314-516-5521, Fax: 314-516-7236. *Application contact:* 314-516-5458, Fax: 314-516-6996, E-mail: gradadm@umsl.edu.
Website: http://www.umsl.edu/~polisci/

University of New Mexico, Graduate Studies, College of Arts and Sciences, Program in American Studies, Albuquerque, NM 87131. Offers MA, PhD. *Program availability:* Part-time. *Faculty:* 12 full-time (7 women). *Students:* 19 full-time (11 women), 31 part-time (23 women); includes 33 minority (5 American Indian or Alaska Native, non-Hispanic/Latino; 22 Hispanic/Latino; 1 Native Hawaiian or other Pacific Islander, non-Hispanic/Latino; 5 Two or more races, non-Hispanic/Latino), 2 international. Average age 37. 37 applicants, 32% accepted, 9 enrolled. In 2017, 5 master's, 2 doctorates awarded. *Degree requirements:* For master's, comprehensive exam (for some programs), thesis (for some programs); for doctorate, one foreign language, comprehensive exam, thesis/dissertation. *Entrance requirements:* For master's, BA in related field; for doctorate, MA in related field, complete dossier. Additional exam requirements/recommendations for international students: Required—TOEFL. *Application deadline:* For fall admission, 1/15 for domestic and international students. Application fee: $50. Electronic applications accepted. *Financial support:* Research assistantships with partial tuition reimbursements, teaching assistantships with partial tuition reimbursements, Federal Work-Study, health care benefits, tuition waivers (partial), and unspecified assistantships available. Support available to part-time students. Financial award application deadline: 2/20; financial award applicants required to submit FAFSA. *Faculty research:* Cultural studies, environment/science/technology, gender, race/class/ethnicity, popular culture, Southwest studies. *Unit head:* Dr. Alex Lubin, Chair, 505-277-3929, Fax: 505-277-1208, E-mail: alubin@unm.edu. *Application contact:* Sandy Rodrigue, Department Administrator, 505-277-3929, Fax: 505-277-1208, E-mail: amstudy@unm.edu.
Website: http://www.unm.edu/~amstudy/

University of New Mexico, Graduate Studies, College of Fine Arts, Program in Art History, Albuquerque, NM 87131. Offers art history (MA); art of the Americas (MA); history of architecture (PhD); history of graphic arts (PhD); history of photography (PhD); modern Latin American art (PhD); Native American art (PhD); Pre-Columbian art and architecture (PhD); Spanish colonial art (PhD). *Program availability:* Part-time. *Faculty:* 7 full-time (5 women). *Students:* 7 full-time (all women), 18 part-time (15 women); includes 8 minority (2 American Indian or Alaska Native, non-Hispanic/Latino; 5 Hispanic/Latino; 1 Two or more races, non-Hispanic/Latino), 2 international. Average age 41. 21 applicants, 33% accepted, 5 enrolled. In 2017, 5 master's, 1 doctorate awarded. *Degree requirements:* For master's, one foreign language, comprehensive exam (for some programs), thesis, symposium; for doctorate, 2 foreign languages, comprehensive exam, thesis/dissertation, symposium. *Entrance requirements:* Additional exam requirements/recommendations for international students: Required—TOEFL (minimum score 550 paper-based), IELTS (minimum score 6). *Application deadline:* For fall admission, 1/15 for domestic students; for spring admission, 1/15 for domestic students. Application fee: $50. Electronic applications accepted. *Financial support:* Fellowships, research assistantships, teaching assistantships with partial tuition reimbursements, Federal Work-Study, institutionally sponsored loans, scholarships/grants, health care benefits, and unspecified assistantships available. Support available to part-time students. Financial award application deadline: 3/1; financial award applicants required to submit FAFSA. *Faculty research:* Native American, modern Latin American, pre-Columbian, architectural, American, medieval, Spanish Colonial, and Latin American art; history of photography. *Unit head:* Prof. Mary Tsiongas, Chair, 505-277-5861, Fax: 505-277-5955, E-mail: tsiongas@unm.edu. *Application contact:* Kat Heatherington, Graduate Advisor, 505-277-6672, Fax: 505-277-5955, E-mail: art255@unm.edu.
Website: http://art.unm.edu/

University of Southern California, Graduate School, Dana and David Dornsife College of Letters, Arts and Sciences, Department of American Studies and Ethnicity, Los Angeles, CA 90089. Offers PhD. *Degree requirements:* For doctorate, one foreign language, thesis/dissertation, qualifying exam. *Entrance requirements:* For doctorate, GRE. Additional exam requirements/recommendations for international students: Recommended—TOEFL. Electronic applications accepted. *Faculty research:* Interdisciplinary study of race and ethnicity, regional focus on Los Angeles and the American West, multidisciplinary exploration of culture, interdisciplinary study of gender and sexuality.

University of Southern Maine, College of Arts, Humanities, and Social Sciences, Program in American and New England Studies, Portland, ME 04103. Offers MA, CGS. *Program availability:* Part-time, evening/weekend. *Degree requirements:* For master's, thesis optional. *Entrance requirements:* For master's, GRE General Test or MAT. Additional exam requirements/recommendations for international students: Required—TOEFL. *Faculty research:* Social history, regional culture, landscape of literature, material culture, art and architecture.

University of South Florida, College of Arts and Sciences, Department of History, Tampa, FL 33620-9951. Offers history (MA, PhD), including American history (MA), ancient history (MA), European history (MA), Latin American history (MA), Medieval history (MA). *Program availability:* Part-time, evening/weekend. *Faculty:* 17 full-time (8 women), 1 (woman) part-time/adjunct. *Students:* 39 full-time (9 women), 19 part-time (9 women); includes 5 minority (1 American Indian or Alaska Native, non-Hispanic/Latino; 4 Hispanic/Latino). Average age 33. 41 applicants, 80% accepted, 24 enrolled. In 2017, 10 master's, 1 doctorate awarded. *Degree requirements:* For master's, one foreign language, comprehensive exam, thesis optional; for doctorate, one foreign language, comprehensive exam, thesis/dissertation. *Entrance requirements:* For master's, GRE General Test, minimum GPA of 3.0, two letters of recommendation, 2-page statement of purpose, writing sample; for doctorate, GRE General Test, minimum GPA of 3.5 in master's degree coursework, three letters of recommendation, statement of purpose, writing sample, foreign language proficiency in the field of study. Additional exam requirements/recommendations for international students: Required—TOEFL (minimum score 550 paper-based; 79 iBT) or IELTS (minimum score 6.5). *Application deadline:* For fall admission, 12/1 priority date for domestic students, 12/1 for international students. Applications are processed on a rolling basis. Application fee: $30. Electronic applications accepted. *Financial support:* In 2017–18, 3 students received support, including 17 teaching assistantships with tuition reimbursements available (averaging $12,750 per year); unspecified assistantships also available. Financial award application deadline: 1/15. *Faculty research:* North American and U.S. history, European history, nineteenth- and twentieth-centuries/modern world, early modern world, ancient history, history of gender/sexuality, Latin American history, history of science and medicine. *Total annual research expenditures:* $194,096. *Unit head:* Dr. Fraser Ottanelli, Professor and Chair, 813-974-6209, Fax: 813-974-6228, E-mail: ottanelli@usf.edu. *Application contact:* Dr. Kees Boterbloem, Professor and Graduate Program Director, 813-974-2807, E-mail: cboterbl@usf.edu.
Website: http://history.usf.edu

University of South Florida, College of Arts and Sciences, Department of Humanities and Cultural Studies, Tampa, FL 33620-9951. Offers liberal arts (MA), including American studies, film studies, humanities. *Program availability:* Part-time, evening/weekend. *Faculty:* 8 full-time (2 women). *Students:* 19 full-time (10 women), 3 part-time (2 women); includes 3 minority (2 Black or African American, non-Hispanic/Latino; 1 Hispanic/Latino), 2 international. Average age 29. 25 applicants, 44% accepted, 7

enrolled. In 2017, 8 master's awarded. *Degree requirements:* For master's, comprehensive exam, thesis, language (for humanities subconcentration). *Entrance requirements:* For master's, GRE General Test, minimum GPA of 3.0 in upper-division courses, personal statement, writing sample. Additional exam requirements/recommendations for international students: Required—TOEFL (minimum score 550 paper-based; 79 iBT) or IELTS (minimum score 6.5). *Application deadline:* For fall admission, 2/15 priority date for domestic students, 2/15 for international students; for spring admission, 10/15 priority date for domestic students, 9/15 for international students; for summer admission, 2/15 for domestic students, 1/15 for international students. Application fee: $30. Electronic applications accepted. *Financial support:* In 2017–18, 2 students received support, including 15 teaching assistantships with tuition reimbursements available (averaging $12,437 per year); scholarships/grants also available. Financial award application deadline: 4/1. *Faculty research:* American South, American autobiography, material culture, critical theory, cultural studies, film studies. *Unit head:* Dr. Andrew Berish, Associate Professor and Chair, 813-974-9380, E-mail: aberish@usf.edu. *Application contact:* Dr. Maria Cizmic, Associate Professor and Graduate Program Director, 813-974-9380, E-mail: mcizmic@usf.edu.
Website: http://humanities.usf.edu/

The University of Texas at Austin, Graduate School, College of Liberal Arts, Department of American Studies, Austin, TX 78712-1111. Offers MA, PhD. *Program availability:* Part-time. *Degree requirements:* For master's, thesis; for doctorate, one foreign language, thesis/dissertation, qualifying oral exam. *Entrance requirements:* For master's and doctorate, GRE General Test, minimum GPA of 3.5. Electronic applications accepted. *Faculty research:* Race, gender, and ethnicity; history of the American West; American design and archaeology; literary cultural history; religion and psychology in American culture.

University of Utah, Graduate School, College of Social and Behavioral Science, Department of Political Science, Program in Political Science, Salt Lake City, UT 84112. Offers American politics (MA, MS, PhD); comparative politics (MA, MS, PhD); international relations (MA, MS, PhD); political theory (MA, MS, PhD); public administration (MA, MS, PhD). *Faculty:* 23 full-time (6 women), 10 part-time/adjunct (2 women). *Students:* 23 full-time (9 women), 28 part-time (8 women); includes 6 minority (2 Asian, non-Hispanic/Latino; 2 Hispanic/Latino; 2 Two or more races, non-Hispanic/Latino), 4 international. Average age 35. 44 applicants, 45% accepted, 11 enrolled. In 2017, 3 master's, 4 doctorates awarded. Terminal master's awarded for partial completion of doctoral program. *Degree requirements:* For master's, variable foreign language requirement, thesis or research paper; for doctorate, comprehensive exam, thesis/dissertation. *Entrance requirements:* For master's and doctorate, GRE General Test, minimum GPA of 3.2. Additional exam requirements/recommendations for international students: Required—TOEFL (minimum score 580 paper-based; 61 iBT), IELTS (minimum score 6). *Application deadline:* For fall admission, 1/15 priority date for domestic and international students. Application fee: $55 ($65 for international students). Electronic applications accepted. *Expenses:* $1,489 for 1 credit hour, $267 for each additional hour (resident); $4,233 for 1 credit hour, $908 for each additional hour (non-resident). *Financial support:* In 2017–18, 10 students received support, including 5 fellowships with full tuition reimbursements available (averaging $15,250 per year), 13 teaching assistantships with full tuition reimbursements available (averaging $15,000 per year); career-related internships or fieldwork, scholarships/grants, health care benefits, and unspecified assistantships also available. Financial award application deadline: 1/15; financial award applicants required to submit FAFSA. *Faculty research:* International politics, comparative politics, political theory, American politics, public administration. *Total annual research expenditures:* $15,000. *Unit head:* Mark Button, Chair, 801-585-7987, Fax: 801-585-6492, E-mail: mark.button@poli-sci.utah.edu. *Application contact:* Sandy Hiskey, Graduate Academic Advisor, 801-581-8608, Fax: 801-585-6492, E-mail: sandy.hiskey@utah.edu.
Website: http://www.poli-sci.utah.edu/

University of West Florida, College of Arts, Social Sciences, and Humanities, Department of History, Pensacola, FL 32514-5750. Offers early American studies (MA); public history (MA); traditional history (MA). *Program availability:* Part-time, evening/weekend. *Degree requirements:* For master's, thesis or alternative. *Entrance requirements:* For master's, GRE (minimum score: verbal 500, writing 3.5) or MAT (minimum score 415), minimum GPA of 3.0; minimum 15 hours of upper-level history courses; official transcripts; letter of intent; writing sample (undergraduate research paper preferred). Additional exam requirements/recommendations for international students: Required—TOEFL (minimum score 550 paper-based).

University of Wisconsin–Madison, Graduate School, College of Letters and Science, Department of History, Madison, WI 53706-1380. Offers African history (MA, PhD); Central Asian history (MA, PhD); comparative world history (MA, PhD); East Asian history (MA, PhD); European history (MA, PhD); gender and women's history (MA, PhD); Latin American and Caribbean history (MA, PhD); Middle Eastern history (MA, PhD); South Asian history (MA, PhD); Southeast Asian history (MA, PhD); United States history (MA, PhD). Terminal master's awarded for partial completion of doctoral program. *Degree requirements:* For master's, thesis (for some programs); for doctorate, variable foreign language requirement, thesis/dissertation. *Entrance requirements:* For master's and doctorate, GRE General Test. Additional exam requirements/recommendations for international students: Required—Michigan English Language Assessment Battery or TOEFL. Electronic applications accepted. *Faculty research:* American, African, European, Asian, Latin American, and Middle Eastern history.

University of Wyoming, College of Arts and Sciences, American Studies Program, Laramie, WY 82071. Offers MA. *Program availability:* Part-time. *Degree requirements:* For master's, thesis optional. *Entrance requirements:* For master's, GRE General Test, minimum GPA of 3.0. *Faculty research:* Material culture, American culture, ethnicity, cultural environments, public culture.

Utah State University, School of Graduate Studies, College of Humanities and Social Sciences, Department of English and Department of History, Program in American Studies, Logan, UT 84322. Offers folklore (MA, MS); western American literature and culture (MA, MS). *Program availability:* Part-time, evening/weekend. *Degree requirements:* For master's, thesis or alternative. *Entrance requirements:* For master's, GRE General Test or MAT, minimum GPA of 3.0, 3 letters of recommendation, writing sample. Additional exam requirements/recommendations for international students: Required—TOEFL. *Faculty research:* Folklore and folklife, American culture, regional studies, material culture, Jewish folklore, Native American folklore.

Washington State University, College of Arts and Sciences, Program in American Studies, Pullman, WA 99164-4010. Offers MA, PhD. Program applications must be made through the Pullman campus. *Program availability:* Part-time. *Degree requirements:* For master's, one foreign language, comprehensive exam, thesis optional, oral exam; for doctorate, one foreign language, comprehensive exam, thesis/dissertation, oral exam. *Entrance requirements:* For master's and doctorate, official college transcripts sent directly from each institution attended, 3-5 page statement of purpose describing areas of interest, minimum GPA of 3.0, writing sample, 3 letters of recommendation. Additional exam requirements/recommendations for international students: Required—TOEFL.

Wilfrid Laurier University, Faculty of Graduate and Postdoctoral Studies, Faculty of Arts, Department of Religion and Culture, Waterloo, ON N2L 3C5, Canada. Offers religion and culture (MA); religious diversity of North America (PhD). *Program availability:* Part-time. *Degree requirements:* For master's, thesis optional; for doctorate, thesis/dissertation. *Entrance requirements:* For master's, honors BA or the equivalent in religious studies or other interdisciplinary social science or humanities program, minimum B average in overall undergraduate course work, B+ average in the undergraduate major; for doctorate, MA in religious studies, minimum A- average. Additional exam requirements/recommendations for international students: Required—TOEFL (minimum score 89 iBT). Electronic applications accepted. *Faculty research:* Religious diversity in North America.

Yale University, Graduate School of Arts and Sciences, Interdisciplinary Program in American Studies, New Haven, CT 06520. Offers PhD. *Degree requirements:* For doctorate, one foreign language, thesis/dissertation. *Entrance requirements:* For doctorate, GRE General Test.

Asian-American Studies

Binghamton University, State University of New York, Graduate School, Harpur College of Arts and Sciences, Department of Asian and Asian American Studies, Binghamton, NY 13902-6000. Offers MA, Certificate. *Program availability:* Part-time. *Faculty:* 20 full-time (11 women). *Students:* 6 full-time (4 women); includes 2 minority (1 Asian, non-Hispanic/Latino; 1 Two or more races, non-Hispanic/Latino), 3 international. Average age 24. 18 applicants, 56% accepted, 3 enrolled. In 2017, 6 master's awarded. *Degree requirements:* For master's, variable foreign language requirement, comprehensive exam (for some programs), thesis (for some programs). *Entrance requirements:* For master's, GRE General Test, writing sample. Additional exam requirements/recommendations for international students: Required—TOEFL (minimum score 80 iBT). *Application deadline:* For fall admission, 1/15 priority date for domestic and international students. Application fee: $75. Electronic applications accepted. *Financial support:* Applicants required to submit FAFSA. *Unit head:* Prof. Robert Ji Song Ku, Chair, 607-777-4517, E-mail: jku@binghamton.edu. *Application contact:* Ben Balkaya, Assistant Dean and Director, 607-777-2151, Fax: 607-777-2501, E-mail: balkaya@binghamton.edu.
Website: http://www.binghamton.edu/aaas/

California State University, Long Beach, Graduate Studies, College of Liberal Arts, Department of Asian and Asian American Studies, Long Beach, CA 90840. Offers Asian studies (MA). *Program availability:* Part-time. *Degree requirements:* For master's, one foreign language, comprehensive exam or thesis. Electronic applications accepted. *Faculty research:* South Asia, China, Japan, Southeast Asia, Asian-Americans in the U.S.

San Francisco State University, Division of Graduate Studies, College of Ethnic Studies, Program in Asian American Studies, San Francisco, CA 94132-1722. Offers MA. *Unit head:* Dr. Russell Yeung, Chair, 415-338-2698, Fax: 415-338-0500, E-mail: aas@sfsu.edu. *Application contact:* Dr. Wei Ming Dariotis, MA Coordinator, 415-338-3494, E-mail: dariotis@sfsu.edu.
Website: http://aas.sfsu.edu/

Stony Brook University, State University of New York, Graduate School, College of Arts and Sciences, Department of Asian and Asian American Studies, Stony Brook, NY 11794. Offers contemporary Asian and Asian American studies (MA). *Faculty:* 15 full-time (10 women), 6 part-time/adjunct (all women). *Students:* 3 full-time (2 women), 5 part-time (all women); includes 4 minority (1 Black or African American, non-Hispanic/Latino; 3 Asian, non-Hispanic/Latino), 1 international. Average age 29. 6 applicants, 83% accepted, 5 enrolled. *Degree requirements:* For master's, thesis or final project. *Entrance requirements:* For master's, GRE, undergraduate transcript, statement of purpose, three letters of recommendation. Additional exam requirements/recommendations for international students: Required—TOEFL (minimum score 85 iBT). *Application deadline:* For fall admission, 1/15 for domestic students; for spring admission, 10/1 for domestic students. Application fee: $100. Electronic applications accepted. *Expenses:* Tuition, state resident: full-time $10,870; part-time $453 per credit. Tuition, nonresident: full-time $22,210; part-time $925 per credit. *Financial support:* Applicants required to submit FAFSA. *Faculty research:* Asian studies, English as a second language, humanities, sociolinguistics. *Total annual research expenditures:* $18,968. *Unit head:* Dr. Agnes He, Chair, 631-632-4041, Fax: 631-632-4098, E-mail: agnes.he@stonybrook.edu. *Application contact:* Melissa Jordan, Assistant Dean for Records and Admission, 631-632-9712, Fax: 631-632-7243, E-mail: melissa.jordan@stonybrook.edu.
Website: http://www.stonybrook.edu/commcms/asianamerican/

University of California, Los Angeles, Graduate Division, College of Letters and Science, Program in Asian-American Studies, Los Angeles, CA 90095. Offers MA, MA/MPH, MA/MSW. *Degree requirements:* For master's, one foreign language, comprehensive exam or thesis. *Entrance requirements:* For master's, bachelor's degree; minimum undergraduate GPA of 3.0 (or its equivalent if letter grade system not used); paper or article preferably on Asian Americans. Additional exam requirements/recommendations for international students: Required—TOEFL. Electronic applications accepted.

Asian Studies

American University, College of Arts and Sciences, Critical Race, Gender, and Culture Studies Collaborative, Washington, DC 20016-8030. Offers Asian studies (Graduate Certificate); women's, gender, and sexuality studies (Graduate Certificate). *Faculty:* 4 full-time (3 women), 10 part-time/adjunct (5 women). In 2017, 3 Graduate Certificates awarded. *Entrance requirements:* Additional exam requirements/recommendations for international students: Required—TOEFL (minimum score 600 paper-based; 100 iBT). *Application deadline:* Applications are processed on a rolling basis. *Expenses: Tuition:* Full-time $29,556. *Required fees:* $690. Tuition and fees vary according to course load and program. *Unit head:* Dr. Peter Starr, Dean, 202-885-2446, Fax: 202-885-2429, E-mail: pstarr@american.edu. *Application contact:* Jonathan Harper, Associate Director, Graduate Recruitment, 202-885-3622, Fax: 202-885-1505, E-mail: jharper@american.edu.
Website: http://www.american.edu/cas/crgc/

Binghamton University, State University of New York, Graduate School, Harpur College of Arts and Sciences, Department of Asian and Asian American Studies, Binghamton, NY 13902-6000. Offers MA, Certificate. *Program availability:* Part-time. *Faculty:* 20 full-time (11 women). *Students:* 6 full-time (4 women); includes 2 minority (1 Asian, non-Hispanic/Latino; 1 Two or more races, non-Hispanic/Latino), 3 international. Average age 24. 18 applicants, 56% accepted, 3 enrolled. In 2017, 6 master's awarded. *Degree requirements:* For master's, variable foreign language requirement, comprehensive exam (for some programs), thesis (for some programs). *Entrance requirements:* For master's, GRE General Test, writing sample. Additional exam requirements/recommendations for international students: Required—TOEFL (minimum score 80 iBT). *Application deadline:* For fall admission, 1/15 priority date for domestic and international students. Application fee: $75. Electronic applications accepted. *Financial support:* Applicants required to submit FAFSA. *Unit head:* Prof. Robert Ji Song Ku, Chair, 607-777-4517, E-mail: jku@binghamton.edu. *Application contact:* Ben Balkaya, Assistant Dean and Director, 607-777-2151, Fax: 607-777-2501, E-mail: balkaya@binghamton.edu.
Website: http://www.binghamton.edu/aaas/

Brown University, Graduate School, Department of Egyptology and Assyriology, Providence, RI 02912. Offers ancient western Asian studies (PhD); Egyptology (PhD); history of the exact sciences in antiquity (PhD). *Degree requirements:* For doctorate, 2 foreign languages, comprehensive exam, thesis/dissertation. *Entrance requirements:* For doctorate, GRE General Test.

Brown University, Graduate School, Department of Religious Studies, Providence, RI 02912. Offers Asian religious traditions (PhD); Islam, society and culture (PhD); religion and critical thought (PhD); religions of the ancient Mediterranean (PhD). *Faculty:* 14 full-time (3 women), 2 part-time/adjunct (1 woman). *Students:* 27 full-time (11 women). 82 applicants, 13% accepted. In 2017, 4 doctorates awarded. *Degree requirements:* For doctorate, variable foreign language requirement, thesis/dissertation. *Entrance requirements:* For doctorate, GRE General Test. Additional exam requirements/ recommendations for international students: Required—TOEFL. *Application deadline:* For fall admission, 1/5 priority date for domestic and international students. Application fee: $75. Electronic applications accepted. *Financial support:* In 2017–18, 27 students received support, including 13 fellowships, 11 teaching assistantships; institutionally sponsored loans, health care benefits, tuition waivers (full and partial), and proctorships also available. Financial award application deadline: 1/5. *Faculty research:* Asian religious traditions; Islam, society, and culture; religions of the ancient Mediterranean; and religion and critical thought. *Unit head:* Mark S. Cladis, Chair, 401-863-3104. *Application contact:* Nicole L. Vadnais, Academic Department and Graduate Program Manager, 401-863-3104, E-mail: religious_studies@brown.edu.
Website: http://www.brown.edu/academics/religious-studies

California Institute of Integral Studies, School of Consciousness and Transformation, San Francisco, CA 94103. Offers anthropology and social change (MA, PhD); Asian philosophies and cultures (MA); creative inquiry/interdisciplinary arts (MFA); East-West psychology (MA, PhD); integral and transpersonal psychology (PhD); philosophy and religion (PhD), including ecology, spirituality, and religion, philosophy, cosmology, and consciousness, women's spirituality; philosophy, cosmology, and consciousness (Certificate); transformative leadership (MA); transformative studies (PhD); women, gender, spirituality and social justice (MA); writing and consciousness (MFA). *Program availability:* Part-time, evening/weekend, 100% online, blended/hybrid learning. *Students:* 392 full-time (265 women), 141 part-time (98 women); includes 145 minority (40 Black or African American, non-Hispanic/Latino; 1 American Indian or Alaska Native, non-Hispanic/Latino; 19 Asian, non-Hispanic/Latino; 54 Hispanic/Latino; 31 Two or more races, non-Hispanic/Latino), 61 international. Average age 43. 212 applicants, 96% accepted, 153 enrolled. In 2017, 49 master's, 36 doctorates awarded. Terminal master's awarded for partial completion of doctoral program. *Degree requirements:* For master's, thesis optional; for doctorate, comprehensive exam, thesis/dissertation, 1 foreign language (for Asian philosophies and cultures). *Entrance requirements:* For master's, minimum GPA of 3.0, letters of recommendation, writing sample; for doctorate, master's degree, minimum GPA of 3.0, letters of recommendation, writing sample. Additional exam requirements/recommendations for international students: Required—TOEFL. *Application deadline:* For fall admission, 2/1 priority date for domestic and international students; for spring admission, 10/15 priority date for domestic and international students. Applications are processed on a rolling basis. Application fee: $65. Electronic applications accepted. *Expenses:* $21,400 tuition and fees (for MA); $28,390 (for MFA); $24,658 (for PhD). *Financial support:* Fellowships, research assistantships, teaching assistantships, career-related internships or fieldwork, Federal Work-Study, and scholarships/grants available. Support available to part-time students. Financial award application deadline: 4/15; financial award applicants required to submit FAFSA. *Faculty research:* Ecology and sustainability, philosophy and religion, East-West psychology, integrative health, social and cultural anthropology, transformative leadership. *Unit head:* Kathy Littles, Academic Dean, 415-575-6100, E-mail: klittles@ciis.edu. *Application contact:* Ellen Durst, Director of Admissions, 415-575-6100, Fax: 415-575-1268, E-mail: admissions@ciis.edu.
Website: http://www.ciis.edu/

California State University, Long Beach, Graduate Studies, College of Liberal Arts, Department of Asian and Asian American Studies, Long Beach, CA 90840. Offers Asian studies (MA). *Program availability:* Part-time. *Degree requirements:* For master's, one foreign language, comprehensive exam or thesis. Electronic applications accepted. *Faculty research:* South Asia, China, Japan, Southeast Asia, Asian-Americans in the U.S.

College of Staten Island of the City University of New York, Graduate Programs, Division of Humanities and Social Sciences, Program in History, Staten Island, NY 10314-6600. Offers history (MA), including Africa and the Middle East, Asia, Europe, Latin America and the Caribbean, United States. *Program availability:* Part-time, evening/weekend. *Faculty:* 2 full-time (1 woman). *Students:* 18. 19 applicants, 79% accepted, 11 enrolled. In 2017, 3 master's awarded. *Degree requirements:* For master's, comprehensive exam (for some programs), 32 credits (total of eight courses); thesis or portfolio. *Entrance requirements:* For master's, bachelor's degree with minimum GPA of 3.0 overall and in undergraduate history courses, two letters of recommendation, letter of interest, research-based writing sample. Additional exam requirements/ recommendations for international students: Required—TOEFL (minimum score 550 paper-based; 79 iBT), IELTS (minimum score 6.5). *Application deadline:* For fall admission, 5/10 priority date for domestic and international students; for spring admission, 12/2 priority date for domestic and international students. Applications are processed on a rolling basis. Application fee: $125. Electronic applications accepted. *Expenses:* Tuition, state resident: full-time $10,450; part-time $440 per credit. Tuition, nonresident: full-time $19,320; part-time $440 per credit. *Required fees:* $181.10 per semester. Tuition and fees vary according to program. *Faculty research:* African and African diaspora history, South Asian history, Middle Eastern history, U.S. history, environmental history. *Unit head:* Dr. John Dixon, Graduate Program Coordinator, 718-982-3307, E-mail: john.dixon@csi.cuny.edu. *Application contact:* Sasha Spence, Associate Director for Graduate Admissions, 718-982-2019, Fax: 718-982-2500, E-mail: sasha.spence@csi.cuny.edu.
Website: https://www.csi.cuny.edu/sites/default/files/pdf/admissions/grad/pdf/History%20Fact%20Sheet.pdf

Columbia University, Graduate School of Arts and Sciences, New York, NY 10027. Offers African-American studies (MA); American studies (MA); anthropology (MA, PhD); art history and archaeology (MA, PhD); astronomy (PhD); biological sciences (PhD); biotechnology (MA); chemical physics (PhD); chemistry (PhD); classical studies (MA, PhD); classics (MA, PhD); climate and society (MA); conservation biology (MA); earth and environmental sciences (PhD); East Asia: regional studies (MA); East Asian languages and cultures (MA, PhD); ecology, evolution and environmental biology (MA), including conservation biology; ecology, evolution, and environmental biology (PhD), including ecology and evolutionary biology, evolutionary primatology; economics (MA, PhD); English and comparative literature (MA, PhD); French and Romance philology (MA, PhD); Germanic languages (MA, PhD); global French studies (MA); global thought (MA); Hispanic cultural studies (MA); history (PhD); history and literature (MA); human rights studies (MA); Islamic studies (MA); Italian (MA, PhD); Japanese pedagogy (MA); Jewish studies (MA); Latin America and the Caribbean: regional studies (MA); Latin American and Iberian cultures (PhD); mathematics (MA, PhD), including finance (MA); medieval and Renaissance studies (MA); Middle Eastern, South Asian, and African studies (MA, PhD); modern art: critical and curatorial studies (MA); modern European studies (MA); museum anthropology (MA); music (DMA, PhD); oral history (MA); philosophical foundations of physics (MA); philosophy (MA, PhD); physics (PhD); political science (MA, PhD); psychology (PhD); quantitative methods in the social sciences (MA); religion (MA, PhD); Russia, Eurasia and East Europe: regional studies (MA); Russian translation (MA); Slavic cultures (MA); Slavic languages (MA, PhD); sociology (MA, PhD); South Asian studies (MA); statistics (MA, PhD); theatre (PhD). Dual-degree programs require admission to both Graduate School of Arts and Sciences and another Columbia school. *Program availability:* Part-time. Terminal master's awarded for partial completion of doctoral program. *Degree requirements:* For master's, variable foreign language requirement, comprehensive exam (for some programs), thesis (for some programs); for doctorate, variable foreign language requirement, comprehensive exam (for some programs), thesis/dissertation. *Entrance requirements:* For master's and doctorate, GRE General Test, GRE Subject Test (for some programs). Additional exam requirements/recommendations for international students: Required—TOEFL, IELTS. Electronic applications accepted. *Expenses: Tuition:* Full-time $44,864; part-time $1704 per credit. *Required fees:* $2370 per semester. One-time fee: $105.

Columbia University, South Asia Institute, New York, NY 10027. Offers MA, Certificate. Students must be enrolled in a separate graduate degree program at Columbia University. *Program availability:* Part-time. *Faculty:* 22 full-time (11 women), 3 part-time/ adjunct (1 woman). *Students:* 6 full-time (4 women); includes 4 minority (all Asian, non-Hispanic/Latino). Average age 28. 18 applicants, 44% accepted, 1 enrolled. In 2017, 8 master's awarded. *Degree requirements:* For master's, thesis, 30 points of coursework. *Entrance requirements:* For master's, BA, BS or equivalent, in any field of study. Additional exam requirements/recommendations for international students: Required—TOEFL. *Application deadline:* For fall admission, 4/6 for domestic and international students; for spring admission, 11/17 for domestic students, 11/18 for international students. Application fee: $100. Electronic applications accepted. *Expenses:* $30,220 per semester. *Financial support:* In 2017–18, 2 students received support, including 3 fellowships (averaging $33,000 per year); Federal Work-Study and tuition waivers (partial) also available. Financial award application deadline: 4/6; financial award applicants required to submit FAFSA. *Faculty research:* Indian art and architecture, history of Indian subcontinent, politics of South Asia, religions of South Asia, women and gender in South Asia. *Unit head:* Prof. Katherine Pratt Ewing, MA Coordinator, E-mail: ke2131@columbia.edu.
Website: http://sai.columbia.edu/

Cornell University, Graduate School, Graduate Fields of Arts and Sciences, Field of Asian Literature, Religion and Culture, Ithaca, NY 14853. Offers Asian religions (MA, PhD); Chinese philosophy (PhD); classical Chinese literature (PhD); classical Japanese literature (PhD); East Asian literature and culture (PhD); Korean literature (PhD); modern Chinese literature (PhD); modern Japanese literature (PhD); South Asian literature and culture (PhD); Southeast Asian literature and culture (PhD). *Degree requirements:* For doctorate, comprehensive exam, thesis/dissertation. *Entrance requirements:* For doctorate, GRE General Test, academic writing sample, 3 letters of recommendation. Additional exam requirements/recommendations for international students: Required—TOEFL (minimum score 600 paper-based; 77 iBT). Electronic applications accepted.

Cornell University, Graduate School, Graduate Fields of Arts and Sciences, Field of Asian Studies, Ithaca, NY 14853. Offers East Asian linguistics (MA); East Asian studies (MA); South Asian linguistics (MA); South Asian studies (MA); Southeast Asian linguistics (MA); Southeast Asian studies (MA). *Degree requirements:* For master's, one foreign language, thesis. *Entrance requirements:* For master's, GRE General Test, 3 letters of recommendation. Additional exam requirements/recommendations for international students: Required—TOEFL (minimum score 550 paper-based; 77 iBT). Electronic applications accepted. *Faculty research:* East Asian studies, South Asian studies, Southeast Asian studies.

Cornell University, Graduate School, Graduate Fields of Arts and Sciences, Field of History, Ithaca, NY 14853. Offers African history (MA, PhD); American history (MA, PhD); ancient Greek history (PhD); ancient history (MA, PhD); ancient Roman history

(PhD); early modern European history (MA, PhD); English history (MA, PhD); French history (MA, PhD); German history (MA, PhD); history of science (MA, PhD); Korean history (PhD); Latin American history (MA, PhD); medieval Chinese history (MA, PhD); medieval history (MA, PhD); modern Chinese history (MA, PhD); modern European history (MA, PhD); modern Japanese history (MA, PhD); modern Middle Eastern history (PhD); premodern Islamic history (MA, PhD); premodern Japanese history (MA, PhD); Renaissance history (MA, PhD); Russian history (MA, PhD); South Asian history (PhD); Southeast Asian history (MA, PhD). Terminal master's awarded for partial completion of doctoral program. *Degree requirements:* For master's, thesis; for doctorate, 2 foreign languages, comprehensive exam, thesis/dissertation, 1 year of teaching experience. *Entrance requirements:* For master's and doctorate, GRE General Test, writing sample, 3 letters of recommendation. Additional exam requirements/recommendations for international students: Required—TOEFL (minimum score 550 paper-based; 77 iBT). Electronic applications accepted.

Cornell University, Graduate School, Graduate Fields of Arts and Sciences, Field of History of Art, Archaeology and Visual Studies, Ithaca, NY 14853. Offers 19th century art (PhD); African, African American and African diaspora (PhD); American art (PhD); ancient art and archaeology (PhD); Asian American art (PhD); Baroque art (PhD); comparative modernities (PhD); digital art (PhD); East Asian art (PhD); history of photography (PhD); Islamic art (PhD); Latin American art (PhD); medieval art (PhD); modern art (PhD); Renaissance art (PhD); Southeast Asian art (PhD); theory and criticism (PhD); visual studies (PhD). *Degree requirements:* For doctorate, one foreign language, comprehensive exam, thesis/dissertation, general exams in 3 areas. *Entrance requirements:* For doctorate, GRE General Test, sample of written work, 3 letters of recommendation. Additional exam requirements/recommendations for international students: Required—TOEFL (minimum score 550 paper-based; 77 iBT). Electronic applications accepted.

Cornell University, Graduate School, Graduate Fields of Arts and Sciences, Field of Linguistics, Ithaca, NY 14853. Offers applied linguistics (MA, PhD); East Asian linguistics (MA, PhD); English linguistics (MA, PhD); general linguistics (MA, PhD); Germanic linguistics (MA, PhD); Indo-European linguistics (MA, PhD); phonetics (MA, PhD); phonological theory (MA, PhD); Romance linguistics (MA, PhD); second language acquisition (MA, PhD); semantics (MA, PhD); Slavic linguistics (MA, PhD); sociolinguistics (MA, PhD); South Asian linguistics (MA, PhD); Southeast Asian linguistics (MA, PhD); syntactic theory (MA, PhD). Terminal master's awarded for partial completion of doctoral program. *Degree requirements:* For master's, one foreign language, thesis; for doctorate, one foreign language, comprehensive exam, thesis/dissertation. *Entrance requirements:* For master's and doctorate, GRE General Test, 2 letters of recommendation. Additional exam requirements/recommendations for international students: Required—TOEFL (minimum score 600 paper-based; 77 iBT). Electronic applications accepted. *Faculty research:* Phonology and phonetics, syntax and semantics, historical linguistics, philosophy of language, language acquisition.

Dallas Baptist University, Gary Cook School of Leadership, Program in International Studies, Dallas, TX 75211-9299. Offers East Asian studies (MA); European studies (MA); general international studies (MA); global business (MA); international immersion (MA); international ministry (MA); international relations (MA). *Program availability:* Part-time, evening/weekend. *Application deadline:* Applications are processed on a rolling basis. Application fee: $25. Electronic applications accepted. Application fee is waived when completed online. *Expenses: Tuition:* Full-time $16,308; part-time $906 per credit hour. *Required fees:* $900; $450 per semester. Tuition and fees vary according to course load and degree level. *Unit head:* Dr. Jack Goodyear, Dean, 214-333-5595, Fax: 214-333-6809, E-mail: jackg@dbu.edu. *Application contact:* Lee Bratcher, Program Director, 214-333-5808, E-mail: leeb@dbu.edu.
Website: http://www4.dbu.edu/leadership/mainternational

Dallas Baptist University, Graduate School of Ministry, Program in Global Leadership, Dallas, TX 75211-9299. Offers church planting (MA); East Asian Studies (MA); English as a second language (MA); general studies (MA); global communication (MA); global studies (MA); international business (MA); leading the nonprofit organization (MA); missions (MA); small group ministry (MA); urban ministry (MA). *Program availability:* Part-time, evening/weekend. *Application deadline:* Applications are processed on a rolling basis. Application fee: $25. Electronic applications accepted. Application fee is waived when completed online. *Expenses: Tuition:* Full-time $16,308; part-time $906 per credit hour. *Required fees:* $900; $450 per semester. Tuition and fees vary according to course load and degree level. *Unit head:* Dr. Robert R. Brooks, Dean, 214-333-5494, Fax: 214-333-5673, E-mail: bobb@dbu.edu. *Application contact:* Dr. Brent Thomason, Program Director, 214-333-5236, E-mail: brentt@dbu.edu.
Website: http://www.dbu.edu/ministry/degree-programs/m-a-in-global-leadership

Dallas Baptist University, Liberal Arts Program, Dallas, TX 75211-9299. Offers art (MLA); Christian studies (MLA); commercial art (MLA); East Asian studies (MLA); English (MLA); English as a second language (MLA); fine arts (MLA); history (MLA); missions (MLA); political science (MLA). *Program availability:* Part-time, evening/weekend. *Application deadline:* Applications are processed on a rolling basis. Application fee: $25. Electronic applications accepted. Application fee is waived when completed online. *Expenses: Tuition:* Full-time $16,308; part-time $906 per credit hour. *Required fees:* $900; $450 per semester. Tuition and fees vary according to course load and degree level. *Unit head:* Jared Ingram, Director, 214-333-5584, E-mail: jaredi@dbu.edu. *Application contact:* Bobby Soto, Director of Admissions, 214-333-5242, E-mail: bobby@dbu.edu.
Website: http://www3.dbu.edu/graduate/mla.asp

Duke University, Graduate School, Department of East Asian Studies, Durham, NC 27708. Offers AM, Certificate. *Program availability:* Part-time. *Entrance requirements:* For master's, GRE General Test. Additional exam requirements/recommendations for international students: Required—TOEFL (minimum score 577 paper-based; 90 iBT) or IELTS (minimum score 7). Electronic applications accepted.

Florida International University, Steven J. Green School of International and Public Affairs, Program in Asian Studies, Miami, FL 33199. Offers MA, MA/PhD. *Program availability:* Part-time, evening/weekend. *Students:* 10 full-time (9 women), 7 part-time (3 women); includes 10 minority (9 Hispanic/Latino; 1 Two or more races, non-Hispanic/Latino), 1 international. Average age 26. 8 applicants, 88% accepted, 5 enrolled. In 2017, 4 master's awarded. *Degree requirements:* For master's, thesis. *Entrance requirements:* For master's, minimum GPA of 3.0, letter of intent, letter of recommendation. Additional exam requirements/recommendations for international students: Required—TOEFL (minimum score 550 paper-based; 80 iBT). *Application deadline:* For fall admission, 6/1 for domestic students, 4/1 for international students; for spring admission, 10/1 for domestic students, 9/1 for international students. Applications are processed on a rolling basis. Application fee: $30. Electronic applications accepted. *Expenses:* Tuition, state resident: full-time $8912; part-time $446 per credit hour. Tuition, nonresident: full-time $21,393; part-time $992 per credit hour. *Required fees:* $390; $195 per semester. *Financial support:* Institutionally sponsored loans, scholarships/grants, and tuition waivers available. Financial award application deadline: 3/1; financial award applicants required to submit FAFSA. *Unit head:* Dr. Steven Heine, Program Director, 305-348-1788, Fax: 305-348-6586, E-mail: asian@fiu.edu. *Application contact:* Nanett Rojas, Manager, Admissions Operations, 305-348-7464, Fax: 305-348-7441, E-mail: gradadm@fiu.edu.

Florida State University, The Graduate School, College of Social Sciences and Public Policy, Program in Asian Studies, Tallahassee, FL 32306. Offers MA. *Program availability:* Part-time. *Faculty:* 4 full-time (all women), 4 part-time/adjunct (0 women). *Students:* 2 full-time (1 woman), 3 part-time (2 women); includes 2 minority (both Black or African American, non-Hispanic/Latino). Average age 30. 8 applicants, 100% accepted, 1 enrolled. In 2017, 1 master's awarded. *Degree requirements:* For master's, one foreign language, comprehensive exam, thesis optional. *Entrance requirements:* For master's, GRE General Test, minimum GPA of 3.0. Additional exam requirements/recommendations for international students: Required—TOEFL (minimum score 550 paper-based, 80 iBT) or IELTS (6.5). *Application deadline:* For fall admission, 7/1 for domestic and international students; for spring admission, 11/1 for domestic and international students; for summer admission, 3/1 for domestic and international students. Applications are processed on a rolling basis. Application fee: $30. Electronic applications accepted. *Expenses:* $479.32 in-state per credit hour; $1,110.72 out-of-state per credit hour. *Financial support:* Research assistantships, teaching assistantships, Federal Work-Study, institutionally sponsored loans, and unspecified assistantships available. Financial award application deadline: 2/1; financial award applicants required to submit FAFSA. *Faculty research:* Art history of the Orient, Asian history and politics, deception in World War II. *Unit head:* Dr. Lee K. Metcalf, Director, 850-644-4418, Fax: 850-645-4981, E-mail: lmetcalf@fsu.edu. *Application contact:* Sabrina Smith, Program Specialist, 850-644-4418, Fax: 850-644-4981, E-mail: ssmith9@fsu.edu.
Website: http://coss.fsu.edu/inaprog/programs/graduate/g-asian

Georgetown University, Graduate School of Arts and Sciences, Walsh School of Foreign Service, Program in Asian Studies, Washington, DC 20057. Offers MA. *Degree requirements:* For master's, comprehensive exam, research project. *Entrance requirements:* Additional exam requirements/recommendations for international students: Required—TOEFL.

The George Washington University, Elliott School of International Affairs, Program in Asian Studies, Washington, DC 20052. Offers MA. *Program availability:* Part-time. *Students:* 22 full-time (12 women), 6 part-time (4 women); includes 8 minority (2 Black or African American, non-Hispanic/Latino; 3 Asian, non-Hispanic/Latino; 2 Hispanic/Latino; 1 Two or more races, non-Hispanic/Latino), 9 international. Average age 26. 66 applicants, 67% accepted, 10 enrolled. In 2017, 15 master's awarded. *Degree requirements:* For master's, one foreign language, capstone project. *Entrance requirements:* For master's, GRE General Test, 2 years (or the equivalent) of an approved Asian language. Additional exam requirements/recommendations for international students: Required—TOEFL (minimum score 100 iBT), IELTS (minimum score 7). *Application deadline:* For fall admission, 1/15 priority date for domestic students; for spring admission, 10/1 for domestic students. Application fee: $75. Electronic applications accepted. *Expenses: Tuition:* Full-time $28,800; part-time $1655 per credit hour. *Required fees:* $45; $2.75 per credit hour. *Financial support:* In 2017–18, 7 students received support. Fellowships with partial tuition reimbursements available and Federal Work-Study available. Financial award application deadline: 1/15; financial award applicants required to submit FAFSA. *Faculty research:* Sino-Soviet studies, Japanese-U.S. relations, Chinese foreign policy, economic development in China. *Unit head:* Prof. Emmanuel Teitelbaum, Director, 202-994-9125, Fax: 202-994-2484, E-mail: ejt@gwu.edu. *Application contact:* Nicole A. Campbell, Director of Graduate Admissions, 202-994-7050, Fax: 202-994-9537, E-mail: esiagrad@gwu.edu.
Website: http://www.gwu.edu/graduate-programs/asian-studies

Harvard University, Graduate School of Arts and Sciences, Committee on Inner Asian and Altaic Studies, Cambridge, MA 02138. Offers PhD. *Degree requirements:* For doctorate, 2 foreign languages, thesis/dissertation, oral general exam. *Entrance requirements:* For doctorate, GRE General Test, proficiency in a related foreign language. Additional exam requirements/recommendations for international students: Required—TOEFL.

Harvard University, Graduate School of Arts and Sciences, Committee on Regional Studies–East Asia, Cambridge, MA 02138. Offers Chinese studies (AM); Japanese studies (AM); Korean studies (AM); Mongolian studies (AM); Vietnamese studies (AM). *Degree requirements:* For master's, one foreign language, seminar paper. *Entrance requirements:* For master's, GRE General Test. Additional exam requirements/recommendations for international students: Required—TOEFL.

Harvard University, Graduate School of Arts and Sciences, Department of Sanskrit and Indian Studies, Cambridge, MA 02138. Offers Indian philosophy (AM, PhD); Pali (AM, PhD); Sanskrit (AM, PhD); Tibetan (AM, PhD); Urdu (AM, PhD). Terminal master's awarded for partial completion of doctoral program. *Degree requirements:* For master's, 3 foreign languages; for doctorate, 3 foreign languages, thesis/dissertation. *Entrance requirements:* For master's, GRE General Test; for doctorate, GRE General Test, proficiency in French and German. Additional exam requirements/recommendations for international students: Required—TOEFL.

Indiana University Bloomington, University Graduate School, College of Arts and Sciences, School of Global and International Studies, Department of Central Eurasian Studies, Bloomington, IN 47405-7000. Offers MA, PhD. Terminal master's awarded for partial completion of doctoral program. *Degree requirements:* For master's, one foreign language, thesis; for doctorate, 2 foreign languages, thesis/dissertation, qualifying exams. *Entrance requirements:* For master's, minimum GPA of 3.0, 2 years of a foreign language; for doctorate, minimum GPA of 3.5, 1 research language. Additional exam requirements/recommendations for international students: Required—TOEFL. Electronic applications accepted. *Faculty research:* Central Asia, Hungarian civilization, Tibetan civilization, Turkish studies, Mongolian philology.

Indiana University Bloomington, University Graduate School, College of Arts and Sciences, School of Global and International Studies, Department of East Asian Languages and Cultures, Bloomington, IN 47408. Offers Chinese (MA, PhD); Chinese language pedagogy (MA); East Asian studies (MA); Japanese (MA, PhD); Japanese language pedagogy (MA). *Program availability:* Part-time. *Degree requirements:* For master's, one foreign language, thesis; for doctorate, 2 foreign languages, comprehensive exam, thesis/dissertation. *Entrance requirements:* Additional exam requirements/recommendations for international students: Required—TOEFL (minimum score 93 iBT). Electronic applications accepted. *Faculty research:* Modern East Asian history; politics and society; traditional Chinese thought and society; medieval and premodern Japanese history, literature and society; modern Chinese and Japanese film and literature; Chinese, Japanese, Korean language and linguistics.

Johns Hopkins University, School of Advanced International Studies, Washington, DC 20036. Offers global risk (MA); international development (MA, Certificate), including international economics (MA); international economics (Certificate); international economics and finance (MA); international public policy (MIPP); international relations (PhD); international studies (Certificate); Japan studies (MA), including international economics; Korea studies (MA), including international economics; South Asia studies (MA), including international economics; Southeast Asia studies (MA), including international economics; JD/MA; MBA/MA; MHS/MA. Terminal master's awarded for

partial completion of doctoral program. *Degree requirements:* For master's, 4-6 international economics courses, 5-6 functional or regional concentration courses, 2 core examinations, proficiency in language other than native language, capstone project; for doctorate, 2 foreign languages, thesis/dissertation, 3 comprehensive exams, economics, quantitative and qualitative course, dissertation prospectus and defense. *Entrance requirements:* For master's, GMAT or GRE General Test, previous course work in economics, foreign language, undergraduate degree; for doctorate, GRE General Test, master's degree. Additional exam requirements/recommendations for international students: Required—TOEFL (minimum score 600 paper-based; 100 iBT) or IELTS (minimum score 7). Electronic applications accepted. *Expenses:* Contact institution. *Faculty research:* International economics; international relations/regional studies; international development; energy, resources, and environment; international security/strategic studies.

Maharishi University of Management, Graduate Studies, Program in Maharishi Vedic Science, Fairfield, IA 52557. Offers MA, PhD. *Program availability:* Evening/weekend. *Degree requirements:* For master's, thesis; for doctorate, thesis/dissertation. *Entrance requirements:* For master's, minimum GPA of 3.0; for doctorate, GRE, minimum GPA of 3.0. Additional exam requirements/recommendations for international students: Required—TOEFL. *Faculty research:* Modern science and Vedic science, unification of knowledge, philosophy of science, Sanskrit.

McGill University, Faculty of Graduate and Postdoctoral Studies, Faculty of Arts, Department of East Asian Studies, Montréal, QC H3A 2T5, Canada. Offers MA, PhD.

New York University, Graduate School of Arts and Science, Department of East Asian Studies, New York, NY 10012-1019. Offers MA, PhD. *Program availability:* Part-time. *Students:* Average age 34. In 2017, 4 master's, 2 doctorates awarded. *Entrance requirements:* Additional exam requirements/recommendations for international students: Required—TOEFL. *Application deadline:* For fall admission, 1/4 for domestic and international students. Application fee: $100. Electronic applications accepted. *Expenses: Tuition:* Full-time $41,352; part-time $19,968 per year. *Required fees:* $2496; $1628 per unit. $814 per term. Tuition and fees vary according to course load and program. *Financial support:* Fellowships, teaching assistantships, Federal Work-Study, institutionally sponsored loans, scholarships/grants, health care benefits, and unspecified assistantships available. Financial award application deadline: 1/4. *Unit head:* Eliot Borenstein, Acting Chair, 212-998-7620, Fax: 212-995-4682, E-mail: gsas.eas.graduate@nyu.edu. *Application contact:* Tom Looser, Director of Graduate Studies, 212-998-7620, Fax: 212-995-4682, E-mail: gsas.eas.graduate@nyu.edu.

The Ohio State University, Graduate School, East Asian Studies Center, Columbus, OH 43210. Offers MA. *Students:* 9 full-time (7 women). Average age 25. In 2017, 5 master's awarded. *Degree requirements:* For master's, thesis optional. *Entrance requirements:* For master's, GRE General Test. Additional exam requirements/ recommendations for international students: Required—TOEFL (minimum score 550 paper-based; 79 iBT), IELTS (minimum score 7). *Application deadline:* For fall admission, 12/13 priority date for domestic students, 11/30 priority date for international students; for spring admission, 12/1 for domestic students, 11/1 for international students; for summer admission, 4/10 for domestic students, 3/13 for international students. Applications are processed on a rolling basis. Application fee: $60 ($70 for international students). Electronic applications accepted. *Unit head:* Dr. Etsuyo Yuasa, Associate Professor, 614-292-5816, E-mail: yuasa.1@osu.edu. *Application contact:* Graduate and Professional Admissions, 614-292-9444, Fax: 614-292-3895, E-mail: gpadmissions@osu.edu.
Website: http://www.easc.osu.edu/

Ohio University, Graduate College, Center for International Studies, Program in Asian Studies, Athens, OH 45701-2979. Offers MA. *Program availability:* Part-time. *Degree requirements:* For master's, one foreign language, thesis optional. *Entrance requirements:* For master's, minimum GPA of 3.0. Additional exam requirements/ recommendations for international students: Required—TOEFL (minimum score 550 paper-based; 80 iBT); Recommended—IELTS (minimum score 6.5). Electronic applications accepted. *Faculty research:* Indonesian and Malaysian political, history, literature, media, Islam, and environmental problems.

Princeton University, Graduate School, Department of East Asian Studies, Princeton, NJ 08544-1019. Offers PhD. *Degree requirements:* For doctorate, 2 foreign languages, thesis/dissertation. *Entrance requirements:* For doctorate, GRE General Test, fluency in Japanese and/or Chinese. Additional exam requirements/recommendations for international students: Required—TOEFL (minimum score 600 paper-based). Electronic applications accepted. *Faculty research:* Modern and classical Japanese literature, premodern Chinese and Japanese history, Chinese narrative and poetry.

Rutgers University–New Brunswick, Graduate School-New Brunswick, Program in East Asian Languages and Cultures, Piscataway, NJ 08854-8097. Offers MA. *Degree requirements:* For master's, one foreign language, final exam. *Entrance requirements:* For master's, GRE, official transcripts, two letters of recommendation, personal statement, writing sample. Additional exam requirements/recommendations for international students: Required—TOEFL or IELTS.

Rutgers University–New Brunswick, Graduate School-New Brunswick, Program in History, Piscataway, NJ 08854-8097. Offers African-American history (PhD); early American history (PhD); early modern European history (PhD); east Asian history (PhD); global and comparative history (PhD); history (PhD); history of diplomacy and foreign relations (PhD); history of technology, environment and health (PhD); history of the Atlantic cultures and African diaspora (PhD); Latin American history (PhD); medieval history (PhD); modern European history (PhD); nineteenth and twentieth century American history (PhD); women's and gender history (PhD). *Degree requirements:* For doctorate, thesis/dissertation. *Entrance requirements:* For doctorate, GRE General Test, sample of written work. Electronic applications accepted. *Faculty research:* American history, European history, Afro-American history, women's history, Latin American history.

St. John's College, Graduate Institute in Liberal Education, Program in Eastern Classics, Santa Fe, NM 87505. Offers MA. *Program availability:* Part-time, evening/ weekend. *Entrance requirements:* For master's, 2 letters of recommendation. Additional exam requirements/recommendations for international students: Required—TOEFL, TWE. *Expenses:* Contact institution.

St. John's University, St. John's College of Liberal Arts and Sciences, Institute of Asian Studies, Queens, NY 11439. Offers Chinese studies (MA); East Asian studies (MA). *Program availability:* Part-time, evening/weekend. *Faculty:* 1 (woman) full-time, 7 part-time/adjunct (3 women). *Students:* 8 full-time (4 women), 2 part-time (both women); includes 2 minority (both Asian, non-Hispanic/Latino), 8 international. Average age 29. 16 applicants, 69% accepted, 6 enrolled. In 2017, 8 master's awarded. *Degree requirements:* For master's, one foreign language, comprehensive exam, thesis optional, 33 major credits including two required courses. *Entrance requirements:* For master's, letters of recommendation, transcripts, resume, personal statement. Additional exam requirements/recommendations for international students: Required—TOEFL (minimum score 80 iBT), IELTS (minimum score 6.5). *Application deadline:* For fall admission, 5/1 for domestic students; for spring admission, 11/1 for domestic students. Applications are processed on a rolling basis. Application fee: $70. Electronic

applications accepted. *Expenses: Tuition:* Full-time $44,280; part-time $1230 per credit. *Required fees:* $340; $340 per credit. Tuition and fees vary according to course load, degree level and program. *Financial support:* Fellowships, research assistantships, teaching assistantships, scholarships/grants, tuition waivers, and unspecified assistantships available. Support available to part-time students. Financial award application deadline: 2/1; financial award applicants required to submit FAFSA. *Faculty research:* East Asian philosophy and religions; government and politics of East Asia; business and economy of East Asia; legal systems and trade relations of East Asian countries; Chinese, Japanese, and Korean languages and civilization. *Unit head:* Dr. Bernadette Li, Director, 718-990-1657, E-mail: lib@stjohns.edu. *Application contact:* Robert Medrano, Director of Graduate Admission, 718-990-1601, Fax: 718-990-5686, E-mail: gradhelp@stjohns.edu.
Website: https://www.stjohns.edu/academics/schools-and-colleges/st-johns-college-liberal-arts-and-sciences/institute-asian-studies

San Diego State University, Graduate and Research Affairs, College of Arts and Letters, Center for Asian Studies, San Diego, CA 92182. Offers MA. *Degree requirements:* For master's, one foreign language, thesis. *Entrance requirements:* For master's, GRE General Test, 3 letters of reference, writing sample. Additional exam requirements/recommendations for international students: Required—TOEFL. Electronic applications accepted. *Faculty research:* Language acquisition process, social organization of Asia, economic development.

Seton Hall University, College of Arts and Sciences, Department of Languages, Literatures and Cultures, South Orange, NJ 07079-2697. Offers Asian studies (MA). *Program availability:* Part-time, evening/weekend. *Degree requirements:* For master's, thesis optional. *Entrance requirements:* For master's, strong background in Asian studies or related discipline. Additional exam requirements/recommendations for international students: Required—TOEFL. Electronic applications accepted. *Faculty research:* Modern Chinese history, contemporary Chinese politics, ancient Chinese history, Hinduism, Asian business, Japanese history.

Stanford University, School of Humanities and Sciences, Center for East Asian Studies, Stanford, CA 94305-2004. Offers MA. *Degree requirements:* For master's, one foreign language, thesis. *Entrance requirements:* For master's, GRE General Test. Additional exam requirements/recommendations for international students: Required—TOEFL. Electronic applications accepted. *Expenses: Tuition:* Full-time $48,987; part-time $10,620 per quarter. One-time fee: $400. Tuition and fees vary according to program.

Stony Brook University, State University of New York, Graduate School, College of Arts and Sciences, Department of Asian and Asian American studies, Stony Brook, NY 11794. Offers contemporary Asian and Asian American studies (MA). *Faculty:* 15 full-time (10 women), 6 part-time/adjunct (all women). *Students:* 3 full-time (2 women), 5 part-time (all women); includes 4 minority (1 Black or African American, non-Hispanic/Latino; 3 Asian, non-Hispanic/Latino), 1 international. Average age 29. 6 applicants, 83% accepted, 5 enrolled. *Degree requirements:* For master's, thesis or final project. *Entrance requirements:* For master's, GRE, undergraduate transcript, statement of purpose, three letters of recommendation. Additional exam requirements/ recommendations for international students: Required—TOEFL (minimum score 85 iBT). *Application deadline:* For fall admission, 1/15 for domestic students; for spring admission, 10/1 for domestic students. Application fee: $100. Electronic applications accepted. *Expenses:* Tuition, state resident: full-time $10,870; part-time $453 per credit. Tuition, nonresident: full-time $22,210; part-time $925 per credit. *Financial support:* Applicants required to submit FAFSA. *Faculty research:* Asian studies, English as a second language, humanities, sociolinguistics. *Total annual research expenditures:* $18,968. *Unit head:* Dr. Agnes He, Chair, 631-632-4041, Fax: 631-632-4098, E-mail: agnes.he@stonybrook.edu. *Application contact:* Melissa Jordan, Assistant Dean for Records and Admission, 631-632-9712, Fax: 631-632-7243, E-mail: melissa.jordan@stonybrook.edu.
Website: http://www.stonybrook.edu/commcms/asianamerican/

United Theological Seminary of the Twin Cities, Graduate Programs, New Brighton, MN 55112-2598. Offers advanced theological studies (Diploma); justice and peace studies (M Div, MA); leadership toward racial justice (M Div, MA, Certificate); Methodist studies (M Div, MA, Certificate); ministry (D Min); ministry renewal and professional development (Certificate); pastoral care and counseling (M Div, MA, MARL); religion and theology (MA); theological and religious studies (Certificate); theology and the arts (M Div, MA); urban ministry (M Div, MA, MARL); women's studies: religion, theology and ministry (M Div, MA). *Accreditation:* ACIPE; ATS. *Program availability:* Part-time, evening/weekend. *Degree requirements:* For master's, thesis; for doctorate, comprehensive exam, thesis/dissertation. *Entrance requirements:* For master's, minimum GPA of 2.75; strong analytical, reflective thinking and writing skills; vocational and academic goals compatible with those of Seminary; for doctorate, M Div or equivalent, minimum GPA of 3.0, 3 years experience in professional ministry; for other advanced degree, BA or equivalent life experience; strong analytical, reflective thinking and writing skills (Certificate); proficiency in English language, previous study of theology at a theological school, recommendation of student's denomination (Diploma). Additional exam requirements/recommendations for international students: Required—TOEFL (minimum score 550 paper-based).

University of Alberta, Faculty of Graduate Studies and Research, Department of East Asian Studies, Edmonton, AB T6G 2E1, Canada. Offers Chinese literature (MA); East Asian interdisciplinary studies (MA); Japanese literature (MA). *Program availability:* Part-time. *Degree requirements:* For master's, one foreign language, thesis. *Entrance requirements:* Additional exam requirements/recommendations for international students: Required—TOEFL. Electronic applications accepted. *Faculty research:* Classical Chinese poetry and poetics, Chinese philosophy, modern/contemporary Chinese literature, modern Japanese literature and culture, Japanese women's writing.

The University of Arizona, College of Humanities, Department of East Asian Studies, Tucson, AZ 85721. Offers MA, PhD. *Program availability:* Part-time. Terminal master's awarded for partial completion of doctoral program. *Degree requirements:* For master's, one foreign language; for doctorate, 2 foreign languages. *Entrance requirements:* For master's, GRE General Test, 2 letters of recommendation; for doctorate, GRE General Test, 2 letters of recommendation, statement of purpose, writing sample. Additional exam requirements/recommendations for international students: Required—TOEFL (minimum score 550 paper-based; 79 iBT). Electronic applications accepted. *Faculty research:* Chinese history; Chinese/Japanese linguistics, literature, and religion.

University of Bridgeport, College of Public and International Affairs, Bridgeport, CT 06604. Offers East Asian and Pacific Rim studies (MA); global development and peace (MA); global media and communication studies (MA). *Program availability:* Part-time, evening/weekend. *Degree requirements:* For master's, thesis. *Entrance requirements:* Additional exam requirements/recommendations for international students: Recommended—TOEFL (minimum score 550 paper-based; 80 iBT), IELTS (minimum score 6.5).

The University of British Columbia, Faculty of Arts, Department of Asian Studies, Vancouver, BC V6T 1Z2, Canada. Offers MA, PhD. *Degree requirements:* For master's, one foreign language, thesis; for doctorate, 2 foreign languages, thesis/dissertation.

Entrance requirements: For master's, BA; for doctorate, master's degree in Asian studies or equivalent. Additional exam requirements/recommendations for international students: Required—TOEFL. Electronic applications accepted. *Expenses:* Contact institution. *Faculty research:* Language; linguistics; literature; religion and philosophy; premodern history of China, Japan, Korea, South and South East Asia.

The University of British Columbia, Institute of Asian Research, Vancouver, BC V6T 1Z2, Canada. Offers Asia Pacific policy studies (MAAPPS); public policy and global affairs (MPPGA). *Degree requirements:* For master's, thesis optional. *Entrance requirements:* Additional exam requirements/recommendations for international students: Required—TOEFL. Electronic applications accepted. *Expenses:* Contact institution. *Faculty research:* Social cohesion, globalization, social safety nets, policy research, research and development alliances, knowledge-based workshops on Asia-Pacific studies.

University of California, Berkeley, Graduate Division, College of Letters and Science, Department of South and Southeast Asian Studies, Berkeley, CA 94720-1500. Offers Hindi (MA, PhD); Indonesian (MA, PhD); Sanskrit (MA, PhD); Tamil (MA, PhD). Terminal master's awarded for partial completion of doctoral program. *Degree requirements:* For master's, 2 foreign languages, thesis; for doctorate, 2 foreign languages, thesis/dissertation, oral qualifying exam. *Entrance requirements:* For master's and doctorate, GRE General Test, minimum GPA of 3.0, 3 letters of recommendation. Electronic applications accepted.

University of California, Berkeley, Graduate Division, College of Letters and Science, Group in Buddhist Studies, Berkeley, CA 94720-1500. Offers PhD. *Degree requirements:* For doctorate, 4 foreign languages, thesis/dissertation, dissertation defense, qualifying exam. *Entrance requirements:* For doctorate, GRE General Test, MA in Japanese, Chinese, or Sanskrit; minimum GPA of 3.0; 3 letters of recommendation. Electronic applications accepted.

University of California, Berkeley, Graduate Division, Group in Asian Studies, Berkeley, CA 94720-1500. Offers East Asian studies (MA); Northeast Asian studies (MA); South Asian studies (MA); Southeast Asian studies (MA); JD/MA; MBA/MA; MJ/MA. *Degree requirements:* For master's, one foreign language, comprehensive exam or thesis. *Entrance requirements:* For master's, GRE General Test, minimum GPA of 3.0, 3 letters of recommendation. Electronic applications accepted.

University of California, Los Angeles, Graduate Division, College of Letters and Science, Department of Asian Languages and Cultures, Los Angeles, CA 90095. Offers MA, PhD. Terminal master's awarded for partial completion of doctoral program. *Degree requirements:* For master's, one foreign language, comprehensive exam or thesis; for doctorate, 2 foreign languages, thesis/dissertation, oral and written qualifying exams. *Entrance requirements:* For master's, GRE General Test, bachelor's degree; minimum undergraduate GPA of 3.0 (or its equivalent if letter grade system not used); writing sample; for doctorate, GRE General Test, master's degree; minimum undergraduate GPA of 3.0 (or its equivalent if letter grade system not used); writing sample. Additional exam requirements/recommendations for international students: Required—TOEFL. Electronic applications accepted.

University of California, Los Angeles, Graduate Division, International Institute, Interdepartmental Program in East Asian Studies, Los Angeles, CA 90095. Offers MA. *Degree requirements:* For master's, one foreign language, comprehensive exam. *Entrance requirements:* For master's, GRE General Test, bachelor's degree; minimum undergraduate GPA of 3.0 (or its equivalent if letter grade system not used). Additional exam requirements/recommendations for international students: Required—TOEFL. Electronic applications accepted.

University of California, Riverside, Graduate Division, Program in Southeast Asian Studies, Riverside, CA 92521. Offers MA. *Degree requirements:* For master's, one foreign language, thesis or comprehensive exam. *Entrance requirements:* For master's, GRE, statement of purpose to indicate serious interest in Southeast Asian Studies (or specific country or area in this region), writing sample. Additional exam requirements/recommendations for international students: Required—TOEFL; Recommended—IELTS (minimum score 7). Electronic applications accepted. *Expenses:* Tuition, state resident: full-time $5746. Tuition, nonresident: full-time $10,780. Tuition and fees vary according to campus/location and program. *Faculty research:* Southeast Asian texts, rituals and performance, music and technoculture, dance ethnography, ethnomusicology.

University of California, Santa Barbara, Graduate Division, College of Letters and Sciences, Division of Humanities and Fine Arts, Department of East Asian Languages and Cultural Studies, Santa Barbara, CA 93106-7075. Offers applied linguistics (PhD); East Asian languages and cultural studies (MA); translation studies (PhD). *Degree requirements:* For master's, one foreign language, comprehensive exam (for some programs), thesis (for some programs); for doctorate, 2 foreign languages, thesis/dissertation, methodology. *Entrance requirements:* For master's and doctorate, GRE General Test. Additional exam requirements/recommendations for international students: Required—TOEFL (minimum score 550 paper-based; 80 iBT), IELTS (minimum score 7). Electronic applications accepted. *Faculty research:* Chinese literature, Chinese film, Japanese society, Japanese literature, East Asian cultural studies.

University of Chicago, Division of the Humanities, Department of East Asian Languages and Civilizations, Chicago, IL 60637. Offers PhD. *Students:* 28 full-time (17 women); includes 5 minority (4 Asian, non-Hispanic/Latino; 1 Two or more races, non-Hispanic/Latino), 16 international. Average age 30. 98 applicants, 7% accepted, 3 enrolled. In 2017, 6 doctorates awarded. Terminal master's awarded for partial completion of doctoral program. *Degree requirements:* For doctorate, 2 foreign languages, comprehensive exam, thesis/dissertation, qualifying exam. *Entrance requirements:* For doctorate, GRE General Test, 15-20 page writing sample, statement of purpose, 3 letters of recommendation, transcripts for all previous degrees and institutions attended. Additional exam requirements/recommendations for international students: Required—TOEFL (minimum score 104 iBT), IELTS (minimum score 7). *Application deadline:* For fall admission, 12/15 for domestic and international students. Application fee: $90. Electronic applications accepted. *Financial support:* In 2017–18, fellowships with full tuition reimbursements (averaging $27,000 per year) were awarded; teaching assistantships with full tuition reimbursements, Federal Work-Study, institutionally sponsored loans, scholarships/grants, traineeships, and health care benefits also available. Financial award application deadline: 12/15. *Faculty research:* East Asian literature, material culture, religious and intellectual history, paleography of early China, performance studies. *Unit head:* Dr. Jacob Eyferth, Chair, 773-834-1323, E-mail: ealc@uchicago.edu. *Application contact:* Michael Beetley, Assistant Dean of Students, Admissions and Fellowships, 773-702-1552, Fax: 773-834-9148, E-mail: humanitiesadmissions@uchicago.edu.
Website: http://ealc.uchicago.edu/

University of Chicago, Division of the Humanities, Department of South Asian Languages and Civilizations, Chicago, IL 60637. Offers South Asian languages and civilizations (PhD), including Bengali, Hindi, Sanskrit, Tamil, Urdu. *Students:* 33 full-time (17 women); includes 5 minority (1 Black or African American, non-Hispanic/Latino; 3 Asian, non-Hispanic/Latino; 1 Two or more races, non-Hispanic/Latino), 19 international. Average age 31. 34 applicants, 15% accepted, 4 enrolled. In 2017, 2 doctorates awarded. Terminal master's awarded for partial completion of doctoral program. *Degree requirements:* For doctorate, 3 foreign languages, comprehensive exam, thesis/dissertation. *Entrance requirements:* For doctorate, GRE General Test, 15-20 page writing sample, statement of purpose, 3 letters of recommendation, transcripts for all previous degrees and institutions attended. Additional exam requirements/recommendations for international students: Required—TOEFL (minimum score 104 iBT), IELTS (minimum score 7). *Application deadline:* For fall admission, 12/15 for domestic and international students. Application fee: $90. Electronic applications accepted. *Financial support:* In 2017–18, fellowships with full tuition reimbursements (averaging $27,000 per year) were awarded; teaching assistantships with full tuition reimbursements, Federal Work-Study, institutionally sponsored loans, scholarships/grants, and health care benefits also available. Financial award application deadline: 12/15. *Unit head:* Gary Tubb, Chair, 773-834-2825, E-mail: salc@lists.uchicago.edu. *Application contact:* Michael Beetley, Assistant Dean of Students, Admissions and Fellowships, 773-702-1552, Fax: 773-834-9148, E-mail: humanitiesadmissions@uchicago.edu.
Website: http://salc.uchicago.edu

University of Chicago, Division of the Humanities, Master of Arts Program in the Humanities, Chicago, IL 60637. Offers art history (MA); cinema and media studies (MA); classic languages (MA); comparative literature (MA); creative writing (MA); cultural policy studies (MA); digital humanities (MA); East Asian languages and civilizations (MA); English language and literature (MA); gender and sexuality studies (MA); Germanic studies (MA); linguistics (MA); music (MA); near Eastern languages and civilizations (MA); philosophy (MA); poetics (MA); race, politics and culture (MA); Romance languages and literatures (MA); Slavic languages and literatures (MA); South Asian languages and civilizations (MA); theater and performance studies (MA). *Students:* 95 full-time (50 women), 6 part-time (4 women); includes 22 minority (1 Black or African American, non-Hispanic/Latino; 10 Asian, non-Hispanic/Latino; 11 Hispanic/Latino), 19 international. Average age 26. 708 applicants, 75% accepted, 101 enrolled. In 2017, 91 master's awarded. *Degree requirements:* For master's, thesis. *Entrance requirements:* For master's, GRE General Test, 10-15 page writing sample, statement of purpose, 3 letters of recommendation, transcripts for all previous degrees and institutions attended. Additional exam requirements/recommendations for international students: Required—TOEFL (minimum score 104 iBT), IELTS (minimum score 7). *Application deadline:* For fall admission, 1/3 priority date for domestic and international students. Application fee: $90. Electronic applications accepted. *Expenses:* Contact institution. *Financial support:* In 2017–18, fellowships with partial tuition reimbursements (averaging $12,000 per year) were awarded; Federal Work-Study, institutionally sponsored loans, scholarships/grants, and tuition waivers (partial) also available. Financial award application deadline: 4/30. *Unit head:* Thomas Christensen, Director, 773-834-1201, Fax: 773-834-7526, E-mail: ma-humanities@uchicago.edu. *Application contact:* Michael Beetley, Assistant Dean of Students for Admissions, 773-834-1552, E-mail: humanitiesadmissions@uchicago.edu.
Website: http://maph.uchicago.edu/

University of Colorado Boulder, Graduate School, College of Arts and Sciences, Department of Asian Languages and Civilizations, Boulder, CO 80309. Offers MA, PhD. *Faculty:* 12 full-time (5 women). *Students:* 20 full-time (13 women), 1 (woman) part-time; includes 6 minority (3 Asian, non-Hispanic/Latino; 2 Hispanic/Latino; 1 Two or more races, non-Hispanic/Latino), 9 international. Average age 28. 53 applicants, 40% accepted, 6 enrolled. In 2017, 7 master's awarded. Terminal master's awarded for partial completion of doctoral program. *Degree requirements:* For master's, comprehensive exam. *Entrance requirements:* For master's, BA in Chinese or Japanese, minimum undergraduate GPA of 3.0. Additional exam requirements/recommendations for international students: Required—TOEFL. *Application deadline:* For fall admission, 12/1 for domestic and international students; for spring admission, 10/1 for domestic and international students. Applications are processed on a rolling basis. Application fee: $60 ($80 for international students). Electronic applications accepted. Application fee is waived when completed online. *Financial support:* In 2017–18, 90 students received support, including 41 fellowships (averaging $1,708 per year), 16 teaching assistantships with full and partial tuition reimbursements available (averaging $28,844 per year); institutionally sponsored loans, scholarships/grants, health care benefits, and unspecified assistantships also available. Financial award application deadline: 2/15; financial award applicants required to submit FAFSA. *Faculty research:* Asian languages/literature; Chinese language/literature; Asian religions; literary criticism; religious literature. *Application contact:* E-mail: dalc@colorado.edu.
Website: http://alc.colorado.edu/

University of Hawaii at Manoa, Office of Graduate Education, School of Pacific and Asian Studies, Program in Asian Studies, Concentration in Korean Studies, Honolulu, HI 96822. Offers Graduate Certificate. *Program availability:* Part-time. *Degree requirements:* For Graduate Certificate, one foreign language. *Entrance requirements:* For degree, GRE. Additional exam requirements/recommendations for international students: Required—TOEFL (minimum score 560 paper-based; 83 iBT), IELTS (minimum score 5).

University of Hawaii at Manoa, Office of Graduate Education, School of Pacific and Asian Studies, Program in Asian Studies, Concentration in Southeast Asian Studies, Honolulu, HI 96822. Offers Graduate Certificate. *Program availability:* Part-time. *Degree requirements:* For Graduate Certificate, one foreign language. *Entrance requirements:* For degree, GRE. Additional exam requirements/recommendations for international students: Required—TOEFL (minimum score 560 paper-based; 83 iBT), IELTS (minimum score 5).

University of Illinois at Urbana–Champaign, Graduate College, College of Liberal Arts and Sciences, Center for South Asian and Middle Eastern Studies, Champaign, IL 61820. Offers MA. *Degree requirements:* For master's, one foreign language, comprehensive exam, thesis or alternative.

University of Illinois at Urbana–Champaign, Graduate College, College of Liberal Arts and Sciences, School of Literatures, Cultures and Linguistics, Department of East Asian Languages and Cultures, Champaign, IL 61820. Offers East Asian languages and cultures (PhD); East Asian studies (MA).

The University of Iowa, Graduate College, College of Liberal Arts and Sciences, Program in Asian Civilizations, Iowa City, IA 52242-1316. Offers Chinese (MA); Hindi (MA); Sanskrit (MA); South Asian studies (MA). *Degree requirements:* For master's, thesis optional, exam. *Entrance requirements:* For master's, GRE General Test, minimum GPA of 3.0. Additional exam requirements/recommendations for international students: Required—TOEFL (minimum score 590 paper-based; 96 iBT). Electronic applications accepted.

The University of Kansas, Graduate Studies, College of Liberal Arts and Sciences, Department of East Asian Languages and Cultures, Lawrence, KS 66045. Offers MA, Graduate Certificate. *Program availability:* Part-time. *Students:* 3 full-time (1 woman); includes 1 minority (Two or more races, non-Hispanic/Latino), 1 international. Average age 26. 3 applicants, 67% accepted, 1 enrolled. In 2017, 3 master's, 2 other advanced degrees awarded. *Entrance requirements:* For master's, GRE, current curriculum vitae,

statement of purpose explaining academic objectives, writing sample that demonstrates writing skills and basic research capacity, three letters of recommendation, transcripts. Additional exam requirements/recommendations for international students: Required—TOEFL. *Application deadline:* For fall admission, 2/1 priority date for domestic and international students. Application fee: $65 ($85 for international students). Electronic applications accepted. *Financial support:* Fellowships, teaching assistantships, and unspecified assistantships available. *Faculty research:* Gender relations in literature, ancient Chinese law, visual culture of modern Japan, Japanese language pedagogy, Chinese paleography, Korean shamanism, folklore, traditional Chinese and Japanese literature, Chinese linguistics and language pedagogy. *Unit head:* Dr. Maggie Childs, Chair, 785-864-9128, E-mail: mgchilds@ku.edu. *Application contact:* Cari Ann Kreienhop, Graduate Programs and Admissions Contact, 785-864-3665, E-mail: ckreienhop@ku.edu.
Website: http://ealc.ku.edu/

The University of Manchester, School of Languages, Linguistics and Cultures, Manchester, United Kingdom. Offers Arab world studies (PhD); Chinese studies (M Phil, PhD); East Asian studies (M Phil, PhD); English language (PhD); French studies (M Phil, PhD); German studies (M Phil, PhD); interpreting studies (PhD); Italian studies (M Phil, PhD); Japanese studies (M Phil, PhD); Latin American cultural studies (M Phil, PhD); linguistics (M Phil, PhD); Middle Eastern studies (M Phil, PhD); Polish studies (M Phil, PhD); Portuguese studies (M Phil, PhD); Russian studies (M Phil, PhD); Spanish studies (M Phil, PhD); translation and intercultural studies (M Phil, PhD).

University of Michigan, Rackham Graduate School, College of Literature, Science, and the Arts, Center for Japanese Studies, Ann Arbor, MI 48109-1106. Offers AM, JD/AM, MBA/AM. *Program availability:* Part-time. *Faculty:* 49 full-time (22 women), 4 part-time/adjunct (2 women). *Students:* 12 full-time (7 women); includes 1 minority (Asian, non-Hispanic/Latino), 4 international. Average age 27. 19 applicants, 74% accepted, 7 enrolled. In 2017, 6 master's awarded. *Degree requirements:* For master's, one foreign language, thesis optional, 24 credits; 6th-term proficiency (3 years) in Japanese language; seminars with independent research/writing component. *Entrance requirements:* For master's, GRE General Test, academic statement of purpose; curriculum vitae; official transcripts of postsecondary education; 3 letters of recommendation. Additional exam requirements/recommendations for international students: Required—TOEFL (minimum score 560 paper-based; 84 iBT); Recommended—IELTS (minimum score 6.5). *Application deadline:* For fall admission, 12/15 for domestic and international students. Application fee: $75 ($90 for international students). Electronic applications accepted. *Expenses:* Tuition, state resident: full-time $22,368; part-time $1201 per credit hour. Tuition, nonresident: full-time $45,156; part-time $2467 per credit hour. *Required fees:* $376 per term. Tuition and fees vary according to course load, degree level and program. *Financial support:* In 2017–18, 14 students received support, including 9 fellowships with full tuition reimbursements available (averaging $15,000 per year); research assistantships with tuition reimbursements available, teaching assistantships with tuition reimbursements available, career-related internships or fieldwork, Federal Work-Study, scholarships/grants, health care benefits, and unspecified assistantships also available. Support available to part-time students. Financial award application deadline: 1/15; financial award applicants required to submit FAFSA. *Faculty research:* Japanese literature; Japanese history (premodern and modern); Japanese linguistics and language pedagogy; modern Japanese society and culture; gender and sexuality in Japan; Japanese art, art history and visual culture; Japanese film; Buddhism and religion in Japan; Japanese law; Japanese health care (medicine, nursing, psychiatry and social work). *Unit head:* Dr. Kiyoteru Tsutsui, Director, 734-764-6307, Fax: 734-936-2948, E-mail: umcjs@umich.edu. *Application contact:* Azumi Ann Takata, Graduate Academic Services Coordinator, 734-763-4528, Fax: 734-615-9058, E-mail: ii-gradadvising@umich.edu.
Website: http://www.ii.umich.edu/cjs/

University of Michigan, Rackham Graduate School, College of Literature, Science, and the Arts, Center for South Asian Studies, Ann Arbor, MI 48109. Offers MA, Certificate, MBA/MA. *Program availability:* Part-time. *Faculty:* 56 full-time (18 women). *Students:* 3 full-time (2 women); includes 1 minority (Two or more races, non-Hispanic/Latino). Average age 34. 11 applicants, 45% accepted, 2 enrolled. In 2017, 1 master's awarded. *Degree requirements:* For master's, one foreign language, thesis, 24 credits; for Certificate, one foreign language. *Entrance requirements:* For master's, GRE General Test, academic statement of purpose; curriculum vitae; writing sample; official transcripts of postsecondary education; 3 letters of recommendation; for Certificate, GRE General Test, academic statement of purpose; official transcripts; letter of recommendation from academic advisor. Additional exam requirements/recommendations for international students: Required—TOEFL (minimum score 560 paper-based; 84 iBT); Recommended—IELTS (minimum score 6.5). *Application deadline:* For fall admission, 12/15 for domestic and international students. Application fee: $75 ($90 for international students). Electronic applications accepted. *Expenses:* Tuition, state resident: full-time $22,368; part-time $1201 per credit hour. Tuition, nonresident: full-time $45,156; part-time $2467 per credit hour. *Required fees:* $376 per term. Tuition and fees vary according to course load, degree level and program. *Financial support:* In 2017–18, 3 students received support, including 3 fellowships with full tuition reimbursements available (averaging $15,000 per year); research assistantships, teaching assistantships, career-related internships or fieldwork, Federal Work-Study, institutionally sponsored loans, scholarships/grants, health care benefits, and unspecified assistantships also available. Support available to part-time students. Financial award application deadline: 1/15; financial award applicants required to submit FAFSA. *Faculty research:* History of Islam in South Asia; British colonialism and the postcolonial predicament; ethnicity and nationalism; global and transnational feminism; South Asian architecture and urbanism. *Unit head:* Dr. Farina Mir, Director, 734-647-5416. *Application contact:* Julie E. Burnett, Graduate Academic Services Coordinator, 734-763-4528, Fax: 734-615-9058, E-mail: ii-gradadvising@umich.edu.
Website: http://www.ii.umich.edu/csas/

University of Michigan, Rackham Graduate School, College of Literature, Science, and the Arts, Center for Southeast Asian Studies, Ann Arbor, MI 48109-1106. Offers MA, Graduate Certificate, MBA/MA, MPP/MA. *Program availability:* Part-time. *Faculty:* 58 full-time (29 women). *Students:* 5 full-time (4 women); includes 3 minority (1 Black or African American, non-Hispanic/Latino; 2 Asian, non-Hispanic/Latino). Average age 28. 7 applicants, 86% accepted, 3 enrolled. In 2017, 1 master's awarded. *Degree requirements:* For master's, one foreign language, thesis, 25 credits; for Graduate Certificate, one foreign language. *Entrance requirements:* For master's, GRE General Test, academic statement of purpose; curriculum vitae; writing sample; official transcript of postsecondary education; 3 letters of recommendation; for Graduate Certificate, GRE General Test, academic statement of purpose; official transcripts; letter of recommendation from academic advisor. Additional exam requirements/recommendations for international students: Required—TOEFL (minimum score 560 paper-based; 84 iBT); Recommended—IELTS (minimum score 6.5). *Application deadline:* For fall admission, 1/15 for domestic and international students. Application fee: $75 ($90 for international students). Electronic applications accepted. *Expenses:* Tuition, state resident: full-time $22,368; part-time $1201 per credit hour. Tuition, nonresident: full-time $45,156; part-time $2467 per credit hour. *Required fees:* $376 per

term. Tuition and fees vary according to course load, degree level and program. *Financial support:* In 2017–18, 5 students received support, including 5 fellowships with full tuition reimbursements available (averaging $15,000 per year); research assistantships, teaching assistantships, career-related internships or fieldwork, Federal Work-Study, institutionally sponsored loans, scholarships/grants, health care benefits, and unspecified assistantships also available. Support available to part-time students. Financial award application deadline: 1/15; financial award applicants required to submit FAFSA. *Faculty research:* Politics, political parties, civil society, the law and human rights in Southeast Asia; nationalism and modernity in late colonial Southeast Asia; Islam, religion, language and media; urbanization, globalization and business; pre-modern Southeast Asia in a global/Eurasian context. *Unit head:* Prof. Christi-Anne Castro, Director, 734-615-4216. *Application contact:* Azumi Ann Takata, Graduate Academic Services Coordinator, 734-763-4528, Fax: 734-615-9058, E-mail: ii-gradadvising@umich.edu.
Website: http://www.ii.umich.edu/cseas

University of Michigan, Rackham Graduate School, College of Literature, Science, and the Arts, Department of Asian Languages and Cultures, Ann Arbor, MI 48104. Offers PhD. *Faculty:* 26 full-time (10 women). *Students:* 18 full-time (11 women); includes 4 minority (3 Asian, non-Hispanic/Latino; 1 Two or more races, non-Hispanic/Latino), 6 international. Average age 32. 79 applicants, 9% accepted, 3 enrolled. In 2017, 3 doctorates awarded. Terminal master's awarded for partial completion of doctoral program. *Degree requirements:* For doctorate, 2 foreign languages, comprehensive exam, thesis/dissertation, preliminary exams, oral defense of dissertation. *Entrance requirements:* Additional exam requirements/recommendations for international students: Required—TOEFL (minimum score 560 paper-based; 84 iBT), IELTS (minimum score 6.5). *Application deadline:* For fall admission, 12/1 for domestic and international students. Application fee: $75 ($90 for international students). Electronic applications accepted. *Expenses:* Tuition, state resident: full-time $22,368; part-time $1201 per credit hour. Tuition, nonresident: full-time $45,156; part-time $2467 per credit hour. *Required fees:* $376 per term. Tuition and fees vary according to course load, degree level and program. *Financial support:* In 2017–18 18 students received support. Fellowships with full tuition reimbursements available, teaching assistantships with full tuition reimbursements available, scholarships/grants, health care benefits, and spring/summer stipends available. Financial award application deadline: 12/1. *Faculty research:* Literature, religion, visual culture, history, modern culture, languages. *Unit head:* Prof. Donald S. Lopez, Jr., Chair, 734-615-6571, Fax: 734-647-0157, E-mail: um-alc@umich.edu. *Application contact:* ALC Student Services, 734-734-8286, Fax: 734-647-0157, E-mail: alc-gradservices@umich.edu.
Website: http://www.lsa.umich.edu/asian/

University of Michigan, Rackham Graduate School, College of Literature, Science, and the Arts, Kenneth G. Lieberthal and Richard H. Rogel Center for Chinese Studies, Ann Arbor, MI 48109. Offers MA, Graduate Certificate, JD/AM, MBA/AM, MPP/AM. *Program availability:* Part-time. *Faculty:* 42 full-time (16 women), 7 part-time/adjunct (3 women). *Students:* 8 full-time (5 women); includes 3 minority (2 Asian, non-Hispanic/Latino; 1 Hispanic/Latino), 3 international. Average age 27. 40 applicants, 35% accepted, 3 enrolled. In 2017, 2 master's awarded. *Degree requirements:* For master's, one foreign language, thesis or alternative, 24 credits; 6th-term proficiency in Chinese language; for Graduate Certificate, one foreign language. *Entrance requirements:* For master's, GRE General Test, academic statement of purpose; curriculum vitae; official transcript of postsecondary education; 3 letters of recommendation. Additional exam requirements/recommendations for international students: Required—TOEFL (minimum score 560 paper-based; 84 iBT); Recommended—IELTS (minimum score 6.5). *Application deadline:* For fall admission, 12/15 for domestic and international students. Application fee: $75 ($90 for international students). Electronic applications accepted. *Expenses:* Tuition, state resident: full-time $22,368; part-time $1201 per credit hour. Tuition, nonresident: full-time $45,156; part-time $2467 per credit hour. *Required fees:* $376 per term. Tuition and fees vary according to course load, degree level and program. *Financial support:* In 2017–18, 7 students received support, including 7 fellowships with full tuition reimbursements available (averaging $15,000 per year); research assistantships, teaching assistantships, Federal Work-Study, scholarships/grants, health care benefits, and unspecified assistantships also available. Support available to part-time students. Financial award application deadline: 1/15; financial award applicants required to submit FAFSA. *Faculty research:* Political and economic reform in China, Chinese religion, history of late Imperial China, Chinese foreign policy, Chinese music and music history. *Unit head:* Mary Gallagher, PhD, Director, 734-764-6308, Fax: 734-764-5540, E-mail: chinese.studies@umich.edu. *Application contact:* Azumi Ann Takata, Graduate Academic Services Coordinator, 734-763-4528, Fax: 734-615-9058, E-mail: ii-gradadvising@umich.edu.
Website: http://www.ii.umich.edu/lrccs

University of Minnesota, Twin Cities Campus, Graduate School, College of Liberal Arts, Department of Asian Languages and Literatures, Minneapolis, MN 55455-0213. Offers Asian literatures, cultures, and media (PhD). *Degree requirements:* For doctorate, comprehensive exam, thesis/dissertation. *Entrance requirements:* For doctorate, GRE, 3 letters of recommendation. Additional exam requirements/recommendations for international students: Required—TOEFL (minimum score 550 paper-based), IELTS (minimum score 6.5). Electronic applications accepted. *Faculty research:* Gender studies, post-colonial theory, poetics and poetic theory, film studies, post modernist thought.

University of Oregon, Graduate School, College of Arts and Sciences, Program in Asian Studies, Eugene, OR 97403. Offers MA. *Program availability:* Part-time. *Degree requirements:* For master's, one foreign language, thesis or alternative. *Entrance requirements:* For master's, GRE General Test. Additional exam requirements/recommendations for international students: Required—TOEFL. *Faculty research:* East and Southeast Asia, Pacific Islands.

University of Pennsylvania, School of Arts and Sciences, Graduate Group in East Asian Languages and Civilizations, Philadelphia, PA 19104. Offers AM, PhD. *Faculty:* 20 full-time (6 women), 3 part-time/adjunct (1 woman). *Students:* 43 full-time (27 women), 12 part-time (10 women); includes 3 minority (2 Asian, non-Hispanic/Latino; 1 Two or more races, non-Hispanic/Latino), 41 international. Average age 28. 125 applicants, 41% accepted, 21 enrolled. In 2017, 13 master's, 7 doctorates awarded.
Website: http://www.sas.upenn.edu/ealc/graduate-program

University of Pennsylvania, School of Arts and Sciences, Graduate Group in South Asian Regional Studies, Philadelphia, PA 19104. Offers AM, PhD. *Faculty:* 16 full-time (4 women), 4 part-time/adjunct (2 women). *Students:* 21 full-time (12 women), 2 part-time (0 women); includes 6 minority (5 Asian, non-Hispanic/Latino; 1 Two or more races, non-Hispanic/Latino), 12 international. Average age 31. 32 applicants, 31% accepted, 4 enrolled. In 2017, 3 master's, 3 doctorates awarded. Terminal master's awarded for partial completion of doctoral program. Application fee: $70.
Website: http://www.southasia.upenn.edu/graduate-programs

University of Pittsburgh, Kenneth P. Dietrich School of Arts and Sciences, Department of East Asian Languages and Literatures, Pittsburgh, PA 15260. Offers Chinese (MA); Japanese (MA). *Program availability:* Part-time. *Faculty:* 18 full-time (11 women), 11 part-time/adjunct (all women). *Students:* 4 full-time (all women); includes 2 minority (both

Asian, non-Hispanic/Latino). Average age 24. 13 applicants, 31% accepted, 3 enrolled. In 2017, 4 master's awarded. *Degree requirements:* For master's, one foreign language, thesis, oral comprehensive exam. *Entrance requirements:* For master's, GRE General Test, 2 years of college-level Chinese or Japanese, minimum QPA of 3.0, writing sample in English. Additional exam requirements/recommendations for international students: Required—TOEFL (minimum score 600 paper-based; 90 iBT), IELTS. *Application deadline:* For fall admission, 1/15 for domestic and international students. Application fee: $50. Electronic applications accepted. *Expenses:* $22,290 tuition, $850 fees. *Financial support:* In 2017–18, 5 students received support, including 1 fellowship with full tuition reimbursement available (averaging $23,262 per year); scholarships/grants and tuition waivers (full and partial) also available. Financial award application deadline: 1/15. *Faculty research:* Chinese literature, film, and poetry; Japanese literature, film, and theater; Chinese society and culture; East Asian foreign policy, security studies, and economic history; Japanese performing arts and fine arts translation studies; cultural studies; intellectual history; language and linguistics; second language acquisition; Japanese government; Japanese and Chinese history; ethnomusicology; religious studies. *Unit head:* Dr. Hiroshi Nara, Chair, 412-624-5579, Fax: 412-624-3458, E-mail: hnara@pitt.edu. *Application contact:* Keanna Cash, Graduate Administrator, 412-624-5227, E-mail: kec176@pitt.edu.
Website: http://deall.pitt.edu/

University of Pittsburgh, University Center for International Studies, Pittsburgh, PA 15260. Offers African studies (Certificate); Asian studies (Certificate); European Union studies (Certificate); global studies (Certificate); Latin American studies (Certificate); Russian and East European studies (Certificate); West European studies (Certificate). *Program availability:* Part-time, evening/weekend, online learning. *Students:* 183 full-time (108 women), 9 part-time (all women); includes 78 minority (6 Black or African American, non-Hispanic/Latino; 23 Asian, non-Hispanic/Latino; 47 Hispanic/Latino; 2 Two or more races, non-Hispanic/Latino). Average age 29. *Degree requirements:* For Certificate, one foreign language, comprehensive exam (for some programs). *Entrance requirements:* Additional exam requirements/recommendations for international students: Required—TOEFL. *Expenses:* No tuition and fees. *Financial support:* In 2017–18, 25 fellowships with full tuition reimbursements (averaging $26,117 per year) were awarded; scholarships/grants, traineeships, health care benefits, and unspecified assistantships also available. *Unit head:* Dr. Ariel Armony, Director, 412-648-7374, Fax: 412-624-4672, E-mail: armony@pitt.edu.
Website: http://www.ucis.pitt.edu

University of San Francisco, College of Arts and Sciences, Program in Asia Pacific Studies, San Francisco, CA 94117-1080. Offers MA, MA/MBA. *Program availability:* Part-time, evening/weekend. *Degree requirements:* For master's, one foreign language, thesis. *Entrance requirements:* For master's, minimum GPA of 3.0. Additional exam requirements/recommendations for international students: Required—TOEFL, IELTS, PTE. Electronic applications accepted. *Faculty research:* History of Christianity in China, U.S.-China policy, East Asian economies and political systems, sociolinguistic aspects of Japanese.

University of Southern California, Graduate School, Dana and David Dornsife College of Letters, Arts and Sciences, Department of East Asian Languages and Cultures, Los Angeles, CA 90089. Offers classical Chinese literature (MA, PhD); classical Japanese literature (MA, PhD); linguistics (MA, PhD); modern Chinese literature (MA, PhD); modern Japanese literature (MA, PhD); modern Korean literature (MA, PhD). *Degree requirements:* For master's, thesis; for doctorate, 2 foreign languages, comprehensive exam, thesis/dissertation. *Entrance requirements:* For master's and doctorate, GRE, BA in relevant field. Additional exam requirements/recommendations for international students: Required—TOEFL. Electronic applications accepted. *Faculty research:* Gender, visual studies, multimedia, ecocriticism, second language acquisition.

University of Southern California, Graduate School, Dana and David Dornsife College of Letters, Arts and Sciences, East Asian Studies Center, Los Angeles, CA 90089. Offers MA, MA/MBA. *Program availability:* Part-time. *Degree requirements:* For master's, one foreign language, thesis, language proficiency in an East Asian language (equivalent to 3 years of study). *Entrance requirements:* For master's, GRE (minimum score 1000). Additional exam requirements/recommendations for international students: Required—TOEFL (minimum score 600 paper-based; 100 iBT). Electronic applications accepted. *Faculty research:* East Asian visual cultures (Chinese, Japanese, and Korean film, culture and art); East Asian politics, society and history; East Asian literature and culture.

The University of Texas at Austin, Graduate School, College of Liberal Arts, Department of Asian Studies, Austin, TX 78712-1111. Offers Asian cultures and languages (MA, PhD); Asian studies (MA). *Program availability:* Part-time. *Degree requirements:* For master's, thesis; for doctorate, 3 foreign languages, thesis/dissertation. *Entrance requirements:* For master's and doctorate, GRE General Test. Electronic applications accepted. *Faculty research:* Modern Taiwanese fiction, modern Japanese literature, religious studies in South Asia during classical period.

University of Toronto, School of Graduate Studies, Faculty of Arts and Science, Department of East Asian Studies, Toronto, ON M5S 1A1, Canada. Offers MA, PhD. *Program availability:* Part-time. *Degree requirements:* For master's, thesis optional; for doctorate, 2 foreign languages, comprehensive exam, thesis/dissertation. *Entrance requirements:* For master's, writing sample, 2 letters of recommendation, BA in a specialist or East Asian studies program, minimum B+ average in final year; for doctorate, writing sample, 3 letters of recommendation, MA in East Asian studies. Additional exam requirements/recommendations for international students: Required—TOEFL (minimum score 600 paper-based), TWE (minimum score 5). Electronic applications accepted.

University of Utah, Graduate School, College of Humanities, Asian Studies Program, Salt Lake City, UT 84112. Offers MA. *Program availability:* Part-time, evening/weekend. *Faculty:* 55 full-time (30 women). *Students:* 2 full-time (0 women); both minorities (both Asian, non-Hispanic/Latino). Average age 23. 12 applicants, 33% accepted, 1 enrolled. In 2017, 1 master's awarded. *Degree requirements:* For master's, one foreign language, thesis, 3rd-year proficiency in one Asian language. *Entrance requirements:* For master's, GRE. Additional exam requirements/recommendations for international students: Required—TOEFL (minimum score 580 paper-based). *Application deadline:* For fall admission, 2/1 for domestic and international students; for spring admission, 9/15 for domestic students. Application fee: $55 ($65 for international students). Electronic applications accepted. *Financial support:* In 2017–18, 6 students received support, including 6 fellowships with full tuition reimbursements available (averaging $15,000 per year). Financial award application deadline: 2/1; financial award applicants required to submit FAFSA. *Faculty research:* Asian health studies, history, literature, culture, politics, economics. *Unit head:* Dr. Kim Korinek, Director, 801-581-6101, Fax: 801-581-6105, E-mail: kim.korinek@soc.utah.edu. *Application contact:* Ashley Glenn, Academic Advisor, 801-581-6101, Fax: 801-581-6105, E-mail: ea.glenn@utah.edu.
Website: http://asia-center.utah.edu/

University of Victoria, Faculty of Graduate Studies, Faculty of Humanities, Department of Pacific and Asian Studies, Victoria, BC V8W 2Y2, Canada. Offers MA. *Degree requirements:* For master's, thesis. *Entrance requirements:* For master's, minimum B+ average, writing sample. Additional exam requirements/recommendations for international students: Required—TOEFL (minimum score 575 paper-based), IELTS (minimum score 7). Electronic applications accepted. *Faculty research:* Culture, ethnicity and identity; economy and society; gender studies; languages and linguistics; literature.

University of Virginia, College and Graduate School of Arts and Sciences, Department of East Asian Languages, Literatures, and Cultures, Charlottesville, VA 22903. Offers East Asian studies (MA); MBA/MA. *Faculty:* 16 full-time (11 women), 1 (woman) part-time/adjunct. *Students:* 3 full-time (0 women); includes 1 minority (Asian, non-Hispanic/Latino), 1 international. Average age 23. 23 applicants, 39% accepted, 3 enrolled. In 2017, 3 master's awarded. *Degree requirements:* For master's, one foreign language, comprehensive exam, thesis. *Entrance requirements:* For master's, GRE General Test, 2 letters of recommendation. Additional exam requirements/recommendations for international students: Required—TOEFL, IELTS. *Application deadline:* For fall admission, 1/15 for domestic and international students; for winter admission, 9/15 for domestic and international students. Applications are processed on a rolling basis. Application fee: $60. Electronic applications accepted. *Financial support:* Applicants required to submit FAFSA. *Unit head:* Charles Laughlin, Chair, 434-924-8950, Fax: 434-243-1528, E-mail: cal5m@virginia.edu.
Website: http://eastasian.virginia.edu/

University of Virginia, College and Graduate School of Arts and Sciences, Department of Middle Eastern and South Asian Languages and Cultures, Charlottesville, VA 22903. Offers Middle Eastern and South Asian studies (MA). *Faculty:* 16 full-time (8 women), 1 (woman) part-time/adjunct. *Students:* 7 full-time (3 women), 2 part-time (0 women); includes 1 minority (Asian, non-Hispanic/Latino). Average age 31. 8 applicants, 100% accepted, 2 enrolled. In 2017, 6 master's awarded. Application fee: $60. *Unit head:* Farzaneh Milani, Chair, 434-243-4930, Fax: 434-243-1528, E-mail: fmm2z@virginia.edu. *Application contact:* Robert Hueckstedt, Director of Graduate Studies, 434-243-8228, Fax: 434-243-1528, E-mail: rah2k@virginia.edu.
Website: http://mesalc.virginia.edu/

University of Washington, Graduate School, College of Arts and Sciences, Department of Asian Languages and Literature, Seattle, WA 98195. Offers Buddhist studies (MA, PhD); Chinese language and literature (MA, PhD); Japanese language and literature (MA, PhD); Korean language and literature (MA, PhD); South Asian language and literature (MA, PhD). *Degree requirements:* For master's, 2 foreign languages, general exam, thesis or 2 research papers; for doctorate, 3 foreign languages, thesis/dissertation, general exam. *Entrance requirements:* For master's, GRE, minimum GPA of 3.0; for doctorate, GRE, master's degree in related field, minimum GPA of 3.0. Additional exam requirements/recommendations for international students: Required—TOEFL. Electronic applications accepted. *Faculty research:* Textual, linguistic, philological, and literary study of languages and literatures of Asia.

University of Washington, Graduate School, College of Arts and Sciences, Henry M. Jackson School of International Studies, China Studies Program, Seattle, WA 98195. Offers MAIS. *Degree requirements:* For master's, one foreign language, thesis optional. *Entrance requirements:* For master's, GRE General Test, minimum GPA of 3.0 in last 2 years. Additional exam requirements/recommendations for international students: Required—TOEFL (minimum score 500 paper-based; 92 iBT), IELTS (minimum score 7). Electronic applications accepted.

University of Washington, Graduate School, College of Arts and Sciences, Henry M. Jackson School of International Studies, Japan Studies Program, Seattle, WA 98195. Offers MAIS. *Degree requirements:* For master's, one foreign language. *Entrance requirements:* For master's, GRE General Test, minimum GPA of 3.0 in last two years. Additional exam requirements/recommendations for international students: Required—TOEFL (minimum score 500 paper-based; 92 iBT), IELTS (minimum score 7). Electronic applications accepted.

University of Washington, Graduate School, College of Arts and Sciences, Henry M. Jackson School of International Studies, Korea Studies Program, Seattle, WA 98195. Offers MAIS. *Degree requirements:* For master's, one foreign language. *Entrance requirements:* For master's, GRE General Test, minimum GPA of 3.0 in last two years. Additional exam requirements/recommendations for international students: Required—TOEFL (minimum score 500 paper-based; 92 iBT), IELTS (minimum score 7). Electronic applications accepted.

University of Washington, Graduate School, College of Arts and Sciences, Henry M. Jackson School of International Studies, Russian, East European and Central Asian Studies Program, Seattle, WA 98195. Offers Central Asian studies (MAIS); East European studies (MAIS); Russian studies (MAIS). *Degree requirements:* For master's, one foreign language, thesis. *Entrance requirements:* For master's, GRE General Test, 2 years of relevant language, minimum GPA of 3.0 in last two years. Additional exam requirements/recommendations for international students: Required—TOEFL (minimum score 500 paper-based; 92 iBT), IELTS (minimum score 7). Electronic applications accepted.

University of Washington, Graduate School, College of Arts and Sciences, Henry M. Jackson School of International Studies, South Asian Studies Program, Seattle, WA 98195. Offers MAIS. *Degree requirements:* For master's, one foreign language, thesis optional. *Entrance requirements:* For master's, GRE General Test, minimum GPA of 3.0 in last two years. Additional exam requirements/recommendations for international students: Required—TOEFL (minimum score 500 paper-based; 92 iBT), IELTS (minimum score 7). Electronic applications accepted.

University of Washington, Graduate School, College of Arts and Sciences, Henry M. Jackson School of International Studies, Southeast Asian Studies Program, Seattle, WA 98195. Offers MAIS. *Degree requirements:* For master's, one foreign language, thesis optional. *Entrance requirements:* For master's, GRE General Test, minimum GPA of 3.0 in last two years. Additional exam requirements/recommendations for international students: Required—TOEFL (minimum score 500 paper-based; 92 iBT), IELTS (minimum score 7). Electronic applications accepted.

University of Wisconsin–Madison, Graduate School, College of Letters and Science, Center for Southeast Asian Studies, Madison, WI 53706. Offers MA. *Program availability:* Part-time. *Degree requirements:* For master's, one foreign language, oral defense of seminar paper. Electronic applications accepted. *Faculty research:* Economic development, censorship, political change, pedagogical developments in Indonesia, Philippine historical demography, environment photography.

University of Wisconsin–Madison, Graduate School, College of Letters and Science, Department of East Asian Languages and Literature, Madison, WI 53706-1380. Offers Chinese literature (MA, PhD); Chinese thought (MA, PhD); Japanese linguistics (MA, PhD); Japanese literature (MA, PhD). *Program availability:* Part-time. Terminal master's awarded for partial completion of doctoral program. *Degree requirements:* For master's, one foreign language, seminars, written exam; for doctorate, 3 foreign languages, thesis/dissertation, seminars, preliminary exams, oral exams. *Entrance requirements:* For master's, GRE General Test, BA or equivalent in major field; for doctorate, GRE General Test, MA or equivalent in major field. Electronic applications accepted. *Faculty research:* Modern and historical linguistics, literature, literary and cultural history.

University of Wisconsin–Madison, Graduate School, College of Letters and Science, Department of History, Madison, WI 53706-1380. Offers African history (MA, PhD); Central Asian history (MA, PhD); comparative world history (MA, PhD); East Asian history (MA, PhD); European history (MA, PhD); gender and women's history (MA, PhD); Latin American and Caribbean history (MA, PhD); Middle Eastern history (MA, PhD); South Asian history (MA, PhD); Southeast Asian history (MA, PhD); United States history (MA, PhD). Terminal master's awarded for partial completion of doctoral program. *Degree requirements:* For master's, thesis (for some programs); for doctorate, variable foreign language requirement, thesis/dissertation. *Entrance requirements:* For master's and doctorate, GRE General Test. Additional exam requirements/recommendations for international students: Required—Michigan English Language Assessment Battery or TOEFL. Electronic applications accepted. *Faculty research:* American, African, European, Asian, Latin American, and Middle Eastern history.

University of Wisconsin–Madison, Graduate School, College of Letters and Science, Department of Languages and Cultures of Asia, Madison, WI 53706-1380. Offers civilizations and cultures (PhD); languages and cultures of Asia (MA); languages and literatures (PhD); religions of Asia (PhD). *Program availability:* Part-time. Terminal master's awarded for partial completion of doctoral program. *Degree requirements:* For master's, one foreign language, thesis or alternative; for doctorate, 2 foreign languages, thesis/dissertation. *Entrance requirements:* For master's, minimum GPA of 3.0; for doctorate, minimum GPA of 3.25, master's degree. Electronic applications accepted. *Faculty research:* Literature, folklore, religion.

Washington University in St. Louis, The Graduate School, Department of East Asian Languages and Cultures, St. Louis, MO 63130-4899. Offers Chinese (MA); Chinese and comparative literature (PhD); Chinese language and literature (PhD); East Asian studies (MA); Japanese (MA); Japanese and comparative literature (PhD); Japanese language and literature (PhD). Terminal master's awarded for partial completion of doctoral program. *Degree requirements:* For master's, thesis optional; for doctorate, thesis/dissertation. *Entrance requirements:* For master's and doctorate, GRE General Test. Additional exam requirements/recommendations for international students: Required—TOEFL. Electronic applications accepted. *Faculty research:* Chinese; Japanese; Chinese fiction, theater, poetry, modern literature; Japanese modern and classical fiction, translation theory.

Yale University, Graduate School of Arts and Sciences, Program in East Asian Studies, New Haven, CT 06520. Offers MA. *Degree requirements:* For master's, one foreign language. *Entrance requirements:* For master's, GRE General Test.

Canadian Studies

Carleton University, Faculty of Graduate Studies, Faculty of Arts and Social Sciences, School of Canadian Studies, Ottawa, ON K1S 5B6, Canada. Offers MA, PhD. PhD program offered jointly with Trent University. *Degree requirements:* For master's, one foreign language, thesis optional; for doctorate, one foreign language, thesis/dissertation. *Entrance requirements:* For master's, honors degree. Additional exam requirements/recommendations for international students: Required—TOEFL. Electronic applications accepted. *Faculty research:* Modern Canada, cultural studies, women's studies, aboriginal studies and the north, heritage conservation.

Queen's University at Kingston, School of Graduate Studies, Faculty of Arts and Sciences, Department of Political Studies, Kingston, ON K7L 3N6, Canada. Offers Canadian politics (PhD); comparative politics (PhD); gender and politics (PhD); international relations (PhD); political theory (PhD). *Degree requirements:* For master's, thesis or alternative; for doctorate, one foreign language, thesis/dissertation, qualifying exams. *Entrance requirements:* Additional exam requirements/recommendations for international students: Required—TOEFL (minimum score 600 paper-based). *Faculty research:* Canadian politics, comparative politics, political thought, international politics, women and politics.

Saint Mary's University, Faculty of Arts, Program in Atlantic Canada Studies, Halifax, NS B3H 3C3, Canada. Offers MA, Certificate. *Program availability:* Part-time, evening/weekend. *Degree requirements:* For master's, thesis. *Entrance requirements:* For master's, honors degree. Electronic applications accepted. *Expenses:* Contact institution.

Trent University, Graduate Studies, The Frost Centre for Canadian Studies and Indigenous Studies, Peterborough, ON K9J 7B8, Canada. Offers Canadian studies (PhD); Canadian studies and indigenous studies (MA). *Program availability:* Part-time. *Degree requirements:* For master's, thesis. *Entrance requirements:* For master's, honors degree. *Faculty research:* Native community-based socioeconomic development, environmental and social impact inventory, regional studies.

Université de Saint-Boniface, Program in Canadian Studies, Saint-Boniface, MB R2H 0H7, Canada. Offers MA.

Université de Sherbrooke, Faculty of Letters and Human Sciences, Department of Letters and Communications, Sherbrooke, QC J1K 2R1, Canada. Offers comparative Canadian literature (MA, PhD); French literature (MA, PhD); linguistics (MA); theatre (MA). *Degree requirements:* For master's, thesis or alternative; for doctorate, thesis/dissertation. *Entrance requirements:* For master's, minimum GPA of 2.8; for doctorate, minimum GPA of 3.0.

Université du Québec à Chicoutimi, Graduate Programs, Program in Regional Studies, Chicoutimi, QC G7H 2B1, Canada. Offers MA. *Program availability:* Part-time. *Degree requirements:* For master's, thesis. *Entrance requirements:* For master's, appropriate bachelor's degree, proficiency in French.

University at Buffalo, the State University of New York, Graduate School, College of Arts and Sciences, Department of Transnational Studies, Buffalo, NY 14214. Offers American studies (MA, PhD); Canadian studies (MA); global gender studies (MA, PhD). *Program availability:* Part-time. *Faculty:* 16 full-time (8 women), 3 part-time/adjunct (1 woman). *Students:* 71 full-time (42 women); includes 26 minority (9 Black or African American, non-Hispanic/Latino; 6 American Indian or Alaska Native, non-Hispanic/Latino; 9 Asian, non-Hispanic/Latino; 2 Hispanic/Latino). Average age 33. 30 applicants, 70% accepted, 9 enrolled. In 2017, 7 master's, 15 doctorates awarded. Terminal master's awarded for partial completion of doctoral program. *Degree requirements:* For master's, comprehensive exam (for some programs), thesis optional; for doctorate, comprehensive exam, thesis/dissertation. *Entrance requirements:* For master's, minimum GPA of 3.0; for doctorate, GRE, minimum GPA of 3.0. Additional exam requirements/recommendations for international students: Required—TOEFL (minimum score 550 paper-based; 79 iBT), IELTS (minimum score 6.5). *Application deadline:* For fall admission, 8/28 priority date for domestic students, 6/15 priority date for international students; for winter admission, 2/1 for domestic and international students; for spring admission, 1/28 priority date for domestic students, 11/15 priority date for international students. Applications are processed on a rolling basis. Application fee: $75. Electronic applications accepted. *Financial support:* In 2017–18, 20 students received support, including 2 fellowships with full tuition reimbursements available (averaging $13,060 per year), 15 teaching assistantships with full tuition reimbursements available (averaging $13,060 per year); research assistantships, career-related internships or fieldwork, institutionally sponsored loans, scholarships/grants, health care benefits, and unspecified assistantships also available. Financial award application deadline: 1/1. *Faculty research:* Native American, intercultural and indigenous people's studies, border theory, cultural studies, American pop culture, feminist theory, construction of gender in society. *Unit head:* Dr. Cecil Foster, Chair, 716-645-0786, Fax: 716-645-5976, E-mail: cecilfos@buffalo.edu. *Application contact:* Karen M. Reinard, Graduate Coordinator, 716-645-0797, Fax: 716-645-5976, E-mail: kreinard@buffalo.edu.
Website: http://transnationalstudies.buffalo.edu/

University of Lethbridge, School of Graduate Studies, Lethbridge, AB T1K 3M4, Canada. Offers addictions counseling (M Sc); agricultural biotechnology (M Sc); agricultural studies (M Sc, MA); anthropology (MA); archaeology (M Sc, MA); art (MA, MFA); biochemistry (M Sc); biological sciences (M Sc); biomolecular science (PhD); biosystems and biodiversity (PhD); Canadian studies (MA); chemistry (M Sc); computer science (M Sc); computer science and geographical information science (M Sc); counseling (MC); counseling psychology (M Ed); dramatic arts (MA); earth, space, and physical science (PhD); economics (MA); education (MA, PhD); educational leadership (M Ed); English (MA); environmental science (M Sc); evolution and behavior (PhD); exercise science (M Sc); French (MA); French/German (MA); French/Spanish (MA); general education (M Ed); geography (M Sc, MA); German (MA); health sciences (M Sc); individualized multidisciplinary (M Sc, MA); kinesiology (M Sc, MA); management (M Sc), including accounting, finance, human resource management and labor relations, information systems, international management, marketing, policy and strategy; mathematics (M Sc); music (M Mus, MA); Native American studies (MA); neuroscience (M Sc, PhD); new media (MA, MFA); nursing (M Sc, MN); philosophy (MA); physics (M Sc); political science (MA); psychology (M Sc, MA); religious studies (MA); sociology (MA); theatre and dramatic arts (MFA); theoretical and computational science (PhD); urban and regional studies (MA); women and gender studies (MA). *Program availability:* Part-time, evening/weekend. *Degree requirements:* For master's, thesis (for some programs); for doctorate, comprehensive exam, thesis/dissertation. *Entrance requirements:* For master's, GMAT (for M Sc in management), bachelor's degree in related field, minimum GPA of 3.0 during previous 20 graded semester courses, 2 years' teaching or related experience (M Ed); for doctorate, master's degree, minimum graduate GPA of 3.5. Additional exam requirements/recommendations for international students: Required—TOEFL (minimum score 580 paper-based; 93 iBT). Electronic applications accepted. *Faculty research:* Movement and brain plasticity, gibberellin physiology, photosynthesis, carbon cycling, molecular properties of main-group ring components.

University of Manitoba, Faculty of Graduate Studies, College Universitaire de Saint Boniface, Program in Canadian Studies, Winnipeg, MB R3T 2N2, Canada. Offers MA.

University of Ottawa, Faculty of Graduate and Postdoctoral Studies, Faculty of Arts, Institute of Canadian Studies, Ottawa, ON K1N 6N5, Canada. Offers economics (PhD); English (PhD); geography (PhD); history (PhD); lettres Françaises (PhD); linguistics (PhD); philosophy (PhD); political science (PhD); psychology (PhD); religious studies (PhD); translation studies (PhD). *Degree requirements:* For doctorate, comprehensive exam, thesis/dissertation.

University of Regina, Faculty of Graduate Studies and Research, Faculty of Arts, Canadian Plains Studies Program, Regina, SK S4S 0A2, Canada. Offers MA, PhD. Offered as a special case program. *Program availability:* Part-time. *Students:* 2 full-time (1 woman). *Degree requirements:* For master's, thesis; for doctorate, thesis/dissertation. *Entrance requirements:* Additional exam requirements/recommendations for international students: Required—TOEFL (minimum score 580 paper-based; 80 iBT), IELTS (minimum score 6.5), PTE (minimum score 59). *Application deadline:* Applications are processed on a rolling basis. Application fee: $100. Electronic applications accepted. *Expenses:* Tuition, nonresident: full-time $21,330 Canadian dollars; part-time $18,165 Canadian dollars per year. *International tuition:* $24,713 Canadian dollars full-time. *Required fees:* $5136 Canadian dollars; $3118 Canadian dollars per credit hour. $1008 Canadian dollars per semester. Tuition and fees vary according to program. *Financial support:* Fellowships, research assistantships, teaching assistantships, and scholarships/grants available. Financial award application deadline: 6/15. *Unit head:* Dr. Nilgun Onder, Associate Dean of Arts, Research and Graduate Studies, 306-585-4336, Fax: 306-585-5368, E-mail: arts-assocdean-rg@uregina.ca.

University of Saskatchewan, College of Graduate Studies and Research, College of Arts and Science, Department of Native Studies, Saskatoon, SK S7N 5A2, Canada. Offers MA, PhD. *Degree requirements:* For master's, thesis; for doctorate, comprehensive exam (for some programs), thesis/dissertation. *Entrance requirements:* Additional exam requirements/recommendations for international students: Required—TOEFL (minimum score 80 iBT); Recommended—IELTS (minimum score 6.5). Electronic applications accepted.

Wilfrid Laurier University, Faculty of Graduate and Postdoctoral Studies, Faculty of Arts, Department of Political Science, Waterloo, ON N2L 3C5, Canada. Offers Canadian political studies (MA); comparative politics/international relations (MA). *Program availability:* Part-time. *Degree requirements:* For master's, thesis optional. *Entrance requirements:* For master's, honors bachelor's degree or the equivalent in political science, minimum B average in undergraduate course work. Additional exam requirements/recommendations for international students: Required—TOEFL (minimum score 89 iBT). Electronic applications accepted. *Faculty research:* Political behavior/political psychology, Canadian political studies, comparative, politics/relations, public opinion and electoral studies, international.

Wilfrid Laurier University, Faculty of Graduate and Postdoctoral Studies, Lyle S. Hallman Faculty of Social Work, Waterloo, ON N2L 3C5, Canada. Offers Aboriginal studies (MSW); community, policy, planning and organizations (MSW); critical social policy and organizational studies (PhD); individuals, families and groups (MSW); social work practice (individuals, families, groups and communities) (PhD); social work practice: individuals, families, groups and communities (PhD). *Program availability:* Part-

time. *Degree requirements:* For master's, thesis optional; for doctorate, thesis/dissertation. *Entrance requirements:* For master's, course work in social science, research methodology, and statistics; honors BA with a minimum B average; for

doctorate, master's degree in social work, minimum A- average. Additional exam requirements/recommendations for international students: Required—TOEFL (minimum score 89 iBT). Electronic applications accepted. *Expenses:* Contact institution.

Cultural Studies

American University, College of Arts and Sciences, Critical Race, Gender, and Culture Studies Collaborative, Washington, DC 20016-8030. Offers Asian studies (Graduate Certificate); women's, gender, and sexuality studies (Graduate Certificate). *Faculty:* 4 full-time (3 women), 10 part-time/adjunct (5 women). In 2017, 3 Graduate Certificates awarded. *Entrance requirements:* Additional exam requirements/recommendations for international students: Required—TOEFL (minimum score 600 paper-based; 100 iBT). *Application deadline:* Applications are processed on a rolling basis. *Expenses: Tuition:* Full-time $29,556. *Required fees:* $690. Tuition and fees vary according to course load and program. *Unit head:* Dr. Peter Starr, Dean, 202-885-2446, Fax: 202-885-2429, E-mail: pstarr@american.edu. *Application contact:* Jonathan Harper, Associate Director, Graduate Recruitment, 202-885-3622, Fax: 202-885-1505, E-mail: jharper@american.edu.
Website: http://www.american.edu/cas/crgc/

American University, School of International Service, Washington, DC 20016-8071. Offers comparative and regional studies (Certificate); cross-cultural communication (Certificate); development management (MS); ethics, peace, and global affairs (MA); European studies (Certificate); global environmental policy (MA, Certificate); global information technology (Certificate); global media (MA); international affairs (MA), including comparative and regional studies, global governance, politics, and security, international economic relations, natural resources and sustainable development, U.S. foreign policy and national security; international arts management (Certificate); international communication (MA, Certificate); international development (MA); international economic policy (Certificate); international economic relations (Certificate); international economics (MA); international peace and conflict resolution (MA, Certificate); international politics (Certificate); international relations (MA, PhD); international service (MIS); peacebuilding (Certificate); social enterprise (MA); the Americas (Certificate); United States foreign policy (Certificate); JD/MA. *Program availability:* Part-time, evening/weekend, 100% online. *Faculty:* 112 full-time (50 women), 46 part-time/adjunct (19 women). *Students:* 495 full-time (333 women), 518 part-time (276 women); includes 360 minority (95 Black or African American, non-Hispanic/Latino; 2 American Indian or Alaska Native, non-Hispanic/Latino; 60 Asian, non-Hispanic/Latino; 164 Hispanic/Latino; 39 Two or more races, non-Hispanic/Latino), 98 international. Average age 30. 1,559 applicants, 81% accepted, 356 enrolled. In 2017, 427 master's, 9 doctorates, 5 other advanced degrees awarded. Terminal master's awarded for partial completion of doctoral program. *Degree requirements:* For master's, one foreign language, comprehensive exam, thesis or alternative; for doctorate, one foreign language, comprehensive exam, thesis/dissertation. *Entrance requirements:* For master's, GRE; GMAT or GRE (for MA in social enterprise), transcripts, resume, 2 letters of recommendation, statement of purpose; for doctorate, GRE, transcripts, resume, 3 letters of recommendation, statement of purpose. Additional exam requirements/recommendations for international students: Required—TOEFL (minimum score 600 paper-based; 100 iBT). *Application deadline:* For fall admission, 1/15 for domestic students, 1/1 for international students; for spring admission, 10/1 for domestic students, 9/15 for international students. Application fee: $55. Electronic applications accepted. *Expenses:* Contact institution. *Financial support:* Research assistantships, teaching assistantships, institutionally sponsored loans, scholarships/grants, and unspecified assistantships available. Financial award application deadline: 1/15; financial award applicants required to submit FAFSA. *Application contact:* 202-885-1646, Fax: 202-885-1109, E-mail: sisgrad@american.edu.
Website: http://www.american.edu/sis/

The American University of Paris, Graduate Programs, Paris, France. Offers cross-cultural and sustainable business management (MA); cultural translation (MA); global communications (MA); global communications and civil society (MA); international affairs (MA); international affairs, conflict resolution and civil society development (MA); Middle East and Islamic studies (MA); Middle East and Islamic studies and international affairs (MA); public policy and international affairs (MA); public policy and international law (MA). *Degree requirements:* For master's, thesis (for some programs). *Entrance requirements:* For master's, minimum undergraduate GPA of 3.0. Additional exam requirements/recommendations for international students: Recommended—TOEFL, IELTS. Electronic applications accepted.

Appalachian State University, Cratis D. Williams Graduate School, Center for Appalachian Studies, Boone, NC 28608. Offers culture (MA). *Program availability:* Part-time. *Degree requirements:* For master's, one foreign language, comprehensive exam, thesis optional. *Entrance requirements:* For master's, GRE General Test, 3 letters of recommendation. Additional exam requirements/recommendations for international students: Required—TOEFL (minimum score 570 paper-based; 79 iBT), IELTS (minimum score 6.5). Electronic applications accepted. *Faculty research:* Appalachian culture, sustainable development, Appalachian music.

Arizona State University at the Tempe campus, College of Liberal Arts and Sciences, Department of English, Program in Film and Media Studies, Tempe, AZ 85287-0402. Offers American media and popular culture (MAS). *Program availability:* Part-time, evening/weekend, online learning. *Degree requirements:* For master's, integrated project. *Entrance requirements:* For master's, minimum GPA of 3.0 or equivalent in last 2 years of work leading to bachelor's degree. Additional exam requirements/recommendations for international students: Required—TOEFL, IELTS, or PTE. Electronic applications accepted. *Expenses:* Contact institution.

Arizona State University at the Tempe campus, College of Liberal Arts and Sciences, School of International Letters and Cultures, Program in Spanish, Tempe, AZ 85287-0202. Offers cultural studies (PhD); linguistics (MA), including second language acquisition/applied linguistics, sociolinguistics; literature (PhD); literature and culture (MA). *Program availability:* Part-time. Terminal master's awarded for partial completion of doctoral program. *Degree requirements:* For master's, thesis, oral defense; written comprehensive exam (literature and culture); portfolio review (linguistics); interactive Program of Study (iPOS) submitted before completing 50 percent of required credit hours; for doctorate, comprehensive exam, thesis/dissertation, interactive Program of Study (iPOS) submitted before completing 50 percent of required credit hours. *Entrance requirements:* For master's, GRE (recommended), BA in Spanish or close equivalent from accredited institution with minimum GPA of 3.5, 3 letters of recommendation, personal statement, academic writing sample; for doctorate, GRE (recommended), MA in Spanish or equivalent from accredited institution with minimum GPA of 3.75, 3 letters

of recommendation, personal statement, academic writing sample. Additional exam requirements/recommendations for international students: Required—TOEFL (minimum score 550 paper-based; 83 iBT), IELTS (minimum score 6.5). Electronic applications accepted.

Assemblies of God Theological Seminary, Graduate and Professional Programs, Springfield, MO 65802. Offers Biblical interpretation and theology (PhD); Christian ministries (MA); divinity (M Div); intercultural studies (MA, PhD); leadership and ministry (MLM); ministry (D Min); missiology (DAIS); pastoral studies (MPL); theological studies (MA, Th M). *Accreditation:* ATS. *Program availability:* Part-time, evening/weekend, 100% online. *Faculty:* 12 full-time (3 women), 15 part-time/adjunct (4 women). *Students:* 153 full-time (48 women), 159 part-time (41 women); includes 62 minority (20 Black or African American, non-Hispanic/Latino; 4 American Indian or Alaska Native, non-Hispanic/Latino; 14 Asian, non-Hispanic/Latino; 18 Hispanic/Latino; 6 Two or more races, non-Hispanic/Latino), 12 international. Average age 46. 69 applicants, 88% accepted, 48 enrolled. In 2017, 35 master's, 22 doctorates awarded. *Degree requirements:* For master's, variable foreign language requirement, thesis; for doctorate, variable foreign language requirement, comprehensive exam, thesis/dissertation. *Entrance requirements:* For master's, minimum GPA of 2.5; for doctorate, GRE (for PhD in Bible theology), minimum GPA of 3.0. Additional exam requirements/recommendations for international students: Required—TOEFL (minimum score 550 paper-based; 80 iBT). *Application deadline:* For fall admission, 7/1 priority date for domestic students, 6/1 priority date for international students; for spring admission, 12/1 priority date for domestic students, 11/1 priority date for international students. Applications are processed on a rolling basis. Application fee: $75. Electronic applications accepted. *Financial support:* Career-related internships or fieldwork and scholarships/grants available. Support available to part-time students. Financial award application deadline: 7/15; financial award applicants required to submit FAFSA. *Unit head:* Dr. Timothy A. Hager, Dean, 417-268-1000, Fax: 417-268-1001. *Application contact:* Erin Leonard, Seminary Enrollment Coordinator, 417-268-1000, Fax: 417-268-1001, E-mail: info@agts.edu.
Website: http://www.agts.edu

Athabasca University, Centre for Interdisciplinary Studies, Athabasca, AB T9S 3A3, Canada. Offers adult education (MA); community studies (MA); cultural studies (MA); educational studies (MA); global change (MA); heritage resource management (Postbaccalaureate Certificate); legislative drafting (Postbaccalaureate Certificate); work, organization, and leadership (MA). *Program availability:* Part-time, evening/weekend, online learning. *Degree requirements:* For master's, project. *Entrance requirements:* Additional exam requirements/recommendations for international students: Required—TOEFL (minimum score 560 paper-based). Electronic applications accepted. *Faculty research:* Women's history, literature and culture studies, sustainable development, labor and education.

Biola University, Cook School of Intercultural Studies, La Mirada, CA 90639-0001. Offers anthropology (MA); applied linguistics (MA); intercultural education (PhD); intercultural studies (MA, PhD); linguistics (Certificate); linguistics and Biblical languages (MA); missiology (D Miss); missions (MA); teaching English to speakers of other languages (MA, Certificate). *Program availability:* Part-time, 100% online. *Faculty:* 19. *Students:* 127 full-time (64 women), 123 part-time (70 women); includes 72 minority (9 Black or African American, non-Hispanic/Latino; 2 American Indian or Alaska Native, non-Hispanic/Latino; 41 Asian, non-Hispanic/Latino; 17 Hispanic/Latino; 3 Two or more races, non-Hispanic/Latino), 26 international. In 2017, 28 master's, 16 doctorates awarded. *Entrance requirements:* For master's, minimum undergraduate GPA of 3.0; for doctorate, master's degree or equivalent, 3 years of cross-cultural experience, minimum graduate GPA of 3.3. Additional exam requirements/recommendations for international students: Required—TOEFL. *Application deadline:* For fall admission, 7/1 for domestic students, 6/1 for international students; for spring admission, 12/1 for domestic students; for summer admission, 5/1 for domestic students. Applications are processed on a rolling basis. Application fee: $65. Electronic applications accepted. *Financial support:* Scholarships/grants available. Support available to part-time students. Financial award applicants required to submit FAFSA. *Faculty research:* Linguistics, anthropology, intercultural studies, teaching English to speakers of other languages, missions, missiology. *Unit head:* Dr. Bulus Y. Galadima, Dean, 562-903-4844. *Application contact:* Graduate Admissions Office, 562-903-4752, E-mail: graduate.admissions@biola.edu.
Website: http://cook.biola.edu

Biola University, Talbot School of Theology, La Mirada, CA 90639-0001. Offers adult/family ministry (MACE); Bible exposition (MA, Th M); Biblical and theological studies (Certificate); children's ministry (MACE); Christian education (M Div); cross-cultural education ministry (MACE); educational studies (Ed D, PhD); evangelism and discipleship (M Div); general Christian education (MACE); Messianic Jewish studies (M Div, Certificate); missions and intercultural studies (M Div); New Testament (MA, Th M); Old Testament (MA); Old Testament and Semitics (Th M); pastoral and general ministry (M Div); pastoral care and counseling (M Div, MACML); philosophy (MA); preaching and pastoral ministry (MACML); spiritual formation (M Div, Certificate); spiritual formation and soul care (MA); sports ministry (MACML); theology (MA, Th M, D Min, Certificate); youth ministry (MACE). *Program availability:* Part-time, evening/weekend. *Students:* 475 full-time (113 women), 603 part-time (176 women); includes 541 minority (39 Black or African American, non-Hispanic/Latino; 2 American Indian or Alaska Native, non-Hispanic/Latino; 378 Asian, non-Hispanic/Latino; 84 Hispanic/Latino; 1 Native Hawaiian or other Pacific Islander, non-Hispanic/Latino; 37 Two or more races, non-Hispanic/Latino), 105 international. 437 applicants, 78% accepted, 241 enrolled. In 2017, 177 master's, 24 doctorates awarded. *Entrance requirements:* For master's, bachelor's degree from accredited college or university; minimum GPA of 2.6 (for M Div), 3.0 (for MA); for doctorate, M Div or MA. Additional exam requirements/recommendations for international students: Required—TOEFL (minimum score 600 paper-based; 88 iBT). *Application deadline:* For fall admission, 7/1 for domestic students, 6/1 for international students; for spring admission, 12/1 priority date for domestic students. Applications are processed on a rolling basis. Application fee: $65. Electronic applications accepted. *Financial support:* Scholarships/grants and unspecified assistantships available. Support available to part-time students. Financial award applicants required to submit FAFSA. *Faculty research:* New Testament, Old Testament, spiritual formation, Christian education, theological studies, Christian

ministry, preaching and pastoral ministry, language and literature, bible exposition, Christian leadership. *Unit head:* Dr. Clint Arnold, Dean, 562-903-4816, Fax: 562-903-4748. *Application contact:* Graduate Admissions Office, 562-903-4752, E-mail: graduate.admissions@biola.edu.
Website: http://www.talbot.edu/

Boston University, Metropolitan College, Program in Gastronomy, Boston, MA 02215. Offers communications (MLA); history and culture (MLA). *Program availability:* Part-time, evening/weekend. *Faculty:* 3 full-time (2 women), 5 part-time/adjunct (3 women). *Students:* 5 full-time (all women), 68 part-time (58 women); includes 19 minority (6 Black or African American, non-Hispanic/Latino; 4 Asian, non-Hispanic/Latino; 7 Hispanic/Latino; 2 Two or more races, non-Hispanic/Latino), 8 international. Average age 29. 44 applicants, 93% accepted, 17 enrolled. In 2017, 27 master's awarded. *Entrance requirements:* Additional exam requirements/recommendations for international students: Required—TOEFL. *Application deadline:* Applications are processed on a rolling basis. Application fee: $85. Electronic applications accepted. *Expenses:* Contact institution. *Financial support:* In 2017–18, 5 research assistantships (averaging $4,200 per year) were awarded; career-related internships or fieldwork, scholarships/grants, and unspecified assistantships also available. Support available to part-time students. Financial award applicants required to submit FAFSA. *Faculty research:* Food studies. *Unit head:* Dr. Megan Elias, Associate Professor of the Practice and Director, 617-353-6916, Fax: 617-353-4130, E-mail: gastrmla@bu.edu. *Application contact:* Barbara Rotger, Program Manager, 617-353-6916, Fax: 617-353-4130, E-mail: brotger@bu.edu.
Website: http://www.bu.edu/met/gastronomy

Brock University, Faculty of Graduate Studies, Faculty of Social Sciences, Program in Popular Culture, St. Catharines, ON L2S 3A1, Canada. Offers MA. *Program availability:* Part-time. *Degree requirements:* For master's, thesis optional. *Entrance requirements:* For master's, honors BA. Additional exam requirements/recommendations for international students: Required—TOEFL (minimum score 550 paper-based; 80 iBT), IELTS (minimum score 6.5), TWE (minimum score 4). Electronic applications accepted. *Faculty research:* Film and television studies, popular music, historical aspects of popular culture, popular literature.

Carnegie Mellon University, Dietrich College of Humanities and Social Sciences, Department of History, Pittsburgh, PA 15213-3891. Offers African and African-American diaspora (PhD); culture and power (PhD); labor, politics and social movements (PhD); technology, environment, science and health (PhD); women, gender and the family (PhD). *Program availability:* Part-time. *Degree requirements:* For doctorate, oral and written comprehensive exams, dissertation defense. *Entrance requirements:* For doctorate, GRE General Test. Additional exam requirements/recommendations for international students: Required—TOEFL. Electronic applications accepted. *Faculty research:* Anthropology and history, African-American history, technology/environment, cultural history analysis.

Central Michigan University, College of Graduate Studies, College of Humanities and Social and Behavioral Sciences, Program in Humanities, Mount Pleasant, MI 48859. Offers humanities (MA), including contemporary issues in the humanities: race, class, and gender, images and ideas of self, Native American issues in modern culture, popular culture studies, the rise of industrial society. *Program availability:* Part-time, evening/weekend. *Degree requirements:* For master's, thesis or alternative. Electronic applications accepted. *Faculty research:* Rise of industrial society; images and ideas of self; contemporary issues of race, class, and gender; popular culture; Native American issues in modern culture.

Chapman University, Donna Ford Attallah College of Educational Studies, Orange, CA 92866. Offers counseling (MA), including school counseling (MA, Credential); curriculum and instruction (MA), including elementary education, secondary education; education (PhD), including cultural and curricular studies, disability studies, leadership studies, school psychology (PhD, Credential); educational psychology (MA); leadership development (MA); multiple subjects (Credential), including Spanish/English bilingual; pupil personnel services (Credential), including school counseling (MA, Credential), school psychology (PhD, Credential); school psychology (Ed S); single subject (Credential); special education (MA, Credential), including mild/moderate (Credential), moderate/severe (Credential); teaching (MA), including elementary education, secondary education, secondary music education. *Accreditation:* TEAC. *Program availability:* Part-time, evening/weekend. *Faculty:* 32 full-time (18 women), 37 part-time/adjunct (26 women). *Students:* 170 full-time (140 women), 180 part-time (129 women); includes 164 minority (6 Black or African American, non-Hispanic/Latino; 38 Asian, non-Hispanic/Latino; 101 Hispanic/Latino; 1 Native Hawaiian or other Pacific Islander, non-Hispanic/Latino; 18 Two or more races, non-Hispanic/Latino), 10 international. Average age 28. 143 applicants, 63% accepted, 64 enrolled. In 2017, 126 master's, 18 doctorates awarded. *Application deadline:* Applications are processed on a rolling basis. Application fee: $60. Electronic applications accepted. *Expenses:* Contact institution. *Financial support:* Fellowships and scholarships/grants available. Financial award application deadline: 3/2; financial award applicants required to submit FAFSA. *Unit head:* Dr. Margaret Grogan, Dean, 714-516-5968, E-mail: grogan@chapman.edu. *Application contact:* Shannon McCance, Graduate Admission Counselor, 714-516-5236, E-mail: smccance@chapman.edu.
Website: http://www.chapman.edu/CES/

Charlotte Christian College and Theological Seminary, Graduate Program, Charlotte, NC 28206. Offers Biblical studies (MA), including New Testament, Old Testament, theology; chaplaincy (M Div); general pastoral studies (M Div); ministry (D Min); pastoral counseling (M Div); urban Christian ministry (MA), including multicultural studies, youth ministry. *Program availability:* Part-time, evening/weekend. *Faculty:* 5 full-time (0 women), 6 part-time/adjunct (0 women). *Students:* 17 full-time (8 women), 21 part-time (11 women); includes 31 minority (29 Black or African American, non-Hispanic/Latino; 1 Asian, non-Hispanic/Latino; 1 Two or more races, non-Hispanic/Latino), 2 international. Average age 48. 13 applicants, 100% accepted, 9 enrolled. In 2017, 2 master's awarded. *Degree requirements:* For master's, variable foreign language requirement, thesis; for doctorate, thesis/dissertation. *Entrance requirements:* For master's, 1000-2000 word essay. Additional exam requirements/recommendations for international students: Required—TOEFL, IELTS. *Application deadline:* For fall admission, 8/3 for domestic and international students; for spring admission, 12/8 for domestic and international students; for summer admission, 4/7 for domestic and international students. Application fee: $50. Electronic applications accepted. *Expenses:* Contact institution. *Financial support:* In 2017–18, 2 students received support. Teaching assistantships, Federal Work-Study, and scholarships/grants available. Financial award application deadline: 4/1; financial award applicants required to submit FAFSA. *Faculty research:* Pastoral topics, urban ministry topics, Biblical topics. *Unit head:* Dr. Eddie G. Grigg, President, 704-344-6882 Ext. 101, Fax: 704-334-6885, E-mail: egrigg@charlottechristian.edu. *Application contact:* George Shears, Director of Admissions, 704-334-6882 Ext. 115, Fax: 704-334-6885, E-mail: gshears@charlottechristian.edu.
Website: http://www.charlottechristian.edu

Claremont Graduate University, Graduate Programs, School of Arts and Humanities, Department of Cultural Studies, Claremont, CA 91711-6160. Offers Africana studies (Certificate); cultural studies (MA, PhD); media studies (MA, PhD); museum studies (MA). *Program availability:* Part-time. *Entrance requirements:* For master's and doctorate, GRE General Test. Additional exam requirements/recommendations for international students: Required—TOEFL (minimum score 75 iBT). Electronic applications accepted.

Columbia International University, Seminary and School of Ministry, Columbia, SC 29203. Offers academic ministries (M Div); Bible and theology (Certificate); bible exposition (M Div, MABE); Biblical ministry (Certificate); chaplaincy (M Div); intercultural studies (MAIS); leadership (D Min); member care (D Min); missions (D Min); preaching (D Min); theological studies (MA). *Program availability:* Part-time, evening/weekend. *Degree requirements:* For doctorate, comprehensive exam, thesis/dissertation. *Entrance requirements:* For doctorate, 3 years of ministerial experience, M Div. Additional exam requirements/recommendations for international students: Required—TOEFL. Electronic applications accepted.

Concordia University Irvine, School of Theology, Irvine, CA 92612-3299. Offers Christian leadership (MA); research in theology (MA); theology and culture (MA). *Program availability:* Part-time, evening/weekend. *Degree requirements:* For master's, project/thesis or vicarage. *Entrance requirements:* For master's, official college transcript(s), statement of intent, 2 references, interview. Additional exam requirements/recommendations for international students: Required—TOEFL. Electronic applications accepted. *Expenses:* Contact institution.

Cornell University, Graduate School, Graduate Fields of Arts and Sciences, Field of English Language and Literature, Ithaca, NY 14853. Offers African-American literature (PhD); American literature after 1865 (PhD); American literature to 1865 (PhD); American studies (PhD); colonial and postcolonial literatures (PhD); creative writing (MFA); cultural studies (PhD); dramatic literature (PhD); English poetry (PhD); English Renaissance to 1660 (PhD); lesbian, bisexual, and gay literary studies (PhD); literary criticism and theory (PhD); Old and Middle English (PhD); prose fiction (PhD); Restoration and the eighteenth-century (PhD); the nineteenth century (PhD); the twentieth century (PhD); women's literature (PhD); MFA/PhD. Terminal master's awarded for partial completion of doctoral program. *Degree requirements:* For master's, one foreign language, thesis; for doctorate, one foreign language, comprehensive exam, thesis/dissertation, teaching experience. *Entrance requirements:* For master's, GRE General Test, 3 letters of recommendation, creative writing sample; for doctorate, GRE General Test, GRE Subject Test (English), 3 letters of recommendation, writing sample. Additional exam requirements/recommendations for international students: Required—TOEFL (minimum score 600 paper-based; 77 iBT). Electronic applications accepted. *Faculty research:* English and American literature, women's writing, ethnic and post-colonial literature, critical theory, medievalism.

Drew University, Caspersen School of Graduate Studies, Madison, NJ 07940-1493. Offers conflict resolution and leadership (Certificate), including community leadership, moderation, peace building; education (M Ed); finance (MA); history and culture (MA, PhD), including American history, book history, British history, European history, Holocaust and genocide (M Litt, MA, D Litt, PhD), intellectual history, Irish history, print culture, public history; K-12 education (MAT), including art, biology, chemistry, elementary education, English, French, Italian, math, secondary education, special education, teacher of students with disabilities; liberal studies (M Litt, D Litt), including history, Holocaust and genocide (M Litt, MA, D Litt, PhD), Irish/Irish-American studies, literature (M Litt, MMH, D Litt, DMH, CMH), religion, spirituality, teaching in the two-year college, writing; medical humanities (MMH, DMH, CMH), including arts, health, healthcare, literature (M Litt, MMH, D Litt, DMH, CMH), scientific research; poetry (MFA). *Program availability:* Part-time, evening/weekend. *Faculty:* 4 full-time (2 women), 29 part-time/adjunct (15 women). *Students:* 77 full-time (42 women), 175 part-time (114 women); includes 39 minority (12 Black or African American, non-Hispanic/Latino; 6 Asian, non-Hispanic/Latino; 16 Hispanic/Latino; 5 Two or more races, non-Hispanic/Latino), 11 international. Average age 41. 126 applicants, 75% accepted, 52 enrolled. In 2017, 38 master's, 23 doctorates, 35 other advanced degrees awarded. Terminal master's awarded for partial completion of doctoral program. *Degree requirements:* For master's and other advanced degree, thesis (for some programs); for doctorate, one foreign language, comprehensive exam (for some programs), thesis/dissertation. *Entrance requirements:* For master's, PRAXIS Core and Subject Area tests (for MAT), GRE/GMAT (for M Fin), resume, transcripts, writing sample, personal statement, letters of recommendation; for doctorate, GRE (PhD in history and culture), resume, transcripts, writing sample, personal statement, letters of recommendation; for other advanced degree, resume, transcripts, personal statement. Additional exam requirements/recommendations for international students: Required—TOEFL (minimum score 587 paper-based; 80 iBT), IELTS (minimum score 6), TWE (minimum score 4). *Application deadline:* For fall admission, 8/1 for domestic students, 6/1 for international students; for spring admission, 12/1 for domestic students, 10/1 for international students. Applications are processed on a rolling basis. Application fee: $35. Electronic applications accepted. *Financial support:* Fellowships, research assistantships, teaching assistantships, career-related internships or fieldwork, Federal Work-Study, scholarships/grants, and unspecified assistantships available. Support available to part-time students. Financial award applicants required to submit FAFSA. *Faculty research:* Irish history and culture, conflict resolution and leadership. *Application contact:* Leanne Horinko, Director of Caspersen Admissions, 973-408-3280, E-mail: gradm@drew.edu.
Website: http://www.drew.edu/caspersen

Eastern Michigan University, Graduate School, College of Arts and Sciences, Department of Sociology, Anthropology and Criminology, Program in Cultural Museum Studies, Ypsilanti, MI 48197. Offers Graduate Certificate. *Program availability:* Part-time, evening/weekend, online learning. *Students:* 2 part-time (both women). Average age 39. 4 applicants, 50% accepted, 1 enrolled. In 2017, 2 Graduate Certificates awarded. *Entrance requirements:* Additional exam requirements/recommendations for international students: Required—TOEFL. *Application deadline:* Applications are processed on a rolling basis. Application fee: $45. *Financial support:* Fellowships, research assistantships with full tuition reimbursements, teaching assistantships with full tuition reimbursements, career-related internships or fieldwork, Federal Work-Study, institutionally sponsored loans, scholarships/grants, tuition waivers (partial), and unspecified assistantships also available. Support available to part-time students. Financial award applicants required to submit FAFSA. *Application contact:* Dr. Liza Cerroni-Long, Advisor, 734-487-0012, Fax: 734-487-9666, E-mail: liza.cerroni-long@emich.edu.

Florida State University, The Graduate School, College of Fine Arts, Department of Art History, Tallahassee, FL 32306-1233. Offers art history (MA, PhD); museum and cultural heritage studies (MA). *Accreditation:* NASAD. *Program availability:* Part-time. *Faculty:* 11 full-time (4 women), 8 part-time/adjunct (6 women). *Students:* 52 full-time (47 women), 6 part-time (5 women); includes 10 minority (2 Black or African American, non-Hispanic/Latino; 2 Asian, non-Hispanic/Latino; 5 Hispanic/Latino; 1 Two or more races, non-Hispanic/Latino). Average age 31. 67 applicants, 73% accepted, 19 enrolled. In 2017, 12 master's, 3 doctorates awarded. Terminal master's awarded for partial completion of doctoral program. *Degree requirements:* For master's, one foreign language, thesis (for some programs), capstone project (for some programs); for doctorate, 2 foreign languages, comprehensive exam, thesis/dissertation. *Entrance requirements:* For master's, GRE General Test, minimum GPA of 3.0; for doctorate, GRE General Test, minimum GPA of 3.5. Additional exam requirements/

recommendations for international students: Required—TOEFL (minimum score 550 paper-based; 80 iBT), IELTS (minimum score 6.5). *Application deadline:* For fall admission, 6/1 for domestic and international students. Applications are processed on a rolling basis. Application fee: $35. Electronic applications accepted. *Expenses:* Contact institution. *Financial support:* In 2017–18, 36 students received support, including 15 fellowships with full tuition reimbursements available (averaging $5,801 per year), 14 research assistantships with full tuition reimbursements available (averaging $5,038 per year), 9 teaching assistantships with full tuition reimbursements available (averaging $7,140 per year); career-related internships or fieldwork, Federal Work-Study, institutionally sponsored loans, scholarships/grants, tuition waivers (full), and unspecified assistantships also available. Financial award application deadline: 1/1; financial award applicants required to submit FAFSA. *Faculty research:* Modern art and critical theory, contemporary art, medieval, Renaissance and Baroque, pre-Columbian and Spanish Colonial, visual arts of the Americas. *Unit head:* Dr. Adam Jolles, Associate Professor of Art History/Department Chair, 850-644-7066, E-mail: ajolles@fsu.edu. *Application contact:* Juan Barcelo-Gonzalez, Academic Program Specialist/Graduate Student Advisor, 850-644-8207, Fax: 850-644-7065, E-mail: juan.barcelo@fsu.edu.
Website: http://arthistory.fsu.edu/

Gardner-Webb University, School of Divinity, Boiling Springs, NC 28017. Offers biblical studies (M Div); Christian education and formation (M Div); intercultural studies (M Div); ministry (D Min); missiology (M Div); pastoral care and counseling (M Div); pastoral care and counseling/member care for missionaries (D Min); pastoral studies (M Div); M Div/MA; M Div/MBA. *Accreditation:* ACIPE. *Program availability:* Part-time. *Faculty:* 10 full-time (1 woman), 4 part-time/adjunct (2 women). *Students:* 102 full-time (47 women), 56 part-time (15 women); includes 67 minority (63 Black or African American, non-Hispanic/Latino; 3 Asian, non-Hispanic/Latino; 1 Hispanic/Latino). Average age 38. *Entrance requirements:* For master's, minimum GPA of 2.6; for doctorate, minimum GPA of 2.75. Additional exam requirements/recommendations for international students: Required—TOEFL (minimum score 500 paper-based; 61 iBT). *Application deadline:* Applications are processed on a rolling basis. Electronic applications accepted. *Expenses:* Contact institution. *Financial support:* Fellowships, institutionally sponsored loans, and unspecified assistantships available. Support available to part-time students. Financial award application deadline: 5/15. *Faculty research:* Jewish-Christian dialogue, Islam. *Unit head:* Dr. Robert W. Canoy, Sr., Dean, 704-406-4400, Fax: 704-406-3935, E-mail: rcanoy@gardner-webb.edu. *Application contact:* Kheresa Harmon, Director of Admissions, 704-406-3205, Fax: 704-406-3895, E-mail: kharmon@gardner-webb.edu.
Website: http://gardner-webb.edu/academic-programs-and-resources/colleges-and-schools/divinity/index

George Fox University, Portland Seminary, Portland, OR 97223. Offers Biblical studies (M Div, MA); chaplaincy (M Div); Christian history and theology (M Div, MA); creation care (M Div, MA); intercultural studies (M Div, MA); leadership (M Div, MA); leadership and global perspectives (D Min); leadership and spiritual formation (D Min); semiotics and future studies (D Min); spiritual direction (MA, Certificate); spiritual direction supervision (M Div, MA, Certificate); spiritual formation and discipleship (M Div, MA, Certificate). *Accreditation:* ACIPE. *Program availability:* Part-time, evening/weekend, online learning. *Entrance requirements:* For master's, resume, three references (one pastoral, one academic or professional, one personal), one official transcript from each college or university attended; for doctorate, resume, 3 references (1 professional, 1 academic, 1 personal), one official transcript from each college or university attended. Additional exam requirements/recommendations for international students: Required—TOEFL (minimum score 577 paper-based; 90 iBT). Electronic applications accepted. *Expenses:* Contact institution.

George Mason University, College of Humanities and Social Sciences, Program in Cultural Studies, Fairfax, VA 22030. Offers PhD. *Faculty:* 11 full-time (5 women). *Students:* 32 full-time (20 women), 19 part-time (13 women); includes 13 minority (4 Black or African American, non-Hispanic/Latino; 1 American Indian or Alaska Native, non-Hispanic/Latino; 3 Asian, non-Hispanic/Latino; 2 Hispanic/Latino; 3 Two or more races, non-Hispanic/Latino), 3 international. Average age 34. 25 applicants, 48% accepted, 4 enrolled. In 2017, 3 doctorates awarded. *Degree requirements:* For doctorate, one foreign language, comprehensive exam, thesis/dissertation, foreign language exams. *Entrance requirements:* For doctorate, GRE, expanded goals statement; 3 letters of recommendation from academic sources; writing sample; master's degree in relevant field; official transcripts. Additional exam requirements/recommendations for international students: Required—TOEFL (minimum score 575 paper-based; 88 iBT), IELTS (minimum score 6.5), PTE (minimum score 59). *Application deadline:* For fall admission, 1/15 for domestic and international students. Application fee: $75 ($80 for international students). Electronic applications accepted. *Expenses:* Tuition, state resident: full-time $11,228; part-time $459.50 per credit. Tuition, nonresident: full-time $30,932; part-time $1280.50 per credit. *Required fees:* $3252; $135.50 per credit. Part-time tuition and fees vary according to course load and program. *Financial support:* In 2017–18, 25 students received support, including 1 fellowship, 2 research assistantships with tuition reimbursements available, 23 teaching assistantships with tuition reimbursements available (averaging $11,790 per year); career-related internships or fieldwork, Federal Work-Study, scholarships/grants, unspecified assistantships, and health care benefits (for full-time research or teaching assistantship recipients) also available. Support available to part-time students. Financial award application deadline: 3/15; financial award applicants required to submit FAFSA. *Faculty research:* Early modern cultural studies, Shakespeare and film, feminism, Michel Foucault, science and technology studies. *Unit head:* Denise Albanese, Director, 703-993-2869, Fax: 703-993-2852, E-mail: dalbanes@gmu.edu.
Website: http://culturalstudies.gmu.edu

Georgia State University, College of Arts and Sciences, Department of World Languages and Cultures, Atlanta, GA 30302-3083. Offers French (MA), including applied linguistics and pedagogy, French studies, literature and culture; Latin American studies (Certificate); Spanish (MA); translation and interpretation (Certificate), including interpretation, translation. *Program availability:* Part-time. *Faculty:* 36 full-time (20 women). *Students:* 25 full-time (19 women), 9 part-time (5 women); includes 19 minority (8 Black or African American, non-Hispanic/Latino; 10 Hispanic/Latino; 1 Two or more races, non-Hispanic/Latino), 4 international. Average age 39. 36 applicants, 86% accepted, 22 enrolled. In 2017, 10 master's, 2 other advanced degrees awarded. *Entrance requirements:* For master's, GRE, statement of purpose, writing sample in the target language, 2 letters of recommendation, official transcripts; for Certificate, entrance examination involving translating one passage from English to the target language and one passage from the target language to English, 3 letters of recommendation, resume/curriculum vitae, official transcripts. Additional exam requirements/recommendations for international students: Required—TOEFL (minimum score 79 iBT). *Application deadline:* For fall admission, 3/15 priority date for domestic and international students; for spring admission, 11/15 priority date for domestic and international students. Application fee: $50. Electronic applications accepted. *Expenses:* Tuition, state resident: full-time $7020. Tuition, nonresident: full-time $22,518. *Required fees:* $2128. Tuition and fees vary according to degree level and program. *Financial support:* Applicants required to submit FAFSA. *Faculty research:* French literature and culture, Francophone literature and culture, Latin American literature and culture, Spanish literature and culture, Hispanic linguistics. *Unit head:* Dr. Fernando Reati, Department Chair, 404-413-5984, Fax: 404-413-5982, E-mail: freati@gsu.edu. *Application contact:* Amber Amari, Director, Graduate and Scheduling Services, 404-413-5037, E-mail: aamari@gsu.edu.
Website: http://wlc.gsu.edu/

Goucher College, MA and MFA Programs, Baltimore, MD 21204-2794. Offers art and technology (MFA); arts administration (MA); cultural sustainability (MA); digital arts (MA); historic preservation (MA); nonfiction (MFA). *Program availability:* Part-time, evening/weekend, blended/hybrid learning. *Degree requirements:* For master's, thesis, e-portfolio. *Entrance requirements:* For master's, digital portfolio (for MA, MFA in digital arts); writing sample (for MFA in creative nonfiction). Additional exam requirements/recommendations for international students: Required—TOEFL (minimum score 550 paper-based; 80 iBT). *Application deadline:* Applications are processed on a rolling basis. Application fee: $75. Electronic applications accepted. *Expenses:* Contact institution. *Financial support:* Scholarships/grants and unspecified assistantships available. Financial award application deadline: 4/15; financial award applicants required to submit FAFSA. *Unit head:* Leslie Rubinkowski, Acting Assistant Provost for Limited Residency Graduate Programs, 410-337-6200, E-mail: leslie.rubinkowski@goucher.edu. *Application contact:* Carlton E. Surbeck, III, Director of Admissions, 410-337-6100, Fax: 410-337-6200, E-mail: admissions@goucher.edu.
Website: http://www.goucher.edu/grad

Grace Theological Seminary, Graduate and Professional Programs, Winona Lake, IN 46590-9907. Offers biblical studies (Certificate); chaplaincy (M Div); exegetical studies (M Div); intercultural studies (M Div, MA, D Min); local church ministry (MA), including camp administration, women's leadership; pastoral counseling (M Div); pastoral studies (M Div, D Min); theology (Diploma). *Accreditation:* ATS. *Program availability:* Part-time, online learning. *Degree requirements:* For master's, thesis optional; for doctorate, 2 foreign languages, thesis/dissertation. *Entrance requirements:* For master's, MAT, minimum GPA of 2.5. Electronic applications accepted. *Faculty research:* Biblical theology, language, and church ministries.

Graduate Theological Union, Graduate Programs, Berkeley, CA 94709-1212. Offers art and religion (MA, PhD, Th D); biblical languages (MA); biblical studies (MA); Biblical studies (PhD, Th D); Buddhist studies (MA); Christian spirituality (MA, PhD, Th D); cultural and historical studies of religions (MA, PhD, Th D); ethics and social theory (PhD, Th D); history (MA, PhD, Th D); homiletics (MA, PhD, Th D); interdisciplinary studies (PhD, Th D); Jewish studies (MA, PhD, Th D, Certificate); liturgical studies (MA, PhD, Th D); Near Eastern religions (PhD, Th D); Orthodox Christian studies (MA); religion and psychology (MA, PhD, Th D); religion and society/ethics and social theory (MA); systematic and philosophical theology (MA, PhD, Th D). PhD programs in Jewish studies and Near Eastern religions offered jointly with University of California, Berkeley. *Accreditation:* ATS. Terminal master's awarded for partial completion of doctoral program. *Degree requirements:* For master's, one foreign language, thesis; for doctorate, one foreign language, comprehensive exam, thesis/dissertation. *Entrance requirements:* For master's, GRE General Test; for doctorate, GRE General Test, MA or M Div. Additional exam requirements/recommendations for international students: Required—TOEFL. Electronic applications accepted.

Johnson University, Graduate and Professional Programs, Knoxville, TN 37998-1001. Offers biblical interpretation (Graduate Certificate); business administration (MBA); Christian ministries (Graduate Certificate); clinical mental health counseling (MA); educational technology (MA); intercultural studies (MA); leadership (MBA); leadership studies (PhD); New Testament (MA); nonprofit management (MBA); school counseling (MA); spiritual formation and leadership (Graduate Certificate); strategic ministry (MA); teacher education (MA). *Program availability:* Part-time, evening/weekend, 100% online, blended/hybrid learning. *Degree requirements:* For master's, variable foreign language requirement, comprehensive exam, thesis (for some programs), internships; for doctorate, variable foreign language requirement, comprehensive exam, thesis/dissertation, internships. *Entrance requirements:* For master's, PRAXIS (for MA in teacher education); MAT (for counseling); GRE or GMAT (for MBA), interview, 3 references, transcripts, essay, minimum GPA of 2.5 or 3.0 (depending on program); for doctorate, GRE or MAT (taken not less than 5 years prior), interview, 3 references, transcripts, essay, minimum GPA of 3.0; for Graduate Certificate, interview, 3 references, transcripts, essay, minimum GPA of 3.0. Additional exam requirements/recommendations for international students: Required—TOEFL (minimum score 527 paper-based; 71 iBT). Electronic applications accepted. *Expenses:* Contact institution.

Lincoln Christian University, Graduate Programs, Lincoln, IL 62656-2167. Offers Bible and theology (MA); Biblical studies (MA); church history/historical theology (MA); counseling (MA); formative worship (MA); intercultural studies (MA); ministry (MA); organizational leadership (MA); philosophy and apologetics (MA); spiritual formation (MA); theology (MA). MA in spiritual formation offered in Normal, IL. *Program availability:* Online learning. *Faculty:* 21 full-time (3 women), 29 part-time/adjunct (7 women). *Students:* 97 full-time (42 women), 226 part-time (81 women). Average age 39. *Entrance requirements:* For master's, minimum cumulative GPA of 2.5 in undergraduate degree studies. Additional exam requirements/recommendations for international students: Required—TOEFL (minimum score 550 paper-based); Recommended—IELTS (minimum score 6). *Application deadline:* For fall admission, 8/1 for domestic students, 3/1 for international students; for spring admission, 11/15 for domestic students, 11/1 for international students. Application fee: $25 ($50 for international students). Application fee is waived when completed online. *Expenses: Tuition:* Full-time $7920; part-time $5280 per credit hour. *Required fees:* $150; $150 per course. *Financial support:* Applicants required to submit FAFSA. *Application contact:* Lindsey Clark, Associate Director of Graduate Enrollment, 217-732-3168 Ext. 2398, E-mail: lclark@lincolnchristian.edu.
Website: https://lincolnchristian.edu/academics/programs/masters/

Maranatha Baptist University, Master of Arts in Intercultural Studies Program, Watertown, WI 53094. Offers MA. *Program availability:* Part-time. *Entrance requirements:* For master's, BA or BS. Additional exam requirements/recommendations for international students: Required—TOEFL.

McMaster University, School of Graduate Studies, Faculty of Humanities, Department of English and Cultural Studies, Hamilton, ON L8S 4M2, Canada. Offers cultural studies and critical theory (MA); English (MA, PhD). *Program availability:* Part-time. *Degree requirements:* For master's, one foreign language, thesis; for doctorate, one foreign language, comprehensive exam, thesis/dissertation. *Entrance requirements:* For master's, honors degree, minimum B+ average in at least 6 full courses of English beyond year 1; for doctorate, MA; minimum A- average in two of three courses. Additional exam requirements/recommendations for international students: Required—TOEFL (minimum score 580 paper-based). *Faculty research:* Literary theory, feminist theory, literature of migration, Bakhting globalization.

Michigan Technological University, Graduate School, College of Sciences and Arts, Department of Humanities, Houghton, MI 49931. Offers rhetoric, theory and culture (MS, PhD). *Program availability:* Part-time. *Faculty:* 33 full-time (18 women), 2 part-time/adjunct. *Students:* 32 full-time (22 women), 14 part-time (8 women); includes 2 minority (both Two or more races, non-Hispanic/Latino), 21 international. Average age 34. 97

applicants, 20% accepted, 12 enrolled. In 2017, 3 master's, 3 doctorates awarded. Terminal master's awarded for partial completion of doctoral program. *Degree requirements:* For master's, thesis (for some programs); for doctorate, one foreign language, comprehensive exam, thesis/dissertation. *Entrance requirements:* For master's, GRE, statement of purpose, personal statement, official transcripts, 3 letters of recommendation, resume/curriculum vitae, writing sample (10-15 pages); for doctorate, GRE, statement of purpose, personal statement, official transcripts, 3 letters of recommendation, resume/curriculum vitae, writing sample (10-15 pages), master's degree. Additional exam requirements/recommendations for international students: Required—TOEFL (recommended minimum score 100 iBT) or IELTS (recommended minimum score of 7.0). *Application deadline:* For fall admission, 1/15 priority date for domestic and international students. Applications are processed on a rolling basis. Electronic applications accepted. *Expenses:* Tuition, state resident: full-time $17,100; part-time $950 per credit. Tuition, nonresident: full-time $17,100; part-time $950 per credit. *Required fees:* $248; $124 per term. Tuition and fees vary according to course load and program. *Financial support:* In 2017–18, 31 students received support, including fellowships (averaging $15,790 per year), 28 teaching assistantships with tuition reimbursements available (averaging $15,790 per year); career-related internships or fieldwork, Federal Work-Study, scholarships/grants, health care benefits, unspecified assistantships, and cooperative program also available. Financial award applicants required to submit FAFSA. *Faculty research:* Rhetoric and composition; communication and cultural studies; studies of science, technology, and society; technical communication and digital media. *Unit head:* Dr. Ronald L. Strickland, Chair, 906-487-2376, Fax: 906-487-3559, E-mail: rlstrick@mtu.edu. *Application contact:* Alex Renshaw, Administrative Aide, 906-487-2540, Fax: 906-487-3559, E-mail: ajrensha@mtu.edu.
Website: http://www.mtu.edu/humanities/

Nazarene Theological Seminary, Graduate and Professional Programs, Kansas City, MO 64131-1263. Offers Christian formation and discipleship (MA); intercultural studies (MA); pastoral theology (Graduate Certificate); theological studies (MA); theology (M Div, D Min). *Accreditation:* ACIPE; ATS. *Program availability:* Part-time. *Faculty:* 12 full-time (2 women), 16 part-time/adjunct (3 women). *Students:* 54 full-time (25 women), 156 part-time (55 women); includes 22 minority (7 Black or African American, non-Hispanic/Latino; 1 American Indian or Alaska Native, non-Hispanic/Latino; 1 Asian, non-Hispanic/Latino; 9 Hispanic/Latino; 4 Two or more races, non-Hispanic/Latino), 29 international. *Degree requirements:* For master's, comprehensive exam (for some programs), thesis (for some programs); for doctorate, thesis/dissertation. *Entrance requirements:* For master's and Graduate Certificate, three references; for doctorate, three references, interview. Additional exam requirements/recommendations for international students: Required—TOEFL (minimum score 550 paper-based; 80 iBT). *Application deadline:* For fall admission, 2/15 for domestic and international students; for spring admission, 11/1 for domestic and international students. Applications are processed on a rolling basis. Application fee: $50. Electronic applications accepted. *Expenses: Tuition:* Full-time $11,445; part-time $8175 per credit hour. *Required fees:* $200 per semester. *Financial support:* Teaching assistantships, institutionally sponsored loans, and scholarships/grants available. Support available to part-time students. Financial award application deadline: 3/1; financial award applicants required to submit FAFSA. *Unit head:* Dr. Josh Sweeden, Dean of the Faculty, 816-268-5402, Fax: 816-268-5500, E-mail: jsweeden@nts.edu. *Application contact:* Pamala J. Asher, Registrar/Director of Enrollment Services, 816-268-5442, Fax: 816-268-5500, E-mail: pjasher@nts.edu.

New Mexico State University, College of Education, Department of Curriculum and Instruction, Las Cruces, NM 88003. Offers bilingual education (MA); curriculum and instruction (MA, Ed D, PhD); early childhood education (MA); educational diagnostics (Ed S); language, literacy and culture (MA); learning design and technologies (MA); teaching (MAT), including dance, Spanish; teaching English to speakers of other languages (MA). *Accreditation:* NCATE. *Program availability:* Part-time, evening/weekend, 100% online. *Faculty:* 22 full-time (17 women), 7 part-time/adjunct (2 women). *Students:* 113 full-time (79 women), 194 part-time (138 women); includes 171 minority (15 Black or African American, non-Hispanic/Latino; 3 American Indian or Alaska Native, non-Hispanic/Latino; 4 Asian, non-Hispanic/Latino; 142 Hispanic/Latino; 7 Two or more races, non-Hispanic/Latino), 37 international. Average age 36. 106 applicants, 80% accepted, 56 enrolled. In 2017, 82 master's, 15 doctorates, 1 other advanced degree awarded. *Entrance requirements:* For master's, minimum cumulative GPA of 3.0; for doctorate, portfolio, minimum cumulative GPA of 3.0. Additional exam requirements/recommendations for international students: Required—TOEFL (minimum score 550 paper-based; 79 iBT), IELTS (minimum score 6.5). *Application deadline:* For fall admission, 12/15 priority date for domestic and international students; for spring admission, 11/1 for domestic students. Applications are processed on a rolling basis. Application fee: $40 ($50 for international students). Electronic applications accepted. *Expenses:* Tuition, state resident: full-time $4390. Tuition, nonresident: full-time $15,309. *Required fees:* $853. *Financial support:* In 2017–18, 97 students received support, including 2 fellowships (averaging $4,390 per year), 1 research assistantship (averaging $17,368 per year), 10 teaching assistantships (averaging $17,489 per year); career-related internships or fieldwork, Federal Work-Study, scholarships/grants, traineeships, health care benefits, and unspecified assistantships also available. Support available to part-time students. Financial award application deadline: 3/1. *Faculty research:* STEM education, bilingual and English as a second language education, critical pedagogy/multicultural education, learning design and technology, early childhood education. *Total annual research expenditures:* $13,518. *Unit head:* Dr. David Rutledge, Department Head, 575-646-5411, Fax: 575-646-5436, E-mail: rutledge@nmsu.edu. *Application contact:* Dr. David Rutledge, Associate Department Head for Graduate Programs, 575-646-5411, Fax: 575-646-5436, E-mail: rutledge@nmsu.edu.
Website: http://tpal.nmsu.edu/

New York University, Steinhardt School of Culture, Education, and Human Development, New York, NY 10003. Offers MA, MFA, MM, MPH, MS, DPS, DPT, Ed D, PhD, Advanced Certificate, Post Master's Certificate, Postbaccalaureate Certificate, Advanced Certificate/MPH, MA/Advanced Certificate, MA/MA, MA/MS, MLIS/MA. *Accreditation:* TEAC. *Program availability:* Part-time. *Students:* Average age 31. 6,757 applicants, 42% accepted, 1245 enrolled. In 2017, 1,316 master's, 109 doctorates, 36 other advanced degrees awarded. *Entrance requirements:* For doctorate, GRE General Test, interview. Additional exam requirements/recommendations for international students: Required—TOEFL (minimum score 100 iBT). *Application deadline:* Applications are processed on a rolling basis. Application fee: $75. Electronic applications accepted. *Expenses:* Contact institution. *Financial support:* Fellowships, research assistantships, teaching assistantships, career-related internships or fieldwork, Federal Work-Study, institutionally sponsored loans, scholarships/grants, traineeships, tuition waivers (partial), and unspecified assistantships available. Support available to part-time students. Financial award application deadline: 2/1; financial award applicants required to submit FAFSA. *Faculty research:* Equity, urban adolescents, arts in education, globalization, multivariate analysis, psychometrics. *Total annual research expenditures:* $30.4 million. *Unit head:* Dr. Dominic Brewer, Dean, 212-998-5000. *Application contact:* John Myers, Director of Enrollment Management, 212-998-5030,

Fax: 212-995-4328, E-mail: steinhardt.gradadmissions@nyu.edu.
Website: http://steinhardt.nyu.edu/

North Central College, School of Graduate and Professional Studies, Program in Liberal Studies, Naperville, IL 60566-7063. Offers culture and society (MALS). *Program availability:* Part-time, evening/weekend. *Degree requirements:* For master's, thesis optional, project. *Entrance requirements:* For master's, interview. Additional exam requirements/recommendations for international students: Required—TOEFL (minimum score 550 paper-based; 80 iBT), IELTS (minimum score 6.5). Electronic applications accepted. Application fee is waived when completed online. *Expenses:* Contact institution.

Northern Kentucky University, Office of Graduate Programs, College of Arts and Sciences, Program in English, Highland Heights, KY 41099. Offers composition and rhetoric (Certificate); creative writing (Certificate); cultural studies and discourses (Certificate); English (MA); professional writing (Certificate). *Program availability:* Part-time, evening/weekend. *Degree requirements:* For master's, comprehensive exam (for some programs), capstone (thesis, portfolio, project, or exams); 30 hours of credit; for Certificate, 18 hours of credit. *Entrance requirements:* For master's, bachelor's degree in English or related field from regionally-accredited institution with minimum GPA of 3.0 in major or cognate area coursework; official transcripts for all undergraduate and graduate work; two letters of reference; for Certificate, official transcripts for all undergraduate and graduate work; bachelor's degree from regionally-accredited institution; minimum undergraduate GPA of 2.5. Additional exam requirements/recommendations for international students: Required—TOEFL (minimum score 79 iBT); Recommended—IELTS (minimum score 6.5). Electronic applications accepted.

Northwest University, College of Ministry, Kirkland, WA 98033. Offers ministry (MIM); missional leadership (MA); theology and culture (MA). *Program availability:* Part-time, evening/weekend, online learning. *Degree requirements:* For master's, comprehensive exam (for some programs), thesis (for some programs). *Entrance requirements:* Additional exam requirements/recommendations for international students: Required—TOEFL (minimum score 550 paper-based; 75 iBT). Electronic applications accepted.

Old Dominion University, College of Arts and Letters, Graduate Program in International Studies, Norfolk, VA 23529. Offers conflict and cooperation (MA, PhD); interdependence and transnationalism (MA, PhD); international cultural studies (MA, PhD); international political economy and development (MA, PhD); modeling and simulation (MA, PhD); U.S. foreign policy and international relations (MA, PhD). *Program availability:* Part-time. *Faculty:* 15 full-time (4 women). *Students:* 32 full-time (13 women), 40 part-time (16 women); includes 11 minority (7 Black or African American, non-Hispanic/Latino; 2 Hispanic/Latino; 2 Two or more races, non-Hispanic/Latino), 16 international. Average age 37. 95 applicants, 58% accepted, 40 enrolled. In 2017, 2 master's, 7 doctorates awarded. Terminal master's awarded for partial completion of doctoral program. *Degree requirements:* For master's, one foreign language, comprehensive exam, thesis optional; for doctorate, one foreign language, comprehensive exam, thesis/dissertation. *Entrance requirements:* For master's, GRE General Test, sample of written work, 2 letters of recommendation; for doctorate, GRE General Test, sample of written work, 3 letters of recommendation. Additional exam requirements/recommendations for international students: Required—TOEFL (minimum score 570 paper-based). *Application deadline:* For fall admission, 1/15 for domestic and international students; for spring admission, 10/15 for domestic and international students. Application fee: $50. Electronic applications accepted. *Expenses:* Contact institution. *Financial support:* In 2017–18, 12 students received support, including 1 fellowship (averaging $15,000 per year), 5 research assistantships with tuition reimbursements available (averaging $15,000 per year), 4 teaching assistantships with tuition reimbursements available (averaging $15,000 per year); career-related internships or fieldwork, institutionally sponsored loans, and unspecified assistantships also available. Financial award application deadline: 1/15; financial award applicants required to submit FAFSA. *Faculty research:* U.S. foreign policy, international security, transatlantic and transpacific relations, transnational issues, international political economy and development. *Total annual research expenditures:* $330,391. *Unit head:* Dr. Regina Karp, Graduate Program Director, 757-683-5700, Fax: 757-683-5701, E-mail: rkarp@odu.edu. *Application contact:* Dr. Dale Miller, Associate Dean for Research and Graduate Studies, 757-683-3866, E-mail: demiller@odu.edu.
Website: http://www.odu.edu/gpis

Old Dominion University, College of Arts and Letters, Institute for the Humanities, Norfolk, VA 23529. Offers arts and entrepreneurship (Certificate); cultural and human geography (MA); cultural studies (MA); gender and sexuality studies (MA); health, communication and culture (Certificate); media and popular culture studies (MA); philosophy and religious studies (MA); social justice and entrepreneurship (Certificate); visual studies (MA); world cultures (MA). *Program availability:* Part-time, evening/weekend. *Faculty:* 1 full-time (0 women), 1 part-time/adjunct (0 women). *Students:* 20 full-time (16 women), 13 part-time (8 women); includes 15 minority (8 Black or African American, non-Hispanic/Latino; 2 Asian, non-Hispanic/Latino; 2 Hispanic/Latino; 3 Two or more races, non-Hispanic/Latino), 2 international. Average age 35. 27 applicants, 96% accepted, 22 enrolled. In 2017, 3 master's awarded. *Degree requirements:* For master's, thesis optional, project. *Entrance requirements:* For master's, GRE General Test, minimum GPA of 3.25. *Application deadline:* For fall admission, 6/15 for domestic students; for spring admission, 11/15 for domestic students; for summer admission, 4/15 for domestic students. Applications are processed on a rolling basis. Application fee: $50. Electronic applications accepted. *Expenses:* Tuition, state resident: full-time $8928; part-time $496 per credit. Tuition, nonresident: full-time $22,482; part-time $1249 per credit. *Required fees:* $66 per semester. *Financial support:* In 2017–18, 3 students received support, including 5 research assistantships (averaging $10,000 per year); career-related internships or fieldwork, scholarships/grants, and unspecified assistantships also available. Financial award application deadline: 3/15; financial award applicants required to submit FAFSA. *Faculty research:* Media studies, cultural studies, gender studies, American literature, philosophy, art history, cultural geography. *Unit head:* Dr. Avi D. Santo, Graduate Program Director, 757-683-3719, Fax: 757-683-6191, E-mail: humgpd@odu.edu. *Application contact:* Dr. David C. Earnest, Associate Dean, 757-683-6077, Fax: 757-683-5746, E-mail: dearnest@odu.edu.
Website: http://al.odu.edu/hum/

Pacific Northwest College of Art, Program in Critical Theory and Creative Research, Portland, OR 97209. Offers MA, MA/MFA.

Plymouth State University, College of Graduate Studies, Graduate Studies in Education, Program in Integrated Arts, Plymouth, NH 03264-1595. Offers M Ed. *Degree requirements:* For master's, practicum.

Regent University, Graduate School, School of Divinity, Virginia Beach, VA 23464-9800. Offers Christian spirituality and formation (MA); divinity (M Div), including Biblical studies (M Div, MTS, Th M, PhD), chaplain ministry, Christian theology (M Div, MTS, Th M, PhD), church and ministry (M Div, MA), history of Christianity (M Div, MTS, Th M, PhD), inter-cultural studies (M Div, MA), interdisciplinary studies (M Div, MA, MTS), marketplace ministry (M Div, MA), missional discipleship, practical healing ministry (M Div, MA), worship and media (M Div, MA); leadership and renewal (D Min), including Christian leadership and renewal, clinical pastoral education, community transformation,

military ministry, ministry leadership coaching; practical theology (MA), including church and ministry (M Div, MA), cosmogony, inter-cultural studies (M Div, MA), interdisciplinary studies (M Div, MA, MTS), marketplace ministry (M Div, MA), practical healing ministry (M Div, MA), worship and media (M Div, MA); renewal theology (PhD), including Biblical studies (M Div, MTS, Th M, PhD), Christian theology (M Div, MTS, Th M, PhD), history of Christianity (M Div, MTS, Th M, PhD), practical theology; theological studies (MTS), including Biblical studies (M Div, MTS, Th M, PhD), Christian theology (M Div, MTS, Th M, PhD), history of Christianity (M Div, MTS, Th M, PhD), interdisciplinary studies (M Div, MA, MTS); theology (Th M), including Biblical studies (M Div, MTS, Th M, PhD), Christian theology (M Div, MTS, Th M, PhD), history of Christianity (M Div, MTS, Th M, PhD). *Accreditation:* ACIPE; ATS. *Program availability:* Part-time, evening/weekend, 100% online, blended/hybrid learning. *Faculty:* 17 full-time (3 women), 66 part-time/adjunct (9 women). *Students:* 146 full-time (54 women), 917 part-time (404 women); includes 563 minority (470 Black or African American, non-Hispanic/Latino; 1 American Indian or Alaska Native, non-Hispanic/Latino; 17 Asian, non-Hispanic/Latino; 56 Hispanic/Latino; 1 Native Hawaiian or other Pacific Islander, non-Hispanic/Latino; 18 Two or more races, non-Hispanic/Latino), 27 international. Average age 44. 1,321 applicants, 39% accepted, 295 enrolled. In 2017, 146 master's, 25 doctorates awarded. *Degree requirements:* For master's, comprehensive exam, thesis or alternative, internship; for doctorate, thesis/dissertation or alternative. *Entrance requirements:* For master's, minimum undergraduate GPA of 2.75, writing sample, personal goal statement, college transcripts; for doctorate, GRE, minimum graduate GPA of 3.5 (PhD), 3.0 (D Min); clergy recommendations; writing sample; transcripts; resume; interview. Additional exam requirements/recommendations for international students: Required—TOEFL (minimum score 577 paper-based). *Application deadline:* For fall admission, 5/1 priority date for domestic students. Applications are processed on a rolling basis. Application fee: $50. Electronic applications accepted. *Expenses:* $495 per credit (master's); $595 per credit (D Min); $650 per credit (PhD); $300 per semester technology fee. *Financial support:* In 2017–18, 721 students received support. Career-related internships or fieldwork, scholarships/grants, and unspecified assistantships available. Support available to part-time students. *Faculty research:* Greek and Hebrew, theology, spiritual formation, global missions and world Christianity, women in ministry leadership. *Unit head:* Dr. Cornelius Bekker, Dean, 757-352-4401, Fax: 757-352-4597, E-mail: clbekker@regent.edu. *Application contact:* Heidi Cece, Assistant Vice President of Enrollment Management, 800-373-5504, Fax: 757-352-4381, E-mail: admissions@regent.edu.
Website: https://www.regent.edu/school-of-divinity/

St. Francis Xavier University, Graduate Studies, Department of Celtic Studies, Antigonish, NS B2G 2W5, Canada. Offers MA. *Degree requirements:* For master's, thesis. *Entrance requirements:* Additional exam requirements/recommendations for international students: Required—TOEFL (minimum score 580 paper-based). *Faculty research:* Scottish Gaelic in Nova Scotia.

San Francisco State University, Division of Graduate Studies, College of Health and Social Sciences, Department of Sexuality Studies, San Francisco, CA 94132-1722. Offers MA. *Unit head:* Dr. Andreana Clay, Chair, 415-338-1090, Fax: 415-338-2653, E-mail: andreana@sfsu.edu. *Application contact:* Dr. Alexis Martinez, Graduate Coordinator, 415-338-2269, Fax: 415-338-2653, E-mail: alexisnm@sfsu.edu.
Website: http://sxs.sfsu.edu/

School of Visual Arts, Graduate Programs, Critical Theory and the Arts Department, New York, NY 10010-3994. Offers MA. *Degree requirements:* For master's, thesis, 36 credits with minimum cumulative GPA of 3.0. *Entrance requirements:* For master's, writing statement of approximately 1,000 words explaining the development of interest in pursuing an MA; transcripts for previous colleges /universities attended; three letters of recommendation; current resume/curriculum vitae. Additional exam requirements/recommendations for international students: Required—TOEFL (minimum score 600 paper-based; 100 iBT). Electronic applications accepted. *Expenses:* Contact institution.

Simmons College, College of Arts and Sciences, Boston, MA 02115. Offers English (MA); gender/cultural studies (MA); history (MA); public health (MPH); public policy (MPP). *Program availability:* Part-time. *Faculty:* 19 full-time (13 women), 2 part-time/adjunct (both women). *Students:* 4 full-time (3 women), 39 part-time (34 women); includes 11 minority (7 Black or African American, non-Hispanic/Latino; 1 Hispanic/Latino; 3 Two or more races, non-Hispanic/Latino). Average age 26. 99 applicants, 57% accepted, 27 enrolled. In 2017, 23 master's awarded. Terminal master's awarded for partial completion of doctoral program. *Degree requirements:* For master's, thesis optional. *Entrance requirements:* For master's, GRE, bachelor's degree from accredited college or university; minimum B average (preferred). Additional exam requirements/recommendations for international students: Required—TOEFL (minimum score 600 paper-based; 100 iBT). *Application deadline:* For fall admission, 8/1 for domestic and international students; for spring admission, 12/15 for domestic and international students; for summer admission, 5/1 for domestic and international students. Applications are processed on a rolling basis. Application fee: $35. Electronic applications accepted. *Expenses:* $1,052 per credit, $55 activity fee per semester. *Financial support:* In 2017–18, 4 fellowships with partial tuition reimbursements, 22 teaching assistantships with partial tuition reimbursements were awarded; scholarships/grants and unspecified assistantships also available. Support available to part-time students. Financial award applicants required to submit FAFSA. *Faculty research:* Film and media studies, postcolonial literature, critical theory, arts and culture. *Unit head:* Dr. Leanne Doherty, Dean, 617-521-2581, E-mail: leanne.doherty@simmons.edu. *Application contact:* Patricia Flaherty, Director, Graduate Studies Admission, 617-521-3902, Fax: 617-521-3058, E-mail: gsa@simmons.edu.
Website: http://www.simmons.edu/gradstudies/

Simon Fraser University, Office of Graduate Studies and Postdoctoral Fellows, Faculty of Education, Program in Languages, Cultures, and Literacies, Burnaby, BC V5A 1S6, Canada. Offers PhD.

Southern Illinois University Carbondale, Graduate School, College of Liberal Arts, Department of Foreign Languages and Literatures, Carbondale, IL 62901-4701. Offers MA. *Program availability:* Part-time. *Degree requirements:* For master's, one foreign language, thesis. *Entrance requirements:* For master's, minimum GPA of 2.7. Additional exam requirements/recommendations for international students: Required—TOEFL. *Faculty research:* Bibliography, historical linguistics, language pedagogy, philology, commercial facets.

Stanford University, School of Humanities and Sciences, Department of Anthropology, Stanford, CA 94305-2004. Offers anthropology (MA); archaeology (PhD); culture and society (PhD); ecology and environment (PhD). Terminal master's awarded for partial completion of doctoral program. *Degree requirements:* For master's, thesis; for doctorate, one foreign language, thesis/dissertation. *Entrance requirements:* For master's and doctorate, GRE General Test. Additional exam requirements/recommendations for international students: Required—TOEFL. Electronic applications accepted. *Expenses:* Tuition: Full-time $48,987; part-time $10,620 per quarter. One-time fee: $400. Tuition and fees vary according to program.

Stony Brook University, State University of New York, Graduate School, College of Arts and Sciences, Department of Cultural Studies and Comparative Literature, Stony Brook, NY 11794. Offers comparative literature (MA, PhD); cultural studies (PhD, Certificate). *Program availability:* Evening/weekend. *Faculty:* 10 full-time (3 women). *Students:* 49 full-time (35 women), 4 part-time (all women); includes 9 minority (1 Black or African American, non-Hispanic/Latino; 4 Asian, non-Hispanic/Latino; 4 Hispanic/Latino), 17 international. Average age 34. 65 applicants, 29% accepted, 6 enrolled. In 2017, 6 master's, 5 doctorates, 5 other advanced degrees awarded. Terminal master's awarded for partial completion of doctoral program. *Degree requirements:* For master's, 2 foreign languages, exam; for doctorate, 3 foreign languages, comprehensive exam, thesis/dissertation. *Entrance requirements:* For master's and doctorate, GRE General Test, minimum GPA of 3.5 in major, 3.0 overall. Additional exam requirements/recommendations for international students: Required—TOEFL. *Application deadline:* For fall admission, 1/15 for domestic students; for spring admission, 10/1 for domestic students. Application fee: $100. Electronic applications accepted. *Expenses:* Contact institution. *Financial support:* In 2017–18, 17 teaching assistantships were awarded; fellowships and research assistantships also available. *Faculty research:* Humanities, women's studies, literary criticism, gender studies, philosophy. *Unit head:* 631-632-7464, Fax: 631-632-5707. *Application contact:* Mary Moran-Luba, Coordinator, 631-632-7460, Fax: 631-632-5707, E-mail: mary.moran-luba@stonybrook.edu.
Website: http://www.stonybrook.edu/commcms/cat/index.html

Taylor College and Seminary, Graduate and Professional Programs, Edmonton, AB T6J 4T3, Canada. Offers Christian studies (Diploma); intercultural studies (MA, Diploma), including intercultural studies (Diploma), TESOL; theology (M Div, MTS). *Accreditation:* ATS. *Program availability:* Part-time, online learning. *Degree requirements:* For master's, thesis optional. *Entrance requirements:* Additional exam requirements/recommendations for international students: Required—TOEFL (minimum score 550 paper-based; 80 iBT), IELTS (minimum score 6.5). *Faculty research:* Biblical studies, administration and organization, world religions, ethics, missiology.

Texas A&M University, College of Liberal Arts, Department of Performance Studies, College Station, TX 77843. Offers MA. *Faculty:* 11. *Students:* 6 full-time (2 women); includes 2 minority (both Hispanic/Latino), 2 international. Average age 27. 9 applicants, 78% accepted, 6 enrolled. *Degree requirements:* For master's, comprehensive exam (for some programs), thesis or alternative. *Entrance requirements:* For master's, GRE General Test. Additional exam requirements/recommendations for international students: Required—TOEFL (minimum score 550 paper-based; 80 iBT), IELTS (minimum score 6), PTE (minimum score 53). *Application deadline:* For fall admission, 12/1 for domestic students; for spring admission, 10/15 for domestic students. Applications are processed on a rolling basis. Application fee: $50 ($90 for international students). Electronic applications accepted. *Expenses:* Contact institution. *Financial support:* In 2017–18, 6 students received support, including 6 teaching assistantships (averaging $8,944 per year); unspecified assistantships also available. Financial award application deadline: 3/15; financial award applicants required to submit FAFSA. *Unit head:* Dr. Donnlee Dox, Department Head, 979-458-1870, E-mail: dox@tamu.edu. *Application contact:* Dr. Kirsten Pullen, Director of Graduate Studies, 979-845-2899, Fax: 979-845-5164, E-mail: kpullen@tamu.edu.
Website: http://performancestudies.tamu.edu/

Texas A&M University–Kingsville, College of Graduate Studies, College of Arts and Sciences, Department of Language and Literature, Program in Cultural Studies, Kingsville, TX 78363. Offers MA. *Entrance requirements:* Additional exam requirements/recommendations for international students: Required—TOEFL (minimum score 550 paper-based; 79 iBT); Recommended—IELTS. Electronic applications accepted.

Texas Tech University, Graduate School, College of Arts and Sciences, Department of Classical and Modern Languages and Literatures, Lubbock, TX 79409. Offers languages and cultures (MA); Romance languages (MA); Spanish (PhD); MBA/MA. *Program availability:* Part-time. *Faculty:* 58 full-time (39 women), 1 (woman) part-time/adjunct. *Students:* 79 full-time (42 women), 15 part-time (11 women); includes 22 minority (1 Black or African American, non-Hispanic/Latino; 18 Hispanic/Latino; 3 Two or more races, non-Hispanic/Latino), 47 international. Average age 32. 51 applicants, 76% accepted, 27 enrolled. In 2017, 26 master's, 3 doctorates awarded. *Degree requirements:* For master's, comprehensive exam, thesis or alternative; for doctorate, comprehensive exam, thesis/dissertation. *Entrance requirements:* Additional exam requirements/recommendations for international students: Required—TOEFL (minimum score 550 paper-based; 79 iBT). *Application deadline:* For fall admission, 6/1 priority date for domestic students, 1/15 priority date for international students; for spring admission, 9/1 priority date for domestic students, 6/15 priority date for international students. Applications are processed on a rolling basis. Application fee: $60. Electronic applications accepted. *Expenses:* Contact institution. *Financial support:* In 2017–18, 80 students received support, including 52 fellowships (averaging $3,518 per year), 74 teaching assistantships (averaging $12,664 per year); research assistantships, Federal Work-Study, scholarships/grants, and unspecified assistantships also available. Financial award application deadline: 4/15; financial award applicants required to submit FAFSA. *Faculty research:* Literature, comparative literature, linguistics, culture, applied linguistics. *Total annual research expenditures:* $150,379. *Unit head:* Dr. Erin Collopy, Department Chair and Associate Professor, 806-834-8497, Fax: 806-742-3306, E-mail: erin.collopy@ttu.edu. *Application contact:* Carla Burrus, Senior Advisor, 806-834-3282, Fax: 806-742-3306, E-mail: carla.burrus@ttu.edu.
Website: http://www.depts.ttu.edu/classic_modern/

Trent University, Graduate Studies, Program in Cultural Studies, Peterborough, ON K9J 7B8, Canada. Offers PhD.

Trinity College, Graduate Programs, Program in American Studies, Hartford, CT 06106-3100. Offers American culture studies (MA); museums and communities (MA). *Program availability:* Part-time, evening/weekend. *Degree requirements:* For master's, thesis or alternative. *Entrance requirements:* For master's, minimum GPA of 3.0.

Union Institute & University, Master of Arts Program, Cincinnati, OH 45206-1925. Offers creativity studies (MA); health and wellness (MA); history and culture (MA); leadership, public policy, and social issues (MA); literature and writing (MA). *Program availability:* Part-time, online only, 100% online. *Students:* 9 full-time (7 women), 70 part-time (56 women); includes 33 minority (22 Black or African American, non-Hispanic/Latino; 1 American Indian or Alaska Native, non-Hispanic/Latino; 6 Hispanic/Latino; 4 Two or more races, non-Hispanic/Latino). Average age 40. *Degree requirements:* For master's, thesis. *Entrance requirements:* For master's, transcript, essay, 3 letters of recommendation, resume. Additional exam requirements/recommendations for international students: Recommended—TOEFL. *Application deadline:* For spring admission, 3/13 for domestic students. Applications are processed on a rolling basis. Application fee: $50. Electronic applications accepted. *Expenses:* Contact institution. *Financial support:* Career-related internships or fieldwork and tuition waivers available. Financial award applicants required to submit FAFSA. *Unit head:* Elden Golden, Director, 513-487-1153, E-mail: elden.golden@myunion.edu. *Application contact:* Director of Admissions, 800-861-6400.

Union Institute & University, PhD Program in Interdisciplinary Studies, Cincinnati, OH 45206-1925. Offers educational studies (PhD), including Martin Luther King studies; ethical and creative leadership (PhD); humanities and culture (PhD); public policy and

social change (PhD). Program requires participation in brief on-campus residencies twice each year (January and July). *Program availability:* Part-time, online only, blended/hybrid learning. *Degree requirements:* For doctorate, comprehensive exam, thesis/dissertation. *Entrance requirements:* For doctorate, master's degree, three letters of recommendation, statement of purpose. Additional exam requirements/recommendations for international students: Required—TOEFL. *Application deadline:* Applications are processed on a rolling basis. Application fee: $50. Electronic applications accepted. *Expenses:* Contact institution. *Financial support:* Federal Work-Study and scholarships/grants available. Financial award application deadline: 5/1; financial award applicants required to submit FAFSA. *Faculty research:* Social responsibility, ethical leadership, Martin Luther King studies. *Unit head:* Dr. Michael Raffanti, Dean of Graduate College, 800-641-6400 Ext. 1237, E-mail: michael.raffanti@myunion.edu. *Application contact:* Admissions Counselor, 800-486-3116.
Website: https://myunion.edu/academics/doctoral/

Union University, Institute for International and Intercultural Studies, Jackson, TN 38305-3697. Offers MAIS. *Program availability:* Part-time, evening/weekend. *Degree requirements:* For master's, capstone course. *Entrance requirements:* For master's, GRE, minimum undergraduate GPA of 3.0, 3 letters of reference. Additional exam requirements/recommendations for international students: Required—TOEFL (minimum score 560 paper-based). Electronic applications accepted. *Faculty research:* International education, ethnographic field research, intercultural training for professionals and students, language and culture.

University of Alaska Fairbanks, College of Liberal Arts, Department of Cross-Cultural Studies, Fairbanks, AK 99775-6300. Offers MA. *Program availability:* Part-time. *Degree requirements:* For master's, comprehensive exam, project, oral defense of project. *Entrance requirements:* For master's, bachelor's degree from accredited institution with minimum cumulative undergraduate and major GPA of 3.0. Additional exam requirements/recommendations for international students: Required—TOEFL (minimum score 550 paper-based; 79 iBT), IELTS (minimum score 8.5). Electronic applications accepted. *Faculty research:* Alaska native literature, oral traditions, history, law and policy, cultures, art; Native American religion and philosophy.

University of Arkansas, Graduate School, Interdisciplinary Program in Comparative Literature and Cultural Studies, Fayetteville, AR 72701. Offers MA, PhD. *Degree requirements:* For doctorate, 2 foreign languages, comprehensive exam, thesis/dissertation optional. *Entrance requirements:* For doctorate, GRE General Test, official transcripts of all undergraduate and graduate work, three letters of recommendation, writing sample, statement of purpose. Additional exam requirements/recommendations for international students: Required—TOEFL (minimum score 550 paper-based; 80 iBT) or IELTS (minimum score 6.5). *Application deadline:* For fall admission, 8/1 for domestic students, 4/1 for international students; for spring admission, 12/1 for domestic students, 10/1 for international students; for summer admission, 4/15 for domestic students, 3/1 for international students. Application fee: $60. Electronic applications accepted. *Expenses:* Tuition, state resident: full-time $3782. Tuition, nonresident: full-time $10,238. *Financial support:* In 2017–18, 1 research assistantship, 13 teaching assistantships were awarded; fellowships, Federal Work-Study, and institutionally sponsored loans also available. *Faculty research:* Literary and cultural theory, cultural studies, postcolonial theory, gender studies, world literature. *Unit head:* Prof. Luis Fernando Restrepo, Director, 479-575-7580, Fax: 479-575-6795, E-mail: lrestr@uark.edu.
Website: http://www.uark.edu/ua/cplt/

University of California, Davis, Graduate Studies, Graduate Group in Cultural Studies, Davis, CA 95616. Offers MA, PhD. *Degree requirements:* For master's, thesis; for doctorate, thesis/dissertation. *Entrance requirements:* For doctorate, GRE. Additional exam requirements/recommendations for international students: Required—TOEFL (minimum score 550 paper-based). Electronic applications accepted.

University of California, Irvine, School of Humanities, Program in Culture and Theory, Irvine, CA 92697. Offers PhD. *Students:* 13 full-time (9 women); includes 7 minority (2 Black or African American, non-Hispanic/Latino; 3 Asian, non-Hispanic/Latino; 2 Hispanic/Latino). Average age 32. Application fee: $105 ($125 for international students). *Unit head:* Nasrin Rahimieh, Interim Director, 949-824-0406, E-mail: nasrin.rahimieh@uci.edu. *Application contact:* Arielle Hinojosa, Graduate Counselor, 949-824-6441, Fax: 949-824-7006, E-mail: hinojosa@uci.edu.
Website: http://www.humanities.uci.edu/cultureandtheory/

University of California, Riverside, Graduate Division, Department of Ethnic Studies, Riverside, CA 92521. Offers cultural politics and production (PhD). Terminal master's awarded for partial completion of doctoral program. *Degree requirements:* For doctorate, variable foreign language requirement, comprehensive exam, thesis/dissertation. *Entrance requirements:* For doctorate, GRE, writing sample, statement of purpose, personal history statement, 3 letters of recommendation. Additional exam requirements/recommendations for international students: Required—TOEFL (minimum score 550 paper-based; 80 iBT); Recommended—IELTS (minimum score 7). Electronic applications accepted. *Expenses:* Tuition, state resident: full-time $5746. Tuition, nonresident: full-time $10,780. Tuition and fees vary according to campus/location and program. *Faculty research:* The political economy of race, class, gender, sexuality, cultural production, the state, law, criminal justice and grass roots responses.

University of California, Santa Barbara, Graduate Division, College of Letters and Sciences, Division of Social Sciences, Department of Global Studies, Santa Barbara, CA 93106-7065. Offers global culture, ideology, and religion (MA, PhD); global government, human rights, and civil society (MA, PhD); political economy, sustainable development, and the environment (MA, PhD). *Degree requirements:* For master's, one foreign language, thesis, 2 years of a second language; for doctorate, one foreign language, thesis/dissertation, reading proficiency in at least one language other than English. *Entrance requirements:* For master's, GRE, 2 years of a second language with minimum B grade in the final term, statement of purpose, resume or curriculum vitae, 3 letters of recommendation, transcripts (from all post-secondary institutions attended), writing sample (15-20 pages); for doctorate, GRE, statement of purpose, personal achievements/contributions statement, resume or curriculum vitae, 3 letters of recommendation, transcripts from all post-secondary institutions attended, writing sample (15-20 pages). Additional exam requirements/recommendations for international students: Required—TOEFL (minimum score 600 paper-based; 94 iBT), IELTS (minimum score 7). Electronic applications accepted.

University of Dayton, Department of English, Dayton, OH 45469. Offers literary and cultural studies (MA); teaching English to speakers of other languages (TESOL) (MA); writing and rhetoric (MA). *Program availability:* Part-time. *Faculty:* 22 full-time (11 women). *Students:* 20 full-time (14 women), 1 (woman) part-time; includes 2 minority (both Black or African American, non-Hispanic/Latino), 7 international. Average age 26. 35 applicants, 34% accepted. In 2017, 9 master's awarded. *Degree requirements:* For master's, thesis optional. *Entrance requirements:* For master's, 24 undergraduate-level semester hours in literature and/or writing; minimum GPA of 3.0; transcripts; personal statement; 8-10 page writing sample; three professional letters of recommendation. Additional exam requirements/recommendations for international students: Required—TOEFL (minimum score 550 paper-based, 80 iBT) or IELTS. *Application deadline:* For fall admission, 6/15 priority date for domestic and international students; for spring admission, 12/15 priority date for domestic and international students. Applications are processed on a rolling basis. Application fee: $0 ($50 for international students). Electronic applications accepted. Tuition and fees vary according to degree level and program. *Financial support:* In 2017–18, 9 teaching assistantships with full tuition reimbursements (averaging $11,105 per year) were awarded; institutionally sponsored loans also available. Financial award application deadline: 3/1; financial award applicants required to submit FAFSA. *Faculty research:* Gender and Victorian periodicals; literature and human rights; Paul Lawrence Dunbar; the archetype of the Indian princess; Amish country. *Unit head:* Dr. Andrew Slade, Chair, 937-229-3434, Fax: 937-229-3563, E-mail: aslade1@udayton.edu. *Application contact:* Dr. Tereza Szeghi, Director of Graduate Studies, 937-229-3443, E-mail: tszeghi1@udayton.edu.
Website: https://www.udayton.edu/artssciences/academics/english/welcome/index.php

University of Denver, Division of Arts, Humanities and Social Sciences, Department of Media, Film and Journalism Studies, Denver, CO 80208. Offers international and intercultural communication (MA); media and public communication (MA), including media and globalization, strategic communication. *Program availability:* Part-time. *Faculty:* 16 full-time (10 women), 5 part-time/adjunct (4 women). *Students:* 3 full-time (all women), 21 part-time (17 women); includes 5 minority (1 Asian, non-Hispanic/Latino; 4 Hispanic/Latino), 2 international. Average age 26. 34 applicants, 85% accepted, 8 enrolled. In 2017, 12 master's awarded. *Degree requirements:* For master's, thesis (for some programs). *Entrance requirements:* For master's, GRE General Test, bachelor's degree, transcripts, personal statement, three letters of recommendation. Additional exam requirements/recommendations for international students: Required—TOEFL (minimum score 620 paper-based; 105 iBT). *Application deadline:* For fall admission, 2/15 priority date for domestic students, 1/1 priority date for international students. Applications are processed on a rolling basis. Application fee: $65. Electronic applications accepted. *Expenses:* $31,935 per year full-time. *Financial support:* In 2017–18, 18 students received support. Teaching assistantships with tuition reimbursements available, career-related internships or fieldwork, Federal Work-Study, institutionally sponsored loans, scholarships/grants, and unspecified assistantships available. Support available to part-time students. Financial award application deadline: 2/15; financial award applicants required to submit FAFSA. *Faculty research:* Branding; public relations; health communication; social media; international communication. *Unit head:* Dr. Lynn Schofield Clark, Professor and Chair, 303-871-3984, Fax: 303-871-4949, E-mail: lynn.clark@du.edu. *Application contact:* Information Contact, 303-871-2166, E-mail: mfjs@du.edu.
Website: http://www.du.edu/ahss/mfjs

University of Denver, University College, Denver, CO 80208. Offers arts and culture (MA, Certificate); communication management (MS, Certificate), including translation studies (Certificate), world history and culture (Certificate); environmental policy and management (MS); geographic information systems (MS); global affairs (MA, Certificate), including human capital in organizations (Certificate), philanthropic leadership (Certificate), project management (Certificate), strategic innovation and change (Certificate); healthcare leadership (MS); information communications and technology (MS); leadership and organizations (MS); professional creative writing (MA, Certificate), including emergency planning and response (Certificate), organizational security (Certificate); security management (MS, Certificate); strategic human resources (Certificate). *Program availability:* Part-time, evening/weekend, online learning. *Faculty:* 118 part-time/adjunct (62 women). *Students:* 56 full-time (32 women), 1,287 part-time (707 women); includes 330 minority (99 Black or African American, non-Hispanic/Latino; 7 American Indian or Alaska Native, non-Hispanic/Latino; 43 Asian, non-Hispanic/Latino; 141 Hispanic/Latino; 3 Native Hawaiian or other Pacific Islander, non-Hispanic/Latino; 37 Two or more races, non-Hispanic/Latino), 84 international. Average age 34. 783 applicants, 86% accepted, 420 enrolled. In 2017, 461 master's, 173 other advanced degrees awarded. *Degree requirements:* For master's, capstone project. *Entrance requirements:* For master's, transcripts, two letters of recommendation, personal statement, resume. Additional exam requirements/recommendations for international students: Required—TOEFL (minimum score 550 paper-based; 80 iBT). *Application deadline:* For fall admission, 6/21 priority date for domestic students, 5/1 priority date for international students; for winter admission, 9/14 priority date for domestic students, 9/19 priority date for international students; for spring admission, 1/11 priority date for domestic students, 12/12 priority date for international students; for summer admission, 3/29 priority date for domestic students, 3/6 priority date for international students. Applications are processed on a rolling basis. Application fee: $75. Electronic applications accepted. *Expenses:* $7,968 per year half-time. *Financial support:* In 2017–18, 29 students received support. Teaching assistantships available. Financial award applicants required to submit FAFSA. *Unit head:* Dr. Michael McGuire, Dean, 303-871-3518, Fax: 303-871-3303, E-mail: mmcguire@du.edu. *Application contact:* Information Contact, 303-871-2291, E-mail: ucoladm@du.edu.
Website: http://universitycollege.du.edu/

University of Hawaii at Hilo, Program in Hawaiian and Indigenous Language and Culture Revitalization, Hilo, HI 96720-4091. Offers PhD. *Entrance requirements:* Additional exam requirements/recommendations for international students: Required—TOEFL, IELTS. Electronic applications accepted.

University of Hawaii at Hilo, Program in Indigenous Language and Culture Education, Hilo, HI 96720-4091. Offers MA. *Entrance requirements:* Additional exam requirements/recommendations for international students: Required—TOEFL, IELTS. Electronic applications accepted.

University of Hawaii at Manoa, Office of Graduate Education, International Cultural Studies Graduate Certificate Program, Honolulu, HI 96822. Offers Graduate Certificate. *Program availability:* Part-time. *Entrance requirements:* For degree, GRE General Test. Additional exam requirements/recommendations for international students: Required—TOEFL (minimum score 540 paper-based; 76 iBT), IELTS (minimum score 5).

University of Houston, College of Liberal Arts and Social Sciences, Department of Modern and Classical Languages, Houston, TX 77204. Offers world cultures and literatures (MA). *Degree requirements:* For master's, one foreign language, thesis optional. *Entrance requirements:* For master's, GRE General Test, minimum GPA of 3.0 in last 60 hours of course work. Additional exam requirements/recommendations for international students: Required—TOEFL (minimum score 500 paper-based). Electronic applications accepted.

University of Houston–Clear Lake, School of Human Sciences and Humanities, Programs in Human Sciences, Houston, TX 77058-1002. Offers behavioral sciences (MA), including criminology, cross cultural studies, general psychology, sociology; clinical psychology (MA); criminology (MA); cross cultural studies (MA); family therapy (MA); fitness and human performance (MA); school psychology (MA). *Accreditation:* AAMFT/COAMFTE. *Program availability:* Part-time, evening/weekend, online learning. *Degree requirements:* For master's, thesis or alternative. *Entrance requirements:* For master's, GRE General Test. Additional exam requirements/recommendations for international students: Required—TOEFL (minimum score 550 paper-based). Electronic applications accepted. *Faculty research:* Smoking cessation, adolescent sexuality, white collar crime, serial murder, human factors/human computer interaction.

Cultural Studies

The University of Kansas, Graduate Studies, School of Education, Department of Educational Leadership and Policy Studies, Education Leadership and Policy Program, Lawrence, KS 66045-3101. Offers policy studies (PhD); social and cultural studies in education (MSE, PhD). *Program availability:* Part-time, evening/weekend. *Students:* 128 full-time (70 women), 45 part-time (24 women); includes 37 minority (14 Black or African American, non-Hispanic/Latino; 2 American Indian or Alaska Native, non-Hispanic/Latino; 4 Asian, non-Hispanic/Latino; 8 Hispanic/Latino; 9 Two or more races, non-Hispanic/Latino), 30 international. Average age 38. 66 applicants, 68% accepted, 36 enrolled. In 2017, 23 doctorates awarded. *Entrance requirements:* For master's, minimum GPA of 3.0, resume or curriculum vitae, statement of purpose, official academic transcripts, three letters of recommendation; for doctorate, GRE General Test, minimum graduate GPA of 3.5, resume or curriculum vitae, statement of purpose, official academic transcripts, three letters of recommendation, writing sample. *Application deadline:* For fall admission, 7/1 for domestic and international students; for spring admission, 11/1 for domestic and international students; for summer admission, 4/1 for domestic and international students. Application fee: $65 ($85 for international students). Electronic applications accepted. *Financial support:* Fellowships, research assistantships, teaching assistantships, scholarships/grants, and unspecified assistantships available. Financial award application deadline: 3/15. *Faculty research:* Historical and philosophical issues in education, education policy and leadership, higher education faculty, research on college students, education technology. *Unit head:* Dr. Susan B. Twombly, Chair, 785-864-9721, E-mail: stwombly@ku.edu. *Application contact:* Denise Brubaker, Admissions Coordinator, 785-864-7973, E-mail: brubaker@ku.edu.
Website: http://elps.soe.ku.edu/

University of Louisville, Graduate School, College of Arts and Sciences, Department of Comparative Humanities, Louisville, KY 40292-0001. Offers civic leadership (MA); culture, criticism, and contemporary thought (PhD); linguistics (MA); public arts and letters (PhD); traditional humanities (MA); MA/JD; MA/MBA. *Program availability:* Part-time. *Faculty:* 14 full-time (6 women), 8 part-time/adjunct (4 women). *Students:* 33 full-time (21 women), 22 part-time (9 women); includes 7 minority (1 Black or African American, non-Hispanic/Latino; 1 Hispanic/Latino; 5 Two or more races, non-Hispanic/Latino), 4 international. Average age 39. 14 applicants, 79% accepted, 9 enrolled. In 2017, 3 master's, 10 doctorates awarded. *Degree requirements:* For master's, one foreign language, thesis or alternative, directed study culminating project; for doctorate, 2 foreign languages, comprehensive exam, thesis/dissertation, internship. *Entrance requirements:* For master's, GRE General Test, two letters of recommendation, transcripts from all institutions attended; for doctorate, GRE General Test, three letters of recommendation, statement of intent, scholarly writing sample, transcripts from all institutions attended. Additional exam requirements/recommendations for international students: Recommended—TOEFL. *Application deadline:* For fall admission, 1/15 for domestic and international students. Application fee: $65. Electronic applications accepted. *Expenses:* Contact institution. *Financial support:* In 2017–18, 1 fellowship with full tuition reimbursement (averaging $18,000 per year), 10 teaching assistantships with full tuition reimbursements (averaging $18,000 per year) were awarded. Financial award application deadline: 1/15. *Faculty research:* Literary studies, medieval studies;, religious studies, linguistics, translation studies. *Total annual research expenditures:* $7,733. *Unit head:* Dr. Ann Hall, Chair, 502-852-6805, Fax: 502-852-0078, E-mail: ann.hall@louisville.edu. *Application contact:* Latonia Craig, Director of Graduate Recruitment and Diversity Retention, 502-852-5207, Fax: 502-852-6536, E-mail: gradadm@louisville.edu.
Website: http://louisville.edu/humanities/

The University of Manchester, School of Arts, Histories and Cultures, Manchester, United Kingdom. Offers anthropology, media and performance (PhD); applied theatre professional (PhD); archaeology (PhD); art history and visual studies (PhD); arts management and cultural policy (PhD); classics and ancient history (PhD); composition (PhD); creative writing (PhD); drama (PhD); economic and social history (PhD); electroacoustic composition (PhD); English and American studies (PhD); history (PhD); humanitarianism and conflict response (PhD); museology (PhD); music (PhD); musicology (PhD); religions and theology (PhD).

The University of Manchester, School of Languages, Linguistics and Cultures, Manchester, United Kingdom. Offers Arab world studies (PhD); Chinese studies (M Phil, PhD); East Asian studies (M Phil, PhD); English language (PhD); French studies (M Phil, PhD); German studies (M Phil, PhD); interpreting studies (PhD); Italian studies (M Phil, PhD); Japanese studies (M Phil, PhD); Latin American cultural studies (M Phil, PhD); linguistics (M Phil, PhD); Middle Eastern studies (M Phil, PhD); Polish studies (M Phil, PhD); Portuguese studies (M Phil, PhD); Russian studies (M Phil, PhD); Spanish studies (M Phil, PhD); translation and intercultural studies (M Phil, PhD).

The University of Manchester, School of Social Sciences, Manchester, United Kingdom. Offers ethnographic documentary (M Phil); interdisciplinary study of culture (PhD); philosophy (PhD); politics (PhD); social anthropology (PhD); social anthropology with visual media (PhD); social change (PhD); social statistics (PhD); sociology (PhD); visual anthropology (M Phil).

University of Massachusetts Boston, College of Liberal Arts, Program in Transnational, Cultural, and Community Studies, Boston, MA 02125-3393. Offers MS. *Students:* 14 full-time (12 women), 3 part-time (1 woman); includes 13 minority (1 Black or African American, non-Hispanic/Latino; 2 Asian, non-Hispanic/Latino; 8 Hispanic/Latino; 2 Two or more races, non-Hispanic/Latino), 1 international. Average age 28. 17 applicants, 82% accepted, 12 enrolled. *Expenses:* Tuition, state resident: full-time $17,375. Tuition, nonresident: full-time $33,915. *Required fees:* $355. *Unit head:* Dr. Karen L. Suyemoto, Director, 617-287-6370, E-mail: tccs.program@umb.edu. *Application contact:* Graduate Admissions Coordinator, 617-287-6400, Fax: 617-287-6236, E-mail: bos.gadm@dpc.umassp.edu.

University of Minnesota, Twin Cities Campus, Graduate School, College of Liberal Arts, Department of Cultural Studies and Comparative Literature, Program in Comparative Studies in Discourse and Society, Minneapolis, MN 55455-0213. Offers PhD. *Degree requirements:* For doctorate, 2 foreign languages, thesis/dissertation. *Entrance requirements:* For doctorate, GRE General Test, sample of written work. Additional exam requirements/recommendations for international students: Required—TOEFL. *Faculty research:* Cultural theory; music; architecture, space, and urbanism; body and gender; film and popular culture.

University of Montana, Graduate School, Phyllis J. Washington College of Education and Human Sciences, Department of Counselor Education, Missoula, MT 59812. Offers clinical mental health counseling (MA); counseling and supervision (Ed D); counselor education (Ed S); intercultural youth and family development (MA); school counseling (MA). *Accreditation:* ACA. *Degree requirements:* For doctorate, thesis/dissertation. *Entrance requirements:* For master's, doctorate, and Ed S, GRE General Test. Additional exam requirements/recommendations for international students: Required—TOEFL.

University of New Mexico, Graduate Studies, College of Education, Program in Language, Literacy and Sociocultural Studies, Albuquerque, NM 87131. Offers American Indian education (MA); bilingual education (MA, PhD); educational linguistics (PhD); educational thought and sociocultural studies (MA, PhD); literacy/language arts (MA, PhD); social studies (MA); TESOL (MA, PhD). *Faculty:* 16 full-time (10 women), 4 part-time/adjunct (all women). *Students:* 56 full-time (34 women), 129 part-time (97 women); includes 93 minority (7 Black or African American, non-Hispanic/Latino; 15 American Indian or Alaska Native, non-Hispanic/Latino; 9 Asian, non-Hispanic/Latino; 56 Hispanic/Latino; 6 Two or more races, non-Hispanic/Latino), 44 international. Average age 40. 61 applicants, 38% accepted, 23 enrolled. In 2017, 36 master's, 4 doctorates awarded. *Degree requirements:* For master's, comprehensive exam, thesis optional; for doctorate, comprehensive exam, thesis/dissertation, research skills. *Entrance requirements:* For master's, letter of intent, 3 letters of recommendation, resume, BA/BS, department demographic form, transcripts; for doctorate, writing sample, letter of intent, 3 letters of recommendation, resume, BA/BS, MA, department demographic form, transcripts. Additional exam requirements/recommendations for international students: Required—TOEFL. *Application deadline:* For fall admission, 12/1 for domestic and international students; for spring admission, 9/15 for domestic and international students. Application fee: $50. Electronic applications accepted. *Financial support:* Fellowships, research assistantships, teaching assistantships, career-related internships or fieldwork, institutionally sponsored loans, scholarships/grants, and unspecified assistantships available. Support available to part-time students. Financial award application deadline: 3/1; financial award applicants required to submit FAFSA. *Faculty research:* School reform, professional development, history of education, Native American education, politics of education, feminism and issues of sexual identity, critical race theory, bilingualism, literacy reading, adolescent literature, second language acquisition, critical theory and schooling, indigenous languages. *Unit head:* Dr. Lois M. Meyer, Chair, 505-277-7244, Fax: 505-277-8362, E-mail: lsmeyer@unm.edu. *Application contact:* Debra Schaffer, Administrative Assistant, 505-277-0437, Fax: 505-277-8362, E-mail: schaffer@unm.edu.
Website: http://coe.unm.edu/departments-programs/llss/index.html

University of North Carolina at Asheville, Master of Liberal Arts and Sciences Program, Asheville, NC 28804-3299. Offers climate change and society (Graduate Certificate); environmental and cultural sustainability (Graduate Certificate). *Program availability:* Part-time, evening/weekend. *Faculty:* 7 full-time (1 woman), 3 part-time/adjunct (1 woman). *Students:* 1 full-time (0 women), 24 part-time (12 women); includes 3 minority (2 Black or African American, non-Hispanic/Latino; 1 Two or more races, non-Hispanic/Latino). Average age 44. 18 applicants, 83% accepted, 8 enrolled. In 2017, 19 master's awarded. *Degree requirements:* For master's, thesis or alternative. *Entrance requirements:* For master's and Graduate Certificate, essay, 3 letters of recommendation, transcript. Additional exam requirements/recommendations for international students: Required—TOEFL (minimum score 85 iBT), IELTS (minimum score 6.5). *Application deadline:* For fall admission, 4/15 priority date for domestic students; for spring admission, 11/15 priority date for domestic students. Applications are processed on a rolling basis. Application fee: $60. Electronic applications accepted. *Expenses:* $4,914. *Financial support:* Application deadline: 5/1; applicants required to submit FAFSA. *Unit head:* Gerard Voos, Director, Master of Liberal Arts and Sciences Program and the Asheville Graduate Center, 828-232-5040, E-mail: gvoos@unca.edu. *Application contact:* Jordan Dolfi, Program Coordinator, Master of Liberal Arts and Sciences Program and the Asheville Graduate Center, 828-251-6099, E-mail: jdolfi@unca.edu.
Website: https://mlas.unca.edu/

The University of North Carolina at Charlotte, College of Liberal Arts and Sciences, Department of Languages and Culture Studies, Charlotte, NC 28223-0001. Offers languages and culture studies: translating (Graduate Certificate); Spanish (MA). *Program availability:* Part-time, evening/weekend. *Faculty:* 23 full-time (13 women). *Students:* 6 full-time (4 women), 7 part-time (5 women); includes 6 minority (1 Black or African American, non-Hispanic/Latino; 5 Hispanic/Latino). Average age 32. 11 applicants, 73% accepted, 7 enrolled. In 2017, 6 master's, 5 other advanced degrees awarded. *Degree requirements:* For master's, comprehensive exam, thesis, internship; for Graduate Certificate, internship. *Entrance requirements:* For master's, GRE, baccalaureate degree in Spanish or related field with minimum overall GPA of 2.75; essay that addresses the applicant's motivation for enrolling in program, to include particular areas of research interests and career or professional goals; three letters of reference; oral interview; for Graduate Certificate, GRE or MAT, essay in English that addresses applicant's motivation for seeking enrollment in program; three letters of recommendation; portfolio of best writing samples in both English and Spanish or of translations into each language; oral interview. Additional exam requirements/recommendations for international students: Required—TOEFL (minimum score 523 paper-based, 70 iBT) or IELTS (6.5). *Application deadline:* For fall admission, 3/1 priority date for domestic and international students; for spring admission, 10/1 priority date for domestic and international students. Applications are processed on a rolling basis. Application fee: $75. Electronic applications accepted. *Expenses:* Tuition, state resident: full-time $4337. Tuition, nonresident: full-time $17,771. *Required fees:* $3211. Tuition and fees vary according to course load and program. *Financial support:* In 2017–18, 7 students received support, including 4 research assistantships (averaging $7,000 per year), 3 teaching assistantships (averaging $8,667 per year); career-related internships or fieldwork, institutionally sponsored loans, scholarships/grants, and unspecified assistantships also available. Support available to part-time students. Financial award application deadline: 3/1; financial award applicants required to submit FAFSA. *Total annual research expenditures:* $13,367. *Unit head:* Ann Gonzalez, Chair, 704-687-8761, E-mail: abgonzal@uncc.edu. *Application contact:* Kathy B. Giddings, Director of Graduate Admissions, 704-687-5503, Fax: 704-687-1668, E-mail: gradadm@uncc.edu.
Website: https://languages.uncc.edu/

University of Oklahoma, College of Arts and Sciences, Department of English, Norman, OK 73019. Offers literary and cultural studies (MA, PhD); writing and rhetoric studies (MA, PhD). *Program availability:* Part-time. *Faculty:* 25 full-time (13 women), 1 part-time/adjunct (0 women). *Students:* 29 full-time (21 women), 17 part-time (8 women); includes 9 minority (1 American Indian or Alaska Native, non-Hispanic/Latino; 2 Asian, non-Hispanic/Latino; 5 Hispanic/Latino; 1 Two or more races, non-Hispanic/Latino), 2 international. Average age 31. 34 applicants, 71% accepted, 18 enrolled. In 2017, 7 master's, 4 doctorates awarded. *Degree requirements:* For master's, one foreign language, comprehensive exam (for some programs), thesis (for some programs), exam or thesis; for doctorate, one foreign language, comprehensive exam, thesis/dissertation. *Entrance requirements:* For master's, GRE, BA in English or related field; for doctorate, GRE, MA in English or related field. Additional exam requirements/recommendations for international students: Required—TOEFL (minimum score 79 iBT) or IELTS (minimum score 6.5). *Application deadline:* For fall admission, 1/5 priority date for domestic and international students. Application fee: $50 ($100 for international students). Electronic applications accepted. *Expenses:* Tuition, state resident: full-time $5119; part-time $213.30 per credit hour. Tuition, nonresident: full-time $19,778; part-time $824.10 per credit hour. *Required fees:* $3458; $133.55 per credit hour. $126.50 per semester. *Financial support:* In 2017–18, 40 students received support, including 6 research assistantships with full tuition reimbursements available (averaging $14,515 per year), 31 teaching assistantships with full tuition reimbursements available (averaging $12,496 per year); fellowships with full tuition reimbursements available, scholarships/grants,

health care benefits, and unspecified assistantships also available. Financial award application deadline: 6/1; financial award applicants required to submit FAFSA. *Faculty research:* American Indian literature and culture; composition and rhetoric; American literature; British literature; postcolonial literature and culture. *Total annual research expenditures:* $101. *Unit head:* Dr. Daniela Garofalo, Professor and Chair, 405-325-4661, Fax: 405-325-0831, E-mail: dg@ou.edu. *Application contact:* Sara Day, Graduate Assistant, 405-325-0489, Fax: 405-325-0831, E-mail: redpanda@ou.edu.
Website: http://cas.ou.edu/english

University of Pittsburgh, Kenneth P. Dietrich School of Arts and Sciences, Cultural Studies Program, Pittsburgh, PA 15260. Offers Certificate. *Faculty:* 179 full-time (82 women). *Students:* 87 full-time (50 women); includes 31 minority (4 Black or African American, non-Hispanic/Latino; 1 American Indian or Alaska Native, non-Hispanic/Latino; 13 Asian, non-Hispanic/Latino; 12 Hispanic/Latino; 1 Two or more races, non-Hispanic/Latino). Average age 33. 26 applicants, 100% accepted, 26 enrolled. In 2017, 11 Certificates awarded. *Degree requirements:* For Certificate, one foreign language, comprehensive exam (for some programs), thesis. *Entrance requirements:* For degree, good academic standing in a University of Pittsburgh graduate degree-granting department or school. Additional exam requirements/recommendations for international students: Required—TOEFL. *Application deadline:* Applications are processed on a rolling basis. Application fee: $0. Electronic applications accepted. *Financial support:* In 2017–18, 2 fellowships with full tuition reimbursements were awarded; travel grants also available. *Faculty research:* Interdisciplinary research, anthropology, cultures of disability, global literatures, sociology. *Unit head:* Dr. Ronald J. Zboray, Director, 412-624-6969, Fax: 412-624-6492, E-mail: zboray@pitt.edu. *Application contact:* Kathryn Briar Somerville, Graduate Administrator, 412-624-6564, Fax: 412-383-6999, E-mail: kbs47@pitt.edu.
Website: http://www.culturalstudies.pitt.edu

University of Southern California, Graduate School, Dana and David Dornsife College of Letters, Arts and Sciences, Comparative Studies in Literature and Culture Doctoral Program, Los Angeles, CA 90089. Offers comparative literature (PhD); comparative media and culture (PhD); Spanish and Latin American studies (PhD). *Degree requirements:* For doctorate, 2 foreign languages, comprehensive exam, thesis/dissertation. *Entrance requirements:* For doctorate, GRE, competence in language other than English (highly recommended). Additional exam requirements/recommendations for international students: Required—TOEFL. Electronic applications accepted. *Faculty research:* Literary theory, Japanese film and contemporary fiction, Francophone literature and cinema, Latin American and Caribbean literature, Spanish literature and film, nineteenth and twentieth century British and American literature.

University of Southern Indiana, Graduate Studies, College of Liberal Arts, Program in Second Language Acquisition, Policy, and Culture, Evansville, IN 47712-3590. Offers MA. *Program availability:* Part-time. *Faculty:* 2 full-time (0 women). *Students:* 16 full-time (9 women), 3 part-time (all women); includes 4 minority (3 Asian, non-Hispanic/Latino; 1 Hispanic/Latino), 6 international. Average age 35. In 2017, 5 master's awarded. *Entrance requirements:* For master's, minimum GPA of 3.0, letter of intent, 3 letters of recommendation. Additional exam requirements/recommendations for international students: Required—TOEFL (minimum score 550 paper-based; 79 iBT), IELTS (minimum score 6). Application fee: $40. *Expenses:* Tuition, state resident: full-time $9394. Tuition, nonresident: full-time $17,917. *Required fees:* $510. *Financial support:* In 2017–18, 3 students received support. Federal Work-Study, scholarships/grants, tuition waivers (full and partial), and unspecified assistantships available. Financial award application deadline: 3/1; financial award applicants required to submit FAFSA. *Unit head:* Dr. Jessica Jensen, Program Director, 812-465-1292, E-mail: jgjensen@usi.edu. *Application contact:* Dr. Mayola Rowser, Director, Graduate Studies, 812-465-7015, E-mail: mrowser@usi.edu.
Website: http://www.usi.edu/liberal-arts/ma-language/

University of Southern Maine, College of Management and Human Service, School of Education and Human Development, Program in Counselor Education, Portland, ME 04103. Offers clinical mental health counseling (MS); counseling (CAS); culturally responsive practices in education and human development (CGS); mental health rehabilitation technician/community (CGS); rehabilitation counseling (MS); school counseling (MS); substance abuse counseling (CGS). *Accreditation:* ACA (one or more programs are accredited); CORE; TEAC. *Program availability:* Part-time, evening/weekend. *Degree requirements:* For master's, comprehensive exam, thesis or alternative; for other advanced degree, thesis or alternative. *Entrance requirements:* For master's, GRE General Test or MAT, interview; for other advanced degree, master's degree. Additional exam requirements/recommendations for international students: Required—TOEFL (minimum score 550 paper-based; 79 iBT). Electronic applications accepted. *Faculty research:* Counselor licensure, group dynamics, counseling theories, healthy adaptation, counselor educator well-being.

The University of Texas at Austin, Graduate School, College of Education, Department of Curriculum and Instruction, Austin, TX 78712-1111. Offers bilingual/bicultural education (M Ed, MA, PhD); cultural studies in education (M Ed, MA, PhD); early childhood education (M Ed, MA, PhD); language and literacy studies (M Ed, PhD); learning technologies (M Ed, MA, PhD); physical education (M Ed, MA, PhD). Terminal master's awarded for partial completion of doctoral program. *Degree requirements:* For doctorate, thesis/dissertation. *Entrance requirements:* For master's and doctorate, GRE General Test. Electronic applications accepted.

The University of Texas at Austin, Graduate School, College of Liberal Arts, Department of Anthropology, Program in Cultural Forms, Austin, TX 78712-1111. Offers MA, PhD. *Program availability:* Part-time. Terminal master's awarded for partial completion of doctoral program. *Degree requirements:* For master's, one foreign language, thesis, report; for doctorate, one foreign language, thesis/dissertation. *Entrance requirements:* For master's and doctorate, GRE General Test. Electronic applications accepted. *Faculty research:* Expressive culture, gender, genre, folklore and culture of British Isles, ethnography of speaking.

The University of Texas at Austin, Graduate School, College of Liberal Arts, Department of Slavic and Eurasian Studies, Austin, TX 78712-1111. Offers applied linguistics/pedagogy (PhD); literature and culture (PhD); Slavic languages (MA); Slavic linguistics (PhD). *Degree requirements:* For master's, 2 foreign languages, thesis; for doctorate, 3 foreign languages, thesis/dissertation. *Entrance requirements:* For master's and doctorate, GRE General Test. Electronic applications accepted. *Faculty research:* Slavic linguistics; applied linguistics; Russian, Czech, and Slavic literature and culture.

The University of Texas at Austin, Graduate School, College of Liberal Arts, Teresa Lozano Long Institute of Latin American Studies, Austin, TX 78712-1111. Offers cultural politics of Afro-Latin and indigenous peoples (MA); development studies (MA); environmental studies (MA); human rights (MA); Latin American and international law (LL M); JD/MA; MA/MA; MBA/MA; MP Aff/MA; MSCRP/MA. LL M offered jointly with The University of Texas School of Law. *Entrance requirements:* For master's, GRE General Test.

The University of Texas at San Antonio, College of Education and Human Development, Department of Bicultural and Bilingual Studies, San Antonio, TX 78249-0617. Offers bicultural and bilingual studies (MA), including bicultural and bilingual education, bicultural studies; culture, literacy, and language (PhD); teaching English as a second language (MA). *Program availability:* Part-time, evening/weekend. *Faculty:* 18 full-time (16 women). *Students:* 40 full-time (29 women), 82 part-time (68 women); includes 77 minority (2 Black or African American, non-Hispanic/Latino; 2 Asian, non-Hispanic/Latino; 72 Hispanic/Latino; 1 Two or more races, non-Hispanic/Latino), 9 international. Average age 35. 64 applicants, 80% accepted, 28 enrolled. In 2017, 34 master's, 13 doctorates awarded. *Degree requirements:* For master's, one foreign language, comprehensive exam, thesis optional; for doctorate, one foreign language, comprehensive exam, thesis/dissertation. *Entrance requirements:* For master's, bachelor's degree with 18 credit hours in field of study or in another appropriate field of study; for doctorate, GRE General Test, resume or curriculum vitae, 3 letters of recommendation, statement of purpose, master's degree. Additional exam requirements/recommendations for international students: Required—TOEFL (minimum score 550 paper-based; 79 iBT), IELTS (minimum score 6.5). *Application deadline:* For fall admission, 6/15 for domestic students, 3/15 for international students; for spring admission, 10/15 for domestic students, 9/15 for international students. Applications are processed on a rolling basis. Application fee: $50 ($90 for international students). Electronic applications accepted. *Expenses:* Contact institution. *Financial support:* Fellowships, research assistantships, teaching assistantships, scholarships/grants, and unspecified assistantships available. Financial award application deadline: 4/15. *Faculty research:* Bilingual and ESL teacher preparation; transnational communities; applied linguistics; cultural studies; bilingualism, biliteracy and second language acquisition. *Total annual research expenditures:* $2,246. *Unit head:* Dr. Patricia Sanchez, Chair, 210-458-4426, Fax: 210-458-5962, E-mail: patricia.sanchez@utsa.edu. *Application contact:* Rahnuma Islam, Student Development Specialist, 210-458-6619, Fax: 210-458-5576, E-mail: rahnuma.islam@utsa.edu.
Website: http://education.utsa.edu/bicultural-bilingual_studies

University of the Sacred Heart, Graduate Programs, Department of Communication, Program in Contemporary Culture and Media, San Juan, PR 00914-0383. Offers MA. *Degree requirements:* For master's, thesis.

University of Utah, Graduate School, College of Humanities, Department of Communication, Salt Lake City, UT 84112. Offers communicating science, health, environment and risk (MA, MS, PhD); critical cultural studies (MA, MS, PhD); digital media (MA, MS, PhD); rhetoric (MA, MS, PhD). *Faculty:* 26 full-time (13 women), 11 part-time/adjunct (3 women). *Students:* 34 full-time (24 women), 14 part-time (10 women); includes 4 minority (2 Asian, non-Hispanic/Latino; 1 Hispanic/Latino; 1 Two or more races, non-Hispanic/Latino), 3 international. Average age 24. 99 applicants, 31% accepted, 15 enrolled. In 2017, 6 master's, 9 doctorates awarded. Terminal master's awarded for partial completion of doctoral program. *Entrance requirements:* For master's and doctorate, GRE General Test, minimum GPA of 3.0. Additional exam requirements/recommendations for international students: Required—TOEFL (minimum score 500 paper-based; 90 iBT); Recommended—IELTS. *Application deadline:* For fall admission, 12/15 for domestic students, 11/15 for international students. Application fee: $55 ($65 for international students). Electronic applications accepted. *Expenses:* $7,790 resident, $24,804 non-resident. *Financial support:* In 2017–18, 4 students received support, including 1 fellowship with full tuition reimbursement available (averaging $18,000 per year), 25 teaching assistantships with full tuition reimbursements available (averaging $17,700 per year); research assistantships, scholarships/grants, health care benefits, and unspecified assistantships also available. Financial award application deadline: 12/15; financial award applicants required to submit FAFSA. *Faculty research:* CommSHER (communicating science, health, environment, and risk), critical/cultural studies, interpersonal/organizational communication, new media technologies, rhetoric. *Unit head:* Dr. Kent A. Ono, Chair, 801-585-9128, Fax: 801-585-6255, E-mail: kent.ono@utah.edu. *Application contact:* Dr. Helene Shugart, Director of Graduate Studies, 801-581-5686, Fax: 801-585-6255, E-mail: h.shugart@utah.edu.
Website: http://www.communication.utah.edu

University of Washington, Bothell, Master of Arts in Cultural Studies Program, Bothell, WA 98011. Offers MA. *Program availability:* Evening/weekend. *Degree requirements:* For master's, thesis. *Entrance requirements:* Additional exam requirements/recommendations for international students: Required—TOEFL. Electronic applications accepted.

Washington State University, College of Education, Department of Teaching and Learning, Pullman, WA 99164-2132. Offers cultural studies and social thought in education (PhD); curriculum and instruction (Ed M, MA); English language learners (Ed M, MA); language, literacy and technology (PhD); literacy education (Ed M, MA); mathematics education (PhD); special education (Ed M, MA, PhD); teacher leadership (Ed D); teaching (MIT), including elementary education, secondary education. Programs offered at the Pullman, Spokane, Tri-cities, Vancouver and Global (online) campuses. *Program availability:* Part-time, online learning. *Degree requirements:* For master's, comprehensive exam, thesis, oral or written exam; for doctorate, comprehensive exam, thesis/dissertation, oral and written exam. *Entrance requirements:* For master's, GRE General Test, minimum GPA of 3.0, 3 letters of recommendation, letter of intent, transcripts, resume/curriculum vitae; for doctorate, GRE General Test, minimum GPA of 3.0, 3 letters of recommendation, letter of intent, transcripts, writing sample, resume/curriculum vitae. Additional exam requirements/recommendations for international students: Required—TOEFL (minimum score 550 paper-based; 80 iBT). Electronic applications accepted. *Faculty research:* Intersection of gender, youth cultures and schooling; examination of ideology of power in children's literature; early childhood special education; analyzing pre-service and in-service teacher development; second language acquisition.

Wayne State University, College of Liberal Arts and Sciences, Department of English, Detroit, MI 48202. Offers English (MA); film and media studies (PhD); literary and cultural studies (PhD); rhetoric and composition studies (PhD). *Faculty:* 23. *Students:* 68 full-time (34 women), 24 part-time (17 women); includes 22 minority (10 Black or African American, non-Hispanic/Latino; 2 Asian, non-Hispanic/Latino; 6 Hispanic/Latino; 4 Two or more races, non-Hispanic/Latino), 5 international. Average age 33. 110 applicants, 35% accepted, 17 enrolled. In 2017, 15 master's, 15 doctorates awarded. Terminal master's awarded for partial completion of doctoral program. *Degree requirements:* For master's, variable foreign language requirement, essay, thesis, or portfolio of work approved by Director of Graduate Studies; for doctorate, one foreign language, comprehensive exam, thesis/dissertation. *Entrance requirements:* For master's, statement of purpose; two academic letters of reference; sample essay from previous English course; for doctorate, GRE General Test, statement of purpose; two academic letters of reference; sample of scholarly or critical writing. Additional exam requirements/recommendations for international students: Required—TOEFL (minimum score 550 paper-based; 79 iBT), TWE (minimum score 5.5), Michigan English Language Assessment Battery (minimum score 85); Recommended—IELTS (minimum score 6.5). *Application deadline:* For fall admission, 1/15 for domestic students. Applications are processed on a rolling basis. Application fee: $50. Electronic applications accepted. *Expenses:* Tuition, state resident: full-time $10,224; part-time $638.98 per credit hour. Tuition, nonresident: full-time $22,145; part-time $1384.04 per credit hour. Tuition and fees vary according to course load and program. *Financial support:* In 2017–18, 61 students received support, including 6 fellowships with tuition reimbursements available

(averaging $15,583 per year), 30 teaching assistantships with tuition reimbursements available (averaging $18,534 per year); research assistantships with tuition reimbursements available, scholarships/grants, health care benefits, and unspecified assistantships also available. Financial award applicants required to submit FAFSA. *Faculty research:* Literary and cultural studies, film and new media studies, rhetoric and composition studies, linguistics, and creative writing. *Unit head:* Dr. Kenneth Jackson, Chair and Professor, 313-577-7692, E-mail: ai4054@wayne.edu. *Application contact:* Dr. Carolin Maun, Director of Graduate Studies, 313-577-7694, E-mail: caroline.maun@wayne.edu.
Website: http://clas.wayne.edu/english/

West Chester University of Pennsylvania, College of Arts and Humanities, Department of Languages and Cultures, West Chester, PA 19383. Offers French (Teaching Certificate); German (Teaching Certificate); languages and cultures (MA), including French, German, Spanish; Spanish (Teaching Certificate). *Program availability:* Part-time, evening/weekend, minimal on-campus study. *Students:* 8 full-time (all women), 24 part-time (19 women); includes 10 minority (all Hispanic/Latino), 1 international. Average age 30. 8 applicants, 88% accepted, 7 enrolled. In 2017, 10 master's awarded. *Degree requirements:* For master's, one foreign language, comprehensive exam, portfolio defended at oral exit exam, capstone project; for Teaching Certificate, one foreign language. *Entrance requirements:* For master's and Teaching Certificate, ACTFL OPI and WPT. Additional exam requirements/ recommendations for international students: Required—TOEFL or IELTS. *Application deadline:* For fall admission, 5/15 for international students; for spring admission, 10/15 for international students. Applications are processed on a rolling basis. Application fee: $50. Electronic applications accepted. *Expenses:* Tuition, state resident: full-time $9000; part-time $500 per credit. Tuition, nonresident: full-time $13,500; part-time $750 per credit. *Required fees:* $2959; $149.79 per credit. *Financial support:* Scholarships/ grants and unspecified assistantships available. Financial award application deadline: 2/ 15; financial award applicants required to submit FAFSA. *Faculty research:* Language structure, literature, film, culture, pedagogy, technology. *Unit head:* Dr. Mahmoud Amer, Chair, 610-430-5077, Fax: 610-436-3048, E-mail: mamer@wcupa.edu. *Application contact:* Dr. Maria Van Liew, Graduate Coordinator, 610-436-4746, Fax: 610-436-3048, E-mail: mvanliew@wcupa.edu.
Website: http://www.wcupa.edu/arts-humanities/languagesCultures/

Wheaton College, Graduate School, Department of Intercultural Studies, Wheaton, IL 60187-5593. Offers global engagement (Certificate); intercultural studies (MA); intercultural studies/teaching English as a second language (MA); teaching English as a second language (Certificate). *Program availability:* Part-time. *Faculty:* 1 full-time (0 women), 6 part-time/adjunct (all women). *Students:* 18 full-time (13 women), 32 part-time (23 women); includes 8 minority (2 Black or African American, non-Hispanic/Latino; 3 Asian, non-Hispanic/Latino; 2 Hispanic/Latino; 1 Two or more races, non-Hispanic/ Latino), 11 international. Average age 33. 32 applicants, 97% accepted, 12 enrolled. In 2017, 20 master's awarded. *Degree requirements:* For master's, comprehensive exam, thesis or alternative. *Entrance requirements:* For master's, GRE General Test, MAT. Additional exam requirements/recommendations for international students: Required—TOEFL (minimum score 550 paper-based; 80 iBT), IELTS (minimum score 6.5). *Application deadline:* For fall admission, 5/1 for domestic students, 1/1 for international students; for spring admission, 11/1 for domestic students. Applications are processed on a rolling basis. Application fee: $30. Electronic applications accepted. *Expenses: Tuition:* Full-time $19,800; part-time $825 per credit hour. Tuition and fees vary according to degree level and program. *Financial support:* Career-related internships or fieldwork, scholarships/grants, and unspecified assistantships available. Financial award application deadline: 3/1; financial award applicants required to submit FAFSA. *Unit head:* Dr. Robert Gallagher, Chair, 630-752-5948, E-mail: intercultural.studies@wheaton.edu. *Application contact:* Director of Graduate Admissions, 630-752-5195, Fax: 630-752-5047, E-mail: graduate.admissions@wheaton.edu.
Website: https://www.wheaton.edu/graduate-school/degrees/ma-in-intercultural-studies/

Wilfrid Laurier University, Faculty of Graduate and Postdoctoral Studies, Faculty of Arts, Cultural Analysis and Social Theory Program, Waterloo, ON N2L 3C5, Canada. Offers body politics (MA); cultural representation and social theory (MA); gender, sexuality and embodiment (MA); globalization, identity and social movements (MA). *Program availability:* Part-time. *Entrance requirements:* For master's, honours BA in humanities, social science or interdisciplinary program with social theory, minimum B+ in final year of full-time study. Additional exam requirements/recommendations for international students: Required—TOEFL (minimum score 89 iBT). Electronic applications accepted. *Faculty research:* Globalization; identity and social movements; body politics: gender, sexuality and embodiment; cultural representation and social theory.

Wilfrid Laurier University, Faculty of Graduate and Postdoctoral Studies, Faculty of Arts, Department of Communication Studies, Waterloo, ON N2L 3C5, Canada. Offers media, technology and culture (MA); visual communication and culture (MA). *Degree requirements:* For master's, thesis optional. *Entrance requirements:* For master's, honours BA in communication studies or a cognate discipline from an approved university with a minimum B+ overall in last two years of study and in undergraduate major. Additional exam requirements/recommendations for international students: Required—TOEFL (minimum score 89 iBT). Electronic applications accepted. *Faculty research:* Visual communication and culture, media, technology and culture.

Wilson College, Graduate Programs, Chambersburg, PA 17201-1285. Offers accounting (M Acc); choreography and visual art (MFA); education (M Ed); educational technology (MET); healthcare administration (MHA); humanities (MA), including art and culture, critical/cultural theory, English language and literature, women's studies; management (MSM); nursing (MSN), including nursing education, nursing leadership and management; special education (MSE). *Program availability:* Evening/weekend. *Degree requirements:* For master's, project. *Entrance requirements:* For master's, PRAXIS, minimum undergraduate cumulative GPA of 3.0, 2 letters of recommendation, current certification for eligibility to teach in grades K-12, resume, personal interview. Electronic applications accepted.

East European and Russian Studies

Boston College, Graduate School of Arts and Sciences, Department of Slavic and Eastern Languages and Literatures, Program in Slavic Studies, Chestnut Hill, MA 02467-3800. Offers MA, MA/JD, MBA/MA. *Degree requirements:* For master's, 3 foreign languages, comprehensive exam, thesis or alternative. *Entrance requirements:* Additional exam requirements/recommendations for international students: Required—TOEFL (minimum score 600 paper-based; 100 iBT), IELTS (minimum score 8). Electronic applications accepted.

Brown University, Graduate School, Department of Slavic Studies, Providence, RI 02912. Offers Russian language and literature (AM); Slavic linguistics (AM); Slavic studies (PhD). *Degree requirements:* For master's, one foreign language; for doctorate, 2 foreign languages, thesis/dissertation, preliminary exam.

Carleton University, Faculty of Graduate Studies, Faculty of Public Affairs and Management, Institute of European and Russian Studies, Ottawa, ON K1S 5B6, Canada. Offers European and European Union studies (MA); European integration studies (Diploma); Russian, Eurasian and transition studies (MA). *Degree requirements:* For master's, one foreign language, thesis optional. *Entrance requirements:* For master's, honors degree or equivalent; 2 years of Russian, German or other central east European language. Additional exam requirements/recommendations for international students: Required—TOEFL. *Faculty research:* East-West relations, minority rights in Russia and Eastern Europe.

Columbia University, Graduate School of Arts and Sciences, New York, NY 10027. Offers African-American studies (MA); American studies (MA); anthropology (MA, PhD); art history and archaeology (MA, PhD); astronomy (PhD); biological sciences (PhD); biotechnology (MA); chemical physics (PhD); chemistry (PhD); classical studies (MA, PhD); classics (MA, PhD); climate and society (MA); conservation biology (MA); earth and environmental sciences (PhD); East Asia: regional studies (MA); East Asian languages and cultures (MA, PhD); ecology, evolution and environmental biology (MA), including conservation biology; ecology, evolution, and environmental biology (PhD), including ecology and evolutionary biology, evolutionary primatology; economics (MA, PhD); English and comparative literature (MA, PhD); French and Romance philology (MA, PhD); Germanic languages (MA, PhD); global French studies (MA); global thought (MA); Hispanic cultural studies (MA); history (PhD); history and literature (MA); human rights studies (MA); Islamic studies (MA); Italian (MA, PhD); Japanese pedagogy (MA); Jewish studies (MA); Latin America and the Caribbean: regional studies (MA); Latin American and Iberian cultures (PhD); mathematics (MA, PhD), including finance (MA); medieval and Renaissance studies (MA); Middle Eastern, South Asian, and African studies (MA, PhD); modern art: critical and curatorial studies (MA); modern European studies (MA); museum anthropology (MA); music (DMA, PhD); oral history (MA); philosophical foundations of physics (MA); philosophy (MA, PhD); physics (PhD); political science (MA, PhD); psychology (PhD); quantitative methods in the social sciences (MA); religion (MA, PhD); Russia, Eurasia and East Europe: regional studies (MA); Russian translation (MA); Slavic cultures (MA); Slavic languages (MA, PhD); sociology (MA, PhD); South Asian studies (MA); statistics (MA, PhD); theatre (PhD). Dual-degree programs require admission to both Graduate School of Arts and Sciences and another Columbia school. *Program availability:* Part-time. Terminal master's awarded for partial completion of doctoral program. *Degree requirements:* For master's, variable foreign language requirement, comprehensive exam (for some programs), thesis (for some programs); for doctorate, variable foreign language requirement, comprehensive exam (for some programs), thesis/dissertation. *Entrance requirements:* For master's and doctorate, GRE General Test, GRE Subject Test (for some programs). Additional exam requirements/recommendations for international students: Required—TOEFL, IELTS. Electronic applications accepted. *Expenses: Tuition:* Full-time $44,864; part-time $1704 per credit. *Required fees:* $2370 per semester. One-time fee: $105.

Cornell University, Graduate School, Graduate Fields of Arts and Sciences, Field of History, Ithaca, NY 14853. Offers African history (MA, PhD); American history (MA, PhD); ancient Greek history (PhD); ancient history (MA, PhD); ancient Roman history (PhD); early modern European history (MA, PhD); English history (MA, PhD); French history (MA, PhD); German history (MA, PhD); history of science (MA, PhD); Korean history (PhD); Latin American history (MA, PhD); medieval Chinese history (MA, PhD); medieval history (MA, PhD); modern Chinese history (MA, PhD); modern European history (MA, PhD); modern Japanese history (MA, PhD); modern Middle Eastern history (PhD); premodern Islamic history (MA, PhD); premodern Japanese history (MA, PhD); Renaissance history (MA, PhD); Russian history (MA, PhD); South Asian history (PhD); Southeast Asian history (MA, PhD). Terminal master's awarded for partial completion of doctoral program. *Degree requirements:* For master's, thesis; for doctorate, 2 foreign languages, comprehensive exam, thesis/dissertation, 1 year of teaching experience. *Entrance requirements:* For master's and doctorate, GRE General Test, writing sample, 3 letters of recommendation. Additional exam requirements/recommendations for international students: Required—TOEFL (minimum score 550 paper-based; 77 iBT). Electronic applications accepted.

Florida State University, The Graduate School, College of Social Sciences and Public Policy, Program in Russian and East European Studies, Tallahassee, FL 32306. Offers Russian and East European Studies (MA). *Program availability:* Part-time. *Faculty:* 4 full-time (all women), 4 part-time/adjunct (0 women). *Students:* 5 full-time (2 women), 2 part-time (1 woman); includes 2 minority (1 Hispanic/Latino; 1 Two or more races, non-Hispanic/Latino). Average age 30. 6 applicants, 100% accepted, 5 enrolled. In 2017, 4 master's awarded. *Degree requirements:* For master's, one foreign language, comprehensive exam, thesis optional. *Entrance requirements:* For master's, GRE General Test, minimum GPA of 3.0. Additional exam requirements/recommendations for international students: Required—TOEFL (minimum score 550 paper-based, 80 iBT) or IELTS (6.5). *Application deadline:* For fall admission, 7/1 for domestic and international students; for spring admission, 11/1 for domestic and international students; for summer admission, 3/1 for domestic and international students. Applications are processed on a rolling basis. Application fee: $30. Electronic applications accepted. *Expenses:* $479.32 in-state per credit hour; $1,110.72 out-of-state per credit hour. *Financial support:* In 2017–18, 1 student received support, including 1 teaching assistantship with full tuition reimbursement available (averaging $6,100 per year); fellowships, research assistantships, career-related internships or fieldwork, Federal Work-Study, institutionally sponsored loans, and unspecified assistantships also available. Financial award application deadline: 2/1; financial award applicants required to submit FAFSA. *Faculty research:* Deception in World War II. *Unit head:* Dr. Lee K. Metcalf, Director, 850-644-4418, Fax: 850-645-4981, E-mail: lmetcalf@fsu.edu. *Application contact:* Sabrina Smith Bandak, Academic Program Specialist, 850-644-4418, Fax: 850-645-4981, E-mail: ssmith9@fsu.edu.
Website: http://coss.fsu.edu/inaprog/programs/graduate/g-european

Georgetown University, Graduate School of Arts and Sciences, Walsh School of Foreign Service, Center for Eurasian, Russian and East European Studies, Washington, DC 20057. Offers MA, MA/JD, MA/PhD. *Degree requirements:* For master's, one foreign language, comprehensive exam, thesis optional. *Entrance requirements:* For master's, GRE General Test. Additional exam requirements/recommendations for international students: Required—TOEFL. *Faculty research:* East-West trade.

The George Washington University, Elliott School of International Affairs, Program in European and Eurasian Studies, Washington, DC 20052. Offers MA. *Program availability:* Part-time. *Students:* 15 full-time (7 women), 4 part-time (1 woman); includes 3 minority (2 Hispanic/Latino; 1 Two or more races, non-Hispanic/Latino). Average age 27. 66 applicants, 67% accepted, 10 enrolled. In 2017, 10 master's awarded. *Degree requirements:* For master's, one foreign language, capstone project. *Entrance requirements:* For master's, GRE General Test, 2 years (or the equivalent) of a modern European language or Russian, 2 semesters of introductory economics (macro or micro). Additional exam requirements/recommendations for international students: Required—TOEFL (minimum score 100 iBT), IELTS (minimum score 7). *Application deadline:* For fall admission, 1/15 priority date for domestic and international students; for spring admission, 10/1 for domestic students. Application fee: $75. Electronic applications accepted. *Expenses: Tuition:* Full-time $28,800; part-time $1655 per credit hour. *Required fees:* $45; $2.75 per credit hour. *Financial support:* In 2017–18, 3 students received support. Fellowships with partial tuition reimbursements available and Federal Work-Study available. Financial award application deadline: 1/15; financial award applicants required to submit FAFSA. *Faculty research:* NATO, European economics, European history, European Union. *Unit head:* Peter Rollberg, Director, 202-994-7084, E-mail: rgpeter@gwu.edu. *Application contact:* Nicole A. Campbell, Director of Graduate Admissions, 202-994-7050, Fax: 202-994-9537, E-mail: esiagrad@gwu.edu.
Website: http://elliott.gwu.edu/academics/grad/ees/index.cfm

Harvard University, Graduate School of Arts and Sciences, Committee on Regional Studies-Russia, Eastern Europe, and Central Asia, Cambridge, MA 02138. Offers AM. *Degree requirements:* For master's, one foreign language. *Entrance requirements:* For master's, GRE General Test. Additional exam requirements/recommendations for international students: Required—TOEFL. *Faculty research:* Strategic policy, ethnography and demography of U.S.S.R., non-Russian nationality language training.

Indiana University Bloomington, University Graduate School, College of Arts and Sciences, School of Global and International Studies, Russian and East European Institute, Bloomington, IN 47405. Offers MA, Certificate, JD/MA, MA/MA, MBA/MA, MIS/MA, MLS/MA, MPA/MA, MPH/MA, MSSI/MA. *Degree requirements:* For master's, one foreign language, essay, written exams; for Certificate, one foreign language, oral and proficiency exams. *Entrance requirements:* For master's, GRE General Test, minimum 2 years of college Russian (for Russian area studies); for Certificate, GRE General Test. Additional exam requirements/recommendations for international students: Recommended—TOEFL (minimum score 550 paper-based). *Expenses:* Contact institution. *Faculty research:* Political and economic transition of former Soviet Union and eastern Europe, Russian and Soviet history, Slavic literature and linguistics, education and mass media of former Soviet Union and Eastern Europe.

The Ohio State University, Graduate School, Center for Slavic and East European Studies, Columbus, OH 43210. Offers MA. *Students:* 10 full-time (3 women). Average age 26. In 2017, 4 master's awarded. *Degree requirements:* For master's, exam or thesis. *Entrance requirements:* For master's, GRE General Test. Additional exam requirements/recommendations for international students: Required—TOEFL (minimum score 550 paper-based; 79 iBT), Michigan English Language Assessment Battery (minimum score 82); Recommended—IELTS (minimum score 7). *Application deadline:* For fall admission, 12/13 priority date for domestic students, 11/30 priority date for international students; for spring admission, 11/10 for domestic and international students; for summer admission, 3/13 for domestic and international students. Applications are processed on a rolling basis. Application fee: $60 ($70 for international students). Electronic applications accepted. *Financial support:* Fellowships, Federal Work-Study, and institutionally sponsored loans available. Support available to part-time students. *Unit head:* Dr. Yana Hashamova, Director, E-mail: hashamova.1@osu.edu. *Application contact:* Graduate and Professional Admissions, 614-292-9444, Fax: 614-292-3895, E-mail: gpadmissions@osu.edu.
Website: http://slaviccenter.osu.edu

The Ohio State University, Graduate School, College of Arts and Sciences, Division of Arts and Humanities, Department of Slavic and East European Languages and Cultures, Columbus, OH 43210. Offers Slavic linguistics (MA, PhD); Slavic literature, film, and cultural studies (MA, PhD). *Faculty:* 10. *Students:* 16 full-time (11 women). Average age 31. In 2017, 1 master's, 4 doctorates awarded. Terminal master's awarded for partial completion of doctoral program. *Degree requirements:* For master's, variable foreign language requirement, thesis optional; for doctorate, variable foreign language requirement, thesis/dissertation. *Entrance requirements:* For master's and doctorate, GRE General Test, at least 3 years of Russian language study or equivalent. Additional exam requirements/recommendations for international students: Required—TOEFL (minimum score 550 paper-based; 79 iBT), Michigan English Language Assessment Battery (minimum score 82); Recommended—IELTS (minimum score 7). *Application deadline:* For fall admission, 12/12 priority date for domestic students, 11/30 priority date for international students; for spring admission, 3/1 for domestic students, 2/1 for international students. Applications are processed on a rolling basis. Application fee: $60 ($70 for international students). Electronic applications accepted. *Financial support:* Fellowships, teaching assistantships, Federal Work-Study, and institutionally sponsored loans available. Support available to part-time students. *Faculty research:* Polish literature. *Unit head:* Dr. Yana Hashamova, Chair and Professor, 614-292-6733, E-mail: hashamova.1@osu.edu. *Application contact:* Graduate and Professional Admissions, 614-292-9444, Fax: 614-292-3895, E-mail: gpadmissions@osu.edu.
Website: http://slavic.osu.edu/

Stanford University, School of Humanities and Sciences, Center for Russian, East European and Eurasian Studies, Stanford, CA 94305-2004. Offers MA. *Degree requirements:* For master's, one foreign language. *Entrance requirements:* For master's, GRE General Test. Additional exam requirements/recommendations for international students: Required—TOEFL. Electronic applications accepted. *Expenses: Tuition:* Full-time $48,987; part-time $10,620 per quarter. One-time fee: $400. Tuition and fees vary according to program.

University of Alberta, Faculty of Graduate Studies and Research, Department of Modern Languages and Cultural Studies, Edmonton, AB T6G 2E1, Canada. Offers applied linguistics (Germanic, Romance, Slavic) (MA); French language, literatures and linguistics (PhD); French language, literatures, and linguistics (MA); Germanic languages, literatures and linguistics (PhD); Germanic languages, literatures, and linguistics (MA); Italian studies (MA); Slavic languages and literatures (Russian, Ukrainian) (MA, PhD); Slavic linguistics (Russian, Ukrainian) (MA, PhD); Spanish and Latin American studies (MA, PhD); Ukrainian folklore (MA, PhD). *Program availability:* Part-time. *Degree requirements:* For master's, one foreign language, thesis; for doctorate, 2 foreign languages, comprehensive exam, thesis/dissertation. *Entrance requirements:* For master's and doctorate, 1 language other than English. Additional

exam requirements/recommendations for international students: Required—Michigan English Language Assessment Battery or TOEFL (minimum score 550 paper-based). Electronic applications accepted. *Faculty research:* Russian/Ukrainian studies; German studies; contemporary Latin American, French and Francophone studies; Italian studies.

The University of British Columbia, Faculty of Arts and Faculty of Graduate Studies, Department of Central, Eastern and Northern European Studies, Vancouver, BC V6T 1Z1, Canada. Offers Germanic studies (MA, PhD). *Program availability:* Part-time. *Degree requirements:* For master's, one foreign language, thesis optional, exam; for doctorate, one foreign language, comprehensive exam, thesis/dissertation. *Entrance requirements:* For master's, BA in German; for doctorate, MA in German. Additional exam requirements/recommendations for international students: Required—TOEFL. Electronic applications accepted. *Expenses:* Contact institution. *Faculty research:* Second language acquisition, media theory, performance theory, gender studies, cultural studies.

University of Colorado Boulder, Graduate School, College of Arts and Sciences, Russian Studies Program, Boulder, CO 80309. Offers MA. *Students:* 8 full-time (5 women), 1 international. Average age 27. 2 applicants, 50% accepted. *Application deadline:* For fall admission, 1/10 for domestic and international students. Application fee: $60 ($80 for international students). Electronic applications accepted. *Financial support:* In 2017–18, 11 students received support, including 4 fellowships (averaging $2,150 per year), 3 teaching assistantships with full and partial tuition reimbursements available (averaging $33,256 per year); institutionally sponsored loans, scholarships/grants, health care benefits, tuition waivers, and unspecified assistantships also available. Financial award applicants required to submit FAFSA.
Website: https://www.colorado.edu/gsll/russian-program

University of Illinois at Chicago, College of Liberal Arts and Sciences, School of Literatures, Cultural Studies and Linguistics, Department of Slavic and Baltic Languages and Literatures, Chicago, IL 60607-7128. Offers Slavic studies (MA, PhD). *Program availability:* Evening/weekend. Terminal master's awarded for partial completion of doctoral program. *Degree requirements:* For doctorate, one foreign language, thesis/dissertation. *Entrance requirements:* For master's and doctorate, GRE General Test, minimum GPA of 3.0. Additional exam requirements/recommendations for international students: Required—TOEFL. Electronic applications accepted. *Faculty research:* Twentieth-century Polish literature and culture, Russian and Polish modernisms, nineteenth- and twentieth-century Russian literature, Lithuanian language, Polish-Jewish culture and history, Yiddish literature and language.

University of Illinois at Urbana–Champaign, Graduate College, College of Liberal Arts and Sciences, Russian, East European, and Eurasian Center, Champaign, IL 61820. Offers MA.

The University of Kansas, Graduate Studies, College of Liberal Arts and Sciences, Center for Russian, East European and Eurasian Studies, Lawrence, KS 66045. Offers foreign area officer (MA); Russian, East European and Eurasian studies (MA, Graduate Certificate); JD/MA. *Program availability:* Part-time. *Students:* 4 full-time (0 women), 1 part-time (0 women). Average age 27. 6 applicants, 83% accepted, 1 enrolled. In 2017, 5 master's, 1 other advanced degree awarded. *Entrance requirements:* For master's, GRE General Test, two-page statement of educational and professional objectives, three letters of recommendation, official transcripts. Additional exam requirements/recommendations for international students: Required—TOEFL. Application fee: $65 ($85 for international students). Electronic applications accepted. *Financial support:* Fellowships, research assistantships, and scholarships/grants available. Financial award application deadline: 1/1; financial award applicants required to submit FAFSA. *Faculty research:* Russian and East Central European history and culture; Ukrainian, Russian, and Central Asian domestic politics and international security; Slavic languages, linguistics, and literatures. *Unit head:* Vitaly Chernetsky, Acting Director, 785-864-4236, E-mail: vchernetsky@ku.edu. *Application contact:* Alyssa McDonald, Graduate Admissions Contact, 785-864-4236, E-mail: crees@ku.edu.
Website: http://www.crees.ku.edu/

University of Michigan, Rackham Graduate School, College of Literature, Science, and the Arts, Center for Russian, East European, and Eurasian Studies, Ann Arbor, MI 48109-1042. Offers AM, Certificate, JD/AM, MBA/AM, MPP/AM. *Program availability:* Part-time. *Faculty:* 74 full-time (30 women). *Students:* 74 full-time (30 women); includes 2 minority (1 Hispanic/Latino; 1 Two or more races, non-Hispanic/Latino). Average age 28. 23 applicants, 70% accepted, 3 enrolled. In 2017, 4 master's awarded. *Degree requirements:* For master's and Certificate, one foreign language, thesis. *Entrance requirements:* For master's, GRE General Test, academic statement of purpose; curriculum vitae; official transcripts of post-secondary education; 3 letters of recommendation; writing sample. Additional exam requirements/recommendations for international students: Required—TOEFL (minimum score 560 paper-based; 84 iBT). *Application deadline:* For fall admission, 12/15 for domestic and international students. Application fee: $75 ($90 for international students). Electronic applications accepted. *Expenses:* Tuition, state resident: full-time $22,368; part-time $1201 per credit hour. Tuition, nonresident: full-time $45,156; part-time $2467 per credit hour. *Required fees:* $376 per term. Tuition and fees vary according to course load, degree level and program. *Financial support:* In 2017–18, 5 students received support, including 3 fellowships with full tuition reimbursements available (averaging $15,000 per year), 2 teaching assistantships with full tuition reimbursements available (averaging $8,000 per year); career-related internships or fieldwork, scholarships/grants, and health care benefits also available. Financial award application deadline: 1/15; financial award applicants required to submit FAFSA. *Faculty research:* Russia, East Europe, Eurasia, Central Asia, Caucasus. *Unit head:* Dr. Elizabeth King, Associate Director, 734-764-7501, E-mail: ii-gradadvising@umich.edu. *Application contact:* Julie E. Burnett, Academic Services Coordinator, 734-936-1842, Fax: 734-615-9158, E-mail: ii-gradadvising@umich.edu.
Website: http://www.ii.umich.edu/crees

The University of North Carolina at Chapel Hill, Graduate School, College of Arts and Sciences, Center for Slavic, Eurasian and East European Studies, Chapel Hill, NC 27599. Offers global studies (MA). *Program availability:* Part-time. *Degree requirements:* For master's, one foreign language, thesis. *Entrance requirements:* For master's, GRE General Test. Additional exam requirements/recommendations for international students: Required—TOEFL. Electronic applications accepted. *Faculty research:* Language, area studies, social sciences, professional schools.

University of Pittsburgh, University Center for International Studies, Pittsburgh, PA 15260. Offers African studies (Certificate); Asian studies (Certificate); European Union studies (Certificate); global studies (Certificate); Latin American studies (Certificate); Russian and East European studies (Certificate); West European studies (Certificate). *Program availability:* Part-time, evening/weekend, online learning. *Students:* 183 full-time (108 women), 9 part-time (all women); includes 78 minority (6 Black or African American, non-Hispanic/Latino; 23 Asian, non-Hispanic/Latino; 47 Hispanic/Latino; 2 Two or more races, non-Hispanic/Latino). Average age 29. *Degree requirements:* For Certificate, one foreign language, comprehensive exam (for some programs). *Entrance requirements:* Additional exam requirements/recommendations for international students: Required—TOEFL. *Expenses:* No tuition and fees. *Financial support:* In

East European and Russian Studies

2017–18, 25 fellowships with full tuition reimbursements (averaging $26,117 per year) were awarded; scholarships/grants, traineeships, health care benefits, and unspecified assistantships also available. *Unit head:* Dr. Ariel Armony, Director, 412-648-7374, Fax: 412-624-4672, E-mail: armony@pitt.edu.
Website: http://www.ucis.pitt.edu

University of Saskatchewan, College of Graduate Studies and Research, College of Arts and Science, Department of Languages and Linguistics, Saskatoon, SK S7N 5A2, Canada. Offers MA. *Degree requirements:* For master's, 2 foreign languages, thesis. *Entrance requirements:* Additional exam requirements/recommendations for international students: Required—TOEFL (minimum score 80 iBT); Recommended—IELTS (minimum score 6.5). Electronic applications accepted.

The University of Texas at Austin, Graduate School, College of Liberal Arts, Center for Russian, East European, and Eurasian Studies, Austin, TX 78712-1111. Offers MA, JD/MA, MA/MA, MBA/MA, MGPS/MA, MP Aff/MA. *Program availability:* Part-time. *Degree requirements:* For master's, one foreign language, report or thesis. *Entrance requirements:* For master's, GRE General Test, 3 years of formal language training or equivalent, minimum GPA of 3.0. Electronic applications accepted. *Faculty research:* East European gypsies, elite transformation and democracy in Eastern Europe, elite partisanship as an intervening variable in Russian politics, post-Soviet youth in Russia.

University of Toronto, School of Graduate Studies, Munk School of Global Affairs, Centre for European, Russian and Eurasian Studies, Toronto, ON M5S 1A1, Canada. Offers MA, JD/MA. *Degree requirements:* For master's, one foreign language, language proficiency test. *Entrance requirements:* For master's, minimum B+ average in final year, coursework in Russian/East European subjects, 2 years of study in a relevant language. Additional exam requirements/recommendations for international students: Required—TOEFL (minimum score 580 paper-based; 93 iBT), TWE (minimum score 5). Electronic applications accepted.

University of Washington, Graduate School, College of Arts and Sciences, Henry M. Jackson School of International Studies, Russian, East European and Central Asian Studies Program, Seattle, WA 98195. Offers Central Asian studies (MAIS); East European studies (MAIS); Russian studies (MAIS). *Degree requirements:* For master's, one foreign language, thesis. *Entrance requirements:* For master's, GRE General Test, 2 years of relevant language, minimum GPA of 3.0 in last two years. Additional exam requirements/recommendations for international students: Required—TOEFL (minimum score 500 paper-based; 92 iBT), IELTS (minimum score 7). Electronic applications accepted.

Yale University, Graduate School of Arts and Sciences, Department of Slavic Languages and Literatures, New Haven, CT 06520. Offers medieval Slavic literature and philology (PhD); Polish literature (PhD); Russian literature (PhD); Slavic languages and literatures and film studies (PhD). *Degree requirements:* For doctorate, 3 foreign languages, thesis/dissertation. *Entrance requirements:* For doctorate, GRE General Test.

Yale University, Graduate School of Arts and Sciences, Program in Russian and East European Studies, New Haven, CT 06520. Offers MA. *Degree requirements:* For master's, 2 foreign languages. *Entrance requirements:* For master's, GRE General Test.

Ethnic Studies

Colorado State University, College of Liberal Arts, Department of Ethnic Studies, Fort Collins, CO 80523-1790. Offers MA. *Faculty:* 6 full-time (2 women). *Students:* 5 full-time (all women), 9 part-time (5 women); includes 5 minority (2 Asian, non-Hispanic/Latino; 3 Two or more races, non-Hispanic/Latino), 1 international. Average age 32. 14 applicants, 64% accepted, 5 enrolled. In 2017, 6 master's awarded. *Degree requirements:* For master's, thesis (for some programs), professional paper. *Entrance requirements:* For master's, personal statement, resume/curriculum vitae, official transcripts, 3 letters of recommendation, minimum GPA of 3.0. Additional exam requirements/recommendations for international students: Required—TOEFL (minimum score 550 paper-based; 80 iBT). *Application deadline:* For fall admission, 3/15 priority date for domestic and international students. Applications are processed on a rolling basis. Application fee: $60 ($70 for international students). Electronic applications accepted. *Expenses:* Tuition, state resident: full-time $9917. Tuition, nonresident: full-time $24,312. *Required fees:* $2284. Tuition and fees vary according to course load and program. *Financial support:* In 2017–18, 1 fellowship with full and partial tuition reimbursement (averaging $23,760 per year), 4 teaching assistantships with full and partial tuition reimbursements (averaging $14,256 per year) were awarded; scholarships/grants and unspecified assistantships also available. Financial award application deadline: 2/15. *Faculty research:* Political economy of labor; representations of Black life in the slave narratives and other nineteenth-century documents; health disparities; Afro-Caribbean diaspora and feminism; life histories and visual narrative analysis. *Unit head:* Joon K. Kim, Professor/Department Chair, 970-491-6732, Fax: 970-491-2717, E-mail: joon.kim@colostate.edu. *Application contact:* Abby Marweg, Administrative Assistant, 970-491-2418, Fax: 970-491-2717, E-mail: abby.marweg@colostate.edu.
Website: http://ethnicstudies.colostate.edu/

Cornell University, Graduate School, Graduate Fields of Arts and Sciences, Field of Sociology, Ithaca, NY 14853. Offers economy and society (MA, PhD); gender and life course (MA, PhD); methodology (MA, PhD); organizations (MA, PhD); policy analysis (MA, PhD); political sociology/social movements (MA, PhD); racial and ethnic relations (MA, PhD); social networks (MA, PhD); social psychology (MA, PhD); social stratification (MA, PhD). Terminal master's awarded for partial completion of doctoral program. *Degree requirements:* For master's, thesis; for doctorate, thesis/dissertation, 1 year of teaching experience. *Entrance requirements:* For master's and doctorate, GRE General Test, 2 letters of recommendation, writing sample. Additional exam requirements/recommendations for international students: Required—TOEFL (minimum score 550 paper-based; 77 iBT). Electronic applications accepted. *Faculty research:* Comparative societal analysis, work and family, simulations, social class and mobility, racial segregation and inequality.

DePaul University, College of Liberal Arts and Social Sciences, Chicago, IL 60614. Offers Arabic (MA); Chinese (MA); critical ethnic studies (MA); English (MA); French (MA); German (MA); history (MA); interdisciplinary studies (MA, MS); international public service (MS); international studies (MA); Italian (MA); Japanese (MA); liberal studies (MA); nonprofit management (MNM); public administration (MPA); public health (MPH); public policy (MPP); public service management (MS); refugee and forced migration studies (MS); social work (MSW); sociology (MA); Spanish (MA); sustainable urban development (MA); women's and gender studies (MA); writing and publishing (MA); writing, rhetoric and discourse (MA); MA/PhD. *Program availability:* Part-time, evening/weekend, online learning. Terminal master's awarded for partial completion of doctoral program. *Degree requirements:* For master's, variable foreign language requirement, comprehensive exam (for some programs), thesis (for some programs). *Application deadline:* Applications are processed on a rolling basis. Application fee: $40. Electronic applications accepted. *Financial support:* Applicants required to submit FAFSA. *Unit head:* Dr. Guillermo Vasquez de Velasco, Dean, 773-325-7305. *Application contact:* Ann Spittle, Director of Graduate Admission, 773-325-8369, Fax: 312-476-3244, E-mail: graddepaul@depaul.edu.
Website: http://las.depaul.edu/

Minnesota State University Mankato, College of Graduate Studies and Research, College of Social and Behavioral Sciences, Department of Ethnic Studies, Mankato, MN 56001. Offers MS. *Degree requirements:* For master's, thesis optional. *Entrance requirements:* For master's, minimum undergraduate GPA of 3.0, baccalaureate degree, at least 9 undergraduate credits in ethnic and cross-cultural areas, knowledge of or skills in two languages, statement of purpose. Electronic applications accepted.

Northern Arizona University, College of Social and Behavioral Sciences, Ethnic Studies Program, Flagstaff, AZ 86011. Offers Graduate Certificate. *Program availability:* Part-time. *Faculty:* 10 full-time (3 women). *Students:* 1 full-time (0 women), 1 (woman) part-time; includes 1 minority (Hispanic/Latino). Average age 26. 3 applicants, 67% accepted, 2 enrolled. In 2017, 3 Graduate Certificates awarded. *Degree requirements:* For Graduate Certificate, comprehensive exam (for some programs). *Entrance requirements:* For degree, undergraduate degree from regionally-accredited institution with minimum GPA of 3.0, or the equivalent. Additional exam requirements/recommendations for international students: Required—TOEFL (minimum score 80 iBT), IELTS (minimum score 6.5). *Application deadline:* For fall admission, 3/1 for domestic and international students; for spring admission, 10/1 for domestic and international students. Applications are processed on a rolling basis. Application fee: $65. Electronic applications accepted. *Expenses:* Tuition, state resident: full-time $9240; part-time $458 per credit hour. Tuition, nonresident: full-time $21,588; part-time $1199 per credit hour. *Required fees:* $1021; $14 per credit hour. $646 per semester. Tuition and fees vary according to course load, campus/location and program. *Financial support:* In 2017–18, 1 student received support, including 1 teaching assistantship with partial tuition reimbursement available (averaging $6,000 per year); institutionally sponsored loans, health care benefits, and unspecified assistantships also available. Financial award application deadline: 2/1; financial award applicants required to submit FAFSA. *Unit head:* Dr. Sara Aleman, Interim Director, 928-523-3886, Fax: 928-522-6777, E-mail: sara.aleman@nau.edu. *Application contact:* April Peck, Administrative Associate, 928-523-2011, Fax: 928-523-8950, E-mail: april.peck@nau.edu.
Website: http://nau.edu/sbs/ethnic-studies/

San Francisco State University, Division of Graduate Studies, College of Ethnic Studies, Program in Ethnic Studies, San Francisco, CA 94132-1722. Offers MA. *Unit head:* Dr. Amy H. Sueyoshi, Interim Dean, 415-338-1693, Fax: 415-338-1739, E-mail: ethnicst@sfsu.edu. *Application contact:* Dr. Katynka Z. Martinez, Graduate Coordinator, 415-338-3182, Fax: 415-338-1739, E-mail: katynka@sfsu.edu.
Website: http://ethnicstudies.sfsu.edu/

United Theological Seminary of the Twin Cities, Graduate Programs, New Brighton, MN 55112-2598. Offers advanced theological studies (Diploma); justice and peace studies (M Div, MA); leadership toward racial justice (M Div, MA, Certificate); Methodist studies (M Div, MA, Certificate); ministry (D Min); ministry renewal and professional development (Certificate); pastoral care and counseling (M Div, MA, MARL); religion and theology (MA); theological and religious studies (Certificate); theology and the arts (M Div, MA); urban ministry (M Div, MA, MARL); women's studies: religion, theology and ministry (M Div, MA). *Accreditation:* ACIPE; ATS. *Program availability:* Part-time, evening/weekend. *Degree requirements:* For master's, thesis; for doctorate, comprehensive exam, thesis/dissertation. *Entrance requirements:* For master's, minimum GPA of 2.75; strong analytical, reflective thinking and writing skills; vocational and academic goals compatible with those of Seminary; for doctorate, M Div or equivalent, minimum GPA of 3.0, 3 years experience in professional ministry; for other advanced degree, BA or equivalent life experience; strong analytical, reflective thinking and writing skills (Certificate); proficiency in English language, previous study of theology at a theological school, recommendation of student's denomination (Diploma). Additional exam requirements/recommendations for international students: Required—TOEFL (minimum score 550 paper-based).

Université Laval, Faculty of Letters, Department of History, Programs in Ethnology of French-Speaking People in North America, Québec, QC G1K 7P4, Canada. Offers MA, PhD. Terminal master's awarded for partial completion of doctoral program. *Degree requirements:* For master's, thesis; for doctorate, comprehensive exam, thesis/dissertation. *Entrance requirements:* For master's and doctorate, English exam (comprehension of written English), knowledge of French. Electronic applications accepted.

The University of British Columbia, Faculty of Arts, Department of Classical, Near Eastern and Religious Studies, Program in Ancient Culture, Religion and Ethnicity, Vancouver, BC V6T 1Z1, Canada. Offers MA. *Degree requirements:* For master's, thesis.

University of California, Berkeley, Graduate Division, College of Letters and Science, Department of Ethnic Studies, Berkeley, CA 94720-1500. Offers PhD. *Degree requirements:* For doctorate, one foreign language, thesis/dissertation, qualifying exam. *Entrance requirements:* For doctorate, minimum GPA of 3.0, 3 letters of recommendation. Electronic applications accepted. *Faculty research:* Gender and race, Asian American visual art, racial theory and politics, Chicana/o literature and visual arts, history of Native North Americans.

University of California, Riverside, Graduate Division, Department of Ethnic Studies, Riverside, CA 92521. Offers cultural politics and production (PhD). Terminal master's awarded for partial completion of doctoral program. *Degree requirements:* For doctorate, variable foreign language requirement, comprehensive exam, thesis/dissertation. *Entrance requirements:* For doctorate, GRE, writing sample, statement of purpose, personal history statement, 3 letters of recommendation. Additional exam requirements/recommendations for international students: Required—TOEFL (minimum score 550 paper-based; 80 iBT); Recommended—IELTS (minimum score 7). Electronic applications accepted. *Expenses:* Tuition, state resident: full-time $5746. Tuition,

nonresident: full-time $10,780. Tuition and fees vary according to campus/location and program. *Faculty research:* The political economy of race, class, gender, sexuality, cultural production, the state, law, criminal justice and grass roots responses.

University of California, San Diego, Graduate Division, Department of Ethnic Studies, La Jolla, CA 92093. Offers PhD. *Students:* 39 full-time (29 women). 77 applicants, 17% accepted, 5 enrolled. In 2017, 6 doctorates awarded. *Degree requirements:* For doctorate, one foreign language, comprehensive exam, thesis/dissertation. *Entrance requirements:* For doctorate, GRE General Test, writing sample. Additional exam requirements/recommendations for international students: Required—TOEFL (minimum score 550 paper-based; 80 iBT), IELTS (minimum score 7). *Application deadline:* For fall admission, 1/5 for domestic students. Application fee: $105 ($125 for international students). Electronic applications accepted. *Financial support:* Fellowships, teaching assistantships, and scholarships/grants available. Financial award applicants required to submit FAFSA. *Faculty research:* Cultural studies, gender studies, refugee studies, Native American history and culture, theories of performance. *Unit head:* Dayo Gore, Chair, 858-534-8194, E-mail: dgore@ucsd.edu. *Application contact:* Christa Ludeking, Graduate Coordinator, 858-534-6040, E-mail: ethnicstudiesphd@ucsd.edu.
Website: http://ethnicstudies.ucsd.edu

University of Colorado Boulder, Graduate School, College of Arts and Sciences, Department of Ethnic Studies, Boulder, CO 80309. Offers PhD. *Faculty:* 9 full-time (3 women). *Students:* 9 full-time (5 women); includes 8 minority (2 Black or African American, non-Hispanic/Latino; 1 American Indian or Alaska Native, non-Hispanic/Latino; 5 Hispanic/Latino), 1 international. Average age 34. 15 applicants, 40% accepted, 3 enrolled. *Application deadline:* For fall admission, 12/1 for domestic students; for spring admission, 12/1 for domestic students. Application fee: $60 ($80 for international students). Electronic applications accepted. Application fee is waived when completed online. *Financial support:* In 2017-18, 25 students received support, including 8 teaching assistantships with full and partial tuition reimbursements available (averaging $30,056 per year); institutionally sponsored loans, scholarships/grants, health care benefits, and unspecified assistantships also available. Financial award application deadline: 2/15; financial award applicants required to submit FAFSA. *Faculty research:* American history; ethnic studies; history; racism/race relations; social history. *Total annual research expenditures:* $13,500. *Application contact:* E-mail:

grad.ethnst@colorado.edu.
Website: http://ethnicstudies.colorado.edu/

University of New Mexico, Graduate Studies, College of Arts and Sciences, Program in Anthropology, Albuquerque, NM 87131-2039. Offers archaeology (MA, MS, PhD); ethnology (MA, MS, PhD); evolutionary anthropology (PhD); public archaeology (MA, MS, PhD). *Faculty:* 28 full-time (10 women), 2 part-time/adjunct (0 women). *Students:* 47 full-time (34 women), 58 part-time (34 women); includes 25 minority (4 American Indian or Alaska Native, non-Hispanic/Latino; 1 Asian, non-Hispanic/Latino; 15 Hispanic/Latino; 5 Two or more races, non-Hispanic/Latino), 8 international. Average age 34. 58 applicants, 34% accepted, 20 enrolled. In 2017, 18 master's, 14 doctorates awarded. Terminal master's awarded for partial completion of doctoral program. *Degree requirements:* For master's, comprehensive exam (for some programs), thesis or alternative, 1-2 exams; for doctorate, one foreign language, comprehensive exam, thesis/dissertation, exam, proposal, oral defense, skill and/or second language. *Entrance requirements:* For master's and doctorate, GRE General Test, 3 letters of recommendation, letter of interest, transcripts. Additional exam requirements/recommendations for international students: Required—TOEFL (minimum score 550 paper-based), IELTS (minimum score 7). *Application deadline:* For fall admission, 1/4 for domestic and international students. Application fee: $50. Electronic applications accepted. *Financial support:* Fellowships, research assistantships with partial tuition reimbursements, teaching assistantships with partial tuition reimbursements, career-related internships or fieldwork, Federal Work-Study, institutionally sponsored loans, scholarships/grants, traineeships, health care benefits, tuition waivers (partial), and unspecified assistantships available. Support available to part-time students. Financial award application deadline: 3/1; financial award applicants required to submit FAFSA. *Faculty research:* Ethnology, archaeology, evolutionary anthropology, environment, water and land use, gender and social frameworks, Greater Southwest, Latin America, political economy, public anthropology. *Total annual research expenditures:* $875,790. *Unit head:* Michael W. Graves, Chair, 505-277-4524, Fax: 505-277-0874, E-mail: mwgraves@unm.edu. *Application contact:* Erika E. Gerety, Program Advisement Coordinator, 505-277-2732, Fax: 505-277-0874, E-mail: erika@unm.edu.
Website: http://www.unm.edu/~anthro/

Folklore

The George Washington University, Columbian College of Arts and Sciences, Department of American Studies, Washington, DC 20052. Offers American studies (PhD); folk life (MA); historic preservation (MA); material culture (MA). *Program availability:* Part-time, evening/weekend. *Faculty:* 10 full-time (5 women), 1 part-time/adjunct (0 women). *Students:* 18 full-time (14 women), 17 part-time (13 women); includes 13 minority (6 Black or African American, non-Hispanic/Latino; 3 Asian, non-Hispanic/Latino; 2 Hispanic/Latino; 2 Two or more races, non-Hispanic/Latino). Average age 28. 103 applicants, 31% accepted, 12 enrolled. In 2017, 9 master's, 2 doctorates awarded. Terminal master's awarded for partial completion of doctoral program. *Degree requirements:* For master's, comprehensive exam; for doctorate, one foreign language, thesis/dissertation, general exam. *Entrance requirements:* For master's and doctorate, GRE General Test, minimum GPA of 3.0. Additional exam requirements/recommendations for international students: Required—TOEFL (minimum score 550 paper-based; 80 iBT). *Application deadline:* For fall admission, 1/15 priority date for domestic and international students; for spring admission, 10/1 for domestic students. Application fee: $75. *Expenses:* Tuition: Full-time $28,800; part-time $1655 per credit hour. *Required fees:* $45; $2.75 per credit hour. *Financial support:* In 2017-18, 22 students received support. Fellowships, research assistantships, teaching assistantships, career-related internships or fieldwork, Federal Work-Study, institutionally sponsored loans, and tuition waivers available. Financial award application deadline: 1/15. *Unit head:* Melanie McAlister, Chair, 202-994-7244, E-mail: jam@gwu.edu. *Application contact:* Information Contact, 202-994-6070, Fax: 202-994-8651, E-mail: amst@gwu.edu.
Website: http://departments.columbian.gwu.edu/americanstudies/

Indiana University Bloomington, University Graduate School, College of Arts and Sciences, Department of Folklore and Ethnomusicology, Bloomington, IN 47405. Offers ethnomusicology (MA, PhD), including folklore. Terminal master's awarded for partial completion of doctoral program. *Degree requirements:* For master's, one foreign language, comprehensive exam, project, thesis, or exam; for doctorate, 2 foreign languages, comprehensive exam, thesis/dissertation. *Entrance requirements:* For master's, GRE General Test (minimum scores: 151 for Verbal, 150 for Quantitative, 4.5 for Analytical), minimum GPA of 3.0, writing sample, curriculum vitae, 3 letters of recommendation, personal statement; for doctorate, GRE General Test (minimum scores: 151 for Verbal, 150 for Quantitative, 4.5 for Analytical), minimum GPA of 3.0, writing sample, curriculum vitae, 3 letters of recommendation, personal statement, MA. Additional exam requirements/recommendations for international students: Required—TOEFL (minimum score 550 paper-based; 79 iBT). Electronic applications accepted. *Expenses:* Contact institution. *Faculty research:* Narrative, performance studies, material culture, popular culture, music, public practice.

Memorial University of Newfoundland, School of Graduate Studies, Department of Folklore, St. John's, NL A1C 5S7, Canada. Offers MA, PhD. *Program availability:* Part-time. *Degree requirements:* For master's, thesis optional; for doctorate, one foreign language, comprehensive exam, thesis/dissertation, oral thesis defense. *Entrance requirements:* For master's, 36 credit hours of course work in folklore, humanities, or social studies; honors degree; for doctorate, MA in folklore or related field. Electronic applications accepted. *Faculty research:* Narrative, folk life, belief theory, methodology, popular culture.

Penn State Harrisburg, Graduate School, School of Humanities, Middletown, PA 17057. Offers American studies (MA, PhD); communications (MA); folklore and ethnography (Certificate); heritage and museum practice (Certificate); humanities (MA). *Program availability:* Evening/weekend. *Unit head:* Dr. Mukund S. Kulkarni, Chancellor, 717-948-6105, Fax: 717-948-6452. *Application contact:* Robert W. Coffman, Jr., Director of Enrollment Management, Recruitment and Admissions, 717-948-6250, Fax: 717-948-6325, E-mail: hbgadmit@psu.edu.
Website: https://harrisburg.psu.edu/humanities

University of Alberta, Faculty of Graduate Studies and Research, Department of Modern Languages and Cultural Studies, Edmonton, AB T6G 2E1, Canada. Offers applied linguistics (Germanic, Romance, Slavic) (MA); French language, literatures and linguistics (PhD); French language, literatures, and linguistics (MA); Germanic languages, literatures and linguistics (PhD); Germanic languages, literatures, and

linguistics (MA); Italian studies (MA); Slavic languages and literatures (Russian, Ukrainian) (MA, PhD); Slavic linguistics (Russian, Ukrainian) (MA, PhD); Spanish and Latin American studies (MA, PhD); Ukrainian folklore (MA, PhD). *Program availability:* Part-time. *Degree requirements:* For master's, one foreign language, thesis; for doctorate, 2 foreign languages, comprehensive exam, thesis/dissertation. *Entrance requirements:* For master's and doctorate, 1 language other than English. Additional exam requirements/recommendations for international students: Required—Michigan English Language Assessment Battery or TOEFL (minimum score 550 paper-based). Electronic applications accepted. *Faculty research:* Russian/Ukrainian studies; German studies; contemporary Latin American, French and Francophone studies; Italian studies.

University of California, Berkeley, Graduate Division, College of Letters and Science, Department of Anthropology, Group in Folklore, Berkeley, CA 94720-1500. Offers MA. *Entrance requirements:* For master's, GRE General Test, minimum GPA of 3.0, 3 letters of recommendation. Additional exam requirements/recommendations for international students: Recommended—TOEFL (minimum score 570 paper-based; 90 iBT). Electronic applications accepted.

University of Louisiana at Lafayette, College of Liberal Arts, Department of English, Lafayette, LA 70504. Offers British and American literature (MA), including creative writing, folklore, rhetoric; creative writing (PhD); literature (PhD); rhetoric (PhD). *Program availability:* Part-time. Terminal master's awarded for partial completion of doctoral program. *Degree requirements:* For master's, one foreign language, thesis or alternative; for doctorate, 2 foreign languages, comprehensive exam, thesis/dissertation. *Entrance requirements:* For master's, GRE General Test, minimum GPA of 2.75; for doctorate, GRE General Test, minimum GPA of 3.0. Additional exam requirements/recommendations for international students: Required—TOEFL (minimum score 550 paper-based). Electronic applications accepted. *Faculty research:* Composition theory, Southern literature, medieval literature.

The University of North Carolina at Chapel Hill, Graduate School, College of Arts and Sciences, Curriculum in Folklore, Chapel Hill, NC 27599. Offers MA. *Degree requirements:* For master's, one foreign language, comprehensive exam, thesis. *Entrance requirements:* For master's, GRE General Test, minimum GPA of 3.0, writing sample. Electronic applications accepted. *Faculty research:* Public folklore, politics of culture, folklore and feminist theory, belief and health systems, Southern culture.

University of Oregon, Graduate School, College of Arts and Sciences, Folklore Program, Eugene, OR 97403. Offers independent study: folklore (MA, MS). *Program availability:* Part-time. *Degree requirements:* For master's, one foreign language, project or thesis. *Entrance requirements:* For master's, GRE General Test, minimum GPA of 3.0. Additional exam requirements/recommendations for international students: Required—TOEFL. *Faculty research:* American folklore, East European folklore, film and folklore, folk religion and belief, ballad.

The University of Texas at Austin, Graduate School, College of Liberal Arts, Department of Anthropology, Program in Cultural Forms, Austin, TX 78712-1111. Offers MA, PhD. *Program availability:* Part-time. Terminal master's awarded for partial completion of doctoral program. *Degree requirements:* For master's, one foreign language, thesis, report; for doctorate, one foreign language, thesis/dissertation. *Entrance requirements:* For master's and doctorate, GRE General Test. Electronic applications accepted. *Faculty research:* Expressive culture, gender, genre, folklore and culture of British Isles, ethnography of speaking.

University of Wisconsin–Madison, Graduate School, College of Letters and Science, Department of Scandinavian Studies, Madison, WI 53706-1380. Offers area studies (MA); folklore (PhD); literature (MA, PhD); philology (PhD). *Program availability:* Part-time. *Degree requirements:* For master's, 2 foreign languages, exam; for doctorate, thesis/dissertation, exam. *Entrance requirements:* For master's, minimum GPA of 3.25; for doctorate, minimum GPA of 3.5. Electronic applications accepted. *Faculty research:* Historical fiction, Icelandic poetry, nineteenth-century literature, theater, gender studies, folklore.

Utah State University, School of Graduate Studies, College of Humanities and Social Sciences, Department of English and Department of History, Program in American Studies, Logan, UT 84322. Offers folklore (MA, MS); western American literature and

culture (MA, MS). *Program availability:* Part-time, evening/weekend. *Degree requirements:* For master's, thesis or alternative. *Entrance requirements:* For master's, GRE General Test or MAT, minimum GPA of 3.0, 3 letters of recommendation, writing sample. Additional exam requirements/recommendations for international students: Required—TOEFL. *Faculty research:* Folklore and folklife, American culture, regional studies, material culture, Jewish folklore, Native American folklore.

Gender Studies

Adler University, Graduate Programs, MA in Applied Psychology Program, Chicago, IL 60602. Offers gender and sexuality studies (MA). *Program availability:* Online learning. *Degree requirements:* For master's, thesis or capstone.

American University, College of Arts and Sciences, Critical Race, Gender, and Culture Studies Collaborative, Washington, DC 20016-8030. Offers Asian studies (Graduate Certificate); women's, gender, and sexuality studies (Graduate Certificate). *Faculty:* 4 full-time (3 women), 10 part-time/adjunct (5 women). In 2017, 3 Graduate Certificates awarded. *Entrance requirements:* Additional exam requirements/recommendations for international students: Required—TOEFL (minimum score 600 paper-based; 100 iBT). *Application deadline:* Applications are processed on a rolling basis. *Expenses: Tuition:* Full-time $29,556. *Required fees:* $690. Tuition and fees vary according to course load and program. *Unit head:* Dr. Peter Starr, Dean, 202-885-2446, Fax: 202-885-2429, E-mail: pstarr@american.edu. *Application contact:* Jonathan Harper, Associate Director, Graduate Recruitment, 202-885-3622, Fax: 202-885-1505, E-mail: jharper@american.edu.
Website: http://www.american.edu/cas/crgc/

American University, College of Arts and Sciences, Department of Economics, Washington, DC 20016-8029. Offers applied microeconomics (Certificate); economics (MA, PhD); gender analysis in economics (Certificate); international economic relations (Certificate); international economics (MA). *Program availability:* Part-time, evening/weekend, 100% online. *Faculty:* 27 full-time (7 women), 5 part-time/adjunct (2 women). *Students:* 107 full-time (52 women), 59 part-time (21 women); includes 28 minority (10 Black or African American, non-Hispanic/Latino; 1 American Indian or Alaska Native, non-Hispanic/Latino; 8 Asian, non-Hispanic/Latino; 7 Hispanic/Latino; 2 Two or more races, non-Hispanic/Latino), 55 international. Average age 32. 191 applicants, 85% accepted, 38 enrolled. In 2017, 37 master's, 9 doctorates, 1 other advanced degree awarded. Terminal master's awarded for partial completion of doctoral program. *Degree requirements:* For master's, comprehensive exam, thesis or alternative; for doctorate, comprehensive exam, thesis/dissertation. *Entrance requirements:* For master's and doctorate, GRE, statement of purpose, transcripts, 2 letters of recommendation, resume; for Certificate, bachelor's degree, statement of purpose, transcripts, resume. Additional exam requirements/recommendations for international students: Required—TOEFL (minimum score 600 paper-based; 100 iBT). *Application deadline:* For fall admission, 3/1 for domestic students; for spring admission, 11/1 for domestic students. Applications are processed on a rolling basis. Application fee: $55. Electronic applications accepted. *Expenses:* Contact institution. *Financial support:* Research assistantships, teaching assistantships, institutionally sponsored loans, and unspecified assistantships available. Financial award application deadline: 2/1; financial award applicants required to submit FAFSA. *Faculty research:* Political economy, development, labor, gender. *Unit head:* Dr. Mieke Meurs, Department Chair, 202-885-3776, E-mail: mmeurs@american.edu. *Application contact:* Jonathan Harper, Assistant Director, Graduate Recruitment, 202-855-3622, E-mail: jharper@american.edu.
Website: http://www.american.edu/cas/economics/

The American University in Cairo, School of Global Affairs and Public Policy, Cairo, Egypt. Offers gender and women's studies (MA); global affairs (MGA); international and comparative law (LL M); international human rights law (MA); journalism and mass communication (MA); Middle East studies (MA); migration and refugee studies (MA, Diploma); public administration (MPA); public policy (MPP); television and digital journalism (MA). *Program availability:* Part-time, evening/weekend. *Faculty:* 26 full-time (11 women), 4 part-time/adjunct (3 women). *Students:* 65 full-time (50 women), 201 part-time (136 women), 39 international. Average age 29. 357 applicants, 51% accepted, 72 enrolled. In 2017, 94 master's awarded. *Degree requirements:* For master's, comprehensive exam (for some programs), thesis (for some programs). *Entrance requirements:* Additional exam requirements/recommendations for international students: Required—TOEFL (minimum score 450 paper-based; 45 iBT), IELTS (minimum score 5). *Application deadline:* For fall admission, 2/1 for domestic and international students; for spring admission, 10/15 for domestic and international students. Applications are processed on a rolling basis. Application fee: $85. Electronic applications accepted. *Expenses:* Contact institution. *Financial support:* Fellowships with partial tuition reimbursements, scholarships/grants, and unspecified assistantships available. Financial award application deadline: 3/10. *Faculty research:* Law, media and journalism; public policy and public administration; gender studies; Middle East Studies; global affairs; refugees studies. *Unit head:* Dr. Nabil Fahmy, Dean, 20-2-2615-2671, E-mail: nfahmy@aucegypt.edu. *Application contact:* Maha Hegazi, Director for Graduate Admissions, 20-2-2615-1462, E-mail: mahahegazi@aucegypt.edu.
Website: http://www.aucegypt.edu/GAPP/Pages/default.aspx

Arizona State University at the Tempe campus, College of Liberal Arts and Sciences, School of Social Transformation, Tempe, AZ 85287-4902. Offers African studies (Graduate Certificate); gender studies (PhD, Graduate Certificate); justice studies (MS, PhD); social and cultural pedagogy (MA); socio-economic justice (Graduate Certificate); PhD/JD. *Program availability:* Part-time. Terminal master's awarded for partial completion of doctoral program. *Degree requirements:* For master's, thesis or alternative, interactive Program of Study (iPOS) submitted before completing 50 percent of required credit hours; for doctorate, comprehensive exam, thesis/dissertation, interactive Program of Study (iPOS) submitted before completing 50 percent of required credit hours. *Entrance requirements:* For master's, GRE or LSAT, minimum GPA of 3.0 or equivalent in last 2 years of work leading to bachelor's degree; for doctorate, GRE or LSAT (for justice studies program), minimum GPA of 3.0 or equivalent in last 2 years of work leading to bachelor's degree. Additional exam requirements/recommendations for international students: Required—TOEFL, IELTS, or PTE. Electronic applications accepted.

Brandeis University, Graduate School of Arts and Sciences, Department of Anthropology, Waltham, MA 02454-9110. Offers anthropology/women's, gender, and sexuality studies (MA); Mesoamerican archaeology (MA, PhD); sociocultural anthropology (MA, PhD). *Program availability:* Part-time. *Faculty:* 9 full-time (5 women), 4 part-time/adjunct (1 woman). *Students:* 35 full-time (24 women), 1 part-time (0 women); includes 6 minority (3 Black or African American, non-Hispanic/Latino; 1 Hispanic/Latino; 2 Two or more races, non-Hispanic/Latino), 6 international. Average age 28. 50 applicants, 48% accepted, 8 enrolled. In 2017, 11 master's awarded. Terminal master's awarded for partial completion of doctoral program. *Degree requirements:* For master's, thesis; for doctorate, one foreign language, comprehensive exam, thesis/dissertation. *Entrance requirements:* For master's and doctorate, GRE General Test, sample of written work, resume, letters of recommendation, transcript. Additional exam requirements/recommendations for international students: Required—PTE (minimum score 68), TOEFL (minimum score 600 paper-based, 100 iBT) or IELTS (7). *Application deadline:* For fall admission, 1/15 priority date for domestic and international students. Applications are processed on a rolling basis. Application fee: $75. Electronic applications accepted. *Expenses: Tuition:* Full-time $48,720. *Required fees:* $88. Tuition and fees vary according to course load, degree level, program and student level. *Financial support:* In 2017–18, 34 students received support, including 11 fellowships with full tuition reimbursements available (averaging $24,480 per year), 15 teaching assistantships with partial tuition reimbursements available (averaging $3,200 per year); scholarships/grants, health care benefits, and tuition waivers (partial) also available. Support available to part-time students. Financial award application deadline: 4/15; financial award applicants required to submit FAFSA. *Faculty research:* Sociocultural anthropology, archaeology, gender and sexuality, linguistic anthropology, physical anthropology. *Unit head:* Dr. Sarah Lamb, Director of Graduate Studies, 781-736-2210, Fax: 781-736-2232, E-mail: lamb@brandeis.edu. *Application contact:* Laurel Carpenter, Academic Administrator, 781-736-2210, Fax: 781-736-2232, E-mail: lcarpent@brandeis.edu.
Website: http://www.brandeis.edu/gsas/programs/anthropology.html

Brandeis University, Graduate School of Arts and Sciences, Department of English, Waltham, MA 02454-9110. Offers English (MA, PhD); English/women's, gender, and sexuality studies (MA). *Program availability:* Part-time. *Faculty:* 18 full-time (9 women), 12 part-time/adjunct (6 women). *Students:* 40 full-time (22 women), 3 part-time (2 women); includes 8 minority (2 Black or African American, non-Hispanic/Latino; 1 Asian, non-Hispanic/Latino; 3 Hispanic/Latino; 2 Two or more races, non-Hispanic/Latino), 8 international. Average age 33. 134 applicants, 27% accepted, 6 enrolled. In 2017, 3 master's, 5 doctorates awarded. Terminal master's awarded for partial completion of doctoral program. *Degree requirements:* For master's, one foreign language, thesis or alternative; for doctorate, 2 foreign languages, thesis/dissertation, field exam, symposium presentation, prospectus defense. *Entrance requirements:* For master's, GRE, resume, critical writing sample, letters of recommendation, statement of purpose, transcripts; for doctorate, GRE General Test, GRE Subject Test, resume, critical writing sample, letters of recommendation, statement of purpose, transcripts. Additional exam requirements/recommendations for international students: Required—PTE (minimum score 68), TOEFL (minimum score 600 paper-based, 100 iBT) or IELTS (7). *Application deadline:* For fall admission, 1/5 for domestic students. Application fee: $75. Electronic applications accepted. *Expenses: Tuition:* Full-time $48,720. *Required fees:* $88. Tuition and fees vary according to course load, degree level, program and student level. *Financial support:* In 2017–18, 31 students received support, including 24 fellowships with full tuition reimbursements available (averaging $24,480 per year), 3 teaching assistantships with partial tuition reimbursements available (averaging $3,200 per year); Federal Work-Study, scholarships/grants, health care benefits, and tuition waivers (partial) also available. Support available to part-time students. Financial award application deadline: 4/15; financial award applicants required to submit FAFSA. *Faculty research:* Feminist and gender theory, American literature and post-Colonial theory, early modern (Renaissance) English literature, modernism, literature and science, literary theory and philosophy, contemporary poetry. *Unit head:* Dr. David Sherman, Director of Graduate Studies, 781-736-2130, E-mail: chaucer@brandeis.edu. *Application contact:* Lisa Pannella, Department Academic Administrator, 781-736-2130, E-mail: pannella@brandeis.edu.
Website: http://www.brandeis.edu/gsas/programs/english.html

Brandeis University, Graduate School of Arts and Sciences, Department of Near Eastern and Judaic Studies, Waltham, MA 02454-9110. Offers Near Eastern and Judaic studies (MA, PhD); near Eastern and Judaic studies/conflict resolution and coexistence (MA); near Eastern and Judaic studies/Jewish professional leadership (MA); near Eastern and Judaic studies/women's, gender, and sexuality studies (MA); teaching of Hebrew (MAT). Offered jointly with The Heller School of Social Policy and Management. *Program availability:* Part-time. *Faculty:* 24 full-time (10 women), 6 part-time/adjunct (3 women). *Students:* 41 full-time (17 women), 2 part-time (1 woman); includes 7 minority (2 Black or African American, non-Hispanic/Latino; 1 Asian, non-Hispanic/Latino; 4 Hispanic/Latino), 9 international. Average age 33. 47 applicants, 45% accepted, 4 enrolled. In 2017, 8 master's, 3 doctorates awarded. Terminal master's awarded for partial completion of doctoral program. *Degree requirements:* For master's, one foreign language, thesis or alternative, proseminar, capstone; for doctorate, variable foreign language requirement, comprehensive exam, thesis/dissertation. *Entrance requirements:* For master's and doctorate, GRE General Test (recommended), letters of recommendation, transcripts, statement of purpose, writing sample, resume. Additional exam requirements/recommendations for international students: Required—PTE (minimum score 68), TOEFL (minimum score 600 paper-based, 100 iBT) or IELTS (7). *Application deadline:* For fall admission, 1/15 priority date for domestic students. Applications are processed on a rolling basis. Application fee: $75. Electronic applications accepted. *Expenses: Tuition:* Full-time $48,720. *Required fees:* $88. Tuition and fees vary according to course load, degree level, program and student level. *Financial support:* In 2017–18, 29 students received support, including 20 fellowships with full tuition reimbursements available (averaging $24,480 per year), 1 teaching assistantship with partial tuition reimbursement available (averaging $2,500 per year); Federal Work-Study, scholarships/grants, health care benefits, and tuition waivers (partial) also available. Support available to part-time students. Financial award application deadline: 4/15; financial award applicants required to submit FAFSA. *Faculty research:* Bible and ancient Near East, Judaic Studies, Israel Studies, modern Middle East, Arabic and Islamic civilizations. *Unit head:* Dr. Eugene Sheppard, Department Chair, 781-736-2950, E-mail: sheppard@brandeis.edu. *Application contact:* Jean Mannion, Department Administrator, 781-736-2950, E-mail: mannion@brandeis.edu.
Website: http://www.brandeis.edu/gsas/programs/nejs.html

Brandeis University, Graduate School of Arts and Sciences, Program in Women's, Gender, and Sexuality Studies, Waltham, MA 02454-9110. Offers anthropology/women's, gender, and sexuality studies (MA); English/women's, gender, and sexuality studies (MA); near Eastern and Judaic studies /women's, gender, and sexuality studies (MA); public policy/women's, gender, and sexuality studies (MA); sociology/women's,

gender, and sexuality studies (MA); sustainable international development/women's, gender, and sexuality studies (MA); women's, gender, and sexuality studies (MA). Offered jointly with The Heller School of Social Policy and Management. *Students:* 10 full-time (all women); includes 2 minority (1 Hispanic/Latino; 1 Two or more races, non-Hispanic/Latino). Average age 25. 42 applicants, 48% accepted, 8 enrolled. In 2017, 8 master's awarded. *Degree requirements:* For master's, thesis. *Entrance requirements:* For master's, GRE General Test, critical writing sample, resume, statement of purpose, transcripts, letters of recommendation. Additional exam requirements/recommendations for international students: Required—PTE (minimum score 68), TOEFL (minimum score 600 paper-based, 100 iBT) or IELTS (7). *Application deadline:* For fall admission, 1/15 for domestic students. Application fee: $75. Electronic applications accepted. *Expenses: Tuition:* Full-time $48,720. *Required fees:* $88. Tuition and fees vary according to course load, degree level, program and student level. *Financial support:* In 2017–18, 6 students received support, including 7 teaching assistantships with partial tuition reimbursements available (averaging $3,200 per year); fellowships, scholarships/grants, and tuition waivers (partial) also available. Financial award application deadline: 4/15; financial award applicants required to submit FAFSA. *Unit head:* Dr. ChaeRan Freeze, Director of Graduate Study, 781-736-2987, E-mail: cfreeze@brandeis.edu. *Application contact:* Shannon Kearns, Department Administrator, 781-736-3045, E-mail: skearns@brandeis.edu.
Website: http://www.brandeis.edu/gsas/programs/wgs.html

Carnegie Mellon University, Dietrich College of Humanities and Social Sciences, Department of History, Pittsburgh, PA 15213-3891. Offers African and African-American diaspora (PhD); culture and power (PhD); labor, politics and social movements (PhD); technology, environment, science and health (PhD); women, gender and the family (PhD). *Program availability:* Part-time. *Degree requirements:* For doctorate, oral and written comprehensive exams, dissertation defense. *Entrance requirements:* For doctorate, GRE General Test. Additional exam requirements/recommendations for international students: Required—TOEFL. Electronic applications accepted. *Faculty research:* Anthropology and history, African-American history, technology/environment, cultural history analysis.

Central European University, Department of Gender Studies, 1051, Hungary. Offers MA, PhD. *Faculty:* 12 full-time (11 women), 4 part-time/adjunct (all women). *Students:* 77 full-time (60 women). Average age 29. 353 applicants, 14% accepted, 35 enrolled. In 2017, 39 master's, 2 doctorates awarded. *Degree requirements:* For master's, one foreign language, thesis; for doctorate, one foreign language, comprehensive exam, thesis/dissertation. *Entrance requirements:* For master's and doctorate, essay, interview, statement of purpose. Additional exam requirements/recommendations for international students: Required—TOEFL (minimum score 570 paper-based); Recommended—IELTS (minimum score 6.5). *Application deadline:* For fall admission, 2/4 for domestic and international students. Application fee: $30. Electronic applications accepted. *Expenses: Tuition:* Full-time 12,000 euros. *Required fees:* 230 euros. One-time fee: 30 euros full-time. Tuition and fees vary according to course level, course load, degree level and program. *Financial support:* Fellowships, career-related internships or fieldwork, scholarships/grants, health care benefits, and tuition waivers (full and partial) available. Financial award application deadline: 2/4. *Faculty research:* Theories of gender, gendering theory; science and gender; activism, social movements and policy; gender dimensions of post-state socialism; gendered borders, nationalism, and transnational flows; political violence, war and gender; raced and sexed identities; cultural studies; feminist knowledge production. *Unit head:* Jasmina Lukic, Head of Department, 36 1 327-3034, Fax: 36-1-327-3296, E-mail: gender@ceu.edu. *Application contact:* Zsuzsanna Jaszberenyi, Admissions Officer, 361-324-3009, Fax: 367-327-3211, E-mail: admissions@ceu.edu.
Website: http://gender.ceu.edu/

Central Michigan University, College of Graduate Studies, College of Humanities and Social and Behavioral Sciences, Program in Humanities, Mount Pleasant, MI 48859. Offers humanities (MA), including contemporary issues in the humanities: race, class, and gender, images and ideas of self, Native American issues in modern culture, popular culture studies, the rise of industrial society. *Program availability:* Part-time, evening/weekend. *Degree requirements:* For master's, thesis or alternative. Electronic applications accepted. *Faculty research:* Rise of industrial society; images and ideas of self; contemporary issues of race, class, and gender; popular culture; Native American issues in modern culture.

The College of New Jersey, Office of Graduate and Advancing Education, School of Humanities and Social Sciences, Department of Women's and Gender Studies, Ewing, NJ 08628. Offers gender studies (Certificate). *Program availability:* Part-time. *Entrance requirements:* For degree, two letters of recommendation, official transcripts, essay. Additional exam requirements/recommendations for international students: Required—TOEFL. Electronic applications accepted.

Cornell University, Graduate School, Graduate Fields of Arts and Sciences, Field of Sociology, Ithaca, NY 14853. Offers economy and society (MA, PhD); gender and life course (MA, PhD); methodology (MA, PhD); organizations (MA, PhD); policy analysis (MA, PhD); political sociology/social movements (MA, PhD); racial and ethnic relations (MA, PhD); social networks (MA, PhD); social psychology (MA, PhD); social stratification (MA, PhD). Terminal master's awarded for partial completion of doctoral program. *Degree requirements:* For master's, thesis; for doctorate, thesis/dissertation, 1 year of teaching experience. *Entrance requirements:* For master's and doctorate, GRE General Test, 2 letters of recommendation, writing sample. Additional exam requirements/recommendations for international students: Required—TOEFL (minimum score 550 paper-based; 77 iBT). Electronic applications accepted. *Faculty research:* Comparative societal analysis, work and family, simulations, social class and mobility, racial segregation and inequality.

Delta State University, Graduate Programs, College of Arts and Sciences, Program in Liberal Studies, Cleveland, MS 38733-0001. Offers evolving human voices (MALS); gender and diversity studies (MALS); globalization studies (MALS); Mississippi Delta studies (MALS); philosophy (MALS); religious studies (MALS). *Degree requirements:* For master's, oral and/or written comprehensive exam.

DePaul University, College of Liberal Arts and Social Sciences, Chicago, IL 60614. Offers Arabic (MA); Chinese (MA); critical ethnic studies (MA); English (MA); French (MA); German (MA); history (MA); interdisciplinary studies (MA, MS); international public service (MS); international studies (MA); Italian (MA); Japanese (MA); liberal studies (MA); nonprofit management (MNM); public administration (MPA); public health (MPH); public policy (MPP); public service management (MS); refugee and forced migration studies (MS); social work (MSW); sociology (MA); Spanish (MA); sustainable urban development (MA); women's and gender studies (MA); writing and publishing (MA); writing, rhetoric and discourse (MA); MA/PhD. *Program availability:* Part-time, evening/weekend, online learning. Terminal master's awarded for partial completion of doctoral program. *Degree requirements:* For master's, variable foreign language requirement, comprehensive exam (for some programs), thesis (for some programs). *Application deadline:* Applications are processed on a rolling basis. Application fee: $40. Electronic applications accepted. *Financial support:* Applicants required to submit FAFSA. *Unit head:* Dr. Guillermo Vasquez de Velasco, Dean, 773-325-7305. *Application contact:* Ann Spittle, Director of Graduate Admission, 773-325-8369, Fax: 312-476-3244, E-mail: graddepaul@depaul.edu.
Website: http://las.depaul.edu/

Dominican University of California, School of Liberal Arts and Education, Humanities Program, San Rafael, CA 94901-2298. Offers applied music (MA); art history (MA); creative writing (MA); gender studies (MA); history (MA); philosophy (MA); political theory (MA); religion (MA). *Program availability:* Part-time. *Faculty:* 7 full-time (4 women), 1 (woman) part-time/adjunct. *Students:* 6 full-time (5 women), 16 part-time (12 women); includes 8 minority (3 Black or African American, non-Hispanic/Latino; 4 Hispanic/Latino; 1 Two or more races, non-Hispanic/Latino), 2 international. Average age 45. 7 applicants, 100% accepted, 5 enrolled. In 2017, 14 master's awarded. *Degree requirements:* For master's, thesis or alternative. *Entrance requirements:* For master's, minimum GPA of 3.0, interview. Additional exam requirements/recommendations for international students: Required—TOEFL (minimum score 550 paper-based; 80 iBT), IELTS (minimum score 6.5). *Application deadline:* For fall admission, 5/15 priority date for domestic and international students; for spring admission, 11/15 priority date for domestic and international students. Applications are processed on a rolling basis. Application fee: $0. Electronic applications accepted. *Expenses: Tuition:* Full-time $17,370; part-time $965 per credit. *Required fees:* $150 per semester. Tuition and fees vary according to course load and program. *Financial support:* In 2017–18, 4 students received support. Scholarships/grants available. Support available to part-time students. Financial award application deadline: 3/2; financial award applicants required to submit FAFSA. *Unit head:* Joan Baranow, Program Director, 415-485-3264, E-mail: joan.baranow@dominican.edu. *Application contact:* Michael Lavigna, Assistant Director of Graduate Admissions, 415-485-3253, Fax: 415-485-3214, E-mail: gradmissions@dominican.edu.
Website: https://www.dominican.edu/academics/lae/graduate-programs/ma-in-humanities/index_html

Eastern Michigan University, Graduate School, College of Arts and Sciences, Department of Women's and Gender Studies, Ypsilanti, MI 48197. Offers MA, Graduate Certificate. *Program availability:* Part-time, evening/weekend. *Faculty:* 3 full-time (all women). *Students:* 6 full-time (4 women), 10 part-time (all women); includes 5 minority (4 Black or African American, non-Hispanic/Latino; 1 Two or more races, non-Hispanic/Latino), 1 international. Average age 31. 14 applicants, 86% accepted, 8 enrolled. In 2017, 4 master's, 1 other advanced degree awarded. *Degree requirements:* For master's, thesis, research project, or practicum. *Entrance requirements:* Additional exam requirements/recommendations for international students: Required—TOEFL. *Application deadline:* For fall admission, 6/15 for domestic and international students; for winter admission, 9/15 for domestic and international students; for spring admission, 3/1 for domestic and international students. Applications are processed on a rolling basis. Application fee: $45. *Financial support:* Fellowships, research assistantships with full tuition reimbursements, teaching assistantships with full tuition reimbursements, career-related internships or fieldwork, Federal Work-Study, institutionally sponsored loans, scholarships/grants, tuition waivers (partial), and unspecified assistantships available. Support available to part-time students. Financial award applicants required to submit FAFSA. *Unit head:* Dr. Peter Higgins, Interim Department Head, 734-487-1177, Fax: 734-487-5029, E-mail: phiggin1@emich.edu.
Website: http://www.emich.edu/wgstudies/

George Mason University, College of Humanities and Social Sciences, Interdisciplinary Studies Program, Fairfax, VA 22030. Offers computational social science (MAIS); energy and sustainability (MAIS); folklore studies (MAIS); higher education (MAIS); individualized studies (MAIS); religion, culture, and values (MAIS); social entrepreneurship (MAIS); social justice and human rights (MAIS); war and the military in society (MAIS); women and gender studies (MAIS). *Faculty:* 10 full-time (3 women), 15 part-time/adjunct (7 women). *Students:* 29 full-time (23 women), 76 part-time (50 women); includes 39 minority (18 Black or African American, non-Hispanic/Latino; 6 Asian, non-Hispanic/Latino; 11 Hispanic/Latino; 4 Two or more races, non-Hispanic/Latino), 7 international. Average age 32. 71 applicants, 90% accepted, 29 enrolled. In 2017, 23 master's awarded. *Degree requirements:* For master's, thesis or alternative, experiential learning (for some programs). *Entrance requirements:* Additional exam requirements/recommendations for international students: Required—TOEFL (minimum score 575 paper-based; 88 iBT), IELTS (minimum score 6.5), PTE (minimum score 59). *Application deadline:* For fall admission, 3/1 for domestic and international students; for spring admission, 10/15 for domestic and international students. Application fee: $75 ($80 for international students). Electronic applications accepted. *Expenses:* Tuition, state resident: full-time $11,228; part-time $459.50 per credit. Tuition, nonresident: full-time $30,932; part-time $1280.50 per credit. *Required fees:* $3252; $135.50 per credit. Part-time tuition and fees vary according to course load and program. *Financial support:* In 2017–18, 9 students received support, including 2 research assistantships with tuition reimbursements available, 7 teaching assistantships with tuition reimbursements available (averaging $8,599 per year); career-related internships or fieldwork, Federal Work-Study, scholarships/grants, unspecified assistantships, and health care benefits (for full-time research or teaching assistantship recipients) also available. Support available to part-time students. Financial award application deadline: 3/1; financial award applicants required to submit FAFSA. *Faculty research:* Combined English and folklore, religious and cultural studies (Christianity and Muslim society). *Unit head:* Meredith H. Lair, Director, 703-993-2159, Fax: 703-993-1251, E-mail: mlair@gmu.edu. *Application contact:* Morgan Fisher, Graduate Coordinator, 703-993-8762, E-mail: mfisherb@gmu.edu.
Website: http://mais.gmu.edu

The George Washington University, Elliott School of International Affairs, Program in Global Gender Policy, Washington, DC 20052. Offers Graduate Certificate. *Students:* 2 applicants, 100% accepted. *Expenses: Tuition:* Full-time $28,800; part-time $1655 per credit hour. *Required fees:* $45; $2.75 per credit hour. *Unit head:* Michael Brown, Dean, 202-994-1807, Fax: 202-994-0335, E-mail: brownm@gwu.edu. *Application contact:* Nicole A. Campbell, Director of Graduate Admissions, 202-994-7050, Fax: 202-994-9537, E-mail: esiagrad@gwu.edu.

Georgia State University, College of Arts and Sciences, Institute for Women's, Gender, and Sexuality Studies, Atlanta, GA 30302-3083. Offers MA, Graduate Certificate. *Program availability:* Part-time. *Faculty:* 6 full-time (5 women). *Students:* 14 full-time (all women), 2 part-time (both women); includes 11 minority (6 Black or African American, non-Hispanic/Latino; 1 Asian, non-Hispanic/Latino; 4 Two or more races, non-Hispanic/Latino), 2 international. Average age 29. 18 applicants, 89% accepted, 10 enrolled. In 2017, 5 master's, 5 other advanced degrees awarded. *Entrance requirements:* For master's and Graduate Certificate, GRE, two official transcripts from each college or university attended, three letters of recommendation addressing student's ability to undertake graduate study, 750-1000 word statement of purpose, academic writing sample. Additional exam requirements/recommendations for international students: Required—TOEFL (minimum score 550 paper-based; 80 iBT). *Application deadline:* For fall admission, 2/15 for domestic and international students. Application fee: $50. Electronic applications accepted. *Expenses:* Tuition, state resident: full-time $7020. Tuition, nonresident: full-time $22,518. *Required fees:* $2128. Tuition and fees vary according to degree level and program. *Financial support:* In 2017–18, research assistantships with full tuition reimbursements (averaging $7,000 per year), teaching

assistantships with full tuition reimbursements (averaging $7,500 per year) were awarded; career-related internships or fieldwork, health care benefits, and unspecified assistantships also available. Financial award application deadline: 2/15. *Faculty research:* Gender, sexuality, and youth studies; gender and neoliberalism; transnational feminisms; cultural studies; queer theories. *Unit head:* Dr. Susan Talburt, Director, 404-413-6581, Fax: 404-413-6585, E-mail: stalburt@gsu.edu. *Application contact:* Dr. Amira Jarmakani, Director of Graduate Studies, 404-413-6583, Fax: 404-413-6585, E-mail: amira@gsu.edu.
Website: http://www2.gsu.edu/~wwwwsi/

Indiana University Bloomington, University Graduate School, College of Arts and Sciences, Department of Gender Studies, Bloomington, IN 47405. Offers PhD. Terminal master's awarded for partial completion of doctoral program. *Degree requirements:* For doctorate, comprehensive exam. *Entrance requirements:* Additional exam requirements/recommendations for international students: Required—TOEFL (minimum score 550 paper-based, 79 iBT) or IELTS. Electronic applications accepted.

Indiana University Northwest, College of Arts and Sciences, Gary, IN 46408. Offers clinical counseling (MS), including drug and alcohol counseling; community development/urban studies (Graduate Certificate); computer information systems (Graduate Certificate); liberal studies (MLS); race-ethnic studies (Graduate Certificate); women's and gender studies (Graduate Certificate). *Program availability:* Part-time, evening/weekend. *Entrance requirements:* For master's, GRE (recommended for MS), minimum undergraduate GPA of 3.0, bachelor's degree from accredited university (for MS). Electronic applications accepted. *Expenses:* Contact institution.

Instituto Tecnologico de Santo Domingo, Graduate School, Area of Humanities and Social Sciences, Santo Domingo, Dominican Republic. Offers accounting (Certificate); adult education (Certificate); applied linguistics (MA); economics (MA); education (M Ed); educational psychology (MA, Certificate); gender and development (MA, Certificate); humanistic studies (MA); international marketing management (Certificate); international relations in the Caribbean basin (Certificate); intervention systems in family therapy (MA); linguistic and literary communication (Certificate); pedagogical support (MA); social science education (M Ed); sustainable human development (MA); terminal illness and death psychology (Certificate); youth and adult education (M Ed).

Kansas State University, Graduate School, College of Arts and Sciences, Department of Gender, Women and Sexuality Studies, Manhattan, KS 66506. Offers Graduate Certificate. *Entrance requirements:* For degree, minimum GPA of 3.0, letters of recommendation. Additional exam requirements/recommendations for international students: Required—TOEFL, TWE, or IELTS. *Faculty research:* Gender and violence, queer and transgender studies, girls' studies, ecofeminism, animal studies.

Memorial University of Newfoundland, School of Graduate Studies, Department of Sociology, St. John's, NL A1C 5S7, Canada. Offers gender (PhD); maritime sociology (PhD); sociology (M Phil, MA); work and development (PhD). *Program availability:* Part-time. *Degree requirements:* For master's, comprehensive exam, thesis optional, program journal (M Phil); for doctorate, one foreign language, comprehensive exam, thesis/dissertation, oral defense of thesis. *Entrance requirements:* For master's, 2nd class degree from university of recognized standing in area of study; for doctorate, MA, M Phil, or equivalent. Electronic applications accepted. *Faculty research:* Work and development, gender, maritime sociology.

Memorial University of Newfoundland, School of Graduate Studies, Interdisciplinary Program in Gender Studies, St. John's, NL A1C 5S7, Canada. Offers MGS. *Program availability:* Part-time. Electronic applications accepted.

Middle Tennessee State University, College of Graduate Studies, College of Liberal Arts, Program in Women's and Gender Studies, Murfreesboro, TN 37132. Offers Graduate Certificate. *Program availability:* Part-time, evening/weekend, online learning. Electronic applications accepted.

Minnesota State University Mankato, College of Graduate Studies and Research, College of Social and Behavioral Sciences, Department of Gender and Women's Studies, Mankato, MN 56001. Offers MS. *Program availability:* Part-time. *Degree requirements:* For master's, comprehensive exam, thesis or alternative. *Entrance requirements:* For master's, minimum GPA of 3.0, essay. Additional exam requirements/recommendations for international students: Required—TOEFL.

Murray State University, College of Humanities and Fine Arts, Department of English and Philosophy, Murray, KY 42071. Offers creative writing (MFA); English (MA); English pedagogy and technology (DA); gender studies (Certificate); teaching English to speakers of other languages (TESOL) (MA). *Program availability:* Part-time, 100% online, blended/hybrid learning. *Faculty:* 26 full-time (14 women), 1 part-time/adjunct (0 women). *Students:* 31 full-time (12 women), 91 part-time (61 women); includes 11 minority (5 Black or African American, non-Hispanic/Latino; 2 American Indian or Alaska Native, non-Hispanic/Latino; 2 Asian, non-Hispanic/Latino; 2 Two or more races, non-Hispanic/Latino), 23 international. Average age 36. 55 applicants, 95% accepted, 30 enrolled. In 2017, 21 master's awarded. *Entrance requirements:* For master's, doctorate, and Certificate, GRE or GMAT, minimum university GPA of 2.75. Additional exam requirements/recommendations for international students: Required—TOEFL (minimum score 527 paper-based; 71 iBT). *Application deadline:* Applications are processed on a rolling basis. Application fee: $40 ($50 for international students). Electronic applications accepted. *Expenses:* Tuition, state resident: full-time $9504. Tuition, nonresident: full-time $26,811. *International tuition:* $14,400 full-time. Tuition and fees vary according to course load, degree level and reciprocity agreements. *Financial support:* In 2017–18, 3 teaching assistantships were awarded; Federal Work-Study and unspecified assistantships also available. Financial award applicants required to submit FAFSA. *Unit head:* Dr. Sue Sroda, Chair, Department of English and Philosophy, 270-809-4715, Fax: 270-809-4545, E-mail: msroda@murraystate.edu. *Application contact:* Kaitlyn Burzynski, Interim Assistant Director for Graduate Admission and Records, 270-809-5732, Fax: 270-809-3780, E-mail: msu.graduateadmissions@murraystate.edu.
Website: https://www.murraystate.edu/academics/CollegesDepartments/CollegeOfHumanitiesAndFineArts/EnglishAndPhilosophy/index.aspx

New York University, School of Professional Studies, Center for Global Affairs, New York, NY 10012-1019. Offers global affairs (MS), including environment/energy policy, global gender studies, human rights and international law, international development and humanitarian assistance, international relations/global futures, peace building, private sector, transnational security. *Program availability:* Part-time, evening/weekend. *Students:* 143 full-time (90 women), 115 part-time (65 women); includes 73 minority (18 Black or African American, non-Hispanic/Latino; 16 Asian, non-Hispanic/Latino; 32 Hispanic/Latino; 7 Two or more races, non-Hispanic/Latino), 82 international. Average age 28. 285 applicants, 73% accepted, 79 enrolled. In 2017, 238 master's awarded. *Degree requirements:* For master's, thesis. *Entrance requirements:* For master's, GRE or GMAT (only upon request), bachelor's degree, resume with relevant professional work, internship or volunteer experience, two letters of recommendation, statement of purpose. Additional exam requirements/recommendations for international students: Required—TOEFL (minimum score 600 paper-based; 100 iBT), IELTS (minimum score 7). *Application deadline:* For fall admission, 2/1 priority date for domestic and international students; for spring admission, 10/15 priority date for domestic students, 8/15 priority date for international students. Applications are processed on a rolling basis. Application fee: $150. Electronic applications accepted. *Expenses:* $20,244 per term. *Financial support:* Fellowships, career-related internships or fieldwork, Federal Work-Study, scholarships/grants, and health care benefits available. Support available to part-time students. Financial award application deadline: 6/30; financial award applicants required to submit FAFSA. *Unit head:* Vera Jelinek, Divisional Dean and Clinical Associate Professor, 212-992-8380. *Application contact:* Office of Admissions, 212-998-7100, E-mail: sps.gradadmissions@nyu.edu.
Website: http://www.sps.nyu.edu/academics/departments/global-affairs.html

Northern Arizona University, College of Social and Behavioral Sciences, Women's and Gender Studies Program, Flagstaff, AZ 86011. Offers Graduate Certificate. *Program availability:* Part-time. *Faculty:* 5 full-time (all women). *Students:* 1 part-time (0 women). 1 applicant, 100% accepted, 1 enrolled. *Degree requirements:* For Graduate Certificate, comprehensive exam (for some programs). *Entrance requirements:* Additional exam requirements/recommendations for international students: Required—TOEFL (minimum score 80 iBT), IELTS (minimum score 6.5). *Application deadline:* For fall admission, 3/1 for domestic and international students; for spring admission, 10/1 for domestic and international students. Applications are processed on a rolling basis. Application fee: $65. Electronic applications accepted. *Expenses:* Tuition, state resident: full-time $9240; part-time $458 per credit hour. Tuition, nonresident: full-time $21,588; part-time $1199 per credit hour. *Required fees:* $1021; $14 per credit hour. $646 per semester. Tuition and fees vary according to course load, campus/location and program. *Financial support:* In 2017–18, 2 students received support, including 2 teaching assistantships with partial tuition reimbursements available (averaging $6,000 per year); institutionally sponsored loans and unspecified assistantships also available. Financial award application deadline: 2/1; financial award applicants required to submit FAFSA. *Unit head:* Dr. Sheila Nair, Director, 928-523-0180, E-mail: sheila.nair@nau.edu. *Application contact:* Matthew Morse, Administrative Associate, 928-523-2011, E-mail: matthew.morse@nau.edu.
Website: http://nau.edu/sbs/wgs/

Northwestern University, The Graduate School, Program in Gender and Sexuality Studies, Evanston, IL 60208. Offers Graduate Certificate. *Faculty research:* Anthropology, gender in Victorian period, autobiography, performance ethnographies, Slavic literature, women in the law.

The Ohio State University, Graduate School, College of Arts and Sciences, Division of Arts and Humanities, Department of Women's, Gender and Sexuality Studies, Columbus, OH 43210. Offers MA, PhD. *Faculty:* 14. *Students:* 30 (26 women); includes 5 minority (all Black or African American, non-Hispanic/Latino), 8 international. Average age 28. In 2017, 5 master's, 4 doctorates awarded. Terminal master's awarded for partial completion of doctoral program. *Entrance requirements:* For master's and doctorate, GRE (if GPA is less than 3.0 for all work), scholarly writing sample. Additional exam requirements/recommendations for international students: Required—TOEFL (minimum score 550 paper-based; 79 iBT), Michigan English Language Assessment Battery (minimum score 82); Recommended—IELTS (minimum score 7). *Application deadline:* For fall admission, 12/1 priority date for domestic students, 11/15 priority date for international students; for spring admission, 3/1 for domestic students, 2/1 for international students. Applications are processed on a rolling basis. Application fee: $60 ($70 for international students). Electronic applications accepted. *Financial support:* Fellowships, research assistantships, teaching assistantships, career-related internships or fieldwork, Federal Work-Study, institutionally sponsored loans, and unspecified assistantships available. Support available to part-time students. *Unit head:* Dr. Shannon Winnubst, Chair and Professor, 614-292-3915, E-mail: winnubst.1@osu.edu. *Application contact:* Graduate and Professional Admissions, 614-292-9444, Fax: 614-292-3895, E-mail: gpadmissions@osu.edu.
Website: http://wgss.osu.edu/

Old Dominion University, College of Arts and Letters, Institute for the Humanities, Norfolk, VA 23529. Offers arts and entrepreneurship (Certificate); cultural and human geography (MA); cultural studies (MA); gender and sexuality studies (MA); health, communication and culture (Certificate); media and popular culture studies (MA); philosophy and religious studies (MA); social justice and entrepreneurship (Certificate); visual studies (MA); world cultures (MA). *Program availability:* Part-time, evening/weekend. *Faculty:* 1 full-time (0 women), 1 part-time/adjunct (0 women). *Students:* 20 full-time (16 women), 13 part-time (8 women); includes 15 minority (8 Black or African American, non-Hispanic/Latino; 2 Asian, non-Hispanic/Latino; 2 Hispanic/Latino; 3 Two or more races, non-Hispanic/Latino), 2 international. Average age 35. 27 applicants, 96% accepted, 22 enrolled. In 2017, 3 master's awarded. *Degree requirements:* For master's, thesis optional, project. *Entrance requirements:* For master's, GRE General Test, minimum GPA of 3.25. *Application deadline:* For fall admission, 6/15 for domestic students; for spring admission, 11/15 for domestic students; for summer admission, 4/15 for domestic students. Applications are processed on a rolling basis. Application fee: $50. Electronic applications accepted. *Expenses:* Tuition, state resident: full-time $8928; part-time $496 per credit. Tuition, nonresident: full-time $22,482; part-time $1249 per credit. *Required fees:* $66 per semester. *Financial support:* In 2017–18, 3 students received support, including 5 research assistantships (averaging $10,000 per year); career-related internships or fieldwork, scholarships/grants, and unspecified assistantships also available. Financial award application deadline: 3/15; financial award applicants required to submit FAFSA. *Faculty research:* Media studies, cultural studies, gender studies, American literature, philosophy, art history, cultural geography. *Unit head:* Dr. Avi D. Santo, Graduate Program Director, 757-683-3719, Fax: 757-683-6191, E-mail: humgpd@odu.edu. *Application contact:* Dr. David C. Earnest, Associate Dean, 757-683-6077, Fax: 757-683-5746, E-mail: dearnest@odu.edu.
Website: http://al.odu.edu/hum/

Oregon State University, College of Liberal Arts, Program in Women, Gender, and Sexuality Studies, Corvallis, OR 97331. Offers feminist leadership (PhD). *Program availability:* Part-time. *Degree requirements:* For master's, one foreign language; for doctorate, thesis/dissertation. *Entrance requirements:* Additional exam requirements/recommendations for international students: Required—TOEFL (minimum score 80 iBT), IELTS (minimum score 6.5). *Application deadline:* For fall admission, 12/1 for domestic and international students. Application fee: $75 ($85 for international students). *Financial support:* Application deadline: 4/1. *Unit head:* Qwo-Li Driskill, Director of Graduate Studies, E-mail: qwo-li.driskill@oregonstate.edu. *Application contact:* Dr. Qwo-Li Driskill, Director of Graduate Studies, 541-737-1114, E-mail: qwo-li.driskill@oregonstate.edu.
Website: http://liberalarts.oregonstate.edu/slcs/wgss/

Queen's University at Kingston, School of Graduate Studies, Faculty of Arts and Sciences, Department of Political Studies, Kingston, ON K7L 3N6, Canada. Offers Canadian politics (PhD); comparative politics (PhD); gender and politics (PhD); international relations (PhD); political theory (PhD). *Degree requirements:* For master's, thesis or alternative; for doctorate, one foreign language, thesis/dissertation, qualifying exams. *Entrance requirements:* Additional exam requirements/recommendations for international students: Required—TOEFL (minimum score 600 paper-based). *Faculty research:* Canadian politics, comparative politics, political thought, international politics, women and politics.

Rutgers University–New Brunswick, Graduate School-New Brunswick, Program in Women's and Gender Studies, Piscataway, NJ 08854-8097. Offers MA, PhD. *Program availability:* Part-time. *Degree requirements:* For master's, thesis or alternative; for doctorate, comprehensive exam, thesis/dissertation. *Entrance requirements:* For master's and doctorate, GRE General Test, writing sample, 3 letters of recommendation. Additional exam requirements/recommendations for international students: Required—TOEFL. *Faculty research:* Feminist theory, gender and sexuality, global and cultural studies, women in history, literature, and politics, feminist politics.

Saint Mary's University, Faculty of Arts, Program in Women and Gender Studies, Halifax, NS B3H 3C3, Canada. Offers MA. Program offered jointly with Mount Saint Vincent University. *Program availability:* Part-time. *Degree requirements:* For master's, thesis. *Entrance requirements:* For master's, honors degree.

San Diego State University, Graduate and Research Affairs, College of Arts and Letters, Program in Lesbian, Gay, Bisexual and Transgender Studies, San Diego, CA 92182. Offers Graduate Certificate.

Simmons College, College of Arts and Sciences, Boston, MA 02115. Offers English (MA); gender/cultural studies (MA); history (MA); public health (MPH); public policy (MPP). *Program availability:* Part-time. *Faculty:* 19 full-time (13 women), 2 part-time/adjunct (both women). *Students:* 4 full-time (3 women), 39 part-time (34 women); includes 11 minority (7 Black or African American, non-Hispanic/Latino; 1 Hispanic/Latino; 3 Two or more races, non-Hispanic/Latino). Average age 26. 99 applicants, 57% accepted, 27 enrolled. In 2017, 23 master's awarded. Terminal master's awarded for partial completion of doctoral program. *Degree requirements:* For master's, thesis optional. *Entrance requirements:* For master's, GRE, bachelor's degree from accredited college or university; minimum B average (preferred). Additional exam requirements/recommendations for international students: Required—TOEFL (minimum score 600 paper-based; 100 iBT). *Application deadline:* For fall admission, 8/1 for domestic and international students; for spring admission, 12/15 for domestic and international students; for summer admission, 5/1 for domestic and international students. Applications are processed on a rolling basis. Application fee: $35. Electronic applications accepted. *Expenses:* $1,052 per credit, $55 activity fee per semester. *Financial support:* In 2017–18, 4 fellowships with partial tuition reimbursements, 22 teaching assistantships with partial tuition reimbursements were awarded; scholarships/grants and unspecified assistantships also available. Support available to part-time students. Financial award applicants required to submit FAFSA. *Faculty research:* Film and media studies, postcolonial literature, critical theory, arts and culture. *Unit head:* Dr. Leanne Doherty, Dean, 617-521-2581, E-mail: leanne.doherty@simmons.edu. *Application contact:* Patricia Flaherty, Director, Graduate Studies Admission, 617-521-3902, Fax: 617-521-3058, E-mail: gsa@simmons.edu.
Website: http://www.simmons.edu/gradstudies/

Simon Fraser University, Office of Graduate Studies and Postdoctoral Fellows, Faculty of Arts and Social Sciences, Department of Gender, Sexuality and Women's Studies, Burnaby, BC V5A 1S6, Canada. Offers MA, PhD. *Degree requirements:* For master's, thesis or alternative; for doctorate, comprehensive exam, thesis/dissertation. *Entrance requirements:* For master's, minimum GPA of 3.0 (on scale of 4.33) or 3.33 based on last 60 credits of undergraduate courses; for doctorate, minimum GPA of 3.5 (on scale of 4.33). Additional exam requirements/recommendations for international students: Recommended—TOEFL (minimum score 580 paper-based; 93 iBT), IELTS (minimum score 7), TWE (minimum score 5). Electronic applications accepted. *Faculty research:* Gender history, feminist labor studies/economics, queer theory, women and media, feminist research methods.

Stony Brook University, State University of New York, Graduate School, College of Arts and Sciences, Program in Women's, Gender, and Sexuality Studies, Stony Brook, NY 11794. Offers Certificate. *Faculty:* 8 full-time (7 women). In 2017, 3 Certificates awarded. *Degree requirements:* For Certificate, interdisciplinary research colloquium. *Entrance requirements:* For degree, GRE, minimum GPA of 2.75, 3 letters of recommendation. Additional exam requirements/recommendations for international students: Required—TOEFL. *Application deadline:* For fall admission, 1/15 for domestic students; for spring admission, 10/1 for domestic students. *Expenses:* Contact institution. *Faculty research:* Exercise, gender studies, humanities, literary criticism, women's studies. *Unit head:* Prof. Mary Jo Bona, Chair, 631-632-6355, E-mail: maryjo.bona@stonybrook.edu. *Application contact:* Graduate Program Director, 631-632-7461.
Website: http://www.stonybrook.edu/commcms/wgss/

Texas Woman's University, Graduate School, College of Arts and Sciences, Department of Multicultural Women's and Gender Studies, Denton, TX 76204. Offers MA, PhD. *Program availability:* Part-time. *Faculty:* 5 full-time (4 women), 1 part-time/adjunct (0 women). *Students:* 10 full-time (all women), 36 part-time (34 women); includes 22 minority (9 Black or African American, non-Hispanic/Latino; 1 American Indian or Alaska Native, non-Hispanic/Latino; 3 Asian, non-Hispanic/Latino; 6 Hispanic/Latino; 3 Two or more races, non-Hispanic/Latino), 4 international. Average age 36. 14 applicants, 93% accepted, 8 enrolled. In 2017, 5 master's, 3 doctorates awarded. Terminal master's awarded for partial completion of doctoral program. *Degree requirements:* For master's, comprehensive exam, thesis (for some programs), thesis or coursework; for doctorate, comprehensive exam, thesis/dissertation. *Entrance requirements:* For master's, 2 letters of reference, personal essay, minimum GPA of 3.0, writing sample; for doctorate, statement of purpose, writing sample, curriculum vitae/resume, 2 reference letters, minimum GPA of 3.5 in prior graduate level course work. Additional exam requirements/recommendations for international students: Required—TOEFL (minimum score 550 paper-based; 79 iBT); Recommended—IELTS (minimum score 6.5), TSE (minimum score 53). *Application deadline:* For fall admission, 3/1 priority date for domestic and international students; for spring admission, 11/1 priority date for domestic students, 7/1 priority date for international students. Applications are processed on a rolling basis. Application fee: $50 ($75 for international students). Electronic applications accepted. *Expenses:* $7,520 per year full-time in-state; $16,820 per year full-time out-of-state. *Financial support:* In 2017–18, 20 students received support, including 9 teaching assistantships (averaging $27,404 per year); career-related internships or fieldwork, Federal Work-Study, institutionally sponsored loans, scholarships/grants, traineeships, health care benefits, and unspecified assistantships also available. Support available to part-time students. Financial award application deadline: 3/1; financial award applicants required to submit FAFSA. *Faculty research:* Feminist/womanist theories and epistemologies, history of U.S. feminism, U.S. women of color, feminism and religion/spirituality, critical race theories. *Unit head:* Dr. AnaLouise Keating, Interim Chair, 940-898-2119, Fax: 940-898-2101, E-mail: womenstudies@twu.edu. *Application contact:* Korie Hawkins, Associate Director of Admissions, Graduate Recruitment, 940-898-3188, Fax: 940-898-3081, E-mail: admissions@twu.edu.
Website: http://www.twu.edu/ws/

University at Albany, State University of New York, College of Arts and Sciences, Department of Women's, Gender and Sexuality Studies, Albany, NY 12222-0001. Offers MA. *Faculty:* 6 full-time (all women). *Students:* 10 full-time (all women), 5 part-time (all women); includes 2 minority (1 Hispanic/Latino; 1 Two or more races, non-Hispanic/Latino), 3 international. 21 applicants, 67% accepted, 5 enrolled. In 2017, 12 master's awarded. *Entrance requirements:* Additional exam requirements/recommendations for international students: Required—TOEFL (minimum score 550 paper-based). *Application deadline:* For fall admission, 8/1 for domestic students, 5/1 for international students. Applications are processed on a rolling basis. Application fee: $75. Electronic applications accepted. *Expenses:* Tuition, state resident: full-time $10,870; part-time $453 per credit hour. Tuition, nonresident: full-time $22,210; part-time $925 per credit hour. *Required fees:* $84.68 per credit hour. $508.06 per semester. Part-time tuition and fees vary according to course load and program. *Faculty research:* Feminist pedagogy, lesbian and gay studies, women in the African diaspora, women's health policy, literature of feminism. *Unit head:* Janell Hobson, Chair, 518-442-4220, Fax: 518-442-4419, E-mail: jhobson@albany.edu. *Application contact:* Michael DeRensis, Director, Graduate Admissions, 518-442-3980, Fax: 518-442-3922, E-mail: graduate@albany.edu.
Website: http://www.albany.edu/ws/

University at Buffalo, the State University of New York, Graduate School, College of Arts and Sciences, Department of Transnational Studies, Buffalo, NY 14214. Offers American studies (MA, PhD); Canadian studies (MA); global gender studies (MA, PhD). *Program availability:* Part-time. *Faculty:* 16 full-time (8 women), 3 part-time/adjunct (1 woman). *Students:* 71 full-time (42 women); includes 26 minority (9 Black or African American, non-Hispanic/Latino; 6 American Indian or Alaska Native, non-Hispanic/Latino; 9 Asian, non-Hispanic/Latino; 2 Hispanic/Latino). Average age 33. 30 applicants, 70% accepted, 9 enrolled. In 2017, 7 master's, 15 doctorates awarded. Terminal master's awarded for partial completion of doctoral program. *Degree requirements:* For master's, comprehensive exam (for some programs), thesis optional; for doctorate, comprehensive exam, thesis/dissertation. *Entrance requirements:* For master's, minimum GPA of 3.0; for doctorate, GRE, minimum GPA of 3.0. Additional exam requirements/recommendations for international students: Required—TOEFL (minimum score 550 paper-based; 79 iBT), IELTS (minimum score 6.5). *Application deadline:* For fall admission, 8/28 priority date for domestic students, 6/15 priority date for international students; for winter admission, 2/1 for domestic and international students; for spring admission, 1/28 priority date for domestic students, 11/15 priority date for international students. Applications are processed on a rolling basis. Application fee: $75. Electronic applications accepted. *Financial support:* In 2017–18, 20 students received support, including 2 fellowships with full tuition reimbursements available (averaging $13,060 per year), 15 teaching assistantships with full tuition reimbursements available (averaging $13,060 per year); research assistantships, career-related internships or fieldwork, institutionally sponsored loans, scholarships/grants, health care benefits, and unspecified assistantships also available. Financial award application deadline: 1/1. *Faculty research:* Native American, intercultural and indigenous people's studies, border theory, cultural studies, American pop culture, feminist theory, construction of gender in society. *Unit head:* Dr. Cecil Foster, Chair, 716-645-0786, Fax: 716-645-5976, E-mail: cecilfos@buffalo.edu. *Application contact:* Karen M. Reinard, Graduate Coordinator, 716-645-0797, Fax: 716-645-5976, E-mail: kreinard@buffalo.edu.
Website: http://transnationalstudies.buffalo.edu/

The University of Arizona, College of Social and Behavioral Sciences, Department of Gender and Women's Studies, Tucson, AZ 85721. Offers MA, PhD, Certificate. *Program availability:* Part-time. *Degree requirements:* For master's, thesis/project. *Entrance requirements:* For master's and doctorate, GRE (minimum score: 500 verbal, 500 quantitative, 4.5 analytical), 3 letters of recommendation. Additional exam requirements/recommendations for international students: Required—TOEFL (minimum score 600 paper-based; 100 iBT). Electronic applications accepted. *Faculty research:* Gender, race and border studies; sexuality and the body; gender health and science; cultural representation and theory; public policy and social movements.

The University of British Columbia, Faculty of Arts, Institute for Gender, Race, Sexuality, and Social Justice, Vancouver, BC V6T 1Z2, Canada. Offers MA, PhD. *Expenses:* Contact institution.

University of California, Los Angeles, Graduate Division, College of Letters and Science, Program in Gender Studies, Los Angeles, CA 90095. Offers MA, PhD. Terminal master's awarded for partial completion of doctoral program. *Degree requirements:* For master's, comprehensive exam, thesis; for doctorate, one foreign language, thesis/dissertation, written and oral qualifying exams. *Entrance requirements:* For doctorate, GRE General Test, bachelor's degree; minimum undergraduate GPA of 3.0 (or its equivalent if letter grade system not used); writing sample. Additional exam requirements/recommendations for international students: Required—TOEFL. Electronic applications accepted.

University of Chicago, Division of the Humanities, Master of Arts Program in the Humanities, Chicago, IL 60637. Offers art history (MA); cinema and media studies (MA); classic languages (MA); comparative literature (MA); creative writing (MA); cultural policy studies (MA); digital humanities (MA); East Asian languages and civilizations (MA); English language and literature (MA); gender and sexuality studies (MA); Germanic studies (MA); linguistics (MA); music (MA); near Eastern languages and civilizations (MA); philosophy (MA); poetics (MA); race, politics and culture (MA); Romance languages and literatures (MA); Slavic languages and literatures (MA); South Asian languages and civilizations (MA); theater and performance studies (MA). *Students:* 95 full-time (50 women), 6 part-time (4 women); includes 22 minority (1 Black or African American, non-Hispanic/Latino; 10 Asian, non-Hispanic/Latino; 11 Hispanic/Latino), 19 international. Average age 26. 708 applicants, 75% accepted, 101 enrolled. In 2017, 91 master's awarded. *Degree requirements:* For master's, thesis. *Entrance requirements:* For master's, GRE General Test, 10-15 page writing sample, statement of purpose, 3 letters of recommendation, transcripts for all previous degrees and institutions attended. Additional exam requirements/recommendations for international students: Required—TOEFL (minimum score 104 iBT), IELTS (minimum score 7). *Application deadline:* For fall admission, 1/3 priority date for domestic and international students. Application fee: $90. Electronic applications accepted. *Expenses:* Contact institution. *Financial support:* In 2017–18, fellowships with partial tuition reimbursements (averaging $12,000 per year) were awarded; Federal Work-Study, institutionally sponsored loans, scholarships/grants, and tuition waivers (partial) also available. Financial award application deadline: 4/30. *Unit head:* Thomas Christensen, Director, 773-834-1201, Fax: 773-834-7526, E-mail: ma-humanities@uchicago.edu. *Application contact:* Michael Beetley, Assistant Dean of Students for Admissions, 773-834-1552, E-mail: humanitiesadmissions@uchicago.edu.
Website: http://maph.uchicago.edu/

University of Colorado Denver, College of Liberal Arts and Sciences, Program in Humanities, Denver, CO 80217. Offers community health science (MSS); humanities (MH); international studies (MSS); philosophy and theory (MH); social justice (MSS); society and the environment (MSS); visual studies (MH); women's and gender studies (MSS). *Program availability:* Part-time, evening/weekend. *Degree requirements:* For master's, 36 credit hours, project or thesis. *Entrance requirements:* For master's, writing sample, statement of purpose/letter of intent, three letters of recommendation. Additional exam requirements/recommendations for international students: Required—TOEFL (minimum score 537 paper-based; 75 iBT); Recommended—IELTS (minimum score 6.5). Electronic applications accepted. *Faculty research:* Women and gender in the classical Mediterranean, communication theory and democracy, relationship between psychology and philosophy.

Gender Studies

University of Florida, Graduate School, College of Liberal Arts and Sciences, Center for Women's Studies and Gender Research, Gainesville, FL 32611. Offers gender and development (Graduate Certificate); women's studies (MA, Graduate Certificate); MA/JD; MA/MA. Terminal master's awarded for partial completion of doctoral program. *Degree requirements:* For master's, thesis or project. *Entrance requirements:* For master's, GRE General Test (minimum score 1000), minimum GPA of 3.2. Additional exam requirements/recommendations for international students: Required—TOEFL (minimum score 550 paper-based; 80 iBT), IELTS (minimum score 6). Electronic applications accepted. *Faculty research:* Prejudice, discrimination, intersections, resistance, history.

University of Lethbridge, School of Graduate Studies, Lethbridge, AB T1K 3M4, Canada. Offers addictions counseling (M Sc); agricultural biotechnology (M Sc); agricultural studies (M Sc, MA); anthropology (MA); archaeology (M Sc, MA); art (MA, MFA); biochemistry (M Sc); biological sciences (M Sc); biomolecular science (PhD); biosystems and biodiversity (PhD); Canadian studies (MA); chemistry (M Sc); computer science (M Sc); computer science and geographical information science (M Sc); counseling (MC); counseling psychology (M Ed); dramatic arts (MA); earth, space, and physical science (PhD); economics (MA); education (MA, PhD); educational leadership (M Ed); English (MA); environmental science (M Sc); evolution and behavior (PhD); exercise science (M Sc); French (MA); French/German (MA); French/Spanish (MA); general education (M Ed); geography (M Sc, MA); German (MA); health sciences (M Sc); individualized multidisciplinary (M Sc, MA); kinesiology (M Sc, MA); management (M Sc), including accounting, finance, human resource management and labor relations, information systems, international management, marketing, policy and strategy; mathematics (M Sc); music (M Mus, MA); Native American studies (MA); neuroscience (M Sc, PhD); new media (MA, MFA); nursing (M Sc, MN); philosophy (MA); physics (M Sc); political science (MA); psychology (M Sc, MA); religious studies (MA); sociology (MA); theatre and dramatic arts (MFA); theoretical and computational science (PhD); urban and regional studies (MA); women and gender studies (MA). *Program availability:* Part-time, evening/weekend. *Degree requirements:* For master's, thesis (for some programs); for doctorate, comprehensive exam, thesis/dissertation. *Entrance requirements:* For master's, GMAT (for M Sc in management), bachelor's degree in related field, minimum GPA of 3.0 during previous 20 graded semester courses, 2 years' teaching or related experience (M Ed); for doctorate, master's degree, minimum graduate GPA of 3.5. Additional exam requirements/recommendations for international students: Required—TOEFL (minimum score 580 paper-based; 93 iBT). Electronic applications accepted. *Faculty research:* Movement and brain plasticity, gibberellin physiology, photosynthesis, carbon cycling, molecular properties of main-group ring components.

University of Memphis, Graduate School, College of Arts and Sciences, Program in Interdisciplinary Studies, Memphis, TN 38152. Offers museum studies (Graduate Certificate); women's and gender studies (Graduate Certificate). *Faculty:* 3 full-time (1 woman). *Students:* 7 full-time (1 woman), 13 part-time (7 women); includes 9 minority (6 Black or African American, non-Hispanic/Latino; 3 Asian, non-Hispanic/Latino), 4 international. Average age 32. 22 applicants, 82% accepted, 14 enrolled. *Degree requirements:* For Graduate Certificate, minimum GPA of 3.0. *Entrance requirements:* For degree, GRE, letter of interest, undergraduate transcript. Additional exam requirements/recommendations for international students: Required—TOEFL (minimum score 550 paper-based). *Application deadline:* For fall admission, 4/3 for domestic students. Application fee: $35 ($60 for international students). *Expenses:* Contact institution. *Financial support:* In 2017–18, 11 students received support, including 13 research assistantships with full tuition reimbursements available (averaging $12,420 per year); teaching assistantships with full tuition reimbursements available, Federal Work-Study, scholarships/grants, and unspecified assistantships also available. Financial award application deadline: 2/1; financial award applicants required to submit FAFSA. *Unit head:* Dr. Henry A. Kurtz, Dean, 901-678-2251, Fax: 901-678-4831, E-mail: hkurtz@memphis.edu. *Application contact:* Dr. Kathy Schultz, Director of Women's and Gender Studies, 901-678-2651, E-mail: klschltz@memphis.edu.
Website: http://www.memphis.edu/isc/

University of Michigan–Flint, College of Arts and Sciences, Program in Social Sciences, Flint, MI 48502-1950. Offers gender studies (MA); global studies (MA); U.S. history and politics (MA). *Program availability:* Part-time. *Faculty:* 12 full-time (7 women), 6 part-time/adjunct (4 women). *Students:* 2 full-time (1 woman), 12 part-time (6 women); includes 4 minority (3 Black or African American, non-Hispanic/Latino; 1 Hispanic/Latino). Average age 43. 8 applicants, 88% accepted, 6 enrolled. In 2017, 11 master's awarded. *Entrance requirements:* For master's, bachelor's degree from regionally-accredited institution, minimum overall undergraduate GPA of 3.0. Additional exam requirements/recommendations for international students: Required—TOEFL (minimum score 84 iBT), IELTS (minimum score 6.5). *Application deadline:* For fall admission, 8/1 for domestic students, 5/1 for international students; for winter admission, 11/15 for domestic students, 9/1 for international students; for spring admission, 3/15 for domestic students, 1/1 for international students; for summer admission, 5/15 for domestic students. Applications are processed on a rolling basis. Application fee: $55. Electronic applications accepted. *Expenses:* Contact institution. *Financial support:* Federal Work-Study, scholarships/grants, and unspecified assistantships available. Financial award application deadline: 3/1; financial award applicants required to submit FAFSA. *Unit head:* Dr. Adam Lutzker, Director, 810-762-3470, Fax: 810-762-3281, E-mail: alutzker@umflint.edu. *Application contact:* Bradley T. Maki, Director of Graduate Admissions, 810-762-3171, Fax: 810-766-6789, E-mail: bmaki@umflint.edu.
Website: http://www.umflint.edu/graduateprograms/social-sciences-ma

The University of North Carolina at Charlotte, College of Liberal Arts and Sciences, Interdisciplinary Liberal Arts and Sciences Programs, Charlotte, NC 28223-0001. Offers gender, sexuality, and women's studies (Graduate Certificate); gerontology (MA, Graduate Certificate); Latin American studies (MA); liberal studies (MA); organizational science (PhD); public policy (PhD). *Program availability:* Part-time, evening/weekend. *Faculty:* 1 full-time (0 women). *Students:* 66 full-time (48 women), 66 part-time (52 women); includes 41 minority (14 Black or African American, non-Hispanic/Latino; 2 Asian, non-Hispanic/Latino; 24 Hispanic/Latino; 1 Two or more races, non-Hispanic/Latino), 16 international. Average age 27. 129 applicants, 53% accepted, 43 enrolled. In 2017, 22 master's, 10 doctorates, 9 other advanced degrees awarded. *Degree requirements:* For master's, comprehensive exam (for some programs), thesis (for some programs), practicum, project; for doctorate, comprehensive exam, thesis/dissertation; for Graduate Certificate, practicum (for gerontology). *Entrance requirements:* For master's, GRE General Test or MAT, bachelor's degree from accredited college or university; official transcripts of all previous academic work attempted beyond high school with minimum overall GPA of 3.0; statement of purpose; recommendation letters; for doctorate, GRE or GMAT, statement of purpose discussing interest in program and objectives for pursuing degree, current resume or curriculum vitae, unofficial transcripts; for Graduate Certificate, bachelor's degree from accredited university and either enrolled and in good standing in a graduate degree program at UNC Charlotte or have a minimum undergraduate GPA of 3.0. Additional exam requirements/recommendations for international students: Required—TOEFL (minimum score 523 paper-based, 70 iBT) or IELTS (6.5). *Application deadline:* For fall admission, 2/15 for domestic and international students; for spring admission, 10/1 for domestic and international students; for summer admission, 4/1 for domestic and international students. Applications are processed on a rolling basis. Application fee: $75. Electronic applications accepted. *Expenses:* Tuition, state resident: full-time $4337. Tuition, nonresident: full-time $17,771. *Required fees:* $3211. Tuition and fees vary according to course load and program. *Financial support:* In 2017–18, 21 students received support, including 19 research assistantships (averaging $12,011 per year), 1 teaching assistantship (averaging $18,600 per year); career-related internships or fieldwork, institutionally sponsored loans, scholarships/grants, unspecified assistantships, and administrative assistantships also available. Support available to part-time students. Financial award application deadline: 3/1; financial award applicants required to submit FAFSA. *Unit head:* Dr. Nancy A. Gutierrez, Dean, 704-687-0081, E-mail: ngutierr@uncc.edu. *Application contact:* Kathy B. Giddings, Director of Graduate Admissions, 704-687-5503, Fax: 704-687-3279, E-mail: gradadm@uncc.edu.
Website: http://clas.uncc.edu/academics

The University of North Carolina at Greensboro, Graduate School, College of Arts and Sciences, Program in Women's and Gender Studies, Greensboro, NC 27412-5001. Offers MA, Certificate. Electronic applications accepted.

University of Northern British Columbia, Office of Graduate Studies, Prince George, BC V2N 4Z9, Canada. Offers business administration (Diploma); community health science (M Sc); disability management (MA); education (M Ed); first nations studies (MA); gender studies (MA); history (MA); interdisciplinary studies (MA); international studies (MA); mathematical, computer and physical sciences (M Sc); natural resources and environmental studies (M Sc, MA, MNRES, PhD); political science (MA); psychology (M Sc, PhD); social work (MSW). *Program availability:* Part-time, evening/weekend, online learning. *Degree requirements:* For master's, thesis; for doctorate, thesis/dissertation. *Entrance requirements:* For master's, GRE, minimum B average in undergraduate course work; for doctorate, candidacy exam, minimum A average in graduate course work.

University of Northern Iowa, Graduate College, MA Program in Women's and Gender Studies, Cedar Falls, IA 50614. Offers MA. *Degree requirements:* For master's, comprehensive exam (for some programs), thesis or alternative. *Entrance requirements:* For master's, minimum GPA of 3.0. Additional exam requirements/recommendations for international students: Required—TOEFL (minimum score 500 paper-based; 61 iBT). Electronic applications accepted.

University of Oklahoma, College of Arts and Sciences, Women's and Gender Studies Department, Norman, OK 73019. Offers Graduate Certificate. *Program availability:* Part-time. *Faculty:* 1 (woman) full-time. *Students:* 2 full-time (1 woman), 10 part-time (9 women); includes 3 minority (1 Black or African American, non-Hispanic/Latino; 1 American Indian or Alaska Native, non-Hispanic/Latino; 1 Hispanic/Latino), 1 international. Average age 40. In 2017, 6 Graduate Certificates awarded. *Entrance requirements:* Additional exam requirements/recommendations for international students: Required—TOEFL (minimum score 79 iBT) or IELTS (minimum score 6.5). *Application deadline:* Applications are processed on a rolling basis. Application fee: $50 ($100 for international students). Electronic applications accepted. *Expenses:* Tuition, state resident: full-time $5119; part-time $213.30 per credit hour. Tuition, nonresident: full-time $19,778; part-time $824.10 per credit hour. *Required fees:* $3458; $133.55 per credit hour. $126.50 per semester. *Financial support:* Application deadline: 6/1; applicants required to submit FAFSA. *Faculty research:* Black feminism, terrorism, popular culture, indigenous studies, reproductive justice. *Total annual research expenditures:* $197,283. *Unit head:* Dr. Maria Lupe Davidson, Chair, 405-325-3481, E-mail: mdavidson@ou.edu.
Website: http://wgs.ou.edu

University of Rhode Island, Graduate School, College of Arts and Sciences, Department of English, Kingston, RI 02881. Offers American literature and culture (PhD); British literature and culture (PhD); creative writing (PhD); critical theories (PhD); English (MA); film (PhD); gender studies (PhD); MLIS/MA. *Program availability:* Part-time. *Faculty:* 17 full-time (10 women). *Students:* 36 full-time (27 women), 7 part-time (4 women); includes 2 minority (both Black or African American, non-Hispanic/Latino), 7 international. 34 applicants, 65% accepted, 10 enrolled. In 2017, 4 master's, 8 doctorates awarded. *Entrance requirements:* Additional exam requirements/recommendations for international students: Required—TOEFL (minimum score 91 iBT). *Application deadline:* For fall admission, 1/15 for domestic and international students. Application fee: $65. Electronic applications accepted. *Expenses:* Tuition, state resident: full-time $12,706; part-time $786 per credit. Tuition, nonresident: full-time $25,216; part-time $1401 per credit. *Required fees:* $1598; $45 per credit. One-time fee: $30 part-time. *Financial support:* In 2017–18, 28 teaching assistantships with tuition reimbursements (averaging $17,158 per year) were awarded. Financial award application deadline: 1/15; financial award applicants required to submit FAFSA. *Unit head:* Dr. Travis Williams, Chair, 401-874-9501, E-mail: tdwilliams@uri.edu. *Application contact:* Dr. David Faflik, Director of Graduate Studies, 401-874-4670, E-mail: faflik@uri.edu.
Website: http://www.uri.edu/artsci/eng/

University of Rhode Island, Graduate School, College of Arts and Sciences, Program in Gender and Women's Studies, Kingston, RI 02881. Offers Graduate Certificate. In 2017, 3 Graduate Certificates awarded. Application fee: $65. Electronic applications accepted. *Expenses:* Tuition, state resident: full-time $12,706; part-time $786 per credit. Tuition, nonresident: full-time $25,216; part-time $1401 per credit. *Required fees:* $1598; $45 per credit. One-time fee: $30 part-time. *Financial support:* In 2017–18, 1 teaching assistantship (averaging $18,080 per year) was awarded. *Unit head:* Dr. Rosaria Pisa, Director, 401-874-2482, E-mail: rpisa@uri.edu.
Website: http://web.uri.edu/gws/graduate-certificate-program/

University of Saskatchewan, College of Graduate Studies and Research, College of Arts and Science, Department of Women's and Gender Studies, Saskatoon, SK S7N 5A2, Canada. Offers MA, PhD. *Degree requirements:* For master's, thesis; for doctorate, comprehensive exam (for some programs), thesis/dissertation. *Entrance requirements:* Additional exam requirements/recommendations for international students: Required—TOEFL (minimum score 80 iBT); Recommended—IELTS (minimum score 6.5). Electronic applications accepted.

University of South Florida, College of Arts and Sciences, Department of Women's and Gender Studies, Tampa, FL 33620-9951. Offers women's and gender studies (MA). *Program availability:* Part-time. *Faculty:* 4 full-time (3 women). *Students:* 8 full-time (all women), 3 part-time (2 women); includes 3 minority (2 Black or African American, non-Hispanic/Latino; 1 Hispanic/Latino). Average age 24. 9 applicants, 78% accepted, 4 enrolled. In 2017, 6 master's awarded. *Degree requirements:* For master's, comprehensive exam, thesis (for some programs), thesis or internship. *Entrance requirements:* For master's, GRE General Test, minimum GPA of 3.0, three letters of recommendation, personal narrative statement of purpose, scholarly writing sample (examples include term paper or research paper); undergraduate major or minor in women's studies (recommended). Additional exam requirements/recommendations for international students: Required—TOEFL (minimum score 550 paper-based; 79 iBT) or IELTS (minimum score 6.5). *Application deadline:* For fall admission, 2/15 priority date for domestic and international students; for spring admission, 10/15 priority date for

domestic students, 9/15 priority date for international students; for summer admission, 2/15 priority date for domestic students, 1/15 priority date for international students. Applications are processed on a rolling basis. Application fee: $30. Electronic applications accepted. *Financial support:* In 2017–18, 3 students received support. Teaching assistantships with tuition reimbursements available available. Financial award application deadline: 3/1. *Faculty research:* Performance studies, feminist theory and pedagogy; constructions of gender in public discourse, including education, mass media, and popular culture; women's health, reproductive justice, and sexuality; bodies and cultural representations; feminist theory as it relates to learning disabilities, critical race theory, postmodernist and queer theory; hiring practices in higher education, mothering; women of color feminisms. *Unit head:* Dr. Diane Price Herndl, Professor and Chairperson, 813-974-0987, Fax: 813-974-0336, E-mail: priceherndl@usf.edu. *Application contact:* Dr. Kim Golombisky, Associate Professor and Graduate Director, 813-974-0986, Fax: 813-974-0336, E-mail: kgolombi@usf.edu.
Website: http://wgs.usf.edu/

University of South Florida, Innovative Education, Tampa, FL 33620-9951. Offers adult, career and higher education (Graduate Certificate), including college teaching, leadership in developing human resources, leadership in higher education; Africana studies (Graduate Certificate), including diasporas and health disparities, genocide and human rights; aging studies (Graduate Certificate), including gerontology; art research (Graduate Certificate), including museum studies; business foundations (Graduate Certificate); chemical and biomedical engineering (Graduate Certificate), including materials science and engineering, water, health and sustainability; child and family studies (Graduate Certificate), including positive behavior support; civil and industrial engineering (Graduate Certificate), including transportation systems analysis; community and family health (Graduate Certificate), including maternal and child health, social marketing and public health, violence and injury: prevention and intervention, women's health; criminology (Graduate Certificate), including criminal justice administration; data science for public administration (Graduate Certificate); digital humanities (Graduate Certificate); educational measurement and research (Graduate Certificate), including evaluation; English (Graduate Certificate), including comparative literary studies, creative writing, professional and technical communication; entrepreneurship (Graduate Certificate); environmental health (Graduate Certificate), including safety management; epidemiology and biostatistics (Graduate Certificate), including applied biostatistics, biostatistics, concepts and tools of epidemiology, epidemiology, epidemiology of infectious diseases; geography, environment and planning (Graduate Certificate), including community development, environmental policy and management, geographical information systems; geology (Graduate Certificate), including hydrogeology; global health (Graduate Certificate), including disaster management, global health and Latin American and Caribbean studies, global health practice, humanitarian assistance, infection control; government and international affairs (Graduate Certificate), including Cuban studies, globalization studies; health policy and management (Graduate Certificate), including health management and leadership, public health policy and programs; hearing specialist: early intervention (Graduate Certificate); industrial and management systems engineering (Graduate Certificate), including systems engineering, technology management; information studies (Graduate Certificate), including school library media specialist; information systems/decision sciences (Graduate Certificate), including analytics and business intelligence; instructional technology (Graduate Certificate), including distance education, Florida digital/virtual educator, instructional design, multimedia design, Web design; internal medicine, bioethics and medical humanities (Graduate Certificate), including biomedical ethics; Latin American and Caribbean studies (Graduate Certificate); leadership for coastal resiliency planning (Graduate Certificate); mass communications (Graduate Certificate), including multimedia journalism; mathematics and statistics (Graduate Certificate), including mathematics; medicine (Graduate Certificate), including aging and neuroscience, bioinformatics, biotechnology, brain fitness and memory management, clinical investigation, hand and upper limb rehabilitation, health informatics, health sciences, integrative weight management, intellectual property, medicine and gender, metabolic and nutritional medicine, metabolic cardiology, pharmacy sciences; national and competitive intelligence (Graduate Certificate); nursing (Graduate Certificate), including simulation based academic fellowship in advanced pain management; psychological and social foundations (Graduate Certificate), including career counseling, college teaching, diversity in education, mental health counseling, school counseling; public affairs (Graduate Certificate), including nonprofit management, public management, research administration; public health (Graduate Certificate), including assessing chemical toxicity and public health risks, health equity, pharmacoepidemiology, public health generalist, toxicology, translational research in adolescent behavioral health; public health practices (Graduate Certificate), including planning for healthy communities; rehabilitation and mental health counseling (Graduate Certificate), including integrative mental health care, marriage and family therapy, rehabilitation technology; secondary education (Graduate Certificate), including ESOL, foreign language education: culture and content, foreign language education: professional; social work (Graduate Certificate), including geriatric social work/clinical gerontology; special education (Graduate Certificate), including autism spectrum disorder, disabilities education: severe/profound; world languages (Graduate Certificate), including teaching English as a second language (TESL) or foreign language. *Unit head:* Dr. Cynthia DeLuca, Associate Vice President and Assistant Vice Provost, 813-974-3077, Fax: 813-974-7061, E-mail: deluca@usf.edu. *Application contact:* Owen Hooper, Director, Summer and Alternative Calendar Programs, 813-974-6917, E-mail: hooper@usf.edu.
Website: http://www.usf.edu/innovative-education/

The University of Toledo, College of Graduate Studies, College of Languages, Literature and Social Sciences, Department of Women's and Gender Studies, Toledo, OH 43606-3390. Offers Certificate. *Program availability:* Part-time.

University of Toronto, School of Graduate Studies, Faculty of Arts and Science, Women and Gender Studies Institute, Toronto, ON M5S 1A1, Canada. Offers MA, PhD. *Entrance requirements:* For master's, minimum B+ in final year of undergraduate study. Additional exam requirements/recommendations for international students: Required—TOEFL (minimum score 580 paper-based; 93 iBT), TWE (minimum score 5). Electronic applications accepted.

University of Wisconsin–Milwaukee, Graduate School, College of Letters and Science, Department of Women's and Gender Studies, Milwaukee, WI 53201-0413. Offers MA, Graduate Certificate. *Program availability:* Part-time. *Students:* 2 full-time (both women), 4 part-time (all women); includes 2 minority (1 Black or African American, non-Hispanic/Latino; 1 Two or more races, non-Hispanic/Latino). Average age 37. 9 applicants, 100% accepted, 2 enrolled. In 2017, 3 master's, 2 other advanced degrees awarded. *Entrance requirements:* For master's, three letters of recommendation, sample of written work, letter of intent. Application fee: $56 ($96 for international students). Electronic applications accepted. *Financial support:* Fellowships, research assistantships, teaching assistantships with full tuition reimbursements, health care benefits, and unspecified assistantships available. Financial award applicants required to submit FAFSA. *Unit head:* Dr. Gwynne Kennedy, Director, 414-229-5918, E-mail: gkennedy@uwm.edu. *Application contact:* General Information Contact, 414-229-4982, Fax: 414-229-6967, E-mail: gradschool@uwm.edu.
Website: http://uwm.edu/womens-gender-studies/

Wayne State University, College of Liberal Arts and Sciences, Department of History, Detroit, MI 48202. Offers history (MA, PhD); public history (MA), including African American history and culture, cultural resource management, gender, sexuality, and women's studies, labor and urban history, museum studies, public policy; world history (Graduate Certificate); JD/MA; M Ed/MA; MLIS/MA. Doctoral program admits for fall only. *Program availability:* Evening/weekend. *Faculty:* 17. *Students:* 21 full-time (7 women), 20 part-time (7 women); includes 9 minority (5 Black or African American, non-Hispanic/Latino; 1 Hispanic/Latino; 3 Two or more races, non-Hispanic/Latino). Average age 40. 50 applicants, 16% accepted, 5 enrolled. In 2017, 11 master's, 2 doctorates awarded. *Degree requirements:* For master's, comprehensive exam, thesis (for some programs), final oral exam on thesis or essay and seminar; internship and project (for public history); for doctorate, variable foreign language requirement, comprehensive exam, thesis/dissertation, qualifying exam in 4 fields of history. *Entrance requirements:* For master's, GRE General Test, minimum undergraduate GPA of 3.25 in history, 3.0 overall; at least 18 credits in history and related subjects at the advanced undergraduate level; foreign language; letter of intent; research paper; at least two letters of recommendation from former instructors; for doctorate, GRE General Test, minimum GPA of 3.0, 3.25 in minimum of 18 semester credits in history and related subjects; letter of intent; research paper; at least three letters of recommendation from former professors; for Graduate Certificate, baccalaureate degree from accredited college or university; minimum GPA of 3.0, 3.25 in a minimum of eighteen semester credits in history and related subjects at the advanced undergraduate level. Additional exam requirements/recommendations for international students: Required—TOEFL (minimum score 550 paper-based; 79 iBT), TWE (minimum score 5.5), Michigan English Language Assessment Battery (minimum score 85); Recommended—IELTS (minimum score 6.5). *Application deadline:* For fall admission, 2/1 priority date for domestic and international students; for winter admission, 11/1 for domestic students, 10/1 priority date for international students; for spring admission, 2/1 for domestic students, 1/1 priority date for international students. Application fee: $50. Electronic applications accepted. *Expenses:* Tuition, state resident: full-time $10,224; part-time $638.98 per credit hour. Tuition, nonresident: full-time $22,145; part-time $1384.04 per credit hour. Tuition and fees vary according to course load and program. *Financial support:* In 2017–18, 17 students received support, including 3 fellowships with tuition reimbursements available (averaging $17,198 per year), 1 research assistantship with tuition reimbursement available (averaging $22,241 per year), 6 teaching assistantships with tuition reimbursements available (averaging $18,534 per year); scholarships/grants, health care benefits, and unspecified assistantships also available. Financial award applicants required to submit FAFSA. *Faculty research:* Urban history, labor, political history, history of gender and women. *Unit head:* Dr. Elizabeth V. Faue, Professor/Chair, 313-577-2525, E-mail: evfaue@wayne.edu. *Application contact:* Dr. Eric Ash, Associate Professor and Director of Graduate Studies, 313-577-2525, E-mail: ericash@wayne.edu.
Website: http://clas.wayne.edu/history/

Wilfrid Laurier University, Faculty of Graduate and Postdoctoral Studies, Faculty of Arts, Cultural Analysis and Social Theory Program, Waterloo, ON N2L 3C5, Canada. Offers body politics (MA); cultural representation and social theory (MA); gender, sexuality and embodiment (MA); globalization, identity and social movements (MA). *Program availability:* Part-time. *Entrance requirements:* For master's, honours BA in humanities, social science or interdisciplinary program with social theory, minimum B+ in final year of full-time study. Additional exam requirements/recommendations for international students: Required—TOEFL (minimum score 89 iBT). Electronic applications accepted. *Faculty research:* Globalization; identity and social movements; body politics: gender, sexuality and embodiment; cultural representation and social theory.

York University, Faculty of Graduate Studies, Faculty of Liberal Arts and Professional Studies, Program in Gender, Feminist and Women's Studies, Toronto, ON M3J 1P3, Canada. Offers MA, PhD. *Degree requirements:* For master's, thesis or alternative; for doctorate, comprehensive exam, thesis/dissertation. Electronic applications accepted.

Hispanic Studies

Brown University, Graduate School, Department of Hispanic Studies, Providence, RI 02912. Offers PhD. *Degree requirements:* For doctorate, 2 foreign languages, thesis/dissertation, preliminary exam.

California State University, Los Angeles, Graduate Studies, College of Natural and Social Sciences, Department of Chicano Studies, Los Angeles, CA 90032-8530. Offers Mexican-American studies (MA). *Program availability:* Part-time, evening/weekend. *Degree requirements:* For master's, one foreign language, comprehensive exam or thesis. *Entrance requirements:* For master's, undergraduate major in Mexican-American studies or related area, 20 upper-division units in Chicano studies, minimum GPA of 2.75 in last 90 quarter units. Additional exam requirements/recommendations for international students: Required—TOEFL (minimum score 500 paper-based). Electronic applications accepted. *Faculty research:* U.S.-Mexican relations, Chicano literature,

community organization among Chicanos and Hispanics, Spanish language in the American Southwest.

California State University, Northridge, Graduate Studies, College of Humanities, Department of Chicana and Chicano Studies, Northridge, CA 91330. Offers MA. *Students:* 19 full-time (6 women), 12 part-time (10 women); includes 29 minority (28 Hispanic/Latino; 1 Two or more races, non-Hispanic/Latino). Average age 29. 27 applicants, 81% accepted, 13 enrolled. In 2017, 5 master's awarded. *Degree requirements:* For master's, thesis, project. *Entrance requirements:* Additional exam requirements/recommendations for international students: Required—TOEFL. *Application deadline:* For fall admission, 11/30 for domestic students. Application fee: $55. *Financial support:* Application deadline: 3/1. *Unit head:* Dr. Gabriel Gutierrez, Chair, 818-677-2734.
Website: http://www.csun.edu/chicanostudies/

Hispanic Studies

California State University, San Marcos, College of Humanities, Arts, Behavioral and Social Sciences, Program in Spanish, San Marcos, CA 92096-0001. Offers Hispanic cultures and society (MA); Hispanic language and linguistics (MA); Hispanic literatures and literary theory (MA). *Program availability:* Part-time, evening/weekend. *Degree requirements:* For master's, 2 foreign languages, exam. *Entrance requirements:* For master's, GRE General Test, minimum GPA of 3.0 overall and in upper-division Spanish courses, official transcripts, three letters of recommendation, 750-word statement of purpose (in English), academic writing sample (in Spanish). Additional exam requirements/recommendations for international students: Required—TOEFL (minimum score 500 paper-based), TWE (minimum score 4.5). *Application deadline:* For fall admission, 3/15 priority date for domestic students. Applications are processed on a rolling basis. Application fee: $55. Electronic applications accepted. *Expenses:* Tuition, state resident: full-time $7176. Tuition, nonresident: full-time $9504. *Faculty research:* Applied linguistics, Golden Age Spanish literature, Latin American literature, poetry, Chicano studies. *Unit head:* Dr. Silvia Rolle-Rissetto, Graduate Coordinator, 760-750-4115, E-mail: srolle@csusm.edu.
Website: http://www.csusm.edu/modernlanguages/masters_degree/

The Catholic University of America, School of Arts and Sciences, Department of Modern Languages and Literatures, Washington, DC 20064. Offers Hispanic studies (MA, PhD). *Program availability:* Part-time. *Faculty:* 22 full-time (17 women), 3 part-time/adjunct (2 women). *Students:* 3 full-time (1 woman), 4 part-time (3 women), 6 international. Average age 34. 7 applicants, 43% accepted, 3 enrolled. In 2017, 4 master's, 1 doctorate awarded. *Degree requirements:* For master's, comprehensive exam; for doctorate, one foreign language, comprehensive exam, thesis/dissertation, annotated bibliography; oral defense of the proposal; oral defense of the dissertation. *Entrance requirements:* For master's, GRE General Test, statement of purpose, official copies of academic transcripts, two letters of recommendation, sample of academic writing; for doctorate, GRE General Test, statement of purpose, official copies of academic transcripts, three letters of recommendation, sample of academic writing (20-25-pages long). Additional exam requirements/recommendations for international students: Required—TOEFL (minimum score 550 paper-based; 80 iBT). *Application deadline:* For fall admission, 7/15 priority date for domestic students, 7/1 for international students; for spring admission, 11/15 priority date for domestic students, 11/1 for international students. Applications are processed on a rolling basis. Application fee: $55. Electronic applications accepted. *Expenses:* Contact institution. *Financial support:* Fellowships, research assistantships, teaching assistantships, Federal Work-Study, scholarships/grants, tuition waivers (full and partial), and unspecified assistantships available. Financial award application deadline: 2/1; financial award applicants required to submit FAFSA. *Faculty research:* Golden age Spain; 18th-21st-century Spain; colonial/postcolonial Latin American and transatlantic studies; modern and contemporary Latin America; theory, criticism, and language teaching methodology. *Total annual research expenditures:* $32,340. *Unit head:* Dr. Claudia Bornholdt, Chair, 202-319-5240, Fax: 202-319-6077, E-mail: kassen@cua.edu. *Application contact:* Dr. Steven Brown, Director of Graduate Admissions, 202-319-5057, Fax: 202-319-6533, E-mail: cua-admissions@cua.edu.
Website: http://modernlanguages.cua.edu/

The Citadel, The Military College of South Carolina, Citadel Graduate College, School of Humanities and Social Sciences, Department of Modern Languages, Literatures and Cultures, Charleston, SC 29409. Offers Hispanic studies (Graduate Certificate). *Entrance requirements:* Additional exam requirements/recommendations for international students: Required—TOEFL (minimum score 550 paper-based; 79 iBT). Electronic applications accepted. *Expenses:* Tuition, state resident: part-time $587 per credit hour. Tuition, nonresident: part-time $988 per credit hour. *Required fees:* $90 per term.

Columbia University, Graduate School of Arts and Sciences, New York, NY 10027. Offers African-American studies (MA); American studies (MA); anthropology (MA, PhD); art history and archaeology (MA, PhD); astronomy (PhD); biological sciences (PhD); biotechnology (MA); chemical physics (PhD); chemistry (PhD); classical studies (MA, PhD); classics (MA, PhD); climate and society (MA); conservation biology (MA); earth and environmental sciences (PhD); East Asia: regional studies (MA); East Asian languages and cultures (MA, PhD); ecology, evolution and environmental biology (MA), including conservation biology; ecology, evolution, and environmental biology (PhD), including ecology and evolutionary biology, evolutionary primatology; economics (MA, PhD); English and comparative literature (MA, PhD); French and Romance philology (MA, PhD); Germanic languages (MA, PhD); global French studies (MA); global thought (MA); Hispanic cultural studies (MA); history (PhD); history and literature (MA); human rights studies (MA); Islamic studies (MA); Italian (MA, PhD); Japanese pedagogy (MA); Jewish studies (MA); Latin America and the Caribbean: regional studies (MA); Latin American and Iberian cultures (PhD); mathematics (MA, PhD), including finance (MA); medieval and Renaissance studies (MA); Middle Eastern, South Asian, and African studies (MA, PhD); modern art: critical and curatorial studies (MA); modern European studies (MA); museum anthropology (MA); music (DMA, PhD); oral history (MA); philosophical foundations of physics (MA); philosophy (MA, PhD); physics (PhD); political science (MA, PhD); psychology (PhD); quantitative methods in the social sciences (MA); religion (MA, PhD); Russia, Eurasia and East Europe: regional studies (MA); Russian translation (MA); Slavic cultures (MA); Slavic languages (MA, PhD); sociology (MA, PhD); South Asian studies (MA); statistics (MA, PhD); theatre (PhD). Dual-degree programs require admission to both Graduate School of Arts and Sciences and another Columbia school. *Program availability:* Part-time. Terminal master's awarded for partial completion of doctoral program. *Degree requirements:* For master's, variable foreign language requirement, comprehensive exam (for some programs), thesis (for some programs); for doctorate, variable foreign language requirement, comprehensive exam (for some programs), thesis/dissertation. *Entrance requirements:* For master's and doctorate, GRE General Test, GRE Subject Test (for some programs). Additional exam requirements/recommendations for international students: Required—TOEFL, IELTS. Electronic applications accepted. *Expenses: Tuition:* Full-time $44,864; part-time $1704 per credit. *Required fees:* $2370 per semester. One-time fee: $105.

La Salle University, School of Arts and Sciences, Hispanic Institute, Philadelphia, PA 19141-1199. Offers bilingual/bicultural studies (MA); ESL program specialist (Certificate); interpretation: English/Spanish-Spanish/English (Certificate); teaching English to speakers of other languages (MA); translation and interpretation (MA); translation: English/Spanish-Spanish/English (Certificate). *Program availability:* Part-time, evening/weekend. *Faculty:* 2 full-time (1 woman), 5 part-time/adjunct (1 woman). *Students:* 1 (woman) full-time, 37 part-time (26 women); includes 21 minority (7 Black or African American, non-Hispanic/Latino; 1 American Indian or Alaska Native, non-Hispanic/Latino; 1 Asian, non-Hispanic/Latino; 10 Hispanic/Latino; 2 Two or more races, non-Hispanic/Latino), 2 international. Average age 33. 24 applicants, 79% accepted, 11 enrolled. In 2017, 4 master's, 1 other advanced degree awarded. *Degree requirements:* For master's, one foreign language, project or thesis. *Entrance requirements:* For master's, GRE, MAT, or GMAT, professional resume; two letters of recommendation; for Certificate, GRE, MAT, or GMAT, professional resume; two letters of recommendation; evidence of an advanced level in Spanish. Additional exam requirements/recommendations for international students: Required—TOEFL. *Application deadline:* For fall admission, 8/15 priority date for domestic students, 7/15 for international students; for spring admission, 12/15 priority date for domestic students, 11/15 for international students; for summer admission, 4/15 priority date for domestic students, 3/15 for international students. Applications are processed on a rolling basis. Application fee: $35. Electronic applications accepted. Application fee is waived when completed online. *Expenses:* Contact institution. *Financial support:* In 2017–18, 10 students received support. Scholarships/grants available. Support available to part-time students. Financial award application deadline: 8/31; financial award applicants required to submit FAFSA. *Faculty research:* Puerto Rican literature, cross-cultural communication, English as a second language methodology, Spanish language. *Unit head:* Guadalupe Da Costa Montesinos, Director, 215-951-1209, Fax: 215-991-3506, E-mail: montesin@lasalle.edu. *Application contact:* Elizabeth Heenan, Director, Graduate and Adult Enrollment, 215-951-1100, Fax: 215-951-1462, E-mail: heenan@lasalle.edu.
Website: http://www.lasalle.edu/hispanic-institute/

Louisiana State University and Agricultural & Mechanical College, Graduate School, College of Humanities and Social Sciences, Department of Foreign Languages and Literatures, Baton Rouge, LA 70803. Offers Hispanic studies (MA). *Faculty:* 20 full-time (10 women). *Students:* 8 full-time (7 women), 1 part-time (0 women); includes 6 minority (1 Asian, non-Hispanic/Latino; 5 Hispanic/Latino), 2 international. Average age 31. 8 applicants, 75% accepted, 5 enrolled. In 2017, 8 master's awarded. *Financial support:* In 2017–18, 9 teaching assistantships (averaging $17,000 per year) were awarded. *Total annual research expenditures:* $1,164.

McGill University, Faculty of Graduate and Postdoctoral Studies, Faculty of Arts, Department of Hispanic Studies, Montréal, QC H3A 2T5, Canada. Offers MA, PhD.

Michigan State University, The Graduate School, College of Arts and Letters, Department of Spanish and Portuguese, East Lansing, MI 48824. Offers applied Spanish linguistics (MA); Hispanic cultural studies (PhD); Hispanic literatures (MA). *Entrance requirements:* Additional exam requirements/recommendations for international students: Required—TOEFL. Electronic applications accepted.

Oregon State University, College of Liberal Arts, Program in Contemporary Hispanic Studies, Corvallis, OR 97331. Offers MA. *Entrance requirements:* For master's, ACTFL OPI (Oral Proficiency Interview). Application fee: $75 ($85 for international students). *Unit head:* Dr. Juan Trujillo, Contemporary Hispanic Studies Advisor, 541-737-3956, E-mail: jtrujillo@oregonstate.edu. *Application contact:* Dr. Juan Trujillo, Contemporary Hispanic Studies Advisor, 541-737-3956, E-mail: jtrujillo@oregonstate.edu.
Website: http://liberalarts.oregonstate.edu/slcs

Pontifical Catholic University of Puerto Rico, College of Arts and Humanities, Department of Hispanic Studies, Ponce, PR 00717-0777. Offers grammar and writing (Professional Certificate); Hispanic studies (MA). *Program availability:* Part-time, evening/weekend. *Degree requirements:* For master's, variable foreign language requirement, comprehensive exam, thesis or alternative. *Entrance requirements:* For master's, GRE General Test, 2 letters of recommendation, interview, minimum GPA of 2.75. Electronic applications accepted.

Queen's University at Kingston, School of Graduate Studies, Faculty of Arts and Sciences, Department of Spanish and Italian, Kingston, ON K7L 3N6, Canada. Offers Spanish language and literature (MA). *Program availability:* Part-time. *Degree requirements:* For master's, one foreign language, thesis. *Entrance requirements:* Additional exam requirements/recommendations for international students: Required—TOEFL. Electronic applications accepted. *Faculty research:* Golden Age, nineteenth- and twentieth-century Peninsular novel, literary theory, colonial Latin America, nineteenth-and-twentieth century Latin America.

St. Thomas University, School of Leadership Studies, Program in Hispanic Media, Miami Gardens, FL 33054-6459. Offers MA, Certificate. *Program availability:* Part-time, evening/weekend. *Degree requirements:* For master's, comprehensive exam. *Entrance requirements:* Additional exam requirements/recommendations for international students: Required—TOEFL (minimum score 550 paper-based; 79 iBT). Electronic applications accepted.

San Jose State University, Graduate Studies and Research, College of Social Sciences, San Jose, CA 95192-0107. Offers applied anthropology (MA); communication studies (MA); economics (MA), including applied economics, economics; environmental studies (MS); geography (MA); history (MA), including history, history education; Mexican American studies (MA); psychology (MA, MS), including clinical psychology (MS), industrial/organizational psychology (MS), research and experimental psychology (MA); public administration (MPA); social sciences (MS); sociology (MA). *Faculty:* 59 full-time (29 women), 18 part-time/adjunct (5 women). *Students:* 181 full-time (126 women), 221 part-time (127 women); includes 228 minority (15 Black or African American, non-Hispanic/Latino; 48 Asian, non-Hispanic/Latino; 112 Hispanic/Latino; 3 Native Hawaiian or other Pacific Islander, non-Hispanic/Latino; 50 Two or more races, non-Hispanic/Latino), 38 international. Average age 30. 532 applicants, 44% accepted, 156 enrolled. In 2017, 139 master's awarded. *Degree requirements:* For master's, one foreign language, comprehensive exam, thesis (for some programs), project, field work, professional work experience. *Entrance requirements:* Additional exam requirements/recommendations for international students: Required—TOEFL (minimum score 550 paper-based; 80 iBT), IELTS (minimum score 6.5), PTE (minimum score 53). *Application deadline:* For fall admission, 2/1 for domestic and international students. Applications are processed on a rolling basis. Application fee: $55. Electronic applications accepted. *Expenses:* Tuition, state resident: full-time $7176. Tuition, nonresident: full-time $16,680. Tuition and fees vary according to course load and program. *Financial support:* Fellowships, research assistantships, career-related internships or fieldwork, Federal Work-Study, scholarships/grants, tuition waivers (full and partial), and unspecified assistantships available. Support available to part-time students. Financial award application deadline: 4/28; financial award applicants required to submit FAFSA. *Unit head:* Dr. Walt Jacobs, Dean, 408-924-5300, Fax: 408-924-5303, E-mail: walter.jacobs@sjsu.edu.
Website: http://www.sjsu.edu/socialsciences/

Texas A&M International University, Office of Graduate Studies and Research, College of Arts and Sciences, Department of Humanities, Laredo, TX 78041. Offers English (MA); Hispanic studies (PhD); history and political thought (MA); language, literature and translation (MA). *Degree requirements:* For master's, comprehensive exam (for some programs), thesis (for some programs). *Entrance requirements:* For master's, GRE General Test. Additional exam requirements/recommendations for international students: Required—TOEFL (minimum score 550 paper-based; 79 iBT).

Texas A&M University–Kingsville, College of Graduate Studies, College of Arts and Sciences, Department of Language and Literature, Interdisciplinary Program in Hispanic Culture, Kingsville, TX 78363. Offers PhD. *Degree requirements:* For doctorate, variable foreign language requirement, comprehensive exam, thesis/dissertation. *Entrance requirements:* For doctorate, GRE, MAT, GMAT, minimum GPA of 3.2, at least three letters of recommendation, demonstrated oral and written proficiency in Spanish. Additional exam requirements/recommendations for international students: Required—TOEFL (minimum score 550 paper-based; 79 iBT). Electronic applications accepted.

University of Alberta, Faculty of Graduate Studies and Research, Department of Modern Languages and Cultural Studies, Edmonton, AB T6G 2E1, Canada. Offers

applied linguistics (Germanic, Romance, Slavic) (MA); French language, literatures and linguistics (PhD); French language, literatures, and linguistics (MA); Germanic languages, literatures and linguistics (PhD); Germanic languages, literatures, and linguistics (MA); Italian studies (MA); Slavic languages and literatures (Russian, Ukrainian) (MA, PhD); Slavic linguistics (Russian, Ukrainian) (MA, PhD); Spanish and Latin American studies (MA, PhD); Ukrainian folklore (MA, PhD). *Program availability:* Part-time. *Degree requirements:* For master's, one foreign language, thesis; for doctorate, 2 foreign languages, comprehensive exam, thesis/dissertation. *Entrance requirements:* For master's and doctorate, 1 language other than English. Additional exam requirements/recommendations for international students: Required—Michigan English Language Assessment Battery or TOEFL (minimum score 550 paper-based). Electronic applications accepted. *Faculty research:* Russian/Ukrainian studies; German studies; contemporary Latin American, French and Francophone studies; Italian studies.

The University of British Columbia, Faculty of Arts and Faculty of Graduate Studies, Department of French, Hispanic and Italian Studies, Vancouver, BC V6T 1Z1, Canada. Offers French (MA, PhD); Hispanic studies (MA, PhD). *Program availability:* Part-time. *Degree requirements:* For master's, thesis optional; for doctorate, 2 foreign languages, comprehensive exam, thesis/dissertation. *Entrance requirements:* For doctorate, MA. Additional exam requirements/recommendations for international students: Required—TOEFL. Electronic applications accepted. *Expenses:* Contact institution. *Faculty research:* Medieval and Renaissance literature, modern literature, romance philology and linguistics, cultural studies, women's literature.

University of California, Riverside, Graduate Division, Department of Hispanic Studies, Riverside, CA 92521-0102. Offers Spanish (MA, PhD). Terminal master's awarded for partial completion of doctoral program. *Degree requirements:* For master's, one foreign language, comprehensive exam; for doctorate, one foreign language, thesis/dissertation, qualifying exams, 1 quarter of teaching experience. *Entrance requirements:* For master's and doctorate, GRE General Test, minimum GPA of 3.0. Additional exam requirements/recommendations for international students: Required—TOEFL (minimum score 550 paper-based; 80 iBT). Electronic applications accepted. *Expenses:* Tuition, state resident: full-time $5746. Tuition, nonresident: full-time $10,780. Tuition and fees vary according to campus/location and program. *Faculty research:* Spanish literature of the sixteenth-, seventeenth- and twentieth-century; pre-Columbian and colonial Latin American literature; nineteenth- and twentieth-century Latin American literature.

University of California, Santa Barbara, Graduate Division, College of Letters and Sciences, Division of Humanities and Fine Arts, Department of Spanish and Portuguese, Santa Barbara, CA 93106-4150. Offers Hispanic languages and literatures (PhD), including European medieval studies, feminist studies, Hispanic linguistics, Hispanic literature, Luso-Brazilian literature; Hispanic linguistics (MA); Luso-Brazilian literature (MA); Spanish or Spanish-American literature (MA); MA/PhD. Terminal master's awarded for partial completion of doctoral program. *Degree requirements:* For master's, 2 foreign languages, comprehensive exam (for some programs), thesis optional; for doctorate, 3 foreign languages, comprehensive exam, thesis/dissertation. *Entrance requirements:* For master's and doctorate, GRE. Additional exam requirements/recommendations for international students: Required—TOEFL (minimum score 550 paper-based; 80 iBT), IELTS (minimum score 7). Electronic applications accepted. *Faculty research:* Nineteenth-century Spanish and Portuguese literature, Spanish and Spanish-American literature, nineteenth- and twentieth-century Portuguese and Brazilian literatures, Hispanic linguistics, Catalan language and culture.

University of California, Santa Barbara, Graduate Division, College of Letters and Sciences, Division of Social Sciences, Department of Chicana and Chicano Studies, Santa Barbara, CA 93106-4120. Offers MA/PhD. *Entrance requirements:* Additional exam requirements/recommendations for international students: Required—TOEFL (minimum score 550 paper-based; 80 iBT), IELTS (minimum score 7). Electronic applications accepted. *Faculty research:* History and narrative, cultural production, social processes, gender and sexuality studies.

University of Houston, College of Liberal Arts and Social Sciences, Department of Hispanic Studies, Houston, TX 77204. Offers Hispanic literature and linguistics (PhD); Spanish (MA, PhD), including creative writing (PhD). *Program availability:* Part-time. *Degree requirements:* For master's, comprehensive exam, thesis optional; for doctorate, 2 foreign languages, comprehensive exam, thesis/dissertation. *Entrance requirements:* For master's and doctorate, GRE. Additional exam requirements/recommendations for international students: Required—TOEFL (minimum score 550 paper-based; 79 iBT); Recommended—IELTS (minimum score 6.5). Electronic applications accepted.

University of Illinois at Chicago, College of Liberal Arts and Sciences, School of Literatures, Cultural Studies and Linguistics, Department of Hispanic and Italian Studies, Chicago, IL 60607-7128. Offers Hispanic linguistics (PhD). *Program availability:* Part-time. Terminal master's awarded for partial completion of doctoral program. *Degree requirements:* For master's, one foreign language, departmental qualifying exam. *Entrance requirements:* For master's, GRE General Test, minimum GPA of 2.75, undergraduate major in Spanish. Additional exam requirements/recommendations for international students: Required—TOEFL. Electronic applications accepted. *Faculty research:* Linguistic competence of bilingual speakers as a window to understanding the human faculty of language, neurocognitive processing of language among different speakers and learners, how languages are used within their social contexts.

University of Kentucky, Graduate School, College of Arts and Sciences, Program in Hispanic Studies, Lexington, KY 40506-0032. Offers MA, PhD. *Degree requirements:* For master's, one foreign language, comprehensive exam, thesis optional; for doctorate, 2 foreign languages, comprehensive exam, thesis/dissertation. *Entrance requirements:* For master's, GRE General Test, minimum undergraduate GPA of 2.75; for doctorate, GRE General Test, minimum graduate GPA of 3.0. Additional exam requirements/recommendations for international students: Required—TOEFL (minimum score 550 paper-based). Electronic applications accepted. *Faculty research:* Hispanic linguistics, medieval Spanish literature and civilization, Renaissance and Golden Age literature and civilization, Spanish American literature and civilization.

The University of Manchester, School of Languages, Linguistics and Cultures, Manchester, United Kingdom. Offers Arab world studies (PhD); Chinese studies (M Phil, PhD); East Asian studies (M Phil, PhD); English language (PhD); French studies (M Phil, PhD); German studies (M Phil, PhD); interpreting studies (PhD); Italian studies (M Phil, PhD); Japanese studies (M Phil, PhD); Latin American cultural studies (M Phil, PhD); linguistics (M Phil, PhD); Middle Eastern studies (M Phil, PhD); Polish studies (M Phil, PhD); Portuguese studies (M Phil, PhD); Russian studies (M Phil, PhD); Spanish studies (M Phil, PhD); translation and intercultural studies (M Phil, PhD).

University of Nevada, Las Vegas, Graduate College, College of Liberal Arts, Department of World Languages and Cultures, Las Vegas, NV 89154-5047. Offers Hispanic studies (MA); Spanish translation (Certificate). *Program availability:* Part-time. *Faculty:* 3 full-time (2 women), 1 (woman) part-time/adjunct. *Students:* 4 full-time (3 women), 8 part-time (5 women); includes 9 minority (all Hispanic/Latino), 1 international. Average age 35. 6 applicants, 50% accepted, 3 enrolled. In 2017, 1 master's awarded. *Degree requirements:* For master's, one foreign language, comprehensive exam, final research project. *Entrance requirements:* For master's, minimum GPA of 3.0; 2 letters of recommendation. Additional exam requirements/recommendations for international students: Required—TOEFL (minimum score 550 paper-based; 80 iBT), IELTS (minimum score 7). *Application deadline:* For fall admission, 5/1 for domestic students; for spring admission, 11/15 for domestic students. Application fee: $60 ($95 for international students). Electronic applications accepted. *Expenses:* Contact institution. *Financial support:* In 2017–18, 4 students received support, including 4 teaching assistantships with full and partial tuition reimbursements available (averaging $11,250 per year); institutionally sponsored loans, scholarships/grants, health care benefits, and unspecified assistantships also available. Financial award application deadline: 3/15; financial award applicants required to submit FAFSA. *Faculty research:* Spanish Golden Age poetry, prose and theater; Miguel de Cervantes; history of ideas in creative letters, historical linguistics (French/Spanish), Spanish sociolinguistics, second language acquisition, women narrators of Mexico and Spain, translation studies, Mexican film and culture. *Unit head:* Dr. Susan Byrne, Chair, 702-895-3464, Fax: 702-895-1226, E-mail: susan.byrne@unlv.edu. *Application contact:* Dr. Margarita Jara, Graduate Coordinator, 702-895-1690, Fax: 702-895-1226, E-mail: margarita.jara@unlv.edu.
Website: http://liberalarts.unlv.edu/Foreign_Languages/graduates.html

The University of North Carolina at Greensboro, Graduate School, College of Arts and Sciences, Department of Languages, Literatures, and Cultures, Program in Spanish, Greensboro, NC 27412-5001. Offers advanced Spanish language and Hispanic cultural studies (Certificate); Spanish (MA). *Degree requirements:* For master's, one foreign language, comprehensive exam, thesis or alternative. *Entrance requirements:* For master's, GRE General Test, 3-5 minute tape demonstrating foreign language proficiency, composition in Spanish, sample paper in English. Additional exam requirements/recommendations for international students: Required—TOEFL. Electronic applications accepted.

The University of North Carolina Wilmington, College of Arts and Sciences, Department of World Languages and Cultures, Wilmington, NC 28403-3297. Offers Hispanic studies (Postbaccalaureate Certificate); Spanish (MA). *Program availability:* Part-time. *Faculty:* 15 full-time (7 women). *Students:* 6 full-time (5 women), 10 part-time (7 women); includes 5 minority (all Hispanic/Latino), 2 international. Average age 28. 12 applicants, 75% accepted, 7 enrolled. In 2017, 6 master's awarded. *Degree requirements:* For master's, one foreign language, comprehensive exam, thesis (for some programs). *Entrance requirements:* For master's, 3 letters of recommendation, 2 three- to five-minute recorded speaking samples (both in English and Spanish), writing sample (both in English and Spanish). Additional exam requirements/recommendations for international students: Required—TOEFL (minimum score 550 paper-based; 79 iBT), IELTS (minimum score 6.5). *Application deadline:* For fall admission, 5/15 for domestic students; for spring admission, 11/1 for domestic students; for summer admission, 3/1 for domestic students. Applications are processed on a rolling basis. Application fee: $75. Electronic applications accepted. *Expenses:* Tuition, state resident: full-time $4626; part-time $226.76 per credit hour. Tuition, nonresident: full-time $17,834; part-time $874.22 per credit hour. *Required fees:* $2124. Tuition and fees vary according to program. *Financial support:* Teaching assistantships and scholarships/grants available. Financial award application deadline: 1/1; financial award applicants required to submit FAFSA. *Unit head:* Dr. Derrick Miller, Interim Chair, 910-962-2538, Fax: 910-962-7712, E-mail: millerd@uncw.edu. *Application contact:* Dr. Brian Chandler, Graduate Coordinator, 910-962-2299, Fax: 910-962-7712, E-mail: chandlerb@uncw.edu.
Website: http://www.uncw.edu/fll/spanish/spngraduate.html

University of Puerto Rico–Mayagüez, Graduate Studies, College of Arts and Sciences, Department of Hispanic Studies, Mayagüez, PR 00681-9000. Offers MA. *Program availability:* Part-time. *Degree requirements:* For master's, comprehensive exam, thesis. *Entrance requirements:* For master's, minimum GPA of 2.75, BA in Hispanic studies or its equivalent. Electronic applications accepted. *Faculty research:* Spanish literature, Hispanic-American literature, Puerto Rican literature, stylistics, linguistics.

University of Puerto Rico–Río Piedras, College of Humanities, Department of Hispanic Studies, San Juan, PR 00931-3300. Offers Hispanic linguistics (PhD); Hispanic studies (MA); Latin American literature (PhD); Puerto Rican literature (PhD); Spanish literature (PhD). *Program availability:* Part-time. *Degree requirements:* For master's, one foreign language, comprehensive exam, thesis; for doctorate, one foreign language, comprehensive exam, thesis/dissertation. *Entrance requirements:* For master's, PAEG or GRE, interview, minimum GPA of 3.0, letter of recommendation (2); for doctorate, PAEG or GRE, interview, master's degree, minimum GPA of 3.0, letter of recommendation (2). *Faculty research:* Poetry of Luis Palés Matos, short stories in Puerto Rico, language in the social process, "Decima Popular", Anglicism.

The University of Texas at Austin, Graduate School, College of Liberal Arts, Center for Mexican American Studies, Austin, TX 78712-1111. Offers MA.

University of Victoria, Faculty of Graduate Studies, Faculty of Humanities, Department of Hispanic and Italian Studies, Victoria, BC V8W 2Y2, Canada. Offers Hispanic and Italian studies (MA); Hispanic studies (MA). *Degree requirements:* For master's, one foreign language, comprehensive exam, thesis (for some programs). *Entrance requirements:* For master's, undergraduate major in Hispanic studies, minimum B+ average. Additional exam requirements/recommendations for international students: Required—TOEFL (minimum score 575 paper-based), IELTS (minimum score 7). Electronic applications accepted. *Faculty research:* Medieval/Renaissance Spanish and Italian literature, Golden Age literature, Latin American literature.

Villanova University, Graduate School of Liberal Arts and Sciences, Department of Romance Languages and Literatures, Villanova, PA 19085-1699. Offers Hispanic studies (MA). *Program availability:* Part-time, evening/weekend. *Faculty:* 3. *Students:* 10 applicants, 100% accepted, 5 enrolled. In 2017, 7 master's awarded. *Degree requirements:* For master's, one foreign language, comprehensive exam. *Entrance requirements:* For master's, minimum GPA of 3.0, writing sample in Spanish. Additional exam requirements/recommendations for international students: Required—TOEFL. *Application deadline:* For fall admission, 3/1 for domestic students, 5/1 for international students; for spring admission, 11/15 for domestic students, 10/15 for international students; for summer admission, 5/1 for domestic students. Applications are processed on a rolling basis. Application fee: $50. Electronic applications accepted. *Financial support:* Teaching assistantships with tuition reimbursements, scholarships/grants, and unspecified assistantships available. Financial award applicants required to submit FAFSA. *Unit head:* Dr. Christine Palus, Dean, 610-519-7090, Fax: 610-519-7096.
Website: http://www1.villanova.edu/villanova/artsci/romancelanglit/academics/graduateprograminhispanicstudies.html

Holocaust and Genocide Studies

Chapman University, Wilkinson College of Arts, Humanities, and Social Sciences, War and Society Program, Orange, CA 92866. Offers MA. *Program availability:* Part-time, evening/weekend. *Faculty:* 9 full-time (3 women), 8 part-time/adjunct (3 women). *Students:* 10 full-time (7 women), 7 part-time (2 women); includes 3 minority (1 Black or African American, non-Hispanic/Latino; 2 Hispanic/Latino). Average age 32. 8 applicants, 88% accepted, 5 enrolled. In 2017, 3 master's awarded. *Degree requirements:* For master's, thesis. *Entrance requirements:* For master's, GRE (if undergraduate GPA less than 3.0). *Application deadline:* For fall admission, 2/1 priority date for domestic students. Applications are processed on a rolling basis. Application fee: $60. Electronic applications accepted. *Expenses:* Contact institution. *Financial support:* Fellowships, teaching assistantships, Federal Work-Study, scholarships/grants, and unspecified assistantships available. *Unit head:* Dr. Gregory A. Daddis, Director, 714-997-6834, E-mail: daddis@chapman.edu.
Website: https://www.chapman.edu/wilkinson/graduate-studies/ma-warsociety.aspx

Clark University, Graduate School, Department of History, Program in Holocaust History and Genocide Studies, Worcester, MA 01610-1477. Offers genocide studies (PhD); history of the Holocaust (PhD). *Students:* 21 full-time (13 women), 10 international. Average age 33. 31 applicants, 13% accepted, 4 enrolled. In 2017, 2 doctorates awarded. *Degree requirements:* For doctorate, thesis/dissertation. *Entrance requirements:* For doctorate, GRE. Additional exam requirements/recommendations for international students: Required—TOEFL (minimum score 575 paper-based; 90 iBT), IELTS (minimum score 6.5). *Application deadline:* For fall admission, 1/15 priority date for domestic students. Application fee: $75. Electronic applications accepted. *Financial support:* Fellowships, research assistantships, teaching assistantships, and tuition waivers (partial) available. *Faculty research:* Jewish persecution, children and survivors, Germany's role in the Holocaust. *Unit head:* Shelly Tenenbaum, 508-793-7241, E-mail: stenenbaum@clarku.edu. *Application contact:* Mary Jane Rein, Executive Director, 508-793-8897, Fax: 508-793-8827, E-mail: mrein@clarku.edu.

College of Saint Elizabeth, Program in Education, Morristown, NJ 07960-6989. Offers assistive technology (Certificate); education (MA); ESL (Certificate); Holocaust/genocide education (Certificate); middle school science (Certificate); online teaching in the 21st century (Certificate); teaching (Certificate), including K-12, K-6, teacher of students with disabilities. *Program availability:* Part-time. *Faculty:* 3 full-time (2 women), 8 part-time/adjunct (6 women). *Students:* 1 (woman) full-time, 34 part-time (29 women); includes 1 minority (Hispanic/Latino). Average age 32. 25 applicants, 100% accepted, 24 enrolled. In 2017, 23 master's awarded. *Degree requirements:* For master's and Certificate, thesis. *Entrance requirements:* For master's, certification. Additional exam requirements/recommendations for international students: Required—TOEFL (minimum score 550 paper-based; 79 iBT), IELTS (minimum score 6.5). *Application deadline:* For fall admission, 5/1 for international students. Applications are processed on a rolling basis. Application fee: $35. Electronic applications accepted. Application fee is waived when completed online. *Financial support:* Career-related internships or fieldwork, scholarships/grants, and unspecified assistantships available. Financial award applicants required to submit FAFSA. *Unit head:* Dr. Joseph Ciccone, 973-290-4383, Fax: 973-290-4389, E-mail: jciccone@cse.edu. *Application contact:* Lori J. Fragoso, Director of Graduate and Continuing Studies Admissions, 973-290-4413, Fax: 973-290-4710, E-mail: apply@cse.edu.
Website: http://www.cse.edu/academics/prof-studies/education/

Gratz College, Graduate Programs, Programs in Holocaust and Genocide Studies, Melrose Park, PA 19027. Offers MA, PhD. *Program availability:* Online learning.

Kean University, College of Liberal Arts, Program in Holocaust and Genocide Studies, Union, NJ 07083. Offers MA. *Program availability:* Part-time. *Faculty:* 14 full-time (7 women). *Students:* 3 full-time (2 women), 13 part-time (6 women), 1 international. Average age 39. 13 applicants, 100% accepted, 6 enrolled. In 2017, 8 master's awarded. *Degree requirements:* For master's, thesis. *Entrance requirements:* For master's, minimum cumulative GPA of 3.0, official transcripts from all institutions attended, two letters of recommendation from professional associates, personal statement, professional resume/curriculum vitae. Additional exam requirements/recommendations for international students: Required—TOEFL (minimum score 550 paper-based; 79 iBT), IELTS (minimum score 6.5). *Application deadline:* For fall admission, 6/30 for domestic and international students; for spring admission, 12/1 for domestic and international students. Applications are processed on a rolling basis. Application fee: $75. Electronic applications accepted. *Expenses:* Tuition, state resident: full-time $13,419; part-time $653 per credit. Tuition, nonresident: full-time $18,188; part-time $801 per credit. *Required fees:* $3382; $154 per credit. Tuition and fees vary according to course level, course load, degree level and program. *Financial support:* Scholarships/grants and unspecified assistantships available. Financial award applicants required to submit FAFSA. *Unit head:* Dr. Dennis Klein, Program Coordinator, 908-737-0256, E-mail: dklein@kean.edu. *Application contact:* Amy Clark, Program Assistant, 908-737-7100, E-mail: gradadmissions@kean.edu.
Website: http://grad.kean.edu/mahgs

Stockton University, Office of Graduate Studies, Program in Holocaust and Genocide Studies, Galloway, NJ 08205-9441. Offers MA. *Program availability:* Part-time, evening/weekend, online only, 100% online. *Faculty:* 5 full-time (2 women), 1 part-time/adjunct (0 women). *Students:* 2 full-time (both women), 39 part-time (30 women); includes 5

minority (1 Black or African American, non-Hispanic/Latino; 2 Hispanic/Latino; 2 Two or more races, non-Hispanic/Latino), 11 international. Average age 35. 37 applicants, 86% accepted, 25 enrolled. In 2017, 6 master's awarded. *Entrance requirements:* Additional exam requirements/recommendations for international students: Required—TOEFL. *Application deadline:* For fall admission, 7/1 for domestic and international students; for spring admission, 12/1 for domestic students, 11/1 for international students. Applications are processed on a rolling basis. Application fee: $50. Electronic applications accepted. *Expenses:* Contact institution. *Financial support:* Fellowships, research assistantships, career-related internships or fieldwork, Federal Work-Study, scholarships/grants, and unspecified assistantships available. Financial award application deadline: 3/1; financial award applicants required to submit FAFSA. *Faculty research:* Women and the Holocaust, survivor perspectives, liberty and persecution. *Unit head:* Dr. Elisa Forgey, Program Director, 609-626-3640, Fax: 609-626-6050, E-mail: mahg@stockton.edu. *Application contact:* Tara Williams, Assistant Director of Graduate Enrollment Management, 609-626-3640, Fax: 609-626-6050, E-mail: gradschool@stockton.edu.

Texas A&M University–Commerce, College of Humanities, Social Sciences and Arts, Commerce, TX 75429. Offers applied criminology (MS); applied linguistics (MA, MS); art (MA, MFA); computational linguistics (Graduate Certificate); creative writing (Graduate Certificate); criminal justice management (Graduate Certificate); criminal justice studies (Graduate Certificate); English (MA, MS, PhD); film studies (Graduate Certificate); history (MA, MS); history of Christianity (Graduate Certificate); Holocaust studies (Graduate Certificate); homeland security (Graduate Certificate); music education (MM); music performance (MM); political science (MA, MS); public history (Graduate Certificate); sociology (MS); Spanish (MA); studies in children's and adolescent literature and culture (Graduate Certificate); teaching English to speakers of other languages (Graduate Certificate); theater (MA, MS); world history (Graduate Certificate). *Program availability:* Part-time. *Faculty:* 56 full-time (26 women), 10 part-time/adjunct (5 women). *Students:* 133 full-time (85 women), 439 part-time (311 women); includes 204 minority (79 Black or African American, non-Hispanic/Latino; 4 American Indian or Alaska Native, non-Hispanic/Latino; 9 Asian, non-Hispanic/Latino; 98 Hispanic/Latino; 14 Two or more races, non-Hispanic/Latino), 26 international. Average age 36. 261 applicants, 50% accepted, 113 enrolled. In 2017, 105 master's, 5 doctorates awarded. *Degree requirements:* For master's, one foreign language, comprehensive exam, thesis (for some programs); for doctorate, one foreign language, comprehensive exam, thesis/dissertation, departmental qualifying exam. *Entrance requirements:* For master's and doctorate, GRE General Test. Additional exam requirements/recommendations for international students: Required—TOEFL (minimum score 550 paper-based; 79 iBT), IELTS (minimum score 6). *Application deadline:* Applications are processed on a rolling basis. Application fee: $50. Electronic applications accepted. *Expenses:* Contact institution. *Financial support:* In 2017–18, 43 students received support, including 9 research assistantships with partial tuition reimbursements available (averaging $9,000 per year), 68 teaching assistantships with partial tuition reimbursements available (averaging $9,000 per year); Federal Work-Study, institutionally sponsored loans, scholarships/grants, health care benefits, and unspecified assistantships also available. Financial award application deadline: 5/1; financial award applicants required to submit FAFSA. *Unit head:* Dr. William F. Kuracina, Interim Dean, 903-886-5166, Fax: 903-886-5774, E-mail: william.kuracina@tamuc.edu. *Application contact:* Vicky Turner, Doctoral Degree and Special Programs Coordinator, 903-886-5167, E-mail: vicky.turner@tamuc.edu.
Website: http://www.tamuc.edu/academics/graduateSchool/programs/humanitiesSocialScienceArts/default.aspx

West Chester University of Pennsylvania, College of Arts and Humanities, Program in Holocaust and Genocide Studies, West Chester, PA 19383. Offers Holocaust and genocide studies (MA, Certificate). *Program availability:* Part-time, evening/weekend. *Students:* 3 full-time (2 women), 7 part-time (5 women). Average age 35. 9 applicants, 100% accepted, 3 enrolled. In 2017, 3 master's awarded. *Degree requirements:* For master's, comprehensive exam (for some programs), thesis or comprehensive exam; for Certificate, 18 hours of coursework. *Entrance requirements:* For master's and Certificate, statement of professional goals, two letters of recommendation, minimum GPA of 2.8. Additional exam requirements/recommendations for international students: Required—TOEFL or IELTS. *Application deadline:* For fall admission, 5/15 for international students; for spring admission, 10/15 for international students. Applications are processed on a rolling basis. Application fee: $50. Electronic applications accepted. *Expenses:* Tuition, state resident: full-time $9000; part-time $500 per credit. Tuition, nonresident: full-time $13,500; part-time $750 per credit. *Required fees:* $2959; $149.79 per credit. *Financial support:* Scholarships/grants and unspecified assistantships available. Financial award application deadline: 3/15; financial award applicants required to submit FAFSA. *Faculty research:* Holocaust, genocide history, German history, human rights studies, Jewish history. *Unit head:* Dr. Jonathan Friedman, Director and Graduate Coordinator, 610-436-2972, Fax: 610-436-3150, E-mail: jfriedman@wcupa.edu. *Application contact:* Office of Graduate Studies and Extended Education, 610-436-2943, Fax: 610-436-2763, E-mail: gradstudy@wcupa.edu.
Website: http://www.wcupa.edu/arts-humanities/holocaust/

Jewish Studies

Academy for Jewish Religion California, Graduate Programs, Los Angeles, CA 90024. Offers MJS. Application fee: $300. *Expenses:* $826 per credit. *Application contact:* Robin Federman, Director of Admissions, 213-884-4133, E-mail: rfederman@ajrca.edu.
Website: https://ajrca.edu/programs/masters-programs/

American Jewish University, Graduate School of Nonprofit Management, Program in Jewish Communal Studies, Bel Air, CA 90077-1599. Offers MAJCS. *Degree requirements:* For master's, thesis. *Entrance requirements:* For master's, GMAT or GRE General Test, interview.

Biola University, Talbot School of Theology, La Mirada, CA 90639-0001. Offers adult/family ministry (MACE); Bible exposition (MA, Th M); Biblical and theological studies

(Certificate); children's ministry (MACE); Christian education (M Div); cross-cultural education ministry (MACE); educational studies (Ed D, PhD); evangelism and discipleship (M Div); general Christian education (MACE); Messianic Jewish studies (M Div, Certificate); missions and intercultural studies (M Div); New Testament (MA, Th M); Old Testament (MA); Old Testament and Semitics (Th M); pastoral and general ministry (M Div); pastoral care and counseling (M Div, MACML); philosophy (MA); preaching and pastoral ministry (MACML); spiritual formation (M Div, Certificate); spiritual formation and soul care (MA); sports ministry (MACML); theology (MA, Th M, D Min, Certificate); youth ministry (MACE). *Program availability:* Part-time, evening/weekend. *Students:* 475 full-time (113 women), 603 part-time (176 women); includes 541 minority (39 Black or African American, non-Hispanic/Latino; 2 American Indian or

Alaska Native, non-Hispanic/Latino; 378 Asian, non-Hispanic/Latino; 84 Hispanic/Latino; 1 Native Hawaiian or other Pacific Islander, non-Hispanic/Latino; 37 Two or more races, non-Hispanic/Latino), 105 international. 437 applicants, 78% accepted, 241 enrolled. In 2017, 177 master's, 24 doctorates awarded. *Entrance requirements:* For master's, bachelor's degree from accredited college or university; minimum GPA of 2.6 (for M Div), 3.0 (for MA); for doctorate, M Div or MA. Additional exam requirements/recommendations for international students: Required—TOEFL (minimum score 600 paper-based; 88 iBT). *Application deadline:* For fall admission, 7/1 for domestic students, 6/1 for international students; for spring admission, 12/1 priority date for domestic students. Applications are processed on a rolling basis. Application fee: $65. Electronic applications accepted. *Financial support:* Scholarships/grants and unspecified assistantships available. Support available to part-time students. Financial award applicants required to submit FAFSA. *Faculty research:* New Testament, Old Testament, spiritual formation, Christian education, theological studies, Christian ministry, preaching and pastoral ministry, language and literature, bible exposition, Christian leadership. *Unit head:* Dr. Clint Arnold, Dean, 562-903-4816, Fax: 562-903-4748. *Application contact:* Graduate Admissions Office, 562-903-4752, E-mail: graduate.admissions@biola.edu.
Website: http://www.talbot.edu/

Brandeis University, Graduate School of Arts and Sciences, Department of Near Eastern and Judaic Studies, Waltham, MA 02454-9110. Offers Near Eastern and Judaic studies (MA, PhD); near Eastern and Judaic studies/conflict resolution and coexistence (MA); near Eastern and Judaic studies/Jewish professional leadership (MA); near Eastern and Judaic studies/women's, gender, and sexuality studies (MA); teaching of Hebrew (MAT). Offered jointly with The Heller School of Social Policy and Management. *Program availability:* Part-time. *Faculty:* 24 full-time (10 women), 6 part-time/adjunct (3 women). *Students:* 41 full-time (17 women), 2 part-time (1 woman); includes 7 minority (2 Black or African American, non-Hispanic/Latino; 1 Asian, non-Hispanic/Latino; 4 Hispanic/Latino), 9 international. Average age 33. 47 applicants, 45% accepted, 4 enrolled. In 2017, 8 master's, 3 doctorates awarded. Terminal master's awarded for partial completion of doctoral program. *Degree requirements:* For master's, one foreign language, thesis or alternative, proseminar, capstone; for doctorate, variable foreign language requirement, comprehensive exam, thesis/dissertation. *Entrance requirements:* For master's and doctorate, GRE General Test (recommended), letters of recommendation, transcripts, statement of purpose, writing sample, resume. Additional exam requirements/recommendations for international students: Required—PTE (minimum score 68), TOEFL (minimum score 600 paper-based, 100 iBT) or IELTS (7). *Application deadline:* For fall admission, 1/15 priority date for domestic students. Applications are processed on a rolling basis. Application fee: $75. Electronic applications accepted. *Expenses: Tuition:* Full-time $48,720. *Required fees:* $88. Tuition and fees vary according to course load, degree level, program and student level. *Financial support:* In 2017–18, 29 students received support, including 20 fellowships with full tuition reimbursements available (averaging $24,480 per year), 1 teaching assistantship with partial tuition reimbursement available (averaging $2,500 per year); Federal Work-Study, scholarships/grants, health care benefits, and tuition waivers (partial) also available. Support available to part-time students. Financial award application deadline: 4/15; financial award applicants required to submit FAFSA. *Faculty research:* Bible and ancient Near East, Judaic Studies, Israel Studies, modern Middle East, Arabic and Islamic civilizations. *Unit head:* Dr. Eugene Sheppard, Department Chair, 781-736-2950, E-mail: sheppard@brandeis.edu. *Application contact:* Jean Mannion, Department Administrator, 781-736-2950, E-mail: mannion@brandeis.edu.
Website: http://www.brandeis.edu/gsas/programs/nejs.html

Brandeis University, Graduate School of Arts and Sciences, Hornstein: Jewish Professional Leadership Program, Waltham, MA 02454-9110. Offers MA/MA, MBA/MA, MPP/MA. Offered jointly with The Heller School of Social Policy and Management. *Faculty:* 3 full-time (1 woman), 2 part-time/adjunct (0 women). *Students:* 13 full-time (8 women), 2 international. Average age 26. 14 applicants, 86% accepted, 6 enrolled. *Entrance requirements:* Additional exam requirements/recommendations for international students: Required—PTE (minimum score 68), TOEFL (minimum score 600 paper-based, 100 iBT) or IELTS (7). *Application deadline:* For fall admission, 1/15 priority date for domestic students. Applications are processed on a rolling basis. Application fee: $75. Electronic applications accepted. *Expenses:* $60,900 tuition, $382 fees. *Financial support:* In 2017–18, 3 students received support. Federal Work-Study, scholarships/grants, and tuition waivers (partial) available. Financial award application deadline: 4/15; financial award applicants required to submit FAFSA. *Faculty research:* Leadership, Jewish professional leadership, business administration, non-profit management, public policy, Near Eastern and Judaic studies, Israel-Diaspora relations. *Unit head:* Dr. Ellen Smith, Director of Graduate Studies, 781-736-2998, E-mail: esmith2@brandeis.edu. *Application contact:* Carol Hengerle, Department Administrator, 781-736-2990, Fax: 781-736-2070, E-mail: hornstein@brandeis.edu.
Website: http://www.brandeis.edu/gsas/programs/hornstein.html

Brandeis University, Graduate School of Arts and Sciences, Program in Women's, Gender, and Sexuality Studies, Waltham, MA 02454-9110. Offers anthropology/women's, gender, and sexuality studies (MA); English/women's, gender, and sexuality studies (MA); near Eastern and Judaic studies /women's, gender, and sexuality studies (MA); public policy/women's, gender, and sexuality studies (MA); sociology/women's, gender, and sexuality studies (MA); sustainable international development/women's, gender, and sexuality studies (MA); women's, gender, and sexuality studies (MA). Offered jointly with The Heller School of Social Policy and Management. *Students:* 10 full-time (all women); includes 2 minority (1 Hispanic/Latino; 1 Two or more races, non-Hispanic/Latino). Average age 25. 42 applicants, 48% accepted, 8 enrolled. In 2017, 8 master's awarded. *Degree requirements:* For master's, thesis. *Entrance requirements:* For master's, GRE General Test, critical writing sample, resume, statement of purpose, transcripts, letters of recommendation. Additional exam requirements/recommendations for international students: Required—PTE (minimum score 68), TOEFL (minimum score 600 paper-based, 100 iBT) or IELTS (7). *Application deadline:* For fall admission, 1/15 for domestic students. Application fee: $75. Electronic applications accepted. *Expenses: Tuition:* Full-time $48,720. *Required fees:* $88. Tuition and fees vary according to course load, degree level, program and student level. *Financial support:* In 2017–18, 6 students received support, including 7 teaching assistantships with partial tuition reimbursements available (averaging $3,200 per year); fellowships, scholarships/grants, and tuition waivers (partial) also available. Financial award application deadline: 4/15; financial award applicants required to submit FAFSA. *Unit head:* Dr. ChaeRan Freeze, Director of Graduate Study, 781-736-2987, E-mail: cfreeze@brandeis.edu. *Application contact:* Shannon Kearns, Department Administrator, 781-736-3045, E-mail: skearns@brandeis.edu.
Website: http://www.brandeis.edu/gsas/programs/wgs.html

Brooklyn College of the City University of New York, School of Humanities and Social Sciences, Department of Judaic Studies, Brooklyn, NY 11210-2889. Offers MA. *Program availability:* Part-time, evening/weekend. *Degree requirements:* For master's, 2 foreign languages, comprehensive exam or thesis. *Entrance requirements:* For master's, 18 upper-level credits in Judaic studies, interview, 2 letters of recommendation. Additional exam requirements/recommendations for international students: Required—TOEFL (minimum score 525 paper-based; 70 iBT). Electronic applications accepted. *Faculty research:* Biblical studies, Talmud and Midrash, modern Jewish history and thought.

Central Yeshiva Tomchei Tmimim-Lubavitch, Graduate Programs, Brooklyn, NY 11230. Offers Jewish/Judaic studies (MA); Talmudic studies (MA). *Accreditation:* AARTS.

Columbia University, Graduate School of Arts and Sciences, New York, NY 10027. Offers African-American studies (MA); American studies (MA); anthropology (MA, PhD); art history and archaeology (MA, PhD); astronomy (PhD); biological sciences (PhD); biotechnology (MA); chemical physics (PhD); chemistry (PhD); classical studies (MA, PhD); classics (MA, PhD); climate and society (MA); conservation biology (MA); earth and environmental sciences (PhD); East Asia: regional studies (MA); East Asian languages and cultures (MA, PhD); ecology, evolution and environmental biology (MA), including conservation biology; ecology, evolution, and environmental biology (PhD), including ecology and evolutionary biology, evolutionary primatology; economics (MA, PhD); English and comparative literature (MA, PhD); French and Romance philology (MA, PhD); Germanic languages (MA, PhD); global French studies (MA); global thought (MA); Hispanic cultural studies (MA); history (PhD); history and literature (MA); human rights studies (MA); Islamic studies (MA); Italian (MA, PhD); Japanese pedagogy (MA); Jewish studies (MA); Latin America and the Caribbean: regional studies (MA); Latin American and Iberian cultures (PhD); mathematics (MA, PhD), including finance (MA); medieval and Renaissance studies (MA); Middle Eastern, South Asian, and African studies (MA, PhD); modern art: critical and curatorial studies (MA); modern European studies (MA); museum anthropology (MA); music (DMA, PhD); oral history (MA); philosophical foundations of physics (MA); philosophy (MA, PhD); physics (PhD); political science (MA, PhD); psychology (PhD); quantitative methods in the social sciences (MA); religion (MA, PhD); Russia, Eurasia and East Europe: regional studies (MA); Russian translation (MA); Slavic cultures (MA); Slavic languages (MA, PhD); sociology (MA, PhD); South Asian studies (MA); statistics (MA, PhD); theatre (PhD). Dual-degree programs require admission to both Graduate School of Arts and Sciences and another Columbia school. *Program availability:* Part-time. Terminal master's awarded for partial completion of doctoral program. *Degree requirements:* For master's, variable foreign language requirement, comprehensive exam (for some programs), thesis (for some programs); for doctorate, variable foreign language requirement, comprehensive exam (for some programs), thesis/dissertation. *Entrance requirements:* For master's and doctorate, GRE General Test, GRE Subject Test (for some programs). Additional exam requirements/recommendations for international students: Required—TOEFL, IELTS. Electronic applications accepted. *Expenses: Tuition:* Full-time $44,864; part-time $1704 per credit. *Required fees:* $2370 per semester. One-time fee: $105.

Concordia University, School of Graduate Studies, Faculty of Arts and Science, Department of Religion, Program in Judaic Studies, Montréal, QC H3G 1M8, Canada. Offers MA. *Degree requirements:* For master's, one foreign language, comprehensive exam, thesis optional. *Entrance requirements:* For master's, Hebrew exam, honors degree in Judaic studies or equivalent. Additional exam requirements/recommendations for international students: Required—TOEFL. *Faculty research:* Jewish religious reflections and modern philosophy of religion, Judaism and modernity, Judaism in late antiquity.

Cornell University, Graduate School, Graduate Fields of Arts and Sciences, Field of Near Eastern Studies, Ithaca, NY 14853. Offers ancient Near Eastern studies (MA, PhD); Arabic and Islamic studies (MA, PhD); biblical studies (MA, PhD); Hebrew and Judaic studies (MA, PhD). Terminal master's awarded for partial completion of doctoral program. *Degree requirements:* For master's, one foreign language, thesis; for doctorate, 2 foreign languages, comprehensive exam, thesis/dissertation. *Entrance requirements:* For master's and doctorate, GRE General Test, 2 years of 1 Near Eastern language, 3 letters of recommendation, writing sample. Additional exam requirements/recommendations for international students: Required—TOEFL (minimum score 550 paper-based; 77 iBT). Electronic applications accepted. *Faculty research:* Ancient Near East (including archeology), Hebrew and Judaic studies (including Bible), early Christianity, Arabic and Islamic studies, modern Middle East.

Criswell College, Graduate School of the Bible, Dallas, TX 75246-1537. Offers biblical studies (M Div); Christian leadership (MA); counseling (MA); Jewish studies (MA); ministry (MA); theological and biblical studies (MA). *Program availability:* Part-time. *Degree requirements:* For master's, 2 foreign languages, thesis optional. *Entrance requirements:* For master's, GRE General Test, minimum GPA of 2.5. Electronic applications accepted. *Faculty research:* Emphasis on biblical languages (Hebrew and Greek), expository preaching and evangelism in the local church.

Dallas Theological Seminary, Graduate Programs, Dallas, TX 75204-6499. Offers adult education (Th M); apologetics (Th M); Bible backgrounds (Th M); Bible translation (Th M); Biblical and theological studies (Certificate); biblical counseling (MA); Biblical exegesis and linguistics (MA); biblical exposition (PhD); biblical studies (MA); Biblical theology (Th M); children's education (Th M); Christian education (MA, D Min); Christian leadership (MA); cross-cultural ministries (MA); educational administration (Th M); educational leadership (Th M); evangelism and discipleship (Th M); exposition of Biblical books (Th M); family life education (Th M); general studies (Th M); Hebrew and cognate studies (Th M); hermeneutics (Th M); historical theology (Th M); homiletics (Th M); intercultural ministries (Th M); Jesus studies (Th M); leadership studies (Th M); media and communication (MA); media arts (Th M); ministry (D Min); ministry with women (Th M); New Testament studies (Th M, PhD); Old Testament studies (Th M, PhD); parachurch ministries (Th M); pastoral care and counseling (Th M); pastoral theology and practice (Th M); philosophy (Th M); sacred theology (STM); spiritual formation (Th M); systematic theology (Th M); teaching in Christian institutions (Th M); theological studies (PhD); urban ministries (Th M); worship studies (Th M); youth education (Th M). *Program availability:* Part-time, online learning. *Degree requirements:* For master's, variable foreign language requirement, thesis (for some programs); for doctorate, 2 foreign languages, thesis/dissertation. *Entrance requirements:* For master's, GRE or MAT (if minimum undergraduate cumulative GPA is below 2.5 or undergraduate degree is unaccredited). Additional exam requirements/recommendations for international students: Required—TOEFL (minimum score 575 paper-based; 85 iBT), TWE. Electronic applications accepted.

Graduate Theological Union, Graduate Programs, Berkeley, CA 94709-1212. Offers art and religion (MA, PhD, Th D); biblical languages (MA); biblical studies (MA); Biblical studies (PhD, Th D); Buddhist studies (MA); Christian spirituality (MA, PhD, Th D); cultural and historical studies of religions (MA, PhD, Th D); ethics and social theory (PhD, Th D); history (MA, PhD, Th D); homiletics (MA, PhD, Th D); interdisciplinary studies (PhD, Th D); Jewish studies (MA, PhD, Th D, Certificate); liturgical studies (MA, PhD, Th D); Near Eastern religions (PhD, Th D); Orthodox Christian studies (MA); religion and psychology (MA, PhD, Th D); religion and society/ethics and social theory (MA); systematic and philosophical theology (MA, PhD, Th D). PhD programs in Jewish studies and Near Eastern religions offered jointly with University of California, Berkeley. *Accreditation:* ATS. Terminal master's awarded for partial completion of doctoral program. *Degree requirements:* For master's, one foreign language, thesis; for doctorate, one foreign language, comprehensive exam, thesis/dissertation. *Entrance requirements:* For master's, GRE General Test; for doctorate, GRE General Test, MA or M Div. Additional exam requirements/recommendations for international students: Required—TOEFL. Electronic applications accepted.

Jewish Studies

Gratz College, Graduate Programs, Program in Jewish Christian Studies, Melrose Park, PA 19027. Offers Graduate Certificate. *Program availability:* Online learning.

Gratz College, Graduate Programs, Program in Jewish Studies, Melrose Park, PA 19027. Offers MA. *Program availability:* Part-time, online learning. *Degree requirements:* For master's, one foreign language, comprehensive exam, thesis optional.

Harvard University, Graduate School of Arts and Sciences, Department of Near Eastern Languages and Civilizations, Cambridge, MA 02138. Offers Akkadian and Sumerian (AM, PhD); Arabic (AM, PhD); Armenian (AM, PhD); biblical history (AM, PhD); Hebrew (AM, PhD); Indo-Muslim culture (AM, PhD); Iranian (AM, PhD); Jewish history and literature (AM, PhD); Persian (AM, PhD); Semitic philology (AM, PhD); Syro-Palestinian archaeology (AM, PhD); Turkish (AM, PhD). *Degree requirements:* For doctorate, variable foreign language requirement, thesis/dissertation, general exams. *Entrance requirements:* For master's, GRE General Test; for doctorate, GRE General Test, proficiency in a Near Eastern language. Additional exam requirements/recommendations for international students: Required—TOEFL.

Hebrew College, Cantor Educator Program, Newton Centre, MA 02459. Offers MJ Ed. *Entrance requirements:* For master's, GRE, interview. Additional exam requirements/recommendations for international students: Required—TOEFL.

Hebrew College, Program in Jewish Studies, Newton Centre, MA 02459. Offers Jewish liturgical music (Certificate); Jewish music education (Certificate); Jewish studies (MA). *Program availability:* Part-time, evening/weekend, online learning. *Degree requirements:* For master's, one foreign language. *Entrance requirements:* For master's, GRE, interview. Additional exam requirements/recommendations for international students: Required—TOEFL.

Hebrew Union College–Jewish Institute of Religion, School of Graduate Studies, Program in Judaic Studies, New York, NY 10012-1186. Offers MAJS. *Program availability:* Part-time. *Degree requirements:* For master's, one foreign language, thesis. *Entrance requirements:* For master's, GRE, minimum 2 years of college-level Hebrew. *Faculty research:* Philosophy and theology, Bible, Hebrew, history and Rabbinics.

Indiana University Bloomington, University Graduate School, College of Arts and Sciences, Robert A. and Sandra S. Borns Jewish Studies Program, Bloomington, IN 47405. Offers Jewish studies (MA), including nonprofit management; Jewish studies and history (MA). *Degree requirements:* For master's, one foreign language, thesis. *Entrance requirements:* Additional exam requirements/recommendations for international students: Required—TOEFL. Electronic applications accepted. *Faculty research:* Jewish studies, religious studies, history, Holocaust study.

The Jewish Theological Seminary, The Graduate School, New York, NY 10027-4649. Offers ancient Judaism (MA, DHL, PhD); Bible and ancient Semitic languages (MA, DHL, PhD); interdepartmental studies (MA); Jewish art and visual culture (MA); Jewish gender and women's studies (MA); Jewish history (MA, DHL, PhD); Jewish literature (MA, DHL, PhD); Jewish philosophy (DHL); Jewish thought (MA, PhD); liturgy (MA, DHL, PhD); medieval Jewish studies (MA, DHL, PhD); Midrash (DHL); Midrash and scriptural interpretation (MA, PhD); modern Jewish studies (MA, DHL, PhD); Talmud and rabbinics (MA, DHL, PhD); MA/MSW. MA/MSW offered jointly with Columbia University. *Accreditation:* ACIPE. *Program availability:* Part-time. Terminal master's awarded for partial completion of doctoral program. *Degree requirements:* For master's, one foreign language, comprehensive exam (for some programs), thesis (for some programs); for doctorate, 3 foreign languages, comprehensive exam (for some programs), thesis/dissertation. *Entrance requirements:* For master's, GRE or MAT, 3 letters of recommendation, writing sample; for doctorate, GRE or MAT, 3 letters of recommendation, writing research sample. Additional exam requirements/recommendations for international students: Required—TOEFL.

The Jewish Theological Seminary, William Davidson Graduate School of Jewish Education, New York, NY 10027-4649. Offers MA, Ed D. Offered in conjunction with The Rabbinical School; H. L. Miller Cantorial School and College of Jewish Music; Teacher's College, Columbia University; and Union Theological Seminary. *Program availability:* Part-time, online learning. *Degree requirements:* For master's, one foreign language, thesis optional; for doctorate, one foreign language, comprehensive exam, thesis/dissertation. *Entrance requirements:* For master's, GRE or MAT, 3 letters of recommendation; for doctorate, GRE or MAT, writing sample, 3 letters of recommendation. Additional exam requirements/recommendations for international students: Recommended—TOEFL.

McGill University, Faculty of Graduate and Postdoctoral Studies, Faculty of Arts, Department of Jewish Studies, Montréal, QC H3A 2T5, Canada. Offers MA.

New York University, Graduate School of Arts and Science, Program in Museum Studies, New York, NY 10012-1019. Offers museum studies (MA, Advanced Certificate), including Africana studies (MA), Hebrew and Judaic studies (MA), Latin American and Caribbean studies (MA), Near Eastern studies (MA). *Program availability:* Part-time, evening/weekend. *Students:* Average age 26. 123 applicants, 81% accepted, 29 enrolled. In 2017, 35 master's, 1 other advanced degree awarded. *Entrance requirements:* For master's, GRE General Test; for Advanced Certificate, master's degree or PhD. Additional exam requirements/recommendations for international students: Required—TOEFL. *Application deadline:* For fall admission, 2/15 for domestic and international students; for spring admission, 11/1 for domestic and international students. Application fee: $100. *Expenses: Tuition:* Full-time $41,352; part-time $19,968 per year. *Required fees:* $2496; $1628 per unit. $814 per term. Tuition and fees vary according to course load and program. *Financial support:* Application deadline: 2/15. *Faculty research:* Modern and contemporary art, history of museums and exhibitions, conservation of cultural materials, museum anthropology, ethnography. *Unit head:* Bruce Altshuler, Director, 212-998-8080, Fax: 212-995-4185, E-mail: museum.studies@nyu.edu. *Application contact:* Tatiana Kamorina, Department Administrator, 212-998-8080, Fax: 212-995-4185, E-mail: museum.studies@nyu.edu.
Website: http://www.nyu.edu/fas/program/museumstudies/

New York University, Graduate School of Arts and Science, Skirball Department of Hebrew and Judaic Studies, New York, NY 10012-1019. Offers Hebrew and Judaic studies (MA, PhD); Hebrew and Judaic studies/museum studies (MA). *Program availability:* Part-time. *Students:* Average age 30. 75 applicants, 51% accepted, 16 enrolled. In 2017, 18 master's, 13 doctorates awarded. Terminal master's awarded for partial completion of doctoral program. *Degree requirements:* For master's, 2 foreign languages, comprehensive exam, thesis optional; for doctorate, 4 foreign languages, comprehensive exam, thesis/dissertation. *Entrance requirements:* For master's and doctorate, GRE General Test. Additional exam requirements/recommendations for international students: Required—TOEFL. *Application deadline:* For fall admission, 1/4 priority date for domestic students, 1/4 for international students. Application fee: $100. *Expenses: Tuition:* Full-time $41,352; part-time $19,968 per year. *Required fees:* $2496; $1628 per unit. $814 per term. Tuition and fees vary according to course load and program. *Financial support:* Fellowships, teaching assistantships, Federal Work-Study, and institutionally sponsored loans available. Financial award application deadline: 1/4; financial award applicants required to submit FAFSA. *Faculty research:* Post-Biblical and Talmudic literature and history, mysticism, Bible and ancient Near East, medieval and modern Jewish history, medieval and modern Jewish philosophy. *Unit head:* David Engel, Chair, 212-998-8980, Fax: 212-995-4178, E-mail: gsas.hebrewjudaic@nyu.edu. *Application contact:* Jeffrey Rubenstein, Director of Graduate Studies, 212-998-8980, Fax: 212-995-4178, E-mail: gsas.hebrewjudaic@nyu.edu.
Website: http://www.nyu.edu/gsas/dept/hebrew/

New York University, Steinhardt School of Culture, Education, and Human Development, Department of Humanities and Social Sciences in the Professions, Program in Education and Jewish Studies, New York, NY 10012-1019. Offers MA, PhD, MA/MA. *Program availability:* Part-time. *Students:* Average age 29. 14 applicants, 79% accepted, 7 enrolled. In 2017, 5 master's, 2 doctorates awarded. *Entrance requirements:* For doctorate, GRE General Test, interview. Additional exam requirements/recommendations for international students: Required—TOEFL (minimum score 100 iBT). *Application deadline:* For fall admission, 12/1 priority date for domestic and international students. Applications are processed on a rolling basis. Application fee: $75. Electronic applications accepted. *Expenses: Tuition:* Full-time $41,352; part-time $19,968 per year. *Required fees:* $2496; $1628 per unit. $814 per term. Tuition and fees vary according to course load and program. *Financial support:* Fellowships with full and partial tuition reimbursements, teaching assistantships with partial tuition reimbursements, career-related internships or fieldwork, Federal Work-Study, institutionally sponsored loans, scholarships/grants, tuition waivers (partial), and unspecified assistantships available. Support available to part-time students. Financial award application deadline: 2/1; financial award applicants required to submit FAFSA. *Faculty research:* Jewish education, educational history, Judaic studies. *Unit head:* Prof. Harold Wechsler, Director, 212-992-9423, Fax: 212-995-4178, E-mail: hw29@nyu.edu. *Application contact:* 212-998-5030, Fax: 212-995-4328, E-mail: steinhardt.gradadmissions@nyu.edu.
Website: http://steinhardt.nyu.edu/humsocsci/jewish

Reconstructionist Rabbinical College, Graduate Programs, Wyncote, PA 19095-1898. Offers Jewish studies (MAJS); rabbinics (MAHL, DHL); women's studies (Certificate). Certificate offered jointly with Temple University. *Program availability:* Part-time. *Degree requirements:* For master's, one foreign language, thesis (MAJS), completion of rabbinical program (MAHL); for doctorate, one foreign language. *Entrance requirements:* For master's, GRE General Test; placement examinations in Hebrew and Judaism (MAHL); for doctorate, GRE General Test, placement examinations in Hebrew and Judaism. *Faculty research:* Bible, Hebrew Semitic texts, contemporary Judaism.

Rice University, Graduate Programs, School of Humanities, Department of Religious Studies, Houston, TX 77251-1892. Offers African religions (PhD); African-American religions (PhD); contemplative studies (PhD); ghosticism, esotericism, mysticism (PhD); Islam (PhD); Jewish thought and philosophy (PhD); modern Christianity in thought and popular culture (PhD); psychology of religion (PhD); the Bible and beyond (PhD). *Degree requirements:* For doctorate, 2 foreign languages, comprehensive exam, thesis/dissertation. *Entrance requirements:* For doctorate, GRE, letters of recommendation, writing sample. Additional exam requirements/recommendations for international students: Required—TOEFL (minimum score 600 paper-based; 90 iBT). Electronic applications accepted. *Faculty research:* Origins and historical development of Islam, history of Christianity, the study of comparative religion, African-American religion, religion and culture.

Rutgers University–New Brunswick, Graduate School-New Brunswick, Department of Jewish Studies, New Brunswick, NJ 08901. Offers MA, Certificate. *Program availability:* Part-time.

Seton Hall University, College of Arts and Sciences, Department of Religion, South Orange, NJ 07079-2697. Offers Jewish-Christian studies (MA). *Program availability:* Part-time, evening/weekend. *Degree requirements:* For master's, thesis optional. *Entrance requirements:* For master's, interview or suitable correspondence with department chair. Additional exam requirements/recommendations for international students: Required—TOEFL. Electronic applications accepted. *Faculty research:* Jewish-Christian issues, Biblical studies, Holocaust studies.

Southern Evangelical Seminary, Graduate Programs, Matthews, NC 28105. Offers apologetics (MA, D Min, Certificate); Christian education (MA); church ministry (MA, Certificate); divinity (Certificate), including apologetics (M Div, Certificate); Islamic studies (MA, Certificate); Jewish studies (MA); philosophy (MA); philosophy of religion (PhD); religion (MA); theology (M Div), including apologetics (M Div, Certificate), Biblical studies; youth ministry (MA). *Program availability:* Part-time, evening/weekend, online learning. *Degree requirements:* For master's, thesis (for some programs); for doctorate, 2 foreign languages, comprehensive exam (for some programs), thesis/dissertation. *Entrance requirements:* Additional exam requirements/recommendations for international students: Required—TOEFL (minimum score 600 paper-based).

Spertus Institute for Jewish Learning and Leadership, Program in Jewish Studies, Chicago, IL 60605-1901. Offers MAJPS, MAJS, DJS, DSJS. *Program availability:* Part-time, evening/weekend, online learning. *Degree requirements:* For master's, one foreign language, thesis (for some programs); for doctorate, one foreign language, thesis/dissertation. *Entrance requirements:* For master's, interview, BAJS (for MAJS); for doctorate, MAJS.

Telshe Yeshiva–Chicago, Graduate Program, Chicago, IL 60625-5598. Offers Second Talmudic Degree. *Accreditation:* AARTS.

Touro College, Graduate School of Jewish Studies, New York, NY 10010. Offers MA. *Program availability:* Part-time. *Faculty:* 4 full-time (2 women), 5 part-time/adjunct (2 women). *Students:* 23 full-time (22 women), 28 part-time (26 women); includes 1 minority (Hispanic/Latino), 4 international. Average age 38. *Degree requirements:* For master's, one foreign language, thesis. *Entrance requirements:* For master's, previous course work in Jewish studies, proficiency in Hebrew. Additional exam requirements/recommendations for international students: Required—TOEFL (minimum score 550 paper-based; 80 iBT), IELTS (minimum score 6.5), PTE (minimum score 58). Application fee: $50. *Financial support:* Tuition waivers (full and partial) available. Support available to part-time students. *Faculty research:* Medieval and modern Jewish history, Jewish philosophy, Holocaust studies, Jewish education. *Unit head:* Dr. Michael Shmidman, Dean, 212-213-2230. *Application contact:* Karen Rubin, Executive Assistant to the Dean, 212-463-0400 Ext. 5581, E-mail: karen.rubin@touro.edu.

Towson University, College of Liberal Arts, Program in Leadership and Jewish Studies, Towson, MD 21252-0001. Offers Jewish communal service (Postbaccalaureate Certificate). *Students:* 3 full-time (1 woman), 14 part-time (7 women); includes 3 minority (1 Black or African American, non-Hispanic/Latino; 1 Hispanic/Latino; 1 Two or more races, non-Hispanic/Latino), 1 international. *Entrance requirements:* For master's, bachelor's degree, minimum GPA of 3.0, letters of recommendation, statement of intent, sample of work, interview, resume; for Postbaccalaureate Certificate, bachelor's degree, minimum GPA of 3.0, statement of intent, sample of work, interview, 2 letters of recommendation, resume. Additional exam requirements/recommendations for international students: Required—TOEFL. *Application deadline:* For fall admission, 1/17 for domestic students, 5/15 for international students; for spring admission, 10/15 for domestic students, 12/1 for international students. Applications are processed on a rolling basis. Application fee: $45. Electronic applications accepted. *Expenses:* Tuition, state resident: full-time $7960; part-time $398 per unit. Tuition, nonresident: full-time $16,480; part-time $824 per unit. *Required fees:* $2600; $130 per year. $390 per term.

Unit head: Jill Max, Program Director, 410-704-7120, E-mail: jmax@towson.edu. *Application contact:* Coverley Beidleman, Assistant Director of Graduate Admissions, 410-704-5630, Fax: 410-704-3030, E-mail: grads@towson.edu.
Website: http://www.towson.edu/cla/centers/baltimorehebrewinstitute

University of California, San Diego, Graduate Division, Department of History, La Jolla, CA 92093. Offers history (MA, PhD); Judaic studies (MA). *Students:* 83 full-time (34 women), 3 part-time (2 women). 114 applicants, 15% accepted, 8 enrolled. In 2017, 9 master's, 5 doctorates awarded. *Degree requirements:* For master's, one foreign language, comprehensive exam; for doctorate, one foreign language, comprehensive exam, thesis/dissertation. *Entrance requirements:* For master's, GRE General Test, minimum GPA of 3.0; for doctorate, GRE General Test, writing sample (7-15 pages long), preferably in a history course. Additional exam requirements/recommendations for international students: Required—TOEFL (minimum score 550 paper-based; 80 iBT), IELTS (minimum score 7). *Application deadline:* For fall admission, 1/12 for domestic students. Application fee: $105 ($125 for international students). Electronic applications accepted. *Financial support:* Fellowships, research assistantships, teaching assistantships, career-related internships or fieldwork, scholarships/grants, and readerships available. Financial award applicants required to submit FAFSA. *Faculty research:* Ancient history, east Asian history, history of science, Jewish studies, global transnational studies. *Unit head:* Pamela Radcliff, Chair, 858-534-8919, E-mail: pradcliff@ucsd.edu. *Application contact:* Sally Hargate, Graduate Coordinator, 858-822-0664, E-mail: shargate@ucsd.edu.
Website: http://history.ucsd.edu

University of Connecticut, Graduate School, College of Liberal Arts and Sciences, Field of International Studies, Program in Judaic Studies, Storrs, CT 06269. Offers MA. *Entrance requirements:* Additional exam requirements/recommendations for international students: Required—TOEFL (minimum score 550 paper-based). Electronic applications accepted.

University of Florida, Graduate School, College of Liberal Arts and Sciences, Department of History, Gainesville, FL 32611. Offers historic preservation (MA, PhD); history (MA, PhD); Jewish studies (MA); women's and gender studies (PhD); JD/MA; JD/PhD. *Program availability:* Part-time. Terminal master's awarded for partial completion of doctoral program. *Degree requirements:* For master's, variable foreign language requirement, thesis optional, 30 credit hours; for doctorate, variable foreign language requirement, comprehensive exam, thesis/dissertation, 90 credit hours. *Entrance requirements:* For master's and doctorate, GRE General Test, minimum GPA of 3.0. Additional exam requirements/recommendations for international students: Required—TOEFL (minimum score 550 paper-based; 80 iBT), IELTS (minimum score 6). Electronic applications accepted. *Faculty research:* Latin American and Caribbean history, nineteenth century U.S. history, medieval European history, African history and Atlantic world history.

University of Florida, Graduate School, College of Liberal Arts and Sciences, Department of Religion, Gainesville, FL 32611. Offers Jewish studies (MA); religion (MA, PhD); tropical conservation and development (MA, PhD); women's and gender studies (MA, PhD). *Program availability:* Part-time. *Degree requirements:* For master's, one foreign language, thesis optional; for doctorate, one foreign language, comprehensive exam, thesis/dissertation. *Entrance requirements:* For master's, GRE General Test, minimum GPA of 3.0. Additional exam requirements/recommendations for international students: Required—TOEFL (minimum score 550 paper-based; 80 iBT), IELTS (minimum score 6). Electronic applications accepted. *Faculty research:* Religion in America, Christian thought, Islam, religions of India, comparative religion.

University of Maryland, College Park, Academic Affairs, College of Arts and Humanities, Meyerhoff Center for Jewish Studies, College Park, MD 20742. Offers MA. *Degree requirements:* For master's, thesis or 2 major research papers. *Entrance requirements:* For master's, GRE General Test, 3 letters of recommendation, writing sample. Additional exam requirements/recommendations for international students: Required—TOEFL.

University of Michigan, Rackham Graduate School, College of Literature, Science, and the Arts, Department of Near Eastern Studies, Ann Arbor, MI 48109. Offers ancient Near Eastern studies (AM, PhD); Arabic for professional purposes (AM); Arabic language and literature (AM, PhD); Armenian studies (AM, PhD); Christianity in late antiquity (AM, PhD); Egyptology (AM, PhD); Hebrew Bible and ancient Israel (AM, PhD); Hebrew literature (AM, PhD); Islamic studies (AM, PhD); Jewish cultural studies (AM, PhD); Jewish mysticism (AM, PhD); Persian and Iranian studies (AM, PhD); Rabbinic literature (AM, PhD); Second Temple Judaism (AM, PhD); teaching Arabic as a foreign language (AM); Turkish studies (AM, PhD). *Faculty:* 27 full-time (8 women). *Students:* 31 full-time (12 women); includes 2 minority (1 Black or African American, non-Hispanic/Latino; 1 Asian, non-Hispanic/Latino), 13 international. Average age 33. 76 applicants, 11% accepted, 5 enrolled. In 2017, 4 master's, 4 doctorates awarded. Terminal master's awarded for partial completion of doctoral program. *Degree requirements:* For master's, 2 foreign languages; for doctorate, 4 foreign languages, comprehensive exam, thesis/dissertation, preliminary exams, oral defense of dissertation. *Entrance requirements:* For master's, ACTFL (for teaching Arabic as a foreign language MA program). Additional exam requirements/recommendations for international students: Required—TOEFL (minimum score 560 paper-based; 84 iBT), IELTS (minimum score 6.5). *Application deadline:* For fall admission, 12/1 for domestic and international students. Application fee: $75 ($90 for international students). Electronic applications accepted. *Expenses:*

Tuition, state resident: full-time $22,368; part-time $1201 per credit hour. Tuition, nonresident: full-time $45,156; part-time $2467 per credit hour. *Required fees:* $376 per term. Tuition and fees vary according to course load, degree level and program. *Financial support:* In 2017-18, 31 students received support. Fellowships with full tuition reimbursements available, teaching assistantships with full tuition reimbursements available, scholarships/grants, health care benefits, unspecified assistantships, and spring/summer stipends available. Financial award application deadline: 12/1. *Faculty research:* Middle and Near Eastern literatures, languages, cultures from ancient times to the present. *Unit head:* Prof. Gottfried Hagen, Chair, 734-764-0314, E-mail: nes-chair@umich.edu. *Application contact:* Student Services, 734-764-0315, E-mail: nes-gradservices@umich.edu.
Website: http://www.lsa.umich.edu/neareast/

University of Michigan, Rackham Graduate School, College of Literature, Science, and the Arts, Jean and Samuel Frankel Center for Judaic Studies, Ann Arbor, MI 48178. Offers MA, Graduate Certificate. *Program availability:* Part-time. *Faculty:* 31 full-time (12 women). *Students:* 19 full-time (7 women); includes 2 minority (1 Black or African American, non-Hispanic/Latino; 1 Hispanic/Latino). Average age 31. 3 applicants, 100% accepted. In 2017, 1 master's, 2 other advanced degrees awarded. *Degree requirements:* For master's, thesis; for Graduate Certificate, one foreign language, capstone course (including public lecture), reading knowledge of 1 Jewish language. *Entrance requirements:* For master's, GRE General Test; for Graduate Certificate, currently enrolled in a PhD or professional degree program at the University of Michigan. Additional exam requirements/recommendations for international students: Required—TOEFL (minimum score 560 paper-based). *Application deadline:* For fall admission, 1/10 for domestic and international students; for winter admission, 9/1 for domestic and international students. Application fee: $75 ($90 for international students). Electronic applications accepted. *Expenses:* Tuition, state resident: full-time $22,368; part-time $1201 per credit hour. Tuition, nonresident: full-time $45,156; part-time $2467 per credit hour. *Required fees:* $376 per term. Tuition and fees vary according to course load, degree level and program. *Financial support:* In 2017-18, 14 students received support, including 2 fellowships with full tuition reimbursements available, research assistantships, scholarships/grants, and health care benefits also available. *Faculty research:* Jewish culture and history; Jews in modern Europe; Jewish languages; Bible and ancient Judaism; Mediterranean and Sephardic. *Unit head:* Prof. Jeffrey Veidlinger, Director, 734-763-9047, Fax: 734-936-2186, E-mail: jveidlin@umich.edu. *Application contact:* Michael Goldberg, Student Services Coordinator, 734-615-6097, Fax: 734-936-2186, E-mail: js-student-services@umich.edu.
Website: http://www.lsa.umich.edu/judaic

University of St. Michael's College, Faculty of Theology, Toronto, ON M5S 1J4, Canada. Offers Catholic leadership (MA); eastern Christian studies (Diploma); religious education (Diploma); theological studies (Diploma); theology (M Div, MA, MRE, MTS, D Min, PhD, Th D); theology and Jewish studies (MA). Th D offered jointly with University of Toronto. *Accreditation:* ATS (one or more programs are accredited). *Program availability:* Part-time. *Degree requirements:* For master's, thesis (for some programs), 1 foreign language (MA), 2 foreign languages (Th M); for doctorate, 3 foreign languages, comprehensive exam, thesis/dissertation; for other advanced degree, thesis optional. *Entrance requirements:* For master's, M Div or BA, course work in an ancient or modern language, minimum GPA of 3.3; for doctorate, MA in theology, Th M, or M Div with thesis, minimum GPA of 3.7; for other advanced degree, minimum GPA of 2.7. Additional exam requirements/recommendations for international students: Required—TOEFL (minimum score 600 paper-based). Electronic applications accepted. *Expenses:* Contact institution. *Faculty research:* Patristics, eastern Christianity, ecology and theology, ecumenism, Jewish Christian studies.

University of Wisconsin–Madison, Graduate School, College of Letters and Science, Department of Hebrew and Semitic Studies, Madison, WI 53706-1380. Offers MA, PhD. Terminal master's awarded for partial completion of doctoral program. *Degree requirements:* For master's, 2 foreign languages; for doctorate, thesis/dissertation. *Entrance requirements:* For master's and doctorate, GRE. Electronic applications accepted. *Faculty research:* Biblical language and literature, Northwest Semitic languages.

Washington University in St. Louis, The Graduate School, Department of Jewish, Islamic, and Near Eastern Languages and Cultures, St. Louis, MO 63130-4899. Offers Islamic and Near Eastern studies (MA); Jewish studies (MA). *Degree requirements:* For master's, one foreign language, thesis (for some programs). *Entrance requirements:* For master's, GRE General Test. Additional exam requirements/recommendations for international students: Required—TOEFL. Electronic applications accepted. *Faculty research:* Islamic and Near Eastern studies (Islamic history; Arabic language and literature, modern Middle East history); Jewish studies (Hebrew Bible, Rabbinic literature, Jewish history, modern Hebrew literature).

Yeshiva University, Bernard Revel Graduate School of Jewish Studies, New York, NY 10033-3201. Offers MA, PhD. *Program availability:* Part-time. Terminal master's awarded for partial completion of doctoral program. *Degree requirements:* For master's, comprehensive exam; for doctorate, 2 foreign languages, comprehensive exam, thesis/dissertation. *Entrance requirements:* For master's and doctorate, GRE General Test (recommended), reading knowledge of Hebrew, minimum GPA of 3.0. *Faculty research:* Bible, Jewish history, Jewish philosophy and mysticism, Talmud, Semitic languages.

Latin American Studies

American University, College of Arts and Sciences, Department of World Languages and Cultures, Washington, DC 20016-8045. Offers Spanish: Latin American studies (MA); teaching English as a foreign language (MA); teaching English to speakers of other languages (MA, Certificate); translation: French (Certificate); translation: Russian (Certificate); translation: Spanish (Certificate). *Program availability:* Part-time, evening/weekend. *Faculty:* 43 full-time (33 women), 23 part-time/adjunct (17 women). *Students:* 17 full-time (14 women), 19 part-time (15 women); includes 10 minority (2 Black or African American, non-Hispanic/Latino; 6 Hispanic/Latino; 2 Two or more races, non-Hispanic/Latino), 5 international. Average age 32. 39 applicants, 97% accepted, 9 enrolled. In 2017, 16 master's, 11 other advanced degrees awarded. *Degree requirements:* For master's, one foreign language, comprehensive exam, thesis or alternative. *Entrance requirements:* For master's, GRE, writing sample, statement of purpose, transcripts, 2 letters of recommendation, resume; for Certificate, bachelor's degree, statement of purpose, transcripts, resume. Additional exam requirements/recommendations for international students: Required—TOEFL (minimum score 600 paper-based; 100 iBT). *Application deadline:* For fall admission, 2/1 priority date for

domestic students; for spring admission, 11/1 priority date for domestic students. Application fee: $55. *Expenses:* Contact institution. *Financial support:* Institutionally sponsored loans, scholarships/grants, and unspecified assistantships available. Financial award application deadline: 2/1; financial award applicants required to submit FAFSA. *Unit head:* Henry Gerfen, Chair, 202-885-2385, Fax: 202-885-1076, E-mail: gerfen@american.edu. *Application contact:* Jonathan Harper, Director of Graduate Recruitment, 202-885-3622, E-mail: jharper@american.edu.
Website: http://www.american.edu/cas/wlc/

Boricua College, Program in Latin American and Caribbean Studies, New York, NY 10032-1560. Offers MA. Program offered in Brooklyn and Manhattan. *Program availability:* Evening/weekend. *Degree requirements:* For master's, thesis. *Entrance requirements:* For master's, interview by the faculty.

Boston University, Graduate School of Arts and Sciences, Frederick S. Pardee School of Global Studies, Boston, MA 02215. Offers global policy (MA); international affairs (MA); international relations (MA); Latin American studies (MA); MA/JD; MBA/MA.

Latin American Studies

Faculty: 33 full-time (8 women), 10 part-time/adjunct (4 women). *Students:* 100 full-time (62 women), 10 part-time (4 women); includes 17 minority (5 Black or African American, non-Hispanic/Latino; 6 Asian, non-Hispanic/Latino; 5 Hispanic/Latino; 1 Two or more races, non-Hispanic/Latino), 45 international. Average age 25. 377 applicants, 79% accepted, 41 enrolled. In 2017, 31 master's awarded. *Degree requirements:* For master's, one foreign language, thesis (for some programs), capstone. *Entrance requirements:* For master's, GRE General Test, 3 letters of recommendation, transcript of all prior college coursework, personal statement, resume or curriculum vitae (recommended). Additional exam requirements/recommendations for international students: Required—TOEFL (minimum score 550 paper-based; 84 iBT). *Application deadline:* For fall admission, 1/15 priority date for domestic and international students; for spring admission, 12/15 for domestic and international students. Applications are processed on a rolling basis. Application fee: $95. Electronic applications accepted. *Financial support:* In 2017–18, 55 students received support. Federal Work-Study, scholarships/grants, and unspecified assistantships available. Financial award application deadline: 1/15. *Faculty research:* International relations, area studies, political economy, global development policy, global climate. *Unit head:* Adil Najam, Dean, 617-358-0988, Fax: 617-353-9290, E-mail: anajam@bu.edu. *Application contact:* Holly Chase, Graduate Affairs Manager, 617-358-8625, Fax: 617-353-9290, E-mail: psgsgrad@bu.edu.
Website: http://www.bu.edu/PardeeSchool

See Display on page 911 and Close-Up on page 957.

Brown University, Graduate School, Department of Portuguese and Brazilian Studies, Providence, RI 02912. Offers Brazilian studies (AM); English as a second language and cross-cultural studies (AM); Portuguese and Brazilian studies (AM, PhD); Portuguese bilingual education and cross-cultural studies (AM). *Degree requirements:* For doctorate, thesis/dissertation.

California State University, Los Angeles, Graduate Studies, College of Natural and Social Sciences, Department of Latin American Studies, Los Angeles, CA 90032-8530. Offers MA. *Program availability:* Part-time, evening/weekend. *Degree requirements:* For master's, one foreign language, comprehensive exam, thesis. *Entrance requirements:* For master's, minimum GPA of 2.5. Additional exam requirements/recommendations for international students: Required—TOEFL (minimum score 500 paper-based). Electronic applications accepted. *Faculty research:* Central America, Cuba, Third World development, labor history, redemocratization.

Centro de Estudios Avanzados de Puerto Rico y el Caribe, Graduate Program in Puerto Rican and Caribbean Studies, Old San Juan, PR 00902-3970. Offers Puerto Rican and Caribbean history (MA, PhD); Puerto Rican and Caribbean literature (MA, PhD); Puerto Rican studies (MA). *Program availability:* Part-time, evening/weekend. *Degree requirements:* For master's, comprehensive exam, thesis; for doctorate, 2 foreign languages, comprehensive exam, thesis/dissertation. *Entrance requirements:* For master's and doctorate, interview. *Faculty research:* Literature, history, art, folklore, and culture of Puerto Rico and Caribbean countries.

College of Staten Island of the City University of New York, Graduate Programs, Division of Humanities and Social Sciences, Program in History, Staten Island, NY 10314-6600. Offers history (MA), including Africa and the Middle East, Asia, Europe, Latin America and the Caribbean, United States. *Program availability:* Part-time, evening/weekend. *Faculty:* 2 full-time (1 woman). *Students:* 18. 19 applicants, 79% accepted, 11 enrolled. In 2017, 3 master's awarded. *Degree requirements:* For master's, comprehensive exam (for some programs), 32 credits (total of eight courses); thesis or portfolio. *Entrance requirements:* For master's, bachelor's degree with minimum GPA of 3.0 overall and in undergraduate history courses, two letters of recommendation, letter of interest, research-based writing sample. Additional exam requirements/recommendations for international students: Required—TOEFL (minimum score 550 paper-based; 79 iBT), IELTS (minimum score 6.5). *Application deadline:* For fall admission, 5/10 priority date for domestic and international students; for spring admission, 12/2 priority date for domestic and international students. Applications are processed on a rolling basis. Application fee: $125. Electronic applications accepted. *Expenses:* Tuition, state resident: full-time $10,450; part-time $440 per credit. Tuition, nonresident: full-time $19,320; part-time $440 per credit. *Required fees:* $181.10 per semester. Tuition and fees vary according to program. *Faculty research:* African and African diaspora history, South Asian history, Middle Eastern history, U.S. history, environmental history. *Unit head:* Dr. John Dixon, Graduate Program Coordinator, 718-982-3307, E-mail: john.dixon@csi.cuny.edu. *Application contact:* Sasha Spence, Associate Director for Graduate Admissions, 718-982-2019, Fax: 718-982-2500, E-mail: sasha.spence@csi.cuny.edu.
Website: https://www.csi.cuny.edu/sites/default/files/pdf/admissions/grad/pdf/History%20Fact%20Sheet.pdf

Columbia University, Graduate School of Arts and Sciences, New York, NY 10027. Offers African-American studies (MA); American studies (MA); anthropology (MA, PhD); art history and archaeology (MA, PhD); astronomy (PhD); biological sciences (PhD); biotechnology (MA); chemical physics (PhD); chemistry (PhD); classical studies (MA, PhD); classics (MA, PhD); climate and society (MA); conservation biology (MA); earth and environmental sciences (PhD); East Asia: regional studies (MA); East Asian languages and cultures (MA, PhD); ecology, evolution and environmental biology (MA), including conservation biology; ecology, evolution, and environmental biology (PhD), including ecology and evolutionary biology, evolutionary primatology; economics (MA, PhD); English and comparative literature (MA, PhD); French and Romance philology (MA, PhD); Germanic languages (MA, PhD); global French studies (MA); global thought (MA); Hispanic cultural studies (MA); history (PhD); history and literature (MA); human rights studies (MA); Islamic studies (MA); Italian (MA, PhD); Japanese pedagogy (MA); Jewish studies (MA); Latin America and the Caribbean: regional studies (MA); Latin American and Iberian cultures (PhD); mathematics (MA, PhD), including finance (MA); medieval and Renaissance studies (MA); Middle Eastern, South Asian, and African studies (MA, PhD); modern art: critical and curatorial studies (MA); modern European studies (MA); museum anthropology (MA); music (DMA, PhD); oral history (MA); philosophical foundations of physics (MA); philosophy (MA, PhD); physics (PhD); political science (MA, PhD); psychology (PhD); quantitative methods in the social sciences (MA); religion (MA, PhD); Russia, Eurasia and East Europe: regional studies (MA); Russian translation (MA); Slavic cultures (MA); Slavic languages (MA, PhD); sociology (MA, PhD); South Asian studies (MA); statistics (MA, PhD); theatre (PhD). Dual-degree programs require admission to both Graduate School of Arts and Sciences and another Columbia school. *Program availability:* Part-time. Terminal master's awarded for partial completion of doctoral program. *Degree requirements:* For master's, variable foreign language requirement, comprehensive exam (for some programs), thesis (for some programs); for doctorate, variable foreign language requirement, comprehensive exam (for some programs), thesis/dissertation. *Entrance requirements:* For master's and doctorate, GRE General Test, GRE Subject Test (for some programs). Additional exam requirements/recommendations for international students: Required—TOEFL, IELTS. Electronic applications accepted. *Expenses: Tuition:* Full-time $44,864; part-time $1704 per credit. *Required fees:* $2370 per semester. One-time fee: $105.

Cornell University, Graduate School, Graduate Fields of Arts and Sciences, Field of Archaeology, Ithaca, NY 14853. Offers environmental archaeology (MA); historical archaeology (MA); Latin American archaeology (MA); medieval archaeology (MA); Mediterranean and Near Eastern archaeology (MA); Stone Age archaeology (MA). *Degree requirements:* For master's, one foreign language, thesis. *Entrance requirements:* For master's, GRE General Test, 3 letters of recommendation, sample of written work. Additional exam requirements/recommendations for international students: Required—TOEFL (minimum score 550 paper-based; 77 iBT). Electronic applications accepted. *Faculty research:* Anatolia, Lydia, Sardis, classical and Hellenistic Greece, science in archaeology, North American Indians, Stone Age Africa, Mayan trade.

Cornell University, Graduate School, Graduate Fields of Arts and Sciences, Field of History, Ithaca, NY 14853. Offers African history (MA, PhD); American history (MA, PhD); ancient Greek history (PhD); ancient history (MA, PhD); ancient Roman history (PhD); early modern European history (MA, PhD); English history (MA, PhD); French history (MA, PhD); German history (MA, PhD); history of science (MA, PhD); Korean history (PhD); Latin American history (MA, PhD); medieval Chinese history (MA, PhD); medieval history (MA, PhD); modern Chinese history (MA, PhD); modern European history (MA, PhD); modern Japanese history (MA, PhD); modern Middle Eastern history (PhD); premodern Islamic history (MA, PhD); premodern Japanese history (MA, PhD); Renaissance history (MA, PhD); Russian history (MA, PhD); South Asian history (PhD); Southeast Asian history (MA, PhD). Terminal master's awarded for partial completion of doctoral program. *Degree requirements:* For master's, thesis; for doctorate, 2 foreign languages, comprehensive exam, thesis/dissertation, 1 year of teaching experience. *Entrance requirements:* For master's and doctorate, GRE General Test, writing sample, 3 letters of recommendation. Additional exam requirements/recommendations for international students: Required—TOEFL (minimum score 550 paper-based; 77 iBT). Electronic applications accepted.

Cornell University, Graduate School, Graduate Fields of Arts and Sciences, Field of History of Art, Archaeology and Visual Studies, Ithaca, NY 14853. Offers 19th century art (PhD); African, African American and African diaspora (PhD); American art (PhD); ancient art and archaeology (PhD); Asian American art (PhD); Baroque art (PhD); comparative modernities (PhD); digital art (PhD); East Asian art (PhD); history of photography (PhD); Islamic art (PhD); Latin American art (PhD); medieval art (PhD); modern art (PhD); Renaissance art (PhD); Southeast Asian art (PhD); theory and criticism (PhD); visual studies (PhD). *Degree requirements:* For doctorate, one foreign language, comprehensive exam, thesis/dissertation, general exams in 3 areas. *Entrance requirements:* For doctorate, GRE General Test, sample of written work, 3 letters of recommendation. Additional exam requirements/recommendations for international students: Required—TOEFL (minimum score 550 paper-based; 77 iBT). Electronic applications accepted.

Duke University, Graduate School, Department of History, Durham, NC 27708. Offers history (AM, PhD); Latin American studies (PhD); JD/AM. *Degree requirements:* For doctorate, 2 foreign languages, thesis/dissertation. *Entrance requirements:* For doctorate, GRE General Test. Additional exam requirements/recommendations for international students: Required—TOEFL (minimum score 577 paper-based; 90 iBT) or IELTS (minimum score 7). Electronic applications accepted.

Florida International University, Steven J. Green School of International and Public Affairs, Program in Latin American and Caribbean Studies, Miami, FL 33199. Offers MA. *Program availability:* Part-time, evening/weekend. *Faculty:* 2 full-time (0 women), 1 (woman) part-time/adjunct. *Students:* 5 full-time (2 women), 4 part-time (2 women); includes 5 minority (1 Black or African American, non-Hispanic/Latino; 4 Hispanic/Latino), 3 international. Average age 35. 18 applicants, 72% accepted, 3 enrolled. In 2017, 8 master's awarded. *Degree requirements:* For master's, one foreign language, thesis or alternative. *Entrance requirements:* For master's, GRE General Test (minimum score 1000); GMAT, LSAT, or EXADEP (minimum 62nd percentile), minimum GPA of 3.0, 3 letters of recommendation, letter of intent. Additional exam requirements/recommendations for international students: Required—TOEFL (minimum score 550 paper-based; 80 iBT). *Application deadline:* For fall admission, 2/1 for domestic and international students; for spring admission, 10/1 for domestic students, 9/1 for international students. Applications are processed on a rolling basis. Application fee: $30. Electronic applications accepted. *Expenses:* Tuition, state resident: full-time $8912; part-time $446 per credit hour. Tuition, nonresident: full-time $21,393; part-time $992 per credit hour. *Required fees:* $390; $195 per semester. *Financial support:* Institutionally sponsored loans and scholarships/grants available. Financial award application deadline: 3/1; financial award applicants required to submit FAFSA. *Unit head:* Dr. Frank Mora, Director, 305-348-2894, Fax: 305-348-3593, E-mail: francisco.mora6@fiu.edu. *Application contact:* Nanett Rojas, Manager, Admissions Operations, 305-348-7464, Fax: 305-348-7441, E-mail: gradadm@fiu.edu.

Georgetown University, Graduate School of Arts and Sciences, Walsh School of Foreign Service, Center for Latin American Studies, Washington, DC 20057-1026. Offers MA, MA/JD, MA/PhD. *Program availability:* Part-time, evening/weekend. *Degree requirements:* For master's, one foreign language, comprehensive exam, thesis optional. *Entrance requirements:* For master's, GRE General Test, minimum B average. Additional exam requirements/recommendations for international students: Required—TOEFL. Electronic applications accepted.

The George Washington University, Elliott School of International Affairs, Program in Latin American and Hemispheric Studies, Washington, DC 20052. Offers MA. *Program availability:* Part-time. *Students:* 13 full-time (7 women), 5 part-time (2 women); includes 8 minority (all Hispanic/Latino). Average age 27. 24 applicants, 83% accepted, 6 enrolled. In 2017, 3 master's awarded. *Degree requirements:* For master's, one foreign language, capstone project. *Entrance requirements:* For master's, GRE General Test, 2 years (or the equivalent) of Spanish or Portuguese. Additional exam requirements/recommendations for international students: Required—TOEFL (minimum score 100 iBT), IELTS (minimum score 7). *Application deadline:* For fall admission, 1/15 priority date for domestic and international students; for spring admission, 10/1 for domestic students. Application fee: $75. Electronic applications accepted. *Expenses: Tuition:* Full-time $28,800; part-time $1655 per credit hour. *Required fees:* $45; $2.75 per credit hour. *Financial support:* In 2017–18, 4 students received support. Fellowships with partial tuition reimbursements available, Federal Work-Study, and scholarships/grants available. Financial award application deadline: 1/15; financial award applicants required to submit FAFSA. *Faculty research:* Democracy and change in Andean nations, rural economic development, peasant cooperatives and political change. *Unit head:* Robert Maguire, Director, 202-994-4060, E-mail: lasp@gwu.edu. *Application contact:* Nicole A. Campbell, Director of Graduate Admissions, 202-994-7050, Fax: 202-994-9537, E-mail: esiagrad@gwu.edu.
Website: http://elliott.gwu.edu/latin-american-studies

Georgia State University, College of Arts and Sciences, Department of World Languages and Cultures, Atlanta, GA 30302-3083. Offers French (MA), including applied linguistics and pedagogy, French studies, literature and culture; Latin American studies (Certificate); Spanish (MA); translation and interpretation (Certificate), including interpretation, translation. *Program availability:* Part-time. *Faculty:* 36 full-time (20 women). *Students:* 25 full-time (19 women), 9 part-time (5 women); includes 19 minority (8 Black or African American, non-Hispanic/Latino; 10 Hispanic/Latino; 1 Two or more

races, non-Hispanic/Latino), 4 international. Average age 39. 36 applicants, 86% accepted, 22 enrolled. In 2017, 10 master's, 2 other advanced degrees awarded. *Entrance requirements:* For master's, GRE, statement of purpose, writing sample in the target language, 2 letters of recommendation, official transcripts; for Certificate, entrance examination involving translating one passage from English to the target language and one passage from the target language to English, 3 letters of recommendation, resume/curriculum vitae, official transcripts. Additional exam requirements/recommendations for international students: Required—TOEFL (minimum score 79 iBT). *Application deadline:* For fall admission, 3/15 priority date for domestic and international students; for spring admission, 11/15 priority date for domestic and international students. Application fee: $50. Electronic applications accepted. *Expenses:* Tuition, state resident: full-time $7020. Tuition, nonresident: full-time $22,518. *Required fees:* $2128. Tuition and fees vary according to degree level and program. *Financial support:* Applicants required to submit FAFSA. *Faculty research:* French literature and culture, Francophone literature and culture, Latin American literature and culture, Spanish literature and culture, Hispanic linguistics. *Unit head:* Dr. Fernando Reati, Department Chair, 404-413-5984, Fax: 404-413-5982, E-mail: freati@gsu.edu. *Application contact:* Amber Amari, Director, Graduate and Scheduling Services, 404-413-5037, E-mail: aamari@gsu.edu.
Website: http://wlc.gsu.edu/

Indiana University Bloomington, University Graduate School, College of Arts and Sciences, School of Global and International Studies, Center for Latin American and Caribbean Studies, Bloomington, IN 47405. Offers MA, MBA/MA, MIS/MA, MLS/MA, MPA/MA, MPH/MA. *Program availability:* Part-time. *Degree requirements:* For master's, one foreign language, oral and written exam. *Entrance requirements:* For master's, GRE General Test. Additional exam requirements/recommendations for international students: Required—TOEFL. Electronic applications accepted.

La Salle University, School of Arts and Sciences, Hispanic Institute, Philadelphia, PA 19141-1199. Offers bilingual/bicultural studies (MA); ESL program specialist (Certificate); interpretation: English/Spanish-Spanish/English (Certificate); teaching English to speakers of other languages (MA); translation and interpretation (MA); translation: English/Spanish-Spanish/English (Certificate). *Program availability:* Part-time, evening/weekend. *Faculty:* 2 full-time (1 woman), 5 part-time/adjunct (1 woman). *Students:* 1 (woman) full-time, 37 part-time (26 women); includes 21 minority (7 Black or African American, non-Hispanic/Latino; 1 American Indian or Alaska Native, non-Hispanic/Latino; 1 Asian, non-Hispanic/Latino; 10 Hispanic/Latino; 2 Two or more races, non-Hispanic/Latino), 2 international. Average age 33. 24 applicants, 79% accepted, 11 enrolled. In 2017, 4 master's, 1 other advanced degree awarded. *Degree requirements:* For master's, one foreign language, project or thesis. *Entrance requirements:* For master's, GRE, MAT, or GMAT, professional resume; two letters of recommendation; for Certificate, GRE, MAT, or GMAT, professional resume; two letters of recommendation; evidence of an advanced level in Spanish. Additional exam requirements/recommendations for international students: Required—TOEFL. *Application deadline:* For fall admission, 8/15 priority date for domestic students, 7/15 for international students; for spring admission, 12/15 priority date for domestic students, 11/15 for international students; for summer admission, 4/15 priority date for domestic students, 3/15 for international students. Applications are processed on a rolling basis. Application fee: $35. Electronic applications accepted. Application fee is waived when completed online. *Expenses:* Contact institution. *Financial support:* In 2017–18, 10 students received support. Scholarships/grants available. Support available to part-time students. Financial award application deadline: 8/31; financial award applicants required to submit FAFSA. *Faculty research:* Puerto Rican literature, cross-cultural communication, English as a second language methodology, Spanish language. *Unit head:* Guadalupe Da Costa Montesinos, Director, 215-951-1209, Fax: 215-991-3506, E-mail: montesin@lasalle.edu. *Application contact:* Elizabeth Heenan, Director, Graduate and Adult Enrollment, 215-951-1100, Fax: 215-951-1462, E-mail: heenan@lasalle.edu.
Website: http://www.lasalle.edu/hispanic-institute/

Michigan State University, The Graduate School, College of Social Science, Program in Chicano/Latino Studies, East Lansing, MI 48824. Offers PhD. *Entrance requirements:* Additional exam requirements/recommendations for international students: Required—TOEFL. Electronic applications accepted.

New York University, Graduate School of Arts and Science, Center for Latin American and Caribbean Studies, New York, NY 10012-1019. Offers MA, JD/MA. *Program availability:* Part-time. *Students:* 20 full-time (13 women), 5 part-time (4 women); includes 15 minority (1 Black or African American, non-Hispanic/Latino; 13 Hispanic/Latino; 1 Two or more races, non-Hispanic/Latino), 5 international. Average age 27. 41 applicants, 93% accepted, 14 enrolled. In 2017, 12 master's awarded. *Degree requirements:* For master's, one foreign language, thesis or alternative, major project. *Entrance requirements:* For master's, GRE General Test, knowledge of Portuguese or Spanish. Additional exam requirements/recommendations for international students: Required—TOEFL. *Application deadline:* For fall admission, 2/1 priority date for domestic students, 2/1 for international students. Application fee: $100. *Expenses:* Tuition: Full-time $41,352; part-time $19,968 per year. *Required fees:* $2496; $1628 per unit. $814 per term. Tuition and fees vary according to course load and program. *Financial support:* Fellowships with tuition reimbursements, teaching assistantships with tuition reimbursements, Federal Work-Study, institutionally sponsored loans, scholarships/grants, health care benefits, and unspecified assistantships available. Financial award application deadline: 2/1; financial award applicants required to submit FAFSA. *Faculty research:* Latin American politics, Caribbean societies, Andean history, political economy of cultural policies. *Unit head:* Jill Lane, Director, 212-998-8686, Fax: 212-995-4163, E-mail: clacs.info@nyu.edu. *Application contact:* Amalia Cordova, Program Administrator, 212-998-8686, Fax: 212-995-4163, E-mail: clacs.info@nyu.edu.
Website: http://clacs.as.nyu.edu/

New York University, Graduate School of Arts and Science, Program in Museum Studies, New York, NY 10012-1019. Offers museum studies (MA, Advanced Certificate), including Africana studies (MA), Hebrew and Judaic studies (MA), Latin American and Caribbean studies (MA), Near Eastern studies (MA). *Program availability:* Part-time, evening/weekend. *Students:* Average age 26. 123 applicants, 81% accepted, 29 enrolled. In 2017, 35 master's, 1 other advanced degree awarded. *Entrance requirements:* For master's, GRE General Test; for Advanced Certificate, master's degree or PhD. Additional exam requirements/recommendations for international students: Required—TOEFL. *Application deadline:* For fall admission, 2/15 for domestic and international students; for spring admission, 11/1 for domestic and international students. Application fee: $100. *Expenses:* Tuition: Full-time $41,352; part-time $19,968 per year. *Required fees:* $2496; $1628 per unit. $814 per term. Tuition and fees vary according to course load and program. *Financial support:* Application deadline: 2/15. *Faculty research:* Modern and contemporary art, history of museums and exhibitions, conservation of cultural materials, museum anthropology, ethnography. *Unit head:* Bruce Altshuler, Director, 212-998-8080, Fax: 212-995-4185, E-mail: museum.studies@nyu.edu. *Application contact:* Tatiana Kamorina, Department Administrator, 212-998-8080, Fax: 212-995-4185, E-mail: museum.studies@nyu.edu.
Website: http://www.nyu.edu/fas/program/museumstudies/

Northeastern Illinois University, College of Graduate Studies and Research, College of Arts and Sciences, Program in Latin American Literatures and Cultures, Chicago, IL 60625. Offers MA. *Expenses:* Tuition, state resident: full-time $7274; part-time $404.11 per credit hour. Tuition, nonresident: full-time $14,548; part-time $808.23 per credit hour. *Required fees:* $1284. *Unit head:* Dr. Paul Schroeder-Rodriguez, Department Chair, 773-442-4279, E-mail: p-schroeder-rodriguez@neiu.edu. *Application contact:* Martha Narvaez, Graduate Admission Representative, 773-442-6006, E-mail: m-narvaez@neiu.edu.
Website: http://www.neiu.edu/~fldept/grad_program.htm

The Ohio State University, Graduate School, Center for Latin American Studies, Columbus, OH 43210. Offers MA. *Students:* 1. *Entrance requirements:* For master's, GRE General Test. Additional exam requirements/recommendations for international students: Required—TOEFL (minimum score 550 paper-based; 79 iBT), IELTS (minimum score 7). *Application deadline:* For fall admission, 12/13 priority date for domestic students, 11/30 priority date for international students; for spring admission, 12/12 for domestic students, 11/10 for international students; for summer admission, 4/10 for domestic students, 3/13 for international students. Applications are processed on a rolling basis. Application fee: $60 ($70 for international students). Electronic applications accepted. *Financial support:* Fellowships with tuition reimbursements available. *Unit head:* Dr. Terrell Morgan, Director, 614-292-9555, E-mail: morgan.3@osu.edu. *Application contact:* Graduate and Professional Admissions, 614-292-9444, Fax: 614-292-3895, E-mail: gpadmissions@osu.edu.
Website: http://clas.osu.edu

Ohio University, Graduate College, Center for International Studies, Program in Latin American Studies, Athens, OH 45701-2979. Offers MA. *Program availability:* Part-time. *Degree requirements:* For master's, one foreign language, thesis optional. *Entrance requirements:* For master's, minimum GPA of 3.0. Additional exam requirements/recommendations for international students: Required—TOEFL (minimum score 550 paper-based; 80 iBT), IELTS (minimum score 6.5). Electronic applications accepted. *Faculty research:* Central America, Ecuador, Brazil, transnational migration, microfinance.

San Diego State University, Graduate and Research Affairs, College of Arts and Letters, Center for Latin American Studies, San Diego, CA 92182. Offers MA, MBA/MA. *Degree requirements:* For master's, 2 foreign languages, thesis or alternative. *Entrance requirements:* For master's, GRE General Test, 3 letters of reference. Additional exam requirements/recommendations for international students: Required—TOEFL. Electronic applications accepted. *Faculty research:* Latin American politics and economics.

Simon Fraser University, Office of Graduate Studies and Postdoctoral Fellows, Faculty of Arts and Social Sciences, Latin American Studies Program, Vancouver, BC V6B 5K3, Canada. Offers MA, Graduate Certificate. *Degree requirements:* For master's, one foreign language, thesis; for Graduate Certificate, one foreign language, Spanish or Portuguese language exam. *Entrance requirements:* For master's, minimum GPA of 3.0 (on scale of 4.33) or 3.33 based on last 60 credits of undergraduate courses; for Graduate Certificate, current enrollment in a master's or doctoral program. Additional exam requirements/recommendations for international students: Recommended—TOEFL (minimum score 580 paper-based; 93 iBT), IELTS (minimum score 7), TWE (minimum score 5). Electronic applications accepted. *Faculty research:* Theories and strategies of development, political economy, globalization, political sociology, health communications and promotion.

Texas Christian University, AddRan College of Liberal Arts, Department of History, Fort Worth, TX 76129. Offers Latin America (MA, PhD); United States (MA, PhD). *Faculty:* 18 full-time (6 women). *Students:* 50 full-time (20 women); includes 6 minority (5 Hispanic/Latino; 1 Two or more races, non-Hispanic/Latino), 1 international. Average age 34. 21 applicants, 57% accepted, 9 enrolled. In 2017, 1 master's, 6 doctorates awarded. Terminal master's awarded for partial completion of doctoral program. *Degree requirements:* For master's, comprehensive exam, thesis or alternative; for doctorate, one foreign language, comprehensive exam, thesis/dissertation. *Entrance requirements:* For master's and doctorate, GRE General Test. Additional exam requirements/recommendations for international students: Recommended—TOEFL. *Application deadline:* 2/1 for domestic and international students; for summer admission, 2/1 for domestic and international students. Application fee: $60. Electronic applications accepted. *Financial support:* In 2017–18, 50 students received support, including 3 fellowships with full tuition reimbursements available (averaging $20,000 per year), 15 research assistantships with full tuition reimbursements available (averaging $17,500 per year), 5 teaching assistantships with full tuition reimbursements available (averaging $17,500 per year); tuition waivers (full) also available. Financial award application deadline: 2/1. *Faculty research:* U.S. South, Latin American history, Atlantic World history, American West. *Total annual research expenditures:* $140,000. *Unit head:* Dr. Jodi Campbell, Professor, 817-257-5882, Fax: 817-257-5650, E-mail: j.campbell@tcu.edu. *Application contact:* Heather Confessore, Administrative Assistant, 817-257-7288, Fax: 817-257-5650, E-mail: h.confessore@tcu.edu.
Website: http://www.his.tcu.edu/graduate.asp

Tulane University, School of Liberal Arts, Roger Thayer Stone Center for Latin American Studies, New Orleans, LA 70118-5669. Offers MA, PhD, MBA/MA, MCL/MA. Terminal master's awarded for partial completion of doctoral program. *Degree requirements:* For master's, one foreign language, thesis optional; for doctorate, 2 foreign languages, thesis/dissertation. *Entrance requirements:* For master's, GRE General Test, minimum B average in undergraduate course work; for doctorate, GRE General Test. Additional exam requirements/recommendations for international students: Required—TOEFL. Electronic applications accepted. *Expenses:* Tuition: Full-time $50,920; part-time $2829 per credit hour. *Required fees:* $2040; $44.50 per credit hour. $580 per term. Tuition and fees vary according to course load, degree level and program.

University at Albany, State University of New York, College of Arts and Sciences, Department of Latin American, Caribbean, and U.S. Latino Studies, Albany, NY 12222-0001. Offers MA, PhD, Certificate. *Program availability:* Part-time. *Faculty:* 10 full-time (7 women). *Students:* 9 full-time (5 women), 15 part-time (10 women); includes 22 minority (1 Black or African American, non-Hispanic/Latino; 20 Hispanic/Latino; 1 Two or more races, non-Hispanic/Latino). 12 applicants, 75% accepted, 4 enrolled. In 2017, 1 master's, 1 doctorate, 1 other advanced degree awarded. *Degree requirements:* For master's, thesis. *Entrance requirements:* For master's, ability to read and write Spanish. Additional exam requirements/recommendations for international students: Required—TOEFL (minimum score 550 paper-based). *Application deadline:* For fall admission, 3/15 for domestic students, 5/1 for international students; for spring admission, 11/1 for international students. Applications are processed on a rolling basis. Application fee: $75. Electronic applications accepted. *Expenses:* Tuition, state resident: full-time $10,870; part-time $453 per credit hour. Tuition, nonresident: full-time $22,210; part-time $925 per credit hour. *Required fees:* $84.68 per credit hour. $508.06 per semester. Part-time tuition and fees vary according to course load and program. *Financial support:* Fellowships, research assistantships, and teaching assistantships available. Financial award application deadline: 3/15. *Faculty research:* Meso-American anthropology, Latin American women's studies, Latinos in the U.S. *Unit head:* Pedro Caban, Chair, 518-442-

4890, Fax: 518-442-4790, E-mail: pcaban@albany.edu. *Application contact:* Michael DeRensis, Director, Graduate Admissions, 518-442-3980, Fax: 518-442-3922, E-mail: graduate@albany.edu.
Website: http://www.albany.edu/lacs/

The University of Arizona, College of Social and Behavioral Sciences, Center for Latin American Studies, Tucson, AZ 85721. Offers MA. *Program availability:* Part-time. *Degree requirements:* For master's, 2 foreign languages, comprehensive exam, thesis optional. *Entrance requirements:* For master's, GRE, 2 letters of recommendation, resume. Additional exam requirements/recommendations for international students: Required—TOEFL (minimum score 550 paper-based; 79 iBT). Electronic applications accepted. *Faculty research:* Comparative analyses of national identities and of democratization across Latin America, environmental problems and management along the U.S.-Mexican border, integration efforts along the Peru/Ecuador border, social justice issues in Guatemala.

University of California, Los Angeles, Graduate Division, International Institute, Interdepartmental Program in Latin American Studies, Los Angeles, CA 90095. Offers MA, M Ed/MA, MA/MA, MBA/MA, MLIS/MA, MPH/MA. *Degree requirements:* For master's, 2 foreign languages, comprehensive exam or thesis. *Entrance requirements:* For master's, GRE General Test, bachelor's degree; minimum undergraduate GPA of 3.0 (or its equivalent if letter grade system not used); language requirement. Additional exam requirements/recommendations for international students: Required—TOEFL. Electronic applications accepted.

University of California, San Diego, Graduate Division, Latin American Studies Program, La Jolla, CA 92093. Offers MA. *Students:* 16 full-time (9 women), 1 (woman) part-time. 25 applicants, 76% accepted, 10 enrolled. In 2017, 3 master's awarded. *Degree requirements:* For master's, one foreign language, thesis. *Entrance requirements:* For master's, GRE General Test, minimum GPA of 3.0; writing sample; statement of purpose. Additional exam requirements/recommendations for international students: Required—TOEFL (minimum score 550 paper-based; 80 iBT), IELTS (minimum score 7). Application fee: $105 ($125 for international students). Electronic applications accepted. *Financial support:* Fellowships, research assistantships, teaching assistantships, scholarships/grants, unspecified assistantships, and readerships available. Financial award applicants required to submit FAFSA. *Faculty research:* Cultural studies, gender studies, history, international migration, sociology. *Unit head:* Scott Desposato, Director, E-mail: las-director@ucsd.edu. *Application contact:* Jessica Cassidy, Graduate Coordinator, 858-534-7967, E-mail: las@ucsd.edu.

University of California, Santa Barbara, Graduate Division, College of Letters and Sciences, Division of Humanities and Fine Arts, Program in Latin American and Iberian Studies, Santa Barbara, CA 93106-4150. Offers MA. *Degree requirements:* For master's, one foreign language, comprehensive exam (for some programs), thesis. *Entrance requirements:* For master's, GRE. Additional exam requirements/recommendations for international students: Required—TOEFL (minimum score 550 paper-based; 80 iBT), IELTS (minimum score 7). Electronic applications accepted. *Faculty research:* Political science, anthropology, history, sociology, Portuguese.

University of Chicago, Division of the Social Sciences and Division of the Humanities, Center for Latin American Studies, Chicago, IL 60637. Offers MA. *Faculty:* 54. *Students:* 6 full-time (0 women). 20 applicants, 85% accepted, 6 enrolled. In 2017, 3 master's awarded. *Degree requirements:* For master's, one foreign language, thesis. *Entrance requirements:* For master's, GRE General Test, 3 letters of recommendation, writing sample (dependent on program), statement of purpose, resume or curriculum vitae. Additional exam requirements/recommendations for international students: Required—TOEFL (minimum score 104 iBT), IELTS (minimum score 7). *Application deadline:* For fall admission, 1/4 priority date for domestic and international students. Application fee: $90. Electronic applications accepted. *Expenses:* $57,996 tuition. *Financial support:* In 2017–18, 6 students received support. Federal Work-Study, institutionally sponsored loans, and scholarships/grants available. Financial award application deadline: 1/4. *Unit head:* Prof. Brodwyn Fischer, Director, E-mail: clas@uchicago.edu. *Application contact:* Office of the Dean of Students, 773-702-8415, E-mail: ssd-admissions@uchicago.edu.
Website: http://clas.uchicago.edu

University of Connecticut, Graduate School, College of Liberal Arts and Sciences, Field of International Studies, Program in International Studies, Storrs, CT 06269. Offers European studies (MA); Italian history and culture (MA); Latino and Latin American studies (MA). *Degree requirements:* For master's, comprehensive exam. *Entrance requirements:* For master's, GRE General Test. Additional exam requirements/recommendations for international students: Required—TOEFL (minimum score 550 paper-based). Electronic applications accepted.

University of Florida, Graduate School, College of Liberal Arts and Sciences, Center for Latin American Studies, Gainesville, FL 32611. Offers Latin American studies (MA, Certificate); sustainable development practice (MDP); tropical conservation and development (MA); JD/MA. *Program availability:* Part-time. *Degree requirements:* For master's, thesis. *Entrance requirements:* For master's, GRE General Test, minimum GPA of 3.0. Additional exam requirements/recommendations for international students: Required—TOEFL (minimum score 550 paper-based; 80 iBT), IELTS (minimum score 6). Electronic applications accepted. *Faculty research:* Tropical conservation and development; ethnicity in the Americas, Brazil, and Cuba; North American Free Trade Agreement (NAFTA).

University of Illinois at Chicago, College of Liberal Arts and Sciences, Latin American and Latino Studies Program, Chicago, IL 60607-7128. Offers MA. *Faculty research:* Representation of nation, race, gender and labor in film; Colonial political discourse and social resistance; social structures and religious rituals among the Maya; rural development and ecology in Mexico; Latina reproductive rights; youth activism; transnational Cuban migration; globalization and labor strategies of women in Brazil; Mexican hometown associations; local, national and global immigrant rights struggles.

University of Illinois at Urbana–Champaign, Graduate College, College of Liberal Arts and Sciences, Center for Latin American and Caribbean Studies, Champaign, IL 61820. Offers Latin American studies (MA).

The University of Kansas, Graduate Studies, College of Liberal Arts and Sciences, Latin American and Caribbean Studies Program, Lawrence, KS 66045. Offers Brazilian studies (Graduate Certificate); Central American and Mexican studies (Graduate Certificate); Latin American and Caribbean studies (Graduate Certificate); Latin American studies (MA). *Program availability:* Part-time. *Students:* 3 full-time (1 woman), 2 part-time (1 woman), 3 international. Average age 30. 3 applicants, 100% accepted, 2 enrolled. In 2017, 2 master's awarded. *Entrance requirements:* For master's, GRE, minimum GPA of 3.0; three letters of recommendation; 10-page writing sample, preferably in one of the social sciences or humanities; resume; language proficiency in either Spanish or Portuguese. Additional exam requirements/recommendations for international students: Required—TOEFL. Application fee: $65 ($85 for international students). Electronic applications accepted. *Financial support:* Fellowships, research assistantships, teaching assistantships, scholarships/grants, and unspecified assistantships available. *Faculty research:* New migration studies; analysis and implementation of sustainable rural water projects in the developing world; develop research collaborations involving institutions in Campinas, São Paulo in Brazil *Unit head:* Marta Caminero-Santangelo, Interim Director, Center for Latin American and Caribbean Studies, 785-979-2513, E-mail: camsan@ku.edu. *Application contact:* Alyssa McDonald, Graduate Admissions Contact, 785-864-9814, E-mail: mcdonalda@ku.edu.
Website: https://latamst.ku.edu/

The University of Manchester, School of Languages, Linguistics and Cultures, Manchester, United Kingdom. Offers Arab world studies (PhD); Chinese studies (M Phil, PhD); East Asian studies (M Phil, PhD); English language (PhD); French studies (M Phil, PhD); German studies (M Phil, PhD); interpreting studies (PhD); Italian studies (M Phil, PhD); Japanese studies (M Phil, PhD); Latin American cultural studies (M Phil, PhD); linguistics (M Phil, PhD); Middle Eastern studies (M Phil, PhD); Polish studies (M Phil, PhD); Portuguese studies (M Phil, PhD); Russian studies (M Phil, PhD); Spanish studies (M Phil, PhD); translation and intercultural studies (M Phil, PhD).

University of Massachusetts Dartmouth, Graduate School, College of Arts and Sciences, Department of Portuguese, North Dartmouth, MA 02747-2300. Offers Luso-Afro Brazilian studies and theory (PhD); Portuguese studies (MA). *Program availability:* Part-time. *Faculty:* 5 full-time (2 women), 2 part-time/adjunct (0 women). *Students:* 6 full-time (5 women), 5 part-time (3 women); includes 4 minority (3 Hispanic/Latino; 1 Two or more races, non-Hispanic/Latino), 3 international. Average age 41. 4 applicants, 50% accepted. In 2017, 1 master's, 2 doctorates awarded. Terminal master's awarded for partial completion of doctoral program. *Degree requirements:* For master's, comprehensive exam, thesis, written exam or project; for doctorate, comprehensive exam, thesis/dissertation. *Entrance requirements:* For master's, GRE (recommended), statement of purpose (minimum of 300 words), resume, 3 letters of recommendation, official transcripts, writing samples in Portuguese (minimum of 10 pages of writing); for doctorate, GRE (recommended), statement of purpose (minimum of 300 words), resume, 3 letters of recommendation, official transcripts, scholarly writing sample (minimum of 10 pages). Additional exam requirements/recommendations for international students: Required—TOEFL (minimum score 500 paper-based; 61 iBT). *Application deadline:* For fall admission, 2/1 priority date for domestic students, 1/1 priority date for international students; for spring admission, 11/15 priority date for domestic students, 10/15 priority date for international students. Application fee: $60. Electronic applications accepted. *Expenses:* Tuition, state resident: full-time $15,449; part-time $643.71 per credit. Tuition, nonresident: full-time $27,880; part-time $1161.67 per credit. *Required fees:* $405; $25.88 per credit. Tuition and fees vary according to course load and reciprocity agreements. *Financial support:* In 2017–18, 8 fellowships (averaging $18,750 per year) were awarded; research assistantships, teaching assistantships, tuition waivers (full), and unspecified assistantships also available. Support available to part-time students. Financial award application deadline: 3/1; financial award applicants required to submit FAFSA. *Faculty research:* Teaching and learning Portuguese as a heritage language, literature in Luso-Afro-Brazilian studies, studies in ethnicity and migration, bi- and multi-linguicism, histories of translation and gender in romance literary traditions. *Total annual research expenditures:* $308,000. *Unit head:* Victor Mendes, Director of Graduate Studies, Department of Portuguese, 508-999-8338, Fax: 508-910-9272, E-mail: vmendes@umassd.edu. *Application contact:* Steven Briggs, Director of Marketing and Recruitment for Graduate Studies, 508-999-8604, Fax: 508-999-8183, E-mail: graduate@umassd.edu.
Website: http://www.umassd.edu/cas/departmentsanddegreeprograms/portguese

University of Miami, Graduate School, College of Arts and Sciences, Department of Latin American and Caribbean Studies, Coral Gables, FL 33124. Offers Latin American studies (MA). *Program availability:* Part-time. *Degree requirements:* For master's, comprehensive exam (for some programs), thesis, linguistic competency in Spanish or Portuguese, reading competency in a second Latin American language. *Entrance requirements:* For master's, GRE, 3 letters of recommendation. Additional exam requirements/recommendations for international students: Required—TOEFL. Electronic applications accepted. *Faculty research:* Literary, media, religious, visual and cultural studies; environment and tourism studies; US-Latin American Relations and drug trafficking; migration, globalization, and social movements; democratization, regime transitions, and citizenship.

University of New Mexico, Graduate Studies, College of Arts and Sciences, Program in Latin American Studies, Albuquerque, NM 87131. Offers MA, PhD, JD/MA, MA/MA, MA/MPH, MBA/MA, MCRP/MA. *Program availability:* Part-time. *Faculty:* 6 full-time (4 women). *Students:* 12 full-time (6 women), 8 part-time (6 women); includes 7 minority (all Hispanic/Latino), 9 international. Average age 36. 12 applicants, 67% accepted, 7 enrolled. In 2017, 9 master's awarded. *Degree requirements:* For master's, one foreign language, comprehensive exam (for some programs), thesis (for some programs); for doctorate, 2 foreign languages, comprehensive exam, thesis/dissertation. *Entrance requirements:* For master's, GRE General Test, intermediate competence in Spanish, Portuguese or indigenous Latin American language; for doctorate, GRE General Test, master's degree in related field, one Latin American language. Additional exam requirements/recommendations for international students: Required—TOEFL. *Application deadline:* For fall admission, 2/1 priority date for domestic and international students; for spring admission, 11/1 for domestic and international students. Application fee: $50. Electronic applications accepted. *Financial support:* Fellowships with full tuition reimbursements, research assistantships with full tuition reimbursements, teaching assistantships with full tuition reimbursements, Federal Work-Study, scholarships/grants, health care benefits, tuition waivers (full), and unspecified assistantships available. Financial award application deadline: 2/1; financial award applicants required to submit FAFSA. *Unit head:* Dr. Susan Tiano, Director, 505-277-2961, Fax: 505-277-5989, E-mail: stiano@unm.edu. *Application contact:* Matias Fontenla, Associate Director for Academic Programs, 505-277-2961, Fax: 505-277-5989, E-mail: fontenla@unm.edu.
Website: http://laii.unm.edu

University of New Mexico, Graduate Studies, College of Fine Arts, Program in Art History, Albuquerque, NM 87131. Offers art history (MA); art of the Americas (MA); history of architecture (PhD); history of graphic arts (PhD); history of photography (PhD); modern Latin American art (PhD); Native American art (PhD); Pre-Columbian art and architecture (PhD); Spanish colonial art (PhD). *Program availability:* Part-time. *Faculty:* 7 full-time (5 women). *Students:* 7 full-time (all women), 18 part-time (15 women); includes 8 minority (2 American Indian or Alaska Native, non-Hispanic/Latino; 5 Hispanic/Latino; 1 Two or more races, non-Hispanic/Latino), 2 international. Average age 41. 21 applicants, 33% accepted, 5 enrolled. In 2017, 5 master's, 1 doctorate awarded. *Degree requirements:* For master's, one foreign language, comprehensive exam (for some programs), thesis, symposium; for doctorate, 2 foreign languages, comprehensive exam, thesis/dissertation, symposium. *Entrance requirements:* Additional exam requirements/recommendations for international students: Required—TOEFL (minimum score 550 paper-based), IELTS (minimum score 6). *Application deadline:* For fall admission, 1/15 for domestic students; for spring admission, 1/15 for domestic students. Application fee: $50. Electronic applications accepted. *Financial support:* Fellowships, research assistantships, teaching assistantships with partial tuition reimbursements, Federal Work-Study, institutionally sponsored loans, scholarships/grants, health care benefits, and unspecified assistantships available. Support available to part-time students. Financial award application deadline: 3/1; financial award applicants required to submit FAFSA. *Faculty research:* Native American, modern Latin American, pre-

Columbian, architectural, American, medieval, Spanish Colonial, and Latin American art; history of photography. *Unit head:* Prof. Mary Tsiongas, Chair, 505-277-5861, Fax: 505-277-5955, E-mail: tsiongas@unm.edu. *Application contact:* Kat Heatherington, Graduate Advisor, 505-277-6672, Fax: 505-277-5955, E-mail: art255@unm.edu. Website: http://art.unm.edu/

The University of North Carolina at Chapel Hill, Graduate School, College of Arts and Sciences, Department of Political Science, Chapel Hill, NC 27599. Offers Latin American studies (Certificate); political science (MA, PhD); trans-Atlantic studies (MA). *Degree requirements:* For master's, comprehensive exam; for doctorate, one foreign language, comprehensive exam, thesis/dissertation. *Entrance requirements:* For master's and doctorate, GRE General Test, minimum GPA of 3.0 recommended. Electronic applications accepted.

The University of North Carolina at Charlotte, College of Liberal Arts and Sciences, Interdisciplinary Liberal Arts and Sciences Programs, Charlotte, NC 28223-0001. Offers gender, sexuality, and women's studies (Graduate Certificate); gerontology (MA, Graduate Certificate); Latin American studies (MA); liberal studies (MA); organizational science (PhD); public policy (PhD). *Program availability:* Part-time, evening/weekend. *Faculty:* 1 full-time (0 women). *Students:* 66 full-time (48 women), 66 part-time (52 women); includes 41 minority (14 Black or African American, non-Hispanic/Latino; 2 Asian, non-Hispanic/Latino; 24 Hispanic/Latino; 1 Two or more races, non-Hispanic/Latino), 16 international. Average age 27. 129 applicants, 53% accepted, 43 enrolled. In 2017, 22 master's, 10 doctorates, 9 other advanced degrees awarded. *Degree requirements:* For master's, comprehensive exam (for some programs), thesis (for some programs), practicum, project; for doctorate, comprehensive exam, thesis/dissertation; for Graduate Certificate, practicum (for gerontology). *Entrance requirements:* For master's, GRE General Test or MAT, bachelor's degree from accredited college or university; official transcripts of all previous academic work attempted beyond high school with minimum overall GPA of 3.0; statement of purpose; recommendation letters; for doctorate, GRE or GMAT, statement of purpose discussing interest in program and objectives for pursuing degree, current resume or curriculum vitae, unofficial transcripts; for Graduate Certificate, bachelor's degree from accredited university and either enrolled and in good standing in a graduate degree program at UNC Charlotte or have a minimum undergraduate GPA of 3.0. Additional exam requirements/recommendations for international students: Required—TOEFL (minimum score 523 paper-based, 70 iBT) or IELTS (6.5). *Application deadline:* For fall admission, 2/15 for domestic and international students; for spring admission, 10/1 for domestic and international students; for summer admission, 4/1 for domestic and international students. Applications are processed on a rolling basis. Application fee: $75. Electronic applications accepted. *Expenses:* Tuition, state resident: full-time $4337. Tuition, nonresident: full-time $17,771. *Required fees:* $3211. Tuition and fees vary according to course load and program. *Financial support:* In 2017–18, 21 students received support, including 19 research assistantships (averaging $12,011 per year), 1 teaching assistantship (averaging $18,600 per year); career-related internships or fieldwork, institutionally sponsored loans, scholarships/grants, unspecified assistantships, and administrative assistantships also available. Support available to part-time students. Financial award application deadline: 3/1; financial award applicants required to submit FAFSA. *Unit head:* Dr. Nancy A. Gutierrez, Dean, 704-687-0081, E-mail: ngutierr@uncc.edu. *Application contact:* Kathy B. Giddings, Director of Graduate Admissions, 704-687-5503, Fax: 704-687-3279, E-mail: gradadm@uncc.edu. Website: http://clas.uncc.edu/academics

University of Notre Dame, Graduate School, College of Arts and Letters, Division of Humanities, Department of Romance Languages and Literatures, Notre Dame, IN 46556. Offers French and Francophone studies (MA); Iberian and Latin American studies (MA); Italian studies (MA); Romance literatures (MA). *Degree requirements:* For master's, 2 foreign languages, comprehensive exam, thesis optional. *Entrance requirements:* For master's, GRE General Test, BA in target language. Additional exam requirements/recommendations for international students: Required—TOEFL (minimum score 600 paper-based; 80 iBT). Electronic applications accepted. *Faculty research:* Literature of discovery and exploration, modern literature, literary criticism, medieval literature, feminist critical theory.

University of Pittsburgh, University Center for International Studies, Pittsburgh, PA 15260. Offers African studies (Certificate); Asian studies (Certificate); European Union studies (Certificate); global studies (Certificate); Latin American studies (Certificate); Russian and East European studies (Certificate); West European studies (Certificate). *Program availability:* Part-time, evening/weekend, online learning. *Students:* 183 full-time (108 women), 9 part-time (all women); includes 78 minority (6 Black or African American, non-Hispanic/Latino; 23 Asian, non-Hispanic/Latino; 47 Hispanic/Latino; 2 Two or more races, non-Hispanic/Latino). Average age 29. *Degree requirements:* For Certificate, one foreign language, comprehensive exam (for some programs). *Entrance requirements:* Additional exam requirements/recommendations for international students: Required—TOEFL. *Expenses:* No tuition and fees. *Financial support:* In 2017–18, 25 fellowships with full tuition reimbursements (averaging $26,117 per year) were awarded; scholarships/grants, traineeships, health care benefits, and unspecified assistantships also available. *Unit head:* Dr. Ariel Armony, Director, 412-648-7374, Fax: 412-624-4672, E-mail: armony@pitt.edu. Website: http://www.ucis.pitt.edu

University of Southern California, Graduate School, Dana and David Dornsife College of Letters, Arts and Sciences, Comparative Studies in Literature and Culture Doctoral Program, Los Angeles, CA 90089. Offers comparative literature (PhD); comparative media and culture (PhD); Spanish and Latin American studies (PhD). *Degree requirements:* For doctorate, 2 foreign languages, comprehensive exam, thesis/dissertation. *Entrance requirements:* For doctorate, GRE, competence in language other than English (highly recommended). Additional exam requirements/recommendations for international students: Required—TOEFL. Electronic applications accepted. *Faculty research:* Literary theory, Japanese film and contemporary fiction, Francophone literature and cinema, Latin American and Caribbean literature, Spanish literature and film, nineteenth and twentieth century British and American literature.

University of South Florida, College of Arts and Sciences, Department of History, Tampa, FL 33620-9951. Offers history (MA, PhD), including American history (MA), ancient history (MA), European history (MA), Latin American history (MA), Medieval history (MA). *Program availability:* Part-time, evening/weekend. *Faculty:* 17 full-time (8 women), 1 (woman) part-time/adjunct. *Students:* 39 full-time (9 women), 19 part-time (9 women); includes 5 minority (1 American Indian or Alaska Native, non-Hispanic/Latino; 4 Hispanic/Latino). Average age 33. 41 applicants, 80% accepted, 24 enrolled. In 2017, 10 master's, 1 doctorate awarded. *Degree requirements:* For master's, one foreign language, comprehensive exam, thesis optional; for doctorate, one foreign language, comprehensive exam, thesis/dissertation. *Entrance requirements:* For master's, GRE General Test, minimum GPA of 3.0, two letters of recommendation, 2-page statement of purpose, writing sample; for doctorate, GRE General Test, minimum GPA of 3.5 in master's degree coursework, three letters of recommendation, statement of purpose, writing sample, foreign language proficiency in the field of study. Additional exam requirements/recommendations for international students: Required—TOEFL (minimum score 550 paper-based; 79 iBT) or IELTS (minimum score 6.5). *Application deadline:* For fall admission, 12/1 priority date for domestic students, 12/1

for international students. Applications are processed on a rolling basis. Application fee: $30. Electronic applications accepted. *Financial support:* In 2017–18, 3 students received support, including 17 teaching assistantships with tuition reimbursements available (averaging $12,750 per year); unspecified assistantships also available. Financial award application deadline: 1/15. *Faculty research:* North American and U.S. history, European history, nineteenth- and twentieth-centuries/modern world, early modern world, ancient history, history of gender/sexuality, Latin American history, history of science and medicine. *Total annual research expenditures:* $194,096. *Unit head:* Dr. Fraser Ottanelli, Professor and Chair, 813-974-6209, Fax: 813-974-6228, E-mail: ottanelli@usf.edu. *Application contact:* Dr. Kees Boterbloem, Professor and Graduate Program Director, 813-974-2807, E-mail: cboterbl@usf.edu. Website: http://history.usf.edu

University of South Florida, College of Arts and Sciences, School of Interdisciplinary Global Studies, Tampa, FL 33620-9951. Offers government (PhD); Latin American, Caribbean and Latino studies (MA); liberal arts (MA), including Africana studies; political science (MA), including comparative government and politics. *Accreditation:* NASPAA. *Program availability:* Part-time, evening/weekend. *Faculty:* 14 full-time (2 women). *Students:* 3 applicants. In 2017, 9 master's, 1 doctorate awarded. *Degree requirements:* For master's, comprehensive exam, thesis; for doctorate, comprehensive exam, thesis/dissertation. *Entrance requirements:* For master's, GRE General Test, minimum GPA of 3.0 in upper-division undergraduate course work; letters of recommendation (2 for MPA, 3 for MS); 500-word personal statement and undergraduate background in political science or related fields (for MS); one-page career statement (for MPA); for doctorate, GRE General Test, 500-word personal statement, three letters of recommendation, transcripts of MA/BA coursework, writing sample. Additional exam requirements/recommendations for international students: Required—TOEFL (minimum score 550 paper-based; 79 iBT) or IELTS (minimum score 6.5). *Application deadline:* For fall admission, 1/5 for domestic and international students; for spring admission, 10/15 for domestic students, 9/15 for international students. Applications are processed on a rolling basis. Application fee: $30. Electronic applications accepted. *Financial support:* In 2017–18, 3 students received support, including 18 teaching assistantships with tuition reimbursements available (averaging $12,390 per year); unspecified assistantships also available. Financial award application deadline: 4/1. *Faculty research:* Citizenship and identity, social movements, global governance, American politics, public policy. *Total annual research expenditures:* $195,426. *Unit head:* Dr. Steven Tauber, Associate Professor/Interim Chair, 813-974-2278, Fax: 813-974-0832, E-mail: stauber@usf.edu. *Application contact:* Dr. Bernd Reiter, Associate Professor and Director of Graduate Studies, 813-974-3583, Fax: 813-974-0832, E-mail: breiter@usf.edu. Website: http://gia.usf.edu/

University of South Florida, Innovative Education, Tampa, FL 33620-9951. Offers adult, career and higher education (Graduate Certificate), including college teaching, leadership in developing human resources, leadership in higher education; Africana studies (Graduate Certificate), including diasporas and health disparities, genocide and human rights; aging studies (Graduate Certificate), including gerontology; art research (Graduate Certificate), including museum studies; business foundations (Graduate Certificate); chemical and biomedical engineering (Graduate Certificate), including materials science and engineering, water, health and sustainability; child and family studies (Graduate Certificate), including positive behavior support; civil and industrial engineering (Graduate Certificate), including transportation systems analysis; community and family health (Graduate Certificate), including maternal and child health, social marketing and public health, violence and injury: prevention and intervention, women's health; criminology (Graduate Certificate), including criminal justice administration; data science for public administration (Graduate Certificate); digital humanities (Graduate Certificate); educational measurement and research (Graduate Certificate), including evaluation; English (Graduate Certificate), including comparative literary studies, creative writing, professional and technical communication; entrepreneurship (Graduate Certificate); environmental health (Graduate Certificate), including safety management; epidemiology and biostatistics (Graduate Certificate), including applied biostatistics, biostatistics, concepts and tools of epidemiology, epidemiology, epidemiology of infectious diseases; geography, environment and planning (Graduate Certificate), including community development, environmental policy and management, geographical information systems; geology (Graduate Certificate), including hydrogeology; global health (Graduate Certificate), including disaster management, global health and Latin American and Caribbean studies, global health practice, humanitarian assistance, infection control; government and international affairs (Graduate Certificate), including Cuban studies, globalization studies; health policy and management (Graduate Certificate), including health management and leadership, public health policy and programs; hearing specialist: early intervention (Graduate Certificate); industrial and management systems engineering (Graduate Certificate), including systems engineering, technology management; information studies (Graduate Certificate), including school library media specialist; information systems/decision sciences (Graduate Certificate), including analytics and business intelligence; instructional technology (Graduate Certificate), including distance education, Florida digital/virtual educator, instructional design, multimedia design, Web design; internal medicine, bioethics and medical humanities (Graduate Certificate), including biomedical ethics; Latin American and Caribbean studies (Graduate Certificate); leadership for coastal resiliency planning (Graduate Certificate); mass communications (Graduate Certificate), including multimedia journalism; mathematics and statistics (Graduate Certificate), including mathematics; medicine (Graduate Certificate), including aging and neuroscience, bioinformatics, biotechnology, brain fitness and memory management, clinical investigation, hand and upper limb rehabilitation, health informatics, health sciences, integrative weight management, intellectual property, medicine and gender, metabolic and nutritional medicine, metabolic cardiology, pharmacy sciences; national and competitive intelligence (Graduate Certificate); nursing (Graduate Certificate), including simulation based academic fellowship in advanced pain management; psychological and social foundations (Graduate Certificate), including career counseling, college teaching, diversity in education, mental health counseling, school counseling; public affairs (Graduate Certificate), including nonprofit management, public management, research administration; public health (Graduate Certificate), including assessing chemical toxicity and public health risks, health equity, pharmacoepidemiology, public health generalist, toxicology, translational research in adolescent behavioral health; public health practices (Graduate Certificate), including planning for healthy communities; rehabilitation and mental health counseling (Graduate Certificate), including integrative mental health care, marriage and family therapy, rehabilitation technology; secondary education (Graduate Certificate), including ESOL, foreign language education: culture and content, foreign language education: professional; social work (Graduate Certificate), including geriatric social work/clinical gerontology; special education (Graduate Certificate), including autism spectrum disorder, disabilities education: severe/profound; world languages (Graduate Certificate), including teaching English as a second language (TESL) or foreign language. *Unit head:* Dr. Cynthia DeLuca, Associate Vice President and Assistant Vice Provost, 813-974-3077, Fax: 813-974-7061, E-mail: deluca@usf.edu. *Application contact:* Owen Hooper, Director, Summer and Alternative Calendar Programs, 813-974-6917, E-mail: hooper@usf.edu. Website: http://www.usf.edu/innovative-education/

Latin American Studies

The University of Texas at Austin, Graduate School, College of Liberal Arts, Teresa Lozano Long Institute of Latin American Studies, Austin, TX 78712-1111. Offers cultural politics of Afro-Latin and indigenous peoples (MA); development studies (MA); environmental studies (MA); human rights (MA); Latin American and international law (LL M); JD/MA; MA/MA; MBA/MA; MP Aff/MA; MSCRP/MA. LL M offered jointly with The University of Texas School of Law. *Entrance requirements:* For master's, GRE General Test.

The University of Texas at Dallas, School of Arts and Humanities, Richardson, TX 75080. Offers art history (MA); history (MA); humanities (MA, PhD), including aesthetic studies, history of ideas, studies in literature; Latin American studies (MA). *Program availability:* Part-time, evening/weekend. *Faculty:* 47 full-time (17 women), 4 part-time/adjunct (2 women). *Students:* 132 full-time (83 women), 117 part-time (71 women); includes 62 minority (11 Black or African American, non-Hispanic/Latino; 3 American Indian or Alaska Native, non-Hispanic/Latino; 10 Asian, non-Hispanic/Latino; 25 Hispanic/Latino; 13 Two or more races, non-Hispanic/Latino), 29 international. Average age 40. 127 applicants, 55% accepted, 43 enrolled. In 2017, 17 master's, 18 doctorates awarded. *Degree requirements:* For master's, one foreign language, portfolio; for doctorate, one foreign language, thesis/dissertation. *Entrance requirements:* For master's and doctorate, minimum GPA of 3.0 in undergraduate course work in field. Additional exam requirements/recommendations for international students: Required—TOEFL (minimum score 550 paper-based). *Application deadline:* For fall admission, 7/15 for domestic students, 5/1 priority date for international students; for spring admission, 11/15 for domestic students, 9/1 priority date for international students. Applications are processed on a rolling basis. Application fee: $50 ($100 for international students). Electronic applications accepted. *Expenses:* Tuition, state resident: full-time $12,916; part-time $718 per credit hour. Tuition, nonresident: full-time $25,252; part-time $1403 per credit hour. *Financial support:* In 2017–18, 136 students received support, including 12 research assistantships with partial tuition reimbursements available (averaging $22,710 per year), 71 teaching assistantships with partial tuition reimbursements available (averaging $15,000 per year); fellowships, Federal Work-Study, institutionally sponsored loans, scholarships/grants, and unspecified assistantships also available. Support available to part-time students. Financial award application deadline: 4/30; financial award applicants required to submit FAFSA. *Faculty research:* Science and the arts and humanities, intellectual and philosophical history, cultural studies, translation studies. *Total annual research expenditures:* $183,441. *Unit head:* Dr. Dennis M. Kratz, Dean, 972-883-2984, Fax: 972-883-2989, E-mail: dkratz@utdallas.edu. *Application contact:* Dr. John Gooch, Associate Dean of Graduate Studies, 972-883-2756, Fax: 972-883-2989, E-mail: john.gooch@utdallas.edu.
Website: http://www.utdallas.edu/ah/

University of Utah, Graduate School, College of Humanities, Latin American Studies Program, Salt Lake City, UT 84112. Offers MA. *Program availability:* Part-time, evening/weekend. *Faculty:* 49 full-time (28 women). *Students:* 1 full-time (0 women). 3 applicants, 67% accepted, 1 enrolled. In 2017, 2 master's awarded. *Degree requirements:* For master's, 2 foreign languages, thesis, third-year proficiency in one of the two major Latin American languages, first-year proficiency in the other (Spanish or Portuguese). *Entrance requirements:* For master's, GRE, minimum undergraduate GPA of 3.0, graduate 3.4. Additional exam requirements/recommendations for international students: Required—TOEFL (minimum score 580 paper-based). *Application deadline:* For fall admission, 2/1 priority date for domestic and international students. Application fee: $55 ($65 for international students). Electronic applications accepted. *Financial support:* Fellowships and research assistantships available. Financial award application deadline: 4/15. *Faculty research:* Latin American health studies, history, literature, culture, politics, economics. *Unit head:* Dr. Claudio Holzner, Director, 801-581-6101, E-mail: claudio.holzner@poli-sci.utah.edu. *Application contact:* Ashley Glenn, Academic Coordinator, 801-584-6101, Fax: 801-581-6105, E-mail: ea.glenn@utah.edu.
Website: http://latin-american-studies.utah.edu/

University of Wisconsin–Madison, Graduate School, College of Letters and Science, Department of History, Madison, WI 53706-1380. Offers African history (MA, PhD); Central Asian history (MA, PhD); comparative world history (MA, PhD); East Asian history (MA, PhD); European history (MA, PhD); gender and women's history (MA, PhD); Latin American and Caribbean history (MA, PhD); Middle Eastern history (MA, PhD); South Asian history (MA, PhD); Southeast Asian history (MA, PhD); United States history (MA, PhD). Terminal master's awarded for partial completion of doctoral program. *Degree requirements:* For master's, thesis (for some programs); for doctorate, variable foreign language requirement, thesis/dissertation. *Entrance requirements:* For master's and doctorate, GRE General Test. Additional exam requirements/recommendations for international students: Required—Michigan English Language Assessment Battery or TOEFL. Electronic applications accepted. *Faculty research:* American, African, European, Asian, Latin American, and Middle Eastern history.

University of Wisconsin–Madison, Graduate School, College of Letters and Science, Latin American, Caribbean and Iberian Studies Program, Madison, WI 53706-1380. Offers MA, MA/JD. *Degree requirements:* For master's, 2 foreign languages, thesis. *Entrance requirements:* For master's, minimum GPA of 3.0. Electronic applications accepted. *Faculty research:* Development, gender, social movements, cultural studies, history.

University of Wisconsin–Milwaukee, Graduate School, College of Letters and Science, Department of Foreign Languages and Literature, Milwaukee, WI 53201-0413. Offers foreign languages and literature (MA), including classic Greek, classics, comparative literature, French/Francophone language, literature, and culture, German language, literature, and culture, interpreting, Latin, linguistics, Spanish language, literature, and culture, translation; interpreting (Graduate Certificate); language, literature, and translation (MA, MALLT); translation (Graduate Certificate). *Program availability:* Part-time. *Students:* 11 full-time (6 women), 40 part-time (29 women); includes 10 minority (2 Black or African American, non-Hispanic/Latino; 3 Hispanic/Latino; 5 Two or more races, non-Hispanic/Latino), 4 international. Average age 35. 37 applicants, 68% accepted, 20 enrolled. In 2017, 5 master's awarded. *Degree requirements:* For master's, 2 foreign languages, thesis or alternative. *Entrance requirements:* Additional exam requirements/recommendations for international students: Required—TOEFL (minimum score 550 paper-based; 79 iBT), IELTS (minimum score 6.5). *Application deadline:* For fall admission, 1/1 priority date for domestic students; for spring admission, 9/1 for domestic students. Application fee: $56 ($96 for international students). Electronic applications accepted. *Financial support:* Fellowships, research assistantships, teaching assistantships, career-related internships or fieldwork, health care benefits, unspecified assistantships, and project assistantships available. Support available to part-time students. Financial award application deadline: 4/15; financial award applicants required to submit FAFSA. *Unit head:* Kevin Muse, Department Chair, 414-229-5213, E-mail: kmuse@uwm.edu. *Application contact:* General Information Contact, 414-229-4982, Fax: 414-229-6967, E-mail: gradschool@uwm.edu.
Website: http://uwm.edu/foreign-languages-literature/

Vanderbilt University, Program in Latin American Studies, Nashville, TN 37240-1001. Offers MA, LL M/MA, MBA/MA. *Faculty:* 62 full-time (22 women). *Students:* 8 full-time (3 women); includes 3 minority (1 Black or African American, non-Hispanic/Latino; 2 Hispanic/Latino), 2 international. Average age 25. 17 applicants, 35% accepted, 4 enrolled. In 2017, 4 master's awarded. *Degree requirements:* For master's, 2 foreign languages, thesis or alternative. *Entrance requirements:* For master's, GRE General Test. Additional exam requirements/recommendations for international students: Required—TOEFL (minimum score 570 paper-based; 88 iBT). *Application deadline:* For fall admission, 1/15 for domestic and international students. Application fee: $0. Electronic applications accepted. *Financial support:* Teaching assistantships with full tuition reimbursements, Federal Work-Study, institutionally sponsored loans, and health care benefits available. Financial award application deadline: 1/15; financial award applicants required to submit CSS PROFILE or FAFSA. *Faculty research:* Latin American and Iberian studies, anthropology, history, Spanish and Portuguese, social and political science. *Unit head:* Dr. Edward Fischer, Director, 615-322-2527, Fax: 615-343-6002, E-mail: edward.f.fischer@vanderbilt.edu. *Application contact:* Nicolette M. Kostiw, Assistant Director/Director of Graduate Studies, 615-322-2527, Fax: 615-343-6002, E-mail: nicolette.m.wilhide@vanderbilt.edu.
Website: http://www.vanderbilt.edu/clas/graduate-programs/

Yale University, Graduate School of Arts and Sciences, Department of Spanish and Portuguese, New Haven, CT 06520. Offers Latin American literature (PhD); Luso-Brazilian and Spanish/Spanish American literatures (PhD); Spanish peninsular literature (PhD). Terminal master's awarded for partial completion of doctoral program. *Degree requirements:* For doctorate, 3 foreign languages, thesis/dissertation. *Entrance requirements:* For doctorate, GRE General Test.

Near and Middle Eastern Studies

The American University in Cairo, School of Humanities and Social Sciences, Cairo, Egypt. Offers Arab and Islamic civilizations (Graduate Diploma); Arabic studies (MA); comparative literary studies (Graduate Diploma); Egyptology and Coptology (MA); English and comparative literature (MA); humanities and social sciences (Graduate Diploma); philosophy (MA); psychology (MA); sociology and anthropology (MA); teaching Arabic as a foreign language (MA); teaching English to speakers of other languages (MA). *Program availability:* Part-time, evening/weekend. *Faculty:* 52 full-time (27 women), 7 part-time/adjunct (3 women). *Students:* 52 full-time (41 women), 159 part-time (119 women), 38 international. Average age 31. 209 applicants, 36% accepted, 39 enrolled. In 2017, 73 master's awarded. *Degree requirements:* For master's, comprehensive exam (for some programs), thesis (for some programs). *Entrance requirements:* Additional exam requirements/recommendations for international students: Required—TOEFL (minimum score 450 paper-based; 45 iBT), IELTS (minimum score 5). *Application deadline:* For fall admission, 2/1 priority date for domestic and international students; for spring admission, 10/15 priority date for domestic and international students. Applications are processed on a rolling basis. Application fee: $85. Electronic applications accepted. *Financial support:* Fellowships with partial tuition reimbursements, scholarships/grants, tuition waivers (partial), and unspecified assistantships available. Financial award application deadline: 3/10. *Faculty research:* English literature, political science, psychology, sociology, anthropology and Egyptology, philosophy, Arabic studies, history, teaching Arabic as a foreign language, teaching English to speakers of other languages. *Unit head:* Dr. Robert Switzer, Interim Dean, 20-2-2615-1068, E-mail: nbowditch@aucegypt.edu. *Application contact:* Maha Hegazi, Director for Graduate Admissions, 20-2-2615-1462, E-mail: mahahegazi@aucegypt.edu.
Website: http://www.aucegypt.edu/huss/Pages/default.aspx

American University of Beirut, Graduate Programs, Faculty of Arts and Sciences, 1107 2020, Lebanon. Offers anthropology (MA); Arab and Middle Eastern history (PhD); Arabic language and literature (MA, PhD); archaeology (MA); art history and curating (MA); biology (MS); cell and molecular biology (PhD); chemistry (MS); clinical psychology (MA); computational sciences (MS); computer science (MS); economics (MA); education (MA), including administration and policy studies, elementary education, mathematics education, psychology school guidance, psychology test and measurements, science education, teaching English as a foreign language; English language (MA); English literature (MA); environmental policy planning (MS); financial economics (MAFE); general psychology (MA); geology (MS); history (MA); Islamic studies (MA); mathematics (MS); media studies (MA); Middle East studies (MA); philosophy (MA); physics (MS); political studies (MA); public administration (MA); public policy and international affairs (MA); sociology (MA); theoretical physics (PhD). *Program availability:* Part-time. *Faculty:* 108 full-time (36 women), 5 part-time/adjunct (4 women). *Students:* 251 full-time (180 women), 233 part-time (172 women). Average age 26. 425 applicants, 65% accepted, 121 enrolled. In 2017, 47 master's, 2 doctorates awarded. *Degree requirements:* For master's, one foreign language, comprehensive exam, thesis (for some programs), project; for doctorate, one foreign language, comprehensive exam, thesis/dissertation. *Entrance requirements:* For master's, GRE General Test (for some programs); for doctorate, GRE General Test (GRE Subject Test for theoretical physics). Additional exam requirements/recommendations for international students: Required—TOEFL (minimum score 583 paper-based; 97 iBT), IELTS (minimum score 7). *Application deadline:* For fall admission, 2/8 for domestic students; for spring admission, 11/3 for domestic students. Application fee: $50. Electronic applications accepted. *Expenses:* Contact institution. *Financial support:* In 2017–18, 29 fellowships, 40 research assistantships were awarded; teaching assistantships, scholarships/grants, tuition waivers (full and partial), and unspecified assistantships also available. Financial award application deadline: 4/4. *Unit head:* Dr. Nadia Maria El Cheikh, Dean, Faculty of Arts and Sciences, 961-1-374374 Ext. 3800, Fax: 961-1-744461, E-mail: nmcheikh@aub.edu.lb. *Application contact:* Rima Rassi, Graduate Studies Officer, 961-1-350000 Ext. 3833, Fax: 961-1-744461, E-mail: rr46@aub.edu.lb.
Website: http://www.aub.edu.lb/fas/pages/default.aspx

The American University of Paris, Graduate Programs, Paris, France. Offers cross-cultural and sustainable business management (MA); cultural translation (MA); global

communications (MA); global communications and civil society (MA); international affairs (MA); international affairs, conflict resolution and civil society development (MA); Middle East and Islamic studies (MA); Middle East and Islamic studies and international affairs (MA); public policy and international affairs (MA); public policy and international law (MA). *Degree requirements:* For master's, thesis (for some programs). *Entrance requirements:* For master's, minimum undergraduate GPA of 3.0. Additional exam requirements/recommendations for international students: Recommended—TOEFL, IELTS. Electronic applications accepted.

Brandeis University, Graduate School of Arts and Sciences, Department of Near Eastern and Judaic Studies, Waltham, MA 02454-9110. Offers Near Eastern and Judaic studies (MA, PhD); near Eastern and Judaic studies/conflict resolution and coexistence (MA); near Eastern and Judaic studies/Jewish professional leadership (MA); near Eastern and Judaic studies/women's, gender, and sexuality studies (MA); teaching of Hebrew (MAT). Offered jointly with The Heller School of Social Policy and Management. *Program availability:* Part-time. *Faculty:* 24 full-time (10 women), 6 part-time/adjunct (3 women). *Students:* 41 full-time (17 women), 2 part-time (1 woman); includes 7 minority (2 Black or African American, non-Hispanic/Latino; 1 Asian, non-Hispanic/Latino; 4 Hispanic/Latino), 9 international. Average age 33. 47 applicants, 45% accepted, 4 enrolled. In 2017, 8 master's, 3 doctorates awarded. Terminal master's awarded for partial completion of doctoral program. *Degree requirements:* For master's, one foreign language, thesis or alternative, proseminar, capstone; for doctorate, variable foreign language requirement, comprehensive exam, thesis/dissertation. *Entrance requirements:* For master's and doctorate, GRE General Test (recommended), letters of recommendation, transcripts, statement of purpose, writing sample, resume. Additional exam requirements/recommendations for international students: Required—PTE (minimum score 68), TOEFL (minimum score 600 paper-based, 100 iBT) or IELTS (7). *Application deadline:* For fall admission, 1/15 priority date for domestic students. Applications are processed on a rolling basis. Application fee: $75. Electronic applications accepted. *Expenses: Tuition:* Full-time $48,720. *Required fees:* $88. Tuition and fees vary according to course load, degree level, program and student level. *Financial support:* In 2017–18, 29 students received support, including 20 fellowships with full tuition reimbursements available (averaging $24,480 per year), 1 teaching assistantship with partial tuition reimbursement available (averaging $2,500 per year); Federal Work-Study, scholarships/grants, health care benefits, and tuition waivers (partial) also available. Support available to part-time students. Financial award application deadline: 4/15; financial award applicants required to submit FAFSA. *Faculty research:* Bible and ancient Near East, Judaic Studies, Israel Studies, modern Middle East, Arabic and Islamic civilizations. *Unit head:* Dr. Eugene Sheppard, Department Chair, 781-736-2950, E-mail: sheppard@brandeis.edu. *Application contact:* Jean Mannion, Department Administrator, 781-736-2950, E-mail: mannion@brandeis.edu.
Website: http://www.brandeis.edu/gsas/programs/nejs.html

Brown University, Graduate School, Department of Egyptology and Assyriology, Providence, RI 02912. Offers ancient western Asian studies (PhD); Egyptology (PhD); history of the exact sciences in antiquity (PhD). *Degree requirements:* For doctorate, 2 foreign languages, comprehensive exam, thesis/dissertation. *Entrance requirements:* For doctorate, GRE General Test.

California State University, Long Beach, Graduate Studies, College of Liberal Arts, Department of History, Long Beach, CA 90840. Offers Africa and the Middle East (MA). *Program availability:* Part-time, evening/weekend. *Degree requirements:* For master's, one foreign language, comprehensive exam or thesis. Electronic applications accepted. *Faculty research:* All periods of European and American history, recent Asian and African history.

The Catholic University of America, School of Arts and Sciences, Department of Semitic and Egyptian Languages and Literatures, Washington, DC 20064. Offers ancient Near East (Biblical Hebrew/Aramaic) (MA, PhD); Arabic (PhD); Christian Near East (Biblical Hebrew/Aramaic) (MA); Coptic (MA, PhD); Syriac (MA, PhD). *Program availability:* Part-time. *Faculty:* 3 full-time (0 women), 2 part-time/adjunct (1 woman). *Students:* 16 full-time (1 woman), 17 part-time (6 women); includes 3 minority (1 Asian, non-Hispanic/Latino; 2 Two or more races, non-Hispanic/Latino), 4 international. Average age 35. 15 applicants, 87% accepted, 4 enrolled. In 2017, 6 master's, 3 doctorates awarded. Terminal master's awarded for partial completion of doctoral program. *Degree requirements:* For master's, one foreign language, comprehensive exam; for doctorate, 2 foreign languages, comprehensive exam, thesis/dissertation. *Entrance requirements:* For master's, GRE General Test, statement of purpose, official copies of academic transcripts, three letters of recommendation; for doctorate, GRE General Test, statement of purpose, official copies of academic transcripts, three letters of recommendation, successful completion of MA field. Additional exam requirements/recommendations for international students: Required—TOEFL (minimum score 550 paper-based; 80 iBT). *Application deadline:* For fall admission, 7/15 priority date for domestic students, 7/1 for international students; for spring admission, 11/15 priority date for domestic students, 11/1 for international students. Applications are processed on a rolling basis. Application fee: $55. Electronic applications accepted. *Expenses:* Contact institution. *Financial support:* Fellowships, research assistantships, teaching assistantships, Federal Work-Study, scholarships/grants, tuition waivers (full and partial), and unspecified assistantships available. Financial award application deadline: 2/1; financial award applicants required to submit FAFSA. *Faculty research:* Christian history and literature of the Near East, Biblical Hebrew, Arabic Christianity, Coptic, Syriac. *Unit head:* Dr. Andrew D. Gross, Chair, 202-319-5083, Fax: 202-319-4735, E-mail: grossa@cua.edu. *Application contact:* Dr. Steven Brown, Director of Graduate Admissions, 202-319-5057, Fax: 202-319-6533, E-mail: cua-admissions@cua.edu.
Website: http://semitics.cua.edu/

The Catholic University of America, School of Arts and Sciences, Program in Medieval and Byzantine Studies, Washington, DC 20064. Offers Byzantine and Orthodox studies (MA); Medieval and Byzantine studies (PhD, Certificate); the Islamic world (MA); the Medieval West (MA). *Program availability:* Part-time. *Students:* Average age 31. 13 applicants, 54% accepted, 3 enrolled. In 2017, 2 master's awarded. *Degree requirements:* For master's, one foreign language, comprehensive exam, thesis or alternative; for doctorate, 2 foreign languages, comprehensive exam, thesis/dissertation. *Entrance requirements:* For master's and doctorate, GRE General Test, statement of purpose, official copies of academic transcripts, three letters of recommendation, writing sample; for Certificate, bachelor's degree. Additional exam requirements/recommendations for international students: Required—TOEFL (minimum score 550 paper-based; 80 iBT). *Application deadline:* For fall admission, 7/15 priority date for domestic students, 7/1 for international students; for spring admission, 11/15 priority date for domestic students, 11/1 for international students. Applications are processed on a rolling basis. Application fee: $55. Electronic applications accepted. *Expenses:* Contact institution. *Financial support:* Fellowships, research assistantships, teaching assistantships, Federal Work-Study, scholarships/grants, tuition waivers (full and partial), and unspecified assistantships available. Financial award application deadline: 2/1; financial award applicants required to submit FAFSA. *Faculty research:* Scholasticism and medieval theology; early and late medieval history; medieval philosophy; liturgical studies; medieval English literature. *Unit head:* Dr. Lilla Kopar, Director, 202-319-5794, Fax: 202-319-6609, E-mail: kopar@cua.edu. *Application contact:* Director of Graduate Admissions, 202-319-5057, Fax: 202-319-6533, E-mail: cua-admissions@cua.edu.
Website: http://mbs.cua.edu/

College of Staten Island of the City University of New York, Graduate Programs, Division of Humanities and Social Sciences, Program in History, Staten Island, NY 10314-6600. Offers history (MA), including Africa and the Middle East, Asia, Europe, Latin America and the Caribbean, United States. *Program availability:* Part-time, evening/weekend. *Faculty:* 2 full-time (1 woman). *Students:* 18. 19 applicants, 79% accepted, 11 enrolled. In 2017, 3 master's awarded. *Degree requirements:* For master's, comprehensive exam (for some programs), 32 credits (total of eight courses); thesis or portfolio. *Entrance requirements:* For master's, bachelor's degree with minimum GPA of 3.0 overall and in undergraduate history courses, two letters of recommendation, letter of interest, research-based writing sample. Additional exam requirements/recommendations for international students: Required—TOEFL (minimum score 550 paper-based; 79 iBT), IELTS (minimum score 6.5). *Application deadline:* For fall admission, 5/10 priority date for domestic and international students; for spring admission, 12/2 priority date for domestic and international students. Applications are processed on a rolling basis. Application fee: $125. Electronic applications accepted. *Expenses:* Tuition, state resident: full-time $10,450; part-time $440 per credit. Tuition, nonresident: full-time $19,320; part-time $440 per credit. *Required fees:* $181.10 per semester. Tuition and fees vary according to program. *Faculty research:* African and African diaspora history, South Asian history, Middle Eastern history, U.S. history, environmental history. *Unit head:* Dr. John Dixon, Graduate Program Coordinator, 718-982-3307, E-mail: john.dixon@csi.cuny.edu. *Application contact:* Sasha Spence, Associate Director for Graduate Admissions, 718-982-2019, Fax: 718-982-2500, E-mail: sasha.spence@csi.cuny.edu.
Website: https://www.csi.cuny.edu/sites/default/files/pdf/admissions/grad/pdf/History%20Fact%20Sheet.pdf

Columbia University, Graduate School of Arts and Sciences, New York, NY 10027. Offers African-American studies (MA); American studies (MA); anthropology (MA, PhD); art history and archaeology (MA, PhD); astronomy (PhD); biological sciences (PhD); biotechnology (MA); chemical physics (PhD); chemistry (PhD); classical studies (MA, PhD); classics (MA, PhD); climate and society (MA); conservation biology (MA); earth and environmental sciences (PhD); East Asia: regional studies (MA); East Asian languages and cultures (MA, PhD); ecology, evolution and environmental biology (MA), including conservation biology; ecology, evolution, and environmental biology (PhD), including ecology and evolutionary biology, evolutionary primatology; economics (MA, PhD); English and comparative literature (MA, PhD); French and Romance philology (MA, PhD); Germanic languages (MA, PhD); global French studies (MA); global thought (MA); Hispanic cultural studies (MA); history (PhD); history and literature (MA); human rights studies (MA); Islamic studies (MA); Italian (MA, PhD); Japanese pedagogy (MA); Jewish studies (MA); Latin America and the Caribbean: regional studies (MA); Latin American and Iberian cultures (PhD); mathematics (MA, PhD), including finance (MA); medieval and Renaissance studies (MA); Middle Eastern, South Asian, and African studies (MA, PhD); modern art: critical and curatorial studies (MA); modern European studies (MA); museum anthropology (MA); music (DMA, PhD); oral history (MA); philosophical foundations of physics (MA); philosophy (MA, PhD); physics (PhD); political science (MA, PhD); psychology (PhD); quantitative methods in the social sciences (MA); religion (MA, PhD); Russia, Eurasia and East Europe: regional studies (MA); Russian translation (MA); Slavic cultures (MA); Slavic languages (MA, PhD); sociology (MA, PhD); South Asian studies (MA); statistics (MA, PhD); theatre (PhD). Dual-degree programs require admission to both Graduate School of Arts and Sciences and another Columbia school. *Program availability:* Part-time. Terminal master's awarded for partial completion of doctoral program. *Degree requirements:* For master's, variable foreign language requirement, comprehensive exam (for some programs), thesis (for some programs); for doctorate, variable foreign language requirement, comprehensive exam (for some programs), thesis/dissertation. *Entrance requirements:* For master's and doctorate, GRE General Test, GRE Subject Test (for some programs). Additional exam requirements/recommendations for international students: Required—TOEFL, IELTS. Electronic applications accepted. *Expenses: Tuition:* Full-time $44,864; part-time $1704 per credit. *Required fees:* $2370 per semester. One-time fee: $105.

Cornell University, Graduate School, Graduate Fields of Arts and Sciences, Field of Archaeology, Ithaca, NY 14853. Offers environmental archaeology (MA); historical archaeology (MA); Latin American archaeology (MA); medieval archaeology (MA); Mediterranean and Near Eastern archaeology (MA); Stone Age archaeology (MA). *Degree requirements:* For master's, one foreign language, thesis. *Entrance requirements:* For master's, GRE General Test, 3 letters of recommendation, sample of written work. Additional exam requirements/recommendations for international students: Required—TOEFL (minimum score 550 paper-based; 77 iBT). Electronic applications accepted. *Faculty research:* Anatolia, Lydia, Sardis, classical and Hellenistic Greece, science in archaeology, North American Indians, Stone Age Africa, Mayan trade.

Cornell University, Graduate School, Graduate Fields of Arts and Sciences, Field of History, Ithaca, NY 14853. Offers African history (MA, PhD); American history (MA, PhD); ancient Greek history (PhD); ancient history (MA, PhD); ancient Roman history (PhD); early modern European history (MA, PhD); English history (MA, PhD); French history (MA, PhD); German history (MA, PhD); history of science (MA, PhD); Korean history (PhD); Latin American history (MA, PhD); medieval Chinese history (MA, PhD); medieval history (MA, PhD); modern Chinese history (MA, PhD); modern European history (MA, PhD); modern Japanese history (MA, PhD); modern Middle Eastern history (PhD); premodern Islamic history (MA, PhD); premodern Japanese history (MA, PhD); Renaissance history (MA, PhD); Russian history (MA, PhD); South Asian history (PhD); Southeast Asian history (MA, PhD). Terminal master's awarded for partial completion of doctoral program. *Degree requirements:* For master's, thesis; for doctorate, 2 foreign languages, comprehensive exam, thesis/dissertation, 1 year of teaching experience. *Entrance requirements:* For master's and doctorate, GRE General Test, writing sample, 3 letters of recommendation. Additional exam requirements/recommendations for international students: Required—TOEFL (minimum score 550 paper-based; 77 iBT). Electronic applications accepted.

Cornell University, Graduate School, Graduate Fields of Arts and Sciences, Field of History of Art, Archaeology and Visual Studies, Ithaca, NY 14853. Offers 19th century art (PhD); African, African American and African diaspora (PhD); American art (PhD); ancient art and archaeology (PhD); Asian American art (PhD); Baroque art (PhD); comparative modernities (PhD); digital art (PhD); East Asian art (PhD); history of photography (PhD); Islamic art (PhD); Latin American art (PhD); medieval art (PhD); modern art (PhD); Renaissance art (PhD); Southeast Asian art (PhD); theory and criticism (PhD); visual studies (PhD). *Degree requirements:* For doctorate, one foreign language, comprehensive exam, thesis/dissertation, general exams in 3 areas. *Entrance requirements:* For doctorate, GRE General Test, sample of written work, 3 letters of recommendation. Additional exam requirements/recommendations for international students: Required—TOEFL (minimum score 550 paper-based; 77 iBT). Electronic applications accepted.

Cornell University, Graduate School, Graduate Fields of Arts and Sciences, Field of Near Eastern Studies, Ithaca, NY 14853. Offers ancient Near Eastern studies (MA,

PhD); Arabic and Islamic studies (MA, PhD); biblical studies (MA, PhD); Hebrew and Judaic studies (MA, PhD). Terminal master's awarded for partial completion of doctoral program. *Degree requirements:* For master's, one foreign language, thesis; for doctorate, 2 foreign languages, comprehensive exam, thesis/dissertation. *Entrance requirements:* For master's and doctorate, GRE General Test, 2 years of 1 Near Eastern language, 3 letters of recommendation, writing sample. Additional exam requirements/recommendations for international students: Required—TOEFL (minimum score 550 paper-based; 77 iBT). Electronic applications accepted. *Faculty research:* Ancient Near East (including archeology), Hebrew and Judaic studies (including Bible), early Christianity, Arabic and Islamic studies, modern Middle East.

George Mason University, College of Humanities and Social Sciences, Program in Middle East and Islamic Studies, Fairfax, VA 22030. Offers MA, Certificate. *Faculty:* 17 full-time (7 women), 1 (woman) part-time/adjunct. *Students:* 5 full-time (2 women), 11 part-time (6 women); includes 2 minority (1 Asian, non-Hispanic/Latino; 1 Hispanic/Latino). Average age 27. 19 applicants, 95% accepted, 6 enrolled. In 2017, 4 master's awarded. *Degree requirements:* For master's, one foreign language, thesis optional. *Entrance requirements:* For master's, GRE, resume, 3 letters of recommendation, goals statement, writing sample, official transcripts. Additional exam requirements/recommendations for international students: Required—TOEFL (minimum score 575 paper-based; 88 iBT), IELTS (minimum score 6.5), PTE (minimum score 59). *Application deadline:* For fall admission, 2/15 for domestic and international students; for spring admission, 10/15 for domestic and international students. Application fee: $75 ($80 for international students). Electronic applications accepted. *Expenses:* Tuition, state resident: full-time $11,228; part-time $459.50 per credit. Tuition, nonresident: full-time $30,932; part-time $1280.50 per credit. *Required fees:* $3252; $135.50 per credit. Part-time tuition and fees vary according to course load and program. *Financial support:* Career-related internships or fieldwork, Federal Work-Study, institutionally sponsored loans, scholarships/grants, unspecified assistantships, and health care benefits (for full-time research or teaching assistantship recipients) available. *Unit head:* Bassam S. Haddad, Middle East Studies Program Director, 703-993-2962, Fax: 703-993-1399, E-mail: bhaddad@gmu.edu.
Website: http://meis.gmu.edu

Georgetown University, Graduate School of Arts and Sciences, Walsh School of Foreign Service, The Center for Contemporary Arab Studies, Washington, DC 20057. Offers MA, Certificate, MA/JD, MA/PhD. *Degree requirements:* For master's, one foreign language, comprehensive exam, thesis or alternative, proficiency in Arabic. *Entrance requirements:* For master's, GRE, minimum GPA of 3.0. Additional exam requirements/recommendations for international students: Required—TOEFL (minimum score 600 paper-based; 100 iBT). Electronic applications accepted. *Faculty research:* Contemporary Arab world.

The George Washington University, Columbian College of Arts and Sciences, Department of Religion, Washington, DC 20052. Offers Islam (MA), including Hinduism and Islam. *Program availability:* Part-time, evening/weekend. *Faculty:* 7 full-time (3 women), 7 part-time/adjunct (2 women). *Students:* 10 full-time (7 women), 4 part-time (3 women); includes 2 minority (1 Black or African American, non-Hispanic/Latino; 1 Asian, non-Hispanic/Latino), 6 international. Average age 31. 26 applicants, 73% accepted, 6 enrolled. In 2017, 4 master's awarded. *Degree requirements:* For master's, one foreign language, comprehensive exam, thesis. *Entrance requirements:* For master's, GRE General Test, interview, minimum GPA of 3.0. Additional exam requirements/recommendations for international students: Required—TOEFL (minimum score 550 paper-based; 80 iBT). *Application deadline:* For fall admission, 4/1 priority date for domestic students, 1/15 priority date for international students; for spring admission, 10/1 priority date for domestic students, 9/1 priority date for international students. Applications are processed on a rolling basis. Application fee: $75. Electronic applications accepted. *Expenses: Tuition:* Full-time $28,800; part-time $1655 per credit hour. *Required fees:* $45; $2.75 per credit hour. *Financial support:* In 2017–18, 1 student received support. Federal Work-Study and tuition waivers available. *Unit head:* Dr. Robert Eisen, Chair, 202-994-6327, Fax: 202-994-9379, E-mail: eisen@gwu.edu. *Application contact:* Information Contact, 202-994-6325, Fax: 202-994-9379, E-mail: religion@gwu.edu.
Website: http://religion.columbian.gwu.edu/

The George Washington University, Elliott School of International Affairs, Program in Middle East Studies, Washington, DC 20052. Offers MA. *Program availability:* Part-time. *Students:* 24 full-time (13 women), 16 part-time (8 women); includes 7 minority (3 Black or African American, non-Hispanic/Latino; 1 Asian, non-Hispanic/Latino; 1 Hispanic/Latino; 2 Two or more races, non-Hispanic/Latino). Average age 27. 56 applicants, 64% accepted, 10 enrolled. In 2017, 13 master's awarded. *Degree requirements:* For master's, one foreign language, capstone project. *Entrance requirements:* For master's, GRE General Test, 2 years (or equivalent) of an approved regional language. Additional exam requirements/recommendations for international students: Required—TOEFL (minimum score 100 iBT), IELTS (minimum score 7). *Application deadline:* For fall admission, 1/15 priority date for domestic and international students; for spring admission, 10/1 for domestic students. Application fee: $75. Electronic applications accepted. *Expenses: Tuition:* Full-time $28,800; part-time $1655 per credit hour. *Required fees:* $45; $2.75 per credit hour. *Financial support:* In 2017–18, 7 students received support. Fellowships with partial tuition reimbursements available, Federal Work-Study, and scholarships/grants available. Financial award application deadline: 1/15; financial award applicants required to submit FAFSA. *Unit head:* Prof. Marc Lynch, Director, 202-994-7757, Fax: 202-994-2484, E-mail: atia@gwu.edu. *Application contact:* Nicole A. Campbell, Director of Graduate Admissions, 202-994-7050, Fax: 202-994-9537, E-mail: esiagrad@gwu.edu.
Website: http://elliott.gwu.edu/middle-east-studies

Harvard University, Graduate School of Arts and Sciences, Committee on Middle Eastern Studies, Cambridge, MA 02138. Offers anthropology and Middle Eastern studies (PhD); economics and Middle Eastern studies (PhD); fine arts and Middle Eastern studies (PhD); history and Middle Eastern studies (PhD); regional studies–Middle East (AM). Terminal master's awarded for partial completion of doctoral program. *Degree requirements:* For master's, one foreign language; for doctorate, 2 foreign languages, thesis/dissertation. *Entrance requirements:* For master's, GRE General Test; for doctorate, GRE General Test, 1 year of course work in Middle Eastern regional studies, proficiency in a related language. Additional exam requirements/recommendations for international students: Required—TOEFL.

Harvard University, Graduate School of Arts and Sciences, Department of Near Eastern Languages and Civilizations, Cambridge, MA 02138. Offers Akkadian and Sumerian (AM, PhD); Arabic (AM, PhD); Armenian (AM, PhD); biblical history (AM, PhD); Hebrew (AM, PhD); Indo-Muslim culture (AM, PhD); Iranian (AM, PhD); Jewish history and literature (AM, PhD); Persian (AM, PhD); Semitic philology (AM, PhD); Syro-Palestinian archaeology (AM, PhD); Turkish (AM, PhD). *Degree requirements:* For doctorate, variable foreign language requirement, thesis/dissertation, general exams. *Entrance requirements:* For master's, GRE General Test; for doctorate, GRE General Test, proficiency in a Near Eastern language. Additional exam requirements/recommendations for international students: Required—TOEFL.

Johns Hopkins University, Zanvyl Krieger School of Arts and Sciences, Department of Near Eastern Studies, Baltimore, MD 21218. Offers archaeology (PhD); Assyriology (PhD); Egyptology (PhD); Hebrew Bible/Northwest Semitics (PhD). *Faculty:* 8 full-time (2 women), 1 part-time/adjunct (0 women). *Students:* 22 full-time (13 women); includes 3 minority (1 Black or African American, non-Hispanic/Latino; 1 Asian, non-Hispanic/Latino; 1 Hispanic/Latino), 5 international. Average age 31. 54 applicants, 15% accepted, 4 enrolled. In 2017, 4 doctorates awarded. *Degree requirements:* For doctorate, 2 foreign languages, comprehensive exam, thesis/dissertation. *Entrance requirements:* For doctorate, GRE. Additional exam requirements/recommendations for international students: Required—TOEFL (minimum score 600 paper-based; 100 iBT); Recommended—IELTS. *Application deadline:* For fall admission, 12/15 for domestic and international students. Application fee: $75. Electronic applications accepted. *Expenses:* $10,434. *Financial support:* In 2017–18, 17 students received support, including 17 fellowships with full tuition reimbursements available (averaging $27,000 per year); teaching assistantships, career-related internships or fieldwork, Federal Work-Study, scholarships/grants, and health care benefits also available. Financial award application deadline: 4/15; financial award applicants required to submit FAFSA. *Faculty research:* Egyptology, Assyriology, Hebrew Bible/Northwest Semitic languages, Demotic Egyptian, archaeology. *Total annual research expenditures:* $64,479. *Unit head:* Dr. Glenn Schwartz, Chair, 410-516-8492, Fax: 410-516-5218, E-mail: schwartz@jhu.edu. *Application contact:* Glenda Hogan, Academic Program Coordinator, 410-516-7394, Fax: 410-516-5218, E-mail: ghogan@jhu.edu.
Website: http://neareast.jhu.edu/

McGill University, Faculty of Graduate and Postdoctoral Studies, Faculty of Arts, Institute of Islamic Studies, Montréal, QC H3A 2T5, Canada. Offers MA, PhD, Diploma.

New York University, Graduate School of Arts and Science, Hagop Kevorkian Center for Near Eastern Studies, Department of Middle Eastern and Islamic Studies, New York, NY 10012-1019. Offers Middle Eastern and Islamic studies (MA, PhD); Middle Eastern and Islamic studies/history (PhD). *Program availability:* Part-time. *Students:* Average age 32. 101 applicants, 7% accepted, 4 enrolled. In 2017, 9 doctorates awarded. Terminal master's awarded for partial completion of doctoral program. *Degree requirements:* For master's, 2 foreign languages, thesis; for doctorate, 4 foreign languages, comprehensive exam, thesis/dissertation. *Entrance requirements:* For doctorate, GRE General Test. Additional exam requirements/recommendations for international students: Required—TOEFL. *Application deadline:* For fall admission, 12/18 for domestic and international students. Application fee: $100. *Expenses: Tuition:* Full-time $41,352; part-time $19,968 per year. *Required fees:* $2496; $1628 per unit. $814 per term. Tuition and fees vary according to course load and program. *Financial support:* Fellowships, teaching assistantships, Federal Work-Study, and institutionally sponsored loans available. Financial award application deadline: 12/18; financial award applicants required to submit FAFSA. *Faculty research:* Middle Eastern history, Arabic/Persian/Turkish language and literature, cultures and societies of Middle East, Islamic studies. *Unit head:* Zvi Ben-Dor Benite, Chair, 212-998-8880, Fax: 212-995-4689, E-mail: mideast.studies@nyu.edu. *Application contact:* Everett Rowson, Acting Director of Graduate Studies, 212-998-8880, Fax: 212-995-4689, E-mail: mideast.studies@nyu.edu.
Website: http://www.nyu.edu/gsas/dept/mideast/

New York University, Graduate School of Arts and Science, Hagop Kevorkian Center for Near Eastern Studies, Program in Near Eastern Studies, New York, NY 10012-1019. Offers Near Eastern studies (MA); Near Eastern studies/journalism (MA); Near Eastern studies/museum studies (MA). *Program availability:* Part-time. *Students:* Average age 26. 73 applicants, 79% accepted, 22 enrolled. In 2017, 22 master's awarded. *Degree requirements:* For master's, one foreign language, thesis. *Entrance requirements:* For master's, GRE General Test. Additional exam requirements/recommendations for international students: Required—TOEFL. *Application deadline:* For fall admission, 1/4 for domestic and international students. Application fee: $100. *Expenses: Tuition:* Full-time $41,352; part-time $19,968 per year. *Required fees:* $2496; $1628 per unit. $814 per term. Tuition and fees vary according to course load and program. *Financial support:* Fellowships, teaching assistantships, Federal Work-Study, and institutionally sponsored loans available. Financial award application deadline: 1/4; financial award applicants required to submit FAFSA. *Faculty research:* Politics, political economy, anthropology, history and culture of the Middle East. *Unit head:* Helga Tawil-Souri, Acting Director, 212-998-8877, Fax: 212-995-4144, E-mail: kevorkian.center@nyu.edu. *Application contact:* Greta Scharnweber, Associate Director, 212-998-8877, Fax: 212-995-4144, E-mail: kevorkian.center@nyu.edu.
Website: http://neareaststudies.as.nyu.edu/

New York University, Graduate School of Arts and Science, Program in Museum Studies, New York, NY 10012-1019. Offers museum studies (MA, Advanced Certificate), including Africana studies (MA), Hebrew and Judaic studies (MA), Latin American and Caribbean studies (MA), Near Eastern studies (MA). *Program availability:* Part-time, evening/weekend. *Students:* Average age 26. 123 applicants, 81% accepted, 29 enrolled. In 2017, 35 master's, 1 other advanced degree awarded. *Entrance requirements:* For master's, GRE General Test; for Advanced Certificate, master's degree or PhD. Additional exam requirements/recommendations for international students: Required—TOEFL. *Application deadline:* For fall admission, 2/15 for domestic and international students; for spring admission, 11/1 for domestic and international students. Application fee: $100. *Expenses: Tuition:* Full-time $41,352; part-time $19,968 per year. *Required fees:* $2496; $1628 per unit. $814 per term. Tuition and fees vary according to course load and program. *Financial support:* Application deadline: 2/15. *Faculty research:* Modern and contemporary art, history of museums and exhibitions, conservation of cultural materials, museum anthropology, ethnography. *Unit head:* Bruce Altshuler, Director, 212-998-8080, Fax: 212-995-4185, E-mail: museum.studies@nyu.edu. *Application contact:* Tatiana Kamorina, Department Administrator, 212-998-8080, Fax: 212-995-4185, E-mail: museum.studies@nyu.edu.
Website: http://www.nyu.edu/fas/program/museumstudies/

Princeton University, Graduate School, Department of Near Eastern Studies, Princeton, NJ 08544-1019. Offers MA, PhD. *Degree requirements:* For master's, one foreign language, thesis; for doctorate, 2 foreign languages, thesis/dissertation. *Entrance requirements:* For master's and doctorate, GRE General Test. Additional exam requirements/recommendations for international students: Required—TOEFL. Electronic applications accepted.

Rice University, Graduate Programs, School of Humanities, Department of Religious Studies, Houston, TX 77251-1892. Offers African religions (PhD); African-American religions (PhD); contemplative studies (PhD); ghosticism, esotericism, mysticism (PhD); Islam (PhD); Jewish thought and philosophy (PhD); modern Christianity in thought and popular culture (PhD); psychology of religion (PhD); the Bible and beyond (PhD). *Degree requirements:* For doctorate, 2 foreign languages, comprehensive exam, thesis/dissertation. *Entrance requirements:* For doctorate, GRE, letters of recommendation, writing sample. Additional exam requirements/recommendations for international students: Required—TOEFL (minimum score 600 paper-based; 90 iBT). Electronic applications accepted. *Faculty research:* Origins and historical development of Islam, history of Christianity, the study of comparative religion, African-American religion, religion and culture.

Southern Evangelical Seminary, Graduate Programs, Matthews, NC 28105. Offers apologetics (MA, D Min, Certificate); Christian education (MA); church ministry (MA, Certificate); divinity (Certificate), including apologetics (M Div, Certificate); Islamic studies (MA, Certificate); Jewish studies (MA); philosophy (MA); philosophy of religion (PhD); religion (MA); theology (M Div), including apologetics (M Div, Certificate), Biblical studies; youth ministry (MA). *Program availability:* Part-time, evening/weekend, online learning. *Degree requirements:* For master's, thesis (for some programs); for doctorate, 2 foreign languages, comprehensive exam (for some programs), thesis/dissertation. *Entrance requirements:* Additional exam requirements/recommendations for international students: Required—TOEFL (minimum score 600 paper-based).

Southwestern Baptist Theological Seminary, Roy Fish School of Evangelism and Missions, Fort Worth, TX 76122-0000. Offers cross-cultural missions (MTS); evangelism (M Div); evangelism and missions (D Min); international church planting (M Div); Islamic studies (M Div, MA Islamic); missiology (MA Miss); missions (M Div); North American church planting (M Div); North American evangelism and international missions (D Min); theology (Th M); world Christian studies (PhD).

The University of Arizona, College of Social and Behavioral Sciences, School of Middle Eastern and North African Studies, Tucson, AZ 85721. Offers MA, PhD, Graduate Certificate. *Program availability:* Part-time, evening/weekend. Terminal master's awarded for partial completion of doctoral program. *Degree requirements:* For master's, one foreign language; for doctorate, 3 foreign languages, thesis/dissertation. *Entrance requirements:* For master's, GRE General Test, 3 letters of recommendation, statement of purpose, curriculum vitae, writing sample; for doctorate, GRE General Test, 3 letters of recommendation, curriculum vitae, writing sample. Additional exam requirements/recommendations for international students: Required—TOEFL (minimum score 550 paper-based; 79 iBT). Electronic applications accepted.

University of California, Berkeley, Graduate Division, College of Letters and Science, Department of Near Eastern Studies, Berkeley, CA 94720-1500. Offers Near Eastern studies (MA, PhD). *Degree requirements:* For doctorate, 2 foreign languages, thesis/dissertation, qualifying exam. *Entrance requirements:* For master's and doctorate, GRE General Test, minimum GPA of 3.0, 3 letters of recommendation. Electronic applications accepted.

University of California, Los Angeles, Graduate Division, College of Letters and Science, Department of Near Eastern Languages and Cultures, Los Angeles, CA 90034. Offers MA, PhD. *Degree requirements:* For master's, one foreign language, comprehensive exam; for doctorate, 2 foreign languages, thesis/dissertation, oral and written qualifying exams. *Entrance requirements:* For master's, GRE General Test, bachelor's degree; minimum undergraduate GPA of 3.25 (or its equivalent if letter grade system not used); for doctorate, GRE General Test, master's degree; minimum undergraduate GPA of 3.25 (or its equivalent if letter grade system not used). Additional exam requirements/recommendations for international students: Required—TOEFL. Electronic applications accepted.

University of California, Los Angeles, Graduate Division, College of Letters and Science, Interdepartmental Program in Indo-European Studies, Los Angeles, CA 90095. Offers PhD. *Degree requirements:* For doctorate, 2 foreign languages, thesis/dissertation, oral and written qualifying exams. *Entrance requirements:* For doctorate, bachelor's degree; minimum undergraduate GPA of 3.0 (or its equivalent if letter grade system not used); writing sample; competence in Latin. Additional exam requirements/recommendations for international students: Required—TOEFL. Electronic applications accepted.

University of California, Los Angeles, Graduate Division, International Institute, Interdepartmental Program in Islamic Studies, Los Angeles, CA 90095. Offers MA, PhD, MPH/MA. *Degree requirements:* For master's, one foreign language, comprehensive exam; for doctorate, one foreign language, thesis/dissertation, oral and written qualifying exams. *Entrance requirements:* For master's, GRE General Test, bachelor's degree; minimum undergraduate GPA of 3.0 (or its equivalent if letter grade system not used); language requirement; for doctorate, GRE General Test, master's degree; minimum undergraduate GPA of 3.0 (or its equivalent if letter grade system not used); proficiency in Arabic. Additional exam requirements/recommendations for international students: Required—TOEFL. Electronic applications accepted.

University of Chicago, Divinity School, PhD Program, Chicago, IL 60637. Offers anthropology and sociology of religions (PhD); Bible (PhD); history of Christianity (PhD); history of Judaism (PhD); history of religions (PhD); Islamic studies (PhD); philosophy of religions (PhD); religion, literature, and visual culture (PhD); religions in America (PhD); religious ethics (PhD); theology (PhD). *Students:* 157 full-time (59 women); includes 23 minority (6 Black or African American, non-Hispanic/Latino; 11 Asian, non-Hispanic/Latino; 3 Hispanic/Latino; 3 Two or more races, non-Hispanic/Latino), 24 international. Average age 33. 184 applicants, 11% accepted, 17 enrolled. In 2017, 12 doctorates awarded. *Degree requirements:* For doctorate, 2 foreign languages, comprehensive exam, thesis/dissertation. *Entrance requirements:* For doctorate, GRE General Test, 3 letters of recommendation; transcripts; curriculum vitae or resume; writing sample. Additional exam requirements/recommendations for international students: Required—TOEFL (minimum score 600 paper-based; 104 iBT), IELTS (minimum score 7). *Application deadline:* For fall admission, 12/15 for domestic and international students. Application fee: $75. Electronic applications accepted. *Financial support:* In 2017–18, fellowships with full tuition reimbursements (averaging $27,000 per year), teaching assistantships with full tuition reimbursements (averaging $27,000 per year) were awarded; Federal Work-Study, institutionally sponsored loans, scholarships/grants, and health care benefits also available. Financial award application deadline: 12/15. *Faculty research:* Constructive studies (philosophy of religion, religious ethics, and theology); historical studies (Bible, history of Christianity, and history of Judaism); religion and the human sciences (anthropology and sociology of religion, history of religions, and religion, literature, and visual culture); Islamic studies; religions in America. *Unit head:* Dr. David Nirenberg, Interim Dean/Executive Vice Provost, 773-702-8200, E-mail: divinityadmissions@uchicago.edu. *Application contact:* Anita Lumpkin, Associate Dean of Students, 773-702-8249, E-mail: divinityadmissions@uchicago.edu. Website: http://divinity.uchicago.edu/doctoral-program-phd

University of Chicago, Division of the Humanities, Department of Near Eastern Languages and Civilizations, Chicago, IL 60637. Offers PhD. *Students:* 103 full-time (37 women); includes 13 minority (1 Black or African American, non-Hispanic/Latino; 5 Asian, non-Hispanic/Latino; 4 Hispanic/Latino; 3 Two or more races, non-Hispanic/Latino), 24 international. Average age 31. 136 applicants, 11% accepted, 12 enrolled. In 2017, 16 doctorates awarded. Terminal master's awarded for partial completion of doctoral program. *Degree requirements:* For doctorate, 2 foreign languages, comprehensive exam, thesis/dissertation. *Entrance requirements:* For doctorate, GRE General Test, 15-20 page writing sample, statement of purpose, 3 letters of recommendation, transcripts for all previous degrees and institutions attended. Additional exam requirements/recommendations for international students: Required—TOEFL (minimum score 104 iBT), IELTS (minimum score 7). *Application deadline:* For fall admission, 12/15 for domestic and international students. Application fee: $90. Electronic applications accepted. *Financial support:* In 2017–18, fellowships with full tuition reimbursements (averaging $27,000 per year) were awarded; teaching

assistantships with full tuition reimbursements, Federal Work-Study, institutionally sponsored loans, scholarships/grants, and health care benefits also available. Financial award application deadline: 12/15. *Faculty research:* Archaeology and history of the ancient near East, Middle Eastern history and civilization, Semitic language and literature, Middle Eastern languages and literatures. *Unit head:* Dr. Frank Lewis, Chair, E-mail: ne-lc@uchicago.edu. *Application contact:* Michael Beetley, Assistant Dean of Students, Admissions and Fellowships, 773-702-1552, Fax: 773-834-9148, E-mail: humanitiesadmissions@uchicago.edu. Website: http://nelc.uchicago.edu/

University of Chicago, Division of the Social Sciences and Division of the Humanities, Center for Middle Eastern Studies, Chicago, IL 60637. Offers MA. *Faculty:* 18. *Students:* 61 full-time (30 women), 1 (woman) part-time; includes 7 minority (1 Black or African American, non-Hispanic/Latino; 3 Asian, non-Hispanic/Latino; 2 Hispanic/Latino; 1 Two or more races, non-Hispanic/Latino), 6 international. Average age 25. 91 applicants, 96% accepted, 30 enrolled. In 2017, 29 master's awarded. *Degree requirements:* For master's, one foreign language, thesis. *Entrance requirements:* For master's, GRE General Test, 3 letters of recommendation, statement of purpose, transcripts, resume or curriculum vitae, writing sample (dependent on department). Additional exam requirements/recommendations for international students: Required—TOEFL (minimum score 104 iBT), IELTS (minimum score 7). *Application deadline:* For fall admission, 1/4 priority date for domestic and international students. Application fee: $90. Electronic applications accepted. *Expenses:* $57,996 tuition. *Financial support:* In 2017–18, 8 students received support. Federal Work-Study, institutionally sponsored loans, and scholarships/grants available. Financial award application deadline: 1/4. *Unit head:* Prof. Orit Bashkin, Director, E-mail: oritb@uchicago.edu. *Application contact:* Office of the Dean of Students, 773-702-8415, E-mail: ssd-admissions@uchicago.edu. Website: http://cmes.uchicago.edu

University of Illinois at Urbana–Champaign, Graduate College, College of Liberal Arts and Sciences, Center for South Asian and Middle Eastern Studies, Champaign, IL 61820. Offers MA. *Degree requirements:* For master's, one foreign language, comprehensive exam, thesis or alternative.

The University of Kansas, Graduate Studies, College of Liberal Arts and Sciences, Center for Russian, East European and Eurasian Studies, Lawrence, KS 66045. Offers foreign area officer (MA); Russian, East European and Eurasian studies (MA, Graduate Certificate); JD/MA. *Program availability:* Part-time. *Students:* 4 full-time (0 women), 1 part-time (0 women). Average age 27. 6 applicants, 83% accepted, 1 enrolled. In 2017, 5 master's, 1 other advanced degree awarded. *Entrance requirements:* For master's, GRE General Test, two-page statement of educational and professional objectives, three letters of recommendation, official transcripts. Additional exam requirements/recommendations for international students: Required—TOEFL. Application fee: $65 ($85 for international students). Electronic applications accepted. *Financial support:* Fellowships, research assistantships, and scholarships/grants available. Financial award application deadline: 1/1; financial award applicants required to submit FAFSA. *Faculty research:* Russian and East Central European history and culture; Ukrainian, Russian, and Central Asian domestic politics and international security; Slavic languages, linguistics, and literatures. *Unit head:* Vitaly Chernetsky, Acting Director, 785-864-4236, E-mail: vchernetsky@ku.edu. *Application contact:* Alyssa McDonald, Graduate Admissions Contact, 785-864-4236, E-mail: crees@ku.edu. Website: http://www.crees.ku.edu/

The University of Manchester, Faculty of Life Sciences, Manchester, United Kingdom. Offers adaptive organismal biology (M Phil, PhD); animal biology (M Phil, PhD); biochemistry (M Phil, PhD); bioinformatics (M Phil, PhD); biomolecular sciences (M Phil, PhD); biotechnology (M Phil, PhD); cell biology (M Phil, PhD); cell matrix research (M Phil, PhD); channels and transporters (M Phil, PhD); developmental biology (M Phil, PhD); Egyptology (M Phil, PhD); environmental biology (M Phil, PhD); evolutionary biology (M Phil, PhD); gene expression (M Phil, PhD); genetics (M Phil, PhD); history of science, technology and medicine (M Phil, PhD); immunology (M Phil, PhD); integrative neurobiology and behavior (M Phil, PhD); membrane trafficking (M Phil, PhD); microbiology (M Phil, PhD); molecular and cellular neuroscience (M Phil, PhD); molecular biology (M Phil, PhD); molecular cancer studies (M Phil, PhD); neuroscience (M Phil, PhD); ophthalmology (M Phil, PhD); optometry (M Phil, PhD); organelle function (M Phil, PhD); pharmacology (M Phil, PhD); physiology (M Phil, PhD); plant sciences (M Phil, PhD); stem cell research (M Phil, PhD); structural biology (M Phil, PhD); systems neuroscience (M Phil, PhD); toxicology (M Phil, PhD).

The University of Manchester, School of Languages, Linguistics and Cultures, Manchester, United Kingdom. Offers Arab world studies (PhD); Chinese studies (M Phil, PhD); East Asian studies (M Phil, PhD); English language (PhD); French studies (M Phil, PhD); German studies (M Phil, PhD); interpreting studies (PhD); Italian studies (M Phil, PhD); Japanese studies (M Phil, PhD); Latin American cultural studies (M Phil, PhD); linguistics (M Phil, PhD); Middle Eastern studies (M Phil, PhD); Polish studies (M Phil, PhD); Portuguese studies (M Phil, PhD); Russian studies (M Phil, PhD); Spanish studies (M Phil, PhD); translation and intercultural studies (M Phil, PhD).

University of Memphis, Graduate School, College of Arts and Sciences, Department of History, Memphis, TN 38152. Offers ancient Egyptian history (MA, PhD). *Program availability:* 100% online. *Faculty:* 20 full-time (8 women), 1 (woman) part-time/adjunct. *Students:* 31 full-time (20 women), 46 part-time (26 women); includes 16 minority (11 Black or African American, non-Hispanic/Latino; 2 Hispanic/Latino; 3 Two or more races, non-Hispanic/Latino), 2 international. Average age 35. 33 applicants, 82% accepted, 22 enrolled. In 2017, 7 master's, 3 doctorates awarded. *Degree requirements:* For master's, comprehensive exam, thesis optional; for doctorate, one foreign language, comprehensive exam, thesis/dissertation, 60 credits plus 12 dissertation credits, 2 research seminars. *Entrance requirements:* For master's, GRE General Test or MAT, 18 undergraduate hours of course work in history with minimum GPA of 3.0, 2 letters of recommendation, writing sample, statement of research interest; for doctorate, GRE General Test, GRE Subject Test, MA in history or related field, three letters of recommendation, writing sample, statement of purpose. Additional exam requirements/recommendations for international students: Required—TOEFL (minimum score 550 paper-based; 79 iBT). *Application deadline:* For fall admission, 1/15 for domestic students; for spring admission, 9/15 for domestic students. Applications are processed on a rolling basis. Application fee: $35 ($60 for international students). Electronic applications accepted. *Expenses:* Contact institution. *Financial support:* In 2017–18, 54 students received support, including 4 research assistantships with full tuition reimbursements available (averaging $12,000 per year), 21 teaching assistantships with full tuition reimbursements available (averaging $18,142 per year); career-related internships or fieldwork, Federal Work-Study, scholarships/grants, and unspecified assistantships also available. Financial award application deadline: 2/1; financial award applicants required to submit FAFSA. *Faculty research:* African/African-American history; U.S. history; ancient Egyptian history; modern European history; women, gender, and family studies. *Unit head:* Dr. Aram Goudsouzian, Chair, 901-678-2516, Fax: 901-678-2720, E-mail: agoudszn@memphis.edu. *Application contact:* Dr. Daniel Unowsky, Coordinator of Graduate Studies, 901-678-3385, Fax: 901-678-2720, E-mail: dunowsky@memphis.edu. Website: http://history.memphis.edu/

Near and Middle Eastern Studies

University of Michigan, Rackham Graduate School, College of Literature, Science, and the Arts, Center for Middle Eastern and North African Studies, Ann Arbor, MI 48109-1106. Offers AM, JD/AM, MBA/AM. *Program availability:* Part-time. *Faculty:* 78 full-time (24 women), 1 (woman) part-time/adjunct. *Students:* 11 full-time (7 women); includes 2 minority (1 Black or African American, non-Hispanic/Latino; 1 Asian, non-Hispanic/Latino). Average age 30. 20 applicants, 75% accepted, 5 enrolled. In 2017, 3 master's awarded. *Degree requirements:* For master's, one foreign language, thesis or alternative. *Entrance requirements:* For master's, GRE General Test. Additional exam requirements/recommendations for international students: Required—TOEFL (minimum score 560 paper-based; 84 iBT). *Application deadline:* For fall admission, 12/15 for domestic and international students. Application fee: $75 ($90 for international students). Electronic applications accepted. *Expenses:* Tuition, state resident: full-time $22,368; part-time $1201 per credit hour. Tuition, nonresident: full-time $45,156; part-time $2467 per credit hour. *Required fees:* $376 per term. Tuition and fees vary according to course load, degree level and program. *Financial support:* In 2017–18, 4 students received support, including 4 fellowships with tuition reimbursements available (averaging $15,000 per year); teaching assistantships, career-related internships or fieldwork, Federal Work-Study, scholarships/grants, health care benefits, and Richard P. Mitchell Memorial Prize also available. Support available to part-time students. Financial award application deadline: 1/15; financial award applicants required to submit FAFSA. *Faculty research:* Middle East and North Africa. *Unit head:* Dr. Samer Mahdy Ali, Director, 734-764-1401, E-mail: ii-gradadvising@umich.edu. *Application contact:* Julie E. Burnett, Graduate Academic Services Coordinator, 734-936-1842, Fax: 734-615-9158, E-mail: ii-gradadvising@umich.edu.
Website: https://www.ii.umich.edu/cmenas/

University of Michigan, Rackham Graduate School, College of Literature, Science, and the Arts, Department of Near Eastern Studies, Ann Arbor, MI 48109. Offers ancient Near Eastern studies (AM, PhD); Arabic for professional purposes (AM); Arabic language and literature (AM, PhD); Armenian studies (AM, PhD); Christianity in late antiquity (AM, PhD); Egyptology (AM, PhD); Hebrew Bible and ancient Israel (AM, PhD); Hebrew literature (AM, PhD); Islamic studies (AM, PhD); Jewish cultural studies (AM, PhD); Jewish mysticism (AM, PhD); Persian and Iranian studies (AM, PhD); Rabbinic literature (AM, PhD); Second Temple Judaism (AM, PhD); teaching Arabic as a foreign language (AM); Turkish studies (AM, PhD). *Faculty:* 27 full-time (8 women). *Students:* 31 full-time (12 women); includes 2 minority (1 Black or African American, non-Hispanic/Latino; 1 Asian, non-Hispanic/Latino), 13 international. Average age 33. 76 applicants, 11% accepted, 5 enrolled. In 2017, 4 master's, 4 doctorates awarded. Terminal master's awarded for partial completion of doctoral program. *Degree requirements:* For master's, 2 foreign languages; for doctorate, 4 foreign languages, comprehensive exam, thesis/dissertation, preliminary exams, oral defense of dissertation. *Entrance requirements:* For master's, ACTFL (for teaching Arabic as a foreign language MA program). Additional exam requirements/recommendations for international students: Required—TOEFL (minimum score 560 paper-based; 84 iBT), IELTS (minimum score 6.5). *Application deadline:* For fall admission, 12/1 for domestic and international students. Application fee: $75 ($90 for international students). Electronic applications accepted. *Expenses:* Tuition, state resident: full-time $22,368; part-time $1201 per credit hour. Tuition, nonresident: full-time $45,156; part-time $2467 per credit hour. *Required fees:* $376 per term. Tuition and fees vary according to course load, degree level and program. *Financial support:* In 2017–18, 31 students received support. Fellowships with full tuition reimbursements available, teaching assistantships with full tuition reimbursements available, scholarships/grants, health care benefits, unspecified assistantships, and spring/summer stipends available. Financial award application deadline: 12/1. *Faculty research:* Middle and Near Eastern literatures, languages, cultures from ancient times to the present. *Unit head:* Prof. Gottfried Hagen, Chair, 734-764-0314, E-mail: nes-chair@umich.edu. *Application contact:* Student Services, 734-764-0315, E-mail: nes-gradservices@umich.edu.
Website: http://www.lsa.umich.edu/neareast/

University of Pennsylvania, School of Arts and Sciences, Graduate Group in Near Eastern Languages and Civilizations, Philadelphia, PA 19104. Offers AM, PhD. *Faculty:* 24 full-time (11 women), 4 part-time/adjunct (0 women). *Students:* 18 full-time (8 women), 5 part-time (3 women); includes 2 minority (1 Asian, non-Hispanic/Latino; 1 Two or more races, non-Hispanic/Latino), 6 international. Average age 32. 58 applicants, 14% accepted, 3 enrolled. In 2017, 6 master's, 3 doctorates awarded. Application fee: $70.
Website: http://www.sas.upenn.edu/nelc/grad_programs/grad_programs.html

University of South Africa, College of Human Sciences, Pretoria, South Africa. Offers adult education (M Ed); African languages (MA, PhD); African politics (MA, PhD); Afrikaans (MA, PhD); ancient history (MA, PhD); ancient Near Eastern studies (MA, PhD); anthropology (MA, PhD); applied linguistics (MA); Arabic (MA, PhD); archaeology (MA); art history (MA); Biblical archaeology (MA); Biblical studies (M Th, D Th, PhD); Christian spirituality (M Th, D Th); church history (M Th, D Th); classical studies (MA, PhD); clinical psychology (MA); communication (MA, PhD); comparative education (M Ed, Ed D); consulting psychology (D Admin, D Com, PhD); curriculum studies (M Ed, Ed D); development studies (M Admin, MA, D Admin, PhD); didactics (M Ed, Ed D); education (M Tech); education management (M Ed, Ed D); educational psychology (M Ed); English (MA); environmental education (M Ed); French (MA, PhD); German (MA, PhD); Greek (MA); guidance and counseling (M Ed); health studies (MA, PhD), including health sciences education (MA), health services management (MA), medical and surgical nursing science (critical care general) (MA), midwifery and neonatal nursing science (MA), trauma and emergency care (MA); history (MA, PhD); history of education (Ed D); inclusive education (M Ed, Ed D); information and communications technology policy and regulation (MA); information science (MA, MIS, PhD); international politics (MA, PhD); Islamic studies (MA, PhD); Italian (MA, PhD); Judaica (MA, PhD); linguistics (MA, PhD); mathematical education (M Ed); mathematics education (MA); missiology (M Th, D Th); modern Hebrew (MA, PhD); musicology (MA, MMus, D Mus, PhD); natural science education (M Ed); New Testament (M Th, D Th); Old Testament (D Th); pastoral therapy (M Th, D Th); philosophy (MA); philosophy of education (M Ed, Ed D); politics (MA, PhD); Portuguese (MA, PhD); practical theology (M Th, D Th); psychology (MA, MS, PhD); psychology of education (M Ed, Ed D); public health (MA); religious studies (MA, D Th, PhD); Romance languages (MA); Russian (MA, PhD); Semitic languages (MA, PhD); social behavior studies in HIV/AIDS (MA); social science (mental health) (MA); social science in development studies (MA); social science in psychology (MA); social science in social work (MA); social science in sociology (MA); social work (MSW, DSW, PhD); socio-education (M Ed, Ed D); sociolinguistics (MA); sociology (MA, PhD); Spanish (MA, PhD); systematic theology (M Th, D Th); TESOL (teaching English to speakers of other languages) (MA); theological ethics (M Th, D Th); theory of literature (MA, PhD); urban ministries (D Th); urban ministry (M Th).

The University of Texas at Austin, Graduate School, College of Liberal Arts, Department of Middle Eastern Studies, Austin, TX 78712-1111. Offers Middle Eastern languages and cultures (MA, PhD); Middle Eastern studies (MA); JD/MA; MA/M Sc; MA/MA; MBA/MA; MPA/MA. *Degree requirements:* For master's, one foreign language, comprehensive exam, thesis; for doctorate, 2 foreign languages, comprehensive exam, thesis/dissertation. *Entrance requirements:* For master's and doctorate, GRE General Test. Additional exam requirements/recommendations for international students: Required—TOEFL. Electronic applications accepted. *Faculty research:* Islamic studies, Persian language and literature, Hebrew language, Jewish studies, Arabic literature and language.

University of Toronto, School of Graduate Studies, Faculty of Arts and Science, Department of Near and Middle Eastern Civilizations, Toronto, ON M5S 1A1, Canada. Offers MA, PhD. *Program availability:* Part-time. *Degree requirements:* For master's, thesis optional; for doctorate, 2 foreign languages, thesis/dissertation, language proficiency exams. *Entrance requirements:* For master's, BA in relevant area, minimum B+ average in final year, prior coursework in ancient Near Eastern or Islamic civilizations, 2 letters of reference; for doctorate, MA in relevant area with a minimum A-average, 2 letters of reference. Additional exam requirements/recommendations for international students: Required—TOEFL (minimum score 580 paper-based; 93 iBT), TWE (minimum score 5). Electronic applications accepted.

University of Utah, Graduate School, College of Humanities, Program in Middle East Studies, Salt Lake City, UT 84112. Offers Arabic (MA, PhD); Hebrew (MA); history (MA, PhD); Persian (MA, PhD); political science (MA, PhD). *Students:* 2 part-time (1 woman); includes 1 minority (Asian, non-Hispanic/Latino). In 2017, 1 doctorate awarded. *Entrance requirements:* For master's, GRE General Test, minimum GPA of 3.2; for doctorate, GRE General Test, MA in Middle East studies or equivalent, minimum GPA of 3.2. Additional exam requirements/recommendations for international students: Required—TOEFL (minimum score 580 paper-based; 92 iBT); Recommended—IELTS (minimum score 7). Application fee: $55 ($65 for international students). Electronic applications accepted. *Financial support:* In 2017–18, 5 students received support, including 2 teaching assistantships with full tuition reimbursements available (averaging $13,500 per year); fellowships and unspecified assistantships also available. Financial award application deadline: 1/15. *Faculty research:* Islamic studies; Middle Eastern history; political science; Judaic studies; anthropology; Arabic, Persian, Hebrew, and Turkish language and literature. *Unit head:* Johanna Watzinger-Tharp, Director, 801-581-7148, Fax: 801-581-6105, E-mail: j.tharp@utah.edu. *Application contact:* Kellie Hubbard, Academic Advisor, 801-581-5362, Fax: 801-581-6105, E-mail: kellie.hubbard@utah.edu.
Website: http://www.mec.utah.edu

University of Virginia, College and Graduate School of Arts and Sciences, Department of Middle Eastern and South Asian Languages and Cultures, Charlottesville, VA 22903. Offers Middle Eastern and South Asian studies (MA). *Faculty:* 16 full-time (8 women), 1 (woman) part-time/adjunct. *Students:* 7 full-time (3 women), 2 part-time (0 women); includes 1 minority (Asian, non-Hispanic/Latino). Average age 31. 8 applicants, 100% accepted, 2 enrolled. In 2017, 6 master's awarded. Application fee: $60. *Unit head:* Farzaneh Milani, Chair, 434-243-4930, Fax: 434-243-1528, E-mail: fmm2z@virginia.edu. *Application contact:* Robert Hueckstedt, Director of Graduate Studies, 434-243-8228, Fax: 434-243-1528, E-mail: rah2k@virginia.edu.
Website: http://mesalc.virginia.edu/

University of Washington, Graduate School, College of Arts and Sciences, Department of Near Eastern Languages and Civilization, Seattle, WA 98195. Offers MA. *Degree requirements:* For master's, 2 foreign languages, exams. *Entrance requirements:* For master's, GRE, minimum GPA of 3.0. Additional exam requirements/recommendations for international students: Required—TOEFL. Electronic applications accepted. *Faculty research:* Arabic, Hebrew, Persian, and Turkish literature; Islamic civilization and religion; Central Asian Turkic language and literature; Hebrew Bible and ancient Near East; ancient Christianity.

University of Washington, Graduate School, College of Arts and Sciences, Henry M. Jackson School of International Studies, Middle East Studies Program, Seattle, WA 98195. Offers MAIS. *Degree requirements:* For master's, one foreign language, thesis optional. *Entrance requirements:* For master's, GRE General Test, minimum GPA of 3.0 in last two years. Additional exam requirements/recommendations for international students: Required—TOEFL (minimum score 500 paper-based; 92 iBT), IELTS (minimum score 7). Electronic applications accepted.

University of Washington, Graduate School, Interdisciplinary Program in Near and Middle Eastern Studies, Seattle, WA 98195. Offers PhD. *Degree requirements:* For doctorate, 3 foreign languages, thesis/dissertation. *Entrance requirements:* For doctorate, GRE General Test, minimum GPA of 3.0. Additional exam requirements/recommendations for international students: Required—TOEFL. Electronic applications accepted.

University of Waterloo, Graduate Studies, Faculty of Arts, Department of Classical Studies, Waterloo, ON N2L 3G1, Canada. Offers ancient Mediterranean cultures (MA). *Degree requirements:* For master's, one foreign language. *Faculty research:* Ancient history, philosophy, anthropology, religion, culture.

University of Wisconsin–Madison, Graduate School, College of Letters and Science, Department of History, Madison, WI 53706-1380. Offers African history (MA, PhD); Central Asian history (MA, PhD); comparative world history (MA, PhD); East Asian history (MA, PhD); European history (MA, PhD); gender and women's history (MA, PhD); Latin American and Caribbean history (MA, PhD); Middle Eastern history (MA, PhD); South Asian history (MA, PhD); Southeast Asian history (MA, PhD); United States history (MA, PhD). Terminal master's awarded for partial completion of doctoral program. *Degree requirements:* For master's, thesis (for some programs); for doctorate, variable foreign language requirement, thesis/dissertation. *Entrance requirements:* For master's and doctorate, GRE General Test. Additional exam requirements/recommendations for international students: Required—Michigan English Language Assessment Battery or TOEFL. Electronic applications accepted. *Faculty research:* American, African, European, Asian, Latin American, and Middle Eastern history.

Washington University in St. Louis, The Graduate School, Department of Jewish, Islamic, and Near Eastern Languages and Cultures, St. Louis, MO 63130-4899. Offers Islamic and Near Eastern studies (MA); Jewish studies (MA). *Degree requirements:* For master's, one foreign language, thesis (for some programs). *Entrance requirements:* For master's, GRE General Test. Additional exam requirements/recommendations for international students: Required—TOEFL. Electronic applications accepted. *Faculty research:* Islamic and Near Eastern studies (Islamic history; Arabic language and literature, modern Middle East history); Jewish studies (Hebrew Bible, Rabbinic literature, Jewish history, modern Hebrew literature).

Wayne State University, College of Liberal Arts and Sciences, Department of Classical and Modern Languages, Literatures, and Cultures, Detroit, MI 48202. Offers classics (MA), including ancient Greek and Latin, ancient studies, classics, Latin; German (MA); language learning (MALL), including Arabic (MA, MALL), French (MA, MALL, PhD), German (MALL, PhD), Italian (MA, MALL), Spanish (MA, MALL, PhD); modern languages (PhD), including French (MA, MALL, PhD), German (MALL, PhD), Spanish (MA, MALL, PhD); Near Eastern languages (MA), including Arabic (MA, MALL), Hebrew; Romance languages (MA), including French (MA, MALL, PhD), Italian (MA, MALL), Spanish (MA, MALL, PhD). *Faculty:* 22. *Students:* 24 full-time (18 women), 21 part-time (15 women); includes 11 minority (4 Black or African American, non-Hispanic/Latino; 1 American Indian or Alaska Native, non-Hispanic/Latino; 2 Asian, non-Hispanic/Latino; 2 Hispanic/Latino; 2 Two or more races, non-Hispanic/Latino), 3 international. Average age 37. 32 applicants, 63% accepted, 14 enrolled. In 2017, 10 master's awarded.

Degree requirements: For master's, variable foreign language requirement, comprehensive exam (for some programs), thesis (for some programs); for doctorate, one foreign language, comprehensive exam, thesis/dissertation. *Entrance requirements:* Additional exam requirements/recommendations for international students: Required—TOEFL (minimum score 550 paper-based; 79 iBT), TWE (minimum score 5.5), Michigan English Language Assessment Battery (minimum score 85); Recommended—IELTS (minimum score 6.5). Application fee: $50. Electronic applications accepted. *Expenses:* Tuition, state resident: full-time $10,224; part-time $638.98 per credit hour. Tuition, nonresident: full-time $22,145; part-time $1384.04 per credit hour. Tuition and fees vary according to course load and program. *Financial support:* In 2017–18, 25 students received support, including 4 fellowships with tuition reimbursements available (averaging $13,500 per year), 17 teaching assistantships with tuition reimbursements available (averaging $18,591 per year); research assistantships, scholarships/grants, health care benefits, and unspecified assistantships also available. Financial award applicants required to submit FAFSA. *Faculty research:* Classical and modern literature

and culture (Greek, Latin, Arabic, Chinese, French, German, Russian, Spanish) including colonial studies and exile and Holocaust studies; critical theory (French, German, Slavic, Spanish); theoretical and applied linguistics (Arabic, Chinese, French, Spanish); area studies (Arabic, Near Eastern, classical, Islamic, and Judaic studies). *Unit head:* Dr. Anne Duggan, Department Chair, 313-577-6244, Fax: 313-577-6243, E-mail: a.duggan@wayne.edu.
Website: http://clas.wayne.edu/languages/

Yale University, Graduate School of Arts and Sciences, Department of Near Eastern Languages and Civilizations, New Haven, CT 06520. Offers Arabic and Islamic studies (MA, PhD); archaeology of the ancient Near East (MA, PhD); Assyriology (MA, PhD); Egyptology (MA, PhD); Graeco-Arabic studies (MA, PhD); Northwest Semitic, Bible, comparative Semitics (MA, PhD). *Degree requirements:* For doctorate, 2 foreign languages, thesis/dissertation. *Entrance requirements:* For doctorate, GRE General Test.

Northern Studies

University of Alaska Fairbanks, College of Liberal Arts, Department of Arctic and Northern Studies, Fairbanks, AK 99775-6460. Offers Arctic policy (MA); environmental politics and policy (MA); Northern history (MA). *Program availability:* Part-time. *Degree requirements:* For master's, comprehensive exam, oral defense of project or thesis. *Entrance requirements:* For master's, bachelor's degree from accredited institution with minimum cumulative undergraduate and major GPA of 3.0. Additional exam

requirements/recommendations for international students: Required—TOEFL (minimum score 550 paper-based; 79 iBT), IELTS (minimum score 6.5). Electronic applications accepted.

University of Manitoba, Faculty of Graduate Studies, Faculty of Arts, Department of Icelandic Language and Literature, Winnipeg, MB R3T 2N2, Canada. Offers MA.

Pacific Area/Pacific Rim Studies

The University of British Columbia, Institute of Asian Research, Vancouver, BC V6T 1Z2, Canada. Offers Asia Pacific policy studies (MAAPPS); public policy and global affairs (MPPGA). *Degree requirements:* For master's, thesis optional. *Entrance requirements:* Additional exam requirements/recommendations for international students: Required—TOEFL. Electronic applications accepted. *Expenses:* Contact institution. *Faculty research:* Social cohesion, globalization, social safety nets, policy research, research and development alliances, knowledge-based workshops on Asia-Pacific studies.

University of Guam, Office of Graduate Studies, College of Liberal Arts and Social Sciences, Micronesian Studies Program, Mangilao, GU 96923. Offers MA. *Degree requirements:* For master's, thesis. *Entrance requirements:* For master's, GRE General Test. Additional exam requirements/recommendations for international students: Required—TOEFL. *Faculty research:* Adolescent suicide in Micronesia, history of Micronesia, traditional agriculture in the Pacific, Micronesian languages, health and cultural practices.

University of Hawaii at Manoa, Office of Graduate Education, School of Pacific and Asian Studies, Program in Pacific Island Studies, Honolulu, HI 96822. Offers MA, Graduate Certificate. *Program availability:* Part-time. *Degree requirements:* For

master's, thesis optional. *Entrance requirements:* Additional exam requirements/recommendations for international students: Required—TOEFL (minimum score 580 paper-based; 92 iBT), IELTS (minimum score 5).

University of San Francisco, College of Arts and Sciences, Program in Asia Pacific Studies, San Francisco, CA 94117-1080. Offers MA, MA/MBA. *Program availability:* Part-time, evening/weekend. *Degree requirements:* For master's, one foreign language, thesis. *Entrance requirements:* For master's, minimum GPA of 3.0. Additional exam requirements/recommendations for international students: Required—TOEFL, IELTS, PTE. Electronic applications accepted. *Faculty research:* History of Christianity in China, U.S.-China policy, East Asian economies and political systems, sociolinguistic aspects of Japanese.

University of Victoria, Faculty of Graduate Studies, Faculty of Humanities, Department of Pacific and Asian Studies, Victoria, BC V8W 2Y2, Canada. Offers MA. *Degree requirements:* For master's, thesis. *Entrance requirements:* For master's, minimum B+ average, writing sample. Additional exam requirements/recommendations for international students: Required—TOEFL (minimum score 575 paper-based), IELTS (minimum score 7). Electronic applications accepted. *Faculty research:* Culture, ethnicity and identity; economy and society; gender studies; languages and linguistics; literature.

Western European Studies

American University, School of International Service, Washington, DC 20016-8071. Offers comparative and regional studies (Certificate); cross-cultural communication (Certificate); development management (MS); ethics, peace, and global affairs (MA); European studies (Certificate); global environmental policy (MA, Certificate); global information technology (Certificate); global media (MA); international affairs (MA), including comparative and regional studies, global governance, politics, and security, international economic relations, natural resources and sustainable development, U.S. foreign policy and national security; international arts management (Certificate); international communication (MA, Certificate); international development (MA); international economic policy (Certificate); international economic relations (Certificate); international economics (MA); international peace and conflict resolution (MA, Certificate); international politics (Certificate); international relations (MA, PhD); international service (MIS); peacebuilding (Certificate); social enterprise (MA); the Americas (Certificate); United States foreign policy (Certificate); JD/MA. *Program availability:* Part-time, evening/weekend, 100% online. *Faculty:* 112 full-time (50 women), 46 part-time/adjunct (19 women). *Students:* 495 full-time (333 women), 518 part-time (276 women); includes 360 minority (95 Black or African American, non-Hispanic/Latino; 2 American Indian or Alaska Native, non-Hispanic/Latino; 60 Asian, non-Hispanic/Latino; 164 Hispanic/Latino; 39 Two or more races, non-Hispanic/Latino), 98 international. Average age 30. 1,559 applicants, 81% accepted, 356 enrolled. In 2017, 427 master's, 9 doctorates, 5 other advanced degrees awarded. Terminal master's awarded for partial completion of doctoral program. *Degree requirements:* For master's, one foreign language, comprehensive exam, thesis or alternative; for doctorate, one foreign language, comprehensive exam, thesis/dissertation. *Entrance requirements:* For master's, GRE; GMAT or GRE (for MA in social enterprise), transcripts, resume, 2 letters of recommendation, statement of purpose; for doctorate, GRE, transcripts, resume, 3 letters of recommendation, statement of purpose. Additional exam requirements/recommendations for international students: Required—TOEFL (minimum score 600 paper-based; 100 iBT). *Application deadline:* For fall admission, 1/15 for domestic students, 1/1 for international students; for spring admission, 10/1 for domestic students, 9/15 for international students. Application fee: $55. Electronic applications accepted. *Expenses:* Contact institution. *Financial support:* Research assistantships, teaching assistantships, institutionally sponsored loans, scholarships/grants, and unspecified assistantships available. Financial award application deadline:

1/15; financial award applicants required to submit FAFSA. *Application contact:* 202-885-1646, Fax: 202-885-1109, E-mail: sisgrad@american.edu.
Website: http://www.american.edu/sis/

Boston College, Graduate School of Arts and Sciences, Department of History, Chestnut Hill, MA 02467-3800. Offers European national studies (MA); history (MA, PhD); medieval studies (MA). Terminal master's awarded for partial completion of doctoral program. *Degree requirements:* For master's, one foreign language, comprehensive exam, thesis optional; for doctorate, 2 foreign languages, comprehensive exam, thesis/dissertation. *Entrance requirements:* For master's and doctorate, GRE General Test, writing sample. Additional exam requirements/recommendations for international students: Required—TOEFL (minimum score 600 paper-based; 100 iBT), IELTS (minimum score 8). Electronic applications accepted. *Faculty research:* U.S. history, medieval history, early modern European history, modern European history, British and Irish history, Latin American history, Asian history, Middle eastern history, international and global history, transnational history.

Brown University, Graduate School, Department of Portuguese and Brazilian Studies, Providence, RI 02912. Offers Brazilian studies (AM); English as a second language and cross-cultural studies (AM); Portuguese and Brazilian studies (AM, PhD); Portuguese bilingual education and cross-cultural studies (AM). *Degree requirements:* For doctorate, thesis/dissertation.

Carleton University, Faculty of Graduate Studies, Faculty of Public Affairs and Management, Institute of European and Russian Studies, Ottawa, ON K1S 5B6, Canada. Offers European and European Union studies (MA); European integration studies (Diploma); Russian, Eurasian and transition studies (MA). *Degree requirements:* For master's, one foreign language, thesis optional. *Entrance requirements:* For master's, honors degree or equivalent; 2 years of Russian, German or other central east European language. Additional exam requirements/recommendations for international students: Required—TOEFL. *Faculty research:* East-West relations, minority rights in Russia and Eastern Europe.

The Catholic University of America, School of Arts and Sciences, Department of History, Washington, DC 20064. Offers history (MA, PhD), including early modern European history, medieval history, modern European history, U.S. history; religion and society in the late medieval and early modern world (MA); MA/JD; MSLS/MA. *Program*

availability: Part-time. *Faculty:* 15 full-time (6 women), 1 part-time/adjunct (0 women). *Students:* 6 full-time (0 women), 19 part-time (7 women); includes 3 minority (all Two or more races, non-Hispanic/Latino), 2 international. Average age 31. 11 applicants, 82% accepted, 3 enrolled. In 2017, 4 master's, 2 doctorates awarded. Terminal master's awarded for partial completion of doctoral program. *Degree requirements:* For master's, one foreign language, comprehensive exam, thesis optional, 2 languages (for medievalists), one of which must be Latin; for doctorate, 2 foreign languages, comprehensive exam, thesis/dissertation, 3 languages (for medievalists), one of which must be Latin. *Entrance requirements:* For master's and doctorate, GRE General Test, statement of purpose, official copies of academic transcripts, three letters of recommendation, writing sample. Additional exam requirements/recommendations for international students: Required—TOEFL (minimum score 550 paper-based; 80 iBT). *Application deadline:* For fall admission, 7/15 priority date for domestic students, 7/1 for international students; for spring admission, 11/15 priority date for domestic students, 11/1 for international students. Applications are processed on a rolling basis. Application fee: $55. Electronic applications accepted. *Expenses:* Contact institution. *Financial support:* Fellowships, research assistantships, teaching assistantships, Federal Work-Study, scholarships/grants, tuition waivers (full and partial), and unspecified assistantships available. Financial award application deadline: 2/1; financial award applicants required to submit FAFSA. *Faculty research:* Medieval history, including the Islamic Middle East, with particular expertise in later medieval religious, social, and economic history and early medieval and late antique history; European and American intellectual history; renaissance, reformation, catholic reformation; U.S. Catholic history; history of immigration. *Unit head:* Dr. Katherine Jansen, Chair, 202-319-5484, Fax: 202-319-5569, E-mail: jansen@cua.edu. *Application contact:* Dr. Steven Brown, Director of Graduate Admissions, 202-319-5057, Fax: 202-319-6533, E-mail: cua-admissions@cua.edu.
Website: http://history.cua.edu/

Central Michigan University, College of Graduate Studies, College of Humanities and Social and Behavioral Sciences, Department of History, Mount Pleasant, MI 48859. Offers European history (Graduate Certificate); history (MA); modern history (Graduate Certificate); United States history (Graduate Certificate); MA/PhD. *Program availability:* Part-time. *Degree requirements:* For master's, thesis or alternative. Electronic applications accepted. *Faculty research:* Colonial and revolutionary United States history, modern European history, Latin American and transatlantic history, transnational and comparative history, United States social history.

Claremont Graduate University, Graduate Programs, School of Arts and Humanities, Department of History, Claremont, CA 91711-6160. Offers Africana history (Certificate); American studies and U.S. history (MA, PhD); archival studies (MA); early modern studies (MA, PhD); European studies (MA, PhD); oral history (MA, PhD); MBA/MA; MBA/PhD. Terminal master's awarded for partial completion of doctoral program. *Entrance requirements:* For master's and doctorate, GRE General Test. Additional exam requirements/recommendations for international students: Required—TOEFL (minimum score 75 iBT). Electronic applications accepted. *Faculty research:* Intellectual and social history, cultural studies, gender studies, Western history, Chicano history.

College of Staten Island of the City University of New York, Graduate Programs, Division of Humanities and Social Sciences, Program in History, Staten Island, NY 10314-6600. Offers history (MA), including Africa and the Middle East, Asia, Europe, Latin America and the Caribbean, United States. *Program availability:* Part-time, evening/weekend. *Faculty:* 2 full-time (1 woman). *Students:* 18. 19 applicants, 79% accepted, 11 enrolled. In 2017, 3 master's awarded. *Degree requirements:* For master's, comprehensive exam (for some programs), 32 credits (total of eight courses); thesis or portfolio. *Entrance requirements:* For master's, bachelor's degree with minimum GPA of 3.0 overall and in undergraduate history courses, two letters of recommendation, letter of interest, research-based writing sample. Additional exam requirements/recommendations for international students: Required—TOEFL (minimum score 550 paper-based; 79 iBT), IELTS (minimum score 6.5). *Application deadline:* For fall admission, 5/10 priority date for domestic and international students; for spring admission, 12/2 priority date for domestic and international students. Applications are processed on a rolling basis. Application fee: $125. Electronic applications accepted. *Expenses:* Tuition, state resident: full-time $10,450; part-time $440 per credit. Tuition, nonresident: full-time $19,320; part-time $440 per credit. *Required fees:* $181.10 per semester. Tuition and fees vary according to program. *Faculty research:* African and African diaspora history, South Asian history, Middle Eastern history, U.S. history, environmental history. *Unit head:* Dr. John Dixon, Graduate Program Coordinator, 718-982-3307, E-mail: john.dixon@csi.cuny.edu. *Application contact:* Sasha Spence, Associate Director for Graduate Admissions, 718-982-2019, Fax: 718-982-2500, E-mail: sasha.spence@csi.cuny.edu.
Website: https://www.csi.cuny.edu/sites/default/files/pdf/admissions/grad/pdf/History%20Fact%20Sheet.pdf

Columbia University, Graduate School of Arts and Sciences, New York, NY 10027. Offers African-American studies (MA); American studies (MA); anthropology (MA, PhD); art history and archaeology (MA, PhD); astronomy (PhD); biological sciences (PhD); biotechnology (MA); chemical physics (PhD); chemistry (PhD); classical studies (MA, PhD); classics (MA, PhD); climate and society (MA); conservation biology (MA); earth and environmental sciences (PhD); East Asia: regional studies (MA); East Asian languages and cultures (MA, PhD); ecology, evolution and environmental biology (MA), including conservation biology; ecology, evolution, and environmental biology (PhD), including ecology and evolutionary biology, evolutionary primatology; economics (MA, PhD); English and comparative literature (MA, PhD); French and Romance philology (MA, PhD); Germanic languages (MA, PhD); global French studies (MA); global thought (MA); Hispanic cultural studies (MA); history (PhD); history and literature (MA); human rights studies (MA); Islamic studies (MA); Italian (MA, PhD); Japanese pedagogy (MA); Jewish studies (MA); Latin America and the Caribbean: regional studies (MA); Latin American and Iberian cultures (PhD); mathematics (MA, PhD), including finance (MA); medieval and Renaissance studies (MA); Middle Eastern, South Asian, and African studies (MA, PhD); modern art: critical and curatorial studies (MA); modern European studies (MA); museum anthropology (MA); music (DMA, PhD); oral history (MA); philosophical foundations of physics (MA); philosophy (MA, PhD); physics (PhD); political science (MA, PhD); psychology (PhD); quantitative methods in the social sciences (MA); religion (MA, PhD); Russia, Eurasia and East Europe: regional studies (MA); Russian translation (MA); Slavic cultures (MA); Slavic languages (MA, PhD); sociology (MA, PhD); South Asian studies (MA); statistics (MA, PhD); theatre (PhD). Dual-degree programs require admission to both Graduate School of Arts and Sciences and another Columbia school. *Program availability:* Part-time. Terminal master's awarded for partial completion of doctoral program. *Degree requirements:* For master's, variable foreign language requirement, comprehensive exam (for some programs), thesis (for some programs); for doctorate, variable foreign language requirement, comprehensive exam (for some programs), thesis/dissertation. *Entrance requirements:* For master's and doctorate, GRE General Test, GRE Subject Test (for some programs). Additional exam requirements/recommendations for international students: Required—TOEFL, IELTS. Electronic applications accepted. *Expenses: Tuition:* Full-time $44,864; part-time $1704 per credit. *Required fees:* $2370 per semester. One-time fee: $105.

Cornell University, Graduate School, Graduate Fields of Arts and Sciences, Field of History, Ithaca, NY 14853. Offers African history (MA, PhD); American history (MA, PhD); ancient Greek history (PhD); ancient history (MA, PhD); ancient Roman history (PhD); early modern European history (MA, PhD); English history (MA, PhD); French history (MA, PhD); German history (MA, PhD); history of science (MA, PhD); Korean history (PhD); Latin American history (MA, PhD); medieval Chinese history (MA, PhD); medieval history (MA, PhD); modern Chinese history (MA, PhD); modern European history (MA, PhD); modern Japanese history (MA, PhD); modern Middle Eastern history (PhD); premodern Islamic history (MA, PhD); premodern Japanese history (MA, PhD); Renaissance history (MA, PhD); Russian history (MA, PhD); South Asian history (PhD); Southeast Asian history (MA, PhD). Terminal master's awarded for partial completion of doctoral program. *Degree requirements:* For master's, thesis; for doctorate, 2 foreign languages, comprehensive exam, thesis/dissertation, 1 year of teaching experience. *Entrance requirements:* For master's and doctorate, GRE General Test, writing sample, 3 letters of recommendation. Additional exam requirements/recommendations for international students: Required—TOEFL (minimum score 550 paper-based; 77 iBT). Electronic applications accepted.

Dallas Baptist University, Gary Cook School of Leadership, Program in International Studies, Dallas, TX 75211-9299. Offers East Asian studies (MA); European studies (MA); general international studies (MA); global business (MA); international immersion (MA); international ministry (MA); international relations (MA). *Program availability:* Part-time, evening/weekend. *Application deadline:* Applications are processed on a rolling basis. Application fee: $25. Electronic applications accepted. Application fee is waived when completed online. *Expenses: Tuition:* Full-time $16,308; part-time $906 per credit hour. *Required fees:* $900; $450 per semester. Tuition and fees vary according to course load and degree level. *Unit head:* Dr. Jack Goodyear, Dean, 214-333-5595, Fax: 214-333-6809, E-mail: jackg@dbu.edu. *Application contact:* Lee Bratcher, Program Director, 214-333-5808, E-mail: leeb@dbu.edu.
Website: http://www4.dbu.edu/leadership/maintemational

Drew University, Caspersen School of Graduate Studies, Madison, NJ 07940-1493. Offers conflict resolution and leadership (Certificate), including community leadership, moderation, peace building; education (M Ed); finance (MA); history and culture (MA, PhD), including American history, book history, British history, European history, Holocaust and genocide (M Litt, MA, D Litt, PhD), intellectual history, Irish history, print culture, public history; K-12 education (MAT), including art, biology, chemistry, elementary education, English, French, Italian, math, secondary education, special education, teacher of students with disabilities; liberal studies (M Litt, D Litt), including history, Holocaust and genocide (M Litt, MA, D Litt, PhD), Irish/Irish-American studies, literature (M Litt, MMH, D Litt, DMH, CMH), religion, spirituality, teaching in the two-year college, writing; medical humanities (MMH, DMH, CMH), including arts, health, healthcare, literature (M Litt, MMH, D Litt, DMH, CMH), scientific research; poetry (MFA). *Program availability:* Part-time, evening/weekend. *Faculty:* 4 full-time (2 women), 29 part-time/adjunct (15 women). *Students:* 77 full-time (42 women), 175 part-time (114 women); includes 39 minority (12 Black or African American, non-Hispanic/Latino; 6 Asian, non-Hispanic/Latino; 16 Hispanic/Latino; 5 Two or more races, non-Hispanic/Latino), 11 international. Average age 41. 126 applicants, 75% accepted, 52 enrolled. In 2017, 38 master's, 23 doctorates, 35 other advanced degrees awarded. Terminal master's awarded for partial completion of doctoral program. *Degree requirements:* For master's and other advanced degree, thesis (for some programs); for doctorate, one foreign language, comprehensive exam (for some programs), thesis/dissertation. *Entrance requirements:* For master's, PRAXIS Core and Subject Area tests (for MAT), GRE/GMAT (for M Fin), resume, transcripts, writing sample, personal statement, letters of recommendation; for doctorate, GRE (PhD in history and culture), resume, transcripts, writing sample, personal statement, letters of recommendation; for other advanced degree, resume, transcripts, personal statement. Additional exam requirements/recommendations for international students: Required—TOEFL (minimum score 587 paper-based; 80 iBT), IELTS (minimum score 6), TWE (minimum score 4). *Application deadline:* For fall admission, 8/1 for domestic students, 6/1 for international students; for spring admission, 12/1 for domestic students, 10/1 for international students. Applications are processed on a rolling basis. Application fee: $35. Electronic applications accepted. *Financial support:* Fellowships, research assistantships, teaching assistantships, career-related internships or fieldwork, Federal Work-Study, scholarships/grants, and unspecified assistantships available. Support available to part-time students. Financial award applicants required to submit FAFSA. *Faculty research:* Irish history and culture, conflict resolution and leadership. *Application contact:* Leanne Horinko, Director of Caspersen Admissions, 973-408-3280, E-mail: gradm@drew.edu.
Website: http://www.drew.edu/caspersen

East Carolina University, Graduate School, Thomas Harriot College of Arts and Sciences, Department of History, Greenville, NC 27858-4353. Offers American history (MA); Atlantic world (MA); European history (MA); maritime studies (MA); military history (MA); public history (MA). *Program availability:* Part-time. *Students:* 39 full-time (16 women), 49 part-time (21 women); includes 11 minority (2 Black or African American, non-Hispanic/Latino; 1 Asian, non-Hispanic/Latino; 5 Hispanic/Latino; 3 Two or more races, non-Hispanic/Latino), 1 international. Average age 29. 35 applicants, 83% accepted, 19 enrolled. In 2017, 15 master's awarded. *Degree requirements:* For master's, one foreign language, comprehensive exam, thesis. *Entrance requirements:* For master's, GRE General Test. Additional exam requirements/recommendations for international students: Recommended—TOEFL (minimum score 78 iBT), IELTS (minimum score 6.5). *Application deadline:* For fall admission, 4/1 priority date for domestic and international students; for spring admission, 10/15 priority date for domestic and international students. Applications are processed on a rolling basis. Application fee: $75. Electronic applications accepted. *Expenses:* Tuition, state resident: full-time $4749; part-time $297 per credit hour. Tuition, nonresident: full-time $17,898; part-time $1119 per credit hour. *Required fees:* $2691; $224 per credit hour. Part-time tuition and fees vary according to course load and program. *Financial support:* Fellowships, research assistantships with partial tuition reimbursements, teaching assistantships with partial tuition reimbursements, and Federal Work-Study available. Support available to part-time students. Financial award application deadline: 1/15. *Unit head:* Dr. Christopher Oakley, Chair, 252-328-1025, E-mail: oakleyc@ecu.edu. *Application contact:* Dean of Graduate School, 252-328-6012, E-mail: gradschool@ecu.edu.
Website: http://www.ecu.edu/cs-cas/history/

Georgetown University, Graduate School of Arts and Sciences, Walsh School of Foreign Service, BMW Center for German and European Studies, Washington, DC 20057. Offers MA, MA/JD, MA/PhD. *Degree requirements:* For master's, 2 foreign languages, comprehensive exam. *Entrance requirements:* For master's, GRE General Test. Additional exam requirements/recommendations for international students: Required—TOEFL. Electronic applications accepted. *Faculty research:* Transatlantic relations, European Union, German and European Studies.

The George Washington University, Elliott School of International Affairs, Program in European and Eurasian Studies, Washington, DC 20052. Offers MA. *Program availability:* Part-time. *Students:* 15 full-time (7 women), 4 part-time (1 woman); includes 3 minority (2 Hispanic/Latino; 1 Two or more races, non-Hispanic/Latino). Average age

27. 66 applicants, 67% accepted, 10 enrolled. In 2017, 10 master's awarded. *Degree requirements:* For master's, one foreign language, capstone project. *Entrance requirements:* For master's, GRE General Test, 2 years (or the equivalent) of a modern European language or Russian, 2 semesters of introductory economics (macro or micro). Additional exam requirements/recommendations for international students: Required—TOEFL (minimum score 100 iBT), IELTS (minimum score 7). *Application deadline:* For fall admission, 1/15 priority date for domestic and international students; for spring admission, 10/1 for domestic students. Application fee: $75. Electronic applications accepted. *Expenses: Tuition:* Full-time $28,800; part-time $1655 per credit hour. *Required fees:* $45; $2.75 per credit hour. *Financial support:* In 2017–18, 3 students received support. Fellowships with partial tuition reimbursements available and Federal Work-Study available. Financial award application deadline: 1/15; financial award applicants required to submit FAFSA. *Faculty research:* NATO, European economics, European history, European Union. *Unit head:* Peter Rollberg, Director, 202-994-7084, E-mail: rgpeter@gwu.edu. *Application contact:* Nicole A. Campbell, Director of Graduate Admissions, 202-994-7050, Fax: 202-994-9537, E-mail: esiagrad@gwu.edu.
Website: http://elliott.gwu.edu/academics/grad/ees/index.cfm

Georgia Southern University–Armstrong Campus, College of Graduate Studies, Program in History, Savannah, GA 31419-1997. Offers American and European history (MA); public history (MA). *Program availability:* Part-time, evening/weekend. *Faculty:* 11 full-time (3 women), 1 (woman) part-time/adjunct. *Students:* 7 full-time (3 women), 10 part-time (5 women); includes 3 minority (all Black or African American, non-Hispanic/Latino). Average age 43. 14 applicants, 43% accepted, 5 enrolled. In 2017, 5 master's awarded. *Degree requirements:* For master's, one foreign language, comprehensive exam (for some programs), thesis (for some programs), thesis, internship, or advanced fieldwork. *Entrance requirements:* For master's, GRE General Test, minimum GPA of 3.0, letters of recommendation, BA in history or equivalent. Additional exam requirements/recommendations for international students: Required—TOEFL (minimum score 523 paper-based; 70 iBT). *Application deadline:* For fall admission, 6/30 priority date for domestic students, 5/1 priority date for international students; for spring admission, 11/15 priority date for domestic students, 9/15 priority date for international students; for summer admission, 4/15 priority date for domestic students, 9/15 for international students. Applications are processed on a rolling basis. Application fee: $30. Electronic applications accepted. *Expenses: Tuition:* state resident: part-time $211 per credit hour. Tuition, nonresident: part-time $782 per credit hour. *Required fees:* $737 per semester. Tuition and fees vary according to course load, degree level, campus/location and program. *Financial support:* In 2017–18, research assistantships with full tuition reimbursements (averaging $5,000 per year) were awarded; career-related internships or fieldwork, Federal Work-Study, and unspecified assistantships also available. Support available to part-time students. Financial award application deadline: 3/15; financial award applicants required to submit FAFSA. *Faculty research:* Public history; European, Latin American, African, and United States history. *Unit head:* Dr. Christopher Hendricks, Interim Department Head, 912-344-2725, Fax: 912-344-3451, E-mail: chris.hendricks@armstrong.edu. *Application contact:* McKenzie Peterman, Graduate Admissions Specialist, 912-478-5678, Fax: 912-478-0740, E-mail: mpeterman@georgiasouthern.edu.
Website: http://www.armstrong.edu/Liberal_Arts/history/history_graduate_program

Indiana University Bloomington, University Graduate School, College of Arts and Sciences, School of Global and International Studies, Institute for European Studies, Bloomington, IN 47405. Offers MA, MA/MBA, MPA/MA. *Program availability:* Part-time. *Degree requirements:* For master's, one foreign language, thesis. *Entrance requirements:* For master's, GRE General Test. Additional exam requirements/recommendations for international students: Required—TOEFL. Electronic applications accepted. *Faculty research:* European integration, economics of Europe, European Union, European culture and identity, expansion of European Union.

Indiana University–Purdue University Indianapolis, School of Liberal Arts, Department of History, Indianapolis, IN 46202. Offers European history (MA); public history (MA); United States history (MA); MA/MA; MA/MLS. *Program availability:* Part-time, evening/weekend. *Degree requirements:* For master's, one foreign language, thesis. *Entrance requirements:* For master's, GRE General Test, minimum GPA of 3.0. Electronic applications accepted.

La Salle University, School of Arts and Sciences, Program in History, Philadelphia, PA 19141-1199. Offers American history (Certificate); European history (Certificate); history (MA); history for educators (MA); public history (MA); teaching advanced placement history (Certificate); world history (Certificate). *Program availability:* Part-time. *Faculty:* 4 full-time (1 woman), 2 part-time/adjunct (0 women). *Students:* 2 full-time (0 women), 10 part-time (5 women); includes 1 minority (Asian, non-Hispanic/Latino). Average age 37. 9 applicants, 78% accepted, 2 enrolled. In 2017, 7 master's awarded. *Degree requirements:* For master's, thesis or comprehensive exam. *Entrance requirements:* For master's, GRE or MAT, 18 hours of undergraduate coursework in history or a related discipline with minimum GPA of 3.0; two letters of recommendation; brief personal statement (250 to 500 words); writing sample (preferably from an undergraduate research paper). Additional exam requirements/recommendations for international students: Required—TOEFL. *Application deadline:* For fall admission, 8/15 priority date for domestic students, 7/15 for international students; for spring admission, 12/15 priority date for domestic students, 11/15 for international students; for summer admission, 4/15 priority date for domestic students, 3/15 for international students. Applications are processed on a rolling basis. Application fee: $35. Electronic applications accepted. Application fee is waived when completed online. *Expenses:* Contact institution. *Financial support:* In 2017–18, 1 student received support. Scholarships/grants available. Support available to part-time students. Financial award application deadline: 8/31; financial award applicants required to submit FAFSA. *Unit head:* Dr. George B. Stow, Director, 215-951-1097, E-mail: grahis@lasalle.edu. *Application contact:* Elizabeth Heenan, Director, Graduate and Adult Enrollment, 215-951-1100, Fax: 215-951-1462, E-mail: heenan@lasalle.edu.
Website: http://www.lasalle.edu/master-history/

Monmouth University, Graduate Studies, Program in History, West Long Branch, NJ 07764-1898. Offers European history (MA); United States history (MA); world history (MA). *Program availability:* Part-time, evening/weekend. *Faculty:* 4 full-time (2 women). *Students:* 3 full-time (2 women), 22 part-time (7 women); includes 4 minority (all Hispanic/Latino). Average age 33. In 2017, 14 master's awarded. *Degree requirements:* For master's, comprehensive exam (for some programs), thesis (for some programs). *Entrance requirements:* For master's, minimum GPA of 3.0 in major, 2.5 overall; two letters of recommendation; statement describing historical areas of interest and how graduate study will contribute to professional and academic goals. Additional exam requirements/recommendations for international students: Required—TOEFL (minimum score 550 paper-based; 79 iBT), IELTS (minimum score 6) or Michigan English Language Assessment Battery (minimum score 77). *Application deadline:* For fall admission, 7/15 priority date for domestic students, 6/1 for international students; for spring admission, 12/15 priority date for domestic students, 11/1 for international students. Applications are processed on a rolling basis. Application fee: $50. Electronic applications accepted. *Expenses: Tuition:* Full-time $21,366; part-time $7122 per credit.

Required fees: $700; $175 per term. *Financial support:* In 2017–18, 4 students received support. Institutionally sponsored loans, scholarships/grants, and unspecified assistantships available. Support available to part-time students. Financial award applicants required to submit FAFSA. *Faculty research:* British, German, and French Revolutions; Soviet Union; Africa; English history; U.S. military; women's history. *Unit head:* Dr. Maryann Rhett, Director, 732-263-5768, Fax: 732-263-5112, E-mail: mrhett@monmouth.edu. *Application contact:* Andrea Thompson, Graduate Admission Counselor, 732-571-3452, Fax: 732-263-5123, E-mail: gradadm@monmouth.edu.
Website: https://www.monmouth.edu/graduate/ma-history/

New York University, Graduate School of Arts and Science, Center for European Studies, New York, NY 10012-1019. Offers MA. *Faculty:* 4 full-time (0 women). *Students:* 10 full-time (7 women), 1 (woman) part-time; includes 2 minority (both Two or more races, non-Hispanic/Latino), 3 international. Average age 27. 14 applicants, 93% accepted, 8 enrolled. In 2017, 4 master's awarded. *Entrance requirements:* For master's, GRE General Test. Additional exam requirements/recommendations for international students: Required—TOEFL. *Application deadline:* For fall admission, 2/1 priority date for domestic students, 2/1 for international students. Application fee: $100. Electronic applications accepted. *Expenses: Tuition:* Full-time $41,352; part-time $19,968 per year. *Required fees:* $2496; $1628 per unit. $814 per term. Tuition and fees vary according to course load and program. *Financial support:* Fellowships with tuition reimbursements, teaching assistantships, career-related internships or fieldwork, Federal Work-Study, institutionally sponsored loans, and scholarships/grants available. Financial award application deadline: 2/1; financial award applicants required to submit FAFSA. *Faculty research:* Xenophobia, migration, and identity politics in Europe; European Union and political economy; Central Eastern Europe. *Unit head:* Larry Wolff, Director, 212-998-3838, Fax: 212-995-4188, E-mail: european.studies@nyu.edu. *Application contact:* Mikhala Stein, Administrator, 212-998-3838, Fax: 212-995-4188, E-mail: european.studies@nyu.edu.
Website: http://www.nyu.edu/gsas/dept/europe/

San Diego State University, Graduate and Research Affairs, College of Arts and Letters, Department of European Studies, San Diego, CA 92182. Offers MA. *Degree requirements:* For master's, one foreign language. *Entrance requirements:* For master's, GRE General Test. Additional exam requirements/recommendations for international students: Required—TOEFL. Electronic applications accepted.

University of Colorado Denver, College of Liberal Arts and Sciences, Department of History, Denver, CO 80217. Offers European history (MA); global history (MA); public history (MA); U.S. history (MA). *Program availability:* Part-time, evening/weekend. *Degree requirements:* For master's, comprehensive exam, thesis optional, 36 semester hours (12 courses). *Entrance requirements:* For master's, GRE General Test, writing sample, minimum undergraduate GPA of 3.25, three letters of recommendation, statement of purpose addressing any weaknesses in academic record. Additional exam requirements/recommendations for international students: Required—TOEFL (minimum score 537 paper-based; 75 iBT); Recommended—IELTS (minimum score 6.5). Electronic applications accepted. *Faculty research:* Uses of pre-modern Islamic heritage in modern India; relationship between liberal understandings of democracy, crime, and police discretion; relationships between gender, class, health, and welfare in nineteenth and early twentieth century England; U.S. business cultures and their influences on marketing and personnel practices; intersection of business and political ideologies; social and environmental history of the Rocky Mountain West.

University of Connecticut, Graduate School, College of Liberal Arts and Sciences, Field of International Studies, Program in International Studies, Storrs, CT 06269. Offers European studies (MA); Italian history and culture (MA); Latino and Latin American studies (MA). *Degree requirements:* For master's, comprehensive exam. *Entrance requirements:* For master's, GRE General Test. Additional exam requirements/recommendations for international students: Required—TOEFL (minimum score 550 paper-based). Electronic applications accepted.

University of Guelph, Graduate Studies, College of Arts, School of Languages and Literatures, Program in European Studies, Guelph, ON N1G 2W1, Canada. Offers MA. *Degree requirements:* For master's, research paper. *Entrance requirements:* For master's, curriculum vitae, writing sample, 2 letters of recommendation.

University of Illinois at Urbana–Champaign, Graduate College, College of Liberal Arts and Sciences, European Union Center, Champaign, IL 61820. Offers MA. *Degree requirements:* For master's, one foreign language.

University of Nevada, Reno, Graduate School, Interdisciplinary Program in Basque Studies, Reno, NV 89557. Offers PhD. *Degree requirements:* For doctorate, thesis/dissertation. *Entrance requirements:* For doctorate, GRE General Test, master's degree in related field, minimum GPA of 3.0. Additional exam requirements/recommendations for international students: Required—TOEFL (minimum score 500 paper-based; 61 iBT), IELTS (minimum score 6). Electronic applications accepted. *Faculty research:* Ethnic groups, Basque society, migration studies, symbolic anthropology, terrorism.

University of Pittsburgh, University Center for International Studies, Pittsburgh, PA 15260. Offers African studies (Certificate); Asian studies (Certificate); European Union studies (Certificate); global studies (Certificate); Latin American studies (Certificate); Russian and East European studies (Certificate); West European studies (Certificate). *Program availability:* Part-time, evening/weekend, online learning. *Students:* 183 full-time (108 women), 9 part-time (all women); includes 78 minority (6 Black or African American, non-Hispanic/Latino; 23 Asian, non-Hispanic/Latino; 47 Hispanic/Latino; 2 Two or more races, non-Hispanic/Latino). Average age 29. *Degree requirements:* For Certificate, one foreign language, comprehensive exam (for some programs). *Entrance requirements:* Additional exam requirements/recommendations for international students: Required—TOEFL. *Expenses:* No tuition and fees. *Financial support:* In 2017–18, 25 fellowships with full tuition reimbursements (averaging $26,117 per year) were awarded; scholarships/grants, traineeships, health care benefits, and unspecified assistantships also available. *Unit head:* Dr. Ariel Armony, Director, 412-648-7374, Fax: 412-624-4672, E-mail: armony@pitt.edu.
Website: http://www.ucis.pitt.edu

University of South Florida, College of Arts and Sciences, Department of History, Tampa, FL 33620-9951. Offers history (MA, PhD), including American history (MA), ancient history (MA), European history (MA), Latin American history (MA), Medieval history (MA). *Program availability:* Part-time, evening/weekend. *Faculty:* 17 full-time (8 women), 1 (woman) part-time/adjunct. *Students:* 39 full-time (9 women), 19 part-time (9 women); includes 5 minority (1 American Indian or Alaska Native, non-Hispanic/Latino; 4 Hispanic/Latino). Average age 33. 41 applicants, 80% accepted, 24 enrolled. In 2017, 10 master's, 1 doctorate awarded. *Degree requirements:* For master's, one foreign language, comprehensive exam, thesis optional; for doctorate, one foreign language, comprehensive exam, thesis/dissertation. *Entrance requirements:* For master's, GRE General Test, minimum GPA of 3.0, two letters of recommendation, 2-page statement of purpose, writing sample; for doctorate, GRE General Test, minimum GPA of 3.5 in master's degree coursework, three letters of recommendation, statement of purpose, writing sample, foreign language proficiency in the field of study. Additional exam requirements/recommendations for international students: Required—TOEFL (minimum score 550 paper-based; 79 iBT) or IELTS (minimum score 6.5). *Application deadline:*

For fall admission, 12/1 priority date for domestic students, 12/1 for international students. Applications are processed on a rolling basis. Application fee: $30. Electronic applications accepted. *Financial support:* In 2017–18, 3 students received support, including 17 teaching assistantships with tuition reimbursements available (averaging $12,750 per year); unspecified assistantships also available. Financial award application deadline: 1/15. *Faculty research:* North American and U.S. history, European history, nineteenth- and twentieth-centuries/modern world, early modern world, ancient history, history of gender/sexuality, Latin American history, history of science and medicine. *Total annual research expenditures:* $194,096. *Unit head:* Dr. Fraser Ottanelli, Professor and Chair, 813-974-6209, Fax: 813-974-6228, E-mail: ottanelli@usf.edu. *Application contact:* Dr. Kees Boterbloem, Professor and Graduate Program Director, 813-974-2807, E-mail: cboterbl@usf.edu.
Website: http://history.usf.edu

University of Virginia, College and Graduate School of Arts and Sciences, Program in European Studies, Charlottesville, VA 22903. Offers MA. *Students:* 1 (woman) full-time; minority (Black or African American, non-Hispanic/Latino). Average age 21. 4 applicants, 75% accepted, 1 enrolled. *Unit head:* Janet Horne, Director, 434-924-7742, E-mail: jrh9e@virginia.edu.
Website: http://europeanstudies.as.virginia.edu/

Women's Studies

American University, College of Arts and Sciences, Critical Race, Gender, and Culture Studies Collaborative, Washington, DC 20016-8030. Offers Asian studies (Graduate Certificate); women's, gender, and sexuality studies (Graduate Certificate). *Faculty:* 4 full-time (3 women), 10 part-time/adjunct (5 women). In 2017, 3 Graduate Certificates awarded. *Entrance requirements:* Additional exam requirements/recommendations for international students: Required—TOEFL (minimum score 600 paper-based; 100 iBT). *Application deadline:* Applications are processed on a rolling basis. *Expenses: Tuition:* Full-time $29,556. *Required fees:* $690. Tuition and fees vary according to course load and program. *Unit head:* Dr. Peter Starr, Dean, 202-885-2446, Fax: 202-885-2429, E-mail: pstarr@american.edu. *Application contact:* Jonathan Harper, Associate Director, Graduate Recruitment, 202-885-3622, Fax: 202-885-1505, E-mail: jharper@american.edu.
Website: http://www.american.edu/cas/crgc/

The American University in Cairo, School of Global Affairs and Public Policy, Cairo, Egypt. Offers gender and women's studies (MA); global affairs (MGA); international and comparative law (LL M); international human rights law (MA); journalism and mass communication (MA); Middle East studies (MA); migration and refugee studies (MA, Diploma); public administration (MPA); public policy (MPP); television and digital journalism (MA). *Program availability:* Part-time, evening/weekend. *Faculty:* 26 full-time (11 women), 4 part-time/adjunct (3 women). *Students:* 65 full-time (50 women), 201 part-time (136 women), 39 international. Average age 29. 357 applicants, 51% accepted, 72 enrolled. In 2017, 94 master's awarded. *Degree requirements:* For master's, comprehensive exam (for some programs), thesis (for some programs). *Entrance requirements:* Additional exam requirements/recommendations for international students: Required—TOEFL (minimum score 450 paper-based; 45 iBT), IELTS (minimum score 5). *Application deadline:* For fall admission, 2/1 for domestic and international students; for spring admission, 10/15 for domestic and international students. Applications are processed on a rolling basis. Application fee: $85. Electronic applications accepted. *Expenses:* Contact institution. *Financial support:* Fellowships with partial tuition reimbursements, scholarships/grants, and unspecified assistantships available. Financial award application deadline: 3/10. *Faculty research:* Law, media and journalism; public policy and public administration; gender studies; Middle East Studies; global affairs; refugees studies. *Unit head:* Dr. Nabil Fahmy, Dean, 20-2-2615-2671, E-mail: nfahmy@aucegypt.edu. *Application contact:* Maha Hegazi, Director for Graduate Admissions, 20-2-2615-1462, E-mail: mahahegazi@aucegypt.edu.
Website: http://www.aucegypt.edu/GAPP/Pages/default.aspx

Benedictine University, Graduate Programs, Program in Leadership, Lisle, IL 60532. Offers MS. *Degree requirements:* For master's, capstone.

Brandeis University, Graduate School of Arts and Sciences, Department of Anthropology, Waltham, MA 02454-9110. Offers anthropology/women's, gender, and sexuality studies (MA); Mesoamerican archaeology (MA, PhD); sociocultural anthropology (MA, PhD). *Program availability:* Part-time. *Faculty:* 9 full-time (5 women), 4 part-time/adjunct (1 woman). *Students:* 35 full-time (24 women), 1 part-time (0 women); includes 6 minority (3 Black or African American, non-Hispanic/Latino; 1 Hispanic/Latino; 2 Two or more races, non-Hispanic/Latino), 6 international. Average age 28. 50 applicants, 48% accepted, 8 enrolled. In 2017, 11 master's awarded. Terminal master's awarded for partial completion of doctoral program. *Degree requirements:* For master's, thesis; for doctorate, one foreign language, comprehensive exam, thesis/dissertation. *Entrance requirements:* For master's and doctorate, GRE General Test, sample of written work, resume, letters of recommendation, transcript. Additional exam requirements/recommendations for international students: Required—PTE (minimum score 68), TOEFL (minimum score 600 paper-based, 100 iBT) or IELTS (7). *Application deadline:* For fall admission, 1/15 priority date for domestic and international students. Applications are processed on a rolling basis. Application fee: $75. Electronic applications accepted. *Expenses: Tuition:* Full-time $48,720. *Required fees:* $88. Tuition and fees vary according to course load, degree level, program and student level. *Financial support:* In 2017–18, 34 students received support, including 11 fellowships with full tuition reimbursements available (averaging $24,480 per year), 15 teaching assistantships with partial tuition reimbursements available (averaging $3,200 per year); scholarships/grants, health care benefits, and tuition waivers (partial) also available. Support available to part-time students. Financial award application deadline: 4/15; financial award applicants required to submit FAFSA. *Faculty research:* Sociocultural anthropology, archaeology, gender and sexuality, linguistic anthropology, physical anthropology. *Unit head:* Dr. Sarah Lamb, Director of Graduate Studies, 781-736-2210, Fax: 781-736-2232, E-mail: lamb@brandeis.edu. *Application contact:* Laurel Carpenter, Academic Administrator, 781-736-2210, Fax: 781-736-2232, E-mail: lcarpent@brandeis.edu.
Website: http://www.brandeis.edu/gsas/programs/anthropology.html

Brandeis University, Graduate School of Arts and Sciences, Department of English, Waltham, MA 02454-9110. Offers English (MA, PhD); English/women's, gender, and sexuality studies (MA). *Program availability:* Part-time. *Faculty:* 18 full-time (9 women), 12 part-time/adjunct (6 women). *Students:* 40 full-time (22 women), 3 part-time (2 women); includes 8 minority (2 Black or African American, non-Hispanic/Latino; 1 Asian, non-Hispanic/Latino; 3 Hispanic/Latino; 2 Two or more races, non-Hispanic/Latino), 8 international. Average age 33. 134 applicants, 27% accepted, 6 enrolled. In 2017, 3 master's, 5 doctorates awarded. Terminal master's awarded for partial completion of doctoral program. *Degree requirements:* For master's, one foreign language, thesis or alternative; for doctorate, 2 foreign languages, thesis/dissertation, field exam, symposium presentation, prospectus defense. *Entrance requirements:* For master's, GRE, resume, critical writing sample, letters of recommendation, statement of purpose, transcripts; for doctorate, GRE General Test, GRE Subject Test, resume, critical writing sample, letters of recommendation, statement of purpose, transcripts. Additional exam requirements/recommendations for international students: Required—PTE (minimum score 68), TOEFL (minimum score 600 paper-based, 100 iBT) or IELTS (7). *Application deadline:* For fall admission, 1/5 for domestic students. Application fee: $75. Electronic applications accepted. *Expenses: Tuition:* Full-time $48,720. *Required fees:* $88. Tuition and fees vary according to course load, degree level, program and student level. *Financial support:* In 2017–18, 31 students received support, including 24 fellowships with full tuition reimbursements available (averaging $24,480 per year), 3 teaching assistantships with partial tuition reimbursements available (averaging $3,200 per year); Federal Work-Study, scholarships/grants, health care benefits, and tuition waivers (partial) also available. Support available to part-time students. Financial award application deadline: 4/15; financial award applicants required to submit FAFSA. *Faculty research:* Feminist and gender theory, American literature and post-Colonial theory, early modern (Renaissance) English literature, modernism, literature and science, literary theory and philosophy, contemporary poetry. *Unit head:* Dr. David Sherman, Director of Graduate Studies, 781-736-2130, E-mail: chaucer@brandeis.edu. *Application contact:* Lisa Pannella, Department Academic Administrator, 781-736-2130, E-mail: pannella@brandeis.edu.
Website: http://www.brandeis.edu/gsas/programs/english.html

Brandeis University, Graduate School of Arts and Sciences, Department of Near Eastern and Judaic Studies, Waltham, MA 02454-9110. Offers Near Eastern and Judaic studies (MA, PhD); near Eastern and Judaic studies/conflict resolution and coexistence (MA); near Eastern and Judaic studies/Jewish professional leadership (MA); near Eastern and Judaic studies/women's, gender, and sexuality studies (MA); teaching of Hebrew (MAT). Offered jointly with The Heller School of Social Policy and Management. *Program availability:* Part-time. *Faculty:* 24 full-time (10 women), 6 part-time/adjunct (3 women). *Students:* 41 full-time (17 women), 2 part-time (1 woman); includes 7 minority (2 Black or African American, non-Hispanic/Latino; 1 Asian, non-Hispanic/Latino; 4 Hispanic/Latino), 9 international. Average age 33. 47 applicants, 45% accepted, 4 enrolled. In 2017, 8 master's, 3 doctorates awarded. Terminal master's awarded for partial completion of doctoral program. *Degree requirements:* For master's, one foreign language, thesis or alternative, proseminar, capstone; for doctorate, variable foreign language requirement, comprehensive exam, thesis/dissertation. *Entrance requirements:* For master's and doctorate, GRE General Test (recommended), letters of recommendation, transcripts, statement of purpose, writing sample, resume. Additional exam requirements/recommendations for international students: Required—PTE (minimum score 68), TOEFL (minimum score 600 paper-based, 100 iBT) or IELTS (7). *Application deadline:* For fall admission, 1/15 priority date for domestic students. Applications are processed on a rolling basis. Application fee: $75. Electronic applications accepted. *Expenses: Tuition:* Full-time $48,720. *Required fees:* $88. Tuition and fees vary according to course load, degree level, program and student level. *Financial support:* In 2017–18, 29 students received support, including 20 fellowships with full tuition reimbursements available (averaging $24,480 per year), 1 teaching assistantship with partial tuition reimbursement available (averaging $2,500 per year); Federal Work-Study, scholarships/grants, health care benefits, and tuition waivers (partial) also available. Support available to part-time students. Financial award application deadline: 4/15; financial award applicants required to submit FAFSA. *Faculty research:* Bible and ancient Near East, Judaic Studies, Israel Studies, modern Middle East, Arabic and Islamic civilizations. *Unit head:* Dr. Eugene Sheppard, Department Chair, 781-736-2950, E-mail: sheppard@brandeis.edu. *Application contact:* Jean Mannion, Department Administrator, 781-736-2950, E-mail: mannion@brandeis.edu.
Website: http://www.brandeis.edu/gsas/programs/nejs.html

Brandeis University, Graduate School of Arts and Sciences, Department of Sociology, Waltham, MA 02454-9110. Offers social policy and sociology (PhD); sociology (PhD); sociology/women's, gender, and sexuality studies (MA). Offered jointly with The Heller School of Social Policy and Management. *Program availability:* Part-time. *Faculty:* 8 full-time (6 women), 7 part-time/adjunct (5 women). *Students:* 22 full-time (20 women); includes 5 minority (3 Asian, non-Hispanic/Latino; 2 Hispanic/Latino), 2 international. Average age 30. 81 applicants, 14% accepted, 5 enrolled. In 2017, 6 master's awarded. Terminal master's awarded for partial completion of doctoral program. *Degree requirements:* For master's, thesis, project or exam; for doctorate, comprehensive exam, thesis/dissertation, qualifying exam. *Entrance requirements:* For master's and doctorate, GRE General Test, resume, letters of recommendation, statement of purpose, critical writing sample, transcripts. Additional exam requirements/recommendations for international students: Required—PTE (minimum score 68), TOEFL (minimum score 600 paper-based, 100 iBT) or IELTS (7). *Application deadline:* For fall admission, 12/15 for domestic and international students. Applications are processed on a rolling basis. Application fee: $75. Electronic applications accepted. *Expenses: Tuition:* Full-time $48,720. *Required fees:* $88. Tuition and fees vary according to course load, degree level, program and student level. *Financial support:* In 2017–18, 14 students received support, including 10 fellowships with full tuition reimbursements available (averaging $24,480 per year), 6 teaching assistantships with partial tuition reimbursements available (averaging $3,200 per year); Federal Work-Study, scholarships/grants, health care benefits, and tuition waivers (partial) also available. Support available to part-time students. Financial award application deadline: 4/15; financial award applicants required to submit FAFSA. *Faculty research:* Gender and feminist studies; medical sociology; politics and social change; culture and religion. *Unit head:* Dr. Wendy Cadge, Director of Graduate Studies, 781-736-2641, E-mail: wcadge@brandeis.edu. *Application contact:* Lauren Jordahl, Department Administrator, 781-736-2644, E-mail: ljordahl@brandeis.edu.
Website: http://www.brandeis.edu/gsas/programs/sociology.html

Brandeis University, Graduate School of Arts and Sciences, Program in Women's, Gender, and Sexuality Studies, Waltham, MA 02454-9110. Offers anthropology/women's, gender, and sexuality studies (MA); English/women's, gender, and sexuality studies (MA); near Eastern and Judaic studies /women's, gender, and sexuality studies (MA); public policy/women's, gender, and sexuality studies (MA); sociology/women's,

gender, and sexuality studies (MA); sustainable international development/women's, gender, and sexuality studies (MA); women's, gender, and sexuality studies (MA). Offered jointly with The Heller School of Social Policy and Management. *Students:* 10 full-time (all women); includes 2 minority (1 Hispanic/Latino; 1 Two or more races, non-Hispanic/Latino). Average age 25. 42 applicants, 48% accepted, 8 enrolled. In 2017, 8 master's awarded. *Degree requirements:* For master's, thesis. *Entrance requirements:* For master's, GRE General Test, critical writing sample, resume, statement of purpose, transcripts, letters of recommendation. Additional exam requirements/recommendations for international students: Required—PTE (minimum score 68), TOEFL (minimum score 600 paper-based, 100 iBT) or IELTS (7). *Application deadline:* For fall admission, 1/15 for domestic students. Application fee: $75. Electronic applications accepted. *Expenses: Tuition:* Full-time $48,720. *Required fees:* $88. Tuition and fees vary according to course load, degree level, program and student level. *Financial support:* In 2017–18, 6 students received support, including 7 teaching assistantships with partial tuition reimbursements available (averaging $3,200 per year); fellowships, scholarships/grants, and tuition waivers (partial) also available. Financial award application deadline: 4/15; financial award applicants required to submit FAFSA. *Unit head:* Dr. ChaeRan Freeze, Director of Graduate Study, 781-736-2987, E-mail: cfreeze@brandeis.edu. *Application contact:* Shannon Kearns, Department Administrator, 781-736-3045, E-mail: skearns@brandeis.edu.
Website: http://www.brandeis.edu/gsas/programs/wgs.html

California Institute of Integral Studies, School of Consciousness and Transformation, San Francisco, CA 94103. Offers anthropology and social change (MA, PhD); Asian philosophies and cultures (MA); creative inquiry/interdisciplinary arts (MFA); East-West psychology (MA, PhD); integral and transpersonal psychology (PhD); philosophy and religion (PhD), including ecology, spirituality, and religion, philosophy, cosmology, and consciousness, women's spirituality; philosophy, cosmology, and consciousness (Certificate); transformative leadership (MA); transformative studies (PhD); women, gender, spirituality and social justice (MA); writing and consciousness (MFA). *Program availability:* Part-time, evening/weekend, 100% online, blended/hybrid learning. *Students:* 392 full-time (265 women), 141 part-time (98 women); includes 145 minority (40 Black or African American, non-Hispanic/Latino; 1 American Indian or Alaska Native, non-Hispanic/Latino; 19 Asian, non-Hispanic/Latino; 54 Hispanic/Latino; 31 Two or more races, non-Hispanic/Latino), 61 international. Average age 43. 212 applicants, 96% accepted, 153 enrolled. In 2017, 49 master's, 36 doctorates awarded. Terminal master's awarded for partial completion of doctoral program. *Degree requirements:* For master's, thesis optional; for doctorate, comprehensive exam, thesis/dissertation, 1 foreign language (for Asian philosophies and cultures). *Entrance requirements:* For master's, minimum GPA of 3.0, letters of recommendation, writing sample; for doctorate, master's degree, minimum GPA of 3.0, letters of recommendation, writing sample. Additional exam requirements/recommendations for international students: Required—TOEFL. *Application deadline:* For fall admission, 2/1 priority date for domestic and international students; for spring admission, 10/15 priority date for domestic and international students. Applications are processed on a rolling basis. Application fee: $65. Electronic applications accepted. *Expenses:* $21,400 tuition and fees (for MA); $28,390 (for MFA); $24,658 (for PhD). *Financial support:* Fellowships, research assistantships, teaching assistantships, career-related internships or fieldwork, Federal Work-Study, and scholarships/grants available. Support available to part-time students. Financial award application deadline: 4/15; financial award applicants required to submit FAFSA. *Faculty research:* Ecology and sustainability, philosophy and religion, East-West psychology, integrative health, social and cultural anthropology, transformative leadership. *Unit head:* Kathy Littles, Academic Dean, 415-575-6100, E-mail: klittles@ciis.edu. *Application contact:* Ellen Durst, Director of Admissions, 415-575-6100, Fax: 415-575-1268, E-mail: admissions@ciis.edu.
Website: http://www.ciis.edu/

Carnegie Mellon University, Dietrich College of Humanities and Social Sciences, Department of History, Pittsburgh, PA 15213-3891. Offers African and African-American diaspora (PhD); culture and power (PhD); labor, politics and social movements (PhD); technology, environment, science and health (PhD); women, gender and the family (PhD). *Program availability:* Part-time. *Degree requirements:* For doctorate, oral and written comprehensive exams, dissertation defense. *Entrance requirements:* For doctorate, GRE General Test. Additional exam requirements/recommendations for international students: Required—TOEFL. Electronic applications accepted. *Faculty research:* Anthropology and history, African-American history, technology/environment, cultural history analysis.

Chatham University, Program in Business Administration, Pittsburgh, PA 15232-2826. Offers business administration (MBA); healthcare management (MBA); sustainability (MBA); women's leadership (MBA). *Program availability:* Part-time, evening/weekend. *Faculty:* 6 part-time/adjunct (2 women). *Students:* 19 full-time (12 women), 36 part-time (20 women); includes 8 minority (4 Black or African American, non-Hispanic/Latino; 3 Asian, non-Hispanic/Latino; 1 Hispanic/Latino), 5 international. Average age 31. 57 applicants, 56% accepted, 24 enrolled. In 2017, 20 master's awarded. *Entrance requirements:* For master's, minimum GPA of 3.0, letters of recommendation. Additional exam requirements/recommendations for international students: Required—TOEFL (minimum score 600 paper-based; 100 iBT), IELTS (minimum score 7), TWE. *Application deadline:* For fall admission, 4/1 for domestic and international students; for spring admission, 11/1 for domestic students, 10/1 for international students. Applications are processed on a rolling basis. Application fee: $45. Electronic applications accepted. Application fee is waived when completed online. *Expenses:* Contact institution. *Financial support:* Applicants required to submit FAFSA. *Unit head:* Dr. Rachel Chung, Director of Business and Entrepreneurship Program, 412-365-2433. *Application contact:* Katie Noel, Assistant Director of Graduate Admission, 412-365-2758, Fax: 412-365-1609, E-mail: gradadmissions@chatham.edu.
Website: http://www.chatham.edu/mba

Claremont Graduate University, Graduate Programs, School of Arts and Humanities, Department of Religion, Claremont, CA 91711-6160. Offers Hebrew Bible (MA, PhD); history of Christianity and religions of North America (MA, PhD); New Testament (MA, PhD); philosophy of religion and theology (MA, PhD); theology, ethics and culture (MA, PhD); women's studies in religion (MA, PhD); MA/PhD; MBA/PhD. *Program availability:* Part-time. Terminal master's awarded for partial completion of doctoral program. *Entrance requirements:* For master's and doctorate, GRE General Test. Additional exam requirements/recommendations for international students: Required—TOEFL (minimum score 75 iBT). Electronic applications accepted.

Claremont Graduate University, Graduate Programs, School of Arts and Humanities, Program in Applied Women's Studies, Claremont, CA 91711-6160. Offers MA. *Entrance requirements:* For master's, GRE General Test. Additional exam requirements/recommendations for international students: Required—TOEFL (minimum score 75 iBT). Electronic applications accepted.

Cornell University, Graduate School, Graduate Fields of Arts and Sciences, Field of English Language and Literature, Ithaca, NY 14853. Offers African-American literature (PhD); American literature after 1865 (PhD); American literature to 1865 (PhD); American studies (PhD); colonial and postcolonial literatures (PhD); creative writing (MFA); cultural studies (PhD); dramatic literature (PhD); English poetry (PhD); English

Renaissance to 1660 (PhD); lesbian, bisexual, and gay literary studies (PhD); literary criticism and theory (PhD); Old and Middle English (PhD); prose fiction (PhD); Restoration and the eighteenth-century (PhD); the nineteenth century (PhD); the twentieth century (PhD); women's literature (PhD); MFA/PhD. Terminal master's awarded for partial completion of doctoral program. *Degree requirements:* For master's, one foreign language, thesis; for doctorate, one foreign language, comprehensive exam, thesis/dissertation, teaching experience. *Entrance requirements:* For master's, GRE General Test, 3 letters of recommendation, creative writing sample; for doctorate, GRE General Test, GRE Subject Test (English), 3 letters of recommendation, writing sample. Additional exam requirements/recommendations for international students: Required—TOEFL (minimum score 600 paper-based; 77 iBT). Electronic applications accepted. *Faculty research:* English and American literature, women's writing, ethnic and post-colonial literature, critical theory, medievalism.

DePaul University, College of Liberal Arts and Social Sciences, Chicago, IL 60614. Offers Arabic (MA); Chinese (MA); critical ethnic studies (MA); English (MA); French (MA); German (MA); history (MA); interdisciplinary studies (MA, MS); international public service (MS); international studies (MA); Italian (MA); Japanese (MA); liberal studies (MA); nonprofit management (MNM); public administration (MPA); public health (MPH); public policy (MPP); public service management (MS); refugee and forced migration studies (MS); social work (MSW); sociology (MA); Spanish (MA); sustainable urban development (MA); women's and gender studies (MA); writing and publishing (MA); writing, rhetoric and discourse (MA); MA/PhD. *Program availability:* Part-time, evening/weekend, online learning. Terminal master's awarded for partial completion of doctoral program. *Degree requirements:* For master's, variable foreign language requirement, comprehensive exam (for some programs), thesis (for some programs). *Application deadline:* Applications are processed on a rolling basis. Application fee: $40. Electronic applications accepted. *Financial support:* Applicants required to submit FAFSA. *Unit head:* Dr. Guillermo Vasquez de Velasco, Dean, 773-325-7305. *Application contact:* Ann Spittle, Director of Graduate Admission, 773-325-8369, Fax: 312-476-3244, E-mail: graddepaul@depaul.edu.
Website: http://las.depaul.edu/

Eastern Michigan University, Graduate School, College of Arts and Sciences, Department of Women's and Gender Studies, Ypsilanti, MI 48197. Offers MA, Graduate Certificate. *Program availability:* Part-time, evening/weekend. *Faculty:* 3 full-time (all women). *Students:* 6 full-time (4 women), 10 part-time (all women); includes 5 minority (4 Black or African American, non-Hispanic/Latino; 1 Two or more races, non-Hispanic/Latino), 1 international. Average age 31. 14 applicants, 86% accepted, 8 enrolled. In 2017, 4 master's, 1 other advanced degree awarded. *Degree requirements:* For master's, thesis, research project, or practicum. *Entrance requirements:* Additional exam requirements/recommendations for international students: Required—TOEFL. *Application deadline:* For fall admission, 6/15 for domestic and international students; for winter admission, 9/15 for domestic and international students; for spring admission, 3/1 for domestic and international students. Applications are processed on a rolling basis. Application fee: $45. *Financial support:* Fellowships, research assistantships with full tuition reimbursements, teaching assistantships with full tuition reimbursements, career-related internships or fieldwork, Federal Work-Study, institutionally sponsored loans, scholarships/grants, tuition waivers (partial), and unspecified assistantships available. Support available to part-time students. Financial award applicants required to submit FAFSA. *Unit head:* Dr. Peter Higgins, Interim Department Head, 734-487-1177, Fax: 734-487-5029, E-mail: phiggin1@emich.edu.
Website: http://www.emich.edu/wgstudies/

Emory University, Laney Graduate School, Department of Comparative Literature, Atlanta, GA 30322-1100. Offers comparative literature (PhD); philosophy (Certificate); psychoanalytic studies (PhD); women's studies (Certificate). *Degree requirements:* For doctorate, 2 foreign languages, comprehensive exam, thesis/dissertation. *Entrance requirements:* For doctorate, GRE General Test, minimum GPA of 3.0. Additional exam requirements/recommendations for international students: Required—TOEFL. Electronic applications accepted. *Faculty research:* Literary theory, psychoanalysis trauma and testimony, literature and religion, literature and technology, literature and philosophy, politics and global culture, literature and aesthetics.

Emory University, Laney Graduate School, Department of Spanish and Portuguese, Atlanta, GA 30322-1100. Offers comparative literature (Certificate); film studies (Certificate); Spanish (PhD); women's studies (Certificate). *Degree requirements:* For doctorate, 2 foreign languages, comprehensive exam, thesis/dissertation. *Entrance requirements:* For doctorate, GRE General Test. Additional exam requirements/recommendations for international students: Required—TOEFL. Electronic applications accepted. *Faculty research:* Spanish literature, Spanish American literature, literary theory, criticism, cultural studies.

Emory University, Laney Graduate School, Department of Women's, Gender, and Sexuality Studies, Atlanta, GA 30322-1100. Offers PhD. *Degree requirements:* For doctorate, comprehensive exam, thesis/dissertation. *Entrance requirements:* For doctorate, GRE General Test, writing sample. Additional exam requirements/recommendations for international students: Required—TOEFL. Electronic applications accepted. *Faculty research:* Feminist theory, women's literature, African-American literature, gender in cross-cultural perspective, public policy and globalization.

Florida Atlantic University, Dorothy F. Schmidt College of Arts and Letters, Center for Women, Gender and Sexuality Studies, Boca Raton, FL 33431-0991. Offers MA. *Program availability:* Part-time. *Faculty:* 2 full-time (both women). *Students:* 6 full-time (4 women), 3 part-time (2 women); includes 4 minority (2 Hispanic/Latino; 2 Two or more races, non-Hispanic/Latino). Average age 28. 6 applicants, 67% accepted, 4 enrolled. In 2017, 5 master's awarded. *Degree requirements:* For master's, comprehensive exam, thesis or alternative. *Entrance requirements:* For master's, GRE General Test, minimum GPA of 3.0. Additional exam requirements/recommendations for international students: Required—TOEFL (minimum score 500 paper-based; 61 iBT), IELTS (minimum score 6). *Application deadline:* For fall admission, 7/1 for domestic students, 2/15 for international students; for spring admission, 11/1 for domestic students, 7/15 for international students. Applications are processed on a rolling basis. Application fee: $30. Electronic applications accepted. *Expenses:* Tuition, state resident: full-time $7400; part-time $369.82 per credit. Tuition, nonresident: full-time $20,496; part-time $1042.81 per credit. *Financial support:* Fellowships with tuition reimbursements, teaching assistantships with tuition reimbursements, career-related internships or fieldwork, Federal Work-Study, institutionally sponsored loans, scholarships/grants, and unspecified assistantships available. Support available to part-time students. Financial award applicants required to submit FAFSA. *Faculty research:* Women and science/technology, feminist theory, violence against women, women and international development, feminist medical anthropology. *Unit head:* Barclay Barrious, Associate Dean/Director, 561-297-4573, E-mail: bbarrios@fau.edu.
Website: http://www.fau.edu/WomensStudies/

George Mason University, College of Humanities and Social Sciences, Interdisciplinary Studies Program, Fairfax, VA 22030. Offers computational social science (MAIS); energy and sustainability (MAIS); folklore studies (MAIS); higher education (MAIS); individualized studies (MAIS); religion, culture, and values (MAIS); social entrepreneurship (MAIS); social justice and human rights (MAIS); war and the

military in society (MAIS); women and gender studies (MAIS). *Faculty:* 10 full-time (3 women), 15 part-time/adjunct (7 women). *Students:* 29 full-time (23 women), 76 part-time (50 women); includes 39 minority (18 Black or African American, non-Hispanic/Latino; 6 Asian, non-Hispanic/Latino; 11 Hispanic/Latino; 4 Two or more races, non-Hispanic/Latino), 7 international. Average age 32. 71 applicants, 90% accepted, 29 enrolled. In 2017, 23 master's awarded. *Degree requirements:* For master's, thesis or alternative, experiential learning (for some programs). *Entrance requirements:* Additional exam requirements/recommendations for international students: Required—TOEFL (minimum score 575 paper-based; 88 iBT), IELTS (minimum score 6.5), PTE (minimum score 59). *Application deadline:* For fall admission, 3/1 for domestic and international students; for spring admission, 10/15 for domestic and international students. Application fee: $75 ($80 for international students). Electronic applications accepted. *Expenses:* Tuition, state resident: full-time $11,228; part-time $459.50 per credit. Tuition, nonresident: full-time $30,932; part-time $1280.50 per credit. *Required fees:* $3252; $135.50 per credit. Part-time tuition and fees vary according to course load and program. *Financial support:* In 2017–18, 9 students received support, including 2 research assistantships with tuition reimbursements available, 7 teaching assistantships with tuition reimbursements available (averaging $8,599 per year); career-related internships or fieldwork, Federal Work-Study, scholarships/grants, unspecified assistantships, and health care benefits (for full-time research or teaching assistantship recipients) also available. Support available to part-time students. Financial award application deadline: 3/1; financial award applicants required to submit FAFSA. *Faculty research:* Combined English and folklore, religious and cultural studies (Christianity and Muslim society). *Unit head:* Meredith H. Lair, Director, 703-993-2159, Fax: 703-993-1251, E-mail: mlair@gmu.edu. *Application contact:* Morgan Fisher, Graduate Coordinator, 703-993-8762, E-mail: mfisherb@gmu.edu.
Website: http://mais.gmu.edu

The George Washington University, Columbian College of Arts and Sciences, Department of Women's Studies, Washington, DC 20052. Offers MA, Certificate. *Program availability:* Part-time, evening/weekend. *Faculty:* 3 full-time (all women), 2 part-time/adjunct (both women). *Students:* 19 full-time (17 women), 8 part-time (all women); includes 6 minority (2 Black or African American, non-Hispanic/Latino; 3 Hispanic/Latino; 1 Two or more races, non-Hispanic/Latino), 3 international. Average age 27. 52 applicants, 77% accepted, 17 enrolled. In 2017, 11 master's, 4 other advanced degrees awarded. *Degree requirements:* For master's, comprehensive exam, thesis or alternative. *Entrance requirements:* For master's, GRE General Test, minimum GPA of 3.0. Additional exam requirements/recommendations for international students: Required—TOEFL (minimum score 550 paper-based; 80 iBT). *Application deadline:* For fall admission, 4/1 priority date for domestic students, 1/15 priority date for international students; for spring admission, 10/1 priority date for domestic students, 9/1 priority date for international students. Applications are processed on a rolling basis. Application fee: $75. Electronic applications accepted. *Expenses: Tuition:* Full-time $28,800; part-time $1655 per credit hour. *Required fees:* $45; $2.75 per credit hour. *Financial support:* In 2017–18, 2 students received support. Fellowships with tuition reimbursements available, teaching assistantships with tuition reimbursements available, Federal Work-Study, institutionally sponsored loans, and tuition waivers available. Financial award application deadline: 1/15. *Unit head:* Dr. Daniel Moshenberg, Director, 202-994-9086, Fax: 202-994-7249. *Application contact:* Information Contact, 202-994-6942, Fax: 202-994-2249, E-mail: wgss@gwu.edu.
Website: http://womensstudies.columbian.gwu.edu/

Georgia State University, College of Arts and Sciences, Institute for Women's, Gender, and Sexuality Studies, Atlanta, GA 30302-3083. Offers MA, Graduate Certificate. *Program availability:* Part-time. *Faculty:* 6 full-time (5 women). *Students:* 14 full-time (all women), 2 part-time (both women); includes 11 minority (6 Black or African American, non-Hispanic/Latino; 1 Asian, non-Hispanic/Latino; 4 Two or more races, non-Hispanic/Latino), 2 international. Average age 29. 18 applicants, 89% accepted, 10 enrolled. In 2017, 5 master's, 5 other advanced degrees awarded. *Entrance requirements:* For master's and Graduate Certificate, GRE, two official transcripts from each college or university attended, three letters of recommendation addressing student's ability to undertake graduate study, 750-1000 word statement of purpose, academic writing sample. Additional exam requirements/recommendations for international students: Required—TOEFL (minimum score 550 paper-based; 80 iBT). *Application deadline:* For fall admission, 2/15 for domestic and international students. Application fee: $50. Electronic applications accepted. *Expenses:* Tuition, state resident: full-time $7020. Tuition, nonresident: full-time $22,518. *Required fees:* $2128. Tuition and fees vary according to degree level and program. *Financial support:* In 2017–18, research assistantships with full tuition reimbursements (averaging $7,000 per year), teaching assistantships with full tuition reimbursements (averaging $7,500 per year) were awarded; career-related internships or fieldwork, health care benefits, and unspecified assistantships also available. Financial award application deadline: 2/15. *Faculty research:* Gender, sexuality, and youth studies; gender and neoliberalism; transnational feminisms; cultural studies; queer theories. *Unit head:* Dr. Susan Talburt, Director, 404-413-6581, Fax: 404-413-6585, E-mail: stalburt@gsu.edu. *Application contact:* Dr. Amira Jarmakani, Director of Graduate Studies, 404-413-6583, Fax: 404-413-6585, E-mail: amira@gsu.edu.
Website: http://www2.gsu.edu/~wwwwsi/

Grace Theological Seminary, Graduate and Professional Programs, Winona Lake, IN 46590-9907. Offers biblical studies (Certificate); chaplaincy (M Div); exegetical studies (M Div); intercultural studies (M Div, MA, D Min); local church ministry (MA), including camp administration, women's leadership; pastoral counseling (M Div); pastoral studies (M Div, D Min); theology (Diploma). *Accreditation:* ATS. *Program availability:* Part-time, online learning. *Degree requirements:* For master's, thesis optional; for doctorate, 2 foreign languages, thesis/dissertation. *Entrance requirements:* For master's, MAT, minimum GPA of 2.5. Electronic applications accepted. *Faculty research:* Biblical theology, language, and church ministries.

Inter American University of Puerto Rico, Metropolitan Campus, Graduate Programs, Program in Women's and Gender Studies, San Juan, PR 00919-1293. Offers MA.

The Jewish Theological Seminary, The Graduate School, New York, NY 10027-4649. Offers ancient Judaism (MA, DHL, PhD); Bible and ancient Semitic languages (MA, DHL, PhD); interdepartmental studies (MA); Jewish art and visual culture (MA); Jewish gender and women's studies (MA); Jewish history (MA, DHL, PhD); Jewish literature (MA, DHL, PhD); Jewish philosophy (DHL); Jewish thought (MA, PhD); liturgy (MA, DHL, PhD); medieval Jewish studies (MA, DHL, PhD); Midrash (DHL); Midrash and scriptural interpretation (MA, PhD); modern Jewish studies (MA, DHL, PhD); Talmud and rabbinics (MA, DHL, PhD); MA/MSW. MA/MSW offered jointly with Columbia University. *Accreditation:* ACIPE. *Program availability:* Part-time. Terminal master's awarded for partial completion of doctoral program. *Degree requirements:* For master's, one foreign language, comprehensive exam (for some programs), thesis (for some programs); for doctorate, 3 foreign languages, comprehensive exam (for some programs), thesis/dissertation. *Entrance requirements:* For master's, GRE or MAT, 3 letters of recommendation, writing sample; for doctorate, GRE or MAT, 3 letters of recommendation, writing research sample. Additional exam requirements/recommendations for international students: Required—TOEFL.

Kansas State University, Graduate School, College of Arts and Sciences, Department of Gender, Women and Sexuality Studies, Manhattan, KS 66506. Offers Graduate Certificate. *Entrance requirements:* For degree, minimum GPA of 3.0, letters of recommendation. Additional exam requirements/recommendations for international students: Required—TOEFL, TWE, or IELTS. *Faculty research:* Gender and violence, queer and transgender studies, girls' studies, ecofeminism, animal studies.

Lakehead University, Graduate Studies, Department of History, Thunder Bay, ON P7B 5E1, Canada. Offers gerontology (MA); history (MA); women's studies (MA). *Program availability:* Part-time. *Degree requirements:* For master's, one foreign language, thesis. *Entrance requirements:* For master's, minimum B average. Additional exam requirements/recommendations for international students: Required—TOEFL. *Faculty research:* Canadian history, British history, Russian/German history, women's studies.

Lakehead University, Graduate Studies, Faculty of Education, Thunder Bay, ON P7B 5E1, Canada. Offers educational studies (PhD); gerontology (M Ed); women's studies (M Ed). *Program availability:* Part-time, evening/weekend. *Degree requirements:* For master's, project or thesis. *Entrance requirements:* For master's, minimum B average. Additional exam requirements/recommendations for international students: Required—TOEFL. *Faculty research:* Art education, AIDS education, language arts education, gerontology, women's studies.

Lakehead University, Graduate Studies, Faculty of Social Sciences and Humanities, Department of English, Thunder Bay, ON P7B 5E1, Canada. Offers English (MA); women's studies (MA). *Program availability:* Part-time, evening/weekend. *Degree requirements:* For master's, one foreign language, thesis optional. *Entrance requirements:* For master's, minimum B average. Additional exam requirements/recommendations for international students: Required—TOEFL. *Faculty research:* Rhetoric and literary studies, children's literature, nineteenth- and twentieth-century American literature, modern literature, women's studies.

Lakehead University, Graduate Studies, Faculty of Social Sciences and Humanities, Department of Sociology, Thunder Bay, ON P7B 5E1, Canada. Offers gerontology (MA); health services and policy research (MA); sociology (MA); women's studies (MA). *Program availability:* Part-time, evening/weekend. *Degree requirements:* For master's, research project or thesis. *Entrance requirements:* For master's, minimum B average. Additional exam requirements/recommendations for international students: Required—TOEFL. *Faculty research:* Sociology of medicine, cultural and social change, health human resources, gerontology, women's studies.

Lakehead University, Graduate Studies, School of Social Work, Thunder Bay, ON P7B 5E1, Canada. Offers gerontology (MSW); social work (MSW); women's studies (MSW). *Program availability:* Part-time. *Degree requirements:* For master's, thesis or project. *Entrance requirements:* For master's, minimum B average. Additional exam requirements/recommendations for international students: Required—TOEFL. *Faculty research:* Clinical psychology, social work and practice theory, long-term care, health care for frail elderly, women's studies.

Lakehead University, Graduate Studies, Women's Studies Collaborative Program, Thunder Bay, ON P7B 5E1, Canada. Offers M Ed, MA, MSW. *Program availability:* Part-time. *Degree requirements:* For master's, thesis (for some programs). *Entrance requirements:* Additional exam requirements/recommendations for international students: Required—TOEFL. *Faculty research:* Feminist thought, feminist pedagogy, women of literature, Canadian women's history, well-being of women.

Lesley University, Graduate School of Arts and Social Sciences, Cambridge, MA 02138-2790. Offers clinical mental health counseling (MA), including holistic counseling, school and community counseling, trauma studies; counseling psychology (MA, CAGS), including professional counseling (MA), school counseling (MA); creative writing (MFA); expressive therapies (MA, PhD, CAGS), including art (MA), clinical mental health counseling (MA), dance (MA), expressive therapies (MA), music (MA); independent studies (CAGS); independent study (MA); intercultural relations (MA, CAGS); interdisciplinary studies (MA), including individualized studies, integrative holistic health, mindfulness studies, peace and conflict transformation, trauma sensitive assessment, intervention, and consultation, women's studies; urban environmental leadership (MA). *Program availability:* Part-time, online learning. *Degree requirements:* For master's, internship, practicum, thesis (for expressive therapies); for doctorate, thesis/dissertation, arts apprenticeship, field placement; for CAGS, thesis, internship (for counseling psychology, expressive therapies). *Entrance requirements:* For master's, MAT (counseling psychology), interview, writing samples, art portfolio; for doctorate, GRE or MAT, interview, master's degree; for CAGS, interview, master's degree. Additional exam requirements/recommendations for international students: Required—TOEFL (minimum score 550 paper-based; 80 iBT). Electronic applications accepted. *Faculty research:* Psychotherapy and culture; psychotherapy and psychological trauma; women's issues in art, teaching and psychotherapy; community-based art, psycho-spiritual inquiry.

London Metropolitan University, Graduate Programs, London, United Kingdom. Offers applied psychology (M Sc); architecture (MA); biomedical science (M Sc); blood science (M Sc); cancer pharmacology (M Sc); computer networking and cyber security (M Sc); computing and information systems (M Sc); conference interpreting (MA); counter-terrorism studies (M Sc); creative, digital and professional writing (MA); crime, violence and prevention (M Sc); criminology (M Sc); curating contemporary art (MA); data analytics (M Sc); digital media (MA); early childhood studies (MA); education (MA, Ed D); financial services law, regulation and compliance (LL M); food science (M Sc); forensic psychology (M Sc); health and social care management and policy (M Sc); human nutrition (M Sc); human resource management (MA); human rights and international conflict (MA); information technology (M Sc); intelligence and security studies (M Sc); international oil, gas and energy law (LL M); international relations (MA); interpreting (MA); learning and teaching in higher education (MA); legal practice (LL M); media and entertainment law (LL M); organizational and consumer psychology (M Sc); psychological therapy (M Sc); psychology of mental health (M Sc); public health (M Sc); public policy and management (MPA); security studies (M Sc); social work (M Sc); spatial planning and urban design (MA); sports therapy (M Sc); supporting older children and young people with dyslexia (MA); teaching languages (MA), including Arabic, English; translation (MA); woman and child abuse (MA).

Middle Tennessee State University, College of Graduate Studies, College of Liberal Arts, Program in Women's and Gender Studies, Murfreesboro, TN 37132. Offers Graduate Certificate. *Program availability:* Part-time, evening/weekend, online learning. Electronic applications accepted.

Minnesota State University Mankato, College of Graduate Studies and Research, College of Social and Behavioral Sciences, Department of Gender and Women's Studies, Mankato, MN 56001. Offers MS. *Program availability:* Part-time. *Degree requirements:* For master's, comprehensive exam, thesis or alternative. *Entrance requirements:* For master's, minimum GPA of 3.0, essay. Additional exam requirements/recommendations for international students: Required—TOEFL.

Mount Saint Vincent University, Graduate Programs, Department of Women's Studies, Halifax, NS B3M 2J6, Canada. Offers MA. Program offered jointly with Dalhousie University, Saint Mary's University. *Program availability:* Part-time. *Degree requirements:* For master's, thesis. Electronic applications accepted.

Northern Arizona University, College of Social and Behavioral Sciences, Women's and Gender Studies Program, Flagstaff, AZ 86011. Offers Graduate Certificate. *Program availability:* Part-time. *Faculty:* 5 full-time (all women). *Students:* 1 part-time (0 women). 1 applicant, 100% accepted, 1 enrolled. *Degree requirements:* For Graduate Certificate, comprehensive exam (for some programs). *Entrance requirements:* Additional exam requirements/recommendations for international students: Required—TOEFL (minimum score 80 iBT), IELTS (minimum score 6.5). *Application deadline:* For fall admission, 3/1 for domestic and international students; for spring admission, 10/1 for domestic and international students. Applications are processed on a rolling basis. Application fee: $65. Electronic applications accepted. *Expenses:* Tuition, state resident: full-time $9240; part-time $458 per credit hour. Tuition, nonresident: full-time $21,588; part-time $1199 per credit hour. *Required fees:* $1021; $14 per credit hour. $646 per semester. Tuition and fees vary according to course load, campus/location and program. *Financial support:* In 2017–18, 2 students received support, including 2 teaching assistantships with partial tuition reimbursements available (averaging $6,000 per year); institutionally sponsored loans and unspecified assistantships also available. Financial award application deadline: 2/1; financial award applicants required to submit FAFSA. *Unit head:* Dr. Sheila Nair, Director, 928-523-0180, E-mail: sheila.nair@nau.edu. *Application contact:* Matthew Morse, Administrative Associate, 928-523-2011, E-mail: matthew.morse@nau.edu.
Website: http://nau.edu/sbs/wgs/

The Ohio State University, Graduate School, College of Arts and Sciences, Division of Arts and Humanities, Department of Women's, Gender and Sexuality Studies, Columbus, OH 43210. Offers MA, PhD. *Faculty:* 14. *Students:* 30 (26 women); includes 5 minority (all Black or African American, non-Hispanic/Latino), 8 international. Average age 28. In 2017, 5 master's, 4 doctorates awarded. Terminal master's awarded for partial completion of doctoral program. *Entrance requirements:* For master's and doctorate, GRE (if GPA is less than 3.0 for all work), scholarly writing sample. Additional exam requirements/recommendations for international students: Required—TOEFL (minimum score 550 paper-based; 79 iBT), Michigan English Language Assessment Battery (minimum score 82); Recommended—IELTS (minimum score 7). *Application deadline:* For fall admission, 12/1 priority date for domestic students, 11/15 priority date for international students; for spring admission, 3/1 for domestic students, 2/1 for international students. Applications are processed on a rolling basis. Application fee: $60 ($70 for international students). Electronic applications accepted. *Financial support:* Fellowships, research assistantships, teaching assistantships, career-related internships or fieldwork, Federal Work-Study, institutionally sponsored loans, and unspecified assistantships available. Support available to part-time students. *Unit head:* Dr. Shannon Winnubst, Chair and Professor, 614-292-3915, E-mail: winnubst.1@osu.edu. *Application contact:* Graduate and Professional Admissions, 614-292-9444, Fax: 614-292-3895, E-mail: gpadmissions@osu.edu.
Website: http://wgss.osu.edu/

Old Dominion University, College of Arts and Letters, Program in Applied Sociology, Norfolk, VA 23529. Offers criminal justice (MA); general sociology (MA); women's studies (MA). *Program availability:* Part-time, evening/weekend. *Faculty:* 19 full-time (11 women). *Students:* 18 full-time (13 women), 2 part-time (1 woman); includes 10 minority (4 Black or African American, non-Hispanic/Latino; 1 Hispanic/Latino; 5 Two or more races, non-Hispanic/Latino). Average age 26. 26 applicants, 65% accepted, 12 enrolled. In 2017, 3 master's awarded. *Degree requirements:* For master's, thesis. *Entrance requirements:* For master's, GRE General Test, minimum GPA of 3.0; 12 credits in criminal justice, sociology, or women's studies. Additional exam requirements/recommendations for international students: Required—TOEFL. *Application deadline:* For fall admission, 3/1 for domestic and international students. Application fee: $50. Electronic applications accepted. *Expenses:* Contact institution. *Financial support:* In 2017–18, 8 students received support, including 2 research assistantships (averaging $10,000 per year), 6 teaching assistantships (averaging $10,000 per year); career-related internships or fieldwork, scholarships/grants, and unspecified assistantships also available. Financial award application deadline: 2/15. *Faculty research:* Quantitative methodology, theory, family, gender/class/race, crime. *Total annual research expenditures:* $350,000. *Unit head:* Dr. Ingrid Whitaker, Graduate Program Director, 757-683-3811, Fax: 757-683-5634, E-mail: iwhitake@odu.edu. *Application contact:* Dr. David C. Earnest, Associate Dean, 757-683-6077, Fax: 757-683-5746, E-mail: dearnest@odu.edu.
Website: http://al.odu.edu/sociology/gradprogram/graduatehome.shtml

Oregon State University, College of Liberal Arts, Program in Women, Gender, and Sexuality Studies, Corvallis, OR 97331. Offers feminist leadership (PhD). *Program availability:* Part-time. *Degree requirements:* For master's, one foreign language; for doctorate, thesis/dissertation. *Entrance requirements:* Additional exam requirements/recommendations for international students: Required—TOEFL (minimum score 80 iBT), IELTS (minimum score 6.5). *Application deadline:* For fall admission, 12/1 for domestic and international students. Application fee: $75 ($85 for international students). *Financial support:* Application deadline: 4/1. *Unit head:* Qwo-Li Driskill, Director of Graduate Studies, E-mail: qwo-li.driskill@oregonstate.edu. *Application contact:* Dr. Qwo-Li Driskill, Director of Graduate Studies, 541-737-1114, E-mail: quo-li.driskill@oregonstate.edu.
Website: http://liberalarts.oregonstate.edu/slcs/wgss/

Queen's University at Kingston, School of Graduate Studies, Faculty of Arts and Sciences, Department of Sociology, Kingston, ON K7L 3N6, Canada. Offers communication and Information technology (MA, PhD); feminist sociology (MA, PhD); socio-legal studies (MA, PhD); sociological theory (MA, PhD). *Program availability:* Part-time. *Degree requirements:* For master's, thesis; for doctorate, comprehensive exam, thesis/dissertation. *Entrance requirements:* For master's, honors bachelors degree in sociology; for doctorate, honors bachelors degree, masters degree in sociology. Additional exam requirements/recommendations for international students: Required—TOEFL. *Faculty research:* Social change and modernization, social control, deviance and criminology, surveillance.

Reconstructionist Rabbinical College, Graduate Programs, Wyncote, PA 19095-1898. Offers Jewish studies (MAJS); rabbinics (MAHL, DHL); women's studies (Certificate). Certificate offered jointly with Temple University. *Program availability:* Part-time. *Degree requirements:* For master's, one foreign language, thesis (MAJS), completion of rabbinical program (MAHL); for doctorate, one foreign language. *Entrance requirements:* For master's, GRE General Test; placement examinations in Hebrew and Judaism (MAHL); for doctorate, GRE General Test, placement examinations in Hebrew and Judaism. *Faculty research:* Bible, Hebrew Semitic texts, contemporary Judaism.

Rutgers University–New Brunswick, Graduate School-New Brunswick, Department of Political Science, Piscataway, NJ 08854-8097. Offers American politics (PhD); comparative politics (PhD); international relations (PhD); political theory (PhD); public law (PhD); United Nations and global policy studies (MA); women and politics (PhD). *Degree requirements:* For doctorate, one foreign language, comprehensive exam, thesis/dissertation. *Entrance requirements:* For master's, bachelor's degree from accredited U.S. college or university or a comparable institution in another country; for doctorate, GRE General Test. Additional exam requirements/recommendations for international students: Required—TOEFL.

Rutgers University–New Brunswick, Graduate School-New Brunswick, Program in Women's and Gender Studies, Piscataway, NJ 08854-8097. Offers MA, PhD. *Program availability:* Part-time. *Degree requirements:* For master's, thesis or alternative; for doctorate, comprehensive exam, thesis/dissertation. *Entrance requirements:* For master's and doctorate, GRE General Test, writing sample, 3 letters of recommendation. Additional exam requirements/recommendations for international students: Required—TOEFL. *Faculty research:* Feminist theory, gender and sexuality, global and cultural studies, women in history, literature, and politics, feminist politics.

Saint Mary's University, Faculty of Arts, Program in Women and Gender Studies, Halifax, NS B3H 3C3, Canada. Offers MA. Program offered jointly with Mount Saint Vincent University. *Program availability:* Part-time. *Degree requirements:* For master's, thesis. *Entrance requirements:* For master's, honors degree.

San Diego State University, Graduate and Research Affairs, College of Arts and Letters, Department of Women's Studies, San Diego, CA 92182. Offers MA. *Entrance requirements:* For master's, GRE General Test, 2 letters of reference. Additional exam requirements/recommendations for international students: Required—TOEFL. Electronic applications accepted.

San Francisco State University, Division of Graduate Studies, College of Liberal and Creative Arts, Department of Women and Gender Studies, San Francisco, CA 94132-1722. Offers MA. *Program availability:* Part-time, evening/weekend. *Unit head:* Dr. Julietta Hua, Chair, 415-338-3065, Fax: 415-338-6159, E-mail: jyhua@sfsu.edu. *Application contact:* Dr. Evren Savci, Graduate Coordinator, 415-338-1238, Fax: 415-338-6159, E-mail: savci@sfsu.edu.
Website: http://wgsdept.sfsu.edu/

Sarah Lawrence College, Graduate Studies, Program in Women's History, Bronxville, NY 10708-5999. Offers MA. *Program availability:* Part-time. *Degree requirements:* For master's, thesis. *Entrance requirements:* For master's, previous course work in history, minimum B average in undergraduate course work. Additional exam requirements/recommendations for international students: Required—TOEFL (minimum score 600 paper-based). Electronic applications accepted.

Simon Fraser University, Office of Graduate Studies and Postdoctoral Fellows, Faculty of Arts and Social Sciences, Department of Gender, Sexuality and Women's Studies, Burnaby, BC V5A 1S6, Canada. Offers MA, PhD. *Degree requirements:* For master's, thesis or alternative; for doctorate, comprehensive exam, thesis/dissertation. *Entrance requirements:* For master's, minimum GPA of 3.0 (on scale of 4.33) or 3.33 based on last 60 credits of undergraduate courses; for doctorate, minimum GPA of 3.5 (on scale of 4.33). Additional exam requirements/recommendations for international students: Recommended—TOEFL (minimum score 580 paper-based; 93 iBT), IELTS (minimum score 7), TWE (minimum score 5). Electronic applications accepted. *Faculty research:* Gender history, feminist labor studies/economics, queer theory, women and media, feminist research methods.

Smith College, Graduate and Special Programs, Center for Women in Mathematics Post-Baccalaureate Program, Northampton, MA 01063. Offers Postbaccalaureate Certificate. *Students:* 11 full-time (all women); includes 5 minority (1 Black or African American, non-Hispanic/Latino; 4 Asian, non-Hispanic/Latino), 1 international. Average age 26. 40 applicants, 35% accepted, 11 enrolled. In 2017, 10 Postbaccalaureate Certificates awarded. *Entrance requirements:* Additional exam requirements/recommendations for international students: Required—TOEFL (minimum score 595 paper-based; 97 iBT), IELTS (minimum score 7.5). *Application deadline:* For fall admission, 3/15 for domestic students; for spring admission, 10/15 for domestic students. Application fee: $60. *Expenses: Tuition:* Full-time $37,440; part-time $1560 per credit. Tuition and fees vary according to course load and program. *Financial support:* In 2017–18, 11 students received support. Scholarships/grants and tuition waivers (full) available. Financial award application deadline: 3/15. *Unit head:* Ruth Haas, Director, 413-585-3872, E-mail: rhaas@smith.edu. *Application contact:* Ruth Morgan, Program Assistant, 413-585-3050, Fax: 413-585-3054, E-mail: rmorgan@smith.edu.

Southeastern Baptist Theological Seminary, Graduate and Professional Programs, Wake Forest, NC 27587. Offers advanced biblical studies (M Div); Christian education (M Div, MACE); Christian ethics (PhD); Christian ministry (M Div); Christian planting (M Div); church music (MACM); counseling (MACO); evangelism (PhD); language (M Div); ministry (D Min); New Testament (PhD); Old Testament (PhD); philosophy (PhD); theology (Th M, PhD); women's studies (M Div). *Accreditation:* ACIPE; ATS (one or more programs are accredited). *Degree requirements:* For master's, thesis (for some programs), oral exam; for doctorate, thesis/dissertation, fieldwork. *Entrance requirements:* For master's, Cooperative English Test, minimum GPA of 2.0, M Div or equivalent (Th M); for doctorate, GRE General Test or MAT, Cooperative English Test, M Div or equivalent, 3 years of professional experience.

Southern Connecticut State University, School of Graduate Studies, School of Arts and Sciences, Program in Women's Studies, New Haven, CT 06515-1355. Offers MA. *Program availability:* Part-time, evening/weekend. *Degree requirements:* For master's, thesis or alternative. *Entrance requirements:* For master's, interview. Electronic applications accepted.

Stony Brook University, State University of New York, Graduate School, College of Arts and Sciences, Program in Women's, Gender, and Sexuality Studies, Stony Brook, NY 11794. Offers Certificate. *Faculty:* 8 full-time (7 women). In 2017, 3 Certificates awarded. *Degree requirements:* For Certificate, interdisciplinary research colloquium. *Entrance requirements:* For degree, GRE, minimum GPA of 2.75, 3 letters of recommendation. Additional exam requirements/recommendations for international students: Required—TOEFL. *Application deadline:* For fall admission, 1/15 for domestic students; for spring admission, 10/1 for domestic students. *Expenses:* Contact institution. *Faculty research:* Exercise, gender studies, humanities, literary criticism, women's studies. *Unit head:* Prof. Mary Jo Bona, Chair, 631-632-6355, E-mail: maryjo.bona@stonybrook.edu. *Application contact:* Graduate Program Director, 631-632-7461.
Website: http://www.stonybrook.edu/commcms/wgss/

Texas Woman's University, Graduate School, College of Arts and Sciences, Department of Multicultural Women's and Gender Studies, Denton, TX 76204. Offers MA, PhD. *Program availability:* Part-time. *Faculty:* 5 full-time (4 women), 1 part-time/adjunct (0 women). *Students:* 10 full-time (all women), 36 part-time (34 women); includes 22 minority (9 Black or African American, non-Hispanic/Latino; 1 American Indian or Alaska Native, non-Hispanic/Latino; 3 Asian, non-Hispanic/Latino; 6 Hispanic/Latino; 3 Two or more races, non-Hispanic/Latino), 4 international. Average age 36. 14 applicants, 93% accepted, 8 enrolled. In 2017, 5 master's, 3 doctorates awarded. Terminal master's awarded for partial completion of doctoral program. *Degree requirements:* For master's, comprehensive exam, thesis (for some programs), thesis or coursework; for doctorate, comprehensive exam, thesis/dissertation. *Entrance requirements:* For master's, 2 letters of reference, personal essay, minimum GPA of 3.0, writing sample; for doctorate, statement of purpose, writing sample, curriculum vitae/resume, 2 reference letters, minimum GPA of 3.5 in prior graduate level course work. Additional exam requirements/recommendations for international students: Required—TOEFL (minimum score 550 paper-based; 79 iBT); Recommended—IELTS (minimum

score 6.5), TSE (minimum score 53). *Application deadline:* For fall admission, 3/1 priority date for domestic and international students; for spring admission, 11/1 priority date for domestic students, 7/1 priority date for international students. Applications are processed on a rolling basis. Application fee: $50 ($75 for international students). Electronic applications accepted. *Expenses:* $7,520 per year full-time in-state; $16,820 per year full-time out-of-state. *Financial support:* In 2017–18, 20 students received support, including 9 teaching assistantships (averaging $27,404 per year); career-related internships or fieldwork, Federal Work-Study, institutionally sponsored loans, scholarships/grants, traineeships, health care benefits, and unspecified assistantships also available. Support available to part-time students. Financial award application deadline: 3/1; financial award applicants required to submit FAFSA. *Faculty research:* Feminist/womanist theories and epistemologies, history of U.S. feminism, U.S. women of color, feminism and religion/spirituality, critical race theories. *Unit head:* Dr. AnaLouise Keating, Interim Chair, 940-898-2119, Fax: 940-898-2101, E-mail: womenstudies@twu.edu. *Application contact:* Korie Hawkins, Associate Director of Admissions, Graduate Recruitment, 940-898-3188, Fax: 940-898-3081, E-mail: admissions@twu.edu.
Website: http://www.twu.edu/ws/

Towson University, College of Liberal Arts, Program in Women's Studies, Towson, MD 21252-0001. Offers MS, Postbaccalaureate Certificate. *Students:* 8 full-time (7 women), 5 part-time (all women); includes 3 minority (all Black or African American, non-Hispanic/Latino), 3 international. *Degree requirements:* For master's, thesis optional. *Entrance requirements:* For master's, bachelor's degree with minimum GPA of 3.0, 9 credits of course work in women's studies and/or the social sciences, essay, 2 letters of recommendation; for Postbaccalaureate Certificate, bachelor's degree, 9 units in women's studies and/or the social sciences, 2 letters of recommendation, essay. *Application deadline:* For fall admission, 1/17 for domestic students, 5/15 for international students; for spring admission, 10/15 for domestic students, 12/1 for international students. Applications are processed on a rolling basis. Application fee: $45. Electronic applications accepted. *Expenses:* Tuition, state resident: full-time $7960; part-time $398 per unit. Tuition, nonresident: full-time $16,480; part-time $824 per unit. *Required fees:* $2600; $130 per year. $390 per term. *Financial support:* Application deadline: 4/1. *Unit head:* Dr. Cindy Gissendanner, Department Chair, 410-704-5456, E-mail: ewangari@towson.edu. *Application contact:* Coverley Beidleman, Assistant Director of Graduate Admissions, 410-704-5630, Fax: 410-704-3030, E-mail: cbeidleman@towson.edu.
Website: http://www.towson.edu/cla/departments/womengender/grad/womengender/

United Theological Seminary of the Twin Cities, Graduate Programs, New Brighton, MN 55112-2598. Offers advanced theological studies (Diploma); justice and peace studies (M Div, MA); leadership toward racial justice (M Div, MA, Certificate); Methodist studies (M Div, MA, Certificate); ministry (D Min); ministry renewal and professional development (Certificate); pastoral care and counseling (M Div, MA, MARL); religion and theology (MA); theological and religious studies (Certificate); theology and the arts (M Div, MA); urban ministry (M Div, MA, MARL); women's studies: religion, theology and ministry (M Div, MA). *Accreditation:* ACIPE; ATS. *Program availability:* Part-time, evening/weekend. *Degree requirements:* For master's, thesis; for doctorate, comprehensive exam, thesis/dissertation. *Entrance requirements:* For master's, minimum GPA of 2.75; strong analytical, reflective thinking and writing skills; vocational and academic goals compatible with those of Seminary; for doctorate, M Div or equivalent, minimum GPA of 3.0, 3 years experience in professional ministry; for other advanced degree, BA or equivalent life experience; strong analytical, reflective thinking and writing skills (Certificate); proficiency in English language, previous study of theology at a theological school, recommendation of student's denomination (Diploma). Additional exam requirements/recommendations for international students: Required—TOEFL (minimum score 550 paper-based).

Université Laval, Faculty of Social Sciences, Program in Feminist Studies, Québec, QC G1K 7P4, Canada. Offers Diploma. *Program availability:* Part-time. *Entrance requirements:* For degree, knowledge of French, comprehension of written English. Electronic applications accepted.

University at Albany, State University of New York, College of Arts and Sciences, Department of Women's, Gender and Sexuality Studies, Albany, NY 12222-0001. Offers MA. *Faculty:* 6 full-time (all women). *Students:* 10 full-time (all women), 5 part-time (all women); includes 2 minority (1 Hispanic/Latino; 1 Two or more races, non-Hispanic/Latino), 3 international. 21 applicants, 67% accepted, 5 enrolled. In 2017, 12 master's awarded. *Entrance requirements:* Additional exam requirements/recommendations for international students: Required—TOEFL (minimum score 550 paper-based). *Application deadline:* For fall admission, 8/1 for domestic students, 5/1 for international students. Applications are processed on a rolling basis. Application fee: $75. Electronic applications accepted. *Expenses:* Tuition, state resident: full-time $10,870; part-time $453 per credit hour. Tuition, nonresident: full-time $22,210; part-time $925 per credit hour. *Required fees:* $84.68 per credit hour. $508.06 per semester. Part-time tuition and fees vary according to course load and program. *Faculty research:* Feminist pedagogy, lesbian and gay studies, women in the African diaspora, women's health policy, literature of feminism. *Unit head:* Janell Hobson, Chair, 518-442-4220, Fax: 518-442-4419, E-mail: jhobson@albany.edu. *Application contact:* Michael DeRensis, Director, Graduate Admissions, 518-442-3980, Fax: 518-442-3922, E-mail: graduate@albany.edu.
Website: http://www.albany.edu/ws/

The University of Alabama, Graduate School, College of Arts and Sciences, Department of Gender and Race Studies, Tuscaloosa, AL 35487. Offers women's studies (MA). *Program availability:* Part-time. *Faculty:* 5 full-time (3 women). *Students:* 17 full-time (12 women), 4 part-time (2 women); includes 14 minority (13 Black or African American, non-Hispanic/Latino; 1 Hispanic/Latino). Average age 27. 13 applicants, 85% accepted, 8 enrolled. In 2017, 5 master's awarded. *Degree requirements:* For master's, comprehensive exam, thesis optional. *Entrance requirements:* For master's, MAT or GRE. Additional exam requirements/recommendations for international students: Required—TOEFL. *Application deadline:* For fall admission, 3/7 priority date for domestic students, 3/7 for international students. Applications are processed on a rolling basis. Application fee: $50 ($60 for international students). Electronic applications accepted. *Financial support:* In 2017–18, 10 students received support, including research assistantships with tuition reimbursements available (averaging $10,908 per year), teaching assistantships with tuition reimbursements available (averaging $10,908 per year); health care benefits and unspecified assistantships also available. Financial award application deadline: 4/1. *Faculty research:* Black feminist theory, African-American women's discursive practices, black women's leadership, feminist theory, queer theory. *Unit head:* Dr. Utz McKnight, Chair, 205-348-5528, E-mail: umcknigh@bama.ua.edu. *Application contact:* Patrick D. Fuller, Senior Graduate Admissions Counselor, 205-348-5923, Fax: 205-348-0400, E-mail: patrick.d.fuller@ua.edu.
Website: http://www.as.ua.edu/grs/

The University of Arizona, College of Social and Behavioral Sciences, Department of Gender and Women's Studies, Tucson, AZ 85721. Offers MA, PhD, Certificate. *Program availability:* Part-time. *Degree requirements:* For master's, thesis/project. *Entrance requirements:* For master's and doctorate, GRE (minimum score: 500 verbal, 500 quantitative, 4.5 analytical), 3 letters of recommendation. Additional exam requirements/recommendations for international students: Required—TOEFL (minimum score 600 paper-based; 100 iBT). Electronic applications accepted. *Faculty research:* Gender, race and border studies; sexuality and the body; gender health and science; cultural representation and theory; public policy and social movements.

University of California, Santa Barbara, Graduate Division, College of Letters and Sciences, Division of Humanities and Fine Arts, Department of English, Santa Barbara, CA 93106-3170. Offers English (PhD), including environment and society, European medieval studies, feminist studies, global studies, technology and society, translation studies, writing studies; MA/PhD. Terminal master's awarded for partial completion of doctoral program. *Degree requirements:* For doctorate, one foreign language, comprehensive exam, thesis/dissertation. *Entrance requirements:* For doctorate, GRE General Test, GRE Subject Test (English literature). Additional exam requirements/recommendations for international students: Required—TOEFL (minimum score 550 paper-based; 80 iBT), IELTS (minimum score 7). Electronic applications accepted. *Faculty research:* Medieval, Romantic and Victorian studies; gender studies and feminist theory; literature and the mind; American literature; literature and new media/information culture.

University of California, Santa Barbara, Graduate Division, College of Letters and Sciences, Division of Humanities and Fine Arts, Department of History, Santa Barbara, CA 93106-9410. Offers European medieval studies (PhD); global studies (PhD); public historical studies (PhD); technology and society (PhD); women's studies (PhD); MA/PhD. *Degree requirements:* For doctorate, variable foreign language requirement, comprehensive exam, thesis/dissertation. *Entrance requirements:* For doctorate, GRE. Additional exam requirements/recommendations for international students: Required—TOEFL (minimum score 550 paper-based; 80 iBT), IELTS (minimum score 7). Electronic applications accepted. *Faculty research:* Europe, United States, Latin America, Africa, Middle East, East Asia.

University of California, Santa Barbara, Graduate Division, College of Letters and Sciences, Division of Humanities and Fine Arts, Department of History of Art and Architecture, Santa Barbara, CA 93106-2014. Offers art history (PhD), including art history, European medieval studies, feminist studies; MA/PhD. Terminal master's awarded for partial completion of doctoral program. *Degree requirements:* For doctorate, 2 foreign languages, comprehensive exam, thesis/dissertation. *Entrance requirements:* For doctorate, GRE. Additional exam requirements/recommendations for international students: Required—TOEFL (minimum score 550 paper-based; 80 iBT), IELTS (minimum score 7). Electronic applications accepted. *Faculty research:* History of architecture, Renaissance-Italian, Baroque, American, Chinese, Japanese, contemporary, Northern Renaissance.

University of California, Santa Barbara, Graduate Division, College of Letters and Sciences, Division of Humanities and Fine Arts, Department of Religious Studies, Santa Barbara, CA 93106-3130. Offers ancient Mediterranean studies (PhD); cognitive science (PhD); European medieval studies (PhD); feminist studies (PhD); global studies (PhD); religious studies (MA, PhD); translation studies (PhD); MA/PhD. Terminal master's awarded for partial completion of doctoral program. *Degree requirements:* For master's, one foreign language, comprehensive exam (for some programs), thesis (for some programs); for doctorate, 2 foreign languages, thesis/dissertation, methodology. *Entrance requirements:* For master's and doctorate, GRE General Test. Additional exam requirements/recommendations for international students: Required—TOEFL (minimum score 550 paper-based; 80 iBT), IELTS (minimum score 7). Electronic applications accepted. *Faculty research:* Area studies; religious traditions; theory and method in the study of religion; religion, culture, and politics; spirituality and religious experience.

University of California, Santa Barbara, Graduate Division, College of Letters and Sciences, Division of Humanities and Fine Arts, Department of Spanish and Portuguese, Santa Barbara, CA 93106-4150. Offers Hispanic languages and literatures (PhD), including European medieval studies, feminist studies, Hispanic linguistics, Hispanic literature, Luso-Brazilian literature; Hispanic linguistics (MA); Luso-Brazilian literature (MA); Spanish or Spanish-American literature (MA); MA/PhD. Terminal master's awarded for partial completion of doctoral program. *Degree requirements:* For master's, 2 foreign languages, comprehensive exam (for some programs), thesis optional; for doctorate, 3 foreign languages, comprehensive exam, thesis/dissertation. *Entrance requirements:* For master's and doctorate, GRE. Additional exam requirements/recommendations for international students: Required—TOEFL (minimum score 550 paper-based; 80 iBT), IELTS (minimum score 7). Electronic applications accepted. *Faculty research:* Nineteenth-century Spanish and Portuguese literature, Spanish and Spanish-American literature, nineteenth- and twentieth-century Portuguese and Brazilian literatures, Hispanic linguistics, Catalan language and culture.

University of California, Santa Barbara, Graduate Division, College of Letters and Sciences, Division of Humanities and Fine Arts, Department of Theater and Dance, Santa Barbara, CA 93106-7060. Offers theater studies (MA, PhD), including European medieval studies (PhD), feminist studies (PhD), theatre studies (PhD); MA/PhD. Terminal master's awarded for partial completion of doctoral program. *Degree requirements:* For master's, comprehensive exam, thesis; for doctorate, one foreign language, comprehensive exam, thesis/dissertation. *Entrance requirements:* For master's and doctorate, GRE. Additional exam requirements/recommendations for international students: Required—TOEFL (minimum score 550 paper-based; 80 iBT), IELTS (minimum score 7). Electronic applications accepted. *Faculty research:* English and American theater and Ancient Greek; Spanish, Latin American and Caribbean performance; Renaissance and Baroque drama and intercultural theory; East Asian performance, gender and nationalism; Korean cultural studies, Russian literature, and Slavic folklore; history of German theater, Shakespeare, and European opera; postcolonialism, performance-based ethnography, globalism and national identity formation in Africa.

University of California, Santa Barbara, Graduate Division, College of Letters and Sciences, Division of Humanities and Fine Arts, Program in Comparative Literature, Santa Barbara, CA 93106-4130. Offers comparative literature (PhD); East Asian literatures (PhD); feminist studies (PhD); French (PhD); global studies (PhD); translation studies (PhD); MA/PhD. *Degree requirements:* For doctorate, 2 foreign languages, comprehensive exam, thesis/dissertation. *Entrance requirements:* For doctorate, GRE. Additional exam requirements/recommendations for international students: Required—TOEFL (minimum score 550 paper-based; 80 iBT), IELTS (minimum score 7). Electronic applications accepted. *Faculty research:* Comparative literary studies in global context, critical theory, translation studies, media technological studies, trauma studies.

University of California, Santa Barbara, Graduate Division, College of Letters and Sciences, Division of Social Sciences, Department of Communication, Santa Barbara, CA 93106-4020. Offers cognitive science (PhD); communication (PhD); feminist studies (PhD); language, interaction and social organization (PhD); quantitative methods in the social sciences (PhD); society and technology (PhD); MA/PhD. Terminal master's awarded for partial completion of doctoral program. *Degree requirements:* For doctorate, comprehensive exam, thesis/dissertation. *Entrance requirements:* For doctorate, GRE. Additional exam requirements/recommendations for international students: Required—

TOEFL (minimum score 80 iBT), IELTS (minimum score 7). Electronic applications accepted. *Faculty research:* Interpersonal, intergroup, intercultural, organizational, health, media.

University of California, Santa Barbara, Graduate Division, College of Letters and Sciences, Division of Social Sciences, Department of Feminist Studies, Santa Barbara, CA 93106-7110. Offers MA, PhD, MA/PhD. Terminal master's awarded for partial completion of doctoral program. *Degree requirements:* For master's, thesis (for some programs); for doctorate, one foreign language, comprehensive exam, thesis/dissertation. *Entrance requirements:* For master's and doctorate, GRE. Additional exam requirements/recommendations for international students: Required—TOEFL (minimum score 550 paper-based; 80 iBT), IELTS (minimum score 7). Electronic applications accepted. *Faculty research:* Genders and sexualities, productive and reproductive labors, race and nation, discourse and theory, media and new technologies.

University of California, Santa Barbara, Graduate Division, College of Letters and Sciences, Division of Social Sciences, Department of Sociology, Santa Barbara, CA 93106-9430. Offers interdisciplinary emphasis: Black studies (PhD); interdisciplinary emphasis: environment and society (PhD); interdisciplinary emphasis: feminist studies (PhD); interdisciplinary emphasis: global studies (PhD); interdisciplinary emphasis: language, interaction and social organization (PhD); interdisciplinary emphasis: quantitative methods in the social sciences (PhD); interdisciplinary emphasis: technology and society (PhD); sociology (PhD); MA/PhD. Terminal master's awarded for partial completion of doctoral program. *Degree requirements:* For doctorate, comprehensive exam, thesis/dissertation. *Entrance requirements:* For doctorate, GRE General Test. Additional exam requirements/recommendations for international students: Required—TOEFL (minimum score 550 paper-based; 80 iBT), IELTS (minimum score 7). Electronic applications accepted. *Faculty research:* Gender and sexualities, race/ethnicity, social movements, conversation analysis, global sociology.

University of Cincinnati, Graduate School, McMicken College of Arts and Sciences, Department of Women's, Gender, and Sexuality Studies, Cincinnati, OH 45221-0164. Offers MA, Certificate, MA/JD. *Program availability:* Part-time. Terminal master's awarded for partial completion of doctoral program. *Degree requirements:* For master's, comprehensive exam, final paper/project. *Entrance requirements:* For master's, GRE General Test, 3 letters of recommendation. Additional exam requirements/recommendations for international students: Required—TOEFL (minimum score 600 paper-based), IELTS (minimum score 6.5). Electronic applications accepted. *Expenses:* Tuition, area resident: Full-time $14,468. Tuition, state resident: full-time $14,968; part-time $754 per credit hour. Tuition, nonresident: full-time $24,210; part-time $1311 per credit hour. *International tuition:* $26,460 full-time. *Required fees:* $3958; $84 per credit hour. One-time fee: $85 full-time. Tuition and fees vary according to course load, degree level and program. *Faculty research:* Feminist legal issues, sexuality, international political economy, Latin America, cultural/literary and environmental studies.

University of Colorado Denver, College of Liberal Arts and Sciences, Program in Humanities, Denver, CO 80217. Offers community health science (MSS); humanities (MH); international studies (MSS); philosophy and theory (MH); social justice (MSS); society and the environment (MSS); visual studies (MH); women's and gender studies (MSS). *Program availability:* Part-time, evening/weekend. *Degree requirements:* For master's, 36 credit hours, project or thesis. *Entrance requirements:* For master's, writing sample, statement of purpose/letter of intent, three letters of recommendation. Additional exam requirements/recommendations for international students: Required—TOEFL (minimum score 537 paper-based; 75 iBT); Recommended—IELTS (minimum score 6.5). Electronic applications accepted. *Faculty research:* Women and gender in the classical Mediterranean, communication theory and democracy, relationship between psychology and philosophy.

University of Florida, Graduate School, College of Liberal Arts and Sciences, Center for Women's Studies and Gender Research, Gainesville, FL 32611. Offers gender and development (Graduate Certificate); women's studies (MA, Graduate Certificate); MA/JD; MA/MA. Terminal master's awarded for partial completion of doctoral program. *Degree requirements:* For master's, thesis or project. *Entrance requirements:* For master's, GRE General Test (minimum score 1000), minimum GPA of 3.2. Additional exam requirements/recommendations for international students: Required—TOEFL (minimum score 550 paper-based; 80 iBT), IELTS (minimum score 6). Electronic applications accepted. *Faculty research:* Prejudice, discrimination, intersections, resistance, history.

University of Georgia, Franklin College of Arts and Sciences, Institute for Women's Studies, Athens, GA 30602. Offers Certificate.

University of Hawaii at Manoa, Office of Graduate Education, College of Social Sciences, Advanced Women's Studies Program, Honolulu, HI 96822. Offers Graduate Certificate. *Program availability:* Part-time. *Entrance requirements:* Additional exam requirements/recommendations for international students: Required—TOEFL (minimum score 500 paper-based; 61 iBT), IELTS (minimum score 5).

The University of Iowa, Graduate College, College of Liberal Arts and Sciences, Department of Gender, Women's and Sexuality Studies, Iowa City, IA 52242-1316. Offers Certificate. *Entrance requirements:* Additional exam requirements/recommendations for international students: Required—TOEFL (minimum score 550 paper-based; 81 iBT).

University of Lethbridge, School of Graduate Studies, Lethbridge, AB T1K 3M4, Canada. Offers addictions counseling (M Sc); agricultural biotechnology (M Sc); agricultural studies (M Sc, MA); anthropology (MA); archaeology (M Sc, MA); art (MA, MFA); biochemistry (M Sc); biological sciences (M Sc); biomolecular science (PhD); biosystems and biodiversity (PhD); Canadian studies (MA); chemistry (M Sc); computer science (M Sc); computer science and geographical information science (M Sc); counseling (MC); counseling psychology (M Ed); dramatic arts (MA); earth, space, and physical science (PhD); economics (MA); education (MA, PhD); educational leadership (M Ed); English (MA); environmental science (M Sc); evolution and behavior (PhD); exercise science (M Sc); French (MA); French/German (MA); French/Spanish (MA); general education (M Ed); geography (M Sc, MA); German (MA); health sciences (M Sc); individualized multidisciplinary (M Sc, MA); kinesiology (M Sc, MA); management (M Sc), including accounting, finance, human resource management and labor relations, information systems, international management, marketing, policy and strategy; mathematics (M Sc); music (M Mus, MA); Native American studies (MA); neuroscience (M Sc, PhD); new media (MA, MFA); nursing (M Sc, MN); philosophy (MA); physics (M Sc); political science (MA); psychology (M Sc, MA); religious studies (MA); sociology (MA); theatre and dramatic arts (MFA); theoretical and computational science (PhD); urban and regional studies (MA); women and gender studies (MA). *Program availability:* Part-time, evening/weekend. *Degree requirements:* For master's, thesis (for some programs); for doctorate, comprehensive exam, thesis/dissertation. *Entrance requirements:* For master's, GMAT (for M Sc in management), bachelor's degree in related field, minimum GPA of 3.0 during previous 20 graded semester courses, 2 years' teaching or related experience (M Ed); for doctorate, master's degree, minimum graduate GPA of 3.5. Additional exam requirements/recommendations for international students: Required—TOEFL (minimum score 580 paper-based; 93 iBT). Electronic applications accepted. *Faculty research:* Movement and brain plasticity,

gibberellin physiology, photosynthesis, carbon cycling, molecular properties of main-group ring components.

University of Louisville, Graduate School, College of Arts and Sciences, Department of Women's and Gender Studies, Louisville, KY 40292. Offers MA, Certificate, MSSW/MA. *Program availability:* Part-time. *Faculty:* 6 full-time (all women), 6 part-time/adjunct (all women). *Students:* 11 full-time (10 women), 5 part-time (3 women); includes 3 minority (2 Black or African American, non-Hispanic/Latino; 1 Two or more races, non-Hispanic/Latino). Average age 31. 3 applicants, 100% accepted, 1 enrolled. In 2017, 4 master's awarded. *Degree requirements:* For master's, thesis or alternative. *Entrance requirements:* For master's, undergraduate degree; two letters of recommendation; writing sample; letter of intent. Additional exam requirements/recommendations for international students: Required—TOEFL. *Application deadline:* For fall admission, 7/15 for domestic students, 7/16 priority date for international students; for spring admission, 12/5 for domestic students, 11/5 priority date for international students; for summer admission, 4/1 for domestic students, 4/1 priority date for international students. Applications are processed on a rolling basis. Application fee: $65. *Expenses:* Tuition, state resident: full-time $12,246; part-time $681 per credit hour. Tuition, nonresident: full-time $25,486; part-time $1417 per credit hour. *Required fees:* $196. Tuition and fees vary according to course load, program and reciprocity agreements. *Financial support:* In 2017–18, 1 teaching assistantship with full tuition reimbursement (averaging $12,000 per year) was awarded; scholarships/grants, health care benefits, and tuition waivers (full) also available. Support available to part-time students. Financial award application deadline: 3/15; financial award applicants required to submit FAFSA. *Faculty research:* History of gender/sexualities/social justice, gender in popular culture/media/literature/music, black feminisms/black lesbian studies/queer studies, girl cultures, feminism and art. *Total annual research expenditures:* $67,720. *Unit head:* Dr. Diane Pecknold, Chairperson, 502-852-1254, E-mail: depeck01@louisville.edu. *Application contact:* Latonia Craig, Director of Graduate Recruitment and Diversity Retention, 502-852-5207, E-mail: gradadm@louisville.edu.
Website: http://louisville.edu/wgs/

University of Maryland, College Park, Academic Affairs, College of Arts and Humanities, Department of Women's Studies, College Park, MD 20742. Offers MA, PhD. *Degree requirements:* For master's, thesis or alternative; for doctorate, one foreign language, thesis/dissertation or alternative. *Entrance requirements:* For master's, GRE General Test, writing sample, 3 letters of recommendation. Additional exam requirements/recommendations for international students: Required—TOEFL. *Faculty research:* Gender roles, national and global diversity, sexuality.

University of Michigan, Rackham Graduate School, College of Literature, Science, and the Arts, Department of Women's Studies, Ann Arbor, MI 48109. Offers English and women's studies (PhD); history and women's studies (PhD); LGBTQ studies (Certificate); psychology and women's studies (PhD); women's studies (Certificate). *Degree requirements:* For doctorate, variable foreign language requirement, comprehensive exam (for some programs), thesis/dissertation. *Entrance requirements:* For doctorate, GRE General Test, previous undergraduate coursework in women's studies. Electronic applications accepted. *Expenses:* Tuition, state resident: full-time $22,368; part-time $1201 per credit hour. Tuition, nonresident: full-time $45,156; part-time $2467 per credit hour. *Required fees:* $376 per term. Tuition and fees vary according to course load, degree level and program. *Faculty research:* LGBTQ studies, sexuality studies, feminist science studies, global feminism, health studies, international studies, cultural studies.

University of Minnesota, Twin Cities Campus, Graduate School, College of Liberal Arts, Department of Gender, Women, and Sexuality Studies, Minneapolis, MN 55455-0213. Offers feminist studies (PhD). *Degree requirements:* For doctorate, comprehensive exam, thesis/dissertation. *Entrance requirements:* For doctorate, GRE. Additional exam requirements/recommendations for international students: Required—TOEFL (minimum score 550 paper-based). Electronic applications accepted. *Faculty research:* Transnational feminist theories, critical development theory, feminist postcolonialisms, feminist science studies and studying of health, literature, Asian diasporas, sexuality and queer theory.

University of New Hampshire, Graduate School, Interdisciplinary Programs, Program in Feminist Studies, Durham, NH 03824. Offers Postbaccalaureate Certificate. *Entrance requirements:* Additional exam requirements/recommendations for international students: Required—TOEFL (minimum score 550 paper-based; 80 iBT). *Application deadline:* For fall admission, 7/1 for domestic students; for spring admission, 12/1 for domestic students; for summer admission, 4/1 for domestic students. Application fee: $25. Electronic applications accepted. *Financial support:* Application deadline: 2/15. *Unit head:* Siobhan Senier, Coordinator, 603-862-2466, Fax: 603-862-3563, E-mail: siobhan.senier@unh.edu. *Application contact:* Julia Pond, Administrative Assistant, 603-862-2194.
Website: https://cola.unh.edu/womens-studies/program/feminist-studies-certificate

The University of North Carolina at Charlotte, College of Liberal Arts and Sciences, Interdisciplinary Liberal Arts and Sciences Programs, Charlotte, NC 28223-0001. Offers gender, sexuality, and women's studies (Graduate Certificate); gerontology (MA, Graduate Certificate); Latin American studies (MA); liberal studies (MA); organizational science (PhD); public policy (PhD). *Program availability:* Part-time, evening/weekend. *Faculty:* 1 full-time (0 women). *Students:* 66 full-time (48 women), 66 part-time (52 women); includes 41 minority (14 Black or African American, non-Hispanic/Latino; 2 Asian, non-Hispanic/Latino; 24 Hispanic/Latino; 1 Two or more races, non-Hispanic/Latino), 16 international. Average age 27. 129 applicants, 53% accepted, 43 enrolled. In 2017, 22 master's, 10 doctorates, 9 other advanced degrees awarded. *Degree requirements:* For master's, comprehensive exam (for some programs), thesis (for some programs), practicum, project; for doctorate, comprehensive exam, thesis/dissertation; for Graduate Certificate, practicum (for gerontology). *Entrance requirements:* For master's, GRE General Test or MAT, bachelor's degree from accredited college or university; official transcripts of all previous academic work attempted beyond high school with minimum overall GPA of 3.0; statement of purpose; recommendation letters; for doctorate, GRE or GMAT, statement of purpose discussing interest in program and objectives for pursuing degree, current resume or curriculum vitae, unofficial transcripts; for Graduate Certificate, bachelor's degree from accredited university and either enrolled and in good standing in a graduate degree program at UNC Charlotte or have a minimum undergraduate GPA of 3.0. Additional exam requirements/recommendations for international students: Required—TOEFL (minimum score 523 paper-based, 70 iBT) or IELTS (6.5). *Application deadline:* For fall admission, 2/15 for domestic and international students; for spring admission, 10/1 for domestic and international students; for summer admission, 4/1 for domestic and international students. Applications are processed on a rolling basis. Application fee: $75. Electronic applications accepted. *Expenses:* Tuition, state resident: full-time $4337. Tuition, nonresident: full-time $17,771. *Required fees:* $3211. Tuition and fees vary according to course load and program. *Financial support:* In 2017–18, 21 students received support, including 19 research assistantships (averaging $12,011 per year), 1 teaching assistantship (averaging $18,600 per year); career-related internships or fieldwork, institutionally sponsored loans, scholarships/grants, unspecified assistantships, and administrative assistantships also available. Support available to part-time students.

Financial award application deadline: 3/1; financial award applicants required to submit FAFSA. *Unit head:* Dr. Nancy A. Gutierrez, Dean, 704-687-0081, E-mail: ngutierr@uncc.edu. *Application contact:* Kathy B. Giddings, Director of Graduate Admissions, 704-687-5503, Fax: 704-687-3279, E-mail: gradadm@uncc.edu.
Website: http://clas.uncc.edu/academics

The University of North Carolina at Greensboro, Graduate School, College of Arts and Sciences, Department of English, Greensboro, NC 27412-5001. Offers creative writing (MFA); English (M Ed, MA, PhD, Certificate), including American literature (PhD), English (M Ed, MA), English literature (PhD), rhetoric and composition (PhD), technical writing (Certificate), women's studies (Certificate). *Degree requirements:* For master's, comprehensive exam; for doctorate, variable foreign language requirement, thesis/dissertation, preliminary exam. *Entrance requirements:* For master's, GRE General Test, minimum GPA of 3.0; for doctorate, GRE General Test, GRE Subject Test, critical writing sample, minimum GPA of 3.0. Additional exam requirements/recommendations for international students: Required—TOEFL. Electronic applications accepted.

The University of North Carolina at Greensboro, Graduate School, College of Arts and Sciences, Program in Women's and Gender Studies, Greensboro, NC 27412-5001. Offers MA, Certificate. Electronic applications accepted.

University of Northern Iowa, Graduate College, MA Program in Women's and Gender Studies, Cedar Falls, IA 50614. Offers MA. *Degree requirements:* For master's, comprehensive exam (for some programs), thesis or alternative. *Entrance requirements:* For master's, minimum GPA of 3.0. Additional exam requirements/recommendations for international students: Required—TOEFL (minimum score 500 paper-based; 61 iBT). Electronic applications accepted.

University of Oklahoma, College of Arts and Sciences, Women's and Gender Studies Department, Norman, OK 73019. Offers Graduate Certificate. *Program availability:* Part-time. *Faculty:* 1 (woman) full-time. *Students:* 2 full-time (1 woman), 10 part-time (9 women); includes 3 minority (1 Black or African American, non-Hispanic/Latino; 1 American Indian or Alaska Native, non-Hispanic/Latino; 1 Hispanic/Latino), 1 international. Average age 40. In 2017, 6 Graduate Certificates awarded. *Entrance requirements:* Additional exam requirements/recommendations for international students: Required—TOEFL (minimum score 79 iBT) or IELTS (minimum score 6.5). *Application deadline:* Applications are processed on a rolling basis. Application fee: $50 ($100 for international students). Electronic applications accepted. *Expenses:* Tuition, state resident: full-time $5119; part-time $213.30 per credit hour. Tuition, nonresident: full-time $19,778; part-time $824.10 per credit hour. *Required fees:* $3458; $133.55 per credit hour. $126.50 per semester. *Financial support:* Application deadline: 6/1; applicants required to submit FAFSA. *Faculty research:* Black feminism, terrorism, popular culture, indigenous studies, reproductive justice. *Total annual research expenditures:* $197,283. *Unit head:* Dr. Maria Lupe Davidson, Chair, 405-325-3481, E-mail: mdavidson@ou.edu.
Website: http://wgs.ou.edu

University of Ottawa, Faculty of Graduate and Postdoctoral Studies, Faculty of Social Sciences, Institute of Women's Studies, Ottawa, ON K1N 6N5, Canada. Offers criminology (MA, MCA); education (MA); English (MA); history (MA); human kinetics (MA); law (LL M); lettres Françaises (MA); nursing (M Sc); pastoral studies (MA); political science (MA); religious studies (MA); sociology (MA). *Degree requirements:* For master's, thesis or alternative.

University of Pittsburgh, Kenneth P. Dietrich School of Arts and Sciences, Gender, Sexuality, and Women's Studies Program, Pittsburgh, PA 15260. Offers Doctoral Certificate, Master's Certificate. *Program availability:* Part-time. *Faculty:* 104 full-time (78 women), 5 part-time/adjunct (4 women). *Students:* 71 full-time (49 women); includes 19 minority (6 Black or African American, non-Hispanic/Latino; 1 American Indian or Alaska Native, non-Hispanic/Latino; 3 Asian, non-Hispanic/Latino; 7 Hispanic/Latino; 2 Two or more races, non-Hispanic/Latino). Average age 31. 20 applicants, 100% accepted, 20 enrolled. *Entrance requirements:* For degree, good academic standing in a University of Pittsburgh graduate degree-granting department. Additional exam requirements/recommendations for international students: Required—TOEFL. *Application deadline:* Applications are processed on a rolling basis. Application fee: $0. Electronic applications accepted. *Financial support:* Teaching assistantships available. Financial award application deadline: 2/9. *Faculty research:* Global feminisms; intersectionality; masculinities; queer theory. *Unit head:* Dr. Todd Reeser, Director, 412-624-6486, E-mail: reeser@pitt.edu.
Website: http://www.gsws.pitt.edu/

University of Regina, Faculty of Graduate Studies and Research, Faculty of Arts, Department of Women's and Gender Studies, Regina, SK S4S 0A2, Canada. Offers MA. Offered as a special case program. *Program availability:* Part-time. *Faculty:* 3 full-time (all women), 7 part-time/adjunct (all women). *Students:* 3 full-time (all women). 1 applicant, 100% accepted. *Degree requirements:* For master's, thesis. *Entrance requirements:* Additional exam requirements/recommendations for international students: Required—TOEFL (minimum score 580 paper-based; 80 iBT), IELTS (minimum score 6.5), PTE (minimum score 59). *Application deadline:* Applications are processed on a rolling basis. Application fee: $100. Electronic applications accepted. *Expenses:* $10,681. *Financial support:* In 2017–18, 1 teaching assistantship (averaging $2,562 per year) was awarded; fellowships, research assistantships, and scholarships/grants also available. Financial award application deadline: 6/15. *Faculty research:* Feminist theory; mapping sexualities; mapping gender; women, feminism, and globalization. *Unit head:* Dr. Darlene Juschka, Department Head, 306-585-5280, E-mail: darlene.juschka@uregina.ca. *Application contact:* Bettyann Paterson, Administrative Assistant, 306-585-4972, E-mail: bettyann.paterson@uregina.ca.
Website: http://www.uregina.ca/arts/womens-gender-studies

University of Rhode Island, Graduate School, College of Arts and Sciences, Program in Gender and Women's Studies, Kingston, RI 02881. Offers Graduate Certificate. In 2017, 3 Graduate Certificates awarded. Application fee: $65. Electronic applications accepted. *Expenses:* Tuition, state resident: full-time $12,706; part-time $786 per credit. Tuition, nonresident: full-time $25,216; part-time $1401 per credit. *Required fees:* $1598; $45 per credit. One-time fee: $30 part-time. *Financial support:* In 2017–18, 1 teaching assistantship (averaging $18,080 per year) was awarded. *Unit head:* Dr. Rosaria Pisa, Director, 401-874-2482, E-mail: rpisa@uri.edu.
Website: http://web.uri.edu/gws/graduate-certificate-program/

University of Saskatchewan, College of Graduate Studies and Research, College of Arts and Science, Department of Women's and Gender Studies, Saskatoon, SK S7N 5A2, Canada. Offers MA, PhD. *Degree requirements:* For master's, thesis; for doctorate, comprehensive exam (for some programs), thesis/dissertation. *Entrance requirements:* Additional exam requirements/recommendations for international students: Required—TOEFL (minimum score 80 iBT); Recommended—IELTS (minimum score 6.5). Electronic applications accepted.

University of South Carolina, The Graduate School, College of Arts and Sciences, Program in Women's Studies, Columbia, SC 29208. Offers Certificate. *Program availability:* Part-time. *Entrance requirements:* For degree, GRE General Test or MAT. Additional exam requirements/recommendations for international students: Required—TOEFL. Electronic applications accepted. *Faculty research:* Health; pedagogy; intersection of race, class, gender; public policy; politics of culture and representations, feminist political economics.

University of South Florida, College of Arts and Sciences, Department of Women's and Gender Studies, Tampa, FL 33620-9951. Offers women's and gender studies (MA). *Program availability:* Part-time. *Faculty:* 4 full-time (3 women). *Students:* 8 full-time (all women), 3 part-time (2 women); includes 3 minority (2 Black or African American, non-Hispanic/Latino; 1 Hispanic/Latino). Average age 24. 9 applicants, 78% accepted, 4 enrolled. In 2017, 6 master's awarded. *Degree requirements:* For master's, comprehensive exam, thesis (for some programs), thesis or internship. *Entrance requirements:* For master's, GRE General Test, minimum GPA of 3.0, three letters of recommendation, personal narrative statement of purpose, scholarly writing sample (examples include term paper or research paper); undergraduate major or minor in women's studies (recommended). Additional exam requirements/recommendations for international students: Required—TOEFL (minimum score 550 paper-based; 79 iBT) or IELTS (minimum score 6.5). *Application deadline:* For fall admission, 2/15 priority date for domestic and international students; for spring admission, 10/15 priority date for domestic students, 9/15 priority date for international students; for summer admission, 2/15 priority date for domestic students, 1/15 priority date for international students. Applications are processed on a rolling basis. Application fee: $30. Electronic applications accepted. *Financial support:* In 2017–18, 3 students received support. Teaching assistantships with tuition reimbursements available available. Financial award application deadline: 3/1. *Faculty research:* Performance studies, feminist theory and pedagogy; constructions of gender in public discourse, including education, mass media, and popular culture; women's health, reproductive justice, and sexuality; bodies and cultural representations; feminist theory as it relates to learning disabilities, critical race theory, postmodernist and queer theory; hiring practices in higher education, mothering; women of color feminisms. *Unit head:* Dr. Diane Price Herndl, Professor and Chairperson, 813-974-0987, Fax: 813-974-0336, E-mail: priceherndl@usf.edu. *Application contact:* Dr. Kim Golombisky, Associate Professor and Graduate Director, 813-974-0986, Fax: 813-974-0336, E-mail: kgolombi@usf.edu.
Website: http://wgs.usf.edu/

The University of Toledo, College of Graduate Studies, College of Languages, Literature and Social Sciences, Department of Women's and Gender Studies, Toledo, OH 43606-3390. Offers Certificate. *Program availability:* Part-time.

University of Toronto, School of Graduate Studies, Faculty of Arts and Science, Women and Gender Studies Institute, Toronto, ON M5S 1A1, Canada. Offers MA, PhD. *Entrance requirements:* For master's, minimum B+ in final year of undergraduate study. Additional exam requirements/recommendations for international students: Required—TOEFL (minimum score 580 paper-based; 93 iBT), TWE (minimum score 5). Electronic applications accepted.

University of Washington, Graduate School, College of Arts and Sciences, Department of Gender, Women and Sexuality Studies, Seattle, WA 98195. Offers PhD. Terminal master's awarded for partial completion of doctoral program. *Degree requirements:* For doctorate, one foreign language, thesis/dissertation, exam. *Entrance requirements:* For doctorate, GRE General Test. Additional exam requirements/recommendations for international students: Required—TOEFL. Electronic applications accepted. *Faculty research:* Women's history in U.S. and China; Native American ethnography and identity; women, science, and technology; political economy of development, feminism and nationalism.

University of Wisconsin–Madison, Graduate School, College of Letters and Science, Department of History, Madison, WI 53706-1380. Offers African history (MA, PhD); Central Asian history (MA, PhD); comparative world history (MA, PhD); East Asian history (MA, PhD); European history (MA, PhD); gender and women's history (MA, PhD); Latin American and Caribbean history (MA, PhD); Middle Eastern history (MA, PhD); South Asian history (MA, PhD); Southeast Asian history (MA, PhD); United States history (MA, PhD). Terminal master's awarded for partial completion of doctoral program. *Degree requirements:* For master's, thesis (for some programs); for doctorate, variable foreign language requirement, thesis/dissertation. *Entrance requirements:* For master's and doctorate, GRE General Test. Additional exam requirements/recommendations for international students: Required—Michigan English Language Assessment Battery or TOEFL. Electronic applications accepted. *Faculty research:* American, African, European, Asian, Latin American, and Middle Eastern history.

University of Wisconsin–Milwaukee, Graduate School, College of Letters and Science, Department of Women's and Gender Studies, Milwaukee, WI 53201-0413. Offers MA, Graduate Certificate. *Program availability:* Part-time. *Students:* 2 full-time (both women), 4 part-time (all women); includes 2 minority (1 Black or African American, non-Hispanic/Latino; 1 Two or more races, non-Hispanic/Latino). Average age 37. 9 applicants, 100% accepted, 2 enrolled. In 2017, 3 master's, 2 other advanced degrees awarded. *Entrance requirements:* For master's, three letters of recommendation, sample of written work, letter of intent. Application fee: $56 ($96 for international students). Electronic applications accepted. *Financial support:* Fellowships, research assistantships, teaching assistantships with full tuition reimbursements, health care benefits, and unspecified assistantships available. Financial award applicants required to submit FAFSA. *Unit head:* Dr. Gwynne Kennedy, Director, 414-229-5918, E-mail: gkennedy@uwm.edu. *Application contact:* General Information Contact, 414-229-4982, Fax: 414-229-6967, E-mail: gradschool@uwm.edu.
Website: http://uwm.edu/womens-gender-studies/

Wayne State University, College of Liberal Arts and Sciences, Department of History, Detroit, MI 48202. Offers history (MA, PhD); public history (MA), including African American history and culture, cultural resource management, gender, sexuality, and women's studies, labor and urban history, museum studies, public policy; world history (Graduate Certificate); JD/MA; M Ed/MA; MLIS/MA. Doctoral program admits for fall only. *Program availability:* Evening/weekend. *Faculty:* 17. *Students:* 21 full-time (7 women), 20 part-time (7 women); includes 9 minority (5 Black or African American, non-Hispanic/Latino; 1 Hispanic/Latino; 3 Two or more races, non-Hispanic/Latino). Average age 40. 50 applicants, 16% accepted, 5 enrolled. In 2017, 11 master's, 2 doctorates awarded. *Degree requirements:* For master's, comprehensive exam, thesis (for some programs), final oral exam on thesis or essay and seminar; internship and project (for public history); for doctorate, variable foreign language requirement, comprehensive exam, thesis/dissertation, qualifying exam in 4 fields of history. *Entrance requirements:* For master's, GRE General Test, minimum undergraduate GPA of 3.25 in history, 3.0 overall; at least 18 credits in history and related subjects at the advanced undergraduate level; foreign language; letter of intent; research paper; at least two letters of recommendation from former instructors; for doctorate, GRE General Test, minimum GPA of 3.0, 3.25 in minimum of 18 semester credits in history and related subjects; letter of intent; research paper; at least three letters of recommendation from former professors; for Graduate Certificate, baccalaureate degree from accredited college or university; minimum GPA of 3.0, 3.25 in a minimum of eighteen semester credits in history and related subjects at the advanced undergraduate level. Additional exam requirements/recommendations for international students: Required—TOEFL (minimum score 550 paper-based; 79 iBT), TWE (minimum score 5.5), Michigan English Language Assessment Battery (minimum score 85); Recommended—IELTS (minimum score 6.5). *Application deadline:* For fall admission, 2/1 priority date for domestic and international

students; for winter admission, 11/1 for domestic students, 10/1 priority date for international students; for spring admission, 2/1 for domestic students, 1/1 priority date for international students. Application fee: $50. Electronic applications accepted. *Expenses:* Tuition, state resident: full-time $10,224; part-time $638.98 per credit hour. Tuition, nonresident: full-time $22,145; part-time $1384.04 per credit hour. Tuition and fees vary according to course load and program. *Financial support:* In 2017–18, 17 students received support, including 3 fellowships with tuition reimbursements available (averaging $17,198 per year), 1 research assistantship with tuition reimbursement available (averaging $22,241 per year), 6 teaching assistantships with tuition reimbursements available (averaging $18,534 per year); scholarships/grants, health care benefits, and unspecified assistantships also available. Financial award applicants required to submit FAFSA. *Faculty research:* Urban history, labor, political history, history of gender and women. *Unit head:* Dr. Elizabeth V. Faue, Professor/Chair, 313-577-2525, E-mail: evfaue@wayne.edu. *Application contact:* Dr. Eric Ash, Associate Professor and Director of Graduate Studies, 313-577-2525, E-mail: ericash@wayne.edu.
Website: http://clas.wayne.edu/history/

Western Seminary, Graduate Programs, Program in Ministry and Leadership, Portland, OR 97215-3367. Offers chaplaincy (MA); coaching (MA); Jewish ministry (MA); pastoral care to women (MA); youth ministry (MA). *Degree requirements:* For master's, practicum. *Entrance requirements:* Additional exam requirements/recommendations for international students: Required—TOEFL.

Western Seminary–Sacramento Campus, Graduate Certificate Programs, Rocklin, CA 95765. Offers Bible (Graduate Certificate); coaching (Graduate Certificate); pastoral care to women (Graduate Certificate); theology (Graduate Certificate); youth and family (Graduate Certificate). *Program availability:* Online learning. *Entrance requirements:* For degree, essays, undergraduate transcripts, 4 recommendations. Additional exam requirements/recommendations for international students: Required—TOEFL.

Western Seminary–Sacramento Campus, Graduate Diploma Programs, Rocklin, CA 95765. Offers Bible and theology (Graduate Diploma); ministry (Graduate Diploma); pastoral care to women (Graduate Diploma). *Entrance requirements:* For degree, essays, undergraduate transcripts, 4 recommendations. Additional exam requirements/ recommendations for international students: Required—TOEFL.

Western Seminary–San Jose Campus, Graduate Programs, Milpitas, CA 95035. Offers Bible and theology (Graduate Diploma); Bible, camp and conference ministry (CGS); Biblical and theological studies (MA), including exegetical track, theological track; coaching (CGS); expositional ministry (M Div); marital and family therapy (MA); ministry (Graduate Diploma); ministry and leadership (MA), including camp and conference ministry, coaching, pastoral care to women, youth ministry; pastoral care to women (CGS, Graduate Diploma); pastoral ministry (M Div); theology (CGS); youth and family (CGS). *Program availability:* Part-time, evening/weekend, online learning. *Entrance requirements:* For master's, minimum GPA of 3.0. Electronic applications accepted.

Wilson College, Graduate Programs, Chambersburg, PA 17201-1285. Offers accounting (M Acc); choreography and visual art (MFA); education (M Ed); educational technology (MET); healthcare administration (MHA); humanities (MA), including art and culture, critical/cultural theory, English language and literature, women's studies; management (MSM); nursing (MSN), including nursing education, nursing leadership and management; special education (MSE). *Program availability:* Evening/weekend. *Degree requirements:* For master's, project. *Entrance requirements:* For master's, PRAXIS, minimum undergraduate cumulative GPA of 3.0, 2 letters of recommendation, current certification for eligibility to teach in grades K-12, resume, personal interview. Electronic applications accepted.

York University, Faculty of Graduate Studies, Faculty of Liberal Arts and Professional Studies, Program in Gender, Feminist and Women's Studies, Toronto, ON M3J 1P3, Canada. Offers MA, PhD. *Degree requirements:* For master's, thesis or alternative; for doctorate, comprehensive exam, thesis/dissertation. Electronic applications accepted.

Section 16
Communication and Media

This section contains a directory of institutions offering graduate work in communication and media, followed by an in-depth entry submitted by an institution that chose to prepare a detailed program description. Additional information about programs listed in the directory but not augmented by an in-depth entry may be obtained by writing directly to the dean of a graduate school or chair of a department at the address given in the directory.

For programs offering related work, see also in this book *Film, Television, and Video; Language and Literature;* and *Psychology and Counseling.* In the other guides in this series:

Graduate Programs in Engineering & Applied Sciences

See *Computer Science and Information Technology* and *Telecommunications*

Graduate Programs in Business, Education, Information Studies, Law & Social Work

See *Advertising and Public Relations*

CONTENTS

Communication—General

Abilene Christian University, Graduate Programs, College of Arts and Sciences, Department of Communication, Abilene, TX 79699. Offers corporate communication (MA). *Program availability:* Part-time. *Faculty:* 13 part-time/adjunct (7 women). *Students:* 6 full-time (5 women), 2 part-time (both women); includes 4 minority (1 Black or African American, non-Hispanic/Latino; 2 American Indian or Alaska Native, non-Hispanic/Latino; 1 Hispanic/Latino). 16 applicants, 13% accepted, 2 enrolled. In 2017, 4 master's awarded. *Degree requirements:* For master's, comprehensive exam, thesis. *Entrance requirements:* For master's, GRE General Test. Additional exam requirements/recommendations for international students: Required—TOEFL (minimum score 80 iBT), IELTS (minimum score 6), PTE. *Application deadline:* For fall admission, 4/1 priority date for domestic students; for spring admission, 11/1 for domestic students. Applications are processed on a rolling basis. Application fee: $50. Electronic applications accepted. *Expenses:* $1,148 per hour. *Financial support:* In 2017–18, 13 students received support, including 3 research assistantships with partial tuition reimbursements available (averaging $5,800 per year), 6 teaching assistantships with partial tuition reimbursements available (averaging $5,800 per year); Federal Work-Study also available. Support available to part-time students. Financial award application deadline: 4/1; financial award applicants required to submit FAFSA. *Faculty research:* Intercultural communication, family communication, forensics, interpersonal communication. *Unit head:* Dr. Lauren Lemley, Graduate Director, 325-674-2136, E-mail: lauren.lemley@acu.edu. *Application contact:* Graduate Admissions, 325-674-6911, Fax: 325-674-6717, E-mail: gradinfo@acu.edu.
Website: http://www.acu.edu/graduate/academics/communication.html

American University, School of Communication, Washington, DC 20016. Offers MA, MFA, PhD. *Accreditation:* ACEJMC (one or more programs are accredited). *Program availability:* Part-time, evening/weekend, 100% online. *Faculty:* 59 full-time (32 women), 33 part-time/adjunct (19 women). *Students:* 188 full-time (117 women), 229 part-time (163 women); includes 144 minority (81 Black or African American, non-Hispanic/Latino; 2 American Indian or Alaska Native, non-Hispanic/Latino; 14 Asian, non-Hispanic/Latino; 35 Hispanic/Latino; 2 Native Hawaiian or other Pacific Islander, non-Hispanic/Latino; 10 Two or more races, non-Hispanic/Latino), 37 international. 955 applicants, 30% accepted, 139 enrolled. In 2017, 137 master's, 2 doctorates awarded. *Degree requirements:* For master's, comprehensive exam, thesis or alternative; for doctorate, comprehensive exam, thesis/dissertation. *Entrance requirements:* For doctorate, GRE General Test. Additional exam requirements/recommendations for international students: Required—TOEFL (minimum score 600 paper-based; 100 iBT), IELTS (minimum score 7). *Application deadline:* For fall admission, 2/1 priority date for domestic and international students; for spring admission, 11/1 for domestic and international students. Applications are processed on a rolling basis. Application fee: $55. Electronic applications accepted. *Expenses: Tuition:* Full-time $29,556. *Required fees:* $690. Tuition and fees vary according to course load and program. *Financial support:* In 2017–18, 150 students received support, including 3 fellowships with partial tuition reimbursements available (averaging $20,000 per year), 46 research assistantships with partial tuition reimbursements available (averaging $10,000 per year), 45 teaching assistantships with partial tuition reimbursements available (averaging $10,000 per year); career-related internships or fieldwork, Federal Work-Study, institutionally sponsored loans, scholarships/grants, health care benefits, tuition waivers (partial), and unspecified assistantships also available. Support available to part-time students. Financial award application deadline: 2/1; financial award applicants required to submit FAFSA. *Faculty research:* New communication technology; documentaries and public broadcasting; litigation and public relations; dissident media; race, gender, and the media; international journalism and human rights; social media. *Unit head:* Dr. Jeffrey Rutenbeck, Dean, 202-885-2058, Fax: 202-885-2099, E-mail: jeff@american.edu. *Application contact:* Christine Rials, Assistant Director for Graduate Admissions, 202-885-2040, Fax: 202-885-2019, E-mail: gradcomm@american.edu.
Website: http://www.soc.american.edu/

The American University in Cairo, School of Sciences and Engineering, Cairo, Egypt. Offers biotechnology (MS); chemistry (MS); computer science (MS); computing (M Comp); construction engineering (M Eng, MS); electronics and communications engineering (M Eng); environmental engineering (MS); environmental system design (M Eng); mechanical engineering (M Eng, MS); nanotechnology (MS); physics (MS); robotics, control and smart systems (MS); sciences and engineering (PhD); sustainable development (MS, Graduate Diploma). *Program availability:* Part-time, evening/weekend. *Faculty:* 53 full-time (8 women), 12 part-time/adjunct (0 women). *Students:* 62 full-time (26 women), 210 part-time (104 women), 14 international. Average age 28. 252 applicants, 39% accepted, 51 enrolled. In 2017, 71 master's, 10 doctorates awarded. *Degree requirements:* For master's, comprehensive exam (for some programs), thesis (for some programs); for doctorate, comprehensive exam (for some programs), thesis/dissertation. *Entrance requirements:* Additional exam requirements/recommendations for international students: Required—TOEFL (minimum score 450 paper-based; 45 iBT), IELTS (minimum score 5). *Application deadline:* For fall admission, 2/1 priority date for domestic and international students; for spring admission, 10/15 priority date for domestic and international students. Applications are processed on a rolling basis. Application fee: $85. Electronic applications accepted. *Financial support:* Fellowships with partial tuition reimbursements, scholarships/grants, and unspecified assistantships available. Financial award application deadline: 3/10. *Faculty research:* Construction, mechanical, and electronics engineering; physics; computer science; biotechnology; nanotechnology; chemistry; robotics. *Unit head:* Dr. Hassan El Fawal, Dean, 20-2-2615-2926, E-mail: hassan.elfawal@aucegypt.edu. *Application contact:* Maha Hegazi, Director for Graduate Admissions, 20-2-2615-1462, E-mail: mahahegazi@aucegypt.edu.
Website: http://www.aucegypt.edu/sse/Pages/default.aspx

The American University of Paris, Graduate Programs, Paris, France. Offers cross-cultural and sustainable business management (MA); cultural translation (MA); global communications (MA); global communications and civil society (MA); international affairs (MA); international affairs, conflict resolution and civil society development (MA); Middle East and Islamic studies (MA); Middle East and Islamic studies and international affairs (MA); public policy and international affairs (MA); public policy and international law (MA). *Degree requirements:* For master's, thesis (for some programs). *Entrance requirements:* For master's, minimum undergraduate GPA of 3.0. Additional exam requirements/recommendations for international students: Recommended—TOEFL, IELTS. Electronic applications accepted.

Andrews University, School of Graduate Studies, College of Arts and Sciences, Interdisciplinary Studies in Communication Program, Berrien Springs, MI 49104. Offers MA. *Faculty:* 3 full-time (all women). *Students:* 3 full-time (2 women), 1 (woman) part-time; includes 2 minority (both Black or African American, non-Hispanic/Latino), 2 international. Average age 35. 14 applicants, 29% accepted, 2 enrolled. In 2017, 4 master's awarded. *Application deadline:* Applications are processed on a rolling basis. Application fee: $40. *Unit head:* Steve Hanson, Chair, 269-471-3126. *Application contact:* Justina Clayburn, Supervisor of Graduate Admission, 800-253-2874, Fax: 269-471-3228, E-mail: graduate@andrews.edu.
Website: https://www.andrews.edu/wp/comm/graduate-degrees/program-information.html

Angelo State University, College of Graduate Studies and Research, College of Arts and Humanities, Department of Communication and Mass Media, San Angelo, TX 76909. Offers communication (MA). *Program availability:* Part-time, evening/weekend. *Students:* 9 full-time (4 women), 10 part-time (5 women); includes 9 minority (3 Black or African American, non-Hispanic/Latino; 6 Hispanic/Latino), 5 international. Average age 29. *Degree requirements:* For master's, comprehensive exam, thesis optional. *Entrance requirements:* Additional exam requirements/recommendations for international students: Required—TOEFL or IELTS. *Application deadline:* For fall admission, 7/15 priority date for domestic students, 6/10 for international students; for spring admission, 12/1 priority date for domestic students, 11/1 for international students. Applications are processed on a rolling basis. Application fee: $40 ($50 for international students). Electronic applications accepted. *Expenses:* Tuition, state resident: full-time $3856. Tuition, nonresident: full-time $11,324. *Required fees:* $2650. *Financial support:* Teaching assistantships, career-related internships or fieldwork, Federal Work-Study, scholarships/grants, and unspecified assistantships available. Support available to part-time students. Financial award application deadline: 3/1; financial award applicants required to submit FAFSA. *Unit head:* Dr. Herman Otis Howard, Chair, 325-942-2031, Fax: 325-942-2551, E-mail: herman.howard@angelo.edu. *Application contact:* Dr. June H. Smith, Graduate Advisor, 325-486-6088, Fax: 325-942-2551, E-mail: june.smith@angelo.edu.
Website: http://www.angelo.edu/dept/communication-mass-media/

Arizona State University at the Tempe campus, College of Liberal Arts and Sciences, Hugh Downs School of Human Communication, Tempe, AZ 85287. Offers communication (PhD). *Program availability:* Evening/weekend. *Degree requirements:* For doctorate, comprehensive exam, thesis/dissertation, interactive Program of Study (iPOS) submitted before completing 50 percent of required credit hours. *Entrance requirements:* For doctorate, GRE, minimum GPA of 3.0 or equivalent in last 2 years of work leading to bachelor's degree. Additional exam requirements/recommendations for international students: Required—TOEFL, IELTS, or PTE. Electronic applications accepted.

Arizona State University at the Tempe campus, New College of Interdisciplinary Arts and Sciences, Program in Communication Studies, Phoenix, AZ 85069-7100. Offers MA. *Program availability:* Part-time, evening/weekend. *Degree requirements:* For master's, thesis, applied project or written comprehensive exam; interactive Program of Study (iPOS) submitted before completing 50 percent of required credit hours. *Entrance requirements:* For master's, GRE (if GPA less than 3.0 in last 60 hours of undergraduate study), minimum GPA of 3.0 or equivalent in last 2 years of work leading to bachelor's degree, 3 letters of recommendation, official transcripts, writing sample of scholarly work or example of professional activities. Additional exam requirements/recommendations for international students: Required—TOEFL, IELTS, or PTE. Electronic applications accepted. *Faculty research:* Organizational, applied, and environmental communication; intergenerational family communication and its connectedness to wellness; communication in personal and work relationships; popular culture; technology and culture; cultural dimensions of new mobile communication and computing technologies.

Arkansas State University, Graduate School, College of Media and Communication, Department of Communication, State University, AR 72467. Offers communication studies (MA, SCCT); health communications (Graduate Certificate). *Program availability:* Part-time. *Degree requirements:* For master's, one foreign language, comprehensive exam, thesis or alternative; for other advanced degree, comprehensive exam. *Entrance requirements:* For master's, GRE General Test or MAT, appropriate bachelor's degree, writing sample, letter of recommendation, official transcripts, immunization records; for other advanced degree, GRE or MAT, appropriate master's degree, interview, official transcript, immunization records. Additional exam requirements/recommendations for international students: Required—TOEFL (minimum score 550 paper-based; 79 iBT), IELTS (minimum score 6), PTE (minimum score 56). Electronic applications accepted.

Ashland University, College of Arts and Sciences, Program in Corporate and Strategic Communication, Ashland, OH 44805-3702. Offers communication (MA). *Program availability:* Online learning. *Application deadline:* Applications are processed on a rolling basis. Electronic applications accepted. *Expenses: Tuition:* Full-time $9621; part-time $4707 per credit hour. *Required fees:* $15 per semester. *Unit head:* Shawn Orr, Interim Director, 419-207-6929, E-mail: sorr3@ashland.edu. *Application contact:* Bernie Bannin, Director, Graduate, Online, and Adult Admissions, 419-289-5291, E-mail: grad-admissions@ashland.edu.

Auburn University, Graduate School, College of Liberal Arts, School of Communication and Journalism, Auburn University, AL 36849. Offers MA, Graduate Certificate. *Program availability:* Part-time. *Faculty:* 31 full-time (17 women), 9 part-time/adjunct (4 women). *Students:* 17 full-time (13 women), 2 part-time (both women); includes 6 minority (2 Black or African American, non-Hispanic/Latino; 1 Asian, non-Hispanic/Latino; 2 Hispanic/Latino; 1 Two or more races, non-Hispanic/Latino), 3 international. Average age 25. 20 applicants, 65% accepted, 9 enrolled. In 2017, 14 master's awarded. *Degree requirements:* For master's, thesis (for some programs). *Entrance requirements:* For master's, GRE General Test. *Application deadline:* Applications are processed on a rolling basis. Application fee: $50 ($60 for international students). Electronic applications accepted. *Expenses:* Tuition, state resident: full-time $10,974; part-time $519 per credit hour. Tuition, nonresident: full-time $29,658; part-time $1557 per credit hour. *Required fees:* $816 per semester. Tuition and fees vary according to degree level and program. *Financial support:* Teaching assistantships and Federal Work-Study available. Support available to part-time students. Financial award application deadline: 3/15; financial award applicants required to submit FAFSA. *Unit head:* Dr. Jennifer Adams, Director, 334-844-2751. *Application contact:* Dr. George Flowers, Dean of the Graduate School, 334-844-2125.
Website: http://www.cla.auburn.edu/cmjn/

Austin Peay State University, College of Graduate Studies, College of Arts and Letters, Department of Communication, Clarksville, TN 37044. Offers marketing communication (MA); media management (MA). *Program availability:* Part-time, evening/weekend, online learning. *Faculty:* 4 full-time (2 women), 1 (woman) part-time/adjunct. *Students:* 45 part-time (32 women); includes 14 minority (11 Black or African American, non-Hispanic/Latino; 2 Hispanic/Latino; 1 Two or more races, non-Hispanic/Latino). Average age 29. 27 applicants, 96% accepted, 19 enrolled. In 2017, 27 master's

awarded. *Degree requirements:* For master's, comprehensive exam, thesis (for some programs). *Entrance requirements:* For master's, GRE General Test, minimum GPA of 2.5. Additional exam requirements/recommendations for international students: Required—TOEFL (minimum score 500 paper-based). *Application deadline:* For fall admission, 8/8 priority date for domestic students. Applications are processed on a rolling basis. Application fee: $45 ($55 for international students). Electronic applications accepted. *Expenses:* Tuition, state resident: full-time $7686; part-time $427 per credit hour. Tuition, nonresident: full-time $20,268; part-time $1126 per credit hour. *Required fees:* $1529; $76.45 per credit hour. *Financial support:* Research assistantships with full tuition reimbursements, career-related internships or fieldwork, Federal Work-Study, institutionally sponsored loans, scholarships/grants, and unspecified assistantships available. Support available to part-time students. Financial award application deadline: 4/1; financial award applicants required to submit FAFSA. *Unit head:* Dr. Kathy Heuston, Interim Chair, 931-221-7554, Fax: 931-221-7265, E-mail: leek@apsu.edu. *Application contact:* Megan Mitchell, Coordinator of Graduate Admissions, 931-221-6189, Fax: 931-221-7641, E-mail: mitchellm@apsu.edu.
Website: http://www.apsu.edu/communication/index.php

Ball State University, Graduate School, College of Communication, Information, and Media, Muncie, IN 47306. Offers MA, MS, Certificate. *Program availability:* Part-time, 100% online, blended/hybrid learning. *Students:* 115 full-time (66 women), 100 part-time (59 women); includes 42 minority (21 Black or African American, non-Hispanic/Latino; 1 Asian, non-Hispanic/Latino; 11 Hispanic/Latino; 9 Two or more races, non-Hispanic/Latino), 15 international. Average age 28. 202 applicants, 71% accepted, 117 enrolled. In 2017, 97 master's, 10 other advanced degrees awarded. *Degree requirements:* For master's, comprehensive exam (for some programs), thesis (for some programs). *Entrance requirements:* For master's, GRE (for some programs), minimum baccalaureate GPA of 2.75 or 3.0 in latter half of baccalaureate. Additional exam requirements/recommendations for international students: Required—TOEFL (minimum score 550 paper-based; 79 iBT), IELTS (minimum score 6.5). *Application deadline:* For fall admission, 1/1 priority date for international students; for spring admission, 7/1 priority date for international students. Applications are processed on a rolling basis. Application fee: $60. Electronic applications accepted. *Financial support:* In 2017–18, 68 students received support, including 26 research assistantships with partial tuition reimbursements available (averaging $8,911 per year), 38 teaching assistantships with partial tuition reimbursements available (averaging $11,503 per year); unspecified assistantships also available. Financial award application deadline: 3/1; financial award applicants required to submit FAFSA. *Unit head:* Roger Lavery, Dean, 765-285-6000, Fax: 765-285-6002, E-mail: rlavery@bsu.edu.
Website: http://www.bsu.edu/ccim

Barry University, College of Arts and Sciences, Department of Communication, Miami Shores, FL 33161-6695. Offers broadcasting (Certificate); communication (MA), including broadcast communication, public relations and corporate communications; organizational communication (MS). *Program availability:* Part-time, evening/weekend. *Degree requirements:* For master's, thesis (for some programs). *Entrance requirements:* For master's, GRE General Test, MAT, minimum GPA of 3.0. Electronic applications accepted. *Faculty research:* Organizational communication, broadcast communication, intercultural communication, advertising, leadership.

Baylor University, Graduate School, College of Arts and Sciences, Department of Communication, Waco, TX 76798. Offers MA. *Program availability:* Part-time. *Students:* 25 full-time (10 women), 2 part-time (1 woman); includes 10 minority (2 Black or African American, non-Hispanic/Latino; 1 Asian, non-Hispanic/Latino; 5 Hispanic/Latino; 2 Two or more races, non-Hispanic/Latino), 1 international. Average age 24. 42 applicants, 48% accepted, 18 enrolled. In 2017, 10 master's awarded. *Entrance requirements:* For master's, GRE General Test, transcripts; 3 letters of recommendation; personal statement of intent; scholarly writing sample. Additional exam requirements/recommendations for international students: Required—TOEFL, IELTS, PTE. *Application deadline:* Applications are processed on a rolling basis. Application fee: $50. Electronic applications accepted. *Financial support:* In 2017–18, 14 students received support. Research assistantships, teaching assistantships, career-related internships or fieldwork, Federal Work-Study, institutionally sponsored loans, scholarships/grants, and tuition waivers (full and partial) available. Financial award application deadline: 2/1; financial award applicants required to submit CSS PROFILE. *Faculty research:* Rhetoric, interpersonal and family communication, organizational communication, film and digital media, new technology. *Unit head:* Dr. Mark T. Morman, Graduate Program Director, 254-710-1621, Fax: 254-710-1563, E-mail: mark_morman@baylor.edu. *Application contact:* Marilyn Spivey, Office Manager, 254-710-1621, Fax: 254-710-1563, E-mail: marilyn_spivey@baylor.edu.
Website: http://www.baylor.edu/comm_studies/

Bellarmine University, School of Communication, Louisville, KY 40205. Offers MA, MSDM. *Program availability:* Part-time, evening/weekend. *Faculty:* 6 full-time (3 women). *Students:* 9 full-time (6 women), 29 part-time (15 women); includes 4 minority (all Black or African American, non-Hispanic/Latino), 5 international. Average age 26. In 2017, 10 master's awarded. *Degree requirements:* For master's, thesis optional. *Entrance requirements:* For master's, personal statement; professional/academic writing sample; essay; letters of recommendation; resume. Additional exam requirements/recommendations for international students: Required—TOEFL (minimum score 550 paper-based; 80 iBT). *Application deadline:* Applications are processed on a rolling basis. Application fee: $40. Electronic applications accepted. Tuition and fees vary according to program. *Financial support:* Applicants required to submit FAFSA. *Unit head:* Dr. Lara Needham, Dean, 502-272-7965, E-mail: lneedham@bellarmine.edu. *Application contact:* Dr. Sara Pettingill, Dean of Graduate Admission, 502-272-8401, Fax: 502-272-8002, E-mail: spettingill@bellarmine.edu.
Website: https://www.bellarmine.edu/communication/

Boise State University, College of Arts and Sciences, Department of Communication, Boise, ID 83725-0399. Offers MA. *Program availability:* Part-time. *Faculty:* 8. *Students:* 10 full-time (5 women), 11 part-time (8 women); includes 5 minority (1 Asian, non-Hispanic/Latino; 3 Hispanic/Latino; 1 Two or more races, non-Hispanic/Latino). Average age 34. 20 applicants, 45% accepted, 6 enrolled. In 2017, 3 master's awarded. *Degree requirements:* For master's, thesis. *Entrance requirements:* For master's, GRE General Test, minimum GPA of 3.0, writing sample. Additional exam requirements/recommendations for international students: Required—TOEFL (minimum score 550 paper-based; 80 iBT), IELTS (minimum score 6). *Application deadline:* For fall admission, 2/15 for domestic and international students. Application fee: $65 ($95 for international students). Electronic applications accepted. *Expenses:* Tuition, state resident: full-time $6471; part-time $390 per credit. Tuition, nonresident: full-time $21,787; part-time $685 per credit. *Required fees:* $2283; $100 per term. Part-time tuition and fees vary according to course load and program. *Financial support:* Research assistantships, teaching assistantships, and unspecified assistantships available. Financial award application deadline: 2/15; financial award applicants required to submit FAFSA. *Unit head:* Todd Norton, Department Chair, 208-426-1922, E-mail: toddnorton@boisestate.edu. *Application contact:* Dr. John McClellan, Director of Graduate Studies, 208-426-2450, E-mail: johnmcclellan@boisestate.edu.
Website: http://communication.boisestate.edu/

Boston University, College of Communication, Department of Mass Communication, Advertising, and Public Relations, Boston, MA 02215. Offers advertising (MS); mass communication (MS), including communication studies, marketing communication research; public relations (MS); JD/MS. *Program availability:* Part-time. *Faculty:* 26 full-time, 33 part-time/adjunct. *Students:* 231 full-time (195 women), 8 part-time (6 women); includes 22 minority (8 Black or African American, non-Hispanic/Latino; 2 Asian, non-Hispanic/Latino; 8 Hispanic/Latino; 4 Two or more races, non-Hispanic/Latino), 173 international. Average age 23. 529 applicants, 67% accepted, 126 enrolled. In 2017, 106 master's awarded. *Degree requirements:* For master's, comprehensive exam (for some programs), thesis (for some programs). *Entrance requirements:* For master's, GRE General Test, resume, letters of recommendation, personal statement. Additional exam requirements/recommendations for international students: Required—TOEFL (minimum score 600 paper-based; 100 iBT), IELTS (minimum score 7). *Application deadline:* For fall admission, 5/1 for domestic and international students. Applications are processed on a rolling basis. Application fee: $95. Electronic applications accepted. *Financial support:* Research assistantships, teaching assistantships with partial tuition reimbursements, career-related internships or fieldwork, Federal Work-Study, scholarships/grants, and unspecified assistantships available. Support available to part-time students. Financial award application deadline: 5/1; financial award applicants required to submit FAFSA. *Unit head:* Christopher Beaudoin, Chairperson, 617-353-3482, E-mail: mcadvpr@bu.edu. *Application contact:* Jackie Cummings, Admission and Financial Aid Counselor, 617-353-3481, E-mail: comgrad@bu.edu.
Website: http://www.bu.edu/com/academics/masscomm-ad-pr/

Bowling Green State University, Graduate College, College of Arts and Sciences, School of Media and Communication, Bowling Green, OH 43403. Offers media and communication (MA, PhD); strategic communication (MA). *Program availability:* Part-time. Terminal master's awarded for partial completion of doctoral program. *Degree requirements:* For master's, thesis or alternative; for doctorate, comprehensive exam, thesis/dissertation. *Entrance requirements:* For master's and doctorate, GRE General Test. Additional exam requirements/recommendations for international students: Required—TOEFL. Electronic applications accepted.

Brigham Young University, Graduate Studies, College of Fine Arts and Communications, School of Communications, Provo, UT 84602. Offers mass communications (MA). *Faculty:* 18 full-time (2 women). *Students:* 19 full-time (13 women), 16 part-time (10 women); includes 6 minority (2 Asian, non-Hispanic/Latino; 4 Hispanic/Latino), 4 international. Average age 30. 15 applicants, 87% accepted, 12 enrolled. In 2017, 15 master's awarded. *Degree requirements:* For master's, comprehensive exam, thesis. *Entrance requirements:* For master's, GRE, minimum GPA of 3.0 in last 60 hours of course work. Additional exam requirements/recommendations for international students: Required—TOEFL (minimum score 580 paper-based; 85 iBT). *Application deadline:* For fall admission, 3/31 priority date for domestic and international students. Applications are processed on a rolling basis. Application fee: $50. Electronic applications accepted. *Expenses: Tuition:* Full-time $6880; part-time $405 per credit hour. Tuition and fees vary according to course load, program and student's religious affiliation. *Financial support:* In 2017–18, 19 students received support, including 30 research assistantships with full and partial tuition reimbursements available (averaging $3,101 per year), 1 teaching assistantship with full tuition reimbursement available (averaging $2,752 per year); scholarships/grants and supplementary awards also available. Financial award application deadline: 4/30; financial award applicants required to submit FAFSA. *Faculty research:* Ethics, international, magazine, newspaper, media effects, social media. *Unit head:* Edward Carter, Director, 801-422-2997, Fax: 801-422-0160, E-mail: comms_secretary@byu.edu. *Application contact:* Debby Jackson, Graduate Program Manager, 801-422-2632, Fax: 801-422-0160, E-mail: debby_jackson@byu.edu.
Website: http://cfac.byu.edu/departments/communications

Bryant University, College of Arts and Sciences, Smithfield, RI 02917. Offers applied economics (MS, Graduate Certificate); communication (MA, Graduate Certificate), including general communication (MA), health care communication (MA), organizational communication (MA), professional communication (Graduate Certificate); organizational communication (Graduate Certificate), including managerial communication, public communication; sustainability practices (Graduate Certificate). *Program availability:* Part-time-only, evening/weekend. *Faculty:* 3 full-time (0 women), 2 part-time/adjunct (0 women). *Students:* 8 full-time (4 women), 10 part-time (8 women); includes 3 minority (2 Black or African American, non-Hispanic/Latino; 1 Two or more races, non-Hispanic/Latino), 2 international. Average age 25. 25 applicants, 32% accepted, 6 enrolled. In 2017, 4 master's awarded. *Degree requirements:* For master's, thesis. *Entrance requirements:* For master's, GRE. Additional exam requirements/recommendations for international students: Required—TOEFL (minimum score 550 paper-based; 80 iBT). *Application deadline:* For fall admission, 8/15 for domestic and international students; for spring admission, 1/15 for domestic and international students; for summer admission, 5/15 for domestic and international students. Applications are processed on a rolling basis. Application fee: $80. Electronic applications accepted. *Expenses:* $932 per credit hour. *Financial support:* In 2017–18, 15 fellowships with full and partial tuition reimbursements (averaging $10,483 per year) were awarded; research assistantships, scholarships/grants, and unspecified assistantships also available. Financial award application deadline: 2/15; financial award applicants required to submit FAFSA. *Faculty research:* Mass media and social construction of reality; development and improvement of media literacy skills; sociocultural influences on cognition and learning in K-12 populations, oil pollution impacts on marine and estuarine microbial communities; wetlands ecology. *Unit head:* Bradford Martin, Dean, College of Arts and Sciences, 401-232-6929, E-mail: bmartin@bryant.edu. *Application contact:* Terri Rogers, Admission Assistant, Graduate School, 401-232-6230, E-mail: graduateprograms@bryant.edu.
Website: http://gradschool.bryant.edu/arts-and-sciences/

Cabrini University, Academic Affairs, Radnor, PA 19087. Offers accounting (M Acc); autism spectrum disorder (M Ed); biological sciences (MS), including civic leadership; criminology and criminal justice (MA); curriculum, instruction, and assessment (M Ed); educational leadership (M Ed, Ed D), including curriculum and instructional leadership (Ed D), preK-12 leadership (Ed D); English as a second language (M Ed); organizational leadership (DBA, PhD); preK to 4 (M Ed); reading specialist (M Ed); secondary education (M Ed), including biology, chemistry, English, English/communication, mathematics, social studies; special education grades 7-12 (M Ed); special education preK-8 (M Ed); teaching and learning (M Ed). *Program availability:* Part-time, evening/weekend. *Faculty:* 23 full-time (17 women), 46 part-time/adjunct (38 women). *Students:* 60 full-time (35 women), 559 part-time (435 women); includes 93 minority (66 Black or African American, non-Hispanic/Latino; 1 American Indian or Alaska Native, non-Hispanic/Latino; 8 Asian, non-Hispanic/Latino; 15 Hispanic/Latino; 3 Two or more races, non-Hispanic/Latino), 4 international. Average age 33. 290 applicants, 82% accepted, 154 enrolled. In 2017, 283 master's awarded. *Degree requirements:* For master's, comprehensive exam (for some programs), thesis (for some programs); for doctorate, comprehensive exam (for some programs), thesis/dissertation. *Entrance requirements:* For master's, professional resume, personal statement, two recommendations, official transcripts; for doctorate, official transcripts, minimum master's GPA of 3.0, two recommendations, interview with admissions committee. Additional exam requirements/recommendations for international students: Required—TOEFL (minimum score 80

iBT). *Application deadline:* For fall admission, 8/26 for domestic students, 8/1 for international students; for winter admission, 1/13 for domestic students, 12/20 for international students; for spring admission, 1/13 for domestic students, 12/20 for international students; for summer admission, 5/20 for domestic students, 4/30 for international students. Applications are processed on a rolling basis. Application fee: $50. Electronic applications accepted. Application fee is waived when completed online. *Expenses:* Contact institution. *Financial support:* In 2017–18, 1,459 students received support. Tuition waivers and unspecified assistantships available. Financial award application deadline: 5/1; financial award applicants required to submit FAFSA. *Unit head:* Dr. Maliha Zaman, 610-902-8502, Fax: 610-902-8797, E-mail: msz37@cabrini.edu. *Application contact:* Diane Greenwood, Director of Graduate Admissions, 610-902-8291, E-mail: diane.l.greenwood@cabrini.edu.
Website: http://cabrini.edu/graduate

California Baptist University, Program in Communication, Riverside, CA 92503. Offers MA. *Program availability:* Part-time, evening/weekend. *Faculty:* 2 full-time (both women), 1 (woman) part-time/adjunct. *Students:* 10 full-time (9 women), 4 part-time (3 women); includes 10 minority (3 Black or African American, non-Hispanic/Latino; 1 Asian, non-Hispanic/Latino; 3 Hispanic/Latino; 3 Two or more races, non-Hispanic/Latino). Average age 28. 14 applicants, 71% accepted, 4 enrolled. In 2017, 13 master's awarded. *Degree requirements:* For master's, thesis or alternative, comprehensive project, defended paper. *Entrance requirements:* For master's, bachelor's degree, official transcripts, 2 recommendations, current resume, 500-word essay, minimum GPA of 2.5. Additional exam requirements/recommendations for international students: Required—TOEFL (minimum score 80 iBT). *Application deadline:* For fall admission, 8/1 priority date for domestic students, 7/1 priority date for international students; for spring admission, 12/1 priority date for domestic students, 11/1 priority date for international students. Applications are processed on a rolling basis. Application fee: $45. Electronic applications accepted. *Expenses:* Contact institution. *Financial support:* In 2017–18, 2 students received support. Federal Work-Study and scholarships/grants available. Financial award applicants required to submit CSS PROFILE or FAFSA. *Faculty research:* Millennials, social media, new media, convergent media. *Unit head:* Dr. Sandra Romo, Program Director, MA in Communication, 951-343-2173, E-mail: sromo@calbaptist.edu. *Application contact:* Ted Meyer, Dean of Enrollment Services, Online and Professional Studies, 951-343-3909, E-mail: tmeyer@calbaptist.edu.
Website: https://www.cbuonline.edu/degrees/master-of-arts-in-communication

California State University, Chico, Office of Graduate Studies, College of Communication and Education, Department of Communication Arts and Sciences, Program in Communication Studies, Chico, CA 95929-0722. Offers MA. *Degree requirements:* For master's, thesis or project. *Entrance requirements:* For master's, GRE, three letters of recommendation, example of writing, one-page statement of purpose, minimum GPA of 3.0. Additional exam requirements/recommendations for international students: Required—TOEFL (minimum score 550 paper-based; 80 iBT), IELTS (minimum score 6.5), PTE (minimum score 59). Electronic applications accepted.

California State University, East Bay, Office of Graduate Studies, College of Letters, Arts, and Social Sciences, Department of Communication, Hayward, CA 94542-3000. Offers MA. *Program availability:* Part-time. *Faculty:* 8 full-time (5 women), 18 part-time/adjunct (12 women). *Students:* 5 full-time (4 women), 20 part-time (14 women); includes 19 minority (7 Black or African American, non-Hispanic/Latino; 3 Asian, non-Hispanic/Latino; 7 Hispanic/Latino; 2 Two or more races, non-Hispanic/Latino), 3 international. Average age 33. 39 applicants, 64% accepted, 16 enrolled. In 2017, 14 master's awarded. *Degree requirements:* For master's, comprehensive exam, project, thesis, or exam. *Entrance requirements:* For master's, GRE, minimum GPA of 3.0 in field; 3 letters of recommendation; sample of scholarly writing. Additional exam requirements/recommendations for international students: Required—TOEFL (minimum score 550 paper-based). *Application deadline:* For fall admission, 6/1 for domestic and international students. Applications are processed on a rolling basis. Application fee: $55. Electronic applications accepted. *Financial support:* Fellowships, teaching assistantships, career-related internships or fieldwork, Federal Work-Study, institutionally sponsored loans, scholarships/grants, and unspecified assistantships available. Support available to part-time students. Financial award application deadline: 3/2; financial award applicants required to submit FAFSA. *Unit head:* Dr. Mary Cardaras, Chair, 510-885-3925, Fax: 510-885-4099, E-mail: mary.cardaras@csueastbay.edu. *Application contact:* Philip Cole-Regis, Administrative Support Coordinator, 510-885-3286, E-mail: philip.coleregis@csueastbay.edu.
Website: http://www20.csueastbay.edu/class/departments/communication/

California State University, Fresno, Division of Research and Graduate Studies, College of Arts and Humanities, Department of Communication, Fresno, CA 93740-8027. Offers MA. *Program availability:* Part-time, evening/weekend. *Degree requirements:* For master's, thesis or alternative. *Entrance requirements:* For master's, GRE General Test, minimum GPA of 3.1. Additional exam requirements/recommendations for international students: Required—TOEFL. Electronic applications accepted. *Faculty research:* Learning styles, education, critical thinking.

California State University, Fullerton, Graduate Studies, College of Communications, Department of Communications, Fullerton, CA 92831-3599. Offers communications in tourism and entertainment (MA); mass communications research and theory (MA); professional communications (MA). *Program availability:* Part-time. *Faculty:* 4 full-time (3 women), 1 part-time/adjunct (0 women). *Students:* 23 full-time (18 women), 17 part-time (8 women); includes 21 minority (4 Black or African American, non-Hispanic/Latino; 1 Asian, non-Hispanic/Latino; 15 Hispanic/Latino; 1 Two or more races, non-Hispanic/Latino), 2 international. Average age 27. 41 applicants, 56% accepted, 13 enrolled. *Entrance requirements:* For master's, GRE General Test. Application fee: $55. *Financial support:* Teaching assistantships, career-related internships or fieldwork, Federal Work-Study, institutionally sponsored loans, and scholarships/grants available. Support available to part-time students. Financial award application deadline: 3/1; financial award applicants required to submit FAFSA. *Unit head:* Jason Shepard, Chair, 657-278-5301, E-mail: jshepard@fullerton.edu. *Application contact:* Coordinator, 657-278-3832.

California State University, Fullerton, Graduate Studies, College of Communications, Department of Human Communication Studies, Fullerton, CA 92831-3599. Offers communication studies (MA). *Program availability:* Part-time. *Faculty:* 9 full-time (6 women), 1 part-time/adjunct (0 women). *Students:* 10 full-time (7 women), 24 part-time (17 women); includes 15 minority (1 Black or African American, non-Hispanic/Latino; 5 Asian, non-Hispanic/Latino; 8 Hispanic/Latino; 1 Native Hawaiian or other Pacific Islander, non-Hispanic/Latino), 2 international. Average age 31. 33 applicants, 48% accepted, 13 enrolled. *Degree requirements:* For master's, comprehensive exam, thesis or alternative. *Entrance requirements:* For master's, minimum GPA of 3.0 in major. Application fee: $55. *Financial support:* Teaching assistantships, career-related internships or fieldwork, Federal Work-Study, institutionally sponsored loans, and scholarships/grants available. Support available to part-time students. Financial award application deadline: 3/1; financial award applicants required to submit FAFSA. *Faculty research:* Speech therapy. *Unit head:* Gary Ruud, Chair, 657-278-4198, E-mail: gruud@fullerton.edu. *Application contact:* Admissions/Applications, 657-278-2371.
Website: http://communications.fullerton.edu/hcom/

California State University, Long Beach, Graduate Studies, College of Liberal Arts, Department of Communication Studies, Long Beach, CA 90840. Offers MA. *Program availability:* Part-time. *Degree requirements:* For master's, comprehensive exam or thesis. *Entrance requirements:* For master's, GRE. Electronic applications accepted. *Faculty research:* Rhetoric, public address, communication theory, interpersonal communication, intercultural communication.

California State University, Los Angeles, Graduate Studies, College of Arts and Letters, Department of Communication Studies, Los Angeles, CA 90032-8530. Offers MA, MFA. *Program availability:* Part-time, evening/weekend. *Degree requirements:* For master's, comprehensive exam or thesis. *Entrance requirements:* For master's, minimum GPA of 2.75 in last 90 units of course work. Additional exam requirements/recommendations for international students: Required—TOEFL (minimum score 500 paper-based). Electronic applications accepted. *Faculty research:* Organizational, interpersonal, intercultural, and instructional communication; rhetorical theories.

California State University, Northridge, Graduate Studies, Mike Curb College of Arts, Media, and Communication, Northridge, CA 91330. Offers MA, MFA, MM. *Program availability:* Part-time, evening/weekend. *Students:* 121 full-time (69 women), 79 part-time (45 women); includes 75 minority (9 Black or African American, non-Hispanic/Latino; 1 American Indian or Alaska Native, non-Hispanic/Latino; 14 Asian, non-Hispanic/Latino; 40 Hispanic/Latino; 11 Two or more races, non-Hispanic/Latino), 33 international. Average age 31. 368 applicants, 42% accepted, 85 enrolled. *Entrance requirements:* Additional exam requirements/recommendations for international students: Required—TOEFL. *Application deadline:* For fall admission, 11/30 for domestic students. Application fee: $55. *Financial support:* Teaching assistantships, career-related internships or fieldwork, Federal Work-Study, and unspecified assistantships available. Support available to part-time students. Financial award application deadline: 3/1. *Unit head:* Dan Hosken, Dean, 818-677-2246.
Website: http://www.csun.edu/mike-curb-arts-media-communication

California State University, Sacramento, College of Arts and Letters, Department of Communication Studies, Sacramento, CA 95819. Offers MA. *Program availability:* Part-time. *Students:* 3 full-time (2 women), 18 part-time (11 women); includes 6 minority (1 Black or African American, non-Hispanic/Latino; 2 Asian, non-Hispanic/Latino; 3 Hispanic/Latino). Average age 30. 22 applicants, 45% accepted, 5 enrolled. In 2017, 7 master's awarded. *Degree requirements:* For master's, thesis or project; writing proficiency exam. *Entrance requirements:* For master's, GRE, minimum GPA of 3.25 during previous 2 years. Additional exam requirements/recommendations for international students: Required—TOEFL (minimum score 550 paper-based; 80 iBT). *Application deadline:* For fall admission, 1/3 for domestic students, 3/1 for international students; for spring admission, 9/15 for domestic students, 9/30 for international students. Applications are processed on a rolling basis. Application fee: $55. Electronic applications accepted. *Expenses:* Contact institution. *Financial support:* Teaching assistantships, career-related internships or fieldwork, Federal Work-Study, and scholarships/grants available. Support available to part-time students. Financial award application deadline: 3/1; financial award applicants required to submit FAFSA. *Faculty research:* Hypermedia development; information literacy in higher education; representations of race and ethnicity; the definition of "newsworthy" as it relates to front-page newspaper coverage; journalism ethics. *Unit head:* Dr. Gerri Smith, Chair, 916-278-6688, E-mail: smithg@csus.edu. *Application contact:* Jose Martinez, Outreach and Graduate Diversity Coordinator, 916-278-6470, Fax: 916-278-5669, E-mail: martinj@skymail.csus.edu.
Website: http://www.al.csus.edu/coms

California State University, San Bernardino, Graduate Studies, College of Arts and Letters, Program in Communication Studies, San Bernardino, CA 92407. Offers communication studies (MA); integrated marketing communication (MA). *Faculty:* 6 full-time (3 women). *Students:* 7 full-time (all women), 30 part-time (19 women); includes 19 minority (4 Black or African American, non-Hispanic/Latino; 2 Asian, non-Hispanic/Latino; 12 Hispanic/Latino; 1 Two or more races, non-Hispanic/Latino), 3 international. Average age 31. 33 applicants, 52% accepted, 12 enrolled. In 2017, 3 master's awarded. *Degree requirements:* For master's, comprehensive exam. *Entrance requirements:* Additional exam requirements/recommendations for international students: Required—TOEFL. *Application deadline:* For fall admission, 5/15 for domestic students. Application fee: $55. *Unit head:* Ahlam Muhtaseb, Graduate Coordinator, 909-537-5897, Fax: 909-537-7585, E-mail: amuhtase@csusb.edu. *Application contact:* Dr. Dorota Huizinga, Dean of Graduate Studies, 909-537-3064, Fax: 909-537-7034, E-mail: dorota.huizinga@csusb.edu.

Carleton University, Faculty of Graduate Studies, Faculty of Public Affairs and Management, School of Journalism and Communication, Program in Communication, Ottawa, ON K1S 5B6, Canada. Offers MA, PhD. *Degree requirements:* For master's, thesis optional; for doctorate, comprehensive exam, thesis/dissertation. *Entrance requirements:* For master's, honors degree. Additional exam requirements/recommendations for international students: Required—TOEFL. *Faculty research:* History of communication and media systems, communication/information technologies and society, communication and social relations, communication policy and political economy.

Carnegie Mellon University, Dietrich College of Humanities and Social Sciences, Department of English, Pittsburgh, PA 15213-3891. Offers communication planning and design (M Des); literary and cultural studies (MA, PhD); professional writing (MAPW), including editing and publishing, policy and non-profit communication, public and media relations / corporate communications, science or healthcare communication, technical writing, writing for new media, writing for print media; rhetoric (MA, PhD). *Program availability:* Part-time. Terminal master's awarded for partial completion of doctoral program. *Degree requirements:* For doctorate, 2 foreign languages, comprehensive exam, thesis/dissertation. *Entrance requirements:* For master's and doctorate, GRE General Test. Additional exam requirements/recommendations for international students: Required—TOEFL, TWE. *Faculty research:* Cognitive processes in discourse with emphasis on writing, testing, and evaluation.

Central Connecticut State University, School of Graduate Studies, College of Liberal Arts and Social Sciences, Department of Communication, New Britain, CT 06050-4010. Offers communication (MS); public relations/promotions (Certificate). *Program availability:* Part-time, evening/weekend. *Faculty:* 6 full-time (1 woman). *Students:* 8 full-time (3 women), 24 part-time (19 women); includes 11 minority (5 Black or African American, non-Hispanic/Latino; 6 Hispanic/Latino), 2 international. Average age 28. 22 applicants, 77% accepted, 10 enrolled. In 2017, 9 master's awarded. *Degree requirements:* For master's, comprehensive exam, thesis or alternative, special project; for Certificate, qualifying exam. *Entrance requirements:* For master's, minimum undergraduate GPA of 3.0, resume, references, essay. Additional exam requirements/recommendations for international students: Required—TOEFL (minimum score 550 paper-based; 79 iBT); Recommended—IELTS (minimum score 6.5). *Application deadline:* For fall admission, 8/1 for domestic students, 5/1 for international students; for spring admission, 11/1 for domestic and international students. Applications are processed on a rolling basis. Application fee: $50. Electronic applications accepted. *Expenses: Tuition, area resident:* Full-time $6757. Tuition, state resident: full-time $9750; part-time $374 per credit. Tuition, nonresident: full-time $18,102; part-time $374

per credit. *Required fees:* $4635; $255 per credit. *Financial support:* In 2017–18, 5 students received support. Career-related internships or fieldwork, Federal Work-Study, scholarships/grants, and unspecified assistantships available. Support available to part-time students. Financial award application deadline: 3/1; financial award applicants required to submit FAFSA. *Faculty research:* Organizational communication, mass communication, intercultural communication, political communication, information management. *Unit head:* Dr. Christopher Pudlinski, Chair, 860-832-2690, E-mail: pudlinskic@ccsu.edu. *Application contact:* Patricia Gardner, Associate Director of Graduate Studies, 860-832-2350, Fax: 860-832-2362.
Website: http://comm.ccsu.edu/

Central Michigan University, College of Graduate Studies, College of Communication and Fine Arts, Department of Communication and Dramatic Arts, Mount Pleasant, MI 48859. Offers communication (MA), including communication and dramatic arts. *Program availability:* Part-time. *Degree requirements:* For master's, thesis. *Entrance requirements:* Additional exam requirements/recommendations for international students: Recommended—TOEFL (minimum score 100 iBT), IELTS. Electronic applications accepted. *Faculty research:* Communication theory, interpersonal/nonverbal communication, organizational communication, family and interpersonal communication, political communication.

Chapman University, School of Communication, Orange, CA 92866. Offers MS. *Program availability:* Evening/weekend. *Faculty:* 18 full-time (12 women), 14 part-time/adjunct (7 women). *Students:* 6 full-time (all women), 3 part-time (2 women); includes 2 minority (1 Asian, non-Hispanic/Latino; 1 Hispanic/Latino), 2 international. Average age 24. 10 applicants, 100% accepted, 7 enrolled. In 2017, 6 master's awarded. *Degree requirements:* For master's, capstone research project. *Entrance requirements:* For master's, GRE, minimum undergraduate GPA of 3.0. *Application deadline:* Applications are processed on a rolling basis. Application fee: $60. Electronic applications accepted. *Expenses:* Contact institution. *Financial support:* Fellowships, research assistantships, Federal Work-Study, scholarships/grants, and unspecified assistantships available. Financial award applicants required to submit FAFSA. *Unit head:* Dr. Lisa Sparks, Dean, 714-744-7088, E-mail: ditommas@chapman.edu. *Application contact:* Shannon McCance, Admission Counselor, 714-997-6711, E-mail: smccance@chapman.edu. Website: https://www.chapman.edu/communication/index.aspx

Chatham University, Program in Communication, Pittsburgh, PA 15232-2826. Offers environmental communication (M Comm); health communication (M Comm); strategic communication (M Comm). *Program availability:* Part-time, online learning. *Faculty:* 3 part-time/adjunct (2 women). *Students:* 4 full-time (1 woman), 9 part-time (all women); includes 1 minority (Black or African American, non-Hispanic/Latino), 1 international. Average age 28. 16 applicants, 50% accepted, 7 enrolled. *Entrance requirements:* Additional exam requirements/recommendations for international students: Required—TOEFL, IELTS. *Application deadline:* Applications are processed on a rolling basis. Application fee: $35. Electronic applications accepted. Application fee is waived when completed online. *Expenses: Tuition:* Full-time $16,740; part-time $930 per credit. *Required fees:* $486; $27 per credit. $243 per semester. *Financial support:* Applicants required to submit FAFSA. *Application contact:* Athena Wintruba, Graduate Admission Recruiter, 412-365-1141, E-mail: awintruba@chatham.edu.
Website: http://www.chatham.edu/mcomm/

Clarion University of Pennsylvania, College of Arts, Education and Sciences, MS Program in Mass Media Arts and Journalism, Clarion, PA 16214. Offers MS. *Program availability:* Part-time, evening/weekend, online only, 100% online. *Faculty:* 5 full-time (3 women). *Students:* 9 full-time (6 women), 8 part-time (4 women); includes 6 minority (all Black or African American, non-Hispanic/Latino). Average age 33. 10 applicants, 80% accepted, 4 enrolled. In 2017, 6 master's awarded. *Entrance requirements:* For master's, statement of purpose, short essay, minimum undergraduate QPA of 3.0. Additional exam requirements/recommendations for international students: Required—TOEFL (minimum score 600 paper-based, 80 iBT) or IELTS (7). *Application deadline:* For fall admission, 8/15 priority date for domestic students, 7/15 priority date for international students; for winter admission, 11/1 priority date for domestic students; for spring admission, 1/7 priority date for domestic students, 11/15 priority date for international students; for summer admission, 4/1 priority date for domestic students. Applications are processed on a rolling basis. Application fee: $40. Electronic applications accepted. *Expenses:* $655.05 per credit. *Financial support:* Career-related internships or fieldwork, scholarships/grants, and unspecified assistantships available. Support available to part-time students. Financial award application deadline: 3/1; financial award applicants required to submit FAFSA. *Unit head:* Dr. Steven Harris, Interim Dean, 814-393-2328, E-mail: harris@clarion.edu. *Application contact:* Dana Bearer, Associate Director for Transfer, Adult and Graduate Admissions, 814-393-2337, Fax: 814-393-2772, E-mail: gradstudies@clarion.edu.

Clarks Summit University, Baptist Bible Seminary, South Abington Township, PA 18411. Offers Biblical apologetics (MA); Biblical studies (MA); church education (M Min); church planting (M Div, M Min); communication (D Min); counseling and spiritual development (D Min); global ministry (M Min, D Min); ministry (PhD); missions (M Min); organizational leadership (M Min); outreach pastor (M Min); pastoral counseling (M Min); pastoral leadership (M Div, M Min); pastoral ministry (D Min); theological studies (D Min); theology (Th M); youth pastor (M Min). M Min in missions available only for Association of Baptists for World Evangelism missionary personnel. *Program availability:* Part-time, evening/weekend, online learning. Terminal master's awarded for partial completion of doctoral program. *Degree requirements:* For master's, 2 foreign languages, thesis, oral exam (for M Div); for doctorate, 2 foreign languages, comprehensive exam (for some programs), thesis/dissertation, oral exam. *Entrance requirements:* For doctorate, Greek and Hebrew entrance exams (for PhD). *Application deadline:* Applications are processed on a rolling basis. Application fee: $30. Electronic applications accepted. *Financial support:* Career-related internships or fieldwork and scholarships/grants available. Support available to part-time students. *Unit head:* Dr. Wayne Slusser, Dean, 570-585-9348, Fax: 570-585-4057, E-mail: wslusser@clarkssummitu.edu. *Application contact:* Dr. Wayne Slusser, Dean, 570-585-9348, Fax: 570-585-4057, E-mail: wslusser@clarkssummitu.edu.
Website: https://www.clarkssummitu.edu/seminary/

Clark University, Graduate School, School of Professional Studies, Program in Professional Communication, Worcester, MA 01610-1477. Offers MSPC. *Program availability:* Part-time, evening/weekend. *Students:* 33 full-time (26 women), 3 part-time (all women); includes 2 minority (1 Asian, non-Hispanic/Latino; 1 Hispanic/Latino), 25 international. Average age 24. 123 applicants, 58% accepted, 22 enrolled. In 2017, 42 master's awarded. *Degree requirements:* For master's, thesis optional. *Entrance requirements:* For master's, 2 references, resume or curriculum vitae, personal statement. Additional exam requirements/recommendations for international students: Required—TOEFL (minimum score 575 paper-based; 90 iBT), IELTS (minimum score 6.5). *Application deadline:* Applications are processed on a rolling basis. Application fee: $75. Electronic applications accepted. *Expenses:* $2,750 tuition per 14-week course; $40 activity fee (full-time students only); $40 miscellaneous one-time fee; $300 student services fee. *Unit head:* Mary Piecewicz, Assistant Dean, 508-793-7212, E-mail: mpiecewicz@clarku.edu.
Website: http://www.clarku.edu/programs/masters-professional-communication

Clemson University, Graduate School, College of Behavioral, Social and Health Sciences, Department of Communication, Clemson, SC 29634. Offers communication, technology and society (MA). *Program availability:* Part-time. *Faculty:* 27 full-time (18 women), 3 part-time/adjunct (1 woman). *Students:* 15 full-time (8 women), 1 (woman) part-time; includes 2 minority (both Black or African American, non-Hispanic/Latino), 2 international. Average age 25. 35 applicants, 37% accepted, 8 enrolled. In 2017, 7 master's awarded. *Degree requirements:* For master's, comprehensive exam (for some programs), thesis (for some programs). *Entrance requirements:* For master's, GRE General Test, resume, unofficial transcripts, letters of recommendation. Additional exam requirements/recommendations for international students: Required—TOEFL (minimum score 80 iBT), IELTS (minimum score 6.5), PTE (minimum score 54). *Application deadline:* For fall admission, 2/1 priority date for domestic and international students; for spring admission, 9/1 priority date for domestic and international students. Applications are processed on a rolling basis. Application fee: $80 ($90 for international students). Electronic applications accepted. *Expenses:* $5,174 per semester full-time resident, $9,714 per semester full-time non-resident, $511 per credit hour part-time resident, $1,017 per credit hour part-time non-resident; $741 per credit hour online; other fees may apply per session. *Financial support:* In 2017–18, 14 students received support, including 14 teaching assistantships with partial tuition reimbursements available (averaging $12,000 per year); career-related internships or fieldwork also available. Financial award application deadline: 2/1. *Total annual research expenditures:* $23,955. *Unit head:* Dr. Bryan Denham, Department Chair, 864-656-1567, E-mail: bdenham@clemson.edu. *Application contact:* Dr. D. Travers Scott, Director of Graduate Studies, 864-656-1567, E-mail: dscott3@clemson.edu.
Website: http://www.clemson.edu/cbshs/departments/communication/index.html

Clemson University, Graduate School, College of Business, Department of Graphic Communications, Clemson, SC 29634. Offers MS. *Program availability:* Part-time. *Faculty:* 13 full-time (5 women), 2 part-time/adjunct (0 women). *Students:* 39 full-time (24 women); includes 6 minority (all Black or African American, non-Hispanic/Latino), 6 international. Average age 25. 16 applicants, 100% accepted, 9 enrolled. In 2017, 6 master's awarded. *Degree requirements:* For master's, thesis optional. *Entrance requirements:* For master's, GRE General Test, unofficial transcripts, letters of recommendation, personal statement, resume. Additional exam requirements/recommendations for international students: Required—TOEFL (minimum score 80 iBT), IELTS (minimum score 6.5), PTE (minimum score 54). *Application deadline:* For fall admission, 5/15 for domestic and international students; for spring admission, 10/15 for domestic and international students. Applications are processed on a rolling basis. Application fee: $80 ($90 for international students). Electronic applications accepted. *Expenses:* $5,174 per semester full-time resident, $9,714 per semester full-time non-resident, $511 per credit hour part-time resident, $1,017 per credit hour part-time non-resident; $741 per credit hour online; other fees may apply per session. *Financial support:* In 2017–18, 10 students received support, including 1 research assistantship with partial tuition reimbursement available (averaging $14,784 per year); career-related internships or fieldwork and unspecified assistantships also available. Financial award application deadline: 5/15. *Total annual research expenditures:* $54,125. *Unit head:* Dr. Chip Tonkin, Department Chair, 864-656-3447, E-mail: tonkin@clemson.edu. *Application contact:* Dr. Nona Woolbright, Graduate Coordinator, 864-656-0105, E-mail: nwoolbr@clemson.edu.
Website: https://www.clemson.edu/business/departments/graphics/

Cleveland State University, College of Graduate Studies, College of Liberal Arts and Social Sciences, School of Communication, Cleveland, OH 44115. Offers applied communication theory and methodology (MA). *Program availability:* Part-time, evening/weekend. *Faculty:* 10 full-time (5 women), 1 part-time/adjunct (0 women). *Students:* 10 full-time (9 women), 4 part-time (3 women); includes 5 minority (4 Black or African American, non-Hispanic/Latino; 1 Two or more races, non-Hispanic/Latino), 4 international. Average age 27. 16 applicants, 81% accepted, 7 enrolled. In 2017, 5 master's awarded. *Degree requirements:* For master's, comprehensive exam (for some programs), thesis, project, comprehensive exam, or collaborative project. *Entrance requirements:* For master's, GRE or MAT, minimum undergraduate GPA of 2.75, 2 letters of recommendation, statement of interest. Additional exam requirements/recommendations for international students: Required—TOEFL (minimum score 550 paper-based; 78 iBT). *Application deadline:* For fall admission, 7/1 priority date for domestic students, 5/15 priority date for international students; for spring admission, 11/15 priority date for domestic students, 11/1 priority date for international students; for summer admission, 4/1 for domestic students, 3/15 for international students. Applications are processed on a rolling basis. Application fee: $40. Electronic applications accepted. *Expenses:* Contact institution. *Financial support:* In 2017–18, 14 students received support, including 8 teaching assistantships with partial tuition reimbursements available (averaging $6,960 per year); tuition waivers (full and partial) also available. Financial award application deadline: 8/1; financial award applicants required to submit FAFSA. *Faculty research:* Interpersonal, organizational, and mass communication; health communication. *Unit head:* Dr. Cheryl Bracken, Professor and Graduate Program Director, 216-687-4512, Fax: 216-687-5435, E-mail: c.bracken@csuohio.edu. *Application contact:* Sandra M. Thorp, Administrative Secretary, 216-687-2116, Fax: 216-687-5435, E-mail: s.m.thorp@csuohio.edu.
Website: http://www.csuohio.edu/class/communication/communication

Cleveland State University, College of Graduate Studies, Maxine Goodman Levin College of Urban Affairs, Program in Urban Studies and Public Affairs, Cleveland, OH 44115. Offers communication (PhD); public administration (PhD); urban policy and development (PhD). *Program availability:* Part-time, evening/weekend. *Faculty:* 16 full-time (8 women), 13 part-time/adjunct (5 women). *Students:* 3 full-time (2 women), 24 part-time (14 women); includes 6 minority (4 Black or African American, non-Hispanic/Latino; 1 Hispanic/Latino; 1 Two or more races, non-Hispanic/Latino), 4 international. Average age 41. 32 applicants, 34% accepted, 2 enrolled. In 2017, 4 doctorates awarded. *Degree requirements:* For doctorate, comprehensive exam, thesis/dissertation. *Entrance requirements:* For doctorate, GRE General Test (minimum score: verbal and quantitative 50th percentile, analytical writing 4.0), minimum GPA of 3.5. Additional exam requirements/recommendations for international students: Required—TOEFL (minimum score 550 paper-based; 78 iBT), IELTS (6.0), or International Test of English Proficiency (iTEP). *Application deadline:* For fall admission, 1/31 for domestic and international students. Application fee: $40. Electronic applications accepted. *Expenses:* Contact institution. *Financial support:* In 2017–18, 15 students received support, including 1 research assistantship with full tuition reimbursement available (averaging $11,800 per year), 2 teaching assistantships with full tuition reimbursements available (averaging $11,800 per year); scholarships/grants, tuition waivers (full and partial), and unspecified assistantships also available. Support available to part-time students. Financial award application deadline: 3/1; financial award applicants required to submit FAFSA. *Faculty research:* Urban and public policy, public affairs. *Unit head:* Dr. Bill Bowen, Professor/PhD Program Director, 216-687-9226, E-mail: w.bowen@csuohio.edu. *Application contact:* David Arrighi, Graduate Academic Advisor, 216-523-7522, Fax: 216-687-5398, E-mail: d.arrighi@csuohio.edu.
Website: http://urban.csuohio.edu/academics/graduate/phd/

The College at Brockport, State University of New York, School of Arts and Sciences, Department of Communication, Brockport, NY 14420-2997. Offers MA.

Communication—General

Program availability: Part-time, evening/weekend. *Faculty:* 6 full-time (3 women). *Students:* 8 full-time (5 women), 11 part-time (8 women); includes 6 minority (2 Black or African American, non-Hispanic/Latino; 2 Hispanic/Latino; 2 Two or more races, non-Hispanic/Latino), 1 international. 15 applicants, 67% accepted, 4 enrolled. In 2017, 10 master's awarded. *Degree requirements:* For master's, thesis or alternative, research project. *Entrance requirements:* For master's, minimum GPA of 3.0, letters of recommendation. Additional exam requirements/recommendations for international students: Required—TOEFL (minimum score 550 paper-based; 79 iBT), IELTS (minimum score 6.5). *Application deadline:* For fall admission, 7/15 priority date for domestic and international students; for spring admission, 11/15 priority date for domestic and international students; for summer admission, 4/1 priority date for domestic and international students. Application fee: $50. Electronic applications accepted. *Expenses:* Tuition, state resident: full-time $10,870; part-time $453 per credit hour. Tuition, nonresident: full-time $22,210. *Required fees:* $988; $246 per semester. *Financial support:* In 2017–18, 1 fellowship with full tuition reimbursement (averaging $7,500 per year), 2 teaching assistantships with full tuition reimbursements (averaging $6,000 per year) were awarded; Federal Work-Study, scholarships/grants, and unspecified assistantships also available. Support available to part-time students. Financial award application deadline: 3/15; financial award applicants required to submit FAFSA. *Faculty research:* Organizational communication, rhetorical theory and criticism, media theory and criticism, interpersonal communication, communication theory. *Unit head:* Dr. Monica Brasted, Chairperson, 585-395-2511, Fax: 585-395-5771, E-mail: mbrasted@brockport.edu. *Application contact:* Dr. Alex Lyon, Graduate Director, 585-395-5772, Fax: 585-395-5771, E-mail: alyon@brockport.edu.
Website: http://www.brockport.edu/cmc/grad/

The College of New Rochelle, Graduate School, Division of Art and Communication Studies, Program in Communication Studies, New Rochelle, NY 10805-2308. Offers MS, Certificate. *Program availability:* Part-time, evening/weekend. *Degree requirements:* For master's, thesis or alternative, thesis or comprehensive exam. *Entrance requirements:* For master's, GRE General Test, interview, minimum GPA of 3.0. Additional exam requirements/recommendations for international students: Required—TOEFL. *Expenses: Tuition:* Full-time $17,406. *Required fees:* $1120.

Columbia College Chicago, School of Graduate Studies, Communication Department, Chicago, IL 60605-1996. Offers civic media (MA). *Students:* 10 full-time (7 women), 5 part-time (4 women); includes 9 minority (6 Black or African American, non-Hispanic/Latino; 3 Hispanic/Latino), 2 international. 26 applicants, 69% accepted, 8 enrolled. *Degree requirements:* For master's, thesis. *Entrance requirements:* For master's, self-assessment essay, work sample, interview, letters of recommendation, transcripts, resume. Additional exam requirements/recommendations for international students: Required—TOEFL, IELTS. *Application deadline:* For fall admission, 1/15 for domestic and international students. Applications are processed on a rolling basis. Application fee: $55 ($100 for international students). Electronic applications accepted. *Expenses:* Contact institution. *Financial support:* In 2017–18, 8 students received support. Career-related internships or fieldwork, Federal Work-Study, scholarships/grants, and unspecified assistantships available. Financial award application deadline: 1/16. *Unit head:* Suzanne McBride, Chair, 312-369-8907, E-mail: smcbride@colum.edu. *Application contact:* Emily Schmidt, Graduate Admissions, 312-369-7298, E-mail: eschmidt@colum.edu.
Website: https://www.colum.edu/academics/media-arts/communication/index.html

Columbia University, Graduate School of Business, Doctoral Program in Business, New York, NY 10027. Offers business (PhD), including accounting, decision, risk, and operations, finance and economics, management, marketing. *Accreditation:* AACSB. *Degree requirements:* For doctorate, comprehensive exam, thesis/dissertation, major field exam, research paper, thesis proposal. *Entrance requirements:* For doctorate, GMAT or GRE (finance), 2 letters of reference, resume. Additional exam requirements/recommendations for international students: Required—TOEFL. Electronic applications accepted. *Expenses:* Contact institution. *Faculty research:* Human decision making and behavioral research; real estate market and mortgage defaults; financial crisis and corporate governance; international business; security analysis and accounting.

Columbia University, School of Professional Studies, Program in Communications Practice, New York, NY 10027. Offers MS. Electronic applications accepted. *Expenses: Tuition:* Full-time $44,864; part-time $1704 per credit. *Required fees:* $2370 per semester. One-time fee: $105.

Concordia University, School of Graduate Studies, Faculty of Arts and Science, Department of Communication Studies, Montréal, QC H3G 1M8, Canada. Offers communication (PhD); communication studies (Diploma); media studies (MA). PhD program offered jointly with Universityé de Montréal and Universityé du Quebec à Montréal. *Degree requirements:* For master's, thesis optional; for doctorate, one foreign language, comprehensive exam, thesis/dissertation, research practicum, seminar. *Entrance requirements:* For master's, bachelor's degree in communications, 2 years of media-related experience; for doctorate, MA in communications. *Faculty research:* Communication and development, organizational communication, cultural studies, rhetoric, future studies.

Cornell University, Graduate School, Graduate Fields of Agriculture and Life Sciences, Field of Communication, Ithaca, NY 14853. Offers communication (MS, PhD); human-computer interaction (MS, PhD); language and communication (MS, PhD); media communication and society (MS, PhD); organizational communication (MS, PhD); science, environment and health communication (MS, PhD); social psychology of communication (MS, PhD). *Degree requirements:* For master's, thesis (MS); for doctorate, comprehensive exam, thesis/dissertation. *Entrance requirements:* For master's and doctorate, GRE General Test, 3 letters of recommendation. Additional exam requirements/recommendations for international students: Required—TOEFL (minimum score 600 paper-based; 100 iBT). Electronic applications accepted. *Faculty research:* Mass communication, communication technologies, science and environmental communication.

Dallas Baptist University, College of Fine Arts, Dallas, TX 75211-9299. Offers worship studies (MA), including communication for ministry, communication leadership, communication studies, marketing communication, organizational communication management, worship studies. *Program availability:* Part-time, evening/weekend. *Application deadline:* Applications are processed on a rolling basis. Application fee: $25. Electronic applications accepted. Application fee is waived when completed online. *Expenses: Tuition:* Full-time $16,308; part-time $906 per credit hour. *Required fees:* $900; $450 per semester. Tuition and fees vary according to course load and degree level. *Unit head:* Dr. Ronald Bowles, Dean, 214-333-5316, E-mail: ronb@dbu.edu. *Application contact:* Dr. Joanne Morgan, Program Director, 214-333-6854, E-mail: joannem@dbu.edu.
Website: http://www3.dbu.edu/graduate/macoma.asp

Dallas Baptist University, Graduate School of Ministry, Program in Global Leadership, Dallas, TX 75211-9299. Offers church planting (MA); East Asian Studies (MA); English as a second language (MA); general studies (MA); global communication (MA); global studies (MA); international business (MA); leading the nonprofit organization (MA); missions (MA); small group ministry (MA); urban ministry (MA). *Program availability:*

Part-time, evening/weekend. *Application deadline:* Applications are processed on a rolling basis. Application fee: $25. Electronic applications accepted. Application fee is waived when completed online. *Expenses: Tuition:* Full-time $16,308; part-time $906 per credit hour. *Required fees:* $900; $450 per semester. Tuition and fees vary according to course load and degree level. *Unit head:* Dr. Robert R. Brooks, Dean, 214-333-5494, Fax: 214-333-5673, E-mail: bobb@dbu.edu. *Application contact:* Dr. Brent Thomason, Program Director, 214-333-5236, E-mail: brentt@dbu.edu.
Website: http://www.dbu.edu/ministry/degree-programs/m-a-in-global-leadership

Dallas Baptist University, Professional Development Program, Dallas, TX 75211-9299. Offers accounting (MA); church leadership (MA); communication (MA); counseling (MA); criminal justice (MA); English as a second language (MA); finance (MA); higher education (MA); leadership studies (MA); management (MA). *Program availability:* Part-time, evening/weekend. *Application deadline:* Applications are processed on a rolling basis. Application fee: $25. Electronic applications accepted. Application fee is waived when completed online. *Expenses: Tuition:* Full-time $16,308; part-time $906 per credit hour. *Required fees:* $900; $450 per semester. Tuition and fees vary according to course load and degree level. *Unit head:* Jared Ingram, Program Director, 214-333-5584, E-mail: jaredi@dbu.edu. *Application contact:* Bobby Soto, Director of Admissions, 214-333-5242, E-mail: bobby@dbu.edu.
Website: http://www3.dbu.edu/graduate/mapd.asp

DePaul University, College of Communication, Chicago, IL 60604. Offers digital communication and media arts (MA); health communication (MA); journalism (MA); media and cinema studies (MA); multicultural communication (MA); organizational communication (MA); public relations and advertising (MA); relational communication (MA). *Program availability:* Part-time, evening/weekend. *Entrance requirements:* Additional exam requirements/recommendations for international students: Required—TOEFL (minimum score 590 paper-based; 96 iBT), IELTS (minimum score 7.5) or PTE. *Application deadline:* For fall admission, 6/1 priority date for domestic students; for winter admission, 10/1 priority date for domestic students; for spring admission, 2/15 priority date for domestic students. Applications are processed on a rolling basis. Application fee: $40. Electronic applications accepted. *Financial support:* Applicants required to submit FAFSA. *Unit head:* Salma Ghanem, Dean, 312-362-8600, Fax: 312-362-8620. *Application contact:* Ann Spittle, Director of Graduate Admission, 773-325-7315, Fax: 312-362-8620, E-mail: graddepaul@depaul.edu.
Website: http://communication.depaul.edu/

DEREE - The American College of Greece, Graduate Programs, Athens, Greece. Offers applied psychology (MS); communication (MA); leadership (MS); marketing (MS).

Drake University, School of Journalism and Mass Communication, Des Moines, IA 50311-4516. Offers brand communication (MCL); communication leadership (MCL); public affairs and advocacy (MCL). *Program availability:* Part-time, evening/weekend. *Expenses: Tuition:* Part-time $600 per credit hour. *Required fees:* $120 per credit hour. Tuition and fees vary according to course load and program. *Unit head:* Dr. Kathleen Richardson, Dean, 515-271-2295, Fax: 515-271-4518, E-mail: kathleen.richardson@drake.edu.
Website: http://www.drake.edu/sjmc/

Drexel University, College of Arts and Sciences, Department of Communication, Culture and Media, Philadelphia, PA 19104-2875. Offers communication (MS), including public communication, science communication, technical communication. *Program availability:* Part-time, evening/weekend. *Degree requirements:* For master's, internship, professional portfolio. *Entrance requirements:* Additional exam requirements/recommendations for international students: Required—TOEFL. Electronic applications accepted. *Faculty research:* Science information and attitudes, science influence on literature, process of technical writing, document design, software documentation.

Drury University, Master of Arts in Communication Program, Springfield, MO 65802. Offers integrated marketing communications (MA); organizational leadership and change (MA). *Program availability:* Part-time, evening/weekend. *Entrance requirements:* For master's, GRE. Additional exam requirements/recommendations for international students: Required—TOEFL (minimum score 80 iBT); Recommended—IELTS (minimum score 6.5). Electronic applications accepted. *Expenses:* Contact institution. *Faculty research:* Nonprofit leadership, organizational change, leadership accountability, digital media, health communication.

Duquesne University, Graduate School of Liberal Arts, Department of Communication and Rhetorical Studies, Pittsburgh, PA 15282-0001. Offers communication (MA); rhetoric (PhD). *Program availability:* Part-time, evening/weekend, 100% online. *Faculty:* 10 full-time (4 women), 5 part-time/adjunct (3 women). *Students:* 96 full-time (56 women), 8 part-time (6 women); includes 13 minority (10 Black or African American, non-Hispanic/Latino; 1 Asian, non-Hispanic/Latino; 2 Hispanic/Latino), 20 international. Average age 35. 39 applicants, 97% accepted, 18 enrolled. In 2017, 18 master's, 6 doctorates awarded. Terminal master's awarded for partial completion of doctoral program. *Degree requirements:* For master's, thesis optional, practicum; for doctorate, 2 foreign languages, comprehensive exam, thesis/dissertation. *Entrance requirements:* For master's and doctorate, GRE General Test. Additional exam requirements/recommendations for international students: Required—TOEFL. *Application deadline:* For fall admission, 2/1 priority date for domestic and international students; for spring admission, 11/1 priority date for domestic and international students. Applications are processed on a rolling basis. Application fee: $0. Electronic applications accepted. *Expenses:* $958 per credit. *Financial support:* In 2017–18, 24 students received support, including 7 research assistantships with full tuition reimbursements available (averaging $8,000 per year), 14 teaching assistantships with full tuition reimbursements available (averaging $17,000 per year); career-related internships or fieldwork, Federal Work-Study, institutionally sponsored loans, scholarships/grants, tuition waivers (full and partial), and unspecified assistantships also available. Financial award application deadline: 5/1. *Unit head:* Dr. Ronald Arnett, Chair, 412-396-5076, E-mail: arnett@duq.edu. *Application contact:* Linda Rendulic, Assistant to the Dean, 412-396-6400, Fax: 412-396-5265, E-mail: rendulic@duq.edu.
Website: http://www.duq.edu/academics/schools/liberal-arts/graduate-school/programs/communication-

Eastern Illinois University, Graduate School, College of Liberal Arts and Sciences, Department of Communication Studies, Charleston, IL 61920. Offers communication pedagogy (MA). *Program availability:* Part-time, evening/weekend. *Degree requirements:* For master's, comprehensive exam (for some programs), thesis (for some programs). *Entrance requirements:* For master's, GMAT or GRE. Additional exam requirements/recommendations for international students: Required—TOEFL (minimum score 500 paper-based; 61 iBT), IELTS (minimum score 6). *Application deadline:* For fall admission, 5/15 for domestic and international students; for spring admission, 10/15 for domestic and international students. Applications are processed on a rolling basis. Application fee: $30. Electronic applications accepted. *Financial support:* Teaching assistantships with full tuition reimbursements, career-related internships or fieldwork, Federal Work-Study, and unspecified assistantships available. Support available to part-time students. Financial award application deadline: 3/1; financial award applicants required to submit FAFSA. *Unit head:* Matthew J. Gill, Chair, 217-581-6306, Fax: 217-581-5718, E-mail: mjgill@eiu.edu. *Application contact:* Dr. Angela S. Jacobs, Graduate

Coordinator, 217-581-2020, Fax: 217-581-5718, E-mail: asjacobs@eiu.edu. Website: http://www.eiu.edu/commstudiesgrad/index.php

Eastern Michigan University, Graduate School, College of Arts and Sciences, School of Communication, Media and Theatre Arts, Program in Communication, Ypsilanti, MI 48197. Offers MA. *Program availability:* Part-time, evening/weekend, online learning. *Students:* 7 full-time (4 women), 27 part-time (18 women); includes 17 minority (14 Black or African American, non-Hispanic/Latino; 3 Hispanic/Latino). Average age 28. 34 applicants, 62% accepted, 11 enrolled. In 2017, 16 master's awarded. *Degree requirements:* For master's, thesis or alternative. *Entrance requirements:* Additional exam requirements/recommendations for international students: Required—TOEFL. *Application deadline:* Applications are processed on a rolling basis. Application fee: $45. *Financial support:* Fellowships, research assistantships with full tuition reimbursements, teaching assistantships with full tuition reimbursements, career-related internships or fieldwork, Federal Work-Study, institutionally sponsored loans, scholarships/grants, tuition waivers (partial), and unspecified assistantships available. Support available to part-time students. Financial award applicants required to submit FAFSA. *Application contact:* Dr. Doris Fields, Coordinator, 734-487-4199, Fax: 734-487-3443, E-mail: dfields1@emich.edu.

Eastern New Mexico University, Graduate School, College of Fine Arts, Portales, NM 88130. Offers communication (MA). *Program availability:* Part-time, online learning. *Degree requirements:* For master's, comprehensive exam, thesis optional. *Entrance requirements:* For master's, minimum GPA of 3.0, writing sample. Additional exam requirements/recommendations for international students: Required—TOEFL (minimum score 550 paper-based; 79 iBT), IELTS (minimum score 6). *Application deadline:* For fall admission, 7/20 priority date for domestic students, 6/20 priority date for international students; for spring admission, 12/15 priority date for domestic students, 11/15 priority date for international students. Applications are processed on a rolling basis. Application fee: $10. Electronic applications accepted. *Financial support:* Applicants required to submit FAFSA. *Unit head:* Dr. Patricia Dobson, Graduate Coordinator, 575-562-2778, E-mail: patricia.dobson@enmu.edu. *Application contact:* Gail Crozier, Receptionist/Records Clerk, 575-562-2147, Fax: 575-562-2500, E-mail: gail.crozier@enmu.edu. Website: http://fine-arts.enmu.edu/

Eastern University, Graduate Education Programs, St. Davids, PA 19087-3696. Offers ESL program specialist (K-12) (Certificate); general supervisor (PreK-12) (Certificate); health and physical education (K-12) (Certificate); middle level (4-8) (Certificate); multicultural education (M Ed); music (K-12) (Certificate); Pre K-4 (Certificate); Pre K-4 with special education (Certificate); reading (M Ed); reading specialist (K-12) (Certificate); reading supervisor (K-12) (Certificate); school counseling (MA, CAGS); school principalship (preK-12) (Certificate); school psychology (MS, CAGS); secondary biology education (7-12) (Certificate); secondary chemistry education (7-12) (Certificate); secondary communication education (7-12) (Certificate); secondary English education (7-12) (Certificate); secondary math education (7-12) (Certificate); secondary social studies education (7-12) (Certificate); special education (M Ed); special education (7-12) (Certificate); special education (Pre K-8) (Certificate); special education supervisor (K-12) (Certificate); TESOL (M Ed); world language (Certificate), including Spanish. *Program availability:* Part-time, evening/weekend, online learning. *Students:* 46 full-time (40 women), 115 part-time (93 women); includes 65 minority (42 Black or African American, non-Hispanic/Latino; 3 Asian, non-Hispanic/Latino; 14 Hispanic/Latino; 6 Two or more races, non-Hispanic/Latino), 1 international. Average age 32. In 2017, 72 master's awarded. *Entrance requirements:* Additional exam requirements/recommendations for international students: Required—TOEFL. *Application deadline:* Applications are processed on a rolling basis. Application fee: $35. Electronic applications accepted. Application fee is waived when completed online. *Expenses:* Contact institution. *Unit head:* Michael Dziedziak, Executive Director of Enrollment, 800-452-0996, E-mail: gpsadmissions@eastern.edu. Website: https://www.eastern.edu/academics/programs/education-department-graduate-programs/graduate-programs

Eastern Washington University, Graduate Studies, College of Social Sciences, Department of Communication Studies, Cheney, WA 99004-2431. Offers MSC. *Program availability:* Part-time, evening/weekend. *Faculty:* 5. *Students:* 14 full-time (7 women), 3 part-time (all women); includes 2 minority (1 American Indian or Alaska Native, non-Hispanic/Latino; 1 Hispanic/Latino), 1 international. Average age 35. 23 applicants, 30% accepted, 7 enrolled. In 2017, 13 master's awarded. *Degree requirements:* For master's, comprehensive exam, thesis or alternative. *Entrance requirements:* For master's, GRE General Test, minimum GPA of 3.0. Additional exam requirements/recommendations for international students: Required—TOEFL (minimum score 580 paper-based; 92 iBT), IELTS (minimum score 7), TWE, PTE (minimum score 63). *Application deadline:* For fall admission, 4/1 priority date for domestic students; for spring admission, 1/15 for domestic students. Applications are processed on a rolling basis. Application fee: $75. Electronic applications accepted. *Expenses:* Tuition, state resident: full-time $11,191; part-time $373.06 per credit. Tuition, nonresident: full-time $25,995; part-time $866.52 per credit. *Financial support:* Teaching assistantships with partial tuition reimbursements, career-related internships or fieldwork, Federal Work-Study, institutionally sponsored loans, scholarships/grants, health care benefits, tuition waivers (partial), and unspecified assistantships available. Support available to part-time students. Financial award application deadline: 2/1; financial award applicants required to submit FAFSA. *Unit head:* Dr. Peter Shields, 509-359-4947. *Application contact:* Kathy White, Advisor/Recruiter for Graduate Studies, 509-359-6297, Fax: 509-359-6044, E-mail: gradprograms@ewu.edu.

East Tennessee State University, School of Graduate Studies, College of Arts and Sciences, Department of Communication and Performance, Johnson City, TN 37614. Offers communication and storytelling studies (MA), including communication studies; storytelling (Postbaccalaureate Certificate). *Program availability:* Part-time. *Degree requirements:* For master's, comprehensive exam, thesis optional, admission to candidacy after completion of core semester hours. *Entrance requirements:* For master's, GRE General Test, minimum GPA of 3.0; three letters of recommendation; for Postbaccalaureate Certificate, essay, official transcript from each undergraduate and graduate institution attended, three letters of recommendation from academic or professional mentors or associates. Additional exam requirements/recommendations for international students: Required—TOEFL (minimum score 550 paper-based; 79 iBT). *Application deadline:* For fall admission, 6/1 for domestic students, 4/29 for international students; for spring admission, 11/1 for domestic students, 9/29 for international students. Application fee: $55 ($65 for international students). Electronic applications accepted. *Financial support:* Research assistantships with full tuition reimbursements, teaching assistantships with full tuition reimbursements, career-related internships or fieldwork, institutionally sponsored loans, scholarships/grants, and unspecified assistantships available. Financial award application deadline: 7/1; financial award applicants required to submit FAFSA. *Faculty research:* Political communications, visual communication, depictions of gender and ethnicity in print and online media and online corporate media, presidential rhetoric and newspaper coverage of presidential speeches. *Unit head:* Dr. Amber Kinser, Chair, 423-439-7676, E-mail: kinsera@etsu.edu. *Application contact:* Dr. Amber Kinser, Chair, 423-439-7676, E-mail: kinsera@etsu.edu. Website: http://www.etsu.edu/cas/comm_perform/

Edinboro University of Pennsylvania, Department of Communication Studies, Edinboro, PA 16444. Offers MA. *Program availability:* Part-time, evening/weekend. *Degree requirements:* For master's, thesis or alternative, competency exam. *Entrance requirements:* For master's, GRE or MAT, minimum QPA of 2.5. Electronic applications accepted.

Fairfield University, College of Arts and Sciences, Fairfield, CT 06824. Offers American studies (MA); communication (MA); creative writing (MFA); mathematics (MS); public administration (MPA). *Program availability:* Part-time, evening/weekend, online learning. *Faculty:* 16 full-time (8 women), 12 part-time/adjunct (8 women). *Students:* 67 full-time (46 women), 64 part-time (35 women); includes 27 minority (8 Black or African American, non-Hispanic/Latino; 1 Asian, non-Hispanic/Latino; 14 Hispanic/Latino; 4 Two or more races, non-Hispanic/Latino), 10 international. Average age 32. 80 applicants, 81% accepted, 43 enrolled. In 2017, 38 master's awarded. *Degree requirements:* For master's, capstone research course. *Entrance requirements:* For master's, minimum GPA of 3.0, 2 letters of recommendation, resume, personal statement. Additional exam requirements/recommendations for international students: Required—TOEFL (minimum score 550 paper-based; 80 iBT) or IELTS (minimum score 6.5). *Application deadline:* For fall admission, 5/15 for international students; for spring admission, 10/15 for international students. Applications are processed on a rolling basis. Application fee: $60. Electronic applications accepted. *Expenses:* $725 per credit hour (for American studies, communication and math programs); $575 per credit hour (for MFA); $775 per credit hour (for MPA). *Financial support:* In 2017–18, 11 students received support. Scholarships/grants and unspecified assistantships available. Financial award applicants required to submit FAFSA. *Faculty research:* Nutrition and physiology, media industries, community-based teaching and learning, non commutative algebra and partial differential equations, cancer research in biology and physics. *Unit head:* Dr. Richard Greenwald, Dean, 203-254-4000 Ext. 2221, Fax: 203-254-4119, E-mail: rgreenwald@fairfield.edu. *Application contact:* Marianne Gumpper, Director of Graduate Admission, 203-254-4184, Fax: 203-254-4073, E-mail: gradadmis@fairfield.edu. Website: http://www.fairfield.edu/cas

Fairleigh Dickinson University, Metropolitan Campus, University College: Arts, Sciences, and Professional Studies, School of Art and Media Studies, Program in Media and Communications, Teaneck, NJ 07666-1914. Offers MA.

Fitchburg State University, Division of Graduate and Continuing Education, Program in Applied Communications, Fitchburg, MA 01420-2697. Offers applied communication studies (MS); technical and professional writing (MS). *Program availability:* Part-time, evening/weekend. *Faculty:* 6 full-time (4 women). *Students:* 1 (woman) full-time, 18 part-time (11 women); includes 3 minority (1 Hispanic/Latino; 2 Two or more races, non-Hispanic/Latino). Average age 36. 6 applicants, 100% accepted, 4 enrolled. In 2017, 6 master's awarded. *Entrance requirements:* Additional exam requirements/recommendations for international students: Required—TOEFL (minimum score 550 paper-based; 79 iBT). *Application deadline:* For fall admission, 7/15 for international students; for spring admission, 12/1 for international students. Applications are processed on a rolling basis. Application fee: $50. Electronic applications accepted. *Expenses:* Contact institution. *Financial support:* In 2017–18, research assistantships with partial tuition reimbursements (averaging $5,500 per year) were awarded; Federal Work-Study, scholarships/grants, and unspecified assistantships also available. Support available to part-time students. Financial award application deadline: 3/1; financial award applicants required to submit FAFSA. *Unit head:* Dr. Viera Lorencova, Chair, 978-665-4856, Fax: 978-665-3658, E-mail: gce@fitchburgstate.edu. *Application contact:* Jinawa McNeil, Director of Admissions, 978-665-3140, Fax: 978-665-4540, E-mail: admissions@fitchburgstate.edu.

Fitchburg State University, Division of Graduate and Continuing Education, Program in Interdisciplinary Studies, Fitchburg, MA 01420-2697. Offers applied communications (CAGS); counseling/psychology (CAGS); individualized track (CAGS); reading specialist (CAGS). *Program availability:* Part-time, evening/weekend. *Students:* 11 full-time (all women), 14 part-time (13 women); includes 3 minority (all Hispanic/Latino). Average age 36. 5 applicants, 100% accepted, 5 enrolled. In 2017, 14 CAGSs awarded. *Entrance requirements:* Additional exam requirements/recommendations for international students: Required—TOEFL (minimum score 550 paper-based; 79 iBT). *Application deadline:* For fall admission, 7/15 for international students; for spring admission, 12/1 for international students. Applications are processed on a rolling basis. Application fee: $50. Electronic applications accepted. *Expenses:* Contact institution. *Financial support:* In 2017–18, research assistantships with partial tuition reimbursements (averaging $5,500 per year) were awarded; Federal Work-Study, scholarships/grants, and unspecified assistantships also available. Support available to part-time students. Financial award application deadline: 3/1; financial award applicants required to submit FAFSA. *Unit head:* Dr. Jessica Robey, Chair, 978-665-3386, Fax: 978-665-3658, E-mail: gce@fitchburgstate.edu. *Application contact:* Jinawa McNeil, Director of Admissions, 978-665-3140, Fax: 978-665-4540, E-mail: admissions@fitchburgstate.edu.

Florida Atlantic University, Dorothy F. Schmidt College of Arts and Letters, School of Communication and Multimedia Studies, Boca Raton, FL 33431-0991. Offers communication studies (MA); film and video (Certificate); media, technology and entertainment (MFA). *Program availability:* Part-time. *Faculty:* 24 full-time (8 women). *Students:* 21 full-time (15 women), 16 part-time (9 women); includes 19 minority (11 Black or African American, non-Hispanic/Latino; 1 Asian, non-Hispanic/Latino; 6 Hispanic/Latino; 1 Two or more races, non-Hispanic/Latino), 2 international. Average age 32. 29 applicants, 52% accepted, 13 enrolled. In 2017, 15 master's awarded. *Degree requirements:* For master's, one foreign language, comprehensive exam (for some programs), thesis (for some programs). *Entrance requirements:* For master's, GRE General Test, minimum GPA of 3.0, essay, letters of recommendation. *Application deadline:* For fall admission, 7/1 priority date for domestic students, 4/1 for international students; for spring admission, 11/1 for domestic students, 10/1 for international students. Applications are processed on a rolling basis. Application fee: $30. Electronic applications accepted. *Expenses:* Tuition, state resident: full-time $7400; part-time $369.82 per credit. Tuition, nonresident: full-time $20,496; part-time $1042.81 per credit. *Financial support:* Teaching assistantships with partial tuition reimbursements, Federal Work-Study, institutionally sponsored loans, scholarships/grants, and unspecified assistantships available. Support available to part-time students. Financial award application deadline: 3/1; financial award applicants required to submit FAFSA. *Faculty research:* Cultural studies, gender studies, film, communication theory, journalism, new media. *Unit head:* Dr. David Williams, Director, 561-297-0045, Fax: 561-297-2615, E-mail: dcwill@fau.edu. *Application contact:* Dr. Stephen Charbonneau, Graduate Director, 561-297-3856, Fax: 561-297-2615, E-mail: efreedma@fau.edu. Website: http://www.fau.edu/scms/

Florida Institute of Technology, College of Psychology and Liberal Arts, Program in Global Strategic Communication, Melbourne, FL 32901-6975. Offers MS. *Program availability:* Part-time. *Students:* Average age 27. 27 applicants, 59% accepted, 3 enrolled. In 2017, 6 master's awarded. *Degree requirements:* For master's, comprehensive exam, thesis optional, minimum of 36 credit hours. *Entrance*

requirements: For master's, GRE General Test (recommended), 2 letters of recommendation, statement of objectives, previous work experience. Additional exam requirements/recommendations for international students: Required—TOEFL (minimum score 550 paper-based; 79 iBT). *Application deadline:* Applications are processed on a rolling basis. Electronic applications accepted. *Expenses:* Tuition: Part-time $1241 per credit hour. Part-time tuition and fees vary according to campus/location. *Financial support:* Applicants required to submit FAFSA. *Unit head:* Dr. Judith B. Strother, Professor/Chair, MS in Global Strategic Communication, 321-674-7358, Fax: 321-674-8109, E-mail: strother@fit.edu. *Application contact:* Cheryl A. Brown, Associate Director of Graduate Admissions, 321-674-7581, Fax: 321-723-9468, E-mail: cbrown@fit.edu. Website: http://cpla.fit.edu/sac/global-strategic-communication/

Florida International University, College of Communication, Architecture and The Arts, School of Communication and Journalism, Miami, FL 33199. Offers mass communication (MS), including global strategic communications, Spanish language journalism. *Program availability:* Part-time, evening/weekend. *Faculty:* 35 full-time (24 women), 59 part-time/adjunct (38 women). *Students:* 91 full-time (63 women), 65 part-time (47 women); includes 112 minority (20 Black or African American, non-Hispanic/Latino; 3 Asian, non-Hispanic/Latino; 84 Hispanic/Latino; 5 Two or more races, non-Hispanic/Latino), 31 international. Average age 28. 122 applicants, 68% accepted, 67 enrolled. In 2017, 86 master's awarded. *Degree requirements:* For master's, thesis optional. *Entrance requirements:* For master's, 2 letters of recommendation; minimum GPA of 3.0 during last 60 hours of upper-level work; resume. Additional exam requirements/recommendations for international students: Required—TOEFL (minimum score 550 paper-based; 80 iBT). *Application deadline:* For fall admission, 6/1 for domestic students, 4/1 for international students; for spring admission, 10/1 for domestic students, 9/1 for international students. Applications are processed on a rolling basis. Application fee: $30. Electronic applications accepted. *Expenses:* Tuition, state resident: full-time $8912; part-time $446 per credit hour. Tuition, nonresident: full-time $21,393; part-time $992 per credit hour. *Required fees:* $390; $195 per semester. *Financial support:* Institutionally sponsored loans and scholarships/grants available. Financial award application deadline: 3/1; financial award applicants required to submit FAFSA. *Unit head:* Dr. Maria Elena Villar, Chair, 305-919-5795, Fax: 305-919-5215, E-mail: mariaelena.villar@fiu.edu. *Application contact:* Nanett Rojas, Assistant Director, Graduate Admissions, 305-348-7442, Fax: 305-348-7441, E-mail: gradadm@fiu.edu. Website: https://scj.fiu.edu/

Florida State University, The Graduate School, College of Communication and Information, School of Communication, Tallahassee, FL 32306. Offers communication theory and research (PhD); integrated marketing communication (MA, MS); media and communication studies (MA, MS); public interest media and communication (MA, MS). *Program availability:* Part-time. *Faculty:* 20 full-time (11 women), 1 part-time/adjunct (0 women). *Students:* 104 full-time (74 women), 38 part-time (27 women); includes 81 minority (20 Black or African American, non-Hispanic/Latino; 24 Asian, non-Hispanic/Latino; 26 Hispanic/Latino; 1 Native Hawaiian or other Pacific Islander, non-Hispanic/Latino; 10 Two or more races, non-Hispanic/Latino). Average age 24. 184 applicants, 59% accepted, 46 enrolled. In 2017, 59 master's, 5 doctorates awarded. *Degree requirements:* For master's, thesis (for some programs); for doctorate, comprehensive exam, thesis/dissertation. *Entrance requirements:* For master's, GRE General Test, minimum GPA of 3.0; for doctorate, GRE General Test, minimum GPA of 3.3 in graduate course work. Additional exam requirements/recommendations for international students: Required—TOEFL (minimum score 600 paper-based; 100 iBT), IELTS (minimum score 7). *Application deadline:* For fall admission, 7/1 priority date for domestic students, 5/1 priority date for international students; for spring admission, 11/1 priority date for domestic and international students; for summer admission, 3/1 priority date for domestic and international students. Applications are processed on a rolling basis. Application fee: $30. Electronic applications accepted. *Expenses:* Contact institution. *Financial support:* In 2017–18, 112 students received support, including 28 research assistantships with full tuition reimbursements available (averaging $11,752 per year), 81 teaching assistantships with full tuition reimbursements available (averaging $10,109 per year); scholarships/grants, tuition waivers (full and partial), and unspecified assistantships also available. Financial award application deadline: 11/1; financial award applicants required to submit FAFSA. *Faculty research:* Communication in the public interest; strategic communication; media and technology; multicultural, intercultural, and international communication. *Total annual research expenditures:* $41,657. *Unit head:* Dr. Jennifer Proffitt, Director, 850-644-5034, Fax: 850-644-8642, E-mail: jennifer.proffitt@cci.fsu.edu. *Application contact:* Natashia Hinson-Turner, Graduate Coordinator, 850-644-5034, Fax: 850-644-8642, E-mail: comgradadvising@cci.fsu.edu. Website: http://www.cci.fsu.edu

Fordham University, Gabelli School of Business, New York, NY 10023. Offers accounting (MBA, MS); applied statistics and decision-making (MS); business economics (DPS); capital markets (DPS); communications and media management (MBA); electronic business (MBA); entrepreneurship (MBA); finance (MBA, PhD); global finance (MS); global sustainability (MBA); health administration (MS); healthcare management (MBA); information systems (MBA, MS); investor relations (MS); management (EMBA, MBA, MS, PhD); marketing (MBA); marketing intelligence (MS); media management (MS); nonprofit leadership (MS); quantitative finance (MS); strategy and decision-making (DPS); taxation (MS); JD/MBA; MS/MBA. *Accreditation:* AACSB. *Program availability:* Part-time, evening/weekend. *Faculty:* 130 full-time (46 women), 42 part-time/adjunct (5 women). *Students:* 1,051 full-time (570 women), 563 part-time (313 women); includes 190 minority (48 Black or African American, non-Hispanic/Latino; 72 Asian, non-Hispanic/Latino; 69 Hispanic/Latino; 1 Native Hawaiian or other Pacific Islander, non-Hispanic/Latino), 1,106 international. Average age 27. 4,577 applicants, 58% accepted, 794 enrolled. In 2017, 937 master's awarded. Terminal master's awarded for partial completion of doctoral program. *Degree requirements:* For master's, internships (for some degrees); for doctorate, comprehensive exam (for some programs), thesis/dissertation. *Entrance requirements:* For master's, GMAT/GRE, 2 letters of recommendation, resume, 2 essays, transcripts, interview. Additional exam requirements/recommendations for international students: Required—TOEFL (minimum score 100 iBT), IELTS (minimum score 7). *Application deadline:* For fall admission, 11/15 priority date for domestic and international students; for winter admission, 1/19 priority date for domestic students, 1/1 priority date for international students; for spring admission, 4/15 for domestic students, 3/1 for international students; for summer admission, 6/1 for domestic students. Application fee: $130. Electronic applications accepted. *Expenses:* $1,495 per credit. *Financial support:* Career-related internships or fieldwork, institutionally sponsored loans, scholarships/grants, and unspecified assistantships available. Support available to part-time students. Financial award application deadline: 6/30; financial award applicants required to submit FAFSA. *Unit head:* Dr. Donna Rapaccioli, Dean, 212-636-6165, Fax: 212-307-1779, E-mail: rapaccioli@fordham.edu. *Application contact:* Lawrence Murray, Senior Assistant Dean of Graduate Admissions and Advising, 212-636-6200, Fax: 212-636-7076, E-mail: admissionsgb@fordham.edu. Website: http://www.fordham.edu/gabelli

Fordham University, Graduate School of Arts and Sciences, Department of Communication and Media Studies, New York, NY 10458. Offers public media (MA).

Program offered in collaboration with WFUV and WNET. *Program availability:* Part-time, evening/weekend. *Faculty:* 11 full-time (3 women). *Students:* 17 full-time (10 women), 1 part-time (0 women); includes 10 minority (4 Black or African American, non-Hispanic/Latino; 1 American Indian or Alaska Native, non-Hispanic/Latino; 1 Asian, non-Hispanic/Latino; 4 Hispanic/Latino), 1 international. Average age 25. 91 applicants, 49% accepted, 18 enrolled. In 2017, 17 master's awarded. *Degree requirements:* For master's, thesis, internship. *Entrance requirements:* For master's, GRE General Test. Additional exam requirements/recommendations for international students: Required—TOEFL (minimum score 600 paper-based). *Application deadline:* For fall admission, 1/4 priority date for domestic students; for spring admission, 11/1 for domestic students. Application fee: $70. Electronic applications accepted. *Financial support:* In 2017–18, 3 students received support, including 2 research assistantships with full and partial tuition reimbursements available (averaging $23,200 per year); career-related internships or fieldwork, Federal Work-Study, institutionally sponsored loans, scholarships/grants, tuition waivers (full and partial), and unspecified assistantships also available. Financial award application deadline: 1/4. *Total annual research expenditures:* $1.1 million. *Unit head:* Jacqueline Reich, Chair, 718-817-4850, E-mail: jreich8@fordham.edu. *Application contact:* Travis Strattion, Interim Director of Graduate Admissions, 718-817-4417, Fax: 718-817-3566, E-mail: tstrattion@fordham.edu.

Fort Hays State University, Graduate School, College of Arts and Sciences, Department of Communication Studies, Hays, KS 67601-4099. Offers communication (MS). *Program availability:* Part-time. *Degree requirements:* For master's, comprehensive exam, thesis optional. *Entrance requirements:* Additional exam requirements/recommendations for international students: Required—TOEFL (minimum score 550 paper-based). Electronic applications accepted. *Faculty research:* Listening skills development, oral sensory motor skills, speech, reading, articulation in preschool children.

George Mason University, College of Humanities and Social Sciences, Department of Communication, Fairfax, VA 22030. Offers communication (MA, PhD, Certificate); science communication (Certificate). *Faculty:* 40 full-time (14 women), 28 part-time/adjunct (17 women). *Students:* 40 full-time (29 women), 27 part-time (21 women); includes 17 minority (5 Black or African American, non-Hispanic/Latino; 2 American Indian or Alaska Native, non-Hispanic/Latino; 5 Asian, non-Hispanic/Latino; 4 Hispanic/Latino; 1 Two or more races, non-Hispanic/Latino), 5 international. Average age 32. 85 applicants, 67% accepted, 25 enrolled. In 2017, 19 master's, 6 doctorates, 2 other advanced degrees awarded. *Degree requirements:* For master's, comprehensive exam, thesis or project; for doctorate, comprehensive exam, thesis/dissertation; for Certificate, 15-18 credits. *Entrance requirements:* For master's, GRE, expanded goals statement; 2 letters of recommendation; resume; official transcripts; writing sample; for doctorate, GRE, 3 letters of recommendation; expanded goals statement; resume; official transcript; writing sample; for Certificate, GRE, expanded goals statement, resume, 2 letters of recommendation, official transcripts. Additional exam requirements/recommendations for international students: Required—TOEFL (minimum score 570 paper-based; 88 iBT), IELTS (minimum score 6.5), PTE (minimum score 59). Application fee: $75 ($80 for international students). Electronic applications accepted. *Expenses:* Tuition, state resident: full-time $11,228; part-time $459.50 per credit. Tuition, nonresident: full-time $30,932; part-time $1280.50 per credit. *Required fees:* $3252; $135.50 per credit. Part-time tuition and fees vary according to course load and program. *Financial support:* In 2017–18, 26 students received support, including 6 research assistantships with tuition reimbursements available (averaging $15,805 per year), 23 teaching assistantships with tuition reimbursements available (averaging $11,356 per year); career-related internships or fieldwork, Federal Work-Study, scholarships/grants, unspecified assistantships, and health care benefits (for full-time research or teaching assistantship recipients) also available. Support available to part-time students. Financial award application deadline: 3/1; financial award applicants required to submit FAFSA. *Faculty research:* Theoretical and multi-methodological promotion, disease prevention, quality of care, risk assessment, crisis management, consumer/provider relationships, health campaigns, communication policy. *Total annual research expenditures:* $2 million. *Unit head:* Dr. Anne M. Nicotera, Chair, 703-993-8296, Fax: 703-993-1096, E-mail: anicoter@gmu.edu. *Application contact:* Brittany Sanders, Graduate Programs Coordinator, 703-993-1090, Fax: 703-993-1096, E-mail: bsander7@gmu.edu. Website: http://communication.gmu.edu

Georgetown University, Graduate School of Arts and Sciences, Program in Communication, Culture, and Technology, Washington, DC 20057. Offers MA. *Program availability:* Part-time, evening/weekend. *Degree requirements:* For master's, thesis (for some programs). *Entrance requirements:* For master's, GRE General Test, 3 letters of recommendation, writing sample. Additional exam requirements/recommendations for international students: Required—TOEFL (minimum score 600 paper-based). Electronic applications accepted.

The George Washington University, Elliott School of International Affairs, Program in Global Communication, Washington, DC 20052. Offers MA. *Program availability:* Part-time. *Students:* 21 full-time (17 women), 13 part-time (10 women); includes 8 minority (3 Black or African American, non-Hispanic/Latino; 3 Asian, non-Hispanic/Latino; 2 Hispanic/Latino), 9 international. Average age 26. 86 applicants, 67% accepted, 13 enrolled. In 2017, 20 master's awarded. *Degree requirements:* For master's, one foreign language, capstone project. *Entrance requirements:* For master's, GRE General Test, 2 years (or equivalent) of a modern, spoken foreign language; introductory microeconomics/macroeconomics. Additional exam requirements/recommendations for international students: Required—TOEFL (minimum score 100 iBT), IELTS (minimum score 7). *Application deadline:* For fall admission, 1/15 priority date for domestic and international students; for spring admission, 10/1 for domestic students. Electronic applications accepted. *Expenses:* Tuition: Full-time $28,800; part-time $1655 per credit hour. *Required fees:* $45; $2.75 per credit hour. *Financial support:* Fellowships, Federal Work-Study, and scholarships/grants available. Financial award application deadline: 1/15; financial award applicants required to submit FAFSA. *Unit head:* Janet Steele, Director, 202-994-2004, Fax: 202-994-5806, E-mail: jesteele@gwu.edu. *Application contact:* Nicole A. Campbell, Director of Graduate Admissions, 202-994-7050, Fax: 202-994-9537, E-mail: esiagrad@gwu.edu. Website: http://www.gwu.edu/~elliott/academics/grad/gc/

Georgia State University, College of Arts and Sciences, Department of Communication, Atlanta, GA 30302-3083. Offers film, video, and digital imaging (MA), including critical studies, production, screenwriting; human communication and social influence (MA); mass communication (MA); media and society (PhD); moving image studies (PhD); public communication (PhD); rhetoric and politics (PhD). *Program availability:* Part-time. *Faculty:* 57 full-time (34 women). *Students:* 71 full-time (51 women), 17 part-time (9 women); includes 36 minority (28 Black or African American, non-Hispanic/Latino; 1 Asian, non-Hispanic/Latino; 4 Hispanic/Latino; 1 Native Hawaiian or other Pacific Islander, non-Hispanic/Latino; 2 Two or more races, non-Hispanic/Latino), 15 international. Average age 33. 63 applicants, 54% accepted, 17 enrolled. In 2017, 20 master's, 10 doctorates awarded. *Degree requirements:* For master's, variable foreign language requirement, thesis (for some programs); for doctorate, comprehensive exam, thesis/dissertation. *Entrance requirements:* For master's and doctorate, GRE. Additional exam requirements/recommendations for international students: Required—TOEFL (minimum score 550 paper-based; 80 iBT), IELTS (minimum score 6.5).

Application deadline: For fall admission, 2/10 for domestic and international students; for spring admission, 10/15 for domestic and international students. Application fee: $50. Electronic applications accepted. *Expenses:* Tuition, state resident: full-time $7020. Tuition, nonresident: full-time $22,518. *Required fees:* $2128. Tuition and fees vary according to degree level and program. *Financial support:* In 2017–18, fellowships with tuition reimbursements (averaging $15,000 per year), teaching assistantships with tuition reimbursements (averaging $15,000 per year) were awarded; career-related internships or fieldwork and unspecified assistantships also available. Financial award applicants required to submit FAFSA. *Faculty research:* New media, mass media and journalism, rhetoric, film and media studies, film production. *Unit head:* Dr. Greg Lisby, Chair, 404-413-5639, Fax: 404-413-5634, E-mail: glisby@gsu.edu. Website: http://communication.gsu.edu

Governors State University, College of Arts and Sciences, Program in Communication and Training, University Park, IL 60484. Offers communication studies (MA). *Program availability:* Part-time. *Faculty:* 60 full-time (34 women), 115 part-time/adjunct (58 women). *Students:* 8 full-time (7 women), 45 part-time (33 women); includes 42 minority (39 Black or African American, non-Hispanic/Latino; 1 Asian, non-Hispanic/Latino; 2 Two or more races, non-Hispanic/Latino). Average age 43. 25 applicants, 60% accepted, 13 enrolled. In 2017, 23 master's awarded. *Application deadline:* For fall admission, 4/1 for domestic students. Applications are processed on a rolling basis. Application fee: $50. Electronic applications accepted. *Expenses:* Tuition, state resident: full-time $8472; part-time $353 per credit hour. Tuition, nonresident: full-time $16,944; part-time $706 per credit hour. *Required fees:* $1824; $76 per credit hour. $38 per term. Tuition and fees vary according to course load, degree level and program. *Financial support:* Application deadline: 5/1; applicants required to submit FAFSA. *Unit head:* Lori Montalbano, Chair, Division of Arts and Letters, 708-534-5000 Ext. 2802, E-mail: lmontalbano@govst.edu.

Grand Valley State University, College of Liberal Arts and Sciences, School of Communications, Allendale, MI 49401-9403. Offers MS. *Program availability:* Part-time, evening/weekend. *Faculty:* 2 full-time (0 women), 1 part-time/adjunct (0 women). *Students:* 18 full-time (9 women), 35 part-time (21 women); includes 11 minority (4 Black or African American, non-Hispanic/Latino; 1 Asian, non-Hispanic/Latino; 4 Hispanic/Latino; 2 Two or more races, non-Hispanic/Latino), 11 international. Average age 29. 34 applicants, 97% accepted, 17 enrolled. In 2017, 24 master's awarded. *Degree requirements:* For master's, project or thesis. *Entrance requirements:* For master's, minimum GPA of 3.0 in last 60 hours, 2 letters of recommendation, interview, essay or personal statement. Additional exam requirements/recommendations for international students: Required—TOEFL (minimum iBT score of 80), IELTS (6.5), or Michigan English Language Assessment Battery (77). *Application deadline:* For fall admission, 8/15 priority date for domestic students; for winter admission, 12/15 priority date for domestic students; for spring admission, 4/15 priority date for domestic students. Applications are processed on a rolling basis. Application fee: $30. Electronic applications accepted. *Expenses:* $627 per credit hour. *Financial support:* In 2017–18, 12 students received support, including 8 fellowships; research assistantships, career-related internships or fieldwork, Federal Work-Study, and institutionally sponsored loans also available. Support available to part-time students. Financial award application deadline: 4/15. *Faculty research:* Communication technology, databases, organizational communication, systems theory, public relations and advertising. *Unit head:* Dr. Jonathan Hodge, Department Director, 616-331-3668, Fax: 616-895-2700, E-mail: hodgejo@gvsu.edu. *Application contact:* Dr. Alex Nesterenko, Graduate Program Director, 616-331-3667, Fax: 616-331-2700, E-mail: nesterea@gvsu.edu.

Harvard University, Extension School, Cambridge, MA 02138-3722. Offers applied sciences (CAS); biotechnology (ALM); educational technologies (ALM); educational technology (CET); English for graduate and professional studies (DGP); environmental management (ALM, CEM); information technology (ALM); journalism (ALM); liberal arts (ALM); management (ALM, CM); mathematics for teaching (ALM); museum studies (ALM); premedical studies (Diploma); publication and communication (CPC). *Program availability:* Part-time, evening/weekend. *Degree requirements:* For master's, thesis. *Entrance requirements:* For master's, 3 completed graduate courses with grade of B or higher. Additional exam requirements/recommendations for international students: Required—TOEFL (minimum score 600 paper-based), TWE (minimum score 5). *Expenses:* Contact institution.

Hawai`i Pacific University, College of Liberal Arts, Program in Communication, Honolulu, HI 96813. Offers MA. *Program availability:* Part-time, evening/weekend. *Faculty:* 5 full-time (2 women), 2 part-time/adjunct (both women). *Students:* 22 full-time (14 women), 7 part-time (4 women); includes 13 minority (2 Black or African American, non-Hispanic/Latino; 3 Asian, non-Hispanic/Latino; 5 Hispanic/Latino; 3 Two or more races, non-Hispanic/Latino), 10 international. Average age 32. 25 applicants, 92% accepted, 13 enrolled. In 2017, 19 master's awarded. *Entrance requirements:* For master's, transcripts, personal statement, letter of recommendation, resume. Additional exam requirements/recommendations for international students: Recommended—TOEFL (minimum score 550 paper-based; 80 iBT), IELTS (minimum score 6), TWE (minimum score 5). *Application deadline:* For fall admission, 1/15 priority date for domestic students; for spring admission, 10/15 priority date for domestic students. Applications are processed on a rolling basis. Application fee: $50. Electronic applications accepted. *Expenses: Tuition:* Full-time $18,000; part-time $1000 per credit. *Required fees:* $200; $26 per credit. Tuition and fees vary according to course load and program. *Financial support:* In 2017–18, 10 students received support. Career-related internships or fieldwork, Federal Work-Study, scholarships/grants, tuition waivers (partial), and unspecified assistantships available. Financial award application deadline: 3/1; financial award applicants required to submit FAFSA. *Unit head:* Dr. John Hart, Department Chair, 808-544-0805, E-mail: jhart@hpu.edu. *Application contact:* Danny Lam, Assistant Director of Graduate Admissions, 808-544-1135, E-mail: graduate@hpu.edu. Website: https://www.hpu.edu/cla/communication/ma-comm.html

Howard University, Cathy Hughes School of Communications, Washington, DC 20059-0002. Offers MA, MFA, MS, PhD. *Program availability:* Part-time, evening/weekend. Terminal master's awarded for partial completion of doctoral program. *Degree requirements:* For master's, comprehensive exam (for some programs), thesis optional; for doctorate, one foreign language, comprehensive exam, thesis/dissertation. *Entrance requirements:* For master's, GRE General Test, minimum GPA of 3.0; for doctorate, GRE General Test, minimum GPA of 3.2. Additional exam requirements/recommendations for international students: Required—TOEFL. Electronic applications accepted. *Expenses:* Contact institution. *Faculty research:* Communication disorders, intercultural communication, communication skills, race and media.

Idaho State University, Office of Graduate Studies, College of Arts and Letters, Department of Communication, Media, and Persuasion, Pocatello, ID 83209-8115. Offers communication (MA). *Program availability:* Part-time. *Degree requirements:* For master's, comprehensive exam, paper or thesis. *Entrance requirements:* For master's, GRE General Test, minimum GPA of 3.0 in all upper-level courses. Additional exam requirements/recommendations for international students: Required—TOEFL (minimum score 550 paper-based; 80 iBT). Electronic applications accepted. *Faculty research:* Metaphor and cognition in organizational groups and teams; rhetorical criticism of

contemporary culture, including music, film, television, and advertising; communication pedagogy; the effect of language on organizational identification and commitment; risk communication and crisis communication.

Illinois Institute of Technology, Graduate College, Lewis College of Human Sciences, Department of Humanities, Chicago, IL 60616. Offers information architecture (MS); technical communication (PhD); technical communication and information design (MS). *Program availability:* Part-time. *Degree requirements:* For master's, comprehensive exam, thesis or alternative; for doctorate, comprehensive exam, thesis/dissertation. *Entrance requirements:* For master's, GRE General Test (minimum score 144 Quantitative, 153 Verbal, and 4.0 Analytical Writing), minimum undergraduate GPA of 3.0; 2 letters of recommendation from faculty or supervisors; professional statement discussing academic goals; for doctorate, GRE General Test (minimum score 144 Quantitative, 153 Verbal, and 4.0 Analytical Writing), bachelor's or master's degree in a field that, in combination with the 27-credit hour technical core, would provide a solid basis for advanced academic work leading to original research in the field; 3 letters of recommendation from faculty or supervisors; professional statement discussing academic goals. Additional exam requirements/recommendations for international students: Required—TOEFL (minimum score 95 iBT); Recommended—IELTS (minimum score 7). Electronic applications accepted. *Faculty research:* Linguistics, punishment theory, political communication, gender and technology, philosophical and ethical issues in neuroscience.

Illinois State University, Graduate School, College of Arts and Sciences, School of Communication, Normal, IL 61790. Offers MA, MS. *Degree requirements:* For master's, thesis or alternative. *Entrance requirements:* For master's, GRE General Test, minimum GPA of 2.8 in last 60 hours of course work. Additional exam requirements/recommendations for international students: Required—TOEFL.

Indiana State University, College of Graduate and Professional Studies, College of Arts and Sciences, Department of Communication, Terre Haute, IN 47809. Offers communication studies (MA); radio, television and film (MA). *Program availability:* Part-time. *Degree requirements:* For master's, thesis (for some programs), oral and written exam. *Entrance requirements:* For master's, GRE General Test. Additional exam requirements/recommendations for international students: Required—TOEFL. *Faculty research:* Women in media, communication apprehension, media history.

Indiana University of Pennsylvania, School of Graduate Studies and Research, College of Education and Communications, Department of Communications Media, Indiana, PA 15705. Offers communications media and instructional technology (PhD). *Program availability:* Part-time, evening/weekend. *Faculty:* 8 full-time (4 women). *Students:* 12 full-time (6 women), 39 part-time (15 women); includes 10 minority (4 Black or African American, non-Hispanic/Latino; 1 Asian, non-Hispanic/Latino; 3 Hispanic/Latino; 2 Two or more races, non-Hispanic/Latino), 6 international. Average age 39. 41 applicants, 41% accepted, 10 enrolled. In 2017, 10 doctorates awarded. Terminal master's awarded for partial completion of doctoral program. *Degree requirements:* For doctorate, comprehensive exam, thesis/dissertation. *Entrance requirements:* For doctorate, GRE, goal statement, resume, writing sample, two letters of recommendation. Additional exam requirements/recommendations for international students: Required—TOEFL (minimum score 540 paper-based). *Application deadline:* Applications are processed on a rolling basis. Application fee: $50. Electronic applications accepted. *Expenses:* Tuition, state resident: full-time $12,000; part-time $500 per credit. Tuition, nonresident: full-time $18,000; part-time $750 per credit. *Required fees:* $4073; $165.55 per credit. $64 per term. *Financial support:* In 2017–18, 2 fellowships with full tuition reimbursements (averaging $2,296 per year), 7 research assistantships with tuition reimbursements (averaging $5,769 per year), 3 teaching assistantships with partial tuition reimbursements (averaging $23,305 per year) were awarded; career-related internships or fieldwork, Federal Work-Study, scholarships/grants, tuition waivers (full), and unspecified assistantships also available. Support available to part-time students. Financial award application deadline: 4/15; financial award applicants required to submit FAFSA. *Unit head:* Dr. Gail Wilson, Chairperson, 724-357-2492, Fax: 724-357-5503, E-mail: bgwilson@iup.edu. *Application contact:* Dr. Zachary Stiegler, Graduate Coordinator, 724-357-3219, E-mail: zachary.stiegler@iup.edu. Website: http://www.iup.edu/commmedia/

Indiana University–Purdue University Fort Wayne, College of Arts and Sciences, Department of Communication, Fort Wayne, IN 46805-1499. Offers professional communication (MA, MS). *Program availability:* Part-time. *Entrance requirements:* For master's, minimum GPA of 3.0. Additional exam requirements/recommendations for international students: Required—TOEFL (minimum score 550 paper-based; 79 iBT); Recommended—TWE. Electronic applications accepted. *Faculty research:* Cosmetic surgery and Chinese women, First Amendment and online information.

Indiana University–Purdue University Indianapolis, School of Liberal Arts, Department of Communication Studies, Indianapolis, IN 46202. Offers applied communication (MA); health communication (PhD). *Program availability:* Part-time. *Degree requirements:* For master's, comprehensive exam, thesis; for doctorate, thesis/dissertation. *Entrance requirements:* For doctorate, master's degree. Additional exam requirements/recommendations for international students: Required—TOEFL; Recommended—IELTS. Electronic applications accepted.

Indiana University South Bend, Ernestine M. Raclin School of the Arts, South Bend, IN 46615. Offers communication studies (MA); music (MM), including composition, performance; music performance (AD). *Accreditation:* NASM. *Program availability:* Part-time. *Entrance requirements:* For master's, performance audition. Additional exam requirements/recommendations for international students: Required—TOEFL (minimum score 600 paper-based; 90 iBT). Electronic applications accepted. *Expenses:* Contact institution. *Faculty research:* Orchestral conducting.

Instituto Tecnologico de Santo Domingo, Graduate School, Area of Humanities and Social Sciences, Santo Domingo, Dominican Republic. Offers accounting (Certificate); adult education (Certificate); applied linguistics (MA); economics (MA); education (M Ed); educational psychology (MA, Certificate); gender and development (MA, Certificate); humanistic studies (MA); international marketing management (Certificate); international relations in the Caribbean basin (Certificate); intervention systems in family therapy (MA); linguistic and literary communication (Certificate); pedagogical support (MA); social science education (M Ed); sustainable human development (MA); terminal illness and death psychology (Certificate); youth and adult education (M Ed).

Instituto Tecnológico y de Estudios Superiores de Monterrey, Campus Ciudad Obregón, Programs in Education, Program in Communications, Ciudad Obregón, Mexico. Offers ME.

Instituto Tecnológico y de Estudios Superiores de Monterrey, Campus Monterrey, Graduate and Research Division, Program in Natural and Social Sciences, Monterrey, Mexico. Offers biotechnology (MS); chemistry (MS, PhD); communications (MS); education (MA). *Program availability:* Part-time. *Degree requirements:* For master's, one foreign language, thesis; for doctorate, one foreign language, thesis/dissertation. *Entrance requirements:* For master's, EXADEP; for doctorate, EXADEP, master's degree in related field. Additional exam requirements/recommendations for international students: Required—TOEFL. *Faculty research:* Cultural industries, mineral substances, bioremediation, food processing, CQ in industrial chemical processing.

Communication—General

International University in Geneva, Leadership Programs, Geneva, Switzerland. Offers international relations and diplomacy (MIRD); media and communication (MA); public administration (DPA). *Degree requirements:* For master's, comprehensive exam. *Entrance requirements:* Additional exam requirements/recommendations for international students: Required—TOEFL. Electronic applications accepted.

James Madison University, The Graduate School, College of Arts and Letters, Program in Communication and Advocacy, Harrisonburg, VA 22801. Offers environmental communication (MA); health communication (MA); strategic communication (MA). *Program availability:* Part-time, evening/weekend. *Students:* 27 full-time (18 women), 4 part-time (all women); includes 11 minority (6 Black or African American, non-Hispanic/Latino; 2 Asian, non-Hispanic/Latino; 1 Hispanic/Latino; 2 Two or more races, non-Hispanic/Latino), 2 international. Average age 30. In 2017, 7 master's awarded. Application fee: $55. Electronic applications accepted. *Expenses:* Tuition, state resident: full-time $10,512; part-time $438 per credit hour. Tuition, nonresident: full-time $28,358; part-time $1162 per credit hour. *Required fees:* $1128. *Financial support:* In 2017–18, 21 students received support, including 14 fellowships, 7 teaching assistantships with full tuition reimbursements available (averaging $9,284 per year); Federal Work-Study and assistantships (averaging $7911) also available. Financial award application deadline: 3/1; financial award applicants required to submit FAFSA. *Unit head:* Dr. Eric M. Fife, Director of the School of Communication Studies, 540-568-6449, E-mail: fifeem@jmu.edu. *Application contact:* Lynette D. Michael, Director of Graduate Admissions, 540-568-6131 Ext. 6395, Fax: 540-568-7860, E-mail: michaeld@jmu.edu.
Website: http://www.jmu.edu/commstudies/

Johns Hopkins University, Engineering Program for Professionals, Part-time Program in Computer Science, Baltimore, MD 21218. Offers communications and networking (MS); computer science (Post-Master's Certificate). *Program availability:* Part-time, evening/weekend, 100% online, blended/hybrid learning. *Entrance requirements:* Additional exam requirements/recommendations for international students: Required—TOEFL (minimum score 600 paper-based; 100 iBT). Electronic applications accepted.

Johns Hopkins University, Engineering Program for Professionals, Part-time Program in Electrical and Computer Engineering, Baltimore, MD 21218. Offers communications and networking (MS); electrical and computer engineering (Graduate Certificate, Post-Master's Certificate); photonics (MS). *Program availability:* Part-time, evening/weekend, 100% online, blended/hybrid learning. *Degree requirements:* For master's and other advanced degree, thesis optional. *Entrance requirements:* Additional exam requirements/recommendations for international students: Required—TOEFL (minimum score 600 paper-based; 100 iBT). Electronic applications accepted.

Johns Hopkins University, Zanvyl Krieger School of Arts and Sciences, Advanced Academic Programs, Program in Communication, Washington, DC 20036. Offers MA, MA/MBA. *Program availability:* Part-time, evening/weekend, online learning. *Degree requirements:* For master's, thesis. *Entrance requirements:* For master's, minimum GPA of 3.0, strong writing skills. Additional exam requirements/recommendations for international students: Required—TOEFL (minimum score 100 iBT). Electronic applications accepted.

Kansas State University, Graduate School, College of Arts and Sciences, A.Q. Miller School of Journalism and Mass Communications, Manhattan, KS 66506. Offers advertising (MS); community journalism (MS); global communication (MS); health communication (MS); media management (MS); public relations (MS). *Program availability:* Part-time, evening/weekend. *Degree requirements:* For master's, comprehensive exam, thesis. *Entrance requirements:* For master's, GRE General Test, minimum GPA of 3.0. Additional exam requirements/recommendations for international students: Required—TOEFL (minimum score 79 iBT). Electronic applications accepted. *Faculty research:* Health communication, risk communication, strategic communications, community journalism, global communication.

Kansas State University, Graduate School, College of Arts and Sciences, Department of Communication Studies, Manhattan, KS 66505. Offers MA. *Degree requirements:* For master's, thesis or alternative. *Entrance requirements:* For master's, GRE General Test (recommended), minimum GPA of 3.0. Additional exam requirements/recommendations for international students: Required—TOEFL. Electronic applications accepted. *Faculty research:* Conflict, public deliberation, political communication, intercultural communication, relational communication.

Kansas State University, Graduate School, College of Arts and Sciences, Department of English, Manhattan, KS 66506. Offers English (MA); technical writing and professional communication (Graduate Certificate). *Program availability:* Part-time. *Degree requirements:* For master's, one foreign language, thesis optional. *Entrance requirements:* For master's, GRE, minimum B average in English. Additional exam requirements/recommendations for international students: Required—TOEFL. Electronic applications accepted. *Faculty research:* Cultural studies, children's literature, American literature, rhetorical and composition theory, British literature.

Kansas State University, Graduate School, College of Engineering, Department of Electrical and Computer Engineering, Manhattan, KS 66506. Offers electrical engineering (MS), including bioengineering, communication systems, design of computer systems, electrical engineering, energy and power systems, integrated circuits and devices, real time embedded systems, renewable energy, signal processing. *Program availability:* Part-time, evening/weekend, online learning. *Degree requirements:* For master's, thesis or alternative, final exam; for doctorate, thesis/dissertation, final exam, preliminary exams. *Entrance requirements:* For master's, GRE General Test, bachelor's degree in electrical engineering or computer science, minimum GPA of 3.0; for doctorate, GRE General Test. Additional exam requirements/recommendations for international students: Required—TOEFL (minimum score 600 paper-based; 85 iBT). Electronic applications accepted. *Faculty research:* Energy systems and renewable energy, computer systems and real time embedded systems, communication systems and signal processing, integrated circuits and devices, bioengineering.

Kean University, College of Liberal Arts, Program in Communication Studies, Union, NJ 07083. Offers MA. *Program availability:* Part-time. *Faculty:* 14 full-time (6 women). *Students:* 6 full-time (4 women), 10 part-time (8 women); includes 7 minority (4 Black or African American, non-Hispanic/Latino; 2 Hispanic/Latino; 1 Two or more races, non-Hispanic/Latino). Average age 33. 8 applicants, 100% accepted, 5 enrolled. In 2017, 15 master's awarded. *Degree requirements:* For master's, comprehensive exam, thesis optional. *Entrance requirements:* For master's, GRE General Test, minimum cumulative GPA of 3.0, official transcripts from all institutions attended, three letters of recommendation, professional resume/curriculum vitae, personal statement. Additional exam requirements/recommendations for international students: Required—TOEFL (minimum score 550 paper-based; 79 iBT), IELTS (minimum score 6.5). *Application deadline:* For fall admission, 6/30 for domestic and international students; for spring admission, 12/1 for domestic and international students. Applications are processed on a rolling basis. Application fee: $75. Electronic applications accepted. *Expenses:* Tuition, state resident: full-time $13,419; part-time $653 per credit. Tuition, nonresident: full-time $18,188; part-time $801 per credit. *Required fees:* $3382; $154 per credit. Tuition and fees vary according to course level, course load, degree level and program. *Financial support:* Scholarships/grants and unspecified assistantships available. Financial award applicants required to submit FAFSA. *Unit head:* Dr. Wenli Yuan, Program Coordinator, 908-737-0471, E-mail: wyuan@kean.edu. *Application contact:* Amy Clark, Program Assistant, 908-737-7100, E-mail: grad-adm@kean.edu.
Website: http://grad.kean.edu/masters-programs/communication-studies

Kennesaw State University, College of Humanities and Social Sciences, Program in Integrated Global Communication, Kennesaw, GA 30144. Offers MA. *Entrance requirements:* For master's, GRE, BA or BS in communication or related field from accredited college or university; official transcripts; two-page resume; 500-word personal statement; three letters of recommendation. Additional exam requirements/recommendations for international students: Required—TOEFL (minimum score 550 paper-based; 80 iBT), IELTS (minimum score 6.5). Electronic applications accepted.

Kent State University, College of Communication and Information, School of Communication Studies, Kent, OH 44242-0001. Offers communication studies (MA); MBA/MA. *Program availability:* Part-time. *Faculty:* 9 full-time (5 women). *Students:* 27 full-time (22 women), 4 part-time (2 women); includes 1 minority (Black or African American, non-Hispanic/Latino), 10 international. Average age 27. 26 applicants, 92% accepted, 12 enrolled. In 2017, 11 master's awarded. *Degree requirements:* For master's, thesis, coursework, project, or internship. *Entrance requirements:* For master's, GRE General Test (for applicants seeking assistantship), minimum GPA of 3.0, goal statement, undergraduate major/minor in communication, writing sample, 3 letters of recommendation, curriculum vitae/resume. Additional exam requirements/recommendations for international students: Required—TOEFL (minimum score 587 paper-based; 94 iBT), IELTS (minimum score 7), PTE (minimum score 65), Michigan English Language Assessment Battery (minimum score 82). *Application deadline:* For fall admission, 1/15 for domestic students, 12/25 for international students; for spring admission, 11/15 for domestic students, 10/25 for international students. Applications are processed on a rolling basis. Application fee: $45 ($70 for international students). Electronic applications accepted. *Expenses:* Tuition, state resident: full-time $11,310; part-time $515 per credit hour. Tuition, nonresident: full-time $20,396; part-time $928 per credit hour. *International tuition:* $18,544 full-time. *Financial support:* Research assistantships with full tuition reimbursements, teaching assistantships with full tuition reimbursements, career-related internships or fieldwork, and unspecified assistantships available. Financial award application deadline: 1/15. *Unit head:* Dr. Elizabeth E. Graham, Director, 330-672-3087, E-mail: egraha18@kent.edu. *Application contact:* Dr. Suzy D'Enbeau, Associate Professor and Graduate Coordinator, 330-672-3802, E-mail: sdenbeau@kent.edu.
Website: http://www.kent.edu/comm/

La Salle University, School of Arts and Sciences, Program in Strategic Communication, Philadelphia, PA 19141-1199. Offers communication consulting and development (MA); communication management (MA); general professional communication (MA); professional and business communication (Certificate); public relations (MA); social and new media (Certificate). *Program availability:* Part-time, evening/weekend, online learning. *Faculty:* 4 full-time (3 women), 1 (woman) part-time/adjunct. *Students:* 11 full-time (4 women), 22 part-time (16 women); includes 10 minority (9 Black or African American, non-Hispanic/Latino; 1 Two or more races, non-Hispanic/Latino). Average age 27. 40 applicants, 93% accepted, 23 enrolled. In 2017, 34 master's, 1 other advanced degree awarded. *Degree requirements:* For master's, practicum. *Entrance requirements:* For master's, writing assessment, professional resume; minimum overall B average; two letters of recommendation (if GPA below 3.25); brief personal statement (about 500 words); interview; for Certificate, writing assessment, minimum GPA of 2.75 in undergraduate studies; brief personal statement (about 500 words); interview. Additional exam requirements/recommendations for international students: Required—TOEFL. *Application deadline:* For fall admission, 8/15 priority date for domestic students, 7/15 for international students; for spring admission, 12/15 priority date for domestic students, 11/15 for international students; for summer admission, 4/15 priority date for domestic students, 3/15 for international students. Applications are processed on a rolling basis. Application fee: $35. Electronic applications accepted. Application fee is waived when completed online. *Expenses:* Contact institution. *Financial support:* In 2017–18, 12 students received support. Scholarships/grants available. Support available to part-time students. Financial award application deadline: 8/31; financial award applicants required to submit FAFSA. *Unit head:* Dr. Pamela Lannutti, Director, 215-951-1935, Fax: 215-951-5043, E-mail: annutti95@lasalle.edu. *Application contact:* Elizabeth Heenan, Director, Graduate and Adult Enrollment, 215-951-1100, Fax: 214-951-1462, E-mail: heenan@lasalle.edu.
Website: http://www.lasalle.edu/strategic-communication/

Lasell College, Graduate and Professional Studies in Communication, Newton, MA 02466-2709. Offers health communication (MSC, Graduate Certificate); integrated marketing communication (MSC, Graduate Certificate); public relations (MSC, Graduate Certificate). *Program availability:* Part-time, evening/weekend, 100% online, blended/hybrid learning. *Faculty:* 3 full-time (2 women), 7 part-time/adjunct (5 women). *Students:* 25 full-time (16 women), 35 part-time (28 women); includes 12 minority (6 Black or African American, non-Hispanic/Latino; 1 Asian, non-Hispanic/Latino; 4 Hispanic/Latino; 1 Two or more races, non-Hispanic/Latino), 16 international. Average age 30. 53 applicants, 45% accepted, 22 enrolled. In 2017, 28 master's awarded. *Degree requirements:* For master's, comprehensive exam, thesis or alternative, minimum GPA of 3.0; special project or internship. *Entrance requirements:* For master's, one-page personal statement, 2 letters of recommendation, resume, bachelor's degree transcript; for Graduate Certificate, bachelor's degree transcript, 2 letters of recommendation, 1-page personal statement, resume. Additional exam requirements/recommendations for international students: Required—TOEFL (minimum score 550 paper-based, 79 iBT) or IELTS (minimum score 6). *Application deadline:* For fall admission, 8/31 priority date for domestic students, 6/30 priority date for international students; for spring admission, 12/31 priority date for domestic students, 10/31 priority date for international students. Applications are processed on a rolling basis. Electronic applications accepted. *Expenses:* $600 per credit. *Financial support:* Federal Work-Study, scholarships/grants, and tuition discounts available. Support available to part-time students. Financial award application deadline: 8/31; financial award applicants required to submit FAFSA. *Faculty research:* Terrorists' use of the Internet; refugees' use of cell phones as means of communication in Jordan and Germany; political communication; analysis of the media coverage of the conflict and peace process in northern Ireland; interpersonal communication; strategies to address bullying in online communities, in schools and in the workplace. *Unit head:* Eric Turner, Vice President of Graduate and Professional Studies, 617-243-2071, Fax: 617-243-2450, E-mail: gradinfo@lasell.edu. *Application contact:* Adrienne Franciosi, Director of Graduate Enrollment, 617-243-2214, Fax: 617-243-2450, E-mail: gradinfo@lasell.edu.
Website: http://www.lasell.edu/academics/graduate-and-professional-studies/programs-of-study/master-of-science-in-communication.html

La Sierra University, College of Arts and Sciences, Department of English and Communication, Riverside, CA 92505. Offers communication (MA), including public relations/advertising, theory emphasis; English (MA), including literary emphasis, writing emphasis. *Program availability:* Part-time. *Degree requirements:* For master's, one foreign language. *Entrance requirements:* For master's, GRE General Test.

Lawrence Technological University, College of Arts and Sciences, Southfield, MI 48075-1058. Offers bioinformatics (Graduate Certificate); computer science (MS), including data science, big data, and data mining, intelligent systems; educational technology (MA), including robotics; instructional design, communication, and presentation (Graduate Certificate); integrated science (MA); science education (MA); technical and professional communication (MS, Graduate Certificate); writing for the digital age (Graduate Certificate). *Program availability:* Part-time, evening/weekend. *Faculty:* 6 full-time (2 women), 7 part-time/adjunct (3 women). *Students:* 34 part-time (15 women); includes 4 minority (1 Black or African American, non-Hispanic/Latino; 2 Asian, non-Hispanic/Latino; 1 Hispanic/Latino), 7 international. Average age 31. 84 applicants, 15% accepted, 10 enrolled. In 2017, 14 master's awarded. *Degree requirements:* For master's, thesis (for some programs). *Entrance requirements:* Additional exam requirements/recommendations for international students: Required—TOEFL (minimum score 550 paper-based; 79 iBT), IELTS (minimum score 6.5). *Application deadline:* For fall admission, 5/27 for international students; for spring admission, 10/8 for international students; for summer admission, 2/14 for international students. Applications are processed on a rolling basis. Application fee: $50. Electronic applications accepted. *Expenses: Tuition:* Full-time $15,274; part-time $1091 per credit. One-time fee: $150. *Financial support:* In 2017–18, 8 students received support. Scholarships/grants and tuition reduction available. Financial award application deadline: 4/1; financial award applicants required to submit FAFSA. *Faculty research:* Computer analysis of music, machine learning of literature and lyrics, customer sentiments and response analysis through social media, peta-scale computing in astronomical databases, early detection of diseases with pattern recognition. *Total annual research expenditures:* $242,460. *Unit head:* Glen Bauer, Interim Dean, 248-204-3532, Fax: 248-204-3518, E-mail: scidean@ltu.edu. *Application contact:* Jane Rohrback, Director of Admissions, 248-204-3160, Fax: 248-204-2228, E-mail: admissions@ltu.edu.

Liberty University, School of Communication and Digital Content, Lynchburg, VA 24515. Offers communication (MA); promotion and video content (MA); social media management (MS); strategic communication (MA). *Program availability:* Part-time. *Students:* 118 full-time (90 women), 137 part-time (95 women); includes 60 minority (37 Black or African American, non-Hispanic/Latino; 1 American Indian or Alaska Native, non-Hispanic/Latino; 1 Asian, non-Hispanic/Latino; 11 Hispanic/Latino; 10 Two or more races, non-Hispanic/Latino), 7 international. Average age 31. 329 applicants, 50% accepted, 95 enrolled. In 2017, 38 master's awarded. *Degree requirements:* For master's, thesis (for some programs). *Entrance requirements:* For master's, minimum undergraduate GPA of 3.0, faculty recommendation, written statement of purpose, writing sample. Additional exam requirements/recommendations for international students: Required—TOEFL (minimum score 600 paper-based; 100 iBT). *Application deadline:* For fall admission, 6/1 for domestic students; for spring admission, 11/1 for domestic students. Applications are processed on a rolling basis. Application fee: $50. Electronic applications accepted. *Financial support:* Federal Work-Study and unspecified assistantships available. Financial award applicants required to submit FAFSA. *Unit head:* Dr. Norman Mintle, Dean, 434-582-2077, E-mail: cvkramer@liberty.edu. *Application contact:* Dr. Terry Elam, Director of Graduate Admissions, 434-582-2111, Fax: 434-582-7836, E-mail: gradadmissions@liberty.edu.

Lindenwood University, Graduate Programs, School of Accelerated Degree Programs, St. Charles, MO 63301-1695. Offers administration (MSA), including management, marketing, project management; business administration (MBA); communications (MA), including digital and multimedia, media management, promotions, training and development; criminal justice and administration (MS); healthcare administration (MS); human resource management (MS); information technology (Certificate); managing information security (MS); managing information technology (MS); managing virtualization and cloud computing (MS); writing (MFA). *Program availability:* Part-time, evening/weekend, 100% online. *Faculty:* 12 full-time (5 women), 90 part-time/adjunct (37 women). *Students:* 597 full-time (383 women), 202 part-time (138 women); includes 248 minority (206 Black or African American, non-Hispanic/Latino; 3 American Indian or Alaska Native, non-Hispanic/Latino; 6 Asian, non-Hispanic/Latino; 21 Hispanic/Latino; 1 Native Hawaiian or other Pacific Islander, non-Hispanic/Latino; 11 Two or more races, non-Hispanic/Latino), 69 international. Average age 36. 526 applicants, 46% accepted, 204 enrolled. In 2017, 537 master's awarded. *Degree requirements:* For master's, thesis (for some programs), minimum cumulative GPA of 3.0; for Certificate, minimum cumulative GPA of 3.0. *Entrance requirements:* For master's, resume, personal statement, official undergraduate transcript, minimum undergraduate cumulative GPA of 3.0. Additional exam requirements/recommendations for international students: Required—TOEFL (minimum score 550 paper-based; 80 iBT); Recommended—IELTS (minimum score 6.5). *Application deadline:* For fall admission, 9/24 priority date for domestic and international students; for winter admission, 1/7 priority date for domestic and international students; for spring admission, 4/8 priority date for domestic and international students; for summer admission, 7/8 priority date for domestic and international students. Applications are processed on a rolling basis. Application fee: $30 ($100 for international students). Electronic applications accepted. *Expenses: Tuition:* Full-time $16,300; part-time $460 per credit. *Required fees:* $660; $330 per credit. Tuition and fees vary according to degree level and program. *Financial support:* In 2017–18, 738 students received support. Career-related internships or fieldwork, institutionally sponsored loans, scholarships/grants, tuition waivers (partial), and unspecified assistantships available. Financial award application deadline: 6/30; financial award applicants required to submit FAFSA. *Unit head:* Dr. Gina Ganahl, Dean, Accelerated Degree Programs, 636-949-4501, Fax: 636-949-4505, E-mail: gganahl@lindenwood.edu. *Application contact:* Kara Schilli, Director, Evening and Graduate Admissions, 636-949-4349, Fax: 636-949-4109, E-mail: adultadmissions@lindenwood.edu.
Website: http://www.lindenwood.edu/academics/academic-schools/school-of-accelerated-degree-programs/

Lindenwood University–Belleville, Graduate Programs, Belleville, IL 62226. Offers business administration (MBA); communications (MA), including digital and multimedia, media management, promotions, training and development; counseling (MA); criminal justice administration (MS); education (MA); healthcare administration (MS); human resource management (MS); school administration (MA); teaching (MAT).

Louisiana State University and Agricultural & Mechanical College, Graduate School, College of Humanities and Social Sciences, Department of Communication Studies, Baton Rouge, LA 70803. Offers MA, PhD. *Faculty:* 11 full-time (6 women). *Students:* 28 full-time (17 women), 6 part-time (2 women); includes 5 minority (4 Black or African American, non-Hispanic/Latino; 1 Hispanic/Latino). Average age 31. 24 applicants, 46% accepted, 7 enrolled. In 2017, 5 master's, 5 doctorates awarded. *Financial support:* In 2017–18, 28 teaching assistantships (averaging $19,398 per year) were awarded. *Total annual research expenditures:* $6,013.

Loyola Marymount University, College of Communication and Fine Arts, Los Angeles, CA 90045-2659. Offers MA. *Faculty:* 5 full-time (4 women), 14 part-time/adjunct (13 women). *Students:* 50 full-time (47 women); includes 24 minority (1 Black or African American, non-Hispanic/Latino; 7 Asian, non-Hispanic/Latino; 13 Hispanic/Latino; 3 Two or more races, non-Hispanic/Latino). Average age 28. 53 applicants, 53% accepted, 23 enrolled. In 2017, 24 master's awarded. *Entrance requirements:* For master's, official

transcripts, letters of recommendation. Additional exam requirements/recommendations for international students: Required—TOEFL, IELTS. Application fee: $50. Electronic applications accepted. *Financial support:* Research assistantships, career-related internships or fieldwork, institutionally sponsored loans, scholarships/grants, and unspecified assistantships available. Financial award application deadline: 5/1; financial award applicants required to submit FAFSA. *Unit head:* Dr. Bryant Keith Alexander, Dean, College of Communication and Fine Arts, 310-338-7430, E-mail: bryantkeithalexander@lmu.edu. *Application contact:* Chake H. Kouyoumjian, Associate Dean of Graduate Studies, 310-338-2721, Fax: 310-338-6086, E-mail: graduateinfo@lmu.edu.
Website: http://cfa.lmu.edu

Loyola University Chicago, Graduate School, School of Communication, Chicago, IL 60660. Offers digital storytelling (MC); global strategic communication (MS). *Students:* 36 full-time (24 women), 20 part-time (14 women); includes 22 minority (12 Black or African American, non-Hispanic/Latino; 1 Asian, non-Hispanic/Latino; 9 Hispanic/Latino), 9 international. Average age 29. 104 applicants, 60% accepted, 29 enrolled. In 2017, 29 master's awarded. *Expenses:* $1,033 per credit hour tuition, $432 pere semester mandatory fees. *Financial support:* Applicants required to submit FAFSA. *Unit head:* Dr. Don Heider, Dean, 312-915-6548, E-mail: dheider@luc.edu. *Application contact:* Ron Martin, Associate Director of Enrollment Management, 312-915-8950, Fax: 312-915-8905, E-mail: gradapp@luc.edu.
Website: http://www.luc.edu/soc/

Lynn University, Eugene M. and Christine E. Lynn College of Communication and Design, Boca Raton, FL 33431-5598. Offers communication and media (MS), including design strategies for Web development, digital media, media studies and practice; digital media (Certificate); graphic and Web design (MFA); visual effects animation (MFA); Web design and technology (MS). *Program availability:* Part-time, evening/weekend. *Faculty:* 14 full-time (9 women), 7 part-time/adjunct (1 woman). *Students:* 35 full-time (21 women), 33 part-time (13 women); includes 31 minority (12 Black or African American, non-Hispanic/Latino; 2 American Indian or Alaska Native, non-Hispanic/Latino; 2 Asian, non-Hispanic/Latino; 14 Hispanic/Latino; 1 Two or more races, non-Hispanic/Latino), 12 international. Average age 27. 59 applicants, 92% accepted, 44 enrolled. In 2017, 17 master's awarded. *Degree requirements:* For master's, thesis (for some programs), completion of degree in four calendar years; minimum cumulative GPA of 3.0 and C grade or higher in each course; orientation seminar (one credit); 36 credits of foundation and specialization or a thesis. *Entrance requirements:* For master's, bachelor's degree from accredited institution, minimum undergraduate GPA of 3.0, official undergraduate transcripts, letter of recommendation from academic or professional source, writing sample demonstrating capacity to perform at graduate level. Additional exam requirements/recommendations for international students: Required—TOEFL (minimum score 550 paper-based; 80 iBT), IELTS (minimum score 6.5). *Application deadline:* For fall admission, 8/18 for domestic students, 8/4 for international students; for spring admission, 12/15 for domestic students, 12/1 for international students; for summer admission, 4/17 for domestic students, 4/3 for international students. Applications are processed on a rolling basis. Application fee: $45. Electronic applications accepted. *Expenses:* $740 per credit. *Financial support:* Career-related internships or fieldwork, Federal Work-Study, institutionally sponsored loans, scholarships/grants, tuition waivers (partial), and unspecified assistantships available. Support available to part-time students. Financial award application deadline: 8/1; financial award applicants required to submit FAFSA. *Unit head:* Dr. David L. Jaffe, Dean, 561-237-7099, Fax: 561-237-7097, E-mail: djaffe@lynn.edu. *Application contact:* Steven Pruitt, Director of Graduate Admission, 561-237-7834, Fax: 561-237-7100, E-mail: admission@lynn.edu.
Website: https://www.lynn.edu/academics/colleges-schools/communication-and-design

Marist College, Graduate Programs, School of Communication and the Arts, Poughkeepsie, NY 12601-1387. Offers communication (MA); integrated marketing communication (MA); museum studies (MA). *Program availability:* Part-time, online learning. *Degree requirements:* For master's, thesis or comprehensive exam. *Entrance requirements:* For master's, GRE, minimum undergraduate GPA of 3.0, resume, 3 letters of recommendation. Additional exam requirements/recommendations for international students: Required—TOEFL (minimum score 550 paper-based; 80 iBT); Recommended—IELTS (minimum score 6.5). Electronic applications accepted.

Marquette University, Graduate School, College of Communication, Milwaukee, WI 53201-1881. Offers advertising and public relations (MA); communication studies (MA); digital storytelling (Certificate); journalism (MA); mass communication (MA); science, health and environmental communication (MA). *Accreditation:* ACEJMC (one or more programs are accredited). *Program availability:* Part-time, evening/weekend. *Degree requirements:* For master's, comprehensive exam, thesis or alternative. *Entrance requirements:* For master's, GRE, official transcripts from all current and previous colleges/universities except Marquette, three letters of recommendation, statement of academic and professional goals. Additional exam requirements/recommendations for international students: Required—TOEFL (minimum score 530 paper-based). Electronic applications accepted. *Faculty research:* Urban journalism, gender and communication, intercultural communication, religious communication.

Marshall University, Academic Affairs Division, College of Liberal Arts, Department of Communication Studies, Huntington, WV 25755. Offers MA. *Students:* 9 full-time (8 women); includes 2 minority (1 Black or African American, non-Hispanic/Latino; 1 Two or more races, non-Hispanic/Latino). Average age 24. In 2017, 6 master's awarded. *Degree requirements:* For master's, thesis optional. *Entrance requirements:* For master's, GRE General Test. Application fee: $40. *Financial support:* Fellowships available. *Unit head:* Dr. Camilla Brammer, Chair, 304-696-2810, E-mail: brammer@marshall.edu. *Application contact:* Fax: 304-746-1902, E-mail: services@marshall.edu.

Marywood University, Academic Affairs, Insalaco College of Creative and Performing Arts, Department of Communication Arts, Scranton, PA 18509-1598. Offers MA. *Program availability:* Part-time. Electronic applications accepted.

McGill University, Faculty of Graduate and Postdoctoral Studies, Faculty of Arts, Department of Art History and Communication Studies, Montréal, QC H3A 2T5, Canada. Offers MA, PhD.

Michigan State University, The Graduate School, College of Communication Arts and Sciences, Department of Communication, East Lansing, MI 48824. Offers MA, PhD. *Entrance requirements:* Additional exam requirements/recommendations for international students: Required—TOEFL (minimum score 580 paper-based). Electronic applications accepted.

Minnesota State University Mankato, College of Graduate Studies and Research, College of Arts and Humanities, Department of Communication Studies, Mankato, MN 56001. Offers communication education (Certificate); communication studies (MA, MS); forensics (MFA); professional communication (Certificate). *Degree requirements:* For master's, one foreign language, comprehensive exam, thesis. *Entrance requirements:* For master's, minimum GPA of 3.0 during previous 2 years, writing sample. Electronic applications accepted.

Communication—General

Minnesota State University Mankato, College of Graduate Studies and Research, College of Arts and Humanities, Department of English, Mankato, MN 56001. Offers communication and composition (MA); creative writing (MFA); English studies (MA); teaching English as a second language (MA, Certificate); technical communication (MA, Certificate). *Program availability:* Part-time. *Degree requirements:* For master's, one foreign language, comprehensive exam, thesis or alternative. *Entrance requirements:* For master's, minimum GPA of 3.0 during previous 2 years, writing sample (MFA). Additional exam requirements/recommendations for international students: Required—TOEFL (minimum score 500 paper-based; 61 iBT). Electronic applications accepted.

Mississippi College, Graduate School, College of Arts and Sciences, School of Christian Studies and the Arts, Department of Communication, Clinton, MS 39058. Offers applied communication (MSC); public relations and corporate communication (MSC). *Program availability:* Part-time. *Degree requirements:* For master's, comprehensive exam, thesis optional. *Entrance requirements:* For master's, GRE or NTE, minimum GPA of 2.5. Additional exam requirements/recommendations for international students: Recommended—TOEFL, IELTS. Electronic applications accepted.

Mississippi State University, College of Agriculture and Life Sciences, School of Human Sciences, Mississippi State, MS 39762. Offers agriculture and extension education (MS), including communication, leadership; agriculture science (PhD), including agriculture and extension education; fashion design and merchandising (MS), including design and product development, merchandising; human development and family studies (MS, PhD). *Accreditation:* NCATE (one or more programs are accredited). *Program availability:* Part-time. *Faculty:* 20 full-time (11 women). *Students:* 31 full-time (23 women), 54 part-time (38 women); includes 19 minority (15 Black or African American, non-Hispanic/Latino; 1 Hispanic/Latino; 3 Two or more races, non-Hispanic/Latino), 5 international. Average age 36. 26 applicants, 65% accepted, 15 enrolled. In 2017, 19 master's, 2 doctorates awarded. *Degree requirements:* For master's, thesis optional, comprehensive oral or written exam. *Entrance requirements:* For master's, GRE, minimum GPA of 2.75 in last 4 semesters of course work; for doctorate, minimum GPA of 3.0 on prior graduate work. Additional exam requirements/recommendations for international students: Required—TOEFL (minimum score 477 paper-based; 53 iBT); Recommended—IELTS (minimum score 4.5). *Application deadline:* For fall admission, 7/1 for domestic students, 5/1 for international students; for spring admission, 11/1 for domestic students, 9/1 for international students. Applications are processed on a rolling basis. Application fee: $60 ($80 for international students). Electronic applications accepted. *Expenses:* Tuition, state resident: full-time $8318; part-time $462.12 per credit hour. Tuition, nonresident: full-time $22,358; part-time $1242.12 per credit hour. *Required fees:* $110; $12.24 per credit hour. $6.12 per semester. *Financial support:* In 2017–18, 13 research assistantships (averaging $13,718 per year) were awarded; Federal Work-Study, institutionally sponsored loans, and unspecified assistantships also available. Financial award application deadline: 4/1; financial award applicants required to submit FAFSA. *Faculty research:* Animal welfare, agroscience, information technology, learning styles, problem solving. *Unit head:* Dr. Michael Newman, Professor and Director, 662-325-2950, E-mail: mnewman@humansci.msstate.edu. *Application contact:* Marina Hunt, Admissions and Enrollment Assistant, 662-325-5188, E-mail: mhunt@grad.msstate.edu.
Website: http://www.humansci.msstate.edu

Missouri State University, Graduate College, College of Arts and Letters, Department of Communication, Springfield, MO 65897. Offers MA. *Program availability:* Part-time, 100% online, blended/hybrid learning. *Faculty:* 13 full-time (8 women). *Students:* 12 full-time (6 women), 38 part-time (32 women); includes 12 minority (6 Black or African American, non-Hispanic/Latino; 1 Asian, non-Hispanic/Latino; 2 Hispanic/Latino; 3 Two or more races, non-Hispanic/Latino), 2 international. Average age 23. 51 applicants, 31% accepted, 16 enrolled. In 2017, 41 master's awarded. *Degree requirements:* For master's, comprehensive exam, thesis or alternative. *Entrance requirements:* For master's, GRE General Test or MAT, minimum GPA of 3.0 for last 60 credit hours of academic work. Additional exam requirements/recommendations for international students: Required—TOEFL (minimum score 550 paper-based; 79 iBT), IELTS (minimum score 6). *Application deadline:* For fall admission, 6/1 priority date for domestic students, 5/1 for international students; for spring admission, 11/1 priority date for domestic students, 9/1 for international students. Applications are processed on a rolling basis. Application fee: $35 ($50 for international students). Electronic applications accepted. *Expenses:* Tuition, state resident: full-time $2915; part-time $2021 per credit hour. Tuition, nonresident: full-time $5354; part-time $3647 per credit hour. *International tuition:* $11,992 full-time. *Required fees:* $173; $173 per credit hour. Tuition and fees vary according to class time, course level, course load, degree level, campus/location and program. *Financial support:* In 2017–18, 10 teaching assistantships with full tuition reimbursements (averaging $8,772 per year) were awarded; career-related internships or fieldwork, Federal Work-Study, institutionally sponsored loans, scholarships/grants, and unspecified assistantships also available. Support available to part-time students. Financial award application deadline: 3/31; financial award applicants required to submit FAFSA. *Faculty research:* Conflict resolution, media analysis, intercultural communication, political communication, communication theory and organizational praxis. *Unit head:* Dr. Isabelle Bauman, Interim Department Head, 417-836-4423, Fax: 417-836-4774, E-mail: communication@missouristate.edu. *Application contact:* Stephanie Praschan, Director, Graduate Enrollment Management, 417-836-5330, Fax: 417-836-6200, E-mail: michaeledwards@missouristate.edu.
Website: http://communication.missouristate.edu/

Missouri State University, Graduate College, Interdisciplinary Program in Professional Studies, Springfield, MO 65897. Offers administrative studies (Certificate); applied communication (MS); criminal justice (MS); environmental management (MS); homeland security (MS); individualized (MS); professional studies (MS); screenwriting and producing (MS); sports management (MS). *Program availability:* Part-time, evening/weekend, 100% online, blended/hybrid learning. *Students:* 51 full-time (33 women), 95 part-time (41 women); includes 21 minority (8 Black or African American, non-Hispanic/Latino; 1 Asian, non-Hispanic/Latino; 7 Hispanic/Latino; 5 Two or more races, non-Hispanic/Latino), 37 international. Average age 24. 71 applicants, 69% accepted, 35 enrolled. In 2017, 50 master's awarded. *Degree requirements:* For master's, comprehensive exam, thesis or alternative. *Entrance requirements:* For master's, GRE, GMAT (if GPA less than 3.0). Additional exam requirements/recommendations for international students: Required—TOEFL (minimum score 550 paper-based; 79 iBT), IELTS (minimum score 6). *Application deadline:* For fall admission, 7/15 priority date for domestic students; for spring admission, 12/1 priority date for domestic students; for summer admission, 5/1 for domestic students. Applications are processed on a rolling basis. Application fee: $35 ($50 for international students). Electronic applications accepted. *Expenses:* Tuition, state resident: full-time $2915; part-time $2021 per credit hour. Tuition, nonresident: full-time $5354; part-time $3647 per credit hour. *International tuition:* $11,992 full-time. *Required fees:* $173; $173 per credit hour. Tuition and fees vary according to class time, course level, course load, degree level, campus/location and program. *Financial support:* Career-related internships or fieldwork, Federal Work-Study, institutionally sponsored loans, scholarships/grants, and unspecified assistantships available. Support available to part-time students. Financial award application deadline: 3/31; financial award applicants required to submit FAFSA. *Unit*

head: Dr. Gerald Masterson, Program Director, 417-836-5251, Fax: 417-836-6888, E-mail: mps@missouristate.edu. *Application contact:* Stephanie Praschan, Director, Graduate Enrollment Management, 417-836-5330, Fax: 417-836-6200, E-mail: stephaniepraschan@missouristate.edu.
Website: http://mps.missouristate.edu

Monmouth University, Graduate Studies, Department of Communication, West Long Branch, NJ 07764-1898. Offers corporate and public communication (MA); human resources management and communication (Certificate); public service communication specialist (Certificate); strategic public relations and new media (Certificate). *Program availability:* Part-time, evening/weekend, online learning. *Faculty:* 4 full-time (3 women), 2 part-time/adjunct (both women). *Students:* 10 full-time (7 women), 18 part-time (14 women); includes 9 minority (5 Black or African American, non-Hispanic/Latino; 1 Asian, non-Hispanic/Latino; 3 Hispanic/Latino). Average age 28. In 2017, 18 master's, 1 other advanced degree awarded. Terminal master's awarded for partial completion of doctoral program. *Degree requirements:* For master's, comprehensive exam (for some programs), thesis (for some programs), project. *Entrance requirements:* For master's, GRE, baccalaureate degree with minimum GPA of 3.0 in major, 2.75 overall; two letters of recommendation; personal essay (750 words or less describing preparation for study and personal objectives); digital or hard copy portfolio of select samples of work including writing sample; resume. Additional exam requirements/recommendations for international students: Required—TOEFL (minimum score 550 paper-based; 79 iBT), IELTS (minimum score 6), Michigan English Language Assessment Battery (minimum score 77). *Application deadline:* For fall admission, 7/15 priority date for domestic students, 6/1 for international students; for spring admission, 12/1 priority date for domestic students, 11/1 for international students; for summer admission, 5/1 for domestic students. Applications are processed on a rolling basis. Application fee: $50. Electronic applications accepted. *Expenses:* Tuition: Full-time $21,366; part-time $7122 per credit. *Required fees:* $700; $175 per term. *Financial support:* In 2017–18, 2 students received support. Institutionally sponsored loans, scholarships/grants, and unspecified assistantships available. Support available to part-time students. Financial award applicants required to submit FAFSA. *Faculty research:* Service-learning, history of television, feminism and the media, executive communication, public relations pedagogy. *Unit head:* Dr. Marina Vujnovic, Program Director, 732-263-5667, Fax: 732-571-5667, E-mail: mvujnovi@monmouth.edu. *Application contact:* Andrea Thompson, Graduate Admission Counselor, 732-571-3452, Fax: 732-263-5123, E-mail: gradadm@monmouth.edu.
Website: http://www.monmouth.edu/cpc

Montana State University Billings, College of Arts and Sciences, Department of Communication and Theatre, Billings, MT 59101. Offers public relations (MS). *Program availability:* Part-time, 100% online, blended/hybrid learning. *Degree requirements:* For master's, comprehensive exam, thesis optional. *Entrance requirements:* For master's, GRE General Test, minimum undergraduate GPA of 3.0, letters of recommendation, letter of intent, resume. Additional exam requirements/recommendations for international students: Required—TOEFL (minimum score 79 iBT), IELTS (minimum score 6.5). *Application deadline:* For fall admission, 3/15 for domestic students, 7/15 for international students; for spring admission, 10/15 for domestic students, 12/1 for international students. Applications are processed on a rolling basis. Application fee: $40. Electronic applications accepted. *Expenses:* Tuition, state resident: full-time $11,740; part-time $7880 per year. Tuition, nonresident: full-time $32,200; part-time $24,140 per year. *Financial support:* Research assistantships with partial tuition reimbursements, teaching assistantships with partial tuition reimbursements, career-related internships or fieldwork, Federal Work-Study, institutionally sponsored loans, scholarships/grants, and unspecified assistantships available. Support available to part-time students. Financial award application deadline: 5/1; financial award applicants required to submit FAFSA. *Unit head:* Dr. Stephen L. Coffman, Chair, 406-657-1726, E-mail: scoffman@msubillings.edu. *Application contact:* Dr. Stephen L. Coffman, Chair, 406-657-1726, E-mail: scoffman@msubillings.edu.
Website: http://www.msubillings.edu/cas/comt/

Moore College of Art & Design, Program in Social Engagement, Philadelphia, PA 19103. Offers MA. *Program availability:* Part-time. *Degree requirements:* For master's, thesis.

Morehead State University, Graduate Programs, Caudill College of Arts, Humanities and Social Sciences, Department of Communication, Media and Leadership Studies, Morehead, KY 40351. Offers communication (MA). *Program availability:* Part-time, evening/weekend. *Degree requirements:* For master's, comprehensive exam, exit assessment, written examination, oral interview. *Entrance requirements:* For master's, GRE General Test, bachelor's degree in communications or closely related field. Additional exam requirements/recommendations for international students: Required—TOEFL (minimum score 500 paper-based). Electronic applications accepted. *Faculty research:* Mass media effects, organizational communications, advertising/public relations.

New Mexico State University, College of Arts and Sciences, Department of Communication Studies, Las Cruces, NM 88003. Offers MA. *Program availability:* Part-time. *Faculty:* 6 full-time (3 women), 1 part-time/adjunct (0 women). *Students:* 17 full-time (10 women), 4 part-time (3 women); includes 9 minority (1 Black or African American, non-Hispanic/Latino; 6 Hispanic/Latino; 2 Two or more races, non-Hispanic/Latino), 6 international. Average age 33. 18 applicants, 67% accepted, 5 enrolled. In 2017, 6 master's awarded. *Entrance requirements:* For master's, minimum GPA of 3.25. Additional exam requirements/recommendations for international students: Required—TOEFL (minimum score 550 paper-based; 79 iBT), IELTS (minimum score 6.5). *Application deadline:* For fall admission, 2/15 priority date for domestic students; for spring admission, 11/15 priority date for domestic students. Applications are processed on a rolling basis. Application fee: $40 ($50 for international students). Electronic applications accepted. *Expenses:* Tuition, state resident: full-time $4390. Tuition, nonresident: full-time $15,309. *Required fees:* $853. *Financial support:* In 2017–18, 16 students received support, including 2 fellowships (averaging $450 per year), 12 teaching assistantships (averaging $16,964 per year); career-related internships or fieldwork, Federal Work-Study, scholarships/grants, traineeships, health care benefits, and unspecified assistantships also available. Support available to part-time students. Financial award application deadline: 3/1. *Faculty research:* Interpersonal, organizational, intercultural, political, and health communication. *Total annual research expenditures:* $14,152. *Unit head:* Dr. Kenneth Hacker, Department Head, 575-646-2801, Fax: 575-646-4642, E-mail: khacker@nmsu.edu. *Application contact:* 575-646-2801, Fax: 575-646-4642, E-mail: comstudy@nmsu.edu.
Website: http://commstudies.nmsu.edu

New York Institute of Technology, College of Arts and Sciences, Department of Communication Arts, Old Westbury, NY 11568-8000. Offers MA. *Program availability:* Part-time, evening/weekend. *Faculty:* 9 full-time (4 women), 17 part-time/adjunct (7 women). *Students:* 84 full-time (54 women), 36 part-time (21 women); includes 22 minority (12 Black or African American, non-Hispanic/Latino; 1 Asian, non-Hispanic/Latino; 7 Hispanic/Latino; 2 Two or more races, non-Hispanic/Latino), 82 international. Average age 25. 112 applicants, 80% accepted, 37 enrolled. In 2017, 96 master's awarded. *Degree requirements:* For master's, thesis or alternative. *Entrance*

requirements: For master's, minimum undergraduate GPA of 2.85. Additional exam requirements/recommendations for international students: Required—TOEFL (minimum score 79 iBT), IELTS (minimum score 6). *Application deadline:* Applications are processed on a rolling basis. Application fee: $50. Electronic applications accepted. *Expenses:* $1,285 per credit plus fees. *Financial support:* Career-related internships or fieldwork, Federal Work-Study, scholarships/grants, tuition waivers (full and partial), and unspecified assistantships available. Support available to part-time students. Financial award application deadline: 2/15; financial award applicants required to submit FAFSA. *Faculty research:* Effects of new media, interactive technology for promoting healthy behavior, video games and virtual reality, social media, health communications. *Unit head:* Don Fizzinoglia, Department Chair, 516-686-1468, E-mail: dfizzino@nyit.edu. *Application contact:* Alice Dolitsky, Director, Graduate Admissions, 516-686-7520, Fax: 516-686-1116, E-mail: nyitgrad@nyit.edu.
Website: http://www.nyit.edu/degrees/communication_arts_ma

New York University, Steinhardt School of Culture, Education, and Human Development, Department of Media, Culture and Communication, New York, NY 10012. Offers media, culture and communication (MA, PhD); MLIS/MA. *Program availability:* Part-time. *Students:* Average age 33. 550 applicants, 24% accepted, 46 enrolled. In 2017, 57 master's, 6 doctorates awarded. Terminal master's awarded for partial completion of doctoral program. *Entrance requirements:* For master's, GRE General Test; for doctorate, GRE General Test, interview. Additional exam requirements/ recommendations for international students: Required—TOEFL (minimum score 100 iBT). *Application deadline:* For fall admission, 12/1 priority date for domestic and international students; for spring admission, 10/1 for domestic and international students. Applications are processed on a rolling basis. Application fee: $75. Electronic applications accepted. *Expenses:* Tuition: Full-time $41,352; part-time $19,968 per year. *Required fees:* $2496; $1628 per unit. $814 per term. Tuition and fees vary according to course load and program. *Financial support:* Fellowships with full and partial tuition reimbursements, teaching assistantships with full and partial tuition reimbursements, career-related internships or fieldwork, Federal Work-Study, institutionally sponsored loans, scholarships/grants, tuition waivers (partial), and unspecified assistantships available. Support available to part-time students. Financial award application deadline: 2/1; financial award applicants required to submit FAFSA. *Faculty research:* Digital media and new technologies, media criticism, flow of media and culture transnationally and transculturally. *Unit head:* Prof. Lisa Gitelman, Chairperson, 212-998-5191, Fax: 212-995-4046, E-mail: lg91@nyu.edu. *Application contact:* 212-998-5030, Fax: 212-995-4328, E-mail: steinhardt.gradadmissions@nyu.edu.
Website: http://steinhardt.nyu.edu/mcc

Norfolk State University, School of Graduate Studies, School of Liberal Arts, Department of Media and Communication, Norfolk, VA 23504. Offers MA. *Program availability:* Part-time. *Degree requirements:* For master's, thesis. *Entrance requirements:* For master's, GRE, minimum GPA of 2.5, letters of recommendation. Additional exam requirements/recommendations for international students: Required—TOEFL.

North Carolina State University, Graduate School, College of Humanities and Social Sciences, Department of Communication, Raleigh, NC 27695. Offers MS. *Program availability:* Part-time. *Degree requirements:* For master's, thesis optional. *Entrance requirements:* For master's, GRE, minimum undergraduate GPA of 3.0 during last 60 hours. Electronic applications accepted. *Faculty research:* Instructional communication, political communication, organizational conflict management, intercultural communication, communication technology.

North Dakota State University, College of Graduate and Interdisciplinary Studies, College of Arts, Humanities and Social Sciences, Department of Communication, Fargo, ND 58102. Offers communication (PhD); mass communication (MA, MS); speech communication (MA, MS). *Program availability:* Part-time, online learning. Terminal master's awarded for partial completion of doctoral program. *Degree requirements:* For master's, thesis (for some programs); for doctorate, comprehensive exam, thesis/ dissertation, 2-3 publications. *Entrance requirements:* For master's, GRE, minimum undergraduate GPA of 3.25; for doctorate, GRE, minimum undergraduate GPA of 3.5. Additional exam requirements/recommendations for international students: Required— TOEFL (minimum score 600 paper-based; 100 iBT), IELTS (minimum score 7). Electronic applications accepted. *Faculty research:* Communication and rhetorical theory, organizational communication, broadcast and print journalism, international communication, public relations and advertising.

Northeastern State University, College of Liberal Arts, Department of Communication, Art and Theatre, Tahlequah, OK 74464-2399. Offers communication arts (MA). *Program availability:* Part-time, evening/weekend. *Faculty:* 3 full-time (2 women). *Students:* 5 full-time (3 women), 9 part-time (6 women); includes 3 minority (1 American Indian or Alaska Native, non-Hispanic/Latino; 2 Two or more races, non-Hispanic/Latino). Average age 32. In 2017, 2 master's awarded. *Degree requirements:* For master's, comprehensive exam. *Entrance requirements:* For master's, GRE, MAT, minimum GPA of 2.5. Additional exam requirements/recommendations for international students: Required— TOEFL. *Application deadline:* For fall admission, 6/1 priority date for domestic students. Applications are processed on a rolling basis. Application fee: $25. Electronic applications accepted. *Expenses:* Tuition, state resident: part-time $222 per credit hour. Tuition, nonresident: part-time $501.75 per credit hour. *Required fees:* $37.40 per credit hour. Tuition and fees vary according to degree level. *Financial support:* Teaching assistantships and Federal Work-Study available. Financial award application deadline: 3/1. *Unit head:* Dr. Sydney Yueh, Director of Master's of Communication, 918-444-4725, E-mail: yueh@nsuok.edu. *Application contact:* Josh McCollum, Graduate Coordinator, 918-444-2093, E-mail: mccolluj@nsuok.edu.
Website: http://academics.nsuok.edu/communicationstudies/MasterofArts.aspx

Northern Arizona University, College of Social and Behavioral Sciences, School of Communication, Flagstaff, AZ 86011. Offers communication (MA); communication studies (Graduate Certificate); science communication (Graduate Certificate). *Program availability:* Part-time, 100% online, blended/hybrid learning. *Faculty:* 55 full-time (30 women), 4 part-time/adjunct (2 women). *Students:* 15 full-time (9 women), 19 part-time (15 women); includes 9 minority (3 Black or African American, non-Hispanic/Latino; 1 American Indian or Alaska Native, non-Hispanic/Latino; 4 Hispanic/Latino; 1 Two or more races, non-Hispanic/Latino), 1 international. Average age 31. 25 applicants, 80% accepted, 18 enrolled. In 2017, 13 master's, 1 other advanced degree awarded. *Degree requirements:* For master's, variable foreign language requirement, comprehensive exam (for some programs), thesis (for some programs); for Graduate Certificate, comprehensive exam (for some programs). *Entrance requirements:* For master's, GRE General Test. Additional exam requirements/recommendations for international students: Required—TOEFL (minimum score 80 iBT), IELTS (minimum score 6.5). *Application deadline:* For fall admission, 3/1 for domestic and international students; for spring admission, 10/1 for domestic and international students. Applications are processed on a rolling basis. Application fee: $65. Electronic applications accepted. *Expenses:* Tuition, state resident: full-time $9240; part-time $458 per credit hour. Tuition, nonresident: full-time $21,588; part-time $1199 per credit hour. *Required fees:* $1021; $14 per credit hour. $646 per semester. Tuition and fees vary according to course load, campus/location and program. *Financial support:* In 2017–18, 11 students

received support, including 2 research assistantships with full and partial tuition reimbursements available (averaging $12,000 per year), 9 teaching assistantships with full and partial tuition reimbursements available (averaging $12,000 per year); institutionally sponsored loans, health care benefits, and unspecified assistantships also available. Financial award application deadline: 2/1; financial award applicants required to submit FAFSA. *Unit head:* Dr. Norman Medoff, Professor/Director, 928-523-8257, Fax: 928-523-1505, E-mail: norm.medoff@nau.edu. *Application contact:* Patricia Johnson, Administrative Associate, 928-523-0030, Fax: 928-523-1505, E-mail: comgrad@nau.edu.
Website: http://www.nau.edu/sbs/communication/

Northern Illinois University, Graduate School, College of Liberal Arts and Sciences, Department of Communication, De Kalb, IL 60115-2854. Offers communication studies (MA). *Program availability:* Part-time. *Faculty:* 24 full-time (11 women), 1 part-time/ adjunct (0 women). *Students:* 16 full-time (10 women), 3 part-time (all women); includes 3 minority (1 Black or African American, non-Hispanic/Latino; 1 Hispanic/Latino; 1 Two or more races, non-Hispanic/Latino), 2 international. Average age 26. 14 applicants, 79% accepted, 4 enrolled. In 2017, 14 master's awarded. *Degree requirements:* For master's, comprehensive exam, thesis optional. *Entrance requirements:* For master's, GRE General Test, minimum GPA of 2.75. Additional exam requirements/ recommendations for international students: Required—TOEFL (minimum score 550 paper-based). *Application deadline:* For fall admission, 6/1 for domestic students, 5/1 for international students; for spring admission, 11/1 for domestic students, 10/1 for international students. Applications are processed on a rolling basis. Application fee: $40. Electronic applications accepted. *Financial support:* In 2017–18, 2 research assistantships with full tuition reimbursements, 20 teaching assistantships with full tuition reimbursements were awarded; fellowships with full tuition reimbursements, career-related internships or fieldwork, Federal Work-Study, scholarships/grants, tuition waivers (full), and unspecified assistantships also available. Support available to part-time students. Financial award applicants required to submit FAFSA. *Faculty research:* Journalism, history film studies, rhetoric or criticism, globalization, mass media law. *Unit head:* Dr. Mehdi Semati, Acting Chair, 815-753-7028, Fax: 815-753-7109, E-mail: msemati@niu.edu. *Application contact:* Dr. Kathleen Valde, Director, Graduate Studies, 815-753-7005, E-mail: kvalde@niu.edu.
Website: http://www.comm.niu.edu/

Northern Kentucky University, Office of Graduate Programs, College of Informatics, Program in Communication, Highland Heights, KY 41099. Offers communication (MA); communication teaching (Certificate); documentary studies (Certificate); public relations (Certificate); relationships (Certificate). *Program availability:* Part-time, evening/ weekend. Terminal master's awarded for partial completion of doctoral program. *Degree requirements:* For master's, comprehensive exams, thesis or applied capstone project. *Entrance requirements:* For master's, GRE, minimum GPA of 3.0, 3 letters of recommendation, letter of intent. Additional exam requirements/recommendations for international students: Required—TOEFL (minimum score 79 iBT); Recommended— IELTS (minimum score 6.5). Electronic applications accepted. *Faculty research:* Mediating effect of health communication, organizational communication, quantitative and qualitative research methods, family and interpersonal communication.

Northwestern University, The Graduate School, School of Communication, Department of Communication Studies, Evanston, IL 60208. Offers communication studies (PhD), including interaction and social influence, rhetoric and public culture; managerial communication (MSC); media, technology and society (PhD); technology and social behavior (PhD). PhD admissions and degree offered through The Graduate School. Terminal master's awarded for partial completion of doctoral program. *Degree requirements:* For doctorate, thesis/dissertation. *Entrance requirements:* For master's and doctorate, GRE General Test. Additional exam requirements/recommendations for international students: Required—TOEFL. Electronic applications accepted.

Notre Dame of Maryland University, Graduate Studies, Program in Contemporary Communication, Baltimore, MD 21210-2476. Offers MA. *Program availability:* Part-time, evening/weekend. *Degree requirements:* For master's, thesis optional. *Entrance requirements:* For master's, minimum GPA of 3.0. Additional exam requirements/ recommendations for international students: Required—TOEFL (minimum score 500 paper-based; 61 iBT). Electronic applications accepted.

The Ohio State University, Graduate School, College of Arts and Sciences, Division of Social and Behavioral Sciences, School of Communication, Columbus, OH 43210. Offers MA, PhD. *Faculty:* 30. *Students:* 53 full-time (34 women), 13 international. Average age 28. In 2017, 8 master's, 6 doctorates awarded. *Entrance requirements:* For master's and doctorate, GRE. Additional exam requirements/recommendations for international students: Required—TOEFL (minimum score 640 paper-based; 111 iBT); Recommended—IELTS (minimum score 8.5). *Application deadline:* For fall admission, 12/1 for domestic and international students. Applications are processed on a rolling basis. Application fee: $60 ($70 for international students). Electronic applications accepted. *Financial support:* Fellowships, research assistantships, and teaching assistantships available. *Unit head:* Dr. Daniel McDonald, Professor and Director, 614-292-0451, E-mail: mcdonald.221@osu.edu. *Application contact:* Graduate and Professional Admissions, 614-292-9444, Fax: 614-292-3895, E-mail: gpadmissions@osu.edu.
Website: http://www.comm.osu.edu/

Ohio University, Graduate College, Scripps College of Communication, Athens, OH 45701-2979. Offers MA, MCTP, MFA, MS, PhD. *Program availability:* Part-time. *Degree requirements:* For master's, comprehensive exam (for some programs), thesis or alternative; for doctorate, comprehensive exam, thesis/dissertation. *Entrance requirements:* For master's and doctorate, GRE General Test. Additional exam requirements/recommendations for international students: Required—TOEFL or IELTS. Electronic applications accepted. *Expenses:* Contact institution.

Old Dominion University, College of Arts and Letters, Institute for the Humanities, Norfolk, VA 23529. Offers arts and entrepreneurship (Certificate); cultural and human geography (MA); cultural studies (MA); gender and sexuality studies (MA); health, communication and culture (Certificate); media and popular culture studies (MA); philosophy and religious studies (MA); social justice and entrepreneurship (Certificate); visual studies (MA); world cultures (MA). *Program availability:* Part-time, evening/ weekend. *Faculty:* 1 full-time (0 women), 1 part-time/adjunct (0 women). *Students:* 20 full-time (16 women), 13 part-time (8 women); includes 15 minority (8 Black or African American, non-Hispanic/Latino; 2 Asian, non-Hispanic/Latino; 2 Hispanic/Latino; 3 Two or more races, non-Hispanic/Latino), 2 international. Average age 35. 27 applicants, 96% accepted, 22 enrolled. In 2017, 3 master's awarded. *Degree requirements:* For master's, thesis optional, project. *Entrance requirements:* For master's, GRE General Test, minimum GPA of 3.25. *Application deadline:* For fall admission, 6/15 for domestic students; for spring admission, 11/15 for domestic students; for summer admission, 4/15 for domestic students. Applications are processed on a rolling basis. Application fee: $50. Electronic applications accepted. *Expenses:* Tuition, state resident: full-time $8928; part-time $496 per credit. Tuition, nonresident: full-time $22,482; part-time $1249 per credit. *Required fees:* $66 per semester. *Financial support:* In 2017–18, 3 students received support, including 5 research assistantships (averaging $10,000 per year); career-related internships or fieldwork, scholarships/grants, and unspecified

assistantships also available. Financial award application deadline: 3/15; financial award applicants required to submit FAFSA. *Faculty research:* Media studies, cultural studies, gender studies, American literature, philosophy, art history, cultural geography. *Unit head:* Dr. Avi D. Santo, Graduate Program Director, 757-683-3719, Fax: 757-683-6191, E-mail: humgpd@odu.edu. *Application contact:* Dr. David C. Earnest, Associate Dean, 757-683-6077, Fax: 757-683-5746, E-mail: dearnest@odu.edu.
Website: http://al.odu.edu/hum/

Pace University, Dyson College of Arts and Sciences, MA Program in Media and Communication Arts, New York, NY 10038. Offers MA. *Program availability:* Part-time, evening/weekend. *Students:* 6 full-time (2 women), 20 part-time (15 women); includes 13 minority (6 Black or African American, non-Hispanic/Latino; 1 Asian, non-Hispanic/Latino; 5 Hispanic/Latino; 1 Two or more races, non-Hispanic/Latino), 5 international. Average age 25. In 2017, 14 master's awarded. *Degree requirements:* For master's, comprehensive exam, thesis, internship. *Entrance requirements:* For master's, portfolio containing examples of prior work (press releases, advertisements, presentations, writing samples, etc.) and official transcripts. Additional exam requirements/recommendations for international students: Required—TOEFL (minimum score 100 iBT). *Application deadline:* For fall admission, 8/1 priority date for domestic students, 6/1 for international students; for spring admission, 12/1 priority date for domestic students, 10/1 for international students. Applications are processed on a rolling basis. Application fee: $70. Electronic applications accepted. *Financial support:* Career-related internships or fieldwork, scholarships/grants, and unspecified assistantships available. Financial award application deadline: 2/15; financial award applicants required to submit FAFSA. *Unit head:* Dr. Maria Luskay, Program Director, 914-773-3353, E-mail: mluskay@pace.edu. *Application contact:* Susan Ford-Goldschein, Director of Admissions, 914-422-4283, Fax: 212-346-1585, E-mail: graduateadmission@pace.edu.
Website: http://www.pace.edu/dyson/programs/ma-media-communication-arts-plv

Penn State Harrisburg, Graduate School, School of Humanities, Middletown, PA 17057. Offers American studies (MA, PhD); communications (MA); folklore and ethnography (Certificate); heritage and museum practice (Certificate); humanities (MA). *Program availability:* Evening/weekend. *Unit head:* Dr. Mukund S. Kulkarni, Chancellor, 717-948-6105, Fax: 717-948-6452. *Application contact:* Robert W. Coffman, Jr., Director of Enrollment Management, Recruitment and Admissions, 717-948-6250, Fax: 717-948-6325, E-mail: hbgadmit@psu.edu.
Website: https://harrisburg.psu.edu/humanities

Penn State University Park, Graduate School, College of the Liberal Arts, Department of Communication Arts and Sciences, University Park, PA 16802. Offers MA, PhD. *Unit head:* Dr. Susan Welch, Dean, 814-865-7691, Fax: 814-863-2085. *Application contact:* Lori Hawn, Director, Graduate Student Services, 814-865-1795, Fax: 814-863-4627, E-mail: l-gswww@lists.psu.edu.
Website: http://cas.la.psu.edu/

Pepperdine University, Seaver College, Division of Communication, Malibu, CA 90263. Offers cinematic media production (MFA); strategic communication (MA). *Program availability:* Part-time. *Students:* 8 full-time (3 women), 15 part-time (9 women); includes 9 minority (4 Black or African American, non-Hispanic/Latino; 1 American Indian or Alaska Native, non-Hispanic/Latino; 3 Asian, non-Hispanic/Latino; 1 Hispanic/Latino), 3 international. Average age 27. In 2017, 6 master's awarded. *Entrance requirements:* For master's, GRE General Test, letters of recommendation, writing sample. Additional exam requirements/recommendations for international students: Required—TOEFL. *Application deadline:* For fall admission, 2/1 priority date for domestic students, 2/1 for international students. Applications are processed on a rolling basis. Application fee: $65. Electronic applications accepted. *Financial support:* Research assistantships, teaching assistantships, career-related internships or fieldwork, and scholarships/grants available. Support available to part-time students. Financial award applicants required to submit FAFSA. *Unit head:* Dr. Kenneth E. Waters, Divisional Dean/Professor of Journalism, 310-506-4245, E-mail: ken.waters@pepperdine.edu. *Application contact:* Hayley Wolf, Director of Admission, 310-506-4392, E-mail: hayley.wolf@pepperdine.edu.

Pittsburg State University, Graduate School, College of Arts and Sciences, Department of Communication, Pittsburg, KS 66762. Offers MA. *Program availability:* Part-time. *Students:* 18 (12 women); includes 4 minority (1 American Indian or Alaska Native, non-Hispanic/Latino; 1 Asian, non-Hispanic/Latino; 1 Hispanic/Latino; 1 Two or more races, non-Hispanic/Latino), 2 international. In 2017, 13 master's awarded. *Degree requirements:* For master's, thesis or alternative. *Entrance requirements:* Additional exam requirements/recommendations for international students: Required—TOEFL (minimum score 550 paper-based; 79 iBT), IELTS (minimum score 6.5), PTE (minimum score 53). *Application deadline:* For fall admission, 7/15 for domestic students, 6/1 for international students; for spring admission, 12/15 for domestic students, 10/15 for international students; for summer admission, 5/15 for domestic students, 4/1 for international students. Applications are processed on a rolling basis. Application fee: $35 ($60 for international students). Electronic applications accepted. *Expenses:* Contact institution. *Financial support:* In 2017–18, 9 teaching assistantships with full tuition reimbursements (averaging $5,500 per year) were awarded; career-related internships or fieldwork, Federal Work-Study, and unspecified assistantships also available. Financial award application deadline: 2/1; financial award applicants required to submit FAFSA. *Unit head:* Dr. Cynthia Allan, Chairperson, 620-235-4724, E-mail: callan@pittstate.edu. *Application contact:* Lisa Allen, Assistant Director of Graduate and Continuing Studies, 620-235-4223, Fax: 620-235-4219, E-mail: lallen@pittstate.edu.

Point Park University, School of Communication, Pittsburgh, PA 15222-1984. Offers communication technology (MA); media communication (MA). *Program availability:* Part-time, evening/weekend. *Degree requirements:* For master's, comprehensive exam (for some programs), thesis or alternative. *Entrance requirements:* For master's, GRE (if GPA less than 2.75), minimum GPA of 2.75, 2 letters of recommendation, statement of intent. Additional exam requirements/recommendations for international students: Required—TOEFL (minimum score 570 paper-based; 88 iBT), IELTS (minimum score 6.5); Recommended—TWE (minimum score 5). Electronic applications accepted.

Purdue University, Graduate School, College of Liberal Arts, Department of Communication, West Lafayette, IN 47907. Offers MA, MS, PhD. *Faculty:* 28 full-time (12 women). *Students:* 54 full-time (40 women), 430 part-time (312 women); includes 123 minority (52 Black or African American, non-Hispanic/Latino; 1 American Indian or Alaska Native, non-Hispanic/Latino; 11 Asian, non-Hispanic/Latino; 43 Hispanic/Latino; 2 Native Hawaiian or other Pacific Islander, non-Hispanic/Latino; 14 Two or more races, non-Hispanic/Latino), 21 international. Average age 34. 320 applicants, 58% accepted, 166 enrolled. In 2017, 75 master's, 10 doctorates awarded. *Degree requirements:* For master's, comprehensive exams or thesis; for doctorate, thesis/dissertation. *Entrance requirements:* For master's and doctorate, GRE General Test, minimum undergraduate GPA of 3.0 or equivalent. Additional exam requirements/recommendations for international students: Required—TOEFL (minimum score 600 paper-based; 77 iBT). *Application deadline:* For fall admission, 1/1 priority date for domestic students, 1/1 for international students; for spring admission, 8/1 for domestic and international students. Applications are processed on a rolling basis. Application fee: $60 ($75 for international students). Electronic applications accepted. *Financial support:* In 2017–18, 70 students received support. Fellowships, research assistantships, teaching assistantships, and scholarships/grants available. Financial award application deadline: 1/1; financial award applicants required to submit FAFSA. *Faculty research:* Interpersonal communication, mass communication, organizational communication, public affairs and issue management, rhetorical studies. *Unit head:* Dr. Marifran Mattson, Head, 765-494-7596, E-mail: mmattson@purdue.edu. *Application contact:* Melanie Morgan, Chair of the Graduate Committee, 765-494-3305, E-mail: morgan3@purdue.edu.
Website: http://www.cla.purdue.edu/communication

Purdue University Northwest, Graduate Studies Office, School of Liberal Arts and Social Sciences, Department of Communication and Creative Arts, Hammond, IN 46323-2094. Offers communication (MA). *Program availability:* Part-time, evening/weekend. *Degree requirements:* For master's, comprehensive exam, thesis or extended course work. *Entrance requirements:* For master's, minimum GPA of 3.0. Additional exam requirements/recommendations for international students: Required—TOEFL. Electronic applications accepted. *Faculty research:* International communication, gender studies, political rhetoric, media effects, media accountability.

Queen's University at Kingston, School of Graduate Studies, Faculty of Arts and Sciences, Department of Sociology, Kingston, ON K7L 3N6, Canada. Offers communication and information technology (MA, PhD); feminist sociology (MA, PhD); socio-legal studies (MA, PhD); sociological theory (MA, PhD). *Program availability:* Part-time. *Degree requirements:* For master's, thesis; for doctorate, comprehensive exam, thesis/dissertation. *Entrance requirements:* For master's, honors bachelors degree in sociology; for doctorate, honors bachelors degree, masters degree in sociology. Additional exam requirements/recommendations for international students: Required—TOEFL. *Faculty research:* Social change and modernization, social control, deviance and criminology, surveillance.

Queens University of Charlotte, Knight School of Communication, Charlotte, NC 28274-0002. Offers organizational and strategic communication (MA). *Program availability:* Part-time, evening/weekend, online learning. *Degree requirements:* For master's, capstone course. *Entrance requirements:* Additional exam requirements/recommendations for international students: Required—TOEFL. *Expenses:* Contact institution.

Quinnipiac University, School of Communications, Hamden, CT 06518-1940. Offers MS. *Program availability:* Part-time, evening/weekend, online learning. *Faculty:* 12 full-time (9 women), 15 part-time/adjunct (6 women). *Students:* 41 full-time (24 women), 84 part-time (59 women); includes 30 minority (14 Black or African American, non-Hispanic/Latino; 3 Asian, non-Hispanic/Latino; 10 Hispanic/Latino; 3 Two or more races, non-Hispanic/Latino), 4 international. 112 applicants, 84% accepted, 65 enrolled. In 2017, 55 master's awarded. *Entrance requirements:* Additional exam requirements/recommendations for international students: Required—TOEFL (minimum score 575 paper-based; 90 iBT), IELTS (minimum score 6.5). *Application deadline:* For fall admission, 7/30 priority date for domestic students, 4/30 priority date for international students; for spring admission, 12/15 priority date for domestic students, 9/30 priority date for international students. Applications are processed on a rolling basis. Application fee: $45. Electronic applications accepted. *Financial support:* Career-related internships or fieldwork, Federal Work-Study, scholarships/grants, and unspecified assistantships available. Financial award application deadline: 6/1; financial award applicants required to submit FAFSA. *Unit head:* Phillip Simon, Program Director, 203-582-8274.
Website: http://www.qu.edu/gradprograms

Regent University, Graduate School, School of Communication and the Arts, Virginia Beach, VA 23464-9800. Offers acting (MFA); communication (MA, PhD), including media and arts management and promotion (MA), political communication (MA), strategic communication (MA), technical communication (MA); film and TV (MA), including producing (MA, MFA), production, script writing; film-television (MFA), including directing, producing (MA, MFA), script and screenwriting; journalism (MA); theatre (MA). *Program availability:* Part-time, evening/weekend, 100% online, blended/hybrid learning. *Faculty:* 15 full-time (2 women), 66 part-time/adjunct (23 women). *Students:* 101 full-time (65 women), 342 part-time (237 women); includes 177 minority (127 Black or African American, non-Hispanic/Latino; 4 American Indian or Alaska Native, non-Hispanic/Latino; 9 Asian, non-Hispanic/Latino; 25 Hispanic/Latino; 12 Two or more races, non-Hispanic/Latino), 11 international. Average age 37. 498 applicants, 36% accepted, 124 enrolled. In 2017, 93 master's, 22 doctorates awarded. *Degree requirements:* For master's, thesis or alternative; for doctorate, thesis/dissertation. *Entrance requirements:* For master's, transcripts, writing sample, resume, audition (for MFA programs); for doctorate, GRE General Test, resume, writing sample, recommendations, interview, transcripts, personal goals statement. Additional exam requirements/recommendations for international students: Required—TOEFL (minimum score 577 paper-based). *Application deadline:* For fall admission, 3/1 priority date for domestic students; for spring admission, 10/1 priority date for domestic students. Applications are processed on a rolling basis. Application fee: $50. Electronic applications accepted. *Expenses:* $650 per credit (MA, MFA); $885 per credit (PhD); $300 per semester technology fee. *Financial support:* In 2017–18, 234 students received support, including 2 fellowships (averaging $10,000 per year); career-related internships or fieldwork, scholarships/grants, and unspecified assistantships also available. Support available to part-time students. *Faculty research:* Screenwriting, digital media production, communication, acting, directing. *Unit head:* Dr. Robert Herron, Dean, 757-352-4500, E-mail: rherron@regent.edu. *Application contact:* Heidi Cece, Assistant Vice President of Enrollment Management, 800-373-5504, Fax: 757-352-4381, E-mail: admissions@regent.edu.
Website: https://www.regent.edu/school-of-communication-and-the-arts/

Rochester Institute of Technology, Graduate Enrollment Services, College of Imaging Arts and Sciences, School of Media Sciences, Rochester, NY 14623-5603. Offers MS. *Program availability:* Part-time. *Students:* 25 full-time (12 women), 6 part-time (3 women); includes 3 minority (1 Black or African American, non-Hispanic/Latino; 2 Asian, non-Hispanic/Latino), 21 international. Average age 26. 26 applicants, 77% accepted, 17 enrolled. In 2017, 1 master's awarded. *Entrance requirements:* For master's, GRE, minimum GPA of 3.0 (recommended). *Application deadline:* For fall admission, 2/15 priority date for domestic and international students; for spring admission, 12/15 priority date for domestic and international students. Applications are processed on a rolling basis. Application fee: $65. Electronic applications accepted. *Expenses:* $1,815 per credit hour. *Financial support:* In 2017–18, 21 students received support. Research assistantships with partial tuition reimbursements available, teaching assistantships with partial tuition reimbursements available, career-related internships or fieldwork, scholarships/grants, and unspecified assistantships available. Support available to part-time students. Financial award applicants required to submit FAFSA. *Faculty research:* Digital publishing and digital content management; media distribution and media business transformation; 3D, functional, and packaging print processes; color management; cross-media publishing; digital printing. *Unit head:* Dr. Bruce Myers, Interim Administrative Chair, 585-475-5224, E-mail: blmppr@rit.edu. *Application contact:* Diane Ellison, Senior Associate Vice President, Graduate Enrollment Services, 585-475-2229, Fax: 585-475-7164, E-mail: gradinfo@rit.edu.
Website: http://cias.rit.edu/schools/media-sciences

Rochester Institute of Technology, Graduate Enrollment Services, College of Liberal Arts, School of Communication, MS Program in Communication and Media Technologies, Rochester, NY 14623. Offers MS. *Program availability:* Part-time. *Students:* 11 full-time (10 women), 6 part-time (5 women); includes 1 minority (Black or African American, non-Hispanic/Latino), 9 international. Average age 25. 33 applicants, 48% accepted, 10 enrolled. In 2017, 13 master's awarded. *Degree requirements:* For master's, thesis. *Entrance requirements:* For master's, minimum GPA of 3.0 (recommended), writing sample. Additional exam requirements/recommendations for international students: Required—TOEFL (minimum score 570 paper-based; 88 iBT), IELTS (minimum score 6.5), PTE (minimum score 61). *Application deadline:* For fall admission, 2/15 priority date for domestic and international students; for spring admission, 12/15 priority date for domestic and international students. Applications are processed on a rolling basis. Application fee: $65. Electronic applications accepted. *Expenses:* $1,815 per credit hour. *Financial support:* Research assistantships with partial tuition reimbursements, teaching assistantships with partial tuition reimbursements, career-related internships or fieldwork, scholarships/grants, and unspecified assistantships available. Support available to part-time students. Financial award applicants required to submit FAFSA. *Faculty research:* Media and culture, visual communication, mass media, technology and media. *Unit head:* Dr. Grant Cos, Graduate Program Director, 585-475-6646, Fax: 585-475-7732, E-mail: communication@rit.edu. *Application contact:* Diane Ellison, Senior Associate Vice President, Graduate Enrollment Services, 585-475-2229, Fax: 585-475-7164, E-mail: gradinfo@rit.edu.
Website: http://www.rit.edu/cla/communication/graduate-programs/ms-communication-media-technologies/overview

Roosevelt University, Graduate Division, College of Arts and Sciences, Department of Communication, Chicago, IL 60605. Offers integrated marketing communications (MSIMC). *Program availability:* Part-time, evening/weekend. *Students:* 38 full-time (28 women), 25 part-time (19 women); includes 28 minority (19 Black or African American, non-Hispanic/Latino; 3 Asian, non-Hispanic/Latino; 5 Hispanic/Latino; 1 Two or more races, non-Hispanic/Latino), 24 international. Average age 27. 43 applicants, 95% accepted, 15 enrolled. In 2017, 38 master's awarded. *Application deadline:* Applications are processed on a rolling basis. Application fee: $40. Electronic applications accepted. *Financial support:* Career-related internships or fieldwork, scholarships/grants, and unspecified assistantships available. *Unit head:* Marian Azzaro, Chair, 312-281-3239. *Application contact:* Sivling Lam, Graduate Admission Counselor, 312-281-3252, E-mail: slam02@roosevelt.edu.

Rutgers University–New Brunswick, School of Communication and Information, Program in Communication, Information and Library Studies, Piscataway, NJ 08854-8097. Offers PhD. *Program availability:* Part-time. *Degree requirements:* For doctorate, comprehensive exam, thesis/dissertation, qualifying exams. *Entrance requirements:* For doctorate, GRE General Test, proficiency in statistics. Additional exam requirements/recommendations for international students: Required—TOEFL (minimum score 600 paper-based). Electronic applications accepted. *Faculty research:* Information science, media studies.

Sacred Heart University, Graduate Programs, College of Arts and Sciences, Department of Communication, Fairfield, CT 06825. Offers corporate communications and public relations (MA Comm); digital multimedia journalism (MA Comm); digital multimedia production (MA Comm); film and television production (MA); media literacy and digital culture (MA), including children, health and media, media and social justice, political action and media production; sports communication and media (MA), including athletic communications and promotions, sports broadcasting. *Program availability:* Part-time, evening/weekend. *Faculty:* 9 full-time (1 woman), 6 part-time/adjunct (1 woman). *Students:* 70 full-time (36 women), 52 part-time (28 women); includes 36 minority (18 Black or African American, non-Hispanic/Latino; 16 Hispanic/Latino; 2 Two or more races, non-Hispanic/Latino), 20 international. Average age 26. 155 applicants, 89% accepted, 66 enrolled. In 2017, 71 master's awarded. *Degree requirements:* For master's, thesis or alternative. *Entrance requirements:* For master's, bachelor's degree. Additional exam requirements/recommendations for international students: Required—TOEFL (minimum score 570 paper-based, 80 iBT), TWE, or IELTS (6.5). *Application deadline:* Applications are processed on a rolling basis. Application fee: $75. Electronic applications accepted. *Expenses:* Contact institution. *Financial support:* Unspecified assistantships available. Financial award applicants required to submit FAFSA. *Unit head:* Dr. Andrew Miller, Director of Graduate Programs, 203-396-8087, E-mail: millera@sacredheart.edu. *Application contact:* Pam Pillo, Executive Director of Graduate Admissions, 203-365-7619, Fax: 203-365-4732, E-mail: graduatestudies@sacredheart.edu.
Website: http://www.sacredheart.edu/academics/collegeofartssciences/academicdepartments/communicationmediastudies/

Saginaw Valley State University, College of Arts and Behavioral Sciences, Program in Communication and Media Administration, University Center, MI 48710. Offers MA. *Program availability:* Part-time, evening/weekend. *Students:* 18 full-time (8 women), 8 part-time (6 women); includes 3 minority (1 Black or African American, non-Hispanic/Latino; 2 Asian, non-Hispanic/Latino), 20 international. Average age 27. 22 applicants, 82% accepted, 12 enrolled. In 2017, 24 master's awarded. *Degree requirements:* For master's, thesis. *Entrance requirements:* For master's, minimum GPA of 3.0. Additional exam requirements/recommendations for international students: Required—TOEFL (minimum score 540 paper-based; 76 iBT). *Application deadline:* For fall admission, 7/15 for international students; for winter admission, 11/15 for international students; for spring admission, 4/15 for international students. Applications are processed on a rolling basis. Application fee: $30 ($90 for international students). Electronic applications accepted. *Expenses:* Tuition, state resident: full-time $10,156; part-time $564.20 per credit hour. Tuition, nonresident: full-time $19,336; part-time $1074.20 per credit hour. *Required fees:* $263; $14.60 per credit hour. Tuition and fees vary according to degree level and program. *Financial support:* Federal Work-Study and scholarships/grants available. Support available to part-time students. Financial award application deadline: 4/1; financial award applicants required to submit FAFSA. *Unit head:* Dr. Robert Drew, Professor of Communication, 989-964-7495, E-mail: rdrew@svsu.edu. *Application contact:* Jenna Briggs, Director, Graduate and International Admissions, 989-964-6096, Fax: 989-964-2788, E-mail: gradadm@svsu.edu.

Saint Louis University, Graduate Programs, College of Arts and Sciences and Graduate Programs, Department of Communication, St. Louis, MO 63103. Offers MA, MA-R. *Program availability:* Part-time. *Degree requirements:* For master's, thesis (for some programs), comprehensive oral and written exams. *Entrance requirements:* For master's, GRE General Test, letters of recommendation, resume, interview. Additional exam requirements/recommendations for international students: Required—TOEFL (minimum score 525 paper-based). Electronic applications accepted. *Faculty research:* Media studies, organizational communication, dialogue, intercultural communication, qualitative research methods.

St. Mary's University, Graduate Studies, Program in Communication Studies, San Antonio, TX 78228. Offers communication studies (MA); JD/MA. *Program availability:* Part-time, evening/weekend, online learning. *Students:* 6 full-time (4 women), 8 part-time (5 women); includes 9 minority (2 Black or African American, non-Hispanic/Latino;

7 Hispanic/Latino), 2 international. Average age 27. 13 applicants, 15% accepted, 1 enrolled. In 2017, 9 master's awarded. *Degree requirements:* For master's, thesis (for some programs). *Entrance requirements:* For master's, GRE General Test, MAT, minimum GPA of 3.1; professional experience. Additional exam requirements/recommendations for international students: Required—TOEFL (minimum score 550 paper-based; 80 iBT), IELTS (minimum score 6). *Application deadline:* For fall admission, 7/1 priority date for domestic students; for spring admission, 11/15 for domestic students; for summer admission, 4/1 for domestic students. Applications are processed on a rolling basis. Application fee: $0. Electronic applications accepted. *Expenses:* Tuition: Full-time $16,200; part-time $900 per credit hour. *Required fees:* $810; $405 per semester. *Financial support:* Research assistantships, career-related internships or fieldwork, Federal Work-Study, institutionally sponsored loans, scholarships/grants, and health care benefits available. Financial award application deadline: 3/31; financial award applicants required to submit FAFSA. *Faculty research:* Interpersonal communication, rhetorical communication. *Unit head:* Dr. Amanda Kennedy, Graduate Program Director, 210-431-2263, E-mail: akennedy4@stmarytx.edu. *Application contact:* Kim Thornton, Director of Graduate Admission, 210-436-3101, E-mail: kthornton@stmarytx.edu.
Website: https://www.stmarytx.edu/academics/programs/master-communication-studies/

St. Thomas University, School of Leadership Studies, Miami Gardens, FL 33054-6459. Offers MA, MPS, MS, Ed D, Certificate. *Program availability:* Part-time, evening/weekend. *Entrance requirements:* Additional exam requirements/recommendations for international students: Required—TOEFL (minimum score 550 paper-based; 79 iBT).

Sam Houston State University, College of Humanities and Social Sciences, Department of Communication Studies, Huntsville, TX 77341. Offers MA. *Program availability:* Part-time, evening/weekend, online learning. *Degree requirements:* For master's, comprehensive exam, thesis optional. *Entrance requirements:* For master's, GRE General Test, three letters of recommendation. Additional exam requirements/recommendations for international students: Required—TOEFL (minimum score 550 paper-based; 79 iBT), IELTS (minimum score 6.5). Electronic applications accepted.

San Diego State University, Graduate and Research Affairs, College of Professional Studies and Fine Arts, School of Communication, San Diego, CA 92182. Offers advertising and public relations (MA); critical-cultural studies (MA); interaction studies (MA); intercultural and international studies (MA); new media studies (MA); news and information studies (MA); telecommunications and media management (MA). *Degree requirements:* For master's, thesis. *Entrance requirements:* For master's, GRE General Test, 3 letters of recommendation. Additional exam requirements/recommendations for international students: Required—TOEFL. Electronic applications accepted.

San Jose State University, Graduate Studies and Research, College of Social Sciences, San Jose, CA 95192-0107. Offers applied anthropology (MA); communication studies (MA); economics (MA), including applied economics, economics; environmental studies (MS); geography (MA); history (MA), including history, history education; Mexican American studies (MA); psychology (MA, MS), including clinical psychology (MS), industrial/organizational psychology (MS), research and experimental psychology (MA); public administration (MPA); social sciences (MS); sociology (MA). *Faculty:* 59 full-time (29 women), 18 part-time/adjunct (5 women). *Students:* 181 full-time (126 women), 221 part-time (127 women); includes 228 minority (15 Black or African American, non-Hispanic/Latino; 48 Asian, non-Hispanic/Latino; 112 Hispanic/Latino; 3 Native Hawaiian or other Pacific Islander, non-Hispanic/Latino; 50 Two or more races, non-Hispanic/Latino), 38 international. Average age 30. 532 applicants, 44% accepted, 156 enrolled. In 2017, 139 master's awarded. *Degree requirements:* For master's, one foreign language, comprehensive exam, thesis (for some programs), project, field work, professional work experience. *Entrance requirements:* Additional exam requirements/recommendations for international students: Required—TOEFL (minimum score 550 paper-based; 80 iBT), IELTS (minimum score 6.5), PTE (minimum score 53). *Application deadline:* For fall admission, 2/1 for domestic and international students. Applications are processed on a rolling basis. Application fee: $55. Electronic applications accepted. *Expenses:* Tuition, state resident: full-time $7176. Tuition, nonresident: full-time $16,680. Tuition and fees vary according to course load and program. *Financial support:* Fellowships, research assistantships, career-related internships or fieldwork, Federal Work-Study, scholarships/grants, tuition waivers (full and partial), and unspecified assistantships available. Support available to part-time students. Financial award application deadline: 4/28; financial award applicants required to submit FAFSA. *Unit head:* Dr. Walt Jacobs, Dean, 408-924-5300, Fax: 408-924-5303, E-mail: walter.jacobs@sjsu.edu.
Website: http://www.sjsu.edu/socialsciences/

Seton Hall University, College of Communication and the Arts, South Orange, NJ 07079-2697. Offers museum professions (MA), including exhibition development, museum management, museum registration; public relations (MA); strategic communication (MA). *Program availability:* Part-time, evening/weekend, online learning. *Degree requirements:* For master's, thesis (for some programs). *Entrance requirements:* For master's, GRE or MAT, official transcripts, resume, personal statement, 3 letters of recommendation. Additional exam requirements/recommendations for international students: Required—TOEFL (minimum iBT score 80) or IELTS (6.5). Electronic applications accepted. *Faculty research:* Organizational communication, digital communication, leadership, art history.

Shippensburg University of Pennsylvania, School of Graduate Studies, College of Arts and Sciences, Department of Communication/Journalism, Shippensburg, PA 17257-2299. Offers communication studies (MS). *Program availability:* Part-time, evening/weekend. *Faculty:* 6 full-time (3 women), 2 part-time/adjunct (1 woman). *Students:* 12 full-time (8 women), 10 part-time (9 women); includes 2 minority (both Black or African American, non-Hispanic/Latino), 7 international. Average age 26. 31 applicants, 39% accepted, 4 enrolled. In 2017, 9 master's awarded. *Degree requirements:* For master's, 6-credit thesis or 3-credit professional project, candidacy. *Entrance requirements:* For master's, GRE or MAT (if GPA less than 2.75), 3 professional references, resume, essay, 500-word statement of purpose. Additional exam requirements/recommendations for international students: Required—TOEFL (minimum score 550 paper-based, 68 iBT) or IELTS (minimum score 6). *Application deadline:* For fall admission, 4/30 for international students; for spring admission, 9/30 for international students. Applications are processed on a rolling basis. Application fee: $45. Electronic applications accepted. *Expenses:* Tuition, state resident: part-time $500 per credit. Tuition, nonresident: part-time $750 per credit. *Required fees:* $145 per credit. *Financial support:* In 2017–18, 9 students received support. Career-related internships or fieldwork, scholarships/grants, unspecified assistantships, and resident hall director and student payroll positions available. Support available to part-time students. Financial award application deadline: 3/1; financial award applicants required to submit FAFSA. *Unit head:* Dr. Kyle R. Heim, Assistant Professor and Program Coordinator, 717-477-1521, Fax: 717-477-4013, E-mail: krheim@ship.edu. *Application contact:* Maya T. Mapp, Director of Admissions, 717-477-1231, Fax: 717-477-4016, E-mail: mtmapp@ship.edu.
Website: http://www.ship.edu/communication_journalism/

Communication—General

Simmons College, School of Management, Boston, MA 02115. Offers business administration (MBA); health care (MBA); management (MS, MSM), including communications management (MS), non-profit management (MS); MBA/MSW; MS/MA. *Accreditation:* AACSB. *Program availability:* Part-time, evening/weekend, 100% online, blended/hybrid learning. *Faculty:* 23 full-time (15 women), 5 part-time/adjunct (all women). *Students:* 7 full-time (all women), 130 part-time (118 women); includes 34 minority (14 Black or African American, non-Hispanic/Latino; 8 Asian, non-Hispanic/Latino; 10 Hispanic/Latino; 2 Two or more races, non-Hispanic/Latino), 1 international. Average age 32. 53 applicants, 68% accepted, 19 enrolled. In 2017, 77 master's awarded. *Entrance requirements:* For master's, GMAT or GRE. Additional exam requirements/recommendations for international students: Required—TOEFL. *Application deadline:* For fall admission, 7/18 priority date for domestic students; for summer admission, 4/24 priority date for domestic students. Applications are processed on a rolling basis. Application fee: $75. Electronic applications accepted. *Expenses:* $1,295 per credit hour, $3,885 per course, $123 activity fee per semester. *Financial support:* Scholarships/grants and unspecified assistantships available. Financial award applicants required to submit FAFSA. *Faculty research:* Gender and organizations, leadership, health care management. *Unit head:* Patricia Deyton, Associate Dean for Graduate Programs, 617-521-3876.
Website: http://www.simmons.edu/som

Simon Fraser University, Office of Graduate Studies and Postdoctoral Fellows, Faculty of Communication, Art and Technology, School of Communication, Burnaby, BC V5A 1S6, Canada. Offers MA, PhD, MA/MA. MA/MA program in global communication offered jointly with the Communication University of China. *Degree requirements:* For master's, thesis or alternative, annual formal review; for doctorate, comprehensive exam, thesis/dissertation, annual formal review. *Entrance requirements:* For master's, minimum GPA of 3.0 (on scale of 4.33) or 3.33 based on last 60 credits of undergraduate courses; for doctorate, minimum GPA of 3.5 (on scale of 4.33). Additional exam requirements/recommendations for international students: Recommended—TOEFL (minimum score 580 paper-based; 93 iBT), IELTS (minimum score 7), TWE (minimum score 5). Electronic applications accepted. *Faculty research:* Cultural policy and politics; globalization, social change, and social justice; history and theory of communication; media and cultural studies; technology and society.

South Dakota State University, Graduate School, College of Arts and Science, Department of Journalism and Mass Communication, Brookings, SD 57007. Offers communication studies and journalism (MS). *Accreditation:* ACEJMC. *Program availability:* Part-time, evening/weekend. *Degree requirements:* For master's, thesis, oral exam. *Entrance requirements:* Additional exam requirements/recommendations for international students: Required—TOEFL (minimum score 550 paper-based; 79 iBT). *Faculty research:* Mass communication applications.

Southeastern Louisiana University, College of Arts, Humanities and Social Sciences, Department of Languages and Communication, Hammond, LA 70402. Offers health communications (MA); journalism (MA); marketing (MA); public relations (MA); sociology (MA). *Program availability:* Part-time, evening/weekend. *Faculty:* 5 full-time (3 women). *Students:* 7 full-time (6 women), 11 part-time (7 women); includes 10 minority (5 Black or African American, non-Hispanic/Latino; 3 Hispanic/Latino; 2 Two or more races, non-Hispanic/Latino). Average age 28. 133 applicants, 51% accepted, 10 enrolled. In 2017, 36 master's awarded. *Degree requirements:* For master's, comprehensive exam. *Entrance requirements:* For master's, GRE (minimum score 148 on Verbal section, 3.5 Written). Additional exam requirements/recommendations for international students: Required—TOEFL (minimum score 525 paper-based; 75 iBT). *Application deadline:* For fall admission, 7/15 priority date for domestic students, 6/1 priority date for international students; for spring admission, 12/1 priority date for domestic students, 10/1 priority date for international students. Applications are processed on a rolling basis. Application fee: $20 ($30 for international students). Electronic applications accepted. *Expenses:* Tuition, state resident: full-time $6684. Tuition, nonresident: full-time $19,162. *Required fees:* $2088. *Financial support:* In 2017–18, 12 students received support, including 7 research assistantships (averaging $6,082 per year); career-related internships or fieldwork, Federal Work-Study, institutionally sponsored loans, scholarships/grants, traineeships, health care benefits, tuition waivers, and unspecified assistantships also available. Financial award application deadline: 5/1; financial award applicants required to submit FAFSA. *Faculty research:* Communicate with the millennial generation to enhance organizational effectiveness, conflict resolution and mediation among nations, journalism history, media law, media writing, media convergence, external compliances accreditation and strategic planning. *Unit head:* Dr. Lucia Harrison, Department Head, 985-549-2105, Fax: 985-549-5014, E-mail: lharrison@southeastern.edu. *Application contact:* Amanda Harper, Graduate Admissions Analyst, 985-549-5620, Fax: 985-549-5632, E-mail: admissions@southeastern.edu.
Website: http://www.southeastern.edu/acad_research/depts/lang_comm/index.html

Southern Illinois University Carbondale, Graduate School, College of Mass Communication and Media Arts, Carbondale, IL 62901-4701. Offers MA, MFA, MS, PhD, MBA/MA. *Program availability:* Part-time. *Degree requirements:* For doctorate, thesis/dissertation. *Entrance requirements:* For doctorate, GRE General Test, minimum GPA of 3.25. Additional exam requirements/recommendations for international students: Required—TOEFL.

Southern Utah University, Program in Communication, Cedar City, UT 84720-2498. Offers MA. *Program availability:* Part-time, 100% online. *Faculty:* 6 full-time (1 woman), 1 (woman) part-time/adjunct. *Students:* 18 full-time (13 women), 36 part-time (21 women); includes 4 minority (3 Black or African American, non-Hispanic/Latino; 1 Two or more races, non-Hispanic/Latino), 1 international. Average age 31. 21 applicants, 76% accepted, 15 enrolled. In 2017, 25 master's awarded. *Entrance requirements:* For master's, GRE. Additional exam requirements/recommendations for international students: Required—TOEFL (minimum score 550 paper-based, 79 iBT) or IELTS (minimum score 6). *Application deadline:* For fall admission, 6/15 for domestic and international students; for spring admission, 10/15 for domestic and international students. Applications are processed on a rolling basis. Application fee: $60 ($65 for international students). Electronic applications accepted. *Expenses:* Contact institution. *Financial support:* Teaching assistantships with tuition reimbursements and unspecified assistantships available. Financial award application deadline: 3/15. *Unit head:* Dr. Arthur Challis, Department Chair, 435-586-7861, Fax: 435-865-8352, E-mail: challis@suu.edu. *Application contact:* Dr. Matthew Barton, Graduate Coordinator, 435-586-7970, Fax: 435-865-8352, E-mail: bartonm@suu.edu.
Website: https://www.suu.edu/hss/comm/masters/

Spring Arbor University, School of Arts and Sciences, Spring Arbor, MI 49283-9799. Offers communication (MA); spiritual formation and leadership (MA). *Program availability:* Part-time, online learning. *Degree requirements:* For master's, thesis (for some programs). *Entrance requirements:* For master's, GRE (minimum score of 40th percentile and taken within last 5 years), bachelor's degree from regionally-accredited college or university, minimum GPA of 3.0 for at least the last two years of the bachelor's degree, at least two recommendations from professional/academic individuals. Additional exam requirements/recommendations for international students: Required—TOEFL (minimum score 600 paper-based). *Expenses:* Contact institution.

Stanford University, School of Humanities and Sciences, Department of Communication, Stanford, CA 94305-2050. Offers MA, PhD. *Faculty:* 12 full-time (3 women), 4 part-time/adjunct (3 women). *Students:* 65 full-time (38 women). Average age 29. 176 applicants, 12% accepted, 12 enrolled. In 2017, 40 master's, 7 doctorates awarded. Terminal master's awarded for partial completion of doctoral program. *Degree requirements:* For master's, thesis, project; for doctorate, thesis/dissertation, qualifying examination, area examination, 2 projects. *Entrance requirements:* For master's and doctorate, GRE General Test. Additional exam requirements/recommendations for international students: Required—TOEFL (minimum score 650 paper-based; 115 iBT). *Application deadline:* For fall admission, 12/4 for domestic and international students. Application fee: $125. Electronic applications accepted. *Expenses: Tuition:* Full-time $48,987; part-time $10,620 per quarter. One-time fee: $400. Tuition and fees vary according to program. *Financial support:* Fellowships, research assistantships, and teaching assistantships available. *Faculty research:* Virtual reality, deliberative democracy, computational journalism, technology and deception, journalism ethics, political campaigns, survey methodology, censorship in authoritarian regimes, media psychology, social impact of digital media. *Unit head:* Fred Turner, Chair, 650-723-0706, E-mail: fturner@stanford.edu. *Application contact:* Katrin Wheeler, Student Services Manager, 650-724-8920, Fax: 650-725-2472, E-mail: comm-studentservices@stanford.edu.
Website: http://communication.stanford.edu/

State University of New York at Oswego, Graduate Studies, School of Communication, Media and the Arts, Oswego, NY 13126. Offers strategic communication (MA), including health communication, integrated media and social networks, organizational communication. *Entrance requirements:* For master's, GRE, official transcript, statement of purpose, resume, two letters of recommendation.

State University of New York College at Potsdam, School of Arts and Sciences, Department of English and Communication, Potsdam, NY 13676. Offers MA. *Program availability:* Part-time, evening/weekend. *Degree requirements:* For master's, one foreign language, thesis or alternative. *Entrance requirements:* For master's, minimum GPA of 3.0 in last 60 hours of undergraduate course work. Additional exam requirements/recommendations for international students: Required—TOEFL (minimum score 550 paper-based; 80 iBT), IELTS (minimum score 6). Electronic applications accepted.

Stephen F. Austin State University, Graduate School, College of Applied Arts and Science, Department of Communication, Nacogdoches, TX 75962. Offers communication (MA); mass communication (MA). *Program availability:* Part-time. *Degree requirements:* For master's, comprehensive exam, thesis optional. *Entrance requirements:* For master's, GRE General Test. Additional exam requirements/recommendations for international students: Required—TOEFL (minimum score 550 paper-based).

Stevens Institute of Technology, Graduate School, Charles V. Schaefer Jr. School of Engineering and Science, Department of Electrical and Computer Engineering, Program in Electrical Engineering, Hoboken, NJ 07030. Offers autonomous robotics (Certificate); electrical engineering (M Eng, PhD, Certificate), including computer architecture and digital systems (M Eng), microelectronics and photonics science and technology (M Eng), signal processing for communications (M Eng), telecommunications systems engineering (M Eng), wireless communications (M Eng, Certificate). *Program availability:* Part-time, evening/weekend. *Students:* 147 full-time (24 women), 27 part-time (6 women); includes 14 minority (4 Black or African American, non-Hispanic/Latino; 10 Asian, non-Hispanic/Latino), 139 international. Average age 25. 737 applicants, 65% accepted, 70 enrolled. In 2017, 91 master's, 5 doctorates, 6 other advanced degrees awarded. *Degree requirements:* For master's, thesis optional, minimum B average in major field and overall; for doctorate, comprehensive exam (for some programs), thesis/dissertation; for Certificate, minimum B average. *Entrance requirements:* Additional exam requirements/recommendations for international students: Required—TOEFL (minimum score 74 iBT), IELTS (minimum score 6). *Application deadline:* For fall admission, 7/1 for domestic students, 4/15 for international students; for spring admission, 12/1 for domestic and international students. Applications are processed on a rolling basis. Application fee: $60. Electronic applications accepted. *Expenses: Tuition:* Full-time $34,494; part-time $1554 per credit. *Required fees:* $291 per semester. *Financial support:* Fellowships, research assistantships, teaching assistantships, career-related internships or fieldwork, Federal Work-Study, scholarships/grants, and unspecified assistantships available. Financial award application deadline: 2/15; financial award applicants required to submit FAFSA. *Unit head:* Cristina Comaniciu, Program Director, 201-216-5606, Fax: 201-216-8246, E-mail: ccomanic@stevens.edu. *Application contact:* Graduate Admissions, 888-783-8367, Fax: 888-511-1306, E-mail: graduate@stevens.edu.

Stevenson University, Program in Communication Studies, Stevenson, MD 21153. Offers MS. *Program availability:* Part-time, online only, 100% online, blended/hybrid learning. *Faculty:* 5 part-time/adjunct (3 women). *Students:* 6 full-time (4 women), 22 part-time (17 women); includes 14 minority (12 Black or African American, non-Hispanic/Latino; 1 Asian, non-Hispanic/Latino; 1 Two or more races, non-Hispanic/Latino). Average age 28. 18 applicants, 94% accepted, 13 enrolled. In 2017, 16 master's awarded. *Degree requirements:* For master's, project or thesis. *Entrance requirements:* For master's, bachelor's degree from regionally-accredited institution; official college transcripts from all previous academic work; minimum cumulative GPA of 3.0 in past academic work; 250-350 word personal statement. *Application deadline:* Applications are processed on a rolling basis. Electronic applications accepted. *Expenses:* Contact institution. *Financial support:* Unspecified assistantships available. Financial award applicants required to submit FAFSA. *Unit head:* Dr. Nadene Vevea, Associate Dean, Communications Studies, 443-394-9498, E-mail: nvevea@stevenson.edu. *Application contact:* Amanda Courter, Senior Enrollment Counselor, 443-352-4243, Fax: 443-352-4440, E-mail: acourter@stevenson.edu.
Website: http://www.stevenson.edu/online/academics/online-graduate-programs/communication-studies/

Syracuse University, College of Visual and Performing Arts, MA Program in Communication and Rhetorical Studies, Syracuse, NY 13244. Offers MA. *Program availability:* Part-time. *Degree requirements:* For master's, comprehensive exam (for some programs), thesis (for some programs). *Entrance requirements:* For master's, GRE General Test, three letters of recommendation, writing sample, transcripts, personal statement, resume. Additional exam requirements/recommendations for international students: Required—TOEFL (minimum score 90 iBT). *Application deadline:* For fall admission, 2/1 priority date for domestic and international students. Application fee: $75. Electronic applications accepted. *Financial support:* In 2017–18, 9 students received support. Fellowships with full tuition reimbursements available, teaching assistantships with tuition reimbursements available, and tuition waivers available. Financial award application deadline: 1/1; financial award applicants required to submit FAFSA. *Faculty research:* Language and social interaction, communication and critical/cultural studies, rhetorical theory and criticism. *Unit head:* Dr. Dana Cloud, Graduate Program Director, 315-443-5140, E-mail: dlcloud@syr.edu. *Application contact:* Caitlin Jarvis, Graduate Recruitment Specialist, 315-443-2769, E-mail: admissg@syr.edu.
Website: http://vpa.syr.edu/prospective-students/graduate-students/programs/communication-rhetorical-studies

Syracuse University, S. I. Newhouse School of Public Communications, Syracuse, NY 13244. Offers MA, MS, PhD, JD/MA, JD/MS, MS/MA. *Accreditation:* ACEJMC (one or more programs are accredited). *Program availability:* Online learning. *Faculty:* 81 full-time (34 women), 56 part-time/adjunct (26 women). *Students:* 252 full-time (166 women), 259 part-time (202 women); includes 169 minority (95 Black or African American, non-Hispanic/Latino; 4 American Indian or Alaska Native, non-Hispanic/Latino; 15 Asian, non-Hispanic/Latino; 39 Hispanic/Latino; 1 Native Hawaiian or other Pacific Islander, non-Hispanic/Latino; 15 Two or more races, non-Hispanic/Latino), 107 international. Average age 29. 796 applicants, 67% accepted, 250 enrolled. In 2017, 258 master's, 3 doctorates awarded. *Degree requirements:* For master's, comprehensive exam (for some programs); for doctorate, thesis/dissertation, qualifying exams. *Entrance requirements:* For master's and doctorate, GRE General Test, resume, official transcripts, personal statement, three letters of recommendation. Additional exam requirements/recommendations for international students: Required—TOEFL (minimum score 100 iBT), IELTS (minimum score 7). *Application deadline:* For fall admission, 1/15 priority date for domestic and international students; for summer admission, 1/15 priority date for domestic and international students. Application fee: $45. Electronic applications accepted. *Financial support:* Fellowships with full tuition reimbursements, research assistantships with partial tuition reimbursements, scholarships/grants, and instructional associate positions with partial tuition reimbursements available. Financial award application deadline: 2/1. *Faculty research:* Media convergence, political reporting, interactive multimedia, popular television, advertising effectiveness. *Unit head:* Lorraine Branham, Dean, 315-443-3372, E-mail: lbranham@syr.edu. *Application contact:* Martha Coria, Graduate Records Office, 315-443-4039, Fax: 315-443-1834, E-mail: pcgrad@syr.edu.
Website: http://newhouse.syr.edu/

Tarleton State University, College of Graduate Studies, College of Liberal and Fine Arts, Department of Communication Studies, Stephenville, TX 76402. Offers MA. *Program availability:* Part-time. *Faculty:* 3 full-time (1 woman), 2 part-time/adjunct (both women). *Students:* 8 full-time (all women), 25 part-time (21 women); includes 14 minority (5 Black or African American, non-Hispanic/Latino; 1 Asian, non-Hispanic/Latino; 8 Hispanic/Latino). Average age 29. 21 applicants, 81% accepted, 12 enrolled. In 2017, 8 master's awarded. *Degree requirements:* For master's, comprehensive exam, thesis (for some programs). *Entrance requirements:* For master's, GRE, minimum overall GPA of 3.0. Additional exam requirements/recommendations for international students: Required—TOEFL (minimum score 550 paper-based; 80 iBT), IELTS (minimum score 6). *Application deadline:* For fall admission, 8/15 for domestic students; for spring admission, 1/5 for domestic students. Applications are processed on a rolling basis. Application fee: $45 ($145 for international students). Electronic applications accepted. *Expenses:* Contact institution. *Financial support:* Applicants required to submit FAFSA. *Unit head:* Dr. Lora Helvie-Mason, Department Head, 254-918-7620, E-mail: helviemason@tarleton.edu. *Application contact:* Information Contact, 254-968-9104, Fax: 254-968-9670, E-mail: gradoffice@tarleton.edu.
Website: http://www.tarleton.edu/degrees/masters/ma-communication-studies/index.html

Teachers College, Columbia University, Department of Mathematics, Science and Technology, New York, NY 10027-6696. Offers biology 7-12 (MA); chemistry 7-12 (MA); communication and education (MA, Ed D); computing in education (MA); earth science 7-12 (MA); instructional technology and media (Ed M, MA, Ed D); mathematics education (Ed M, MA, Ed D, Ed DCT, PhD); physics 7-12 (MA); science and dental education (MA); science education (Ed M, MS, Ed DCT, PhD); supervisor/teacher of science education (MA); technology specialist (MA). *Program availability:* Part-time, evening/weekend, online learning. *Students:* 187 full-time (129 women), 228 part-time (153 women); includes 143 minority (42 Black or African American, non-Hispanic/Latino; 64 Asian, non-Hispanic/Latino; 25 Hispanic/Latino; 12 Two or more races, non-Hispanic/Latino), 125 international. Average age 32. 484 applicants, 59% accepted, 141 enrolled. Terminal master's awarded for partial completion of doctoral program. *Degree requirements:* For doctorate, thesis/dissertation. *Unit head:* Prof. Erica Walker, Chair, E-mail: ewalker@tc.columbia.edu. *Application contact:* David Estrella, Director of Admission, 212-678-3305, E-mail: estrella@tc.columbia.edu.
Website: http://www.tc.columbia.edu/mathematics-science-and-technology/

Temple University, Klein College of Media and Communication, Department of Communication, Philadelphia, PA 19122-6096. Offers communication management (MS); globalization and development communication (MS); media and communication (PhD). *Program availability:* Part-time, evening/weekend. *Faculty:* 10 full-time (3 women). *Students:* 2 full-time (1 woman), 15 part-time (10 women); includes 6 minority (4 Black or African American, non-Hispanic/Latino; 1 Asian, non-Hispanic/Latino; 1 Two or more races, non-Hispanic/Latino). 8 applicants, 88% accepted, 4 enrolled. In 2017, 7 master's awarded. *Entrance requirements:* For master's, GRE General Test. Additional exam requirements/recommendations for international students: Required—TOEFL (minimum score 620 paper-based; 105 iBT). *Application deadline:* For fall admission, 2/15 for domestic and international students; for spring admission, 11/1 for domestic and international students. Application fee: $60. Electronic applications accepted. *Expenses:* Contact institution. *Financial support:* Career-related internships or fieldwork and Federal Work-Study available. Financial award application deadline: 1/15; financial award applicants required to submit FAFSA. *Unit head:* Dr. R. Lance Holbert, Chair, 215-204-3152, E-mail: r.lance.holbert@temple.edu. *Application contact:* Nicole McKenna, Director, Office of Research and Graduate Studies, 215-204-1497, Fax: 215-204-0310, E-mail: nmckenna@temple.edu.
Website: https://klein.temple.edu/degree/communication

Texas A&M University, College of Liberal Arts, Department of Communication, College Station, TX 77843. Offers MA, PhD. *Faculty:* 21. *Students:* 38 full-time (26 women), 6 part-time (2 women); includes 7 minority (2 Black or African American, non-Hispanic/Latino; 1 Asian, non-Hispanic/Latino; 3 Hispanic/Latino; 1 Two or more races, non-Hispanic/Latino), 11 international. Average age 31. 45 applicants, 49% accepted, 9 enrolled. In 2017, 11 doctorates awarded. *Degree requirements:* For master's, thesis or alternative; for doctorate, thesis/dissertation. *Entrance requirements:* For master's, GRE General Test. Additional exam requirements/recommendations for international students: Required—TOEFL (minimum score 550 paper-based; 80 iBT), IELTS (minimum score 6), PTE (minimum score 53). *Application deadline:* For fall admission, 12/15 for domestic students. Applications are processed on a rolling basis. Application fee: $50 ($90 for international students). Electronic applications accepted. *Expenses:* Contact institution. *Financial support:* In 2017–18, 38 students received support, including 5 fellowships with tuition reimbursements available (averaging $10,544 per year), 2 research assistantships with tuition reimbursements available (averaging $12,172 per year), 35 teaching assistantships with tuition reimbursements available (averaging $13,354 per year); career-related internships or fieldwork, institutionally sponsored loans, scholarships/grants, traineeships, health care benefits, tuition waivers (full and partial), and unspecified assistantships also available. Support available to part-time students. Financial award application deadline: 3/15; financial award applicants required to submit FAFSA. *Faculty research:* Rhetoric and public affairs, communication and health, communication and organizations. *Unit head:* Dr. J. Kevin Barge, Head, 979-845-5514, E-mail: kbarge@tamu.edu. *Application contact:* Kristan Poirot, Graduate Program Director, 979-845-2842, E-mail: poirot@tamu.edu.
Website: http://comm.tamu.edu/

Texas A&M University–Corpus Christi, College of Graduate Studies, College of Liberal Arts, Corpus Christi, TX 78412. Offers communication (MA); English (MA); history (MA); psychology (MA), including clinical psychology, general psychology; public administration (MPA); studio art (MFA). *Program availability:* Part-time, evening/weekend. *Faculty:* 76 full-time (39 women), 9 part-time/adjunct (4 women). *Students:* 83 full-time (56 women), 109 part-time (78 women); includes 112 minority (9 Black or African American, non-Hispanic/Latino; 100 Hispanic/Latino; 3 Two or more races, non-Hispanic/Latino). Average age 32. 119 applicants, 67% accepted, 65 enrolled. In 2017, 65 master's awarded. *Degree requirements:* For master's, comprehensive exam (for some programs). *Entrance requirements:* For master's, portfolio. Additional exam requirements/recommendations for international students: Required—TOEFL (minimum score 550 paper-based; 79 iBT), IELTS (minimum score 6.5). *Application deadline:* For fall admission, 7/15 for domestic students, 5/1 for international students; for spring admission, 11/15 priority date for domestic students, 9/1 priority date for international students. Applications are processed on a rolling basis. Application fee: $50 ($70 for international students). Electronic applications accepted. *Expenses:* Tuition, state resident: full-time $3568; part-time $198.24 per credit hour. Tuition, nonresident: full-time $11,038; part-time $613.24 per credit hour. *Required fees:* $2129; $1422.58 per semester. Tuition and fees vary according to program. *Financial support:* Research assistantships, teaching assistantships, career-related internships or fieldwork, Federal Work-Study, institutionally sponsored loans, scholarships/grants, health care benefits, and unspecified assistantships available. Support available to part-time students. Financial award application deadline: 3/15; financial award applicants required to submit FAFSA. *Unit head:* Dr. Mark Hartlaub, Dean, 361-825-2659, Fax: 361-825-5844, E-mail: mark.hartlaub@tamucc.edu. *Application contact:* Graduate Admissions Coordinator, 361-825-2177, Fax: 361-825-2755, E-mail: gradweb@tamucc.edu.
Website: http://cla.tamucc.edu/

Texas Christian University, Bob Schieffer College of Communication, Fort Worth, TX 76129. Offers communication studies (MS); strategic communication (MS). *Program availability:* Part-time. *Faculty:* 26 full-time (12 women). *Students:* 21 full-time (18 women), 2 part-time (1 woman); includes 5 minority (1 Asian, non-Hispanic/Latino; 4 Hispanic/Latino). Average age 25. 24 applicants, 71% accepted, 12 enrolled. In 2017, 16 master's awarded. *Degree requirements:* For master's, comprehensive exam (for some programs), thesis (for some programs). *Entrance requirements:* For master's, GRE General Test. Additional exam requirements/recommendations for international students: Required—TOEFL (minimum score 550 paper-based; 80 iBT). *Application deadline:* For fall admission, 2/15 for domestic and international students; for spring admission, 10/15 for domestic and international students. Application fee: $60. Electronic applications accepted. *Expenses:* Contact institution. *Financial support:* In 2017–18, 25 students received support, including 18 teaching assistantships with full tuition reimbursements available (averaging $10,000 per year); research assistantships, health care benefits, tuition waivers (full and partial), and unspecified assistantships also available. Financial award application deadline: 2/15. *Faculty research:* Interpersonal communication, family communication, social networking, media history, media studies, media law, media ethics, mobile communications. *Unit head:* Dr. Daxton Stewart, Associate Dean, 817-257-5911, Fax: 817-257-5921, E-mail: d.stewart@tcu.edu. *Application contact:* Alicia E. Craff, Academic Program Specialist, 817-257-5917, Fax: 817-257-5921, E-mail: a.e.craff@tcu.edu.
Website: http://www.schieffercollege.tcu.edu/

Texas Southern University, Tavis Smiley School of Communication, Houston, TX 77004-4584. Offers MA. *Program availability:* Part-time. *Degree requirements:* For master's, comprehensive exam, thesis. *Entrance requirements:* For master's, GRE General Test, minimum GPA of 2.5. Additional exam requirements/recommendations for international students: Required—TOEFL. Electronic applications accepted.

Texas State University, The Graduate College, College of Fine Arts and Communication, Program in Communication Studies, San Marcos, TX 78666. Offers MA. *Program availability:* Part-time, evening/weekend. *Faculty:* 15 full-time (12 women), 1 part-time/adjunct (0 women). *Students:* 29 full-time (22 women), 8 part-time (6 women); includes 9 minority (3 Black or African American, non-Hispanic/Latino; 5 Hispanic/Latino; 1 Two or more races, non-Hispanic/Latino), 3 international. Average age 25. 32 applicants, 63% accepted, 12 enrolled. In 2017, 28 master's awarded. *Degree requirements:* For master's, comprehensive exam, thesis optional. *Entrance requirements:* For master's, baccalaureate degree from regionally-accredited institution with minimum GPA of 3.2 in last 60 hours of undergraduate course work, 3 letters of recommendation, statement of purpose, 18 hours of undergraduate course work in communication studies. Additional exam requirements/recommendations for international students: Required—TOEFL (minimum score 550 paper-based; 78 iBT), IELTS (minimum score 6), TOEFL (minimum iBT scores: 19 listening, 19 reading, 19 speaking, 18 writing). *Application deadline:* For fall admission, 3/1 priority date for domestic and international students; for spring admission, 10/15 priority date for domestic students, 10/1 priority date for international students; for summer admission, 3/1 for domestic and international students. Applications are processed on a rolling basis. Application fee: $40 ($90 for international students). Electronic applications accepted. *Expenses:* Tuition, state resident: full-time $7868; part-time $3934 per semester. Tuition, nonresident: full-time $17,828; part-time $8914 per semester. *Required fees:* $2092; $1435 per semester. Tuition and fees vary according to course load. *Financial support:* In 2017–18, 17 students received support, including 28 teaching assistantships (averaging $14,400 per year); research assistantships, career-related internships or fieldwork, Federal Work-Study, institutionally sponsored loans, scholarships/grants, and unspecified assistantships also available. Support available to part-time students. Financial award application deadline: 3/1; financial award applicants required to submit FAFSA. *Faculty research:* Parent-child processes affecting long term post-disaster psycho-social adjustment, sexual health assessment and risk. *Total annual research expenditures:* $423,218. *Unit head:* Dr. Maureen Keeley, Graduate Adviser, 512-245-3133, Fax: 512-245-3138, E-mail: mk09@txstate.edu. *Application contact:* Dr. Andrea Golato, Dean of Graduate School, 512-245-2581, Fax: 512-245-8365, E-mail: gradcollege@txstate.edu.
Website: http://www.finearts.txstate.edu/commstudies/

Texas Tech University, Graduate School, College of Media and Communication, Department of Communication Studies, Lubbock, TX 79409. Offers MA. *Program availability:* Part-time. *Faculty:* 16 full-time (9 women), 4 part-time/adjunct (2 women). *Students:* 18 full-time (10 women), 1 (woman) part-time; includes 4 minority (all Hispanic/Latino), 1 international. Average age 24. 26 applicants, 54% accepted, 11 enrolled. In 2017, 6 master's awarded. *Degree requirements:* For master's, comprehensive exam (for some programs), thesis or alternative. *Entrance requirements:* For master's, GRE (only if GPA is under 3.0), minimum undergraduate GPA of 3.0. Additional exam requirements/recommendations for international students: Required—TOEFL (minimum score 550 paper-based; 79 iBT). *Application deadline:* For fall admission, 6/1 priority date for domestic students, 1/15 priority date for international

students; for spring admission, 9/1 priority date for domestic students, 6/15 priority date for international students. Applications are processed on a rolling basis. Application fee: $60. Electronic applications accepted. *Expenses:* Contact institution. *Financial support:* In 2017–18, 21 students received support, including 10 fellowships (averaging $3,236 per year), 20 teaching assistantships (averaging $8,673 per year); scholarships/grants and unspecified assistantships also available. Financial award application deadline: 4/15; financial award applicants required to submit FAFSA. *Faculty research:* Organizational communication, interpersonal communication, instructional communication, intercultural communication, rhetorical and media studies. *Unit head:* Dr. Brian L. Ott, Professor/Chair, 806-834-2928, E-mail: brian.ott@ttu.edu. *Application contact:* Dr. Mark A. Gring, Associate Professor/Assistant Graduate Director for the College of Media and Communication, 806-843-3913, E-mail: mark.gring@ttu.edu.
Website: http://www.depts.ttu.edu/comc/programs/commstudies/

Tiffin University, Program in Humanities, Tiffin, OH 44883-2161. Offers art and visual media (MH); communication (MH); creative writing (MH); English (MH); film studies (MH); humanities (MH); individualized studies (MH). *Program availability:* Part-time, evening/weekend, online only, 100% online, blended/hybrid learning. *Entrance requirements:* For master's, work experience. Additional exam requirements/recommendations for international students: Required—TOEFL (minimum score 550 paper-based; 79 iBT). Electronic applications accepted. Application fee is waived when completed online. *Expenses:* Contact institution.

Towson University, College of Fine Arts and Communication, Program in Communication Management, Towson, MD 21252-0001. Offers MS. *Students:* 3 full-time (2 women), 12 part-time (9 women); includes 7 minority (all Black or African American, non-Hispanic/Latino). *Degree requirements:* For master's, thesis. *Entrance requirements:* For master's, bachelor's degree with 24 credits in mass communications, public relations, advertising or communication studies; advanced writing and basic statistics courses; professional experience; minimum GPA of 3.0; letter of recommendation; resume. Additional exam requirements/recommendations for international students: Required—TOEFL. *Application deadline:* For fall admission, 1/17 for domestic students, 5/15 for international students; for spring admission, 10/15 for domestic students, 12/1 for international students. Applications are processed on a rolling basis. Application fee: $45. Electronic applications accepted. *Expenses:* Tuition, state resident: full-time $7960; part-time $398 per unit. Tuition, nonresident: full-time $16,480; part-time $824 per unit. *Required fees:* $2600; $130 per year. $390 per term. *Financial support:* Application deadline: 4/1. *Unit head:* Dr. Lingling Zhang, Graduate Program Director, 410-704-3458, E-mail: lizhang@towson.edu. *Application contact:* Coverley Beidleman, Assistant Director of Graduate Admissions, 410-704-5630, Fax: 410-704-3030, E-mail: cbeidleman@towson.edu.
Website: http://www.towson.edu/cofac/departments/communication/gradcommunicationmgmt/

Trinity Washington University, School of Business and Graduate Studies, Washington, DC 20017-1094. Offers business administration (MBA); communication (MA); international security studies (MA); organizational management (MSA), including federal program management, human resource management, nonprofit management, organizational development, public and community health. *Program availability:* Part-time, evening/weekend. *Degree requirements:* For master's, thesis (for some programs), capstone project (MSA). *Entrance requirements:* For master's, minimum GPA of 2.5. Additional exam requirements/recommendations for international students: Required—TOEFL (minimum score 550 paper-based).

Troy University, Graduate School, College of Communication and Fine Arts, Troy, AL 36082. Offers strategic communication (MS). *Program availability:* Part-time, evening/weekend. *Faculty:* 5 full-time (3 women). *Students:* 47 full-time (33 women), 76 part-time (60 women); includes 29 minority (26 Black or African American, non-Hispanic/Latino; 1 Hispanic/Latino; 1 Native Hawaiian or other Pacific Islander, non-Hispanic/Latino; 1 Two or more races, non-Hispanic/Latino). Average age 27. 52 applicants, 100% accepted, 42 enrolled. In 2017, 44 master's awarded. *Degree requirements:* For master's, comprehensive exam, thesis optional, minimum GPA of 3.0, admission to candidacy. *Entrance requirements:* For master's, GRE (minimum score of 850 on old exam or 290 on new exam), MAT (minimum score of 385) or GMAT (minimum score of 380), bachelor's degree; minimum undergraduate GPA of 2.5 or 3.0 on last 30 semester hours. Additional exam requirements/recommendations for international students: Required—TOEFL (minimum score 523 paper-based; 70 iBT), IELTS (minimum score 6). *Application deadline:* For fall admission, 6/1 for international students; for spring admission, 10/15 for international students. Applications are processed on a rolling basis. Application fee: $50. Electronic applications accepted. *Expenses:* Tuition, state resident: part-time $417 per credit hour. Tuition, nonresident: part-time $834 per credit hour. *Required fees:* $42 per credit hour. $50 per semester. Tuition and fees vary according to campus/location. *Financial support:* Fellowships, career-related internships or fieldwork, and scholarships/grants available. Support available to part-time students. Financial award applicants required to submit FAFSA. *Unit head:* Dr. Larry Blocher, Dean, 334-670-3869, Fax: 334-670-3858, E-mail: lblocher@troy.edu. *Application contact:* Jessica A. Kimbro, Director of Graduate Admissions, 334-670-3178, E-mail: jacord@troy.edu.

Université de Montréal, Faculty of Arts and Sciences, Department of Communication, Montréal, QC H3C 3J7, Canada. Offers communication (PhD); communication sciences (M Sc). *Degree requirements:* For master's, thesis; for doctorate, one foreign language, thesis/dissertation, general exam. *Entrance requirements:* For doctorate, proficiency in French. Electronic applications accepted. *Faculty research:* Mass media/new communication technologies, organizational communication.

Université du Québec à Montréal, Graduate Programs, Program in Communications, Montréal, QC H3C 3P8, Canada. Offers MA, PhD. PhD offered jointly with Concordia University and Université de Montréal. *Program availability:* Part-time. *Degree requirements:* For master's, thesis; for doctorate, thesis/dissertation. *Entrance requirements:* For master's, appropriate bachelor's degree or equivalent, proficiency in French; for doctorate, appropriate master's degree or equivalent, proficiency in French.

Université du Québec à Trois-Rivières, Graduate Programs, Program in Social Communication, Trois-Rivières, QC G9A 5H7, Canada. Offers MA, DESS.

University at Albany, State University of New York, College of Arts and Sciences, Department of Communication, Albany, NY 12222-0001. Offers communication (MA); sociology and communication (PhD). *Program availability:* Part-time. *Faculty:* 11 full-time (6 women). *Students:* 31 full-time (26 women), 32 part-time (25 women); includes 13 minority (8 Black or African American, non-Hispanic/Latino; 2 Asian, non-Hispanic/Latino; 2 Hispanic/Latino; 1 Two or more races, non-Hispanic/Latino), 9 international. 71 applicants, 54% accepted, 19 enrolled. In 2017, 15 master's awarded. *Degree requirements:* For master's, comprehensive exam, thesis or alternative; for doctorate, comprehensive exam, thesis/dissertation. *Entrance requirements:* For master's, minimum GPA of 3.0; for doctorate, GRE, minimum GPA of 3.0. Additional exam requirements/recommendations for international students: Required—TOEFL (minimum score 550 paper-based). *Application deadline:* For fall admission, 2/20 priority date for domestic students, 5/1 for international students. Applications are processed on a rolling basis. Application fee: $75. Electronic applications accepted. *Expenses:* Tuition, state resident: full-time $10,870; part-time $453 per credit hour. Tuition, nonresident: full-time $22,210; part-time $925 per credit hour. *Required fees:* $84.68 per credit hour. $508.06 per semester. Part-time tuition and fees vary according to course load and program. *Financial support:* Fellowships, teaching assistantships, career-related internships or fieldwork, and institutionally sponsored loans available. Financial award application deadline: 3/1. *Faculty research:* Language and social interaction, campaign communication, media agenda-setting, high-speed management, organizational boundary-spanning. *Unit head:* Annis Golden, Chair, 518-442-4871, Fax: 518-442-3884, E-mail: agolden@albany.edu. *Application contact:* Michael DeRensis, Director, Graduate Admissions, 518-442-3980, Fax: 518-442-3922, E-mail: graduate@albany.edu.
Website: http://www.albany.edu/communication/

University at Buffalo, the State University of New York, Graduate School, College of Arts and Sciences, Department of Communication, Buffalo, NY 14260. Offers MA, PhD. *Faculty:* 16 full-time (5 women), 16 part-time/adjunct (9 women). *Students:* 23 full-time (12 women), 12 part-time (9 women); includes 12 minority (1 Black or African American, non-Hispanic/Latino; 11 Asian, non-Hispanic/Latino), 1 international. Average age 30. 78 applicants, 47% accepted, 14 enrolled. In 2017, 7 master's, 1 doctorate awarded. Terminal master's awarded for partial completion of doctoral program. *Degree requirements:* For master's, thesis; for doctorate, comprehensive exam, thesis/dissertation. *Entrance requirements:* For master's, minimum GPA of 3.0; for doctorate, GRE General Test, minimum GPA of 3.0. Additional exam requirements/recommendations for international students: Required—TOEFL (minimum score 600 paper-based; 100 iBT), IELTS (minimum score 7), GRE; Recommended—TWE. *Application deadline:* For fall admission, 1/15 priority date for domestic students, 4/1 priority date for international students. Applications are processed on a rolling basis. Application fee: $75. Electronic applications accepted. Application fee is waived when completed online. *Financial support:* In 2017–18, 2 students received support, including 2 research assistantships with full tuition reimbursements available (averaging $19,000 per year), 13 teaching assistantships with full tuition reimbursements available (averaging $13,650 per year); fellowships, career-related internships or fieldwork, institutionally sponsored loans, scholarships/grants, health care benefits, and unspecified assistantships also available. Financial award application deadline: 1/15; financial award applicants required to submit FAFSA. *Faculty research:* Technology, health communication, global communication, media. *Total annual research expenditures:* $70,000. *Unit head:* Dr. Mark G. Frank, Chairman, 716-645-1170, Fax: 716-645-2086, E-mail: mfrank83@buffalo.edu. *Application contact:* Rose Gryckiewicz, Graduate Program Coordinator, 716-645-1505, Fax: 716-645-2086, E-mail: rfg@buffalo.edu.
Website: http://www.cas.buffalo.edu/communication

The University of Akron, Graduate School, Buchtel College of Arts and Sciences, School of Communication, Akron, OH 44325. Offers MA. *Program availability:* Part-time, evening/weekend. *Faculty:* 11 full-time (6 women). *Students:* 8 full-time (5 women), 5 part-time (all women); includes 3 minority (all Black or African American, non-Hispanic/Latino), 1 international. Average age 24. 12 applicants, 100% accepted, 6 enrolled. In 2017, 6 master's awarded. *Degree requirements:* For master's, thesis, project or written comprehensive exam. *Entrance requirements:* For master's, baccalaureate degree in communication, journalism, or related field; essay of no more than 500 words outlining reasons for choosing graduate program in communication at The University of Akron. Additional exam requirements/recommendations for international students: Required—TOEFL (minimum score 79 iBT), IELTS (minimum score 6.5). *Application deadline:* For fall admission, 5/1 for domestic and international students. Application fee: $45 ($70 for international students). Electronic applications accepted. *Financial support:* In 2017–18, 6 teaching assistantships with full tuition reimbursements were awarded. *Faculty research:* Communications theory, business and organization communications, criticism of communications, film and video studies, interpersonal and intercultural communications. *Total annual research expenditures:* $41,020. *Unit head:* Dr. Heather Walter, School Director, 330-972-6486, E-mail: hlwalter@uakron.edu. *Application contact:* Dr. Tang Tang, Graduate Director, 330-972-7606, E-mail: tang@uakron.edu.
Website: http://www.uakron.edu/schlcomm/

The University of Alabama, Graduate School, College of Communication and Information Sciences, Tuscaloosa, AL 35487-0172. Offers MA, MFA, MLIS, PhD. *Accreditation:* ACEJMC (one or more programs are accredited at the [master's] level). *Faculty:* 68 full-time (33 women), 2 part-time/adjunct (both women). *Students:* 137 full-time (94 women), 234 part-time (182 women); includes 53 minority (25 Black or African American, non-Hispanic/Latino; 1 American Indian or Alaska Native, non-Hispanic/Latino; 2 Asian, non-Hispanic/Latino; 11 Hispanic/Latino; 14 Two or more races, non-Hispanic/Latino), 31 international. Average age 32. 279 applicants, 70% accepted, 137 enrolled. In 2017, 117 master's, 15 doctorates awarded. *Degree requirements:* For master's, comprehensive exam, thesis or alternative; for doctorate, comprehensive exam, thesis/dissertation. *Entrance requirements:* For master's, GRE; for doctorate, GRE, minimum graduate GPA of 3.0, master's degree. Additional exam requirements/recommendations for international students: Required—TOEFL (minimum score 600 paper-based; 100 iBT). *Application deadline:* For fall admission, 2/15 priority date for domestic and international students; for winter admission, 11/1 priority date for international students; for spring admission, 11/1 priority date for domestic students. Applications are processed on a rolling basis. Application fee: $50 ($60 for international students). Electronic applications accepted. *Financial support:* In 2017–18, 70 students received support. Fellowships with tuition reimbursements available, research assistantships with tuition reimbursements available, teaching assistantships with tuition reimbursements available, institutionally sponsored loans, health care benefits, and unspecified assistantships available. Financial award application deadline: 2/15. *Faculty research:* Mass media research; media effects; information studies; cultural, critical, and rhetorical studies; electronic media; law and policy. *Total annual research expenditures:* $1,935. *Unit head:* Dr. Mark Nelson, Dean, 205-348-4787, E-mail: mnelson@ua.edu. *Application contact:* Marylou Cox, Information Contact, 205-348-8593, Fax: 205-348-6774, E-mail: mcox@ua.edu.
Website: http://www.cis.ua.edu

The University of Alabama at Birmingham, College of Arts and Sciences, Program in Communication Management, Birmingham, AL 35294. Offers MA. *Program availability:* Part-time, evening/weekend. Terminal master's awarded for partial completion of doctoral program. *Degree requirements:* For master's, comprehensive exam, thesis or alternative. *Entrance requirements:* For master's, GRE (recommended) or MAT, minimum undergraduate GPA of 3.0, letters of reference. Additional exam requirements/recommendations for international students: Required—TOEFL (minimum score 550 paper-based; 80 iBT), IELTS (minimum score 6.5). Electronic applications accepted. *Faculty research:* Deception, political communication, nonverbal communication, virtual world, game theory.

University of Alaska Fairbanks, College of Liberal Arts, Department of Communications, Fairbanks, AK 99775-5680. Offers professional communication (MA). *Program availability:* Part-time. *Degree requirements:* For master's, comprehensive exam, thesis, oral defense of thesis. *Entrance requirements:* For master's, bachelor's degree from accredited institution with minimum cumulative undergraduate and major

GPA of 3.0, academic writing sample. Additional exam requirements/recommendations for international students: Required—TOEFL (minimum score 550 paper-based; 79 iBT), IELTS (minimum score 6.5). Electronic applications accepted. *Faculty research:* Interpersonal communications, health communications, intercultural communications, politeness and face management in conversation, gender communication.

University of Alberta, Faculty of Extension, Edmonton, AB T6G 2E1, Canada. Offers communications and technology (MA).

University of Alberta, Faculty of Graduate Studies and Research, Program in Communications and Technology, Edmonton, AB T6G 2E1, Canada. Offers MACT.

The University of Arizona, College of Social and Behavioral Sciences, Department of Communication, Tucson, AZ 85721. Offers MA, PhD. *Program availability:* Part-time. Terminal master's awarded for partial completion of doctoral program. *Degree requirements:* For master's, thesis optional; for doctorate, comprehensive exam, thesis/dissertation. *Entrance requirements:* For master's, GRE General Test, minimum GPA of 3.25, writing sample, 3 letters of recommendation; for doctorate, GRE General Test, minimum GPA of 3.5, writing sample, 3 letters of recommendation, statement of purpose. Additional exam requirements/recommendations for international students: Required—TOEFL (minimum score 600 paper-based; 90 iBT). Electronic applications accepted. *Faculty research:* Health communication, new communication technologies.

University of Arkansas, Graduate School, J. William Fulbright College of Arts and Sciences, Department of Communication, Fayetteville, AR 72701. Offers MA. *Program availability:* Part-time. In 2017, 12 master's awarded. *Degree requirements:* For master's, thesis. *Entrance requirements:* For master's, GRE General Test. *Application deadline:* For fall admission, 8/1 for domestic students, 4/1 for international students; for spring admission, 12/1 for domestic students, 10/1 for international students; for summer admission, 4/15 for domestic students, 3/1 for international students. Applications are processed on a rolling basis. Application fee: $60. Electronic applications accepted. *Expenses:* Tuition, state resident: full-time $3782. Tuition, nonresident: full-time $10,238. *Financial support:* In 2017–18, 21 teaching assistantships were awarded; fellowships, research assistantships, career-related internships or fieldwork, and Federal Work-Study also available. Support available to part-time students. Financial award application deadline: 4/1; financial award applicants required to submit FAFSA. *Unit head:* Dr. Robert Brady, Department Chair, 479-575-3048, Fax: 479-575-6734, E-mail: rbrady@uark.edu. *Application contact:* Dr. Myria Allen, Graduate Coordinator, 479-575-5952, E-mail: myria@uark.edu.
Website: https://fulbright.uark.edu/departments/communication/

University of Bridgeport, College of Public and International Affairs, Bridgeport, CT 06604. Offers East Asian and Pacific Rim studies (MA); global development and peace (MA); global media and communication studies (MA). *Program availability:* Part-time, evening/weekend. *Degree requirements:* For master's, thesis. *Entrance requirements:* Additional exam requirements/recommendations for international students: Recommended—TOEFL (minimum score 550 paper-based; 80 iBT), IELTS (minimum score 6.5).

University of Calgary, Faculty of Graduate Studies, Faculty of Arts, Department of Communication and Culture, Calgary, AB T2N 1N4, Canada. Offers MA, MCS, PhD. *Program availability:* Part-time, evening/weekend. *Degree requirements:* For master's, project (MCS), thesis (MA); for doctorate, thesis/dissertation. *Entrance requirements:* For master's, minimum GPA of 3.0; for doctorate, master's degree, minimum GPA of 3.0, BA degree, min GPA of 3.0. Additional exam requirements/recommendations for international students: Required—TOEFL (minimum score 600 paper-based); Recommended—IELTS (minimum score 8). Electronic applications accepted. *Faculty research:* Science communications, structuration theory, organizational communication, communication theory, media law.

University of California, Davis, Graduate Studies, Program in Communication, Davis, CA 95616. Offers MA. *Degree requirements:* For master's, comprehensive exam (for some programs), thesis (for some programs). *Entrance requirements:* For master's, GRE. Additional exam requirements/recommendations for international students: Required—TOEFL (minimum score 550 paper-based).

University of California, San Diego, Graduate Division, Department of Communication, La Jolla, CA 92093. Offers PhD. *Students:* 37 full-time (23 women). 87 applicants, 20% accepted, 7 enrolled. In 2017, 10 doctorates awarded. *Degree requirements:* For doctorate, one foreign language, comprehensive exam, thesis/dissertation, 2 quarters of teaching assistantship. *Entrance requirements:* For doctorate, GRE General Test, demonstrated competence in a natural language other than English, writing samples, letters of recommendation. Additional exam requirements/recommendations for international students: Required—TOEFL (minimum score 550 paper-based; 80 iBT), IELTS (minimum score 7), PTE. *Application deadline:* For fall admission, 12/15 for domestic students. Application fee: $105 ($125 for international students). Electronic applications accepted. *Financial support:* Fellowships, research assistantships, teaching assistantships, and scholarships/grants available. Financial award applicants required to submit FAFSA. *Faculty research:* Communication and culture, communication as a social force, communication and the person, communications and science and technology studies, digital media, political communication and journalism studies, language, cognition, media systems. *Unit head:* Valerie Hartouni, Chair, 858-534-2366, E-mail: vhartouni@ucsd.edu. *Application contact:* Melanie Lynn, Graduate Coordinator, 858-534-2379, E-mail: comm-gradadmit@ucsd.edu.
Website: http://communication.ucsd.edu

University of California, Santa Barbara, Graduate Division, College of Letters and Sciences, Division of Social Sciences, Department of Communication, Santa Barbara, CA 93106-4020. Offers cognitive science (PhD); communication (PhD); feminist studies (PhD); language, interaction and social organization (PhD); quantitative methods in the social sciences (PhD); society and technology (PhD); MA/PhD. Terminal master's awarded for partial completion of doctoral program. *Degree requirements:* For doctorate, comprehensive exam, thesis/dissertation. *Entrance requirements:* For doctorate, GRE. Additional exam requirements/recommendations for international students: Required—TOEFL (minimum score 80 iBT), IELTS (minimum score 7). Electronic applications accepted. *Faculty research:* Interpersonal, intergroup, intercultural, organizational, health, media.

University of California, Santa Cruz, Division of Graduate Studies, Division of Physical and Biological Sciences, Program in Science Communication, Santa Cruz, CA 95064. Offers Certificate. *Entrance requirements:* For degree, GRE General Test, GRE Subject Test, bachelor's degree in science. Additional exam requirements/recommendations for international students: Required—TOEFL (minimum score 550 paper-based; 83 iBT); Recommended—IELTS (minimum score 8). Electronic applications accepted. *Faculty research:* Science writing.

University of Central Florida, College of Sciences, Nicholson School of Communication, Orlando, FL 32816. Offers communication (MA); corporate communication (Certificate). *Program availability:* Part-time, evening/weekend. *Students:* 32 full-time (23 women), 25 part-time (20 women); includes 14 minority (5 Black or African American, non-Hispanic/Latino; 1 Asian, non-Hispanic/Latino; 5 Hispanic/Latino; 3 Two or more races, non-Hispanic/Latino), 8 international. Average age 28. 52 applicants, 75% accepted, 27 enrolled. In 2017, 27 master's, 17 other advanced degrees awarded. *Degree requirements:* For master's, thesis or alternative. *Entrance requirements:* For master's, GRE General Test, minimum GPA of 3.0 in last 60 hours of course work, letters of recommendation, personal/professional statement. Additional exam requirements/recommendations for international students: Required—TOEFL. *Application deadline:* For fall admission, 6/1 for domestic students; for spring admission, 11/1 for domestic students. Application fee: $30. Electronic applications accepted. *Expenses:* Tuition, state resident: part-time $288.16 per credit hour. Tuition, nonresident: part-time $1073.31 per credit hour. Tuition and fees vary according to program. *Financial support:* In 2017–18, 21 students received support, including 4 fellowships with partial tuition reimbursements available (averaging $2,000 per year), 4 research assistantships with partial tuition reimbursements available (averaging $5,339 per year), 18 teaching assistantships with partial tuition reimbursements available (averaging $9,407 per year); career-related internships or fieldwork, Federal Work-Study, institutionally sponsored loans, health care benefits, tuition waivers (partial), and unspecified assistantships also available. Financial award application deadline: 3/1; financial award applicants required to submit FAFSA. *Faculty research:* Persuasion, interpersonal communication, nonverbal communication, conflict resolution. *Unit head:* Dr. Robert Littlefield, Director, 407-823-1708, E-mail: robert.littlefield@ucf.edu. *Application contact:* Associate Director, Graduate Admissions, 407-823-2766, Fax: 407-823-6442, E-mail: gradadmissions@ucf.edu.
Website: http://communication.cos.ucf.edu/

University of Central Missouri, The Graduate School, Warrensburg, MO 64093. Offers accountancy (MA); accounting (MBA); applied mathematics (MS); aviation safety (MA); biology (MS); business administration (MBA); career and technical education leadership (MS); college student personnel administration (MS); communication (MA); computer science (MS); counseling (MS); criminal justice (MS); educational leadership (Ed D); educational technology (MS); elementary and early childhood education (MSE); English (MA); environmental studies (MA); finance (MBA); history (MA); human services/educational technology (Ed S); human services/learning resources (Ed S); human services/professional counseling (Ed S); industrial hygiene (MS); industrial management (MS); information systems (MBA); information technology (MS); kinesiology (MS); library science and information services (MS); literacy education (MSE); marketing (MBA); mathematics (MS); music (MA); occupational safety management (MS); psychology (MS); rural family nursing (MS); school administration (MSE); social gerontology (MS); sociology (MA); special education (MSE); speech language pathology (MS); superintendency (Ed S); teaching (MAT); teaching English as a second language (MA); technology (MS); technology management (PhD); theatre (MA). *Program availability:* Part-time, 100% online, blended/hybrid learning. *Faculty:* 337 full-time (145 women), 41 part-time/adjunct (28 women). *Students:* 785 full-time (398 women), 1,633 part-time (1,063 women); includes 231 minority (102 Black or African American, non-Hispanic/Latino; 4 American Indian or Alaska Native, non-Hispanic/Latino; 16 Asian, non-Hispanic/Latino; 52 Hispanic/Latino; 57 Two or more races, non-Hispanic/Latino), 692 international. Average age 30. In 2017, 2,605 master's, 122 other advanced degrees awarded. *Degree requirements:* For master's and Ed S, comprehensive exam (for some programs), thesis (for some programs). *Entrance requirements:* Additional exam requirements/recommendations for international students: Required—TOEFL (minimum score 550 paper-based; 79 iBT). *Application deadline:* For fall admission, 6/1 priority date for domestic and international students; for spring admission, 10/1 priority date for domestic and international students; for summer admission, 4/1 priority date for domestic and international students. Applications are processed on a rolling basis. Application fee: $30 ($75 for international students). Electronic applications accepted. *Expenses:* Tuition, state resident: full-time $8771; part-time $292.35 per credit hour. Tuition, nonresident: full-time $17,541; part-time $584.70 per credit hour. *Required fees:* $372; $24.78 per credit hour. *Financial support:* In 2017–18, 99 students received support. Research assistantships, teaching assistantships, career-related internships or fieldwork, Federal Work-Study, scholarships/grants, and administrative and laboratory assistantships available. Support available to part-time students. Financial award application deadline: 3/1; financial award applicants required to submit FAFSA. *Unit head:* Shellie Hewitt, Director of Graduate and International Student Services, 660-543-4621, Fax: 660-543-4778, E-mail: hewitt@ucmo.edu. *Application contact:* 660-543-4621, E-mail: admit_intl@ucmo.edu.
Website: http://www.ucmo.edu/graduate/

University of Cincinnati, Graduate School, McMicken College of Arts and Sciences, Department of Communication, Cincinnati, OH 45221. Offers MA. *Program availability:* Part-time. *Degree requirements:* For master's, comprehensive exam, thesis or alternative. *Entrance requirements:* For master's, GRE General Test, undergraduate course work in communication. Additional exam requirements/recommendations for international students: Required—TOEFL. Electronic applications accepted. *Expenses: Tuition, area resident:* Full-time $14,468. Tuition, state resident: full-time $14,968; part-time $754 per credit hour. Tuition, nonresident: full-time $24,210; part-time $1311 per credit hour. *International tuition:* $26,460 full-time. *Required fees:* $3958; $84 per credit hour. One-time fee: $85 full-time. Tuition and fees vary according to course load, degree level and program. *Faculty research:* Political communication, health communication, organizational communication, interpersonal communication.

University of Colorado Boulder, Graduate School, College of Media, Communication and Information, Program in Communication, Boulder, CO 80309. Offers MA, PhD. *Faculty:* 19 full-time (11 women). *Students:* 47 full-time (27 women), 3 part-time (1 woman); includes 5 minority (1 Black or African American, non-Hispanic/Latino; 3 Hispanic/Latino; 1 Two or more races, non-Hispanic/Latino), 4 international. Average age 30. 68 applicants, 28% accepted, 9 enrolled. In 2017, 5 master's, 10 doctorates awarded. Terminal master's awarded for partial completion of doctoral program. *Degree requirements:* For master's, comprehensive exam, thesis optional; for doctorate, comprehensive exam, thesis/dissertation. *Entrance requirements:* For master's and doctorate, GRE General Test, minimum undergraduate GPA of 3.2. *Application deadline:* For fall admission, 12/1 for domestic and international students; for spring admission, 9/15 for domestic students, 10/1 for international students. Applications are processed on a rolling basis. Application fee: $60 ($80 for international students). Electronic applications accepted. Application fee is waived when completed online. *Financial support:* In 2017–18, 210 students received support, including 87 fellowships (averaging $1,181 per year), 20 research assistantships with full and partial tuition reimbursements available (averaging $22,042 per year), 39 teaching assistantships with full and partial tuition reimbursements available (averaging $28,881 per year); institutionally sponsored loans, scholarships/grants, health care benefits, and unspecified assistantships also available. Financial award application deadline: 2/15; financial award applicants required to submit FAFSA. *Faculty research:* Communications; ethnography; organizational theory and behavior; culture; democracy. *Application contact:* E-mail: larry.frey@colorado.edu.
Website: http://www.colorado.edu/communication/

University of Colorado Colorado Springs, College of Letters, Arts and Sciences, Department of Communication, Colorado Springs, CO 80918. Offers MA. *Program availability:* Part-time, 100% online, blended/hybrid learning. *Faculty:* 14 full-time (10 women), 18 part-time/adjunct (11 women). *Students:* 10 full-time (7 women), 15 part-

time (7 women); includes 8 minority (1 Black or African American, non-Hispanic/Latino; 3 Hispanic/Latino; 4 Two or more races, non-Hispanic/Latino). Average age 29. 16 applicants, 100% accepted, 8 enrolled. In 2017, 12 master's awarded. *Degree requirements:* For master's, thesis optional. *Entrance requirements:* For master's, GRE. Additional exam requirements/recommendations for international students: Recommended—TOEFL (minimum score 550 paper-based; 80 iBT), IELTS (minimum score 6.5). *Application deadline:* Applications are processed on a rolling basis. Application fee: $60 ($100 for international students). Electronic applications accepted. *Expenses:* $10,350 per year resident tuition, $20,935 nonresident, $11,961 nonresidential online; annual costs vary depending on program, course-load, and residency status. *Financial support:* In 2017–18, 8 students received support. Career-related internships or fieldwork, Federal Work-Study, scholarships/grants, and unspecified assistantships available. Support available to part-time students. Financial award application deadline: 3/1; financial award applicants required to submit FAFSA. *Faculty research:* Instructional communication, popular culture, strategic communication efforts in public relations, the impact of gender and culture on leadership behavior, leadership succession, organizational trust, intercultural communication, psychological and social effects of media, organizational communication. *Unit head:* Dr. Chris Bell, Director of Graduate Studies, 719-255-8193, Fax: 719-255-4030, E-mail: cbell3@uccs.edu. *Application contact:* Debbie MacDonald, Program Assistant, 719-255-4114, Fax: 719-255-4030, E-mail: debbie.macdonald@uccs.edu.
Website: http://www.uccs.edu/comm/

University of Colorado Denver, College of Liberal Arts and Sciences, Department of Communication, Denver, CO 80217. Offers MA. *Program availability:* Part-time, evening/weekend. *Degree requirements:* For master's, comprehensive exam, 33 credits; thesis or substantial writing project. *Entrance requirements:* For master's, GRE General Test (minimum score of 153) or LSAT (minimum score of 150), minimum undergraduate GPA of 3.25, three letters of recommendation, two official transcripts, resume, academic writing sample. Additional exam requirements/recommendations for international students: Required—TOEFL (minimum score 80 iBT); Recommended—IELTS (minimum score 6.5). Electronic applications accepted. *Faculty research:* Diversity, difference, and intercultural communication; health communication/medical rhetoric; organizational communication; rhetoric and public affairs; social justice and civic engagement.

University of Connecticut, Graduate School, College of Liberal Arts and Sciences, Department of Communication Sciences, Program in Communication Processes, Storrs, CT 06269. Offers MA. *Degree requirements:* For master's, comprehensive exam. *Entrance requirements:* For master's, GRE General Test. Additional exam requirements/recommendations for international students: Required—TOEFL (minimum score 550 paper-based). Electronic applications accepted.

University of Dayton, Department of Communication, Dayton, OH 45469. Offers communication (MA); interdisciplinary communication (MA). *Program availability:* Part-time, 100% online. *Faculty:* 11 full-time (5 women). *Students:* 14 full-time (13 women), 4 part-time (2 women); includes 1 minority (Black or African American, non-Hispanic/Latino), 3 international. Average age 30. 33 applicants, 30% accepted, 4 enrolled. In 2017, 6 master's awarded. *Degree requirements:* For master's, comprehensive exam (for some programs), thesis optional, 36 credit hours of course work. *Entrance requirements:* For master's, GRE, minimum undergraduate GPA of 3.0, 3 letters of recommendation, personal statement, curriculum vitae/resume, transcripts, writing samples (if applying for a graduate assistantship). Additional exam requirements/recommendations for international students: Required—TOEFL (minimum score 550 paper-based; 80 iBT). *Application deadline:* Applications are processed on a rolling basis. Application fee: $0 ($50 for international students). Electronic applications accepted. Tuition and fees vary according to degree level and program. *Financial support:* In 2017–18, 4 research assistantships with full tuition reimbursements (averaging $11,105 per year), 7 teaching assistantships with full tuition reimbursements (averaging $11,105 per year) were awarded; institutionally sponsored loans and unspecified assistantships also available. Financial award application deadline: 3/9; financial award applicants required to submit FAFSA. *Faculty research:* International public relations, health communication, corporate social responsibility, patient provider communication, media effects and persuasion. *Unit head:* Dr. Joseph Valenzano, III, Chair, 937-229-2028, E-mail: jvalenzano1@udayton.edu. *Application contact:* Dr. JeeHee Han, Graduate Program Director, 937-229-2486, E-mail: jhan01@udayton.edu.
Website: https://www.udayton.edu/artssciences/academics/communication/welcome/index.php

University of Delaware, College of Arts and Sciences, Department of Communication, Newark, DE 19716. Offers MA. *Program availability:* Part-time, evening/weekend. *Degree requirements:* For master's, comprehensive exam (for some programs), thesis (for some programs). *Entrance requirements:* For master's, GRE General Test, minimum GPA of 3.0. Additional exam requirements/recommendations for international students: Required—TOEFL (minimum score 600 paper-based). Electronic applications accepted. *Faculty research:* Politics and the media, online social interaction technologies, mass communication law, media and the perceptions of reality, the role of communication in public opinion processes, small group research, communication during resource dilemmas.

University of Denver, Division of Arts, Humanities and Social Sciences, Department of Communication Studies, Denver, CO 80208. Offers culture and communication (MA, PhD); interpersonal and family communication (MA, PhD); rhetoric and communication ethics (MA, PhD). Tuition and fees vary according to course load, campus/location and program.

University of Denver, University College, Denver, CO 80208. Offers arts and culture (MA, Certificate); communication management (MS, Certificate), including translation studies (Certificate), world history and culture (Certificate); environmental policy and management (MS); geographic information systems (MS); global affairs (MA, Certificate), including human capital in organizations (Certificate), philanthropic leadership (Certificate), project management (Certificate), strategic innovation and change (Certificate); healthcare leadership (MS); information communications and technology (MS); leadership and organizations (MS); professional creative writing (MA, Certificate), including emergency planning and response (Certificate), organizational security (Certificate); security management (MS, Certificate); strategic human resources (Certificate). *Program availability:* Part-time, evening/weekend, online learning. *Faculty:* 118 part-time/adjunct (62 women). *Students:* 56 full-time (32 women), 1,287 part-time (707 women); includes 330 minority (99 Black or African American, non-Hispanic/Latino; 7 American Indian or Alaska Native, non-Hispanic/Latino; 43 Asian, non-Hispanic/Latino; 141 Hispanic/Latino; 3 Native Hawaiian or other Pacific Islander, non-Hispanic/Latino; 37 Two or more races, non-Hispanic/Latino), 84 international. Average age 34. 783 applicants, 86% accepted, 420 enrolled. In 2017, 461 master's, 173 other advanced degrees awarded. *Degree requirements:* For master's, capstone project. *Entrance requirements:* For master's, transcripts, two letters of recommendation, personal statement, resume. Additional exam requirements/recommendations for international students: Required—TOEFL (minimum score 550 paper-based; 80 iBT). *Application deadline:* For fall admission, 6/21 priority date for domestic students, 5/1 priority date for international students; for winter admission, 9/14 priority date for domestic students, 9/19 priority date for international students; for spring admission, 1/11 priority date for domestic students, 12/12 priority date for international students; for summer admission, 3/29 priority date for domestic students, 3/6 priority date for international students. Applications are processed on a rolling basis. Application fee: $75. Electronic applications accepted. *Expenses:* $7,968 per year half-time. *Financial support:* In 2017–18, 29 students received support. Teaching assistantships available. Financial award applicants required to submit FAFSA. *Unit head:* Dr. Michael McGuire, Dean, 303-871-3518, Fax: 303-871-3303, E-mail: mmcguire@du.edu. *Application contact:* Information Contact, 303-871-2291, E-mail: ucoladm@du.edu.
Website: http://universitycollege.du.edu/

University of Dubuque, Program in Communication, Dubuque, IA 52001-5099. Offers information technologies communication (MAC); leadership and management (MAC); strategic and corporate communication (MAC). *Program availability:* Part-time, evening/weekend. *Degree requirements:* For master's, thesis optional. *Entrance requirements:* For master's, GRE, minimum GPA of 2.5, 3 recommendations. Additional exam requirements/recommendations for international students: Required—TOEFL (minimum score 550 paper-based). Electronic applications accepted. *Faculty research:* Intercultural communication, management communication.

University of Florida, Graduate School, College of Journalism and Communications, Gainesville, FL 32611. Offers advertising (M Adv); mass communication (MAMC, PhD), including international/intercultural communication (MAMC), journalism (MAMC), mass communication, public relations (MAMC), science/health communication (MAMC), telecommunication (MAMC); JD/MAMC; JD/PhD. *Accreditation:* ACEJMC (one or more programs are accredited). *Program availability:* Part-time, online learning. *Degree requirements:* For master's, comprehensive exam (for some programs), thesis; for doctorate, comprehensive exam (for some programs), thesis/dissertation. *Entrance requirements:* For master's and doctorate, GRE General Test (minimum scores: 156 Verbal, 146 Quantitative), minimum GPA of 3.0, resume, statement of goals, 3 letters of recommendation. Additional exam requirements/recommendations for international students: Required—TOEFL (minimum score 550 paper-based; 80 iBT), IELTS (minimum score 6). Electronic applications accepted. *Faculty research:* Translational communication in science, technology, engineering, medicine, and health; international and intercultural communication; audience analysis and media effects; social interest communication, grassroots activism, and civic engagement; corporate social responsibility.

University of Georgia, Grady College of Journalism and Mass Communication, Athens, GA 30602. Offers journalism and mass communication (MA); mass communication (PhD). *Degree requirements:* For master's, comprehensive exam, thesis (MA); for doctorate, comprehensive exam, thesis/dissertation. *Entrance requirements:* For master's and doctorate, GRE General Test. Additional exam requirements/recommendations for international students: Required—TOEFL, TWE for PhD. Electronic applications accepted.

University of Hartford, College of Arts and Sciences, Program in Communication, West Hartford, CT 06117-1599. Offers MA. *Program availability:* Part-time, evening/weekend. *Degree requirements:* For master's, comprehensive exam, thesis optional. *Entrance requirements:* For master's, GRE, 3 letters of recommendation. Additional exam requirements/recommendations for international students: Required—TOEFL (minimum score 550 paper-based). Electronic applications accepted. *Expenses:* Contact institution. *Faculty research:* Communication reticence, relational communication, media literacy, journalism history, media audience attitude and behavior.

University of Hawaii at Manoa, Office of Graduate Education, College of Social Sciences, School of Communications, Honolulu, HI 96822. Offers communication (MA); telecommunication and information resource management (Graduate Certificate). *Program availability:* Part-time. *Degree requirements:* For master's, thesis optional. *Entrance requirements:* Additional exam requirements/recommendations for international students: Required—TOEFL (minimum score 600 paper-based; 100 iBT), IELTS (minimum score 7). *Faculty research:* Communication technology policy and development, intercultural communication, organizational communication.

University of Houston, College of Liberal Arts and Social Sciences, Jack J. Valenti School of Communication, Houston, TX 77204. Offers health communication (MA); mass communication studies (MA); public relations studies (MA); speech communication (MA). *Program availability:* Part-time. *Degree requirements:* For master's, comprehensive exam (for some programs), thesis (for some programs), 30-33 hours. *Entrance requirements:* For master's, GRE. Additional exam requirements/recommendations for international students: Required—TOEFL. Electronic applications accepted.

University of Illinois at Chicago, College of Liberal Arts and Sciences, Department of Communication, Chicago, IL 60607-7128. Offers MA, PhD. *Program availability:* Evening/weekend. *Degree requirements:* For master's, thesis. *Entrance requirements:* For master's, GRE General Test, minimum GPA of 3.0 in last 90 hours. Additional exam requirements/recommendations for international students: Required—TOEFL. Electronic applications accepted. *Faculty research:* Organizational, political, and interpersonal communication; public relations.

University of Illinois at Springfield, Graduate Programs, College of Liberal Arts and Sciences, Program in Communication, Springfield, IL 62703-5407. Offers MA. *Program availability:* Part-time, evening/weekend. *Faculty:* 9 full-time (5 women). *Students:* 3 full-time (1 woman), 8 part-time (all women); includes 3 minority (all Black or African American, non-Hispanic/Latino). Average age 27. 13 applicants, 31% accepted, 2 enrolled. In 2017, 9 master's awarded. *Degree requirements:* For master's, comprehensive exam, thesis, or project. *Entrance requirements:* For master's, in-house writing exam, departmental writing proficiency exam, minimum undergraduate GPA of 3.0; two letters of recommendation, including one from an academic source; one- to two-page personal statement of purpose. Additional exam requirements/recommendations for international students: Required—TOEFL (minimum score 580 paper-based). *Application deadline:* Applications are processed on a rolling basis. Application fee: $60 ($75 for international students). Electronic applications accepted. *Expenses:* Tuition, state resident: full-time $7896; part-time $329 per credit hour. Tuition, nonresident: full-time $16,200; part-time $675 per credit hour. Tuition and fees vary according to program. *Financial support:* In 2017–18, research assistantships with full tuition reimbursements (averaging $10,249 per year), teaching assistantships with full tuition reimbursements (averaging $10,303 per year) were awarded; fellowships, career-related internships or fieldwork, Federal Work-Study, scholarships/grants, health care benefits, and unspecified assistantships also available. Support available to part-time students. Financial award application deadline: 11/15; financial award applicants required to submit FAFSA. *Unit head:* Dr. Amie Kincaid, Program Administrator, 217-206-8415, Fax: 217-206-6217, E-mail: akinc2@uis.edu.

University of Illinois at Urbana–Champaign, Graduate College, College of Liberal Arts and Sciences, Department of Communication, Champaign, IL 61820. Offers MA, PhD. *Program availability:* Part-time, evening/weekend, online learning. Terminal master's awarded for partial completion of doctoral program.

University of Illinois at Urbana–Champaign, Graduate College, College of Media, Institute of Communications Research, Champaign, IL 61820. Offers communications and media (PhD). *Faculty research:* Feminist cultural studies, media technology, international communications, Latino studies, economics of media.

The University of Iowa, Graduate College, College of Liberal Arts and Sciences, Department of Communication Studies, Iowa City, IA 52242-1316. Offers interpersonal communication and relationships (MA, PhD); media studies (MA, PhD); rhetoric and public advocacy (MA, PhD). *Degree requirements:* For master's, thesis optional; exam; for doctorate, comprehensive exam, thesis/dissertation. *Entrance requirements:* For master's and doctorate, GRE General Test, minimum GPA of 3.0. Additional exam requirements/recommendations for international students: Required—TOEFL (minimum score 550 paper-based; 81 iBT). Electronic applications accepted.

The University of Kansas, Graduate Studies, College of Liberal Arts and Sciences, Department of Communication Studies, Lawrence, KS 66045-7574. Offers communication studies (MA, PhD); professional workplace communication (Graduate Certificate). *Program availability:* Part-time, evening/weekend. *Students:* 60 full-time (33 women), 10 part-time (9 women); includes 8 minority (5 Black or African American, non-Hispanic/Latino; 1 Asian, non-Hispanic/Latino; 1 Hispanic/Latino; 1 Two or more races, non-Hispanic/Latino), 10 international. Average age 30. 52 applicants, 77% accepted, 24 enrolled. In 2017, 10 master's, 7 doctorates, 1 other advanced degree awarded. *Entrance requirements:* For master's and doctorate, GRE General Test, official transcript, three letters of recommendation, two- to three-page statement of purpose, resume, research writing sample. Additional exam requirements/recommendations for international students: Required—TOEFL. *Application deadline:* For fall admission, 5/5 for domestic and international students; for spring admission, 11/15 for domestic and international students; for summer admission, 4/15 for domestic and international students. Application fee: $65 ($85 for international students). Electronic applications accepted. *Financial support:* Fellowships, research assistantships, teaching assistantships, and unspecified assistantships available. Financial award application deadline: 1/15; financial award applicants required to submit FAFSA. *Faculty research:* Rhetoric, interpersonal communication, organizational communication, intercultural communication, legal communication. *Unit head:* Tom D. Beisecker, Chair, 785-864-9882, E-mail: south40@ku.edu. *Application contact:* Michelle Reames, Graduate Admission Contact/Senior Graduate Academic Advisor, 913-897-8510, E-mail: michelle.reames@ku.edu.
Website: http://www.coms.ku.edu

University of Kentucky, Graduate School, College of Communication and Information, Program in Communication, Lexington, KY 40506-0032. Offers MA, PhD. *Degree requirements:* For master's, comprehensive exam, thesis optional; for doctorate, comprehensive exam, thesis/dissertation. *Entrance requirements:* For master's, GRE General Test, minimum undergraduate GPA of 2.75; for doctorate, GRE General Test, minimum graduate GPA of 3.0, undergraduate 2.75. Additional exam requirements/recommendations for international students: Required—TOEFL (minimum score 550 paper-based). Electronic applications accepted. *Faculty research:* Public service campaigns, health communication, mass media law and public policy, political communication, international and intercultural communication.

University of Louisiana at Lafayette, College of Liberal Arts, Department of Communication, Lafayette, LA 70504. Offers mass communications (MS). *Program availability:* Part-time. *Degree requirements:* For master's, thesis optional. *Entrance requirements:* For master's, GRE General Test, minimum GPA of 2.75. Additional exam requirements/recommendations for international students: Required—TOEFL (minimum score 550 paper-based). Electronic applications accepted. *Faculty research:* Mass media problems, issues and ethics, mass communication, historical studies, conflict of interest and law and ethics in journalism, contemporary issues and trends in publications.

University of Louisiana at Monroe, Graduate School, College of Arts, Education, and Sciences, Department of Communication, Monroe, LA 71209-0001. Offers MA. *Faculty:* 4 full-time (2 women). *Students:* 12 full-time (8 women), 5 part-time (3 women); includes 2 minority (both Black or African American, non-Hispanic/Latino), 5 international. Average age 27. 16 applicants, 56% accepted, 7 enrolled. In 2017, 5 master's awarded. *Degree requirements:* For master's, thesis. *Entrance requirements:* For master's, GRE (minimum verbal and quantitative score: 900). Additional exam requirements/recommendations for international students: Required—TOEFL (minimum score 500 paper-based; 61 iBT). *Application deadline:* For fall admission, 8/24 priority date for domestic students, 7/1 for international students; for winter admission, 12/14 priority date for domestic students; for spring admission, 1/19 priority date for domestic students, 11/1 for international students. Applications are processed on a rolling basis. Application fee: $20 ($30 for international students). Electronic applications accepted. *Expenses:* Tuition, state resident: full-time $6489; part-time $479 per hour. Tuition, nonresident: full-time $12,100; part-time $479 per hour. *Required fees:* $8860; $802 per hour. $3273 per semester. *Financial support:* In 2017–18, 11 students received support. Career-related internships or fieldwork, Federal Work-Study, and unspecified assistantships available. Financial award application deadline: 4/1; financial award applicants required to submit FAFSA. *Faculty research:* Interactive media, rhetoric progress, interpersonal, journalism history, gender/multicultural issues, forensics. *Unit head:* Dr. Lesli Pace, Head, 318-342-1165, Fax: 318-342-1422, E-mail: pace@ulm.edu. *Application contact:* Dr. Leslie Pace, 318-342-1165, Fax: 318-342-1422, E-mail: pace@ulm.edu.
Website: http://www.ulm.edu/communication

University of Louisville, Graduate School, College of Arts and Sciences, Department of Communication, Louisville, KY 40292-0001. Offers MA. *Program availability:* Part-time, evening/weekend, online learning. *Faculty:* 24 full-time (13 women), 28 part-time/adjunct (18 women). *Students:* 5 full-time (4 women), 8 part-time (5 women); includes 3 minority (2 Black or African American, non-Hispanic/Latino; 1 Hispanic/Latino). Average age 30. 6 applicants, 83% accepted, 3 enrolled. In 2017, 6 master's awarded. *Degree requirements:* For master's, comprehensive exam (for some programs), thesis or alternative. *Entrance requirements:* For master's, GRE General Test. Additional exam requirements/recommendations for international students: Required—TOEFL (minimum score 550 paper-based; 79 iBT). *Application deadline:* For fall admission, 7/1 for domestic students, 5/1 priority date for international students; for spring admission, 11/1 for domestic students, 11/1 priority date for international students; for summer admission, 4/1 priority date for international students. Applications are processed on a rolling basis. Application fee: $65. Electronic applications accepted. *Expenses:* Tuition, state resident: full-time $12,246; part-time $681 per credit hour. Tuition, nonresident: full-time $25,486; part-time $1417 per credit hour. *Required fees:* $196. Tuition and fees vary according to course load, program and reciprocity agreements. *Financial support:* Research assistantships with full tuition reimbursements, teaching assistantships with tuition reimbursements, scholarships/grants, tuition waivers (partial), and unspecified assistantships available. Support available to part-time students. Financial award applicants required to submit FAFSA. *Faculty research:* Health communication, interpersonal communication, computer-mediated communication, strategic communication, mass communication. *Total annual research expenditures:* $744. *Unit head:* Dr. Al Futrell, Chair, 502-852-6976, E-mail: al@louisville.edu. *Application contact:* Latonia Craig, Director of Graduate Recruitment and Diversity Retention, 502-852-5207, Fax: 502-852-6536, E-mail: gradadm@louisville.edu.
Website: http://louisville.edu/communication

University of Maine, Graduate School, College of Liberal Arts and Sciences, Department of Communication and Journalism, Orono, ME 04469. Offers MA, PhD. *Program availability:* Part-time. *Faculty:* 8 full-time (3 women), 7 part-time/adjunct (3 women). *Students:* 14 full-time (6 women), 1 part-time (0 women); includes 2 minority (both Hispanic/Latino), 2 international. Average age 27. 18 applicants, 44% accepted, 6 enrolled. In 2017, 8 master's, 1 doctorate awarded. *Degree requirements:* For master's, thesis (for some programs); for doctorate, comprehensive exam, thesis/dissertation. *Entrance requirements:* For master's, GRE General Test. Additional exam requirements/recommendations for international students: Required—TOEFL. *Application deadline:* For fall admission, 2/1 priority date for domestic students. Applications are processed on a rolling basis. Application fee: $65. Electronic applications accepted. *Expenses:* Tuition, state resident: full-time $7722; part-time $429 per credit hour. Tuition, nonresident: full-time $25,146; part-time $1397 per credit hour. *Required fees:* $1162; $581 per credit hour. *Financial support:* In 2017–18, 16 students received support, including 3 research assistantships (averaging $21,200 per year), 12 teaching assistantships with full tuition reimbursements available (averaging $15,200 per year); career-related internships or fieldwork, Federal Work-Study, institutionally sponsored loans, tuition waivers (full and partial), and unspecified assistantships also available. Support available to part-time students. Financial award application deadline: 3/1. *Faculty research:* Rhetorical theory, semiotics, discourse analysis, gender and communication, children's talk/communication disorders. *Total annual research expenditures:* $104,293. *Unit head:* Dr. Nathan Stormer, Chair, 207-581-1938, Fax: 207-581-1286, E-mail: nathan@maine.edu. *Application contact:* Scott G. Delcourt, Assistant Vice President for Graduate Studies and Senior Associate Dean, 207-581-3291, Fax: 207-581-3232, E-mail: graduate@maine.edu.
Website: http://cmj.umaine.edu/graduate-program/

University of Maryland, Baltimore County, The Graduate School, College of Arts, Humanities and Social Sciences, Department of Modern Languages and Linguistics, Program in Intercultural Communication, Baltimore, MD 21250. Offers MA. *Program availability:* Part-time, evening/weekend. *Faculty:* 16 full-time (9 women). *Students:* 10 full-time (6 women), 2 part-time (1 woman); includes 2 minority (both Hispanic/Latino), 3 international. Average age 29. 10 applicants, 70% accepted, 4 enrolled. In 2017, 4 master's awarded. *Degree requirements:* For master's, one foreign language, comprehensive exam (for some programs), thesis (for some programs). *Entrance requirements:* For master's, GRE General Test, minimum GPA of 3.0, 3 letters of recommendation, self-evaluation and statement of support, resume, writing sample in modern language. Additional exam requirements/recommendations for international students: Required—TOEFL (minimum score 550 paper-based, 80 iBT) or IELTS. *Application deadline:* For fall admission, 1/31 for domestic and international students. Application fee: $50. Electronic applications accepted. *Expenses:* Contact institution. *Financial support:* In 2017–18, 7 students received support, including 5 teaching assistantships with full tuition reimbursements available (averaging $12,874 per year); Federal Work-Study, scholarships/grants, health care benefits, and tuition waivers (full) also available. Financial award application deadline: 1/31; financial award applicants required to submit FAFSA. *Faculty research:* Comparative television research-cross-cultural; cultural studies; social developments in Latin America; intercultural communication; French civilization and cultural studies; language, gender and sexuality; sociolinguistics; African linguistics; immigrants in U.S. and Latin American societies. *Unit head:* Dr. Edward Larkey, Interim Director, 410-455-2104, Fax: 410-455-1025, E-mail: larkey@umbc.edu.
Website: http://www.umbc.edu/mll/incc/

University of Maryland, College Park, Academic Affairs, College of Arts and Humanities, Department of Communication, College Park, MD 20742. Offers MA, PhD. *Degree requirements:* For master's, thesis optional; for doctorate, comprehensive exam, thesis/dissertation. *Entrance requirements:* For master's, GRE General Test, minimum GPA of 3.0, sample of scholarly writing, 3 letters of recommendation, statement of goals and experiences; for doctorate, GRE General Test. Additional exam requirements/recommendations for international students: Required—TOEFL. Electronic applications accepted. *Faculty research:* Health communication, interpersonal communication, persuasion, intercultural communication, contemporary rhetoric theory.

University of Massachusetts Amherst, Graduate School, College of Social and Behavioral Sciences, Department of Communication, Amherst, MA 01003. Offers MA, PhD. *Program availability:* Part-time. Terminal master's awarded for partial completion of doctoral program. *Degree requirements:* For master's, thesis or alternative; for doctorate, comprehensive exam, thesis/dissertation. *Entrance requirements:* For master's and doctorate, GRE General Test, 3 letters of recommendation. Additional exam requirements/recommendations for international students: Required—TOEFL (minimum score 550 paper-based; 80 iBT), IELTS (minimum score 6.5). Electronic applications accepted.

University of Memphis, Graduate School, College of Communication and Fine Arts, Department of Communication, Memphis, TN 38152. Offers communication (MA); communication arts (PhD); film and video production (MA). *Program availability:* Part-time. *Faculty:* 13 full-time (6 women). *Students:* 18 full-time (11 women), 24 part-time (11 women); includes 11 minority (8 Black or African American, non-Hispanic/Latino; 3 Two or more races, non-Hispanic/Latino), 2 international. Average age 36. 19 applicants, 79% accepted, 9 enrolled. In 2017, 3 master's, 3 doctorates awarded. *Degree requirements:* For master's, comprehensive exam, thesis or alternative, culminating project; for doctorate, comprehensive exam, thesis/dissertation. *Entrance requirements:* For master's and doctorate, GRE General Test, personal goal statement, letters of recommendation, writing sample. Additional exam requirements/recommendations for international students: Required—TOEFL (minimum score 600 paper-based). *Application deadline:* For fall admission, 1/13 priority date for domestic students. Applications are processed on a rolling basis. Application fee: $35 ($60 for international students). *Expenses:* Contact institution. *Financial support:* In 2017–18, 27 students received support, including 2 research assistantships with full tuition reimbursements available (averaging $12,000 per year), 17 teaching assistantships with full tuition reimbursements available (averaging $22,406 per year); Federal Work-Study, scholarships/grants, and unspecified assistantships also available. Financial award application deadline: 2/1; financial award applicants required to submit FAFSA. *Faculty research:* Rhetoric, media studies, applied communication (health communication). *Unit head:* Dr. Sandra Sarkela, Interim Department Chair, 901-678-2565, Fax: 901-678-4331, E-mail: ssarkela@memphis.edu. *Application contact:* Dr. Antonio de Velasco, Coordinator of Graduate Studies, 901-678-3185, Fax: 901-678-4331, E-mail: adevelsc@memphis.edu.
Website: http://www.memphis.edu/ccfa/index.php

University of Miami, Graduate School, School of Communication, Coral Gables, FL 33124. Offers communication (PhD); communication studies (MA); film studies (MA, PhD); motion pictures (MFA), including production, producing, and screenwriting; print journalism (MA); public relations (MA); Spanish language journalism (MA); television broadcast journalism (MA). *Program availability:* Part-time. *Degree requirements:* For

master's, comprehensive exam (for some programs), thesis (for some programs); for doctorate, comprehensive exam, thesis/dissertation. *Entrance requirements:* For master's, GRE General Test; for doctorate, GRE General Test, master's thesis or scholarly research. Additional exam requirements/recommendations for international students: Required—TOEFL (minimum score 600 paper-based; 100 iBT). Electronic applications accepted. *Faculty research:* Communication studies, mass communication, international/interpersonal communication, film studies, journalism.

University of Michigan, Rackham Graduate School, College of Literature, Science, and the Arts, Department of Communication Studies, Ann Arbor, MI 48109-1285. Offers PhD. *Faculty:* 21 full-time (8 women). *Students:* 37 full-time (24 women); includes 10 minority (6 Black or African American, non-Hispanic/Latino; 2 Hispanic/Latino; 2 Two or more races, non-Hispanic/Latino), 11 international. Average age 29. 80 applicants, 13% accepted, 9 enrolled. In 2017, 3 doctorates awarded. *Degree requirements:* For doctorate, comprehensive exam, thesis/dissertation, first-year research project, 2 terms in student instructor position, publications, presentations. *Entrance requirements:* For doctorate, GRE, U.S. bachelor's degree or its equivalent from accredited institution. Additional exam requirements/recommendations for international students: Required—TOEFL (minimum score 600 paper-based; 102 iBT). *Application deadline:* For fall admission, 12/1 for domestic and international students. Application fee: $75 ($90 for international students). Electronic applications accepted. *Expenses:* $11,184 resident; $22,578 non-resident; $164.19 fees. *Financial support:* In 2017–18, 36 students received support. Fellowships with full tuition reimbursements available, research assistantships with full tuition reimbursements available, teaching assistantships with full tuition reimbursements available, scholarships/grants, traineeships, and health care benefits available. Financial award application deadline: 4/30; financial award applicants required to submit FAFSA. *Faculty research:* Media psychology; political communication; global and comparative media; media, technology, and society; critical media studies. *Unit head:* Prof. Nojin Kwak, Professor and Chair, 734-764-0420, Fax: 734-764-3288, E-mail: commchair@umich.edu. *Application contact:* Amy B. Eaton, Graduate Program Coordinator, 734-615-8974, Fax: 734-764-3288, E-mail: lsa-commphd@umich.edu.
Website: http://www.lsa.umich.edu/comm/

University of Michigan–Flint, College of Arts and Sciences, Program in Applied Communication, Flint, MI 48502-1950. Offers MA. *Program availability:* Part-time, evening/weekend, 100% online. *Faculty:* 11 full-time (6 women), 4 part-time/adjunct (2 women). *Students:* 26 part-time (15 women); includes 8 minority (all Black or African American, non-Hispanic/Latino). Average age 41. 22 applicants, 68% accepted, 13 enrolled. *Entrance requirements:* For master's, bachelor's degree from accredited institution, minimum overall undergraduate GPA of 3.0. Additional exam requirements/recommendations for international students: Required—TOEFL (minimum score 84 iBT), IELTS (minimum score 6.5). *Application deadline:* For fall admission, 8/1 for domestic students, 5/1 for international students. Applications are processed on a rolling basis. Application fee: $55. Electronic applications accepted. *Expenses:* Contact institution. *Financial support:* Fellowships, Federal Work-Study, scholarships/grants, and unspecified assistantships available. Support available to part-time students. Financial award application deadline: 3/1; financial award applicants required to submit FAFSA. *Unit head:* Dr. Dan Lair, Director, 810-424-5348, E-mail: danlair@umflint.edu. *Application contact:* Bradley T. Maki, Director of Graduate Admissions, 810-762-3171, Fax: 810-766-6789, E-mail: bmaki@umflint.edu.

University of Minnesota, Twin Cities Campus, Graduate School, College of Design, Department of Design, Housing, and Apparel, Minneapolis, MN 55455-0213. Offers apparel (MA, MS, PhD); design communication (MA, MS, PhD); housing studies (MA, MS, PhD, Postbaccalaureate Certificate); interactive design (MFA); interior design (MA, MS, PhD). *Program availability:* Part-time. *Degree requirements:* For master's and Postbaccalaureate Certificate, comprehensive exam, thesis (for some programs); for doctorate, comprehensive exam, thesis/dissertation. *Entrance requirements:* For master's, GRE General Test, minimum GPA of 3.0 (preferred), portfolio, 3 letters of recommendation; for doctorate, GRE General Test, minimum GPA of 3.0 (preferred), portfolio, 3 letters of recommendation, writing sample; for Postbaccalaureate Certificate, GRE General Test, minimum GPA of 3.0 (preferred). Additional exam requirements/recommendations for international students: Required—TOEFL (minimum score 550 paper-based; 79 iBT). Electronic applications accepted. *Faculty research:* Housing policy and community development; consumer behavior; interactive design; design history; social, cultural, and behavioral issues related to designed environments.

University of Minnesota, Twin Cities Campus, Graduate School, College of Liberal Arts, Department of Communication Studies, Minneapolis, MN 55455-0213. Offers MA, PhD. *Degree requirements:* For master's, thesis or alternative; for doctorate, thesis/dissertation. *Entrance requirements:* For master's, GRE General Test, minimum GPA of 3.0; for doctorate, GRE General Test, minimum graduate GPA of 3.5. Additional exam requirements/recommendations for international students: Required—TOEFL. Electronic applications accepted. *Faculty research:* Rhetorical studies, communication theory, media studies, gender and communication, public address.

University of Missouri, Office of Research and Graduate Studies, College of Arts and Science, Department of Communication, Columbia, MO 65211. Offers MA, PhD. Terminal master's awarded for partial completion of doctoral program. *Degree requirements:* For doctorate, comprehensive exam, thesis/dissertation. *Entrance requirements:* For master's and doctorate, GRE General Test (minimum score 500 verbal, 500 quantitative, 4.0 analytical preferred), minimum GPA of 3.0. Additional exam requirements/recommendations for international students: Required—TOEFL (minimum score 600 paper-based; 100 iBT). Electronic applications accepted. *Faculty research:* Interpersonal, mass media, organizational, and political communication.

University of Missouri–St. Louis, College of Arts and Sciences, Department of Communication and Media, St. Louis, MO 63121. Offers communication (MA). *Program availability:* Part-time, evening/weekend. *Faculty:* 7 full-time (6 women), 1 (woman) part-time/adjunct. *Students:* 4 full-time (all women), 6 part-time (5 women); includes 2 minority (both Black or African American, non-Hispanic/Latino), 3 international. 11 applicants, 55% accepted, 3 enrolled. *Degree requirements:* For master's, thesis optional. *Entrance requirements:* For master's, 3 letters of recommendation, minimum GPA of 3.25, BA in communication or related discipline. Additional exam requirements/recommendations for international students: Required—TOEFL (minimum score 600 paper-based). *Application deadline:* For fall admission, 7/1 for domestic students, 5/1 for international students; for spring admission, 12/1 for domestic students, 10/1 for international students. Application fee: $50 ($40 for international students). Electronic applications accepted. *Expenses:* Tuition, state resident: part-time $476.50 per credit hour. Tuition, nonresident: part-time $1169.70 per credit hour. *Financial support:* Teaching assistantships available. Financial award application deadline: 4/1; financial award applicants required to submit FAFSA. *Faculty research:* Theory and methodology: intercultural, interpersonal, and mass organizational. *Unit head:* Dr. Alice Hall, Chair, 314-516-6662, Fax: 314-516-5816, E-mail: halla@umsl.edu. *Application contact:* 314-516-5458, Fax: 314-516-6996, E-mail: gradadm@umsl.edu.
Website: http://www.umsl.edu/~comm/

University of Montana, Graduate School, College of Humanities and Sciences, Department of Communication Studies, Missoula, MT 59812. Offers MA. *Degree requirements:* For master's, thesis (for some programs). *Entrance requirements:* For master's, GRE General Test. Additional exam requirements/recommendations for international students: Required—TOEFL (minimum score 525 paper-based). *Faculty research:* Conflict management, organizational communication, language, personal relationships, rhetoric.

University of Nebraska at Omaha, Graduate Studies, College of Communication, Fine Arts and Media, School of Communication, Omaha, NE 68182. Offers communication (MA); human resources and training (Certificate); technical communication (Certificate). *Program availability:* Part-time, evening/weekend. *Degree requirements:* For master's, comprehensive exam, thesis (for some programs). *Entrance requirements:* For master's, minimum GPA of 3.0, 15 undergraduate communication courses, resume, statement of purpose, 3 letters of recommendation. Additional exam requirements/recommendations for international students: Required—TOEFL, IELTS, PTE. Electronic applications accepted.

University of Nebraska–Lincoln, Graduate College, College of Arts and Sciences, Department of Communication Studies, Lincoln, NE 68588. Offers instructional communication (MA, PhD); interpersonal communication (MA, PhD); marketing, communication studies, and advertising (MA, PhD); organizational communication (MA, PhD); rhetoric and culture (MA, PhD). *Degree requirements:* For master's, thesis optional; for doctorate, comprehensive exam, thesis/dissertation. *Entrance requirements:* For master's and doctorate, GRE General Test, writing sample. Additional exam requirements/recommendations for international students: Required—TOEFL (minimum score 600 paper-based). Electronic applications accepted. *Faculty research:* Message strategies, gender communication, political communication, organizational communication, instructional communication.

University of Nevada, Las Vegas, Graduate College, Greenspun College of Urban Affairs, Department of Communication Studies, Las Vegas, NV 89154-4052. Offers MA. *Program availability:* Part-time. *Faculty:* 5 full-time (3 women), 2 part-time/adjunct (0 women). *Students:* 16 full-time (9 women); includes 7 minority (2 Black or African American, non-Hispanic/Latino; 3 Hispanic/Latino; 2 Two or more races, non-Hispanic/Latino), 1 international. Average age 29. 11 applicants, 64% accepted, 6 enrolled. In 2017, 11 master's awarded. *Degree requirements:* For master's, comprehensive exam (for some programs), thesis optional. *Entrance requirements:* For master's, GRE General Test, writing sample; 3 letters of recommendation; statement of purpose. Additional exam requirements/recommendations for international students: Required—TOEFL (minimum score 550 paper-based; 80 iBT), IELTS (minimum score 7). *Application deadline:* For fall admission, 1/15 for domestic students. Application fee: $60 ($95 for international students). Electronic applications accepted. *Expenses:* Contact institution. *Financial support:* In 2017–18, 15 students received support, including 2 research assistantships with full and partial tuition reimbursements available (averaging $11,800 per year), 13 teaching assistantships with full and partial tuition reimbursements available (averaging $11,250 per year); institutionally sponsored loans, scholarships/grants, health care benefits, and unspecified assistantships also available. Financial award application deadline: 3/15; financial award applicants required to submit FAFSA. *Faculty research:* Rhetoric/public address and persuasion, argumentation, debate; interpersonal, family and health communication, conflict resolution; media and political communication; sex and gender, inter-cultural communication; cultural studies, memory studies, food studies. *Unit head:* Dr. Michael Bruner, Professor/Chair, 702-895-5125, E-mail: michael.bruner@unlv.edu. *Application contact:* Dr. Donovan Conley, Graduate Coordinator, 702-895-5137, Fax: 702-895-4805, E-mail: donovan.conley@unlv.edu.
Website: http://communicationstudies.unlv.edu/

University of New Mexico, Graduate Studies, College of Arts and Sciences, Program in Communication, Albuquerque, NM 87131-2039. Offers MA, PhD. *Program availability:* Part-time. *Faculty:* 11 full-time (8 women). *Students:* 32 full-time (20 women), 20 part-time (17 women); includes 23 minority (1 Black or African American, non-Hispanic/Latino; 1 American Indian or Alaska Native, non-Hispanic/Latino; 2 Asian, non-Hispanic/Latino; 15 Hispanic/Latino; 4 Two or more races, non-Hispanic/Latino), 5 international. Average age 35. 26 applicants, 50% accepted, 12 enrolled. In 2017, 9 master's, 7 doctorates awarded. *Degree requirements:* For master's, 30 hours of class work and 6-hour thesis or project, or 36 hours of class work and comprehensive exam; for doctorate, 2 foreign languages, comprehensive exam, thesis/dissertation. *Entrance requirements:* For master's, GRE General Test, letters of recommendation, letter of intent, curriculum vitae, transcripts; for doctorate, GRE General Test, letters of recommendation, writing sample, letter of intent, curriculum vitae, transcripts. Additional exam requirements/recommendations for international students: Required—TOEFL (minimum score 550 paper-based). *Application deadline:* For fall admission, 1/15 for domestic and international students. Application fee: $50. Electronic applications accepted. *Financial support:* Fellowships with tuition reimbursements, research assistantships, teaching assistantships with tuition reimbursements, career-related internships or fieldwork, scholarships/grants, health care benefits, and unspecified assistantships available. Financial award application deadline: 3/1; financial award applicants required to submit FAFSA. *Faculty research:* Health communication, intercultural communication, interpersonal/organizational communication, mass communication. *Total annual research expenditures:* $82,797. *Unit head:* Dr. Karen Foss, Chair, 505-277-5305, Fax: 505-277-2068, E-mail: kfoss@unm.edu. *Application contact:* Gregoria Arienda Cavazos, Student Advisement Coordinator, 505-277-5305, Fax: 505-277-2068, E-mail: cjadvise@unm.edu.
Website: http://www.unm.edu/~cjdept/

The University of North Carolina at Chapel Hill, Graduate School, College of Arts and Sciences, Department of Communication Studies, Chapel Hill, NC 27599. Offers PhD. *Degree requirements:* For doctorate, comprehensive exam, thesis/dissertation. *Entrance requirements:* For doctorate, GRE General Test, minimum GPA of 3.0. Additional exam requirements/recommendations for international students: Required—TOEFL (minimum score 550 paper-based; 79 iBT). Electronic applications accepted.

The University of North Carolina at Chapel Hill, Graduate School, School of Media and Journalism, Chapel Hill, NC 27599. Offers digital communication (MA, Certificate); media and communication (MA, PhD), including interdisciplinary health communication (MA), journalism (MA), strategic communication (MA), theory and research (MA), visual communication (MA); JD/PhD; MA/JD. MA/JD and JD/PhD offered jointly with School of Law. *Accreditation:* ACEJMC (one or more programs are accredited). *Program availability:* Part-time, all course instruction online, plus two on-campus experiences totaling seven days. *Faculty:* 51 full-time (22 women), 4 part-time/adjunct (2 women). *Students:* 75 full-time (50 women), 63 part-time (41 women); includes 44 minority (10 Black or African American, non-Hispanic/Latino; 11 Asian, non-Hispanic/Latino; 5 Hispanic/Latino; 18 Two or more races, non-Hispanic/Latino), 6 international. Average age 31. 207 applicants, 41% accepted, 63 enrolled. In 2017, 32 master's, 9 doctorates, 17 other advanced degrees awarded. *Degree requirements:* For master's, comprehensive exam, thesis; for doctorate, comprehensive exam, thesis/dissertation. *Entrance requirements:* For master's and doctorate, GRE General Test, minimum GPA of 3.0. Additional exam requirements/recommendations for international students: Required—TOEFL (minimum iBT score of 105) or IELTS (7.5). Application fee: $88. Electronic applications accepted. *Expenses:* Contact institution. *Financial support:* In 2017–18, 73 students received support, including 47 fellowships with full tuition

reimbursements available (averaging $16,006 per year), 6 research assistantships with full tuition reimbursements available (averaging $17,405 per year); scholarships/grants and health care benefits also available. Financial award application deadline: 12/4; financial award applicants required to submit FAFSA. *Faculty research:* Media processes and production; legal and regulatory issues in communication; media uses and effects; health communication; political, social, and strategic communication. *Total annual research expenditures:* $1 million. *Unit head:* Susan King, Dean, 919-962-1204, Fax: 919-962-0620, E-mail: susanking@unc.edu. *Application contact:* Casey Hart, Marketing and Instructional Design Coordinator, 919-843-9471, Fax: 919-962-0620, E-mail: mjgrad@unc.edu.
Website: http://mj.unc.edu/

The University of North Carolina at Charlotte, College of Liberal Arts and Sciences, Department of Communication Studies, Charlotte, NC 28223-0001. Offers MA. *Program availability:* Part-time, evening/weekend. *Faculty:* 17 full-time (10 women). *Students:* 14 full-time (11 women), 10 part-time (all women); includes 4 minority (2 Black or African American, non-Hispanic/Latino; 1 Hispanic/Latino; 1 Two or more races, non-Hispanic/Latino), 2 international. Average age 26. 24 applicants, 79% accepted, 14 enrolled. In 2017, 4 master's awarded. Terminal master's awarded for partial completion of doctoral program. *Degree requirements:* For master's, project, thesis, or comprehensive exam. *Entrance requirements:* For master's, GRE General Test, bachelor's degree from accredited institution; transcripts from all post-secondary educational institutions in which the candidate was enrolled; minimum overall GPA of 3.0 as undergraduate and in junior and senior years; three letters of recommendation; personal statement; writing sample. Additional exam requirements/recommendations for international students: Required—TOEFL (minimum score 523 paper-based, 70 iBT) or IELTS (6.5). *Application deadline:* For fall admission, 1/15 priority date for domestic and international students. Applications are processed on a rolling basis. Application fee: $75. Electronic applications accepted. *Expenses:* Tuition, state resident: full-time $4337. Tuition, nonresident: full-time $17,771. *Required fees:* $3211. Tuition and fees vary according to course load and program. *Financial support:* In 2017–18, 17 students received support, including 17 teaching assistantships (averaging $13,588 per year); career-related internships or fieldwork, institutionally sponsored loans, scholarships/grants, and unspecified assistantships also available. Support available to part-time students. Financial award application deadline: 3/1; financial award applicants required to submit FAFSA. *Total annual research expenditures:* $39,189. *Unit head:* Dr. Jason Black, Chair, 704-687-0783, E-mail: jblac143@uncc.edu. *Application contact:* Kathy B. Giddings, Director of Graduate Admissions, 704-687-5503, Fax: 704-687-1668, E-mail: gradadm@uncc.edu.
Website: http://communication.uncc.edu/

The University of North Carolina at Greensboro, Graduate School, College of Arts and Sciences, Department of Communication Studies, Greensboro, NC 27412-5001. Offers MA. *Program availability:* Part-time. *Degree requirements:* For master's, thesis or alternative. *Entrance requirements:* For master's, GRE General Test, MAT, or PRAXIS. Additional exam requirements/recommendations for international students: Required—TOEFL. Electronic applications accepted.

University of North Dakota, Graduate School, College of Arts and Sciences, School of Communication, Grand Forks, ND 58202. Offers communication and public discourse (PhD). *Program availability:* Part-time. *Degree requirements:* For doctorate, thesis/dissertation. *Entrance requirements:* For doctorate, GRE General Test, minimum GPA of 3.0. Additional exam requirements/recommendations for international students: Required—TOEFL (minimum score 550 paper-based; 79 iBT), IELTS (minimum score 6.5). Electronic applications accepted. *Faculty research:* Communication technologies, mass communication in diverse society, acculturation and socialization functions.

University of Northern Colorado, Graduate School, College of Humanities and Social Sciences, School of Communication, Greeley, CO 80639. Offers MA. *Program availability:* Part-time. *Degree requirements:* For master's, comprehensive exam, thesis or alternative. *Entrance requirements:* For master's, GRE General Test, 3 letters of recommendation. Electronic applications accepted.

University of Northern Iowa, Graduate College, College of Humanities, Arts and Sciences, Department of Communication Studies, Cedar Falls, IA 50614. Offers MA. *Program availability:* Part-time, evening/weekend. *Degree requirements:* For master's, comprehensive exam, thesis or alternative. *Entrance requirements:* For master's, minimum GPA of 3.0. Additional exam requirements/recommendations for international students: Required—TOEFL (minimum score 500 paper-based; 61 iBT). Electronic applications accepted.

University of North Texas, Robert B. Toulouse School of Graduate Studies, Denton, TX 76203-5459. Offers accounting (MS); applied anthropology (MA, MS); applied behavior analysis (Certificate); applied geography (MA); applied technology and performance improvement (M Ed, MS); art education (MA); art history (MA); art museum education (Certificate); arts leadership (Certificate); audiology (Au D); behavior analysis (MS); behavioral science (PhD); biochemistry and molecular biology (MS); biology (MA, MS); biomedical engineering (MS); business analysis (MS); chemistry (MS); clinical health psychology (PhD); communication studies (MA, MS); computer engineering (MS); computer science (MS); counseling (M Ed, MS), including clinical mental health counseling (MS), college and university counseling, elementary school counseling, secondary school counseling; creative writing (MA); criminal justice (MS); curriculum and instruction (M Ed); decision sciences (MBA); design (MA, MFA), including fashion design (MFA), innovation studies, interior design (MFA); early childhood studies (MS); economics (MS); educational leadership (M Ed, Ed D); educational psychology (MS, PhD), including family studies (MS), gifted and talented (MS), human development (MS), learning and cognition (MS), research, measurement and evaluation (MS); electrical engineering (MS); emergency management (MPA); engineering technology (MS); English (MA); English as a second language (MA); environmental science (MS); finance (MBA, MS); financial management (MPA); French (MA); health services management (MBA); higher education (M Ed, Ed D); history (MA, MS); hospitality management (MS); human resources management (MPA); information science (MS); information systems (PhD); information technologies (MBA); interdisciplinary studies (MA, MS); international studies (MA); international sustainable tourism (MS); jazz studies (MM); journalism (MA, MJ, Graduate Certificate), including interactive and virtual digital communication (Graduate Certificate), narrative journalism (Graduate Certificate), public relations (Graduate Certificate); kinesiology (MS); linguistics (MA); local government management (MPA); logistics (PhD); logistics and supply chain management (MBA); long-term care, senior housing, and aging services (MA); management (PhD); marketing (MBA); mathematics (MA, MS); mechanical and energy engineering (MS, PhD); music (MA), including ethnomusicology, music theory, musicology, performance; music composition (PhD); music education (MM Ed, PhD); nonprofit management (MPA); operations and supply chain management (MBA); performance (MM, DMA); philosophy (MA); political science (MA); professional and technical communication (MA); radio, television and film (MA, MFA); rehabilitation counseling (Certificate); sociology (MA); Spanish (MA); special education (M Ed); speech-language pathology (MA); strategic management (MBA); studio art (MFA); teaching (M Ed); MBA/MS. *Program availability:* Part-time, evening/weekend, online learning. Terminal master's awarded for partial completion of doctoral program. *Degree requirements:* For master's, variable foreign

language requirement, comprehensive exam (for some programs), thesis (for some programs); for doctorate, variable foreign language requirement, comprehensive exam (for some programs), thesis/dissertation; for other advanced degree, variable foreign language requirement, comprehensive exam (for some programs). *Entrance requirements:* For master's and doctorate, GRE, GMAT. Additional exam requirements/ recommendations for international students: Required—TOEFL (minimum score 550 paper-based; 79 iBT). Electronic applications accepted.

University of Oklahoma, College of Arts and Sciences, Department of Communication, Norman, OK 73019. Offers communication (MA); communication technology (PhD); health communication (PhD); intercultural/international communication (PhD); organizational communication (PhD); political/mass communication (PhD); social influence/interpersonal communication (PhD). *Program availability:* Part-time. *Faculty:* 18 full-time (8 women). *Students:* 27 full-time (17 women), 36 part-time (17 women); includes 23 minority (8 Black or African American, non-Hispanic/Latino; 3 American Indian or Alaska Native, non-Hispanic/Latino; 1 Asian, non-Hispanic/Latino; 10 Hispanic/Latino; 1 Two or more races, non-Hispanic/Latino), 5 international. Average age 35. 45 applicants, 49% accepted, 10 enrolled. In 2017, 14 master's, 6 doctorates awarded. *Degree requirements:* For master's, comprehensive exam (for some programs), thesis (for some programs), comprehensive exams or thesis; for doctorate, comprehensive exam, thesis/dissertation. *Entrance requirements:* For master's, GRE (for assistantship), statement of purpose, transcripts, writing sample, letters of recommendation; for doctorate, GRE, statement of purpose, transcripts, writing sample, letters of recommendation. Additional exam requirements/recommendations for international students: Required—TOEFL (minimum score 79 iBT) or IELTS (minimum score 6.5). *Application deadline:* For fall admission, 1/15 priority date for domestic students, 1/15 for international students; for spring admission, 10/15 for domestic and international students. Application fee: $50 ($100 for international students). Electronic applications accepted. *Expenses:* Tuition, state resident: full-time $5119; part-time $213.30 per credit hour. Tuition, nonresident: full-time $19,778; part-time $824.10 per credit hour. *Required fees:* $3458; $133.55 per credit hour. $126.50 per semester. *Financial support:* In 2017–18, 29 students received support, including 1 research assistantship with full tuition reimbursement available (averaging $10,373 per year), 25 teaching assistantships with full tuition reimbursements available (averaging $16,350 per year); health care benefits also available. Financial award application deadline: 6/1; financial award applicants required to submit FAFSA. *Faculty research:* Interpersonal/social influence, organizational, political/mass communication, health communication, intercultural/international. *Total annual research expenditures:* $242,423. *Unit head:* Dr. Michael W. Kramer, Professor and Chair, 405-325-9503, Fax: 405-325-7625, E-mail: mkramer@ou.edu. *Application contact:* Shay Glover, Academic Advisor, 405-325-7710, Fax: 405-325-7625, E-mail: shay.glover@ou.edu.
Website: http://www.ou.edu/cas/comm

University of Oklahoma, Jeannine Rainbolt College of Education, Department of General Education, Norman, OK 73019. Offers communication, culture and pedagogy for Hispanic (ESL/ELL) populations in educational settings (Graduate Certificate). *Program availability:* Part-time, online learning. *Students:* 4 full-time (3 women), 15 part-time (12 women); includes 1 minority (American Indian or Alaska Native, non-Hispanic/Latino). Average age 36. 5 applicants, 80% accepted, 2 enrolled. *Entrance requirements:* Additional exam requirements/recommendations for international students: Required—TOEFL (minimum score 79 iBT) or IELTS (minimum score 6.5). Application fee: $50 ($100 for international students). Electronic applications accepted. *Expenses:* Tuition, state resident: full-time $5119; part-time $213.30 per credit hour. Tuition, nonresident: full-time $19,778; part-time $824.10 per credit hour. *Required fees:* $3458; $133.55 per credit hour. $126.50 per semester. *Financial support:* Research assistantships with full tuition reimbursements, scholarships/grants, and tuition waivers available. Support available to part-time students. Financial award application deadline: 6/1; financial award applicants required to submit FAFSA. *Faculty research:* Teacher effectiveness in the PreK-12 classroom, immersion-style teaching, language advocacy, English as a second language, SIOP and communicative classroom. *Unit head:* Rebecca Borden, Instructor/Program Area Coordinator, 405-325-1498, Fax: 405-325-4061, E-mail: rborden@ou.edu.
Website: http://www.ou.edu/education.html

University of Oregon, Graduate School, School of Journalism and Communication, Eugene, OR 97403. Offers journalism (MA, MS); media studies (MA, MS, PhD); multimedia journalism (MA, MS); strategic communication (MA, MS). *Accreditation:* ASHA. *Program availability:* Part-time. *Degree requirements:* For master's, thesis or alternative. *Entrance requirements:* For master's, GRE General Test; for doctorate, master's degree. *Faculty research:* Impact of mass communication, media technology, media accountability, craft attitudes, media economics.

University of Ottawa, Faculty of Graduate and Postdoctoral Studies, Faculty of Arts, Department of Communication, Ottawa, ON K1N 6N5, Canada. Offers MA. Electronic applications accepted. *Faculty research:* Media studies, organizational communications.

University of Pennsylvania, Annenberg School for Communication, Philadelphia, PA 19104. Offers PhD. *Faculty:* 17 full-time (7 women), 7 part-time/adjunct (2 women). *Students:* 80 full-time (42 women), 1 part-time (0 women); includes 9 minority (2 Black or African American, non-Hispanic/Latino; 3 Asian, non-Hispanic/Latino; 2 Hispanic/Latino; 2 Two or more races, non-Hispanic/Latino), 29 international. Average age 30. 257 applicants, 7% accepted, 11 enrolled. In 2017, 6 doctorates awarded. *Entrance requirements:* Additional exam requirements/recommendations for international students: Required—TOEFL. *Financial support:* In 2017–18, 80 students received support. *Application contact:* Joanne Murray, Assistant Dean for Graduate Studies, 215-573-6349, Fax: 215-898-2024, E-mail: joanne.murray@asc.upenn.edu.
Website: http://www.asc.upenn.edu/

University of Pittsburgh, Kenneth P. Dietrich School of Arts and Sciences, Department of Communication, Pittsburgh, PA 15260. Offers MA, PhD. *Faculty:* 12 full-time (3 women). *Students:* 34 full-time (18 women); includes 7 minority (2 Black or African American, non-Hispanic/Latino; 1 American Indian or Alaska Native, non-Hispanic/Latino; 2 Asian, non-Hispanic/Latino; 1 Hispanic/Latino; 1 Two or more races, non-Hispanic/Latino). Average age 30. 66 applicants, 3% accepted, 2 enrolled. In 2017, 1 master's, 8 doctorates awarded. *Degree requirements:* For master's, comprehensive exam, thesis optional; for doctorate, comprehensive exam, thesis/dissertation. *Entrance requirements:* For master's and doctorate, GRE General Test, sample of written work, curriculum vitae. Additional exam requirements/recommendations for international students: Required—TOEFL (minimum score 577 paper-based; 90 iBT), IELTS (minimum score 7). *Application deadline:* For fall admission, 1/4 priority date for domestic and international students. Application fee: $50. Electronic applications accepted. *Expenses:* Contact institution. *Financial support:* In 2017–18, 30 students received support, including 27 fellowships with full tuition reimbursements available (averaging $18,700 per year), 2 teaching assistantships with full tuition reimbursements available (averaging $18,450 per year); research assistantships, Federal Work-Study, institutionally sponsored loans, scholarships/grants, traineeships, health care benefits, and tuition waivers (full) also available. Financial award application deadline: 1/4; financial award applicants required to submit FAFSA. *Faculty research:* Media and cultural studies, public argument and discourse, rhetoric of science, history, criticism and

theory of rhetoric. *Unit head:* Dr. Lester Olson, Department Chair, 412-624-1564, Fax: 412-624-1878, E-mail: olson@pitt.edu. *Application contact:* Dr. Brenton Malin, Director of Graduate Studies, 412-624-6798, Fax: 412-624-1878, E-mail: bmalin@pitt.edu.
Website: http://www.comm.pitt.edu/

University of Portland, Department of Communication Studies, Portland, OR 97203-5798. Offers communication (MA); management communication (MS). *Program availability:* Part-time, evening/weekend. *Degree requirements:* For master's, thesis optional. *Entrance requirements:* For master's, GRE General Test, minimum GPA of 3.25, 3 letters of recommendation, resume, statement of goals, official transcripts. Additional exam requirements/recommendations for international students: Required—TOEFL (minimum score 600 paper-based; 100 iBT), IELTS (minimum score 7.5).

University of Puerto Rico–Río Piedras, School of Communication, Program in Communication Theory and Research, San Juan, PR 00931-3300. Offers MA.

University of Rhode Island, Graduate School, College of Arts and Sciences, Department of Communication Studies, Kingston, RI 02881. Offers MA. *Program availability:* Part-time. *Faculty:* 33 full-time (17 women). *Students:* 8 full-time (6 women), 5 part-time (4 women); includes 2 minority (1 Black or African American, non-Hispanic/Latino; 1 Native Hawaiian or other Pacific Islander, non-Hispanic/Latino), 1 international. 16 applicants, 81% accepted, 7 enrolled. In 2017, 8 master's awarded. *Entrance requirements:* For master's, GRE. Additional exam requirements/recommendations for international students: Required—TOEFL. *Application deadline:* Applications are processed on a rolling basis. Application fee: $65. Electronic applications accepted. *Expenses:* Tuition, state resident: full-time $12,706; part-time $786 per credit. Tuition, nonresident: full-time $25,216; part-time $1401 per credit. *Required fees:* $1598; $45 per credit. One-time fee: $30 part-time. *Financial support:* In 2017–18, 1 research assistantship with tuition reimbursement (averaging $8,862 per year), 5 teaching assistantships with tuition reimbursements (averaging $15,952 per year) were awarded. Financial award application deadline: 2/1; financial award applicants required to submit FAFSA. *Unit head:* Dr. Kevin McClure, Chair, 401-874-4726, Fax: 401-874-4722, E-mail: kmcclure@uri.edu. *Application contact:* Dr. Abran Salazar, Director of Graduate Studies, 401-874-9015, E-mail: abran_salazar@uri.edu.
Website: http://www.uri.edu/artsci/com/

University of San Francisco, College of Arts and Sciences, Program in Professional Communication, San Francisco, CA 94117-1080. Offers MA.

University of South Africa, College of Human Sciences, Pretoria, South Africa. Offers adult education (M Ed); African languages (MA, PhD); African politics (MA, PhD); Afrikaans (MA, PhD); ancient history (MA, PhD); ancient Near Eastern studies (MA, PhD); anthropology (MA, PhD); applied linguistics (MA); Arabic (MA, PhD); archaeology (MA); art history (MA); Biblical archaeology (MA); Biblical studies (M Th, D Th, PhD); Christian spirituality (M Th, D Th); church history (M Th, D Th); classical studies (MA, PhD); clinical psychology (MA); communication (MA, PhD); comparative education (M Ed, Ed D); consulting psychology (D Admin, D Com, PhD); curriculum studies (M Ed, Ed D); development studies (M Admin, MA, D Admin, PhD); didactics (M Ed, Ed D); education (M Tech); education management (M Ed, Ed D); educational psychology (M Ed); English (MA); environmental education (M Ed); French (MA, PhD); German (MA, PhD); Greek (MA); guidance and counseling (M Ed); health studies (MA, PhD), including health sciences education (MA), health services management (MA), medical and surgical nursing science (critical care general) (MA), midwifery and neonatal nursing science (MA), trauma and emergency care (MA); history (MA, PhD); history of education (Ed D); inclusive education (M Ed, Ed D); information and communications technology policy and regulation (MA); information science (MA, MIS, PhD); international politics (MA, PhD); Islamic studies (MA, PhD); Italian (MA, PhD); Judaica (MA, PhD); linguistics (MA, PhD); mathematical education (M Ed); mathematics education (MA); missiology (M Th, D Th); modern Hebrew (MA, PhD); musicology (MA, MMus, D Mus, PhD); natural science education (M Ed); New Testament (M Th, D Th); Old Testament (D Th); pastoral therapy (M Th, D Th); philosophy (MA); philosophy of education (M Ed, Ed D); politics (MA, PhD); Portuguese (MA, PhD); practical theology (M Th, D Th); psychology (MA, MS, PhD); psychology of education (M Ed, Ed D); public health (MA); religious studies (MA, D Th, PhD); Romance languages (MA); Russian (MA, PhD); Semitic languages (MA, PhD); social behavior studies in HIV/AIDS (MA); social science (mental health) (MA); social science in development studies (MA); social science in psychology (MA); social science in social work (MA); social science in sociology (MA); social work (MSW, DSW, PhD); socio-education (M Ed, Ed D); sociolinguistics (MA); sociology (MA, PhD); Spanish (MA, PhD); systematic theology (M Th, D Th); TESOL (teaching English to speakers of other languages) (MA); theological ethics (M Th, D Th); theory of literature (MA, PhD); urban ministries (D Th); urban ministry (M Th).

University of South Alabama, College of Arts and Sciences, Department of Communication, Mobile, AL 36688. Offers MA. *Program availability:* Part-time, evening/weekend. *Faculty:* 6 full-time (2 women). *Students:* 16 full-time (13 women), 4 part-time (2 women); includes 5 minority (all Black or African American, non-Hispanic/Latino). Average age 27. 10 applicants, 90% accepted, 6 enrolled. In 2017, 6 master's awarded. *Degree requirements:* For master's, comprehensive exam, thesis optional, minimum of 33 semesters hours, including 6 hours of thesis or project work; minimum of 27 semester hours in communication. *Entrance requirements:* For master's, GRE, GMAT, minimum GPA of 3.0, BA in communication or 15 semester hours. Additional exam requirements/recommendations for international students: Required—TOEFL (minimum score 525 paper-based; 71 iBT). *Application deadline:* For fall admission, 7/1 priority date for domestic students, 6/1 priority date for international students; for spring admission, 12/1 priority date for domestic students, 11/1 priority date for international students; for summer admission, 5/1 for domestic students, 4/1 for international students. Applications are processed on a rolling basis. Application fee: $35. Electronic applications accepted. *Expenses:* Tuition, state resident: full-time $10,104; part-time $421 per semester hour. Tuition, nonresident: full-time $20,208; part-time $842 per semester hour. *Financial support:* Fellowships, research assistantships, teaching assistantships, career-related internships or fieldwork, Federal Work-Study, institutionally sponsored loans, scholarships/grants, and unspecified assistantships available. Support available to part-time students. Financial award application deadline: 3/31; financial award applicants required to submit FAFSA. *Faculty research:* Mass media ethics, literary journalism, film and television history, advertising, and technology policy. *Unit head:* Dr. James Aucoin, Chair, 251-380-2800, Fax: 251-380-2850, E-mail: jaucoin@southalabama.edu. *Application contact:* Dr. Steve Rockwell, Graduate Studies Chair, 251-380-2801, E-mail: srockwell@southalabama.edu.
Website: http://comm.southalabama.edu/colleges/artsandsci/communication/

University of South Dakota, Graduate School, College of Arts and Sciences, Department of Communication Studies, Vermillion, SD 57069. Offers MA. *Program availability:* Part-time. *Degree requirements:* For master's, comprehensive exam (for some programs), thesis (for some programs). *Entrance requirements:* For master's, minimum GPA of 3.0. Additional exam requirements/recommendations for international students: Required—TOEFL (minimum score 575 paper-based; 79 iBT). *Application deadline:* Applications are processed on a rolling basis. Application fee: $35. Electronic applications accepted. *Financial support:* Teaching assistantships with partial tuition reimbursements, career-related internships or fieldwork, Federal Work-Study, and unspecified assistantships available. Support available to part-time students. Financial award applicants required to submit FAFSA. *Faculty research:* Male/female communication, interpersonal communication, relational communication, rhetoric and public address, organizational communication. *Application contact:* Graduate School, 605-658-6140, Fax: 605-677-6118, E-mail: grad@usd.edu.
Website: http://www.usd.edu/arts-and-sciences/communication-studies

University of Southern California, Graduate School, Annenberg School for Communication and Journalism, School of Communication, Program in Communication, Los Angeles, CA 90089. Offers culture and community (PhD); global and transnational communication (PhD); groups, organizations and networks (PhD); health communication and social dynamics (PhD); information, political economy and entertainment (PhD); new media and technology (PhD); rhetoric, politics and public media (PhD). *Degree requirements:* For doctorate, thesis/dissertation. *Entrance requirements:* For doctorate, GRE General Test, resume or curriculum vitae, scholarly writing, 3 letters of recommendation, statement of purpose. Additional exam requirements/recommendations for international students: Required—TOEFL (minimum score 114 iBT), IELTS (minimum score 8); Recommended—TWE. Electronic applications accepted. *Faculty research:* Computer-mediated communication, public health campaigns, communication democracy and the public sphere, new communication technologies in organizations, communication and community.

University of Southern California, Graduate School, Annenberg School for Communication and Journalism, School of Communication, Program in Global Communication, Los Angeles, CA 90089. Offers MA/M Sc. Program offered jointly with London School of Economics and Political Science (LSE); first year is at LSE and second year at USC. *Entrance requirements:* Additional exam requirements/recommendations for international students: Required—TOEFL (minimum score 114 iBT), IELTS (minimum score 8). Electronic applications accepted. *Faculty research:* New technology, audience analysis, globalization, entertainment industry, integrated communication.

University of Southern California, Graduate School, Annenberg School for Communication and Journalism, School of Communication, Program in Public Diplomacy, Los Angeles, CA 90089. Offers MPD. *Program availability:* Part-time. *Degree requirements:* For master's, thesis. *Entrance requirements:* For master's, GRE, resume, writing samples, statement of purpose, recommendation letters. Additional exam requirements/recommendations for international students: Required—TOEFL (minimum score 114 iBT), IELTS (minimum score 8). Electronic applications accepted.

University of Southern Indiana, Graduate Studies, College of Liberal Arts, Program in Communication, Evansville, IN 47712-3590. Offers MA. *Program availability:* Part-time, evening/weekend. *Faculty:* 6 full-time (2 women), 1 part-time/adjunct (0 women). *Students:* 12 full-time (9 women), 7 part-time (4 women); includes 1 minority (Black or African American, non-Hispanic/Latino), 3 international. Average age 35. In 2017, 7 master's awarded. *Entrance requirements:* For master's, GRE, written letter of intent, three professional letters of recommendation. Additional exam requirements/recommendations for international students: Required—TOEFL (minimum score 550 paper-based; 79 iBT), IELTS (minimum score 6). *Application deadline:* For fall admission, 7/1 for domestic and international students; for spring admission, 11/1 for domestic and international students. Applications are processed on a rolling basis. Application fee: $40. Electronic applications accepted. *Expenses:* Tuition, state resident: full-time $9394. Tuition, nonresident: full-time $17,917. *Required fees:* $510. *Financial support:* In 2017–18, 2 students received support. Federal Work-Study, scholarships/grants, and unspecified assistantships available. Financial award application deadline: 3/1; financial award applicants required to submit FAFSA. *Unit head:* Dr. Leigh Anne Howard, Program Director, 812-464-1741, E-mail: lahoward@usi.edu. *Application contact:* Dr. Mayola Rowser, Director, Graduate Studies, 812-465-7015, E-mail: mrowser@usi.edu.
Website: http://www.usi.edu/liberalarts/master-of-arts-in-communication

University of South Florida, College of Arts and Sciences, Department of Communication, Tampa, FL 33620-9951. Offers MA, PhD. *Program availability:* Part-time. *Faculty:* 13 full-time (7 women). *Students:* 35 full-time (23 women), 14 part-time (6 women); includes 17 minority (5 Black or African American, non-Hispanic/Latino; 3 Asian, non-Hispanic/Latino; 7 Hispanic/Latino; 2 Two or more races, non-Hispanic/Latino), 7 international. Average age 34. 63 applicants, 32% accepted, 13 enrolled. In 2017, 5 master's, 6 doctorates awarded. *Degree requirements:* For master's, comprehensive exam, thesis (for some programs); for doctorate, comprehensive exam, thesis/dissertation. *Entrance requirements:* For master's and doctorate, GRE General Test, minimum GPA of 3.0, three letters of recommendation, writing sample, statement of purpose, resume/curriculum vitae. Additional exam requirements/recommendations for international students: Required—TOEFL (minimum score 550 paper-based; 79 iBT), IELTS. *Application deadline:* For fall admission, 1/15 for domestic and international students; for spring admission, 10/15 for domestic students, 9/15 for international students. Applications are processed on a rolling basis. Application fee: $30. Electronic applications accepted. *Financial support:* In 2017–18, 3 students received support, including 32 teaching assistantships with full tuition reimbursements available (averaging $9,875 per year); unspecified assistantships also available. Financial award application deadline: 1/15; financial award applicants required to submit FAFSA. *Faculty research:* Organizational, interpersonal, and health communication; media and cultural studies; rhetoric; performance studies; qualitative research methods. *Total annual research expenditures:* $224,881. *Unit head:* Dr. Patrice Buzzanell, Associate Professor/Interim Chair, 813-974-2145, E-mail: pmbuzzanell@usf.edu. *Application contact:* Dr. Ambar Basu, Associate Professor and Graduate Program Director, 813-974-2145, Fax: 813-974-6817, E-mail: abasu@usf.edu.
Website: http://communication.usf.edu/

The University of Tennessee, Graduate School, College of Communication and Information, Knoxville, TN 37996. Offers advertising (MS, PhD); broadcasting (MS, PhD); communications (MS, PhD); information sciences (MS, PhD); journalism (MS, PhD); public relations (MS, PhD); speech communication (MS, PhD). *Program availability:* Part-time, evening/weekend, online learning. *Degree requirements:* For master's, thesis or alternative; for doctorate, thesis/dissertation. *Entrance requirements:* For master's and doctorate, GRE General Test, minimum GPA of 2.7. Additional exam requirements/recommendations for international students: Required—TOEFL. Electronic applications accepted.

The University of Tennessee at Martin, Graduate Programs, College of Humanities and Fine Arts, Martin, TN 38238. Offers strategic communication (MASC). *Program availability:* Part-time, blended/hybrid learning. *Faculty:* 20 full-time (7 women). *Students:* 15 part-time (12 women). Average age 34. 10 applicants, 50% accepted, 5 enrolled. *Degree requirements:* For master's, comprehensive exam. *Entrance requirements:* For master's, GRE. Additional exam requirements/recommendations for international students: Required—TOEFL (minimum score 525 paper-based; 71 iBT). *Application deadline:* For fall admission, 7/27 priority date for domestic and international students; for spring admission, 12/15 priority date for domestic and international students; for summer admission, 5/10 priority date for domestic and international students. Applications are processed on a rolling basis. Application fee: $30 ($130 for international students). Electronic applications accepted. *Expenses:* Tuition, state resident: full-time $8658; part-time $481 per credit hour. Tuition, nonresident: full-time

$14,418; part-time $801 per credit hour. *International tuition:* $22,602 full-time. *Required fees:* $1404; $79 per credit hour. Part-time tuition and fees vary according to course load. *Financial support:* In 2017–18, 11 students received support, including 1 research assistantship with full tuition reimbursement available (averaging $9,048 per year); teaching assistantships, scholarships/grants, and tuition waivers (full and partial) also available. Financial award application deadline: 2/1; financial award applicants required to submit FAFSA. *Unit head:* Dr. Lynn Alexander, Dean, 731-881-7490, Fax: 731-881-7276, E-mail: lalexand@utm.edu. *Application contact:* Jolene L. Cunningham, Student Services Specialist, 731-881-7012, Fax: 731-881-7499, E-mail: jcunningham@utm.edu.
Website: http://www.utm.edu/departments/chfa/

The University of Texas at Arlington, Graduate School, College of Liberal Arts, Department of Communication, Arlington, TX 76019. Offers MA. *Program availability:* Part-time, evening/weekend. *Degree requirements:* For master's, comprehensive exam (for some programs), thesis or alternative. *Entrance requirements:* For master's, GRE General Test. Additional exam requirements/recommendations for international students: Required—TOEFL (minimum score 550 paper-based). Electronic applications accepted.

The University of Texas at Austin, Graduate School, College of Communication, Department of Communication Studies, Austin, TX 78712-1111. Offers MA, PhD. *Entrance requirements:* For master's and doctorate, GRE General Test. Electronic applications accepted.

The University of Texas at Dallas, School of Behavioral and Brain Sciences, Program in Communication Sciences and Disorders, Richardson, TX 75080. Offers audiology (Au D); communication disorders (MS); communication sciences and disorders (PhD). *Program availability:* Part-time, evening/weekend. *Faculty:* 16 full-time (10 women), 11 part-time/adjunct (10 women). *Students:* 276 full-time (262 women), 14 part-time (12 women); includes 71 minority (3 Black or African American, non-Hispanic/Latino; 1 American Indian or Alaska Native, non-Hispanic/Latino; 19 Asian, non-Hispanic/Latino; 30 Hispanic/Latino; 18 Two or more races, non-Hispanic/Latino), 14 international. Average age 25. 715 applicants, 15% accepted, 70 enrolled. In 2017, 116 master's, 14 doctorates awarded. *Degree requirements:* For doctorate, thesis/dissertation. *Entrance requirements:* For master's and doctorate, GRE General Test, minimum GPA of 3.0 in upper-level course work in field. Additional exam requirements/recommendations for international students: Required—TOEFL (minimum score 550 paper-based). *Application deadline:* For fall admission, 7/15 for domestic students, 5/1 priority date for international students; for spring admission, 11/15 for domestic students, 9/1 priority date for international students. Applications are processed on a rolling basis. Application fee: $50 ($100 for international students). Electronic applications accepted. *Expenses:* Tuition, state resident: full-time $12,916; part-time $718 per credit hour. Tuition, nonresident: full-time $25,252; part-time $1403 per credit hour. *Financial support:* In 2017–18, 221 students received support, including 1 fellowship (averaging $1,500 per year), 10 research assistantships with partial tuition reimbursements available (averaging $24,181 per year), 21 teaching assistantships with partial tuition reimbursements available (averaging $18,335 per year); Federal Work-Study, institutionally sponsored loans, scholarships/grants, and unspecified assistantships also available. Support available to part-time students. Financial award application deadline: 4/30; financial award applicants required to submit FAFSA. *Faculty research:* Developmental neurolinguistics, brain plasticity and biofeedback treatment, autism spectrum disorders, speech production, neurogenic speech and language disorders. *Unit head:* Dr. Robert D. Stillman, Area Head, 214-905-3106, Fax: 972-883-3022, E-mail: stillman@utdallas.edu.
Website: http://www.utdallas.edu/bbs/degrees/csd-degrees/

The University of Texas at El Paso, Graduate School, College of Liberal Arts, Department of Communication, El Paso, TX 79968. Offers MA. *Program availability:* Part-time, evening/weekend. Terminal master's awarded for partial completion of doctoral program. *Degree requirements:* For master's, thesis optional. *Entrance requirements:* For master's, GRE General Test, minimum GPA of 3.0. Additional exam requirements/recommendations for international students: Required—TOEFL. Electronic applications accepted. *Faculty research:* Intercultural communication, international communication, rhetorical theories, cultural and media studies, health communication.

The University of Texas at San Antonio, College of Liberal and Fine Arts, Department of Communication, San Antonio, TX 78249-0617. Offers MA. *Program availability:* Part-time, evening/weekend, online learning. *Faculty:* 6 full-time (3 women). *Students:* 16 full-time (11 women), 20 part-time (13 women); includes 31 minority (1 Black or African American, non-Hispanic/Latino; 29 Hispanic/Latino; 1 Two or more races, non-Hispanic/Latino), 1 international. Average age 28. 39 applicants, 67% accepted, 21 enrolled. In 2017, 8 master's awarded. *Degree requirements:* For master's, comprehensive exam, thesis optional, 36 course hours. *Entrance requirements:* For master's, GRE, minimum GPA of 3.0 in last 60 hours, statement of purpose, two academic letters of recommendation. Additional exam requirements/recommendations for international students: Required—TOEFL (minimum score 550 paper-based; 79 iBT), IELTS (minimum score 6.5). *Application deadline:* For fall admission, 6/15 for domestic students, 3/1 priority date for international students; for spring admission, 10/15 for domestic students, 9/15 for international students. Applications are processed on a rolling basis. Application fee: $50 ($90 for international students). Electronic applications accepted. *Expenses:* Contact institution. *Financial support:* Fellowships, research assistantships, teaching assistantships, career-related internships or fieldwork, Federal Work-Study, institutionally sponsored loans, scholarships/grants, traineeships, health care benefits, and unspecified assistantships available. Support available to part-time students. Financial award applicants required to submit FAFSA. *Faculty research:* Organizational communication, health communication, interpersonal communication, intercultural communication, new media and digital media. *Total annual research expenditures:* $5,908. *Unit head:* Dr. Paul LeBlanc, Department Chair, 210-458-5990, Fax: 210-458-5991, E-mail: paul.leblanc@utsa.edu. *Application contact:* Mary Tutor, Program Coordinator, 210-458-7750, E-mail: mary.tutor@utsa.edu.
Website: http://communication.utsa.edu/

The University of Texas at Tyler, College of Arts and Sciences, Department of Communication, Tyler, TX 75799-0001. Offers communication (MA); interdisciplinary studies (MAIS, MSIS). *Program availability:* Part-time. *Degree requirements:* For master's, comprehensive exam. *Entrance requirements:* For master's, GRE General Test, minimum GPA of 2.5. Additional exam requirements/recommendations for international students: Required—TOEFL. Electronic applications accepted. *Faculty research:* Organizational communication, feminist criticism, religions communication, mass media.

The University of Texas Rio Grande Valley, College of Liberal Arts, Department of Communication, Edinburg, TX 78539. Offers communication (MA). *Accreditation:* NAST. *Program availability:* Part-time. *Faculty:* 5 full-time (2 women). *Students:* 12 full-time (9 women), 18 part-time (15 women); includes 29 minority (all Hispanic/Latino), 1 international. Average age 30. 16 applicants, 94% accepted, 11 enrolled. In 2017, 18 master's awarded. *Degree requirements:* For master's, comprehensive exam, thesis or alternative. *Entrance requirements:* For master's, minimum GPA of 3.0. Additional exam requirements/recommendations for international students: Required—TOEFL or IELTS. Application fee: $50 ($100 for international students). *Expenses:* Tuition, state resident: full-time $5550; part-time $417 per credit hour. Tuition, nonresident: full-time $13,020; part-time $832 per credit hour. *Required fees:* $1169. *Financial support:* Application deadline: 6/1. *Faculty research:* Rhetorical theory, intercultural and mass communication, American theatre, multicultural theatre and drama, television and film. *Unit head:* John Cook, Chair, 956-882-8851, E-mail: john.cook@utrgv.edu.

University of the Incarnate Word, School of Media and Design, San Antonio, TX 78209-6397. Offers communication arts (MA); fashion design (MA). *Program availability:* Part-time, evening/weekend. *Faculty:* 10 full-time (6 women). *Students:* 27 full-time (15 women), 9 part-time (5 women); includes 26 minority (4 Black or African American, non-Hispanic/Latino; 22 Hispanic/Latino), 3 international. In 2017, 15 master's awarded. *Degree requirements:* For master's, thesis or alternative, capstone. *Entrance requirements:* For master's, GRE, interview, writing sample. Additional exam requirements/recommendations for international students: Required—TOEFL (minimum score 560 paper-based; 83 iBT). *Application deadline:* Applications are processed on a rolling basis. Application fee: $20. Electronic applications accepted. *Expenses: Tuition:* Full-time $16,470; part-time $915 per credit hour. Tuition and fees vary according to degree level, program and student level. *Financial support:* Federal Work-Study, scholarships/grants, tuition waivers (partial), and unspecified assistantships available. Financial award applicants required to submit FAFSA. *Faculty research:* Representation of minority groups on screen, communication effectiveness and human relationships, philosophy of communication and social theories, spirituality in higher education, examining the role of race, gender and sexuality in political cartoons. *Unit head:* Dr. Sharon Welkey, Dean, 210-829-6091, Fax: 210-829-3196, E-mail: welkey@uiwtx.edu. *Application contact:* Johnny Garcia, Graduate Admissions Counselor, 210-805-3554, Fax: 210-829-3921, E-mail: admis@uiwtx.edu.
Website: http://www.uiw.edu/simd/index.htm

University of the Incarnate Word, School of Professional Studies, San Antonio, TX 78209-6397. Offers communication arts (MAA), including applied administration, communication arts, healthcare administration, industrial and organizational psychology, organizational development; organizational development and leadership (MS); professional studies (DBA). *Program availability:* Part-time, evening/weekend, 100% online, blended/hybrid learning. *Faculty:* 9 full-time (3 women), 25 part-time/adjunct (10 women). *Students:* 528 full-time (263 women), 348 part-time (141 women); includes 543 minority (122 Black or African American, non-Hispanic/Latino; 3 American Indian or Alaska Native, non-Hispanic/Latino; 26 Asian, non-Hispanic/Latino; 365 Hispanic/Latino; 6 Native Hawaiian or other Pacific Islander, non-Hispanic/Latino; 21 Two or more races, non-Hispanic/Latino). In 2017, 377 master's, 10 doctorates awarded. *Degree requirements:* For master's, comprehensive exam (for some programs), thesis or alternative. *Entrance requirements:* For master's, GMAT, GRE, official transcripts from all other colleges attended. Additional exam requirements/recommendations for international students: Required—TOEFL (minimum score 560 paper-based; 83 iBT). *Application deadline:* Applications are processed on a rolling basis. Electronic applications accepted. *Expenses:* $915 per credit hour (for master's programs); $940 per credit hour (for doctoral program). *Financial support:* Scholarships/grants and unspecified assistantships available. Financial award applicants required to submit FAFSA. *Unit head:* Dr. Cyndi Porter, Vice President, 877-603-1130, E-mail: porter@uiwtx.edu. *Application contact:* Julie Weber, Director of Marketing and Recruitment, 210-318-1876, Fax: 210-829-2756, E-mail: eapadmission@uiwtx.edu.
Website: http://sps.uiw.edu/

University of the Pacific, College of the Pacific, Department of Communication, Stockton, CA 95211-0197. Offers MA. *Faculty:* 16 full-time (5 women), 2 part-time/adjunct (1 woman). *Students:* 18 part-time (9 women); includes 8 minority (3 Black or African American, non-Hispanic/Latino; 3 Hispanic/Latino; 2 Two or more races, non-Hispanic/Latino), 1 international. Average age 29. 15 applicants, 73% accepted, 6 enrolled. In 2017, 1 master's awarded. *Degree requirements:* For master's, thesis. *Entrance requirements:* For master's, GRE General Test. Additional exam requirements/recommendations for international students: Required—TOEFL. *Application deadline:* For fall admission, 3/1 priority date for domestic students; for spring admission, 10/1 for domestic students. Applications are processed on a rolling basis. Application fee: $75. *Financial support:* Teaching assistantships available. Support available to part-time students. Financial award application deadline: 3/1; financial award applicants required to submit FAFSA. *Unit head:* Dr. Teresa Bergman, 209-946-7602. *Application contact:* Information Contact, 209-946-2261.
Website: http://www.pacific.edu/Documents/school-graduate/acrobat/Pacific-MA-Communication-Fact-Sheet-17-18.pdf

University of the Sacred Heart, Graduate Programs, Department of Communication, San Juan, PR 00914-0383. Offers contemporary culture and media (MA); digital journalism (MA, Certificate); editing for media (MA, Certificate); public relations (MA, Certificate); publicity (MA, Certificate); scriptwriting (MA, Certificate). *Program availability:* Part-time, evening/weekend. *Degree requirements:* For master's, thesis.

The University of Toledo, College of Graduate Studies, College of Communication and the Arts, Department of Communication, Toledo, OH 43606-3390. Offers Certificate. *Program availability:* Part-time. *Entrance requirements:* For degree, minimum GPA of 2.7 for all prior academic work, transcripts from all prior institutions attended; statement of purpose. Electronic applications accepted.

University of Utah, Graduate School, College of Humanities, Department of Communication, Salt Lake City, UT 84112. Offers communicating science, health, environment and risk (MA, MS, PhD); critical cultural studies (MA, MS, PhD); digital media (MA, MS, PhD); rhetoric (MA, MS, PhD). *Faculty:* 26 full-time (13 women), 11 part-time/adjunct (3 women). *Students:* 34 full-time (24 women), 14 part-time (10 women); includes 4 minority (2 Asian, non-Hispanic/Latino; 1 Hispanic/Latino; 1 Two or more races, non-Hispanic/Latino), 3 international. Average age 24. 99 applicants, 31% accepted, 15 enrolled. In 2017, 6 master's, 9 doctorates awarded. Terminal master's awarded for partial completion of doctoral program. *Entrance requirements:* For master's and doctorate, GRE General Test, minimum GPA of 3.0. Additional exam requirements/recommendations for international students: Required—TOEFL (minimum score 500 paper-based; 90 iBT); Recommended—IELTS. *Application deadline:* For fall admission, 12/15 for domestic students, 11/15 for international students. Application fee: $55 ($65 for international students). Electronic applications accepted. *Expenses:* $7,790 resident, $24,804 non-resident. *Financial support:* In 2017–18, 4 students received support, including 1 fellowship with full tuition reimbursement available (averaging $18,000 per year), 25 teaching assistantships with full tuition reimbursement available (averaging $17,700 per year); research assistantships, scholarships/grants, health care benefits, and unspecified assistantships also available. Financial award application deadline: 12/15; financial award applicants required to submit FAFSA. *Faculty research:* CommSHER (communicating science, health, environment, and risk), critical/cultural studies, interpersonal/organizational communication, new media technologies, rhetoric. *Unit head:* Dr. Kent A. Ono, Chair, 801-585-9128, Fax: 801-585-6255, E-mail: kent.ono@utah.edu. *Application contact:* Dr. Helene Shugart, Director of Graduate Studies, 801-581-5686, Fax: 801-585-6255, E-mail: h.shugart@utah.edu.
Website: http://www.communication.utah.edu

Communication—General

University of Washington, Graduate School, College of Arts and Sciences, Department of Communication, Seattle, WA 98195. Offers MA, MC, PhD. *Program availability:* Part-time. Terminal master's awarded for partial completion of doctoral program. *Degree requirements:* For master's, thesis, project (MC); for doctorate, thesis/dissertation. *Entrance requirements:* For master's and doctorate, GRE, minimum GPA of 3.0, writing sample. Additional exam requirements/recommendations for international students: Required—TOEFL. Electronic applications accepted. *Faculty research:* Communication and culture, communication technology and society, international communication, political communication, rhetoric and critical studies.

University of Washington, Graduate School, College of Arts and Sciences, School of Art, Division of Design, Seattle, WA 98195. Offers industrial design (MFA); visual communication design (MFA).

University of West Florida, College of Arts, Social Sciences, and Humanities, Department of Communication, Pensacola, FL 32514-5750. Offers strategic communication and leadership (MA). *Program availability:* Part-time, evening/weekend. *Degree requirements:* For master's, thesis or alternative. *Entrance requirements:* For master's, GRE (minimum score: verbal 470, writing 4.0), MAT (minimum score 413), or GMAT (minimum score of 400), minimum GPA of 3.2; official transcripts; undergraduate degree in related field; three letters of reference; current curriculum vitae/resume. Additional exam requirements/recommendations for international students: Required—TOEFL (minimum score 550 paper-based). *Faculty research:* Equity studies.

University of Windsor, Faculty of Graduate Studies, Faculty of Arts and Social Sciences, Department of Communication Studies, Windsor, ON N9B 3P4, Canada. Offers communication and social justice (MA). *Degree requirements:* For master's, thesis. *Entrance requirements:* For master's, writing sample/media production or multimedia portfolio. Additional exam requirements/recommendations for international students: Required—TOEFL (minimum score 600 paper-based). Electronic applications accepted. *Faculty research:* Sociology of news, media ownership and control, communication networks and social movements, issues of media representation.

University of Wisconsin–Madison, Graduate School, College of Letters and Science, Department of Communication Arts, Madison, WI 53706-1380. Offers communication science (MA, PhD); film (MA, PhD); media and cultural studies (MA, PhD); rhetoric (MA, PhD). Terminal master's awarded for partial completion of doctoral program. *Degree requirements:* For master's, one foreign language, thesis (for some programs); for doctorate, one foreign language, thesis/dissertation. *Entrance requirements:* For master's and doctorate, GRE General Test, minimum GPA of 3.5. Electronic applications accepted.

University of Wisconsin–Madison, Graduate School, College of Letters and Science, School of Journalism and Mass Communication, Madison, WI 53706-1380. Offers family and consumer journalism (PhD); journalism and mass communication (MA); mass communication (PhD). *Program availability:* Part-time. *Degree requirements:* For master's, thesis (for some programs); for doctorate, thesis/dissertation. *Entrance requirements:* For master's, GRE General Test, minimum GPA of 3.0; for doctorate, GRE General Test, minimum GPA of 3.5. Additional exam requirements/recommendations for international students: Required—TOEFL. Electronic applications accepted. *Faculty research:* International/development communication; strategic mass communication; mass communication and the individual; science, technology, and environment communication; mass communication and societal institutions.

University of Wisconsin–Milwaukee, Graduate School, College of Letters and Science, Department of Communication, Milwaukee, WI 53201-0413. Offers communication (MA, PhD), including rhetorical leadership; rhetorical leadership (Graduate Certificate). *Program availability:* Part-time. *Students:* 23 full-time (16 women), 16 part-time (13 women); includes 5 minority (2 Black or African American, non-Hispanic/Latino; 2 Asian, non-Hispanic/Latino; 1 Two or more races, non-Hispanic/Latino), 6 international. Average age 31. 45 applicants, 51% accepted, 17 enrolled. In 2017, 3 doctorates awarded. *Degree requirements:* For master's, thesis or alternative; for doctorate, comprehensive exam. *Entrance requirements:* For master's, GRE General Test, minimum GPA of 3.0. Additional exam requirements/recommendations for international students: Required—TOEFL (minimum score 550 paper-based; 79 iBT), IELTS (minimum score 6). *Application deadline:* For fall admission, 1/1 priority date for domestic students; for spring admission, 9/1 for domestic students. Application fee: $56. Electronic applications accepted. *Financial support:* Fellowships, research assistantships, teaching assistantships, career-related internships or fieldwork, unspecified assistantships, and project assistantships available. Support available to part-time students. Financial award application deadline: 4/15; financial award applicants required to submit FAFSA. *Unit head:* Mike Allen, Department Chair, 414-229-4510, E-mail: mikealle@uwm.edu. *Application contact:* General Information Contact, 414-229-4982, Fax: 414-229-6967, E-mail: gradschool@uwm.edu. Website: https://uwm.edu/communication/

University of Wisconsin–Stevens Point, College of Fine Arts and Communication, Division of Communication, Stevens Point, WI 54481-3897. Offers interpersonal communication (MA); media studies (MA); organizational communication (MA); public relations (MA). *Program availability:* Part-time. *Degree requirements:* For master's, thesis or alternative. *Entrance requirements:* For master's, GRE. Additional exam requirements/recommendations for international students: Required—TOEFL (minimum score 575 paper-based). *Faculty research:* Communication theory and research, film history.

University of Wisconsin–Superior, Graduate Division, Department of Communicating Arts, Superior, WI 54880-4500. Offers mass communication (MA); speech communication (MA); theater (MA). *Program availability:* Part-time. *Degree requirements:* For master's, comprehensive exam, thesis or alternative, position paper or project. *Entrance requirements:* For master's, minimum GPA of 2.75. Electronic applications accepted. *Faculty research:* Multimedia technology, ethics in journalism, diversity, electronic portfolio assessment.

University of Wisconsin–Whitewater, School of Graduate Studies, College of Arts and Communications, Department of Communication, Whitewater, WI 53190-1790. Offers corporate communication (MS); mass communication (MS). *Program availability:* Part-time, evening/weekend, online learning. *Degree requirements:* For master's, thesis or alternative. *Entrance requirements:* For master's, 2 letters of recommendation, goal statement. Additional exam requirements/recommendations for international students: Required—TOEFL (minimum score 550 paper-based; 80 iBT), IELTS (minimum score 6). Electronic applications accepted.

University of Wyoming, College of Arts and Sciences, Department of Communication and Journalism, Laramie, WY 82071. Offers communication (MA). *Program availability:* Part-time. *Degree requirements:* For master's, thesis. *Entrance requirements:* For master's, GRE General Test, minimum GPA of 3.0. *Faculty research:* Personal relations, nonverbal behavior, media management, communication technology, conversation analysis.

Utah State University, School of Graduate Studies, College of Humanities and Social Sciences, Department of Journalism and Communication, Logan, UT 84322. Offers MA, MS. *Program availability:* Part-time. *Degree requirements:* For master's, comprehensive exam, thesis. *Entrance requirements:* For master's, GRE General Test or MAT, minimum GPA of 3.0. Additional exam requirements/recommendations for international students: Required—TOEFL. Electronic applications accepted. *Faculty research:* Race and gender and media, history of censorship, internet design and advertising, technology gap.

Valparaiso University, Graduate School and Continuing Education, Program in English Studies and Communication, Valparaiso, IN 46383. Offers English studies and communication (MA). *Program availability:* Part-time, evening/weekend. *Entrance requirements:* For master's, minimum GPA of 3.0. Additional exam requirements/recommendations for international students: Required—TOEFL (minimum score 550 paper-based; 80 iBT), IELTS (minimum score 6). Electronic applications accepted. *Expenses: Tuition:* Full-time $11,340; part-time $630 per credit hour. *Required fees:* $520; $250 per year. $125 per semester. Tuition and fees vary according to program and reciprocity agreements.

Valparaiso University, Graduate School and Continuing Education, Program in Media and Communication, Valparaiso, IN 46383. Offers digital media (MS, Certificate); sports media (MS, Certificate). *Program availability:* Part-time, evening/weekend. *Entrance requirements:* For master's, minimum GPA of 3.0, undergraduate minor in communication. Additional exam requirements/recommendations for international students: Required—TOEFL (minimum score 550 paper-based; 80 iBT), IELTS (minimum score 6). Electronic applications accepted. *Expenses: Tuition:* Full-time $11,340; part-time $630 per credit hour. *Required fees:* $520; $250 per year. $125 per semester. Tuition and fees vary according to program and reciprocity agreements.

Villanova University, Graduate School of Liberal Arts and Sciences, Department of Communication, Villanova, PA 19085-1699. Offers MA. *Program availability:* Part-time, evening/weekend. *Faculty:* 7. *Students:* 25 full-time (20 women), 17 part-time (15 women); includes 3 minority (1 Black or African American, non-Hispanic/Latino; 2 Two or more races, non-Hispanic/Latino), 6 international. Average age 29. 38 applicants, 84% accepted, 12 enrolled. In 2017, 13 master's awarded. *Degree requirements:* For master's, comprehensive exam (for some programs), thesis optional. *Entrance requirements:* For master's, GRE or GMAT, minimum GPA of 3.0, writing sample, statement of goals, 3 letters of recommendation. Additional exam requirements/recommendations for international students: Required—TOEFL. *Application deadline:* For fall admission, 5/1 priority date for international students; for spring admission, 10/15 priority date for international students. Applications are processed on a rolling basis. Application fee: $50. Electronic applications accepted. *Financial support:* Research assistantships, teaching assistantships, scholarships/grants, and unspecified assistantships available. Financial award applicants required to submit FAFSA. *Unit head:* Dr. Thomas Ksiazek, Program Director, 610-519-8944. Website: http://www1.villanova.edu/villanova/artsci/communication/academic/graduate.html

Virginia Commonwealth University, Graduate School, College of Humanities and Sciences, Richard T. Robertson School of Media and Culture, Program in Media, Art, and Text, Richmond, VA 23284-9005. Offers PhD. *Entrance requirements:* For doctorate, GRE. Additional exam requirements/recommendations for international students: Required—TOEFL (minimum score 600 paper-based; 100 iBT); Recommended—IELTS (minimum score 6.5). Electronic applications accepted.

Virginia Polytechnic Institute and State University, Graduate School, College of Liberal Arts and Human Sciences, Blacksburg, VA 24061. Offers career and technical education (MS Ed, Ed S); communication (MA); counselor education (MA); creative writing (MFA); curriculum and instruction (MA Ed, Ed S); educational leadership and policy studies (Ed S); educational research and evaluation (PhD); English (MA); social, political, ethical, and cultural thought (PhD); Ed D/PhD. *Faculty:* 411 full-time (213 women), 3 part-time/adjunct (all women). *Students:* 623 full-time (427 women), 431 part-time (278 women); includes 203 minority (115 Black or African American, non-Hispanic/Latino; 4 American Indian or Alaska Native, non-Hispanic/Latino; 29 Asian, non-Hispanic/Latino; 33 Hispanic/Latino; 2 Native Hawaiian or other Pacific Islander, non-Hispanic/Latino; 20 Two or more races, non-Hispanic/Latino), 87 international. Average age 34. 898 applicants, 50% accepted, 329 enrolled. In 2017, 314 master's, 102 doctorates awarded. *Degree requirements:* For master's, comprehensive exam (for some programs), thesis (for some programs); for doctorate, comprehensive exam (for some programs), thesis/dissertation (for some programs). *Entrance requirements:* For master's and doctorate, GRE/GMAT. Additional exam requirements/recommendations for international students: Required—TOEFL (minimum score 80 iBT). *Application deadline:* For fall admission, 8/1 for domestic students, 4/1 for international students; for spring admission, 1/1 for domestic students, 9/1 for international students. Applications are processed on a rolling basis. Application fee: $75. Electronic applications accepted. *Expenses:* Tuition, state resident: full-time $15,072; part-time $718.50 per credit hour. Tuition, nonresident: full-time $28,810; part-time $1448.25 per credit hour. *Required fees:* $2741; $502 per semester. Tuition and fees vary according to course load, campus/location and program. *Financial support:* In 2017–18, 19 research assistantships with full tuition reimbursements (averaging $19,611 per year), 226 teaching assistantships with full tuition reimbursements (averaging $16,220 per year) were awarded. Financial award application deadline: 3/1; financial award applicants required to submit FAFSA. *Total annual research expenditures:* $7.9 million. *Unit head:* Dr. Rosemary Blieszner, Dean, 540-231-6779, Fax: 540-231-7157, E-mail: rmb@vt.edu. *Application contact:* Chelsea Blanchet, Executive Assistant, 540-231-6779, Fax: 540-231-7157, E-mail: bchels1@vt.edu. Website: http://www.liberalarts.vt.edu/

Wake Forest University, Graduate School of Arts and Sciences, Department of Communication, Winston-Salem, NC 27109. Offers speech communication (MA). *Program availability:* Part-time. *Degree requirements:* For master's, one foreign language, thesis. *Entrance requirements:* For master's, GRE General Test, writing sample. Additional exam requirements/recommendations for international students: Required—TOEFL (minimum score 79 iBT). Electronic applications accepted.

Walden University, Graduate Programs, School of Management, Minneapolis, MN 55401. Offers accounting (MBA, MS, DBA), including accounting for the professional (MS), accounting with CPA emphasis (MS), self-designed (MS); advanced project management (Graduate Certificate); applied project management (Graduate Certificate); auditing (Graduate Certificate); bridge to business administration (Post-Doctoral Certificate); bridge to management (Post-Doctoral Certificate); business management (Graduate Certificate); communication (MBA); corporate finance (MBA); digital marketing (Graduate Certificate); entrepreneurship (DBA); entrepreneurship and small business (MBA); finance (MS, DBA), including finance for the professional (MS), finance with CFA/investment (MS), finance with CPA emphasis (MS); global supply chain management (DBA); healthcare management (MBA, DBA); human resource management (MBA, MS, Graduate Certificate), including functional human resource management (MS), general program (MS), integrating functional and strategic human resource management (MS), organizational strategy (MS); human resources management (DBA); information systems management (DBA); international business (MBA, DBA); leadership (MBA, MS, DBA, Graduate Certificate), including general program (MS), human resource leadership (MS), leader development (MS), self-designed (MS); management (MS, PhD), including communications (MS), finance

(PhD), general program (MS), healthcare management (MS), human resource management (MS), human resources management (PhD), information systems management (PhD), international business (MS), leadership (MS), leadership and organizational change (PhD), marketing (MS), project management (MS), strategy and operations (MS); managerial accounting (Graduate Certificate); marketing (MBA, MS, DBA); project management (MBA, MS, DBA); self-designed (MBA, DBA); social impact management (DBA); technology entrepreneurship (DBA). *Accreditation:* ACBSP. *Program availability:* Part-time, evening/weekend, online only, 100% online. *Degree requirements:* For master's, thesis (for some programs), residency (for EMBA); for doctorate, thesis/dissertation (for some programs), residency. *Entrance requirements:* For master's, bachelor's degree or higher; minimum GPA of 2.5; official transcripts; goal statement (for some programs); access to computer and Internet; for doctorate, master's degree or higher; three years of related professional or academic experience (preferred); minimum GPA of 3.0; goal statement and current resume (for select programs); official transcripts; access to computer and Internet; for other advanced degree, relevant work experience; access to computer and Internet. Additional exam requirements/recommendations for international students: Required—TOEFL (minimum score 550 paper-based, 79 iBT), IELTS (minimum score 6.5), Michigan English Language Assessment Battery (minimum score 82), or PTE (minimum score 53). Electronic applications accepted.

Walla Walla University, Graduate Studies, Center for Cinema, Religion, and Worldview, College Place, WA 99324. Offers Web and interactive media (MA). *Entrance requirements:* For master's, three professional references, transcripts, personal statement. *Application deadline:* For fall admission, 8/15 for domestic students. Application fee: $50. *Unit head:* Lynelle Ellis, Director, 509-527-2843, Fax: 509-527-2237, E-mail: lynelle.ellis@wallawalla.edu. *Application contact:* Rachel Scribner, Coordinator, 509-527-2832, Fax: 509-527-2237, E-mail: rachel.scribner@wallawalla.edu.
Website: https://www.wallawalla.edu/academics/grad-studies/cinema-religion-worldview/

Washington State University, The Edward R. Murrow College of Communication, Pullman, WA 99164-2520. Offers communication (MA, PhD); strategic communication (MA). MA in strategic communication offered at the Global (online) campus. *Degree requirements:* For master's, comprehensive exam (for some programs), thesis optional, oral exam; for doctorate, comprehensive exam, thesis/dissertation. *Entrance requirements:* For master's, GRE General Test, minimum GPA of 3.25, 3 letters of recommendation; for doctorate, GRE General Test, minimum undergraduate GPA of 3.25, graduate 3.5; MA in communication; 3 letters of recommendation. Additional exam requirements/recommendations for international students: Required—TOEFL (minimum score 580 paper-based). Electronic applications accepted. *Faculty research:* Communication technology, health communication, science communication, political communication, intercultural communication.

Wayne State College, School of Education and Counseling, Department of Educational Foundations and Leadership, Program in Curriculum and Instruction, Wayne, NE 68787. Offers alternative education (MSE); business and information technology education (MSE); communication arts education (MSE); early childhood education (MSE); elementary education (MSE); English as a second language (MSE); English education (MSE); family and consumer sciences education (MSE); industrial technology and vocational education (MSE); learning communities (MSE); mathematics education (MSE); music education (MSE); science education (MSE); social science education (MSE). *Accreditation:* NCATE. *Program availability:* Part-time, evening/weekend. *Degree requirements:* For master's, comprehensive exam, thesis optional. *Entrance requirements:* For master's, GRE General Test. Additional exam requirements/recommendations for international students: Required—TOEFL (minimum score 550 paper-based).

Wayne State University, College of Fine, Performing and Communication Arts, Department of Communication, Detroit, MI 48202. Offers communication (PhD), including democratic participation and culture, identity and representation, media, society and culture, risk, crisis and conflict, wellness, work life and relationships; communication and new media (Graduate Certificate); communication studies (MA); dispute resolution (MADR, Graduate Certificate), including community and urban studies (MADR), conflict area studies (MADR), health and family (MADR), international conflict and cooperation (MADR), professional practice (MADR), theory of conflict (MADR), workplace (MADR); health communication (Graduate Certificate); journalism (MA); media arts (MA); media studies (MA); public relations and organizational communication (MA); JD/MADR. Doctoral program admits for fall only. *Program availability:* Online learning. *Faculty:* 21. *Students:* 63 full-time (35 women), 87 part-time (55 women); includes 54 minority (39 Black or African American, non-Hispanic/Latino; 2 Asian, non-Hispanic/Latino; 7 Hispanic/Latino; 6 Two or more races, non-Hispanic/Latino), 10 international. Average age 34. 153 applicants, 39% accepted, 27 enrolled. In 2017, 26 master's, 7 doctorates, 8 other advanced degrees awarded. *Degree requirements:* For master's, thesis (for some programs), thesis or essay; for doctorate, thesis/dissertation. *Entrance requirements:* For master's, GRE (for MA if undergraduate GPA less than 3.2), personal statement; BA or BS in communication or related field with minimum upper-division GPA of 3.2 and minimum upper-division undergraduate GPA of 3.0, and sample of academic writing (for MA); undergraduate degree with minimum upper-division GPA of 3.0 and three letters of recommendation (for MADR); for doctorate, GRE, undergraduate degree in communication or related field; master's degree in communication or related field with minimum GPA of 3.5; letters of recommendation; personal statement; sample of written scholarship. Additional exam requirements/recommendations for international students: Required—TOEFL (minimum score 100 iBT), IELTS, TWE. Application fee: $50. Electronic applications accepted. *Expenses:* Contact institution. *Financial support:* In 2017–18, 57 students received support, including 5 fellowships with tuition reimbursements available (averaging $17,400 per year), 2 research assistantships with tuition reimbursements available (averaging $20,388 per year), 20 teaching assistantships with tuition reimbursements available (averaging $18,534 per year); scholarships/grants and unspecified assistantships also available. Financial award applicants required to submit FAFSA. *Faculty research:* Democratic participation and culture; identity and representation; media, society and culture; risk, crisis and conflict; wellness, work life, and relationships. *Unit head:* Dr. Lee Wilkins, Professor and Chair, 313-577-2943, E-mail: eh8899@wayne.edu. *Application contact:* E-mail: communication@wayne.edu.
Website: http://comm.wayne.edu/

Weber State University, Telitha E. Lindquist College of Arts and Humanities, Department of Communication, Ogden, UT 84408-1001. Offers MPC. *Program availability:* Part-time, evening/weekend. *Faculty:* 10 full-time (7 women). *Students:* 14 full-time (10 women), 42 part-time (25 women); includes 7 minority (1 Black or African American, non-Hispanic/Latino; 5 Hispanic/Latino; 1 Two or more races, non-Hispanic/Latino). Average age 34. In 2017, 15 master's awarded. *Degree requirements:* For master's, thesis optional. *Entrance requirements:* For master's, GRE. Additional exam requirements/recommendations for international students: Required—TOEFL (minimum score 550 paper-based; 85 iBT). *Application deadline:* For fall admission, 4/1 for domestic students. Application fee: $60 ($90 for international students). Electronic

applications accepted. *Expenses:* Tuition, state resident: full-time $7283. Tuition, nonresident: full-time $17,166. *Required fees:* $898. Tuition and fees vary according to program. *Financial support:* In 2017–18, 4 students received support. Scholarships/grants and tuition waivers (full and partial) available. Financial award application deadline: 4/1; financial award applicants required to submit FAFSA. *Unit head:* Dr. Sarah Steimel, Program Director, 801-626-6535, Fax: 801-626-7760, E-mail: sarahsteimel@weber.edu. *Application contact:* Shari Love, Office Specialist, 801-626-7499, Fax: 801-626-7975, E-mail: slove@weber.edu.
Website: http://www.weber.edu/mpc

Webster University, School of Communications, St. Louis, MO 63119-3194. Offers MA. *Program availability:* Part-time, evening/weekend, online learning. *Degree requirements:* For master's, thesis (for some programs). *Entrance requirements:* For master's, 36 hours of graduate course work. Additional exam requirements/recommendations for international students: Required—TOEFL.

Webster University, School of Education, Department of Multidisciplinary Studies, St. Louis, MO 63119-3194. Offers applied educational psychology (MA, Ed S); communication arts (MA); early childhood education (MA, MAT); education and innovation (MA); educational technology (MET); elementary education (MAT); mathematics for educators (MA); middle school education (MAT); multidisciplinary studies (MAT); multimodal literacy for global impact (MA); reading (MA); secondary school education (MAT); special education (MA, MAT); teaching English as a second language (MA); transformative learning in the global community (Ed S). *Program availability:* Part-time. *Entrance requirements:* For master's, minimum GPA of 2.5. Additional exam requirements/recommendations for international students: Required—TOEFL.

West Chester University of Pennsylvania, College of Arts and Humanities, Department of Communication Studies, West Chester, PA 19383. Offers MA. *Program availability:* Part-time, evening/weekend. *Students:* 9 full-time (6 women), 13 part-time (8 women); includes 6 minority (4 Black or African American, non-Hispanic/Latino; 1 Hispanic/Latino; 1 Two or more races, non-Hispanic/Latino). Average age 30. 11 applicants, 82% accepted, 6 enrolled. In 2017, 8 master's awarded. *Degree requirements:* For master's, comprehensive exam, thesis optional. *Entrance requirements:* For master's, GRE General Test (minimum scores in two of three tested areas in 50th percentile) or GPA of 3.5 or better, minimum GPA of 2.8 overall, 3.0 in major; writing sample; statement of goals; two letters of reference; courses or experience that indicate skill in public speaking, communication theory, and communication (or related) research. Additional exam requirements/recommendations for international students: Required—TOEFL or IELTS. *Application deadline:* For fall admission, 5/15 for international students; for spring admission, 10/1 for international students. Applications are processed on a rolling basis. Application fee: $50. Electronic applications accepted. *Expenses:* Tuition, state resident: full-time $9000; part-time $500 per credit. Tuition, nonresident: full-time $13,500; part-time $750 per credit. *Required fees:* $2959; $149.79 per credit. *Financial support:* Scholarships/grants and unspecified assistantships available. Financial award application deadline: 2/15; financial award applicants required to submit FAFSA. *Faculty research:* Rhetorical communication, media/social media, intercultural communication, interpersonal communication, and organization communication. *Unit head:* Dr. Denise M. Polk, Chair, 610-436-2500, E-mail: dpolk@wcupa.edu. *Application contact:* Dr. Matthew R. Meier, Graduate Coordinator, 610-436-6987, E-mail: mmeier@wcupa.edu.
Website: http://communicationstudies.org/

Western Illinois University, School of Graduate Studies, College of Fine Arts and Communication, Department of Communication, Macomb, IL 61455-1390. Offers MA. *Program availability:* Part-time. *Students:* 20 full-time (14 women), 5 part-time (4 women); includes 12 minority (8 Black or African American, non-Hispanic/Latino; 4 Hispanic/Latino). Average age 24. 25 applicants, 96% accepted, 13 enrolled. In 2017, 9 master's awarded. *Degree requirements:* For master's, comprehensive exam (for some programs), thesis or alternative. *Entrance requirements:* Additional exam requirements/recommendations for international students: Required—TOEFL (minimum score 580 paper-based; 92 iBT). *Application deadline:* Applications are processed on a rolling basis. Application fee: $30. Electronic applications accepted. *Financial support:* In 2017–18, research assistantships with full tuition reimbursements (averaging $7,544 per year), teaching assistantships with full tuition reimbursements (averaging $8,688 per year) were awarded; unspecified assistantships also available. Financial award applicants required to submit FAFSA. *Unit head:* Dr. Pete Jorgensen, Chairperson, 309-298-1507. *Application contact:* Dr. Nancy Parsons, Associate Provost and Director of Graduate Studies, 309-298-1806, Fax: 309-298-2345, E-mail: grad-office@wiu.edu.
Website: http://wiu.edu/comm

Western Kentucky University, Graduate Studies, Potter College of Arts and Letters, Department of Communication, Bowling Green, KY 42101. Offers communication (MA); organizational communication (Graduate Certificate). *Program availability:* Part-time, evening/weekend. *Degree requirements:* For master's, comprehensive exam, thesis optional, final exam. *Entrance requirements:* For master's, GRE General Test, minimum GPA of 2.75. Additional exam requirements/recommendations for international students: Required—TOEFL (minimum score 555 paper-based; 79 iBT). *Faculty research:* Public rhetoric and public address organization communication, teamwork in communication, intercultural crisis communication.

Western Michigan University, Graduate College, College of Arts and Sciences, School of Communication, Kalamazoo, MI 49008. Offers MA.

Western New England University, College of Arts and Sciences, Program in Communication, Springfield, MA 01119. Offers public relations (MA). *Program availability:* Part-time, evening/weekend. *Faculty:* 6 full-time (5 women). *Students:* 11 part-time (6 women); includes 3 minority (1 Black or African American, non-Hispanic/Latino; 1 Asian, non-Hispanic/Latino; 1 Hispanic/Latino). Average age 31. 7 applicants, 100% accepted, 5 enrolled. In 2017, 7 master's awarded. *Degree requirements:* For master's, independent study or thesis. *Entrance requirements:* For master's, official transcript, personal statement, resume, three letters of recommendation. Additional exam requirements/recommendations for international students: Required—TOEFL (minimum score 79 iBT). *Application deadline:* Applications are processed on a rolling basis. Application fee: $30. Electronic applications accepted. *Expenses:* Contact institution. *Financial support:* Application deadline: 4/15; applicants required to submit FAFSA. *Unit head:* Dr. Saeed Ghahramani, Dean, 413-782-1218, Fax: 413-796-2118, E-mail: sghahram@wne.edu. *Application contact:* Matthew Fox, Director of Graduate Admissions, Enrollment Management Group, 413-782-1410, Fax: 413-782-1777, E-mail: study@wne.edu.
Website: http://www1.wne.edu/academics/graduate/ma-communication.cfm

Westminster College, Program in Professional Communication, Salt Lake City, UT 84105-3697. Offers MPC, MSC. *Faculty:* 3 full-time (2 women), 2 part-time/adjunct (both women). *Students:* 29 full-time (19 women), 6 part-time (all women); includes 11 minority (2 Asian, non-Hispanic/Latino; 5 Hispanic/Latino; 4 Two or more races, non-Hispanic/Latino), 1 international. Average age 34. 18 applicants, 89% accepted, 15 enrolled. In 2017, 22 master's awarded. *Degree requirements:* For master's, capstone project. *Entrance requirements:* For master's, GRE, resume, personal statement of

intent, official transcripts, two letters of recommendation, writing sample. Additional exam requirements/recommendations for international students: Required—TOEFL (minimum score 84 iBT), IELTS (minimum score 7). *Application deadline:* Applications are processed on a rolling basis. Application fee: $50. Electronic applications accepted. Application fee is waived when completed online. *Expenses:* $850 per credit hour (for MSC); $1,010 per credit hour (for MPC); $13 student fee per credit hour. *Financial support:* In 2017–18, 13 students received support. Career-related internships or fieldwork, scholarships/grants, unspecified assistantships, and tuition remission available. Financial award applicants required to submit FAFSA. *Faculty research:* Diversity in higher education, communication pedagogy, mass media law and ethics, impact of new technologies on society, rhetorical theory, feminism and popular culture, critical communication pedagogy. *Unit head:* Dr. Curtis Newbold, Director, 801-832-2827, Fax: 801-832-3102, E-mail: cnewbold@westminstercollege.edu. *Application contact:* Lauren Erlacher, Associate Director, Graduate Admissions, 801-832-2208, Fax: 801-832-3101, E-mail: lerlacher@westminstercollege.edu.
Website: https://www.westminstercollege.edu/graduate/programs

West Texas A&M University, College of Fine Arts and Humanities, Department of Communication, Canyon, TX 79015. Offers MA. *Program availability:* Part-time. *Degree requirements:* For master's, comprehensive exam, thesis optional. *Entrance requirements:* For master's, GRE General Test, 24 hours of undergraduate communications courses, letter of recommendation, interview with communication advisor. Additional exam requirements/recommendations for international students: Required—TOEFL (minimum score 550 paper-based). Electronic applications accepted. *Faculty research:* Comparison student learning in basic public speaking in traditional versus online format, impact of supervisor immediacy and power on organizational outcomes, storytelling, gender, nonverbal.

West Virginia University, Eberly College of Arts and Sciences, Morgantown, WV 26506. Offers biology (MS, PhD); chemistry (MS, PhD); communication studies (MA, PhD); computational statistics (PhD); creative writing (MFA); English (MA, PhD); forensic and investigative science (MS); forensic science (PhD); geography (MA); geology (MA, PhD); history (MA, PhD); legal studies (MLS); math (MS); physics (MS, PhD); political science (MA, PhD); professional writing and editing (MA); psychology (MA); public administration (MPA); social work (MSW); sociology (MA, PhD); statistics (MS). *Program availability:* Part-time, evening/weekend, online learning. *Students:* 831 full-time (437 women), 236 part-time (142 women); includes 112 minority (35 Black or African American, non-Hispanic/Latino; 15 Asian, non-Hispanic/Latino; 29 Hispanic/Latino; 33 Two or more races, non-Hispanic/Latino), 235 international. Terminal master's awarded for partial completion of doctoral program. *Degree requirements:* For master's, thesis (for some programs); for doctorate, comprehensive exam, thesis/dissertation. *Entrance requirements:* For master's and doctorate, GRE. Additional exam requirements/recommendations for international students: Required—TOEFL (minimum score 600 paper-based); Recommended—TWE. *Application deadline:* For spring admission, 2/15 priority date for domestic and international students. Applications are processed on a rolling basis. Application fee: $45. Electronic applications accepted. *Expenses:* Tuition, state resident: full-time $9450. Tuition, nonresident: full-time $24,390. *Financial support:* Fellowships with full tuition reimbursements, research assistantships with full tuition reimbursements, teaching assistantships with full tuition reimbursements, career-related internships or fieldwork, Federal Work-Study, institutionally sponsored loans, scholarships/grants, health care benefits, tuition waivers (full and partial), unspecified assistantships, and administrative assistantships available. Financial award application deadline: 2/1; financial award applicants required to submit FAFSA. *Faculty research:* Humanities, social sciences, life science, physical sciences, mathematics. *Unit head:* Dr. Mary Ellen Mazey, Dean, 304-293-4611, Fax: 304-293-6858, E-mail: mary.mazey@mail.wvu.edu. *Application contact:* Dr. Fred L. King, Associate Dean for Graduate Studies, 304-293-4611 Ext. 5205, Fax: 304-293-6858, E-mail: fred.king@mail.wvu.edu.
Website: http://www.as.wvu.edu/

Wichita State University, Graduate School, Fairmount College of Liberal Arts and Sciences, Elliott School of Communication, Wichita, KS 67260. Offers MA. *Program availability:* Part-time. *Unit head:* Dr. Jeffrey Jarman, Interim Director, 316-978-3185, Fax: 316-978-3006, E-mail: jeffrey.jarman@wichita.edu. *Application contact:* Jordan Oleson, Admissions Coordinator, 316-978-3095, E-mail: jordan.oleson@wichita.edu.
Website: http://www.wichita.edu/esc

Wilfrid Laurier University, Faculty of Graduate and Postdoctoral Studies, Faculty of Arts, Department of Communication Studies, Waterloo, ON N2L 3C5, Canada. Offers media, technology and culture (MA); visual communication and culture (MA). *Degree requirements:* For master's, thesis optional. *Entrance requirements:* For master's, honours BA in communication studies or a cognate discipline from an approved university with a minimum B+ overall in last two years of study and in undergraduate major. Additional exam requirements/recommendations for international students: Required—TOEFL (minimum score 89 iBT). Electronic applications accepted. *Faculty research:* Visual communication and culture, media, technology and culture.

York University, Faculty of Graduate Studies, Program in Communication and Culture, Toronto, ON M3J 1P3, Canada. Offers MA, PhD. Program offered jointly with Ryerson University. *Degree requirements:* For master's, thesis or alternative; for doctorate, comprehensive exam, thesis/dissertation. Electronic applications accepted.

Arts Journalism

Academy of Art University, Graduate Programs, Program in Fashion Journalism, San Francisco, CA 94105-3410. Offers MA. *Program availability:* Part-time, evening/weekend, 100% online. *Faculty:* 26 full-time (17 women), 54 part-time/adjunct (44 women). *Students:* 26 full-time (24 women), 26 part-time (24 women); includes 17 minority (12 Black or African American, non-Hispanic/Latino; 4 Asian, non-Hispanic/Latino; 1 Two or more races, non-Hispanic/Latino), 15 international. Average age 29. 21 applicants, 100% accepted, 16 enrolled. In 2017, 20 master's awarded. *Degree requirements:* For master's, final review. *Entrance requirements:* For master's, statement of intent; resume; portfolio/reel; official college transcripts. *Application deadline:* Applications are processed on a rolling basis. Application fee: $50. Electronic applications accepted. *Expenses: Tuition:* Part-time $982 per unit. *Financial support:* Career-related internships or fieldwork, Federal Work-Study, and scholarships/grants available. Financial award application deadline: 8/10; financial award applicants required to submit FAFSA. *Unit head:* 800-544-ARTS, E-mail: info@academyart.edu. *Application contact:* 800-544-ARTS, E-mail: info@academyart.edu.
Website: http://www.academyart.edu/academics/fashion/graduate-degrees

School of the Art Institute of Chicago, Graduate Division, Program in New Arts Journalism, Chicago, IL 60603-3103. Offers MA. *Entrance requirements:* Additional exam requirements/recommendations for international students: Required—TOEFL, IELTS.

Syracuse University, S. I. Newhouse School of Public Communications, MA Program in Arts Journalism, Syracuse, NY 13244. Offers MA. *Accreditation:* ACEJMC. *Students:* Average age 24. *Entrance requirements:* For master's, GRE General Test, resume, official transcripts, personal statement, three letters of recommendation. Additional exam requirements/recommendations for international students: Required—TOEFL (minimum score 600 paper-based; 100 iBT). *Application deadline:* For summer admission, 1/15 for domestic students, 1/15 priority date for international students. Application fee: $45. Electronic applications accepted. *Financial support:* Fellowships with full tuition reimbursements, research assistantships with partial tuition reimbursements, and teaching assistantships with partial tuition reimbursements available. Financial award application deadline: 2/1. *Faculty research:* Arts journalism, communications, online journalism, television, radio, film. *Unit head:* Eric Grode, Director, 315-443-2305, E-mail: ejgrode@syr.edu. *Application contact:* Martha Coria, Graduate Records Office, 315-443-4039, Fax: 315-443-1834, E-mail: pcgrad@syr.edu.
Website: http://newhouse.syr.edu/academics/degrees/masters/arts-journalism-masters

Broadcast Journalism

The American University in Cairo, School of Global Affairs and Public Policy, Cairo, Egypt. Offers gender and women's studies (MA); global affairs (MGA); international and comparative law (LL M); international human rights law (MA); journalism and mass communication (MA); Middle East studies (MA); migration and refugee studies (MA, Diploma); public administration (MPA); public policy (MPP); television and digital journalism (MA). *Program availability:* Part-time, evening/weekend. *Faculty:* 26 full-time (11 women), 4 part-time/adjunct (3 women). *Students:* 65 full-time (50 women), 201 part-time (136 women), 39 international. Average age 29. 357 applicants, 51% accepted, 72 enrolled. In 2017, 94 master's awarded. *Degree requirements:* For master's, comprehensive exam (for some programs), thesis (for some programs). *Entrance requirements:* Additional exam requirements/recommendations for international students: Required—TOEFL (minimum score 450 paper-based; 45 iBT), IELTS (minimum score 5). *Application deadline:* For fall admission, 2/1 for domestic and international students; for spring admission, 10/15 for domestic and international students. Applications are processed on a rolling basis. Application fee: $85. Electronic applications accepted. *Expenses:* Contact institution. *Financial support:* Fellowships with partial tuition reimbursements, scholarships/grants, and unspecified assistantships available. Financial award application deadline: 3/10. *Faculty research:* Law, media and journalism; public policy and public administration; gender studies; Middle East Studies; global affairs; refugees studies. *Unit head:* Dr. Nabil Fahmy, Dean, 20-2-2615-2671, E-mail: nfahmy@aucegypt.edu. *Application contact:* Maha Hegazi, Director for Graduate Admissions, 20-2-2615-1462, E-mail: mahahegazi@aucegypt.edu.
Website: http://www.aucegypt.edu/GAPP/Pages/default.aspx

Northwestern University, Medill School of Journalism, Media, and Integrated Marketing Communications, Evanston, IL 60208. Offers integrated marketing communications (MSIMC), including brand strategy, content marketing, direct and interactive marketing, marketing analytics, strategic communications; interactive publishing (MSJ); magazine writing/editing (MSJ); reporting (MSJ); video/broadcast (MSJ). *Entrance requirements:* For master's, GRE General Test, GMAT or LSAT (for MSJ). Additional exam requirements/recommendations for international students: Required—TOEFL. Electronic applications accepted. *Expenses:* Contact institution. *Faculty research:* Web business journalism, cultural stereotypes, voter apathy, digital television.

Quinnipiac University, School of Communications, Program in Journalism, Hamden, CT 06518-1940. Offers journalism (MS), including broadcast/multimedia, writing; sports journalism (MS), including broadcast/multimedia. *Program availability:* Part-time, evening/weekend. *Faculty:* 5 full-time (4 women), 6 part-time/adjunct (1 woman). *Students:* 3 full-time (1 woman), 4 part-time (2 women); includes 1 minority (Hispanic/Latino), 1 international. 9 applicants, 56% accepted, 2 enrolled. In 2017, 9 master's awarded. *Degree requirements:* For master's, project. *Entrance requirements:* For master's, minimum GPA of 3.0, portfolio or writing sample. Additional exam requirements/recommendations for international students: Required—TOEFL (minimum score 575 paper-based; 90 iBT), IELTS (minimum score 6.5). *Application deadline:* For fall admission, 7/30 priority date for domestic students, 4/15 priority date for international students. Applications are processed on a rolling basis. Application fee: $45. Electronic applications accepted. *Financial support:* Federal Work-Study, scholarships/grants, and unspecified assistantships available. Financial award application deadline: 6/1; financial award applicants required to submit FAFSA. *Faculty research:* Journalism history, federal law enforcement and journalism, social media and journalism, online journalism, sports journalism, American football history and media, journalism and film, McCarthyism and journalism. *Unit head:* Phillip Simon, Program Director, 203-582-8672, E-mail: graduate@qu.edu. *Application contact:* Office of Graduate Admissions, 800-462-

1944, Fax: 203-582-3443, E-mail: graduate@qu.edu.
Website: http://www.qu.edu/gradjournalism

Quinnipiac University, School of Communications, Program in Sports Journalism, Hamden, CT 06518-1940. Offers MS. *Program availability:* Part-time, evening/weekend. *Faculty:* 5 full-time (4 women), 6 part-time/adjunct (1 woman). *Students:* 13 full-time (5 women), 5 part-time (0 women); includes 5 minority (4 Black or African American, non-Hispanic/Latino; 1 Hispanic/Latino). 31 applicants, 87% accepted, 16 enrolled. In 2017, 9 master's awarded. *Entrance requirements:* For master's, minimum GPA of 3.0, portfolio or writing sample. Additional exam requirements/recommendations for international students: Required—TOEFL (minimum score 575 paper-based; 90 iBT), IELTS (minimum score 6.5). *Application deadline:* For fall admission, 7/30 priority date for domestic students, 4/30 priority date for international students. Applications are processed on a rolling basis. Application fee: $45. Electronic applications accepted. *Financial support:* Federal Work-Study, scholarships/grants, and unspecified assistantships available. Financial award application deadline: 6/1; financial award applicants required to submit FAFSA. *Unit head:* Phillip Simon, Director of Graduate Programs, School of Communications, 203-582-8672, E-mail: graduate@qu.edu. *Application contact:* Office of Graduate Admissions, 203-582-8672, Fax: 203-582-3443, E-mail: graduate@qu.edu.
Website: http://www.qu.edu/gradsportsjournalism

Syracuse University, S. I. Newhouse School of Public Communications, MS Program in Broadcast and Digital Journalism, Syracuse, NY 13244. Offers MS. *Accreditation:* ACEJMC. *Entrance requirements:* For master's, GRE General Test, resume, official transcripts, personal statement, three letters of recommendation. Additional exam requirements/recommendations for international students: Required—TOEFL (minimum score 100 iBT). *Application deadline:* For summer admission, 1/15 for domestic and international students. Application fee: $45. Electronic applications accepted. *Financial support:* Fellowships with full tuition reimbursements, research assistantships with partial tuition reimbursements, and teaching assistantships with partial tuition reimbursements available. Financial award application deadline: 2/1. *Faculty research:* Electronic journalism, broadcast and digital journalism, anchoring in traditional and new platforms, producing. *Unit head:* Prof. Chris Tuohey, Chair, 315-443-4118, E-mail: cptuohey@syr.edu. *Application contact:* Martha Coria, Graduate Records Office, 315-443-5749, Fax: 315-443-1834, E-mail: pcgrad@syr.edu.
Website: http://newhouse.syr.edu/

University of Maryland, College Park, Academic Affairs, Philip Merrill College of Journalism, College Park, MD 20742. Offers broadcast journalism (MA); journalism (MA); journalism and media studies (PhD); online news (MA); public affairs reporting (MA). *Accreditation:* ACEJMC (one or more programs are accredited). *Program availability:* Part-time, evening/weekend. *Degree requirements:* For doctorate, thesis/dissertation, preliminary written and oral comprehensive exams. *Entrance requirements:* For master's and doctorate, GRE General Test, minimum GPA of 3.0, 3 letters of recommendation. Additional exam requirements/recommendations for international students: Required—TOEFL. Electronic applications accepted. *Faculty research:* Mass communication theory, specialized journalism, new telecommunication technologies, press integration.

University of Miami, Graduate School, School of Communication, Coral Gables, FL 33124. Offers communication (PhD); communication studies (MA); film studies (MA, PhD); motion pictures (MFA), including production, producing, and screenwriting; print journalism (MA); public relations (MA); Spanish language journalism (MA); television broadcast journalism (MA). *Program availability:* Part-time. *Degree requirements:* For master's, comprehensive exam (for some programs), thesis (for some programs); for doctorate, comprehensive exam, thesis/dissertation. *Entrance requirements:* For master's, GRE General Test; for doctorate, GRE General Test, master's thesis or scholarly research. Additional exam requirements/recommendations for international students: Required—TOEFL (minimum score 600 paper-based; 100 iBT). Electronic applications accepted. *Faculty research:* Communication studies, mass communication, international/interpersonal communication, film studies, journalism.

University of the Sacred Heart, Graduate Programs, Department of Communication, San Juan, PR 00914-0383. Offers contemporary culture and media (MA); digital journalism (MA, Certificate); editing for media (MA, Certificate); public relations (MA, Certificate); publicity (MA, Certificate); scriptwriting (MA, Certificate). *Program availability:* Part-time, evening/weekend. *Degree requirements:* For master's, thesis.

Corporate and Organizational Communication

American University, School of Communication, Division of Public Communication, Washington, DC 20016-8001. Offers advocacy and social impact (MA); corporate communication and reputation management (MA); digital strategies and analytics (MA); poltical communication (MA); strategic communication (MA). *Accreditation:* ACEJMC. *Program availability:* Part-time, evening/weekend. *Faculty:* 23 full-time (15 women), 18 part-time/adjunct (10 women). *Students:* 52 full-time (42 women), 34 part-time (20 women); includes 31 minority (19 Black or African American, non-Hispanic/Latino; 4 Asian, non-Hispanic/Latino; 7 Hispanic/Latino; 1 Two or more races, non-Hispanic/Latino), 6 international. 282 applicants, 38% accepted, 55 enrolled. In 2017, 105 master's awarded. *Degree requirements:* For master's, comprehensive exam, thesis or alternative. *Entrance requirements:* Additional exam requirements/recommendations for international students: Required—TOEFL (minimum score 600 paper-based; 100 iBT), IELTS (minimum score 7). *Application deadline:* For fall admission, 2/1 priority date for domestic and international students. Applications are processed on a rolling basis. Application fee: $50. Electronic applications accepted. *Expenses: Tuition:* Full-time $29,556. *Required fees:* $690. Tuition and fees vary according to course load and program. *Financial support:* In 2017–18, 45 students received support, including 11 research assistantships with partial tuition reimbursements available (averaging $13,000 per year), 15 teaching assistantships with partial tuition reimbursements available (averaging $13,000 per year); career-related internships or fieldwork, Federal Work-Study, institutionally sponsored loans, scholarships/grants, tuition waivers (partial), and unspecified assistantships also available. Financial award application deadline: 2/1; financial award applicants required to submit FAFSA. *Faculty research:* Litigation and public relations, cross-cultural and intercultural communication, statistical public relations, African-Americans and women in public communication, international public relations. *Unit head:* Pallavi Kumar, Public Communication Division Director, 202-885-2047, E-mail: kumar@american.edu. *Application contact:* Christine Rials, Assistant Director of Graduate Admissions, 202-885-2040, Fax: 202-885-2019, E-mail: gradcomm@american.edu.
Website: http://www.american.edu/soc/communication/degrees/MA-SCOM.cfm

Ashland University, College of Arts and Sciences, Program in Corporate and Strategic Communication, Ashland, OH 44805-3702. Offers communication (MA). *Program availability:* Online learning. *Application deadline:* Applications are processed on a rolling basis. Electronic applications accepted. *Expenses: Tuition:* Full-time $9621; part-time $4707 per credit hour. *Required fees:* $15 per semester. *Unit head:* Shawn Orr, Interim Director, 419-207-6929, E-mail: sorr3@ashland.edu. *Application contact:* Bernie Bannin, Director, Graduate, Online, and Adult Admissions, 419-289-5291, E-mail: grad-admissions@ashland.edu.

Austin Peay State University, College of Graduate Studies, College of Arts and Letters, Department of Communication, Clarksville, TN 37044. Offers marketing communication (MA); media management (MA). *Program availability:* Part-time, evening/weekend, online learning. *Faculty:* 4 full-time (2 women), 1 (woman) part-time/adjunct. *Students:* 45 part-time (32 women); includes 14 minority (11 Black or African American, non-Hispanic/Latino; 2 Hispanic/Latino; 1 Two or more races, non-Hispanic/Latino). Average age 29. 27 applicants, 96% accepted, 19 enrolled. In 2017, 27 master's awarded. *Degree requirements:* For master's, comprehensive exam, thesis (for some programs). *Entrance requirements:* For master's, GRE General Test, minimum GPA of 2.5. Additional exam requirements/recommendations for international students: Required—TOEFL (minimum score 500 paper-based). *Application deadline:* For fall admission, 8/8 priority date for domestic students. Applications are processed on a rolling basis. Application fee: $45 ($55 for international students). Electronic applications accepted. *Expenses:* Tuition, state resident: full-time $7686; part-time $427 per credit hour. Tuition, nonresident: full-time $20,268; part-time $1126 per credit hour. *Required fees:* $1529; $76.45 per credit hour. *Financial support:* Research assistantships with full tuition reimbursements, career-related internships or fieldwork, Federal Work-Study, institutionally sponsored loans, scholarships/grants, and unspecified assistantships available. Support available to part-time students. Financial award application deadline: 4/1; financial award applicants required to submit FAFSA. *Unit head:* Dr. Kathy Heuston, Interim Chair, 931-221-7554, Fax: 931-221-7265, E-mail: leek@apsu.edu. *Application contact:* Megan Mitchell, Coordinator of Graduate Admissions, 931-221-6189, Fax: 931-221-7641, E-mail: mitchellm@apsu.edu.
Website: http://www.apsu.edu/communication/index.php

Barry University, College of Arts and Sciences, Department of Communication, Miami Shores, FL 33161-6695. Offers broadcasting (Certificate); communication (MA), including broadcast communication, public relations and corporate communications; organizational communication (MS). *Program availability:* Part-time, evening/weekend. *Degree requirements:* For master's, thesis (for some programs). *Entrance requirements:* For master's, GRE General Test, MAT, minimum GPA of 3.0. Electronic applications accepted. *Faculty research:* Organizational communication, broadcast communication, intercultural communication, advertising, leadership.

Baruch College of the City University of New York, Weissman School of Arts and Sciences, Program in Corporate Communication, New York, NY 10010-5585. Offers MA. *Program availability:* Part-time, evening/weekend. *Degree requirements:* For master's, thesis or alternative. *Entrance requirements:* For master's, GRE/GMAT, 3 letters of recommendation; personal essay; resume; official transcripts. Additional exam requirements/recommendations for international students: Required—TOEFL. Electronic applications accepted. *Faculty research:* Media history; cultural studies; film studies; social implications of contemporary digital media; improving public argument; intercultural and international aspects of communication; intercultural friendship formation; use of technology in communication education; strategic corporate communication; immersive spectatorship; global corporate communication; communications strategy development; public and media relations; crisis management; work and life balance.

Bellevue University, Graduate School, College of Arts and Sciences, Bellevue, NE 68005-3098. Offers clinical counseling (MS); healthcare administration (MHA); human services (MA); international security and intelligence studies (MS); managerial communication (MA). *Program availability:* Online learning.

Boston University, Metropolitan College, Program in Gastronomy, Boston, MA 02215. Offers communications (MLA); history and culture (MLA). *Program availability:* Part-time, evening/weekend. *Faculty:* 3 full-time (2 women), 5 part-time/adjunct (3 women). *Students:* 5 full-time (all women), 68 part-time (58 women); includes 19 minority (6 Black or African American, non-Hispanic/Latino; 4 Asian, non-Hispanic/Latino; 7 Hispanic/Latino; 2 Two or more races, non-Hispanic/Latino), 8 international. Average age 29. 44 applicants, 93% accepted, 17 enrolled. In 2017, 27 master's awarded. *Entrance requirements:* Additional exam requirements/recommendations for international students: Required—TOEFL. *Application deadline:* Applications are processed on a rolling basis. Application fee: $85. Electronic applications accepted. *Expenses:* Contact institution. *Financial support:* In 2017–18, 5 research assistantships (averaging $4,200 per year) were awarded; career-related internships or fieldwork, scholarships/grants, and unspecified assistantships also available. Support available to part-time students. Financial award applicants required to submit FAFSA. *Faculty research:* Food studies. *Unit head:* Dr. Megan Elias, Associate Professor of the Practice and Director, 617-353-6916, Fax: 617-353-4130, E-mail: gastrmla@bu.edu. *Application contact:* Barbara Rotger, Program Manager, 617-353-6916, Fax: 617-353-4130, E-mail: brotger@bu.edu.
Website: http://www.bu.edu/met/gastronomy

Bowie State University, Graduate Programs, Program in Organizational Communication, Bowie, MD 20715-9465. Offers MA, Certificate. *Program availability:* Part-time, evening/weekend. *Degree requirements:* For master's, comprehensive exam, thesis optional, research paper. *Entrance requirements:* For master's, minimum GPA of 2.5. Electronic applications accepted. *Faculty research:* International telecommunications, developmental communications.

Bryant University, College of Arts and Sciences, Smithfield, RI 02917. Offers applied economics (MS, Graduate Certificate); communication (MA, Graduate Certificate), including general communication (MA), health care communication (MA), organizational communication (MA), professional communication (Graduate Certificate); organizational communication (Graduate Certificate), including managerial communication, public communication; sustainability practices (Graduate Certificate). *Program availability:* Part-time-only, evening/weekend. *Faculty:* 3 full-time (0 women), 2 part-time/adjunct (0 women). *Students:* 8 full-time (4 women), 10 part-time (8 women); includes 3 minority (2 Black or African American, non-Hispanic/Latino; 1 Two or more races, non-Hispanic/

Latino), 2 international. Average age 25. 25 applicants, 32% accepted, 6 enrolled. In 2017, 4 master's awarded. *Degree requirements:* For master's, thesis. *Entrance requirements:* For master's, GRE. Additional exam requirements/recommendations for international students: Required—TOEFL (minimum score 550 paper-based; 80 iBT). *Application deadline:* For fall admission, 8/15 for domestic and international students; for spring admission, 1/15 for domestic and international students; for summer admission, 5/15 for domestic and international students. Applications are processed on a rolling basis. Application fee: $80. Electronic applications accepted. *Expenses:* $932 per credit hour. *Financial support:* In 2017–18, 15 fellowships with full and partial tuition reimbursements (averaging $10,483 per year) were awarded; research assistantships, scholarships/grants, and unspecified assistantships also available. Financial award application deadline: 2/15; financial award applicants required to submit FAFSA. *Faculty research:* Mass media and social construction of reality; development and improvement of media literacy skills; sociocultural influences on cognition and learning in K-12 populations, oil pollution impacts on marine and estuarine microbial communities; wetlands ecology. *Unit head:* Bradford Martin, Dean, College of Arts and Sciences, 401-232-6929, E-mail: bmartin@bryant.edu. *Application contact:* Terri Rogers, Admission Assistant, Graduate School, 401-232-6230, E-mail: graduateprograms@bryant.edu.
Website: http://gradschool.bryant.edu/arts-and-sciences/

California State University, San Bernardino, Graduate Studies, College of Arts and Letters, Program in Communication Studies, San Bernardino, CA 92407. Offers communication studies (MA); integrated marketing communication (MA). *Faculty:* 6 full-time (3 women). *Students:* 7 full-time (all women), 30 part-time (19 women); includes 19 minority (4 Black or African American, non-Hispanic/Latino; 2 Asian, non-Hispanic/Latino; 12 Hispanic/Latino; 1 Two or more races, non-Hispanic/Latino), 3 international. Average age 31. 33 applicants, 52% accepted, 12 enrolled. In 2017, 3 master's awarded. *Degree requirements:* For master's, comprehensive exam. *Entrance requirements:* Additional exam requirements/recommendations for international students: Required—TOEFL. *Application deadline:* For fall admission, 5/15 for domestic students. Application fee: $55. *Unit head:* Ahlam Muhtaseb, Graduate Coordinator, 909-537-5897, Fax: 909-537-7585, E-mail: amuhtase@csusb.edu. *Application contact:* Dr. Dorota Huizinga, Dean of Graduate Studies, 909-537-3064, Fax: 909-537-7034, E-mail: dorota.huizinga@csusb.edu.

Canisius College, Graduate Division, College of Arts and Sciences, Department of Communication Studies, Buffalo, NY 14208-1098. Offers communication and leadership (MS). *Program availability:* Part-time, evening/weekend. *Faculty:* 1 (woman) full-time, 3 part-time/adjunct (2 women). *Students:* 6 full-time (4 women), 13 part-time (9 women); includes 3 minority (2 Black or African American, non-Hispanic/Latino; 1 Hispanic/Latino). Average age 27. 18 applicants, 72% accepted, 5 enrolled. In 2017, 10 master's awarded. *Degree requirements:* For master's, thesis. *Entrance requirements:* For master's, GRE (recommended), BA, minimum GPA of 3.0, official transcript of all college work, 2 letters of recommendation. Additional exam requirements/recommendations for international students: Required—TOEFL (minimum score 550 paper-based, 80 iBT), IELTS (minimum score 6.5), or CAEL (minimum score 70). *Application deadline:* For fall admission, 7/15 priority date for domestic students; for spring admission, 4/15 priority date for domestic students. Applications are processed on a rolling basis. Application fee: $0. Electronic applications accepted. *Expenses: Tuition:* Full-time $22,860; part-time $820 per credit. *Required fees:* $720; $25 per credit. $65 per semester. One-time fee: $425. *Financial support:* Career-related internships or fieldwork, Federal Work-Study, scholarships/grants, tuition waivers (partial), and unspecified assistantships available. Support available to part-time students. Financial award application deadline: 4/30; financial award applicants required to submit FAFSA. *Faculty research:* Conflict and communication, health and communication, leadership. *Unit head:* Dr. Rosanne L. Hartman, Graduate Program Director/Professor, Communication and Leadership, 716-888-2589, Fax: 716-888-3118, E-mail: hartmanr@canisius.edu.
Website: http://www.canisius.edu/graduate/

Carnegie Mellon University, Dietrich College of Humanities and Social Sciences, Department of English, Program in Professional Writing, Pittsburgh, PA 15213-3891. Offers editing and publishing (MAPW); policy and non-profit communication (MAPW); public and media relations/corporate communications (MAPW); science or healthcare communication (MAPW); technical writing (MAPW); writing for new media (MAPW); writing for print media (MAPW). *Program availability:* Part-time. *Entrance requirements:* For master's, GRE General Test. Additional exam requirements/recommendations for international students: Required—TOEFL, TWE.

City College of the City University of New York, Graduate School, Division of Humanities and the Arts, Department of Media and Communication Arts, Program in Branding and Integrated Communications, New York, NY 10031. Offers MPS. *Entrance requirements:* Additional exam requirements/recommendations for international students: Required—TOEFL (minimum score 90 iBT).

Columbia University, Graduate School of Business, MBA Program, New York, NY 10027. Offers accounting (MBA); decision, risk, and operations (MBA); entrepreneurship (MBA); finance and economics (MBA); healthcare and pharmaceutical management (MBA); human resource management (MBA); international business (MBA); leadership and ethics (MBA); management (MBA); marketing (MBA); media (MBA); private equity (MBA); real estate (MBA); social enterprise (MBA); value investing (MBA); DDS/MBA; JD/MBA; MBA/MIA; MBA/MPH; MBA/MS; MD/MBA. *Entrance requirements:* For master's, GMAT, 2 letters of recommendation. Additional exam requirements/recommendations for international students: Required—TOEFL. Electronic applications accepted. *Expenses:* Contact institution. *Faculty research:* Human decision making and behavioral research; real estate market and mortgage defaults; financial crisis and corporate governance; international business; security analysis and accounting.

Columbia University, School of Professional Studies, Program in Strategic Communications, New York, NY 10027. Offers MS. *Program availability:* Part-time, evening/weekend. *Entrance requirements:* For master's, minimum undergraduate GPA of 3.0. Additional exam requirements/recommendations for international students: Required—American Language Program placement test. Electronic applications accepted. *Expenses: Tuition:* Full-time $44,864; part-time $1704 per credit. *Required fees:* $2370 per semester. One-time fee: $105. *Faculty research:* Marketing communications, public relations, crisis management.

Concordia University, St. Paul, College of Business and Technology, St. Paul, MN 55104-5494. Offers business administration (MBA), including cyber-security leadership; health care management (MBA); human resource management (MA); information technology (MBA); leadership and management (MA); strategic communication management (MA). *Accreditation:* ACBSP. *Program availability:* Part-time, evening/weekend, 100% online, blended/hybrid learning. *Faculty:* 12 full-time (5 women), 33 part-time/adjunct (16 women). *Students:* 475 full-time (293 women), 35 part-time (17 women); includes 122 minority (57 Black or African American, non-Hispanic/Latino; 1 American Indian or Alaska Native, non-Hispanic/Latino; 34 Asian, non-Hispanic/Latino; 12 Hispanic/Latino; 1 Native Hawaiian or other Pacific Islander, non-Hispanic/Latino; 17 Two or more races, non-Hispanic/Latino), 47 international. Average age 33. 203 applicants, 70% accepted, 136 enrolled. In 2017, 172 master's awarded. *Degree requirements:* For master's, thesis (for some programs). *Entrance requirements:* For master's, official transcripts from regionally-accredited institution stating the conferral of a bachelor's degree with minimum cumulative GPA of 3.0; personal statement; professional resume. Additional exam requirements/recommendations for international students: Recommended—TOEFL (minimum score 547 paper-based; 78 iBT), IELTS (minimum score 6). *Application deadline:* For fall admission, 8/1 for domestic and international students; for spring admission, 12/1 for domestic and international students; for summer admission, 5/1 for domestic and international students. Applications are processed on a rolling basis. Application fee: $0. Electronic applications accepted. *Expenses:* $625 per credit (for MBA); $475 per credit (for MA). *Financial support:* In 2017–18, 292 students received support. Scholarships/grants and unspecified assistantships available. Financial award applicants required to submit FAFSA. *Faculty research:* Alternative dispute resolution, franchising, entrepreneurship, applied business ethics, strategic leadership development. *Unit head:* Dr. Kevin Hall, Dean, 651-603-6165, Fax: 651-641-8807, E-mail: khall@csp.edu. *Application contact:* Amber Faletti, Director of Enrollment Management, 651-641-8838, Fax: 651-603-6320, E-mail: faletti@csp.edu.

Concordia University Wisconsin, Graduate Programs, School of Business Administration, MBA Program, Mequon, WI 53097-2402. Offers finance (MBA); health care administration (MBA); human resource management (MBA); international business (MBA); international business-bilingual English/Chinese (MBA); management (MBA); management information systems (MBA); managerial communications (MBA); marketing (MBA); public administration (MBA); risk management (MBA). *Program availability:* Online learning. *Degree requirements:* For master's, comprehensive exam, thesis or alternative. *Entrance requirements:* Additional exam requirements/recommendations for international students: Required—TOEFL. *Expenses:* Contact institution.

Cornell University, Graduate School, Graduate Fields of Agriculture and Life Sciences, Field of Communication, Ithaca, NY 14853. Offers communication (MS, PhD); human-computer interaction (MS, PhD); language and communication (MS, PhD); media communication and society (MS, PhD); organizational communication (MS, PhD); science, environment and health communication (MS, PhD); social psychology of communication (MS, PhD). *Degree requirements:* For master's, thesis (MS); for doctorate, comprehensive exam, thesis/dissertation. *Entrance requirements:* For master's and doctorate, GRE General Test, 3 letters of recommendation. Additional exam requirements/recommendations for international students: Required—TOEFL (minimum score 600 paper-based; 100 iBT). Electronic applications accepted. *Faculty research:* Mass communication, communication technologies, science and environmental communication.

Dallas Baptist University, College of Business, Management Program, Dallas, TX 75211-9299. Offers conflict resolution management (MA); general management (MA, MS); health care management (MA); human resource management (MA); organizational communication (MA); performance management (MA); professional sales and management optimization (MA). *Program availability:* Part-time, evening/weekend, online learning. *Application deadline:* Applications are processed on a rolling basis. Application fee: $25. Electronic applications accepted. Application fee is waived when completed online. *Expenses: Tuition:* Full-time $16,308; part-time $906 per credit hour. *Required fees:* $900; $450 per semester. Tuition and fees vary according to course load and degree level. *Unit head:* Dr. Sandra Reid, Chair, Graduate School of Business, 214-333-6860, E-mail: sandra@dbu.edu. *Application contact:* Richard Nassar, Director, 214-333-6801, E-mail: richardn@dbu.edu.
Website: http://www.dbu.edu/gsb/ma-in-management

Dallas Baptist University, College of Business, Master of Business Administration Program, Dallas, TX 75211-9299. Offers accounting (MBA); business communication (MBA); conflict resolution management (MBA); entrepreneurship (MBA); finance (MBA); health care management (MBA); international business (MBA); leading the non-profit organization (MBA); management (MBA); management information systems (MBA); marketing (MBA); project management (MBA); technology and engineering management (MBA). *Accreditation:* ACBSP. *Program availability:* Part-time, evening/weekend, 100% online, blended/hybrid learning. *Application deadline:* Applications are processed on a rolling basis. Application fee: $25. Electronic applications accepted. Application fee is waived when completed online. *Expenses: Tuition:* Full-time $16,308; part-time $906 per credit hour. *Required fees:* $900; $450 per semester. Tuition and fees vary according to course load and degree level. *Unit head:* Dr. Sandra Reid, Chair of Graduate Business Programs, 214-333-5280, E-mail: sandra@dbu.edu. *Application contact:* Bobby Soto, Director of Admissions, 214-333-5242, E-mail: graduate@dbu.edu.
Website: http://www.dbu.edu/gsb/mba

DePaul University, College of Communication, Chicago, IL 60604. Offers digital communication and media arts (MA); health communication (MA); journalism (MA); media and cinema studies (MA); multicultural communication (MA); organizational communication (MA); public relations and advertising (MA); relational communication (MA). *Program availability:* Part-time, evening/weekend. *Entrance requirements:* Additional exam requirements/recommendations for international students: Required—TOEFL (minimum score 590 paper-based; 96 iBT), IELTS (minimum score 7.5) or PTE. *Application deadline:* For fall admission, 6/1 priority date for domestic students; for winter admission, 10/1 priority date for domestic students; for spring admission, 2/15 priority date for domestic students. Applications are processed on a rolling basis. Application fee: $40. Electronic applications accepted. *Financial support:* Applicants required to submit FAFSA. *Unit head:* Salma Ghanem, Dean, 312-362-8600, Fax: 312-362-8620. *Application contact:* Ann Spittle, Director of Graduate Admission, 773-325-7315, Fax: 312-362-8620, E-mail: graddepaul@depaul.edu.
Website: http://communication.depaul.edu/

Drexel University, College of Arts and Sciences, Department of Communication, Culture and Media, Program in Communication, Philadelphia, PA 19104-2875. Offers public communication (MS); science communication (MS); technical communication (MS). *Program availability:* Part-time, evening/weekend. *Degree requirements:* For master's, internship, professional portfolio. *Entrance requirements:* For master's, GRE or minimum GPA of 3.0. Additional exam requirements/recommendations for international students: Required—TOEFL. Electronic applications accepted.

East Carolina University, Graduate School, Thomas Harriot College of Arts and Sciences, Department of English, Greenville, NC 27858-4353. Offers creative writing (MA); English studies (MA); linguistics (MA); literature (MA); multicultural and transnational literatures (MA, Certificate); professional communication (Certificate); rhetoric and composition (MA); rhetoric, writing, and professional communication (PhD); teaching English in the two-year college (Certificate); teaching English to speakers of other languages (MA, Certificate); technical and professional communication (MA). *Program availability:* Part-time, evening/weekend, online learning. *Students:* 40 full-time (27 women), 74 part-time (57 women); includes 33 minority (23 Black or African American, non-Hispanic/Latino; 2 Asian, non-Hispanic/Latino; 4 Hispanic/Latino; 4 Two or more races, non-Hispanic/Latino). Average age 35. 36 applicants, 94% accepted, 25 enrolled. In 2017, 23 master's, 4 doctorates, 24 other advanced degrees awarded. *Degree requirements:* For master's, comprehensive exam, thesis optional; for doctorate, comprehensive exam, thesis/dissertation. *Entrance requirements:* For master's, GRE General Test or MAT; for doctorate, GRE General Test or MAT, writing samples. Additional exam requirements/recommendations for international students:

Recommended—TOEFL (minimum score 78 iBT), IELTS (minimum score 6.5), TWE. *Application deadline:* For fall admission, 7/31 priority date for domestic students, 2/1 priority date for international students; for spring admission, 11/30 priority date for domestic students, 10/1 priority date for international students. Applications are processed on a rolling basis. Application fee: $75. Electronic applications accepted. *Expenses:* Tuition, state resident: full-time $4749; part-time $297 per credit hour. Tuition, nonresident: full-time $17,898; part-time $1119 per credit hour. *Required fees:* $2691; $224 per credit hour. Part-time tuition and fees vary according to course load and program. *Financial support:* Research assistantships with partial tuition reimbursements, teaching assistantships with partial tuition reimbursements, and Federal Work-Study available. Support available to part-time students. Financial award application deadline: 3/1. *Faculty research:* Technical and professional communication, rhetoric/composition, multicultural and transnational literature, creative writing, film studies. *Unit head:* Dr. Marianne Montgomery, Chair, 252-328-6687, E-mail: montgomerym@ecu.edu. *Application contact:* Dean of Graduate School, 252-328-6012, Fax: 252-328-6071, E-mail: gradschool@ecu.edu.
Website: http://www.ecu.edu/cs-cas/engl/

Eastern Michigan University, Graduate School, Academic and Student Affairs Division, Ypsilanti, MI 48197. Offers individualized studies (MA, MS); integrated marketing communications (MS). *Students:* 4 full-time (2 women), 36 part-time (25 women); includes 6 minority (2 Asian, non-Hispanic/Latino; 1 Hispanic/Latino; 3 Two or more races, non-Hispanic/Latino). Average age 35. 64 applicants, 84% accepted, 26 enrolled. In 2017, 1 master's awarded. *Entrance requirements:* Additional exam requirements/recommendations for international students: Required—TOEFL. Application fee: $45. *Unit head:* Dr. Wade Tornquist, Interim Dean, 734-487-0042, Fax: 734-487-0050, E-mail: wade.tornquist@emich.edu. *Application contact:* Graduate Admissions, 734-487-2400, Fax: 734-487-6559, E-mail: graduate.admissions@emich.edu.

Eastern Michigan University, Graduate School, College of Business, Department of Marketing, Program in Integrated Marketing Communications, Ypsilanti, MI 48197. Offers MS, Postbaccalaureate Certificate. *Students:* 24 full-time (20 women), 33 part-time (26 women); includes 15 minority (11 Black or African American, non-Hispanic/Latino; 3 Hispanic/Latino; 1 Two or more races, non-Hispanic/Latino). Average age 31. 41 applicants, 66% accepted, 23 enrolled. In 2017, 22 master's, 1 other advanced degree awarded. Application fee: $45. *Application contact:* K. Michelle Henry, Director, Graduate Business Programs, 734-487-4444, Fax: 734-478-1316, E-mail: cob.graduate@emich.edu.

Fairleigh Dickinson University, Florham Campus, Maxwell Becton College of Arts and Sciences, Department of English, Communication and Philosophy, Program in Corporate and Organizational Communication, Madison, NJ 07940-1099. Offers MA, MA/MBA. *Entrance requirements:* For master's, GRE General Test.

Florida State University, The Graduate School, College of Communication and Information, School of Communication, Tallahassee, FL 32306. Offers communication theory and research (PhD); integrated marketing communication (MA, MS); media and communication studies (MA, MS); public interest media and communication (MA, MS). *Program availability:* Part-time. *Faculty:* 20 full-time (11 women), 1 part-time/adjunct (0 women). *Students:* 104 full-time (74 women), 38 part-time (27 women); includes 81 minority (20 Black or African American, non-Hispanic/Latino; 24 Asian, non-Hispanic/Latino; 26 Hispanic/Latino; 1 Native Hawaiian or other Pacific Islander, non-Hispanic/Latino; 10 Two or more races, non-Hispanic/Latino). Average age 24. 184 applicants, 59% accepted, 46 enrolled. In 2017, 59 master's, 5 doctorates awarded. *Degree requirements:* For master's, thesis (for some programs); for doctorate, comprehensive exam, thesis/dissertation. *Entrance requirements:* For master's, GRE General Test, minimum GPA of 3.0; for doctorate, GRE General Test, minimum GPA of 3.3 in graduate course work. Additional exam requirements/recommendations for international students: Required—TOEFL (minimum score 600 paper-based; 100 iBT), IELTS (minimum score 7). *Application deadline:* For fall admission, 7/1 priority date for domestic students, 5/1 priority date for international students; for spring admission, 11/1 priority date for domestic and international students; for summer admission, 3/1 priority date for domestic and international students. Applications are processed on a rolling basis. Application fee: $30. Electronic applications accepted. *Expenses:* Contact institution. *Financial support:* In 2017–18, 112 students received support, including 28 research assistantships with full tuition reimbursements available (averaging $11,752 per year), 81 teaching assistantships with full tuition reimbursements available (averaging $10,109 per year); scholarships/grants, tuition waivers (full and partial), and unspecified assistantships also available. Financial award application deadline: 11/1; financial award applicants required to submit FAFSA. *Faculty research:* Communication in the public interest; strategic communication; media and technology; multicultural, intercultural, and international communication. *Total annual research expenditures:* $41,657. *Unit head:* Dr. Jennifer Proffitt, Director, 850-644-5034, Fax: 850-644-8642, E-mail: jennifer.proffitt@cci.fsu.edu. *Application contact:* Natashia Hinson-Turner, Graduate Coordinator, 850-644-5034, Fax: 850-644-8642, E-mail: comgradadvising@cci.fsu.edu.
Website: http://www.cci.fsu.edu

Franklin University, Marketing and Communication Program, Columbus, OH 43215-5399. Offers MS. *Program availability:* Part-time, evening/weekend. *Entrance requirements:* For master's, minimum undergraduate GPA of 2.75. Additional exam requirements/recommendations for international students: Required—TOEFL (minimum score 550 paper-based). Electronic applications accepted.

Georgia Southern University–Armstrong Campus, College of Graduate Studies, Program in Professional Communication and Leadership, Savannah, GA 31419-1997. Offers MA, Certificate. *Program availability:* Part-time, evening/weekend. *Faculty:* 2 full-time (1 woman), 1 (woman) part-time/adjunct. *Students:* 26 full-time (16 women), 48 part-time (37 women); includes 46 minority (39 Black or African American, non-Hispanic/Latino; 7 Hispanic/Latino). Average age 35. 53 applicants, 53% accepted, 21 enrolled. In 2017, 29 master's awarded. *Degree requirements:* For master's, comprehensive exam, project. *Entrance requirements:* For master's, minimum GPA of 2.5, letters of recommendation, letter of intent, resume. Additional exam requirements/recommendations for international students: Required—TOEFL (minimum score 523 paper-based; 70 iBT). *Application deadline:* For fall admission, 6/1 priority date for domestic students, 5/1 priority date for international students; for spring admission, 11/15 priority date for domestic students, 9/15 priority date for international students; for summer admission, 4/15 for domestic students, 9/15 priority date for international students. Applications are processed on a rolling basis. Application fee: $30. Electronic applications accepted. *Expenses:* Tuition, state resident: part-time $211 per credit hour. Tuition, nonresident: part-time $782 per credit hour. *Required fees:* $737 per semester. Tuition and fees vary according to course load, degree level, campus/location and program. *Financial support:* In 2017–18, research assistantships with full tuition reimbursements (averaging $5,000 per year) were awarded; scholarships/grants and unspecified assistantships also available. Financial award application deadline: 3/15; financial award applicants required to submit FAFSA. *Faculty research:* Organizational communication, conflict resolution and mediation, rhetoric and language identity, brand identity and marketing, communication theory. *Unit head:* Dr. Kimberly Martin, Program Coordinator, 912-344-2698, E-mail: kimberly.martin@armstrong.edu. *Application contact:* McKenzie Peterman, Graduate Admissions Specialist, 912-478-5678, Fax: 912-

478-0740, E-mail: mpeterman@georgiasouthern.edu.
Website: http://www.armstrong.edu/Majors/degree/master_professional_communication_leadership

HEC Montreal, School of Business Administration, Graduate Diploma Programs in Administration, Program in Marketing Communication, Montréal, QC H3T 2A7, Canada. Offers Graduate Diploma. All courses are given in French. *Program availability:* Part-time-only, evening/weekend. *Students:* 3 full-time (2 women), 81 part-time (59 women). 59 applicants, 71% accepted, 39 enrolled. In 2017, 32 Graduate Diplomas awarded. *Entrance requirements:* For degree, bachelor's degree in administration (marketing option), work experience. *Application deadline:* For fall admission, 4/15 for domestic and international students. Application fee: $88 Canadian dollars ($184 Canadian dollars for international students). Electronic applications accepted. *Expenses:* Tuition, state resident: full-time $2869 Canadian dollars; part-time $79.70 Canadian dollars per credit. Tuition, nonresident: full-time $8883 Canadian dollars; part-time $246.76 Canadian dollars per credit. *International tuition:* $19,648 Canadian dollars full-time. *Required fees:* $41.20 Canadian dollars per credit. $67.94 Canadian dollars per term. Tuition and fees vary according to degree level and program. *Financial support:* Research assistantships, teaching assistantships, and scholarships/grants available. Financial award application deadline: 9/2. *Unit head:* Renaud Lachance, Director, 514-340-7165, E-mail: renaud.lachance@hec.ca. *Application contact:* Anny Caron, Administrative Director, 514-340-6151, Fax: 514-340-6411, E-mail: aide@hec.ca.
Website: http://www.hec.ca/programmes/dess/dess-gestion-communication-marketing/index.html

High Point University, Norcross Graduate School, High Point, NC 27268. Offers athletic training (MSAT); business administration (MBA); educational leadership (M Ed, Ed D); elementary education (M Ed, MAT); pharmacy (Pharm D); physical therapy (DPT); physician assistant studies (MPAS); secondary mathematics (M Ed, MAT); special education (M Ed); strategic communication (MA). *Accreditation:* NCATE. *Program availability:* Part-time, evening/weekend. *Degree requirements:* For master's, comprehensive exam (for some programs), thesis (for some programs). *Entrance requirements:* For master's, GMAT (MBA), GRE, MAT, minimum GPA of 3.0. Additional exam requirements/recommendations for international students: Required—TOEFL (minimum score 550 paper-based). Electronic applications accepted.

Howard University, Cathy Hughes School of Communications, Department of Strategic, Legal and Management Communication, Washington, DC 20059-0002. Offers intercultural communication (MA, PhD); organizational communication (MA, PhD). Offered through the Graduate School of Arts and Sciences. *Program availability:* Part-time. Terminal master's awarded for partial completion of doctoral program. *Degree requirements:* For master's, comprehensive exam or thesis; for doctorate, one foreign language, comprehensive exam, thesis/dissertation. *Entrance requirements:* For master's, English proficiency exam, GRE General Test, minimum GPA of 3.0; for doctorate, English proficiency exam, GRE General Test, master's degree in related field, minimum GPA of 3.5. Additional exam requirements/recommendations for international students: Required—TOEFL. *Faculty research:* Media effects, black discourse, development communication, African-American organizations.

Illinois Institute of Technology, Stuart School of Business, Program in Marketing Analytics and Communication, Chicago, IL 60661. Offers MS, MBA/MS. *Program availability:* Part-time, evening/weekend. *Entrance requirements:* For master's, GRE (minimum score 1000) or GMAT (500). Additional exam requirements/recommendations for international students: Required—TOEFL (minimum score 600 paper-based; 85 iBT); Recommended—IELTS (minimum score 7). Electronic applications accepted. *Expenses:* Contact institution.

Iowa State University of Science and Technology, Department of English, Ames, IA 50011. Offers creative writing (MFA); English (MA); rhetoric and professional communication (PhD). *Degree requirements:* For master's, thesis or alternative; for doctorate, thesis/dissertation. *Entrance requirements:* For master's, GRE General Test, sample of written work, resume, portfolio in creative writing; for doctorate, GRE General Test, sample of written work, resume. Additional exam requirements/recommendations for international students: Required—TOEFL (minimum score 600 paper-based; 100 iBT), IELTS (minimum score 7). Electronic applications accepted. *Faculty research:* Creative writing, literature, rhetoric, composition and professional communication, teaching English as a second language, applied linguistics.

Iowa State University of Science and Technology, Program in Rhetoric and Professional Communication, Ames, IA 50011. Offers PhD. *Entrance requirements:* For doctorate, GRE, official academic transcripts, resume, three letters of recommendation, writing sample. Additional exam requirements/recommendations for international students: Required—TOEFL (minimum score 640 paper-based; 111 iBT), IELTS (minimum score 7.5). Electronic applications accepted.

Iowa State University of Science and Technology, Program in Rhetoric, Composition, and Professional Communication, Ames, IA 50011. Offers MA. *Entrance requirements:* For master's, GRE, official academic transcripts, resume, three letters of recommendation, writing sample. Additional exam requirements/recommendations for international students: Required—TOEFL (minimum score 600 paper-based; 100 iBT), IELTS (minimum score 7). Electronic applications accepted.

La Salle University, School of Arts and Sciences, Program in Strategic Communication, Philadelphia, PA 19141-1199. Offers communication consulting and development (MA); communication management (MA); general professional communication (MA); professional and business communication (Certificate); public relations (MA); social and new media (Certificate). *Program availability:* Part-time, evening/weekend, online learning. *Faculty:* 4 full-time (3 women), 1 (woman) part-time/adjunct. *Students:* 11 full-time (4 women), 22 part-time (16 women); includes 10 minority (9 Black or African American, non-Hispanic/Latino; 1 Two or more races, non-Hispanic/Latino). Average age 27. 40 applicants, 93% accepted, 23 enrolled. In 2017, 34 master's, 1 other advanced degree awarded. *Degree requirements:* For master's, practicum. *Entrance requirements:* For master's, writing assessment, professional resume; minimum overall B average; two letters of recommendation (if GPA below 3.25); brief personal statement (about 500 words); interview; for Certificate, writing assessment, minimum GPA of 2.75 in undergraduate studies; brief personal statement (about 500 words); interview. Additional exam requirements/recommendations for international students: Required—TOEFL. *Application deadline:* For fall admission, 8/15 priority date for domestic students, 7/15 for international students; for spring admission, 12/15 priority date for domestic students, 11/15 for international students; for summer admission, 4/15 priority date for domestic students, 3/15 for international students. Applications are processed on a rolling basis. Application fee: $35. Electronic applications accepted. Application fee is waived when completed online. *Expenses:* Contact institution. *Financial support:* In 2017–18, 12 students received support. Scholarships/grants available. Support available to part-time students. Financial award application deadline: 8/31; financial award applicants required to submit FAFSA. *Unit head:* Dr. Pamela Lannutti, Director, 215-951-1935, Fax: 215-951-5043, E-mail: annutti95@lasalle.edu. *Application contact:* Elizabeth Heenan, Director, Graduate and Adult Enrollment, 215-951-1100, Fax: 214-951-1462, E-mail: heenan@lasalle.edu.
Website: http://www.lasalle.edu/strategic-communication/

Corporate and Organizational Communication

Lasell College, Graduate and Professional Studies in Communication, Newton, MA 02466-2709. Offers health communication (MSC, Graduate Certificate); integrated marketing communication (MSC, Graduate Certificate); public relations (MSC, Graduate Certificate). *Program availability:* Part-time, evening/weekend, 100% online, blended/hybrid learning. *Faculty:* 3 full-time (2 women), 7 part-time/adjunct (5 women). *Students:* 25 full-time (16 women), 35 part-time (28 women); includes 12 minority (6 Black or African American, non-Hispanic/Latino; 1 Asian, non-Hispanic/Latino; 4 Hispanic/Latino; 1 Two or more races, non-Hispanic/Latino), 16 international. Average age 30. 53 applicants, 45% accepted, 22 enrolled. In 2017, 28 master's awarded. *Degree requirements:* For master's, comprehensive exam, thesis or alternative, minimum GPA of 3.0; special project or internship. *Entrance requirements:* For master's, one-page personal statement, 2 letters of recommendation, resume, bachelor's degree transcript; for Graduate Certificate, bachelor's degree transcript, 2 letters of recommendation, 1-page personal statement, resume. Additional exam requirements/recommendations for international students: Required—TOEFL (minimum score 550 paper-based, 79 iBT) or IELTS (minimum score 6). *Application deadline:* For fall admission, 8/31 priority date for domestic students, 6/30 priority date for international students; for spring admission, 12/31 priority date for domestic students, 10/31 priority date for international students. Applications are processed on a rolling basis. Electronic applications accepted. *Expenses:* $600 per credit. *Financial support:* Federal Work-Study, scholarships/grants, and tuition discounts available. Support available to part-time students. Financial award application deadline: 8/31; financial award applicants required to submit FAFSA. *Faculty research:* Terrorists' use of the Internet; refugees' use of cell phones as means of communication in Jordan and Germany; political communication; analysis of the media coverage of the conflict and peace process in northern Ireland; interpersonal communication; strategies to address bullying in online communities, in schools and in the workplace. *Unit head:* Eric Turner, Vice President of Graduate and Professional Studies, 617-243-2071, Fax: 617-243-2450, E-mail: gradinfo@lasell.edu. *Application contact:* Adrienne Franciosi, Director of Graduate Enrollment, 617-243-2214, Fax: 617-243-2450, E-mail: gradinfo@lasell.edu.
Website: http://www.lasell.edu/academics/graduate-and-professional-studies/programs-of-study/master-of-science-in-communication.html

Loyola University Chicago, Quinlan School of Business, Master of Science in Integrated Marketing Communications Program, Chicago, IL 60611. Offers MS. *Program availability:* Part-time, evening/weekend. *Faculty:* 13 full-time (11 women), 5 part-time/adjunct (1 woman). *Students:* 24 full-time (20 women), 3 part-time (1 woman); includes 6 minority (3 Black or African American, non-Hispanic/Latino; 1 Asian, non-Hispanic/Latino; 2 Hispanic/Latino), 14 international. Average age 27. 93 applicants, 68% accepted, 12 enrolled. In 2017, 23 master's awarded. *Entrance requirements:* For master's, GMAT or GRE, official transcripts, two letters of recommendation, statement of purpose, resume. Additional exam requirements/recommendations for international students: Required—TOEFL (minimum score 90 iBT) or IELTS (minimum score 6.5). *Application deadline:* For fall admission, 7/15 for domestic and international students; for winter admission, 10/1 for domestic and international students; for spring admission, 1/15 for domestic and international students; for summer admission, 4/1 for domestic and international students. Applications are processed on a rolling basis. Application fee: $50. Electronic applications accepted. Application fee is waived when completed online. *Expenses:* $4,488 per course. *Financial support:* In 2017–18, 2 students received support. Research assistantships, career-related internships or fieldwork, Federal Work-Study, scholarships/grants, and health care benefits available. *Faculty research:* Brand strategy, consumer behavior, digital/interactive marketing, international marketing. *Unit head:* Dr. Mary Ann McGrath, Chair, 312-915-6136, E-mail: mmcgrat@luc.edu.
Website: http://luc.edu/quinlan/mba/masters-in-marketing/

Manhattanville College, School of Business, Master of Science in International Management Program, Purchase, NY 10577-2132. Offers international management (MS, Advanced Certificate), including business leadership (MS), finance (MS), human resource management (MS), marketing communication management (MS). *Program availability:* Part-time, evening/weekend. *Faculty:* 2 part-time/adjunct (0 women). *Students:* 6 full-time (3 women), 2 part-time (1 woman); includes 2 minority (1 Black or African American, non-Hispanic/Latino; 1 Two or more races, non-Hispanic/Latino), 2 international. Average age 34. 6 applicants, 67% accepted, 1 enrolled. In 2017, 2 master's awarded. *Degree requirements:* For master's, thesis (for some programs), final project. *Entrance requirements:* For master's, personal essay, transcripts, 2 letters of recommendation (academic or professional), resume, health form with proof of immunization (for those born after 1957). Additional exam requirements/recommendations for international students: Required—TOEFL (minimum score 563 paper-based, 85 iBT), IELTS (7), or iTEP (B2). *Application deadline:* Applications are processed on a rolling basis. Application fee: $75. Electronic applications accepted. *Expenses:* $915 per credit. *Financial support:* Federal Work-Study, institutionally sponsored loans, scholarships/grants, and unspecified assistantships available. Financial award application deadline: 3/15; financial award applicants required to submit FAFSA. *Unit head:* Laura Persky, Graduate Program Director, 914-323-5188, E-mail: laura.persky@mville.edu. *Application contact:* Monika Pottgen, Assistant Director, Recruitment and Admissions, 914-323-5150, E-mail: business@mville.edu.
Website: https://www.mville.edu/programs/ms-international-management

Manhattanville College, School of Business, Master of Science in Marketing Communication Management Program, Purchase, NY 10577-2132. Offers MS, Advanced Certificate. *Program availability:* Part-time, evening/weekend. *Faculty:* 3 part-time/adjunct (1 woman). *Students:* 13 full-time (8 women), 6 part-time (4 women); includes 6 minority (1 Asian, non-Hispanic/Latino; 5 Hispanic/Latino), 2 international. Average age 30. 20 applicants, 30% accepted, 5 enrolled. In 2017, 4 master's awarded. *Degree requirements:* For master's, thesis (for some programs), final project. *Entrance requirements:* For master's, personal essay, transcripts, 2 letters of recommendation (academic or professional), resume, health form with proof of immunization (for those born after 1957). Additional exam requirements/recommendations for international students: Required—TOEFL (minimum score 563 paper-based, 85 iBT), IELTS (7), or iTEP (B2). *Application deadline:* Applications are processed on a rolling basis. Application fee: $75. Electronic applications accepted. *Expenses:* $915 per credit. *Financial support:* Federal Work-Study, institutionally sponsored loans, scholarships/grants, and unspecified assistantships available. Financial award application deadline: 3/15; financial award applicants required to submit FAFSA. *Unit head:* Laura Persky, Graduate Program Director, 914-323-5188, E-mail: laura.persky@mville.edu. *Application contact:* Monika Pottgen, Assistant Director, Recruitment and Admissions, 914-323-5150, E-mail: business@mville.edu.
Website: https://www.mville.edu/programs/ms-marketing-communication-management

Marist College, Graduate Programs, School of Communication and the Arts, Program in Integrated Marketing Communication, Poughkeepsie, NY 12601-1387. Offers MA. *Entrance requirements:* For master's, GRE or GMAT, official undergraduate/graduate transcripts from all institutions attended; current resume; completed recommendation forms for three references; personal statement.

Minnesota State University Mankato, College of Graduate Studies and Research, College of Arts and Humanities, Department of Communication Studies, Mankato, MN 56001. Offers communication education (Certificate); communication studies (MA, MS);

forensics (MFA); professional communication (Certificate). *Degree requirements:* For master's, one foreign language, comprehensive exam, thesis. *Entrance requirements:* For master's, minimum GPA of 3.0 during previous 2 years, writing sample. Electronic applications accepted.

Mississippi College, Graduate School, College of Arts and Sciences, School of Christian Studies and the Arts, Department of Communication, Clinton, MS 39058. Offers applied communication (MSC); public relations and corporate communication (MSC). *Program availability:* Part-time. *Degree requirements:* For master's, comprehensive exam, thesis optional. *Entrance requirements:* For master's, GRE or NTE, minimum GPA of 2.5. Additional exam requirements/recommendations for international students: Recommended—TOEFL, IELTS. Electronic applications accepted.

Monmouth University, Graduate Studies, Department of Communication, West Long Branch, NJ 07764-1898. Offers corporate and public communication (MA); human resources management and communication (Certificate); public service communication specialist (Certificate); strategic public relations and new media (Certificate). *Program availability:* Part-time, evening/weekend, online learning. *Faculty:* 4 full-time (3 women), 2 part-time/adjunct (both women). *Students:* 10 full-time (7 women), 18 part-time (14 women); includes 9 minority (5 Black or African American, non-Hispanic/Latino; 1 Asian, non-Hispanic/Latino; 3 Hispanic/Latino). Average age 28. In 2017, 18 master's, 1 other advanced degree awarded. Terminal master's awarded for partial completion of doctoral program. *Degree requirements:* For master's, comprehensive exam (for some programs), thesis (for some programs), project. *Entrance requirements:* For master's, GRE, baccalaureate degree with minimum GPA of 3.0 in major, 2.75 overall; two letters of recommendation; personal essay (750 words or less describing preparation for study and personal objectives); digital or hard copy portfolio of select samples of work including writing sample; resume. Additional exam requirements/recommendations for international students: Required—TOEFL (minimum score 550 paper-based; 79 iBT), IELTS (minimum score 6), Michigan English Language Assessment Battery (minimum score 77). *Application deadline:* For fall admission, 7/15 priority date for domestic students, 6/1 for international students; for spring admission, 12/1 priority date for domestic students, 11/1 for international students; for summer admission, 5/1 for domestic students. Applications are processed on a rolling basis. Application fee: $50. Electronic applications accepted. *Expenses: Tuition:* Full-time $21,366; part-time $7122 per credit. *Required fees:* $700; $175 per term. *Financial support:* In 2017–18, 2 students received support. Institutionally sponsored loans, scholarships/grants, and unspecified assistantships available. Support available to part-time students. Financial award applicants required to submit FAFSA. *Faculty research:* Service-learning, history of television, feminism and the media, executive communication, public relations pedagogy. *Unit head:* Dr. Marina Vujnovic, Program Director, 732-263-5667, Fax: 732-571-5667, E-mail: mvujnovi@monmouth.edu. *Application contact:* Andrea Thompson, Graduate Admission Counselor, 732-571-3452, Fax: 732-263-5123, E-mail: gradadm@monmouth.edu.
Website: http://www.monmouth.edu/cpc

Montclair State University, The Graduate School, College of the Arts, MA Program in Public and Organizational Relations, Montclair, NJ 07043-1624. Offers MA. *Program availability:* Part-time, evening/weekend. *Degree requirements:* For master's, comprehensive exam. *Entrance requirements:* For master's, GRE General Test, 2 letters of recommendation. Additional exam requirements/recommendations for international students: Required—TOEFL (minimum score 83 iBT) or IELTS (minimum score 6.5). Electronic applications accepted. *Faculty research:* Organizational problem solving and innovation, social media, health communication, globalization, organizational change management.

Murray State University, Arthur J. Bauernfeind College of Business, Department of Organizational Communication, Murray, KY 42071. Offers nursing education (MA). *Program availability:* Part-time, evening/weekend, 100% online, blended/hybrid learning. *Faculty:* 6 full-time (2 women), 1 part-time/adjunct (0 women). *Students:* 15 full-time (9 women), 46 part-time (31 women); includes 13 minority (7 Black or African American, non-Hispanic/Latino; 2 Asian, non-Hispanic/Latino; 1 Hispanic/Latino; 3 Two or more races, non-Hispanic/Latino), 4 international. Average age 33. 35 applicants, 86% accepted, 15 enrolled. In 2017, 6 master's awarded. *Entrance requirements:* For master's, GRE or GMAT, minimum university GPA of 2.75. Additional exam requirements/recommendations for international students: Required—TOEFL (minimum score 527 paper-based; 71 iBT). *Application deadline:* Applications are processed on a rolling basis. Application fee: $40 ($50 for international students). Electronic applications accepted. *Expenses:* Tuition, state resident: full-time $9504. Tuition, nonresident: full-time $26,811. *International tuition:* $14,400 full-time. Tuition and fees vary according to course load, degree level and reciprocity agreements. *Financial support:* In 2017–18, 4 teaching assistantships were awarded; Federal Work-Study and unspecified assistantships also available. Financial award applicants required to submit FAFSA. *Faculty research:* Organizational learning, organizational culture, leadership, health communication, interpersonal communication. *Unit head:* Dr. Michael Bokeno, Chair, Department of Organizational Communication, 270-809-4463, Fax: 270-809-4484, E-mail: rbokeno@murraystate.edu. *Application contact:* Kathy Garrison, Assistant Director for Graduate Admission and Records, 270-809-3779, Fax: 270-809-3780, E-mail: kgarrison@murraystate.edu.
Website: http://www.murraystate.edu/academics/CollegesDepartments/CollegeOfBusiness/Programs/OrganizationalCommunication/index.aspx

New Mexico State University, College of Arts and Sciences, Department of English, Las Cruces, NM 88003. Offers creative writing (MFA); English (MA), including creative writing, English studies for teachers, literature, rhetoric and professional communication; rhetoric and professional communication (PhD). *Program availability:* Part-time. *Faculty:* 17 full-time (9 women), 3 part-time/adjunct (1 woman). *Students:* 50 full-time (32 women), 21 part-time (14 women); includes 19 minority (2 Black or African American, non-Hispanic/Latino; 2 Asian, non-Hispanic/Latino; 14 Hispanic/Latino; 1 Two or more races, non-Hispanic/Latino), 8 international. Average age 35. 68 applicants, 50% accepted, 12 enrolled. In 2017, 13 master's, 1 doctorate awarded. *Entrance requirements:* For master's and doctorate, sample of written work. Additional exam requirements/recommendations for international students: Required—TOEFL (minimum score 550 paper-based; 79 iBT), IELTS (minimum score 6.5). *Application deadline:* For fall admission, 2/1 for domestic and international students. Application fee: $40 ($50 for international students). Electronic applications accepted. *Expenses:* Tuition, state resident: full-time $4390. Tuition, nonresident: full-time $15,309. *Required fees:* $853. *Financial support:* In 2017–18, 49 students received support, including 6 fellowships (averaging $4,390 per year); 41 teaching assistantships (averaging $17,317 per year); career-related internships or fieldwork, Federal Work-Study, scholarships/grants, traineeships, health care benefits, and unspecified assistantships also available. Support available to part-time students. Financial award application deadline: 3/1. *Faculty research:* Composition research, history and theory of rhetoric, technical/professional communication, creative writing, English and American literature. *Total annual research expenditures:* $10,666. *Unit head:* Dr. Elizabeth Schirmer, Interim Department Head, 575-646-3931, Fax: 575-646-7725, E-mail: eschirme@nmsu.edu. *Application contact:* Dr. Tracey Eileen Miller-Tomlinson, Director of Graduate Studies,

575-646-2213, Fax: 575-646-7725, E-mail: tomlin@nmsu.edu.
Website: http://english.nmsu.edu

New York University, School of Professional Studies, Division of Programs in Business, Program in Integrated Marketing, New York, NY 10012-1019. Offers integrated marketing (MS), including brand management, digital marketing, marketing analytics. *Program availability:* Part-time, evening/weekend. *Students:* 821 full-time (611 women), 176 part-time (134 women); includes 70 minority (12 Black or African American, non-Hispanic/Latino; 1 American Indian or Alaska Native, non-Hispanic/Latino; 38 Asian, non-Hispanic/Latino; 17 Hispanic/Latino; 2 Two or more races, non-Hispanic/Latino), 865 international. Average age 25. 1,688 applicants, 61% accepted, 416 enrolled. In 2017, 744 master's awarded. *Degree requirements:* For master's, thesis, capstone project. *Entrance requirements:* For master's, GRE or GMAT (only upon request), bachelor's degree, resume with relevant professional work, internship or volunteer experience, two letters of recommendation, statement of purpose. Additional exam requirements/recommendations for international students: Required—TOEFL (minimum score 600 paper-based; 100 iBT), IELTS (minimum score 7). *Application deadline:* For fall admission, 2/1 priority date for domestic and international students; for spring admission, 10/15 priority date for domestic students, 8/15 priority date for international students. Applications are processed on a rolling basis. Application fee: $150. Electronic applications accepted. *Expenses:* $20,244 per term. *Financial support:* Fellowships, career-related internships or fieldwork, Federal Work-Study, scholarships/grants, and health care benefits available. Support available to part-time students. Financial award application deadline: 6/30; financial award applicants required to submit FAFSA. *Unit head:* Martin Ihrig, Associate Dean/Clinical Professor, 212-992-3228. *Application contact:* Admissions Office, 212-998-7100, E-mail: scps.gradadmissions@nyu.edu.
Website: http://www.sps.nyu.edu/academics/departments/marketing-and-pr.html

New York University, School of Professional Studies, Division of Programs in Business, Programs in Marketing and Public Relations, New York, NY 10012-1019. Offers public relations and corporate communication (MS), including corporate and organizational communication, public relations management. *Program availability:* Part-time, evening/weekend. *Students:* 224 full-time (197 women), 62 part-time (56 women); includes 40 minority (18 Black or African American, non-Hispanic/Latino; 1 American Indian or Alaska Native, non-Hispanic/Latino; 7 Asian, non-Hispanic/Latino; 11 Hispanic/Latino; 3 Two or more races, non-Hispanic/Latino), 219 international. Average age 25. 355 applicants, 69% accepted, 110 enrolled. In 2017, 316 master's awarded. *Degree requirements:* For master's, thesis. *Entrance requirements:* For master's, GRE or GMAT (only upon request), bachelor's degree, resume with relevant professional work, internship or volunteer experience, two letters of recommendation, statement of purpose. Additional exam requirements/recommendations for international students: Required—TOEFL (minimum score 600 paper-based; 100 iBT), IELTS (minimum score 7). *Application deadline:* For fall admission, 2/1 priority date for domestic and international students; for spring admission, 10/15 priority date for domestic students, 8/15 priority date for international students. Applications are processed on a rolling basis. Application fee: $150. Electronic applications accepted. *Expenses:* $20,244 per term. *Financial support:* Fellowships, career-related internships or fieldwork, Federal Work-Study, scholarships/grants, and health care benefits available. Support available to part-time students. Financial award application deadline: 6/30; financial award applicants required to submit FAFSA. *Unit head:* Martin Ihrig, Associate Dean/Clinical Professor, 212-992-3288. *Application contact:* Admissions Office, 212-998-7100, E-mail: sps.gradadmissions@nyu.edu.
Website: http://www.sps.nyu.edu/academics/departments/marketing-and-pr.html

Northeastern University, College of Professional Studies, Boston, MA 02115-5096. Offers applied nutrition (MS); college athletics administration (MSL); commerce and economic development (MS); corporate and organizational communication (MS); criminal justice (MS); digital media (MPS); elearning and instructional design (M Ed); elementary education (MAT); geographic information technology (MPS); global studies and international relations (MS); higher education administration (M Ed); homeland security (MA); human services (MS); informatics (MPS); leadership (MS); learning analytics (M Ed); learning and instruction (M Ed); nonprofit management (MS); professional sports administration (MSL); project management (MS); regulatory affairs for drugs, biologics, and medical devices (MS); respiratory care leadership (MS); special education (M Ed); technical communication (MS). *Program availability:* Part-time, evening/weekend, 100% online, blended/hybrid learning. *Faculty:* 82 full-time (51 women), 853 part-time/adjunct (366 women). *Students:* 5,278 part-time (3,230 women). In 2017, 1,586 master's awarded. *Application deadline:* Applications are processed on a rolling basis. Application fee: $0. Electronic applications accepted. *Expenses:* Contact institution. *Financial support:* Applicants required to submit FAFSA. *Unit head:* Dr. Mary Loeffelholz, Dean of the College of Professional Studies. *Application contact:* E-mail: cpsadmissions@northeastern.edu.
Website: https://cps.northeastern.edu/

Northwestern University, The Graduate School, School of Communication, Department of Communication Studies, Evanston, IL 60208. Offers communication studies (PhD), including interaction and social influence, rhetoric and public culture; managerial communication (MSC); media, technology and society (PhD); technology and social behavior (PhD). PhD admissions and degree offered through The Graduate School. Terminal master's awarded for partial completion of doctoral program. *Degree requirements:* For doctorate, thesis/dissertation. *Entrance requirements:* For master's and doctorate, GRE General Test. Additional exam requirements/recommendations for international students: Required—TOEFL. Electronic applications accepted.

Northwestern University, Medill School of Journalism, Media, and Integrated Marketing Communications, Integrated Marketing Communications Program, Evanston, IL 60208. Offers brand strategy (MSIMC); content marketing (MSIMC); direct and interactive marketing (MSIMC); marketing analytics (MSIMC); strategic communications (MSIMC). *Program availability:* Part-time. *Entrance requirements:* For master's, GRE General Test or GMAT, full-time work experience (preferred). Additional exam requirements/recommendations for international students: Required—TOEFL. Electronic applications accepted. *Faculty research:* Data mining, business to business marketing, values in advertising, political advertising.

Ohio University, Graduate College, Scripps College of Communication, School of Communication Studies, Athens, OH 45701-2979. Offers health communication (PhD); organizational communication (MA); relating and organizing (PhD); rhetoric and public culture (PhD). *Program availability:* Part-time, online learning. Terminal master's awarded for partial completion of doctoral program. *Degree requirements:* For master's, capstone; for doctorate, comprehensive exam, thesis/dissertation. *Entrance requirements:* For master's, GRE; for doctorate, GRE General Test, minimum GPA of 3.0. Additional exam requirements/recommendations for international students: Required—TOEFL (minimum score 550 paper-based; 80 iBT) or IELTS (minimum score 6.5). Electronic applications accepted. *Faculty research:* Rhetoric and public culture, relating and organizing, health communication.

Radford University, College of Graduate Studies and Research, Program in Strategic Communication, Radford, VA 24142. Offers MS. *Program availability:* Part-time, evening/weekend. *Faculty:* 9 full-time (4 women). *Students:* 20 full-time (15 women); includes 2 minority (both Black or African American, non-Hispanic/Latino), 2 international. Average age 26. 14 applicants, 86% accepted, 8 enrolled. In 2017, 10 master's awarded. *Degree requirements:* For master's, comprehensive exam, thesis optional. *Entrance requirements:* For master's, GRE, minimum GPA of 2.75, short essay, 3 letters of reference, resume, official transcripts. Additional exam requirements/recommendations for international students: Required—TOEFL (minimum score 550 paper-based; 79 iBT), IELTS (minimum score 6.5). *Application deadline:* For fall admission, 2/1 priority date for domestic students, 12/1 for international students; for spring admission, 9/15 priority date for domestic students, 7/1 for international students. Applications are processed on a rolling basis. Application fee: $50. Electronic applications accepted. *Expenses:* Tuition, state resident: full-time $8336; part-time $347 per credit hour. Tuition, nonresident: full-time $16,862; part-time $702 per credit hour. *Required fees:* $3220; $135 per credit hour. Tuition and fees vary according to course load and program. *Financial support:* In 2017–18, 15 students received support, including 5 research assistantships (averaging $10,000 per year), 8 teaching assistantships (averaging $10,500 per year); career-related internships or fieldwork, scholarships/grants, and unspecified assistantships also available. Support available to part-time students. Financial award application deadline: 3/1; financial award applicants required to submit FAFSA. *Faculty research:* Rhetoric and persuasion in organizations, media relations, organizational legitimacy, issues management, social capital. *Unit head:* Dr. Scott Dunn, Graduate Coordinator, 540-831-1058, Fax: 540-831-5883, E-mail: comm@radford.edu.
Website: http://www.radford.edu/content/grad/home/academics/graduate-programs/strategic-comm.html

Regent University, Graduate School, School of Communication and the Arts, Virginia Beach, VA 23464-9800. Offers acting (MFA); communication (MA, PhD), including media and arts management and promotion (MA), political communication (MA), strategic communication (MA), technical communication (MA); film and TV (MA), including producing (MA, MFA), production, script writing; film-television (MFA), including directing, producing (MA, MFA), script and screenwriting; journalism (MA); theatre (MA). *Program availability:* Part-time, evening/weekend, 100% online, blended/hybrid learning. *Faculty:* 15 full-time (2 women), 66 part-time/adjunct (23 women). *Students:* 101 full-time (65 women), 342 part-time (237 women); includes 177 minority (127 Black or African American, non-Hispanic/Latino; 4 American Indian or Alaska Native, non-Hispanic/Latino; 9 Asian, non-Hispanic/Latino; 25 Hispanic/Latino; 12 Two or more races, non-Hispanic/Latino), 11 international. Average age 37. 498 applicants, 36% accepted, 124 enrolled. In 2017, 93 master's, 22 doctorates awarded. *Degree requirements:* For master's, thesis or alternative; for doctorate, thesis/dissertation. *Entrance requirements:* For master's, transcripts, writing sample, resume, audition (for MFA programs); for doctorate, GRE General Test, resume, writing sample, recommendations, interview, transcripts, personal goals statement. Additional exam requirements/recommendations for international students: Required—TOEFL (minimum score 577 paper-based). *Application deadline:* For fall admission, 3/1 priority date for domestic students; for spring admission, 10/1 priority date for domestic students. Applications are processed on a rolling basis. Application fee: $50. Electronic applications accepted. *Expenses:* $650 per credit (MA, MFA); $885 per credit (PhD); $300 per semester technology fee. *Financial support:* In 2017–18, 234 students received support, including 2 fellowships (averaging $10,000 per year); career-related internships or fieldwork, scholarships/grants, and unspecified assistantships also available. Support available to part-time students. *Faculty research:* Screenwriting, digital media production, communication, acting, directing. *Unit head:* Dr. Robert Herron, Dean, 757-352-4500, E-mail: rherron@regent.edu. *Application contact:* Heidi Cece, Assistant Vice President of Enrollment Management, 800-373-5504, Fax: 757-352-4381, E-mail: admissions@regent.edu.
Website: https://www.regent.edu/school-of-communication-and-the-arts/

Regis College, Strategic Communication Program, Weston, MA 02493. Offers MA. *Program availability:* Part-time, evening/weekend. *Degree requirements:* For master's, thesis. *Entrance requirements:* For master's, GRE or MAT, official transcripts, recommendations, personal statement, resume, interview. Additional exam requirements/recommendations for international students: Required—TOEFL (minimum score 560 paper-based; 79 iBT); Recommended—IELTS (minimum score 6.5). *Application deadline:* Applications are processed on a rolling basis. Application fee: $65. Electronic applications accepted. *Financial support:* Federal Work-Study and unspecified assistantships available. Financial award applicants required to submit FAFSA. *Unit head:* Dr. Colleen Malachowski, Director, 781-768-7373, E-mail: colleen.malachowski@regiscollege.edu.

Rider University, College of Liberal Arts and Sciences, Program in Business Communication, Lawrenceville, NJ 08648-3001. Offers business communication studies (MA); health communication (MA). *Program availability:* Online learning.

Roosevelt University, Graduate Division, College of Arts and Sciences, Department of Communication, Chicago, IL 60605. Offers integrated marketing communications (MSIMC). *Program availability:* Part-time, evening/weekend. *Students:* 38 full-time (28 women), 25 part-time (19 women); includes 28 minority (19 Black or African American, non-Hispanic/Latino; 3 Asian, non-Hispanic/Latino; 5 Hispanic/Latino; 1 Two or more races, non-Hispanic/Latino), 24 international. Average age 27. 43 applicants, 95% accepted, 15 enrolled. In 2017, 38 master's awarded. *Application deadline:* Applications are processed on a rolling basis. Application fee: $40. Electronic applications accepted. *Financial support:* Career-related internships or fieldwork, scholarships/grants, and unspecified assistantships available. *Unit head:* Marian Azzaro, Chair, 312-281-3239. *Application contact:* Sivling Lam, Graduate Admission Counselor, 312-281-3252, E-mail: slam02@roosevelt.edu.

Rowan University, Graduate School, College of Communication and Creative Arts, Integrated Marketing Communication and New Media Certificate of Graduate Study Program, Glassboro, NJ 08028-1701. Offers CGS. Electronic applications accepted. *Expenses:* Tuition, state resident: full-time $15,020; part-time $751 per semester hour. Tuition, nonresident: full-time $15,020; part-time $751 per semester hour. *Required fees:* $3158; $157.90 per semester hour. Tuition and fees vary according to course load, campus/location and program.

St. Bonaventure University, School of Graduate Studies, Jandoli School of Communication, Program in Integrated Marketing Communications, St. Bonaventure, NY 14778-2284. Offers MA. *Program availability:* Part-time, evening/weekend, 100% online. *Faculty:* 5 full-time (3 women), 6 part-time/adjunct (4 women). *Students:* 31 full-time (17 women), 45 part-time (33 women); includes 14 minority (4 Black or African American, non-Hispanic/Latino; 1 American Indian or Alaska Native, non-Hispanic/Latino; 7 Hispanic/Latino; 2 Two or more races, non-Hispanic/Latino), 4 international. Average age 27. 32 applicants, 91% accepted, 20 enrolled. In 2017, 17 master's awarded. *Degree requirements:* For master's, campaign project. *Entrance requirements:* For master's, transcripts, personal statement describing desire to pursue the IMC program. Additional exam requirements/recommendations for international students: Required—TOEFL (minimum score 550 paper-based; 79 iBT). *Application deadline:* For fall admission, 6/5 for domestic students, 2/1 for international students; for spring admission, 10/15 for domestic students, 7/1 for international students. Applications are processed on a rolling basis. Application fee: $0. Electronic applications accepted.

Expenses: $733 per credit hour, $100 graduation fee. *Financial support:* Federal Work-Study, scholarships/grants, health care benefits, and unspecified assistantships available. Support available to part-time students. Financial award application deadline: 4/15; financial award applicants required to submit FAFSA. *Faculty research:* Network analysis of internal and external communication networks in organizations, organizational behavior, student engagement in active learning. *Unit head:* Dr. Richard Lee, Director, 716-375-2563, Fax: 716-375-2588, E-mail: rlee@sbu.edu. *Application contact:* Bruce Campbell, Director of Graduate Admissions, 716-375-2429, Fax: 716-375-4015, E-mail: gradsch@sbu.edu.
Website: http://www.sbu.edu/academics/schools/journalism-and-mass-communications/graduate-degrees/ma-integrated-marketing-communications

St. Bonaventure University, School of Graduate Studies, Jandoli School of Communication, Program in Strategic Leadership, St. Bonaventure, NY 14778-2284. Offers MA. *Program availability:* Part-time, online only, 100% online. *Faculty:* 1 (woman) full-time, 1 (woman) part-time/adjunct. *Students:* 5 full-time (2 women), 30 part-time (14 women); includes 10 minority (5 Black or African American, non-Hispanic/Latino; 1 Asian, non-Hispanic/Latino; 2 Hispanic/Latino; 2 Two or more races, non-Hispanic/Latino). Average age 38. 24 applicants, 79% accepted, 16 enrolled. In 2017, 20 master's awarded. *Degree requirements:* For master's, portfolio, project. *Entrance requirements:* For master's, transcripts, three years of work experience, current resume, short essay (500 words) on candidate's goals for engaging in such a learning experience. Additional exam requirements/recommendations for international students: Required—TOEFL (minimum score 550 paper-based; 79 iBT). *Application deadline:* For fall admission, 6/15 for domestic students, 2/1 for international students; for spring admission, 10/15 for domestic students, 7/1 for international students. Applications are processed on a rolling basis. Application fee: $0. Electronic applications accepted. *Expenses:* $733 per credit, $100 graduation fee. *Financial support:* Federal Work-Study, scholarships/grants, and health care benefits available. Support available to part-time students. Financial award application deadline: 4/15; financial award applicants required to submit FAFSA. *Faculty research:* Internet addiction. *Unit head:* Dr. Kimberly Young, Director, 716-375-2076, Fax: 716-375-2588, E-mail: kyoung@sbu.edu. *Application contact:* Bruce Campbell, Director of Graduate Admissions, 716-375-2429, Fax: 716-375-4015, E-mail: gradsch@sbu.edu.
Website: https://online.sbu.edu/programs/master/msl?schoolsrc=42787

Seton Hall University, College of Communication and the Arts, Program in Strategic Communication, South Orange, NJ 07079-2697. Offers MA. *Program availability:* Part-time, evening/weekend, online learning. *Degree requirements:* For master's, thesis (for some programs). *Entrance requirements:* For master's, GRE or MAT, official transcripts, resume, personal statement, 3 letters of recommendation. Additional exam requirements/recommendations for international students: Required—TOEFL (minimum iBT score 80) or IELTS (6.5). Electronic applications accepted. *Faculty research:* Organizational communication, leadership, digital communication.

Southern Illinois University Edwardsville, Graduate School, College of Arts and Sciences, Department of Applied Communication Studies, Program in Corporate and Organizational Communication, Edwardsville, IL 62026. Offers MA. *Program availability:* Part-time, evening/weekend. *Degree requirements:* For master's, comprehensive exam (for some programs), thesis (for some programs). *Entrance requirements:* Additional exam requirements/recommendations for international students: Required—TOEFL (minimum score 550 paper-based, 79 iBT), IELTS (minimum score 6.5), Michigan Test of English Language Proficiency or PTE. Electronic applications accepted.

Spalding University, Graduate Studies, College of Social Sciences and Humanities, Program in Business and Communication, Louisville, KY 40203-2188. Offers MS. *Program availability:* Part-time, evening/weekend. *Degree requirements:* For master's, project. *Entrance requirements:* For master's, GRE or GMAT, personal essay, interview, letters of recommendation, transcripts, resume. Additional exam requirements/recommendations for international students: Required—TOEFL (minimum score 535 paper-based). *Faculty research:* Curriculum development, consumer behavior, interdisciplinary pedagogy.

State University of New York at Oswego, Graduate Studies, School of Communication, Media and the Arts, Oswego, NY 13126. Offers strategic communication (MA), including health communication, integrated media and social networks, organizational communication. *Entrance requirements:* For master's, GRE, official transcript, statement of purpose, resume, two letters of recommendation.

Stevens Institute of Technology, Graduate School, School of Business, Program in Professional Communications, Hoboken, NJ 07030. Offers Certificate. *Program availability:* Part-time, evening/weekend. *Degree requirements:* For Certificate, minimum B average. *Entrance requirements:* Additional exam requirements/recommendations for international students: Required—TOEFL (minimum score 74 iBT), IELTS (minimum score 6). *Application deadline:* For fall admission, 7/1 for domestic students, 4/15 for international students; for spring admission, 12/1 for domestic and international students. Applications are processed on a rolling basis. Application fee: $60. Electronic applications accepted. *Expenses: Tuition:* Full-time $34,494; part-time $1554 per credit. *Required fees:* $291 per semester. *Financial support:* Fellowships, research assistantships, teaching assistantships, career-related internships or fieldwork, Federal Work-Study, scholarships/grants, and unspecified assistantships available. Financial award application deadline: 2/15; financial award applicants required to submit FAFSA. *Unit head:* Deborah Sinnreich-Levi, Director, 201-216-5403. *Application contact:* Graduate Admissions, 800-496-4935, Fax: 201-216-8044, E-mail: gradadmissions@stevens.edu.

Suffolk University, College of Arts and Sciences, Advertising and Public Relations Department, Boston, MA 02108-2770. Offers communication studies (MAC); integrated marketing communication (MAC); public relations and advertising (MAC). *Program availability:* Part-time, evening/weekend. *Faculty:* 4 full-time (3 women). *Students:* 25 full-time (18 women), 14 part-time (13 women); includes 10 minority (4 Black or African American, non-Hispanic/Latino; 5 Hispanic/Latino; 1 Two or more races, non-Hispanic/Latino), 9 international. Average age 26. 41 applicants, 71% accepted, 2 enrolled. In 2017, 10 master's awarded. *Degree requirements:* For master's, thesis optional. *Entrance requirements:* For master's, GRE General Test, MAT, or GMAT, 2 letters of recommendation, resume. Additional exam requirements/recommendations for international students: Required—TOEFL (minimum score 550 paper-based; 80 iBT). *Application deadline:* For fall admission, 3/15 priority date for domestic and international students; for spring admission, 10/15 priority date for domestic and international students. Applications are processed on a rolling basis. Application fee: $50. Electronic applications accepted. *Expenses:* $29,520 per year full-time tuition; $1,230 per credit part-time. *Financial support:* In 2017–18, 31 students received support, including 4 fellowships (averaging $6,200 per year); career-related internships or fieldwork, Federal Work-Study, institutionally sponsored loans, and scholarships/grants also available. Support available to part-time students. Financial award application deadline: 4/1; financial award applicants required to submit FAFSA. *Faculty research:* Branding law and management, health care communication, gender roles and violence in video games, new media, political communication. *Unit head:* Robert Rosenthal, Chair, 617-573-8502, E-mail: rrosenthal@suffolk.edu. *Application contact:* Mara Marzocchi, Associate Director of Graduate Admissions, 617-573-8302, Fax: 617-305-1733, E-mail: grad.admission@suffolk.edu.
Website: http://www.suffolk.edu/college/graduate/69298.php

Temple University, Klein College of Media and Communication, Department of Communication, Philadelphia, PA 19122-6096. Offers communication management (MS); globalization and development communication (MS); media and communication (PhD). *Program availability:* Part-time, evening/weekend. *Faculty:* 10 full-time (3 women). *Students:* 2 full-time (1 woman), 15 part-time (10 women); includes 6 minority (4 Black or African American, non-Hispanic/Latino; 1 Asian, non-Hispanic/Latino; 1 Two or more races, non-Hispanic/Latino). 8 applicants, 88% accepted, 4 enrolled. In 2017, 7 master's awarded. *Entrance requirements:* For master's, GRE General Test. Additional exam requirements/recommendations for international students: Required—TOEFL (minimum score 620 paper-based; 105 iBT). *Application deadline:* For fall admission, 2/15 for domestic and international students; for spring admission, 11/1 for domestic and international students. Application fee: $60. Electronic applications accepted. *Expenses:* Contact institution. *Financial support:* Career-related internships or fieldwork and Federal Work-Study available. Financial award application deadline: 1/15; financial award applicants required to submit FAFSA. *Unit head:* Dr. R. Lance Holbert, Chair, 215-204-3152, E-mail: r.lance.holbert@temple.edu. *Application contact:* Nicole McKenna, Director, Office of Research and Graduate Studies, 215-204-1497, Fax: 215-204-0310, E-mail: nmckenna@temple.edu.
Website: https://klein.temple.edu/degree/communication

Texas Christian University, Bob Schieffer College of Communication, Fort Worth, TX 76129. Offers communication studies (MS); strategic communication (MS). *Program availability:* Part-time. *Faculty:* 26 full-time (12 women). *Students:* 21 full-time (18 women), 2 part-time (1 woman); includes 5 minority (1 Asian, non-Hispanic/Latino; 4 Hispanic/Latino). Average age 25. 24 applicants, 71% accepted, 12 enrolled. In 2017, 16 master's awarded. *Degree requirements:* For master's, comprehensive exam (for some programs), thesis (for some programs). *Entrance requirements:* For master's, GRE General Test. Additional exam requirements/recommendations for international students: Required—TOEFL (minimum score 550 paper-based; 80 iBT). *Application deadline:* For fall admission, 2/15 for domestic and international students; for spring admission, 10/15 for domestic and international students. Application fee: $60. Electronic applications accepted. *Expenses:* Contact institution. *Financial support:* In 2017–18, 25 students received support, including 18 teaching assistantships with full tuition reimbursements available (averaging $10,000 per year); research assistantships, health care benefits, tuition waivers (full and partial), and unspecified assistantships also available. Financial award application deadline: 2/15. *Faculty research:* Interpersonal communication, family communication, social networking, media history, media studies, media law, media ethics, mobile communications. *Unit head:* Dr. Daxton Stewart, Associate Dean, 817-257-5911, Fax: 817-257-5921, E-mail: d.stewart@tcu.edu. *Application contact:* Alicia E. Craff, Academic Program Specialist, 817-257-5917, Fax: 817-257-5921, E-mail: a.e.craff@tcu.edu.
Website: http://www.schieffercollege.tcu.edu/

Towson University, College of Fine Arts and Communication, Program in Communication Management, Towson, MD 21252-0001. Offers MS. *Students:* 3 full-time (2 women), 12 part-time (9 women); includes 7 minority (all Black or African American, non-Hispanic/Latino). *Degree requirements:* For master's, thesis. *Entrance requirements:* For master's, bachelor's degree with 24 credits in mass communications, public relations, advertising or communication studies; advanced writing and basic statistics courses; professional experience; minimum GPA of 3.0; letter of recommendation; resume. Additional exam requirements/recommendations for international students: Required—TOEFL. *Application deadline:* For fall admission, 1/17 for domestic students, 5/15 for international students; for spring admission, 10/15 for domestic students, 12/1 for international students. Applications are processed on a rolling basis. Application fee: $45. Electronic applications accepted. *Expenses:* Tuition, state resident: full-time $7960; part-time $398 per unit. Tuition, nonresident: full-time $16,480; part-time $824 per unit. *Required fees:* $2600; $130 per year. $390 per term. *Financial support:* Application deadline: 4/1. *Unit head:* Dr. Lingling Zhang, Graduate Program Director, 410-704-3458, E-mail: lizhang@towson.edu. *Application contact:* Coverley Beidleman, Assistant Director of Graduate Admissions, 410-704-5630, Fax: 410-704-3030, E-mail: cbeidleman@towson.edu.
Website: http://www.towson.edu/cofac/departments/communication/gradcommunicationmgmt/

Troy University, Graduate School, College of Communication and Fine Arts, Troy, AL 36082. Offers strategic communication (MS). *Program availability:* Part-time, evening/weekend. *Faculty:* 5 full-time (3 women). *Students:* 47 full-time (33 women), 76 part-time (60 women); includes 29 minority (26 Black or African American, non-Hispanic/Latino; 1 Hispanic/Latino; 1 Native Hawaiian or other Pacific Islander, non-Hispanic/Latino; 1 Two or more races, non-Hispanic/Latino). Average age 27. 52 applicants, 100% accepted, 42 enrolled. In 2017, 44 master's awarded. *Degree requirements:* For master's, comprehensive exam, thesis optional, minimum GPA of 3.0, admission to candidacy. *Entrance requirements:* For master's, GRE (minimum score of 850 on old exam or 290 on new exam), MAT (minimum score of 385) or GMAT (minimum score of 380), bachelor's degree; minimum undergraduate GPA of 2.5 or 3.0 on last 30 semester hours. Additional exam requirements/recommendations for international students: Required—TOEFL (minimum score 523 paper-based; 70 iBT), IELTS (minimum score 6). *Application deadline:* For fall admission, 6/1 for international students; for spring admission, 10/15 for international students. Applications are processed on a rolling basis. Application fee: $50. Electronic applications accepted. *Expenses:* Tuition, state resident: part-time $417 per credit hour. Tuition, nonresident: part-time $834 per credit hour. *Required fees:* $42 per credit hour. $50 per semester. Tuition and fees vary according to campus/location. *Financial support:* Fellowships, career-related internships or fieldwork, and scholarships/grants available. Support available to part-time students. Financial award applicants required to submit FAFSA. *Unit head:* Dr. Larry Blocher, Dean, 334-670-3869, Fax: 334-670-3858, E-mail: lblocher@troy.edu. *Application contact:* Jessica A. Kimbro, Director of Graduate Admissions, 334-670-3178, E-mail: jacord@troy.edu.

Universidad Autonoma de Guadalajara, Graduate Programs, Guadalajara, Mexico. Offers administrative law and justice (LL M); advertising and corporate communications (MA); architecture (M Arch); business (MBA); computational science (MCC); education (Ed M, Ed D); English-Spanish translation (MA); entrepreneurship and management (MBA); integrated management of digital animation (MA); international business (MIB); international corporate law (LL M); internet technologies (MS); manufacturing systems (MMS); occupational health (MS); philosophy (MA, PhD); power electronics (MS); quality systems (MQS); renewable energy (MS); social evaluation of projects (MBA); strategic market research (MBA); tax law (MA); teaching mathematics (MA).

Universidad Iberoamericana, Graduate School, Santo Domingo D.N., Dominican Republic. Offers business administration (MBA, PMBA); constitutional law (LL M); dentistry (DMD); educational management (MA); integrated marketing communication (MA); psychopedagogical intervention (M Ed); real estate law (LL M); strategic management of human talent (MM).

Université de Sherbrooke, Faculty of Administration, Program in Marketing Communications, Sherbrooke, QC J1K 2R1, Canada. Offers M Adm. *Degree*

requirements: For master's, one foreign language, thesis. *Entrance requirements:* For master's, bachelor's degree in related field, minimum GPA of 3.0 (on 4.3 scale). Electronic applications accepted.

University of Alaska Fairbanks, College of Liberal Arts, Department of Communications, Fairbanks, AK 99775-5680. Offers professional communication (MA). *Program availability:* Part-time. *Degree requirements:* For master's, comprehensive exam, thesis, oral defense of thesis. *Entrance requirements:* For master's, bachelor's degree from accredited institution with minimum cumulative undergraduate and major GPA of 3.0, academic writing sample. Additional exam requirements/recommendations for international students: Required—TOEFL (minimum score 550 paper-based; 79 iBT), IELTS (minimum score 6.5). Electronic applications accepted. *Faculty research:* Interpersonal communications, health communications, intercultural communications, politeness and face management in conversation, gender communication.

University of Central Florida, College of Sciences, Nicholson School of Communication, Orlando, FL 32816. Offers communication (MA); corporate communication (Certificate). *Program availability:* Part-time, evening/weekend. *Students:* 32 full-time (23 women), 25 part-time (20 women); includes 14 minority (5 Black or African American, non-Hispanic/Latino; 1 Asian, non-Hispanic/Latino; 5 Hispanic/Latino; 3 Two or more races, non-Hispanic/Latino), 8 international. Average age 28. 52 applicants, 75% accepted, 27 enrolled. In 2017, 27 master's, 17 other advanced degrees awarded. *Degree requirements:* For master's, thesis or alternative. *Entrance requirements:* For master's, GRE General Test, minimum GPA of 3.0 in last 60 hours of course work, letters of recommendation, personal/professional statement. Additional exam requirements/recommendations for international students: Required—TOEFL. *Application deadline:* For fall admission, 6/1 for domestic students; for spring admission, 11/1 for domestic students. Application fee: $30. Electronic applications accepted. *Expenses:* Tuition, state resident: part-time $288.16 per credit hour. Tuition, nonresident: part-time $1073.31 per credit hour. Tuition and fees vary according to program. *Financial support:* In 2017–18, 21 students received support, including 4 fellowships with partial tuition reimbursements available (averaging $2,000 per year), 4 research assistantships with partial tuition reimbursements available (averaging $5,339 per year), 18 teaching assistantships with partial tuition reimbursements available (averaging $9,407 per year); career-related internships or fieldwork, Federal Work-Study, institutionally sponsored loans, health care benefits, tuition waivers (partial), and unspecified assistantships also available. Financial award application deadline: 3/1; financial award applicants required to submit FAFSA. *Faculty research:* Persuasion, interpersonal communication, nonverbal communication, conflict resolution. *Unit head:* Dr. Robert Littlefield, Director, 407-823-1708, E-mail: robert.littlefield@ucf.edu. *Application contact:* Associate Director, Graduate Admissions, 407-823-2766, Fax: 407-823-6442, E-mail: gradadmissions@ucf.edu. Website: http://communication.cos.ucf.edu/

University of Colorado Denver, Business School, Program in Marketing, Denver, CO 80217. Offers brand management and marketing communication (MS); global marketing (MS); high-tech and entrepreneurial marketing (MS); marketing for sustainability (MS); marketing research (MS); sports and entertainment marketing (MS). *Program availability:* Part-time, evening/weekend. *Degree requirements:* For master's, 30 semester hours (21 of marketing core courses, 9 of marketing electives). *Entrance requirements:* For master's, GMAT, resume, essay, two letters of recommendation, financial statements (for international applicants). Additional exam requirements/recommendations for international students: Required—TOEFL (minimum score 525 paper-based; 71 iBT); Recommended—IELTS (minimum score 6.5). Electronic applications accepted. *Expenses:* Contact institution. *Faculty research:* Marketing issues in the Chinese environment, impact of individual difference and contextual factors on the risk-taking behaviors of managers making new-business creation decisions, attribution theory perspective of conflict between marketers and engineers, organizational identity and identification, international market entry strategies.

University of Illinois at Urbana–Champaign, Graduate College, Program in Strategic Brand Communication, Champaign, IL 61820. Offers MS. Program offered jointly between Department of Business Administration and Charles H. Sandage Department of Advertising. *Program availability:* Online learning.

University of Nebraska–Lincoln, Graduate College, College of Arts and Sciences, Department of Communication Studies, Lincoln, NE 68588. Offers instructional communication (MA, PhD); interpersonal communication (MA, PhD); marketing, communication studies, and advertising (MA, PhD); organizational communication (MA, PhD); rhetoric and culture (MA, PhD). *Degree requirements:* For master's, thesis optional; for doctorate, comprehensive exam, thesis/dissertation. *Entrance requirements:* For master's and doctorate, GRE General Test, writing sample. Additional exam requirements/recommendations for international students: Required—TOEFL (minimum score 600 paper-based). Electronic applications accepted. *Faculty research:* Message strategies, gender communication, political communication, organizational communication, instructional communication.

University of Oklahoma, College of Arts and Sciences, Department of Communication, Norman, OK 73019. Offers communication (MA); communication technology (PhD); health communication (PhD); intercultural/international communication (PhD); organizational communication (PhD); political/mass communication (PhD); social influence/interpersonal communication (PhD). *Program availability:* Part-time. *Faculty:* 18 full-time (8 women). *Students:* 27 full-time (17 women), 36 part-time (17 women); includes 23 minority (8 Black or African American, non-Hispanic/Latino; 3 American Indian or Alaska Native, non-Hispanic/Latino; 1 Asian, non-Hispanic/Latino; 10 Hispanic/Latino; 1 Two or more races, non-Hispanic/Latino), 5 international. Average age 35. 45 applicants, 49% accepted, 10 enrolled. In 2017, 14 master's, 6 doctorates awarded. *Degree requirements:* For master's, comprehensive exam (for some programs), thesis (for some programs), comprehensive exams or thesis; for doctorate, comprehensive exam, thesis/dissertation. *Entrance requirements:* For master's, GRE (for assistantship), statement of purpose, transcripts, writing sample, letters of recommendation; for doctorate, GRE, statement of purpose, transcripts, writing sample, letters of recommendation. Additional exam requirements/recommendations for international students: Required—TOEFL (minimum score 79 iBT) or IELTS (minimum score 6.5). *Application deadline:* For fall admission, 1/15 priority date for domestic students, 1/15 for international students; for spring admission, 10/15 for domestic and international students. Application fee: $50 ($100 for international students). Electronic applications accepted. *Expenses:* Tuition, state resident: full-time $5119; part-time $213.30 per credit hour. Tuition, nonresident: full-time $19,778; part-time $824.10 per credit hour. *Required fees:* $3458; $133.55 per credit hour. $126.50 per semester. *Financial support:* In 2017–18, 29 students received support, including 1 research assistantship with full tuition reimbursement available (averaging $10,373 per year), 25 teaching assistantships with full tuition reimbursements available (averaging $16,350 per year); health care benefits also available. Financial award application deadline: 6/1; financial award applicants required to submit FAFSA. *Faculty research:* Interpersonal/social influence, organizational, political/mass communication, health communication, intercultural/international. *Total annual research expenditures:* $242,423. *Unit head:* Dr. Michael W. Kramer, Professor and Chair, 405-325-9503, Fax: 405-325-7625, E-mail: mkramer@ou.edu. *Application contact:* Shay Glover, Academic Advisor, 405-325-7710,

Fax: 405-325-7625, E-mail: shay.glover@ou.edu.
Website: http://www.ou.edu/cas/comm

University of Portland, Department of Communication Studies, Portland, OR 97203-5798. Offers communication (MA); management communication (MS). *Program availability:* Part-time, evening/weekend. *Degree requirements:* For master's, thesis optional. *Entrance requirements:* For master's, GRE General Test, minimum GPA of 3.25, 3 letters of recommendation, resume, statement of goals, official transcripts. Additional exam requirements/recommendations for international students: Required—TOEFL (minimum score 600 paper-based; 100 iBT), IELTS (minimum score 7.5).

University of Southern California, Graduate School, Annenberg School for Communication and Journalism, School of Communication, Program in Communication Management, Los Angeles, CA 90089. Offers MCM, JD/MCM, MCM/MAJCS. *Program availability:* Part-time, evening/weekend, online learning. *Degree requirements:* For master's, professional project. *Entrance requirements:* For master's, GRE General Test or GMAT, resume, writing samples, recommendation letters, statement of purpose. Additional exam requirements/recommendations for international students: Required—TOEFL (minimum score 114 iBT), IELTS (minimum score 8). Electronic applications accepted. *Faculty research:* Global communication, communication law and policy, entertainment management, marketing communication, strategic and corporate communication management.

University of South Florida, College of Arts and Sciences, Zimmerman School of Advertising and Mass Communications, Tampa, FL 33620-9951. Offers mass communications (MA), including media studies, multimedia journalism, strategic communication management. *Program availability:* Part-time, evening/weekend. *Faculty:* 10 full-time (6 women). *Students:* 25 full-time (20 women), 25 part-time (20 women); includes 7 minority (4 Black or African American, non-Hispanic/Latino; 2 Hispanic/Latino; 1 Native Hawaiian or other Pacific Islander, non-Hispanic/Latino), 29 international. Average age 26. 28 applicants, 64% accepted, 15 enrolled. In 2017, 8 master's awarded. *Degree requirements:* For master's, comprehensive exam, thesis optional. *Entrance requirements:* For master's, GRE General Test, minimum GPA of 3.0 in last 60 hours of course work, three letters of recommendation, letter of intent, resume/curriculum vitae. Additional exam requirements/recommendations for international students: Required—TOEFL (minimum score 550 paper-based; 79 iBT) or IELTS (minimum score 6.5). *Application deadline:* For fall admission, 2/15 priority date for domestic and international students. Application fee: $30. Electronic applications accepted. *Financial support:* In 2017–18, 10 students received support, including 9 teaching assistantships with tuition reimbursements available (averaging $10,513 per year); unspecified assistantships also available. Financial award application deadline: 2/28. *Faculty research:* First Amendment analysis, civic journalism, public opinion, media ethics, media effects research in sports public relations, public relations management, advertisement, telecommunications. *Total annual research expenditures:* $78,680. *Unit head:* Dr. Wayne Garcia, Director and Senior Instructor, 813-498-1925, Fax: 813-974-2592, E-mail: wgarcia@usf.edu. *Application contact:* Dr. Artermio Ramirez, Jr., Associate Director, Fax: 813-974-2592, E-mail: aramirez2@usf.edu.
Website: http://masscom.usf.edu/grad/

University of South Florida, Innovative Education, Tampa, FL 33620-9951. Offers adult, career and higher education (Graduate Certificate), including college teaching, leadership in developing human resources, leadership in higher education; Africana studies (Graduate Certificate), including diasporas and health disparities, genocide and human rights; aging studies (Graduate Certificate), including gerontology; art research (Graduate Certificate), including museum studies; business foundations (Graduate Certificate); chemical and biomedical engineering (Graduate Certificate), including materials science and engineering, water, health and sustainability; child and family studies (Graduate Certificate), including positive behavior support; civil and industrial engineering (Graduate Certificate), including transportation systems analysis; community and family health (Graduate Certificate), including maternal and child health, social marketing and public health, violence and injury: prevention and intervention, women's health; criminology (Graduate Certificate), including criminal justice administration; data science for public administration (Graduate Certificate); digital humanities (Graduate Certificate); educational measurement and research (Graduate Certificate), including evaluation; English (Graduate Certificate), including comparative literary studies, creative writing, professional and technical communication; entrepreneurship (Graduate Certificate); environmental health (Graduate Certificate), including safety management; epidemiology and biostatistics (Graduate Certificate), including applied biostatistics, biostatistics, concepts and tools of epidemiology, epidemiology, epidemiology of infectious diseases; geography, environment and planning (Graduate Certificate), including community development, environmental policy and management, geographical information systems; geology (Graduate Certificate), including hydrogeology; global health (Graduate Certificate), including disaster management, global health and Latin American and Caribbean studies, global health practice, humanitarian assistance, infection control; government and international affairs (Graduate Certificate), including Cuban studies, globalization studies; health policy and management (Graduate Certificate), including health management and leadership, public health policy and programs; hearing specialist: early intervention (Graduate Certificate); industrial and management systems engineering (Graduate Certificate), including systems engineering, technology management; information studies (Graduate Certificate), including school library media specialist; information systems/decision sciences (Graduate Certificate), including analytics and business intelligence; instructional technology (Graduate Certificate), including distance education, Florida digital/virtual educator, instructional design, multimedia design, Web design; internal medicine, bioethics and medical humanities (Graduate Certificate), including biomedical ethics; Latin American and Caribbean studies (Graduate Certificate); leadership for coastal resiliency planning (Graduate Certificate); mass communications (Graduate Certificate), including multimedia journalism; mathematics and statistics (Graduate Certificate), including mathematics; medicine (Graduate Certificate), including aging and neuroscience, bioinformatics, biotechnology, brain fitness and memory management, clinical investigation, hand and upper limb rehabilitation, health informatics, health sciences, integrative weight management, intellectual property, medicine and gender, metabolic and nutritional medicine, metabolic cardiology, pharmacy sciences; national and competitive intelligence (Graduate Certificate); nursing (Graduate Certificate), including simulation based academic fellowship in advanced pain management; psychological and social foundations (Graduate Certificate), including career counseling, college teaching, diversity in education, mental health counseling, school counseling; public affairs (Graduate Certificate), including nonprofit management, public management, research administration; public health (Graduate Certificate), including assessing chemical toxicity and public health risks, health equity, pharmacoepidemiology, public health generalist, toxicology, translational research in adolescent behavioral health; public health practices (Graduate Certificate), including planning for healthy communities; rehabilitation and mental health counseling (Graduate Certificate), including integrative mental health care, marriage and family therapy, rehabilitation technology; secondary education (Graduate Certificate), including ESOL, foreign language education: culture and content, foreign language education: professional; social work (Graduate Certificate), including geriatric social work/clinical gerontology; special education (Graduate Certificate), including autism spectrum

disorder, disabilities education: severe/profound; world languages (Graduate Certificate), including teaching English as a second language (TESL) or foreign language. *Unit head:* Dr. Cynthia DeLuca, Associate Vice President and Assistant Vice Provost, 813-974-3077, Fax: 813-974-7061, E-mail: deluca@usf.edu. *Application contact:* Owen Hooper, Director, Summer and Alternative Calendar Programs, 813-974-6917, E-mail: hooper@usf.edu.
Website: http://www.usf.edu/innovative-education/

University of Wisconsin–Stevens Point, College of Fine Arts and Communication, Division of Communication, Stevens Point, WI 54481-3897. Offers interpersonal communication (MA); media studies (MA); organizational communication (MA); public relations (MA). *Program availability:* Part-time. *Degree requirements:* For master's, thesis or alternative. *Entrance requirements:* For master's, GRE. Additional exam requirements/recommendations for international students: Required—TOEFL (minimum score 575 paper-based). *Faculty research:* Communication theory and research, film history.

University of Wisconsin–Whitewater, School of Graduate Studies, College of Arts and Communications, Department of Communication, Whitewater, WI 53190-1790. Offers corporate communication (MS); mass communication (MS). *Program availability:* Part-time, evening/weekend, online learning. *Degree requirements:* For master's, thesis or alternative. *Entrance requirements:* For master's, 2 letters of recommendation, goal statement. Additional exam requirements/recommendations for international students: Required—TOEFL (minimum score 550 paper-based; 80 iBT), IELTS (minimum score 6). Electronic applications accepted.

Washington State University, The Edward R. Murrow College of Communication, Pullman, WA 99164-2520. Offers communication (MA, PhD); strategic communication (MA). MA in strategic communication offered at the Global (online) campus. *Degree requirements:* For master's, comprehensive exam (for some programs), thesis optional, oral exam; for doctorate, comprehensive exam, thesis/dissertation. *Entrance requirements:* For master's, GRE General Test, minimum GPA of 3.25, 3 letters of recommendation; for doctorate, GRE General Test, minimum undergraduate GPA of 3.25, graduate 3.5; MA in communication; 3 letters of recommendation. Additional exam requirements/recommendations for international students: Required—TOEFL (minimum score 580 paper-based). Electronic applications accepted. *Faculty research:* Communication technology, health communication, science communication, political communication, intercultural communication.

Webster University, School of Communications, Program in Communications Management, St. Louis, MO 63119-3194. Offers MA.

Western Kentucky University, Graduate Studies, Potter College of Arts and Letters, Department of Communication, Bowling Green, KY 42101. Offers communication (MA); organizational communication (Graduate Certificate). *Program availability:* Part-time, evening/weekend. *Degree requirements:* For master's, comprehensive exam, thesis optional, final exam. *Entrance requirements:* For master's, GRE General Test, minimum GPA of 2.75. Additional exam requirements/recommendations for international students: Required—TOEFL (minimum score 555 paper-based; 79 iBT). *Faculty research:* Public rhetoric and public address organization communication, teamwork in communication, intercultural crisis communication.

West Virginia University, Reed College of Media, Morgantown, WV 26506-6010. Offers data marketing communications (MS); integrated marketing communications (MS, Graduate Certificate); journalism (MSJ); media solutions and innovation (MSJ). *Program availability:* Part-time, online learning. *Students:* 165 full-time (122 women), 232 part-time (167 women); includes 81 minority (46 Black or African American, non-Hispanic/Latino; 5 Asian, non-Hispanic/Latino; 20 Hispanic/Latino; 10 Two or more races, non-Hispanic/Latino), 6 international. *Degree requirements:* For master's, thesis or alternative. *Entrance requirements:* For master's, GRE General Test, minimum GPA of 3.0, writing samples. Additional exam requirements/recommendations for international students: Required—TOEFL (minimum score 550 paper-based). *Application deadline:* For fall admission, 3/1 priority date for domestic students, 3/1 for international students. Application fee: $60. Electronic applications accepted. *Expenses:* Tuition, state resident: full-time $9450. Tuition, nonresident: full-time $24,390. *Financial support:* Research assistantships, teaching assistantships, career-related internships or fieldwork, Federal Work-Study, institutionally sponsored loans, health care benefits, tuition waivers (full and partial), and administrative assistantships available. Financial award application deadline: 2/1; financial award applicants required to submit FAFSA. *Faculty research:* History, law, and women in media; press management; public opinion; advertising effectiveness; international advertising. *Unit head:* Dr. Maryann Reed, Dean, 304-293-3505 Ext. 5409, Fax: 304-293-3072, E-mail: maryann.reed@mail.wvu.edu. *Application contact:* Dr. Steve Urbanski, Director of Graduate Studies/Associate Professor, 304-293-6797, Fax: 304-293-3072, E-mail: steve.urbanski@mail.wvu.edu.
Website: http://reedcollegeofmedia.wvu.edu/

Health Communication

Arkansas State University, Graduate School, College of Media and Communication, Department of Communication, State University, AR 72467. Offers communication studies (MA, SCCT); health communications (Graduate Certificate). *Program availability:* Part-time. *Degree requirements:* For master's, one foreign language, comprehensive exam, thesis or alternative; for other advanced degree, comprehensive exam. *Entrance requirements:* For master's, GRE General Test or MAT, appropriate bachelor's degree, writing sample, letter of recommendation, official transcripts, immunization records; for other advanced degree, GRE or MAT, appropriate master's degree, interview, official transcript, immunization records. Additional exam requirements/recommendations for international students: Required—TOEFL (minimum score 550 paper-based; 79 iBT), IELTS (minimum score 6), PTE (minimum score 56). Electronic applications accepted.

Boston University, Metropolitan College, Program in Health Communication, Boston, MA 02215. Offers MS. *Program availability:* Part-time, online learning. *Faculty:* 1 full-time (0 women), 9 part-time/adjunct (5 women). *Students:* 53 part-time (46 women); includes 15 minority (8 Black or African American, non-Hispanic/Latino; 1 Asian, non-Hispanic/Latino; 6 Hispanic/Latino), 1 international. Average age 32. 13 applicants, 85% accepted, 3 enrolled. In 2017, 37 master's awarded. *Entrance requirements:* For master's, bachelor's degree, minimum GPA of 3.0. Additional exam requirements/recommendations for international students: Required—TOEFL (minimum score 100 iBT). *Application deadline:* For fall admission, 7/13 for domestic students; for spring admission, 11/21 for domestic students; for summer admission, 3/28 for domestic students. Applications are processed on a rolling basis. Application fee: $85. Electronic applications accepted. *Expenses:* Contact institution. *Financial support:* Unspecified assistantships available. Support available to part-time students. Financial award applicants required to submit FAFSA. *Faculty research:* Public relations and health communication. *Unit head:* Leigh Curtin-Wilding, Director, 617-353-6000.
Website: http://www.bu.edu/online/online_programs/graduate_degree/master_health_communication/

Chatham University, Program in Communication, Pittsburgh, PA 15232-2826. Offers environmental communication (M Comm); health communication (M Comm); strategic communication (M Comm). *Program availability:* Part-time, online learning. *Faculty:* 3 part-time/adjunct (2 women). *Students:* 4 full-time (1 woman), 9 part-time (all women); includes 1 minority (Black or African American, non-Hispanic/Latino), 1 international. Average age 28. 16 applicants, 50% accepted, 7 enrolled. *Entrance requirements:* Additional exam requirements/recommendations for international students: Required—TOEFL, IELTS. *Application deadline:* Applications are processed on a rolling basis. Application fee: $35. Electronic applications accepted. Application fee is waived when completed online. *Expenses: Tuition:* Full-time $16,740; part-time $930 per credit. *Required fees:* $486; $27 per credit. $243 per semester. *Financial support:* Applicants required to submit FAFSA. *Application contact:* Athena Wintruba, Graduate Admission Recruiter, 412-365-1141, E-mail: awintruba@chatham.edu.
Website: http://www.chatham.edu/mcomm/

The College of New Jersey, Office of Graduate and Advancing Education, School of Nursing, Health, and Exercise Science, Program in Public Health, Ewing, NJ 08628. Offers global health (MPH); health communications (MPH); precision health (MPH).

Cornell University, Graduate School, Graduate Fields of Agriculture and Life Sciences, Field of Communication, Ithaca, NY 14853. Offers communication (MS, PhD); human-computer interaction (MS, PhD); language and communication (MS, PhD); media communication and society (MS, PhD); organizational communication (MS, PhD); science, environment and health communication (MS, PhD); social psychology of communication (MS, PhD). *Degree requirements:* For master's, thesis (MS); for doctorate, comprehensive exam, thesis/dissertation. *Entrance requirements:* For master's and doctorate, GRE General Test, 3 letters of recommendation. Additional exam requirements/recommendations for international students: Required—TOEFL (minimum score 600 paper-based; 100 iBT). Electronic applications accepted. *Faculty research:* Mass communication, communication technologies, science and environmental communication.

DePaul University, College of Communication, Chicago, IL 60604. Offers digital communication and media arts (MA); health communication (MA); journalism (MA); media and cinema studies (MA); multicultural communication (MA); organizational communication (MA); public relations and advertising (MA); relational communication (MA). *Program availability:* Part-time, evening/weekend. *Entrance requirements:* Additional exam requirements/recommendations for international students: Required—TOEFL (minimum score 590 paper-based; 96 iBT), IELTS (minimum score 7.5) or PTE. *Application deadline:* For fall admission, 6/1 priority date for domestic students; for winter admission, 10/1 priority date for domestic students; for spring admission, 2/15 priority date for domestic students. Applications are processed on a rolling basis. Application fee: $40. Electronic applications accepted. *Financial support:* Applicants required to submit FAFSA. *Unit head:* Salma Ghanem, Dean, 312-362-8600, Fax: 312-362-8620. *Application contact:* Ann Spittle, Director of Graduate Admission, 773-325-7315, Fax: 312-362-8620, E-mail: graddepaul@depaul.edu.
Website: http://communication.depaul.edu/

East Carolina University, Graduate School, College of Fine Arts and Communication, School of Communication, Greenville, NC 27858-4353. Offers communication (MA); health communication (Certificate). *Students:* 12 full-time (11 women), 32 part-time (25 women); includes 14 minority (11 Black or African American, non-Hispanic/Latino; 1 Asian, non-Hispanic/Latino; 1 Hispanic/Latino; 1 Two or more races, non-Hispanic/Latino), 1 international. Average age 32. 19 applicants, 84% accepted, 13 enrolled. In 2017, 12 master's, 3 other advanced degrees awarded. *Degree requirements:* For master's, thesis or alternative. *Entrance requirements:* For master's, GRE. Additional exam requirements/recommendations for international students: Required—TOEFL. *Application deadline:* For fall admission, 6/1 priority date for domestic students; for spring admission, 10/15 for domestic students. Applications are processed on a rolling basis. Electronic applications accepted. *Expenses:* Tuition, state resident: full-time $4749; part-time $297 per credit hour. Tuition, nonresident: full-time $17,898; part-time $1119 per credit hour. *Required fees:* $2691; $224 per credit hour. Part-time tuition and fees vary according to course load and program. *Financial support:* Teaching assistantships available. *Unit head:* Dr. Linda Kean, Director, 252-328-4227, E-mail: keanl@ecu.edu.
Website: http://www.ecu.edu/comm/

Fontbonne University, Graduate Programs, St. Louis, MO 63105-3098. Offers accounting (MBA, MS); art (MA); art (K-12) (MAT); business (MBA); computer science (MS); deaf education (MA); early intervention in deaf education (MA); education (MA), including autism spectrum disorders, curriculum and instruction, diverse learners, early childhood education, reading, special education; elementary education (MAT); family and consumer sciences (MA), including multidisciplinary health communication studies; fine arts (MFA); instructional design and technology (MS); management and leadership (MM); middle school education (MAT); secondary education (MAT); special education (MAT); speech-language pathology (MS); supply chain management (MS); theatre (MA). *Program availability:* Part-time, evening/weekend, online learning. *Degree requirements:* For master's, comprehensive exam (for some programs), thesis (for some programs). *Entrance requirements:* Additional exam requirements/recommendations for international students: Required—TOEFL (minimum score 500 paper-based; 65 iBT). Electronic applications accepted.

Gannon University, School of Graduate Studies, College of Humanities, Education, and Social Sciences, School of Humanities, Program in Health Communication, Erie, PA 16541-0001. Offers MA. *Entrance requirements:* For master's, bachelor's degree from accredited college or university, transcripts, 3 professional letters of recommendation, statement of professional and career goals. Additional exam requirements/recommendations for international students: Required—TOEFL (minimum score 79 iBT). Electronic applications accepted. Application fee is waived when completed online.

The George Washington University, Milken Institute School of Public Health, Department of Global Health, Washington, DC 20052. Offers global health (Dr PH); global health communication (MPH). *Students:* 16 full-time (15 women), 21 part-time (12 women); includes 16 minority (6 Black or African American, non-Hispanic/Latino; 7 Asian, non-Hispanic/Latino; 2 Hispanic/Latino; 1 Two or more races, non-Hispanic/Latino), 4 international. Average age 37. 126 applicants, 61% accepted, 14 enrolled. In 2017, 6 master's awarded. *Entrance requirements:* For master's, GMAT, GRE General Test, or MCAT. Additional exam requirements/recommendations for international students: Required—TOEFL. *Application deadline:* For fall admission, 4/15 priority date for domestic students, 4/15 for international students; for spring admission, 11/1 for domestic and international students. Applications are processed on a rolling basis. Application fee: $75. *Expenses: Tuition:* Full-time $28,800; part-time $1655 per credit hour. *Required fees:* $45; $2.75 per credit hour. *Financial support:* In 2017–18, 24 students received support. Tuition waivers available. Financial award application deadline: 2/15. *Unit head:* Prof. James Tielsch, Chair, 202-994-4124, Fax: 202-994-1955, E-mail: jtielsch@gwu.edu. *Application contact:* Jane Smith, Director of Admissions, 202-994-0248, Fax: 202-994-1860, E-mail: sphhsinfo@gwumc.edu.

Indiana University–Purdue University Indianapolis, School of Liberal Arts, Department of Communication Studies, Indianapolis, IN 46202. Offers applied communication (MA); health communication (PhD). *Program availability:* Part-time. *Degree requirements:* For master's, comprehensive exam, thesis; for doctorate, thesis/dissertation. *Entrance requirements:* For doctorate, master's degree. Additional exam requirements/recommendations for international students: Required—TOEFL; Recommended—IELTS. Electronic applications accepted.

Johns Hopkins University, Bloomberg School of Public Health, Department of Health, Behavior and Society, Baltimore, MD 21218. Offers genetic counseling (Sc M); health education and health communication (MSPH); social and behavioral sciences (PhD); social factors in health (MHS). *Students:* 86 full-time (76 women), 5 part-time (4 women); includes 33 minority (8 Black or African American, non-Hispanic/Latino; 13 Asian, non-Hispanic/Latino; 7 Hispanic/Latino; 5 Two or more races, non-Hispanic/Latino), 13 international. Average age 28. 312 applicants, 29% accepted, 28 enrolled. In 2017, 27 master's, 10 doctorates awarded. *Degree requirements:* For master's, comprehensive exam (for some programs), thesis (for some programs); for doctorate, comprehensive exam, thesis/dissertation. *Entrance requirements:* For master's, GRE, curriculum vitae, 3 letters of recommendation; for doctorate, GRE, transcripts, curriculum vitae, 3 recommendation letters. Additional exam requirements/recommendations for international students: Required—TOEFL (minimum score 100 iBT), IELTS (minimum score 7). *Application deadline:* Applications are processed on a rolling basis. Application fee: $135. Electronic applications accepted. *Financial support:* Fellowships with tuition reimbursements, research assistantships, teaching assistantships, career-related internships or fieldwork, Federal Work-Study, scholarships/grants, traineeships, health care benefits, unspecified assistantships, and stipends available. *Faculty research:* Social determinants of health and structural and community-level inventions to improve health, communication and health education, behavioral and social aspects of genetic counseling. *Unit head:* Margaret Ensminger, Interim Chair, 410-502-4076, Fax: 410-502-4080. *Application contact:* Shenay Johnson, Academic Program Administrator, 410-502-4415, E-mail: shejohns@jhu.edu.
Website: http://jhsph.edu/dept/hbs

Kansas State University, Graduate School, College of Arts and Sciences, A.Q. Miller School of Journalism and Mass Communications, Manhattan, KS 66506. Offers advertising (MS); community journalism (MS); global communication (MS); health communication (MS); media management (MS); public relations (MS). *Program availability:* Part-time, evening/weekend. *Degree requirements:* For master's, comprehensive exam, thesis. *Entrance requirements:* For master's, GRE General Test, minimum GPA of 3.0. Additional exam requirements/recommendations for international students: Required—TOEFL (minimum score 79 iBT). Electronic applications accepted. *Faculty research:* Health communication, risk communication, strategic communications, community journalism, global communication.

Lasell College, Graduate and Professional Studies in Communication, Newton, MA 02466-2709. Offers health communication (MSC, Graduate Certificate); integrated marketing communication (MSC, Graduate Certificate); public relations (MSC, Graduate Certificate). *Program availability:* Part-time, evening/weekend, 100% online, blended/hybrid learning. *Faculty:* 3 full-time (2 women), 7 part-time/adjunct (5 women). *Students:* 25 full-time (16 women), 35 part-time (28 women); includes 12 minority (6 Black or African American, non-Hispanic/Latino; 1 Asian, non-Hispanic/Latino; 4 Hispanic/Latino; 1 Two or more races, non-Hispanic/Latino), 16 international. Average age 30. 53 applicants, 45% accepted, 22 enrolled. In 2017, 28 master's awarded. *Degree requirements:* For master's, comprehensive exam, thesis or alternative, minimum GPA of 3.0; special project or internship. *Entrance requirements:* For master's, one-page personal statement, 2 letters of recommendation, resume, bachelor's degree transcript; for Graduate Certificate, bachelor's degree transcript, 2 letters of recommendation, 1-page personal statement, resume. Additional exam requirements/recommendations for international students: Required—TOEFL (minimum score 550 paper-based, 79 iBT) or IELTS (minimum score 6). *Application deadline:* For fall admission, 8/31 priority date for domestic students, 6/30 priority date for international students; for spring admission, 12/31 priority date for domestic students, 10/31 priority date for international students. Applications are processed on a rolling basis. Electronic applications accepted. *Expenses:* $600 per credit. *Financial support:* Federal Work-Study, scholarships/grants, and tuition discounts available. Support available to part-time students. Financial award application deadline: 8/31; financial award applicants required to submit FAFSA. *Faculty research:* Terrorists' use of the Internet; refugees' use of cell phones as means of communication in Jordan and Germany; political communication; analysis of the media coverage of the conflict and peace process in northern Ireland; interpersonal communication; strategies to address bullying in online communities, in schools and in the workplace. *Unit head:* Eric Turner, Vice President of Graduate and Professional Studies, 617-243-2071, Fax: 617-243-2450, E-mail: gradinfo@lasell.edu. *Application contact:* Adrienne Franciosi, Director of Graduate Enrollment, 617-243-2214, Fax: 617-243-2450, E-mail: gradinfo@lasell.edu.
Website: http://www.lasell.edu/academics/graduate-and-professional-studies/programs-of-study/master-of-science-in-communication.html

Marquette University, Graduate School, College of Communication, Milwaukee, WI 53201-1881. Offers advertising and public relations (MA); communication studies (MA); digital storytelling (Certificate); journalism (MA); mass communication (MA); science, health and environmental communication (MA). *Accreditation:* ACEJMC (one or more programs are accredited). *Program availability:* Part-time, evening/weekend. *Degree requirements:* For master's, comprehensive exam, thesis or alternative. *Entrance requirements:* For master's, GRE, official transcripts from all current and previous colleges/universities except Marquette, three letters of recommendation, statement of academic and professional goals. Additional exam requirements/recommendations for international students: Required—TOEFL (minimum score 530 paper-based). Electronic applications accepted. *Faculty research:* Urban journalism, gender and communication, intercultural communication, religious communication.

Michigan State University, The Graduate School, College of Communication Arts and Sciences, Program in Health Communication, East Lansing, MI 48824. Offers MA. *Entrance requirements:* Additional exam requirements/recommendations for international students: Required—TOEFL. Electronic applications accepted. *Faculty research:* Mass communication and public health, health communication for diverse populations, descriptive and analytical epidemiology.

Ohio University, Graduate College, Scripps College of Communication, School of Communication Studies, Athens, OH 45701-2979. Offers health communication (PhD); organizational communication (MA); relating and organizing (PhD); rhetoric and public culture (PhD). *Program availability:* Part-time, online learning. Terminal master's awarded for partial completion of doctoral program. *Degree requirements:* For master's, capstone; for doctorate, comprehensive exam, thesis/dissertation. *Entrance requirements:* For master's, GRE; for doctorate, GRE General Test, minimum GPA of 3.0. Additional exam requirements/recommendations for international students: Required—TOEFL (minimum score 550 paper-based; 80 iBT) or IELTS (minimum score 6.5). Electronic applications accepted. *Faculty research:* Rhetoric and public culture, relating and organizing, health communication.

Rider University, College of Liberal Arts and Sciences, Program in Business Communication, Lawrenceville, NJ 08648-3001. Offers business communication studies (MA); health communication (MA). *Program availability:* Online learning.

Southeastern Louisiana University, College of Arts, Humanities and Social Sciences, Department of Languages and Communication, Hammond, LA 70402. Offers health communications (MA); journalism (MA); marketing (MA); public relations (MA); sociology (MA). *Program availability:* Part-time, evening/weekend. *Faculty:* 5 full-time (3 women). *Students:* 7 full-time (6 women), 11 part-time (7 women); includes 10 minority (5 Black or African American, non-Hispanic/Latino; 3 Hispanic/Latino; 2 Two or more races, non-Hispanic/Latino). Average age 28. 133 applicants, 51% accepted, 10 enrolled. In 2017, 36 master's awarded. *Degree requirements:* For master's, comprehensive exam. *Entrance requirements:* For master's, GRE (minimum score 148 on Verbal section, 3.5 Written). Additional exam requirements/recommendations for international students: Required—TOEFL (minimum score 525 paper-based; 75 iBT). *Application deadline:* For fall admission, 7/15 priority date for domestic students, 6/1 priority date for international students; for spring admission, 12/1 priority date for domestic students, 10/1 priority date for international students. Applications are processed on a rolling basis. Application fee: $20 ($30 for international students). Electronic applications accepted. *Expenses:* Tuition, state resident: full-time $6684. Tuition, nonresident: full-time $19,162. *Required fees:* $2088. *Financial support:* In 2017–18, 12 students received support, including 7 research assistantships (averaging $6,082 per year); career-related internships or fieldwork, Federal Work-Study, institutionally sponsored loans, scholarships/grants, traineeships, health care benefits, tuition waivers, and unspecified assistantships also available. Financial award application deadline: 5/1; financial award applicants required to submit FAFSA. *Faculty research:* Communicate with the millennial generation to enhance organizational effectiveness, conflict resolution and mediation among nations, journalism history, media law, media writing, media convergence, external compliances accreditation and strategic planning. *Unit head:* Dr. Lucia Harrison, Department Head, 985-549-2105, Fax: 985-549-5014, E-mail: lharrison@southeastern.edu. *Application contact:* Amanda Harper, Graduate Admissions Analyst, 985-549-5620, Fax: 985-549-5632, E-mail: admissions@southeastern.edu.
Website: http://www.southeastern.edu/acad_research/depts/lang_comm/index.html

Southern Illinois University Edwardsville, Graduate School, College of Arts and Sciences, Department of Applied Communication Studies, Program in Health Communication, Edwardsville, IL 62026. Offers MA. *Program availability:* Part-time, evening/weekend. *Degree requirements:* For master's, comprehensive exam (for some programs), thesis (for some programs). *Entrance requirements:* Additional exam requirements/recommendations for international students: Required—TOEFL (minimum score 550 paper-based, 79 iBT), IELTS (minimum score 6.5), Michigan Test of English Language Proficiency or PTE. Electronic applications accepted.

State University of New York at Oswego, Graduate Studies, School of Communication, Media and the Arts, Oswego, NY 13126. Offers strategic communication (MA), including health communication, integrated media and social networks, organizational communication. *Entrance requirements:* For master's, GRE, official transcript, statement of purpose, resume, two letters of recommendation.

Stony Brook University, State University of New York, School of Journalism, Stony Brook, NY 11794. Offers health communication (Certificate); journalism (MS). *Faculty:* 9 full-time (3 women), 23 part-time/adjunct (8 women). *Students:* 2 part-time (both women). Average age 30. In 2017, 5 master's awarded. *Entrance requirements:* For master's, GRE, MCAT, DAT, or GMAT, bachelor's degree with minimum GPA of 3.0. Additional exam requirements/recommendations for international students: Required—TOEFL (minimum score 600 paper-based; 100 iBT). *Application deadline:* For fall admission, 1/15 for domestic students; for spring admission, 10/1 for domestic students. Application fee: $100. *Expenses:* Contact institution. *Financial support:* Teaching assistantships available. *Faculty research:* Journalism, newspaper journalism, non-fiction, children's literature, Constitutional law. *Total annual research expenditures:* $132,282. *Unit head:* Prof. Howard Schneider, Dean, 631-632-7403, E-mail: howard.schneider@stonybrook.edu. *Application contact:* Maureen Robinson, Coordinator, 631-632-7403, Fax: 631-632-7550, E-mail: maureen.robinson@stonybrook.edu.
Website: https://journalism.cc.stonybrook.edu/

Stony Brook University, State University of New York, Stony Brook Medicine, School of Medicine, Program in Public Health, Stony Brook, NY 11794. Offers community health (MPH); evaluation sciences (MPH); family violence (MPH); health communication (Certificate); health economics (MPH); health education and promotion (Certificate); population health (MPH); substance abuse (MPH). *Accreditation:* CEPH. *Program availability:* Part-time, evening/weekend. *Students:* 32 full-time (24 women), 11 part-time (10 women); includes 18 minority (4 Black or African American, non-Hispanic/Latino; 10 Asian, non-Hispanic/Latino; 4 Hispanic/Latino), 2 international. Average age 29. 128 applicants, 71% accepted, 29 enrolled. In 2017, 25 master's, 1 other advanced degree awarded. *Entrance requirements:* For master's, GRE, 3 references, bachelor's degree from accredited college or university with minimum GPA of 3.0, essays, interview. Additional exam requirements/recommendations for international students: Required—TOEFL (minimum score 90 iBT). *Application deadline:* For fall admission, 7/15 for domestic students, 3/15 for international students. Application fee: $100. Electronic applications accepted. *Expenses:* Contact institution. *Financial support:* Fellowships available. *Faculty research:* Abnormal psychology, academic achievement, broadcast media, communications, communications systems, public health. *Total annual research expenditures:* $422,408. *Unit head:* Dr. Lisa A. Benz Scott, Director, 631-444-8811, E-mail: lisa.benzscott@stonybrook.edu. *Application contact:* Joanie Maniaci, Assistant Director for Student Affairs, 631-444-2074, Fax: 631-444-6035, E-mail: joanmarie.maniaci@stonybrook.edu.
Website: http://publichealth.stonybrookmedicine.edu/

Tufts University, School of Medicine, Public Health and Professional Degree Programs, Boston, MA 02111. Offers biomedical sciences (MS); health communication

(MS, Certificate); pain research, education and policy (MS, Certificate); physician assistant (MS); public health (MPH, Dr PH), including behavioral science (MPH), biostatistics (MPH), epidemiology (MPH), health communication (MPH), health services (MPH), management and policy (MPH), nutrition (MPH); DMD/MPH; DVM/MPH; JD/MPH; MD/MPH; MMS/MPH; MS/MBA; MS/MPH. *Accreditation:* CEPH (one or more programs are accredited). *Program availability:* Part-time, evening/weekend. *Faculty:* 62 full-time (25 women), 50 part-time/adjunct (25 women). *Students:* 449 full-time (280 women), 60 part-time (46 women); includes 188 minority (23 Black or African American, non-Hispanic/Latino; 112 Asian, non-Hispanic/Latino; 35 Hispanic/Latino; 18 Two or more races, non-Hispanic/Latino), 23 international. Average age 27. 1,750 applicants, 46% accepted, 252 enrolled. In 2017, 283 master's awarded. Terminal master's awarded for partial completion of doctoral program. *Degree requirements:* For master's, thesis (for some programs); for doctorate, thesis/dissertation. *Entrance requirements:* For master's, GRE General Test, MCAT, or GMAT; for doctorate, GRE General Test or MCAT. Additional exam requirements/recommendations for international students: Required—TOEFL (minimum score 100 iBT); Recommended—IELTS (minimum score 7). *Application deadline:* For fall admission, 1/15 priority date for domestic and international students; for spring admission, 10/25 priority date for domestic and international students. Applications are processed on a rolling basis. Application fee: $70. Electronic applications accepted. *Expenses:* Contact institution. *Financial support:* In 2017–18, 13 students received support, including 1 fellowship (averaging $3,000 per year), 50 research assistantships (averaging $1,000 per year), 65 teaching assistantships (averaging $2,000 per year); Federal Work-Study and scholarships/grants also available. Financial award application deadline: 2/23; financial award applicants required to submit FAFSA. *Faculty research:* Environmental and occupational health, nutrition, epidemiology, health communication, biostatics, obesity/chronic disease, health policy and health care delivery, global health, health inequality and social determinants of health. *Unit head:* Dr. Aviva Must, Dean, 617-636-0935, Fax: 617-636-0898, E-mail: aviva.must@tufts.edu. *Application contact:* Emily Keily, Director of Admissions, 617-636-0935, Fax: 617-636-0898, E-mail: med-phpd@tufts.edu.
Website: http://publichealth.tufts.edu

University of Florida, Graduate School, College of Health and Human Performance, Department of Health Education and Behavior, Gainesville, FL 32611. Offers health and human performance (PhD), including health behavior; health communication (Graduate Certificate); health education and behavior (MS). *Accreditation:* NCATE (one or more programs are accredited). *Program availability:* Part-time. Terminal master's awarded for partial completion of doctoral program. *Degree requirements:* For master's, comprehensive exam, thesis (for some programs); for doctorate, comprehensive exam, thesis/dissertation. *Entrance requirements:* For master's and doctorate, GRE General Test (minimum score 293), minimum GPA of 3.0. Additional exam requirements/recommendations for international students: Required—TOEFL (minimum score 550 paper-based; 80 iBT), IELTS (minimum score 6). Electronic applications accepted. *Faculty research:* Community-based participatory research; health disparities issues; health; cancer prevention and control; obesity-related issues; community capacity building; training community health workers; use of community based research principles to design, implement, an evaluate community health worker interventions; obesity; weight management; health literacy; health disparities (ethnic, gender, age, urban/rural); tailored health messages; entertainment education; COPD.

University of Florida, Graduate School, College of Journalism and Communications, Program in Mass Communication, Gainesville, FL 32611. Offers international/intercultural communication (MAMC); journalism (MAMC); mass communication (MAMC, PhD), including clinical translational science (MAMC); public relations (MAMC); science/health communication (MAMC); telecommunication (MAMC). *Accreditation:* ACEJMC. *Entrance requirements:* For master's and doctorate, GRE General Test, minimum GPA of 3.0.

University of Houston, College of Liberal Arts and Social Sciences, Jack J. Valenti School of Communication, Houston, TX 77204. Offers health communication (MA); mass communication studies (MA); public relations studies (MA); speech communication (MA). *Program availability:* Part-time. *Degree requirements:* For master's, comprehensive exam (for some programs), thesis (for some programs), 30-33 hours. *Entrance requirements:* For master's, GRE. Additional exam requirements/recommendations for international students: Required—TOEFL. Electronic applications accepted.

University of Missouri, Office of Research and Graduate Studies, School of Journalism, Columbia, MO 65211. Offers health communications (MA); journalism (PhD). *Accreditation:* ACEJMC (one or more programs are accredited). *Program availability:* Part-time. Terminal master's awarded for partial completion of doctoral program. *Degree requirements:* For master's, thesis (for some programs); for doctorate, 2 foreign languages, thesis/dissertation. *Entrance requirements:* For master's and doctorate, GRE General Test, minimum GPA of 3.0. Additional exam requirements/recommendations for international students: Required—TOEFL (minimum score 600 paper-based; 100 iBT), IELTS (minimum score 7). Electronic applications accepted.

The University of North Carolina at Chapel Hill, Graduate School, School of Media and Journalism, Chapel Hill, NC 27599. Offers digital communication (MA, Certificate); media and communication (MA, PhD), including interdisciplinary health communication (MA), journalism (MA), strategic communication (MA), theory and research (MA), visual communication (MA); JD/PhD; MA/JD. MA/JD and JD/PhD offered jointly with School of Law. *Accreditation:* ACEJMC (one or more programs are accredited). *Program availability:* Part-time, all course instruction online, plus two on-campus experiences totaling seven days. *Faculty:* 51 full-time (22 women), 4 part-time/adjunct (2 women). *Students:* 75 full-time (50 women), 63 part-time (41 women); includes 44 minority (10 Black or African American, non-Hispanic/Latino; 11 Asian, non-Hispanic/Latino; 5 Hispanic/Latino; 18 Two or more races, non-Hispanic/Latino), 6 international. Average age 31. 207 applicants, 41% accepted, 63 enrolled. In 2017, 32 master's, 9 doctorates, 17 other advanced degrees awarded. *Degree requirements:* For master's, comprehensive exam, thesis; for doctorate, comprehensive exam, thesis/dissertation. *Entrance requirements:* For master's and doctorate, GRE General Test, minimum GPA of 3.0. Additional exam requirements/recommendations for international students: Required—TOEFL (minimum iBT score of 105) or IELTS (7.5). Application fee: $88. Electronic applications accepted. *Expenses:* Contact institution. *Financial support:* In 2017–18, 73 students received support, including 47 fellowships with full tuition reimbursements available (averaging $16,006 per year), 6 research assistantships with full tuition reimbursements available (averaging $17,405 per year); scholarships/grants and health care benefits also available. Financial award application deadline: 12/4; financial award applicants required to submit FAFSA. *Faculty research:* Media processes and production; legal and regulatory issues in communication; media uses and effects; health communication; political, social, and strategic communication. *Total annual research expenditures:* $1 million. *Unit head:* Susan King, Dean, 919-962-1204, Fax: 919-962-0620, E-mail: susanking@unc.edu. *Application contact:* Casey Hart, Marketing and Instructional Design Coordinator, 919-843-9471, Fax: 919-962-0620, E-mail: mjgrad@unc.edu.
Website: http://mj.unc.edu/

University of Oklahoma, College of Arts and Sciences, Department of Communication, Norman, OK 73019. Offers communication (MA); communication technology (PhD); health communication (PhD); intercultural/international communication (PhD); organizational communication (PhD); political/mass communication (PhD); social influence/interpersonal communication (PhD). *Program availability:* Part-time. *Faculty:* 18 full-time (8 women). *Students:* 27 full-time (17 women), 36 part-time (17 women); includes 23 minority (8 Black or African American, non-Hispanic/Latino; 3 American Indian or Alaska Native, non-Hispanic/Latino; 1 Asian, non-Hispanic/Latino; 10 Hispanic/Latino; 1 Two or more races, non-Hispanic/Latino), 5 international. Average age 35. 45 applicants, 49% accepted, 10 enrolled. In 2017, 14 master's, 6 doctorates awarded. *Degree requirements:* For master's, comprehensive exam (for some programs), thesis (for some programs), comprehensive exams or thesis; for doctorate, comprehensive exam, thesis/dissertation. *Entrance requirements:* For master's, GRE (for assistantship), statement of purpose, transcripts, writing sample, letters of recommendation; for doctorate, GRE, statement of purpose, transcripts, writing sample, letters of recommendation. Additional exam requirements/recommendations for international students: Required—TOEFL (minimum score 79 iBT) or IELTS (minimum score 6.5). *Application deadline:* For fall admission, 1/15 priority date for domestic students, 1/15 for international students; for spring admission, 10/15 for domestic and international students. Application fee: $50 ($100 for international students). Electronic applications accepted. *Expenses:* Tuition, state resident: full-time $5119; part-time $213.30 per credit hour. Tuition, nonresident: full-time $19,778; part-time $824.10 per credit hour. *Required fees:* $3458; $133.55 per credit hour. $126.50 per semester. *Financial support:* In 2017–18, 29 students received support, including 1 research assistantship with full tuition reimbursement available (averaging $10,373 per year), 25 teaching assistantships with full tuition reimbursements available (averaging $16,350 per year); health care benefits also available. Financial award application deadline: 6/1; financial award applicants required to submit FAFSA. *Faculty research:* Interpersonal/social influence, organizational, political/mass communication, health communication, intercultural/international. *Total annual research expenditures:* $242,423. *Unit head:* Dr. Michael W. Kramer, Professor and Chair, 405-325-9503, Fax: 405-325-7625, E-mail: mkramer@ou.edu. *Application contact:* Shay Glover, Academic Advisor, 405-325-7710, Fax: 405-325-7625, E-mail: shay.glover@ou.edu.
Website: http://www.ou.edu/cas/comm

University of St. Thomas, Opus College of Business, Master of Science in Health Care Communication Program, Minneapolis, MN 55403. Offers MS. *Program availability:* Part-time, evening/weekend. *Application deadline:* Applications are processed on a rolling basis. Electronic applications accepted. Tuition and fees vary according to course load, degree level, campus/location and program. *Unit head:* Sandy Bauer, Coordinator, 651-962-8800, Fax: 651-962-4020, E-mail: healthcarecomm@stthomas.edu.
Website: http://www.stthomas.edu/mbc

University of Southern California, Graduate School, Annenberg School for Communication and Journalism, School of Communication, Program in Communication, Los Angeles, CA 90089. Offers culture and community (PhD); global and transnational communication (PhD); groups, organizations and networks (PhD); health communication and social dynamics (PhD); information, political economy and entertainment (PhD); new media and technology (PhD); rhetoric, politics and public media (PhD). *Degree requirements:* For doctorate, thesis/dissertation. *Entrance requirements:* For doctorate, GRE General Test, resume or curriculum vitae, scholarly writing, 3 letters of recommendation, statement of purpose. Additional exam requirements/recommendations for international students: Required—TOEFL (minimum score 114 iBT), IELTS (minimum score 8); Recommended—TWE. Electronic applications accepted. *Faculty research:* Computer-mediated communication, public health campaigns, communication democracy and the public sphere, new communication technologies in organizations, communication and community.

University of Southern California, Keck School of Medicine and Graduate School, Graduate Programs in Medicine, Department of Preventive Medicine, Master of Public Health Program, Los Angeles, CA 90032. Offers biostatistics and epidemiology (MPH); child and family health (MPH); environmental health (MPH); geohealth (MPH); global health leadership (MPH); health communication (MPH); health education and promotion (MPH); public health policy (MPH). *Accreditation:* CEPH. *Program availability:* Part-time, evening/weekend. *Faculty:* 47 full-time (35 women), 13 part-time/adjunct (8 women). *Students:* 258 full-time (204 women), 61 part-time (50 women); includes 167 minority (28 Black or African American, non-Hispanic/Latino; 1 American Indian or Alaska Native, non-Hispanic/Latino; 61 Asian, non-Hispanic/Latino; 64 Hispanic/Latino; 4 Native Hawaiian or other Pacific Islander, non-Hispanic/Latino; 9 Two or more races, non-Hispanic/Latino), 28 international. Average age 26. 378 applicants, 53% accepted, 87 enrolled. In 2017, 91 master's awarded. *Degree requirements:* For master's, practicum, final report, oral presentation. *Entrance requirements:* For master's, GRE General Test, MCAT, GMAT, minimum GPA of 3.0. Additional exam requirements/recommendations for international students: Required—TOEFL (minimum score 600 paper-based; 90 iBT). *Application deadline:* For fall admission, 12/1 priority date for domestic students, 5/1 priority date for international students; for spring admission, 9/1 priority date for domestic and international students; for summer admission, 3/1 for domestic and international students. Applications are processed on a rolling basis. Application fee: $90. Electronic applications accepted. *Expenses:* Contact institution. *Financial support:* Career-related internships or fieldwork, Federal Work-Study, institutionally sponsored loans, and scholarships/grants available. Support available to part-time students. Financial award application deadline: 5/4; financial award applicants required to submit CSS PROFILE or FAFSA. *Faculty research:* Cancer and heart disease epidemiology and prevention, mass media and health communication research, effects of air pollution on health, tobacco control, global health. *Total annual research expenditures:* $7 million. *Unit head:* Dr. Louise A. Rohrbach, Director, 323-442-8237, Fax: 323-442-8297, E-mail: rohrbac@usc.edu. *Application contact:* Valerie Burris, Admissions Counselor, 323-442-7257, Fax: 323-442-8297, E-mail: valeriem@usc.edu.
Website: http://mph.usc.edu/

Wayne State University, College of Fine, Performing and Communication Arts, Department of Communication, Detroit, MI 48202. Offers communication (PhD), including democratic participation and culture, identity and representation, media, society and culture, risk, crisis and conflict, wellness, work life and relationships; communication and new media (Graduate Certificate); communication studies (MA); dispute resolution (MADR, Graduate Certificate), including community and urban studies (MADR), conflict area studies (MADR), health and family (MADR), international conflict and cooperation (MADR), professional practice (MADR), theory of conflict (MADR), workplace (MADR); health communication (Graduate Certificate); journalism (MA); media arts (MA); media studies (MA); public relations and organizational communication (MA); JD/MADR. Doctoral program admits for fall only. *Program availability:* Online learning. *Faculty:* 21. *Students:* 63 full-time (35 women), 87 part-time (55 women); includes 54 minority (39 Black or African American, non-Hispanic/Latino; 2 Asian, non-Hispanic/Latino; 7 Hispanic/Latino; 6 Two or more races, non-Hispanic/Latino), 10 international. Average age 34. 153 applicants, 39% accepted, 27 enrolled. In 2017, 26 master's, 7 doctorates, 8 other advanced degrees awarded. *Degree requirements:* For master's, thesis (for some programs), thesis or essay; for doctorate, thesis/dissertation. *Entrance requirements:* For master's, GRE (for MA if undergraduate GPA less than 3.2),

personal statement; BA or BS in communication or related field with minimum upper-division GPA of 3.2 and minimum upper-division undergraduate GPA of 3.0, and sample of academic writing (for MA); undergraduate degree with minimum upper-division GPA of 3.0 and three letters of recommendation (for MADR); for doctorate, GRE, undergraduate degree in communication or related field; master's degree in communication or related field with minimum GPA of 3.5; letters of recommendation; personal statement; sample of written scholarship. Additional exam requirements/recommendations for international students: Required—TOEFL (minimum score 100 iBT), IELTS, TWE. Application fee: $50. Electronic applications accepted. *Expenses:* Contact institution. *Financial support:* In 2017–18, 57 students received support,

including 5 fellowships with tuition reimbursements available (averaging $17,400 per year), 2 research assistantships with tuition reimbursements available (averaging $20,388 per year), 20 teaching assistantships with tuition reimbursements available (averaging $18,534 per year); scholarships/grants and unspecified assistantships also available. Financial award applicants required to submit FAFSA. *Faculty research:* Democratic participation and culture; identity and representation; media, society and culture; risk, crisis and conflict; wellness, work life, and relationships. *Unit head:* Dr. Lee Wilkins, Professor and Chair, 313-577-2943, E-mail: eh8899@wayne.edu. *Application contact:* E-mail: communication@wayne.edu.
Website: http://comm.wayne.edu/

Internet and Interactive Multimedia

Academy of Art University, Graduate Programs, School of Communications and Media Technologies, San Francisco, CA 94105-3410. Offers communications and media technologies (MA). *Program availability:* Part-time, 100% online. *Faculty:* 2 full-time (0 women), 12 part-time/adjunct (4 women). *Students:* 45 full-time (29 women), 15 part-time (8 women); includes 7 minority (2 Black or African American, non-Hispanic/Latino; 2 Asian, non-Hispanic/Latino; 3 Hispanic/Latino), 40 international. Average age 29. 34 applicants, 100% accepted, 16 enrolled. In 2017, 44 master's awarded. *Degree requirements:* For master's, final review. *Entrance requirements:* For master's, statement of intent; resume; portfolio/reel; official college transcripts. *Application deadline:* Applications are processed on a rolling basis. Application fee: $50. Electronic applications accepted. *Expenses: Tuition:* Part-time $982 per unit. *Financial support:* Career-related internships or fieldwork, Federal Work-Study, and scholarships/grants available. Financial award application deadline: 8/10; financial award applicants required to submit FAFSA. *Unit head:* 800-544-ARTS, E-mail: info@academyart.edu. *Application contact:* 800-544-ARTS, E-mail: info@academyart.edu.
Website: http://www.academyart.edu/multimedia-communications-school/

Alfred University, Graduate School, College of Ceramics, School of Art and Design, Alfred, NY 14802. Offers ceramic art (MFA); electronic integrated arts (MFA); painting (MFA); sculpture/dimensional studies (MFA). *Accreditation:* NASAD. *Degree requirements:* For master's, thesis, exhibit. *Entrance requirements:* For master's, portfolio. Additional exam requirements/recommendations for international students: Required—TOEFL (minimum score 550 paper-based; 80 iBT), IELTS (minimum score 6). Electronic applications accepted. *Expenses:* Contact institution. *Faculty research:* Ceramic art, sculpture, glass art, new media, time-based media.

Ball State University, Graduate School, College of Communication, Information, and Media, Department of Journalism, Program in Emerging Media Design and Development, Muncie, IN 47306. Offers MA. *Program availability:* Part-time, evening/weekend. *Students:* 24 full-time (18 women), 25 part-time (19 women); includes 8 minority (4 Black or African American, non-Hispanic/Latino; 4 Hispanic/Latino), 4 international. Average age 28. 36 applicants, 92% accepted, 31 enrolled. In 2017, 9 master's awarded. *Entrance requirements:* For master's, GRE General Test (minimum score 150 verbal), minimum baccalaureate GPA of 2.75 or 3.0 in latter half of baccalaureate, transcripts of all prior course work, three letters of recommendation, current resume, statement of purpose, writing sample, portfolio. Additional exam requirements/recommendations for international students: Required—TOEFL (minimum score 550 paper-based; 79 iBT), IELTS (minimum score 6.5). *Application deadline:* Applications are processed on a rolling basis. Application fee: $60. Electronic applications accepted. *Financial support:* Research assistantships with partial tuition reimbursements and unspecified assistantships available. Financial award application deadline: 3/1; financial award applicants required to submit FAFSA. *Unit head:* Dr. Johnny Sparks, Chairperson, 765-285-8278, E-mail: jvsparks@bsu.edu.
Website: http://cms.bsu.edu/academics/collegesanddepartments/journalism/graduateprograms/emerging-media-design-and-development

Boston University, Metropolitan College, Department of Computer Science, Boston, MA 02215. Offers computer information systems (MS), including computer networks, data analytics, database management and business intelligence, health informatics, IT project management, security, Web application development; computer networks (Certificate); computer science (MS); data analytics (Certificate); digital forensics (Certificate); health informatics (Certificate); information technology project management (Certificate); software development (MS); software engineering in health care systems (Certificate); telecommunications (MS), including security. *Program availability:* Part-time, evening/weekend, online learning. *Faculty:* 10 full-time (2 women), 51 part-time/adjunct (5 women). *Students:* 109 full-time (39 women), 985 part-time (268 women); includes 286 minority (64 Black or African American, non-Hispanic/Latino; 3 American Indian or Alaska Native, non-Hispanic/Latino; 131 Asian, non-Hispanic/Latino; 73 Hispanic/Latino; 1 Native Hawaiian or other Pacific Islander, non-Hispanic/Latino; 14 Two or more races, non-Hispanic/Latino), 253 international. Average age 32. 952 applicants, 65% accepted, 230 enrolled. In 2017, 392 master's awarded. *Entrance requirements:* For master's and Certificate, official transcripts from regionally-accredited bachelor's degree program, 3 letters of recommendation, professional resume, personal statement. Additional exam requirements/recommendations for international students: Required—TOEFL (minimum score 84 iBT), IELTS. *Application deadline:* For fall admission, 6/1 priority date for international students; for spring admission, 10/1 priority date for international students. Applications are processed on a rolling basis. Application fee: $85. Electronic applications accepted. *Expenses:* Contact institution. *Financial support:* In 2017–18, 11 research assistantships (averaging $8,400 per year), 3 teaching assistantships (averaging $5,000 per year) were awarded; unspecified assistantships also available. Support available to part-time students. Financial award applicants required to submit FAFSA. *Faculty research:* Medical informatics, Web technologies, telecom and networks, security and forensics, software engineering, programming languages, multimedia and artificial intelligence (AI), information systems and IT project management. *Unit head:* Dr. Anatoly Temkin, Chair, 617-353-2566, Fax: 617-353-2367, E-mail: csinfo@bu.edu. *Application contact:* Lesley Moreau, Academic Program Coordinator, 617-353-2566, Fax: 617-353-2367, E-mail: metcs@bu.edu.
Website: http://www.bu.edu/csmet/

Brandeis University, Rabb School of Continuing Studies, Division of Graduate Professional Studies, Master of Science in Digital Marketing and Design Program, Waltham, MA 02454-9110. Offers MS. *Program availability:* Part-time-only. *Faculty:* 55 part-time/adjunct (18 women). *Students:* 31 part-time (22 women); includes 5 minority (1 Black or African American, non-Hispanic/Latino; 1 Asian, non-Hispanic/Latino; 3 Hispanic/Latino). Average age 31. 13 applicants, 100% accepted, 11 enrolled. *Entrance requirements:* For master's, undergraduate degree with at least 2 marketing courses and/or 2 years of relevant work experience; four-year bachelor's degree from U.S.

accredited institution or equivalent; statement of goals; resume or curriculum vitae; letter of recommendation. Additional exam requirements/recommendations for international students: Required—TWE (minimum score 4.5), TOEFL (minimum scores: 600 paper-based, 100 iBT), IELTS (7), or PTE (68). *Application deadline:* For fall admission, 6/20 priority date for domestic and international students; for winter admission, 9/12 priority date for domestic and international students; for spring admission, 12/19 priority date for domestic and international students; for summer admission, 3/13 for domestic students, 3/13 priority date for international students. Applications are processed on a rolling basis. Application fee: $75. Electronic applications accepted. *Expenses:* $1,178 per credit. *Financial support:* Applicants required to submit FAFSA. *Unit head:* Steven Dupree, Program Chair, 781-736-8787, E-mail: sdupree@brandeis.edu. *Application contact:* Frances Stearns, Director of Student and Faculty Operations, 781-736-8785, E-mail: fstearns@brandeis.edu.

Brooklyn College of the City University of New York, School of Visual, Media and Performing Arts, Program in Performance and Interactive Media Arts, Brooklyn, NY 11210-2889. Offers MFA. *Entrance requirements:* For master's, 2 letters of recommendation, resume, portfolio, interview. Additional exam requirements/recommendations for international students: Required—TOEFL (minimum score 550 paper-based; 61 iBT). Electronic applications accepted.

California State University, East Bay, Office of Graduate Studies, College of Letters, Arts, and Social Sciences, Multimedia Graduate Program, Hayward, CA 94542-3000. Offers MA. *Program availability:* Part-time. *Students:* 12 full-time (7 women), 5 part-time (1 woman); includes 7 minority (2 Black or African American, non-Hispanic/Latino; 2 Asian, non-Hispanic/Latino; 3 Hispanic/Latino), 5 international. Average age 32. 15 applicants, 87% accepted, 7 enrolled. In 2017, 11 master's awarded. *Degree requirements:* For master's, multimedia project or thesis. *Entrance requirements:* For master's, minimum GPA of 2.5; resume; 2 letters of recommendation; multimedia portfolio; statement of purpose. Additional exam requirements/recommendations for international students: Required—TOEFL (minimum score 550 paper-based). *Application deadline:* For fall admission, 5/15 for domestic and international students. Application fee: $55. Electronic applications accepted. *Expenses:* Contact institution. *Financial support:* Fellowships, teaching assistantships, Federal Work-Study, institutionally sponsored loans, and scholarships/grants available. Support available to part-time students. Financial award application deadline: 3/2; financial award applicants required to submit FAFSA. *Unit head:* Ian Pollock, Director, 510-885-2427, E-mail: ian.pollock@csueastbay.edu.
Website: http://multimedia.csueastbay.edu

Champlain College, Graduate Studies, Burlington, VT 05402-0670. Offers business (MBA); digital forensic science (MS); early childhood education (M Ed); emergent media (MFA, MS); executive leadership (MS); health care administration (MS); information security operations (MS); law (MS); mediation and applied conflict studies (MS). MS in emergent media program held in Shanghai. *Program availability:* Part-time, online learning. *Degree requirements:* For master's, capstone project. *Entrance requirements:* Additional exam requirements/recommendations for international students: Required—TOEFL (minimum score 550 paper-based; 80 iBT). Electronic applications accepted.

College of Saint Elizabeth, Program in Social Media Design and Management, Morristown, NJ 07960-6989. Offers MA. *Program availability:* Part-time. *Degree requirements:* For master's, thesis. *Entrance requirements:* Additional exam requirements/recommendations for international students: Required—TOEFL (minimum score 550 paper-based; 79 iBT), IELTS (minimum score 6.5). *Application deadline:* For fall admission, 5/1 for international students. Applications are processed on a rolling basis. Application fee: $35. Electronic applications accepted. Application fee is waived when completed online. *Financial support:* Career-related internships or fieldwork, scholarships/grants, and unspecified assistantships available. Financial award applicants required to submit FAFSA. *Unit head:* Dr. Virginia Butera, Chair, 973-290-4315, E-mail: vbutera@cse.edu. *Application contact:* Lori J. Fragoso, Director of Graduate and Continuing Studies Admissions, Fax: 973-290-4710, E-mail: apply@cse.edu.
Website: http://www.cse.edu/academics/aas/social-media-design-and-management/ma-in-social-media-design-and-management

Concordia University, School of Graduate Studies, Faculty of Engineering and Computer Science, Concordia Institute for Information Systems Engineering (CIISE), Montréal, QC H3G 1M8, Canada. Offers 3D graphics and game development (Certificate); information and systems engineering (PhD); information systems security (M Eng, MA Sc); quality systems engineering (M Eng, MA Sc); service engineering and network management (Certificate).

DePaul University, College of Computing and Digital Media, Chicago, IL 60604. Offers animation (MA, MFA); applied technology (MS); business information technology (MS); computational finance (MS); computer and information sciences (PhD); computer science (MS); creative producing (MFA); cybersecurity (MS); data science (MS); digital communication and media arts (MA); documentary (MFA); e-commerce technology (MS); experience design (MA); film and television (MS); film and television directing (MFA); game design (MFA); game programming (MS); health informatics (MS); human centered design (PhD); human-computer interaction (MS); information systems (MS); network engineering and security (MS); product innovation and computing (MS); screenwriting (MFA); software engineering (MS); JD/MS. *Program availability:* Part-time, evening/weekend, online learning. *Degree requirements:* For master's, thesis (for some programs); for doctorate, comprehensive exam, thesis/dissertation. *Entrance requirements:* For master's, GRE or GMAT (for MS in computational finance only), bachelor's degree, resume (MS in predictive analytics only), IT experience (MS in information technology project management only), portfolio review (all MFA programs and MA in animation); for doctorate, GRE, master's degree in computer science. Additional exam requirements/recommendations for international students: Required—

TOEFL (minimum score 590 paper-based; 80 iBT), IELTS (minimum score 6.5), PTE (minimum score 53). *Application deadline:* For fall admission, 8/1 priority date for domestic students, 6/15 priority date for international students; for winter admission, 12/1 priority date for domestic students, 10/15 priority date for international students; for spring admission, 3/1 priority date for domestic students, 1/15 priority date for international students; for summer admission, 5/1 for domestic students, 4/15 for international students. Applications are processed on a rolling basis. Application fee: $25. Electronic applications accepted. *Expenses:* Contact institution. *Financial support:* Fellowships with full tuition reimbursements, research assistantships with full and partial tuition reimbursements, teaching assistantships with full and partial tuition reimbursements, Federal Work-Study, scholarships/grants, tuition waivers (full and partial), and unspecified assistantships available. Support available to part-time students. Financial award application deadline: 4/20; financial award applicants required to submit FAFSA. *Faculty research:* Data mining, computer science, human-computer interaction, security, animation and film. *Unit head:* Elly Kafritsas-Wessels, Communications Manager, 312-362-5816, Fax: 312-362-5185, E-mail: ekafrits@cdm.depaul.edu. *Application contact:* Office of Admission, 312-362-8714, E-mail: admission@cdm.depaul.edu.
Website: http://cdm.depaul.edu

Elon University, Program in Interactive Media, Elon, NC 27244-2010. Offers MA. *Faculty:* 10 full-time (3 women). *Students:* 26 full-time (15 women); includes 13 minority (11 Black or African American, non-Hispanic/Latino; 2 Hispanic/Latino). Average age 23. 41 applicants, 85% accepted, 26 enrolled. In 2017, 24 master's awarded. *Degree requirements:* For master's, 6-hour capstone. *Entrance requirements:* For master's, GRE. Additional exam requirements/recommendations for international students: Required—TOEFL (minimum score 550 paper-based; 79 iBT). *Application deadline:* For fall admission, 5/1 priority date for domestic students. Applications are processed on a rolling basis. Application fee: $50. Electronic applications accepted. *Financial support:* Federal Work-Study and scholarships/grants available. Support available to part-time students. Financial award application deadline: 3/15; financial award applicants required to submit FAFSA. *Faculty research:* Effects of service-learning (local and international) on the quality of learning for interactive media students, pedagogy for visual communication, impact of reviewer comments on consumer product and news perceptions, visual communication, social media in pedagogy. *Unit head:* Dr. Paul Parsons, Dean of the School of Communications, 336-278-5724, E-mail: pparsons@elon.edu. *Application contact:* Art Fadde, Director of Graduate Admissions, 800-334-8448 Ext. 3, Fax: 336-278-7699, E-mail: afadde@elon.edu.
Website: http://www.elon.edu/imedia

Excelsior College, School of Business and Technology, Albany, NY 12203-5159. Offers business administration (MBA); cybersecurity - information assurance (MS); cybersecurity - medical data security (MS); cybersecurity - policy administration (MS); cybersecurity management (MBA, Graduate Certificate); general business management (MS); health care management (MBA); human performance technology (MBA); human resource management (MS); human resources management (MBA); leadership (MBA, MS); mediation and arbitration (MBA, MS); social media management (MBA); technology management (MBA). *Program availability:* Part-time, evening/weekend, online learning. *Faculty:* 30 part-time/adjunct (12 women). *Students:* 1,204 part-time (333 women); includes 560 minority (310 Black or African American, non-Hispanic/Latino; 7 American Indian or Alaska Native, non-Hispanic/Latino; 42 Asian, non-Hispanic/Latino; 140 Hispanic/Latino; 10 Native Hawaiian or other Pacific Islander, non-Hispanic/Latino; 51 Two or more races, non-Hispanic/Latino). Average age 40. In 2017, 294 master's awarded. *Application deadline:* Applications are processed on a rolling basis. Application fee: $50. Electronic applications accepted. *Expenses: Tuition:* Part-time $645 per credit. *Required fees:* $265 per credit. *Financial support:* Scholarships/grants available. *Unit head:* Dr. Lifang Shih, Dean, 888-647-2388. *Application contact:* Admissions, 888-647-2388 Ext. 133, Fax: 518-464-8777, E-mail: admissions@excelsior.edu.

Fairfield University, School of Engineering, Fairfield, CT 06824. Offers database management (CAS); electrical and computer engineering (MS); information security (CAS); management of technology (MS); mechanical engineering (MS); network technology (CAS); software engineering (MS); Web application development (CAS). *Program availability:* Part-time, evening/weekend. *Faculty:* 9 full-time (2 women), 9 part-time/adjunct (0 women). *Students:* 40 full-time (12 women), 69 part-time (19 women); includes 23 minority (10 Black or African American, non-Hispanic/Latino; 7 Asian, non-Hispanic/Latino; 5 Hispanic/Latino; 1 Two or more races, non-Hispanic/Latino), 51 international. Average age 28. 91 applicants, 78% accepted, 30 enrolled. In 2017, 100 master's awarded. *Degree requirements:* For master's, capstone course. *Entrance requirements:* For master's, resume, 2 recommendations. Additional exam requirements/recommendations for international students: Required—TOEFL (minimum score 550 paper-based; 80 iBT) or IELTS (minimum score 6.5). *Application deadline:* For fall admission, 5/15 for international students; for spring admission, 10/15 for international students. Applications are processed on a rolling basis. Application fee: $60. Electronic applications accepted. *Expenses:* $825 per credit hour. *Financial support:* In 2017–18, 20 students received support. Scholarships/grants and unspecified assistantships available. Financial award applicants required to submit FAFSA. *Faculty research:* Artificial intelligence and information visualization, natural language processing, thermofluids, microwaves and electromagnetics, micro-/nano-manufacturing. *Unit head:* Dr. Bruce Berdanier, Dean, 203-254-4147, Fax: 203-254-4013, E-mail: bberdanier@fairfield.edu. *Application contact:* Marianne Gumpper, Director of Graduate and Continuing Studies Admission, 203-254-4184, Fax: 203-254-4073, E-mail: gradadmis@fairfield.edu.
Website: http://www.fairfield.edu/soe

Full Sail University, Education Media Design and Technology Master of Science Program - Online, Winter Park, FL 32792-7437. Offers MS. *Program availability:* Online learning. *Entrance requirements:* Additional exam requirements/recommendations for international students: Required—TOEFL (minimum score 550 paper-based; 79 iBT).

Full Sail University, Game Design Master of Science Program - Campus, Winter Park, FL 32792-7437. Offers MS.

Full Sail University, Internet Marketing Master of Science Program - Online, Winter Park, FL 32792-7437. Offers MS. *Program availability:* Online learning.

Georgetown University, Graduate School of Arts and Sciences, Program in Communication, Culture, and Technology, Washington, DC 20057. Offers MA. *Program availability:* Part-time, evening/weekend. *Degree requirements:* For master's, thesis (for some programs). *Entrance requirements:* For master's, GRE General Test, 3 letters of recommendation, writing sample. Additional exam requirements/recommendations for international students: Required—TOEFL (minimum score 600 paper-based). Electronic applications accepted.

Georgia Institute of Technology, Graduate Studies, Ivan Allen College of Liberal Arts, School of Literature, Media, and Communication, Atlanta, GA 30332-0001. Offers digital media (MS, PhD). *Program availability:* Part-time. Terminal master's awarded for partial completion of doctoral program. *Degree requirements:* For master's, thesis optional, project studio, paid internship, responsible conduct of research training; for doctorate, comprehensive exam, thesis/dissertation, portfolio review, responsible conduct of research training. *Entrance requirements:* For master's and doctorate, GRE, three letters of recommendation, transcripts from each college/university attended, design portfolio, statement of purpose. Additional exam requirements/recommendations for international students: Required—TOEFL (minimum score 650 paper-based; 114 iBT). Electronic applications accepted. *Faculty research:* New media studies.

Ithaca College, Roy H. Park School of Communications, Executive Master's in Communications Innovation Program, Ithaca, NY 14850. Offers MS. *Faculty:* 9 full-time (2 women). *Students:* 5 part-time (2 women), 1 international. Average age 40. 6 applicants, 50% accepted. In 2017, 4 master's awarded. *Entrance requirements:* Additional exam requirements/recommendations for international students: Required—TOEFL (minimum score 550 paper-based; 80 iBT). *Application deadline:* For fall admission, 3/15 for domestic and international students; for spring admission, 12/1 for domestic and international students. Applications are processed on a rolling basis. Application fee: $40. Electronic applications accepted. *Expenses:* Contact institution. *Financial support:* In 2017–18, 5 students received support, including 3 fellowships (averaging $9,167 per year); career-related internships or fieldwork, Federal Work-Study, and scholarships/grants also available. Support available to part-time students. Financial award application deadline: 2/1; financial award applicants required to submit FAFSA. *Unit head:* Dr. Diane Gayeski, Dean, 607-274-3895, E-mail: gayeski@ithaca.edu. *Application contact:* Nicole Eversley Bradwell, Director, Office of Admission, 607-274-3124, Fax: 607-274-1263, E-mail: admission@ithaca.edu.
Website: http://www.ithaca.edu/gradprograms/innovation/

Kutztown University of Pennsylvania, College of Visual and Performing Arts, Program in Communication Design, Kutztown, PA 19530-0730. Offers MFA. *Program availability:* Part-time. *Faculty:* 7 full-time (4 women). *Students:* 3 full-time (2 women), 8 part-time (7 women), 1 international. Average age 35. 10 applicants, 90% accepted, 4 enrolled. In 2017, 2 master's awarded. *Degree requirements:* For master's, thesis optional. *Entrance requirements:* For master's, resume documenting a minimum of 3 years professional experience in the field, artist's statement, porfolio. Additional exam requirements/recommendations for international students: Required—TOEFL (minimum score 550 paper-based, 79 iBT), IELTS (minimum score 6.5), or PTE (minimum score 53). *Application deadline:* For fall admission, 3/1 priority date for domestic and international students. Application fee: $35. Electronic applications accepted. *Expenses:* Tuition, state resident: part-time $500 per credit. Tuition, nonresident: part-time $750 per credit. *Required fees:* $115 per credit. One-time fee: $50 part-time. Tuition and fees vary according to degree level. *Financial support:* Career-related internships or fieldwork, Federal Work-Study, and unspecified assistantships available. Support available to part-time students. Financial award application deadline: 3/1; financial award applicants required to submit FAFSA. *Unit head:* Denise Bosler, Department Chair, 610-683-4531, Fax: 610-683-4619, E-mail: bosler@kutztown.edu. *Application contact:* Kathy Sue Traylor, Department Secretary, 610-683-4530, E-mail: traylor@kutztown.edu.
Website: http://kucd.kutztown.edu

Liberty University, School of Communication and Digital Content, Lynchburg, VA 24515. Offers communication (MA); promotion and video content (MA); social media management (MS); strategic communication (MA). *Program availability:* Part-time. *Students:* 118 full-time (90 women), 137 part-time (95 women); includes 60 minority (37 Black or African American, non-Hispanic/Latino; 1 American Indian or Alaska Native, non-Hispanic/Latino; 1 Asian, non-Hispanic/Latino; 11 Hispanic/Latino; 10 Two or more races, non-Hispanic/Latino), 7 international. Average age 31. 329 applicants, 50% accepted, 95 enrolled. In 2017, 38 master's awarded. *Degree requirements:* For master's, thesis (for some programs). *Entrance requirements:* For master's, minimum undergraduate GPA of 3.0, faculty recommendation, written statement of purpose, writing sample. Additional exam requirements/recommendations for international students: Required—TOEFL (minimum score 600 paper-based; 100 iBT). *Application deadline:* For fall admission, 6/1 for domestic students; for spring admission, 11/1 for domestic students. Applications are processed on a rolling basis. Application fee: $50. Electronic applications accepted. *Financial support:* Federal Work-Study and unspecified assistantships available. Financial award applicants required to submit FAFSA. *Unit head:* Dr. Norman Mintle, Dean, 434-582-2077, E-mail: cvkramer@liberty.edu. *Application contact:* Dr. Terry Elam, Director of Graduate Admissions, 434-582-2111, Fax: 434-582-7836, E-mail: gradadmissions@liberty.edu.

Lindenwood University, Graduate Programs, School of Arts, Media, and Communications, St. Charles, MO 63301-1695. Offers advertising (MA); art history (MA); cinema and media arts (MFA); communications (MA); digital and Web design (MA); fashion and business design (MS); journalism (MA); mass communications (MA); social media and digital content (MS). *Program availability:* Part-time. *Faculty:* 23 full-time (6 women), 8 part-time/adjunct (4 women). *Students:* 26 full-time (13 women), 11 part-time (8 women); includes 3 minority (1 American Indian or Alaska Native, non-Hispanic/Latino; 2 Hispanic/Latino), 7 international. Average age 33. 60 applicants, 45% accepted, 16 enrolled. In 2017, 11 master's awarded. *Degree requirements:* For master's, thesis (for some programs), minimum cumulative GPA of 3.0. *Entrance requirements:* For master's, audition or interview, minimum GPA of 3.0, portfolio, letter of recommendation. Additional exam requirements/recommendations for international students: Required—TOEFL (minimum score 550 paper-based; 80 iBT); Recommended—IELTS (minimum score 6.5). *Application deadline:* For fall admission, 8/27 priority date for domestic and international students; for spring admission, 1/14 for domestic students, 1/14 priority date for international students; for summer admission, 6/4 priority date for domestic and international students. Applications are processed on a rolling basis. Application fee: $30 ($100 for international students). Electronic applications accepted. *Expenses: Tuition:* Full-time $16,300; part-time $460 per credit. *Required fees:* $660; $330 per credit. Tuition and fees vary according to degree level and program. *Financial support:* In 2017–18, 34 students received support. Career-related internships or fieldwork, institutionally sponsored loans, scholarships/grants, tuition waivers (partial), and unspecified assistantships available. Financial award application deadline: 6/30; financial award applicants required to submit FAFSA. *Unit head:* Dr. Joseph Alsobrook, Dean, School of Arts, Media, and Communications, 636-949-4164, Fax: 636-949-4910, E-mail: jalsobrook@lindenwood.edu. *Application contact:* Kara Schilli, Director, Evening and Graduate Admissions, 636-949-4349, Fax: 636-949-4109, E-mail: adultadmissions@lindenwood.edu.
Website: http://www.lindenwood.edu/academics/academic-schools/school-of-arts-media-and-communications/

Lindenwood University–Belleville, Graduate Programs, Belleville, IL 62226. Offers business administration (MBA); communications (MA), including digital and multimedia, media management, promotions, training and development; counseling (MA); criminal justice administration (MS); education (MA); healthcare administration (MS); human resource management (MS); school administration (MA); teaching (MAT).

Lindsey Wilson College, Louisville Center for Design, Columbia, KY 42728. Offers interactive design (MA). *Program availability:* Online learning.

London Metropolitan University, Graduate Programs, London, United Kingdom. Offers applied psychology (M Sc); architecture (MA); biomedical science (M Sc); blood science (M Sc); cancer pharmacology (M Sc); computer networking and cyber security

(M Sc); computing and information systems (M Sc); conference interpreting (MA); counter-terrorism studies (M Sc); creative, digital and professional writing (MA); crime, violence and prevention (M Sc); criminology (M Sc); curating contemporary art (MA); data analytics (M Sc); digital media (MA); early childhood studies (MA); education (MA, Ed D); financial services law, regulation and compliance (LL M); food science (M Sc); forensic psychology (M Sc); health and social care management and policy (M Sc); human nutrition (M Sc); human resource management (MA); human rights and international conflict (MA); information technology (M Sc); intelligence and security studies (M Sc); international oil, gas and energy law (LL M); international relations (MA); interpreting (MA); learning and teaching in higher education (MA); legal practice (LL M); media and entertainment law (LL M); organizational and consumer psychology (M Sc); psychological therapy (M Sc); psychology of mental health (M Sc); public health (M Sc); public policy and management (MPA); security studies (M Sc); social work (M Sc); spatial planning and urban design (MA); sports therapy (M Sc); supporting older children and young people with dyslexia (MA); teaching languages (MA), including Arabic, English; translation (MA); woman and child abuse (MA).

Long Island University–LIU Post, College of Arts, Communications and Design, Brookville, NY 11548-1300. Offers art (MA); clinical art therapy (MA); clinical art therapy and counseling (MA); digital game design and development (MA); fine arts and design (MFA); interactive multimedia arts (MA); museum studies (MA); music (MA); theatre (MFA). *Faculty:* 22 full-time (10 women), 44 part-time/adjunct (24 women). *Students:* 99 full-time (80 women), 14 part-time (12 women); includes 22 minority (7 Black or African American, non-Hispanic/Latino; 4 Asian, non-Hispanic/Latino; 9 Hispanic/Latino; 2 Two or more races, non-Hispanic/Latino), 23 international. Average age 28. 125 applicants, 70% accepted, 42 enrolled. In 2017, 55 master's awarded. *Degree requirements:* For master's, variable foreign language requirement, comprehensive exam (for some programs), thesis. *Entrance requirements:* For master's, performance audition or portfolio. Additional exam requirements/recommendations for international students: Required—TOEFL (minimum score 550 paper-based; 79 iBT). *Application deadline:* Applications are processed on a rolling basis. Application fee: $50. Electronic applications accepted. *Expenses: Tuition:* Full-time $21,618; part-time $1201 per credit. *Required fees:* $1840; $920 per term. Tuition and fees vary according to course load. *Financial support:* In 2017–18, 78 students received support. Career-related internships or fieldwork, scholarships/grants, tuition waivers (full and partial), and unspecified assistantships available. Support available to part-time students. Financial award application deadline: 2/15; financial award applicants required to submit FAFSA. *Faculty research:* Creative writing, playwriting, music composition, music performance, international impact of art therapy, artistic creation. *Unit head:* Steven Breese, Dean, 516-299-2309, E-mail: steven.breese@liu.edu. *Application contact:* Rita Langdon, Graduate Admissions, 516-299-2334, Fax: 516-299-2137, E-mail: post-enroll@liu.edu.
Website: http://www.liu.edu/CWPost/Academics/School-of-Visual-Arts-Communications-and-Digital-Technologies

Louisiana State University and Agricultural & Mechanical College, Graduate School, College of Engineering, Program in Digital Media Arts and Engineering, Baton Rouge, LA 70803. Offers M Sc. *Students:* 10 full-time (7 women); includes 2 minority (both Black or African American, non-Hispanic/Latino), 2 international. Average age 31. 8 applicants, 75% accepted, 4 enrolled. In 2017, 4 master's awarded. *Entrance requirements:* For master's, GRE, digital portfolio. *Unit head:* Marc Aubanel, Director, 225-578-8907, Fax: 225-578-5040, E-mail: maubanel@cct.lsu.edu. *Application contact:* Theresa Mooney, Academic Counselor, 225-578-5400, Fax: 225-578-5040, E-mail: deacon1@lsu.edu.
Website: http://master.dmae.lsu.edu/

Lynn University, Eugene M. and Christine E. Lynn College of Communication and Design, Boca Raton, FL 33431-5598. Offers communication and media (MS), including design strategies for Web development, digital media, media studies and practice; digital media (Certificate); graphic and Web design (MFA); visual effects animation (MFA); Web design and technology (MS). *Program availability:* Part-time, evening/weekend. *Faculty:* 14 full-time (9 women), 7 part-time/adjunct (1 woman). *Students:* 35 full-time (21 women), 33 part-time (13 women); includes 31 minority (12 Black or African American, non-Hispanic/Latino; 2 American Indian or Alaska Native, non-Hispanic/Latino; 2 Asian, non-Hispanic/Latino; 14 Hispanic/Latino; 1 Two or more races, non-Hispanic/Latino), 12 international. Average age 27. 59 applicants, 92% accepted, 44 enrolled. In 2017, 17 master's awarded. *Degree requirements:* For master's, thesis (for some programs), completion of degree in four calendar years; minimum cumulative GPA of 3.0 and C grade or higher in each course; orientation seminar (one credit); 36 credits of foundation and specialization or a thesis. *Entrance requirements:* For master's, bachelor's degree from accredited institution, minimum undergraduate GPA of 3.0, official undergraduate transcripts, letter of recommendation from academic or professional source, writing sample demonstrating capacity to perform at graduate level. Additional exam requirements/recommendations for international students: Required—TOEFL (minimum score 550 paper-based; 80 iBT), IELTS (minimum score 6.5). *Application deadline:* For fall admission, 8/18 for domestic students, 8/4 for international students; for spring admission, 12/15 for domestic students, 12/1 for international students; for summer admission, 4/17 for domestic students, 4/3 for international students. Applications are processed on a rolling basis. Application fee: $45. Electronic applications accepted. *Expenses:* $740 per credit. *Financial support:* Career-related internships or fieldwork, Federal Work-Study, institutionally sponsored loans, scholarships/grants, tuition waivers (partial), and unspecified assistantships available. Support available to part-time students. Financial award application deadline: 8/1; financial award applicants required to submit FAFSA. *Unit head:* Dr. David L. Jaffe, Dean, 561-237-7099, Fax: 561-237-7097, E-mail: djaffe@lynn.edu. *Application contact:* Steven Pruitt, Director of Graduate Admission, 561-237-7834, Fax: 561-237-7100, E-mail: admission@lynn.edu.
Website: https://www.lynn.edu/academics/colleges-schools/communication-and-design

Minneapolis College of Art and Design, Program in Graphic and Web Design, Minneapolis, MN 55404-4347. Offers MA. *Expenses: Tuition:* Full-time $38,670. *Required fees:* $450. One-time fee: $300 full-time.

Mount Mary University, Graduate Programs, Program in English, Milwaukee, WI 53222-4597. Offers creative writing (MA); professional and new media writing (MA). *Program availability:* Part-time, evening/weekend. *Degree requirements:* For master's, comprehensive exam, thesis or alternative. *Entrance requirements:* For master's, minimum GPA of 2.75. Additional exam requirements/recommendations for international students: Required—TOEFL (minimum score 550 paper-based; 80 iBT); Recommended—IELTS (minimum score 6.5). Electronic applications accepted. *Expenses:* Contact institution.

National University, Academic Affairs, School of Professional Studies, La Jolla, CA 92037-1011. Offers criminal justice (MCJ); digital cinema production (MFA); digital journalism (MA); homeland security and emergency management (MS); juvenile justice (MS); professional screenwriting (MFA); public administration (MPA), including human resource management, organizational leadership. *Program availability:* Part-time, evening/weekend, 100% online, blended/hybrid learning. *Degree requirements:* For master's, thesis (for some programs). *Entrance requirements:* For master's, interview, minimum GPA of 2.5. Additional exam requirements/recommendations for international students: Required—TOEFL (minimum score 550 paper-based; 79 iBT), IELTS (minimum score 6). *Application deadline:* Applications are processed on a rolling basis. Application fee: $60 ($65 for international students). Electronic applications accepted. *Expenses: Tuition:* Part-time $430 per quarter hour. *Financial support:* Career-related internships or fieldwork, institutionally sponsored loans, scholarships/grants, and tuition waivers (partial) available. Support available to part-time students. Financial award application deadline: 6/30; financial award applicants required to submit FAFSA. *Unit head:* Dr. Daniel Donaldson, Dean, 858-642-8480, E-mail: sops@nu.edu. *Application contact:* Brandon Jouganatos, Vice President for Enrollment Services, 800-628-8648, E-mail: advisor@nu.edu.
Website: http://www.nu.edu/OurPrograms/School-of-Professional-Studies.html

New Mexico Highlands University, Graduate Studies, College of Arts and Sciences, Department of Computer Sciences, Las Vegas, NM 87701. Offers media arts and computer science (MS), including computer science. *Degree requirements:* For master's, comprehensive exam, thesis. *Entrance requirements:* For master's, minimum undergraduate GPA of 3.0. Additional exam requirements/recommendations for international students: Required—TOEFL (minimum score 540 paper-based). *Faculty research:* Advanced digital compositing, photographic installations and exhibition design, pattern recognition, parallel and distributed computing, computer security education.

The New School, Parsons School of Design, Program in Communication Design, New York, NY 10011. Offers MPS. *Program availability:* Part-time. *Faculty:* 1 full-time (0 women), 3 part-time/adjunct (1 woman). *Students:* 13 full-time (10 women); includes 8 minority (1 Black or African American, non-Hispanic/Latino; 6 Asian, non-Hispanic/Latino; 1 Hispanic/Latino). Average age 28. 47 applicants, 53% accepted, 13 enrolled. *Degree requirements:* For master's, thesis or alternative. *Entrance requirements:* For master's, transcripts, resume, statement of purpose, recommendation letters, portfolio. Additional exam requirements/recommendations for international students: Required—TOEFL (minimum score 92 iBT), IELTS (minimum score 7), PTE (minimum score 63). *Application deadline:* For fall admission, 1/1 priority date for domestic and international students. Applications are processed on a rolling basis. Application fee: $50. Electronic applications accepted. *Expenses:* $24,922 per semester full-time, $1,744 per credit part-time, $100 maintenance of status fee. *Financial support:* In 2017–18, 9 students received support. Career-related internships or fieldwork, Federal Work-Study, and scholarships/grants available. Support available to part-time students. Financial award application deadline: 2/1; financial award applicants required to submit FAFSA. *Unit head:* Brendan Griffiths, Program Director, 212-229-8900 Ext. 1544, E-mail: brendan@newschool.edu. *Application contact:* Courtney Malenius, Director of Graduate Admission, 212-229-5150 Ext. 4011, E-mail: thinkparsonsgrad@newschool.edu.
Website: https://www.newschool.edu/parsons/mps-communication-design/

New York University, Tandon School of Engineering, Department of Technology, Culture and Society, Major in Integrated Digital Media, New York, NY 10012-1019. Offers MS. *Program availability:* Part-time. *Students:* 55 full-time (31 women), 25 part-time (16 women); includes 16 minority (5 Black or African American, non-Hispanic/Latino; 4 Asian, non-Hispanic/Latino; 5 Hispanic/Latino; 2 Two or more races, non-Hispanic/Latino), 44 international. Average age 27. 189 applicants, 41% accepted, 37 enrolled. In 2017, 23 master's awarded. *Degree requirements:* For master's, comprehensive exam (for some programs), thesis (for some programs). *Entrance requirements:* Additional exam requirements/recommendations for international students: Required—TOEFL (minimum score 550 paper-based; 90 iBT); Recommended—IELTS (minimum score 7). *Application deadline:* For fall admission, 2/15 priority date for domestic and international students; for spring admission, 11/1 priority date for domestic and international students. Applications are processed on a rolling basis. Application fee: $75. Electronic applications accepted. *Expenses: Tuition:* Full-time $41,352; part-time $19,968 per year. *Required fees:* $2496; $1628 per unit. $814 per term. Tuition and fees vary according to course load and program. *Financial support:* Institutionally sponsored loans, scholarships/grants, and unspecified assistantships available. Support available to part-time students. Financial award applicants required to submit FAFSA. *Unit head:* Dr. R. Luke DuBois, Program Director, 646-997-0719, E-mail: dubois@nyu.edu. *Application contact:* Elizabeth Ensweiler, Senior Director of Graduate Enrollment and Graduate Admissions, 646-997-3182, E-mail: elizabeth.ensweiler@nyu.edu.
Website: http://engineering.nyu.edu/academics/programs/integrated-digital-media-ms

New York University, Tisch School of the Arts, Interactive Telecommunications Program, New York, NY 10012-1019. Offers MPS. *Faculty:* 9 full-time, 40 part-time/adjunct. *Students:* 229 full-time (129 women); includes 47 minority (7 Black or African American, non-Hispanic/Latino; 20 Asian, non-Hispanic/Latino; 13 Hispanic/Latino; 7 Two or more races, non-Hispanic/Latino), 130 international. 361 applicants, 63% accepted, 117 enrolled. In 2017, 103 master's awarded. *Degree requirements:* For master's, thesis. Application fee: $60. Electronic applications accepted. *Expenses: Tuition:* Full-time $41,352; part-time $19,968 per year. *Required fees:* $2496; $1628 per unit. $814 per term. Tuition and fees vary according to course load and program. *Financial support:* In 2017–18, 90 students received support, including 24 fellowships with full and partial tuition reimbursements available; career-related internships or fieldwork, Federal Work-Study, institutionally sponsored loans, scholarships/grants, and tuition waivers (partial) also available. Financial award application deadline: 2/15; financial award applicants required to submit FAFSA. *Faculty research:* Interactive narrative/storytelling, interactive media, Web technology, physical computing, ubiquitous computing. *Unit head:* Dan O'Sullivan, Chair, 212-998-1880, Fax: 212-998-1898, E-mail: itp.inquiries@nyu.edu. *Application contact:* Dan Sandford, Director of Graduate Admissions, 212-998-1918, Fax: 212-995-4060, E-mail: tisch.gradadmissions@nyu.edu.
Website: http://www.itp.tisch.nyu.edu/

Northeastern University, College of Professional Studies, Boston, MA 02115-5096. Offers applied nutrition (MS); college athletics administration (MSL); commerce and economic development (MS); corporate and organizational communication (MS); criminal justice (MS); digital media (MPS); elearning and instructional design (M Ed); elementary education (MAT); geographic information technology (MPS); global studies and international relations (MS); higher education administration (M Ed); homeland security (MA); human services (MS); informatics (MPS); leadership (MS); learning analytics (M Ed); learning and instruction (M Ed); nonprofit management (MS); professional sports administration (MSL); project management (MS); regulatory affairs for drugs, biologics, and medical devices (MS); respiratory care leadership (MS); special education (M Ed); technical communication (MS). *Program availability:* Part-time, evening/weekend, 100% online, blended/hybrid learning. *Faculty:* 82 full-time (51 women), 853 part-time/adjunct (366 women). *Students:* 5,278 part-time (3,230 women). In 2017, 1,586 master's awarded. *Application deadline:* Applications are processed on a rolling basis. Application fee: $0. Electronic applications accepted. *Expenses:* Contact institution. *Financial support:* Applicants required to submit FAFSA. *Unit head:* Dr. Mary Loeffelholz, Dean of the College of Professional Studies. *Application contact:* E-mail: cpsadmissions@northeastern.edu.
Website: https://cps.northeastern.edu/

Internet and Interactive Multimedia

Northwestern University, School of Professional Studies, Program in Information Systems, Evanston, IL 60208. Offers analytics and business intelligence (MS); database and Internet technologies (MS); information systems (MS); information systems management (MS); information systems security (MS); medical informatics (MS); software project management and development (MS). *Program availability:* Part-time, evening/weekend.
Website: https://sps.northwestern.edu/masters/information-systems/index.php

The Ohio State University, Graduate School, College of Arts and Sciences, Division of Arts and Humanities, Department of Design, Columbus, OH 43210. Offers design (MA); design research and development (MFA); digital animation and interactive media (MFA). *Accreditation:* NASAD. *Program availability:* Part-time. *Faculty:* 16. *Students:* 25 (15 women), 8 international. Average age 28. In 2017, 10 master's awarded. *Entrance requirements:* For master's, GRE General Test (for all applicants with cumulative GPA below 3.0), portfolio. Additional exam requirements/recommendations for international students: Recommended—TOEFL (minimum score 550 paper-based; 79 iBT). *Application deadline:* For fall admission, 12/13 priority date for domestic students, 11/30 priority date for international students; for spring admission, 3/1 for domestic students, 2/1 for international students. Applications are processed on a rolling basis. Application fee: $60 ($70 for international students). Electronic applications accepted. *Financial support:* Fellowships, research assistantships, teaching assistantships, career-related internships or fieldwork, Federal Work-Study, institutionally sponsored loans, and unspecified assistantships available. Support available to part-time students. Financial award application deadline: 5/1. *Unit head:* Dr. Mary Anne Beecher, Chair, 614-688-6746, E-mail: beecher.17@osu.edu. *Application contact:* Graduate and Professional Admissions, 614-292-9444, Fax: 614-292-3895, E-mail: gpadmissions@osu.edu.
Website: http://design.osu.edu/

Ohio University, Graduate College, Scripps College of Communication, School of Visual Communication, Athens, OH 45701-2979. Offers MA. *Entrance requirements:* For master's, minimum GPA of 2.5, portfolio. Additional exam requirements/recommendations for international students: Required—TOEFL (minimum score 600 paper-based; 100 iBT) or IELTS (minimum score 7). Electronic applications accepted. *Faculty research:* Photojournalism (including documentary photography), commercial photography (including illustrative photography), picture editing, informational graphics/publication design, interactive multimedia, visual media management.

Pace University, Lubin School of Business, Marketing Program, New York, NY 10038. Offers analytics and customer intelligence (MS); marketing management (MBA); social media and mobile marketing (MS). *Program availability:* Part-time, evening/weekend. *Students:* 31 full-time (22 women), 19 part-time (15 women); includes 8 minority (1 Black or African American, non-Hispanic/Latino; 2 Asian, non-Hispanic/Latino; 4 Hispanic/Latino; 1 Two or more races, non-Hispanic/Latino), 24 international. Average age 26. 84 applicants, 60% accepted, 18 enrolled. In 2017, 34 master's awarded. *Entrance requirements:* For master's, GMAT, GRE, undergraduate degree, transcripts from all accredited colleges/universities attended, two letters of recommendation, resume, personal statement. Additional exam requirements/recommendations for international students: Required—TOEFL (minimum score 90 iBT), IELTS (minimum score 7) or PTE (minimum score 61). *Application deadline:* For fall admission, 8/1 priority date for domestic students, 6/1 for international students; for spring admission, 12/1 for domestic students, 10/1 for international students. Applications are processed on a rolling basis. Application fee: $70. Electronic applications accepted. *Financial support:* Research assistantships, career-related internships or fieldwork, and Federal Work-Study available. Support available to part-time students. Financial award application deadline: 2/15; financial award applicants required to submit FAFSA. *Unit head:* Dr. Ipshita Ray, Chairperson, 212-618-6505, E-mail: iray@pace.edu. *Application contact:* Susan Ford-Goldschein, Director of Graduate Admissions, 212-346-1531, Fax: 212-346-1585, E-mail: graduateadmission@pace.edu.
Website: http://www.pace.edu/lubin/mba-in-marketing-management

Pace University, Seidenberg School of Computer Science and Information Systems, New York, NY 10038. Offers chief information security officer (APC); computer science (MS, PhD); enterprise analytics (MS); information and communication technology strategy and innovation (APC); information systems (MS, APC); Internet technology (MS); professional studies in computing (DPS); secure software and information engineering (APC); security and information assurance (Certificate); software development and engineering (MS, Certificate); telecommunications systems and networks (MS, Certificate). *Program availability:* Part-time, evening/weekend, online only, 100% online, blended/hybrid learning. *Faculty:* 26 full-time (7 women), 7 part-time/adjunct (2 women). *Students:* 569 full-time (203 women), 319 part-time (95 women); includes 186 minority (73 Black or African American, non-Hispanic/Latino; 3 American Indian or Alaska Native, non-Hispanic/Latino; 56 Asian, non-Hispanic/Latino; 43 Hispanic/Latino; 11 Two or more races, non-Hispanic/Latino), 541 international. Average age 30. 871 applicants, 90% accepted, 272 enrolled. In 2017, 311 master's, 10 doctorates, 2 other advanced degrees awarded. *Degree requirements:* For master's, thesis or alternative, capstone course; for doctorate, comprehensive exam (for some programs), thesis/dissertation. *Entrance requirements:* For master's, GRE General Test. Additional exam requirements/recommendations for international students: Required—TOEFL (minimum score 78 iBT), IELTS (minimum score 6.5) or PTE (minimum score 52). *Application deadline:* For fall admission, 8/1 priority date for domestic students, 6/1 for international students; for spring admission, 12/1 for domestic students, 10/1 for international students. Applications are processed on a rolling basis. Application fee: $70. Electronic applications accepted. *Expenses:* Contact institution. *Financial support:* In 2017–18, 45 students received support. Research assistantships, career-related internships or fieldwork, scholarships/grants, and unspecified assistantships available. Support available to part-time students. Financial award application deadline: 2/15; financial award applicants required to submit FAFSA. *Faculty research:* Cyber security/digital forensics; mobile app development; big data/enterprise analytics; artificial intelligence; software development. *Total annual research expenditures:* $314,545. *Unit head:* Dr. Jonathan Hill, Dean, Seidenberg School of Computer Science and Information Systems, 212-346-1864, E-mail: jhill@pace.edu. *Application contact:* Susan Ford-Goldschein, Director of Graduate Admissions, 914-422-4283, Fax: 212-346-1585, E-mail: graduateadmission@pace.edu.
Website: http://www.pace.edu/seidenberg

Pratt Institute, School of Art, Program in Digital Arts, Brooklyn, NY 11205-3899. Offers MFA, MS/MFA. *Accreditation:* NASAD. *Students:* 47 full-time (34 women), 5 part-time (3 women); includes 2 minority (1 Asian, non-Hispanic/Latino; 1 Hispanic/Latino), 42 international. Average age 26. 218 applicants, 34% accepted, 18 enrolled. In 2017, 26 master's awarded. *Degree requirements:* For master's, thesis, exhibit. *Entrance requirements:* For master's, portfolio or video, letters of recommendation. Additional exam requirements/recommendations for international students: Required—TOEFL (minimum score 550 paper-based; 79 iBT). *Application deadline:* For fall admission, 1/5 for domestic and international students; for spring admission, 10/1 for domestic and international students. Application fee: $50 ($90 for international students). Electronic applications accepted. *Expenses:* Tuition: Full-time $30,834. *Required fees:* $1974. *Financial support:* Career-related internships or fieldwork, Federal Work-Study, institutionally sponsored loans, scholarships/grants, health care benefits, and

unspecified assistantships available. Support available to part-time students. Financial award application deadline: 2/1; financial award applicants required to submit FAFSA. *Unit head:* Peter Patchen, Chair, 718-636-3693, Fax: 718-399-4494, E-mail: ppatchen@pratt.edu. *Application contact:* Natalie Capannelli, Director of Graduate Admissions, 718-636-3551, Fax: 718-399-4242, E-mail: ncapanne@pratt.edu.
Website: https://www.pratt.edu/academics/school-of-art/graduate-school-of-art/digital-arts-grad/

See Display on page 141 and Close-Up on page 189.

Quinnipiac University, School of Communications, Program in Interactive Media and Communications, Hamden, CT 06518-1940. Offers interactive media (MS); media design (MS); social media (MS); UX design (MS). *Program availability:* Part-time, evening/weekend, online only, 100% online. *Faculty:* 2 full-time (1 woman), 10 part-time/adjunct (5 women). *Students:* 5 full-time (3 women), 74 part-time (51 women); includes 23 minority (13 Black or African American, non-Hispanic/Latino; 2 Asian, non-Hispanic/Latino; 6 Hispanic/Latino; 2 Two or more races, non-Hispanic/Latino). 50 applicants, 86% accepted, 38 enrolled. In 2017, 48 master's awarded. *Entrance requirements:* For master's, minimum GPA of 3.0, portfolio or writing sample. Additional exam requirements/recommendations for international students: Required—TOEFL (minimum score 575 paper-based; 90 iBT), IELTS (minimum score 6.5). *Application deadline:* For fall admission, 7/30 priority date for domestic students, 4/30 priority date for international students; for spring admission, 12/30 priority date for domestic students, 9/30 priority date for international students. Applications are processed on a rolling basis. Application fee: $45. Electronic applications accepted. *Expenses:* Contact institution. *Financial support:* Federal Work-Study and unspecified assistantships available. Financial award application deadline: 6/1; financial award applicants required to submit FAFSA. *Faculty research:* User experience, social media, semiotics and communication, online distribution of news, Web-based interventions for research. *Unit head:* Phillip Simon, Director, 203-582-8274, E-mail: phillip.simon@qu.edu. *Application contact:* Quinnipiac University Online Admissions Office, 800-462-1944, E-mail: quonlineadmissions@qu.edu.
Website: https://quonline.quinnipiac.edu/online-programs/online-graduate-programs/ms-in-interactive-media/

Robert Morris University, School of Communications and Information Systems, Moon Township, PA 15108-1189. Offers communication and information systems (MS); cyber security (MS); data analytics (MS); information security and assurance (MS); information systems and communications (D Sc); information systems management (MS); information technology project management (MS); Internet information systems (MS); organizational leadership (MS). *Program availability:* Part-time, evening/weekend, online learning. *Faculty:* 23 full-time (10 women), 10 part-time/adjunct (3 women). *Students:* 258 part-time (99 women); includes 46 minority (22 Black or African American, non-Hispanic/Latino; 16 Asian, non-Hispanic/Latino; 5 Hispanic/Latino; 3 Two or more races, non-Hispanic/Latino), 46 international. Average age 35. 226 applicants, 52% accepted, 79 enrolled. In 2017, 148 master's, 12 doctorates awarded. *Degree requirements:* For doctorate, thesis/dissertation. *Entrance requirements:* For doctorate, employer letter of endorsement, interview. Additional exam requirements/recommendations for international students: Required—TOEFL (minimum score 550 paper-based; 79 iBT). *Application deadline:* For fall admission, 7/1 priority date for domestic and international students; for spring admission, 11/1 priority date for domestic and international students. Applications are processed on a rolling basis. Application fee: $35. Electronic applications accepted. Application fee is waived when completed online. *Expenses:* $920 per credit tuition plus university fees of $80 per credit. *Financial support:* Institutionally sponsored loans available. Support available to part-time students. Financial award application deadline: 5/1. *Unit head:* Ann Marie M. Le Blanc, Dean, 412-397-6433, Fax: 412-397-6469, E-mail: leblanc@rmu.edu. *Application contact:* E-mail: graduateadmissions@rmu.edu.
Website: http://www.rmu.edu/web/cms/schools/scis/Pages/default.aspx

Rochester Institute of Technology, Graduate Enrollment Services, College of Imaging Arts and Sciences, School of Design, Advanced Certificate Program in User Experience Design and Development, Rochester, NY 14623-5603. Offers Advanced Certificate. *Program availability:* Part-time, evening/weekend, online only, 100% online. *Students:* 5 part-time (3 women); includes 1 minority (Two or more races, non-Hispanic/Latino). Average age 38. 7 applicants, 57% accepted, 2 enrolled. In 2017, 6 Advanced Certificates awarded. *Entrance requirements:* Additional exam requirements/recommendations for international students: Required—TOEFL (minimum score 550 paper-based; 79 iBT), IELTS (minimum score 6.5), PTE (minimum score 58). *Application deadline:* Applications are processed on a rolling basis. Application fee: $65. Electronic applications accepted. *Expenses:* $1,035 per credit hour (online study). *Financial support:* Available to part-time students. Applicants required to submit FAFSA. *Faculty research:* User experience planning and process, visual design for interactive design, interaction modeling and prototyping. *Unit head:* Adam Smith, Graduate Director, 585-475-4552, E-mail: aesfaa@rit.edu. *Application contact:* Diane Ellison, Senior Associate Vice President, Graduate Enrollment Services, 585-475-2229, Fax: 585-475-7164, E-mail: gradinfo@rit.edu.
Website: https://www.rit.edu/ritonline/program/UXDE-ACT

Rochester Institute of Technology, Graduate Enrollment Services, College of Liberal Arts, School of Communication, Advanced Certificate Program in Communication and Digital Media, Rochester, NY 14623-5603. Offers Advanced Certificate. *Program availability:* Part-time, evening/weekend, online only, 100% online. *Students:* 4 part-time (3 women); includes 1 minority (Black or African American, non-Hispanic/Latino). Average age 45. 6 applicants, 33% accepted, 1 enrolled. *Entrance requirements:* Additional exam requirements/recommendations for international students: Required—TOEFL (minimum score 570 paper-based; 88 iBT), IELTS (minimum score 6.5), PTE (minimum score 61). *Application deadline:* Applications are processed on a rolling basis. Application fee: $65. Electronic applications accepted. *Expenses:* $1,035 per credit hour (online study). *Financial support:* Available to part-time students. Applicants required to submit FAFSA. *Unit head:* Dr. Grant Cos, Director of Graduate Programs, 585-475-6646, E-mail: gccgpt@rit.edu. *Application contact:* Diane Ellison, Senior Associate Vice President, Graduate Enrollment Services, 585-475-2229, Fax: 585-475-7164, E-mail: gradinfo@rit.edu.
Website: https://www.rit.edu/ritonline/program/COMTCH-ACT

Rochester Institute of Technology, Graduate Enrollment Services, Golisano College of Computing and Information Sciences, Information Science and Technologies Department, Advanced Certificate Program in Web Development, Rochester, NY 14623. Offers Advanced Certificate. *Program availability:* Part-time, evening/weekend. *Students:* 1 (woman) part-time. Average age 41. 5 applicants, 40% accepted. *Entrance requirements:* For degree, minimum GPA of 3.0. Additional exam requirements/recommendations for international students: Required—TOEFL (minimum score 570 paper-based; 88 iBT), IELTS (minimum score 6.5), PTE (minimum score 61). *Application deadline:* Applications are processed on a rolling basis. Application fee: $65. Electronic applications accepted. *Expenses:* $1,815 per credit hour. *Financial support:* In 2017–18, 1 student received support. Available to part-time students. Applicants required to submit FAFSA. *Faculty research:* Web development, mobile computing, service computing, advanced software development, health informatics. *Unit head:* Qi

Yu, Graduate Program Director, 585-475-2700, Fax: 585-475-6584, E-mail: informaticsgrad@rit.edu. *Application contact:* Diane Ellison, Senior Associate Vice President, Graduate Enrollment Services, 585-475-2229, Fax: 585-475-7164, E-mail: gradinfo@rit.edu.
Website: http://www.ist.rit.edu/degrees/graduate/advanced-cert.php

Rocky Mountain College of Art + Design, Program in Education, Leadership + Emerging Technologies, Lakewood, CO 80214. Offers MA. *Accreditation:* NASAD. *Program availability:* Online learning.

Sam Houston State University, College of Fine Arts and Mass Communication, Department of Mass Communication, Huntsville, TX 77341. Offers digital media (MA). *Program availability:* Part-time. *Degree requirements:* For master's, comprehensive exam (for some programs), thesis optional. *Entrance requirements:* For master's, GRE General Test, personal statement, digital media portfolio. Electronic applications accepted.

San Diego State University, Graduate and Research Affairs, College of Professional Studies and Fine Arts, School of Communication, San Diego, CA 92182. Offers advertising and public relations (MA); critical-cultural studies (MA); interaction studies (MA); intercultural and international studies (MA); new media studies (MA); news and information studies (MA); telecommunications and media management (MA). *Degree requirements:* For master's, thesis. *Entrance requirements:* For master's, GRE General Test, 3 letters of recommendation. Additional exam requirements/recommendations for international students: Required—TOEFL. Electronic applications accepted.

Savannah College of Art and Design, Program in Interactive Design and Game Development, Savannah, GA 31402-3146. Offers MA, MFA. *Program availability:* Part-time, 100% online. *Faculty:* 16 full-time (4 women), 4 part-time/adjunct (1 woman). *Students:* 74 full-time (28 women), 27 part-time (9 women); includes 11 minority (3 Black or African American, non-Hispanic/Latino; 6 Asian, non-Hispanic/Latino; 2 Hispanic/Latino), 58 international. Average age 27. 145 applicants, 41% accepted, 26 enrolled. In 2017, 34 master's awarded. *Degree requirements:* For master's, final project (for MA); thesis (for MFA). *Entrance requirements:* For master's, GRE (recommended), portfolio (submitted in digital format), audition or writing submission, resume, statement of purpose, two letters of recommendation. Additional exam requirements/recommendations for international students: Recommended—TOEFL (minimum score 550 paper-based; 85 iBT), IELTS (minimum score 6.5). *Application deadline:* For fall admission, 4/1 for domestic and international students. Applications are processed on a rolling basis. Application fee: $40. Electronic applications accepted. *Expenses: Tuition:* Full-time $36,765; part-time $817 per credit hour. One-time fee: $500. *Financial support:* Career-related internships or fieldwork, Federal Work-Study, and scholarships/grants available. Financial award application deadline: 4/1; financial award applicants required to submit FAFSA. *Unit head:* SuAnne Fu, Chair, Interactive Design and Game Development. *Application contact:* Jenny Jaquillard, Executive Director of Admissions, Recruitment and Events, 912-525-5100, Fax: 912-525-5985, E-mail: admission@scad.edu.
Website: http://www.scad.edu/academics/programs/interactive-design-and-game-development

School of Visual Arts, Graduate Programs, Interaction Design Department, New York, NY 10010-3994. Offers MFA. *Degree requirements:* For master's, thesis, 60 credits, residency of two academic years, thesis project. *Entrance requirements:* For master's, portfolio, statement of purpose, resume. Additional exam requirements/recommendations for international students: Required—TOEFL (minimum score 550 paper-based; 79 iBT). Electronic applications accepted. *Faculty research:* Data analysis and visualization, service design, interaction design.

School of Visual Arts, Graduate Programs, Program in Photography, Video and Related Media, New York, NY 10010-3994. Offers MFA. *Accreditation:* NASAD. *Degree requirements:* For master's, thesis, 60 credits and all course requirements; minimum GPA of 3.3; thesis project. *Entrance requirements:* For master's, portfolio (still images and/or videos) through SlideRoom. Additional exam requirements/recommendations for international students: Required—TOEFL (minimum score 550 paper-based; 79 iBT). Electronic applications accepted. *Faculty research:* Contemporary and responsible creative initiatives, including experimental, narrative or documentary video, installation and conceptual art, tableau and real-world-witness photography.

Southern New Hampshire University, School of Business, Manchester, NH 03106-1045. Offers accounting (MBA, Graduate Certificate); accounting finance (MS); accounting/auditing (MS); accounting/forensic accounting (MS); accounting/management accounting (MS); accounting/taxation (MS); applied economics (MS); athletic administration (MBA, Graduate Certificate); business administration (IMBA, Certificate), including business information systems (Certificate), human resource management (Certificate); business analytics (MBA); business intelligence (MBA); communication (MA), including new media and marketing, public relations; community economic development (MBA); criminal justice (MBA); data analytics (MS); economics (MBA); engineering management (MBA); entrepreneurship (MBA); finance (MBA, MS, Graduate Certificate); finance/corporate finance (MS); finance/investments (MS); forensic accounting (MBA); forensic accounting and fraud examination (Graduate Certificate); healthcare informatics (MBA); healthcare management (MBA); human resource management (MS); human resources (MBA); information technology (MS); information technology management (MBA); international business (PhD); Internet marketing (MBA); leadership (MBA); leadership of nonprofit organizations (Graduate Certificate); management (MS); marketing (MBA, MS, Graduate Certificate); music business (MBA); operations and project management (MS); operations and supply chain management (MBA, Graduate Certificate); organizational leadership (MS); project management (MBA, Graduate Certificate); public administration (MBA, Graduate Certificate); quantitative analysis (MBA); Six Sigma (Graduate Certificate); Six Sigma quality (MBA); social media marketing (MBA, Graduate Certificate); sport management (MBA, MS, Graduate Certificate); sustainability and environmental compliance (MBA); MBA/Certificate. *Accreditation:* ACBSP. *Program availability:* Part-time, evening/weekend, online learning. Terminal master's awarded for partial completion of doctoral program. *Degree requirements:* For master's, one foreign language, comprehensive exam (for some programs), thesis or alternative; for doctorate, one foreign language, comprehensive exam, thesis/dissertation. *Entrance requirements:* For master's, minimum GPA of 2.5; for doctorate, GMAT. Additional exam requirements/recommendations for international students: Required—TOEFL (minimum score 500 paper-based). *Application deadline:* Applications are processed on a rolling basis. Application fee: $40. Electronic applications accepted. *Expenses: Tuition:* Part-time $627 per credit hour. Part-time tuition and fees vary according to campus/location and program. *Financial support:* Career-related internships or fieldwork, Federal Work-Study, institutionally sponsored loans, scholarships/grants, tuition waivers (partial), and unspecified assistantships available. Support available to part-time students. Financial award applicants required to submit FAFSA. *Unit head:* Dr. Bill Lightfoot, Dean, 603-644-3102, Fax: 603-644-3144. *Application contact:* Office of Graduate Admission, 888-327-SNHU, Fax: 603-644-3144, E-mail: enroll@snhu.edu.

State University of New York at Oswego, Graduate Studies, Department of Art, Oswego, NY 13126. Offers art (MA); graphic design and digital media (MA). *Accreditation:* NASAD. *Program availability:* Part-time. *Degree requirements:* For master's, exhibit, final presentation. *Entrance requirements:* For master's, slides of previous work. Additional exam requirements/recommendations for international students: Required—TOEFL (minimum score 560 paper-based). *Faculty research:* Ancient and primitive art, nineteenth century art, medieval art, Renaissance art.

Stevens Institute of Technology, Graduate School, Charles V. Schaefer Jr. School of Engineering and Science, Department of Computer Science, Hoboken, NJ 07030. Offers computer graphics (Certificate), including computer graphics; computer science (MS, PhD); computer systems (Certificate), including computer systems; cybersecurity (MS); database management systems (Certificate), including databases; distributed systems (Certificate), including distributed systems; elements of computer science (Certificate), including cybersecurity; enterprise and cloud computing (MS); enterprise computing (Certificate), including enterprise and cloud computing; enterprise security and information assurance (Certificate), including enterprise security and information assurance; health informatics (Certificate), including health informatics; multimedia experience and management (Certificate), including multimedia experience and management; networks and systems administration (Certificate), including cloud computing; service oriented computing (Certificate), including service oriented computing. *Program availability:* Part-time, evening/weekend. *Faculty:* 20 full-time (4 women), 13 part-time/adjunct (3 women). *Students:* 462 full-time (100 women), 65 part-time (13 women); includes 27 minority (4 Black or African American, non-Hispanic/Latino; 22 Asian, non-Hispanic/Latino; 1 Hispanic/Latino), 427 international. Average age 25. 1,354 applicants, 57% accepted, 181 enrolled. In 2017, 269 master's, 7 doctorates, 8 other advanced degrees awarded. Terminal master's awarded for partial completion of doctoral program. *Degree requirements:* For master's, thesis optional, minimum B average in major field and overall; for doctorate, comprehensive exam (for some programs), thesis/dissertation; for Certificate, minimum B average. *Entrance requirements:* Additional exam requirements/recommendations for international students: Required—TOEFL (minimum score 74 iBT), IELTS (minimum score 6). *Application deadline:* For fall admission, 7/1 for domestic students, 4/15 for international students; for spring admission, 12/1 for domestic and international students. Applications are processed on a rolling basis. Application fee: $60. Electronic applications accepted. *Expenses: Tuition:* Full-time $34,494; part-time $1554 per credit. *Required fees:* $291 per semester. *Financial support:* Fellowships, research assistantships, teaching assistantships, career-related internships or fieldwork, Federal Work-Study, scholarships/grants, and unspecified assistantships available. Financial award application deadline: 2/15; financial award applicants required to submit FAFSA. *Faculty research:* Computer security, computer vision, dynamic scene analysis, privacy-preserving data mining, visualization. *Unit head:* Giuseppe Ateniese, Director, 201-216-3741, E-mail: gatenies@stevens.edu. *Application contact:* Graduate Admissions, 888-783-8367, Fax: 888-511-1306, E-mail: graduate@stevens.edu.
Website: https://www.stevens.edu/schaefer-school-engineering-science/departments/computer-science

Tennessee Technological University, College of Graduate Studies, College of Engineering, Department of Computer Science, Cookeville, TN 38505. Offers Internet-based computing (MS). *Program availability:* Part-time. *Students:* 14 full-time (2 women), 10 part-time (2 women); includes 2 minority (both Black or African American, non-Hispanic/Latino), 11 international. 61 applicants, 57% accepted, 13 enrolled. In 2017, 8 master's awarded. *Degree requirements:* For master's, thesis or alternative. *Entrance requirements:* For master's, GRE. Additional exam requirements/recommendations for international students: Required—TOEFL (minimum score 550 paper-based; 79 iBT), IELTS (minimum score 5.5), PTE (minimum score 53), or TOEIC (Test of English as an International Communication). *Application deadline:* For fall admission, 8/1 for domestic students, 5/1 for international students; for spring admission, 12/1 for domestic students, 10/1 for international students; for summer admission, 5/1 for domestic students, 2/1 for international students. Applications are processed on a rolling basis. Application fee: $35 ($40 for international students). Electronic applications accepted. *Expenses:* Tuition, state resident: full-time $9925; part-time $565 per credit hour. Tuition, nonresident: full-time $22,993; part-time $1291 per credit hour. *Financial support:* Research assistantships and teaching assistantships available. Financial award application deadline: 4/1. *Unit head:* Dr. Jerry Gannod, Chairperson, 931-372-3691, Fax: 931-372-3686, E-mail: jgannod@tntech.edu. *Application contact:* Shelia K. Kendrick, Coordinator of Graduate Studies, 931-372-3808, Fax: 931-372-3497, E-mail: skendrick@tntech.edu.

Texas Woman's University, Graduate School, College of Arts and Sciences, School of the Arts, Department of Visual Arts, Denton, TX 76204. Offers art (MA, MAT, MFA), including art education (MA, MAT), art history (MA), ceramics (MFA), graphic design (MA), intermedia (MFA), painting (MFA), photography (MFA), sculpture (MFA). MFA degrees are granted through the Federation of North Texas Area Universities (The University of North Texas, Texas A&M Commerce, and Texas Woman's University). *Faculty:* 6 full-time (3 women). *Students:* 8 full-time (6 women), 9 part-time (8 women); includes 7 minority (1 Black or African American, non-Hispanic/Latino; 1 American Indian or Alaska Native, non-Hispanic/Latino; 4 Hispanic/Latino; 1 Two or more races, non-Hispanic/Latino). Average age 33. 10 applicants, 50% accepted, 2 enrolled. In 2017, 10 master's awarded. *Degree requirements:* For master's, comprehensive exam, thesis (for some programs), exhibit (MFA), oral exam, thesis or professional paper (MA). *Entrance requirements:* For master's, portfolio, interview, current curriculum vitae, letter of intent, 3 letters of recommendation, artist statement, 2 research papers (for art history or art education). Additional exam requirements/recommendations for international students: Required—TOEFL (minimum score 550 paper-based; 79 iBT); Recommended—IELTS (minimum score 6.5), TSE (minimum score 53). *Application deadline:* For fall admission, 1/31 priority date for domestic and international students; for spring admission, 10/15 priority date for domestic students, 7/1 priority date for international students. Applications are processed on a rolling basis. Application fee: $50 ($75 for international students). Electronic applications accepted. *Expenses:* $7,520 per year full-time in-state; $16,820 per year full-time out-of-state. *Financial support:* In 2017–18, 9 students received support, including 5 teaching assistantships (averaging $9,780 per year); career-related internships or fieldwork, Federal Work-Study, institutionally sponsored loans, scholarships/grants, traineeships, health care benefits, and unspecified assistantships also available. Support available to part-time students. Financial award application deadline: 3/1; financial award applicants required to submit FAFSA. *Faculty research:* Art education and electronic technology, film noir, one-of-a kind art books, new media, early video art from 1960-1980. *Unit head:* Dr. Vagner Whitehead, Chair, 940-898-2530, Fax: 940-898-2496, E-mail: visualarts@twu.edu. *Application contact:* Korie Hawkins, Associate Director of Admissions, Graduate Recruitment, 940-898-3188, Fax: 940-898-3081, E-mail: admissions@twu.edu.
Website: http://www.twu.edu/visual-arts/

Thomas Jefferson University, Kanbar College of Design, Engineering and Commerce, Program in User Experience and Interaction Design, Philadelphia, PA 19107. Offers MS. *Entrance requirements:* For master's, portfolio. Additional exam requirements/recommendations for international students: Required—TOEFL (minimum score 550 paper-based; 79 iBT). Electronic applications accepted.

Internet and Interactive Multimedia

Touro College, Graduate School of Technology, New York, NY 10010. Offers information systems (MS); instructional technology (MS); Web and multimedia design (MA). *Faculty:* 18 part-time/adjunct (6 women). *Students:* 125 full-time (122 women), 177 part-time (163 women); includes 79 minority (39 Black or African American, non-Hispanic/Latino; 23 Asian, non-Hispanic/Latino; 14 Hispanic/Latino; 3 Two or more races, non-Hispanic/Latino), 150 international. Average age 34. *Entrance requirements:* Additional exam requirements/recommendations for international students: Required—TOEFL (minimum score 83 iBT), IELTS (minimum score 6.5), PTE (minimum score 58). Application fee: $50. *Unit head:* Dr. Issac Herskowitz, Dean of the Graduate School of Technology, 202-463-0400 Ext. 5231, E-mail: issac.herskowitz@touro.edu. *Application contact:* Jack Romano, Program Director, 212-463-0400 Ext. 5462.
Website: http://www.touro.edu/gst/

Towson University, College of Fine Arts and Communication, Program in Interactive Media Design, Towson, MD 21252-0001. Offers Postbaccalaureate Certificate. *Program availability:* Online learning. *Students:* 1 (woman) full-time, 6 part-time (3 women); includes 1 minority (Black or African American, non-Hispanic/Latino). *Entrance requirements:* For degree, minimum GPA of 3.0; resume; letter of intent; bachelor's degree in art or art education, or a bachelor's degree in another discipline with a minimum of 9 credits of course work in studio art and/or professional experience working in the field of art education or graphic design. *Application deadline:* For fall admission, 1/17 for domestic students, 5/15 for international students; for spring admission, 10/15 for domestic students, 12/1 for international students. Applications are processed on a rolling basis. Application fee: $45. Electronic applications accepted. *Expenses:* Tuition, state resident: full-time $7960; part-time $398 per unit. Tuition, nonresident: full-time $16,480; part-time $824 per unit. *Required fees:* $2600; $130 per year. $390 per term. *Unit head:* Prof. Bridget Sullivan, Graduate Program Director, 410-704-2802, E-mail: bsullivan@towson.edu. *Application contact:* Coverley Beidleman, Assistant Director of Graduate Admissions, 410-704-5630, Fax: 410-704-3030, E-mail: cbeidleman@towson.edu.
Website: http://www.towson.edu/cofac/departments/art/grad/interactivemediadesign/index.html

Towson University, Jess and Mildred Fisher College of Science and Mathematics, Program in Applied Information Technology, Towson, MD 21252-0001. Offers applied information technology (MS); Internet applications development (Postbaccalaureate Certificate). *Students:* 79 full-time (33 women), 126 part-time (43 women); includes 113 minority (77 Black or African American, non-Hispanic/Latino; 23 Asian, non-Hispanic/Latino; 5 Hispanic/Latino; 8 Two or more races, non-Hispanic/Latino), 36 international. *Entrance requirements:* For master's and Postbaccalaureate Certificate, bachelor's degree, minimum GPA of 3.0. Additional exam requirements/recommendations for international students: Required—TOEFL. *Application deadline:* For fall admission, 1/17 for domestic students, 5/15 for international students; for spring admission, 10/15 for domestic students, 12/1 for international students. Applications are processed on a rolling basis. Application fee: $45. Electronic applications accepted. *Expenses:* Tuition, state resident: full-time $7960; part-time $398 per unit. Tuition, nonresident: full-time $16,480; part-time $824 per unit. *Required fees:* $2600; $130 per year. $390 per term. *Unit head:* Dr. Suranjan Charkraborty, Graduate Program Director, 410-704-4769, E-mail: ait@towson.edu. *Application contact:* Coverley Beidleman, Assistant Director of Graduate Admissions, 410-704-5630, Fax: 410-704-3030, E-mail: cbeidleman@towson.edu.
Website: https://www.towson.edu/fcsm/departments/emergingtech/

Universidad Autonoma de Guadalajara, Graduate Programs, Guadalajara, Mexico. Offers administrative law and justice (LL M); advertising and corporate communications (MA); architecture (M Arch); business (MBA); computational science (MCC); education (Ed M, Ed D); English-Spanish translation (MA); entrepreneurship and management (MBA); integrated management of digital animation (MA); international business (MIB); international corporate law (LL M); internet technologies (MS); manufacturing systems (MMS); occupational health (MS); philosophy (MA, PhD); power electronics (MS); quality systems (MQS); renewable energy (MS); social evaluation of projects (MBA); strategic market research (MBA); tax law (MA); teaching mathematics (MA).

University of Advancing Technology, Master of Science Program in Technology, Tempe, AZ 85283-1042. Offers advancing computer science (MS); emerging technologies (MS); game production and management (MS); information assurance (MS); technology leadership (MS). *Degree requirements:* For master's, project or thesis. *Entrance requirements:* Additional exam requirements/recommendations for international students: Required—TOEFL (minimum score 550 paper-based). Electronic applications accepted. *Faculty research:* Artificial intelligence, fractals, organizational management.

The University of British Columbia, Faculty of Arts, Center for Digital Media, Vancouver, BC V6T 1Z1, Canada. Offers MDM.

University of California, Santa Cruz, Jack Baskin School of Engineering, Department of Computational Media, Santa Cruz, CA 95064. Offers computational media (MS, PhD); games and playable media (MS).

University of Chicago, Division of the Humanities, Program in Digital Studies of Language, Culture, and History, Chicago, IL 60637-1513. Offers MA. *Entrance requirements:* For master's, BA in the humanities, arts, or history. *Unit head:* David Schloen, Director, 773-702-1552, E-mail: d-schloen@uchicago.edu. *Application contact:* Michael Beetley, Assistant Dean of Students, 773-702-1552, Fax: 773-834-9148, E-mail: humanitiesadmissions@uchicago.edu.
Website: https://digitalstudies.uchicago.edu/

University of Colorado Boulder, Graduate School, College of Media, Communication and Information, Program in Intermedia Art, Writing and Performance, Boulder, CO 80309. Offers PhD. *Students:* 9 full-time (5 women); includes 3 minority (2 Asian, non-Hispanic/Latino; 1 Hispanic/Latino). Average age 38. 24 applicants, 17% accepted, 2 enrolled. *Application deadline:* For fall admission, 1/10 for domestic students; for spring admission, 12/1 for domestic students. Application fee: $60 ($80 for international students). Electronic applications accepted. Application fee is waived when completed online. *Financial support:* In 2017–18, 23 students received support, including 5 fellowships (averaging $1,400 per year), 1 research assistantship with full and partial tuition reimbursement available (averaging $26,474 per year), 7 teaching assistantships with full and partial tuition reimbursements available (averaging $33,065 per year); institutionally sponsored loans, scholarships/grants, health care benefits, and unspecified assistantships also available. Financial award application deadline: 2/15; financial award applicants required to submit FAFSA. *Application contact:* E-mail: cmci.iawp@colorado.edu.
Website: http://www.colorado.edu/cmci/academics/phd-intermedia-art-writing-and-

University of Miami, Graduate School, College of Arts and Sciences, Department of Art and Art History, Coral Gables, FL 33124. Offers art history (MA); ceramics/glass (MFA); graphic design/multimedia (MFA); painting (MFA); photography/digital imaging (MFA); printmaking (MFA); sculpture (MFA). *Program availability:* Part-time. *Degree requirements:* For master's, variable foreign language requirement, thesis, exhibit (MFA), comprehensive exam (MA). *Entrance requirements:* For master's, GRE General Test (MA), research paper (MA), slide portfolio (MFA). Additional exam requirements/recommendations for international students: Required—TOEFL. Electronic applications accepted. *Faculty research:* Installation art, public art.

University of Montana, Graduate School, College of Visual and Performing Arts, School of Media Arts, Missoula, MT 59812. Offers digital filmmaking (MFA); integrated digital media (MFA).

University of North Texas, Robert B. Toulouse School of Graduate Studies, Denton, TX 76203-5459. Offers accounting (MS); applied anthropology (MA, MS); applied behavior analysis (Certificate); applied geography (MA); applied technology and performance improvement (M Ed, MS); art education (MA); art history (MA); art museum education (Certificate); arts leadership (Certificate); audiology (Au D); behavior analysis (MS); behavioral science (PhD); biochemistry and molecular biology (MS); biology (MA, MS); biomedical engineering (MS); business analysis (MS); chemistry (MS); clinical health psychology (PhD); communication studies (MA, MS); computer engineering (MS); computer science (MS); counseling (M Ed, MS), including clinical mental health counseling (MS), college and university counseling, elementary school counseling, secondary school counseling; creative writing (MA); criminal justice (MS); curriculum and instruction (M Ed); decision sciences (MBA); design (MA, MFA), including fashion design (MFA), innovation studies, interior design (MFA); early childhood studies (MS); economics (MS); educational leadership (M Ed, Ed D); educational psychology (MS, PhD), including family studies (MS), gifted and talented (MS), human development (MS), learning and cognition (MS), research, measurement and evaluation (MS); electrical engineering (MS); emergency management (MPA); engineering technology (MS); English (MA); English as a second language (MA); environmental science (MS); finance (MBA, MS); financial management (MPA); French (MA); health services management (MBA); higher education (M Ed, Ed D); history (MA, MS); hospitality management (MS); human resources management (MPA); information science (MS); information systems (PhD); information technologies (MBA); interdisciplinary studies (MA, MS); international studies (MA); international sustainable tourism (MS); jazz studies (MM); journalism (MA, MJ, Graduate Certificate), including interactive and virtual digital communication (Graduate Certificate), narrative journalism (Graduate Certificate), public relations (Graduate Certificate); kinesiology (MS); linguistics (MA); local government management (MPA); logistics (PhD); logistics and supply chain management (MBA); long-term care, senior housing, and aging services (MA); management (PhD); marketing (MBA); mathematics (MA, MS); mechanical and energy engineering (MS, PhD); music (MA), including ethnomusicology, music theory, musicology, performance; music composition (PhD); music education (MM Ed, PhD); nonprofit management (MPA); operations and supply chain management (MBA); performance (MM, DMA); philosophy (MA); political science (MA); professional and technical communication (MA); radio, television and film (MA, MFA); rehabilitation counseling (Certificate); sociology (MA); Spanish (MA); special education (M Ed); speech-language pathology (MA); strategic management (MBA); studio art (MFA); teaching (M Ed); MBA/MS. *Program availability:* Part-time, evening/weekend, online learning. Terminal master's awarded for partial completion of doctoral program. *Degree requirements:* For master's, variable foreign language requirement, comprehensive exam (for some programs), thesis (for some programs); for doctorate, variable foreign language requirement, comprehensive exam (for some programs), thesis/dissertation; for other advanced degree, variable foreign language requirement, comprehensive exam (for some programs). *Entrance requirements:* For master's and doctorate, GRE, GMAT. Additional exam requirements/recommendations for international students: Required—TOEFL (minimum score 550 paper-based; 79 iBT). Electronic applications accepted.

University of Pennsylvania, School of Design, Department of Fine Arts, Philadelphia, PA 19104. Offers emerging design and research (Certificate); fine arts (MFA); time-based and interactive media (Certificate). *Faculty:* 8 full-time (4 women), 1 part-time/adjunct (0 women). *Students:* 25 full-time (11 women); includes 8 minority (3 Black or African American, non-Hispanic/Latino; 1 Asian, non-Hispanic/Latino; 3 Hispanic/Latino; 1 Two or more races, non-Hispanic/Latino), 10 international. Average age 30. 123 applicants, 41% accepted, 15 enrolled. In 2017, 16 master's, 1 other advanced degree awarded. *Degree requirements:* For master's, thesis. *Application deadline:* Applications are processed on a rolling basis. Electronic applications accepted. *Financial support:* In 2017–18, 30 students received support, including teaching assistantships (averaging $6,000 per year); fellowships with full tuition reimbursements available, research assistantships, Federal Work-Study, scholarships/grants, health care benefits, and unspecified assistantships also available. Financial award applicants required to submit FAFSA. *Faculty research:* Performance art, photography and video, drawing and painting, sculpture, animation and creative research. *Unit head:* Joshua Mosley, Professor/Chair/Director of Graduate Program, 215-898-8374, E-mail: jmosley@design.upenn.edu. *Application contact:* Leighann Bogner, Administrative Assistant, 215-898-8374, Fax: 215-573-2459, E-mail: mfa@pobox.upenn.edu.
Website: http://www.design.upenn.edu/mfa

University of Southern California, Graduate School, School of Cinematic Arts, Interactive Media Division, Los Angeles, CA 90089. Offers interactive media (MFA); media arts and practice (PhD). *Degree requirements:* For master's, thesis, thesis project. *Entrance requirements:* Additional exam requirements/recommendations for international students: Required—TOEFL (minimum score 600 paper-based; 100 iBT). Electronic applications accepted. *Expenses:* Contact institution. *Faculty research:* Immersive media, mobile media, stereoscopic, game design and development, serious games and games for health and learning, experiments in game play.

University of Southern California, Graduate School, Viterbi School of Engineering, Department of Computer Science, Los Angeles, CA 90089. Offers computer networks (MS); computer science (MS, PhD); computer security (MS); game development (MS); high performance computing and simulations (MS); human language technology (MS); intelligent robotics (MS); multimedia and creative technologies (MS); software engineering (MS). *Program availability:* Part-time, evening/weekend, online learning. *Entrance requirements:* For master's and doctorate, GRE General Test. Additional exam requirements/recommendations for international students: Required—TOEFL. Electronic applications accepted. *Faculty research:* Databases, computer graphics and computer vision, software engineering, networks and security, robotics, multimedia and virtual reality.

University of Southern California, Graduate School, Viterbi School of Engineering, Ming Hsieh Department of Electrical Engineering, Los Angeles, CA 90089. Offers computer engineering (MS, PhD); electric power (MS); electrical engineering (MS, PhD, Engr); engineering technology commercialization (Graduate Certificate); multimedia and creative technologies (MS); telecommunications (MS); VLSI design (MS); wireless health technology (MS). *Program availability:* Part-time, online learning. Terminal master's awarded for partial completion of doctoral program. *Degree requirements:* For master's, thesis optional; for doctorate, thesis/dissertation. *Entrance requirements:* For master's and doctorate, GRE General Test. Additional exam requirements/recommendations for international students: Recommended—TOEFL. Electronic applications accepted. *Faculty research:* Communications, computer engineering and networks, control systems, integrated circuits and systems, electromagnetics and energy conversion, micro electro-mechanical systems and nanotechnology, photonics and quantum electronics, plasma research, signal and image processing.

University of South Florida, College of Arts and Sciences, Zimmerman School of Advertising and Mass Communications, Tampa, FL 33620-9951. Offers mass communications (MA), including media studies, multimedia journalism, strategic communication management. *Program availability:* Part-time, evening/weekend. *Faculty:* 10 full-time (6 women). *Students:* 25 full-time (20 women), 25 part-time (20 women); includes 7 minority (4 Black or African American, non-Hispanic/Latino; 2 Hispanic/Latino; 1 Native Hawaiian or other Pacific Islander, non-Hispanic/Latino), 29 international. Average age 26. 28 applicants, 64% accepted, 15 enrolled. In 2017, 8 master's awarded. *Degree requirements:* For master's, comprehensive exam, thesis optional. *Entrance requirements:* For master's, GRE General Test, minimum GPA of 3.0 in last 60 hours of course work, three letters of recommendation, letter of intent, resume/curriculum vitae. Additional exam requirements/recommendations for international students: Required—TOEFL (minimum score 550 paper-based; 79 iBT) or IELTS (minimum score 6.5). *Application deadline:* For fall admission, 2/15 priority date for domestic and international students. Application fee: $30. Electronic applications accepted. *Financial support:* In 2017–18, 10 students received support, including 9 teaching assistantships with tuition reimbursements available (averaging $10,513 per year); unspecified assistantships also available. Financial award application deadline: 2/28. *Faculty research:* First Amendment analysis, civic journalism, public opinion, media ethics, media effects research in sports public relations, public relations management, advertisement, telecommunications. *Total annual research expenditures:* $78,680. *Unit head:* Dr. Wayne Garcia, Director and Senior Instructor, 813-498-1925, Fax: 813-974-2592, E-mail: wgarcia@usf.edu. *Application contact:* Dr. Artermio Ramirez, Jr., Associate Director, Fax: 813-974-2592, E-mail: aramirez2@usf.edu.
Website: http://masscom.usf.edu/grad/

University of South Florida, Innovative Education, Tampa, FL 33620-9951. Offers adult, career and higher education (Graduate Certificate), including college teaching, leadership in developing human resources, leadership in higher education; Africana studies (Graduate Certificate), including diasporas and health disparities, genocide and human rights; aging studies (Graduate Certificate), including gerontology; art research (Graduate Certificate), including museum studies; business foundations (Graduate Certificate); chemical and biomedical engineering (Graduate Certificate), including materials science and engineering, water, health and sustainability; child and family studies (Graduate Certificate), including positive behavior support; civil and industrial engineering (Graduate Certificate), including transportation systems analysis; community and family health (Graduate Certificate), including maternal and child health, social marketing and public health, violence and injury: prevention and intervention, women's health; criminology (Graduate Certificate), including criminal justice administration; data science for public administration (Graduate Certificate); digital humanities (Graduate Certificate); educational measurement and research (Graduate Certificate), including evaluation; English (Graduate Certificate), including comparative literary studies, creative writing, professional and technical communication; entrepreneurship (Graduate Certificate); environmental health (Graduate Certificate), including safety management; epidemiology and biostatistics (Graduate Certificate), including applied biostatistics, biostatistics, concepts and tools of epidemiology, epidemiology, epidemiology of infectious diseases; geography, environment and planning (Graduate Certificate), including community development, environmental policy and management, geographical information systems; geology (Graduate Certificate), including hydrogeology; global health (Graduate Certificate), including disaster management, global health and Latin American and Caribbean studies, global health practice, humanitarian assistance, infection control; government and international affairs (Graduate Certificate), including Cuban studies, globalization studies; health policy and management (Graduate Certificate), including health management and leadership, public health policy and programs; hearing specialist: early intervention (Graduate Certificate); industrial and management systems engineering (Graduate Certificate), including systems engineering, technology management; information studies (Graduate Certificate), including school library media specialist; information systems/decision sciences (Graduate Certificate), including analytics and business intelligence; instructional technology (Graduate Certificate), including distance education, Florida digital/virtual educator, instructional design, multimedia design, Web design; internal medicine, bioethics and medical humanities (Graduate Certificate), including biomedical ethics; Latin American and Caribbean studies (Graduate Certificate); leadership for coastal resiliency planning (Graduate Certificate); mass communications (Graduate Certificate), including multimedia journalism; mathematics and statistics (Graduate Certificate), including mathematics; medicine (Graduate Certificate), including aging and neuroscience, bioinformatics, biotechnology, brain fitness and memory management, clinical investigation, hand and upper limb rehabilitation, health informatics, health sciences, integrative weight management, intellectual property, medicine and gender, metabolic and nutritional medicine, metabolic cardiology, pharmacy sciences; national and competitive intelligence (Graduate Certificate); nursing (Graduate Certificate), including simulation based academic fellowship in advanced pain management; psychological and social foundations (Graduate Certificate), including career counseling, college teaching, diversity in education, mental health counseling, school counseling; public affairs (Graduate Certificate), including nonprofit management, public management, research administration; public health (Graduate Certificate), including assessing chemical toxicity and public health risks, health equity, pharmacoepidemiology, public health generalist, toxicology, translational research in adolescent behavioral health; public health practices (Graduate Certificate), including planning for healthy communities; rehabilitation and mental health counseling (Graduate Certificate), including integrative mental health care, marriage and family therapy, rehabilitation technology; secondary education (Graduate Certificate), including ESOL, foreign language education: culture and content, foreign language education: professional; social work (Graduate Certificate), including geriatric social work/clinical gerontology; special education (Graduate Certificate), including autism spectrum disorder, disabilities education: severe/profound; world languages (Graduate Certificate), including teaching English as a second language (TESL) or foreign language. *Unit head:* Dr. Cynthia DeLuca, Associate Vice President and Assistant Vice Provost, 813-974-3077, Fax: 813-974-7061, E-mail: deluca@usf.edu. *Application contact:* Owen Hooper, Director, Summer and Alternative Calendar Programs, 813-974-6917, E-mail: hooper@usf.edu.
Website: http://www.usf.edu/innovative-education/

The University of Texas at Dallas, School of Arts, Technology, and Emerging Communication, Richardson, TX 75080. Offers arts and technology (MA, MFA, PhD); emerging media and communication (MA). *Faculty:* 25 full-time (10 women), 2 part-time/adjunct (0 women). *Students:* 56 full-time (23 women), 37 part-time (17 women); includes 24 minority (7 Black or African American, non-Hispanic/Latino; 6 Asian, non-Hispanic/Latino; 8 Hispanic/Latino; 3 Two or more races, non-Hispanic/Latino), 15 international. Average age 32. 143 applicants, 15% accepted, 11 enrolled. In 2017, 40 master's, 5 doctorates awarded. *Degree requirements:* For master's and doctorate, portfolio, thesis, or capstone project. *Entrance requirements:* For master's and doctorate, minimum GPA of 3.3 in upper-level coursework in field. Additional exam requirements/recommendations for international students: Required—TOEFL (minimum score 550 paper-based). *Application deadline:* For fall admission, 7/15 for domestic students, 5/1 priority date for international students; for spring admission, 11/15 for domestic students, 9/1 priority date for international students. Applications are processed on a rolling basis. Application fee: $50 ($100 for international students). Electronic applications accepted. *Expenses:* Tuition, state resident: full-time $12,916; part-time $718 per credit hour. Tuition, nonresident: full-time $25,252; part-time $1403 per credit hour. *Financial support:* In 2017–18, 58 students received support, including 8 research assistantships with partial tuition reimbursements available (averaging $27,884 per year), 26 teaching assistantships with partial tuition reimbursements available (averaging $14,653 per year); career-related internships or fieldwork, Federal Work-Study, institutionally sponsored loans, scholarships/grants, and unspecified assistantships also available. Support available to part-time students. Financial award application deadline: 4/30; financial award applicants required to submit FAFSA. *Faculty research:* Motion capture, conversational/interactive robotics, simulations as modern teaching tools. *Total annual research expenditures:* $1.3 million. *Unit head:* Dr. Anne Balsamo, Dean, 972-883-4376, E-mail: atecdean@utdallas.edu. *Application contact:* Dr. Kim Knight, Associate Dean for Graduate Studies, 972-883-4346, E-mail: kak102020@utdallas.edu.
Website: http://www.utdallas.edu/atec/

University of the Sacred Heart, Graduate Programs, Department of Communication, San Juan, PR 00914-0383. Offers contemporary culture and media (MA); digital journalism (MA, Certificate); editing for media (MA, Certificate); public relations (MA, Certificate); publicity (MA, Certificate); scriptwriting (MA, Certificate). *Program availability:* Part-time, evening/weekend. *Degree requirements:* For master's, thesis.

University of the Sacred Heart, Graduate Programs, Department of Education, San Juan, PR 00914-0383. Offers early childhood education (M Ed); information technology and multimedia (Certificate); instruction systems and education technology (M Ed), including English, information technology and multimedia, instructional design, mathematics, Spanish. *Program availability:* Part-time, evening/weekend. *Degree requirements:* For master's, thesis. *Entrance requirements:* For master's, EXADEP, minimum undergraduate GPA of 2.75, interview.

University of Utah, Graduate School, College of Engineering, Program in Entertainment Arts and Engineering, Salt Lake City, UT 84112. Offers game art (MEAE); game engineering (MEAE); game production (MEAE); technical art (MEAE). *Program availability:* Part-time. *Faculty:* 10 full-time (1 woman), 14 part-time/adjunct (2 women). *Students:* 120 full-time (29 women), 3 part-time (0 women); includes 15 minority (4 Black or African American, non-Hispanic/Latino; 4 Asian, non-Hispanic/Latino; 5 Hispanic/Latino; 2 Two or more races, non-Hispanic/Latino), 55 international. Average age 25. 200 applicants, 45% accepted, 60 enrolled. In 2017, 49 master's awarded. *Entrance requirements:* For master's, GRE (recommended for game engineering and game production track applicants). Additional exam requirements/recommendations for international students: Required—TOEFL (minimum score 550 paper-based; 80 iBT), IELTS (minimum score 6.5). *Application deadline:* For fall admission, 2/28 for domestic and international students. Application fee: $55 ($65 for international students). Electronic applications accepted. *Expenses:* Contact institution. *Financial support:* In 2017–18, 91 students received support, including 60 research assistantships with partial tuition reimbursements available (averaging $7,500 per year), 31 teaching assistantships with partial tuition reimbursements available (averaging $7,500 per year); career-related internships or fieldwork, scholarships/grants, health care benefits, and unspecified assistantships also available. Financial award application deadline: 2/28; financial award applicants required to submit FAFSA. *Faculty research:* Games for health, simulation, user research/user interface. *Unit head:* Hallie Huber, Academic Program Manager, 801-581-5460, E-mail: hallie.huber@utah.edu. *Application contact:* Hallie Huber, Academic Program Manager, 801-581-5460, E-mail: hallie.huber@utah.edu.
Website: http://eae.utah.edu/

University of Utah, Graduate School, College of Humanities, Department of Communication, Salt Lake City, UT 84112. Offers communicating science, health, environment and risk (MA, MS, PhD); critical cultural studies (MA, MS, PhD); digital media (MA, MS, PhD); rhetoric (MA, MS, PhD). *Faculty:* 26 full-time (13 women), 11 part-time/adjunct (3 women). *Students:* 34 full-time (24 women), 14 part-time (10 women); includes 4 minority (2 Asian, non-Hispanic/Latino; 1 Hispanic/Latino; 1 Two or more races, non-Hispanic/Latino), 3 international. Average age 24. 99 applicants, 31% accepted, 15 enrolled. In 2017, 6 master's, 9 doctorates awarded. Terminal master's awarded for partial completion of doctoral program. *Entrance requirements:* For master's and doctorate, GRE General Test, minimum GPA of 3.0. Additional exam requirements/recommendations for international students: Required—TOEFL (minimum score 500 paper-based; 90 iBT); Recommended—IELTS. *Application deadline:* For fall admission, 12/15 for domestic students, 11/15 for international students. Application fee: $55 ($65 for international students). Electronic applications accepted. *Expenses:* $7,790 resident, $24,804 non-resident. *Financial support:* In 2017–18, 4 students received support, including 1 fellowship with full tuition reimbursement available (averaging $18,000 per year), 25 teaching assistantships with full tuition reimbursements available (averaging $17,700 per year); research assistantships, scholarships/grants, health care benefits, and unspecified assistantships also available. Financial award application deadline: 12/15; financial award applicants required to submit FAFSA. *Faculty research:* CommSHER (communicating science, health, environment, and risk), critical/cultural studies, interpersonal/organizational communication, new media technologies, rhetoric. *Unit head:* Dr. Kent A. Ono, Chair, 801-585-9128, Fax: 801-585-6255, E-mail: kent.ono@utah.edu. *Application contact:* Dr. Helene Shugart, Director of Graduate Studies, 801-581-5686, Fax: 801-585-6255, E-mail: h.shugart@utah.edu.
Website: http://www.communication.utah.edu

Virginia Polytechnic Institute and State University, Graduate School, College of Architecture and Urban Studies, Blacksburg, VA 24061. Offers architecture (M Arch, MS); architecture and design research (PhD); building construction science management (MS); creative technologies (MFA); environmental design and planning (PhD); government and international affairs (MPIA); landscape architecture (MLA, PhD); planning, governance, and globalization (PhD); public administration and public affairs (MPA, PhD); urban and regional planning (MURPL). *Accreditation:* ASLA (one or more programs are accredited). *Faculty:* 139 full-time (58 women), 1 (woman) part-time/adjunct. *Students:* 339 full-time (165 women), 210 part-time (97 women); includes 115 minority (49 Black or African American, non-Hispanic/Latino; 1 American Indian or Alaska Native, non-Hispanic/Latino; 30 Asian, non-Hispanic/Latino; 29 Hispanic/Latino; 6 Two or more races, non-Hispanic/Latino), 136 international. Average age 32. 649 applicants, 49% accepted, 105 enrolled. In 2017, 142 master's, 18 doctorates awarded. *Degree requirements:* For master's, comprehensive exam (for some programs), thesis (for some programs); for doctorate, comprehensive exam (for some programs), thesis/dissertation (for some programs). *Entrance requirements:* For master's and doctorate, GRE/GMAT. Additional exam requirements/recommendations for international students: Required—TOEFL (minimum score 80 iBT). *Application deadline:* For fall admission, 8/1 for domestic students, 4/1 for international students; for spring admission, 1/1 for domestic students, 9/1 for international students. Applications are processed on a rolling basis. Application fee: $75. Electronic applications accepted. *Expenses:* Tuition, state resident: full-time $15,072; part-time $718.50 per credit hour. Tuition, nonresident: full-time $28,810; part-time $1448.25 per credit hour. *Required fees:* $2741; $502 per

semester. Tuition and fees vary according to course load, campus/location and program. *Financial support:* In 2017–18, 17 research assistantships with full tuition reimbursements (averaging $18,561 per year), 41 teaching assistantships with full tuition reimbursements (averaging $17,340 per year) were awarded. Financial award application deadline: 3/1; financial award applicants required to submit FAFSA. *Total annual research expenditures:* $3.1 million. *Unit head:* Dr. Richard Blythe, Dean, 540-231-6416, Fax: 540-231-6332, E-mail: richbl1@vt.edu. *Application contact:* Christine Mattsson-Coon, Executive Assistant, 540-231-6416, Fax: 540-231-6332, E-mail: cmattsso@vt.edu.
Website: http://www.caus.vt.edu/

Walla Walla University, Graduate Studies, Center for Cinema, Religion, and Worldview, College Place, WA 99324. Offers Web and interactive media (MA). *Entrance requirements:* For master's, three professional references, transcripts, personal statement. *Application deadline:* For fall admission, 8/15 for domestic students. Application fee: $50. *Unit head:* Lynelle Ellis, Director, 509-527-2843, Fax: 509-527-2237, E-mail: lynelle.ellis@wallawalla.edu. *Application contact:* Rachel Scribner, Coordinator, 509-527-2832, Fax: 509-527-2237, E-mail: rachel.scribner@wallawalla.edu.
Website: https://www.wallawalla.edu/academics/grad-studies/cinema-religion-worldview/

Webster University, School of Communications, Program in New Media Production, St. Louis, MO 63119-3194. Offers MA.

Wilmington University, College of Technology, New Castle, DE 19720-6491. Offers cybersecurity (MS); information assurance (MS); information systems technologies (MS); management and management information systems (MS); technology project management (MS); Web design (MS). *Program availability:* Part-time, evening/weekend. *Faculty:* 5 full-time (2 women), 99 part-time/adjunct (31 women). *Students:* 631 full-time (159 women), 486 part-time (141 women); includes 91 minority (53 Black or African American, non-Hispanic/Latino; 3 American Indian or Alaska Native, non-Hispanic/Latino; 22 Asian, non-Hispanic/Latino; 5 Hispanic/Latino; 2 Native Hawaiian or other Pacific Islander, non-Hispanic/Latino; 6 Two or more races, non-Hispanic/Latino),

917 international. Average age 26. 774 applicants, 45% accepted, 307 enrolled. In 2017, 965 master's awarded. *Entrance requirements:* Additional exam requirements/recommendations for international students: Required—TOEFL (minimum score 500 paper-based). *Application deadline:* Applications are processed on a rolling basis. Application fee: $35. Electronic applications accepted. *Expenses: Tuition:* Part-time $466 per credit. *Required fees:* $25 per semester. Tuition and fees vary according to degree level and campus/location. *Unit head:* Dr. Mary Ann K. Westerfield, Dean. *Application contact:* Laura Morris, Director of Admissions, 877-967-5464, E-mail: infocenter@wilmu.edu.
Website: http://www.wilmu.edu/technology/

Worcester Polytechnic Institute, Graduate Admissions, Program in Interactive Media and Game Development, Worcester, MA 01609-2280. Offers MS. *Program availability:* Part-time, evening/weekend. *Students:* 16 full-time (3 women); includes 1 minority (Asian, non-Hispanic/Latino), 8 international. Average age 27. 47 applicants, 49% accepted, 4 enrolled. In 2017, 3 master's awarded. *Entrance requirements:* For master's, GRE (recommended), 3 letters of recommendation, statement of purpose, portfolio (recommended). Additional exam requirements/recommendations for international students: Required—TOEFL (minimum score 563 paper-based; 84 iBT), IELTS (minimum score 7). *Application deadline:* For fall admission, 1/1 for domestic and international students; for spring admission, 10/1 for domestic and international students. Applications are processed on a rolling basis. Application fee: $70. Electronic applications accepted. *Expenses: Tuition:* Full-time $26,226; part-time $1457 per credit. *Required fees:* $60; $30 per credit. One-time fee: $15. Tuition and fees vary according to course load. *Financial support:* Research assistantships, teaching assistantships, and health care benefits available. Financial award application deadline: 1/1. *Unit head:* Jennifer DeWinter, Graduate Coordinator, 508-831-4977, Fax: 508-831-5776, E-mail: jdewinter@wpi.edu. *Application contact:* Alison Darling, Administrative Assistant, 508-831-4977, E-mail: ajdarling@wpi.edu.
Website: https://www.wpi.edu/academics/departments/interactive-media-game-development

Journalism

American University, School of Communication, Division of Journalism, Washington, DC 20016-8001. Offers broadcast journalism (MA); international journalism (MA); investigative journalism (MA); journalism and digital storytelling (MA). *Accreditation:* ACEJMC. *Program availability:* Part-time, evening/weekend. *Faculty:* 14 full-time (7 women), 4 part-time/adjunct (3 women). *Students:* 30 full-time (20 women), 17 part-time (14 women); includes 31 minority (18 Black or African American, non-Hispanic/Latino; 3 Asian, non-Hispanic/Latino; 7 Hispanic/Latino; 3 Two or more races, non-Hispanic/Latino), 2 international. 277 applicants, 33% accepted, 39 enrolled. In 2017, 36 master's awarded. *Degree requirements:* For master's, comprehensive exam, thesis or alternative. *Entrance requirements:* Additional exam requirements/recommendations for international students: Required—TOEFL (minimum score 600 paper-based; 100 iBT), IELTS (minimum score 7). *Application deadline:* For fall admission, 2/1 priority date for domestic and international students. Applications are processed on a rolling basis. Application fee: $55. Electronic applications accepted. *Expenses: Tuition:* Full-time $29,556. *Required fees:* $690. Tuition and fees vary according to course load and program. *Financial support:* In 2017–18, 37 students received support, including 3 fellowships with tuition reimbursements available (averaging $27,000 per year), 6 research assistantships with partial tuition reimbursements available (averaging $10,000 per year), 5 teaching assistantships with partial tuition reimbursements available (averaging $10,000 per year); career-related internships or fieldwork, Federal Work-Study, institutionally sponsored loans, scholarships/grants, tuition waivers (partial), and unspecified assistantships also available. Financial award application deadline: 2/1; financial award applicants required to submit FAFSA. *Faculty research:* Government and media effects of journalistic practices and policies; race, gender, and the media; investigative reporting; computer-assisted reporting; data driven journalism. *Unit head:* Prof. Amy Eisman, Division Director, 202-885-2106, E-mail: aeisman@american.edu. *Application contact:* Christine Rials, Assistant Director for Graduate Admissions, 202-885-2040, Fax: 202-885-2019, E-mail: crials@american.edu.
Website: http://www.american.edu/soc/journalism/index.cfm

The American University in Cairo, School of Global Affairs and Public Policy, Cairo, Egypt. Offers gender and women's studies (MA); global affairs (MGA); international and comparative law (LL M); international human rights law (MA); journalism and mass communication (MA); Middle East studies (MA); migration and refugee studies (MA, Diploma); public administration (MPA); public policy (MPP); television and digital journalism (MA). *Program availability:* Part-time, evening/weekend. *Faculty:* 26 full-time (11 women), 4 part-time/adjunct (3 women). *Students:* 65 full-time (50 women), 201 part-time (136 women), 39 international. Average age 29. 357 applicants, 51% accepted, 72 enrolled. In 2017, 94 master's awarded. *Degree requirements:* For master's, comprehensive exam (for some programs), thesis (for some programs). *Entrance requirements:* Additional exam requirements/recommendations for international students: Required—TOEFL (minimum score 450 paper-based; 45 iBT), IELTS (minimum score 5). *Application deadline:* For fall admission, 2/1 for domestic and international students; for spring admission, 10/15 for domestic and international students. Applications are processed on a rolling basis. Application fee: $85. Electronic applications accepted. *Expenses:* Contact institution. *Financial support:* Fellowships with partial tuition reimbursements, scholarships/grants, and unspecified assistantships available. Financial award application deadline: 3/10. *Faculty research:* Law, media and journalism; public policy and public administration; gender studies; Middle East Studies; global affairs; refugees studies. *Unit head:* Dr. Nabil Fahmy, Dean, 20-2-2615-2671, E-mail: nfahmy@aucegypt.edu. *Application contact:* Maha Hegazi, Director for Graduate Admissions, 20-2-2615-1462, E-mail: mahahegazi@aucegypt.edu.
Website: http://www.aucegypt.edu/GAPP/Pages/default.aspx

Arizona State University at the Tempe campus, Walter Cronkite School of Journalism and Mass Communication, Phoenix, AZ 85004. Offers journalism and mass communication (PhD); mass communication (MMC). *Accreditation:* ACEJMC. Terminal master's awarded for partial completion of doctoral program. *Degree requirements:* For master's, 9-hour professional capstone experience; interactive Program of Study (iPOS) submitted before completing 50 percent of required credit hours; for doctorate, comprehensive exam, thesis/dissertation, interactive Program of Study (iPOS) submitted before completing 50 percent of required credit hours. *Entrance requirements:* For master's and doctorate, GRE, minimum GPA of 3.0 or equivalent in last 2 years of work leading to bachelor's degree. Additional exam requirements/recommendations for

international students: Required—TOEFL, IELTS, or PTE. Electronic applications accepted. *Expenses:* Contact institution.

Arkansas State University, Graduate School, College of Media and Communication, Department of Media, State University, AR 72467. Offers mass communications (MSMC). *Accreditation:* ACEJMC. *Program availability:* Part-time. *Degree requirements:* For master's, comprehensive exam, thesis or alternative. *Entrance requirements:* For master's, GRE General Test or MAT, appropriate bachelor's degree, letters of reference, educational experience, professional experience, official transcripts, immunization records. Additional exam requirements/recommendations for international students: Required—TOEFL (minimum score 550 paper-based; 79 iBT), IELTS (minimum score 6), PTE (minimum score 56). Electronic applications accepted.

Arkansas Tech University, College of Arts and Humanities, Russellville, AR 72801. Offers applied sociology (MS); English (M Ed, MA); history (MA); liberal arts (MLA); multi-media journalism (MA); psychology (MS); teaching English as a second language (MA). *Program availability:* Part-time, 100% online, blended/hybrid learning. *Students:* 35 full-time (22 women), 122 part-time (94 women); includes 34 minority (11 Black or African American, non-Hispanic/Latino; 2 Asian, non-Hispanic/Latino; 19 Hispanic/Latino; 2 Two or more races, non-Hispanic/Latino), 19 international. Average age 34. In 2017, 85 master's awarded. *Degree requirements:* For master's, comprehensive exam (for some programs), thesis (for some programs), project. *Entrance requirements:* Additional exam requirements/recommendations for international students: Required—TOEFL (minimum score 550 paper-based; 79 iBT), IELTS (minimum score 6.5), PTE (minimum score 58). *Application deadline:* For fall admission, 3/1 priority date for domestic students, 5/1 priority date for international students; for spring admission, 10/1 priority date for domestic and international students. Applications are processed on a rolling basis. Application fee: $40 ($90 for international students). Electronic applications accepted. *Expenses:* Tuition, state resident: full-time $6816; part-time $284 per credit hour. Tuition, nonresident: full-time $13,632; part-time $568 per credit hour. *Required fees:* $420 per semester. Tuition and fees vary according to course load. *Financial support:* In 2017–18, research assistantships with full and partial tuition reimbursements (averaging $4,800 per year), teaching assistantships with full and partial tuition reimbursements (averaging $4,800 per year) were awarded; career-related internships or fieldwork, Federal Work-Study, scholarships/grants, health care benefits, and unspecified assistantships also available. Support available to part-time students. Financial award application deadline: 4/15; financial award applicants required to submit FAFSA. *Unit head:* Dr. Jeffrey Woods, Dean, 479-968-0274, Fax: 479-964-0812, E-mail: jwoods@atu.edu. *Application contact:* Dr. Mary B. Gunter, Dean of Graduate College, 479-968-0398, Fax: 479-964-0542, E-mail: gradcollege@atu.edu.
Website: http://www.atu.edu/humanities/

Ball State University, Graduate School, College of Communication, Information, and Media, Department of Journalism, Program in Journalism, Muncie, IN 47306. Offers MA. *Program availability:* Online only, 100% online. *Students:* 4 full-time (3 women), 17 part-time (11 women); includes 7 minority (4 Black or African American, non-Hispanic/Latino; 1 Hispanic/Latino; 2 Two or more races, non-Hispanic/Latino). Average age 32. 14 applicants, 71% accepted, 9 enrolled. In 2017, 2 master's awarded. *Entrance requirements:* For master's, GRE General Test (minimum score 150 verbal), minimum baccalaureate GPA of 2.75 or 3.0 in latter half of baccalaureate, transcripts of all prior course work, current resume or curriculum vitae, 1000-word statement of purpose, writing sample. Additional exam requirements/recommendations for international students: Required—TOEFL (minimum score 550 paper-based; 79 iBT), IELTS (minimum score 6.5). *Application deadline:* Applications are processed on a rolling basis. Application fee: $60. Electronic applications accepted. *Financial support:* Unspecified assistantships available. Financial award application deadline: 3/1; financial award applicants required to submit FAFSA. *Unit head:* Dr. Johnny Sparks, Chairperson, 765-285-8728, Fax: 765-285-7997, E-mail: jvsparks@bsu.edu. *Application contact:* Dr. Robin Blom, Assistant Professor of Journalism, 765-285-8737, Fax: 765-285-7997, E-mail: rblom@bsu.edu.
Website: http://cms.bsu.edu/academics/collegesanddepartments/journalism/graduateprograms/majournalism

Baylor University, Graduate School, College of Arts and Sciences, Department of Journalism, Public Relations and New Media, Waco, TX 76798. Offers journalism, public

relations and new media (MIJ); news editorial public relations (MA). *Students:* 6 full-time (all women), 8 part-time (5 women); includes 4 minority (1 Black or African American, non-Hispanic/Latino; 2 Hispanic/Latino; 1 Two or more races, non-Hispanic/Latino), 1 international. Average age 24. 12 applicants, 75% accepted, 8 enrolled. In 2017, 1 master's awarded. *Degree requirements:* For master's, thesis, proficiency in 1 foreign language (for MIJ). *Entrance requirements:* For master's, academic/scholarly writing sample (i.e., research paper from previous course); portfolio with ten or more samples of work (press releases, feature stories, brochures, newspaper clippings, newspaper articles, flyers, etc.). Additional exam requirements/recommendations for international students: Required—TOEFL (minimum score 550 paper-based). *Application deadline:* For fall admission, 2/15 for domestic and international students; for spring admission, 12/1 for domestic and international students; for summer admission, 5/1 for domestic and international students. Application fee: $25. Electronic applications accepted. *Expenses:* Contact institution. *Financial support:* In 2017–18, 11 students received support, including 10 teaching assistantships with full and partial tuition reimbursements available (averaging $1,800 per year); research assistantships, career-related internships or fieldwork, Federal Work-Study, and institutionally sponsored loans also available. Support available to part-time students. Financial award application deadline: 5/1; financial award applicants required to submit FAFSA. *Faculty research:* International politics, mass media and society, journalism history, editing practices. *Unit head:* Dr. Mia N. Moody-Ramirez, Graduate Program Director, 254-710-7247, Fax: 254-710-7347, E-mail: mia_moody@baylor.edu. *Application contact:* Jan Loosier, Administrative Assistant, 254-710-3261, Fax: 254-710-3870, E-mail: jan_loosier@baylor.edu.
Website: http://www.baylor.edu/journalism/

Bob Jones University, Graduate Programs, Greenville, SC 29614. Offers accountancy (MS); Bible (MA); Bible translation (MA); Biblical studies (Certificate); broadcast management (MS); business administration (MBA); church history (MA, PhD); church ministries (MA); church music (MM); cinema and video production (MA); counseling (MS); curriculum and instruction (Ed D); divinity (M Div); dramatic production (MA); educational leadership (MS, Ed D, Ed S); elementary education (M Ed, MAT); English (M Ed, MA, MAT); fine arts (MA); graphic design (MA); history (M Ed, MA); illustration (MA); interpretative speech (MA); mathematics (M Ed, MAT); medical missions (Certificate); ministry (MM, D Min); multi-categorical special education (M Ed, MAT); music (M Ed); New Testament interpretation (PhD); Old Testament interpretation (PhD); orchestral instrument performance (MM); organ performance (MM); pastoral studies (MA); personnel services (MS, Ed S); piano pedagogy (MM); piano performance (MM); platform arts (MA); radio and television broadcasting (MS); rhetoric and public address (MA); secondary education (M Ed); studio art (MA); teaching Bible (MA); theology (MA, PhD); voice performance (MM); youth ministries (MA); M Div/MM.

Boston University, College of Communication, Department of Journalism, Boston, MA 02215. Offers MS. *Program availability:* Part-time. *Faculty:* 24 full-time, 15 part-time/adjunct. *Students:* 60 full-time (42 women), 3 part-time (2 women); includes 11 minority (5 Black or African American, non-Hispanic/Latino; 1 Asian, non-Hispanic/Latino; 5 Hispanic/Latino), 22 international. Average age 25. 170 applicants, 73% accepted, 34 enrolled. In 2017, 75 master's awarded. *Degree requirements:* For master's, thesis, professional project. *Entrance requirements:* For master's, GRE General Test, resume, writing samples, letters of recommendation. Additional exam requirements/recommendations for international students: Required—TOEFL (minimum score 600 paper-based; 100 iBT), IELTS (minimum score 7). *Application deadline:* For fall admission, 5/1 for domestic and international students. Applications are processed on a rolling basis. Application fee: $95. Electronic applications accepted. *Financial support:* Teaching assistantships with partial tuition reimbursements, career-related internships or fieldwork, Federal Work-Study, scholarships/grants, and unspecified assistantships available. Support available to part-time students. Financial award application deadline: 5/1; financial award applicants required to submit FAFSA. *Unit head:* William McKeen, Chairman, 617-353-3484, Fax: 617-353-1086, E-mail: wmckeen@bu.edu. *Application contact:* Jackie Cummings, Admission and Financial Aid Counselor, 617-353-3481, E-mail: comgrad@bu.edu.
Website: http://www.bu.edu/com/academics/journalism/

California State University, Northridge, Graduate Studies, Mike Curb College of Arts, Media, and Communication, Department of Journalism, Northridge, CA 91330. Offers mass communication (MA). *Program availability:* Part-time, evening/weekend. *Students:* 12 full-time (6 women), 9 part-time (5 women); includes 11 minority (1 Black or African American, non-Hispanic/Latino; 2 American Indian or Alaska Native, non-Hispanic/Latino; 8 Hispanic/Latino), 4 international. Average age 31. 27 applicants, 56% accepted, 8 enrolled. In 2017, 21 master's awarded. *Degree requirements:* For master's, thesis. *Entrance requirements:* For master's, GRE General Test. Additional exam requirements/recommendations for international students: Required—TOEFL. *Application deadline:* For fall admission, 11/30 for domestic students. *Financial support:* Career-related internships or fieldwork and Federal Work-Study available. Financial award application deadline: 3/1. *Unit head:* Linda Bowen, Chair, 818-677-3135.
Website: http://www.csun.edu/journalism/

Carleton University, Faculty of Graduate Studies, Faculty of Public Affairs and Management, School of Journalism and Communication, Ottawa, ON K1S 5B6, Canada. Offers communication (MA, PhD); journalism (MJ). *Degree requirements:* For master's, thesis optional; for doctorate, comprehensive exam, thesis/dissertation. *Entrance requirements:* For master's, honors degree. Additional exam requirements/recommendations for international students: Required—TOEFL. *Faculty research:* Specialized print reporting, broadcast journalism, journalism studies.

Clarion University of Pennsylvania, College of Arts, Education and Sciences, MS Program in Mass Media Arts and Journalism, Clarion, PA 16214. Offers MS. *Program availability:* Part-time, evening/weekend, online only, 100% online. *Faculty:* 5 full-time (3 women). *Students:* 9 full-time (6 women), 8 part-time (4 women); includes 6 minority (all Black or African American, non-Hispanic/Latino). Average age 33. 10 applicants, 80% accepted, 4 enrolled. In 2017, 6 master's awarded. *Entrance requirements:* For master's, statement of purpose, short essay, minimum undergraduate QPA of 3.0. Additional exam requirements/recommendations for international students: Required—TOEFL (minimum score 600 paper-based, 80 iBT) or IELTS (7). *Application deadline:* For fall admission, 8/15 priority date for domestic students, 7/15 priority date for international students; for winter admission, 11/1 priority date for domestic students; for spring admission, 1/7 priority date for domestic students, 11/15 priority date for international students; for summer admission, 4/1 priority date for domestic students. Applications are processed on a rolling basis. Application fee: $40. Electronic applications accepted. *Expenses:* $655.05 per credit. *Financial support:* Career-related internships or fieldwork, scholarships/grants, and unspecified assistantships available. Support available to part-time students. Financial award application deadline: 3/1; financial award applicants required to submit FAFSA. *Unit head:* Dr. Steven Harris, Interim Dean, 814-393-2328, E-mail: harris@clarion.edu. *Application contact:* Dana Bearer, Associate Director for Transfer, Adult and Graduate Admissions, 814-393-2337, Fax: 814-393-2772, E-mail: gradstudies@clarion.edu.

Columbia University, Graduate School of Journalism, New York, NY 10027. Offers MA, MS, PhD, JD/MS, MIA/MS, MS/MBA. *Accreditation:* ACEJMC. *Program availability:*

Part-time. *Degree requirements:* For master's, thesis; for doctorate, thesis/dissertation. *Entrance requirements:* For master's, writing test, 2-3 samples of journalistic work, minimum typing speed of 50 words per minute; for doctorate, GRE. Additional exam requirements/recommendations for international students: Required—TOEFL. *Expenses:* Contact institution. *Faculty research:* International communication, communication technologies, ethics in journalism, journalism history.

Concordia University, School of Graduate Studies, Faculty of Arts and Science, Department of Journalism, Montréal, QC H3G 1M8, Canada. Offers journalism (Graduate Diploma); journalism studies (MA); visual journalism (Diploma). *Degree requirements:* For other advanced degree, one foreign language. *Entrance requirements:* Additional exam requirements/recommendations for international students: Required—departmental English test or TOEFL.

CUNY Graduate School of Journalism, Graduate Program, New York, NY 10018. Offers entrepreneurial journalism (MA); journalism (MA); social journalism (MA). *Accreditation:* ACEJMC. *Degree requirements:* For master's, internship, final or capstone project. *Entrance requirements:* For master's, 3 letters of recommendation, personal statement, resume, interview, 3 writing samples. Additional exam requirements/recommendations for international students: Required—TOEFL (minimum score 105 iBT). Electronic applications accepted.

DePaul University, College of Communication, Chicago, IL 60604. Offers digital communication and media arts (MA); health communication (MA); journalism (MA); media and cinema studies (MA); multicultural communication (MA); organizational communication (MA); public relations and advertising (MA); relational communication (MA). *Program availability:* Part-time, evening/weekend. *Entrance requirements:* Additional exam requirements/recommendations for international students: Required—TOEFL (minimum score 590 paper-based; 96 iBT), IELTS (minimum score 7.5) or PTE. *Application deadline:* For fall admission, 6/1 priority date for domestic students; for winter admission, 10/1 priority date for domestic students; for spring admission, 2/15 priority date for domestic students. Applications are processed on a rolling basis. Application fee: $40. Electronic applications accepted. *Financial support:* Applicants required to submit FAFSA. *Unit head:* Salma Ghanem, Dean, 312-362-8600, Fax: 312-362-8620. *Application contact:* Ann Spittle, Director of Graduate Admission, 773-325-7315, Fax: 312-362-8620, E-mail: graddepaul@depaul.edu.
Website: http://communication.depaul.edu/

Florida Agricultural and Mechanical University, Division of Graduate Studies, Research, and Continuing Education, School of Journalism and Graphic Communication, Tallahassee, FL 32307-3200. Offers journalism (MS). *Degree requirements:* For master's, comprehensive exam, thesis (for some programs). *Entrance requirements:* For master's, GRE General Test, minimum GPA of 3.0. Additional exam requirements/recommendations for international students: Required—TOEFL.

Florida International University, College of Communication, Architecture and The Arts, School of Communication and Journalism, Miami, FL 33199. Offers mass communication (MS), including global strategic communications, Spanish language journalism. *Program availability:* Part-time, evening/weekend. *Faculty:* 35 full-time (24 women), 59 part-time/adjunct (38 women). *Students:* 91 full-time (63 women), 65 part-time (47 women); includes 112 minority (20 Black or African American, non-Hispanic/Latino; 3 Asian, non-Hispanic/Latino; 84 Hispanic/Latino; 5 Two or more races, non-Hispanic/Latino), 31 international. Average age 28. 122 applicants, 68% accepted, 67 enrolled. In 2017, 86 master's awarded. *Degree requirements:* For master's, thesis optional. *Entrance requirements:* For master's, 2 letters of recommendation; minimum GPA of 3.0 during last 60 hours of upper-level work; resume. Additional exam requirements/recommendations for international students: Required—TOEFL (minimum score 550 paper-based; 80 iBT). *Application deadline:* For fall admission, 6/1 for domestic students, 4/1 for international students; for spring admission, 10/1 for domestic students, 9/1 for international students. Applications are processed on a rolling basis. Application fee: $30. Electronic applications accepted. *Expenses:* Tuition, state resident: full-time $8912; part-time $446 per credit hour. Tuition, nonresident: full-time $21,393; part-time $992 per credit hour. *Required fees:* $390; $195 per semester. *Financial support:* Institutionally sponsored loans and scholarships/grants available. Financial award application deadline: 3/1; financial award applicants required to submit FAFSA. *Unit head:* Dr. Maria Elena Villar, Chair, 305-919-5795, Fax: 305-919-5215, E-mail: mariaelena.villar@fiu.edu. *Application contact:* Nanett Rojas, Assistant Director, Graduate Admissions, 305-348-7442, Fax: 305-348-7441, E-mail: gradadm@fiu.edu.
Website: https://scj.fiu.edu/

Full Sail University, New Media Journalism Master of Arts Program - Online, Winter Park, FL 32792-7437. Offers MA.

Georgetown University, Graduate School of Arts and Sciences, School of Continuing Studies, Washington, DC 20057. Offers American studies (MALS); applied intelligence (MPS); Catholic studies (MALS); classical civilizations (MALS); emergency and disaster management (MPS); ethics and the professions (MALS); global strategic communications (MPS); hospitality management (MPS); human resources management (MPS); humanities (MALS); individualized study (MALS); integrated marketing communications (MPS); international affairs (MALS); Islam and Muslim-Christian relations (MALS); journalism (MPS); liberal studies (DLS); literature and society (MALS); medieval and early modern European studies (MALS); public relations and corporate communications (MPS); real estate (MPS); religious studies (MALS); social and public policy (MALS); sports industry management (MPS); systems engineering management (MPS); technology management (MPS); the theory and practice of American democracy (MALS); urban and regional planning (MPS); visual culture (MALS). MPS in systems engineering management offered jointly with Stevens Institute of Technology. *Entrance requirements:* Additional exam requirements/recommendations for international students: Required—TOEFL.

Harvard University, Extension School, Cambridge, MA 02138-3722. Offers applied sciences (CAS); biotechnology (ALM); educational technologies (ALM); educational technology (CET); English for graduate and professional studies (DGP); environmental management (ALM, CEM); information technology (ALM); journalism (ALM); liberal arts (ALM); management (ALM, CM); mathematics for teaching (ALM); museum studies (ALM); premedical studies (Diploma); publication and communication (CPC). *Program availability:* Part-time, evening/weekend. *Degree requirements:* For master's, thesis. *Entrance requirements:* For master's, 3 completed graduate courses with grade of B or higher. Additional exam requirements/recommendations for international students: Required—TOEFL (minimum score 600 paper-based), TWE (minimum score 5). *Expenses:* Contact institution.

Hofstra University, Lawrence Herbert School of Communication, Programs in Journalism and Public Relations, Hempstead, NY 11549. Offers journalism (MA); public relations (MA). *Program availability:* Part-time, evening/weekend. *Students:* 46 full-time (29 women), 19 part-time (14 women); includes 38 minority (20 Black or African American, non-Hispanic/Latino; 2 Asian, non-Hispanic/Latino; 14 Hispanic/Latino; 1 Native Hawaiian or other Pacific Islander, non-Hispanic/Latino; 1 Two or more races, non-Hispanic/Latino), 3 international. Average age 27. 61 applicants, 85% accepted, 25 enrolled. In 2017, 42 master's awarded. *Degree requirements:* For master's, thesis. *Entrance requirements:* For master's, minimum GPA of 2.75; bachelor's degree.

Additional exam requirements/recommendations for international students: Required—TOEFL (minimum score 550 paper-based; 95 iBT). *Application deadline:* Applications are processed on a rolling basis. Application fee: $75. Electronic applications accepted. *Expenses: Tuition:* Full-time $1292. *Required fees:* $970. Tuition and fees vary according to program. *Financial support:* In 2017–18, 42 students received support, including 32 fellowships with full and partial tuition reimbursements available (averaging $3,199 per year), 2 research assistantships with full and partial tuition reimbursements available (averaging $7,045 per year); career-related internships or fieldwork, Federal Work-Study, institutionally sponsored loans, scholarships/grants, tuition waivers (full and partial), and unspecified assistantships also available. Support available to part-time students. Financial award applicants required to submit FAFSA. *Faculty research:* Hybrid media theory, particularly as it relates to journalism and politics; political communication, public relations and international communication; impact of convergence and interactive-based technologies and the impact of immigration and globalization on health information campaigns; mediated message design; rational and emotional appeals in strategic messaging; crisis communications; public relations; persuasion; the crossroads of popular culture, politics, new media, and civic engagement. *Unit head:* Dr. Cliff Jernigan, Chairperson, 516-463-4873, E-mail: cliff.jernigan@hofstra.edu. *Application contact:* Sunil Samuel, Assistant Vice President of Admissions, 516-463-4723, Fax: 516-463-4664, E-mail: graduateadmission@hofstra.edu.
Website: http://www.hofstra.edu/academics/colleges/soc/

Iowa State University of Science and Technology, Greenlee School of Journalism and Communication, Ames, IA 50011. Offers journalism and mass communication (MS). *Entrance requirements:* For master's, GRE General Test. Additional exam requirements/recommendations for international students: Required—TOEFL (minimum score 570 paper-based; 88 iBT), IELTS (minimum score 6.5). Electronic applications accepted.

Kansas State University, Graduate School, College of Arts and Sciences, A.Q. Miller School of Journalism and Mass Communications, Manhattan, KS 66506. Offers advertising (MS); community journalism (MS); global communication (MS); health communication (MS); media management (MS); public relations (MS). *Program availability:* Part-time, evening/weekend. *Degree requirements:* For master's, comprehensive exam, thesis. *Entrance requirements:* For master's, GRE General Test, minimum GPA of 3.0. Additional exam requirements/recommendations for international students: Required—TOEFL (minimum score 79 iBT). Electronic applications accepted. *Faculty research:* Health communication, risk communication, strategic communications, community journalism, global communication.

Kent State University, College of Communication and Information, School of Journalism and Mass Communication, Kent, OH 44242-0001. Offers journalism and mass communication (MA), including media management, public relations, reporting and editing-broadcast, reporting and editing-convergence, reporting and editing-journalism educators, reporting and editing-magazine, reporting and editing-newspaper. *Program availability:* Part-time, online learning. *Faculty:* 15 full-time (8 women), 14 part-time/adjunct (7 women). *Students:* 13 full-time (8 women), 74 part-time (51 women); includes 14 minority (11 Black or African American, non-Hispanic/Latino; 2 Hispanic/Latino; 1 Two or more races, non-Hispanic/Latino), 4 international. Average age 35. 24 applicants, 71% accepted, 13 enrolled. In 2017, 58 master's awarded. *Degree requirements:* For master's, thesis or project. *Entrance requirements:* For master's, GRE, minimum GPA of 3.0, statement of purpose, 3 online recommendations, resume. Additional exam requirements/recommendations for international students: Required—TOEFL (minimum score 587 paper-based, 94 iBT), Michigan English Language Assessment Battery (minimum score 82), IELTS (minimum score 7.0) or PTE (minimum score 65). *Application deadline:* For fall admission, 7/1 for domestic and international students. Applications are processed on a rolling basis. Application fee: $45 ($70 for international students). Electronic applications accepted. *Expenses:* Tuition, state resident: full-time $11,310; part-time $515 per credit hour. Tuition, nonresident: full-time $20,396; part-time $928 per credit hour. *International tuition:* $18,544 full-time. *Financial support:* Research assistantships with full tuition reimbursements, teaching assistantships with full tuition reimbursements, scholarships/grants, and unspecified assistantships available. Financial award application deadline: 2/16. *Unit head:* Jeff Fruit, Interim Director and Professor, 330-672-2572, E-mail: jmc@kent.edu. *Application contact:* Mark Goodman, Graduate Coordinator/Professor, 330-672-6239, E-mail: mgoodm10@kent.edu.
Website: http://www.kent.edu/jmc

Lindenwood University, Graduate Programs, School of Arts, Media, and Communications, St. Charles, MO 63301-1695. Offers advertising (MA); art history (MA); cinema and media arts (MFA); communications (MA); digital and Web design (MA); fashion and business design (MS); journalism (MA); mass communications (MA); social media and digital content (MS). *Program availability:* Part-time. *Faculty:* 23 full-time (6 women), 8 part-time/adjunct (4 women). *Students:* 26 full-time (13 women), 11 part-time (8 women); includes 3 minority (1 American Indian or Alaska Native, non-Hispanic/Latino; 2 Hispanic/Latino), 7 international. Average age 33. 60 applicants, 45% accepted, 16 enrolled. In 2017, 11 master's awarded. *Degree requirements:* For master's, thesis (for some programs), minimum cumulative GPA of 3.0. *Entrance requirements:* For master's, audition or interview, minimum GPA of 3.0, portfolio, letter of recommendation. Additional exam requirements/recommendations for international students: Required—TOEFL (minimum score 550 paper-based; 80 iBT); Recommended—IELTS (minimum score 6.5). *Application deadline:* For fall admission, 8/27 priority date for domestic and international students; for spring admission, 1/14 for domestic students, 1/14 priority date for international students; for summer admission, 6/4 priority date for domestic and international students. Applications are processed on a rolling basis. Application fee: $30 ($100 for international students). Electronic applications accepted. *Expenses: Tuition:* Full-time $16,300; part-time $460 per credit. *Required fees:* $660; $330 per credit. Tuition and fees vary according to degree level and program. *Financial support:* In 2017–18, 34 students received support. Career-related internships or fieldwork, institutionally sponsored loans, scholarships/grants, tuition waivers (partial), and unspecified assistantships available. Financial award application deadline: 6/30; financial award applicants required to submit FAFSA. *Unit head:* Dr. Joseph Alsobrook, Dean, School of Arts, Media, and Communications, 636-949-4164, Fax: 636-949-4910, E-mail: jalsobrook@lindenwood.edu. *Application contact:* Kara Schilli, Director, Evening and Graduate Admissions, 636-949-4349, Fax: 636-949-4109, E-mail: adultadmissions@lindenwood.edu.
Website: http://www.lindenwood.edu/academics/academic-schools/school-of-arts-media-and-communications/

Marquette University, Graduate School, College of Communication, Milwaukee, WI 53201-1881. Offers advertising and public relations (MA); communication studies (MA); digital storytelling (Certificate); journalism (MA); mass communication (MA); science, health and environmental communication (MA). *Accreditation:* ACEJMC (one or more programs are accredited). *Program availability:* Part-time, evening/weekend. *Degree requirements:* For master's, comprehensive exam, thesis or alternative. *Entrance requirements:* For master's, GRE, official transcripts from all current and previous colleges/universities except Marquette, three letters of recommendation, statement of academic and professional goals. Additional exam requirements/recommendations for

international students: Required—TOEFL (minimum score 530 paper-based). Electronic applications accepted. *Faculty research:* Urban journalism, gender and communication, intercultural communication, religious communication.

Marshall University, Academic Affairs Division, College of Arts and Media, Program in Journalism, Huntington, WV 25755. Offers journalism (MAJ, Certificate), including health care public relations (MAJ). *Faculty:* 6 full-time (2 women). *Students:* 8 full-time (3 women), 4 part-time (0 women); includes 1 minority (Two or more races, non-Hispanic/Latino). Average age 33. In 2017, 5 master's awarded. *Degree requirements:* For master's, thesis optional. *Entrance requirements:* For master's, GRE General Test. Application fee: $40. *Unit head:* Dr. Janet Dooley, Chair, 304-696-2734, E-mail: dooley@marshall.edu. *Application contact:* Dr. Robert Rabe, Graduate Coordinator, 304-696-4636, E-mail: rabe@marshall.edu.

Michigan State University, The Graduate School, College of Communication Arts and Sciences, School of Journalism, East Lansing, MI 48824. Offers MA. *Entrance requirements:* Additional exam requirements/recommendations for international students: Required—TOEFL. Electronic applications accepted.

Murray State University, Arthur J. Bauernfeind College of Business, Department of Journalism and Mass Communications, Murray, KY 42071. Offers mass communications (MA, MS), including public relations. *Program availability:* Part-time. *Faculty:* 7 full-time (4 women), 2 part-time/adjunct (0 women). *Students:* 18 full-time (6 women), 11 part-time (9 women); includes 1 minority (Two or more races, non-Hispanic/Latino), 15 international. Average age 28. 41 applicants, 90% accepted, 10 enrolled. In 2017, 6 master's awarded. *Entrance requirements:* For master's, GRE or GMAT, minimum university GPA of 2.75. Additional exam requirements/recommendations for international students: Required—TOEFL (minimum score 527 paper-based; 51 iBT). *Application deadline:* Applications are processed on a rolling basis. Application fee: $40 ($50 for international students). Electronic applications accepted. *Expenses:* Tuition, state resident: full-time $9504. Tuition, nonresident: full-time $26,811. *International tuition:* $14,400 full-time. Tuition and fees vary according to course load, degree level and reciprocity agreements. *Financial support:* Research assistantships, Federal Work-Study, and unspecified assistantships available. Financial award applicants required to submit FAFSA. *Faculty research:* Mass media, audience analysis, press and politics, government open records laws, public relations. *Unit head:* Dr. Debbie Owens, Associate Professor/Interim Chair, 270-809-6318, Fax: 270-809-2390, E-mail: dowens@murraystate.edu. *Application contact:* Kaitlyn Burzysnki, Interim Assistant Director for Graduate Admission and Records, 270-809-5732, Fax: 270-809-3780, E-mail: msu.graduateadmissions@murraystate.edu.
Website: http://www.murraystate.edu/academics/CollegesDepartments/CollegeOfBusiness/Programs/JournalismAndMassCommunications/graduate/masscomm.aspx

National University, Academic Affairs, School of Professional Studies, La Jolla, CA 92037-1011. Offers criminal justice (MCJ); digital cinema production (MFA); digital journalism (MA); homeland security and emergency management (MS); juvenile justice (MS); professional screenwriting (MFA); public administration (MPA), including human resource management, organizational leadership. *Program availability:* Part-time, evening/weekend, 100% online, blended/hybrid learning. *Degree requirements:* For master's, thesis (for some programs). *Entrance requirements:* For master's, interview, minimum GPA of 2.5. Additional exam requirements/recommendations for international students: Required—TOEFL (minimum score 550 paper-based; 79 iBT), IELTS (minimum score 6). *Application deadline:* Applications are processed on a rolling basis. Application fee: $60 ($65 for international students). Electronic applications accepted. *Expenses: Tuition:* Part-time $430 per quarter hour. *Financial support:* Career-related internships or fieldwork, institutionally sponsored loans, scholarships/grants, and tuition waivers (partial) available. Support available to part-time students. Financial award application deadline: 6/30; financial award applicants required to submit FAFSA. *Unit head:* Dr. Daniel Donaldson, Dean, 858-642-8480, E-mail: sops@nu.edu. *Application contact:* Brandon Jouganatos, Vice President for Enrollment Services, 800-628-8648, E-mail: advisor@nu.edu.
Website: http://www.nu.edu/OurPrograms/School-of-Professional-Studies.html

New York University, Graduate School of Arts and Science, Arthur L. Carter Journalism Institute, New York, NY 10012-1019. Offers biomedical journalism (MS); cultural reporting and criticism (MA); French studies/journalism (MA); journalism (MA); Latin American and Caribbean studies/journalism (MA); Near Eastern studies/journalism (MA); science and environmental reporting (Advanced Certificate); MA/Advanced Certificate. *Accreditation:* ACEJMC. *Program availability:* Part-time. *Students:* Average age 26. 314 applicants, 70% accepted, 90 enrolled. In 2017, 111 master's, 25 other advanced degrees awarded. *Entrance requirements:* For master's, GRE General Test, sample of written work. Additional exam requirements/recommendations for international students: Required—TOEFL. *Application deadline:* For fall admission, 1/4 priority date for domestic students, 1/4 for international students. Application fee: $100. *Expenses: Tuition:* Full-time $41,352; part-time $19,968 per year. *Required fees:* $2496; $1628 per unit. $814 per term. Tuition and fees vary according to course load and program. *Financial support:* Fellowships, teaching assistantships, Federal Work-Study, institutionally sponsored loans, scholarships/grants, and tuition waivers (partial) available. Financial award application deadline: 1/4; financial award applicants required to submit FAFSA. *Faculty research:* Newspaper, magazine, and broadcast journalism; business and financial reporting; media studies. *Unit head:* Perri Klass, Chair, 212-998-7980, Fax: 212-995-4148, E-mail: graduate.journalism@nyu.edu. *Application contact:* Charles Seife, Director of Graduate Studies, 212-998-7980, Fax: 212-995-4148, E-mail: graduate.journalism@nyu.edu.
Website: http://journalism.nyu.edu/graduate/

New York University, Graduate School of Arts and Science, Department of Biology, New York, NY 10012-1019. Offers biology (PhD); biomedical journalism (MS); cancer and molecular biology (PhD); computational biology (PhD); computers in biological research (MS); developmental genetics (PhD); general biology (MS); immunology and microbiology (PhD); molecular genetics (PhD); neurobiology (PhD); oral biology (MS); plant biology (PhD); recombinant DNA technology (MS); MS/MBA. *Program availability:* Part-time. *Students:* Average age 27. 394 applicants, 56% accepted, 77 enrolled. In 2017, 68 master's, 9 doctorates awarded. Terminal master's awarded for partial completion of doctoral program. *Degree requirements:* For master's, thesis or alternative, qualifying paper; for doctorate, comprehensive exam, thesis/dissertation. *Entrance requirements:* For master's and doctorate, GRE General Test. Additional exam requirements/recommendations for international students: Required—TOEFL. *Application deadline:* For fall admission, 12/1 priority date for domestic students, 12/1 for international students. Application fee: $100. *Expenses: Tuition:* Full-time $41,352; part-time $19,968 per year. *Required fees:* $2496; $1628 per unit. $814 per term. Tuition and fees vary according to course load and program. *Financial support:* Fellowships, research assistantships, teaching assistantships, career-related internships or fieldwork, Federal Work-Study, institutionally sponsored loans, scholarships/grants, health care benefits, and unspecified assistantships available. Financial award application deadline: 12/1; financial award applicants required to submit FAFSA. *Faculty research:* Genomics, molecular and cell biology, development and molecular genetics, molecular evolution of plants and animals. *Unit head:* Stephen Small, Chair, 212-998-8200, Fax: 212-995-

4015, E-mail: biology.admissions@nyu.edu. *Application contact:* Ken Birnbaum, Director of Graduate Studies, PhD Programs, 212-998-8200, Fax: 212-995-4015, E-mail: biology.admissions@nyu.edu.
Website: http://biology.as.nyu.edu/

Northeastern University, College of Arts, Media and Design, Boston, MA 02115-5096. Offers architecture (M Arch); game science and design (MS); information design and visualization (MFA); interdisciplinary arts (MFA); journalism (MA); music industry leadership (MS); studio art (MFA); sustainable building systems (MS); sustainable urban environments (M Des). *Faculty:* 145. *Students:* 259. In 2017, 83 master's awarded. Application fee: $75. Electronic applications accepted. *Expenses:* Contact institution. *Financial support:* Applicants required to submit FAFSA. *Unit head:* Dr. Elizabeth Hudson, Dean, 617-373-5088, E-mail: n.elysse@northeastern.edu. *Application contact:* Jane Amidon, Associate Dean for Graduate Programs and Research, 617-373-4614, E-mail: gscamd@northeastern.edu.
Website: http://www.northeastern.edu/camd/

Northwestern University, Medill School of Journalism, Media, and Integrated Marketing Communications, Evanston, IL 60208. Offers integrated marketing communications (MSIMC), including brand strategy, content marketing, direct and interactive marketing, marketing analytics, strategic communications; interactive publishing (MSJ); magazine writing/editing (MSJ); reporting (MSJ); video/broadcast (MSJ). *Entrance requirements:* For master's, GRE General Test, GMAT or LSAT (for MSJ). Additional exam requirements/recommendations for international students: Required—TOEFL. Electronic applications accepted. *Expenses:* Contact institution. *Faculty research:* Web business journalism, cultural stereotypes, voter apathy, digital television.

Ohio University, Graduate College, Scripps College of Communication, E.W. Scripps School of Journalism, Athens, OH 45701-2979. Offers journalism (MS); mass communication (PhD). PhD offered in cooperation with the School of Media Arts and Studies. *Program availability:* Part-time. *Degree requirements:* For master's, thesis or alternative; for doctorate, comprehensive exam, thesis/dissertation. *Entrance requirements:* For master's and doctorate, GRE General Test, minimum GPA of 3.0. Additional exam requirements/recommendations for international students: Required—TOEFL (minimum score 550 paper-based; 80 iBT) or IELTS (minimum score 6.5). Electronic applications accepted. *Faculty research:* Newspaper, magazine, broadcasting, public relations, advertising.

Point Park University, School of Communication, Pittsburgh, PA 15222-1984. Offers communication technology (MA); media communication (MA). *Program availability:* Part-time, evening/weekend. *Degree requirements:* For master's, comprehensive exam (for some programs), thesis or alternative. *Entrance requirements:* For master's, GRE (if GPA less than 2.75), minimum GPA of 2.75, 2 letters of recommendation, statement of intent. Additional exam requirements/recommendations for international students: Required—TOEFL (minimum score 570 paper-based; 88 iBT), IELTS (minimum score 6.5); Recommended—TWE (minimum score 5). Electronic applications accepted.

Quinnipiac University, School of Communications, Program in Journalism, Hamden, CT 06518-1940. Offers journalism (MS), including broadcast/multimedia, writing; sports journalism (MS), including broadcast/multimedia. *Program availability:* Part-time, evening/weekend. *Faculty:* 5 full-time (4 women), 6 part-time/adjunct (1 woman). *Students:* 3 full-time (1 woman), 4 part-time (2 women); includes 1 minority (Hispanic/Latino), 1 international. 9 applicants, 56% accepted, 2 enrolled. In 2017, 9 master's awarded. *Degree requirements:* For master's, project. *Entrance requirements:* For master's, minimum GPA of 3.0, portfolio or writing sample. Additional exam requirements/recommendations for international students: Required—TOEFL (minimum score 575 paper-based; 90 iBT), IELTS (minimum score 6.5). *Application deadline:* For fall admission, 7/30 priority date for domestic students, 4/15 priority date for international students. Applications are processed on a rolling basis. Application fee: $45. Electronic applications accepted. *Financial support:* Federal Work-Study, scholarships/grants, and unspecified assistantships available. Financial award application deadline: 6/1; financial award applicants required to submit FAFSA. *Faculty research:* Journalism history, federal law enforcement and journalism, social media and journalism, online journalism, sports journalism, American football history and media, journalism and film, McCarthyism and journalism. *Unit head:* Phillip Simon, Program Director, 203-582-8672, E-mail: graduate@qu.edu. *Application contact:* Office of Graduate Admissions, 800-462-1944, Fax: 203-582-3443, E-mail: graduate@qu.edu.
Website: http://www.qu.edu/gradjournalism

Regent University, Graduate School, School of Communication and the Arts, Virginia Beach, VA 23464-9800. Offers acting (MFA); communication (MA, PhD), including media and arts management and promotion (MA), political communication (MA), strategic communication (MA), technical communication (MA); film and TV (MA), including producing (MA, MFA), production, script writing; film-television (MFA), including directing, producing (MA, MFA), script and screenwriting; journalism (MA); theatre (MA). *Program availability:* Part-time, evening/weekend, 100% online, blended/hybrid learning. *Faculty:* 15 full-time (2 women), 66 part-time/adjunct (23 women). *Students:* 101 full-time (65 women), 342 part-time (237 women); includes 177 minority (127 Black or African American, non-Hispanic/Latino; 4 American Indian or Alaska Native, non-Hispanic/Latino; 9 Asian, non-Hispanic/Latino; 25 Hispanic/Latino; 12 Two or more races, non-Hispanic/Latino), 11 international. Average age 37. 498 applicants, 36% accepted, 124 enrolled. In 2017, 93 master's, 22 doctorates awarded. *Degree requirements:* For master's, thesis or alternative; for doctorate, thesis/dissertation. *Entrance requirements:* For master's, transcripts, writing sample, resume, audition (for MFA programs); for doctorate, GRE General Test, resume, writing sample, recommendations, interview, transcripts, personal goals statement. Additional exam requirements/recommendations for international students: Required—TOEFL (minimum score 577 paper-based). *Application deadline:* For fall admission, 3/1 priority date for domestic students; for spring admission, 10/1 priority date for domestic students. Applications are processed on a rolling basis. Application fee: $50. Electronic applications accepted. *Expenses:* $650 per credit (MA, MFA); $885 per credit (PhD); $300 per semester technology fee. *Financial support:* In 2017–18, 234 students received support, including 2 fellowships (averaging $10,000 per year); career-related internships or fieldwork, scholarships/grants, and unspecified assistantships also available. Support available to part-time students. *Faculty research:* Screenwriting, digital media production, communication, acting, directing. *Unit head:* Dr. Robert Herron, Dean, 757-352-4500, E-mail: rherron@regent.edu. *Application contact:* Heidi Cece, Assistant Vice President of Enrollment Management, 800-373-5504, Fax: 757-352-4381, E-mail: admissions@regent.edu.
Website: https://www.regent.edu/school-of-communication-and-the-arts/

Sacred Heart University, Graduate Programs, College of Arts and Sciences, Department of Communication, Fairfield, CT 06825. Offers corporate communications and public relations (MA Comm); digital multimedia journalism (MA Comm); digital multimedia production (MA Comm); film and television production (MA); media literacy and digital culture (MA), including children, health and media, media and social justice, political action and media production; sports communication and media (MA), including athletic communications and promotions, sports broadcasting. *Program availability:* Part-time, evening/weekend. *Faculty:* 9 full-time (1 woman), 6 part-time/adjunct (1 woman). *Students:* 70 full-time (36 women), 52 part-time (28 women); includes 36 minority (18 Black or African American, non-Hispanic/Latino; 16 Hispanic/Latino; 2 Two or more races, non-Hispanic/Latino), 20 international. Average age 26. 155 applicants, 89% accepted, 66 enrolled. In 2017, 71 master's awarded. *Degree requirements:* For master's, thesis or alternative. *Entrance requirements:* For master's, bachelor's degree. Additional exam requirements/recommendations for international students: Required—TOEFL (minimum score 570 paper-based, 80 iBT), TWE, or IELTS (6.5). *Application deadline:* Applications are processed on a rolling basis. Application fee: $75. Electronic applications accepted. *Expenses:* Contact institution. *Financial support:* Unspecified assistantships available. Financial award applicants required to submit FAFSA. *Unit head:* Dr. Andrew Miller, Director of Graduate Programs, 203-396-8087, E-mail: millera@sacredheart.edu. *Application contact:* Pam Pillo, Executive Director of Graduate Admissions, 203-365-7619, Fax: 203-365-4732, E-mail: graduatestudies@sacredheart.edu.
Website: http://www.sacredheart.edu/academics/collegeofartssciences/academicdepartments/communicationmediastudies/

School of the Art Institute of Chicago, Graduate Division, Program in New Arts Journalism, Chicago, IL 60603-3103. Offers MA. *Entrance requirements:* Additional exam requirements/recommendations for international students: Required—TOEFL, IELTS.

South Dakota State University, Graduate School, College of Arts and Science, Department of Journalism and Mass Communication, Brookings, SD 57007. Offers communication studies and journalism (MS). *Accreditation:* ACEJMC. *Program availability:* Part-time, evening/weekend. *Degree requirements:* For master's, thesis, oral exam. *Entrance requirements:* Additional exam requirements/recommendations for international students: Required—TOEFL (minimum score 550 paper-based; 79 iBT). *Faculty research:* Mass communication applications.

Southeastern Louisiana University, College of Arts, Humanities and Social Sciences, Department of Languages and Communication, Hammond, LA 70402. Offers health communications (MA); journalism (MA); marketing (MA); public relations (MA); sociology (MA). *Program availability:* Part-time, evening/weekend. *Faculty:* 5 full-time (3 women). *Students:* 7 full-time (6 women), 11 part-time (7 women); includes 10 minority (5 Black or African American, non-Hispanic/Latino; 3 Hispanic/Latino; 2 Two or more races, non-Hispanic/Latino). Average age 28. 133 applicants, 51% accepted, 10 enrolled. In 2017, 36 master's awarded. *Degree requirements:* For master's, comprehensive exam. *Entrance requirements:* For master's, GRE (minimum score 148 on Verbal section, 3.5 Written). Additional exam requirements/recommendations for international students: Required—TOEFL (minimum score 525 paper-based; 75 iBT). *Application deadline:* For fall admission, 7/15 priority date for domestic students, 6/1 priority date for international students; for spring admission, 12/1 priority date for domestic students, 10/1 priority date for international students. Applications are processed on a rolling basis. Application fee: $20 ($30 for international students). Electronic applications accepted. *Expenses:* Tuition, state resident: full-time $6684. Tuition, nonresident: full-time $19,162. *Required fees:* $2088. *Financial support:* In 2017–18, 12 students received support, including 7 research assistantships (averaging $6,082 per year); career-related internships or fieldwork, Federal Work-Study, institutionally sponsored loans, scholarships/grants, traineeships, health care benefits, tuition waivers, and unspecified assistantships also available. Financial award application deadline: 5/1; financial award applicants required to submit FAFSA. *Faculty research:* Communicate with the millennial generation to enhance organizational effectiveness, conflict resolution and mediation among nations, journalism history, media law, media writing, media convergence, external compliances accreditation and strategic planning. *Unit head:* Dr. Lucia Harrison, Department Head, 985-549-2105, Fax: 985-549-5014, E-mail: lharrison@southeastern.edu. *Application contact:* Amanda Harper, Graduate Admissions Analyst, 985-549-5620, Fax: 985-549-5632, E-mail: admissions@southeastern.edu.
Website: http://www.southeastern.edu/acad_research/depts/lang_comm/index.html

Stony Brook University, State University of New York, School of Journalism, Stony Brook, NY 11794. Offers health communication (Certificate); journalism (MS). *Faculty:* 9 full-time (3 women), 23 part-time/adjunct (8 women). *Students:* 2 part-time (both women). Average age 30. In 2017, 5 master's awarded. *Entrance requirements:* For master's, GRE, MCAT, DAT, or GMAT, bachelor's degree with minimum GPA of 3.0. Additional exam requirements/recommendations for international students: Required—TOEFL (minimum score 600 paper-based; 100 iBT). *Application deadline:* For fall admission, 1/15 for domestic students; for spring admission, 10/1 for domestic students. Application fee: $100. *Expenses:* Contact institution. *Financial support:* Teaching assistantships available. *Faculty research:* Journalism, newspaper journalism, non-fiction, children's literature, Constitutional law. *Total annual research expenditures:* $132,282. *Unit head:* Prof. Howard Schneider, Dean, 631-632-7403, E-mail: howard.schneider@stonybrook.edu. *Application contact:* Maureen Robinson, Coordinator, 631-632-7403, Fax: 631-632-7550, E-mail: maureen.robinson@stonybrook.edu.
Website: https://journalism.cc.stonybrook.edu/

Syracuse University, S. I. Newhouse School of Public Communications, MA Program in Magazine, Newspaper and Online Journalism, Syracuse, NY 13244. Offers MA. *Accreditation:* ACEJMC. *Students:* Average age 24. *Entrance requirements:* For master's, GRE General Test, resume, official transcripts, personal statement, three letters of recommendation. Additional exam requirements/recommendations for international students: Required—TOEFL (minimum score 600 paper-based; 100 iBT). *Application deadline:* For summer admission, 1/15 priority date for domestic and international students. Application fee: $45. Electronic applications accepted. *Financial support:* Fellowships with full tuition reimbursements, research assistantships with partial tuition reimbursements, and teaching assistantships with partial tuition reimbursements available. Financial award application deadline: 2/1; financial award applicants required to submit FAFSA. *Faculty research:* Media law, content management, reporting and writing, magazine and newspaper editing. *Unit head:* Melissa Chessher, Director, 315-443-4004, Fax: 315-443-3946, E-mail: pcgrad@syr.edu. *Application contact:* Graduate Records Office, 315-443-4039, Fax: 315-443-1834, E-mail: pcgrad@syr.edu.
Website: http://newhouse.syr.edu/academics/degrees/masters/magazine-newspaper-and-online-journalism

Syracuse University, S. I. Newhouse School of Public Communications, MS Program in Broadcast and Digital Journalism, Syracuse, NY 13244. Offers MS. *Accreditation:* ACEJMC. *Entrance requirements:* For master's, GRE General Test, resume, official transcripts, personal statement, three letters of recommendation. Additional exam requirements/recommendations for international students: Required—TOEFL (minimum score 100 iBT). *Application deadline:* For summer admission, 1/15 for domestic and international students. Application fee: $45. Electronic applications accepted. *Financial support:* Fellowships with full tuition reimbursements, research assistantships with partial tuition reimbursements, and teaching assistantships with partial tuition reimbursements available. Financial award application deadline: 2/1. *Faculty research:* Electronic journalism, broadcast and digital journalism, anchoring in traditional and new platforms, producing. *Unit head:* Prof. Chris Tuohey, Chair, 315-443-4118, E-mail: cptuohey@syr.edu. *Application contact:* Martha Coria, Graduate Records Office, 315-443-5749, Fax: 315-443-1834, E-mail: pcgrad@syr.edu.
Website: http://newhouse.syr.edu/

Temple University, Klein College of Media and Communication, Department of Journalism, Philadelphia, PA 19122-6096. Offers MJ. *Program availability:* Part-time, evening/weekend. *Faculty:* 19 full-time (10 women), 18 part-time/adjunct (6 women). *Students:* 4 full-time (1 woman), 6 part-time (3 women); includes 4 minority (3 Black or African American, non-Hispanic/Latino; 1 Hispanic/Latino), 2 international. 17 applicants, 41% accepted, 1 enrolled. In 2017, 3 master's awarded. *Entrance requirements:* For master's, GRE General Test, minimum GPA of 3.0. Additional exam requirements/recommendations for international students: Required—TOEFL (minimum score 620 paper-based; 105 iBT). *Application deadline:* For fall admission, 3/1 for domestic and international students; for spring admission, 11/1 for domestic and international students. Applications are processed on a rolling basis. Application fee: $60. Electronic applications accepted. *Expenses:* Contact institution. *Financial support:* Career-related internships or fieldwork and Federal Work-Study available. Financial award application deadline: 1/15; financial award applicants required to submit FAFSA. *Faculty research:* Journalism history, advertising research, media law, media institutions. *Unit head:* Dr. Carolyn Kitch, Chair, 215-204-8346, Fax: 215-204-1974, E-mail: ckitch@temple.edu. *Application contact:* Nicole McKenna, Director, Office of Research and Graduate Studies, 215-204-1497, Fax: 215-204-0310, E-mail: nmckenna@temple.edu.
Website: https://klein.temple.edu/journalism

Université Laval, Faculty of Letters, Department of Information and Communication, Program in International Journalism, Québec, QC G1K 7P4, Canada. Offers Diploma. Offered jointly with École Supérieure De Journalisme De Lille (France). *Entrance requirements:* For degree, English exam, French exam, test on international current events, interview, knowledge of French, knowledge of English. Electronic applications accepted.

The University of Alabama, Graduate School, College of Communication and Information Sciences, Department of Journalism and Creative Media, Tuscaloosa, AL 35487-0172. Offers journalism and creative media (MA). *Program availability:* Part-time, evening/weekend. *Faculty:* 5 full-time (2 women). *Students:* 12 full-time (5 women), 10 part-time (3 women); includes 6 minority (4 Black or African American, non-Hispanic/Latino; 2 Two or more races, non-Hispanic/Latino), 2 international. Average age 30. 21 applicants, 62% accepted, 10 enrolled. In 2017, 12 master's awarded. *Degree requirements:* For master's, comprehensive exam (for some programs), thesis. *Entrance requirements:* For master's, GRE (minimum score 300, Writing 4.5), writing sample, 3 references, minimum undergraduate GPA of 3.0. Additional exam requirements/recommendations for international students: Required—TOEFL (minimum score 550 paper-based; 79 iBT). *Application deadline:* For fall admission, 3/31 priority date for domestic students, 2/15 priority date for international students; for spring admission, 11/1 priority date for domestic students, 9/15 priority date for international students. Applications are processed on a rolling basis. Application fee: $50 ($60 for international students). Electronic applications accepted. *Financial support:* In 2017–18, 9 students received support. Application deadline: 3/1; applicants required to submit FAFSA. *Faculty research:* Journalistic processes, practices and ethics, media effects, media sociology, history, law. *Unit head:* Dr. Cory Armstrong, Department Chair, 205-348-9684, Fax: 205-348-9684, E-mail: cory.i.armstrong@ua.edu. *Application contact:* Dr. Chris Roberts, Graduate Coordinator, 205-348-8619, Fax: 205-348-9684, E-mail: croberts@ua.edu.
Website: http://www.jcm.ua.edu/

The University of Arizona, College of Social and Behavioral Sciences, School of Journalism, Tucson, AZ 85721. Offers international journalism studies (MA); professional journalism (MA). *Program availability:* Part-time. *Degree requirements:* For master's, project. *Entrance requirements:* For master's, GRE, minimum GPA of 3.0. Additional exam requirements/recommendations for international students: Required—TOEFL. Electronic applications accepted. *Faculty research:* Press law, military censorship, Latin American press, media and minorities, reporting public affairs.

University of Arkansas, Graduate School, J. William Fulbright College of Arts and Sciences, Department of Journalism, Fayetteville, AR 72701. Offers MA. In 2017, 4 master's awarded. *Application deadline:* For fall admission, 8/1 for domestic students, 4/1 for international students; for spring admission, 12/1 for domestic students, 10/1 for international students; for summer admission, 4/15 for domestic students, 3/1 for international students. Application fee: $60. Electronic applications accepted. *Expenses:* Tuition, state resident: full-time $3782. Tuition, nonresident: full-time $10,238. *Financial support:* In 2017–18, 4 research assistantships, 3 teaching assistantships were awarded; fellowships with tuition reimbursements, career-related internships or fieldwork, and Federal Work-Study also available. Support available to part-time students. Financial award application deadline: 4/1; financial award applicants required to submit FAFSA. *Unit head:* Dr. Larry Foley, Department Chair, 479-575-3601, Fax: 479-575-4341, E-mail: lfoley@uark.edu. *Application contact:* Dr. Patsy Watkins, Graduate Coordinator, 479-575-5964, Fax: 479-575-4314, E-mail: pwatkins@uark.edu.
Website: https://fulbright.uark.edu/departments/journalism/

The University of British Columbia, Faculty of Arts and Faculty of Graduate Studies, School of Journalism, Vancouver, BC V6T 1Z2, Canada. Offers MJ. *Degree requirements:* For master's, thesis, 3-month internship. *Entrance requirements:* For master's, portfolio, resume, letters of reference. Additional exam requirements/recommendations for international students: Required—TOEFL, IELTS. Electronic applications accepted. *Expenses:* Contact institution. *Faculty research:* New media, media coverage, journalistic ethics, international journalism, multimedia.

University of California, Berkeley, Graduate Division, Graduate School of Journalism, Berkeley, CA 94720-1500. Offers MJ, JD/MJ, MJ/MA. *Degree requirements:* For master's, project. *Entrance requirements:* For master's, GRE General Test, 3 work samples, minimum GPA of 3.0, 3 letters of recommendation. Additional exam requirements/recommendations for international students: Required—TOEFL (minimum score 600 paper-based). Electronic applications accepted. *Faculty research:* Documentary, new media, print (newspaper and magazine), broadcast (television and radio), photography.

University of Colorado Boulder, Graduate School, College of Media, Communication and Information, Program in Journalism, Boulder, CO 80309. Offers journalism (MA); media research and practice (PhD). *Accreditation:* ACEJMC. *Faculty:* 13 full-time (7 women). *Students:* 23 full-time (18 women), 1 (woman) part-time; includes 3 minority (1 Black or African American, non-Hispanic/Latino; 2 Hispanic/Latino), 3 international. Average age 30. 50 applicants, 78% accepted, 8 enrolled. In 2017, 10 master's awarded. *Application deadline:* For fall admission, 1/10 for domestic students; for spring admission, 12/1 for domestic students. Application fee: $60 ($80 for international students). Electronic applications accepted. Application fee is waived when completed online. *Financial support:* In 2017–18, 38 students received support, including 9 fellowships (averaging $1,365 per year), 11 teaching assistantships with full and partial tuition reimbursements available (averaging $22,425 per year); research assistantships, institutionally sponsored loans, scholarships/grants, health care benefits, and unspecified assistantships also available. Financial award application deadline: 2/15; financial award applicants required to submit FAFSA. *Faculty research:* Journalism; mass communication/media; print media; cinema/video; content analysis. *Application contact:* E-mail: paul.voakes@colorado.edu.
Website: http://www.colorado.edu/cmci/academics/journalism

University of Florida, Graduate School, College of Journalism and Communications, Program in Mass Communication, Gainesville, FL 32611. Offers international/intercultural communication (MAMC); journalism (MAMC); mass communication (MAMC, PhD), including clinical translational science (MAMC); public relations (MAMC); science/health communication (MAMC); telecommunication (MAMC). *Accreditation:* ACEJMC. *Entrance requirements:* For master's and doctorate, GRE General Test, minimum GPA of 3.0.

University of Georgia, Grady College of Journalism and Mass Communication, Athens, GA 30602. Offers journalism and mass communication (MA); mass communication (PhD). *Degree requirements:* For master's, comprehensive exam, thesis (MA); for doctorate, comprehensive exam, thesis/dissertation. *Entrance requirements:* For master's and doctorate, GRE General Test. Additional exam requirements/recommendations for international students: Required—TOEFL, TWE for PhD. Electronic applications accepted.

University of Illinois at Springfield, Graduate Programs, College of Public Affairs and Administration, Public Affairs Reporting Program, Springfield, IL 62703-5407. Offers MA. *Program availability:* Part-time, evening/weekend. *Faculty:* 1 full-time (0 women). *Students:* 12 full-time (6 women); includes 2 minority (both Black or African American, non-Hispanic/Latino). Average age 23. 19 applicants, 74% accepted, 12 enrolled. In 2017, 10 master's awarded. *Degree requirements:* For master's, internship, professional portfolio. *Entrance requirements:* For master's, literacy/competency writing test, interview, written work sample, narrative statement on qualifications and interest in program, 3 letters of reference. Additional exam requirements/recommendations for international students: Required—TOEFL (minimum score 500 paper-based; 61 iBT). *Application deadline:* Applications are processed on a rolling basis. Application fee: $60 ($75 for international students). Electronic applications accepted. *Expenses:* Tuition, state resident: full-time $7896; part-time $329 per credit hour. Tuition, nonresident: full-time $16,200; part-time $675 per credit hour. Tuition and fees vary according to program. *Financial support:* In 2017–18, research assistantships with full tuition reimbursements (averaging $10,249 per year), teaching assistantships with full tuition reimbursements (averaging $10,303 per year) were awarded; fellowships, career-related internships or fieldwork, Federal Work-Study, scholarships/grants, health care benefits, and unspecified assistantships also available. Support available to part-time students. Financial award application deadline: 11/15; financial award applicants required to submit FAFSA. *Unit head:* Dr. Charles Wheeler, Director, 217-206-6535, Fax: 217-206-7807, E-mail: cwhee1@uis.edu.
Website: http://www.uis.edu/publicaffairsreporting/

University of Illinois at Urbana–Champaign, Graduate College, College of Media, Department of Journalism, Champaign, IL 61820. Offers MS, MS/JD, MS/MBA.

The University of Iowa, Graduate College, College of Liberal Arts and Sciences, School of Journalism and Mass Communication, Iowa City, IA 52242-1316. Offers journalism and media communication (MA); mass communication (PhD); strategic communication (MA); JD/MA; JD/PhD. *Degree requirements:* For master's, thesis optional, exam; for doctorate, comprehensive exam, thesis/dissertation. *Entrance requirements:* For master's and doctorate, GRE General Test, minimum GPA of 3.0. Additional exam requirements/recommendations for international students: Required—TOEFL (minimum score 637 paper-based; 110 iBT). Electronic applications accepted. *Faculty research:* Verbal and visual aspects of historical, legal, social, and cross-cultural communication.

The University of Kansas, Graduate Studies, William Allen White School of Journalism and Mass Communications, Lawrence, KS 66045. Offers journalism (MS); journalism and mass communications (PhD); JD/MS. *Program availability:* Part-time. *Students:* 39 full-time (27 women), 60 part-time (44 women); includes 19 minority (9 Black or African American, non-Hispanic/Latino; 2 Asian, non-Hispanic/Latino; 1 Hispanic/Latino; 1 Native Hawaiian or other Pacific Islander, non-Hispanic/Latino; 6 Two or more races, non-Hispanic/Latino), 10 international. Average age 33. 74 applicants, 82% accepted, 42 enrolled. In 2017, 8 master's, 6 doctorates awarded. Terminal master's awarded for partial completion of doctoral program. *Entrance requirements:* For master's and doctorate, GRE, minimum GPA of 3.0; official transcript; current resume; two writing samples, preferably academic, or samples of professional work that reflect years of experience; statement of academic interests and professional goals; three letters of reference. *Application deadline:* For fall admission, 1/1 priority date for domestic and international students; for spring admission, 11/1 for domestic and international students. Application fee: $65 ($85 for international students). Electronic applications accepted. *Financial support:* Fellowships, research assistantships, teaching assistantships, career-related internships or fieldwork, scholarships/grants, and unspecified assistantships available. Support available to part-time students. Financial award application deadline: 2/1; financial award applicants required to submit FAFSA. *Faculty research:* Advertising, creativity, public relations, integrated marketing communication; media economics, online journalism; new media, visual communication; health communication, sports communication; political journalism, press law. *Unit head:* Ann Brill, Dean, 785-864-4755, E-mail: abrill@ku.edu. *Application contact:* Jammie A. Johnson, Graduate Advisor/Administrative Assistant, 785-864-7649, E-mail: jamjohn@ku.edu.
Website: http://www.journalism.ku.edu/

University of King's College, Graduate and Advanced Programs, Halifax, NS B3H 2A1, Canada. Offers creative nonfiction (MFA); journalism (MJ).

University of Maryland, College Park, Academic Affairs, Philip Merrill College of Journalism, College Park, MD 20742. Offers broadcast journalism (MA); journalism (MA); journalism and media studies (PhD); online news (MA); public affairs reporting (MA). *Accreditation:* ACEJMC (one or more programs are accredited). *Program availability:* Part-time, evening/weekend. *Degree requirements:* For doctorate, thesis/dissertation, preliminary written and oral comprehensive exams. *Entrance requirements:* For master's and doctorate, GRE General Test, minimum GPA of 3.0, 3 letters of recommendation. Additional exam requirements/recommendations for international students: Required—TOEFL. Electronic applications accepted. *Faculty research:* Mass communication theory, specialized journalism, new telecommunication technologies, press integration.

University of Memphis, Graduate School, College of Communication and Fine Arts, Department of Journalism and Strategic Media, Memphis, TN 38152. Offers entrepreneurial journalism (Graduate Certificate); journalism and strategic media (MA). *Program availability:* Part-time, evening/weekend, online learning. *Faculty:* 7 full-time (3 women). *Students:* 10 full-time (7 women), 22 part-time (14 women); includes 11 minority (9 Black or African American, non-Hispanic/Latino; 2 Two or more races, non-Hispanic/Latino). Average age 34. 16 applicants, 88% accepted, 12 enrolled. In 2017, 8 master's awarded. *Degree requirements:* For master's, comprehensive exam, thesis (for some programs), culminating experience: project, thesis, or referred paper. *Entrance requirements:* For master's, GRE General Test, MAT, transcripts, resume, goal statement. Additional exam requirements/recommendations for international students: Required—TOEFL (minimum score 600 paper-based). *Application deadline:* For fall

admission, 6/1 for domestic and international students; for spring admission, 10/1 for domestic and international students; for summer admission, 2/1 for domestic and international students. Applications are processed on a rolling basis. Application fee: $35 ($60 for international students). Electronic applications accepted. *Expenses:* Contact institution. *Financial support:* In 2017–18, 25 students received support, including 5 research assistantships with full tuition reimbursements available (averaging $12,000 per year); Federal Work-Study, scholarships/grants, and unspecified assistantships also available. Support available to part-time students. Financial award application deadline: 2/1; financial award applicants required to submit FAFSA. *Faculty research:* Spirit of libel law, statistical software packages, college yearbooks, computer-assisted grammar project, newspaper in education. *Unit head:* Dr. David Arant, Chair, 901-678-2401, Fax: 901-678-4287, E-mail: darant@memphis.edu. *Application contact:* Dr. Thomas Hrach, Coordinator of Graduate Studies, 901-678-4779, Fax: 901-678-4287, E-mail: thrach@memphis.edu.
Website: http://www.memphis.edu/jrsm/

University of Miami, Graduate School, School of Communication, Coral Gables, FL 33124. Offers communication (PhD); communication studies (MA); film studies (MA, PhD); motion pictures (MFA), including production, producing, and screenwriting; print journalism (MA); public relations (MA); Spanish language journalism (MA); television broadcast journalism (MA). *Program availability:* Part-time. *Degree requirements:* For master's, comprehensive exam (for some programs), thesis (for some programs); for doctorate, comprehensive exam, thesis/dissertation. *Entrance requirements:* For master's, GRE General Test; for doctorate, GRE General Test, master's thesis or scholarly research. Additional exam requirements/recommendations for international students: Required—TOEFL (minimum score 600 paper-based; 100 iBT). Electronic applications accepted. *Faculty research:* Communication studies, mass communication, international/interpersonal communication, film studies, journalism.

University of Mississippi, Graduate School, Meek School of Journalism and New Media, University, MS 38677. Offers integrated marketing communications (MA); journalism (MA). *Faculty:* 30 full-time (15 women), 19 part-time/adjunct (11 women). *Students:* 39 full-time (18 women), 7 part-time (1 woman); includes 6 minority (4 Black or African American, non-Hispanic/Latino; 1 Asian, non-Hispanic/Latino; 1 Two or more races, non-Hispanic/Latino), 5 international. Average age 26. In 2017, 11 master's awarded. *Degree requirements:* For master's, thesis. *Application deadline:* For fall admission, 3/31 priority date for domestic and international students. Applications are processed on a rolling basis. Application fee: $40. *Unit head:* Dr. Will Norton, Jr., Dean, 662-915-7146, Fax: 662-915-7765, E-mail: meekschool@olemiss.edu. *Application contact:* Dr. Joseph Atkins, Professor of Journalism, 662-915-5510, E-mail: jbatkins@olemiss.edu.
Website: http://meek.olemiss.edu/

University of Missouri, Office of Research and Graduate Studies, School of Journalism, Columbia, MO 65211. Offers health communications (MA); journalism (PhD). *Accreditation:* ACEJMC (one or more programs are accredited). *Program availability:* Part-time. Terminal master's awarded for partial completion of doctoral program. *Degree requirements:* For master's, thesis (for some programs); for doctorate, 2 foreign languages, thesis/dissertation. *Entrance requirements:* For master's and doctorate, GRE General Test, minimum GPA of 3.0. Additional exam requirements/recommendations for international students: Required—TOEFL (minimum score 600 paper-based; 100 iBT), IELTS (minimum score 7). Electronic applications accepted.

University of Montana, Graduate School, School of Journalism, Missoula, MT 59812. Offers MA. *Degree requirements:* For master's, thesis or alternative, professional project. *Entrance requirements:* For master's, GRE. Additional exam requirements/recommendations for international students: Required—TOEFL (minimum score 580 paper-based). Electronic applications accepted. *Faculty research:* Native American issues, natural resources, public affairs, economy, photojournalism, multimedia, media law.

University of Nebraska–Lincoln, Graduate College, College of Journalism and Mass Communications, Lincoln, NE 68588. Offers marketing, communication and advertising (MA); professional journalism (MA). *Program availability:* Online learning. *Degree requirements:* For master's, thesis. *Entrance requirements:* For master's, samples of work. Additional exam requirements/recommendations for international students: Required—TOEFL (minimum score 600 paper-based). Electronic applications accepted. *Faculty research:* Interactive media and the Internet, community newspapers, children's radio, advertising involvement, telecommunications policy.

University of Nevada, Las Vegas, Graduate College, Greenspun College of Urban Affairs, Hank Greenspun School of Journalism and Media Studies, Las Vegas, NV 89154-5007. Offers MA. *Program availability:* Part-time. *Faculty:* 3 full-time (0 women). *Students:* 8 full-time (6 women), 1 part-time (0 women); includes 3 minority (1 Black or African American, non-Hispanic/Latino; 1 Hispanic/Latino; 1 Two or more races, non-Hispanic/Latino), 1 international. Average age 29. 14 applicants, 57% accepted, 5 enrolled. In 2017, 5 master's awarded. *Degree requirements:* For master's, comprehensive exam, thesis optional, oral exam. *Entrance requirements:* For master's, GRE General Test, bachelor's degree with minimum GPA 3.0; 3 letters of recommendation; statement of purpose; writing sample. Additional exam requirements/recommendations for international students: Required—TOEFL (minimum score 550 paper-based; 80 iBT), IELTS (minimum score 7). *Application deadline:* For fall admission, 3/15 for domestic students. Application fee: $60 ($95 for international students). Electronic applications accepted. *Expenses:* $275 per credit, $850 per course, $7,969 per year resident, $22,157 per year non-resident, $7,094 non-resident fee (7 credits or more), $1,307 annual health insurance fee. *Financial support:* In 2017–18, 7 students received support, including 7 teaching assistantships with full and partial tuition reimbursements available (averaging $11,250 per year); institutionally sponsored loans, scholarships/grants, health care benefits, and unspecified assistantships also available. Financial award application deadline: 3/15; financial award applicants required to submit FAFSA. *Faculty research:* Journalism, media, social and digital media, media history, media ethics, media law, First Amendment theory, First Amendment law, visual literacy, social psychology of visually mediated world, global media, audience reception theory and research, video criticism, advertising, media technology and society, emerging media, children and media. *Unit head:* Dr. Joel Lieberman, Interim Director/Professor, 702-895-0249, Fax: 702-895-0252, E-mail: joel.lieberman@unlv.edu. *Application contact:* Dr. Julian Kilker, Graduate Coordinator, 702-895-3729, Fax: 702-895-5189, E-mail: julian.kilker@unlv.edu.
Website: http://journalism.unlv.edu/

University of Nevada, Reno, Graduate School, Donald W. Reynolds School of Journalism, Reno, NV 89557. Offers MA. *Degree requirements:* For master's, thesis. *Entrance requirements:* For master's, GRE General Test, minimum GPA of 2.75. Additional exam requirements/recommendations for international students: Required—TOEFL (minimum score 500 paper-based; 61 iBT), IELTS (minimum score 6). Electronic applications accepted. *Faculty research:* Interactive environmental journalism.

The University of North Carolina at Chapel Hill, Graduate School, School of Media and Journalism, Chapel Hill, NC 27599. Offers digital communication (MA, Certificate); media and communication (MA, PhD), including interdisciplinary health communication (MA), journalism (MA), strategic communication (MA), theory and research (MA), visual communication (MA); JD/PhD; MA/JD. MA/JD and JD/PhD offered jointly with School of Law. *Accreditation:* ACEJMC (one or more programs are accredited). *Program availability:* Part-time, all course instruction online, plus two on-campus experiences totaling seven days. *Faculty:* 51 full-time (22 women), 4 part-time/adjunct (2 women). *Students:* 75 full-time (50 women), 63 part-time (41 women); includes 44 minority (10 Black or African American, non-Hispanic/Latino; 11 Asian, non-Hispanic/Latino; 5 Hispanic/Latino; 18 Two or more races, non-Hispanic/Latino), 6 international. Average age 31. 207 applicants, 41% accepted, 63 enrolled. In 2017, 32 master's, 9 doctorates, 17 other advanced degrees awarded. *Degree requirements:* For master's, comprehensive exam, thesis; for doctorate, comprehensive exam, thesis/dissertation. *Entrance requirements:* For master's and doctorate, GRE General Test, minimum GPA of 3.0. Additional exam requirements/recommendations for international students: Required—TOEFL (minimum iBT score of 105) or IELTS (7.5). Application fee: $88. Electronic applications accepted. *Expenses:* Contact institution. *Financial support:* In 2017–18, 73 students received support, including 47 fellowships with full tuition reimbursements available (averaging $16,006 per year), 6 research assistantships with full tuition reimbursements available (averaging $17,405 per year); scholarships/grants and health care benefits also available. Financial award application deadline: 12/4; financial award applicants required to submit FAFSA. *Faculty research:* Media processes and production; legal and regulatory issues in communication; media uses and effects; health communication; political, social, and strategic communication. *Total annual research expenditures:* $1 million. *Unit head:* Susan King, Dean, 919-962-1204, Fax: 919-962-0620, E-mail: susanking@unc.edu. *Application contact:* Casey Hart, Marketing and Instructional Design Coordinator, 919-843-9471, Fax: 919-962-0620, E-mail: mjgrad@unc.edu.
Website: http://mj.unc.edu/

University of North Texas, Robert B. Toulouse School of Graduate Studies, Denton, TX 76203-5459. Offers accounting (MS); applied anthropology (MA, MS); applied behavior analysis (Certificate); applied geography (MA); applied technology and performance improvement (M Ed, MS); art education (MA); art history (MA); art museum education (Certificate); arts leadership (Certificate); audiology (Au D); behavior analysis (MS); behavioral science (PhD); biochemistry and molecular biology (MS); biology (MA, MS); biomedical engineering (MS); business analysis (MS); chemistry (MS); clinical health psychology (PhD); communication studies (MA, MS); computer engineering (MS); computer science (MS); counseling (M Ed, MS), including clinical mental health counseling (MS), college and university counseling, elementary school counseling, secondary school counseling; creative writing (MA); criminal justice (MS); curriculum and instruction (M Ed); decision sciences (MBA); design (MA, MFA), including fashion design (MFA), innovation studies, interior design (MFA); early childhood studies (MS); economics (MS); educational leadership (M Ed, Ed D); educational psychology (MS, PhD), including family studies (MS), gifted and talented (MS), human development (MS), learning and cognition (MS), research, measurement and evaluation (MS); electrical engineering (MS); emergency management (MPA); engineering technology (MS); English (MA); English as a second language (MA); environmental science (MS); finance (MBA, MS); financial management (MPA); French (MA); health services management (MBA); higher education (M Ed, Ed D); history (MA, MS); hospitality management (MS); human resources management (MPA); information science (MS); information systems (PhD); information technologies (MBA); interdisciplinary studies (MA, MS); international studies (MA); international sustainable tourism (MS); jazz studies (MM); journalism (MA, MJ, Graduate Certificate), including interactive and virtual digital communication (Graduate Certificate), narrative journalism (Graduate Certificate), public relations (Graduate Certificate); kinesiology (MS); linguistics (MA); local government management (MPA); logistics (PhD); logistics and supply chain management (MBA); long-term care, senior housing, and aging services (MA); management (PhD); marketing (MBA); mathematics (MA, MS); mechanical and energy engineering (MS, PhD); music (MA), including ethnomusicology, music theory, musicology, performance; music composition (PhD); music education (MM Ed, PhD); nonprofit management (MPA); operations and supply chain management (MBA); performance (MM, DMA); philosophy (MA); political science (MA); professional and technical communication (MA); radio, television and film (MA, MFA); rehabilitation counseling (Certificate); sociology (MA); Spanish (MA); special education (M Ed); speech-language pathology (MA); strategic management (MBA); studio art (MFA); teaching (M Ed); MBA/MS. *Program availability:* Part-time, evening/weekend, online learning. Terminal master's awarded for partial completion of doctoral program. *Degree requirements:* For master's, variable foreign language requirement, comprehensive exam (for some programs), thesis (for some programs); for doctorate, variable foreign language requirement, comprehensive exam (for some programs), thesis/dissertation; for other advanced degree, variable foreign language requirement, comprehensive exam (for some programs). *Entrance requirements:* For master's and doctorate, GRE, GMAT. Additional exam requirements/recommendations for international students: Required—TOEFL (minimum score 550 paper-based; 79 iBT). Electronic applications accepted.

University of Oklahoma, Gaylord College of Journalism and Mass Communication, Program in Journalism and Mass Communication, Norman, OK 73019. Offers broadcast and electronic media (MA); journalism (MA); media arts (PhD); media management (MA); news and information (PhD); strategic communication (MA, PhD). *Program availability:* Part-time. *Students:* 24 full-time (11 women), 19 part-time (10 women); includes 5 minority (2 Black or African American, non-Hispanic/Latino; 1 Asian, non-Hispanic/Latino; 2 Hispanic/Latino), 18 international. Average age 33. 22 applicants, 64% accepted, 7 enrolled. In 2017, 10 master's awarded. *Degree requirements:* For master's, comprehensive exam (for some programs), thesis (for some programs); for doctorate, comprehensive exam, thesis/dissertation. *Entrance requirements:* For master's, GRE, resume, statement of purpose, two letters of recommendation, official transcript, minimum GPA of 3.2; for doctorate, GRE, resume, statement of purpose, three letters of recommendation, official transcript. Additional exam requirements/recommendations for international students: Required—TOEFL (minimum score 79 iBT) or IELTS (minimum score 6.5). *Application deadline:* For fall admission, 5/1 for domestic students, 3/1 for international students; for spring admission, 11/1 for domestic students, 10/1 for international students; for summer admission, 3/1 for domestic students. Applications are processed on a rolling basis. Application fee: $50 ($100 for international students). Electronic applications accepted. *Expenses:* Tuition, state resident: full-time $5119; part-time $213.30 per credit hour. Tuition, nonresident: full-time $19,778; part-time $824.10 per credit hour. *Required fees:* $3458; $133.55 per credit hour. $126.50 per semester. *Financial support:* In 2017–18, 31 students received support. Research assistantships with full tuition reimbursements available, teaching assistantships with full tuition reimbursements available, career-related internships or fieldwork, institutionally sponsored loans, scholarships/grants, health care benefits, unspecified assistantships, and McNair fellowships available. Financial award application deadline: 6/1; financial award applicants required to submit FAFSA. *Faculty research:* Digital advertising, interactivity and user experience; news sociology and journalism ethics; media management and digital change; corporate, non-profit and global public relations; media psychology and media effects. *Unit head:* Dr. Peter Gade, Director of Graduate Studies/Professor of Journalism, 405-325-5528, Fax: 405-325-7565, E-mail: pgade@ou.edu. *Application contact:* Larry Laneer, Administrative Assistant to Director/Graduate Advisor, 405-325-2722, Fax: 405-325-7565, E-mail: llaneer@ou.edu.
Website: http://www.ou.edu/content/gaylord/graduate

Journalism

University of Oregon, Graduate School, School of Journalism and Communication, Eugene, OR 97403. Offers journalism (MA, MS); media studies (MA, MS, PhD); multimedia journalism (MA, MS); strategic communication (MA, MS). *Accreditation:* ASHA. *Program availability:* Part-time. *Degree requirements:* For master's, thesis or alternative. *Entrance requirements:* For master's, GRE General Test; for doctorate, master's degree. *Faculty research:* Impact of mass communication, media technology, media accountability, craft attitudes, media economics.

University of Puerto Rico–Río Piedras, School of Communication, Program in Journalism, San Juan, PR 00931-3300. Offers MA.

University of Regina, Faculty of Graduate Studies and Research, Faculty of Arts, School of Journalism, Regina, SK S4S 0A2, Canada. Offers MJ. *Program availability:* Part-time. *Faculty:* 5 full-time (2 women). *Students:* 8 full-time (6 women). 24 applicants, 25% accepted. In 2017, 7 master's awarded. *Degree requirements:* For master's, project. *Entrance requirements:* For master's, written project concept; statement of interest; statement of ability. Additional exam requirements/recommendations for international students: Required—TOEFL (minimum score 580 paper-based; 80 iBT), IELTS (minimum score 6.5), PTE (minimum score 59). *Application deadline:* For fall admission, 1/15 for domestic and international students. Application fee: $100. Electronic applications accepted. *Expenses:* $10,681. *Financial support:* In 2017–18, 2 fellowships (averaging $6,000 per year), 2 teaching assistantships (averaging $2,562 per year) were awarded; research assistantships and scholarships/grants also available. Financial award application deadline: 6/15. *Unit head:* Dr. Gennadiy Chernov, Department Head, 306-585-4090, Fax: 306-585-4867, E-mail: gennadiy.chernov@uregina.ca. *Application contact:* Patricia Elliot, Graduate Program Coordinator, 306-585-4449, Fax: 306-585-4867, E-mail: patricia.elliott@uregina.ca. Website: http://www.uregina.ca/arts/journalism/

University of South Carolina, The Graduate School, College of Mass Communications and Information Studies, School of Journalism and Mass Communications, Columbia, SC 29208. Offers MA, MMC, PhD. *Accreditation:* ACEJMC. *Program availability:* Part-time. *Degree requirements:* For master's, comprehensive exam, thesis (for some programs); for doctorate, one foreign language, comprehensive exam, thesis/dissertation. *Entrance requirements:* For master's and doctorate, GRE General Test, minimum GPA of 3.0. Additional exam requirements/recommendations for international students: Required—TOEFL (minimum score 600 paper-based; 75 iBT). Electronic applications accepted. *Faculty research:* Ethics, communications law, international communications, science/health/environmental/risk communications, convergent media.

University of Southern California, Graduate School, Annenberg School for Communication and Journalism, School of Journalism, Program in Journalism, Los Angeles, CA 90089. Offers MS. Program enrolls new students to Summer term only. *Accreditation:* ACEJMC. *Program availability:* Part-time. *Degree requirements:* For master's, professional project. *Entrance requirements:* For master's, GRE General Test, resume, writing samples, letters of recommendation, statement of purpose. Additional exam requirements/recommendations for international students: Required—TOEFL (minimum score 114 iBT), IELTS (minimum score 8). Electronic applications accepted.

University of Southern California, Graduate School, Annenberg School for Communication and Journalism, School of Journalism, Program in Specialized Journalism, Los Angeles, CA 90089. Offers specialized journalism (MA); specialized journalism (the arts) (MA). Program enrolls new students to Summer term only. *Accreditation:* ACEJMC. *Program availability:* Part-time. *Degree requirements:* For master's, thesis or alternative, professional project. *Entrance requirements:* For master's, GRE General Test, resume, portfolio of professional work, letters of recommendation, statement of purpose. Additional exam requirements/recommendations for international students: Required—TOEFL (minimum score 114 iBT), IELTS (minimum score 8). Electronic applications accepted.

University of South Florida, College of Arts and Sciences, Zimmerman School of Advertising and Mass Communications, Tampa, FL 33620-9951. Offers mass communications (MA), including media studies, multimedia journalism, strategic communication management. *Program availability:* Part-time, evening/weekend. *Faculty:* 10 full-time (6 women). *Students:* 25 full-time (20 women), 25 part-time (20 women); includes 7 minority (4 Black or African American, non-Hispanic/Latino; 2 Hispanic/Latino; 1 Native Hawaiian or other Pacific Islander, non-Hispanic/Latino), 29 international. Average age 26. 28 applicants, 64% accepted, 15 enrolled. In 2017, 8 master's awarded. *Degree requirements:* For master's, comprehensive exam, thesis optional. *Entrance requirements:* For master's, GRE General Test, minimum GPA of 3.0 in last 60 hours of course work, three letters of recommendation, letter of intent, resume/curriculum vitae. Additional exam requirements/recommendations for international students: Required—TOEFL (minimum score 550 paper-based; 79 iBT) or IELTS (minimum score 6.5). *Application deadline:* For fall admission, 2/15 priority date for domestic and international students. Application fee: $30. Electronic applications accepted. *Financial support:* In 2017–18, 10 students received support, including 9 teaching assistantships with tuition reimbursements available (averaging $10,513 per year); unspecified assistantships also available. Financial award application deadline: 2/28. *Faculty research:* First Amendment analysis, civic journalism, public opinion, media ethics, media effects research in sports public relations, public relations management, advertisement, telecommunications. *Total annual research expenditures:* $78,680. *Unit head:* Dr. Wayne Garcia, Director and Senior Instructor, 813-498-1925, Fax: 813-974-2592, E-mail: wgarcia@usf.edu. *Application contact:* Dr. Artermio Ramirez, Jr., Associate Director, Fax: 813-974-2592, E-mail: aramirez2@usf.edu. Website: http://masscom.usf.edu/grad/

University of South Florida, Innovative Education, Tampa, FL 33620-9951. Offers adult, career and higher education (Graduate Certificate), including college teaching, leadership in developing human resources, leadership in higher education; Africana studies (Graduate Certificate), including diasporas and health disparities, genocide and human rights; aging studies (Graduate Certificate), including gerontology; art research (Graduate Certificate), including museum studies; business foundations (Graduate Certificate); chemical and biomedical engineering (Graduate Certificate), including materials science and engineering, water, health and sustainability; child and family studies (Graduate Certificate), including positive behavior support; civil and industrial engineering (Graduate Certificate), including transportation systems analysis; community and family health (Graduate Certificate), including maternal and child health, social marketing and public health, violence and injury: prevention and intervention, women's health; criminology (Graduate Certificate), including criminal justice administration; data science for public administration (Graduate Certificate); digital humanities (Graduate Certificate); educational measurement and research (Graduate Certificate), including evaluation; English (Graduate Certificate), including comparative literary studies, creative writing, professional and technical communication; entrepreneurship (Graduate Certificate); environmental health (Graduate Certificate), including safety management; epidemiology and biostatistics (Graduate Certificate), including applied biostatistics, biostatistics, concepts and tools of epidemiology, epidemiology, epidemiology of infectious diseases; geography, environment and planning (Graduate Certificate), including community development, environmental policy and management, geographical information systems; geology (Graduate Certificate), including hydrogeology; global health (Graduate Certificate), including disaster management, global health and Latin American and Caribbean studies, global health practice, humanitarian assistance, infection control; government and international affairs (Graduate Certificate), including Cuban studies, globalization studies; health policy and management (Graduate Certificate), including health management and leadership, public health policy and programs; hearing specialist: early intervention (Graduate Certificate); industrial and management systems engineering (Graduate Certificate), including systems engineering, technology management; information studies (Graduate Certificate), including school library media specialist; information systems/decision sciences (Graduate Certificate), including analytics and business intelligence; instructional technology (Graduate Certificate), including distance education, Florida digital/virtual educator, instructional design, multimedia design, Web design; internal medicine, bioethics and medical humanities (Graduate Certificate), including biomedical ethics; Latin American and Caribbean studies (Graduate Certificate); leadership for coastal resiliency planning (Graduate Certificate); mass communications (Graduate Certificate), including multimedia journalism; mathematics and statistics (Graduate Certificate), including mathematics; medicine (Graduate Certificate), including aging and neuroscience, bioinformatics, biotechnology, brain fitness and memory management, clinical investigation, hand and upper limb rehabilitation, health informatics, health sciences, integrative weight management, intellectual property, medicine and gender, metabolic and nutritional medicine, metabolic cardiology, pharmacy sciences; national and competitive intelligence (Graduate Certificate); nursing (Graduate Certificate), including simulation based academic fellowship in advanced pain management; psychological and social foundations (Graduate Certificate), including career counseling, college teaching, diversity in education, mental health counseling, school counseling; public affairs (Graduate Certificate), including nonprofit management, public management, research administration; public health (Graduate Certificate), including assessing chemical toxicity and public health risks, health equity, pharmacoepidemiology, public health generalist, toxicology, translational research in adolescent behavioral health; public health practices (Graduate Certificate), including planning for healthy communities; rehabilitation and mental health counseling (Graduate Certificate), including integrative mental health care, marriage and family therapy, rehabilitation technology; secondary education (Graduate Certificate), including ESOL, foreign language education: culture and content, foreign language education: professional; social work (Graduate Certificate), including geriatric social work/clinical gerontology; special education (Graduate Certificate), including autism spectrum disorder, disabilities education: severe/profound; world languages (Graduate Certificate), including teaching English as a second language (TESL) or foreign language. *Unit head:* Dr. Cynthia DeLuca, Associate Vice President and Assistant Vice Provost, 813-974-3077, Fax: 813-974-7061, E-mail: deluca@usf.edu. *Application contact:* Owen Hooper, Director, Summer and Alternative Calendar Programs, 813-974-6917, E-mail: hooper@usf.edu.
Website: http://www.usf.edu/innovative-education/

University of South Florida, St. Petersburg, College of Arts and Sciences, St. Petersburg, FL 33701. Offers digital journalism and design (MA); environmental science and policy (MA, MS); Florida studies (MLA); journalism and media studies (MA); liberal studies (MLA); psychology (MA). *Program availability:* Part-time, online learning. *Degree requirements:* For master's, comprehensive exam, thesis or project. *Entrance requirements:* For master's, GRE, LSAT, MCAT (varies by program), letter of intent, 3 letters of recommendation, writing samples, bachelor's degree from regionally-accredited institution with minimum GPA of 3.0 overall or in upper two years. Additional exam requirements/recommendations for international students: Required—TOEFL (minimum score 550 paper-based; 79 iBT); Recommended—IELTS. Electronic applications accepted.

The University of Tennessee, Graduate School, College of Communication and Information, Knoxville, TN 37996. Offers advertising (MS, PhD); broadcasting (MS, PhD); communications (MS, PhD); information sciences (MS, PhD); journalism (MS, PhD); public relations (MS, PhD); speech communication (MS, PhD). *Program availability:* Part-time, evening/weekend, online learning. *Degree requirements:* For master's, thesis or alternative; for doctorate, thesis/dissertation. *Entrance requirements:* For master's and doctorate, GRE General Test, minimum GPA of 2.7. Additional exam requirements/recommendations for international students: Required—TOEFL. Electronic applications accepted.

The University of Texas at Austin, Graduate School, College of Communication, School of Journalism, Austin, TX 78712-1111. Offers MA, PhD, MA/MA, MBA/MA, MP Aff/MA. *Program availability:* Part-time. *Degree requirements:* For master's, thesis; for doctorate, one foreign language, thesis/dissertation. *Entrance requirements:* For master's and doctorate, GRE General Test. Electronic applications accepted. *Faculty research:* Politics of race, gender, and sexuality; visual ethics; media law and ethics; national television violence study; agenda setting and public opinion.

The University of Western Ontario, Faculty of Graduate Studies, Faculty of Information and Media Studies, Program in Journalism, London, ON N6A 5B8, Canada. Offers MA. *Degree requirements:* For master's, internship. *Entrance requirements:* For master's, honors degree, minimum B average during previous 2 years of course work. Additional exam requirements/recommendations for international students: Required—TOEFL (minimum score 640 paper-based), TWE (minimum score 5). Electronic applications accepted.

University of Wisconsin–Madison, Graduate School, College of Agricultural and Life Sciences, Department of Life Sciences Communication, Madison, WI 53706-1380. Offers life sciences communication (MPS, MS); mass communications (PhD). *Program availability:* Part-time. Terminal master's awarded for partial completion of doctoral program. *Degree requirements:* For master's, thesis (for some programs); for doctorate, thesis/dissertation. *Entrance requirements:* For master's, GRE; for doctorate, GRE, master's degree in a communication field or related area of study. Additional exam requirements/recommendations for international students: Required—TOEFL. Electronic applications accepted. *Faculty research:* Science and risk communication, new communication technologies, health communication, mass communication, political communication, history of communication, indigenous communication.

University of Wisconsin–Madison, Graduate School, College of Letters and Science, School of Journalism and Mass Communication, Program in Journalism and Mass Communication, Madison, WI 53706-1380. Offers MA.

Virginia Commonwealth University, Graduate School, College of Humanities and Sciences, Richard T. Robertson School of Media and Culture, Program in Mass Communications, Richmond, VA 23284-9005. Offers multimedia journalism (MS); strategic public relations (MS). *Degree requirements:* For master's, comprehensive exam, thesis optional. *Entrance requirements:* For master's, GRE General Test. Additional exam requirements/recommendations for international students: Required—TOEFL (minimum score 600 paper-based; 100 iBT); Recommended—IELTS (minimum score 6.5). Electronic applications accepted. *Faculty research:* Multimedia journalism, strategic public relations.

Wayne State University, College of Fine, Performing and Communication Arts, Department of Communication, Detroit, MI 48202. Offers communication (PhD), including democratic participation and culture, identity and representation, media,

society and culture, risk, crisis and conflict, wellness, work life and relationships; communication and new media (Graduate Certificate); communication studies (MA); dispute resolution (MADR, Graduate Certificate), including community and urban studies (MADR), conflict area studies (MADR), health and family (MADR), international conflict and cooperation (MADR), professional practice (MADR), theory of conflict (MADR), workplace (MADR); health communication (Graduate Certificate); journalism (MA); media arts (MA); media studies (MA); public relations and organizational communication (MA); JD/MADR. Doctoral program admits for fall only. *Program availability:* Online learning. *Faculty:* 21. *Students:* 63 full-time (35 women), 87 part-time (55 women); includes 54 minority (39 Black or African American, non-Hispanic/Latino; 2 Asian, non-Hispanic/Latino; 7 Hispanic/Latino; 6 Two or more races, non-Hispanic/Latino), 10 international. Average age 34. 153 applicants, 39% accepted, 27 enrolled. In 2017, 26 master's, 7 doctorates, 8 other advanced degrees awarded. *Degree requirements:* For master's, thesis (for some programs), thesis or essay; for doctorate, thesis/dissertation. *Entrance requirements:* For master's, GRE (for MA if undergraduate GPA less than 3.2), personal statement; BA or BS in communication or related field with minimum upper-division GPA of 3.2 and minimum upper-division undergraduate GPA of 3.0, and sample of academic writing (for MA); undergraduate degree with minimum upper-division GPA of 3.0 and three letters of recommendation (for MADR); for doctorate, GRE, undergraduate degree in communication or related field; master's degree in communication or related field with minimum GPA of 3.5; letters of recommendation; personal statement; sample of written scholarship. Additional exam requirements/recommendations for international students: Required—TOEFL (minimum score 100 iBT), IELTS, TWE. Application fee: $50. Electronic applications accepted. *Expenses:* Contact institution. *Financial support:* In 2017–18, 57 students received support, including 5 fellowships with tuition reimbursements available (averaging $17,400 per year), 2 research assistantships with tuition reimbursements available (averaging $20,388 per year), 20 teaching assistantships with tuition reimbursements available (averaging $18,534 per year); scholarships/grants and unspecified assistantships also available. Financial award applicants required to submit FAFSA. *Faculty research:* Democratic participation and culture; identity and representation; media, society and culture; risk, crisis and conflict; wellness, work life, and relationships. *Unit head:* Dr. Lee Wilkins, Professor and Chair, 313-577-2943, E-mail: eh8899@wayne.edu. *Application contact:* E-mail: communication@wayne.edu.
Website: http://comm.wayne.edu/

West Virginia University, Reed College of Media, Morgantown, WV 26506-6010. Offers data marketing communications (MS); integrated marketing communications (MS, Graduate Certificate); journalism (MSJ); media solutions and innovation (MSJ). *Program availability:* Part-time, online learning. *Students:* 165 full-time (122 women), 232 part-time (167 women); includes 81 minority (46 Black or African American, non-Hispanic/Latino; 5 Asian, non-Hispanic/Latino; 20 Hispanic/Latino; 10 Two or more races, non-Hispanic/Latino), 6 international. *Degree requirements:* For master's, thesis or alternative. *Entrance requirements:* For master's, GRE General Test, minimum GPA of 3.0, writing samples. Additional exam requirements/recommendations for international students: Required—TOEFL (minimum score 550 paper-based). *Application deadline:* For fall admission, 3/1 priority date for domestic students, 3/1 for international students. Application fee: $60. Electronic applications accepted. *Expenses:* Tuition, state resident: full-time $9450. Tuition, nonresident: full-time $24,390. *Financial support:* Research assistantships, teaching assistantships, career-related internships or fieldwork, Federal Work-Study, institutionally sponsored loans, health care benefits, tuition waivers (full and partial), and administrative assistantships available. Financial award application deadline: 2/1; financial award applicants required to submit FAFSA. *Faculty research:* History, law, and women in media; press management; public opinion; advertising effectiveness; international advertising. *Unit head:* Dr. Maryann Reed, Dean, 304-293-3505 Ext. 5409, Fax: 304-293-3072, E-mail: maryann.reed@mail.wvu.edu. *Application contact:* Dr. Steve Urbanski, Director of Graduate Studies/Associate Professor, 304-293-6797, Fax: 304-293-3072, E-mail: steve.urbanski@mail.wvu.edu.
Website: http://reedcollegeofmedia.wvu.edu/

Mass Communication

American University, School of Communication, Division of Public Communication, Washington, DC 20016-8001. Offers advocacy and social impact (MA); corporate communication and reputation management (MA); digital strategies and analytics (MA); poltical communication (MA); strategic communication (MA). *Accreditation:* ACEJMC. *Program availability:* Part-time, evening/weekend. *Faculty:* 23 full-time (15 women), 18 part-time/adjunct (10 women). *Students:* 52 full-time (42 women), 34 part-time (20 women); includes 31 minority (19 Black or African American, non-Hispanic/Latino; 4 Asian, non-Hispanic/Latino; 7 Hispanic/Latino; 1 Two or more races, non-Hispanic/Latino), 6 international. 282 applicants, 38% accepted, 55 enrolled. In 2017, 105 master's awarded. *Degree requirements:* For master's, comprehensive exam, thesis or alternative. *Entrance requirements:* Additional exam requirements/recommendations for international students: Required—TOEFL (minimum score 600 paper-based; 100 iBT), IELTS (minimum score 7). *Application deadline:* For fall admission, 2/1 priority date for domestic and international students. Applications are processed on a rolling basis. Application fee: $50. Electronic applications accepted. *Expenses: Tuition:* Full-time $29,556. *Required fees:* $690. Tuition and fees vary according to course load and program. *Financial support:* In 2017–18, 45 students received support, including 11 research assistantships with partial tuition reimbursements available (averaging $13,000 per year), 15 teaching assistantships with partial tuition reimbursements available (averaging $13,000 per year); career-related internships or fieldwork, Federal Work-Study, institutionally sponsored loans, scholarships/grants, tuition waivers (partial), and unspecified assistantships also available. Financial award application deadline: 2/1; financial award applicants required to submit FAFSA. *Faculty research:* Litigation and public relations, cross-cultural and intercultural communication, statistical public relations, African-Americans and women in public communication, international public relations. *Unit head:* Pallavi Kumar, Public Communication Division Director, 202-885-2047, E-mail: kumar@american.edu. *Application contact:* Christine Rials, Assistant Director of Graduate Admissions, 202-885-2040, Fax: 202-885-2019, E-mail: gradcomm@american.edu.
Website: http://www.american.edu/soc/communication/degrees/MA-SCOM.cfm

American University, School of Communication, Program in Global Media, Washington, DC 20016-8001. Offers MA. *Program availability:* Part-time. *Faculty:* 6 full-time (3 women), 2 part-time/adjunct (1 woman). *Students:* 12 full-time (9 women), 1 (woman) part-time; includes 3 minority (1 Black or African American, non-Hispanic/Latino; 1 Hispanic/Latino; 1 Two or more races, non-Hispanic/Latino), 3 international. 53 applicants, 30% accepted, 8 enrolled. In 2017, 6 master's awarded. *Degree requirements:* For master's, one foreign language, comprehensive exam, thesis or alternative. *Entrance requirements:* For master's, GRE General Test for applicants who studied within the U.S., Canada (except Quebec), UK, Australia, New Zealand, and Ireland. Additional exam requirements/recommendations for international students: Required—TOEFL (minimum score 600 paper-based; 100 iBT), IELTS (minimum score 7). *Application deadline:* For fall admission, 2/1 priority date for domestic and international students. Applications are processed on a rolling basis. Application fee: $55. Electronic applications accepted. *Expenses: Tuition:* Full-time $29,556. *Required fees:* $690. Tuition and fees vary according to course load and program. *Financial support:* In 2017–18, 10 students received support, including 1 fellowship with partial tuition reimbursement available (averaging $12,000 per year), 10 research assistantships with partial tuition reimbursements available (averaging $8,000 per year); career-related internships or fieldwork, Federal Work-Study, scholarships/grants, and unspecified assistantships also available. Financial award application deadline: 2/1; financial award applicants required to submit FAFSA. *Unit head:* Prof. Rhonda Zaharna, Program Director, 202-885-3995, Fax: 202-885-2019, E-mail: zaharna@american.edu. *Application contact:* Christine Rials, Assistant Director for Graduate Admissions, 202-885-2040, Fax: 202-885-2019, E-mail: crials@american.edu.

American University, School of International Service, Washington, DC 20016-8071. Offers comparative and regional studies (Certificate); cross-cultural communication (Certificate); development management (MS); ethics, peace, and global affairs (MA); European studies (Certificate); global environmental policy (MA, Certificate); global information technology (Certificate); global media (MA); international affairs (MA), including comparative and regional studies, global governance, politics, and security, international economic relations, natural resources and sustainable development, U.S. foreign policy and national security; international arts management (Certificate); international communication (MA, Certificate); international development (MA); international economic policy (Certificate); international economic relations (Certificate); international economics (MA); international peace and conflict resolution (MA, Certificate); international politics (Certificate); international relations (MA, PhD); international service (MIS); peacebuilding (Certificate); social enterprise (MA); the Americas (Certificate); United States foreign policy (Certificate); JD/MA. *Program availability:* Part-time, evening/weekend, 100% online. *Faculty:* 112 full-time (50 women), 46 part-time/adjunct (19 women). *Students:* 495 full-time (333 women), 518 part-time (276 women); includes 360 minority (95 Black or African American, non-Hispanic/Latino; 2 American Indian or Alaska Native, non-Hispanic/Latino; 60 Asian, non-Hispanic/Latino; 164 Hispanic/Latino; 39 Two or more races, non-Hispanic/Latino), 98 international. Average age 30. 1,559 applicants, 81% accepted, 356 enrolled. In 2017, 427 master's, 9 doctorates, 5 other advanced degrees awarded. Terminal master's awarded for partial completion of doctoral program. *Degree requirements:* For master's, one foreign language, comprehensive exam, thesis or alternative; for doctorate, one foreign language, comprehensive exam, thesis/dissertation. *Entrance requirements:* For master's, GRE; GMAT or GRE (for MA in social enterprise), transcripts, resume, 2 letters of recommendation, statement of purpose; for doctorate, GRE, transcripts, resume, 3 letters of recommendation, statement of purpose. Additional exam requirements/recommendations for international students: Required—TOEFL (minimum score 600 paper-based; 100 iBT). *Application deadline:* For fall admission, 1/15 for domestic students, 1/1 for international students; for spring admission, 10/1 for domestic students, 9/15 for international students. Application fee: $55. Electronic applications accepted. *Expenses:* Contact institution. *Financial support:* Research assistantships, teaching assistantships, institutionally sponsored loans, scholarships/grants, and unspecified assistantships available. Financial award application deadline: 1/15; financial award applicants required to submit FAFSA. *Application contact:* 202-885-1646, Fax: 202-885-1109, E-mail: sisgrad@american.edu.
Website: http://www.american.edu/sis/

The American University in Cairo, School of Global Affairs and Public Policy, Cairo, Egypt. Offers gender and women's studies (MA); global affairs (MGA); international and comparative law (LL M); international human rights law (MA); journalism and mass communication (MA); Middle East studies (MA); migration and refugee studies (MA, Diploma); public administration (MPA); public policy (MPP); television and digital journalism (MA). *Program availability:* Part-time, evening/weekend. *Faculty:* 26 full-time (11 women), 4 part-time/adjunct (3 women). *Students:* 65 full-time (50 women), 201 part-time (136 women), 39 international. Average age 29. 357 applicants, 51% accepted, 72 enrolled. In 2017, 94 master's awarded. *Degree requirements:* For master's, comprehensive exam (for some programs), thesis (for some programs). *Entrance requirements:* Additional exam requirements/recommendations for international students: Required—TOEFL (minimum score 450 paper-based; 45 iBT), IELTS (minimum score 5). *Application deadline:* For fall admission, 2/1 for domestic and international students; for spring admission, 10/15 for domestic and international students. Applications are processed on a rolling basis. Application fee: $85. Electronic applications accepted. *Expenses:* Contact institution. *Financial support:* Fellowships with partial tuition reimbursements, scholarships/grants, and unspecified assistantships available. Financial award application deadline: 3/10. *Faculty research:* Law, media and journalism; public policy and public administration; gender studies; Middle East Studies; global affairs; refugees studies. *Unit head:* Dr. Nabil Fahmy, Dean, 20-2-2615-2671, E-mail: nfahmy@aucegypt.edu. *Application contact:* Maha Hegazi, Director for Graduate Admissions, 20-2-2615-1462, E-mail: mahahegazi@aucegypt.edu.
Website: http://www.aucegypt.edu/GAPP/Pages/default.aspx

Arizona State University at the Tempe campus, Walter Cronkite School of Journalism and Mass Communication, Phoenix, AZ 85004. Offers journalism and mass communication (PhD); mass communication (MMC). *Accreditation:* ACEJMC. Terminal master's awarded for partial completion of doctoral program. *Degree requirements:* For master's, 9-hour professional capstone experience; interactive Program of Study (iPOS) submitted before completing 50 percent of required credit hours; for doctorate, comprehensive exam, thesis/dissertation, interactive Program of Study (iPOS) submitted before completing 50 percent of required credit hours. *Entrance requirements:* For master's and doctorate, GRE, minimum GPA of 3.0 or equivalent in last 2 years of work leading to bachelor's degree. Additional exam requirements/recommendations for international students: Required—TOEFL, IELTS, or PTE. Electronic applications accepted. *Expenses:* Contact institution.

Arkansas State University, Graduate School, College of Media and Communication, Department of Media, State University, AR 72467. Offers mass communications

(MSMC). *Accreditation:* ACEJMC. *Program availability:* Part-time. *Degree requirements:* For master's, comprehensive exam, thesis or alternative. *Entrance requirements:* For master's, GRE General Test or MAT, appropriate bachelor's degree, letters of reference, educational experience, professional experience, official transcripts, immunization records. Additional exam requirements/recommendations for international students: Required—TOEFL (minimum score 550 paper-based; 79 iBT), IELTS (minimum score 6), PTE (minimum score 56). Electronic applications accepted.

Boston University, College of Communication, Department of Mass Communication, Advertising, and Public Relations, Boston, MA 02215. Offers advertising (MS); mass communication (MS), including communication studies, marketing communication research; public relations (MS); JD/MS. *Program availability:* Part-time. *Faculty:* 26 full-time, 33 part-time/adjunct. *Students:* 231 full-time (195 women), 8 part-time (6 women); includes 22 minority (8 Black or African American, non-Hispanic/Latino; 2 Asian, non-Hispanic/Latino; 8 Hispanic/Latino; 4 Two or more races, non-Hispanic/Latino), 173 international. Average age 23. 529 applicants, 67% accepted, 126 enrolled. In 2017, 106 master's awarded. *Degree requirements:* For master's, comprehensive exam (for some programs), thesis (for some programs). *Entrance requirements:* For master's, GRE General Test, resume, letters of recommendation, personal statement. Additional exam requirements/recommendations for international students: Required—TOEFL (minimum score 600 paper-based; 100 iBT), IELTS (minimum score 7). *Application deadline:* For fall admission, 5/1 for domestic and international students. Applications are processed on a rolling basis. Application fee: $95. Electronic applications accepted. *Financial support:* Research assistantships, teaching assistantships with partial tuition reimbursements, career-related internships or fieldwork, Federal Work-Study, scholarships/grants, and unspecified assistantships available. Support available to part-time students. Financial award application deadline: 5/1; financial award applicants required to submit FAFSA. *Unit head:* Christopher Beaudoin, Chairperson, 617-353-3482, E-mail: mcadvpr@bu.edu. *Application contact:* Jackie Cummings, Admission and Financial Aid Counselor, 617-353-3481, E-mail: comgrad@bu.edu.
Website: http://www.bu.edu/com/academics/masscomm-ad-pr/

Brigham Young University, Graduate Studies, College of Fine Arts and Communications, School of Communications, Provo, UT 84602. Offers mass communications (MA). *Faculty:* 18 full-time (2 women). *Students:* 19 full-time (13 women), 16 part-time (10 women); includes 6 minority (2 Asian, non-Hispanic/Latino; 4 Hispanic/Latino), 4 international. Average age 30. 15 applicants, 87% accepted, 12 enrolled. In 2017, 15 master's awarded. *Degree requirements:* For master's, comprehensive exam, thesis. *Entrance requirements:* For master's, GRE, minimum GPA of 3.0 in last 60 hours of course work. Additional exam requirements/recommendations for international students: Required—TOEFL (minimum score 580 paper-based; 85 iBT). *Application deadline:* For fall admission, 3/31 priority date for domestic and international students. Applications are processed on a rolling basis. Application fee: $50. Electronic applications accepted. *Expenses: Tuition:* Full-time $6880; part-time $405 per credit hour. Tuition and fees vary according to course load, program and student's religious affiliation. *Financial support:* In 2017–18, 19 students received support, including 30 research assistantships with full and partial tuition reimbursements available (averaging $3,101 per year), 1 teaching assistantship with full tuition reimbursement available (averaging $2,752 per year); scholarships/grants and supplementary awards also available. Financial award application deadline: 4/30; financial award applicants required to submit FAFSA. *Faculty research:* Ethics, international, magazine, newspaper, media effects, social media. *Unit head:* Edward Carter, Director, 801-422-2997, Fax: 801-422-0160, E-mail: comms_secretary@byu.edu. *Application contact:* Debby Jackson, Graduate Program Manager, 801-422-2632, Fax: 801-422-0160, E-mail: debby_jackson@byu.edu.
Website: http://cfac.byu.edu/departments/communications

Bryant University, College of Arts and Sciences, Smithfield, RI 02917. Offers applied economics (MS, Graduate Certificate); communication (MA, Graduate Certificate), including general communication (MA), health care communication (MA), organizational communication (MA), professional communication (Graduate Certificate); organizational communication (Graduate Certificate), including managerial communication, public communication; sustainability practices (Graduate Certificate). *Program availability:* Part-time-only, evening/weekend. *Faculty:* 3 full-time (0 women), 2 part-time/adjunct (0 women). *Students:* 8 full-time (4 women), 10 part-time (8 women); includes 3 minority (2 Black or African American, non-Hispanic/Latino; 1 Two or more races, non-Hispanic/Latino), 2 international. Average age 25. 25 applicants, 32% accepted, 6 enrolled. In 2017, 4 master's awarded. *Degree requirements:* For master's, thesis. *Entrance requirements:* For master's, GRE. Additional exam requirements/recommendations for international students: Required—TOEFL (minimum score 550 paper-based; 80 iBT). *Application deadline:* For fall admission, 8/15 for domestic and international students; for spring admission, 1/15 for domestic and international students; for summer admission, 5/15 for domestic and international students. Applications are processed on a rolling basis. Application fee: $80. Electronic applications accepted. *Expenses:* $932 per credit hour. *Financial support:* In 2017–18, 15 fellowships with full and partial tuition reimbursements (averaging $10,483 per year) were awarded; research assistantships, scholarships/grants, and unspecified assistantships also available. Financial award application deadline: 2/15; financial award applicants required to submit FAFSA. *Faculty research:* Mass media and social construction of reality; development and improvement of media literacy skills; sociocultural influences on cognition and learning in K-12 populations, oil pollution impacts on marine and estuarine microbial communities; wetlands ecology. *Unit head:* Bradford Martin, Dean, College of Arts and Sciences, 401-232-6929, E-mail: bmartin@bryant.edu. *Application contact:* Terri Rogers, Admission Assistant, Graduate School, 401-232-6230, E-mail: graduateprograms@bryant.edu.
Website: http://gradschool.bryant.edu/arts-and-sciences/

California State University, Fullerton, Graduate Studies, College of Communications, Department of Communications, Fullerton, CA 92831-3599. Offers communications in tourism and entertainment (MA); mass communications research and theory (MA); professional communications (MA). *Program availability:* Part-time. *Faculty:* 4 full-time (3 women), 1 part-time/adjunct (0 women). *Students:* 23 full-time (18 women), 17 part-time (8 women); includes 21 minority (4 Black or African American, non-Hispanic/Latino; 1 Asian, non-Hispanic/Latino; 15 Hispanic/Latino; 1 Two or more races, non-Hispanic/Latino), 2 international. Average age 27. 41 applicants, 56% accepted, 13 enrolled. *Entrance requirements:* For master's, GRE General Test. Application fee: $55. *Financial support:* Teaching assistantships, career-related internships or fieldwork, Federal Work-Study, institutionally sponsored loans, and scholarships/grants available. Support available to part-time students. Financial award application deadline: 3/1; financial award applicants required to submit FAFSA. *Unit head:* Jason Shepard, Chair, 657-278-5301, E-mail: jshepard@fullerton.edu. *Application contact:* Coordinator, 657-278-3832.

California State University, Northridge, Graduate Studies, Mike Curb College of Arts, Media, and Communication, Department of Journalism, Northridge, CA 91330. Offers mass communication (MA). *Program availability:* Part-time, evening/weekend. *Students:* 12 full-time (6 women), 9 part-time (5 women); includes 11 minority (1 Black or African American, non-Hispanic/Latino; 2 American Indian or Alaska Native, non-Hispanic/Latino; 8 Hispanic/Latino), 4 international. Average age 31. 27 applicants, 56% accepted, 8 enrolled. In 2017, 21 master's awarded. *Degree requirements:* For master's, thesis. *Entrance requirements:* For master's, GRE General Test. Additional exam requirements/recommendations for international students: Required—TOEFL. *Application deadline:* For fall admission, 11/30 for domestic students. *Financial support:* Career-related internships or fieldwork and Federal Work-Study available. Financial award application deadline: 3/1. *Unit head:* Linda Bowen, Chair, 818-677-3135.
Website: http://www.csun.edu/journalism/

Clarion University of Pennsylvania, College of Arts, Education and Sciences, MS Program in Mass Media Arts and Journalism, Clarion, PA 16214. Offers MS. *Program availability:* Part-time, evening/weekend, online only, 100% online. *Faculty:* 5 full-time (3 women). *Students:* 9 full-time (6 women), 8 part-time (4 women); includes 6 minority (all Black or African American, non-Hispanic/Latino). Average age 33. 10 applicants, 80% accepted, 4 enrolled. In 2017, 6 master's awarded. *Entrance requirements:* For master's, statement of purpose, short essay, minimum undergraduate QPA of 3.0. Additional exam requirements/recommendations for international students: Required—TOEFL (minimum score 600 paper-based, 80 iBT) or IELTS (7). *Application deadline:* For fall admission, 8/15 priority date for domestic students, 7/15 priority date for international students; for winter admission, 11/1 priority date for domestic students; for spring admission, 1/7 priority date for domestic students, 11/15 priority date for international students; for summer admission, 4/1 priority date for domestic students. Applications are processed on a rolling basis. Application fee: $40. Electronic applications accepted. *Expenses:* $655.05 per credit. *Financial support:* Career-related internships or fieldwork, scholarships/grants, and unspecified assistantships available. Support available to part-time students. Financial award application deadline: 3/1; financial award applicants required to submit FAFSA. *Unit head:* Dr. Steven Harris, Interim Dean, 814-393-2328, E-mail: harris@clarion.edu. *Application contact:* Dana Bearer, Associate Director for Transfer, Adult and Graduate Admissions, 814-393-2337, Fax: 814-393-2772, E-mail: gradstudies@clarion.edu.

Drexel University, College of Arts and Sciences, Department of Communication, Culture and Media, Program in Communication, Philadelphia, PA 19104-2875. Offers public communication (MS); science communication (MS); technical communication (MS). *Program availability:* Part-time, evening/weekend. *Degree requirements:* For master's, internship, professional portfolio. *Entrance requirements:* For master's, GRE or minimum GPA of 3.0. Additional exam requirements/recommendations for international students: Required—TOEFL. Electronic applications accepted.

Florida International University, College of Communication, Architecture and The Arts, School of Communication and Journalism, Miami, FL 33199. Offers mass communication (MS), including global strategic communications, Spanish language journalism. *Program availability:* Part-time, evening/weekend. *Faculty:* 35 full-time (24 women), 59 part-time/adjunct (38 women). *Students:* 91 full-time (63 women), 65 part-time (47 women); includes 112 minority (20 Black or African American, non-Hispanic/Latino; 3 Asian, non-Hispanic/Latino; 84 Hispanic/Latino; 5 Two or more races, non-Hispanic/Latino), 31 international. Average age 28. 122 applicants, 68% accepted, 67 enrolled. In 2017, 86 master's awarded. *Degree requirements:* For master's, thesis optional. *Entrance requirements:* For master's, 2 letters of recommendation; minimum GPA of 3.0 during last 60 hours of upper-level work; resume. Additional exam requirements/recommendations for international students: Required—TOEFL (minimum score 550 paper-based; 80 iBT). *Application deadline:* For fall admission, 6/1 for domestic students, 4/1 for international students; for spring admission, 10/1 for domestic students, 9/1 for international students. Applications are processed on a rolling basis. Application fee: $30. Electronic applications accepted. *Expenses:* Tuition, state resident: full-time $8912; part-time $446 per credit hour. Tuition, nonresident: full-time $21,393; part-time $992 per credit hour. *Required fees:* $390; $195 per semester. *Financial support:* Institutionally sponsored loans and scholarships/grants available. Financial award application deadline: 3/1; financial award applicants required to submit FAFSA. *Unit head:* Dr. Maria Elena Villar, Chair, 305-919-5795, Fax: 305-919-5215, E-mail: mariaelena.villar@fiu.edu. *Application contact:* Nanett Rojas, Assistant Director, Graduate Admissions, 305-348-7442, Fax: 305-348-7441, E-mail: gradadm@fiu.edu.
Website: https://scj.fiu.edu/

Fordham University, Graduate School of Arts and Sciences, Department of Communication and Media Studies, New York, NY 10458. Offers public media (MA). Program offered in collaboration with WFUV and WNET. *Program availability:* Part-time, evening/weekend. *Faculty:* 11 full-time (3 women). *Students:* 17 full-time (10 women), 1 part-time (0 women); includes 10 minority (4 Black or African American, non-Hispanic/Latino; 1 American Indian or Alaska Native, non-Hispanic/Latino; 1 Asian, non-Hispanic/Latino; 4 Hispanic/Latino), 1 international. Average age 25. 91 applicants, 49% accepted, 18 enrolled. In 2017, 17 master's awarded. *Degree requirements:* For master's, thesis, internship. *Entrance requirements:* For master's, GRE General Test. Additional exam requirements/recommendations for international students: Required—TOEFL (minimum score 600 paper-based). *Application deadline:* For fall admission, 1/4 priority date for domestic students; for spring admission, 11/1 for domestic students. Application fee: $70. Electronic applications accepted. *Financial support:* In 2017–18, 3 students received support, including 2 research assistantships with full and partial tuition reimbursements available (averaging $23,200 per year); career-related internships or fieldwork, Federal Work-Study, institutionally sponsored loans, scholarships/grants, tuition waivers (full and partial), and unspecified assistantships also available. Financial award application deadline: 1/4. *Total annual research expenditures:* $1.1 million. *Unit head:* Jacqueline Reich, Chair, 718-817-4850, E-mail: jreich8@fordham.edu. *Application contact:* Travis Strattion, Interim Director of Graduate Admissions, 718-817-4417, Fax: 718-817-3566, E-mail: tstrattion@fordham.edu.

The George Washington University, Columbian College of Arts and Sciences, School of Media and Public Affairs, Washington, DC 20052. Offers MA, Graduate Certificate. *Faculty:* 24 full-time (10 women), 27 part-time/adjunct (7 women). *Students:* 33 full-time (20 women), 17 part-time (13 women); includes 11 minority (4 Black or African American, non-Hispanic/Latino; 5 Hispanic/Latino; 2 Two or more races, non-Hispanic/Latino), 7 international. Average age 27. 98 applicants, 55% accepted, 20 enrolled. In 2017, 23 master's, 13 other advanced degrees awarded. *Entrance requirements:* For master's, GRE General Test. Additional exam requirements/recommendations for international students: Required—TOEFL (minimum score 550 paper-based; 80 iBT). *Application deadline:* For fall admission, 4/1 priority date for domestic students, 1/15 priority date for international students; for spring admission, 10/1 priority date for domestic students, 9/1 priority date for international students. Applications are processed on a rolling basis. Application fee: $75. Electronic applications accepted. *Expenses: Tuition:* Full-time $28,800; part-time $1655 per credit hour. *Required fees:* $45; $2.75 per credit hour. *Financial support:* In 2017–18, fellowships with tuition reimbursements (averaging $10,000 per year), teaching assistantships with tuition reimbursements (averaging $5,000 per year) were awarded. Financial award application deadline: 1/15. *Unit head:* Frank Sesno, Director, 202-994-9553, E-mail: sesno@gwu.edu. *Application contact:* Information Contact, 202-994-6227, Fax: 202-994-5806, E-mail: smpa@gwu.edu.
Website: http://smpa.gwu.edu/

Georgia State University, College of Arts and Sciences, Department of Communication, Atlanta, GA 30302-3083. Offers film, video, and digital imaging (MA), including critical studies, production, screenwriting; human communication and social

influence (MA); mass communication (MA); media and society (PhD); moving image studies (PhD); public communication (PhD); rhetoric and politics (PhD). *Program availability:* Part-time. *Faculty:* 57 full-time (34 women). *Students:* 71 full-time (51 women), 17 part-time (9 women); includes 36 minority (28 Black or African American, non-Hispanic/Latino; 1 Asian, non-Hispanic/Latino; 4 Hispanic/Latino; 1 Native Hawaiian or other Pacific Islander, non-Hispanic/Latino; 2 Two or more races, non-Hispanic/Latino), 15 international. Average age 33. 63 applicants, 54% accepted, 17 enrolled. In 2017, 20 master's, 10 doctorates awarded. *Degree requirements:* For master's, variable foreign language requirement, thesis (for some programs); for doctorate, comprehensive exam, thesis/dissertation. *Entrance requirements:* For master's and doctorate, GRE. Additional exam requirements/recommendations for international students: Required—TOEFL (minimum score 550 paper-based; 80 iBT), IELTS (minimum score 6.5). *Application deadline:* For fall admission, 2/10 for domestic and international students; for spring admission, 10/15 for domestic and international students. Application fee: $50. Electronic applications accepted. *Expenses:* Tuition, state resident: full-time $7020. Tuition, nonresident: full-time $22,518. *Required fees:* $2128. Tuition and fees vary according to degree level and program. *Financial support:* In 2017–18, fellowships with tuition reimbursements (averaging $15,000 per year), teaching assistantships with tuition reimbursements (averaging $15,000 per year) were awarded; career-related internships or fieldwork and unspecified assistantships also available. Financial award applicants required to submit FAFSA. *Faculty research:* New media, mass media and journalism, rhetoric, film and media studies, film production. *Unit head:* Dr. Greg Lisby, Chair, 404-413-5639, Fax: 404-413-5634, E-mail: glisby@gsu.edu. Website: http://communication.gsu.edu

Grambling State University, School of Graduate Studies and Research, College of Professional Studies, Department of Mass Communication, Grambling, LA 71245. Offers MA. *Program availability:* Part-time. *Degree requirements:* For master's, comprehensive exam, thesis optional. *Entrance requirements:* For master's, GRE, minimum GPA of 2.5 on last degree. Additional exam requirements/recommendations for international students: Required—TOEFL (minimum score 500 paper-based; 62 iBT). Electronic applications accepted.

Howard University, Cathy Hughes School of Communications, Department of Communication, Culture and Media Studies, Washington, DC 20059-0002. Offers mass communication (MA, PhD); media studies (MA, PhD). *Program availability:* Part-time, evening/weekend. *Degree requirements:* For master's, comprehensive exam (for some programs), thesis optional; for doctorate, one foreign language, comprehensive exam, thesis/dissertation. *Entrance requirements:* For master's, GRE, minimum GPA of 3.0; for doctorate, GRE, minimum graduate GPA of 3.5. Additional exam requirements/recommendations for international students: Required—TOEFL. Electronic applications accepted. *Faculty research:* Advertising, public relations, journalism new media.

Iona College, School of Arts and Science, Department of Mass Communication, New Rochelle, NY 10801-1890. Offers non-profit public relations (Certificate); public relations (MA); sports communication and media (MA). *Accreditation:* ACEJMC (one or more programs are accredited). *Program availability:* Part-time, evening/weekend. *Faculty:* 4 full-time (1 woman), 5 part-time/adjunct (0 women). *Students:* 21 full-time (12 women), 13 part-time (8 women); includes 16 minority (11 Black or African American, non-Hispanic/Latino; 1 Asian, non-Hispanic/Latino; 4 Hispanic/Latino), 1 international. Average age 27. 18 applicants, 100% accepted, 11 enrolled. In 2017, 18 master's, 3 other advanced degrees awarded. *Degree requirements:* For master's, comprehensive exam (for some programs), thesis or alternative. *Entrance requirements:* For master's, GRE General Test if undergraduate GPA is below 3.0. Additional exam requirements/recommendations for international students: Required—TOEFL (minimum score 550 paper-based; 80 iBT), IELTS (minimum score 6). *Application deadline:* For fall admission, 8/1 for domestic students, 5/1 for international students; for spring admission, 1/1 for domestic students, 9/1 for international students. Applications are processed on a rolling basis. Electronic applications accepted. *Expenses:* Contact institution. *Financial support:* In 2017–18, 8 students received support. Scholarships/grants, tuition waivers (partial), and unspecified assistantships available. Support available to part-time students. Financial award application deadline: 4/15; financial award applicants required to submit FAFSA. *Faculty research:* Media ecology, new media, corporate communication, media images, organizational learning in public relations, media law, medicine ethics. *Unit head:* Anthony Kelso, PhD, Chair, 914-633-7795, E-mail: akelso@iona.edu. *Application contact:* Katelyn Brunck, Assistant Director of Graduate Admissions, 914-633-2492, Fax: 914-633-2277, E-mail: kbrunck@iona.edu. Website: http://www.iona.edu/Academics/School-of-Arts-Science/Departments/Mass-Communication/Graduate-Programs.aspx

Iowa State University of Science and Technology, Greenlee School of Journalism and Communication, Ames, IA 50011. Offers journalism and mass communication (MS). *Entrance requirements:* For master's, GRE General Test. Additional exam requirements/recommendations for international students: Required—TOEFL (minimum score 570 paper-based; 88 iBT), IELTS (minimum score 6.5). Electronic applications accepted.

Kansas State University, Graduate School, College of Arts and Sciences, A.Q. Miller School of Journalism and Mass Communications, Manhattan, KS 66506. Offers advertising (MS); community journalism (MS); global communication (MS); health communication (MS); media management (MS); public relations (MS). *Program availability:* Part-time, evening/weekend. *Degree requirements:* For master's, comprehensive exam, thesis. *Entrance requirements:* For master's, GRE General Test, minimum GPA of 3.0. Additional exam requirements/recommendations for international students: Required—TOEFL (minimum score 79 iBT). Electronic applications accepted. *Faculty research:* Health communication, risk communication, strategic communications, community journalism, global communication.

Kent State University, College of Communication and Information, School of Journalism and Mass Communication, Kent, OH 44242-0001. Offers journalism and mass communication (MA), including media management, public relations, reporting and editing-broadcast, reporting and editing-convergence, reporting and editing-journalism educators, reporting and editing-magazine, reporting and editing-newspaper. *Program availability:* Part-time, online learning. *Faculty:* 15 full-time (8 women), 14 part-time/adjunct (7 women). *Students:* 13 full-time (8 women), 74 part-time (51 women); includes 14 minority (11 Black or African American, non-Hispanic/Latino; 2 Hispanic/Latino; 1 Two or more races, non-Hispanic/Latino), 4 international. Average age 35. 24 applicants, 71% accepted, 13 enrolled. In 2017, 58 master's awarded. *Degree requirements:* For master's, thesis or project. *Entrance requirements:* For master's, GRE, minimum GPA of 3.0, statement of purpose, 3 online recommendations, resume. Additional exam requirements/recommendations for international students: Required—TOEFL (minimum score 587 paper-based, 94 iBT), Michigan English Language Assessment Battery (minimum score 82), IELTS (minimum score 7.0) or PTE (minimum score 65). *Application deadline:* For fall admission, 7/1 for domestic and international students. Applications are processed on a rolling basis. Application fee: $45 ($70 for international students). Electronic applications accepted. *Expenses:* Tuition, state resident: full-time $11,310; part-time $515 per credit hour. Tuition, nonresident: full-time $20,396; part-time $928 per credit hour. *International tuition:* $18,544 full-time. *Financial support:* Research assistantships with full tuition reimbursements, teaching assistantships with full tuition reimbursements, scholarships/grants, and unspecified

assistantships available. Financial award application deadline: 2/16. *Unit head:* Jeff Fruit, Interim Director and Professor, 330-672-2572, E-mail: jmc@kent.edu. *Application contact:* Mark Goodman, Graduate Coordinator/Professor, 330-672-6239, E-mail: mgoodm10@kent.edu.
Website: http://www.kent.edu/jmc

Lindenwood University, Graduate Programs, School of Arts, Media, and Communications, St. Charles, MO 63301-1695. Offers advertising (MA); art history (MA); cinema and media arts (MFA); communications (MA); digital and Web design (MA); fashion and business design (MS); journalism (MA); mass communications (MA); social media and digital content (MS). *Program availability:* Part-time. *Faculty:* 23 full-time (6 women), 8 part-time/adjunct (4 women). *Students:* 26 full-time (13 women), 11 part-time (8 women); includes 3 minority (1 American Indian or Alaska Native, non-Hispanic/Latino; 2 Hispanic/Latino), 7 international. Average age 33. 60 applicants, 45% accepted, 16 enrolled. In 2017, 11 master's awarded. *Degree requirements:* For master's, thesis (for some programs), minimum cumulative GPA of 3.0. *Entrance requirements:* For master's, audition or interview, minimum GPA of 3.0, portfolio, letter of recommendation. Additional exam requirements/recommendations for international students: Required—TOEFL (minimum score 550 paper-based; 80 iBT); Recommended—IELTS (minimum score 6.5). *Application deadline:* For fall admission, 8/27 priority date for domestic and international students; for spring admission, 1/14 for domestic students, 1/14 priority date for international students; for summer admission, 6/4 priority date for domestic and international students. Applications are processed on a rolling basis. Application fee: $30 ($100 for international students). Electronic applications accepted. *Expenses:* Tuition: Full-time $16,300; part-time $460 per credit. *Required fees:* $660; $330 per credit. Tuition and fees vary according to degree level and program. *Financial support:* In 2017–18, 34 students received support. Career-related internships or fieldwork, institutionally sponsored loans, scholarships/grants, tuition waivers (partial), and unspecified assistantships available. Financial award application deadline: 6/30; financial award applicants required to submit FAFSA. *Unit head:* Dr. Joseph Alsobrook, Dean, School of Arts, Media, and Communications, 636-949-4164, Fax: 636-949-4910, E-mail: jalsobrook@lindenwood.edu. *Application contact:* Kara Schilli, Director, Evening and Graduate Admissions, 636-949-4349, Fax: 636-949-4109, E-mail: adultadmissions@lindenwood.edu.
Website: http://www.lindenwood.edu/academics/academic-schools/school-of-arts-media-and-communications/

Louisiana State University and Agricultural & Mechanical College, Graduate School, Manship School of Mass Communication, Baton Rouge, LA 70803. Offers MMC, PhD, JD/MMC. *Accreditation:* ACEJMC. *Faculty:* 24 full-time (10 women). *Students:* 50 full-time (34 women), 9 part-time (5 women); includes 17 minority (16 Black or African American, non-Hispanic/Latino; 1 Two or more races, non-Hispanic/Latino), 9 international. Average age 27. 51 applicants, 65% accepted, 22 enrolled. In 2017, 16 master's, 6 doctorates awarded. *Financial support:* In 2017–18, 29 research assistantships (averaging $21,011 per year), 13 teaching assistantships (averaging $25,523 per year) were awarded. *Total annual research expenditures:* $93,684.

Lynn University, Eugene M. and Christine E. Lynn College of Communication and Design, Boca Raton, FL 33431-5598. Offers communication and media (MS), including design strategies for Web development, digital media, media studies and practice; digital media (Certificate); graphic and Web design (MFA); visual effects animation (MFA); Web design and technology (MS). *Program availability:* Part-time, evening/weekend. *Faculty:* 14 full-time (9 women), 7 part-time/adjunct (1 woman). *Students:* 35 full-time (21 women), 33 part-time (13 women); includes 31 minority (12 Black or African American, non-Hispanic/Latino; 2 American Indian or Alaska Native, non-Hispanic/Latino; 2 Asian, non-Hispanic/Latino; 14 Hispanic/Latino; 1 Two or more races, non-Hispanic/Latino), 12 international. Average age 27. 59 applicants, 92% accepted, 44 enrolled. In 2017, 17 master's awarded. *Degree requirements:* For master's, thesis (for some programs), completion of degree in four calendar years; minimum cumulative GPA of 3.0 and C grade or higher in each course; orientation seminar (one credit); 36 credits of foundation and specialization or a thesis. *Entrance requirements:* For master's, bachelor's degree from accredited institution, minimum undergraduate GPA of 3.0, official undergraduate transcripts, letter of recommendation from academic or professional source, writing sample demonstrating capacity to perform at graduate level. Additional exam requirements/recommendations for international students: Required—TOEFL (minimum score 550 paper-based; 80 iBT), IELTS (minimum score 6.5). *Application deadline:* For fall admission, 8/18 for domestic students, 8/4 for international students; for spring admission, 12/15 for domestic students, 12/1 for international students; for summer admission, 4/17 for domestic students, 4/3 for international students. Applications are processed on a rolling basis. Application fee: $45. Electronic applications accepted. *Expenses:* $740 per credit. *Financial support:* Career-related internships or fieldwork, Federal Work-Study, institutionally sponsored loans, scholarships/grants, tuition waivers (partial), and unspecified assistantships available. Support available to part-time students. Financial award application deadline: 8/1; financial award applicants required to submit FAFSA. *Unit head:* Dr. David L. Jaffe, Dean, 561-237-7099, Fax: 561-237-7097, E-mail: djaffe@lynn.edu. *Application contact:* Steven Pruitt, Director of Graduate Admission, 561-237-7834, Fax: 561-237-7100, E-mail: admission@lynn.edu.
Website: https://www.lynn.edu/academics/colleges-schools/communication-and-design

Marquette University, Graduate School, College of Communication, Milwaukee, WI 53201-1881. Offers advertising and public relations (MA); communication studies (MA); digital storytelling (Certificate); journalism (MA); mass communication (MA); science, health and environmental communication (MA). *Accreditation:* ACEJMC (one or more programs are accredited). *Program availability:* Part-time, evening/weekend. *Degree requirements:* For master's, comprehensive exam, thesis or alternative. *Entrance requirements:* For master's, GRE, official transcripts from all current and previous colleges/universities except Marquette, three letters of recommendation, statement of academic and professional goals. Additional exam requirements/recommendations for international students: Required—TOEFL (minimum score 530 paper-based). Electronic applications accepted. *Faculty research:* Urban journalism, gender and communication, intercultural communication, religious communication.

Middle Tennessee State University, College of Graduate Studies, College of Mass Communication, Program in Mass Communication, Murfreesboro, TN 37132. Offers MS. *Program availability:* Part-time, evening/weekend, online learning. *Degree requirements:* For master's, comprehensive exam, thesis optional. *Entrance requirements:* For master's, GRE. Additional exam requirements/recommendations for international students: Required—TOEFL (minimum score 525 paper-based; 71 iBT) or IELTS (minimum score 6).

Murray State University, Arthur J. Bauernfeind College of Business, Department of Journalism and Mass Communications, Murray, KY 42071. Offers mass communications (MA, MS), including public relations. *Program availability:* Part-time. *Faculty:* 7 full-time (4 women), 2 part-time/adjunct (0 women). *Students:* 18 full-time (6 women), 11 part-time (9 women); includes 1 minority (Two or more races, non-Hispanic/Latino), 15 international. Average age 28. 41 applicants, 90% accepted, 10 enrolled. In 2017, 6 master's awarded. *Entrance requirements:* For master's, GRE or GMAT, minimum university GPA of 2.75. Additional exam requirements/recommendations for

international students: Required—TOEFL (minimum score 527 paper-based; 51 iBT). *Application deadline:* Applications are processed on a rolling basis. Application fee: $40 ($50 for international students). Electronic applications accepted. *Expenses:* Tuition, state resident: full-time $9504. Tuition, nonresident: full-time $26,811. *International tuition:* $14,400 full-time. Tuition and fees vary according to course load, degree level and reciprocity agreements. *Financial support:* Research assistantships, Federal Work-Study, and unspecified assistantships available. Financial award applicants required to submit FAFSA. *Faculty research:* Mass media, audience analysis, press and politics, government open records laws, public relations. *Unit head:* Dr. Debbie Owens, Associate Professor/Interim Chair, 270-809-6318, Fax: 270-809-2390, E-mail: dowens@murraystate.edu. *Application contact:* Kaitlyn Burzysnki, Interim Assistant Director for Graduate Admission and Records, 270-809-5732, Fax: 270-809-3780, E-mail: msu.graduateadmissions@murraystate.edu.
Website: http://www.murraystate.edu/academics/CollegesDepartments/CollegeOfBusiness/Programs/JournalismAndMassCommunications/graduate/masscomm.aspx

North Dakota State University, College of Graduate and Interdisciplinary Studies, College of Arts, Humanities and Social Sciences, Department of Communication, Fargo, ND 58102. Offers communication (PhD); mass communication (MA, MS); speech communication (MA, MS). *Program availability:* Part-time, online learning. Terminal master's awarded for partial completion of doctoral program. *Degree requirements:* For master's, thesis (for some programs); for doctorate, comprehensive exam, thesis/dissertation, 2-3 publications. *Entrance requirements:* For master's, GRE, minimum undergraduate GPA of 3.25; for doctorate, GRE, minimum undergraduate GPA of 3.5. Additional exam requirements/recommendations for international students: Required—TOEFL (minimum score 600 paper-based; 100 iBT), IELTS (minimum score 7). Electronic applications accepted. *Faculty research:* Communication and rhetorical theory, organizational communication, broadcast and print journalism, international communication, public relations and advertising.

Oklahoma State University, College of Arts and Sciences, School of Media and Strategic Communications, Stillwater, OK 74078. Offers mass communication (MS). *Faculty:* 17 full-time (6 women), 5 part-time/adjunct (1 woman). *Students:* 16 full-time (13 women), 13 part-time (7 women); includes 7 minority (1 Black or African American, non-Hispanic/Latino; 3 American Indian or Alaska Native, non-Hispanic/Latino; 1 Hispanic/Latino; 2 Two or more races, non-Hispanic/Latino), 2 international. Average age 27. 12 applicants, 83% accepted, 9 enrolled. In 2017, 15 master's awarded. *Entrance requirements:* For master's, GRE, minimum GPA of 3.0. Additional exam requirements/recommendations for international students: Required—TOEFL (minimum score 550 paper-based; 79 iBT). *Application deadline:* For fall admission, 3/1 priority date for international students; for spring admission, 8/1 priority date for international students. Applications are processed on a rolling basis. Application fee: $40 ($75 for international students). Electronic applications accepted. *Expenses:* Tuition, state resident: full-time $4019; part-time $2679.60 per year. Tuition, nonresident: full-time $15,286; part-time $10,190.40 per year. *Required fees:* $2129; $1419 per unit. Tuition and fees vary according to program. *Financial support:* Research assistantships, teaching assistantships, career-related internships or fieldwork, Federal Work-Study, scholarships/grants, health care benefits, tuition waivers (partial), and unspecified assistantships available. Support available to part-time students. Financial award application deadline: 3/1; financial award applicants required to submit FAFSA. *Unit head:* Dr. Craig Freem, Director, 405-744-7676, Fax: 405-744-7104, E-mail: freemanc@okstate.edu.
Website: http://media.okstate.edu

Penn State University Park, Graduate School, Donald P. Bellisario College of Communications, Department of Communications, University Park, PA 16802. Offers mass communications (PhD); media studies (MA). *Unit head:* Dr. Marie C. Hardin, Dean, 814-863-1484, Fax: 814-863-8044. *Application contact:* Lori Hawn, Director, Graduate Student Services, 814-865-1795, Fax: 814-863-4627, E-mail: l-gswww@lists.psu.edu.
Website: http://comm.psu.edu/

Point Park University, School of Communication, Pittsburgh, PA 15222-1984. Offers communication technology (MA); media communication (MA). *Program availability:* Part-time, evening/weekend. *Degree requirements:* For master's, comprehensive exam (for some programs), thesis or alternative. *Entrance requirements:* For master's, GRE (if GPA less than 2.75), minimum GPA of 2.75, 2 letters of recommendation, statement of intent. Additional exam requirements/recommendations for international students: Required—TOEFL (minimum score 570 paper-based; 88 iBT), IELTS (minimum score 6.5); Recommended—TWE (minimum score 5). Electronic applications accepted.

St. Cloud State University, School of Graduate Studies, College of Liberal Arts, Department of Mass Communications, St. Cloud, MN 56301-4498. Offers MS. *Degree requirements:* For master's, thesis or alternative. *Entrance requirements:* For master's, minimum GPA of 2.75. Additional exam requirements/recommendations for international students: Required—Michigan English Language Assessment Battery; Recommended—TOEFL (minimum score 600 paper-based), IELTS (minimum score 6.5). Electronic applications accepted.

St. John's University, College of Professional Studies, Department of Mass Communications, Queens, NY 11439. Offers international communications (MS). *Faculty:* 15 full-time (7 women), 51 part-time/adjunct (31 women). *Students:* 43 full-time (29 women), 7 part-time (5 women); includes 24 minority (16 Black or African American, non-Hispanic/Latino; 2 Asian, non-Hispanic/Latino; 6 Hispanic/Latino), 15 international. Average age 25. 63 applicants, 75% accepted, 25 enrolled. In 2017, 19 master's awarded. *Entrance requirements:* For master's, letters of recommendation, transcripts, resume, personal statement, proficiency in a foreign language. Additional exam requirements/recommendations for international students: Required—TOEFL (minimum score 90 iBT), IELTS (minimum score 6.5). *Application deadline:* For fall admission, 5/1 for domestic students; for spring admission, 11/1 for domestic students. Applications are processed on a rolling basis. Application fee: $70. Electronic applications accepted. *Expenses:* *Tuition:* Full-time $44,280; part-time $1230 per credit. *Required fees:* $340; $340 per credit. Tuition and fees vary according to course load, degree level and program. *Financial support:* Research assistantships, teaching assistantships, scholarships/grants, and unspecified assistantships available. Financial award application deadline: 2/1; financial award applicants required to submit FAFSA. *Unit head:* Prof. Alla Baeva, Chair, 718-990-2036, E-mail: baevaa@stjohns.edu. *Application contact:* Robert Medrano, Director of Graduate Admission, 718-990-1601, Fax: 718-990-5686, E-mail: gradhelp@stjohns.edu.
Website: https://www.stjohns.edu/academics/schools-and-colleges/college-professional-studies/mass-communication

San Jose State University, Graduate Studies and Research, College of Health and Human Sciences, San Jose, CA 95192-0049. Offers criminology (MS), including global criminology, law and justice; justice studies (MS); kinesiology (MA), including athletic training, exercise physiology, interdisciplinary, sport studies, sports management; library and information science (MLIS); mass communications (MS); nursing (MS), including family nurse practitioner; nutritional science (MS); occupational therapy (MS); public health (MPH); social work (MSW); MD/M Div. *Program availability:* Part-time, 100% online, blended/hybrid learning. *Faculty:* 15 full-time (7 women), 6 part-time/adjunct (3 women). *Students:* 517 full-time (407 women), 405 part-time (302 women); includes 523 minority (39 Black or African American, non-Hispanic/Latino; 2 American Indian or Alaska Native, non-Hispanic/Latino; 141 Asian, non-Hispanic/Latino; 226 Hispanic/Latino; 2 Native Hawaiian or other Pacific Islander, non-Hispanic/Latino; 113 Two or more races, non-Hispanic/Latino), 14 international. Average age 32. 1,250 applicants, 45% accepted, 375 enrolled. In 2017, 808 master's awarded. *Degree requirements:* For master's, thesis (for some programs), graduate writing assessment. *Entrance requirements:* Additional exam requirements/recommendations for international students: Required—TOEFL (minimum score 550 paper-based; 80 iBT), IELTS (minimum score 6.5), PTE (minimum score 53). *Application deadline:* For fall admission, 2/1 for domestic and international students. Applications are processed on a rolling basis. Application fee: $55. Electronic applications accepted. *Expenses:* Tuition, state resident: full-time $7176. Tuition, nonresident: full-time $16,680. Tuition and fees vary according to course load and program. *Financial support:* Fellowships, research assistantships, teaching assistantships, career-related internships or fieldwork, Federal Work-Study, scholarships/grants, and tuition waivers (full and partial) available. Support available to part-time students. Financial award application deadline: 4/24; financial award applicants required to submit FAFSA. *Unit head:* Dr. Mary Schutten, Dean, College of Health and Human Sciences, 408-924-2900, Fax: 408-924-2901, E-mail: mary.schutten@sjsu.edu.
Website: http://www.sjsu.edu/casa/

Southern Illinois University Carbondale, Graduate School, College of Mass Communication and Media Arts, Department of Mass Communication and Media Arts, Carbondale, IL 62901-4701. Offers MFA, PhD. *Degree requirements:* For doctorate, thesis/dissertation. *Entrance requirements:* For master's, minimum GPA of 2.7; for doctorate, GRE, minimum GPA of 3.25. Additional exam requirements/recommendations for international students: Required—TOEFL (minimum score 100 iBT).

Southern Illinois University Edwardsville, Graduate School, College of Arts and Sciences, Department of Mass Communications, Program in Mass Communications, Edwardsville, IL 62026. Offers MS. *Program availability:* Part-time, evening/weekend. *Degree requirements:* For master's, comprehensive exam (for some programs), thesis (for some programs). *Entrance requirements:* Additional exam requirements/recommendations for international students: Required—TOEFL (minimum score 550 paper-based; 79 iBT), IELTS (minimum score 6.5). Electronic applications accepted.

Southern University and Agricultural and Mechanical College, Graduate School, College of Arts and Humanities, Department of Mass Communication, Baton Rouge, LA 70813. Offers MA. *Degree requirements:* For master's, comprehensive exam, thesis. *Entrance requirements:* For master's, GRE General Test. Additional exam requirements/recommendations for international students: Required—TOEFL (minimum score 525 paper-based). *Faculty research:* Photojournalism, textbook on broadcast.

Stephen F. Austin State University, Graduate School, College of Applied Arts and Science, Department of Communication, Nacogdoches, TX 75962. Offers communication (MA); mass communication (MA). *Program availability:* Part-time. *Degree requirements:* For master's, comprehensive exam, thesis optional. *Entrance requirements:* For master's, GRE General Test. Additional exam requirements/recommendations for international students: Required—TOEFL (minimum score 550 paper-based).

Syracuse University, S. I. Newhouse School of Public Communications, MS Program in Communications Management, Syracuse, NY 13244. Offers MS. *Accreditation:* ACEJMC. *Program availability:* Part-time, evening/weekend, online learning. *Students:* Average age 43. In 2017, 22 master's awarded. *Degree requirements:* For master's, comprehensive exam, internship. *Entrance requirements:* For master's, GRE General Test, minimum 5 years of experience in public relations or related field; portfolio; 3 letters of recommendation including 1 from current employer, client, or business partner; resume. Additional exam requirements/recommendations for international students: Required—TOEFL (minimum score 100 iBT). *Application deadline:* For fall admission, 1/15 priority date for domestic and international students. Application fee: $45. Electronic applications accepted. *Financial support:* Fellowships, research assistantships, and teaching assistantships available. Financial award application deadline: 1/1; financial award applicants required to submit FAFSA. *Faculty research:* Public relations theory, public opinion research, communications law, public relations management, measurement and evaluation in communication. *Unit head:* Anthony D'Angelo, Professor of Practice/Director, 315-443-3858, E-mail: dangeloa@syr.edu. *Application contact:* Martha Coria, Graduate Records Office, 315-443-5749, E-mail: pcgrad@syr.edu.
Website: http://newhouse.syr.edu/academics/degrees/masters/communications-management

Syracuse University, S. I. Newhouse School of Public Communications, PhD Program in Mass Communications, Syracuse, NY 13244. Offers PhD. *Students:* Average age 33. In 2017, 4 doctorates awarded. *Degree requirements:* For doctorate, comprehensive exam, thesis/dissertation, qualifying exams. *Entrance requirements:* For doctorate, GRE General Test, resume, personal statement, official transcript, three letters of recommendation, writing sample. Additional exam requirements/recommendations for international students: Required—TOEFL (minimum score 100 iBT). *Application deadline:* For fall admission, 12/1 priority date for domestic and international students. Application fee: $45. Electronic applications accepted. *Financial support:* Fellowships with full tuition reimbursements, research assistantships with partial tuition reimbursements, teaching assistantships with partial tuition reimbursements, career-related internships or fieldwork, and tuition waivers (partial) available. Financial award application deadline: 12/10. *Faculty research:* Communications theory, social effects of television, theories of media content, quantitative methods for mass communications research. *Unit head:* Dr. Dennis Kinsey, Director of Doctoral Studies, 315-443-3372, Fax: 315-443-3946, E-mail: masscomm@syr.edu. *Application contact:* Amy Arends, Doctoral Office, 315-443-3372, E-mail: masscomm@syr.edu.
Website: http://newhouse.syr.edu/academics/degrees/doctoral/mass-communications

Texas Christian University, Bob Schieffer College of Communication, Department of Strategic Communication, Fort Worth, TX 76129. Offers MS. *Program availability:* Part-time. *Faculty:* 8 full-time (6 women). *Students:* 12 full-time (11 women), 2 part-time (1 woman); includes 2 minority (both Hispanic/Latino). Average age 26. 13 applicants, 69% accepted, 7 enrolled. In 2017, 10 master's awarded. *Degree requirements:* For master's, thesis or capstone project. *Entrance requirements:* For master's, GRE General Test, 15 semester hours (five courses) in undergraduate journalism, advertising or public relations, or substantial professional experience in a communication discipline as determined by the graduate faculty. Additional exam requirements/recommendations for international students: Required—TOEFL (minimum score 100 iBT). *Application deadline:* For fall admission, 7/1 for domestic and international students; for spring admission, 10/15 for domestic and international students. Applications are processed on a rolling basis. Application fee: $60. Electronic applications accepted. *Expenses:* $1,555 per credit hour. *Financial support:* In 2017–18, 12 students received support, including 11 teaching assistantships with full tuition reimbursements available (averaging $9,000 per year); tuition waivers (full) also available. Financial award application deadline: 6/15.

Faculty research: Social and digital media, advertising and public relations, health communication, crisis communication, ethics. *Unit head:* Dr. Jacque Lambiase, Department Chair, 817-257-6552, Fax: 817-257-7322, E-mail: j.lambiase@tcu.edu. *Application contact:* Dr. Julie O'Neil, Graduate Director, 817-257-6966, Fax: 817-257-7322, E-mail: j.oneil@tcu.edu.
Website: http://stco.tcu.edu/

Texas State University, The Graduate College, College of Fine Arts and Communication, Program in Mass Communication, San Marcos, TX 78666. Offers MA. *Program availability:* Part-time. *Faculty:* 18 full-time (9 women), 4 part-time/adjunct (3 women). *Students:* 29 full-time (26 women), 16 part-time (8 women); includes 24 minority (7 Black or African American, non-Hispanic/Latino; 1 American Indian or Alaska Native, non-Hispanic/Latino; 15 Hispanic/Latino; 1 Two or more races, non-Hispanic/Latino), 1 international. Average age 28. 34 applicants, 56% accepted, 9 enrolled. In 2017, 19 master's awarded. *Degree requirements:* For master's, comprehensive exam, thesis optional. *Entrance requirements:* For master's, GRE General Test (minimum preferred score of 303 with no less than 153 on the verbal section, 150 on the quantitative section, and 4.5 on the analytical writing section), baccalaureate degree from regionally-accredited institution with minimum GPA of 3.0 in last 60 hours of course work, statement of purpose, 2 letters of recommendation, current resume. Additional exam requirements/recommendations for international students: Required—TOEFL (minimum score 100 iBT), IELTS (minimum score 6.5). *Application deadline:* For fall admission, 2/1 for domestic and international students; for spring admission, 10/1 for domestic and international students. Applications are processed on a rolling basis. Application fee: $40 ($90 for international students). Electronic applications accepted. *Expenses:* Tuition, state resident: full-time $7868; part-time $3934 per semester. Tuition, nonresident: full-time $17,828; part-time $8914 per semester. *Required fees:* $2092; $1435 per semester. Tuition and fees vary according to course load. *Financial support:* In 2017–18, 30 students received support, including 12 teaching assistantships (averaging $12,475 per year); research assistantships, career-related internships or fieldwork, Federal Work-Study, institutionally sponsored loans, and unspecified assistantships also available. Support available to part-time students. Financial award application deadline: 3/1; financial award applicants required to submit FAFSA. *Faculty research:* Medicare improvements for patients. *Total annual research expenditures:* $53,256. *Unit head:* Dr. Judith Oskam, Graduate Advisor, 512-245-2656, Fax: 512-245-7649, E-mail: jo18@txstate.edu. *Application contact:* Dr. Andrea Golato, Dean of the Graduate College, 512-245-2581, Fax: 512-245-8365, E-mail: gradcollege@txstate.edu.
Website: http://www.masscomm.txstate.edu/

Texas Tech University, Graduate School, College of Media and Communication, Department of Media and Communication, Lubbock, TX 79409. Offers mass communications (MA); media and communication (PhD); strategic communication and innovation (MA). *Program availability:* Part-time, evening/weekend, 100% online, blended/hybrid learning. *Faculty:* 7 full-time (2 women), 3 part-time/adjunct (all women). *Students:* 84 full-time (43 women), 128 part-time (91 women); includes 62 minority (10 Black or African American, non-Hispanic/Latino; 2 Asian, non-Hispanic/Latino; 42 Hispanic/Latino; 8 Two or more races, non-Hispanic/Latino), 11 international. Average age 30. 163 applicants, 63% accepted, 83 enrolled. In 2017, 64 master's, 5 doctorates awarded. *Degree requirements:* For master's, thesis optional; for doctorate, comprehensive exam, thesis/dissertation. *Entrance requirements:* For doctorate, GRE. Additional exam requirements/recommendations for international students: Required—TOEFL (minimum score 550 paper-based; 79 iBT), GRE. *Application deadline:* For fall admission, 6/1 priority date for domestic students, 1/15 priority date for international students; for spring admission, 9/1 priority date for domestic students, 6/15 priority date for international students. Applications are processed on a rolling basis. Application fee: $60. Electronic applications accepted. *Expenses:* Contact institution. *Financial support:* In 2017–18, 119 students received support, including 95 fellowships (averaging $4,110 per year), 35 research assistantships (averaging $8,745 per year), 72 teaching assistantships (averaging $8,545 per year); career-related internships or fieldwork, scholarships/grants, and unspecified assistantships also available. Support available to part-time students. Financial award application deadline: 4/15; financial award applicants required to submit FAFSA. *Faculty research:* Media effects, political communication, health/science communication, critical/cultural/rhetorical, Hispanic and international communication. *Unit head:* Dr. Coy Callison, Associate Dean for Graduate Studies, 806-834-5344, E-mail: coy.callison@ttu.edu. *Application contact:* Bridget Christopherson, Graduate Program Administrative, 806-834-1619, E-mail: bridget.christopherson@ttu.edu.
Website: http://www.depts.ttu.edu/comc/

Université Laval, Faculty of Letters, Department of Information and Communication, Program in Public Communication, Québec, QC G1K 7P4, Canada. Offers MA, PhD. *Program availability:* Part-time. *Degree requirements:* For master's, thesis (for some programs). *Entrance requirements:* For master's, knowledge of French, knowledge of English. Electronic applications accepted.

The University of Alabama, Graduate School, College of Communication and Information Sciences, Communication and Information Sciences Program, Tuscaloosa, AL 35487-0172. Offers PhD. *Accreditation:* ACEJMC. *Students:* Average age 33. 22 applicants, 55% accepted, 8 enrolled. In 2017, 8 doctorates awarded. *Degree requirements:* For doctorate, comprehensive exam, thesis/dissertation. *Entrance requirements:* For doctorate, GRE, master's degree, minimum undergraduate and graduate GPA of 3.0. Additional exam requirements/recommendations for international students: Required—TOEFL (minimum score 100 iBT). *Application deadline:* For fall admission, 2/15 priority date for domestic students, 2/15 for international students; for winter admission, 11/1 priority date for domestic students, 11/1 for international students. Applications are processed on a rolling basis. Application fee: $50 ($60 for international students). Electronic applications accepted. *Financial support:* In 2017–18, 28 students received support, including fellowships with full tuition reimbursements available (averaging $15,000 per year), research assistantships with full tuition reimbursements available (averaging $13,045 per year), teaching assistantships with full tuition reimbursements available (averaging $13,045 per year); institutionally sponsored loans, health care benefits, and unspecified assistantships also available. Financial award application deadline: 3/1. *Faculty research:* Mass media; mass media effects; information studies; cultural, critical and rhetorical studies; policy and law; electronic media. *Unit head:* Dr. William Evans, Associate Dean for Graduate Studies, 205-348-3176, Fax: 205-348-6774, E-mail: wevans@ua.edu. *Application contact:* Marylou Cox, Program Assistant, 205-348-8593, E-mail: mcox@ua.edu.
Website: http://www.cis.ua.edu/graduate

University of Arkansas at Little Rock, Graduate School, College of Social Sciences and Communication, School of Mass Communication, Little Rock, AR 72204-1099. Offers MA. *Program availability:* Part-time, evening/weekend. *Degree requirements:* For master's, comprehensive exam, thesis optional. *Entrance requirements:* For master's, GRE General Test, minimum GPA of 2.7. *Faculty research:* Theory and practice of mass communication, social role of the mass media.

University of Colorado Boulder, Graduate School, College of Media, Communication and Information, Boulder, CO 80309. Offers MA, MFA, PhD. *Faculty:* 67 full-time (36 women). *Students:* 139 full-time (85 women), 7 part-time (5 women); includes 19 minority (3 Black or African American, non-Hispanic/Latino; 4 Asian, non-Hispanic/Latino; 10 Hispanic/Latino; 2 Two or more races, non-Hispanic/Latino), 16 international. Average age 31. 279 applicants, 44% accepted, 55 enrolled. In 2017, 35 master's, 10 doctorates awarded. Terminal master's awarded for partial completion of doctoral program. *Degree requirements:* For master's, comprehensive exam, thesis or alternative; for doctorate, comprehensive exam, thesis/dissertation. *Entrance requirements:* For master's, GRE General Test, minimum undergraduate GPA of 2.75; for doctorate, GRE General Test, minimum undergraduate GPA of 3.2, graduate 3.5. *Application deadline:* Applications are processed on a rolling basis. Application fee: $60 ($80 for international students). Electronic applications accepted. Application fee is waived when completed online. *Financial support:* In 2017–18, 393 students received support, including 125 fellowships (averaging $1,542 per year), 23 research assistantships with full and partial tuition reimbursements available (averaging $23,508 per year), 90 teaching assistantships with full and partial tuition reimbursements available (averaging $30,255 per year); institutionally sponsored loans, scholarships/grants, health care benefits, and unspecified assistantships also available. Financial award application deadline: 3/1; financial award applicants required to submit FAFSA. *Faculty research:* Mass communication/media; communications; journalism; electronic media; culture. *Application contact:* E-mail: cmcigrad@colorado.edu.
Website: http://www.colorado.edu/cmci/

University of Denver, Division of Arts, Humanities and Social Sciences, Department of Media, Film and Journalism Studies, Denver, CO 80208. Offers international and intercultural communication (MA); media and public communication (MA), including media and globalization, strategic communication. *Program availability:* Part-time. *Faculty:* 16 full-time (10 women), 5 part-time/adjunct (4 women). *Students:* 3 full-time (all women), 21 part-time (17 women); includes 5 minority (1 Asian, non-Hispanic/Latino; 4 Hispanic/Latino), 2 international. Average age 26. 34 applicants, 85% accepted, 8 enrolled. In 2017, 12 master's awarded. *Degree requirements:* For master's, thesis (for some programs). *Entrance requirements:* For master's, GRE General Test, bachelor's degree, transcripts, personal statement, three letters of recommendation. Additional exam requirements/recommendations for international students: Required—TOEFL (minimum score 620 paper-based; 105 iBT). *Application deadline:* For fall admission, 2/15 priority date for domestic students, 1/1 priority date for international students. Applications are processed on a rolling basis. Application fee: $65. Electronic applications accepted. *Expenses:* $31,935 per year full-time. *Financial support:* In 2017–18, 18 students received support. Teaching assistantships with tuition reimbursements available, career-related internships or fieldwork, Federal Work-Study, institutionally sponsored loans, scholarships/grants, and unspecified assistantships available. Support available to part-time students. Financial award application deadline: 2/15; financial award applicants required to submit FAFSA. *Faculty research:* Branding; public relations; health communication; social media; international communication. *Unit head:* Dr. Lynn Schofield Clark, Professor and Chair, 303-871-3984, Fax: 303-871-4949, E-mail: lynn.clark@du.edu. *Application contact:* Information Contact, 303-871-2166, E-mail: mfjs@du.edu.
Website: http://www.du.edu/ahss/mfjs

University of Florida, Graduate School, College of Journalism and Communications, Program in Mass Communication, Gainesville, FL 32611. Offers international/intercultural communication (MAMC); journalism (MAMC); mass communication (MAMC, PhD), including clinical translational science (MAMC); public relations (MAMC); science/health communication (MAMC); telecommunication (MAMC). *Accreditation:* ACEJMC. *Entrance requirements:* For master's and doctorate, GRE General Test, minimum GPA of 3.0.

University of Georgia, Grady College of Journalism and Mass Communication, Athens, GA 30602. Offers journalism and mass communication (MA); mass communication (PhD). *Degree requirements:* For master's, comprehensive exam, thesis (MA); for doctorate, comprehensive exam, thesis/dissertation. *Entrance requirements:* For master's and doctorate, GRE General Test. Additional exam requirements/recommendations for international students: Required—TOEFL, TWE for PhD. Electronic applications accepted.

University of Houston, College of Liberal Arts and Social Sciences, Jack J. Valenti School of Communication, Houston, TX 77204. Offers health communication (MA); mass communication studies (MA); public relations studies (MA); speech communication (MA). *Program availability:* Part-time. *Degree requirements:* For master's, comprehensive exam (for some programs), thesis (for some programs), 30-33 hours. *Entrance requirements:* For master's, GRE. Additional exam requirements/recommendations for international students: Required—TOEFL. Electronic applications accepted.

The University of Iowa, Graduate College, College of Liberal Arts and Sciences, School of Journalism and Mass Communication, Iowa City, IA 52242-1316. Offers journalism and media communication (MA); mass communication (PhD); strategic communication (MA); JD/MA; JD/PhD. *Degree requirements:* For master's, thesis optional, exam; for doctorate, comprehensive exam, thesis/dissertation. *Entrance requirements:* For master's and doctorate, GRE General Test, minimum GPA of 3.0. Additional exam requirements/recommendations for international students: Required—TOEFL (minimum score 637 paper-based; 110 iBT). Electronic applications accepted. *Faculty research:* Verbal and visual aspects of historical, legal, social, and cross-cultural communication.

University of Louisiana at Lafayette, College of Liberal Arts, Department of Communication, Lafayette, LA 70504. Offers mass communications (MS). *Program availability:* Part-time. *Degree requirements:* For master's, thesis optional. *Entrance requirements:* For master's, GRE General Test, minimum GPA of 2.75. Additional exam requirements/recommendations for international students: Required—TOEFL (minimum score 550 paper-based). Electronic applications accepted. *Faculty research:* Mass media problems, issues and ethics, mass communication, historical studies, conflict of interest and law and ethics in journalism, contemporary issues and trends in publications.

University of Minnesota, Twin Cities Campus, Graduate School, College of Liberal Arts, School of Journalism and Mass Communication, Minneapolis, MN 55455-0213. Offers mass communication (MA, PhD); strategic communication (professional program) (MA). *Degree requirements:* For master's, thesis; for doctorate, comprehensive exam, thesis/dissertation. *Entrance requirements:* For master's, GRE; GMAT (for strategic communications program), letters of recommendation, minimum undergraduate GPA of 3.0, writing sample; two years professional experience (for strategic communications program); for doctorate, GRE, letters of recommendation, minimum undergraduate GPA of 3.0, writing sample. Additional exam requirements/recommendations for international students: Required—TOEFL (minimum score 79 iBT). Electronic applications accepted. *Faculty research:* Communication law, regulation, and ethics; history; mass media effects; new media, health communication.

University of Nebraska–Lincoln, Graduate College, College of Journalism and Mass Communications, Lincoln, NE 68588. Offers marketing, communication and advertising (MA); professional journalism (MA). *Program availability:* Online learning. *Degree requirements:* For master's, thesis. *Entrance requirements:* For master's, samples of

work. Additional exam requirements/recommendations for international students: Required—TOEFL (minimum score 600 paper-based). Electronic applications accepted. *Faculty research:* Interactive media and the Internet, community newspapers, children's radio, advertising involvement, telecommunications policy.

University of Oklahoma, College of Arts and Sciences, Department of Communication, Norman, OK 73019. Offers communication (MA); communication technology (PhD); health communication (PhD); intercultural/international communication (PhD); organizational communication (PhD); political/mass communication (PhD); social influence/interpersonal communication (PhD). *Program availability:* Part-time. *Faculty:* 18 full-time (8 women). *Students:* 27 full-time (17 women), 36 part-time (17 women); includes 23 minority (8 Black or African American, non-Hispanic/Latino; 3 American Indian or Alaska Native, non-Hispanic/Latino; 1 Asian, non-Hispanic/Latino; 10 Hispanic/Latino; 1 Two or more races, non-Hispanic/Latino), 5 international. Average age 35. 45 applicants, 49% accepted, 10 enrolled. In 2017, 14 master's, 6 doctorates awarded. *Degree requirements:* For master's, comprehensive exam (for some programs), thesis (for some programs), comprehensive exams or thesis; for doctorate, comprehensive exam, thesis/dissertation. *Entrance requirements:* For master's, GRE (for assistantship), statement of purpose, transcripts, writing sample, letters of recommendation; for doctorate, GRE, statement of purpose, transcripts, writing sample, letters of recommendation. Additional exam requirements/recommendations for international students: Required—TOEFL (minimum score 79 iBT) or IELTS (minimum score 6.5). *Application deadline:* For fall admission, 1/15 priority date for domestic students, 1/15 for international students; for spring admission, 10/15 for domestic and international students. Application fee: $50 ($100 for international students). Electronic applications accepted. *Expenses:* Tuition, state resident: full-time $5119; part-time $213.30 per credit hour. Tuition, nonresident: full-time $19,778; part-time $824.10 per credit hour. *Required fees:* $3458; $133.55 per credit hour. $126.50 per semester. *Financial support:* In 2017–18, 29 students received support, including 1 research assistantship with full tuition reimbursement available (averaging $10,373 per year), 25 teaching assistantships with full tuition reimbursements available (averaging $16,350 per year); health care benefits also available. Financial award application deadline: 6/1; financial award applicants required to submit FAFSA. *Faculty research:* Interpersonal/social influence, organizational, political/mass communication, health communication, intercultural/international. *Total annual research expenditures:* $242,423. *Unit head:* Dr. Michael W. Kramer, Professor and Chair, 405-325-9503, Fax: 405-325-7625, E-mail: mkramer@ou.edu. *Application contact:* Shay Glover, Academic Advisor, 405-325-7710, Fax: 405-325-7625, E-mail: shay.glover@ou.edu.
Website: http://www.ou.edu/cas/comm

University of Oklahoma, Gaylord College of Journalism and Mass Communication, Program in Journalism and Mass Communication, Norman, OK 73019. Offers broadcast and electronic media (MA); journalism (MA); media arts (PhD); media management (MA); news and information (PhD); strategic communication (MA, PhD). *Program availability:* Part-time. *Students:* 24 full-time (11 women), 19 part-time (10 women); includes 5 minority (2 Black or African American, non-Hispanic/Latino; 1 Asian, non-Hispanic/Latino; 2 Hispanic/Latino), 18 international. Average age 33. 22 applicants, 64% accepted, 7 enrolled. In 2017, 10 master's awarded. *Degree requirements:* For master's, comprehensive exam (for some programs), thesis (for some programs); for doctorate, comprehensive exam, thesis/dissertation. *Entrance requirements:* For master's, GRE, resume, statement of purpose, two letters of recommendation, official transcript, minimum GPA of 3.2; for doctorate, GRE, resume, statement of purpose, three letters of recommendation, official transcript. Additional exam requirements/recommendations for international students: Required—TOEFL (minimum score 79 iBT) or IELTS (minimum score 6.5). *Application deadline:* For fall admission, 5/1 for domestic students, 3/1 for international students; for spring admission, 11/1 for domestic students, 10/1 for international students; for summer admission, 3/1 for domestic students. Applications are processed on a rolling basis. Application fee: $50 ($100 for international students). Electronic applications accepted. *Expenses:* Tuition, state resident: full-time $5119; part-time $213.30 per credit hour. Tuition, nonresident: full-time $19,778; part-time $824.10 per credit hour. *Required fees:* $3458; $133.55 per credit hour. $126.50 per semester. *Financial support:* In 2017–18, 31 students received support. Research assistantships with full tuition reimbursements available, teaching assistantships with full tuition reimbursements available, career-related internships or fieldwork, institutionally sponsored loans, scholarships/grants, health care benefits, unspecified assistantships, and McNair fellowships available. Financial award application deadline: 6/1; financial award applicants required to submit FAFSA. *Faculty research:* Digital advertising, interactivity and user experience; news sociology and journalism ethics; media management and digital change; corporate, non-profit and global public relations; media psychology and media effects. *Unit head:* Dr. Peter Gade, Director of Graduate Studies/Professor of Journalism, 405-325-5528, Fax: 405-325-7565, E-mail: pgade@ou.edu. *Application contact:* Larry Laneer, Administrative Assistant to Director/Graduate Advisor, 405-325-2722, Fax: 405-325-7565, E-mail: llaneer@ou.edu.
Website: http://www.ou.edu/content/gaylord/graduate

University of Puerto Rico–Río Piedras, School of Communication, San Juan, PR 00931-3300. Offers MA. *Program availability:* Part-time. *Degree requirements:* For master's, comprehensive exam, thesis. *Entrance requirements:* For master's, GRE, PAEG, minimum GPA of 3.0, 2 letters of recommendation, interview.

University of South Florida, College of Arts and Sciences, Zimmerman School of Advertising and Mass Communications, Tampa, FL 33620-9951. Offers mass communications (MA), including media studies, multimedia journalism, strategic communication management. *Program availability:* Part-time, evening/weekend. *Faculty:* 10 full-time (6 women). *Students:* 25 full-time (20 women), 25 part-time (20 women); includes 7 minority (4 Black or African American, non-Hispanic/Latino; 2 Hispanic/Latino; 1 Native Hawaiian or other Pacific Islander, non-Hispanic/Latino), 29 international. Average age 26. 28 applicants, 64% accepted, 15 enrolled. In 2017, 8 master's awarded. *Degree requirements:* For master's, comprehensive exam, thesis optional. *Entrance requirements:* For master's, GRE General Test, minimum GPA of 3.0 in last 60 hours of course work, three letters of recommendation, letter of intent, resume/curriculum vitae. Additional exam requirements/recommendations for international students: Required—TOEFL (minimum score 550 paper-based; 79 iBT) or IELTS (minimum score 6.5). *Application deadline:* For fall admission, 2/15 priority date for domestic and international students. Application fee: $30. Electronic applications accepted. *Financial support:* In 2017–18, 10 students received support, including 9 teaching assistantships with tuition reimbursements available (averaging $10,513 per year); unspecified assistantships also available. Financial award application deadline: 2/28. *Faculty research:* First Amendment analysis, civic journalism, public opinion, media ethics, media effects research in sports public relations, public relations management, advertisement, telecommunications. *Total annual research expenditures:* $78,680. *Unit head:* Dr. Wayne Garcia, Director and Senior Instructor, 813-498-1925, Fax: 813-974-2592, E-mail: wgarcia@usf.edu. *Application contact:* Dr. Artermio Ramirez, Jr., Associate Director, Fax: 813-974-2592, E-mail: aramirez2@usf.edu.
Website: http://masscom.usf.edu/grad/

University of South Florida, Innovative Education, Tampa, FL 33620-9951. Offers adult, career and higher education (Graduate Certificate), including college teaching, leadership in developing human resources, leadership in higher education; Africana studies (Graduate Certificate), including diasporas and health disparities, genocide and human rights; aging studies (Graduate Certificate), including gerontology; art research (Graduate Certificate), including museum studies; business foundations (Graduate Certificate); chemical and biomedical engineering (Graduate Certificate), including materials science and engineering, water, health and sustainability; child and family studies (Graduate Certificate), including positive behavior support; civil and industrial engineering (Graduate Certificate), including transportation systems analysis; community and family health (Graduate Certificate), including maternal and child health, social marketing and public health, violence and injury: prevention and intervention, women's health; criminology (Graduate Certificate), including criminal justice administration; data science for public administration (Graduate Certificate); digital humanities (Graduate Certificate); educational measurement and research (Graduate Certificate), including evaluation; English (Graduate Certificate), including comparative literary studies, creative writing, professional and technical communication; entrepreneurship (Graduate Certificate); environmental health (Graduate Certificate), including safety management; epidemiology and biostatistics (Graduate Certificate), including applied biostatistics, biostatistics, concepts and tools of epidemiology, epidemiology, epidemiology of infectious diseases; geography, environment and planning (Graduate Certificate), including community development, environmental policy and management, geographical information systems; geology (Graduate Certificate), including hydrogeology; global health (Graduate Certificate), including disaster management, global health and Latin American and Caribbean studies, global health practice, humanitarian assistance, infection control; government and international affairs (Graduate Certificate), including Cuban studies, globalization studies; health policy and management (Graduate Certificate), including health management and leadership, public health policy and programs; hearing specialist: early intervention (Graduate Certificate); industrial and management systems engineering (Graduate Certificate), including systems engineering, technology management; information studies (Graduate Certificate), including school library media specialist; information systems/decision sciences (Graduate Certificate), including analytics and business intelligence; instructional technology (Graduate Certificate), including distance education, Florida digital/virtual educator, instructional design, multimedia design, Web design; internal medicine, bioethics and medical humanities (Graduate Certificate), including biomedical ethics; Latin American and Caribbean studies (Graduate Certificate); leadership for coastal resiliency planning (Graduate Certificate); mass communications (Graduate Certificate), including multimedia journalism; mathematics and statistics (Graduate Certificate), including mathematics; medicine (Graduate Certificate), including aging and neuroscience, bioinformatics, biotechnology, brain fitness and memory management, clinical investigation, hand and upper limb rehabilitation, health informatics, health sciences, integrative weight management, intellectual property, medicine and gender, metabolic and nutritional medicine, metabolic cardiology, pharmacy sciences; national and competitive intelligence (Graduate Certificate); nursing (Graduate Certificate), including simulation based academic fellowship in advanced pain management; psychological and social foundations (Graduate Certificate), including career counseling, college teaching, diversity in education, mental health counseling, school counseling; public affairs (Graduate Certificate), including nonprofit management, public management, research administration; public health (Graduate Certificate), including assessing chemical toxicity and public health risks, health equity, pharmacoepidemiology, public health generalist, toxicology, translational research in adolescent behavioral health; public health practices (Graduate Certificate), including planning for healthy communities; rehabilitation and mental health counseling (Graduate Certificate), including integrative mental health care, marriage and family therapy, rehabilitation technology; secondary education (Graduate Certificate), including ESOL, foreign language education: culture and content, foreign language education: professional; social work (Graduate Certificate), including geriatric social work/clinical gerontology; special education (Graduate Certificate), including autism spectrum disorder, disabilities education: severe/profound; world languages (Graduate Certificate), including teaching English as a second language (TESL) or foreign language. *Unit head:* Dr. Cynthia DeLuca, Associate Vice President and Assistant Vice Provost, 813-974-3077, Fax: 813-974-7061, E-mail: deluca@usf.edu. *Application contact:* Owen Hooper, Director, Summer and Alternative Calendar Programs, 813-974-6917, E-mail: hooper@usf.edu.
Website: http://www.usf.edu/innovative-education/

University of Wisconsin–Madison, Graduate School, College of Letters and Science, School of Journalism and Mass Communication, Program in Journalism and Mass Communication, Madison, WI 53706-1380. Offers MA.

University of Wisconsin–Madison, Graduate School, College of Letters and Science, School of Journalism and Mass Communication, Program in Mass Communication, Madison, WI 53706-1380. Offers PhD. *Degree requirements:* For doctorate, thesis/dissertation.

University of Wisconsin–Superior, Graduate Division, Department of Communicating Arts, Superior, WI 54880-4500. Offers mass communication (MA); speech communication (MA); theater (MA). *Program availability:* Part-time. *Degree requirements:* For master's, comprehensive exam, thesis or alternative, position paper or project. *Entrance requirements:* For master's, minimum GPA of 2.75. Electronic applications accepted. *Faculty research:* Multimedia technology, ethics in journalism, diversity, electronic portfolio assessment.

University of Wisconsin–Whitewater, School of Graduate Studies, College of Arts and Communications, Department of Communication, Whitewater, WI 53190-1790. Offers corporate communication (MS); mass communication (MS). *Program availability:* Part-time, evening/weekend, online learning. *Degree requirements:* For master's, thesis or alternative. *Entrance requirements:* For master's, 2 letters of recommendation, goal statement. Additional exam requirements/recommendations for international students: Required—TOEFL (minimum score 550 paper-based; 80 iBT), IELTS (minimum score 6). Electronic applications accepted.

Virginia Commonwealth University, Graduate School, College of Humanities and Sciences, Richard T. Robertson School of Media and Culture, Program in Mass Communications, Richmond, VA 23284-9005. Offers multimedia journalism (MS); strategic public relations (MS). *Degree requirements:* For master's, comprehensive exam, thesis optional. *Entrance requirements:* For master's, GRE General Test. Additional exam requirements/recommendations for international students: Required—TOEFL (minimum score 600 paper-based; 100 iBT); Recommended—IELTS (minimum score 6.5). Electronic applications accepted. *Faculty research:* Multimedia journalism, strategic public relations.

Media Studies

Adler University, Graduate Programs, MA in Media and Communications Program, Chicago, IL 60602. Offers MA. *Program availability:* Online learning.

American University, School of Communication, Division of Communication Studies, Washington, DC 20016-8001. Offers media industries and institutions (PhD); media, public issues, and engagement (PhD); media, technology, and culture (PhD). *Faculty:* 6 full-time (3 women), 2 part-time/adjunct (1 woman). *Students:* 24 full-time (14 women); includes 5 minority (2 Black or African American, non-Hispanic/Latino; 3 Hispanic/Latino), 8 international. 136 applicants, 7% accepted, 6 enrolled. In 2017, 3 doctorates awarded. *Degree requirements:* For doctorate, comprehensive exam, thesis/dissertation. *Entrance requirements:* For doctorate, GRE General Test. Additional exam requirements/recommendations for international students: Required—TOEFL (minimum score 600 paper-based; 100 iBT), IELTS (minimum score 7). *Application deadline:* For fall admission, 12/15 priority date for domestic and international students. Applications are processed on a rolling basis. Application fee: $55. Electronic applications accepted. *Expenses: Tuition:* Full-time $29,556. *Required fees:* $690. Tuition and fees vary according to course load and program. *Financial support:* In 2017–18, 5 students received support, including 15 research assistantships with full tuition reimbursements available (averaging $52,000 per year); scholarships/grants, health care benefits, and unspecified assistantships also available. Financial award application deadline: 12/15; financial award applicants required to submit FAFSA. *Faculty research:* Public policy advocacy; social impact of mass media and communication policies; science, health, and environmental communication; intercultural and international strategic communication. *Unit head:* Prof. Kathryn Montgomery, Division Director, 202-885-2680, Fax: 202-885-2099, E-mail: kcm@american.edu. *Application contact:* Leila Hernandez, Recruitment Coordinator, Graduate Programs, 202-885-2040, Fax: 202-885-2019, E-mail: leila@american.edu. Website: http://www.american.edu/soc/communication-studies/degrees/phd-in-communication.cfm

American University, School of Communication, Film and Media Arts Division, Washington, DC 20016-8001. Offers art in entertainment (MFA); environmental and wildlife filmmaking (MFA); film and media arts (MFA); game design (MA); games and interactive media (MFA); games and interactivity (MFA); political, cultural, and social impact (MFA); producing film, television and video (MA). *Program availability:* Part-time, evening/weekend. *Faculty:* 16 full-time (6 women), 9 part-time/adjunct (5 women). *Students:* 57 full-time (32 women), 75 part-time (32 women); includes 71 minority (42 Black or African American, non-Hispanic/Latino; 8 Asian, non-Hispanic/Latino; 16 Hispanic/Latino; 5 Two or more races, non-Hispanic/Latino), 7 international. 258 applicants, 29% accepted, 41 enrolled. In 2017, 71 master's awarded. *Degree requirements:* For master's, comprehensive exam, thesis or alternative. *Entrance requirements:* Additional exam requirements/recommendations for international students: Required—TOEFL (minimum score 600 paper-based; 100 iBT), IELTS (minimum score 7). *Application deadline:* For fall admission, 2/1 priority date for domestic and international students. Applications are processed on a rolling basis. Application fee: $50. Electronic applications accepted. *Expenses: Tuition:* Full-time $29,556. *Required fees:* $690. Tuition and fees vary according to course load and program. *Financial support:* In 2017–18, 58 students received support, including 35 teaching assistantships with partial tuition reimbursements available (averaging $10,000 per year); career-related internships or fieldwork, Federal Work-Study, institutionally sponsored loans, scholarships/grants, tuition waivers (partial), and unspecified assistantships also available. Support available to part-time students. Financial award application deadline: 2/1; financial award applicants required to submit FAFSA. *Faculty research:* Documentary film production, social media, media and public policy, visual literacy, new technology. *Unit head:* Prof. Brigid Maher, Director, Film and Media Arts Division, 202-885-2664, Fax: 202-885-2019, E-mail: bmaher@american.edu. *Application contact:* Leila Hernandez, Recruitment Coordinator, Graduate Programs, 202-885-2040, Fax: 202-885-2019, E-mail: leila@american.edu. Website: https://www.american.edu/soc/film/index.cfm

American University of Beirut, Graduate Programs, Faculty of Arts and Sciences, 1107 2020, Lebanon. Offers anthropology (MA); Arab and Middle Eastern history (PhD); Arabic language and literature (MA, PhD); archaeology (MA); art history and curating (MA); biology (MS); cell and molecular biology (PhD); chemistry (MS); clinical psychology (MA); computational sciences (MS); computer science (MS); economics (MA); education (MA), including administration and policy studies, elementary education, mathematics education, psychology school guidance, psychology test and measurements, science education, teaching English as a foreign language; English language (MA); English literature (MA); environmental policy planning (MS); financial economics (MAFE); general psychology (MA); geology (MS); history (MA); Islamic studies (MA); mathematics (MS); media studies (MA); Middle East studies (MA); philosophy (MA); physics (MS); political studies (MA); public administration (MA); public policy and international affairs (MA); sociology (MA); theoretical physics (PhD). *Program availability:* Part-time. *Faculty:* 108 full-time (36 women), 5 part-time/adjunct (4 women). *Students:* 251 full-time (180 women), 233 part-time (172 women). Average age 26. 425 applicants, 65% accepted, 121 enrolled. In 2017, 47 master's, 2 doctorates awarded. *Degree requirements:* For master's, one foreign language, comprehensive exam, thesis (for some programs), project; for doctorate, one foreign language, comprehensive exam, thesis/dissertation. *Entrance requirements:* For master's, GRE General Test (for some programs); for doctorate, GRE General Test (GRE Subject Test for theoretical physics). Additional exam requirements/recommendations for international students: Required—TOEFL (minimum score 583 paper-based; 97 iBT), IELTS (minimum score 7). *Application deadline:* For fall admission, 2/8 for domestic students; for spring admission, 11/3 for domestic students. Application fee: $50. Electronic applications accepted. *Expenses:* Contact institution. *Financial support:* In 2017–18, 29 fellowships, 40 research assistantships were awarded; teaching assistantships, scholarships/grants, tuition waivers (full and partial), and unspecified assistantships also available. Financial award application deadline: 4/4. *Unit head:* Dr. Nadia Maria El Cheikh, Dean, Faculty of Arts and Sciences, 961-1-374374 Ext. 3800, Fax: 961-1-744461, E-mail: nmcheikh@aub.edu.lb. *Application contact:* Rima Rassi, Graduate Studies Officer, 961-1-350000 Ext. 3833, Fax: 961-1-744461, E-mail: rr46@aub.edu.lb. Website: http://www.aub.edu.lb/fas/pages/default.aspx

Angelo State University, College of Graduate Studies and Research, College of Arts and Humanities, Department of Communication and Mass Media, San Angelo, TX 76909. Offers communication (MA). *Program availability:* Part-time, evening/weekend. *Students:* 9 full-time (4 women), 10 part-time (5 women); includes 9 minority (3 Black or African American, non-Hispanic/Latino; 6 Hispanic/Latino), 5 international. Average age 29. *Degree requirements:* For master's, comprehensive exam, thesis optional. *Entrance requirements:* Additional exam requirements/recommendations for international students: Required—TOEFL or IELTS. *Application deadline:* For fall admission, 7/15 priority date for domestic students, 6/10 for international students; for spring admission, 12/1 priority date

for domestic students, 11/1 for international students. Applications are processed on a rolling basis. Application fee: $40 ($50 for international students). Electronic applications accepted. *Expenses:* Tuition, state resident: full-time $3856. Tuition, nonresident: full-time $11,324. *Required fees:* $2650. *Financial support:* Teaching assistantships, career-related internships or fieldwork, Federal Work-Study, scholarships/grants, and unspecified assistantships available. Support available to part-time students. Financial award application deadline: 3/1; financial award applicants required to submit FAFSA. *Unit head:* Dr. Herman Otis Howard, Chair, 325-942-2031, Fax: 325-942-2551, E-mail: herman.howard@angelo.edu. *Application contact:* Dr. June H. Smith, Graduate Advisor, 325-486-6088, Fax: 325-942-2551, E-mail: june.smith@angelo.edu. Website: http://www.angelo.edu/dept/communication-mass-media/

Arizona State University at the Tempe campus, College of Liberal Arts and Sciences, Department of English, Program in Film and Media Studies, Tempe, AZ 85287-0402. Offers American media and popular culture (MAS). *Program availability:* Part-time, evening/weekend, online learning. *Degree requirements:* For master's, integrated project. *Entrance requirements:* For master's, minimum GPA of 3.0 or equivalent in last 2 years of work leading to bachelor's degree. Additional exam requirements/recommendations for international students: Required—TOEFL, IELTS, or PTE. Electronic applications accepted. *Expenses:* Contact institution.

Arizona State University at the Tempe campus, Herberger Institute for Design and the Arts, School of Arts, Media and Engineering, Tempe, AZ 85287-8709. Offers media arts and sciences (PhD). *Degree requirements:* For doctorate, comprehensive exam, thesis/dissertation, interactive Program of Study (iPOS) submitted before completing 50 percent of required credit hours. *Entrance requirements:* For doctorate, GRE, minimum GPA of 3.25 in last 2 years of work leading to bachelor's degree, portfolio of supporting material, statement of educational/career goals, 3 letters of recommendation, resume/curriculum vitae. Additional exam requirements/recommendations for international students: Required—TOEFL, IELTS, or PTE. Electronic applications accepted.

Arkansas State University, Graduate School, College of Media and Communication, Department of Media, State University, AR 72467. Offers mass communications (MSMC). *Accreditation:* ACEJMC. *Program availability:* Part-time. *Degree requirements:* For master's, comprehensive exam, thesis or alternative. *Entrance requirements:* For master's, GRE General Test or MAT, appropriate bachelor's degree, letters of reference, educational experience, professional experience, official transcripts, immunization records. Additional exam requirements/recommendations for international students: Required—TOEFL (minimum score 550 paper-based; 79 iBT), IELTS (minimum score 6), PTE (minimum score 56). Electronic applications accepted.

Austin Peay State University, College of Graduate Studies, College of Arts and Letters, Department of Communication, Clarksville, TN 37044. Offers marketing communication (MA); media management (MA). *Program availability:* Part-time, evening/weekend, online learning. *Faculty:* 4 full-time (2 women), 1 (woman) part-time/adjunct. *Students:* 45 part-time (32 women); includes 14 minority (11 Black or African American, non-Hispanic/Latino; 2 Hispanic/Latino; 1 Two or more races, non-Hispanic/Latino). Average age 29. 27 applicants, 96% accepted, 19 enrolled. In 2017, 27 master's awarded. *Degree requirements:* For master's, comprehensive exam, thesis (for some programs). *Entrance requirements:* For master's, GRE General Test, minimum GPA of 2.5. Additional exam requirements/recommendations for international students: Required—TOEFL (minimum score 500 paper-based). *Application deadline:* For fall admission, 8/8 priority date for domestic students. Applications are processed on a rolling basis. Application fee: $45 ($55 for international students). Electronic applications accepted. *Expenses:* Tuition, state resident: full-time $7686; part-time $427 per credit hour. Tuition, nonresident: full-time $20,268; part-time $1126 per credit hour. *Required fees:* $1529; $76.45 per credit hour. *Financial support:* Research assistantships with full tuition reimbursements, career-related internships or fieldwork, Federal Work-Study, institutionally sponsored loans, scholarships/grants, and unspecified assistantships available. Support available to part-time students. Financial award application deadline: 4/1; financial award applicants required to submit FAFSA. *Unit head:* Dr. Kathy Heuston, Interim Chair, 931-221-7554, Fax: 931-221-7265, E-mail: leek@apsu.edu. *Application contact:* Megan Mitchell, Coordinator of Graduate Admissions, 931-221-6189, Fax: 931-221-7641, E-mail: mitchellm@apsu.edu. Website: http://www.apsu.edu/communication/index.php

Bob Jones University, Graduate Programs, Greenville, SC 29614. Offers accountancy (MS); Bible (MA); Bible translation (MA); Biblical studies (Certificate); broadcast management (MS); business administration (MBA); church history (MA, PhD); church ministries (MA); church music (MM); cinema and video production (MA); counseling (MS); curriculum and instruction (Ed D); divinity (M Div); dramatic production (MA); educational leadership (MS, Ed D, Ed S); elementary education (M Ed, MAT); English (M Ed, MA, MAT); fine arts (MA); graphic design (MA); history (M Ed, MA); illustration (MA); interpretative speech (MA); mathematics (M Ed, MAT); medical missions (Certificate); ministry (MM, D Min); multi-categorical special education (M Ed, MAT); music (M Ed); New Testament interpretation (PhD); Old Testament interpretation (PhD); orchestral instrument performance (MM); organ performance (MM); pastoral studies (MA); personnel services (MS, Ed S); piano pedagogy (MM); piano performance (MM); platform arts (MA); radio and television broadcasting (MS); rhetoric and public address (MA); secondary education (M Ed); studio art (MA); teaching Bible (MA); theology (MA, PhD); voice performance (MM); youth ministries (MA); M Div/MM.

Boston University, College of Communication, Department of Film and Television, Boston, MA 02215. Offers MFA, MS. *Program availability:* Part-time. *Faculty:* 17 full-time, 25 part-time/adjunct. *Students:* 97 full-time (63 women), 4 part-time (2 women); includes 30 minority (12 Black or African American, non-Hispanic/Latino; 7 Asian, non-Hispanic/Latino; 7 Hispanic/Latino; 4 Two or more races, non-Hispanic/Latino), 15 international. Average age 25. 340 applicants, 40% accepted, 68 enrolled. In 2017, 41 master's awarded. *Degree requirements:* For master's, thesis. *Entrance requirements:* For master's, GRE General Test, resume, writing and creative samples, letters of recommendation. Additional exam requirements/recommendations for international students: Required—TOEFL (minimum score 600 paper-based; 100 iBT), IELTS (minimum score 7). *Application deadline:* For fall admission, 5/1 for domestic and international students. Applications are processed on a rolling basis. Application fee: $95. Electronic applications accepted. *Financial support:* Research assistantships, teaching assistantships with partial tuition reimbursements, career-related internships or fieldwork, Federal Work-Study, scholarships/grants, and unspecified assistantships available. Support available to part-time students. Financial award application deadline: 5/1; financial award applicants required to submit FAFSA. *Unit head:* Paul Schneider, Chairman, 617-353-3483, Fax: 617-353-1084, E-mail: ftvchair@bu.edu. *Application contact:* Jackie Cummings, Admission and Financial Aid Counselor, 617-353-3481, E-mail: comgrad@bu.edu. Website: http://www.bu.edu/com/academics/film-tv/

Media Studies

Boston University, College of Communication, Division of Emerging Media Studies, Boston, MA 02215. Offers MA, PhD. *Program availability:* Part-time. *Faculty:* 4 full-time (1 woman). *Students:* 29 full-time (21 women), 4 part-time (3 women); includes 3 minority (2 Hispanic/Latino; 1 Two or more races, non-Hispanic/Latino), 21 international. Average age 25. 143 applicants, 32% accepted, 20 enrolled. In 2017, 36 master's awarded. *Degree requirements:* For master's, thesis; for doctorate, comprehensive exam, thesis/dissertation. *Entrance requirements:* For master's and doctorate, GRE, resume, writing samples, letters of recommendation. Additional exam requirements/recommendations for international students: Required—TOEFL (minimum score 600 paper-based; 100 iBT), IELTS (minimum score 7). *Application deadline:* For fall admission, 5/1 for domestic and international students. Applications are processed on a rolling basis. Application fee: $95. Electronic applications accepted. *Financial support:* In 2017–18, 3 fellowships with full tuition reimbursements were awarded; research assistantships, teaching assistantships, career-related internships or fieldwork, Federal Work-Study, scholarships/grants, health care benefits, and unspecified assistantships also available. Financial award application deadline: 5/1; financial award applicants required to submit FAFSA. *Unit head:* Dr. James Katz, Professor of Emerging Media/Chair of the Division of Emerging Media Studies, 617-353-7733, E-mail: dems@bu.edu. *Application contact:* Jackie Cummings, Admission and Financial Aid Counselor, 617-353-3481, E-mail: comgrad@bu.edu.
Website: http://www.bu.edu/com/academics/emerging-media/

Bowling Green State University, Graduate College, College of Arts and Sciences, School of Media and Communication, Bowling Green, OH 43403. Offers media and communication (MA, PhD); strategic communication (MA). *Program availability:* Part-time. Terminal master's awarded for partial completion of doctoral program. *Degree requirements:* For master's, thesis or alternative; for doctorate, comprehensive exam, thesis/dissertation. *Entrance requirements:* For master's and doctorate, GRE General Test. Additional exam requirements/recommendations for international students: Required—TOEFL. Electronic applications accepted.

Brooklyn College of the City University of New York, School of Visual, Media and Performing Arts, Department of Television and Radio, Brooklyn, NY 11210-2889. Offers media studies (MS); television production (MFA). *Program availability:* Part-time, evening/weekend. *Degree requirements:* For master's, comprehensive exam. *Entrance requirements:* For master's, GRE General Test or MAT, 12 credits in television/radio with a minimum B average, 2 letters of recommendation. Additional exam requirements/recommendations for international students: Required—TOEFL (minimum score 580 paper-based; 92 iBT). Electronic applications accepted. *Faculty research:* Criticism, research methods, audience behavior, policy and regulation, program history, international television and radio.

Carnegie Mellon University, School of Computer Science and College of Fine Arts, Program in Entertainment Technology, Pittsburgh, PA 15213-3891. Offers MET.

Central Michigan University, College of Graduate Studies, College of Communication and Fine Arts, School of Broadcasting and Cinematic Arts, Mount Pleasant, MI 48859. Offers electronic media management (MA); electronic media production (MA); electronic media studies (MA); film theory and criticism (MA). *Program availability:* Part-time. *Degree requirements:* For master's, thesis or alternative. *Entrance requirements:* For master's, undergraduate degree in broadcasting, film studies, or an associated discipline with minimum GPA of 2.7. Electronic applications accepted. *Faculty research:* Multimedia production, film history and criticism, writing and promotions, international broadcasting and media systems, history of American broadcasting.

Champlain College, Graduate Studies, Burlington, VT 05402-0670. Offers business (MBA); digital forensic science (MS); early childhood education (M Ed); emergent media (MFA, MS); executive leadership (MS); health care administration (MS); information security operations (MS); law (MS); mediation and applied conflict studies (MS). MS in emergent media program held in Shanghai. *Program availability:* Part-time, online learning. *Degree requirements:* For master's, capstone project. *Entrance requirements:* Additional exam requirements/recommendations for international students: Required—TOEFL (minimum score 550 paper-based; 80 iBT). Electronic applications accepted.

City College of the City University of New York, Graduate School, Division of Humanities and the Arts, Department of Media and Communication Arts, Program in Film, New York, NY 10031-9198. Offers MFA. *Entrance requirements:* For master's, BA or BFA with minimum GPA of 3.0, undergraduate training in film and video or equivalent work/industry experience, online video portfolio, 2 letters of recommendation, official transcripts, resume. Additional exam requirements/recommendations for international students: Required—TOEFL (minimum score 575 paper-based; 91 iBT), IELTS (minimum score 6.5). Electronic applications accepted.

Claremont Graduate University, Graduate Programs, School of Arts and Humanities, Department of Cultural Studies, Claremont, CA 91711-6160. Offers Africana studies (Certificate); cultural studies (MA, PhD); media studies (MA, PhD); museum studies (MA). *Program availability:* Part-time. *Entrance requirements:* For master's and doctorate, GRE General Test. Additional exam requirements/recommendations for international students: Required—TOEFL (minimum score 75 iBT). Electronic applications accepted.

Clarion University of Pennsylvania, College of Arts, Education and Sciences, MS Program in Mass Media Arts and Journalism, Clarion, PA 16214. Offers MS. *Program availability:* Part-time, evening/weekend, online only, 100% online. *Faculty:* 5 full-time (3 women). *Students:* 9 full-time (6 women), 8 part-time (4 women); includes 6 minority (all Black or African American, non-Hispanic/Latino). Average age 33. 10 applicants, 80% accepted, 4 enrolled. In 2017, 6 master's awarded. *Entrance requirements:* For master's, statement of purpose, short essay, minimum undergraduate QPA of 3.0. Additional exam requirements/recommendations for international students: Required—TOEFL (minimum score 600 paper-based, 80 iBT) or IELTS (7). *Application deadline:* For fall admission, 8/15 priority date for domestic students, 7/15 priority date for international students; for winter admission, 11/1 priority date for domestic students; for spring admission, 1/7 priority date for domestic students, 11/15 priority date for international students; for summer admission, 4/1 priority date for domestic students. Applications are processed on a rolling basis. Application fee: $40. Electronic applications accepted. *Expenses:* $655.05 per credit. *Financial support:* Career-related internships or fieldwork, scholarships/grants, and unspecified assistantships available. Support available to part-time students. Financial award application deadline: 3/1; financial award applicants required to submit FAFSA. *Unit head:* Dr. Steven Harris, Interim Dean, 814-393-2328, E-mail: harris@clarion.edu. *Application contact:* Dana Bearer, Associate Director for Transfer, Adult and Graduate Admissions, 814-393-2337, Fax: 814-393-2772, E-mail: gradstudies@clarion.edu.

College of Staten Island of the City University of New York, Graduate Programs, Division of Humanities and Social Sciences, Program in Cinema and Media Studies, Staten Island, NY 10314-6600. Offers MA. *Program availability:* Part-time, evening/weekend. *Faculty:* 3 full-time (all women). *Students:* 7. 12 applicants, 42% accepted, 2 enrolled. In 2017, 1 master's awarded. *Degree requirements:* For master's, comprehensive exam (for some programs), 36 credits in cinema and media studies courses; written thesis, production thesis, or examination. *Entrance requirements:* For master's, bachelor's degree with minimum B average in undergraduate cinema studies or communications courses; 10-12 page writing sample; three letters of recommendation; 1-2 page statement of intent detailing interest in the field, background in film and media studies, and/or research interests; three letters of recommendation. Additional exam requirements/recommendations for international students: Required—TOEFL (minimum score 550 paper-based; 79 iBT), IELTS (minimum score 6.5). *Application deadline:* For fall admission, 6/15 priority date for domestic and international students; for spring admission, 11/25 priority date for domestic and international students. Applications are processed on a rolling basis. Application fee: $125. Electronic applications accepted. *Expenses:* Tuition, state resident: full-time $10,450; part-time $440 per credit. Tuition, nonresident: full-time $19,320; part-time $440 per credit. *Required fees:* $181.10 per semester. Tuition and fees vary according to program. *Faculty research:* Political communication, Latino/a media and audience, gender and sexuality, representation of race and ethnicity, video surveillance. *Unit head:* Dr. Edward Miller, Graduate Program Coordinator, 718-982-2474, E-mail: edward.miller@csi.cuny.edu. *Application contact:* Sasha Spence, Associate Director for Graduate Admissions, 718-982-2019, Fax: 718-982-2500, E-mail: sasha.spence@csi.cuny.edu.
Website: https://www.csi.cuny.edu/sites/default/files/pdf/admissions/grad/pdf/Cinema%20and%20Media%20Fact%20Sheet.pdf

Colorado State University, College of Liberal Arts, Department of Journalism and Media Communication, Fort Collins, CO 80523-1785. Offers communications and media management (MCMM); public communication and technology (MS, PhD). *Program availability:* Part-time, blended/hybrid learning. *Faculty:* 12 full-time (7 women), 2 part-time/adjunct (both women). *Students:* 27 full-time (22 women), 38 part-time (25 women); includes 11 minority (1 Black or African American, non-Hispanic/Latino; 2 American Indian or Alaska Native, non-Hispanic/Latino; 1 Asian, non-Hispanic/Latino; 5 Hispanic/Latino; 2 Two or more races, non-Hispanic/Latino), 12 international. Average age 32. 40 applicants, 73% accepted, 20 enrolled. In 2017, 11 master's, 4 doctorates awarded. Terminal master's awarded for partial completion of doctoral program. *Degree requirements:* For master's, thesis (for some programs), research project; for doctorate, comprehensive exam, thesis/dissertation. *Entrance requirements:* For master's, GRE General Test (for MS program only), minimum GPA of 3.0; transcripts; letters of recommendation; writing sample, curriculum vitae/resume; statement of purpose; for doctorate, GRE General Test, minimum GPA of 3.0; transcripts; letters of recommendation; writing sample, curriculum vitae/resume; statement of purpose. Additional exam requirements/recommendations for international students: Required—TOEFL (minimum score 550 paper-based; 80 iBT), IELTS (minimum score 6.5); Recommended—TWE. Application fee: $60 ($70 for international students). Electronic applications accepted. *Expenses:* Contact institution. *Financial support:* In 2017–18, 2 research assistantships with full and partial tuition reimbursements (averaging $14,102 per year), 33 teaching assistantships with full and partial tuition reimbursements (averaging $14,861 per year) were awarded; scholarships/grants, health care benefits, and unspecified assistantships also available. *Faculty research:* Food marketing communication models of influence; sports media and journalism; health and science communication; social interaction in online contexts; public discourse and media sociology. *Total annual research expenditures:* $668,408. *Unit head:* Greg Luft, Professor and Department Chair, 970-491-1979, Fax: 970-491-2908, E-mail: greg.luft@colostate.edu. *Application contact:* Linda Kidder, Graduate Program Administrator, 970-491-5132, Fax: 970-491-2908, E-mail: linda.kidder@colostate.edu.
Website: http://journalism.colostate.edu/

Columbia University, School of the Arts, Film and Media Studies Program, New York, NY 10027. Offers MA. *Program availability:* Part-time. *Faculty:* 7 full-time (3 women), 3 part-time/adjunct (0 women). *Students:* 36 full-time (19 women); includes 6 minority (1 Black or African American, non-Hispanic/Latino; 2 Asian, non-Hispanic/Latino; 3 Hispanic/Latino), 17 international. Average age 25. 81 applicants, 52% accepted, 14 enrolled. In 2017, 17 master's awarded. Terminal master's awarded for partial completion of doctoral program. *Degree requirements:* For master's, thesis. *Entrance requirements:* Additional exam requirements/recommendations for international students: Required—TOEFL (minimum score 600 paper-based; 100 iBT). *Application deadline:* For fall admission, 2/1 for domestic and international students. Application fee: $110. Electronic applications accepted. *Expenses:* Contact institution. *Financial support:* In 2017–18, 1 student received support, including 2 teaching assistantships with full and partial tuition reimbursements available; fellowships, research assistantships, Federal Work-Study, and scholarships/grants also available. Financial award application deadline: 2/1; financial award applicants required to submit FAFSA. *Unit head:* Carol Becker, Dean, 212-854-9847. *Application contact:* Kenny Wong, Director of Admissions and Financial Aid, 212-854-2134, E-mail: admissions-arts@columbia.edu.
Website: https://arts.columbia.edu/film/ma

Concordia University, School of Graduate Studies, Faculty of Arts and Science, Department of Communication Studies, Montréal, QC H3G 1M8, Canada. Offers communication (PhD); communication studies (Diploma); media studies (MA). PhD program offered jointly with Universityé de Montréal and Universityé du Quebec à Montréal. *Degree requirements:* For master's, thesis optional; for doctorate, one foreign language, comprehensive exam, thesis/dissertation, research practicum, seminar. *Entrance requirements:* For master's, bachelor's degree in communications, 2 years of media-related experience; for doctorate, MA in communications. *Faculty research:* Communication and development, organizational communication, cultural studies, rhetoric, future studies.

Concordia University, School of Graduate Studies, Faculty of Fine Arts, Department of Studio Arts, Montréal, QC H3G 1M8, Canada. Offers studio arts (MFA), including fibers and material practices, film production, intermedia, painting and drawing, photography, print media, sculpture. *Degree requirements:* For master's, thesis or alternative. *Entrance requirements:* For master's, portfolio.

Cornell University, Graduate School, Graduate Fields of Agriculture and Life Sciences, Field of Communication, Ithaca, NY 14853. Offers communication (MS, PhD); human-computer interaction (MS, PhD); language and communication (MS, PhD); media communication and society (MS, PhD); organizational communication (MS, PhD); science, environment and health communication (MS, PhD); social psychology of communication (MS, PhD). *Degree requirements:* For master's, thesis (MS); for doctorate, comprehensive exam, thesis/dissertation. *Entrance requirements:* For master's and doctorate, GRE General Test, 3 letters of recommendation. Additional exam requirements/recommendations for international students: Required—TOEFL (minimum score 600 paper-based; 100 iBT). Electronic applications accepted. *Faculty research:* Mass communication, communication technologies, science and environmental communication.

Dallas Theological Seminary, Graduate Programs, Dallas, TX 75204-6499. Offers adult education (Th M); apologetics (Th M); Bible backgrounds (Th M); Bible translation (Th M); Biblical and theological studies (Certificate); biblical counseling (MA); biblical exegesis and linguistics (MA); biblical exposition (PhD); biblical studies (MA); Biblical theology (Th M); children's education (Th M); Christian education (MA, D Min); Christian leadership (MA); cross-cultural ministries (MA); educational administration (Th M); educational leadership (Th M); evangelism and discipleship (Th M); exposition of Biblical books (Th M); family life education (Th M); general studies (Th M); Hebrew and cognate

studies (Th M); hermeneutics (Th M); historical theology (Th M); homiletics (Th M); intercultural ministries (Th M); Jesus studies (Th M); leadership studies (Th M); media and communication (MA); media arts (Th M); ministry (D Min); ministry with women (Th M); New Testament studies (Th M, PhD); Old Testament studies (Th M, PhD); parachurch ministries (Th M); pastoral care and counseling (Th M); pastoral theology and practice (Th M); philosophy (Th M); sacred theology (STM); spiritual formation (Th M); systematic theology (Th M); teaching in Christian institutions (Th M); theological studies (PhD); urban ministries (Th M); worship studies (Th M); youth education (Th M). *Program availability:* Part-time, online learning. *Degree requirements:* For master's, variable foreign language requirement, thesis (for some programs); for doctorate, 2 foreign languages, thesis/dissertation. *Entrance requirements:* For master's, GRE or MAT (if minimum undergraduate cumulative GPA is below 2.5 or undergraduate degree is unaccredited). Additional exam requirements/recommendations for international students: Required—TOEFL (minimum score 575 paper-based; 85 iBT), TWE. Electronic applications accepted.

DePaul University, College of Communication, Chicago, IL 60604. Offers digital communication and media arts (MA); health communication (MA); journalism (MA); media and cinema studies (MA); multicultural communication (MA); organizational communication (MA); public relations and advertising (MA); relational communication (MA). *Program availability:* Part-time, evening/weekend. *Entrance requirements:* Additional exam requirements/recommendations for international students: Required—TOEFL (minimum score 590 paper-based; 96 iBT), IELTS (minimum score 7.5) or PTE. *Application deadline:* For fall admission, 6/1 priority date for domestic students; for winter admission, 10/1 priority date for domestic students; for spring admission, 2/15 priority date for domestic students. Applications are processed on a rolling basis. Application fee: $40. Electronic applications accepted. *Financial support:* Applicants required to submit FAFSA. *Unit head:* Salma Ghanem, Dean, 312-362-8600, Fax: 312-362-8620. *Application contact:* Ann Spittle, Director of Graduate Admission, 773-325-7315, Fax: 312-362-8620, E-mail: graddepaul@depaul.edu.
Website: http://communication.depaul.edu/

Drexel University, College of Arts and Sciences, Department of Communication, Culture and Media, Philadelphia, PA 19104-2875. Offers communication (MS), including public communication, science communication, technical communication. *Program availability:* Part-time, evening/weekend. *Degree requirements:* For master's, internship, professional portfolio. *Entrance requirements:* Additional exam requirements/recommendations for international students: Required—TOEFL. Electronic applications accepted. *Faculty research:* Science information and attitudes, science influence on literature, process of technical writing, document design, software documentation.

Duke University, Graduate School, Master of Fine Arts in Experimental and Documentary Arts Program, Durham, NC 27708. Offers MFA. *Degree requirements:* For master's, thesis, final project. *Entrance requirements:* For master's, portfolio. Additional exam requirements/recommendations for international students: Required—TOEFL (minimum score 577 paper-based; 90 iBT) or IELTS (minimum score 7). Electronic applications accepted.

Fairleigh Dickinson University, Metropolitan Campus, University College: Arts, Sciences, and Professional Studies, School of Art and Media Studies, Program in Media and Communications, Teaneck, NJ 07666-1914. Offers MA.

Fielding Graduate University, Graduate Programs, School of Psychology, Programs in Media Psychology, Santa Barbara, CA 93105-3814. Offers MA, PhD, Graduate Certificate. *Program availability:* Part-time, evening/weekend, 100% online, blended/hybrid learning. *Faculty:* 4 full-time (3 women), 18 part-time/adjunct (9 women). *Students:* 83 full-time (58 women), 23 part-time (17 women); includes 34 minority (11 Black or African American, non-Hispanic/Latino; 2 Asian, non-Hispanic/Latino; 13 Hispanic/Latino; 8 Two or more races, non-Hispanic/Latino). Average age 42. 34 applicants, 100% accepted, 22 enrolled. In 2017, 18 master's, 16 doctorates, 4 other advanced degrees awarded. Terminal master's awarded for partial completion of doctoral program. *Degree requirements:* For master's, thesis or alternative, capstone; for doctorate, comprehensive exam, thesis/dissertation. *Entrance requirements:* For master's, bachelor's degree from regionally-accredited U.S. institution or equivalent, resume, statement of purpose, official transcript; for doctorate, bachelor's or master's degree from regionally-accredited U.S. institution or equivalent, curriculum vitae, statement of purpose, critical thinking writing sample, 2 letters of recommendation, official transcript; for Graduate Certificate, bachelor's degree from regionally-accredited U.S. institution or equivalent. *Application deadline:* For fall admission, 7/16 for domestic and international students; for spring admission, 11/1 for domestic and international students; for summer admission, 3/1 for domestic and international students. Application fee: $75. Electronic applications accepted. *Expenses:* Contact institution. *Financial support:* In 2017–18, 26 students received support, including 1 teaching assistantship (averaging $1,700 per year); research assistantships and scholarships/grants also available. Support available to part-time students. Financial award applicants required to submit FAFSA. *Unit head:* Dr. Jerri Lynn Hogg, E-mail: jhogg@fielding.edu. *Application contact:* Enrollment Coordinator, 800-340-1099 Ext. 4098, Fax: 805-687-9793, E-mail: psyadmission@fielding.edu.
Website: http://www.fielding.edu/our-programs/school-of-psychology/

Florida Atlantic University, Dorothy F. Schmidt College of Arts and Letters, School of Communication and Multimedia Studies, Boca Raton, FL 33431-0991. Offers communication studies (MA); film and video (Certificate); media, technology and entertainment (MFA). *Program availability:* Part-time. *Faculty:* 24 full-time (8 women). *Students:* 21 full-time (15 women), 16 part-time (9 women); includes 19 minority (11 Black or African American, non-Hispanic/Latino; 1 Asian, non-Hispanic/Latino; 6 Hispanic/Latino; 1 Two or more races, non-Hispanic/Latino), 2 international. Average age 32. 29 applicants, 52% accepted, 13 enrolled. In 2017, 15 master's awarded. *Degree requirements:* For master's, one foreign language, comprehensive exam (for some programs), thesis (for some programs). *Entrance requirements:* For master's, GRE General Test, minimum GPA of 3.0, essay, letters of recommendation. *Application deadline:* For fall admission, 7/1 priority date for domestic students, 4/1 for international students; for spring admission, 11/1 for domestic students, 10/1 for international students. Applications are processed on a rolling basis. Application fee: $30. Electronic applications accepted. *Expenses:* Tuition, state resident: full-time $7400; part-time $369.82 per credit. Tuition, nonresident: full-time $20,496; part-time $1042.81 per credit. *Financial support:* Teaching assistantships with partial tuition reimbursements, Federal Work-Study, institutionally sponsored loans, scholarships/grants, and unspecified assistantships available. Support available to part-time students. Financial award application deadline: 3/1; financial award applicants required to submit FAFSA. *Faculty research:* Cultural studies, gender studies, film, communication theory, journalism, new media. *Unit head:* Dr. David Williams, Director, 561-297-0045, Fax: 561-297-2615, E-mail: dcwill@fau.edu. *Application contact:* Dr. Stephen Charbonneau, Graduate Director, 561-297-3856, Fax: 561-297-2615, E-mail: efreedma@fau.edu.
Website: http://www.fau.edu/scms/

Florida State University, The Graduate School, College of Communication and Information, School of Communication, Tallahassee, FL 32306. Offers communication theory and research (PhD); integrated marketing communication (MA, MS); media and communication studies (MA, MS); public interest media and communication (MA, MS). *Program availability:* Part-time. *Faculty:* 20 full-time (11 women), 1 part-time/adjunct (0 women). *Students:* 104 full-time (74 women), 38 part-time (27 women); includes 81 minority (20 Black or African American, non-Hispanic/Latino; 24 Asian, non-Hispanic/Latino; 26 Hispanic/Latino; 1 Native Hawaiian or other Pacific Islander, non-Hispanic/Latino; 10 Two or more races, non-Hispanic/Latino). Average age 24. 184 applicants, 59% accepted, 46 enrolled. In 2017, 59 master's, 5 doctorates awarded. *Degree requirements:* For master's, thesis (for some programs); for doctorate, comprehensive exam, thesis/dissertation. *Entrance requirements:* For master's, GRE General Test, minimum GPA of 3.0; for doctorate, GRE General Test, minimum GPA of 3.3 in graduate course work. Additional exam requirements/recommendations for international students: Required—TOEFL (minimum score 600 paper-based; 100 iBT), IELTS (minimum score 7). *Application deadline:* For fall admission, 7/1 priority date for domestic students, 5/1 priority date for international students; for spring admission, 11/1 priority date for domestic and international students; for summer admission, 3/1 priority date for domestic and international students. Applications are processed on a rolling basis. Application fee: $30. Electronic applications accepted. *Expenses:* Contact institution. *Financial support:* In 2017–18, 112 students received support, including 28 research assistantships with full tuition reimbursements available (averaging $11,752 per year), 81 teaching assistantships with full tuition reimbursements available (averaging $10,109 per year); scholarships/grants, tuition waivers (full and partial), and unspecified assistantships also available. Financial award application deadline: 11/1; financial award applicants required to submit FAFSA. *Faculty research:* Communication in the public interest; strategic communication; media and technology; multicultural, intercultural, and international communication. *Total annual research expenditures:* $41,657. *Unit head:* Dr. Jennifer Proffitt, Director, 850-644-5034, Fax: 850-644-8642, E-mail: jennifer.proffitt@cci.fsu.edu. *Application contact:* Natashia Hinson-Turner, Graduate Coordinator, 850-644-5034, Fax: 850-644-8642, E-mail: comgradadvising@cci.fsu.edu.
Website: http://www.cci.fsu.edu

Fordham University, Gabelli School of Business, New York, NY 10023. Offers accounting (MBA, MS); applied statistics and decision-making (MS); business economics (DPS); capital markets (DPS); communications and media management (MBA); electronic business (MBA); entrepreneurship (MBA); finance (MBA, PhD); global finance (MS); global sustainability (MBA); health administration (MS); healthcare management (MBA); information systems (MBA, MS); investor relations (MS); management (EMBA, MBA, MS, PhD); marketing (MBA); marketing intelligence (MS); media management (MS); nonprofit leadership (MS); quantitative finance (MS); strategy and decision-making (DPS); taxation (MS); JD/MBA; MS/MBA. *Accreditation:* AACSB. *Program availability:* Part-time, evening/weekend. *Faculty:* 130 full-time (46 women), 42 part-time/adjunct (5 women). *Students:* 1,051 full-time (570 women), 563 part-time (313 women); includes 190 minority (48 Black or African American, non-Hispanic/Latino; 72 Asian, non-Hispanic/Latino; 69 Hispanic/Latino; 1 Native Hawaiian or other Pacific Islander, non-Hispanic/Latino), 1,106 international. Average age 27. 4,577 applicants, 58% accepted, 794 enrolled. In 2017, 937 master's awarded. Terminal master's awarded for partial completion of doctoral program. *Degree requirements:* For master's, internships (for some degrees); for doctorate, comprehensive exam (for some programs), thesis/dissertation. *Entrance requirements:* For master's, GMAT/GRE, 2 letters of recommendation, resume, 2 essays, transcripts, interview. Additional exam requirements/recommendations for international students: Required—TOEFL (minimum score 100 iBT), IELTS (minimum score 7). *Application deadline:* For fall admission, 11/15 priority date for domestic and international students; for winter admission, 1/19 priority date for domestic students, 1/1 priority date for international students; for spring admission, 4/15 for domestic students, 3/1 for international students; for summer admission, 6/1 for domestic students. Application fee: $130. Electronic applications accepted. *Expenses:* $1,495 per credit. *Financial support:* Career-related internships or fieldwork, institutionally sponsored loans, scholarships/grants, and unspecified assistantships available. Support available to part-time students. Financial award application deadline: 6/30; financial award applicants required to submit FAFSA. *Unit head:* Dr. Donna Rapaccioli, Dean, 212-636-6165, Fax: 212-307-1779, E-mail: rapaccioli@fordham.edu. *Application contact:* Lawrence Murray, Senior Assistant Dean of Graduate Admissions and Advising, 212-636-6200, Fax: 212-636-7076, E-mail: admissionsgb@fordham.edu.
Website: http://www.fordham.edu/gabelli

Fordham University, Graduate School of Arts and Sciences, Department of Communication and Media Studies, New York, NY 10458. Offers public media (MA). Program offered in collaboration with WFUV and WNET. *Program availability:* Part-time, evening/weekend. *Faculty:* 11 full-time (3 women). *Students:* 17 full-time (10 women), 1 part-time (0 women); includes 10 minority (4 Black or African American, non-Hispanic/Latino; 1 American Indian or Alaska Native, non-Hispanic/Latino; 1 Asian, non-Hispanic/Latino; 4 Hispanic/Latino), 1 international. Average age 25. 91 applicants, 49% accepted, 18 enrolled. In 2017, 17 master's awarded. *Degree requirements:* For master's, thesis, internship. *Entrance requirements:* For master's, GRE General Test. Additional exam requirements/recommendations for international students: Required—TOEFL (minimum score 600 paper-based). *Application deadline:* For fall admission, 1/4 priority date for domestic students; for spring admission, 11/1 for domestic students. Application fee: $70. Electronic applications accepted. *Financial support:* In 2017–18, 3 students received support, including 2 research assistantships with full and partial tuition reimbursements available (averaging $23,200 per year); career-related internships or fieldwork, Federal Work-Study, institutionally sponsored loans, scholarships/grants, tuition waivers (full and partial), and unspecified assistantships also available. Financial award application deadline: 1/4. *Total annual research expenditures:* $1.1 million. *Unit head:* Jacqueline Reich, Chair, 718-817-4850, E-mail: jreich8@fordham.edu. *Application contact:* Travis Stratton, Interim Director of Graduate Admissions, 718-817-4417, Fax: 718-817-3566, E-mail: tstrattion@fordham.edu.

Full Sail University, Media Design Master of Fine Arts Program - Online, Winter Park, FL 32792-7437. Offers MFA. *Program availability:* Online learning.

Georgetown University, Graduate School of Arts and Sciences, School of Continuing Studies, Washington, DC 20057. Offers American studies (MALS); applied intelligence (MPS); Catholic studies (MALS); classical civilizations (MALS); emergency and disaster management (MPS); ethics and the professions (MALS); global strategic communications (MPS); hospitality management (MPS); human resources management (MPS); humanities (MALS); individualized study (MALS); integrated marketing communications (MPS); international affairs (MALS); Islam and Muslim-Christian relations (MALS); journalism (MPS); liberal studies (DLS); literature and society (MALS); medieval and early modern European studies (MALS); public relations and corporate communications (MPS); real estate (MPS); religious studies (MALS); social and public policy (MALS); sports industry management (MPS); systems engineering management (MPS); technology management (MPS); the theory and practice of American democracy (MALS); urban and regional planning (MPS); visual culture (MALS). MPS in systems engineering management offered jointly with Stevens Institute of Technology. *Entrance requirements:* Additional exam requirements/recommendations for international students: Required—TOEFL.

Media Studies

Georgia State University, College of Arts and Sciences, Department of Communication, Atlanta, GA 30302-3083. Offers film, video, and digital imaging (MA), including critical studies, production, screenwriting; human communication and social influence (MA); mass communication (MA); media and society (PhD); moving image studies (PhD); public communication (PhD); rhetoric and politics (PhD). *Program availability:* Part-time. *Faculty:* 57 full-time (34 women). *Students:* 71 full-time (51 women), 17 part-time (9 women); includes 36 minority (28 Black or African American, non-Hispanic/Latino; 1 Asian, non-Hispanic/Latino; 4 Hispanic/Latino; 1 Native Hawaiian or other Pacific Islander, non-Hispanic/Latino; 2 Two or more races, non-Hispanic/Latino), 15 international. Average age 33. 63 applicants, 54% accepted, 17 enrolled. In 2017, 20 master's, 10 doctorates awarded. *Degree requirements:* For master's, variable foreign language requirement, thesis (for some programs); for doctorate, comprehensive exam, thesis/dissertation. *Entrance requirements:* For master's and doctorate, GRE. Additional exam requirements/recommendations for international students: Required—TOEFL (minimum score 550 paper-based; 80 iBT), IELTS (minimum score 6.5). *Application deadline:* For fall admission, 2/10 for domestic and international students; for spring admission, 10/15 for domestic and international students. Application fee: $50. Electronic applications accepted. *Expenses:* Tuition, state resident: full-time $7020. Tuition, nonresident: full-time $22,518. *Required fees:* $2128. Tuition and fees vary according to degree level and program. *Financial support:* In 2017–18, fellowships with tuition reimbursements (averaging $15,000 per year), teaching assistantships with tuition reimbursements (averaging $15,000 per year) were awarded; career-related internships or fieldwork and unspecified assistantships also available. Financial award applicants required to submit FAFSA. *Faculty research:* New media, mass media and journalism, rhetoric, film and media studies, film production. *Unit head:* Dr. Greg Lisby, Chair, 404-413-5639, Fax: 404-413-5634, E-mail: glisby@gsu.edu. Website: http://communication.gsu.edu

Howard University, Cathy Hughes School of Communications, Department of Communication, Culture and Media Studies, Washington, DC 20059-0002. Offers mass communication (MA, PhD); media studies (MA, PhD). *Program availability:* Part-time, evening/weekend. *Degree requirements:* For master's, comprehensive exam (for some programs), thesis optional; for doctorate, one foreign language, comprehensive exam, thesis/dissertation. *Entrance requirements:* For master's, GRE, minimum GPA of 3.0; for doctorate, GRE, minimum graduate GPA of 3.5. Additional exam requirements/recommendations for international students: Required—TOEFL. Electronic applications accepted. *Faculty research:* Advertising, public relations, journalism new media.

Hunter College of the City University of New York, Graduate School, School of Arts and Sciences, Department of Film and Media Studies, Program in Integrated Media Arts, New York, NY 10065-5085. Offers MFA. *Program availability:* Part-time, evening/weekend. *Entrance requirements:* For master's, GRE General Test, 3 letters of recommendation, portfolio of media works, minimum GPA of 3.0. Additional exam requirements/recommendations for international students: Required—TOEFL, TWE. *Faculty research:* Nonfiction production, Internet as medium, public interest journalism, social and historical roots of media arts.

Indiana State University, College of Graduate and Professional Studies, College of Arts and Sciences, Department of Communication, Terre Haute, IN 47809. Offers communication studies (MA); radio, television and film (MA). *Program availability:* Part-time. *Degree requirements:* For master's, thesis (for some programs), oral and written exam. *Entrance requirements:* For master's, GRE General Test. Additional exam requirements/recommendations for international students: Required—TOEFL. *Faculty research:* Women in media, communication apprehension, media history.

Indiana University Bloomington, University Graduate School, College of Arts and Sciences, The Media School, Bloomington, IN 47405-7000. Offers media (MS); media arts and sciences (MA, PhD). *Degree requirements:* For master's, comprehensive exam (for some programs), thesis (for some programs); for doctorate, comprehensive exam, thesis/dissertation. *Entrance requirements:* Additional exam requirements/recommendations for international students: Required—TOEFL. Electronic applications accepted. *Faculty research:* Film and cinema studies, communication science, journalism, media design and production.

Indiana University of Pennsylvania, School of Graduate Studies and Research, College of Education and Communications, Department of Communications Media, Program in Communications Media and Instructional Technology, Indiana, PA 15705. Offers PhD. *Faculty:* 8 full-time (4 women). *Students:* 12 full-time (6 women), 38 part-time (15 women); includes 10 minority (4 Black or African American, non-Hispanic/Latino; 1 Asian, non-Hispanic/Latino; 3 Hispanic/Latino; 2 Two or more races, non-Hispanic/Latino), 5 international. Average age 39. 41 applicants, 41% accepted, 10 enrolled. In 2017, 10 doctorates awarded. Application fee: $50. *Expenses:* Contact institution. *Financial support:* In 2017–18, 2 fellowships with full tuition reimbursements (averaging $2,296 per year), 7 research assistantships with tuition reimbursements (averaging $5,769 per year), 3 teaching assistantships with partial tuition reimbursements (averaging $23,305 per year) were awarded. *Unit head:* Dr. Zachary Stiegler, Coordinator, 724-357-3219, E-mail: zachary.stiegler@iup.edu. Website: http://www.iup.edu/commmedia/programs/phdcmit/

International University in Geneva, Leadership Programs, Geneva, Switzerland. Offers international relations and diplomacy (MIRD); media and communication (MA); public administration (DPA). *Degree requirements:* For master's, comprehensive exam. *Entrance requirements:* Additional exam requirements/recommendations for international students: Required—TOEFL. Electronic applications accepted.

Johns Hopkins University, Zanvyl Krieger School of Arts and Sciences, Advanced Academic Programs, Program in Film and Media, Baltimore, MD 21218. Offers MA. Students choose two concentrations from business, sound, and writing. *Program availability:* Part-time.

Kent State University, College of Communication and Information, School of Journalism and Mass Communication, Kent, OH 44242-0001. Offers journalism and mass communication (MA), including media management, public relations, reporting and editing-broadcast, reporting and editing-convergence, reporting and editing-journalism educators, reporting and editing-magazine, reporting and editing-newspaper. *Program availability:* Part-time, online learning. *Faculty:* 15 full-time (8 women), 14 part-time/adjunct (7 women). *Students:* 13 full-time (8 women), 74 part-time (51 women); includes 14 minority (11 Black or African American, non-Hispanic/Latino; 2 Hispanic/Latino; 1 Two or more races, non-Hispanic/Latino), 4 international. Average age 35. 24 applicants, 71% accepted, 13 enrolled. In 2017, 58 master's awarded. *Degree requirements:* For master's, thesis or project. *Entrance requirements:* For master's, GRE, minimum GPA of 3.0, statement of purpose, 3 online recommendations, resume. Additional exam requirements/recommendations for international students: Required—TOEFL (minimum score 587 paper-based, 94 iBT), Michigan English Language Assessment Battery (minimum score 82), IELTS (minimum score 7.0) or PTE (minimum score 65). *Application deadline:* For fall admission, 7/1 for domestic and international students. Applications are processed on a rolling basis. Application fee: $45 ($70 for international students). Electronic applications accepted. *Expenses:* Tuition, state resident: full-time $11,310; part-time $515 per credit hour. Tuition, nonresident: full-time $20,396; part-time $928 per credit hour. *International tuition:* $18,544 full-time. *Financial support:* Research assistantships with full tuition reimbursements, teaching assistantships with full tuition reimbursements, scholarships/grants, and unspecified assistantships available. Financial award application deadline: 2/16. *Unit head:* Jeff Fruit, Interim Director and Professor, 330-672-2572, E-mail: jmc@kent.edu. *Application contact:* Mark Goodman, Graduate Coordinator/Professor, 330-672-6239, E-mail: mgoodm10@kent.edu. Website: http://www.kent.edu/jmc

La Salle University, School of Arts and Sciences, Program in Strategic Communication, Philadelphia, PA 19141-1199. Offers communication consulting and development (MA); communication management (MA); general professional communication (MA); professional and business communication (Certificate); public relations (MA); social and new media (Certificate). *Program availability:* Part-time, evening/weekend, online learning. *Faculty:* 4 full-time (3 women), 1 (woman) part-time/adjunct. *Students:* 11 full-time (4 women), 22 part-time (16 women); includes 10 minority (9 Black or African American, non-Hispanic/Latino; 1 Two or more races, non-Hispanic/Latino). Average age 27. 40 applicants, 93% accepted, 23 enrolled. In 2017, 34 master's, 1 other advanced degree awarded. *Degree requirements:* For master's, practicum. *Entrance requirements:* For master's, writing assessment, professional resume; minimum overall B average; two letters of recommendation (if GPA below 3.25); brief personal statement (about 500 words); interview; for Certificate, writing assessment, minimum GPA of 2.75 in undergraduate studies; brief personal statement (about 500 words); interview. Additional exam requirements/recommendations for international students: Required—TOEFL. *Application deadline:* For fall admission, 8/15 priority date for domestic students, 7/15 for international students; for spring admission, 12/15 priority date for domestic students, 11/15 for international students; for summer admission, 4/15 priority date for domestic students, 3/15 for international students. Applications are processed on a rolling basis. Application fee: $35. Electronic applications accepted. Application fee is waived when completed online. *Expenses:* Contact institution. *Financial support:* In 2017–18, 12 students received support. Scholarships/grants available. Support available to part-time students. Financial award application deadline: 8/31; financial award applicants required to submit FAFSA. *Unit head:* Dr. Pamela Lannutti, Director, 215-951-1935, Fax: 215-951-5043, E-mail: annutti95@lasalle.edu. *Application contact:* Elizabeth Heenan, Director, Graduate and Adult Enrollment, 215-951-1100, Fax: 214-951-1462, E-mail: heenan@lasalle.edu. Website: http://www.lasalle.edu/strategic-communication/

Lindenwood University, Graduate Programs, School of Accelerated Degree Programs, St. Charles, MO 63301-1695. Offers administration (MSA), including management, marketing, project management; business administration (MBA); communications (MA), including digital and multimedia, media management, promotions, training and development; criminal justice and administration (MS); healthcare administration (MS); human resource management (MS); information technology (Certificate); managing information security (MS); managing information technology (MS); managing virtualization and cloud computing (MS); writing (MFA). *Program availability:* Part-time, evening/weekend, 100% online. *Faculty:* 12 full-time (5 women), 90 part-time/adjunct (37 women). *Students:* 597 full-time (383 women), 202 part-time (138 women); includes 248 minority (206 Black or African American, non-Hispanic/Latino; 3 American Indian or Alaska Native, non-Hispanic/Latino; 6 Asian, non-Hispanic/Latino; 21 Hispanic/Latino; 1 Native Hawaiian or other Pacific Islander, non-Hispanic/Latino; 11 Two or more races, non-Hispanic/Latino), 69 international. Average age 36. 526 applicants, 46% accepted, 204 enrolled. In 2017, 537 master's awarded. *Degree requirements:* For master's, thesis (for some programs), minimum cumulative GPA of 3.0; for Certificate, minimum cumulative GPA of 3.0. *Entrance requirements:* For master's, resume, personal statement, official undergraduate transcript, minimum undergraduate cumulative GPA of 3.0. Additional exam requirements/recommendations for international students: Required—TOEFL (minimum score 550 paper-based; 80 iBT); Recommended—IELTS (minimum score 6.5). *Application deadline:* For fall admission, 9/24 priority date for domestic and international students; for winter admission, 1/7 priority date for domestic and international students; for spring admission, 4/8 priority date for domestic and international students; for summer admission, 7/8 priority date for domestic and international students. Applications are processed on a rolling basis. Application fee: $30 ($100 for international students). Electronic applications accepted. *Expenses: Tuition:* Full-time $16,300; part-time $460 per credit. *Required fees:* $660; $330 per credit. Tuition and fees vary according to degree level and program. *Financial support:* In 2017–18, 738 students received support. Career-related internships or fieldwork, institutionally sponsored loans, scholarships/grants, tuition waivers (partial), and unspecified assistantships available. Financial award application deadline: 6/30; financial award applicants required to submit FAFSA. *Unit head:* Dr. Gina Ganahl, Dean, Accelerated Degree Programs, 636-949-4501, Fax: 636-949-4505, E-mail: gganahl@lindenwood.edu. *Application contact:* Kara Schilli, Director, Evening and Graduate Admissions, 636-949-4349, Fax: 636-949-4109, E-mail: adultadmissions@lindenwood.edu. Website: http://www.lindenwood.edu/academics/academic-schools/school-of-accelerated-degree-programs/

Lindenwood University, Graduate Programs, School of Arts, Media, and Communications, St. Charles, MO 63301-1695. Offers advertising (MA); art history (MA); cinema and media arts (MFA); communications (MA); digital and Web design (MA); fashion and business design (MS); journalism (MA); mass communications (MA); social media and digital content (MS). *Program availability:* Part-time. *Faculty:* 23 full-time (6 women), 8 part-time/adjunct (4 women). *Students:* 26 full-time (13 women), 11 part-time (8 women); includes 3 minority (1 American Indian or Alaska Native, non-Hispanic/Latino; 2 Hispanic/Latino), 7 international. Average age 33. 60 applicants, 45% accepted, 16 enrolled. In 2017, 11 master's awarded. *Degree requirements:* For master's, thesis (for some programs), minimum cumulative GPA of 3.0. *Entrance requirements:* For master's, audition or interview, minimum GPA of 3.0, portfolio, letter of recommendation. Additional exam requirements/recommendations for international students: Required—TOEFL (minimum score 550 paper-based; 80 iBT); Recommended—IELTS (minimum score 6.5). *Application deadline:* For fall admission, 8/27 priority date for domestic and international students; for spring admission, 1/14 for domestic students, 1/14 priority date for international students; for summer admission, 6/4 priority date for domestic and international students. Applications are processed on a rolling basis. Application fee: $30 ($100 for international students). Electronic applications accepted. *Expenses: Tuition:* Full-time $16,300; part-time $460 per credit. *Required fees:* $660; $330 per credit. Tuition and fees vary according to degree level and program. *Financial support:* In 2017–18, 34 students received support. Career-related internships or fieldwork, institutionally sponsored loans, scholarships/grants, tuition waivers (partial), and unspecified assistantships available. Financial award application deadline: 6/30; financial award applicants required to submit FAFSA. *Unit head:* Dr. Joseph Alsobrook, Dean, School of Arts, Media, and Communications, 636-949-4164, Fax: 636-949-4910, E-mail: jalsobrook@lindenwood.edu. *Application contact:* Kara Schilli, Director, Evening and Graduate Admissions, 636-949-4349, Fax: 636-949-4109, E-mail: adultadmissions@lindenwood.edu. Website: http://www.lindenwood.edu/academics/academic-schools/school-of-arts-media-and-communications/

Lindenwood University–Belleville, Graduate Programs, Belleville, IL 62226. Offers business administration (MBA); communications (MA), including digital and multimedia, media management, promotions, training and development; counseling (MA); criminal justice administration (MS); education (MA); healthcare administration (MS); human resource management (MS); school administration (MA); teaching (MAT).

Long Island University–LIU Brooklyn, Richard L. Conolly College of Liberal Arts and Sciences, Brooklyn, NY 11201-8423. Offers biology (MS); chemistry (MS); clinical psychology (PhD); creative writing (MFA); English (MA); media arts (MA, MFA); political science (MA); psychology (MA); social science (MS); United Nations (Advanced Certificate); urban studies (MA); writing and production for television (MFA). *Program availability:* Part-time. *Faculty:* 32 full-time (13 women), 17 part-time/adjunct (6 women). *Students:* 178 full-time (123 women), 143 part-time (96 women); includes 128 minority (65 Black or African American, non-Hispanic/Latino; 22 Asian, non-Hispanic/Latino; 31 Hispanic/Latino; 10 Two or more races, non-Hispanic/Latino), 54 international. Average age 30. 629 applicants, 38% accepted, 74 enrolled. In 2017, 147 master's, 9 doctorates, 8 other advanced degrees awarded. Terminal master's awarded for partial completion of doctoral program. *Degree requirements:* For master's, comprehensive exam (for some programs), thesis (for some programs); for doctorate, thesis/dissertation. *Entrance requirements:* For doctorate, GRE. Additional exam requirements/recommendations for international students: Required—TOEFL (minimum score 550 paper-based, 79 iBT) or IELTS. *Application deadline:* Applications are processed on a rolling basis. Application fee: $50. Electronic applications accepted. *Expenses: Tuition:* Full-time $21,618; part-time $1201 per credit. *Required fees:* $1840; $920 per term. Tuition and fees vary according to course load. *Financial support:* In 2017–18, 214 students received support, including 120 fellowships with full and partial tuition reimbursements available (averaging $915 per year), 5 research assistantships with full and partial tuition reimbursements available (averaging $2,300 per year), 136 teaching assistantships with full and partial tuition reimbursements available (averaging $2,300 per year); career-related internships or fieldwork, Federal Work-Study, institutionally sponsored loans, scholarships/grants, and unspecified assistantships also available. Support available to part-time students. Financial award application deadline: 2/15; financial award applicants required to submit FAFSA. *Faculty research:* Quantum gravity and astrophysics; string theory; pharmaceutical biotechnology with a focus on molecular details of drug susceptibility/resistance mechanisms; entomology, population and community ecology, agroecology, and biodiversity; psychotherapy process-outcome, particularly therapeutic alliance development, the role of common factors, and the study of treatment failures; personality pathology, borderline personality disorder and pathological narcissism. *Unit head:* Dr. Scott Krawczyk, Dean, 718-488-1003, E-mail: scott.krawczyk@liu.edu. *Application contact:* Bayu Sutrisno, Graduate Admissions Counselor, 718-488-1564, Fax: 718-780-6110, E-mail: bayu.sutrisno@liu.edu.

Louisiana State University and Agricultural & Mechanical College, Graduate School, Manship School of Mass Communication, Baton Rouge, LA 70803. Offers MMC, PhD, JD/MMC. *Accreditation:* ACEJMC. *Faculty:* 24 full-time (10 women). *Students:* 50 full-time (34 women), 9 part-time (5 women); includes 17 minority (16 Black or African American, non-Hispanic/Latino; 1 Two or more races, non-Hispanic/Latino), 9 international. Average age 27. 51 applicants, 65% accepted, 22 enrolled. In 2017, 16 master's, 6 doctorates awarded. *Financial support:* In 2017–18, 29 research assistantships (averaging $21,011 per year), 13 teaching assistantships (averaging $25,523 per year) were awarded. *Total annual research expenditures:* $93,684.

Loyola University Maryland, Graduate Programs, Loyola College of Arts and Sciences, Emerging Media Department, Baltimore, MD 21210-2699. Offers emerging media (MA). *Program availability:* Part-time, evening/weekend, blended/hybrid learning. *Faculty:* 64 full-time (37 women), 31 part-time/adjunct (20 women). *Students:* 13 full-time (9 women), 41 part-time (26 women); includes 20 minority (17 Black or African American, non-Hispanic/Latino; 3 Hispanic/Latino). Average age 31. In 2017, 25 master's awarded. *Application deadline:* For fall admission, 8/1 for domestic students. Applications are processed on a rolling basis. Application fee: $60. Electronic applications accepted. *Expenses:* Contact institution. *Financial support:* Career-related internships or fieldwork, scholarships/grants, and tuition waivers available. Financial award application deadline: 4/15; financial award applicants required to submit FAFSA. *Unit head:* Erin Richardson, Director of Program Operations, 410-617-2462, E-mail: erichardson@loyola.edu. *Application contact:* Office of Graduate Admission, 410-617-5020, E-mail: graduate@loyola.edu.
Website: http://www.loyola.edu/academic/communication/

Lynn University, College of Business and Management, Boca Raton, FL 33431-5598. Offers business administration (MBA), including aviation management, entrepreneurial management, financial valuation and investment management, hospitality management, human resource management, international business management, marketing, media management, social innovation management, sports management, Web development. *Program availability:* Part-time, evening/weekend, 100% online, blended/hybrid learning. *Faculty:* 29 full-time (11 women), 19 part-time/adjunct (7 women). *Students:* 287 full-time (124 women), 195 part-time (105 women); includes 110 minority (44 Black or African American, non-Hispanic/Latino; 2 American Indian or Alaska Native, non-Hispanic/Latino; 11 Asian, non-Hispanic/Latino; 47 Hispanic/Latino; 6 Two or more races, non-Hispanic/Latino), 135 international. Average age 28. 293 applicants, 94% accepted, 192 enrolled. In 2017, 236 master's awarded. *Degree requirements:* For master's, thesis, minimum GPA of 3.0, strategic management seminar, written presentation reflecting the integration and application of theory to practice. *Entrance requirements:* For master's, bachelor's degree from accrediated institution, minimum undergraduate GPA of 2.5, official undergraduate transcripts, resume, personal statement, letter of recommendation from academic or professional sources, writing sample demonstrating capacity to perform at graduate level. Additional exam requirements/recommendations for international students: Required—TOEFL (minimum score 550 paper-based; 80 iBT), IELTS (minimum score 6.5). *Application deadline:* For fall admission, 8/18 for domestic students, 8/4 for international students; for spring admission, 12/15 for domestic students, 12/1 for international students; for summer admission, 4/17 for domestic students, 4/3 for international students. Applications are processed on a rolling basis. Application fee: $45. Electronic applications accepted. *Expenses:* $740 per credit. *Financial support:* Career-related internships or fieldwork, Federal Work-Study, scholarships/grants, tuition waivers (full and partial), and unspecified assistantships available. Support available to part-time students. Financial award application deadline: 3/1; financial award applicants required to submit FAFSA. *Faculty research:* Knowledge economy, urban economy, U.S. manufacturing industries, leadership personality, stock market reactions to terrorism, personality psychology, industrial/organizational psychology. *Unit head:* Dr. RT Good, Dean of the College of Business and Management, 561-237-7458, E-mail: rgood@lynn.edu. *Application contact:* Steven Pruitt, Director of Graduate and Undergraduate Evening Admission, 561-237-7834, Fax: 561-237-7100, E-mail: spruitt@lynn.edu.
Website: http://www.lynn.edu/academics/colleges/business-and-management

Lynn University, Eugene M. and Christine E. Lynn College of Communication and Design, Boca Raton, FL 33431-5598. Offers communication and media (MS), including design strategies for Web development, digital media, media studies and practice; digital media (Certificate); graphic and Web design (MFA); visual effects animation (MFA); Web design and technology (MS). *Program availability:* Part-time, evening/weekend. *Faculty:* 14 full-time (9 women), 7 part-time/adjunct (1 woman). *Students:* 35 full-time (21 women), 33 part-time (13 women); includes 31 minority (12 Black or African American, non-Hispanic/Latino; 2 American Indian or Alaska Native, non-Hispanic/Latino; 2 Asian, non-Hispanic/Latino; 14 Hispanic/Latino; 1 Two or more races, non-Hispanic/Latino), 12 international. Average age 27. 59 applicants, 92% accepted, 44 enrolled. In 2017, 17 master's awarded. *Degree requirements:* For master's, thesis (for some programs), completion of degree in four calendar years; minimum cumulative GPA of 3.0 and C grade or higher in each course; orientation seminar (one credit); 36 credits of foundation and specialization or a thesis. *Entrance requirements:* For master's, bachelor's degree from accredited institution, minimum undergraduate GPA of 3.0, official undergraduate transcripts, letter of recommendation from academic or professional source, writing sample demonstrating capacity to perform at graduate level. Additional exam requirements/recommendations for international students: Required—TOEFL (minimum score 550 paper-based; 80 iBT), IELTS (minimum score 6.5). *Application deadline:* For fall admission, 8/18 for domestic students, 8/4 for international students; for spring admission, 12/15 for domestic students, 12/1 for international students; for summer admission, 4/17 for domestic students, 4/3 for international students. Applications are processed on a rolling basis. Application fee: $45. Electronic applications accepted. *Expenses:* $740 per credit. *Financial support:* Career-related internships or fieldwork, Federal Work-Study, institutionally sponsored loans, scholarships/grants, tuition waivers (partial), and unspecified assistantships available. Support available to part-time students. Financial award application deadline: 8/1; financial award applicants required to submit FAFSA. *Unit head:* Dr. David L. Jaffe, Dean, 561-237-7099, Fax: 561-237-7097, E-mail: djaffe@lynn.edu. *Application contact:* Steven Pruitt, Director of Graduate Admission, 561-237-7834, Fax: 561-237-7100, E-mail: admission@lynn.edu.
Website: https://www.lynn.edu/academics/colleges-schools/communication-and-design

Massachusetts College of Art and Design, Graduate Programs, MFA Program, Boston, MA 02115-5882. Offers 2D fine arts (MFA), including painting, printmaking; 3D fine arts (MFA), including ceramics, fibers, glass, jewelry and metalsmithing, sculpture; design (MFA, Postbaccalaureate Certificate), including dynamic media; fine arts (MFA), including interdisciplinary; media arts (MFA, Postbaccalaureate Certificate), including film/video (MFA), photography. *Accreditation:* NASAD. *Faculty:* 28 full-time (8 women), 28 part-time/adjunct (17 women). *Students:* 44 full-time (26 women), 28 part-time (17 women); includes 8 minority (5 Asian, non-Hispanic/Latino; 3 Hispanic/Latino), 18 international. 247 applicants, 52% accepted, 47 enrolled. In 2017, 42 master's, 5 other advanced degrees awarded. *Degree requirements:* For master's, thesis, thesis exhibition (for fine arts programs); thesis project and document (for design/dynamic media program). *Entrance requirements:* For master's, portfolio, college transcripts, resume, statement of purpose, letters of reference, interview, 6 credits of art history taken prior to or during MFA program; for Postbaccalaureate Certificate, portfolio, college transcripts, resume, statement of purpose, letters of reference, interview. Additional exam requirements/recommendations for international students: Required—TOEFL (minimum score 550 paper-based, 85 iBT) or IELTS (6). *Application deadline:* For fall admission, 1/4 priority date for domestic and international students; for summer admission, 1/4 priority date for domestic and international students. Applications are processed on a rolling basis. Application fee: $90. Electronic applications accepted. *Expenses:* $780 per credit. *Financial support:* In 2017–18, 51 students received support, including 1 research assistantship (averaging $2,160 per year), 33 teaching assistantships (averaging $2,160 per year); fellowships, career-related internships or fieldwork, scholarships/grants, tuition waivers (partial), unspecified assistantships, and adjunct co-teaching positions also available. Support available to part-time students. Financial award application deadline: 1/4; financial award applicants required to submit FAFSA. *Faculty research:* Painting and printmaking, sculpture, photography, film and video, dynamic media design. *Unit head:* Paul Paturzo, Dean of Graduate Studies, 617-879-7166, E-mail: pjpaturzo@massart.edu. *Application contact:* Lauren O'Neill, Assistant Director of Graduate Admissions, 617-879-7222, E-mail: gradadmissions@massart.edu.
Website: http://www.massart.edu/Admissions/Graduate_Programs.html

Massachusetts Institute of Technology, School of Architecture and Planning, Program in Media Arts and Sciences, Cambridge, MA 02139. Offers media arts and sciences (SM, PhD); media technology (SM). Terminal master's awarded for partial completion of doctoral program. *Degree requirements:* For master's, thesis; for doctorate, comprehensive exam, thesis/dissertation. *Entrance requirements:* Additional exam requirements/recommendations for international students: Required—IELTS. Electronic applications accepted. *Faculty research:* Human machine interaction; new media technologies; learning and creativity; design and fabrication; biological interfaces.

Massachusetts Institute of Technology, School of Humanities, Arts, and Social Sciences, Program in Comparative Media Studies/Writing, Program in Comparative Media Studies, Cambridge, MA 02139. Offers SM. *Degree requirements:* For master's, thesis. *Entrance requirements:* For master's, GRE General Test. Additional exam requirements/recommendations for international students: Required—IELTS. Electronic applications accepted. *Faculty research:* Media history and theory; game design, learning games, and creative computing; civic media; digital humanities; TV/film/Internet studies.

Metropolitan College of New York, Program in Business Administration, New York, NY 10006. Offers financial services (MBA); general management (MBA); healthcare systems and risk management (MBA); media management (MBA). *Accreditation:* ACBSP. *Program availability:* Evening/weekend. *Students:* 164 full-time (106 women), 37 part-time (31 women); includes 153 minority (112 Black or African American, non-Hispanic/Latino; 3 American Indian or Alaska Native, non-Hispanic/Latino; 10 Asian, non-Hispanic/Latino; 24 Hispanic/Latino; 1 Native Hawaiian or other Pacific Islander, non-Hispanic/Latino; 3 Two or more races, non-Hispanic/Latino), 31 international. Average age 37. 133 applicants, 62% accepted, 66 enrolled. In 2017, 100 master's awarded. *Degree requirements:* For master's, thesis, 10-day study abroad. *Entrance requirements:* For master's, GMAT. Additional exam requirements/recommendations for international students: Required—TOEFL (minimum score 600 paper-based). *Application deadline:* For fall admission, 7/15 priority date for domestic students; for winter admission, 11/15 priority date for domestic students; for spring admission, 3/30 priority date for domestic students. Applications are processed on a rolling basis. Application fee: $45. Electronic applications accepted. *Expenses:* $926 per credit, $395 fee per semester. *Financial support:* Scholarships/grants available. Financial award application deadline: 8/15; financial award applicants required to submit FAFSA. *Unit head:* Dr. Tilokie Depoo, Dean and Professor, School for Business, 212-343-1234 Ext. 2204. *Application contact:* Steebo Varghese, Assistant Director of Admissions, 212-343-1234 Ext. 2708, Fax: 212-343-8470.

Michigan State University, The Graduate School, College of Communication Arts and Sciences, Department of Telecommunication, Information Studies, and Media, East Lansing, MI 48824. Offers digital media arts and technology (MA); information and telecommunication management (MA); information, policy and society (MA); serious game design (MA). *Entrance requirements:* Additional exam requirements/recommendations for international students: Required—TOEFL. Electronic applications accepted.

Media Studies

Michigan State University, The Graduate School, College of Communication Arts and Sciences, Program in Communication Arts and Sciences–Media and Information Studies, East Lansing, MI 48824. Offers PhD. *Entrance requirements:* Additional exam requirements/recommendations for international students: Required—TOEFL. Electronic applications accepted. *Faculty research:* Mass media, comparative media.

Missouri Western State University, Program in Digital Media, St. Joseph, MO 64507-2294. Offers MAA, Graduate Certificate. *Program availability:* Part-time. *Students:* 5 full-time (2 women), 7 part-time (2 women), 6 international. Average age 30. 5 applicants, 40% accepted, 1 enrolled. In 2017, 7 master's awarded. *Entrance requirements:* For master's, minimum GPA of 2.75, curriculum vitae, interview, 3 letters of reference, letter of intent, portfolio. Additional exam requirements/recommendations for international students: Recommended—TOEFL (minimum score 79 iBT), IELTS (minimum score 6). *Application deadline:* For fall admission, 7/15 for domestic and international students; for spring admission, 10/1 for domestic and international students; for summer admission, 3/15 for domestic students. Applications are processed on a rolling basis. Application fee: $45 ($50 for international students). Electronic applications accepted. *Expenses:* Tuition: state resident: full-time $6391; part-time $336 per credit hour. Tuition, nonresident: full-time $11,483; part-time $604 per credit hour. *Required fees:* $542; $99 per credit hour. $176 per semester. One-time fee: $45. Tuition and fees vary according to course load and program. *Financial support:* Scholarships/grants and unspecified assistantships available. Support available to part-time students. Unit head: Dr. Bob Bergland, Professor, 816-271-4446, E-mail: bergland@missouriwestern.edu. *Application contact:* Dr. Benjamin D. Caldwell, Dean of the Graduate School, 816-271-4394, Fax: 816-271-4525, E-mail: graduate@missouriwestern.edu.
Website: http://www.missouriwestern.edu/digitalmedia/

Monmouth University, Graduate Studies, Department of Communication, West Long Branch, NJ 07764-1898. Offers corporate and public communication (MA); human resources management and communication (Certificate); public service communication specialist (Certificate); strategic public relations and new media (Certificate). *Program availability:* Part-time, evening/weekend, online learning. *Faculty:* 4 full-time (3 women), 2 part-time/adjunct (both women). *Students:* 10 full-time (7 women), 18 part-time (14 women); includes 9 minority (5 Black or African American, non-Hispanic/Latino; 1 Asian, non-Hispanic/Latino; 3 Hispanic/Latino). Average age 28. In 2017, 18 master's, 1 other advanced degree awarded. Terminal master's awarded for partial completion of doctoral program. *Degree requirements:* For master's, comprehensive exam (for some programs), thesis (for some programs), project. *Entrance requirements:* For master's, GRE, baccalaureate degree with minimum GPA of 3.0 in major, 2.75 overall; two letters of recommendation; personal essay (750 words or less describing preparation for study and personal objectives); digital or hard copy portfolio of select samples of work including writing sample; resume. Additional exam requirements/recommendations for international students: Required—TOEFL (minimum score 550 paper-based; 79 iBT), IELTS (minimum score 6), Michigan English Language Assessment Battery (minimum score 77). *Application deadline:* For fall admission, 7/15 priority date for domestic students, 6/1 for international students; for spring admission, 12/1 priority date for domestic students, 11/1 for international students; for summer admission, 5/1 for domestic students. Applications are processed on a rolling basis. Application fee: $50. Electronic applications accepted. *Expenses:* Tuition: Full-time $21,366; part-time $7122 per credit. *Required fees:* $700; $175 per term. *Financial support:* In 2017–18, 2 students received support. Institutionally sponsored loans, scholarships/grants, and unspecified assistantships available. Support available to part-time students. Financial award applicants required to submit FAFSA. *Faculty research:* Service-learning, history of television, feminism and the media, executive communication, public relations pedagogy. *Unit head:* Dr. Marina Vujnovic, Program Director, 732-263-5667, Fax: 732-571-5667, E-mail: mvujnovi@monmouth.edu. *Application contact:* Andrea Thompson, Graduate Admission Counselor, 732-571-3452, Fax: 732-263-5123, E-mail: gradadm@monmouth.edu.
Website: http://www.monmouth.edu/cpc

New Mexico Highlands University, Graduate Studies, College of Arts and Sciences, Department of Computer Sciences, Las Vegas, NM 87701. Offers media arts and computer science (MS), including computer science. *Degree requirements:* For master's, comprehensive exam, thesis. *Entrance requirements:* For master's, minimum undergraduate GPA of 3.0. Additional exam requirements/recommendations for international students: Required—TOEFL (minimum score 540 paper-based). *Faculty research:* Advanced digital compositing, photographic installations and exhibition design, pattern recognition, parallel and distributed computing, computer security education.

The New School, Schools of Public Engagement, Program in Media Studies, New York, NY 10003. Offers documentary media studies (Graduate Certificate); media management (MS, Graduate Certificate); media studies (MA). *Program availability:* Part-time, 100% online. *Faculty:* 17 full-time (8 women), 22 part-time/adjunct (5 women). *Students:* 218 full-time (162 women), 142 part-time (99 women); includes 128 minority (68 Black or African American, non-Hispanic/Latino; 3 American Indian or Alaska Native, non-Hispanic/Latino; 6 Asian, non-Hispanic/Latino; 39 Hispanic/Latino; 1 Native Hawaiian or other Pacific Islander, non-Hispanic/Latino; 11 Two or more races, non-Hispanic/Latino), 115 international. Average age 29. 268 applicants, 94% accepted, 124 enrolled. In 2017, 162 master's, 52 other advanced degrees awarded. *Degree requirements:* For master's, thesis, capstone project (for MS); for Graduate Certificate, thesis optional, synthesis paper (for media management). *Entrance requirements:* For master's, two letters of recommendation, statement of purpose, resume, transcripts, writing sample (strongly encouraged). Additional exam requirements/recommendations for international students: Required—TOEFL (minimum score 92 iBT), IELTS (minimum score 7), PTE (minimum score 68). *Application deadline:* For fall admission, 2/5 priority date for domestic and international students; for spring admission, 10/15 priority date for domestic and international students. Applications are processed on a rolling basis. Application fee: $50. Electronic applications accepted. *Expenses:* $1,567 per credit. *Financial support:* In 2017–18, 244 students received support, including 6 teaching assistantships (averaging $5,644 per year); career-related internships or fieldwork, Federal Work-Study, scholarships/grants, and unspecified assistantships also available. Support available to part-time students. Financial award application deadline: 2/1; financial award applicants required to submit FAFSA. *Application contact:* Karl Ramos, Assistant Director of Graduate Admission, 212-229-5630 Ext. 2330, E-mail: ramosk@newschool.edu.
Website: https://www.newschool.edu/public-engagement/ma-media-studies/

New York University, Graduate School of Arts and Science, Department of Anthropology, Program in Culture and Media, New York, NY 10012-1019. Offers MA/Advanced Certificate, PhD/Advanced Certificate. *Students:* Average age 30. 25 applicants, 8% accepted, 1 enrolled. *Entrance requirements:* Additional exam requirements/recommendations for international students: Required—TOEFL. *Application deadline:* For fall admission, 12/18 priority date for domestic students, 12/18 for international students. Application fee: $100. *Expenses:* Tuition: Full-time $41,352; part-time $19,968 per year. *Required fees:* $2496; $1628 per unit. $814 per term. Tuition and fees vary according to course load and program. *Financial support:* Fellowships, research assistantships, teaching assistantships, career-related internships or fieldwork,

institutionally sponsored loans, scholarships/grants, health care benefits, and unspecified assistantships available. Financial award application deadline: 12/18. *Faculty research:* Critical history of ethnographic film, ethnography of media, indigenous media, politics of reproduction and disability, social movements. *Unit head:* Faye Ginsburg, Director, 212-998-3759, Fax: 212-995-4730, E-mail: anthropology@nyu.edu. *Application contact:* Pegi Vail, Associate Director, 212-998-3759, Fax: 212-995-4730, E-mail: anthropology@nyu.edu.
Website: http://www.nyu.edu/gsas/dept/anthro/

New York University, School of Professional Studies, Preston Robert Tisch Institute for Global Sport, New York, NY 10012-1019. Offers sports business (MS), including global sports media, professional and collegiate sports operations, sports law, sports marketing and sales. *Program availability:* Part-time, evening/weekend. *Students:* 70 full-time (21 women), 38 part-time (13 women); includes 21 minority (6 Black or African American, non-Hispanic/Latino; 7 Asian, non-Hispanic/Latino; 5 Hispanic/Latino; 1 Native Hawaiian or other Pacific Islander, non-Hispanic/Latino; 2 Two or more races, non-Hispanic/Latino), 52 international. Average age 26. 145 applicants, 67% accepted, 46 enrolled. In 2017, 78 master's awarded. *Degree requirements:* For master's, thesis. *Entrance requirements:* For master's, GRE or GMAT (only upon request), bachelor's degree, resume with relevant professional work, internship or volunteer experience, two letters of recommendation, statement of purpose. Additional exam requirements/recommendations for international students: Required—TOEFL (minimum score 600 paper-based; 100 iBT), IELTS (minimum score 7). *Application deadline:* For fall admission, 2/1 priority date for domestic and international students; for spring admission, 10/15 priority date for domestic students, 8/15 priority date for international students. Applications are processed on a rolling basis. Application fee: $150. Electronic applications accepted. *Expenses:* $20,244 per term. *Financial support:* Fellowships, career-related internships or fieldwork, Federal Work-Study, scholarships/grants, and health care benefits available. Support available to part-time students. Financial award application deadline: 6/30; financial award applicants required to submit FAFSA. *Unit head:* Vince Gennaro, Associate Dean/Clinical Associate Professor, 212-995-4676. *Application contact:* Admissions Office, 212-998-7100, E-mail: sps.gradadmissions@nyu.edu.
Website: http://www.sps.nyu.edu/content/scps/academics/departments/tisch-institute.html

New York University, Steinhardt School of Culture, Education, and Human Development, Department of Media, Culture and Communication, New York, NY 10012. Offers media, culture and communication (MA, PhD); MLIS/MA. *Program availability:* Part-time. *Students:* Average age 33. 550 applicants, 24% accepted, 46 enrolled. In 2017, 57 master's, 6 doctorates awarded. Terminal master's awarded for partial completion of doctoral program. *Entrance requirements:* For master's, GRE General Test; for doctorate, GRE General Test, interview. Additional exam requirements/recommendations for international students: Required—TOEFL (minimum score 100 iBT). *Application deadline:* For fall admission, 12/1 priority date for domestic and international students; for spring admission, 10/1 for domestic and international students. Applications are processed on a rolling basis. Application fee: $75. Electronic applications accepted. *Expenses:* Tuition: Full-time $41,352; part-time $19,968 per year. *Required fees:* $2496; $1628 per unit. $814 per term. Tuition and fees vary according to course load and program. *Financial support:* Fellowships with full and partial tuition reimbursements, teaching assistantships with full and partial tuition reimbursements, career-related internships or fieldwork, Federal Work-Study, institutionally sponsored loans, scholarships/grants, tuition waivers (partial), and unspecified assistantships available. Support available to part-time students. Financial award application deadline: 2/1; financial award applicants required to submit FAFSA. *Faculty research:* Digital media and new technologies, media criticism, flow of media and culture transnationally and transculturally. *Unit head:* Prof. Lisa Gitelman, Chairperson, 212-998-5191, Fax: 212-995-4046, E-mail: lg91@nyu.edu. *Application contact:* 212-998-5030, Fax: 212-995-4328, E-mail: steinhardt.gradadmissions@nyu.edu.
Website: http://steinhardt.nyu.edu/mcc

Norfolk State University, School of Graduate Studies, School of Liberal Arts, Department of Media and Communication, Norfolk, VA 23504. Offers MA. *Program availability:* Part-time. *Degree requirements:* For master's, thesis. *Entrance requirements:* For master's, GRE, minimum GPA of 2.5, letters of recommendation. Additional exam requirements/recommendations for international students: Required—TOEFL.

Northern Kentucky University, Office of Graduate Programs, College of Informatics, Program in Communication, Highland Heights, KY 41099. Offers communication (MA); communication teaching (Certificate); documentary studies (Certificate); public relations (Certificate); relationships (Certificate). *Program availability:* Part-time, evening/weekend. Terminal master's awarded for partial completion of doctoral program. *Degree requirements:* For master's, comprehensive exams, thesis or applied capstone project. *Entrance requirements:* For master's, GRE, minimum GPA of 3.0, 3 letters of recommendation, letter of intent. Additional exam requirements/recommendations for international students: Required—TOEFL (minimum score 79 iBT); Recommended—IELTS (minimum score 6.5). Electronic applications accepted. *Faculty research:* Mediating effect of health communication, organizational communication, quantitative and qualitative research methods, family and interpersonal communication.

Northwestern University, The Graduate School, Kellogg School of Management, Management Programs, Evanston, IL 60208. Offers accounting information and management (MBA, PhD); analytical finance (MBA); business administration (MBA); decision sciences (MBA); entrepreneurship and innovation (MBA); finance (MBA, PhD); health enterprise management (MBA); human resources management (MBA); international business (MBA); management and organizations (MBA, PhD); management and organizations and sociology (PhD); management and strategy (MBA); management studies (MS); managerial analytics (MBA); managerial economics (MBA); managerial economics and strategy (PhD); marketing (MBA, PhD); marketing management (MBA); media management (MBA); operations management (MBA, PhD); real estate (MBA); social enterprise at Kellogg (MBA); JD/MBA. *Program availability:* Part-time, evening/weekend. Terminal master's awarded for partial completion of doctoral program. *Degree requirements:* For doctorate, thesis/dissertation, 2 years of coursework, qualifying (field) exam and candidacy, summer research papers and presentations to faculty, proposal defense, final exam/defense. *Entrance requirements:* For master's, GMAT, GRE, interview, 2 letters of recommendation, college transcripts, resume, essays, Kellogg honor code; for doctorate, GMAT, GRE, statement of purpose, transcripts, 2 letters of recommendation, resume, interview. Additional exam requirements/recommendations for international students: Required—TOEFL, IELTS. Electronic applications accepted. *Expenses:* Contact institution. *Faculty research:* Business cycles and international finance, health policy, networks, non-market strategy, consumer psychology.

Northwestern University, The Graduate School, School of Communication, Department of Communication Studies, Evanston, IL 60208. Offers communication studies (PhD), including interaction and social influence, rhetoric and public culture; managerial communication (MSC); media, technology and society (PhD); technology and social behavior (PhD). PhD admissions and degree offered through The Graduate

School. Terminal master's awarded for partial completion of doctoral program. *Degree requirements:* For doctorate, thesis/dissertation. *Entrance requirements:* For master's and doctorate, GRE General Test. Additional exam requirements/recommendations for international students: Required—TOEFL. Electronic applications accepted.

Northwestern University, The Graduate School, School of Communication, Department of Radio, Television and Film, Evanston, IL 60208. Offers documentary media (MFA); screen cultures (MA, PhD); writing for the screen and stage (MFA). Admissions and degrees offered through The Graduate School. *Program availability:* Part-time. Terminal master's awarded for partial completion of doctoral program. *Degree requirements:* For master's, comprehensive exam or thesis; for doctorate, thesis/dissertation, qualifying exam. *Entrance requirements:* For master's and doctorate, GRE General Test. Additional exam requirements/recommendations for international students: Required—TOEFL. Electronic applications accepted. *Faculty research:* Art and new media, media theory and criticism, gender, media history, documentary.

Ohio University, Graduate College, Scripps College of Communication, School of Media Arts and Studies, Athens, OH 45701-2979. Offers communication media arts (MFA); mass communication (PhD); media arts and studies (MA). PhD offered jointly with E.W. Scripps School of Journalism; MFA offered in partnership with School of Visual Communication. *Degree requirements:* For master's, comprehensive exam (for some programs), thesis or alternative; for doctorate, comprehensive exam, thesis/dissertation. *Entrance requirements:* For master's, GRE General Test or MAT, minimum GPA of 3.0; for doctorate, GRE General Test or MAT. Additional exam requirements/recommendations for international students: Required—TOEFL (minimum score 600 paper-based; 100 iBT) or IELTS (minimum score 7). Electronic applications accepted. *Faculty research:* Media and development communication, new media and society, industry studies.

Old Dominion University, College of Arts and Letters, Institute for the Humanities, Norfolk, VA 23529. Offers arts and entrepreneurship (Certificate); cultural and human geography (MA); cultural studies (MA); gender and sexuality studies (MA); health, communication and culture (Certificate); media and popular culture studies (MA); philosophy and religious studies (MA); social justice and entrepreneurship (Certificate); visual studies (MA); world cultures (MA). *Program availability:* Part-time, evening/weekend. *Faculty:* 1 full-time (0 women), 1 part-time/adjunct (0 women). *Students:* 20 full-time (16 women), 13 part-time (8 women); includes 15 minority (8 Black or African American, non-Hispanic/Latino; 2 Asian, non-Hispanic/Latino; 2 Hispanic/Latino; 3 Two or more races, non-Hispanic/Latino), 2 international. Average age 35. 27 applicants, 96% accepted, 22 enrolled. In 2017, 3 master's awarded. *Degree requirements:* For master's, thesis optional, project. *Entrance requirements:* For master's, GRE General Test, minimum GPA of 3.25. *Application deadline:* For fall admission, 6/15 for domestic students; for spring admission, 11/15 for domestic students; for summer admission, 4/15 for domestic students. Applications are processed on a rolling basis. Application fee: $50. Electronic applications accepted. *Expenses:* Tuition, state resident: full-time $8928; part-time $496 per credit. Tuition, nonresident: full-time $22,482; part-time $1249 per credit. *Required fees:* $66 per semester. *Financial support:* In 2017–18, 3 students received support, including 5 research assistantships (averaging $10,000 per year); career-related internships or fieldwork, scholarships/grants, and unspecified assistantships also available. Financial award application deadline: 3/15; financial award applicants required to submit FAFSA. *Faculty research:* Media studies, cultural studies, gender studies, American literature, philosophy, art history, cultural geography. *Unit head:* Dr. Avi D. Santo, Graduate Program Director, 757-683-3719, Fax: 757-683-6191, E-mail: humgpd@odu.edu. *Application contact:* Dr. David C. Earnest, Associate Dean, 757-683-6077, Fax: 757-683-5746, E-mail: dearnest@odu.edu.
Website: http://al.odu.edu/hum/

Pace University, Dyson College of Arts and Sciences, MA Program in Media and Communication Arts, New York, NY 10038. Offers MA. *Program availability:* Part-time, evening/weekend. *Students:* 6 full-time (2 women), 20 part-time (15 women); includes 13 minority (6 Black or African American, non-Hispanic/Latino; 1 Asian, non-Hispanic/Latino; 5 Hispanic/Latino; 1 Two or more races, non-Hispanic/Latino), 5 international. Average age 25. In 2017, 14 master's awarded. *Degree requirements:* For master's, comprehensive exam, thesis, internship. *Entrance requirements:* For master's, portfolio containing examples of prior work (press releases, advertisements, presentations, writing samples, etc.) and official transcripts. Additional exam requirements/recommendations for international students: Required—TOEFL (minimum score 100 iBT). *Application deadline:* For fall admission, 8/1 priority date for domestic students, 6/1 for international students; for spring admission, 12/1 priority date for domestic students, 10/1 for international students. Applications are processed on a rolling basis. Application fee: $70. Electronic applications accepted. *Financial support:* Career-related internships or fieldwork, scholarships/grants, and unspecified assistantships available. Financial award application deadline: 2/15; financial award applicants required to submit FAFSA. *Unit head:* Dr. Maria Luskay, Program Director, 914-773-3353, E-mail: mluskay@pace.edu. *Application contact:* Susan Ford-Goldschein, Director of Admissions, 914-422-4283, Fax: 212-346-1585, E-mail: graduateadmission@pace.edu.
Website: http://www.pace.edu/dyson/programs/ma-media-communication-arts-plv

Paris College of Art, Graduate Programs, Paris, France. Offers accessories design (MA); fashion design: new materials and technologies (MA); fashion film and photography (MA); interior design (MA); transdisciplinary new media (MA, MFA). *Entrance requirements:* Additional exam requirements/recommendations for international students: Required—TOEFL or IELTS.

Penn State University Park, Graduate School, Donald P. Bellisario College of Communications, Department of Communications, University Park, PA 16802. Offers mass communications (PhD); media studies (MA). *Unit head:* Dr. Marie C. Hardin, Dean, 814-863-1484, Fax: 814-863-8044. *Application contact:* Lori Hawn, Director, Graduate Student Services, 814-865-1795, Fax: 814-863-4627, E-mail: l-gswww@lists.psu.edu.
Website: http://comm.psu.edu/

Pepperdine University, Seaver College, Division of Communication, Malibu, CA 90263. Offers cinematic media production (MFA); strategic communication (MA). *Program availability:* Part-time. *Students:* 8 full-time (3 women), 15 part-time (9 women); includes 9 minority (4 Black or African American, non-Hispanic/Latino; 1 American Indian or Alaska Native, non-Hispanic/Latino; 3 Asian, non-Hispanic/Latino; 1 Hispanic/Latino), 3 international. Average age 27. In 2017, 6 master's awarded. *Entrance requirements:* For master's, GRE General Test, letters of recommendation, writing sample. Additional exam requirements/recommendations for international students: Required—TOEFL. *Application deadline:* For fall admission, 2/1 priority date for domestic students, 2/1 for international students. Applications are processed on a rolling basis. Application fee: $65. Electronic applications accepted. *Financial support:* Research assistantships, teaching assistantships, career-related internships or fieldwork, and scholarships/grants available. Support available to part-time students. Financial award applicants required to submit FAFSA. *Unit head:* Dr. Kenneth E. Waters, Divisional Dean/Professor of Journalism, 310-506-4245, E-mail: ken.waters@pepperdine.edu. *Application contact:* Hayley Wolf, Director of Admission, 310-506-4392, E-mail: hayley.wolf@pepperdine.edu.

Point Park University, School of Communication, Pittsburgh, PA 15222-1984. Offers communication technology (MA); media communication (MA). *Program availability:* Part-time, evening/weekend. *Degree requirements:* For master's, comprehensive exam (for some programs), thesis or alternative. *Entrance requirements:* For master's, GRE (if GPA less than 2.75), minimum GPA of 2.75, 2 letters of recommendation, statement of intent. Additional exam requirements/recommendations for international students: Required—TOEFL (minimum score 570 paper-based; 88 iBT), IELTS (minimum score 6.5); Recommended—TWE (minimum score 5). Electronic applications accepted.

Pratt Institute, School of Liberal Arts and Sciences, Program in Media Studies, Brooklyn, NY 11205-3899. Offers MA. *Students:* 14 full-time (10 women), 2 part-time (1 woman); includes 7 minority (3 Black or African American, non-Hispanic/Latino; 1 Asian, non-Hispanic/Latino; 2 Hispanic/Latino; 1 Two or more races, non-Hispanic/Latino), 4 international. Average age 27. 44 applicants, 93% accepted, 7 enrolled. In 2017, 6 master's awarded. *Degree requirements:* For master's, thesis. *Entrance requirements:* For master's, BA, BS, or BFA from accredited institution; statement of purpose; 10-20 pages of relevant writing samples; transcripts of undergraduate coursework; three letters of recommendation. Additional exam requirements/recommendations for international students: Required—TOEFL (minimum score 600 paper-based; 100 iBT). *Application deadline:* For fall admission, 1/5 for domestic and international students; for spring admission, 10/1 for domestic and international students. Application fee: $50 ($90 for international students). Electronic applications accepted. *Expenses: Tuition:* Full-time $30,834. *Required fees:* $1974. *Financial support:* Career-related internships or fieldwork, Federal Work-Study, institutionally sponsored loans, scholarships/grants, health care benefits, and unspecified assistantships available. Support available to part-time students. Financial award application deadline: 2/1; financial award applicants required to submit FAFSA. *Unit head:* Arlene Keizer, Chair, 718-636-3421, E-mail: akeizer@pratt.edu. *Application contact:* Natalie Capannelli, Director of Graduate Admissions, 718-636-3551, Fax: 718-399-4242, E-mail: ncapanne@pratt.edu.
Website: https://www.pratt.edu/academics/liberal-arts-and-sciences/graduate-media-studies/

See Display on the next page and Close-Up on page 749.

Purchase College, State University of New York, School of Film and Media Studies, Purchase, NY 10577-1400. Offers media arts and culture (MFA). *Unit head:* Agustin Zarzosa, Chair, 914-251-6860, E-mail: fms@purchase.edu. *Application contact:* Sabrina Johnston, Admissions Counselor, 914-251-6479, Fax: 914-251-6314, E-mail: admissn@purchase.edu.
Website: https://www.purchase.edu/academics/school-of-film-and-media-studies/

Queens College of the City University of New York, Arts and Humanities Division, Department of Media Studies, Queens, NY 11367-1597. Offers MA. *Faculty:* 14 full-time (7 women), 11 part-time/adjunct (6 women). *Students:* 5 full-time (3 women), 11 part-time (3 women); includes 5 minority (2 Asian, non-Hispanic/Latino; 3 Hispanic/Latino), 2 international. Average age 28. 27 applicants, 52% accepted, 8 enrolled. In 2017, 5 master's awarded. *Degree requirements:* For master's, thesis. *Entrance requirements:* For master's, GRE General Test, minimum GPA of 3.0. Additional exam requirements/recommendations for international students: Required—TOEFL. *Application deadline:* For fall admission, 4/1 for domestic students; for spring admission, 11/1 for domestic students. Applications are processed on a rolling basis. Application fee: $50. *Financial support:* Career-related internships or fieldwork, Federal Work-Study, institutionally sponsored loans, and tuition waivers (partial) available. Support available to part-time students. Financial award application deadline: 4/1; financial award applicants required to submit FAFSA. *Unit head:* Dr. Richard Maxwell, Chair, 718-997-2950, E-mail: richard.maxwell@qc.cuny.edu. *Application contact:* Elizabeth D'Amico-Ramirez, Assistant Director of Graduate Admissions, 718-997-5203, E-mail: elizabeth.damicoramirez@qc.cuny.edu.

Rhode Island School of Design, Department of Digital and Media, Providence, RI 02903-2784. Offers MFA. *Faculty:* 2 full-time (0 women), 11 part-time/adjunct (5 women). *Students:* 19 full-time (9 women); includes 2 minority (1 Asian, non-Hispanic/Latino; 1 Two or more races, non-Hispanic/Latino), 10 international. Average age 26. 143 applicants, 18% accepted, 11 enrolled. In 2017, 15 master's awarded. *Degree requirements:* For master's, thesis, exhibition. *Entrance requirements:* For master's, portfolio, statement of purpose, 3 letters of recommendation. Additional exam requirements/recommendations for international students: Required—TOEFL (minimum score 580 paper-based; 93 iBT). *Application deadline:* For fall admission, 1/10 for domestic and international students. Application fee: $60. Electronic applications accepted. *Expenses: Tuition:* Full-time $48,210. *Required fees:* $260. *Financial support:* Fellowships, research assistantships, teaching assistantships, Federal Work-Study, scholarships/grants, and unspecified assistantships available. Financial award application deadline: 2/15; financial award applicants required to submit FAFSA. *Unit head:* Shona Kitchen, Department Head and Graduate Program Director, 401-454-6139, Fax: 401-277-4966, E-mail: digital@risd.edu. *Application contact:* Molly Pettengill, Assistant Director for Graduate Recruitment, 401-454-6312, Fax: 401-454-6309, E-mail: mpetteng@risd.edu.
Website: http://www.risd.edu/academics/digital-media/

Rochester Institute of Technology, Graduate Enrollment Services, College of Imaging Arts and Sciences, School of Media Sciences, MS Program in Media Arts and Technology, Rochester, NY 14623-5603. Offers MS. *Program availability:* Part-time, evening/weekend. *Students:* 14 full-time (7 women); includes 2 minority (1 Black or African American, non-Hispanic/Latino; 1 Asian, non-Hispanic/Latino), 8 international. Average age 25. 20 applicants, 85% accepted, 14 enrolled. *Degree requirements:* For master's, capstone project. *Entrance requirements:* For master's, minimum GPA of 3.0 (recommended). Additional exam requirements/recommendations for international students: Required—TOEFL (minimum score 79 iBT), IELTS (minimum score 6.5), PTE (minimum score 58). *Application deadline:* Applications are processed on a rolling basis. Application fee: $65. Electronic applications accepted. *Expenses:* $1,815 per credit hour. *Financial support:* In 2017–18, 14 students received support. Research assistantships with partial tuition reimbursements available, teaching assistantships with partial tuition reimbursements available, career-related internships or fieldwork, scholarships/grants, and unspecified assistantships available. Support available to part-time students. Financial award applicants required to submit FAFSA. *Faculty research:* Digital publishing, digital content management, media distribution, consumer preferences, media business transformation. *Unit head:* Christine Heusner, Graduate Program Director, 585-475-4627, E-mail: cxhppr@rit.edu. *Application contact:* Diane Ellison, Senior Associate Vice President, Graduate Enrollment Services, 585-475-2229, Fax: 585-475-7164, E-mail: gradinfo@rit.edu.
Website: http://cias.rit.edu/schools/media-sciences/graduate-media-arts-and-technology

Rochester Institute of Technology, Graduate Enrollment Services, College of Liberal Arts, School of Communication, MS Program in Communication and Media Technologies, Rochester, NY 14623. Offers MS. *Program availability:* Part-time. *Students:* 11 full-time (10 women), 6 part-time (5 women); includes 1 minority (Black or African American, non-Hispanic/Latino), 9 international. Average age 25. 33 applicants, 48% accepted, 10 enrolled. In 2017, 13 master's awarded. *Degree requirements:* For

master's, thesis. *Entrance requirements:* For master's, minimum GPA of 3.0 (recommended), writing sample. Additional exam requirements/recommendations for international students: Required—TOEFL (minimum score 570 paper-based; 88 iBT), IELTS (minimum score 6.5), PTE (minimum score 61). *Application deadline:* For fall admission, 2/15 priority date for domestic and international students; for spring admission, 12/15 priority date for domestic and international students. Applications are processed on a rolling basis. Application fee: $65. Electronic applications accepted. *Expenses:* $1,815 per credit hour. *Financial support:* Research assistantships with partial tuition reimbursements, teaching assistantships with partial tuition reimbursements, career-related internships or fieldwork, scholarships/grants, and unspecified assistantships available. Support available to part-time students. Financial award applicants required to submit FAFSA. *Faculty research:* Media and culture, visual communication, mass media, technology and media. *Unit head:* Dr. Grant Cos, Graduate Program Director, 585-475-6646, Fax: 585-475-7732, E-mail: communication@rit.edu. *Application contact:* Diane Ellison, Senior Associate Vice President, Graduate Enrollment Services, 585-475-2229, Fax: 585-475-7164, E-mail: gradinfo@rit.edu.
Website: http://www.rit.edu/cla/communication/graduate-programs/ms-communication-media-technologies/overview

Rowan University, Graduate School, College of Communication and Creative Arts, Integrated Marketing Communication and New Media Certificate of Graduate Study Program, Glassboro, NJ 08028-1701. Offers CGS. Electronic applications accepted. *Expenses:* Tuition, state resident: full-time $15,020; part-time $751 per semester hour. Tuition, nonresident: full-time $15,020; part-time $751 per semester hour. *Required fees:* $3158; $157.90 per semester hour. Tuition and fees vary according to course load, campus/location and program.

Saginaw Valley State University, College of Arts and Behavioral Sciences, Program in Communication and Media Administration, University Center, MI 48710. Offers MA. *Program availability:* Part-time, evening/weekend. *Students:* 18 full-time (8 women), 8 part-time (6 women); includes 3 minority (1 Black or African American, non-Hispanic/Latino; 2 Asian, non-Hispanic/Latino), 20 international. Average age 27. 22 applicants, 82% accepted, 12 enrolled. In 2017, 24 master's awarded. *Degree requirements:* For master's, thesis. *Entrance requirements:* For master's, minimum GPA of 3.0. Additional exam requirements/recommendations for international students: Required—TOEFL (minimum score 540 paper-based; 76 iBT). *Application deadline:* For fall admission, 7/15 for international students; for winter admission, 11/15 for international students; for spring admission, 4/15 for international students. Applications are processed on a rolling basis. Application fee: $30 ($90 for international students). Electronic applications accepted. *Expenses:* Tuition, state resident: full-time $10,156; part-time $564.20 per credit hour. Tuition, nonresident: full-time $19,336; part-time $1074.20 per credit hour. *Required fees:* $263; $14.60 per credit hour. Tuition and fees vary according to degree level and program. *Financial support:* Federal Work-Study and scholarships/grants available. Support available to part-time students. Financial award application deadline: 4/1; financial award applicants required to submit FAFSA. *Unit head:* Dr. Robert Drew, Professor of Communication, 989-964-7495, E-mail: rdrew@svsu.edu. *Application contact:* Jenna Briggs, Director, Graduate and International Admissions, 989-964-6096, Fax: 989-964-2788, E-mail: gradadm@svsu.edu.

San Diego State University, Graduate and Research Affairs, College of Professional Studies and Fine Arts, School of Communication, San Diego, CA 92182. Offers advertising and public relations (MA); critical-cultural studies (MA); interaction studies (MA); intercultural and international studies (MA); new media studies (MA); news and information studies (MA); telecommunications and media management (MA). *Degree requirements:* For master's, thesis. *Entrance requirements:* For master's, GRE General Test, 3 letters of recommendation. Additional exam requirements/recommendations for international students: Required—TOEFL. Electronic applications accepted.

San Diego State University, Graduate and Research Affairs, College of Professional Studies and Fine Arts, School of Theater, Television and Film, Program in Television, Film, and New Media Production, San Diego, CA 92182. Offers MA. *Entrance requirements:* For master's, GRE General Test, 3 letters of recommendation, resume, sample reel, influential book list, influential films list, hobby list. Additional exam requirements/recommendations for international students: Required—TOEFL. Electronic applications accepted. *Faculty research:* Experimental film and television programs, documentary film, television research and production.

San Francisco State University, Division of Graduate Studies, College of Liberal and Creative Arts, Department of Broadcast and Electronic Communication Arts, San Francisco, CA 94132-1722. Offers MA. *Unit head:* Dr. Vinay Shrivastava, Chair, 415-338-1787, Fax: 415-338-1168, E-mail: vinay@sfsu.edu. *Application contact:* Dr. Nancy Reist, Graduate Coordinator, 415-338-1787, Fax: 415-338-1168, E-mail: sami@sfsu.edu.
Website: http://beca.sfsu.edu/

San Jose State University, Graduate Studies and Research, College of Humanities and the Arts, San Jose, CA 95192-0088. Offers art (MA, MFA), including digital media art (MFA), history and visual culture (MA), photography (MFA), pictorial art (MFA), spatial art (MFA); English (MA, MFA), including creative writing (MFA); linguistics (MA); music (MM); music education (MA); philosophy (MA); Spanish (MA); teaching English to speakers of other languages (MA). *Program availability:* Part-time. *Faculty:* 35 full-time (17 women), 19 part-time/adjunct (11 women). *Students:* 129 full-time (79 women), 106 part-time (71 women); includes 117 minority (5 Black or African American, non-Hispanic/Latino; 29 Asian, non-Hispanic/Latino; 44 Hispanic/Latino; 39 Two or more races, non-Hispanic/Latino), 28 international. Average age 35. 204 applicants, 65% accepted, 79 enrolled. In 2017, 85 master's awarded. *Degree requirements:* For master's, one foreign language, comprehensive exam (for some programs), thesis (for some programs), graduate writing assessment, special study/project, recital. *Entrance requirements:* Additional exam requirements/recommendations for international students: Required—TOEFL (minimum score 550 paper-based; 80 iBT), IELTS (minimum score 6.5), PTE (minimum score 53). *Application deadline:* For fall admission, 2/1 for domestic and international students. Applications are processed on a rolling basis. Application fee: $55. Electronic applications accepted. *Expenses:* Tuition, state resident: full-time $7176. Tuition, nonresident: full-time $16,680. Tuition and fees vary according to course load and program. *Financial support:* Fellowships, research assistantships, Federal Work-Study, scholarships/grants, traineeships, tuition waivers (full and partial), and unspecified assistantships available. Support available to part-time students. Financial award application deadline: 4/28; financial award applicants required to submit FAFSA. *Unit head:* Dr. Shannon Miller, Dean, 408-924-4300, Fax: 408-924-4365, E-mail: shannon.miller@sjsu.edu.
Website: http://www.sjsu.edu/humanitiesandarts/

Savannah College of Art and Design, Program in Motion Media Design, Savannah, GA 31402-3146. Offers MA, MFA. *Program availability:* Part-time, 100% online. *Faculty:* 16 full-time (3 women), 7 part-time/adjunct (5 women). *Students:* 49 full-time (29 women), 28 part-time (12 women); includes 12 minority (7 Black or African American, non-Hispanic/Latino; 1 Asian, non-Hispanic/Latino; 4 Hispanic/Latino), 38 international. Average age 30. 34 applicants, 53% accepted, 13 enrolled. In 2017, 23 master's awarded. *Degree requirements:* For master's, final project (for MA); thesis (for MFA).

Entrance requirements: For master's, GRE (recommended), portfolio (submitted in digital format), audition or writing submission, resume, statement of purpose, two letters of recommendation. Additional exam requirements/recommendations for international students: Recommended—TOEFL (minimum score 550 paper-based; 85 iBT), IELTS (minimum score 6.5). *Application deadline:* For fall admission, 4/1 for domestic and international students. Applications are processed on a rolling basis. Application fee: $40. Electronic applications accepted. *Expenses: Tuition:* Full-time $36,765; part-time $817 per credit hour. One-time fee: $500. *Financial support:* Career-related internships or fieldwork, Federal Work-Study, and scholarships/grants available. Financial award application deadline: 4/1; financial award applicants required to submit FAFSA. *Unit head:* Kelly Carlton, Chair, Motion Media Design. *Application contact:* Jenny Jaquillard, Executive Director of Admissions, Recruitment and Events, 912-525-5100, Fax: 912-525-5985, E-mail: admission@scad.edu.
Website: http://www.scad.edu/academics/programs/motion-media-design

Savannah College of Art and Design, Program in Performing Arts, Savannah, GA 31402-3146. Offers MFA. *Program availability:* Part-time. *Faculty:* 10 full-time (4 women), 7 part-time/adjunct (5 women). *Students:* 45 full-time (30 women), 5 part-time (3 women); includes 25 minority (18 Black or African American, non-Hispanic/Latino; 1 American Indian or Alaska Native, non-Hispanic/Latino; 1 Asian, non-Hispanic/Latino; 5 Hispanic/Latino), 1 international. Average age 27. 97 applicants, 47% accepted, 21 enrolled. In 2017, 14 master's awarded. *Degree requirements:* For master's, thesis. *Entrance requirements:* For master's, GRE (recommended), portfolio (submitted in digital format), audition or writing submission, resume, statement of purpose, two letters of recommendation. Additional exam requirements/recommendations for international students: Recommended—TOEFL (minimum score 550 paper-based; 85 iBT), IELTS (minimum score 6.5). *Application deadline:* For fall admission, 4/1 for domestic and international students. Applications are processed on a rolling basis. Application fee: $40. Electronic applications accepted. *Expenses: Tuition:* Full-time $36,765; part-time $817 per credit hour. One-time fee: $500. *Financial support:* Career-related internships or fieldwork, Federal Work-Study, and scholarships/grants available. Financial award application deadline: 4/1; financial award applicants required to submit FAFSA. *Unit head:* Mark Tymchyshyn, Chair, Performing Arts. *Application contact:* Jenny Jaquillard, Executive Director of Admissions, Recruitment and Events, 912-525-5100, Fax: 912-525-5985, E-mail: admission@scad.edu.
Website: http://www.scad.edu/academics/programs/performing-arts

Southern Illinois University Carbondale, Graduate School, College of Mass Communication and Media Arts, Department of Mass Communication and Media Arts, Carbondale, IL 62901-4701. Offers MFA, PhD. *Degree requirements:* For doctorate, thesis/dissertation. *Entrance requirements:* For master's, minimum GPA of 2.7; for doctorate, GRE, minimum GPA of 3.25. Additional exam requirements/recommendations for international students: Required—TOEFL (minimum score 100 iBT).

Southern Illinois University Carbondale, Graduate School, College of Mass Communication and Media Arts, Department of Professional Media and Media Management Studies, Carbondale, IL 62901-4701. Offers MS. *Entrance requirements:* Additional exam requirements/recommendations for international students: Required—TOEFL (minimum score 100 iBT).

Southern Illinois University Carbondale, Graduate School, College of Mass Communication and Media Arts, Program in Media Theory and Research, Carbondale, IL 62901-4701. Offers MA. *Entrance requirements:* For master's, GRE, minimum GPA of 2.7. Additional exam requirements/recommendations for international students: Required—TOEFL (minimum score 100 iBT).

Southern Illinois University Edwardsville, Graduate School, College of Arts and Sciences, Department of Mass Communications, Program in Media Literacy, Edwardsville, IL 62026. Offers Postbaccalaureate Certificate. *Program availability:* Part-time, evening/weekend. *Entrance requirements:* Additional exam requirements/recommendations for international students: Required—TOEFL (minimum score 550 paper-based; 79 iBT), IELTS (minimum score 6.5). Electronic applications accepted.

Stevens Institute of Technology, Graduate School, Charles V. Schaefer Jr. School of Engineering and Science, Interdisciplinary Program in Media and Broadcast Engineering, Hoboken, NJ 07030. Offers MS. *Students:* 3 applicants, 33% accepted. *Degree requirements:* For master's, thesis optional, minimum B average in major field and overall. *Entrance requirements:* Additional exam requirements/recommendations for international students: Required—TOEFL (minimum score 74 iBT), IELTS (minimum score 6). *Application deadline:* For fall admission, 6/1 for domestic students, 4/15 for international students; for spring admission, 11/30 for domestic students, 11/1 for international students. *Expenses: Tuition:* Full-time $34,494; part-time $1554 per credit. *Required fees:* $291 per semester. *Unit head:* Dr. Keith G. Sheppard, Interim Dean, 201-216-5263. *Application contact:* Graduate Admissions, 888-783-8367, Fax: 888-555-1306, E-mail: graduate@stevens.edu.

Syracuse University, S. I. Newhouse School of Public Communications, MA Program in Media Studies, Syracuse, NY 13244. Offers MA. *Students:* Average age 25. *Entrance requirements:* For master's, GRE General Test, resume, official transcripts, personal statement, three letters of recommendation. Additional exam requirements/recommendations for international students: Required—TOEFL (minimum score 600 paper-based; 100 iBT). *Application deadline:* For fall admission, 1/15 priority date for domestic and international students. Application fee: $45. Electronic applications accepted. *Financial support:* Fellowships with full tuition reimbursements, research assistantships with partial tuition reimbursements, and teaching assistantships with partial tuition reimbursements available. Financial award application deadline: 1/1. *Faculty research:* Media law, communications theory, global persuasion, mass communications, media and diversity. *Unit head:* Bradley Gorham, Director, 315-443-3372, Fax: 315-443-3946, E-mail: masscomm@syr.edu. *Application contact:* Martha Coria, Graduate Records Office, 315-443-4039, E-mail: pcgrad@syr.edu.
Website: http://newhouse.syr.edu/academics/degrees/masters/media-studies

Syracuse University, S. I. Newhouse School of Public Communications, MS Program in New Media Management, Syracuse, NY 13244. Offers MS. *Students:* Average age 24. *Degree requirements:* For master's, thesis optional, capstone course. *Entrance requirements:* For master's, GRE General Test or GMAT, resume, official transcripts, personal statement, three letters of recommendation. Additional exam requirements/recommendations for international students: Required—TOEFL (minimum score 600 paper-based; 100 iBT). *Application deadline:* For summer admission, 1/15 priority date for domestic and international students. Application fee: $45. Electronic applications accepted. *Financial support:* Fellowships with full tuition reimbursements, research assistantships with partial tuition reimbursements, and teaching assistantships with partial tuition reimbursements available. Financial award application deadline: 2/1. *Faculty research:* Emerging enterprise consulting, communications industry frontiers, issues in media management, telecommunications law and policy, media law. *Unit head:* Prof. Stephen Masiclat, Director, 315-443-9243, Fax: 315-443-3946, E-mail: pcgrad@syr.edu. *Application contact:* Martha Coria, Graduate Records Office, 315-443-4039, Fax: 315-334-1834, E-mail: pcgrad@syr.edu.
Website: http://newhouse.syr.edu/academics/degrees/masters/new-media-management

Syracuse University, S. I. Newhouse School of Public Communications, Program in Television, Radio, and Film, Syracuse, NY 13244. Offers MA. In 2017, 36 master's awarded. *Entrance requirements:* For master's, GRE General Test, resume, official transcripts, personal statement, three letters of recommendation. Additional exam requirements/recommendations for international students: Required—TOEFL (minimum score 600 paper-based; 100 iBT). *Application deadline:* For summer admission, 1/15 priority date for domestic and international students. Application fee: $45. Electronic applications accepted. *Financial support:* Fellowships with full tuition reimbursements, research assistantships with partial tuition reimbursements, and teaching assistantships with partial tuition reimbursements available. Financial award application deadline: 1/15. *Faculty research:* Communications industry frontiers, sound for picture, media studies, television, radio, film. *Unit head:* Michael Schoonmaker, Chair of Television, Radio and Film/Associate Professor, 315-443-9240, E-mail: msschoon@syr.edu. *Application contact:* Martha Coria, Graduate Records Office, 315-443-4039, E-mail: pcgrad@syr.edu.
Website: http://newhouse.syr.edu/academics/degrees/masters/television-radio-and-film

Temple University, Klein College of Media and Communication, Department of Media Studies and Production, Philadelphia, PA 19122-6096. Offers MA. *Program availability:* Part-time. *Students:* 131 applicants, 42% accepted, 27 enrolled. In 2017, 11 master's awarded. *Entrance requirements:* For master's, GRE General Test, minimum GPA of 3.0. Additional exam requirements/recommendations for international students: Required—TOEFL (minimum score 600 paper-based; 100 iBT). *Application deadline:* For fall admission, 2/15 for domestic and international students. Application fee: $60. Electronic applications accepted. *Expenses:* Contact institution. *Financial support:* Career-related internships or fieldwork and Federal Work-Study available. Financial award application deadline: 1/15; financial award applicants required to submit FAFSA. *Faculty research:* Media institutions, international communications, communication policy, media theory. *Unit head:* Dr. Geoffrey Baym, Chair, 215-204-5475, E-mail: gdbaym@temple.edu. *Application contact:* Nicole McKenna, Director, Office of Research and Graduate Studies, 215-204-1497, Fax: 215-204-0310, E-mail: nmckenna@temple.edu.
Website: https://klein.temple.edu/media-studies-and-production

Texas Tech University, Graduate School, College of Media and Communication, Department of Media and Communication, Lubbock, TX 79409. Offers mass communications (MA); media and communication (PhD); strategic communication and innovation (MA). *Program availability:* Part-time, evening/weekend, 100% online, blended/hybrid learning. *Faculty:* 7 full-time (2 women), 3 part-time/adjunct (all women). *Students:* 84 full-time (43 women), 128 part-time (91 women); includes 62 minority (10 Black or African American, non-Hispanic/Latino; 2 Asian, non-Hispanic/Latino; 42 Hispanic/Latino; 8 Two or more races, non-Hispanic/Latino), 11 international. Average age 30. 163 applicants, 63% accepted, 83 enrolled. In 2017, 64 master's, 5 doctorates awarded. *Degree requirements:* For master's, thesis optional; for doctorate, comprehensive exam, thesis/dissertation. *Entrance requirements:* For doctorate, GRE. Additional exam requirements/recommendations for international students: Required—TOEFL (minimum score 550 paper-based; 79 iBT), GRE. *Application deadline:* For fall admission, 6/1 priority date for domestic students, 1/15 priority date for international students; for spring admission, 9/1 priority date for domestic students, 6/15 priority date for international students. Applications are processed on a rolling basis. Application fee: $60. Electronic applications accepted. *Expenses:* Contact institution. *Financial support:* In 2017–18, 119 students received support, including 95 fellowships (averaging $4,110 per year), 35 research assistantships (averaging $8,745 per year), 72 teaching assistantships (averaging $8,545 per year); career-related internships or fieldwork, scholarships/grants, and unspecified assistantships also available. Support available to part-time students. Financial award application deadline: 4/15; financial award applicants required to submit FAFSA. *Faculty research:* Media effects, political communication, health/science communication, critical/cultural/rhetorical, Hispanic and international communication. *Unit head:* Dr. Coy Callison, Associate Dean for Graduate Studies, 806-834-5344, E-mail: coy.callison@ttu.edu. *Application contact:* Bridget Christopherson, Graduate Program Administrative, 806-834-1619, E-mail: bridget.christopherson@ttu.edu.
Website: http://www.depts.ttu.edu/comc/

Trinity College, Graduate Programs, Program in English, Hartford, CT 06106-3100. Offers literary studies (MA); writing, rhetoric, and media arts (MA). *Program availability:* Part-time, evening/weekend. *Degree requirements:* For master's, thesis (for some programs). *Entrance requirements:* For master's, minimum GPA of 3.0.

University at Buffalo, the State University of New York, Graduate School, College of Arts and Sciences, Department of Media Study, Buffalo, NY 14260. Offers film and media study (MAH); media arts production (MFA); media study (PhD); new media design (Certificate); social media (MAH); M Arch/MFA. *Faculty:* 9 full-time (5 women), 3 part-time/adjunct (1 woman). *Students:* 46 full-time (24 women); includes 17 minority (3 Black or African American, non-Hispanic/Latino; 13 Asian, non-Hispanic/Latino; 1 Hispanic/Latino). Average age 32. 84 applicants, 29% accepted, 9 enrolled. In 2017, 5 master's awarded. Terminal master's awarded for partial completion of doctoral program. *Degree requirements:* For master's, thesis, media project; for doctorate, thesis/dissertation, qualifying exam, media project. *Entrance requirements:* For master's, portfolio; for doctorate, GRE, portfolio. Additional exam requirements/recommendations for international students: Required—TOEFL (minimum score 550 paper-based; 79 iBT). *Application deadline:* For fall admission, 1/5 priority date for domestic students, 1/7 priority date for international students. Applications are processed on a rolling basis. Application fee: $75. Electronic applications accepted. *Expenses:* Contact institution. *Financial support:* In 2017–18, 14 students received support, including 11 teaching assistantships with full tuition reimbursements available (averaging $13,733 per year); fellowships, career-related internships or fieldwork, Federal Work-Study, scholarships/grants, health care benefits, and unspecified assistantships also available. Support available to part-time students. Financial award application deadline: 1/5; financial award applicants required to submit FAFSA. *Faculty research:* Digital arts, video, documentary, film, game design, digital poetics, locative media. *Unit head:* Prof. Tom Feeley, Chair, 716-645-6902, Fax: 716-645-6979, E-mail: thfeeley@buffalo.edu. *Application contact:* Bradley Hendricks, Assistant to the Chair for Student Programs, 716-645-0945, Fax: 716-645-6979, E-mail: bhendric@buffalo.edu.
Website: http://mediastudy.buffalo.edu/

University of Bridgeport, College of Public and International Affairs, Bridgeport, CT 06604. Offers East Asian and Pacific Rim studies (MA); global development and peace (MA); global media and communication studies (MA). *Program availability:* Part-time, evening/weekend. *Degree requirements:* For master's, thesis. *Entrance requirements:* Additional exam requirements/recommendations for international students: Recommended—TOEFL (minimum score 550 paper-based; 80 iBT), IELTS (minimum score 6.5).

University of California, Los Angeles, Graduate Division, School of Theater, Film and Television, Department of Film, Television, and Digital Media, Los Angeles, CA 90034. Offers animation (MFA); cinema and media studies (MA, PhD); cinematography (MFA);

production (MFA); screenwriting (MFA). *Degree requirements:* For master's, comprehensive exam; for doctorate, one foreign language, thesis/dissertation, oral and written qualifying exams. *Entrance requirements:* For master's, GRE General Test (for MA applicants), bachelor's degree; minimum undergraduate GPA of 3.0 (or its equivalent if letter grade system not used); writing sample (for MA); for doctorate, GRE General Test, master's degree; minimum undergraduate GPA of 3.0 (or its equivalent if letter grade system not used); writing sample. Additional exam requirements/recommendations for international students: Required—TOEFL. Electronic applications accepted. *Expenses:* Contact institution.

University of California, Santa Barbara, Graduate Division, College of Letters and Sciences, Division of Humanities and Fine Arts, Department of Film and Media Studies, Santa Barbara, CA 93106-4010. Offers PhD, MA/PhD. Terminal master's awarded for partial completion of doctoral program. *Degree requirements:* For doctorate, one foreign language, comprehensive exam, thesis/dissertation. *Entrance requirements:* For doctorate, GRE, MA in film/media studies or equivalent. Additional exam requirements/recommendations for international students: Required—TOEFL (minimum score 600 paper-based; 100 iBT), IELTS (minimum score 7). Electronic applications accepted. *Faculty research:* Classical film theory, film and television history, historiography, cultural studies, global media, media industries, regulation and policy.

University of California, Santa Barbara, Graduate Division, College of Letters and Sciences, Division of Humanities and Fine Arts, Department of Media Arts and Technology, Santa Barbara, CA 93106-6065. Offers MS, PhD. Terminal master's awarded for partial completion of doctoral program. *Degree requirements:* For master's, thesis; for doctorate, comprehensive exam, thesis/dissertation. *Entrance requirements:* For master's and doctorate, GRE. Additional exam requirements/recommendations for international students: Required—TOEFL (minimum score 550 paper-based; 80 iBT), IELTS (minimum score 7). Electronic applications accepted. *Faculty research:* Transarchitectures and world making, virtual and mixed reality, visualization, intelligent space and interactive installation, human-computer interaction.

University of Chicago, Division of the Humanities, Department of Cinema and Media Studies, Chicago, IL 60637. Offers PhD. *Students:* 40 full-time (25 women); includes 12 minority (3 Black or African American, non-Hispanic/Latino; 4 Asian, non-Hispanic/Latino; 3 Hispanic/Latino; 2 Two or more races, non-Hispanic/Latino), 14 international. Average age 31. 119 applicants, 5% accepted, 4 enrolled. In 2017, 8 doctorates awarded. *Degree requirements:* For doctorate, 2 foreign languages, comprehensive exam, thesis/dissertation. *Entrance requirements:* For doctorate, GRE General Test, 15-20 page writing sample, statement of purpose, 3 letters of recommendation, transcripts for all previous degrees and institutions attended. Additional exam requirements/recommendations for international students: Required—TOEFL (minimum score 104 iBT), IELTS (minimum score 7). *Application deadline:* For fall admission, 12/15 for domestic and international students. Application fee: $90. Electronic applications accepted. *Financial support:* In 2017–18, fellowships with full tuition reimbursements (averaging $27,000 per year), 4 teaching assistantships with full tuition reimbursements (averaging $27,000 per year) were awarded; Federal Work-Study, institutionally sponsored loans, scholarships/grants, and health care benefits also available. Financial award application deadline: 12/15. *Unit head:* Daniel Morgan, Chair, 773-702-3317, E-mail: cinema@uchicago.edu. *Application contact:* Michael Beetley, Assistant Dean of Students, Admissions and Fellowships, 773-702-1552, Fax: 773-834-9148, E-mail: humanitiesadmissions@uchicago.edu.
Website: https://cms.uchicago.edu/

University of Chicago, Division of the Humanities, Master of Arts Program in the Humanities, Chicago, IL 60637. Offers art history (MA); cinema and media studies (MA); classic languages (MA); comparative literature (MA); creative writing (MA); cultural policy studies (MA); digital humanities (MA); East Asian languages and civilizations (MA); English language and literature (MA); gender and sexuality studies (MA); Germanic studies (MA); linguistics (MA); music (MA); near Eastern languages and civilizations (MA); philosophy (MA); poetics (MA); race, politics and culture (MA); Romance languages and literatures (MA); Slavic languages and literatures (MA); South Asian languages and civilizations (MA); theater and performance studies (MA). *Students:* 95 full-time (50 women), 6 part-time (4 women); includes 22 minority (1 Black or African American, non-Hispanic/Latino; 10 Asian, non-Hispanic/Latino; 11 Hispanic/Latino), 19 international. Average age 26. 708 applicants, 75% accepted, 101 enrolled. In 2017, 91 master's awarded. *Degree requirements:* For master's, thesis. *Entrance requirements:* For master's, GRE General Test, 10-15 page writing sample, statement of purpose, 3 letters of recommendation, transcripts for all previous degrees and institutions attended. Additional exam requirements/recommendations for international students: Required—TOEFL (minimum score 104 iBT), IELTS (minimum score 7). *Application deadline:* For fall admission, 1/3 priority date for domestic and international students. Application fee: $90. Electronic applications accepted. *Expenses:* Contact institution. *Financial support:* In 2017–18, fellowships with partial tuition reimbursements (averaging $12,000 per year) were awarded; Federal Work-Study, institutionally sponsored loans, scholarships/grants, and tuition waivers (partial) also available. Financial award application deadline: 4/30. *Unit head:* Thomas Christensen, Director, 773-834-1201, Fax: 773-834-7526, E-mail: ma-humanities@uchicago.edu. *Application contact:* Michael Beetley, Assistant Dean of Students for Admissions, 773-834-1552, E-mail: humanitiesadmissions@uchicago.edu.
Website: http://maph.uchicago.edu/

University of Colorado Boulder, Graduate School, College of Engineering and Applied Science, Alliance for Technology, Learning, and Society Program, Boulder, CO 80309. Offers MS, PhD. *Students:* 36 full-time (23 women), 7 part-time (6 women); includes 10 minority (2 Black or African American, non-Hispanic/Latino; 4 Asian, non-Hispanic/Latino; 3 Hispanic/Latino; 1 Two or more races, non-Hispanic/Latino), 8 international. Average age 31. 42 applicants, 57% accepted, 13 enrolled. In 2017, 15 master's, 3 doctorates awarded. *Entrance requirements:* For master's, minimum undergraduate GPA of 3.0. *Application deadline:* For fall admission, 1/10 for domestic students; for spring admission, 1/10 for domestic students. Application fee: $60 ($80 for international students). Electronic applications accepted. Application fee is waived when completed online. *Financial support:* In 2017–18, 57 students received support, including 22 fellowships (averaging $4,669 per year), 11 research assistantships with full and partial tuition reimbursements available (averaging $46,933 per year), 2 teaching assistantships with full and partial tuition reimbursements available (averaging $23,768 per year); institutionally sponsored loans, scholarships/grants, health care benefits, and unspecified assistantships also available. Financial award application deadline: 2/15; financial award applicants required to submit FAFSA. *Faculty research:* Evaluation of the Dissector Tool based on the Visible Human Data Project, assessing student outcomes for SENCER (an NSF-sponsored program using civic engagement to increase the interest and learning in undergraduate science at over 300 U.S. universities). *Total annual research expenditures:* $3.1 million. *Application contact:* E-mail: cuatlas@colorado.edu.
Website: http://www.colorado.edu/ATLAS/

University of Colorado Boulder, Graduate School, College of Media, Communication and Information, Program in Media Studies, Boulder, CO 80309. Offers PhD. *Faculty:* 9 full-time (4 women). *Students:* 25 full-time (18 women), 1 (woman) part-time; includes 4 minority (1 Black or African American, non-Hispanic/Latino; 2 Hispanic/Latino; 1 Two or more races, non-Hispanic/Latino), 3 international. Average age 32. 37 applicants, 49% accepted, 8 enrolled. *Entrance requirements:* For doctorate, GRE General Test, minimum undergraduate GPA of 3.25. Additional exam requirements/recommendations for international students: Required—TOEFL. *Application deadline:* For fall admission, 1/10 for domestic students; for spring admission, 12/1 for domestic students. Application fee: $60 ($80 for international students). Electronic applications accepted. Application fee is waived when completed online. *Financial support:* In 2017–18, 62 students received support, including 9 fellowships (averaging $1,251 per year), 1 research assistantship with full and partial tuition reimbursement available (averaging $36,573 per year), 18 teaching assistantships with full and partial tuition reimbursements available (averaging $32,913 per year); institutionally sponsored loans, scholarships/grants, health care benefits, and unspecified assistantships also available. Financial award application deadline: 2/15; financial award applicants required to submit FAFSA. *Faculty research:* Mass communication/media; electronic media; journalism; cultural history; television. *Application contact:* E-mail: mediastudies@colorado.edu.
Website: http://www.colorado.edu/cmci/academics/media-studies

University of Denver, Division of Arts, Humanities and Social Sciences, Department of Media, Film and Journalism Studies, Denver, CO 80208. Offers international and intercultural communication (MA); media and public communication (MA), including media and globalization, strategic communication. *Program availability:* Part-time. *Faculty:* 16 full-time (10 women), 5 part-time/adjunct (4 women). *Students:* 3 full-time (all women), 21 part-time (17 women); includes 5 minority (1 Asian, non-Hispanic/Latino; 4 Hispanic/Latino), 2 international. Average age 26. 34 applicants, 85% accepted, 8 enrolled. In 2017, 12 master's awarded. *Degree requirements:* For master's, thesis (for some programs). *Entrance requirements:* For master's, GRE General Test, bachelor's degree, transcripts, personal statement, three letters of recommendation. Additional exam requirements/recommendations for international students: Required—TOEFL (minimum score 620 paper-based; 105 iBT). *Application deadline:* For fall admission, 2/15 priority date for domestic students, 1/1 priority date for international students. Applications are processed on a rolling basis. Application fee: $65. Electronic applications accepted. *Expenses:* $31,935 per year full-time. *Financial support:* In 2017–18, 18 students received support. Teaching assistantships with tuition reimbursements available, career-related internships or fieldwork, Federal Work-Study, institutionally sponsored loans, scholarships/grants, and unspecified assistantships available. Support available to part-time students. Financial award application deadline: 2/15; financial award applicants required to submit FAFSA. *Faculty research:* Branding; public relations; health communication; social media; international communication. *Unit head:* Dr. Lynn Schofield Clark, Professor and Chair, 303-871-3984, Fax: 303-871-4949, E-mail: lynn.clark@du.edu. *Application contact:* Information Contact, 303-871-2166, E-mail: mfjs@du.edu.
Website: http://www.du.edu/ahss/mfjs

University of Illinois at Urbana–Champaign, Graduate College, College of Fine and Applied Arts, School of Art and Design, Program in Design and Media, Champaign, IL 61820. Offers art and design (MFA), including new media; graphic design (MFA); industrial design (MFA). *Accreditation:* NASAD.

University of Illinois at Urbana–Champaign, Graduate College, College of Media, Institute of Communications Research, Champaign, IL 61820. Offers communications and media (PhD). *Faculty research:* Feminist cultural studies, media technology, international communications, Latino studies, economics of media.

The University of Iowa, Graduate College, College of Liberal Arts and Sciences, Department of Communication Studies, Iowa City, IA 52242-1316. Offers interpersonal communication and relationships (MA, PhD); media studies (MA, PhD); rhetoric and public advocacy (MA, PhD). *Degree requirements:* For master's, thesis optional, exam; for doctorate, comprehensive exam, thesis/dissertation. *Entrance requirements:* For master's and doctorate, GRE General Test, minimum GPA of 3.0. Additional exam requirements/recommendations for international students: Required—TOEFL (minimum score 550 paper-based; 81 iBT). Electronic applications accepted.

The University of Iowa, Graduate College, College of Liberal Arts and Sciences, School of Journalism and Mass Communication, Iowa City, IA 52242-1316. Offers journalism and media communication (MA); mass communication (PhD); strategic communication (MA); JD/MA; JD/PhD. *Degree requirements:* For master's, thesis optional, exam; for doctorate, comprehensive exam, thesis/dissertation. *Entrance requirements:* For master's and doctorate, GRE General Test, minimum GPA of 3.0. Additional exam requirements/recommendations for international students: Required—TOEFL (minimum score 637 paper-based; 110 iBT). Electronic applications accepted. *Faculty research:* Verbal and visual aspects of historical, legal, social, and cross-cultural communication.

The University of Kansas, Graduate Studies, College of Liberal Arts and Sciences, Department of Film and Media Studies, Lawrence, KS 66045. Offers MA, PhD. *Students:* 16 full-time (6 women), 1 (woman) part-time; includes 5 minority (2 Black or African American, non-Hispanic/Latino; 1 American Indian or Alaska Native, non-Hispanic/Latino; 2 Asian, non-Hispanic/Latino), 3 international. Average age 32. 5 applicants, 40% accepted, 2 enrolled. In 2017, 2 master's, 2 doctorates awarded. *Entrance requirements:* For master's, GRE General Test, three recent letters of recommendation, current resume, statement of personal goals, writing sample; for doctorate, GRE General Test, MA in film or related field; three recent letters of recommendation; current resume; statement of personal goals; writing sample; minimum GPA of 3.2 undergraduate, 3.5 graduate. Additional exam requirements/recommendations for international students: Required—TOEFL or IELTS. *Application deadline:* For fall admission, 1/1 priority date for domestic and international students. Application fee: $65 ($85 for international students). Electronic applications accepted. *Financial support:* Fellowships, research assistantships, teaching assistantships, scholarships/grants, and unspecified assistantships available. Financial award application deadline: 1/1; financial award applicants required to submit FAFSA. *Faculty research:* Latin American cinema, Japanese and East Asian cinema, new media/cultural geography of media, film history, film theory and visual culture. *Unit head:* Dr. Michael Baskett, Chair, 785-864-1384, E-mail: eiga@ku.edu. *Application contact:* Karla Conrad, Graduate Secretary, 785-864-1340, E-mail: kmconrad@ku.edu.
Website: http://film.ku.edu/

University of Lethbridge, School of Graduate Studies, Lethbridge, AB T1K 3M4, Canada. Offers addictions counseling (M Sc); agricultural biotechnology (M Sc); agricultural studies (M Sc, MA); anthropology (MA); archaeology (M Sc, MA); art (MA, MFA); biochemistry (M Sc); biological sciences (M Sc); biomolecular science (PhD); biosystems and biodiversity (PhD); Canadian studies (MA); chemistry (M Sc); computer science (M Sc); computer science and geographical information science (M Sc); counseling (MC); counseling psychology (M Ed); dramatic arts (MA); earth, space, and physical science (PhD); economics (MA); education (MA, PhD); educational leadership (M Ed); English (MA); environmental science (M Sc); evolution and behavior (PhD); exercise science (M Sc); French (MA); French/German (MA); French/Spanish (MA); general education (M Ed); geography (M Sc, MA); German (MA); health sciences (M Sc); individualized multidisciplinary (M Sc, MA); kinesiology (M Sc, MA); management (M Sc), including accounting, finance, human resource management and

labor relations, information systems, international management, marketing, policy and strategy; mathematics (M Sc); music (M Mus, MA); Native American studies (MA); neuroscience (M Sc, PhD); new media (MA, MFA); nursing (M Sc, MN); philosophy (MA); physics (M Sc); political science (MA); psychology (M Sc, MA); religious studies (MA); sociology (MA); theatre and dramatic arts (MFA); theoretical and computational science (PhD); urban and regional studies (MA); women and gender studies (MA). *Program availability:* Part-time, evening/weekend. *Degree requirements:* For master's, thesis (for some programs); for doctorate, comprehensive exam, thesis/dissertation. *Entrance requirements:* For master's, GMAT (for M Sc in management), bachelor's degree in related field, minimum GPA of 3.0 during previous 20 graded semester courses, 2 years' teaching or related experience (M Ed); for doctorate, master's degree, minimum graduate GPA of 3.5. Additional exam requirements/recommendations for international students: Required—TOEFL (minimum score 580 paper-based; 93 iBT). Electronic applications accepted. *Faculty research:* Movement and brain plasticity, gibberellin physiology, photosynthesis, carbon cycling, molecular properties of main-group ring components.

University of Maryland, College Park, Academic Affairs, Philip Merrill College of Journalism, College Park, MD 20742. Offers broadcast journalism (MA); journalism (MA); journalism and media studies (PhD); online news (MA); public affairs reporting (MA). *Accreditation:* ACEJMC (one or more programs are accredited). *Program availability:* Part-time, evening/weekend. *Degree requirements:* For doctorate, thesis/dissertation, preliminary written and oral comprehensive exams. *Entrance requirements:* For master's and doctorate, GRE General Test, minimum GPA of 3.0, 3 letters of recommendation. Additional exam requirements/recommendations for international students: Required—TOEFL. Electronic applications accepted. *Faculty research:* Mass communication theory, specialized journalism, new telecommunication technologies, press integration.

University of Massachusetts Dartmouth, Graduate School, College of Visual and Performing Arts, Department of Art Education, Art History and Media Studies, North Dartmouth, MA 02747-2300. Offers MAE. *Accreditation:* NASAD. *Program availability:* Part-time. *Faculty:* 7 full-time (6 women), 1 (woman) part-time/adjunct. *Students:* 4 full-time (all women), 22 part-time (18 women); includes 2 minority (1 Asian, non-Hispanic/Latino; 1 Hispanic/Latino). Average age 32. 11 applicants, 100% accepted, 9 enrolled. In 2017, 2 master's awarded. *Degree requirements:* For master's, thesis. *Entrance requirements:* For master's, MTEL (Communication Literacy and Visual Arts), statement of purpose (minimum of 300 words), resume, 2 letters of recommendation, official transcripts, portfolio (20 images representing applicant's art work, process of thinking, implementation of concepts and studio production). Additional exam requirements/recommendations for international students: Required—TOEFL (minimum score 533 paper-based; 72 iBT), IELTS (minimum score 6). *Application deadline:* For fall admission, 8/1 priority date for domestic students, 7/1 priority date for international students; for spring admission, 10/15 priority date for domestic students, 9/15 priority date for international students. Application fee: $60. Electronic applications accepted. *Expenses:* Tuition, state resident: full-time $15,449; part-time $643.71 per credit. Tuition, nonresident: full-time $27,880; part-time $1161.67 per credit. *Required fees:* $405; $25.88 per credit. Tuition and fees vary according to course load and reciprocity agreements. *Financial support:* In 2017–18, 1 teaching assistantship (averaging $4,000 per year) was awarded; tuition waivers (partial) and unspecified assistantships also available. Support available to part-time students. Financial award application deadline: 3/1; financial award applicants required to submit FAFSA. *Faculty research:* Contemporary art, design and architectural history, curatorial studies, film studies, theory of photography. *Unit head:* Cathy Smilan, Graduate Program Director, 508-910-6594, Fax: 508-999-8901, E-mail: csmilan@umassd.edu. *Application contact:* Steven Briggs, Director of Marketing and Recruitment for Graduate Studies, 508-999-8604, Fax: 508-999-8183, E-mail: graduate@umassd.edu.
Website: http://www.umassd.edu/cvpa/programs

University of Michigan, Rackham Graduate School, School of Music, Theatre, and Dance, Program in Media Arts, Ann Arbor, MI 48109-2085. Offers MA. *Entrance requirements:* For master's, GRE, portfolio. Additional exam requirements/recommendations for international students: Required—TOEFL. *Expenses:* Tuition, state resident: full-time $22,368; part-time $1201 per credit hour. Tuition, nonresident: full-time $45,156; part-time $2467 per credit hour. *Required fees:* $376 per term. Tuition and fees vary according to course load, degree level and program.

University of Nevada, Las Vegas, Graduate College, Greenspun College of Urban Affairs, Hank Greenspun School of Journalism and Media Studies, Las Vegas, NV 89154-5007. Offers MA. *Program availability:* Part-time. *Faculty:* 3 full-time (0 women). *Students:* 8 full-time (6 women), 1 part-time (0 women); includes 3 minority (1 Black or African American, non-Hispanic/Latino; 1 Hispanic/Latino; 1 Two or more races, non-Hispanic/Latino), 1 international. Average age 29. 14 applicants, 57% accepted, 5 enrolled. In 2017, 5 master's awarded. *Degree requirements:* For master's, comprehensive exam, thesis optional, oral exam. *Entrance requirements:* For master's, GRE General Test, bachelor's degree with minimum GPA 3.0; 3 letters of recommendation; statement of purpose; writing sample. Additional exam requirements/recommendations for international students: Required—TOEFL (minimum score 550 paper-based; 80 iBT), IELTS (minimum score 7). *Application deadline:* For fall admission, 3/15 for domestic students. Application fee: $60 ($95 for international students). Electronic applications accepted. *Expenses:* $275 per credit, $850 per course, $7,969 per year resident, $22,157 per year non-resident, $7,094 non-resident fee (7 credits or more), $1,307 annual health insurance fee. *Financial support:* In 2017–18, 7 students received support, including 7 teaching assistantships with full and partial tuition reimbursements available (averaging $11,250 per year); institutionally sponsored loans, scholarships/grants, health care benefits, and unspecified assistantships also available. Financial award application deadline: 3/15; financial award applicants required to submit FAFSA. *Faculty research:* Journalism, media, social and digital media, media history, media ethics, media law, First Amendment theory, First Amendment law, visual literacy, social psychology of visually mediated world, global media, audience reception theory and research, video criticism, advertising, media technology and society, emerging media, children and media. *Unit head:* Dr. Joel Lieberman, Interim Director/Professor, 702-895-0249, Fax: 702-895-0252, E-mail: joel.lieberman@unlv.edu. *Application contact:* Dr. Julian Kilker, Graduate Coordinator, 702-895-3729, Fax: 702-895-5189, E-mail: julian.kilker@unlv.edu.
Website: http://journalism.unlv.edu/

The University of North Carolina at Chapel Hill, Graduate School, School of Media and Journalism, Chapel Hill, NC 27599. Offers digital communication (MA, Certificate); media and communication (MA, PhD), including interdisciplinary health communication (MA), journalism (MA), strategic communication (MA), theory and research (MA), visual communication (MA); JD/PhD; MA/JD. MA/JD and JD/PhD offered jointly with School of Law. *Accreditation:* ACEJMC (one or more programs are accredited). *Program availability:* Part-time, all course instruction online, plus two on-campus experiences totaling seven days. *Faculty:* 51 full-time (22 women), 4 part-time/adjunct (2 women). *Students:* 75 full-time (50 women), 63 part-time (41 women); includes 44 minority (10 Black or African American, non-Hispanic/Latino; 11 Asian, non-Hispanic/Latino; 5 Hispanic/Latino; 18 Two or more races, non-Hispanic/Latino), 6 international. Average

age 31. 207 applicants, 41% accepted, 63 enrolled. In 2017, 32 master's, 9 doctorates, 17 other advanced degrees awarded. *Degree requirements:* For master's, comprehensive exam, thesis; for doctorate, comprehensive exam, thesis/dissertation. *Entrance requirements:* For master's and doctorate, GRE General Test, minimum GPA of 3.0. Additional exam requirements/recommendations for international students: Required—TOEFL (minimum iBT score of 105) or IELTS (7.5). Application fee: $88. Electronic applications accepted. *Expenses:* Contact institution. *Financial support:* In 2017–18, 73 students received support, including 47 fellowships with full tuition reimbursements available (averaging $16,006 per year), 6 research assistantships with full tuition reimbursements available (averaging $17,405 per year); scholarships/grants and health care benefits also available. Financial award application deadline: 12/4; financial award applicants required to submit FAFSA. *Faculty research:* Media processes and production; legal and regulatory issues in communication; media uses and effects; health communication; political, social, and strategic communication. *Total annual research expenditures:* $1 million. *Unit head:* Susan King, Dean, 919-962-1204, Fax: 919-962-0620, E-mail: susanking@unc.edu. *Application contact:* Casey Hart, Marketing and Instructional Design Coordinator, 919-843-9471, Fax: 919-962-0620, E-mail: mjgrad@unc.edu.
Website: http://mj.unc.edu/

The University of North Carolina at Greensboro, Graduate School, College of Arts and Sciences, Department of Media Studies, Greensboro, NC 27412-5001. Offers film and video production (MFA).

University of Oklahoma, Gaylord College of Journalism and Mass Communication, Program in Journalism and Mass Communication, Norman, OK 73019. Offers broadcast and electronic media (MA); journalism (MA); media arts (PhD); media management (MA); news and information (PhD); strategic communication (MA, PhD). *Program availability:* Part-time. *Students:* 24 full-time (11 women), 19 part-time (10 women); includes 5 minority (2 Black or African American, non-Hispanic/Latino; 1 Asian, non-Hispanic/Latino; 2 Hispanic/Latino), 18 international. Average age 33. 22 applicants, 64% accepted, 7 enrolled. In 2017, 10 master's awarded. *Degree requirements:* For master's, comprehensive exam (for some programs), thesis (for some programs); for doctorate, comprehensive exam, thesis/dissertation. *Entrance requirements:* For master's, GRE, resume, statement of purpose, two letters of recommendation, official transcript, minimum GPA of 3.2; for doctorate, GRE, resume, statement of purpose, three letters of recommendation, official transcript. Additional exam requirements/recommendations for international students: Required—TOEFL (minimum score 79 iBT) or IELTS (minimum score 6.5). *Application deadline:* For fall admission, 5/1 for domestic students, 3/1 for international students; for spring admission, 11/1 for domestic students, 10/1 for international students; for summer admission, 3/1 for domestic students. Applications are processed on a rolling basis. Application fee: $50 ($100 for international students). Electronic applications accepted. *Expenses:* Tuition, state resident: full-time $5119; part-time $213.30 per credit hour. Tuition, nonresident: full-time $19,778; part-time $824.10 per credit hour. *Required fees:* $3458; $133.55 per credit hour. $126.50 per semester. *Financial support:* In 2017–18, 31 students received support. Research assistantships with full tuition reimbursements available, teaching assistantships with full tuition reimbursements available, career-related internships or fieldwork, institutionally sponsored loans, scholarships/grants, health care benefits, unspecified assistantships, and McNair fellowships available. Financial award application deadline: 6/1; financial award applicants required to submit FAFSA. *Faculty research:* Digital advertising, interactivity and user experience; news sociology and journalism ethics; media management and digital change; corporate, non-profit and global public relations; media psychology and media effects. *Unit head:* Dr. Peter Gade, Director of Graduate Studies/Professor of Journalism, 405-325-5528, Fax: 405-325-7565, E-mail: pgade@ou.edu. *Application contact:* Larry Laneer, Administrative Assistant to Director/Graduate Advisor, 405-325-2722, Fax: 405-325-7565, E-mail: llaneer@ou.edu.
Website: http://www.ou.edu/content/gaylord/graduate

University of Oregon, Graduate School, School of Journalism and Communication, Eugene, OR 97403. Offers journalism (MA, MS); media studies (MA, MS, PhD); multimedia journalism (MA, MS); strategic communication (MA, MS). *Accreditation:* ASHA. *Program availability:* Part-time. *Degree requirements:* For master's, thesis or alternative. *Entrance requirements:* For master's, GRE General Test; for doctorate, master's degree. *Faculty research:* Impact of mass communication, media technology, media accountability, craft attitudes, media economics.

University of South Carolina, The Graduate School, College of Arts and Sciences, Department of Art, Division of Media Arts, Columbia, SC 29208. Offers MMA. *Degree requirements:* For master's, thesis. *Entrance requirements:* For master's, GRE General Test, interview, portfolio. Additional exam requirements/recommendations for international students: Required—TOEFL. Electronic applications accepted. *Faculty research:* Three dimensional imaging, script writing.

University of Southern California, Graduate School, Annenberg School for Communication and Journalism, School of Communication, Program in Communication, Los Angeles, CA 90089. Offers culture and community (PhD); global and transnational communication (PhD); groups, organizations and networks (PhD); health communication and social dynamics (PhD); information, political economy and entertainment (PhD); new media and technology (PhD); rhetoric, politics and public media (PhD). *Degree requirements:* For doctorate, thesis/dissertation. *Entrance requirements:* For doctorate, GRE General Test, resume or curriculum vitae, scholarly writing, 3 letters of recommendation, statement of purpose. Additional exam requirements/recommendations for international students: Required—TOEFL (minimum score 114 iBT), IELTS (minimum score 8); Recommended—TWE. Electronic applications accepted. *Faculty research:* Computer-mediated communication, public health campaigns, communication democracy and the public sphere, new communication technologies in organizations, communication and community.

University of Southern California, Graduate School, Annenberg School for Communication and Journalism, School of Communication, Program in Communication Management, Los Angeles, CA 90089. Offers MCM, JD/MCM, MCM/MAJCS. *Program availability:* Part-time, evening/weekend, online learning. *Degree requirements:* For master's, professional project. *Entrance requirements:* For master's, GRE General Test or GMAT, resume, writing samples, recommendation letters, statement of purpose. Additional exam requirements/recommendations for international students: Required—TOEFL (minimum score 114 iBT), IELTS (minimum score 8). Electronic applications accepted. *Faculty research:* Global communication, communication law and policy, entertainment management, marketing communication, strategic and corporate communication management.

University of Southern California, Graduate School, Annenberg School for Communication and Journalism, School of Communication, Program in Digital Social Media, Los Angeles, CA 90089. Offers MS. *Program availability:* Part-time, evening/weekend. *Degree requirements:* For master's, dynamic digital media site or app launch. *Entrance requirements:* For master's, GRE General Test, resume, statement of purpose, writing sample, two letters of recommendation. Additional exam requirements/recommendations for international students: Required—TOEFL (minimum score 114 iBT), IELTS (minimum score 8). Electronic applications accepted.

Media Studies

University of Southern California, Graduate School, Dana and David Dornsife College of Letters, Arts and Sciences, Comparative Studies in Literature and Culture Doctoral Program, Los Angeles, CA 90089. Offers comparative literature (PhD); comparative media and culture (PhD); Spanish and Latin American studies (PhD). *Degree requirements:* For doctorate, 2 foreign languages, comprehensive exam, thesis/dissertation. *Entrance requirements:* For doctorate, GRE, competence in language other than English (highly recommended). Additional exam requirements/recommendations for international students: Required—TOEFL. Electronic applications accepted. *Faculty research:* Literary theory, Japanese film and contemporary fiction, Francophone literature and cinema, Latin American and Caribbean literature, Spanish literature and film, nineteenth and twentieth century British and American literature.

University of Southern California, Graduate School, School of Cinematic Arts, Interactive Media Division, Los Angeles, CA 90089. Offers interactive media (MFA); media arts and practice (PhD). *Degree requirements:* For master's, thesis, thesis project. *Entrance requirements:* Additional exam requirements/recommendations for international students: Required—TOEFL (minimum score 600 paper-based; 100 iBT). Electronic applications accepted. *Expenses:* Contact institution. *Faculty research:* Immersive media, mobile media, stereoscopic, game design and development, serious games and games for health and learning, experiments in game play.

University of Southern California, Graduate School, School of Cinematic Arts, Interdivisional Program in Media Arts and Practice, Los Angeles, CA 90089. Offers PhD. *Degree requirements:* For doctorate, 2 foreign languages, thesis/dissertation. *Entrance requirements:* For doctorate, GRE, portfolio. Additional exam requirements/recommendations for international students: Required—TOEFL. Electronic applications accepted. *Faculty research:* Transmedia, theory and history of emerging technologies; documentary and experimental film and video; interactive media design; telepresence research and mobile media.

University of South Florida, College of Arts and Sciences, Zimmerman School of Advertising and Mass Communications, Tampa, FL 33620-9951. Offers mass communications (MA), including media studies, multimedia journalism, strategic communication management. *Program availability:* Part-time, evening/weekend. *Faculty:* 10 full-time (6 women). *Students:* 25 full-time (20 women), 25 part-time (20 women); includes 7 minority (4 Black or African American, non-Hispanic/Latino; 2 Hispanic/Latino; 1 Native Hawaiian or other Pacific Islander, non-Hispanic/Latino), 29 international. Average age 26. 28 applicants, 64% accepted, 15 enrolled. In 2017, 8 master's awarded. *Degree requirements:* For master's, comprehensive exam, thesis optional. *Entrance requirements:* For master's, GRE General Test, minimum GPA of 3.0 in last 60 hours of course work, three letters of recommendation, letter of intent, resume/curriculum vitae. Additional exam requirements/recommendations for international students: Required—TOEFL (minimum score 550 paper-based; 79 iBT) or IELTS (minimum score 6.5). *Application deadline:* For fall admission, 2/15 priority date for domestic and international students. Application fee: $30. Electronic applications accepted. *Financial support:* In 2017–18, 10 students received support, including 9 teaching assistantships with tuition reimbursements available (averaging $10,513 per year); unspecified assistantships also available. Financial award application deadline: 2/28. *Faculty research:* First Amendment analysis, civic journalism, public opinion, media ethics, media effects research in sports public relations, public relations management, advertisement, telecommunications. *Total annual research expenditures:* $78,680. *Unit head:* Dr. Wayne Garcia, Director and Senior Instructor, 813-498-1925, Fax: 813-974-2592, E-mail: wgarcia@usf.edu. *Application contact:* Dr. Artermio Ramirez, Jr., Associate Director, Fax: 813-974-2592, E-mail: aramirez2@usf.edu.
Website: http://masscom.usf.edu/grad/

University of South Florida, St. Petersburg, College of Arts and Sciences, St. Petersburg, FL 33701. Offers digital journalism and design (MA); environmental science and policy (MA, MS); Florida studies (MLA); journalism and media studies (MA); liberal studies (MLA); psychology (MA). *Program availability:* Part-time, online learning. *Degree requirements:* For master's, comprehensive exam, thesis or project. *Entrance requirements:* For master's, GRE, LSAT, MCAT (varies by program), letter of intent, 3 letters of recommendation, writing samples, bachelor's degree from regionally-accredited institution with minimum GPA of 3.0 overall or in upper two years. Additional exam requirements/recommendations for international students: Required—TOEFL (minimum score 550 paper-based; 79 iBT); Recommended—IELTS. Electronic applications accepted.

The University of Tennessee, Graduate School, College of Communication and Information, Knoxville, TN 37996. Offers advertising (MS, PhD); broadcasting (MS, PhD); communications (MS, PhD); information sciences (MS, PhD); journalism (MS, PhD); public relations (MS, PhD); speech communication (MS, PhD). *Program availability:* Part-time, evening/weekend, online learning. *Degree requirements:* For master's, thesis or alternative; for doctorate, thesis/dissertation. *Entrance requirements:* For master's and doctorate, GRE General Test, minimum GPA of 2.7. Additional exam requirements/recommendations for international students: Required—TOEFL. Electronic applications accepted.

The University of Texas at Austin, Graduate School, College of Communication, Department of Radio-Television-Film, Austin, TX 78712-1111. Offers film and media production (MFA); media studies (MA, PhD); screenwriting (MFA). *Degree requirements:* For master's, thesis (for some programs); for doctorate, thesis/dissertation. *Entrance requirements:* For master's and doctorate, GRE General Test. Electronic applications accepted. *Faculty research:* International communication, film studies, media and culture, telecommunication and new media, gender and sexuality.

The University of Western Ontario, Faculty of Graduate Studies, Faculty of Information and Media Studies, Programs in Media Studies, London, ON N6A 5B8, Canada. Offers MA, PhD. *Program availability:* Part-time. *Degree requirements:* For master's, thesis; for doctorate, comprehensive exam, thesis/dissertation. *Entrance requirements:* For master's, 2 letters of reference; for doctorate, MA in media studies, communications or related field. Additional exam requirements/recommendations for international students: Required—TOEFL (minimum score 625 paper-based), TWE (minimum score 5). Electronic applications accepted. *Faculty research:* Media cultures, media industries, media technologies.

University of Wisconsin–Madison, Graduate School, College of Letters and Science, Department of Communication Arts, Madison, WI 53706-1380. Offers communication science (MA, PhD); film (MA, PhD); media and cultural studies (MA, PhD); rhetoric (MA, PhD). Terminal master's awarded for partial completion of doctoral program. *Degree requirements:* For master's, one foreign language, thesis (for some programs); for doctorate, one foreign language, thesis/dissertation. *Entrance requirements:* For master's and doctorate, GRE General Test, minimum GPA of 3.5. Electronic applications accepted.

University of Wisconsin–Milwaukee, Graduate School, College of Letters and Science, Department of English, Milwaukee, WI 53201-0413. Offers English (MA, PhD), including creative writing, English language and linguistics, English secondary education, literary and critical studies, literature and cultural theory (PhD), literature and language studies, literature, culture, and media, media, cinema and digital studies, professional and technical communication (MA), professional and technical writing, professional writing (PhD), rhetoric and composition (PhD), rhetoric and writing. *Students:* 90 full-time (54 women), 42 part-time (17 women); includes 12 minority (2 Black or African American, non-Hispanic/Latino; 1 American Indian or Alaska Native, non-Hispanic/Latino; 4 Asian, non-Hispanic/Latino; 1 Hispanic/Latino; 4 Two or more races, non-Hispanic/Latino), 9 international. Average age 34. 166 applicants, 21% accepted, 27 enrolled. In 2017, 10 master's, 12 doctorates awarded. *Degree requirements:* For master's, thesis or alternative; for doctorate, one foreign language, thesis/dissertation. *Entrance requirements:* For master's, GRE General Test, GRE Subject Test; for doctorate, GRE. Additional exam requirements/recommendations for international students: Required—TOEFL (minimum score 550 paper-based; 79 iBT), IELTS (minimum score 6.5). *Application deadline:* For fall admission, 1/1 priority date for domestic students; for spring admission, 9/1 for domestic students. Application fee: $56 ($96 for international students). Electronic applications accepted. *Financial support:* Fellowships, research assistantships, teaching assistantships, career-related internships or fieldwork, unspecified assistantships, and project assistantships available. Support available to part-time students. Financial award application deadline: 4/15; financial award applicants required to submit FAFSA. *Unit head:* Mark Netzloff, Department Chair, 414-229-4511, E-mail: netzloff@uwm.edu. *Application contact:* General Information Contact, 414-229-4982, Fax: 414-229-6967, E-mail: gradschool@uwm.edu.
Website: https://uwm.edu/english/

University of Wisconsin–Milwaukee, Graduate School, College of Letters and Science, Department of Journalism, Advertising, and Media Studies, Milwaukee, WI 53201-0413. Offers media studies (MA). *Students:* 7 full-time (3 women), 10 part-time (6 women); includes 5 minority (3 Black or African American, non-Hispanic/Latino; 2 Two or more races, non-Hispanic/Latino), 3 international. Average age 27. 15 applicants, 47% accepted, 7 enrolled. *Entrance requirements:* Additional exam requirements/recommendations for international students: Required—TOEFL (minimum score 550 paper-based; 79 iBT), IELTS (minimum score 6.5). *Application deadline:* For fall admission, 1/1 priority date for domestic students; for spring admission, 9/1 for domestic students. Application fee: $56 ($96 for international students). Electronic applications accepted. *Financial support:* Fellowships, research assistantships, teaching assistantships, career-related internships or fieldwork, unspecified assistantships, and project assistantships available. Support available to part-time students. Financial award application deadline: 4/15; financial award applicants required to submit FAFSA. *Application contact:* General Information Contact, 414-229-4982, Fax: 414-229-6967, E-mail: gradschool@uwm.edu.

University of Wisconsin–Stevens Point, College of Fine Arts and Communication, Division of Communication, Stevens Point, WI 54481-3897. Offers interpersonal communication (MA); media studies (MA); organizational communication (MA); public relations (MA). *Program availability:* Part-time. *Degree requirements:* For master's, thesis or alternative. *Entrance requirements:* For master's, GRE. Additional exam requirements/recommendations for international students: Required—TOEFL (minimum score 575 paper-based). *Faculty research:* Communication theory and research, film history.

Valparaiso University, Graduate School and Continuing Education, Program in Media and Communication, Valparaiso, IN 46383. Offers digital media (MS, Certificate); sports media (MS, Certificate). *Program availability:* Part-time, evening/weekend. *Entrance requirements:* For master's, minimum GPA of 3.0, undergraduate minor in communication. Additional exam requirements/recommendations for international students: Required—TOEFL (minimum score 550 paper-based; 80 iBT), IELTS (minimum score 6). Electronic applications accepted. *Expenses: Tuition:* Full-time $11,340; part-time $630 per credit hour. *Required fees:* $520; $250 per year. $125 per semester. Tuition and fees vary according to program and reciprocity agreements.

Virginia Commonwealth University, Graduate School, College of Humanities and Sciences, Department of English, Richmond, VA 23284-9005. Offers creative writing (MFA), including dual genre, fiction, poetry; English (MA), including literature; media, art, and text (PhD). *Program availability:* Part-time. *Degree requirements:* For master's, thesis optional. *Entrance requirements:* For master's, GRE General Test, portfolio (MFA); for doctorate, GRE General Test. Additional exam requirements/recommendations for international students: Required—TOEFL (minimum score 600 paper-based; 100 iBT) or IELTS (minimum score 6.5). Electronic applications accepted.

Virginia Commonwealth University, Graduate School, College of Humanities and Sciences, Richard T. Robertson School of Media and Culture, Program in Media, Art, and Text, Richmond, VA 23284-9005. Offers PhD. *Entrance requirements:* For doctorate, GRE. Additional exam requirements/recommendations for international students: Required—TOEFL (minimum score 600 paper-based; 100 iBT); Recommended—IELTS (minimum score 6.5). Electronic applications accepted.

Virginia State University, College of Graduate Studies, College of Humanities and Social Sciences, Department of Mass Communications, Petersburg, VA 23806-0001. Offers media management (MA).

Wagner College, Division of Graduate Studies, Nicolais School of Business, Staten Island, NY 10301-4495. Offers accounting (MS); business administration (MBA); finance (MBA); management (Exec MBA); marketing (MBA); media management (MS). *Accreditation:* ACBSP. *Program availability:* Part-time, evening/weekend. *Faculty:* 8 full-time (3 women), 17 part-time/adjunct (5 women). *Students:* 90 full-time (41 women), 27 part-time (9 women); includes 18 minority (10 Black or African American, non-Hispanic/Latino; 2 Asian, non-Hispanic/Latino; 4 Hispanic/Latino; 2 Two or more races, non-Hispanic/Latino), 14 international. Average age 27. 85 applicants, 92% accepted, 58 enrolled. In 2017, 72 master's awarded. *Degree requirements:* For master's, thesis optional. *Entrance requirements:* For master's, minimum GPA of 2.75, proficiency in computers and math. Additional exam requirements/recommendations for international students: Required—TOEFL (minimum score 550 paper-based; 79 iBT), IELTS (minimum score 6.5). *Application deadline:* For fall admission, 5/1 priority date for domestic students, 3/1 priority date for international students; for spring admission, 12/1 for domestic students, 11/1 for international students. Applications are processed on a rolling basis. Application fee: $60. *Financial support:* In 2017–18, 93 students received support. Career-related internships or fieldwork, unspecified assistantships, and alumni fellowship grants available. Financial award application deadline: 4/1; financial award applicants required to submit FAFSA. *Unit head:* Dr. Donald Crooks, Director, 718-390-3429, Fax: 718-390-3429, E-mail: dcrooks@wagner.edu. *Application contact:* Patricia Clancy, Assistant Director for Enrollment, 718-420-4464, Fax: 718-390-3105, E-mail: patricia.clancy@wagner.edu.

Wayne State University, College of Fine, Performing and Communication Arts, Department of Communication, Detroit, MI 48202. Offers communication (PhD), including democratic participation and culture, identity and representation, media, society and culture, risk, crisis and conflict, wellness, work life and relationships; communication and new media (Graduate Certificate); communication studies (MA); dispute resolution (MADR, Graduate Certificate), including community and urban studies (MADR), conflict area studies (MADR), health and family (MADR), international conflict and cooperation (MADR), professional practice (MADR), theory of conflict (MADR), workplace (MADR); health communication (Graduate Certificate); journalism (MA);

media arts (MA); media studies (MA); public relations and organizational communication (MA); JD/MADR. Doctoral program admits for fall only. *Program availability:* Online learning. *Faculty:* 21. *Students:* 63 full-time (35 women), 87 part-time (55 women); includes 54 minority (39 Black or African American, non-Hispanic/Latino; 2 Asian, non-Hispanic/Latino; 7 Hispanic/Latino; 6 Two or more races, non-Hispanic/Latino), 10 international. Average age 34. 153 applicants, 39% accepted, 27 enrolled. In 2017, 26 master's, 7 doctorates, 8 other advanced degrees awarded. *Degree requirements:* For master's, thesis (for some programs), thesis or essay; for doctorate, thesis/dissertation. *Entrance requirements:* For master's, GRE (for MA if undergraduate GPA less than 3.2), personal statement; BA or BS in communication or related field with minimum upper-division GPA of 3.2 and minimum upper-division undergraduate GPA of 3.0, and sample of academic writing (for MA); undergraduate degree with minimum upper-division GPA of 3.0 and three letters of recommendation (for MADR); for doctorate, GRE, undergraduate degree in communication or related field; master's degree in communication or related field with minimum GPA of 3.5; letters of recommendation; personal statement; sample of written scholarship. Additional exam requirements/recommendations for international students: Required—TOEFL (minimum score 100 iBT), IELTS, TWE. *Application fee:* $50. Electronic applications accepted. *Expenses:* Contact institution. *Financial support:* In 2017–18, 57 students received support, including 5 fellowships with tuition reimbursements available (averaging $17,400 per year), 2 research assistantships with tuition reimbursements available (averaging $20,388 per year), 20 teaching assistantships with tuition reimbursements available (averaging $18,534 per year); scholarships/grants and unspecified assistantships also available. Financial award applicants required to submit FAFSA. *Faculty research:* Democratic participation and culture; identity and representation; media, society and culture; risk, crisis and conflict; wellness, work life, and relationships. *Unit head:* Dr. Lee Wilkins, Professor and Chair, 313-577-2943, E-mail: eh8899@wayne.edu. *Application contact:* E-mail: communication@wayne.edu.
Website: http://comm.wayne.edu/

Wayne State University, College of Liberal Arts and Sciences, Department of English, Detroit, MI 48202. Offers English (MA); film and media studies (PhD); literary and cultural studies (PhD); rhetoric and composition studies (PhD). *Faculty:* 23. *Students:* 68 full-time (34 women), 24 part-time (17 women); includes 22 minority (10 Black or African American, non-Hispanic/Latino; 2 Asian, non-Hispanic/Latino; 6 Hispanic/Latino; 4 Two or more races, non-Hispanic/Latino), 5 international. Average age 33. 110 applicants, 35% accepted, 17 enrolled. In 2017, 15 master's, 15 doctorates awarded. Terminal master's awarded for partial completion of doctoral program. *Degree requirements:* For master's, variable foreign language requirement, essay, thesis, or portfolio of work approved by Director of Graduate Studies; for doctorate, one foreign language, comprehensive exam, thesis/dissertation. *Entrance requirements:* For master's, statement of purpose; two academic letters of reference; sample essay from previous English course; for doctorate, GRE General Test, statement of purpose; two academic letters of reference; sample of scholarly or critical writing. Additional exam requirements/recommendations for international students: Required—TOEFL (minimum score 550 paper-based; 79 iBT), TWE (minimum score 5.5), Michigan English Language Assessment Battery (minimum score 85); Recommended—IELTS (minimum score 6.5). *Application deadline:* For fall admission, 1/15 for domestic students. Applications are processed on a rolling basis. *Application fee:* $50. Electronic applications accepted. *Expenses:* Tuition, state resident: full-time $10,224; part-time $638.98 per credit hour. Tuition, nonresident: full-time $22,145; part-time $1384.04 per credit hour. Tuition and fees vary according to course load and program. *Financial support:* In 2017–18, 61 students received support, including 6 fellowships with tuition reimbursements available (averaging $15,583 per year), 30 teaching assistantships with tuition reimbursements available (averaging $18,534 per year); research assistantships with tuition reimbursements available, scholarships/grants, health care benefits, and unspecified assistantships also available. Financial award applicants required to submit FAFSA. *Faculty research:* Literary and cultural studies, film and new media studies, rhetoric and composition studies, linguistics, and creative writing. *Unit head:* Dr. Kenneth Jackson, Chair and Professor, 313-577-7692, E-mail: ai4054@wayne.edu. *Application contact:*

Dr. Carolin Maun, Director of Graduate Studies, 313-577-7694, E-mail: caroline.maun@wayne.edu.
Website: http://clas.wayne.edu/english/

Webster University, George Herbert Walker School of Business and Technology, Department of Business, St. Louis, MO 63119-3194. Offers business and organizational security management (MBA); decision support systems (MBA); environmental management (MBA); finance (MBA, MS); forensic accounting (MS); gerontology (MBA); human resources development (MBA); human resources management (MBA); information technology management (MBA); international business (MA, MBA); international relations (MBA); management and leadership (MBA); marketing (MBA); media communications (MBA); procurement and acquisitions management (MBA); Web services (MBA). *Accreditation:* ACBSP. *Program availability:* Part-time, evening/weekend, online learning. *Degree requirements:* For master's, comprehensive exam (for some programs), thesis (for some programs). *Entrance requirements:* Additional exam requirements/recommendations for international students: Required—TOEFL.

Webster University, School of Communications, Program in Media Communications, St. Louis, MO 63119-3194. Offers MA.

Webster University, School of Communications, Program in Media Literacy, St. Louis, MO 63119-3194. Offers MA.

West Virginia State University, Media Studies Graduate Program, Institute, WV 25112-1000. Offers MA. *Degree requirements:* For master's, thesis, Comprehensive exam may be taken in lieu of a thesis. *Entrance requirements:* For master's, GRE (950), Undergraduate GPA of 3.0, Letters of Recommendation. Additional exam requirements/recommendations for international students: Required—TOEFL (minimum score 550 paper-based). Electronic applications accepted.

West Virginia University, Reed College of Media, Morgantown, WV 26506-6010. Offers data marketing communications (MS); integrated marketing communications (MS, Graduate Certificate); journalism (MSJ); media solutions and innovation (MSJ). *Program availability:* Part-time, online learning. *Students:* 165 full-time (122 women), 232 part-time (167 women); includes 81 minority (46 Black or African American, non-Hispanic/Latino; 5 Asian, non-Hispanic/Latino; 20 Hispanic/Latino; 10 Two or more races, non-Hispanic/Latino), 6 international. *Degree requirements:* For master's, thesis or alternative. *Entrance requirements:* For master's, GRE General Test, minimum GPA of 3.0, writing samples. Additional exam requirements/recommendations for international students: Required—TOEFL (minimum score 550 paper-based). *Application deadline:* For fall admission, 3/1 priority date for domestic students, 3/1 for international students. *Application fee:* $60. Electronic applications accepted. *Expenses:* Tuition, state resident: full-time $9450. Tuition, nonresident: full-time $24,390. *Financial support:* Research assistantships, teaching assistantships, career-related internships or fieldwork, Federal Work-Study, institutionally sponsored loans, health care benefits, tuition waivers (full and partial), and administrative assistantships available. Financial award application deadline: 2/1; financial award applicants required to submit FAFSA. *Faculty research:* History, law, and women in media; press management; public opinion; advertising effectiveness; international advertising. *Unit head:* Dr. Maryann Reed, Dean, 304-293-3505 Ext. 5409, Fax: 304-293-3072, E-mail: maryann.reed@mail.wvu.edu. *Application contact:* Dr. Steve Urbanski, Director of Graduate Studies/Associate Professor, 304-293-6797, Fax: 304-293-3072, E-mail: steve.urbanski@mail.wvu.edu. Website: http://reedcollegeofmedia.wvu.edu/

Wilfrid Laurier University, Faculty of Graduate and Postdoctoral Studies, Faculty of Arts, Department of Communication Studies, Waterloo, ON N2L 3C5, Canada. Offers media, technology and culture (MA); visual communication and culture (MA). *Degree requirements:* For master's, thesis optional. *Entrance requirements:* For master's, honours BA in communication studies or a cognate discipline from an approved university with a minimum B+ overall in last two years of study and in undergraduate major. Additional exam requirements/recommendations for international students: Required—TOEFL (minimum score 89 iBT). Electronic applications accepted. *Faculty research:* Visual communication and culture, media, technology and culture.

Publishing

Arizona State University at the Tempe campus, College of Liberal Arts and Sciences, School of Historical, Philosophical and Religious Studies, Tempe, AZ 85287-4301. Offers European history (MA, PhD); medieval studies (Graduate Certificate); North American history (MA, PhD); philosophy (MA, PhD); public history (MA); religious studies (MA, PhD); Renaissance studies (Graduate Certificate); scholarly publishing (Graduate Certificate). *Program availability:* Part-time. Terminal master's awarded for partial completion of doctoral program. *Degree requirements:* For master's, thesis or alternative, interactive Program of Study (iPOS) submitted before completing 50 percent of required credit hours; for doctorate, variable foreign language requirement, comprehensive exam, thesis/dissertation, interactive Program of Study (iPOS) submitted before completing 50 percent of required credit hours. *Entrance requirements:* For master's and doctorate, GRE, minimum GPA of 3.0 or equivalent in last 2 years of work leading to bachelor's degree. Additional exam requirements/recommendations for international students: Required—TOEFL, IELTS, or PTE. Electronic applications accepted.

Brown University, Graduate School, School of Engineering, Providence, RI 02912. Offers biomedical engineering (Sc M, PhD); chemical and biochemical engineering (Sc M, PhD); electrical sciences and computer engineering (Sc M, PhD); fluid and thermal sciences (Sc M, PhD); materials science and engineering (Sc M, PhD); mechanics of solids and structures (Sc M, PhD). *Degree requirements:* For doctorate, thesis/dissertation, preliminary exam.

Carnegie Mellon University, Dietrich College of Humanities and Social Sciences, Department of English, Program in Professional Writing, Pittsburgh, PA 15213-3891. Offers editing and publishing (MAPW); policy and non-profit communication (MAPW); public and media relations/corporate communications (MAPW); science or healthcare communication (MAPW); technical writing (MAPW); writing for new media (MAPW); writing for print media (MAPW). *Program availability:* Part-time. *Entrance requirements:* For master's, GRE General Test. Additional exam requirements/recommendations for international students: Required—TOEFL, TWE.

DePaul University, College of Liberal Arts and Social Sciences, Chicago, IL 60614. Offers Arabic (MA); Chinese (MA); critical ethnic studies (MA); English (MA); French (MA); German (MA); history (MA); interdisciplinary studies (MA, MS); international public service (MS); international studies (MA); Italian (MA); Japanese (MA); liberal studies (MA); nonprofit management (MNM); public administration (MPA); public health (MPH);

public policy (MPP); public service management (MS); refugee and forced migration studies (MS); social work (MSW); sociology (MA); Spanish (MA); sustainable urban development (MA); women's and gender studies (MA); writing and publishing (MA); writing, rhetoric and discourse (MA); MA/PhD. *Program availability:* Part-time, evening/weekend, online learning. Terminal master's awarded for partial completion of doctoral program. *Degree requirements:* For master's, variable foreign language requirement, comprehensive exam (for some programs), thesis (for some programs). *Application deadline:* Applications are processed on a rolling basis. *Application fee:* $40. Electronic applications accepted. *Financial support:* Applicants required to submit FAFSA. *Unit head:* Dr. Guillermo Vasquez de Velasco, Dean, 773-325-7305. *Application contact:* Ann Spittle, Director of Graduate Admission, 773-325-8369, Fax: 312-476-3244, E-mail: graddepaul@depaul.edu.
Website: http://las.depaul.edu/

Emerson College, Graduate Studies, Boston, MA 02116-4624. Offers civic media (MA), including art and practice; communication disorders (MS); creative writing (MFA); digital marketing (MA), including data analytics; film and media art (MFA); journalism (MA); popular fiction writing and publishing (MFA); public relations (MA); publishing and writing (MA); strategic communication for marketing (MA); theatre education (MA); writing for film and television (MFA). *Program availability:* Part-time, evening/weekend. *Faculty:* 202 full-time (86 women), 252 part-time/adjunct (125 women). *Students:* 571 full-time (423 women), 82 part-time (60 women); includes 102 minority (24 Black or African American, non-Hispanic/Latino; 19 Asian, non-Hispanic/Latino; 38 Hispanic/Latino; 1 Native Hawaiian or other Pacific Islander, non-Hispanic/Latino; 20 Two or more races, non-Hispanic/Latino), 170 international. Average age 27. 1,578 applicants, 57% accepted, 297 enrolled. In 2017, 271 master's awarded. *Entrance requirements:* For master's, GRE or GMAT (for certain programs). Additional exam requirements/recommendations for international students: Required—TOEFL (minimum score 550 paper-based; 80 iBT), IELTS (minimum score 6.5). *Application deadline:* Applications are processed on a rolling basis. *Application fee:* $60 ($75 for international students). Electronic applications accepted. *Expenses:* Tuition: Full-time $20,016; part-time $1251 per credit. *Required fees:* $624; $232 per credit. $116 per semester. *Financial support:* In 2017–18, 382 students received support, including 382 fellowships with partial tuition reimbursements available (averaging $7,551 per year); research assistantships with partial tuition reimbursements available, Federal Work-Study, scholarships/grants, and unspecified assistantships also available. Financial award application deadline: 3/1;

financial award applicants required to submit FAFSA. *Application contact:* Leanda Ferland, Director of Graduate Admission, 617-824-8610, Fax: 617-824-8614, E-mail: gradadmission@emerson.edu.
Website: http://www.emerson.edu/academics/graduate-degrees

The George Washington University, College of Professional Studies, Program in Publishing, Washington, DC 20052. Offers MPS. Program offered in Alexandria, VA. *Students:* 90 part-time (81 women); includes 24 minority (13 Black or African American, non-Hispanic/Latino; 4 Asian, non-Hispanic/Latino; 5 Hispanic/Latino; 2 Two or more races, non-Hispanic/Latino). Average age 31. 87 applicants, 92% accepted, 47 enrolled. In 2017, 39 master's awarded. *Entrance requirements:* For master's, minimum cumulative GPA of 3.0. *Application deadline:* For fall admission, 4/1 for domestic and international students. Electronic applications accepted. *Expenses: Tuition:* Full-time $28,800; part-time $1655 per credit hour. *Required fees:* $45; $2.75 per credit hour. *Unit head:* Dr. Arnold Grossblatt, Director, 202-994-7220, E-mail: arnieg@gwu.edu. *Application contact:* Kristin Williams, Associate Provost, Graduate Enrollment, 202-994-0467, Fax: 202-994-0371, E-mail: ksw@gwu.edu.
Website: http://nearyou.gwu.edu/pubs/

New York University, School of Professional Studies, Center for Publishing, New York, NY 10012-1019. Offers publishing: digital and print media (MS). *Program availability:* Part-time, evening/weekend. *Students:* 55 full-time (48 women), 33 part-time (31 women); includes 20 minority (3 Black or African American, non-Hispanic/Latino; 3 Asian, non-Hispanic/Latino; 10 Hispanic/Latino; 4 Two or more races, non-Hispanic/Latino), 22 international. Average age 25. 84 applicants, 82% accepted, 39 enrolled. In 2017, 72 master's awarded. *Degree requirements:* For master's, thesis. *Entrance requirements:* For master's, GRE or GMAT (only upon request), bachelor's degree, resume with relevant professional work, internship or volunteer experience, two letters of recommendation, statement of purpose. Additional exam requirements/recommendations for international students: Required—TOEFL (minimum score 600 paper-based; 100 iBT), IELTS (minimum score 7). *Application deadline:* For fall admission, 2/1 priority date for domestic and international students; for spring admission, 10/15 priority date for domestic students, 8/15 priority date for international students. Applications are processed on a rolling basis. Application fee: $150. Electronic applications accepted. *Expenses:* $20,244 per term. *Financial support:* Fellowships, career-related internships or fieldwork, Federal Work-Study, scholarships/grants, and health care benefits available. Support available to part-time students. Financial award application deadline: 6/30; financial award applicants required to submit FAFSA. *Unit head:* Andrea Chambers, Academic Director and Clinical Assistant Professor, 212-992-3232. *Application contact:* Admissions Office, 212-998-7100, E-mail: sps.gradadmissions@nyu.edu.
Website: http://www.sps.nyu.edu/academics/departments/publishing.html

Northwestern University, Medill School of Journalism, Media, and Integrated Marketing Communications, Evanston, IL 60208. Offers integrated marketing communications (MSIMC), including brand strategy, content marketing, direct and interactive marketing, marketing analytics, strategic communications; interactive publishing (MSJ); magazine writing/editing (MSJ); reporting (MSJ); video/broadcast (MSJ). *Entrance requirements:* For master's, GRE General Test, GMAT or LSAT (for MSJ). Additional exam requirements/recommendations for international students: Required—TOEFL. Electronic applications accepted. *Expenses:* Contact institution. *Faculty research:* Web business journalism, cultural stereotypes, voter apathy, digital television.

Pace University, Dyson College of Arts and Sciences, Program in Publishing, New York, NY 10038. Offers book publishing (Certificate); business side of publishing (Certificate); digital publishing (Certificate); magazine publishing (Certificate); publishing (MS). *Program availability:* Part-time, evening/weekend, 100% online. *Faculty:* 2 full-time (1 woman), 13 part-time/adjunct (7 women). *Students:* 47 full-time (42 women), 31 part-time (27 women); includes 32 minority (14 Black or African American, non-Hispanic/Latino; 3 Asian, non-Hispanic/Latino; 10 Hispanic/Latino; 5 Two or more races, non-Hispanic/Latino), 5 international. Average age 27. In 2017, 33 master's, 2 other advanced degrees awarded. *Degree requirements:* For master's, internship or thesis. *Entrance requirements:* For master's, GRE General Test, two letters of recommendation, personal statement, resume, all official transcripts. Additional exam requirements/recommendations for international students: Required—TOEFL (minimum score 88 iBT), IELTS (minimum score 7) or PTE (minimum score 60). *Application deadline:* For fall admission, 8/1 priority date for domestic students, 6/1 for international students; for spring admission, 12/1 priority date for domestic students, 10/1 for international students. Applications are processed on a rolling basis. Application fee: $70. Electronic applications accepted. *Financial support:* Research assistantships, career-related internships or fieldwork, scholarships/grants, and unspecified assistantships available. Financial award application deadline: 2/15; financial award applicants required to submit FAFSA. *Unit head:* Prof. Manuela Soares, MS in Publishing Program Director, 212-346-1513, E-mail: msoares@pace.edu. *Application contact:* Susan Ford-Goldschein, Director of Graduate Admissions, 212-346-1531, Fax: 212-346-1585, E-mail: graduateadmission@pace.edu.
Website: http://www.pace.edu/dyson/academic-departments-and-programs/publishing

Rosemont College, Schools of Graduate and Professional Studies, Publishing Program, Rosemont, PA 19010-1699. Offers MA. *Program availability:* Part-time, online learning. *Degree requirements:* For master's, comprehensive exam (for some programs), thesis. *Entrance requirements:* For master's, 3 letters of recommendation. Additional exam requirements/recommendations for international students: Required—TOEFL. Electronic applications accepted. Application fee is waived when completed online.

Rowan University, Graduate School, College of Communication and Creative Arts, Program in Editing and Publishing, Glassboro, NJ 08028-1701. Offers CGS. Electronic applications accepted. *Expenses:* Tuition, state resident: full-time $15,020; part-time $751 per semester hour. Tuition, nonresident: full-time $15,020; part-time $751 per semester hour. *Required fees:* $3158; $157.90 per semester hour. Tuition and fees vary according to course load, campus/location and program.

Sam Houston State University, College of Humanities and Social Sciences, Department of English, Huntsville, TX 77341. Offers creative writing, editing, and publishing (MFA); English (MA). *Program availability:* Part-time. *Degree requirements:* For master's, comprehensive exam, thesis optional. *Entrance requirements:* For master's, GRE General Test, creative writing sample, letters of recommendation. Additional exam requirements/recommendations for international students: Required—TOEFL (minimum score 550 paper-based; 79 iBT), IELTS (minimum score 6.5). Electronic applications accepted.

Simon Fraser University, Office of Graduate Studies and Postdoctoral Fellows, Faculty of Communication, Art and Technology, Canadian Institute for Studies in Publishing, Vancouver, BC V6B 5K3, Canada. Offers M Pub. *Degree requirements:* For master's, internship, internship project report. *Entrance requirements:* For master's, minimum GPA of 3.0 (on scale of 4.33) or 3.33 based on last 60 credits of undergraduate courses. Additional exam requirements/recommendations for international students: Recommended—TOEFL (minimum score 580 paper-based; 93 iBT), IELTS (minimum score 7), TWE (minimum score 5). Electronic applications accepted. *Expenses:* Contact institution. *Faculty research:* History of publishing, electronic publishing, editing, multimedia, publication design, communications technology, copyright and intellectual property.

University of Baltimore, Graduate School, Yale Gordon College of Arts and Sciences, Program in Creative Writing and Publishing Arts, Baltimore, MD 21201-5779. Offers MFA. *Program availability:* Part-time, evening/weekend. *Entrance requirements:* Additional exam requirements/recommendations for international students: Required—TOEFL.

University of Baltimore, Graduate School, Yale Gordon College of Arts and Sciences, Program in Publications Design, Baltimore, MD 21201-5779. Offers MA. *Program availability:* Part-time, evening/weekend. *Degree requirements:* For master's, seminar project. *Entrance requirements:* For master's, minimum GPA of 3.0, portfolio, interview. Additional exam requirements/recommendations for international students: Required—TOEFL (minimum score 550 paper-based). Electronic applications accepted. *Faculty research:* Communication theory, graphic design, media technology.

University of Houston–Victoria, School of Arts and Sciences, Program in Publishing, Victoria, TX 77901-4450. Offers MS. *Entrance requirements:* For master's, GMAT or GRE, 2 letters of recommendation, writing sample. Additional exam requirements/recommendations for international students: Required—TOEFL. Electronic applications accepted.

University of St. Thomas, College of Arts and Sciences, Graduate Program in English, St. Paul, MN 55105. Offers creative writing and publishing (MA); English literature (MA); teaching college English (Certificate). *Program availability:* Part-time, evening/weekend. *Faculty:* 24 full-time (15 women). *Students:* 41 full-time (29 women); includes 4 minority (3 Black or African American, non-Hispanic/Latino; 1 Asian, non-Hispanic/Latino). Average age 30. 9 applicants, 89% accepted, 8 enrolled. In 2017, 16 master's awarded. *Degree requirements:* For master's, essay. *Entrance requirements:* For master's, minimum GPA of 3.0, minimum 5 upper-level undergraduate courses in literature, sample of written work, personal statement, BA from accredited university, transcripts. Additional exam requirements/recommendations for international students: Required—TOEFL (minimum score 80 iBT), IELTS (minimum score 6.5). *Application deadline:* For fall admission, 3/1 priority date for domestic and international students; for spring admission, 10/1 priority date for domestic and international students; for summer admission, 3/1 priority date for domestic and international students. Applications are processed on a rolling basis. Application fee: $0. Electronic applications accepted. *Expenses:* $2,572.50 per course, $857.50 per credit; $55 technology fee per semester part-time, $111 full-time. *Financial support:* In 2017–18, 23 students received support, including 18 fellowships with partial tuition reimbursements available (averaging $5,145 per year), 3 research assistantships (averaging $2,000 per year), 4 teaching assistantships (averaging $750 per year); institutionally sponsored loans, scholarships/grants, traineeships, and unspecified assistantships also available. Support available to part-time students. Financial award application deadline: 3/1; financial award applicants required to submit FAFSA. *Faculty research:* Multicultural literature, literature and theory, regional writers, creative writing, 19th-century American literature. *Unit head:* Dr. Alexis Easley, Director, 651-962-5653, Fax: 651-962-5623, E-mail: maeasley@stthomas.edu. *Application contact:* Soren Hoeger-Lerdal, Coordinator, 651-962-5628, Fax: 651-962-5623, E-mail: gradenglish@stthomas.edu.
Website: http://www.stthomas.edu/english/graduate/

Vermont College of Fine Arts, MFA in Writing and Publishing Program, Montpelier, VT 05602. Offers MFA. *Faculty:* 5 full-time (3 women). *Students:* 25 full-time (17 women), 1 (woman) part-time; includes 6 minority (1 American Indian or Alaska Native, non-Hispanic/Latino; 2 Asian, non-Hispanic/Latino; 2 Hispanic/Latino; 1 Two or more races, non-Hispanic/Latino), 3 international. Average age 31. In 2017, 6 master's awarded. *Expenses:* Contact institution. *Financial support:* In 2017–18, 26 students received support, including 6 fellowships (averaging $3,000 per year); scholarships/grants also available. *Unit head:* Miciah Gault, Director, 802-828-8534. *Application contact:* David Markow, Director of Enrollment Management, 802-828-8535, E-mail: admissions@vcfa.edu.
Website: http://vcfa.edu/writing-publishing

Rhetoric

Abilene Christian University, Graduate Programs, College of Arts and Sciences, Department of English, Abilene, TX 79699. Offers composition/rhetoric (MA); literature (MA); writing (MA). *Program availability:* Part-time. *Faculty:* 16 part-time/adjunct (6 women). *Students:* 4 full-time (3 women), 1 (woman) part-time. 8 applicants, 50% accepted, 1 enrolled. In 2017, 8 master's awarded. *Degree requirements:* For master's, one foreign language, comprehensive exam (for some programs), thesis (for some programs). *Entrance requirements:* For master's, GRE General Test. Additional exam requirements/recommendations for international students: Required—TOEFL (minimum score 80 iBT), IELTS (minimum score 6), PTE. *Application deadline:* For fall admission, 8/11 for domestic students; for spring admission, 11/1 for domestic students. Applications are processed on a rolling basis. Application fee: $50. Electronic applications accepted. *Expenses:* $1,148 per hour. *Financial support:* In 2017–18, 4 students received support, including 4 teaching assistantships with partial tuition reimbursements available (averaging $5,800 per year); Federal Work-Study and scholarships/grants also available. Support available to part-time students. Financial award application deadline: 4/1; financial award applicants required to submit FAFSA. *Faculty research:* Feminism, Shakespearean dimensions of new literature, poetic consciousness, deconstruction myths. *Unit head:* Dr. William Carroll, Graduate Director, 325-674-2556, Fax: 325-674-2408, E-mail: william.carroll@acu.edu. *Application contact:* Graduate Admissions, 325-674-6911, Fax: 325-674-6717, E-mail: gradinfo@acu.edu.
Website: http://www.acu.edu/graduate/academics/english.html

Arizona State University at the Tempe campus, College of Liberal Arts and Sciences, Department of English, Tempe, AZ 85287-0302. Offers applied linguistics (PhD); creative writing (MFA); English (MA, PhD), including comparative literature (MA), linguistics (MA), literature, rhetoric and composition (MA), rhetoric, composition, and linguistics (PhD); film and media studies (MAS), including American media and popular culture; linguistics (Graduate Certificate); teaching English to speakers of other languages (MTESOL); translation studies (Graduate Certificate). Terminal master's awarded for partial completion of doctoral program. *Degree requirements:* For master's, variable foreign language requirement, comprehensive exam (for some programs), thesis (for some programs), interactive Program of Study (iPOS) submitted before completing 50 percent of required credit hours; for doctorate, variable foreign language requirement, comprehensive exam, thesis/dissertation, interactive Program of Study (iPOS) submitted before completing 50 percent of required credit hours. *Entrance requirements:* For master's and doctorate, GRE, minimum GPA of 3.0 or equivalent in last 2 years of work leading to bachelor's degree. Additional exam requirements/recommendations for international students: Required—TOEFL, IELTS, or PTE. Electronic applications accepted.

Ball State University, Graduate School, College of Sciences and Humanities, Department of English, Muncie, IN 47306. Offers English (MA, PhD), including composition (MA), creative writing (MA), literature, rhetoric and composition; linguistics (MA), including linguistics, teaching English to speakers of other languages (TESOL) and linguistics. *Program availability:* Part-time. *Faculty:* 20 full-time (15 women), 2 part-time/adjunct (both women). *Students:* 45 full-time (30 women), 30 part-time (17 women); includes 5 minority (2 Asian, non-Hispanic/Latino; 3 Hispanic/Latino), 17 international. Average age 29. 93 applicants, 61% accepted, 32 enrolled. In 2017, 20 master's, 7 doctorates awarded. *Degree requirements:* For doctorate, variable foreign language requirement, thesis/dissertation. *Entrance requirements:* For master's, GRE General Test, minimum baccalaureate GPA of 2.75 or 3.0 in latter half of baccalaureate, statement of purpose, writing sample, three letters of recommendation; for doctorate, GRE General Test, GRE Subject Test, minimum graduate GPA of 3.2, statement of purpose, writing sample, three letters of recommendation. Additional exam requirements/recommendations for international students: Required—TOEFL (minimum score 550 paper-based; 79 iBT), IELTS (minimum score 6.5). *Application deadline:* Applications are processed on a rolling basis. Application fee: $60. Electronic applications accepted. *Financial support:* In 2017–18, 46 students received support, including 5 research assistantships with partial tuition reimbursements available (averaging $15,132 per year), 28 teaching assistantships with partial tuition reimbursements available (averaging $13,595 per year); unspecified assistantships also available. Financial award application deadline: 3/1; financial award applicants required to submit FAFSA. *Faculty research:* American literature; literary editing; medieval, Renaissance, and eighteenth-century British literature; rhetoric. *Unit head:* Dr. Deborah Mix, Assistant Chair of Programs, 765-285-8401, Fax: 765-285-3765, E-mail: dmmix@bsu.edu. *Application contact:* Dr. Deborah Mix, Assistant Chair of Programs, 765-285-8401, Fax: 765-285-3765, E-mail: dmmix@bsu.edu.
Website: http://www.bsu.edu/english/

Bob Jones University, Graduate Programs, Greenville, SC 29614. Offers accountancy (MS); Bible (MA); Bible translation (MA); Biblical studies (Certificate); broadcast management (MS); business administration (MBA); church history (MA, PhD); church ministries (MA); church music (MM); cinema and video production (MA); counseling (MS); curriculum and instruction (Ed D); divinity (M Div); dramatic production (MA); educational leadership (MS, Ed D, Ed S); elementary education (M Ed, MAT); English (M Ed, MA, MAT); fine arts (MA); graphic design (MA); history (M Ed, MA); illustration (MA); interpretative speech (MA); mathematics (M Ed, MAT); medical missions (Certificate); ministry (MM, D Min); multi-categorical special education (M Ed, MAT); music (M Ed); New Testament interpretation (PhD); Old Testament interpretation (PhD); orchestral instrument performance (MM); organ performance (MM); pastoral studies (MA); personnel services (MS, Ed S); piano pedagogy (MM); piano performance (MM); platform arts (MA); radio and television broadcasting (MS); rhetoric and public address (MA); secondary education (M Ed); studio art (MA); teaching Bible (MA); theology (MA, PhD); voice performance (MM); youth ministries (MA); M Div/MM.

Boise State University, College of Arts and Sciences, Department of English, Boise, ID 83725-0399. Offers English literature (MA); English, rhetoric and composition (MA); teaching English language (MA); technical communication (MA). *Program availability:* Part-time. *Faculty:* 26. *Students:* 44 full-time (28 women), 38 part-time (29 women); includes 6 minority (2 American Indian or Alaska Native, non-Hispanic/Latino; 2 Asian, non-Hispanic/Latino; 1 Hispanic/Latino; 1 Two or more races, non-Hispanic/Latino), 3 international. Average age 33. 242 applicants, 15% accepted, 28 enrolled. In 2017, 29 master's awarded. *Degree requirements:* For master's, thesis (for some programs). *Entrance requirements:* For master's, GRE General Test, minimum GPA of 3.0. Additional exam requirements/recommendations for international students: Required—TOEFL (minimum score 550 paper-based; 80 iBT), IELTS (minimum score 6). *Application deadline:* For fall admission, 4/15 for domestic and international students; for spring admission, 10/15 for domestic and international students. Application fee: $65 ($95 for international students). Electronic applications accepted. *Expenses:* Tuition, state resident: full-time $6471; part-time $390 per credit. Tuition, nonresident: full-time $21,787; part-time $685 per credit. *Required fees:* $2283; $100 per term. Part-time tuition and fees vary according to course load and program. *Financial support:* Teaching assistantships, scholarships/grants, and unspecified assistantships available. Financial award application deadline: 1/15; financial award applicants required to submit FAFSA. *Unit head:* Dr. Michelle Payne, Chair, 208-426-3426, Fax: 208-426-4373, E-mail: mpayne@boisestate.edu. *Application contact:* Dr. Tom Hillard, Director, 208-426-2991, E-mail: thomashillard@boisestate.edu.
Website: http://english.boisestate.edu/graduate-programs/

Bowling Green State University, Graduate College, College of Arts and Sciences, Department of English, Program in English, Bowling Green, OH 43403. Offers English (MA, PhD); literature (MA); rhetoric and writing (PhD); scientific and technical communication (MA). *Program availability:* Part-time. *Degree requirements:* For master's, thesis or alternative; for doctorate, comprehensive exam, thesis/dissertation, foreign language or proficiency in Old English. *Entrance requirements:* For master's and doctorate, GRE General Test. Additional exam requirements/recommendations for international students: Required—TOEFL. Electronic applications accepted. *Faculty research:* Postmodern literary theory, rhetorical theory, ethnic American literature, literature and culture, composition pedagogy.

Brigham Young University, Graduate Studies, College of Humanities, Department of English, Provo, UT 84602. Offers creative writing (MFA); literature (MA); rhetoric/composition (MA). *Faculty:* 53 full-time (15 women). *Students:* 68 full-time (44 women), 1 part-time (0 women); includes 3 minority (1 Asian, non-Hispanic/Latino; 2 Hispanic/Latino). Average age 28. 44 applicants, 64% accepted, 24 enrolled. In 2017, 31 master's awarded. *Degree requirements:* For master's, variable foreign language requirement, comprehensive exam, thesis. *Entrance requirements:* For master's, GRE General Test, creative portfolio (for MFA). *Application deadline:* For fall admission, 1/15 for domestic and international students. Application fee: $50. Electronic applications accepted. *Expenses:* Tuition: Full-time $6880; part-time $405 per credit hour. Tuition and fees vary according to course load, program and student's religious affiliation. *Financial support:* In 2017–18, 67 students received support, including 10 research assistantships (averaging $4,000 per year), 62 teaching assistantships (averaging $6,700 per year); career-related internships or fieldwork, institutionally sponsored loans, and scholarships/grants also available. Support available to part-time students. Financial award application deadline: 3/15. *Faculty research:* English literature, American literature, rhetoric, creative writing. *Unit head:* Prof. Phillip Snyder, Head, 801-422-2487, Fax: 801-422-0221, E-mail: phillip_snyder@byu.edu. *Application contact:* Danielle N. Steed, Graduate Secretary and English Program Manager, 801-422-8673, Fax: 801-422-0221, E-mail: danielle-steed@byu.edu.
Website: http://english.byu.edu/

California State University, Dominguez Hills, College of Arts and Humanities, Department of English, Carson, CA 90747-0001. Offers English literature (MA); rhetoric and composition (Certificate); teaching English as a second language (MA, Certificate). *Program availability:* Part-time, evening/weekend. *Degree requirements:* For master's, comprehensive exam (for some programs), thesis or alternative. *Entrance requirements:* For master's, minimum GPA of 3.0 in last 60 units. Additional exam requirements/recommendations for international students: Required—TOEFL (minimum score 550 paper-based). Electronic applications accepted. *Faculty research:* Gender studies, transnationalism, discourse analysis, visual culture, Shakespeare.

California State University, Fresno, Division of Research and Graduate Studies, College of Arts and Humanities, Department of English, Fresno, CA 93740-8027. Offers creative writing (MFA); literature (MA); rhetoric and writing studies (MA). *Program availability:* Part-time, evening/weekend. *Degree requirements:* For master's, one foreign language, thesis. *Entrance requirements:* For master's, GRE General Test, minimum GPA of 3.0, writing sample. Additional exam requirements/recommendations for international students: Required—TOEFL. Electronic applications accepted. *Faculty research:* American literature, Renaissance literature, foreign literature.

California State University, Northridge, Graduate Studies, College of Humanities, Department of English, Northridge, CA 91330. Offers creative writing (MA); literature (MA); rhetoric and composition theory (MA). *Program availability:* Part-time, evening/weekend. *Students:* 24 full-time (19 women), 66 part-time (40 women); includes 39 minority (4 Black or African American, non-Hispanic/Latino; 5 Asian, non-Hispanic/Latino; 23 Hispanic/Latino; 1 Native Hawaiian or other Pacific Islander, non-Hispanic/Latino; 6 Two or more races, non-Hispanic/Latino), 1 international. Average age 34. 74 applicants, 77% accepted, 33 enrolled. In 2017, 42 master's awarded. *Degree requirements:* For master's, thesis or alternative. *Entrance requirements:* For master's, writing proficiency test, GRE General Test or minimum GPA of 3.0. Additional exam requirements/recommendations for international students: Required—TOEFL. *Application deadline:* For fall admission, 11/30 for domestic students. Application fee: $55. *Financial support:* Teaching assistantships available. Financial award application deadline: 3/1. *Faculty research:* Reading improvement, professional writing, Dickens, Shaw, English as a second language. *Unit head:* Kent Baxter, Chair, 818-677-3431.
Website: http://www.csun.edu/english/index.php

California State University, Stanislaus, College of the Arts, Humanities and Social Sciences, MA Program in English, Turlock, CA 95382. Offers literature (Certificate); rhetoric and teaching writing (MA); teaching English to speakers of other languages (MA). *Program availability:* Part-time. *Degree requirements:* For master's, comprehensive exam, thesis or alternative. *Entrance requirements:* For master's, GRE, minimum GPA of 3.0, 2 letters of reference, personal statement. Additional exam requirements/recommendations for international students: Required—TOEFL (minimum score 575 paper-based), TWE (minimum score 4). Electronic applications accepted. *Faculty research:* Transnational literacies, Renaissance and medieval literature, abolition writings and slave narratives, qualitative writing.

Carnegie Mellon University, Dietrich College of Humanities and Social Sciences, Department of English, Pittsburgh, PA 15213-3891. Offers communication planning and design (M Des); literary and cultural studies (MA, PhD); professional writing (MAPW), including editing and publishing, policy and non-profit communication, public and media relations / corporate communications, science or healthcare communication, technical writing, writing for new media, writing for print media; rhetoric (MA, PhD). *Program availability:* Part-time. Terminal master's awarded for partial completion of doctoral program. *Degree requirements:* For doctorate, 2 foreign languages, comprehensive exam, thesis/dissertation. *Entrance requirements:* For master's and doctorate, GRE General Test. Additional exam requirements/recommendations for international students: Required—TOEFL, TWE. *Faculty research:* Cognitive processes in discourse with emphasis on writing, testing, and evaluation.

The Catholic University of America, School of Arts and Sciences, Department of English Language and Literature, Washington, DC 20064. Offers English (MA, PhD); rhetoric (Certificate). *Program availability:* Part-time. *Faculty:* 14 full-time (6 women), 2 part-time/adjunct (1 woman). *Students:* 7 full-time (6 women), 29 part-time (14 women); includes 4 minority (3 Hispanic/Latino; 1 Two or more races, non-Hispanic/Latino), 3 international. Average age 30. 35 applicants, 49% accepted. In 2017, 2 master's, 6 doctorates awarded. *Degree requirements:* For master's, one foreign language, comprehensive exam; for doctorate, 2 foreign languages, comprehensive exam, thesis/dissertation. *Entrance requirements:* For master's and doctorate, GRE General Test, statement of purpose, official copies of academic transcripts, three letters of recommendation, writing sample. Additional exam requirements/recommendations for international students: Required—TOEFL (minimum score 550 paper-based; 80 iBT). *Application deadline:* For fall admission, 7/15 priority date for domestic students, 7/1 for international students; for spring admission, 11/15 priority date for domestic students, 11/1 for international students. Applications are processed on a rolling basis. Application fee: $55. Electronic applications accepted. *Expenses:* Contact institution. *Financial support:* Fellowships, research assistantships, teaching assistantships, Federal Work-Study, scholarships/grants, tuition waivers (full and partial), and unspecified assistantships available. Financial award application deadline: 2/1; financial award applicants required to submit FAFSA. *Faculty research:* Medieval literature, theory and history of rhetoric, Renaissance literature, religion and literature, English and American drama. *Total annual research expenditures:* $4,035. *Unit head:* Dr. Ernest Suarez, Chair, 202-319-5488, Fax: 202-319-4188, E-mail: johnsong@cua.edu. *Application contact:* Dr. Steven Brown, Director of Graduate Admissions, 202-319-5057, Fax: 202-319-6533, E-mail: cua-admissions@cua.edu.
Website: http://english.cua.edu/

Clemson University, Graduate School, College of Architecture, Arts, and Humanities, Department of English, Clemson, SC 29634. Offers English (MA); rhetoric, communication and information design (PhD); writing, rhetoric and media (MA). *Program availability:* Part-time. *Faculty:* 66 full-time (32 women), 7 part-time/adjunct (5 women). *Students:* 51 full-time (34 women), 16 part-time (9 women); includes 4 minority (1 Asian, non-Hispanic/Latino; 2 Hispanic/Latino; 1 Two or more races, non-Hispanic/Latino), 5 international. Average age 32. 30 applicants, 67% accepted, 9 enrolled. In 2017, 8 master's, 8 doctorates awarded. *Degree requirements:* For master's, variable foreign language requirement, thesis (for some programs). *Entrance requirements:* For master's, GRE General Test, unofficial transcripts, personal statement, writing sample, letters of recommendation. Additional exam requirements/recommendations for

international students: Required—TOEFL (minimum score 80 iBT), IELTS (minimum score 6.5), PTE (minimum score 54). *Application deadline:* For fall admission, 2/1 priority date for domestic and international students. Application fee: $80 ($90 for international students). Electronic applications accepted. *Expenses:* $5,174 per semester full-time resident, $9,714 per semester full-time non-resident, $511 per credit hour part-time resident, $1,017 per credit hour part-time non-resident; $741 per credit hour online; other fees may apply per session. *Financial support:* In 2017–18, 13 students received support, including 8 teaching assistantships with partial tuition reimbursements available (averaging $12,843 per year); unspecified assistantships also available. Financial award application deadline: 2/1. *Faculty research:* English literature, British literature, American literature, literary theory. *Total annual research expenditures:* $20,544. *Unit head:* Dr. Susanna Ashton, Department Chair, 864-656-3151, E-mail: sashton@clemson.edu. *Application contact:* Dr. William Stockton, Graduate Program Coordinator, 864-656-3151, E-mail: wstockt@clemson.edu.
Website: https://www.clemson.edu/caah/departments/english/

Colorado State University, College of Liberal Arts, Department of English, Fort Collins, CO 80523-1773. Offers creative writing (MFA); rhetoric and composition (MA). *Faculty:* 17 full-time (7 women), 10 part-time/adjunct (9 women). *Students:* 64 full-time (44 women), 33 part-time (28 women); includes 6 minority (2 Black or African American, non-Hispanic/Latino; 1 Asian, non-Hispanic/Latino; 3 Hispanic/Latino), 12 international. Average age 30. 207 applicants, 38% accepted, 23 enrolled. In 2017, 33 master's awarded. *Degree requirements:* For master's, thesis (for some programs), portfolio, project or thesis. *Entrance requirements:* For master's, BA/BS or equivalent with minimum cumulative undergraduate GPA of 3.0, transcripts, writing sample, statement of purpose, 3 letters of recommendation. Additional exam requirements/recommendations for international students: Recommended—TOEFL (minimum score 550 paper-based; 80 iBT), IELTS (minimum score 6.5). Application fee: $60 ($70 for international students). Electronic applications accepted. *Expenses:* Tuition, state resident: full-time $9917. Tuition, nonresident: full-time $24,312. *Required fees:* $2284. Tuition and fees vary according to course load and program. *Financial support:* In 2017–18, 1 fellowship with full and partial tuition reimbursement (averaging $14,256 per year), 40 teaching assistantships with full and partial tuition reimbursements (averaging $14,678 per year) were awarded; scholarships/grants and unspecified assistantships also available. *Faculty research:* Narratives written in new media; racial, gender, and sexual identity in the United States; the rhetoric of social change; pedagogical potential of graphic narratives. *Total annual research expenditures:* $134,319. *Unit head:* Louann Reid, Professor, 970-491-6428, E-mail: louann.reid@colostate.edu. *Application contact:* Marnie Leonard, Administrative Assistant, 970-491-2403, E-mail: marnie.leonard@colostate.edu.
Website: http://english.colostate.edu/

DePaul University, College of Liberal Arts and Social Sciences, Chicago, IL 60614. Offers Arabic (MA); Chinese (MA); critical ethnic studies (MA); English (MA); French (MA); German (MA); history (MA); interdisciplinary studies (MA, MS); international public service (MS); international studies (MA); Italian (MA); Japanese (MA); liberal studies (MA); nonprofit management (MNM); public administration (MPA); public health (MPH); public policy (MPP); public service management (MS); refugee and forced migration studies (MS); social work (MSW); sociology (MA); Spanish (MA); sustainable urban development (MA); women's and gender studies (MA); writing and publishing (MA); writing, rhetoric and discourse (MA); MA/PhD. *Program availability:* Part-time, evening/weekend, online learning. Terminal master's awarded for partial completion of doctoral program. *Degree requirements:* For master's, variable foreign language requirement, comprehensive exam (for some programs), thesis (for some programs). *Application deadline:* Applications are processed on a rolling basis. Application fee: $40. Electronic applications accepted. *Financial support:* Applicants required to submit FAFSA. *Unit head:* Dr. Guillermo Vasquez de Velasco, Dean, 773-325-7305. *Application contact:* Ann Spittle, Director of Graduate Admission, 773-325-8369, Fax: 312-476-3244, E-mail: graddepaul@depaul.edu.
Website: http://las.depaul.edu/

Duquesne University, Graduate School of Liberal Arts, Department of Communication and Rhetorical Studies, Pittsburgh, PA 15282-0001. Offers communication (MA); rhetoric (PhD). *Program availability:* Part-time, evening/weekend, 100% online. *Faculty:* 10 full-time (4 women), 5 part-time/adjunct (3 women). *Students:* 96 full-time (56 women), 8 part-time (6 women); includes 13 minority (10 Black or African American, non-Hispanic/Latino; 1 Asian, non-Hispanic/Latino; 2 Hispanic/Latino), 20 international. Average age 35. 39 applicants, 97% accepted, 18 enrolled. In 2017, 18 master's, 6 doctorates awarded. Terminal master's awarded for partial completion of doctoral program. *Degree requirements:* For master's, thesis optional, practicum; for doctorate, 2 foreign languages, comprehensive exam, thesis/dissertation. *Entrance requirements:* For master's and doctorate, GRE General Test. Additional exam requirements/recommendations for international students: Required—TOEFL. *Application deadline:* For fall admission, 2/1 priority date for domestic and international students; for spring admission, 11/1 priority date for domestic and international students. Applications are processed on a rolling basis. Application fee: $0. Electronic applications accepted. *Expenses:* $958 per credit. *Financial support:* In 2017–18, 24 students received support, including 7 research assistantships with full tuition reimbursements available (averaging $8,000 per year), 14 teaching assistantships with full tuition reimbursements available (averaging $17,000 per year); career-related internships or fieldwork, Federal Work-Study, institutionally sponsored loans, scholarships/grants, tuition waivers (full and partial), and unspecified assistantships also available. Financial award application deadline: 5/1. *Unit head:* Dr. Ronald Arnett, Chair, 412-396-5076, E-mail: arnett@duq.edu. *Application contact:* Linda Rendulic, Assistant to the Dean, 412-396-6400, Fax: 412-396-5265, E-mail: rendulic@duq.edu.
Website: http://www.duq.edu/academics/schools/liberal-arts/graduate-school/programs/communication-

East Carolina University, Graduate School, Thomas Harriot College of Arts and Sciences, Department of English, Greenville, NC 27858-4353. Offers creative writing (MA); English studies (MA); linguistics (MA); literature (MA); multicultural and transnational literatures (MA, Certificate); professional communication (Certificate); rhetoric and composition (MA); rhetoric, writing, and professional communication (PhD); teaching English in the two-year college (Certificate); teaching English to speakers of other languages (MA, Certificate); technical and professional communication (MA). *Program availability:* Part-time, evening/weekend, online learning. *Students:* 40 full-time (27 women), 74 part-time (57 women); includes 33 minority (23 Black or African American, non-Hispanic/Latino; 2 Asian, non-Hispanic/Latino; 4 Hispanic/Latino; 4 Two or more races, non-Hispanic/Latino). Average age 35. 36 applicants, 94% accepted, 25 enrolled. In 2017, 23 master's, 4 doctorates, 24 other advanced degrees awarded. *Degree requirements:* For master's, comprehensive exam, thesis optional; for doctorate, comprehensive exam, thesis/dissertation. *Entrance requirements:* For master's, GRE General Test or MAT; for doctorate, GRE General Test or MAT, writing samples. Additional exam requirements/recommendations for international students: Recommended—TOEFL (minimum score 78 iBT), IELTS (minimum score 6.5), TWE. *Application deadline:* For fall admission, 7/31 priority date for domestic students, 2/1 priority date for international students; for spring admission, 11/30 priority date for domestic students, 10/1 priority date for international students. Applications are processed on a rolling basis. Application fee: $75. Electronic applications accepted. *Expenses:* Tuition, state resident: full-time $4749; part-time $297 per credit hour. Tuition, nonresident: full-time $17,898; part-time $1119 per credit hour. *Required fees:* $2691; $224 per credit hour. Part-time tuition and fees vary according to course load and program. *Financial support:* Research assistantships with partial tuition reimbursements, teaching assistantships with partial tuition reimbursements, and Federal Work-Study available. Support available to part-time students. Financial award application deadline: 3/1. *Faculty research:* Technical and professional communication, rhetoric/composition, multicultural and transnational literature, creative writing, film studies. *Unit head:* Dr. Marianne Montgomery, Chair, 252-328-6687, E-mail: montgomerym@ecu.edu. *Application contact:* Dean of Graduate School, 252-328-6012, Fax: 252-328-6071, E-mail: gradschool@ecu.edu.
Website: http://www.ecu.edu/cs-cas/engl/

Eastern Washington University, Graduate Studies, College of Arts, Letters and Education, Department of English, Cheney, WA 99004-2431. Offers literature (MA); rhetoric, composition, and technical communication (MA); teaching English as a second language (MA). *Faculty:* 14. *Students:* 61 full-time (40 women), 11 part-time (9 women); includes 3 minority (1 Asian, non-Hispanic/Latino; 2 Hispanic/Latino), 7 international. Average age 34. 91 applicants, 52% accepted, 33 enrolled. In 2017, 32 master's awarded. *Degree requirements:* For master's, comprehensive exam, thesis or alternative. *Entrance requirements:* For master's, GRE General Test, minimum GPA of 3.0. Additional exam requirements/recommendations for international students: Required—TOEFL (minimum score 580 paper-based; 92 iBT), IELTS (minimum score 7), PTE (minimum score 6). *Application deadline:* For fall admission, 4/1 priority date for domestic students; for spring admission, 1/15 for domestic students. Applications are processed on a rolling basis. Application fee: $50. *Expenses:* Tuition, state resident: full-time $11,191; part-time $373.06 per credit. Tuition, nonresident: full-time $25,995; part-time $866.52 per credit. *Financial support:* Teaching assistantships with partial tuition reimbursements, career-related internships or fieldwork, Federal Work-Study, institutionally sponsored loans, scholarships/grants, health care benefits, tuition waivers (partial), and unspecified assistantships available. Support available to part-time students. Financial award application deadline: 2/1; financial award applicants required to submit FAFSA. *Application contact:* Kathy White, Advisor/Recruiter for Graduate Studies, 509-359-2491, E-mail: gradprograms@ewu.edu.
Website: http://www.ewu.edu/CALE/Programs/English.xml

Florida State University, The Graduate School, College of Arts and Sciences, Department of English, Tallahassee, FL 32312. Offers English (MA, MFA, PhD), including creative writing (MFA, PhD), literature (MA, PhD), rhetoric and composition (MA, PhD). *Program availability:* Part-time. *Faculty:* 47 full-time (24 women), 2 part-time/adjunct (1 woman). *Students:* 142 full-time (80 women), 31 part-time (23 women); includes 44 minority (17 Black or African American, non-Hispanic/Latino; 1 American Indian or Alaska Native, non-Hispanic/Latino; 12 Asian, non-Hispanic/Latino; 5 Hispanic/Latino; 9 Two or more races, non-Hispanic/Latino), 9 international. Average age 30. 307 applicants, 22% accepted, 47 enrolled. In 2017, 21 master's, 24 doctorates awarded. *Degree requirements:* For master's, one foreign language, 33 hours of coursework including capstone essay, thesis or portfolio (MA); 45 hours of coursework including 9-12 thesis hours (MFA); for doctorate, one foreign language, comprehensive exam, thesis/dissertation, 27 hours of coursework, 24 hours of dissertation work. *Entrance requirements:* For master's and doctorate, GRE General Test, sample of written work, 3 letters of recommendation, resume. Additional exam requirements/recommendations for international students: Required—TOEFL. *Application deadline:* For fall admission, 12/17 priority date for domestic and international students. Application fee: $30. Electronic applications accepted. *Financial support:* In 2017–18, 132 students received support, including 5 fellowships with tuition reimbursements available, teaching assistantships with tuition reimbursements available (averaging $13,500 per year); career-related internships or fieldwork, Federal Work-Study, and institutionally sponsored loans also available. Financial award application deadline: 8/1; financial award applicants required to submit FAFSA. *Faculty research:* British and Irish literature, American literature, creative writing, rhetoric and composition, multiethnic transnational literature, history of text technologies. *Unit head:* Dr. Gary Taylor, Chair, 850-644-4230, Fax: 850-644-0811, E-mail: gtaylor@fsu.edu. *Application contact:* Ginger Martin, Senior Graduate Academic Coordinator, 850-644-1081, Fax: 850-644-9656, E-mail: vmartin@fsu.edu.
Website: http://english.fsu.edu/

George Mason University, College of Humanities and Social Sciences, Department of English, Fairfax, VA 22030. Offers college teaching (Certificate), including higher education pedagogy; creative writing (MFA), including fiction, nonfiction writing, poetry; English (MA), including cultural studies, linguistics, literature, professional writing and rhetoric, teaching of writing and literature; English pedagogy (Certificate); folklore studies (Certificate); linguistics (PhD); writing and rhetoric (PhD). *Program availability:* Part-time. *Faculty:* 78 full-time (40 women), 45 part-time/adjunct (30 women). *Students:* 120 full-time (84 women), 116 part-time (94 women); includes 43 minority (13 Black or African American, non-Hispanic/Latino; 8 Asian, non-Hispanic/Latino; 14 Hispanic/Latino; 1 Native Hawaiian or other Pacific Islander, non-Hispanic/Latino; 7 Two or more races, non-Hispanic/Latino), 19 international. Average age 32. 224 applicants, 61% accepted, 68 enrolled. In 2017, 60 master's, 1 doctorate, 17 other advanced degrees awarded. *Degree requirements:* For master's, thesis (for some programs), proficiency in a foreign language by course work or translation test; for doctorate, comprehensive exam, thesis/dissertation, 2 papers. *Entrance requirements:* For master's, official transcripts; expanded goals statement; writing sample; portfolio; 2 letters of recommendation; resume; for doctorate, GRE (for linguistics), expanded goals statement; 2 letters of recommendation (writing and rhetoric); 3 letters of recommendation (linguistics); writing sample; introductory course in linguistics; official transcripts; master's degree in relevant field; for Certificate, official transcripts; expanded goals statement; 2 letters of recommendation; writing sample; resume. Additional exam requirements/recommendations for international students: Required—TOEFL (minimum score 575 paper-based; 88 iBT), IELTS (minimum score 6.5), PTE (minimum score 59). *Application deadline:* For fall admission, 3/15 for domestic and international students; for spring admission, 10/15 for domestic and international students. Application fee: $75 ($80 for international students). Electronic applications accepted. *Expenses:* Tuition, state resident: full-time $11,228; part-time $459.50 per credit. Tuition, nonresident: full-time $30,932; part-time $1280.50 per credit. *Required fees:* $3252; $135.50 per credit. Part-time tuition and fees vary according to course load and program. *Financial support:* In 2017–18, 84 students received support, including 9 research assistantships with tuition reimbursements available (averaging $17,199 per year), 76 teaching assistantships with tuition reimbursements available (averaging $11,917 per year); career-related internships or fieldwork, Federal Work-Study, scholarships/grants, unspecified assistantships, and health care benefits (for full-time research or teaching assistantship recipients) also available. Support available to part-time students. Financial award application deadline: 3/1; financial award applicants required to submit FAFSA. *Faculty research:* Literature, professional writing and editing, writing of fiction or poetry. *Total annual research expenditures:* $68,592. *Unit head:* Debra Lattanzi-Shutika, Chair, 703-993-1170, Fax: 703-993-1161, E-mail: dshutika@gmu.edu. *Application contact:* Alex Walsh, Graduate Admissions Coordinator, 703-993-1185, Fax: 703-993-

1161, E-mail: awalsh7@gmu.edu.
Website: http://english.gmu.edu

Georgia State University, College of Arts and Sciences, Department of Communication, Atlanta, GA 30302-3083. Offers film, video, and digital imaging (MA), including critical studies, production, screenwriting; human communication and social influence (MA); mass communication (MA); media and society (PhD); moving image studies (PhD); public communication (PhD); rhetoric and politics (PhD). *Program availability:* Part-time. *Faculty:* 57 full-time (34 women). *Students:* 71 full-time (51 women), 17 part-time (9 women); includes 36 minority (28 Black or African American, non-Hispanic/Latino; 1 Asian, non-Hispanic/Latino; 4 Hispanic/Latino; 1 Native Hawaiian or other Pacific Islander, non-Hispanic/Latino; 2 Two or more races, non-Hispanic/Latino), 15 international. Average age 33. 63 applicants, 54% accepted, 17 enrolled. In 2017, 20 master's, 10 doctorates awarded. *Degree requirements:* For master's, variable foreign language requirement, thesis (for some programs); for doctorate, comprehensive exam, thesis/dissertation. *Entrance requirements:* For master's and doctorate, GRE. Additional exam requirements/recommendations for international students: Required—TOEFL (minimum score 550 paper-based; 80 iBT), IELTS (minimum score 6.5). *Application deadline:* For fall admission, 2/10 for domestic and international students; for spring admission, 10/15 for domestic and international students. Application fee: $50. Electronic applications accepted. *Expenses:* Tuition, state resident: full-time $7020. Tuition, nonresident: full-time $22,518. *Required fees:* $2128. Tuition and fees vary according to degree level and program. *Financial support:* In 2017–18, fellowships with tuition reimbursements (averaging $15,000 per year), teaching assistantships with tuition reimbursements (averaging $15,000 per year) were awarded; career-related internships or fieldwork and unspecified assistantships also available. Financial award applicants required to submit FAFSA. *Faculty research:* New media, mass media and journalism, rhetoric, film and media studies, film production. *Unit head:* Dr. Greg Lisby, Chair, 404-413-5639, Fax: 404-413-5634, E-mail: glisby@gsu.edu.
Website: http://communication.gsu.edu

Georgia State University, College of Arts and Sciences, Department of English, Atlanta, GA 30302-3083. Offers creative writing (MA, MFA, PhD), including creative writing (PhD), fiction (MA, MFA), poetry (MA, MFA); English (MA, PhD); literary studies (MA, PhD); rhetoric and composition (MA, PhD). *Program availability:* Part-time. *Faculty:* 47 full-time (24 women). *Students:* 122 full-time (77 women), 63 part-time (39 women); includes 26 minority (16 Black or African American, non-Hispanic/Latino; 4 Asian, non-Hispanic/Latino; 1 Hispanic/Latino; 5 Two or more races, non-Hispanic/Latino), 12 international. Average age 36. 168 applicants, 58% accepted, 38 enrolled. In 2017, 16 master's, 18 doctorates awarded. *Entrance requirements:* For master's and doctorate, GRE. Additional exam requirements/recommendations for international students: Required—TOEFL (minimum score 550 paper-based; 80 iBT). *Application deadline:* For fall admission, 1/15 for domestic and international students. Application fee: $50. Electronic applications accepted. *Expenses:* Tuition, state resident: full-time $7020. Tuition, nonresident: full-time $22,518. *Required fees:* $2128. Tuition and fees vary according to degree level and program. *Financial support:* In 2017–18, research assistantships with full tuition reimbursements (averaging $6,000 per year), teaching assistantships with full tuition reimbursements (averaging $15,000 per year) were awarded; career-related internships or fieldwork, traineeships, and health care benefits also available. Financial award application deadline: 2/15. *Faculty research:* British and American literature and transnational literatures in English, literary theory and cultural studies, creative writing (fiction and poetry), rhetoric and composition, new media and digital humanities. *Unit head:* Dr. Lynnee Lewis Gaillet, Chair, 404-413-5842, Fax: 404-413-5830, E-mail: lgaillet@gsu.edu.
Website: http://www.english.gsu.edu

Indiana University Bloomington, University Graduate School, College of Arts and Sciences, Department of English, Bloomington, IN 47405. Offers creative writing (MA, MFA), including fiction (MFA), poetry (MFA); literature (PhD); rhetoric (PhD). *Degree requirements:* For master's, 30-36 credit hours plus one language proficiency (for MA); 60 credit hours plus thesis (for MFA); for doctorate, thesis/dissertation, qualifying exam; 90 credit hours; 2nd language proficiency or one language only if acquired at in-depth level. *Entrance requirements:* For master's, GRE General Test, GRE Subject Test (for all but MFA and MA in creative writing), minimum GPA of 3.5; for doctorate, GRE General Test, GRE Subject Test, minimum GPA of 3.7. Additional exam requirements/recommendations for international students: Required—TOEFL (minimum score 550 paper-based; 79 iBT), IELTS (minimum score 6.5). Electronic applications accepted.

Iowa State University of Science and Technology, Department of English, Ames, IA 50011. Offers creative writing (MFA); English (MA); rhetoric and professional communication (PhD). *Degree requirements:* For master's, thesis or alternative; for doctorate, thesis/dissertation. *Entrance requirements:* For master's, GRE General Test, sample of written work, resume, portfolio in creative writing; for doctorate, GRE General Test, sample of written work, resume. Additional exam requirements/recommendations for international students: Required—TOEFL (minimum score 600 paper-based; 100 iBT), IELTS (minimum score 7). Electronic applications accepted. *Faculty research:* Creative writing, literature, rhetoric, composition and professional communication, teaching English as a second language, applied linguistics.

Iowa State University of Science and Technology, Program in Rhetoric and Professional Communication, Ames, IA 50011. Offers PhD. *Entrance requirements:* For doctorate, GRE, official academic transcripts, resume, three letters of recommendation, writing sample. Additional exam requirements/recommendations for international students: Required—TOEFL (minimum score 640 paper-based; 111 iBT), IELTS (minimum score 7.5). Electronic applications accepted.

Iowa State University of Science and Technology, Program in Rhetoric, Composition, and Professional Communication, Ames, IA 50011. Offers MA. *Entrance requirements:* For master's, GRE, official academic transcripts, resume, three letters of recommendation, writing sample. Additional exam requirements/recommendations for international students: Required—TOEFL (minimum score 600 paper-based; 100 iBT), IELTS (minimum score 7). Electronic applications accepted.

James Madison University, The Graduate School, College of Arts and Letters, Program in Writing, Rhetoric, and Technical Communication, Harrisonburg, VA 22801. Offers MA, MS. *Program availability:* Part-time. *Students:* 9 full-time (8 women), 3 part-time (all women); includes 1 minority (Asian, non-Hispanic/Latino), 1 international. Average age 30. In 2017, 13 master's awarded. Application fee: $55. Electronic applications accepted. *Expenses:* Tuition, state resident: full-time $10,512; part-time $438 per credit hour. Tuition, nonresident: full-time $28,358; part-time $1162 per credit hour. *Required fees:* $1128. *Financial support:* In 2017–18, 8 students received support, including 5 fellowships, 3 teaching assistantships with full tuition reimbursements available (averaging $9,284 per year); career-related internships or fieldwork, Federal Work-Study, and assistantships (averaging $7911) also available. Financial award application deadline: 3/1; financial award applicants required to submit FAFSA. *Unit head:* Dr. Traci A. Zimmerman, Director of the School of Writing, Rhetoric and Technical Communication, 540-568-2334, E-mail: zimmerta@jmu.edu. *Application contact:* Lynette D. Michael, Director of Graduate Admissions, 540-568-6131 Ext. 6395, Fax: 540-568-7860, E-mail: michaeld@jmu.edu.
Website: http://www.jmu.edu/wrtc/

Kent State University, College of Arts and Sciences, Department of English, Kent, OH 44242-0001. Offers creative writing (MFA); English (MA, PhD); English for teachers (MA); literature and writing (MA); rhetoric and composition (PhD); teaching English as a second language (MA). MFA program offered jointly with Cleveland State University, The University of Akron, and Youngstown State University. *Program availability:* Part-time. *Faculty:* 25 full-time (13 women), 2 part-time/adjunct (1 woman). *Students:* 101 full-time (69 women), 19 part-time (11 women); includes 10 minority (4 Black or African American, non-Hispanic/Latino; 1 Asian, non-Hispanic/Latino; 2 Hispanic/Latino; 3 Two or more races, non-Hispanic/Latino), 20 international. Average age 34. 63 applicants, 76% accepted, 18 enrolled. In 2017, 37 master's, 6 doctorates awarded. *Degree requirements:* For master's, one foreign language, thesis (for some programs), final portfolio, final exam, or thesis (for MA in teaching English as a second language); for doctorate, one foreign language, comprehensive exam, thesis/dissertation. *Entrance requirements:* For master's, GRE General Test, goal statement, 3 letters of recommendation, 8-15 page writing sample relevant to the field of study (waived for MA in English for teachers concentration), transcripts; for doctorate, GRE General Test, statement of purpose, 3 letters of recommendation, 8-15 page writing sample relevant to field of study, transcripts. Additional exam requirements/recommendations for international students: Required—TOEFL (minimum score 587 paper-based, 94 iBT), Michigan English Language Assessment Battery (minimum score 82), IELTS (minimum score 7.0) or PTE (minimum score 65). *Application deadline:* For fall admission, 1/15 for domestic and international students. Applications are processed on a rolling basis. Application fee: $45 ($70 for international students). Electronic applications accepted. *Expenses:* Tuition, state resident: full-time $11,310; part-time $515 per credit hour. Tuition, nonresident: full-time $20,396; part-time $928 per credit hour. *International tuition:* $18,544 full-time. *Financial support:* Fellowships with full tuition reimbursements, teaching assistantships with full tuition reimbursements, and unspecified assistantships available. Financial award application deadline: 1/15. *Unit head:* Dr. Robert Trogdon, Chair, 330-672-2676, E-mail: rtrogdon@kent.edu. *Application contact:* Wesley Raabe, Graduate Studies Coordinator, E-mail: wraabe@kent.edu.
Website: http://www.kent.edu/english/

Michigan State University, The Graduate School, College of Arts and Letters, Program in Rhetoric and Writing, East Lansing, MI 48824. Offers critical studies in literacy and pedagogy (MA); digital rhetoric and professional writing (MA); rhetoric and writing (PhD). *Entrance requirements:* Additional exam requirements/recommendations for international students: Required—TOEFL. Electronic applications accepted. *Faculty research:* Rhetoric, writing and communication studies; media studies; technical communication, writing for digital environments.

Michigan Technological University, Graduate School, College of Sciences and Arts, Department of Humanities, Houghton, MI 49931. Offers rhetoric, theory and culture (MS, PhD). *Program availability:* Part-time. *Faculty:* 33 full-time (18 women), 2 part-time/adjunct. *Students:* 32 full-time (22 women), 14 part-time (8 women); includes 2 minority (both Two or more races, non-Hispanic/Latino), 21 international. Average age 34. 97 applicants, 20% accepted, 12 enrolled. In 2017, 3 master's, 3 doctorates awarded. Terminal master's awarded for partial completion of doctoral program. *Degree requirements:* For master's, thesis (for some programs); for doctorate, one foreign language, comprehensive exam, thesis/dissertation. *Entrance requirements:* For master's, GRE, statement of purpose, personal statement, official transcripts, 3 letters of recommendation, resume/curriculum vitae, writing sample (10-15 pages); for doctorate, GRE, statement of purpose, personal statement, official transcripts, 3 letters of recommendation, resume/curriculum vitae, writing sample (10-15 pages), master's degree. Additional exam requirements/recommendations for international students: Required—TOEFL (recommended minimum score 100 iBT) or IELTS (recommended minimum score of 7.0). *Application deadline:* For fall admission, 1/15 priority date for domestic and international students. Applications are processed on a rolling basis. Electronic applications accepted. *Expenses:* Tuition, state resident: full-time $17,100; part-time $950 per credit. Tuition, nonresident: full-time $17,100; part-time $950 per credit. *Required fees:* $248; $124 per term. Tuition and fees vary according to course load and program. *Financial support:* In 2017–18, 31 students received support, including fellowships (averaging $15,790 per year), 28 teaching assistantships with tuition reimbursements available (averaging $15,790 per year); career-related internships or fieldwork, Federal Work-Study, scholarships/grants, health care benefits, unspecified assistantships, and cooperative program also available. Financial award applicants required to submit FAFSA. *Faculty research:* Rhetoric and composition; communication and cultural studies; studies of science, technology, and society; technical communication and digital media. *Unit head:* Dr. Ronald L. Strickland, Chair, 906-487-2376, Fax: 906-487-3559, E-mail: rlstrick@mtu.edu. *Application contact:* Alex Renshaw, Administrative Aide, 906-487-2540, Fax: 906-487-3559, E-mail: ajrensha@mtu.edu.
Website: http://www.mtu.edu/humanities/

Missouri Western State University, Program in Assessment, St. Joseph, MO 64507-2294. Offers K-12 cross-categorical special education (MAS); TESOL (MAS, Graduate Certificate); writing (MAS). *Program availability:* Part-time. *Students:* 29 part-time (25 women); includes 1 minority (Black or African American, non-Hispanic/Latino). Average age 38. 8 applicants, 100% accepted, 4 enrolled. In 2017, 9 master's, 3 other advanced degrees awarded. *Entrance requirements:* For master's, minimum GPA of 2.75. Additional exam requirements/recommendations for international students: Recommended—TOEFL (minimum score 79 iBT), IELTS (minimum score 6). *Application deadline:* For fall admission, 7/15 for domestic and international students; for spring admission, 10/1 for domestic and international students; for summer admission, 3/15 for domestic students. Applications are processed on a rolling basis. Application fee: $45 ($50 for international students). Electronic applications accepted. *Expenses:* Tuition, state resident: full-time $6391; part-time $336 per credit hour. Tuition, nonresident: full-time $11,483; part-time $604 per credit hour. *Required fees:* $542; $99 per credit hour. $176 per semester. One-time fee: $45. Tuition and fees vary according to course load and program. *Financial support:* Scholarships/grants and unspecified assistantships available. Support available to part-time students. *Unit head:* Dr. Susan Bashinski, Director of Graduate Programs in Education, 816-271-5629, E-mail: sbashinski@missouriwestern.edu. *Application contact:* Dr. Benjamin D. Caldwell, Dean of the Graduate School, 816-271-4394, Fax: 816-271-4525, E-mail: graduate@missouriwestern.edu.
Website: https://www.missouriwestern.edu/masa/

Monmouth University, Graduate Studies, Department of English, West Long Branch, NJ 07764-1898. Offers creative writing (MA); literature (MA); rhetoric and writing (MA). *Program availability:* Part-time, evening/weekend. *Faculty:* 5 full-time (3 women). *Students:* 1 full-time (0 women), 28 part-time (21 women); includes 2 minority (1 Hispanic/Latino; 1 Two or more races, non-Hispanic/Latino). Average age 30. In 2017, 9 master's awarded. *Degree requirements:* For master's, comprehensive exam (for some programs), thesis. *Entrance requirements:* For master's, minimum overall GPA of 2.75, fifteen or more credits in literature or related field, essay of 1000 words describing interest and goals, two letters of recommendation, creative writing sample. Additional exam requirements/recommendations for international students: Required—TOEFL (minimum score 550 paper-based, 79 iBT), IELTS (minimum score 6), Michigan English

Language Assessment Battery (minimum score 77) or Certificate of Advanced English (minimum score of 160). *Application deadline:* For fall admission, 7/15 for domestic students, 6/1 for international students; for spring admission, 12/1 for domestic students, 11/1 for international students; for summer admission, 5/1 for domestic students. Applications are processed on a rolling basis. Application fee: $50. Electronic applications accepted. *Expenses: Tuition:* Full-time $21,366; part-time $7122 per credit. *Required fees:* $700; $175 per term. *Financial support:* In 2017–18, 7 students received support. Institutionally sponsored loans, scholarships/grants, and unspecified assistantships available. Support available to part-time students. Financial award applicants required to submit FAFSA. *Faculty research:* Renaissance and medieval literature, nineteenth-century American literature, eighteenth-century British literature and women's studies, Old and Middle English, African diaspora and African post-colonial literature. *Unit head:* Dr. Kristin Bluemel, Program Director, 732-571-3622, Fax: 732-263-5242, E-mail: kbluemel@monmouth.edu. *Application contact:* Andrea Thompson, Graduate Admission Counselor, 732-571-3452, Fax: 732-263-5123, E-mail: gradadm@monmouth.edu.
Website: https://www.monmouth.edu/graduate/ma-english/

New Mexico Highlands University, Graduate Studies, College of Arts and Sciences, Department of English, Las Vegas, NM 87701. Offers English (MA), including creative writing, language, rhetoric and composition, literature. *Degree requirements:* For master's, comprehensive exam, thesis. *Entrance requirements:* For master's, minimum undergraduate GPA of 3.0. Additional exam requirements/recommendations for international students: Required—TOEFL (minimum score 540 paper-based). *Faculty research:* Twentieth-century literature, life path writing in homeless shelters, native American philosophy, medieval intellectual and cultural history, creating pedagogical tools for teaching law.

New Mexico State University, College of Arts and Sciences, Department of English, Las Cruces, NM 88003. Offers creative writing (MFA); English (MA), including creative writing, English studies for teachers, literature, rhetoric and professional communication; rhetoric and professional communication (PhD). *Program availability:* Part-time. *Faculty:* 17 full-time (9 women), 3 part-time/adjunct (1 woman). *Students:* 50 full-time (32 women), 21 part-time (14 women); includes 19 minority (2 Black or African American, non-Hispanic/Latino; 2 Asian, non-Hispanic/Latino; 14 Hispanic/Latino; 1 Two or more races, non-Hispanic/Latino), 8 international. Average age 35. 68 applicants, 50% accepted, 12 enrolled. In 2017, 13 master's, 1 doctorate awarded. *Entrance requirements:* For master's and doctorate, sample of written work. Additional exam requirements/recommendations for international students: Required—TOEFL (minimum score 550 paper-based; 79 iBT), IELTS (minimum score 6.5). *Application deadline:* For fall admission, 2/1 for domestic and international students. Application fee: $40 ($50 for international students). Electronic applications accepted. *Expenses:* Tuition, state resident: full-time $4390. Tuition, nonresident: full-time $15,309. *Required fees:* $853. *Financial support:* In 2017–18, 49 students received support, including 6 fellowships (averaging $4,390 per year), 41 teaching assistantships (averaging $17,317 per year); career-related internships or fieldwork, Federal Work-Study, scholarships/grants, traineeships, health care benefits, and unspecified assistantships also available. Support available to part-time students. Financial award application deadline: 3/1. *Faculty research:* Composition research, history and theory of rhetoric, technical/professional communication, creative writing, English and American literature. *Total annual research expenditures:* $10,666. *Unit head:* Dr. Elizabeth Schirmer, Interim Department Head, 575-646-3931, Fax: 575-646-7725, E-mail: eschirme@nmsu.edu. *Application contact:* Dr. Tracey Eileen Miller-Tomlinson, Director of Graduate Studies, 575-646-2213, Fax: 575-646-7725, E-mail: tomlin@nmsu.edu.
Website: http://english.nmsu.edu

North Carolina State University, Graduate School, College of Humanities and Social Sciences, Program in Communication, Rhetoric, and Digital Media, Raleigh, NC 27695. Offers PhD.

★ **North Dakota State University,** College of Graduate and Interdisciplinary Studies, College of Arts, Humanities and Social Sciences, Department of English, Fargo, ND 58102. Offers composition (MA); literature (MA); rhetoric, writing and culture (PhD). *Program availability:* Part-time. *Degree requirements:* For master's, one foreign language, thesis. *Entrance requirements:* Additional exam requirements/recommendations for international students: Required—TOEFL (minimum score 600 paper-based; 100 iBT), IELTS (minimum score 7). Electronic applications accepted. *Faculty research:* American and English literature, women's studies, language attitudes, composition practices, computers and composition.

See Display below and Close-Up on page 747.

Northern Arizona University, College of Arts and Letters, Department of English, Flagstaff, AZ 86011. Offers applied linguistics (PhD); creative writing (MFA), including creative writing; English (MA), including literature, professional writing, rhetoric, writing, and digital media studies, secondary education; professional writing (Graduate Certificate); rhetoric, writing and digital media studies (Graduate Certificate); teaching English as a second language (MA, Graduate Certificate). *Program availability:* Part-time, 100% online, blended/hybrid learning. *Faculty:* 62 full-time (43 women), 3 part-time/adjunct (2 women). *Students:* 115 full-time (78 women), 115 part-time (89 women); includes 57 minority (11 Black or African American, non-Hispanic/Latino; 3 American Indian or Alaska Native, non-Hispanic/Latino; 4 Asian, non-Hispanic/Latino; 26 Hispanic/Latino; 13 Two or more races, non-Hispanic/Latino), 19 international. Average age 35. 189 applicants, 56% accepted, 92 enrolled. In 2017, 82 master's, 5 doctorates, 15 other advanced degrees awarded. *Degree requirements:* For master's, variable foreign language requirement, comprehensive exam (for some programs), thesis (for some programs); for doctorate, variable foreign language requirement, comprehensive exam (for some programs), thesis/dissertation (for some programs); for Graduate Certificate, comprehensive exam (for some programs). *Entrance requirements:* Additional exam requirements/recommendations for international students: Required—TOEFL (minimum score 80 iBT), IELTS (minimum score 6.5). *Application deadline:* For fall admission, 1/30 for domestic and international students; for spring admission, 10/1 for domestic and international students. Application fee: $65. Electronic applications accepted. *Expenses:* Tuition, state resident: full-time $9240; part-time $458 per credit hour. Tuition, nonresident: full-time $21,588; part-time $1199 per credit hour. *Required fees:* $1021; $14 per credit hour. $646 per semester. Tuition and fees vary according to course load, campus/location and program. *Financial support:* In 2017–18, 69 students received support, including 4 fellowships with full and partial tuition reimbursements available (averaging $16,250 per year), 2 research assistantships with full and partial tuition reimbursements available (averaging $16,250 per year), 65 teaching assistantships with full and partial tuition reimbursements available (averaging $16,250 per year); institutionally sponsored loans, health care benefits, tuition waivers (full and partial), and unspecified assistantships also available. Financial award application deadline: 2/1; financial award applicants required to submit FAFSA. *Unit head:* Dr. Steven Rosendale, Chair, 928-523-4911, Fax: 928-523-7074, E-mail: steven.rosendale@nau.edu. *Application contact:* Tina Sutton, Coordinator, Graduate College, 928-523-4348, Fax: 928-523-8950, E-mail: graduate@nau.edu.
Website: https://nau.edu/cal/english/

Northern Kentucky University, Office of Graduate Programs, College of Arts and Sciences, Program in English, Highland Heights, KY 41099. Offers composition and rhetoric (Certificate); creative writing (Certificate); cultural studies and discourses

(Certificate); English (MA); professional writing (Certificate). *Program availability:* Part-time, evening/weekend. *Degree requirements:* For master's, comprehensive exam (for some programs), capstone (thesis, portfolio, project, or exams); 30 hours of credit; for Certificate, 18 hours of credit. *Entrance requirements:* For master's, bachelor's degree in English or related field from regionally-accredited institution with minimum GPA of 3.0 in major or cognate area coursework; official transcripts for all undergraduate and graduate work; two letters of reference; for Certificate, official transcripts for all undergraduate and graduate work; bachelor's degree from regionally-accredited institution; minimum undergraduate GPA of 2.5. Additional exam requirements/recommendations for international students: Required—TOEFL (minimum score 79 iBT); Recommended—IELTS (minimum score 6.5). Electronic applications accepted.

Northwestern University, The Graduate School, School of Communication, Department of Communication Studies, Evanston, IL 60208. Offers communication studies (PhD), including interaction and social influence, rhetoric and public culture; managerial communication (MSC); media, technology and society (PhD); technology and social behavior (PhD). PhD admissions and degree offered through The Graduate School. Terminal master's awarded for partial completion of doctoral program. *Degree requirements:* For doctorate, thesis/dissertation. *Entrance requirements:* For master's and doctorate, GRE General Test. Additional exam requirements/recommendations for international students: Required—TOEFL. Electronic applications accepted.

Ohio University, Graduate College, Scripps College of Communication, School of Communication Studies, Athens, OH 45701-2979. Offers health communication (PhD); organizational communication (MA); relating and organizing (PhD); rhetoric and public culture (PhD). *Program availability:* Part-time, online learning. Terminal master's awarded for partial completion of doctoral program. *Degree requirements:* For master's, capstone; for doctorate, comprehensive exam, thesis/dissertation. *Entrance requirements:* For master's, GRE; for doctorate, GRE General Test, minimum GPA of 3.0. Additional exam requirements/recommendations for international students: Required—TOEFL (minimum score 550 paper-based; 80 iBT) or IELTS (minimum score 6.5). Electronic applications accepted. *Faculty research:* Rhetoric and public culture, relating and organizing, health communication.

Old Dominion University, College of Arts and Letters, Master of Arts in English Program, Norfolk, VA 23529. Offers literature (MA); professional writing (MA); rhetoric and composition (MA). *Program availability:* Part-time, evening/weekend. *Faculty:* 15 full-time (7 women). *Students:* 7 full-time (4 women), 16 part-time (13 women); includes 9 minority (2 Black or African American, non-Hispanic/Latino; 1 American Indian or Alaska Native, non-Hispanic/Latino; 3 Hispanic/Latino; 3 Two or more races, non-Hispanic/Latino). Average age 34. 12 applicants, 67% accepted, 7 enrolled. In 2017, 11 master's awarded. Terminal master's awarded for partial completion of doctoral program. *Degree requirements:* For master's, comprehensive exam, thesis optional. *Entrance requirements:* For master's, GRE General Test, 24 hours in English, sample of written work, BA. Additional exam requirements/recommendations for international students: Required—TOEFL. *Application deadline:* For fall admission, 3/15 priority date for domestic and international students; for winter admission, 11/1 for domestic students, 10/1 for international students; for spring admission, 11/1 priority date for domestic students, 11/1 for international students. Applications are processed on a rolling basis. Application fee: $50. Electronic applications accepted. *Expenses:* Tuition, state resident: full-time $8928; part-time $496 per credit. Tuition, nonresident: full-time $22,482; part-time $1249 per credit. *Required fees:* $66 per semester. *Financial support:* In 2017–18, 9 students received support, including 4 research assistantships (averaging $10,000 per year), 6 teaching assistantships (averaging $10,000 per year); career-related internships or fieldwork and unspecified assistantships also available. Financial award application deadline: 2/15; financial award applicants required to submit FAFSA. *Faculty research:* Literary theory, composition theory, professional writing, rhetoric, British and American literature. *Total annual research expenditures:* $3,451. *Unit head:* Dr. Drew Lopenzina, Graduate Program Director, 757-683-4033, E-mail: alopenzi@odu.edu. *Application contact:* Dr. Dale Miller, Associate Dean, 757-683-6077, Fax: 757-683-5746, E-mail: demiller@odu.edu.

Oregon State University, College of Liberal Arts, Program in English, Corvallis, OR 97331. Offers film and visual studies (MA); literature and culture (MA); rhetoric, writing and composition (MA). *Program availability:* Part-time. *Entrance requirements:* For master's, GRE (recommended). Additional exam requirements/recommendations for international students: Required—TOEFL (minimum score 80 iBT), IELTS (minimum score 6.5). *Application deadline:* For fall admission, 1/3 for domestic and international students. Application fee: $75 ($85 for international students). *Financial support:* Application deadline: 1/3. *Unit head:* Molly McFerran, Office Specialist, 541-737-1635, E-mail: molly.mcferran@oregonstate.edu. *Application contact:* Dr. Raymond Malewitz, Assistant Professor and Director, 541-737-1656, E-mail: raymond.malewitz@oregonstate.edu.
Website: http://liberalarts.oregonstate.edu/wlf/ma

Rensselaer Polytechnic Institute, Graduate School, School of Humanities, Arts, and Social Sciences, Program in Communication and Rhetoric, Troy, NY 12180-3590. Offers MS, PhD. *Faculty:* 9 full-time (6 women). *Students:* 13 full-time (8 women), 3 part-time (2 women); includes 1 minority (Hispanic/Latino). Average age 32. 17 applicants, 41% accepted, 3 enrolled. In 2017, 1 master's, 2 doctorates awarded. Terminal master's awarded for partial completion of doctoral program. *Degree requirements:* For master's, thesis optional; for doctorate, comprehensive exam, thesis/dissertation. *Entrance requirements:* For master's and doctorate, GRE, writing sample. Additional exam requirements/recommendations for international students: Required—TOEFL (minimum score 570 paper-based; 88 iBT), IELTS (minimum score 6.5), PTE (minimum score 60). *Application deadline:* For fall admission, 1/1 priority date for domestic and international students; for spring admission, 8/15 priority date for domestic and international students. Applications are processed on a rolling basis. Application fee: $75. Electronic applications accepted. *Expenses: Tuition:* Full-time $52,550; part-time $2125 per credit hour. *Required fees:* $2890. *Financial support:* In 2017–18, research assistantships with full tuition reimbursements (averaging $23,000 per year), teaching assistantships with full tuition reimbursements (averaging $23,000 per year) were awarded; fellowships also available. Financial award application deadline: 1/1. *Faculty research:* Communication, game studies, human computer interaction, literary theory, media studies, rhetoric, visual design, writing studies. *Total annual research expenditures:* $13,688. *Unit head:* Dr. Audrey Bennett, Graduate Program Director, 518-276-6933, E-mail: bennett@rpi.edu.
Website: http://www.cm.rpi.edu/pl/graduate

Rowan University, Graduate School, College of Communication and Creative Arts, Writing, Composition, and Rhetoric Certificate of Graduate Study Program, Glassboro, NJ 08028-1701. Offers CGS. *Expenses:* Tuition, state resident: full-time $15,020; part-time $751 per semester hour. Tuition, nonresident: full-time $15,020; part-time $751 per semester hour. *Required fees:* $3158; $157.90 per semester hour. Tuition and fees vary according to course load, campus/location and program.

San Diego State University, Graduate and Research Affairs, College of Arts and Letters, Department of Rhetoric and Writing Studies, San Diego, CA 92182. Offers MA. *Program availability:* Part-time. *Degree requirements:* For master's, thesis. *Entrance requirements:* For master's, GRE General Test, writing sample, 3 letters of reference. Additional exam requirements/recommendations for international students: Required—TOEFL. Electronic applications accepted.

Southern Illinois University Carbondale, Graduate School, College of Liberal Arts, Department of English, Carbondale, IL 62901-4701. Offers composition (MA, PhD), including composition, literature, rhetoric; creative writing (MFA). *Degree requirements:* For master's, one foreign language, thesis; for doctorate, 2 foreign languages, thesis/dissertation. *Entrance requirements:* For master's, GRE General Test, GRE Subject Test, minimum GPA of 2.7; for doctorate, GRE General Test, GRE Subject Test, minimum GPA of 3.25. Additional exam requirements/recommendations for international students: Required—TOEFL. *Faculty research:* British literature, English literature, modern Continental literature, literary criticism and theory, film studies, Irish studies.

Syracuse University, College of Arts and Sciences, PhD Program in Composition and Cultural Rhetoric, Syracuse, NY 13244. Offers PhD. *Degree requirements:* For doctorate, comprehensive exam, thesis/dissertation. *Entrance requirements:* For doctorate, GRE, three letters of recommendation, essay on intellectual history and academic interests, statement about teaching interests and practical experience, resume, transcripts. Additional exam requirements/recommendations for international students: Required—TOEFL (minimum score 100 iBT). *Application deadline:* For fall admission, 1/15 for domestic and international students. Application fee: $75. Electronic applications accepted. *Financial support:* Fellowships with tuition reimbursements, teaching assistantships with tuition reimbursements, scholarships/grants, and unspecified assistantships available. Financial award application deadline: 1/15; financial award applicants required to submit FAFSA. *Faculty research:* American ethnic rhetorics, authorship studies, composition studies and pedagogies, studies of gender and sexuality, transnational rhetorics and globalization. *Unit head:* Prof. Eileen Schell, Associate Professor, Writing and Rhetoric/Director of Graduate Studies, 315-443-1067, E-mail: eeschell@syr.edu. *Application contact:* Kristen Krause, Graduate Program Coordinator, 315-443-5146, E-mail: ccr@syr.edu.
Website: http://wrt.syr.edu/graduate/welcome.html

Syracuse University, College of Visual and Performing Arts, MA Program in Communication and Rhetorical Studies, Syracuse, NY 13244. Offers MA. *Program availability:* Part-time. *Degree requirements:* For master's, comprehensive exam (for some programs), thesis (for some programs). *Entrance requirements:* For master's, GRE General Test, three letters of recommendation, writing sample, transcripts, personal statement, resume. Additional exam requirements/recommendations for international students: Required—TOEFL (minimum score 90 iBT). *Application deadline:* For fall admission, 2/1 priority date for domestic and international students. Application fee: $75. Electronic applications accepted. *Financial support:* In 2017–18, 9 students received support. Fellowships with full tuition reimbursements available, teaching assistantships with tuition reimbursements available, and tuition waivers available. Financial award application deadline: 1/1; financial award applicants required to submit FAFSA. *Faculty research:* Language and social interaction, communication and critical/cultural studies, rhetorical theory and criticism. *Unit head:* Dr. Dana Cloud, Graduate Program Director, 315-443-5140, E-mail: dlcloud@syr.edu. *Application contact:* Caitlin Jarvis, Graduate Recruitment Specialist, 315-443-2769, E-mail: admissg@syr.edu.
Website: http://vpa.syr.edu/prospective-students/graduate-students/programs/communication-rhetorical-studies

Texas Christian University, AddRan College of Liberal Arts, Department of English, Fort Worth, TX 76129. Offers English (MA, PhD); rhetoric and composition (PhD). *Faculty:* 16 full-time (11 women), 1 (woman) part-time/adjunct. *Students:* 60 full-time (48 women); includes 12 minority (3 Black or African American, non-Hispanic/Latino; 6 Hispanic/Latino; 3 Two or more races, non-Hispanic/Latino), 3 international. Average age 29. 29 applicants, 34% accepted, 10 enrolled. In 2017, 1 master's, 5 doctorates awarded. *Degree requirements:* For master's, one foreign language, thesis; for doctorate, one foreign language, comprehensive exam, thesis/dissertation. *Entrance requirements:* For master's and doctorate, GRE General Test. Additional exam requirements/recommendations for international students: Required—TOEFL. *Application deadline:* 1/10 for domestic and international students. Application fee: $60. Electronic applications accepted. *Expenses:* Contact institution. *Financial support:* In 2017–18, 55 students received support, including 4 fellowships with full tuition reimbursements available (averaging $21,000 per year), 6 research assistantships with full tuition reimbursements available, 25 teaching assistantships with full tuition reimbursements available (averaging $17,000 per year); Federal Work-Study, tuition waivers (full and partial), and unspecified assistantships also available. Financial award application deadline: 1/10; financial award applicants required to submit FAFSA. *Faculty research:* Literary studies, rhetoric and composition, new media and digital humanities, print culture, women and gender studies. *Total annual research expenditures:* $10,000. *Unit head:* Dr. Brad E. Lucas, Director of Graduate Studies, 817-257-6981, Fax: 817-257-6238, E-mail: b.e.lucas2@tcu.edu. *Application contact:* Merry Roberts, English Department Office Manager, 817-257-6890, Fax: 817-257-6238, E-mail: m.roberts@tcu.edu.
Website: http://www.eng.tcu.edu/

Texas State University, The Graduate College, College of Liberal Arts, Program in Rhetoric and Composition, San Marcos, TX 78666. Offers MA. *Program availability:* Part-time. *Faculty:* 7 full-time (4 women), 1 (woman) part-time/adjunct. *Students:* 7 full-time (5 women), 5 part-time (2 women); includes 2 minority (1 Asian, non-Hispanic/Latino; 1 Hispanic/Latino). Average age 29. 12 applicants, 75% accepted, 4 enrolled. In 2017, 5 master's awarded. *Degree requirements:* For master's, comprehensive exam, thesis optional. *Entrance requirements:* For master's, baccalaureate degree from regionally-accredited institution with minimum GPA of 2.75 on last 60 undergraduate semester hours, 3.0 in minimum of 12 hours of undergraduate English courses; 3 letters of recommendation; portfolio; 2 non-fiction documents, one of which demonstrates academic research; statement of purpose. Additional exam requirements/recommendations for international students: Required—TOEFL (minimum score 550 paper-based; 78 iBT), IELTS (minimum score 6.5). *Application deadline:* For fall admission, 1/15 priority date for domestic and international students; for spring admission, 11/1 for domestic students, 10/1 for international students; for summer admission, 4/15 for domestic students, 3/15 for international students. Applications are processed on a rolling basis. Application fee: $40 ($90 for international students). Electronic applications accepted. *Expenses:* Tuition, state resident: full-time $7868; part-time $3934 per semester. Tuition, nonresident: full-time $17,828; part-time $8914 per semester. *Required fees:* $2092; $1435 per semester. Tuition and fees vary according to course load. *Financial support:* In 2017–18, 10 students received support, including 1 research assistantship (averaging $16,755 per year), 8 teaching assistantships (averaging $14,756 per year); Federal Work-Study, institutionally sponsored loans, scholarships/grants, health care benefits, and unspecified assistantships also available. Support available to part-time students. Financial award application deadline: 3/1; financial award applicants required to submit FAFSA. *Unit head:* Dr. Rebecca Jackson, Graduate Advisor, 512-245-8975, E-mail: rj10@txstate.edu. *Application contact:* Dr. Andrea Golato, Dean of Graduate School, 512-245-2581, Fax: 512-245-8365, E-mail: gradcollege@txstate.edu.
Website: http://marc.english.txstate.edu/

Rhetoric

Texas Tech University, Graduate School, College of Arts and Sciences, Department of English, Lubbock, TX 79409-3091. Offers English (MA, PhD); technical communication (MA); technical communication and rhetoric (PhD). *Program availability:* Part-time, 100% online, blended/hybrid learning. *Faculty:* 79 full-time (46 women), 9 part-time/adjunct (4 women). *Students:* 80 full-time (46 women), 88 part-time (60 women); includes 32 minority (9 Black or African American, non-Hispanic/Latino; 1 American Indian or Alaska Native, non-Hispanic/Latino; 3 Asian, non-Hispanic/Latino; 13 Hispanic/Latino; 6 Two or more races, non-Hispanic/Latino), 8 international. Average age 35. 136 applicants, 32% accepted, 32 enrolled. In 2017, 28 master's, 16 doctorates awarded. Terminal master's awarded for partial completion of doctoral program. *Degree requirements:* For master's, variable foreign language requirement, comprehensive exam, thesis optional; for doctorate, variable foreign language requirement, comprehensive exam, thesis/dissertation. *Entrance requirements:* For master's and doctorate, GRE General Test. Additional exam requirements/recommendations for international students: Required—TOEFL (minimum score 550 paper-based; 79 iBT), IELTS (minimum score 6.5). *Application deadline:* For fall admission, 6/1 priority date for domestic students, 1/15 priority date for international students; for spring admission, 9/1 priority date for domestic students, 6/15 priority date for international students. Applications are processed on a rolling basis. Application fee: $60. Electronic applications accepted. *Expenses:* Contact institution. *Financial support:* In 2017–18, 101 students received support, including 84 fellowships (averaging $2,712 per year), 6 research assistantships (averaging $17,139 per year), 76 teaching assistantships (averaging $15,638 per year); career-related internships or fieldwork, Federal Work-Study, scholarships/grants, and unspecified assistantships also available. Financial award application deadline: 1/8; financial award applicants required to submit FAFSA. *Faculty research:* American, British, and comparative literature; creative writing; linguistics; film; technical communication and rhetoric. *Total annual research expenditures:* $21,274. *Unit head:* Dr. Brian Still, Department Chair, 806-834-6439, Fax: 806-742-0989, E-mail: brian.still@ttu.edu. *Application contact:* Dr. Julie Nelson Couch, Director of Graduate Studies, 806-834-1742, Fax: 806-742-0989, E-mail: english.gradadvisor@ttu.edu.
Website: http://www.english.ttu.edu/

Texas Woman's University, Graduate School, College of Arts and Sciences, Department of English, Speech, and Foreign Languages, Denton, TX 76204. Offers English (MA, MAT); rhetoric (PhD). *Program availability:* Part-time. *Faculty:* 9 full-time (4 women). *Students:* 6 full-time (5 women), 38 part-time (30 women); includes 10 minority (4 Black or African American, non-Hispanic/Latino; 2 Asian, non-Hispanic/Latino; 2 Hispanic/Latino; 2 Two or more races, non-Hispanic/Latino), 1 international. Average age 39. 8 applicants, 63% accepted, 4 enrolled. In 2017, 7 master's, 4 doctorates awarded. *Degree requirements:* For master's, comprehensive exam, thesis (for some programs), professional paper, thesis or coursework; for doctorate, comprehensive exam, thesis/dissertation, residency for at least 2 consecutive semesters (strongly encouraged). *Entrance requirements:* For master's, GRE General Test (preferred minimum score 153 [500 old version] verbal, 138 [350 old version] quantitative), 3 letters of reference, minimum GPA of 3.0 on previous upper-division and graduate work, writing sample, statement of purpose; for doctorate, GRE General Test (preferred minimum score 153 [500 old version] verbal, 138 [350 old version] quantitative), writing sample, 3 letters of reference, interview (for graduate assistants), minimum GPA of 3.0 on previous upper-division and graduate work, statement of purpose. Additional exam requirements/recommendations for international students: Required—TOEFL (minimum score 600 paper-based; 79 iBT); Recommended—IELTS (minimum score 6.5). *Application deadline:* For fall admission, 7/1 for domestic students, 3/1 priority date for international students; for spring admission, 11/1 for domestic students, 7/1 priority date for international students; for summer admission, 4/1 for domestic students, 2/1 priority date for international students. Applications are processed on a rolling basis. Application fee: $50 ($75 for international students). Electronic applications accepted. *Expenses:* $7,520 per year full-time in-state; $16,820 per year full-time out-of-state. *Financial support:* In 2017–18, 20 students received support, including 13 teaching assistantships (averaging $23,215 per year); career-related internships or fieldwork, Federal Work-Study, institutionally sponsored loans, scholarships/grants, traineeships, health care benefits, and unspecified assistantships also available. Support available to part-time students. Financial award application deadline: 3/1; financial award applicants required to submit FAFSA. *Faculty research:* American literature, medieval literature, history of the English language, rhetoric, world literature. *Unit head:* Dr. Genevieve West, Chair, 940-898-2324, Fax: 940-898-2297, E-mail: engspfl@twu.edu. *Application contact:* Korie Hawkins, Associate Director of Admissions, Graduate Recruitment, 940-898-3188, Fax: 940-898-3081, E-mail: admissions@twu.edu.
Website: http://www.twu.edu/english-speech-foreign-languages/

The University of Alabama, Graduate School, College of Arts and Sciences, Department of English, Tuscaloosa, AL 35487. Offers composition and rhetoric (PhD); creative writing (MFA), including fiction, poetry; literature (MA, PhD); rhetoric and composition (MA); teaching English as a second language (MATESOL). *Faculty:* 37 full-time (21 women). *Students:* 123 full-time (71 women), 11 part-time (8 women); includes 22 minority (10 Black or African American, non-Hispanic/Latino; 1 Asian, non-Hispanic/Latino; 6 Hispanic/Latino; 5 Two or more races, non-Hispanic/Latino), 2 international. Average age 29. 378 applicants, 17% accepted, 44 enrolled. In 2017, 32 master's, 7 doctorates awarded. *Degree requirements:* For master's, one foreign language, comprehensive exam, thesis; for doctorate, 2 foreign languages, comprehensive exam, thesis/dissertation. *Entrance requirements:* For master's, GRE (minimum score of 300, except for MFA), minimum GPA of 3.0, critical writing sample; for doctorate, GRE (minimum score of 300), minimum GPA of 3.5 on master's or equivalent graduate work, critical writing sample. Additional exam requirements/recommendations for international students: Recommended—TOEFL (minimum score 550 paper-based; 79 iBT). *Application deadline:* For fall admission, 12/20 for domestic and international students. Application fee: $50 ($60 for international students). Electronic applications accepted. *Financial support:* In 2017–18, 113 students received support, including fellowships with full tuition reimbursements available (averaging $15,000 per year), research assistantships with full tuition reimbursements available (averaging $13,500 per year), teaching assistantships with full tuition reimbursements available (averaging $13,500 per year); career-related internships or fieldwork, scholarships/grants, health care benefits, and unspecified assistantships also available. Financial award application deadline: 12/20. *Faculty research:* American literature, British literature, composition/rhetoric, applied linguistics, creative writing. *Unit head:* Prof. Joel Brouwer, Department Chair, 205-348-5065, Fax: 205-348-1388, E-mail: joel.brouwer@ua.edu. *Application contact:* Jennifer Fuqua, Graduate Coordinator, 205-348-0766, Fax: 205-348-1388, E-mail: jfuqua@ua.edu.

The University of Alabama at Birmingham, College of Arts and Sciences, Program in English, Birmingham, AL 35294. Offers creative writing (MA); literature (MA); rhetoric and composition (MA). *Program availability:* Part-time. *Degree requirements:* For master's, one foreign language, comprehensive exam, thesis or alternative. *Entrance requirements:* For master's, GRE General Test or MAT, minimum GPA of 2.75. Electronic applications accepted.

The University of Arizona, College of Humanities, Department of English, Rhetoric, Composition and the Teaching of English Program, Tucson, AZ 85721. Offers MA, PhD. *Accreditation:* NASM. *Degree requirements:* For master's, one foreign language, comprehensive exam; for doctorate, one foreign language, comprehensive exam, thesis/dissertation. *Entrance requirements:* For doctorate, GRE General Test, 3 letters of recommendation, writing sample. Additional exam requirements/recommendations for international students: Required—TOEFL (minimum score 550 paper-based; 79 iBT). Electronic applications accepted.

University of Arkansas at Little Rock, Graduate School, College of Social Sciences and Communication, Department of Rhetoric and Writing, Little Rock, AR 72204-1099. Offers professional and technical writing (MA). *Program availability:* Part-time, evening/weekend. *Degree requirements:* For master's, thesis or alternative, oral defense of final project. *Entrance requirements:* For master's, GRE, minimum GPA of 3.0, writing portfolio. *Faculty research:* Writing for industry, science, business, and government; composition and rhetorical theory; writing nonfiction; teaching of writing.

University of California, Berkeley, Graduate Division, College of Letters and Science, Department of Rhetoric, Berkeley, CA 94720-1500. Offers PhD. *Degree requirements:* For doctorate, 2 foreign languages, thesis/dissertation, qualifying exam. *Entrance requirements:* For doctorate, GRE General Test, minimum GPA of 3.0, 3 letters of recommendation. Electronic applications accepted. *Faculty research:* History and theory of rhetoric, public discourse (law, politics, and science), literature and philosophy, film.

University of Central Oklahoma, The Jackson College of Graduate Studies, College of Liberal Arts, Department of English, Edmond, OK 73034-5209. Offers composition and rhetoric (MA); creative writing (MA); literature (MA); teaching English as a second language (MA). *Program availability:* Part-time. *Faculty:* 21 full-time (14 women). *Students:* 30 full-time (17 women), 45 part-time (23 women); includes 17 minority (3 Black or African American, non-Hispanic/Latino; 3 American Indian or Alaska Native, non-Hispanic/Latino; 2 Asian, non-Hispanic/Latino; 3 Hispanic/Latino; 2 Native Hawaiian or other Pacific Islander, non-Hispanic/Latino; 4 Two or more races, non-Hispanic/Latino), 13 international. Average age 32. 34 applicants, 76% accepted, 18 enrolled. In 2017, 30 master's awarded. *Degree requirements:* For master's, variable foreign language requirement, comprehensive exam (for some programs), thesis (for some programs), portfolio. *Entrance requirements:* For master's, 18-24 hours of course work in English language and literature; writing sample; essay. Additional exam requirements/recommendations for international students: Required—TOEFL (minimum score 550 paper-based; 79 iBT), IELTS (minimum score 6.5). *Application deadline:* For fall admission, 7/15 for international students; for spring admission, 11/15 for international students. Applications are processed on a rolling basis. Application fee: $60. Electronic applications accepted. *Expenses:* Tuition, state resident: full-time $5375; part-time $268.75 per credit hour. Tuition, nonresident: full-time $13,295; part-time $664.75 per credit hour. *Required fees:* $626; $31.30 per credit hour. One-time fee: $50. Tuition and fees vary according to program. *Financial support:* In 2017–18, 22 students received support, including 4 research assistantships with partial tuition reimbursements available (averaging $11,830 per year), 8 teaching assistantships with partial tuition reimbursements available (averaging $11,830 per year); career-related internships or fieldwork, Federal Work-Study, scholarships/grants, tuition waivers (partial), and unspecified assistantships also available. Financial award application deadline: 3/31; financial award applicants required to submit FAFSA. *Unit head:* Dr. Matt Hollrah, Chairperson, 405-974-5540, Fax: 405-974-3823, E-mail: gradcoll@uco.edu.
Website: http://www.uco.edu/la/english/

University of Colorado Denver, College of Liberal Arts and Sciences, Department of English, Denver, CO 80217. Offers applied linguistics (MA); literature (MA); rhetoric and teaching of writing (MA). *Program availability:* Part-time, evening/weekend. *Degree requirements:* For master's, variable foreign language requirement, comprehensive exam (for some programs), thesis (for some programs), minimum of 33 credit hours (for literature program), 30 (for rhetoric and teaching of writing and applied linguistics programs). *Entrance requirements:* For master's, GRE General Test, minimum GPA of 3.0 in undergraduate courses, critical writing sample, letters of recommendation, completion of 24 semester hours in English courses (at least 16 at the upper-division level), statement of purpose. Additional exam requirements/recommendations for international students: Required—TOEFL (minimum score 537 paper-based; 75 iBT); Recommended—IELTS (minimum score 6.5). Electronic applications accepted. *Faculty research:* Literature, rhetoric, teaching of writing, applied linguistics.

University of Dayton, Department of English, Dayton, OH 45469. Offers literary and cultural studies (MA); teaching English to speakers of other languages (TESOL) (MA); writing and rhetoric (MA). *Program availability:* Part-time. *Faculty:* 22 full-time (11 women). *Students:* 20 full-time (14 women), 1 (woman) part-time; includes 2 minority (both Black or African American, non-Hispanic/Latino), 7 international. Average age 26. 35 applicants, 34% accepted. In 2017, 9 master's awarded. *Degree requirements:* For master's, thesis optional. *Entrance requirements:* For master's, 24 undergraduate-level semester hours in literature and/or writing; minimum GPA of 3.0; transcripts; personal statement; 8-10 page writing sample; three professional letters of recommendation. Additional exam requirements/recommendations for international students: Required—TOEFL (minimum score 550 paper-based, 80 iBT) or IELTS. *Application deadline:* For fall admission, 6/15 priority date for domestic and international students; for spring admission, 12/15 priority date for domestic and international students. Applications are processed on a rolling basis. Application fee: $0 ($50 for international students). Electronic applications accepted. Tuition and fees vary according to degree level and program. *Financial support:* In 2017–18, 9 teaching assistantships with full tuition reimbursements (averaging $11,105 per year) were awarded; institutionally sponsored loans also available. Financial award application deadline: 3/1; financial award applicants required to submit FAFSA. *Faculty research:* Gender and Victorian periodicals; literature and human rights; Paul Lawrence Dunbar; the archetype of the Indian princess; Amish country. *Unit head:* Dr. Andrew Slade, Chair, 937-229-3434, Fax: 937-229-3563, E-mail: aslade1@udayton.edu. *Application contact:* Dr. Tereza Szeghi, Director of Graduate Studies, 937-229-3443, E-mail: tszeghi1@udayton.edu.
Website: https://www.udayton.edu/artssciences/academics/english/welcome/index.php

University of Denver, Division of Arts, Humanities and Social Sciences, Department of Communication Studies, Denver, CO 80208. Offers culture and communication (MA, PhD); interpersonal and family communication (MA, PhD); rhetoric and communication ethics (MA, PhD). Tuition and fees vary according to course load, campus/location and program.

The University of Findlay, Office of Graduate Admissions, Findlay, OH 45840. Offers applied security and analytics (MSAS); athletic training (MAT); business (MBA), including certified management accountant, certified public accountant, health care management, hospitality management; education (MA Ed, Ed D), including children's literature (MA Ed), curriculum and teaching (MA Ed), education (MA Ed), educational administration (MA Ed), human resource development (MA Ed), mathematics (MA Ed), reading (MA Ed), science education (MA Ed), superintendent (Ed D), teaching (Ed D), technology (MA Ed); environmental, safety, and health management (MSEM); health informatics (MS); occupational therapy (MOT); pharmacy (Pharm D); physical therapy (DPT); physician assistant (MPA); rhetoric and writing (MA); teaching English to speakers of other languages (TESOL) and applied linguistics (MA). *Program availability:* Part-time, evening/weekend, 100% online, blended/hybrid learning. *Students:* 688 full-time (430 women), 553 part-time (308 women), 170 international. Average age 28. In

2017, 366 master's, 137 doctorates awarded. *Degree requirements:* For master's, comprehensive exam (for some programs), thesis (for some programs), cumulative project, capstone project; for doctorate, thesis/dissertation (for some programs). *Entrance requirements:* For master's, GRE/GMAT, bachelor's degree from accredited institution, minimum undergraduate GPA of 2.5 in last 64 hours of course work; for doctorate, GRE, MAT, minimum cumulative GPA of 3.0. Additional exam requirements/recommendations for international students: Required—TOEFL (minimum score 79 iBT), IELTS (minimum score 7), PTE (minimum score 61). *Application deadline:* Applications are processed on a rolling basis. Electronic applications accepted. *Financial support:* In 2017–18, 10 research assistantships with partial tuition reimbursements (averaging $7,200 per year), 35 teaching assistantships with partial tuition reimbursements (averaging $7,200 per year) were awarded; Federal Work-Study, institutionally sponsored loans, and unspecified assistantships also available. Financial award applicants required to submit FAFSA. *Unit head:* Christopher M. Harris, Director of Admissions, 419-434-4347, E-mail: harrisc1@findlay.edu. *Application contact:* Madeline Fauser Brennan, Graduate Admissions Counselor, 419-434-4636, Fax: 419-434-4898, E-mail: fauserbrennan@findlay.edu.
Website: http://www.findlay.edu/admissions/graduate/Pages/default.aspx

University of Houston–Downtown, College of Humanities and Social Sciences, Department of English, Program in Rhetoric and Composition, Houston, TX 77002. Offers MA. *Program availability:* Part-time, evening/weekend. *Faculty:* 4 full-time (1 woman). *Students:* 8 full-time (6 women), 23 part-time (15 women); includes 16 minority (5 Black or African American, non-Hispanic/Latino; 1 American Indian or Alaska Native, non-Hispanic/Latino; 1 Asian, non-Hispanic/Latino; 9 Hispanic/Latino), 1 international. Average age 43. 8 applicants, 75% accepted, 6 enrolled. In 2017, 4 master's awarded. *Entrance requirements:* For master's, essay, resume, 2 letters of recommendation, transcripts, 10-15 page sample of academic writing. Additional exam requirements/recommendations for international students: Required—TOEFL (minimum score 550 paper-based; 50 iBT). *Application deadline:* For fall admission, 7/15 for domestic and international students; for spring admission, 12/1 for domestic and international students; for summer admission, 4/20 for domestic and international students. Application fee: $35 ($60 for international students). Electronic applications accepted. *Expenses:* $335 per credit resident; $700 per credit non-resident. *Financial support:* Federal Work-Study and scholarships/grants available. Financial award application deadline: 4/1; financial award applicants required to submit FAFSA. *Unit head:* Dr. Paul Kintzele, Chair, 713-221-8090, Fax: 713-226-5205, E-mail: kintzelep@uhd.edu. *Application contact:* Ceshia Love, Director of Admissions, 713-221-8093, Fax: 713-223-7408, E-mail: gradadmissions@uhd.edu.
Website: https://www.uhd.edu/academics/humanities/graduate-programs/masters-arts-rhetoric-composition/Pages/marc-index.aspx

The University of Iowa, Graduate College, College of Liberal Arts and Sciences, Department of Communication Studies, Iowa City, IA 52242-1316. Offers interpersonal communication and relationships (MA, PhD); media studies (MA, PhD); rhetoric and public advocacy (MA, PhD). *Degree requirements:* For master's, thesis optional, exam; for doctorate, comprehensive exam, thesis/dissertation. *Entrance requirements:* For master's and doctorate, GRE General Test, minimum GPA of 3.0. Additional exam requirements/recommendations for international students: Required—TOEFL (minimum score 550 paper-based; 81 iBT). Electronic applications accepted.

University of Louisiana at Lafayette, College of Liberal Arts, Department of English, Lafayette, LA 70504. Offers British and American literature (MA), including creative writing, folklore, rhetoric; creative writing (PhD); literature (PhD); rhetoric (PhD). *Program availability:* Part-time. Terminal master's awarded for partial completion of doctoral program. *Degree requirements:* For master's, one foreign language, thesis or alternative; for doctorate, 2 foreign languages, comprehensive exam, thesis/dissertation. *Entrance requirements:* For master's, GRE General Test, minimum GPA of 2.75; for doctorate, GRE General Test, minimum GPA of 3.0. Additional exam requirements/recommendations for international students: Required—TOEFL (minimum score 550 paper-based). Electronic applications accepted. *Faculty research:* Composition theory, Southern literature, medieval literature.

University of Louisville, Graduate School, College of Arts and Sciences, Department of English, Louisville, KY 40292. Offers English (MA), including creative writing, literature, rhetoric and composition (MA, PhD); rhetoric and composition (PhD), including rhetoric and composition (MA, PhD). *Program availability:* Part-time, evening/weekend. *Faculty:* 37 full-time (20 women), 3 part-time/adjunct (2 women). *Students:* 43 full-time (24 women), 12 part-time (9 women); includes 5 minority (2 Black or African American, non-Hispanic/Latino; 1 Asian, non-Hispanic/Latino; 1 Hispanic/Latino; 1 Two or more races, non-Hispanic/Latino). Average age 31. 47 applicants, 66% accepted, 15 enrolled. In 2017, 12 master's, 6 doctorates awarded. *Degree requirements:* For master's, one foreign language, thesis optional, culminating project of 25-30 pages; for doctorate, one foreign language, comprehensive exam, thesis/dissertation. *Entrance requirements:* For master's and doctorate, GRE General Test. Additional exam requirements/recommendations for international students: Required—TOEFL (minimum score 600 paper-based) or IELTS (6.5). *Application deadline:* Applications are processed on a rolling basis. Application fee: $65. Electronic applications accepted. *Expenses:* Contact institution. *Financial support:* In 2017–18, 3 fellowships with full tuition reimbursements (averaging $20,000 per year), 2 research assistantships (averaging $17,750 per year), 34 teaching assistantships with full tuition reimbursements (averaging $17,750 per year) were awarded; health care benefits and unspecified assistantships also available. Financial award application deadline: 1/5. *Faculty research:* Rhetoric and composition, creative writing, Eighteenth- and Nineteenth-Century British literature, Nineteenth-Century American literature, critical theory. *Total annual research expenditures:* $124,449. *Unit head:* Dr. Glynis Ridley, Chair, 502-852-6803, E-mail: glynis.ridley@louisville.edu. *Application contact:* Annelise Gray, Senior Program Assistant, 502-852-0505, E-mail: annelise.gray@louisville.edu.
Website: http://www.louisville.edu/english/graduate

University of Massachusetts Amherst, Graduate School, College of Humanities and Fine Arts, Department of English, Amherst, MA 01003. Offers American studies (PhD); composition and rhetoric (PhD); creative writing (MFA); English and American literature (MA, PhD). *Program availability:* Part-time. Terminal master's awarded for partial completion of doctoral program. *Degree requirements:* For master's, one foreign language, thesis optional; for doctorate, one foreign language, comprehensive exam, thesis/dissertation. *Entrance requirements:* For master's, manuscript; for doctorate, GRE General Test, manuscript. Additional exam requirements/recommendations for international students: Required—TOEFL (minimum score 550 paper-based; 80 iBT), IELTS (minimum score 6.5). Electronic applications accepted.

University of Michigan–Flint, College of Arts and Sciences, Program in English Language and Literature, Flint, MI 48502-1950. Offers literature (MA); writing and rhetoric (MA). *Program availability:* Part-time. *Faculty:* 26 full-time (17 women), 3 part-time/adjunct (2 women). *Students:* 7 full-time (6 women), 16 part-time (13 women); includes 6 minority (1 Black or African American, non-Hispanic/Latino; 3 Hispanic/Latino; 2 Two or more races, non-Hispanic/Latino), 1 international. Average age 37. 16 applicants, 69% accepted, 9 enrolled. In 2017, 4 master's awarded. *Degree requirements:* For master's, thesis optional. *Entrance requirements:* For master's, bachelor's degree with major or significant coursework in English or related fields from regionally-accredited institution; minimum overall undergraduate GPA of 3.0. Additional exam requirements/recommendations for international students: Required—TOEFL (minimum score 84 iBT), IELTS (minimum score 6.5). *Application deadline:* For fall admission, 8/1 for domestic students, 5/1 for international students; for winter admission, 11/15 for domestic students, 9/1 for international students; for spring admission, 3/15 for domestic students, 1/1 for international students; for summer admission, 5/15 for domestic students. Applications are processed on a rolling basis. Application fee: $55. Electronic applications accepted. *Expenses:* Contact institution. *Financial support:* Career-related internships or fieldwork, Federal Work-Study, scholarships/grants, and unspecified assistantships available. Support available to part-time students. Financial award application deadline: 3/1; financial award applicants required to submit FAFSA. *Unit head:* Dr. Suzanne Knight, Director, 810-762-0145, E-mail: suknight@umflint.edu. *Application contact:* Bradley T. Maki, Director of Graduate Admissions, 810-762-3171, Fax: 810-766-6789, E-mail: bmaki@umflint.edu.
Website: http://www.umflint.edu/graduateprograms/english-language-and-literature-ma

University of Nebraska–Lincoln, Graduate College, College of Arts and Sciences, Department of Communication Studies, Lincoln, NE 68588. Offers instructional communication (MA, PhD); interpersonal communication (MA, PhD); marketing, communication studies, and advertising (MA, PhD); organizational communication (MA, PhD); rhetoric and culture (MA, PhD). *Degree requirements:* For master's, thesis optional; for doctorate, comprehensive exam, thesis/dissertation. *Entrance requirements:* For master's and doctorate, GRE General Test, writing sample. Additional exam requirements/recommendations for international students: Required—TOEFL (minimum score 600 paper-based). Electronic applications accepted. *Faculty research:* Message strategies, gender communication, political communication, organizational communication, instructional communication.

University of Nebraska–Lincoln, Graduate College, College of Arts and Sciences, Department of English, Lincoln, NE 68588-0333. Offers composition and rhetoric (MA, PhD); creative writing (MA, PhD); literature studies (MA, PhD). *Degree requirements:* For master's, thesis optional; for doctorate, one foreign language, comprehensive exam, thesis/dissertation. *Entrance requirements:* For master's, writing sample; for doctorate, GRE General Test, writing sample. Additional exam requirements/recommendations for international students: Required—TOEFL (minimum score 600 paper-based). Electronic applications accepted. *Faculty research:* Creative writing, composition and rhetoric, women's studies, North American literature, medieval/Renaissance studies.

University of North Alabama, College of Arts and Sciences, Department of English, Program in Writing, Florence, AL 35632-0001. Offers creative writing (MA); rhetoric and composition (MA); technical writing (MA). *Program availability:* Part-time, 100% online. *Faculty:* 12 full-time (8 women). *Students:* 5 part-time (4 women). Average age 31. 5 applicants, 60% accepted, 3 enrolled. *Degree requirements:* For master's, comprehensive exam (for some programs), thesis (for some programs). *Entrance requirements:* For master's, GRE, MAT, three letters of recommendation; writing sample. Additional exam requirements/recommendations for international students: Required—TOEFL (minimum score 79 iBT), IELTS (minimum score 6), PTE (minimum score 54). *Application deadline:* Applications are processed on a rolling basis. Application fee: $50 ($100 for international students). Electronic applications accepted. *Expenses:* Tuition, state resident: full-time $7824; part-time $5943 per year. Tuition, nonresident: full-time $15,648; part-time $11,736 per year. *Required fees:* $3064; $2298 per unit. Tuition and fees vary according to course load and reciprocity agreements. *Financial support:* In 2017–18, 2 students received support. Federal Work-Study, scholarships/grants, and unspecified assistantships available. Financial award application deadline: 2/1; financial award applicants required to submit FAFSA. *Unit head:* Dr. Tammy Winner, Coordinator, 256-660-9026, E-mail: twinner@una.edu. *Application contact:* Hillary N. Coats, Graduate Admissions Coordinator, 256-765-4447, E-mail: graduate@una.edu.
Website: https://www.una.edu/english/master-of-arts-in-writing.html

The University of North Carolina at Greensboro, Graduate School, College of Arts and Sciences, Department of English, Program in English, Greensboro, NC 27412-5001. Offers American literature (PhD); English (M Ed, MA); English literature (PhD); rhetoric and composition (PhD). *Degree requirements:* For master's, comprehensive exam, thesis or alternative; for doctorate, variable foreign language requirement, thesis/dissertation, preliminary exam. *Entrance requirements:* For master's, GRE General Test, GRE Subject Test, minimum GPA of 3.0; for doctorate, GRE General Test, GRE Subject Test, critical writing sample, minimum GPA of 3.0. Additional exam requirements/recommendations for international students: Required—TOEFL. Electronic applications accepted.

University of Oklahoma, College of Arts and Sciences, Department of English, Norman, OK 73019. Offers literary and cultural studies (MA, PhD); writing and rhetoric studies (MA, PhD). *Program availability:* Part-time. *Faculty:* 25 full-time (13 women), 1 part-time/adjunct (0 women). *Students:* 29 full-time (21 women), 17 part-time (8 women); includes 9 minority (1 American Indian or Alaska Native, non-Hispanic/Latino; 2 Asian, non-Hispanic/Latino; 5 Hispanic/Latino; 1 Two or more races, non-Hispanic/Latino), 2 international. Average age 31. 34 applicants, 71% accepted, 18 enrolled. In 2017, 7 master's, 4 doctorates awarded. *Degree requirements:* For master's, one foreign language, comprehensive exam (for some programs), thesis (for some programs), exam or thesis; for doctorate, one foreign language, comprehensive exam, thesis/dissertation. *Entrance requirements:* For master's, GRE, BA in English or related field; for doctorate, GRE, MA in English or related field. Additional exam requirements/recommendations for international students: Required—TOEFL (minimum score 79 iBT) or IELTS (minimum score 6.5). *Application deadline:* For fall admission, 1/5 priority date for domestic and international students. Application fee: $50 ($100 for international students). Electronic applications accepted. *Expenses:* Tuition, state resident: full-time $5119; part-time $213.30 per credit hour. Tuition, nonresident: full-time $19,778; part-time $824.10 per credit hour. *Required fees:* $3458; $133.55 per credit hour. $126.50 per semester. *Financial support:* In 2017–18, 40 students received support, including 6 research assistantships with full tuition reimbursements available (averaging $14,515 per year), 31 teaching assistantships with full tuition reimbursements available (averaging $12,496 per year); fellowships with full tuition reimbursements available, scholarships/grants, health care benefits, and unspecified assistantships also available. Financial award application deadline: 6/1; financial award applicants required to submit FAFSA. *Faculty research:* American Indian literature and culture; composition and rhetoric; American literature; British literature; postcolonial literature and culture. *Total annual research expenditures:* $101. *Unit head:* Dr. Daniela Garofalo, Professor and Chair, 405-325-4661, Fax: 405-325-0831, E-mail: dg@ou.edu. *Application contact:* Sara Day, Graduate Assistant, 405-325-0489, Fax: 405-325-0831, E-mail: redpanda@ou.edu.
Website: http://cas.ou.edu/english

University of Southern California, Graduate School, Annenberg School for Communication and Journalism, School of Communication, Program in Communication, Los Angeles, CA 90089. Offers culture and community (PhD); global and transnational communication (PhD); groups, organizations and networks (PhD); health communication and social dynamics (PhD); information, political economy and entertainment (PhD); new media and technology (PhD); rhetoric, politics and public

media (PhD). *Degree requirements:* For doctorate, thesis/dissertation. *Entrance requirements:* For doctorate, GRE General Test, resume or curriculum vitae, scholarly writing, 3 letters of recommendation, statement of purpose. Additional exam requirements/recommendations for international students: Required—TOEFL (minimum score 114 iBT), IELTS (minimum score 8); Recommended—TWE. Electronic applications accepted. *Faculty research:* Computer-mediated communication, public health campaigns, communication democracy and the public sphere, new communication technologies in organizations, communication and community.

University of South Florida, College of Arts and Sciences, Department of English, Tampa, FL 33620-9951. Offers creative writing (MFA), including fiction, poetry; English (MA, PhD), including literature, rhetoric and composition. *Program availability:* Part-time, evening/weekend. *Faculty:* 24 full-time (13 women). *Students:* 70 full-time (51 women), 17 part-time (15 women); includes 14 minority (6 Black or African American, non-Hispanic/Latino; 3 Asian, non-Hispanic/Latino; 3 Hispanic/Latino; 2 Two or more races, non-Hispanic/Latino). Average age 32. 74 applicants, 54% accepted, 25 enrolled. In 2017, 22 master's, 10 doctorates awarded. *Degree requirements:* For master's, comprehensive exam, thesis (for MFA); thesis or portfolio (for MA); for doctorate, one foreign language, comprehensive exam, thesis/dissertation. *Entrance requirements:* For master's, GRE General Test, minimum undergraduate GPA of 3.5 (for MA), 3.2 (for MFA); three letters of recommendation; personal statement; writing sample from 10 to 20 pages (depending on genre); for doctorate, GRE General Test, minimum graduate GPA of 3.7; three letters of recommendation; 2-3 page personal statement; 2500-word writing sample from English coursework. Additional exam requirements/recommendations for international students: Required—TOEFL minimum score 550 paper-based; 79 iBT or IELTS minimum score 6.5 (for MA and PhD); TOEFL minimum score 600 paper-based (for MFA). *Application deadline:* For fall admission, 1/1 for domestic and international students. Applications are processed on a rolling basis. Application fee: $30. Electronic applications accepted. *Financial support:* In 2017–18, 20 students received support, including 2 research assistantships (averaging $17,221 per year), 79 teaching assistantships with tuition reimbursements available (averaging $11,576 per year); unspecified assistantships also available. Financial award application deadline: 6/30; financial award applicants required to submit FAFSA. *Faculty research:* British and American literature, rhetoric and composition, world and comparative literatures, creative writing, gender and sexuality studies, women's literature, film and genre studies, literary theory, popular and visual culture, textual and translation studies. *Total annual research expenditures:* $202,166. *Unit head:* Dr. Laura Runge, Professor and Chairperson, 813-974-9496, E-mail: runge@usf.edu. *Application contact:* Dr. John Lennon, Associate Professor and Graduate Director, 813-974-2663, Fax: 813-974-2270, E-mail: jflennon@usf.edu.
Website: http://english.usf.edu/

The University of Tennessee at Chattanooga, Program in English, Chattanooga, TN 37403. Offers creative writing (MA); literary study (MA); rhetoric and writing (MA). *Program availability:* Part-time. *Students:* 12 full-time (8 women), 14 part-time (11 women); includes 4 minority (1 Black or African American, non-Hispanic/Latino; 1 Asian, non-Hispanic/Latino; 1 Hispanic/Latino; 1 Two or more races, non-Hispanic/Latino). Average age 27. 10 applicants, 100% accepted, 7 enrolled. In 2017, 12 master's awarded. *Degree requirements:* For master's, comprehensive exam, thesis. *Entrance requirements:* For master's, minimum GPA of 3.0 in English, two letters of recommendation. Additional exam requirements/recommendations for international students: Required—TOEFL (minimum score 550 paper-based; 79 iBT), IELTS (minimum score 6). *Application deadline:* For fall admission, 6/15 priority date for domestic students, 7/1 for international students; for spring admission, 11/1 priority date for domestic students, 11/1 for international students. Applications are processed on a rolling basis. Application fee: $35 ($40 for international students). Electronic applications accepted. *Expenses:* Contact institution. *Financial support:* Research assistantships, teaching assistantships, career-related internships or fieldwork, scholarships/grants, health care benefits, and unspecified assistantships available. Support available to part-time students. Financial award application deadline: 7/1; financial award applicants required to submit FAFSA. *Faculty research:* Technical writing, African-American literature, Milton, creative writing and poetry, American modernism and gender theory. *Total annual research expenditures:* $6,000. *Unit head:* Dr. Christopher Stuart, Department Head, 423-425-2140, Fax: 423-425-2282, E-mail: chris-stuart@utc.edu. *Application contact:* Dr. Joanne Romagni, Dean of the Graduate School, 423-425-4478, Fax: 423-425-5223, E-mail: joanne-romagni@utc.edu.
Website: http://www.utc.edu/english/

The University of Texas at El Paso, Graduate School, College of Liberal Arts, Department of English, El Paso, TX 79968-0001. Offers bilingual professional writing (Certificate); English and American literature (MA); rhetoric and composition (PhD); rhetoric and writing studies (MA); teaching English (MAT). *Program availability:* Part-time, evening/weekend. *Degree requirements:* For master's, thesis optional. *Entrance requirements:* For master's, GRE General Test, minimum GPA of 3.0. Additional exam requirements/recommendations for international students: Required—TOEFL. Electronic applications accepted. *Faculty research:* Literature, creative writing, literary theory.

University of Utah, Graduate School, College of Humanities, Department of Communication, Salt Lake City, UT 84112. Offers communicating science, health, environment and risk (MA, MS, PhD); critical cultural studies (MA, MS, PhD); digital media (MA, MS, PhD); rhetoric (MA, MS, PhD). *Faculty:* 26 full-time (13 women), 11 part-time/adjunct (3 women). *Students:* 34 full-time (24 women), 14 part-time (10 women); includes 4 minority (2 Asian, non-Hispanic/Latino; 1 Hispanic/Latino; 1 Two or more races, non-Hispanic/Latino), 3 international. Average age 24. 99 applicants, 31% accepted, 15 enrolled. In 2017, 6 master's, 9 doctorates awarded. Terminal master's awarded for partial completion of doctoral program. *Entrance requirements:* For master's and doctorate, GRE General Test, minimum GPA of 3.0. Additional exam requirements/recommendations for international students: Required—TOEFL (minimum score 500 paper-based; 90 iBT); Recommended—IELTS. *Application deadline:* For fall admission, 12/15 for domestic students, 11/15 for international students. Application fee: $55 ($65 for international students). Electronic applications accepted. *Expenses:* $7,790 resident, $24,804 non-resident. *Financial support:* In 2017–18, 4 students received support, including 1 fellowship with full tuition reimbursement available (averaging $18,000 per year), 25 teaching assistantships with full tuition reimbursements available (averaging $17,700 per year); research assistantships, scholarships/grants, health care benefits, and unspecified assistantships also available. Financial award application deadline: 12/15; financial award applicants required to submit FAFSA. *Faculty research:* CommSHER (communicating science, health, environment, and risk), critical/cultural studies, interpersonal/organizational communication, new media technologies, rhetoric. *Unit head:* Dr. Kent A. Ono, Chair, 801-585-9128, Fax: 801-585-6255, E-mail: kent.ono@utah.edu. *Application contact:* Dr. Helene Shugart, Director of Graduate Studies, 801-581-5686, Fax: 801-585-6255, E-mail: h.shugart@utah.edu.
Website: http://www.communication.utah.edu

University of Utah, Graduate School, College of Humanities, Department of English, Salt Lake City, UT 84112. Offers English (MA, MFA, PhD), including creative writing (MFA, PhD), literary and cultural studies (MA, PhD), rhetoric and composition (MA,

PhD). *Program availability:* Part-time. *Faculty:* 31 full-time (13 women), 5 part-time/adjunct (2 women). *Students:* 43 full-time (24 women), 25 part-time (15 women); includes 13 minority (5 Asian, non-Hispanic/Latino; 5 Hispanic/Latino; 3 Two or more races, non-Hispanic/Latino), 3 international. Average age 26. 225 applicants, 17% accepted, 14 enrolled. In 2017, 1 master's, 8 doctorates awarded. Terminal master's awarded for partial completion of doctoral program. *Entrance requirements:* For master's and doctorate, GRE General Test, minimum GPA of 3.2. Additional exam requirements/recommendations for international students: Required—TOEFL (minimum score 650 paper-based; 115 iBT); Recommended—IELTS (minimum score 9), TSE. *Application deadline:* For fall admission, 12/15 for domestic and international students. Application fee: $55 ($65 for international students). Electronic applications accepted. *Financial support:* In 2017–18, 39 students received support, including 10 fellowships (averaging $18,600 per year), 29 teaching assistantships with full tuition reimbursements available (averaging $18,600 per year); health care benefits also available. Financial award application deadline: 12/15; financial award applicants required to submit FAFSA. *Faculty research:* Creative writing including poetics and modern poetry, fiction, and experimental forms; nineteenth- and twentieth-century British and American literature; American Studies, the American West, and environmental studies; critical theory and practice; race and gender studies. *Total annual research expenditures:* $126,500. *Unit head:* Prof. Barry L. Weller, Department Chair, 801-581-6168, Fax: 801-585-5167, E-mail: barry.weller@utah.edu. *Application contact:* Prof. Andrew Franta, Director of Graduate Studies, 801-581-7850, Fax: 801-585-5167, E-mail: a.franta@utah.edu.
Website: http://english.utah.edu/

University of Wisconsin–Madison, Graduate School, College of Letters and Science, Department of Communication Arts, Madison, WI 53706-1380. Offers communication science (MA, PhD); film (MA, PhD); media and cultural studies (MA, PhD); rhetoric (MA, PhD). Terminal master's awarded for partial completion of doctoral program. *Degree requirements:* For master's, one foreign language, thesis (for some programs); for doctorate, one foreign language, thesis/dissertation. *Entrance requirements:* For master's and doctorate, GRE General Test, minimum GPA of 3.5. Electronic applications accepted.

University of Wisconsin–Milwaukee, Graduate School, College of Letters and Science, Department of Communication, Milwaukee, WI 53201-0413. Offers communication (MA, PhD), including rhetorical leadership; rhetorical leadership (Graduate Certificate). *Program availability:* Part-time. *Students:* 23 full-time (16 women), 16 part-time (13 women); includes 5 minority (2 Black or African American, non-Hispanic/Latino; 2 Asian, non-Hispanic/Latino; 1 Two or more races, non-Hispanic/Latino), 6 international. Average age 31. 45 applicants, 51% accepted, 17 enrolled. In 2017, 3 doctorates awarded. *Degree requirements:* For master's, thesis or alternative; for doctorate, comprehensive exam. *Entrance requirements:* For master's, GRE General Test, minimum GPA of 3.0. Additional exam requirements/recommendations for international students: Required—TOEFL (minimum score 550 paper-based; 79 iBT), IELTS (minimum score 6). *Application deadline:* For fall admission, 1/1 priority date for domestic students; for spring admission, 9/1 for domestic students. Application fee: $56. Electronic applications accepted. *Financial support:* Fellowships, research assistantships, teaching assistantships, career-related internships or fieldwork, unspecified assistantships, and project assistantships available. Support available to part-time students. Financial award application deadline: 4/15; financial award applicants required to submit FAFSA. *Unit head:* Mike Allen, Department Chair, 414-229-4510, E-mail: mikealle@uwm.edu. *Application contact:* General Information Contact, 414-229-4982, Fax: 414-229-6967, E-mail: gradschool@uwm.edu.
Website: https://uwm.edu/communication/

University of Wisconsin–Milwaukee, Graduate School, College of Letters and Science, Department of English, Milwaukee, WI 53201-0413. Offers English (MA, PhD), including creative writing, English language and linguistics, English secondary education, literary and critical studies, literature and cultural theory (PhD), literature and language studies, literature, culture, and media, media, cinema and digital studies, professional and technical communication (MA), professional and technical writing, professional writing (PhD), rhetoric and composition (PhD), rhetoric and writing. *Students:* 90 full-time (54 women), 42 part-time (17 women); includes 12 minority (2 Black or African American, non-Hispanic/Latino; 1 American Indian or Alaska Native, non-Hispanic/Latino; 4 Asian, non-Hispanic/Latino; 1 Hispanic/Latino; 4 Two or more races, non-Hispanic/Latino), 9 international. Average age 34. 166 applicants, 21% accepted, 27 enrolled. In 2017, 10 master's, 12 doctorates awarded. *Degree requirements:* For master's, thesis or alternative; for doctorate, one foreign language, thesis/dissertation. *Entrance requirements:* For master's, GRE General Test, GRE Subject Test; for doctorate, GRE. Additional exam requirements/recommendations for international students: Required—TOEFL (minimum score 550 paper-based; 79 iBT), IELTS (minimum score 6.5). *Application deadline:* For fall admission, 1/1 priority date for domestic students; for spring admission, 9/1 for domestic students. Application fee: $56 ($96 for international students). Electronic applications accepted. *Financial support:* Fellowships, research assistantships, teaching assistantships, career-related internships or fieldwork, unspecified assistantships, and project assistantships available. Support available to part-time students. Financial award application deadline: 4/15; financial award applicants required to submit FAFSA. *Unit head:* Mark Netzloff, Department Chair, 414-229-4511, E-mail: netzloff@uwm.edu. *Application contact:* General Information Contact, 414-229-4982, Fax: 414-229-6967, E-mail: gradschool@uwm.edu.
Website: https://uwm.edu/english/

Wayne State University, College of Liberal Arts and Sciences, Department of English, Detroit, MI 48202. Offers English (MA); film and media studies (PhD); literary and cultural studies (PhD); rhetoric and composition studies (PhD). *Faculty:* 23. *Students:* 68 full-time (34 women), 24 part-time (17 women); includes 22 minority (10 Black or African American, non-Hispanic/Latino; 2 Asian, non-Hispanic/Latino; 6 Hispanic/Latino; 4 Two or more races, non-Hispanic/Latino), 5 international. Average age 33. 110 applicants, 35% accepted, 17 enrolled. In 2017, 15 master's, 15 doctorates awarded. Terminal master's awarded for partial completion of doctoral program. *Degree requirements:* For master's, variable foreign language requirement, essay, thesis, or portfolio of work approved by Director of Graduate Studies; for doctorate, one foreign language, comprehensive exam, thesis/dissertation. *Entrance requirements:* For master's, statement of purpose, two academic letters of reference; sample essay from previous English course; for doctorate, GRE General Test, statement of purpose; two academic letters of reference; sample of scholarly or critical writing. Additional exam requirements/recommendations for international students: Required—TOEFL (minimum score 550 paper-based; 79 iBT), TWE (minimum score 5.5), Michigan English Language Assessment Battery (minimum score 85); Recommended—IELTS (minimum score 6.5). *Application deadline:* For fall admission, 1/15 for domestic students. Applications are processed on a rolling basis. Application fee: $50. Electronic applications accepted. *Expenses:* Tuition, state resident: full-time $10,224; part-time $638.98 per credit hour. Tuition, nonresident: full-time $22,145; part-time $1384.04 per credit hour. Tuition and fees vary according to course load and program. *Financial support:* In 2017–18, 61 students received support, including 6 fellowships with tuition reimbursements available (averaging $15,583 per year), 30 teaching assistantships with tuition reimbursements

available (averaging $18,534 per year); research assistantships with tuition reimbursements available, scholarships/grants, health care benefits, and unspecified assistantships also available. Financial award applicants required to submit FAFSA. *Faculty research:* Literary and cultural studies, film and new media studies, rhetoric and composition studies, linguistics, and creative writing. *Unit head:* Dr. Kenneth Jackson, Chair and Professor, 313-577-7692, E-mail: ai4054@wayne.edu. *Application contact:* Dr. Carolin Maun, Director of Graduate Studies, 313-577-7694, E-mail: caroline.maun@wayne.edu.
Website: http://clas.wayne.edu/english/

Western Carolina University, Graduate School, College of Arts and Sciences, Department of English, Cullowhee, NC 28723. Offers literature (MA); professional writing (MA); rhetoric and composition (MA); teaching English to speakers of other languages (Certificate); technical and professional writing (Certificate). *Program availability:* Part-time, evening/weekend. *Students:* 31. *Degree requirements:* For master's, one foreign language, comprehensive exam, thesis (for some programs). *Entrance requirements:* For master's, appropriate undergraduate degree, writing sample, 3 letters of recommendation. Additional exam requirements/recommendations for international students: Required—TOEFL (minimum score 550 paper-based, 79 iBT) or IELTS (6.5). *Application deadline:* For fall admission, 2/15 priority date for domestic and international students; for spring admission, 11/15 priority date for domestic students, 10/15 priority date for international students. Applications are processed on a rolling basis. Application fee: $65. Electronic applications accepted. *Expenses:* $10,000 per year in-state full-time; $20,308 per year out-of-state full-time. *Financial support:* In 2017–18, 1 research assistantship with full and partial tuition reimbursement (averaging $9,000 per year), 16 teaching assistantships with full and partial tuition reimbursements (averaging $9,500 per year) were awarded; career-related internships or fieldwork, institutionally sponsored loans, scholarships/grants, and unspecified assistantships also available. Financial award application deadline: 2/15; financial award applicants required to submit FAFSA. *Faculty research:* Teaching English to speakers of other languages (TESOL), language assessment, applied linguistics, poetry, folk and fairy tales, post World War II British literature, Appalachian and Southern literature. *Unit head:* Dr. Brent Kinser, Department Head, E-mail: bkinser@wcu.edu. *Application contact:* Bobbi Smith, Graduate Admissions Coordinator, E-mail: bobbismith@email.wcu.edu.
Website: https://www.wcu.edu/learn/departments-schools-colleges/cas/humanities/english/enggrad/index.aspx

Speech and Interpersonal Communication

Ball State University, Graduate School, College of Communication, Information, and Media, Department of Communication Studies, Muncie, IN 47306. Offers communication studies (MA), including communication liberal arts and sciences, organization and professional communication and development. *Program availability:* Part-time. *Faculty:* 7 full-time (5 women). *Students:* 17 full-time (11 women), 9 part-time (6 women); includes 6 minority (3 Black or African American, non-Hispanic/Latino; 1 Hispanic/Latino; 2 Two or more races, non-Hispanic/Latino), 1 international. Average age 27. 26 applicants, 54% accepted, 10 enrolled. In 2017, 12 master's awarded. *Degree requirements:* For master's, comprehensive exam (for some programs), thesis (for some programs). *Entrance requirements:* For master's, GRE General Test, minimum baccalaureate GPA of 2.75 or 3.0 in latter half of baccalaureate, goal statement, writing sample, three letters of reference. Additional exam requirements/recommendations for international students: Required—TOEFL (minimum score 550 paper-based; 79 iBT), IELTS (minimum score 6.5). *Application deadline:* Applications are processed on a rolling basis. Application fee: $60. Electronic applications accepted. *Financial support:* In 2017–18, 31 students received support, including 31 teaching assistantships with partial tuition reimbursements available (averaging $11,649 per year); unspecified assistantships also available. Financial award application deadline: 3/1; financial award applicants required to submit FAFSA. *Unit head:* Dr. Glen Stamp, Chairperson, 765-285-1882, Fax: 765-285-2736, E-mail: gstamp@bsu.edu.
Website: http://www.bsu.edu/commstudies

Bob Jones University, Graduate Programs, Greenville, SC 29614. Offers accountancy (MS); Bible (MA); Bible translation (MA); Biblical studies (Certificate); broadcast management (MS); business administration (MBA); church history (MA, PhD); church ministries (MA); church music (MM); cinema and video production (MA); counseling (MS); curriculum and instruction (Ed D); divinity (M Div); dramatic production (MA); educational leadership (MS, Ed D, Ed S); elementary education (M Ed, MAT); English (M Ed, MA, MAT); fine arts (MA); graphic design (MA); history (M Ed, MA); illustration (MA); interpretative speech (MA); mathematics (M Ed, MAT); medical missions (Certificate); ministry (MM, D Min); multi-categorical special education (M Ed, MAT); music (M Ed); New Testament interpretation (PhD); Old Testament interpretation (PhD); orchestral instrument performance (MM); organ performance (MM); pastoral studies (MA); personnel services (MS, Ed S); piano pedagogy (MM); piano performance (MM); platform arts (MA); radio and television broadcasting (MS); rhetoric and public address (MA); secondary education (M Ed); studio art (MA); teaching Bible (MA); theology (MA, PhD); voice performance (MM); youth ministries (MA); M Div/MM.

Brooklyn College of the City University of New York, School of Humanities and Social Sciences, Department of Speech Communication Arts and Sciences, Brooklyn, NY 11210-2889. Offers audiology (Au D); speech (MA), including public communication; speech-language pathology (MS). Au D offered jointly with Hunter College of the City University of New York. *Accreditation:* ASHA (one or more programs are accredited). *Program availability:* Part-time. Terminal master's awarded for partial completion of doctoral program. *Degree requirements:* For master's, comprehensive exam, NTE. *Entrance requirements:* For master's, GRE, minimum GPA of 3.0, interview, essay. Additional exam requirements/recommendations for international students: Required—TOEFL (minimum score 500 paper-based; 61 iBT). Electronic applications accepted. *Faculty research:* Language and learning disorders, aphasia, auditory disorders, public and business communication, voice and fluency disorders.

California State University, Fullerton, Graduate Studies, College of Communications, Department of Human Communication Studies, Fullerton, CA 92831-3599. Offers communication studies (MA). *Program availability:* Part-time. *Faculty:* 9 full-time (6 women), 1 part-time/adjunct (0 women). *Students:* 10 full-time (7 women), 24 part-time (17 women); includes 15 minority (1 Black or African American, non-Hispanic/Latino; 5 Asian, non-Hispanic/Latino; 8 Hispanic/Latino; 1 Native Hawaiian or other Pacific Islander, non-Hispanic/Latino), 2 international. Average age 31. 33 applicants, 48% accepted, 13 enrolled. *Degree requirements:* For master's, comprehensive exam, thesis or alternative. *Entrance requirements:* For master's, minimum GPA of 3.0 in major. Application fee: $55. *Financial support:* Teaching assistantships, career-related internships or fieldwork, Federal Work-Study, institutionally sponsored loans, and scholarships/grants available. Support available to part-time students. Financial award application deadline: 3/1; financial award applicants required to submit FAFSA. *Faculty research:* Speech therapy. *Unit head:* Gary Ruud, Chair, 657-278-4198, E-mail: gruud@fullerton.edu. *Application contact:* Admissions/Applications, 657-278-2371.
Website: http://communications.fullerton.edu/hcom/

California State University, Northridge, Graduate Studies, Mike Curb College of Arts, Media, and Communication, Department of Communication Studies, Northridge, CA 91330. Offers MA. *Students:* 22 full-time (14 women), 10 part-time (5 women); includes 14 minority (2 Black or African American, non-Hispanic/Latino; 2 Asian, non-Hispanic/Latino; 8 Hispanic/Latino; 2 Two or more races, non-Hispanic/Latino), 4 international. Average age 28. 61 applicants, 44% accepted, 19 enrolled. In 2017, 19 master's awarded. *Entrance requirements:* For master's, GRE General Test. Additional exam requirements/recommendations for international students: Required—TOEFL. *Application deadline:* For fall admission, 11/30 for domestic students. Application fee: $55. *Financial support:* Teaching assistantships available. Financial award application deadline: 3/1. *Unit head:* Kathryn Sorrells, Chair, 818-677-2853.
Website: http://www.csun.edu/CommunicationStudies/

Colorado State University, College of Liberal Arts, Department of Communication Studies, Fort Collins, CO 80523-1783. Offers communication (PhD); communication studies (MA), including deliberative practices. *Faculty:* 12 full-time (8 women). *Students:* 21 full-time (14 women), 9 part-time (all women); includes 5 minority (3 Hispanic/Latino; 2 Two or more races, non-Hispanic/Latino), 1 international. Average age 25. 59 applicants, 41% accepted, 15 enrolled. In 2017, 9 master's awarded. *Degree requirements:* For master's, variable foreign language requirement, comprehensive exam (for some programs), thesis (for some programs), conference submission, colloquium, prospectus and thesis or project defense; for doctorate, variable foreign language requirement, comprehensive exam, thesis/dissertation (for some programs), conference submission, colloquium, prospectus and thesis or project defense. *Entrance requirements:* For master's, GRE, minimum GPA of 3.0, writing sample, 3 letters of reference, statement of purpose, curriculum vitae or resume, transcripts; for doctorate, GRE, minimum GPA of 3.0, writing sample, 3 letters of reference, statement of purpose, transcripts, curriculum vitae or resume. Additional exam requirements/recommendations for international students: Required—TOEFL (minimum score 550 paper-based; 80 iBT), IELTS (minimum score 6.5), PTE (minimum score 58). *Application deadline:* For fall admission, 1/5 priority date for domestic and international students. Application fee: $60 ($70 for international students). Electronic applications accepted. *Expenses:* Tuition, state resident: full-time $9917. Tuition, nonresident: full-time $24,312. *Required fees:* $2284. Tuition and fees vary according to course load and program. *Financial support:* In 2017–18, 24 students received support, including 24 teaching assistantships with full tuition reimbursements available (averaging $14,864 per year); fellowships with full tuition reimbursements available, research assistantships with full tuition reimbursements available, scholarships/grants, health care benefits, and unspecified assistantships also available. Financial award application deadline: 1/5. *Faculty research:* Rhetoric and civic engagement; media and visual culture; organizational, deliberative practices studies, and relational communication. *Total annual research expenditures:* $55,122. *Unit head:* Dr. Karrin Anderson, Director of Graduate Studies, 970-491-6893, E-mail: karrin.anderson@colostate.edu. *Application contact:* Carly Hennegan, Graduate Studies Support Coordinator, 970-491-4123, E-mail: carly.hennegan@colostate.edu.
Website: http://communicationstudies.colostate.edu/

Georgia State University, College of Arts and Sciences, Department of Communication, Atlanta, GA 30302-3083. Offers film, video, and digital imaging (MA), including critical studies, production, screenwriting; human communication and social influence (MA); mass communication (MA); media and society (PhD); moving image studies (PhD); public communication (PhD); rhetoric and politics (PhD). *Program availability:* Part-time. *Faculty:* 57 full-time (34 women). *Students:* 71 full-time (51 women), 17 part-time (9 women); includes 36 minority (28 Black or African American, non-Hispanic/Latino; 1 Asian, non-Hispanic/Latino; 4 Hispanic/Latino; 1 Native Hawaiian or other Pacific Islander, non-Hispanic/Latino; 2 Two or more races, non-Hispanic/Latino), 15 international. Average age 33. 63 applicants, 54% accepted, 17 enrolled. In 2017, 20 master's, 10 doctorates awarded. *Degree requirements:* For master's, variable foreign language requirement, thesis (for some programs); for doctorate, comprehensive exam, thesis/dissertation. *Entrance requirements:* For master's and doctorate, GRE. Additional exam requirements/recommendations for international students: Required—TOEFL (minimum score 550 paper-based; 80 iBT), IELTS (minimum score 6.5). *Application deadline:* For fall admission, 2/10 for domestic and international students; for spring admission, 10/15 for domestic and international students. Application fee: $50. Electronic applications accepted. *Expenses:* Tuition, state resident: full-time $7020. Tuition, nonresident: full-time $22,518. *Required fees:* $2128. Tuition and fees vary according to degree level and program. *Financial support:* In 2017–18, fellowships with tuition reimbursements (averaging $15,000 per year), teaching assistantships with tuition reimbursements (averaging $15,000 per year) were awarded; career-related internships or fieldwork and unspecified assistantships also available. Financial award applicants required to submit FAFSA. *Faculty research:* New media, mass media and journalism, rhetoric, film and media studies, film production. *Unit head:* Dr. Greg Lisby, Chair, 404-413-5639, Fax: 404-413-5634, E-mail: glisby@gsu.edu.
Website: http://communication.gsu.edu

Marquette University, Graduate School, College of Communication, Milwaukee, WI 53201-1881. Offers advertising and public relations (MA); communication studies (MA); digital storytelling (Certificate); journalism (MA); mass communication (MA); science, health and environmental communication (MA). *Accreditation:* ACEJMC (one or more programs are accredited). *Program availability:* Part-time, evening/weekend. *Degree requirements:* For master's, comprehensive exam, thesis or alternative. *Entrance requirements:* For master's, GRE, official transcripts from all current and previous colleges/universities except Marquette, three letters of recommendation, statement of academic and professional goals. Additional exam requirements/recommendations for international students: Required—TOEFL (minimum score 530 paper-based). Electronic applications accepted. *Faculty research:* Urban journalism, gender and communication, intercultural communication, religious communication.

Speech and Interpersonal Communication

New York University, Steinhardt School of Culture, Education, and Human Development, Department of Media, Culture and Communication, New York, NY 10012. Offers media, culture and communication (MA, PhD); MLIS/MA. *Program availability:* Part-time. *Students:* Average age 33. 550 applicants, 24% accepted, 46 enrolled. In 2017, 57 master's, 6 doctorates awarded. Terminal master's awarded for partial completion of doctoral program. *Entrance requirements:* For master's, GRE General Test; for doctorate, GRE General Test, interview. Additional exam requirements/recommendations for international students: Required—TOEFL (minimum score 100 iBT). *Application deadline:* For fall admission, 12/1 priority date for domestic and international students; for spring admission, 10/1 for domestic and international students. Applications are processed on a rolling basis. Application fee: $75. Electronic applications accepted. *Expenses: Tuition:* Full-time $41,352; part-time $19,968 per year. *Required fees:* $2496; $1628 per unit. $814 per term. Tuition and fees vary according to course load and program. *Financial support:* Fellowships with full and partial tuition reimbursements, teaching assistantships with full and partial tuition reimbursements, career-related internships or fieldwork, Federal Work-Study, institutionally sponsored loans, scholarships/grants, tuition waivers (partial), and unspecified assistantships available. Support available to part-time students. Financial award application deadline: 2/1; financial award applicants required to submit FAFSA. *Faculty research:* Digital media and new technologies, media criticism, flow of media and culture transnationally and transculturally. *Unit head:* Prof. Lisa Gitelman, Chairperson, 212-998-5191, Fax: 212-995-4046, E-mail: lg91@nyu.edu. *Application contact:* 212-998-5030, Fax: 212-995-4328, E-mail: steinhardt.gradadmissions@nyu.edu.
Website: http://steinhardt.nyu.edu/mcc

North Dakota State University, College of Graduate and Interdisciplinary Studies, College of Arts, Humanities and Social Sciences, Department of Communication, Fargo, ND 58102. Offers communication (PhD); mass communication (MA, MS); speech communication (MA, MS). *Program availability:* Part-time, online learning. Terminal master's awarded for partial completion of doctoral program. *Degree requirements:* For master's, thesis (for some programs); for doctorate, comprehensive exam, thesis/dissertation, 2-3 publications. *Entrance requirements:* For master's, GRE, minimum undergraduate GPA of 3.25; for doctorate, GRE, minimum undergraduate GPA of 3.5. Additional exam requirements/recommendations for international students: Required—TOEFL (minimum score 600 paper-based; 100 iBT), IELTS (minimum score 7). Electronic applications accepted. *Faculty research:* Communication and rhetorical theory, organizational communication, broadcast and print journalism, international communication, public relations and advertising.

Northeastern Illinois University, College of Graduate Studies and Research, College of Arts and Sciences, Program in Communication, Media and Theatre, Chicago, IL 60625. Offers MA. *Program availability:* Part-time, evening/weekend. *Degree requirements:* For master's, comprehensive exam, oral exams, thesis or 3 term papers. *Entrance requirements:* For master's, 15 undergraduate hours in speech and performing arts, minimum GPA of 2.75. Additional exam requirements/recommendations for international students: Required—TOEFL (minimum score 550 paper-based; 79 iBT). *Application deadline:* Applications are processed on a rolling basis. Application fee: $25. Electronic applications accepted. *Expenses:* Tuition, state resident: full-time $7274; part-time $404.11 per credit hour. Tuition, nonresident: full-time $14,548; part-time $808.23 per credit hour. *Required fees:* $1284. *Financial support:* Applicants required to submit FAFSA. *Faculty research:* Creative drama, family communication, fine arts and general education, playwriting techniques, interpersonal communications. *Unit head:* Dr. Katrina E. Bell-Jordan, Department Chair, 773-442-5957, E-mail: k-bell1@neiu.edu. *Application contact:* Martha Narvaez, Graduate Admission Representative, 773-442-6006, E-mail: m-narvaez@neiu.edu.

Northwestern University, The Graduate School, School of Communication, Department of Performance Studies, Evanston, IL 60208. Offers MA, PhD. Admissions and degrees offered through The Graduate School. *Program availability:* Part-time. Terminal master's awarded for partial completion of doctoral program. *Degree requirements:* For master's, recital; for doctorate, one foreign language, thesis/dissertation, recital. *Entrance requirements:* For master's and doctorate, GRE General Test. Additional exam requirements/recommendations for international students: Required—TOEFL. *Faculty research:* Adaptation/performance of literature, ethnography of performance, critical cultural studies, performance theory, intercultural performance, gender studies.

Ohio University, Graduate College, Scripps College of Communication, School of Communication Studies, Athens, OH 45701-2979. Offers health communication (PhD); organizational communication (MA); relating and organizing (PhD); rhetoric and public culture (PhD). *Program availability:* Part-time, online learning. Terminal master's awarded for partial completion of doctoral program. *Degree requirements:* For master's, capstone; for doctorate, comprehensive exam, thesis/dissertation. *Entrance requirements:* For master's, GRE; for doctorate, GRE General Test, minimum GPA of 3.0. Additional exam requirements/recommendations for international students: Required—TOEFL (minimum score 550 paper-based; 80 iBT) or IELTS (minimum score 6.5). Electronic applications accepted. *Faculty research:* Rhetoric and public culture, relating and organizing, health communication.

Old Dominion University, College of Arts and Letters, Program in Lifespan and Digital Communication, Norfolk, VA 23529. Offers MA. *Accreditation:* NASAD. *Program availability:* Part-time, evening/weekend. *Faculty:* 11 full-time (3 women). *Students:* 9 full-time (5 women), 16 part-time (12 women); includes 14 minority (7 Black or African American, non-Hispanic/Latino; 1 Asian, non-Hispanic/Latino; 3 Hispanic/Latino; 3 Two or more races, non-Hispanic/Latino), 1 international. Average age 34. 14 applicants, 86% accepted, 12 enrolled. In 2017, 5 master's awarded. *Degree requirements:* For master's, thesis or capstone project. *Entrance requirements:* For master's, GRE. Additional exam requirements/recommendations for international students: Required—TOEFL (minimum score 550 paper-based; 79 iBT). *Application deadline:* For fall admission, 6/15 for domestic students, 4/15 for international students. Applications are processed on a rolling basis. Application fee: $50. Electronic applications accepted. *Expenses:* $8,928 in-state tuition, $300 in-state fees. *Financial support:* In 2017–18, 10 students received support, including 10 research assistantships (averaging $10,000 per year), 10 teaching assistantships (averaging $10,000 per year); 10 assistantships (averaging $5000) also available. Financial award application deadline: 6/15. *Faculty research:* Lifespan digital media studies, lifespan relational communication, social media, screenwriting, media industries. *Unit head:* Dr. Thomas J. Socha, Graduate Program Director, 757-683-3833, E-mail: tsocha@odu.edu. *Application contact:* Dr. Dale Miller, Associate Dean for Research and Graduate Studies, 757-683-3866, E-mail: demiller@odu.edu.
Website: http://www.odu.edu/commtheatre/graduate#.WtdfPme-YSk

Portland State University, Graduate Studies, College of Liberal Arts and Sciences, Department of Communication, Portland, OR 97207-0751. Offers general speech communication (MA, MS, Certificate). *Program availability:* Part-time. *Faculty:* 12 full-time (6 women), 9 part-time/adjunct (2 women). *Students:* 16 full-time (12 women), 9 part-time (6 women); includes 4 minority (2 Black or African American, non-Hispanic/Latino; 1 Hispanic/Latino; 1 Two or more races, non-Hispanic/Latino), 2 international. Average age 32. 17 applicants, 47% accepted, 6 enrolled. In 2017, 6 master's awarded.

Degree requirements: For master's, variable foreign language requirement, thesis optional. *Entrance requirements:* For master's, GRE (for students who select the thesis option and/or who receive an assistantship), minimum GPA of 3.0 in upper-division course work or 2.75 overall, 3 letters of recommendation, statement of purpose, writing samples. Additional exam requirements/recommendations for international students: Required—TOEFL (minimum score 600 paper-based; 100 iBT). *Application deadline:* For fall admission, 2/1 priority date for domestic and international students. Applications are processed on a rolling basis. Application fee: $65. Electronic applications accepted. *Expenses:* Tuition, state resident: full-time $14,436; part-time $401 per credit. Tuition, nonresident: full-time $21,780; part-time $605 per credit. *Required fees:* $1380; $22 per credit. $119 per quarter. One-time fee: $325. Tuition and fees vary according to program. *Financial support:* In 2017–18, 12 students received support, including 8 teaching assistantships with full and partial tuition reimbursements available (averaging $6,390 per year); research assistantships, career-related internships or fieldwork, Federal Work-Study, and scholarships/grants also available. Support available to part-time students. Financial award application deadline: 3/1; financial award applicants required to submit FAFSA. *Total annual research expenditures:* $82,153. *Unit head:* Dr. Jeffrey Robinson, Chair, 503-725-3599, Fax: 503-725-3599, E-mail: jeffreyr@pdx.edu. *Application contact:* Seyrra Crow, Department Coordinator, 503-725-5378, E-mail: croy@pdx.edu.
Website: http://www.pdx.edu/communication/home

Rensselaer Polytechnic Institute, Graduate School, School of Humanities, Arts, and Social Sciences, Program in Communication and Rhetoric, Troy, NY 12180-3590. Offers MS, PhD. *Faculty:* 9 full-time (6 women). *Students:* 13 full-time (8 women), 3 part-time (2 women); includes 1 minority (Hispanic/Latino). Average age 32. 17 applicants, 41% accepted, 3 enrolled. In 2017, 1 master's, 2 doctorates awarded. Terminal master's awarded for partial completion of doctoral program. *Degree requirements:* For master's, thesis optional; for doctorate, comprehensive exam, thesis/dissertation. *Entrance requirements:* For master's and doctorate, GRE, writing sample. Additional exam requirements/recommendations for international students: Required—TOEFL (minimum score 570 paper-based; 88 iBT), IELTS (minimum score 6.5), PTE (minimum score 60). *Application deadline:* For fall admission, 1/1 priority date for domestic and international students; for spring admission, 8/15 priority date for domestic and international students. Applications are processed on a rolling basis. Application fee: $75. Electronic applications accepted. *Expenses: Tuition:* Full-time $52,550; part-time $2125 per credit hour. *Required fees:* $2890. *Financial support:* In 2017–18, research assistantships with full tuition reimbursements (averaging $23,000 per year), teaching assistantships with full tuition reimbursements (averaging $23,000 per year) were awarded; fellowships also available. Financial award application deadline: 1/1. *Faculty research:* Communication, game studies, human computer interaction, literary theory, media studies, rhetoric, visual design, writing studies. *Total annual research expenditures:* $13,688. *Unit head:* Dr. Audrey Bennett, Graduate Program Director, 518-276-6933, E-mail: bennett@rpi.edu.
Website: http://www.cm.rpi.edu/pl/graduate

San Francisco State University, Division of Graduate Studies, College of Liberal and Creative Arts, Department of Communication Studies, San Francisco, CA 94132-1722. Offers MA. *Program availability:* Part-time. *Application deadline:* Applications are processed on a rolling basis. *Financial support:* Teaching assistantships available. *Unit head:* Prof. Joseph Tuman, Chair, 415-338-1597, Fax: 415-338-6159, E-mail: joetuman@sfsu.edu. *Application contact:* Prof. Leah Wingard, Graduate Coordinator, 415-338-3171, Fax: 415-338-6159, E-mail: wingard@sfsu.edu.
Website: http://communicationstudies.sfsu.edu/

Seton Hall University, School of Health and Medical Sciences, Program in Speech-Language Pathology, South Orange, NJ 07079-2697. Offers MS. *Accreditation:* ASHA. *Entrance requirements:* For master's, GRE, bachelor's degree, clinical experience; minimum GPA of 3.0, undergraduate preprofessional coursework in communication sciences and disorders. Additional exam requirements/recommendations for international students: Recommended—TOEFL. Electronic applications accepted. *Faculty research:* Child language disorders, motor speech control, voice disorders, dysphagia, early intervention/teaming.

Southern Illinois University Carbondale, Graduate School, College of Liberal Arts, Department of Communication Studies, Carbondale, IL 62901-4701. Offers MA, MS, PhD. *Degree requirements:* For master's, one foreign language, thesis or alternative; for doctorate, one foreign language, thesis/dissertation. *Entrance requirements:* For master's, GRE General Test or MAT, minimum GPA of 2.7; for doctorate, GRE General Test or MAT, minimum GPA of 3.25. Additional exam requirements/recommendations for international students: Required—TOEFL (minimum score 100 iBT).

Southern Illinois University Edwardsville, Graduate School, College of Arts and Sciences, Department of Applied Communication Studies, Program in Interpersonal Communication, Edwardsville, IL 62026. Offers MA. *Program availability:* Part-time, evening/weekend. *Degree requirements:* For master's, comprehensive exam (for some programs), thesis (for some programs). *Entrance requirements:* Additional exam requirements/recommendations for international students: Required—TOEFL (minimum score 550 paper-based, 79 iBT), IELTS (minimum score 6.5), Michigan Test of English Language Proficiency or PTE. Electronic applications accepted.

Texas Christian University, Bob Schieffer College of Communication, Department of Communication Studies, Fort Worth, TX 76129. Offers MS. *Program availability:* Part-time. *Faculty:* 12 full-time (5 women). *Students:* 9 full-time (7 women); includes 3 minority (1 Asian, non-Hispanic/Latino; 2 Hispanic/Latino). Average age 23. 11 applicants, 73% accepted, 5 enrolled. In 2017, 6 master's awarded. *Degree requirements:* For master's, comprehensive exams or thesis. *Entrance requirements:* For master's, GRE General Test. Additional exam requirements/recommendations for international students: Required—TOEFL (minimum score 550 paper-based; 80 iBT). *Application deadline:* For fall and spring admission, 2/15 for domestic and international students. Application fee: $60. Electronic applications accepted. *Financial support:* In 2017–18, 9 students received support, including 9 teaching assistantships with full tuition reimbursements available (averaging $12,500 per year); tuition waivers (full) also available. Financial award application deadline: 2/15. *Faculty research:* Interpersonal communication, social media, organizational communication, persuasion, health communication. *Unit head:* Dr. Melissa Schroeder, Associate Professor/Chair, 817-257-7784, Fax: 817-257-6580, E-mail: m.y.schroeder@tcu.edu. *Application contact:* Dr. Paul Schrodt, Professor and Graduate Director, 817-257-5674, Fax: 817-257-6580, E-mail: p.schrodt@tcu.edu.
Website: http://www.commstudies.tcu.edu

The University of Alabama, Graduate School, College of Communication and Information Sciences, Department of Communication Studies, Tuscaloosa, AL 35487. Offers MA. *Program availability:* Part-time, 100% online, blended/hybrid learning. *Faculty:* 19 full-time (12 women), 1 (woman) part-time/adjunct. *Students:* 23 full-time (16 women), 40 part-time (26 women); includes 13 minority (5 Black or African American, non-Hispanic/Latino; 1 American Indian or Alaska Native, non-Hispanic/Latino; 4 Hispanic/Latino; 3 Two or more races, non-Hispanic/Latino), 2 international. Average age 31. 75 applicants, 61% accepted, 27 enrolled. In 2017, 17 master's awarded. *Degree requirements:* For master's, comprehensive exam (for some programs), thesis

(for some programs), capstone portfolio (for some programs), graduate showcase. *Entrance requirements:* For master's, GRE, MAT, minimum GPA of 3.0. Additional exam requirements/recommendations for international students: Required—TOEFL (minimum score 550 paper-based). *Application deadline:* For fall admission, 5/1 for domestic students, 4/1 for international students; for spring admission, 11/1 for domestic students, 10/1 for international students; for summer admission, 3/1 for domestic and international students. Applications are processed on a rolling basis. Application fee: $50 ($60 for international students). Electronic applications accepted. *Financial support:* In 2017–18, 9 students received support, including teaching assistantships with full tuition reimbursements available (averaging $12,366 per year); fellowships with full tuition reimbursements available, health care benefits, unspecified assistantships, and teaching stipends (averaging $3000 per semester) also available. Financial award application deadline: 3/1. *Faculty research:* Rhetorical studies, organizational communication, interpersonal communication, gender and communication, health communication. *Unit head:* Dr. Beth S. Bennett, Department Chair, 205-348-8073, E-mail: bbennett@ua.edu. *Application contact:* Dr. Carol Bishop Mills, Graduate Program Coordinator, 205-348-6165, E-mail: cbmills@ua.edu. Website: http://www.comstudies.ua.edu/

University of Arkansas at Little Rock, Graduate School, College of Social Sciences and Communication, Department of Speech Communication, Little Rock, AR 72204-1099. Offers applied communication studies (MA). *Program availability:* Part-time, evening/weekend. *Degree requirements:* For master's, comprehensive exam, internship, paper, or thesis. *Entrance requirements:* For master's, GRE General Test, MAT, minimum GPA of 2.7. *Faculty research:* Communication theory and applications, managerial communication, human resource training and development, relational communication.

University of California, Santa Barbara, Graduate Division, College of Letters and Sciences, Division of Social Sciences, Department of Sociology, Santa Barbara, CA 93106-9430. Offers interdisciplinary emphasis: Black studies (PhD); interdisciplinary emphasis: environment and society (PhD); interdisciplinary emphasis: feminist studies (PhD); interdisciplinary emphasis: global studies (PhD); interdisciplinary emphasis: language, interaction and social organization (PhD); interdisciplinary emphasis: quantitative methods in the social sciences (PhD); interdisciplinary emphasis: technology and society (PhD); sociology (PhD); MA/PhD. Terminal master's awarded for partial completion of doctoral program. *Degree requirements:* For doctorate, comprehensive exam, thesis/dissertation. *Entrance requirements:* For doctorate, GRE General Test. Additional exam requirements/recommendations for international students: Required—TOEFL (minimum score 550 paper-based; 80 iBT), IELTS (minimum score 7). Electronic applications accepted. *Faculty research:* Gender and sexualities, race/ethnicity, social movements, conversation analysis, global sociology.

University of Denver, Division of Arts, Humanities and Social Sciences, Department of Communication Studies, Denver, CO 80208. Offers culture and communication (MA, PhD); interpersonal and family communication (MA, PhD); rhetoric and communication ethics (MA, PhD). Tuition and fees vary according to course load, campus/location and program.

University of Hawaii at Manoa, Office of Graduate Education, College of Arts and Humanities, Department of Communicology, Honolulu, HI 96822. Offers MA. *Program availability:* Part-time. *Degree requirements:* For master's, thesis optional. *Entrance requirements:* For master's, GRE General Test. Additional exam requirements/recommendations for international students: Required—TOEFL (minimum score 600 paper-based; 100 iBT), IELTS (minimum score 7). *Faculty research:* Social influence, relational management, message processing, intercultural communication.

University of Houston, College of Liberal Arts and Social Sciences, Jack J. Valenti School of Communication, Houston, TX 77204. Offers health communication (MA); mass communication studies (MA); public relations studies (MA); speech communication (MA). *Program availability:* Part-time. *Degree requirements:* For master's, comprehensive exam (for some programs), thesis (for some programs), 30-33 hours. *Entrance requirements:* For master's, GRE. Additional exam requirements/recommendations for international students: Required—TOEFL. Electronic applications accepted.

The University of Iowa, Graduate College, College of Liberal Arts and Sciences, Department of Communication Studies, Iowa City, IA 52242-1316. Offers interpersonal communication and relationships (MA, PhD); media studies (MA, PhD); rhetoric and public advocacy (MA, PhD). *Degree requirements:* For master's, thesis optional, exam; for doctorate, comprehensive exam, thesis/dissertation. *Entrance requirements:* For master's and doctorate, GRE General Test, minimum GPA of 3.0. Additional exam requirements/recommendations for international students: Required—TOEFL (minimum score 550 paper-based; 81 iBT). Electronic applications accepted.

University of Maryland, College Park, Academic Affairs, College of Behavioral and Social Sciences, Department of Hearing and Speech Sciences, College Park, MD 20742. Offers audiology (MA, PhD); hearing and speech sciences (Au D); language pathology (MA, PhD); neuroscience (PhD); speech (MA, PhD). *Accreditation:* ASHA (one or more programs are accredited). *Degree requirements:* For master's, thesis optional; for doctorate, thesis/dissertation, written and oral exams. *Entrance requirements:* For master's, GRE General Test, minimum GPA of 3.5, 3 letters of recommendation; for doctorate, GRE General Test, minimum GPA of 3.5. Additional exam requirements/recommendations for international students: Required—TOEFL. Electronic applications accepted. *Faculty research:* Speech perception, language acquisition, bilingualism, hearing loss.

University of Nebraska–Lincoln, Graduate College, College of Arts and Sciences, Department of Communication Studies, Lincoln, NE 68588. Offers instructional communication (MA, PhD); interpersonal communication (MA, PhD); marketing, communication studies, and advertising (MA, PhD); organizational communication (MA, PhD); rhetoric and culture (MA, PhD). *Degree requirements:* For master's, thesis optional; for doctorate, comprehensive exam, thesis/dissertation. *Entrance requirements:* For master's and doctorate, GRE General Test, writing sample. Additional exam requirements/recommendations for international students: Required—TOEFL (minimum score 600 paper-based). Electronic applications accepted. *Faculty research:* Message strategies, gender communication, political communication, organizational communication, instructional communication.

University of Nevada, Reno, Graduate School, College of Liberal Arts, Department of Speech Communications, Reno, NV 89557. Offers MA. *Degree requirements:* For master's, thesis optional. *Entrance requirements:* For master's, GRE General Test, minimum GPA of 2.75. Additional exam requirements/recommendations for international students: Required—TOEFL (minimum score 500 paper-based; 61 iBT), IELTS (minimum score 6). Electronic applications accepted. *Faculty research:* Rhetorical theory and criticism; communications/sex roles; judicial, legal, contextual, and behavioral approaches to communication theory.

University of South Carolina, The Graduate School, College of Education, Department of Instruction and Teacher Education, Program in Secondary Education, Columbia, SC 29208. Offers art education (IMA, MAT); business education (IMA, MAT); English (MAT); foreign language (MAT); health education (MAT); mathematics (MAT); science (IMA, MAT); secondary (Ed D); secondary education (MT, PhD); social studies (MAT); theatre and speech (MAT). IMA and MT offered jointly with the subject areas. *Accreditation:* NCATE. *Degree requirements:* For master's, comprehensive exam, thesis (for some programs), foreign language (MA); for doctorate, one foreign language, comprehensive exam, thesis/dissertation. *Entrance requirements:* For master's, GRE General Test or MAT, teaching certificate (IMA, M Ed), interview; for doctorate, GRE General Test or MAT, interview. *Faculty research:* Middle school programs, professional development, school collaboration.

University of Southern Mississippi, College of Arts and Letters, Department of Communication Studies, Hattiesburg, MS 39406-0001. Offers MA, PhD. *Program availability:* Part-time. *Students:* 14 full-time (11 women), 1 (woman) part-time. 34 applicants, 59% accepted, 15 enrolled. In 2017, 37 master's, 4 doctorates awarded. *Degree requirements:* For master's, comprehensive exam, thesis optional; for doctorate, comprehensive exam, thesis/dissertation. *Entrance requirements:* For master's, GRE General Test, minimum GPA of 3.0 in last 60 hours and in major; for doctorate, GRE General Test, minimum GPA of 3.5. Additional exam requirements/recommendations for international students: Required—TOEFL, IELTS. *Application deadline:* For fall admission, 3/1 priority date for domestic students, 3/1 for international students; for spring admission, 1/10 priority date for domestic and international students. Applications are processed on a rolling basis. Application fee: $60. Electronic applications accepted. *Expenses:* Tuition, state resident: full-time $3830. *Financial support:* Fellowships with full tuition reimbursements, research assistantships, teaching assistantships with full tuition reimbursements, Federal Work-Study, institutionally sponsored loans, scholarships/grants, health care benefits, and unspecified assistantships available. Financial award application deadline: 3/15; financial award applicants required to submit FAFSA. *Faculty research:* Persuasion and social influence, interpersonal communication, organizational communication, political communication, crisis communication, public advocacy. *Unit head:* Dr. Wendy Atkins-Sayre, Chair, 601-266-4271, Fax: 601-266-4275, E-mail: wendy.atkinssayre@usm.edu. Website: https://www.usm.edu/communication-studies

The University of Tennessee, Graduate School, College of Communication and Information, Knoxville, TN 37996. Offers advertising (MS, PhD); broadcasting (MS, PhD); communications (MS, PhD); information sciences (MS, PhD); journalism (MS, PhD); public relations (MS, PhD); speech communication (MS, PhD). *Program availability:* Part-time, evening/weekend, online learning. *Degree requirements:* For master's, thesis or alternative; for doctorate, thesis/dissertation. *Entrance requirements:* For master's and doctorate, GRE General Test, minimum GPA of 2.7. Additional exam requirements/recommendations for international students: Required—TOEFL. Electronic applications accepted.

University of Wisconsin–Madison, Graduate School, College of Letters and Science, Department of Communication Sciences and Disorders, Madison, WI 53706-1380. Offers audiology (Au D); normal aspects of speech, language and hearing (MS, PhD); speech-language pathology (MS, PhD); MS/PhD. *Accreditation:* ASHA (one or more programs are accredited). *Degree requirements:* For doctorate, thesis/dissertation. *Entrance requirements:* For master's and doctorate, GRE. Electronic applications accepted. *Faculty research:* Language disorders in children and adults, disorders of speech production, intelligibility, fluency, hearing impairment, deafness.

University of Wisconsin–Stevens Point, College of Fine Arts and Communication, Division of Communication, Stevens Point, WI 54481-3897. Offers interpersonal communication (MA); media studies (MA); organizational communication (MA); public relations (MA). *Program availability:* Part-time. *Degree requirements:* For master's, thesis or alternative. *Entrance requirements:* For master's, GRE. Additional exam requirements/recommendations for international students: Required—TOEFL (minimum score 575 paper-based). *Faculty research:* Communication theory and research, film history.

University of Wisconsin–Superior, Graduate Division, Department of Communicating Arts, Superior, WI 54880-4500. Offers mass communication (MA); speech communication (MA); theater (MA). *Program availability:* Part-time. *Degree requirements:* For master's, comprehensive exam, thesis or alternative, position paper or project. *Entrance requirements:* For master's, minimum GPA of 2.75. Electronic applications accepted. *Faculty research:* Multimedia technology, ethics in journalism, diversity, electronic portfolio assessment.

Wake Forest University, Graduate School of Arts and Sciences, Department of Communication, Winston-Salem, NC 27109. Offers speech communication (MA). *Program availability:* Part-time. *Degree requirements:* For master's, one foreign language, thesis. *Entrance requirements:* For master's, GRE General Test, writing sample. Additional exam requirements/recommendations for international students: Required—TOEFL (minimum score 79 iBT). Electronic applications accepted.

Washington University in St. Louis, School of Medicine, Program in Audiology and Communication Sciences, St. Louis, MO 63110. Offers audiology (Au D); deaf education (MS); speech and hearing sciences (PhD). *Accreditation:* ASHA (one or more programs are accredited). *Faculty:* 22 full-time (12 women), 18 part-time/adjunct (12 women). *Students:* 67 full-time (61 women). Average age 24. 129 applicants, 34% accepted, 20 enrolled. In 2017, 8 master's, 14 doctorates awarded. *Degree requirements:* For master's, comprehensive exam, thesis, independent study project, oral exam; for doctorate, comprehensive exam, thesis/dissertation, capstone project. *Entrance requirements:* For master's and doctorate, GRE General Test, minimum B average in previous college/university coursework (recommended). Additional exam requirements/recommendations for international students: Required—TOEFL (minimum score 100 iBT). *Application deadline:* For fall admission, 2/15 for domestic and international students. Application fee: $25. Electronic applications accepted. *Expenses:* $38,000 per academic year (all-inclusive). *Financial support:* In 2017–18, 67 students received support, including 67 fellowships with full and partial tuition reimbursements available (averaging $17,879 per year), 6 teaching assistantships with partial tuition reimbursements available (averaging $1,500 per year); Federal Work-Study, scholarships/grants, traineeships, health care benefits, tuition waivers (partial), and unspecified assistantships also available. Financial award application deadline: 2/15; financial award applicants required to submit FAFSA. *Faculty research:* Audiology, deaf education, speech and hearing sciences, sensory neuroscience. *Unit head:* Dr. William W. Clark, Program Director, 314-747-0104, Fax: 314-747-0105. *Application contact:* Beth Elliott, Director, Finance and Student/Academic Affairs, 314-747-0104, Fax: 314-747-0105, E-mail: elliottb@wustl.edu. Website: http://pacs.wustl.edu/

Technical Communication

Auburn University, Graduate School, College of Liberal Arts, Department of English, Auburn University, AL 36849. Offers MA, MTPC, PhD, Graduate Certificate. *Program availability:* Part-time. *Faculty:* 66 full-time (33 women), 8 part-time/adjunct (4 women). *Students:* 25 full-time (14 women), 29 part-time (18 women); includes 6 minority (5 Black or African American, non-Hispanic/Latino; 1 Hispanic/Latino), 1 international. Average age 30. 57 applicants, 60% accepted, 17 enrolled. In 2017, 14 master's, 7 doctorates, 1 other advanced degree awarded. *Degree requirements:* For master's, one foreign language, thesis optional, written exam; for doctorate, 2 foreign languages, thesis/dissertation, oral and written exams. *Entrance requirements:* For master's, GRE General Test, sample of written work; for doctorate, GRE General Test, GRE Subject Test, sample of written work. *Application deadline:* Applications are processed on a rolling basis. Application fee: $50 ($60 for international students). Electronic applications accepted. *Expenses:* Tuition, state resident: full-time $10,974; part-time $519 per credit hour. Tuition, nonresident: full-time $29,658; part-time $1557 per credit hour. *Required fees:* $816 per semester. Tuition and fees vary according to degree level and program. *Financial support:* Fellowships, teaching assistantships, and Federal Work-Study available. Support available to part-time students. Financial award application deadline: 3/15; financial award applicants required to submit FAFSA. *Faculty research:* English literature, American literature, linguistics, rhetoric and composition, literary theory. *Unit head:* Dr. Jeremy M. Downes, Chair, 334-844-9079. *Application contact:* Dr. George Flowers, Dean of the Graduate School, 334-844-2125.

See Display on page 339 and Close-Up on page 433.

Boise State University, College of Arts and Sciences, Department of English, Boise, ID 83725-0399. Offers English literature (MA); English, rhetoric and composition (MA); teaching English language (MA); technical communication (MA). *Program availability:* Part-time. *Faculty:* 26. *Students:* 44 full-time (28 women), 38 part-time (29 women); includes 6 minority (2 American Indian or Alaska Native, non-Hispanic/Latino; 2 Asian, non-Hispanic/Latino; 1 Hispanic/Latino; 1 Two or more races, non-Hispanic/Latino), 3 international. Average age 33. 242 applicants, 15% accepted, 28 enrolled. In 2017, 29 master's awarded. *Degree requirements:* For master's, thesis (for some programs). *Entrance requirements:* For master's, GRE General Test, minimum GPA of 3.0. Additional exam requirements/recommendations for international students: Required—TOEFL (minimum score 550 paper-based; 80 iBT), IELTS (minimum score 6). *Application deadline:* For fall admission, 4/15 for domestic and international students; for spring admission, 10/15 for domestic and international students. Application fee: $65 ($95 for international students). Electronic applications accepted. *Expenses:* Tuition, state resident: full-time $6471; part-time $390 per credit. Tuition, nonresident: full-time $21,787; part-time $685 per credit. *Required fees:* $2283; $100 per term. Part-time tuition and fees vary according to course load and program. *Financial support:* Teaching assistantships, scholarships/grants, and unspecified assistantships available. Financial award application deadline: 1/15; financial award applicants required to submit FAFSA. *Unit head:* Dr. Michelle Payne, Chair, 208-426-3426, Fax: 208-426-4373, E-mail: mpayne@boisestate.edu. *Application contact:* Dr. Tom Hillard, Director, 208-426-2991, E-mail: thomashillard@boisestate.edu.
Website: http://english.boisestate.edu/graduate-programs/

Bowling Green State University, Graduate College, College of Arts and Sciences, Department of English, Program in English, Bowling Green, OH 43403. Offers English (MA, PhD); literature (MA); rhetoric and writing (PhD); scientific and technical communication (MA). *Program availability:* Part-time. *Degree requirements:* For master's, thesis or alternative; for doctorate, comprehensive exam, thesis/dissertation, foreign language or proficiency in Old English. *Entrance requirements:* For master's and doctorate, GRE General Test. Additional exam requirements/recommendations for international students: Required—TOEFL. Electronic applications accepted. *Faculty research:* Postmodern literary theory, rhetorical theory, ethnic American literature, literature and culture, composition pedagogy.

Drexel University, College of Arts and Sciences, Department of Communication, Culture and Media, Program in Communication, Philadelphia, PA 19104-2875. Offers public communication (MS); science communication (MS); technical communication (MS). *Program availability:* Part-time, evening/weekend. *Degree requirements:* For master's, internship, professional portfolio. *Entrance requirements:* For master's, GRE or minimum GPA of 3.0. Additional exam requirements/recommendations for international students: Required—TOEFL. Electronic applications accepted.

East Carolina University, Graduate School, Thomas Harriot College of Arts and Sciences, Department of English, Greenville, NC 27858-4353. Offers creative writing (MA); English studies (MA); linguistics (MA); literature (MA); multicultural and transnational literatures (MA, Certificate); professional communication (Certificate); rhetoric and composition (MA); rhetoric, writing, and professional communication (PhD); teaching English in the two-year college (Certificate); teaching English to speakers of other languages (MA, Certificate); technical and professional communication (MA). *Program availability:* Part-time, evening/weekend, online learning. *Students:* 40 full-time (27 women), 74 part-time (57 women); includes 33 minority (23 Black or African American, non-Hispanic/Latino; 2 Asian, non-Hispanic/Latino; 4 Hispanic/Latino; 4 Two or more races, non-Hispanic/Latino). Average age 35. 36 applicants, 94% accepted, 25 enrolled. In 2017, 23 master's, 4 doctorates, 24 other advanced degrees awarded. *Degree requirements:* For master's, comprehensive exam, thesis optional; for doctorate, comprehensive exam, thesis/dissertation. *Entrance requirements:* For master's, GRE General Test or MAT; for doctorate, GRE General Test or MAT, writing samples. Additional exam requirements/recommendations for international students: Recommended—TOEFL (minimum score 78 iBT), IELTS (minimum score 6.5), TWE. *Application deadline:* For fall admission, 7/31 priority date for domestic students, 2/1 priority date for international students; for spring admission, 11/30 priority date for domestic students, 10/1 priority date for international students. Applications are processed on a rolling basis. Application fee: $75. Electronic applications accepted. *Expenses:* Tuition, state resident: full-time $4749; part-time $297 per credit hour. Tuition, nonresident: full-time $17,898; part-time $1119 per credit hour. *Required fees:* $2691; $224 per credit hour. Part-time tuition and fees vary according to course load and program. *Financial support:* Research assistantships with partial tuition reimbursements, teaching assistantships with partial tuition reimbursements, and Federal Work-Study available. Support available to part-time students. Financial award application deadline: 3/1. *Faculty research:* Technical and professional communication, rhetoric/composition, multicultural and transnational literature, creative writing, film studies. *Unit head:* Dr. Marianne Montgomery, Chair, 252-328-6687, E-mail: montgomerym@ecu.edu. *Application contact:* Dean of Graduate School, 252-328-6012, Fax: 252-328-6071, E-mail: gradschool@ecu.edu.
Website: http://www.ecu.edu/cs-cas/engl/

Eastern Michigan University, Graduate School, College of Arts and Sciences, Department of English Language and Literature, Programs in Written Communication, Ypsilanti, MI 48197. Offers technical communication (Graduate Certificate); written communication (MA). *Program availability:* Part-time, evening/weekend, online learning. *Students:* 1 full-time (0 women), 18 part-time (14 women); includes 5 minority (3 Black or African American, non-Hispanic/Latino; 1 Asian, non-Hispanic/Latino; 1 Hispanic/Latino). Average age 36. 8 applicants, 88% accepted, 6 enrolled. In 2017, 8 master's awarded. *Entrance requirements:* Additional exam requirements/recommendations for international students: Required—TOEFL. *Application deadline:* Applications are processed on a rolling basis. Application fee: $45. *Financial support:* Fellowships, research assistantships with full tuition reimbursements, teaching assistantships with full tuition reimbursements, career-related internships or fieldwork, Federal Work-Study, institutionally sponsored loans, scholarships/grants, tuition waivers (partial), and unspecified assistantships available. Support available to part-time students. Financial award applicants required to submit FAFSA. *Application contact:* Dr. Steve Benninghoff, Program Coordinator, 734-487-2075, Fax: 734-483-9744, E-mail: steve.benninghoff@emich.edu.

Eastern Washington University, Graduate Studies, College of Arts, Letters and Education, Department of English, Cheney, WA 99004-2431. Offers literature (MA); rhetoric, composition, and technical communication (MA); teaching English as a second language (MA). *Faculty:* 14. *Students:* 61 full-time (40 women), 11 part-time (9 women); includes 3 minority (1 Asian, non-Hispanic/Latino; 2 Hispanic/Latino), 7 international. Average age 34. 91 applicants, 52% accepted, 33 enrolled. In 2017, 32 master's awarded. *Degree requirements:* For master's, comprehensive exam, thesis or alternative. *Entrance requirements:* For master's, GRE General Test, minimum GPA of 3.0. Additional exam requirements/recommendations for international students: Required—TOEFL (minimum score 580 paper-based; 92 iBT), IELTS (minimum score 7), PTE (minimum score 6). *Application deadline:* For fall admission, 4/1 priority date for domestic students; for spring admission, 1/15 for domestic students. Applications are processed on a rolling basis. Application fee: $50. *Expenses:* Tuition, state resident: full-time $11,191; part-time $373.06 per credit. Tuition, nonresident: full-time $25,995; part-time $866.52 per credit. *Financial support:* Teaching assistantships with partial tuition reimbursements, career-related internships or fieldwork, Federal Work-Study, institutionally sponsored loans, scholarships/grants, health care benefits, tuition waivers (partial), and unspecified assistantships available. Support available to part-time students. Financial award application deadline: 2/1; financial award applicants required to submit FAFSA. *Application contact:* Kathy White, Advisor/Recruiter for Graduate Studies, 509-359-2491, E-mail: gradprograms@ewu.edu.
Website: http://www.ewu.edu/CALE/Programs/English.xml

Harvard University, Harvard Graduate School of Education, Master's Programs in Education, Cambridge, MA 02138. Offers arts in education (Ed M); education policy and management (Ed M); higher education (Ed M); human development and psychology (Ed M); international education policy (Ed M); language and literacy (Ed M); learning and teaching (Ed M); mind, brain, and education (Ed M); prevention science and practice (Ed M); school leadership (Ed M); special studies (Ed M); teacher education (Ed M); technology, innovation, and education (Ed M). *Program availability:* Part-time. *Entrance requirements:* For master's, GRE General Test, statement of purpose, 3 letters of recommendation, resume, official transcripts. Additional exam requirements/recommendations for international students: Required—TOEFL (minimum score 613 paper-based; 104 iBT), TWE (minimum score 5). Electronic applications accepted. *Faculty research:* Learning and development, educational leadership and organizations, education policy analysis.

Indiana University–Purdue University Indianapolis, School of Engineering and Technology, MS in Technology Program, Indianapolis, IN 46202. Offers applied data management and analytics (MS); facilities management (MS); information security and assurance (MS); motorsports (MS); organizational leadership (MS); technical communication (MS). *Program availability:* Online learning.

Lawrence Technological University, College of Arts and Sciences, Southfield, MI 48075-1058. Offers bioinformatics (Graduate Certificate); computer science (MS), including data science, big data, and data mining, intelligent systems; educational technology (MA), including robotics; instructional design, communication, and presentation (Graduate Certificate); integrated science (MA); science education (MA); technical and professional communication (MS, Graduate Certificate); writing for the digital age (Graduate Certificate). *Program availability:* Part-time, evening/weekend. *Faculty:* 6 full-time (2 women), 7 part-time/adjunct (3 women). *Students:* 34 part-time (15 women); includes 4 minority (1 Black or African American, non-Hispanic/Latino; 2 Asian, non-Hispanic/Latino; 1 Hispanic/Latino), 7 international. Average age 31. 84 applicants, 15% accepted, 10 enrolled. In 2017, 14 master's awarded. *Degree requirements:* For master's, thesis (for some programs). *Entrance requirements:* Additional exam requirements/recommendations for international students: Required—TOEFL (minimum score 550 paper-based; 79 iBT), IELTS (minimum score 6.5). *Application deadline:* For fall admission, 5/27 for international students; for spring admission, 10/8 for international students; for summer admission, 2/14 for international students. Applications are processed on a rolling basis. Application fee: $50. Electronic applications accepted. *Expenses:* Tuition: Full-time $15,274; part-time $1091 per credit. One-time fee: $150. *Financial support:* In 2017–18, 8 students received support. Scholarships/grants and tuition reduction available. Financial award application deadline: 4/1; financial award applicants required to submit FAFSA. *Faculty research:* Computer analysis of music, machine learning of literature and lyrics, customer sentiments and response analysis through social media, peta-scale computing in astronomical databases, early detection of diseases with pattern recognition. *Total annual research expenditures:* $242,460. *Unit head:* Glen Bauer, Interim Dean, 248-204-3532, Fax: 248-204-3518, E-mail: scidean@ltu.edu. *Application contact:* Jane Rohrback, Director of Admissions, 248-204-3160, Fax: 248-204-2228, E-mail: admissions@ltu.edu.

Minnesota State University Mankato, College of Graduate Studies and Research, College of Arts and Humanities, Department of English, Mankato, MN 56001. Offers communication and composition (MA); creative writing (MFA); English studies (MA); teaching English as a second language (MA, Certificate); technical communication (MA, Certificate). *Program availability:* Part-time. *Degree requirements:* For master's, one foreign language, comprehensive exam, thesis or alternative. *Entrance requirements:* For master's, minimum GPA of 3.0 during previous 2 years, writing sample (MFA). Additional exam requirements/recommendations for international students: Required—TOEFL (minimum score 500 paper-based; 61 iBT). Electronic applications accepted.

Missouri University of Science and Technology, Department of English and Technical Communication, Rolla, MO 65409. Offers technical communication (MS). *Expenses:* Tuition, state resident: full-time $7391; part-time $3696 per year. Tuition,

nonresident: full-time $21,712; part-time $10,857 per year. *Required fees:* $728; $564 per unit. Tuition and fees vary according to course load.

Missouri Western State University, Program in Written Communication, St. Joseph, MO 64507-2294. Offers teaching of writing (Graduate Certificate); technical communication (MAA); writing studies (MAA). *Program availability:* Part-time. *Students:* 6 full-time (5 women), 6 part-time (4 women), 6 international. Average age 31. 4 applicants, 100% accepted, 4 enrolled. In 2017, 2 master's, 2 other advanced degrees awarded. *Entrance requirements:* For master's, minimum undergraduate GPA of 3.0, portfolio, 3 letters of reference. Additional exam requirements/recommendations for international students: Recommended—TOEFL (minimum score 79 iBT), IELTS (minimum score 6). *Application deadline:* For fall admission, 7/15 for domestic and international students; for spring admission, 10/1 for domestic and international students; for summer admission, 3/15 for domestic students. Applications are processed on a rolling basis. Application fee: $45 ($50 for international students). Electronic applications accepted. *Expenses:* Tuition, state resident: full-time $6391; part-time $336 per credit hour. Tuition, nonresident: full-time $11,483; part-time $604 per credit hour. *Required fees:* $542; $99 per credit hour. $176 per semester. One-time fee: $45. Tuition and fees vary according to course load and program. *Financial support:* Scholarships/grants and unspecified assistantships available. Support available to part-time students. *Unit head:* Dr. Michael Charlton, Associate Professor, 816-271-4310, E-mail: mcharlton@missouriwestern.edu. *Application contact:* Dr. Benjamin D. Caldwell, Dean of the Graduate School, 816-271-4394, Fax: 816-271-4525, E-mail: graduate@missouriwestern.edu.
Website: https://www.missouriwestern.edu/eml/maawc/

Montana Tech of The University of Montana, Department of Technical Communication, Butte, MT 59701-8997. Offers MS. *Program availability:* Part-time. *Degree requirements:* For master's, project or thesis. *Entrance requirements:* For master's, GRE General Test, minimum GPA of 3.0. Additional exam requirements/recommendations for international students: Required—TOEFL (minimum score 545 paper-based; 78 iBT), IELTS (minimum score 6.5). Electronic applications accepted. *Faculty research:* Environmental concerns and the Big Hole River, history of Butte mining, African studies, multicultural communications.

New Jersey Institute of Technology, College of Science and Liberal Arts, Newark, NJ 07102. Offers applied mathematics (MS); applied physics (MS, PhD); applied statistics (MS, Certificate); biology (MS, PhD); biostatistics (MS); chemistry (MS, PhD); environmental and sustainability policy (MS); environmental science (MS, PhD); history (MA, MAT); materials science and engineering (MS, PhD); mathematical and computational finance (MS); mathematical sciences (PhD); pharmaceutical chemistry (MS); professional and technical communications (MS); technical communication essentials (Certificate). *Program availability:* Part-time, evening/weekend. *Students:* Average age 28. 504 applicants, 64% accepted, 65 enrolled. In 2017, 81 master's, 18 doctorates, 1 other advanced degree awarded. Terminal master's awarded for partial completion of doctoral program. *Entrance requirements:* For master's, GRE General Test; for doctorate, GRE General Test, minimum graduate GPA of 3.5. Additional exam requirements/recommendations for international students: Required—TOEFL (minimum score 550 paper-based; 79 iBT). *Application deadline:* For fall admission, 6/1 priority date for domestic students, 5/1 priority date for international students; for spring admission, 11/15 priority date for domestic and international students. Applications are processed on a rolling basis. Application fee: $75. Electronic applications accepted. *Expenses:* Contact institution. *Financial support:* In 2017–18, 106 students received support, including 8 fellowships (averaging $3,436 per year), 51 research assistantships (averaging $23,452 per year), 91 teaching assistantships (averaging $25,553 per year); scholarships/grants, traineeships, and unspecified assistantships also available. Financial award application deadline: 1/15. *Faculty research:* Biophotonics and bioimaging, morphogenetic patterning, embryogenesis, biological fluid dynamics, applied research in the mathematical sciences. *Unit head:* Dr. Kevin Belfield, Dean, 973-596-3676, Fax: 973-565-0586, E-mail: kevin.d.belfield@njit.edu. *Application contact:* Stephen Eck, Director of Admissions, 973-596-3300, Fax: 973-596-3461, E-mail: admissions@njit.edu.
Website: http://csla.njit.edu/

North Carolina State University, Graduate School, College of Humanities and Social Sciences, Department of English, Program in Technical Communication, Raleigh, NC 27695. Offers MS. *Degree requirements:* For master's, thesis optional. *Entrance requirements:* For master's, GRE General Test. Electronic applications accepted. *Faculty research:* Workplace writing, organizational socialization and power, integrated and multimedia documentation systems, technical communication management, usability testing theories.

Northeastern University, College of Professional Studies, Boston, MA 02115-5096. Offers applied nutrition (MS); college athletics administration (MSL); commerce and economic development (MS); corporate and organizational communication (MS); criminal justice (MS); digital media (MPS); elearning and instructional design (M Ed); elementary education (MAT); geographic information technology (MPS); global studies and international relations (MS); higher education administration (M Ed); homeland security (MA); human services (MS); informatics (MPS); leadership (MS); learning analytics (M Ed); learning and instruction (M Ed); nonprofit management (MS); professional sports administration (MSL); project management (MS); regulatory affairs for drugs, biologics, and medical devices (MS); respiratory care leadership (MS); special education (M Ed); technical communication (MS). *Program availability:* Part-time, evening/weekend, 100% online, blended/hybrid learning. *Faculty:* 82 full-time (51 women), 853 part-time/adjunct (366 women). *Students:* 5,278 part-time (3,230 women). In 2017, 1,586 master's awarded. *Application deadline:* Applications are processed on a rolling basis. Application fee: $0. Electronic applications accepted. *Expenses:* Contact institution. *Financial support:* Applicants required to submit FAFSA. *Unit head:* Dr. Mary Loeffelholz, Dean of the College of Professional Studies. *Application contact:* E-mail: cpsadmissions@northeastern.edu.
Website: https://cps.northeastern.edu/

Texas State University, The Graduate College, College of Liberal Arts, Program in Technical Communication, San Marcos, TX 78666. Offers MA. *Program availability:* Part-time. *Faculty:* 7 full-time (3 women), 1 (woman) part-time/adjunct. *Students:* 5 full-time (2 women), 19 part-time (14 women); includes 5 minority (1 Black or African American, non-Hispanic/Latino; 4 Hispanic/Latino). Average age 30. 10 applicants, 100% accepted, 4 enrolled. In 2017, 14 master's awarded. *Degree requirements:* For master's, comprehensive exam, thesis optional. *Entrance requirements:* For master's, baccalaureate degree from regionally-accredited institution with minimum GPA of 2.75 on last 60 undergraduate semester hours, 3.0 in minimum of 12 hours of undergraduate English courses; portfolio; 2 non-fiction prose documents with one academic research paper. Additional exam requirements/recommendations for international students: Required—TOEFL (minimum score 550 paper-based; 78 iBT), IELTS (minimum score 6.5). *Application deadline:* For fall admission, 1/15 priority date for domestic and international students; for spring admission, 11/1 for domestic students, 10/1 for international students; for summer admission, 4/15 for domestic students, 3/15 for international students. Applications are processed on a rolling basis. Application fee: $40 ($90 for international students). Electronic applications accepted. *Expenses:* Tuition, state resident: full-time $7868; part-time $3934 per semester. Tuition, nonresident: full-time $17,828; part-time $8914 per semester. *Required fees:* $2092; $1435 per semester. Tuition and fees vary according to course load. *Financial support:* In 2017–18, 11 students received support, including 2 teaching assistantships (averaging $14,425 per year); research assistantships, Federal Work-Study, institutionally sponsored loans, scholarships/grants, health care benefits, and unspecified assistantships also available. Support available to part-time students. Financial award application deadline: 3/1; financial award applicants required to submit FAFSA. *Unit head:* Dr. Miriam Williams, Graduate Advisor, 512-245-3015, Fax: 512-245-8546, E-mail: mw32@txstate.edu. *Application contact:* Dr. Andrea Golato, Dean of Graduate School, 512-245-2581, Fax: 512-245-8365, E-mail: gradcollege@txstate.edu.
Website: http://matc.english.txstate.edu/

University of Houston–Downtown, College of Humanities and Social Sciences, Department of English, Program in Technical Communication, Houston, TX 77002. Offers MS. *Program availability:* Part-time, evening/weekend. *Faculty:* 4 full-time (2 women). *Students:* 9 full-time (3 women), 19 part-time (14 women); includes 14 minority (7 Black or African American, non-Hispanic/Latino; 1 Asian, non-Hispanic/Latino; 6 Hispanic/Latino). Average age 35. 8 applicants, 88% accepted, 6 enrolled. In 2017, 2 master's awarded. *Entrance requirements:* For master's, GRE (for students with lower than 3.0 GPA), essay, resume, 2 letters of recommendation, transcripts. Additional exam requirements/recommendations for international students: Required—TOEFL (minimum score 600 paper-based; 86 iBT). *Application deadline:* For fall admission, 7/15 for domestic and international students; for spring admission, 11/15 for domestic and international students; for summer admission, 4/20 for domestic and international students. Application fee: $35 ($60 for international students). Electronic applications accepted. *Expenses:* $335 per credit resident; $700 per credit non-resident. *Financial support:* Federal Work-Study and scholarships/grants available. Financial award application deadline: 4/1; financial award applicants required to submit FAFSA. *Faculty research:* Environmental rhetoric, instructional design, usability, assessment, presentation slides. *Unit head:* Dr. Paul Kintzele, Chair, 713-221-8090, Fax: 713-226-5205, E-mail: kintzelep@uhd.edu. *Application contact:* Ceshia Love, Director of Admissions, 713-221-8093, Fax: 713-223-7408, E-mail: gradadmissions@uhd.edu.
Website: https://www.uhd.edu/academics/humanities/graduate-programs/master-science-technical-communication/Pages/mstc-index.aspx

University of Nebraska at Omaha, Graduate Studies, College of Arts and Sciences, Department of English, Omaha, NE 68182. Offers advanced writing (Certificate); English (MA); teaching English to speakers of other languages (Certificate); technical communication (Certificate). *Program availability:* Part-time, evening/weekend. *Degree requirements:* For master's, comprehensive exam, thesis (for some programs). *Entrance requirements:* For master's, GRE or MAT, minimum GPA of 3.0, transcripts, 3 letters of recommendation, statement of purpose, writing sample; for Certificate, minimum GPA of 3.0, transcripts, statement of purpose. Additional exam requirements/recommendations for international students: Required—TOEFL, IELTS, PTE. Electronic applications accepted.

University of Nebraska at Omaha, Graduate Studies, College of Communication, Fine Arts and Media, School of Communication, Omaha, NE 68182. Offers communication (MA); human resources and training (Certificate); technical communication (Certificate). *Program availability:* Part-time, evening/weekend. *Degree requirements:* For master's, comprehensive exam, thesis (for some programs). *Entrance requirements:* For master's, minimum GPA of 3.0, 15 undergraduate communication courses, resume, statement of purpose, 3 letters of recommendation. Additional exam requirements/recommendations for international students: Required—TOEFL, IELTS, PTE. Electronic applications accepted.

University of South Florida, Innovative Education, Tampa, FL 33620-9951. Offers adult, career and higher education (Graduate Certificate), including college teaching, leadership in developing human resources, leadership in higher education; Africana studies (Graduate Certificate), including diasporas and health disparities, genocide and human rights; aging studies (Graduate Certificate), including gerontology; art research (Graduate Certificate), including museum studies; business foundations (Graduate Certificate); chemical and biomedical engineering (Graduate Certificate), including materials science and engineering, water, health and sustainability; child and family studies (Graduate Certificate), including positive behavior support; civil and industrial engineering (Graduate Certificate), including transportation systems analysis; community and family health (Graduate Certificate), including maternal and child health, social marketing and public health, violence and injury: prevention and intervention, women's health; criminology (Graduate Certificate), including criminal justice administration; data science for public administration (Graduate Certificate); digital humanities (Graduate Certificate); educational measurement and research (Graduate Certificate), including evaluation; English (Graduate Certificate), including comparative literary studies, creative writing, professional and technical communication; entrepreneurship (Graduate Certificate); environmental health (Graduate Certificate), including safety management; epidemiology and biostatistics (Graduate Certificate), including applied biostatistics, biostatistics, concepts and tools of epidemiology, epidemiology, epidemiology of infectious diseases; geography, environment and planning (Graduate Certificate), including community development, environmental policy and management, geographical information systems; geology (Graduate Certificate), including hydrogeology; global health (Graduate Certificate), including disaster management, global health and Latin American and Caribbean studies, global health practice, humanitarian assistance, infection control; government and international affairs (Graduate Certificate), including Cuban studies, globalization studies; health policy and management (Graduate Certificate), including health management and leadership, public health policy and programs; hearing specialist: early intervention (Graduate Certificate); industrial and management systems engineering (Graduate Certificate), including systems engineering, technology management; information studies (Graduate Certificate), including school library media specialist; information systems/decision sciences (Graduate Certificate), including analytics and business intelligence; instructional technology (Graduate Certificate), including distance education, Florida digital/virtual educator, instructional design, multimedia design, Web design; internal medicine, bioethics and medical humanities (Graduate Certificate), including biomedical ethics; Latin American and Caribbean studies (Graduate Certificate); leadership for coastal resiliency planning (Graduate Certificate); mass communications (Graduate Certificate), including multimedia journalism; mathematics and statistics (Graduate Certificate), including mathematics; medicine (Graduate Certificate), including aging and neuroscience, bioinformatics, biotechnology, brain fitness and memory management, clinical investigation, hand and upper limb rehabilitation, health informatics, health sciences, integrative weight management, intellectual property, medicine and gender, metabolic and nutritional medicine, metabolic cardiology, pharmacy sciences; national and competitive intelligence (Graduate Certificate); nursing (Graduate Certificate), including simulation based academic fellowship in advanced pain management; psychological and social foundations (Graduate Certificate), including career counseling, college teaching, diversity in education, mental health counseling, school counseling; public affairs (Graduate Certificate), including nonprofit management, public management, research administration; public health (Graduate Certificate), including assessing chemical toxicity and public health risks, health equity,

Technical Communication

pharmacoepidemiology, public health generalist, toxicology, translational research in adolescent behavioral health; public health practices (Graduate Certificate), including planning for healthy communities; rehabilitation and mental health counseling (Graduate Certificate), including integrative mental health care, marriage and family therapy, rehabilitation technology; secondary education (Graduate Certificate), including ESOL, foreign language education: culture and content, foreign language education: professional; social work (Graduate Certificate), including geriatric social work/clinical gerontology; special education (Graduate Certificate), including autism spectrum disorder, disabilities education: severe/profound; world languages (Graduate Certificate), including teaching English as a second language (TESL) or foreign language. *Unit head:* Dr. Cynthia DeLuca, Associate Vice President and Assistant Vice Provost, 813-974-3077, Fax: 813-974-7061, E-mail: deluca@usf.edu. *Application contact:* Owen Hooper, Director, Summer and Alternative Calendar Programs, 813-974-6917, E-mail: hooper@usf.edu.
Website: http://www.usf.edu/innovative-education/

University of Wisconsin–Stout, Graduate School, College of Arts, Humanities and Social Sciences, Menomonie, WI 54751. Offers design (MFA); technical and professional communication (MS). *Accreditation:* NASAD.

NORTH DAKOTA STATE UNIVERSITY
College of Arts, Humanities and Social Sciences

NDSU GRADUATE SCHOOL

 For more information, visit http://petersons.to/ndstateartshumanities

Programs of Study

The College of Arts, Humanities and Social Sciences at North Dakota State University equips students with the skills and knowledge to thrive in their professional and personal lives, including the following:

- Ability to think critically
- Ability to effectively communicate in all media
- Understanding the diverse ideas that constitute the intellectual marketplace
- Recognition of the significance of all traditions in creating cultures throughout the world

The college offers several graduate programs through eight of its twelve departments: Architecture and Landscape Architecture; Communication; Criminal Justice and Political Science; Emergency Management; English; History, Philosophy, and Religious Studies; Music; and Sociology and Anthropology.

Department of Architecture and Landscape Architecture: The Department of Architecture and Landscape Architecture focuses on the challenges related to designing landscapes and built environments. It offers a nationally accredited Master of Architecture (M.Arch.) program as well as a Master of Landscape Architecture (m.L.A.) for individuals interested in pursuing advanced careers in these fields.

Department of Communication: The Department of Communication provides students with the expertise to build rewarding careers in a wide variety of professions. Its graduate programs include the Master of Arts (M.A.) and Master of Science (M.S.) in Mass Communication and in Speech Communication, and the Doctor of Philosophy (Ph.D.) in Communication.

Department of Criminal Justice and Political Science: The Department of Criminal Justice and Political Science prepares students for positions that protect and serve people and communities, create and strengthen political and social systems, and enhance quality of life. It offers both M.S. and Ph.D. degrees in Criminal Justice.

Department of Emergency Management: The Department of Emergency Management trains students to protect people and communities, and it facilitates research that strengthens theory and practice in the field. It has two graduate programs: the M.S. in Emergency Management and Ph.D. in Emergency Management.

Department of English: The Department of English cultivates students' appreciation, knowledge, and understanding of the English language. It offers the following graduate programs: the M.A. in English Composition; M.A. in English Literature; and Ph.D. in English: Rhetoric, Writing, and Culture.

Department of History, Philosophy, and Religious Studies: The Department of History, Philosophy, and Religious Studies encourages active learning and provides diverse learning opportunities. It provides the M.A. in History and Ph.D. in History programs.

Challey School of Music: The Challey School of Music prepares students for excellence in musical performance and scholarship. It provides a Master of Music program with options in performance, conducting, and music education, as well as a Doctor of Musical Arts program with options in performance and conducting.

Department of Sociology and Anthropology: The Department of Sociology and Anthropology provides comprehensive study of human behavior in social settings. It has six graduate programs: the M.A. in Anthropology, M.S. in Anthropology, M.S. in Natural Resources Management (social science option), Ph.D. in Natural Resources Management (social science option), M.S. in Sociology, and an online master's in Community Development.

Research

Faculty members and students actively engage in research regarding a wide range of subjects. Faculty members are awarded millions of dollars in research grants and contracts annually, and their work is published in more than 100 peer-reviewed publications each year.

Students assist faculty members with their research and conduct individual research that contributes to the body of knowledge in their fields.

Financial Aid

Graduate students in the College of Arts, Humanities and Social Sciences may receive financial aid from employer tuition reimbursement programs, fellowships, graduate assistantships (teaching or research), loans (through federal programs or private lenders), military and veteran assistance, and scholarships from the university and private funders.

Cost of Study

The most current information on tuition and fees can be found online at https://www.ndsu.edu/onestop/accounts/tuition/.

Living and Housing Costs

Information about on-campus housing for graduate students can be found at www.ndsu.edu/reslife/general_apartment_information. While there is no specific residence hall for graduate students, they are able to live in the University apartments. There are also numerous housing options in the Fargo community.

Faculty

Faculty members, like Stephenson J. Beck, Ph.D., are talented teachers and scholars. Dr. Beck is an associate professor and the director of graduate studies in the Department of Communication. His research focuses on relational communication in groups, communication strategy, and macro-cognition. His goal is to understand how people alter messages to achieve individual and group goals and to examine how this process influences group processes and message perception.

Dr. Beck has authored and co-authored many articles and books about his research. He has also presented his work at several conferences, colloquia, and symposia. In addition, he has served on editorial boards of journals, participated in policy and planning and other committees, and operated a consulting practice.

Student Life

North Dakota State University provides students with the resources and opportunities to create vibrant and fulfilling college careers. They receive academic, career, support, and wellness services from the Career Center, Center for Writers, Office of International Student and Study Abroad Services, Office of Multicultural Programs, the Wallman Wellness Center, and others.

Social resources include arts and culture, community outreach, intramural sports, recreational programs, and student organizations.

Location

North Dakota State University is located on the eastern edge of North Dakota in Fargo, the state's largest community. With its sister city, Moorhead, Minnesota, directly across the Red River, Fargo is one of the largest metropolitan centers between Minneapolis and Seattle and offers a family-friendly environment with excellent schools, safe neighborhoods, and a low crime rate; an active arts and cultural scene, including a symphony, civic opera company, art museums, and community theater; and many places to shop and eat, including numerous restaurants, coffee shops, and a newly refurbished downtown district.

The University

In 1890, North Dakota State University became North Dakota's first land-grant university. Today, this esteemed research institution offers more than 14,300 students nearly 100 undergraduate majors, 86 master's programs, and 53 doctoral programs.

It is recognized nationally and internationally for providing high quality education, excellent service, and innovative research. In fact, the National Science Foundation determined that several of its programs rank within the top 100.

Applying

The North Dakota State University graduate school application procedure places responsibility on the applicant to gather all supporting credentials and verifying that the application file is complete. The deadline for submission is dependent upon the program. If no deadline is listed on the program's bulletin page, all application materials are due at least one month prior to the start of the semester.

Prospective students must file their application online. There is a $35 nonrefundable application fee. A statement of purpose—covering reasons for pursuing graduate study, special interests within the chosen discipline, and preparation, skills, and experience in the proposed field of study—is required for admission consideration and must be uploaded with the online application. Other requirements include three letters of recommendation; official transcripts from each college or university attended; and official GRE or GMAT scores if required. Some programs may have additional requirements, as stated on the individual program pages.

The online application and additional details regarding the application process are available at https://www.ndsu.edu/gradschool/prospective_students.

Correspondence and Information

College of Arts, Humanities and Social Sciences
Graduate School
North Dakota State University
Department 2820, P.O. Box 6050
Fargo, North Dakota 58108-6050
Phone: 701-231-7033
      800-608-6378 (toll-free)
E-mail: ndsu.grad.school@ndsu.edu
Website: www.ndsu.edu/gradschool
    facebook.com/ndsugradschool (Facebook)
    @NDSUGradSchool (Twitter)

The College of Arts, Humanities and Social Sciences is at the center of the Liberal and Fine Arts on the campus of NDSU. The departments in this college offer high-quality graduate degree programs in the humanities, social sciences, and the fine arts.

PRATT INSTITUTE
School of Liberal Arts

 For more information, visit http://petersons.to/prattmediastudies

Programs of Study

Pratt has been educating professionals for productive careers since its founding in 1887. Pratt's School of Liberal Arts offers an outstanding professional art and design education taught by a faculty of working professionals who bring high standards and current practices to the classroom. Faculty members have received more than eighteen Tiffany, Fulbright, and Guggenheim awards as well as other prestigious professional honors.

Pratt offers master's degrees in a variety of programs, including Master of Arts in Media Studies; Master of Fine Arts in Performance and Performance Studies; Master of Fine Arts in Writing, and Master of Art in History of Art and Design. Pratt also offers a dual degree in Art History and Library Science and a dual degree in Art History and Fine Art.

Graduates of Pratt's liberal arts programs have the competitive edge needed to obtain top administrative and creative positions in design studios, businesses, various industries, and arts organizations; Students can choose from a wide array of course offerings, including art and design history, comparative literature, philosophy, foreign languages, and social sciences. The graduate programs require the completion of 30 to 68 credits (75 credits for the M.A./M.F.A. dual-degree program) and last from 1-1/2 to 3 years, depending on the curriculum and the number of prerequisites that have been met at the time of admission. For the granting of degrees, all of the graduate programs require the submission of a thesis or a comparable effort.

Media Studies at Pratt is an intensive 30-credit, three-semester theory and practice M.A., shaped in relation to Pratt's art/design/architecture environment and to the lively social space and theoretical scene of Brooklyn and New York City. Classes in media theory and media practice are small, following seminar and workshop formats, and all are taught by professors on Pratt Institute's Brooklyn campus.

The graduate degree offers students the freedom and flexibility to design their own program of study. The M.A. in Media Studies at Pratt is designed to train students to think and work critically, whether their final destination is a Ph.D. program or a professional career in the arts, media, or communication.

The curriculum emphasizes studies of media in their various forms, including film, video, television, radio, writing, smart phones, and other computerized forms of media convergence. Alongside their theoretical investigations, students are also encouraged to become media makers. Guided by a diverse and exceptional faculty, students study the logics and processes of media, and they explore cultural technologies of expression, representation, and manipulation. Students learn to analyze a variety of media forms (cinema, photography, audio-phonic, and social media), along with the aesthetic, social, economic and political contexts in which these media operate. They also work also work on textual analysis, interpretation, and semiotics and gain expertise in media history and theory.

Research Facilities

The Pratt Library contains 186,589 bound volumes, serial backfiles, and other material (including government documents); 251,603 audiovisual materials; and 3,996 microforms. The library also subscribes to 925 periodicals.

Pratt maintains numerous studios, shops, and technical facilities for work in all media as well as state-of-the-art computer facilities. Digital arts labs include state-of-the-art Macintosh, PC/NT, and UNIX operating systems as well as digital video and audio systems. Pratt also has extensive gallery space for exhibitions.

Financial Aid

Financial aid awards are offered through a variety of institutional, state, and federally funded programs. These include Graduate Scholarships awarded by departments to incoming students on the basis of merit, endowed and restricted scholarships for continuing students, and student employment. Assistantships are awarded on a competitive basis to continuing students in all departments. Special alumni-sponsored fellowships are also available.

Cost of Study

Graduate tuition for 2018–19 is $32,004 per year (full-time, 18 credits, $1,778 per credit) and student fees are $1,980 per year. The cost of books and supplies varies widely, depending on the program in which the student is enrolled.

Living and Housing Costs

Campus housing continues to be expanded to meet students' needs and is available for single students on a first-come, first-served basis. Housing costs average $19,950 per academic year. Pratt offers limited graduate student housing two blocks away from the campus. There is a plentiful supply of moderately priced rentals in the immediate area and in adjacent neighborhoods for married students seeking housing and for those students choosing to reside off campus.

Student Group

In educating more than four generations of students to be creative, technically skilled, and adaptable professionals, Pratt has gained an international reputation that attracts about 4,800 undergraduate and graduate students annually from forty-eight states and eighty-four countries.

Location

Pratt Institute's 25-acre, parklike main campus is situated among the turn-of-the-century mansions, Victorian brownstones, and wide, tree-lined boulevards of Clinton Hill, one of Brooklyn's historic neighborhoods. Midtown Manhattan, the heart of New York City, is only 25 minutes away by subway and offers students a vast array of professional, cultural, and recreational opportunities. Pratt also maintains a satellite facility in Manhattan's Chelsea district. Pratt Manhattan houses the Institute's graduate arts and cultural management, communications/packaging design, design management, facilities management, and library and information science; it also offers Associate of Occupational Studies (A.O.S.) and Associate of Applied Science (A.A.S.) degree programs.

The Institute

A private, nonsectarian institute of higher education, Pratt Institute was founded by industrialist and philanthropist Charles Pratt. Changing with the needs and requirements of the professional world for which it prepares its graduates, Pratt today educates 3,439 undergraduate and 1,390 graduate students for careers in art and design, architecture, and library and information science.

Applying

The deadline for applications and all supporting materials, including portfolio, is January 5. Applicants should complete the application process online. Early submission of applications with all necessary credentials is highly desirable. Applications received after these dates are considered if openings exist in a particular program. For applicants who intend to file for financial aid, the FAFSA should be filed by March 1 for fall entrance and by October 1 for spring entrance.

Correspondence and Information

Graduate Admissions Office
Pratt Institute
200 Willoughby Avenue
Brooklyn, New York 11205
United States
Phone: 718-636-3514
     800-331-0834 (toll-free)
Fax: 718-399-4242
E-mail: admissions@pratt.edu
Websites: www.pratt.edu
     www.pratt.edu/admissions/request-information

THE FACULTY

Andrew Barnes, Dean of the School of Liberal Arts and Sciences
Sincere Brooks, Assistant to the Dean

HISTORY OF ART AND DESIGN
John Decker, Chair; Ph.D., UC Santa Barbara.
Evan Neely, Assistant Chair, Adjunct Assistant Professor; Ph.D., Columbia.
Sonya Abrego, Visiting Assistant Instructor; Ph.D., Bard.
Kira Albinsky, Visiting Instructor; M.A., Rutgers.
Kelly Rae Aldridge, Visiting Instructor; M.A., Stony Brook, SUNY.
Karen Bachmann, Visiting Assistant Professor; M.A., SUNY Purchase.
Lisa Banner, Visiting Associate Professor; Ph.D., NYU.
Agnes Berecz, Visiting Assistant Professor; Ph.D., Universite Paris I.
Liam Considine, Visiting Assistant Professor; Ph.D., NYU.
Corey D'Augustine, Visiting Assistant Professor; M.A., NYU.
Ed DeCarbo, Adjunct Associate Professor; Ph.D., Indiana.
Peter De Staebler, Assistant Professor, Ph.D., NYU.
Eva Diaz, Associate Professor; Ph.D., Princeton.
Mary Douglas Edwards, Adjunct Professor; Ph.D., Columbia.
Diana Gisolfi, Professor; Ph.D., Chicago.
Frima Fox Hofrichter, Professor; Ph.D., Rutgers.
Heather Horton, Visiting Assistant Professor; Ph.D., NYU.
Susan Karnet, Visiting Instructor; M.F.A., Hunter.
Dara Kiese, Visiting Assistant Professor; Ph.D., CUNY Graduate Center.
Vivien Knussi, Adjunct Instructor; Ph.D., Columbia.
Joseph Reid Kopta, Visiting Instructor; M.S., Pratt.

Pratt Institute

Gayle Rodda Kurtz, Adjunct Associate Professor; Ph.D., CUNY Graduate Center.
Tiffany Lambert, Visiting Instructor.
Thomas La Padula, Adjunct Professor, M.F.A., Syracuse.
Anca Lasc, Assistant Professor; Ph.D., USC.
Michele Licalsi, Visiting Assistant Professor; M.A., NYU.
William Lorenzo, Visiting Assistant Professor; B.F.A., CUNY, Brooklyn.
Elizabeth Meggs, Visiting Assistant Professor; B.F.A., Virginia Commonwealth.
Juan Monroy, Visiting Assistant Professor; Ph.D., NYU.
Marsha Morton, Professor; Ph.D., NYU.
Caterina Pierre, Visiting Associate Professor; Ph.D., The Graduate Center, CUNY.
Joyce Polistena, Adjunct Professor; Ph.D., CUNY Graduate Center, CCE.
Elena Rossi-Snook, Visiting Assistant Professor; M.A., University of East Anglia.
Ann Schoenfeld, Adjunct Assistant Professor; Ph.D., CUNY Graduate Center.
Dorothy Shepard, Adjunct Associate Professor; Ph.D., Bryn Mawr.
Elizabeth St. George, Visiting Instructor; M.A., Bard.
Adedoyin Teriba, Visiting Assistant Professor; M.A., Princeton.
Jack Toolin, Visiting Assistant Professor; M.F.A., San Jose State.
Alice Walkiewicz, Visiting Instructor; M.Phil., CUNY Graduate Center.
Bor-Hua Wang, Adjunct Assistant Professor; Ph.D., Columbia.
Sarah Wilkins, Visiting Assistant Professor; Ph.D., Rutgers.
Karyn Zieve, Visiting Assistant Professor; Ph.D., NYU.

MEDIA STUDIES

Mendi Obadike, Coordinator of Media Studies program, Assistant Professor, Ph.D., Duke.
Jonathan Beller, Professor; Ph.D., Duke.
Jayna Brown, Professor, Ph.D., Yale.
Allen Feldman, Visiting Professor; Ph.D., New School.
Ira Livingston, Professor; Ph.D., Stanford.
Minh-Ha Pham, Associate Professor; Ph.D., Berkeley.
Ethan Spigland, Professor; M.F.A., NYU.

PERFORMANCE AND PERFORMANCE STUDIES

Jennifer Miller, Coordinator of Performance and Performance Studies program, Professor.
Donald Andreasen, Adjunct Associate Professor; M.F.A., New School.
Youmna Chlala, Associate Professor; M.F.A., California College of the Arts.
Steven Doloff, Professor; Ph.D., CUNY Graduate Center.
Lisabeth During, Associate Professor; Ph.D., Cambridge (U.K.).
Ann Holder, Associate Professor; Ph.D. Boston College.
May Joseph, Professor, Global Studies.
Ira Livingston, Professor; Ph.D., Stanford.
Tracie Morris, Professor, Ph.D., NYU.
Mendi Obadike, Associate Professor; Ph.D., Duke.
Martha Wilson, Visiting Associate Professor; Artist and Gallery Director.

WRITING

Beth Loffreda, Chair.
Emily Beall, Adjunct Assistant Professor with CCE; M.A., Washington (Seattle).
Priscilla Becker, Adjunct Assistant Professor; M.F.A., Columbia.
Peter Catalanotto, Visiting Associate Professor; B.F.A., Pratt.
Diane Cohen, Visiting Instructor; M.A.. CUNY, Brooklyn.
Gabriel Cohen, Adjunct Assistant Professor; B.A., Wesleyan.
Jon Cotner, Visiting Instructor; M.A., St. John's.
Maria Damon, Professor; Ph.D., Stanford.
Amanda Davidson, Adjunct Assistant Professor; M.F.A., San Francisco State.
Steven Doloff, Professor; B.A., Stony Brook, SUNY.
Claire Donato, Visiting Assistant Professor; M.F.A., Brown.
Laura Elrick, Associate Professor; M.A., NYU.
David Gordon, Adjunct Associate Professor; M.F.A., Columbia.
James Hannaham, Associate Professor; M.F.A., Texas at Austin.
Christian Hawkey, Professor; M.F.A., University of Massachusetts.
Jason Helm, Visiting Assistant Professor; M.F.A., Sarah Lawrence.
Mary-Beth Hughes, Visiting Assistant Professor; B.A., Marymount Manhattan.
Samantha Hunt, Professor; M.F.A., Warren Wilson.
Lucy Ives, Visiting Assistant Professor; M.F.A., Iowa Writer's Workshop.
Jeff T. Johnson, Visiting Assistant Professor; M.F.A., New School.
Rachel Levitsky, Professor; M.F.A., Naropa.
Robert Lopez, Assistant Adjunct Professor; M.F.A., New School.
Max Ludington, Visiting Instructor; M.F.A., Columbia.
Anna Moschovakis, Adjunct Associate Professor; M.F.A., Bard.
Cecilia Muhlstein, Adjunct Assistant Professor, Tutor; UCLA.
Shelly Orla, Visiting Professor; M.F.A., Sarah Lawrence.
Eric Rosenblum, Adjunct Assistant Professor; M.F.A., Syracuse.
Jonathan Santlofer, Visiting Assistant Professor; M.F.A., Pratt.
Adrian Shirk, Visiting Instructor; M.F.A., Wyoming.
Ellery Washington, Associate Professor; M.A. equivalent, Sorbonne (Paris).
Uljana Wolf, Visting Assistant Professor; M.A., Berlin (Germany).
Gina Zucker, Visiting Assistant Professor; M.F.A., New School.

© 2017 Bob Handelman

© 2017 Bob Handelman

Section 17
Conflict Resolution and Mediation/Peace Studies

This section contains a directory of institutions offering graduate work in conflict resolution and mediation/peace studies, followed by an in-depth entry submitted by an institution that chose to prepare a detailed program description. Additional information about programs listed in the directory but not augmented by an in-depth entry may be obtained by writing directly to the dean of a graduate school or chair of a department at the address given in the directory.

For programs offering related work, see also in this book *Political Science and International Affairs* and *Public, Regional, and Industrial Affairs*. In another guide in this series:

Graduate Programs in Business, Education, Information Studies, Law & Social Work

See *Business Administration and Management* and *Law*

CONTENTS

Program Directory

Featured School: Display and Close-Up

See:

Conflict Resolution and Mediation/Peace Studies

Abilene Christian University, College of Graduate and Professional Studies, Conflict Management and Resolution Program, Addison, TX 75001. Offers conflict management (Certificate); conflict management and resolution (MA). *Program availability:* Part-time, evening/weekend, online learning. *Faculty:* 2 full-time (1 woman), 5 part-time/adjunct (1 woman). *Students:* 37 full-time (18 women), 18 part-time (10 women); includes 26 minority (19 Black or African American, non-Hispanic/Latino; 1 American Indian or Alaska Native, non-Hispanic/Latino; 3 Asian, non-Hispanic/Latino; 3 Hispanic/Latino). 45 applicants, 58% accepted, 22 enrolled. In 2017, 21 master's, 7 other advanced degrees awarded. *Degree requirements:* For master's, practicum. *Entrance requirements:* Additional exam requirements/recommendations for international students: Required—TOEFL (minimum score 80 iBT), IELTS (minimum score 6), PTE. *Application deadline:* For fall admission, 8/11 for domestic students; for winter admission, 10/1 for domestic students; for spring admission, 12/15 for domestic students; for summer admission, 4/15 for domestic students. Applications are processed on a rolling basis. Application fee: $50. Electronic applications accepted. *Expenses:* $831 per hour. *Financial support:* In 2017–18, 4 students received support. Available to part-time students. Application deadline: 4/1; applicants required to submit FAFSA. *Unit head:* Dr. Kipi Fleming, Program Director, 214-305-9500, E-mail: conflictresolution@acu.edu. *Application contact:* Graduate Advisor, 855-219-7300, E-mail: gradonline@acu.edu.
Website: http://www.acu.edu/online/academics/conflict-resolution-and-reconciliation.html

Abilene Christian University, College of Graduate and Professional Studies, Instruction and Learning Program, Abilene, TX 79699. Offers conflict management (M Ed); learning with emerging technologies (M Ed, Certificate). *Program availability:* Part-time, online only. *Faculty:* 2 full-time (1 woman), 1 part-time/adjunct (0 women). *Students:* 14 full-time (11 women); includes 3 minority (all Black or African American, non-Hispanic/Latino). 25 applicants, 44% accepted, 5 enrolled. *Degree requirements:* For master's, comprehensive exam, practicum. *Entrance requirements:* Additional exam requirements/recommendations for international students: Required—TOEFL (minimum score 80 iBT), IELTS (minimum score 6), PTE. *Application deadline:* For fall admission, 8/15 priority date for domestic students; for winter admission, 10/1 priority date for domestic students; for spring admission, 12/15 priority date for domestic students; for summer admission, 4/15 for domestic students. Applications are processed on a rolling basis. Application fee: $50. Electronic applications accepted. *Expenses:* $600 per hour. *Financial support:* Application deadline: 4/1; applicants required to submit FAFSA. *Unit head:* Dr. Peter Williams, Program Director, 214-721-0685, E-mail: peter.williams@acu.edu. *Application contact:* Graduate Admissions, 855-219-7300, E-mail: gradonline@acu.edu.
Website: http://www.acu.edu/online/academics/master-of-education-in-instructional-leadership.html

Abilene Christian University, College of Graduate and Professional Studies, Program in Higher Education, Addison, TX 75001. Offers conflict management (M Ed); enrollment management (M Ed). *Program availability:* Part-time, online only. *Faculty:* 1 full-time (0 women). *Students:* 34 full-time (24 women), 16 part-time (12 women); includes 21 minority (15 Black or African American, non-Hispanic/Latino; 1 American Indian or Alaska Native, non-Hispanic/Latino; 2 Asian, non-Hispanic/Latino; 3 Hispanic/Latino). 24 applicants, 67% accepted, 11 enrolled. In 2017, 28 master's awarded. *Degree requirements:* For master's, internship, capstone. *Entrance requirements:* Additional exam requirements/recommendations for international students: Required—TOEFL (minimum score 80 iBT), IELTS (minimum score 6), PTE. *Application deadline:* For fall admission, 8/15 priority date for domestic students; for winter admission, 10/1 priority date for domestic students; for spring admission, 12/15 priority date for domestic students; for summer admission, 4/15 for domestic students. Applications are processed on a rolling basis. Application fee: $50. Electronic applications accepted. *Expenses:* $726 per hour. *Financial support:* In 2017–18, 2 students received support. Scholarships/grants available. Financial award application deadline: 4/1; financial award applicants required to submit FAFSA. *Unit head:* Dr. Jason Morris, Graduate Director, 325-674-2830, Fax: 325-674-2123, E-mail: morrisj@acu.edu. *Application contact:* Graduate Advisor, 855-219-7300, E-mail: gradonline@acu.edu.
Website: http://www.acu.edu/online/academics/higher-education.html

American Public University System, AMU/APU Graduate Programs, Charles Town, WV 25414. Offers accounting (MS); applied business analytics (MS); business administration (MBA); criminal justice (MA); cybersecurity studies (MS); educational leadership (M Ed); environmental policy and management (MS); global security (DGS); health information management (MS); history (MA), including American military history, American Revolution, civil war, war since 1945, World War II; information technology (MS); international relations and conflict resolution (MA), including American politics and government, comparative government and development, general, international relations, public policy; national security studies (MA); nursing (MSN); political science (MA); public policy (MPP); reverse logistics management (MA), including comparative and security issues, conflict resolution, international and transnational security issues, peacekeeping; space studies (MS); sports management (MS); strategic intelligence (DSI); teaching (M Ed), including secondary social studies; transportation and logistics management (MA). *Program availability:* Part-time, evening/weekend, online only, 100% online. *Students:* 455 full-time (227 women), 7,939 part-time (3,353 women); includes 2,793 minority (1,429 Black or African American, non-Hispanic/Latino; 48 American Indian or Alaska Native, non-Hispanic/Latino; 205 Asian, non-Hispanic/Latino; 766 Hispanic/Latino; 62 Native Hawaiian or other Pacific Islander, non-Hispanic/Latino; 283 Two or more races, non-Hispanic/Latino), 101 international. Average age 37. In 2017, 2,977 master's awarded. *Degree requirements:* For master's, comprehensive exam or practicum. *Entrance requirements:* For master's, official transcript showing earned bachelor's degree from institution accredited by recognized accrediting body. Additional exam requirements/recommendations for international students: Required—TOEFL (minimum score 550 paper-based), IELTS (minimum score 6.5). *Application deadline:* Applications are processed on a rolling basis. Application fee: $0. Electronic applications accepted. *Expenses:* Tuition: Full-time $6300; part-time $350 per credit. *Required fees:* $300; $50 per course. *Financial support:* Scholarships/grants available. Financial award applicants required to submit FAFSA. *Unit head:* Dr. Wallace Boston, President, 877-468-6268, Fax: 304-728-2348, E-mail: president@apus.edu. *Application contact:* Yoci Deal, Associate Vice President, Graduate and International Admissions, 877-468-6268, Fax: 304-724-3764, E-mail: info@apus.edu.
Website: http://www.apus.edu

American University, School of International Service, Washington, DC 20016-8071. Offers comparative and regional studies (Certificate); cross-cultural communication (Certificate); development management (MS); ethics, peace, and global affairs (MA); European studies (Certificate); global environmental policy (MA, Certificate); global information technology (Certificate); global media (MA); international affairs (MA), including comparative and regional studies, global governance, politics, and security, international economic relations, natural resources and sustainable development, U.S. foreign policy and national security; international arts management (Certificate); international communication (MA, Certificate); international development (MA); international economic policy (Certificate); international economic relations (Certificate); international economics (MA); international peace and conflict resolution (MA, Certificate); international politics (Certificate); international relations (MA, PhD); international service (MIS); peacebuilding (Certificate); social enterprise (MA); the Americas (Certificate); United States foreign policy (Certificate); JD/MA. *Program availability:* Part-time, evening/weekend, 100% online. *Faculty:* 112 full-time (50 women), 46 part-time/adjunct (19 women). *Students:* 495 full-time (333 women), 518 part-time (276 women); includes 360 minority (95 Black or African American, non-Hispanic/Latino; 2 American Indian or Alaska Native, non-Hispanic/Latino; 60 Asian, non-Hispanic/Latino; 164 Hispanic/Latino; 39 Two or more races, non-Hispanic/Latino), 98 international. Average age 30. 1,559 applicants, 81% accepted, 356 enrolled. In 2017, 427 master's, 9 doctorates, 5 other advanced degrees awarded. Terminal master's awarded for partial completion of doctoral program. *Degree requirements:* For master's, one foreign language, comprehensive exam, thesis or alternative; for doctorate, one foreign language, comprehensive exam, thesis/dissertation. *Entrance requirements:* For master's, GRE; GMAT or GRE (for MA in social enterprise), transcripts, resume, 2 letters of recommendation, statement of purpose; for doctorate, GRE, transcripts, resume, 3 letters of recommendation, statement of purpose. Additional exam requirements/recommendations for international students: Required—TOEFL (minimum score 600 paper-based; 100 iBT). *Application deadline:* For fall admission, 1/15 for domestic students, 1/1 for international students; for spring admission, 10/1 for domestic students, 9/15 for international students. Application fee: $55. Electronic applications accepted. *Expenses:* Contact institution. *Financial support:* Research assistantships, teaching assistantships, institutionally sponsored loans, scholarships/grants, and unspecified assistantships available. Financial award application deadline: 1/15; financial award applicants required to submit FAFSA. *Application contact:* 202-885-1646, Fax: 202-885-1109, E-mail: sisgrad@american.edu.
Website: http://www.american.edu/sis/

The American University of Paris, Graduate Programs, Paris, France. Offers cross-cultural and sustainable business management (MA); cultural translation (MA); global communications (MA); global communications and civil society (MA); international affairs (MA); international affairs, conflict resolution and civil society development (MA); Middle East and Islamic studies (MA); Middle East and Islamic studies and international affairs (MA); public policy and international affairs (MA); public policy and international law (MA). *Degree requirements:* For master's, thesis (for some programs). *Entrance requirements:* For master's, minimum undergraduate GPA of 3.0. Additional exam requirements/recommendations for international students: Recommended—TOEFL, IELTS. Electronic applications accepted.

Anabaptist Mennonite Biblical Seminary, Graduate and Professional Programs, Elkhart, IN 46517-1999. Offers chaplaincy (M Div); Christian faith formation (M Div); Christian formation (MA); Christian spiritual formation (Certificate); divinity (M Div); pastoral ministry (M Div); pastoral theology for financial professionals (Certificate); peace studies (M Div), including environmental sustainability leadership (M Div, MA); theological studies (M Div, Certificate), including peace studies (M Div), theology and ethics (M Div); theology and peace studies (MA), including conflict transformation, environmental sustainability leadership (M Div, MA), international development administration; United Methodist leadership (M Div). Conflict transformation and environmental sustainability leadership concentrations offered in cooperation with Goshen College; international development administration offered in cooperation with Andrews University. *Accreditation:* ACIPE; ATS. *Program availability:* Part-time, 100% online, blended/hybrid learning. *Degree requirements:* For master's, variable foreign language requirement, comprehensive exam (for some programs), thesis optional, senior interview. *Entrance requirements:* For master's, undergraduate degree transcripts, 3 letters of reference, essay. Additional exam requirements/recommendations for international students: Required—TOEFL (minimum score 90 iBT); Recommended—IELTS (minimum score 7). Electronic applications accepted. *Faculty research:* Biblical studies, peace studies, theology, ethics, creation care or environmental ethics, church history, church leadership, mission, ministry, preaching, pastoral leadership, social justice, peacemaking, Jesus Christ, Christianity, Anabaptism, Mennonite, Scripture, Bible, Old Testament, New Testament, spirituality, clinical pastoral education, teaching, faith formation, pastoral care, Koine Greek, Hebrew, Aramaic, Syriac, Ugaritic.

Arcadia University, College of Arts and Sciences, Program in International Peace and Conflict Resolution, Glenside, PA 19038-3295. Offers MA. *Program availability:* Part-time, evening/weekend. *Degree requirements:* For master's, capstone project. *Entrance requirements:* Additional exam requirements/recommendations for international students: Required—TOEFL or IELTS. *Expenses:* Contact institution.

Bethany Theological Seminary, Graduate and Professional Programs, Richmond, IN 47374-4019. Offers biblical studies (MA Th); ministry studies (M Div); peace studies (M Div, MA Th); theological studies (MA Th, CATS); youth ministry (M Div). *Accreditation:* ACIPE; ATS. *Program availability:* Part-time, online learning. *Degree requirements:* For master's, thesis (for some programs). *Entrance requirements:* For master's, letters of reference. Additional exam requirements/recommendations for international students: Required—TOEFL (minimum score 550 paper-based).

Bethel University, Graduate Programs, McKenzie, TN 38201. Offers administration and supervision (MA Ed); business administration (MBA); conflict resolution (MA); physician assistant studies (MS). *Program availability:* Part-time, evening/weekend. *Degree requirements:* For master's, thesis (for some programs). *Entrance requirements:* For master's, GRE General Test or MAT, minimum undergraduate GPA of 2.5.

Brandeis University, Graduate School of Arts and Sciences, Department of Near Eastern and Judaic Studies, Waltham, MA 02454-9110. Offers Near Eastern and Judaic studies (MA, PhD); near Eastern and Judaic studies/conflict resolution and coexistence (MA); near Eastern and Judaic studies/Jewish professional leadership (MA); near Eastern and Judaic studies/women's, gender, and sexuality studies (MA); teaching of Hebrew (MAT). Offered jointly with The Heller School of Social Policy and Management. *Program availability:* Part-time. *Faculty:* 24 full-time (10 women), 6 part-time/adjunct (3 women). *Students:* 41 full-time (17 women), 2 part-time (1 woman); includes 7 minority (2 Black or African American, non-Hispanic/Latino; 1 Asian, non-Hispanic/Latino; 4 Hispanic/Latino), 9 international. Average age 33. 47 applicants, 45% accepted, 4 enrolled. In 2017, 8 master's, 3 doctorates awarded. Terminal master's awarded for partial completion of doctoral program. *Degree requirements:* For master's, one foreign language, thesis or alternative, proseminar, capstone; for doctorate, variable foreign

language requirement, comprehensive exam, thesis/dissertation. *Entrance requirements:* For master's and doctorate, GRE General Test (recommended), letters of recommendation, transcripts, statement of purpose, writing sample, resume. Additional exam requirements/recommendations for international students: Required—PTE (minimum score 68), TOEFL (minimum score 600 paper-based, 100 iBT) or IELTS (7). *Application deadline:* For fall admission, 1/15 priority date for domestic students. Applications are processed on a rolling basis. Application fee: $75. Electronic applications accepted. *Expenses: Tuition:* Full-time $48,720. *Required fees:* $88. Tuition and fees vary according to course load, degree level, program and student level. *Financial support:* In 2017–18, 29 students received support, including 20 fellowships with full tuition reimbursements available (averaging $24,480 per year), 1 teaching assistantship with partial tuition reimbursement available (averaging $2,500 per year); Federal Work-Study, scholarships/grants, health care benefits, and tuition waivers (partial) also available. Support available to part-time students. Financial award application deadline: 4/15; financial award applicants required to submit FAFSA. *Faculty research:* Bible and ancient Near East, Judaic Studies, Israel Studies, modern Middle East, Arabic and Islamic civilizations. *Unit head:* Dr. Eugene Sheppard, Department Chair, 781-736-2950, E-mail: sheppard@brandeis.edu. *Application contact:* Jean Mannion, Department Administrator, 781-736-2950, E-mail: mannion@brandeis.edu.
Website: http://www.brandeis.edu/gsas/programs/nejs.html

Brandeis University, The Heller School for Social Policy and Management, Program in Coexistence and Conflict, Waltham, MA 02454-9110. Offers MA, MA/MA. MA/MA program offered in conjunction with Program in Sustainable International Development. *Degree requirements:* For master's, thesis, internship. *Entrance requirements:* For master's, 3 letters of recommendation, curriculum vitae or resume, 5 years of field experience. Additional exam requirements/recommendations for international students: Required—TOEFL (minimum score 600 paper-based; 100 iBT). Electronic applications accepted. *Expenses: Tuition:* Full-time $48,720. *Required fees:* $88. Tuition and fees vary according to course load, degree level, program and student level. *Faculty research:* Intercommunal conflicts, strategic intervention, conflict resolution, coexistence and conflict, international and inter-governmental organizations.

California State University, Dominguez Hills, College of Arts and Humanities, Program in Negotiation, Conflict Resolution and Peacebuilding, Carson, CA 90747-0001. Offers MA. *Program availability:* Part-time, evening/weekend, online learning. *Degree requirements:* For master's, portfolio. *Entrance requirements:* For master's, minimum GPA of 3.0, 3 letters of recommendation. Additional exam requirements/recommendations for international students: Required—TOEFL (minimum score 550 paper-based). Electronic applications accepted. *Faculty research:* Ethnic conflict, mediator ethics, teacher training, global conflict resolution (including role of ombuds), optimal multicultural process.

California University of Pennsylvania, School of Graduate Studies and Research, College of Liberal Arts, Department of Criminal Justice, California, PA 15419-1394. Offers conflict resolution (MA); criminal justice studies (MA). *Program availability:* Part-time, evening/weekend. *Degree requirements:* For master's, comprehensive exam, thesis optional. *Entrance requirements:* For master's, MAT, minimum GPA of 3.0. Additional exam requirements/recommendations for international students: Required—TOEFL (minimum score 550 paper-based; 80 iBT). *Application deadline:* For fall admission, 8/1 priority date for domestic and international students; for spring admission, 5/1 priority date for domestic and international students. Applications are processed on a rolling basis. Application fee: $25. Electronic applications accepted. *Financial support:* Applicants required to submit FAFSA. *Faculty research:* Ethics and law, ethics in police practice, law and morality, police policy, St. Thomas Aquinas and crime. *Unit head:* Dr. John R. Cencich, Director, 724-938-1576, E-mail: cencich@calu.edu. *Application contact:* Suzanne C. Powers, Director of Graduate Admissions and Recruitment, 724-938-4029, Fax: 724-938-5712, E-mail: powers_s@cup.edu.
Website: http://www.calu.edu/academics/colleges/liberal-arts/criminal-justice/

Cambridge College, School of Management, Boston, MA 02129. Offers business negotiation and conflict resolution (M Mgt); general business (M Mgt); health care informatics (M Mgt); health care management (M Mgt); leadership in human and organizational dynamics (M Mgt); non-profit and public organization management (M Mgt); small business development (M Mgt); technology management (M Mgt). *Program availability:* Part-time, evening/weekend. *Degree requirements:* For master's, thesis, seminars. *Entrance requirements:* For master's, resume, 2 professional references. Additional exam requirements/recommendations for international students: Required—TOEFL (minimum score 550 paper-based; 79 iBT), Michigan English Language Assessment Battery (minimum score 85); Recommended—IELTS (minimum score 6). Electronic applications accepted. *Expenses:* Contact institution. *Faculty research:* Negotiation, mediation and conflict resolution; leadership; management of diverse organizations; case studies and simulation methodologies for management education, digital as a second language: social networking for digital immigrants, non-profit and public management.

Carleton University, Faculty of Graduate Studies, Faculty of Public Affairs and Management, Department of Law, Ottawa, ON K1S 5B6, Canada. Offers conflict resolution (Certificate); legal studies (MA). *Degree requirements:* For master's, thesis. *Entrance requirements:* For master's, honors degree. Additional exam requirements/recommendations for international students: Required—TOEFL. *Faculty research:* Legal and social theory; women, law, and gender relations; law, crime, and social order; political economy of law; international law.

Champlain College, Graduate Studies, Burlington, VT 05402-0670. Offers business (MBA); digital forensic science (MS); early childhood education (M Ed); emergent media (MFA, MS); executive leadership (MS); health care administration (MS); information security operations (MS); law (MS); mediation and applied conflict studies (MS). MS in emergent media program held in Shanghai. *Program availability:* Part-time, online learning. *Degree requirements:* For master's, capstone project. *Entrance requirements:* Additional exam requirements/recommendations for international students: Required—TOEFL (minimum score 550 paper-based; 80 iBT). Electronic applications accepted.

Colgate Rochester Crozer Divinity School, Graduate and Professional Programs, Rochester, NY 14620-2530. Offers divinity (M Div, MA, Certificate); peace building and interfaith dialogue (D Min); prophetic preaching (D Min); transformative leadership (D Min). *Accreditation:* ACIPE; ATS (one or more programs are accredited). *Program availability:* Part-time, evening/weekend. *Faculty:* 7 full-time (3 women), 15 part-time/adjunct (7 women). *Students:* 70 full-time, 24 part-time; includes 58 minority (48 Black or African American, non-Hispanic/Latino; 3 Asian, non-Hispanic/Latino; 3 Hispanic/Latino; 4 Two or more races, non-Hispanic/Latino). Average age 43. 23 applicants, 96% accepted, 21 enrolled. In 2017, 21 master's, 3 doctorates awarded. *Degree requirements:* For master's, thesis (for some programs), supervised ministry year (for M Div); for doctorate, thesis/dissertation. *Entrance requirements:* For master's, BA/BS, personal statement, 4 recommendations; for doctorate, M Div, 3 years' professional experience, writing sample, personal statement, curriculum vitae, 4 recommendations. Additional exam requirements/recommendations for international students: Required—TOEFL (minimum score 600 paper-based; 93 iBT). *Application deadline:* For fall admission, 7/1 priority date for domestic students, 3/1 for international students; for spring admission, 12/1 priority date for domestic students, 9/1 for international students. Applications are processed on a rolling basis. Application fee: $35. Electronic applications accepted. *Expenses:* $11,030. *Financial support:* In 2017–18, 26 students received support. Scholarships/grants available. Financial award application deadline: 9/1; financial award applicants required to submit FAFSA. *Faculty research:* Book of Jeremiah, postcolonial Asian feminist biblical interpretation, Charles Wesley, Christian ethics, black church studies. *Unit head:* Rev. Marvin A. McMickle, PhD, President, 585-271-1320 Ext. 680, Fax: 585-271-8013. *Application contact:* Rev. Melissa M. Morral, Vice President for Enrollment Services, 585-340-9633, Fax: 585-340-9644, E-mail: mmorral@crcds.edu.
Website: http://www.crcds.edu

Colorado Technical University Aurora, Programs in Business Administration and Management, Aurora, CO 80014. Offers accounting (MBA); business administration (MBA); business administration and management (EMBA); finance (MBA); human resource management (MBA); marketing (MBA); mediation and dispute resolution (MBA); operations management (MBA); project management (MBA); technology management (MBA). *Program availability:* Part-time, evening/weekend. *Degree requirements:* For master's, thesis or alternative. *Entrance requirements:* For master's, minimum undergraduate GPA of 3.0, resume.

Colorado Technical University Colorado Springs, Graduate Studies, Program in Management, Colorado Springs, CO 80907. Offers accounting (MBA, MSA); business administration (MBA); finance (MBA); human resources management (MBA); logistics/supply chain management (MBA); management (DM); marketing (MBA); mediation and dispute resolution (MBA); operations management (MBA); project management (MBA); technology management (MBA). *Accreditation:* ACBSP. *Program availability:* Part-time, evening/weekend, online learning. *Degree requirements:* For master's, thesis or alternative; for doctorate, thesis/dissertation. *Entrance requirements:* For doctorate, minimum graduate GPA of 3.0, 5 years of related work experience. *Faculty research:* Sexual harassment, performance evaluation, critical thinking.

Columbia University, School of Professional Studies, Program in Negotiation and Conflict Resolution, New York, NY 10027. Offers MS. *Program availability:* Part-time. *Entrance requirements:* For master's, 2 letters of recommendation, professional resume. Electronic applications accepted. *Expenses: Tuition:* Full-time $44,864; part-time $1704 per credit. *Required fees:* $2370 per semester. One-time fee: $105.

Cornell University, Graduate School, Graduate Fields of Architecture, Art and Planning, Field of Regional Science, Ithaca, NY 14853. Offers environmental studies (MA, MS, PhD); international spatial problems (MA, MS, PhD); location theory (MA, MS, PhD); multiregional economic analysis (MA, MS, PhD); peace science (MA, MS, PhD); planning methods (MA, MS, PhD); urban and regional economics (MA, MS, PhD). Terminal master's awarded for partial completion of doctoral program. *Degree requirements:* For master's, thesis; for doctorate, comprehensive exam, thesis/dissertation. *Entrance requirements:* For master's and doctorate, GRE General Test, 2 letters of recommendation. Additional exam requirements/recommendations for international students: Required—TOEFL (minimum score 600 paper-based; 77 iBT). Electronic applications accepted. *Faculty research:* Urban and regional growth, spatial economics, formation of spatial patterns by socioeconomic systems, non-linear dynamics and complex systems, environmental-economic systems.

Creighton University, Graduate School, Department of Interdisciplinary Studies, Omaha, NE 68178-0001. Offers health and wellness coaching (MS); health care ethics (MS); healthcare management (MHM); leadership (Ed D); negotiation and conflict resolution (MS); organizational leadership (MS); public health (MPH). *Program availability:* Part-time, online only, blended/hybrid learning. *Faculty:* 26 full-time (18 women). *Students:* 95 full-time (67 women), 531 part-time (313 women); includes 79 minority (49 Black or African American, non-Hispanic/Latino; 7 American Indian or Alaska Native, non-Hispanic/Latino; 12 Asian, non-Hispanic/Latino; 10 Hispanic/Latino; 1 Native Hawaiian or other Pacific Islander, non-Hispanic/Latino), 10 international. Average age 39. 190 applicants, 82% accepted, 94 enrolled. In 2017, 148 master's, 44 doctorates awarded. *Degree requirements:* For master's, capstone project or practicum; for doctorate, thesis/dissertation. *Entrance requirements:* Additional exam requirements/recommendations for international students: Required—TOEFL (minimum score 90 iBT). *Application deadline:* For fall admission, 8/1 for domestic students, 6/1 for international students; for spring admission, 11/15 for domestic students, 10/15 for international students; for summer admission, 3/1 for domestic students, 2/1 for international students. Applications are processed on a rolling basis. Application fee: $50. Electronic applications accepted. *Expenses:* Contact institution. *Financial support:* Scholarships/grants available. Financial award applicants required to submit FAFSA. *Unit head:* Dr. Cindy Costanzo, Professor, 402-280-2041, E-mail: cindycostanzo@creighton.edu. *Application contact:* Lindsay Johnson, Director of Graduate and Adult Recruitment, 402-280-2703, Fax: 402-280-2423, E-mail: gradschool@creighton.edu.

Creighton University, School of Law, Program in Negotiation and Conflict Resolution, Omaha, NE 68178-0001. Offers MS, Certificate. *Program availability:* Part-time, evening/weekend, 100% online, blended/hybrid learning. *Degree requirements:* For master's, thesis or alternative, practicum. *Entrance requirements:* For master's, baccalaureate degree, two letters of recommendation, statement of purpose (500-750 words), short writing sample, resume, interview with faculty member, transcripts. Additional exam requirements/recommendations for international students: Required—TOEFL (minimum score 90 iBT). Electronic applications accepted. *Expenses:* Contact institution. *Faculty research:* Structural violence; online pedagogy; identity conflict; healthcare conflict engagement and inter professional team building; community engagement of difficult conversations.

Dallas Baptist University, College of Business, Management Program, Dallas, TX 75211-9299. Offers conflict resolution management (MA); general management (MA, MS); health care management (MA); human resource management (MA); organizational communication (MA); performance management (MA); professional sales and management optimization (MA). *Program availability:* Part-time, evening/weekend, online learning. *Application deadline:* Applications are processed on a rolling basis. Application fee: $25. Electronic applications accepted. Application fee is waived when completed online. *Expenses: Tuition:* Full-time $16,308; part-time $906 per credit hour. *Required fees:* $900; $450 per semester. Tuition and fees vary according to course load and degree level. *Unit head:* Dr. Sandra Reid, Chair, Graduate School of Business, 214-333-6860, E-mail: sandra@dbu.edu. *Application contact:* Richard Nassar, Director, 214-333-6801, E-mail: richardn@dbu.edu.
Website: http://www.dbu.edu/gsb/ma-in-management

Dallas Baptist University, College of Business, Master of Business Administration Program, Dallas, TX 75211-9299. Offers accounting (MBA); business communication (MBA); conflict resolution management (MBA); entrepreneurship (MBA); finance (MBA); health care management (MBA); international business (MBA); leading the non-profit organization (MBA); management (MBA); management information systems (MBA); marketing (MBA); project management (MBA); technology and engineering management (MBA). *Accreditation:* ACBSP. *Program availability:* Part-time, evening/weekend, 100% online, blended/hybrid learning. *Application deadline:* Applications are

processed on a rolling basis. Application fee: $25. Electronic applications accepted. Application fee is waived when completed online. *Expenses: Tuition:* Full-time $16,308; part-time $906 per credit hour. *Required fees:* $900; $450 per semester. Tuition and fees vary according to course load and degree level. *Unit head:* Dr. Sandra Reid, Chair of Graduate Business Programs, 214-333-5280, E-mail: sandra@dbu.edu. *Application contact:* Bobby Soto, Director of Admissions, 214-333-5242, E-mail: graduate@dbu.edu.
Website: http://www.dbu.edu/gsb/mba

Drew University, Caspersen School of Graduate Studies, Madison, NJ 07940-1493. Offers conflict resolution and leadership (Certificate), including community leadership, moderation, peace building; education (M Ed); finance (MA); history and culture (MA, PhD), including American history, book history, British history, European history, Holocaust and genocide (M Litt, MA, D Litt, PhD), intellectual history, Irish history, print culture, public history; K-12 education (MAT), including art, biology, chemistry, elementary education, English, French, Italian, math, secondary education, special education, teacher of students with disabilities; liberal studies (M Litt, D Litt), including history, Holocaust and genocide (M Litt, MA, D Litt, PhD), Irish/Irish-American studies, literature (M Litt, MMH, D Litt, DMH, CMH), religion, spirituality, teaching in the two-year college, writing; medical humanities (MMH, DMH, CMH), including arts, health, healthcare, literature (M Litt, MMH, D Litt, DMH, CMH), scientific research; poetry (MFA). *Program availability:* Part-time, evening/weekend. *Faculty:* 4 full-time (2 women), 29 part-time/adjunct (15 women). *Students:* 77 full-time (42 women), 175 part-time (114 women); includes 39 minority (12 Black or African American, non-Hispanic/Latino; 6 Asian, non-Hispanic/Latino; 16 Hispanic/Latino; 5 Two or more races, non-Hispanic/Latino), 11 international. Average age 41. 126 applicants, 75% accepted, 52 enrolled. In 2017, 38 master's, 23 doctorates, 35 other advanced degrees awarded. Terminal master's awarded for partial completion of doctoral program. *Degree requirements:* For master's and other advanced degree, thesis (for some programs); for doctorate, one foreign language, comprehensive exam (for some programs), thesis/dissertation. *Entrance requirements:* For master's, PRAXIS Core and Subject Area tests (for MAT), GRE/GMAT (for M Fin), resume, transcripts, writing sample, personal statement, letters of recommendation; for doctorate, GRE (PhD in history and culture), resume, transcripts, writing sample, personal statement, letters of recommendation; for other advanced degree, resume, transcripts, personal statement. Additional exam requirements/recommendations for international students: Required—TOEFL (minimum score 587 paper-based; 80 iBT), IELTS (minimum score 6), TWE (minimum score 4). *Application deadline:* For fall admission, 8/1 for domestic students, 6/1 for international students; for spring admission, 12/1 for domestic students, 10/1 for international students. Applications are processed on a rolling basis. Application fee: $35. Electronic applications accepted. *Financial support:* Fellowships, research assistantships, teaching assistantships, career-related internships or fieldwork, Federal Work-Study, scholarships/grants, and unspecified assistantships available. Support available to part-time students. Financial award applicants required to submit FAFSA. *Faculty research:* Irish history and culture, conflict resolution and leadership. *Application contact:* Leanne Horinko, Director of Caspersen Admissions, 973-408-3280, E-mail: gradm@drew.edu.
Website: http://www.drew.edu/caspersen

Eastern Mennonite University, Program in Conflict Transformation, Harrisonburg, VA 22802-2462. Offers MA, Graduate Certificate. *Program availability:* Part-time. *Degree requirements:* For master's, practicum. *Entrance requirements:* For master's, minimum undergraduate GPA of 2.75. Additional exam requirements/recommendations for international students: Required—TOEFL (minimum score 550 paper-based). *Application deadline:* For fall admission, 2/15 priority date for domestic and international students. Applications are processed on a rolling basis. Application fee: $50. Electronic applications accepted. *Expenses:* Contact institution. *Financial support:* Scholarships/grants available. Financial award application deadline: 6/30; financial award applicants required to submit FAFSA. *Faculty research:* Restorative justice, negotiation, security in an age of terror, trauma recovery, development, peacebuilding. *Unit head:* Dr. Jayne Docherty, Program Director, 540-432-4627, Fax: 540-432-4449, E-mail: jayne.docherty@emu.edu. *Application contact:* Lora Steiner, Coordinator of Admissions and Marketing, 540-432-4689, Fax: 540-432-4449, E-mail: lora.steiner@emu.edu.
Website: https://emu.edu/cjp/grad/conflict-transformation/

Excelsior College, School of Business and Technology, Albany, NY 12203-5159. Offers business administration (MBA); cybersecurity - information assurance (MS); cybersecurity - medical data security (MS); cybersecurity - policy administration (MS); cybersecurity management (MBA, Graduate Certificate); general business management (MS); health care management (MBA); human performance technology (MBA); human resource management (MS); human resources management (MBA); leadership (MBA, MS); mediation and arbitration (MBA, MS); social media management (MBA); technology management (MBA). *Program availability:* Part-time, evening/weekend, online learning. *Faculty:* 30 part-time/adjunct (12 women). *Students:* 1,204 part-time (333 women); includes 560 minority (310 Black or African American, non-Hispanic/Latino; 7 American Indian or Alaska Native, non-Hispanic/Latino; 42 Asian, non-Hispanic/Latino; 140 Hispanic/Latino; 10 Native Hawaiian or other Pacific Islander, non-Hispanic/Latino; 51 Two or more races, non-Hispanic/Latino). Average age 40. In 2017, 294 master's awarded. *Application deadline:* Applications are processed on a rolling basis. Application fee: $50. Electronic applications accepted. *Expenses: Tuition:* Part-time $645 per credit. *Required fees:* $265 per credit. *Financial support:* Scholarships/grants available. *Unit head:* Dr. Lifang Shih, Dean, 888-647-2388. *Application contact:* Admissions, 888-647-2388 Ext. 133, Fax: 518-464-8777, E-mail: admissions@excelsior.edu.

Excelsior College, School of Public Service, Albany, NY 12203-5159. Offers criminal justice (MSCI); homeland security and emergency management (MSCJ); justice administration (MSCI); mediation and arbitration (MPA); public administration (MPA). *Program availability:* Part-time, evening/weekend, online learning. *Faculty:* 6 part-time/adjunct (5 women). *Students:* 173 part-time (49 women); includes 70 minority (32 Black or African American, non-Hispanic/Latino; 1 American Indian or Alaska Native, non-Hispanic/Latino; 3 Asian, non-Hispanic/Latino; 28 Hispanic/Latino; 1 Native Hawaiian or other Pacific Islander, non-Hispanic/Latino; 5 Two or more races, non-Hispanic/Latino). Average age 40. In 2017, 45 master's awarded. *Application deadline:* Applications are processed on a rolling basis. Application fee: $50. Electronic applications accepted. *Expenses: Tuition:* Part-time $645 per credit. *Required fees:* $265 per credit. *Financial support:* Scholarships/grants available. *Unit head:* Dr. Robert Waters, Dean, School of Public Service, 518-464-8500, Fax: 518-464-8777. *Application contact:* Admissions Counselor, 888-647-2388, Fax: 518-464-8777, E-mail: gradadmissions@excelsior.edu.
Website: http://www.excelsior.edu/programs/public-service

Fresno Pacific University, Graduate Programs, Program in Peacemaking and Conflict Studies, Fresno, CA 93702-4709. Offers church conflict and peacemaking (Certificate); mediation (Certificate); peacemaking and conflict studies (MA); restorative justice (Certificate). *Program availability:* Part-time, evening/weekend. *Degree requirements:* For master's, thesis. *Entrance requirements:* For master's, GMAT, MAT, GRE, interview, writing sample, three references. Additional exam requirements/recommendations for international students: Required—TOEFL (minimum score 550 paper-based). Electronic applications accepted. *Expenses:* Contact institution.

George Mason University, School for Conflict Analysis and Resolution, Arlington, VA 22201. Offers MS, PhD, Certificate. *Program availability:* Part-time, evening/weekend, blended/hybrid learning. *Faculty:* 19 full-time (10 women), 24 part-time/adjunct (11 women). *Students:* 119 full-time (68 women), 154 part-time (89 women); includes 84 minority (37 Black or African American, non-Hispanic/Latino; 13 Asian, non-Hispanic/Latino; 24 Hispanic/Latino; 1 Native Hawaiian or other Pacific Islander, non-Hispanic/Latino; 9 Two or more races, non-Hispanic/Latino), 34 international. Average age 35. 231 applicants, 51% accepted, 50 enrolled. In 2017, 75 master's, 13 doctorates, 5 other advanced degrees awarded. *Degree requirements:* For master's, thesis optional; for doctorate, variable foreign language requirement, comprehensive exam, thesis/dissertation, oral defense of dissertation. *Entrance requirements:* For master's and Certificate, goals statement, two letters of recommendation, curriculum vitae or resume, transcripts; for doctorate, goals statement, three letters of recommendation, curriculum vitae or resume, transcripts, writing sample. Additional exam requirements/recommendations for international students: Required—TOEFL (minimum score 575 paper-based; 88 iBT), IELTS (minimum score 6.5), PTE (minimum score 59). Application fee: $75 ($80 for international students). Electronic applications accepted. *Expenses:* Tuition, state resident: full-time $11,228; part-time $459.50 per credit. Tuition, nonresident: full-time $30,932; part-time $1280.50 per credit. *Required fees:* $3252; $135.50 per credit. Part-time tuition and fees vary according to course load and program. *Financial support:* In 2017–18, 29 students received support, including 21 research assistantships with tuition reimbursements available (averaging $14,607 per year), 8 teaching assistantships with tuition reimbursements available (averaging $11,298 per year); career-related internships or fieldwork, Federal Work-Study, scholarships/grants, unspecified assistantships, and health care benefits (for full-time research or teaching assistantship recipients) also available. Support available to part-time students. Financial award application deadline: 3/1; financial award applicants required to submit FAFSA. *Faculty research:* Social justice advocacy and activism; dynamics of violence; inclusive conflict engagement; conflict sensitive development and resilience; media, narrative and public discourse. *Total annual research expenditures:* $570,918. *Unit head:* Kevin Avruch, Dean, 703-993-3607, Fax: 703-993-1302, E-mail: kavruch@gmu.edu. *Application contact:* Monique Barner, Assistant Director for Graduate Admissions, 703-993-1300, Fax: 703-993-1302, E-mail: mwilli43@gmu.edu.
Website: http://scar.gmu.edu

Georgetown University, Graduate School of Arts and Sciences, Department of Government, Program in Conflict Resolution, Washington, DC 20057. Offers MA.

Georgetown University, Graduate School of Arts and Sciences, Walsh School of Foreign Service, Center for Security Studies, Washington, DC 20057. Offers MA, MA/JD, MA/PhD.

Henley-Putnam School of Strategic Security, Master of Science Program in Strategic Security and Protection Management, Rapid City, SD 57701. Offers extremist organizations (MS). *Program availability:* Part-time, online learning. *Degree requirements:* For master's, comprehensive exam, thesis. *Entrance requirements:* For master's, bachelor's degree from institution accredited by an agency recognized by the U.S. Department of Education and/or the Council for Higher Education Accreditation, background check. Additional exam requirements/recommendations for international students: Required—TOEFL (minimum score 650 paper-based; 79 iBT); Recommended—IELTS. *Expenses:* Contact institution.

Henley-Putnam School of Strategic Security, Master of Science Program in Terrorism and Counterterrorism Studies, Rapid City, SD 57701. Offers intelligence operations (MS); protective intelligence (MS). *Program availability:* Part-time, online learning. *Degree requirements:* For master's, thesis. *Entrance requirements:* For master's, bachelor's degree from institution accredited by an agency recognized by the U.S. Department of Education and/or the Council for Higher Education Accreditation, background check. Additional exam requirements/recommendations for international students: Required—TOEFL (minimum score 650 paper-based; 79 iBT); Recommended—IELTS (minimum score 7). *Expenses:* Contact institution.

Kansas State University, Graduate School, College of Human Ecology, School of Family Studies and Human Services, Manhattan, KS 66506-1403. Offers applied family sciences (MS); communication sciences and disorders (MS); conflict resolution (Graduate Certificate); couple and family therapy (MS); early childhood education (MS); family and community service (MS); life-span human development (MS); personal financial planning (MS, PhD, Graduate Certificate); youth development (MS, Graduate Certificate). *Accreditation:* AAMFT/COAMFTE; ASHA. *Program availability:* Part-time, online learning. *Degree requirements:* For master's, comprehensive exam (for some programs), thesis optional. *Entrance requirements:* For master's, GRE, minimum GPA of 3.0 in last 2 years (60 semester hours) of undergraduate study; for doctorate, GRE. Additional exam requirements/recommendations for international students: Required—TOEFL (minimum score 600 paper-based). Electronic applications accepted. *Faculty research:* Health and security of military families, training in and evaluation of professional human services (marriage and couple therapy, family life education, treatment of speech and swallowing disorders, financial therapy), disorders of communication and swallowing, family and relationship development and health, financial decision-making.

Kennesaw State University, College of Humanities and Social Sciences, PhD Program in International Conflict Management, Kennesaw, GA 30144. Offers PhD. *Degree requirements:* For doctorate, one foreign language, thesis/dissertation. *Entrance requirements:* For doctorate, GRE, portfolio of documents, copy of transcripts from all universities previously attended, resume, statement of goals and objectives, academic writing sample, three letters of recommendation. Additional exam requirements/recommendations for international students: Required—TOEFL (minimum score 90 iBT), IELTS (minimum score 7). Electronic applications accepted.

Kennesaw State University, College of Humanities and Social Sciences, Program in Conflict Management, Kennesaw, GA 30144. Offers MSCM. *Program availability:* Evening/weekend. *Entrance requirements:* For master's, GMAT, GRE, LSAT. Additional exam requirements/recommendations for international students: Required—TOEFL (minimum score 550 paper-based; 80 iBT), IELTS (minimum score 6.5). Electronic applications accepted.

Kent State University, College of Arts and Sciences, Department of Political Science, Kent, OH 44242-0001. Offers political science (MA, PhD), including American politics and policy, conflict analysis and management, transnational and comparative politics and policy; public administration (MPA). *Accreditation:* NASPAA. *Program availability:* Part-time, online learning. *Faculty:* 16 full-time (4 women), 3 part-time/adjunct (2 women). *Students:* 28 full-time (11 women), 58 part-time (36 women); includes 13 minority (8 Black or African American, non-Hispanic/Latino; 1 American Indian or Alaska Native, non-Hispanic/Latino; 3 Asian, non-Hispanic/Latino; 1 Hispanic/Latino), 9 international. Average age 35. 46 applicants, 83% accepted, 24 enrolled. In 2017, 34 master's, 4 doctorates awarded. *Degree requirements:* For master's, thesis optional; for doctorate, comprehensive exam, thesis/dissertation. *Entrance requirements:* For master's, GRE, goal statement, transcripts, writing sample, 3 letters of recommendation, minimum GPA of 3.0, resume; for doctorate, GRE, goal statement, transcripts, writing sample, 3 letters of recommendation, minimum GPA of 3.0. Additional exam

requirements/recommendations for international students: Required—TOEFL (minimum score 550 paper-based, 79 iBT), Michigan English Language Assessment Battery (minimum score 77), IELTS (minimum score 6.5) or PTE (minimum score 58). *Application deadline:* For fall admission, 1/31 for domestic and international students. Applications are processed on a rolling basis. Application fee: $45 ($70 for international students). Electronic applications accepted. *Expenses:* Tuition, state resident: full-time $11,310; part-time $515 per credit hour. Tuition, nonresident: full-time $20,396; part-time $928 per credit hour. *International tuition:* $18,544 full-time. *Financial support:* Research assistantships with full tuition reimbursements, teaching assistantships with full tuition reimbursements, and unspecified assistantships available. Financial award application deadline: 1/31. *Unit head:* Dr. Andrew Barnes, Associate Professor and Chair, 330-672-2060, E-mail: abarnes3@kent.edu. *Application contact:* Julie Mazzei, Associate Professor and Graduate Coordinator, 330-672-8934, E-mail: jmazzei@kent.edu.
Website: http://www.kent.edu/polisci

Lesley University, Graduate School of Arts and Social Sciences, Cambridge, MA 02138-2790. Offers clinical mental health counseling (MA), including holistic counseling, school and community counseling, trauma studies; counseling psychology (MA, CAGS), including professional counseling (MA), school counseling (MA); creative writing (MFA); expressive therapies (MA, PhD, CAGS), including art (MA), clinical mental health counseling (MA), dance (MA), expressive therapies (MA), music (MA); independent studies (CAGS); independent study (MA); intercultural relations (MA, CAGS); interdisciplinary studies (MA), including individualized studies, integrative holistic health, mindfulness studies, peace and conflict transformation, trauma sensitive assessment, intervention, and consultation, women's studies; urban environmental leadership (MA). *Program availability:* Part-time, online learning. *Degree requirements:* For master's, internship, practicum, thesis (for expressive therapies); for doctorate, thesis/dissertation, arts apprenticeship, field placement; for CAGS, thesis, internship (for counseling psychology, expressive therapies). *Entrance requirements:* For master's, MAT (counseling psychology), interview, writing samples, art portfolio; for doctorate, GRE or MAT, interview, master's degree; for CAGS, interview, master's degree. Additional exam requirements/recommendations for international students: Required—TOEFL (minimum score 550 paper-based; 80 iBT). Electronic applications accepted. *Faculty research:* Psychotherapy and culture; psychotherapy and psychological trauma; women's issues in art, teaching and psychotherapy; community-based art, psycho-spiritual inquiry.

Lipscomb University, Institute for Conflict Management, Nashville, TN 37204-3951. Offers MA, Certificate. *Program availability:* Part-time, evening/weekend. *Faculty:* 3 full-time (1 woman), 4 part-time/adjunct (3 women). *Students:* 24 full-time (18 women), 16 part-time (11 women); includes 12 minority (7 Black or African American, non-Hispanic/Latino; 1 Hispanic/Latino; 4 Two or more races, non-Hispanic/Latino), 1 international. Average age 41. 27 applicants, 70% accepted, 15 enrolled. In 2017, 12 master's, 8 other advanced degrees awarded. *Degree requirements:* For master's, thesis optional, externship. *Entrance requirements:* For master's, GRE, GMAT, LSAT or equivalent, 3 years of work experience. Additional exam requirements/recommendations for international students: Required—TOEFL (minimum score 570 paper-based; 80 iBT). *Application deadline:* For fall admission, 7/15 for domestic students; for spring admission, 12/15 for domestic students. Applications are processed on a rolling basis. Application fee: $50 ($75 for international students). Electronic applications accepted. *Expenses:* $1,290. *Financial support:* Tuition waivers (full) available. Financial award applicants required to submit FAFSA. *Faculty research:* Generationally generated conflict, cross-cultural conflict, risk and injury reduction in healthcare, spiritual formation. *Unit head:* Dr. Steve Joiner, Director, 615-966-7141, Fax: 615-966-7143, E-mail: phyllis.hildreth@lipscomb.edu. *Application contact:* Dr. Phyllis Hildreth, Academic Director, 615-966-5695, Fax: 615-966-7143, E-mail: phyllis.hildreth@lipscomb.edu.
Website: http://lipscomb.edu/icm

London Metropolitan University, Graduate Programs, London, United Kingdom. Offers applied psychology (M Sc); architecture (MA); biomedical science (M Sc); blood science (M Sc); cancer pharmacology (M Sc); computer networking and cyber security (M Sc); computing and information systems (M Sc); conference interpreting (MA); counter-terrorism studies (M Sc); creative, digital and professional writing (MA); crime, violence and prevention (M Sc); criminology (M Sc); curating contemporary art (MA); data analytics (M Sc); digital media (MA); early childhood studies (MA); education (MA, Ed D); financial services law, regulation and compliance (LL M); food science (M Sc); forensic psychology (M Sc); health and social care management and policy (M Sc); human nutrition (M Sc); human resource management (MA); human rights and international conflict (MA); information technology (M Sc); intelligence and security studies (M Sc); international oil, gas and energy law (LL M); international relations (MA); interpreting (MA); learning and teaching in higher education (MA); legal practice (LL M); media and entertainment law (LL M); organizational and consumer psychology (M Sc); psychological therapy (M Sc); psychology of mental health (M Sc); public health (M Sc); public policy and management (MPA); security studies (M Sc); social work (M Sc); spatial planning and urban design (MA); sports therapy (M Sc); supporting older children and young people with dyslexia (MA); teaching languages (MA), including Arabic, English; translation (MA); woman and child abuse (MA).

Middlebury Institute of International Studies at Monterey, Graduate School of International Policy and Management, Program in Nonproliferation and Terrorism Studies, Monterey, CA 93940-2691. Offers MA. *Degree requirements:* For master's, one foreign language. *Entrance requirements:* For master's, minimum GPA of 3.0, proficiency in a foreign language. Additional exam requirements/recommendations for international students: Required—TOEFL (minimum score 550 paper-based; 80 iBT). Application fee is waived when completed online.

Montclair State University, The Graduate School, College of Humanities and Social Sciences, Conflict Management in the Workplace Certificate Program, Montclair, NJ 07043-1624. Offers Certificate.

Montclair State University, The Graduate School, College of Humanities and Social Sciences, MA Program in Law and Governance, Montclair, NJ 07043-1624. Offers conflict management and peace studies (MA); governance, compliance and regulation (MA); intellectual property (MA); law and governance (MA); legal management (MA). *Program availability:* Part-time, evening/weekend. *Degree requirements:* For master's, thesis or comprehensive exam. *Entrance requirements:* For master's, GRE General Test, minimum cumulative GPA of 2.75 for undergraduate work, 2 letters of recommendation, essay. Additional exam requirements/recommendations for international students: Required—TOEFL (minimum score 83 iBT) or IELTS (minimum score 6.5). Electronic applications accepted.

Naval Postgraduate School, Departments and Academic Groups, Department of National Security Affairs, Monterey, CA 93943. Offers national security affairs (MA); security studies (MA), including civil-military relations, combating terrorism: policy and strategy, defense decision-making and planning, Europe and Eurasia, Far East, Southeast Asia, the Pacific, homeland security and defense, Middle East, South Asia, Sub-Saharan Africa, stabilization and reconstruction, western hemisphere. Program only open to commissioned officers of the United States and friendly nations and selected United States federal civilian employees. *Program availability:* Part-time. *Degree requirements:* For master's, thesis (for some programs). *Faculty research:* Privatizing welfare in the Middle East; social construction of Russia's resurgence; institutions, ethnicity and political mobilization in South Africa; Hezbollah; China's strategic interests in Cambodia.

New York University, School of Professional Studies, Center for Global Affairs, New York, NY 10012-1019. Offers global affairs (MS), including environment/energy policy, global gender studies, human rights and international law, international development and humanitarian assistance, international relations/global futures, peace building, private sector, transnational security. *Program availability:* Part-time, evening/weekend. *Students:* 143 full-time (90 women), 115 part-time (65 women); includes 73 minority (18 Black or African American, non-Hispanic/Latino; 16 Asian, non-Hispanic/Latino; 32 Hispanic/Latino; 7 Two or more races, non-Hispanic/Latino), 82 international. Average age 28. 285 applicants, 73% accepted, 79 enrolled. In 2017, 238 master's awarded. *Degree requirements:* For master's, thesis. *Entrance requirements:* For master's, GRE or GMAT (only upon request), bachelor's degree, resume with relevant professional work, internship or volunteer experience, two letters of recommendation, statement of purpose. Additional exam requirements/recommendations for international students: Required—TOEFL (minimum score 600 paper-based; 100 iBT), IELTS (minimum score 7). *Application deadline:* For fall admission, 2/1 priority date for domestic and international students; for spring admission, 10/15 priority date for domestic students, 8/15 priority date for international students. Applications are processed on a rolling basis. Application fee: $150. Electronic applications accepted. *Expenses:* $20,244 per term. *Financial support:* Fellowships, career-related internships or fieldwork, Federal Work-Study, scholarships/grants, and health care benefits available. Support available to part-time students. Financial award application deadline: 6/30; financial award applicants required to submit FAFSA. *Unit head:* Vera Jelinek, Divisional Dean and Clinical Associate Professor, 212-992-8380. *Application contact:* Office of Admissions, 212-998-7100, E-mail: sps.gradadmissions@nyu.edu.
Website: http://www.sps.nyu.edu/academics/departments/global-affairs.html

Norwich University, College of Graduate and Continuing Studies, Master of Arts in Diplomacy Program, Northfield, VT 05663. Offers diplomacy (MA), including cyber diplomacy - policy, cyber diplomacy - technical, international commerce, international conflict management, international terrorism. *Program availability:* Evening/weekend, online only, mostly all online with a week-long residency requirement. *Degree requirements:* For master's, comprehensive exam, thesis optional. *Entrance requirements:* For master's, minimum undergraduate GPA of 2.75. Additional exam requirements/recommendations for international students: Required—TOEFL (minimum score 550 paper-based; 80 iBT), IELTS (minimum score 6.5). Electronic applications accepted. *Expenses:* Contact institution.

Nova Southeastern University, College of Arts, Humanities, and Social Sciences, Fort Lauderdale, FL 33314-7796. Offers advanced conflict resolution practice (Graduate Certificate); child protection (MHS); college student affairs (MS); conflict analysis and resolution (MS, PhD); criminal justice (MS, PhD); cross-disciplinary studies (MA); developmental disabilities (MS); family studies (Graduate Certificate); family systems health care (Graduate Certificate); family therapy (MS, PhD); marriage and family therapy (DMFT); peace studies (Graduate Certificate); qualitative research (Graduate Certificate); solution focused coaching (Graduate Certificate). *Accreditation:* AAMFT/COAMFTE (one or more programs are accredited). *Program availability:* Part-time, evening/weekend, 100% online, blended/hybrid learning. *Faculty:* 29 full-time (18 women), 27 part-time/adjunct (21 women). *Students:* 303 full-time (238 women), 903 part-time (677 women); includes 689 minority (385 Black or African American, non-Hispanic/Latino; 4 American Indian or Alaska Native, non-Hispanic/Latino; 31 Asian, non-Hispanic/Latino; 234 Hispanic/Latino; 1 Native Hawaiian or other Pacific Islander, non-Hispanic/Latino; 34 Two or more races, non-Hispanic/Latino), 60 international. Average age 37. 624 applicants, 61% accepted, 285 enrolled. In 2017, 277 master's, 62 doctorates, 25 other advanced degrees awarded. *Degree requirements:* For master's, thesis optional, comprehensive exams, portfolios (for some programs), table-top exams (for some programs); for doctorate, comprehensive exam, thesis/dissertation, qualifying exams, portfolios (for some programs). *Entrance requirements:* For master's, interview, minimum GPA of 3.0, writing sample; for doctorate, interview, minimum GPA of 3.5, master's degree in related field, writing sample; for Graduate Certificate, minimum GPA of 3.0. Additional exam requirements/recommendations for international students: Required—TOEFL. *Application deadline:* For fall admission, 5/17 priority date for domestic and international students; for winter admission, 12/1 priority date for domestic and international students; for spring admission, 4/1 priority date for domestic and international students. Applications are processed on a rolling basis. Application fee: $50. Electronic applications accepted. *Expenses:* Contact institution. *Financial support:* In 2017–18, 170 students received support. Career-related internships or fieldwork, Federal Work-Study, scholarships/grants, and unspecified assistantships available. Financial award application deadline: 4/1; financial award applicants required to submit CSS PROFILE. *Faculty research:* Conflict resolution, family therapy, peace research, international conflict, multi-disciplinary studies, college student affairs, national security affairs, health care conflict resolution, family systems health care, advanced family systems, qualitative research, solution-focused coaching. *Unit head:* Dr. Honggang Yang, Dean, 954-262-3016, Fax: 954-262-3968, E-mail: yangh@nova.edu. *Application contact:* Marcia Arango, Student Recruitment Coordinator, 954-262-3006, Fax: 954-262-3968, E-mail: marango@nsu.nova.edu.
Website: http://cahss.nova.edu/

Old Dominion University, College of Arts and Letters, Graduate Program in International Studies, Norfolk, VA 23529. Offers conflict and cooperation (MA, PhD); interdependence and transnationalism (MA, PhD); international cultural studies (MA, PhD); international political economy and development (MA, PhD); modeling and simulation (MA, PhD); U.S. foreign policy and international relations (MA, PhD). *Program availability:* Part-time. *Faculty:* 15 full-time (4 women). *Students:* 32 full-time (13 women), 40 part-time (16 women); includes 11 minority (7 Black or African American, non-Hispanic/Latino; 2 Hispanic/Latino; 2 Two or more races, non-Hispanic/Latino), 16 international. Average age 37. 95 applicants, 58% accepted, 40 enrolled. In 2017, 2 master's, 7 doctorates awarded. Terminal master's awarded for partial completion of doctoral program. *Degree requirements:* For master's, one foreign language, comprehensive exam, thesis optional; for doctorate, one foreign language, comprehensive exam, thesis/dissertation. *Entrance requirements:* For master's, GRE General Test, sample of written work, 2 letters of recommendation; for doctorate, GRE General Test, sample of written work, 3 letters of recommendation. Additional exam requirements/recommendations for international students: Required—TOEFL (minimum score 570 paper-based). *Application deadline:* For fall admission, 1/15 for domestic and international students; for spring admission, 10/15 for domestic and international students. Application fee: $50. Electronic applications accepted. *Expenses:* Contact institution. *Financial support:* In 2017–18, 12 students received support, including 1 fellowship (averaging $15,000 per year), 5 research assistantships with tuition reimbursements available (averaging $15,000 per year), 4 teaching assistantships with tuition reimbursements available (averaging $15,000 per year); career-related internships or fieldwork, institutionally sponsored loans, and unspecified assistantships also available. Financial award application deadline: 1/15; financial award applicants required to submit FAFSA. *Faculty research:* U.S. foreign policy, international security, transatlantic and transpacific relations, transnational issues, international political

economy and development. *Total annual research expenditures:* $330,391. *Unit head:* Dr. Regina Karp, Graduate Program Director, 757-683-5700, Fax: 757-683-5701, E-mail: rkarp@odu.edu. *Application contact:* Dr. Dale Miller, Associate Dean for Research and Graduate Studies, 757-683-3866, E-mail: demiller@odu.edu.
Website: http://www.odu.edu/gpis

Pepperdine University, School of Law, Master of Dispute Resolution Program, Malibu, CA 90263. Offers MDR, JD/MDR, MDR/MBA, MDR/MPP. *Students:* 4 full-time (3 women), 40 part-time (23 women); includes 14 minority (5 Black or African American, non-Hispanic/Latino; 3 Asian, non-Hispanic/Latino; 6 Hispanic/Latino), 7 international. Average age 37. 115 applicants, 95% accepted, 44 enrolled. In 2017, 28 master's awarded. *Entrance requirements:* For master's, GRE/LSAT, letters of recommendation. *Application deadline:* For fall admission, 2/15 for domestic students; for spring admission, 8/15 for domestic students. Application fee: $60. *Unit head:* Dr. Peter Robinson, Managing Director, Straus Institute for Dispute Resolution, 310-506-4655, E-mail: peter.robinson@pepperdine.edu. *Application contact:* Seth Hackett, Admissions and Student Services Coordinator, 310-506-4655, E-mail: seth.hackett@pepperdine.edu.
Website: http://law.pepperdine.edu/degrees-programs/master-of-dispute-resolution/

Pepperdine University, School of Law, Master of Laws Programs, Malibu, CA 90263. Offers dispute resolution (LL M); entertainment, media, and sports law (LL M); international commercial arbitration (LL M); international commercial law and arbitration (LL M); international commercial law and dispute resolution (LL M); U.S. law and dispute resolution (LL M); United States law (LL M). *Students:* 34 full-time (19 women), 33 part-time (17 women); includes 7 minority (2 Black or African American, non-Hispanic/Latino; 2 Asian, non-Hispanic/Latino; 3 Hispanic/Latino), 42 international. Average age 34. In 2017, 18 master's awarded. *Entrance requirements:* For master's, GRE General Test or LSAT, JD from ABA-accredited institution. Additional exam requirements/recommendations for international students: Required—TOEFL. *Application deadline:* For fall admission, 2/15 for domestic and international students; for spring admission, 8/15 for domestic and international students. Applications are processed on a rolling basis. Application fee: $60. Electronic applications accepted. *Expenses:* Contact institution. *Financial support:* Career-related internships or fieldwork, Federal Work-Study, institutionally sponsored loans, and scholarships/grants available. Support available to part-time students. Financial award application deadline: 4/1; financial award applicants required to submit FAFSA. *Unit head:* Dr. Peter Robinson, Director, Institute for Dispute Resolution, 310-506-4655, Fax: 310-506-4266, E-mail: peter.robinson@pepperdine.edu. *Application contact:* Shellee S. Warnes, Assistant Director, Academic Programs, 310-506-7455, Fax: 310-506-4266, E-mail: shellee.warnes@pepperdine.edu.
Website: https://law.pepperdine.edu/degrees-programs/master-of-laws/

Portland State University, Graduate Studies, College of Liberal Arts and Sciences, Program in Conflict Resolution, Portland, OR 97207-0751. Offers MA, MS. *Faculty:* 8 full-time (4 women), 4 part-time/adjunct (2 women). *Students:* 22 full-time (14 women), 19 part-time (15 women); includes 10 minority (4 Black or African American, non-Hispanic/Latino; 1 Asian, non-Hispanic/Latino; 3 Hispanic/Latino; 2 Two or more races, non-Hispanic/Latino), 3 international. Average age 36. 23 applicants, 91% accepted, 14 enrolled. In 2017, 21 master's awarded. *Degree requirements:* For master's, variable foreign language requirement, thesis or alternative, practicum, culminating experience. *Entrance requirements:* For master's, personal statement, writing samples, transcripts, 3 letters of recommendation. Additional exam requirements/recommendations for international students: Required—TOEFL (minimum score 550 paper-based; 80 iBT), IELTS (minimum score 6.5). *Application deadline:* For fall admission, 3/30 for domestic students, 3/1 for international students; for winter admission, 9/1 for domestic students, 8/1 for international students; for spring admission, 11/1 for domestic and international students. Application fee: $65. *Expenses:* Tuition, state resident: full-time $14,436; part-time $401 per credit. Tuition, nonresident: full-time $21,780; part-time $605 per credit. *Required fees:* $1380; $22 per credit. $119 per quarter. One-time fee: $325. Tuition and fees vary according to program. *Financial support:* Teaching assistantships and Federal Work-Study available. Financial award application deadline: 2/1; financial award applicants required to submit FAFSA. *Total annual research expenditures:* $163,547. *Unit head:* Dr. Harry Anastasiou, Director/Chair, 503-725-9711, E-mail: harrya@pdx.edu. *Application contact:* Aislyn Matias, Program Administrator, 503-725-9175, E-mail: aislyn.matias@pdx.edu.
Website: http://www.pdx.edu/conflict-resolution/

Regent University, Graduate School, School of Law, Virginia Beach, VA 23464. Offers American legal studies (LL M); human rights (LL M); law (MA, JD), including advanced paralegal studies (MA), alternative dispute resolution (MA), business (MA), criminal justice (MA), general legal studies (MA), human resources management (MA), human rights and rule of law (MA), national security (MA), non-profit organizational law (MA), regulatory compliance (MA), wealth management and financial planning (MA); JD/MA; JD/MBA. *Accreditation:* ABA. *Program availability:* Part-time, 100% online, blended/hybrid learning. *Faculty:* 16 full-time (5 women), 76 part-time/adjunct (22 women). *Students:* 313 full-time (181 women), 248 part-time (175 women); includes 240 minority (155 Black or African American, non-Hispanic/Latino; 3 American Indian or Alaska Native, non-Hispanic/Latino; 15 Asian, non-Hispanic/Latino; 45 Hispanic/Latino; 2 Native Hawaiian or other Pacific Islander, non-Hispanic/Latino; 20 Two or more races, non-Hispanic/Latino), 59 international. Average age 35. 923 applicants, 36% accepted, 188 enrolled. In 2017, 138 master's, 80 doctorates awarded. *Entrance requirements:* For master's, college transcripts, resume, personal statement; for doctorate, LSAT, minimum undergraduate GPA of 3.0, official transcripts, 2 letters of recommendation, resume, personal statement. Additional exam requirements/recommendations for international students: Required—TOEFL (minimum score 600 paper-based). *Application deadline:* For fall admission, 3/1 for domestic students. Applications are processed on a rolling basis. Application fee: $50. Electronic applications accepted. *Expenses:* $650 per credit (MA, LL M); $1,140 per credit (JD); $300 per semester technology fee. *Financial support:* In 2017–18, 459 students received support. Career-related internships or fieldwork, scholarships/grants, and unspecified assistantships available. Support available to part-time students. *Faculty research:* Family law, Constitutional law, law and culture, evidence and practice, intellectual property. *Unit head:* Michael Hernandez, Dean, 757-352-4040, Fax: 757-352-4595, E-mail: michher@regent.edu. *Application contact:* Ernie Walton, Assistant Dean of Admissions, 757-352-4315, E-mail: lawschool@regent.edu.
Website: https://www.regent.edu/school-of-law/

Royal Roads University, Graduate Studies, Peace and Conflict Studies Program, Victoria, BC V9B 5Y2, Canada. Offers conflict analysis (G Dip); conflict analysis and management (MA); disaster and emergency management (MA, G Dip); human security and peacebuilding (MA, G Dip); justice studies (G Dip); peace and conflict studies (MAIS). *Program availability:* Blended/hybrid learning. *Degree requirements:* For master's, thesis. *Entrance requirements:* For master's, 5-7 years of related work experience. Additional exam requirements/recommendations for international students: Required—TOEFL (minimum score 570 paper-based) or IELTS (7) recommended. *Application deadline:* Applications are processed on a rolling basis. Application fee: $120 ($240 for international students). Electronic applications accepted. *Financial support:* Federal Work-Study, institutionally sponsored loans, and scholarships/grants available. Support available to part-time students. *Faculty research:* Conflict analysis, ethno-political conflict reconciliation, international relations, displaced persons, resiliency. *Unit head:* Dr. Brigitte Harris, Dean, 250-391-2511, E-mail: admissions@royalroads.ca. *Application contact:* E-mail: admissions@royalroads.ca.
Website: http://www.royalroads.ca/

Saint Mary's College of California, Kalmanovitz School of Education, Leadership Programs, Moraga, CA 94556. Offers coaching and facilitation (MA); organizational leadership and change (MA); peacebuilding and conflict transformation (MA); social justice (MA). *Accreditation:* AACSB. *Program availability:* Part-time, evening/weekend, online learning. *Degree requirements:* For master's, research project. *Entrance requirements:* For master's, letters of recommendation, interview. Electronic applications accepted. *Expenses:* Contact institution. *Faculty research:* Leadership, organizational change, values, adult learning, transformative learning.

St. Mary's University, Graduate Studies, Program in International Relations, San Antonio, TX 78228. Offers conflict transformation (Certificate); international conflict resolution (MA); international development (MA); international relations (MA); security policy (MA); JD/MA. *Program availability:* Part-time, evening/weekend, 100% online. *Students:* 22 full-time (12 women), 48 part-time (16 women); includes 38 minority (5 Black or African American, non-Hispanic/Latino; 1 American Indian or Alaska Native, non-Hispanic/Latino; 1 Asian, non-Hispanic/Latino; 30 Hispanic/Latino; 1 Two or more races, non-Hispanic/Latino), 5 international. Average age 31. 89 applicants, 39% accepted, 19 enrolled. In 2017, 36 master's awarded. *Degree requirements:* For master's, one foreign language, comprehensive exam (for some programs), thesis (for some programs), thesis or comprehensive exam. *Entrance requirements:* For master's, minimum undergraduate cumulative GPA of 3.0. Additional exam requirements/recommendations for international students: Required—TOEFL (minimum score 550 paper-based; 80 iBT), IELTS (minimum score 6). *Application deadline:* For fall admission, 7/1 for domestic students; for spring admission, 11/15 for domestic students; for summer admission, 4/1 for domestic students. Applications are processed on a rolling basis. Application fee: $0. Electronic applications accepted. *Expenses: Tuition:* Full-time $16,200; part-time $900 per credit hour. *Required fees:* $810; $405 per semester. *Financial support:* Research assistantships, Federal Work-Study, tuition waivers (full), unspecified assistantships, and grants for active-duty and retired military, DOD employees, and their spouses available. Financial award application deadline: 3/31; financial award applicants required to submit FAFSA. *Faculty research:* Anthropology and ethics, states in crisis and socioeconomic development, politics and society of South Asia, political psychology, international relations theory. *Unit head:* Dr. Larry Hufford, Graduate International Relations, 210-431-6790, E-mail: lhufford@stmarytx.edu. *Application contact:* Kim Thornton, Director of Graduate Admission, 210-436-3101, E-mail: kthornton@stmarytx.edu.
Website: https://www.stmarytx.edu/academics/programs/master-international-relations/

Saint Paul University, Faculty of Human Sciences, Program in Conflict Studies, Ottawa, ON K1S 1C4, Canada. Offers MA. *Program availability:* Part-time. *Entrance requirements:* For master's, H=honors BA, B average.

Salisbury University, Department of Conflict Analysis and Dispute Resolution, Salisbury, MD 21801-6837. Offers MA. *Program availability:* Part-time. *Faculty:* 5 full-time (0 women). *Students:* 37 full-time (23 women), 3 part-time (2 women); includes 15 minority (11 Black or African American, non-Hispanic/Latino; 1 Asian, non-Hispanic/Latino; 1 Hispanic/Latino; 2 Two or more races, non-Hispanic/Latino), 1 international. Average age 31. 28 applicants, 75% accepted, 21 enrolled. In 2017, 18 master's awarded. *Degree requirements:* For master's, thesis optional. *Entrance requirements:* For master's, three letters of recommendation; transcripts from all colleges and universities attended; personal statement; undergraduate degree; minimum GPA of 3.0; resume; writing sample. Additional exam requirements/recommendations for international students: Required—TOEFL (minimum score 550 paper-based; 79 iBT), IELTS (minimum score 6.5). *Application deadline:* For fall admission, 4/14 priority date for domestic and international students. Applications are processed on a rolling basis. Application fee: $65. Electronic applications accepted. *Expenses:* $392 per credit hour resident; $703 per credit hour non-resident; $92 per credit hour fees. *Financial support:* In 2017–18, 12 students received support, including 8 teaching assistantships with full tuition reimbursements available (averaging $8,185 per year); career-related internships or fieldwork and scholarships/grants also available. Support available to part-time students. Financial award application deadline: 3/1; financial award applicants required to submit FAFSA. *Faculty research:* International conflict and transitional justice (Africa, South Asia, South America, Middle East, Europe); alternative dispute resolution, restorative justice and the field of conflict resolution; environmental change and conflicts stemming from ecologic issues and human interactions, non-violent; organizational conflict and non-profit management; indigenous conflict resolution, religious and cultural conflict. *Unit head:* Dr. Ignaciyas Soosaipillai, Graduate Program Director, Conflict Analysis and Dispute Resolution, 410-543-6435, E-mail: iksoosaipillai@salisbury.edu. *Application contact:* Dr. Vitus Ozoke, Faculty, Conflict Analysis and Dispute Resolution, 410-677-0276, E-mail: vaozoke@salisbury.edu.
Website: http://www.salisbury.edu/gsr/gradstudies/CADRPage.html

Salve Regina University, Program in Humanities, Newport, RI 02840-4192. Offers humanitarian assistance (MA); humanities (PhD); public humanities (MA); religion, peace and justice (MA). *Program availability:* Part-time, evening/weekend, online learning. *Degree requirements:* For master's, thesis optional; for doctorate, one foreign language, comprehensive exam, thesis/dissertation. *Entrance requirements:* For master's, GMAT, GRE General Test, or MAT; for doctorate, GRE General Test. Additional exam requirements/recommendations for international students: Required—TOEFL (minimum score 600 paper-based; 100 iBT) or IELTS. Electronic applications accepted.

SIT Graduate Institute, Graduate Programs, Master's Programs in Intercultural Service, Leadership, and Management, Master's Program in Peace and Justice Leadership, Brattleboro, VT 05302-0676. Offers MA.

Southern Methodist University, Annette Caldwell Simmons School of Education and Human Development, Department of Dispute Resolution and Counseling, Dallas, TX 75275. Offers counseling (MS); dispute resolution (MA). *Program availability:* Part-time. *Degree requirements:* For master's, practica experience, 2 internships (counseling). *Entrance requirements:* For master's, minimum undergraduate GPA of 2.75 (for dispute resolution), 3.0 (for counseling); 3 letters of recommendation. Additional exam requirements/recommendations for international students: Required—TOEFL. Electronic applications accepted.

Syracuse University, Maxwell School of Citizenship and Public Affairs, CAS Program in Conflict Resolution, Syracuse, NY 13244. Offers CAS. *Program availability:* Part-time. In 2017, 39 CASs awarded. *Entrance requirements:* For degree, resume, three letters of recommendation, personal statement, official transcripts. Additional exam requirements/recommendations for international students: Required—TOEFL (minimum score 100 iBT). *Application deadline:* For fall admission, 2/1 priority date for domestic and international students; for spring admission, 8/15 priority date for domestic and international students. Applications are processed on a rolling basis. Application fee:

$75. Electronic applications accepted. *Financial support:* Application deadline: 2/1. *Faculty research:* Applied dispute resolution and conflict management, advocacy and social movements, collaborative governance, environmental public participation and conflict, transnational conflicts. *Unit head:* Steven Lux, Director, 315-443-3759, E-mail: cgerard@maxwell.syr.edu. *Application contact:* Margaret Lane, Assistant Director, Executive Education, 315-443-8708, E-mail: melane02@maxwell.syr.edu.
Website: https://www.maxwell.syr.edu/exed/certificates/sa-conflict_resolution/overview/

Trident University International, College of Business Administration, Program in Business Administration, Cypress, CA 90630. Offers business administration (PhD); conflict and negotiation management (MBA); criminal justice administration (MBA); entrepreneurship (MBA); finance (MBA); general management (MBA); government accounting (MBA); human resource management (MBA); information security and digital assurance management (MBA); information technology management (MBA); international business (MBA); logistics management (MBA); marketing (MBA); project management (MBA); public management (MBA); quality management (MBA); strategic leadership (MBA). *Program availability:* Part-time, evening/weekend, online learning. *Degree requirements:* For doctorate, comprehensive exam, thesis/dissertation, defense of dissertation. *Entrance requirements:* For master's, minimum GPA of 2.5 (students with GPA 3.0 or greater may transfer up to 30% of graduate level credits); for doctorate, minimum GPA of 3.4, curriculum vitae, course work in research methods or statistics. Additional exam requirements/recommendations for international students: Required—TOEFL. Electronic applications accepted.

United States International University–Africa, School of Arts and Sciences, Nairobi, Kenya. Offers counseling psychology (MA), including chemical dependency, health psychology; international relations (MA), including development studies, diplomacy and foreign policy, peace and conflict studies. *Program availability:* Part-time, evening/weekend. *Degree requirements:* For master's, thesis, practicum. *Entrance requirements:* For master's, GRE General Test, 2 letters of recommendation, resume. Additional exam requirements/recommendations for international students: Required—TOEFL. *Faculty research:* Trauma in children, African intellectualism, psychological assessment tools.

United Theological Seminary of the Twin Cities, Graduate Programs, New Brighton, MN 55112-2598. Offers advanced theological studies (Diploma); justice and peace studies (M Div, MA); leadership toward racial justice (M Div, MA, Certificate); Methodist studies (M Div, MA, Certificate); ministry (D Min); ministry renewal and professional development (Certificate); pastoral care and counseling (M Div, MA, MARL); religion and theology (MA); theological and religious studies (Certificate); theology and the arts (M Div, MA); urban ministry (M Div, MA, MARL); women's studies: religion, theology and ministry (M Div, MA). *Accreditation:* ACIPE; ATS. *Program availability:* Part-time, evening/weekend. *Degree requirements:* For master's, thesis; for doctorate, comprehensive exam, thesis/dissertation. *Entrance requirements:* For master's, minimum GPA of 2.75; strong analytical, reflective thinking and writing skills; vocational and academic goals compatible with those of Seminary; for doctorate, M Div or equivalent, minimum GPA of 3.0, 3 years experience in professional ministry; for other advanced degree, BA or equivalent life experience; strong analytical, reflective thinking and writing skills (Certificate); proficiency in English language, previous study of theology at a theological school, recommendation of student's denomination (Diploma). Additional exam requirements/recommendations for international students: Required—TOEFL (minimum score 550 paper-based).

Universidad del Turabo, Graduate Programs, School of Social Sciences and Humanities, Programs in Public Affairs, Gurabo, PR 00778-3030. Offers arts administration (MPA); conflict and mediation studies (MPA); criminal justice studies (MPA); forensic science (MPA); human services administration (MPA). *Entrance requirements:* For master's, GRE, EXADEP, interview, essay, official transcript, recommendation letters. Electronic applications accepted.

Université de Sherbrooke, Faculty of Law, Sherbrooke, QC J1K 2R1, Canada. Offers alternative dispute resolution (LL M, Diploma); business law (Diploma); common law (JD); criminal and penal law (Diploma); health law (LL M, Diploma); international law (LL M); law (LL D); legal management (Diploma); notarial law (Diploma); transnational law (Diploma). *Program availability:* Part-time, evening/weekend. *Degree requirements:* For master's, thesis; for Diploma, one foreign language. *Entrance requirements:* For master's and Diploma, LL B. Electronic applications accepted.

University of Arkansas at Little Rock, Graduate School, College of Social Sciences and Communication, Program in Conflict Mediation, Little Rock, AR 72204-1099. Offers Graduate Certificate.

University of Baltimore, Graduate School, College of Public Affairs, Program in Negotiations and Conflict Management, Baltimore, MD 21201-5779. Offers MS. *Program availability:* Part-time, evening/weekend. *Degree requirements:* For master's, thesis optional, internship. *Entrance requirements:* For master's, minimum GPA of 3.0. Additional exam requirements/recommendations for international students: Required—TOEFL (minimum score 550 paper-based). Electronic applications accepted. *Faculty research:* Communication and conflict, conflict management systems theory.

University of Bridgeport, College of Public and International Affairs, Bridgeport, CT 06604. Offers East Asian and Pacific Rim studies (MA); global development and peace (MA); global media and communication studies (MA). *Program availability:* Part-time, evening/weekend. *Degree requirements:* For master's, thesis. *Entrance requirements:* Additional exam requirements/recommendations for international students: Recommended—TOEFL (minimum score 550 paper-based; 80 iBT), IELTS (minimum score 6.5).

University of Denver, Josef Korbel School of International Studies, Program in Conflict Resolution, Denver, CO 80208. Offers MA. *Program availability:* Part-time. *Faculty:* 1 (woman) full-time, 2 part-time/adjunct (1 woman). *Students:* 13 full-time (6 women), 2 part-time (1 woman); includes 1 minority (Asian, non-Hispanic/Latino). Average age 28. 28 applicants, 86% accepted, 9 enrolled. In 2017, 9 master's awarded. *Degree requirements:* For master's, thesis optional, internship. *Entrance requirements:* For master's, GRE General Test or GMAT, bachelor's degree, transcripts, statement of purpose, writing sample, two letters of recommendation. Additional exam requirements/recommendations for international students: Required—TOEFL (minimum score 587 paper-based; 95 iBT). *Application deadline:* For fall admission, 1/15 priority date for domestic and international students; for winter admission, 11/1 priority date for domestic and international students. Applications are processed on a rolling basis. Application fee: $65. Electronic applications accepted. *Expenses:* $47,823 per year full-time. *Financial support:* In 2017–18, 13 students received support. Research assistantships with tuition reimbursements available, career-related internships or fieldwork, Federal Work-Study, scholarships/grants, tuition waivers (partial), and unspecified assistantships available. Support available to part-time students. Financial award application deadline: 2/15; financial award applicants required to submit FAFSA. *Unit head:* Dr. Karen Feste, Director, 303-871-2418, Fax: 303-871-2456, E-mail: kfeste@du.edu. *Application contact:* Information Contact, 303-871-6477, E-mail: cri@du.edu.
Website: http://www.du.edu/conflictresolution

University of Hawaii at Manoa, Office of Graduate Education, College of Social Sciences, Matsunaga Institute for Peace and Conflict Resolution, Honolulu, HI 96822. Offers conflict resolution (Graduate Certificate). *Program availability:* Part-time. *Entrance requirements:* For degree, GRE General Test. Additional exam requirements/recommendations for international students: Required—TOEFL (minimum score 540 paper-based; 76 iBT), IELTS (minimum score 5).

The University of Manchester, School of Arts, Histories and Cultures, Manchester, United Kingdom. Offers anthropology, media and performance (PhD); applied theatre professional (PhD); archaeology (PhD); art history and visual studies (PhD); arts management and cultural policy (PhD); classics and ancient history (PhD); composition (PhD); creative writing (PhD); drama (PhD); economic and social history (PhD); electroacoustic composition (PhD); English and American studies (PhD); history (PhD); humanitarianism and conflict response (PhD); museology (PhD); music (PhD); musicology (PhD); religions and theology (PhD).

University of Massachusetts Amherst, Graduate School, College of Natural Sciences, Department of Psychological and Brain Sciences, Amherst, MA 01003. Offers clinical psychology (MS, PhD); cognitive psychology (MS, PhD); developmental science (MS, PhD); psychology of peace and violence (MS, PhD); social psychology (MS, PhD). *Accreditation:* APA (one or more programs are accredited). Terminal master's awarded for partial completion of doctoral program. *Degree requirements:* For master's, thesis; for doctorate, comprehensive exam, thesis/dissertation. *Entrance requirements:* For master's and doctorate, GRE General Test, 3 letters of recommendation. Additional exam requirements/recommendations for international students: Required—TOEFL (minimum score 550 paper-based; 80 iBT), IELTS (minimum score 6.5). Electronic applications accepted.

University of Massachusetts Boston, McCormack Graduate School of Policy and Global Studies, Program in Conflict Resolution, Boston, MA 02125-3393. Offers MA, Certificate. MA program accepts applications for fall admission only; Certificate program accepts applications for spring admission only. *Faculty:* 7 full-time (2 women), 4 part-time/adjunct (2 women). *Students:* 15 full-time (5 women), 22 part-time (12 women); includes 11 minority (6 Black or African American, non-Hispanic/Latino; 3 Asian, non-Hispanic/Latino; 1 Hispanic/Latino; 1 Two or more races, non-Hispanic/Latino), 3 international. Average age 40. 30 applicants, 70% accepted, 13 enrolled. In 2017, 10 master's, 3 other advanced degrees awarded. *Entrance requirements:* For master's, MAT or GRE, minimum GPA of 2.75; for Certificate, minimum GPA of 2.75. *Application deadline:* For fall admission, 3/1 for domestic students; for spring admission, 11/1 for domestic students. *Expenses:* Tuition, state resident: full-time $17,375. Tuition, nonresident: full-time $33,915. *Required fees:* $355. *Financial support:* Research assistantships, teaching assistantships, career-related internships or fieldwork, Federal Work-Study, and unspecified assistantships available. Support available to part-time students. Financial award application deadline: 3/1. *Faculty research:* Mediation and negotiation, justice and conflict, cross-cultural mediation, environmental fairness, dispute resolution theory and ethics. *Unit head:* Dr. Darren Kew, Executive Director of Peace, Democracy, and Development, 617-287-7489. *Application contact:* Graduate Admissions Coordinator, 617-287-6400, Fax: 617-287-6236, E-mail: bos.gadm@dpc.umassp.edu.

University of Massachusetts Boston, McCormack Graduate School of Policy and Global Studies, Program in Global Governance and Human Security, Boston, MA 02125-3393. Offers MA. *Students:* 20 full-time (10 women), 31 part-time (19 women); includes 9 minority (2 Black or African American, non-Hispanic/Latino; 2 Asian, non-Hispanic/Latino; 3 Hispanic/Latino; 2 Two or more races, non-Hispanic/Latino), 22 international. Average age 35. 43 applicants, 33% accepted, 11 enrolled. In 2017, 7 master's awarded. *Expenses:* Tuition, state resident: full-time $17,375. Tuition, nonresident: full-time $33,915. *Required fees:* $355. *Unit head:* Dr. David Cash, Dean, 617-287-5000. *Application contact:* Graduate Admissions Coordinator, 617-287-6400, Fax: 617-287-6236, E-mail: bos.gadm@dpc.umassp.edu.

University of Massachusetts Lowell, College of Fine Arts, Humanities and Social Sciences, Program in Peace and Conflict Studies, Lowell, MA 01854. Offers MA. *Degree requirements:* For master's, practicum, project, or thesis. *Entrance requirements:* For master's, GRE, GMAT, or LSAT, bachelor's degree from accredited college or university, minimum undergraduate GPA of 3.0, 18 credits of peace and conflict studies related coursework, three letters of reference, personal statement, resume or curriculum vitae. Additional exam requirements/recommendations for international students: Required—TOEFL.

University of Missouri, Office of Research and Graduate Studies and School of Law, Program in Dispute Resolution, Columbia, MO 65211. Offers LL M, Certificate, Graduate Certificate. *Entrance requirements:* Additional exam requirements/recommendations for international students: Required—TOEFL (minimum score 600 paper-based; 100 iBT). Electronic applications accepted.

University of Missouri, School of Law, Columbia, MO 65211. Offers dispute resolution (LL M); law (JD); JD/MA; JD/MBA; JD/MPA. *Accreditation:* ABA. *Entrance requirements:* For doctorate, LSAT. Additional exam requirements/recommendations for international students: Required—TOEFL (minimum score 600 paper-based; 100 iBT), IELTS (minimum score 7). *Expenses:* Contact institution.

University of New Brunswick Fredericton, School of Graduate Studies, Policy Studies Program, Fredericton, NB E3B 5A3, Canada. Offers citizen engagement/dispute resolution (M Phil); community development (M Phil); international development (M Phil); leadership (M Phil); sustainability/environmental issues (M Phil); worldviews (M Phil). *Program availability:* Part-time. *Degree requirements:* For master's, thesis, report. *Entrance requirements:* For master's, minimum GPA of 3.5. Additional exam requirements/recommendations for international students: Required—TWE (minimum score 5.5), TOEFL (minimum score 600 paper-based; 100 iBT) or IELTS (minimum score 7). Electronic applications accepted. *Faculty research:* International development, worldviews, citizenship/dispute resolution, sustainability/environmental issues, leadership, community development.

University of New Haven, Graduate School, College of Arts and Sciences, Program in Industrial and Organizational Psychology, West Haven, CT 06516. Offers conflict management (MA); industrial organizational psychology (MA); industrial-human resources psychology (MA); organizational development and consultation (MA); psychology of conflict management (Graduate Certificate). *Program availability:* Part-time, evening/weekend. *Students:* 80 full-time (53 women), 10 part-time (6 women); includes 17 minority (8 Black or African American, non-Hispanic/Latino; 4 Asian, non-Hispanic/Latino; 5 Hispanic/Latino), 3 international. Average age 26. 116 applicants, 89% accepted, 47 enrolled. In 2017, 45 master's awarded. *Degree requirements:* For master's, thesis or alternative, internship or practicum. *Entrance requirements:* Additional exam requirements/recommendations for international students: Required—TOEFL (minimum score 80 iBT), IELTS, PTE. *Application deadline:* Applications are processed on a rolling basis. Application fee: $50. Electronic applications accepted. Application fee is waived when completed online. *Expenses:* Contact institution. *Financial support:* Research assistantships with partial tuition reimbursements, teaching assistantships with partial tuition reimbursements, career-related internships or fieldwork, Federal Work-Study, scholarships/grants, and unspecified assistantships

available. Support available to part-time students. Financial award applicants required to submit FAFSA. *Unit head:* Dr. Eric Marcus, Coordinator, 203-932-1242, E-mail: emarcus@newhaven.edu. *Application contact:* Michelle Mason, Director of Graduate Enrollment, 203-932-7067.
Website: http://www.newhaven.edu/4730/

See Display on page 1139 and Close-Up on page 1207.

The University of North Carolina at Greensboro, Graduate School, School of Health and Human Sciences, Department of Peace and Conflict Studies, Greensboro, NC 27412-5001. Offers MA, Certificate. Electronic applications accepted.

The University of North Carolina Wilmington, College of Arts and Sciences, Department of Public and International Affairs, Wilmington, NC 28403-3297. Offers coastal and ocean policy (MS); conflict management and resolution (MA); public administration (MPA), including coastal management. *Accreditation:* NASPAA. *Program availability:* Blended/hybrid learning. *Faculty:* 10 full-time (6 women). *Students:* 50 full-time (30 women), 52 part-time (30 women); includes 22 minority (9 Black or African American, non-Hispanic/Latino; 1 American Indian or Alaska Native, non-Hispanic/Latino; 1 Asian, non-Hispanic/Latino; 6 Hispanic/Latino; 5 Two or more races, non-Hispanic/Latino), 1 international. Average age 32. 46 applicants, 74% accepted, 27 enrolled. In 2017, 64 master's awarded. *Degree requirements:* For master's, thesis (for some programs), internship, practicum, capstone project. *Entrance requirements:* For master's, GRE, GMAT, 3 letters of recommendation, statement of interest, resume, essay. Additional exam requirements/recommendations for international students: Required—TOEFL (minimum score 550 paper-based; 79 iBT), IELTS (minimum score 6.5). *Application deadline:* For fall admission, 4/15 for domestic students; for spring admission, 11/15 for domestic students. Applications are processed on a rolling basis. Application fee: $75. Electronic applications accepted. *Expenses:* Tuition, state resident: full-time $4626; part-time $226.76 per credit hour. Tuition, nonresident: full-time $17,834; part-time $874.22 per credit hour. *Required fees:* $2124. Tuition and fees vary according to program. *Financial support:* Teaching assistantships and scholarships/grants available. Financial award application deadline: 1/1; financial award applicants required to submit FAFSA. *Unit head:* Dr. Raymond Burt, Interim Chair, 910-962-3220, Fax: 910-962-3286, E-mail: burtr@uncw.edu. *Application contact:* Dr. Mark Imperial, MPA Program Director, 910-962-7928, Fax: 910-962-3286, E-mail: imperialm@uncw.edu.
Website: http://www.uncw.edu/pia/graduate/index.html

University of Notre Dame, Graduate School, College of Arts and Letters, Division of Social Science, Joan B. Kroc Institute for International Peace Studies, Notre Dame, IN 46556. Offers MA, PhD. *Degree requirements:* For master's, one foreign language, comprehensive exam, thesis optional; for doctorate, one foreign language, comprehensive exam, thesis/dissertation. *Entrance requirements:* For master's, GRE General Test. Additional exam requirements/recommendations for international students: Required—TOEFL (minimum score 600 paper-based; 80 iBT). Electronic applications accepted. *Faculty research:* The role of international norms and institutions in peacemaking; the impact of religious, philosophical, and cultural influences on peace; the dynamics of intergroup conflict and conflict transformation; the promotion of social, economic, and environmental justice.

University of Notre Dame, Graduate School, Keough School of Global Affairs, Notre Dame, IN 46556. Offers global affairs (MGA); international peace studies (MGA); sustainable development (MGA).

University of Phoenix–Online Campus, College of Social Science, Phoenix, AZ 85034-7209. Offers mediation (Certificate); psychology (MS), including behavioral health, industrial-organizational, psychology. *Program availability:* Evening/weekend, online learning. *Entrance requirements:* Additional exam requirements/recommendations for international students: Required—TOEFL, TOEIC (Test of English as an International Communication), Berlitz Online English Proficiency Exam, PTE, or IELTS. Electronic applications accepted. *Expenses:* Contact institution.

University of San Diego, Joan B. Kroc School of Peace Studies, San Diego, CA 92110-2492. Offers conflict management and resolution (MS); peace and justice (MA); social innovation (MA). *Faculty:* 6 full-time (3 women), 3 part-time/adjunct (1 woman). *Students:* 71 full-time (58 women), 14 part-time (13 women); includes 33 minority (1 Black or African American, non-Hispanic/Latino; 3 Asian, non-Hispanic/Latino; 25 Hispanic/Latino; 4 Two or more races, non-Hispanic/Latino), 12 international. Average age 29. In 2017, 17 master's awarded. *Degree requirements:* For master's, capstone project. *Entrance requirements:* For master's, minimum GPA of 3.0. Additional exam requirements/recommendations for international students: Required—TOEFL (minimum score 580 paper-based; 83 iBT), TWE. Application fee: $45. Electronic applications accepted. *Financial support:* In 2017–18, 35 students received support. Career-related internships or fieldwork, Federal Work-Study, institutionally sponsored loans, scholarships/grants, and unspecified assistantships available. Support available to part-time students. Financial award application deadline: 4/1; financial award applicants required to submit FAFSA. *Faculty research:* Conflict analysis and resolution, human security and peacebuilding, development and peacebuilding, human rights and transitional justice, religion and peacebuilding. *Unit head:* Dr. Patricia Marquez, Dean, 619-260-7919, E-mail: krocschool@sandiego.edu. *Application contact:* Monica Mahon, Associate Director of Graduate Admissions, 619-260-4524, Fax: 619-260-4158, E-mail: grads@sandiego.edu.
Website: http://www.sandiego.edu/peace/

University of the Sacred Heart, Graduate Programs, Program in Systems of Justice, San Juan, PR 00914-0383. Offers human rights and anti-discriminatory processes (MASJ); mediation and transformation of conflicts (MASJ).

University of Victoria, Faculty of Graduate Studies, Faculty of Human and Social Development, School of Public Administration, Victoria, BC V8W 2Y2, Canada. Offers dispute resolution (MADR); public administration (MPA, PhD); MPA/LL B. *Program availability:* Part-time, evening/weekend, online learning. *Degree requirements:* For master's, thesis (for some programs), report; for doctorate, thesis/dissertation, candidacy exam. *Entrance requirements:* For master's, GMAT or GRE General Test, professional resume; for doctorate, GMAT or GRE General Test. Additional exam requirements/recommendations for international students: Required—TOEFL (minimum score 610 paper-based). Electronic applications accepted. *Faculty research:* Policy analysis, local government, performance management, energy markets, labor markets.

University of Wisconsin–Milwaukee, Graduate School, College of Letters and Science, Interdepartmental Program in Human Resources and Labor Relations, Milwaukee, WI 53201-0413. Offers human resources and labor relations (MHRLR); international human resources and labor relations (Graduate Certificate); mediation and negotiation (Graduate Certificate). *Program availability:* Part-time. *Students:* 14 full-time (10 women), 18 part-time (13 women); includes 8 minority (6 Black or African American, non-Hispanic/Latino; 1 Asian, non-Hispanic/Latino; 1 Two or more races, non-Hispanic/Latino), 1 international. Average age 31. 17 applicants, 65% accepted, 10 enrolled. In 2017, 13 master's awarded. *Entrance requirements:* For master's, GMAT or GRE General Test. Additional exam requirements/recommendations for international students: Required—TOEFL (minimum score 80 iBT), IELTS (minimum score 6.5). Application fee: $56 ($96 for international students). Electronic applications accepted. *Financial support:* Career-related internships or fieldwork available. Support available to part-time students. Financial award application deadline: 4/15; financial award applicants required to submit FAFSA. *Unit head:* Susan M. Donohue-Davies, Assistant Director, 414-299-4009, Fax: 414-229-5915, E-mail: suedono@uwm.edu.
Website: http://uwm.edu/human-resources-labor-relations/

University of Wisconsin–Milwaukee, Graduate School, College of Nursing, Milwaukee, WI 53201. Offers clinical nurse specialist (Graduate Certificate); family nurse practitioner (Graduate Certificate); nursing (MN, DNP, PhD); sustainable peacebuilding (MSP). *Accreditation:* AACN. *Program availability:* Part-time. *Students:* 181 full-time (153 women), 128 part-time (117 women); includes 203 minority (23 Black or African American, non-Hispanic/Latino; 1 American Indian or Alaska Native, non-Hispanic/Latino; 147 Asian, non-Hispanic/Latino; 3 Hispanic/Latino; 29 Two or more races, non-Hispanic/Latino), 11 international. Average age 36. 154 applicants, 59% accepted, 60 enrolled. In 2017, 26 master's, 54 doctorates, 2 other advanced degrees awarded. *Entrance requirements:* For master's, GRE General Test or MAT, autobiographical sketch; for doctorate, GRE, minimum GPA of 3.2. Additional exam requirements/recommendations for international students: Required—TOEFL (minimum score 550 paper-based; 79 iBT), IELTS (minimum score 6.5). *Application deadline:* For fall admission, 1/1 priority date for domestic students; for spring admission, 9/1 for domestic students. Application fee: $56 ($96 for international students). Electronic applications accepted. *Financial support:* Fellowships, research assistantships, teaching assistantships, career-related internships or fieldwork, Federal Work-Study, health care benefits, unspecified assistantships, and project assistantships available. Support available to part-time students. Financial award application deadline: 4/15; financial award applicants required to submit FAFSA. *Unit head:* Dr. Kim Litwack, Interim Dean, 414-229-4189, E-mail: litwack@uwm.edu. *Application contact:* Student Affairs Office, 414-229-5047, E-mail: uwmnurse@uwm.edu.
Website: http://uwm.edu/nursing/

Walden University, Graduate Programs, School of Public Policy and Administration, Minneapolis, MN 55401. Offers criminal justice (MPA, MPP, MS, Graduate Certificate), including emergency management (MS, PhD), general program (MS), global leadership (MS, PhD), homeland security and policy coordination (MS, PhD), law and public policy (MS, PhD), policy analysis (MS, PhD), public management and leadership (MS, PhD), self-designed (MS), terrorism, mediation, and peace (MS, PhD); criminal justice and executive management (MS), including global leadership (MS, PhD); criminal justice leadership and executive management (MS), including emergency management (MS, PhD), general program, homeland security and policy coordination (MS, PhD), law and public policy (MS, PhD), policy analysis (MS, PhD), public management and leadership (MS, PhD), self-designed, terrorism, mediation, and peace (MS, PhD); emergency management (MPA, MPP, MS), including criminal justice (MS, PhD), general program (MS), homeland security (MS), public management and leadership (MS, PhD), terrorism and emergency management (MS); general program (MPA, MPP); global leadership (MPA, MPP); government management (Graduate Certificate); health policy (MPA, MPP); homeland security (Graduate Certificate); homeland security and policy coordination (MPA, MPP); international nongovernmental organizations (MPA, MPP); law and public policy (MPA, MPP); local government management for sustainable communities (MPA, MPP); nonprofit management (Graduate Certificate); nonprofit management and leadership (MPA, MPP, MS), including global leadership (MS, PhD), international nongovernmental organization (MS), local government for sustainable communities (MS), self designed (MS); online teaching in higher education (Post-Master's Certificate); policy analysis (MPA); public management and leadership (MPA, MPP, Graduate Certificate); public policy (Graduate Certificate); public policy and administration (PhD), including criminal justice (MS, PhD), emergency management (MS, PhD), global leadership (MS, PhD), health policy, homeland security and policy coordination (MS, PhD), international nongovernmental organizations, law and public policy (MS, PhD), local government management for sustainable communities, nonprofit management and leadership, policy analysis (MS, PhD), public management and leadership (MS, PhD), terrorism, mediation, and peace (MS, PhD); strategic planning and public policy (Graduate Certificate); terrorism, mediation, and peace (MPA, MPP). *Program availability:* Part-time, evening/weekend, online only, 100% online. *Degree requirements:* For doctorate, thesis/dissertation, residency. *Entrance requirements:* For master's, bachelor's degree or higher; minimum GPA of 2.5; official transcripts; goal statement (for some programs); access to computer and Internet; for doctorate, master's degree or higher; three years of related professional or academic experience (preferred); minimum GPA of 3.0; goal statement and current resume (for select programs); official transcripts; access to computer and Internet; for other advanced degree, relevant work experience; access to computer and Internet. Additional exam requirements/recommendations for international students: Required—TOEFL (minimum score 550 paper-based, 79 iBT), IELTS (minimum score 6.5), Michigan English Language Assessment Battery (minimum score 82), or PTE (minimum score 53). Electronic applications accepted.

Walden University, Graduate Programs, School of Social Work and Human Services, Minneapolis, MN 55401. Offers addictions and social work (DSW); advanced clinical practice (MSW); clinical expertise (DSW); criminal justice (DSW); disaster, crisis, and intervention (DSW); family studies and interventions (DSW); human and social services (PhD), including advanced research, community and social services, community intervention and leadership, conflict management, criminal justice, disaster crisis and intervention, family studies and intervention, gerontology, global social services, higher education, human services and nonprofit administration, mental health facilitation; medical social work (DSW); military social work (MSW); policy practice (DSW); social work (PhD), including addictions and social work, clinical expertise, criminal justice, disaster, crisis and intervention, family studies and interventions, medical social work, policy practice, social work administration; social work administration (DSW); social work in healthcare (MSW); social work with children and families (MSW). *Accreditation:* CSWE. *Program availability:* Part-time, evening/weekend, online only, 100% online. *Degree requirements:* For master's, residency (for some programs); for doctorate, thesis/dissertation, residency. *Entrance requirements:* For master's, bachelor's degree or higher; minimum GPA of 2.5; official transcripts; goal statement (for some programs); access to computer and Internet; for doctorate, master's degree or higher; three years of related professional or academic experience (preferred); minimum GPA of 3.0; goal statement and current resume (for select programs); official transcripts; access to computer and Internet. Additional exam requirements/recommendations for international students: Required—TOEFL (minimum score 550 paper-based, 79 iBT), IELTS (minimum score 6.5), Michigan English Language Assessment Battery (minimum score 82), or PTE (minimum score 53). Electronic applications accepted.

Wayne State University, College of Fine, Performing and Communication Arts, Department of Communication, Detroit, MI 48202. Offers communication (PhD), including democratic participation and culture, identity and representation, media, society and culture, risk, crisis and conflict, wellness, work life and relationships; communication and new media (Graduate Certificate); communication studies (MA); dispute resolution (MADR, Graduate Certificate), including community and urban studies (MADR), conflict area studies (MADR), health and family (MADR), international conflict and cooperation (MADR), professional practice (MADR), theory of conflict (MADR),

workplace (MADR); health communication (Graduate Certificate); journalism (MA); media arts (MA); media studies (MA); public relations and organizational communication (MA); JD/MADR. Doctoral program admits for fall only. *Program availability:* Online learning. *Faculty:* 21. *Students:* 63 full-time (35 women), 87 part-time (55 women); includes 54 minority (39 Black or African American, non-Hispanic/Latino; 2 Asian, non-Hispanic/Latino; 7 Hispanic/Latino; 6 Two or more races, non-Hispanic/Latino), 10 international. Average age 34. 153 applicants, 39% accepted, 27 enrolled. In 2017, 26 master's, 7 doctorates, 8 other advanced degrees awarded. *Degree requirements:* For master's, thesis (for some programs), thesis or essay; for doctorate, thesis/dissertation. *Entrance requirements:* For master's, GRE (for MA if undergraduate GPA less than 3.2), personal statement; BA or BS in communication or related field with minimum upper-division GPA of 3.2 and minimum upper-division undergraduate GPA of 3.0, and sample of academic writing (for MA); undergraduate degree with minimum upper-division GPA of 3.0 and three letters of recommendation (for MADR); for doctorate, GRE, undergraduate degree in communication or related field; master's degree in communication or related field with minimum GPA of 3.5; letters of recommendation; personal statement; sample of written scholarship. Additional exam requirements/recommendations for international students: Required—TOEFL (minimum score 100 iBT), IELTS, TWE. Application fee: $50. Electronic applications accepted. *Expenses:* Contact institution. *Financial support:* In 2017–18, 57 students received support, including 5 fellowships with tuition reimbursements available (averaging $17,400 per year), 2 research assistantships with tuition reimbursements available (averaging $20,388 per year), 20 teaching assistantships with tuition reimbursements available (averaging $18,534 per year); scholarships/grants and unspecified assistantships also available. Financial award applicants required to submit FAFSA. *Faculty research:* Democratic participation and culture; identity and representation; media, society and culture; risk, crisis and conflict; wellness, work life, and relationships. *Unit head:* Dr. Lee Wilkins, Professor and Chair, 313-577-2943, E-mail: eh8899@wayne.edu. *Application contact:* E-mail: communication@wayne.edu.
Website: http://comm.wayne.edu/

Wayne State University, College of Liberal Arts and Sciences, Center for Peace and Conflict Studies, Detroit, MI 48202. Offers peace and security studies (Graduate Certificate). *Degree requirements:* For Graduate Certificate, internship or practicum. *Entrance requirements:* For degree, admission to master's degree program at WSU or University of Windsor, or graduate of master's degree program in approved discipline at an accredited institution. Additional exam requirements/recommendations for international students: Required—TOEFL (minimum score 550 paper-based; 79 iBT), Michigan English Language Assessment Battery (minimum score 85); Recommended—IELTS (minimum score 6.5). *Application deadline:* For fall admission, 6/1 priority date for domestic students, 5/1 priority date for international students; for winter admission, 10/1 priority date for domestic students, 9/1 priority date for international students; for spring admission, 2/1 priority date for domestic students, 1/1 priority date for international students; for summer admission, 2/1 priority date for domestic students, 1/1 priority date for international students. Applications are processed on a rolling basis. Application fee: $50. Electronic applications accepted. *Expenses:* Contact institution. *Financial support:* Scholarships/grants available. Financial award applicants required to submit FAFSA. *Unit head:* Dr. Fred Pearson, Professor and Program Director, 313-577-3453, E-mail: ab3440@wayne.edu.
Website: http://clas.wayne.edu/cpcs/

Wilfrid Laurier University, Faculty of Graduate and Postdoctoral Studies, School of International Policy and Governance, Global Governance Program, Waterloo, ON N2L 3C5, Canada. Offers conflict and security (PhD); global environment (PhD); global justice and human rights (PhD); global political economy (PhD); global social governance (PhD); multilateral institutions and diplomacy (PhD). Offered jointly with University of Waterloo. *Degree requirements:* For doctorate, thesis/dissertation. *Entrance requirements:* For doctorate, MA in political science, history, economics, international development studies, international peace studies, globalization studies, environmental studies or related field with minimum A-. Additional exam requirements/recommendations for international students: Required—TOEFL (minimum score 89 iBT). Electronic applications accepted. *Faculty research:* Global political economy, global environment, conflict and security, global justice and human rights, multilateral institutions and diplomacy.

Willamette University, College of Law, Salem, OR 97301-3922. Offers dispute resolution (LL M); law (MLS, JD); transnational law (LL M); JD/MBA. *Accreditation:* ABA. *Program availability:* Part-time. *Degree requirements:* For master's, thesis, 25 credit hours (for LL M); 26 credit hours (for MLS); for doctorate, thesis/dissertation, 90 credit hours. *Entrance requirements:* For master's, bachelor's degree (for MLS); domestic or foreign JD (for LL M); for doctorate, LSAT. Additional exam requirements/recommendations for international students: Required—TOEFL (minimum score 480 paper-based; 45 iBT); Recommended—IELTS (minimum score 5). Electronic applications accepted. Application fee is waived when completed online. *Expenses:* Contact institution. *Faculty research:* Dispute resolution, international law, business law, law and government, sustainability.

Yeshiva University, Benjamin N. Cardozo School of Law, New York, NY 10003-4301. Offers comparative legal thought (LL M); dispute resolution and advocacy (LL M); general studies (LL M); intellectual property law (LL M); law (JD). *Accreditation:* ABA. *Program availability:* Part-time. *Faculty:* 61 full-time (24 women), 92 part-time/adjunct (38 women). *Students:* 994 full-time (530 women), 107 part-time (56 women); includes 218 minority (40 Black or African American, non-Hispanic/Latino; 84 Asian, non-Hispanic/Latino; 74 Hispanic/Latino; 20 Two or more races, non-Hispanic/Latino), 96 international. Average age 25. 2,755 applicants, 52% accepted, 419 enrolled. In 2017, 70 master's, 391 doctorates awarded. *Entrance requirements:* For doctorate, LSAT, 2 letters of recommendation. Additional exam requirements/recommendations for international students: Required—TOEFL (minimum score 100 iBT); Recommended—IELTS (minimum score 7). *Application deadline:* For fall admission, 4/1 priority date for domestic students; for spring admission, 12/1 for domestic students. Applications are processed on a rolling basis. Application fee: $50. Electronic applications accepted. *Expenses:* Contact institution. *Financial support:* In 2017–18, 845 students received support, including 115 research assistantships (averaging $1,429 per year); career-related internships or fieldwork, Federal Work-Study, institutionally sponsored loans, scholarships/grants, health care benefits, and tuition waivers (full and partial) also available. Support available to part-time students. Financial award application deadline: 3/1; financial award applicants required to submit FAFSA. *Faculty research:* Corporate and commercial law, intellectual property law, criminal law and litigation, Constitutional law, legal theory and jurisprudence. *Unit head:* David G. Martinidez, Dean of Admissions, 212-790-0357, Fax: 212-790-0482, E-mail: lawinfo@yu.edu.
Website: http://www.cardozo.yu.edu/

Section 18
Criminology and Forensics

This section contains a directory of institutions offering graduate work in criminology and forensics, followed by an in-depth entry submitted by an institution that chose to prepare a detailed program description. Additional information about programs listed in the directory but not augmented by an in-depth entry may be obtained by writing directly to the dean of a graduate school or chair of a department at the address given in the directory.

For programs offering related work, see also in this book *Political Science and International Affairs, Psychology and Counseling,* and *Sociology, Anthropology, and Archaeology.* In another guide in this series:

Graduate Programs in Business, Education, Information Studies, Law & Social Work
See *Law* and *Social Work*

CONTENTS

Program Directories

Featured School: Display and Close-Up

Criminal Justice and Criminology

Adler University, Graduate Programs, MA in Criminology and Criminal Justice Program, Chicago, IL 60602. Offers MA. *Program availability:* Online learning.

Adler University, Graduate Programs, Master of Public Administration Program, Chicago, IL 60602. Offers criminal justice (MPA); sustainable communities (MPA). *Program availability:* Part-time, evening/weekend.

Adrian College, Graduate Programs, Adrian, MI 49221-2575. Offers accounting (MS); athletic training (MS); criminal justice (MA). *Degree requirements:* For master's, comprehensive exam (for some programs), thesis (for some programs), thesis, internship or practicum with corresponding in-depth paper and/or presentation. *Entrance requirements:* For master's, appropriate undergraduate degree, minimum cumulative and major GPA of 3.0, personal statement.

Albany State University, College of Arts and Humanities, Albany, GA 31705-2717. Offers criminal justice (MS); English education (M Ed); public administration (MPA), including community and economic development, criminal justice administration, health administration and policy, human resources management, public management, public policy, water resources management and policy; social work (MSW). *Accreditation:* NASPAA. *Program availability:* Part-time. *Degree requirements:* For master's, comprehensive exam, professional portfolio (for MPA), internship, capstone report. *Entrance requirements:* For master's, GRE, MAT, minimum GPA of 3.0, official transcript, pre-medical record/certificate of immunization, letters of reference. Electronic applications accepted. *Faculty research:* HIV prevention for minority students.

Albertus Magnus College, Master of Science in Criminal Justice Program, New Haven, CT 06511-1189. Offers corrections administration (MS); juvenile justice (MS). *Program availability:* Part-time, evening/weekend, 100% online, blended/hybrid learning. *Degree requirements:* For master's, thesis, capstone. *Entrance requirements:* For master's, bachelor's degree from regionally-accredited college or university with minimum GPA of 3.0 in criminal justice, 2.8 overall; undergraduate major in criminal justice or completion of 18 criminal justice credits; interview; two letters of recommendation; one-page personal statement. Additional exam requirements/recommendations for international students: Recommended—TOEFL (minimum score 550 paper-based; 80 iBT). Application fee: $50. *Expenses:* Contact institution. *Financial support:* Federal Work-Study and unspecified assistantships available. Support available to part-time students. Financial award applicants required to submit FAFSA. *Unit head:* John Lawrie, Coordinator, 203-773-6142, E-mail: jnlawrie@albertus.edu. *Application contact:* John Lawrie, Coordinator, 203-773-6142, E-mail: jnlawrie@albertus.edu. Website: http://www.albertus.edu/criminal-justice/ms/

Alliant International University–San Francisco, California School of Forensic Studies, Program in Applied Criminology, San Francisco, CA 94133. Offers victimology (MS). *Entrance requirements:* For master's, 3 essays, resume. Additional exam requirements/recommendations for international students: Required—TOEFL (minimum score 550 paper-based; 80 iBT). Electronic applications accepted.

American Public University System, AMU/APU Graduate Programs, Charles Town, WV 25414. Offers accounting (MS); applied business analytics (MS); business administration (MBA); criminal justice (MA); cybersecurity studies (MS); educational leadership (M Ed); environmental policy and management (MS); global security (DGS); health information management (MS); history (MA), including American military history, American Revolution, civil war, war since 1945, World War II; information technology (MS); international relations and conflict resolution (MA), including American politics and government, comparative government and development, general, international relations, public policy; national security studies (MA); nursing (MSN); political science (MA); public policy (MPP); reverse logistics management (MA), including comparative and security issues, conflict resolution, international and transnational security issues, peacekeeping; space studies (MS); sports management (MS); strategic intelligence (DSI); teaching (M Ed), including secondary social studies; transportation and logistics management (MA). *Program availability:* Part-time, evening/weekend, online only, 100% online. *Students:* 455 full-time (227 women), 7,939 part-time (3,353 women); includes 2,793 minority (1,429 Black or African American, non-Hispanic/Latino; 48 American Indian or Alaska Native, non-Hispanic/Latino; 205 Asian, non-Hispanic/Latino; 766 Hispanic/Latino; 62 Native Hawaiian or other Pacific Islander, non-Hispanic/Latino; 283 Two or more races, non-Hispanic/Latino), 101 international. Average age 37. In 2017, 2,977 master's awarded. *Degree requirements:* For master's, comprehensive exam or practicum. *Entrance requirements:* For master's, official transcript showing earned bachelor's degree from institution accredited by recognized accrediting body. Additional exam requirements/recommendations for international students: Required—TOEFL (minimum score 550 paper-based), IELTS (minimum score 6.5). *Application deadline:* Applications are processed on a rolling basis. Application fee: $0. Electronic applications accepted. *Expenses: Tuition:* Full-time $6300; part-time $350 per credit. *Required fees:* $300; $50 per course. *Financial support:* Scholarships/grants available. Financial award applicants required to submit FAFSA. *Unit head:* Dr. Wallace Boston, President, 877-468-6268, Fax: 304-728-2348, E-mail: president@apus.edu. *Application contact:* Yoci Deal, Associate Vice President, Graduate and International Admissions, 877-468-6268, Fax: 304-724-3764, E-mail: info@apus.edu. Website: http://www.apus.edu

American University, School of Public Affairs, Department of Justice, Law and Criminology, Washington, DC 20016-8043. Offers justice, law and criminology (MS, PhD); terrorism, homeland security and policy (MS); JD/MS. *Program availability:* Part-time, evening/weekend. *Faculty:* 23 full-time (9 women), 16 part-time/adjunct (5 women). *Students:* 94 full-time (64 women), 27 part-time (17 women); includes 30 minority (13 Black or African American, non-Hispanic/Latino; 5 Asian, non-Hispanic/Latino; 11 Hispanic/Latino; 1 Two or more races, non-Hispanic/Latino), 2 international. Average age 27. 157 applicants, 80% accepted, 49 enrolled. In 2017, 30 master's, 7 doctorates awarded. *Degree requirements:* For master's, comprehensive exam; for doctorate, comprehensive exam, thesis/dissertation. *Entrance requirements:* For master's, GRE, 2 recommendations, statement of purpose, resume, transcript; for doctorate, GRE, 3 recommendations, statement of purpose, resume, writing sample, transcript. Additional exam requirements/recommendations for international students: Required—TOEFL (minimum score 600 paper-based; 100 iBT). *Application deadline:* For fall admission, 2/15 for domestic students, 5/1 for international students; for spring admission, 11/1 for domestic students, 9/15 for international students. Application fee: $55. *Expenses:* Contact institution. *Financial support:* Research assistantships, teaching assistantships, institutionally sponsored loans, scholarships/grants, and unspecified assistantships available. Financial award application deadline: 2/1; financial award applicants required to submit FAFSA. *Unit head:* Dr. Joseph Young, Department Chair, 202-885-2618, Fax: 202-885-2907, E-mail: jyoung@american.edu. *Application contact:* Jennifer Forney, Assistant Dean, Graduate Enrollment, E-mail: forney@american.edu.
Website: http://www.american.edu/spa/jlc/

American University of Puerto Rico, Program in Criminal Justice, Bayamon, PR 00960-2037. Offers MA. *Program availability:* Part-time, evening/weekend. *Faculty:* 4 part-time/adjunct (1 woman). *Students:* 1 full-time (0 women), 8 part-time (3 women); all minorities (all Hispanic/Latino). Average age 32. 2 applicants, 100% accepted, 2 enrolled. In 2017, 2 master's awarded. *Degree requirements:* For master's, comprehensive exam. *Entrance requirements:* For master's, interviews; recommendations. *Application deadline:* For fall admission, 8/1 for domestic students; for winter admission, 10/15 for domestic students; for spring admission, 3/22 for domestic students. Applications are processed on a rolling basis. Application fee: $25. Tuition and fees vary according to course load and degree level. *Financial support:* In 2017–18, 8 students received support, including 9 fellowships (averaging $500 per year). Financial award applicants required to submit FAFSA. *Unit head:* Prof. Bolivar Ramirez-Carlo, III, Dean of Faculty, 787-620-2040 Ext. 2011, Fax: 787-785-7377, E-mail: bramirez@aupr.edu. *Application contact:* Keren I. Llanos-Figueroa, Information Contact, 787-620-2040 Ext. 2021, Fax: 787-785-7377, E-mail: kllanos@aupr.edu.

Anderson University, Command College of South Carolina, Anderson, SC 29621-4035. Offers criminal justice (MCJ). *Program availability:* Blended/hybrid learning. *Entrance requirements:* For master's, minimum undergraduate GPA of 2.75, 5 years of experience working in criminal justice field, resume. *Expenses:* $1,612 tuition per course, $350 fees/books/materials per course. *Financial support:* Application deadline: 3/1; applicants required to submit FAFSA. *Application contact:* Mallory Knight, Graduate Admission Counselor, 864-231-2182, Fax: 864-231-2115, E-mail: malloryknight@andersonuniversity.edu.
Website: https://www.andersonuniversity.edu/graduate/programs/criminal-justice/command-college

Angelo State University, College of Graduate Studies and Research, College of Arts and Humanities, Department of Security Studies and Criminal Justice, San Angelo, TX 76909. Offers criminal justice (MS); homeland security (MS); intelligence, security studies, and analysis (MSS); security studies (MSS). *Program availability:* Part-time, evening/weekend, online learning. *Students:* 56 full-time (28 women), 146 part-time (44 women); includes 81 minority (27 Black or African American, non-Hispanic/Latino; 2 American Indian or Alaska Native, non-Hispanic/Latino; 10 Asian, non-Hispanic/Latino; 35 Hispanic/Latino; 7 Two or more races, non-Hispanic/Latino). Average age 32. *Degree requirements:* For master's, comprehensive exam. *Entrance requirements:* For master's, essay, letters of recommendation. Additional exam requirements/recommendations for international students: Required—TOEFL or IELTS. *Application deadline:* For fall admission, 7/15 priority date for domestic students, 6/10 for international students; for spring admission, 12/1 priority date for domestic students, 11/1 for international students. Applications are processed on a rolling basis. Application fee: $40 ($50 for international students). Electronic applications accepted. *Expenses:* Tuition, state resident: full-time $3856. Tuition, nonresident: full-time $11,324. *Required fees:* $2650. *Financial support:* Federal Work-Study and scholarships/grants available. Support available to part-time students. Financial award application deadline: 3/1; financial award applicants required to submit FAFSA. *Unit head:* Dr. William A. Taylor, Chair, 325-486-6689, Fax: 325-942-2544, E-mail: william.taylor@angelo.edu.
Website: http://www.angelo.edu/dept/security_studies_criminal_justice/

Anna Maria College, Graduate Division, Program in Criminal Justice, Paxton, MA 01612. Offers criminal justice (MS). *Program availability:* Part-time, evening/weekend. *Degree requirements:* For master's, capstone project or thesis. *Entrance requirements:* For master's, bachelor's degree in related field, minimum GPA of 2.7. Additional exam requirements/recommendations for international students: Required—TOEFL (minimum score 500 paper-based). Electronic applications accepted.

Arizona State University at the Tempe campus, College of Public Programs, School of Criminology and Criminal Justice, Phoenix, AZ 85004. Offers corrections management (Graduate Certificate); criminal justice (MA); criminology and criminal justice (MS, PhD); law enforcement administration (Graduate Certificate). *Program availability:* Part-time, evening/weekend, online learning. Terminal master's awarded for partial completion of doctoral program. *Degree requirements:* For master's, thesis or alternative, policy analysis project, interactive Program of Study (iPOS) submitted before completing 50 percent of required credit hours; for doctorate, comprehensive exam, thesis/dissertation, interactive Program of Study (iPOS) submitted before completing 50 percent of required credit hours. *Entrance requirements:* For master's, GRE (MS), minimum GPA of 3.0 or equivalent in last 2 years of work leading to bachelor's degree; for doctorate, GRE, minimum GPA of 3.0 or equivalent in last 2 years of work leading to bachelor's degree, 2 letters of recommendation, resume, personal statement. Additional exam requirements/recommendations for international students: Required—TOEFL, IELTS, or PTE. Electronic applications accepted.

Arkansas State University, Graduate School, College of Humanities and Social Sciences, Department of Criminology, Sociology, and Geography, State University, AR 72467. Offers criminal justice (MA); sociology (MA); sociology education (SCCT). *Program availability:* Part-time. *Degree requirements:* For master's, one foreign language, comprehensive exam, thesis or alternative; for SCCT, comprehensive exam. *Entrance requirements:* For master's, GRE General Test or MAT, appropriate bachelor's degree, letters of recommendation, official transcripts, immunization records; for SCCT, GRE General Test or MAT, interview, master's degree, official transcript, immunization records. Additional exam requirements/recommendations for international students: Required—TOEFL (minimum score 550 paper-based; 79 iBT), IELTS (minimum score 6), PTE (minimum score 56). Electronic applications accepted.

Ashworth College, Graduate Programs, Norcross, GA 30092. Offers business administration (MBA); criminal justice (MS); health care administration (MBA, MS); human resource management (MBA, MS); international business (MBA); management (MS); marketing (MBA, MS).

Auburn University at Montgomery, College of Public Policy and Justice, Department of Justice and Public Safety, Montgomery, AL 36124-4023. Offers criminal studies (MSJPS); homeland security (MSJPS); homeland security and emergency management (MS); legal studies (MSJPS); organizational leadership (MSJPS). *Program availability:* Part-time, evening/weekend. *Faculty:* 5 full-time (2 women). *Students:* 9 full-time (3 women), 33 part-time (20 women); includes 23 minority (22 Black or African American, non-Hispanic/Latino; 1 Asian, non-Hispanic/Latino). Average age 30. 24 applicants, 75% accepted, 9 enrolled. In 2017, 23 master's awarded. *Degree requirements:* For master's, comprehensive exam, thesis optional. *Entrance requirements:* For master's, GRE General Test or MAT. Additional exam requirements/recommendations for international students: Recommended—TOEFL (minimum score 500 paper-based; 61 iBT), IELTS (minimum score 5.5), TSE (minimum score 44). *Application deadline:* For fall admission,

7/15 for international students; for spring admission, 11/15 for international students; for summer admission, 4/15 for international students. Applications are processed on a rolling basis. Application fee: $25. Electronic applications accepted. *Expenses:* Tuition, state resident: full-time $6930; part-time $385 per credit hour. Tuition, nonresident: full-time $15,588; part-time $866 per credit hour. *Required fees:* $640. *Financial support:* Career-related internships or fieldwork and scholarships/grants available. Support available to part-time students. Financial award application deadline: 3/1; financial award applicants required to submit FAFSA. *Faculty research:* Law enforcement, corrections, juvenile justice. *Unit head:* Dr. Ralph Ioimo, Head, 334-244-3691, Fax: 334-244-3244, E-mail: rioimo@aum.edu.
Website: http://cppj.aum.edu/departments/justice-and-public-safety

Ball State University, Graduate School, College of Sciences and Humanities, Department of Political Science, Program in Public Administration, Muncie, IN 47306. Offers public administration (MPA, Certificate), including community and economic development (MPA), criminal justice (MPA), emergency management and homeland security (MPA), information and communication technology (MPA). *Program availability:* Part-time. *Students:* 20 full-time (7 women), 14 part-time (8 women); includes 4 minority (2 Black or African American, non-Hispanic/Latino; 2 Hispanic/Latino), 1 international. Average age 29. 28 applicants, 89% accepted, 15 enrolled. In 2017, 10 master's awarded. *Degree requirements:* For master's, comprehensive exam. *Entrance requirements:* For master's, GRE General Test, minimum baccalaureate GPA of 2.8, two letters of recommendation. Additional exam requirements/recommendations for international students: Required—TOEFL (minimum score 550 paper-based; 79 iBT), IELTS (minimum score 6.5). *Application deadline:* Applications are processed on a rolling basis. Application fee: $60. Electronic applications accepted. *Financial support:* Research assistantships with partial tuition reimbursements and unspecified assistantships available. Financial award application deadline: 3/1; financial award applicants required to submit FAFSA. *Faculty research:* Employment training programs, personnel and labor relations, planning. *Unit head:* Dr. Daniel Reagan, Chairperson, 765-285-8789, Fax: 765-285-5345, E-mail: jlosco@bsu.edu. *Application contact:* Dr. Charles Taylor, Associate Professor/Graduate Advisor, 765-285-8794, Fax: 765-285-5345, E-mail: cdtaylor@bsu.edu.
Website: http://www.bsu.edu/poli-sci

Bellevue University, Graduate School, College of Information Technology, Bellevue, NE 68005-3098. Offers computer information systems (MS); cybersecurity (MS); management of information systems (MS); project management (MPM).

Bellevue University, Graduate School, College of Professional Studies, Bellevue, NE 68005-3098. Offers instructional design and development (MS); justice administration and criminal management (MS); leadership (MA); organizational performance (MS); public administration (MPA); security management (MS).

Boise State University, School of Public Service, Department of Criminal Justice, Boise, ID 83725-0399. Offers MA. *Program availability:* Part-time. *Faculty:* 8. *Students:* 9 full-time (7 women), 12 part-time (6 women); includes 4 minority (1 Asian, non-Hispanic/Latino; 3 Hispanic/Latino). Average age 31. 15 applicants, 53% accepted, 5 enrolled. In 2017, 13 master's awarded. *Degree requirements:* For master's, thesis optional. *Entrance requirements:* For master's, GRE General Test, minimum GPA of 3.0. Additional exam requirements/recommendations for international students: Required—TOEFL (minimum score 550 paper-based; 80 iBT), IELTS (minimum score 6). *Application deadline:* For fall admission, 4/1 for domestic and international students; for spring admission, 10/1 for domestic and international students. Application fee: $65 ($95 for international students). Electronic applications accepted. *Expenses:* Tuition, state resident: full-time $6471; part-time $390 per credit. Tuition, nonresident: full-time $21,787; part-time $685 per credit. *Required fees:* $2283; $100 per term. Part-time tuition and fees vary according to course load and program. *Financial support:* Scholarships/grants and unspecified assistantships available. Financial award application deadline: 2/15; financial award applicants required to submit FAFSA. *Application contact:* Lisa Growett Bostaph, Program Coordinator, 208-426-3886, E-mail: lisabostaph@boisestate.edu.
Website: http://sps.boisestate.edu/criminaljustice/

Boston University, Metropolitan College, Program in Criminal Justice, Boston, MA 02215. Offers cybercrime investigation and cybersecurity (MCJ); strategic management (MCJ). *Program availability:* Part-time, evening/weekend, online learning. *Faculty:* 5 full-time (2 women), 6 part-time/adjunct (1 woman). *Students:* 14 full-time (5 women), 294 part-time (170 women); includes 99 minority (40 Black or African American, non-Hispanic/Latino; 2 American Indian or Alaska Native, non-Hispanic/Latino; 8 Asian, non-Hispanic/Latino; 40 Hispanic/Latino; 9 Two or more races, non-Hispanic/Latino), 18 international. Average age 30. 104 applicants, 79% accepted, 59 enrolled. In 2017, 155 master's awarded. *Degree requirements:* For master's, comprehensive examination (for on-campus program only). *Entrance requirements:* Additional exam requirements/recommendations for international students: Required—TOEFL (minimum score 84 iBT). *Application deadline:* Applications are processed on a rolling basis. Application fee: $85. Electronic applications accepted. *Expenses:* Contact institution. *Financial support:* In 2017–18, 8 research assistantships (averaging $4,200 per year) were awarded; scholarships/grants and unspecified assistantships also available. Support available to part-time students. Financial award applicants required to submit FAFSA. *Faculty research:* Criminal justice administration and planning, criminology, police, corrections, collective violence, juvenile issues, cybersecurity, forensic psychology. *Unit head:* Dr. Mary Ellen Mastrorilli, Assistant Professor and Associate Chair, 617-353-3025, Fax: 617-358-3595, E-mail: memastro@bu.edu. *Application contact:* Dr. Mary Ellen Mastrorilli, Assistant Professor and Associate Chair, 617-353-3025, E-mail: memastro@bu.edu.
Website: http://www.bu.edu/met/cj/

Bowling Green State University, Graduate College, College of Health and Human Services, Program in Criminal Justice, Bowling Green, OH 43403. Offers MSCJ. *Program availability:* Part-time, evening/weekend, online learning. *Degree requirements:* For master's, thesis or alternative. *Entrance requirements:* For master's, GRE General Test. Additional exam requirements/recommendations for international students: Required—TOEFL. Electronic applications accepted.

Bridgewater State University, College of Graduate Studies, College of Humanities and Social Sciences, Department of Criminal Justice, Bridgewater, MA 02325. Offers MS. *Entrance requirements:* For master's, GRE General Test.

Buffalo State College, State University of New York, The Graduate School, Faculty of Applied Science and Education, Department of Criminal Justice, Buffalo, NY 14222-1095. Offers MS. *Program availability:* Part-time, evening/weekend. *Degree requirements:* For master's, comprehensive exam, project. *Entrance requirements:* For master's, minimum GPA of 3.0. Additional exam requirements/recommendations for international students: Required—TOEFL (minimum score 550 paper-based).

Cabrini University, Academic Affairs, Radnor, PA 19087. Offers accounting (M Acc); autism spectrum disorder (M Ed); biological sciences (MS), including civic leadership; criminology and criminal justice (MA); curriculum, instruction, and assessment (M Ed); educational leadership (M Ed, Ed D), including curriculum and instructional leadership (Ed D), preK-12 leadership (Ed D); English as a second language (M Ed); organizational leadership (DBA, PhD); preK to 4 (M Ed); reading specialist (M Ed); secondary education (M Ed), including biology, chemistry, English, English/communication, mathematics, social studies; special education grades 7-12 (M Ed); special education preK-8 (M Ed); teaching and learning (M Ed). *Program availability:* Part-time, evening/weekend. *Faculty:* 23 full-time (17 women), 46 part-time/adjunct (38 women). *Students:* 60 full-time (35 women), 559 part-time (435 women); includes 93 minority (66 Black or African American, non-Hispanic/Latino; 1 American Indian or Alaska Native, non-Hispanic/Latino; 8 Asian, non-Hispanic/Latino; 15 Hispanic/Latino; 3 Two or more races, non-Hispanic/Latino), 4 international. Average age 33. 290 applicants, 82% accepted, 154 enrolled. In 2017, 283 master's awarded. *Degree requirements:* For master's, comprehensive exam (for some programs), thesis (for some programs); for doctorate, comprehensive exam (for some programs), thesis/dissertation. *Entrance requirements:* For master's, professional resume, personal statement, two recommendations, official transcripts; for doctorate, official transcripts, minimum master's GPA of 3.0, two recommendations, interview with admissions committee. Additional exam requirements/recommendations for international students: Required—TOEFL (minimum score 80 iBT). *Application deadline:* For fall admission, 8/26 for domestic students, 8/1 for international students; for winter admission, 1/13 for domestic students, 12/20 for international students; for spring admission, 1/13 for domestic students, 12/20 for international students; for summer admission, 5/20 for domestic students, 4/30 for international students. Applications are processed on a rolling basis. Application fee: $50. Electronic applications accepted. Application fee is waived when completed online. *Expenses:* Contact institution. *Financial support:* In 2017–18, 1,459 students received support. Tuition waivers and unspecified assistantships available. Financial award application deadline: 5/1; financial award applicants required to submit FAFSA. *Unit head:* Dr. Maliha Zaman, 610-902-8502, Fax: 610-902-8797, E-mail: msz37@cabrini.edu. *Application contact:* Diane Greenwood, Director of Graduate Admissions, 610-902-8291, E-mail: diane.l.greenwood@cabrini.edu.
Website: http://cabrini.edu/graduate

California Coast University, School of Criminal Justice, Santa Ana, CA 92701. Offers MS.

California State University, Fresno, Division of Research and Graduate Studies, College of Social Sciences, Department of Criminology, Fresno, CA 93740-8027. Offers MS. *Program availability:* Part-time, evening/weekend. *Degree requirements:* For master's, thesis project or comprehensive examination. *Entrance requirements:* For master's, GRE General Test, minimum GPA of 3.0, personal essay. Additional exam requirements/recommendations for international students: Required—TOEFL. Electronic applications accepted. *Faculty research:* Substance abuse, gangs vs. law enforcement, needs of female offenders, battered women, crime victims.

California State University, Long Beach, Graduate Studies, College of Health and Human Services, Department of Criminal Justice, Long Beach, CA 90840. Offers criminal justice (MS); emergency services administration (MS). *Program availability:* Part-time. *Degree requirements:* For master's, comprehensive course or thesis. *Entrance requirements:* For master's, minimum GPA of 3.0. Electronic applications accepted.

California State University, Los Angeles, Graduate Studies, College of Health and Human Services, Department of Criminal Justice and Criminalistics, Los Angeles, CA 90032-8530. Offers criminal justice (MS); criminalistics (MS). *Program availability:* Part-time, evening/weekend. *Degree requirements:* For master's, thesis. *Entrance requirements:* For master's, minimum GPA of 2.75. Additional exam requirements/recommendations for international students: Required—TOEFL (minimum score 500 paper-based).

California State University, Sacramento, College of Health and Human Services, Division of Criminal Justice, Sacramento, CA 95819. Offers MS. *Program availability:* Part-time. *Students:* 6 full-time (5 women), 17 part-time (11 women); includes 10 minority (2 Black or African American, non-Hispanic/Latino; 3 Asian, non-Hispanic/Latino; 5 Hispanic/Latino). Average age 27. 18 applicants, 44% accepted, 8 enrolled. In 2017, 8 master's awarded. *Degree requirements:* For master's, thesis or project. *Entrance requirements:* For master's, GRE, BA in criminal justice or equivalent; minimum GPA of 3.0 during previous 2 years of course work and in major field. Additional exam requirements/recommendations for international students: Required—TOEFL (minimum score 550 paper-based; 80 iBT); Recommended—IELTS, TSE. *Application deadline:* For fall admission, 3/1 for domestic and international students; for spring admission, 9/15 for domestic students, 9/30 for international students. Applications are processed on a rolling basis. Application fee: $55. Electronic applications accepted. *Expenses:* Contact institution. *Financial support:* Teaching assistantships, career-related internships or fieldwork, Federal Work-Study, and scholarships/grants available. Support available to part-time students. Financial award application deadline: 3/1; financial award applicants required to submit FAFSA. *Unit head:* Dr. Ernest Uwazie, Chair, 916-278-6282, E-mail: uwazieee@csus.edu. *Application contact:* Jose Martinez, Graduate Admissions Supervisor, 916-278-7871, E-mail: martinj@skymail.csus.edu.
Website: http://www.csus.edu/hhs/cj

California State University, San Bernardino, Graduate Studies, College of Social and Behavioral Sciences, Program in Criminal Justice, San Bernardino, CA 92407. Offers MA. *Program availability:* Part-time. *Faculty:* 4 full-time (3 women). *Students:* 3 full-time (1 woman), 23 part-time (18 women); includes 13 minority (2 Asian, non-Hispanic/Latino; 10 Hispanic/Latino; 1 Two or more races, non-Hispanic/Latino), 2 international. Average age 29. 28 applicants, 71% accepted, 8 enrolled. In 2017, 8 master's awarded. *Entrance requirements:* Additional exam requirements/recommendations for international students: Required—TOEFL. *Application deadline:* For fall admission, 4/1 for domestic students; for winter admission, 9/1 for domestic students; for spring admission, 12/15 for domestic students. Application fee: $55. *Financial support:* Institutionally sponsored loans available. *Faculty research:* Crime seriousness, fear of crime, victimization, corrections management, crime correlates. *Unit head:* Dr. Larry Gaines, Chair, 909-537-5508, Fax: 909-537-7025, E-mail: lgaines@csusb.edu. *Application contact:* Dr. Dorota Huizinga, Dean of Graduate Studies, 909-537-3064, E-mail: dorota.huizinga@csusb.edu.

California State University, Stanislaus, College of the Arts, Humanities and Social Sciences, Master's in Criminal Justice Program, Turlock, CA 95382. Offers MA. *Program availability:* Part-time. *Degree requirements:* For master's, comprehensive exam, thesis or alternative. *Entrance requirements:* For master's, minimum GPA of 3.0, 3 letters of reference, personal statement. Electronic applications accepted. *Faculty research:* Police gerontology services, hate crimes, juvenile justice, masculinities and modern society, nutrition and criminal behavior.

California University of Pennsylvania, School of Graduate Studies and Research, College of Liberal Arts, Department of Criminal Justice, California, PA 15419-1394. Offers conflict resolution (MA); criminal justice studies (MA). *Program availability:* Part-time, evening/weekend. *Degree requirements:* For master's, comprehensive exam, thesis optional. *Entrance requirements:* For master's, MAT, minimum GPA of 3.0. Additional exam requirements/recommendations for international students: Required—TOEFL (minimum score 550 paper-based; 80 iBT). *Application deadline:* For fall

admission, 8/1 priority date for domestic and international students; for spring admission, 5/1 priority date for domestic and international students. Applications are processed on a rolling basis. Application fee: $25. Electronic applications accepted. *Financial support:* Applicants required to submit FAFSA. *Faculty research:* Ethics and law, ethics in police practice, law and morality, police policy, St. Thomas Aquinas and crime. *Unit head:* Dr. John R. Cencich, Director, 724-938-1576, E-mail: cencich@calu.edu. *Application contact:* Suzanne C. Powers, Director of Graduate Admissions and Recruitment, 724-938-4029, Fax: 724-938-5712, E-mail: powers_s@cup.edu.
Website: http://www.calu.edu/academics/colleges/liberal-arts/criminal-justice/

California University of Pennsylvania, School of Graduate Studies and Research, College of Liberal Arts, Department of History, Politics, Society and Law, California, PA 15419-1394. Offers legal studies (MS), including criminal justice, homeland security, law and public policy. *Program availability:* Part-time, evening/weekend, online learning. *Faculty:* 2 part-time/adjunct (both women). *Degree requirements:* For master's, thesis optional. *Entrance requirements:* For master's, interview, minimum GPA of 3.0. Additional exam requirements/recommendations for international students: Required—TOEFL (minimum score 550 paper-based; 80 iBT). *Application deadline:* For fall admission, 8/1 priority date for domestic and international students; for winter admission, 12/1 priority date for domestic and international students; for spring admission, 5/1 priority date for domestic and international students. Applications are processed on a rolling basis. Application fee: $25. Electronic applications accepted. *Financial support:* Career-related internships or fieldwork, scholarships/grants, traineeships, and unspecified assistantships available. Financial award applicants required to submit FAFSA. *Faculty research:* Ethics in political practice, ethics and law, law and morality, St. Thomas Aquinas and crime, police policy. *Unit head:* Dr. Christina A. Toras, Chair, 724-938-4761, E-mail: toras@calu.edu. *Application contact:* Suzanne C. Powers, Director of Graduate Admissions and Recruitment, 724-938-4029, Fax: 724-938-5712, E-mail: powers_s@cup.edu.

Calumet College of Saint Joseph, Program in Public Safety Administration, Whiting, IN 46394-2195. Offers MS.

Capella University, School of Public Service Leadership, Doctoral Programs in Healthcare, Minneapolis, MN 55402. Offers criminal justice (PhD); emergency management (PhD); epidemiology (Dr PH); general health administration (DHA); general public administration (DPA); health advocacy and leadership (Dr PH); health care administration (PhD); health care leadership (DHA); health policy advocacy (DHA); multidisciplinary human services (PhD); nonprofit management and leadership (PhD); public safety leadership (PhD); social and community services (PhD).

Capella University, School of Public Service Leadership, Master's Programs in Healthcare, Minneapolis, MN 55402. Offers criminal justice (MS); emergency management (MS); general public health (MPH); gerontology (MS); health administration (MHA); health care operations (MHA); health management policy (MPH); health policy (MHA); homeland security (MS); multidisciplinary human services (MS); public administration (MPA); public safety leadership (MS); social and community services (MS); social behavioral sciences (MPH); MS/MPA.

Cardinal Stritch University, College of Business and Management, Milwaukee, WI 53217-3985. Offers cyber security (MBA); healthcare management (MBA); justice administration (MBA); marketing (MBA). *Accreditation:* ACBSP. *Program availability:* Part-time, evening/weekend, 100% online, blended/hybrid learning. *Students:* 133 full-time (72 women), 98 part-time (54 women); includes 88 minority (64 Black or African American, non-Hispanic/Latino; 1 American Indian or Alaska Native, non-Hispanic/Latino; 12 Asian, non-Hispanic/Latino; 10 Hispanic/Latino; 1 Two or more races, non-Hispanic/Latino), 8 international. Average age 36. 144 applicants, 100% accepted, 57 enrolled. In 2017, 118 master's awarded. *Degree requirements:* For master's, thesis. *Entrance requirements:* For master's, 3 years of management or related experience, minimum GPA of 2.5. Additional exam requirements/recommendations for international students: Required—TOEFL (minimum score 79 iBT), IELTS (minimum score 6.5). *Application deadline:* Applications are processed on a rolling basis. Application fee: $0. Electronic applications accepted. *Expenses:* $665 per credit. *Financial support:* Career-related internships or fieldwork, Federal Work-Study, and scholarships/grants available. Financial award applicants required to submit FAFSA. *Unit head:* Janette Braverman, Dean, 414-410-4004, E-mail: jmbraverman1@stritch.edu. *Application contact:* Graduate Admissions, 414-410-4042, E-mail: admissions@stritch.edu.
Website: http://www.stritch.edu/cbm

Caribbean University, Graduate School, Bayamón, PR 00960-0493. Offers administration and supervision (MA Ed); criminal justice (MA); curriculum and instruction (MA Ed, PhD), including elementary education (MA Ed), English education (MA Ed), history education (MA Ed), mathematics education (MA Ed), primary education (MA Ed), science education (MA Ed), Spanish education (MA Ed); educational technology in instructional systems (MA Ed); gerontology (MSN); human resources (MBA); museology, archiving and art history (MA Ed); neonatal pediatrics (MSN); physical education (MA Ed); special education (MA Ed). *Entrance requirements:* For master's, interview, minimum GPA of 2.5.

Carnegie Mellon University, Heinz College, School of Information Systems and Management, Master of Science in Information Security Policy and Management Program, Pittsburgh, PA 15213-3891. Offers MSISPM. *Entrance requirements:* For master's, GRE or GMAT, college-level course in advanced algebra/pre-calculus; college-level courses in economics and statistics (recommended). Additional exam requirements/recommendations for international students: Required—TOEFL or IELTS.

The Catholic University of America, School of Arts and Sciences, Department of Sociology, Washington, DC 20064. Offers crime and justice studies (MA); global and comparative sociology (MA); public policy (MA). *Program availability:* Part-time. *Faculty:* 3 full-time (2 women), 3 part-time/adjunct (0 women). *Students:* 1 (woman) full-time, 1 (woman) part-time; includes 1 minority (Hispanic/Latino). Average age 24. 2 applicants. *Degree requirements:* For master's, comprehensive exam, thesis or alternative, two seminar papers. *Entrance requirements:* For master's, GRE General Test, statement of purpose, official copies of academic transcripts, three letters of recommendation. Additional exam requirements/recommendations for international students: Required—TOEFL (minimum score 550 paper-based; 80 iBT). *Application deadline:* For fall admission, 7/15 priority date for domestic students, 7/1 for international students; for spring admission, 11/15 priority date for domestic students, 11/1 for international students. Applications are processed on a rolling basis. Application fee: $55. Electronic applications accepted. *Expenses:* Contact institution. *Financial support:* Fellowships, research assistantships, teaching assistantships, Federal Work-Study, scholarships/grants, tuition waivers (full and partial), and unspecified assistantships available. Financial award application deadline: 2/1; financial award applicants required to submit FAFSA. *Faculty research:* Social movements, gender structure, political sociology, race and ethnic relations, evaluation methodologies. *Unit head:* Dr. David Walsh, Chair, 202-319-5445, Fax: 202-319-4980, E-mail: pumar@cua.edu. *Application contact:* Dr. Steven Brown, Director of Graduate Admissions, 202-319-5057, Fax: 202-319-6533, E-mail: cua-admissions@cua.edu.
Website: http://sociology.cua.edu/

Central Connecticut State University, School of Graduate Studies, College of Liberal Arts and Social Sciences, Department of Criminology and Criminal Justice, New Britain, CT 06050-4010. Offers criminal justice (MS). *Program availability:* Part-time, evening/weekend. *Faculty:* 9 full-time (5 women), 1 part-time/adjunct (0 women). *Students:* 6 full-time (all women), 21 part-time (9 women); includes 12 minority (5 Black or African American, non-Hispanic/Latino; 3 Asian, non-Hispanic/Latino; 3 Hispanic/Latino; 1 Two or more races, non-Hispanic/Latino). Average age 26. 19 applicants, 74% accepted, 8 enrolled. In 2017, 14 master's awarded. *Degree requirements:* For master's, comprehensive exam, thesis or alternative. *Entrance requirements:* For master's, minimum undergraduate GPA of 3.0, essay, resume. Additional exam requirements/recommendations for international students: Required—TOEFL (minimum score 550 paper-based; 79 iBT); Recommended—IELTS (minimum score 6.5). *Application deadline:* For fall admission, 6/1 for domestic students, 5/1 for international students; for spring admission, 11/1 for domestic and international students. Applications are processed on a rolling basis. Application fee: $50. Electronic applications accepted. *Expenses: Tuition, area resident:* Full-time $6757. Tuition, state resident: full-time $9750; part-time $374 per credit. Tuition, nonresident: full-time $18,102; part-time $374 per credit. *Required fees:* $4635; $255 per credit. *Financial support:* In 2017–18, 6 students received support. Career-related internships or fieldwork, Federal Work-Study, scholarships/grants, and unspecified assistantships available. Support available to part-time students. Financial award application deadline: 3/1; financial award applicants required to submit FAFSA. *Unit head:* Dr. Kathleen Bantley, Chair, 860-832-3005, E-mail: bantleyk@ccsu.edu. *Application contact:* Patricia Gardner, Associate Director of Graduate Studies, 860-832-2350, Fax: 860-832-2362.
Website: http://www.ccsu.edu/criminology/index.html

Chaminade University of Honolulu, Office of Professional and Continuing Education, Program in Criminal Justice Administration, Honolulu, HI 96816-1578. Offers correctional (MSCJA); criminal justice (MSCJA); law enforcement (MSCJA). *Program availability:* Part-time, evening/weekend, 100% online, blended/hybrid learning. *Faculty:* 2 full-time (0 women), 3 part-time/adjunct (all women). *Students:* 34 full-time (20 women), 12 part-time (9 women); includes 36 minority (5 Black or African American, non-Hispanic/Latino; 12 Asian, non-Hispanic/Latino; 6 Hispanic/Latino; 11 Native Hawaiian or other Pacific Islander, non-Hispanic/Latino; 2 Two or more races, non-Hispanic/Latino). Average age 30. 9 applicants, 78% accepted, 4 enrolled. In 2017, 28 master's awarded. *Degree requirements:* For master's, comprehensive exam. *Entrance requirements:* For master's, minimum undergraduate GPA of 3.0, 3 letters of recommendation, interview, resume. Additional exam requirements/recommendations for international students: Required—TOEFL (minimum score 550 paper-based; 79 iBT). *Application deadline:* Applications are processed on a rolling basis. Application fee: $40. Electronic applications accepted. *Expenses:* $860 per credit hour plus $93 fee per online course. *Financial support:* Applicants required to submit FAFSA. *Unit head:* Ronald Becker, Director, 808-735-4703, Fax: 808-739-4614, E-mail: mscja@chaminade.edu. *Application contact:* 808-735-4755, E-mail: gradserv@chaminade.edu.
Website: https://pace.chaminade.edu/graduate-programs/mscja-program/

Charleston Southern University, Department of Criminal Justice, Charleston, SC 29423-8087. Offers MSCJ. *Program availability:* Part-time, evening/weekend, online learning. *Degree requirements:* For master's, comprehensive exam, thesis optional. *Entrance requirements:* For master's, GRE or MAT, bachelor's degree in criminal justice. Additional exam requirements/recommendations for international students: Required—TOEFL (minimum score 550 paper-based; 79 iBT). *Application deadline:* Applications are processed on a rolling basis. Application fee: $40. Electronic applications accepted. *Expenses: Tuition:* Part-time $500 per credit hour. One-time fee: $30. Tuition and fees vary according to program. *Financial support:* Research assistantships with full tuition reimbursements available. Financial award application deadline: 4/15; financial award applicants required to submit FAFSA. *Unit head:* Gary Metts, Interim Chair, 843-863-7330, Fax: 843-863-7198, E-mail: gmetts@csuniv.edu.
Website: http://www.csuniv.edu/criminaljustice/

Chicago State University, School of Graduate and Professional Studies, College of Arts and Sciences, Department of Criminal Justice, Philosophy, and Political Science, Chicago, IL 60628. Offers criminal justice (MS). *Program availability:* Part-time, evening/weekend. *Entrance requirements:* For master's, minimum GPA of 2.75. *Application deadline:* For fall admission, 7/1 for domestic students; for spring admission, 11/10 for domestic students. Applications are processed on a rolling basis. Application fee: $25. *Faculty research:* Gang crime. *Unit head:* Emmett L. Bradbury, III, Chairperson, 773-995-2343, Fax: 773-995-3819, E-mail: ebradbur@csu.edu. *Application contact:* Graduate Studies Office, 773-995-2404.
Website: http://www.csu.edu/cas/criminalphilosophypolitical/

Clark Atlanta University, School of Arts and Sciences, Department of Sociology and Criminal Justice, Atlanta, GA 30314. Offers MA. *Program availability:* Part-time. *Faculty:* 5 full-time (4 women), 6 part-time/adjunct (1 woman). *Students:* 20 full-time (15 women), 3 part-time (1 woman); includes 14 minority (all Black or African American, non-Hispanic/Latino), 7 international. Average age 26. 8 applicants, 88% accepted, 5 enrolled. In 2017, 8 master's awarded. *Degree requirements:* For master's, one foreign language, comprehensive exam, thesis. *Entrance requirements:* For master's, GRE General Test, minimum GPA of 2.5. Additional exam requirements/recommendations for international students: Required—TOEFL (minimum score 500 paper-based; 61 iBT). *Application deadline:* For fall admission, 4/1 for domestic and international students; for spring admission, 11/1 for domestic and international students. Applications are processed on a rolling basis. Application fee: $40 ($55 for international students). Electronic applications accepted. *Financial support:* Scholarships/grants and unspecified assistantships available. Financial award application deadline: 4/30; financial award applicants required to submit FAFSA. *Faculty research:* Gerontology, geriatric education. *Unit head:* Dr. Obie Clayton, Chairperson, 404-880-8681, E-mail: oclayton@cau.edu.

Clayton State University, School of Graduate Studies, College of Arts and Sciences, Program in Criminal Justice, Morrow, GA 30260-0285. Offers administration of justice (MS); criminology, law, and society (MS).

Clemson University, Graduate School, College of Behavioral, Social and Health Sciences, Department of Sociology, Anthropology and Criminal Justice, Clemson, SC 29634. Offers applied sociology (MS). *Program availability:* Part-time. *Faculty:* 17 full-time (12 women). *Students:* 14 full-time (8 women), 2 part-time (both women); includes 2 minority (both Black or African American, non-Hispanic/Latino), 6 international. Average age 28. 13 applicants, 77% accepted, 5 enrolled. In 2017, 8 master's awarded. *Degree requirements:* For master's, thesis optional. *Entrance requirements:* For master's, GRE General Test, unofficial transcripts, letters of recommendation. Additional exam requirements/recommendations for international students: Required—TOEFL (minimum score 80 iBT), IELTS (minimum score 6.5), PTE (minimum score 54). *Application deadline:* For fall admission, 2/1 priority date for domestic and international students. Applications are processed on a rolling basis. Application fee: $80 ($90 for international students). Electronic applications accepted. *Expenses:* $5,174 per semester full-time resident, $9,714 per semester full-time non-resident, $511 per credit hour part-time resident, $1,017 per credit hour part-time non-resident; $741 per credit hour online; other fees may apply per session. *Financial support:* In 2017–18, 5 students received

support, including 5 teaching assistantships with partial tuition reimbursements available (averaging $11,000 per year); career-related internships or fieldwork also available. Financial award application deadline: 2/1. *Faculty research:* Environmental issues; social inequalities; health and medical development; sociology of food, nutrition, and food security. *Total annual research expenditures:* $36,371. *Unit head:* Dr. Catherine Weisensee, Interim Department Chair, 864-656-3238, E-mail: kweisen@clemson.edu. *Application contact:* Dr. William Haller, Graduate Program Coordinator, 864-656-3814, E-mail: whaller@clemson.edu.
Website: http://www.clemson.edu/cbshs/departments/sociology/

Coker College, Graduate Programs, Hartsville, SC 29550. Offers college athletic administration (MS); criminal and social justice policy (MS); curriculum and instructional technology (M Ed); literacy studies (M Ed); management and leadership (MS). *Program availability:* Part-time, 100% online. *Faculty:* 9 full-time (4 women), 3 part-time/adjunct (2 women). *Students:* 77 full-time (47 women), 9 part-time (4 women); includes 21 minority (15 Black or African American, non-Hispanic/Latino; 1 American Indian or Alaska Native, non-Hispanic/Latino; 1 Hispanic/Latino; 4 Two or more races, non-Hispanic/Latino), 1 international. Average age 30. *Degree requirements:* For master's, comprehensive exam, portfolio. *Entrance requirements:* For master's, GRE or GMAT, minimum overall GPA of 2.85 in bachelor's program, official transcripts, resume, three letters of recommendation, teacher licensure. *Application deadline:* Applications are processed on a rolling basis. Application fee: $25. Electronic applications accepted. *Expenses: Tuition:* Full-time $14,424; part-time $601 per credit hour. *Required fees:* $176; $176 per credit hour. Tuition and fees vary according to course load and program. *Financial support:* Unspecified assistantships available. Financial award application deadline: 6/30; financial award applicants required to submit FAFSA. *Application contact:* Lacey Rice-Serafin, Director of Graduate Programs, 843-857-4128, E-mail: lriceserafin@coker.edu.

College of Saint Elizabeth, Program in Justice Administration and Public Service, Morristown, NJ 07960-6989. Offers counter terrorism (Certificate); cyber security investigation (Certificate); justice administration and public service (MA); leadership in community policing (Certificate). *Program availability:* Part-time, 100% online, blended/hybrid learning. *Faculty:* 3 full-time (1 woman), 1 (woman) part-time/adjunct. *Students:* 4 full-time (2 women), 21 part-time (12 women); includes 12 minority (8 Black or African American, non-Hispanic/Latino; 1 Asian, non-Hispanic/Latino; 2 Hispanic/Latino; 1 Two or more races, non-Hispanic/Latino). Average age 31. 15 applicants, 100% accepted, 10 enrolled. In 2017, 13 master's awarded. *Degree requirements:* For master's, thesis. *Entrance requirements:* Additional exam requirements/recommendations for international students: Required—TOEFL (minimum score 550 paper-based; 79 iBT), IELTS (minimum score 6.5). *Application deadline:* For fall admission, 5/1 for international students. Applications are processed on a rolling basis. Application fee: $35. Electronic applications accepted. Application fee is waived when completed online. *Expenses:* Contact institution. *Financial support:* Career-related internships or fieldwork, scholarships/grants, and unspecified assistantships available. Support available to part-time students. Financial award applicants required to submit FAFSA. *Unit head:* Dr. James Ford, Associate Professor, 973-290-4324, E-mail: jford@cse.edu. *Application contact:* Lori J. Fragoso, Director of Graduate and Continuing Studies Admissions, 973-290-4413, Fax: 973-290-4710, E-mail: apply@cse.edu.
Website: http://www.cse.edu/academics/prof-studies/criminal-justice/

Colorado State University–Global Campus, Graduate Programs, Greenwood Village, CO 80111. Offers criminal justice and law enforcement administration (MS); education leadership (MS); finance (MS); healthcare administration and management (MS); human resource management (MHRM); information technology management (MITM); international management (MS); management (MS); organizational leadership (MS); professional accounting (MPA); project management (MS); teaching and learning (MS). *Accreditation:* ACBSP. *Program availability:* Online learning.

Colorado Technical University Aurora, Program in Computer Science, Aurora, CO 80014. Offers computer systems security (MSCS); database systems (MSCS); software engineering (MSCS). *Program availability:* Part-time, evening/weekend. *Degree requirements:* For master's, thesis or alternative. *Entrance requirements:* For master's, minimum undergraduate GPA of 3.0, resume.

Colorado Technical University Colorado Springs, Graduate Studies, Program in Criminal Justice, Colorado Springs, CO 80907. Offers MSM. *Program availability:* Online learning.

Columbia College, Graduate Programs, Program in Criminal Justice, Columbia, SC 29203-5998. Offers MA. *Expenses: Tuition:* Full-time $15,840; part-time $480 per semester hour. Full-time tuition and fees vary according to course load.

Columbia College, Master of Science in Criminal Justice Program, Columbia, MO 65216-0002. Offers MSCJ. *Program availability:* Part-time, evening/weekend, 100% online, blended/hybrid learning. *Faculty:* 3 full-time (0 women), 26 part-time/adjunct (13 women). *Students:* 10 full-time (4 women), 100 part-time (62 women); includes 42 minority (27 Black or African American, non-Hispanic/Latino; 1 American Indian or Alaska Native, non-Hispanic/Latino; 12 Hispanic/Latino; 2 Two or more races, non-Hispanic/Latino). Average age 40. 80 applicants, 76% accepted, 27 enrolled. In 2017, 42 master's awarded. *Degree requirements:* For master's, final exams, culminating experience (intensive writing seminar). *Entrance requirements:* Additional exam requirements/recommendations for international students: Required—TOEFL (minimum score 550 paper-based; 79 iBT). *Application deadline:* For fall admission, 8/9 priority date for domestic and international students; for spring admission, 12/27 priority date for domestic and international students. Applications are processed on a rolling basis. Application fee: $55. Electronic applications accepted. *Expenses:* Contact institution. *Financial support:* In 2017–18, 9 students received support. Federal Work-Study and scholarships/grants available. Financial award application deadline: 3/1; financial award applicants required to submit FAFSA. *Unit head:* Dr. David Roebuck, Dean of the School of Humanities, 573-875-7570, E-mail: cdroebuck@ccis.edu. *Application contact:* Stephanie Johnson, Director of Admissions, 573-875-7352, Fax: 573-875-7506, E-mail: sgjohnson@ccis.edu.
Website: http://www.ccis.edu/graduate/academics/degrees.asp?MSCJ

Columbia Southern University, College of Safety and Emergency Services, Orange Beach, AL 36561. Offers criminal justice administration (MS); emergency services management (MS); occupational safety and health (MS), including environmental management. *Program availability:* Part-time, evening/weekend, online learning. *Entrance requirements:* For master's, bachelor's degree from accredited/approved institution. Additional exam requirements/recommendations for international students: Required—TOEFL. Electronic applications accepted.

Columbus State University, Graduate Studies, College of Letters and Sciences, Department of Political Science and Public Administration, Columbus, GA 31907-5645. Offers public administration (MPA), including criminal justice, environmental policy, government administration, health services administration, political campaigning, urban policy. *Program availability:* Part-time, evening/weekend, 100% online, blended/hybrid learning. *Faculty:* 15 full-time (6 women), 14 part-time/adjunct (0 women). *Students:* 34 full-time (21 women), 44 part-time (24 women); includes 40 minority (32 Black or African American, non-Hispanic/Latino; 2 Asian, non-Hispanic/Latino; 3 Hispanic/Latino; 1

Native Hawaiian or other Pacific Islander, non-Hispanic/Latino; 2 Two or more races, non-Hispanic/Latino), 3 international. Average age 33. 68 applicants, 43% accepted, 21 enrolled. In 2017, 38 master's awarded. *Degree requirements:* For master's, comprehensive exam. *Entrance requirements:* For master's, GRE General Test, minimum GPA of 2.75, three letters of recommendation. Additional exam requirements/recommendations for international students: Required—TOEFL (minimum score 550 paper-based; 79 iBT). *Application deadline:* For fall admission, 6/30 for domestic students, 5/1 for international students; for spring admission, 11/1 for domestic and international students; for summer admission, 3/1 for domestic and international students. Applications are processed on a rolling basis. Application fee: $50. Electronic applications accepted. *Expenses:* Tuition, state resident: full-time $3708; part-time $2472 per year. Tuition, nonresident: full-time $14,418; part-time $9612 per year. *International tuition:* $19,218 full-time. *Required fees:* $1605. Tuition and fees vary according to program. *Financial support:* In 2017–18, 4 students received support, including 6 research assistantships with partial tuition reimbursements available (averaging $3,000 per year); career-related internships or fieldwork, Federal Work-Study, institutionally sponsored loans, scholarships/grants, tuition waivers (partial), and unspecified assistantships also available. Support available to part-time students. Financial award application deadline: 5/1; financial award applicants required to submit FAFSA. *Unit head:* Dr. Frederick Gordon, Director, 706-565-7875, E-mail: gordon_frederick@colstate.edu. *Application contact:* Catrina Smith-Edmond, Assistant Director for Graduate and Global Admission, 706-507-8824, Fax: 706-568-5091, E-mail: smithedmond_catrina@columbusstate.edu.
Website: http://politicalscience.columbusstate.edu/

Coppin State University, Division of Graduate Studies, Division of Arts and Sciences, Department of Criminal Justice and Law Enforcement, Baltimore, MD 21216-3698. Offers criminal justice (MS). *Program availability:* Part-time, evening/weekend. *Degree requirements:* For master's, thesis optional. *Entrance requirements:* For master's, GRE, minimum GPA of 3.0.

Curry College, Graduate Studies, Program in Criminal Justice, Milton, MA 02186-9984. Offers MA. *Program availability:* Part-time, evening/weekend. *Degree requirements:* For master's, thesis. *Entrance requirements:* For master's, resume, recommendations, interview. Additional exam requirements/recommendations for international students: Required—TOEFL (minimum score 550 paper-based; 80 iBT). *Expenses:* Contact institution.

Dallas Baptist University, Professional Development Program, Dallas, TX 75211-9299. Offers accounting (MA); church leadership (MA); communication (MA); counseling (MA); criminal justice (MA); English as a second language (MA); finance (MA); higher education (MA); leadership studies (MA); management (MA). *Program availability:* Part-time, evening/weekend. *Application deadline:* Applications are processed on a rolling basis. Application fee: $25. Electronic applications accepted. Application fee is waived when completed online. *Expenses: Tuition:* Full-time $16,308; part-time $906 per credit hour. *Required fees:* $900; $450 per semester. Tuition and fees vary according to course load and degree level. *Unit head:* Jared Ingram, Program Director, 214-333-5584, E-mail: jaredi@dbu.edu. *Application contact:* Bobby Soto, Director of Admissions, 214-333-5242, E-mail: bobby@dbu.edu.
Website: http://www3.dbu.edu/graduate/mapd.asp

Delta State University, Graduate Programs, College of Arts and Sciences, Division of Social Sciences and History, Program in Social Justice and Criminology, Cleveland, MS 38733-0001. Offers MSJC. *Program availability:* Part-time, online learning. *Degree requirements:* For master's, thesis or alternative.

DeSales University, Division of Liberal Arts and Social Sciences, Center Valley, PA 18034-9568. Offers criminal justice (MCJ); digital forensics (MCJ, Postbaccalaureate Certificate); education (M Ed), including instructional technology, secondary education, special education, teaching English to speakers of other languages; investigative forensics (MCJ, Postbaccalaureate Certificate). *Program availability:* Part-time, 100% online, blended/hybrid learning. *Faculty:* 5 full-time (3 women), 15 part-time/adjunct (9 women). *Students:* 54 full-time (36 women), 112 part-time (68 women); includes 23 minority (3 Black or African American, non-Hispanic/Latino; 1 Asian, non-Hispanic/Latino; 17 Hispanic/Latino; 2 Two or more races, non-Hispanic/Latino), 1 international. Average age 33. 114 applicants, 64% accepted, 41 enrolled. In 2017, 41 master's awarded. *Entrance requirements:* For master's, bachelor's degree from accredited institution, minimum undergraduate GPA of 3.0, personal statement showing potential of graduate work, three letters of recommendation, professional goal statement. Additional exam requirements/recommendations for international students: Required—TOEFL. *Application deadline:* Applications are processed on a rolling basis. Application fee: $50. Electronic applications accepted. *Expenses: Tuition:* Part-time $840 per credit. Full-time tuition and fees vary according to course load, degree level and program. *Financial support:* Applicants required to submit FAFSA. *Unit head:* Ronald Nordone, Dean of Graduate Education, 610-282-1100 Ext. 1289, E-mail: ronald.nordone@desales.edu. *Application contact:* Julia Ferraro, Director of Graduate Admissions, 610-282-1100 Ext. 1768, E-mail: gradadmissions@desales.edu.

East Carolina University, Graduate School, Thomas Harriot College of Arts and Sciences, Department of Criminal Justice, Greenville, NC 27858-4353. Offers criminal justice (MS); criminal justice education (Certificate). *Program availability:* Part-time, evening/weekend, online learning. *Students:* 19 full-time (9 women), 54 part-time (21 women); includes 24 minority (20 Black or African American, non-Hispanic/Latino; 1 American Indian or Alaska Native, non-Hispanic/Latino; 3 Hispanic/Latino). Average age 33. 23 applicants, 100% accepted, 18 enrolled. In 2017, 14 master's, 14 other advanced degrees awarded. *Entrance requirements:* For master's, GRE. Additional exam requirements/recommendations for international students: Recommended—TOEFL (minimum score 78 iBT), IELTS (minimum score 6.5). *Application deadline:* For fall admission, 4/1 priority date for domestic and international students; for spring admission, 10/1 priority date for domestic and international students. Applications are processed on a rolling basis. Application fee: $75. Electronic applications accepted. *Expenses:* Tuition, state resident: full-time $4749; part-time $297 per credit hour. Tuition, nonresident: full-time $17,898; part-time $1119 per credit hour. *Required fees:* $2691; $224 per credit hour. Part-time tuition and fees vary according to course load and program. *Financial support:* Research assistantships with tuition reimbursements, career-related internships or fieldwork, Federal Work-Study, institutionally sponsored loans, scholarships/grants, and unspecified assistantships available. Financial award application deadline: 3/1. *Faculty research:* Corrections, policing, international criminal justice, terrorism. *Unit head:* Dr. William P. Bloss, Chair, 252-328-4192, Fax: 252-328-4196, E-mail: blossw@ecu.edu. *Application contact:* Dean of Graduate School, 252-328-6012, Fax: 252-328-6071, E-mail: gradschool@ecu.edu.
Website: http://www.ecu.edu/cs-cas/just/index.cfm

East Carolina University, Graduate School, Thomas Harriot College of Arts and Sciences, Department of Political Science, Greenville, NC 27858-4353. Offers public administration (MPA); security studies (MS, Certificate). *Accreditation:* NASPAA. *Program availability:* Part-time, evening/weekend, online learning. *Students:* 29 full-time (13 women), 76 part-time (30 women); includes 27 minority (16 Black or African American, non-Hispanic/Latino; 1 American Indian or Alaska Native, non-Hispanic/Latino; 1 Asian, non-Hispanic/Latino; 9 Hispanic/Latino), 1 international. Average age

34. 28 applicants, 100% accepted, 18 enrolled. In 2017, 21 master's, 10 other advanced degrees awarded. *Degree requirements:* For master's, internship, professional paper. *Entrance requirements:* For master's, GRE General Test. Additional exam requirements/recommendations for international students: Recommended—TOEFL (minimum score 78 iBT), IELTS (minimum score 6.5). *Application deadline:* For fall admission, 6/1 priority date for domestic students; for spring admission, 10/15 for domestic students. Applications are processed on a rolling basis. Application fee: $75. Electronic applications accepted. *Expenses:* Tuition, state resident: full-time $4749; part-time $297 per credit hour. Tuition, nonresident: full-time $17,898; part-time $1119 per credit hour. *Required fees:* $2691; $224 per credit hour. Part-time tuition and fees vary according to course load and program. *Financial support:* Research assistantships with partial tuition reimbursements, teaching assistantships with partial tuition reimbursements, and Federal Work-Study available. Support available to part-time students. Financial award application deadline: 3/1. *Unit head:* Dr. Alethia Cook, Chair, 252-328-5869, E-mail: cooka@ecu.edu. *Application contact:* Dean of Graduate School, 252-328-6012, Fax: 252-328-6071, E-mail: gradschool@ecu.edu.
Website: http://www.ecu.edu/polsci/

East Central University, School of Graduate Studies, Department of Professional Programs in Human Services, Ada, OK 74820. Offers clinical rehabilitation and clinical mental health counseling (MSHR); criminal justice (MSHR); human resources (MSHR). *Accreditation:* CORE. *Program availability:* Part-time, evening/weekend. *Degree requirements:* For master's, thesis optional. *Entrance requirements:* For master's, GRE General Test, MAT, minimum GPA of 2.5. *Application deadline:* Applications are processed on a rolling basis. Application fee: $0 ($50 for international students). Electronic applications accepted. *Unit head:* Regina Robertson, Chair, 580-559-5647, E-mail: rrobrtsn@ecok.edu. *Application contact:* Regina Robertson, Chair, 580-559-5647, E-mail: rrobrtsn@ecok.edu.
Website: http://www.ecok.edu/academics/colleges-and-schools/college-liberal-arts-and-social-sciences/department-human-resources

Eastern Kentucky University, The Graduate School, College of Justice and Safety, Program in Correctional and Juvenile Justice Studies, Richmond, KY 40475-3102. Offers MS. *Degree requirements:* For master's, comprehensive exam (for some programs), thesis (for some programs). *Entrance requirements:* For master's, GRE.

Eastern Kentucky University, The Graduate School, College of Justice and Safety, Program in Criminal Justice and Police Studies, Richmond, KY 40475-3102. Offers criminal justice (MS); criminal justice education (MS); police studies (MS). *Program availability:* Part-time. *Degree requirements:* For master's, thesis optional. *Entrance requirements:* For master's, GRE General Test, minimum GPA of 3.0.

Eastern Kentucky University, The Graduate School, College of Justice and Safety, Program in Loss Prevention and Safety, Richmond, KY 40475-3102. Offers MS. *Entrance requirements:* For master's, GRE.

Eastern Michigan University, Graduate School, College of Arts and Sciences, Department of Sociology, Anthropology and Criminology, Program in Criminology and Criminal Justice, Ypsilanti, MI 48197. Offers MA. *Students:* 2 full-time (1 woman), 8 part-time (6 women); includes 4 minority (2 Black or African American, non-Hispanic/Latino; 1 Hispanic/Latino; 1 Two or more races, non-Hispanic/Latino). Average age 33. 11 applicants, 45% accepted, 1 enrolled. In 2017, 1 master's awarded. Application fee: $45. *Application contact:* Dr. Brian Sellers, Advisor, 734-487-0012, Fax: 734-487-9666, E-mail: bseller3@emich.edu.

East Tennessee State University, School of Graduate Studies, College of Arts and Sciences, Department of Criminal Justice and Criminology, Johnson City, TN 37614. Offers criminal justice and criminology (MA); forensic document examination (Postbaccalaureate Certificate). *Program availability:* Part-time, evening/weekend. *Degree requirements:* For master's, comprehensive exam, thesis optional; for Postbaccalaureate Certificate, practicum. *Entrance requirements:* For master's, GRE General Test, minimum GPA of 3.0; for Postbaccalaureate Certificate, minimum GPA of 2.5, three letters of recommendation. Additional exam requirements/recommendations for international students: Required—TOEFL (minimum score 550 paper-based; 79 iBT). *Application deadline:* For fall admission, 6/1 for domestic students, 4/29 for international students; for spring admission, 11/1 for domestic students, 9/29 for international students. Application fee: $55 ($65 for international students). Electronic applications accepted. *Financial support:* Research assistantships with tuition reimbursements, teaching assistantships with full tuition reimbursements, career-related internships or fieldwork, institutionally sponsored loans, scholarships/grants, and unspecified assistantships available. Financial award application deadline: 7/1; financial award applicants required to submit FAFSA. *Faculty research:* Adolescent work experience and delinquency, violence against women, prisons and inmates, death penalty, women and crime, juvenile justice and alternative education. *Unit head:* Dr. Larry Miller, Chair, 423-439-5964, Fax: 423-439-4660, E-mail: millerls@etsu.edu. *Application contact:* Dr. Dustin Osborne, Graduate Coordinator, 423-439-4324, Fax: 423-439-5624, E-mail: osbornedl@etsu.edu.
Website: http://www.etsu.edu/cas/cj/

Excelsior College, School of Business and Technology, Albany, NY 12203-5159. Offers business administration (MBA); cybersecurity - information assurance (MS); cybersecurity - medical data security (MS); cybersecurity - policy administration (MS); cybersecurity management (MBA, Graduate Certificate); general business management (MS); health care management (MBA); human performance technology (MBA); human resource management (MS); human resources management (MBA); leadership (MBA, MS); mediation and arbitration (MBA, MS); social media management (MBA); technology management (MBA). *Program availability:* Part-time, evening/weekend, online learning. *Faculty:* 30 part-time/adjunct (12 women). *Students:* 1,204 part-time (333 women); includes 560 minority (310 Black or African American, non-Hispanic/Latino; 7 American Indian or Alaska Native, non-Hispanic/Latino; 42 Asian, non-Hispanic/Latino; 140 Hispanic/Latino; 10 Native Hawaiian or other Pacific Islander, non-Hispanic/Latino; 51 Two or more races, non-Hispanic/Latino). Average age 40. In 2017, 294 master's awarded. *Application deadline:* Applications are processed on a rolling basis. Application fee: $50. Electronic applications accepted. *Expenses: Tuition:* Part-time $645 per credit. *Required fees:* $265 per credit. *Financial support:* Scholarships/grants available. *Unit head:* Dr. Lifang Shih, Dean, 888-647-2388. *Application contact:* Admissions, 888-647-2388 Ext. 133, Fax: 518-464-8777, E-mail: admissions@excelsior.edu.

Excelsior College, School of Public Service, Albany, NY 12203-5159. Offers criminal justice (MSCJ); homeland security and emergency management (MSCJ); justice administration (MSCJ); mediation and arbitration (MPA); public administration (MPA). *Program availability:* Part-time, evening/weekend, online learning. *Faculty:* 6 part-time/adjunct (5 women). *Students:* 173 part-time (49 women); includes 70 minority (32 Black or African American, non-Hispanic/Latino; 1 American Indian or Alaska Native, non-Hispanic/Latino; 3 Asian, non-Hispanic/Latino; 28 Hispanic/Latino; 1 Native Hawaiian or other Pacific Islander, non-Hispanic/Latino; 5 Two or more races, non-Hispanic/Latino). Average age 40. In 2017, 45 master's awarded. *Application deadline:* Applications are processed on a rolling basis. Application fee: $50. Electronic applications accepted. *Expenses: Tuition:* Part-time $645 per credit. *Required fees:* $265 per credit. *Financial support:* Scholarships/grants available. *Unit head:* Dr. Robert Waters, Dean, School of Public Service, 518-464-8500, Fax: 518-464-8777. *Application contact:* Admissions Counselor, 888-647-2388, Fax: 518-464-8777, E-mail: gradadmissions@excelsior.edu.
Website: http://www.excelsior.edu/programs/public-service

Fairleigh Dickinson University, Metropolitan Campus, University College: Arts, Sciences, and Professional Studies, School of Criminal Justice and Legal Studies, Program in Criminal Justice, Teaneck, NJ 07666-1914. Offers MA.

Fairmont State University, Program in Criminal Justice, Fairmont, WV 26554. Offers MS. *Program availability:* Part-time, evening/weekend, 100% online. *Degree requirements:* For master's, thesis or comprehensive exam. *Entrance requirements:* For master's, GRE, minimum GPA of 3.0. Additional exam requirements/recommendations for international students: Required—TOEFL (minimum score 80 iBT), IELTS (minimum score 6.5). Electronic applications accepted.

Faulkner University, Alabama Christian College of Arts and Sciences, Department of Criminal Justice, Montgomery, AL 36109-3398. Offers justice administration (MJA). *Program availability:* Part-time, evening/weekend, online only, 100% online. *Faculty:* 4 full-time (1 woman), 2 part-time/adjunct (1 woman). *Students:* 63 full-time (35 women), 7 part-time (4 women); includes 38 minority (36 Black or African American, non-Hispanic/Latino; 1 American Indian or Alaska Native, non-Hispanic/Latino; 1 Hispanic/Latino). Average age 34. 81 applicants, 52% accepted, 38 enrolled. In 2017, 38 master's awarded. *Degree requirements:* For master's, research project. *Entrance requirements:* For master's, MAT, bachelor's degree from regionally-accredited college or university; official transcripts from all colleges and universities attended; minimum GPA of 2.5 on undergraduate degree, 3.0 from field of study; letter of intent (300-word minimum); resume; three professional letters of recommendation. Additional exam requirements/recommendations for international students: Required—TOEFL (minimum score 500 paper-based). *Application deadline:* Applications are processed on a rolling basis. Application fee: $35. Electronic applications accepted. *Expenses:* $515 per hour tuition, $220 per semester fees. *Financial support:* Applicants required to submit FAFSA. *Unit head:* Dr. Cathy L. Davis, Chair, Criminal Justice Department, 334-386-7132, Fax: 334-386-7147, E-mail: cdavis@faulkner.edu. *Application contact:* Dr. Robert M. Thetford, Director, Justice Administration Program, 334-386-7132, Fax: 334-386-7147, E-mail: rthetford@faulkner.edu.
Website: https://www.faulkner.edu/online/academics/master-justice-administration/

Fayetteville State University, Graduate School, Program in Criminal Justice, Fayetteville, NC 28301-4298. Offers MA. *Program availability:* Part-time. *Faculty:* 5 full-time (3 women). *Students:* 9 full-time (6 women), 22 part-time (18 women); includes 21 minority (18 Black or African American, non-Hispanic/Latino; 3 Hispanic/Latino). Average age 34. 14 applicants, 57% accepted, 4 enrolled. In 2017, 19 master's awarded. *Entrance requirements:* Additional exam requirements/recommendations for international students: Required—TOEFL. *Application deadline:* For fall admission, 4/15 for domestic students; for spring admission, 10/15 for domestic students. Application fee: $40. *Expenses:* Tuition, state resident: full-time $8604. Tuition, nonresident: full-time $19,669. *Financial support:* Application deadline: 3/1; applicants required to submit FAFSA. *Unit head:* Dr. Joe Brown, Interim Chair, 910-672-1478, Fax: 910-672-1908, E-mail: jbrown25@uncfsu.edu. *Application contact:* Dr. Lori Guevara, Graduate Coordinator, 910-672-2190, Fax: 910-672-1908, E-mail: lguevara@uncfsu.edu.

Ferris State University, College of Education and Human Services, School of Criminal Justice, Big Rapids, MI 49307. Offers criminal justice administration (MSCJ). *Program availability:* Part-time, evening/weekend. *Faculty:* 8 full-time (2 women). *Students:* 6 full-time (5 women), 32 part-time (18 women); includes 14 minority (9 Black or African American, non-Hispanic/Latino; 2 Hispanic/Latino; 3 Two or more races, non-Hispanic/Latino). Average age 35. 23 applicants, 100% accepted, 17 enrolled. In 2017, 17 master's awarded. *Degree requirements:* For master's, comprehensive exam or thesis/dissertation. *Entrance requirements:* For master's, bachelor's degree in criminal justice or related field, minimum GPA of 3.0. Additional exam requirements/recommendations for international students: Required—TOEFL (minimum score 500 paper-based; 61 iBT). *Application deadline:* For fall admission, 8/15 for domestic students; for winter admission, 12/15 for domestic students; for spring admission, 3/15 for domestic students. Applications are processed on a rolling basis. Application fee: $0. Electronic applications accepted. *Financial support:* In 2017–18, 1 research assistantship (averaging $4,850 per year) was awarded; Federal Work-Study and unspecified assistantships also available. Support available to part-time students. Financial award applicants required to submit FAFSA. *Faculty research:* Policy enactment, health and safety issues, criminological theory, juvenile justice, policy techniques, problem-based learning. *Unit head:* Dr. Nancy L. Hogan, Professor/Graduate Program Coordinator, 231-591-2664, Fax: 231-591-3792, E-mail: hogann@ferris.edu. *Application contact:* Sara P. Rasmussen, Secretary, 231-591-3652, Fax: 231-591-3792, E-mail: sararasmussen@ferris.edu.
Website: http://www.ferris.edu/education/cj/

Florida Agricultural and Mechanical University, Division of Graduate Studies, Research, and Continuing Education, College of Social Sciences, Arts and Humanities, Department of History and Political Science, Program in Applied Social Science, Tallahassee, FL 32307-3200. Offers criminal justice (MASS); history (MASS); political science (MASS); public administration (MASS). *Program availability:* Part-time. *Degree requirements:* For master's, thesis optional. *Entrance requirements:* For master's, GRE General Test, minimum GPA of 3.0. *Faculty research:* Southern history, black history, election trends, Presidential history.

Florida Atlantic University, College for Design and Social Inquiry, School of Criminology and Criminal Justice, Boca Raton, FL 33431-0991. Offers MS. *Program availability:* Part-time, evening/weekend, online learning. *Faculty:* 9 full-time (2 women). *Students:* 20 full-time (16 women), 29 part-time (22 women); includes 33 minority (21 Black or African American, non-Hispanic/Latino; 1 Asian, non-Hispanic/Latino; 10 Hispanic/Latino; 1 Two or more races, non-Hispanic/Latino). Average age 27. 57 applicants, 35% accepted, 15 enrolled. In 2017, 38 master's awarded. *Entrance requirements:* For master's, GRE General Test, minimum GPA of 3.0, undergraduate course work in statistics and criminology. Additional exam requirements/recommendations for international students: Required—TOEFL (minimum score 550 paper-based; 61 iBT), IELTS (minimum score 6). *Application deadline:* For fall admission, 5/1 priority date for domestic students, 2/15 for international students; for spring admission, 11/1 priority date for domestic students, 7/15 for international students. Applications are processed on a rolling basis. Application fee: $30. Electronic applications accepted. *Expenses:* Tuition, state resident: full-time $7400; part-time $369.82 per credit. Tuition, nonresident: full-time $20,496; part-time $1042.81 per credit. *Financial support:* Research assistantships, institutionally sponsored loans, scholarships/grants, and unspecified assistantships available. Financial award application deadline: 4/1. *Faculty research:* Restorative, justice corrections, logic modeling, criminal justice management, crime causation. *Unit head:* Sigal Rubin, Assistant Graduate Coordinator, 561-297-4936, E-mail: rubins@fau.edu.
Website: http://cdsi.fau.edu/sccj/

Florida Gulf Coast University, College of Arts and Sciences, Program in Criminal Justice, Fort Myers, FL 33965-6565. Offers MS. *Faculty:* 238 full-time (97 women), 158

part-time/adjunct (62 women). *Students:* 6 full-time (4 women), 8 part-time (4 women); includes 3 minority (all Black or African American, non-Hispanic/Latino). Average age 26. 10 applicants, 70% accepted, 6 enrolled. In 2017, 3 master's awarded. *Entrance requirements:* For master's, GRE General Test, minimum GPA of 3.0. Additional exam requirements/recommendations for international students: Required—TOEFL (minimum score 550 paper-based). *Application deadline:* For fall admission, 3/1 for domestic students; for spring admission, 11/1 for domestic students. Applications are processed on a rolling basis. Application fee: $30. Electronic applications accepted. *Expenses:* Tuition, state resident: part-time $290 per credit hour. Tuition, nonresident: part-time $1173 per credit hour. *Required fees:* $127 per credit hour. Tuition and fees vary according to course load. *Financial support:* In 2017–18, 2 students received support. Application deadline: 3/1; applicants required to submit FAFSA. *Unit head:* Shawn Keller, Program Chair, 239-590-4248, E-mail: skeller@fgcu.edu. *Application contact:* Mary Zager, Associate Professor/Chair, Division of Justice Studies, 239-590-7832, Fax: 239-590-7843, E-mail: mzager@fgcu.edu.

Florida International University, Steven J. Green School of International and Public Affairs, Department of Criminal Justice, Miami, FL 33199. Offers criminal justice (MS); international crime and justice (PhD). *Program availability:* Part-time, evening/weekend. *Faculty:* 15 full-time (7 women), 33 part-time/adjunct (8 women). *Students:* 48 full-time (32 women), 53 part-time (30 women); includes 74 minority (18 Black or African American, non-Hispanic/Latino; 1 Asian, non-Hispanic/Latino; 52 Hispanic/Latino; 3 Two or more races, non-Hispanic/Latino), 6 international. Average age 28. 146 applicants, 38% accepted, 32 enrolled. In 2017, 27 master's awarded. *Degree requirements:* For master's, thesis optional. *Entrance requirements:* For master's, minimum undergraduate GPA of 3.0. Additional exam requirements/recommendations for international students: Required—TOEFL (minimum score 550 paper-based; 80 iBT). *Application deadline:* For fall admission, 6/1 for domestic students, 4/1 for international students; for spring admission, 10/1 for domestic students, 9/1 for international students. Applications are processed on a rolling basis. Application fee: $30. Electronic applications accepted. *Expenses:* Tuition, state resident: full-time $8912; part-time $446 per credit hour. Tuition, nonresident: full-time $21,393; part-time $992 per credit hour. *Required fees:* $390; $195 per semester. *Financial support:* Institutionally sponsored loans and scholarships/grants available. Financial award application deadline: 3/1; financial award applicants required to submit FAFSA. *Unit head:* Dr. Lisa Stolzenberg, Chair, 305-348-5892, E-mail: stolzenb@fiu.edu. *Application contact:* Nanett Rojas, Manager, Admissions Operations, 305-348-7464, Fax: 305-348-7441, E-mail: gradadm@fiu.edu.
Website: http://cj.fiu.edu/

Florida State University, The Graduate School, College of Criminology and Criminal Justice, Tallahassee, FL 32306-1127. Offers criminology and criminal justice (MA, MSC, PhD); MPA/MSC; MS/MSW. *Program availability:* Part-time, 100% online. *Faculty:* 18 full-time (7 women). *Students:* 92 full-time (59 women), 123 part-time (60 women); includes 80 minority (37 Black or African American, non-Hispanic/Latino; 1 American Indian or Alaska Native, non-Hispanic/Latino; 7 Asian, non-Hispanic/Latino; 29 Hispanic/Latino; 6 Two or more races, non-Hispanic/Latino). Average age 33. 201 applicants, 57% accepted, 59 enrolled. In 2017, 83 master's, 3 doctorates awarded. Terminal master's awarded for partial completion of doctoral program. *Degree requirements:* For master's, thesis optional, minimum GPA of 3.0, minimum grade of C in all required courses; for doctorate, comprehensive exam, thesis/dissertation, minimum GPA of 3.0, minimum grade of B in all required courses, minimum of 24 dissertation hours. *Entrance requirements:* For master's, GRE General Test; for doctorate, GRE General Test, area paper or thesis. Additional exam requirements/recommendations for international students: Required—TOEFL (minimum score 600 paper-based; 100 iBT). *Application deadline:* For fall admission, 7/1 for domestic and international students; for spring admission, 11/1 for domestic and international students; for summer admission, 3/1 for domestic and international students. Applications are processed on a rolling basis. Application fee: $30. Electronic applications accepted. *Financial support:* In 2017–18, 44 students received support, including 3 fellowships with full tuition reimbursements available (averaging $12,000 per year), 29 research assistantships with full tuition reimbursements available (averaging $17,100 per year), 15 teaching assistantships with full tuition reimbursements available (averaging $16,000 per year); career-related internships or fieldwork, institutionally sponsored loans, scholarships/grants, health care benefits, tuition waivers (full), and unspecified assistantships also available. Financial award application deadline: 1/15; financial award applicants required to submit FAFSA. *Faculty research:* Criminological theory, criminal justice administration and planning, criminal justice policy and evaluation, law and social control, biosocial criminology. *Total annual research expenditures:* $781,433. *Unit head:* Dr. Thomas G. Blomberg, Dean, 850-644-7365, Fax: 850-644-9614. *Application contact:* Meghan Martinez, Graduate Coordinator, 850-645-9169, Fax: 850-644-9614, E-mail: mhm1991@fsu.edu.
Website: http://www.criminology.fsu.edu/

Gannon University, School of Graduate Studies, College of Humanities, Education, and Social Sciences, School of Humanities, Program in Criminalistics, Erie, PA 16541-0001. Offers MSC. *Program availability:* Online only, 100% online. *Entrance requirements:* For master's, bachelor's degree from accredited college or university; transcripts; minimum overall GPA of 2.75, 3.0 in prerequisite courses; resume; three letters of recommendation; background check. Additional exam requirements/recommendations for international students: Required—TOEFL (minimum score 79 iBT). Electronic applications accepted. Application fee is waived when completed online.

George Mason University, College of Humanities and Social Sciences, Department of Criminology, Law and Society, Fairfax, VA 22030. Offers criminal justice (MS); criminology, law, and society (MA, PhD). *Program availability:* Part-time. *Faculty:* 28 full-time (19 women), 46 part-time/adjunct (12 women). *Students:* 34 full-time (27 women), 29 part-time (19 women); includes 14 minority (6 Black or African American, non-Hispanic/Latino; 1 American Indian or Alaska Native, non-Hispanic/Latino; 2 Asian, non-Hispanic/Latino; 3 Hispanic/Latino; 2 Two or more races, non-Hispanic/Latino), 6 international. Average age 31. 71 applicants, 69% accepted, 15 enrolled. In 2017, 11 master's, 4 doctorates awarded. Terminal master's awarded for partial completion of doctoral program. *Degree requirements:* For master's, thesis (for some programs); for doctorate, comprehensive exam (for some programs), thesis/dissertation, major area paper (depends on catalog year). *Entrance requirements:* For master's, GRE (for MA), college transcripts, goals statement, two letters of recommendation, resume, writing sample; for doctorate, GRE, college transcripts, goals statement, three letters of recommendation, resume, writing sample. Additional exam requirements/recommendations for international students: Required—TOEFL (minimum score 575 paper-based; 88 iBT), IELTS (minimum score 6.5), PTE (minimum score 59). Application fee: $75 ($80 for international students). Electronic applications accepted. *Expenses:* Tuition, state resident: full-time $11,228; part-time $459.50 per credit. Tuition, nonresident: full-time $30,932; part-time $1280.50 per credit. *Required fees:* $3252; $135.50 per credit. Part-time tuition and fees vary according to course load and program. *Financial support:* In 2017–18, 24 students received support, including 19 research assistantships with tuition reimbursements available (averaging $17,916 per year), 5 teaching assistantships with tuition reimbursements available (averaging $20,520 per year); career-related internships or fieldwork, Federal Work-Study, scholarships/grants, unspecified assistantships, and health care benefits (for full-time research or teaching assistantship recipients) also available. Support available to part-time students. Financial award application deadline: 3/1; financial award applicants required to submit FAFSA. *Faculty research:* Wrongful convictions; violence, firearms, and public policy; public opinion and justice issues; evidence-based policing and crime policy; corrections, probation, parole, and reentry. *Total annual research expenditures:* $3.4 million. *Unit head:* David B. Wilson, Chair, 703-993-4701, Fax: 703-993-8316, E-mail: dwilsonb@gmu.edu. *Application contact:* Mary Schifferli, Graduate Coordinator, 703-993-9417, Fax: 703-993-8316, E-mail: mschiffe@gmu.edu.
Website: http://cls.gmu.edu/

The George Washington University, Columbian College of Arts and Sciences, Department of Forensic Sciences, Washington, DC 20052. Offers crime scene investigation (MFS); forensic chemistry (MFS); forensic molecular biology (MFS); forensic toxicology (MFS); high-technology crime investigation (MS); security management (MFS). MFS programs in high-technology crime investigation and in security management offered in Arlington, VA. *Program availability:* Part-time, evening/weekend. *Faculty:* 10 full-time (1 woman), 12 part-time/adjunct (3 women). *Students:* 65 full-time (54 women), 23 part-time (15 women); includes 41 minority (14 Black or African American, non-Hispanic/Latino; 12 Asian, non-Hispanic/Latino; 13 Hispanic/Latino; 1 Native Hawaiian or other Pacific Islander, non-Hispanic/Latino; 1 Two or more races, non-Hispanic/Latino), 5 international. Average age 25. 192 applicants, 67% accepted, 44 enrolled. In 2017, 43 master's, 1 other advanced degree awarded. *Degree requirements:* For master's, comprehensive exam. *Entrance requirements:* For master's, GRE General Test, minimum GPA of 3.0. Additional exam requirements/recommendations for international students: Required—TOEFL (minimum score 550 paper-based; 80 iBT). *Application deadline:* For fall admission, 1/16 priority date for international students; for spring admission, 10/1 priority date for domestic students, 9/1 priority date for international students. Applications are processed on a rolling basis. Application fee: $75. Electronic applications accepted. *Expenses: Tuition:* Full-time $28,800; part-time $1655 per credit hour. *Required fees:* $45; $2.75 per credit hour. *Financial support:* In 2017–18, 19 students received support. Fellowships with partial tuition reimbursements available, Federal Work-Study, and tuition waivers available. *Unit head:* Dr. Walter F. Rowe, Chair, 202-242-5757, E-mail: wfrowe@gwu.edu. *Application contact:* 202-242-5758, Fax: 202-994-6213, E-mail: forsc@gwu.edu.
Website: http://forensicsciences.columbian.gwu.edu/

The George Washington University, Columbian College of Arts and Sciences, Department of Sociology, Program in Criminology, Washington, DC 20052. Offers MA. *Students:* 9 full-time (all women), 3 part-time (all women); includes 5 minority (1 Black or African American, non-Hispanic/Latino; 2 Hispanic/Latino; 2 Two or more races, non-Hispanic/Latino), 2 international. Average age 24. 23 applicants, 52% accepted, 5 enrolled. In 2017, 3 master's awarded. *Degree requirements:* For master's, comprehensive exam. *Entrance requirements:* For master's, GRE General Test, minimum GPA of 3.0. Additional exam requirements/recommendations for international students: Required—TOEFL (minimum score 550 paper-based). *Application deadline:* For fall admission, 4/1 priority date for domestic and international students; for spring admission, 10/1 priority date for domestic and international students. Applications are processed on a rolling basis. Application fee: $75. Electronic applications accepted. *Expenses: Tuition:* Full-time $28,800; part-time $1655 per credit hour. *Required fees:* $45; $2.75 per credit hour. *Financial support:* In 2017–18, fellowships with full tuition reimbursements (averaging $10,000 per year), teaching assistantships (averaging $5,000 per year) were awarded. Financial award application deadline: 2/1. *Unit head:* Ronald Weitzer, Director, 202-994-6895. *Application contact:* Information Contact, 202-994-6345, Fax: 202-994-3239, E-mail: soc@gwu.edu.
Website: http://www.gwu.edu/graduate-programs/criminology

Georgia College & State University, Graduate School, College of Arts and Sciences, Department of Government and Sociology, Program in Criminal Justice, Milledgeville, GA 31061. Offers MSCJ. *Program availability:* Part-time, evening/weekend. *Students:* 5 full-time (3 women), 10 part-time (8 women); includes 6 minority (3 Black or African American, non-Hispanic/Latino; 2 Hispanic/Latino; 1 Two or more races, non-Hispanic/Latino). Average age 31. 8 applicants, 100% accepted, 7 enrolled. In 2017, 4 master's awarded. *Degree requirements:* For master's, comprehensive exam. *Entrance requirements:* For master's, resume with relevant work experience; minimum undergraduate GPA of 3.0. *Application deadline:* For fall admission, 7/1 priority date for domestic students, 4/1 priority date for international students; for spring admission, 11/1 priority date for domestic students, 9/1 priority date for international students; for summer admission, 4/1 priority date for domestic students. Applications are processed on a rolling basis. Application fee: $40. Electronic applications accepted. *Expenses:* $288 per semester hour full-time, $2,592 per term; $343 per semester fees. *Financial support:* In 2017–18, 3 students received support. Unspecified assistantships available. Financial award application deadline: 3/1; financial award applicants required to submit FAFSA. *Unit head:* Dr. Sara Doude, Program Coordinator, 478-445-4262, E-mail: sara.doude@gcsu.edu. *Application contact:* Kate Marshall, Graduate Admissions Coordinator, 478-445-1184, Fax: 478-445-1336, E-mail: grad-admit@gcsu.edu.
Website: http://www.gcsu.edu/artsandsciences/gov/criminal-justice-ms

Georgian Court University, School of Arts and Sciences, Lakewood, NJ 08701-2697. Offers applied behavior analysis (MA); autism spectrum disorders (Certificate); clinical mental health counseling (MA); criminal justice and human rights (MS); holistic health studies (MA, Certificate); homeland security (Certificate); instructional technology (CPC); mercy spirituality (Certificate); parish business management (Certificate); professional counselor (Certificate); school psychology (MA, Certificate); theology (MA, Certificate). *Program availability:* Part-time, evening/weekend. *Faculty:* 18 full-time (11 women), 8 part-time/adjunct (4 women). *Students:* 100 full-time (86 women), 92 part-time (67 women); includes 34 minority (9 Black or African American, non-Hispanic/Latino; 1 Asian, non-Hispanic/Latino; 20 Hispanic/Latino; 4 Two or more races, non-Hispanic/Latino), 2 international. Average age 34. 187 applicants, 56% accepted, 78 enrolled. In 2017, 58 master's, 20 other advanced degrees awarded. *Degree requirements:* For master's, comprehensive exam (for some programs), thesis (for some programs). *Entrance requirements:* For master's, GRE, GMAT, or NTE/PRAXIS, 3 letters of recommendation. Additional exam requirements/recommendations for international students: Required—TOEFL (minimum score 550 paper-based). *Application deadline:* For fall admission, 8/15 for domestic students, 5/1 for international students; for spring admission, 1/15 for domestic students, 10/1 for international students. Applications are processed on a rolling basis. Application fee: $40. Electronic applications accepted. *Expenses: Tuition:* Part-time $839 per credit. *Required fees:* $248 per semester. Tuition and fees vary according to campus/location and program. *Financial support:* Scholarships/grants, health care benefits, and unspecified assistantships available. Financial award application deadline: 4/15; financial award applicants required to submit FAFSA. *Unit head:* Dr. Mary Chinery, Dean, 732-987-2493, Fax: 732-987-2007, E-mail: mchinery@georgian.edu. *Application contact:* Patrick Givens, Director of Graduate and Professional Studies Admissions, 732-987-2736, Fax: 732-987-2000, E-mail: gps@georgian.edu.
Website: https://georgian.edu/academics/school-of-arts-sciences/

Georgia Southern University–Armstrong Campus, College of Graduate Studies, Program in Criminal Justice, Savannah, GA 31419-1997. Offers criminal justice (MS); cyber crime (Certificate). *Program availability:* Part-time, online learning. *Faculty:* 6 full-

time (2 women), 2 part-time/adjunct (both women). *Students:* 5 full-time (3 women), 11 part-time (8 women); includes 8 minority (all Black or African American, non-Hispanic/ Latino). Average age 31. 35 applicants, 23% accepted, 5 enrolled. In 2017, 6 master's, 4 other advanced degrees awarded. *Degree requirements:* For master's, comprehensive exam, field practicum or thesis. *Entrance requirements:* For master's, GRE General Test (minimum score 150 on verbal, 141 on quantitative, or 4 on analytical section) or MAT, minimum GPA of 2.5, 2 letters of recommendation, letter of intent (500-1000 words). Additional exam requirements/recommendations for international students: Required—TOEFL (minimum score 523 paper-based; 70 iBT). *Application deadline:* For fall admission, 6/1 priority date for domestic students, 5/1 priority date for international students; for spring admission, 11/15 priority date for domestic students, 9/15 priority date for international students; for summer admission, 4/15 priority date for domestic students, 9/15 for international students. Applications are processed on a rolling basis. Application fee: $30. Electronic applications accepted. *Expenses:* Tuition, state resident: part-time $211 per credit hour. Tuition, nonresident: part-time $782 per credit hour. *Required fees:* $737 per semester. Tuition and fees vary according to course load, degree level, campus/location and program. *Financial support:* In 2017–18, research assistantships with full tuition reimbursements (averaging $5,000 per year) were awarded; career-related internships or fieldwork, Federal Work-Study, scholarships/ grants, and unspecified assistantships also available. Support available to part-time students. Financial award application deadline: 3/15; financial award applicants required to submit FAFSA. *Faculty research:* International crime/globalization, cyber-crime, influence of social science research on judicial decision-making. *Unit head:* Dr. Daniel Skidmore-Hess, Department Head, 912-344-2532, Fax: 912-344-3438, E-mail: daniel.skidmore-hess@armstrong.edu. *Application contact:* McKenzie Peterman, Graduate Admissions Specialist, 912-478-5678, Fax: 912-478-0740, E-mail: mpeterman@georgiasouthern.edu.
Website: https://www.armstrong.edu/academic-departments/cjsps-master-of-science-in-criminal-justice

Georgia State University, Andrew Young School of Policy Studies, Department of Criminal Justice and Criminology, Atlanta, GA 30302. Offers criminal justice (MS); criminal justice and criminology (PhD). *Program availability:* Part-time. *Faculty:* 14 full-time (5 women). *Students:* 33 full-time (28 women), 10 part-time (4 women); includes 22 minority (11 Black or African American, non-Hispanic/Latino; 2 Asian, non-Hispanic/ Latino; 4 Hispanic/Latino; 5 Two or more races, non-Hispanic/Latino). Average age 29. 60 applicants, 28% accepted, 11 enrolled. In 2017, 5 master's, 3 doctorates awarded. Terminal master's awarded for partial completion of doctoral program. *Degree requirements:* For master's, thesis optional; for doctorate, comprehensive exam, thesis/ dissertation. *Entrance requirements:* For master's and doctorate, GRE. Additional exam requirements/recommendations for international students: Required—TOEFL (minimum score 603 paper-based; 100 iBT) or IELTS (minimum score 7). *Application deadline:* For fall admission, 1/15 for domestic and international students. Application fee: $50. Electronic applications accepted. *Expenses:* Tuition, state resident: full-time $7020. Tuition, nonresident: full-time $22,518. *Required fees:* $2128. Tuition and fees vary according to degree level and program. *Financial support:* In 2017–18, fellowships with full tuition reimbursements (averaging $22,000 per year), research assistantships with full tuition reimbursements (averaging $14,000 per year), teaching assistantships with full tuition reimbursements (averaging $14,000 per year) were awarded; career-related internships or fieldwork, Federal Work-Study, scholarships/grants, traineeships, health care benefits, and unspecified assistantships also available. Financial award application deadline: 2/15. *Faculty research:* Urban violence, drugs, victimization, criminal justice, criminology. *Unit head:* Dr. Richard Wright, Professor of Criminal Justice and Criminology/Department Chair, 404-413-1015, Fax: 404-413-1030, E-mail: rwright28@gsu.edu.
Website: http://aysps.gsu.edu/cj/

Georgia State University, Andrew Young School of Policy Studies, Department of Public Management and Policy, Atlanta, GA 30303. Offers criminal justice (MPA); disaster management (Certificate); disaster policy (MPA); environmental policy (PhD); health policy (PhD); management and finance (MPA); nonprofit management (MPA, Certificate); nonprofit policy (MPA); planning and economic development (MPP, Certificate); policy analysis and evaluation (MPA), including planning and economic development; public and nonprofit management (PhD); public finance and budgeting (PhD), including science and technology policy, urban and regional economic development; public finance policy (MPA), including social policy; public health (MPA). *Accreditation:* NASPAA (one or more programs are accredited). *Program availability:* Part-time. *Faculty:* 17 full-time (9 women). *Students:* 125 full-time (75 women), 78 part-time (51 women); includes 90 minority (67 Black or African American, non-Hispanic/ Latino; 5 Asian, non-Hispanic/Latino; 9 Hispanic/Latino; 9 Two or more races, non-Hispanic/Latino), 34 international. Average age 30. 275 applicants, 62% accepted, 88 enrolled. In 2017, 71 master's, 5 doctorates, 12 other advanced degrees awarded. Terminal master's awarded for partial completion of doctoral program. *Degree requirements:* For master's, thesis optional; for doctorate, comprehensive exam, thesis/ dissertation. *Entrance requirements:* For master's and doctorate, GRE. Additional exam requirements/recommendations for international students: Required—TOEFL (minimum score 603 paper-based; 100 iBT) or IELTS (minimum score 7). *Application deadline:* For fall admission, 1/15 for domestic and international students. Application fee: $50. Electronic applications accepted. *Expenses:* Tuition, state resident: full-time $7020. Tuition, nonresident: full-time $22,518. *Required fees:* $2128. Tuition and fees vary according to degree level and program. *Financial support:* In 2017–18, fellowships (averaging $8,194 per year), research assistantships (averaging $8,068 per year), teaching assistantships (averaging $3,600 per year) were awarded; institutionally sponsored loans, scholarships/grants, health care benefits, and unspecified assistantships also available. Financial award application deadline: 2/1. *Faculty research:* Public budgeting and finance, public management, nonprofit management, performance measurement and management, urban development. *Unit head:* Dr. Carolyn Bourdeaux, Chair and Professor, 404-413-0013, Fax: 404-413-0104, E-mail: cbourdeaux@gsu.edu.
Website: http://aysps.gsu.edu/pmap/

Governors State University, College of Arts and Sciences, Program in Criminal Justice, University Park, IL 60484. Offers MA. *Program availability:* Part-time. *Faculty:* 60 full-time (34 women), 115 part-time/adjunct (58 women). *Students:* 7 full-time (4 women), 24 part-time (12 women); includes 14 minority (12 Black or African American, non-Hispanic/Latino; 1 Hispanic/Latino; 1 Two or more races, non-Hispanic/Latino). Average age 37. 21 applicants, 33% accepted, 5 enrolled. In 2017, 12 master's awarded. *Application deadline:* For fall admission, 4/1 for domestic students. Applications are processed on a rolling basis. Application fee: $50. Electronic applications accepted. *Expenses:* Tuition, state resident: full-time $8472; part-time $353 per credit hour. Tuition, nonresident: full-time $16,944; part-time $706 per credit hour. *Required fees:* $1824; $76 per credit hour. $38 per term. Tuition and fees vary according to course load, degree level and program. *Financial support:* Application deadline: 5/1; applicants required to submit FAFSA. *Unit head:* Lori Montalbano, Chair, Division of Arts and Letters, 708-534-5000 Ext. 2802, E-mail: lmontalbano@govst.edu.

The Graduate Center, City University of New York, Graduate Studies, Program in Criminal Justice, New York, NY 10016-4039. Offers PhD. *Faculty:* 28 full-time (6 women). *Students:* 87 full-time (48 women), 5 part-time (0 women); includes 26 minority (4 Black or African American, non-Hispanic/Latino; 4 Asian, non-Hispanic/Latino; 17 Hispanic/Latino; 1 Two or more races, non-Hispanic/Latino), 18 international. Average age 36. 79 applicants, 20% accepted, 12 enrolled. In 2017, 17 doctorates awarded. *Degree requirements:* For doctorate, one foreign language, thesis/dissertation. *Entrance requirements:* For doctorate, GRE General Test, writing sample. Additional exam requirements/recommendations for international students: Required—TOEFL. *Application deadline:* For fall admission, 1/15 for domestic students. Application fee: $125. Electronic applications accepted. *Financial support:* In 2017–18, 70 students received support, including 54 fellowships, 5 teaching assistantships; research assistantships, career-related internships or fieldwork, Federal Work-Study, institutionally sponsored loans, and tuition waivers (full and partial) also available. Financial award application deadline: 2/1; financial award applicants required to submit FAFSA. *Unit head:* Dr. Deborah Koetzle, Executive Officer, 212-237-8040, Fax: 212-237-8940, E-mail: dkoetzle@jjay.cuny.edu. *Application contact:* Les Gribben, Director of Admissions, 212-817-7470, Fax: 212-817-1624, E-mail: lgribben@gc.cuny.edu.

Grambling State University, School of Graduate Studies and Research, College of Professional Studies, Department of Criminal Justice, Grambling, LA 71245. Offers MS. *Program availability:* Part-time. *Degree requirements:* For master's, comprehensive exam, thesis optional. *Entrance requirements:* For master's, GRE, minimum GPA of 2.5 on last degree and in four core courses. Additional exam requirements/ recommendations for international students: Required—TOEFL (minimum score 500 paper-based; 62 iBT). Electronic applications accepted.

Grand Valley State University, College of Community and Public Service, School of Criminal Justice, Allendale, MI 49401-9403. Offers MS. *Program availability:* Part-time, evening/weekend. *Faculty:* 4 full-time (3 women). *Students:* 5 full-time (4 women), 17 part-time (7 women); includes 8 minority (2 Black or African American, non-Hispanic/ Latino; 6 Hispanic/Latino). Average age 29. 11 applicants, 91% accepted, 5 enrolled. In 2017, 11 master's awarded. *Degree requirements:* For master's, comprehensive exam or thesis. *Entrance requirements:* For master's, minimum GPA of 3.0, three letters of recommendation, personal statement, essay, oral interview. Additional exam requirements/recommendations for international students: Required—TOEFL (minimum iBT score of 80), IELTS (6.5), or Michigan English Language Assessment Battery (77). *Application deadline:* For fall admission, 5/1 priority date for domestic students; for winter admission, 11/1 priority date for domestic students; for spring admission, 4/1 priority date for domestic students. Applications are processed on a rolling basis. Application fee: $30. Electronic applications accepted. *Expenses:* $627 per credit hour. *Financial support:* In 2017–18, 9 students received support, including 1 fellowship, 10 research assistantships with full and partial tuition reimbursements available (averaging $4,000 per year); career-related internships or fieldwork, Federal Work-Study, scholarships/grants, and unspecified assistantships also available. Financial award application deadline: 5/1. *Faculty research:* Correctional administration, juvenile justice issues/gangs, women's issues, leadership, program/policy evaluation. *Unit head:* Dr. Kathleen Bailey, Director, 616-331-7148, Fax: 616-331-7155, E-mail: baileyk@gvsu.edu. *Application contact:* Tonisha Jones, Graduate Program Director/ Recruiting Contact, 616-331-7187, Fax: 616-331-7155, E-mail: jontonis@gvsu.edu.
Website: http://www.gvsu.edu/cj/

Hilbert College, Program in Criminal Justice Administration, Hamburg, NY 14075-1597. Offers MS. *Program availability:* Evening/weekend. *Faculty:* 6 full-time (3 women), 5 part-time/adjunct (2 women). *Students:* 15 full-time (6 women), 3 part-time (1 woman); includes 3 minority (1 Black or African American, non-Hispanic/Latino; 2 Two or more races, non-Hispanic/Latino). Average age 31. In 2017, 13 master's awarded. *Degree requirements:* For master's, final capstone project. *Entrance requirements:* For master's, essay, official transcripts from all prior colleges, two letters of recommendation, current resume, relevant work experience, baccalaureate degree from accredited college or university with minimum cumulative GPA of 3.0, personal interview. Additional exam requirements/recommendations for international students: Recommended—TOEFL. *Application deadline:* Applications are processed on a rolling basis. Application fee: $25. Electronic applications accepted. Application fee is waived when completed online. *Expenses:* $800 per credit hour; $20 technology fee per course; $20 one-time orientation fee; $50 one-time graduation fee. *Financial support:* Scholarships/grants and tuition waivers (partial) available. Financial award application deadline: 7/1; financial award applicants required to submit FAFSA. *Unit head:* Kathryn Eskew, Director for Adult and Graduate Studies, 716-649-7900 Ext. 305, Fax: 716-649-0702, E-mail: keskew@hilbert.edu. *Application contact:* Kim Chiarmonte, Director for Adult and Graduate Recruitment, 716-926-8948, Fax: 716-649-0702, E-mail: kchiarmonte@hilbert.edu.
Website: http://www.hilbert.edu/grad/ms-cja

Holy Family University, Graduate and Professional Programs, School of Arts and Sciences, Program in Criminal Justice, Philadelphia, PA 19114. Offers MA. *Program availability:* Part-time, evening/weekend. *Degree requirements:* For master's, thesis or alternative. *Entrance requirements:* For master's, 2 letters of recommendation, official transcripts of all college or university work, writing sample. Additional exam requirements/recommendations for international students: Required—TOEFL (minimum score 550 paper-based; 79 iBT), IELTS (minimum score 6), PTE (minimum score 54). Electronic applications accepted. *Expenses: Tuition:* Full-time $13,518; part-time $9012 per credit hour. Tuition and fees vary according to degree level and program.

Howard Payne University, Program in Criminal Justice, Brownwood, TX 76801-2715. Offers criminal justice (MS), including corrections, law enforcement. *Program availability:* Part-time, evening/weekend, online only, 100% online. *Entrance requirements:* For master's, baccalaureate degree, minimum cumulative GPA of 3.0, 800-1200 word written essay, official transcripts, three letters of reference. Electronic applications accepted. *Expenses:* Contact institution.

Husson University, Master of Science in Criminal Justice Administration Program, Bangor, ME 04401-2999. Offers MS. *Program availability:* Part-time, evening/weekend. *Faculty:* 5 full-time (2 women), 2 part-time/adjunct (0 women). *Students:* 6 full-time (2 women), 11 part-time (3 women); includes 1 minority (American Indian or Alaska Native, non-Hispanic/Latino). Average age 34. 12 applicants, 100% accepted, 6 enrolled. In 2017, 17 master's awarded. *Degree requirements:* For master's, thesis optional. *Entrance requirements:* For master's, letter of recommendation. Additional exam requirements/recommendations for international students: Required—TOEFL (minimum score 550 paper-based; 80 iBT), IELTS (minimum score 6.5). *Application deadline:* For fall admission, 8/1 for domestic students. Applications are processed on a rolling basis. Application fee: $50 ($0 for international students). Electronic applications accepted. *Expenses:* $464 per credit; fees dependent on number of credits enrolled. *Financial support:* Career-related internships or fieldwork, scholarships/grants, and unspecified assistantships available. Financial award application deadline: 4/15; financial award applicants required to submit FAFSA. *Faculty research:* Jury's attitudes towards forensic evidence. *Unit head:* John Michaud, Director, School of Legal Studies, 207-941-7037, E-mail: michaudj@husson.edu. *Application contact:* Kristen Card, Director of Graduate Admissions, 207-404-5660, E-mail: cardk@husson.edu.
Website: http://www.husson.edu/college-of-business/school-of-legal-studies/criminal-justice/masterofscienceincriminaljustice

Illinois State University, Graduate School, College of Applied Science and Technology, Department of Criminal Justice Sciences, Normal, IL 61790. Offers MA, MS. *Degree requirements:* For master's, thesis or alternative. *Entrance requirements:* For master's, GRE General Test, minimum GPA of 2.6 in last 60 hours of course work. *Faculty research:* Graduate practicum for victim assistance and advocacy, graduate practicum in adult probation cases, graduate practicum in youth intervention program.

Indiana State University, College of Graduate and Professional Studies, College of Arts and Sciences, Department of Criminology and Criminal Justice, Terre Haute, IN 47809. Offers MA, MS. *Program availability:* Part-time, online learning. *Degree requirements:* For master's, comprehensive exam, thesis (for some programs). *Entrance requirements:* For master's, minimum GPA of 2.75 in undergraduate work, 3.0 in previous graduate work. Additional exam requirements/recommendations for international students: Required—TOEFL (minimum score 550 paper-based). Electronic applications accepted. *Faculty research:* Violent crime, rape attitudes, classification of offenders, substance abuse, domestic violence.

Indiana University Bloomington, University Graduate School, College of Arts and Sciences, Department of Criminal Justice, Bloomington, IN 47405. Offers crime and youth development (MA, PhD); crime, law and psychology (MA, PhD); criminal justice (MA, PhD); criminal justice institutions and practices (MA, PhD); criminology (MA, PhD); developmental criminology (MA, PhD); interdisciplinary studies in crime and punishment (PhD); interdisciplinary studies of crime and punishment (MA); the relationship between crime and gender, race and ethnicity (MA, PhD); theoretical analyses of criminology (MA, PhD). *Program availability:* Part-time. Terminal master's awarded for partial completion of doctoral program. *Degree requirements:* For master's, thesis optional; for doctorate, comprehensive exam, thesis/dissertation, foreign language or research practicum. *Entrance requirements:* For master's and doctorate, GRE General Test. Additional exam requirements/recommendations for international students: Required—TOEFL (minimum score 600 paper-based; 100 iBT); Recommended—TWE. Electronic applications accepted. *Faculty research:* Violence, crime, juveniles, psychology and law, cross-cultural studies.

Indiana University Northwest, School of Public and Environmental Affairs, Gary, IN 46408. Offers criminal justice (MPA); environmental affairs (Graduate Certificate); health services (MPA); nonprofit management (Certificate); public management (MPA, Graduate Certificate). *Accreditation:* NASPAA (one or more programs are accredited). *Program availability:* Part-time. *Entrance requirements:* For master's, GRE General Test (minimum combined verbal and quantitative score of 280), GMAT, or LSAT, letters of recommendation. Electronic applications accepted. *Faculty research:* Employment in income security policies, evidence in criminal justice, equal employment law, social welfare policy and welfare reform, public finance in developing countries.

Indiana University of Pennsylvania, School of Graduate Studies and Research, College of Health and Human Services, Department of Criminology, Doctoral Program in Criminology, Indiana, PA 15705. Offers PhD. *Program availability:* Part-time. *Faculty:* 11 full-time (6 women). *Students:* 12 full-time (8 women), 17 part-time (11 women); includes 2 minority (1 Black or African American, non-Hispanic/Latino; 1 Asian, non-Hispanic/Latino), 4 international. Average age 31. 17 applicants, 71% accepted, 1 enrolled. In 2017, 2 doctorates awarded. *Degree requirements:* For doctorate, one foreign language, comprehensive exam, thesis/dissertation. *Entrance requirements:* For doctorate, GRE, 3 letters of recommendation, writing sample. Additional exam requirements/recommendations for international students: Required—TOEFL (minimum score 540 paper-based). *Application deadline:* Applications are processed on a rolling basis. Application fee: $50. Electronic applications accepted. *Expenses:* Contact institution. *Financial support:* In 2017–18, 3 fellowships with full tuition reimbursements (averaging $2,018 per year), 11 research assistantships with tuition reimbursements (averaging $11,909 per year), 4 teaching assistantships with partial tuition reimbursements (averaging $23,305 per year) were awarded; Federal Work-Study, scholarships/grants, and unspecified assistantships also available. Support available to part-time students. Financial award application deadline: 4/15; financial award applicants required to submit FAFSA. *Unit head:* Dr. Erika Frenzel, Graduate Coordinator, 724-357-5976, E-mail: e.frenzel@iup.edu.
Website: http://www.iup.edu/grad/criminologyphd/default.aspx

Indiana University of Pennsylvania, School of Graduate Studies and Research, College of Health and Human Services, Department of Criminology, Master's Program in Criminology, Indiana, PA 15705. Offers MA. *Program availability:* Part-time, online learning. *Faculty:* 11 full-time (6 women). *Students:* 48 full-time (27 women), 8 part-time (6 women); includes 12 minority (6 Black or African American, non-Hispanic/Latino; 5 Hispanic/Latino; 1 Two or more races, non-Hispanic/Latino), 2 international. Average age 25. 76 applicants, 79% accepted, 31 enrolled. In 2017, 26 master's awarded. *Degree requirements:* For master's, thesis optional. *Entrance requirements:* For master's, 2 letters of recommendation. Additional exam requirements/recommendations for international students: Required—TOEFL (minimum score 540 paper-based). *Application deadline:* For fall admission, 4/15 priority date for domestic students. Applications are processed on a rolling basis. Application fee: $50. Electronic applications accepted. *Expenses:* Contact institution. *Financial support:* In 2017–18, 17 research assistantships with tuition reimbursements (averaging $2,287 per year) were awarded; fellowships, career-related internships or fieldwork, Federal Work-Study, scholarships/grants, and unspecified assistantships also available. Support available to part-time students. Financial award application deadline: 4/15; financial award applicants required to submit FAFSA. *Unit head:* Dr. Jennifer Gossett, Graduate Coordinator, 724-357-5608, E-mail: jennifer.gossett@iup.edu.
Website: http://www.iup.edu/grad/criminology/default.aspx

Indiana University–Purdue University Indianapolis, School of Public and Environmental Affairs, Indianapolis, IN 46202. Offers criminal justice and public safety (MS); homeland security and emergency management (Graduate Certificate); library management (Graduate Certificate); nonprofit management (Graduate Certificate); public affairs (MPA); public management (Graduate Certificate); social entrepreneurship: nonprofit and public benefit organizations (Graduate Certificate); JD/MPA; MLS/NMC; MLS/PMC; MPA/MA. *Accreditation:* CAHME (one or more programs are accredited); NASPAA. *Program availability:* Part-time, evening/weekend, online learning. *Entrance requirements:* For master's, GRE General Test, GMAT or LSAT, minimum GPA of 3.0 (preferred). Additional exam requirements/recommendations for international students: Required—TOEFL (minimum score 93 iBT), IELTS (minimum score 6.5). Electronic applications accepted. *Faculty research:* Nonprofit and public management, public policy, urban policy, sustainability policy, disaster preparedness and recovery, vehicular safety, homicide, offender rehabilitation and re-entry.

Inter American University of Puerto Rico, Aguadilla Campus, Graduate School, Aguadilla, PR 00605. Offers accounting (MBA); counseling psychology specializing in family (MS); criminal justice (MA); educative management and leadership (MA); elementary education (M Ed); finance (MBA); human resources (MBA); industrial management (MBA); management information systems (MBA); marketing (MBA). *Program availability:* Part-time, evening/weekend. *Degree requirements:* For master's, comprehensive exam. *Entrance requirements:* For master's, EXADEP, 2 letters of recommendation, minimum GPA of 2.5. Electronic applications accepted.

Inter American University of Puerto Rico, Barranquitas Campus, Program in Criminal Justice, Barranquitas, PR 00794. Offers MA. *Program availability:* Evening/weekend. *Faculty:* 2 full-time (0 women). *Students:* 31 full-time (17 women), 2 part-time (both women); all minorities (all Hispanic/Latino). Average age 33. 14 applicants, 86% accepted, 12 enrolled. In 2017, 3 master's awarded. *Degree requirements:* For master's, 2 foreign languages, comprehensive exam (for some programs), thesis optional, minimum GPA of 3.0; comprehensive examination or integration seminar. *Entrance requirements:* For master's, GRE or EXADEP, bachelor's degree or its equivalent from accredited institution, official academic transcript from institution that conferred bachelor's degree, minimum GPA of 2.5, two recommendation letters, interview (for some programs). *Application deadline:* Applications are processed on a rolling basis. Application fee: $31. Electronic applications accepted. *Expenses:* $3,392 full-time tuition plus $652 fees. *Financial support:* Applicants required to submit FAFSA. *Unit head:* Juan A. Negron-Berrios, PhD, Chancellor, 787-857-3600 Ext. 2002, Fax: 787-857-2125, E-mail: janegron@br.inter.edu. *Application contact:* Aramilda Cartagena-Santiago, Dean of Students, 787-857-3600 Ext. 2009, Fax: 787-857-2125, E-mail: aramildacartagena@br.inter.edu.

Inter American University of Puerto Rico, Metropolitan Campus, Graduate Programs, Program in Criminal Justice, San Juan, PR 00919-1293. Offers MA. *Program availability:* Part-time, evening/weekend. *Degree requirements:* For master's, comprehensive exam. *Entrance requirements:* For master's, GRE or EXADEP, interview. Electronic applications accepted.

Inter American University of Puerto Rico, Ponce Campus, Graduate School, Mercedita, PR 00715-1602. Offers accounting (MBA); biology (M Ed); chemistry (M Ed); criminal justice (MA); elementary education (M Ed); English as a Second Language (M Ed); finance (MBA); history (M Ed); human resources (MBA); marketing (MBA); mathematics (M Ed); Spanish (M Ed). *Entrance requirements:* For master's, minimum GPA of 2.5.

Iona College, School of Arts and Science, Department of Criminal Justice, New Rochelle, NY 10801-1890. Offers criminal justice (MS); cybercrime and security (AC); forensic criminology and criminal justice systems (Certificate). *Program availability:* Part-time, evening/weekend. *Faculty:* 3 full-time (1 woman), 4 part-time/adjunct (1 woman). *Students:* 13 full-time (7 women), 7 part-time (1 woman); includes 6 minority (3 Black or African American, non-Hispanic/Latino; 3 Hispanic/Latino). Average age 24. 13 applicants, 92% accepted, 8 enrolled. In 2017, 17 master's, 6 other advanced degrees awarded. *Degree requirements:* For master's, thesis (for some programs), thesis or literature review. *Entrance requirements:* For master's, minimum GPA of 3.0. Additional exam requirements/recommendations for international students: Required—TOEFL (minimum score 550 paper-based; 80 iBT), IELTS (minimum score 6.5). *Application deadline:* For fall admission, 8/1 priority date for domestic students, 5/1 priority date for international students; for spring admission, 1/1 priority date for domestic students, 9/1 priority date for international students. Applications are processed on a rolling basis. Electronic applications accepted. Tuition and fees vary according to program. *Financial support:* In 2017–18, 1 student received support. Unspecified assistantships available. Financial award application deadline: 4/15; financial award applicants required to submit FAFSA. *Faculty research:* Juvenile justice, criminology, victimology, policing, social justice, security threat assessment. *Unit head:* Cathryn Lavery, PhD, Chair, 914-633-2597, E-mail: clavery@iona.edu. *Application contact:* Katelyn Brunck, Assistant Director of Graduate Admissions, 914-633-2451, Fax: 914-633-2277, E-mail: kbrunck@iona.edu. Website: http://www.iona.edu/Academics/School-of-Arts-Science/Departments/Criminal-Justice/Graduate-Programs.aspx

Jackson State University, Graduate School, College of Liberal Arts, Department of Criminal Justice and Sociology, Jackson, MS 39217. Offers criminology and justice services (MA); sociology (MA). *Program availability:* Part-time, evening/weekend. *Degree requirements:* For master's, comprehensive exam, thesis or alternative. *Entrance requirements:* For master's, GRE General Test. Additional exam requirements/recommendations for international students: Required—TOEFL (minimum score 520 paper-based; 67 iBT).

Jacksonville State University, College of Graduate Studies and Continuing Education, College of Arts and Sciences, Department of Criminal Justice, Jacksonville, AL 36265-1602. Offers MS. *Program availability:* Part-time, evening/weekend. *Degree requirements:* For master's, comprehensive exam, thesis (for some programs). *Entrance requirements:* For master's, GRE General Test or MAT. Additional exam requirements/recommendations for international students: Required—TOEFL (minimum score 500 paper-based; 61 iBT). Electronic applications accepted.

John Jay College of Criminal Justice of the City University of New York, Graduate Studies, Program in Protection Management, New York, NY 10019. Offers MS. *Program availability:* Part-time, evening/weekend. *Degree requirements:* For master's, thesis or alternative. *Entrance requirements:* For master's, minimum B average. Additional exam requirements/recommendations for international students: Required—TOEFL (minimum score 500 paper-based).

John Jay College of Criminal Justice of the City University of New York, Graduate Studies, Programs in Criminal Justice, New York, NY 10019. Offers criminal justice (MA, PhD); criminology and deviance (PhD); forensic psychology (PhD); forensic science (PhD); international crime and justice (MA); law and philosophy (PhD); organizational behavior (PhD); public policy (PhD). *Program availability:* Part-time, evening/weekend. Terminal master's awarded for partial completion of doctoral program. *Degree requirements:* For master's, thesis or alternative; for doctorate, one foreign language, thesis/dissertation. *Entrance requirements:* For master's, GRE General Test, minimum B average; for doctorate, GRE General Test. Additional exam requirements/recommendations for international students: Required—TOEFL (minimum score 500 paper-based).

Johnson & Wales University, Graduate Studies, MS Program in Criminal Justice, Providence, RI 02903-3703. Offers MS. *Program availability:* Online only, 100% online. *Expenses:* Tuition: Full-time $12,636; part-time $702 per credit hour. *Application contact:* Graduate School Admissions, 401-598-1015, Fax: 401-598-1286, E-mail: pvdgrad@admissions.jwu.edu.

Kean University, College of Business and Public Management, Program in Criminal Justice, Union, NJ 07083. Offers MA. *Program availability:* Part-time. *Faculty:* 14 full-time (4 women). *Students:* 5 full-time (3 women), 3 part-time (all women); includes 3 minority (2 Black or African American, non-Hispanic/Latino; 1 Two or more races, non-Hispanic/Latino). Average age 24. 6 applicants, 67% accepted. In 2017, 9 master's awarded. *Degree requirements:* For master's, comprehensive exam, thesis optional. *Entrance requirements:* For master's, GRE (minimum Analytic Writing score of 3.5), 3 reference letters, minimum GPA of 3.0, writing sample, official transcripts from all institutions attended, personal statement, resume, sample of scholarly work from undergraduate studies. Additional exam requirements/recommendations for international students: Required—TOEFL (minimum score 550 paper-based; 79 iBT), IELTS (minimum score 6.5). *Application deadline:* For fall admission, 6/30 for domestic and international students; for spring admission, 12/1 for domestic and international students. Applications are processed on a rolling basis. Application fee: $75. Electronic applications accepted. *Expenses:* Tuition, state resident: full-time $13,419; part-time

$653 per credit. Tuition, nonresident: full-time $18,188; part-time $801 per credit. *Required fees:* $3382; $154 per credit. Tuition and fees vary according to course level, course load, degree level and program. *Financial support:* Scholarships/grants and unspecified assistantships available. Financial award applicants required to submit FAFSA. *Unit head:* Dr. Pat McManimon, Program Coordinator, 908-737-4309, E-mail: pmcmanim@kean.edu. *Application contact:* Pedro Lopes, Admissions Counselor, 908-737-7100, E-mail: gradadmissions@kean.edu.
Website: http://grad.kean.edu/masters-programs/criminal-justice

Keiser University, MA in Criminal Justice Program, Fort Lauderdale, FL 33309. Offers MA. *Program availability:* Part-time, online learning.
Website: http://www.keiseruniversity.edu/graduateschool/macj.php

Keiser University, MA in Homeland Security Program, Fort Lauderdale, FL 33309. Offers MA.
Website: https://www.keiseruniversity.edu/master-arts-criminal-justice-homeland-security-macjhs/

Kennesaw State University, College of Humanities and Social Sciences, Program in Criminal Justice, Kennesaw, GA 30144. Offers MS. *Program availability:* Part-time. *Degree requirements:* For master's, research project or thesis. *Entrance requirements:* For master's, GRE. Additional exam requirements/recommendations for international students: Required—TOEFL (minimum score 550 paper-based; 80 iBT), IELTS (minimum score 6.5). Electronic applications accepted.

Kent State University, College of Arts and Sciences, Department of Sociology, Kent, OH 44242-0001. Offers criminology and criminal justice (MA), including corrections, global security, policing, victimology; sociology (MA, PhD). PhD offered jointly with The University of Akron. *Program availability:* Part-time, 100% online. *Faculty:* 24 full-time (14 women), 4 part-time/adjunct (2 women). *Students:* 42 full-time (25 women), 51 part-time (36 women); includes 20 minority (15 Black or African American, non-Hispanic/Latino; 1 Asian, non-Hispanic/Latino; 3 Hispanic/Latino; 1 Two or more races, non-Hispanic/Latino). Average age 30. 39 applicants, 67% accepted, 19 enrolled. In 2017, 23 master's, 5 doctorates awarded. Terminal master's awarded for partial completion of doctoral program. *Degree requirements:* For master's, thesis, project, or internship; for doctorate, comprehensive exam, thesis/dissertation. *Entrance requirements:* For master's, minimum undergraduate GPA of 3.0, transcripts, goal statement, 3 letters of recommendation; for doctorate, GRE, minimum GPA of 3.0, transcripts, personal statement, 3 letters of recommendation. Additional exam requirements/recommendations for international students: Required—TOEFL (minimum score 587 paper-based, 94 iBT), Michigan English Language Assessment Battery (minimum score 82), IELTS (minimum score 7.0) or PTE (minimum score 65). *Application deadline:* For fall admission, 12/15 for domestic students, 12/1 for international students. Applications are processed on a rolling basis. Application fee: $45 ($70 for international students). Electronic applications accepted. *Expenses:* Tuition, state resident: full-time $11,310; part-time $515 per credit hour. Tuition, nonresident: full-time $20,396; part-time $928 per credit hour. *International tuition:* $18,544 full-time. *Financial support:* Research assistantships with full tuition reimbursements, teaching assistantships with full tuition reimbursements, scholarships/grants, and unspecified assistantships available. Financial award application deadline: 2/28. *Unit head:* Dr. Richard T. Serpe, Professor and Chair, 330-672-2562, E-mail: rserpe@kent.edu. *Application contact:* Dr. William Kalkhoff, Professor and Graduate Coordinator, 330-672-3712, E-mail: wkalkhof@kent.edu.
Website: http://www.kent.edu/sociology/

Keuka College, Program in Criminal Justice Administration, Keuka Park, NY 14478. Offers MS. *Program availability:* Part-time, evening/weekend. *Degree requirements:* For master's, thesis, action research project. *Entrance requirements:* For master's, bachelor's degree from accredited institution, minimum GPA of 3.0, professional experience in field of criminal justice, essay, letter of recommendation. Additional exam requirements/recommendations for international students: Required—TOEFL (minimum score 550 paper-based). Electronic applications accepted. *Expenses:* Contact institution. *Faculty research:* Re-entry of mentally ill offenders; mentoring in criminal justice profession; police leadership; police decision making.

Lamar University, College of Graduate Studies, College of Arts and Sciences, Department of Sociology, Social Work, and Criminal Justice, Beaumont, TX 77701. Offers criminal justice (MS). *Program availability:* Part-time. *Faculty:* 9 full-time (5 women), 5 part-time/adjunct (0 women). *Students:* 7 full-time (6 women), 126 part-time (66 women); includes 92 minority (64 Black or African American, non-Hispanic/Latino; 28 Hispanic/Latino). Average age 34. 111 applicants, 82% accepted, 45 enrolled. In 2017, 70 master's awarded. *Degree requirements:* For master's, thesis or alternative, applied projects. *Entrance requirements:* For master's, GRE General Test. Additional exam requirements/recommendations for international students: Required—TOEFL (minimum score 550 paper-based; 79 iBT), IELTS (minimum score 6.5). *Application deadline:* For fall admission, 8/10 for domestic students, 7/1 for international students; for spring admission, 1/5 for domestic students, 12/1 for international students. Applications are processed on a rolling basis. Application fee: $25 ($50 for international students). Electronic applications accepted. *Expenses:* Contact institution. *Financial support:* In 2017–18, 3 fellowships with partial tuition reimbursements (averaging $1,000 per year) were awarded; career-related internships or fieldwork, Federal Work-Study, and scholarships/grants also available. Support available to part-time students. Financial award application deadline: 4/1; financial award applicants required to submit FAFSA. *Faculty research:* Corrections, planning and evaluations, juveniles, terrorism, Mexican criminal justice. *Unit head:* Dr. Stuart Wright, Chair, 409-880-8542, Fax: 409-880-2324. *Application contact:* Deidre Mayer, Interim Director, Admissions and Academic Services, 409-880-8888, Fax: 409-880-7419, E-mail: gradmissions@lamar.edu.
Website: http://artssciences.lamar.edu/sociology-social-work-criminal-justice

Lasell College, Graduate and Professional Studies in Criminal Justice, Newton, MA 02466-2709. Offers emergency and crisis management (MS, Certificate); homeland security and global justice (MS, Certificate); violence prevention and advocacy (MS, Certificate). *Program availability:* Part-time, evening/weekend, online only, 100% online. *Faculty:* 2 full-time (1 woman), 2 part-time/adjunct (0 women). *Students:* 20 full-time (9 women), 31 part-time (16 women); includes 11 minority (3 Black or African American, non-Hispanic/Latino; 1 Asian, non-Hispanic/Latino; 5 Hispanic/Latino; 2 Two or more races, non-Hispanic/Latino). Average age 31. 33 applicants, 73% accepted, 23 enrolled. In 2017, 2 master's awarded. *Degree requirements:* For master's, minimum GPA of 3.0; internship or research paper. *Entrance requirements:* For master's, one-page personal statement, 2 letters of recommendation, resume, bachelor's degree transcript; for Certificate, bachelor's transcript, 2 letters of recommendation, 1-page statement, resume. Additional exam requirements/recommendations for international students: Required—TOEFL (minimum score 550 paper-based, 79 iBT) or IELTS (minimum score 6). *Application deadline:* For fall admission, 8/31 priority date for domestic students, 6/30 priority date for international students; for spring admission, 12/31 priority date for domestic students, 10/31 priority date for international students. Applications are processed on a rolling basis. Electronic applications accepted. *Expenses:* $600 per credit. *Financial support:* Federal Work-Study, scholarships/grants, and tuition discounts available. Support available to part-time students. Financial award application deadline: 8/31; financial award applicants required to submit FAFSA. *Faculty research:* Children aging out of foster care and the criminal justice system; police departments' attitudes toward the mentally ill and jail diversion programs for those offenders. *Unit head:* Eric Turner, Vice President of Graduate and Professional Studies, 617-243-2071, Fax: 617-243-2450, E-mail: gradinfo@lasell.edu. *Application contact:* Adrienne Franciosi, Director of Graduate Enrollment, 617-243-2214, Fax: 617-243-2450, E-mail: gradinfo@lasell.edu.
Website: http://www.lasell.edu/academics/graduate-and-professional-studies/programs-of-study/master-of-science-in-criminal-justice-.html

Lewis University, College of Arts and Sciences, Program in Criminal Justice, Romeoville, IL 60446. Offers criminal justice (MS). *Program availability:* Part-time, evening/weekend, 100% online, blended/hybrid learning. *Students:* 23 full-time (18 women), 48 part-time (32 women); includes 29 minority (13 Black or African American, non-Hispanic/Latino; 1 American Indian or Alaska Native, non-Hispanic/Latino; 1 Asian, non-Hispanic/Latino; 11 Hispanic/Latino; 3 Two or more races, non-Hispanic/Latino). Average age 31. *Degree requirements:* For master's, comprehensive exam (for some programs). *Entrance requirements:* For master's, bachelor's degree or a minimum of 12 related hours in criminal/social justice, 2 letters of recommendation, minimum GPA of 3.0, personal statement. Additional exam requirements/recommendations for international students: Required—TOEFL (minimum score 79 iBT), IELTS (minimum score 6). *Application deadline:* For fall admission, 5/1 priority date for international students; for spring admission, 11/15 priority date for international students. Applications are processed on a rolling basis. Application fee: $40. Electronic applications accepted. Tuition and fees vary according to program. *Financial support:* Federal Work-Study, scholarships/grants, tuition waivers (full and partial), and unspecified assistantships available. Financial award application deadline: 5/1; financial award applicants required to submit FAFSA. *Faculty research:* Community policing, management, terrorism, biological warfare, drugs. *Unit head:* Dr. Raymond Garritano, Director of the Public Safety Administration Graduate Program, 815-836-5949, E-mail: garritra@lewisu.edu. *Application contact:* Michelle Mega, Coordinator, 815-838-0500 Ext. 5342, Fax: 815-836-5342, E-mail: megami@lewisu.edu.
Website: http://www.lewisu.edu/academics/masterscrim/index.htm

Liberty University, Helms School of Government, Lynchburg, VA 24515. Offers criminal justice (MS), including forensic psychology, homeland security, public administration (MA, MS); international relations (MS); political science (MS); public administration (MPA), including business and government, healthcare, law and public policy, public and non-profit management; public policy (MA), including campaigns and elections, international affairs, Middle East affairs, public administration (MA, MS). *Program availability:* Part-time, online learning. *Students:* 287 full-time (148 women), 639 part-time (248 women); includes 231 minority (173 Black or African American, non-Hispanic/Latino; 4 American Indian or Alaska Native, non-Hispanic/Latino; 8 Asian, non-Hispanic/Latino; 20 Hispanic/Latino; 1 Native Hawaiian or other Pacific Islander, non-Hispanic/Latino; 25 Two or more races, non-Hispanic/Latino), 7 international. Average age 35. 876 applicants, 64% accepted, 277 enrolled. In 2017, 211 master's awarded. *Entrance requirements:* For master's, minimum undergraduate GPA of 3.0. Additional exam requirements/recommendations for international students: Required—TOEFL (minimum score 600 paper-based; 100 iBT). *Application deadline:* Applications are processed on a rolling basis. Application fee: $50. Electronic applications accepted. *Unit head:* Shawn D. Akers, Dean, 434-592-4986. *Application contact:* Jay Bridge, Director of Admissions, 800-424-9595, Fax: 800-628-7977, E-mail: gradadmissions@liberty.edu.

Liberty University, School of Behavioral Sciences, Lynchburg, VA 24515. Offers applied psychology (MA), including developmental psychology (MA, MS), industrial/organizational psychology (MA, MS); clinical mental health counseling (MA); community care and counseling (Ed D), including marriage and family counseling, pastoral care and counseling, traumatology; counselor education and supervision (PhD); human services counseling (MA), including addictions and recovery, business, child and family law, Christian ministries, criminal justice, crisis response and trauma, executive leadership, health and wellness, life coaching, marriage and family, military resilience; marriage and family counseling (MA); marriage and family therapy (MA); military resilience (Certificate); pastoral counseling (MA), including addictions and recovery, community chaplaincy, crisis response and trauma, discipleship and church ministry, leadership, life coaching, marriage and family, marriage and family studies, military resilience, parenting and child/adolescent, pastoral counseling, theology; professional counseling (MA); psychology (MS), including developmental psychology (MA, MS), industrial/organizational psychology (MA, MS); school counseling (M Ed). *Program availability:* Part-time, online learning. *Students:* 2,649 full-time (2,085 women), 5,086 part-time (4,015 women); includes 2,275 minority (1,784 Black or African American, non-Hispanic/Latino; 44 American Indian or Alaska Native, non-Hispanic/Latino; 67 Asian, non-Hispanic/Latino; 200 Hispanic/Latino; 11 Native Hawaiian or other Pacific Islander, non-Hispanic/Latino; 169 Two or more races, non-Hispanic/Latino), 145 international. Average age 39. 5,839 applicants, 51% accepted, 1710 enrolled. In 2017, 1,626 master's, 7 doctorates, 61 other advanced degrees awarded. *Application deadline:* Applications are processed on a rolling basis. Application fee: $50. Electronic applications accepted. *Financial support:* Applicants required to submit FAFSA. *Unit head:* Dr. Ronald Hawkins, Founding Dean, School of Behavioral Sciences. *Application contact:* Jay Bridge, Director of Admissions, 800-424-9595, Fax: 800-628-7977, E-mail: gradadmissions@liberty.edu.

Liberty University, School of Business, Lynchburg, VA 24515. Offers accounting (MBA, MS), including audit and financial reporting (MS), business (MS), financial services (MS), forensic accounting (MS), leadership (MS), taxation (MS); criminal justice (MBA); cyber security (MS); executive leadership (MA); information systems (MS), including information assurance, technology management; international business (MBA, DBA); leadership (DBA); marketing (MBA, MS, DBA), including digital marketing and advertising (MS), project management (MS), public relations (MS), sports marketing and media (MS); project management (MBA, DBA); public administration (MBA); public relations (MBA). *Program availability:* Part-time, online learning. *Students:* 1,887 full-time (1,003 women), 4,223 part-time (1,950 women); includes 1,570 minority (1,133 Black or African American, non-Hispanic/Latino; 30 American Indian or Alaska Native, non-Hispanic/Latino; 118 Asian, non-Hispanic/Latino; 149 Hispanic/Latino; 13 Native Hawaiian or other Pacific Islander, non-Hispanic/Latino; 127 Two or more races, non-Hispanic/Latino), 109 international. Average age 35. 5,680 applicants, 51% accepted, 1510 enrolled. In 2017, 1,290 master's, 17 doctorates awarded. *Entrance requirements:* For master's, minimum undergraduate GPA of 3.0, 15 hours of upper-level business courses. Additional exam requirements/recommendations for international students: Required—TOEFL (minimum score 600 paper-based; 100 iBT). *Application deadline:* Applications are processed on a rolling basis. Application fee: $50. Electronic applications accepted. *Expenses:* Contact institution. *Financial support:* Applicants required to submit FAFSA. *Unit head:* Dr. Scott Hicks, Dean, 434-592-4808, Fax: 434-582-2366, E-mail: smhicks@liberty.edu. *Application contact:* Jay Bridge, Director of Graduate Admissions, 800-424-9595, Fax: 800-628-7977, E-mail: gradadmissions@liberty.edu.
Website: http://www.liberty.edu/academics/business/index.cfm?PID-149

Lincoln University, Graduate Studies, Jefferson City, MO 65101. Offers business administration (MBA), including accounting, management, management information systems, public administration/policy; elementary teaching (M Ed); environmental science (MS); guidance and counseling (M Ed), including community/agency counseling, elementary school, secondary school; higher education (MA); history (MA); integrated agricultural systems (MS); middle school (M Ed); natural sciences (MS); secondary teaching (M Ed); sociology (MA); sociology/criminal justice (MA). *Program availability:* Part-time, evening/weekend, 100% online, blended/hybrid learning. *Students:* 40 full-time (23 women), 64 part-time (32 women); includes 33 minority (30 Black or African American, non-Hispanic/Latino; 2 Hispanic/Latino; 1 Two or more races, non-Hispanic/Latino), 12 international. Average age 33. 48 applicants, 81% accepted, 22 enrolled. In 2017, 46 master's awarded. *Degree requirements:* For master's, comprehensive exam, thesis optional. *Entrance requirements:* For master's, GRE, MAT, or GMAT, minimum GPA of 2.75 overall, 3.0 in courses related to specialization; 3 letters of recommendation; minimum C average in English composition; personal statement of purpose. Additional exam requirements/recommendations for international students: Required—TOEFL (minimum score 500 paper-based; 61 iBT), IELTS (minimum score 5.5), Michigan English Language Assessment Battery (minimum score 80). *Application deadline:* For fall admission, 7/1 priority date for domestic students, 5/1 priority date for international students; for spring admission, 11/1 priority date for domestic students, 10/1 priority date for international students; for summer admission, 6/1 priority date for domestic students. Applications are processed on a rolling basis. Application fee: $30. Electronic applications accepted. *Expenses:* Tuition, state resident: part-time $291 per credit hour. Tuition, nonresident: part-time $541.50 per credit hour. *Financial support:* In 2017–18, 2 fellowships with tuition reimbursements, 3 research assistantships with tuition reimbursements were awarded; Federal Work-Study, scholarships/grants, and unspecified assistantships also available. Support available to part-time students. Financial award application deadline: 3/1; financial award applicants required to submit FAFSA. *Unit head:* Dr. Debra F. Greene, Interim Provost, 573-681-5247, Fax: 573-681-5106, E-mail: gradschool@lincolnu.edu. *Application contact:* Irasema Steck, Administrative Assistant, 573-681-5247, Fax: 573-681-5106, E-mail: gradschool@lincolnu.edu.
Website: http://www.lincolnu.edu/web/graduate-studies/graduate-studies

Lindenwood University, Graduate Programs, School of Accelerated Degree Programs, St. Charles, MO 63301-1695. Offers administration (MSA), including management, marketing, project management; business administration (MBA); communications (MA), including digital and multimedia, media management, promotions, training and development; criminal justice and administration (MS); healthcare administration (MS); human resource management (MS); information technology (Certificate); managing information security (MS); managing information technology (MS); managing virtualization and cloud computing (MS); writing (MFA). *Program availability:* Part-time, evening/weekend, 100% online. *Faculty:* 12 full-time (5 women), 90 part-time/adjunct (37 women). *Students:* 597 full-time (383 women), 202 part-time (138 women); includes 248 minority (206 Black or African American, non-Hispanic/Latino; 3 American Indian or Alaska Native, non-Hispanic/Latino; 6 Asian, non-Hispanic/Latino; 21 Hispanic/Latino; 1 Native Hawaiian or other Pacific Islander, non-Hispanic/Latino; 11 Two or more races, non-Hispanic/Latino), 69 international. Average age 36. 526 applicants, 46% accepted, 204 enrolled. In 2017, 537 master's awarded. *Degree requirements:* For master's, thesis (for some programs), minimum cumulative GPA of 3.0; for Certificate, minimum cumulative GPA of 3.0. *Entrance requirements:* For master's, resume, personal statement, official undergraduate transcript, minimum undergraduate cumulative GPA of 3.0. Additional exam requirements/recommendations for international students: Required—TOEFL (minimum score 550 paper-based; 80 iBT); Recommended—IELTS (minimum score 6.5). *Application deadline:* For fall admission, 9/24 priority date for domestic and international students; for winter admission, 1/7 priority date for domestic and international students; for spring admission, 4/8 priority date for domestic and international students; for summer admission, 7/8 priority date for domestic and international students. Applications are processed on a rolling basis. Application fee: $30 ($100 for international students). Electronic applications accepted. *Expenses: Tuition:* Full-time $16,300; part-time $460 per credit. *Required fees:* $660; $330 per credit. Tuition and fees vary according to degree level and program. *Financial support:* In 2017–18, 738 students received support. Career-related internships or fieldwork, institutionally sponsored loans, scholarships/grants, tuition waivers (partial), and unspecified assistantships available. Financial award application deadline: 6/30; financial award applicants required to submit FAFSA. *Unit head:* Dr. Gina Ganahl, Dean, Accelerated Degree Programs, 636-949-4501, Fax: 636-949-4505, E-mail: gganahl@lindenwood.edu. *Application contact:* Kara Schilli, Director, Evening and Graduate Admissions, 636-949-4349, Fax: 636-949-4109, E-mail: adultadmissions@lindenwood.edu.
Website: http://www.lindenwood.edu/academics/academic-schools/school-of-accelerated-degree-programs/

Lindenwood University–Belleville, Graduate Programs, Belleville, IL 62226. Offers business administration (MBA); communications (MA), including digital and multimedia, media management, promotions, training and development; counseling (MA); criminal justice administration (MS); education (MA); healthcare administration (MS); human resource management (MS); school administration (MA); teaching (MAT).

Loma Linda University, School of Behavioral Health, Department of Social Work and Social Ecology, Loma Linda, CA 92350. Offers criminal justice (MS); gerontology (MS); social policy and social research (PhD); social work (MSW). *Accreditation:* CSWE. *Degree requirements:* For master's, comprehensive exam, thesis optional; for doctorate, comprehensive exam, thesis/dissertation. *Entrance requirements:* For master's and doctorate, GRE General Test. Additional exam requirements/recommendations for international students: Required—TOEFL, Michigan English Language Assessment Battery. Electronic applications accepted.

London Metropolitan University, Graduate Programs, London, United Kingdom. Offers applied psychology (M Sc); architecture (MA); biomedical science (M Sc); blood science (M Sc); cancer pharmacology (M Sc); computer networking and cyber security (M Sc); computing and information systems (M Sc); conference interpreting (MA); counter-terrorism studies (M Sc); creative, digital and professional writing (MA); crime, violence and prevention (M Sc); criminology (M Sc); curating contemporary art (MA); data analytics (M Sc); digital media (MA); early childhood studies (MA); education (MA, Ed D); financial services law, regulation and compliance (LL M); food science (M Sc); forensic psychology (M Sc); health and social care management and policy (M Sc); human nutrition (M Sc); human resource management (MA); human rights and international conflict (MA); information technology (M Sc); intelligence and security studies (M Sc); international oil, gas and energy law (LL M); international relations (MA); interpreting (MA); learning and teaching in higher education (MA); legal practice (LL M); media and entertainment law (LL M); organizational and consumer psychology (M Sc); psychological therapy (M Sc); psychology of mental health (M Sc); public health (M Sc); public policy and management (MPA); security studies (M Sc); social work (M Sc); spatial planning and urban design (MA); sports therapy (M Sc); supporting older children and young people with dyslexia (MA); teaching languages (MA), including Arabic, English; translation (MA); woman and child abuse (MA).

Long Island University–Brentwood Campus, Graduate Programs, Brentwood, NY 11717. Offers childhood education (MS), including grades 1-6; childhood education/literacy B-6 (MS); childhood education/special education (grades 1-6) (MS); clinical mental health counseling (MS, Advanced Certificate); criminal justice (MS); early childhood education (MS); educational leadership (MS Ed); family nurse practitioner (MS, Advanced Certificate); health administration (MPA); library and information science (MS); literacy (B-6) (MS Ed); school counselor (MS, Advanced Certificate); social work (MSW); special education (MS Ed); students with disabilities generalist (grades 7-12) (Advanced Certificate). *Program availability:* Part-time. *Faculty:* 14 full-time (9 women), 22 part-time/adjunct (11 women). *Students:* 111 full-time (89 women), 47 part-time (34 women); includes 35 minority (8 Black or African American, non-Hispanic/Latino; 1 American Indian or Alaska Native, non-Hispanic/Latino; 3 Asian, non-Hispanic/Latino; 22 Hispanic/Latino; 1 Two or more races, non-Hispanic/Latino), 1 international. Average age 30. 110 applicants, 82% accepted, 63 enrolled. In 2017, 58 master's, 5 other advanced degrees awarded. *Entrance requirements:* For master's and Advanced Certificate, GRE. Additional exam requirements/recommendations for international students: Required—TOEFL or IELTS. *Application deadline:* Applications are processed on a rolling basis. Application fee: $50. Electronic applications accepted. *Expenses: Tuition:* Full-time $21,168; part-time $1201 per credit. *Required fees:* $1840; $920 per term. Tuition and fees vary according to course load. *Financial support:* In 2017–18, 121 students received support. Scholarships/grants available. Support available to part-time students. Financial award application deadline: 2/15; financial award applicants required to submit FAFSA. *Unit head:* Dr. Abby Van Vlerah, Dean and Chief Operating Officer, 631-299-3831, E-mail: abagail.vanvlerah@liu.edu. *Application contact:* Scott Aug, Associate Director of Enrollment Management, 631-287-8506, E-mail: scott.aug@liu.edu.
Website: http://liu.edu/brentwood

Long Island University–LIU Post, College of Liberal Arts and Sciences, Brookville, NY 11548-1300. Offers applied mathematics (MS); behavior analysis (MA); biology (MS); criminal justice (MS); earth science (MS); English (MA); environmental sustainability (MS); genetic counseling (MS); history (MA); interdisciplinary studies (MA, MS); political science (MA); psychology (MA). *Program availability:* Part-time, evening/weekend, blended/hybrid learning. *Faculty:* 41 full-time (21 women), 24 part-time/adjunct (13 women). *Students:* 173 full-time (124 women), 62 part-time (35 women); includes 54 minority (11 Black or African American, non-Hispanic/Latino; 13 Asian, non-Hispanic/Latino; 23 Hispanic/Latino; 7 Two or more races, non-Hispanic/Latino), 12 international. Average age 28. 368 applicants, 54% accepted, 74 enrolled. In 2017, 89 master's, 15 other advanced degrees awarded. Terminal master's awarded for partial completion of doctoral program. *Degree requirements:* For master's, comprehensive exam (for some programs), thesis (for some programs). *Entrance requirements:* Additional exam requirements/recommendations for international students: Required—TOEFL, IELTS, or PTE. *Application deadline:* Applications are processed on a rolling basis. Application fee: $50. Electronic applications accepted. *Expenses: Tuition:* Full-time $21,618; part-time $1201 per credit. *Required fees:* $1840; $920 per term. Tuition and fees vary according to course load. *Financial support:* In 2017–18, 165 students received support. Fellowships, research assistantships, teaching assistantships, career-related internships or fieldwork, Federal Work-Study, scholarships/grants, tuition waivers (partial), and unspecified assistantships available. Support available to part-time students. Financial award application deadline: 2/15; financial award applicants required to submit FAFSA. *Faculty research:* Biology, environmental sustainability, mathematics, psychology, genetic counseling. *Unit head:* Dr. Nathaniel Bowditch, Dean, 516-299-2234, Fax: 516-299-4140, E-mail: nathaniel.bowditch@liu.edu. *Application contact:* Rita Langdon, Graduate Admissions, 516-299-2900, Fax: 516-299-2137, E-mail: post-enroll@liu.edu.
Website: http://liu.edu/CWPost/Academics/Schools/CLAS

Loyola University Chicago, Graduate School, Department of Criminal Justice and Criminology, Chicago, IL 60660. Offers MA. *Program availability:* Part-time, evening/weekend. *Faculty:* 8 full-time (1 woman), 2 part-time/adjunct (1 woman). *Students:* 20 full-time (13 women), 3 part-time (all women); includes 6 minority (1 Black or African American, non-Hispanic/Latino; 4 Hispanic/Latino; 1 Two or more races, non-Hispanic/Latino). Average age 25. 35 applicants, 66% accepted, 10 enrolled. In 2017, 12 master's awarded. *Degree requirements:* For master's, comprehensive exam or thesis. *Entrance requirements:* For master's, GRE if undergraduate GPA below 3.3, minimum GPA of 3.0. Additional exam requirements/recommendations for international students: Required—TOEFL (minimum score 550 paper-based). *Application deadline:* For fall admission, 2/1 priority date for domestic students. Application fee: $50. Electronic applications accepted. Application fee is waived when completed online. *Expenses:* $1,033 per credit hour tuition, $432 pere semester mandatory fees. *Financial support:* In 2017–18, 5 students received support, including 5 research assistantships with partial tuition reimbursements available (averaging $6,000 per year); career-related internships or fieldwork and scholarships/grants also available. Financial award application deadline: 3/1; financial award applicants required to submit FAFSA. *Faculty research:* Crime and delinquency causation, effectiveness and efficiency of criminal justice system, policy and program evaluation, sentencing, policing, gangs, corrections, ethics. *Total annual research expenditures:* $300,000. *Unit head:* Dr. David Olson, Department Chairperson, 773-508-8594, E-mail: dstemen@luc.edu. *Application contact:* Dr. David Olson, Graduate Program Director, 773-508-8594, E-mail: dolson1@luc.edu.

Loyola University New Orleans, College of Arts and Sciences, Program in Criminology and Justice, New Orleans, LA 70118-6195. Offers MCJ. *Program availability:* Part-time, evening/weekend. *Faculty:* 3 full-time (0 women), 2 part-time/adjunct (1 woman). *Students:* 7 full-time (6 women), 7 part-time (3 women); includes 5 minority (4 Black or African American, non-Hispanic/Latino; 1 Two or more races, non-Hispanic/Latino). Average age 32. 21 applicants, 71% accepted, 9 enrolled. In 2017, 4 master's awarded. *Degree requirements:* For master's, comprehensive exam, research and practicum. *Entrance requirements:* For master's, GRE, resume, interview, letters of recommendation, work experience, transcript from accredited university. Additional exam requirements/recommendations for international students: Required—TOEFL (minimum score 550 paper-based). *Application deadline:* For fall admission, 8/15 priority date for domestic and international students; for spring admission, 1/1 priority date for domestic and international students. Applications are processed on a rolling basis. Application fee: $20. Electronic applications accepted. Application fee is waived when completed online. *Expenses:* $818 per credit hour tuition; $733 full-time fees; $376.50 part-time fees. *Financial support:* Research assistantships, scholarships/grants, and unspecified assistantships available. Financial award application deadline: 5/1; financial award applicants required to submit FAFSA. *Faculty research:* Physical and social aspects of disasters, reconciling interpretations of gang behaviors and processes with viewpoints of actual gang members, examining the social network dynamics of deviant populations, investigating the future of criminal innovation, navigating racial/ethnic dynamics in criminology, human trafficking, criminology and forensic science. *Unit head:* Dr. Rae Taylor, Chair, 504-865-2041, Fax: 504-865-3883, E-mail: crimjust@loyno.edu. *Application contact:* Joy David, Office Manager, 504-865-3228, Fax: 504-865-3612, E-mail: crimjust@loyno.edu.
Website: http://cas.loyno.edu/criminologyjustice/master-criminal-justice

Criminal Justice and Criminology

Lynn University, College of Arts and Sciences, Boca Raton, FL 33431-5598. Offers criminal justice (MS); mental health counseling (MS); psychology (MS), including general psychology, industrial/organizational psychology. *Program availability:* Part-time, evening/weekend, 100% online, blended/hybrid learning. *Faculty:* 59 full-time (26 women), 22 part-time/adjunct (16 women). *Students:* 60 full-time (47 women), 38 part-time (24 women); includes 32 minority (15 Black or African American, non-Hispanic/Latino; 2 Asian, non-Hispanic/Latino; 15 Hispanic/Latino), 6 international. Average age 30. 73 applicants, 82% accepted, 47 enrolled. In 2017, 64 master's awarded. *Degree requirements:* For master's, comprehensive exam (for some programs), thesis (for some programs). *Entrance requirements:* For master's, bachelor's degree from accrediated institution, minimum undergraduate GPA of 3.0, official undergraduate transcripts, two letters of recommendation from academic or professional sources, writing sample demonstrating capacity to perform at graduate level. Additional exam requirements/recommendations for international students: Required—TOEFL (minimum score 550 paper-based; 80 iBT), IELTS (minimum score 6.5). *Application deadline:* For fall admission, 8/18 for domestic students, 8/4 for international students; for spring admission, 12/15 for domestic students, 12/1 for international students; for summer admission, 4/17 for domestic students, 4/3 for international students. Applications are processed on a rolling basis. Application fee: $45. Electronic applications accepted. *Expenses:* $740 per credit. *Financial support:* Career-related internships or fieldwork, Federal Work-Study, scholarships/grants, tuition waivers (full and partial), and unspecified assistantships available. Support available to part-time students. Financial award application deadline: 3/1; financial award applicants required to submit FAFSA. *Faculty research:* Personality and social media, learning strategies, personal health behaviors and compliance, using drums in substance abuse groups, interpersonal behaviors with individuals with autism, case conceptualization, teaching case conceptualization across the curriculum. *Unit head:* Dr. Katrina Carter-Tellison, Dean, 561-237-7412, E-mail: kcartertellison@lynn.edu. *Application contact:* Steven Pruitt, Director of Graduate Admission, 561-237-7834, Fax: 561-237-7100, E-mail: admissionpm@lynn.edu.
Website: https://www.lynn.edu/academics/colleges-schools/arts-and-sciences

Madonna University, School of Business, Livonia, MI 48150-1173. Offers business administration (MBA); international business (MSBA); leadership studies (MSBA); leadership studies in criminal justice (MSBA); quality and operations management (MSBA). *Program availability:* Part-time, evening/weekend, online learning. *Degree requirements:* For master's, thesis (for some programs), foreign language proficiency (international business). *Entrance requirements:* For master's, GMAT, GRE General Test, minimum GPA of 3.0. Electronic applications accepted. *Faculty research:* Management, women in management, future studies.

Marshall University, Academic Affairs Division, College of Science, Department of Criminal Justice, Huntington, WV 25755. Offers MS. *Program availability:* Evening/weekend. *Students:* 10 full-time (5 women), 6 part-time (4 women); includes 1 minority (Hispanic/Latino). Average age 30. In 2017, 4 master's awarded. *Degree requirements:* For master's, thesis optional. *Entrance requirements:* For master's, GRE General Test. Application fee: $40. *Unit head:* Dr. Brian Morgan, Chair, 304-696-6469, E-mail: morgan16@marshall.edu. *Application contact:* Information Contact, Fax: 304-746-1902, E-mail: services@marshall.edu.

Marywood University, Academic Affairs, Munley College of Liberal Arts and Sciences, Department of Social Sciences, Scranton, PA 18509-1598. Offers criminal justice (MS). Electronic applications accepted.

McNeese State University, Doré School of Graduate Studies, College of Liberal Arts, Department of Social Sciences, Lake Charles, LA 70609. Offers criminal justice (MS). *Entrance requirements:* For master's, GRE, minimum undergraduate GPA of 3.0, 3 letters of recommendation, autobiography. *Application deadline:* For fall admission, 5/15 priority date for domestic and international students; for spring admission, 10/15 priority date for domestic and international students. Applications are processed on a rolling basis. Application fee: $20 ($30 for international students). *Financial support:* Application deadline: 5/1. *Unit head:* Dr. Gregory Clark, Department Head, 337-475-5300, E-mail: clark@mcneese.edu. *Application contact:* Dr. Dustin M. Hebert, Director of Dore' School of Graduate Studies, 337-475-5396, Fax: 337-475-5397, E-mail: admissions@mcneese.edu.

Mercer University, Graduate Studies, Cecil B. Day Campus, Penfield College, Atlanta, GA 30341. Offers certified rehabilitation counseling (MS); clinical mental health (MS); counselor education and supervision (PhD); criminal justice and public safety leadership (MS); health informatics (MS); human services (MS), including child and adolescent services, gerontology services; organizational leadership (MS), including leadership for the health care professional, leadership for the nonprofit organization, organizational development and change; school counseling (MS). *Program availability:* Part-time, evening/weekend, 100% online, blended/hybrid learning. *Faculty:* 17 full-time (10 women), 27 part-time/adjunct (24 women). *Students:* 199 full-time (165 women), 266 part-time (218 women); includes 268 minority (226 Black or African American, non-Hispanic/Latino; 1 American Indian or Alaska Native, non-Hispanic/Latino; 19 Asian, non-Hispanic/Latino; 19 Hispanic/Latino; 3 Two or more races, non-Hispanic/Latino). Average age 32. 300 applicants, 45% accepted, 114 enrolled. In 2017, 101 master's, 5 doctorates awarded. *Degree requirements:* For master's, comprehensive exam (for some programs), thesis (for some programs); for doctorate, thesis/dissertation. *Entrance requirements:* For master's, GRE or MAT, Georgia Professional Standards Commission (GPSC) Certification at the SC-5 level; for doctorate, GRE or MAT. Additional exam requirements/recommendations for international students: Recommended—TOEFL (minimum score 550 paper-based; 80 iBT), IELTS (minimum score 6.5). *Application deadline:* For fall admission, 7/1 priority date for domestic and international students; for spring admission, 11/1 priority date for domestic and international students; for summer admission, 4/1 priority date for domestic and international students. Application fee: $35. Electronic applications accepted. Application fee is waived when completed online. *Expenses:* $637 per credit. *Financial support:* In 2017–18, 32 students received support. Federal Work-Study, scholarships/grants, and unspecified assistantships available. Financial award applicants required to submit FAFSA. *Faculty research:* Marriage and families issues, leadership and ethics, cyber-bullying, trauma, narrative counseling and theory. *Total annual research expenditures:* $85,000. *Unit head:* Dr. Priscilla R. Danheiser, Dean, 678-547-6028, Fax: 678-547-6008, E-mail: danheiser_p@mercer.edu. *Application contact:* Dr. Melissa McCants Cruz, Director of Graduate Admissions, 678-547-6024, E-mail: penfield.admissions@mercer.edu.
Website: http://penfield.mercer.edu/programs/graduate-professional/

Mercyhurst University, Graduate Studies, Program in Administration of Justice, Erie, PA 16546. Offers administration of justice (MS). *Program availability:* Part-time, evening/weekend. *Degree requirements:* For master's, thesis optional. *Entrance requirements:* For master's, GRE, resume, essay, three professional references, transcripts. Additional exam requirements/recommendations for international students: Required—TOEFL. Electronic applications accepted. *Faculty research:* Research methods, criminal justice administration, juvenile justice.

Mercyhurst University, Graduate Studies, Program in Applied Intelligence, Erie, PA 16546. Offers MS, Certificate. *Program availability:* Online learning. *Degree requirements:* For master's, internship. *Entrance requirements:* For master's, GRE or MAT, resume, essay, three professional references, transcripts. Additional exam requirements/recommendations for international students: Required—TOEFL. Electronic applications accepted.

Merrimack College, School of Education and Social Policy, North Andover, MA 01845-5800. Offers community engagement (M Ed), including community organizations, higher education, PreK-12 education; criminology and criminal justice (MS); curriculum and instruction (M Ed); early childhood education (M Ed); educational leadership (CAGS), including instructional leadership; elementary education (M Ed); English as a second language (PreK-6) (M Ed); high school education (M Ed); higher education (M Ed), including leadership and organizational development, student affairs; middle school education (M Ed); moderate disabilities (PreK-8) (M Ed); school counseling (M Ed). *Program availability:* Part-time, evening/weekend, 100% online courses with immersion events and in-classroom practicum close to home. *Faculty:* 15 full-time, 36 part-time/adjunct. *Students:* 212 full-time (175 women), 121 part-time (101 women); includes 42 minority (6 Black or African American, non-Hispanic/Latino; 6 Asian, non-Hispanic/Latino; 27 Hispanic/Latino; 3 Two or more races, non-Hispanic/Latino), 3 international. Average age 27. 420 applicants, 84% accepted, 250 enrolled. In 2017, 177 master's awarded. *Degree requirements:* For master's, practicum, portfolio, and state test (for licensure track); capstone (for higher education, curriculum and instruction, and community engagement tracks); for CAGS, capstone. *Entrance requirements:* For master's, Massachusetts Teacher Education Licensure (MTEL), official transcripts from other colleges, resume, personal statement, 2 letters of recommendation. Additional exam requirements/recommendations for international students: Required—TOEFL (minimum score 84 iBT), IELTS (minimum score 6.5), PTE (minimum score 56). *Application deadline:* For fall admission, 8/24 for domestic students, 7/30 for international students; for spring admission, 1/10 for domestic students, 12/10 for international students; for summer admission, 5/10 for domestic students, 4/10 for international students. Applications are processed on a rolling basis. Application fee: $0. Electronic applications accepted. *Expenses:* Contact institution. *Financial support:* Fellowships with full tuition reimbursements, career-related internships or fieldwork, scholarships/grants, and health care benefits available. Support available to part-time students. Financial award application deadline: 5/1; financial award applicants required to submit FAFSA. *Application contact:* Alyssa Orlando, Graduate Admissions Counselor, 978-837-3563, E-mail: orlandoaf@merrimack.edu.
Website: http://www.merrimack.edu/academics/graduate/education/

Methodist University, School of Graduate Studies, Program in Justice Administration, Fayetteville, NC 28311-1498. Offers MJA. *Program availability:* Part-time, evening/weekend. *Entrance requirements:* For master's, bachelor's degree in criminal justice or related discipline with minimum overall GPA of 3.0 from accredited institution. Additional exam requirements/recommendations for international students: Required—TOEFL (minimum score 500 paper-based; 60 iBT).

Metropolitan State University, School of Law Enforcement and Criminal Justice, St. Paul, MN 55106-5000. Offers criminal justice (MS). *Program availability:* Part-time, evening/weekend. *Degree requirements:* For master's, thesis. *Entrance requirements:* For master's, resume, letters of reference, minimum GPA of 3.0. Additional exam requirements/recommendations for international students: Required—TOEFL (minimum score 550 paper-based). *Application deadline:* For fall admission, 8/1 priority date for domestic students; for spring admission, 12/1 priority date for domestic students. Electronic applications accepted. *Expenses:* Tuition, state resident: part-time $388.55 per credit. Tuition, nonresident: part-time $777.11 per credit. *Required fees:* $35.11 per credit. Part-time tuition and fees vary according to campus/location and program. *Financial support:* Applicants required to submit FAFSA. *Unit head:* Everett Doolittle, Interim Dean, 763-657-3754, E-mail: everett.doolittle@metrostate.edu. *Application contact:* Everett Doolittle, Interim Dean, 763-657-3754, E-mail: everett.doolittle@metrostate.edu.
Website: https://www.metrostate.edu/academics/community-studies/law-enforcement-and-criminal-justice

Michigan State University, The Graduate School, College of Social Science, School of Criminal Justice, East Lansing, MI 48824. Offers criminal justice (MS, PhD); forensic science (MS); law enforcement intelligence and analysis (MS). *Program availability:* Online learning. *Entrance requirements:* Additional exam requirements/recommendations for international students: Required—TOEFL. Electronic applications accepted.

Middle Tennessee State University, College of Graduate Studies, College of Behavioral and Health Sciences, Department of Criminal Justice Administration, Murfreesboro, TN 37132. Offers MCJ. Program offered jointly with Tennessee State University. *Program availability:* Part-time, evening/weekend, online learning. *Degree requirements:* For master's, comprehensive exam, thesis. *Entrance requirements:* For master's, GRE or MAT. Additional exam requirements/recommendations for international students: Required—TOEFL (minimum score 525 paper-based; 71 iBT) or IELTS (minimum score 6). Electronic applications accepted.

Midwestern State University, Billie Doris McAda Graduate School, Robert D. and Carol Gunn College of Health Sciences and Human Services, Department of Criminal Justice and Health Services Administration, Wichita Falls, TX 76308. Offers criminal justice (MA); health information management (MHA); health services administration (Graduate Certificate); medical practice management (MHA); public and community sector health care management (MHA); rural and urban hospital management (MHA). *Program availability:* Part-time, evening/weekend. *Degree requirements:* For master's, comprehensive exam, thesis. *Entrance requirements:* For master's, GRE. Additional exam requirements/recommendations for international students: Required—TOEFL (minimum score 550 paper-based). Electronic applications accepted. *Faculty research:* Universal service policy, telehealth, bullying, healthcare financial management, public health ethics.

Minnesota State University Mankato, College of Graduate Studies and Research, College of Social and Behavioral Sciences, Department of Sociology and Corrections, Mankato, MN 56001. Offers sociology (MA); sociology: college teaching (MA); sociology: corrections (MS); sociology: human services planning and administration (MS). *Program availability:* Part-time. *Degree requirements:* For master's, comprehensive exam, thesis or alternative. *Entrance requirements:* For master's, minimum GPA of 3.0 during previous 2 years, 3 letters of reference, resume. Additional exam requirements/recommendations for international students: Required—TOEFL. Electronic applications accepted.

Mississippi College, Graduate School, College of Arts and Sciences, School of Humanities and Social Sciences, Department of History, Political Science, Administration of Justice, and Paralegal Studies, Clinton, MS 39058. Offers administration of justice (MSS); history (M Ed, MA, MSS); paralegal studies (Certificate); political science (MSS); social sciences (M Ed, MSS). *Program availability:* Part-time. *Degree requirements:* For master's, one foreign language, comprehensive exam, thesis (for some programs). *Entrance requirements:* For master's, GRE or NTE, minimum GPA of 2.5. Additional exam requirements/recommendations for international students: Recommended—TOEFL, IELTS. Electronic applications accepted.

Mississippi Valley State University, Department of Criminal Justice, Itta Bena, MS 38941-1400. Offers MS. *Program availability:* Part-time, evening/weekend. *Degree requirements:* For master's, 2 foreign languages, thesis optional. *Entrance requirements:* For master's, minimum GPA of 2.5. Additional exam requirements/recommendations for international students: Recommended—TOEFL (minimum score 525 paper-based). Electronic applications accepted. *Expenses:* Contact institution. *Faculty research:* Police in the criminal justice system, the United States and international terrorism.

Missouri Southern State University, Program in Criminal Justice Administration, Joplin, MO 64801-1595. Offers MS. Program offered jointly with Southeast Missouri State University. *Program availability:* Online learning. *Degree requirements:* For master's, thesis optional. *Entrance requirements:* For master's, minimum undergraduate GPA of 2.5.

Missouri State University, Graduate College, College of Humanities and Public Affairs, Department of Criminology and Criminal Justice, Springfield, MO 65897. Offers community corrections (Certificate); criminology and criminal justice (MS); homeland security and defense (Certificate). *Program availability:* Part-time, 100% online, blended/hybrid learning. *Faculty:* 7 full-time (2 women). *Students:* 19 full-time (12 women), 18 part-time (7 women); includes 2 minority (both Black or African American, non-Hispanic/Latino). Average age 26. 23 applicants, 83% accepted, 11 enrolled. In 2017, 25 master's awarded. *Degree requirements:* For master's, comprehensive exam, thesis or alternative. *Entrance requirements:* For master's, bachelor's degree in criminology, criminal justice, or sociology; minimum undergraduate GPA of 3.0. Additional exam requirements/recommendations for international students: Required—TOEFL (minimum score 550 paper-based; 79 iBT), IELTS (minimum score 6). *Application deadline:* For fall admission, 7/20 priority date for domestic students, 5/1 for international students; for spring admission, 12/20 priority date for domestic students, 9/1 for international students; for summer admission, 5/20 priority date for domestic students. Applications are processed on a rolling basis. Application fee: $35 ($50 for international students). Electronic applications accepted. *Expenses:* Tuition, state resident: full-time $2915; part-time $2021 per credit hour. Tuition, nonresident: full-time $5354; part-time $3647 per credit hour. *International tuition:* $11,992 full-time. *Required fees:* $173; $173 per credit hour. Tuition and fees vary according to class time, course level, course load, degree level, campus/location and program. *Financial support:* Federal Work-Study, institutionally sponsored loans, and unspecified assistantships available. Financial award application deadline: 3/31; financial award applicants required to submit FAFSA. *Faculty research:* Homeland security initiatives, juvenile policy and programs, law enforcement and drug abuse. *Unit head:* Dr. Brett Garland, Department Head, 417-836-6954, E-mail: brettgarland@missouristate.edu. *Application contact:* Stephanie Praschan, Director, Graduate Enrollment Management, 417-836-5388, Fax: 417-836-6200, E-mail: stephaniepraschan@missouristate.edu.
Website: http://criminology.missouristate.edu/

Missouri State University, Graduate College, Interdisciplinary Program in Professional Studies, Springfield, MO 65897. Offers administrative studies (Certificate); applied communication (MS); criminal justice (MS); environmental management (MS); homeland security (MS); individualized (MS); professional studies (MS); screenwriting and producing (MS); sports management (MS). *Program availability:* Part-time, evening/weekend, 100% online, blended/hybrid learning. *Students:* 51 full-time (33 women), 95 part-time (41 women); includes 21 minority (8 Black or African American, non-Hispanic/Latino; 1 Asian, non-Hispanic/Latino; 7 Hispanic/Latino; 5 Two or more races, non-Hispanic/Latino), 37 international. Average age 24. 71 applicants, 69% accepted, 35 enrolled. In 2017, 50 master's awarded. *Degree requirements:* For master's, comprehensive exam, thesis or alternative. *Entrance requirements:* For master's, GRE, GMAT (if GPA less than 3.0). Additional exam requirements/recommendations for international students: Required—TOEFL (minimum score 550 paper-based; 79 iBT), IELTS (minimum score 6). *Application deadline:* For fall admission, 7/15 priority date for domestic students; for spring admission, 12/1 priority date for domestic students; for summer admission, 5/1 for domestic students. Applications are processed on a rolling basis. Application fee: $35 ($50 for international students). Electronic applications accepted. *Expenses:* Tuition, state resident: full-time $2915; part-time $2021 per credit hour. Tuition, nonresident: full-time $5354; part-time $3647 per credit hour. *International tuition:* $11,992 full-time. *Required fees:* $173; $173 per credit hour. Tuition and fees vary according to class time, course level, course load, degree level, campus/location and program. *Financial support:* Career-related internships or fieldwork, Federal Work-Study, institutionally sponsored loans, scholarships/grants, and unspecified assistantships available. Support available to part-time students. Financial award application deadline: 3/31; financial award applicants required to submit FAFSA. *Unit head:* Dr. Gerald Masterson, Program Director, 417-836-5251, Fax: 417-836-6888, E-mail: mps@missouristate.edu. *Application contact:* Stephanie Praschan, Director, Graduate Enrollment Management, 417-836-5330, Fax: 417-836-6200, E-mail: stephaniepraschan@missouristate.edu.
Website: http://mps.missouristate.edu

Molloy College, Criminal Justice Program, Rockville Centre, NY 11571-5002. Offers MS. *Program availability:* Part-time, evening/weekend. *Faculty:* 3 full-time (2 women), 2 part-time/adjunct (0 women). *Students:* 14 full-time (11 women), 18 part-time (8 women); includes 10 minority (4 Black or African American, non-Hispanic/Latino; 1 Asian, non-Hispanic/Latino; 3 Hispanic/Latino; 1 Native Hawaiian or other Pacific Islander, non-Hispanic/Latino; 1 Two or more races, non-Hispanic/Latino). Average age 36. 23 applicants, 70% accepted, 12 enrolled. In 2017, 13 master's awarded. *Entrance requirements:* Additional exam requirements/recommendations for international students: Required—TOEFL (minimum score 550 paper-based; 79 iBT). *Application deadline:* Applications are processed on a rolling basis. Application fee: $60. Electronic applications accepted. *Expenses: Tuition:* Full-time $19,980; part-time $1110 per credit. *Required fees:* $1040. Tuition and fees vary according to course load and degree level. *Financial support:* Application deadline: 3/1; applicants required to submit FAFSA. *Faculty research:* Performance management; policing: higher education, law, deadly physical force; statistical manipulation of official records; violence including serial killers and school shootings; influence of the juvenile justice system on delinquency. *Unit head:* Dr. John Eterno, Associate Dean/Graduate Program Director, 516-323-3804, E-mail: jeterno@molloy.edu. *Application contact:* Jaclyn Machowicz, Assistant Director for Admissions, 516-323-4010, E-mail: jmachowicz@molloy.edu.
Website: http://www.molloy.edu/academics/graduate-programs/graduate-criminal-justice

Monmouth University, Graduate Studies, Department of Criminal Justice, West Long Branch, NJ 07764-1898. Offers criminal justice (MA), including homeland security; criminal justice administration (Certificate). *Program availability:* Part-time, evening/weekend, 100% online. *Faculty:* 5 full-time (1 woman), 2 part-time/adjunct (0 women). *Students:* 12 full-time (8 women), 15 part-time (8 women); includes 9 minority (4 Black or African American, non-Hispanic/Latino; 4 Hispanic/Latino; 1 Two or more races, non-Hispanic/Latino). Average age 29. In 2017, 11 master's, 1 other advanced degree awarded. *Degree requirements:* For master's, comprehensive exam (for some programs), thesis (for some programs). *Entrance requirements:* For master's and Certificate, baccalaureate degree with minimum GPA of 3.0 in major, 2.5 overall; two letters of recommendation; personal essay. Additional exam requirements/recommendations for international students: Required—TOEFL (minimum score 550 paper-based; 79 iBT), IELTS (minimum score 6), Michigan English Language Assessment Battery (minimum score 77) or Certificate of Advanced English (minimum score 160). *Application deadline:* For fall admission, 7/15 priority date for domestic students, 6/1 for international students; for spring admission, 12/1 priority date for domestic students, 11/1 for international students; for summer admission, 5/1 for domestic students. Applications are processed on a rolling basis. Application fee: $50. Electronic applications accepted. *Expenses: Tuition:* Full-time $21,366; part-time $7122 per credit. *Required fees:* $700; $175 per term. *Financial support:* In 2017–18, 7 students received support. Institutionally sponsored loans, scholarships/grants, and unspecified assistantships available. Support available to part-time students. Financial award applicants required to submit FAFSA. *Faculty research:* Violent crimes, criminal pathology, terrorism, computer crime, comparative criminal justice systems, homeland security. *Unit head:* Dr. Brian Lockwood, Program Director, 732-571-7567, Fax: 732-263-5148, E-mail: lockwood@monmouth.edu. *Application contact:* Andrea Thompson, Graduate Admission Counselor, 732-571-3452, Fax: 732-263-5123, E-mail: gradadm@monmouth.edu.
Website: http://www.monmouth.edu/academics/criminal_justice/default.asp

Monroe College, King Graduate School, Bronx, NY 10468. Offers accounting (MS); business administration (MBA), including entrepreneurship, finance, general business administration, healthcare management, human resources, information technology, marketing; computer science (MS); criminal justice (MS); hospitality management (MS); public health (MPH), including biostatistics and epidemiology, community health, health administration and leadership. *Program availability:* Online learning. Application fee: $50.
Website: https://www.monroecollege.edu/Degrees/King-Graduate-School/

Morehead State University, Graduate Programs, Caudill College of Arts, Humanities and Social Sciences, Department of Sociology, Social Work and Criminology, Morehead, KY 40351. Offers criminology (MA); general sociology (MA); gerontology (MA); sociology regional analysis (MA); sociology/chemical dependency (MA). *Program availability:* Part-time, evening/weekend. *Degree requirements:* For master's, comprehensive exam, thesis (for some programs). *Entrance requirements:* For master's, GRE General Test, minimum GPA of 3.0 in sociology, 2.75 overall; 18 hours of course work in sociology, writing sample. Additional exam requirements/recommendations for international students: Required—TOEFL (minimum score 500 paper-based). Electronic applications accepted. *Faculty research:* Death and dying; aging, drinking, and drugs; economic development; adult children of alcoholics.

Mount Mercy University, Program in Criminal Justice, Cedar Rapids, IA 52402-4797. Offers MA. *Program availability:* Evening/weekend, online learning. *Degree requirements:* For master's, capstone.

National American University, Roueche Graduate Center, Austin, TX 78731. Offers accounting (MBA); aviation management (MBA, MM); care coordination (MSN); community college leadership (Ed D); criminal justice (MM); e-marketing (MBA, MM); health care administration (MBA, MM); higher education (MM); human resources management (MBA, MM); information technology management (MBA, MM); international business (MBA); leadership (EMBA); management (MBA); nursing administration (MSN); nursing education (MSN); nursing informatics (MSN); operations and configuration management (MBA, MM); project and process management (MBA, MM). Master's programs offered online through the Harold D. Buckingham Graduate School. *Program availability:* Part-time, evening/weekend, online learning. *Entrance requirements:* For master's, minimum undergraduate GPA of 2.75. Additional exam requirements/recommendations for international students: Required—TOEFL, TWE. Electronic applications accepted. *Faculty research:* Tourism, finance, marketing.

National University, Academic Affairs, School of Professional Studies, La Jolla, CA 92037-1011. Offers criminal justice (MCJ); digital cinema production (MFA); digital journalism (MA); homeland security and emergency management (MS); juvenile justice (MS); professional screenwriting (MFA); public administration (MPA), including human resource management, organizational leadership. *Program availability:* Part-time, evening/weekend, 100% online, blended/hybrid learning. *Degree requirements:* For master's, thesis (for some programs). *Entrance requirements:* For master's, interview, minimum GPA of 2.5. Additional exam requirements/recommendations for international students: Required—TOEFL (minimum score 550 paper-based; 79 iBT), IELTS (minimum score 6). *Application deadline:* Applications are processed on a rolling basis. Application fee: $60 ($65 for international students). Electronic applications accepted. *Expenses: Tuition:* Part-time $430 per quarter hour. *Financial support:* Career-related internships or fieldwork, institutionally sponsored loans, scholarships/grants, and tuition waivers (partial) available. Support available to part-time students. Financial award application deadline: 6/30; financial award applicants required to submit FAFSA. *Unit head:* Dr. Daniel Donaldson, Dean, 858-642-8480, E-mail: sops@nu.edu. *Application contact:* Brandon Jouganatos, Vice President for Enrollment Services, 800-628-8648, E-mail: advisor@nu.edu.
Website: http://www.nu.edu/OurPrograms/School-of-Professional-Studies.html

New Charter University, College of Public Policy and Administration, Program in Criminal Justice, Salt Lake City, UT 84101. Offers MS. *Program availability:* Part-time, evening/weekend, online learning. *Entrance requirements:* For master's, course work in calculus, statistics. Additional exam requirements/recommendations for international students: Required—TOEFL (minimum score 550 paper-based).

New Jersey City University, College of Professional Studies, Department of Criminal Justice, Jersey City, NJ 07305-1597. Offers MS. *Program availability:* Part-time, evening/weekend. *Degree requirements:* For master's, thesis or alternative. *Entrance requirements:* Additional exam requirements/recommendations for international students: Required—TOEFL (minimum score 79 iBT).

New Jersey City University, College of Professional Studies, Program in National Security Studies, Jersey City, NJ 07305-1597. Offers civil security leadership (D Sc); national security studies (MS, Certificate). *Program availability:* Part-time. *Entrance requirements:* Additional exam requirements/recommendations for international students: Required—TOEFL (minimum score 79 iBT).

New Mexico State University, College of Arts and Sciences, Department of Criminal Justice, Las Cruces, NM 88003. Offers MCJ. *Program availability:* Part-time, evening/weekend, 100% online. *Faculty:* 8 full-time (2 women). *Students:* 21 full-time (11 women), 27 part-time (18 women); includes 39 minority (2 Black or African American, non-Hispanic/Latino; 4 American Indian or Alaska Native, non-Hispanic/Latino; 2 Asian, non-Hispanic/Latino; 31 Hispanic/Latino). Average age 31. 28 applicants, 89% accepted, 19 enrolled. In 2017, 11 master's awarded. *Degree requirements:* For master's, comprehensive exam, thesis optional, oral and written exams. *Entrance requirements:* For master's, minimum GPA of 3.0. Additional exam requirements/recommendations for international students: Required—TOEFL (minimum score 550 paper-based; 79 iBT), IELTS (minimum score 6.5). *Application deadline:* For spring admission, 4/1 priority date for domestic students. Application fee: $40 ($50 for international students). Electronic applications accepted. *Expenses:* Tuition, state resident: full-time $4390. Tuition, nonresident: full-time $15,309. *Required fees:* $853.

Financial support: In 2017–18, 12 students received support, including 7 teaching assistantships (averaging $12,117 per year); career-related internships or fieldwork, Federal Work-Study, scholarships/grants, traineeships, health care benefits, and unspecified assistantships also available. Support available to part-time students. Financial award application deadline: 3/1. *Faculty research:* Juvenile justice, jails and prison administration, courts and legal decision-making, victim studies, policy and evaluation research, narcotics and addiction, research methods, and urban studies, borderland studies, race and identity studies, indigenous jurisprudence, immigration and justice, and diversity in higher education scholarship, statistics, crime theory, race and crime, and street crimes, courts and sentencing, immigration and Latino studies. *Total annual research expenditures:* $6,431. *Unit head:* Dr. Dennis Giever, Department Head, 575-646-1632, Fax: 575-646-2827, E-mail: dgiever@nmsu.edu. *Application contact:* Dr. Mike Tapia, Graduate Program Director, 575-646-5386, Fax: 575-646-2827, E-mail: mtapia@nmsu.edu.
Website: http://crimjust.nmsu.edu

Niagara University, Graduate Division of Arts and Sciences, Department of Criminal Justice, Niagara University, NY 14109. Offers criminal justice administration (MS). *Program availability:* Part-time. *Faculty:* 5 full-time, 1 part-time/adjunct. *Students:* 12 full-time (4 women), 11 part-time (6 women); includes 5 minority (2 Black or African American, non-Hispanic/Latino; 1 Asian, non-Hispanic/Latino; 2 Hispanic/Latino), 6 international. Average age 28. In 2017, 19 master's awarded. *Entrance requirements:* For master's, GMAT/GRE (minimum score 600). Additional exam requirements/recommendations for international students: Required—TOEFL (minimum score 550 paper-based; 79 iBT), IELTS (minimum score 6). *Application deadline:* For fall admission, 8/1 for domestic students. Applications are processed on a rolling basis. Electronic applications accepted. *Expenses:* Contact institution. *Financial support:* Research assistantships with tuition reimbursements, teaching assistantships with tuition reimbursements, career-related internships or fieldwork, Federal Work-Study, scholarships/grants, and unspecified assistantships available. Support available to part-time students. Financial award application deadline: 4/15; financial award applicants required to submit FAFSA. *Unit head:* Dr. Peter Butera, Dean, 716-286-8060, Fax: 716-286-8061, E-mail: pbutera@niagara.edu. *Application contact:* Ronald Winkley, Director, 716-286-8089, Fax: 716-286-8061, E-mail: rwinkley@niagara.edu.
Website: http://www.niagara.edu/graduate-crj

Norfolk State University, School of Graduate Studies, School of Liberal Arts, Department of Sociology, Program in Criminal Justice, Norfolk, VA 23504. Offers MA.

North Carolina Central University, College of Behavioral and Social Sciences, Department of Criminal Justice, Durham, NC 27707-3129. Offers MS. *Program availability:* Part-time, evening/weekend. *Degree requirements:* For master's, one foreign language, comprehensive exam, thesis or alternative. *Entrance requirements:* For master's, GRE, minimum GPA of 3.0 in major, 2.5 overall. Additional exam requirements/recommendations for international students: Required—TOEFL. *Application deadline:* For fall admission, 8/1 for domestic students. Application fee: $30. *Expenses:* Tuition, state resident: full-time $2770; part-time $692.50 per credit hour. Tuition, nonresident: full-time $9247; part-time $2311.75 per credit hour. *Financial support:* Application deadline: 5/1; applicants required to submit FAFSA. *Unit head:* Lorna E. Grant, Director, 919-530-5291, E-mail: lgrant@nccu.edu. *Application contact:* Lorna E. Grant, Director, 919-530-5291, E-mail: lgrant@nccu.edu.

North Dakota State University, College of Graduate and Interdisciplinary Studies, College of Arts, Humanities and Social Sciences, Department of Criminal Justice and Political Science, Fargo, ND 58102. Offers criminal justice (PhD); criminal justice administration (MS). *Program availability:* Part-time. Terminal master's awarded for partial completion of doctoral program. *Degree requirements:* For master's, thesis; for doctorate, comprehensive exam, thesis/dissertation. *Entrance requirements:* For master's, minimum GPA of 3.0 in last 60 credit hours, approved bachelor's degree, course work in research methods and statistics; for doctorate, GRE General Test, minimum GPA of 3.0 over last 60 credit hours, 3 letters of recommendation. Additional exam requirements/recommendations for international students: Required—TOEFL (minimum score 525 paper-based; 71 iBT). *Faculty research:* Corrections, policing, drugs and crime, gender and crime, criminology.

Northeastern State University, College of Liberal Arts, Department of Criminal Justice and Legal Studies, Tahlequah, OK 74464-2399. Offers criminal justice (MS). *Program availability:* Part-time, evening/weekend. *Faculty:* 7 full-time (4 women), 1 (woman) part-time/adjunct. *Students:* 15 full-time (8 women), 20 part-time (10 women); includes 19 minority (2 Black or African American, non-Hispanic/Latino; 7 American Indian or Alaska Native, non-Hispanic/Latino; 1 Hispanic/Latino; 9 Two or more races, non-Hispanic/Latino), 2 international. Average age 34. In 2017, 12 master's awarded. *Degree requirements:* For master's, thesis optional, oral exam. *Entrance requirements:* For master's, MAT or GRE, minimum GPA of 2.5. Additional exam requirements/recommendations for international students: Required—TOEFL. *Application deadline:* For fall admission, 6/1 priority date for domestic students. Applications are processed on a rolling basis. Application fee: $25. Electronic applications accepted. *Expenses:* Tuition, state resident: part-time $222 per credit hour. Tuition, nonresident: part-time $501.75 per credit hour. *Required fees:* $37.40 per credit hour. Tuition and fees vary according to degree level. *Financial support:* Teaching assistantships and Federal Work-Study available. Financial award application deadline: 3/1. *Unit head:* Dr. John Clark, Department Chair, 918-444-3518, E-mail: clarkiii@nsuok.edu. *Application contact:* Josh McCollum, Graduate Coordinator, 918-444-2093, E-mail: mccolluj@nsuok.edu.
Website: http://academics.nsuok.edu/criminaljustice/GraduateStudies.aspx

Northeastern University, College of Professional Studies, Boston, MA 02115-5096. Offers applied nutrition (MS); college athletics administration (MSL); commerce and economic development (MS); corporate and organizational communication (MS); criminal justice (MS); digital media (MPS); elearning and instructional design (M Ed); elementary education (MAT); geographic information technology (MPS); global studies and international relations (MS); higher education administration (M Ed); homeland security (MA); human services (MS); informatics (MPS); leadership (MS); learning analytics (M Ed); learning and instruction (M Ed); nonprofit management (MS); professional sports administration (MSL); project management (MS); regulatory affairs for drugs, biologics, and medical devices (MS); respiratory care leadership (MS); special education (M Ed); technical communication (MS). *Program availability:* Part-time, evening/weekend, 100% online, blended/hybrid learning. *Faculty:* 82 full-time (51 women), 853 part-time/adjunct (366 women). *Students:* 5,278 part-time (3,230 women). In 2017, 1,586 master's awarded. *Application deadline:* Applications are processed on a rolling basis. Application fee: $0. Electronic applications accepted. *Expenses:* Contact institution. *Financial support:* Applicants required to submit FAFSA. *Unit head:* Dr. Mary Loeffelholz, Dean of the College of Professional Studies. *Application contact:* E-mail: cpsadmissions@northeastern.edu.
Website: https://cps.northeastern.edu/

Northeastern University, College of Social Sciences and Humanities, Boston, MA 02115. Offers criminology and criminal justice (MSCJ); criminology and justice policy (PhD); economics (MA, PhD); English (MA, PhD); international affairs (MA); law and public policy (PhD); political science (MA, PhD); public administration (MPA); public policy (MPP); security and resilience studies (MS); sociology (MA, PhD); urban and regional policy (MS); urban informatics (MS); world history (MA, PhD). *Program availability:* Online learning. *Faculty:* 242. *Students:* 491. In 2017, 143 master's, 38 doctorates awarded. *Degree requirements:* For doctorate, variable foreign language requirement, comprehensive exam, thesis/dissertation. *Entrance requirements:* For master's and doctorate, GRE. Additional exam requirements/recommendations for international students: Required—TOEFL, IELTS. Application fee: $75. Electronic applications accepted. *Expenses:* Contact institution. *Financial support:* Teaching assistantships, career-related internships or fieldwork, scholarships/grants, health care benefits, tuition waivers (full and partial), and unspecified assistantships available. Support available to part-time students. Financial award applicants required to submit FAFSA. *Unit head:* Dr. Uta Poiger, Dean, 617-373-5173, E-mail: college_of_social_sciences_and_humanities@neu.edu. *Application contact:* 617-373-5990, E-mail: gradcssh@northeastern.edu.
Website: http://www.northeastern.edu/cssh/

Northern Arizona University, College of Social and Behavioral Sciences, Department of Criminology and Criminal Justice, Flagstaff, AZ 86011. Offers applied criminology (MS). *Program availability:* Part-time. *Faculty:* 23 full-time (13 women), 8 part-time/adjunct (2 women). *Students:* 12 full-time (7 women), 1 (woman) part-time; includes 5 minority (1 American Indian or Alaska Native, non-Hispanic/Latino; 3 Hispanic/Latino; 1 Two or more races, non-Hispanic/Latino), 1 international. Average age 29. 14 applicants, 57% accepted, 8 enrolled. In 2017, 10 master's awarded. *Degree requirements:* For master's, variable foreign language requirement, comprehensive exam (for some programs), thesis (for some programs). *Entrance requirements:* For master's, minimum GPA of 3.0 or the equivalent. Additional exam requirements/recommendations for international students: Required—TOEFL (minimum score 80 iBT), IELTS (minimum score 6.5). *Application deadline:* For fall admission, 2/15 for domestic and international students; for spring admission, 10/1 for domestic and international students. Applications are processed on a rolling basis. Application fee: $65. Electronic applications accepted. *Expenses:* Tuition, state resident: full-time $9240; part-time $458 per credit hour. Tuition, nonresident: full-time $21,588; part-time $1199 per credit hour. *Required fees:* $1021; $14 per credit hour. $646 per semester. Tuition and fees vary according to course load, campus/location and program. *Financial support:* In 2017–18, 6 students received support, including 6 teaching assistantships with partial tuition reimbursements available (averaging $9,000 per year); institutionally sponsored loans, health care benefits, tuition waivers (partial), and unspecified assistantships also available. Financial award application deadline: 2/1; financial award applicants required to submit FAFSA. *Unit head:* Phoebe Morgan, Chair, 928-523-8245, Fax: 928-523-6777, E-mail: phoebe.morgan@nau.edu. *Application contact:* Tina Sutton, Coordinator, Graduate College, 928-523-4348, Fax: 928-523-8950, E-mail: graduate@nau.edu.
Website: https://nau.edu/SBS/CCJ/

Northern Arizona University, Office of the Provost, Graduate Certificate in Executive Police Leadership Program, Flagstaff, AZ 86011. Offers Graduate Certificate. Application fee: $65. *Expenses:* Tuition, state resident: full-time $9240; part-time $458 per credit hour. Tuition, nonresident: full-time $21,588; part-time $1199 per credit hour. *Required fees:* $1021; $14 per credit hour. $646 per semester. Tuition and fees vary according to course load, campus/location and program. *Unit head:* Dr. Alex Steenstra, Chair, Department of Business and Administration, 928-317-6083, E-mail: alex.steenstra@nau.edu.

Norwich University, College of Graduate and Continuing Studies, Master of Public Administration Program, Northfield, VT 05663. Offers criminal justice and public safety (MPA); fiscal management (MPA); international development and influence (MPA); municipal governance (MPA); nonprofit management (MPA); policy analysis and analytics (MPA); public administration leadership and crisis management (MPA); public works and sustainability (MPA). *Program availability:* Evening/weekend, online only, mostly all online with a week-long residency requirement. *Degree requirements:* For master's, capstone. *Entrance requirements:* For master's, minimum undergraduate GPA of 2.75. Additional exam requirements/recommendations for international students: Required—TOEFL (minimum score 550 paper-based; 80 iBT), IELTS (minimum score 6.5). Electronic applications accepted. *Expenses:* Contact institution.

Norwich University, College of Graduate and Continuing Studies, Master of Science in Criminal Justice Program, Northfield, VT 05663. Offers MS. *Program availability:* Evening/weekend, online only, mostly all online with a week-long residency requirement. *Entrance requirements:* For master's, minimum GPA of 2.75. Additional exam requirements/recommendations for international students: Required—TOEFL (minimum score 550 paper-based; 80 iBT), IELTS (minimum score 6.5). Electronic applications accepted. *Expenses:* Contact institution.

Nova Southeastern University, College of Arts, Humanities, and Social Sciences, Fort Lauderdale, FL 33314-7796. Offers advanced conflict resolution practice (Graduate Certificate); child protection (MHS); college student affairs (MS); conflict analysis and resolution (MS, PhD); criminal justice (MS, PhD); cross-disciplinary studies (MA); developmental disabilities (MS); family studies (Graduate Certificate); family systems health care (Graduate Certificate); family therapy (MS, PhD); marriage and family therapy (DMFT); peace studies (Graduate Certificate); qualitative research (Graduate Certificate); solution focused coaching (Graduate Certificate). *Accreditation:* AAMFT/COAMFTE (one or more programs are accredited). *Program availability:* Part-time, evening/weekend, 100% online, blended/hybrid learning. *Faculty:* 29 full-time (18 women), 27 part-time/adjunct (21 women). *Students:* 303 full-time (238 women), 903 part-time (677 women); includes 689 minority (385 Black or African American, non-Hispanic/Latino; 4 American Indian or Alaska Native, non-Hispanic/Latino; 31 Asian, non-Hispanic/Latino; 234 Hispanic/Latino; 1 Native Hawaiian or other Pacific Islander, non-Hispanic/Latino; 34 Two or more races, non-Hispanic/Latino), 60 international. Average age 37. 624 applicants, 61% accepted, 285 enrolled. In 2017, 277 master's, 62 doctorates, 25 other advanced degrees awarded. *Degree requirements:* For master's, thesis optional, comprehensive exams, portfolios (for some programs), table-top exams (for some programs); for doctorate, comprehensive exam, thesis/dissertation, qualifying exams, portfolios (for some programs). *Entrance requirements:* For master's, interview, minimum GPA of 3.0, writing sample; for doctorate, interview, minimum GPA of 3.5, master's degree in related field, writing sample; for Graduate Certificate, minimum GPA of 3.0. Additional exam requirements/recommendations for international students: Required—TOEFL. *Application deadline:* For fall admission, 5/17 priority date for domestic and international students; for winter admission, 12/1 priority date for domestic and international students; for spring admission, 4/1 priority date for domestic and international students. Applications are processed on a rolling basis. Application fee: $50. Electronic applications accepted. *Expenses:* Contact institution. *Financial support:* In 2017–18, 170 students received support. Career-related internships or fieldwork, Federal Work-Study, scholarships/grants, and unspecified assistantships available. Financial award application deadline: 4/1; financial award applicants required to submit CSS PROFILE. *Faculty research:* Conflict resolution, family therapy, peace research, international conflict, multi-disciplinary studies, college student affairs, national security affairs, health care conflict resolution, family systems health care, advanced family systems, qualitative research, solution-focused coaching. *Unit head:* Dr. Honggang

Yang, Dean, 954-262-3016, Fax: 954-262-3968, E-mail: yangh@nova.edu. *Application contact:* Marcia Arango, Student Recruitment Coordinator, 954-262-3006, Fax: 954-262-3968, E-mail: marango@nsu.nova.edu.
Website: http://cahss.nova.edu/

Oklahoma City University, Petree College of Arts and Sciences, Oklahoma City, OK 73106-1402. Offers applied behavioral studies (M Ed); applied sociology: nonprofit leadership (MA); creative writing (MFA); criminology (MS); early childhood education (M Ed); elementary education (M Ed); general studies (MLA); leadership/management (MLA); moving image arts (MFA); professional counseling (M Ed); teaching (MA); teaching English to speakers of other languages (MA). *Program availability:* Part-time, evening/weekend. *Faculty:* 6 full-time (2 women), 16 part-time/adjunct (10 women). *Students:* 84 full-time (61 women), 32 part-time (23 women); includes 31 minority (13 Black or African American, non-Hispanic/Latino; 3 American Indian or Alaska Native, non-Hispanic/Latino; 1 Asian, non-Hispanic/Latino; 9 Hispanic/Latino; 5 Two or more races, non-Hispanic/Latino), 30 international. Average age 34. 192 applicants, 67% accepted, 57 enrolled. In 2017, 65 master's awarded. *Degree requirements:* For master's, capstone/practicum. *Entrance requirements:* For master's, bachelor's degree from accredited institution with minimum GPA of 3.0, essay, recommendation letters. Additional exam requirements/recommendations for international students: Required—TOEFL (minimum score 550 paper-based; 80 iBT). *Application deadline:* Applications are processed on a rolling basis. Application fee: $50. Electronic applications accepted. *Expenses:* $8,580. *Financial support:* In 2017–18, 19 students received support. Federal Work-Study, institutionally sponsored loans, scholarships/grants, and tuition waivers (full and partial) available. Support available to part-time students. Financial award application deadline: 6/1; financial award applicants required to submit FAFSA. *Unit head:* Dr. Amy Cataldi, Dean, 405-208-5446, Fax: 405-208-5447, E-mail: acataldi@okcu.edu. *Application contact:* Michael Harrington, Director of Graduate Admissions, 800-633-7242, Fax: 405-208-5356, E-mail: gadmissions@okcu.edu.
Website: https://www.okcu.edu/artsci/home

Old Dominion University, College of Arts and Letters, PhD Program in Criminology and Criminal Justice, Norfolk, VA 23529. Offers criminology and criminal justice (PhD). *Faculty:* 23 full-time (13 women). *Students:* 11 full-time (7 women), 4 part-time (1 woman); includes 6 minority (3 Black or African American, non-Hispanic/Latino; 1 Hispanic/Latino; 2 Two or more races, non-Hispanic/Latino). Average age 29. 11 applicants, 45% accepted, 2 enrolled. In 2017, 3 doctorates awarded. *Degree requirements:* For doctorate, comprehensive exam, thesis/dissertation. *Entrance requirements:* For doctorate, GRE General Test, MA; minimum graduate GPA of 3.25; theory, methods, and statistics graduate coursework; letters of reference; writing sample. Additional exam requirements/recommendations for international students: Required—TOEFL. *Application deadline:* For fall admission, 1/15 for domestic and international students. Application fee: $50. Electronic applications accepted. *Expenses:* Tuition, state resident: full-time $8928; part-time $496 per credit. Tuition, nonresident: full-time $22,482; part-time $1249 per credit. *Required fees:* $66 per semester. *Financial support:* In 2017–18, 10 students received support, including 10 teaching assistantships with full tuition reimbursements available (averaging $15,000 per year). Financial award application deadline: 1/15. *Faculty research:* Inequality, crime and justice; domestic violence; community justice; criminological theory; methods; policing; courts and corrections; juvenile justice. *Unit head:* Dr. Scott R. Maggard, Graduate Program Director, 757-683-5528, Fax: 757-683-5634, E-mail: smaggard@odu.edu.
Website: http://al.odu.edu/sociology/phdprogram/index.shtml

Old Dominion University, College of Arts and Letters, Program in Applied Sociology, Norfolk, VA 23529. Offers criminal justice (MA); general sociology (MA); women's studies (MA). *Program availability:* Part-time, evening/weekend. *Faculty:* 19 full-time (11 women). *Students:* 18 full-time (13 women), 2 part-time (1 woman); includes 10 minority (4 Black or African American, non-Hispanic/Latino; 1 Hispanic/Latino; 5 Two or more races, non-Hispanic/Latino). Average age 26. 26 applicants, 65% accepted, 12 enrolled. In 2017, 3 master's awarded. *Degree requirements:* For master's, thesis. *Entrance requirements:* For master's, GRE General Test, minimum GPA of 3.0; 12 credits in criminal justice, sociology, or women's studies. Additional exam requirements/recommendations for international students: Required—TOEFL. *Application deadline:* For fall admission, 3/1 for domestic and international students. Application fee: $50. Electronic applications accepted. *Expenses:* Contact institution. *Financial support:* In 2017–18, 8 students received support, including 2 research assistantships (averaging $10,000 per year), 6 teaching assistantships (averaging $10,000 per year); career-related internships or fieldwork, scholarships/grants, and unspecified assistantships also available. Financial award application deadline: 2/15. *Faculty research:* Quantitative methodology, theory, family, gender/class/race, crime. *Total annual research expenditures:* $350,000. *Unit head:* Dr. Ingrid Whitaker, Graduate Program Director, 757-683-3811, Fax: 757-683-5634, E-mail: iwhitake@odu.edu. *Application contact:* Dr. David C. Earnest, Associate Dean, 757-683-6077, Fax: 757-683-5746, E-mail: dearnest@odu.edu.
Website: http://al.odu.edu/sociology/gradprogram/graduatehome.shtml

Penn State Harrisburg, Graduate School, School of Public Affairs, Middletown, PA 17057. Offers criminal justice (MA); health administration (MHA); health administration: long term care (Certificate); homeland security (MPS, Certificate); public administration (MPA, PhD); public administration: non-profit administration (Certificate); public budgeting and financial management (Certificate); public sector human resource management (Certificate). *Accreditation:* NASPAA. *Unit head:* Dr. Mukund S. Kulkarni, Chancellor, 717-948-6105, Fax: 717-948-6452. *Application contact:* Robert W. Coffman, Jr., Director of Enrollment Management, Recruitment and Admissions, 717-948-6250, Fax: 717-948-6325, E-mail: hbgadmit@psu.edu.
Website: https://harrisburg.psu.edu/public-affairs

Penn State University Park, Graduate School, College of the Liberal Arts, Department of Sociology and Criminology, University Park, PA 16802. Offers criminology (MA, PhD); sociology (MA, PhD). *Unit head:* Dr. Susan Welch, Dean, 814-865-7691, Fax: 814-863-2085. *Application contact:* Lori Hawn, Director, Graduate Student Services, 814-865-1795, Fax: 814-863-4627, E-mail: l-gswww@lists.psu.edu.
Website: http://sociology.la.psu.edu/

Point Park University, School of Arts and Sciences, Department of Criminal Justice and Intelligence Studies, Pittsburgh, PA 15222-1984. Offers criminal justice administration (MS); intelligence and global security (MA). *Program availability:* Evening/weekend, 100% online. *Degree requirements:* For master's, comprehensive exam (for some programs), thesis or alternative. *Entrance requirements:* For master's, minimum GPA of 2.75, resume, 2 letters of recommendation. Additional exam requirements/recommendations for international students: Required—TOEFL (minimum score 550 paper-based; 79 iBT). Electronic applications accepted.

Pontifical Catholic University of Puerto Rico, College of Graduate Studies in Behavioral Science and Community Affairs, Program in Criminology, Ponce, PR 00717-0777. Offers MA. *Program availability:* Part-time, evening/weekend. *Degree requirements:* For master's, thesis. *Entrance requirements:* For master's, EXADEP, 3 letters of recommendation, interview, minimum GPA of 2.75.

Pontificia Universidad Catolica Madre y Maestra, Graduate School, Faculty of Social and Administrative Sciences, Santiago, Dominican Republic. Offers business administration (MBA), including business development, finance, international business, management skills (M Mgmt, MBA), marketing, operations, strategic cost management, strategy, tourist destination planning and management; law (LL M), including civil law, corporate business law, criminal law, international relations, real estate law; management (M Mgmt), including higher financial management, insurance program administration, management skills (M Mgmt, MBA); psychology (MA), including clinical child and adolescent psychology, forensic psychology; strategic human resources (EMBA).

Portland State University, Graduate Studies, College of Urban and Public Affairs, Hatfield School of Government, Division of Criminology and Criminal Justice, Portland, OR 97207-0751. Offers MS. *Program availability:* Part-time. *Faculty:* 13 full-time (6 women), 11 part-time/adjunct (3 women). *Students:* 27 full-time (19 women), 2 part-time (1 woman); includes 10 minority (2 Black or African American, non-Hispanic/Latino; 2 American Indian or Alaska Native, non-Hispanic/Latino; 1 Asian, non-Hispanic/Latino; 4 Hispanic/Latino; 1 Two or more races, non-Hispanic/Latino), 1 international. Average age 32. 25 applicants, 92% accepted, 13 enrolled. In 2017, 5 master's awarded. *Degree requirements:* For master's, thesis or alternative, specialization field, culminating experience. *Entrance requirements:* For master's, minimum GPA of 3.2 overall or graduate, statement of purpose, resume/curriculum vitae, 2 letters of recommendation. Additional exam requirements/recommendations for international students: Required—TOEFL (minimum score 550 paper-based; 80 iBT). *Application deadline:* For fall admission, 2/1 priority date for domestic and international students. Application fee: $65. *Expenses:* Tuition, state resident: full-time $14,436; part-time $401 per credit. Tuition, nonresident: full-time $21,780; part-time $605 per credit. *Required fees:* $1380; $22 per credit. $119 per quarter. One-time fee: $325. Tuition and fees vary according to program. *Financial support:* In 2017–18, 14 students received support, including 12 teaching assistantships with full and partial tuition reimbursements available (averaging $7,899 per year); research assistantships, career-related internships or fieldwork, Federal Work-Study, scholarships/grants, and unspecified assistantships also available. Support available to part-time students. Financial award application deadline: 3/1; financial award applicants required to submit FAFSA. *Faculty research:* History of criminal justice, mental health issues, international terrorism, offender assessment, domestic violence. *Total annual research expenditures:* $138,501. *Unit head:* Dr. Kris R. Henning, Chair, 503-725-8520, E-mail: khenning@pdx.edu. *Application contact:* Andrew Nolan, Department Manager, 503-725-9586, E-mail: anolan@pdx.edu.
Website: https://www.pdx.edu/hatfieldschool/criminology-criminal-justice

Purdue University Global, School of Criminal Justice, Davenport, IA 52807. Offers corrections (MSCJ); global issues in criminal justice (MSCJ); law (MSCJ); leadership and executive management (MSCJ); policing (MSCJ). *Program availability:* Part-time, evening/weekend, online learning. *Entrance requirements:* Additional exam requirements/recommendations for international students: Required—TOEFL (minimum score 550 paper-based; 80 iBT). Electronic applications accepted.

Radford University, College of Graduate Studies and Research, Program in Criminal Justice, Radford, VA 24142. Offers MA, MS, Certificate. *Program availability:* Part-time. *Faculty:* 10 full-time (5 women). *Students:* 18 full-time (13 women), 6 part-time (3 women); includes 3 minority (1 Black or African American, non-Hispanic/Latino; 1 Hispanic/Latino; 1 Two or more races, non-Hispanic/Latino), 1 international. Average age 24. 15 applicants, 93% accepted, 9 enrolled. In 2017, 4 master's awarded. *Degree requirements:* For master's, comprehensive exam, thesis optional. *Entrance requirements:* For master's, minimum GPA of 2.9, 2 letters of reference, original writing sample, resume, official transcripts. Additional exam requirements/recommendations for international students: Required—TOEFL (minimum score 550 paper-based; 79 iBT), IELTS (minimum score 6.5). *Application deadline:* For fall admission, 2/15 priority date for domestic students, 12/1 for international students; for spring admission, 7/1 for international students. Applications are processed on a rolling basis. Application fee: $50. Electronic applications accepted. *Expenses:* Tuition, state resident: full-time $8336; part-time $347 per credit hour. Tuition, nonresident: full-time $16,862; part-time $702 per credit hour. *Required fees:* $3220; $135 per credit hour. Tuition and fees vary according to course load and program. *Financial support:* In 2017–18, 6 students received support, including 1 research assistantship (averaging $10,000 per year), 5 teaching assistantships (averaging $10,400 per year); career-related internships or fieldwork, scholarships/grants, and unspecified assistantships also available. Support available to part-time students. Financial award application deadline: 3/1; financial award applicants required to submit FAFSA. *Faculty research:* Spatial issues and crime, gun violence, rural crime, gender and criminal issues, interpersonal violence. *Unit head:* Dr. Lori Elis, Graduate Coordinator, 540-831-6775, E-mail: lelis@radford.edu.
Website: http://www.radford.edu/content/chbs/home/criminal-justice/programs/graduate.html

Regent University, Graduate School, School of Law, Virginia Beach, VA 23464. Offers American legal studies (LL M); human rights (LL M); law (MA, JD), including advanced paralegal studies (MA), alternative dispute resolution (MA), business (MA), criminal justice (MA), general legal studies (MA), human resources management (MA), human rights and rule of law (MA), national security (MA), non-profit organizational law (MA), regulatory compliance (MA), wealth management and financial planning (MA); JD/MA; JD/MBA. *Accreditation:* ABA. *Program availability:* Part-time, 100% online, blended/hybrid learning. *Faculty:* 16 full-time (5 women), 76 part-time/adjunct (22 women). *Students:* 313 full-time (181 women), 248 part-time (175 women); includes 240 minority (155 Black or African American, non-Hispanic/Latino; 3 American Indian or Alaska Native, non-Hispanic/Latino; 15 Asian, non-Hispanic/Latino; 45 Hispanic/Latino; 2 Native Hawaiian or other Pacific Islander, non-Hispanic/Latino; 20 Two or more races, non-Hispanic/Latino), 59 international. Average age 35. 923 applicants, 36% accepted, 188 enrolled. In 2017, 138 master's, 80 doctorates awarded. *Entrance requirements:* For master's, college transcripts, resume, personal statement; for doctorate, LSAT, minimum undergraduate GPA of 3.0, official transcripts, 2 letters of recommendation, resume, personal statement. Additional exam requirements/recommendations for international students: Required—TOEFL (minimum score 600 paper-based). *Application deadline:* For fall admission, 3/1 for domestic students. Applications are processed on a rolling basis. Application fee: $50. Electronic applications accepted. *Expenses:* $650 per credit (MA, LL M); $1,140 per credit (JD); $300 per semester technology fee. *Financial support:* In 2017–18, 459 students received support. Career-related internships or fieldwork, scholarships/grants, and unspecified assistantships available. Support available to part-time students. *Faculty research:* Family law, Constitutional law, law and culture, evidence and practice, intellectual property. *Unit head:* Michael Hernandez, Dean, 757-352-4040, Fax: 757-352-4595, E-mail: michher@regent.edu. *Application contact:* Ernie Walton, Assistant Dean of Admissions, 757-352-4315, E-mail: lawschool@regent.edu.
Website: https://www.regent.edu/school-of-law/

Regent University, Graduate School, School of Psychology and Counseling, Virginia Beach, VA 23464-9800. Offers clinical mental health counseling (MA); clinical psychology (Psy D); counseling and psychological studies - clinical (PhD); counseling and psychological studies - research (PhD); counseling studies (CAGS); counselor

education and supervision (PhD); general psychology (MS); human services (MA), including addictions counseling, Biblical counseling, Christian counseling, conflict and mediation ministry, criminal justice and ministry, grief counseling, human services counseling, human services for student affairs, life coaching, marriage and family ministry, trauma and crisis counseling; marriage, couple, and family counseling (MA); pastoral counseling (MA); school counseling (MA); M Div/MA; M Ed/MA; MBA/MA. *Accreditation:* ACA; APA (one or more programs are accredited). *Program availability:* Part-time, evening/weekend, 100% online, blended/hybrid learning. *Faculty:* 28 full-time (16 women), 51 part-time/adjunct (30 women). *Students:* 294 full-time (236 women), 404 part-time (317 women); includes 286 minority (218 Black or African American, non-Hispanic/Latino; 4 American Indian or Alaska Native, non-Hispanic/Latino; 17 Asian, non-Hispanic/Latino; 30 Hispanic/Latino; 17 Two or more races, non-Hispanic/Latino), 13 international. Average age 37. 2,109 applicants, 18% accepted, 233 enrolled. In 2017, 158 master's, 28 doctorates awarded. *Degree requirements:* For master's, thesis or alternative, internship, practicum, written competency exam; for doctorate, thesis/dissertation or alternative. *Entrance requirements:* For master's, GRE General Test (including writing exam) or MAT, minimum undergraduate GPA of 3.0, resume, transcripts, writing sample, personal goals statement; for doctorate, GRE General Test (including writing exam), minimum undergraduate GPA of 3.0, graduate 3.5; writing sample; 3 recommendations; resume; college transcripts; personal goals statement. Additional exam requirements/recommendations for international students: Required—TOEFL (minimum score 577 paper-based). *Application deadline:* For fall admission, 4/1 priority date for domestic students; for spring admission, 11/1 priority date for domestic students. Applications are processed on a rolling basis. Application fee: $50. Electronic applications accepted. *Expenses:* Contact institution. *Financial support:* In 2017–18, 557 students received support, including 5 fellowships (averaging $10,000 per year), 11 research assistantships (averaging $3,200 per year); career-related internships or fieldwork, scholarships/grants, and unspecified assistantships also available. Support available to part-time students. *Faculty research:* Marriage enrichment, clinical psychology, troubled youth, faith and learning, trauma. *Unit head:* Dr. William Hathaway, Dean, 757-352-4294, Fax: 757-352-4282, E-mail: willhat@regent.edu. *Application contact:* Heidi Cece, Assistant Vice President of Enrollment Management, 800-373-5504, Fax: 757-352-4381, E-mail: admissions@regent.edu.
Website: https://www.regent.edu/school-of-psychology-and-counseling/

Regis University, College of Contemporary Liberal Studies, Denver, CO 80221-1099. Offers creative writing (MFA); criminology (M Sc); curriculum, instruction and assessment (M Ed); education - teacher leadership (M Ed); educational leadership (M Ed); elementary education (M Ed); literacy (Certificate); reading (M Ed); secondary education (M Ed); special education (M Ed); teacher academic leadership (Certificate); teacher leadership (MA); teacher/educational leadership (M Ed); teaching the linguistically diverse (M Ed). *Program availability:* Part-time, evening/weekend, 100% online, blended/hybrid learning. *Degree requirements:* For master's, thesis (for some programs). *Entrance requirements:* For master's, official transcript reflecting baccalaureate degree awarded from regionally-accredited college or university, work experience, resume, letters of recommendation. Additional exam requirements/recommendations for international students: Required—TOEFL (minimum score 550 paper-based; 82 iBT). Electronic applications accepted. *Expenses:* Contact institution.

Robert Morris University Illinois, Morris Graduate School of Management, Chicago, IL 60605. Offers accounting (MBA); accounting/finance (MBA); business analytics (MIS); health care administration (MM); higher education administration (MM); human performance (MS); human resource management (MBA); information security (MIS); information systems management (MIS); law enforcement administration (MM); management (MBA); management/finance (MBA); management/human resource management (MBA); sports administration (MM). *Program availability:* Part-time, evening/weekend. *Faculty:* 2 full-time (0 women), 26 part-time/adjunct (8 women). *Students:* 186 full-time (108 women), 114 part-time (57 women); includes 167 minority (88 Black or African American, non-Hispanic/Latino; 15 Asian, non-Hispanic/Latino; 62 Hispanic/Latino; 1 Native Hawaiian or other Pacific Islander, non-Hispanic/Latino; 1 Two or more races, non-Hispanic/Latino), 18 international. Average age 32. 157 applicants, 78% accepted, 72 enrolled. In 2017, 191 master's awarded. *Entrance requirements:* For master's, official transcripts and letters of recommendation (for some programs); written personal statement. Additional exam requirements/recommendations for international students: Required—TOEFL (minimum score 550 paper-based). *Application deadline:* Applications are processed on a rolling basis. Application fee: $20 ($100 for international students). Electronic applications accepted. *Expenses: Tuition:* Full-time $17,100; part-time $2850 per course. *Financial support:* In 2017–18, 381 students received support. Federal Work-Study, scholarships/grants, and unspecified assistantships available. Support available to part-time students. Financial award applicants required to submit FAFSA. *Unit head:* Kayed Akkawi, Dean, 312-935-6050, Fax: 312-935-6020, E-mail: kakkawi@robertmorris.edu. *Application contact:* Mark Daugherty, Director of Admissions, 312-935-4814, Fax: 312-935-6020, E-mail: mdaugherty@robertmorris.edu.

Rochester Institute of Technology, Graduate Enrollment Services, College of Liberal Arts, Criminal Justice Department, MS Program in Criminal Justice, Rochester, NY 14623. Offers MS. *Program availability:* Part-time. *Students:* 6 full-time (3 women), 4 part-time (2 women); includes 3 minority (2 Black or African American, non-Hispanic/Latino; 1 Hispanic/Latino), 1 international. Average age 23. 10 applicants, 70% accepted, 4 enrolled. In 2017, 3 master's awarded. *Degree requirements:* For master's, thesis. *Entrance requirements:* For master's, GRE, minimum GPA of 3.0 (recommended). Additional exam requirements/recommendations for international students: Required—TOEFL (minimum score 570 paper-based; 88 iBT), IELTS (minimum score 6.5), PTE (minimum score 58). *Application deadline:* For fall admission, 2/15 priority date for domestic and international students; for spring admission, 12/15 priority date for domestic and international students. Applications are processed on a rolling basis. Application fee: $65. Electronic applications accepted. *Expenses:* $1,815 per credit hour. *Financial support:* In 2017–18, 6 students received support. Research assistantships with partial tuition reimbursements available, teaching assistantships with partial tuition reimbursements available, career-related internships or fieldwork, scholarships/grants, and unspecified assistantships available. Support available to part-time students. Financial award applicants required to submit FAFSA. *Faculty research:* Criminal justice and the deaf and hard of hearing, community-based criminal justice problem-solving, locally relevant action research, strategic partnerships for violence reduction. *Unit head:* Jason Scott, Graduate Program Director, 585-475-2393, E-mail: jxsgcj@rit.edu. *Application contact:* Diane Ellison, Senior Associate Vice President, Graduate Enrollment Services, 585-475-2229, Fax: 585-475-7164, E-mail: gradinfo@rit.edu.
Website: http://www.rit.edu/cla/criminaljustice/ms/overview

Roger Williams University, School of Justice Studies, Bristol, RI 02809. Offers criminal justice (MS); cybersecurity (MS); leadership (MS), including health care administration (MPA, MS), public management (MPA, MS); public administration (MPA), including health care administration (MPA, MS), public management (MPA, MS); MS/JD. *Program availability:* Part-time, evening/weekend, 100% online, blended/hybrid learning. *Faculty:* 10 full-time (5 women), 7 part-time/adjunct (1 woman). *Students:* 16 full-time (11 women), 114 part-time (57 women); includes 33 minority (14 Black or African American, non-Hispanic/Latino; 1 American Indian or Alaska Native, non-Hispanic/Latino; 1 Asian, non-Hispanic/Latino; 17 Hispanic/Latino), 1 international. Average age 35. 58 applicants, 83% accepted, 33 enrolled. In 2017, 27 master's awarded. *Degree requirements:* For master's, thesis optional. *Entrance requirements:* For master's, 2 letters of recommendation, college transcript, and resume (for MS in leadership and MPA programs); criminal background check (for MS in cybersecurity). Additional exam requirements/recommendations for international students: Required—TOEFL (minimum score 85 iBT), IELTS (minimum score 6.5). *Application deadline:* For fall admission, 8/1 for domestic students; for spring admission, 1/1 for domestic students. Applications are processed on a rolling basis. Application fee: $50. Electronic applications accepted. Application fee is waived when completed online. *Expenses:* Contact institution. *Financial support:* In 2017–18, 1 student received support, including 1 research assistantship (averaging $6,942 per year). Financial award application deadline: 4/1; financial award applicants required to submit FAFSA. *Faculty research:* Opioid addiction and treatment, community policing. *Unit head:* Dr. Eric Bronson, Dean, 401-254-3336, E-mail: ebronson@rwu.edu. *Application contact:* Marcus Hanscom, Director of Graduate Admissions, 401-254-3345, Fax: 401-254-3557, E-mail: gradadmit@rwu.edu.
Website: http://www.rwu.edu/academics/departments/criminaljustice.htm#graduate

Rowan University, Graduate School, College of Humanities and Social Sciences, Department of Law and Justice Studies, Program in Criminal Justice, Glassboro, NJ 08028-1701. Offers MA. *Program availability:* Part-time, evening/weekend. *Degree requirements:* For master's, thesis. *Entrance requirements:* For master's, GRE General Test. Additional exam requirements/recommendations for international students: Required—TOEFL. Electronic applications accepted. *Expenses:* Tuition, state resident: full-time $15,020; part-time $751 per semester hour. Tuition, nonresident: full-time $15,020; part-time $751 per semester hour. *Required fees:* $3158; $157.90 per semester hour. Tuition and fees vary according to course load, campus/location and program.

Rutgers University–Camden, Graduate School of Arts and Sciences, Program in Criminal Justice, Camden, NJ 08102. Offers MA, MPA/MA. *Program availability:* Part-time, evening/weekend. *Degree requirements:* For master's, comprehensive exam, thesis optional, 30 credits. *Entrance requirements:* For master's, GRE, 3 letters of recommendation; statement of personal, professional, and academic goals. Additional exam requirements/recommendations for international students: Required—TOEFL, IELTS. Electronic applications accepted. *Faculty research:* Criminal justice policy, public management, children in the criminal justice system, violence, gender and crime.

Rutgers University–Newark, Graduate School, School of Criminal Justice, Doctoral Program in Criminal Justice, Newark, NJ 07102. Offers PhD. *Degree requirements:* For doctorate, thesis/dissertation. *Entrance requirements:* Additional exam requirements/recommendations for international students: Required—TOEFL.

Rutgers University–Newark, Graduate School, School of Criminal Justice, Master's Program in Criminal Justice, Newark, NJ 07102. Offers MA. *Entrance requirements:* For master's, GRE, minimum undergraduate B average. Additional exam requirements/recommendations for international students: Required—TOEFL.

Sacred Heart University, Graduate Programs, College of Arts and Sciences, Department of Criminal Justice, Fairfield, CT 06825. Offers MA. *Program availability:* Part-time, evening/weekend. *Faculty:* 4 full-time (1 woman), 1 part-time/adjunct (0 women). *Students:* 21 full-time (7 women), 24 part-time (9 women); includes 17 minority (8 Black or African American, non-Hispanic/Latino; 8 Hispanic/Latino; 1 Two or more races, non-Hispanic/Latino), 1 international. Average age 30. 29 applicants, 90% accepted, 19 enrolled. In 2017, 16 master's awarded. *Degree requirements:* For master's, comprehensive exam, thesis optional. *Entrance requirements:* For master's, BA/BS with minimum GPA of 3.0. Additional exam requirements/recommendations for international students: Required—TOEFL (minimum score 570 paper-based, 80 iBT), TWE, or IELTS (6.5). *Application deadline:* For fall admission, 3/1 for domestic students; for spring admission, 11/1 for domestic students. Applications are processed on a rolling basis. Application fee: $75. Electronic applications accepted. *Expenses:* Contact institution. *Financial support:* Unspecified assistantships available. Financial award applicants required to submit FAFSA. *Unit head:* Dr. Patrick Morris, Program Director, 203-396-8002, E-mail: morrisp@sacredheart.edu. *Application contact:* Pam Pillo, Executive Director of Graduate Admissions, 203-365-7619, Fax: 203-365-4732, E-mail: gradstudies@sacredheart.edu.
Website: http://www.sacredheart.edu/academics/collegeofartssciences/academicdepartments/criminaljustice/masterofartsincriminaljustice/

St. Ambrose University, College of Arts and Sciences, Program in Criminal Justice, Davenport, IA 52803-2898. Offers criminal justice (MCJ); juvenile justice education (MCJ). *Program availability:* Part-time, evening/weekend. *Degree requirements:* For master's, thesis (for some programs), practicum or project. *Entrance requirements:* For master's, 2 years of work experience, 2 letters of recommendation, personal interview. Additional exam requirements/recommendations for international students: Required—TOEFL. Electronic applications accepted. *Faculty research:* Community policing.

St. Cloud State University, School of Graduate Studies, College of Social Sciences, Department of Criminal Justice, Program in Criminal Justice, St. Cloud, MN 56301-4498. Offers criminal justice administration (MS). *Program availability:* Part-time, evening/weekend, online learning. *Entrance requirements:* For master's, minimum overall GPA in previous undergraduate and graduate records or in last half of undergraduate work. Electronic applications accepted.

St. John's University, College of Professional Studies, Department of Criminal Justice, Legal Studies, and Homeland Security, Queens, NY 11439. Offers homeland security and criminal justice leadership (MPS). *Faculty:* 22 full-time (5 women), 33 part-time/adjunct (25 women). *Students:* 70 full-time (25 women), 20 part-time (10 women); includes 42 minority (12 Black or African American, non-Hispanic/Latino; 4 Asian, non-Hispanic/Latino; 18 Hispanic/Latino; 8 Two or more races, non-Hispanic/Latino). Average age 29. 52 applicants, 90% accepted, 42 enrolled. In 2017, 35 master's awarded. *Entrance requirements:* For master's, letters of recommendation, transcripts, resume, personal statement, proficiency in a foreign language. Additional exam requirements/recommendations for international students: Required—TOEFL (minimum score 90 iBT), IELTS (minimum score 6.5). *Application deadline:* For fall admission, 5/1 for domestic students; for spring admission, 11/1 for domestic students. Applications are processed on a rolling basis. Application fee: $70. Electronic applications accepted. *Expenses: Tuition:* Full-time $44,280; part-time $1230 per credit. *Required fees:* $340; $340 per credit. Tuition and fees vary according to course load, degree level and program. *Financial support:* Research assistantships, teaching assistantships, scholarships/grants, and unspecified assistantships available. Financial award application deadline: 2/1; financial award applicants required to submit FAFSA. *Unit head:* Dr. Antoinette Collarini-Schlossberg, Acting Chair, 718-990-7531, E-mail: schlossa@stjohns.edu. *Application contact:* Robert Medrano, Director of Graduate Admission, 718-990-1601, Fax: 718-990-5686, E-mail: gradhelp@stjohns.edu.
Website: https://www.stjohns.edu/academics/schools-and-colleges/college-professional-studies/criminal-justice-legal-studies-and-homeland-security

St. John's University, St. John's College of Liberal Arts and Sciences, Department of Sociology and Anthropology, Queens, NY 11439. Offers criminology and justice (MA); sociology (MA). *Program availability:* Part-time, evening/weekend. *Faculty:* 14 full-time

(8 women), 13 part-time/adjunct (4 women). *Students:* 35 full-time (23 women), 11 part-time (8 women); includes 18 minority (12 Black or African American, non-Hispanic/Latino; 2 Asian, non-Hispanic/Latino; 3 Hispanic/Latino; 1 Two or more races, non-Hispanic/Latino), 9 international. Average age 27. 70 applicants, 50% accepted, 15 enrolled. In 2017, 32 master's awarded. *Degree requirements:* For master's, comprehensive exam, thesis optional. *Entrance requirements:* For master's, letters of recommendation, transcripts, resume, personal statement. Additional exam requirements/recommendations for international students: Required—TOEFL (minimum score 80 iBT), IELTS (minimum score 6.5). *Application deadline:* For fall admission, 5/1 for domestic students; for spring admission, 11/1 for domestic students. Applications are processed on a rolling basis. Application fee: $70. Electronic applications accepted. *Expenses: Tuition:* Full-time $44,280; part-time $1230 per credit. *Required fees:* $340; $340 per credit. Tuition and fees vary according to course load, degree level and program. *Financial support:* Fellowships, research assistantships, teaching assistantships, scholarships/grants, tuition waivers, and unspecified assistantships available. Support available to part-time students. Financial award application deadline: 2/1; financial award applicants required to submit FAFSA. *Faculty research:* Community studies and gentrification, global financial crisis, insurance fraud, globalization, immigration and human rights. *Unit head:* Dr. Roberta Villalon, Chair, 718-990-5663, E-mail: villalonr@stjohns.edu. *Application contact:* Robert Medrano, Director of Graduate Admission, 718-990-1601, Fax: 718-990-5686, E-mail: gradhelp@stjohns.edu.
Website: https://www.stjohns.edu/academics/schools-and-colleges/st-johns-college-liberal-arts-and-sciences/sociology-and-anthropology

Saint Joseph's University, College of Arts and Sciences, Department of Criminal Justice, Philadelphia, PA 19131-1395. Offers behavior analysis (MS, Post-Master's Certificate); behavior management (MS); criminal justice (MS); federal law enforcement (MS); intelligence and crime analysis (MS). *Program availability:* Part-time, evening/weekend, 100% online, blended/hybrid learning. *Faculty:* 4 full-time (3 women), 33 part-time/adjunct (16 women). *Students:* 18 full-time (13 women), 371 part-time (272 women); includes 105 minority (83 Black or African American, non-Hispanic/Latino; 2 American Indian or Alaska Native, non-Hispanic/Latino; 4 Asian, non-Hispanic/Latino; 16 Hispanic/Latino). Average age 32. 189 applicants, 66% accepted, 94 enrolled. In 2017, 142 master's, 26 other advanced degrees awarded. *Degree requirements:* For master's, thesis optional. *Entrance requirements:* For master's, 2 letters of recommendation, personal statement, resume, official transcripts, minimum GPA of 3.0. Additional exam requirements/recommendations for international students: Required—TOEFL (minimum score 550 paper-based; 80 iBT). *Application deadline:* For fall admission, 7/15 for international students; for spring admission, 11/1 for international students. Applications are processed on a rolling basis. Application fee: $35. Electronic applications accepted. *Expenses:* Contact institution. *Financial support:* In 2017–18, 5 students received support. Federal Work-Study and unspecified assistantships available. Financial award application deadline: 5/1; financial award applicants required to submit FAFSA. *Faculty research:* Ethics in policing, multiculturalism, behavior analysis. *Total annual research expenditures:* $17,309. *Unit head:* Sylvia M. DeSantis, Director, 610-660-3131, E-mail: gradcas@sju.edu. *Application contact:* Lauren Weiss, Graduate Admissions, College of Arts and Sciences, 610-660-3131, E-mail: gradcas@sju.edu.
Website: http://www.sju.edu/majors-programs/graduate-arts-sciences/masters/criminal-justice-ms

Saint Leo University, Graduate Studies in Public Safety Administration, Saint Leo, FL 33574-6665. Offers criminal justice (MS), including behavioral studies, corrections, criminal investigation, criminal justice, emergency and disaster management, forensic science, legal studies; emergency and disaster management (MS), including emergency and disaster management, fire science. *Program availability:* Part-time, evening/weekend, 100% online, blended/hybrid learning. *Faculty:* 8 full-time (3 women), 32 part-time/adjunct (7 women). *Students:* 7 full-time (6 women), 617 part-time (385 women); includes 313 minority (235 Black or African American, non-Hispanic/Latino; 5 American Indian or Alaska Native, non-Hispanic/Latino; 3 Asian, non-Hispanic/Latino; 54 Hispanic/Latino; 1 Native Hawaiian or other Pacific Islander, non-Hispanic/Latino; 15 Two or more races, non-Hispanic/Latino). Average age 36. 336 applicants, 63% accepted, 197 enrolled. In 2017, 267 master's awarded. *Degree requirements:* For master's, comprehensive project. *Entrance requirements:* For master's, official transcripts, bachelor's degree from regionally-accredited university with minimum GPA of 3.0. Additional exam requirements/recommendations for international students: Required—TOEFL (minimum score 550 paper-based; 78 iBT). *Application deadline:* For fall admission, 7/1 priority date for domestic and international students; for spring admission, 11/1 priority date for domestic and international students. Applications are processed on a rolling basis. Application fee: $80. Electronic applications accepted. *Expenses:* $555 per credit hour. *Financial support:* In 2017–18, 21 students received support. Scholarships/grants, health care benefits, unspecified assistantships, and tuition remission for Saint Leo employees and their dependents available. Financial award application deadline: 3/1; financial award applicants required to submit FAFSA. *Faculty research:* Emergency management, fire science, community policing. *Unit head:* Dr. Robert Diemer, Director of Graduate Studies in Safety Administration, 352-588-8974, Fax: 352-588-8289, E-mail: graduatepublicsafety@saintleo.edu. *Application contact:* Mark Russum, Assistant Vice President, Enrollment, 800-707-8846, Fax: 352-588-7873, E-mail: grad.admissions@saintleo.edu.
Website: https://www.saintleo.edu/criminal-justice-master-degree

Saint Louis University, Graduate Programs, College for Public Health and Social Justice, Program in Criminology and Criminal Justice, St. Louis, MO 63103. Offers administration of justice (MA); emergency management (MA); treatment and rehabilitation (MA). *Program availability:* Part-time. *Degree requirements:* For master's, comprehensive exam. *Entrance requirements:* For master's, GRE General Test, two letters of recommendation, resume, transcripts. Additional exam requirements/recommendations for international students: Required—TOEFL (minimum score 525 paper-based).

Saint Mary's University, Faculty of Arts, Program in Criminology, Halifax, NS B3H 3C3, Canada. Offers MA. *Program availability:* Part-time. *Degree requirements:* For master's, thesis. *Entrance requirements:* For master's, honors degree, official transcripts, sample of academic written work, 2 letters of recommendation. Electronic applications accepted. *Expenses:* Contact institution.

St. Mary's University, School of Law, Master of Jurisprudence Program, San Antonio, TX 78228. Offers business and entrepreneurship law (MJ); commercial law (MJ); compliance, business law and risk (MJ); criminal justice (MJ); education law (MJ); environmental law (MJ); health law (MJ); healthcare compliance (MJ); international comparative law (MJ); military and national security law (MJ); natural resource law (MJ); tax law (MJ). *Program availability:* Part-time, evening/weekend. *Faculty:* 45 full-time (13 women), 68 part-time/adjunct (22 women). *Students:* 10 full-time (7 women), 26 part-time (18 women); includes 25 minority (2 Black or African American, non-Hispanic/Latino; 1 Asian, non-Hispanic/Latino; 22 Hispanic/Latino). Average age 32. 37 applicants, 92% accepted, 22 enrolled. In 2017, 12 master's awarded. *Degree requirements:* For master's, 30 credits, minimum GPA of 2.0. *Entrance requirements:*

For master's, official transcripts, personal statement, resume, 2 letters of recommendation, proof of four-year undergraduate degree from accredited U.S. college/university or foreign institution approved by government or accrediting authority. Additional exam requirements/recommendations for international students: Required—TOEFL (minimum score 550 paper-based; 80 iBT), IELTS (minimum score 6). *Application deadline:* Applications are processed on a rolling basis. Application fee: $0. Electronic applications accepted. *Expenses:* Contact institution. *Financial support:* Fellowships, research assistantships, Federal Work-Study, scholarships/grants, and unspecified assistantships available. Financial award applicants required to submit FAFSA. *Unit head:* Shannon Sevier, Director, Graduate Law Programs, 210-431-4235, E-mail: ssevier@stmarytx.edu. *Application contact:* Shannon Sevier, Director, Graduate Law Programs, 210-431-4235, E-mail: ssevier@stmarytx.edu.
Website: https://law.stmarytx.edu/academics/programs/master-of-jurisprudence/

Saint Peter's University, Program in Criminal Justice Administration, Jersey City, NJ 07306-5997. Offers federal law enforcement administration (MA); police administration (MA). *Program availability:* Part-time, evening/weekend. *Entrance requirements:* Additional exam requirements/recommendations for international students: Required—TOEFL. Electronic applications accepted.

St. Thomas University, School of Business, Department of Management, Miami Gardens, FL 33054-6459. Offers accounting (MBA); general management (MSM, Certificate); health management (MBA, MSM, Certificate); human resource management (MBA, MSM, Certificate); international business (MBA, MIB, MSM, Certificate); justice administration (MSM, Certificate); management accounting (MSM, Certificate); public management (MSM, Certificate); sports administration (MS). *Program availability:* Part-time, evening/weekend. *Degree requirements:* For master's, comprehensive exam. *Entrance requirements:* For master's, interview, minimum GPA of 3.0 or GMAT. Additional exam requirements/recommendations for international students: Required—TOEFL (minimum score 550 paper-based; 79 iBT). Electronic applications accepted.

Salem State University, School of Graduate Studies, Program in Criminal Justice, Salem, MA 01970-5353. Offers MS. *Program availability:* Part-time, evening/weekend. *Entrance requirements:* For master's, GRE or MAT. Additional exam requirements/recommendations for international students: Required—TOEFL (minimum score 550 paper-based; 80 iBT) or IELTS (minimum score 5.5).

Salve Regina University, Program in Administration of Justice and Homeland Security, Newport, RI 02840-4192. Offers administration of justice and homeland security (MS); cybersecurity and intelligence (CGS); digital forensics (CGS); leadership in justice (CGS). *Program availability:* Part-time, evening/weekend, online learning. *Entrance requirements:* For master's, GMAT, GRE General Test, or MAT. Additional exam requirements/recommendations for international students: Required—TOEFL (minimum score 600 paper-based; 100 iBT). Electronic applications accepted.

Sam Houston State University, College of Criminal Justice, Department of Criminal Justice and Criminology, Huntsville, TX 77341. Offers criminal justice (MS, PhD); criminal justice and criminology (MA); criminal justice leadership and management (MS); victim services management (MS). *Program availability:* Part-time, evening/weekend, online learning. *Degree requirements:* For master's, comprehensive exam (for some programs), thesis (for some programs); for doctorate, comprehensive exam, thesis/dissertation. *Entrance requirements:* For master's, GRE, personal essay, official transcripts, three recommendation letters, resume; for doctorate, GRE, personal essay, official transcripts, three recommendation letters, resume, master's degree. Additional exam requirements/recommendations for international students: Required—TOEFL (minimum score 550 paper-based; 79 iBT), IELTS (minimum score 6.5). Electronic applications accepted.

San Diego State University, Graduate and Research Affairs, College of Professional Studies and Fine Arts, School of Public Affairs, Program in Criminal Justice Administration, San Diego, CA 92182. Offers MPA. *Program availability:* Part-time. *Entrance requirements:* For master's, GRE General Test, 2 letters of reference. Additional exam requirements/recommendations for international students: Required—TOEFL. Electronic applications accepted.

San Diego State University, Graduate and Research Affairs, College of Professional Studies and Fine Arts, School of Public Affairs, Program in Criminal Justice and Criminology, San Diego, CA 92182. Offers MS. *Entrance requirements:* For master's, GRE General Test, 2 letters of reference. Additional exam requirements/recommendations for international students: Required—TOEFL. Electronic applications accepted.

San Francisco State University, Division of Graduate Studies, College of Health and Social Sciences, Public Administration Program, San Francisco, CA 94132-1722. Offers criminal justice administration (MPA); environmental administration and policy (MPA); gerontology (MPA); nonprofit administration (MPA); public management (MPA); public policy (MPA); urban administration (MPA). *Accreditation:* NASPAA. *Unit head:* Dr. Jennifer Shea, Graduate Coordinator, 415-817-4462, Fax: 415-817-4464, E-mail: jshea@sfsu.edu.
Website: http://mpa.sfsu.edu/

San Jose State University, Graduate Studies and Research, College of Health and Human Sciences, San Jose, CA 95192-0049. Offers criminology (MS), including global criminology, law and justice; justice studies (MS); kinesiology (MA), including athletic training, exercise physiology, interdisciplinary, sport studies, sports management; library and information science (MLIS); mass communications (MS); nursing (MS), including family nurse practitioner; nutritional science (MS); occupational therapy (MS); public health (MPH); social work (MSW); MD/M Div. *Program availability:* Part-time, 100% online, blended/hybrid learning. *Faculty:* 15 full-time (7 women), 6 part-time/adjunct (3 women). *Students:* 517 full-time (407 women), 405 part-time (302 women); includes 523 minority (39 Black or African American, non-Hispanic/Latino; 2 American Indian or Alaska Native, non-Hispanic/Latino; 141 Asian, non-Hispanic/Latino; 226 Hispanic/Latino; 2 Native Hawaiian or other Pacific Islander, non-Hispanic/Latino; 113 Two or more races, non-Hispanic/Latino), 14 international. Average age 32. 1,250 applicants, 45% accepted, 375 enrolled. In 2017, 808 master's awarded. *Degree requirements:* For master's, thesis (for some programs), graduate writing assessment. *Entrance requirements:* Additional exam requirements/recommendations for international students: Required—TOEFL (minimum score 550 paper-based; 80 iBT), IELTS (minimum score 6.5), PTE (minimum score 53). *Application deadline:* For fall admission, 2/1 for domestic and international students. Applications are processed on a rolling basis. Application fee: $55. Electronic applications accepted. *Expenses:* Tuition, state resident: full-time $7176. Tuition, nonresident: full-time $16,680. Tuition and fees vary according to course load and program. *Financial support:* Fellowships, research assistantships, teaching assistantships, career-related internships or fieldwork, Federal Work-Study, scholarships/grants, and tuition waivers (full and partial) available. Support available to part-time students. Financial award application deadline: 4/24; financial award applicants required to submit FAFSA. *Unit head:* Dr. Mary Schutten, Dean, College of Health and Human Sciences, 408-924-2900, Fax: 408-924-2901, E-mail: mary.schutten@sjsu.edu.
Website: http://www.sjsu.edu/casa/

Criminal Justice and Criminology

Seattle University, College of Arts and Sciences, Department of Criminal Justice, Seattle, WA 98122-1090. Offers crime analysis (Certificate); criminal justice (MACJ). *Program availability:* Part-time, evening/weekend. *Faculty:* 8 full-time (2 women), 4 part-time/adjunct (2 women). *Students:* 19 full-time (13 women), 39 part-time (33 women); includes 23 minority (3 Black or African American, non-Hispanic/Latino; 1 American Indian or Alaska Native, non-Hispanic/Latino; 5 Asian, non-Hispanic/Latino; 5 Hispanic/Latino; 1 Native Hawaiian or other Pacific Islander, non-Hispanic/Latino; 8 Two or more races, non-Hispanic/Latino). Average age 27. 52 applicants, 81% accepted, 24 enrolled. In 2017, 29 master's, 5 Certificates awarded. *Degree requirements:* For master's, comprehensive exam or thesis. *Entrance requirements:* For master's, minimum GPA of 3.0; undergraduate degree in criminal justice or related social, behavioral, or physical science, or related coursework and/or volunteer or supervised experience; letters of recommendation; writing sample. Additional exam requirements/recommendations for international students: Required—TOEFL, IELTS. *Application deadline:* For fall admission, 3/15 for domestic and international students. Application fee: $55. Electronic applications accepted. *Expenses: Tuition:* Full-time $12,960. *Required fees:* $570. Tuition and fees vary according to program. *Financial support:* In 2017–18, 25 students received support. Applicants required to submit FAFSA. *Faculty research:* Criminal justice program evaluation, ex-offender reentry, policing issues, restorative justice, psychopathy. *Unit head:* Dr. Elaine Gunnison, Graduate Program Director, 206-296-2430, E-mail: gunnisone@seattleu.edu. *Application contact:* Janet Shandley, Associate Dean of Graduate Admissions, 206-296-5900, Fax: 206-298-5656, E-mail: grad_admissions@seattleu.edu.
Website: https://www.seattleu.edu/artsci/criminal-graduate/

Shippensburg University of Pennsylvania, School of Graduate Studies, College of Education and Human Services, Department of Criminal Justice, Shippensburg, PA 17257-2299. Offers criminal justice (MS), including administration of justice, juvenile justice. *Program availability:* Part-time, evening/weekend, 100% online. *Faculty:* 7 full-time (4 women). *Students:* 6 full-time (3 women), 11 part-time (3 women); includes 4 minority (3 Black or African American, non-Hispanic/Latino; 1 Hispanic/Latino). Average age 30. 2 applicants, 100% accepted. In 2017, 19 master's awarded. *Degree requirements:* For master's, internship, practicum, or thesis. *Entrance requirements:* For master's, GRE or MAT (if GPA less than 2.75), 500-word statement of interest. Additional exam requirements/recommendations for international students: Required—TOEFL (minimum score 550 paper-based, 68 iBT) or IELTS (minimum score 6). *Application deadline:* For fall admission, 4/30 for international students. Applications are processed on a rolling basis. Application fee: $45. Electronic applications accepted. *Expenses:* Tuition, state resident: part-time $500 per credit. Tuition, nonresident: part-time $750 per credit. *Required fees:* $145 per credit. *Financial support:* In 2017–18, 3 students received support. Career-related internships or fieldwork, scholarships/grants, unspecified assistantships, and resident hall director and student payroll positions available. Support available to part-time students. Financial award application deadline: 3/1; financial award applicants required to submit FAFSA. *Unit head:* Dr. Cyndi A. Koller, Associate Professor and Program Coordinator, 717-477-1599, Fax: 717-477-4087, E-mail: cakoller@ship.edu. *Application contact:* Maya T. Mapp, Director of Admissions, 717-477-1231, Fax: 717-477-4016, E-mail: mtmapp@ship.edu.
Website: http://www.ship.edu/criminal_justice/

Simon Fraser University, Office of Graduate Studies and Postdoctoral Fellows, Faculty of Arts and Social Sciences, School of Criminology, Burnaby, BC V5A 1S6, Canada. Offers applied legal studies (MA); criminology (MA, PhD). *Degree requirements:* For master's, thesis or alternative, practicum; for doctorate, thesis/dissertation. *Entrance requirements:* For master's, minimum GPA of 3.0 (on scale of 4.33) or 3.33 based on last 60 credits of undergraduate courses; for doctorate, minimum GPA of 3.5 (on scale of 4.33). Additional exam requirements/recommendations for international students: Recommended—TOEFL (minimum score 580 paper-based; 93 iBT), IELTS (minimum score 7), TWE (minimum score 5). Electronic applications accepted. *Faculty research:* Media and crime, feminist jurisprudence, policy evaluation, forensic entomology, restorative justice.

Simpson College, Department of Social Sciences, Indianola, IA 50125-1297. Offers criminal justice (MACJ). *Program availability:* Evening/weekend.

Slippery Rock University of Pennsylvania, Graduate Studies (Recruitment), College of Liberal Arts, Department of Criminology and Security Studies, Slippery Rock, PA 16057-1383. Offers criminal justice (MA). *Program availability:* Part-time, evening/weekend, online only, 100% online. *Degree requirements:* For master's, comprehensive exam (for some programs), thesis (for some programs). *Entrance requirements:* For master's, minimum GPA of 2.75, three letters of recommendation, personal statement. Additional exam requirements/recommendations for international students: Required—TOEFL (minimum score 550 paper-based; 80 iBT). Electronic applications accepted. *Expenses:* Contact institution.

Southeast Missouri State University, School of Graduate Studies, Department of Criminal Justice and Sociology, Cape Girardeau, MO 63701-4799. Offers criminal justice (MS). *Program availability:* Part-time, 100% online, blended/hybrid learning. *Faculty:* 6 full-time (3 women), 1 part-time/adjunct (0 women). *Students:* 3 full-time (2 women), 27 part-time (14 women); includes 5 minority (4 Black or African American, non-Hispanic/Latino; 1 Asian, non-Hispanic/Latino), 2 international. Average age 33. 10 applicants, 80% accepted, 7 enrolled. In 2017, 11 master's awarded. *Degree requirements:* For master's, thesis (for some programs), thesis, internship or leadership portfolio. *Entrance requirements:* Additional exam requirements/recommendations for international students: Required—TOEFL (minimum score 550 paper-based; 79 iBT), IELTS (minimum score 6), PTE (minimum score 53). *Application deadline:* For fall admission, 8/1 for domestic students, 6/1 for international students; for spring admission, 11/21 for domestic students, 10/1 for international students; for summer admission, 5/15 for domestic students. Applications are processed on a rolling basis. Application fee: $30 ($40 for international students). Electronic applications accepted. *Expenses:* $270.35 per credit hour in-state tuition, $33.40 per credit hour fees. *Financial support:* In 2017–18, 2 students received support. Career-related internships or fieldwork, Federal Work-Study, scholarships/grants, traineeships, tuition waivers (full), and unspecified assistantships available. Financial award application deadline: 6/30; financial award applicants required to submit FAFSA. *Faculty research:* Law enforcement, corrections, courts, marginalized populations, online learning. *Unit head:* Dr. Jeremy Ball, Department Chair, 573-651-2541, Fax: 573-986-6417, E-mail: jball@semo.edu.
Website: http://www.semo.edu/criminaljustice/

Southern Illinois University Carbondale, Graduate School, College of Liberal Arts, Department of Criminology and Criminal Justice, Carbondale, IL 62901-4701. Offers MA, PhD. *Degree requirements:* For master's, thesis optional; for doctorate, thesis/dissertation. *Entrance requirements:* For master's, GRE General Test, minimum GPA of 2.7; for doctorate, GRE General Test, minimum GPA of 3.25. Additional exam requirements/recommendations for international students: Required—TOEFL. *Faculty research:* Corrections, criminology, law enforcement, crime prevention, victims of crime.

Southern New Hampshire University, School of Arts and Sciences, Manchester, NH 03106-1045. Offers clinical mental health counseling (MS); creative writing (MA); criminal justice (MS); cyber security (MS); English (MA); fiction and nonfiction (MFA); history (MA); political science (MS); psychology (MS). *Program availability:* Part-time, evening/weekend. *Degree requirements:* For master's, one foreign language, thesis. *Entrance requirements:* For master's, minimum GPA of 2.75 (for MS in teaching English as a foreign language), 3.0 (for MFA). Additional exam requirements/recommendations for international students: Required—TOEFL (minimum score 550 paper-based; 79 iBT), IELTS (minimum score 6.5), TWE (minimum score 5). *Application deadline:* For fall admission, 7/1 priority date for domestic students; for winter admission, 11/1 priority date for domestic students; for spring admission, 6/1 priority date for domestic students. Applications are processed on a rolling basis. Application fee: $40. Electronic applications accepted. *Expenses:* Contact institution. *Financial support:* Research assistantships, career-related internships or fieldwork, and scholarships/grants available. Financial award applicants required to submit FAFSA. *Faculty research:* Action research, state of the art practice in behavioral health services, wraparound approaches to working with youth, learning styles. *Unit head:* Steven K. Johnson, Dean, 603-629-4626. *Application contact:* Office of Graduate Admission, 888-327-SNHU, Fax: 603-644-3144, E-mail: enroll@snhu.edu.

Southern University and Agricultural and Mechanical College, Graduate School, Nelson Mandela School of Public Policy and Urban Affairs, Department of Criminal Justice, Baton Rouge, LA 70813. Offers MS. *Entrance requirements:* Additional exam requirements/recommendations for international students: Required—TOEFL (minimum score 525 paper-based).

Southern University at New Orleans, School of Graduate Studies, New Orleans, LA 70126-1009. Offers criminal justice (MA); management information systems (MS); museum studies (MA); social work (MSW). *Accreditation:* CSWE. *Program availability:* Part-time, evening/weekend. *Degree requirements:* For master's, thesis. *Entrance requirements:* For master's, GRE/GMAT. Additional exam requirements/recommendations for international students: Required—TOEFL.

South University, Graduate Programs, College of Arts and Sciences, Program in Criminal Justice, Savannah, GA 31406. Offers MS.

South University, Graduate Programs, College of Business, Savannah, GA 31406. Offers corrections (MBA); entrepreneurship and small business (MBA); healthcare administration (MBA); hospitality management (MBA); leadership (MS); public administration (MPA); sustainability (MBA).

South University, Program in Criminal Justice, Columbia, SC 29203. Offers MS.

South University, Program in Criminal Justice, Montgomery, AL 36116-1120. Offers MS.

South University, Program in Criminal Justice, Tampa, FL 33614. Offers MS.

South University, Program in Criminal Justice, Royal Palm Beach, FL 33411. Offers MS.

Southwestern College, Professional Studies Programs, Wichita, KS 67207. Offers business administration (MBA); leadership (MS); management (MS); security administration (MS); specialized ministries (MA). *Program availability:* Part-time, evening/weekend, online only, 100% online. *Faculty:* 15 part-time/adjunct (6 women). *Students:* 50 part-time (13 women); includes 11 minority (7 Black or African American, non-Hispanic/Latino; 1 American Indian or Alaska Native, non-Hispanic/Latino; 3 Hispanic/Latino). Average age 39. 57 applicants, 74% accepted, 11 enrolled. In 2017, 43 master's awarded. *Degree requirements:* For master's, thesis (for some programs), practicum/capstone project. *Entrance requirements:* For master's, baccalaureate degree; minimum GPA of 3.0. Additional exam requirements/recommendations for international students: Required—TOEFL (minimum score 550 paper-based; 80 iBT). *Application deadline:* Applications are processed on a rolling basis. Application fee: $40. Electronic applications accepted. *Expenses:* $662 per credit hour (for MBA); $599 per credit hour (for MSL, MSSA, MSM, and Graduate Certificates); $476 per credit hour (for MASM and MATS). *Financial support:* In 2017–18, 13 students received support. Unspecified assistantships available. Financial award applicants required to submit FAFSA. *Unit head:* Dennis Russell, Director of Admissions and Student Services, 888-684-5335 Ext. 3372, Fax: 316-688-5218, E-mail: dennis.russell@sckans.edu.
Website: http://www.southwesterncollege.org

Southwest University, Program in Criminal Justice, Kenner, LA 70062. Offers MS.

Stockton University, Office of Graduate Studies, Program in Criminal Justice, Galloway, NJ 08205-9441. Offers MA. *Program availability:* Part-time, evening/weekend. *Faculty:* 7 full-time (4 women), 1 (woman) part-time/adjunct. *Students:* 18 full-time (12 women), 14 part-time (11 women); includes 7 minority (2 Black or African American, non-Hispanic/Latino; 3 Hispanic/Latino; 2 Two or more races, non-Hispanic/Latino). Average age 23. 34 applicants, 74% accepted, 19 enrolled. In 2017, 12 master's awarded. *Degree requirements:* For master's, comprehensive exam (for some programs), thesis, portfolio project. *Entrance requirements:* For master's, GRE General Test, minimum GPA of 3.0. Additional exam requirements/recommendations for international students: Required—TOEFL. *Application deadline:* For fall admission, 7/1 for domestic and international students; for spring admission, 12/1 for domestic students, 11/1 for international students. Applications are processed on a rolling basis. Application fee: $50. Electronic applications accepted. *Expenses:* Contact institution. *Financial support:* In 2017–18, 9 research assistantships with partial tuition reimbursements were awarded; fellowships, career-related internships or fieldwork, Federal Work-Study, scholarships/grants, and unspecified assistantships also available. Support available to part-time students. Financial award application deadline: 3/1; financial award applicants required to submit FAFSA. *Faculty research:* Homeland security, forensic psychology, corrections, sex crimes, violent crimes. *Unit head:* Dr. Christine Tartaro, Director, 609-626-3640, E-mail: christine.tartaro@stockton.edu. *Application contact:* Tara Williams, Assistant Director of Graduate Enrollment Management, 609-626-3640, Fax: 609-626-6050, E-mail: gradschool@stockton.edu.

Suffolk University, College of Arts and Sciences, Department of Sociology, Boston, MA 02108-2770. Offers MSCJS, MSCJS/JD, MSCJS/MPA, MSCJS/MSMHC. *Program availability:* Part-time. *Faculty:* 3 full-time (1 woman). *Students:* 33 full-time (28 women), 25 part-time (23 women); includes 12 minority (1 Black or African American, non-Hispanic/Latino; 7 Asian, non-Hispanic/Latino; 4 Hispanic/Latino), 16 international. Average age 28. 54 applicants, 39% accepted, 8 enrolled. In 2017, 18 master's awarded. *Entrance requirements:* For master's, 2 letters of recommendation, resume. Additional exam requirements/recommendations for international students: Required—TOEFL (minimum score 550 paper-based; 80 iBT). *Application deadline:* For fall admission, 3/15 priority date for domestic students, 3/15 for international students; for spring admission, 10/15 priority date for domestic students, 10/15 for international students. Applications are processed on a rolling basis. Application fee: $50. Electronic applications accepted. *Expenses:* $29,520 per year full-time tuition; $1,230 per credit part-time. *Financial support:* In 2017–18, 20 students received support, including 3 fellowships (averaging $6,108 per year); career-related internships or fieldwork, Federal Work-Study, institutionally sponsored loans, scholarships/grants, and unspecified assistantships also available. Support available to part-time students. Financial award application deadline: 4/1; financial award applicants required to submit FAFSA. *Faculty research:* Restorative justice, anti-gang initiative, healthcare for female ex-offenders, violence against women, juvenile justice and the courts. *Unit head:* Dr. Erika Gebo,

Professor/Chair, 617-557-1594, E-mail: egebo@suffolk.edu. *Application contact:* Mara Marzocchi, Associate Director of Graduate Admissions, 617-573-8302, Fax: 617-305-1733, E-mail: grad.admission@suffolk.edu.
Website: http://www.suffolk.edu/college/graduate/69297.php

Sul Ross State University, College of Professional Studies, Department of Criminal Justice, Alpine, TX 79832. Offers criminal justice (MS); homeland security (MS); MS/MA. *Entrance requirements:* For master's, GRE General Test, minimum GPA of 2.5 in last 60 hours of undergraduate work.

Tarleton State University, College of Graduate Studies, College of Liberal and Fine Arts, Department of Criminal Justice, Stephenville, TX 76402. Offers criminal justice (MCJ). *Program availability:* Part-time, evening/weekend, 100% online, blended/hybrid learning. *Faculty:* 6 full-time (2 women), 2 part-time/adjunct (0 women). *Students:* 15 full-time (7 women), 109 part-time (54 women); includes 52 minority (23 Black or African American, non-Hispanic/Latino; 4 Asian, non-Hispanic/Latino; 25 Hispanic/Latino). Average age 37. 55 applicants, 82% accepted, 38 enrolled. In 2017, 40 master's awarded. *Degree requirements:* For master's, comprehensive exam (for some programs), thesis optional. *Entrance requirements:* For master's, GRE General Test, minimum GPA of 3.0. Additional exam requirements/recommendations for international students: Required—TOEFL (minimum score 550 paper-based; 80 iBT), IELTS (minimum score 6). *Application deadline:* For fall admission, 8/15 priority date for domestic students; for spring admission, 1/7 for domestic students. Applications are processed on a rolling basis. Application fee: $45 ($145 for international students). Electronic applications accepted. *Expenses:* Contact institution. *Financial support:* Research assistantships, career-related internships or fieldwork, and Federal Work-Study available. Support available to part-time students. Financial award application deadline: 5/1; financial award applicants required to submit FAFSA. *Unit head:* Dr. Rhonda Dobbs, Department Head, 254-968-9402, E-mail: dobbs@tarleton.edu. *Application contact:* Information Contact, 254-968-9104, Fax: 254-968-9670, E-mail: gradoffice@tarleton.edu.
Website: http://www.tarleton.edu/COLFAWEB/criminaljustice/index.html

Temple University, College of Liberal Arts, Department of Criminal Justice, Philadelphia, PA 19122-6096. Offers MA, PhD. *Program availability:* Part-time. *Faculty:* 27 full-time (17 women), 16 part-time/adjunct (9 women). *Students:* 34 full-time (25 women), 4 part-time (2 women); includes 10 minority (4 Black or African American, non-Hispanic/Latino; 1 Asian, non-Hispanic/Latino; 2 Hispanic/Latino; 3 Two or more races, non-Hispanic/Latino), 2 international. 41 applicants, 39% accepted, 9 enrolled. In 2017, 8 master's, 2 doctorates awarded. Terminal master's awarded for partial completion of doctoral program. *Degree requirements:* For master's, thesis optional; for doctorate, thesis/dissertation, qualifying exams. *Entrance requirements:* For master's, GRE General Test, minimum GPA of 3.0, 3 letters of recommendation; for doctorate, GRE General Test, 3 letters of recommendation. Additional exam requirements/recommendations for international students: Required—TOEFL (minimum score 550 paper-based; 79 iBT). *Application deadline:* For fall admission, 12/15 for domestic students, 11/30 for international students. Application fee: $60. Electronic applications accepted. *Expenses:* Tuition, state resident: full-time $16,164; part-time $898 per credit hour. Tuition, nonresident: full-time $22,158; part-time $1231 per credit hour. *Required fees:* $890; $445 per semester. Full-time tuition and fees vary according to course load, degree level, campus/location and program. *Financial support:* Research assistantships with tuition reimbursements, teaching assistantships with tuition reimbursements, career-related internships or fieldwork, and Federal Work-Study available. Financial award application deadline: 1/15. *Faculty research:* Policy analysis and program evaluation; geography of crime and justice; criminal behavior; rehabilitation and behavioral change; policing, security, and crime prevention; juvenile delinquency and juvenile justice. *Unit head:* Dr. Jamie Fader, Graduate Chair, 215-204-6523, Fax: 215-204-3872, E-mail: jfader@temple.edu. *Application contact:* LaSaundra Scott, Coordinator, 215-204-1376, Fax: 215-204-3872, E-mail: lscott01@temple.edu.
Website: http://www.cla.temple.edu/cj/

Tennessee State University, The School of Graduate Studies and Research, College of Liberal Arts, Department of Criminal Justice, Nashville, TN 37209-1561. Offers MCJ. Program offered jointly with Middle Tennessee State University. *Degree requirements:* For master's, thesis. *Entrance requirements:* For master's, GRE General Test or MAT. Electronic applications accepted.

Texas A&M International University, Office of Graduate Studies and Research, College of Arts and Sciences, Department of Public Affairs and Social Research, Laredo, TX 78041. Offers criminal justice (MS); history and political thought (MA); political science (MA); public administration (MPA). *Degree requirements:* For master's, comprehensive exam (for some programs), thesis (for some programs). *Entrance requirements:* For master's, GRE General Test. Additional exam requirements/recommendations for international students: Required—TOEFL (minimum score 550 paper-based; 79 iBT).

Texas A&M University–Central Texas, Graduate Studies and Research, Killeen, TX 76549. Offers accounting (MS); business administration (MBA); clinical mental health counseling (MS); criminal justice (MCJ); curriculum and instruction (M Ed); educational administration (M Ed); educational psychology - experimental psychology (MS); history (MA); human resource management (MS); information systems (MS); liberal studies (MS); management and leadership (MS); marriage and family therapy (MS); mathematics (MS); political science (MA); school counseling (M Ed); school psychology (Ed S).

Texas A&M University–Commerce, College of Humanities, Social Sciences and Arts, Commerce, TX 75429. Offers applied criminology (MS); applied linguistics (MA, MS); art (MA, MFA); computational linguistics (Graduate Certificate); creative writing (Graduate Certificate); criminal justice management (Graduate Certificate); criminal justice studies (Graduate Certificate); English (MA, MS, PhD); film studies (Graduate Certificate); history (MA, MS); history of Christianity (Graduate Certificate); Holocaust studies (Graduate Certificate); homeland security (Graduate Certificate); music education (MM); music performance (MM); political science (MA, MS); public history (Graduate Certificate); sociology (MS); Spanish (MA); studies in children's and adolescent literature and culture (Graduate Certificate); teaching English to speakers of other languages (Graduate Certificate); theater (MA, MS); world history (Graduate Certificate). *Program availability:* Part-time. *Faculty:* 56 full-time (26 women), 10 part-time/adjunct (5 women). *Students:* 133 full-time (85 women), 439 part-time (311 women); includes 204 minority (79 Black or African American, non-Hispanic/Latino; 4 American Indian or Alaska Native, non-Hispanic/Latino; 9 Asian, non-Hispanic/Latino; 98 Hispanic/Latino; 14 Two or more races, non-Hispanic/Latino), 26 international. Average age 36. 261 applicants, 50% accepted, 113 enrolled. In 2017, 105 master's, 5 doctorates awarded. *Degree requirements:* For master's, one foreign language, comprehensive exam, thesis (for some programs); for doctorate, one foreign language, comprehensive exam, thesis/dissertation, departmental qualifying exam. *Entrance requirements:* For master's and doctorate, GRE General Test. Additional exam requirements/recommendations for international students: Required—TOEFL (minimum score 550 paper-based; 79 iBT), IELTS (minimum score 6). *Application deadline:* Applications are processed on a rolling basis. Application fee: $50. Electronic applications accepted. *Expenses:* Contact institution. *Financial support:* In 2017–18, 43 students received support, including 9

research assistantships with partial tuition reimbursements available (averaging $9,000 per year), 68 teaching assistantships with partial tuition reimbursements available (averaging $9,000 per year); Federal Work-Study, institutionally sponsored loans, scholarships/grants, health care benefits, and unspecified assistantships also available. Financial award application deadline: 5/1; financial award applicants required to submit FAFSA. *Unit head:* Dr. William F. Kuracina, Interim Dean, 903-886-5166, Fax: 903-886-5774, E-mail: william.kuracina@tamuc.edu. *Application contact:* Vicky Turner, Doctoral Degree and Special Programs Coordinator, 903-886-5167, E-mail: vicky.turner@tamuc.edu.
Website: http://www.tamuc.edu/academics/graduateSchool/programs/humanitiesSocialScienceArts/default.aspx

Texas A&M University–Kingsville, College of Graduate Studies, College of Arts and Sciences, Department of Psychology and Sociology, Program in Criminology, Kingsville, TX 78363. Offers MS. *Entrance requirements:* Additional exam requirements/recommendations for international students: Required—TOEFL (minimum score 550 paper-based; 79 iBT); Recommended—IELTS. Electronic applications accepted.

Texas Christian University, AddRan College of Liberal Arts, Department of Criminal Justice, Fort Worth, TX 76129. Offers criminal justice and criminology (MS). *Program availability:* Online only, 100% online. *Faculty:* 5 full-time (2 women), 1 part-time/adjunct (0 women). *Students:* 37 full-time (18 women); includes 15 minority (3 Black or African American, non-Hispanic/Latino; 1 Asian, non-Hispanic/Latino; 8 Hispanic/Latino; 1 Native Hawaiian or other Pacific Islander, non-Hispanic/Latino; 2 Two or more races, non-Hispanic/Latino). Average age 34. 25 applicants, 96% accepted, 21 enrolled. In 2017, 9 master's awarded. *Degree requirements:* For master's, thesis optional. *Application deadline:* For fall admission, 4/1 for domestic and international students. Application fee: $60. Electronic applications accepted. *Expenses:* Contact institution. *Financial support:* In 2017–18, 12 students received support. Scholarships/grants available. Financial award application deadline: 5/1; financial award applicants required to submit FAFSA. *Faculty research:* Cybercrime, sex offenders, prisoner reentry, criminological theory, policing. *Unit head:* Johnny Nhan, Director/Associate Professor, 626-391-3871, E-mail: j.nhan@tcu.edu. *Application contact:* Pam Carlisle, Administrative Assistant, 817-257-5846, Fax: 817-257-7737, E-mail: p.carlisle@tcu.edu.
Website: http://cj.tcu.edu

Texas Southern University, Barbara Jordan-Mickey Leland School of Public Affairs, Program in Administration of Justice, Houston, TX 77004-4584. Offers MS, PhD. Electronic applications accepted.

Texas State University, The Graduate College, College of Applied Arts, Program in Criminal Justice, San Marcos, TX 78666. Offers MSCJ, PhD. *Program availability:* Part-time, evening/weekend. *Faculty:* 27 full-time (7 women), 1 (woman) part-time/adjunct. *Students:* 39 full-time (22 women), 43 part-time (23 women); includes 32 minority (7 Black or African American, non-Hispanic/Latino; 24 Hispanic/Latino; 1 Two or more races, non-Hispanic/Latino), 5 international. Average age 30. 70 applicants, 50% accepted, 13 enrolled. In 2017, 9 master's, 6 doctorates awarded. *Degree requirements:* For master's, comprehensive exam, thesis (for some programs); for doctorate, comprehensive exam, thesis/dissertation. *Entrance requirements:* For master's, GRE, baccalaureate degree in criminal justice or closely-related field from regionally-accredited university with minimum GPA of 3.0 in last 60 hours of course work; for doctorate, GRE (minimum preferred score of 300 with no less than 150 on the verbal section and 150 on the quantitative section), baccalaureate and master's degrees from regionally-accredited university in criminal justice or related field with minimum GPA of 3.5 in graduate courses; 3 letters of recommendation indicating skills and capacity to be successful in a PhD program; statement of personal history and life goals. Additional exam requirements/recommendations for international students: Required—TOEFL (minimum score 550 paper-based; 78 iBT), IELTS (minimum score 6.5). *Application deadline:* For fall admission, 2/1 priority date for domestic and international students; for spring admission, 8/15 priority date for domestic and international students; for summer admission, 4/15 for domestic students, 3/15 for international students. Applications are processed on a rolling basis. Application fee: $40 ($90 for international students). Electronic applications accepted. *Expenses:* Tuition, state resident: full-time $7868; part-time $3934 per semester. Tuition, nonresident: full-time $17,828; part-time $8914 per semester. *Required fees:* $2092; $1435 per semester. Tuition and fees vary according to course load. *Financial support:* In 2017–18, 56 students received support, including 8 research assistantships (averaging $20,222 per year), 15 teaching assistantships (averaging $19,677 per year); Federal Work-Study, institutionally sponsored loans, scholarships/grants, and unspecified assistantships also available. Support available to part-time students. Financial award application deadline: 3/1; financial award applicants required to submit FAFSA. *Faculty research:* Active shooter response training; juvenile registration and notification policy effects; offender decision-making: decision tree and displacement; preventing violence against law enforcement and ensuring officer resilience; case deconstruction and criminal investigation failures;. *Total annual research expenditures:* $7.2 million. *Unit head:* Dr. Wesley Jennings, Doctoral Program Director, 512-245-3331, Fax: 512-245-8063, E-mail: wgj12@txstate.edu. *Application contact:* Dr. Andrea Golato, Dean of the Graduate College, 512-245-2581, Fax: 512-245-8365, E-mail: gradcollege@txstate.edu.
Website: http://www.cj.txstate.edu/

Texas State University, The Graduate College, College of Liberal Arts, Program in Public Administration, San Marcos, TX 78666. Offers international relations (MPA); legal and judicial administration (MPA). *Accreditation:* NASPAA. *Program availability:* Part-time, evening/weekend. *Faculty:* 7 full-time (3 women), 1 (woman) part-time/adjunct. *Students:* 31 full-time (14 women), 64 part-time (36 women); includes 45 minority (11 Black or African American, non-Hispanic/Latino; 4 Asian, non-Hispanic/Latino; 29 Hispanic/Latino; 1 Two or more races, non-Hispanic/Latino), 2 international. Average age 30. 89 applicants, 76% accepted, 31 enrolled. In 2017, 37 master's awarded. *Degree requirements:* For master's, comprehensive exam, applied research project. *Entrance requirements:* For master's, baccalaureate degree from regionally-accredited university with minimum GPA of 3.0 on last 60 undergraduate semester hours, statement of purpose, 2 letters of recommendation. Additional exam requirements/recommendations for international students: Required—TOEFL (minimum score 550 paper-based; 78 iBT), IELTS (minimum score 6.5). *Application deadline:* For fall admission, 2/1 priority date for domestic and international students; for spring admission, 10/15 for domestic students, 10/1 for international students; for summer admission, 4/15 for domestic students, 3/15 for international students. Applications are processed on a rolling basis. Application fee: $40 ($90 for international students). Electronic applications accepted. *Expenses:* Tuition, state resident: full-time $7868; part-time $3934 per semester. Tuition, nonresident: full-time $17,828; part-time $8914 per semester. *Required fees:* $2092; $1435 per semester. Tuition and fees vary according to course load. *Financial support:* In 2017–18, 51 students received support, including 10 teaching assistantships (averaging $12,194 per year); research assistantships, career-related internships or fieldwork, Federal Work-Study, institutionally sponsored loans, scholarships/grants, and unspecified assistantships also available. Support available to part-time students. Financial award application deadline: 3/1; financial award applicants required to submit FAFSA. *Unit head:* Dr. Patricia Shields, Graduate Advisor, 512-245-3256, Fax: 512-245-7815, E-mail:

ps07@txstate.edu. *Application contact:* Dr. Andrea Golato, Dean of Graduate School, 512-245-2581, Fax: 512-245-8365, E-mail: gradcollege@txstate.edu.
Website: http://mpa.polisci.txstate.edu/

Tiffin University, Program in Criminal Justice, Tiffin, OH 44883-2161. Offers criminal justice (MS), including crime analysis, criminal behavior, forensic psychology, homeland security administration, justice administration. *Program availability:* Part-time, evening/weekend, 100% online, blended/hybrid learning. *Degree requirements:* For master's, thesis optional. *Entrance requirements:* For master's, minimum undergraduate GPA of 2.5, work experience. Additional exam requirements/recommendations for international students: Required—TOEFL (minimum score 550 paper-based; 79 iBT). Electronic applications accepted. *Expenses:* Contact institution. *Faculty research:* Terrorism, intelligence, homeland security, guns and crime.

Trident University International, College of Business Administration, Program in Business Administration, Cypress, CA 90630. Offers business administration (PhD); conflict and negotiation management (MBA); criminal justice administration (MBA); entrepreneurship (MBA); finance (MBA); general management (MBA); government accounting (MBA); human resource management (MBA); information security and digital assurance management (MBA); information technology management (MBA); international business (MBA); logistics management (MBA); marketing (MBA); project management (MBA); public management (MBA); quality management (MBA); strategic leadership (MBA). *Program availability:* Part-time, evening/weekend, online learning. *Degree requirements:* For doctorate, comprehensive exam, thesis/dissertation, defense of dissertation. *Entrance requirements:* For master's, minimum GPA of 2.5 (students with GPA 3.0 or greater may transfer up to 30% of graduate level credits); for doctorate, minimum GPA of 3.4, curriculum vitae, course work in research methods or statistics. Additional exam requirements/recommendations for international students: Required—TOEFL. Electronic applications accepted.

Trine University, Program in Criminal Justice, Angola, IN 46703-1764. Offers emergency management (MS). *Program availability:* Part-time, evening/weekend, online only, 100% online, blended/hybrid learning. *Faculty:* 8. *Students:* 42 (31 women). In 2017, 23 master's awarded. *Entrance requirements:* Additional exam requirements/recommendations for international students: Required—TOEFL. *Application deadline:* Applications are processed on a rolling basis. Electronic applications accepted. *Expenses:* $550 per credit hour tuition. *Financial support:* Application deadline: 3/1; applicants required to submit FAFSA. *Unit head:* Ryan Dombkowski, Dean, College of Graduate and Professional Studies/Associate Professor, 260-203-2695, E-mail: dombkowskir@trine.edu. *Application contact:* Jacqueline Delagrange, Director, Master of Science in Criminal Justice, 260-203-2693, E-mail: delagrangej@trine.edu.
Website: https://www.trine.edu/adult-studies/academics/graduate/ms-criminal-justice.aspx

Troy University, Graduate School, College of Arts and Sciences, Program in Criminal Justice, Troy, AL 36082. Offers MS. *Program availability:* Part-time, evening/weekend. *Faculty:* 7 full-time (3 women), 7 part-time/adjunct (5 women). *Students:* 28 full-time (15 women), 117 part-time (70 women); includes 69 minority (59 Black or African American, non-Hispanic/Latino; 1 American Indian or Alaska Native, non-Hispanic/Latino; 1 Asian, non-Hispanic/Latino; 5 Hispanic/Latino; 3 Two or more races, non-Hispanic/Latino). Average age 36. 72 applicants, 94% accepted, 36 enrolled. In 2017, 62 master's awarded. *Degree requirements:* For master's, comprehensive exam, research course, minimum GPA of 3.0, admission to candidacy. *Entrance requirements:* For master's, GRE (minimum score of 850 on old exam or 290 on new exam), MAT (minimum score of 385) or GMAT (minimum score of 380), bachelor's degree; minimum undergraduate GPA of 2.5 or 3.0 on last 30 semester hours. Additional exam requirements/recommendations for international students: Required—TOEFL (minimum score 523 paper-based; 70 iBT), IELTS (minimum score 6). *Application deadline:* Applications are processed on a rolling basis. Application fee: $50. Electronic applications accepted. *Expenses:* Tuition, state resident: part-time $417 per credit hour. Tuition, nonresident: part-time $834 per credit hour. *Required fees:* $42 per credit hour. $50 per semester. Tuition and fees vary according to campus/location. *Financial support:* Fellowships, career-related internships or fieldwork, and scholarships/grants available. Support available to part-time students. Financial award applicants required to submit FAFSA. *Faculty research:* Crime victims, criminal justice personnel issues, disability issues in criminal justice. *Unit head:* Dr. Xiaoli Su, Assistant Chairman, Department of Criminal Justice, 334-808-6571, Fax: 334-808-6487, E-mail: xiaolisiu@troy.edu. *Application contact:* Jessica A. Kimbro, Director of Graduate Admissions, 334-670-3178, E-mail: jacord@troy.edu.

Troy University, Graduate School, College of Business, Program in Business Administration, Troy, AL 36082. Offers accounting (EMBA, MBA); criminal justice (EMBA); finance (MBA); general management (EMBA, MBA); healthcare management (EMBA); information systems (EMBA, MBA); international economic development (MBA). *Accreditation:* ACBSP. *Program availability:* Part-time, evening/weekend. *Faculty:* 6 full-time (2 women), 1 part-time/adjunct (0 women). *Students:* 43 full-time (22 women), 115 part-time (55 women); includes 50 minority (31 Black or African American, non-Hispanic/Latino; 12 Asian, non-Hispanic/Latino; 6 Hispanic/Latino; 1 Two or more races, non-Hispanic/Latino). Average age 30. 156 applicants, 76% accepted, 36 enrolled. In 2017, 95 master's awarded. *Degree requirements:* For master's, minimum GPA of 3.0, capstone course, research course. *Entrance requirements:* For master's, GMAT (minimum score 500) or GRE (minimum score 900 on old exam or 294 on new exam), bachelor's degree; minimum undergraduate GPA of 2.5 or 3.0 on last 30 semester hours, letter of recommendation. Additional exam requirements/recommendations for international students: Required—TOEFL (minimum score 523 paper-based; 70 iBT), IELTS (minimum score 6). *Application deadline:* Applications are processed on a rolling basis. Application fee: $50. Electronic applications accepted. *Expenses:* Tuition, state resident: part-time $417 per credit hour. Tuition, nonresident: part-time $834 per credit hour. *Required fees:* $42 per credit hour. $50 per semester. Tuition and fees vary according to campus/location. *Financial support:* Fellowships, career-related internships or fieldwork, and scholarships/grants available. Support available to part-time students. Financial award applicants required to submit FAFSA. *Unit head:* Dr. Phillip Mixon, MBA Director, 334-670-3140, Fax: 334-670-3708, E-mail: pamixon@troy.edu. *Application contact:* Jessica A. Kimbro, Director of Graduate Admissions, 334-670-3178, E-mail: jacord@troy.edu.

Universidad del Este, Graduate School, Carolina, PR 00984. Offers accounting (MBA); adult education (M Ed); agribusiness (MBA); criminal justice and criminology (MA); curriculum and instruction - early education (M Ed); curriculum and instruction - elementary (M Ed); curriculum and instruction - English (M Ed); curriculum and instruction - Spanish (M Ed); human resources (MBA); information security management (MBA); information technology and Web business development (MBA); management (MBA); public policy (MPA); social work (MA), including clinical social work; special education (M Ed); strategic leadership (MBA).

Universidad del Turabo, Graduate Programs, School of Social Sciences and Humanities, Programs in Public Affairs, Program in Criminal Justice Studies, Gurabo, PR 00778-3030. Offers MPA. *Entrance requirements:* For master's, GRE, EXADEP or GMAT, interview, essay, official transcript, recommendation letters. Electronic applications accepted.

Université de Montréal, Faculty of Arts and Sciences, School of Criminology, Montréal, QC H3C 3J7, Canada. Offers M Sc, PhD. Terminal master's awarded for partial completion of doctoral program. *Degree requirements:* For master's, thesis; for doctorate, thesis/dissertation, general exam. *Entrance requirements:* For master's, B Sc in criminology or the equivalent; for doctorate, M Sc in criminology or equivalent. Electronic applications accepted. *Faculty research:* Criminal behavior, criminality, prison population, victims of crime, female offenders.

University at Albany, State University of New York, School of Criminal Justice, Albany, NY 12203. Offers MA, PhD, MSW/MA. *Program availability:* Part-time. *Faculty:* 16 full-time (6 women). *Students:* 68 full-time (44 women), 22 part-time (16 women); includes 39 minority (13 Black or African American, non-Hispanic/Latino; 2 Asian, non-Hispanic/Latino; 21 Hispanic/Latino; 3 Two or more races, non-Hispanic/Latino), 7 international. 121 applicants, 55% accepted, 31 enrolled. In 2017, 44 master's, 1 doctorate awarded. *Degree requirements:* For doctorate, thesis/dissertation. *Entrance requirements:* For master's and doctorate, GRE General Test. Additional exam requirements/recommendations for international students: Required—TOEFL (minimum score 550 paper-based). *Application deadline:* For fall admission, 7/1 for domestic students, 5/1 for international students. Applications are processed on a rolling basis. Application fee: $75. Electronic applications accepted. *Expenses:* Tuition, state resident: full-time $10,870; part-time $453 per credit hour. Tuition, nonresident: full-time $22,210; part-time $925 per credit hour. *Required fees:* $84.68 per credit hour. $508.06 per semester. Part-time tuition and fees vary according to course load and program. *Financial support:* Fellowships, research assistantships, teaching assistantships, career-related internships or fieldwork, Federal Work-Study, and institutionally sponsored loans available. Financial award application deadline: 4/1. *Faculty research:* Causes of delinquency, comparative policing, world crime data, correctional policy, family violence. *Unit head:* William Alex Pridemore, Dean, 518-442-5210, E-mail: pridemore@albany.edu. *Application contact:* Jane Champagne, Director, Graduate Admissions, 518-442-3980, Fax: 518-442-3922, E-mail: graduate@albany.edu.
Website: http://www.albany.edu/scj/

The University of Alabama, Graduate School, College of Arts and Sciences, Department of Criminal Justice, Tuscaloosa, AL 35487. Offers MS. *Program availability:* Part-time. *Faculty:* 13 full-time (6 women). *Students:* 22 full-time (19 women), 4 part-time (3 women); includes 4 minority (3 Black or African American, non-Hispanic/Latino; 1 Hispanic/Latino). Average age 25. 27 applicants, 63% accepted, 12 enrolled. In 2017, 16 master's awarded. *Degree requirements:* For master's, comprehensive exam (for some programs), thesis (for some programs), thesis or comprehensive exam. *Entrance requirements:* For master's, GRE. Additional exam requirements/recommendations for international students: Recommended—TOEFL. *Application deadline:* For fall admission, 6/15 for domestic and international students; for winter admission, 11/1 for domestic and international students; for spring admission, 11/1 for domestic and international students. Applications are processed on a rolling basis. Application fee: $50 ($60 for international students). Electronic applications accepted. *Financial support:* In 2017–18, 25 teaching assistantships with partial tuition reimbursements (averaging $6,570 per year) were awarded; fellowships, health care benefits, and unspecified assistantships also available. Financial award application deadline: 6/15. *Faculty research:* Social deviance, sociology of HIV/AIDS, terrorism, cyber crime, juvenile delinquency. *Total annual research expenditures:* $10,064. *Unit head:* Dr. Lesley W. Reid, Department Chair, 205-348-7795, Fax: 205-348-7795, E-mail: lwreid@ua.edu. *Application contact:* Dr. Adam Lankford, Associate Professor and Director of Graduate Studies, 205-348-9901, Fax: 205-348-9901, E-mail: adam.lankford@ua.edu.
Website: http://cj.ua.edu

The University of Alabama at Birmingham, College of Arts and Sciences, Program in Criminal Justice, Birmingham, AL 35294. Offers MSCJ. *Program availability:* Part-time, evening/weekend. *Degree requirements:* For master's, thesis or demonstration project that shows proficiency in the subject. *Entrance requirements:* Additional exam requirements/recommendations for international students: Required—TOEFL, TWE. Electronic applications accepted. *Expenses:* Contact institution. *Faculty research:* Criminology, corrections, police, research methods.

University of Alaska Fairbanks, College of Liberal Arts, Department of Justice, Fairbanks, AK 99775-6120. Offers MA. *Program availability:* Part-time, online only, 100% online. *Degree requirements:* For master's, comprehensive exam, oral defense of project or thesis. *Entrance requirements:* For master's, bachelor's degree from accredited institution with minimum cumulative undergraduate and major GPA of 3.0. Additional exam requirements/recommendations for international students: Required—TOEFL (minimum score 550 paper-based; 79 iBT), IELTS (minimum score 6.5). Electronic applications accepted.

University of Alberta, Faculty of Graduate Studies and Research, Department of Sociology, Edmonton, AB T6G 2E1, Canada. Offers criminal justice (MA); demography (MA, PhD); sociology (MA, PhD). *Program availability:* Part-time. *Degree requirements:* For master's, thesis (for some programs); for doctorate, thesis/dissertation. *Faculty research:* Criminology, knowledge and culture, methods and theory, population studies, stratification.

University of Antelope Valley, Program in Criminal Justice, Lancaster, CA 93534. Offers MS. *Degree requirements:* For master's, capstone project. *Entrance requirements:* For master's, official transcripts documenting earned bachelor's degree from nationally- or regionally-accredited institution with minimum cumulative GPA of 2.0.

University of Arkansas at Little Rock, Graduate School, College of Social Sciences and Communication, Department of Criminal Justice, Little Rock, AR 72204-1099. Offers MA, MS, PhD. MS program is offered by distance education. *Program availability:* Part-time, evening/weekend. *Degree requirements:* For master's, thesis defense or written comprehensive exam; for doctorate, thesis/dissertation. *Entrance requirements:* For master's, GRE General Test or MAT, interview, minimum GPA of 2.75. Additional exam requirements/recommendations for international students: Required—TOEFL (minimum score 550 paper-based; 79 iBT). *Faculty research:* Dissemination and analysis of behavioral science knowledge, leadership and managerial skills, philosophy of individual rights and humane treatment.

University of Baltimore, Graduate School, College of Public Affairs, Program in Criminal Justice, Baltimore, MD 21201-5779. Offers MS, JD/MS. *Program availability:* Part-time, evening/weekend. *Degree requirements:* For master's, thesis or alternative. *Entrance requirements:* For master's, interview, minimum GPA of 2.8. Additional exam requirements/recommendations for international students: Required—TOEFL (minimum score 550 paper-based). Electronic applications accepted. *Faculty research:* Drugs and violence, police and community policing, women and crime, victimization, correction in community.

University of California, Irvine, School of Social Ecology, Department of Criminology, Law and Society, Irvine, CA 92697. Offers MAS, PhD. *Students:* 144 full-time (96 women), 56 part-time (40 women); includes 101 minority (18 Black or African American, non-Hispanic/Latino; 23 Asian, non-Hispanic/Latino; 41 Hispanic/Latino; 19 Two or more races, non-Hispanic/Latino), 6 international. Average age 28. 234 applicants, 56% accepted, 95 enrolled. In 2017, 47 master's, 10 doctorates awarded. *Degree requirements:* For doctorate, thesis/dissertation, research project. *Entrance*

requirements: For master's and doctorate, GRE General Test, minimum GPA of 3.0. Additional exam requirements/recommendations for international students: Required—TOEFL (minimum score 550 paper-based). *Application deadline:* For fall admission, 1/15 priority date for domestic and international students. Application fee: $105 ($125 for international students). Electronic applications accepted. *Financial support:* Fellowships, research assistantships with full tuition reimbursements, teaching assistantships, institutionally sponsored loans, traineeships, health care benefits, and unspecified assistantships available. Financial award application deadline: 3/1; financial award applicants required to submit FAFSA. *Faculty research:* White-collar and corporate crime; immigration, the poor, homelessness, and governmental regulation; sentencing, community corrections, and diversion; mathematical and scientific evidence in jury trials; legal and criminological theory development. *Unit head:* Prof. Cheryl Maxon, Department Chair, 949-824-5150, E-mail: cmaxson@uci.edu. *Application contact:* Leslie Noel, Graduate Coordinator, 949-824-1442, Fax: 949-824-3001, E-mail: lknoel@uci.edu.
Website: http://cls.soceco.uci.edu/

University of Central Florida, College of Community Innovation and Education, Department of Criminal Justice, Orlando, FL 32816. Offers corrections leadership (Certificate); criminal justice (MS, PhD); juvenile justice leadership (Certificate); police leadership (Certificate). *Program availability:* Part-time, evening/weekend. *Students:* 102 full-time (75 women), 172 part-time (108 women); includes 119 minority (47 Black or African American, non-Hispanic/Latino; 8 Asian, non-Hispanic/Latino; 59 Hispanic/Latino; 3 Native Hawaiian or other Pacific Islander, non-Hispanic/Latino; 2 Two or more races, non-Hispanic/Latino), 2 international. Average age 30. 227 applicants, 68% accepted, 117 enrolled. In 2017, 72 master's, 35 other advanced degrees awarded. *Degree requirements:* For master's, thesis or alternative; for doctorate, comprehensive exam, thesis/dissertation. *Entrance requirements:* For master's, minimum GPA of 3.0, letters of recommendation, resume, goal statement; for doctorate, GRE, letters of recommendation, curriculum vitae, goal statement, writing sample. Additional exam requirements/recommendations for international students: Required—TOEFL. *Application deadline:* For fall admission, 7/15 for domestic students; for spring admission, 12/1 for domestic students. Application fee: $30. Electronic applications accepted. *Expenses:* Tuition, state resident: part-time $288.16 per credit hour. Tuition, nonresident: part-time $1073.31 per credit hour. Tuition and fees vary according to program. *Financial support:* In 2017–18, 20 students received support, including 7 fellowships with partial tuition reimbursements available (averaging $5,000 per year), 16 research assistantships with partial tuition reimbursements available (averaging $9,206 per year), 11 teaching assistantships with partial tuition reimbursements available (averaging $7,842 per year); career-related internships or fieldwork, Federal Work-Study, institutionally sponsored loans, health care benefits, tuition waivers (partial), and unspecified assistantships also available. Financial award application deadline: 3/1; financial award applicants required to submit FAFSA. *Unit head:* Dr. Eugene Paoline, III, Program Director, 407-823-2603, E-mail: eugene.paoline@ucf.edu. *Application contact:* Associate Director, Graduate Admissions, 407-823-2766, Fax: 407-823-6442, E-mail: gradadmissions@ucf.edu.
Website: https://www.cohpa.ucf.edu/criminaljustice/

University of Central Missouri, The Graduate School, Warrensburg, MO 64093. Offers accountancy (MA); accounting (MBA); applied mathematics (MS); aviation safety (MA); biology (MS); business administration (MBA); career and technical education leadership (MS); college student personnel administration (MS); communication (MA); computer science (MS); counseling (MS); criminal justice (MS); educational leadership (Ed D); educational technology (MS); elementary and early childhood education (MSE); English (MA); environmental studies (MA); finance (MBA); history (MA); human services/educational technology (Ed S); human services/learning resources (Ed S); human services/professional counseling (Ed S); industrial hygiene (MS); industrial management (MS); information systems (MBA); information technology (MS); kinesiology (MS); library science and information services (MS); literacy education (MSE); marketing (MBA); mathematics (MS); music (MA); occupational safety management (MS); psychology (MS); rural family nursing (MS); school administration (MSE); social gerontology (MS); sociology (MA); special education (MSE); speech language pathology (MS); superintendency (Ed S); teaching (MAT); teaching English as a second language (MA); technology (MS); technology management (PhD); theatre (MA). *Program availability:* Part-time, 100% online, blended/hybrid learning. *Faculty:* 337 full-time (145 women), 41 part-time/adjunct (28 women). *Students:* 785 full-time (398 women), 1,633 part-time (1,063 women); includes 231 minority (102 Black or African American, non-Hispanic/Latino; 4 American Indian or Alaska Native, non-Hispanic/Latino; 16 Asian, non-Hispanic/Latino; 52 Hispanic/Latino; 57 Two or more races, non-Hispanic/Latino), 692 international. Average age 30. In 2017, 2,605 master's, 122 other advanced degrees awarded. *Degree requirements:* For master's and Ed S, comprehensive exam (for some programs), thesis (for some programs). *Entrance requirements:* Additional exam requirements/recommendations for international students: Required—TOEFL (minimum score 550 paper-based; 79 iBT). *Application deadline:* For fall admission, 6/1 priority date for domestic and international students; for spring admission, 10/1 priority date for domestic and international students; for summer admission, 4/1 priority date for domestic and international students. Applications are processed on a rolling basis. Application fee: $30 ($75 for international students). Electronic applications accepted. *Expenses:* Tuition, state resident: full-time $8771; part-time $292.35 per credit hour. Tuition, nonresident: full-time $17,541; part-time $584.70 per credit hour. *Required fees:* $372; $24.78 per credit hour. *Financial support:* In 2017–18, 99 students received support. Research assistantships, teaching assistantships, career-related internships or fieldwork, Federal Work-Study, scholarships/grants, and administrative and laboratory assistantships available. Support available to part-time students. Financial award application deadline: 3/1; financial award applicants required to submit FAFSA. *Unit head:* Shellie Hewitt, Director of Graduate and International Student Services, 660-543-4621, Fax: 660-543-4778, E-mail: hewitt@ucmo.edu. *Application contact:* 660-543-4621, E-mail: admit_intl@ucmo.edu.
Website: http://www.ucmo.edu/graduate/

University of Central Oklahoma, The Jackson College of Graduate Studies, College of Liberal Arts, School of Criminal Justice, Edmond, OK 73034-5209. Offers crime and intelligence analysis (MA); criminal justice management and administration (MA). *Program availability:* Part-time. *Faculty:* 8 full-time (4 women), 4 part-time/adjunct (1 woman). *Students:* 21 full-time (14 women), 14 part-time (10 women); includes 14 minority (4 Black or African American, non-Hispanic/Latino; 5 American Indian or Alaska Native, non-Hispanic/Latino; 4 Hispanic/Latino; 1 Two or more races, non-Hispanic/Latino), 1 international. Average age 30. 27 applicants, 44% accepted, 9 enrolled. In 2017, 11 master's awarded. *Degree requirements:* For master's, comprehensive exam (for some programs), thesis (for some programs). *Entrance requirements:* Additional exam requirements/recommendations for international students: Required—TOEFL (minimum score 550 paper-based; 79 iBT), IELTS (minimum score 6.5). *Application deadline:* For fall admission, 7/15 for international students; for spring admission, 11/15 for international students. Applications are processed on a rolling basis. Application fee: $60. Electronic applications accepted. *Expenses:* Tuition, state resident: full-time $5375; part-time $268.75 per credit hour. Tuition, nonresident: full-time $13,295; part-time $664.75 per credit hour. *Required fees:* $626; $31.30 per credit hour. One-time fee: $50. Tuition and fees vary according to program. *Financial support:* In 2017–18, 11 students received support, including 5 teaching assistantships with partial tuition reimbursements available (averaging $8,873 per year); research assistantships, career-related internships or fieldwork, scholarships/grants, tuition waivers (partial), and unspecified assistantships also available. Financial award application deadline: 3/31; financial award applicants required to submit FAFSA. *Unit head:* Dr. DeWade Langley, Director, 405-974-5501, Fax: 405-974-3816, E-mail: criminaljustice@uco.edu. *Application contact:* Dr. Shawna Cleary, Graduate Advisor, 405-974-5841, Fax: 405-974-3816, E-mail: gradcoll@uco.edu.
Website: http://www.uco.edu/la/criminal-justice/

University of Cincinnati, Graduate School, College of Education, Criminal Justice, and Human Services, School of Criminal Justice, Cincinnati, OH 45221. Offers MS, PhD. *Program availability:* Part-time, online learning. *Students:* 119 full-time (67 women), 566 part-time (316 women); includes 166 minority (121 Black or African American, non-Hispanic/Latino; 2 American Indian or Alaska Native, non-Hispanic/Latino; 10 Asian, non-Hispanic/Latino; 33 Hispanic/Latino), 22 international. In 2017, 233 master's, 4 doctorates awarded. *Degree requirements:* For master's, thesis or alternative; for doctorate, thesis/dissertation. *Entrance requirements:* For master's, GRE or MAT, minimum GPA of 3.0; for doctorate, minimum GPA of 3.5. Additional exam requirements/recommendations for international students: Required—TOEFL (minimum score 550 paper-based). *Application deadline:* For fall admission, 2/1 for domestic students. Application fee: $40. Electronic applications accepted. *Expenses: Tuition, area resident:* Full-time $14,468. Tuition, state resident: full-time $14,968; part-time $754 per credit hour. Tuition, nonresident: full-time $24,210; part-time $1311 per credit hour. *International tuition:* $26,460 full-time. *Required fees:* $3958; $84 per credit hour. One-time fee: $85 full-time. Tuition and fees vary according to course load, degree level and program. *Financial support:* Fellowships, tuition waivers (partial), and unspecified assistantships available. Support available to part-time students. *Total annual research expenditures:* $903,893. *Unit head:* Dr. Edward J. Latessa, Head, 513-556-5836, Fax: 513-556-3303, E-mail: edward.latessa@uc.edu. *Application contact:* Dr. Christopher Sullivan, Director, Graduate Programs, 513-556-3851, E-mail: sullivc6@ucmail.uc.edu.
Website: http://cech.uc.edu/criminaljustice.html

University of Colorado Colorado Springs, School of Public Affairs, Colorado Springs, CO 80918. Offers criminal justice (MCJ); public administration (MPA). *Accreditation:* NASPAA. *Program availability:* Part-time, evening/weekend, 100% online, blended/hybrid learning. *Faculty:* 13 full-time (6 women), 16 part-time/adjunct (3 women). *Students:* 19 full-time (11 women), 164 part-time (101 women); includes 57 minority (6 Black or African American, non-Hispanic/Latino; 1 American Indian or Alaska Native, non-Hispanic/Latino; 5 Asian, non-Hispanic/Latino; 37 Hispanic/Latino; 8 Two or more races, non-Hispanic/Latino). Average age 35. 61 applicants, 95% accepted, 40 enrolled. In 2017, 44 master's awarded. *Degree requirements:* For master's, internship, capstone project, or thesis. *Entrance requirements:* For master's, GRE General Test, GMAT, LSAT, minimum GPA of 3.0. Additional exam requirements/recommendations for international students: Recommended—TOEFL (minimum score 550 paper-based; 80 iBT), IELTS (minimum score 6.5). *Application deadline:* Applications are processed on a rolling basis. Application fee: $60 ($100 for international students). Electronic applications accepted. *Expenses:* $10,350 per year resident tuition, $20,935 nonresident, $11,961 nonresidential online; annual costs vary depending on program, course-load, and residency status. *Financial support:* In 2017–18, 25 students received support. Career-related internships or fieldwork, scholarships/grants, and tuition waivers available. Support available to part-time students. Financial award application deadline: 3/1; financial award applicants required to submit FAFSA. *Faculty research:* Antiquated prison environments; public management; intersections of gender, class, race and crime; national security/U.S. foreign policy; leadership, ethics, organizational theory and behavior. *Total annual research expenditures:* $486,455. *Unit head:* Dr. George Reed, Dean, 719-255-4109, E-mail: george.reed@uccs.edu. *Application contact:* Crista Hill, Outreach Student Services Specialist, 719-255-4993, Fax: 719-255-4183, E-mail: chill12@uccs.edu.
Website: http://www.uccs.edu/spa/

University of Colorado Denver, School of Public Affairs, Program in Criminology and Criminal Justice, Denver, CO 80217. Offers criminal justice (MCJ), including criminal justice, domestic violence, emergency management and homeland security. *Program availability:* Part-time, evening/weekend. *Degree requirements:* For master's, thesis or alternative, 36-39 semester credit hours. *Entrance requirements:* For master's, GRE, GMAT, LSAT, recommendations, official transcripts, current resume, essay. Additional exam requirements/recommendations for international students: Required—TOEFL (minimum score 537 paper-based; 75 iBT); Recommended—IELTS (minimum score 6.5). Electronic applications accepted. *Expenses:* Contact institution. *Faculty research:* White collar crime, women and the criminal justice system, applied family violence issues, intimate partner violence and domestic violence interventions, juvenile delinquency.

University of Colorado Denver, School of Public Affairs, Program in Public Affairs and Administration, Denver, CO 80127. Offers public administration (MPA), including domestic violence, emergency management and homeland security, environmental policy, management and law, homeland security and defense, local government, nonprofit management, public administration; public affairs (PhD). *Accreditation:* NASPAA. *Program availability:* Part-time, evening/weekend, online learning. *Degree requirements:* For master's, thesis or alternative, 36-39 credit hours; for doctorate, comprehensive exam, thesis/dissertation, minimum of 66 semester hours, including at least 30 hours of dissertation. *Entrance requirements:* For master's, GRE, GMAT or LSAT, resume, essay, transcripts, recommendations; for doctorate, GRE, resume, essay, transcripts, recommendations. Additional exam requirements/recommendations for international students: Required—TOEFL (minimum score 550 paper-based; 80 iBT); Recommended—IELTS (minimum score 6.5). Electronic applications accepted. *Expenses:* Contact institution. *Faculty research:* Housing, education and the social and economic issues of vulnerable populations; nonprofit governance and management; education finance, effectiveness and reform; P-20 education initiatives; municipal government accountability.

University of Delaware, College of Arts and Sciences, Department of Sociology and Criminal Justice, Newark, DE 19716. Offers criminology (MA, PhD); sociology (MA, PhD). *Degree requirements:* For master's, thesis; for doctorate, comprehensive exam, thesis/dissertation. *Entrance requirements:* For master's and doctorate, GRE, 3 letters of recommendation. Additional exam requirements/recommendations for international students: Required—TOEFL. Electronic applications accepted. *Faculty research:* Sex and gender, criminology/deviance, theory, methods, collective behavior.

University of Denver, University College, Denver, CO 80208. Offers arts and culture (MA, Certificate); communication management (MS, Certificate), including translation studies (Certificate), world history and culture (Certificate); environmental policy and management (MS); geographic information systems (MS); global affairs (MA, Certificate), including human capital in organizations (Certificate), philanthropic leadership (Certificate), project management (Certificate), strategic innovation and change (Certificate); healthcare leadership (MS); information communications and technology (MS); leadership and organizations (MS); professional creative writing (MA,

Certificate), including emergency planning and response (Certificate), organizational security (Certificate); security management (MS, Certificate); strategic human resources (Certificate). *Program availability:* Part-time, evening/weekend, online learning. *Faculty:* 118 part-time/adjunct (62 women). *Students:* 56 full-time (32 women), 1,287 part-time (707 women); includes 330 minority (99 Black or African American, non-Hispanic/Latino; 7 American Indian or Alaska Native, non-Hispanic/Latino; 43 Asian, non-Hispanic/Latino; 141 Hispanic/Latino; 3 Native Hawaiian or other Pacific Islander, non-Hispanic/Latino; 37 Two or more races, non-Hispanic/Latino), 84 international. Average age 34. 783 applicants, 86% accepted, 420 enrolled. In 2017, 461 master's, 173 other advanced degrees awarded. *Degree requirements:* For master's, capstone project. *Entrance requirements:* For master's, transcripts, two letters of recommendation, personal statement, resume. Additional exam requirements/recommendations for international students: Required—TOEFL (minimum score 550 paper-based; 80 iBT). *Application deadline:* For fall admission, 6/21 priority date for domestic students, 5/1 priority date for international students; for winter admission, 9/14 priority date for domestic students, 9/19 priority date for international students; for spring admission, 1/11 priority date for domestic students, 12/12 priority date for international students; for summer admission, 3/29 priority date for domestic students, 3/6 priority date for international students. Applications are processed on a rolling basis. Application fee: $75. Electronic applications accepted. *Expenses:* $7,968 per year half-time. *Financial support:* In 2017–18, 29 students received support. Teaching assistantships available. Financial award applicants required to submit FAFSA. *Unit head:* Dr. Michael McGuire, Dean, 303-871-3518, Fax: 303-871-3303, E-mail: mmcguire@du.edu. *Application contact:* Information Contact, 303-871-2291, E-mail: ucoladm@du.edu.
Website: http://universitycollege.du.edu/

University of Detroit Mercy, College of Liberal Arts and Education, Detroit, MI 48221. Offers addiction counseling (MA); addiction studies (Certificate); clinical mental health counseling (MA); clinical psychology (MA, PhD); computer and information systems (MS); criminal justice (MA); curriculum and instruction (MA); economics (MA); educational administration (MA); financial economics (MA); industrial/organizational psychology (MA); information assurance (MS); intelligence analysis (MA); liberal studies (MALS); religious studies (MA); school counseling (MA, Certificate); school psychology (Spec); security administration (MS); special education: emotionally impaired/behaviorally disordered (MA); special education: learning disabilities (MA). *Program availability:* Part-time, evening/weekend. *Degree requirements:* For doctorate, departmental qualifying exam. *Faculty research:* Psychology of aging, history of technology, Renaissance humanism, U.S. and Japanese economic relations.

University of Florida, Graduate School, College of Liberal Arts and Sciences, Department of Sociology and Criminology and Law, Gainesville, FL 32611. Offers criminology, law, and society (MA, PhD); sociology (MA, PhD), including sociology, tropical conservation and development, women's and gender studies (PhD); MA/JD. *Program availability:* Part-time. Terminal master's awarded for partial completion of doctoral program. *Degree requirements:* For master's, thesis optional; for doctorate, comprehensive exam, thesis/dissertation. *Entrance requirements:* For master's and doctorate, GRE, minimum GPA of 3.0. Additional exam requirements/recommendations for international students: Required—TOEFL (minimum score 550 paper-based; 80 iBT), IELTS (minimum score 6). Electronic applications accepted. *Faculty research:* Law and society, juvenile justice, criminal investigation procedures, deviance, biosocial criminology, environmental sociology, comparative race and ethnic studies, health and aging, families and gender.

University of Guelph, Graduate Studies, College of Social and Applied Human Sciences, Department of Criminology and Criminal Justice Policy, Guelph, ON N1G 2W1, Canada. Offers MA. *Degree requirements:* For master's, thesis or major paper. *Entrance requirements:* For master's, minimum B+ average during previous 2 years of coursework. Electronic applications accepted.

University of Guelph, Graduate Studies, College of Social and Applied Human Sciences, Department of Sociology and Anthropology, Guelph, ON N1G 2W1, Canada. Offers anthropology (MA); crime and criminal justice policy (MA); sociology (MA, PhD). *Degree requirements:* For master's, thesis or major paper; for doctorate, comprehensive exam, thesis/dissertation. *Entrance requirements:* For master's, minimum B+ average during previous 2 years of course work, honors BA or equivalent; for doctorate, must have an MA in Sociology, must have 80% or higher in graduate level studies. Additional exam requirements/recommendations for international students: Required—TOEFL (minimum score 550 paper-based; 89 iBT) or IELTS (minimum score 6.5). Electronic applications accepted. *Faculty research:* Rural and development sociology; education, employment, and the workplace; race, ethnicity, and native studies; criminology and deviance; social psychology.

University of Houston–Clear Lake, School of Human Sciences and Humanities, Programs in Human Sciences, Houston, TX 77058-1002. Offers behavioral sciences (MA), including criminology, cross cultural studies, general psychology, sociology; clinical psychology (MA); criminology (MA); cross cultural studies (MA); family therapy (MA); fitness and human performance (MA); school psychology (MA). *Accreditation:* AAMFT/COAMFTE. *Program availability:* Part-time, evening/weekend, online learning. *Degree requirements:* For master's, thesis or alternative. *Entrance requirements:* For master's, GRE General Test. Additional exam requirements/recommendations for international students: Required—TOEFL (minimum score 550 paper-based). Electronic applications accepted. *Faculty research:* Smoking cessation, adolescent sexuality, white collar crime, serial murder, human factors/human computer interaction.

University of Houston–Downtown, College of Public Service, Department of Criminal Justice and Social Work, Houston, TX 77002. Offers MS. *Program availability:* Part-time, evening/weekend, 100% online. *Faculty:* 13 full-time (8 women). *Students:* 19 full-time (13 women), 43 part-time (32 women); includes 45 minority (20 Black or African American, non-Hispanic/Latino; 3 Asian, non-Hispanic/Latino; 22 Hispanic/Latino), 1 international. Average age 32. 29 applicants, 59% accepted, 15 enrolled. In 2017, 19 master's awarded. *Degree requirements:* For master's, thesis or project. *Entrance requirements:* For master's, personal statement, 3 letters of recommendation, minimum GPA of 3.0 on last 60 hours. Additional exam requirements/recommendations for international students: Required—TOEFL (minimum score 550 paper-based; 50 iBT). *Application deadline:* For fall admission, 7/15 for domestic and international students; for spring admission, 11/15 for domestic and international students. Application fee: $35 ($60 for international students). Electronic applications accepted. *Expenses:* $335 per credit resident; $700 per credit non-resident. *Financial support:* Federal Work-Study and scholarships/grants available. Financial award application deadline: 4/1; financial award applicants required to submit FAFSA. *Faculty research:* Policing issues, issues in security, community supervision, legal and other issues in prisons, juvenile justice. *Unit head:* Dr. Ashley Blackburn, Chair, 713-222-5326, Fax: 713-221-2726, E-mail: blackburna@uhd.edu. *Application contact:* Ceshia Love, Director of Admissions, 713-221-8093, Fax: 713-223-7408, E-mail: gradadmissions@uhd.edu.
Website: http://www.uhd.edu/mscj/

University of Houston–Downtown, Marilyn Davies College of Business, Master of Security Management Program, Houston, TX 77002. Offers MSM. *Program availability:* Part-time, online only, 100% online. *Faculty:* 3 full-time (1 woman), 2 part-time/adjunct (1 woman). *Students:* 1 (woman) full-time, 39 part-time (11 women); includes 29 minority (18 Black or African American, non-Hispanic/Latino; 3 Asian, non-Hispanic/Latino; 8 Hispanic/Latino). Average age 45. 22 applicants, 86% accepted, 15 enrolled. In 2017, 12 master's awarded. *Degree requirements:* For master's, capstone project. *Entrance requirements:* For master's, letter of intent, 3 letters of recommendation from supervisors indicating probability of applicant's success in program, proof of three years of paid work experience with supervisory or managerial responsibilities. Additional exam requirements/recommendations for international students: Required—TOEFL (minimum score 550 paper-based; 80 iBT). *Application deadline:* For fall admission, 8/1 for domestic students, 5/1 for international students; for spring admission, 11/15 for domestic students. Application fee: $35 ($60 for international students). Electronic applications accepted. *Expenses:* $360 per credit resident; $725 per credit non-resident. *Financial support:* Federal Work-Study and scholarships/grants available. Financial award application deadline: 4/1; financial award applicants required to submit FAFSA. *Unit head:* Dr. Charles E. Gengler, Dean, 713-221-8179, Fax: 713-221-8675. *Application contact:* Ceshia Love, Director of Admissions, 713-221-8093, Fax: 713-223-7408, E-mail: gradadmissions@uhd.edu.
Website: https://www.uhd.edu/academics/business/graduate-programs/Pages/msme-index.aspx

University of Illinois at Chicago, College of Liberal Arts and Sciences, Department of Criminology, Law, and Justice, Chicago, IL 60607-7128. Offers MA, PhD. *Program availability:* Evening/weekend. *Degree requirements:* For master's, thesis. *Entrance requirements:* For master's, GRE General Test, minimum GPA of 3.0. Additional exam requirements/recommendations for international students: Required—TOEFL. Electronic applications accepted. *Faculty research:* Sentencing probation, police and court use of scientific evidence, community mediation and conflict resolution.

University of Louisiana at Monroe, Graduate School, College of Business and Social Sciences, Department of Criminal Justice, Monroe, LA 71209-0001. Offers MA. *Program availability:* Part-time, evening/weekend. *Faculty:* 2 full-time (1 woman). *Students:* 25 full-time (18 women), 3 part-time (2 women); includes 20 minority (19 Black or African American, non-Hispanic/Latino; 1 Asian, non-Hispanic/Latino). Average age 28. 22 applicants, 77% accepted, 10 enrolled. In 2017, 7 master's awarded. *Degree requirements:* For master's, thesis optional. *Entrance requirements:* For master's, GRE General Test, minimum GPA of 2.5. Additional exam requirements/recommendations for international students: Required—TOEFL (minimum score 500 paper-based; 61 iBT). *Application deadline:* For fall admission, 8/24 priority date for domestic students, 7/1 for international students; for winter admission, 12/14 priority date for domestic students; for spring admission, 1/19 for domestic students, 11/1 for international students. Applications are processed on a rolling basis. Application fee: $20 ($30 for international students). Electronic applications accepted. *Expenses:* Tuition, state resident: full-time $6489; part-time $479 per hour. Tuition, nonresident: full-time $12,100; part-time $479 per hour. *Required fees:* $8860; $802 per hour. $3273 per semester. *Financial support:* In 2017–18, 7 students received support. Career-related internships or fieldwork, Federal Work-Study, and unspecified assistantships available. Financial award application deadline: 4/1; financial award applicants required to submit FAFSA. *Unit head:* Dr. Robert D. Hanser, Program Coordinator, 318-342-1443, Fax: 318-342-1458, E-mail: hanser@ulm.edu.
Website: http://www.ulm.edu/criminaljustice

University of Louisville, Graduate School, College of Arts and Sciences, Department of Criminal Justice, Louisville, KY 40292. Offers MS, PhD. *Program availability:* Part-time, evening/weekend, 100% online, blended/hybrid learning. *Faculty:* 15 full-time (7 women), 11 part-time/adjunct (1 woman). *Students:* 64 full-time (25 women), 60 part-time (19 women); includes 23 minority (12 Black or African American, non-Hispanic/Latino; 1 American Indian or Alaska Native, non-Hispanic/Latino; 6 Hispanic/Latino; 4 Two or more races, non-Hispanic/Latino), 2 international. Average age 39. 39 applicants, 44% accepted, 14 enrolled. In 2017, 13 master's, 3 doctorates awarded. *Degree requirements:* For master's, thesis or professional paper; for doctorate, thesis/dissertation, qualifying project. *Entrance requirements:* For master's, GRE General Test, 2 letters of recommendation; personal statement; official transcripts from all colleges attended; for doctorate, GRE General Test, 3 letters of recommendation; personal statement; curriculum vitae or resume; writing sample; official transcripts from all colleges attended. Additional exam requirements/recommendations for international students: Required—TOEFL (minimum score 550 paper-based; 79 iBT), IELTS (minimum score 6.5). *Application deadline:* For fall admission, 7/1 priority date for domestic and international students; for winter admission, 11/1 priority date for domestic students, 11/1 for international students; for spring admission, 11/1 priority date for domestic and international students; for summer admission, 4/1 priority date for domestic and international students. Applications are processed on a rolling basis. Application fee: $65. Electronic applications accepted. *Expenses:* Tuition, state resident: full-time $12,246; part-time $681 per credit hour. Tuition, nonresident: full-time $25,486; part-time $1417 per credit hour. *Required fees:* $196. Tuition and fees vary according to course load, program and reciprocity agreements. *Financial support:* In 2017–18, 2 research assistantships with full tuition reimbursements (averaging $18,000 per year), 8 teaching assistantships with full tuition reimbursements (averaging $18,000 per year) were awarded; health care benefits also available. Financial award application deadline: 2/15; financial award applicants required to submit FAFSA. *Faculty research:* Operations of the elements of the criminal justice system (both theoretical and applied). *Total annual research expenditures:* $152,593. *Unit head:* Dr. Gennaro Vito, Chair, 502-852-6509, Fax: 502-852-0065, E-mail: gfvito01@louisville.edu. *Application contact:* Ginger Brown, Director, Student Services, 502-852-2686, Fax: 502-852-0065, E-mail: vcbrow01@louisville.edu.
Website: https://louisville.edu/justiceadministration/

University of Lynchburg, Graduate Studies, MA Program in Criminal Justice Leadership, Lynchburg, VA 24501-3199. Offers MA. *Program availability:* Part-time. *Faculty:* 4 full-time (2 women), 2 part-time/adjunct (0 women). *Students:* 11 part-time (9 women); includes 5 minority (3 Black or African American, non-Hispanic/Latino; 1 Hispanic/Latino; 1 Two or more races, non-Hispanic/Latino). Average age 27. 17 applicants, 94% accepted, 6 enrolled. In 2017, 5 master's awarded. *Degree requirements:* For master's, thesis, professional project/portfolio. *Entrance requirements:* For master's, GRE. Additional exam requirements/recommendations for international students: Required—TOEFL (minimum score 550 paper-based; 80 iBT), IELTS (minimum score 6). *Application deadline:* For fall admission, 7/31 for domestic and international students; for spring admission, 11/30 for domestic and international students. Applications are processed on a rolling basis. Application fee: $30. Electronic applications accepted. Application fee is waived when completed online. *Expenses:* $510 per credit hour tuition, $100 fees. *Financial support:* Fellowships and unspecified assistantships available. Financial award application deadline: 4/30; financial award applicants required to submit FAFSA. *Unit head:* Dr. Kim McCabe, Director, Criminal Justice Program, 434-544-8129, E-mail: mccabe@lynchburg.edu. *Application contact:* Ellen Thompson, Graduate Admission Counselor, 434-544-8841, E-mail: thompson_e@lynchburg.edu.
Website: https://www.lynchburg.edu/graduate/master-of-criminal-justice-leadership/

University of Management and Technology, Program in Criminal Justice, Arlington, VA 22209-1609. Offers homeland security (MS). *Program availability:* Part-time,

evening/weekend, online learning. *Entrance requirements:* Additional exam requirements/recommendations for international students: Required—TOEFL (minimum score 530 paper-based; 71 iBT).

University of Management and Technology, Program in Management, Arlington, VA 22209-1609. Offers acquisition management (MS, AC); criminal justice administration (MS); general management (MS); project management (MS, AC). *Program availability:* Part-time, evening/weekend, online learning. *Entrance requirements:* For master's, 3 recommendations, resume. Additional exam requirements/recommendations for international students: Required—TOEFL (minimum score 530 paper-based; 71 iBT). Electronic applications accepted.

The University of Manchester, School of Law, Manchester, United Kingdom. Offers bioethics and medical jurisprudence (PhD); criminology (M Phil, PhD); law (M Phil, PhD).

University of Maryland, College Park, Academic Affairs, College of Behavioral and Social Sciences, Department of Criminology and Criminal Justice, College Park, MD 20742. Offers MA, PhD, JD/MA. *Program availability:* Part-time, evening/weekend. Terminal master's awarded for partial completion of doctoral program. *Degree requirements:* For master's, comprehensive exam, thesis optional; for doctorate, comprehensive exam, thesis/dissertation. *Entrance requirements:* For master's, GRE General Test, minimum GPA of 3.0, 3 letters of recommendation; for doctorate, GRE General Test. Additional exam requirements/recommendations for international students: Required—TOEFL. Electronic applications accepted. *Faculty research:* Theory, crime prevention, death penalty, criminal justice technology, policy.

University of Maryland Eastern Shore, Graduate Programs, Department of Criminal Justice, Princess Anne, MD 21853. Offers MS. *Program availability:* Part-time, evening/weekend. *Degree requirements:* For master's, comprehensive exam, thesis optional. *Entrance requirements:* For master's, GRE General Test, interview. Additional exam requirements/recommendations for international students: Required—TOEFL (minimum score 80 iBT).

University of Massachusetts Lowell, College of Fine Arts, Humanities and Social Sciences, School of Criminology and Justice Studies, Lowell, MA 01854. Offers criminal justice (MA). *Program availability:* Part-time, evening/weekend. *Degree requirements:* For master's, thesis optional. *Entrance requirements:* For master's, GRE General Test or MAT. Electronic applications accepted. *Faculty research:* Family violence, criminal justice management, corrections, policing, delinquency.

University of Memphis, Graduate School, College of Arts and Sciences, Department of Criminology and Criminal Justice, Memphis, TN 38152. Offers MA. *Program availability:* Part-time. *Faculty:* 3 full-time (0 women), 2 part-time/adjunct (1 woman). *Students:* 15 full-time (10 women), 8 part-time (4 women); includes 5 minority (3 Black or African American, non-Hispanic/Latino; 1 Asian, non-Hispanic/Latino; 1 Native Hawaiian or other Pacific Islander, non-Hispanic/Latino), 1 international. Average age 29. 19 applicants, 89% accepted, 10 enrolled. In 2017, 7 master's awarded. *Degree requirements:* For master's, comprehensive exam, thesis optional. *Entrance requirements:* For master's, GRE General Test, minimum GPA of 3.0. Additional exam requirements/recommendations for international students: Required—TOEFL (minimum score 550 paper-based; 79 iBT). *Application deadline:* For fall admission, 6/1 for domestic students; for spring admission, 11/1 for domestic students. Application fee: $35 ($60 for international students). Electronic applications accepted. *Expenses:* Contact institution. *Financial support:* In 2017–18, 11 students received support, including 6 research assistantships with full tuition reimbursements available (averaging $14,666 per year), 3 teaching assistantships with full tuition reimbursements available (averaging $16,000 per year); career-related internships or fieldwork, Federal Work-Study, institutionally sponsored loans, scholarships/grants, tuition waivers (partial), and unspecified assistantships also available. Financial award application deadline: 2/1; financial award applicants required to submit FAFSA. *Faculty research:* Violence, crime prevention, crime analysis, survey research, crisis intervention. *Unit head:* Dr. K. B. Turner, Chair, 901-678-3397, Fax: 901-678-5279, E-mail: kbturner@memphis.edu. *Application contact:* Dr. Bert Burraston, Coordinator of Graduate Studies, 901-678-4767, Fax: 901-678-5279, E-mail: bbrrstom@memphis.edu.
Website: http://www.memphis.edu/cjustice/

University of Michigan–Dearborn, College of Arts, Sciences, and Letters, Master of Science in Criminology and Criminal Justice Program, Dearborn, MI 48128. Offers MS. *Program availability:* Part-time, evening/weekend. *Faculty:* 7 full-time (3 women), 10 part-time/adjunct (4 women). *Students:* 9 full-time (7 women), 7 part-time (3 women); includes 5 minority (2 Black or African American, non-Hispanic/Latino; 2 Hispanic/Latino; 1 Two or more races, non-Hispanic/Latino). Average age 30. 24 applicants, 96% accepted, 14 enrolled. *Degree requirements:* For master's, thesis optional. *Entrance requirements:* Additional exam requirements/recommendations for international students: Required—TOEFL (minimum score 84 iBT), IELTS (minimum score 6.5). *Application deadline:* For fall admission, 8/1 for domestic students, 5/1 for international students; for winter admission, 12/1 for domestic students, 9/1 for international students; for spring admission, 4/1 for domestic students, 1/1 for international students. Applications are processed on a rolling basis. Application fee: $60. Electronic applications accepted. *Expenses:* $683 per credit hour in-state; $1,176 per credit hour out-state. *Financial support:* In 2017–18, 18 students received support. Scholarships/grants available. Financial award application deadline: 3/1; financial award applicants required to submit FAFSA. *Faculty research:* Forensic science, immigration, deviance, mindfulness, substance use and misuse, sexual assault. *Unit head:* Dr. Juliette Roddy, Director, 313-436-9180, E-mail: jroddy@umich.edu. *Application contact:* Office of Graduate Studies, 313-583-6321, E-mail: umd-graduatestudies@umich.edu.
Website: https://umdearborn.edu/casl/graduate-programs/programs/master-science-criminology-and-criminal-justice

University of Michigan–Flint, Graduate Programs, Program in Public Administration, Flint, MI 48502-1950. Offers administration of non-profit agencies (MPA); criminal justice administration (MPA); educational administration (MPA); general public administration (MPA); healthcare administration (MPA). *Program availability:* Part-time. *Faculty:* 1 full-time (0 women), 2 part-time/adjunct (both women). *Students:* 13 full-time (6 women), 88 part-time (59 women); includes 38 minority (29 Black or African American, non-Hispanic/Latino; 3 American Indian or Alaska Native, non-Hispanic/Latino; 2 Asian, non-Hispanic/Latino; 4 Two or more races, non-Hispanic/Latino), 3 international. Average age 37. 63 applicants, 81% accepted, 37 enrolled. In 2017, 55 master's awarded. *Degree requirements:* For master's, thesis or alternative, internship. *Entrance requirements:* For master's, bachelor's degree from regionally-accredited institution, minimum overall undergraduate GPA of 3.0. Additional exam requirements/recommendations for international students: Required—TOEFL (minimum score 84 iBT), IELTS (minimum score 6.5). *Application deadline:* For fall admission, 8/1 for domestic students, 5/1 for international students; for winter admission, 11/15 for domestic students, 9/1 for international students; for spring admission, 3/15 for domestic students, 1/1 for international students; for summer admission, 5/15 for domestic students. Applications are processed on a rolling basis. Application fee: $55. Electronic applications accepted. *Expenses:* Contact institution. *Financial support:* Career-related internships or fieldwork, Federal Work-Study, and scholarships/grants available. Support available to part-time students. Financial award application deadline: 3/1; financial award applicants required to submit FAFSA. *Unit head:* Dr. Kathryn Schellenberg, Director, 810-762-3340, E-mail: kathsch@umflint.edu. *Application contact:* Bradley T. Maki, Director of Graduate Admissions, 810-762-3171, Fax: 810-766-6789, E-mail: bmaki@umflint.edu.
Website: http://www.umflint.edu/graduateprograms/public-administration-mpa

University of Minnesota, Duluth, Graduate School, College of Liberal Arts, Department of Sociology/Anthropology, Program in Criminology, Duluth, MN 55812-2496. Offers MA. *Program availability:* Part-time, evening/weekend. *Degree requirements:* For master's, thesis or alternative. *Entrance requirements:* For master's, minimum GPA of 3.0, letter of recommendation, personal statement. Additional exam requirements/recommendations for international students: Required—TOEFL. *Faculty research:* Restorative justice, juvenile delinquency, social justice, program evaluation.

University of Mississippi, Graduate School, School of Applied Sciences, University, MS 38677. Offers communicative disorders (MS); criminal justice (MCJ); exercise science (MS); food and nutrition services (MS); health and kinesiology (PhD); health promotion (MS); nutrition and hospitality management (PhD); park and recreation management (MA); social welfare (PhD); social work (MSW). *Faculty:* 66 full-time (38 women), 33 part-time/adjunct (14 women). *Students:* 182 full-time (139 women), 41 part-time (27 women); includes 49 minority (41 Black or African American, non-Hispanic/Latino; 1 American Indian or Alaska Native, non-Hispanic/Latino; 3 Asian, non-Hispanic/Latino; 3 Hispanic/Latino; 1 Two or more races, non-Hispanic/Latino), 13 international. Average age 26. *Entrance requirements:* For master's, GRE General Test, minimum GPA of 3.0. Additional exam requirements/recommendations for international students: Required—TOEFL. *Application deadline:* For fall admission, 4/1 for domestic students; for spring admission, 10/1 for domestic students. Applications are processed on a rolling basis. Application fee: $50. Electronic applications accepted. *Financial support:* Scholarships/grants available. Financial award application deadline: 3/1; financial award applicants required to submit FAFSA. *Unit head:* Dr. Teresa C. Carithers, Dean, 662-915-1081, Fax: 662-915-5717, E-mail: applsci@olemiss.edu.

University of Missouri–Kansas City, College of Arts and Sciences, Department of Criminal Justice and Criminology, Kansas City, MO 64110-2499. Offers MS. *Program availability:* Part-time, evening/weekend. *Degree requirements:* For master's, thesis optional. *Entrance requirements:* For master's, GRE, minimum GPA of 3.0 in major, 2.7 overall. Additional exam requirements/recommendations for international students: Required—TOEFL (minimum score 550 paper-based; 80 iBT). Electronic applications accepted. *Faculty research:* Death penalty, community corrections, urban community and neighborhoods.

University of Missouri–St. Louis, College of Arts and Sciences, Department of Criminology and Criminal Justice, St. Louis, MO 63121. Offers MA, PhD. *Faculty:* 16 full-time (7 women), 2 part-time/adjunct (0 women). *Students:* 37 full-time (24 women), 14 part-time (9 women); includes 10 minority (4 Black or African American, non-Hispanic/Latino; 3 Hispanic/Latino; 1 Native Hawaiian or other Pacific Islander, non-Hispanic/Latino; 2 Two or more races, non-Hispanic/Latino). 72 applicants, 49% accepted, 17 enrolled. *Degree requirements:* For doctorate, thesis/dissertation. *Entrance requirements:* For master's, essay; 2 letters of recommendation; for doctorate, GRE General Test, writing sample, 3 letters of recommendation. Additional exam requirements/recommendations for international students: Required—TOEFL (minimum score 550 paper-based; 65 iBT), IELTS (minimum score 6.5). *Application deadline:* For fall admission, 2/1 priority date for domestic and international students. Applications are processed on a rolling basis. Application fee: $50 ($40 for international students). Electronic applications accepted. *Expenses:* Tuition, state resident: part-time $476.50 per credit hour. Tuition, nonresident: part-time $1169.70 per credit hour. *Financial support:* Fellowships with full tuition reimbursements, research assistantships with tuition reimbursements, teaching assistantships with tuition reimbursements, and career-related internships or fieldwork available. Financial award applicants required to submit FAFSA. *Faculty research:* Crime control, criminological theory, juvenile delinquency, violence, drugs. *Unit head:* Dr. David Klinger, Chair, 314-516-7012, Fax: 314-516-5048, E-mail: klingerd@umsl.edu. *Application contact:* 314-516-5458, Fax: 314-516-6996, E-mail: gradadm@umsl.edu.
Website: http://www.umsl.edu/ccj/

University of Montana, Graduate School, College of Humanities and Sciences, Department of Sociology, Missoula, MT 59812. Offers criminology (MA); inequality and social justice (MA); rural and environmental change (MA); sociology (MA). *Entrance requirements:* For master's, GRE General Test. Additional exam requirements/recommendations for international students: Required—TOEFL. *Faculty research:* Housing, homelessness, hunger, infant mortality, work safety.

University of Nebraska at Omaha, Graduate Studies, College of Public Affairs and Community Service, School of Criminology and Criminal Justice, Omaha, NE 68182. Offers criminology and criminal justice (MA, MS, PhD); managing juvenile and adult populations (Certificate). *Program availability:* Part-time, evening/weekend. Terminal master's awarded for partial completion of doctoral program. *Degree requirements:* For master's, comprehensive exam, thesis (for some programs); for doctorate, comprehensive exam, thesis/dissertation. *Entrance requirements:* For master's, GRE General Test, previous course work in criminal justice, statistics, and research methods; minimum GPA of 3.0; official transcripts; statement of purpose; 2 letters of recommendation; for doctorate, GRE General Test, master's degree, minimum undergraduate GPA of 3.0, 3 letters of recommendation, statement of purpose, writing sample, resume. Additional exam requirements/recommendations for international students: Required—TOEFL, IELTS, PTE. Electronic applications accepted.

University of Nevada, Las Vegas, Graduate College, Greenspun College of Urban Affairs, Department of Criminal Justice, Las Vegas, NV 89154-5009. Offers criminal justice (MA); criminology and criminal justice (PhD). *Program availability:* Part-time. *Faculty:* 7 full-time (4 women). *Students:* 25 full-time (18 women), 2 part-time (both women); includes 8 minority (1 Black or African American, non-Hispanic/Latino; 4 Hispanic/Latino; 1 Native Hawaiian or other Pacific Islander, non-Hispanic/Latino; 2 Two or more races, non-Hispanic/Latino), 3 international. Average age 27. 37 applicants, 49% accepted, 10 enrolled. In 2017, 11 master's awarded. *Degree requirements:* For master's, comprehensive exam, thesis, oral examination; for doctorate, comprehensive exam, thesis/dissertation. *Entrance requirements:* For master's, GRE General Test, statement of purpose; bachelor's degree; 2 letters of recommendation; for doctorate, GRE General Test (minimum scores: 153 for Quantitative, 155 for Verbal, and 4.5 for Analytical Writing), 3 letters of recommendation; statement of purpose; personal interview. Additional exam requirements/recommendations for international students: Required—TOEFL (minimum score 550 paper-based; 80 iBT), IELTS (minimum score 7). *Application deadline:* For fall admission, 4/15 for domestic students. Application fee: $60 ($95 for international students). Electronic applications accepted. *Expenses:* $275 per credit, $850 per course, $7,969 per year resident, $22,157 per year non-resident, $7,094 non-resident fee (7 credits or more), $1,307 annual health insurance fee. *Financial support:* In 2017–18, 23 students received support, including 1 fellowship with full and partial tuition reimbursement available (averaging $20,000 per year), 4 research assistantships with full and partial tuition reimbursements available (averaging $18,688 per year), 19 teaching assistantships with full and partial tuition reimbursements available (averaging $15,750 per year); institutionally sponsored loans, scholarships/

Criminal Justice and Criminology

grants, health care benefits, and unspecified assistantships also available. Financial award application deadline: 3/15; financial award applicants required to submit FAFSA. *Faculty research:* Administration of justice, corrections, criminological theory, policing, sociology of law. *Total annual research expenditures:* $302,839. *Unit head:* Dr. Joel Lieberman, Chair/Associate Professor, 702-895-0249, Fax: 702-895-0252, E-mail: joel.lieberman@unlv.edu. *Application contact:* Dr. Tamara Madensen, Graduate Coordinator, 702-895-5903, Fax: 702-895-0252, E-mail: tamara.madensen@unlv.edu. Website: http://criminaljustice.unlv.edu/grad/

University of Nevada, Reno, Graduate School, College of Liberal Arts, School of Social Research and Justice Studies, Department of Criminal Justice, Reno, NV 89557. Offers MA. *Degree requirements:* For master's, comprehensive exam, thesis optional. *Entrance requirements:* For master's, GRE or LSAT, undergraduate degree in criminal justice with minimum GPA of 3.0. Additional exam requirements/recommendations for international students: Required—TOEFL (minimum score 500 paper-based; 61 iBT), IELTS (minimum score 6). Electronic applications accepted. *Faculty research:* Criminal justice system, social policy interaction.

University of Nevada, Reno, Graduate School, College of Liberal Arts, School of Social Research and Justice Studies, Program in Justice Management, Reno, NV 89557. Offers MJM. *Program availability:* Part-time, online learning. *Degree requirements:* For master's, thesis optional. *Entrance requirements:* For master's, minimum GPA of 2.75. Additional exam requirements/recommendations for international students: Required—TOEFL (minimum score 500 paper-based; 61 iBT), IELTS (minimum score 6). Electronic applications accepted. *Faculty research:* Justice administration, adult justice management, juvenile justice management.

★ **University of New Haven,** Graduate School, Henry C. Lee College of Criminal Justice and Forensic Sciences, Program in Criminal Justice, West Haven, CT 06516. Offers criminal justice (MS, PhD); criminal justice management (Graduate Certificate). *Program availability:* Part-time, evening/weekend, 100% online, blended/hybrid learning. *Students:* 75 full-time (55 women), 70 part-time (43 women); includes 41 minority (18 Black or African American, non-Hispanic/Latino; 8 Asian, non-Hispanic/Latino; 11 Hispanic/Latino; 4 Two or more races, non-Hispanic/Latino), 10 international. Average age 30. 110 applicants, 75% accepted, 43 enrolled. In 2017, 71 master's awarded. *Degree requirements:* For master's, thesis or alternative. *Entrance requirements:* Additional exam requirements/recommendations for international students: Required—TOEFL (minimum score 80 iBT), IELTS, PTE (minimum score 53). *Application deadline:* Applications are processed on a rolling basis. Application fee: $50. Electronic applications accepted. Application fee is waived when completed online. *Expenses: Tuition:* Full-time $16,020; part-time $890 per credit hour. *Required fees:* $220; $90 per term. *Financial support:* Research assistantships with partial tuition reimbursements, teaching assistantships with partial tuition reimbursements, Federal Work-Study, scholarships/grants, and unspecified assistantships available. Support available to part-time students. Financial award applicants required to submit FAFSA. *Application contact:* Michelle Mason, Director of Graduate Enrollment, 203-932-7067, E-mail: mmason@newhaven.edu. Website: http://www.newhaven.edu/5921/

See Display below and Close-Up on page 799.

★ **University of New Haven,** Graduate School, Henry C. Lee College of Criminal Justice and Forensic Sciences, Program in Investigations, West Haven, CT 06516. Offers criminal investigations (MS); digital forensic investigations (MS); financial crimes investigations (MS). *Program availability:* Part-time, 100% online. *Students:* 51 full-time (30 women), 52 part-time (27 women); includes 34 minority (24 Black or African American, non-Hispanic/Latino; 3 Asian, non-Hispanic/Latino; 6 Hispanic/Latino; 1 Native Hawaiian or other Pacific Islander, non-Hispanic/Latino), 1 international. Average age 31. 97 applicants, 90% accepted, 57 enrolled. In 2017, 15 master's awarded. *Application deadline:* Applications are processed on a rolling basis. Application fee: $50. *Expenses: Tuition:* Full-time $16,020; part-time $890 per credit hour. *Required fees:* $220; $90 per term. *Application contact:* Michelle Mason, Director of Graduate Enrollment, 203-932-7067, E-mail: mmason@newhaven.edu. Website: http://online.newhaven.edu/masters-in-investigations/

See Display below and Close-Up on page 799.

University of North Alabama, College of Arts and Sciences, Department of Interdisciplinary and Professional Studies, Florence, AL 35632-0001. Offers professional studies (MPS), including community development, information technology, security and safety leadership. *Program availability:* Part-time, 100% online. *Faculty:* 4 full-time (1 woman), 1 part-time/adjunct (0 women). *Students:* 19 full-time (9 women), 24 part-time (12 women); includes 7 minority (5 Black or African American, non-Hispanic/Latino; 1 American Indian or Alaska Native, non-Hispanic/Latino; 1 Asian, non-Hispanic/Latino), 13 international. Average age 35. 34 applicants, 65% accepted, 17 enrolled. In 2017, 24 master's awarded. *Entrance requirements:* For master's, ETS PPI, personal statement; three letters of recommendation. Additional exam requirements/recommendations for international students: Required—TOEFL (minimum score 79 iBT), IELTS (minimum score 6), PTE (minimum score 54). *Application deadline:* Applications are processed on a rolling basis. Application fee: $50 ($100 for international students). Electronic applications accepted. *Expenses:* Tuition, state resident: full-time $7824; part-time $5943 per year. Tuition, nonresident: full-time $15,648; part-time $11,736 per year. *Required fees:* $3064; $2298 per unit. Tuition and fees vary according to course load and reciprocity agreements. *Financial support:* In 2017–18, 17 students received support. Federal Work-Study, scholarships/grants, and unspecified assistantships available. Financial award application deadline: 2/1; financial award applicants required to submit FAFSA. *Unit head:* Dr. Craig T. Robertson, Director, 256-765-5003, E-mail: ctrobertson@una.edu. *Application contact:* Hillary N. Coats, Graduate Admissions Coordinator, 256-765-4447, E-mail: graduate@una.edu. Website: https://www.una.edu/interdisciplinary-studies/

University of North Alabama, College of Arts and Sciences, Department of Politics, Justice, and Law, Florence, AL 35632-0001. Offers criminal justice (MSCJ). *Program availability:* Part-time, 100% online. *Faculty:* 4 full-time (0 women), 3 part-time/adjunct (1 woman). *Students:* 5 full-time (4 women), 17 part-time (11 women); includes 9 minority (6 Black or African American, non-Hispanic/Latino; 3 Hispanic/Latino). Average age 30. 18 applicants, 94% accepted, 9 enrolled. In 2017, 6 master's awarded. *Degree requirements:* For master's, comprehensive exam (for some programs), thesis optional. *Entrance requirements:* For master's, GRE General Test, MAT, three letters of recommendation; essay. Additional exam requirements/recommendations for international students: Required—TOEFL (minimum score 79 iBT), IELTS (minimum score 6), PTE (minimum score 54). *Application deadline:* Applications are processed on a rolling basis. Application fee: $50 ($100 for international students). Electronic applications accepted. *Expenses:* Tuition, state resident: full-time $7824; part-time $5943 per year. Tuition, nonresident: full-time $15,648; part-time $11,736 per year. *Required fees:* $3064; $2298 per unit. Tuition and fees vary according to course load and reciprocity agreements. *Financial support:* Federal Work-Study, scholarships/grants, and unspecified assistantships available. Financial award application deadline: 2/1; financial award applicants required to submit FAFSA. *Unit head:* Dr. Tim Collins, Chair, 256-765-5045, E-mail: jtcollins@una.edu. *Application contact:* Hillary N. Coats, Graduate Admissions Coordinator, 256-765-4447, E-mail: graduate@una.edu. Website: http://www.una.edu/criminaljustice/

The University of North Carolina at Charlotte, College of Liberal Arts and Sciences, Department of Criminal Justice and Criminology, Charlotte, NC 28223-0001. Offers MS. *Program availability:* Part-time, evening/weekend. *Faculty:* 15 full-time (8 women). *Students:* 9 full-time (all women), 9 part-time (6 women); includes 6 minority (4 Black or African American, non-Hispanic/Latino; 2 Hispanic/Latino). Average age 23. 14 applicants, 50% accepted, 6 enrolled. In 2017, 6 master's awarded. *Degree requirements:* For master's, thesis or comprehensive exam. *Entrance requirements:* For master's, GRE, official copies of all undergraduate/graduate transcripts; minimum of three letters of recommendation; personal statement; minimum GPA of 3.0 (preferred). Additional exam requirements/recommendations for international students: Required—TOEFL (minimum score 523 paper-based, 70 iBT) or IELTS (6.5). *Application deadline:* For fall admission, 3/1 priority date for domestic and international students; for spring admission, 10/1 priority date for domestic and international students; for summer admission, 4/1 priority date for domestic and international students. Applications are processed on a rolling basis. Application fee: $75. Electronic applications accepted. *Expenses:* Tuition, state resident: full-time $4337. Tuition, nonresident: full-time $17,771. *Required fees:* $3211. Tuition and fees vary according to course load and program. *Financial support:* In 2017–18, 7 students received support, including 1 fellowship (averaging $47,476 per year), 1 research assistantship (averaging $7,500 per year), 5 teaching assistantships (averaging $10,400 per year); career-related internships or fieldwork, Federal Work-Study, institutionally sponsored loans, scholarships/grants, and unspecified assistantships also available. Support available to part-time students. Financial award application deadline: 3/1; financial award applicants required to submit FAFSA. *Total annual research expenditures:* $212,972. *Unit head:* Dr. Michael Turner, Chair, 704-687-0755, E-mail: mgturner@uncc.edu. *Application contact:* Kathy B. Giddings, Director of Graduate Admissions, 704-687-5503, Fax: 704-687-1668, E-mail: gradadm@uncc.edu.
Website: http://criminaljustice.uncc.edu/

The University of North Carolina at Greensboro, Graduate School, College of Arts and Sciences, Department of Sociology, Greensboro, NC 27412-5001. Offers criminology (MA); sociology (MA). *Program availability:* Part-time. *Degree requirements:* For master's, comprehensive exam, thesis. *Entrance requirements:* For master's, GRE General Test. Additional exam requirements/recommendations for international students: Required—TOEFL. Electronic applications accepted.

The University of North Carolina at Pembroke, The Graduate School, Department of Political Science and Public Administration, Pembroke, NC 28372-1510. Offers criminal justice (MPA); emergency management (MPA); health administration (MPA); public management (MPA). *Program availability:* Part-time, evening/weekend, online learning. *Degree requirements:* For master's, comprehensive exam, thesis optional. *Entrance requirements:* For master's, GRE General Test or MAT, minimum GPA of 3.0 in major, 2.5 overall; interview. Additional exam requirements/recommendations for international students: Required—TOEFL. *Application deadline:* Applications are processed on a rolling basis. Application fee: $45 ($60 for international students). *Financial support:* Application deadline: 4/15; applicants required to submit FAFSA. *Unit head:* Dr. Emily Neff-Sharum, Interim Director, 910-775-4409, E-mail: emily.neffsharum@uncp.edu.

The University of North Carolina Wilmington, College of Arts and Sciences, Department of Sociology and Criminology, Wilmington, NC 28403-3297. Offers MA. *Faculty:* 13 full-time (7 women). *Students:* 14 full-time (12 women), 5 part-time (0 women); includes 5 minority (1 Black or African American, non-Hispanic/Latino; 2 Hispanic/Latino; 2 Two or more races, non-Hispanic/Latino). Average age 24. 13 applicants, 54% accepted, 7 enrolled. In 2017, 6 master's awarded. *Degree requirements:* For master's, thesis or internship. *Entrance requirements:* For master's, GRE General Test, 3 letters of recommendation, statement of interest. Additional exam requirements/recommendations for international students: Required—TOEFL (minimum score 550 paper-based, 79 iBT), IELTS (minimum score 6.5). *Application deadline:* For fall admission, 2/15 priority date for domestic students. Applications are processed on a rolling basis. Application fee: $75. Electronic applications accepted. *Expenses:* Tuition, state resident: full-time $4626; part-time $226.76 per credit hour. Tuition, nonresident: full-time $17,834; part-time $874.22 per credit hour. *Required fees:* $2124. Tuition and fees vary according to program. *Financial support:* Research assistantships, teaching assistantships, scholarships/grants, and out-of-state tuition awards available. Financial award application deadline: 1/1; financial award applicants required to submit FAFSA. *Unit head:* Dr. Mike Maume, Chair, 910-962-7749, Fax: 910-962-7385, E-mail: maume@uncw.edu. *Application contact:* Dr. Daniel Buffington, Graduate Coordinator, 910-962-3434, Fax: 910-962-7385, E-mail: buffingtond@uncw.edu.
Website: http://www.uncw.edu/socgrad/index.html

University of North Dakota, Graduate School, College of Arts and Sciences, Program in Criminal Justice, Grand Forks, ND 58202. Offers PhD, JD/PhD. *Program availability:* Part-time. *Entrance requirements:* For doctorate, GRE General Test. Additional exam requirements/recommendations for international students: Required—TOEFL (minimum score 550 paper-based; 79 iBT), IELTS (minimum score 6.5). Electronic applications accepted.

University of Northern Colorado, Graduate School, College of Humanities and Social Sciences, Department of Criminology and Criminal Justice, Greeley, CO 80639. Offers criminal justice (MA).

University of North Florida, College of Arts and Sciences, Department of Criminology and Criminal Justice, Jacksonville, FL 32224. Offers criminal justice (MS). *Degree requirements:* For master's, comprehensive exam, thesis optional. *Entrance requirements:* For master's, GRE General Test, minimum GPA of 3.0 in last 60 hours, letters of recommendation. Additional exam requirements/recommendations for international students: Required—TOEFL (minimum score 500 paper-based; 61 iBT). Electronic applications accepted.

University of North Georgia, Department of Criminal Justice, Dahlonega, GA 30597. Offers MS. *Program availability:* Part-time, evening/weekend, online only, 100% online. *Faculty:* 3 full-time (1 woman). *Students:* 1 (woman) full-time, 14 part-time (10 women); includes 4 minority (3 Black or African American, non-Hispanic/Latino; 1 Two or more races, non-Hispanic/Latino). Average age 30. 14 applicants, 100% accepted, 7 enrolled. In 2017, 12 master's awarded. *Degree requirements:* For master's, comprehensive seminar. *Entrance requirements:* For master's, official transcripts, 3 UNG recommendation forms, letter of intent, professional resume. Additional exam requirements/recommendations for international students: Required—TOEFL (minimum score 550 paper-based; 79 iBT, IELTS (minimum score 6.5). *Application deadline:* For fall admission, 8/10 for domestic students; for spring admission, 12/10 for domestic students; for summer admission, 5/10 for domestic students. Application fee: $40. Electronic applications accepted. *Expenses:* Contact institution. *Financial support:* Fellowships and research assistantships available. Financial award application deadline: 3/17; financial award applicants required to submit FAFSA. *Unit head:* Dr. Brent Paterline, Department Head, 706-864-1914, E-mail: brent.paterline@ung.edu. *Application contact:* Melinda Maxwell, Director of Graduate Admissions, 706-864-1543, E-mail: melinda.maxwell@ung.edu.
Website: http://ung.edu/criminal-justice/

University of North Texas, Robert B. Toulouse School of Graduate Studies, Denton, TX 76203-5459. Offers accounting (MS); applied anthropology (MA, MS); applied behavior analysis (Certificate); applied geography (MA); applied technology and performance improvement (M Ed, MS); art education (MA); art history (MA); art museum education (Certificate); arts leadership (Certificate); audiology (Au D); behavior analysis (MS); behavioral science (PhD); biochemistry and molecular biology (MS); biology (MA, MS); biomedical engineering (MS); business analysis (MS); chemistry (MS); clinical health psychology (PhD); communication studies (MA, MS); computer engineering (MS); computer science (MS); counseling (M Ed, MS), including clinical mental health counseling (MS), college and university counseling, elementary school counseling, secondary school counseling; creative writing (MA); criminal justice (MS); curriculum and instruction (M Ed); decision sciences (MBA); design (MA, MFA), including fashion design (MFA), innovation studies, interior design (MFA); early childhood studies (MS); economics (MS); educational leadership (M Ed, Ed D); educational psychology (MS, PhD), including family studies (MS), gifted and talented (MS), human development (MS); learning and cognition (MS), research, measurement and evaluation (MS); electrical engineering (MS); emergency management (MPA); engineering technology (MS); English (MA); English as a second language (MA); environmental science (MS); finance (MBA, MS); financial management (MPA); French (MA); health services management (MBA); higher education (M Ed, Ed D); history (MA, MS); hospitality management (MS); human resources management (MPA); information science (MS); information systems (PhD); information technologies (MBA); interdisciplinary studies (MA, MS); international studies (MA); international sustainable tourism (MS); jazz studies (MM); journalism (MA, MJ, Graduate Certificate), including interactive and virtual digital communication (Graduate Certificate), narrative journalism (Graduate Certificate), public relations (Graduate Certificate); kinesiology (MS); linguistics (MA); local government management (MPA); logistics (PhD); logistics and supply chain management (MBA); long-term care, senior housing, and aging services (MA); management (PhD); marketing (MBA); mathematics (MA, MS); mechanical and energy engineering (MS, PhD); music (MA), including ethnomusicology, music theory, musicology, performance; music composition (PhD); music education (MM Ed, PhD); nonprofit management (MPA); operations and supply chain management (MBA); performance (MM, DMA); philosophy (MA); political science (MA); professional and technical communication (MA); radio, television and film (MA, MFA); rehabilitation counseling (Certificate); sociology (MA); Spanish (MA); special education (M Ed); speech-language pathology (MA); strategic management (MBA); studio art (MFA); teaching (M Ed); MBA/MS. *Program availability:* Part-time, evening/weekend, online learning. Terminal master's awarded for partial completion of doctoral program. *Degree requirements:* For master's, variable foreign language requirement, comprehensive exam (for some programs), thesis (for some programs); for doctorate, variable foreign language requirement, comprehensive exam (for some programs), thesis/dissertation; for other advanced degree, variable foreign language requirement, comprehensive exam (for some programs). *Entrance requirements:* For master's and doctorate, GRE, GMAT. Additional exam requirements/recommendations for international students: Required—TOEFL (minimum score 550 paper-based; 79 iBT). Electronic applications accepted.

University of North Texas at Dallas, Graduate School, Dallas, TX 75241. Offers accounting (MBA); counseling (M Ed, MS); criminal justice (MS); curriculum and instruction (M Ed); educational administration (M Ed); human resources and organizational behavior (MBA); public leadership (MS); strategic management (MBA).

University of Oklahoma, College of Professional and Continuing Studies, Norman, OK 73019. Offers administrative leadership (MA, Graduate Certificate), including government and military leadership (MA), organizational leadership (MA), volunteer and non-profit leadership (MA); corrections management (Graduate Certificate); criminal justice (MS); integrated studies (MA), including human and health services administration, integrated studies; museum studies (MA); prevention science (MPS); restorative justice administration (Graduate Certificate). *Program availability:* Part-time, 100% online, blended/hybrid learning. *Faculty:* 16 full-time (8 women). *Students:* 64 full-time (39 women), 558 part-time (278 women); includes 191 minority (42 Black or African American, non-Hispanic/Latino; 42 American Indian or Alaska Native, non-Hispanic/Latino; 16 Asian, non-Hispanic/Latino; 46 Hispanic/Latino; 1 Native Hawaiian or other Pacific Islander, non-Hispanic/Latino; 44 Two or more races, non-Hispanic/Latino), 4 international. Average age 35. 151 applicants, 95% accepted, 97 enrolled. In 2017, 202 master's, 11 other advanced degrees awarded. *Degree requirements:* For master's, comprehensive exam, thesis optional, 33 credit hours; project/internship (for museum studies program only); for Graduate Certificate, 12 graduate credit hours (for Graduate Certificate). *Entrance requirements:* For master's and Graduate Certificate, minimum GPA of 3.0 in last 60 undergraduate hours; statement of goals; resume. Additional exam requirements/recommendations for international students: Required—TOEFL (minimum score 79 iBT) or IELTS (minimum score 6.5). *Application deadline:* For fall admission, 7/15 for domestic and international students; for winter admission, 12/1 for domestic and international students; for spring admission, 5/1 for domestic and international students. Applications are processed on a rolling basis. Application fee: $50 ($100 for international students). Electronic applications accepted. *Expenses:* Tuition, state resident: full-time $5119; part-time $213.30 per credit hour. Tuition, nonresident: full-time $19,778; part-time $824.10 per credit hour. *Required fees:* $3458; $133.55 per credit hour. $126.50 per semester. *Financial support:* In 2017–18, 92 students received support. Career-related internships or fieldwork, institutionally sponsored loans, scholarships/grants, health care benefits, and tuition waivers available. Support available to part-time students. Financial award application deadline: 6/1; financial award applicants required to submit FAFSA. *Faculty research:* Change management and leadership; policing and corrections management; neuro-psychology of addiction; disproportionate minority contact; ethnic identity and nationalism. *Unit head:* Dr. Martha L. Banz, Associate Provost for Continuing Education/Interim Dean, College of Professional and Continuing Studies, 405-325-4414, Fax: 405-325-7132, E-mail: mlbanz@ou.edu. *Application contact:* Lindsey Gunderson, Graduate Academic Advisor, 405-325-5827, Fax: 405-325-7132, E-mail: lindsey.gunderson@ou.edu.
Website: https://pacs.ou.edu/

University of Ottawa, Faculty of Graduate and Postdoctoral Studies, Faculty of Social Sciences, Department of Criminology, Ottawa, ON K1N 6N5, Canada. Offers MA, MCA, PhD. *Degree requirements:* For master's, thesis or alternative. *Entrance requirements:* For master's, honors bachelor's degree or equivalent, minimum B average. Electronic applications accepted. *Faculty research:* Creation and reform of criminal policies in Canada.

University of Pennsylvania, School of Arts and Sciences, Graduate Group in Criminology, Philadelphia, PA 19104. Offers MA, MS, PhD. *Faculty:* 15 full-time (2 women), 1 part-time/adjunct (0 women). *Students:* 22 full-time (19 women), 2 part-time (both women); includes 7 minority (2 Asian, non-Hispanic/Latino; 4 Hispanic/Latino; 1 Two or more races, non-Hispanic/Latino), 6 international. Average age 25. 63 applicants, 51% accepted, 20 enrolled. In 2017, 18 master's, 1 doctorate awarded.
Website: http://www.sas.upenn.edu/graduate-division

University of Phoenix–Bay Area Campus, College of Criminal Justice and Security, San Jose, CA 95134-1805. Offers administration of justice and security (MS).

Criminal Justice and Criminology

University of Phoenix–Dallas Campus, College of Criminal Justice and Security, Dallas, TX 75251. Offers administration of justice and security (MS). *Program availability:* Online learning. *Degree requirements:* For master's, thesis (for some programs). *Entrance requirements:* For master's, minimum undergraduate GPA of 2.5, 3 years of work experience. Additional exam requirements/recommendations for international students: Required—TOEFL (minimum score 550 paper-based; 79 iBT). Electronic applications accepted.

University of Phoenix–Online Campus, College of Justice and Security, Phoenix, AZ 85034-7209. Offers administration of justice and security (MS), including administration of justice and security, global and homeland security, law enforcement organizations; public administration (MPA). *Program availability:* Evening/weekend, online learning. *Entrance requirements:* Additional exam requirements/recommendations for international students: Required—TOEFL, TOEIC (Test of English as an International Communication), Berlitz Online English Proficiency Exam, PTE, or IELTS. Electronic applications accepted. *Expenses:* Contact institution.

University of Phoenix–Phoenix Campus, College of Criminal Justice and Security, Tempe, AZ 85282-2371. Offers administration of justice and security (MS); global and homeland security (MS); law enforcement organizations (MS); public administration (MPA). *Program availability:* Evening/weekend, online learning. *Entrance requirements:* Additional exam requirements/recommendations for international students: Required—TOEFL, TOEIC (Test of English as an International Communication), Berlitz Online English Proficiency Exam, PTE, or IELTS. Electronic applications accepted. *Expenses:* Contact institution.

University of Phoenix–San Antonio Campus, College of Criminal Justice and Security, San Antonio, TX 78230. Offers administration of justice and security (MS).

University of Pittsburgh, School of Law, Master of Studies in Law Program, Pittsburgh, PA 15260. Offers biomedical and health services research (MSL); business law (MSL), including commercial law, corporate law, general business law, international business, tax law; Constitutional law (MSL); criminal law and justice (MSL); disability law (MSL); elder and estate planning law (MSL); employment and labor law (MSL); energy law (MSL); environmental and real estate law (MSL); family law (MSL); health law (MSL); intellectual property and technology law (MSL); international and human rights law (MSL); jurisprudence (MSL); regulatory law (MSL); self-designed (MSL). *Program availability:* Part-time. *Faculty:* 47 full-time (22 women), 116 part-time/adjunct (29 women). *Students:* 4 full-time (2 women), 17 part-time (12 women); includes 6 minority (5 Black or African American, non-Hispanic/Latino; 1 Hispanic/Latino). Average age 26. 28 applicants, 75% accepted, 15 enrolled. In 2017, 15 master's awarded. *Entrance requirements:* Additional exam requirements/recommendations for international students: Required—TOEFL (minimum score 600 paper-based; 100 iBT), IELTS (minimum score 7). *Application deadline:* For fall admission, 6/30 for domestic students, 5/1 for international students. Applications are processed on a rolling basis. Application fee: $0. *Faculty research:* Law, health law, business law, contracts, intellectual property, environmental law. *Unit head:* Prof. Alan Meisel, Director, 412-648-1384, Fax: 412-648-2649, E-mail: meisel@pitt.edu. *Application contact:* Beth Ann Pischke, Administrative Coordinator, 412-648-7120, Fax: 412-648-2649, E-mail: pischke@pitt.edu.
Website: http://www.law.pitt.edu/msl

University of Providence, Graduate Studies, Program in Criminal Justice, Great Falls, MT 59405. Offers MSM. *Program availability:* Part-time, evening/weekend. *Degree requirements:* For master's, thesis optional. *Entrance requirements:* For master's, GRE General Test or MAT, 3 letters of recommendation. Additional exam requirements/recommendations for international students: Required—TOEFL (minimum score 500 paper-based). Electronic applications accepted. *Faculty research:* Delinquency, domestic violence law.

University of Regina, Faculty of Graduate Studies and Research, Faculty of Arts, Department of Justice Studies, Regina, SK S4S 0A2, Canada. Offers justice studies (MA); police studies (MA). *Program availability:* Part-time. *Faculty:* 7 full-time (4 women). *Students:* 5 full-time (3 women), 2 part-time (both women). 14 applicants, 21% accepted. In 2017, 3 master's awarded. *Degree requirements:* For master's, thesis. *Entrance requirements:* For master's, writing sample. Additional exam requirements/recommendations for international students: Required—TOEFL (minimum score 580 paper-based; 80 iBT), IELTS (minimum score 6.5), PTE (minimum score 59). *Application deadline:* For fall admission, 1/15 for domestic and international students. Application fee: $100. Electronic applications accepted. *Expenses:* $10,681. *Financial support:* In 2017–18, fellowships (averaging $6,000 per year), 1 teaching assistantship (averaging $2,562 per year) was awarded; research assistantships also available. Financial award application deadline: 6/15. *Faculty research:* Restorative and social justice, policing, public policy, social policy and planning. *Unit head:* Dr. Nick Jones, Department Head, 306-585-4862, Fax: 306-585-4815, E-mail: nick.jones@uregina.ca. *Application contact:* Dr. Sarah Britto, Graduate Program Coordinator, 306-585-4035, Fax: 306-585-4815, E-mail: sarah.britto@uregina.ca.
Website: http://www.uregina.ca/arts/justice-studies

University of San Diego, Division of Professional and Continuing Education, San Diego, CA 92110-2492. Offers cyber security operations and leadership (MS); law enforcement and public safety leadership (MS). *Program availability:* Part-time-only, evening/weekend, 100% online. *Faculty:* 13 part-time/adjunct (1 woman). *Students:* 239 part-time (60 women); includes 88 minority (12 Black or African American, non-Hispanic/Latino; 18 Asian, non-Hispanic/Latino; 55 Hispanic/Latino; 3 Two or more races, non-Hispanic/Latino), 1 international. Average age 39. 197 applicants, 91% accepted, 118 enrolled. *Entrance requirements:* For master's, GMAT, GRE, or LSAT if GPA is under 2.75. Additional exam requirements/recommendations for international students: Required—TOEFL (minimum score 90 iBT). *Application deadline:* For fall admission, 8/7 for domestic students; for spring admission, 12/3 for domestic students; for summer admission, 4/24 for domestic students. Applications are processed on a rolling basis. Application fee: $45. Electronic applications accepted. *Financial support:* Application deadline: 4/1; applicants required to submit FAFSA. *Unit head:* 619-260-4585, Fax: 619-260-2961, E-mail: continuinged@sandiego.edu. *Application contact:* Monica Mahon, Associate Director of Graduate Admissions, 619-260-4524, Fax: 619-260-4158, E-mail: grads@sandiego.edu.
Website: http://pce.sandiego.edu/

University of South Africa, College of Law, Pretoria, South Africa. Offers correctional services management (M Tech); criminology (MA, PhD); law (LL M, LL D); penology (MA, PhD); police science (MA, PhD); policing (M Tech); security risk management (M Tech); social science in criminology (MA).

University of South Carolina, The Graduate School, College of Arts and Sciences, Department of Criminology and Criminal Justice, Columbia, SC 29208. Offers MA, PhD, JD/MA. *Program availability:* Part-time, evening/weekend. *Degree requirements:* For master's, comprehensive exam, thesis; for doctorate, comprehensive exam, thesis/dissertation. *Entrance requirements:* For master's and doctorate, GRE. Additional exam requirements/recommendations for international students: Required—TOEFL. Electronic applications accepted. *Faculty research:* Juvenile delinquency, substance abuse, policy development, minority issues, law enforcement services.

University of South Dakota, Graduate School, College of Arts and Sciences, Program in Administrative Studies, Vermillion, SD 57069. Offers addiction studies (MSA); criminal justice studies (MSA); health services administration (MSA); human resources (MSA); interdisciplinary studies (MSA); long term care administration (MSA); organizational leadership (MSA). *Program availability:* Part-time, evening/weekend, 100% online. *Degree requirements:* For master's, thesis or alternative. *Entrance requirements:* For master's, 3 years of work or experience, minimum GPA of 2.7, resume. Additional exam requirements/recommendations for international students: Required—TOEFL (minimum score 550 paper-based; 79 iBT). *Application deadline:* Applications are processed on a rolling basis. Application fee: $35. Electronic applications accepted. *Financial support:* Teaching assistantships with partial tuition reimbursements available. Financial award applicants required to submit FAFSA. *Application contact:* Graduate School, 605-658-6140, Fax: 605-677-6118, E-mail: grad@usd.edu.
Website: http://www.usd.edu/onlinemsa

University of Southern Mississippi, College of Science and Technology, School of Criminal Justice, Hattiesburg, MS 39406-0001. Offers criminal justice (MA, MS, PhD); forensic science (MS). *Program availability:* Part-time. *Students:* 5 full-time (3 women), 1 (woman) part-time. 7 applicants, 57% accepted, 4 enrolled. *Degree requirements:* For master's, comprehensive exam, thesis; for doctorate, comprehensive exam, thesis/dissertation. *Entrance requirements:* For master's, GRE General Test, minimum GPA of 2.75 in last 60 hours, 3.0 in field of study; for doctorate, GRE General Test, minimum GPA of 3.5. Additional exam requirements/recommendations for international students: Required—TOEFL, IELTS. *Application deadline:* For fall admission, 3/15 priority date for domestic students, 3/15 for international students; for spring admission, 1/10 priority date for domestic and international students. Applications are processed on a rolling basis. Application fee: $60. Electronic applications accepted. *Expenses:* Tuition, state resident: full-time $3830. *Financial support:* Research assistantships with full tuition reimbursements, teaching assistantships with full tuition reimbursements, career-related internships or fieldwork, Federal Work-Study, institutionally sponsored loans, scholarships/grants, health care benefits, and unspecified assistantships available. Financial award application deadline: 3/15; financial award applicants required to submit FAFSA. *Faculty research:* Crime in the family, police training models, humanities and criminal justice. *Unit head:* Dr. Lisa Nored, Director, 601-266-4509, Fax: 601-266-4391. *Application contact:* Tera Wright, Manager of Graduate Admissions, 601-266-4509, Fax: 601-266-4391.
Website: https://www.usm.edu/criminal-justice

University of South Florida, College of Behavioral and Community Sciences, Department of Criminology, Tampa, FL 33620-9951. Offers criminal justice administration (MA); criminology (MA, PhD); cybercrime (MS). *Faculty:* 13 full-time (5 women). *Students:* 36 full-time (23 women), 49 part-time (29 women); includes 22 minority (13 Black or African American, non-Hispanic/Latino; 2 Asian, non-Hispanic/Latino; 6 Hispanic/Latino; 1 Two or more races, non-Hispanic/Latino), 3 international. Average age 31. 114 applicants, 55% accepted, 30 enrolled. In 2017, 26 master's, 4 doctorates awarded. *Degree requirements:* For master's, comprehensive exam, thesis (for some programs); for doctorate, comprehensive exam, thesis/dissertation. *Entrance requirements:* For master's, GRE General Test, statement of purpose; minimum GPA of 3.0 in all upper-division coursework for bachelor's degree, three letters of recommendation, and writing sample (for criminology); minimum undergraduate GPA of 3.0, work experience in the criminal justice field, and two letters of recommendation (for criminal justice administration); for doctorate, GRE General Test, minimum GPA of 3.0 in all upper-division coursework for bachelor's degree or 3.4 in graduate coursework; three letters of recommendation; statement of purpose; sample of academic written work. Additional exam requirements/recommendations for international students: Required—TOEFL (minimum score 550 paper-based; 79 iBT) or IELTS (minimum score 6.5). *Application deadline:* For fall admission, 1/15 for domestic and international students; for spring admission, 9/30 for domestic students, 9/15 for international students. Application fee: $30. Electronic applications accepted. *Financial support:* In 2017–18, 19 students received support, including 2 research assistantships (averaging $14,172 per year), 15 teaching assistantships with tuition reimbursements available (averaging $11,702 per year). *Faculty research:* Juvenile justice and delinquency, substance use and abuse, macro-level models of criminal behavior, race and social control, violence. *Total annual research expenditures:* $412,414. *Unit head:* Dr. Michael Leiber, Professor and Chair, 813-974-9704, Fax: 813-974-2803, E-mail: mjleiber@usf.edu. *Application contact:* Dr. Ojmarrh Mitchell, Associate Professor and Graduate Director, 813-974-2815, Fax: 813-974-2803, E-mail: omitchell@usf.edu.
Website: http://criminology.cbcs.usf.edu/

University of South Florida, Innovative Education, Tampa, FL 33620-9951. Offers adult, career and higher education (Graduate Certificate), including college teaching, leadership in developing human resources, leadership in higher education; Africana studies (Graduate Certificate), including diasporas and health disparities, genocide and human rights; aging studies (Graduate Certificate), including gerontology; art research (Graduate Certificate), including museum studies; business foundations (Graduate Certificate); chemical and biomedical engineering (Graduate Certificate), including materials science and engineering, water, health and sustainability; child and family studies (Graduate Certificate), including positive behavior support; civil and industrial engineering (Graduate Certificate), including transportation systems analysis; community and family health (Graduate Certificate), including maternal and child health, social marketing and public health, violence and injury: prevention and intervention, women's health; criminology (Graduate Certificate), including criminal justice administration; data science for public administration (Graduate Certificate); digital humanities (Graduate Certificate); educational measurement and research (Graduate Certificate), including evaluation; English (Graduate Certificate), including comparative literary studies, creative writing, professional and technical communication; entrepreneurship (Graduate Certificate); environmental health (Graduate Certificate), including safety management; epidemiology and biostatistics (Graduate Certificate), including applied biostatistics, biostatistics, concepts and tools of epidemiology, epidemiology, epidemiology of infectious diseases; geography, environment and planning (Graduate Certificate), including community development, environmental policy and management, geographical information systems; geology (Graduate Certificate), including hydrogeology; global health (Graduate Certificate), including disaster management, global health and Latin American and Caribbean studies, global health practice, humanitarian assistance, infection control; government and international affairs (Graduate Certificate), including Cuban studies, globalization studies; health policy and management (Graduate Certificate), including health management and leadership, public health policy and programs; hearing specialist: early intervention (Graduate Certificate); industrial and management systems engineering (Graduate Certificate), including systems engineering, technology management; information studies (Graduate Certificate), including school library media specialist; information systems/decision sciences (Graduate Certificate), including analytics and business intelligence; instructional technology (Graduate Certificate), including distance education, Florida digital/virtual educator, instructional design, multimedia design, Web design; internal medicine, bioethics and medical humanities (Graduate Certificate), including biomedical ethics; Latin American and Caribbean studies (Graduate Certificate); leadership for coastal resiliency planning (Graduate Certificate); mass communications (Graduate

Certificate), including multimedia journalism; mathematics and statistics (Graduate Certificate), including mathematics; medicine (Graduate Certificate), including aging and neuroscience, bioinformatics, biotechnology, brain fitness and memory management, clinical investigation, hand and upper limb rehabilitation, health informatics, health sciences, integrative weight management, intellectual property, medicine and gender, metabolic and nutritional medicine, metabolic cardiology, pharmacy sciences; national and competitive intelligence (Graduate Certificate); nursing (Graduate Certificate), including simulation based academic fellowship in advanced pain management; psychological and social foundations (Graduate Certificate), including career counseling, college teaching, diversity in education, mental health counseling, school counseling; public affairs (Graduate Certificate), including nonprofit management, public management, research administration; public health (Graduate Certificate), including assessing chemical toxicity and public health risks, health equity, pharmacoepidemiology, public health generalist, toxicology, translational research in adolescent behavioral health; public health practices (Graduate Certificate), including planning for healthy communities; rehabilitation and mental health counseling (Graduate Certificate), including integrative mental health care, marriage and family therapy, rehabilitation technology; secondary education (Graduate Certificate), including ESOL, foreign language education: culture and content, foreign language education: professional; social work (Graduate Certificate), including geriatric social work/clinical gerontology; special education (Graduate Certificate), including autism spectrum disorder, disabilities education: severe/profound; world languages (Graduate Certificate), including teaching English as a second language (TESL) or foreign language. *Unit head:* Dr. Cynthia DeLuca, Associate Vice President and Assistant Vice Provost, 813-974-3077, Fax: 813-974-7061, E-mail: deluca@usf.edu. *Application contact:* Owen Hooper, Director, Summer and Alternative Calendar Programs, 813-974-6917, E-mail: hooper@usf.edu.
Website: http://www.usf.edu/innovative-education/

University of South Florida Sarasota-Manatee, College of Liberal Arts and Social Sciences, Sarasota, FL 34243. Offers criminal justice (MA); education (MA); educational leadership (M Ed), including curriculum leadership, K-12 public school leadership, non-public/charter school leadership; elementary education (MAT); English education (MA); social work (MSW). *Program availability:* Part-time, 100% online, blended/hybrid learning. *Faculty:* 15 full-time (12 women), 8 part-time/adjunct (6 women). *Students:* 11 full-time (10 women), 43 part-time (37 women); includes 17 minority (7 Black or African American, non-Hispanic/Latino; 2 Asian, non-Hispanic/Latino; 8 Hispanic/Latino), 1 international. Average age 35. 62 applicants, 27% accepted, 14 enrolled. In 2017, 32 master's awarded. *Degree requirements:* For master's, comprehensive exam (for some programs). *Entrance requirements:* For master's, GRE. Additional exam requirements/recommendations for international students: Required—TOEFL (minimum score 550 paper-based; 79 iBT), IELTS (minimum score 6.5). *Application deadline:* For fall admission, 3/1 priority date for domestic students, 3/1 for international students; for spring admission, 10/1 priority date for domestic students, 10/1 for international students. Applications are processed on a rolling basis. Application fee: $30. Electronic applications accepted. *Expenses: Tuition,* state resident: full-time $8350; part-time $418 per credit hour. Tuition, nonresident: full-time $19,047; part-time $863 per credit hour. *Required fees:* $1689. Tuition and fees vary according to degree level and program. *Financial support:* In 2017–18, 1 student received support. Career-related internships or fieldwork, institutionally sponsored loans, scholarships/grants, health care benefits, and unspecified assistantships available. Support available to part-time students. Financial award application deadline: 3/1; financial award applicants required to submit FAFSA. *Faculty research:* Educational leadership, secondary education, elementary education, criminal justice, social work. *Total annual research expenditures:* $72,000. *Unit head:* Dr. Jane Rose, Dean, 941-359-4469, Fax: 941-359-4778, E-mail: jane.rose@sar.usf.edu. *Application contact:* Brandon Avery, Assistant Director, Admissions, 941-359-4331, E-mail: bavery@sar.usf.edu.

The University of Tampa, Program in Criminology and Criminal Justice, Tampa, FL 33606-1490. Offers MS. *Faculty:* 3 full-time (1 woman). *Students:* 15 full-time (10 women), 2 part-time (both women); includes 2 minority (1 Black or African American, non-Hispanic/Latino; 1 Two or more races, non-Hispanic/Latino). Average age 27. *Degree requirements:* For master's, thesis optional. *Entrance requirements:* For master's, two letters of recommendation from academic and/or professional sources; writing sample indicating evidence of ability to conduct scholarly research (for thesis option applicants); personal statement; professional resume. *Application deadline:* Applications are processed on a rolling basis. Application fee: $40. Electronic applications accepted. *Expenses: Tuition:* Full-time $7428. *Required fees:* $80. *Financial support:* Fellowships, career-related internships or fieldwork, scholarships/grants, and unspecified assistantships available. *Unit head:* Christopher R. Capsambelis, Coordinator, 813-257-3348, E-mail: ccapsambelis@ut.edu. *Application contact:* Dr. Joshua Stagner, Director of Graduate and Continuing Studies, 813-257-3016, Fax: 813-258-7451, E-mail: jstagner@ut.edu.
Website: http://www.ut.edu/mscriminology/

The University of Tennessee, Graduate School, College of Arts and Sciences, Department of Sociology, Knoxville, TN 37996. Offers criminology (MA, PhD); energy, environment, and resource policy (MA, PhD); political economy (MA, PhD). *Program availability:* Part-time. *Degree requirements:* For master's, thesis or alternative; for doctorate, thesis/dissertation. *Entrance requirements:* For master's, GRE General Test, minimum GPA of 3.0; for doctorate, GRE General Test, minimum GPA of 3.5. Additional exam requirements/recommendations for international students: Required—TOEFL. Electronic applications accepted.

The University of Tennessee at Chattanooga, Program in Criminal Justice, Chattanooga, TN 37403. Offers MSCJ. *Program availability:* Part-time. *Students:* 14 full-time (8 women), 23 part-time (10 women); includes 14 minority (8 Black or African American, non-Hispanic/Latino; 2 Hispanic/Latino; 4 Two or more races, non-Hispanic/Latino). Average age 29. 15 applicants, 93% accepted, 14 enrolled. In 2017, 9 master's awarded. *Degree requirements:* For master's, comprehensive exam, thesis optional. *Entrance requirements:* For master's, GRE General Test or MAT, 2 letters of recommendation. Additional exam requirements/recommendations for international students: Required—TOEFL (minimum score 550 paper-based; 79 iBT), IELTS (minimum score 6). *Application deadline:* For fall admission, 6/15 priority date for domestic students, 7/1 for international students; for spring admission, 11/1 priority date for domestic students, 11/1 for international students. Applications are processed on a rolling basis. Application fee: $35 ($40 for international students). Electronic applications accepted. *Expenses:* Contact institution. *Financial support:* Research assistantships, teaching assistantships, career-related internships or fieldwork, scholarships/grants, and unspecified assistantships available. Support available to part-time students. Financial award application deadline: 7/1; financial award applicants required to submit FAFSA. *Faculty research:* Violence against women, crime prevention, police accountability, criminal justice privatization, public policy. *Total annual research expenditures:* $139,047. *Unit head:* Dr. Tammy Garland, Graduate Coordinator, 423-425-5245, Fax: 423-425-2228, E-mail: tammy-garland@utc.edu. *Application contact:* Dr. Joanne Romagni, Dean of the Graduate School, 423-425-4478, Fax: 423-425-5223, E-mail: joanne-romagni@utc.edu.

Website: http://www.utc.edu/criminal-justice/criminal-justice-graduate-program/graduate-welcome.php

The University of Texas at Arlington, Graduate School, College of Liberal Arts, Department of Criminology and Criminal Justice, Arlington, TX 76019. Offers MA. *Program availability:* Part-time, evening/weekend. *Degree requirements:* For master's, comprehensive exam, thesis or alternative. *Entrance requirements:* For master's, GRE General Test, minimum GPA of 3.0 in last 60 hours of undergraduate course work, 3 letters of recommendation. Additional exam requirements/recommendations for international students: Required—TOEFL (minimum score 550 paper-based).

The University of Texas at Dallas, School of Economic, Political and Policy Sciences, Program in Criminology and Criminal Justice, Richardson, TX 75080. Offers criminology (MS, PhD); justice administration and leadership (MS). *Program availability:* Part-time, evening/weekend. *Faculty:* 11 full-time (4 women), 2 part-time/adjunct (0 women). *Students:* 40 full-time (24 women), 30 part-time (19 women); includes 28 minority (14 Black or African American, non-Hispanic/Latino; 4 Asian, non-Hispanic/Latino; 8 Hispanic/Latino; 2 Two or more races, non-Hispanic/Latino), 6 international. Average age 35. 54 applicants, 33% accepted, 11 enrolled. In 2017, 26 master's, 6 doctorates awarded. *Degree requirements:* For master's, thesis; for doctorate, thesis/dissertation. *Entrance requirements:* For master's, GRE General Test, minimum GPA of 3.0 in upper-level course work in field; for doctorate, GRE (minimum combined verbal and quantitative score of 1200), minimum GPA of 3.2 in upper-level course work in field. Additional exam requirements/recommendations for international students: Required—TOEFL (minimum score 550 paper-based). *Application deadline:* For fall admission, 7/15 for domestic students, 5/1 priority date for international students; for spring admission, 11/15 for domestic students, 9/1 priority date for international students. Applications are processed on a rolling basis. Application fee: $50 ($100 for international students). Electronic applications accepted. *Expenses:* Tuition, state resident: full-time $12,916; part-time $718 per credit hour. Tuition, nonresident: full-time $25,252; part-time $1403 per credit hour. *Financial support:* In 2017–18, 29 students received support, including 3 research assistantships with partial tuition reimbursements available (averaging $18,200 per year), 14 teaching assistantships with partial tuition reimbursements available (averaging $13,100 per year); career-related internships or fieldwork, Federal Work-Study, institutionally sponsored loans, scholarships/grants, and unspecified assistantships also available. Support available to part-time students. Financial award application deadline: 4/30; financial award applicants required to submit FAFSA. *Faculty research:* Developmental criminology, domestic violence, mental health and violence, the death penalty, corrections. *Unit head:* Dr. Denise Paquette Boots, Program Head, 972-883-6468, Fax: 972-883-2735, E-mail: deniseboots@utdallas.edu. *Application contact:* Rita Medford, Graduate Program Administrator, 972-883-4932, Fax: 972-883-2735, E-mail: rmedford@utdallas.edu.
Website: http://www.utdallas.edu/epps/criminology/

The University of Texas at San Antonio, College of Public Policy, Department of Criminal Justice, San Antonio, TX 78207. Offers criminology (MS). *Program availability:* Part-time, evening/weekend. *Faculty:* 6 full-time (2 women). *Students:* 12 full-time (9 women), 27 part-time (19 women); includes 30 minority (1 Black or African American, non-Hispanic/Latino; 1 Asian, non-Hispanic/Latino; 28 Hispanic/Latino). Average age 27. 28 applicants, 68% accepted, 12 enrolled. In 2017, 10 master's awarded. *Degree requirements:* For master's, variable foreign language requirement, minimum of 36 semester credit hours; thesis or written comprehensive exams. *Entrance requirements:* For master's, minimum GPA of 3.0 in last 60 hours of undergraduate course work; 2 letters of recommendation; resume; 18 credit hours in criminal justice, criminology or closely-related discipline. Additional exam requirements/recommendations for international students: Required—TOEFL (minimum score 550 paper-based; 79 iBT), IELTS (minimum score 6.5). *Application deadline:* For fall admission, 6/15 for domestic students, 3/1 for international students; for spring admission, 10/15 for domestic students, 9/15 for international students. Application fee: $50 ($90 for international students). Electronic applications accepted. *Expenses:* Contact institution. *Financial support:* Research assistantships and teaching assistantships available. *Faculty research:* Criminological theory, crime prevention, administration of justice, correctional interventions, evidence-based practices and program evaluation. *Total annual research expenditures:* $32,874. *Unit head:* Dr. Michael Smith, Chair and Professor, 210-458-2686, E-mail: michael.smith@utsa.edu. *Application contact:* Dr. Marie Tillyer, Associate Professor/Graduate Advisor of Record, 210-458-2682, E-mail: marie.tillyer@utsa.edu.
Website: http://copp.utsa.edu/department/about-criminal-justice/

The University of Texas at Tyler, College of Arts and Sciences, Department of Social Sciences, Tyler, TX 75799-0001. Offers criminal justice (MS); public administration (MPA); sociology (MS). *Program availability:* Part-time, evening/weekend. *Degree requirements:* For master's, comprehensive exam, thesis optional. *Entrance requirements:* For master's, GRE General Test, minimum GPA of 3.0. Additional exam requirements/recommendations for international students: Required—TOEFL. *Faculty research:* Urban segregation, minority business, violent crime, gender discrimination.

The University of Texas of the Permian Basin, Office of Graduate Studies, College of Arts and Sciences, Department of Social Sciences, Program in Criminal Justice Administration, Odessa, TX 79762-0001. Offers MS. *Program availability:* Part-time, evening/weekend. *Degree requirements:* For master's, comprehensive exam (for some programs), thesis (for some programs). *Entrance requirements:* For master's, GRE General Test, 3 letters of recommendation. Additional exam requirements/recommendations for international students: Required—TOEFL (minimum score 550 paper-based).

The University of Texas Rio Grande Valley, College of Liberal Arts, Department of Criminal Justice, Edinburg, TX 78539. Offers MS. *Program availability:* Part-time, evening/weekend. *Faculty:* 6 full-time (2 women). *Students:* 12 full-time (4 women), 12 part-time (5 women); includes 20 minority (all Hispanic/Latino). Average age 28. 10 applicants, 100% accepted, 6 enrolled. In 2017, 12 master's awarded. *Degree requirements:* For master's, comprehensive exam, applied project or thesis. *Entrance requirements:* For master's, minimum undergraduate GPA of 3.0, official transcripts, 250-500 word letter of intent, three letters of recommendation. Additional exam requirements/recommendations for international students: Required—TOEFL or IELTS. *Application deadline:* For fall admission, 7/1 for domestic students, 6/1 for international students; for spring admission, 11/15 for domestic students, 11/1 for international students. Applications are processed on a rolling basis. Application fee: $50 ($100 for international students). *Expenses:* Tuition, state resident: full-time $5550; part-time $417 per credit hour. Tuition, nonresident: full-time $13,020; part-time $832 per credit hour. *Required fees:* $1169. *Financial support:* Application deadline: 4/15; applicants required to submit CSS PROFILE or FAFSA. *Faculty research:* Comparative criminal justice systems, death penalty, community policing, Hispanic women. *Unit head:* Benjamin Brown, Interim Chair, E-mail: benjamin.brown@utrgv.edu.

The University of Texas Rio Grande Valley, College of Liberal Arts, Department of Public Affairs and Security Studies, Edinburg, TX 78539. Offers global security studies and leadership (MPA); public administration (MPA); public policy and management (MPA). *Program availability:* Part-time, evening/weekend. *Faculty:* 8 full-time (5 women). *Students:* 6 full-time (3 women), 127 part-time (57 women); includes 96 minority (5 Black or African American, non-Hispanic/Latino; 2 Asian, non-Hispanic/Latino; 89 Hispanic/

Latino), 4 international. Average age 33. 67 applicants, 97% accepted, 40 enrolled. In 2017, 77 master's awarded. *Degree requirements:* For master's, comprehensive exam (for some programs), thesis optional. *Entrance requirements:* For master's, minimum undergraduate GPA of 3.0, official transcripts, personal statement, three recommendations. Additional exam requirements/recommendations for international students: Required—TOEFL or IELTS. *Application deadline:* For fall admission, 7/1 for domestic students, 6/1 for international students; for spring admission, 11/15 for domestic students, 11/1 for international students. Applications are processed on a rolling basis. Application fee: $50 ($100 for international students). Electronic applications accepted. *Expenses:* Tuition, state resident: full-time $5550; part-time $417 per credit hour. Tuition, nonresident: full-time $13,020; part-time $832 per credit hour. *Required fees:* $1169. *Financial support:* Application deadline: 6/1. *Faculty research:* Immigration policy reform, agriculture food policy, social service delivery systems, community development, social welfare policy reform, urban/city management. *Unit head:* Terrence Garett, Chair, E-mail: terence.garrett@utrgv.edu.
Website: http://www.utrgv.edu/pass/

University of the Fraser Valley, Graduate Studies, Abbotsford, BC V2S 7M8, Canada. Offers criminal justice (MA); social work (MSW). *Program availability:* Evening/weekend. *Faculty:* 23 full-time (13 women). *Students:* 41 full-time (24 women), 4 part-time (2 women); includes 4 minority (all American Indian or Alaska Native, non-Hispanic/Latino). Average age 36. 42 applicants, 31% accepted, 13 enrolled. In 2017, 15 master's awarded. *Degree requirements:* For master's, thesis optional, major research paper. *Entrance requirements:* For master's, bachelor's degree, work experience in related field. Additional exam requirements/recommendations for international students: Recommended—TOEFL (minimum score 570 paper-based; 88 iBT), IELTS (minimum score 6.5), TWE (minimum score 4.5), TSE (minimum score 61). *Application deadline:* For fall admission, 1/31 priority date for domestic students, 4/1 priority date for international students; for winter admission, 8/31 priority date for domestic students; for spring admission, 12/31 priority date for domestic students. Application fee: $75 ($250 for international students). Electronic applications accepted. *Expenses:* Contact institution. *Financial support:* Research assistantships, scholarships/grants, health care benefits, and bursaries available. Financial award application deadline: 5/10. *Faculty research:* Criminal justice, criminology, social work, child welfare. *Unit head:* Dr. Adrienne Chan, Associate Vice President for Research, Engagement and Graduate Studies, 604-504-4074, Fax: 778-880-0356, E-mail: adrienne.chan@ufv.ca. *Application contact:* Educational Advisors, 604-854-4528, Fax: 604-855-7614, E-mail: advising@ufv.ca.
Website: http://www.ufv.ca/Graduate_Studies.htm

The University of Toledo, College of Graduate Studies, College of Health and Human Services, School of Social Justice, Toledo, OH 43606-3390. Offers criminal justice (MA); social work (MSW).

The University of Toledo, College of Graduate Studies, College of Social Justice and Human Service, Department of Criminal Justice and Social Work, Toledo, OH 43606-3390. Offers child advocacy (Certificate); criminal justice (MA); elder law (Certificate); juvenile justice (Certificate); patient advocacy (Certificate); social work (MSW); JD/MA. *Accreditation:* CSWE. *Program availability:* Part-time. *Degree requirements:* For master's, comprehensive exam, thesis. *Entrance requirements:* For master's and Certificate, minimum cumulative GPA of 2.7 for all previous academic work, letters of recommendation. Additional exam requirements/recommendations for international students: Required—TOEFL (minimum score 550 paper-based; 80 iBT). Electronic applications accepted.

University of Toronto, School of Graduate Studies, Faculty of Arts and Science, Centre for Criminology and Sociolegal Studies, Toronto, ON M5S 1A1, Canada. Offers MA, PhD, JD/MA. *Program availability:* Part-time. *Degree requirements:* For doctorate, comprehensive exam, thesis/dissertation. *Entrance requirements:* For master's, 2 letters of reference, bachelor's degree in social science or humanities, minimum B+ average in last 2 years of undergraduate study; for doctorate, 2 letters of reference, MA in criminology or equivalent, minimum A- average. Additional exam requirements/recommendations for international students: Required—TOEFL (minimum score 580 paper-based; 93 iBT), TWE (minimum score 5). Electronic applications accepted.

University of West Florida, College of Education and Professional Studies, Department of Criminology and Criminal Justice, Pensacola, FL 32514-5750. Offers criminal justice (MS). *Program availability:* Part-time, evening/weekend. *Degree requirements:* For master's, thesis optional. *Entrance requirements:* For master's, GRE or MAT, official transcripts; minimum undergraduate cumulative GPA of 3.0; 3 letters of recommendation; personal statement. Additional exam requirements/recommendations for international students: Required—TOEFL (minimum score 550 paper-based). Electronic applications accepted.

University of West Georgia, College of Social Sciences, Carrollton, GA 30118. Offers criminology (MA); data analysis and evaluation methods (Postbaccalaureate Certificate); European Union studies (Postbaccalaureate Certificate); integrative health systems (Postbaccalaureate Certificate); nonprofit management and community development (Postbaccalaureate Certificate); psychology (MA, PhD), including consciousness and society (PhD); public administration (MPA); public management (Postbaccalaureate Certificate); sociology (MA). *Program availability:* Part-time, evening/weekend, 100% online, blended/hybrid learning. *Faculty:* 48 full-time (22 women). *Students:* 124 full-time (84 women), 73 part-time (46 women); includes 69 minority (56 Black or African American, non-Hispanic/Latino; 4 Asian, non-Hispanic/Latino; 6 Hispanic/Latino; 3 Two or more races, non-Hispanic/Latino), 10 international. Average age 32. 95 applicants, 89% accepted, 63 enrolled. In 2017, 44 master's, 2 doctorates, 4 other advanced degrees awarded. *Entrance requirements:* Additional exam requirements/recommendations for international students: Required—TOEFL (minimum score 523 paper-based; 69 iBT); Recommended—IELTS (minimum score 6.5). *Application deadline:* For fall admission, 7/15 for domestic students, 6/1 for international students; for spring admission, 11/30 for domestic students, 10/15 for international students; for summer admission, 5/15 for domestic students, 3/30 for international students. Applications are processed on a rolling basis. Application fee: $40. Electronic applications accepted. Tuition and fees vary according to degree level and program. *Financial support:* Fellowships, research assistantships, teaching assistantships, career-related internships or fieldwork, Federal Work-Study, institutionally sponsored loans, scholarships/grants, and unspecified assistantships available. Support available to part-time students. Financial award application deadline: 4/1; financial award applicants required to submit FAFSA. *Unit head:* Dr. N. Jane McCandless, Dean of Social Sciences, 678-839-5170, Fax: 678-839-5171, E-mail: jmccandl@westga.edu. *Application contact:* Dr. Toby Ziglar, Assistant Dean of the Graduate School, 678-839-1394, Fax: 678-839-1395, E-mail: graduate@westga.edu.
Website: https://www.westga.edu/coss

University of Windsor, Faculty of Graduate Studies, Faculty of Arts and Social Sciences, Department of Sociology and Anthropology, Windsor, ON N9B 3P4, Canada. Offers criminology (MA); sociology (MA); sociology-social justice (PhD). *Program availability:* Part-time. *Degree requirements:* For master's, thesis; for doctorate, comprehensive exam, thesis/dissertation. *Entrance requirements:* For master's, minimum B+ average; for doctorate, writing sample, minimum B+ average. Additional exam requirements/recommendations for international students: Required—TOEFL (minimum score 560 paper-based). Electronic applications accepted. *Faculty research:* Power and social change; criminology/deviance; social psychology; comparative development; race and ethnic relations; family, sex, and gender, social justice.

University of Wisconsin–Milwaukee, Graduate School, Helen Bader School of Social Welfare, Department of Criminal Justice, Milwaukee, WI 53201-0413. Offers applied data analysis using SAS (Graduate Certificate); crime analytics (MS); criminal justice (MS). *Program availability:* Part-time. *Students:* 18 full-time (8 women), 15 part-time (5 women); includes 8 minority (2 Black or African American, non-Hispanic/Latino; 1 Asian, non-Hispanic/Latino; 1 Hispanic/Latino; 4 Two or more races, non-Hispanic/Latino), 2 international. Average age 28. 29 applicants, 52% accepted, 10 enrolled. In 2017, 8 master's awarded. *Degree requirements:* For master's, thesis or alternative. *Entrance requirements:* For master's, GRE General Test, MAT. Additional exam requirements/recommendations for international students: Required—TOEFL (minimum score 550 paper-based; 79 iBT), IELTS (minimum score 6.5). *Application deadline:* For fall admission, 1/1 priority date for domestic students; for spring admission, 9/1 for domestic students. Application fee: $56 ($96 for international students). Electronic applications accepted. *Financial support:* Fellowships, research assistantships, teaching assistantships with full tuition reimbursements, career-related internships or fieldwork, health care benefits, unspecified assistantships, and project assistantships available. Support available to part-time students. Financial award application deadline: 4/15; financial award applicants required to submit FAFSA. *Application contact:* Mary Russell, Academic Department Specialist, 414-229-2392, E-mail: russelme@uwm.edu.
Website: http://uwm.edu/socialwelfare/academics/criminal-justice-field-placement/

University of Wisconsin–Platteville, School of Graduate Studies, Distance Learning Center, Online Master of Science in Criminal Justice Program, Platteville, WI 53818-3099. Offers MS. *Program availability:* Part-time, online learning. *Students:* 3 full-time (1 woman), 102 part-time (59 women); includes 19 minority (13 Black or African American, non-Hispanic/Latino; 1 American Indian or Alaska Native, non-Hispanic/Latino; 2 Asian, non-Hispanic/Latino; 3 Hispanic/Latino). 68 applicants, 59% accepted, 28 enrolled. In 2017, 26 master's awarded. *Degree requirements:* For master's, thesis or alternative. *Entrance requirements:* Additional exam requirements/recommendations for international students: Required—TOEFL (minimum score 550 paper-based; 79 iBT), IELTS (minimum score 6.5). *Application deadline:* For fall admission, 7/1 priority date for domestic students; for spring admission, 11/1 priority date for domestic students. Applications are processed on a rolling basis. Application fee: $56. Electronic applications accepted. *Expenses:* Contact institution. *Financial support:* Scholarships/grants available. Support available to part-time students. *Unit head:* Cheryl Banachowski-Fuller, Coordinator, 608-342-1652, Fax: 608-342-1986, E-mail: banachoc@uwplatt.edu. *Application contact:* 608-342-1468, Fax: 608-342-1071, E-mail: disted@uwplatt.edu.
Website: http://www.uwplatt.edu/disted/criminal-justice-MS.html

Urbana University–A Branch Campus of Franklin University, College of Social and Behavioral Sciences, Urbana, OH 43078-2091. Offers criminal justice administration (MA). *Entrance requirements:* For master's, 3 letters of recommendation.

Utica College, Program in Economic Crime and Fraud Management, Utica, NY 13502-4892. Offers MS. *Program availability:* Part-time, evening/weekend, 100% online. *Faculty:* 7 full-time (0 women). *Students:* 1 full-time (0 women), 64 part-time (40 women); includes 16 minority (6 Black or African American, non-Hispanic/Latino; 3 Asian, non-Hispanic/Latino; 6 Hispanic/Latino; 1 Two or more races, non-Hispanic/Latino). Average age 37. 42 applicants, 93% accepted, 37 enrolled. In 2017, 23 master's awarded. *Entrance requirements:* For master's, BS, minimum GPA of 3.0. Additional exam requirements/recommendations for international students: Required—TOEFL (minimum score 525 paper-based). *Application deadline:* Applications are processed on a rolling basis. Application fee: $50. Electronic applications accepted. *Expenses:* Contact institution. *Financial support:* Career-related internships or fieldwork, scholarships/grants, tuition waivers (partial), and unspecified assistantships available. Support available to part-time students. Financial award application deadline: 3/15; financial award applicants required to submit FAFSA. *Unit head:* Dr. R. Bruce McBride, Director of Economic Crime Graduate Programs, 315-792-3808, E-mail: rmcbride@utica.edu. *Application contact:* John D. Rowe, Director of Graduate Admissions, 315-792-3824, Fax: 315-792-3003, E-mail: jrowe@utica.edu.
Website: http://programs.online.utica.edu/programs/mba-fraud-management.asp

Utica College, Program in Economic Crime Management, Utica, NY 13502-4892. Offers MBA. *Program availability:* Part-time, evening/weekend, online learning. *Faculty:* 4 full-time (0 women). *Students:* 2 full-time (1 woman), 81 part-time (46 women); includes 23 minority (13 Black or African American, non-Hispanic/Latino; 1 American Indian or Alaska Native, non-Hispanic/Latino; 2 Asian, non-Hispanic/Latino; 6 Hispanic/Latino; 1 Two or more races, non-Hispanic/Latino). Average age 34. In 2017, 56 master's awarded. *Degree requirements:* For master's, thesis. *Entrance requirements:* For master's, BS, minimum GPA of 3.0. Additional exam requirements/recommendations for international students: Required—TOEFL (minimum score 525 paper-based). *Application deadline:* Applications are processed on a rolling basis. Application fee: $50. Electronic applications accepted. *Expenses:* Contact institution. *Financial support:* Career-related internships or fieldwork, scholarships/grants, tuition waivers (partial), and unspecified assistantships available. Support available to part-time students. Financial award application deadline: 3/15; financial award applicants required to submit FAFSA. *Unit head:* Dr. R. Bruce McBride, Director of Economic Crime Graduate Programs, 315-792-3808, E-mail: rmcbride@utica.edu. *Application contact:* John D. Rowe, Director of Graduate Admissions, 315-792-3824, Fax: 315-792-3003, E-mail: jrowe@utica.edu.
Website: http://programs.online.utica.edu/programs/masters-financial-crime-compliance-management.asp

Virginia Commonwealth University, Graduate School, L. Douglas Wilder School of Government and Public Affairs, Program in Criminal Justice, Richmond, VA 23284-9005. Offers MS, Postbaccalaureate Certificate. *Program availability:* Part-time, evening/weekend. *Degree requirements:* For master's, thesis or comprehensive exam. *Entrance requirements:* For master's, GRE, LSAT or GMAT, minimum cumulative GPA of 3.0. Additional exam requirements/recommendations for international students: Required—TOEFL (minimum score 600 paper-based; 100 iBT); Recommended—IELTS (minimum score 6.5). Electronic applications accepted.

Virginia State University, College of Graduate Studies, College of Humanities and Social Sciences, Department of Sociology and Criminal Justice, Petersburg, VA 23806-0001. Offers criminal justice (MS).

Walden University, Graduate Programs, School of Public Policy and Administration, Minneapolis, MN 55401. Offers criminal justice (MPA, MPP, MS, Graduate Certificate), including emergency management (MS, PhD), general program (MS), global leadership (MS, PhD), homeland security and policy coordination (MS, PhD), law and public policy (MS, PhD), policy analysis (MS, PhD), public management and leadership (MS, PhD), self-designed (MS), terrorism, mediation, and peace (MS, PhD); criminal justice and executive management (MS), including global leadership (MS, PhD); criminal justice leadership and executive management (MS), including emergency management (MS,

PhD), general program, homeland security and policy coordination (MS, PhD), law and public policy (MS, PhD), policy analysis (MS, PhD), public management and leadership (MS, PhD), self-designed, terrorism, mediation, and peace (MS, PhD); emergency management (MPA, MPP, MS), including criminal justice (MS, PhD), general program (MS), homeland security (MS), public management and leadership (MS, PhD), terrorism and emergency management (MS); general program (MPA, MPP); global leadership (MPA, MPP); government management (Graduate Certificate); health policy (MPA, MPP); homeland security (Graduate Certificate); homeland security and policy coordination (MPA, MPP); international nongovernmental organizations (MPA, MPP); law and public policy (MPA, MPP); local government management for sustainable communities (MPA, MPP); nonprofit management (Graduate Certificate); nonprofit management and leadership (MPA, MPP, MS), including global leadership (MS, PhD), international nongovernmental organization (MS), local government for sustainable communities (MS), self designed (MS); online teaching in higher education (Post-Master's Certificate); policy analysis (MPA); public management and leadership (MPA, MPP, Graduate Certificate); public policy (Graduate Certificate); public policy and administration (PhD), including criminal justice (MS, PhD), emergency management (MS, PhD), global leadership (MS, PhD), health policy, homeland security and policy coordination (MS, PhD), international nongovernmental organizations, law and public policy (MS, PhD), local government management for sustainable communities, nonprofit management and leadership, policy analysis (MS, PhD), public management and leadership (MS, PhD), terrorism, mediation, and peace (MS, PhD); strategic planning and public policy (Graduate Certificate); terrorism, mediation, and peace (MPA, MPP). *Program availability:* Part-time, evening/weekend, online only, 100% online. *Degree requirements:* For doctorate, thesis/dissertation, residency. *Entrance requirements:* For master's, bachelor's degree or higher; minimum GPA of 2.5; official transcripts; goal statement (for some programs); access to computer and Internet; for doctorate, master's degree or higher; three years of related professional or academic experience (preferred); minimum GPA of 3.0; goal statement and current resume (for select programs); official transcripts; access to computer and Internet; for other advanced degree, relevant work experience; access to computer and Internet. Additional exam requirements/recommendations for international students: Required—TOEFL (minimum score 550 paper-based, 79 iBT), IELTS (minimum score 6.5), Michigan English Language Assessment Battery (minimum score 82), or PTE (minimum score 53). Electronic applications accepted.

Walden University, Graduate Programs, School of Social Work and Human Services, Minneapolis, MN 55401. Offers addictions and social work (DSW); advanced clinical practice (MSW); clinical expertise (DSW); criminal justice (DSW); disaster, crisis, and intervention (DSW); family studies and interventions (DSW); human and social services (PhD), including advanced research, community and social services, community intervention and leadership, conflict management, criminal justice, disaster crisis and intervention, family studies and intervention, gerontology, global social services, higher education, human services and nonprofit administration, mental health facilitation; medical social work (DSW); military social work (MSW); policy practice (DSW); social work (PhD), including addictions and social work, clinical expertise, criminal justice, disaster, crisis and intervention, family studies and interventions, medical social work, policy practice, social work administration; social work administration (DSW); social work in healthcare (MSW); social work with children and families (MSW). *Accreditation:* CSWE. *Program availability:* Part-time, evening/weekend, online only, 100% online. *Degree requirements:* For master's, residency (for some programs); for doctorate, thesis/dissertation, residency. *Entrance requirements:* For master's, bachelor's degree or higher; minimum GPA of 2.5; official transcripts; goal statement (for some programs); access to computer and Internet; for doctorate, master's degree or higher; three years of related professional or academic experience (preferred); minimum GPA of 3.0; goal statement and current resume (for select programs); official transcripts; access to computer and Internet. Additional exam requirements/recommendations for international students: Required—TOEFL (minimum score 550 paper-based, 79 iBT), IELTS (minimum score 6.5), Michigan English Language Assessment Battery (minimum score 82), or PTE (minimum score 53). Electronic applications accepted.

Waldorf University, Program in Organizational Leadership, Forest City, IA 50436. Offers criminal justice leadership (MA); emergency management leadership (MA); fire/rescue executive leadership (MA); human resource development (MA); public administration (MA); sport management (MA); teacher leader (MA).

Washburn University, School of Applied Studies, Department of Criminal Justice and Legal Studies, Topeka, KS 66621. Offers MCJ. *Program availability:* Part-time, evening/weekend, online learning. *Degree requirements:* For master's, thesis or alternative, continuous enrollment each fall and spring semester, completion of all program requirements within seven years of entry (MCJ). *Entrance requirements:* For master's, GRE, 3 letters of reference, minimum GPA of 3.0 for undergraduate degree, short biography, official transcripts. Additional exam requirements/recommendations for international students: Required—TOEFL (minimum score 80 iBT). Electronic applications accepted. *Faculty research:* Practitioner behavior, police management and training, field and institutional correction administration, terrorism, police training, sex slaves.

Washington State University, College of Arts and Sciences, Department of Criminal Justice and Criminology, Pullman, WA 99164. Offers MA, PhD. MA program also offered at Spokane and Global (online) campuses. *Program availability:* Online learning. *Degree requirements:* For master's, comprehensive exam (for some programs), thesis, oral exam; for doctorate, comprehensive exam, thesis/dissertation, oral or written exam. *Entrance requirements:* For master's, GRE General Test, major in criminal justice, sociology, psychology, liberal arts, or a related field; strong writing and analytical skills; minimum GPA of 3.0; for doctorate, GRE General Test, major in criminal justice, sociology, psychology, liberal arts, or a related field; strong writing and analytical skills. Additional exam requirements/recommendations for international students: Required—TOEFL, IELTS. Electronic applications accepted. *Faculty research:* Community policing, community justice, corrections policy, crime prevention policy, criminal justice management.

Wayland Baptist University, Graduate Programs, Programs in Behavioral and Social Sciences, Plainview, TX 79072-6998. Offers counseling (MA); criminal justice (MACJ); government administration (MPA); history (MA); homeland security (MPA); humanities (MAH); justice administration (MPA). *Program availability:* Part-time, evening/weekend, 100% online, blended/hybrid learning. *Faculty:* 19 full-time (5 women), 18 part-time/adjunct (8 women). *Students:* 16 full-time (10 women), 322 part-time (183 women); includes 207 minority (82 Black or African American, non-Hispanic/Latino; 8 American Indian or Alaska Native, non-Hispanic/Latino; 8 Asian, non-Hispanic/Latino; 84 Hispanic/Latino; 5 Native Hawaiian or other Pacific Islander, non-Hispanic/Latino; 20 Two or more races, non-Hispanic/Latino), 1 international. Average age 40. 56 applicants, 93% accepted, 39 enrolled. In 2017, 141 master's awarded. *Degree requirements:* For master's, comprehensive exam. *Entrance requirements:* For master's, GRE, MAT. Additional exam requirements/recommendations for international students: Required—TOEFL (minimum score 500 paper-based; 61 iBT). *Application deadline:* Applications are processed on a rolling basis. Application fee: $50. Electronic applications accepted. *Expenses: Tuition:* Full-time $11,250; part-time $625 per credit hour. *Required fees:* $1200. *Financial support:* Federal Work-Study, institutionally sponsored loans, and scholarships/grants available. Support available to part-time students. Financial award application deadline: 5/1; financial award applicants required to submit FAFSA. *Unit head:* Dr. Peter Bowen, Dean, 806-291-1179, Fax: 806-291-1972, E-mail: pbowen@wbu.edu. *Application contact:* Amanda Stanton, Graduate Studies, 806-291-3423, Fax: 806-291-1950, E-mail: stanton@wbu.edu.

Waynesburg University, Graduate and Professional Studies, Canonsburg, PA 15370. Offers business (MBA), including energy management, finance, health systems, human resources, leadership, market development; counseling (MA), including addictions counseling, clinical mental health; counselor education and supervision (PhD); criminal investigation (MA); education (M Ed), including autism, curriculum and instruction, educational leadership, online teaching; nursing (MSN), including administration, education, informatics; nursing practice (DNP); special education (M Ed); technology (M Ed); MSN/MBA. *Accreditation:* AACN. *Program availability:* Part-time, evening/weekend. *Degree requirements:* For doctorate, thesis/dissertation. *Entrance requirements:* Additional exam requirements/recommendations for international students: Required—TOEFL. Electronic applications accepted.

Wayne State University, College of Liberal Arts and Sciences, Department of Criminal Justice, Detroit, MI 48202. Offers MS, MS/JD. *Program availability:* 100% online. *Faculty:* 8. *Students:* 9 full-time (6 women), 31 part-time (22 women); includes 11 minority (8 Black or African American, non-Hispanic/Latino; 3 Hispanic/Latino). Average age 35. 57 applicants, 35% accepted, 15 enrolled. In 2017, 16 master's awarded. *Degree requirements:* For master's, comprehensive exam, three-credit essay, thesis, or capstone seminar. *Entrance requirements:* For master's, GRE (for applicants with a GPA of 2.75-2.99), minimum GPA of 3.0 or written statement and writing sample; bachelor's degree from accredited college or university; two letters of recommendation; personal statement. Additional exam requirements/recommendations for international students: Required—TOEFL (minimum score 550 paper-based; 79 iBT), TWE (minimum score 5.5), Michigan English Language Assessment Battery (minimum score 85); Recommended—IELTS (minimum score 6.5). *Application deadline:* For fall admission, 6/1 for domestic students, 5/1 priority date for international students; for winter admission, 10/1 for domestic students, 9/1 priority date for international students. Application fee: $50. Electronic applications accepted. *Expenses:* Tuition, state resident: full-time $10,224; part-time $638.98 per credit hour. Tuition, nonresident: full-time $22,145; part-time $1384.04 per credit hour. Tuition and fees vary according to course load and program. *Financial support:* In 2017–18, 11 students received support, including 1 teaching assistantship with tuition reimbursement available (averaging $18,534 per year); fellowships with tuition reimbursements available, research assistantships with tuition reimbursements available, scholarships/grants, health care benefits, and unspecified assistantships also available. Financial award applicants required to submit FAFSA. *Faculty research:* Comparative/international criminal justice and criminology, corrections, criminal justice policy, deviant behavior, life-course criminology, juvenile justice, corrections, and delinquency, mental health and crime, policing, positive psychology, suicide, wrongful convictions. *Unit head:* Dr. Shanhe Jiang, Chair, 313-577-2705, E-mail: fx6954@wayne.edu. *Application contact:* Dr. Jennifer Wareham, Associate Professor/Graduate Director, 313-577-3286, Fax: 313-577-9977, E-mail: ay3167@wayne.edu.
Website: http://clas.wayne.edu/CRJ/

Webber International University, Graduate School of Business, Babson Park, FL 33827-0096. Offers accounting (MBA); business (MBA); criminal justice management (MBA); international business (MBA); sport business management (MBA). *Program availability:* Part-time, evening/weekend, 100% online. *Faculty:* 10 full-time (4 women), 1 part-time/adjunct (0 women). *Students:* 50 full-time (29 women), 6 part-time (2 women); includes 19 minority (12 Black or African American, non-Hispanic/Latino; 6 Hispanic/Latino; 1 Two or more races, non-Hispanic/Latino), 6 international. Average age 24. 64 applicants, 61% accepted, 32 enrolled. In 2017, 29 master's awarded. *Degree requirements:* For master's, class trip (for international business); practicum (for criminal justice management). *Entrance requirements:* For master's, three recommendation letters, résumé, essay, official transcripts from all colleges and universities attended. Additional exam requirements/recommendations for international students: Recommended—TOEFL (minimum score 500 paper-based; 61 iBT), IELTS (minimum score 6). *Application deadline:* For fall admission, 7/1 for international students. Applications are processed on a rolling basis. Application fee: $50 ($75 for international students). Electronic applications accepted. *Expenses: Tuition:* Part-time $688 per hour. *Financial support:* In 2017–18, 11 students received support. Scholarships/grants and unspecified assistantships available. Financial award application deadline: 8/1; financial award applicants required to submit FAFSA. *Unit head:* Dr. Nikos Orphanoudakis, Dean, 863-638-2910, Fax: 863-638-1591, E-mail: orphanoudakisn@webber.edu. *Application contact:* Lacy Edwards, Admissions Counselor and MBA Coordinator, 863-638-2910, Fax: 863-638-1591, E-mail: admissions@webber.edu.

Webster University, George Herbert Walker School of Business and Technology, Department of Business, St. Louis, MO 63119-3194. Offers business and organizational security management (MBA); decision support systems (MBA); environmental management (MBA); finance (MBA, MS); forensic accounting (MS); gerontology (MBA); human resources development (MBA); human resources management (MBA); information technology management (MBA); international business (MA, MBA); international relations (MBA); management and leadership (MBA); marketing (MBA); media communications (MBA); procurement and acquisitions management (MBA); Web services (MBA). *Accreditation:* ACBSP. *Program availability:* Part-time, evening/weekend, online learning. *Degree requirements:* For master's, comprehensive exam (for some programs), thesis (for some programs). *Entrance requirements:* Additional exam requirements/recommendations for international students: Required—TOEFL.

Webster University, George Herbert Walker School of Business and Technology, Department of Management, St. Louis, MO 63119-3194. Offers business and organizational security management (MA); digital marketing management (Graduate Certificate); government contracting (Graduate Certificate); health administration (MHA); health care management (MA); health services management (MA); human resources development (MA); human resources management (MA); information technology management (MA, MS); management (D Mgt); management and leadership (MA); marketing (MA); nonprofit leadership (MA); nonprofit revenue development (Graduate Certificate); organizational development (Graduate Certificate); procurement and acquisitions management (MA); public administration (MPA); space systems operations management (MS). *Program availability:* Part-time, evening/weekend, online learning. *Degree requirements:* For master's, thesis (for some programs); for doctorate, thesis/dissertation, written exam. *Entrance requirements:* For doctorate, GMAT, 3 years of work experience, MBA. Additional exam requirements/recommendations for international students: Required—TOEFL.

West Chester University of Pennsylvania, College of Business and Public Management, Department of Criminal Justice, West Chester, PA 19383. Offers MS. *Program availability:* Part-time, evening/weekend. *Students:* 17 full-time (12 women), 40 part-time (22 women); includes 18 minority (14 Black or African American, non-Hispanic/Latino; 1 Asian, non-Hispanic/Latino; 2 Hispanic/Latino; 1 Two or more races, non-Hispanic/Latino). Average age 29. 34 applicants, 85% accepted, 23 enrolled. In 2017,

17 master's awarded. *Degree requirements:* For master's, 15-credit core (law, research, ethics, theories, and capstone independent research project); 15 additional credits of criminal justice electives. *Entrance requirements:* For master's, minimum GPA of 3.0; two letters of recommendation. Additional exam requirements/recommendations for international students: Required—TOEFL or IELTS. *Application deadline:* For fall admission, 5/15 for international students; for spring admission, 10/15 for international students. Applications are processed on a rolling basis. Application fee: $50. Electronic applications accepted. *Expenses:* Tuition, state resident: full-time $9000; part-time $500 per credit. Tuition, nonresident: full-time $13,500; part-time $750 per credit. *Required fees:* $2959; $149.79 per credit. *Financial support:* Scholarships/grants and unspecified assistantships available. Financial award application deadline: 2/15; financial award applicants required to submit FAFSA. *Faculty research:* Criminal law, criminal procedure, Constitutional interpretation, drug and alcohol prevention, drug courts, mental health courts, legislation related to sex offending, animal cruelty, pharmaceutical battery, terrorism, law enforcement. *Unit head:* Dr. Mary Brewster, Chair, 610-436-2630, Fax: 610-738-0491, E-mail: mbrewster@wcupa.edu. *Application contact:* Dr. Shannon Grugan, Graduate Coordinator, 610-436-2659, Fax: 610-738-0491, E-mail: sgrugan@wcupa.edu.
Website: http://www.wcupa.edu/business-publicManagement/criminalJustice/

Western Illinois University, School of Graduate Studies, College of Education and Human Services, School of Law Enforcement and Justice Administration, Macomb, IL 61455-1390. Offers law enforcement and justice administration (MA); police executive administration (Certificate). *Program availability:* Part-time. *Degree requirements:* For master's, thesis or alternative. *Entrance requirements:* For master's, GRE or MAT, minimum GPA of 3.0. Additional exam requirements/recommendations for international students: Required—TOEFL (minimum score 520 paper-based; 68 iBT). *Application deadline:* Applications are processed on a rolling basis. Application fee: $30. Electronic applications accepted. *Financial support:* Unspecified assistantships available. Financial award applicants required to submit FAFSA. *Unit head:* Dr. Jill Myers, Director, 309-298-1038. *Application contact:* Dr. Nancy Parsons, Associate Provost and Director of Graduate Studies, 309-298-1806, Fax: 309-298-2345, E-mail: grad-office@wiu.edu.
Website: http://wiu.edu/leja

Western Kentucky University, Graduate Studies, Potter College of Arts and Letters, Department of Sociology, Bowling Green, KY 42101. Offers criminology (MA); sociology (MA). *Program availability:* Online learning. *Degree requirements:* For master's, comprehensive exam, thesis optional, final exam. *Entrance requirements:* For master's, GRE General Test, minimum GPA of 3.0. Additional exam requirements/recommendations for international students: Required—TOEFL (minimum score 555 paper-based; 79 iBT). *Faculty research:* Criminology/delinquency, quantitative and survey research methodology, occupations/professions, sex and gender, demography.

Western Oregon University, Graduate Programs, College of Liberal Arts and Sciences, Division of Social Science, Monmouth, OR 97361. Offers criminal justice (MA, MS). *Program availability:* Part-time, evening/weekend. *Degree requirements:* For master's, thesis optional, written exams. *Entrance requirements:* For master's, minimum GPA of 3.0. Additional exam requirements/recommendations for international students: Required—TOEFL (minimum score 550 paper-based; 79 iBT), IELTS (minimum score 6.5). *Faculty research:* Prison to community transition of adult felons, community justice, restorative justice, parole and probation.

Westfield State University, College of Graduate and Continuing Education, Department of Criminal Justice, Westfield, MA 01086. Offers MS. *Program availability:* Part-time, evening/weekend. *Faculty:* 4 full-time (1 woman). *Students:* 3 full-time (1 woman), 21 part-time (7 women); includes 3 minority (1 Black or African American, non-Hispanic/Latino; 2 Hispanic/Latino). Average age 33. 8 applicants, 88% accepted, 6 enrolled. In 2017, 13 master's awarded. *Degree requirements:* For master's, comprehensive exam, thesis (for some programs). *Entrance requirements:* For master's, GRE General Test or MAT, minimum undergraduate GPA of 2.8. Additional exam requirements/recommendations for international students: Recommended—TOEFL (minimum score 550 paper-based; 79 iBT). *Application deadline:* For fall admission, 7/1 for domestic students; for spring admission, 11/1 for domestic students; for summer admission, 4/1 for domestic students. Applications are processed on a rolling basis. Application fee: $50. *Expenses:* Tuition, state resident: part-time $332 per credit. Tuition, nonresident: part-time $332 per credit. *Required fees:* $75 per semester. Tuition and fees vary according to program. *Financial support:* Unspecified assistantships available. Financial award application deadline: 3/1; financial award applicants required to submit FAFSA. *Unit head:* Dr. Christopher Kudlac, Professor/Graduate Coordinator, 413-572-5728, E-mail: ckudlac@westfield.ma.edu. *Application contact:* Shelly Henrichon, Coordinator of College of Graduate and Continuing Education Admissions, 413-572-8022, Fax: 413-572-5227, E-mail: mhenrichon@westfield.ma.edu.
Website: http://www.westfield.ma.edu/academics/degrees/criminal-justice-graduate-programs

Westfield State University, College of Graduate and Continuing Education, Department of Political Science, Westfield, MA 01086. Offers criminal justice administration (MPA); non-profit management (MPA); public management (MPA). *Program availability:* Part-time, evening/weekend. *Faculty:* 3 full-time (1 woman), 3 part-time/adjunct (2 women). *Students:* 9 full-time (2 women), 40 part-time (17 women); includes 13 minority (2 Black or African American, non-Hispanic/Latino; 2 American Indian or Alaska Native, non-Hispanic/Latino; 8 Hispanic/Latino; 1 Two or more races, non-Hispanic/Latino). Average age 33. 19 applicants, 100% accepted, 14 enrolled. In 2017, 16 master's awarded. *Degree requirements:* For master's, comprehensive exam, thesis (for some programs). *Entrance requirements:* For master's, GRE General Test or MAT, minimum undergraduate GPA of 2.8. Additional exam requirements/recommendations for international students: Recommended—TOEFL (minimum score 550 paper-based; 79 iBT). *Application deadline:* For fall admission, 7/1 for domestic students; for spring admission, 11/1 for domestic students; for summer admission, 4/1 for domestic students. Applications are processed on a rolling basis. Application fee: $50. *Expenses:* Tuition, state resident: part-time $332 per credit. Tuition, nonresident: part-time $332 per credit. *Required fees:* $75 per semester. Tuition and fees vary according to program. *Financial support:* Unspecified assistantships available. Financial award application deadline: 3/1; financial award applicants required to submit FAFSA.

Unit head: Dr. Hugh Jo, Chair, 413-572-8806, Fax: 413-572-8168, E-mail: hjo@westfield.ma.edu. *Application contact:* Shelly Henrichon, Admissions Coordinator, 413-572-8022, Fax: 413-572-5227, E-mail: mhenrichon@westfield.ma.edu.

West Texas A&M University, College of Education and Social Sciences, Department of Political Science and Criminal Justice, Canyon, TX 79015. Offers criminal justice (MA). *Program availability:* Part-time, evening/weekend. *Degree requirements:* For master's, comprehensive exam, thesis optional. *Entrance requirements:* For master's, GRE General Test. Additional exam requirements/recommendations for international students: Required—TOEFL. Electronic applications accepted.

West Virginia State University, Master of Science Program in Law Enforcement and Administration, Institute, WV 25112-1000. Offers MS. *Degree requirements:* For master's, comprehensive exam, internship, paper. *Entrance requirements:* For master's, GRE (50th Percentile) or MAT (50th Percentile), minimum undergraduate GPA of 2.7, 3 letters of recommendation, completion of course in statistics/research methods, interview. Additional exam requirements/recommendations for international students: Required—TOEFL (minimum score 550 paper-based). Electronic applications accepted.

Wichita State University, Graduate School, Fairmount College of Liberal Arts and Sciences, School of Community Affairs, Wichita, KS 67260. Offers criminal justice (MA). *Program availability:* Part-time, 100% online, blended/hybrid learning. *Unit head:* Dr. Andra Bannister, Interim Director, 316-978-7200, Fax: 316-978-3626, E-mail: andra.bannister@wichita.edu. *Application contact:* Jordan Oleson, Admissions Coordinator, 316-978-3095, Fax: 316-978-3253, E-mail: jordan.oleson@wichita.edu.
Website: http://www.wichita.edu/cj

Widener University, College of Arts and Sciences, Program in Criminal Justice, Chester, PA 19013-5792. Offers MA, Psy D/MA. *Program availability:* Part-time, evening/weekend. *Faculty:* 1 full-time (0 women), 2 part-time/adjunct (0 women). *Students:* 12 part-time (6 women); includes 8 minority (7 Black or African American, non-Hispanic/Latino; 1 Two or more races, non-Hispanic/Latino). Average age 31. 21 applicants, 90% accepted. In 2017, 1 master's awarded. *Degree requirements:* For master's, project. *Entrance requirements:* For master's, interview, minimum undergraduate GPA of 3.0. *Application deadline:* For fall admission, 3/1 priority date for domestic students. Applications are processed on a rolling basis. Application fee: $25 ($300 for international students). *Expenses:* Contact institution. *Financial support:* Career-related internships or fieldwork and institutionally sponsored loans available. Support available to part-time students. Financial award application deadline: 5/1. *Faculty research:* Criminal law and procedure, corrections, domestic violence. *Unit head:* Dr. William E. Harver, Director, 610-499-4554, Fax: 510-499-4605, E-mail: william.e.harver@widener.edu.

Wilfrid Laurier University, Laurier Brantford, Brantford, ON N3T 2Y3, Canada. Offers criminology (MA), including culture, crime and policy, international crime and justice, media criminology. *Degree requirements:* For master's, thesis. *Entrance requirements:* For master's, honours bachelor's degree with major in criminology or equivalent degree; minimum B+ average in final year and in all criminology courses. Additional exam requirements/recommendations for international students: Required—TOEFL (minimum score 89 iBT). Electronic applications accepted.

Wilmington University, College of Social and Behavioral Sciences, New Castle, DE 19720-6491. Offers administration of human services (MS); administration of justice (MS); clinical mental health counseling (MS); homeland security (MS). *Accreditation:* ACA. *Program availability:* Part-time, evening/weekend. *Faculty:* 11 full-time (6 women), 74 part-time/adjunct (34 women). *Students:* 174 full-time (132 women), 428 part-time (334 women); includes 269 minority (229 Black or African American, non-Hispanic/Latino; 5 American Indian or Alaska Native, non-Hispanic/Latino; 7 Asian, non-Hispanic/Latino; 17 Hispanic/Latino; 11 Two or more races, non-Hispanic/Latino), 11 international. Average age 35. 541 applicants, 81% accepted, 292 enrolled. In 2017, 271 master's awarded. *Entrance requirements:* Additional exam requirements/recommendations for international students: Required—TOEFL (minimum score 500 paper-based). *Application deadline:* Applications are processed on a rolling basis. Application fee: $35. Electronic applications accepted. *Expenses:* Tuition: Part-time $466 per credit. *Required fees:* $25 per semester. Tuition and fees vary according to degree level and campus/location. *Financial support:* Applicants required to submit FAFSA. *Unit head:* Dr. Edward L. Guthrie, Dean, 302-356-6870. *Application contact:* Laura Morris, Director of Admissions, 877-967-5464, E-mail: inquire@wilmcoll.edu.
Website: http://www.wilmu.edu/behavioralscience/

Wright State University, Graduate School, College of Liberal Arts, Program in Applied Behavioral Science, Criminal Justice and Social Problems, Dayton, OH 45435. Offers criminal justice and social problems (MA). *Degree requirements:* For master's, thesis optional. *Entrance requirements:* Additional exam requirements/recommendations for international students: Required—TOEFL. *Faculty research:* Training and development, criminal justice and social problems, community systems, human factors, industrial/organizational psychology.

Xavier University, College of Social Sciences, Health and Education, Department of Criminal Justice, Cincinnati, OH 45207. Offers MS. *Program availability:* Part-time, evening/weekend. *Degree requirements:* For master's, comprehensive exam, thesis. *Entrance requirements:* For master's, MAT, GRE, or LSAT, minimum GPA of 2.7; official transcript; 2 letters of recommendation. Additional exam requirements/recommendations for international students: Required—TOEFL (minimum score 550 paper-based; 79 iBT). Electronic applications accepted. Application fee is waived when completed online. *Expenses:* Contact institution. *Faculty research:* Women and crime, crime policy, policing.

Youngstown State University, Graduate School, Bitonte College of Health and Human Services, Department of Criminal Justice, Youngstown, OH 44555-0001. Offers MS. *Program availability:* Part-time, evening/weekend. *Degree requirements:* For master's, thesis optional. *Entrance requirements:* For master's, minimum GPA of 2.7. Additional exam requirements/recommendations for international students: Required—TOEFL. *Faculty research:* Police human resource allocation, police administration, computerized test development, criminal law.

Forensic Sciences

Alabama State University, College of Science, Mathematics and Technology, Department of Physical Sciences, Montgomery, AL 36101-0271. Offers forensic science (MS). *Faculty:* 4 full-time (1 woman). *Students:* 5 full-time (all women), 1 (woman) part-time; all minorities (all Black or African American, non-Hispanic/Latino). Average age 22. 3 applicants, 100% accepted, 3 enrolled. In 2017, 5 master's awarded. *Degree requirements:* For master's, comprehensive exam, thesis or alternative. *Entrance requirements:* Additional exam requirements/recommendations for international students: Required—TOEFL (minimum score 500 paper-based). *Application deadline:* For fall admission, 4/15 for domestic and international students; for spring admission, 11/15 for domestic and international students; for summer admission, 3/15 for domestic and international students. Application fee: $25. Electronic applications accepted. *Expenses:* Tuition, state resident: part-time $412 per credit hour. Tuition, nonresident: part-time $824 per credit hour. *Required fees:* $685 per semester. *Financial support:* Research assistantships and unspecified assistantships available. Financial award application deadline: 6/30; financial award applicants required to submit FAFSA. *Unit head:* Dr. Azriel Gorski, Dean, 334-229-6705, Fax: 334-229-6103, E-mail: agorski@alasu.edu. *Application contact:* Dr. William Person, Dean of Graduate Studies, 334-229-4274, Fax: 334-229-4928, E-mail: wperson@alasu.edu.
Website: http://www.alasu.edu/academics/colleges—departments/science-mathematics-technology/physical-sciences/index.aspx

Alliant International University–Irvine, California School of Forensic Studies, Irvine, CA 92606. Offers Psy D. *Degree requirements:* For doctorate, comprehensive exam, thesis/dissertation, internship. *Entrance requirements:* For doctorate, minimum GPA of 3.0, recommendations, essay. Additional exam requirements/recommendations for international students: Required—TOEFL (minimum score 80 iBT), TWE (minimum score 5). Electronic applications accepted. *Faculty research:* Detecting deception, psychological safety of undercover police officers, domestic violence, risk assessment, competency evaluations.

Arcadia University, College of Arts and Sciences, Program in Forensic Science, Glenside, PA 19038-3295. Offers MSFS. *Expenses:* Contact institution.

Bay Path University, Program in Applied Laboratory Science and Operations, Longmeadow, MA 01106-2292. Offers MS. *Program availability:* Part-time, evening/weekend. *Faculty:* 39 full-time (34 women), 155 part-time/adjunct (118 women). *Students:* 9 full-time (all women), 5 part-time (all women); includes 5 minority (1 Black or African American, non-Hispanic/Latino; 3 Hispanic/Latino; 1 Two or more races, non-Hispanic/Latino). Average age 32. *Degree requirements:* For master's, 40 credits with minimum B- grade in all coursework; final portfolio. *Entrance requirements:* For master's, BS in forensic science or a natural science, minimum cumulative GPA of 3.0. *Application deadline:* Applications are processed on a rolling basis. Application fee: $45. Electronic applications accepted. Application fee is waived when completed online. *Expenses:* $825 per credit. *Financial support:* Unspecified assistantships available. Financial award applicants required to submit FAFSA. *Unit head:* Dr. Thomas Mennella, Program Director, 413-565-1318, E-mail: tmennella@baypath.edu. *Application contact:* Diane Ranaldi, Dean of Graduate Admissions, 413-565-1332, Fax: 413-565-1250, E-mail: dranaldi@baypath.edu.
Website: http://graduate.baypath.edu/Graduate-Programs/Programs-On-Campus/MS-Programs/Forensics

Boston University, School of Medicine, Division of Graduate Medical Sciences, Program in Biomedical Forensic Sciences, Boston, MA 02118. Offers MS. *Program availability:* Part-time, evening/weekend, online learning. *Degree requirements:* For master's, thesis. *Application deadline:* For fall admission, 7/1 for domestic and international students. *Unit head:* Dr. Robin Cotton, Director, 617-638-1950, E-mail: rwcotton@bu.edu. *Application contact:* GMS Admissions Office, 617-638-5255, E-mail: askgms@bu.edu.
Website: http://www.bumc.bu.edu/biomedforensic/

Boston University, School of Medicine, Division of Graduate Medical Sciences, Program in Forensic Anthropology, Boston, MA 02215. Offers MS. *Financial support:* Applicants required to submit FAFSA. *Unit head:* Dr. Tara L. Moore, Program Director, 617-638-4054, Fax: 617-638-4922, E-mail: tlmoore@bu.edu. *Application contact:* GMS Admissions Office, 617-638-5255, E-mail: askgms@bu.edu.
Website: http://www.bumc.bu.edu/gms/forensicanthropology/

Carlow University, College of Leadership and Social Change, MBA Program, Pittsburgh, PA 15213-3165. Offers fraud and forensics (MBA); healthcare management (MBA); human resource management (MBA); leadership and management (MBA); project management (MBA). *Program availability:* Part-time, evening/weekend, 100% online, blended/hybrid learning. *Students:* 81 full-time (62 women), 28 part-time (18 women); includes 32 minority (26 Black or African American, non-Hispanic/Latino; 2 Asian, non-Hispanic/Latino; 1 Hispanic/Latino; 3 Two or more races, non-Hispanic/Latino). Average age 32. 46 applicants, 98% accepted, 32 enrolled. In 2017, 57 master's awarded. *Entrance requirements:* For master's, minimum undergraduate GPA of 3.0 (preferred); personal essay; resume; official transcripts; two professional recommendations. Additional exam requirements/recommendations for international students: Required—TOEFL (minimum score 550 paper-based). *Application deadline:* Applications are processed on a rolling basis. Electronic applications accepted. *Expenses: Tuition:* Full-time $12,103; part-time $825 per credit hour. Tuition and fees vary according to program. *Financial support:* Application deadline: 4/1; applicants required to submit FAFSA. *Unit head:* Dr. Howard Stern, Chair, MBA Program, 412-578-8828, E-mail: hastern@carlow.edu. *Application contact:* 412-578-6059, Fax: 412-578-6321, E-mail: gradstudies@carlow.edu.
Website: http://www.carlow.edu/Business_Administration.aspx

Cedar Crest College, Program in Forensic Science, Allentown, PA 18104-6196. Offers MS. *Faculty:* 4 full-time (2 women), 2 part-time/adjunct (1 woman). *Students:* 19 full-time (14 women), 7 part-time (5 women); includes 4 minority (1 American Indian or Alaska Native, non-Hispanic/Latino; 3 Asian, non-Hispanic/Latino). Average age 25. In 2017, 11 master's awarded. *Degree requirements:* For master's, thesis. *Entrance requirements:* For master's, GRE. *Application deadline:* For fall admission, 1/2 priority date for domestic students. Applications are processed on a rolling basis. Electronic applications accepted. *Expenses:* Contact institution. *Financial support:* In 2017–18, 4 students received support. Unspecified assistantships available. *Faculty research:* Genotyping of low copy number DNA, presumptive and confirmatory testing of gamma hydroxyl butyrate (GHB) and gamma-butyrolactone (GBL). *Unit head:* Dr. Lawrence A. Quarino, Director and Associate Professor, 610-606-4666 Ext. 3507, Fax: 610-740-3787, E-mail: laquarin@cedarcrest.edu. *Application contact:* Nancy Wunderly, Director of School of Adult and Graduate Education, 610-606-4666, E-mail: sage@cedarcrest.edu.

Champlain College, Graduate Studies, Burlington, VT 05402-0670. Offers business (MBA); digital forensic science (MS); early childhood education (M Ed); emergent media (MFA, MS); executive leadership (MS); health care administration (MS); information security operations (MS); law (MS); mediation and applied conflict studies (MS). MS in emergent media program held in Shanghai. *Program availability:* Part-time, online learning. *Degree requirements:* For master's, capstone project. *Entrance requirements:* Additional exam requirements/recommendations for international students: Required—TOEFL (minimum score 550 paper-based; 80 iBT). Electronic applications accepted.

DeSales University, Division of Liberal Arts and Social Sciences, Center Valley, PA 18034-9568. Offers criminal justice (MCJ); digital forensics (MCJ, Postbaccalaureate Certificate); education (M Ed), including instructional technology, secondary education, special education, teaching English to speakers of other languages; investigative forensics (MCJ, Postbaccalaureate Certificate). *Program availability:* Part-time, 100% online, blended/hybrid learning. *Faculty:* 5 full-time (3 women), 15 part-time/adjunct (9 women). *Students:* 54 full-time (36 women), 112 part-time (68 women); includes 23 minority (3 Black or African American, non-Hispanic/Latino; 1 Asian, non-Hispanic/Latino; 17 Hispanic/Latino; 2 Two or more races, non-Hispanic/Latino), 1 international. Average age 33. 114 applicants, 64% accepted, 41 enrolled. In 2017, 41 master's awarded. *Entrance requirements:* For master's, bachelor's degree from accredited institution, minimum undergraduate GPA of 3.0, personal statement showing potential of graduate work, three letters of recommendation, professional goal statement. Additional exam requirements/recommendations for international students: Required—TOEFL. *Application deadline:* Applications are processed on a rolling basis. Application fee: $50. Electronic applications accepted. *Expenses: Tuition:* Part-time $840 per credit. Full-time tuition and fees vary according to course load, degree level and program. *Financial support:* Applicants required to submit FAFSA. *Unit head:* Ronald Nordone, Dean of Graduate Education, 610-282-1100 Ext. 1289, E-mail: ronald.nordone@desales.edu. *Application contact:* Julia Ferraro, Director of Graduate Admissions, 610-282-1100 Ext. 1768, E-mail: gradadmissions@desales.edu.

DeSales University, Division of Science and Mathematics, Center Valley, PA 18034-9568. Offers cyber security (Postbaccalaureate Certificate); data analytics (Postbaccalaureate Certificate); information systems (MS), including cyber security, digital forensics, healthcare information management, project management. *Program availability:* Part-time, evening/weekend, 100% online, blended/hybrid learning. *Faculty:* 1 (woman) full-time, 2 part-time/adjunct (0 women). *Students:* 8 full-time (0 women), 12 part-time (6 women); includes 3 minority (1 Asian, non-Hispanic/Latino; 1 Hispanic/Latino; 1 Two or more races, non-Hispanic/Latino), 1 international. Average age 35. 35 applicants, 31% accepted, 5 enrolled. In 2017, 6 master's awarded. *Entrance requirements:* For master's, GRE or GMAT, bachelor's degree in computer-related discipline from accredited college or university, minimum undergraduate GPA of 3.0, personal statement, three letters of recommendation. Additional exam requirements/recommendations for international students: Required—TOEFL. *Application deadline:* Applications are processed on a rolling basis. Application fee: $50. Electronic applications accepted. *Expenses:* Contact institution. *Financial support:* Applicants required to submit FAFSA. *Unit head:* Dr. Patricia Riola, Director/Assistant Professor of Computer Science, 610-282-1100 Ext. 1647, E-mail: patricia.riola@desales.edu. *Application contact:* Julia Ferraro, Director of Graduate Admissions, 610-282-1100 Ext. 1768, E-mail: gradadmissions@desales.edu.
Website: http://www.desales.edu/home/academics/graduate-studies/programs-of-study/msis—-master-of-science-in-information-systems

Duquesne University, Bayer School of Natural and Environmental Sciences, Program in Forensic Science and Law, Pittsburgh, PA 15282-0001. Offers MS. *Faculty:* 5 full-time (3 women), 15 part-time/adjunct (9 women). *Students:* 16 full-time (11 women); includes 2 minority (1 Hispanic/Latino; 1 Two or more races, non-Hispanic/Latino), 1 international. Average age 23. In 2017, 21 master's awarded. *Degree requirements:* For master's, comprehensive exam. *Entrance requirements:* For master's, SAT or ACT, recommendation form; minimum total QPA of 3.0, 2.5 in math and science. *Application deadline:* For fall admission, 7/1 for domestic and international students. Applications are processed on a rolling basis. Application fee: $0. Electronic applications accepted. *Expenses:* $1,312 per credit. *Financial support:* In 2017–18, 10 students received support. Career-related internships or fieldwork and scholarships/grants available. Financial award application deadline: 5/1. *Faculty research:* Extraction protocols, mass spectrometry, synthetic fiber analysis, synthetic polymer characterization, trace analysis, amplification of DNA, methods for labeling DNA, construction of a genetic profile, experiential exploration of mitochondrial DNA, the Y-chromosome, amelogenin. *Total annual research expenditures:* $50,419. *Unit head:* Dr. Federick W. Fochtman, Director, 412-396-6373, E-mail: fochtman@duq.edu. *Application contact:* Valerie L. Lijewski, Assistant Director/Academic Advisor, 412-396-1084, E-mail: lijewski@duq.edu.
Website: http://www.duq.edu/academics/schools/natural-and-environmental-sciences/academic-programs/forensic-science-and-law

Emporia State University, Department of Biological Sciences, Emporia, KS 66801-5415. Offers botany (MS); environmental biology (MS); forensic science (MS); general biology (MS); microbial and cellular biology (MS); zoology (MS). *Program availability:* Part-time. *Faculty:* 13 full-time (3 women), 1 part-time/adjunct (0 women). *Students:* 20 full-time (11 women), 15 part-time (3 women); includes 3 minority (2 Hispanic/Latino; 1 Two or more races, non-Hispanic/Latino), 17 international. 17 applicants, 59% accepted, 8 enrolled. In 2017, 21 master's awarded. *Degree requirements:* For master's, comprehensive exam or thesis. *Entrance requirements:* For master's, GRE, appropriate undergraduate degree, interview, letters of reference. Additional exam requirements/recommendations for international students: Required—TOEFL (minimum score 520 paper-based; 68 iBT). *Application deadline:* For fall admission, 8/15 priority date for domestic students. Applications are processed on a rolling basis. Application fee: $30 ($75 for international students). Electronic applications accepted. *Expenses:* Tuition, state resident: full-time $6084; part-time $253.50 per credit hour. Tuition, nonresident: full-time $18,924; part-time $788.50 per credit hour. *Required fees:* $1943; $80.95 per credit hour. Tuition and fees vary according to campus/location. *Financial support:* In 2017–18, 7 research assistantships with full tuition reimbursements (averaging $9,747 per year), 15 teaching assistantships with full tuition reimbursements (averaging $7,499 per year) were awarded; career-related internships or fieldwork, Federal Work-Study, institutionally sponsored loans, health care benefits, and unspecified assistantships also available. Financial award application deadline: 3/15; financial award applicants required to submit FAFSA. *Faculty research:* Fisheries, range, and wildlife management; aquatic, plant, grassland, vertebrate, and invertebrate ecology; mammalian and plant systematics, taxonomy, and evolution; immunology, virology, and molecular biology. *Unit head:* Dr. Tim Burnett, Interim Chair, 620-341-5910, Fax: 620-341-5608, E-mail: tburnett@emporia.edu.
Website: http://www.emporia.edu/info/degrees-courses/grad/biology

Emporia State University, Department of Physical Sciences, Emporia, KS 66801-5415. Offers forensic science (MS); geospatial analysis (Postbaccalaureate Certificate);

physical science (MS). *Program availability:* Part-time, online learning. *Faculty:* 14 full-time (6 women), 3 part-time/adjunct (0 women). *Students:* 7 full-time (5 women), 15 part-time (8 women); includes 3 minority (all Two or more races, non-Hispanic/Latino), 7 international. 18 applicants, 50% accepted, 5 enrolled. In 2017, 15 master's, 1 other advanced degree awarded. *Degree requirements:* For master's, comprehensive exam or thesis; qualifying exam. *Entrance requirements:* For master's, appropriate undergraduate degree. Additional exam requirements/recommendations for international students: Required—TOEFL (minimum score 520 paper-based; 68 iBT). *Application deadline:* For fall admission, 8/15 priority date for domestic students. Applications are processed on a rolling basis. Application fee: $30 ($75 for international students). Electronic applications accepted. *Expenses:* Tuition, state resident: full-time $6084; part-time $253.50 per credit hour. Tuition, nonresident: full-time $18,924; part-time $788.50 per credit hour. *Required fees:* $1943; $80.95 per credit hour. Tuition and fees vary according to campus/location. *Financial support:* In 2017–18, 6 teaching assistantships with full tuition reimbursements (averaging $7,190 per year) were awarded; research assistantships with full tuition reimbursements, Federal Work-Study, institutionally sponsored loans, health care benefits, and unspecified assistantships also available. Financial award application deadline: 3/15; financial award applicants required to submit FAFSA. *Faculty research:* Bredigite, larnite, and dicalcium silicates from Marble Canyon. *Unit head:* Dr. Kim Simons, Chair, 620-341-5330, Fax: 620-341-6055, E-mail: ksimons@emporia.edu. *Application contact:* Mary Sewell, Admissions Coordinator, 800-950-GRAD, Fax: 620-341-5909, E-mail: msewell@emporia.edu.
Website: http://www.emporia.edu/physci/

Emporia State University, Program in Forensic Science, Emporia, KS 66801-5415. Offers MS. *Program availability:* Part-time. *Faculty:* 13 full-time (3 women), 1 part-time/adjunct (0 women). *Students:* 21 full-time (13 women), 1 (woman) part-time; includes 2 minority (1 Hispanic/Latino; 1 Two or more races, non-Hispanic/Latino), 7 international. 22 applicants, 82% accepted, 13 enrolled. In 2017, 10 master's awarded. *Entrance requirements:* For master's, bachelor's degree in a natural science or in forensic science (recommended), three letters of reference, official transcripts, minimum undergraduate GPA of 3.0. Additional exam requirements/recommendations for international students: Required—TOEFL. *Application deadline:* For fall admission, 4/15 for domestic students. Applications are processed on a rolling basis. Application fee: $40. Electronic applications accepted. *Expenses:* Tuition, state resident: full-time $6084; part-time $253.50 per credit hour. Tuition, nonresident: full-time $18,924; part-time $788.50 per credit hour. *Required fees:* $1943; $80.95 per credit hour. Tuition and fees vary according to campus/location. *Financial support:* In 2017–18, 7 research assistantships (averaging $9,747 per year), 15 teaching assistantships with full tuition reimbursements (averaging $7,499 per year) were awarded; unspecified assistantships also available. Financial award applicants required to submit FAFSA. *Unit head:* Dr. Melissa M. Bailey, Interim Director, 620-341-5619, E-mail: mbailey4@emporia.edu. *Application contact:* April Huddleston, Recruitment and Development Specialist, 800-950-GRAD, Fax: 620-341-5909, E-mail: ahuddles@emporia.edu.
Website: http://www.emporia.edu/physci/forensicscience/

Florida Gulf Coast University, College of Arts and Sciences, Program in Forensic Studies, Fort Myers, FL 33965-6565. Offers MS. *Program availability:* Part-time. *Faculty:* 245 full-time (104 women), 155 part-time/adjunct (71 women). *Students:* 18 full-time (16 women), 18 part-time (13 women); includes 12 minority (1 Asian, non-Hispanic/Latino; 10 Hispanic/Latino; 1 Two or more races, non-Hispanic/Latino), 1 international. Average age 27. 9 applicants, 78% accepted, 7 enrolled. In 2017, 3 master's awarded. *Entrance requirements:* For master's, GRE General Test, minimum GPA of 3.0. Additional exam requirements/recommendations for international students: Required—TOEFL (minimum score 550 paper-based). *Application deadline:* For fall admission, 2/15 priority date for domestic students, 5/1 for international students; for spring admission, 12/1 for domestic students, 9/15 for international students. Applications are processed on a rolling basis. Application fee: $30. Electronic applications accepted. *Expenses:* Tuition, state resident: part-time $290 per credit hour. Tuition, nonresident: part-time $1173 per credit hour. *Required fees:* $127 per credit hour. Tuition and fees vary according to course load. *Financial support:* In 2017–18, 3 students received support. Application deadline: 6/30; applicants required to submit FAFSA. *Unit head:* Heather Walsh-Haney, Professor, 239-590-7693, Fax: 239-590-7846, E-mail: hwalsh@fgcu.edu.

Florida International University, College of Arts, Sciences, and Education, Department of Chemistry and Biochemistry, Miami, FL 33199. Offers chemistry (MS, PhD); forensic science (MS, PSM, PhD). *Program availability:* Part-time, evening/weekend. *Faculty:* 34 full-time (11 women), 7 part-time/adjunct (3 women). *Students:* 131 full-time (70 women), 11 part-time (5 women); includes 55 minority (13 Black or African American, non-Hispanic/Latino; 3 Asian, non-Hispanic/Latino; 38 Hispanic/Latino; 1 Two or more races, non-Hispanic/Latino), 54 international. Average age 29. 199 applicants, 18% accepted, 28 enrolled. In 2017, 58 master's, 19 doctorates awarded. *Degree requirements:* For master's, thesis (for some programs); for doctorate, comprehensive exam, thesis/dissertation. *Entrance requirements:* For master's and doctorate, GRE General Test, minimum GPA of 3.0, 3 letters of recommendation, resume, letter of intent. Additional exam requirements/recommendations for international students: Required—TOEFL (minimum score 550 paper-based; 80 iBT). *Application deadline:* For fall admission, 6/1 for domestic students, 4/1 for international students; for spring admission, 10/1 for domestic students, 9/1 for international students. Applications are processed on a rolling basis. Application fee: $30. Electronic applications accepted. *Expenses:* Tuition, state resident: full-time $8912; part-time $446 per credit hour. Tuition, nonresident: full-time $21,393; part-time $992 per credit hour. *Required fees:* $390; $195 per semester. *Financial support:* Institutionally sponsored loans and scholarships/grants available. Financial award application deadline: 3/1; financial award applicants required to submit FAFSA. *Faculty research:* Organic synthesis and reaction catalysis, environmental chemistry, molecular beam studies, organic geochemistry, bioinorganic and organometallic chemistry. *Unit head:* Dr. Yong Cai, Chair, 305-348-6210, Fax: 305-348-3772, E-mail: yong.cai@fiu.edu. *Application contact:* Nanett Rojas, Assistant Director, Graduate Admissions, 305-348-7464, E-mail: gradadm@fiu.edu.

George Mason University, College of Science, Program in Forensic Science, Fairfax, VA 22030. Offers MS. *Faculty:* 6 full-time (4 women), 7 part-time/adjunct (3 women). *Students:* 37 full-time (30 women), 51 part-time (42 women); includes 44 minority (17 Black or African American, non-Hispanic/Latino; 8 Asian, non-Hispanic/Latino; 14 Hispanic/Latino; 1 Native Hawaiian or other Pacific Islander, non-Hispanic/Latino; 4 Two or more races, non-Hispanic/Latino), 4 international. Average age 27. 56 applicants, 95% accepted, 39 enrolled. In 2017, 34 master's awarded. *Degree requirements:* For master's, comprehensive exam (for some programs), research project or thesis; capstone course; 36 credits, minimum GPA of 3.0. *Entrance requirements:* For master's, undergraduate transcript; 3 letters of recommendation; interest letter; minimum GPA of 3.0. Additional exam requirements/recommendations for international students: Required—TOEFL (minimum score 575 paper-based; 88 iBT), IELTS (minimum score 6.5), PTE (minimum score 59). *Application deadline:* For fall admission, 2/1 priority date for domestic students. Application fee: $75 ($80 for international students). Electronic applications accepted. *Expenses:* $695 per credit in-state tuition, $1,516 out-of-state. *Financial support:* In 2017–18, 2 students received support, including 2 teaching assistantships with tuition reimbursements available; career-related internships or fieldwork, Federal Work-Study, scholarships/grants, and unspecified assistantships also available. Support available to part-time students. Financial award application deadline: 3/1; financial award applicants required to submit FAFSA. *Faculty research:* Forensic serology; probalistic genotyping; automated DNA mixture interpretation; biometrics (future); scent research (with dogs). *Unit head:* Mary E. O'Toole, Director, 703-993-5059, Fax: 703-993-3535, E-mail: motoole2@gmu.edu. *Application contact:* Emily Rancourt, Graduate Program Coordinator, 703-993-5234, Fax: 703-993-1993, E-mail: erancour@gmu.edu.
Website: http://forensicscience.gmu.edu/

The George Washington University, Columbian College of Arts and Sciences, Department of Forensic Sciences, Washington, DC 20052. Offers crime scene investigation (MFS); forensic chemistry (MFS); forensic molecular biology (MFS); forensic toxicology (MFS); high-technology crime investigation (MS); security management (MFS). MFS programs in high-technology crime investigation and in security management offered in Arlington, VA. *Program availability:* Part-time, evening/weekend. *Faculty:* 10 full-time (1 woman), 12 part-time/adjunct (3 women). *Students:* 65 full-time (54 women), 23 part-time (15 women); includes 41 minority (14 Black or African American, non-Hispanic/Latino; 12 Asian, non-Hispanic/Latino; 13 Hispanic/Latino; 1 Native Hawaiian or other Pacific Islander, non-Hispanic/Latino; 1 Two or more races, non-Hispanic/Latino), 5 international. Average age 25. 192 applicants, 67% accepted, 44 enrolled. In 2017, 43 master's, 1 other advanced degree awarded. *Degree requirements:* For master's, comprehensive exam. *Entrance requirements:* For master's, GRE General Test, minimum GPA of 3.0. Additional exam requirements/recommendations for international students: Required—TOEFL (minimum score 550 paper-based; 80 iBT). *Application deadline:* For fall admission, 1/16 priority date for international students; for spring admission, 10/1 priority date for domestic students, 9/1 priority date for international students. Applications are processed on a rolling basis. Application fee: $75. Electronic applications accepted. *Expenses: Tuition:* Full-time $28,800; part-time $1655 per credit hour. *Required fees:* $45; $2.75 per credit hour. *Financial support:* In 2017–18, 19 students received support. Fellowships with partial tuition reimbursements available, Federal Work-Study, and tuition waivers available. *Unit head:* Dr. Walter F. Rowe, Chair, 202-242-5757, E-mail: wfrowe@gwu.edu. *Application contact:* 202-242-5758, Fax: 202-994-6213, E-mail: forsc@gwu.edu.
Website: http://forensicsciences.columbian.gwu.edu/

Georgia State University, Andrew Young School of Policy Studies, School of Social Work, Atlanta, GA 30294. Offers child welfare leadership (Certificate); community partnerships (MSW); forensic social work (Certificate). *Accreditation:* CSWE. *Program availability:* Part-time. *Faculty:* 17 full-time (12 women). *Students:* 117 full-time (107 women), 8 part-time (6 women); includes 77 minority (63 Black or African American, non-Hispanic/Latino; 2 Asian, non-Hispanic/Latino; 7 Hispanic/Latino; 5 Two or more races, non-Hispanic/Latino), 1 international. Average age 30. 168 applicants, 42% accepted, 47 enrolled. In 2017, 59 master's awarded. *Entrance requirements:* For master's and Certificate, GRE. Additional exam requirements/recommendations for international students: Required—TOEFL (minimum score 550 paper-based; 100 iBT) or IELTS (minimum score 7). *Application deadline:* For fall admission, 2/1 priority date for domestic and international students. Application fee: $50. Electronic applications accepted. *Expenses:* Tuition, state resident: full-time $7020. Tuition, nonresident: full-time $22,518. *Required fees:* $2128. Tuition and fees vary according to degree level and program. *Financial support:* In 2017–18, research assistantships with tuition reimbursements (averaging $4,000 per year), teaching assistantships with tuition reimbursements (averaging $4,000 per year) were awarded; career-related internships or fieldwork, institutionally sponsored loans, scholarships/grants, tuition waivers, and unspecified assistantships also available. Financial award application deadline: 2/1; financial award applicants required to submit FAFSA. *Faculty research:* Community partnership, non-profit organizations, child welfare practice and policy, gerontological practice and policy, restorative justice. *Unit head:* Brian Bride, Director of School of Social Work, 404-413-1052, Fax: 404-413-1075, E-mail: bbride@gsu.edu.
Website: http://aysps.gsu.edu/socialwork

Golden Gate University, School of Accounting, San Francisco, CA 94105-2968. Offers financial accounting and reporting (M Ac, MSA, Graduate Certificate); forensic accounting (M Ac, MSA, Graduate Certificate); internal auditing (M Ac, MSA, Certificate); management accounting (M Ac, MSA); taxation (M Ac, MSA). *Program availability:* Part-time, evening/weekend. *Faculty:* 3 full-time (1 woman), 64 part-time/adjunct (21 women). *Students:* 76 full-time (51 women), 136 part-time (87 women); includes 63 minority (7 Black or African American, non-Hispanic/Latino; 35 Asian, non-Hispanic/Latino; 18 Hispanic/Latino; 1 Native Hawaiian or other Pacific Islander, non-Hispanic/Latino; 2 Two or more races, non-Hispanic/Latino), 76 international. Average age 32. 94 applicants, 69% accepted, 38 enrolled. *Entrance requirements:* For master's, minimum GPA of 3.0. Additional exam requirements/recommendations for international students: Required—TOEFL (minimum score 550 paper-based), IELTS (minimum score 6.5). *Application deadline:* For fall admission, 5/15 for international students; for winter admission, 1/15 for international students; for spring admission, 9/15 for international students. Applications are processed on a rolling basis. Application fee: $65 ($95 for international students). Electronic applications accepted. *Expenses:* $3,150 per 3-unit course. *Financial support:* Career-related internships or fieldwork, Federal Work-Study, institutionally sponsored loans, and scholarships/grants available. Support available to part-time students. Financial award applicants required to submit FAFSA. *Faculty research:* Forensic accounting, audit, tax, CPA exam. *Unit head:* Fred Sroka, Dean, 415-369-5285, Fax: 415-543-2607. *Application contact:* Angela Melero, Enrollment Services, 415-442-7800, Fax: 415-442-7807, E-mail: info@ggu.edu.

Indiana University–Purdue University Indianapolis, School of Science, Forensic and Investigative Sciences Program, Indianapolis, IN 46202. Offers MS. *Degree requirements:* For master's, thesis optional. *Entrance requirements:* For master's, GRE General Test, bachelor's degree in chemistry, biology, forensic science, pharmacology/toxicology, or related science from accredited institution; minimum GPA of 3.0 for all undergraduate work.

Iona College, School of Arts and Science, Department of Criminal Justice, New Rochelle, NY 10801-1890. Offers criminal justice (MS); cybercrime and security (AC); forensic criminology and criminal justice systems (Certificate). *Program availability:* Part-time, evening/weekend. *Faculty:* 3 full-time (1 woman), 4 part-time/adjunct (1 woman). *Students:* 13 full-time (7 women), 7 part-time (1 woman); includes 6 minority (3 Black or African American, non-Hispanic/Latino; 3 Hispanic/Latino). Average age 24. 13 applicants, 92% accepted, 8 enrolled. In 2017, 17 master's, 6 other advanced degrees awarded. *Degree requirements:* For master's, thesis (for some programs), thesis or literature review. *Entrance requirements:* For master's, minimum GPA of 3.0. Additional exam requirements/recommendations for international students: Required—TOEFL (minimum score 550 paper-based; 80 iBT), IELTS (minimum score 6.5). *Application deadline:* For fall admission, 8/1 priority date for domestic students, 5/1 priority date for international students; for spring admission, 1/1 priority date for domestic students, 9/1 priority date for international students. Applications are processed on a rolling basis. Electronic applications accepted. Tuition and fees vary according to program. *Financial support:* In 2017–18, 1 student received support. Unspecified assistantships available. Financial award application deadline: 4/15; financial award applicants required to submit

FAFSA. *Faculty research:* Juvenile justice, criminology, victimology, policing, social justice, security threat assessment. *Unit head:* Cathryn Lavery, PhD, Chair, 914-633-2597, E-mail: clavery@iona.edu. *Application contact:* Katelyn Brunck, Assistant Director of Graduate Admissions, 914-633-2451, Fax: 914-633-2277, E-mail: kbrunck@iona.edu. Website: http://www.iona.edu/Academics/School-of-Arts-Science/Departments/Criminal-Justice/Graduate-Programs.aspx

James Madison University, The Graduate School, College of Integrated Science and Engineering, Program in Computer Science, Harrisonburg, VA 22801. Offers digital forensics (MS); information security (MS). *Program availability:* Online learning. *Students:* 7 full-time (1 woman), 34 part-time (10 women); includes 5 minority (2 Black or African American, non-Hispanic/Latino; 1 Asian, non-Hispanic/Latino; 1 Hispanic/Latino; 1 Two or more races, non-Hispanic/Latino), 1 international. Average age 30. In 2017, 9 master's awarded. Application fee: $55. Electronic applications accepted. *Expenses:* Tuition, state resident: full-time $10,512; part-time $438 per credit hour. Tuition, nonresident: full-time $28,358; part-time $1162 per credit hour. *Required fees:* $1128. *Financial support:* In 2017–18, 4 students received support. Fellowships, Federal Work-Study, and 4 assistantships (averaging $7911) available. Financial award application deadline: 3/1; financial award applicants required to submit FAFSA. *Unit head:* Dr. Sharon J. Simmons, Department Head, 540-568-4196, E-mail: simmonsj@jmu.edu. *Application contact:* Lynette D. Michael, Director of Graduate Admissions, 540-568-6131 Ext. 6395, Fax: 540-568-7860, E-mail: michaeld@jmu.edu. Website: http://www.jmu.edu/cs/

John Jay College of Criminal Justice of the City University of New York, Graduate Studies, Program in Forensic Computing, New York, NY 10019. Offers MS. *Program availability:* Part-time, evening/weekend. *Degree requirements:* For master's, thesis or alternative. *Entrance requirements:* For master's, GRE General Test, minimum B average. Additional exam requirements/recommendations for international students: Required—TOEFL (minimum score 500 paper-based).

John Jay College of Criminal Justice of the City University of New York, Graduate Studies, Program in Forensic Science, New York, NY 10019. Offers MS. *Program availability:* Part-time, evening/weekend. *Degree requirements:* For master's, thesis. *Entrance requirements:* For master's, GRE, minimum B average. Additional exam requirements/recommendations for international students: Required—TOEFL (minimum score 500 paper-based).

John Jay College of Criminal Justice of the City University of New York, Graduate Studies, Programs in Criminal Justice, New York, NY 10019. Offers criminal justice (MA, PhD); criminology and deviance (PhD); forensic psychology (PhD); forensic science (PhD); international crime and justice (MA); law and philosophy (PhD); organizational behavior (PhD); public policy (PhD). *Program availability:* Part-time, evening/weekend. Terminal master's awarded for partial completion of doctoral program. *Degree requirements:* For master's, thesis or alternative; for doctorate, one foreign language, thesis/dissertation. *Entrance requirements:* For master's, GRE General Test, minimum B average; for doctorate, GRE General Test. Additional exam requirements/recommendations for international students: Required—TOEFL (minimum score 500 paper-based).

La Salle University, School of Arts and Sciences, Program in Economic Crime Forensics, Philadelphia, PA 19141-1199. Offers corporate fraud (MS); fraud and forensic accounting (Certificate); network security (MS). *Program availability:* Part-time, evening/weekend, online only, 100% online. *Faculty:* 6 part-time/adjunct (1 woman). *Students:* 1 full-time (0 women), 43 part-time (25 women); includes 21 minority (16 Black or African American, non-Hispanic/Latino; 2 Asian, non-Hispanic/Latino; 2 Hispanic/Latino; 1 Native Hawaiian or other Pacific Islander, non-Hispanic/Latino), 2 international. Average age 38. 10 applicants, 30% accepted, 3 enrolled. In 2017, 13 master's, 7 other advanced degrees awarded. *Entrance requirements:* For master's, minimum GPA of 3.0; professional resume; letters of recommendation; personal interview; for Certificate, professional resume, 200-word essay. Additional exam requirements/recommendations for international students: Required—TOEFL. *Application deadline:* For fall admission, 8/15 priority date for domestic students; for spring admission, 12/15 priority date for domestic students; for summer admission, 4/15 priority date for domestic students. Applications are processed on a rolling basis. Application fee: $35. Electronic applications accepted. Application fee is waived when completed online. *Expenses:* Contact institution. *Financial support:* In 2017–18, 10 students received support. Scholarships/grants available. Support available to part-time students. Financial award application deadline: 8/31; financial award applicants required to submit FAFSA. *Unit head:* Margaret M. McCoey, Director, 215-951-1136, Fax: 215-951-1805, E-mail: mccoey@lasalle.edu. *Application contact:* Elizabeth Heenan, Director, Graduate and Adult Enrollment, 215-951-1100, Fax: 215-951-1462, E-mail: heenan@lasalle.edu. Website: http://www.lasalle.edu/economic-crime-forensics/

Long Island University–LIU Brooklyn, School of Health Professions, Brooklyn, NY 11201-8423. Offers athletic training and sport sciences (MS); community health (MS Ed); exercise science (MS); forensic social work (Advanced Certificate); occupational therapy (MS); physical therapy (DPT); physician assistant (MS); public health (MPH); social work (MSW); speech-language pathology (MS). *Faculty:* 33 full-time (23 women), 82 part-time/adjunct (55 women). *Students:* 690 full-time (508 women), 86 part-time (74 women); includes 259 minority (120 Black or African American, non-Hispanic/Latino; 1 American Indian or Alaska Native, non-Hispanic/Latino; 52 Asian, non-Hispanic/Latino; 76 Hispanic/Latino; 10 Two or more races, non-Hispanic/Latino), 65 international. Average age 27. 1,241 applicants, 45% accepted, 255 enrolled. In 2017, 249 master's, 42 doctorates, 8 other advanced degrees awarded. *Degree requirements:* For master's, comprehensive exam (for some programs), thesis (for some programs); for doctorate, comprehensive exam (for some programs). *Entrance requirements:* For master's and doctorate, GRE. Additional exam requirements/recommendations for international students: Required—TOEFL (minimum score 550 paper-based; 79 iBT). *Application deadline:* Applications are processed on a rolling basis. Application fee: $50. Electronic applications accepted. *Expenses:* Tuition: Full-time $21,618; part-time $1201 per credit. *Required fees:* $1840; $920 per term. Tuition and fees vary according to course load. *Financial support:* In 2017–18, 187 students received support. Research assistantships, teaching assistantships, career-related internships or fieldwork, Federal Work-Study, scholarships/grants, and unspecified assistantships available. Support available to part-time students. Financial award application deadline: 2/15; financial award applicants required to submit FAFSA. *Faculty research:* Pediatric physical therapy, complementary and alternative medicine, global health and human rights, sport leadership and entrepreneurship, feminist sport psychology. *Unit head:* Dr. Barry S. Eckert, Dean, 718-780-6578, Fax: 718-780-4561, E-mail: barry.eckert@liu.edu. *Application contact:* Dr. Dominick Fortugno, Associate Dean, 718-488-1496, Fax: 718-780-4561, E-mail: dominick.fortugno@liu.edu. Website: http://liu.edu/brooklyn/academics/school-of-health-professions

Marshall University, Academic Affairs Division, Forensic Science Center, Huntington, WV 25755. Offers MS, Graduate Certificate. *Students:* 33 full-time (28 women), 1 part-time (0 women); includes 5 minority (1 American Indian or Alaska Native, non-Hispanic/Latino; 2 Asian, non-Hispanic/Latino; 1 Hispanic/Latino; 1 Two or more races, non-Hispanic/Latino). Average age 23. In 2017, 16 master's awarded. *Degree requirements:* For master's, comprehensive exam, thesis optional. *Entrance requirements:* For

master's, GRE General Test, undergraduate degree in a natural science, forensic science, or equivalent course work in a related field; 1 year of undergraduate coursework in general chemistry, organic chemistry, physics and biology, with 1 year of associated laboratory for each course. Additional exam requirements/recommendations for international students: Required—TOEFL. *Application deadline:* For fall admission, 3/1 for domestic and international students. Application fee: $40. *Expenses:* Contact institution. *Financial support:* In 2017–18, 12 research assistantships with full tuition reimbursements (averaging $4,000 per year), teaching assistantships with full tuition reimbursements (averaging $6,000 per year) were awarded; career-related internships or fieldwork, Federal Work-Study, institutionally sponsored loans, tuition waivers (partial), and unspecified assistantships also available. Financial award application deadline: 8/27; financial award applicants required to submit FAFSA. *Faculty research:* STR analysis of DNA for human identification, forensic analytical chemistry, digital forensics/computer forensics examination, microbial source tracking. *Total annual research expenditures:* $6.5 million. *Unit head:* Dr. Terry W. Fenger, Director, 304-690-4373, Fax: 304-690-4360, E-mail: fenger@marshall.edu. *Application contact:* Kelly Preston, Senior Administrative Secretary, 304-690-4363 Ext. 248, Fax: 304-690-4371, E-mail: forensics@marshall.edu. Website: http://forensics.marshall.edu/

McGill University, Faculty of Graduate and Postdoctoral Studies, Faculty of Dentistry, Montréal, QC H3A 2T5, Canada. Offers forensic dentistry (Certificate); oral and maxillofacial surgery (M Sc, PhD).

Mercyhurst University, Graduate Studies, Program in Anthropology, Erie, PA 16546. Offers archaeology and geological archaeology (MS); forensic and biological anthropology (MS). *Entrance requirements:* For master's, GRE or MAT, undergraduate degree in related field, interview, resume, essay, three professional references, transcripts. Additional exam requirements/recommendations for international students: Required—TOEFL.

Michigan State University, The Graduate School, College of Social Science, School of Criminal Justice, East Lansing, MI 48824. Offers criminal justice (MS, PhD); forensic science (MS); law enforcement intelligence and analysis (MS). *Program availability:* Online learning. *Entrance requirements:* Additional exam requirements/recommendations for international students: Required—TOEFL. Electronic applications accepted.

Middle Georgia State University, Office of Graduate Studies, Macon, GA 31206. Offers adult/gerontology acute care nurse practitioner (MSN); information technology (MS), including health informatics, information security and digital forensics, software development. *Entrance requirements:* For master's, GRE. Additional exam requirements/recommendations for international students: Required—TOEFL (minimum score 523 paper-based; 69 iBT). *Expenses:* Contact institution.

Missouri Western State University, Program in Forensic Investigations, St. Joseph, MO 64507-2294. Offers MAS, Graduate Certificate. *Program availability:* Part-time. *Students:* 10 full-time (9 women), 12 part-time (10 women); includes 6 minority (4 Black or African American, non-Hispanic/Latino; 1 American Indian or Alaska Native, non-Hispanic/Latino; 1 Two or more races, non-Hispanic/Latino), 1 international. Average age 30. 6 applicants, 100% accepted, 6 enrolled. In 2017, 5 master's awarded. *Entrance requirements:* For master's, minimum GPA of 2.75, personal statement, 2 letters of recommendation. Additional exam requirements/recommendations for international students: Recommended—TOEFL (minimum score 79 iBT), IELTS (minimum score 6). *Application deadline:* For fall admission, 7/15 for domestic and international students; for spring admission, 10/1 for domestic and international students; for summer admission, 3/15 for domestic students. Applications are processed on a rolling basis. Application fee: $45 ($50 for international students). Electronic applications accepted. *Expenses:* Tuition, state resident: full-time $6391; part-time $336 per credit hour. Tuition, nonresident: full-time $11,483; part-time $604 per credit hour. *Required fees:* $542; $99 per credit hour. $176 per semester. One-time fee: $45. Tuition and fees vary according to course load and program. *Financial support:* Scholarships/grants and unspecified assistantships available. Support available to part-time students. *Unit head:* Dr. Monty Smith, Forensics Graduate Program Director, 816-271-4434, E-mail: msmith84@missouriwestern.edu. *Application contact:* Dr. Benjamin D. Caldwell, Dean of the Graduate School, 816-271-4394, Fax: 816-271-4525, E-mail: graduate@missouriwestern.edu. Website: https://www.missouriwestern.edu/cj-ls-swk/forensic-investigation/

National University, Academic Affairs, College of Letters and Sciences, La Jolla, CA 92037-1011. Offers biology (MS); counseling psychology (MA), including licensed professional clinical counseling, marriage and family therapy; creative writing (MFA); english (MA); film studies (MA); forensic and crime scene investigations (Certificate); forensic sciences (MFS); human behavior (MA); mathematics for educators (MS); performance psychology (MA); strategic communications (MA). *Program availability:* Part-time, evening/weekend, 100% online, blended/hybrid learning. *Degree requirements:* For master's, thesis (for some programs). *Entrance requirements:* For master's, interview, minimum GPA of 2.5. Additional exam requirements/recommendations for international students: Required—TOEFL (minimum score 550 paper-based; 79 iBT), IELTS (minimum score 6). *Application deadline:* Applications are processed on a rolling basis. Application fee: $60 ($65 for international students). Electronic applications accepted. *Expenses:* Tuition: Part-time $430 per quarter hour. *Financial support:* Career-related internships or fieldwork, institutionally sponsored loans, scholarships/grants, and tuition waivers (partial) available. Support available to part-time students. Financial award application deadline: 6/30; financial award applicants required to submit FAFSA. *Unit head:* Dr. Carol Richardson, Dean, 858-642-8450, E-mail: cols@nu.edu. *Application contact:* Brandon Jouganatos, Interim Vice President for Enrollment Services, 800-628-8648, E-mail: advisor@nu.edu. Website: http://www.nu.edu/OurPrograms/CollegeOfLettersAndSciences.html

Nebraska Wesleyan University, University College, Program in Forensic Science, Lincoln, NE 68504-2796. Offers MFS. *Program availability:* Part-time, evening/weekend.

Niagara University, Graduate Division of Arts and Sciences, Niagara University, NY 14109. Offers criminal justice (MS), including criminal justice administration; information security and digital forensics (MS); interdisciplinary studies (MA). *Program availability:* Part-time, evening/weekend. *Faculty:* 9 full-time, 1 part-time/adjunct. *Students:* 34 full-time (14 women), 21 part-time (13 women); includes 11 minority (4 Black or African American, non-Hispanic/Latino; 3 Asian, non-Hispanic/Latino; 4 Hispanic/Latino), 16 international. Average age 29. In 2017, 21 master's awarded. *Entrance requirements:* For master's, GRE. Additional exam requirements/recommendations for international students: Required—TOEFL (minimum score 550 paper-based; 79 iBT), IELTS (minimum score 6). *Application deadline:* For fall admission, 8/1 for domestic students. Applications are processed on a rolling basis. *Expenses:* Contact institution. *Financial support:* Research assistantships with tuition reimbursements, teaching assistantships with tuition reimbursements, career-related internships or fieldwork, Federal Work-Study, scholarships/grants, and unspecified assistantships available. Support available to part-time students. Financial award application deadline: 4/15; financial award applicants required to submit FAFSA. *Unit head:* Dr. Peter Butera, Dean, 716-286-8060, Fax: 716-286-8061, E-mail: pbutera@niagara.edu. *Application contact:* Evan Pierce, Associate Dean for Graduate Recruitment, 716-286-8769, Fax: 716-286-8170. Website: http://www.niagara.edu/coas-graduate

Forensic Sciences

Oklahoma State University Center for Health Sciences, Graduate Program in Forensic Sciences, Tulsa, OK 74107-1898. Offers forensic sciences (MS), including arson and explosives investigation, forensic biology/DNA, forensic document examination, forensic pathology/death scene investigations, forensic psychology, forensic science administration, forensic toxicology/trace evidence. *Program availability:* Part-time, evening/weekend, 100% online, blended/hybrid learning. *Degree requirements:* For master's, comprehensive exam, thesis (for some programs), thesis or creative component. *Entrance requirements:* For master's, GRE (for thesis tracks); GRE or MAT (for options in arson and explosives investigation, forensic science administration, and forensic document examination), professional experience (for options in arson and explosives investigation, forensic science administration and forensic document examination). Additional exam requirements/recommendations for international students: Required—TOEFL (minimum score 100 iBT) or IELTS (minimum score 7.0). Electronic applications accepted. *Faculty research:* Studies on the variability in chromosomal DNA; development/ enhancement of accessory methods useful for forensic DNA typing; forensic chemistry in the areas of controlled substances, explosives, and technology; research on explosives and IEDs (non-chemistry); therapeutic jurisprudence, issues involving inmates and their families, institutional stress suicide.

Pace University, Dyson College of Arts and Sciences, Program in Forensic Science, New York, NY 10038. Offers MS. *Program availability:* Part-time, evening/weekend. *Faculty:* 1 full-time (0 women), 5 part-time/adjunct (3 women). *Students:* 20 full-time (17 women), 8 part-time (6 women); includes 15 minority (4 Black or African American, non-Hispanic/Latino; 4 Asian, non-Hispanic/Latino; 4 Hispanic/Latino; 3 Two or more races, non-Hispanic/Latino), 1 international. Average age 25. In 2017, 9 master's awarded. *Degree requirements:* For master's, thesis. *Entrance requirements:* For master's, two letters of recommendation, personal statement, resume, official transcripts. Additional exam requirements/recommendations for international students: Required—TOEFL (minimum score 88 iBT). *Application deadline:* For fall admission, 8/1 priority date for domestic students, 6/1 for international students; for spring admission, 12/1 priority date for domestic students, 10/1 for international students. Applications are processed on a rolling basis. Application fee: $70. Electronic applications accepted. *Financial support:* Career-related internships or fieldwork, Federal Work-Study, and scholarships/grants available. Financial award application deadline: 2/15; financial award applicants required to submit FAFSA. *Unit head:* Dr. Demos Athanasopolous, Director, Forensic Science Program, 212-346-1763, E-mail: dathanasopolous@pace.edu. *Application contact:* Susan Ford-Goldschein, Director of Graduate Admissions, 212-346-1531, Fax: 212-346-1585, E-mail: gradnyc@pace.edu.
Website: http://www.pace.edu/dyson/academic-departments-and-programs/forensic-science

Penn State University Park, Graduate School, Eberly College of Science, Program in Forensic Science, University Park, PA 16802. Offers MPS. *Unit head:* Reena Roy, Director, 814-867-2054, E-mail: rxr34@psu.edu. *Application contact:* Cynthia E. Nicosia, Director, Graduate Enrollment Services, 814-865-1795, Fax: 814-865-4627, E-mail: cey1@psu.edu. Website: http://forensics.psu.edu/program/masters-in-forensic-science

Philadelphia College of Osteopathic Medicine, Graduate and Professional Programs, Programs in Forensic Medicine, Philadelphia, PA 19131-1694. Offers MS. *Program availability:* Evening/weekend. *Faculty:* 2 full-time (0 women), 2 part-time/adjunct (1 woman). *Students:* 63 full-time (53 women); includes 20 minority (9 Black or African American, non-Hispanic/Latino; 2 Asian, non-Hispanic/Latino; 9 Two or more races, non-Hispanic/Latino), 1 international. Average age 28. 75 applicants, 40% accepted, 25 enrolled. In 2017, 20 master's awarded. *Degree requirements:* For master's, capstone project. *Entrance requirements:* For master's, minimum GPA of 3.0; coursework in biology, chemistry, anatomy and physiology or completion of PCOM pathway program. Additional exam requirements/recommendations for international students: Required—TOEFL (minimum score 79 iBT). *Application deadline:* Applications are processed on a rolling basis. Application fee: $75. Electronic applications accepted. *Expenses:* Contact institution. *Financial support:* In 2017–18, 11 students received support. Federal Work-Study, institutionally sponsored loans, and scholarships/grants available. Financial award application deadline: 3/15; financial award applicants required to submit FAFSA. *Unit head:* Dr. Gregory McDonald, Chair, 215-871-6760, Fax: 215-871-6792. *Application contact:* Brianna Rojas, Admissions Recruiter, 215-871-6700, Fax: 215-871-6719, E-mail: briannaro@pcom.edu.
Website: http://www.pcom.edu

St. Joseph's College, Long Island Campus, Program in Forensic Computing, Patchogue, NY 11772-2399. Offers MS. *Program availability:* Part-time, evening/ weekend, 100% online, blended/hybrid learning. *Students:* 3 full-time (1 woman), 7 part-time (0 women); includes 2 minority (1 Black or African American, non-Hispanic/Latino; 1 Hispanic/Latino). Average age 25. 12 applicants, 100% accepted, 10 enrolled. *Entrance requirements:* For master's, Official transcripts, 2 letters of reference, resume, and written statement. Additional exam requirements/recommendations for international students: Required—TOEFL (minimum score 80 iBT). *Application deadline:* Applications are processed on a rolling basis. Application fee: $25. Electronic applications accepted. *Expenses:* Tuition: Full-time $17,550; part-time $975 per credit. *Required fees:* $362. *Financial support:* In 2017–18, 2 students received support. *Unit head:* Victoria Hong, Chairperson/Assistant Professor/Director, 631-687-2646, E-mail: vhong@sjcny.edu. Website: https://www.sjcny.edu/long-island/academics/graduate/degree/forensic-computing

St. Joseph's College, New York, Program in Forensic Computing, Brooklyn, NY 11205-3688. Offers MS. *Program availability:* Part-time, evening/weekend, online learning. *Faculty:* 2 full-time (0 women), 1 (woman) part-time/adjunct. *Students:* 4 full-time (1 woman), 4 part-time (2 women); includes 4 minority (2 Black or African American, non-Hispanic/Latino; 2 Hispanic/Latino). Average age 27. 11 applicants, 82% accepted, 3 enrolled. *Entrance requirements:* For master's, official transcripts, 2 letters of reference, resume, written statement. Additional exam requirements/ recommendations for international students: Required—TOEFL (minimum score 80 iBT). *Application deadline:* Applications are processed on a rolling basis. Application fee: $25. Electronic applications accepted. *Expenses:* Tuition: Full-time $17,550; part-time $975 per credit. *Required fees:* $362. *Financial support:* In 2017–18, 3 students received support. *Unit head:* Dr. Joseph Pascarella, Associate Professor, 718-940-5775, E-mail: jpascarella2@sjcny.edu. *Application contact:* Roberto Figueroa, Director, Graduate and Adult Admissions, 718-940-5828, E-mail: rfigueroa@sjcny.edu.
Website: https://www.sjcny.edu/brooklyn/academics/graduate/graduate-degrees/forensic-computing

Saint Leo University, Graduate Studies in Public Safety Administration, Saint Leo, FL 33574-6665. Offers criminal justice (MS), including behavioral studies, corrections, criminal investigation, criminal justice, emergency and disaster management, forensic science, legal studies; emergency and disaster management (MS), including emergency and disaster management, fire science. *Program availability:* Part-time, evening/ weekend, 100% online, blended/hybrid learning. *Faculty:* 8 full-time (3 women), 32 part-time/adjunct (7 women). *Students:* 7 full-time (6 women), 617 part-time (385 women); includes 313 minority (235 Black or African American, non-Hispanic/Latino; 5 American Indian or Alaska Native, non-Hispanic/Latino; 3 Asian, non-Hispanic/Latino; 54 Hispanic/ Latino; 1 Native Hawaiian or other Pacific Islander, non-Hispanic/Latino; 15 Two or more races, non-Hispanic/Latino). Average age 36. 336 applicants, 63% accepted, 197 enrolled. In 2017, 267 master's awarded. *Degree requirements:* For master's, comprehensive project. *Entrance requirements:* For master's, official transcripts, bachelor's degree from regionally-accredited university with minimum GPA of 3.0. Additional exam requirements/recommendations for international students: Required— TOEFL (minimum score 550 paper-based; 78 iBT). *Application deadline:* For fall admission, 7/1 priority date for domestic and international students; for spring admission, 11/1 priority date for domestic and international students. Applications are processed on a rolling basis. Application fee: $80. Electronic applications accepted. *Expenses:* $555 per credit hour. *Financial support:* In 2017–18, 21 students received support. Scholarships/grants, health care benefits, unspecified assistantships, and tuition remission for Saint Leo employees and their dependents available. Financial award application deadline: 3/1; financial award applicants required to submit FAFSA. *Faculty research:* Emergency management, fire science, community policing. *Unit head:* Dr. Robert Diemer, Director of Graduate Studies in Safety Administration, 352-588-8974, Fax: 352-588-8289, E-mail: graduatepublicsafety@saintleo.edu. *Application contact:* Mark Russum, Assistant Vice President, Enrollment, 800-707-8846, Fax: 352-588-7873, E-mail: grad.admissions@saintleo.edu.
Website: https://www.saintleo.edu/criminal-justice-master-degree

Salve Regina University, Program in Administration of Justice and Homeland Security, Newport, RI 02840-4192. Offers administration of justice and homeland security (MS); cybersecurity and intelligence (CGS); digital forensics (CGS); leadership in justice (CGS). *Program availability:* Part-time, evening/weekend, online learning. *Entrance requirements:* For master's, GMAT, GRE General Test, or MAT. Additional exam requirements/recommendations for international students: Required—TOEFL (minimum score 600 paper-based; 100 iBT). Electronic applications accepted.

Sam Houston State University, College of Criminal Justice, Department of Forensic Science, Huntsville, TX 77341. Offers MS. *Program availability:* Part-time. *Degree requirements:* For master's, comprehensive exam. *Entrance requirements:* For master's, GRE, official transcripts, three letters of recommendation, personal essay. Additional exam requirements/recommendations for international students: Required— TOEFL (minimum score 550 paper-based; 79 iBT), IELTS (minimum score 6.5). Electronic applications accepted.

Sam Houston State University, College of Sciences, Department of Computer Science, Huntsville, TX 77341. Offers computing and information science (MS); digital forensics (MS); information assurance and security (MS). *Program availability:* Part-time. *Degree requirements:* For master's, comprehensive exam, thesis optional, internship; for doctorate, comprehensive exam, thesis/dissertation. *Entrance requirements:* For master's, GRE General Test, letters of recommendation. Additional exam requirements/ recommendations for international students: Required—TOEFL (minimum score 550 paper-based; 79 iBT), IELTS (minimum score 6.5). Electronic applications accepted.

Seattle University, College of Arts and Sciences, Department of Criminal Justice, Seattle, WA 98122-1090. Offers crime analysis (Certificate); criminal justice (MACJ). *Program availability:* Part-time, evening/weekend. *Faculty:* 8 full-time (2 women), 4 part-time/adjunct (2 women). *Students:* 19 full-time (13 women), 39 part-time (33 women); includes 23 minority (3 Black or African American, non-Hispanic/Latino; 1 American Indian or Alaska Native, non-Hispanic/Latino; 5 Asian, non-Hispanic/Latino; 5 Hispanic/ Latino; 1 Native Hawaiian or other Pacific Islander, non-Hispanic/Latino; 8 Two or more races, non-Hispanic/Latino). Average age 27. 52 applicants, 81% accepted, 24 enrolled. In 2017, 29 master's, 5 Certificates awarded. *Degree requirements:* For master's, comprehensive exam or thesis. *Entrance requirements:* For master's, minimum GPA of 3.0; undergraduate degree in criminal justice or related social, behavioral, or physical science, or related coursework and/or volunteer or supervised experience; letters of recommendation; writing sample. Additional exam requirements/recommendations for international students: Required—TOEFL, IELTS. *Application deadline:* For fall admission, 3/15 for domestic and international students. Application fee: $55. Electronic applications accepted. *Expenses:* Tuition: Full-time $12,960. *Required fees:* $570. Tuition and fees vary according to program. *Financial support:* In 2017–18, 25 students received support. Applicants required to submit FAFSA. *Faculty research:* Criminal justice program evaluation, ex-offender reentry, policing issues, restorative justice, psychopathy. *Unit head:* Dr. Elaine Gunnison, Graduate Program Director, 206-296-2430, E-mail: gunnisone@seattleu.edu. *Application contact:* Janet Shandley, Associate Dean of Graduate Admissions, 206-296-5900, Fax: 206-298-5656, E-mail: grad_admissions@seattleu.edu.
Website: https://www.seattleu.edu/artsci/criminal-graduate/

Stevenson University, Program in Forensic Science, Owings Mills, MD 21153. Offers biology (MS); chemistry (MS); crime scene investigation (MS). Program offered in partnership with Maryland State Police Forensic Sciences Division. *Program availability:* Part-time. *Faculty:* 4 full-time (3 women), 4 part-time/adjunct (2 women). *Students:* 22 full-time (16 women), 21 part-time (18 women); includes 23 minority (19 Black or African American, non-Hispanic/Latino; 1 American Indian or Alaska Native, non-Hispanic/ Latino; 3 Two or more races, non-Hispanic/Latino). Average age 28. 18 applicants, 100% accepted, 18 enrolled. In 2017, 26 master's awarded. *Degree requirements:* For master's, capstone course. *Entrance requirements:* For master's, bachelor's degree in a natural science from regionally-accredited institution; official college transcripts from all previous academic work; minimum cumulative GPA of 3.0 in past academic work. *Application deadline:* Applications are processed on a rolling basis. Application fee: $0. Electronic applications accepted. *Expenses:* Contact institution. *Financial support:* Unspecified assistantships available. Financial award applicants required to submit FAFSA. *Unit head:* John Tobin, PhD, Coordinator, 443-352-4142, Fax: 443-394-0538, E-mail: jtobin@stevenson.edu. *Application contact:* William Wellein, Enrollment Counselor, 443-352-5843, Fax: 443-394-0538, E-mail: wwellein@stevenson.edu.
Website: http://www.stevenson.edu

Stevenson University, Program in Forensic Studies, Owings Mills, MD 21153. Offers computer forensics (MS); criminalistics (MS); forensic accounting (MS); forensic legal professional (MS); interdisciplinary track (MS); investigations (MS). *Program availability:* Part-time, blended/hybrid learning. *Faculty:* 3 full-time (all women), 10 part-time/adjunct (1 woman). *Students:* 22 full-time (15 women), 103 part-time (85 women); includes 61 minority (51 Black or African American, non-Hispanic/Latino; 3 Asian, non-Hispanic/ Latino; 7 Two or more races, non-Hispanic/Latino). Average age 30. 42 applicants, 90% accepted, 34 enrolled. In 2017, 34 master's awarded. *Degree requirements:* For master's, capstone course. *Entrance requirements:* For master's, bachelor's degree from regionally-accredited institution, official college transcripts from all previous academic work, minimum cumulative GPA of 3.0 in past academic work, personal statement (250-350 words). *Application deadline:* Applications are processed on a rolling basis. Application fee: $0. Electronic applications accepted. *Expenses:* Contact institution. *Financial support:* Unspecified assistantships available. Financial award applicants required to submit FAFSA. *Unit head:* Thomas Coogan, JD, Associate Dean, 443-352-4075, Fax: 443-394-0538, E-mail: tcoogan@stevenson.edu. *Application contact:* William Wellein, Enrollment Counselor, 443-352-5843, Fax: 443-394-0538, E-mail: wwellein@stevenson.edu.
Website: http://www.stevenson.edu/online/academics/online-graduate-programs/forensic-studies/

Stratford University, School of Graduate Studies, Falls Church, VA 22043. Offers accounting (MS); business administration (MBA, DBA); cyber security (MS); cyber security leadership and policy (MS); digital forensics (MS); healthcare administration (MS); information systems (MS); information technology (DIT); networking and telecommunications (MS); software engineering (MS). *Program availability:* Part-time, evening/weekend, 100% online, blended/hybrid learning. *Students:* 272 full-time (110 women), 204 part-time (89 women). *Degree requirements:* For master's, comprehensive exam, capstone project. *Entrance requirements:* For master's, GRE or GMAT, baccalaureate degree. Additional exam requirements/recommendations for international students: Required—TOEFL (minimum score 79 iBT), IELTS (minimum score 6.5), PTE (minimum score 5). *Application deadline:* Applications are processed on a rolling basis. Application fee: $50. Electronic applications accepted. *Expenses: Tuition:* Full-time $33,405; part-time $11,135 per credit hour. One-time fee: $385 full-time. Tuition and fees vary according to degree level and program. *Financial support:* Federal Work-Study and scholarships/grants available. Financial award applicants required to submit FAFSA. *Unit head:* Dr. Valarie Trimarchi, Campus President, 703-539-6890, Fax: 703-539-6960. *Application contact:* Lori Smith, Admissions, 214-649-7113, E-mail: lasmith@stratford.edu.

Syracuse University, College of Arts and Sciences, Programs in Forensic Science, Syracuse, NY 13244. Offers advanced forensic science (MS); biomedical forensic science (MS); firearm and tool mark examination (CAS); general forensic science (MS); medicolegal death investigation (MS, CAS); nuclear forensics (MS); MS/JD. *Degree requirements:* For master's, internship. *Entrance requirements:* For master's, GRE General Test, personal statement, three letters of recommendation, transcripts, telephone interview. Additional exam requirements/recommendations for international students: Required—TOEFL (minimum score 100 iBT). *Application deadline:* For fall admission, 2/15 priority date for domestic and international students; for summer admission, 2/15 for domestic students, 2/16 priority date for international students. Applications are processed on a rolling basis. Application fee: $75. Electronic applications accepted. *Financial support:* Research assistantships, teaching assistantships, scholarships/grants, and unspecified assistantships available. Financial award application deadline: 1/1; financial award applicants required to submit FAFSA. *Faculty research:* Chemical analysis, molecular genetics, forensic biochemical analysis, forensic entomology, human osteology. *Unit head:* Dr. Kevin Sweder, Director of Research and Operations/Professor, Forensics, 315-443-3396, E-mail: kssweder@syr.edu. *Application contact:* Christine Woods Heslin, Academic Support Coordinator, 315-443-0360, E-mail: forensics@syr.edu.
Website: http://forensics.syr.edu/

Texas Tech University, Graduate School, College of Arts and Sciences, Program in Forensic Science, Lubbock, TX 79409. Offers MS. *Students:* 14 full-time (12 women), 7 part-time (2 women); includes 8 minority (2 Black or African American, non-Hispanic/Latino; 1 Asian, non-Hispanic/Latino; 5 Hispanic/Latino), 1 international. Average age 25. 17 applicants, 41% accepted, 7 enrolled. In 2017, 10 master's awarded. *Degree requirements:* For master's, thesis (for some programs), internship with comprehensive exam. *Entrance requirements:* Additional exam requirements/recommendations for international students: Required—TOEFL (minimum score 550 paper-based; 79 iBT). *Application deadline:* For fall admission, 6/1 priority date for domestic students, 1/15 priority date for international students; for spring admission, 9/1 priority date for domestic students, 6/15 priority date for international students. Applications are processed on a rolling basis. Application fee: $60. Electronic applications accepted. *Expenses:* Contact institution. *Financial support:* In 2017–18, 10 students received support, including 10 fellowships (averaging $2,034 per year); research assistantships also available. Financial award application deadline: 4/15; financial award applicants required to submit FAFSA. *Faculty research:* Forensic sciences; including toxicology, DNA, chemistry, psychology, and biology. *Unit head:* Dr. Megan A. Thoen, Graduate Program Director, 806-834-1687, Fax: 806-743-7932, E-mail: megan.thoen@ttu.edu.
Website: https://www.depts.ttu.edu/ifs/program-info.php

Towson University, Jess and Mildred Fisher College of Science and Mathematics, Program in Forensic Science, Towson, MD 21252-0001. Offers MS. *Students:* 43 full-time (35 women), 8 part-time (all women); includes 17 minority (10 Black or African American, non-Hispanic/Latino; 5 Asian, non-Hispanic/Latino; 2 Hispanic/Latino), 2 international. *Entrance requirements:* For master's, minimum GPA of 3.0; bachelor's degree in biological sciences, chemistry, forensic chemistry, or related field. *Application deadline:* For fall admission, 1/17 for domestic students, 5/15 for international students; for spring admission, 10/15 for domestic students, 12/1 for international students. Applications are processed on a rolling basis. Application fee: $45. Electronic applications accepted. *Expenses:* Tuition, state resident: full-time $7960; part-time $398 per unit. Tuition, nonresident: full-time $16,480; part-time $824 per unit. *Required fees:* $2600; $130 per year. $390 per term. *Unit head:* Mark Profili, Graduate Program Director, 410-704-2668, E-mail: mprofili@towson.edu. *Application contact:* Coverley Beidleman, Assistant Director of Graduate Admissions, 410-704-5630, Fax: 410-704-3030, E-mail: cbeidleman@towson.edu.
Website: http://www.towson.edu/fcsm/departments/chemistry/grad/forensic/

Universidad del Turabo, Graduate Programs, School of Social Sciences and Humanities, Programs in Public Affairs, Program in Forensic Science, Gurabo, PR 00778-3030. Offers MPA. *Entrance requirements:* For master's, GRE, GMAT or EXADEP, interview, essay, official transcript, recommendation letters. Electronic applications accepted.

University at Albany, State University of New York, College of Arts and Sciences, Department of Biological Sciences, Albany, NY 12222-0001. Offers forensic biology (MS). *Faculty:* 22 full-time (8 women). *Students:* 28 full-time (18 women), 36 part-time (20 women); includes 8 minority (2 Black or African American, non-Hispanic/Latino; 4 Asian, non-Hispanic/Latino; 1 Hispanic/Latino; 1 Two or more races, non-Hispanic/Latino), 10 international. 88 applicants, 31% accepted, 18 enrolled. In 2017, 4 master's awarded. *Degree requirements:* For master's, one foreign language. *Entrance requirements:* For master's, GRE General Test. Additional exam requirements/recommendations for international students: Required—TOEFL (minimum score 550 paper-based). *Application deadline:* For fall admission, 2/15 priority date for domestic students, 5/1 for international students; for spring admission, 11/1 for domestic and international students. Applications are processed on a rolling basis. Application fee: $75. Electronic applications accepted. *Expenses:* Tuition, state resident: full-time $10,870; part-time $453 per credit hour. Tuition, nonresident: full-time $22,210; part-time $925 per credit hour. *Required fees:* $84.68 per credit hour. $508.06 per semester. Part-time tuition and fees vary according to course load and program. *Financial support:* Fellowships, research assistantships, teaching assistantships, and minority assistantships available. Financial award application deadline: 5/1. *Faculty research:* Interferon, neural development, RNA self-splicing, behavioral ecology, DNA repair enzymes. *Unit head:* Glyne Griffith, Chair, 518-442-4300, Fax: 518-442-4354, E-mail: ggriffith@albany.edu. *Application contact:* Michael DeRensis, Director, Graduate Admissions, 518-442-3980, Fax: 518-442-3922, E-mail: graduate@albany.edu.
Website: http://www.albany.edu/biology/

The University of Alabama at Birmingham, College of Arts and Sciences, Program in Computer Forensics and Security Management, Birmingham, AL 35294. Offers MS. Interdisciplinary program offered jointly with College of Arts and Sciences and School of Business. *Degree requirements:* For master's, field practicum (internship). *Entrance requirements:* For master's, GRE General Test (minimum combined score of 320) or GMAT (minimum total score of 550), minimum GPA of 3.0. Electronic applications accepted.

The University of Alabama at Birmingham, College of Arts and Sciences, Program in Forensic Science, Birmingham, AL 35294. Offers MSFS. *Entrance requirements:* For master's, GRE, minimum GPA of 3.0. Additional exam requirements/recommendations for international students: Required—TOEFL, TWE. Electronic applications accepted.

University of California, Davis, Graduate Studies, Graduate Group in Forensic Science, Davis, CA 95616. Offers MS. *Degree requirements:* For master's, thesis. *Entrance requirements:* Additional exam requirements/recommendations for international students: Required—TOEFL (minimum score 550 paper-based), IELTS (minimum score 7). Electronic applications accepted.

University of Central Florida, College of Engineering and Computer Science, Department of Computer Science, Orlando, FL 32816. Offers computer science (MS, PhD); digital forensics (MS). *Program availability:* Part-time, evening/weekend. *Students:* 264 full-time (65 women), 153 part-time (38 women); includes 93 minority (21 Black or African American, non-Hispanic/Latino; 23 Asian, non-Hispanic/Latino; 47 Hispanic/Latino; 2 Two or more races, non-Hispanic/Latino), 198 international. Average age 30. 559 applicants, 63% accepted, 132 enrolled. In 2017, 91 master's, 10 doctorates awarded. *Degree requirements:* For master's, thesis or alternative; for doctorate, thesis/dissertation, candidacy exam, departmental qualifying exam. *Entrance requirements:* For master's, GRE General Test, GRE Subject Test, minimum GPA of 3.0 in last 60 hours, letters of recommendation, resume; for doctorate, GRE Subject Test, minimum GPA of 3.0 in last 60 hours, letters of recommendation, resume, goal statement. Additional exam requirements/recommendations for international students: Required—TOEFL. *Application deadline:* For fall admission, 7/15 for domestic students; for spring admission, 12/1 for domestic students. Application fee: $30. Electronic applications accepted. *Expenses:* Tuition, state resident: part-time $288.16 per credit hour. Tuition, nonresident: part-time $1073.31 per credit hour. Tuition and fees vary according to program. *Financial support:* In 2017–18, 145 students received support, including 26 fellowships with partial tuition reimbursements available (averaging $8,246 per year), 92 research assistantships with partial tuition reimbursements available (averaging $11,681 per year), 64 teaching assistantships with partial tuition reimbursements available (averaging $13,619 per year); career-related internships or fieldwork, Federal Work-Study, institutionally sponsored loans, health care benefits, tuition waivers (partial), and unspecified assistantships also available. Financial award application deadline: 3/1; financial award applicants required to submit FAFSA. *Faculty research:* Image and video processing, computer vision, artificial intelligence and machine learning, virtual reality, software engineering and systems. *Unit head:* Dr. Gary Leavens, Chair, 407-823-4758, Fax: 407-823-1488, E-mail: leavens@eecs.ucf.edu. *Application contact:* Associate Director, Graduate Admissions, 407-823-2766, Fax: 407-823-6442, E-mail: gradadmissions@ucf.edu.
Website: http://www.cs.ucf.edu/

University of Central Oklahoma, The Jackson College of Graduate Studies, College of Liberal Arts, School of Criminal Justice, Edmond, OK 73034-5209. Offers crime and intelligence analysis (MA); criminal justice management and administration (MA). *Program availability:* Part-time. *Faculty:* 8 full-time (4 women), 4 part-time/adjunct (1 woman). *Students:* 21 full-time (14 women), 14 part-time (10 women); includes 14 minority (4 Black or African American, non-Hispanic/Latino; 5 American Indian or Alaska Native, non-Hispanic/Latino; 4 Hispanic/Latino; 1 Two or more races, non-Hispanic/Latino), 1 international. Average age 30. 27 applicants, 44% accepted, 9 enrolled. In 2017, 11 master's awarded. *Degree requirements:* For master's, comprehensive exam (for some programs), thesis (for some programs). *Entrance requirements:* Additional exam requirements/recommendations for international students: Required—TOEFL (minimum score 550 paper-based; 79 iBT), IELTS (minimum score 6.5). *Application deadline:* For fall admission, 7/15 for international students; for spring admission, 11/15 for international students. Applications are processed on a rolling basis. Application fee: $60. Electronic applications accepted. *Expenses:* Tuition, state resident: full-time $5375; part-time $268.75 per credit hour. Tuition, nonresident: full-time $13,295; part-time $664.75 per credit hour. *Required fees:* $626; $31.30 per credit hour. One-time fee: $50. Tuition and fees vary according to program. *Financial support:* In 2017–18, 11 students received support, including 5 teaching assistantships with partial tuition reimbursements available (averaging $8,873 per year); research assistantships, career-related internships or fieldwork, scholarships/grants, tuition waivers (partial), and unspecified assistantships also available. Financial award application deadline: 3/31; financial award applicants required to submit FAFSA. *Unit head:* Dr. DeWade Langley, Director, 405-974-5501, Fax: 405-974-3816, E-mail: criminaljustice@uco.edu. *Application contact:* Dr. Shawna Cleary, Graduate Advisor, 405-974-5841, Fax: 405-974-3816, E-mail: gradcoll@uco.edu.
Website: http://www.uco.edu/la/criminal-justice/

University of Central Oklahoma, The Jackson College of Graduate Studies, Forensic Science Institute, Edmond, OK 73034-5209. Offers biology/chemistry (MS); forensic science (MS). *Faculty:* 8 full-time (2 women), 3 part-time/adjunct (2 women). *Students:* 14 full-time (13 women), 17 part-time (14 women); includes 3 minority (1 Asian, non-Hispanic/Latino; 1 Hispanic/Latino; 1 Two or more races, non-Hispanic/Latino), 1 international. Average age 28. 19 applicants, 37% accepted, 6 enrolled. In 2017, 5 master's awarded. *Degree requirements:* For master's, thesis. *Entrance requirements:* For master's, GRE, official transcripts. Additional exam requirements/recommendations for international students: Required—TOEFL (minimum score 550 paper-based; 79 iBT), IELTS (minimum score 6.5). *Application deadline:* For fall admission, 4/15 for domestic and international students; for spring admission, 11/15 for international students. Application fee: $60. Electronic applications accepted. *Expenses:* Tuition, state resident: full-time $5375; part-time $268.75 per credit hour. Tuition, nonresident: full-time $13,295; part-time $664.75 per credit hour. *Required fees:* $626; $31.30 per credit hour. One-time fee: $50. Tuition and fees vary according to program. *Financial support:* In 2017–18, 6 students received support, including 1 research assistantship with partial tuition reimbursement available (averaging $2,958 per year); teaching assistantships and scholarships/grants also available. Financial award application deadline: 3/31; financial award applicants required to submit FAFSA. *Unit head:* Dr. Dwight Adams, Director, 405-974-6911, Fax: 405-974-3804. *Application contact:* Dr. John Mabry, Graduate Advisor, 405-974-6913, Fax: 405-974-3804, E-mail: gradcoll@uco.edu.
Website: http://www.uco.edu/forensics/

University of Charleston, Master of Forensic Accounting Program, Charleston, WV 25304-1099. Offers EMFA. *Program availability:* Part-time, blended/hybrid learning. *Entrance requirements:* Additional exam requirements/recommendations for international students: Required—TOEFL. Electronic applications accepted.

University of Colorado Denver, Business School, Program in Accounting, Denver, CO 80217. Offers accounting and information systems audit control (MS); auditing and forensic accounting (MS); controllership and financial leadership (MS). *Accreditation:* AACSB. *Program availability:* Part-time, evening/weekend. *Degree requirements:* For master's, 30 semester hours. *Entrance requirements:* For master's, GMAT (waived for

students who already hold a graduate degree, or an undergraduate degree from CU Denver), essay, resume, two letters of recommendation; financial statements (for international students). Additional exam requirements/recommendations for international students: Required—TOEFL (minimum score 537 paper-based; 75 iBT); Recommended—IELTS (minimum score 6.5). Electronic applications accepted. *Expenses:* Contact institution. *Faculty research:* Transportation, energy, communications, healthcare, nano-science and engineering, unmanned aircraft systems, biomedical applications, aerosol mechanics, interface mechanics during rapid evaporation, low SWAP-C inertial navigation systems.

University of Colorado Denver, College of Arts and Media, Denver, CO 80217. Offers recording arts (MS), including media forensics, recording arts. *Accreditation:* NASM. *Program availability:* Part-time, evening/weekend. *Degree requirements:* For master's, 34 credits, thesis/portfolio. *Entrance requirements:* For master's, GRE General Test (minimum scores higher than 50th percentile for all sections), minimum undergraduate GPA of 3.0, portfolio, resume, interview, 3 letters of recommendation. Additional exam requirements/recommendations for international students: Required—TOEFL (minimum score 70 iBT). Electronic applications accepted. *Expenses:* Contact institution. *Faculty research:* Audio forensics, audio pedagogy, concert recordings, digital audio workstations, music law.

University of Detroit Mercy, College of Business Administration, Detroit, MI 48221. Offers business administration (MBA); business fundamentals (Certificate); business turnaround management (Certificate); ethical leadership and change management (Certificate); finance (Certificate); forensic accounting (Certificate); JD/MBA; MBA/MHSA. *Program availability:* Part-time, evening/weekend, 100% online, blended/hybrid learning. *Entrance requirements:* For master's, GMAT, resume, letter of recommendation, transcripts; for Certificate, resume, letter of recommendation, transcripts. Electronic applications accepted. Application fee is waived when completed online. *Expenses:* Contact institution. *Faculty research:* Ethics, international finance, trade policy, leadership, information technology.

University of Florida, Graduate School, College of Pharmacy, Programs in Forensic Science, Gainesville, FL 32611. Offers clinical toxicology (Certificate); drug chemistry (Certificate); environmental forensics (Certificate); forensic death investigation (Certificate); forensic DNA and serology (MSP, Certificate); forensic drug chemistry (MSP); forensic science (MSP); forensic toxicology (Certificate). *Program availability:* Part-time, evening/weekend, online learning. *Degree requirements:* For master's, comprehensive exam. *Entrance requirements:* For master's, GRE General Test, minimum GPA of 3.0. Additional exam requirements/recommendations for international students: Required—TOEFL (minimum score 550 paper-based; 80 iBT), IELTS (minimum score 6).

University of Houston–Victoria, School of Arts and Sciences, Program in Biomedical Sciences, Victoria, TX 77901-4450. Offers biological sciences (MS); biomedical sciences (MS); forensic science (MS).

University of Illinois at Chicago, College of Pharmacy and Graduate College, Graduate Programs in Pharmacy, Program in Forensic Science, Chicago, IL 60607-7128. Offers MS. *Degree requirements:* For master's, thesis. *Entrance requirements:* For master's, GRE General Test. Additional exam requirements/recommendations for international students: Required—TOEFL. *Faculty research:* Interpretation of physical evidence, utilization of physical evidence, analytical toxicology of controlled substances, automated fingerprint systems, dye and ink characterizations.

University of Maryland, Baltimore, Graduate School, Program in Forensic Medicine, Baltimore, MD 21201. Offers MS. *Students:* 10 full-time (8 women), 4 part-time (all women); includes 6 minority (5 Black or African American, non-Hispanic/Latino; 1 Hispanic/Latino), 3 international. Average age 26. 18 applicants, 56% accepted, 6 enrolled. *Degree requirements:* For master's, comprehensive exam, thesis optional. *Entrance requirements:* For master's, GRE, minimum GPA of 3.0, curriculum vitae, 3 letters of recommendation, essay. Additional exam requirements/recommendations for international students: Required—TOEFL (minimum score 80 iBT); Recommended—IELTS (minimum score 7). *Application deadline:* For fall admission, 5/1 for domestic students, 2/15 for international students. Application fee: $75. Electronic applications accepted. *Expenses:* Tuition, state resident: full-time $13,990; part-time $661 per credit. Tuition, nonresident: full-time $30,484; part-time $1310 per credit. *Required fees:* $1894; $94 per credit. $415 per semester. Part-time tuition and fees vary according to course load, degree level and program. *Unit head:* Dr. Bruce E. Jarrell, Chief Academic and Research Officer/Dean of the Graduate School, 410-706-2304, Fax: 410-706-0500, E-mail: bjarrell@som.umaryland.edu. *Application contact:* Keith T. Brooks, Assistant Dean, 410-706-7131, Fax: 410-706-3473, E-mail: kbrooks@umaryland.edu.

★ **University of New Haven,** Graduate School, Henry C. Lee College of Criminal Justice and Forensic Sciences, Program in Fire Science, West Haven, CT 06516. Offers fire science (MS); fire/arson investigation (MS, Graduate Certificate); forensic science (Graduate Certificate); public safety management (MS). *Program availability:* Part-time, evening/weekend. *Students:* 14 full-time (4 women), 4 part-time (0 women); includes 1 minority (Hispanic/Latino), 9 international. Average age 29. 12 applicants, 100% accepted, 6 enrolled. In 2017, 9 master's, 1 other advanced degree awarded. *Degree requirements:* For master's, thesis or alternative, research project or internship. *Entrance requirements:* Additional exam requirements/recommendations for international students: Required—TOEFL (minimum score 80 iBT), IELTS, PTE (minimum score 53). *Application deadline:* Applications are processed on a rolling basis. Application fee: $50. Electronic applications accepted. Application fee is waived when completed online. *Expenses:* Tuition: Full-time $16,020; part-time $890 per credit hour. *Required fees:* $220; $90 per term. *Financial support:* Research assistantships with partial tuition reimbursements, teaching assistantships with partial tuition reimbursements, Federal Work-Study, scholarships/grants, and unspecified assistantships available. Support available to part-time students. Financial award applicants required to submit FAFSA. *Unit head:* Dr. Sorin Iliescu, Director, 203-932-7239, E-mail: silliescu@newhaven.edu. *Application contact:* Michelle Mason, Director of Graduate Enrollment, 203-932-7067, E-mail: mmason@newhaven.edu. Website: http://www.newhaven.edu/5922/

See Display on page 784 and Close-Up on page 799.

★ **University of New Haven,** Graduate School, Henry C. Lee College of Criminal Justice and Forensic Sciences, Program in Forensic Science, West Haven, CT 06516. Offers forensic computer investigation (Graduate Certificate); forensic science (MS); forensic science/fire science (Graduate Certificate). *Program availability:* Part-time, evening/weekend. *Students:* 22 full-time (19 women), 2 part-time (1 woman); includes 5 minority (2 Black or African American, non-Hispanic/Latino; 1 Asian, non-Hispanic/Latino; 2 Hispanic/Latino), 1 international. Average age 25. 50 applicants, 56% accepted, 13 enrolled. In 2017, 13 master's awarded. *Entrance requirements:* For master's, GRE. Additional exam requirements/recommendations for international students: Required—TOEFL (minimum score 80 iBT), IELTS, PTE (minimum score 53). *Application deadline:* Applications are processed on a rolling basis. Application fee: $50. Electronic applications accepted. Application fee is waived when completed online. *Expenses:* Tuition: Full-time $16,020; part-time $890 per credit hour. *Required fees:* $220; $90 per term. *Financial support:* Research

assistantships with partial tuition reimbursements, teaching assistantships with partial tuition reimbursements, Federal Work-Study, scholarships/grants, and unspecified assistantships available. Support available to part-time students. Financial award applicants required to submit FAFSA. *Unit head:* Dr. Virginia Maxwell, Assistant Dean, 203-479-4599, E-mail: vmaxwell@newhaven.edu. *Application contact:* Michelle Mason, Director of Graduate Enrollment, 203-932-7067, E-mail: mmason@newhaven.edu. Website: http://www.newhaven.edu/5923/

See Display on page 784 and Close-Up on page 799.

★ **University of New Haven,** Graduate School, Henry C. Lee College of Criminal Justice and Forensic Sciences, Program in Forensic Technology, West Haven, CT 06516. Offers MS. *Program availability:* Part-time. *Students:* 46 full-time (34 women), 6 part-time (all women); includes 10 minority (3 Black or African American, non-Hispanic/Latino; 1 Asian, non-Hispanic/Latino; 5 Hispanic/Latino; 1 Two or more races, non-Hispanic/Latino), 3 international. Average age 25. 46 applicants, 89% accepted, 24 enrolled. In 2017, 18 master's awarded. *Application deadline:* Applications are processed on a rolling basis. Application fee: $50. *Expenses:* Tuition: Full-time $16,020; part-time $890 per credit hour. *Required fees:* $220; $90 per term. *Unit head:* Dr. Lisa Dadio, Coordinator, 203-479-4845, E-mail: ldadio@newhaven.edu. *Application contact:* Michelle Mason, Director of Graduate Enrollment, 203-932-7067, E-mail: mmason@newhaven.edu.

See Display on page 784 and Close-Up on page 799.

University of North Texas Health Science Center at Fort Worth, Graduate School of Biomedical Sciences, Fort Worth, TX 76107-2699. Offers biochemistry and cancer biology (MS, PhD); biotechnology (MS); cell biology, immunology and microbiology (MS, PhD); clinical research management (MS); forensic genetics (MS); genetics (MS, PhD); integrative physiology (MS, PhD); medical sciences (MS); pharmaceutical sciences and pharmacotherapy (MS, PhD); pharmacology and neuroscience (MS, PhD); structural anatomy and rehabilitation sciences (MS, PhD); DO/MS; DO/PhD. Terminal master's awarded for partial completion of doctoral program. *Degree requirements:* For master's, thesis; for doctorate, thesis/dissertation. *Entrance requirements:* For master's and doctorate, GRE General Test. Additional exam requirements/recommendations for international students: Required—TOEFL. *Expenses:* Contact institution. *Faculty research:* Alzheimer's disease, aging, eye diseases, cancer, cardiovascular disease.

University of Rhode Island, Graduate School, College of Arts and Sciences, Department of Computer Science and Statistics, Kingston, RI 02881. Offers computer science (MS, PhD); cyber security (PSM, Graduate Certificate); digital forensics (Graduate Certificate). *Program availability:* Part-time, evening/weekend, 100% online, blended/hybrid learning. *Faculty:* 19 full-time (6 women). *Students:* 36 full-time (14 women), 111 part-time (28 women); includes 18 minority (6 Black or African American, non-Hispanic/Latino; 8 Asian, non-Hispanic/Latino; 3 Hispanic/Latino; 1 Two or more races, non-Hispanic/Latino), 19 international. 104 applicants, 73% accepted, 60 enrolled. In 2017, 9 master's, 3 doctorates, 13 other advanced degrees awarded. Terminal master's awarded for partial completion of doctoral program. *Entrance requirements:* Additional exam requirements/recommendations for international students: Required—TOEFL. *Application deadline:* For fall admission, 7/15 for domestic students, 2/1 for international students; for spring admission, 11/15 for domestic students, 7/15 for international students. Application fee: $65. Electronic applications accepted. *Expenses:* Tuition, state resident: full-time $12,706; part-time $786 per credit. Tuition, nonresident: full-time $25,216; part-time $1401 per credit. *Required fees:* $1598; $45 per credit. One-time fee: $30 part-time. *Financial support:* In 2017–18, 7 research assistantships with tuition reimbursements (averaging $15,553 per year), 9 teaching assistantships with tuition reimbursements (averaging $14,534 per year) were awarded; unspecified assistantships also available. Financial award application deadline: 2/1; financial award applicants required to submit FAFSA. *Unit head:* Dr. Lisa DiPippo, Chair, 401-874-2701, Fax: 401-874-4617, E-mail: dipippo@cs.uri.edu. *Application contact:* Lutz Hamel, Graduate Program Director, 401-874-2701, E-mail: lutzhamel@uri.edu. Website: http://www.cs.uri.edu/

University of St. Francis, College of Arts and Sciences, Joliet, IL 60435-6169. Offers forensic social work (Post-Master's Certificate); physician assistant practice (MS); social work (MSW). *Program availability:* Part-time. *Faculty:* 7 full-time (5 women), 5 part-time/adjunct (4 women). *Students:* 107 full-time (82 women), 24 part-time (22 women); includes 40 minority (13 Black or African American, non-Hispanic/Latino; 3 Asian, non-Hispanic/Latino; 20 Hispanic/Latino; 2 Native Hawaiian or other Pacific Islander, non-Hispanic/Latino; 2 Two or more races, non-Hispanic/Latino), 6 international. Average age 28. 69 applicants, 48% accepted, 26 enrolled. In 2017, 64 master's awarded. *Entrance requirements:* For master's, GRE (for MS). Additional exam requirements/recommendations for international students: Required—TOEFL (minimum score 550 paper-based; 79 iBT), IELTS (minimum score 6). *Application deadline:* Applications are processed on a rolling basis. Application fee: $30. Electronic applications accepted. Application fee is waived when completed online. *Expenses:* $748 per credit. *Financial support:* In 2017–18, 10 students received support. Scholarships/grants and unspecified assistantships available. Support available to part-time students. Financial award applicants required to submit FAFSA. *Unit head:* Dr. Robert Kase, Dean, 815-740-3367, Fax: 815-740-6366. *Application contact:* Sandra Sloka, Director of Admissions for Graduate and Degree Completion Programs, 800-735-7500, Fax: 815-740-3431, E-mail: ssloka@stfrancis.edu. Website: http://www.stfrancis.edu/academics/cas

University of Southern Mississippi, College of Science and Technology, School of Criminal Justice, Hattiesburg, MS 39406-0001. Offers criminal justice (MA, MS, PhD); forensic science (MS). *Program availability:* Part-time. *Students:* 5 full-time (3 women), 1 (woman) part-time. 7 applicants, 57% accepted, 4 enrolled. *Degree requirements:* For master's, comprehensive exam, thesis; for doctorate, comprehensive exam, thesis/dissertation. *Entrance requirements:* For master's, GRE General Test, minimum GPA of 2.75 in last 60 hours, 3.0 in field of study; for doctorate, GRE General Test, minimum GPA of 3.5. Additional exam requirements/recommendations for international students: Required—TOEFL, IELTS. *Application deadline:* For fall admission, 3/15 priority date for domestic students, 3/15 for international students; for spring admission, 1/10 priority date for domestic and international students. Applications are processed on a rolling basis. Application fee: $60. Electronic applications accepted. *Expenses:* Tuition, state resident: full-time $3830. *Financial support:* Research assistantships with full tuition reimbursements, teaching assistantships with full tuition reimbursements, career-related internships or fieldwork, Federal Work-Study, institutionally sponsored loans, scholarships/grants, health care benefits, and unspecified assistantships available. Financial award application deadline: 3/15; financial award applicants required to submit FAFSA. *Faculty research:* Crime in the family, police training models, humanities and criminal justice. *Unit head:* Dr. Lisa Nored, Director, 601-266-4509, Fax: 601-266-4391. *Application contact:* Tera Wright, Manager of Graduate Admissions, 601-266-4509, Fax: 601-266-4391. Website: https://www.usm.edu/criminal-justice

University of South Florida, College of Arts and Sciences, Department of Anthropology, Tampa, FL 33620-9951. Offers applied anthropology (MA, PhD),

including archaeological and forensic sciences, biocultural medical anthropology, cultural resource management, heritage studies; medical anthropology (Graduate Certificate). *Program availability:* Part-time. *Faculty:* 22 full-time (15 women). *Students:* 73 full-time (50 women), 42 part-time (33 women); includes 30 minority (6 Black or African American, non-Hispanic/Latino; 2 Asian, non-Hispanic/Latino; 18 Hispanic/Latino; 1 Native Hawaiian or other Pacific Islander, non-Hispanic/Latino; 3 Two or more races, non-Hispanic/Latino), 6 international. Average age 32. 117 applicants, 36% accepted, 26 enrolled. In 2017, 16 master's, 7 doctorates awarded. *Degree requirements:* For master's, one foreign language, comprehensive exam, thesis; for doctorate, one foreign language, comprehensive exam, thesis/dissertation. *Entrance requirements:* For master's and doctorate, GRE, minimum GPA of 3.0, 3 letters of recommendation, statement of purpose, signed research ethics statement, resume or curriculum vitae; for Graduate Certificate, bachelor's degree with minimum GPA of 3.0. Additional exam requirements/recommendations for international students: Required—TOEFL (minimum score 550 paper-based; 79 iBT) or IELTS (minimum score 6.5). *Application deadline:* For fall admission, 12/15 priority date for domestic and international students. Application fee: $30. Electronic applications accepted. *Financial support:* In 2017–18, 19 students received support, including 14 research assistantships with tuition reimbursements available (averaging $14,475 per year), 52 teaching assistantships with partial tuition reimbursements available (averaging $12,540 per year); scholarships/grants and tuition waivers (partial) also available. Financial award application deadline: 1/15; financial award applicants required to submit FAFSA. *Faculty research:* Biocultural medical anthropology; archaeology and culture resource management in the Americas; community identity and heritage; urban community issues; verbal and nonverbal communications in media and education; global dynamics of sustainable resource management and economic development; social and cultural constructions of race, ethnicity, and gender. *Total annual research expenditures:* $1.1 million. *Unit head:* Dr. David Himmelgreen, Professor/Chair, 813-974-5455, E-mail: dhimmelg@usf.edu. *Application contact:* Dr. Rebecca Zarger, Associate Professor and Graduate Director, 813-974-0069, E-mail: rzarger@usf.edu.
Website: http://anthropology.usf.edu/graduate/

University of South Florida, College of Graduate Studies, Tampa, FL 33620-9951. Offers cybersecurity (MS), including computer security fundamentals, cyber intelligence, digital forensics, information assurance. *Program availability:* Part-time, evening/weekend, online learning. *Faculty:* 1 (woman) full-time. *Students:* 79 full-time (12 women), 167 part-time (50 women); includes 95 minority (34 Black or African American, non-Hispanic/Latino; 1 American Indian or Alaska Native, non-Hispanic/Latino; 12 Asian, non-Hispanic/Latino; 42 Hispanic/Latino; 1 Native Hawaiian or other Pacific Islander, non-Hispanic/Latino; 5 Two or more races, non-Hispanic/Latino), 2 international. Average age 36. 117 applicants, 66% accepted, 61 enrolled. In 2017, 112 master's awarded. Terminal master's awarded for partial completion of doctoral program. *Degree requirements:* For master's, variable foreign language requirement, comprehensive exam, thesis (for some programs), practicum. *Entrance requirements:* For master's, GRE General Test, minimum GPA of 3.0; official transcripts with confirmation that applicant has received bachelor's degree from regionally-accredited university; 250-500 word essay in which student describes academic and professional background, reasons for pursuing degree, and professional goals pertaining to cybersecurity; two letters of recommendation. Additional exam requirements/recommendations for international students: Required—TOEFL (minimum score 550 paper-based; 79 iBT) or IELTS (minimum score 6.5). *Application deadline:* For fall admission, 2/15 for domestic and international students; for spring admission, 10/15 for domestic students, 9/15 for international students; for summer admission, 2/15 for domestic and international students. Application fee: $30. Electronic applications accepted. *Financial support:* In 2017–18, 11 students received support. Teaching assistantships available. Financial award application deadline: 2/1; financial award applicants required to submit FAFSA. *Faculty research:* Integrated neuroscience, diabetes, sustainability of populations/environment, drug design and delivery, marine science. *Total annual research expenditures:* $851,732. *Unit head:* Dr. Dwayne Smith, Senior Vice Provost and Dean of the Office of Graduate Studies, 813-974-7359, Fax: 813-974-5762, E-mail: mdsmith8@usf.edu. *Application contact:* Paul Crawford, Associate Director for Graduate Admissions, 813-974-8800, E-mail: pjcrawford@usf.edu.
Website: http://www.grad.usf.edu/

Virginia Commonwealth University, Graduate School, College of Humanities and Sciences, Department of Forensic Science, Richmond, VA 23284-9005. Offers forensic biology (MS); forensic chemistry/drugs and toxicology (MS); forensic chemistry/trace evidence (MS); forensic physical analysis (MS). *Program availability:* Part-time. *Entrance requirements:* For master's, GRE General Test, bachelor's degree in a natural science discipline, including forensic science, or a degree with equivalent work. Additional exam requirements/recommendations for international students: Required—

TOEFL (minimum score 600 paper-based; 100 iBT) or IELTS (minimum score 6.5). Electronic applications accepted.

Webster University, George Herbert Walker School of Business and Technology, Department of Business, St. Louis, MO 63119-3194. Offers business and organizational security management (MBA); decision support systems (MBA); environmental management (MBA); finance (MBA, MS); forensic accounting (MS); gerontology (MBA); human resources development (MBA); human resources management (MBA); information technology management (MBA); international business (MA, MBA); international relations (MBA); management and leadership (MBA); marketing (MBA); media communications (MBA); procurement and acquisitions management (MBA); Web services (MBA). *Accreditation:* ACBSP. *Program availability:* Part-time, evening/weekend, online learning. *Degree requirements:* For master's, comprehensive exam (for some programs), thesis (for some programs). *Entrance requirements:* Additional exam requirements/recommendations for international students: Required—TOEFL.

West Virginia University, College of Law, Morgantown, WV 26506-6130. Offers energy law and sustainable development (LL M); forensic justice (LL M); law (JD); white collar forensic justice (LL M). *Accreditation:* ABA. *Program availability:* Part-time. *Students:* 306 full-time (138 women), 1 part-time (0 women); includes 33 minority (10 Black or African American, non-Hispanic/Latino; 4 Asian, non-Hispanic/Latino; 11 Hispanic/Latino; 8 Two or more races, non-Hispanic/Latino), 1 international. *Entrance requirements:* For doctorate, LSAT. Additional exam requirements/recommendations for international students: Required—TOEFL (minimum score 600 paper-based; 100 iBT). *Application deadline:* For fall admission, 2/1 for domestic and international students. Applications are processed on a rolling basis. Application fee: $60. Electronic applications accepted. *Expenses:* Contact institution. *Financial support:* Fellowships, research assistantships, teaching assistantships, career-related internships or fieldwork, Federal Work-Study, institutionally sponsored loans, scholarships/grants, health care benefits, tuition waivers (full), unspecified assistantships, and administrative assistantships, resident assistantships available. Support available to part-time students. Financial award application deadline: 3/1; financial award applicants required to submit FAFSA. *Faculty research:* Constitutional law, public interest law, corporate law, environment and natural resources innocence project, professional skills, leadership, intellectual property, entrepreneurship, labor, sustainable development, family law, IR human rights, immigration. *Unit head:* Beth Pierpont, Assistant Dean for Admissions and Student Financial Support, 304-293-7320, E-mail: beth.pierpont@mail.wvu.edu.
Website: https://law.wvu.edu

West Virginia University, Eberly College of Arts and Sciences, Morgantown, WV 26506. Offers biology (MS, PhD); chemistry (MS, PhD); communication studies (MA, PhD); computational statistics (PhD); creative writing (MFA); English (MA, PhD); forensic and investigative science (MS); forensic science (PhD); geography (MA); geology (MA, PhD); history (MA, PhD); legal studies (MLS); math (MS); physics (MS, PhD); political science (MA, PhD); professional writing and editing (MA); psychology (MA); public administration (MPA); social work (MSW); sociology (MA, PhD); statistics (MS). *Program availability:* Part-time, evening/weekend, online learning. *Students:* 831 full-time (437 women), 236 part-time (142 women); includes 112 minority (35 Black or African American, non-Hispanic/Latino; 15 Asian, non-Hispanic/Latino; 29 Hispanic/Latino; 33 Two or more races, non-Hispanic/Latino), 235 international. Terminal master's awarded for partial completion of doctoral program. *Degree requirements:* For master's, thesis (for some programs); for doctorate, comprehensive exam, thesis/dissertation. *Entrance requirements:* For master's and doctorate, GRE. Additional exam requirements/recommendations for international students: Required—TOEFL (minimum score 600 paper-based); Recommended—TWE. *Application deadline:* For spring admission, 2/15 priority date for domestic and international students. Applications are processed on a rolling basis. Application fee: $45. Electronic applications accepted. *Expenses:* Tuition, state resident: full-time $9450. Tuition, nonresident: full-time $24,390. *Financial support:* Fellowships with full tuition reimbursements, research assistantships with full tuition reimbursements, teaching assistantships with full tuition reimbursements, career-related internships or fieldwork, Federal Work-Study, institutionally sponsored loans, scholarships/grants, health care benefits, tuition waivers (full and partial), unspecified assistantships, and administrative assistantships available. Financial award application deadline: 2/1; financial award applicants required to submit FAFSA. *Faculty research:* Humanities, social sciences, life science, physical sciences, mathematics. *Unit head:* Dr. Mary Ellen Mazey, Dean, 304-293-4611, Fax: 304-293-6858, E-mail: mary.mazey@mail.wvu.edu. *Application contact:* Dr. Fred L. King, Associate Dean for Graduate Studies, 304-293-4611 Ext. 5205, Fax: 304-293-6858, E-mail: fred.king@mail.wvu.edu.
Website: http://www.as.wvu.edu/

UNIVERSITY OF NEW HAVEN
The Henry C. Lee School of Criminal Justice and Forensic Sciences

University of
New Haven

Programs of Study

The Henry C. Lee School of Criminal Justice and Forensic Sciences at the University of New Haven is named for the world-renowned forensic scientist who has consulted on more than 8,000 cases worldwide, including the O.J. Simpson trial and the Jon Benet Ramsey investigation. Dr. Lee, who previously served as chief criminalist for the State of Connecticut and director of the Connecticut State Police Forensic Science Laboratory, joined the University of New Haven forensic sciences program in 1975 and helped build it into one of the foremost forensic academic programs in the world.

The University of New Haven campus is also home to the Henry C. Lee Institute of Forensic Science, which conducts advanced forensic research and trains law enforcement professionals from around the globe. Through the Lee College and the Lee Institute, University of New Haven students have the opportunity to interact with Lee and other distinguished forensic scientists and law enforcement professionals.

The Henry C. Lee School at the University of New Haven offers graduate degree programs in Forensic Science and Forensic Technology. The programs are designed for students continuing beyond their undergraduate work or working professionals in criminal justice-related fields seeking additional focus and training in a scientific or technical sub-specialty.

M.S. in Forensic Science: This degree program is one of the foremost forensic science programs in the nation, focusing on up-to-date analytical and scientific methods and a broad understanding of the concepts of the forensic sciences as applied to physical evidence in law and criminal investigations. Accredited by the Forensic Science Education Programs Accreditation Commission (FEPAC), the 42-credit, four-semester program offers flexible class times and course delivery options for working professionals.

Students complete a sequence of coursework and a series of electives. Core courses include Survey of Forensic Science, Forensic Expert Testimony, Advanced Criminalistics, Physical Analysis in Forensic Science, Forensic DNA Analysis, and Thesis I and II. Among the electives are Capillary Electrophoresis, Advanced Crime Scene Investigation, Wildlife Forensics, Drug Chemistry and Identification, Forensic Anthropology, and Forensic Toxicology.

Through immersive, concentrated study in the laboratory, students gain hands-on experience immediately applicable to their chosen careers. Students learn from expert faculty with professional experience in key positions such as lab directors and crime scene bench analysts.

Graduates of the University of New Haven M.S .in Forensic Science program have gone on to pursue careers with organizations and agencies that include FBI Lab Division, Bristol-Myers Squibb, California Los Angeles Crime Lab, New York City Police Department, U.S. Dept. of Agriculture Bioforensics Unit, NCIS; and American Regulation of Pathology Armed Forces DNA Lab.

M.S. in Forensic Technology: This program is the first graduate-level forensic science curriculum of its kind in the nation. It combines traditional crime scene techniques with advanced instrumentation and measurements. The program is designed for students continuing from their undergraduate work or working professionals. Students can complete all required courses during evening hours, Monday through Friday.

Students in the program master various forms of field technology including ground penetrating radar, laser scanners, portable instruments, and biometric devices. In addition, the students benefit from the strong connections that the University of New Haven has forged with local and state police as well as the state medical examiner.

Students complete 42 credits of coursework, a capstone or internship project, and restricted electives that allow them to develop specialized knowledge in areas such as bloodstain pattern analysis, firearms evidence, and forensic anthropology. Core courses include Advanced Crime Scene Investigation, Crime Scene Reconstruction, Forensic Field Technology, Medicolegal Investigation and Identification, Law and Evidence, Criminal Procedure, and Forensic Photography.

Career Support

All graduate students at the University of New Haven have access to the University's top-rated Career Development Center, which offers internship location help, interview practice, and other services.

Financial Aid

The University is committed to assisting graduate students by offering a comprehensive financial aid program. The financial aid that is offered generally consists of student loans and, when applicable, grants and student employment.

A number of merit-based assistantships are available for full-time graduate students to defray the cost of tuition and provide an earned wage. These include the Provost's Assistantship, which offsets 75 percent of tuition expenses and provides 15 to 20 hours per week of research or teaching experience, and the Dean's Scholarship, which covers up to half of the recipients' tuition.

Cost of Study

Full-time graduate tuition for the 2018–19 academic year is $16,470; half-time tuition is $10,980. Books are estimated at $400–$600 and fees are $220 for full-time students, $180 for half-time students.

Living and Housing

There are two graduate student housing options sponsored by the University. The Atwood Apartments are located just across the street from the northeast end of campus and the Savin Court apartments are located approximately 1.5 miles from campus. Other off-campus housing is also available.

The University's Office of Graduate Student Services offers many resources to assist participants in the program.

Location

The University's main campus is located on 82 acres in West Haven, Connecticut, a suburban hillside community minutes from the bustling city of New Haven and miles of Connecticut shoreline and beaches. The campus is 90 minutes from New York City and 2 1/2 hours from Boston and is also accessible by train from those cities.

Situated on 82 acres atop a hill overlooking the New Haven skyline with views of Long Island Sound, this residential campus is conveniently located a mile north of Interstate 95. The campus has experienced significant growth in the last decade with more than $220 million in construction projects completed or underway.

The University

The University of New Haven is a small private, secular school established in 1920 in West Haven, Connecticut. Today, the university has four campuses in Connecticut as well as one in Italy. It has been named one of *U.S. News & World Report*'s "Best Regional Universities–North" and one of The Princeton Review's "Best 382 Colleges" and "Best Northeastern Colleges." The Princeton Review has also named the University of New Haven to its top-20 U.S. colleges for "Best Career Services." The institution has also been recognized by multiple organizations for its service to military veteran students.

The Graduate School offers nearly 50 graduate degree and certificate programs to help prepare students for success in their careers and lives.

University of New Haven

The various courses of study deliver skills and experiences that will help students make the most of real-world opportunities and maximize your career potential. Graduate programs follow a semester schedule. Courses are generally in the evenings, offering flexibility for those continuing to work while pursuing their studies.

Faculty

The University of New Haven is a recognized leader in experiential education, promoting a philosophy and methodology of education in which educators purposefully engage with learners in direct experience and focused reflection in order to increase knowledge, develop skills, and clarify values.

In addition to the distinguished Dr. Henry C. Lee, other notable forensic science faculty at University of New Haven include Dr. Clare R. Glynn, whose research interests are forensic biology focused on body fluid identification, DNA degradation, and RNA analysis; Dr. Brooke Weinger Kammrath, whose research interests comprise the identification and characterization of microscopic samples of forensic interest, the statistical analysis of trace, pattern, and impression evidence, and investigations into the significance of physical evidence; and Dr. Alyssa Marsico, an expert in mass spectrometry and its use for the forensic analysis of both trace and biological evidence.

Applying

The Office of Graduate Admissions strives to provide a personalized admission process. Interested students are welcome to visit campus, meet with a graduate admissions counselor, go on a campus tour, meet a faculty advisor in the program, and meet with a financial aid officer.

Applicants to the Forensic Science programs must submit the following:

- Online application

- $50 nonrefundable fee

- Official university transcripts and proof of bachelor's degree completion. An explanation of the grading system that conferred the degree must be provided with the transcripts.

- Two letters of recommendation from professors or employers

- A statement of purpose is required. A resume is highly recommended.

Applications are considered on a rolling basis, but there are recommended deadlines: June 1 (domestic) and May 1 (international) for fall admission and November 15 for spring admission.

Conditional acceptance is offered in most majors to those who are academically admissible but who have not met the University's required English test scores. Students who do not submit proof of English proficiency will be recommended to enroll in the Academic Preparatory Program (APP).

Contact

University of New Haven

Office of Graduate Admissions

Maxcy Hall 129

300 Boston Post Road

West Haven, Connecticut 06516

Phone: 800-342-5864

      203-932-7440

E-mail: SOToole@newhaven.edu

Website: https://www.newhaven.edu/lee-college/graduate-programs/forensic-science/index.php

Section 19
Economics

This section contains a directory of institutions offering graduate work in economics. Additional information about programs listed in the directory may be obtained by writing directly to the dean of a graduate school or chair of a department at the address given in the directory.

For programs offering related work, see also in this book *Family and Consumer Sciences, Political Science and International Affairs,* and *Public, Regional, and Industrial Affairs.* In the other guides in this series:

Graduate Programs in the Physical Sciences, Mathematics, Agricultural Sciences, the Environment & Natural Resources

See *Agricultural and Food Sciences* and *Mathematical Sciences*

Graduate Programs in Engineering & Applied Sciences

See *Computer Science and Information Technology; Geological, Mineral/Mining, and Petroleum Engineering;* and *Industrial Engineering*

Graduate Programs in Business, Education, Information Studies, Law & Social Work

See *Business Administration and Management*

CONTENTS

Agricultural Economics and Agribusiness

Alcorn State University, School of Graduate Studies, School of Agriculture and Applied Science, Lorman, MS 39096-7500. Offers agricultural economics (MS Ag); agronomy (MS Ag); animal science (MS Ag). *Degree requirements:* For master's, thesis optional. *Faculty research:* Aquatic systems, dairy herd improvement, fruit production, alternative farming practices.

American University of Beirut, Graduate Programs, Faculty of Agricultural and Food Sciences, Beirut, Lebanon. Offers agricultural economics (MS); animal science (MS); ecosystem management (MSES); food safety (MS); food security (MS); food technology (MS); irrigation (MS); nutrition (MS); plant protection (MS); plant science (MS); poultry science (MS); public health nutrition (MS); rural community development (MS). *Program availability:* Part-time. *Faculty:* 16 full-time (4 women), 1 part-time/adjunct (0 women). *Students:* 76 full-time (58 women), 19 part-time (13 women); includes 6 minority (all Black or African American, non-Hispanic/Latino). Average age 25. 142 applicants, 72% accepted, 32 enrolled. In 2017, 20 master's awarded. *Degree requirements:* For master's, one foreign language, comprehensive exam, thesis (for some programs). *Entrance requirements:* Additional exam requirements/recommendations for international students: Required—TOEFL (minimum score 600 paper-based; 100 iBT), IELTS (minimum score 7.5). *Application deadline:* For fall admission, 2/10 for domestic and international students; for spring admission, 11/2 for domestic and international students. Application fee: $50. Electronic applications accepted. *Expenses: Tuition:* Full-time $17,244; part-time $958 per credit. *Required fees:* $740. Tuition and fees vary according to course load and program. *Financial support:* In 2017–18, 9 research assistantships with partial tuition reimbursements (averaging $1,800 per year), 47 teaching assistantships with full and partial tuition reimbursements (averaging $1,400 per year) were awarded; scholarships/grants, health care benefits, and unspecified assistantships also available. Financial award application deadline: 2/2. *Faculty research:* Refugee socio-economic vulnerability, nutrition in emergencies, forest and landscape restoration, broiler immunological response, vegetated infrastructure in deserts. *Total annual research expenditures:* $600,000. *Unit head:* Rabi Hassan Mohtar, Dean of Faculty of Agricultural and Food Sciences, 961-1-350000 Ext. 4400, Fax: 961-1-744460, E-mail: mohtar@aub.edu.lb. *Application contact:* Prof. Zaher Dawy, Graduate Council Chairperson, 961-1-374374 Ext. 4386, Fax: 961-1-374376, E-mail: graduate.council@aub.edu.lb.
Website: http://www.aub.edu.lb/fafs/Pages/default.aspx

Arizona State University at the Tempe campus, W. P. Carey School of Business, Morrison School of Agribusiness, Mesa, AZ 85212. Offers PhD. *Program availability:* Part-time, evening/weekend. *Entrance requirements:* Additional exam requirements/recommendations for international students: Required—TOEFL (minimum score 550 paper-based; 80 iBT), IELTS (minimum score 6.5); Recommended—TWE. Electronic applications accepted. *Faculty research:* Consumer behavior and marketing strategies in food markets, supply-chain management, derivatives and risk management, international agricultural trade and policy.

Auburn University, Graduate School, College of Agriculture, Department of Agricultural Economics and Rural Sociology, Auburn University, AL 36849. Offers agricultural economics (M Ag). *Program availability:* Part-time. *Faculty:* 13 full-time (6 women). *Students:* 4 full-time (2 women), 1 part-time (0 women); includes 3 minority (all Black or African American, non-Hispanic/Latino). Average age 24. 23 applicants, 48% accepted, 2 enrolled. In 2017, 7 master's awarded. *Degree requirements:* For master's, thesis (for some programs). *Entrance requirements:* For master's, GRE General Test. *Application deadline:* Applications are processed on a rolling basis. Application fee: $50 ($60 for international students). Electronic applications accepted. *Expenses:* Tuition, state resident: full-time $10,974; part-time $519 per credit hour. Tuition, nonresident: full-time $29,658; part-time $1557 per credit hour. *Required fees:* $816 per semester. Tuition and fees vary according to degree level and program. *Financial support:* Research assistantships, teaching assistantships, and Federal Work-Study available. Support available to part-time students. Financial award application deadline: 3/15; financial award applicants required to submit FAFSA. *Unit head:* Deacue Fields, Chair, 334-844-4800. *Application contact:* Dr. George Flowers, Dean of the Graduate School, 334-844-2125.
Website: http://www.ag.auburn.edu/agec/

Colorado State University, College of Agricultural Sciences, Department of Agricultural and Resource Economics, Fort Collins, CO 80523-1172. Offers MS, PhD. *Faculty:* 17 full-time (5 women), 2 part-time/adjunct (both women). *Students:* 29 full-time (18 women), 7 part-time (1 woman); includes 2 minority (1 Hispanic/Latino; 1 Two or more races, non-Hispanic/Latino), 11 international. Average age 27. 77 applicants, 68% accepted, 14 enrolled. In 2017, 4 master's, 6 doctorates awarded. *Degree requirements:* For master's, thesis; for doctorate, thesis/dissertation. *Entrance requirements:* For master's and doctorate, GRE, intermediate microeconomics, intermediate econometrics. Additional exam requirements/recommendations for international students: Required—TOEFL (minimum score 550 paper-based). *Application deadline:* For fall admission, 2/15 priority date for domestic and international students. Applications are processed on a rolling basis. Application fee: $60 ($70 for international students). Electronic applications accepted. *Expenses:* Tuition, state resident: full-time $9917. Tuition, nonresident: full-time $24,312. *Required fees:* $2284. Tuition and fees vary according to course load and program. *Financial support:* In 2017–18, 29 students received support, including 16 research assistantships with full and partial tuition reimbursements available (averaging $16,125 per year), 9 teaching assistantships with full and partial tuition reimbursements available (averaging $15,238 per year); scholarships/grants and health care benefits also available. Financial award application deadline: 2/15. *Faculty research:* Agri-food system analysis; impact of perception, values, and ideology on education and society; energy, climate and the environment; rural-urban linkages in food and resource management; water and resource economics. *Total annual research expenditures:* $1.6 million. *Unit head:* Dr. Hayley Chouinard, Department Head, 970-491-6955, Fax: 970-491-2067, E-mail: hayley.chouinard@colostate.edu. *Application contact:* Denise Davis, Program Assistant II, 970-491-6955, Fax: 970-491-2067, E-mail: denise.davis@colostate.edu.
Website: http://dare.agsci.colostate.edu/

Cornell University, Graduate School, Graduate Fields of Agriculture and Life Sciences, Field of Applied Economics and Management, Ithaca, NY 14853. Offers agricultural finance (MS, PhD); applied econometrics and qualitative analysis (MS, PhD); economics of development (MS, PhD); environmental economics (MS, PhD); environmental management (MPS); farm management and production economics (MS, PhD); marketing and food distribution (MS, PhD); public policy analysis (MS, PhD); resource economics (PhD). *Entrance requirements:* For master's and doctorate, GRE. Additional exam requirements/recommendations for international students: Required—TOEFL.

Cornell University, Graduate School, Graduate Fields of Agriculture and Life Sciences, Field of Global Development, Ithaca, NY 14853. Offers development policy (MPS); international agriculture and development (MPS); international development (MPS); international nutrition (MPS); international planning (MPS); international population (MPS); science and technology policy (MPS). *Degree requirements:* For master's, project paper. *Entrance requirements:* For master's, GRE General Test (recommended), 2 years of development experience, 2 letters of recommendation. Additional exam requirements/recommendations for international students: Required—TOEFL (minimum score 550 paper-based; 77 iBT). Electronic applications accepted.

Delaware Valley University, MBA Program, Doylestown, PA 18901-2697. Offers accounting (MBA); entrepreneurship (MBA); finance (MBA); food and agribusiness (MBA); general business (MBA); global executive leadership (MBA); human resource management (MBA); supply chain management (MBA). *Program availability:* Part-time, evening/weekend, online learning. *Entrance requirements:* For master's, minimum undergraduate GPA of 3.0. Electronic applications accepted. *Expenses:* Contact institution.

Illinois State University, Graduate School, College of Applied Science and Technology, Department of Agriculture, Normal, IL 61790. Offers agribusiness (MS). *Degree requirements:* For master's, thesis optional. *Entrance requirements:* For master's, GRE General Test, minimum GPA of 3.0 in last 60 hours. *Faculty research:* Engineering-economic system models for rural ethanol production facilities, development and evaluation of a propane-fueled, production scale, on-site thermal destruction system C-FAR 2007; field scale evaluation and technology transfer of economically, ecologically systems; sound liquid swine manure treatment and application.

Instituto Centroamericano de Administración de Empresas, Graduate Programs, La Garita, Costa Rica. Offers agribusiness management (MIAM); business administration (EMBA); finance (MBA); real estate management (MGREM); sustainable development (MBA); technology (MBA). *Degree requirements:* For master's, comprehensive exam, essay. *Entrance requirements:* For master's, GMAT or GRE General Test, fluency in Spanish, interview, letters of recommendation, minimum 1 year of work experience. Additional exam requirements/recommendations for international students: Recommended—TOEFL. Electronic applications accepted. *Faculty research:* Competitiveness, production.

Iowa State University of Science and Technology, Department of Economics, Ames, IA 50011. Offers agricultural economics (MS, PhD); economics (MS, PhD); JD/MS; JD/PhD. JD/MS and JD/PhD offered jointly with Drake University and The University of Iowa. *Degree requirements:* For master's, thesis or alternative; for doctorate, thesis/dissertation. *Entrance requirements:* For master's and doctorate, GRE General Test. Additional exam requirements/recommendations for international students: Required—TOEFL (minimum score 570 paper-based; 88 iBT), IELTS (minimum score 6.5). Electronic applications accepted.

Iowa State University of Science and Technology, Program in Agricultural Economics, Ames, IA 50011. Offers MS, PhD. *Degree requirements:* For master's, thesis or alternative; for doctorate, thesis/dissertation. *Entrance requirements:* For master's and doctorate, GRE General Test. Additional exam requirements/recommendations for international students: Required—TOEFL (minimum score 570 paper-based; 88 iBT), IELTS (minimum score 6.5). Electronic applications accepted.

Iowa State University of Science and Technology, Program in Seed Technology and Business, Ames, IA 50011. Offers MS. *Degree requirements:* For master's, thesis or alternative. *Entrance requirements:* For master's, resume, 3 letters of recommendation. Additional exam requirements/recommendations for international students: Required—TOEFL (minimum score 570 paper-based; 85 iBT), IELTS (minimum score 6.5). Electronic applications accepted.

Kansas State University, Graduate School, College of Agriculture, Department of Agricultural Economics, Manhattan, KS 66506. Offers MAB, MS, PhD. *Program availability:* Part-time, online learning. Terminal master's awarded for partial completion of doctoral program. *Degree requirements:* For master's, thesis or alternative, oral exam; for doctorate, thesis/dissertation, preliminary exams. *Entrance requirements:* For master's and doctorate, GRE General Test. Additional exam requirements/recommendations for international students: Required—TOEFL (minimum score 550 paper-based; 79 iBT), IELTS (minimum score 6.5). Electronic applications accepted. *Expenses:* Contact institution. *Faculty research:* Livestock marketing, biofuels research, natural resources, agribusiness industry, international development and trade.

Louisiana State University and Agricultural & Mechanical College, Graduate School, College of Agriculture, Department of Agricultural Economics and Agribusiness, Baton Rouge, LA 70803. Offers MS, PhD. *Faculty:* 15 full-time (4 women). *Students:* 16 full-time (3 women), 1 (woman) part-time; includes 1 minority (Hispanic/Latino), 14 international. Average age 31. 22 applicants, 23% accepted, 2 enrolled. In 2017, 7 master's, 2 doctorates awarded. *Financial support:* In 2017–18, 15 research assistantships (averaging $19,973 per year) were awarded. *Total annual research expenditures:* $3,304.

McGill University, Faculty of Graduate and Postdoctoral Studies, Faculty of Agricultural and Environmental Sciences, Department of Agricultural Economics, Montréal, QC H3A 2T5, Canada. Offers M Sc.

Michigan State University, The Graduate School, College of Agriculture and Natural Resources, Department of Agricultural, Food, and Resource Economics, East Lansing, MI 48824. Offers agricultural economics (MS, PhD); agricultural, food, and resource economics (MS, PhD). *Entrance requirements:* Additional exam requirements/recommendations for international students: Required—TOEFL (minimum score 550 paper-based), Michigan State University ELT (minimum score 85), Michigan English Language Assessment Battery (minimum score 83). Electronic applications accepted.

Mississippi State University, College of Agriculture and Life Sciences, Department of Agricultural Economics, Mississippi State, MS 39762. Offers agricultural economics (MS). MABM offered jointly with College of Business. *Program availability:* Part-time. *Faculty:* 21 full-time (3 women), 1 (woman) part-time/adjunct. *Students:* 13 full-time (6 women), 1 part-time (0 women); includes 2 minority (1 Black or African American, non-Hispanic/Latino; 1 Asian, non-Hispanic/Latino), 2 international. Average age 25. 19 applicants, 58% accepted, 6 enrolled. In 2017, 10 master's awarded. *Degree requirements:* For master's, comprehensive exam, thesis (for some programs), thesis defense. *Entrance requirements:* For master's, GRE, minimum GPA of 3.0. Additional exam requirements/recommendations for international students: Required—TOEFL (minimum score 575 paper-based; 84 iBT). Recommended—IELTS (minimum score 7). *Application deadline:* For fall admission, 7/1 for domestic students, 5/1 for international students; for spring admission, 11/1 for domestic students, 9/1 for international students.

Applications are processed on a rolling basis. Application fee: $60 ($80 for international students). Electronic applications accepted. *Expenses:* Tuition, state resident: full-time $8318; part-time $462.12 per credit hour. Tuition, nonresident: full-time $22,358; part-time $1242.12 per credit hour. *Required fees:* $110; $12.24 per credit hour. $6.12 per semester. *Financial support:* In 2017–18, 10 research assistantships with full tuition reimbursements (averaging $13,906 per year), 1 teaching assistantship (averaging $18,000 per year) were awarded; career-related internships or fieldwork, Federal Work-Study, institutionally sponsored loans, and unspecified assistantships also available. Financial award application deadline: 4/1; financial award applicants required to submit FAFSA. *Faculty research:* Production economics, policy, resource economics, international trade, agribusiness management. *Unit head:* Dr. Keith Coble, Professor and Head, 662-325-6670, Fax: 662-325-8777, E-mail: coble@aegcon.msstate.edu. *Application contact:* Marina Hunt, Admissions and Enrollment Assistant, 662-325-5188, E-mail: mhunt@grad.msstate.edu.
Website: http://www.agecon.msstate.edu/

New Mexico State University, College of Agricultural, Consumer and Environmental Sciences, Department of Agricultural Economics and Agricultural Business, Las Cruces, NM 88003. Offers agribusiness (MBA); economic development (DED); water science management (MS). *Program availability:* Part-time. *Faculty:* 5 full-time (0 women), 1 part-time/adjunct (0 women). *Students:* 6 full-time (2 women), 1 (woman) part-time; includes 3 minority (all Hispanic/Latino), 3 international. Average age 26. 11 applicants, 82% accepted, 3 enrolled. In 2017, 5 master's awarded. *Degree requirements:* For master's, thesis (for some programs); for doctorate, comprehensive exam, thesis/dissertation. *Entrance requirements:* For master's, GRE; GMAT (for MBA), previous course work in intermediate microeconomics, intermediate macroeconomics, college-level calculus, statistics; for doctorate, previous course work in intermediate microeconomics, intermediate macroeconomics, college-level calculus, statistics, related MS or equivalent, minimum GPA of 3.0. Additional exam requirements/recommendations for international students: Required—TOEFL (minimum score 550 paper-based; 79 iBT), IELTS (minimum score 6.5). *Application deadline:* For fall admission, 7/1 priority date for domestic and international students; for spring admission, 11/1 priority date for domestic and international students. Applications are processed on a rolling basis. Application fee: $40 ($50 for international students). Electronic applications accepted. *Expenses:* Tuition, state resident: full-time $4390. Tuition, nonresident: full-time $15,309. *Required fees:* $853. *Financial support:* In 2017–18, 7 students received support, including 3 research assistantships (averaging $15,678 per year), 3 teaching assistantships (averaging $16,964 per year); career-related internships or fieldwork, Federal Work-Study, scholarships/grants, traineeships, health care benefits, and unspecified assistantships also available. Support available to part-time students. Financial award application deadline: 3/1. *Faculty research:* Natural resource policy, production economics and farm/ranch management, agribusiness and marketing, international marketing and trade, agricultural risk management. *Total annual research expenditures:* $702,551. *Unit head:* Dr. Jay Lillywhite, Department Head, 575-646-3215, Fax: 575-646-3808, E-mail: lillywhi@nmsu.edu. *Application contact:* Dr. Ram Acharya, Graduate Committee Chair, 575-646-2524, Fax: 575-646-3808, E-mail: acharyar@nmsu.edu.
Website: http://aces.nmsu.edu/academics/aeab/

New Mexico State University, College of Business, MBA Program, Las Cruces, NM 88003. Offers agribusiness (MBA); finance (MBA); information systems (MBA). *Accreditation:* AACSB. *Program availability:* Part-time-only, evening/weekend, online with required 2-3 day orientation and 2-3 day concluding session in Las Cruces. *Students:* 47 full-time (24 women), 123 part-time (74 women); includes 98 minority (2 Black or African American, non-Hispanic/Latino; 3 American Indian or Alaska Native, non-Hispanic/Latino; 4 Asian, non-Hispanic/Latino; 85 Hispanic/Latino; 1 Native Hawaiian or other Pacific Islander, non-Hispanic/Latino; 3 Two or more races, non-Hispanic/Latino), 6 international. Average age 33. 166 applicants, 82% accepted, 19 enrolled. In 2017, 79 master's awarded. *Entrance requirements:* For master's, GMAT or GRE (depending upon undergraduate or graduate degree institution and GPA), minimum GPA of 3.5 from AACSB international or ACBSP-accredited institution or graduate degree from regionally-accredited U.S. university (without GMAT or GRE). Additional exam requirements/recommendations for international students: Required—TOEFL (minimum score 550 paper-based; 79 iBT), IELTS (minimum score 6.5). *Application deadline:* For fall admission, 7/15 priority date for domestic students, 4/15 priority date for international students; for spring admission, 4/15 priority date for domestic students, 9/15 priority date for international students; for summer admission, 4/15 for domestic students, 1/15 for international students. Applications are processed on a rolling basis. Application fee: $40 ($50 for international students). Electronic applications accepted. *Expenses:* Tuition, state resident: full-time $4390. Tuition, nonresident: full-time $15,309. *Required fees:* $853. *Financial support:* In 2017–18, 29 students received support. Fellowships, Federal Work-Study, institutionally sponsored loans, scholarships/grants, health care benefits, and unspecified assistantships available. Financial award application deadline: 3/1. *Unit head:* Dr. Kathy Brook, Associate Dean, 575-646-8003, Fax: 575-646-7977, E-mail: kbrook@nmsu.edu. *Application contact:* John Shonk, MBA Advisor, 575-646-8003, Fax: 575-646-7977, E-mail: mbaprog@nmsu.edu.
Website: http://business.nmsu.edu/mba

North Carolina Agricultural and Technical State University, School of Graduate Studies, School of Agriculture and Environmental Sciences, Department of Agribusiness, Applied Economics, and Agriscience Education, Greensboro, NC 27411. Offers agricultural economics (MS); agricultural education (MS). *Accreditation:* NCATE. *Program availability:* Part-time, evening/weekend. *Degree requirements:* For master's, comprehensive exam, thesis or alternative, qualifying exam. *Entrance requirements:* For master's, GRE General Test, minimum GPA of 3.0. *Faculty research:* Aid for small farmers, agricultural technology resources, labor force mobility, agrology.

North Carolina State University, Graduate School, College of Agriculture and Life Sciences, Program in Agricultural and Resource Economics, Raleigh, NC 27695. Offers MS. *Program availability:* Part-time. *Degree requirements:* For master's, thesis. *Entrance requirements:* Additional exam requirements/recommendations for international students: Required—TOEFL. Electronic applications accepted. *Faculty research:* Resource economics, international economics, labor economics, econometrics, environmental economics.

North Dakota State University, College of Graduate and Interdisciplinary Studies, College of Agriculture, Food Systems, and Natural Resources, Department of Agribusiness and Applied Economics, Fargo, ND 58102. Offers agribusiness and applied economics (MS); international agribusiness (MS). *Program availability:* Part-time. *Degree requirements:* For master's, thesis. *Entrance requirements:* For master's, minimum GPA of 3.0. Additional exam requirements/recommendations for international students: Required—TOEFL (minimum score 525 paper-based; 79 iBT). Electronic applications accepted. *Faculty research:* Agribusiness, transportation, marketing, microeconomics, trade.

Northwest Missouri State University, Graduate School, Melvin and Valorie Booth College of Business and Professional Studies, Maryville, MO 64468-6001. Offers agricultural economics (MBA); business decision and analytics (MBA); general

management (MBA); human resource management (MBA); marketing (MBA). *Program availability:* Part-time. *Faculty:* 17 full-time (6 women). *Students:* 40 full-time (13 women), 95 part-time (48 women); includes 16 minority (8 Black or African American, non-Hispanic/Latino; 1 American Indian or Alaska Native, non-Hispanic/Latino; 2 Asian, non-Hispanic/Latino; 3 Hispanic/Latino; 2 Two or more races, non-Hispanic/Latino), 15 international. Average age 31. 142 applicants, 66% accepted, 70 enrolled. In 2017, 53 master's awarded. *Degree requirements:* For master's, comprehensive exam. *Entrance requirements:* For master's, GMAT, GRE, minimum GPA of 2.5. Additional exam requirements/recommendations for international students: Required—TOEFL (minimum score 550 paper-based). *Application deadline:* For fall admission, 7/1 for domestic and international students; for spring admission, 11/15 for domestic and international students; for summer admission, 4/1 for domestic and international students. Applications are processed on a rolling basis. Application fee: $0 ($50 for international students). Electronic applications accepted. *Expenses:* $389.11 per credit in-state tuition; $641.97 per credit out-of-state tuition. *Financial support:* Research assistantships with full tuition reimbursements, teaching assistantships with full tuition reimbursements, career-related internships or fieldwork, and administrative assistantships, tutorial assistantships available. Financial award application deadline: 4/1; financial award applicants required to submit FAFSA. *Unit head:* Dr. Steve Ludwig, Director of the Melvin And Valorie Booth School of Business, 660-562-1749, Fax: 660-562-1096, E-mail: sludwig@nwmissouri.edu.
Website: https://www.nwmissouri.edu/business/index.htm

Northwest Missouri State University, Graduate School, School of Agricultural Sciences, Maryville, MO 64468-6001. Offers agricultural economics (MBA); agricultural education (MS Ed); agriculture (MS); teaching: agriculture (MS Ed). *Program availability:* Part-time. *Faculty:* 7 full-time (1 woman). *Students:* 7 full-time (4 women), 4 part-time (1 woman), 3 international. Average age 26. 11 applicants, 64% accepted, 3 enrolled. In 2017, 3 master's awarded. *Degree requirements:* For master's, comprehensive exam, thesis (for some programs). *Entrance requirements:* For master's, GRE General Test, minimum undergraduate GPA of 2.5, writing sample. Additional exam requirements/recommendations for international students: Required—TOEFL (minimum score 550 paper-based). *Application deadline:* For fall admission, 7/1 for domestic and international students; for spring admission, 11/15 for domestic and international students. Applications are processed on a rolling basis. Application fee: $0 ($50 for international students). Electronic applications accepted. *Expenses:* Tuition, state resident: full-time $4551; part-time $252.86 per credit hour. Tuition, nonresident: full-time $9103; part-time $505.72 per credit hour. *Required fees:* $2453; $136.25 per credit hour. Tuition and fees vary according to course load and program. *Financial support:* Research assistantships with full tuition reimbursements, teaching assistantships with full tuition reimbursements, and unspecified assistantships available. Financial award application deadline: 4/1; financial award applicants required to submit FAFSA. *Unit head:* Rodney Barr, Director, 660-562-1620.
Website: http://www.nwmissouri.edu/ag/

The Ohio State University, Graduate School, College of Food, Agricultural, and Environmental Sciences, Department of Agricultural, Environmental, and Development Economics, Columbus, OH 43210. Offers MS, PhD. *Faculty:* 19. *Students:* 70 full-time (26 women), 5 part-time (4 women), 46 international. Average age 27. In 2017, 20 master's, 14 doctorates awarded. *Entrance requirements:* For master's, GRE General Test (preferred minimum score: 156 quantitative, 153 verbal), minimum undergraduate GPA of 3.1 (recommended); for doctorate, GRE General Test (minimum score: 163 quantitative, 163 verbal), minimum GPA of 3.3 undergraduate, 3.5 graduate (recommended). Additional exam requirements/recommendations for international students: Required—TOEFL minimum score 600 paper-based; 100 IBT (for PhD); Recommended—TOEFL (minimum score 550 paper-based; 80 iBT). *Application deadline:* For fall admission, 12/15 priority date for domestic students, 11/30 priority date for international students. Applications are processed on a rolling basis. Application fee: $60 ($70 for international students). Electronic applications accepted. *Financial support:* Fellowships, research assistantships, teaching assistantships, Federal Work-Study, and institutionally sponsored loans available. Support available to part-time students. *Unit head:* Dr. Tim Haab, Chair, 614-292-7911, E-mail: haab.1@osu.edu. *Application contact:* Holly Hall, Graduate Recruitment Coordinator, 614-292-3599, E-mail: aedegradservices@osu.edu.
Website: http://aede.osu.edu/

Oklahoma State University, College of Agricultural Science and Natural Resources, Department of Agricultural Economics, Stillwater, OK 74078. Offers M Ag, MS, PhD. *Faculty:* 28 full-time (5 women). *Students:* 26 full-time (9 women), 22 part-time (10 women); includes 2 minority (1 American Indian or Alaska Native, non-Hispanic/Latino; 1 Two or more races, non-Hispanic/Latino), 23 international. Average age 29. 50 applicants, 50% accepted, 13 enrolled. In 2017, 11 master's, 9 doctorates awarded. *Degree requirements:* For master's, thesis or report, oral exam; for doctorate, comprehensive exam, thesis/dissertation. *Entrance requirements:* For master's and doctorate, GRE or GMAT. Additional exam requirements/recommendations for international students: Required—TOEFL (minimum score 550 paper-based; 79 iBT). *Application deadline:* For fall admission, 3/1 priority date for international students; for spring admission, 8/1 priority date for international students. Applications are processed on a rolling basis. Application fee: $40 ($75 for international students). Electronic applications accepted. *Expenses:* Tuition, state resident: full-time $4019; part-time $2679.60 per year. Tuition, nonresident: full-time $15,286; part-time $10,190.40 per year. *Required fees:* $2129; $1419 per unit. Tuition and fees vary according to program. *Financial support:* In 2017–18, 42 research assistantships (averaging $17,637 per year), 4 teaching assistantships (averaging $18,999 per year) were awarded; career-related internships or fieldwork, Federal Work-Study, scholarships/grants, health care benefits, tuition waivers (partial), and unspecified assistantships also available. Support available to part-time students. Financial award application deadline: 3/1; financial award applicants required to submit FAFSA. *Faculty research:* Marketing and agribusiness, production and farm management, policy and natural resources, community and rural development, international trade and development. *Unit head:* Dr. Mike Woods, Department Head, 405-744-6161, Fax: 405-744-8210, E-mail: mike.woods@okstate.edu.
Website: http://agecon.okstate.edu

Penn State University Park, Graduate School, College of Agricultural Sciences, Department of Agricultural Economics, Sociology, and Education, University Park, PA 16802. Offers agricultural and extension education (M Ed, MS, PhD, Certificate); applied youth, family and community education (M Ed); energy, environmental, and food economics (MS, PhD); rural sociology (MS, PhD). *Unit head:* Dr. Richard T. Roush, Dean, 814-865-2541, Fax: 814-865-3103. *Application contact:* Lori Hawn, Director, Graduate Student Services, 814-865-1795, Fax: 814-863-4627, E-mail: l-gswww@lists.psu.edu.
Website: http://aese.psu.edu/

Purdue University, Graduate School, College of Agriculture, Department of Agricultural Economics, West Lafayette, IN 47907. Offers EMBA, MS, PhD. *Program availability:* Part-time. *Faculty:* 47 full-time (6 women), 2 part-time/adjunct (0 women). *Students:* 85 full-time (37 women), 58 part-time (19 women); includes 11 minority (4 Black or African

American, non-Hispanic/Latino; 3 Asian, non-Hispanic/Latino; 3 Hispanic/Latino; 1 Two or more races, non-Hispanic/Latino), 57 international. Average age 29. 188 applicants, 47% accepted, 56 enrolled. In 2017, 42 master's, 10 doctorates awarded. Terminal master's awarded for partial completion of doctoral program. *Degree requirements:* For master's, thesis (for some programs); for doctorate, thesis/dissertation. *Entrance requirements:* For master's and doctorate, GRE General Test, minimum undergraduate GPA of 3.0 or equivalent. Additional exam requirements/recommendations for international students: Required—TOEFL (minimum score 550 paper-based; 77 iBT). *Application deadline:* For fall admission, 4/1 priority date for domestic students, 3/1 for international students; for spring admission, 10/1 for domestic students, 8/1 for international students. Applications are processed on a rolling basis. Application fee: $60 ($75 for international students). Electronic applications accepted. *Financial support:* In 2017–18, fellowships with tuition reimbursements (averaging $22,000 per year), research assistantships with tuition reimbursements (averaging $18,000 per year), teaching assistantships with tuition reimbursements (averaging $15,900 per year) were awarded. Financial award application deadline: 3/1; financial award applicants required to submit FAFSA. *Faculty research:* Marketing, international trade, policy and development, production, resources. *Unit head:* Jayson L. Lusk, Head of the Graduate Program, 765-494-4191, E-mail: jlusk@purdue.edu. *Application contact:* Lou Ann Baugh, Graduate Contact, 765-494-4196, E-mail: baughl@purdue.edu.
Website: https://ag.purdue.edu/agecon

Rutgers University–New Brunswick, Graduate School-New Brunswick, Program in Food and Business Economics, Piscataway, NJ 08854-8097. Offers MS. *Degree requirements:* For master's, comprehensive exam, thesis or alternative. *Entrance requirements:* Additional exam requirements/recommendations for international students: Required—TOEFL. Electronic applications accepted. *Faculty research:* Science policy, land use, nutrition policy, food industry, international development.

South Carolina State University, College of Graduate and Professional Studies, School of Business, Orangeburg, SC 29117-0001. Offers agribusiness (MBA); entrepreneurship (MBA); general business administration (MBA); healthcare management (MBA). *Program availability:* Part-time, evening/weekend. *Faculty:* 7 full-time (3 women), 2 part-time/adjunct (0 women). *Students:* 20 full-time (10 women), 11 part-time (7 women); all minorities (all Black or African American, non-Hispanic/Latino). Average age 27. 12 applicants, 92% accepted, 11 enrolled. In 2017, 10 master's awarded. *Degree requirements:* For master's, comprehensive exam, business plan. *Entrance requirements:* For master's, GMAT, minimum GPA of 2.8. Additional exam requirements/recommendations for international students: Required—TOEFL. *Application deadline:* For fall admission, 6/15 for domestic and international students; for spring admission, 11/1 for domestic and international students. Application fee: $25. Electronic applications accepted. *Expenses:* Tuition, state resident: full-time $9388; part-time $607 per credit hour. Tuition, nonresident: full-time $19,968; part-time $1194 per credit hour. *Required fees:* $766; $766 per credit hour. *Financial support:* Fellowships, research assistantships, career-related internships or fieldwork, Federal Work-Study, scholarships/grants, and unspecified assistantships available. Financial award application deadline: 6/1. *Unit head:* Dr. David Jamison, Interim Chair, 803-536-8443, Fax: 803-536-8078, E-mail: djamison@scsu.edu. *Application contact:* Ellen R. Ricoma, MBA Program Director, 803-533-3777, Fax: 803-516-4651, E-mail: ericoma1@scsu.edu.

Southern Illinois University Carbondale, Graduate School, College of Agriculture, Department of Agribusiness Economics, Carbondale, IL 62901-4701. Offers MS, MBA/MS. *Program availability:* Part-time. *Degree requirements:* For master's, thesis. *Entrance requirements:* For master's, minimum GPA of 2.7. Additional exam requirements/recommendations for international students: Required—TOEFL (minimum score 550 paper-based; 80 iBT). Electronic applications accepted. *Faculty research:* Agricultural finance and credit, agribusiness management, resource use, rural area economic development, marketing and price analysis.

Texas A&M University, College of Agriculture and Life Sciences, Department of Agricultural Economics, College Station, TX 77843. Offers M Agr, MS, PhD. *Program availability:* Part-time. *Faculty:* 33. *Students:* 128 full-time (54 women), 13 part-time (6 women); includes 14 minority (3 Asian, non-Hispanic/Latino; 10 Hispanic/Latino; 1 Two or more races, non-Hispanic/Latino), 71 international. Average age 28. 111 applicants, 65% accepted, 40 enrolled. In 2017, 37 master's, 13 doctorates awarded. Terminal master's awarded for partial completion of doctoral program. *Degree requirements:* For master's, comprehensive exam (for some programs), thesis (for some programs); for doctorate, comprehensive exam, thesis/dissertation. *Entrance requirements:* For master's and doctorate, GRE General Test. Additional exam requirements/recommendations for international students: Required—TOEFL (minimum score 550 paper-based; 80 iBT), IELTS (minimum score 6), PTE (minimum score 53). *Application deadline:* For fall admission, 3/1 for domestic students; for spring admission, 8/1 for domestic students. Applications are processed on a rolling basis. Application fee: $50 ($90 for international students). Electronic applications accepted. *Expenses:* Contact institution. *Financial support:* In 2017–18, 111 students received support, including 14 fellowships with tuition reimbursements available (averaging $13,602 per year), 25 research assistantships with tuition reimbursements available (averaging $9,398 per year), 40 teaching assistantships with tuition reimbursements available (averaging $8,749 per year); career-related internships or fieldwork, institutionally sponsored loans, scholarships/grants, traineeships, health care benefits, tuition waivers (full and partial), and unspecified assistantships also available. Support available to part-time students. Financial award application deadline: 3/15; financial award applicants required to submit FAFSA. *Faculty research:* Production economics, agricultural finance, resources, marketing and policy, agribusiness. *Unit head:* Dr. C. Parr Rosson, III, Professor and Head, 979-845-2116, Fax: 979-847-9378, E-mail: prosson@tamu.edu. *Application contact:* Brandi Blankenship, Program Coordinator, 979-845-5222, Fax: 979-862-1563, E-mail: brandi.blankenship@tamu.edu.
Website: http://agecon.tamu.edu/

Texas A&M University–Kingsville, College of Graduate Studies, Dick and Mary Lewis Kleberg College of Agriculture, Natural Resources and Human Sciences, Department of Agriculture, Agribusiness, and Environmental Sciences, Kingsville, TX 78363. Offers agribusiness (MS); agricultural science (MS); horticulture (PhD); plant and soil science (MS); ranch management (MS). Electronic applications accepted.

Texas Tech University, Graduate School, College of Agricultural Sciences and Natural Resources, Department of Agricultural and Applied Economics, Lubbock, TX 79409. Offers agribusiness (MAB); agricultural and applied economics (MS, PhD); JD/MS. *Program availability:* Part-time. *Faculty:* 21 full-time (5 women), 2 part-time/adjunct (0 women). *Students:* 50 full-time (27 women), 4 part-time (1 woman); includes 4 minority (all Hispanic/Latino), 33 international. Average age 30. 63 applicants, 68% accepted, 13 enrolled. In 2017, 19 master's, 4 doctorates awarded. Terminal master's awarded for partial completion of doctoral program. *Degree requirements:* For master's, thesis or alternative; for doctorate, comprehensive exam, thesis/dissertation. *Entrance requirements:* For master's and doctorate, GRE General Test, formal approval from departmental committee. Additional exam requirements/recommendations for international students: Required—TOEFL (minimum score 550 paper-based; 79 iBT). *Application deadline:* For fall admission, 6/1 priority date for domestic students, 1/15 priority date for international students; for spring admission, 9/1 priority date for domestic students, 6/15 priority date for international students. Applications are processed on a rolling basis. Application fee: $60. Electronic applications accepted. *Expenses:* Contact institution. *Financial support:* In 2017–18, 53 students received support, including 45 fellowships (averaging $3,593 per year), 43 research assistantships (averaging $14,523 per year); teaching assistantships, institutionally sponsored loans, scholarships/grants, health care benefits, and unspecified assistantships also available. Financial award application deadline: 5/1; financial award applicants required to submit FAFSA. *Faculty research:* Economics of the United States cotton and textile industries, natural resource management in semi-arid climates, commodity policy analysis, international trade in agricultural products, agribusiness analysis. *Total annual research expenditures:* $585,282. *Unit head:* Dr. Phillip N. Johnson, Professor/Chairman, 806-834-0474, Fax: 806-742-1099, E-mail: phil.johnson@ttu.edu. *Application contact:* Dr. Darren Hudson, Graduate Adviser, 806-742-2821, Fax: 806-742-1099, E-mail: darren.hudson@ttu.edu.
Website: http://www.aaec.ttu.edu

Tropical Agriculture Research and Higher Education Center, Graduate School, Turrialba, Costa Rica. Offers agribusiness management (MS); agroforestry systems (PhD); development practices (MS); ecological agriculture (MS); environmental socioeconomics (MS); forestry in tropical and subtropical zones (PhD); integrated watershed management (MS); international sustainable tourism (MS); management and conservation of tropical rainforests and biodiversity (MS); tropical agriculture (PhD); tropical agroforestry (MS). *Entrance requirements:* For master's, GRE, 2 years of related professional experience, letters of recommendation; for doctorate, GRE, 4 letters of recommendation, letter of support from employing organization, master's degree in agronomy, biological sciences, forestry, natural resources or related field. Additional exam requirements/recommendations for international students: Required—TOEFL (minimum score 550 paper-based). Electronic applications accepted. *Faculty research:* Biodiversity in fragmented landscapes, ecosystem management, integrated pest management, environmental livestock production, biotechnology carbon balances in diverse land uses.

Tuskegee University, Graduate Programs, College of Agriculture, Environment and Nutrition Sciences, Department of Agricultural and Environmental Sciences, Program in Agricultural and Resource Economics, Tuskegee, AL 36088. Offers MS. *Degree requirements:* For master's, thesis. *Entrance requirements:* For master's, GRE General Test. Additional exam requirements/recommendations for international students: Required—TOEFL (minimum score 500 paper-based).

Universidad del Este, Graduate School, Carolina, PR 00984. Offers accounting (MBA); adult education (M Ed); agribusiness (MBA); criminal justice and criminology (MA); curriculum and instruction - early education (M Ed); curriculum and instruction - elementary (M Ed); curriculum and instruction - English (M Ed); curriculum and instruction - Spanish (M Ed); human resources (MBA); information security management (MBA); information technology and Web business development (MBA); management (MBA); public policy (MPA); social work (MA), including clinical social work; special education (M Ed); strategic leadership (MBA).

Université Laval, Faculty of Agricultural and Food Sciences, Department of Agricultural Economics and Consumer Sciences, Program in Agricultural Economics, Québec, QC G1K 7P4, Canada. Offers M Sc. *Program availability:* Part-time. *Degree requirements:* For master's, thesis (for some programs). *Entrance requirements:* For master's, knowledge of French. Electronic applications accepted.

University of Alberta, Faculty of Graduate Studies and Research, Department of Rural Economy, Edmonton, AB T6G 2E1, Canada. Offers agricultural economics (M Ag, M Sc, PhD); forest economics (M Ag, M Sc, PhD); rural sociology (M Ag, M Sc); MBA/M Ag. *Program availability:* Part-time. *Degree requirements:* For doctorate, thesis/dissertation. *Entrance requirements:* Additional exam requirements/recommendations for international students: Required—TOEFL. *Faculty research:* Agroforestry, development, extension education, marketing and trade, natural resources and environment, policy, production economics.

The University of Arizona, College of Agriculture and Life Sciences, Department of Agricultural and Resource Economics, Tucson, AZ 85721. Offers applied econometrics and data analytics (MS); applied economics and policy analysis (MS). *Program availability:* Part-time. *Degree requirements:* For master's, thesis or alternative. *Entrance requirements:* For master's, GRE General Test, 3 letters of recommendation, minimum GPA of 3.0. Additional exam requirements/recommendations for international students: Required—TOEFL (minimum score 550 paper-based; 79 iBT). Electronic applications accepted. *Faculty research:* Natural resources, international development trade, production and marketing, agricultural policy, rural development.

University of Arkansas, Graduate School, Dale Bumpers College of Agricultural, Food and Life Sciences, Department of Agricultural Economics and Agribusiness, Fayetteville, AR 72701. Offers MS. *Students:* 28 applicants, 100% accepted. In 2017, 26 master's awarded. *Degree requirements:* For master's, thesis optional. *Application deadline:* For fall admission, 8/1 for domestic students, 4/1 for international students; for spring admission, 12/1 for domestic students, 10/1 for international students; for summer admission, 4/15 for domestic students, 3/1 for international students. Applications are processed on a rolling basis. Application fee: $60. Electronic applications accepted. *Expenses:* Tuition, state resident: full-time $3782. Tuition, nonresident: full-time $10,238. *Financial support:* In 2017–18, 8 research assistantships, 1 teaching assistantship were awarded; fellowships with tuition reimbursements, career-related internships or fieldwork, and Federal Work-Study also available. Support available to part-time students. Financial award application deadline: 4/1; financial award applicants required to submit FAFSA. *Unit head:* Dr. Robert Bacon, Interim Head, 479-575-7726, Fax: 479-575-5306, E-mail: rbacon@uark.edu. *Application contact:* Dr. Daniel Rainey, Graduate Coordinator, 479-575-5584, E-mail: rainey@uark.edu.
Website: https://agribusiness.uark.edu/index.php

The University of British Columbia, Faculty of Land and Food Systems, Program in Food and Resource Economics, Vancouver, BC V6T 1Z1, Canada. Offers MFRE.

University of California, Berkeley, Graduate Division, College of Natural Resources, Department of Agricultural and Resource Economics, Berkeley, CA 94720-1500. Offers PhD. *Degree requirements:* For doctorate, thesis/dissertation, qualifying exam. *Entrance requirements:* For doctorate, GRE General Test, minimum GPA of 3.0, 3 letters of recommendation. Electronic applications accepted. *Faculty research:* Agricultural economics and policy, environmental and resource economics and policy, international agricultural development and trade.

University of California, Davis, Graduate Studies, Program in Agricultural and Resource Economics, Davis, CA 95616. Offers MS, PhD, MBA/MS. Terminal master's awarded for partial completion of doctoral program. *Degree requirements:* For master's, thesis optional; for doctorate, thesis/dissertation. *Entrance requirements:* For master's, GRE General Test, minimum GPA of 3.0; for doctorate, GRE General Test, minimum GPA of 3.3. Additional exam requirements/recommendations for international students: Required—TOEFL (minimum score 550 paper-based). Electronic applications accepted. *Faculty research:* Applied microeconomics, international trade, development, econometrics, environmental economics.

University of California, Santa Barbara, Graduate Division, Donald Bren School of Environmental Science and Management, Santa Barbara, CA 93106-5131. Offers economics and environmental science (PhD); environmental science and management (MESM, PhD); technology and society (PhD). *Degree requirements:* For master's, thesis; for doctorate, thesis/dissertation. *Entrance requirements:* For master's and doctorate, GRE. Additional exam requirements/recommendations for international students: Required—TOEFL (minimum score 550 paper-based; 80 iBT), IELTS (minimum score 7). Electronic applications accepted. *Faculty research:* Coastal marine resources management, conservation planning, corporate environmental management, economics and politics of the environment, energy and climate, pollution prevention and remediation, water resources management.

University of Connecticut, Graduate School, College of Agriculture, Health and Natural Resources, Department of Agricultural and Resource Economics, Storrs, CT 06269. Offers MS, PhD. Terminal master's awarded for partial completion of doctoral program. *Degree requirements:* For master's, comprehensive exam; for doctorate, thesis/dissertation. *Entrance requirements:* For master's and doctorate, GRE General Test. Additional exam requirements/recommendations for international students: Required—TOEFL (minimum score 550 paper-based). Electronic applications accepted. *Faculty research:* Food marketing, international agricultural development.

University of Delaware, College of Agriculture and Natural Resources, Department of Food and Resource Economics, Newark, DE 19716. Offers agricultural and resource economics (MS); agricultural education (MA); operations research (MS); statistics (MS). *Program availability:* Part-time. *Degree requirements:* For master's, thesis. *Entrance requirements:* For master's, GRE General Test, 3 letters of recommendation. Additional exam requirements/recommendations for international students: Required—TOEFL (minimum score 550 paper-based). Electronic applications accepted. *Faculty research:* Experimental economics, environmental and resource economics, land use, law and economics.

University of Florida, Graduate School, College of Agricultural and Life Sciences, Department of Food and Resource Economics, Gainesville, FL 32611. Offers agribusiness (MS); food and resource economics (MAB, MS, PhD); hydrologic sciences (MS, PhD); toxicology (MS, PhD); tropical conservation and development (MAB, MS, PhD). *Program availability:* Part-time. *Degree requirements:* For master's, comprehensive exam, thesis; for doctorate, comprehensive exam, thesis/dissertation. *Entrance requirements:* For master's, GRE (combined minimum score of 300 overall, 145 on quantitative), minimum GPA of 3.0, minimum B grade in prerequisites; for doctorate, GRE (combined minimum score of 305 overall, 150 on quantitative), minimum GPA of 3.0, minimum B grade in prerequisites. Additional exam requirements/recommendations for international students: Required—TOEFL (minimum score 550 paper-based; 80 iBT), IELTS (minimum score 6). Electronic applications accepted. *Faculty research:* Economics of agriculture marketing, production, international trade, and policy; environmental and resource economics, development economics.

University of Georgia, College of Agricultural and Environmental Sciences, Department of Agricultural and Applied Economics, Athens, GA 30602. Offers agricultural economics (MAE, MS, PhD); environmental economics (MS). *Degree requirements:* For master's, thesis (MS); for doctorate, thesis/dissertation. *Entrance requirements:* For master's and doctorate, GRE General Test. Electronic applications accepted.

University of Guelph, Graduate Studies, College of Management and Economics, MBA Program, Guelph, ON N1G 2W1, Canada. Offers food and agribusiness management (MBA); hospitality and tourism management (MBA). *Program availability:* Part-time, evening/weekend, online learning. *Entrance requirements:* For master's, minimum B-average, minimum of 3 years of relevant work experience. Additional exam requirements/recommendations for international students: Required—TOEFL (minimum score 550 paper-based). Electronic applications accepted. *Faculty research:* Marketing, operations management, business policy, financial management, organizational behavior.

University of Guelph, Graduate Studies, Ontario Agricultural College, Department of Food, Agricultural and Resource Economics, Guelph, ON N1G 2W1, Canada. Offers agricultural economics (M Sc, PhD); MA/M Sc. *Program availability:* Part-time. *Degree requirements:* For master's, thesis; for doctorate, comprehensive exam, thesis/dissertation. *Entrance requirements:* For master's, minimum B- average during previous 2 years of course work; for doctorate, minimum B standing in recognized master's degree. Additional exam requirements/recommendations for international students: Required—TOEFL (minimum score 550 paper-based), IELTS (minimum score 6.5). Electronic applications accepted. *Faculty research:* Agricultural policy, agribusiness, environmental economics, agricultural marketing, production economics.

University of Idaho, College of Graduate Studies, College of Agricultural and Life Sciences, Department of Agricultural Economics and Rural Sociology, Moscow, ID 83844. Offers MS. *Faculty:* 6 full-time. *Students:* 9. Average age 25. In 2017, 3 master's awarded. *Entrance requirements:* For master's, minimum GPA of 3.0. Additional exam requirements/recommendations for international students: Required—TOEFL (minimum score 79 iBT). *Application deadline:* For fall admission, 8/1 for domestic students; for spring admission, 12/15 for domestic students. Applications are processed on a rolling basis. Application fee: $60. Electronic applications accepted. *Expenses:* Tuition, state resident: full-time $6722; part-time $430 per credit hour. Tuition, nonresident: full-time $23,046; part-time $1337 per credit hour. *Required fees:* $2142; $63 per credit hour. *Financial support:* Research assistantships and teaching assistantships available. Financial award applicants required to submit FAFSA. *Faculty research:* Crops: potatoes, blue grass; livestock: beef, dairy; rural and community development; natural resources and the environment; farm and ranch management. *Unit head:* Dr. Cathy Roheim, Department Head, 208-885-6262, Fax: 208-885-5759, E-mail: cdarby@uidaho.edu. *Application contact:* Sean Scoggin, Graduate Recruitment Coordinator, 208-885-4001, Fax: 208-885-4406, E-mail: graduateadmissions@uidaho.edu.
Website: http://www.uidaho.edu/cals/agricultural-economics-and-rural-sociology.aspx

University of Illinois at Urbana–Champaign, Graduate College, College of Agricultural, Consumer and Environmental Sciences, Department of Agricultural and Consumer Economics, Champaign, IL 61820. Offers agricultural and applied economics (MS, PhD).

University of Kentucky, Graduate School, College of Agriculture, Food and Environment, Program in Agricultural Economics, Lexington, KY 40506-0032. Offers MS, PhD. *Degree requirements:* For master's, comprehensive exam, thesis optional; for doctorate, comprehensive exam, thesis/dissertation. *Entrance requirements:* For master's, GRE General Test, minimum undergraduate GPA of 2.75; for doctorate, GRE General Test, minimum graduate GPA of 3.0. Additional exam requirements/recommendations for international students: Required—TOEFL (minimum score 550 paper-based). Electronic applications accepted. *Faculty research:* Food and agricultural marketing, agricultural and food policy, natural resources and environment, rural economic development.

University of Maine, Graduate School, College of Natural Sciences, Forestry, and Agriculture, School of Economics, Orono, ME 04469. Offers economics (MA); financial economics (MA); resource economics and policy (MS). *Program availability:* Part-time. *Faculty:* 11 full-time (3 women). *Students:* 22 full-time (9 women), 1 (woman) part-time, 9 international. Average age 24. 25 applicants, 84% accepted, 11 enrolled. In 2017, 12 master's awarded. *Degree requirements:* For master's, thesis (for some programs). *Entrance requirements:* For master's, GRE General Test. Additional exam requirements/recommendations for international students: Required—TOEFL (minimum score 580 paper-based; 93 iBT), IELTS (minimum score 6.9), TWE (minimum score 4.9), PTE (minimum score 67). *Application deadline:* For fall admission, 2/15 for domestic students, 2/1 for international students; for spring admission, 9/15 for domestic students, 8/15 for international students. Applications are processed on a rolling basis. Application fee: $65. Electronic applications accepted. *Expenses:* Tuition, state resident: full-time $7722; part-time $429 per credit hour. Tuition, nonresident: full-time $25,146; part-time $1397 per credit hour. *Required fees:* $1162; $581 per credit hour. *Financial support:* In 2017–18, 27 students received support, including 12 research assistantships with full tuition reimbursements available (averaging $20,500 per year), 13 teaching assistantships with full tuition reimbursements available (averaging $15,200 per year); career-related internships or fieldwork, Federal Work-Study, institutionally sponsored loans, scholarships/grants, and tuition waivers (full and partial) also available. Support available to part-time students. Financial award application deadline: 3/1. *Faculty research:* Economics of: health, energy, transportation, marine resource, consumer behavior. *Total annual research expenditures:* $848,400. *Unit head:* Dr. Mario Teisl, Director, 207-581-3151, Fax: 207-581-4278. *Application contact:* Scott G. Delcourt, Assistant Vice President for Graduate Studies and Senior Associate Dean, 207-581-3291, Fax: 207-581-3232, E-mail: graduate@maine.edu.
Website: http://umaine.edu/soe/

University of Manitoba, Faculty of Graduate Studies, Faculty of Agricultural and Food Sciences, Department of Agribusiness and Agricultural Economics, Winnipeg, MB R3T 2N2, Canada. Offers agribusiness (M Sc, PhD). *Degree requirements:* For master's, thesis or alternative; for doctorate, thesis/dissertation.

University of Maryland, College Park, Academic Affairs, College of Agriculture and Natural Resources, Department of Agricultural and Resource Economics, College Park, MD 20742. Offers agriculture economics (MS, PhD); resource economics (MS, PhD). *Program availability:* Part-time, evening/weekend. *Degree requirements:* For master's, variable foreign language requirement, thesis optional, oral exam; for doctorate, variable foreign language requirement, oral dissertation defense. *Entrance requirements:* For master's, GRE General Test, minimum GPA of 3.0, course work in microeconomics and calculus, 3 letters of recommendation; for doctorate, GRE General Test. Additional exam requirements/recommendations for international students: Required—TOEFL. Electronic applications accepted. *Faculty research:* Agricultural development, international trade, agricultural marketing, econometrics, farm management and production economics.

University of Massachusetts Amherst, Graduate School, College of Social and Behavioral Sciences, Department of Resource Economics, Amherst, MA 01003. Offers MS, PhD. *Program availability:* Part-time. Terminal master's awarded for partial completion of doctoral program. *Degree requirements:* For master's, thesis or alternative; for doctorate, comprehensive exam, thesis/dissertation. *Entrance requirements:* For master's and doctorate, GRE General Test. Additional exam requirements/recommendations for international students: Required—TOEFL (minimum score 550 paper-based; 80 iBT), IELTS (minimum score 6.5). Electronic applications accepted.

University of Missouri, Office of Research and Graduate Studies, College of Agriculture, Food and Natural Resources, Department of Agricultural and Applied Economics, Columbia, MO 65211. Offers agricultural economics (MS, PhD); conservation biology (Graduate Certificate). *Degree requirements:* For doctorate, comprehensive exam, thesis/dissertation. *Entrance requirements:* For master's and doctorate, GRE General Test, minimum GPA of 3.0. Additional exam requirements/recommendations for international students: Required—TOEFL (minimum score 550 paper-based; 80 iBT). Electronic applications accepted. *Faculty research:* Agribusiness management, contracting and strategy; collective action and cooperative theory; econometrics and price analysis; entrepreneurship; environmental and natural resource economics; food, biofuel and agricultural policy and regulation; international development; regional economics and rural development policy; science policy and innovation; sustainable agriculture and applied ethics.

University of Nebraska–Lincoln, Graduate College, College of Agricultural Sciences and Natural Resources, Department of Agricultural Economics, Lincoln, NE 68588. Offers agribusiness (MBA); agricultural economics (MS, PhD); community development (M Ag). *Degree requirements:* For master's, thesis optional; for doctorate, comprehensive exam, thesis/dissertation. *Entrance requirements:* For master's and doctorate, GRE General Test. Additional exam requirements/recommendations for international students: Required—TOEFL (minimum score 550 paper-based). Electronic applications accepted. *Faculty research:* Marketing and agribusiness, production economics, resource law, international trade and development, rural policy and revitalization.

University of Nevada, Reno, Graduate School, College of Agriculture, Biotechnology and Natural Resources, Department of Resource Economics, Reno, NV 89557. Offers MS, PhD. Terminal master's awarded for partial completion of doctoral program. *Degree requirements:* For master's, thesis optional; for doctorate, thesis/dissertation. *Entrance requirements:* For master's, GRE General Test, minimum GPA of 2.75; for doctorate, GRE General Test, minimum GPA of 3.0. Additional exam requirements/recommendations for international students: Required—TOEFL (minimum score 500 paper-based; 61 iBT), IELTS (minimum score 6). Electronic applications accepted. *Faculty research:* Econometrics, environmental valuation, natural resource and environmental policy analysis, public lands management.

University of Puerto Rico–Mayagüez, Graduate Studies, College of Agricultural Sciences, Department of Agricultural Economics and Rural Sociology, Mayagüez, PR 00681-9000. Offers MS. *Program availability:* Part-time. *Degree requirements:* For master's, comprehensive exam, thesis. *Entrance requirements:* For master's, bachelor's degree in agricultural economics or its equivalent. Electronic applications accepted. *Faculty research:* Farm management, agricultural development, agrimarketing, natural resource economics.

University of Saskatchewan, College of Graduate Studies and Research, College of Agriculture, Department of Agricultural Economics, Saskatoon, SK S7N 5A2, Canada. Offers M Ag, M Sc, MA, PhD, PGD. *Degree requirements:* For master's, thesis; for doctorate, comprehensive exam (for some programs), thesis/dissertation. *Entrance requirements:* Additional exam requirements/recommendations for international students: Required—TOEFL (minimum score 80 iBT); Recommended—IELTS (minimum score 6.5).

University of Saskatchewan, College of Graduate Studies and Research, Edwards School of Business, Program in Business Administration, Saskatoon, SK S7N 5A2, Canada. Offers agribusiness management (MBA); biotechnology management (MBA); health services management (MBA); indigenous management (MBA); international business management (MBA).

Agricultural Economics and Agribusiness

The University of Tennessee at Martin, Graduate Programs, College of Business and Global Affairs, Program in Business, Martin, TN 38238. Offers agricultural business (MBA); financial services (MBA); general business (MBA). *Accreditation:* AACSB. *Program availability:* Part-time, online only, 100% online, blended/hybrid learning. *Faculty:* 31. *Students:* 12 full-time (5 women), 73 part-time (31 women); includes 12 minority (7 Black or African American, non-Hispanic/Latino; 2 Asian, non-Hispanic/Latino; 2 Hispanic/Latino; 1 Two or more races, non-Hispanic/Latino). Average age 34. 33 applicants, 24% accepted, 6 enrolled. In 2017, 38 master's awarded. *Degree requirements:* For master's, comprehensive exam. *Entrance requirements:* For master's, GMAT, GRE, minimum GPA of 2.5, resume. Additional exam requirements/recommendations for international students: Required—TOEFL (minimum score 525 paper-based; 71 iBT). *Application deadline:* For fall admission, 7/27 priority date for domestic students, 7/27 for international students; for spring admission, 12/17 priority date for domestic students, 12/17 for international students; for summer admission, 5/10 priority date for domestic and international students. Applications are processed on a rolling basis. Application fee: $30 ($130 for international students). Electronic applications accepted. *Expenses:* Tuition, state resident: full-time $8658; part-time $481 per credit hour. Tuition, nonresident: full-time $14,418; part-time $801 per credit hour. *International tuition:* $22,602 full-time. *Required fees:* $1404; $79 per credit hour. Part-time tuition and fees vary according to course load. *Financial support:* In 2017–18, 29 students received support, including 4 research assistantships with full tuition reimbursements available (averaging $7,226 per year), 2 teaching assistantships with full tuition reimbursements available (averaging $7,540 per year); scholarships/grants and tuition waivers (full and partial) also available. Financial award application deadline: 2/1; financial award applicants required to submit FAFSA. *Unit head:* Dr. Ashley Kilburn, Coordinator, 731-881-7245, Fax: 731-881-7231, E-mail: mba@utm.edu. *Application contact:* Jolene L. Cunningham, Student Services Specialist, 731-881-7012, Fax: 731-881-7499, E-mail: jcunningham@utm.edu.

University of Vermont, Graduate College, College of Agriculture and Life Sciences, Program in Community Development and Applied Economics, Burlington, VT 05405. Offers community development and applied economics (MS). *Students:* 14 (7 women). Average age 27. 14 applicants, 93% accepted, 4 enrolled. In 2017, 6 master's awarded. *Degree requirements:* For master's, thesis. *Entrance requirements:* For master's, GRE General Test. Additional exam requirements/recommendations for international students: Required—TOEFL (minimum score 550 paper-based; 90 iBT), IELTS (minimum score 6.5). *Application deadline:* For fall admission, 1/15 priority date for domestic and international students. Applications are processed on a rolling basis. Application fee: $65. Electronic applications accepted. *Expenses:* Tuition, state resident: full-time $11,628; part-time $646 per credit. Tuition, nonresident: full-time $29,340; part-time $1630 per credit. *Required fees:* $1994; $10 per credit. Tuition and fees vary according to course load and program. *Financial support:* In 2017–18, 11 students received support, including 2 research assistantships with full tuition reimbursements available (averaging $23,500 per year), 9 teaching assistantships with full tuition reimbursements available (averaging $23,500 per year); fellowships, career-related internships or fieldwork, and health care benefits also available. Financial award application deadline: 1/15. *Faculty research:* Agricultural production and marketing. *Unit head:* David Conner, Associate Professor, 802-656-2001, E-mail: david.conner@uvm.edu.
Website: https://www.uvm.edu/cals/cdae/ms

University of Wisconsin–Madison, Graduate School, College of Agricultural and Life Sciences, Department of Agricultural and Applied Economics, Madison, WI 53706. Offers MA, MS, PhD. *Program availability:* Part-time. *Degree requirements:* For doctorate, thesis/dissertation, preliminary exams. *Entrance requirements:* For master's and doctorate, GRE General Test. Additional exam requirements/recommendations for international students: Required—TOEFL (minimum score 580 paper-based; 92 iBT). Electronic applications accepted. *Faculty research:* Environmental and resource economics, international development, community economics, energy economics, agricultural technology, food systems, markets and trade.

University of Wyoming, College of Agriculture and Natural Resources, Department of Agricultural and Applied Economics, Laramie, WY 82071. Offers MS. *Program availability:* Part-time. *Degree requirements:* For master's, thesis (for some programs). *Entrance requirements:* For master's, GRE General Test, minimum GPA of 3.0.

Additional exam requirements/recommendations for international students: Required—TOEFL. Electronic applications accepted. *Faculty research:* Farm management, agricultural markets, water economics, community development, agricultural business.

Utah State University, School of Graduate Studies, College of Agriculture and Applied Sciences, Department of Applied Economics, Logan, UT 84322. Offers applied economics (MAE, MS, PhD); international food and agribusiness (MS). *Program availability:* Part-time. *Degree requirements:* For master's, thesis optional. *Entrance requirements:* For master's, GRE General Test, minimum GPA of 3.0.

Virginia Polytechnic Institute and State University, Graduate School, College of Agriculture and Life Sciences, Blacksburg, VA 24061. Offers agricultural and applied economics (MS, PhD); agricultural and life sciences (MS); agriculture, leadership, and community education (MS, PhD); animal and poultry science (MS, PhD); biochemistry (MS, PhD); crop and soil environmental sciences (MS, PhD); dairy science (MS, PhD); entomology (MS, PhD); food science and technology (MS, PhD); horticulture (PhD); human nutrition, foods and exercise (MS, PhD); plant pathology, physiology, and weed science (MS, PhD). *Faculty:* 241 full-time (73 women), 1 (woman) part-time/adjunct. *Students:* 379 full-time (221 women), 126 part-time (75 women); includes 64 minority (21 Black or African American, non-Hispanic/Latino; 15 Asian, non-Hispanic/Latino; 14 Hispanic/Latino; 14 Two or more races, non-Hispanic/Latino), 119 international. Average age 29. 357 applicants, 46% accepted, 118 enrolled. In 2017, 105 master's, 54 doctorates awarded. *Degree requirements:* For master's, comprehensive exam (for some programs), thesis (for some programs); for doctorate, comprehensive exam (for some programs), thesis/dissertation (for some programs). *Entrance requirements:* For master's and doctorate, GRE/GMAT. Additional exam requirements/recommendations for international students: Required—TOEFL (minimum score 80 iBT). *Application deadline:* For fall admission, 8/1 for domestic students, 4/1 for international students; for spring admission, 1/1 for domestic students, 9/1 for international students. Applications are processed on a rolling basis. Application fee: $75. Electronic applications accepted. *Expenses:* Tuition, state resident: full-time $15,072; part-time $718.50 per credit hour. Tuition, nonresident: full-time $28,810; part-time $1448.25 per credit hour. *Required fees:* $2741; $502 per semester. Tuition and fees vary according to course load, campus/location and program. *Financial support:* In 2017–18, 232 research assistantships with full tuition reimbursements (averaging $21,852 per year), 94 teaching assistantships with full tuition reimbursements (averaging $21,643 per year) were awarded. Financial award application deadline: 3/1; financial award applicants required to submit FAFSA. *Total annual research expenditures:* $44.3 million. *Unit head:* Dr. Alan L. Grant, Dean, 540-231-4152, Fax: 540-231-4163, E-mail: algrant@vt.edu. *Application contact:* Crystal Tawney, Administrative Assistant, 540-231-4152, Fax: 540-231-4163, E-mail: cdtawney@vt.edu.
Website: http://www.cals.vt.edu/

Washington State University, College of Agricultural, Human, and Natural Resource Sciences, School of Economic Sciences, Pullman, WA 99164-6210. Offers agricultural economics (PhD); economics (PhD). Programs offered at the Pullman campus. Terminal master's awarded for partial completion of doctoral program. *Degree requirements:* For master's, comprehensive exam (for some programs), thesis (for some programs), oral exam; for doctorate, comprehensive exam, thesis/dissertation, oral exam, written exam, qualifying exams. *Entrance requirements:* For master's and doctorate, GRE, minimum GPA of 3.0, 3 letters of recommendation. Additional exam requirements/recommendations for international students: Required—TOEFL (minimum score 550 paper-based). Electronic applications accepted. *Faculty research:* Agricultural economics, econometrics, natural resource and environmental economics, industrial organization, health economics.

West Texas A&M University, College of Agriculture and Natural Sciences, Department of Agricultural Sciences, Emphasis in Agricultural Business and Economics, Canyon, TX 79015. Offers MS. *Program availability:* Part-time. *Degree requirements:* For master's, comprehensive exam, thesis optional. *Entrance requirements:* For master's, GRE General Test. Additional exam requirements/recommendations for international students: Required—TOEFL (minimum score 550 paper-based). Electronic applications accepted. *Faculty research:* Utilizing expected revenue in selecting optimal marketing alternatives for fixed resource cow/calf operators in the Texas panhandle.

Applied Economics

Auburn University, Graduate School, College of Liberal Arts, Department of Economics, Auburn University, AL 36849. Offers applied economics (PhD); economics (MS). *Program availability:* Part-time. *Faculty:* 16 full-time (5 women), 3 part-time/adjunct (1 woman). *Students:* 14 full-time (6 women), 2 part-time (both women); includes 1 minority (Black or African American, non-Hispanic/Latino), 9 international. Average age 28. 33 applicants, 39% accepted, 6 enrolled. In 2017, 1 master's, 1 doctorate awarded. *Degree requirements:* For master's, thesis. *Entrance requirements:* For master's, GMAT, GRE General Test. Additional exam requirements/recommendations for international students: Required—TOEFL. *Application deadline:* Applications are processed on a rolling basis. Application fee: $50 ($60 for international students). Electronic applications accepted. *Expenses:* Tuition, state resident: full-time $10,974; part-time $519 per credit hour. Tuition, nonresident: full-time $29,658; part-time $1557 per credit hour. *Required fees:* $816 per semester. Tuition and fees vary according to degree level and program. *Financial support:* Teaching assistantships, career-related internships or fieldwork, and Federal Work-Study available. Support available to part-time students. Financial award application deadline: 3/15; financial award applicants required to submit FAFSA. *Unit head:* Dr. Michael Stern, Chair, 334-844-2982. *Application contact:* Dr. George Flowers, Dean of the Graduate School, 334-844-2125.
Website: http://www.cla.auburn.edu/economics/

Auburn University, Graduate School, Interdepartmental Programs, Interdepartmental Program in Applied Economics, Auburn University, AL 36849. Offers PhD. *Students:* 14 full-time (9 women), 1 part-time (0 women), all international. Average age 31. 13 applicants, 46% accepted, 3 enrolled. In 2017, 9 doctorates awarded. *Expenses:* Tuition, state resident: full-time $10,974; part-time $519 per credit hour. Tuition, nonresident: full-time $29,658; part-time $1557 per credit hour. *Required fees:* $816 per semester. Tuition and fees vary according to degree level and program. *Unit head:* Deacue Fields, Chair, 334-844-5614. *Application contact:* Dr. George Flowers, Dean of the Graduate School, 334-844-2125.

Auburn University at Montgomery, College of Public Policy and Justice, Department of Economics, Montgomery, AL 36124-4023. Offers applied economics (MS). *Program availability:* Evening/weekend. *Faculty:* 8 full-time (0 women). *Students:* 15 full-time (9

women); includes 6 minority (5 Black or African American, non-Hispanic/Latino; 1 Asian, non-Hispanic/Latino), 4 international. Average age 31. 20 applicants, 95% accepted, 14 enrolled. *Entrance requirements:* For master's, GMAT or GRE General Test. Additional exam requirements/recommendations for international students: Recommended—TOEFL (minimum score 500 paper-based; 61 iBT), IELTS (minimum score 5.5), TSE (minimum score 44). *Application deadline:* For fall admission, 7/15 for international students; for spring admission, 11/15 for international students; for summer admission, 4/15 for international students. Applications are processed on a rolling basis. Application fee: $25. Electronic applications accepted. *Expenses:* Tuition, state resident: full-time $6930; part-time $385 per credit hour. Tuition, nonresident: full-time $15,588; part-time $866 per credit hour. *Required fees:* $640. *Financial support:* Applicants required to submit FAFSA. *Unit head:* Dr. Carel Ligeon, Head, 334-244-3486, E-mail: cligeon@aum.edu.
Website: http://www.cppj.aum.edu/departments/economics

Brandeis University, International Business School (IBS), Master of Arts in International Economics and Finance Program, Waltham, MA 02454-9110. Offers applied economic analysis (MA). *Faculty:* 40 full-time (16 women), 31 part-time/adjunct (7 women). *Students:* 158 full-time (96 women); includes 8 minority (1 American Indian or Alaska Native, non-Hispanic/Latino; 6 Asian, non-Hispanic/Latino; 1 Hispanic/Latino), 140 international. Average age 23. 649 applicants, 45% accepted, 92 enrolled. In 2017, 103 master's awarded. *Entrance requirements:* For master's, GMAT or GRE. Additional exam requirements/recommendations for international students: Required—TOEFL (minimum score 600 paper-based; 100 iBT), IELTS (minimum score 7), PTE (minimum score 68). *Application deadline:* For fall admission, 11/1 priority date for domestic and international students; for winter admission, 1/15 priority date for domestic and international students; for spring admission, 3/15 priority date for domestic and international students; for summer admission, 4/15 for domestic and international students. Application fee: $100. Electronic applications accepted. *Expenses:* Contact institution. *Financial support:* In 2017–18, 81 students received support. Institutionally sponsored loans and scholarships (averaging $18,384 annually) available. Financial award application deadline: 4/15; financial award applicants required to submit FAFSA.

Faculty research: International economic policy analysis, macroeconomics, econometrics, business economics, economic development. *Unit head:* Peter Petri, Dean, 781-736-2256. *Application contact:* Kelly Sugrue, Assistant Dean of Admissions, 781-736-2252, Fax: 781-736-2263, E-mail: globaladmissions@brandeis.edu.
Website: http://www.brandeis.edu/global/ma

Bryant University, College of Arts and Sciences, Smithfield, RI 02917. Offers applied economics (MS, Graduate Certificate); communication (MA, Graduate Certificate), including general communication (MA), health care communication (MA), organizational communication (MA), professional communication (Graduate Certificate); organizational communication (Graduate Certificate), including managerial communication, public communication; sustainability practices (Graduate Certificate). *Program availability:* Part-time-only, evening/weekend. *Faculty:* 3 full-time (0 women), 2 part-time/adjunct (0 women). *Students:* 8 full-time (4 women), 10 part-time (8 women); includes 3 minority (2 Black or African American, non-Hispanic/Latino; 1 Two or more races, non-Hispanic/Latino), 2 international. Average age 25. 25 applicants, 32% accepted, 6 enrolled. In 2017, 4 master's awarded. *Degree requirements:* For master's, thesis. *Entrance requirements:* For master's, GRE. Additional exam requirements/recommendations for international students: Required—TOEFL (minimum score 550 paper-based; 80 iBT). *Application deadline:* For fall admission, 8/15 for domestic and international students; for spring admission, 1/15 for domestic and international students; for summer admission, 5/15 for domestic and international students. Applications are processed on a rolling basis. Application fee: $80. Electronic applications accepted. *Expenses:* $932 per credit hour. *Financial support:* In 2017–18, 15 fellowships with full and partial tuition reimbursements (averaging $10,483 per year) were awarded; research assistantships, scholarships/grants, and unspecified assistantships also available. Financial award application deadline: 2/15; financial award applicants required to submit FAFSA. *Faculty research:* Mass media and social construction of reality; development and improvement of media literacy skills; sociocultural influences on cognition and learning in K-12 populations, oil pollution impacts on marine and estuarine microbial communities; wetlands ecology. *Unit head:* Bradford Martin, Dean, College of Arts and Sciences, 401-232-6929, E-mail: bmartin@bryant.edu. *Application contact:* Terri Rogers, Admission Assistant, Graduate School, 401-232-6230, E-mail: graduateprograms@bryant.edu.
Website: http://gradschool.bryant.edu/arts-and-sciences/

Buffalo State College, State University of New York, The Graduate School, Faculty of Natural and Social Sciences, Department of Economics and Finance, Buffalo, NY 14222-1095. Offers applied economics (MA). *Degree requirements:* For master's, project. *Entrance requirements:* Additional exam requirements/recommendations for international students: Required—TOEFL (minimum score 550 paper-based).

Clemson University, Graduate School, College of Agriculture, Forestry and Life Sciences, Department of Agricultural Sciences, Clemson, SC 29634. Offers agricultural education (M Ag Ed); applied economics (PhD); applied economics and statistics (MS). *Program availability:* Part-time. *Faculty:* 20 full-time (3 women). *Students:* 30 full-time (20 women), 25 part-time (14 women). Average age 27. 72 applicants, 50% accepted, 17 enrolled. In 2017, 6 master's, 1 doctorate awarded. *Degree requirements:* For master's, thesis optional; for doctorate, comprehensive exam, thesis/dissertation. *Entrance requirements:* For master's and doctorate, GRE General Test, unofficial transcripts, letters of recommendation. Additional exam requirements/recommendations for international students: Required—TOEFL (minimum score 80 iBT), IELTS (minimum score 6.5), PTE (minimum score 5). *Application deadline:* For fall admission, 6/1 for domestic students, 7/1 for international students; for spring admission, 10/1 for domestic students, 11/1 for international students. Applications are processed on a rolling basis. Application fee: $80 ($90 for international students). Electronic applications accepted. *Expenses:* $5,174 per semester full-time resident, $9,714 per semester full-time non-resident, $511 per credit hour part-time resident, $1,017 per credit hour part-time non-resident; $741 per credit hour online; other fees may apply per session. *Financial support:* In 2017–18, 11 students received support, including 7 research assistantships with partial tuition reimbursements available (averaging $11,750 per year), 4 teaching assistantships with partial tuition reimbursements available (averaging $8,307 per year); fellowships, career-related internships or fieldwork, and unspecified assistantships also available. Financial award application deadline: 6/1. *Faculty research:* Agricultural education, agricultural economics, agricultural statistics, agribusiness. *Unit head:* Dr. Charles Privette, Interim Department Head, 864-656-6247, E-mail: privett@clemson.edu.
Website: http://www.clemson.edu/cafls/departments/agricultural-sciences/index.html

Clemson University, Graduate School, College of Business, John E. Walker Department of Economics, Clemson, SC 29634. Offers applied economics (PhD); applied economics and statistics (MS); economics (MA, PhD). *Faculty:* 29 full-time (3 women), 3 part-time/adjunct (1 woman). *Students:* 148 full-time (50 women), 8 part-time (4 women); includes 10 minority (4 Black or African American, non-Hispanic/Latino; 2 Hispanic/Latino; 4 Two or more races, non-Hispanic/Latino), 92 international. Average age 28. 148 applicants, 49% accepted, 14 enrolled. In 2017, 20 master's, 23 doctorates awarded. Terminal master's awarded for partial completion of doctoral program. *Degree requirements:* For master's, thesis, 24 course hours, 6 thesis hours; for doctorate, comprehensive exam, thesis/dissertation, 42 course hours, 18 dissertation hours. *Entrance requirements:* For master's and doctorate, GRE General Test or GMAT, unofficial transcripts, letters of recommendation, courses in intermediate microeconomic theory and multivariable calculus. Additional exam requirements/recommendations for international students: Required—TOEFL (minimum score 80 iBT), IELTS (minimum score 6.5), PTE (minimum score 54). *Application deadline:* For fall admission, 1/15 priority date for domestic and international students. Applications are processed on a rolling basis. Application fee: $80 ($90 for international students). Electronic applications accepted. *Expenses:* $5,174 per semester full-time resident, $9,714 per semester full-time non-resident, $511 per credit hour part-time resident, $1,017 per credit hour part-time non-resident; $741 per credit hour online; other fees may apply per session. *Financial support:* In 2017–18, 66 students received support, including 16 fellowships with partial tuition reimbursements available (averaging $8,813 per year), 13 teaching assistantships with partial tuition reimbursements available (averaging $12,728 per year); unspecified assistantships also available. Financial award application deadline: 1/15. *Faculty research:* Public economics, public choice and political economy; econometrics (focus on data envelope analysis), industrial organization (focus on pricing), labor and development economics, international economics (focus on free trade agreements). *Total annual research expenditures:* $20,956. *Unit head:* Dr. Scott Baier, Department Chair, 864-656-4534, E-mail: sbaier@clemson.edu. *Application contact:* Dr. Curtis Simon, PhD Program Coordinator, 864-656-3966, E-mail: cjsmn@clemson.edu.
Website: http://economics.clemson.edu/

Cornell University, Graduate School, Graduate Fields of Agriculture and Life Sciences, Field of Applied Economics and Management, Ithaca, NY 14853. Offers agricultural finance (MS, PhD); applied econometrics and qualitative analysis (MS, PhD); economics of development (MS, PhD); environmental economics (MS, PhD); environmental management (MPS); farm management and production economics (MS, PhD); marketing and food distribution (MS, PhD); public policy analysis (MS, PhD); resource economics (PhD). *Entrance requirements:* For master's and doctorate, GRE. Additional exam requirements/recommendations for international students: Required—TOEFL.

Cornell University, Graduate School, Graduate Fields of Arts and Sciences, Field of Economics, Ithaca, NY 14853. Offers applied economics (PhD); basic analytical economics (PhD); econometrics and economic statistics (PhD); economic development and planning (PhD); economic theory (PhD); industrial organization and control (PhD); international economics (PhD); labor economics (PhD); monetary and macro economics (PhD); public finance (PhD). *Degree requirements:* For doctorate, comprehensive exam, thesis/dissertation. *Entrance requirements:* For doctorate, GRE General Test, 3 letters of recommendation. Additional exam requirements/recommendations for international students: Required—TOEFL (minimum score 550 paper-based; 77 iBT). Electronic applications accepted. *Faculty research:* Learning and games, economics of education, political economy, transfer payments, time series and nonparametrics.

DePaul University, Kellstadt Graduate School of Business, Chicago, IL 60604. Offers accountancy (MBA, MSA); applied economics (MBA); audit and advisory services (MS); business administration (DBA); business analytics (MS); business strategy and decision-making (MBA); computational finance (MS); economics and policy analysis (MS); enterprise risk management (MS); entrepreneurship (MBA, MS); finance (MBA, MS); general business (MBA); hospitality leadership (MBA); hospitality leadership and operational performance (MS); human resources (MS); international business (MBA); management (MBA, MS); management information systems (MBA); marketing (MBA, MS); marketing analysis (MS); marketing strategy and planning (MBA); real estate (MS); real estate finance and investment (MBA); strategy, execution and valuation (MBA); supply chain management (MS); sustainable management (MS); taxation (MS); JD/MBA. *Accreditation:* AACSB. *Program availability:* Part-time, evening/weekend, online learning. *Entrance requirements:* For master's, GMAT/GRE, 2 letters of recommendation, resume, essay, official transcripts. Additional exam requirements/recommendations for international students: Required—TOEFL (minimum score 550 paper-based; 80 iBT). *Application deadline:* For fall admission, 7/1 for domestic students, 6/1 for international students; for winter admission, 10/1 for domestic students, 9/1 for international students; for spring admission, 2/1 for domestic students, 1/1 for international students. Applications are processed on a rolling basis. Application fee: $60. Electronic applications accepted. *Expenses:* Contact institution. *Financial support:* Application deadline: 4/1; applicants required to submit FAFSA. *Unit head:* Christa Hinton, Assistant Dean and Director, 312-362-8810, Fax: 312-362-6677, E-mail: chinton@depaul.edu. *Application contact:* Garry Cooke, Director of Recruitment and Admissions, 312-362-8810, Fax: 312-362-6677, E-mail: kgsb@depaul.edu.
Website: http://kellstadt.depaul.edu

East Carolina University, Graduate School, Thomas Harriot College of Arts and Sciences, Department of Economics, Greenville, NC 27858-4353. Offers quantitative economics and econometrics (MS). *Program availability:* Part-time. *Students:* 14 full-time (2 women); includes 3 minority (all Black or African American, non-Hispanic/Latino), 3 international. Average age 28. 20 applicants, 100% accepted, 12 enrolled. In 2017, 10 master's awarded. *Degree requirements:* For master's, comprehensive exam. *Entrance requirements:* For master's, GRE General Test. Additional exam requirements/recommendations for international students: Recommended—TOEFL (minimum score 78 iBT), IELTS (minimum score 6.5). *Application deadline:* For fall admission, 8/15 priority date for domestic students, 2/1 priority date for international students; for spring admission, 12/20 priority date for domestic students, 10/1 priority date for international students. Applications are processed on a rolling basis. Application fee: $75. Electronic applications accepted. *Expenses:* Tuition, state resident: full-time $4749; part-time $297 per credit hour. Tuition, nonresident: full-time $17,898; part-time $1119 per credit hour. *Required fees:* $2691; $224 per credit hour. Part-time tuition and fees vary according to course load and program. *Financial support:* Research assistantships with partial tuition reimbursements and teaching assistantships with partial tuition reimbursements available. Financial award application deadline: 3/1. *Faculty research:* Microeconomics, macroeconomics, econometrics, coastal and marine economics. *Unit head:* Dr. Haiyong Liu, Chair, 252-328-1083, E-mail: liuh@ecu.edu. *Application contact:* Dean of Graduate School, 252-328-6012, Fax: 252-328-6071, E-mail: gradschool@ecu.edu.
Website: http://www.ecu.edu/cs-cas/econ/index.cfm

Florida State University, The Graduate School, College of Social Sciences and Public Policy, Department of Economics, Tallahassee, FL 32306-2180. Offers applied economics (MS); economics (PhD); JD/MS. *Faculty:* 30 full-time (3 women), 2 part-time/adjunct (0 women). *Students:* 75 full-time (19 women), 6 part-time (4 women); includes 16 minority (4 Black or African American, non-Hispanic/Latino; 1 Asian, non-Hispanic/Latino; 8 Hispanic/Latino; 3 Two or more races, non-Hispanic/Latino), 4 international. Average age 25. 146 applicants, 75% accepted, 42 enrolled. In 2017, 36 master's, 3 doctorates awarded. *Degree requirements:* For master's, thesis (for some programs), applied project (for some programs); for doctorate, comprehensive exam, thesis/dissertation, dissertation prospectus, workshops. *Entrance requirements:* For master's, GRE General Test, minimum upper-division undergraduate GPA of 3.0, 3.4 on graduate work; minimum 1 course each in statistics and calculus; principles and sufficient upper-level economics courses; for doctorate, GRE General Test, minimum upper-division undergraduate GPA of 3.0, graduate 3.4; minimum 1 course each in statistics and linear algebra, 2 in calculus. Additional exam requirements/recommendations for international students: Required—TOEFL (minimum score 90 iBT). *Application deadline:* For fall admission, 2/15 priority date for domestic and international students. Applications are processed on a rolling basis. Application fee: $30. Electronic applications accepted. *Financial support:* In 2017–18, 55 students received support, including 20 fellowships with full tuition reimbursements available (averaging $25,000 per year), 5 research assistantships with full tuition reimbursements available (averaging $19,000 per year), 23 teaching assistantships with full tuition reimbursements available (averaging $19,000 per year); scholarships/grants, tuition waivers (full), and unspecified assistantships also available. Financial award application deadline: 2/15; financial award applicants required to submit FAFSA. *Faculty research:* Industrial organization, experimental/behavioral, public/urban, law and economics, macroeconomics and financial. *Total annual research expenditures:* $650,000. *Unit head:* Dr. R. Mark Isaac, Chairman, 850-644-5001, Fax: 850-644-4535, E-mail: misaac@fsu.edu. *Application contact:* Dr. Thomas W. Zuehlke, Graduate Director, 850-644-5001, Fax: 850-644-4535, E-mail: tzuehlke@fsu.edu.
Website: http://www.coss.fsu.edu/economics/

Georgia Southern University, Jack N. Averitt College of Graduate Studies, College of Business, Program in Applied Economics, Statesboro, GA 30460. Offers applied economics (MS); information systems (Graduate Certificate). *Program availability:* Part-time-only, online only, 100% online. *Faculty:* 25 full-time (5 women). *Students:* 3 full-time (0 women), 28 part-time (10 women); includes 7 minority (2 Black or African American, non-Hispanic/Latino; 2 Asian, non-Hispanic/Latino; 1 Hispanic/Latino; 2 Two or more races, non-Hispanic/Latino), 4 international. Average age 34. 27 applicants, 100% accepted, 9 enrolled. In 2017, 5 master's, 1 other advanced degree awarded. *Entrance requirements:* For master's, GRE, minimum GPA of 3.0, current knowledge of calculus and statistics, introductory micro and macro courses. Additional exam requirements/recommendations for international students: Required—TOEFL (minimum score 550 paper-based; 80 iBT), IELTS (minimum score 6). *Application deadline:* For fall admission, 3/1 priority date for domestic students, 3/1 for international students; for spring admission, 10/1 priority date for domestic students, 10/1 for international students. Applications are processed on a rolling basis. Application fee: $50. Electronic applications accepted. *Expenses:* Tuition, state resident: full-time $4986; part-time

$3324 per year. Tuition, nonresident: full-time $21,982; part-time $15,352 per year. *Required fees:* $2092; $1802 per credit hour. $901 per semester. Tuition and fees vary according to course load, campus/location and program. *Financial support:* In 2017–18, 1 student received support. Unspecified assistantships available. Financial award application deadline: 4/15; financial award applicants required to submit FAFSA. *Faculty research:* Analytical capabilities in economic development, financial economics, regulatory issues, market analysis, economic development. *Unit head:* 912-478-5767, Fax: 912-478-0710.
Website: http://coba.georgiasouthern.edu/dfe/graduate/master-of-science-in-applied-economics/

HEC Montreal, School of Business Administration, Doctoral Program in Administration, Montréal, QC H3T 2A7, Canada. Offers accounting (PhD); applied economics (PhD); data science (PhD); finance (PhD); financial engineering (PhD); information technology (PhD); international business (PhD); logistics and operations management (PhD); management science (PhD); management, strategy and organizations (PhD); marketing (PhD); organizational behaviour and human resources (PhD). Program offered jointly with Concordia University, McGill University, and Universite du Quebec a Montreal. *Accreditation:* AACSB. *Students:* 114 full-time (47 women). 78 applicants, 42% accepted, 24 enrolled. In 2017, 23 doctorates awarded. *Entrance requirements:* For doctorate, TAGE MAGE, GMAT, or GRE, master's degree in administration or related field. *Application deadline:* For fall admission, 1/15 for domestic and international students. Application fee: $88 ($187 for international students). Electronic applications accepted. *Expenses:* Tuition, state resident: full-time $2869 Canadian dollars; part-time $79.70 Canadian dollars per credit. Tuition, nonresident: full-time $8883 Canadian dollars; part-time $246.76 Canadian dollars per credit. *International tuition:* $19,648 Canadian dollars full-time. *Required fees:* $41.20 Canadian dollars per credit. $67.94 Canadian dollars per term. Tuition and fees vary according to degree level and program. *Financial support:* Research assistantships, teaching assistantships, and scholarships/grants available. Financial award application deadline: 9/2. *Faculty research:* Art management, business policy, entrepreneurship, new technologies, transportation. *Unit head:* Jacques Robert, Director, 514-340-6853, E-mail: jacques.robert@hec.ca. *Application contact:* Julie Bilodeau, PhD Program Analyst, 514-340-6151, Fax: 514-340-6411, E-mail: analyste.phd@hec.ca.
Website: http://www.hec.ca/en/programs/phd/index.html

HEC Montreal, School of Business Administration, Master of Science Programs in Administration, Program in Applied Economics, Montréal, QC H3T 2A7, Canada. Offers M Sc. All courses are given in French. *Students:* 38 full-time (13 women), 1 (woman) part-time. 19 applicants, 89% accepted, 11 enrolled. In 2017, 9 master's awarded. *Entrance requirements:* For master's, BBA, undergraduate degree in another field, degree deemed equivalent by program director and minimum GPA of 3.0 on 4.3 scale. Additional exam requirements/recommendations for international students: Required—TAGE MAGE (minimum recommended score of 283), GMAT (minimum recommended score of 630), or GRE. *Application deadline:* For fall admission, 3/15 for domestic and international students; for winter admission, 9/15 for domestic and international students. Application fee: $88 Canadian dollars ($184 Canadian dollars for international students). Electronic applications accepted. *Expenses:* Tuition, state resident: full-time $2869 Canadian dollars; part-time $79.70 Canadian dollars per credit. Tuition, nonresident: full-time $8883 Canadian dollars; part-time $246.76 Canadian dollars per credit. *International tuition:* $19,648 Canadian dollars full-time. *Required fees:* $41.20 Canadian dollars per credit. $67.94 Canadian dollars per term. Tuition and fees vary according to degree level and program. *Financial support:* Research assistantships, teaching assistantships, and scholarships/grants available. Financial award application deadline: 9/2. *Unit head:* Dr. Marie-Helene Jobin, Director, 514-340-6283, E-mail: marie-helene.jobin@hec.ca. *Application contact:* Marianne de Moura, Administrative Director, 514-340-6151, Fax: 514-340-6411, E-mail: aide@hec.ca.
Website: http://www.hec.ca/programmes/maitrises/maitrise-economie-appliquee/index.html

Johns Hopkins University, Zanvyl Krieger School of Arts and Sciences, Advanced Academic Programs, Program in Applied Economics, Washington, DC 20036. Offers MA. *Program availability:* Part-time, evening/weekend. *Degree requirements:* For master's, thesis (for some programs). *Entrance requirements:* For master's, minimum GPA of 3.0, coursework in microeconomics and macroeconomics. Additional exam requirements/recommendations for international students: Required—TOEFL (minimum score 100 iBT). Electronic applications accepted.

Mills College, Graduate Studies, Lorry I. Lokey Graduate School of Business, Oakland, CA 94613-1000. Offers applied economics (MA); management (MBA, MM). *Program availability:* Part-time. *Faculty:* 4 full-time (3 women), 8 part-time/adjunct (5 women). *Students:* 31 full-time (24 women), 23 part-time (22 women); includes 33 minority (13 Black or African American, non-Hispanic/Latino; 2 American Indian or Alaska Native, non-Hispanic/Latino; 1 Asian, non-Hispanic/Latino; 10 Hispanic/Latino; 7 Two or more races, non-Hispanic/Latino), 1 international. Average age 33. 49 applicants, 84% accepted, 20 enrolled. In 2017, 31 master's awarded. *Entrance requirements:* For master's, GRE, SAT, or ACT, 3 letters of recommendation, 2 transcripts. Additional exam requirements/recommendations for international students: Required—TOEFL (minimum score 550 paper-based; 80 iBT) or IELTS (minimum score 6). *Application deadline:* For fall admission, 2/1 priority date for domestic students, 12/15 for international students; for spring admission, 10/1 for domestic students. Applications are processed on a rolling basis. Application fee: $50. *Expenses:* Contact institution. *Financial support:* In 2017–18, 59 students received support, including 59 fellowships with tuition reimbursements available (averaging $6,398 per year), 19 teaching assistantships with tuition reimbursements available; scholarships/grants and unspecified assistantships also available. Support available to part-time students. Financial award application deadline: 2/1; financial award applicants required to submit FAFSA. *Faculty research:* Diversity and inclusion, applied econometrics, non-profit management, business communication and effective public speaking, social media and Internet marketing. *Unit head:* Dr. Kate Karniouchina, Dean, Lorry I. Lokey School of Business and Public Policy, 510-430-3345, Fax: 510-430-2159, E-mail: kkarniouchina@mills.edu. *Application contact:* Robynne Lofton, Director of Admissions, 510-430-3295, Fax: 510-430-2159, E-mail: grad-admission@mills.edu.
Website: http://www.mills.edu/mba

New York University, Graduate School of Arts and Science, Department of Economics, New York, NY 10012-1019. Offers applied economic analysis (Advanced Certificate); economics (MA, PhD); JD/MA; MD/PhD. *Program availability:* Part-time, evening/weekend. *Faculty:* 35 full-time (2 women). *Students:* 214 full-time (77 women), 21 part-time (7 women); includes 15 minority (13 Asian, non-Hispanic/Latino; 2 Hispanic/Latino), 173 international. Average age 27. 1,531 applicants, 16% accepted, 88 enrolled. In 2017, 83 master's, 18 doctorates awarded. Terminal master's awarded for partial completion of doctoral program. *Degree requirements:* For master's, thesis; for doctorate, one foreign language, thesis/dissertation, 4 qualifying exams. *Entrance requirements:* For master's and doctorate, GRE General Test. Additional exam requirements/recommendations for international students: Required—TOEFL. *Application deadline:* For fall admission, 12/18 priority date for domestic students, 12/18 for international students. Application fee: $100. *Expenses:* *Tuition:* Full-time $41,352; part-time $19,968 per year. *Required fees:* $2496; $1628 per unit. $814 per term. Tuition and fees vary according to course load and program. *Financial support:* Fellowships with tuition reimbursements, research assistantships with tuition reimbursements, teaching assistantships with tuition reimbursements, Federal Work-Study, institutionally sponsored loans, scholarships/grants, health care benefits, and unspecified assistantships available. Financial award application deadline: 12/18; financial award applicants required to submit FAFSA. *Faculty research:* Economic theory, experimental economics, growth and development, macroeconomics and finance, international trade and international finance. *Unit head:* Alessandro Lizzeri, Chair, 212-998-8900, Fax: 212-995-4186, E-mail: admissions@econ.nyu.edu. *Application contact:* Tim Cogley, Director of Graduate Studies, PhD Programs, 212-998-8900, Fax: 212-995-4186, E-mail: admissions@econ.nyu.edu.
Website: http://www.econ.nyu.edu/

North Carolina Agricultural and Technical State University, School of Graduate Studies, School of Agriculture and Environmental Sciences, Department of Agribusiness, Applied Economics, and Agriscience Education, Greensboro, NC 27411. Offers agricultural economics (MS); agricultural education (MS). *Accreditation:* NCATE. *Program availability:* Part-time, evening/weekend. *Degree requirements:* For master's, comprehensive exam, thesis or alternative, qualifying exam. *Entrance requirements:* For master's, GRE General Test, minimum GPA of 3.0. *Faculty research:* Aid for small farmers, agricultural technology resources, labor force mobility, agrology.

Ohio University, Graduate College, College of Arts and Sciences, Department of Economics, Athens, OH 45701-2979. Offers applied economics (MA); financial economics (MFE). *Program availability:* Part-time, evening/weekend. *Degree requirements:* For master's, thesis or alternative. *Entrance requirements:* For master's, GRE or GMAT (recommended), minimum GPA of 3.0. Additional exam requirements/recommendations for international students: Required—TOEFL (minimum score 550 paper-based; 80 iBT) or IELTS (minimum score 6.5). Electronic applications accepted. *Faculty research:* Macroeconomics, public finance, international economics and finance, monetary theory, healthcare economics.

Oregon State University, College of Agricultural Sciences, Program in Applied Economics, Corvallis, OR 97331. Offers public health economics (MA, MS, PhD). *Program availability:* Part-time. Terminal master's awarded for partial completion of doctoral program. *Entrance requirements:* For master's and doctorate, GRE General Test, minimum GPA of 3.0 in last 90 hours. Additional exam requirements/recommendations for international students: Required—TOEFL (minimum score 90 iBT). *Application deadline:* For fall admission, 1/15 for domestic and international students. Application fee: $75 ($85 for international students). *Financial support:* Application deadline: 1/15. *Unit head:* Tjodie Richardson, Applied Economics Advisor, 541-737-1399, E-mail: tjrichardson@oregonstate.edu. *Application contact:* Tjodie Richardson, Applied Economics Advisor, 541-737-1399, E-mail: tjrichardson@oregonstate.edu.
Website: http://oregonstate.edu/aecgradprogram/

St. Cloud State University, School of Graduate Studies, College of Social Sciences, Department of Economics, Program in Applied Economics, St. Cloud, MN 56301-4498. Offers MS.

Southern Methodist University, Dedman College of Humanities and Sciences, Department of Economics, Dallas, TX 75205. Offers applied economics (MA); applied economics and predictive analytics (MS); economics (PhD); law and economics (MA). *Program availability:* Part-time, evening/weekend. Terminal master's awarded for partial completion of doctoral program. *Degree requirements:* For master's, thesis, oral qualifying exam; for doctorate, thesis/dissertation, written exams. *Entrance requirements:* For master's, GRE General Test or GMAT, 12 hours of course work in economics, minimum GPA of 3.0, previous course work in calculus and statistics; for doctorate, GRE General Test, minimum GPA of 3.0; 3 semesters of course work in calculus; 1 semester each of course work in statistics and linear algebra. Additional exam requirements/recommendations for international students: Required—TOEFL (minimum score 550 paper-based). Electronic applications accepted. *Faculty research:* Economic theory, game theory, econometrics, international trade, labor.

Southern New Hampshire University, School of Business, Manchester, NH 03106-1045. Offers accounting (MBA, Graduate Certificate); accounting finance (MS); accounting/auditing (MS); accounting/forensic accounting (MS); accounting/management accounting (MS); accounting/taxation (MS); applied economics (MS); athletic administration (MBA, Graduate Certificate); business administration (IMBA, Certificate), including business information systems (Certificate), human resource management (Certificate); business analytics (MBA); business intelligence (MBA); communication (MA), including new media and marketing, public relations; community economic development (MBA); criminal justice (MBA); data analytics (MS); economics (MBA); engineering management (MBA); entrepreneurship (MBA); finance (MBA, MS, Graduate Certificate); finance/corporate finance (MS); finance/investments (MS); forensic accounting (MBA); forensic accounting and fraud examination (Graduate Certificate); healthcare informatics (MBA); healthcare management (MBA); human resource management (MS); human resources (MBA); information technology (MS); information technology management (MBA); international business (PhD); Internet marketing (MBA); leadership (MBA); leadership of nonprofit organizations (Graduate Certificate); management (MS); marketing (MBA, MS, Graduate Certificate); music business (MBA); operations and project management (MS); operations and supply chain management (MBA, Graduate Certificate); organizational leadership (MS); project management (MBA, Graduate Certificate); public administration (MBA, Graduate Certificate); quantitative analysis (MBA); Six Sigma (Graduate Certificate); Six Sigma quality (MBA); social media marketing (MBA, Graduate Certificate); sport management (MBA, MS, Graduate Certificate); sustainability and environmental compliance (MBA); MBA/Certificate. *Accreditation:* ACBSP. *Program availability:* Part-time, evening/weekend, online learning. Terminal master's awarded for partial completion of doctoral program. *Degree requirements:* For master's, one foreign language, comprehensive exam (for some programs), thesis or alternative; for doctorate, one foreign language, comprehensive exam, thesis/dissertation. *Entrance requirements:* For master's, minimum GPA of 2.5; for doctorate, GMAT. Additional exam requirements/recommendations for international students: Required—TOEFL (minimum score 500 paper-based). *Application deadline:* Applications are processed on a rolling basis. Application fee: $40. Electronic applications accepted. *Expenses:* *Tuition:* Part-time $627 per credit hour. Part-time tuition and fees vary according to campus/location and program. *Financial support:* Career-related internships or fieldwork, Federal Work-Study, institutionally sponsored loans, scholarships/grants, tuition waivers (partial), and unspecified assistantships available. Support available to part-time students. Financial award applicants required to submit FAFSA. *Unit head:* Dr. Bill Lightfoot, Dean, 603-644-3102, Fax: 603-644-3144. *Application contact:* Office of Graduate Admission, 888-327-SNHU, Fax: 603-644-3144, E-mail: enroll@snhu.edu.

Texas Tech University, Graduate School, College of Agricultural Sciences and Natural Resources, Department of Agricultural and Applied Economics, Lubbock, TX 79409. Offers agribusiness (MAB); agricultural and applied economics (MS, PhD); JD/MS. *Program availability:* Part-time. *Faculty:* 21 full-time (5 women), 2 part-time/adjunct (0 women). *Students:* 50 full-time (27 women), 4 part-time (1 woman); includes 4 minority

(all Hispanic/Latino), 33 international. Average age 30. 63 applicants, 68% accepted, 13 enrolled. In 2017, 19 master's, 4 doctorates awarded. Terminal master's awarded for partial completion of doctoral program. *Degree requirements:* For master's, thesis or alternative; for doctorate, comprehensive exam, thesis/dissertation. *Entrance requirements:* For master's and doctorate, GRE General Test, formal approval from departmental committee. Additional exam requirements/recommendations for international students: Required—TOEFL (minimum score 550 paper-based; 79 iBT). *Application deadline:* For fall admission, 6/1 priority date for domestic students, 1/15 priority date for international students; for spring admission, 9/1 priority date for domestic students, 6/15 priority date for international students. Applications are processed on a rolling basis. Application fee: $60. Electronic applications accepted. *Expenses:* Contact institution. *Financial support:* In 2017–18, 53 students received support, including 45 fellowships (averaging $3,593 per year), 43 research assistantships (averaging $14,523 per year); teaching assistantships, institutionally sponsored loans, scholarships/grants, health care benefits, and unspecified assistantships also available. Financial award application deadline: 5/1; financial award applicants required to submit FAFSA. *Faculty research:* Economics of the United States cotton and textile industries, natural resource management in semi-arid climates, commodity policy analysis, international trade in agricultural products, agribusiness analysis. *Total annual research expenditures:* $585,282. *Unit head:* Dr. Phillip N. Johnson, Professor/Chairman, 806-834-0474, Fax: 806-742-1099, E-mail: phil.johnson@ttu.edu. *Application contact:* Dr. Darren Hudson, Graduate Adviser, 806-742-2821, Fax: 806-742-1099, E-mail: darren.hudson@ttu.edu. Website: http://www.aaec.ttu.edu

Thomas Jefferson University, Jefferson College of Population Health, Philadelphia, PA 19107. Offers applied health economics and outcomes research (MS, PhD, Certificate); behavioral health science (PhD); health policy (MS, Certificate); healthcare quality and safety (MS, PhD); population health (Certificate); public health (MPH, Certificate). *Program availability:* Part-time, evening/weekend, online learning. Terminal master's awarded for partial completion of doctoral program. *Degree requirements:* For master's, thesis; for doctorate, comprehensive exam, thesis/dissertation. *Entrance requirements:* For master's, GRE or other graduate entrance exam (MCAT, LSAT, DAT, etc.), two letters of recommendation, curriculum vitae, transcripts from all undergraduate and graduate institutions; for doctorate, GRE (taken within the last 5 years), three letters of recommendation, curriculum vitae, transcripts from all undergraduate and graduate institutions. Additional exam requirements/recommendations for international students: Required—TOEFL. Electronic applications accepted. *Faculty research:* Applied health economics and outcomes research, behavioral and health sciences, chronic disease management, health policy, healthcare quality and patient safety, wellness and prevention.

The University of Arizona, College of Agriculture and Life Sciences, Department of Agricultural and Resource Economics, Tucson, AZ 85721. Offers applied econometrics and data analytics (MS); applied economics and policy analysis (MS). *Program availability:* Part-time. *Degree requirements:* For master's, thesis or alternative. *Entrance requirements:* For master's, GRE General Test, 3 letters of recommendation, minimum GPA of 3.0. Additional exam requirements/recommendations for international students: Required—TOEFL (minimum score 550 paper-based; 79 iBT). Electronic applications accepted. *Faculty research:* Natural resources, international development trade, production and marketing, agricultural policy, rural development.

University of California, Los Angeles, Graduate Division, College of Letters and Science, Department of Economics, Program in Applied Economics, Los Angeles, CA 90095. Offers MAE. *Faculty:* 51. *Students:* 50 full-time (31 women); includes 43 minority (42 Asian, non-Hispanic/Latino; 1 Hispanic/Latino). 500 applicants, 30% accepted, 50 enrolled. In 2017, 93 master's awarded. *Degree requirements:* For master's, capstone project. *Entrance requirements:* For master's, GRE General Test, bachelor's degree; minimum undergraduate GPA of 3.0 (or equivalent). Additional exam requirements/

recommendations for international students: Required—TOEFL or IELTS. *Application deadline:* For fall admission, 3/15 for domestic students. Applications are processed on a rolling basis. Application fee: $105 ($125 for international students). Electronic applications accepted. *Financial support:* Fellowships available. *Unit head:* Prof. Dora Costa, Department Chair, 310-825-7155, E-mail: mae-office@econ.ucla.edu. *Application contact:* Prof. Dora Costa, Department Chair, 310-825-7155, E-mail: mae-office@econ.ucla.edu.
Website: https://master.econ.ucla.edu/

See Display below and Close-Up on page 841.

University of California, Santa Cruz, Division of Graduate Studies, Division of Social Sciences, Program in Applied Economics and Finance, Santa Cruz, CA 95064. Offers MS. *Degree requirements:* For master's, thesis or alternative, project. *Entrance requirements:* For master's, GRE General Test, GRE Subject Test. Additional exam requirements/recommendations for international students: Required—TOEFL (minimum score 550 paper-based; 83 iBT); Recommended—IELTS (minimum score 8). Electronic applications accepted. *Faculty research:* Economic decision-making skills for the design and operation of complex institutional systems.

University of Cincinnati, Carl H. Lindner College of Business, MS Program, Cincinnati, OH 45221. Offers accounting (MS); applied economics (MS); business analytics (MS); finance (MS); information systems (MS); marketing (MS); taxation (MS). *Program availability:* Part-time, evening/weekend. *Faculty:* 65 full-time (20 women), 27 part-time/adjunct (6 women). *Students:* 324 full-time (132 women), 204 part-time (77 women); includes 50 minority (18 Black or African American, non-Hispanic/Latino; 21 Asian, non-Hispanic/Latino; 5 Hispanic/Latino; 1 Native Hawaiian or other Pacific Islander, non-Hispanic/Latino; 5 Two or more races, non-Hispanic/Latino), 299 international. Average age 28. 1,756 applicants, 24% accepted, 351 enrolled. In 2017, 369 master's awarded. *Degree requirements:* For master's, thesis (for some programs), capstone. *Entrance requirements:* For master's, GMAT, GRE, resume, transcripts, essays, letters of recommendation. Additional exam requirements/recommendations for international students: Required—TOEFL (minimum score 577 paper-based; 90 iBT), IELTS (minimum score 6.5). *Application deadline:* For fall admission, 6/30 priority date for domestic students, 3/15 for international students; for spring admission, 12/15 for domestic students, 9/15 for international students; for summer admission, 4/15 for domestic and international students. Applications are processed on a rolling basis. Application fee: $65 ($70 for international students). Electronic applications accepted. *Expenses:* $10,479 per term full-time resident, $14,398 per term full-time nonresident, $890 per credit hour part-time. *Financial support:* In 2017–18, 251 students received support, including 12 teaching assistantships with full and partial tuition reimbursements available (averaging $3,500 per year); scholarships/grants, tuition waivers (full and partial), and unspecified assistantships also available. Financial award application deadline: 2/1; financial award applicants required to submit FAFSA. *Faculty research:* Business analytics, financial management, organizational behavior, financial accounting, consumer insights. *Total annual research expenditures:* $24,842. *Unit head:* Dr. David Szymanski, Dean, 513-556-7001, Fax: 513-556-4891, E-mail: david.szymanski@uc.edu. *Application contact:* Dona Clary, Executive Director, Graduate Programs, 513-556-3546, Fax: 513-558-7006, E-mail: dona.clary@uc.edu. Website: http://business.uc.edu/graduate/masters.html

University of Georgia, College of Agricultural and Environmental Sciences, Department of Agricultural and Applied Economics, Athens, GA 30602. Offers agricultural economics (MAE, MS, PhD); environmental economics (MS). *Degree requirements:* For master's, thesis (MS); for doctorate, thesis/dissertation. *Entrance requirements:* For master's and doctorate, GRE General Test. Electronic applications accepted.

Applied Economics

University of Houston, College of Liberal Arts and Social Sciences, Department of Economics, Houston, TX 77204. Offers applied economics (MA); economics (MA, PhD). Terminal master's awarded for partial completion of doctoral program. *Degree requirements:* For master's, thesis optional; for doctorate, comprehensive exam, thesis/dissertation. *Entrance requirements:* For master's and doctorate, GRE General Test, minimum GPA of 3.0, statement of purpose, three letters of recommendation. Additional exam requirements/recommendations for international students: Required—TOEFL (minimum score 550 paper-based; 79 iBT), IELTS (minimum score 6.5). Electronic applications accepted. *Faculty research:* Econometrics, labor economics, international economics.

University of Illinois at Urbana–Champaign, Graduate College, College of Agricultural, Consumer and Environmental Sciences, Department of Agricultural and Consumer Economics, Champaign, IL 61820. Offers agricultural and applied economics (MS, PhD).

University of Massachusetts Boston, College of Liberal Arts, Program in Applied Economics, Boston, MA 02125-3393. Offers MA. *Faculty:* 22 full-time (9 women), 7 part-time/adjunct (5 women). *Students:* 9 full-time (5 women), 5 part-time (0 women); includes 4 minority (2 Black or African American, non-Hispanic/Latino; 2 Hispanic/Latino), 4 international. Average age 28. 26 applicants, 54% accepted, 7 enrolled. In 2017, 8 master's awarded. *Expenses:* Tuition, state resident: full-time $17,375. Tuition, nonresident: full-time $33,915. *Required fees:* $355. *Unit head:* Dr. Adugna Lemi, Department Chair, 617-287-6962. *Application contact:* Graduate Admissions Coordinator, 617-287-6400, Fax: 617-287-6236, E-mail: bos.gadm@dpc.umassp.edu.

University of Michigan, Rackham Graduate School, College of Literature, Science, and the Arts, Department of Economics, Program in Applied Economics, Ann Arbor, MI 48109. Offers AM. *Program availability:* Part-time. *Entrance requirements:* For master's, GRE General Test. Additional exam requirements/recommendations for international students: Required—TOEFL (minimum score 600 paper-based). *Expenses:* Tuition, state resident: full-time $22,368; part-time $1201 per credit hour. Tuition, nonresident: full-time $45,156; part-time $2467 per credit hour. *Required fees:* $376 per term. Tuition and fees vary according to course load, degree level and program. *Faculty research:* Econometric analysis transition, macro.

University of Minnesota, Twin Cities Campus, Graduate School, College of Food, Agricultural and Natural Resource Sciences, Applied Economics Graduate Program, St. Paul, MN 55108. Offers MS, PhD. *Faculty:* 55 full-time (14 women), 3 part-time/adjunct (1 woman). *Students:* 103 (36 women). 174 applicants, 50% accepted, 22 enrolled. In 2017, 17 master's, 12 doctorates awarded. Terminal master's awarded for partial completion of doctoral program. *Degree requirements:* For master's, thesis; for doctorate, comprehensive exam, thesis/dissertation. *Entrance requirements:* For master's and doctorate, GRE, minimum GPA of 3.0 (preferred). Additional exam requirements/recommendations for international students: Required—TOEFL (minimum score 550 paper-based; 79 iBT), IELTS (minimum score 6.5). *Application deadline:* For fall admission, 12/10 priority date for domestic and international students. Applications are processed on a rolling basis. Application fee: $75 ($95 for international students). Electronic applications accepted. *Financial support:* Fellowships with full tuition reimbursements, research assistantships with full tuition reimbursements, teaching assistantships with full tuition reimbursements, scholarships/grants, health care benefits, tuition waivers (full and partial), unspecified assistantships, and stipends available. Financial award application deadline: 12/10. *Faculty research:* Production and marketing, labor and population, trade and development, consumer and household, health and policy analysis, resource and environmental. *Unit head:* Prof. Joe Ritter, Director of Graduate Studies, 612-625-0442, Fax: 612-625-6245, E-mail: apecdgs@umn.edu. *Application contact:* Jenna Mead, Graduate Program Coordinator, 612-625-3777, Fax: 612-625-6245, E-mail: apecdgs@umn.edu. Website: http://www.apec.umn.edu/graduate-program

University of Nevada, Las Vegas, Graduate College, Lee Business School, Department of Economics, Las Vegas, NV 89154-6005. Offers applied economics (MA); MA/MS. *Program availability:* Part-time. *Faculty:* 8 full-time (1 woman), 1 part-time/adjunct (0 women). *Students:* 10 full-time (4 women), 10 part-time (1 woman); includes 4 minority (all Hispanic/Latino), 3 international. Average age 32. 23 applicants, 65% accepted, 7 enrolled. In 2017, 13 master's awarded. *Degree requirements:* For master's, thesis optional, oral defense of thesis; internship. *Entrance requirements:* For master's, GRE General Test or GMAT, bachelor's degree with minimum GPA 3.0. Additional exam requirements/recommendations for international students: Required—TOEFL (minimum score 550 paper-based; 80 iBT), IELTS (minimum score 7). *Application deadline:* For fall admission, 6/15 for domestic and international students; for spring admission, 11/15 for domestic and international students. Application fee: $60 ($95 for international students). Electronic applications accepted. *Expenses:* $275 per credit, $850 per course, $7,969 per year resident, $22,157 per year non-resident, $7,094 non-resident fee (7 credits or more), $1,307 annual health insurance fee. *Financial support:* In 2017–18, 9 students received support, including 9 teaching assistantships with full and partial tuition reimbursements available (averaging $13,750 per year); institutionally sponsored loans, scholarships/grants, health care benefits, and unspecified assistantships also available. Financial award application deadline: 3/15; financial award applicants required to submit FAFSA. *Faculty research:* Labor economics/industrial organization; real estate economics; macroeconomics and credit markets; urban, regional and environmental economics; public finance/public policy. *Total annual research expenditures:* $52,500. *Unit head:* Dr. Jeff Waddoups, Chair/Professor, 702-895-3497, Fax: 702-895-1354, E-mail: jeffrey.waddoups@unlv.edu. *Application contact:* Dr. Mary Riddel, Graduate Coordinator, 702-895-2792, Fax: 702-895-1354, E-mail: mary.riddel@unlv.edu. Website: https://www.unlv.edu/economics

University of Nevada, Las Vegas, Graduate College, Lee Business School, Department of Management, Entrepreneurship and Technology, Las Vegas, NV 89154-6034. Offers data analytics (Certificate); data analytics and applied economics (MS); management (Certificate); management information systems (MS, Certificate); new venture management (Certificate); MS/MS. *Program availability:* Part-time, evening/weekend. *Faculty:* 11 full-time (2 women), 2 part-time/adjunct (0 women). *Students:* 35 full-time (13 women), 35 part-time (15 women); includes 22 minority (7 Black or African American, non-Hispanic/Latino; 3 Asian, non-Hispanic/Latino; 6 Hispanic/Latino; 6 Two or more races, non-Hispanic/Latino), 22 international. Average age 31. 57 applicants, 82% accepted, 29 enrolled. In 2017, 14 master's, 11 other advanced degrees awarded. *Degree requirements:* For master's, thesis optional. *Entrance requirements:* For master's, GMAT or GRE, bachelor's degree with minimum GPA 3.0; 2 letters of recommendation; for Certificate, GMAT or GRE. Additional exam requirements/recommendations for international students: Required—TOEFL (minimum score 550 paper-based; 80 iBT), IELTS (minimum score 7). *Application deadline:* For fall admission, 8/1 for domestic students, 5/1 for international students; for spring admission, 11/15 for domestic students, 10/1 for international students. Application fee: $60 ($95 for international students). Electronic applications accepted. *Expenses:* $275 per credit, $850 per course, $7,969 per year resident, $22,157 per year non-resident, $7,094 non-resident fee (7 credits or more), $1,307 annual health insurance fee. *Financial support:* In 2017–18, 10 students received support, including 7 research

assistantships with partial tuition reimbursements available (averaging $11,429 per year), 3 teaching assistantships with partial tuition reimbursements available (averaging $11,250 per year); institutionally sponsored loans, scholarships/grants, health care benefits, and unspecified assistantships also available. Financial award application deadline: 3/15; financial award applicants required to submit FAFSA. *Faculty research:* Decision-making, publish or perish, ethical issues in information systems, IT-enabled decision making, business ethics. *Unit head:* Dr. Sheng Wang, Chair/Associate Professor, 702-895-5394, E-mail: sheng.wang@unlv.edu. *Application contact:* Dr. Greg Moody, Graduate Coordinator, 702-895-1365, Fax: 702-895-4370, E-mail: gregory.moody@unlv.edu. Website: https://www.unlv.edu/met

University of Nevada, Reno, Graduate School, College of Agriculture, Biotechnology and Natural Resources, Department of Resource Economics, Reno, NV 89557. Offers MS, PhD. Terminal master's awarded for partial completion of doctoral program. *Degree requirements:* For master's, thesis optional; for doctorate, thesis/dissertation. *Entrance requirements:* For master's, GRE General Test, minimum GPA of 2.75; for doctorate, GRE General Test, minimum GPA of 3.0. Additional exam requirements/recommendations for international students: Required—TOEFL (minimum score 500 paper-based; 61 iBT), IELTS (minimum score 6). Electronic applications accepted. *Faculty research:* Econometrics, environmental valuation, natural resource and environmental policy analysis, public lands management.

University of New Brunswick Fredericton, School of Graduate Studies, Faculty of Arts, Department of Economics, Fredericton, NB E3B 5A3, Canada. Offers applied economics and finance (M Sc); economics (MA). M Sc offered on Saint John campus. *Entrance requirements:* For master's, minimum GPA of 3.0. Additional exam requirements/recommendations for international students: Required—TWE (minimum score 4), TOEFL (minimum score 580 paper-based) or IELTS (minimum score 7). Electronic applications accepted. *Faculty research:* Epidemiology and population health, micro/macro economics, economics of transportation, regional development, health economics, econometrics.

The University of North Carolina at Charlotte, Belk College of Business, Department of Economics, Charlotte, NC 28223-0001. Offers applied econometrics (Graduate Certificate); economics (MS). *Program availability:* Part-time, evening/weekend. *Faculty:* 17 full-time (7 women), 1 part-time/adjunct (0 women). *Students:* 26 full-time (6 women), 33 part-time (4 women); includes 19 minority (8 Black or African American, non-Hispanic/Latino; 5 Asian, non-Hispanic/Latino; 4 Hispanic/Latino; 2 Two or more races, non-Hispanic/Latino), 7 international. Average age 26. 41 applicants, 90% accepted, 15 enrolled. In 2017, 25 master's, 2 other advanced degrees awarded. *Degree requirements:* For master's, thesis or project. *Entrance requirements:* For master's, GRE General Test, GMAT, undergraduate coursework that includes calculus, econometrics (or equivalent), intermediate macroeconomic theory, intermediate microeconomic theory; for Graduate Certificate, bachelor's degree, or its equivalent, from regionally-accredited college or university; minimum GPA of 2.75 on all previous work completed beyond high school (secondary school); statement of purpose; unofficial transcripts of all college course work. Additional exam requirements/recommendations for international students: Required—TOEFL (minimum score 523 paper-based; 70 iBT) or IELTS (6.5). *Application deadline:* For fall admission, 3/1 priority date for domestic and international students; for spring admission, 10/1 priority date for domestic and international students; for summer admission, 4/1 priority date for domestic and international students. Applications are processed on a rolling basis. Application fee: $75. Electronic applications accepted. *Expenses:* Contact institution. *Financial support:* Career-related internships or fieldwork, institutionally sponsored loans, scholarships/grants, and unspecified assistantships available. Support available to part-time students. Financial award application deadline: 3/1; financial award applicants required to submit FAFSA. *Faculty research:* Health care, taxation, energy, economic growth, monetary policy. *Total annual research expenditures:* $33,366. *Unit head:* Dr. Artie Zillante, Department Chair, 704-687-5375, Fax: 704-687-1384, E-mail: azillant@uncc.edu. *Application contact:* Kathy B. Giddings, Director of Graduate Admissions, 704-687-5503, Fax: 704-687-1668, E-mail: gradadm@uncc.edu. Website: http://msecon.uncc.edu/

The University of North Carolina at Greensboro, Graduate School, Bryan School of Business and Economics, Department of Economics, Program in Applied Economics, Greensboro, NC 27412-5001. Offers MA, MA/PhD. *Degree requirements:* For master's, comprehensive exam, thesis or alternative. *Entrance requirements:* For master's, GRE. Additional exam requirements/recommendations for international students: Required—TOEFL. Electronic applications accepted.

University of North Dakota, Graduate School, College of Business and Public Administration, Applied Economics Program, Grand Forks, ND 58202. Offers MSAE. *Program availability:* Part-time, online learning. *Degree requirements:* For master's, comprehensive exam, thesis or alternative. *Entrance requirements:* For master's, GRE General Test. Additional exam requirements/recommendations for international students: Required—TOEFL (minimum score 550 paper-based; 79 iBT), IELTS (minimum score 6.5). Electronic applications accepted.

University of Oklahoma, College of Arts and Sciences, Department of Economics, Norman, OK 73019. Offers economics (MA, PhD), including applied economics (MA), managerial economics (MA). *Faculty:* 21 full-time (5 women). *Students:* 40 full-time (12 women), 29 part-time (3 women); includes 16 minority (7 Black or African American, non-Hispanic/Latino; 1 American Indian or Alaska Native, non-Hispanic/Latino; 3 Asian, non-Hispanic/Latino; 5 Hispanic/Latino), 20 international. Average age 32. 50 applicants, 64% accepted, 14 enrolled. In 2017, 21 master's, 3 doctorates awarded. Terminal master's awarded for partial completion of doctoral program. *Degree requirements:* For master's, comprehensive exam (for some programs); for doctorate, comprehensive exam, thesis/dissertation. *Entrance requirements:* For master's and doctorate, GRE, undergraduate degree in related field. Additional exam requirements/recommendations for international students: Required—TOEFL (minimum score 79 iBT) or IELTS (minimum score 6.5). *Application deadline:* For fall admission, 2/28 priority date for domestic students, 1/30 priority date for international students. Applications are processed on a rolling basis. Application fee: $50 ($100 for international students). Electronic applications accepted. *Expenses:* Tuition, state resident: full-time $5119; part-time $213.30 per credit hour. Tuition, nonresident: full-time $19,778; part-time $824.10 per credit hour. *Required fees:* $3458; $133.55 per credit hour. $126.50 per semester. *Financial support:* In 2017–18, 28 students received support, including 23 teaching assistantships with partial tuition reimbursements available (averaging $14,507 per year); fellowships with partial tuition reimbursements available, research assistantships with partial tuition reimbursements available, scholarships/grants, and health care benefits also available. Financial award application deadline: 6/1; financial award applicants required to submit FAFSA. *Faculty research:* Public economics, development economics, international economics, industrial organization, labor economics. *Total annual research expenditures:* $50,386. *Unit head:* Dr. Gary Hoover, Department Chair and Professor of Economics, 405-325-5857, E-mail: ghoover@ou.edu. *Application contact:* Prof. Daniel Hicks, Director of Graduate Studies/Associate Professor, 405-325-7049, E-mail: hicksd@ou.edu. Website: http://cas.ou.edu/economics

University of Pennsylvania, Wharton School, Program in Applied Economics, Philadelphia, PA 19104. Offers PhD.

University of Regina, Faculty of Graduate Studies and Research, Faculty of Arts, Department of Economics, Regina, SK S4S 0A2, Canada. Offers applied economics and policy analysis (MA). *Program availability:* Part-time. *Faculty:* 13 full-time (4 women), 6 part-time/adjunct (1 woman). *Students:* 5 full-time (1 woman), 5 part-time (2 women). 16 applicants, 13% accepted. In 2017, 6 master's awarded. *Degree requirements:* For master's, thesis (for some programs), research project. *Entrance requirements:* For master's, writing sample on approved topic. Additional exam requirements/recommendations for international students: Required—TOEFL (minimum score 580 paper-based; 80 iBT), IELTS (minimum score 6.5), PTE (minimum score 59). *Application deadline:* For fall admission, 3/1 for domestic and international students. Application fee: $100. Electronic applications accepted. *Expenses:* $10,681. *Financial support:* In 2017–18, 5 fellowships (averaging $6,400 per year), 2 teaching assistantships (averaging $2,562 per year) were awarded; research assistantships and scholarships/grants also available. *Unit head:* Dr. Monika Cule, Department Head, 306-585-4708, Fax: 306-585-4815, E-mail: monika.cule@uregina.ca. *Application contact:* Dr. Harminder Guliani, Graduate Coordinator, 306-585-4442, Fax: 306-585-4815, E-mail: harminder.guliani@uregina.ca.
Website: http://www.uregina.ca/arts/economics

University of Vermont, Graduate College, College of Agriculture and Life Sciences, Program in Community Development and Applied Economics, Burlington, VT 05405. Offers community development and applied economics (MS). *Students:* 14 (7 women). Average age 27. 14 applicants, 93% accepted, 4 enrolled. In 2017, 6 master's awarded. *Degree requirements:* For master's, thesis. *Entrance requirements:* For master's, GRE General Test. Additional exam requirements/recommendations for international students: Required—TOEFL (minimum score 550 paper-based; 90 iBT), IELTS (minimum score 6.5). *Application deadline:* For fall admission, 1/15 priority date for domestic and international students. Applications are processed on a rolling basis. Application fee: $65. Electronic applications accepted. *Expenses:* Tuition, state resident: full-time $11,628; part-time $646 per credit. Tuition, nonresident: full-time $29,340; part-time $1630 per credit. *Required fees:* $1994; $10 per credit. Tuition and fees vary according to course load and program. *Financial support:* In 2017–18, 11 students received support, including 2 research assistantships with full tuition reimbursements available (averaging $23,500 per year), 9 teaching assistantships with full tuition reimbursements available (averaging $23,500 per year); fellowships, career-related internships or fieldwork, and health care benefits also available. Financial award application deadline: 1/15. *Faculty research:* Agricultural production and marketing. *Unit head:* David Conner, Associate Professor, 802-656-2001, E-mail: david.conner@uvm.edu.
Website: https://www.uvm.edu/cals/cdae/ms

University of Wisconsin–Madison, Graduate School, College of Agricultural and Life Sciences, Department of Agricultural and Applied Economics, Madison, WI 53706. Offers MA, MS, PhD. *Program availability:* Part-time. *Degree requirements:* For doctorate, thesis/dissertation, preliminary exams. *Entrance requirements:* For master's and doctorate, GRE General Test. Additional exam requirements/recommendations for international students: Required—TOEFL (minimum score 580 paper-based; 92 iBT). Electronic applications accepted. *Faculty research:* Environmental and resource economics, international development, community economics, energy economics, agricultural technology, food systems, markets and trade.

University of Wyoming, College of Agriculture and Natural Resources, Department of Agricultural and Applied Economics, Laramie, WY 82071. Offers MS. *Program availability:* Part-time. *Degree requirements:* For master's, thesis (for some programs). *Entrance requirements:* For master's, GRE General Test, minimum GPA of 3.0.

Additional exam requirements/recommendations for international students: Required—TOEFL. Electronic applications accepted. *Faculty research:* Farm management, agricultural markets, water economics, community development, agricultural business.

Utah State University, School of Graduate Studies, College of Agriculture and Applied Sciences, Department of Applied Economics, Logan, UT 84322. Offers applied economics (MAE, MS, PhD); international food and agribusiness (MS). *Program availability:* Part-time. *Degree requirements:* For master's, thesis optional. *Entrance requirements:* For master's, GRE General Test, minimum GPA of 3.0.

Virginia Polytechnic Institute and State University, Graduate School, College of Agriculture and Life Sciences, Blacksburg, VA 24061. Offers agricultural and applied economics (MS, PhD); agricultural and life sciences (MS); agriculture, leadership, and community education (MS, PhD); animal and poultry science (MS, PhD); biochemistry (MS, PhD); crop and soil environmental sciences (MS, PhD); dairy science (MS, PhD); entomology (MS, PhD); food science and technology (MS, PhD); horticulture (PhD); human nutrition, foods and exercise (MS, PhD); plant pathology, physiology, and weed science (MS, PhD). *Faculty:* 241 full-time (73 women), 1 (woman) part-time/adjunct. *Students:* 379 full-time (221 women), 126 part-time (75 women); includes 64 minority (21 Black or African American, non-Hispanic/Latino; 15 Asian, non-Hispanic/Latino; 14 Hispanic/Latino; 14 Two or more races, non-Hispanic/Latino), 119 international. Average age 29. 357 applicants, 46% accepted, 118 enrolled. In 2017, 105 master's, 54 doctorates awarded. *Degree requirements:* For master's, comprehensive exam (for some programs), thesis (for some programs); for doctorate, comprehensive exam (for some programs), thesis/dissertation (for some programs). *Entrance requirements:* For master's and doctorate, GRE/GMAT. Additional exam requirements/recommendations for international students: Required—TOEFL (minimum score 80 iBT). *Application deadline:* For fall admission, 8/1 for domestic students, 4/1 for international students; for spring admission, 1/1 for domestic students, 9/1 for international students. Applications are processed on a rolling basis. Application fee: $75. Electronic applications accepted. *Expenses:* Tuition, state resident: full-time $15,072; part-time $718.50 per credit hour. Tuition, nonresident: full-time $28,810; part-time $1448.25 per credit hour. *Required fees:* $2741; $502 per semester. Tuition and fees vary according to course load, campus/location and program. *Financial support:* In 2017–18, 232 research assistantships with full tuition reimbursements (averaging $21,852 per year), 94 teaching assistantships with full tuition reimbursements (averaging $21,643 per year) were awarded. Financial award application deadline: 3/1; financial award applicants required to submit FAFSA. *Total annual research expenditures:* $44.3 million. *Unit head:* Dr. Alan L. Grant, Dean, 540-231-4152, Fax: 540-231-4163, E-mail: algrant@vt.edu. *Application contact:* Crystal Tawney, Administrative Assistant, 540-231-4152, Fax: 540-231-4163, E-mail: cdtawney@vt.edu.
Website: http://www.cals.vt.edu/

Washington & Jefferson College, Graduate and Continuing Studies, Washington, PA 15301. Offers applied health care economics and outcomes management (MS); professional accounting (MAC); professional writing (Graduate Certificate); thanatology (Graduate Certificate).

Western Kentucky University, Graduate Studies, Gordon Ford College of Business, Program in Applied Economics, Bowling Green, KY 42101. Offers MA.

Western Michigan University, Graduate College, College of Arts and Sciences, Department of Economics, Kalamazoo, MI 49008. Offers applied economics (MA, PhD). *Degree requirements:* For master's, thesis; for doctorate, thesis/dissertation.

Wright State University, Graduate School, Raj Soin College of Business, Department of Economics, Program in Social and Applied Economics, Dayton, OH 45435. Offers MS.

Economic Development

Albany State University, College of Arts and Humanities, Albany, GA 31705-2717. Offers criminal justice (MS); English education (M Ed); public administration (MPA), including community and economic development, criminal justice administration, health administration and policy, human resources management, public management, public policy, water resources management and policy; social work (MSW). *Accreditation:* NASPAA. *Program availability:* Part-time. *Degree requirements:* For master's, comprehensive exam, professional portfolio (for MPA), internship, capstone report. *Entrance requirements:* For master's, GRE, MAT, minimum GPA of 3.0, official transcript, pre-medical record/certificate of immunization, letters of reference. Electronic applications accepted. *Faculty research:* HIV prevention for minority students.

The American University in Cairo, School of Business, Cairo, Egypt. Offers business administration (MBA); economics (MA); economics in international development (MA, Diploma); finance (MS). *Program availability:* Part-time, evening/weekend. *Faculty:* 30 full-time (10 women), 8 part-time/adjunct (3 women). *Students:* 49 full-time (25 women), 67 part-time (38 women), 5 international. Average age 29. 112 applicants, 35% accepted, 26 enrolled. In 2017, 51 master's awarded. *Degree requirements:* For master's, comprehensive exam (for some programs), thesis (for some programs). *Entrance requirements:* For master's, GMAT, GRE. Additional exam requirements/recommendations for international students: Required—TOEFL (minimum score 450 paper-based; 45 iBT), IELTS (minimum score 5). *Application deadline:* For fall admission, 2/1 priority date for domestic and international students; for spring admission, 10/15 priority date for domestic and international students. Applications are processed on a rolling basis. Application fee: $85. Electronic applications accepted. *Expenses:* Contact institution. *Financial support:* Fellowships with partial tuition reimbursements, scholarships/grants, tuition waivers (partial), and unspecified assistantships available. Financial award application deadline: 3/10. *Faculty research:* Marketing and quality management, banking operations management, economics, finance. *Unit head:* Dr. Sherif Kamel, Dean, 20-2-2615-2118, E-mail: skamel@aucegypt.edu. *Application contact:* Maha Hegazi, Director of Graduate Admissions, 20-2-2615-1462, E-mail: mahahegazi@aucegypt.edu.
Website: http://www.aucegypt.edu/Business/Pages/default.aspx

Ball State University, Graduate School, College of Sciences and Humanities, Department of Political Science, Program in Public Administration, Muncie, IN 47306. Offers public administration (MPA, Certificate), including community and economic development (MPA), criminal justice (MPA), emergency management and homeland security (MPA), information and communication technology (MPA). *Program availability:* Part-time. *Students:* 20 full-time (7 women), 14 part-time (8 women); includes 4 minority (2 Black or African American, non-Hispanic/Latino; 2 Hispanic/Latino), 1 international. Average age 29. 28 applicants, 89% accepted, 15 enrolled. In 2017, 10 master's awarded.

Degree requirements: For master's, comprehensive exam. *Entrance requirements:* For master's, GRE General Test, minimum baccalaureate GPA of 2.8, two letters of recommendation. Additional exam requirements/recommendations for international students: Required—TOEFL (minimum score 550 paper-based; 79 iBT), IELTS (minimum score 6.5). *Application deadline:* Applications are processed on a rolling basis. Application fee: $60. Electronic applications accepted. *Financial support:* Research assistantships with partial tuition reimbursements and unspecified assistantships available. Financial award application deadline: 3/1; financial award applicants required to submit FAFSA. *Faculty research:* Employment training programs, personnel and labor relations, planning. *Unit head:* Dr. Daniel Reagan, Chairperson, 765-285-8789, Fax: 765-285-5345, E-mail: jlosco@bsu.edu. *Application contact:* Dr. Charles Taylor, Associate Professor/Graduate Advisor, 765-285-8794, Fax: 765-285-5345, E-mail: cdtaylor@bsu.edu.
Website: http://www.bsu.edu/poli-sci

Ball State University, Graduate School, Miller College of Business, Interdepartmental Program in Business Administration, Muncie, IN 47306. Offers business administration (MBA); business essentials (Graduate Certificate); community and economic development (Certificate). *Accreditation:* AACSB. *Program availability:* Part-time, 100% online, blended/hybrid learning. *Students:* 33 full-time (15 women), 221 part-time (78 women); includes 20 minority (5 Black or African American, non-Hispanic/Latino; 8 Asian, non-Hispanic/Latino; 4 Hispanic/Latino; 1 Native Hawaiian or other Pacific Islander, non-Hispanic/Latino; 2 Two or more races, non-Hispanic/Latino), 8 international. Average age 31. 203 applicants, 41% accepted, 58 enrolled. In 2017, 70 master's awarded. *Entrance requirements:* For master's, GMAT or GRE, minimum baccalaureate GPA of 2.75 or 3.0 in latter half of baccalaureate, resume or curriculum vitae, four professional letters of recommendation. Additional exam requirements/recommendations for international students: Required—TOEFL (minimum score 550 paper-based; 79 iBT), IELTS (minimum score 6.5). *Application deadline:* For fall admission, 7/1 for domestic students; for spring admission, 12/1 for domestic students; for summer admission, 4/1 for domestic students. Applications are processed on a rolling basis. Application fee: $60. Electronic applications accepted. *Expenses:* Contact institution. *Financial support:* Research assistantships with partial tuition reimbursements, teaching assistantships with partial tuition reimbursements, and unspecified assistantships available. Financial award application deadline: 3/1; financial award applicants required to submit FAFSA. *Unit head:* Jason Webber, Director, 765-285-1931, Fax: 765-285-8818, E-mail: jjwebber@bsu.edu.
Website: http://www.bsu.edu/mba

Boston University, Metropolitan College, Department of Administrative Sciences, Boston, MA 02215. Offers applied business analytics (MS); economic development and tourism management (MSAS); enterprise risk management (MS); financial management

(MS); global marketing management (MS); innovation and technology (MSAS); insurance management (MS); project management (MS); supply chain management (MS). *Accreditation:* AACSB. *Program availability:* Part-time, evening/weekend, 100% online, blended/hybrid learning. *Faculty:* 21 full-time (5 women), 34 part-time/adjunct (5 women). *Students:* 297 full-time (156 women), 597 part-time (298 women); includes 183 minority (58 Black or African American, non-Hispanic/Latino; 2 American Indian or Alaska Native, non-Hispanic/Latino; 56 Asian, non-Hispanic/Latino; 51 Hispanic/Latino; 2 Native Hawaiian or other Pacific Islander, non-Hispanic/Latino; 14 Two or more races, non-Hispanic/Latino), 391 international. Average age 30. 963 applicants, 64% accepted, 209 enrolled. In 2017, 372 master's awarded. *Degree requirements:* For master's, thesis optional. *Entrance requirements:* For master's, 1 year of work experience, minimum GPA of 3.0. Additional exam requirements/recommendations for international students: Required—TOEFL (minimum score 84 iBT). *Application deadline:* Applications are processed on a rolling basis. Application fee: $85. Electronic applications accepted. *Expenses:* Contact institution. *Financial support:* In 2017–18, 15 students received support, including 18 research assistantships (averaging $8,400 per year), 12 teaching assistantships (averaging $2,700 per year); career-related internships or fieldwork, Federal Work-Study, and unspecified assistantships also available. Financial award applicants required to submit FAFSA. *Faculty research:* International business, innovative process. *Unit head:* Dr. John Sullivan, Chair, 617-353-3016, E-mail: adminsc@bu.edu. *Application contact:* Fiona Niven, Administrative Sciences Department, 617-353-3016, E-mail: adminsc@bu.edu.
Website: http://www.bu.edu/met/academic-community/departments/administrative-sciences/

The Catholic University of America, Busch School of Business and Economics, Washington, DC 20064. Offers accounting (MS); business analysis (MSBA); integral economic development management (MA); integral economic development policy (MA); management (MS), including Federal contract management, human resource management, leadership and management, project management, sales management. *Program availability:* Part-time. *Faculty:* 27 full-time (6 women), 45 part-time/adjunct (12 women). *Students:* 74 full-time (50 women), 9 part-time (3 women); includes 26 minority (5 Black or African American, non-Hispanic/Latino; 1 American Indian or Alaska Native, non-Hispanic/Latino; 3 Asian, non-Hispanic/Latino; 9 Hispanic/Latino; 8 Two or more races, non-Hispanic/Latino), 18 international. Average age 31. 99 applicants, 86% accepted, 61 enrolled. In 2017, 46 master's awarded. *Degree requirements:* For master's, comprehensive exam (for some programs). *Entrance requirements:* For master's, GRE General Test, statement of purpose, official copies of academic transcripts, three letters of recommendation. Additional exam requirements/recommendations for international students: Required—TOEFL (minimum score 550 paper-based; 80 iBT). *Application deadline:* For fall admission, 7/15 priority date for domestic students, 7/1 for international students; for spring admission, 11/15 priority date for domestic students, 11/1 for international students. Applications are processed on a rolling basis. Application fee: $55. Electronic applications accepted. *Expenses:* Contact institution. *Financial support:* Fellowships, research assistantships, teaching assistantships, Federal Work-Study, scholarships/grants, tuition waivers (full and partial), and unspecified assistantships available. Financial award application deadline: 2/1; financial award applicants required to submit FAFSA. *Faculty research:* Integrity of the marketing process, economics of energy and the environment, emerging markets, social change, international finance and economic development. *Total annual research expenditures:* $31,390. *Unit head:* Dr. William Bowman, Dean, 202-319-5290, Fax: 202-319-4426, E-mail: otey@cua.edu. *Application contact:* Dr. Steven Brown, Director of Graduate Admissions, 202-319-5057, Fax: 202-319-6533, E-mail: cua-admissions@cua.edu.
Website: https://business.catholic.edu/

Claremont Graduate University, Graduate Programs, School of Social Science, Policy and Evaluation, Department of Economics, Claremont, CA 91711-6160. Offers behavioral economics and neuroeconomics (PhD); business and financial economics (MA, PhD); economic development (Certificate); international economic and development policy (PhD); international economics policy and development (MA); international money and finance (PhD); political economy and public economics (PhD); political economy and public policy (MA); MBA/PhD. *Program availability:* Part-time. *Entrance requirements:* For master's and doctorate, GRE General Test or GMAT. Additional exam requirements/recommendations for international students: Required—TOEFL (minimum score 75 iBT). Electronic applications accepted. *Faculty research:* International and financial economics, law and economics, regulation, public choice economics.

Cleveland State University, College of Graduate Studies, Maxine Goodman Levin College of Urban Affairs, Program in Environmental Studies, Cleveland, OH 44115. Offers environmental nonprofit management (MAES); environmental planning (MAES); policy and administration (MAES); sustainable economic development (MAES); urban economic development (Certificate); JD/MAES. *Program availability:* Part-time, evening/weekend. *Faculty:* 16 full-time (8 women), 13 part-time/adjunct (5 women). *Students:* 11 full-time (7 women), 8 part-time (4 women); includes 6 minority (5 Black or African American, non-Hispanic/Latino; 1 Hispanic/Latino). Average age 29. 10 applicants, 100% accepted, 5 enrolled. In 2017, 3 master's awarded. *Degree requirements:* For master's, thesis or alternative, exit project. *Entrance requirements:* For master's, GRE General Test (minimum score: verbal and quantitative combined 40th percentile, analytical writing 4.0), minimum GPA of 3.0. Additional exam requirements/recommendations for international students: Required—TOEFL (minimum score 550 paper-based; 78 iBT), IELTS (6.0), or International Test of English Proficiency (iTEP). *Application deadline:* For fall admission, 7/1 priority date for domestic students, 5/15 for international students; for spring admission, 11/15 for domestic students, 11/1 for international students; for summer admission, 4/1 for domestic students, 3/15 for international students. Applications are processed on a rolling basis. Application fee: $40. Electronic applications accepted. *Expenses:* Contact institution. *Financial support:* In 2017–18, 4 students received support. Research assistantships with tuition reimbursements available, teaching assistantships with partial tuition reimbursements available, scholarships/grants, tuition waivers (full and partial), and unspecified assistantships available. Support available to part-time students. Financial award application deadline: 3/1; financial award applicants required to submit FAFSA. *Faculty research:* Environmental policy and administration, environmental planning, geographic information systems (GIS), urban sustainability planning and management, energy policy, land re-use. *Unit head:* Dr. Sanda Kaufman, Professor/Program Director, 216-687-2367, Fax: 216-687-9239, E-mail: s.kaufman@csuohio.edu. *Application contact:* David Arrighi, Graduate Academic Advisor, 216-523-7522, Fax: 216-687-5398, E-mail: d.arrighi@csuohio.edu.
Website: http://urban.csuohio.edu/academics/graduate/maes/

Cleveland State University, College of Graduate Studies, Maxine Goodman Levin College of Urban Affairs, Program in Public Administration, Cleveland, OH 44115. Offers economic development (MPA); non-profit management (MPA); public management (MPA); JD/MPA. *Accreditation:* NASPAA. *Program availability:* Part-time, evening/weekend. *Faculty:* 16 full-time (8 women), 13 part-time/adjunct (5 women). *Students:* 23 full-time (15 women), 45 part-time (24 women); includes 19 minority (14 Black or African American, non-Hispanic/Latino; 1 Asian, non-Hispanic/Latino; 1 Hispanic/Latino; 3 Two or more races, non-Hispanic/Latino), 3 international. Average age 32. 79 applicants, 77% accepted, 12 enrolled. In 2017, 35 master's awarded. *Degree requirements:* For master's, thesis or alternative, exit project. *Entrance requirements:* For master's, GRE General Test (minimum scores in 40th percentile verbal and quantitative, 4.0 writing), minimum GPA of 3.0. Additional exam requirements/recommendations for international students: Required—TOEFL (minimum score 550 paper-based; 78 iBT), IELTS (6.0), or International Test of English Proficiency (iTEP). *Application deadline:* For fall admission, 7/1 priority date for domestic students, 5/15 for international students; for spring admission, 11/15 for domestic students, 11/1 for international students; for summer admission, 4/1 for domestic students, 3/15 for international students. Applications are processed on a rolling basis. Application fee: $40. Electronic applications accepted. *Expenses:* Contact institution. *Financial support:* In 2017–18, 16 students received support, including 5 research assistantships with full tuition reimbursements available (averaging $7,200 per year), 1 teaching assistantship with partial tuition reimbursement available (averaging $2,400 per year); scholarships/grants, tuition waivers (full and partial), and unspecified assistantships also available. Support available to part-time students. Financial award application deadline: 3/1; financial award applicants required to submit FAFSA. *Faculty research:* City management, nonprofit management, health care administration, public management, economic development. *Unit head:* Dr. Nicholas Zingale, Director, 216-802-3389, Fax: 216-687-9342, E-mail: n.zingale@csuohio.edu. *Application contact:* David Arrighi, Graduate Academic Advisor, 216-523-7522, Fax: 216-687-5398, E-mail: d.arrighi@csuohio.edu.
Website: http://urban.csuohio.edu/academics/graduate/mpa/

Cleveland State University, College of Graduate Studies, Maxine Goodman Levin College of Urban Affairs, Program in Urban Planning and Development, Cleveland, OH 44115. Offers economic development (MUPD); environmental sustainability (MUPD); historic preservation (MUPD); housing and neighborhood development (MUPD); real estate development and finance (MUPD); urban economic development (Certificate); urban geographic information systems (MUPD); JD/MUPDD. *Accreditation:* ACSP. *Program availability:* Part-time, evening/weekend. *Faculty:* 16 full-time (8 women), 13 part-time/adjunct (5 women). *Students:* 20 full-time (7 women), 15 part-time (5 women); includes 1 minority (Black or African American, non-Hispanic/Latino), 2 international. Average age 28. 48 applicants, 56% accepted, 14 enrolled. In 2017, 24 master's awarded. *Degree requirements:* For master's, thesis or alternative, exit project. *Entrance requirements:* For master's, GRE General Test (minimum score: 50th percentile combined verbal and quantitative, 4.0 analytical writing), minimum GPA of 3.0. Additional exam requirements/recommendations for international students: Required—TOEFL (minimum score 550 paper-based; 78 iBT), IELTS (6.0), or International Test of English Proficiency (iTEP). *Application deadline:* For fall admission, 7/1 priority date for domestic students, 5/15 for international students; for spring admission, 11/15 for domestic students, 11/1 for international students; for summer admission, 4/1 for domestic students, 3/15 for international students. Applications are processed on a rolling basis. Application fee: $40. Electronic applications accepted. *Expenses:* Contact institution. *Financial support:* In 2017–18, 10 students received support, including 5 research assistantships with full tuition reimbursements available (averaging $7,200 per year), 3 teaching assistantships with partial tuition reimbursements available (averaging $2,400 per year); scholarships/grants, tuition waivers (full and partial), and unspecified assistantships also available. Support available to part-time students. Financial award application deadline: 3/1; financial award applicants required to submit FAFSA. *Faculty research:* Housing and neighborhood development, urban housing policy, environmental sustainability, economic development, GIS and planning decision support. *Unit head:* Dr. Stephanie Ryberg-Webster, Assistant Professor/Program Director, 216-802-3386, Fax: 216-687-2013, E-mail: s.ryberg@csuohio.edu. *Application contact:* David Arrighi, Graduate Academic Advisor, 216-523-7522, Fax: 216-687-5398, E-mail: d.arrighi@csuohio.edu.
Website: http://www.csuohio.edu/urban/mupd/mupd

Concordia University, School of Graduate Studies, Faculty of Arts and Science, School of Community and Public Affairs, Montréal, QC H3G 1M8, Canada. Offers community economic development (Diploma).

Cornell University, Graduate School, Graduate Fields of Agriculture and Life Sciences, Field of Applied Economics and Management, Ithaca, NY 14853. Offers agricultural finance (MS, PhD); applied econometrics and qualitative analysis (MS, PhD); economics of development (MS, PhD); environmental economics (MS, PhD); environmental management (MPS); farm management and production economics (MS, PhD); marketing and food distribution (MS, PhD); public policy analysis (MS, PhD); resource economics (PhD). *Entrance requirements:* For master's and doctorate, GRE. Additional exam requirements/recommendations for international students: Required—TOEFL.

Cornell University, Graduate School, Graduate Fields of Architecture, Art and Planning, Field of City and Regional Planning, Ithaca, NY 14853. Offers city and regional planning (MRP, PhD); environmental planning and design (MRP, PhD); historic preservation planning (MA); international development planning (MRP, PhD); planning theory and systems analysis (MRP, PhD); regional economics and development planning (MRP, PhD); regional science (MRP, PhD); social and health systems planning (MRP, PhD); urban and regional theory (MRP, PhD); urban planning history (MRP, PhD). *Accreditation:* ACSP (one or more programs are accredited). *Degree requirements:* For master's, thesis (MA); for doctorate, comprehensive exam, thesis/dissertation. *Entrance requirements:* For master's and doctorate, GRE General Test, 2 letters of recommendation. Additional exam requirements/recommendations for international students: Required—TOEFL (minimum score 600 paper-based; 77 iBT). Electronic applications accepted. *Faculty research:* Land use planning, economic development, international development, historic preservation, community development.

Cornell University, Graduate School, Graduate Fields of Arts and Sciences, Field of Economics, Ithaca, NY 14853. Offers applied economics (PhD); basic analytical economics (PhD); econometrics and economic statistics (PhD); economic development and planning (PhD); economic theory (PhD); industrial organization and control (PhD); international economics (PhD); labor economics (PhD); monetary and macro economics (PhD); public finance (PhD). *Degree requirements:* For doctorate, comprehensive exam, thesis/dissertation. *Entrance requirements:* For doctorate, GRE General Test, 3 letters of recommendation. Additional exam requirements/recommendations for international students: Required—TOEFL (minimum score 550 paper-based; 77 iBT). Electronic applications accepted. *Faculty research:* Learning and games, economics of education, political economy, transfer payments, time series and nonparametrics.

East Carolina University, Graduate School, Thomas Harriot College of Arts and Sciences, Department of Geography, Planning, and Environment, Greenville, NC 27858-4353. Offers development and environmental planning (Certificate); economic development (Certificate); geographic information science and technology (Certificate); geography (MA), including geography, planning, rural development. *Program availability:* Part-time, evening/weekend, online learning. *Students:* 15 full-time (8 women), 6 part-time (2 women); includes 4 minority (3 Black or African American, non-Hispanic/Latino; 1 Hispanic/Latino). Average age 27. 14 applicants, 93% accepted, 8 enrolled. In 2017, 5 master's, 1 other advanced degree awarded. *Degree requirements:* For master's, comprehensive exam, thesis optional. *Entrance requirements:* For master's, GRE General Test. Additional exam requirements/recommendations for international students: Recommended—TOEFL (minimum score 78 iBT), IELTS

(minimum score 6.5). *Application deadline:* For fall admission, 4/1 priority date for domestic and international students. Applications are processed on a rolling basis. Application fee: $75. Electronic applications accepted. *Expenses:* Tuition, state resident: full-time $4749; part-time $297 per credit hour. Tuition, nonresident: full-time $17,898; part-time $1119 per credit hour. *Required fees:* $2691; $224 per credit hour. Part-time tuition and fees vary according to course load and program. *Financial support:* Research assistantships with partial tuition reimbursements, teaching assistantships with partial tuition reimbursements, and Federal Work-Study available. Support available to part-time students. Financial award application deadline: 3/1. *Faculty research:* Coastal vulnerability and adaptation, emergency management, public understanding of risk, catastrophic events. *Unit head:* Dr. Thad Wasklewicz, Chair, 252-328-6230, E-mail: wasklewiczt@ecu.edu. *Application contact:* Dean of Graduate School, 252-328-6012, Fax: 252-328-6071, E-mail: gradschool@ecu.edu.
Website: http://www.ecu.edu/geog/

East Tennessee State University, School of Graduate Studies, College of Arts and Sciences, Department of Political Science, International Affairs and Public Administration, Johnson City, TN 37614. Offers economic development (Postbaccalaureate Certificate); economic development and planning (MPA); local government management (MPA); nonprofit and public financial management (MPA); urban planning (Postbaccalaureate Certificate). *Program availability:* Part-time. *Degree requirements:* For master's, internship, capstone. *Entrance requirements:* For master's, GRE General Test, three letters of recommendation. Additional exam requirements/recommendations for international students: Required—TOEFL (minimum score 550 paper-based; 79 iBT). *Application deadline:* For fall admission, 6/1 for domestic students, 4/29 for international students; for spring admission, 11/1 for domestic students, 9/29 for international students. Application fee: $55 ($65 for international students). Electronic applications accepted. *Financial support:* Research assistantships with full tuition reimbursements, teaching assistantships with full tuition reimbursements, career-related internships or fieldwork, institutionally sponsored loans, scholarships/grants, and unspecified assistantships available. Financial award application deadline: 7/1; financial award applicants required to submit FAFSA. *Faculty research:* Labor issues, presidency, public law in American politics, East Asian politics, European politics, Middle Eastern politics, development in comparative politics, international political economy, international relations, world politics in international affairs. *Unit head:* Dr. Andrew Battista, Chair, 423-439-6628, Fax: 423-439-4348, E-mail: battista@etsu.edu. *Application contact:* Dr. Andrew Battista, Chair, 423-439-6628, Fax: 423-439-4348, E-mail: battista@etsu.edu.
Website: http://www.etsu.edu/cas/polisci/

Fordham University, Graduate School of Arts and Sciences, Program in International Political Economy and Development, New York, NY 10458. Offers MA, Certificate. *Program availability:* Part-time, evening/weekend. *Students:* 38 full-time (18 women), 8 part-time (2 women); includes 3 minority (1 Asian, non-Hispanic/Latino; 2 Hispanic/Latino), 15 international. Average age 27. 89 applicants, 60% accepted, 24 enrolled. In 2017, 24 master's, 1 other advanced degree awarded. *Degree requirements:* For master's, comprehensive exam. *Entrance requirements:* For master's, GRE General Test. Additional exam requirements/recommendations for international students: Required—TOEFL (minimum score 600 paper-based). *Application deadline:* For fall admission, 1/4 priority date for domestic students; for spring admission, 11/1 for domestic students. Application fee: $70. Electronic applications accepted. *Financial support:* In 2017–18, 35 students received support, including 4 fellowships with tuition reimbursements available (averaging $17,014 per year); research assistantships with tuition reimbursements available, career-related internships or fieldwork, institutionally sponsored loans, tuition waivers (full and partial), and unspecified assistantships also available. Financial award application deadline: 1/4; financial award applicants required to submit FAFSA. *Faculty research:* International economics, comparative international politics, international banking and finance, international development, emerging markets and country risk analysis. *Unit head:* Dr. Henry Schwalbenberg, Chair, 718-817-3866, Fax: 718-817-3518. *Application contact:* Bernadette Valentino-Morrison, Director of Graduate Admissions, 718-817-4419, Fax: 718-817-3566, E-mail: valentinomor@fordham.edu.

Georgetown University, Graduate School of Arts and Sciences, Department of Economics, Washington, DC 20057. Offers econometrics (PhD); economic development (PhD); economic theory (PhD); industrial organization (PhD); international macro and finance (PhD); international trade (PhD); labor economics (PhD); macroeconomics (PhD); public economics and political economy (PhD); MA/PhD; MS/MA. *Degree requirements:* For doctorate, comprehensive exam, thesis/dissertation. *Entrance requirements:* For doctorate, GRE General Test. Additional exam requirements/recommendations for international students: Required—TOEFL. *Faculty research:* International economics, economic development.

Georgia Institute of Technology, Graduate Studies, College of Design, School of City and Regional Planning, Atlanta, GA 30332-0001. Offers city and regional planning (PhD); economic development (MCRP); environmental planning and management (MCRP); geographic information systems (MCRP); land and community development (MCRP); land use planning (MCRP); transportation (MCRP); urban design (MCRP); MCP/MSCE. *Accreditation:* ACSP. *Degree requirements:* For master's, thesis, internship. *Entrance requirements:* For master's, GRE General Test, minimum GPA of 2.7. Additional exam requirements/recommendations for international students: Required—TOEFL. Electronic applications accepted.

Georgia State University, Andrew Young School of Policy Studies, Department of Public Management and Policy, Atlanta, GA 30303. Offers criminal justice (MPA); disaster management (Certificate); disaster policy (MPA); environmental policy (PhD); health policy (PhD); management and finance (MPA); nonprofit management (MPA, Certificate); nonprofit policy (MPA); planning and economic development (MPP, Certificate); policy analysis and evaluation (MPA), including planning and economic development; public and nonprofit management (PhD); public finance and budgeting (PhD), including science and technology policy, urban and regional economic development; public finance policy (MPA), including social policy; public health (MPA). *Accreditation:* NASPAA (one or more programs are accredited). *Program availability:* Part-time. *Faculty:* 17 full-time (9 women). *Students:* 125 full-time (75 women), 78 part-time (51 women); includes 90 minority (67 Black or African American, non-Hispanic/Latino; 5 Asian, non-Hispanic/Latino; 9 Hispanic/Latino; 9 Two or more races, non-Hispanic/Latino), 34 international. Average age 30. 275 applicants, 62% accepted, 88 enrolled. In 2017, 71 master's, 5 doctorates, 12 other advanced degrees awarded. Terminal master's awarded for partial completion of doctoral program. *Degree requirements:* For master's, thesis optional; for doctorate, comprehensive exam, thesis/dissertation. *Entrance requirements:* For master's and doctorate, GRE. Additional exam requirements/recommendations for international students: Required—TOEFL (minimum score 603 paper-based; 100 iBT) or IELTS (minimum score 7). *Application deadline:* For fall admission, 1/15 for domestic and international students. Application fee: $50. Electronic applications accepted. *Expenses:* Tuition, state resident: full-time $7020. Tuition, nonresident: full-time $22,518. *Required fees:* $2128. Tuition and fees vary according to degree level and program. *Financial support:* In 2017–18, fellowships (averaging $8,194 per year), research assistantships (averaging $8,068 per year), teaching assistantships (averaging $3,600 per year) were awarded; institutionally sponsored loans, scholarships/grants, health care benefits, and unspecified assistantships also available. Financial award application deadline: 2/1. *Faculty research:* Public budgeting and finance, public management, nonprofit management, performance measurement and management, urban development. *Unit head:* Dr. Carolyn Bourdeaux, Chair and Professor, 404-413-0013, Fax: 404-413-0104, E-mail: cbourdeaux@gsu.edu.
Website: http://aysps.gsu.edu/pmap/

Indiana University Bloomington, School of Public and Environmental Affairs, Public Affairs Programs, Bloomington, IN 47405. Offers economic development (MPA); energy (MPA); environmental policy (PhD); environmental policy and natural resource management (MPA); information systems (MPA); international development (MPA); local government management (MPA); nonprofit management (MPA, Certificate); policy analysis (MPA); public budgeting and financial management (Certificate); public finance (PhD); public financial administration (MPA); public management (MPA, PhD, Certificate); public policy analysis (PhD); social entrepreneurship (Certificate); specialized public affairs (MPA); sustainability and sustainable development (MPA); JD/MPA; MPA/MA; MPA/MIS; MPA/MLS; MSES/MPA. *Accreditation:* NASPAA (one or more programs are accredited). *Program availability:* Part-time. *Degree requirements:* For master's, capstone, internship; for doctorate, comprehensive exam, thesis/dissertation. *Entrance requirements:* For master's, GRE General Test or GMAT, official transcripts, 3 letters of recommendation, resume, personal statement; for doctorate, GRE General Test, official transcripts, 3 letters of recommendation, statement of purpose. Additional exam requirements/recommendations for international students: Required—TOEFL (minimum score 600 paper-based; 96 iBT); Recommended—IELTS (minimum score 7). Electronic applications accepted. *Faculty research:* International development, environmental policy and resource management, policy analysis, public finance, public management, urban management, nonprofit management, energy policy, social policy, public finance.

Johnson & Wales University, Graduate Studies, MS Program in Global Tourism and Sustainable Economic Development, Providence, RI 02903-3703. Offers MS. *Program availability:* Online learning. *Expenses: Tuition:* Full-time $12,636; part-time $702 per credit hour. *Unit head:* Dr. Eldad Boker, Director, 401-598-4638, E-mail: eldad.boker@jwu.edu. *Application contact:* Graduate School Admissions, 401-598-1015, Fax: 401-598-1286, E-mail: pvdgrad@admissions.jwu.edu.
Website: https://www.jwu.edu/academics/programs-by-campus/providence-programs/global-tourism-and-sustainable-economic-development-ms.html

Murray State University, Arthur J. Bauernfeind College of Business, Department of Economics and Finance, Murray, KY 42071. Offers economic development (MS); economics (MS), including finance. *Program availability:* Part-time. *Faculty:* 13 full-time (4 women), 1 part-time/adjunct (0 women). *Students:* 10 full-time (6 women), 2 part-time (0 women); includes 2 minority (1 Black or African American, non-Hispanic/Latino; 1 Two or more races, non-Hispanic/Latino), 5 international. Average age 26. 7 applicants, 86% accepted, 1 enrolled. In 2017, 5 master's awarded. *Entrance requirements:* For master's, GRE General Test or GMAT, minimum university GPA of 2.75. Additional exam requirements/recommendations for international students: Required—TOEFL (minimum score 527 paper-based; 71 iBT). *Application deadline:* Applications are processed on a rolling basis. Application fee: $40 ($50 for international students). Electronic applications accepted. *Expenses:* Tuition, state resident: full-time $9504. Tuition, nonresident: full-time $26,811. *International tuition:* $14,400 full-time. Tuition and fees vary according to course load, degree level and reciprocity agreements. *Financial support:* In 2017–18, 1 research assistantship, 1 teaching assistantship were awarded; Federal Work-Study and unspecified assistantships also available. Financial award applicants required to submit FAFSA. *Unit head:* Dr. David Eaton, Chair, Department of Economics and Finance, 270-809-4290, Fax: 270-809-5478, E-mail: deaton@murraystate.edu. *Application contact:* Kaitlyn Burzynski, Interim Assistant Director for Graduate Admission and Records, 270-809-5732, Fax: 270-809-3780, E-mail: msu.graduateadmissions@murraystate.edu.
Website: https://www.murraystate.edu/academics/CollegesDepartments/CollegeOfBusiness/Programs/EconomicsAndFinance/

New Mexico State University, College of Business, Department of Economics, Applied Statistics and International Business, Las Cruces, NM 88003. Offers applied statistics (MS); economic development (DED); economics (MA); public utility regulation and economics (Graduate Certificate). *Program availability:* Part-time. *Faculty:* 17 full-time (4 women). *Students:* 55 full-time (22 women), 24 part-time (10 women); includes 28 minority (3 Black or African American, non-Hispanic/Latino; 2 American Indian or Alaska Native, non-Hispanic/Latino; 1 Asian, non-Hispanic/Latino; 20 Hispanic/Latino; 2 Two or more races, non-Hispanic/Latino), 34 international. Average age 34. 84 applicants, 73% accepted, 27 enrolled. In 2017, 11 master's, 2 doctorates, 9 other advanced degrees awarded. Terminal master's awarded for partial completion of doctoral program. *Entrance requirements:* For master's, minimum GPA of 3.0; for doctorate, appropriate master's degree, minimum GPA of 3.0. Additional exam requirements/recommendations for international students: Required—TOEFL (minimum score 550 paper-based; 79 iBT), IELTS (minimum score 6.5). *Application deadline:* For fall admission, 3/1 priority date for domestic and international students. Applications are processed on a rolling basis. Application fee: $40 ($50 for international students). Electronic applications accepted. *Expenses:* Tuition, state resident: full-time $4390. Tuition, nonresident: full-time $15,309. *Required fees:* $853. *Financial support:* In 2017–18, 43 students received support, including 21 research assistantships (averaging $12,040 per year), 8 teaching assistantships (averaging $15,828 per year); career-related internships or fieldwork, Federal Work-Study, scholarships/grants, traineeships, health care benefits, and unspecified assistantships also available. Support available to part-time students. Financial award application deadline: 3/1. *Faculty research:* Public utilities, environment, linear models, biological sampling, public policy, economic development, energy, regional economics. *Unit head:* Dr. Christopher Erickson, Interim Department Head, 575-646-7211, Fax: 575-646-1915, E-mail: chrerick@nmsu.edu. *Application contact:* 575-646-7211, Fax: 575-646-1915.
Website: http://business.nmsu.edu/departments/economics

Northeastern University, College of Professional Studies, Boston, MA 02115-5096. Offers applied nutrition (MS); college athletics administration (MSL); commerce and economic development (MS); corporate and organizational communication (MS); criminal justice (MS); digital media (MPS); elearning and instructional design (M Ed); elementary education (MAT); geographic information technology (MPS); global studies and international relations (MS); higher education administration (M Ed); homeland security (MA); human services (MS); informatics (MPS); leadership (MS); learning analytics (M Ed); learning and instruction (M Ed); nonprofit management (MS); professional sports administration (MSL); project management (MS); regulatory affairs for drugs, biologics, and medical devices (MS); respiratory care leadership (MS); special education (M Ed); technical communication (MS). *Program availability:* Part-time, evening/weekend, 100% online, blended/hybrid learning. *Faculty:* 82 full-time (51 women), 853 part-time/adjunct (366 women). *Students:* 5,278 part-time (3,230 women). In 2017, 1,586 master's awarded. *Application deadline:* Applications are processed on a rolling basis. Application fee: $0. Electronic applications accepted. *Expenses:* Contact

institution. *Financial support:* Applicants required to submit FAFSA. *Unit head:* Dr. Mary Loeffelholz, Dean of the College of Professional Studies. *Application contact:* E-mail: cpsadmissions@northeastern.edu.
Website: https://cps.northeastern.edu/

Southern New Hampshire University, School of Business, Manchester, NH 03106-1045. Offers accounting (MBA, Graduate Certificate); accounting finance (MS); accounting/auditing (MS); accounting/forensic accounting (MS); accounting/ management accounting (MS); accounting/taxation (MS); applied economics (MS); athletic administration (MBA, Graduate Certificate); business administration (IMBA, Certificate), including business information systems (Certificate), human resource management (Certificate); business analytics (MBA); business intelligence (MBA); communication (MA), including new media and marketing, public relations; community economic development (MBA); criminal justice (MBA); data analytics (MS); economics (MBA); engineering management (MBA); entrepreneurship (MBA); finance (MBA, MS, Graduate Certificate); finance/corporate finance (MS); finance/investments (MS); forensic accounting (MBA); forensic accounting and fraud examination (Graduate Certificate); healthcare informatics (MBA); healthcare management (MBA); human resource management (MS); human resources (MBA); information technology (MS); information technology management (MBA); international business (PhD); Internet marketing (MBA); leadership (MBA); leadership of nonprofit organizations (Graduate Certificate); management (MS); marketing (MBA, MS, Graduate Certificate); music business (MBA); operations and project management (MS); operations and supply chain management (MBA, Graduate Certificate); organizational leadership (MS); project management (MBA, Graduate Certificate); public administration (MBA, Graduate Certificate); quantitative analysis (MBA); Six Sigma (Graduate Certificate); Six Sigma quality (MBA); social media marketing (MBA, Graduate Certificate); sport management (MBA, MS, Graduate Certificate); sustainability and environmental compliance (MBA); MBA/Certificate. *Accreditation:* ACBSP. *Program availability:* Part-time, evening/ weekend, online learning. Terminal master's awarded for partial completion of doctoral program. *Degree requirements:* For master's, one foreign language, comprehensive exam (for some programs), thesis or alternative; for doctorate, one foreign language, comprehensive exam, thesis/dissertation. *Entrance requirements:* For master's, minimum GPA of 2.5; for doctorate, GMAT. Additional exam requirements/ recommendations for international students: Required—TOEFL (minimum score 500 paper-based). *Application deadline:* Applications are processed on a rolling basis. Application fee: $40. Electronic applications accepted. *Expenses: Tuition:* Part-time $627 per credit hour. Part-time tuition and fees vary according to campus/location and program. *Financial support:* Career-related internships or fieldwork, Federal Work-Study, institutionally sponsored loans, scholarships/grants, tuition waivers (partial), and unspecified assistantships available. Support available to part-time students. Financial award applicants required to submit FAFSA. *Unit head:* Dr. Bill Lightfoot, Dean, 603-644-3102, Fax: 603-644-3144. *Application contact:* Office of Graduate Admission, 888-327-SNHU, Fax: 603-644-3144, E-mail: enroll@snhu.edu.

State University of New York Empire State College, School for Graduate Studies, Program in Community and Economic Development, Saratoga Springs, NY 12866-4391. Offers MA. *Program availability:* Part-time, evening/weekend, online learning. *Degree requirements:* For master's, thesis, final project. *Entrance requirements:* For master's, undergraduate-level courses in statistics and macroeconomics, bachelor's degree from regionally-accredited college/university. Additional exam requirements/ recommendations for international students: Required—TOEFL (minimum score 600 paper-based). Electronic applications accepted. *Faculty research:* Business history, applied business statistics, labor/management relations, American social problems and business, effect of government economic policies on business.

Thomas Edison State University, John S. Watson School of Public Service and Continuing Studies, Trenton, NJ 08608. Offers community and economic development (MSM); environmental policy/environmental justice (MSM); homeland security (MSHS, MSM); information and technology for public service (MSM); nonprofit management (MSM); public and municipal finance (MSM); public health (MSM); public service administration and leadership (MSM); public service leadership (MPSL). *Program availability:* Part-time, online learning. *Entrance requirements:* Additional exam requirements/recommendations for international students: Required—TOEFL (minimum score 550 paper-based; 79 iBT). Electronic applications accepted.

Troy University, Graduate School, College of Business, Program in Business Administration, Troy, AL 36082. Offers accounting (EMBA, MBA); criminal justice (EMBA); finance (MBA); general management (EMBA, MBA); healthcare management (EMBA); information systems (EMBA, MBA); international economic development (MBA). *Accreditation:* ACBSP. *Program availability:* Part-time, evening/weekend. *Faculty:* 6 full-time (2 women), 1 part-time/adjunct (0 women). *Students:* 43 full-time (22 women), 115 part-time (55 women); includes 50 minority (31 Black or African American, non-Hispanic/Latino; 12 Asian, non-Hispanic/Latino; 6 Hispanic/Latino; 1 Two or more races, non-Hispanic/Latino). Average age 30. 156 applicants, 76% accepted, 36 enrolled. In 2017, 95 master's awarded. *Degree requirements:* For master's, minimum GPA of 3.0, capstone course, research course. *Entrance requirements:* For master's, GMAT (minimum score 500) or GRE (minimum score 900 on old exam or 294 on new exam), bachelor's degree; minimum undergraduate GPA of 2.5 or 3.0 on last 30 semester hours, letter of recommendation. Additional exam requirements/ recommendations for international students: Required—TOEFL (minimum score 523 paper-based; 70 iBT), IELTS (minimum score 6). *Application deadline:* Applications are processed on a rolling basis. Application fee: $50. Electronic applications accepted. *Expenses:* Tuition, state resident: part-time $417 per credit hour. Tuition, nonresident: part-time $834 per credit hour. *Required fees:* $42 per credit hour. $50 per semester. Tuition and fees vary according to campus/location. *Financial support:* Fellowships, career-related internships or fieldwork, and scholarships/grants available. Support available to part-time students. Financial award applicants required to submit FAFSA. *Unit head:* Dr. Phillip Mixon, MBA Director, 334-670-3140, Fax: 334-670-3708, E-mail: pamixon@troy.edu. *Application contact:* Jessica A. Kimbro, Director of Graduate Admissions, 334-670-3178, E-mail: jacord@troy.edu.

Université de Sherbrooke, Faculty of Administration, PhD Program in Economic Development, Sherbrooke, QC J1K 2R1, Canada. Offers PhD. *Degree requirements:* For doctorate, one foreign language, comprehensive exam, thesis/dissertation, advanced English as a second language. *Entrance requirements:* For doctorate, letters of recommendation, work experience, formal training. *Faculty research:* Impact analysis of economical policies; productivity, competitivity and international commerce; macroeconometric modelisation; environmental economy.

University at Buffalo, the State University of New York, Graduate School, School of Architecture and Planning, Department of Urban and Regional Planning, Buffalo, NY 12414. Offers community health and food systems (MUP); economic development (MUP); environment/land use (MUP); historic preservation (MUP, Certificate); neighborhood/community development (MUP); real estate development (MSRED); urban and regional planning (PhD); urban design (MUP); JD/MUP; M Arch/MUP. *Accreditation:* ACSP. *Program availability:* Part-time. *Faculty:* 13 full-time (6 women), 12 part-time/adjunct (3 women). *Students:* 76 full-time (27 women), 20 part-time (9 women); includes 17 minority (9 Black or African American, non-Hispanic/Latino; 5 Hispanic/Latino; 3 Two or more races, non-Hispanic/Latino), 20 international. Average age 27. 196 applicants, 20% accepted, 32 enrolled. In 2017, 35 master's, 1 doctorate, 5 other advanced degrees awarded. *Degree requirements:* For master's, thesis or alternative, project; for doctorate, comprehensive exam, thesis/dissertation. *Entrance requirements:* For master's, resume, three letters of recommendation, personal statement, transcripts; for doctorate, GRE, transcripts, three letters of recommendation, resume, research statement, writing sample. Additional exam requirements/recommendations for international students: Required—TOEFL (minimum score 79 iBT), IELTS (minimum score 6.5). *Application deadline:* For fall admission, 3/1 priority date for domestic and international students; for spring admission, 10/31 priority date for domestic students, 10/1 priority date for international students. Applications are processed on a rolling basis. Application fee: $75. Electronic applications accepted. *Expenses:* $13,382. *Financial support:* In 2017–18, 45 students received support, including 3 fellowships with full tuition reimbursements available (averaging $15,600 per year), 2 research assistantships with partial tuition reimbursements available (averaging $13,390 per year), 15 teaching assistantships with partial tuition reimbursements available (averaging $4,800 per year); career-related internships or fieldwork, Federal Work-Study, institutionally sponsored loans, scholarships/grants, health care benefits, and unspecified assistantships also available. Financial award application deadline: 3/1; financial award applicants required to submit FAFSA. *Faculty research:* Economic and international development, environmental and land use planning, GIS and spatial analysis, urban design and physical planning, neighborhood planning and community development, historic preservation. *Total annual research expenditures:* $1.3 million. *Unit head:* Dr. Daniel B. Hess, Professor and Chair, 716-829-3671 Ext. 109, Fax: 716-829-3256, E-mail: dbhess@buffalo.edu. *Application contact:* Donna Rogalski, Department Secretary, 716-829-3671, Fax: 716-829-3256, E-mail: dmr1@buffalo.edu.
Website: http://www.ap.buffalo.edu/planning/

University of Central Arkansas, Graduate School, College of Liberal Arts, Department of Geography, Conway, AR 72035-0001. Offers community and economic development (MS); geographic information systems (MGIS, Certificate). *Program availability:* Part-time, online learning. *Entrance requirements:* Additional exam requirements/ recommendations for international students: Required—TOEFL (minimum score 550 paper-based). Electronic applications accepted.

University of Central Arkansas, Graduate School, College of Liberal Arts, Program in Community and Economic Development, Conway, AR 72035-0001. Offers community and economic development (MS); geographic and information systems (MGIS, Graduate Certificate). *Program availability:* Part-time, online learning. *Degree requirements:* For master's, comprehensive exam, thesis. *Entrance requirements:* For master's, GRE General Test, minimum GPA of 2.7. Additional exam requirements/ recommendations for international students: Required—TOEFL (minimum score 550 paper-based). Electronic applications accepted. *Expenses:* Contact institution.

University of Colorado Denver, College of Architecture and Planning, Program in Urban and Regional Planning, Denver, CO 80217. Offers economic and community development planning (MURP); land use and environmental planning (MURP); urban place making (MURP). *Accreditation:* ACSP. *Program availability:* Part-time. *Degree requirements:* For master's, thesis, minimum of 51 semester hours. *Entrance requirements:* For master's, GRE (for students with an undergraduate GPA below 3.0), sample of writing or work project; statement of interest; resume; three letters of recommendation. Additional exam requirements/recommendations for international students: Required—TOEFL (minimum score 75 iBT). Electronic applications accepted. *Expenses:* Contact institution. *Faculty research:* Physical planning, environmental planning, economic development planning.

University of Houston–Victoria, School of Business Administration, Victoria, TX 77901-4450. Offers accounting (MBA); economic development and entrepreneurship (MS); finance (GMBA, MBA); general business (MBA); international business (MBA); management (GMBA, MBA); marketing (MBA). *Accreditation:* AACSB. *Program availability:* Part-time, evening/weekend, online learning. *Entrance requirements:* For master's, GMAT. Additional exam requirements/recommendations for international students: Required—TOEFL (minimum score 550 paper-based). Electronic applications accepted. *Faculty research:* Economic development, marketing, finance.

University of Massachusetts Lowell, College of Fine Arts, Humanities and Social Sciences, Program in Regional Economic and Social Development, Lowell, MA 01854. Offers MA, Graduate Certificate. *Program availability:* Part-time. *Entrance requirements:* For master's, GRE. Electronic applications accepted.

University of New Hampshire, Graduate School, Carsey School of Public Policy, Program in Community Development Policy and Practice, Durham, NH 03824. Offers MA. *Program availability:* Online learning. *Students:* 1 full-time (0 women), 14 part-time (8 women); includes 3 minority (2 Black or African American, non-Hispanic/Latino; 1 Hispanic/Latino), 5 international. Average age 32. 4 applicants, 75% accepted, 1 enrolled. *Entrance requirements:* Additional exam requirements/recommendations for international students: Required—TOEFL (minimum score 80 iBT), IELTS (minimum score 6.5). *Application deadline:* For fall admission, 8/15 for domestic students; for spring admission, 12/15 for domestic students; for summer admission, 4/15 for domestic students. Electronic applications accepted. *Financial support:* Application deadline: 2/ 15; applicants required to submit FAFSA. *Unit head:* Michael Swack, Chair, 603-862-2821, Fax: 603-862-0275, E-mail: michael.swack@unh.edu. *Application contact:* Sarah Dorner, Administrative Assistant, 603-862-2338, E-mail: sarah.dorner@unh.edu.
Website: https://carsey.unh.edu/macdpp

University of North Alabama, College of Arts and Sciences, Department of Interdisciplinary and Professional Studies, Florence, AL 35632-0001. Offers professional studies (MPS), including community development, information technology, security and safety leadership. *Program availability:* Part-time, 100% online. *Faculty:* 4 full-time (1 woman), 1 part-time/adjunct (0 women). *Students:* 19 full-time (9 women), 24 part-time (12 women); includes 7 minority (5 Black or African American, non-Hispanic/ Latino; 1 American Indian or Alaska Native, non-Hispanic/Latino; 1 Asian, non-Hispanic/ Latino), 13 international. Average age 35. 34 applicants, 65% accepted, 17 enrolled. In 2017, 24 master's awarded. *Degree requirements:* For master's, thesis optional. *Entrance requirements:* For master's, ETS PPI, personal statement; three letters of recommendation. Additional exam requirements/recommendations for international students: Required—TOEFL (minimum score 79 iBT), IELTS (minimum score 6), PTE (minimum score 54). *Application deadline:* Applications are processed on a rolling basis. Application fee: $50 ($100 for international students). Electronic applications accepted. *Expenses:* Tuition, state resident: full-time $7824; part-time $5943 per year. Tuition, nonresident: full-time $15,648; part-time $11,736 per year. *Required fees:* $3064; $2298 per unit. Tuition and fees vary according to course load and reciprocity agreements. *Financial support:* In 2017–18, 17 students received support. Federal Work-Study, scholarships/grants, and unspecified assistantships available. Financial award application deadline: 2/1; financial award applicants required to submit FAFSA. *Unit head:* Dr. Craig T. Robertson, Director, 256-765-5003, E-mail: ctrobertson@una.edu. *Application contact:* Hillary N. Coats, Graduate Admissions Coordinator, 256-765-4447, E-mail: graduate@una.edu.
Website: https://www.una.edu/interdisciplinary-studies/

The University of North Carolina at Greensboro, Graduate School, College of Arts and Sciences, Department of Geography, Greensboro, NC 27412-5001. Offers applied geography (MA); geographic information science (Certificate); geography (PhD); urban and economic development (Certificate). *Degree requirements:* For master's, comprehensive exam, thesis or alternative. *Entrance requirements:* For master's, GRE General Test. Additional exam requirements/recommendations for international students: Required—TOEFL. Electronic applications accepted.

The University of North Carolina at Greensboro, Graduate School, College of Arts and Sciences, Department of Political Science, Greensboro, NC 27412-5001. Offers nonprofit management (Certificate); public affairs (MPA); urban and economic development (Certificate). *Accreditation:* NASPAA. *Degree requirements:* For master's, comprehensive exam. *Entrance requirements:* For master's, GRE General Test. Additional exam requirements/recommendations for international students: Required—TOEFL. Electronic applications accepted. *Faculty research:* U.S. Constitution, Canadian parliament, public management, ethical challenge of public service.

University of Oklahoma, Price College of Business, Program in Business Administration, Oklahoma City, OK 73104. Offers business administration (MBA, PhD); including accounting (PhD), business administration, entrepreneurship and economic development (PhD), finance (PhD), management and international business (PhD), management of information systems (PhD), marketing/supply chain (PhD); JD/MBA; MBA/MS. *Accreditation:* AACSB. *Program availability:* Part-time, evening/weekend. *Students:* 100 full-time (27 women), 152 part-time (30 women); includes 36 minority (2 Black or African American, non-Hispanic/Latino; 4 American Indian or Alaska Native, non-Hispanic/Latino; 10 Asian, non-Hispanic/Latino; 13 Hispanic/Latino; 7 Two or more races, non-Hispanic/Latino), 32 international. Average age 31. 247 applicants, 29% accepted, 41 enrolled. In 2017, 118 master's, 9 doctorates awarded. *Degree requirements:* For doctorate, comprehensive exam, thesis/dissertation. *Entrance requirements:* For master's, GMAT or GRE, resume, 2 essays, interview; for doctorate, GMAT or GRE, resume, statement of goals, 3 letters of recommendation. Additional exam requirements/recommendations for international students: Required—TOEFL (minimum score 100 iBT) or IELTS (minimum score 7). *Application deadline:* For fall admission, 11/1 for domestic and international students; for summer admission, 11/1 for domestic and international students. Applications are processed on a rolling basis. Application fee: $50 ($100 for international students). Electronic applications accepted. *Expenses:* Contact institution. *Financial support:* In 2017–18, 107 students received support, including 6 fellowships with partial tuition reimbursements available (averaging $2,500 per year); research assistantships with full and partial tuition reimbursements available, teaching assistantships with full and partial tuition reimbursements available, career-related internships or fieldwork, scholarships/grants, health care benefits, and unspecified assistantships also available. Support available to part-time students. Financial award application deadline: 6/1; financial award applicants required to submit FAFSA. *Faculty research:* Energy finance; international accounting; organizational behavior and entrepreneurship; management information systems; supply chain. *Unit head:* Laku Chidambaram, Associate Dean for Academic Programs and Engagement, 405-325-8013. *Application contact:* Kate Hile, Associate Director of MBA Admissions, 405-325-4572, E-mail: khile@ou.edu.
Website: http://www.ou.edu/price/divisions/graduate-programs/graduate.html

University of Pennsylvania, School of Arts and Sciences, Fels Institute of Government, Philadelphia, PA 19104. Offers economic development and growth (Certificate); government administration (MGA); nonprofit administration (Certificate); organization dynamics (MS); politics (Certificate); public administration (MPA); public finance (Certificate). *Program availability:* Part-time, evening/weekend. *Students:* 44 full-time (27 women), 78 part-time (41 women); includes 30 minority (9 Black or African American, non-Hispanic/Latino; 8 Asian, non-Hispanic/Latino; 10 Hispanic/Latino; 3 Two or more races, non-Hispanic/Latino), 10 international. Average age 31. 333 applicants, 47% accepted, 88 enrolled. In 2017, 57 master's, 9 other advanced degrees awarded. *Financial support:* Application deadline: 1/1.
Website: http://www.fels.upenn.edu/

University of Puerto Rico–Río Piedras, Graduate School of Planning, San Juan, PR 00931-3300. Offers economic planning systems (MP); environmental planning (MP); social policy and planning (MP); urban and territorial planning (MP). *Accreditation:* ACSP. *Program availability:* Part-time. *Degree requirements:* For master's, comprehensive exam, thesis, planning project defense. *Entrance requirements:* For master's, PAEG, GRE, minimum GPA of 3.0, 2 letters of recommendation. *Faculty research:* Municipalities, historic Atlas, Puerto Rico, economic future.

University of Southern California, Graduate School, Dana and David Dornsife College of Letters, Arts and Sciences, Department of Economics, Los Angeles, CA 90089. Offers economic development programming (MA, PhD); mathematical finance (MS); M Pl/MA; MA/JD. Terminal master's awarded for partial completion of doctoral program. *Degree requirements:* For master's, comprehensive exam; for doctorate, comprehensive exam, thesis/dissertation. *Entrance requirements:* For master's and doctorate, GRE. Additional exam requirements/recommendations for international students: Required—TOEFL (minimum score 93 iBT). Electronic applications accepted. *Faculty research:* Macro theory, development economics, econometrics.

University of Southern Mississippi, College of Business, Department of Economic Development, Tourism and Sport Management, Hattiesburg, MS 39406-0001. Offers economic development (MS); sport management (MS). *Program availability:* Part-time, evening/weekend. *Students:* 9 full-time (3 women). 15 applicants, 67% accepted, 9 enrolled. In 2017, 17 master's awarded. *Degree requirements:* For master's, comprehensive exam, thesis optional, internships. *Entrance requirements:* For master's, GMAT or GRE General Test, minimum GPA of 2.75 in last 60 hours. Additional exam requirements/recommendations for international students: Required—TOEFL, IELTS. *Application deadline:* For fall admission, 8/1 for domestic students, 3/1 for international students; for spring admission, 1/3 for domestic and international students. Applications are processed on a rolling basis. Application fee: $60. Electronic applications accepted. *Expenses:* Tuition, state resident: full-time $3830. *Financial support:* Research assistantships with full tuition reimbursements, teaching assistantships with full tuition reimbursements, career-related internships or fieldwork, Federal Work-Study, scholarships/grants, health care benefits, and unspecified assistantships available. Financial award application deadline: 3/1; financial award applicants required to submit FAFSA. *Faculty research:* Economic development, international studies, geography. *Unit head:* Dr. Stacey Hall, Chair, 601-266-6308, Fax: 601-266-6707. *Application contact:* Dr. Chad Miller, Program Coordinator, 601-266-6666, Fax: 601-266-6071.
Website: https://www.usm.edu/business/eco-dev-tourism-sport-management

University of Waterloo, Graduate Studies, Faculty of Environment, Program in Local Economic Development, Waterloo, ON N2L 3G1, Canada. Offers MAES. *Program availability:* Part-time. *Degree requirements:* For master's, internship, research paper. *Entrance requirements:* Additional exam requirements/recommendations for international students: Required—TOEFL, IELTS, PTE. Electronic applications accepted.

Vanderbilt University, Department of Economics, Nashville, TN 37240-1001. Offers economic development (MA); economics (PhD). *Faculty:* 31 full-time (4 women).

Students: 94 full-time (36 women), 2 part-time (1 woman); includes 10 minority (2 Black or African American, non-Hispanic/Latino; 2 Asian, non-Hispanic/Latino; 1 Hispanic/Latino; 5 Two or more races, non-Hispanic/Latino), 57 international. Average age 27. 621 applicants, 28% accepted, 37 enrolled. In 2017, 44 master's, 7 doctorates awarded. Terminal master's awarded for partial completion of doctoral program. *Degree requirements:* For master's, thesis or alternative; for doctorate, thesis/dissertation, final and qualifying exams. *Entrance requirements:* For master's and doctorate, GRE General Test, GRE Subject Test (recommended). Additional exam requirements/recommendations for international students: Required—TOEFL (minimum score 570 paper-based; 88 iBT). *Application deadline:* For fall admission, 1/15 for domestic and international students; for spring admission, 11/1 for domestic students. Applications are processed on a rolling basis. Electronic applications accepted. *Financial support:* Fellowships, teaching assistantships, career-related internships or fieldwork, Federal Work-Study, institutionally sponsored loans, scholarships/grants, and health care benefits available. Financial award application deadline: 1/15; financial award applicants required to submit CSS PROFILE or FAFSA. *Faculty research:* Economic theory, applied fields, developmental economics, environmental economics, health economics and policy. *Unit head:* Dr. Eric Bond, Chair, 615-322-2871, Fax: 615-343-8495, E-mail: k.saggi@vanderbilt.edu. *Application contact:* Jennifer Reinganum, Director of Graduate Studies, 615-322-2871, Fax: 615-343-8495, E-mail: jennifer.f.reinganum@vanderbilt.edu.
Website: http://www.vanderbilt.edu/econ/

Wayne State University, College of Liberal Arts and Sciences, Department of Political Science, Detroit, MI 48202. Offers political science (MA, PhD); public administration (MPA), including economic development policy and management, health and human services policy and management, human and fiscal resource management, nonprofit policy and management, organizational behavior and management, urban and metropolitan policy and management; JD/MA. *Accreditation:* NASPAA. *Faculty:* 18. *Students:* 48 full-time (20 women), 68 part-time (36 women); includes 37 minority (26 Black or African American, non-Hispanic/Latino; 3 Asian, non-Hispanic/Latino; 2 Hispanic/Latino; 6 Two or more races, non-Hispanic/Latino), 6 international. Average age 32. 105 applicants, 39% accepted, 20 enrolled. In 2017, 17 master's, 3 doctorates awarded. *Degree requirements:* For master's, comprehensive exam (for some programs), thesis (for some programs); for doctorate, thesis/dissertation. *Entrance requirements:* For master's, GRE General Test, substantial undergraduate preparation in the social sciences, minimum upper-division undergraduate GPA of 3.0, two letters of recommendation, personal statement; for doctorate, GRE General Test, 3 letters of recommendation, personal statement; interview. Additional exam requirements/recommendations for international students: Required—TOEFL (minimum score 550 paper-based; 79 iBT), TWE (minimum score 5.5), Michigan English Language Assessment Battery (minimum score 85); Recommended—IELTS (minimum score 6.5). *Application deadline:* For fall admission, 5/15 for domestic students, 5/1 priority date for international students; for winter admission, 10/15 for domestic students, 9/1 priority date for international students. Applications are processed on a rolling basis. Application fee: $50. Electronic applications accepted. *Expenses:* Contact institution. *Financial support:* In 2017–18, 44 students received support, including 6 fellowships with tuition reimbursements available (averaging $11,698 per year), 12 teaching assistantships with tuition reimbursements available (averaging $18,534 per year); research assistantships with tuition reimbursements available, scholarships/grants, health care benefits, and unspecified assistantships also available. Financial award applicants required to submit FAFSA. *Faculty research:* American government and politics, comparative politics, political methodology, political theory, public administration, public law, public policy, world politics/international relations, formal theory/modeling, gender and politics, international law, peace research, political economy, political psychology, politics of developing countries, race, religion, and ethnicity, urban politics. *Unit head:* Dr. Daniel Geller, Professor and Chair, 313-577-6328, E-mail: dgeller@wayne.edu. *Application contact:* Dr. Sharon Lean, Graduate Director, 313-577-2630, E-mail: gradpolisci@wayne.edu.
Website: http://clas.wayne.edu/politicalscience/

Wayne State University, College of Liberal Arts and Sciences, Department of Urban Studies and Planning, Detroit, MI 48202. Offers economic development (Graduate Certificate); urban studies and planning (MUP). *Accreditation:* ACSP. *Program availability:* Evening/weekend. *Students:* 12 full-time (9 women), 37 part-time (20 women); includes 21 minority (15 Black or African American, non-Hispanic/Latino; 1 American Indian or Alaska Native, non-Hispanic/Latino; 2 Hispanic/Latino; 3 Two or more races, non-Hispanic/Latino). Average age 30. 62 applicants, 47% accepted, 15 enrolled. In 2017, 16 master's awarded. *Degree requirements:* For master's, thesis or essay. *Entrance requirements:* For degree, graduate degree or actively pursuing a graduate degree at WSU; personal statement of interest. Additional exam requirements/recommendations for international students: Required—TOEFL (minimum score 550 paper-based; 79 iBT), TWE (minimum score 5.5), Michigan English Language Assessment Battery (minimum score 85); Recommended—IELTS (minimum score 6.5). *Application deadline:* For fall admission, 6/1 priority date for domestic students, 5/1 priority date for international students; for winter admission, 10/1 priority date for domestic students, 9/1 priority date for international students; for spring admission, 2/1 priority date for domestic students, 1/1 priority date for international students. Applications are processed on a rolling basis. Application fee: $50. Electronic applications accepted. *Expenses:* Tuition, state resident: full-time $10,224; part-time $638.98 per credit hour. Tuition, nonresident: full-time $22,145; part-time $1384.04 per credit hour. Tuition and fees vary according to course load and program. *Financial support:* In 2017–18, 14 students received support. Research assistantships, scholarships/grants, and unspecified assistantships available. Financial award applicants required to submit FAFSA. *Faculty research:* Community development, economic development, environmental planning, housing policy, land use planning and policy, local fiscal policy, local planning practices, neighborhood change, sustainable food systems. *Unit head:* Dr. Rayman Mohamed, Interim Chair, Associate Professor and Graduate Director, 313-577-3356, E-mail: rayman.mohamed@wayne.edu. *Application contact:* E-mail: dusp@wayne.edu.
Website: http://clas.wayne.edu/dusp/

Western Illinois University, School of Graduate Studies, Illinois Institute for Rural Affairs, Macomb, IL 61455-1390. Offers community and economic development (MA). *Students:* 9 full-time (7 women), 7 part-time (6 women); includes 3 minority (1 Black or African American, non-Hispanic/Latino; 2 Hispanic/Latino). Average age 37. 9 applicants, 89% accepted, 6 enrolled. *Application deadline:* Applications are processed on a rolling basis. Application fee: $30. Electronic applications accepted. *Unit head:* Dr. Christopher Merrett, Director, 309-298-2281, E-mail: cd-merrett@wiu.edu.
Website: http://www.iira.org

Williams College, Graduate Program in the History of Art, Williamstown, MA 01267. Offers development economics (MA); history of art (MA). MA in history of art offered jointly with Sterling and Francine Clark Art Institute. *Faculty:* 24. *Students:* 26 full-time (17 women); includes 7 minority (1 Black or African American, non-Hispanic/Latino; 1 American Indian or Alaska Native, non-Hispanic/Latino; 2 Asian, non-Hispanic/Latino; 3 Hispanic/Latino). 124 applicants, 16% accepted, 12 enrolled. In 2017, 12 master's awarded. *Degree requirements:* For master's, 2 foreign languages, symposium paper

and lecture. *Entrance requirements:* For master's, GRE General Test. Additional exam requirements/recommendations for international students: Required—TOEFL. *Application deadline:* For fall admission, 1/3 for domestic and international students. Application fee: $75. Electronic applications accepted. *Expenses: Tuition:* Full-time $53,240. *Financial support:* In 2017–18, 18 students received support. Fellowships with full and partial tuition reimbursements available and tuition waivers (full and partial) available. Financial award application deadline: 4/1; financial award applicants required

to submit FAFSA. *Application contact:* Karen E. Kowitz, Program Administrator, 413-458-0596, E-mail: kekowitz@williams.edu. Website: http://gradart.williams.edu

Yale University, Graduate School of Arts and Sciences, Department of Economics, Program in International and Development Economics, New Haven, CT 06520. Offers MA. *Entrance requirements:* For master's, GRE General Test.

Economics

Albany State University, College of Arts and Humanities, Albany, GA 31705-2717. Offers criminal justice (MS); English education (M Ed); public administration (MPA), including community and economic development, criminal justice administration, health administration and policy, human resources management, public management, public policy, water resources management and policy; social work (MSW). *Accreditation:* NASPAA. *Program availability:* Part-time. *Degree requirements:* For master's, comprehensive exam, professional portfolio (for MPA), internship, capstone report. *Entrance requirements:* For master's, GRE, MAT, minimum GPA of 3.0, official transcript, pre-medical record/certificate of immunization, letters of reference. Electronic applications accepted. *Faculty research:* HIV prevention for minority students.

American University, College of Arts and Sciences, Department of Economics, Washington, DC 20016-8029. Offers applied microeconomics (Certificate); economics (MA, PhD); gender analysis in economics (Certificate); international economic relations (Certificate); international economics (MA). *Program availability:* Part-time, evening/weekend, 100% online. *Faculty:* 27 full-time (7 women), 5 part-time/adjunct (2 women). *Students:* 107 full-time (52 women), 59 part-time (21 women); includes 28 minority (10 Black or African American, non-Hispanic/Latino; 1 American Indian or Alaska Native, non-Hispanic/Latino; 8 Asian, non-Hispanic/Latino; 7 Hispanic/Latino; 2 Two or more races, non-Hispanic/Latino), 55 international. Average age 32. 191 applicants, 85% accepted, 38 enrolled. In 2017, 37 master's, 9 doctorates, 1 other advanced degree awarded. Terminal master's awarded for partial completion of doctoral program. *Degree requirements:* For master's, comprehensive exam, thesis or alternative; for doctorate, comprehensive exam, thesis/dissertation. *Entrance requirements:* For master's and doctorate, GRE, statement of purpose, transcripts, 2 letters of recommendation, resume; for Certificate, bachelor's degree, statement of purpose, transcripts, resume. Additional exam requirements/recommendations for international students: Required—TOEFL (minimum score 600 paper-based; 100 iBT). *Application deadline:* For fall admission, 3/1 for domestic students; for spring admission, 11/1 for domestic students. Applications are processed on a rolling basis. Application fee: $55. Electronic applications accepted. *Expenses:* Contact institution. *Financial support:* Research assistantships, teaching assistantships, institutionally sponsored loans, and unspecified assistantships available. Financial award application deadline: 2/1; financial award applicants required to submit FAFSA. *Faculty research:* Political economy, development, labor, gender. *Unit head:* Dr. Mieke Meurs, Department Chair, 202-885-3776, E-mail: mmeurs@american.edu. *Application contact:* Jonathan Harper, Assistant Director, Graduate Recruitment, 202-855-3622, E-mail: jharper@american.edu. Website: http://www.american.edu/cas/economics/

American University, School of International Service, Washington, DC 20016-8071. Offers comparative and regional studies (Certificate); cross-cultural communication (Certificate); development management (MS); ethics, peace, and global affairs (MA); European studies (Certificate); global environmental policy (MA, Certificate); global information technology (Certificate); global media (MA); international affairs (MA), including comparative and regional studies, global governance, politics, and security, international economic relations, natural resources and sustainable development, U.S. foreign policy and national security; international arts management (Certificate); international communication (MA, Certificate); international development (MA); international economic policy (Certificate); international economic relations (Certificate); international economics (MA); international peace and conflict resolution (MA, Certificate); international politics (Certificate); international relations (MA, PhD); international service (MIS); peacebuilding (Certificate); social enterprise (MA); the Americas (Certificate); United States foreign policy (Certificate); JD/MA. *Program availability:* Part-time, evening/weekend, 100% online. *Faculty:* 112 full-time (50 women), 46 part-time/adjunct (19 women). *Students:* 495 full-time (333 women), 518 part-time (276 women); includes 360 minority (95 Black or African American, non-Hispanic/Latino; 2 American Indian or Alaska Native, non-Hispanic/Latino; 60 Asian, non-Hispanic/Latino; 164 Hispanic/Latino; 39 Two or more races, non-Hispanic/Latino), 98 international. Average age 30. 1,559 applicants, 81% accepted, 356 enrolled. In 2017, 427 master's, 9 doctorates, 5 other advanced degrees awarded. Terminal master's awarded for partial completion of doctoral program. *Degree requirements:* For master's, one foreign language, comprehensive exam, thesis or alternative; for doctorate, one foreign language, comprehensive exam, thesis/dissertation. *Entrance requirements:* For master's, GRE; GMAT or GRE (for MA in social enterprise), transcripts, resume, 2 letters of recommendation, statement of purpose; for doctorate, GRE, transcripts, resume, 3 letters of recommendation, statement of purpose. Additional exam requirements/recommendations for international students: Required—TOEFL (minimum score 600 paper-based; 100 iBT). *Application deadline:* For fall admission, 1/15 for domestic students, 1/1 for international students; for spring admission, 10/1 for domestic students, 9/15 for international students. Application fee: $55. Electronic applications accepted. *Expenses:* Contact institution. *Financial support:* Research assistantships, teaching assistantships, institutionally sponsored loans, scholarships/grants, and unspecified assistantships available. Financial award application deadline: 1/15; financial award applicants required to submit FAFSA. *Application contact:* 202-885-1646, Fax: 202-885-1109, E-mail: sisgrad@american.edu. Website: http://www.american.edu/sis/

The American University in Cairo, School of Business, Cairo, Egypt. Offers business administration (MBA); economics (MA); economics in international development (MA, Diploma); finance (MS). *Program availability:* Part-time, evening/weekend. *Faculty:* 30 full-time (10 women), 8 part-time/adjunct (3 women). *Students:* 49 full-time (25 women), 67 part-time (38 women), 5 international. Average age 29. 112 applicants, 35% accepted, 26 enrolled. In 2017, 51 master's awarded. *Degree requirements:* For master's, comprehensive exam (for some programs), thesis (for some programs). *Entrance requirements:* For master's, GMAT, GRE. Additional exam requirements/recommendations for international students: Required—TOEFL (minimum score 450 paper-based; 45 iBT), IELTS (minimum score 5). *Application deadline:* For fall admission, 2/1 priority date for domestic and international students; for spring admission, 10/15 priority date for domestic and international students. Applications are processed on a rolling basis. Application fee: $85. Electronic applications accepted.

Expenses: Contact institution. *Financial support:* Fellowships with partial tuition reimbursements, scholarships/grants, tuition waivers (partial), and unspecified assistantships available. Financial award application deadline: 3/10. *Faculty research:* Marketing and quality management, banking operations management, economics, finance. *Unit head:* Dr. Sherif Kamel, Dean, 20-2-2615-2118, E-mail: skamel@aucegypt.edu. *Application contact:* Maha Hegazi, Director of Graduate Admissions, 20-2-2615-1462, E-mail: mahahegazi@aucegypt.edu. Website: http://www.aucegypt.edu/Business/Pages/default.aspx

American University of Armenia, Graduate Programs, Yerevan, Armenia. Offers business administration (MBA); computer and information science (MS), including business management, design and manufacturing, energy (ME, MS), industrial engineering and systems management; economics (MS); industrial engineering and systems management (ME), including business, computer aided design/manufacturing, energy (ME, MS), information technology; law (LL M); political science and international affairs (MPSIA); public health (MPH); teaching English as a foreign language (MA). *Program availability:* Part-time, evening/weekend. *Degree requirements:* For master's, thesis (for some programs), capstone/project. *Entrance requirements:* For master's, GRE, GMAT, or LSAT. Additional exam requirements/recommendations for international students: Recommended—TOEFL (minimum score 79 iBT), IELTS (minimum score 6.5). *Faculty research:* Microfinance, finance (rural/development), international, corporate), firm life cycle theory, TESOL, language proficiency testing, public policy, administrative law, economic development, cryptography, artificial intelligence, energy efficiency/renewable energy, computer-aided design/manufacturing, health financing, tuberculosis control, mother/child health, preventive ophthalmology, post-earthquake psychopathological investigations, tobacco control, environmental health risk assessments.

American University of Beirut, Graduate Programs, Faculty of Arts and Sciences, 1107 2020, Lebanon. Offers anthropology (MA); Arab and Middle Eastern history (PhD); Arabic language and literature (MA, PhD); archaeology (MA); art history and curating (MA); biology (MS); cell and molecular biology (PhD); chemistry (MS); clinical psychology (MA); computational sciences (MS); computer science (MS); economics (MA); education (MA), including administration and policy studies, elementary education, mathematics education, psychology school guidance, psychology test and measurements, science education, teaching English as a foreign language; English language (MA); English literature (MA); environmental policy planning (MS); financial economics (MAFE); general psychology (MA); geology (MS); history (MA); Islamic studies (MA); mathematics (MS); media studies (MA); Middle East studies (MA); philosophy (MA); physics (MS); political studies (MA); public administration (MA); public policy and international affairs (MA); sociology (MA); theoretical physics (PhD). *Program availability:* Part-time. *Faculty:* 108 full-time (36 women), 5 part-time/adjunct (4 women). *Students:* 251 full-time (180 women), 233 part-time (172 women). Average age 26. 425 applicants, 65% accepted, 121 enrolled. In 2017, 47 master's, 2 doctorates awarded. *Degree requirements:* For master's, one foreign language, comprehensive exam, thesis (for some programs), project; for doctorate, one foreign language, comprehensive exam, thesis/dissertation. *Entrance requirements:* For master's, GRE General Test (for some programs); for doctorate, GRE General Test (GRE Subject Test for theoretical physics). Additional exam requirements/recommendations for international students: Required—TOEFL (minimum score 583 paper-based; 97 iBT), IELTS (minimum score 7). *Application deadline:* For fall admission, 2/8 for domestic students; for spring admission, 11/3 for domestic students. Application fee: $50. Electronic applications accepted. *Expenses:* Contact institution. *Financial support:* In 2017–18, 29 fellowships, 40 research assistantships were awarded; teaching assistantships, scholarships/grants, tuition waivers (full and partial), and unspecified assistantships also available. Financial award application deadline: 4/4. *Unit head:* Dr. Nadia Maria El Cheikh, Dean, Faculty of Arts and Sciences, 961-1-374374 Ext. 3800, Fax: 961-1-744461, E-mail: nmcheikh@aub.edu.lb. *Application contact:* Rima Rassi, Graduate Studies Officer, 961-1-350000 Ext. 3833, Fax: 961-1-744461, E-mail: rr46@aub.edu.lb. Website: http://www.aub.edu.lb/fas/pages/default.aspx

Andrews University, School of Graduate Studies, School of Business, Graduate Programs in Business, Berrien Springs, MI 49104. Offers MBA, MSA. *Faculty:* 8 full-time (3 women). *Students:* 23 full-time (13 women), 32 part-time (15 women); includes 21 minority (7 Black or African American, non-Hispanic/Latino; 6 Asian, non-Hispanic/Latino; 6 Hispanic/Latino; 2 Two or more races, non-Hispanic/Latino), 21 international. Average age 31. 83 applicants, 43% accepted, 28 enrolled. In 2017, 23 master's awarded. *Entrance requirements:* For master's, GMAT. Additional exam requirements/recommendations for international students: Required—TOEFL (minimum score 550 paper-based). Application fee: $40. *Unit head:* Dr. Leonard K. Gashugi, Chair, 769-471-3429, E-mail: gashugi@andrews.edu. *Application contact:* Justina Clayburn, Supervisor of Graduate Admission, 800-253-2874, Fax: 269-471-6321, E-mail: graduate@andrews.edu.

Arizona State University at the Tempe campus, W. P. Carey School of Business, Department of Economics, Tempe, AZ 85287-9801. Offers PhD. *Degree requirements:* For doctorate, comprehensive exam, thesis/dissertation, interactive Program of Study (iPOS) submitted before completing 50 percent of required credit hours. *Entrance requirements:* For doctorate, GRE, minimum GPA of 3.0 in last 2 years of work leading to bachelor's degree, 3 letters of recommendation, resume/curriculum vitae, letter of intent, thesis (if applicable), official university transcripts, personal statement. Additional exam requirements/recommendations for international students: Required—TOEFL (minimum score 550 paper-based; 80 iBT), IELTS (minimum score 6.5). Electronic applications accepted. *Faculty research:* Macroeconomics, general equilibrium, business cycles, monetary policy, environmental economics, applied econometrics, economic theory, game theory, procurement and auctions, industrial organization, labor economics, marketing, consumer choice behavior.

Assumption College, Business Studies Program, Worcester, MA 01609-1296. Offers accounting (MBA); business studies (CAGS); finance/economics (MBA); human resources (MBA); international business (MBA); management (MBA); marketing (MBA);

nonprofit leadership (MBA). *Program availability:* Part-time, evening/weekend. *Faculty:* 5 full-time (1 woman), 21 part-time/adjunct (6 women). *Students:* 29 full-time (13 women), 87 part-time (50 women); includes 15 minority (1 Black or African American, non-Hispanic/Latino; 4 Asian, non-Hispanic/Latino; 8 Hispanic/Latino; 2 Two or more races, non-Hispanic/Latino), 4 international. Average age 29. 34 applicants, 100% accepted, 26 enrolled. In 2017, 81 master's, 2 other advanced degrees awarded. *Degree requirements:* For master's, capstone. *Entrance requirements:* For master's, bachelor's degree, three letters of recommendation, official transcripts, personal statement, current resume; for CAGS, MBA or equivalent degree in a closely related field, three letters of recommendation, official transcripts, personal statement, current resume. Additional exam requirements/recommendations for international students: Required—TOEFL (minimum score 540 paper-based; 76 iBT), IELTS (minimum score 6). *Application deadline:* For fall admission, 8/10 priority date for domestic and international students; for spring admission, 1/4 priority date for domestic and international students; for summer admission, 5/10 priority date for domestic and international students. Application fee: $30. Electronic applications accepted. *Expenses:* Tuition: Full-time $11,952; part-time $664 per credit. *Required fees:* $70 per term. *Financial support:* In 2017–18, 19 students received support. Tuition waivers (full and partial), unspecified assistantships, and institutional discounts available. Financial award applicants required to submit FAFSA. *Faculty research:* Workplace diversity, dynamics of team interaction, utilization of leased employees, experiential learning project on due diligence market for prostheses. *Unit head:* Dr. Robin Frkal, Director, 508-767-7622, E-mail: ra.frkal@assumption.edu. *Application contact:* Karen Stoyanoff, Director of Recruitment for Graduate Enrollment, 508-767-7442, Fax: 508-799-4412, E-mail: graduate@assumption.edu.
Website: http://graduate.assumption.edu/mba/assumption-mba

Auburn University, Graduate School, College of Liberal Arts, Department of Economics, Auburn University, AL 36849. Offers applied economics (PhD); economics (MS). *Program availability:* Part-time. *Faculty:* 16 full-time (5 women), 3 part-time/adjunct (1 woman). *Students:* 14 full-time (6 women), 2 part-time (both women); includes 1 minority (Black or African American, non-Hispanic/Latino), 9 international. Average age 28. 33 applicants, 39% accepted, 6 enrolled. In 2017, 1 master's, 1 doctorate awarded. *Degree requirements:* For master's, thesis. *Entrance requirements:* For master's, GMAT, GRE General Test. Additional exam requirements/recommendations for international students: Required—TOEFL. *Application deadline:* Applications are processed on a rolling basis. Application fee: $50 ($60 for international students). Electronic applications accepted. *Expenses:* Tuition, state resident: full-time $10,974; part-time $519 per credit hour. Tuition, nonresident: full-time $29,658; part-time $1557 per credit hour. *Required fees:* $816 per semester. Tuition and fees vary according to degree level and program. *Financial support:* Teaching assistantships, career-related internships or fieldwork, and Federal Work-Study available. Support available to part-time students. Financial award application deadline: 3/15; financial award applicants required to submit FAFSA. *Unit head:* Dr. Michael Stern, Chair, 334-844-2982. *Application contact:* Dr. George Flowers, Dean of the Graduate School, 334-844-2125.
Website: http://www.cla.auburn.edu/economics/

Auburn University at Montgomery, College of Public Policy and Justice, Department of Economics, Montgomery, AL 36124-4023. Offers applied economics (MS). *Program availability:* Evening/weekend. *Faculty:* 8 full-time (0 women). *Students:* 15 full-time (9 women); includes 6 minority (5 Black or African American, non-Hispanic/Latino; 1 Asian, non-Hispanic/Latino), 4 international. Average age 31. 20 applicants, 95% accepted, 14 enrolled. *Entrance requirements:* For master's, GMAT or GRE General Test. Additional exam requirements/recommendations for international students: Recommended—TOEFL (minimum score 500 paper-based; 61 iBT), IELTS (minimum score 5.5), TSE (minimum score 44). *Application deadline:* For fall admission, 7/15 for international students; for spring admission, 11/15 for international students; for summer admission, 4/15 for international students. Applications are processed on a rolling basis. Application fee: $25. Electronic applications accepted. *Expenses:* Tuition, state resident: full-time $6930; part-time $385 per credit hour. Tuition, nonresident: full-time $15,588; part-time $866 per credit hour. *Required fees:* $640. *Financial support:* Applicants required to submit FAFSA. *Unit head:* Dr. Carel Ligeon, Head, 334-244-3486, E-mail: cligeon@aum.edu.
Website: http://www.cppj.aum.edu/departments/economics

Bard College, Levy Economics Institute, Annandale-on-Hudson, NY 12504. Offers economic theory and policy (MS).

Baruch College of the City University of New York, Zicklin School of Business, Department of Economics and Finance, Program in Economics, New York, NY 10010-5585. Offers MBA. *Program availability:* Part-time, evening/weekend. *Entrance requirements:* For master's, GMAT, 2 letters of recommendation, resume, 2 years of work experience. Additional exam requirements/recommendations for international students: Required—TOEFL (minimum score 590 paper-based), TWE (minimum score 5).

Baylor University, Graduate School, Hankamer School of Business, Department of Economics, Waco, TX 76798. Offers MS Eco. *Students:* 12 full-time (7 women), 1 part-time (0 women); includes 1 minority (Asian, non-Hispanic/Latino), 5 international. In 2017, 7 master's awarded. *Entrance requirements:* For master's, GMAT or GRE General Test. Additional exam requirements/recommendations for international students: Required—TOEFL (minimum score 600 paper-based; 100 iBT), IELTS (minimum score 7). Application fee: $25. Electronic applications accepted. *Financial support:* In 2017–18, 12 students received support. Research assistantships, Federal Work-Study, and institutionally sponsored loans available. Financial award application deadline: 3/1. *Faculty research:* Econometrics, international economics, economic development, comparative economic systems, computational economics, health economics, economics of education, monetary economics, labor economics, experimental economics. *Unit head:* Dr. Van Pham, Graduate Program Director, 254-710-3521, Fax: 254-710-6142, E-mail: van_pham@baylor.edu. *Application contact:* Susan Armstrong, Office Manager, 254-710-6177, Fax: 254-710-6142, E-mail: susan_armstrong@baylor.edu.
Website: http://www.baylor.edu/business/economics/

Binghamton University, State University of New York, Graduate School, Harpur College of Arts and Sciences, Department of Economics, Binghamton, NY 13902-6000. Offers MA, PhD. *Program availability:* Part-time. *Faculty:* 25 full-time (7 women). *Students:* 36 full-time (14 women), 26 part-time (14 women); includes 3 minority (1 Black or African American, non-Hispanic/Latino; 1 Asian, non-Hispanic/Latino; 1 Hispanic/Latino), 51 international. Average age 27. 125 applicants, 82% accepted, 25 enrolled. In 2017, 20 master's, 5 doctorates awarded. Terminal master's awarded for partial completion of doctoral program. *Degree requirements:* For doctorate, comprehensive exam, thesis/dissertation. *Entrance requirements:* For master's and doctorate, GRE General Test. Additional exam requirements/recommendations for international students: Required—TOEFL (minimum score 550 paper-based; 80 iBT). *Application deadline:* For fall admission, 2/1 priority date for domestic and international students. Application fee: $75. Electronic applications accepted. *Financial support:* In 2017–18, 31 students received support, including 1 research assistantship with full tuition reimbursement available (averaging $15,000 per year), 29 teaching assistantships with full tuition reimbursements available (averaging $15,000 per year); career-related internships or fieldwork, Federal Work-Study, institutionally sponsored loans, scholarships/grants, health care benefits, tuition waivers (full and partial), and unspecified assistantships also available. Financial award applicants required to submit FAFSA. *Unit head:* Andreas Pape, Director of Graduate Admissions, 607-777-2660, E-mail: apape@binghamton.edu. *Application contact:* Ben Balkaya, Assistant Dean and Director, 607-777-2151, Fax: 607-777-2501, E-mail: balkaya@binghamton.edu.

Boise State University, College of Business and Economics, Department of Economics, Boise, ID 83725-0399. Offers M Ec, MSE. *Expenses:* Tuition, state resident: full-time $6471; part-time $390 per credit. Tuition, nonresident: full-time $21,787; part-time $685 per credit. *Required fees:* $2283; $100 per term. Part-time tuition and fees vary according to course load and program.

Boston College, Graduate School of Arts and Sciences, Department of Economics, Chestnut Hill, MA 02467-3800. Offers PhD. *Degree requirements:* For doctorate, comprehensive exam, thesis/dissertation. *Entrance requirements:* For doctorate, GRE General Test, GRE Subject Test. Additional exam requirements/recommendations for international students: Required—TOEFL (minimum score 600 paper-based; 100 iBT), IELTS (minimum score 8). Electronic applications accepted. *Faculty research:* Economic theory, macroeconomics, microeconomics, econometrics, development economics, industrial organization, labor economics, international economics, public sector economics, monetary economics and finance, urban economics.

Boston University, Graduate School of Arts and Sciences, Department of Economics, Boston, MA 02215. Offers economic policy (MAEP); global development economics (MA); MBA/MA. *Students:* 280 full-time (108 women), 38 part-time (22 women); includes 13 minority (1 Black or African American, non-Hispanic/Latino; 9 Asian, non-Hispanic/Latino; 3 Hispanic/Latino), 261 international. Average age 24. 1,547 applicants, 47% accepted, 127 enrolled. In 2017, 122 master's awarded. Terminal master's awarded for partial completion of doctoral program. *Degree requirements:* For master's, comprehensive exam. *Entrance requirements:* For master's, GRE General Test, 2 letters of recommendation, transcripts, personal statement. Additional exam requirements/recommendations for international students: Required—TOEFL (minimum score 550 paper-based; 84 iBT). *Application deadline:* For fall admission, 1/5 for domestic and international students; for spring admission, 10/1 for domestic and international students. Application fee: $95. Electronic applications accepted. *Financial support:* In 2017–18, 143 students received support, including 25 fellowships with full tuition reimbursements available (averaging $22,000 per year), 38 research assistantships with full tuition reimbursements available (averaging $22,000 per year), 73 teaching assistantships with full tuition reimbursements available (averaging $22,000 per year); Federal Work-Study, scholarships/grants, and health care benefits also available. Financial award application deadline: 1/5. *Unit head:* Barton Lipman, Chair, 617-353-2995, Fax: 617-353-4449, E-mail: blipman@bu.edu. *Application contact:* Andrew Campolieto, PhD Program Administrator, 617-353-4454, Fax: 617-353-4449, E-mail: acamp@bu.edu.
Website: http://www.bu.edu/econ/

Bowling Green State University, Graduate College, College of Business, Program in Financial Economics, Bowling Green, OH 43403. Offers MA. *Program availability:* Part-time. *Degree requirements:* For master's, thesis or alternative. *Entrance requirements:* For master's, GRE General Test. Additional exam requirements/recommendations for international students: Required—TOEFL. Electronic applications accepted. *Faculty research:* Labor economics, monetary economics, economic education, mathematical economics.

Brandeis University, International Business School (IBS), Master of Arts in International Economics and Finance Program, Waltham, MA 02454-9110. Offers applied economic analysis (MA). *Faculty:* 40 full-time (16 women), 31 part-time/adjunct (7 women). *Students:* 158 full-time (96 women); includes 8 minority (1 American Indian or Alaska Native, non-Hispanic/Latino; 6 Asian, non-Hispanic/Latino; 1 Hispanic/Latino), 140 international. Average age 23. 649 applicants, 45% accepted, 92 enrolled. In 2017, 103 master's awarded. *Entrance requirements:* For master's, GMAT or GRE. Additional exam requirements/recommendations for international students: Required—TOEFL (minimum score 600 paper-based; 100 iBT), IELTS (minimum score 7), PTE (minimum score 68). *Application deadline:* For fall admission, 11/1 priority date for domestic and international students; for winter admission, 1/15 priority date for domestic and international students; for spring admission, 3/15 priority date for domestic and international students; for summer admission, 4/15 for domestic and international students. Application fee: $100. Electronic applications accepted. *Expenses:* Contact institution. *Financial support:* In 2017–18, 81 students received support. Institutionally sponsored loans and scholarships (averaging $18,384 annually) available. Financial award application deadline: 4/15; financial award applicants required to submit FAFSA. *Faculty research:* International economic policy analysis, macroeconomics, econometrics, business economics, economic development. *Unit head:* Peter Petri, Dean, 781-736-2256. *Application contact:* Kelly Sugrue, Assistant Dean of Admissions, 781-736-2252, Fax: 781-736-2263, E-mail: globaladmissions@brandeis.edu.
Website: http://www.brandeis.edu/global/ma

Brandeis University, International Business School (IBS), PhD in International Economics and Finance Program, Waltham, MA 02454-9110. Offers advanced macroeconomics (PhD); applied microeconomics (PhD). *Faculty:* 40 full-time (16 women), 31 part-time/adjunct (7 women). *Students:* 20 full-time (7 women); includes 2 minority (1 American Indian or Alaska Native, non-Hispanic/Latino; 1 Hispanic/Latino), 10 international. Average age 32. 107 applicants, 19% accepted, 7 enrolled. In 2017, 5 doctorates awarded. *Degree requirements:* For doctorate, thesis/dissertation. *Entrance requirements:* Additional exam requirements/recommendations for international students: Required—TOEFL (minimum score 600 paper-based; 100 iBT), IELTS (minimum score 7), PTE (minimum score 68). *Application deadline:* For winter admission, 1/15 priority date for domestic and international students. Application fee: $55. *Expenses:* Contact institution. *Financial support:* In 2017–18, 16 students received support, including research assistantships (averaging $6,000 per year), teaching assistantships (averaging $6,000 per year); scholarships/grants and health care benefits also available. Financial award application deadline: 1/15; financial award applicants required to submit FAFSA. *Faculty research:* Global business, global trade, global finance, macroeconomics, development and institutions. *Unit head:* Peter Petri, Interim Dean, 781-736-2256. *Application contact:* Kelly Sugrue, Assistant Dean of Admissions, 781-736-2252, Fax: 781-736-2263, E-mail: globaladmissions@brandeis.edu.
Website: https://www.brandeis.edu/global/academics/phd/

Brock University, Faculty of Graduate Studies, Faculty of Social Sciences, Program in Business Economics, St. Catharines, ON L2S 3A1, Canada. Offers MBE. *Degree requirements:* For master's, thesis or alternative. *Entrance requirements:* For master's, honours degree. Additional exam requirements/recommendations for international students: Required—TOEFL (minimum score 550 paper-based; 80 iBT), IELTS (minimum score 6.5), TWE (minimum score 4). Electronic applications accepted. *Faculty research:* Microeconomic theory, macroeconomics, econometrics, applied econometrics, economic development.

Economics

Brooklyn College of the City University of New York, School of Business, Brooklyn, NY 11210-2889. Offers accounting (MS); business administration (MS), including economic analysis, general business, global business and finance. *Program availability:* Part-time, evening/weekend. *Degree requirements:* For master's, comprehensive exam, thesis or alternative. *Entrance requirements:* For master's, GMAT, 2 letters of recommendation. Additional exam requirements/recommendations for international students: Required—TOEFL (minimum score 550 paper-based; 79 iBT). Electronic applications accepted. *Faculty research:* Econometrics, environmental economics, microeconomics, macroeconomics, taxation.

Brown University, Graduate School, Department of Economics, Providence, RI 02912. Offers PhD. Terminal master's awarded for partial completion of doctoral program. *Degree requirements:* For doctorate, thesis/dissertation. *Entrance requirements:* For doctorate, GRE General Test.

Buffalo State College, State University of New York, The Graduate School, Faculty of Natural and Social Sciences, Department of Economics and Finance, Buffalo, NY 14222-1095. Offers applied economics (MA). *Degree requirements:* For master's, project. *Entrance requirements:* Additional exam requirements/recommendations for international students: Required—TOEFL (minimum score 550 paper-based).

California Polytechnic State University, San Luis Obispo, Orfalea College of Business, Program in Economics, San Luis Obispo, CA 93407. Offers MS. *Students:* 16 full-time (3 women); includes 7 minority (1 Asian, non-Hispanic/Latino; 3 Hispanic/Latino; 3 Two or more races, non-Hispanic/Latino). Average age 23. In 2017, 16 master's awarded. *Degree requirements:* For master's, comprehensive exam (for some programs), thesis (for some programs). *Entrance requirements:* For master's, GMAT. Additional exam requirements/recommendations for international students: Required—TOEFL (minimum score 80 iBT). *Application deadline:* For fall admission, 4/1 for domestic students, 3/1 for international students. Applications are processed on a rolling basis. Application fee: $55. Electronic applications accepted. *Expenses:* Tuition, state resident: full-time $7176; part-time $4164 per year. *Required fees:* $3690; $3219 per year. $1073 per trimester. *Financial support:* Fellowships, career-related internships or fieldwork, Federal Work-Study, institutionally sponsored loans, scholarships/grants, and unspecified assistantships available. Support available to part-time students. Financial award application deadline: 3/2; financial award applicants required to submit FAFSA. *Faculty research:* Management of high-tech firms, Pacific Rim, capital market structures, economics of environmental policy, marketing of services. *Unit head:* Dr. Scott Dawson, Dean, 805-756-2705, E-mail: scdawson@calpoly.edu. *Application contact:* Dr. Sanjiv Jaggia, Associate Dean, Graduate Programs, 805-756-7519, E-mail: sjaggia@calpoly.edu.
Website: http://www.cob.calpoly.edu/gradbusiness/degree-programs/ms-economics/

California State Polytechnic University, Pomona, Program in Economics, Pomona, CA 91768-2557. Offers MS. *Program availability:* Part-time, evening/weekend. *Students:* 6 full-time (3 women), 36 part-time (15 women); includes 15 minority (2 Black or African American, non-Hispanic/Latino; 6 Asian, non-Hispanic/Latino; 5 Hispanic/Latino; 2 Two or more races, non-Hispanic/Latino), 21 international. Average age 29. 40 applicants, 80% accepted, 12 enrolled. In 2017, 8 master's awarded. *Entrance requirements:* Additional exam requirements/recommendations for international students: Required—TOEFL (minimum score 550 paper-based). *Application deadline:* Applications are processed on a rolling basis. Application fee: $55. Electronic applications accepted. *Expenses:* Contact institution. *Financial support:* Application deadline: 3/2; applicants required to submit FAFSA. *Unit head:* Dr. Carsten Lange, Professor/Graduate Coordinator, 909-869-3843, Fax: 909-869-6987, E-mail: clange@cpp.edu. *Application contact:* Deborah L. Brandon, Executive Director of Admissions and Enrollment Planning, 909-869-3427, Fax: 909-869-5315, E-mail: dlbrandon@cpp.edu.
Website: http://www.cpp.edu/~class/economics/graduate-students/

California State University, East Bay, Office of Graduate Studies, College of Business and Economics, Economics Department, Hayward, CA 94542-3000. Offers MA. *Program availability:* Part-time, evening/weekend. *Faculty:* 8 full-time (1 woman), 6 part-time/adjunct (0 women). *Students:* 9 full-time (4 women), 23 part-time (10 women); includes 13 minority (2 Black or African American, non-Hispanic/Latino; 5 Asian, non-Hispanic/Latino; 3 Hispanic/Latino; 3 Two or more races, non-Hispanic/Latino), 7 international. Average age 30. 34 applicants, 74% accepted, 15 enrolled. In 2017, 12 master's awarded. *Degree requirements:* For master's, comprehensive exam, project or thesis. *Entrance requirements:* For master's, GMAT, minimum GPA of 2.75 during previous 2 years of course work. Additional exam requirements/recommendations for international students: Required—TOEFL (minimum score 580 paper-based; 92 iBT). *Application deadline:* For fall admission, 6/1 for domestic and international students. Applications are processed on a rolling basis. Application fee: $55. Electronic applications accepted. *Financial support:* Career-related internships or fieldwork, Federal Work-Study, and institutionally sponsored loans available. Support available to part-time students. Financial award application deadline: 3/2; financial award applicants required to submit FAFSA. *Unit head:* Prof. Jed DeVaro, Chair, 510-885-3289, E-mail: jed.devaro@csueastbay.edu. *Application contact:* Christian Roessler, Graduate Program Director, 510-885-2858, E-mail: christian.roessler@csueastbay.edu.
Website: http://www20.csueastbay.edu/cbe/departments/economics/

California State University, Fullerton, Graduate Studies, College of Business and Economics, Department of Economics, Fullerton, CA 92831-3599. Offers MA, MBA. *Program availability:* Part-time. *Faculty:* 7 full-time (1 woman). *Students:* 22 full-time (9 women), 14 part-time (2 women); includes 15 minority (8 Asian, non-Hispanic/Latino; 7 Hispanic/Latino), 7 international. Average age 28. 29 applicants, 48% accepted, 9 enrolled. *Entrance requirements:* For master's, GMAT, GRE General Test. Application fee: $55. *Financial support:* Career-related internships or fieldwork, Federal Work-Study, institutionally sponsored loans, and scholarships/grants available. Support available to part-time students. Financial award application deadline: 3/1; financial award applicants required to submit FAFSA. *Faculty research:* Environmental and natural resource issues. *Unit head:* Dr. David Wong, Chair, 657-278-3821. *Application contact:* Admissions/Applications, 657-278-2371.

California State University, Long Beach, Graduate Studies, College of Liberal Arts, Department of Economics, Long Beach, CA 90840. Offers economics (MA). *Program availability:* Part-time. *Degree requirements:* For master's, comprehensive exam or thesis. *Entrance requirements:* For master's, GRE General Test, GRE Subject Test, minimum GPA of 3.0. Electronic applications accepted. *Faculty research:* Trade and development, economic forecasting, resource economics.

California State University, Los Angeles, Graduate Studies, College of Business and Economics, Department of Economics and Statistics, Los Angeles, CA 90032-8530. Offers financial economics (MA); global economics (MA). *Program availability:* Part-time, evening/weekend. *Degree requirements:* For master's, comprehensive exam or thesis. *Entrance requirements:* For master's, GMAT, minimum GPA of 2.5 during previous 2 years of course work. Additional exam requirements/recommendations for international students: Required—TOEFL (minimum score 550 paper-based). Electronic applications accepted.

California University of Management and Sciences, Graduate Programs, Anaheim, CA 92801. Offers business administration (MBA, DBA); computer information systems (MS); economics (MS); international business (MS); sports management (MS).

Campbellsville University, School of Business, Economics, and Technology, Campbellsville, KY 42718-2799. Offers business administration (MBA, Professional MBA); information technology management (MS); management (PhD); management and leadership (MML). *Program availability:* Part-time, evening/weekend, 100% online, blended/hybrid learning. *Faculty:* 20 full-time (4 women), 9 part-time/adjunct (3 women). *Students:* 74 full-time (16 women), 3,218 part-time (642 women); includes 28 minority (16 Black or African American, non-Hispanic/Latino; 9 Asian, non-Hispanic/Latino; 3 Hispanic/Latino), 3,164 international. Average age 27. 3,261 applicants, 95% accepted, 2220 enrolled. In 2017, 89 master's awarded. *Degree requirements:* For master's, comprehensive exam (for some programs), thesis optional; for doctorate, comprehensive exam, thesis/dissertation. *Entrance requirements:* For master's, GRE or GMAT, letters of recommendation, college transcripts; for doctorate, GMAT, resume, official transcripts, references, personal essay, interview, completion of course in statistics and research methods. Additional exam requirements/recommendations for international students: Required—TOEFL (minimum score 550 paper-based; 79 iBT); Recommended—IELTS (minimum score 6). *Application deadline:* Applications are processed on a rolling basis. Application fee: $25. Electronic applications accepted. Application fee is waived when completed online. *Expenses:* $479 per credit hour (for MBA and MML); $525 per credit hour (for MSITM and PMBA); $620 per credit hour (for PhD). *Financial support:* In 2017–18, 7 students received support. Unspecified assistantships and employee tuition waivers available. Financial award application deadline: 6/1; financial award applicants required to submit FAFSA. *Unit head:* Dr. Patricia H. Cowherd, Dean, 270-789-5553, Fax: 270-789-5066, E-mail: phcowherd@campbellsville.edu. *Application contact:* Monica Bamwine, Assistant Director of Graduate Admissions, 270-789-5221, Fax: 270-789-5071, E-mail: mkbamwine@campbellsville.edu.
Website: http://www.campbellsville.edu

Carleton University, Faculty of Graduate Studies, Faculty of Public Affairs and Management, Department of Economics, Ottawa, ON K1S 5B6, Canada. Offers MA, PhD. PhD program offered jointly with University of Ottawa. *Degree requirements:* For master's, thesis optional; for doctorate, comprehensive exam, thesis/dissertation. *Entrance requirements:* For master's, honors degree; for doctorate, master's degree. Additional exam requirements/recommendations for international students: Required—TOEFL. *Faculty research:* Monetary economics, economic development, public economics, industrial organization, international trade.

Carleton University, Faculty of Graduate Studies, Faculty of Public Affairs and Management, Institute of Political Economy, Ottawa, ON K1S 5B6, Canada. Offers MA, PhD. *Degree requirements:* For master's, thesis optional. *Entrance requirements:* For master's, honors degree. Additional exam requirements/recommendations for international students: Required—TOEFL. *Faculty research:* Relationships between economy and politics as they affect the political, social and cultural life of societies; historical processes whereby social change is located in the interaction of the economic, political and cultural, and ideological moments of social life.

Carnegie Mellon University, Tepper School of Business, Program in Economics, Pittsburgh, PA 15213-3891. Offers PhD. *Degree requirements:* For doctorate, thesis/dissertation. *Entrance requirements:* For doctorate, GMAT, GRE General Test. *Faculty research:* Research allocation under asymmetric information, monetary theory, estimation of rational expectations models.

Central European University, Department of Economics, 1051, Hungary. Offers business administration (PhD); business analytics (M Sc); economic policy in global markets (MA); economics (MA, PhD); finance (MS); global economic relations (MA); technology management and innovation (MS). *Program availability:* Part-time. *Faculty:* 23 full-time (2 women), 25 part-time/adjunct (4 women). *Students:* 177 full-time (77 women), 125 part-time (39 women). Average age 31. 530 applicants, 49% accepted, 144 enrolled. In 2017, 150 master's, 6 doctorates awarded. *Degree requirements:* For master's, one foreign language, thesis; for doctorate, one foreign language, comprehensive exam, thesis/dissertation. *Entrance requirements:* For master's and doctorate, interview. Additional exam requirements/recommendations for international students: Required—TOEFL (minimum score 570 paper-based); Recommended—IELTS (minimum score 6.5). *Application deadline:* For fall admission, 2/4 for domestic and international students. Application fee: $30. Electronic applications accepted. *Expenses: Tuition:* Full-time 12,000 euros. *Required fees:* 230 euros. One-time fee: 30 euros full-time. Tuition and fees vary according to course level, course load, degree level and program. *Financial support:* Fellowships, teaching assistantships, career-related internships or fieldwork, institutionally sponsored loans, scholarships/grants, health care benefits, and tuition waivers (full and partial) available. *Faculty research:* Economic theory (microeconomics and macroeconomics) and econometrics, as well as study of many applied fields, including labor economics, health economics and economics of education, industrial organization, monetary economics, international economics, law and economics, comparative institutional economics, corporate governance, and economics of transition. *Unit head:* Miklos Koren, Head of Department, 36 1 327-3000 Ext. 2212, E-mail: econbusi@ceu.edu. *Application contact:* Zsuzsanna Jaszberenyi, Admissions Officer, 361-324-3009, Fax: 367-327-3211, E-mail: admissions@ceu.edu.
Website: http://economics.ceu.edu/

Central Michigan University, College of Graduate Studies, College of Business Administration, Department of Economics, Mount Pleasant, MI 48859. Offers MA. *Program availability:* Part-time. *Degree requirements:* For master's, thesis or alternative. Electronic applications accepted. *Faculty research:* Economic development, industrial organization, international trade, monetary theory, public choice/labor.

City College of the City University of New York, Graduate School, Colin Powell School for Civic and Global Leadership, Department of Economics and Business, New York, NY 10031-9198. Offers economics (MA). *Program availability:* Part-time. *Degree requirements:* For master's, comprehensive exam, proficiency in a foreign language or advanced statistics. *Entrance requirements:* Additional exam requirements/recommendations for international students: Required—TOEFL (minimum score 550 paper-based; 79 iBT). Electronic applications accepted. *Faculty research:* International economics, health, banking.

Claremont Graduate University, Graduate Programs, School of Social Science, Policy and Evaluation, Department of Economics, Claremont, CA 91711-6160. Offers behavioral economics and neuroeconomics (PhD); business and financial economics (MA, PhD); economic development (Certificate); international economic and development policy (PhD); international economics policy and development (MA); international money and finance (PhD); political economy and public economics (PhD); political economy and public policy (MA); MBA/PhD. *Program availability:* Part-time. *Entrance requirements:* For master's and doctorate, GRE General Test or GMAT. Additional exam requirements/recommendations for international students: Required—TOEFL (minimum score 75 iBT). Electronic applications accepted. *Faculty research:* International and financial economics, law and economics, regulation, public choice economics.

Claremont Graduate University, Graduate Programs, School of Social Science, Policy and Evaluation, Department of Politics and Policy, Claremont, CA 91711-6160. Offers American politics (MA, PhD); comparative politics (PhD); international political economy (MA); international studies (MA); political philosophy (PhD); political science (PhD); politics, economics and business (MA); public policy (MA, PhD); world politics (PhD); MBA/PhD. *Program availability:* Part-time. Terminal master's awarded for partial completion of doctoral program. *Entrance requirements:* For master's and doctorate, GRE General Test. Additional exam requirements/recommendations for international students: Required—TOEFL (minimum score 75 iBT). Electronic applications accepted. *Faculty research:* Environmental policy, international debt, global democratization, Third World development, public sector discrimination.

Claremont Graduate University, Graduate Programs, School of Social Science, Policy and Evaluation, Program in Politics, Economics, and Business, Claremont, CA 91711-6160. Offers MA. *Program availability:* Part-time. *Entrance requirements:* For master's, GRE General Test. Additional exam requirements/recommendations for international students: Required—TOEFL (minimum score 75 iBT). Electronic applications accepted.

Clark Atlanta University, School of Business Administration, Department of Economics, Atlanta, GA 30314. Offers MA. *Program availability:* Part-time. *Faculty:* 9 full-time (1 woman). *Students:* 2 part-time (both women), both international. Average age 27. 1 applicant. *Degree requirements:* For master's, thesis optional. *Entrance requirements:* For master's, GRE General Test, minimum GPA of 2.5. Additional exam requirements/recommendations for international students: Required—TOEFL (minimum score 500 paper-based; 61 iBT). *Application deadline:* For fall admission, 4/1 for domestic and international students; for spring admission, 11/1 for domestic and international students. Applications are processed on a rolling basis. Application fee: $40 ($55 for international students). Electronic applications accepted. *Financial support:* Career-related internships or fieldwork, Federal Work-Study, scholarships/grants, and unspecified assistantships available. Support available to part-time students. Financial award application deadline: 4/30; financial award applicants required to submit FAFSA. *Faculty research:* Minority energy demand. *Unit head:* Dr. Young Kim, Chairperson, 404-880-8450, E-mail: ykim@cau.edu.

Clark University, Graduate School, Department of Economics, Worcester, MA 01610-1477. Offers PhD. *Faculty:* 11 full-time (3 women), 1 (woman) part-time/adjunct. *Students:* 44 full-time (26 women); includes 2 minority (1 Asian, non-Hispanic/Latino; 1 Hispanic/Latino), 30 international. Average age 30. 49 applicants, 43% accepted, 9 enrolled. In 2017, 5 doctorates awarded. *Degree requirements:* For doctorate, thesis/dissertation. *Entrance requirements:* For doctorate, GRE General Test. Additional exam requirements/recommendations for international students: Required—TOEFL (minimum score 575 paper-based; 90 iBT), IELTS (minimum score 6.5). *Application deadline:* For fall admission, 2/1 priority date for domestic students. Application fee: $75. Electronic applications accepted. *Financial support:* Fellowships, research assistantships, teaching assistantships, career-related internships or fieldwork, institutionally sponsored loans, and tuition waivers (full and partial) available. *Faculty research:* Public finance, economic development, industrial organization, international finance and trade, environmental regulation. *Unit head:* Dr. Jacqueline Geoghegan, Chair, 508-793-7709, E-mail: jgeoghegan@clarku.edu. *Application contact:* Cindy Rice, Managerial Secretary, 508-793-7226, Fax: 508-793-8849, E-mail: crice@clarku.edu. Website: http://www.clarku.edu/departments/economics/

Clemson University, Graduate School, College of Business, John E. Walker Department of Economics, Clemson, SC 29634. Offers applied economics (PhD); applied economics and statistics (MS); economics (MA, PhD). *Faculty:* 29 full-time (3 women), 3 part-time/adjunct (1 woman). *Students:* 148 full-time (50 women), 8 part-time (4 women); includes 10 minority (4 Black or African American, non-Hispanic/Latino; 2 Hispanic/Latino; 4 Two or more races, non-Hispanic/Latino), 92 international. Average age 28. 148 applicants, 49% accepted, 14 enrolled. In 2017, 20 master's, 23 doctorates awarded. Terminal master's awarded for partial completion of doctoral program. *Degree requirements:* For master's, thesis, 24 course hours, 6 thesis hours; for doctorate, comprehensive exam, thesis/dissertation, 42 course hours, 18 dissertation hours. *Entrance requirements:* For master's and doctorate, GRE General Test or GMAT, unofficial transcripts, letters of recommendation, courses in intermediate microeconomic theory and multivariable calculus. Additional exam requirements/recommendations for international students: Required—TOEFL (minimum score 80 iBT), IELTS (minimum score 6.5), PTE (minimum score 54). *Application deadline:* For fall admission, 1/15 priority date for domestic and international students. Applications are processed on a rolling basis. Application fee: $80 ($90 for international students). Electronic applications accepted. *Expenses:* $5,174 per semester full-time resident, $9,714 per semester full-time non-resident, $511 per credit hour part-time resident, $1,017 per credit hour part-time non-resident; $741 per credit hour online; other fees may apply per session. *Financial support:* In 2017–18, 66 students received support, including 16 fellowships with partial tuition reimbursements available (averaging $8,813 per year), 13 teaching assistantships with partial tuition reimbursements available (averaging $12,728 per year); unspecified assistantships also available. Financial award application deadline: 1/15. *Faculty research:* Public economics, public choice and political economy; econometrics (focus on data envelope analysis), industrial organization (focus on pricing), labor and development economics, international economics (focus on free trade agreements). *Total annual research expenditures:* $20,956. *Unit head:* Dr. Scott Baier, Department Chair, 864-656-4534, E-mail: sbaier@clemson.edu. *Application contact:* Dr. Curtis Simon, PhD Program Coordinator, 864-656-3966, E-mail: cjsmn@clemson.edu. Website: http://economics.clemson.edu/

Cleveland State University, College of Graduate Studies, College of Liberal Arts and Social Sciences, Department of Economics, Cleveland, OH 44115. Offers MA. *Program availability:* Part-time, evening/weekend. *Faculty:* 6 full-time (1 woman). *Students:* 6 full-time (2 women), 4 part-time (0 women); includes 3 minority (1 Black or African American, non-Hispanic/Latino; 1 Hispanic/Latino; 1 Two or more races, non-Hispanic/Latino), 1 international. Average age 24. 32 applicants, 72% accepted, 7 enrolled. In 2017, 12 master's awarded. *Entrance requirements:* For master's, minimum GPA of 2.75; coursework in micro theory, macro theory, statistics, and calculus. Additional exam requirements/recommendations for international students: Required—TOEFL (minimum score 550 paper-based; 78 iBT), IELTS (minimum score 6). *Application deadline:* For fall admission, 7/1 priority date for domestic students, 5/15 priority date for international students; for spring admission, 11/15 for domestic students, 11/1 for international students; for summer admission, 4/1 for domestic students, 3/15 for international students. Applications are processed on a rolling basis. Application fee: $40. Electronic applications accepted. *Financial support:* In 2017–18, 4 students received support, including 3 teaching assistantships (averaging $6,960 per year). Financial award application deadline: 4/30; financial award applicants required to submit FAFSA. *Faculty research:* Health economics, monetary economics, computational economics, urban economics, financial economics. *Unit head:* Dr. Billy Kosteas, Department Chairperson/Associate Professor, 216-687-4526, Fax: 216-687-9206, E-mail: b.kosteas@csuohio.edu. *Application contact:* Dr. Myong Hun Chang, Professor, 216-687-4523, Fax: 216-687-9206, E-mail: m.chang@csuohio.edu. Website: http://www.csuohio.edu/class/economics/economics

Cleveland State University, College of Graduate Studies, Maxine Goodman Levin College of Urban Affairs, Program in Urban Planning and Development, Cleveland, OH

44115. Offers economic development (MUPD); environmental sustainability (MUPD); historic preservation (MUPD); housing and neighborhood development (MUPD); real estate development and finance (MUPD); urban economic development (Certificate); urban geographic information systems (MUPD); JD/MUPDD. *Accreditation:* ACSP. *Program availability:* Part-time, evening/weekend. *Faculty:* 16 full-time (8 women), 13 part-time/adjunct (5 women). *Students:* 20 full-time (7 women), 15 part-time (5 women); includes 1 minority (Black or African American, non-Hispanic/Latino), 2 international. Average age 28. 48 applicants, 56% accepted, 14 enrolled. In 2017, 24 master's awarded. *Degree requirements:* For master's, thesis or alternative, exit project. *Entrance requirements:* For master's, GRE General Test (minimum score: 50th percentile combined verbal and quantitative, 4.0 analytical writing), minimum GPA of 3.0. Additional exam requirements/recommendations for international students: Required—TOEFL (minimum score 550 paper-based; 78 iBT), IELTS (6.0), or International Test of English Proficiency (iTEP). *Application deadline:* For fall admission, 7/1 priority date for domestic students, 5/15 for international students; for spring admission, 11/15 for domestic students, 11/1 for international students; for summer admission, 4/1 for domestic students, 3/15 for international students. Applications are processed on a rolling basis. Application fee: $40. Electronic applications accepted. *Expenses:* Contact institution. *Financial support:* In 2017–18, 10 students received support, including 5 research assistantships with full tuition reimbursements available (averaging $7,200 per year), 3 teaching assistantships with partial tuition reimbursements available (averaging $2,400 per year); scholarships/grants, tuition waivers (full and partial), and unspecified assistantships also available. Support available to part-time students. Financial award application deadline: 3/1; financial award applicants required to submit FAFSA. *Faculty research:* Housing and neighborhood development, urban housing policy, environmental sustainability, economic development, GIS and planning decision support. *Unit head:* Dr. Stephanie Ryberg-Webster, Assistant Professor/Program Director, 216-802-3386, Fax: 216-687-2013, E-mail: s.ryberg@csuohio.edu. *Application contact:* David Arrighi, Graduate Academic Advisor, 216-523-7522, Fax: 216-687-5398, E-mail: d.arrighi@csuohio.edu. Website: http://www.csuohio.edu/urban/mupd/mupd

Colorado State University, College of Liberal Arts, Department of Economics, Fort Collins, CO 80523-1771. Offers MA, PhD. *Faculty:* 6 full-time (0 women), 2 part-time/adjunct (0 women). *Students:* 29 full-time (9 women), 40 part-time (13 women); includes 10 minority (3 Black or African American, non-Hispanic/Latino; 2 Asian, non-Hispanic/Latino; 3 Hispanic/Latino; 1 Native Hawaiian or other Pacific Islander, non-Hispanic/Latino; 1 Two or more races, non-Hispanic/Latino), 22 international. Average age 31. 100 applicants, 70% accepted, 17 enrolled. In 2017, 6 master's, 3 doctorates awarded. Terminal master's awarded for partial completion of doctoral program. *Degree requirements:* For master's, thesis, minimum GPA of 3.0; for doctorate, comprehensive exam, thesis/dissertation, minimum GPA of 3.0. *Entrance requirements:* For master's and doctorate, GRE, coursework in intermediate micro, intermediate macro, and calculus; minimum GPA of 3.3. Additional exam requirements/recommendations for international students: Required—TOEFL (minimum score 550 paper-based; 80 iBT), IELTS (minimum score 6.5). *Application deadline:* For fall admission, 2/15 priority date for domestic students, 4/1 for international students. Application fee: $60 ($70 for international students). Electronic applications accepted. *Expenses:* Tuition, state resident: full-time $9917. Tuition, nonresident: full-time $24,312. *Required fees:* $2284. Tuition and fees vary according to course load and program. *Financial support:* In 2017–18, 20 students received support, including 1 research assistantship with full tuition reimbursement available (averaging $14,256 per year), 19 teaching assistantships with full tuition reimbursements available (averaging $16,911 per year); health care benefits also available. Financial award application deadline: 2/15. *Faculty research:* Development economics, environmental economics, international economics, regional economics, political economy, public economics. *Total annual research expenditures:* $225,136. *Unit head:* Dr. Anita Pena, Associate Professor/Department Chair, E-mail: anita.pena@colostate.edu. Website: http://economics.colostate.edu/

Columbia University, Graduate School of Arts and Sciences, New York, NY 10027. Offers African-American studies (MA); American studies (MA); anthropology (MA, PhD); art history and archaeology (MA, PhD); astronomy (PhD); biological sciences (PhD); biotechnology (MA); chemical physics (PhD); chemistry (PhD); classical studies (MA, PhD); classics (MA, PhD); climate and society (MA); conservation biology (MA); earth and environmental sciences (PhD); East Asia: regional studies (MA); East Asian languages and cultures (MA, PhD); ecology, evolution and environmental biology (MA), including conservation biology; ecology, evolution, and environmental biology (PhD), including ecology and evolutionary biology, evolutionary primatology; economics (MA, PhD); English and comparative literature (MA, PhD); French and Romance philology (MA, PhD); Germanic languages (MA, PhD); global French studies (MA); global thought (MA); Hispanic cultural studies (MA); history (PhD); history and literature (MA); human rights studies (MA); Islamic studies (MA); Italian (MA, PhD); Japanese pedagogy (MA); Jewish studies (MA); Latin America and the Caribbean: regional studies (MA); Latin American and Iberian cultures (PhD); mathematics (MA, PhD), including finance (MA); medieval and Renaissance studies (MA); Middle Eastern, South Asian, and African studies (MA, PhD); modern art: critical and curatorial studies (MA); modern European studies (MA); museum anthropology (MA); music (DMA, PhD); oral history (MA); philosophical foundations of physics (MA); philosophy (MA, PhD); physics (PhD); political science (MA, PhD); psychology (PhD); quantitative methods in the social sciences (MA); religion (MA, PhD); Russia, Eurasia and East Europe: regional studies (MA); Russian translation (MA); Slavic cultures (MA); Slavic languages (MA, PhD); sociology (MA, PhD); South Asian studies (MA); statistics (MA, PhD); theatre (PhD). Dual-degree programs require admission to both Graduate School of Arts and Sciences and another Columbia school. *Program availability:* Part-time. Terminal master's awarded for partial completion of doctoral program. *Degree requirements:* For master's, variable foreign language requirement, comprehensive exam (for some programs), thesis (for some programs); for doctorate, variable foreign language requirement, comprehensive exam (for some programs), thesis/dissertation. *Entrance requirements:* For master's and doctorate, GRE General Test, GRE Subject Test (for some programs). Additional exam requirements/recommendations for international students: Required—TOEFL, IELTS. Electronic applications accepted. *Expenses:* Tuition: Full-time $44,864; part-time $1704 per credit. *Required fees:* $2370 per semester. One-time fee: $105.

Columbia University, Graduate School of Business, Doctoral Program in Business, New York, NY 10027. Offers business (PhD), including accounting, decision, risk, and operations, finance and economics, management, marketing. *Accreditation:* AACSB. *Degree requirements:* For doctorate, comprehensive exam, thesis/dissertation, major field exam, research paper, thesis proposal. *Entrance requirements:* For doctorate, GMAT or GRE (finance), 2 letters of reference, resume. Additional exam requirements/recommendations for international students: Required—TOEFL. Electronic applications accepted. *Expenses:* Contact institution. *Faculty research:* Human decision making and behavioral research; real estate market and mortgage defaults; financial crisis and corporate governance; international business; security analysis and accounting.

Columbia University, Graduate School of Business, MBA Program, New York, NY 10027. Offers accounting (MBA); decision, risk, and operations (MBA); entrepreneurship (MBA); finance and economics (MBA); healthcare and pharmaceutical management

(MBA); human resource management (MBA); international business (MBA); leadership and ethics (MBA); management (MBA); marketing (MBA); media (MBA); private equity (MBA); real estate (MBA); social enterprise (MBA); value investing (MBA); DDS/MBA; JD/MBA; MBA/MIA; MBA/MPH; MBA/MS; MD/MBA. *Entrance requirements:* For master's, GMAT, 2 letters of recommendation. Additional exam requirements/recommendations for international students: Required—TOEFL. Electronic applications accepted. *Expenses:* Contact institution. *Faculty research:* Human decision making and behavioral research; real estate market and mortgage defaults; financial crisis and corporate governance; international business; security analysis and accounting.

Concordia University, School of Graduate Studies, Faculty of Arts and Science, Department of Economics, Montréal, QC H3G 1M8, Canada. Offers MA, PhD, Diploma. *Degree requirements:* For master's, thesis or alternative, research paper; for doctorate, one foreign language, comprehensive exam, thesis/dissertation, research seminar. *Entrance requirements:* For master's and doctorate, honors degree in economics or equivalent. *Faculty research:* Trade and industrial adjustment, tax policy and reform, environmental policy, economics of migration, economics of telecommunications.

Copenhagen Business School, Graduate Programs, Copenhagen, Denmark. Offers business administration (Exec MBA, MBA, PhD); business administration and information systems (M Sc); business, language and culture (M Sc); economics and business administration (M Sc); health management (MHM); international business and politics (M Sc); public administration (MPA); shipping and logistics (Exec MBA); technology, market and organization (MBA).

Cornell University, Graduate School, Graduate Fields of Architecture, Art and Planning, Field of Regional Science, Ithaca, NY 14853. Offers environmental studies (MA, MS, PhD); international spatial problems (MA, MS, PhD); location theory (MA, MS, PhD); multiregional economic analysis (MA, MS, PhD); peace science (MA, MS, PhD); planning methods (MA, MS, PhD); urban and regional economics (MA, MS, PhD). Terminal master's awarded for partial completion of doctoral program. *Degree requirements:* For master's, thesis; for doctorate, comprehensive exam, thesis/dissertation. *Entrance requirements:* For master's and doctorate, GRE General Test, 2 letters of recommendation. Additional exam requirements/recommendations for international students: Required—TOEFL (minimum score 600 paper-based; 77 iBT). Electronic applications accepted. *Faculty research:* Urban and regional growth, spatial economics, formation of spatial patterns by socioeconomic systems, non-linear dynamics and complex systems, environmental-economic systems.

Cornell University, Graduate School, Graduate Fields of Arts and Sciences, Field of Economics, Ithaca, NY 14853. Offers applied economics (PhD); basic analytical economics (PhD); econometrics and economic statistics (PhD); economic development and planning (PhD); economic theory (PhD); industrial organization and control (PhD); international economics (PhD); labor economics (PhD); monetary and macro economics (PhD); public finance (PhD). *Degree requirements:* For doctorate, comprehensive exam, thesis/dissertation. *Entrance requirements:* For doctorate, GRE General Test, 3 letters of recommendation. Additional exam requirements/recommendations for international students: Required—TOEFL (minimum score 550 paper-based; 77 iBT). Electronic applications accepted. *Faculty research:* Learning and games, economics of education, political economy, transfer payments, time series and nonparametrics.

Dalhousie University, Faculty of Science, Department of Economics, Halifax, NS B3H 4R2, Canada. Offers MA, MDE, PhD. *Degree requirements:* For master's, thesis; for doctorate, thesis/dissertation. *Entrance requirements:* For master's and doctorate, GRE (recommended). Additional exam requirements/recommendations for international students: Required—TOEFL, IELTS, CANTEST, CAEL, or Michigan English Language Assessment Battery. Electronic applications accepted. *Faculty research:* Applied econometrics, industrial organization, labor and income distribution, economic theory (micro and macro), resource economics (fishing, forestry).

DePaul University, College of Liberal Arts and Social Sciences, Chicago, IL 60614. Offers Arabic (MA); Chinese (MA); critical ethnic studies (MA); English (MA); French (MA); German (MA); history (MA); interdisciplinary studies (MA, MS); international public service (MS); international studies (MA); Italian (MA); Japanese (MA); liberal studies (MA); nonprofit management (MNM); public administration (MPA); public health (MPH); public policy (MPP); public service management (MS); refugee and forced migration studies (MS); social work (MSW); sociology (MA); Spanish (MA); sustainable urban development (MA); women's and gender studies (MA); writing and publishing (MA); writing, rhetoric and discourse (MA); MA/PhD. *Program availability:* Part-time, evening/weekend, online learning. Terminal master's awarded for partial completion of doctoral program. *Degree requirements:* For master's, variable foreign language requirement, comprehensive exam (for some programs), thesis (for some programs). *Application deadline:* Applications are processed on a rolling basis. Application fee: $40. Electronic applications accepted. *Financial support:* Applicants required to submit FAFSA. *Unit head:* Dr. Guillermo Vasquez de Velasco, Dean, 773-325-7305. *Application contact:* Ann Spittle, Director of Graduate Admission, 773-325-8369, Fax: 312-476-3244, E-mail: graddepaul@depaul.edu.
Website: http://las.depaul.edu/

DePaul University, Kellstadt Graduate School of Business, Chicago, IL 60604. Offers accountancy (MBA, MSA); applied economics (MBA); audit and advisory services (MS); business administration (DBA); business analytics (MS); business strategy and decision-making (MBA); computational finance (MS); economics and policy analysis (MS); enterprise risk management (MS); entrepreneurship (MBA, MS); finance (MBA, MS); general business (MBA); hospitality leadership (MBA); hospitality leadership and operational performance (MS); human resources (MS); international business (MBA); management (MBA, MS); management information systems (MBA); marketing (MBA, MS); marketing analysis (MS); marketing strategy and planning (MBA); real estate (MS); real estate finance and investment (MBA); strategy, execution and valuation (MBA); supply chain management (MS); sustainable management (MS); taxation (MS); JD/MBA. *Accreditation:* AACSB. *Program availability:* Part-time, evening/weekend, online learning. *Entrance requirements:* For master's, GMAT/GRE, 2 letters of recommendation, resume, essay, official transcripts. Additional exam requirements/recommendations for international students: Required—TOEFL (minimum score 550 paper-based; 80 iBT). *Application deadline:* For fall admission, 7/1 for domestic students, 6/1 for international students; for winter admission, 10/1 for domestic students, 9/1 for international students; for spring admission, 2/1 for domestic students, 1/1 for international students. Applications are processed on a rolling basis. Application fee: $60. Electronic applications accepted. *Expenses:* Contact institution. *Financial support:* Application deadline: 4/1; applicants required to submit FAFSA. *Unit head:* Christa Hinton, Assistant Dean and Director, 312-362-8810, Fax: 312-362-6677, E-mail: chinton@depaul.edu. *Application contact:* Garry Cooke, Director of Recruitment and Admissions, 312-362-8810, Fax: 312-362-6677, E-mail: kgsb@depaul.edu.
Website: http://kellstadt.depaul.edu

Drexel University, LeBow College of Business, Program in Business Administration, Philadelphia, PA 19104-2875. Offers business administration (MBA, PhD, APC), including accounting (MBA, PhD), decision sciences (PhD), economics (MBA, PhD), finance (MBA, PhD), legal studies (MBA), management (MBA), marketing (MBA, PhD), organizational sciences (PhD), quantitative methods (MBA), strategic management (PhD). *Accreditation:* AACSB. *Program availability:* Part-time, evening/weekend, online learning. Terminal master's awarded for partial completion of doctoral program. *Entrance requirements:* For master's, GMAT, minimum GPA of 2.75; for doctorate, GMAT. Additional exam requirements/recommendations for international students: Required—TOEFL. Electronic applications accepted. *Faculty research:* Decision support systems, individual and group behavior, operations research, techniques and strategy.

Duke University, Graduate School, Department of Economics, Durham, NC 27708. Offers AM, PhD, JD/AM. Spring admission applies to AM program only. *Degree requirements:* For doctorate, thesis/dissertation. *Entrance requirements:* For master's and doctorate, GRE General Test. Additional exam requirements/recommendations for international students: Required—TOEFL (minimum score 577 paper-based; 90 iBT) or IELTS (minimum score 7). Electronic applications accepted.

Duke University, Graduate School, Program in Economics and Computation, Durham, NC 27708-0097. Offers MS. *Entrance requirements:* For master's, GRE General Test. Additional exam requirements/recommendations for international students: Required—TOEFL (minimum score 577 paper-based; 90 iBT) or IELTS (minimum score 7).

Duke University, Graduate School, Program in Statistical and Economic Modeling, Durham, NC 27708. Offers econometrics (MS); financial economics (MS). Program offered jointly by the Departments of Statistical Science and Economics. *Entrance requirements:* For master's, GRE General Test. Additional exam requirements/recommendations for international students: Required—TOEFL (minimum score 577 paper-based; 90 iBT) or IELTS (minimum score 7). Electronic applications accepted.

Eastern Illinois University, Graduate School, College of Liberal Arts and Sciences, Department of Economics, Charleston, IL 61920. Offers MA. *Program availability:* Part-time, evening/weekend. *Degree requirements:* For master's, comprehensive exam (for some programs), thesis (for some programs). *Entrance requirements:* For master's, GMAT or GRE. Additional exam requirements/recommendations for international students: Required—TOEFL (minimum score 500 paper-based; 61 iBT), IELTS (minimum score 6). *Application deadline:* For fall admission, 5/15 for domestic and international students; for spring admission, 10/15 for domestic and international students. Applications are processed on a rolling basis. Application fee: $30. Electronic applications accepted. *Financial support:* Fellowships with full tuition reimbursements, teaching assistantships with full tuition reimbursements, career-related internships or fieldwork, Federal Work-Study, and unspecified assistantships available. Support available to part-time students. Financial award application deadline: 3/1; financial award applicants required to submit FAFSA. *Unit head:* Ali Moshtagh, Chair, 217-581-2916, E-mail: amoshtagh@eiu.edu. *Application contact:* Mukti Upadhyay, Graduate Coordinator, 217-581-3812, E-mail: mpupadhyay@eiu.edu.
Website: http://www.eiu.edu/economicgrad/index.php

Eastern Michigan University, Graduate School, College of Arts and Sciences, Department of Economics, Ypsilanti, MI 48197. Offers MA, Graduate Certificate. *Program availability:* Part-time, evening/weekend, online learning. *Faculty:* 9 full-time (1 woman). *Students:* 19 full-time (10 women), 16 part-time (5 women); includes 6 minority (3 Black or African American, non-Hispanic/Latino; 2 Asian, non-Hispanic/Latino; 1 Hispanic/Latino), 17 international. Average age 27. 47 applicants, 64% accepted, 9 enrolled. In 2017, 13 master's awarded. *Degree requirements:* For master's, thesis or alternative. *Entrance requirements:* Additional exam requirements/recommendations for international students: Required—TOEFL. *Application deadline:* Applications are processed on a rolling basis. Application fee: $45. *Financial support:* Fellowships, research assistantships with full tuition reimbursements, teaching assistantships with full tuition reimbursements, career-related internships or fieldwork, Federal Work-Study, institutionally sponsored loans, scholarships/grants, tuition waivers (partial), and unspecified assistantships available. Support available to part-time students. Financial award applicants required to submit FAFSA. *Unit head:* Dr. James Saunoris, Department Head, 734-487-3395, Fax: 734-487-9666, E-mail: jsaunori@emich.edu. *Application contact:* Dr. Mehmet Yaya, Graduate Coordinator, 734-487-0007, Fax: 734-487-9666, E-mail: myaya@emich.edu.
Website: http://www.emich.edu/economics

Emory University, Laney Graduate School, Department of Economics, Atlanta, GA 30322-1100. Offers PhD. *Degree requirements:* For doctorate, comprehensive exam, thesis/dissertation. *Entrance requirements:* For doctorate, GRE General Test. Additional exam requirements/recommendations for international students: Recommended—TOEFL. Electronic applications accepted. *Faculty research:* Applied microeconomics, econometrics, public choice, macroeconomics, law and economics.

Florida Atlantic University, College of Business, Department of Economics, Boca Raton, FL 33431-0991. Offers MS. *Program availability:* Part-time, evening/weekend. *Faculty:* 14 full-time (4 women). *Students:* 13 full-time (1 woman), 15 part-time (3 women); includes 12 minority (3 Black or African American, non-Hispanic/Latino; 1 Asian, non-Hispanic/Latino; 8 Hispanic/Latino), 4 international. Average age 31. 20 applicants, 75% accepted, 11 enrolled. In 2017, 18 master's awarded. *Degree requirements:* For master's, thesis optional. *Entrance requirements:* For master's, GMAT, GRE General Test, minimum GPA of 3.0. Additional exam requirements/recommendations for international students: Required—TOEFL (minimum score 600 paper-based; 61 iBT), IELTS (minimum score 6). *Application deadline:* For fall admission, 7/1 priority date for domestic students, 2/15 priority date for international students; for spring admission, 4/1 priority date for domestic students, 1/15 priority date for international students. Applications are processed on a rolling basis. Application fee: $30. *Expenses:* Tuition, state resident: full-time $7400; part-time $369.82 per credit. Tuition, nonresident: full-time $20,496; part-time $1042.81 per credit. *Financial support:* Teaching assistantships with tuition reimbursements, tuition waivers (partial), and unspecified assistantships available. Financial award application deadline: 3/1. *Faculty research:* International trade and finance, decision-making, monetary conditions, economic fluctuations and growth. *Unit head:* Dr. Steven B Caudill, Chair, 561-297-2617, E-mail: scaudill@fau.edu.
Website: http://business.fau.edu/departments/economics/index.aspx

Florida International University, Steven J. Green School of International and Public Affairs, Department of Economics, Miami, FL 33199. Offers MA, PhD. *Program availability:* Part-time, evening/weekend. *Faculty:* 15 full-time (3 women), 11 part-time/adjunct (3 women). *Students:* 31 full-time (8 women), 8 part-time (3 women); includes 11 minority (1 Black or African American, non-Hispanic/Latino; 1 Asian, non-Hispanic/Latino; 9 Hispanic/Latino), 25 international. Average age 31. 89 applicants, 16% accepted, 10 enrolled. In 2017, 3 master's, 6 doctorates awarded. *Degree requirements:* For master's, thesis or alternative; for doctorate, comprehensive exam, thesis/dissertation. *Entrance requirements:* For master's, GRE, minimum GPA of 3.0, letters of recommendation; for doctorate, GRE General Test, 3 letters of recommendation, minimum GPA of 3.0. Additional exam requirements/recommendations for international students: Required—TOEFL (minimum score 550 paper-based; 80 iBT). *Application deadline:* For fall admission, 4/1 for domestic and international students. Application fee: $30. Electronic applications accepted. *Expenses:* Tuition, state resident: full-time $8912; part-time $446 per credit hour. Tuition, nonresident: full-time $21,393; part-time $992 per credit hour. *Required fees:* $390; $195 per semester. *Financial support:*

Federal Work-Study, institutionally sponsored loans, and scholarships/grants available. Financial award application deadline: 3/1; financial award applicants required to submit FAFSA. *Faculty research:* Economic development, international economics, urban/regional economics, Latin American economics. *Unit head:* Dr. Cem Karayalcin, Chair, 305-348-3285, E-mail: ali.karayalcin@fiu.edu. *Application contact:* Nanett Rojas, Manager, Admissions Operations, 305-348-7464, Fax: 305-348-7441, E-mail: gradadm@fiu.edu.
Website: http://economics.fiu.edu/

Florida State University, The Graduate School, College of Social Sciences and Public Policy, Department of Economics, Tallahassee, FL 32306-2180. Offers applied economics (MS); economics (PhD); JD/MS. *Faculty:* 30 full-time (3 women), 2 part-time/adjunct (0 women). *Students:* 75 full-time (19 women), 6 part-time (4 women); includes 16 minority (4 Black or African American, non-Hispanic/Latino; 1 Asian, non-Hispanic/Latino; 8 Hispanic/Latino; 3 Two or more races, non-Hispanic/Latino), 4 international. Average age 25. 146 applicants, 75% accepted, 42 enrolled. In 2017, 36 master's, 3 doctorates awarded. *Degree requirements:* For master's, thesis (for some programs), applied project (for some programs); for doctorate, comprehensive exam, thesis/dissertation, dissertation prospectus, workshops. *Entrance requirements:* For master's, GRE General Test, minimum upper-division undergraduate GPA of 3.0, 3.4 on graduate work; minimum 1 course each in statistics and calculus; principles and sufficient upper-level economics courses; for doctorate, GRE General Test, minimum upper-division undergraduate GPA of 3.0, graduate 3.4; minimum 1 course each in statistics and linear algebra, 2 in calculus. Additional exam requirements/recommendations for international students: Required—TOEFL (minimum score 90 iBT). *Application deadline:* For fall admission, 2/15 priority date for domestic and international students. Applications are processed on a rolling basis. Application fee: $30. Electronic applications accepted. *Financial support:* In 2017–18, 55 students received support, including 20 fellowships with full tuition reimbursements available (averaging $25,000 per year), 5 research assistantships with full tuition reimbursements available (averaging $19,000 per year), 23 teaching assistantships with full tuition reimbursements available (averaging $19,000 per year); scholarships/grants, tuition waivers (full), and unspecified assistantships also available. Financial award application deadline: 2/15; financial award applicants required to submit FAFSA. *Faculty research:* Industrial organization, experimental/behavioral, public/urban, law and economics, macroeconomics and financial. *Total annual research expenditures:* $650,000. *Unit head:* Dr. R. Mark Isaac, Chairman, 850-644-5001, Fax: 850-644-4535, E-mail: misaac@fsu.edu. *Application contact:* Dr. Thomas W. Zuehlke, Graduate Director, 850-644-5001, Fax: 850-644-4535, E-mail: tzuehlke@fsu.edu.
Website: http://www.coss.fsu.edu/economics/

Fordham University, Graduate School of Arts and Sciences, Department of Economics, New York, NY 10458. Offers MA, PhD. *Program availability:* Part-time, evening/weekend. *Faculty:* 22 full-time (4 women). *Students:* 48 full-time (24 women), 17 part-time (9 women); includes 10 minority (3 Black or African American, non-Hispanic/Latino; 4 Asian, non-Hispanic/Latino; 3 Hispanic/Latino), 29 international. Average age 32. 140 applicants, 59% accepted, 18 enrolled. In 2017, 27 master's, 9 doctorates awarded. Terminal master's awarded for partial completion of doctoral program. *Degree requirements:* For master's, comprehensive exam; for doctorate, comprehensive exam, thesis/dissertation. *Entrance requirements:* For master's and doctorate, GRE General Test. Additional exam requirements/recommendations for international students: Required—TOEFL (minimum score 600 paper-based). *Application deadline:* For fall admission, 1/4 priority date for domestic students; for spring admission, 11/1 for domestic students. Application fee: $70. Electronic applications accepted. *Financial support:* In 2017–18, 29 students received support, including 1 fellowship with tuition reimbursement available (averaging $15,000 per year), 16 teaching assistantships with tuition reimbursements available (averaging $24,350 per year); career-related internships or fieldwork, institutionally sponsored loans, tuition waivers (full and partial), and unspecified assistantships also available. Financial award application deadline: 1/4; financial award applicants required to submit FAFSA. *Faculty research:* Developmental economics, econometrics. *Total annual research expenditures:* $129,000. *Unit head:* Dr. Johanna Francis, Associate Chair for Graduate Studies, 718-817-4066, Fax: 718-817-4048, E-mail: ajofrancis@fordham.edu. *Application contact:* Travis Strattion, Interim Director of Graduate Admissions, 718-817-4417, Fax: 718-817-3566, E-mail: tstrattion@fordham.edu.

Fordham University, Graduate School of Arts and Sciences, Program in International Political Economy and Development, New York, NY 10458. Offers MA, Certificate. *Program availability:* Part-time, evening/weekend. *Students:* 38 full-time (18 women), 8 part-time (2 women); includes 3 minority (1 Asian, non-Hispanic/Latino; 2 Hispanic/Latino), 15 international. Average age 27. 89 applicants, 60% accepted, 24 enrolled. In 2017, 24 master's, 1 other advanced degree awarded. *Degree requirements:* For master's, comprehensive exam. *Entrance requirements:* For master's, GRE General Test. Additional exam requirements/recommendations for international students: Required—TOEFL (minimum score 600 paper-based). *Application deadline:* For fall admission, 1/4 priority date for domestic students; for spring admission, 11/1 for domestic students. Application fee: $70. Electronic applications accepted. *Financial support:* In 2017–18, 35 students received support, including 4 fellowships with tuition reimbursements available (averaging $17,014 per year); research assistantships with tuition reimbursements available, career-related internships or fieldwork, institutionally sponsored loans, tuition waivers (full and partial), and unspecified assistantships also available. Financial award application deadline: 1/4; financial award applicants required to submit FAFSA. *Faculty research:* International economics, comparative international politics, international banking and finance, international development, emerging markets and country risk analysis. *Unit head:* Dr. Henry Schwalbenberg, Chair, 718-817-3866, Fax: 718-817-3518. *Application contact:* Bernadette Valentino-Morrison, Director of Graduate Admissions, 718-817-4419, Fax: 718-817-3566, E-mail: valentinomor@fordham.edu.

George Mason University, Antonin Scalia Law School, Arlington, VA 22201. Offers global antitrust law and economics (LL M); intellectual property (LL M); law (JD); law and economics (LL M); U.S. law (LL M); JD/MA; JD/MPP; JD/PhD. *Accreditation:* ABA. *Program availability:* Part-time, evening/weekend. *Faculty:* 44 full-time (9 women), 157 part-time/adjunct (41 women). *Students:* 401 full-time (199 women), 138 part-time (56 women); includes 115 minority (17 Black or African American, non-Hispanic/Latino; 40 Asian, non-Hispanic/Latino; 38 Hispanic/Latino; 20 Two or more races, non-Hispanic/Latino), 7 international. Average age 26. 2,452 applicants, 25% accepted, 175 enrolled. In 2017, 142 doctorates awarded. *Entrance requirements:* For master's, JD or international equivalent; for doctorate, LSAT or GRE, baccalaureate degree or international equivalent. Additional exam requirements/recommendations for international students: Required—TOEFL or IELTS (for LL M applicants only). *Application deadline:* For fall admission, 6/15 for domestic and international students. Applications are processed on a rolling basis. Application fee: $0. Electronic applications accepted. *Expenses:* Contact institution. *Financial support:* Fellowships, research assistantships, career-related internships or fieldwork, scholarships/grants, and tuition waivers (full and partial) available. Support available to part-time students. Financial award applicants required to submit FAFSA. *Faculty research:* Law and economics; infrastructure protection, including homeland and national security; intellectual property. *Unit head:* Henry N. Butler, Dean, 703-993-8644, Fax: 703-993-8088. *Application contact:* Tiffany J. Williams, Assistant Dean for Admissions and Enrollment Management, 703-993-8010, Fax: 703-993-8088, E-mail: lawadmit@gmu.edu.
Website: http://www.law.gmu.edu/

George Mason University, College of Humanities and Social Sciences, Department of Economics, Fairfax, VA 22030. Offers MA, PhD. *Faculty:* 28 full-time (1 woman), 13 part-time/adjunct (2 women). *Students:* 134 full-time (35 women), 85 part-time (20 women); includes 28 minority (1 Black or African American, non-Hispanic/Latino; 11 Asian, non-Hispanic/Latino; 12 Hispanic/Latino; 4 Two or more races, non-Hispanic/Latino), 34 international. Average age 30. 220 applicants, 81% accepted, 60 enrolled. In 2017, 50 master's, 24 doctorates awarded. *Degree requirements:* For master's, thesis optional, comprehensive exam in applied economic theory; for doctorate, comprehensive exam, thesis/dissertation, 2 preliminary exams, field exams. *Entrance requirements:* For master's, GRE General Test, expanded goals statement; 2 letters of recommendation; undergraduate degree; intermediate microeconomics and macroeconomics; 1 semester of calculus; 1 semester of statistics; for doctorate, GRE General Test, 2 letters of recommendation; resume; official transcripts; expanded goals statement; undergraduate degree; intermediate microeconomics and macroeconomics; 1 year of calculus and statistics; 1 semester of matrix algebra and econometrics. Additional exam requirements/recommendations for international students: Required—TOEFL (minimum score 570 paper-based; 80 iBT), IELTS (minimum score 6.5), PTE. *Application deadline:* For fall admission, 3/15 priority date for domestic and international students. Application fee: $75 ($80 for international students). Electronic applications accepted. *Expenses:* Tuition, state resident: full-time $11,228; part-time $459.50 per credit. Tuition, nonresident: full-time $30,932; part-time $1280.50 per credit. *Required fees:* $3252; $135.50 per credit. Part-time tuition and fees vary according to course load and program. *Financial support:* In 2017–18, 99 students received support, including 29 fellowships (averaging $2,143 per year), 81 research assistantships with tuition reimbursements available (averaging $18,032 per year), 21 teaching assistantships with tuition reimbursements available (averaging $7,339 per year); career-related internships or fieldwork, Federal Work-Study, scholarships/grants, unspecified assistantships, and health care benefits (for full-time research or teaching assistantship recipients) also available. Support available to part-time students. Financial award application deadline: 3/1; financial award applicants required to submit FAFSA. *Faculty research:* Labor economics and political economy; institutional and comparative economics; monetary theory; Austrian economics; experimental economics. *Total annual research expenditures:* $2.6 million. *Unit head:* Daniel Houser, Director/Professor/Chair, 703-993-4856, Fax: 703-993-4851, E-mail: dhouser@gmu.edu. *Application contact:* Mary Jackson, Graduate Coordinator, 703-993-1135, Fax: 703-993-1133, E-mail: mjacksoq@gmu.edu.
Website: http://economics.gmu.edu

Georgetown University, Graduate School of Arts and Sciences, Department of Economics, Washington, DC 20057. Offers econometrics (PhD); economic development (PhD); economic theory (PhD); industrial organization (PhD); international macro and finance (PhD); international trade (PhD); labor economics (PhD); macroeconomics (PhD); public economics and political economy (PhD); MA/PhD; MS/MA. *Degree requirements:* For doctorate, comprehensive exam, thesis/dissertation. *Entrance requirements:* For doctorate, GRE General Test. Additional exam requirements/recommendations for international students: Required—TOEFL. *Faculty research:* International economics, economic development.

The George Washington University, Columbian College of Arts and Sciences, Department of Economics, Washington, DC 20052. Offers MA, PhD. *Program availability:* Part-time, evening/weekend. *Faculty:* 23 full-time (5 women), 29 part-time/adjunct (10 women). *Students:* 76 full-time (27 women), 62 part-time (21 women); includes 17 minority (6 Black or African American, non-Hispanic/Latino; 1 American Indian or Alaska Native, non-Hispanic/Latino; 5 Asian, non-Hispanic/Latino; 3 Hispanic/Latino; 2 Two or more races, non-Hispanic/Latino), 96 international. Average age 28. 590 applicants, 35% accepted, 14 enrolled. In 2017, 35 master's, 6 doctorates awarded. Terminal master's awarded for partial completion of doctoral program. *Degree requirements:* For master's, comprehensive exam, thesis or alternative; for doctorate, thesis/dissertation, general exam. *Entrance requirements:* For master's and doctorate, GRE General Test, minimum GPA of 3.0. Additional exam requirements/recommendations for international students: Required—TOEFL (minimum score 550 paper-based; 80 iBT). *Application deadline:* For fall admission, 1/15 priority date for domestic and international students; for spring admission, 9/1 for international students. Applications are processed on a rolling basis. Application fee: $75. Electronic applications accepted. *Expenses: Tuition:* Full-time $28,800; part-time $1655 per credit hour. *Required fees:* $45; $2.75 per credit hour. *Financial support:* In 2017–18, 25 students received support. Fellowships with full tuition reimbursements available, teaching assistantships with tuition reimbursements available, and Federal Work-Study available. Financial award application deadline: 1/15. *Unit head:* Barry R. Chiswick, Chair, 202-994-8680, E-mail: brchis@gwu.edu. *Application contact:* Information Contact, 202-994-6150, Fax: 202-994-6147, E-mail: econgrad@gwu.edu.
Website: http://economics.columbian.gwu.edu/

Georgia Institute of Technology, Graduate Studies, Ivan Allen College of Liberal Arts, School of Economics, Atlanta, GA 30332-0001. Offers MS, PhD. *Program availability:* Part-time. Terminal master's awarded for partial completion of doctoral program. *Degree requirements:* For master's, thesis; for doctorate, comprehensive exam, thesis/dissertation, teaching of two undergraduate courses. *Entrance requirements:* For master's and doctorate, GRE. Additional exam requirements/recommendations for international students: Required—TOEFL (minimum score 550 paper-based; 79 iBT). Electronic applications accepted. *Faculty research:* Land use patterns in developing countries, office automation and productivity, dynamic modeling of financial markets.

Georgia State University, Andrew Young School of Policy Studies, Department of Economics, Atlanta, GA 30302. Offers economics (MA); environmental economics (PhD); experimental economics (PhD); labor economics (PhD); policy (MA); public finance (PhD); urban and regional economics (PhD). MA offered through the College of Arts and Sciences. *Program availability:* Part-time. *Faculty:* 26 full-time (4 women). *Students:* 110 full-time (39 women), 14 part-time (5 women); includes 26 minority (14 Black or African American, non-Hispanic/Latino; 4 Asian, non-Hispanic/Latino; 4 Hispanic/Latino; 4 Two or more races, non-Hispanic/Latino), 61 international. Average age 28. 204 applicants, 50% accepted, 37 enrolled. In 2017, 26 master's, 13 doctorates awarded. Terminal master's awarded for partial completion of doctoral program. *Degree requirements:* For master's, thesis optional; for doctorate, comprehensive exam, thesis/dissertation. *Entrance requirements:* For master's and doctorate, GRE. Additional exam requirements/recommendations for international students: Required—TOEFL (minimum score 603 paper-based; 100 iBT) or IELTS (minimum score 7). *Application deadline:* For fall admission, 1/15 for domestic and international students. Application fee: $50. Electronic applications accepted. *Expenses:* Tuition, state resident: full-time $7020. Tuition, nonresident: full-time $22,518. *Required fees:* $2128. Tuition and fees vary according to degree level and program. *Financial support:* In 2017–18, fellowships with full tuition reimbursements (averaging $11,333 per year), research assistantships with full tuition reimbursements (averaging $9,788 per year), teaching assistantships with full tuition reimbursements (averaging $3,000 per year) were awarded; career-related

internships or fieldwork also available. Financial award application deadline: 2/15; financial award applicants required to submit FAFSA. *Faculty research:* Public, experimental, urban/environmental, labor, and health economics. *Unit head:* Dr. Rusty Tchernis, Director of the Doctoral Program, 404-413-0154, Fax: 404-413-0145, E-mail: rtchernis@gsu.edu.
Website: http://economics.gsu.edu/

Georgia State University, College of Education and Human Development, Department of Middle and Secondary Education, Atlanta, GA 30302-3083. Offers curriculum and instruction (Ed D); English education (MAT); mathematics education (M Ed, MAT); middle level education (MAT); reading, language and literacy education (M Ed, MAT), including reading instruction (M Ed); science education (M Ed, MAT), including biology (MAT), broad field science (MAT), chemistry (MAT), earth science (MAT), physics (MAT); social studies education (M Ed, MAT), including economics (MAT), geography (MAT), history (MAT), political science (MAT); teaching and learning (PhD), including language and literacy, mathematics education, music education, science education, social studies education, teaching and teacher education. *Accreditation:* NCATE. *Program availability:* Part-time, evening/weekend, online learning. *Faculty:* 24 full-time (18 women). *Students:* 179 full-time (110 women), 192 part-time (133 women); includes 193 minority (130 Black or African American, non-Hispanic/Latino; 1 American Indian or Alaska Native, non-Hispanic/Latino; 23 Asian, non-Hispanic/Latino; 25 Hispanic/Latino; 14 Two or more races, non-Hispanic/Latino), 6 international. Average age 33. 175 applicants, 58% accepted, 83 enrolled. In 2017, 81 master's, 17 doctorates awarded. *Entrance requirements:* For master's, GRE; GACE I (for initial teacher preparation programs), baccalaureate degree or equivalent, resume, goals statement, two letters of recommendation, minimum undergraduate GPA of 2.5; proof of initial teacher certification in the content area (for M Ed); for doctorate, GRE, resume, goals statement, writing sample, two letters of recommendation, minimum graduate GPA of 3.3, interview. *Application deadline:* For fall admission, 1/15 priority date for domestic and international students; for spring admission, 10/1 for domestic and international students. Application fee: $50. Electronic applications accepted. *Expenses:* Tuition, state resident: full-time $7020. Tuition, nonresident: full-time $22,518. *Required fees:* $2128. Tuition and fees vary according to degree level and program. *Financial support:* In 2017–18, fellowships with full tuition reimbursements (averaging $19,667 per year), research assistantships with full tuition reimbursements (averaging $5,436 per year), teaching assistantships with full tuition reimbursements (averaging $2,779 per year) were awarded; career-related internships or fieldwork, Federal Work-Study, scholarships/grants, health care benefits, tuition waivers (full and partial), and unspecified assistantships also available. Financial award application deadline: 3/15. *Faculty research:* Teacher education in language and literacy, mathematics, science, and social studies in urban middle and secondary school settings; learning technologies in school, community, and corporate settings; multicultural education and education for social justice; urban education; international education. *Unit head:* Dr. Dana L. Fox, Chair, 404-413-8060, Fax: 404-413-8063, E-mail: dfox@gsu.edu. *Application contact:* Bobbie Turner, Administrative Coordinator, 404-413-8405, Fax: 404-413-8063, E-mail: bnturner@gsu.edu.
Website: http://mse.education.gsu.edu/

The Graduate Center, City University of New York, Graduate Studies, Program in Economics, New York, NY 10016-4039. Offers PhD. *Faculty:* 53 full-time (10 women). *Students:* 113 full-time (37 women); includes 19 minority (3 Black or African American, non-Hispanic/Latino; 8 Asian, non-Hispanic/Latino; 8 Hispanic/Latino), 66 international. Average age 34. 135 applicants, 13% accepted, 15 enrolled. In 2017, 5 doctorates awarded. *Degree requirements:* For doctorate, thesis/dissertation. *Entrance requirements:* For doctorate, GRE General Test. Additional exam requirements/recommendations for international students: Required—TOEFL. *Application deadline:* For fall admission, 1/15 priority date for domestic students; for spring admission, 11/15 for domestic students. Application fee: $125. Electronic applications accepted. *Financial support:* In 2017–18, 63 students received support, including 51 fellowships, 10 teaching assistantships; research assistantships, career-related internships or fieldwork, Federal Work-Study, institutionally sponsored loans, and tuition waivers (full and partial) also available. Financial award application deadline: 2/1; financial award applicants required to submit FAFSA. *Unit head:* Dr. Wim Vijverberg, Executive Officer, 212-817-8256, Fax: 212-817-1514, E-mail: wvijverberg@gc.cuny.edu. *Application contact:* Les Gribben, Director of Admissions, 212-817-7470, Fax: 212-817-1624, E-mail: lgribben@gc.cuny.edu.

Harvard University, Graduate School of Arts and Sciences, Committee on Business Economics, Cambridge, MA 02138. Offers PhD. *Degree requirements:* For doctorate, thesis/dissertation. *Entrance requirements:* For doctorate, GMAT or GRE General Test. Additional exam requirements/recommendations for international students: Required—TOEFL.

Harvard University, Graduate School of Arts and Sciences, Department of Economics, Cambridge, MA 02138. Offers PhD. *Degree requirements:* For doctorate, thesis/dissertation, oral exam. *Entrance requirements:* For doctorate, GRE General Test, GRE Subject Test. Additional exam requirements/recommendations for international students: Required—TOEFL. *Faculty research:* Industrial organization, macromonetary issues, international economics.

Howard University, Graduate School, Department of Economics, Washington, DC 20059-0002. Offers MA, PhD. *Program availability:* Part-time. *Degree requirements:* For master's, comprehensive exam, thesis optional; for doctorate, one foreign language, comprehensive exam, thesis/dissertation. *Entrance requirements:* For master's, GRE General Test, minimum GPA of 3.0; for doctorate, GRE General Test, master's degree in economics or related field, minimum GPA of 3.0. Electronic applications accepted. *Faculty research:* Economic development, international trade, urban rentalization.

Hunter College of the City University of New York, Graduate School, School of Arts and Sciences, Department of Economics, Program in Economics, New York, NY 10065-5085. Offers MA. *Degree requirements:* For master's, thesis.

Illinois State University, Graduate School, College of Arts and Sciences, Department of Economics, Normal, IL 61790. Offers MA, MS. *Degree requirements:* For master's, thesis or alternative. *Entrance requirements:* For master's, GRE General Test, minimum GPA of 2.6 in last 60 hours of course work. *Faculty research:* Community/economic development; the social, economic and educational correlates of rural school closure; Stevenson Center AmeriCorps project.

Indiana University Bloomington, University Graduate School, College of Arts and Sciences, Department of Economics, Bloomington, IN 47405-7104. Offers MS, PhD. Terminal master's awarded for partial completion of doctoral program. *Degree requirements:* For doctorate, comprehensive exam, thesis/dissertation, main field exam, two supporting fields, 3rd-year paper, tool skill classes, dissertation proposal presentation, oral defense of dissertation. *Entrance requirements:* For doctorate, GRE General Test, three semesters of calculus, semester of linear algebra, semester of statistics or probability. Additional exam requirements/recommendations for international students: Required—TOEFL (minimum score 600 paper-based; 100 iBT); Recommended—IELTS. Electronic applications accepted. *Faculty research:* Macroeconomics, microeconomic theory, econometrics, experimental economics, economic growth.

Indiana University–Purdue University Indianapolis, School of Liberal Arts, Department of Economics, Indianapolis, IN 46202. Offers MA, MA/MA. *Program availability:* Part-time. *Degree requirements:* For master's, thesis (for some programs). *Entrance requirements:* For master's, GRE, minimum GPA of 3.0; courses in economic theory, statistics, and calculus. Additional exam requirements/recommendations for international students: Required—TOEFL (minimum score 100 iBT), IELTS (minimum score 6.5). Electronic applications accepted. *Faculty research:* Charitable giving.

Instituto Tecnologico de Santo Domingo, Graduate School, Area of Humanities and Social Sciences, Santo Domingo, Dominican Republic. Offers accounting (Certificate); adult education (Certificate); applied linguistics (MA); economics (MA); education (M Ed); educational psychology (MA, Certificate); gender and development (MA, Certificate); humanistic studies (MA); international marketing management (Certificate); international relations in the Caribbean basin (Certificate); intervention systems in family therapy (MA); linguistic and literary communication (Certificate); pedagogical support (MA); social science education (M Ed); sustainable human development (MA); terminal illness and death psychology (Certificate); youth and adult education (M Ed).

Instituto Tecnológico y de Estudios Superiores de Monterrey, Campus Ciudad de México, School of Business Administration, Ciudad de Mexico, Mexico. Offers business administration (EMBA, MBA, PhD); economy (MBA); finance (MBA). EMBA program offered jointly with The University of Texas at Austin. *Program availability:* Part-time, evening/weekend, online learning. *Entrance requirements:* For master's and doctorate, Instituto entrance exam. Additional exam requirements/recommendations for international students: Required—TOEFL.

Iowa State University of Science and Technology, Department of Economics, Ames, IA 50011. Offers agricultural economics (MS, PhD); economics (MS, PhD); JD/MS; JD/PhD. JD/MS and JD/PhD offered jointly with Drake University and The University of Iowa. *Degree requirements:* For master's, thesis or alternative; for doctorate, thesis/dissertation. *Entrance requirements:* For master's and doctorate, GRE General Test. Additional exam requirements/recommendations for international students: Required—TOEFL (minimum score 570 paper-based; 88 iBT), IELTS (minimum score 6.5). Electronic applications accepted.

Johns Hopkins University, Zanvyl Krieger School of Arts and Sciences, Department of Economics, Baltimore, MD 21218. Offers PhD. Terminal master's awarded for partial completion of doctoral program. *Degree requirements:* For doctorate, comprehensive exam, thesis/dissertation. *Entrance requirements:* For doctorate, GRE General Test. Additional exam requirements/recommendations for international students: Required—TOEFL (minimum score 600 paper-based), IELTS. Electronic applications accepted. *Faculty research:* General economic theory, econometrics and mathematical economics, trade and development, game theory, urban economics.

Kansas State University, Graduate School, College of Arts and Sciences, Department of Economics, Manhattan, KS 66506. Offers MA, PhD. Terminal master's awarded for partial completion of doctoral program. *Degree requirements:* For master's, comprehensive exam (for some programs), thesis (for some programs), 30 credit hours, including thesis/report or qualifying exams; for doctorate, comprehensive exam, thesis/dissertation, 90 credit hours, including dissertation, qualifying exams, and field exam. *Entrance requirements:* For master's and doctorate, GRE (highly recommended), minimum GPA of 3.0; course work in microeconomics, macroeconomics, calculus and statistics. Additional exam requirements/recommendations for international students: Required—TOEFL (minimum score 550 paper-based; 79 iBT), IELTS (minimum score 6.5), TWE (minimum score 5), PTE (minimum score 58). Electronic applications accepted. *Faculty research:* Macroeconomics, microeconomics and labor economics, development and growth, international economics, industrial organization.

Kent State University, College of Business Administration, Master of Arts Program in Economics, Kent, OH 44240. Offers MA. *Program availability:* Part-time. *Faculty:* 13 full-time (4 women). *Students:* 24 full-time (8 women), 1 part-time (0 women); includes 2 minority (1 Black or African American, non-Hispanic/Latino; 1 Two or more races, non-Hispanic/Latino), 13 international. Average age 26. 33 applicants, 88% accepted, 13 enrolled. In 2017, 13 master's awarded. *Degree requirements:* For master's, 30 credit hours, minimum GPA of 3.0. *Entrance requirements:* For master's, GMAT or GRE General Test, minimum GPA of 3.0. Additional exam requirements/recommendations for international students: Required—TOEFL (minimum score 550 paper-based; 79 iBT), IELTS (minimum score 6.5). *Application deadline:* For fall admission, 2/15 priority date for domestic students, 2/15 for international students; for spring admission, 10/15 for domestic and international students; for summer admission, 5/1 for domestic and international students. Applications are processed on a rolling basis. Application fee: $45 ($70 for international students). Electronic applications accepted. *Expenses:* $515 per credit resident; $928 per credit non-resident. *Financial support:* In 2017–18, 4 students received support, including 4 research assistantships with full tuition reimbursements available (averaging $4,750 per year); Federal Work-Study and scholarships/grants also available. Financial award application deadline: 2/15; financial award applicants required to submit FAFSA. *Faculty research:* Macro and microeconomic theory, labor economics, international economics, quantitative methods. *Unit head:* Dr. Donald R. Williams, Chair and Professor, 330-672-2366, Fax: 330-672-9808, E-mail: dwilliam@kent.edu. *Application contact:* Louise M. Ditchey, Administrative Director, 330-672-2282, Fax: 330-672-7303, E-mail: gradbus@kent.edu.
Website: http://www.kent.edu/business/ma-economics

Lakehead University, Graduate Studies, Faculty of Social Sciences and Humanities, Department of Economics, Thunder Bay, ON P7B 5E1, Canada. Offers MA. *Program availability:* Part-time, evening/weekend. *Degree requirements:* For master's, thesis or comprehensive exams, research papers. *Entrance requirements:* For master's, minimum B average. Additional exam requirements/recommendations for international students: Required—TOEFL. *Faculty research:* Public finance, economic history, mathematical economics, quantitative economics.

Lee University, Program in Education, Cleveland, TN 37320-3450. Offers art (MAT); curriculum and instruction (M Ed, Ed S); early childhood (MAT); educational leadership (M Ed, Ed S); elementary education (MAT); English and math (MAT); English and science (MAT); English and social studies (MAT); higher education administration (MS); history (MAT); history and economics (MAT); math and science (MAT); math and social studies (MAT); middle grades (MAT); science and social studies (MASW); secondary education (MAT); Spanish (MAT); special education (M Ed, MAT); TESOL (MAT). *Accreditation:* NCATE. *Program availability:* Part-time. *Faculty:* 15 full-time (7 women), 8 part-time/adjunct (3 women). *Students:* 28 full-time (21 women), 77 part-time (48 women); includes 12 minority (7 Black or African American, non-Hispanic/Latino; 2 Hispanic/Latino; 3 Two or more races, non-Hispanic/Latino), 1 international. Average age 31. 35 applicants, 83% accepted, 22 enrolled. In 2017, 54 master's, 4 other advanced degrees awarded. *Degree requirements:* For master's, variable foreign language requirement, thesis optional, internship. *Entrance requirements:* For master's, MAT or GRE General Test, minimum undergraduate GPA of 2.75, 3 letters of recommendation, interview, writing sample, official transcripts, background check; for Ed S, minimum undergraduate and master's GPA of 2.75, official transcripts for undergraduate and master's degrees. Additional exam requirements/recommendations for international students: Required—TOEFL (minimum score 61 iBT). *Application*

deadline: For fall admission, 6/1 priority date for domestic and international students; for spring admission, 11/1 priority date for domestic and international students; for summer admission, 4/1 priority date for domestic and international students. Applications are processed on a rolling basis. Application fee: $25. Electronic applications accepted. *Expenses: Tuition:* Full-time $12,780; part-time $710 per credit hour. *Required fees:* $60; $60 per term. Tuition and fees vary according to program. *Financial support:* In 2017–18, 32 students received support. Career-related internships or fieldwork, Federal Work-Study, institutionally sponsored loans, scholarships/grants, and unspecified assistantships available. Financial award application deadline: 3/1; financial award applicants required to submit FAFSA. *Unit head:* Dr. William Kamm, Director, 423-614-8544, E-mail: wkamm@leeuniversity.edu. *Application contact:* Crystal Keeter, Graduate Education Secretary, 423-614-8544, E-mail: ckeeter@leeuniversity.edu. Website: http://www.leeuniversity.edu/academics/graduate/education

Lehigh University, College of Business and Economics, Department of Economics, Bethlehem, PA 18015. Offers MS, PhD. *Faculty:* 9 full-time (1 woman). *Students:* 27 full-time (12 women), 1 (woman) part-time, 21 international. Average age 26. 39 applicants, 72% accepted, 5 enrolled. In 2017, 7 master's, 4 doctorates awarded. Terminal master's awarded for partial completion of doctoral program. *Degree requirements:* For master's, thesis optional; for doctorate, comprehensive exam, thesis/dissertation, proposal defense. *Entrance requirements:* For master's and doctorate, GMAT or GRE General Test. Additional exam requirements/recommendations for international students: Required—TOEFL (minimum score 600 paper-based; 94 iBT), IELTS (minimum score 7). *Application deadline:* For fall admission, 7/15 for domestic students, 5/1 for international students; for spring admission, 12/1 for domestic students. Application fee: $75. Electronic applications accepted. *Expenses:* Contact institution. *Financial support:* In 2017–18, 18 students received support, including 3 fellowships with full and partial tuition reimbursements available (averaging $22,000 per year), 1 research assistantship with full tuition reimbursement available (averaging $18,900 per year), 13 teaching assistantships with full tuition reimbursements available (averaging $18,000 per year); health care benefits also available. Financial award application deadline: 1/1. *Faculty research:* Public finance, investments, applied econometrics, labor economics, health economics. *Unit head:* Dr. James Dearden, Chair, 610-758-5129, Fax: 610-758-4677, E-mail: jad8@lehigh.edu. *Application contact:* Michael Tarantino, Director of Recruitment and Admissions, 610-758-3418, Fax: 610-758-5283, E-mail: mgt215@lehigh.edu.
Website: http://www4.lehigh.edu/business/academics/depts/economics

Louisiana State University and Agricultural & Mechanical College, Graduate School, E. J. Ourso College of Business, Department of Economics, Baton Rouge, LA 70803. Offers MS, PhD. *Faculty:* 13 full-time (1 woman). *Students:* 25 full-time (12 women), 1 part-time (0 women); includes 3 minority (1 Black or African American, non-Hispanic/Latino; 1 Asian, non-Hispanic/Latino; 1 Hispanic/Latino), 18 international. Average age 27. 57 applicants, 30% accepted, 8 enrolled. In 2017, 1 master's, 3 doctorates awarded. *Financial support:* In 2017–18, 1 fellowship (averaging $18,238 per year), 10 research assistantships (averaging $24,867 per year), 12 teaching assistantships (averaging $24,867 per year) were awarded. *Total annual research expenditures:* $436,250.

Loyola University Chicago, Quinlan School of Business, MBA Programs, Chicago, IL 60611. Offers accounting (MBA); business ethics (MBA); derivative markets (MBA); economics (MBA); entrepreneurship (MBA); finance (MBA); healthcare management (MBA); human resources management (MBA); information systems management (MBA); international business (MBA); management (MBA); marketing (MBA); risk management (MBA); supply chain management (MBA). *Program availability:* Part-time, evening/weekend. *Faculty:* 84 full-time (28 women), 12 part-time/adjunct (3 women). *Students:* 253 full-time (118 women), 76 part-time (35 women); includes 83 minority (21 Black or African American, non-Hispanic/Latino; 1 American Indian or Alaska Native, non-Hispanic/Latino; 33 Asian, non-Hispanic/Latino; 24 Hispanic/Latino; 4 Two or more races, non-Hispanic/Latino), 37 international. Average age 30. 334 applicants, 52% accepted, 80 enrolled. In 2017, 220 master's awarded. *Entrance requirements:* For master's, GMAT or GRE, official transcripts, two letters of recommendation, statement of purpose, resume. Additional exam requirements/recommendations for international students: Required—TOEFL (minimum score 90 iBT) or IELTS (minimum score 6.5). *Application deadline:* For fall admission, 7/15 for domestic and international students; for winter admission, 10/1 for domestic and international students; for spring admission, 1/15 for domestic and international students; for summer admission, 4/1 for domestic and international students. Applications are processed on a rolling basis. Application fee: $50. Electronic applications accepted. Application fee is waived when completed online. *Expenses:* $4,488 per course. *Financial support:* In 2017–18, 11 students received support. Research assistantships, career-related internships or fieldwork, Federal Work-Study, scholarships/grants, and health care benefits available. *Faculty research:* Social enterprise and responsibility, emerging markets, supply chain management, risk management. *Unit head:* Katherine Acles, Assistant Dean for Graduate Programs, 312-915-6124, Fax: 312-915-7207, E-mail: kacles@luc.edu.

Marquette University, Graduate School of Management, Department of Economics, Milwaukee, WI 53201-1881. Offers business economics (MSAE); financial economics (MSAE); international economics (MSAE); marketing research (MSAE); real estate economics (MSAE). *Program availability:* Part-time, evening/weekend. *Degree requirements:* For master's, comprehensive exam, professional project. *Entrance requirements:* For master's, GMAT or GRE General Test. Additional exam requirements/recommendations for international students: Required—TOEFL, IELTS, PTE. Electronic applications accepted. *Faculty research:* Monetary and fiscal policy in open economy, housing and regional migration, political economy of taxation and state/local government.

Marquette University, Graduate School of Management, Executive MBA Program, Milwaukee, WI 53201-1881. Offers economics (MBA); finance (MBA); human resources (MBA); international business (MBA); management information systems (MBA); marketing (MBA); operations and supply chain management (MBA); sports business (MBA). *Accreditation:* AACSB. *Degree requirements:* For master's, international trip. *Entrance requirements:* For master's, GMAT or GRE, two letters of recommendation, official transcripts from current and previous colleges/universities. Additional exam requirements/recommendations for international students: Required—TOEFL (minimum score 550 paper-based; 88 iBT), IELTS (minimum score 6.5), PTE. Electronic applications accepted. *Expenses:* Contact institution. *Faculty research:* International trade and finance, customer relationship management, consumer satisfaction, customer service.

Marquette University, Graduate School of Management, Program in Business Administration, Milwaukee, WI 53201-1881. Offers business administration (MBA); economics (MBA); entrepreneurship (Certificate); finance (MBA); human resources (MBA); international business (MBA); management information systems (MBA); marketing (MBA); operations and supply chain management (MBA); sports business (MBA); JD/MBA; MBA/MA; MBA/MSN. *Accreditation:* AACSB. *Program availability:* Part-time, evening/weekend. *Degree requirements:* For Certificate, business plan. *Entrance requirements:* For master's, GMAT or GRE, letters of recommendation. Additional exam requirements/recommendations for international students: Required—

TOEFL (minimum score 550 paper-based; 88 iBT), IELTS (minimum score 6.5), PTE. Electronic applications accepted. *Faculty research:* Ethics in the professions, services marketing, technology impact on decision-making, mentoring.

Massachusetts Institute of Technology, School of Humanities, Arts, and Social Sciences, Department of Economics, Cambridge, MA 02139. Offers SM, PhD. Terminal master's awarded for partial completion of doctoral program. *Degree requirements:* For master's, thesis; for doctorate, comprehensive exam, thesis/dissertation. *Entrance requirements:* For doctorate, GRE General Test. Additional exam requirements/recommendations for international students: Required—TOEFL, IELTS. Electronic applications accepted. *Faculty research:* Development economics; econometrics; economic theory; financial economics; industrial organization; health economics; international economics; labor economics; macroeconomics; political economy; public economics/public finance.

McGill University, Faculty of Graduate and Postdoctoral Studies, Faculty of Arts, Department of Economics, Montréal, QC H3A 2T5, Canada. Offers economics (MA, PhD); social statistics (MA).

McMaster University, School of Graduate Studies, Faculty of Social Sciences, Department of Economics, Hamilton, ON L8S 4M2, Canada. Offers MA, PhD. *Program availability:* Part-time. *Degree requirements:* For doctorate, comprehensive exam, thesis/dissertation. *Entrance requirements:* For master's, GRE (recommended), honors BA in economics; for doctorate, GRE (recommended), B+ average in a master's degree. Additional exam requirements/recommendations for international students: Required—TOEFL (minimum score 580 paper-based). *Faculty research:* Applied microeconomics, econometrics, health economics, labor economics, public finance.

Memorial University of Newfoundland, School of Graduate Studies, Department of Economics, St. John's, NL A1C 5S7, Canada. Offers MA. *Degree requirements:* For master's, thesis optional. *Entrance requirements:* For master's, honors degree (minimum 2nd class standing). Electronic applications accepted. *Faculty research:* Public sector economics, natural resource economics.

Miami University, Farmer School of Business, Department of Economics, Oxford, OH 45056. Offers MA. *Students:* 11 full-time (7 women), 1 part-time (0 women), 7 international. Average age 25. In 2017, 15 master's awarded. *Expenses:* Tuition, state resident: full-time $13,812; part-time $575 per credit hour. Tuition, nonresident: full-time $30,860; part-time $1286 per credit hour. *Unit head:* George Davis, Chair, 513-529-2836, E-mail: davisgk@miamioh.edu. *Application contact:* Dr. Melissa Thomasson, Director of Graduate Studies, 513-529-2858, E-mail: thomasma@miamioh.edu.
Website: http://www.MiamiOH.edu/economics

Michigan State University, The Graduate School, College of Social Science, Department of Economics, East Lansing, MI 48824. Offers MA, PhD. *Entrance requirements:* Additional exam requirements/recommendations for international students: Required—TOEFL. Electronic applications accepted.

Middle Tennessee State University, College of Graduate Studies, Jennings A. Jones College of Business, Department of Economics and Finance, Murfreesboro, TN 37132. Offers economics (MA, PhD). *Program availability:* Part-time, evening/weekend, online learning. *Degree requirements:* For master's, comprehensive exam, thesis optional; for doctorate, comprehensive exam, thesis/dissertation. *Entrance requirements:* For master's and doctorate, GRE. Additional exam requirements/recommendations for international students: Required—TOEFL (minimum score 525 paper-based; 71 iBT) or IELTS (minimum score 6). Electronic applications accepted.

Mississippi State University, College of Business, Department of Finance and Economics, Mississippi State, MS 39762. Offers applied economics (PhD); economics (MA). PhD in applied economics offered jointly with Department of Agricultural Economics. *Program availability:* Part-time. *Faculty:* 18 full-time (5 women), 1 part-time/adjunct (0 women). *Students:* 11 full-time (3 women), 1 part-time (0 women), 10 international. Average age 30. 36 applicants, 25% accepted, 5 enrolled. In 2017, 1 master's, 1 doctorate awarded. Terminal master's awarded for partial completion of doctoral program. *Degree requirements:* For master's, comprehensive exam, thesis optional; for doctorate, comprehensive exam, thesis/dissertation, written and oral exams. *Entrance requirements:* For master's, GRE, previously-completed intermediate microeconomics and macroeconomics; for doctorate, GRE, BS with minimum GPA of 3.0 cumulative and over last 60 hours of undergraduate work, 3.25 on all graduate work. Additional exam requirements/recommendations for international students: Required—TOEFL (minimum score 575 paper-based; 84 iBT); Recommended—IELTS (minimum score 6.5). *Application deadline:* For fall admission, 7/1 for domestic students, 5/1 for international students; for spring admission, 11/1 for domestic students, 10/1 for international students. Applications are processed on a rolling basis. Application fee: $60 ($80 for international students). Electronic applications accepted. *Expenses:* Tuition, state resident: full-time $8318; part-time $462.12 per credit hour. Tuition, nonresident: full-time $22,358; part-time $1242.12 per credit hour. *Required fees:* $110; $12.24 per credit hour. $6.12 per semester. *Financial support:* Federal Work-Study, scholarships/grants, health care benefits, and unspecified assistantships available. Financial award application deadline: 4/1; financial award applicants required to submit FAFSA. *Faculty research:* Economics development, mergers, event studies, economic education, bank performance. *Total annual research expenditures:* $1 million. *Unit head:* Dr. Mike Highfield, Professor/Head, 662-325-1984, Fax: 662-325-1977, E-mail: m.highfield@msstate.edu. *Application contact:* Lakan Drinker, Admissions and Enrollment Assistant, 662-325-8951, E-mail: ldrinker@grad.msstate.edu.
Website: http://www.business.msstate.edu/programs/fe/index.php

Morgan State University, School of Graduate Studies, College of Liberal Arts, Department of Economics, Baltimore, MD 21251. Offers MA. *Entrance requirements:* For master's, GRE. Additional exam requirements/recommendations for international students: Required—TOEFL (minimum score 550 paper-based). *Application deadline:* For fall admission, 2/1 priority date for domestic students; for spring admission, 10/1 priority date for domestic students. Applications are processed on a rolling basis. Application fee: $0. *Expenses:* Tuition, state resident: part-time $433 per credit. Tuition, nonresident: part-time $851 per credit. *Required fees:* $81.50 per credit. *Financial support:* Application deadline: 2/1. *Unit head:* Dr. Linda Loubert, Interim Chair and Graduate Coordinator, 443-885-1885, E-mail: linda.loubert@morgan.edu. *Application contact:* Dr. Dean Campbell, Graduate Recruitment Specialist, 443-885-3185, Fax: 443-885-8226, E-mail: dean.campbell@morgan.edu.

Murray State University, Arthur J. Bauernfeind College of Business, Department of Economics and Finance, Murray, KY 42071. Offers economic development (MS); economics (MS), including finance. *Program availability:* Part-time. *Faculty:* 13 full-time (4 women), 1 part-time/adjunct (0 women). *Students:* 10 full-time (6 women), 2 part-time (0 women); includes 2 minority (1 Black or African American, non-Hispanic/Latino; 1 Two or more races, non-Hispanic/Latino), 5 international. Average age 26. 7 applicants, 86% accepted, 1 enrolled. In 2017, 5 master's awarded. *Entrance requirements:* For master's, GRE General Test or GMAT, minimum university GPA of 2.75. Additional exam requirements/recommendations for international students: Required—TOEFL (minimum score 527 paper-based; 71 iBT). *Application deadline:* Applications are processed on a rolling basis. Application fee: $40 ($50 for international students). Electronic applications accepted. *Expenses:* Tuition, state resident: full-time $9504.

Tuition, nonresident: full-time $26,811. *International tuition:* $14,400 full-time. Tuition and fees vary according to course load, degree level and reciprocity agreements. *Financial support:* In 2017–18, 1 research assistantship, 1 teaching assistantship were awarded; Federal Work-Study and unspecified assistantships also available. Financial award applicants required to submit FAFSA. *Unit head:* Dr. David Eaton, Chair, Department of Economics and Finance, 270-809-4290, Fax: 270-809-5478, E-mail: deaton@murraystate.edu. *Application contact:* Kaitlyn Burzynski, Interim Assistant Director for Graduate Admission and Records, 270-809-5732, Fax: 270-809-3780, E-mail: msu.graduateadmissions@murraystate.edu.
Website: https://www.murraystate.edu/academics/CollegesDepartments/CollegeOfBusiness/Programs/EconomicsAndFinance/

New Mexico State University, College of Business, Department of Economics, Applied Statistics and International Business, Las Cruces, NM 88003. Offers applied statistics (MS); economic development (DED); economics (MA); public utility regulation and economics (Graduate Certificate). *Program availability:* Part-time. *Faculty:* 17 full-time (4 women). *Students:* 55 full-time (22 women), 24 part-time (10 women); includes 28 minority (3 Black or African American, non-Hispanic/Latino; 2 American Indian or Alaska Native, non-Hispanic/Latino; 1 Asian, non-Hispanic/Latino; 20 Hispanic/Latino; 2 Two or more races, non-Hispanic/Latino), 34 international. Average age 34. 84 applicants, 73% accepted, 27 enrolled. In 2017, 11 master's, 2 doctorates, 9 other advanced degrees awarded. Terminal master's awarded for partial completion of doctoral program. *Entrance requirements:* For master's, minimum GPA of 3.0; for doctorate, appropriate master's degree, minimum GPA of 3.0. Additional exam requirements/recommendations for international students: Required—TOEFL (minimum score 550 paper-based; 79 iBT), IELTS (minimum score 6.5). *Application deadline:* For fall admission, 3/1 priority date for domestic and international students. Applications are processed on a rolling basis. Application fee: $40 ($50 for international students). Electronic applications accepted. *Expenses:* Tuition, state resident: full-time $4390. Tuition, nonresident: full-time $15,309. *Required fees:* $853. *Financial support:* In 2017–18, 43 students received support, including 21 research assistantships (averaging $12,040 per year), 8 teaching assistantships (averaging $15,828 per year); career-related internships or fieldwork, Federal Work-Study, scholarships/grants, traineeships, health care benefits, and unspecified assistantships also available. Support available to part-time students. Financial award application deadline: 3/1. *Faculty research:* Public utilities, environment, linear models, biological sampling, public policy, economic development, energy, regional economics. *Unit head:* Dr. Christopher Erickson, Interim Department Head, 575-646-7211, Fax: 575-646-1915, E-mail: chrerick@nmsu.edu. *Application contact:* 575-646-7211, Fax: 575-646-1915.
Website: http://business.nmsu.edu/departments/economics

The New School, The New School for Social Research, Department of Economics, New York, NY 10003. Offers economics (MA, MS, PhD); global political economy and finance (MA). *Program availability:* Part-time. *Faculty:* 9 full-time (3 women), 2 part-time/adjunct (both women). *Students:* 80 full-time (22 women), 20 part-time (8 women); includes 17 minority (4 Black or African American, non-Hispanic/Latino; 6 Asian, non-Hispanic/Latino; 7 Hispanic/Latino), 53 international. Average age 32. 146 applicants, 66% accepted, 21 enrolled. In 2017, 23 master's, 8 doctorates awarded. Terminal master's awarded for partial completion of doctoral program. *Degree requirements:* For master's, comprehensive exam (for some programs), mentored research/internship; for doctorate, one foreign language, comprehensive exam, thesis/dissertation. *Entrance requirements:* For master's, GRE, letters of recommendation, writing sample, essays, transcript; for doctorate, letters of recommendation, writing sample, essays, transcript. Additional exam requirements/recommendations for international students: Required—TOEFL (minimum score 100 iBT), IELTS (minimum score 7), PTE (minimum score 68). *Application deadline:* For fall admission, 1/5 priority date for domestic and international students; for spring admission, 10/15 priority date for domestic and international students. Applications are processed on a rolling basis. Application fee: $50. Electronic applications accepted. *Expenses:* $2,180 per credit. *Financial support:* In 2017–18, 72 students received support, including 14 fellowships (averaging $16,694 per year), 7 research assistantships (averaging $13,681 per year), 23 teaching assistantships with full and partial tuition reimbursements available (averaging $7,340 per year); career-related internships or fieldwork, Federal Work-Study, scholarships/grants, tuition waivers (full and partial), and unspecified assistantships also available. Support available to part-time students. Financial award application deadline: 2/1; financial award applicants required to submit FAFSA. *Unit head:* Dr. William Milberg, Dean, The New School for Social Research, 212-229-5777, E-mail: milbergw@newschool.edu. *Application contact:* Dana Messinger, Director of Graduate Admission, 212-229-5150 Ext. 2300, E-mail: socialresearchadmit@newschool.edu.
Website: https://www.newschool.edu/nssr/economics/

New York University, Graduate School of Arts and Science, Department of Economics, New York, NY 10012-1019. Offers applied economic analysis (Advanced Certificate); economics (MA, PhD); JD/MA; MD/PhD. *Program availability:* Part-time, evening/weekend. *Faculty:* 35 full-time (2 women). *Students:* 214 full-time (77 women), 21 part-time (7 women); includes 15 minority (13 Asian, non-Hispanic/Latino; 2 Hispanic/Latino), 173 international. Average age 27. 1,531 applicants, 16% accepted, 88 enrolled. In 2017, 83 master's, 18 doctorates awarded. Terminal master's awarded for partial completion of doctoral program. *Degree requirements:* For master's, thesis; for doctorate, one foreign language, thesis/dissertation, 4 qualifying exams. *Entrance requirements:* For master's and doctorate, GRE General Test. Additional exam requirements/recommendations for international students: Required—TOEFL. *Application deadline:* For fall admission, 12/18 priority date for domestic students, 12/18 for international students. Application fee: $100. *Expenses: Tuition:* Full-time $41,352; part-time $19,968 per year. *Required fees:* $2496; $1628 per unit. $814 per term. Tuition and fees vary according to course load and program. *Financial support:* Fellowships with tuition reimbursements, research assistantships with tuition reimbursements, teaching assistantships with tuition reimbursements, Federal Work-Study, institutionally sponsored loans, scholarships/grants, health care benefits, and unspecified assistantships available. Financial award application deadline: 12/18; financial award applicants required to submit FAFSA. *Faculty research:* Economic theory, experimental economics, growth and development, macroeconomics and finance, international trade and international finance. *Unit head:* Alessandro Lizzeri, Chair, 212-998-8900, Fax: 212-995-4186, E-mail: admissions@econ.nyu.edu. *Application contact:* Tim Cogley, Director of Graduate Studies, PhD Programs, 212-998-8900, Fax: 212-995-4186, E-mail: admissions@econ.nyu.edu.
Website: http://www.econ.nyu.edu/

New York University, Leonard N. Stern School of Business, Department of Economics, New York, NY 10012-1019. Offers MBA, PhD. *Expenses: Tuition:* Full-time $41,352; part-time $19,968 per year. *Required fees:* $2496; $1628 per unit. $814 per term. Tuition and fees vary according to course load and program. *Faculty research:* Applied macroeconomics, macroeconomics and macroeconomic policy, international financial markets, international trade and business, game theory.

North Carolina State University, Graduate School, Poole College of Management and College of Agriculture and Life Sciences, Program in Economics, Raleigh, NC 27695. Offers M Econ, MA, PhD. *Program availability:* Part-time. Terminal master's awarded for partial completion of doctoral program. *Degree requirements:* For master's, thesis (for some programs); for doctorate, thesis/dissertation. *Entrance requirements:* For master's and doctorate, GRE General Test. Additional exam requirements/recommendations for international students: Required—TOEFL. Electronic applications accepted. *Faculty research:* Endogenous growth modeling, generalized methods of moments estimation, integration and trade, agricultural policy, path dependence and network externalities.

Northeastern University, College of Social Sciences and Humanities, Boston, MA 02115. Offers criminology and criminal justice (MSCJ); criminology and justice policy (PhD); economics (MA, PhD); English (MA, PhD); international affairs (MA); law and public policy (PhD); political science (MA, PhD); public administration (MPA); public policy (MPP); security and resilience studies (MS); sociology (MA, PhD); urban and regional policy (MS); urban informatics (MS); world history (MA, PhD). *Program availability:* Online learning. *Faculty:* 242. *Students:* 491. In 2017, 143 master's, 38 doctorates awarded. *Degree requirements:* For doctorate, variable foreign language requirement, comprehensive exam, thesis/dissertation. *Entrance requirements:* For master's and doctorate, GRE. Additional exam requirements/recommendations for international students: Required—TOEFL, IELTS. Application fee: $75. Electronic applications accepted. *Expenses:* Contact institution. *Financial support:* Teaching assistantships, career-related internships or fieldwork, scholarships/grants, health care benefits, tuition waivers (full and partial), and unspecified assistantships available. Support available to part-time students. Financial award applicants required to submit FAFSA. *Unit head:* Dr. Uta Poiger, Dean, 617-373-5173, E-mail: college_of_social_sciences_and_humanities@neu.edu. *Application contact:* 617-373-5990, E-mail: gradcssh@northeastern.edu.
Website: http://www.northeastern.edu/cssh/

Northern Illinois University, Graduate School, College of Liberal Arts and Sciences, Department of Economics, De Kalb, IL 60115-2854. Offers MA, PhD. *Program availability:* Part-time. *Faculty:* 15 full-time (3 women). *Students:* 25 full-time (6 women), 7 part-time (3 women); includes 4 minority (1 Black or African American, non-Hispanic/Latino; 2 Hispanic/Latino; 1 Two or more races, non-Hispanic/Latino), 20 international. Average age 31. 62 applicants, 61% accepted, 10 enrolled. In 2017, 3 master's, 4 doctorates awarded. Terminal master's awarded for partial completion of doctoral program. *Degree requirements:* For master's, comprehensive exam, thesis or alternative; for doctorate, thesis/dissertation, candidacy exam, dissertation defense, research seminar. *Entrance requirements:* For master's, GRE General Test, minimum GPA of 2.75; for doctorate, GRE General Test, minimum GPA of 2.75 (undergraduate), 3.2 (graduate). Additional exam requirements/recommendations for international students: Required—TOEFL (minimum score 550 paper-based). *Application deadline:* For fall admission, 6/1 for domestic students, 5/1 for international students; for spring admission, 11/1 for domestic students, 10/1 for international students. Applications are processed on a rolling basis. Application fee: $40. Electronic applications accepted. *Financial support:* In 2017–18, 28 teaching assistantships with full tuition reimbursements were awarded; fellowships with full tuition reimbursements, research assistantships with full tuition reimbursements, career-related internships or fieldwork, Federal Work-Study, scholarships/grants, tuition waivers (full), and unspecified assistantships also available. Support available to part-time students. Financial award applicants required to submit FAFSA. *Faculty research:* Unemployment, behavior under uncertainty, effect of debt on compensation and capital utilization, racial inequality of earnings. *Unit head:* Dr. Carl Campbell, Acting Chair, 815-753-6974, Fax: 815-753-1019, E-mail: carlcamp@niu.edu. *Application contact:* Dr. Jeremy Groves, Director, Graduate Studies, 815-753-6957.
Website: http://www.niu.edu/econ/

Northwestern University, The Graduate School, Judd A. and Marjorie Weinberg College of Arts and Sciences, Department of Economics, Evanston, IL 60208. Offers PhD, JD/PhD. Admissions and degrees offered through The Graduate School. *Degree requirements:* For doctorate, thesis/dissertation, preliminary written exam. *Entrance requirements:* For doctorate, GRE General Test. Additional exam requirements/recommendations for international students: Required—TOEFL. *Faculty research:* Organization of industry, behavior of labor markets, effects of monetary policy, theory of markets.

Northwestern University, The Graduate School, Kellogg School of Management, Department of Managerial Economics and Decision Sciences, Evanston, IL 60208. Offers PhD. Admissions and degree offered through The Graduate School. *Degree requirements:* For doctorate, comprehensive exam, thesis/dissertation. *Entrance requirements:* For doctorate, GMAT or GRE General Test. Additional exam requirements/recommendations for international students: Required—TOEFL. Electronic applications accepted. *Faculty research:* Competitive strategy and organization, managerial economics, decision sciences, game theory, operations management.

Oakland University, Graduate Study and Lifelong Learning, School of Business Administration, Department of Economics, Rochester, MI 48309-4401. Offers economics (MBA, Certificate). *Expenses:* Tuition, state resident: full-time $16,950; part-time $706.25 per credit. Tuition, nonresident: full-time $24,648; part-time $1027 per credit.

The Ohio State University, Graduate School, College of Arts and Sciences, Division of Social and Behavioral Sciences, Department of Economics, Columbus, OH 43210. Offers MA, PhD. *Faculty:* 27. *Students:* 79 full-time (22 women), 56 international. Average age 28. In 2017, 15 master's, 17 doctorates awarded. *Entrance requirements:* For doctorate, GRE. Additional exam requirements/recommendations for international students: Required—TOEFL (minimum score 550 paper-based; 79 iBT), Michigan English Language Assessment Battery (minimum score 82); Recommended—IELTS (minimum score 7). *Application deadline:* For fall admission, 11/30 priority date for domestic and international students. Applications are processed on a rolling basis. Application fee: $60 ($70 for international students). Electronic applications accepted. *Financial support:* Fellowships, research assistantships, teaching assistantships, Federal Work-Study, and institutionally sponsored loans available. Support available to part-time students. *Unit head:* Dr. Trevon Logan, Professor/Chair, 614-292-0762, E-mail: logan.155@osu.edu. *Application contact:* Graduate and Professional Admissions, 614-292-9444, Fax: 614-292-3895, E-mail: gpadmissions@osu.edu.
Website: https://economics.osu.edu/

Ohio University, Graduate College, College of Arts and Sciences, Department of Economics, Athens, OH 45701-2979. Offers applied economics (MA); financial economics (MFE). *Program availability:* Part-time, evening/weekend. *Degree requirements:* For master's, thesis or alternative. *Entrance requirements:* For master's, GRE or GMAT (recommended), minimum GPA of 3.0. Additional exam requirements/recommendations for international students: Required—TOEFL (minimum score 550 paper-based; 80 iBT) or IELTS (minimum score 6.5). Electronic applications accepted. *Faculty research:* Macroeconomics, public finance, international economics and finance, monetary theory, healthcare economics.

Oklahoma State University, Spears School of Business, Department of Economics and Legal Studies in Business, Stillwater, OK 74078. Offers MS, PhD. *Program availability:* Part-time. *Faculty:* 23 full-time (8 women), 3 part-time/adjunct (1 woman). *Students:* 9 full-time (1 woman), 10 part-time (4 women); includes 2 minority (1 Asian,

non-Hispanic/Latino; 1 Hispanic/Latino), 14 international. Average age 30. 27 applicants, 19% accepted, 5 enrolled. In 2017, 2 doctorates awarded. *Entrance requirements:* For master's and doctorate, GRE or GMAT. Additional exam requirements/recommendations for international students: Required—TOEFL (minimum score 550 paper-based; 79 iBT). *Application deadline:* For fall admission, 3/1 priority date for international students; for spring admission, 8/1 priority date for international students. Applications are processed on a rolling basis. Application fee: $40 ($75 for international students). Electronic applications accepted. *Expenses:* Tuition, state resident: full-time $4019; part-time $2679.60 per year. Tuition, nonresident: full-time $15,286; part-time $10,190.40 per year. *Required fees:* $2129; $1419 per unit. Tuition and fees vary according to program. *Financial support:* Research assistantships, teaching assistantships, career-related internships or fieldwork, Federal Work-Study, scholarships/grants, health care benefits, tuition waivers (partial), and unspecified assistantships available. Support available to part-time students. Financial award application deadline: 3/1; financial award applicants required to submit FAFSA. *Faculty research:* Economics and legal studies in business, regional economic modeling/ econometrics, urban/regional economics, monetary economics, international trade/ finance/development, environmental economics. *Unit head:* Dr. Lee Adkins, Head, 405-744-5195, Fax: 405-744-5180, E-mail: lee.adkins@okstate.edu. *Application contact:* Dr. Mary Gade, Graduate Coordinator, 405-744-5197, Fax: 405-744-5180, E-mail: mary.gade@okstate.edu.
Website: https://business.okstate.edu/ecls/

Old Dominion University, Strome College of Business, Program in Economics, Norfolk, VA 23529. Offers MA. *Program availability:* Part-time, evening/weekend. *Faculty:* 11 full-time (1 woman). *Students:* 9 full-time (2 women), 6 part-time (2 women); includes 2 minority (1 Black or African American, non-Hispanic/Latino; 1 Asian, non-Hispanic/Latino), 5 international. Average age 29. 27 applicants, 70% accepted, 12 enrolled. In 2017, 10 master's awarded. *Degree requirements:* For master's, comprehensive exam, thesis optional, independent research. *Entrance requirements:* For master's, GMAT or GRE General Test, minimum GPA of 2.5. Additional exam requirements/recommendations for international students: Required—TOEFL (minimum score 520 paper-based; 79 iBT). *Application deadline:* For fall admission, 8/1 priority date for domestic students, 4/15 for international students; for spring admission, 11/1 priority date for domestic students, 10/1 for international students. Applications are processed on a rolling basis. Application fee: $50. Electronic applications accepted. *Expenses:* Contact institution. *Financial support:* In 2017–18, 8 students received support, including 8 research assistantships with partial tuition reimbursements available (averaging $3,200 per year); unspecified assistantships also available. Financial award application deadline: 8/1; financial award applicants required to submit FAFSA. *Faculty research:* International economics, transportation, public economics, macroeconomics, econometrics. *Unit head:* Dr. Christopher B. Colburn, Director, 757-683-4341, Fax: 757-638-5639, E-mail: dselover@odu.edu.
Website: http://www.odu.edu/business/departments/economics

Pace University, Lubin School of Business, Advanced Professional Certificate Program, New York, NY 10038. Offers business economics (APC); e-business (APC); financial management (APC); international business (APC); international economics (APC); investment management (APC); marketing (APC); public accounting (APC). *Program availability:* Part-time, evening/weekend. *Students:* 1 applicant, 100% accepted. *Entrance requirements:* For degree, MBA or MS in business discipline, relevant professional experience. Additional exam requirements/recommendations for international students: Required—TOEFL (minimum score 90 iBT), IELTS (minimum score 7) or PTE (minimum score 61). *Application deadline:* For fall admission, 8/1 priority date for domestic students, 6/1 for international students; for spring admission, 12/1 for domestic students, 10/1 for international students. Applications are processed on a rolling basis. Application fee: $70. Electronic applications accepted. *Unit head:* Dr. Jack Yurkiewicz, Director, 212-618-6567, E-mail: jyurkiewicz@pace.edu. *Application contact:* Susan Ford-Goldschein, Director of Graduate Admissions, 212-346-1531, Fax: 212-346-1585, E-mail: graduateadmission@pace.edu.
Website: http://www.pace.edu/lubin/agc

Penn State University Park, Graduate School, College of the Liberal Arts, Department of Economics, University Park, PA 16802. Offers MA, PhD. *Unit head:* Dr. Susan Welch, Dean, 814-865-7691, Fax: 814-863-2085. *Application contact:* Lori Hawn, Director, Graduate Student Services, 814-865-1795, Fax: 814-863-4627, E-mail: l-gswww@lists.psu.edu.
Website: http://econ.la.psu.edu/

Pepperdine University, School of Public Policy, Malibu, CA 90263. Offers American politics (MPP); economics (MPP); international relations (MPP); state and local policy (MPP); JD/MPP; MBA/MPP; MDR/MPP. *Students:* Average age 25. 174 applicants, 55% accepted, 29 enrolled. In 2017, 34 master's awarded. *Entrance requirements:* For master's, GRE or GMAT, 2 letters of recommendation, resume, two essays. Additional exam requirements/recommendations for international students: Required—TOEFL. *Application deadline:* For fall admission, 6/15 for domestic students. Applications are processed on a rolling basis. Application fee: $50. Electronic applications accepted. *Expenses:* Contact institution. *Financial support:* Institutionally sponsored loans and scholarships/grants available. Financial award application deadline: 5/1; financial award applicants required to submit FAFSA. *Unit head:* Dr. Pete Peterson, Dean, School of Public Policy, 310-506-7490, Fax: 310-506-7494, E-mail: pete.n.peterson@pepperdine.edu. *Application contact:* Carson Bruno, Assistant Dean for Admission and Program Relations, 310-506-7493, E-mail: carson.bruno@pepperdine.edu.
Website: http://publicpolicy.pepperdine.edu/

Peru State College, Graduate Programs, Program in Organizational Management, Peru, NE 68421. Offers MS. Program offered online only. *Program availability:* Part-time, online learning. *Degree requirements:* For master's, thesis (for some programs). *Expenses:* Contact institution. *Faculty research:* Emotional intelligence.

Portland State University, Graduate Studies, College of Liberal Arts and Sciences, Systems Science Program, Portland, OR 97207-0751. Offers computational intelligence (Certificate); computer modeling and simulation (Certificate); systems science (MS); systems science/anthropology (PhD); systems science/business administration (PhD); systems science/civil engineering (PhD); systems science/economics (PhD); systems science/engineering management (PhD); systems science/general (PhD); systems science/mathematical sciences (PhD); systems science/mechanical engineering (PhD); systems science/psychology (PhD); systems science/sociology (PhD). *Faculty:* 2 full-time (0 women), 4 part-time/adjunct (0 women). *Students:* 12 full-time (4 women), 22 part-time (6 women); includes 6 minority (4 Hispanic/Latino; 2 Two or more races, non-Hispanic/Latino). Average age 37. 18 applicants, 94% accepted, 16 enrolled. In 2017, 6 master's awarded. *Degree requirements:* For master's, comprehensive exam (for some programs), thesis optional; for doctorate, variable foreign language requirement, comprehensive exam (for some programs), thesis/dissertation. *Entrance requirements:* For master's, GRE/GMAT (recommended), minimum GPA of 3.0 on undergraduate or graduate work, 2 letters of recommendation, statement of interest; for doctorate, GMAT, GRE General Test, minimum GPA of 3.0 undergraduate, 3.25 graduate; 3 letters of recommendation; statement of interest. Additional exam requirements/ recommendations for international students: Required—TOEFL (minimum score 550 paper-based; 80 iBT). *Application deadline:* For fall admission, 1/15 for domestic and international students; for spring admission, 11/1 for domestic students. Application fee: $65. Electronic applications accepted. *Expenses:* Tuition, state resident: full-time $14,436; part-time $401 per credit. Tuition, nonresident: full-time $21,780; part-time $605 per credit. *Required fees:* $1380; $22 per credit. $119 per quarter. One-time fee: $325. Tuition and fees vary according to program. *Financial support:* In 2017–18, 1 teaching assistantship with full and partial tuition reimbursement (averaging $7,830 per year) was awarded; research assistantships, career-related internships or fieldwork, Federal Work-Study, scholarships/grants, and unspecified assistantships also available. Support available to part-time students. Financial award application deadline: 3/1; financial award applicants required to submit FAFSA. *Faculty research:* Systems theory and methodology, artificial intelligence neural networks, information theory, nonlinear dynamics/chaos, modeling and simulation. *Total annual research expenditures:* $169,034. *Unit head:* Dr. Wayne Wakeland, Chair, 503-725-4975, E-mail: wakeland@pdx.edu.
Website: http://www.pdx.edu/sysc/

Portland State University, Graduate Studies, College of Urban and Public Affairs, Department of Economics, Portland, OR 97207-0751. Offers economics (MA, MS); environmental and resource economics (Certificate). *Program availability:* Part-time. *Faculty:* 14 full-time (4 women), 5 part-time/adjunct (3 women). *Students:* 18 full-time (6 women), 4 part-time (1 woman); includes 3 minority (1 Black or African American, non-Hispanic/Latino; 1 Asian, non-Hispanic/Latino; 1 Two or more races, non-Hispanic/ Latino), 8 international. Average age 27. 24 applicants, 79% accepted, 11 enrolled. In 2017, 7 master's awarded. *Degree requirements:* For master's, variable foreign language requirement, thesis optional. *Entrance requirements:* For master's, GRE General Test, minimum GPA of 3.0 in economic course work and overall; course work in: calculus, intermediate microeconomics and macroeconomics, statistics, econometrics, linear algebra. Additional exam requirements/recommendations for international students: Required—TOEFL (minimum score 550 paper-based; 80 iBT). *Application deadline:* For fall admission, 2/1 for domestic and international students; for winter admission, 9/1 for domestic and international students; for spring admission, 12/5 for domestic and international students. Applications are processed on a rolling basis. Application fee: $65. *Expenses:* Tuition, state resident: full-time $14,436; part-time $401 per credit. Tuition, nonresident: full-time $21,780; part-time $605 per credit. *Required fees:* $1380; $22 per credit. $119 per quarter. One-time fee: $325. Tuition and fees vary according to program. *Financial support:* In 2017–18, 9 students received support, including 9 teaching assistantships with full and partial tuition reimbursements available (averaging $6,912 per year); career-related internships or fieldwork, Federal Work-Study, and unspecified assistantships also available. Support available to part-time students. Financial award application deadline: 3/1; financial award applicants required to submit FAFSA. *Faculty research:* NAFTA, economies of transition, economics of Eastern Europe, artificial intelligence, comparative economic systems. *Total annual research expenditures:* $443,749. *Unit head:* Dr. Hiro Ito, Chair, 503-725-3930, E-mail: ito@pdx.edu. *Application contact:* Margie Port, Office Coordinator, 503-725-3974, E-mail: mport@pdx.edu.
Website: https://www.pdx.edu/econ/

Princeton University, Graduate School, Department of Economics, Princeton, NJ 08544-1019. Offers PhD. *Degree requirements:* For doctorate, thesis/dissertation. *Entrance requirements:* For doctorate, GRE General Test, GRE Subject Test (recommended), working knowledge of multivariate calculus and matrix algebra. Additional exam requirements/recommendations for international students: Required—TOEFL (minimum score 600 paper-based). Electronic applications accepted.

Princeton University, Graduate School, Program in Population Studies, Princeton, NJ 08544-1019. Offers demography (PhD, Certificate); economics and demography (PhD); public affairs and demography (PhD); sociology and demography (PhD). *Degree requirements:* For doctorate, thesis/dissertation. *Entrance requirements:* For doctorate, GRE General Test. Additional exam requirements/recommendations for international students: Required—TOEFL (minimum score 600 paper-based). Electronic applications accepted. *Faculty research:* Models, fertility, infant and child mortality, migration.

Purdue University, Graduate School, Krannert School of Management, Doctoral Program in Economics, West Lafayette, IN 47907-2056. Offers PhD. *Students:* 36 full-time (12 women); includes 2 minority (1 Asian, non-Hispanic/Latino; 1 Hispanic/Latino), 17 international. Average age 26. 371 applicants, 4% accepted, 9 enrolled. In 2017, 1 doctorate awarded. *Degree requirements:* For doctorate, comprehensive exam, thesis/ dissertation, dissertation proposal in 3rd year of study. *Entrance requirements:* For doctorate, GRE, two semesters of calculus, one semester of linear algebra. Additional exam requirements/recommendations for international students: Required—TOEFL (minimum score 575 paper-based); Recommended—TWE. *Application deadline:* For fall admission, 2/15 priority date for domestic and international students. Application fee: $55. Electronic applications accepted. *Financial support:* In 2017–18, 30 students received support, including 1 fellowship with full and partial tuition reimbursement available (averaging $25,000 per year), 22 research assistantships with partial tuition reimbursements available (averaging $18,000 per year), 12 teaching assistantships with partial tuition reimbursements available (averaging $18,000 per year); institutionally sponsored loans, scholarships/grants, health care benefits, tuition waivers (partial), unspecified assistantships, and travel funds to present at a major conference also available. Financial award application deadline: 2/15. *Faculty research:* Econometrics, experimental economics, international economics, macroeconomic theory, industrial organization. *Unit head:* Dr. David Hummels, Dean/Professor of Economics, 765-494-4366. *Application contact:* Krannert PhD Admissions, 765-494-4375, E-mail: krannertphd@purdue.edu.
Website: http://www.krannert.purdue.edu/programs/phd/

Regent University, Graduate School, School of Business and Leadership, Virginia Beach, VA 23464-9800. Offers business administration (MBA), including accounting, economics, entrepreneurship, finance and investing, general management, healthcare management (MA, MBA), human resource management (MA, MBA), innovation management, leadership, marketing, not-for-profit management (MA, MBA); business analytics (MS); business and design management (MA); church leadership (MA); leadership (Certificate); organizational leadership (MA, PhD), including ecclesial leadership (DSL, PhD), entrepreneurial leadership (PhD), healthcare management (MA, MBA), human resource development (PhD), human resource management (MA, MBA), individualized studies (DSL, PhD), interdisciplinary studies (MA), leadership coaching and mentoring (MA), not-for-profit management (MA, MBA), organizational development consulting (MA), servant leadership (MA, DSL); strategic leadership (DSL), including ecclesial leadership (DSL, PhD), global consulting, healthcare leadership, individualized studies (DSL, PhD), leadership coaching, servant leadership (MA, DSL), strategic foresight. *Program availability:* Part-time, evening/weekend, 100% online, blended/ hybrid learning. *Faculty:* 9 full-time (2 women), 38 part-time/adjunct (11 women). *Students:* 129 full-time (80 women), 1,152 part-time (598 women); includes 685 minority (546 Black or African American, non-Hispanic/Latino; 10 American Indian or Alaska Native, non-Hispanic/Latino; 29 Asian, non-Hispanic/Latino; 65 Hispanic/Latino; 6 Native Hawaiian or other Pacific Islander, non-Hispanic/Latino; 29 Two or more races,

non-Hispanic/Latino), 62 international. Average age 41. 1,721 applicants, 48% accepted, 624 enrolled. In 2017, 125 master's, 69 doctorates awarded. *Degree requirements:* For master's, thesis or alternative, 3-credit hour culminating experience; for doctorate, thesis/dissertation. *Entrance requirements:* For master's, college transcripts, resume, essay; for doctorate, college transcripts, resume, essay, writing sample; for Certificate, writing sample, resume, transcripts. Additional exam requirements/recommendations for international students: Required—TOEFL (minimum score 577 paper-based). *Application deadline:* For fall admission, 5/1 priority date for domestic students; for spring admission, 10/1 priority date for domestic students. Applications are processed on a rolling basis. Application fee: $50. Electronic applications accepted. *Expenses:* $650 per credit (MA, MS, MBA); $995 per credit (PhD); $300 per semester technology fee. *Financial support:* In 2017–18, 829 students received support. Career-related internships or fieldwork, scholarships/grants, and unspecified assistantships available. Support available to part-time students. *Faculty research:* Servant leadership, global business, team effectiveness, technology utilization, leadership development. *Unit head:* Dr. Doris Gomez, Dean, 757-352-4686, Fax: 757-352-4634, E-mail: dorigom@regent.edu. *Application contact:* Heidi Cece, Assistant Vice President of Enrollment Management, 800-373-5504, Fax: 757-352-4381, E-mail: admissions@regent.edu.
Website: https://www.regent.edu/school-of-business-and-leadership/

Regis University, College of Business and Economics, Denver, CO 80221-1099. Offers accounting (MS); executive leadership (Certificate); finance (MS); finance and accounting (MBA); health industry leadership (MBA); human resource management and leadership (MSOL); management (MBA); marketing (MBA); nonprofit leadership (Post-Graduate Certificate); nonprofit management (MNM); nonprofit organizational capacity building (Certificate); operations management (MBA); organizational leadership and management (MSOL); project leadership and management (MS, MSOL); strategic business management (Certificate); strategic human resource integration (Certificate); strategic management (MBA). Programs offered at Colorado Springs Campus, Northwest Denver Campus, Southeast Denver Campus, Fort Collins Campus, Broomfield Campus, Henderson (Nevada) Campus, and Summerlin (Nevada) Campus. *Program availability:* Part-time, evening/weekend, 100% online, blended/hybrid learning. *Degree requirements:* For master's, thesis (for some programs), capstone or final research project. *Entrance requirements:* For master's, official transcript reflecting baccalaureate degree awarded from regionally-accredited college or university, interview, 2 years of full-time related work experience, resume, letters of recommendation. Additional exam requirements/recommendations for international students: Required—TOEFL (minimum score 550 paper-based; 82 iBT). Electronic applications accepted. *Expenses:* Contact institution. *Faculty research:* Impact of information technology on small business regulation of accounting, international project financing, mineral development, delivery of healthcare to rural indigenous communities.

Rice University, Graduate Programs, School of Social Sciences, Department of Economics, Houston, TX 77251-1892. Offers economics (PhD); energy economics (MEECON). *Degree requirements:* For doctorate, comprehensive exam, thesis/dissertation. *Entrance requirements:* For doctorate, GRE. Additional exam requirements/recommendations for international students: Required—TOEFL (minimum score 600 paper-based; 90 iBT). Electronic applications accepted.

Roosevelt University, Graduate Division, College of Arts and Sciences, Department of Economics, Chicago, IL 60605. Offers economics (MA). *Program availability:* Part-time, evening/weekend. *Students:* 9 full-time (1 woman), 6 part-time (4 women); includes 9 minority (4 Black or African American, non-Hispanic/Latino; 5 Hispanic/Latino), 3 international. Average age 30. 12 applicants, 100% accepted, 4 enrolled. In 2017, 8 master's awarded. *Application deadline:* Applications are processed on a rolling basis. Application fee: $40. Electronic applications accepted. *Financial support:* Career-related internships or fieldwork, scholarships/grants, and unspecified assistantships available. *Faculty research:* Labor, gender issues, international trade and development, entrepreneurship, political economy and money. *Application contact:* Sivling Lam, Graduate Admission Counselor, 312-281-3252, E-mail: slam02@roosevelt.edu.
Website: https://www.roosevelt.edu/

Roosevelt University, Graduate Division, College of Arts and Sciences, Department of Math, Actuarial Science, and Economics, Chicago, IL 60605. Offers actuarial science (MS); mathematics (MS), including mathematical sciences. *Students:* 8 full-time (1 woman), 5 part-time (2 women); includes 4 minority (1 Black or African American, non-Hispanic/Latino; 3 Hispanic/Latino), 3 international. Average age 30. 24 applicants, 83% accepted, 2 enrolled. In 2017, 8 master's awarded. *Application deadline:* Applications are processed on a rolling basis. Application fee: $40. Electronic applications accepted. *Financial support:* Career-related internships or fieldwork, scholarships/grants, and unspecified assistantships available. *Application contact:* Sivling Lam, Graduate Admission Counselor, 312-281-3252, E-mail: slam02@roosevelt.edu.

Rutgers University–Newark, Graduate School, Program in Economics, Newark, NJ 07102. Offers MA. *Entrance requirements:* For master's, GRE, minimum undergraduate B average.

Rutgers University–Newark, Rutgers Business School–Newark and New Brunswick, Doctoral Programs in Management, Newark, NJ 07102. Offers accounting (PhD); accounting information systems (PhD); economics (PhD); finance (PhD); individualized study (PhD); information technology (PhD); international business (PhD); management science (PhD); marketing science (PhD); organizational management (PhD); science, technology and management (PhD); supply chain management (PhD). *Degree requirements:* For doctorate, comprehensive exam, thesis/dissertation. *Entrance requirements:* For doctorate, GRE or GMAT. Additional exam requirements/recommendations for international students: Required—TOEFL (minimum score 550 paper-based; 79 iBT). Electronic applications accepted.

Rutgers University–New Brunswick, Graduate School-New Brunswick, Program in Economics, Piscataway, NJ 08854-8097. Offers MA, PhD. Terminal master's awarded for partial completion of doctoral program. *Degree requirements:* For master's, comprehensive exam (for some programs), thesis or alternative; for doctorate, comprehensive exam, thesis/dissertation. *Entrance requirements:* For master's and doctorate, GRE General Test. Additional exam requirements/recommendations for international students: Required—TOEFL. Electronic applications accepted. *Faculty research:* Econometrics, microeconomics, macroeconomics, economichistory.

St. Cloud State University, School of Graduate Studies, College of Social Sciences, Department of Economics, St. Cloud, MN 56301-4498. Offers applied economics (MS); public and nonprofit institutions (MS). *Program availability:* Part-time. *Degree requirements:* For master's, thesis or alternative. *Entrance requirements:* For master's, GRE General Test, minimum GPA of 2.75. Additional exam requirements/recommendations for international students: Recommended—TOEFL (minimum score 550 paper-based), IELTS (minimum score 6.5). Electronic applications accepted.

San Diego State University, Graduate and Research Affairs, College of Arts and Letters, Department of Economics, San Diego, CA 92182. Offers MA. *Entrance requirements:* For master's, GRE General Test, 2 letters of recommendation. Additional exam requirements/recommendations for international students: Required—TOEFL. Electronic applications accepted. *Faculty research:* Financing public education, demand for alternative fuel vehicles, economics of the Gold Rush, interdependence of equity and economic efficiency, economics of welfare.

San Francisco State University, Division of Graduate Studies, College of Business, Department of Economics, San Francisco, CA 94132-1722. Offers MA. *Unit head:* Dr. Sanjit Sengupta, Faculty Director, 415-817-4366, Fax: 415-817-4340, E-mail: sengupta@sfsu.edu. *Application contact:* Dr. Lisa Takeyama, Graduate Coordinator, 415-338-2499, E-mail: takeyama@sfsu.edu.
Website: http://cob.sfsu.edu/economics

San Jose State University, Graduate Studies and Research, College of Social Sciences, San Jose, CA 95192-0107. Offers applied anthropology (MA); communication studies (MA); economics (MA), including applied economics, economics; environmental studies (MS); geography (MA); history (MA), including history, history education; Mexican American studies (MA); psychology (MA, MS), including clinical psychology (MS), industrial/organizational psychology (MS), research and experimental psychology (MA); public administration (MPA); social sciences (MS); sociology (MA). *Faculty:* 59 full-time (29 women), 18 part-time/adjunct (5 women). *Students:* 181 full-time (126 women), 221 part-time (127 women); includes 228 minority (15 Black or African American, non-Hispanic/Latino; 48 Asian, non-Hispanic/Latino; 112 Hispanic/Latino; 3 Native Hawaiian or other Pacific Islander, non-Hispanic/Latino; 50 Two or more races, non-Hispanic/Latino), 38 international. Average age 30. 532 applicants, 44% accepted, 156 enrolled. In 2017, 139 master's awarded. *Degree requirements:* For master's, one foreign language, comprehensive exam, thesis (for some programs), project, field work, professional work experience. *Entrance requirements:* Additional exam requirements/recommendations for international students: Required—TOEFL (minimum score 550 paper-based; 80 iBT), IELTS (minimum score 6.5), PTE (minimum score 53). *Application deadline:* For fall admission, 2/1 for domestic and international students. Applications are processed on a rolling basis. Application fee: $55. Electronic applications accepted. *Expenses:* Tuition, state resident: full-time $7176. Tuition, nonresident: full-time $16,680. Tuition and fees vary according to course load and program. *Financial support:* Fellowships, research assistantships, career-related internships or fieldwork, Federal Work-Study, scholarships/grants, tuition waivers (full and partial), and unspecified assistantships available. Support available to part-time students. Financial award application deadline: 4/28; financial award applicants required to submit FAFSA. *Unit head:* Dr. Walt Jacobs, Dean, 408-924-5300, Fax: 408-924-5303, E-mail: walter.jacobs@sjsu.edu.
Website: http://www.sjsu.edu/socialsciences/

Simon Fraser University, Office of Graduate Studies and Postdoctoral Fellows, Faculty of Arts and Social Sciences, Department of Economics, Burnaby, BC V5A 1S6, Canada. Offers MA, PhD. *Degree requirements:* For master's, thesis (for some programs); for doctorate, comprehensive exam, thesis/dissertation. *Entrance requirements:* For master's, GRE, minimum GPA of 3.0 (on scale of 4.33) or 3.33 based on last 60 credits of undergraduate courses; for doctorate, GRE, minimum GPA of 3.5 (on scale of 4.33). Additional exam requirements/recommendations for international students: Recommended—TOEFL (minimum score 580 paper-based; 93 iBT), IELTS (minimum score 7), TWE (minimum score 5). *Faculty research:* Industrial organization, international trade, econometrics, labor, macroeconomics.

South Dakota State University, Graduate School, College of Agriculture and Biological Sciences, Department of Economics, Brookings, SD 57007. Offers MS. *Degree requirements:* For master's, comprehensive exam, thesis (for some programs), oral exam. *Entrance requirements:* For master's, minimum GPA of 2.75. Additional exam requirements/recommendations for international students: Required—TOEFL (minimum score 550 paper-based; 79 iBT). *Faculty research:* Sustainable agriculture, rural finance, grain and livestock marketing, agricultural policy, applied economics.

Southern Illinois University Carbondale, Graduate School, College of Liberal Arts, Department of Economics, Carbondale, IL 62901-4701. Offers MA, MS, PhD. *Degree requirements:* For master's, thesis; for doctorate, thesis/dissertation. *Entrance requirements:* For master's, GRE General Test, minimum GPA of 2.7; for doctorate, GRE General Test, minimum GPA of 3.25. Additional exam requirements/recommendations for international students: Required—TOEFL. *Faculty research:* Advanced economic theory, applied microeconomics, economic development, finance, international economics, monetary theory and policy.

Southern Illinois University Edwardsville, Graduate School, School of Business, Department of Economics and Finance, Edwardsville, IL 62026. Offers MA, MS. *Program availability:* Part-time, evening/weekend. *Degree requirements:* For master's, thesis or alternative, final exam, portfolio. *Entrance requirements:* For master's, GMAT or GRE. Additional exam requirements/recommendations for international students: Required—TOEFL (minimum score 550 paper-based; 79 iBT), IELTS (minimum score 6.5). Electronic applications accepted.

Southern Methodist University, Dedman College of Humanities and Sciences, Department of Economics, Dallas, TX 75205. Offers applied economics (MA); applied economics and predictive analytics (MS); economics (PhD); law and economics (MA). *Program availability:* Part-time, evening/weekend. Terminal master's awarded for partial completion of doctoral program. *Degree requirements:* For master's, thesis, oral qualifying exam; for doctorate, thesis/dissertation, written exams. *Entrance requirements:* For master's, GRE General Test or GMAT, 12 hours of course work in economics, minimum GPA of 3.0, previous course work in calculus and statistics; for doctorate, GRE General Test, minimum GPA of 3.0; 3 semesters of course work in calculus; 1 semester each of course work in statistics and linear algebra. Additional exam requirements/recommendations for international students: Required—TOEFL (minimum score 550 paper-based). Electronic applications accepted. *Faculty research:* Economic theory, game theory, econometrics, international trade, labor.

Southern New Hampshire University, School of Business, Manchester, NH 03106-1045. Offers accounting (MBA, Graduate Certificate); accounting finance (MS); accounting/auditing (MS); accounting/forensic accounting (MS); accounting/management accounting (MS); accounting/taxation (MS); applied economics (MS); athletic administration (MBA, Graduate Certificate); business administration (IMBA, Certificate), including business information systems (Certificate), human resource management (Certificate); business analytics (MBA); business intelligence (MBA); communication (MA), including new media and marketing, public relations; community economic development (MBA); criminal justice (MBA); data analytics (MS); economics (MBA); engineering management (MBA); entrepreneurship (MBA); finance (MBA, MS, Graduate Certificate); finance/corporate finance (MS); finance/investments (MS); forensic accounting (MBA); forensic accounting and fraud examination (Graduate Certificate); healthcare informatics (MBA); healthcare management (MBA); human resource management (MS); human resources (MBA); information technology (MS); information technology management (MBA); international business (PhD); Internet marketing (MBA); leadership (MBA); leadership of nonprofit organizations (Graduate Certificate); management (MS); marketing (MBA, MS, Graduate Certificate); music business (MBA); operations and project management (MS); operations and supply chain management (MBA, Graduate Certificate); organizational leadership (MS); project management (MBA, Graduate Certificate); public administration (MBA, Graduate Certificate); quantitative analysis (MBA); Six Sigma (Graduate Certificate); Six Sigma

quality (MBA); social media marketing (MBA, Graduate Certificate); sport management (MBA, MS, Graduate Certificate); sustainability and environmental compliance (MBA); MBA/Certificate. *Accreditation:* ACBSP. *Program availability:* Part-time, evening/ weekend, online learning. Terminal master's awarded for partial completion of doctoral program. *Degree requirements:* For master's, one foreign language, comprehensive exam (for some programs), thesis or alternative; for doctorate, one foreign language, comprehensive exam, thesis/dissertation. *Entrance requirements:* For master's, minimum GPA of 2.5; for doctorate, GMAT. Additional exam requirements/ recommendations for international students: Required—TOEFL (minimum score 500 paper-based). *Application deadline:* Applications are processed on a rolling basis. Application fee: $40. Electronic applications accepted. *Expenses: Tuition:* Part-time $627 per credit hour. Part-time tuition and fees vary according to campus/location and program. *Financial support:* Career-related internships or fieldwork, Federal Work-Study, institutionally sponsored loans, scholarships/grants, tuition waivers (partial), and unspecified assistantships available. Support available to part-time students. Financial award applicants required to submit FAFSA. *Unit head:* Dr. Bill Lightfoot, Dean, 603-644-3102, Fax: 603-644-3144. *Application contact:* Office of Graduate Admission, 888-327-SNHU, Fax: 603-644-3144, E-mail: enroll@snhu.edu.

Stanford University, School of Humanities and Sciences, Department of Economics, Stanford, CA 94305-2004. Offers PhD. *Degree requirements:* For doctorate, comprehensive exam, thesis/dissertation. *Entrance requirements:* For doctorate, GRE General Test. Additional exam requirements/recommendations for international students: Required—TOEFL. Electronic applications accepted. *Expenses: Tuition:* Full-time $48,987; part-time $10,620 per quarter. One-time fee: $400. Tuition and fees vary according to program.

State University of New York College of Environmental Science and Forestry, Program in Environmental Science, Syracuse, NY 13210-2779. Offers biophysical and ecological economics (MPS); coupled natural and human systems (MPS); ecosystem restoration (MPS); environmental and community land planning (MPS, MS); environmental and natural resources policy (PhD); environmental communication and participatory processes (PhD); environmental monitoring and modeling (MPS); water and wetland resource studies (MPS, MS). *Program availability:* Part-time. *Faculty:* 1 full-time (0 women), 1 (woman) part-time/adjunct. *Students:* 57 full-time (36 women), 13 part-time (9 women); includes 5 minority (1 Black or African American, non-Hispanic/ Latino; 2 Asian, non-Hispanic/Latino; 2 Hispanic/Latino), 26 international. Average age 30. 64 applicants, 63% accepted, 15 enrolled. In 2017, 15 master's, 4 doctorates awarded. Terminal master's awarded for partial completion of doctoral program. *Degree requirements:* For master's, thesis (for some programs); for doctorate, comprehensive exam, thesis/dissertation. *Entrance requirements:* For master's and doctorate, GRE General Test, minimum GPA of 3.0. Additional exam requirements/recommendations for international students: Required—TOEFL (minimum score 550 paper-based; 80 iBT), IELTS (minimum score 6). *Application deadline:* For fall admission, 2/1 priority date for domestic and international students; for spring admission, 11/1 priority date for domestic and international students. Applications are processed on a rolling basis. Application fee: $60. Electronic applications accepted. *Expenses:* Tuition, state resident: full-time $10,870; part-time $453 per credit. Tuition, nonresident: full-time $22,210; part-time $925 per credit. *Required fees:* $1435; $70.85 per credit. One-time fee: $25 full-time. Part-time tuition and fees vary according to course load. *Financial support:* In 2017–18, 20 students received support. Unspecified assistantships available. Financial award application deadline: 6/30; financial award applicants required to submit FAFSA. *Faculty research:* Environmental education/communications, water resources, land resources, waste management. *Total annual research expenditures:* $47,415. *Unit head:* Dr. Russell Briggs, Director of the Division of Environmental Science, 315-470-6989, Fax: 315-470-6700, E-mail: rdbriggs@esf.edu. *Application contact:* Scott Shannon, Associate Provost for Instruction/Dean of the Graduate School, 315-470-6599, Fax: 315-470-6978, E-mail: esfgrad@esf.edu.
Website: http://www.esf.edu/environmentalscience/graduate/

Stony Brook University, State University of New York, Graduate School, College of Arts and Sciences, Department of Economics, Stony Brook, NY 11794. Offers MA, PhD. *Faculty:* 14 full-time (6 women), 6 part-time/adjunct (1 woman). *Students:* 62 full-time (28 women); includes 1 minority (Hispanic/Latino), 56 international. Average age 28. 162 applicants, 53% accepted, 17 enrolled. In 2017, 13 master's, 7 doctorates awarded. *Degree requirements:* For doctorate, comprehensive exam, thesis/dissertation. *Entrance requirements:* For master's and doctorate, GRE General Test. Additional exam requirements/recommendations for international students: Required—TOEFL (minimum score 90 iBT). *Application deadline:* For fall admission, 1/15 for domestic students; for spring admission, 10/1 for domestic students. Application fee: $100. Electronic applications accepted. *Expenses:* Contact institution. *Financial support:* In 2017–18, 34 teaching assistantships were awarded; fellowships and research assistantships also available. *Faculty research:* Economics, economic theory, macroeconomics, industrial organization, labor economics. *Total annual research expenditures:* $140,773. *Unit head:* Prof. Juan Carlos Conesa, Chair, 631-632-7549, Fax: 631-632-7516, E-mail: juan.conesa@stonybrook.edu. *Application contact:* Maryann Calvacca, Graduate Program Coordinator, 631-632-7537, Fax: 631-632-7516, E-mail: graduate_economics@stonybrook.edu.
Website: http://www.sunysb.edu/economics/

Syracuse University, Maxwell School of Citizenship and Public Affairs, Dual MA Program in Economics and International Relations, Syracuse, NY 13244. Offers MA/MA. *Entrance requirements:* Additional exam requirements/recommendations for international students: Required—TOEFL (minimum score 100 iBT). *Application deadline:* For fall admission, 2/1 priority date for domestic and international students. Application fee: $75. Electronic applications accepted. *Financial support:* Fellowships with full tuition reimbursements, research assistantships, and teaching assistantships available. Financial award application deadline: 1/1. *Faculty research:* Economic concepts, urban and regional economics, policy-oriented settings, public and international affairs, comparative foreign policy. *Unit head:* Dr. Robert Bifulco, Associate Dean and Chair, Public Administration and International Affairs, 315-443-3232, E-mail: rbifulco@maxwell.syr.edu. *Application contact:* Christine Omolino, Associate Director, 315-443-4000, Fax: 315-443-3423, E-mail: comolino@syr.edu.
Website: https://www.maxwell.syr.edu/paia/degrees/MAIR/Economics_Overview/

Syracuse University, Maxwell School of Citizenship and Public Affairs, Programs in Economics, Syracuse, NY 13244. Offers MA, PhD. In 2017, 35 master's, 5 doctorates awarded. *Degree requirements:* For doctorate, comprehensive exam, thesis/ dissertation. *Entrance requirements:* For master's and doctorate, GRE General Test, personal statement, three letters of recommendation, resume, official transcripts. Additional exam requirements/recommendations for international students: Required—TOEFL (minimum score 100 iBT). *Application deadline:* For fall admission, 1/15 priority date for domestic and international students. Applications are processed on a rolling basis. Application fee: $75. Electronic applications accepted. *Financial support:* Fellowships with full tuition reimbursements, research assistantships, and teaching assistantships available. Financial award application deadline: 1/1. *Faculty research:* International economics, labor economics, public finance, urban economics. *Unit head:* Dr. Stuart Rosenthal, Department Chair, 315-443-3809, E-mail: ssrosent@maxwell.syr.edu. *Application contact:* Sue Lewis, Recruiting Contact, 315-443-5763, E-mail: swlewis@syr.edu.
Website: https://www.maxwell.syr.edu/econ/Graduate_Programs/

Teachers College, Columbia University, Department of Education Policy and Social Analysis, New York, NY 10027-6696. Offers economics and education (Ed M, MA, PhD); education policy (Ed M, MA, Ed D, PhD); politics and education (Ed M, MA, Ed D, PhD); sociology and education (Ed M, MA, Ed D, PhD). *Students:* 144 full-time (109 women), 107 part-time (85 women); includes 100 minority (43 Black or African American, non-Hispanic/Latino; 17 Asian, non-Hispanic/Latino; 33 Hispanic/Latino; 7 Two or more races, non-Hispanic/Latino), 69 international. Average age 29. 524 applicants, 53% accepted, 104 enrolled. *Unit head:* Dr. Aaron Pallas, Chair, E-mail: amp155@tc.columbia.edu. *Application contact:* David Estrella, Director of Admissions, 212-678-3305, E-mail: estrella@tc.columbia.edu.
Website: http://www.tc.columbia.edu/education-policy-and-social-analysis/

Temple University, College of Liberal Arts, Department of Economics, Philadelphia, PA 19122-6096. Offers MA, PhD. *Program availability:* Part-time, evening/weekend. *Faculty:* 21 full-time (3 women), 3 part-time/adjunct (0 women). *Students:* 39 full-time (17 women), 6 part-time (2 women); includes 4 minority (all Black or African American, non-Hispanic/Latino), 23 international. 76 applicants, 57% accepted, 14 enrolled. In 2017, 8 master's, 11 doctorates awarded. *Entrance requirements:* For master's and doctorate, GRE, minimum GPA of 3.0, 3 letters of recommendation. Additional exam requirements/recommendations for international students: Required—TOEFL (minimum score 550 paper-based; 79 iBT). *Application deadline:* For fall admission, 3/1 for domestic students, 12/15 for international students; for spring admission, 11/1 for domestic students, 8/1 for international students. Application fee: $60. Electronic applications accepted. *Expenses:* Tuition, state resident: full-time $16,164; part-time $898 per credit hour. Tuition, nonresident: full-time $22,158; part-time $1231 per credit hour. *Required fees:* $890; $445 per semester. Full-time tuition and fees vary according to course load, degree level, campus/location and program. *Financial support:* Application deadline: 1/15; applicants required to submit FAFSA. *Faculty research:* Applied econometrics, health economics, labor economics, macroeconomic theory, microeconomic theory. *Unit head:* Dr. Dimitrios I. Diamantaras, Acting Graduate Director, 215-204-8169. *Application contact:* Linda Wyatt, Graduate Program Coordinator, 215-204-6638, E-mail: ldwyatt@temple.edu.
Website: http://www.cla.temple.edu/economics/

Texas A&M University, College of Liberal Arts, Department of Economics, College Station, TX 77843. Offers MS, PhD. *Program availability:* Part-time. *Faculty:* 29. *Students:* 266 full-time (116 women), 9 part-time (5 women); includes 24 minority (6 Black or African American, non-Hispanic/Latino; 9 Asian, non-Hispanic/Latino; 8 Hispanic/Latino; 1 Two or more races, non-Hispanic/Latino), 208 international. Average age 25. 358 applicants, 51% accepted, 108 enrolled. In 2017, 96 master's, 13 doctorates awarded. Terminal master's awarded for partial completion of doctoral program. *Degree requirements:* For master's, comprehensive exam, thesis optional; for doctorate, comprehensive exam, thesis/dissertation. *Entrance requirements:* For master's and doctorate, GRE General Test. Additional exam requirements/ recommendations for international students: Required—TOEFL (minimum score 550 paper-based; 80 iBT), IELTS (minimum score 6), PTE (minimum score 53). *Application deadline:* For fall admission, 3/1 for domestic students. Applications are processed on a rolling basis. Application fee: $50 ($90 for international students). Electronic applications accepted. *Expenses:* Contact institution. *Financial support:* In 2017–18, 157 students received support, including 7 fellowships with tuition reimbursements available (averaging $25,429 per year), 12 research assistantships with tuition reimbursements available (averaging $13,844 per year), 49 teaching assistantships with tuition reimbursements available (averaging $13,939 per year); career-related internships or fieldwork, institutionally sponsored loans, scholarships/grants, traineeships, health care benefits, tuition waivers (full and partial), and unspecified assistantships also available. Support available to part-time students. Financial award application deadline: 3/15; financial award applicants required to submit FAFSA. *Faculty research:* Tax policy, state tax, labor, international economics, macroeconomics. *Unit head:* Dr. Timothy Gronberg, Head, 979-845-7351, E-mail: tjg@econmail.tamu.edu. *Application contact:* Dr. Dennis W. Jansen, Director of Doctoral Program, 979-845-7351, Fax: 979-847-8557, E-mail: d-jansen@tamu.edu.
Website: http://econ.tamu.edu/

Texas Tech University, Graduate School, College of Arts and Sciences, Department of Economics, Lubbock, TX 79409. Offers MA, PhD. *Faculty:* 13 full-time (1 woman). *Students:* 47 full-time (19 women), 6 part-time (1 woman); includes 2 minority (both Hispanic/Latino), 48 international. Average age 31. 50 applicants, 42% accepted, 11 enrolled. In 2017, 4 master's, 1 doctorate awarded. Terminal master's awarded for partial completion of doctoral program. *Degree requirements:* For master's, variable foreign language requirement, comprehensive exam (for some programs), thesis (for some programs); for doctorate, variable foreign language requirement, comprehensive exam, thesis/dissertation. *Entrance requirements:* Additional exam requirements/ recommendations for international students: Required—TOEFL (minimum score 550 paper-based; 79 iBT). *Application deadline:* For fall admission, 6/1 priority date for domestic students, 1/15 priority date for international students; for spring admission, 9/1 priority date for domestic students, 6/15 priority date for international students. Applications are processed on a rolling basis. Application fee: $75. Electronic applications accepted. *Expenses:* Contact institution. *Financial support:* In 2017–18, 40 students received support, including 37 fellowships (averaging $1,838 per year), 40 teaching assistantships (averaging $14,150 per year); research assistantships, scholarships/grants, unspecified assistantships, and partial tuition and fee waivers also available. Financial award application deadline: 3/1; financial award applicants required to submit FAFSA. *Faculty research:* Industrial organization, labor economics, public finance, monetary economics, international economics. *Total annual research expenditures:* $1,411. *Unit head:* Dr. Klaus G. Becker, Associate Professor/Chair, 806-834-7275, Fax: 806-742-1137, E-mail: klaus.becker@ttu.edu. *Application contact:* Rosie Carrillo, Business Manager, 806-742-2201, Fax: 806-742-1137, E-mail: rosie.carrillo@ttu.edu.
Website: http://www.depts.ttu.edu/economics/

Troy University, Graduate School, College of Business, Program in Economics, Troy, AL 36082. Offers MA. *Program availability:* Part-time, evening/weekend. *Faculty:* 8 full-time (3 women). *Students:* 6 full-time (3 women), 2 part-time (1 woman); includes 1 minority (Black or African American, non-Hispanic/Latino). Average age 24. 10 applicants, 70% accepted, 4 enrolled. In 2017, 4 master's awarded. *Degree requirements:* For master's, thesis or alternative, minimum GPA of 3.0, capstone course, research course, admission to candidacy. *Entrance requirements:* For master's, GRE (minimum score of 850 on old exam or 290 on new exam), GMAT (minimum score of 380) or MAT (minimum score of 385), official transcripts; bachelor's degree; minimum GPA of 2.5 in all undergraduate work or 3.0 for last 30 semester hours; letter of recommendation. Additional exam requirements/recommendations for international students: Required—TOEFL (minimum score 523 paper-based; 70 iBT), IELTS (minimum score 6). *Application deadline:* Applications are processed on a rolling basis. Application fee: $50. Electronic applications accepted. *Expenses:* Tuition, state

resident: part-time $417 per credit hour. Tuition, nonresident: part-time $834 per credit hour. *Required fees:* $42 per credit hour. $50 per semester. Tuition and fees vary according to campus/location. *Financial support:* Fellowships, career-related internships or fieldwork, and scholarships/grants available. Support available to part-time students. Financial award applicants required to submit FAFSA. *Unit head:* Dr. George Crowley, Chairman, Economics, 334-670-3525, Fax: 334-670-3708, E-mail: grcrowley@troy.edu. *Application contact:* Jessica A. Kimbro, Director of Graduate Admissions, 334-670-3178, Fax: 334-670-3733, E-mail: bcamp@troy.edu.

Tufts University, The Fletcher School of Law and Diplomacy, Medford, MA 02155. Offers economics and public policy (PhD); international affairs (PhD); international business (MIB); international law (LL M); law and diplomacy (MA, MALD); transatlantic affairs (MA); DVM/MA; JD/MALD; MALD/MA; MALD/MBA; MALD/MS; MD/MA. MA in transatlantic affairs offered jointly with The College of Europe; PhD in economics and public policy with Tufts' Graduate School of Arts and Sciences. *Program availability:* Online learning. *Degree requirements:* For master's, one foreign language, thesis; for doctorate, one foreign language, comprehensive exam, thesis/dissertation, dissertation defense. *Entrance requirements:* For master's and doctorate, GMAT or GRE General Test. Additional exam requirements/recommendations for international students: Required—TOEFL (minimum score 600 paper-based; 100 iBT), IELTS (minimum score 7). Electronic applications accepted. *Expenses:* Contact institution. *Faculty research:* Negotiation and conflict resolution, international organizations, international business and economic law, security studies, development economics.

Tufts University, Graduate School of Arts and Sciences, Department of Economics, Medford, MA 02155. Offers economics (MS); economics and public policy (PhD). Program offered jointly with The Fletcher School of Law and Diplomacy. *Program availability:* Part-time. *Students:* 41 full-time (18 women), 37 international. Average age 24. 217 applicants, 49% accepted, 28 enrolled. In 2017, 14 master's awarded. *Degree requirements:* For master's, thesis optional. *Entrance requirements:* For master's, GRE General Test. Additional exam requirements/recommendations for international students: Required—TOEFL (minimum score 550 paper-based; 80 iBT), IELTS (minimum score 6.5). *Application deadline:* For fall admission, 2/15 for domestic and international students. Applications are processed on a rolling basis. Application fee: $85. Electronic applications accepted. *Expenses:* Contact institution. *Financial support:* Teaching assistantships, Federal Work-Study, scholarships/grants, tuition waivers (full and partial), and unspecified assistantships available. Financial award application deadline: 1/15. *Unit head:* Dr. Gilbert Metcalf, Graduate Program Director. *Application contact:* Office of Graduate Admissions, 617-627-3395, E-mail: gradadmissions@tufts.edu.
Website: http://ase.tufts.edu/econ

Tulane University, School of Liberal Arts, Department of Economics, New Orleans, LA 70118-5669. Offers MA, PhD. *Degree requirements:* For master's, thesis or alternative; for doctorate, one foreign language, thesis/dissertation. *Entrance requirements:* For master's, GRE General Test, minimum B average in undergraduate course work; for doctorate, GRE General Test. Additional exam requirements/recommendations for international students: Required—TOEFL. Electronic applications accepted. *Expenses: Tuition:* Full-time $50,920; part-time $2829 per credit hour. *Required fees:* $2040; $44.50 per credit hour. $580 per term. Tuition and fees vary according to course load, degree level and program. *Faculty research:* Economic development, public finance, labor economics, international and regional economics, industrial organization.

Universidad de las Américas Puebla, Division of Graduate Studies, School of Social Sciences, Program in Economics, Puebla, Mexico. Offers economics (MA); finance (M Adm). *Program availability:* Part-time, evening/weekend. *Degree requirements:* For master's, one foreign language, thesis. *Faculty research:* Economic models (mathematics), industrial organization, assets and values market.

Université de Moncton, Faculty of Arts and Social Sciences, Department of Economics, Moncton, NB E1A 3E9, Canada. Offers MA. *Degree requirements:* For master's, one foreign language, thesis. *Entrance requirements:* For master's, minimum GPA of 3.0. *Faculty research:* Free trade, public finance, small and medium size businesses, regional development, demography and development.

Université de Montréal, Faculty of Arts and Sciences, Department of Economic Sciences, Montréal, QC H3C 3J7, Canada. Offers economics (M Sc, PhD); mathematical and computational finance (M Sc). *Degree requirements:* For master's, one foreign language, thesis; for doctorate, one foreign language, thesis/dissertation, general exam. Electronic applications accepted. *Faculty research:* Applied and economic theory, public choice, international trade, labor economics, industrial organization.

Université de Sherbrooke, Faculty of Administration, Program in Economics, Sherbrooke, QC J1K 2R1, Canada. Offers M Sc. Terminal master's awarded for partial completion of doctoral program. *Degree requirements:* For master's, one foreign language, thesis. *Entrance requirements:* For master's, minimum GPA of 3.0 (on 4.3 scale). Electronic applications accepted. *Faculty research:* Poverty and inequality analysis, wellbeing analysis, international trade, econometrics.

Université de Sherbrooke, Faculty of Letters and Human Sciences, Department of Economics, Sherbrooke, QC J1K 2R1, Canada. Offers MA. *Degree requirements:* For master's, thesis. *Faculty research:* Economic development, public finance, macroeconomics.

Université du Québec à Montréal, Graduate Programs, Program in Economics, Montréal, QC H3C 3P8, Canada. Offers M Sc, PhD. *Program availability:* Part-time. *Degree requirements:* For master's, thesis; for doctorate, thesis/dissertation. *Entrance requirements:* For master's, appropriate bachelor's degree or equivalent, proficiency in French; for doctorate, appropriate master's degree or equivalent, proficiency in French.

Université Laval, Faculty of Social Sciences, Department of Economics, Programs in Economics, Québec, QC G1K 7P4, Canada. Offers MA, PhD. Terminal master's awarded for partial completion of doctoral program. *Degree requirements:* For master's, thesis (for some programs); for doctorate, comprehensive exam, thesis/dissertation. *Entrance requirements:* For master's and doctorate, knowledge of French. Electronic applications accepted.

University at Albany, State University of New York, College of Arts and Sciences, Department of Economics, Albany, NY 12222-0001. Offers economic forecasting (MA); economics (MA, PhD). *Program availability:* Part-time. *Faculty:* 18 full-time (3 women). *Students:* 48 full-time (17 women), 41 part-time (21 women); includes 10 minority (1 Black or African American, non-Hispanic/Latino; 5 Asian, non-Hispanic/Latino; 3 Hispanic/Latino; 1 Two or more races, non-Hispanic/Latino), 64 international. 159 applicants, 44% accepted, 30 enrolled. In 2017, 14 master's, 3 doctorates awarded. Terminal master's awarded for partial completion of doctoral program. *Degree requirements:* For doctorate, one foreign language, thesis/dissertation. *Entrance requirements:* For doctorate, GRE General Test, GRE Subject Test. Additional exam requirements/recommendations for international students: Required—TOEFL (minimum score 550 paper-based). *Application deadline:* For fall admission, 2/15 for domestic students, 5/1 for international students. Applications are processed on a rolling basis. Application fee: $75. Electronic applications accepted. *Expenses:* Tuition, state resident: full-time $10,870; part-time $453 per credit hour. Tuition, nonresident: full-time $22,210; part-time $925 per credit hour. *Required fees:* $84.68 per credit hour. $508.06 per semester. Part-time tuition and fees vary according to course load and program. *Financial support:* Fellowships, research assistantships, teaching assistantships, career-related internships or fieldwork, institutionally sponsored loans, and lectureships available. Financial award application deadline: 2/15. *Faculty research:* Expectations of inflation and interest rates, diffusion of new technology, labor markets in developing countries, government deficits and international exchange markets. *Unit head:* Betty Daniel, Chair, 518-442-4735, Fax: 518-442-4736, E-mail: bdaniel@albany.edu. *Application contact:* Michael DeRensis, Director, Graduate Admissions, 518-442-3980, Fax: 518-442-3922, E-mail: graduate@albany.edu.
Website: http://www.albany.edu/econ/

University at Albany, State University of New York, Nelson A. Rockefeller College of Public Affairs and Policy, Department of Public Administration and Policy, Albany, NY 12222-0001. Offers financial management and public economics (MPA); financial market regulation (MPA); health policy (MPA); healthcare management (MPA); homeland security (MPA); human resources management (MPA); information strategy and management (MPA); local government management (MPA); nonprofit management (MPA); nonprofit management and leadership (Certificate); organizational behavior and theory (MPA, PhD); planning and policy analysis (CAS); policy analysis (MPA); politics and administration (PhD); public finance (PhD); public management (PhD); public policy (PhD); public sector management (Certificate); women and public policy (Certificate); JD/MPA. JD/MPA offered jointly with Albany Law School. *Accreditation:* NASPAA (one or more programs are accredited). *Faculty:* 21 full-time (7 women), 14 part-time/adjunct (7 women). *Students:* 115 full-time (59 women), 93 part-time (56 women); includes 41 minority (11 Black or African American, non-Hispanic/Latino; 9 Asian, non-Hispanic/Latino; 18 Hispanic/Latino; 3 Two or more races, non-Hispanic/Latino), 32 international. 236 applicants, 69% accepted, 86 enrolled. In 2017, 57 master's, 1 doctorate, 14 other advanced degrees awarded. *Degree requirements:* For doctorate, one foreign language, thesis/dissertation. *Entrance requirements:* For doctorate, GRE General Test. Additional exam requirements/recommendations for international students: Required—TOEFL (minimum score 550 paper-based). *Application deadline:* For fall admission, 2/1 priority date for domestic students, 5/1 for international students; for spring admission, 12/1 for domestic students. Applications are processed on a rolling basis. Application fee: $75. Electronic applications accepted. *Expenses:* Tuition, state resident: full-time $10,870; part-time $453 per credit hour. Tuition, nonresident: full-time $22,210; part-time $925 per credit hour. *Required fees:* $84.68 per credit hour. $508.06 per semester. Part-time tuition and fees vary according to course load and program. *Financial support:* Application deadline: 2/1. *Unit head:* Victor Asal, Chair, 518-591-8729, E-mail: vasal@albany.edu.
Website: http://www.albany.edu/rockefeller/pad.shtml

University at Buffalo, the State University of New York, Graduate School, College of Arts and Sciences, Department of Economics, Buffalo, NY 14260. Offers econometrics and quantitative economics (MS); economics (MA, PhD); financial economics (Certificate); health services (Certificate); information and Internet economics (Certificate); international economics (Certificate); law and regulation (Certificate); urban and regional economics (Certificate). *Program availability:* Part-time. *Faculty:* 17 full-time (3 women), 5 part-time/adjunct (2 women). *Students:* 119 full-time (42 women); includes 14 minority (8 Black or African American, non-Hispanic/Latino; 6 Asian, non-Hispanic/Latino), 75 international. Average age 27. 229 applicants, 28% accepted, 30 enrolled. In 2017, 28 master's, 5 doctorates, 2 other advanced degrees awarded. Terminal master's awarded for partial completion of doctoral program. *Degree requirements:* For master's, comprehensive exam; for doctorate, comprehensive exam, thesis/dissertation, field and theory exams. *Entrance requirements:* For master's, GRE General Test or GMAT; for doctorate, GRE General Test. Additional exam requirements/recommendations for international students: Required—TOEFL (minimum score 550 paper-based; 79 iBT), TWE. *Application deadline:* For fall admission, 1/15 priority date for domestic and international students. Applications are processed on a rolling basis. Application fee: $75. Electronic applications accepted. *Financial support:* In 2017–18, 8 students received support, including 3 fellowships with full tuition reimbursements available (averaging $13,594 per year), 1 research assistantship with full tuition reimbursement available (averaging $13,594 per year), 20 teaching assistantships with full tuition reimbursements available (averaging $13,594 per year); Federal Work-Study, health care benefits, and unspecified assistantships also available. Financial award application deadline: 2/1; financial award applicants required to submit FAFSA. *Faculty research:* Human capital, international economics, econometrics, applied economics, urban economics, economic growth and development. *Unit head:* Dr. Alex Anas, Chair, 716-645-8663, Fax: 716-645-2127, E-mail: alexanas@buffalo.edu. *Application contact:* Dr. Nagesh Revankar, Director of Graduate Studies, 716-645-2121 Ext. 428, Fax: 716-645-2127, E-mail: ecorevan@buffalo.edu.
Website: http://www.economics.buffalo.edu/

University at Buffalo, the State University of New York, Graduate School, Graduate School of Education, Department of Educational Leadership and Policy, Buffalo, NY 14260. Offers economics and education policy analysis (MA); education studies (Ed M); educational administration (Ed M, Ed D, PhD); educational culture, policy and society (PhD); higher education administration (Ed M, PhD); school building leadership (Certificate); school business and human resource administration (Certificate); school district business leadership (Certificate); school district leadership (Certificate). *Program availability:* Part-time, evening/weekend. *Faculty:* 16 full-time (10 women), 9 part-time/adjunct (6 women). *Students:* 65 full-time (44 women), 125 part-time (82 women); includes 29 minority (23 Black or African American, non-Hispanic/Latino; 3 Asian, non-Hispanic/Latino; 3 Hispanic/Latino), 19 international. Average age 35. 153 applicants, 75% accepted, 59 enrolled. In 2017, 45 master's, 4 doctorates, 23 other advanced degrees awarded. *Degree requirements:* For master's, comprehensive exam (for some programs), thesis optional; for doctorate, comprehensive exam, thesis/dissertation. *Entrance requirements:* For master's, interview, letters of reference; for doctorate, GRE General Test or MAT, writing sample, letters of reference. Additional exam requirements/recommendations for international students: Required—TOEFL (minimum score 550 paper-based; 79 iBT). *Application deadline:* For fall admission, 2/1 priority date for domestic students, 2/1 for international students; for spring admission, 11/15 priority date for domestic students, 10/1 for international students. Applications are processed on a rolling basis. Application fee: $50. Electronic applications accepted. *Financial support:* In 2017–18, 18 fellowships (averaging $5,673 per year), 34 research assistantships with tuition reimbursements (averaging $12,055 per year) were awarded; career-related internships or fieldwork, Federal Work-Study, institutionally sponsored loans, scholarships/grants, health care benefits, tuition waivers (full and partial), and unspecified assistantships also available. Financial award application deadline: 3/15; financial award applicants required to submit FAFSA. *Faculty research:* College access and choice, school leadership preparation and practice, public policy, curriculum and pedagogy, comparative and international education. *Total annual research expenditures:* $637,951. *Unit head:* Dr. Janina C. Brutt-Griffler, Chair, 716-645-2471, Fax: 716-645-2481, E-mail: bruttg@buffalo.edu. *Application contact:* Veronica Kase, Admission Assistant, 716-645-2110, Fax: 716-645-7937, E-mail: vakase@buffalo.edu.
Website: http://gse.buffalo.edu/elp

The University of Akron, Graduate School, College of Business Administration, Department of Economics, Akron, OH 44325. Offers MA. *Program availability:* Part-time. *Faculty:* 5 full-time (2 women). *Students:* 11 full-time (3 women), 3 part-time (0 women); includes 2 minority (both Asian, non-Hispanic/Latino), 8 international. Average age 26. 25 applicants, 68% accepted, 5 enrolled. In 2017, 2 master's awarded. *Degree requirements:* For master's, thesis optional. *Entrance requirements:* For master's, GRE or GMAT (recommended), three letters of recommendation (preferably from academics), statement of purpose, resume. Additional exam requirements/recommendations for international students: Required—TOEFL (minimum score 79 iBT), IELTS (minimum score 6.5), GRE or GMAT. *Application deadline:* For fall admission, 2/15 priority date for domestic and international students; for spring admission, 10/15 priority date for domestic and international students. Application fee: $45 ($70 for international students). Electronic applications accepted. *Financial support:* In 2017–18, 10 teaching assistantships with full and partial tuition reimbursements were awarded. Financial award application deadline: 2/15. *Faculty research:* Regional economic performance, effects of addiction on labor market outcomes, programmatic assessment, regional trading arrangements, agriculture production in early twentieth-century South. *Total annual research expenditures:* $3,323. *Unit head:* Dr. Michael Nelson, Chair, 330-972-7939, E-mail: nelson2@uakron.edu. *Application contact:* Dr. Sucharita Ghosh, Director of Graduate Studies, 330-972-7549, E-mail: sghosh@uakron.edu.
Website: http://www.uakron.edu/economics/

The University of Alabama, Graduate School, Manderson Graduate School of Business, Economics, Finance and Legal Studies Department, Tuscaloosa, AL 35487. Offers economics (MA, PhD); finance (MS, PhD). *Faculty:* 37 full-time (6 women), 1 part-time/adjunct (0 women). *Students:* 49 full-time (14 women), 6 part-time (1 woman); includes 2 minority (1 Asian, non-Hispanic/Latino; 1 Two or more races, non-Hispanic/Latino), 35 international. Average age 29. 117 applicants, 33% accepted, 14 enrolled. In 2017, 26 master's, 6 doctorates awarded. Terminal master's awarded for partial completion of doctoral program. *Degree requirements:* For master's, comprehensive exam (MA), thesis (MS); for doctorate, comprehensive exam, thesis/dissertation. *Entrance requirements:* For master's, GMAT, GRE; for doctorate, GRE or GMAT. Additional exam requirements/recommendations for international students: Required—TOEFL (minimum score 550 paper-based; 79 iBT). *Application deadline:* For fall admission, 7/1 priority date for domestic students, 1/15 for international students; for spring admission, 11/1 priority date for domestic students, 6/1 for international students. Applications are processed on a rolling basis. Application fee: $50 ($60 for international students). Electronic applications accepted. *Financial support:* In 2017–18, 41 students received support, including research assistantships with tuition reimbursements available (averaging $15,000 per year), teaching assistantships with tuition reimbursements available (averaging $15,000 per year); fellowships, Federal Work-Study, institutionally sponsored loans, and unspecified assistantships also available. Financial award application deadline: 1/15. *Faculty research:* Taxation, futures market, monetary theory and policy, income distribution. *Unit head:* Dr. Laura Razzolini, Department Head, 205-348-6683, E-mail: kcwise@cba.ua.edu. *Application contact:* Debra F. Wheatley, Graduate Programs Secretary, 205-348-6683, Fax: 205-348-0590, E-mail: dwheatle@cba.ua.edu.
Website: http://www.cba.ua.edu/

University of Alaska Fairbanks, School of Management, Department of Economics, Fairbanks, AK 99775-6080. Offers resource and applied economics (MS). *Program availability:* Part-time. *Degree requirements:* For master's, comprehensive exam, oral defense of project or thesis. *Entrance requirements:* For master's, bachelor's degree from accredited institution with minimum cumulative undergraduate and major GPA of 3.0, intermediate microeconomics, intermediate macroeconomics, basic statistics, calculus. Additional exam requirements/recommendations for international students: Required—TOEFL (minimum score 550 paper-based; 79 iBT), IELTS (minimum score 6.5). Electronic applications accepted. *Expenses:* Contact institution. *Faculty research:* Statistics; resource and agriculture economics; oil, gas, and energy; sustainability; public land management.

University of Alberta, Faculty of Graduate Studies and Research, Department of Economics, Edmonton, AB T6G 2E1, Canada. Offers economics (MA, PhD); economics and finance (MA); environmental and natural resource economics (PhD). *Program availability:* Part-time. *Degree requirements:* For doctorate, thesis/dissertation. *Entrance requirements:* For master's and doctorate, GRE. Additional exam requirements/recommendations for international students: Required—TOEFL. *Faculty research:* Public finance, international trade, industrial organization, Pacific Rim economics, monetary economics.

The University of Arizona, Eller College of Management, Department of Economics, Tucson, AZ 85721. Offers MA, PhD. Terminal master's awarded for partial completion of doctoral program. *Degree requirements:* For master's, comprehensive exam; for doctorate, thesis/dissertation. *Entrance requirements:* For doctorate, GRE General Test, 3 letters of recommendation. Additional exam requirements/recommendations for international students: Required—TOEFL (minimum score 550 paper-based; 79 iBT). Electronic applications accepted. *Faculty research:* Applied microeconomics, experimental economics, economic history, microeconomic theory, property rights, industrial organization.

University of Arkansas, Graduate School, Sam M. Walton College of Business Administration, Department of Economics, Fayetteville, AR 72701. Offers MA, PhD. In 2017, 4 master's, 1 doctorate awarded. *Degree requirements:* For doctorate, variable foreign language requirement, thesis/dissertation. *Entrance requirements:* For master's and doctorate, GRE General Test. *Application deadline:* For fall admission, 8/1 for domestic students, 4/1 for international students; for spring admission, 12/1 for domestic students, 10/1 for international students; for summer admission, 4/15 for domestic students, 3/1 for international students. Application fee: $60. Electronic applications accepted. *Expenses:* Tuition, state resident: full-time $3782. Tuition, nonresident: full-time $10,238. *Financial support:* In 2017–18, 5 research assistantships, 8 teaching assistantships were awarded; fellowships with tuition reimbursements, career-related internships or fieldwork, and Federal Work-Study also available. Support available to part-time students. Financial award application deadline: 4/1; financial award applicants required to submit FAFSA. *Unit head:* Dr. Bill Curington, Department Chair, 479-575-6354, E-mail: bcurington@walton.uark.edu.
Website: https://economics.uark.edu/

The University of British Columbia, Faculty of Arts, Vancouver School of Economics, Vancouver, BC V6T 1Z1, Canada. Offers MA, PhD. *Degree requirements:* For master's, thesis (for some programs); for doctorate, comprehensive exam, thesis/dissertation. *Entrance requirements:* For master's and doctorate, GRE General Test. Additional exam requirements/recommendations for international students: Required—TOEFL. Electronic applications accepted. *Expenses:* Contact institution. *Faculty research:* Economic theory, international economics, labor economics, public finance, economic development.

University of Calgary, Faculty of Graduate Studies, Faculty of Arts, Department of Economics, Calgary, AB T2N 1N4, Canada. Offers MA, PhD. *Program availability:* Part-time, evening/weekend. *Degree requirements:* For master's, thesis (for some programs); for doctorate, thesis/dissertation, candidacy exam. *Entrance requirements:* Additional exam requirements/recommendations for international students: Required—TOEFL. *Faculty research:* Energy economics, public finance/public choice, resource economics, international trade, monetary economics.

University of California, Berkeley, Graduate Division, College of Letters and Science, Department of Economics, Berkeley, CA 94720-1500. Offers PhD, JD/MA. *Degree requirements:* For doctorate, thesis/dissertation, field exams, oral qualifying exam. *Entrance requirements:* For doctorate, GRE General Test, minimum GPA of 3.0, 3 letters of recommendation. Additional exam requirements/recommendations for international students: Required—TOEFL (minimum score 570 paper-based; 90 iBT). Electronic applications accepted.

University of California, Davis, Graduate Studies, Program in Economics, Davis, CA 95616. Offers MA, PhD. Terminal master's awarded for partial completion of doctoral program. *Degree requirements:* For master's, comprehensive exam (for some programs), thesis (for some programs); for doctorate, thesis/dissertation. *Entrance requirements:* For master's, GRE General Test, minimum GPA of 3.0; for doctorate, GRE General Test, minimum GPA of 3.25. Additional exam requirements/recommendations for international students: Required—TOEFL (minimum score 550 paper-based). Electronic applications accepted. *Faculty research:* Applied microeconomics, macroeconomics, international studies, economic theory, economic history.

University of California, Irvine, School of Social Sciences, Department of Economics, Irvine, CA 92697. Offers economics (MA, PhD); public choice (MA, PhD); transportation economics (MA, PhD). *Students:* 91 full-time (26 women); includes 19 minority (1 Black or African American, non-Hispanic/Latino; 6 Asian, non-Hispanic/Latino; 8 Hispanic/Latino; 4 Two or more races, non-Hispanic/Latino), 36 international. Average age 28. 222 applicants, 23% accepted, 22 enrolled. In 2017, 24 master's, 12 doctorates awarded. *Entrance requirements:* For master's and doctorate, GRE General Test, minimum GPA of 3.0. Additional exam requirements/recommendations for international students: Required—TOEFL (minimum score 550 paper-based). *Application deadline:* For fall admission, 1/15 priority date for domestic and international students. Applications are processed on a rolling basis. Application fee: $105 ($125 for international students). Electronic applications accepted. *Financial support:* Fellowships, research assistantships with full tuition reimbursements, teaching assistantships, institutionally sponsored loans, traineeships, health care benefits, and unspecified assistantships available. Financial award application deadline: 3/1; financial award applicants required to submit FAFSA. *Faculty research:* Econometrics, urban economics, applied microeconomics. *Unit head:* Prof. Jan Brueckner, Chair, 949-824-0083, E-mail: jkbrueck@uci.edu. *Application contact:* Prof. John Duffy, Graduate Program Director, 949-824-8341, E-mail: duffy@uci.edu.
Website: http://www.economics.uci.edu/

University of California, Los Angeles, Graduate Division, College of Letters and Science, Department of Economics, Program in Economics, Los Angeles, CA 90095. Offers PhD.

University of California, Riverside, Graduate Division, Department of Economics, Riverside, CA 92521-0102. Offers MA, PhD. Terminal master's awarded for partial completion of doctoral program. *Degree requirements:* For master's, comprehensive exam; for doctorate, thesis/dissertation, qualifying exams. *Entrance requirements:* For master's and doctorate, GRE General Test, minimum GPA of 3.2. Additional exam requirements/recommendations for international students: Required—TOEFL (minimum score 550 paper-based; 80 iBT). Electronic applications accepted. *Expenses:* Tuition, state resident: full-time $5746. Tuition, nonresident: full-time $10,780. Tuition and fees vary according to campus/location and program. *Faculty research:* Advanced political economy; resource and environmental economics; advanced econometrics; labor economics; advanced microeconomics theory; advanced macroeconomics theory; development economics; economic history; international trade theory; money, credit and business cycles; public economics.

University of California, San Diego, Graduate Division, Department of Economics, La Jolla, CA 92093. Offers PhD. *Students:* 119 full-time (39 women). 819 applicants, 10% accepted, 26 enrolled. In 2017, 27 doctorates awarded. *Degree requirements:* For doctorate, comprehensive exam, thesis/dissertation. *Entrance requirements:* For doctorate, GRE General Test, minimum GPA of 3.5, letters of recommendation, statement of purpose. Additional exam requirements/recommendations for international students: Required—TOEFL (minimum score 550 paper-based; 80 iBT), IELTS (minimum score 7), PTE. *Application deadline:* For fall admission, 12/15 for domestic students. Application fee: $105 ($125 for international students). Electronic applications accepted. *Financial support:* Fellowships, research assistantships, teaching assistantships, and scholarships/grants available. Financial award applicants required to submit FAFSA. *Faculty research:* Behavioral/experimental economics, development economics, econometrics, environment and resource economics, finance, health economics, industrial organization, international, labor, macroeconomics, microeconomic theory, public economics. *Unit head:* Eli Berman, Chair, 858-534-2858, E-mail: econchair@ucsd.edu. *Application contact:* Cathy Pugh, Graduate Coordinator, 858-534-1867, E-mail: econ-phdadmissions@ucsd.edu.
Website: http://economics.ucsd.edu

University of California, Santa Barbara, Graduate Division, College of Letters and Sciences, Division of Social Sciences, Department of Economics, Santa Barbara, CA 93106-9210. Offers economics (MA); mathematical economics (PhD); public finance (PhD); MA/PhD. Terminal master's awarded for partial completion of doctoral program. *Degree requirements:* For master's, comprehensive exam; for doctorate, comprehensive exam, thesis/dissertation. *Entrance requirements:* For master's and doctorate, GRE General Test, 3 letters of recommendation, statement of purpose, personal achievements/contributions statement, resume/curriculum vitae, transcripts for post-secondary institutions attended. Additional exam requirements/recommendations for international students: Required—TOEFL (minimum score 550 paper-based; 80 iBT), IELTS (minimum score 7), TOEFL (minimum score 600 paper-based or 100 iBT) for PhD. Electronic applications accepted. *Faculty research:* Labor economics, econometrics, macroeconomic theory and policy, environmental and natural resources economics, experimental and behavioral economics.

University of California, Santa Barbara, Graduate Division, College of Letters and Sciences, Division of Social Sciences, Department of Global Studies, Santa Barbara, CA 93106-7065. Offers global culture, ideology, and religion (MA, PhD); global government, human rights, and civil society (MA, PhD); political economy, sustainable development, and the environment (MA, PhD). *Degree requirements:* For master's, one foreign language, thesis, 2 years of a second language; for doctorate, one foreign language, thesis/dissertation, reading proficiency in at least one language other than English. *Entrance requirements:* For master's, GRE, 2 years of a second language with minimum B grade in the final term, statement of purpose, resume or curriculum vitae, 3 letters of recommendation, transcripts (from all post-secondary institutions attended), writing sample (15-20 pages); for doctorate, GRE, statement of purpose, personal achievements/contributions statement, resume or curriculum vitae, 3 letters of recommendation, transcripts from all post-secondary institutions attended, writing sample (15-20 pages). Additional exam requirements/recommendations for international students: Required—TOEFL (minimum score 600 paper-based; 94 iBT), IELTS (minimum score 7). Electronic applications accepted.

Economics

University of California, Santa Barbara, Graduate Division, Donald Bren School of Environmental Science and Management, Santa Barbara, CA 93106-5131. Offers economics and environmental science (PhD); environmental science and management (MESM, PhD); technology and society (PhD). *Degree requirements:* For master's, thesis; for doctorate, thesis/dissertation. *Entrance requirements:* For master's and doctorate, GRE. Additional exam requirements/recommendations for international students: Required—TOEFL (minimum score 550 paper-based; 80 iBT), IELTS (minimum score 7). Electronic applications accepted. *Faculty research:* Coastal marine resources management, conservation planning, corporate environmental management, economics and politics of the environment, energy and climate, pollution prevention and remediation, water resources management.

University of California, Santa Cruz, Division of Graduate Studies, Division of Social Sciences, Program in International Economics, Santa Cruz, CA 95064. Offers PhD. *Degree requirements:* For doctorate, thesis/dissertation, 4 field exams, field papers, econometrics project, qualifying exams. *Entrance requirements:* For doctorate, GRE General Test. Additional exam requirements/recommendations for international students: Required—TOEFL (minimum score 550 paper-based; 83 iBT); Recommended—IELTS (minimum score 8). Electronic applications accepted. *Faculty research:* Current and emerging issues in taxation, industrial policy, environmental regulation, market structure, labor economics focus on behavior and adjustment in an interdependent world economy.

University of Central Arkansas, Graduate School, College of Liberal Arts, Program in Community and Economic Development, Conway, AR 72035-0001. Offers community and economic development (MS); geographic and information systems (MGIS, Graduate Certificate). *Program availability:* Part-time, online learning. *Degree requirements:* For master's, comprehensive exam, thesis. *Entrance requirements:* For master's, GRE General Test, minimum GPA of 2.7. Additional exam requirements/recommendations for international students: Required—TOEFL (minimum score 550 paper-based). Electronic applications accepted. *Expenses:* Contact institution.

University of Chicago, Booth School of Business, Full-Time MBA Program, Chicago, IL 60637. Offers accounting (MBA); analytic finance (MBA); analytic management (MBA); econometrics and statistics (MBA); economics (MBA); entrepreneurship (MBA); finance (MBA); general management (MBA); health administration and policy (Certificate); international business (MBA); managerial and organizational behavior (MBA); marketing analytics (MBA); marketing management (MBA); operations management (MBA); strategic management (MBA); MBA/AM; MBA/JD; MBA/MA; MBA/MD; MBA/MPP. *Accreditation:* AACSB. *Faculty:* 154 full-time (26 women), 61 part-time/adjunct (12 women). *Students:* 1,176 full-time (481 women). In 2017, 586 master's awarded. *Entrance requirements:* For master's, GMAT or GRE, transcripts, resume, 2 letters of recommendation, essays, interview. Additional exam requirements/recommendations for international students: Required—TOEFL, IELTS, or PTE. *Application deadline:* For fall admission, 9/1 for domestic and international students; for winter admission, 1/1 for domestic and international students; for spring admission, 4/1 for domestic and international students. Application fee: $250. Electronic applications accepted. *Expenses:* Contact institution. *Unit head:* Stacey Kole, Deputy Dean for Alumni, Corporate Relations, and the Full-time MBA Program, 773-702-7121. *Application contact:* Kurt Ahlm, Associate Dean for Student Recruitment and Admissions, 773-702-7369, Fax: 773-702-9085, E-mail: admissions@chicagobooth.edu. Website: https://www.chicagobooth.edu/programs/full-time

University of Chicago, Division of the Social Sciences, The Kenneth C. Griffin Department of Economics, Chicago, IL 60637. Offers PhD. *Faculty:* 41. *Students:* 178 full-time (34 women); includes 13 minority (10 Asian, non-Hispanic/Latino; 2 Hispanic/Latino; 1 Two or more races, non-Hispanic/Latino), 134 international. Average age 28. 625 applicants, 10% accepted, 21 enrolled. In 2017, 28 doctorates awarded. *Degree requirements:* For doctorate, one foreign language, thesis/dissertation, written exams in 2 fields. *Entrance requirements:* For doctorate, GRE General Test, 3 letters of recommendation, statement of purpose, transcripts, resume or curriculum vitae, writing sample (dependent on department). Additional exam requirements/recommendations for international students: Required—TOEFL (minimum score 104 iBT), IELTS (minimum score 7). *Application deadline:* For fall admission, 12/15 for domestic and international students. Application fee: $135. Electronic applications accepted. *Financial support:* In 2017–18, 30 students received support, including 19 fellowships with full tuition reimbursements available (averaging $27,000 per year); research assistantships, teaching assistantships, Federal Work-Study, institutionally sponsored loans, scholarships/grants, health care benefits, and tuition waivers (full) also available. Financial award application deadline: 12/15. *Unit head:* Prof. John List, Chair, 773-702-8176, E-mail: ssd-admissions@uchicago.edu. *Application contact:* Office of the Dean of Students, 773-702-8415, E-mail: ssd-admissions@uchicago.edu. Website: http://economics.uchicago.edu

University of Cincinnati, Carl H. Lindner College of Business, PhD Programs, Cincinnati, OH 45221. Offers accounting (PhD); business analytics (PhD); economics (PhD); finance (PhD); information systems (PhD); management (PhD); marketing (PhD); operations and business analytics (PhD); operations research (PhD). *Faculty:* 37 full-time (13 women). *Students:* 29 full-time (12 women), 12 part-time (6 women); includes 5 minority (1 Black or African American, non-Hispanic/Latino; 4 Asian, non-Hispanic/Latino), 20 international. Average age 30. 123 applicants, 16% accepted, 11 enrolled. In 2017, 5 doctorates awarded. *Degree requirements:* For doctorate, comprehensive exam, thesis/dissertation. *Entrance requirements:* For doctorate, GMAT, GRE, transcripts, essays, resume, letters of recommendation. Additional exam requirements/recommendations for international students: Required—TOEFL (minimum score 600 paper-based; 100 iBT), IELTS (minimum score 7). *Application deadline:* For fall admission, 1/15 for domestic and international students. Application fee: $65 ($70 for international students). Electronic applications accepted. *Expenses:* $7,234 resident per term, $13,105 nonresident per term. *Financial support:* In 2017–18, 41 students received support, including 29 research assistantships with full tuition reimbursements available (averaging $23,250 per year); scholarships/grants, health care benefits, tuition waivers (full), and unspecified assistantships also available. Financial award application deadline: 1/15; financial award applicants required to submit FAFSA. *Faculty research:* Bayesian Prediction Theory, organizational fairness, consumer insight and market research, consumer insight and market research, density estimation from correlated data. *Unit head:* Dr. Suzanne Masterson, Director, 513-556-7125, Fax: 513-556-5499, E-mail: suzanne.masterson@uc.edu. *Application contact:* Angel Elvin, Assistant Director, 513-556-7190, Fax: 513-558-7006, E-mail: angel.elvin@uc.edu. Website: http://business.uc.edu/graduate/phd.html

University of Colorado Boulder, Graduate School, College of Arts and Sciences, Department of Economics, Boulder, CO 80309. Offers MA, PhD. *Faculty:* 33 full-time (8 women). *Students:* 62 full-time (18 women), 1 part-time (0 women); includes 9 minority (6 Asian, non-Hispanic/Latino; 3 Hispanic/Latino), 19 international. Average age 29. 138 applicants, 32% accepted, 13 enrolled. In 2017, 13 master's, 9 doctorates awarded. Terminal master's awarded for partial completion of doctoral program. *Degree requirements:* For master's, comprehensive exam, thesis or alternative; for doctorate, comprehensive exam, thesis/dissertation, preliminary exam. *Entrance requirements:* For master's, GRE General Test, minimum undergraduate GPA of 2.75; for doctorate, GRE

General Test. Additional exam requirements/recommendations for international students: Required—TOEFL. *Application deadline:* For fall admission, 1/10 for domestic students; for spring admission, 12/1 for domestic students. Applications are processed on a rolling basis. Application fee: $60 ($80 for international students). Electronic applications accepted. Application fee is waived when completed online. *Financial support:* In 2017–18, 182 students received support, including 23 fellowships (averaging $5,718 per year), 4 research assistantships with full and partial tuition reimbursements available (averaging $23,473 per year), 55 teaching assistantships with full and partial tuition reimbursements available (averaging $25,961 per year); institutionally sponsored loans, scholarships/grants, health care benefits, and unspecified assistantships also available. Financial award application deadline: 2/15; financial award applicants required to submit FAFSA. *Faculty research:* Economics; economics of the environment; microeconomics; labor economics; international economics. *Total annual research expenditures:* $156,484. *Application contact:* E-mail: econ@colorado.edu. Website: http://www.colorado.edu/Economics/graduate/index.html

University of Colorado Denver, Business School, Program in Finance, Denver, CO 80217. Offers economics (MS); finance (MS); financial analysis and management (MS); financial and commodities risk management (MS); risk management and insurance (MS); MS/MA; MS/MBA. *Program availability:* Part-time, evening/weekend. *Degree requirements:* For master's, 30 semester hours (18 of required core courses, 9 of finance electives, and 3 of free elective). *Entrance requirements:* For master's, GMAT, essay, resume, two letters of recommendation; financial statements (for international students). Additional exam requirements/recommendations for international students: Required—TOEFL (minimum score 537 paper-based; 75 iBT); Recommended—IELTS (minimum score 6.5). Electronic applications accepted. *Expenses:* Contact institution. *Faculty research:* Corporate governance, debt maturity policies, regulation and financial markets, option management strategies.

University of Colorado Denver, College of Liberal Arts and Sciences, Department of Economics, Denver, CO 80217. Offers MA. *Program availability:* Part-time, evening/weekend. *Degree requirements:* For master's, thesis or alternative, 30 credit hours, including 21 of core courses and 9 of electives. *Entrance requirements:* For master's, GRE General Test, 15 hours of course work in economics, minimum GPA of 2.5, three letters of recommendation, calculus and statistics course. Additional exam requirements/recommendations for international students: Required—TOEFL (minimum score 537 paper-based; 75 iBT); Recommended—IELTS (minimum score 6.5). Electronic applications accepted. *Faculty research:* Economic/income inequality, poverty and mobility measurement; international finance and monetary policy; economics of philanthropy; history of economic thought; health and labor economics.

University of Connecticut, Graduate School, College of Liberal Arts and Sciences, Department of Economics, Storrs, CT 06269-1063. Offers MA, PhD. Terminal master's awarded for partial completion of doctoral program. *Degree requirements:* For master's, comprehensive exam; for doctorate, thesis/dissertation. *Entrance requirements:* For master's and doctorate, GRE General Test, GRE Subject Test. Additional exam requirements/recommendations for international students: Required—TOEFL (minimum score 550 paper-based). Electronic applications accepted.

University of Delaware, Alfred Lerner College of Business and Economics, Department of Economics, Newark, DE 19716. Offers economic education (PhD); economics (MA, MS, PhD); economics for entrepreneurship and educators (MA); MA/MBA. *Program availability:* Part-time. *Degree requirements:* For master's, comprehensive exam, thesis (for some programs), mathematics review exam, research project; for doctorate, comprehensive exam, thesis/dissertation, field exam. *Entrance requirements:* For master's, GMAT or GRE General Test, minimum GPA of 2.5; for doctorate, GRE General Test, minimum GPA of 3.5 in graduate economics course work. Additional exam requirements/recommendations for international students: Required—TOEFL (minimum score 550 paper-based). Electronic applications accepted. *Faculty research:* Applied quantitative economics, industrial organization, resource economics, monetary economics, labor economics.

University of Denver, Division of Arts, Humanities and Social Sciences, Department of Economics, Denver, CO 80208. Offers MA. *Program availability:* Part-time. *Faculty:* 10 full-time (3 women), 1 part-time/adjunct (0 women). *Students:* 1 full-time (0 women), 12 part-time (4 women); includes 4 minority (1 Black or African American, non-Hispanic/Latino; 1 Asian, non-Hispanic/Latino; 1 Hispanic/Latino; 1 Two or more races, non-Hispanic/Latino), 5 international. Average age 28. 47 applicants, 81% accepted, 7 enrolled. In 2017, 3 master's awarded. *Degree requirements:* For master's, thesis. *Entrance requirements:* For master's, GRE General Test, bachelor's degree with major or minor in economics, 20 quarter hours of economics coursework, or departmental waiver; transcripts; personal statement; three letters of recommendation. Additional exam requirements/recommendations for international students: Required—TOEFL (minimum score 550 paper-based; 80 iBT). *Application deadline:* For fall admission, 2/15 priority date for domestic and international students. Applications are processed on a rolling basis. Application fee: $65. Electronic applications accepted. *Expenses:* $31,935 per year full-time. *Financial support:* In 2017–18, 7 students received support. Teaching assistantships with tuition reimbursements available, career-related internships or fieldwork, Federal Work-Study, scholarships/grants, and unspecified assistantships available. Support available to part-time students. Financial award application deadline: 2/15; financial award applicants required to submit FAFSA. *Faculty research:* Trade and policy effects on economic development; income distribution, inequality, and the macroeconomy; history of economic thought; the Chinese economy; problems of neo-liberalism. *Unit head:* Dr. Peter Sai-Wing Ho, Associate Professor and Chair, 303-871-2259, Fax: 303-871-2605, E-mail: peter.ho@du.edu. *Application contact:* Jamie Dinneen, Program Coordinator, 303-871-2243, E-mail: jamie.dinneen@du.edu. Website: http://www.du.edu/ahss/economics

University of Detroit Mercy, College of Liberal Arts and Education, Detroit, MI 48221. Offers addiction counseling (MA); addiction studies (Certificate); clinical mental health counseling (MA); clinical psychology (MA, PhD); computer and information systems (MS); criminal justice (MA); curriculum and instruction (MA); economics (MA); educational administration (MA); financial economics (MA); industrial/organizational psychology (MA); information assurance (MS); intelligence analysis (MA); liberal studies (MALS); religious studies (MA); school counseling (MA, Certificate); school psychology (Spec); security administration (MS); special education: emotionally impaired/behaviorally disordered (MA); special education: learning disabilities (MA). *Program availability:* Part-time, evening/weekend. *Degree requirements:* For doctorate, departmental qualifying exam. *Faculty research:* Psychology of aging, history of technology, Renaissance humanism, U.S. and Japanese economic relations.

University of Florida, Graduate School, Warrington College of Business Administration, Hough Graduate School of Business, Department of Economics, Gainesville, FL 32611. Offers MA, PhD. Terminal master's awarded for partial completion of doctoral program. *Degree requirements:* For master's, thesis optional; for doctorate, comprehensive exam, thesis/dissertation. *Entrance requirements:* For master's and doctorate, GMAT (minimum score of 465) or GRE General Test, minimum GPA of 3.0. Additional exam requirements/recommendations for international students: Required—TOEFL (minimum score 550 paper-based; 80 iBT), IELTS (minimum score

6). Electronic applications accepted. *Faculty research:* Econometrics, international economics, industrial organization, public finance, economic theory.

University of Georgia, Terry College of Business, Department of Economics, Athens, GA 30602. Offers MA, PhD. *Degree requirements:* For master's, thesis; for doctorate, thesis/dissertation. *Entrance requirements:* For master's and doctorate, GRE General Test. Electronic applications accepted.

University of Guelph, Graduate Studies, College of Management and Economics, Department of Economics, Guelph, ON N1G 2W1, Canada. Offers MA, PhD. *Program availability:* Part-time. *Degree requirements:* For master's, thesis or alternative; for doctorate, comprehensive exam, thesis/dissertation. *Entrance requirements:* For master's, minimum B+ average during previous 2 years of course work; for doctorate, minimum A- average, MA in economics. Additional exam requirements/recommendations for international students: Required—TOEFL (minimum score 550 paper-based; 89 iBT), IELTS (minimum score 6.5). Electronic applications accepted. *Faculty research:* Resource and environmental economics, econometrics, labor economics, micro and macro economics.

University of Hawaii at Manoa, Office of Graduate Education, College of Social Sciences, Department of Economics, Honolulu, HI 96822. Offers MA, PhD. *Program availability:* Part-time. Terminal master's awarded for partial completion of doctoral program. *Degree requirements:* For master's, thesis optional; for doctorate, comprehensive exam, thesis/dissertation. *Entrance requirements:* For master's and doctorate, GRE General Test. Additional exam requirements/recommendations for international students: Required—TOEFL (minimum score 500 paper-based; 61 iBT), IELTS (minimum score 5). *Faculty research:* Trade, development, demography, labor, resource economics.

University of Houston, College of Liberal Arts and Social Sciences, Department of Economics, Houston, TX 77204. Offers applied economics (MA); economics (MA, PhD). Terminal master's awarded for partial completion of doctoral program. *Degree requirements:* For master's, thesis optional; for doctorate, comprehensive exam, thesis/dissertation. *Entrance requirements:* For master's and doctorate, GRE General Test, minimum GPA of 3.0, statement of purpose, three letters of recommendation. Additional exam requirements/recommendations for international students: Required—TOEFL (minimum score 550 paper-based; 79 iBT), IELTS (minimum score 6.5). Electronic applications accepted. *Faculty research:* Econometrics, labor economics, international economics.

University of Illinois at Chicago, College of Liberal Arts and Sciences, Department of Economics, Chicago, IL 60607-7128. Offers MA, PhD, MBA/MA. Terminal master's awarded for partial completion of doctoral program. *Degree requirements:* For master's, comprehensive exam; for doctorate, thesis/dissertation. *Entrance requirements:* For master's and doctorate, GRE General Test, minimum GPA of 2.75. Additional exam requirements/recommendations for international students: Required—TOEFL. Electronic applications accepted. *Faculty research:* International, labor, and urban economics.

University of Illinois at Urbana–Champaign, Graduate College, College of Liberal Arts and Sciences, Department of Economics, Champaign, IL 61820. Offers economics (MS, PhD); policy economics (MS). Terminal master's awarded for partial completion of doctoral program.

The University of Iowa, Tippie College of Business, Department of Economics, Iowa City, IA 52242-1316. Offers PhD. *Faculty:* 12 full-time (3 women), 2 part-time/adjunct (0 women). *Students:* 26 full-time (15 women), 18 international. Average age 27. 119 applicants. In 2017, 6 doctorates awarded. *Degree requirements:* For doctorate, comprehensive exam, thesis/dissertation. *Entrance requirements:* For doctorate, GRE General Test. Additional exam requirements/recommendations for international students: Required—TOEFL (minimum score 100 iBT). *Application deadline:* For fall admission, 1/15 priority date for domestic and international students. Application fee: $60 ($100 for international students). Electronic applications accepted. *Financial support:* In 2017–18, 26 students received support, including 25 fellowships (averaging $2,000 per year), 1 research assistantship with full tuition reimbursement available (averaging $19,016 per year), 25 teaching assistantships with full tuition reimbursements available (averaging $19,016 per year); health care benefits and unspecified assistantships also available. Financial award application deadline: 1/15. *Faculty research:* Political economy, macroeconomics, econometrics, game theory, economic development. *Unit head:* Prof. Jarjisu Sa-Aadu, Interim Department Executive Officer, 319-335-0829, Fax: 319-335-1956, E-mail: jsa-aadu@uiowa.edu. *Application contact:* Renea L. Jay, Associate Director, Non-MBA Graduate Programs, 319-335-0830, Fax: 319-335-1956, E-mail: renea-jay@uiowa.edu.
Website: https://tippie.uiowa.edu/economics

The University of Kansas, Graduate Studies, College of Liberal Arts and Sciences, Department of Economics, Lawrence, KS 66045. Offers MA, PhD, JD/MA. *Program availability:* Part-time. *Students:* 62 full-time (24 women), 1 part-time (0 women); includes 2 minority (both Asian, non-Hispanic/Latino), 19 international. Average age 29. 102 applicants, 51% accepted, 16 enrolled. In 2017, 17 master's, 9 doctorates awarded. Terminal master's awarded for partial completion of doctoral program. *Degree requirements:* For doctorate, thesis/dissertation or alternative. *Entrance requirements:* For master's and doctorate, statement of personal goals, resume or curriculum vitae, official transcripts, three letters of recommendation. Additional exam requirements/recommendations for international students: Required—TOEFL, IELTS. *Application deadline:* For fall admission, 2/1 priority date for domestic and international students; for spring admission, 11/1 priority date for domestic and international students. Application fee: $65 ($85 for international students). Electronic applications accepted. *Financial support:* Fellowships, research assistantships, teaching assistantships, institutionally sponsored loans, scholarships/grants, health care benefits, and unspecified assistantships available. Financial award application deadline: 2/1. *Faculty research:* Macroeconomics, econometrics, industrial organization, microeconomics, economic development, international economics, financial economics. *Unit head:* Ted Juhl, Chair, 785-864-2849, E-mail: juhl@ku.edu. *Application contact:* Michelle Huslig-Lowrance, Graduate Secretary, 785-864-2841, E-mail: econgrad@ku.edu.
Website: http://www.economics.ku.edu/

University of Kentucky, Graduate School, Gatton College of Business and Economics, Program in Economics, Lexington, KY 40506-0032. Offers MS, PhD. *Degree requirements:* For master's, comprehensive exam; for doctorate, comprehensive exam, thesis/dissertation. *Entrance requirements:* For master's, GMAT, minimum undergraduate GPA of 2.75; for doctorate, GMAT, minimum undergraduate GPA of 3.0. Additional exam requirements/recommendations for international students: Required—TOEFL (minimum score 550 paper-based). Electronic applications accepted. *Faculty research:* Public economics, international economics and economic development, labor economics, environmental economics, industrial economics.

University of Lethbridge, School of Graduate Studies, Lethbridge, AB T1K 3M4, Canada. Offers addictions counseling (M Sc); agricultural biotechnology (M Sc); agricultural studies (M Sc, MA); anthropology (MA); archaeology (M Sc, MA); art (MA, MFA); biochemistry (M Sc); biological sciences (M Sc); biomolecular science (PhD); biosystems and biodiversity (PhD); Canadian studies (MA); chemistry (M Sc); computer science (M Sc); computer science and geographical information science (M Sc); counseling (MC); counseling psychology (M Ed); dramatic arts (MA); earth, space, and physical science (PhD); economics (MA); education (MA, PhD); educational leadership (M Ed); English (MA); environmental science (M Sc); evolution and behavior (PhD); exercise science (M Sc); French (MA); French/German (MA); French/Spanish (MA); general education (M Ed); geography (M Sc, MA); German (MA); health sciences (M Sc); individualized multidisciplinary (M Sc, MA); kinesiology (M Sc, MA); management (M Sc), including accounting, finance, human resource management and labor relations, information systems, international management, marketing, policy and strategy; mathematics (M Sc); music (M Mus, MA); Native American studies (MA); neuroscience (M Sc, PhD); new media (MA, MFA); nursing (M Sc, MN); philosophy (MA); physics (M Sc); political science (MA); psychology (M Sc, MA); religious studies (MA); sociology (MA); theatre and dramatic arts (MFA); theoretical and computational science (PhD); urban and regional studies (MA); women and gender studies (MA). *Program availability:* Part-time, evening/weekend. *Degree requirements:* For master's, thesis (for some programs); for doctorate, comprehensive exam, thesis/dissertation. *Entrance requirements:* For master's, GMAT (for M Sc in management); bachelor's degree in related field, minimum GPA of 3.0 during previous 20 graded semester courses, 2 years' teaching or related experience (M Ed); for doctorate, master's degree, minimum graduate GPA of 3.5. Additional exam requirements/recommendations for international students: Required—TOEFL (minimum score 580 paper-based; 93 iBT). Electronic applications accepted. *Faculty research:* Movement and brain plasticity, gibberellin physiology, photosynthesis, carbon cycling, molecular properties of main-group ring components.

University of Maine, Graduate School, College of Natural Sciences, Forestry, and Agriculture, School of Economics, Orono, ME 04469. Offers economics (MA); financial economics (MA); resource economics and policy (MS). *Program availability:* Part-time. *Faculty:* 11 full-time (3 women). *Students:* 22 full-time (9 women), 1 (woman) part-time, 9 international. Average age 24. 25 applicants, 84% accepted, 11 enrolled. In 2017, 12 master's awarded. *Degree requirements:* For master's, thesis (for some programs). *Entrance requirements:* For master's, GRE General Test. Additional exam requirements/recommendations for international students: Required—TOEFL (minimum score 580 paper-based; 93 iBT), IELTS (minimum score 6.9), TWE (minimum score 4.9), PTE (minimum score 67). *Application deadline:* For fall admission, 2/15 for domestic students, 2/1 for international students; for spring admission, 9/15 for domestic students, 8/15 for international students. Applications are processed on a rolling basis. Application fee: $65. Electronic applications accepted. *Expenses:* Tuition, state resident: full-time $7722; part-time $429 per credit hour. Tuition, nonresident: full-time $25,146; part-time $1397 per credit hour. *Required fees:* $1162; $581 per credit hour. *Financial support:* In 2017–18, 27 students received support, including 12 research assistantships with full tuition reimbursements available (averaging $20,500 per year), 13 teaching assistantships with full tuition reimbursements available (averaging $15,200 per year); career-related internships or fieldwork, Federal Work-Study, institutionally sponsored loans, scholarships/grants, and tuition waivers (full and partial) also available. Support available to part-time students. Financial award application deadline: 3/1. *Faculty research:* Economics of: health, energy, transportation, marine resource, consumer behavior. *Total annual research expenditures:* $848,400. *Unit head:* Dr. Mario Teisl, Director, 207-581-3151, Fax: 207-581-4278. *Application contact:* Scott G. Delcourt, Assistant Vice President for Graduate Studies and Senior Associate Dean, 207-581-3291, Fax: 207-581-3232, E-mail: graduate@maine.edu.
Website: http://umaine.edu/soe/

The University of Manchester, School of Arts, Histories and Cultures, Manchester, United Kingdom. Offers anthropology, media and performance (PhD); applied theatre professional (PhD); archaeology (PhD); art history and visual studies (PhD); arts management and cultural policy (PhD); classics and ancient history (PhD); composition (PhD); creative writing (PhD); drama (PhD); economic and social history (PhD); electroacoustic composition (PhD); English and American studies (PhD); history (PhD); humanitarianism and conflict response (PhD); museology (PhD); music (PhD); musicology (PhD); religions and theology (PhD).

University of Manitoba, Faculty of Graduate Studies, Faculty of Arts, Department of Economics, Winnipeg, MB R3T 2N2, Canada. Offers MA, PhD. *Degree requirements:* For master's, thesis or alternative; for doctorate, one foreign language, thesis/dissertation.

University of Maryland, Baltimore County, The Graduate School, College of Arts, Humanities and Social Sciences, Program in Economic Policy Analysis, Baltimore, MD 21250. Offers MA. *Program availability:* Part-time. *Faculty:* 17 full-time (6 women), 4 part-time/adjunct (2 women). *Students:* 6 full-time (2 women), 8 part-time (4 women); includes 1 minority (Black or African American, non-Hispanic/Latino), 2 international. Average age 26. 17 applicants, 88% accepted, 6 enrolled. In 2017, 4 master's awarded. *Degree requirements:* For master's, comprehensive exam, capstone research project. *Entrance requirements:* For master's, GRE General Test, undergraduate coursework in economic theory, econometrics, and calculus; letters of reference; statement of purpose; transcripts. Additional exam requirements/recommendations for international students: Required—TOEFL (minimum score 80 iBT). *Application deadline:* For fall admission, 7/1 priority date for domestic students, 3/1 priority date for international students; for spring admission, 1/1 priority date for domestic students, 9/15 priority date for international students. Applications are processed on a rolling basis. Application fee: $45. Electronic applications accepted. *Expenses:* Contact institution. *Financial support:* In 2017–18, 6 students received support, including 5 research assistantships with tuition reimbursements available (averaging $12,560 per year), 1 teaching assistantship with partial tuition reimbursement available (averaging $6,500 per year); Federal Work-Study, health care benefits, tuition waivers (full and partial), and unspecified assistantships also available. Support available to part-time students. Financial award application deadline: 4/15; financial award applicants required to submit FAFSA. *Faculty research:* Health and hospital policy evaluation, environmental policy analysis, economics of education, economic growth and development, cost-benefit and risk analysis. *Total annual research expenditures:* $28,539. *Unit head:* Dr. David F. Mitch, Chair, 410-455-2157, Fax: 410-455-1054, E-mail: mitch@umbc.edu. *Application contact:* Dr. Tim H. Gindling, Graduate Program Director, 410-455-3629, Fax: 410-455-1054, E-mail: econ-masters@umbc.edu.
Website: http://www.umbc.edu/economics/grad_intro.html

University of Maryland, Baltimore County, The Graduate School, College of Arts, Humanities and Social Sciences, School of Public Policy, Baltimore, MD 21250. Offers public policy (MPP, PhD), including economics (PhD), educational policy, emergency services (PhD), environmental policy (MPP), evaluation and analytical methods, health policy, policy history (PhD), public management, urban policy. *Program availability:* Part-time, evening/weekend. *Faculty:* 10 full-time (5 women). *Students:* 50 full-time (24 women), 69 part-time (37 women); includes 35 minority (17 Black or African American, non-Hispanic/Latino; 1 American Indian or Alaska Native, non-Hispanic/Latino; 8 Asian, non-Hispanic/Latino; 5 Hispanic/Latino; 1 Native Hawaiian or other Pacific Islander, non-Hispanic/Latino; 3 Two or more races, non-Hispanic/Latino), 6 international. Average age 37. 60 applicants, 68% accepted, 25 enrolled. In 2017, 15 master's, 3 doctorates awarded. Terminal master's awarded for partial completion of doctoral program. *Degree*

requirements: For master's, thesis, policy analysis paper, internship for pre-service; for doctorate, comprehensive exam, thesis/dissertation, comprehensive and field qualifying exams. *Entrance requirements:* For master's, GRE General Test, 3 academic letters of reference, resume, official transcripts; for doctorate, GRE General Test, 3 academic letters of reference, resume, research paper, official transcripts. Additional exam requirements/recommendations for international students: Required—TOEFL (minimum score 550 paper-based; 80 iBT), IELTS (minimum score 6.5). *Application deadline:* For fall admission, 1/15 priority date for domestic students, 1/1 priority date for international students; for spring admission, 11/1 priority date for domestic students, 5/1 priority date for international students. Applications are processed on a rolling basis. Application fee: $50. Electronic applications accepted. *Expenses:* $28,061 in-state, $39,356 out-of-state to complete the degree (for MPP); $43,823 in-state, $61,508 out-of-state to complete the degree (for PhD). *Financial support:* In 2017–18, 26 students received support, including 26 research assistantships with full tuition reimbursements available (averaging $20,000 per year); Federal Work-Study, scholarships/grants, health care benefits, and unspecified assistantships also available. Financial award application deadline: 1/1; financial award applicants required to submit FAFSA. *Faculty research:* Education policy, health policy, urban and environmental policy, public management, evaluation and analytical method. *Unit head:* Dr. Susan Sterett, Director, 410-455-2140, Fax: 410-455-1172, E-mail: ssterett@umbc.edu. *Application contact:* Sally F. Helms, Administrator of Academic Affairs, 410-455-3202, Fax: 410-455-1172, E-mail: gradpubpol@umbc.edu.
Website: http://publicpolicy.umbc.edu/

University of Maryland, College Park, Academic Affairs, College of Behavioral and Social Sciences, Department of Economics, College Park, MD 20742. Offers MA, PhD. *Program availability:* Part-time, evening/weekend. Terminal master's awarded for partial completion of doctoral program. *Degree requirements:* For master's, comprehensive exam, thesis optional; for doctorate, comprehensive exam, thesis/dissertation, exams. *Entrance requirements:* For master's, GRE General Test, minimum GPA of 3.0, course work in calculus and mathematics, 3 letters of recommendation; for doctorate, GRE General Test, calculus background. Additional exam requirements/recommendations for international students: Required—TOEFL. Electronic applications accepted. *Faculty research:* International economics, natural resource and environmental economics, forecasting and policy analysis, economic growth, demography of inequality.

University of Maryland, College Park, Academic Affairs, College of Behavioral and Social Sciences, Department of Government and Politics, College Park, MD 20742. Offers American politics (PhD); comparative politics (PhD); international relations (PhD); political economy (PhD); political theory (PhD). *Program availability:* Part-time, evening/weekend. *Degree requirements:* For doctorate, comprehensive exam, thesis/dissertation, written exams in 2 fields. *Entrance requirements:* For doctorate, GRE General Test, minimum GPA of 3.5, writing sample. Additional exam requirements/recommendations for international students: Required—TOEFL. Electronic applications accepted. *Faculty research:* International development/conflict, international security, post-communist society, public service, dynamics of conflict and conflict resolution.

University of Massachusetts Amherst, Graduate School, College of Social and Behavioral Sciences, Department of Economics, Amherst, MA 01003. Offers MA, PhD. *Program availability:* Part-time. Terminal master's awarded for partial completion of doctoral program. *Degree requirements:* For master's, thesis or alternative; for doctorate, comprehensive exam, thesis/dissertation. *Entrance requirements:* For master's and doctorate, GRE General Test. Additional exam requirements/recommendations for international students: Required—TOEFL (minimum score 550 paper-based; 80 iBT), IELTS (minimum score 6.5). Electronic applications accepted.

University of Massachusetts Lowell, College of Fine Arts, Humanities and Social Sciences, Program in Regional Economic and Social Development, Lowell, MA 01854. Offers MA, Graduate Certificate. *Program availability:* Part-time. *Entrance requirements:* For master's, GRE. Electronic applications accepted.

University of Memphis, Graduate School, Fogelman College of Business and Economics, Department of Economics, Memphis, TN 38152. Offers MA, PhD. *Program availability:* Part-time. *Faculty:* 8 full-time (1 woman). *Students:* 7 full-time (0 women), 4 part-time (0 women); includes 1 minority (Two or more races, non-Hispanic/Latino), 1 international. Average age 30. 10 applicants, 90% accepted, 4 enrolled. In 2017, 7 master's awarded. Terminal master's awarded for partial completion of doctoral program. *Degree requirements:* For master's, comprehensive exam, thesis or alternative; for doctorate, comprehensive exam, thesis/dissertation, paper presentation. *Entrance requirements:* For master's, GMAT or GRE General Test, previous course work in statistics, intermediate micro and macro theory; one semester of calculus and statistics and matrix or linear algebra; for doctorate, GMAT or GRE, two letters of reference, personal statement, curriculum vitae, interview, minimum GPA of 3.4. Additional exam requirements/recommendations for international students: Required—TOEFL (minimum score 550 paper-based; 79 iBT). *Application deadline:* For fall admission, 8/1 for domestic students; for spring admission, 12/1 for domestic students. Application fee: $35 ($60 for international students). Electronic applications accepted. *Expenses:* Contact institution. *Financial support:* In 2017–18, 3 students received support, including 7 research assistantships with full tuition reimbursements available (averaging $15,786 per year), 3 teaching assistantships with full tuition reimbursements available (averaging $26,000 per year); Federal Work-Study, scholarships/grants, and unspecified assistantships also available. Financial award application deadline: 2/1; financial award applicants required to submit FAFSA. *Faculty research:* Tax research, medical economics, law and economics, labor economics, U.S. and Japanese economic relations. *Unit head:* Dr. William Smith, Chair, 901-678-2785, E-mail: wtsmith@memphis.edu. *Application contact:* Dr. Albert Okunade, PhD Program Coordinator, 901-678-2672, Fax: 901-678-4705, E-mail: aokunade@memphis.edu.
Website: http://economics.memphis.edu/

University of Memphis, Graduate School, Fogelman College of Business and Economics, Program in Business Administration, Memphis, TN 38152. Offers accounting (MBA, PhD); business administration (IMBA); economics (PhD); executive business administration (MBA); finance (PhD); management (PhD); marketing (MS); marketing and supply chain management (PhD); real estate development (MS); JD/MBA. *Accreditation:* AACSB. *Faculty:* 2 part-time/adjunct (0 women). *Students:* 166 full-time (76 women), 361 part-time (142 women); includes 161 minority (91 Black or African American, non-Hispanic/Latino; 51 Asian, non-Hispanic/Latino; 10 Hispanic/Latino; 9 Two or more races, non-Hispanic/Latino), 89 international. Average age 32. 263 applicants, 83% accepted, 157 enrolled. In 2017, 186 master's, 14 doctorates awarded. *Degree requirements:* For master's, comprehensive exam; for doctorate, comprehensive exam, thesis/dissertation. *Entrance requirements:* For master's, GMAT, resume; for doctorate, GMAT, interview, minimum GPA of 3.4, resume, letter of recommendation. Additional exam requirements/recommendations for international students: Required—TOEFL (minimum score 550 paper-based). *Application deadline:* For fall admission, 8/1 for domestic students; for spring admission, 12/1 for domestic students. Application fee: $35 ($60 for international students). *Financial support:* In 2017–18, 164 students received support, including 17 research assistantships with full tuition reimbursements available (averaging $53,750 per year), 13 teaching assistantships with full tuition reimbursements available (averaging $20,798 per year); career-related internships or fieldwork, Federal Work-Study, scholarships/grants, and unspecified assistantships also available. Financial award application deadline: 2/15; financial award applicants required to submit FAFSA. *Faculty research:* Competitive business strategy, finance microstructures, supply chain management innovations, health care economics, litigation risks and corporate audits. *Unit head:* Dr. Rajiv Grover, Dean, 901-678-3759, E-mail: rgrover@memphis.edu. *Application contact:* Dr. Carol V. Danehower, Associate Dean, 901-678-5402, Fax: 901-678-3579, E-mail: fcbegp@memphis.edu.
Website: https://web0.memphis.edu/gradcatalog/degreeprog/fcbe/fcbe.php

University of Michigan, Rackham Graduate School, College of Literature, Science, and the Arts, Department of Economics, Ann Arbor, MI 48109. Offers applied economics (AM); economics (AM, PhD); public policy and economics (PhD); social work and economics (PhD); JD/PhD; MPP/AM. Terminal master's awarded for partial completion of doctoral program. *Degree requirements:* For doctorate, comprehensive exam, thesis/dissertation, oral defense of dissertation; preliminary exams in microeconomics, macroeconomics, and 2 fields. *Entrance requirements:* For master's and doctorate, GRE General Test. Additional exam requirements/recommendations for international students: Required—TOEFL (minimum score 600 paper-based; 100 iBT). Electronic applications accepted. *Expenses:* Tuition, state resident: full-time $22,368; part-time $1201 per credit hour. Tuition, nonresident: full-time $45,156; part-time $2467 per credit hour. *Required fees:* $376 per term. Tuition and fees vary according to course load, degree level and program. *Faculty research:* Econometric analysis, finance, industrial organization, international trade, public finance, economic development, economic history, health, labor, natural resources, population studies, macro theory, micro theory.

University of Michigan, School of Social Work, Interdisciplinary PhD Program in Social Work and Social Science, Ann Arbor, MI 48109. Offers social work and anthropology (PhD); social work and economics (PhD); social work and political science (PhD); social work and psychology (PhD); social work and sociology (PhD). Programs offered through the Rackham Graduate School. *Faculty:* 57 full-time (36 women). *Students:* 53 full-time (38 women); includes 27 minority (10 Black or African American, non-Hispanic/Latino; 2 American Indian or Alaska Native, non-Hispanic/Latino; 9 Asian, non-Hispanic/Latino; 6 Hispanic/Latino). Average age 32. 124 applicants, 6% accepted, 7 enrolled. In 2017, 10 doctorates awarded. *Degree requirements:* For doctorate, thesis/dissertation, oral defense of dissertation, preliminary exam. *Entrance requirements:* For doctorate, GRE General Test. Additional exam requirements/recommendations for international students: Required—TOEFL (minimum score 620 paper-based, 88 iBT) or IELTS. *Application deadline:* For fall admission, 12/1 for domestic and international students. Application fee: $75 ($90 for international students). Electronic applications accepted. *Expenses:* Contact institution. *Financial support:* In 2017–18, 59 students received support, including 24 fellowships with full tuition reimbursements available (averaging $17,600 per year), 7 research assistantships with full tuition reimbursements available (averaging $20,399 per year), 21 teaching assistantships with full tuition reimbursements available (averaging $20,399 per year); career-related internships or fieldwork, scholarships/grants, traineeships, health care benefits, tuition waivers (full and partial), and unspecified assistantships also available. Financial award application deadline: 12/1; financial award applicants required to submit FAFSA. *Faculty research:* Children and family, aging, community organization, health and mental health, police and evaluation. *Total annual research expenditures:* $4.1 million. *Unit head:* Dr. William Elliott, III, Director, 734-763-5768, E-mail: willelli@umich.edu. *Application contact:* Todd Huynh, Graduate Coordinator, 734-647-2554, Fax: 734-615-3192, E-mail: ssw.phd.info@umich.edu.
Website: https://ssw.umich.edu/offices/phd

University of Minnesota, Twin Cities Campus, Graduate School, College of Liberal Arts, Department of Economics, Minneapolis, MN 55455. Offers MA, PhD. *Faculty:* 19 full-time (3 women), 6 part-time/adjunct (3 women). *Students:* 121 full-time (27 women), 3 part-time (1 woman); includes 10 minority (6 Asian, non-Hispanic/Latino; 3 Hispanic/Latino; 1 Two or more races, non-Hispanic/Latino), 85 international. Average age 25. 356 applicants, 17% accepted, 22 enrolled. In 2017, 14 master's, 16 doctorates awarded. Terminal master's awarded for partial completion of doctoral program. *Degree requirements:* For master's, comprehensive exam; for doctorate, comprehensive exam, thesis/dissertation, preliminary written and oral exams. *Entrance requirements:* For doctorate, GRE General Test. Additional exam requirements/recommendations for international students: Required—TOEFL (minimum score 100 iBT), IELTS (minimum score 7). *Application deadline:* For fall admission, 12/13 priority date for domestic and international students. Application fee: $75 ($95 for international students). Electronic applications accepted. *Expenses:* Contact institution. *Financial support:* In 2017–18, 100 students received support, including 15 fellowships with full tuition reimbursements available (averaging $24,000 per year), 4 research assistantships with full tuition reimbursements available (averaging $18,500 per year), 76 teaching assistantships with full tuition reimbursements available (averaging $18,500 per year); scholarships/grants, health care benefits, and unspecified assistantships also available. Financial award application deadline: 12/13. *Faculty research:* Macroeconomics, monetary economics, econometrics, mathematical economics, industrial organization, applied microeconomic theory. *Unit head:* Prof. Christopher Phelan, Chair, 612-625-6353, Fax: 612-624-0209. *Application contact:* Prof. Amil Petrin, Director of Graduate Studies, 612-625-6833, Fax: 612-624-0209, E-mail: econdgs@umn.edu.
Website: https://cla.umn.edu/economics

University of Mississippi, Graduate School, College of Liberal Arts, University, MS 38677. Offers anthropology (MA); biology (MS, PhD); chemistry (MS, DA, PhD); creative writing (MFA); documentary expression (MFA); economics (MA, PhD); English (MA, PhD); experimental psychology (PhD); history (MA, PhD); mathematics (MS, PhD); modern languages (MA); music (MM); philosophy (MA); physics (MA, MS, PhD); political science (MA, PhD); Southern studies (MA); studio art (MFA). *Program availability:* Part-time. *Faculty:* 465 full-time (207 women), 82 part-time/adjunct (46 women). *Students:* 466 full-time (229 women), 72 part-time (34 women); includes 87 minority (38 Black or African American, non-Hispanic/Latino; 18 Asian, non-Hispanic/Latino; 24 Hispanic/Latino; 7 Two or more races, non-Hispanic/Latino), 121 international. Average age 29. *Degree requirements:* For doctorate, thesis/dissertation. *Entrance requirements:* For master's, GRE General Test, minimum GPA of 3.0; for doctorate, GRE General Test. Additional exam requirements/recommendations for international students: Required—TOEFL. *Application deadline:* For fall admission, 2/1 priority date for domestic students; for spring admission, 10/1 for domestic students. Applications are processed on a rolling basis. Application fee: $50. Electronic applications accepted. *Financial support:* Fellowships, research assistantships, teaching assistantships, career-related internships or fieldwork, Federal Work-Study, institutionally sponsored loans, scholarships/grants, and unspecified assistantships available. Financial award application deadline: 3/1; financial award applicants required to submit FAFSA. *Unit head:* Dr. Lee Michael Cohen, Dean, 662-915-7177, Fax: 662-915-5792, E-mail: libarts@olemiss.edu. *Application contact:* Dr. Christy M. Wyandt, Associate Dean of Graduate School, 662-915-7474, Fax: 662-915-7577, E-mail: cwyandt@olemiss.edu.

University of Missouri, Office of Research and Graduate Studies, College of Arts and Science, Department of Economics, Columbia, MO 65211. Offers MA, PhD. Terminal master's awarded for partial completion of doctoral program. *Degree requirements:* For

doctorate, comprehensive exam, thesis/dissertation. *Entrance requirements:* For master's, GRE General Test (minimum score 700 quantitative, 400 verbal), minimum GPA of 3.0; bachelor's degree in any field; for doctorate, GRE General Test (minimum score 700 quantitative, 400 verbal), minimum GPA of 3.0. Additional exam requirements/recommendations for international students: Required—TOEFL (minimum score 550 paper-based; 80 iBT), IELTS (minimum score 6.5). Electronic applications accepted. *Faculty research:* Monetary economics, econometrics, macroeconomics, public economics, industrial organization, game theory, labor economics, microeconomic theory, teacher labor markets, international trade.

University of Missouri–Kansas City, College of Arts and Sciences, Department of Economics, Kansas City, MO 64110-2499. Offers MA, PhD. PhD (interdisciplinary) offered through the School of Graduate Studies. *Program availability:* Part-time, evening/weekend. *Degree requirements:* For doctorate, comprehensive exam, thesis/dissertation. *Entrance requirements:* For master's, GRE or minimum undergraduate GPA of 2.5; for doctorate, GRE, master's degree in economics or equivalent. Additional exam requirements/recommendations for international students: Required—TOEFL (minimum score 550 paper-based; 80 iBT). Electronic applications accepted. *Faculty research:* International trade, general theory, institutions/utilities, forensic economics, human resources.

University of Missouri–St. Louis, College of Arts and Sciences, Department of Economics, St. Louis, MO 63121. Offers MA. *Program availability:* Part-time, evening/weekend. *Faculty:* 11 full-time (3 women), 2 part-time/adjunct (1 woman). *Students:* 7 full-time (1 woman), 8 part-time (2 women); includes 2 minority (1 Black or African American, non-Hispanic/Latino; 1 Asian, non-Hispanic/Latino). 8 applicants, 88% accepted, 4 enrolled. *Entrance requirements:* For master's, GRE General Test, 2 letters of recommendation. Additional exam requirements/recommendations for international students: Required—TOEFL (minimum score 550 paper-based; 79 iBT), IELTS (minimum score 6.5). *Application deadline:* For fall admission, 7/1 priority date for domestic and international students; for spring admission, 12/1 priority date for domestic and international students. Applications are processed on a rolling basis. Application fee: $50 ($40 for international students). Electronic applications accepted. *Expenses:* Tuition, state resident: part-time $476.50 per credit hour. Tuition, nonresident: part-time $1169.70 per credit hour. *Financial support:* Research assistantships and teaching assistantships with tuition reimbursements available. Financial award applicants required to submit FAFSA. *Faculty research:* Health economics, public policy analysis, econometrics, public choice, telecommunications and forensic economics. *Unit head:* Anne Winkler, Chair, 314-516-5563, Fax: 314-516-5562, E-mail: awinkler@umsl.edu. *Application contact:* 314-516-5458, Fax: 314-516-6996, E-mail: gradadm@umsl.edu. Website: http://www.umsl.edu/~econ/

University of Montana, Graduate School, College of Humanities and Sciences, Department of Economics, Missoula, MT 59812. Offers MA. *Degree requirements:* For master's, thesis. *Entrance requirements:* For master's, GRE General Test. Additional exam requirements/recommendations for international students: Required—TOEFL (minimum score 525 paper-based). *Faculty research:* Resource economics, public policy, environmental economics, economic development, regional economics.

University of Nebraska at Omaha, Graduate Studies, College of Business Administration, Department of Economics, Omaha, NE 68182. Offers MA, MS. *Program availability:* Part-time, evening/weekend. *Degree requirements:* For master's, comprehensive exam, thesis (for some programs). *Entrance requirements:* For master's, minimum GPA of 2.7, official transcripts. Additional exam requirements/recommendations for international students: Required—TOEFL, IELTS, PTE. Electronic applications accepted.

University of Nebraska–Lincoln, Graduate College, College of Business Administration, Department of Economics, Lincoln, NE 68588. Offers MA, PhD, JD/MA. *Degree requirements:* For master's, thesis optional; for doctorate, comprehensive exam, thesis/dissertation. *Entrance requirements:* For master's and doctorate, GRE General Test. Additional exam requirements/recommendations for international students: Required—TOEFL (minimum score 550 paper-based). Electronic applications accepted. *Faculty research:* Applied microeconomics, economic education, international trade and finance, public finance, regional and institutional economics.

University of Nevada, Las Vegas, Graduate College, Lee Business School, Department of Economics, Las Vegas, NV 89154-6005. Offers applied economics (MA); MA/MS. *Program availability:* Part-time. *Faculty:* 8 full-time (1 woman), 1 part-time/adjunct (0 women). *Students:* 10 full-time (4 women), 10 part-time (1 woman); includes 4 minority (all Hispanic/Latino), 3 international. Average age 32. 23 applicants, 65% accepted, 7 enrolled. In 2017, 13 master's awarded. *Degree requirements:* For master's, thesis optional, oral defense of thesis; internship. *Entrance requirements:* For master's, GRE General Test or GMAT, bachelor's degree with minimum GPA 3.0. Additional exam requirements/recommendations for international students: Required—TOEFL (minimum score 550 paper-based; 80 iBT), IELTS (minimum score 7). *Application deadline:* For fall admission, 6/15 for domestic and international students; for spring admission, 11/15 for domestic and international students. Application fee: $60 ($95 for international students). Electronic applications accepted. *Expenses:* $275 per credit, $850 per course, $7,969 per year resident, $22,157 per year non-resident, $7,094 non-resident fee (7 credits or more), $1,307 annual health insurance fee. *Financial support:* In 2017–18, 9 students received support, including 9 teaching assistantships with full and partial tuition reimbursements available (averaging $13,750 per year); institutionally sponsored loans, scholarships/grants, health care benefits, and unspecified assistantships also available. Financial award application deadline: 3/15; financial award applicants required to submit FAFSA. *Faculty research:* Labor economics/industrial organization; real estate economics; macroeconomics and credit markets; urban, regional and environmental economics; public finance/public policy. *Total annual research expenditures:* $52,500. *Unit head:* Dr. Jeff Waddoups, Chair/Professor, 702-895-3497, Fax: 702-895-1354, E-mail: jeffrey.waddoups@unlv.edu. *Application contact:* Dr. Mary Riddel, Graduate Coordinator, 702-895-2792, Fax: 702-895-1354, E-mail: mary.riddel@unlv.edu. Website: https://www.unlv.edu/economics

University of Nevada, Reno, Graduate School, College of Business Administration, Department of Economics, Reno, NV 89557. Offers MA, MS. *Degree requirements:* For master's, thesis. *Entrance requirements:* For master's, GMAT or GRE, minimum GPA of 2.75. Additional exam requirements/recommendations for international students: Required—TOEFL (minimum score 500 paper-based; 61 iBT), IELTS (minimum score 6). Electronic applications accepted. *Faculty research:* Applied microeconomics, public finance, development, labor.

University of New Brunswick Fredericton, School of Graduate Studies, Faculty of Arts, Department of Economics, Fredericton, NB E3B 5A3, Canada. Offers applied economics and finance (M Sc); economics (MA). M Sc offered on Saint John campus. *Entrance requirements:* For master's, minimum GPA of 3.0. Additional exam requirements/recommendations for international students: Required—TWE (minimum score 4), TOEFL (minimum score 580 paper-based) or IELTS (minimum score 7). Electronic applications accepted. *Faculty research:* Epidemiology and population health, micro/macro economics, economics of transportation, regional development, health economics, econometrics.

University of New Hampshire, Graduate School, Peter T. Paul College of Business and Economics, Department of Economics, Durham, NH 03824. Offers MA, PhD. *Program availability:* Part-time. *Students:* 26 full-time (13 women), 2 part-time (0 women); includes 1 minority (Hispanic/Latino), 16 international. Average age 27. 67 applicants, 70% accepted, 17 enrolled. In 2017, 11 master's, 3 doctorates awarded. Terminal master's awarded for partial completion of doctoral program. *Entrance requirements:* For master's and doctorate, GRE General Test. Additional exam requirements/recommendations for international students: Required—TOEFL (minimum score 550 paper-based; 80 iBT). *Application deadline:* For fall admission, 4/15 for domestic and international students. Application fee: $65. Electronic applications accepted. *Financial support:* In 2017–18, 25 students received support, including 4 research assistantships, 12 teaching assistantships; fellowships, career-related internships or fieldwork, Federal Work-Study, scholarships/grants, and tuition waivers (full and partial) also available. Support available to part-time students. Financial award application deadline: 2/15. *Unit head:* Dr. Jim Wible, Chair, 603-862-3324. *Application contact:* Wendy Harris, Administrative Assistant, 603-862-3326, E-mail: econ.info@unh.edu. Website: http://paulcollege.unh.edu/academics/graduate-programs/ma-phd-economics

University of New Mexico, Graduate Studies, College of Arts and Sciences, Program in Economics, Albuquerque, NM 87131-2039. Offers econometrics (MA); economic theory (MA); environmental/natural resource economics (MA, PhD); international/development and sustainability economics (MA, PhD); public economics (MA, PhD). *Program availability:* Part-time. *Faculty:* 12 full-time (5 women), 1 (woman) part-time/adjunct. *Students:* 28 full-time (6 women), 22 part-time (8 women); includes 5 minority (all Hispanic/Latino), 31 international. Average age 33. 49 applicants, 20% accepted, 10 enrolled. In 2017, 7 master's, 4 doctorates awarded. Terminal master's awarded for partial completion of doctoral program. *Degree requirements:* For master's, comprehensive exam, thesis (for some programs); for doctorate, comprehensive exam, thesis/dissertation. *Entrance requirements:* For master's and doctorate, GRE General Test, 3 letters of recommendation, letter of intent, curriculum vitae. Additional exam requirements/recommendations for international students: Required—TOEFL (minimum score 520 paper-based; 68 iBT). *Application deadline:* For fall admission, 3/1 priority date for domestic students, 3/1 for international students. Applications are processed on a rolling basis. Application fee: $50. Electronic applications accepted. *Financial support:* Fellowships with tuition reimbursements, research assistantships with tuition reimbursements, teaching assistantships with tuition reimbursements, career-related internships or fieldwork, Federal Work-Study, scholarships/grants, health care benefits, and unspecified assistantships available. Support available to part-time students. Financial award application deadline: 3/1; financial award applicants required to submit FAFSA. *Faculty research:* Core theory, econometrics, public finance, international/development economics, labor/human resource economics, environmental/natural resource economics. *Total annual research expenditures:* $167,690. *Unit head:* Dr. Janie Chermak, Chair, 505-277-2037, Fax: 505-277-9445, E-mail: jchermak@unm.edu. *Application contact:* Jeff Newcomer Miller, Academic Advisor, 505-277-3056, Fax: 505-277-9445, E-mail: econgrad@unm.edu. Website: http://econ.unm.edu

University of New Orleans, Graduate School, College of Business Administration, Department of Economics and Finance, Program in Financial Economics, New Orleans, LA 70148. Offers PhD. Terminal master's awarded for partial completion of doctoral program. *Degree requirements:* For doctorate, one foreign language, comprehensive exam, thesis/dissertation, general exams. *Entrance requirements:* For doctorate, GRE General Test, minimum GPA of 3.0. Additional exam requirements/recommendations for international students: Required—TOEFL (minimum score 550 paper-based; 79 iBT). Electronic applications accepted. *Faculty research:* Urban and regional economics, economic development, monetary theory and policy, international finance.

The University of North Carolina at Chapel Hill, Graduate School, College of Arts and Sciences, Department of Economics, Chapel Hill, NC 27599. Offers MS, PhD. Terminal master's awarded for partial completion of doctoral program. *Degree requirements:* For master's, comprehensive exam, thesis or alternative; for doctorate, comprehensive exam, thesis/dissertation. *Entrance requirements:* For master's, GRE General Test, minimum GPA of 3.0; for doctorate, GRE General Test, minimum GPA of 3.5. Additional exam requirements/recommendations for international students: Required—TOEFL (minimum score 550 paper-based). Electronic applications accepted. *Faculty research:* Health economics, micro theory/IO, labor economics, economic history, financial econometrics.

The University of North Carolina at Charlotte, Belk College of Business, Department of Economics, Charlotte, NC 28223-0001. Offers applied econometrics (Graduate Certificate); economics (MS). *Program availability:* Part-time, evening/weekend. *Faculty:* 17 full-time (7 women), 1 part-time/adjunct (0 women). *Students:* 26 full-time (6 women), 33 part-time (4 women); includes 19 minority (8 Black or African American, non-Hispanic/Latino; 5 Asian, non-Hispanic/Latino; 4 Hispanic/Latino; 2 Two or more races, non-Hispanic/Latino), 7 international. Average age 26. 41 applicants, 90% accepted, 15 enrolled. In 2017, 25 master's, 2 other advanced degrees awarded. *Degree requirements:* For master's, thesis or project. *Entrance requirements:* For master's, GRE General Test, GMAT, undergraduate coursework that includes calculus, econometrics (or equivalent), intermediate macroeconomic theory, intermediate microeconomic theory; for Graduate Certificate, bachelor's degree, or its equivalent, from regionally-accredited college or university; minimum GPA of 2.75 on all previous work completed beyond high school (secondary school); statement of purpose; unofficial transcripts of all college course work. Additional exam requirements/recommendations for international students: Required—TOEFL (minimum score 523 paper-based, 70 iBT) or IELTS (6.5). *Application deadline:* For fall admission, 3/1 priority date for domestic and international students; for spring admission, 10/1 priority date for domestic and international students; for summer admission, 4/1 priority date for domestic and international students. Applications are processed on a rolling basis. Application fee: $75. Electronic applications accepted. *Expenses:* Contact institution. *Financial support:* Career-related internships or fieldwork, institutionally sponsored loans, scholarships/grants, and unspecified assistantships available. Support available to part-time students. Financial award application deadline: 3/1; financial award applicants required to submit FAFSA. *Faculty research:* Health care, taxation, energy, economic growth, monetary policy. *Total annual research expenditures:* $33,366. *Unit head:* Dr. Artie Zillante, Department Chair, 704-687-5375, Fax: 704-687-1384, E-mail: azillant@uncc.edu. *Application contact:* Kathy B. Giddings, Director of Graduate Admissions, 704-687-5503, Fax: 704-687-1668, E-mail: gradadm@uncc.edu. Website: http://msecon.uncc.edu/

The University of North Carolina at Greensboro, Graduate School, Bryan School of Business and Economics, Department of Economics, Program in Economics, Greensboro, NC 27412-5001. Offers PhD. *Degree requirements:* For doctorate, comprehensive exam, thesis/dissertation. *Entrance requirements:* Additional exam requirements/recommendations for international students: Required—TOEFL. Electronic applications accepted.

University of North Florida, Coggin College of Business, MBA Program, Jacksonville, FL 32224. Offers accounting (MBA); construction management (MBA); e-commerce

(MBA); economics (MBA); finance (MBA); human resource management (MBA); international business (MBA); logistics (MBA); management applications (MBA). *Accreditation:* AACSB. *Program availability:* Part-time, evening/weekend. *Entrance requirements:* For master's, GMAT or GRE, U.S. bachelor's degree from regionally-accredited university or equivalent foreign degree. Additional exam requirements/recommendations for international students: Required—TOEFL (minimum score 550 paper-based; 79 iBT). *Faculty research:* Performance measures, costing, and inventory issues in logistics and supply chain management; inter-organizational systems; international management and marketing practices; e-commerce; organizational learning and socialization processes.

University of North Texas, Robert B. Toulouse School of Graduate Studies, Denton, TX 76203-5459. Offers accounting (MS); applied anthropology (MA, MS); applied behavior analysis (Certificate); applied geography (MA); applied technology and performance improvement (M Ed, MS); art education (MA); art history (MA); art museum education (Certificate); arts leadership (Certificate); audiology (Au D); behavior analysis (MS); behavioral science (PhD); biochemistry and molecular biology (MS); biology (MA, MS); biomedical engineering (MS); business analysis (MS); chemistry (MS); clinical health psychology (PhD); communication studies (MA, MS); computer engineering (MS); computer science (MS); counseling (M Ed, MS), including clinical mental health counseling (MS), college and university counseling, elementary school counseling, secondary school counseling; creative writing (MA); criminal justice (MS); curriculum and instruction (M Ed); decision sciences (MBA); design (MA, MFA), including fashion design (MFA), innovation studies, interior design (MFA); early childhood studies (MS); economics (MS); educational leadership (M Ed, Ed D); educational psychology (MS, PhD), including family studies (MS), gifted and talented (MS), human development (MS), learning and cognition (MS), research, measurement and evaluation (MS); electrical engineering (MS); emergency management (MPA); engineering technology (MS); English (MA); English as a second language (MA); environmental science (MS); finance (MBA, MS); financial management (MPA); French (MA); health services management (MBA); higher education (M Ed, Ed D); history (MA, MS); hospitality management (MS); human resources management (MPA); information science (MS); information systems (PhD); information technologies (MBA); interdisciplinary studies (MA, MS); international studies (MA); international sustainable tourism (MS); jazz studies (MM); journalism (MA, MJ, Graduate Certificate), including interactive and virtual digital communication (Graduate Certificate), narrative journalism (Graduate Certificate), public relations (Graduate Certificate); kinesiology (MS); linguistics (MA); local government management (MPA); logistics (PhD); logistics and supply chain management (MBA); long-term care, senior housing, and aging services (MA); management (PhD); marketing (MBA); mathematics (MA, MS); mechanical and energy engineering (MS, PhD); music (MA), including ethnomusicology, music theory, musicology, performance; music composition (PhD); music education (MM Ed, PhD); nonprofit management (MPA); operations and supply chain management (MBA); performance (MM, DMA); philosophy (MA); political science (MA); professional and technical communication (MA); radio, television and film (MA, MFA); rehabilitation counseling (Certificate); sociology (MA); Spanish (MA); special education (M Ed); speech-language pathology (MA); strategic management (MBA); studio art (MFA); teaching (M Ed); MBA/MS. *Program availability:* Part-time, evening/weekend, online learning. Terminal master's awarded for partial completion of doctoral program. *Degree requirements:* For master's, variable foreign language requirement, comprehensive exam (for some programs), thesis (for some programs); for doctorate, variable foreign language requirement, comprehensive exam (for some programs), thesis/dissertation; for other advanced degree, variable foreign language requirement, comprehensive exam (for some programs). *Entrance requirements:* For master's and doctorate, GRE, GMAT. Additional exam requirements/recommendations for international students: Required—TOEFL (minimum score 550 paper-based; 79 iBT). Electronic applications accepted.

University of Notre Dame, Graduate School, College of Arts and Letters, Division of Social Science, Department of Economics and Econometrics, Notre Dame, IN 46556. Offers MA, PhD. Terminal master's awarded for partial completion of doctoral program. *Degree requirements:* For master's, comprehensive exam (for some programs), thesis optional; for doctorate, thesis/dissertation, candidacy exam. *Entrance requirements:* For doctorate, GRE General Test. Additional exam requirements/recommendations for international students: Required—TOEFL (minimum score 600 paper-based; 80 iBT). Electronic applications accepted.

University of Oklahoma, College of Arts and Sciences, Department of Economics, Norman, OK 73019. Offers economics (MA, PhD), including applied economics (MA), managerial economics (MA). *Faculty:* 21 full-time (5 women). *Students:* 40 full-time (12 women), 29 part-time (3 women); includes 16 minority (7 Black or African American, non-Hispanic/Latino; 1 American Indian or Alaska Native, non-Hispanic/Latino; 3 Asian, non-Hispanic/Latino; 5 Hispanic/Latino), 20 international. Average age 32. 50 applicants, 64% accepted, 14 enrolled. In 2017, 21 master's, 3 doctorates awarded. Terminal master's awarded for partial completion of doctoral program. *Degree requirements:* For master's, comprehensive exam (for some programs); for doctorate, comprehensive exam, thesis/dissertation. *Entrance requirements:* For master's and doctorate, GRE, undergraduate degree in related field. Additional exam requirements/recommendations for international students: Required—TOEFL (minimum score 79 iBT) or IELTS (minimum score 6.5). *Application deadline:* For fall admission, 2/28 priority date for domestic students, 1/30 priority date for international students. Applications are processed on a rolling basis. Application fee: $50 ($100 for international students). Electronic applications accepted. *Expenses:* Tuition, state resident: full-time $5119; part-time $213.30 per credit hour. Tuition, nonresident: full-time $19,778; part-time $824.10 per credit hour. *Required fees:* $3458; $133.55 per credit hour. $126.50 per semester. *Financial support:* In 2017–18, 28 students received support, including 23 teaching assistantships with partial tuition reimbursements available (averaging $14,507 per year); fellowships with partial tuition reimbursements available, research assistantships with partial tuition reimbursements available, scholarships/grants, and health care benefits also available. Financial award application deadline: 6/1; financial award applicants required to submit FAFSA. *Faculty research:* Public economics, development economics, international economics, industrial organization, labor economics. *Total annual research expenditures:* $50,386. *Unit head:* Dr. Gary Hoover, Department Chair and Professor of Economics, 405-325-5857, E-mail: ghoover@ou.edu. *Application contact:* Prof. Daniel Hicks, Director of Graduate Studies/Associate Professor, 405-325-7049, E-mail: hicksd@ou.edu.
Website: http://cas.ou.edu/economics

University of Oklahoma, College of International Studies, Norman, OK 73019. Offers economics and development (MAIS), including global economics and development, global security studies (MA, MAIS); global affairs (MA), including economics and development, global security studies (MA, MAIS); JD/MAIS; MAIS/MSW. *Program availability:* Part-time, online courses with an 8-10 day study abroad. *Faculty:* 20 full-time (7 women), 1 part-time/adjunct (0 women). *Students:* 80 full-time (35 women), 307 part-time (97 women); includes 118 minority (33 Black or African American, non-Hispanic/Latino; 2 American Indian or Alaska Native, non-Hispanic/Latino; 15 Asian, non-Hispanic/Latino; 45 Hispanic/Latino; 1 Native Hawaiian or other Pacific Islander, non-Hispanic/Latino; 22 Two or more races, non-Hispanic/Latino), 7 international. Average age 32. 121 applicants, 89% accepted, 68 enrolled. In 2017, 73 master's awarded. Terminal master's awarded for partial completion of doctoral program. *Degree requirements:* For master's, variable foreign language requirement, 36 credit hours (33 online); thesis, policy paper or internship project; faculty-led overseas travel program of 8-10 days that will vary in location (online). *Entrance requirements:* For master's, GRE. Additional exam requirements/recommendations for international students: Required—TOEFL (minimum score 79 iBT) or IELTS (minimum score 6.5). *Application deadline:* For fall admission, 2/15 for domestic and international students. Applications are processed on a rolling basis. Application fee: $50 ($100 for international students). Electronic applications accepted. *Expenses:* Tuition, state resident: full-time $5119; part-time $213.30 per credit hour. Tuition, nonresident: full-time $19,778; part-time $824.10 per credit hour. *Required fees:* $3458; $133.55 per credit hour. $126.50 per semester. *Financial support:* In 2017–18, 31 students received support, including 4 research assistantships with full tuition reimbursements available (averaging $13,500 per year), 4 teaching assistantships with full tuition reimbursements available (averaging $13,500 per year); fellowships with full tuition reimbursements available, career-related internships or fieldwork, scholarships/grants, health care benefits, and unspecified assistantships also available. Financial award application deadline: 6/1; financial award applicants required to submit FAFSA. *Faculty research:* Area studies, including the Middle East, China, East and South Asia, Latin America, and Europe; political economy and development; international security; identity and nationalism; global history and culture. *Total annual research expenditures:* $1,502. *Unit head:* Dr. Mitchell Smith, Professor/Associate Dean for Academic Affairs, 405-325-1584, Fax: 405-325-7738, E-mail: mps@ou.edu. *Application contact:* Katie Watkins, Academic Advisor, 405-325-2337, Fax: 405-325-7738, E-mail: kwatkins@ou.edu.
Website: http://www.ou.edu/dias

University of Oregon, Graduate School, College of Arts and Sciences, Department of Economics, Eugene, OR 97403. Offers MA, MS, PhD. Terminal master's awarded for partial completion of doctoral program. *Degree requirements:* For master's, thesis or alternative; for doctorate, thesis/dissertation, qualifying exam. *Entrance requirements:* For master's and doctorate, GRE General Test, minimum GPA of 3.0. Additional exam requirements/recommendations for international students: Required—TOEFL. *Faculty research:* Labor economics, macroeconomics, international economics, industrial organization, public finance.

University of Ottawa, Faculty of Graduate and Postdoctoral Studies, Faculty of Social Sciences, Department of Economics, Ottawa, ON K1N 6N5, Canada. Offers MA, PhD. PhD offered jointly with Carleton University. *Program availability:* Part-time. *Degree requirements:* For master's, thesis or alternative; for doctorate, comprehensive exam, thesis/dissertation. *Entrance requirements:* For master's, honors bachelor's degree or equivalent, minimum B average; for doctorate, master's degree, minimum B+ average. Electronic applications accepted. *Faculty research:* Public economics, industrial organizations, monetary economics, international economics, economic development.

University of Pennsylvania, School of Arts and Sciences, Graduate Group in Economics, Philadelphia, PA 19104. Offers AM, PhD, JD/AM, JD/PhD. *Faculty:* 41 full-time (6 women), 6 part-time/adjunct (0 women). *Students:* 112 full-time (25 women), 1 (woman) part-time; includes 9 minority (1 Black or African American, non-Hispanic/Latino; 4 Asian, non-Hispanic/Latino; 2 Hispanic/Latino; 2 Two or more races, non-Hispanic/Latino), 85 international. Average age 28. 714 applicants, 16% accepted, 32 enrolled. In 2017, 7 master's, 16 doctorates awarded. *Degree requirements:* For doctorate, thesis/dissertation. *Entrance requirements:* For doctorate, GRE General Test.
Website: http://economics.sas.upenn.edu/graduate-program

University of Pittsburgh, Graduate School of Public and International Affairs, Master of Public and International Affairs Program, Pittsburgh, PA 15260. Offers human security (MPIA); international political economy (MPIA); security and intelligence studies (MPIA); JD/MPIA; MBA/MPIA; MPH/MPIA; MPIA/MSW; MSIS/MPIA. *Program availability:* Part-time, evening/weekend. *Faculty:* 30 full-time (11 women), 14 part-time/adjunct (5 women). *Students:* 87 full-time (42 women), 14 part-time (7 women); includes 15 minority (6 Black or African American, non-Hispanic/Latino; 3 Asian, non-Hispanic/Latino; 6 Hispanic/Latino), 14 international. Average age 27. 173 applicants, 88% accepted, 37 enrolled. In 2017, 54 master's awarded. *Degree requirements:* For master's, thesis optional, capstone seminar. *Entrance requirements:* For master's, GRE General Test or GMAT, 2 letters of recommendation, resume, undergraduate transcripts, personal statement. Additional exam requirements/recommendations for international students: Required—TOEFL (minimum score 80 iBT); Recommended—IELTS (minimum score 7). *Application deadline:* For fall admission, 2/1 priority date for domestic students, 1/15 priority date for international students; for spring admission, 11/1 priority date for domestic students, 8/1 priority date for international students. Application fee: $50. Electronic applications accepted. *Expenses:* $23,140 per year in-state, $37,830 out-of-state. *Financial support:* In 2017–18, 47 students received support, including 7 fellowships with full tuition reimbursements available (averaging $37,000 per year), 8 research assistantships with full tuition reimbursements available (averaging $37,000 per year); scholarships/grants also available. Financial award application deadline: 2/1; financial award applicants required to submit FAFSA. *Faculty research:* International political economy, human security, security and intelligence studies. *Total annual research expenditures:* $1.6 million. *Unit head:* Dr. John Keeler, Dean, 412-648-7605, Fax: 412-648-7601, E-mail: gspia@pitt.edu. *Application contact:* Dr. Michael Rizzi, Director of Student Services, 412-648-7643, Fax: 412-648-7641, E-mail: rizzim@pitt.edu.
Website: http://www.gspia.pitt.edu/

University of Pittsburgh, Kenneth P. Dietrich School of Arts and Sciences, Department of Economics, Pittsburgh, PA 15260. Offers MA, PhD. *Faculty:* 22 full-time (6 women). *Students:* 50 full-time (22 women); includes 27 minority (25 Asian, non-Hispanic/Latino; 2 Hispanic/Latino). Average age 27. 320 applicants, 8% accepted, 15 enrolled. *Degree requirements:* For doctorate, comprehensive exam, thesis/dissertation, comprehensive research paper. *Entrance requirements:* For doctorate, GRE, 3 letters of recommendation. Additional exam requirements/recommendations for international students: Required—TOEFL (minimum score 90 iBT). *Application deadline:* For fall admission, 1/15 for domestic and international students. Application fee: $50. Electronic applications accepted. *Financial support:* In 2017–18, 12 fellowships with full tuition reimbursements (averaging $22,042 per year), 5 research assistantships with full tuition reimbursements (averaging $18,815 per year), 24 teaching assistantships with full tuition reimbursements (averaging $18,815 per year) were awarded; scholarships/grants, tuition waivers (full), and unspecified assistantships also available. Financial award application deadline: 1/15. *Faculty research:* Game theory, experimental economics, econometrics, labor, experimental trade. *Total annual research expenditures:* $213,755. *Unit head:* Dr. Lise Vesterlund, Chair, 412-648-1794, E-mail: vester@pitt.edu. *Application contact:* Brian Deutsch, Graduate Administrator, 412-648-1399, E-mail: brd51@pitt.edu.
Website: http://www.econ.pitt.edu/

University of Puerto Rico–Río Piedras, College of Social Sciences, Department of Economics, San Juan, PR 00931-3300. Offers MA. *Program availability:* Part-time. *Degree requirements:* For master's, comprehensive exam, thesis. *Entrance requirements:* For master's, GRE, PAEG, interview, minimum GPA of 3.0, letter of recommendation.

University of Regina, Faculty of Graduate Studies and Research, Johnson-Shoyama Graduate School of Public Policy, Regina, SK S4S 0A2, Canada. Offers economic analysis for public policy (Master's Certificate); health administration (MHA); health systems management (Master's Certificate); public management (MPA, Master's Certificate); public policy (MPA, MPP, PhD); public policy analysis (Master's Certificate). *Program availability:* Part-time. *Faculty:* 9 full-time (4 women), 26 part-time/adjunct (10 women). *Students:* 104 full-time (65 women), 189 part-time (123 women). 285 applicants, 52% accepted. In 2017, 30 master's awarded. *Degree requirements:* For master's, thesis (for some programs); for doctorate, thesis/dissertation. *Entrance requirements:* For doctorate, master's degree, intended research program in an area of public policy. Additional exam requirements/recommendations for international students: Required—TOEFL (minimum score 580 paper-based; 80 iBT), IELTS (minimum score 6.5), PTE (minimum score 59). *Application deadline:* For fall admission, 5/1 for domestic and international students; for winter admission, 11/1 for domestic and international students; for spring admission, 3/15 for domestic and international students. Application fee: $100. Electronic applications accepted. *Expenses:* CAD$10,626 per year (for master's degrees); CAD$8,783 per year (for PhD). *Financial support:* In 2017–18, fellowships (averaging $6,059 per year), teaching assistantships (averaging $2,562 per year) were awarded; research assistantships, career-related internships or fieldwork, and scholarships/grants also available. Financial award application deadline: 6/15. *Faculty research:* Governance and administration, public finance, public policy analysis, non-governmental organizations and alternative service delivery, micro-economics for policy analysis. *Unit head:* Dr. Kathleen McNutt, Executive Director, Main Campus, 306-585-4759, Fax: 306-585-5461, E-mail: kathy.mcnutt@uregina.ca. *Application contact:* John Bird, Manager, Main Campus, 306-585-5469, Fax: 306-585-5461, E-mail: john.bird@uregina.ca.
Website: http://www.schoolofpublicpolicy.sk.ca/

University of Rhode Island, Graduate School, College of the Environment and Life Sciences, Department of Environmental and Natural Resource Economics, Kingston, RI 02881. Offers MS, PhD. *Program availability:* Part-time. *Faculty:* 7 full-time (2 women). *Students:* 15 full-time (5 women), 5 part-time (1 woman); includes 1 minority (Asian, non-Hispanic/Latino), 9 international. 22 applicants, 91% accepted, 4 enrolled. In 2017, 4 master's, 2 doctorates awarded. *Entrance requirements:* Additional exam requirements/recommendations for international students: Required—TOEFL. *Application deadline:* For fall admission, 2/1 for domestic and international students. Application fee: $65. Electronic applications accepted. *Expenses:* Tuition, state resident: full-time $12,706; part-time $786 per credit. Tuition, nonresident: full-time $25,216; part-time $1401 per credit. *Required fees:* $1598; $45 per credit. One-time fee: $30 part-time. *Financial support:* In 2017–18, 12 research assistantships with tuition reimbursements (averaging $14,872 per year), 1 teaching assistantship with tuition reimbursement (averaging $9,040 per year) were awarded. Financial award application deadline: 2/1; financial award applicants required to submit FAFSA. *Unit head:* Dr. James Opaluch, Chair, 401-874-4590, Fax: 401-874-4766, E-mail: jimo@uri.edu.
Website: http://web.uri.edu/enre/

University of Rochester, School of Arts and Sciences, Department of Economics, Rochester, NY 14627. Offers PhD. *Faculty:* 19 full-time (6 women). *Students:* 60 full-time (17 women), 1 part-time (0 women), 51 international. Average age 27. 307 applicants, 24% accepted, 19 enrolled. In 2017, 6 doctorates awarded. Terminal master's awarded for partial completion of doctoral program. *Degree requirements:* For doctorate, comprehensive exam, thesis/dissertation, qualifying exam. *Entrance requirements:* For doctorate, GRE General Test, transcripts, three letters of recommendation. Additional exam requirements/recommendations for international students: Required—TOEFL. *Application deadline:* For fall admission, 1/3 for domestic and international students. Application fee: $60. Electronic applications accepted. *Expenses:* $1,596 per credit hour. *Financial support:* In 2017–18, 39 students received support, including 4 fellowships (averaging $60,000 per year), 5 research assistantships (averaging $15,000 per year), 26 teaching assistantships (averaging $70,000 per year); health care benefits, tuition waivers (full), and unspecified assistantships also available. Financial award application deadline: 1/3. *Faculty research:* Macroeconomics, labor market dynamics, political economics, applied econometrics, financial econometrics. *Total annual research expenditures:* $57,483. *Unit head:* Srihari Govindan, Chair, 585-275-7241, E-mail: s.govindan@rochester.edu. *Application contact:* Pamela Young, Administrative Assistant, 585-275-8625, E-mail: pamela.l.young@rochester.edu.
Website: http://www.sas.rochester.edu/eco/graduate/index.html

University of San Francisco, College of Arts and Sciences, Economics Program, San Francisco, CA 94117-1080. Offers MA, MS, MS/MBA. *Program availability:* Part-time, evening/weekend. *Degree requirements:* For master's, comprehensive exam, thesis or alternative. *Entrance requirements:* For master's, GRE General Test (recommended), BA in economics (preferred). Additional exam requirements/recommendations for international students: Required—TOEFL, IELTS, PTE. *Faculty research:* Economic development, forecasting and planning, labor markets, Pacific Rim, financial markets.

University of Saskatchewan, College of Graduate Studies and Research, College of Arts and Science, Department of Economics, Saskatoon, SK S7N 5A2, Canada. Offers MA, Diploma. *Degree requirements:* For master's, thesis (for some programs). *Entrance requirements:* Additional exam requirements/recommendations for international students: Required—TOEFL (minimum score 80 iBT); Recommended—IELTS (minimum score 6.5). Electronic applications accepted.

University of South Africa, College of Economic and Management Sciences, Pretoria, South Africa. Offers accounting (D Admin, D Com); accounting science (DA); auditing (D Admin, D Com); business administration (M Tech); business economics (D Admin); business leadership (DBL); business management (D Admin, D Com); economic management analysis (M Tech); economics (D Admin, D Com, PhD); human resource development (M Tech); industrial psychology (D Admin, D Com, PhD); logistics (D Com); marketing (M Tech); public administration (D Admin, D Com, DPA, PhD); public management (M Tech); quantitative management (D Admin, D Com); real estate (M Tech); statistics (D Admin, PhD); tourism management (D Admin, D Com); transport economics (D Admin, D Com).

University of South Carolina, The Graduate School, Darla Moore School of Business, Doctoral Program in Business Administration, Columbia, SC 29208. Offers business administration (PhD); economics (PhD). *Degree requirements:* For doctorate, thesis/dissertation, qualifying and comprehensive exams. *Entrance requirements:* For doctorate, GRE or GMAT. Additional exam requirements/recommendations for international students: Required—TOEFL (minimum score 600 paper-based; 100 iBT), IELTS (minimum score 7). Electronic applications accepted. *Expenses:* Contact institution. *Faculty research:* International competitiveness of U.S. textiles, international compensation, exchange rates, international finance.

University of South Carolina, The Graduate School, Darla Moore School of Business, Master of Arts in Economics Program, Columbia, SC 29208. Offers MA, JD/MA. *Degree requirements:* For master's, thesis optional. *Entrance requirements:* For master's, GMAT or GRE General Test. Additional exam requirements/recommendations for international students: Required—TOEFL (minimum score 100 iBT); Recommended—IELTS. Electronic applications accepted. *Faculty research:* Monetary theory, labor economics, international economics, industrial organization.

University of Southern California, Graduate School, Dana and David Dornsife College of Letters, Arts and Sciences, Department of Economics, Los Angeles, CA 90089. Offers economic development programming (MA, PhD); mathematical finance (MS); M Pl/MA; MA/JD. Terminal master's awarded for partial completion of doctoral program. *Degree requirements:* For master's, comprehensive exam; for doctorate, comprehensive exam, thesis/dissertation. *Entrance requirements:* For master's and doctorate, GRE. Additional exam requirements/recommendations for international students: Required—TOEFL (minimum score 93 iBT). Electronic applications accepted. *Faculty research:* Macro theory, development economics, econometrics.

University of Southern Mississippi, College of Business, Department of Economic Development, Tourism and Sport Management, Hattiesburg, MS 39406-0001. Offers economic development (MS); sport management (MS). *Program availability:* Part-time, evening/weekend. *Students:* 9 full-time (3 women). 15 applicants, 67% accepted, 9 enrolled. In 2017, 17 master's awarded. *Degree requirements:* For master's, comprehensive exam, thesis optional, internships. *Entrance requirements:* For master's, GMAT or GRE General Test, minimum GPA of 2.75 in last 60 hours. Additional exam requirements/recommendations for international students: Required—TOEFL, IELTS. *Application deadline:* For fall admission, 8/1 for domestic students, 3/1 for international students; for spring admission, 1/3 for domestic and international students. Applications are processed on a rolling basis. Application fee: $60. Electronic applications accepted. *Expenses:* Tuition, state resident: full-time $3830. *Financial support:* Research assistantships with full tuition reimbursements, teaching assistantships with full tuition reimbursements, career-related internships or fieldwork, Federal Work-Study, scholarships/grants, health care benefits, and unspecified assistantships available. Financial award application deadline: 3/1; financial award applicants required to submit FAFSA. *Faculty research:* Economic development, international studies, geography. *Unit head:* Dr. Stacey Hall, Chair, 601-266-6308, Fax: 601-266-6707. *Application contact:* Dr. Chad Miller, Program Coordinator, 601-266-6666, Fax: 601-266-6071.
Website: https://www.usm.edu/business/eco-dev-tourism-sport-management

University of South Florida, College of Arts and Sciences, Department of Economics, Tampa, FL 33620-9951. Offers MA, PhD. *Program availability:* Part-time, evening/weekend. *Faculty:* 11 full-time (4 women), 1 part-time/adjunct (0 women). *Students:* 33 full-time (14 women), 12 part-time (3 women); includes 5 minority (1 Black or African American, non-Hispanic/Latino; 1 Asian, non-Hispanic/Latino; 3 Hispanic/Latino), 18 international. Average age 29. 83 applicants, 58% accepted, 25 enrolled. In 2017, 51 master's, 4 doctorates awarded. *Degree requirements:* For master's, comprehensive exam, oral exam; for doctorate, comprehensive exam, thesis/dissertation. *Entrance requirements:* For master's, GRE General Test, minimum GPA of 3.0 in last 60 hours of course work; minimum B grade in calculus, statistics, undergraduate-level intermediate microeconomics, and undergraduate-level intermediate macroeconomics; for doctorate, GRE General Test, minimum GPA of 3.0 in last 60 hours of undergraduate and graduate coursework; minimum B grade in calculus (two courses), probability and statistics, undergraduate intermediate-level microeconomics and undergraduate intermediate-level macroeconomics. Additional exam requirements/recommendations for international students: Required—TOEFL (minimum score 550 paper-based; 79 iBT) or IELTS (minimum score 6.5). *Application deadline:* For fall admission, 6/1 for domestic and international students; for spring admission, 10/15 for domestic students, 9/15 for international students. Applications are processed on a rolling basis. Application fee: $30. Electronic applications accepted. *Financial support:* In 2017–18, 17 students received support, including 1 research assistantship (averaging $13,082 per year), 15 teaching assistantships with tuition reimbursements available (averaging $11,393 per year); unspecified assistantships also available. Financial award application deadline: 2/1; financial award applicants required to submit FAFSA. *Faculty research:* Applied microeconomics, health economics, industrial organization, development economics, public economics. *Total annual research expenditures:* $11,733. *Unit head:* Dr. Bradley Kamp, Associate Professor and Chairperson, 813-974-6549, Fax: 813-974-6510, E-mail: bkamp@usf.edu. *Application contact:* Dr. Michael Loewy, Associate Professor and Graduate Director, 813-974-6532, Fax: 813-974-6510, E-mail: mloewy@usf.edu.
Website: http://www.economics.usf.edu

The University of Tennessee, Graduate School, College of Arts and Sciences, Department of Sociology, Knoxville, TN 37996. Offers criminology (MA, PhD); energy, environment, and resource policy (MA, PhD); political economy (MA, PhD). *Program availability:* Part-time. *Degree requirements:* For master's, thesis or alternative; for doctorate, thesis/dissertation. *Entrance requirements:* For master's, GRE General Test, minimum GPA of 3.0; for doctorate, GRE General Test, minimum GPA of 3.5. Additional exam requirements/recommendations for international students: Required—TOEFL. Electronic applications accepted.

The University of Tennessee, Graduate School, College of Business Administration, Department of Economics, Knoxville, TN 37996. Offers MA, PhD. *Degree requirements:* For master's, thesis or alternative; for doctorate, thesis/dissertation. *Entrance requirements:* For master's and doctorate, GRE General Test or GMAT, minimum GPA of 2.7. Additional exam requirements/recommendations for international students: Required—TOEFL. Electronic applications accepted.

The University of Texas at Arlington, Graduate School, College of Business, Economics Department, Arlington, TX 76019. Offers MA. *Program availability:* Part-time, evening/weekend. *Degree requirements:* For master's, thesis optional. *Entrance requirements:* For master's, GMAT or GRE. Additional exam requirements/recommendations for international students: Required—TOEFL (minimum score 550 paper-based; 79 iBT).

The University of Texas at Austin, Graduate School, College of Liberal Arts, Department of Economics, Austin, TX 78712-1111. Offers MA, MS Econ, PhD. *Program availability:* Part-time. *Degree requirements:* For master's, thesis; for doctorate, comprehensive exam, thesis/dissertation. *Entrance requirements:* For master's and doctorate, GRE General Test, minimum GPA of 3.5 (based on upper-division undergraduate and graduate course work). Additional exam requirements/recommendations for international students: Required—TOEFL. Electronic applications accepted. *Faculty research:* Industrial organization, game theory, monetary economics, labor economics, public economics.

The University of Texas at Dallas, School of Economic, Political and Policy Sciences, Program in Economics, Richardson, TX 75080. Offers MS, PhD. *Program availability:* Part-time, evening/weekend. *Faculty:* 12 full-time (3 women), 1 part-time/adjunct (0 women). *Students:* 49 full-time (20 women), 13 part-time (4 women); includes 15 minority (6 Black or African American, non-Hispanic/Latino; 4 Asian, non-Hispanic/Latino; 2 Hispanic/Latino; 3 Two or more races, non-Hispanic/Latino), 37 international. Average age 29. 104 applicants, 48% accepted, 20 enrolled. In 2017, 12 master's, 3 doctorates awarded. *Degree requirements:* For master's, internship; for doctorate, thesis/dissertation. *Entrance requirements:* For master's, GRE (minimum combined verbal and quantitative score of 1200), minimum GPA of 3.0 in upper-level course work in field; for doctorate, GRE (minimum combined verbal and quantitative score of 1200, writing 4.5), minimum GPA of 3.25 in upper-level and graduate course work in field. Additional exam requirements/recommendations for international students: Required—TOEFL (minimum score 550 paper-based). *Application deadline:* For fall admission, 7/15 for domestic students, 5/1 priority date for international students; for spring

admission, 11/15 for domestic students, 9/1 priority date for international students. Applications are processed on a rolling basis. Application fee: $50 ($100 for international students). Electronic applications accepted. *Expenses:* Tuition, state resident: full-time $12,916; part-time $718 per credit hour. Tuition, nonresident: full-time $25,252; part-time $1403 per credit hour. *Financial support:* In 2017–18, 28 students received support, including 5 research assistantships with partial tuition reimbursements available (averaging $21,211 per year), 20 teaching assistantships with partial tuition reimbursements available (averaging $13,100 per year); career-related internships or fieldwork, Federal Work-Study, institutionally sponsored loans, scholarships/grants, and unspecified assistantships also available. Support available to part-time students. Financial award application deadline: 4/30; financial award applicants required to submit FAFSA. *Faculty research:* Bargaining and negotiation, experimental economics, judgment and decision-making, game theory, terrorism. *Unit head:* Dr. Daniel G. Arce, Program Head, 972-883-6857, Fax: 972-883-2735, E-mail: darce@utdallas.edu. *Application contact:* Judy Du, Graduate Program Administrator, 972-883-4964, Fax: 972-883-2735, E-mail: judy.du@utdallas.edu.
Website: http://www.utdallas.edu/epps/economics/

The University of Texas at Dallas, School of Economic, Political and Policy Sciences, Program in Public Policy and Political Economy, Richardson, TX 75080. Offers international political economy (MS); public policy (MPP); public policy and political economy (PhD); social data analytics and research (MS). *Program availability:* Part-time, evening/weekend. *Faculty:* 12 full-time (1 woman), 1 part-time/adjunct (0 women). *Students:* 46 full-time (22 women), 33 part-time (14 women); includes 27 minority (8 Black or African American, non-Hispanic/Latino; 8 Asian, non-Hispanic/Latino; 10 Hispanic/Latino; 1 Two or more races, non-Hispanic/Latino), 21 international. Average age 33. 69 applicants, 52% accepted, 22 enrolled. In 2017, 21 master's, 3 doctorates awarded. *Degree requirements:* For doctorate, thesis/dissertation. *Entrance requirements:* For master's and doctorate, GRE General Test, minimum GPA of 3.0 in upper-level course work in field. Additional exam requirements/recommendations for international students: Required—TOEFL (minimum score 550 paper-based). *Application deadline:* For fall admission, 7/15 for domestic students, 5/1 priority date for international students; for spring admission, 11/15 for domestic students, 9/1 priority date for international students. Applications are processed on a rolling basis. Application fee: $50 ($100 for international students). Electronic applications accepted. *Expenses:* Tuition, state resident: full-time $12,916; part-time $718 per credit hour. Tuition, nonresident: full-time $25,252; part-time $1403 per credit hour. *Financial support:* In 2017–18, 46 students received support, including 4 research assistantships with partial tuition reimbursements available (averaging $17,697 per year), 14 teaching assistantships with partial tuition reimbursements available (averaging $13,100 per year); career-related internships or fieldwork, Federal Work-Study, institutionally sponsored loans, scholarships/grants, and unspecified assistantships also available. Support available to part-time students. Financial award application deadline: 4/30; financial award applicants required to submit FAFSA. *Faculty research:* Ethnicity, community and local public good provision; community mental health policy; Texas Schools Project; biological and chemical arms control; cross-disciplinary applications of quantitative methodology. *Unit head:* Dr. Jennifer Holmes, Program Head, 972-883-6843, Fax: 972-883-6297, E-mail: jholmes@utdallas.edu. *Application contact:* Marjorie McDonald, Graduate Program Administrator, 972-883-6406, Fax: 972-883-6297, E-mail: pppe@utdallas.edu.
Website: http://www.utdallas.edu/epps/public-policy-and-political-economy/

The University of Texas at El Paso, Graduate School, College of Business Administration, Department of Economics and Finance, El Paso, TX 79968-0001. Offers economics (MS). *Program availability:* Part-time, evening/weekend. *Degree requirements:* For master's, thesis optional, at least 24 credit hours with minimum cumulative GPA of 3.0. *Entrance requirements:* For master's, GRE, undergraduate degree from accredited college or university. Additional exam requirements/recommendations for international students: Required—TOEFL. Electronic applications accepted. *Faculty research:* Border economics, public utility economics, urban economics, international economics, applied econometrics.

The University of Texas at San Antonio, College of Business, Department of Economics, San Antonio, TX 78249-0617. Offers business economics (MBA); economics (MA). *Program availability:* Part-time, evening/weekend. *Faculty:* 10 full-time (3 women), 1 part-time/adjunct (0 women). *Students:* 30 full-time (11 women), 31 part-time (8 women); includes 26 minority (1 Black or African American, non-Hispanic/Latino; 2 Asian, non-Hispanic/Latino; 22 Hispanic/Latino; 1 Two or more races, non-Hispanic/Latino), 6 international. Average age 28. 33 applicants, 79% accepted, 20 enrolled. In 2017, 5 master's awarded. *Degree requirements:* For master's, comprehensive exam, thesis optional. *Entrance requirements:* For master's, GMAT or GRE, transcripts, statement of purpose. Additional exam requirements/recommendations for international students: Required—TOEFL (minimum score 550 paper-based; 79 iBT), IELTS (minimum score 6.5). *Application deadline:* For fall admission, 7/31 for domestic students, 3/1 for international students; for spring admission, 10/15 for domestic students, 9/15 for international students. Applications are processed on a rolling basis. Application fee: $50 ($90 for international students). Electronic applications accepted. *Expenses:* Tuition, state resident: full-time $5495. Tuition, nonresident: full-time $21,938. *Required fees:* $1915. Tuition and fees vary according to program. *Faculty research:* Game theory, international trade, monetary policy, panel data, exchange and interest rates. *Total annual research expenditures:* $104,897. *Unit head:* Dr. Melody Lo, Department Chair, 210-458-4315, Fax: 210-458-5837, E-mail: melody.lo@utsa.edu. *Application contact:* Katherine Pope, Economics Graduate Advisor of Record, 210-458-7316, Fax: 210-458-4398, E-mail: katherine.pope@utsa.edu.
Website: http://business.utsa.edu/economics/

The University of Toledo, College of Graduate Studies, College of Languages, Literature and Social Sciences, Department of Economics, Toledo, OH 43606-3390. Offers applied econometric specialization (MA); economics (MA). *Program availability:* Part-time. *Degree requirements:* For master's, comprehensive exam, paper or thesis. *Entrance requirements:* For master's, GRE General Test, minimum cumulative GPA of 2.7 on all previous academic work, three letters of recommendation, statement of purpose, transcripts from all prior institutions attended. Additional exam requirements/recommendations for international students: Required—TOEFL (minimum score 550 paper-based; 80 iBT). Electronic applications accepted. *Faculty research:* Economic development.

The University of Toledo, College of Graduate Studies, Judith Herb College of Education, Department of Curriculum and Instruction, Toledo, OH 43606-3390. Offers art education (ME); career and technical education (ME, Ed S); curriculum and instruction (ME, PhD, Ed S); early childhood education (Ed S); education and anthropology (MAE); education and biology (MES); education and chemistry (MES); education and classics (MAE); education and economics (MAE); education and English (MAE); education and French (MAE); education and geology (MES); education and German (MAE); education and history (MAE); education and mathematics (MAE, MES); education and physics (MES); education and political science (MAE); education and sociology (MAE); education and Spanish (MAE); educational media (PhD); educational technology (ME); educational technology: virtual educator (Certificate); elementary education (PhD); English as a second language (MAE); gifted and talented education (PhD); middle childhood education (ME); secondary education (ME, PhD); special education (PhD). *Accreditation:* NCATE. *Program availability:* Part-time, evening/weekend. *Degree requirements:* For master's, comprehensive exam, thesis or alternative; for doctorate, comprehensive exam, thesis/dissertation; for other advanced degree, thesis optional. *Entrance requirements:* For master's, doctorate, and other advanced degree, minimum cumulative GPA of 2.7 for all previous academic work, letters of recommendation. Additional exam requirements/recommendations for international students: Required—TOEFL (minimum score 550 paper-based; 80 iBT). Electronic applications accepted.

University of Toronto, School of Graduate Studies, Faculty of Arts and Science, Department of Economics, Toronto, ON M5S 1A1, Canada. Offers economics (MA, PhD); financial economics (MFE); JD/MA; JD/PhD. *Program availability:* Part-time. *Degree requirements:* For doctorate, comprehensive exam, thesis/dissertation. *Entrance requirements:* For master's, GRE (for applicants without a degree from a Canadian university), minimum B average in final year, 2 letters of reference; for doctorate, GRE (for applicants without a degree from a Canadian university), master's degree in economics, minimum B+ average, 3 letters of reference. Additional exam requirements/recommendations for international students: Required—TOEFL (minimum 580 paper-based; 93 iBT), IELTS (minimum score 7), TWE (minimum score 5), or Michigan English Language Assessment Battery (minimum score 85). Electronic applications accepted.

University of Utah, Graduate School, College of Social and Behavioral Science, Department of Economics, Salt Lake City, UT 84112. Offers econometrics (M Stat); economics (M Phil, MA, MS, PhD). *Faculty:* 20 full-time (5 women), 32 part-time/adjunct (8 women). *Students:* 48 full-time (14 women), 30 part-time (9 women). Average age 33. 89 applicants, 35% accepted, 15 enrolled. In 2017, 21 master's, 8 doctorates awarded. *Degree requirements:* For master's, thesis or alternative, oral presentation, research project; for doctorate, comprehensive exam, thesis/dissertation, qualifying exams, final defense. *Entrance requirements:* For master's, GRE General Test; GRE Subject Test (for M Stat), undergraduate course work in economics, minimum GPA of 3.0; for doctorate, GRE General Test, minimum GPA of 3.0, course work in calculus and statistics. Additional exam requirements/recommendations for international students: Required—TOEFL (minimum score 550 paper-based; 80 iBT), IELTS (minimum score 6.5). *Application deadline:* For fall admission, 2/1 priority date for domestic and international students. Application fee: $55 ($65 for international students). Electronic applications accepted. *Expenses:* Contact institution. *Financial support:* In 2017–18, 27 students received support, including 1 fellowship with full tuition reimbursement available (averaging $16,000 per year), 1 research assistantship with full tuition reimbursement available (averaging $16,000 per year), 32 teaching assistantships with full tuition reimbursements available (averaging $16,000 per year); scholarships/grants, traineeships, health care benefits, tuition waivers (partial), and unspecified assistantships also available. Financial award application deadline: 2/1. *Faculty research:* Globalization, inequality, sustainability, development, history. *Total annual research expenditures:* $380,178. *Unit head:* Dr. Norman Waitzman, Chair, 801-581-7481, E-mail: waitzman@economics.utah.edu. *Application contact:* Alex Francis, Academic Advisor, 801-581-7481, E-mail: grad-advising@economics.utah.edu.
Website: http://www.economics.utah.edu

University of Vermont, Graduate College, The Rubenstein School of Environment and Natural Resources, Program in Natural Resources, Burlington, VT 05405. Offers ecological economics (Certificate); natural resources (MS), including aquatic ecology and watershed science, environment thought and culture, environment, science and public affairs, forestry; natural resources (PhD); MELP/MS. MELP/MS offered in collaboration with Vermont Law School. *Students:* 77 (49 women). 116 applicants, 22% accepted, 21 enrolled. In 2017, 18 master's, 9 other advanced degrees awarded. *Degree requirements:* For master's, thesis or alternative; for doctorate, thesis/dissertation. *Entrance requirements:* For master's and doctorate, GRE General Test. Additional exam requirements/recommendations for international students: Required—TOEFL (minimum score 550 paper-based; 90 iBT), IELTS (minimum score 6.5). *Application deadline:* For fall admission, 2/1 for domestic and international students; for spring admission, 11/1 for domestic and international students; for summer admission, 4/1 for domestic and international students. Application fee: $65. Electronic applications accepted. *Expenses:* Tuition, state resident: full-time $11,628; part-time $646 per credit. Tuition, nonresident: full-time $29,340; part-time $1630 per credit. *Required fees:* $1994; $10 per credit. Tuition and fees vary according to course load and program. *Financial support:* In 2017–18, 31 research assistantships with full and partial tuition reimbursements (averaging $18,600 per year), 19 teaching assistantships with full and partial tuition reimbursements (averaging $14,000 per year) were awarded; fellowships also available. Financial award application deadline: 3/1. *Unit head:* Dr. Kimberly Wallin, Associate Dean for Research and Graduate Programs, 802-656-2517, E-mail: kimberly.wallin@uvm.edu. *Application contact:* Carolyn Goodwin-Kueffner, Graduate Program Student Services Specialist, 802-656-2911, E-mail: rsenr@uvm.edu.
Website: https://www.uvm.edu/rsenr/graduate_programs

University of Victoria, Faculty of Graduate Studies, Faculty of Social Sciences, Department of Economics, Victoria, BC V8W 2Y2, Canada. Offers MA, PhD. *Program availability:* Part-time. *Degree requirements:* For master's, comprehensive exam (for some programs), thesis optional; for doctorate, comprehensive exam, thesis/dissertation, candidacy exam. *Entrance requirements:* For master's and doctorate, GRE. Additional exam requirements/recommendations for international students: Required—TOEFL (minimum score 575 paper-based), IELTS (minimum score 7). Electronic applications accepted. *Faculty research:* Industrial organization, cost/benefit, applied economics, econometrics, airline economics, health economics.

University of Virginia, College and Graduate School of Arts and Sciences, Department of Economics, Charlottesville, VA 22903. Offers MA, PhD. *Faculty:* 30 full-time (5 women), 3 part-time/adjunct (1 woman). *Students:* 84 full-time (36 women), 2 part-time (1 woman); includes 3 minority (2 Asian, non-Hispanic/Latino; 1 Two or more races, non-Hispanic/Latino), 57 international. Average age 27. 507 applicants, 9% accepted, 20 enrolled. In 2017, 24 master's, 12 doctorates awarded. *Degree requirements:* For master's, comprehensive exam (for some programs), thesis (for some programs), thesis or comprehensive exam; for doctorate, comprehensive exam, thesis/dissertation. *Entrance requirements:* For master's and doctorate, GRE General Test. Additional exam requirements/recommendations for international students: Required—TOEFL (minimum score 600 paper-based; 90 iBT), IELTS (minimum score 7). *Application deadline:* For fall admission, 4/1 for domestic and international students. Applications are processed on a rolling basis. Application fee: $60. Electronic applications accepted. *Financial support:* Fellowships, research assistantships, teaching assistantships, and tuition waivers (full and partial) available. Financial award application deadline: 2/1; financial award applicants required to submit FAFSA. *Faculty research:* Macroeconomics, public economics, labor, industrial organization, economic history. *Unit head:* John Pepper, Chair, 434-924-3177, Fax: 434-982-2904, E-mail: econ@virginia.edu. *Application contact:* Sheetal Sekhri, Graduate Director, 434-924-3177, Fax: 434-982-2904, E-mail: ss5mj@virginia.edu.
Website: http://economics.virginia.edu/

University of Washington, Graduate School, College of Arts and Sciences, Department of Economics, Seattle, WA 98195. Offers PhD. Terminal master's awarded for partial completion of doctoral program. *Degree requirements:* For doctorate, comprehensive exam, thesis/dissertation. *Entrance requirements:* For doctorate, GRE General Test, minimum GPA of 3.0. Additional exam requirements/recommendations for international students: Required—TOEFL. Electronic applications accepted. *Faculty research:* Microeconomic theory; macroeconomic theory; econometrics; natural resource economics; international, development, and industrial organization.

University of Waterloo, Graduate Studies, Faculty of Arts, Department of Economics, Waterloo, ON N2L 3G1, Canada. Offers MA, PhD. *Program availability:* Part-time. *Entrance requirements:* For master's, honors degree, minimum B average. Additional exam requirements/recommendations for international students: Required—TOEFL, IELTS, PTE. Electronic applications accepted. *Faculty research:* Applied microeconomics, applied macroeconomics, public finance, international trade and finance, wage inflation and consumer problems.

The University of Western Ontario, Faculty of Graduate Studies, Social Sciences Division, Department of Economics, London, ON N6A 5B8, Canada. Offers MA, PhD. *Degree requirements:* For doctorate, thesis/dissertation. *Entrance requirements:* For master's, GRE, honours BA with B+ average. Additional exam requirements/recommendations for international students: Required—TOEFL.

University of Windsor, Faculty of Graduate Studies, Faculty of Science, Department of Economics, Windsor, ON N9B 3P4, Canada. Offers MA. *Program availability:* Part-time. *Degree requirements:* For master's, thesis or alternative. *Entrance requirements:* For master's, minimum B average. Additional exam requirements/recommendations for international students: Required—TOEFL (minimum score 560 paper-based). Electronic applications accepted. *Faculty research:* International trade, economic growth, microeconomic theory.

University of Wisconsin–Madison, Graduate School, College of Letters and Science, Department of Economics, Madison, WI 53706-1380. Offers PhD. *Degree requirements:* For doctorate, thesis/dissertation. *Entrance requirements:* For doctorate, GRE General Test, 3 semesters of course work in calculus, 1 semester of course work in algebra and mathematics/statistics. Electronic applications accepted.

University of Wisconsin–Milwaukee, Graduate School, College of Letters and Science, Department of Economics, Milwaukee, WI 53201-0413. Offers MA, PhD. *Students:* 51 full-time (13 women), 6 part-time (1 woman); includes 2 minority (both Asian, non-Hispanic/Latino), 37 international. Average age 30. 82 applicants, 40% accepted, 22 enrolled. In 2017, 8 master's, 7 doctorates awarded. *Degree requirements:* For master's, comprehensive exam; for doctorate, comprehensive exam, thesis/dissertation. *Entrance requirements:* For master's, GRE General Test; for doctorate, GRE General Test, GRE Subject Test, minimum GPA of 3.0. Additional exam requirements/recommendations for international students: Required—TOEFL (minimum score 550 paper-based; 79 iBT), IELTS (minimum score 6.5). *Application deadline:* For fall admission, 1/1 priority date for domestic students; for spring admission, 9/1 for domestic students. Application fee: $56 ($96 for international students). Electronic applications accepted. *Financial support:* Teaching assistantships, career-related internships or fieldwork, and unspecified assistantships available. Support available to part-time students. Financial award application deadline: 4/15; financial award applicants required to submit FAFSA. *Unit head:* Scott J. Adams, Department Chair, 414-229-4811, E-mail: sjadams@uwm.edu. *Application contact:* General Information Contact, 414-229-4982, Fax: 414-229-6967, E-mail: gradschool@uwm.edu. Website: https://uwm.edu/economics/

University of Wyoming, College of Business, Department of Economics and Finance, Program in Economics, Laramie, WY 82071. Offers MS, PhD. *Program availability:* Part-time. *Degree requirements:* For master's, thesis; for doctorate, comprehensive exam, thesis/dissertation. *Entrance requirements:* For master's, GRE General Test or GMAT, minimum GPA of 3.0; for doctorate, GRE General Test, minimum GPA of 3.0. Additional exam requirements/recommendations for international students: Required—TOEFL (minimum score 525 paper-based). *Faculty research:* Resource and environmental economics, industrial organization, regulation.

University of Wyoming, College of Business, Department of Economics and Finance, Program in Economics and Finance, Laramie, WY 82071. Offers MS. *Degree requirements:* For master's, thesis. *Entrance requirements:* For master's, GRE, minimum GPA of 3.0. Additional exam requirements/recommendations for international students: Required—TOEFL (minimum score 540 paper-based; 76 iBT). *Faculty research:* Financial economics.

Utah State University, School of Graduate Studies, Jon M. Huntsman School of Business, Department of Economics and Finance, Logan, UT 84322. Offers economics (MS); financial economics (MS). *Degree requirements:* For master's, thesis (for some programs). *Entrance requirements:* For master's, GRE General Test, GMAT, minimum GPA of 3.0. Additional exam requirements/recommendations for international students: Required—TOEFL. Electronic applications accepted. *Faculty research:* Resource economics, economic theory, international trade, industrial organization, development

Vanderbilt University, Department of Economics, Nashville, TN 37240-1001. Offers economic development (MA); economics (PhD). *Faculty:* 31 full-time (4 women). *Students:* 94 full-time (36 women), 2 part-time (1 woman); includes 10 minority (2 Black or African American, non-Hispanic/Latino; 2 Asian, non-Hispanic/Latino; 1 Hispanic/Latino; 5 Two or more races, non-Hispanic/Latino), 57 international. Average age 27. 621 applicants, 28% accepted, 37 enrolled. In 2017, 44 master's, 7 doctorates awarded. Terminal master's awarded for partial completion of doctoral program. *Degree requirements:* For master's, thesis or alternative; for doctorate, thesis/dissertation, final and qualifying exams. *Entrance requirements:* For master's and doctorate, GRE General Test, GRE Subject Test (recommended). Additional exam requirements/recommendations for international students: Required—TOEFL (minimum score 570 paper-based; 88 iBT). *Application deadline:* For fall admission, 1/15 for domestic and international students; for spring admission, 11/1 for domestic students. Applications are processed on a rolling basis. Electronic applications accepted. *Financial support:* Fellowships, teaching assistantships, career-related internships or fieldwork, Federal Work-Study, institutionally sponsored loans, scholarships/grants, and health care benefits available. Financial award application deadline: 1/15; financial award applicants required to submit CSS PROFILE or FAFSA. *Faculty research:* Economic theory, applied fields, developmental economics, environmental economics, health economics and policy. *Unit head:* Dr. Eric Bond, Chair, 615-322-2871, Fax: 615-343-8495, E-mail: k.saggi@vanderbilt.edu. *Application contact:* Jennifer Reinganum, Director of Graduate Studies, 615-322-2871, Fax: 615-343-8495, E-mail: jennifer.f.reinganum@vanderbilt.edu. Website: http://www.vanderbilt.edu/econ/

Vanderbilt University, Vanderbilt Law School, Nashville, TN 37203. Offers law (LL M, JD); law and economics (PhD); JD/M Div; JD/MA; JD/MBA; JD/MD; JD/MPP; JD/MTS; JD/PhD; LL M/MA. *Accreditation:* ABA. *Degree requirements:* For doctorate, comprehensive exam (for some programs), thesis/dissertation (for some programs), 72 hours of coursework and research (for PhD). *Entrance requirements:* For master's, foreign law degree; for doctorate, GRE (for PhD), LSAT, advanced undergraduate

economics (for PhD). Additional exam requirements/recommendations for international students: Required—TOEFL. Electronic applications accepted. *Expenses:* Contact institution.

Virginia Commonwealth University, Graduate School, School of Business, Program in Economics, Richmond, VA 23284-9005. Offers MA. *Degree requirements:* For master's, thesis optional. *Entrance requirements:* For master's, GRE General Test (preferred) or GMAT. Additional exam requirements/recommendations for international students: Required—TOEFL (minimum score 600 paper-based; 100 iBT). Electronic applications accepted.

Virginia Polytechnic Institute and State University, Graduate School, College of Science, Blacksburg, VA 24061. Offers biological sciences (MS, PhD); biomedical technology development and management (MS); chemistry (MS, PhD); data analysis and applied statistics (MA); economics (PhD); geosciences (MS, PhD); mathematics (MS, PhD); physics (MS, PhD); psychology (MS, PhD); statistics (MS, PhD). *Faculty:* 321 full-time (103 women). *Students:* 557 full-time (205 women), 39 part-time (18 women); includes 68 minority (13 Black or African American, non-Hispanic/Latino; 1 American Indian or Alaska Native, non-Hispanic/Latino; 14 Asian, non-Hispanic/Latino; 32 Hispanic/Latino; 8 Two or more races, non-Hispanic/Latino), 238 international. Average age 27. 1,060 applicants, 15% accepted, 121 enrolled. In 2017, 75 master's, 89 doctorates awarded. *Degree requirements:* For master's, comprehensive exam (for some programs), thesis (for some programs); for doctorate, comprehensive exam (for some programs), thesis/dissertation (for some programs). *Entrance requirements:* For master's and doctorate, GRE/GMAT. Additional exam requirements/recommendations for international students: Required—TOEFL (minimum score 80 iBT). *Application deadline:* For fall admission, 8/1 for domestic students, 4/1 for international students; for spring admission, 1/1 for domestic students, 9/1 for international students. Applications are processed on a rolling basis. Application fee: $75. Electronic applications accepted. *Expenses:* Tuition, state resident: full-time $15,072; part-time $718.50 per credit hour. Tuition, nonresident: full-time $28,810; part-time $1448.25 per credit hour. *Required fees:* $2741; $502 per semester. Tuition and fees vary according to course load, campus/location and program. *Financial support:* In 2017–18, 2 fellowships with full tuition reimbursements (averaging $12,267 per year), 140 research assistantships with full tuition reimbursements (averaging $23,004 per year), 351 teaching assistantships with full tuition reimbursements (averaging $20,157 per year) were awarded. Financial award application deadline: 3/1; financial award applicants required to submit FAFSA. *Total annual research expenditures:* $24.3 million. *Unit head:* Dr. Sally C. Morton, Dean, 540-231-5422, Fax: 540-231-3380, E-mail: scmorton@vt.edu. *Application contact:* Allison Craft, Executive Assistant, 540-231-6394, Fax: 540-231-3380, E-mail: crafta@vt.edu. Website: http://www.science.vt.edu/

Virginia State University, College of Graduate Studies, College of Humanities and Social Sciences, Department of Political Science, Public Administration and Economics, Petersburg, VA 23806-0001. Offers economics (MA). *Degree requirements:* For master's, thesis optional. *Entrance requirements:* For master's, GRE General Test.

Washington State University, College of Agricultural, Human, and Natural Resource Sciences, School of Economic Sciences, Pullman, WA 99164-6210. Offers agricultural economics (PhD); economics (PhD). Programs offered at the Pullman campus. Terminal master's awarded for partial completion of doctoral program. *Degree requirements:* For master's, comprehensive exam (for some programs), thesis (for some programs), oral exam; for doctorate, comprehensive exam, thesis/dissertation, oral exam, written exam, qualifying exams. *Entrance requirements:* For master's and doctorate, GRE, minimum GPA of 3.0, 3 letters of recommendation. Additional exam requirements/recommendations for international students: Required—TOEFL (minimum score 550 paper-based). Electronic applications accepted. *Faculty research:* Agricultural economics, econometrics, natural resource and environmental economics, industrial organization, health economics.

Washington University in St. Louis, The Graduate School, Department of Economics, St. Louis, MO 63130-4899. Offers PhD. Terminal master's awarded for partial completion of doctoral program. *Degree requirements:* For doctorate, one foreign language, thesis/dissertation. *Entrance requirements:* For doctorate, GRE General Test. Additional exam requirements/recommendations for international students: Required—TOEFL. Electronic applications accepted. *Faculty research:* Economic theory; industrial organization; political economy; public economics; macroeconomics; public finance, development economics.

Wayne State University, College of Liberal Arts and Sciences, Department of Economics, Detroit, MI 48202. Offers applied macroeconomics (MA, PhD); health economics (MA, PhD); industrial organization (MA, PhD); international economics (MA, PhD); labor and human resources (MA, PhD); JD/MA. *Faculty:* 11. *Students:* 34 full-time (8 women), 9 part-time (3 women); includes 5 minority (4 Black or African American, non-Hispanic/Latino; 1 Asian, non-Hispanic/Latino), 17 international. Average age 30. 90 applicants, 30% accepted, 13 enrolled. In 2017, 10 master's, 6 doctorates awarded. *Degree requirements:* For master's, comprehensive exam; for doctorate, comprehensive exam, thesis/dissertation, oral examination on research, completion of course work in quantitative methods, final lecture. *Entrance requirements:* For master's, minimum upper-division GPA of 3.0; prior coursework in intermediate microeconomic and macroeconomic theory, statistics, and elementary calculus; for doctorate, GRE, minimum upper-division GPA of 3.0, prior coursework in intermediate microeconomic and macroeconomic theory, statistics, two courses in calculus, three letters of recommendation from officials or teaching staff at institution(s) most recently attended, statement of purpose. Additional exam requirements/recommendations for international students: Required—TOEFL (minimum score 550 paper-based; 79 iBT), TWE (minimum score 5.5), Michigan English Language Assessment Battery (minimum score 85); Recommended—IELTS (minimum score 6.5). *Application deadline:* For fall admission, 5/1 for domestic and international students; for winter admission, 10/1 priority date for domestic students, 9/1 priority date for international students; for spring admission, 1/1 priority date for domestic and international students. Applications are processed on a rolling basis. Application fee: $50. Electronic applications accepted. *Expenses:* Tuition, state resident: full-time $10,224; part-time $638.98 per credit hour. Tuition, nonresident: full-time $22,145; part-time $1384.04 per credit hour. Tuition and fees vary according to course load and program. *Financial support:* In 2017–18, 25 students received support, including 2 fellowships with tuition reimbursements available (averaging $16,000 per year), 17 teaching assistantships with tuition reimbursements available (averaging $18,534 per year); research assistantships with tuition reimbursements available, scholarships/grants, health care benefits, and unspecified assistantships also available. Support available to part-time students. Financial award applicants required to submit FAFSA. *Faculty research:* Health economics, international economics, macroeconomics, urban and labor economics, econometrics. *Unit head:* Dr. Kevin Cotter, Interim Chair, 313-577-3345, E-mail: kevin.cotter@wayne.edu. *Application contact:* Dr. Li Way Lee, Professor and Director of Graduate Studies, 313-577-3345, E-mail: aa1313@wayne.edu. Website: http://clas.wayne.edu/economics/

Western Illinois University, School of Graduate Studies, College of Business and Technology, Department of Economics and Decision Sciences, Program in Economics,

Macomb, IL 61455-1390. Offers MA. *Students:* 24 full-time (10 women), 3 part-time (1 woman); includes 6 minority (3 Black or African American, non-Hispanic/Latino; 2 Asian, non-Hispanic/Latino; 1 Two or more races, non-Hispanic/Latino), 14 international. Average age 29. 25 applicants, 72% accepted, 6 enrolled. In 2017, 8 master's awarded. *Application deadline:* Applications are processed on a rolling basis. Application fee: $30. Electronic applications accepted. *Financial support:* Unspecified assistantships available. *Unit head:* Dr. Tej Kaul, Chairperson, 309-298-1153. *Application contact:* Dr. Nancy Parsons, Assistant Director of Graduate Studies, 309-298-1806, Fax: 309-298-2345, E-mail: grad-office@wiu.edu.
Website: http://www.wiu.edu/cbt/eds/graduate-economics.php

Western Michigan University, Graduate College, College of Arts and Sciences, Department of Economics, Kalamazoo, MI 49008. Offers applied economics (MA, PhD). *Degree requirements:* For master's, thesis; for doctorate, thesis/dissertation.

West Texas A&M University, College of Business, Department of Accounting, Economics and Finance, Canyon, TX 79015. Offers accounting (MPA); finance and economics (MS). *Program availability:* Part-time, evening/weekend, online learning. *Degree requirements:* For master's, comprehensive exam, thesis optional. *Entrance requirements:* For master's, GMAT. Additional exam requirements/recommendations for international students: Required—TOEFL (minimum score 550 paper-based). Electronic applications accepted. *Faculty research:* Texas economy, decision report service learning and entrepreneurship, small business, trade effects of financial flow.

West Virginia University, College of Business and Economics, Morgantown, WV 26506. Offers accountancy (M Acc); accounting (PhD); business administration (MBA); business cyber security management (MS); business data analytics (MS); economics (MA, PhD); finance (MS, PhD); forensic and fraud examination (MS); industrial relations (MS); management (PhD); marketing (PhD). *Program availability:* Part-time, online learning. *Students:* 343 full-time (141 women), 43 part-time (12 women); includes 59 minority (22 Black or African American, non-Hispanic/Latino; 11 Asian, non-Hispanic/Latino; 12 Hispanic/Latino; 14 Two or more races, non-Hispanic/Latino), 54 international. Terminal master's awarded for partial completion of doctoral program. *Degree requirements:* For master's, thesis optional; for doctorate, comprehensive exam, thesis/dissertation. *Entrance requirements:* For doctorate, GRE General Test, minimum GPA of 3.0. Additional exam requirements/recommendations for international students: Required—TOEFL (minimum score 550 paper-based; 92 iBT). *Application deadline:* For fall admission, 10/15 priority date for domestic and international students; for spring admission, 3/1 priority date for domestic and international students. Applications are processed on a rolling basis. Application fee: $60. Electronic applications accepted. *Expenses:* Contact institution. *Financial support:* Fellowships, research assistantships, teaching assistantships, career-related internships or fieldwork, Federal Work-Study, institutionally sponsored loans, scholarships/grants, health care benefits, tuition waivers (full and partial), unspecified assistantships, and administrative assistantships available. Financial award application deadline: 2/1; financial award applicants required to submit FAFSA. *Faculty research:* Regional labor market studies, economic development, market research, economic forecasting, energy analysis. *Unit head:* Dr. Javier Reyes, Dean, 304-293-7800, Fax: 304-293-4056, E-mail: javier.reyes@mail.wvu.edu. *Application contact:* Dr. Mark Gavin, Associate Dean for Graduate Programs, 304-293-7952, Fax: 304-293-7188, E-mail: mark.gavin@mail.wvu.edu.
Website: http://www.be.wvu.edu

Wichita State University, Graduate School, W. Frank Barton School of Business, Department of Economics, Wichita, KS 67260. Offers economic analysis (MA); financial economics (MA); international economics (MA). *Program availability:* Part-time, evening/weekend. *Unit head:* Dr. Jen-Chi Cheng, Chair, 316-978-3220, Fax: 316-978-3845, E-mail: jenchi.cheng@wichita.edu. *Application contact:* Jordan Oleson, Admissions Coordinator, 316-978-3095, Fax: 316-978-3253, E-mail: jordan.oleson@wichita.edu.
Website: http://www.wichita.edu/econ

Wilfrid Laurier University, Faculty of Graduate and Postdoctoral Studies, School of Business and Economics, Department of Business, Waterloo, ON N2L 3C5, Canada. Offers accounting (PhD); finance (M Fin); financial economics (PhD); marketing (PhD); operations and supply chain management (PhD); organizational behavior and human resource management (M Sc); organizational behaviour and human resource management (PhD); supply chain management (M Sc); technology management (EMTM). *Accreditation:* AACSB. *Program availability:* Part-time, evening/weekend. *Degree requirements:* For master's, thesis optional; for doctorate, comprehensive exam, thesis/dissertation. *Entrance requirements:* For master's, GMAT, 4-year honors degree with minimum B+ average; for doctorate, GMAT, master's degree, minimum B+ average. Additional exam requirements/recommendations for international students: Required—TOEFL (minimum score 89 iBT). Electronic applications accepted. *Faculty research:* Financial economics, management and organizational behavior, operations and supply chain management.

Wilfrid Laurier University, Faculty of Graduate and Postdoctoral Studies, School of Business and Economics, Department of Economics, Waterloo, ON N2L 3C5, Canada. Offers MA. *Entrance requirements:* For master's, honors BA or the equivalent in economics, minimum B average in undergraduate course work. Additional exam requirements/recommendations for international students: Required—TOEFL (minimum score 89 iBT). Electronic applications accepted. *Faculty research:* Economic forecasting, economic policy analysis, industry and market studies, financial economics, strategic planning, public policy and business.

Wilfrid Laurier University, Faculty of Graduate and Postdoctoral Studies, School of International Policy and Governance, Global Governance Program, Waterloo, ON N2L 3C5, Canada. Offers conflict and security (PhD); global environment (PhD); global justice and human rights (PhD); global political economy (PhD); global social governance (PhD); multilateral institutions and diplomacy (PhD). Offered jointly with University of Waterloo. *Degree requirements:* For doctorate, thesis/dissertation. *Entrance requirements:* For doctorate, MA in political science, history, economics, international development studies, international peace studies, globalization studies, environmental studies or related field with minimum A-. Additional exam requirements/recommendations for international students: Required—TOEFL (minimum score 89 iBT). Electronic applications accepted. *Faculty research:* Global political economy, global environment, conflict and security, global justice and human rights, multilateral institutions and diplomacy.

Wright State University, Graduate School, Raj Soin College of Business, Department of Economics, Dayton, OH 45435. Offers social and applied economics (MS). *Entrance requirements:* For master's, GRE General Test. Additional exam requirements/recommendations for international students: Required—TOEFL.

Yale University, Graduate School of Arts and Sciences, Department of Economics, New Haven, CT 06520. Offers economics (PhD); international and development economics (MA). *Degree requirements:* For doctorate, thesis/dissertation. *Entrance requirements:* For master's, GRE General Test; for doctorate, GRE General Test, GRE Subject Test. *Faculty research:* Economic history of Western Europe, environmental economics, economic growth and development.

Yeshiva University, The Katz School, Program in Quantitative Economics, New York, NY 10033-3201. Offers MS.

York University, Faculty of Graduate Studies, Faculty of Liberal Arts and Professional Studies, Program in Economics, Toronto, ON M3J 1P3, Canada. Offers MA, PhD. *Program availability:* Part-time. *Degree requirements:* For doctorate, comprehensive exam, thesis/dissertation. Electronic applications accepted.

Youngstown State University, Graduate School, College of Liberal Arts and Social Sciences, Department of Economics, Youngstown, OH 44555-0001. Offers economics (MA); financial economics (MA). *Program availability:* Part-time. *Degree requirements:* For master's, comprehensive exam, thesis optional. *Entrance requirements:* For master's, minimum GPA of 2.7, 21 hours in economics. Additional exam requirements/recommendations for international students: Required—TOEFL. *Faculty research:* Forecasting, applied econometrics, labor economics, applied macroeconomics, industrial organization.

International Economics

American University, College of Arts and Sciences, Department of Economics, Washington, DC 20016-8029. Offers applied microeconomics (Certificate); economics (MA, PhD); gender analysis in economics (Certificate); international economic relations (Certificate); international economics (MA). *Program availability:* Part-time, evening/weekend, 100% online. *Faculty:* 27 full-time (7 women), 5 part-time/adjunct (2 women). *Students:* 107 full-time (52 women), 59 part-time (21 women); includes 28 minority (10 Black or African American, non-Hispanic/Latino; 1 American Indian or Alaska Native, non-Hispanic/Latino; 8 Asian, non-Hispanic/Latino; 7 Hispanic/Latino; 2 Two or more races, non-Hispanic/Latino), 55 international. Average age 32. 191 applicants, 85% accepted, 38 enrolled. In 2017, 37 master's, 9 doctorates, 1 other advanced degree awarded. Terminal master's awarded for partial completion of doctoral program. *Degree requirements:* For master's, comprehensive exam, thesis or alternative; for doctorate, comprehensive exam, thesis/dissertation. *Entrance requirements:* For master's and doctorate, GRE, statement of purpose, transcripts, 2 letters of recommendation, resume; for Certificate, bachelor's degree, statement of purpose, transcripts, resume. Additional exam requirements/recommendations for international students: Required—TOEFL (minimum score 600 paper-based; 100 iBT). *Application deadline:* For fall admission, 3/1 for domestic students; for spring admission, 11/1 for domestic students. Applications are processed on a rolling basis. Application fee: $55. Electronic applications accepted. *Expenses:* Contact institution. *Financial support:* Research assistantships, teaching assistantships, institutionally sponsored loans, and unspecified assistantships available. Financial award application deadline: 2/1; financial award applicants required to submit FAFSA. *Faculty research:* Political economy, development, labor, gender. *Unit head:* Dr. Mieke Meurs, Department Chair, 202-885-3776, E-mail: mmeurs@american.edu. *Application contact:* Jonathan Harper, Assistant Director, Graduate Recruitment, 202-855-3622, E-mail: jharper@american.edu.
Website: http://www.american.edu/cas/economics/

American University, School of International Service, Washington, DC 20016-8071. Offers comparative and regional studies (Certificate); cross-cultural communication (Certificate); development management (MS); ethics, peace, and global affairs (MA); European studies (Certificate); global environmental policy (MA, Certificate); global information technology (Certificate); global media (MA); international affairs (MA), including comparative and regional studies, global governance, politics, and security, international economic relations, natural resources and sustainable development, U.S. foreign policy and national security; international arts management (Certificate); international communication (MA, Certificate); international development (MA); international economic policy (Certificate); international economic relations (Certificate); international economics (MA); international peace and conflict resolution (MA, Certificate); international politics (Certificate); international relations (MA, PhD); international service (MIS); peacebuilding (Certificate); social enterprise (MA); the Americas (Certificate); United States foreign policy (Certificate); JD/MA. *Program availability:* Part-time, evening/weekend, 100% online. *Faculty:* 112 full-time (50 women), 46 part-time/adjunct (19 women). *Students:* 495 full-time (333 women), 518 part-time (276 women); includes 360 minority (95 Black or African American, non-Hispanic/Latino; 2 American Indian or Alaska Native, non-Hispanic/Latino; 60 Asian, non-Hispanic/Latino; 164 Hispanic/Latino; 39 Two or more races, non-Hispanic/Latino), 98 international. Average age 30. 1,559 applicants, 81% accepted, 356 enrolled. In 2017, 427 master's, 9 doctorates, 5 other advanced degrees awarded. Terminal master's awarded for partial completion of doctoral program. *Degree requirements:* For master's, one foreign language, comprehensive exam, thesis or alternative; for doctorate, one foreign language, comprehensive exam, thesis/dissertation. *Entrance requirements:* For master's, GRE; GMAT or GRE (for MA in social enterprise), transcripts, resume, 2 letters of recommendation, statement of purpose; for doctorate, GRE, transcripts, resume, 3 letters of recommendation, statement of purpose. Additional exam requirements/recommendations for international students: Required—TOEFL (minimum score 600 paper-based; 100 iBT). *Application deadline:* For fall admission, 1/15 for domestic students, 1/1 for international students; for spring admission, 10/1 for domestic students, 9/15 for international students. Application fee: $55. Electronic applications accepted. *Expenses:* Contact institution. *Financial support:* Research assistantships, teaching assistantships, institutionally sponsored loans, scholarships/grants, and unspecified assistantships available. Financial award application deadline: 1/15; financial award applicants required to submit FAFSA. *Application contact:* 202-885-1646, Fax: 202-885-1109, E-mail: sisgrad@american.edu.
Website: http://www.american.edu/sis/

Baruch College of the City University of New York, Austin W. Marxe School of Public and International Affairs, Program in International Affairs, New York, NY 10010-5585. Offers international nongovernmental organizations (MIA); trade policy and global economic governance (MIA); Western Hemisphere affairs (MIA). *Program availability:* Part-time.

See Display on page 910 and Close-Up on page 955.

Bryant University, Graduate School of Business, Smithfield, RI 02917. Offers accounting (MPAC); business administration (MBA), including business analytics, general management, global finance, global supply chain management, international business; taxation (MST). *Program availability:* Part-time, 100% online. *Faculty:* 30 full-time (5 women), 7 part-time/adjunct (2 women). *Students:* 84 full-time (31 women), 91 part-time (35 women); includes 24 minority (4 Black or African American, non-Hispanic/Latino; 1 American Indian or Alaska Native, non-Hispanic/Latino; 6 Asian, non-Hispanic/Latino; 8 Hispanic/Latino; 5 Two or more races, non-Hispanic/Latino), 6 international. Average age 26. 215 applicants, 66% accepted, 96 enrolled. In 2017, 118 master's awarded. *Degree requirements:* For master's, comprehensive exam (for some programs). *Entrance requirements:* For master's, GMAT, resume, recommendation, college transcripts. Additional exam requirements/recommendations for international students: Required—TOEFL (minimum score 580 paper-based; 95 iBT). *Application deadline:* For fall admission, 7/15 for domestic and international students; for spring admission, 11/15 for domestic and international students; for summer admission, 4/15 for domestic and international students. Applications are processed on a rolling basis. Application fee: $80. Electronic applications accepted. *Expenses:* $45,102 total, $1,118 per credit hour, $1,500 study abroad fee (for full-time MBA); $40,248 total, $1,118 per credit hour (for part-time MBA); $30,280 total, $1,176 per credit hour (for MP Ac and MST); $13,146, $1,118 per credit hour (for CGS). *Financial support:* In 2017–18, 95 fellowships with full and partial tuition reimbursements (averaging $9,825 per year), 9 research assistantships with full and partial tuition reimbursements (averaging $7,100 per year) were awarded; scholarships/grants and unspecified assistantships also available. Support available to part-time students. Financial award application deadline: 2/15; financial award applicants required to submit FAFSA. *Faculty research:* International business, public sector auditing, taxation of partnerships, information systems security, financial markets microstructure. *Unit head:* Bjorn Carlsson, Graduate Program Director, 401-232-6707, E-mail: bcarlsson@bryant.edu. *Application contact:* Terri Rogers, Admissions Assistant, 401-232-6230, Fax: 401-232-6494, E-mail: graduateprograms@bryant.edu.
Website: http://gradschool.bryant.edu/business/

Claremont Graduate University, Graduate Programs, School of Social Science, Policy and Evaluation, Department of Economics, Claremont, CA 91711-6160. Offers behavioral economics and neuroeconomics (PhD); business and financial economics (MA, PhD); economic development (Certificate); international economic and development policy (PhD); international economics policy and development (MA); international money and finance (PhD); political economy and public economics (PhD); political economy and public policy (MA); MBA/PhD. *Program availability:* Part-time. *Entrance requirements:* For master's and doctorate, GRE General Test or GMAT. Additional exam requirements/recommendations for international students: Required—TOEFL (minimum score 75 iBT). Electronic applications accepted. *Faculty research:* International and financial economics, law and economics, regulation, public choice economics.

Cleveland State University, College of Graduate Studies, College of Liberal Arts and Social Sciences, Department of Political Science, Cleveland, OH 44115. Offers global interactions (MA), including global business interactions, global political interactions. *Faculty:* 3 full-time (1 woman). *Students:* 15 full-time (10 women), 6 part-time (1 woman); includes 8 minority (5 Black or African American, non-Hispanic/Latino; 3 Two or more races, non-Hispanic/Latino), 4 international. Average age 26. 33 applicants, 100% accepted, 5 enrolled. In 2017, 11 master's awarded. *Entrance requirements:* For master's, minimum undergraduate GPA of 3.0 or GRE (50th percentile or above); two letters of recommendation; undergraduate degree in economics, political science, international relations, or a related discipline; completion of undergraduate macro and micro economics course. Additional exam requirements/recommendations for international students: Required—TOEFL (minimum score 550 paper-based; 78 iBT). *Application deadline:* Applications are processed on a rolling basis. Application fee: $40. Electronic applications accepted. *Expenses:* Contact institution. *Financial support:* Research assistantships, tuition waivers (full), and unspecified assistantships available. Financial award applicants required to submit FAFSA. *Faculty research:* International political economy, globalization, new regionalism, European integration, adaptation to climate change. *Unit head:* Dr. Rodger M. Govea, Associate Professor/Chairperson, 216-687-4554, E-mail: r.govea@csuohio.edu. *Application contact:* Janice McCowan, Public Inquiries Assistant, 216-523-7473, Fax: 216-687-9210, E-mail: j.c.mccowan@csuohio.edu.
Website: http://www.csuohio.edu/class/politicalscience/

Fordham University, Gabelli School of Business, New York, NY 10023. Offers accounting (MBA, MS); applied statistics and decision-making (MS); business economics (DPS); capital markets (DPS); communications and media management (MBA); electronic business (MBA); entrepreneurship (MBA); finance (MBA, PhD); global finance (MS); global sustainability (MBA); health administration (MS); healthcare management (MBA); information systems (MBA, MS); investor relations (MS); management (EMBA, MBA, MS, PhD); marketing (MBA); marketing intelligence (MS); media management (MS); nonprofit leadership (MS); quantitative finance (MS); strategy and decision-making (DPS); taxation (MS); JD/MBA; MS/MBA. *Accreditation:* AACSB. *Program availability:* Part-time, evening/weekend. *Faculty:* 130 full-time (46 women), 42 part-time/adjunct (5 women). *Students:* 1,051 full-time (570 women), 563 part-time (313 women); includes 190 minority (48 Black or African American, non-Hispanic/Latino; 72 Asian, non-Hispanic/Latino; 69 Hispanic/Latino; 1 Native Hawaiian or other Pacific Islander, non-Hispanic/Latino), 1,106 international. Average age 27. 4,577 applicants, 58% accepted, 794 enrolled. In 2017, 937 master's awarded. Terminal master's awarded for partial completion of doctoral program. *Degree requirements:* For master's, internships (for some degrees); for doctorate, comprehensive exam (for some programs), thesis/dissertation. *Entrance requirements:* For master's, GMAT/GRE, 2 letters of recommendation, resume, 2 essays, transcripts, interview. Additional exam requirements/recommendations for international students: Required—TOEFL (minimum score 100 iBT), IELTS (minimum score 7). *Application deadline:* For fall admission, 11/15 priority date for domestic and international students; for winter admission, 1/19 priority date for domestic students; 1/1 priority date for international students; for spring admission, 4/15 for domestic students, 3/1 for international students; for summer admission, 6/1 for domestic students. Application fee: $130. Electronic applications accepted. *Expenses:* $1,495 per credit. *Financial support:* Career-related internships or fieldwork, institutionally sponsored loans, scholarships/grants, and unspecified assistantships available. Support available to part-time students. Financial award application deadline: 6/30; financial award applicants required to submit FAFSA. *Unit head:* Dr. Donna Rapaccioli, Dean, 212-636-6165, Fax: 212-307-1779, E-mail: rapaccioli@fordham.edu. *Application contact:* Lawrence Murray, Senior Assistant Dean of Graduate Admissions and Advising, 212-636-6200, Fax: 212-636-7076, E-mail: admissionsgb@fordham.edu.
Website: http://www.fordham.edu/gabelli

Fordham University, Graduate School of Arts and Sciences, Program in International Political Economy and Development, New York, NY 10458. Offers MA, Certificate. *Program availability:* Part-time, evening/weekend. *Students:* 38 full-time (18 women), 8 part-time (2 women); includes 3 minority (1 Asian, non-Hispanic/Latino; 2 Hispanic/Latino), 15 international. Average age 27. 89 applicants, 60% accepted, 24 enrolled. In

2017, 24 master's, 1 other advanced degree awarded. *Degree requirements:* For master's, comprehensive exam. *Entrance requirements:* For master's, GRE General Test. Additional exam requirements/recommendations for international students: Required—TOEFL (minimum score 600 paper-based). *Application deadline:* For fall admission, 1/4 priority date for domestic students; for spring admission, 11/1 for domestic students. Application fee: $70. Electronic applications accepted. *Financial support:* In 2017–18, 35 students received support, including 4 fellowships with tuition reimbursements available (averaging $17,014 per year); research assistantships with tuition reimbursements available, career-related internships or fieldwork, institutionally sponsored loans, tuition waivers (full and partial), and unspecified assistantships also available. Financial award application deadline: 1/4; financial award applicants required to submit FAFSA. *Faculty research:* International economics, comparative international politics, international banking and finance, international development, emerging markets and country risk analysis. *Unit head:* Dr. Henry Schwalbenberg, Chair, 718-817-3866, Fax: 718-817-3518. *Application contact:* Bernadette Valentino-Morrison, Director of Graduate Admissions, 718-817-4419, Fax: 718-817-3566, E-mail: valentinomor@fordham.edu.

Johns Hopkins University, School of Advanced International Studies, Washington, DC 20036. Offers global risk (MA); international development (MA, Certificate), including international economics (MA); international economics (Certificate); international economics and finance (MA); international public policy (MIPP); international relations (PhD); international studies (Certificate); Japan studies (MA), including international economics; Korea studies (MA), including international economics; South Asia studies (MA), including international economics; Southeast Asia studies (MA), including international economics; JD/MA; MBA/MA; MHS/MA. Terminal master's awarded for partial completion of doctoral program. *Degree requirements:* For master's, 4-6 international economics courses, 5-6 functional or regional concentration courses, 2 core examinations, proficiency in language other than native language, capstone project; for doctorate, 2 foreign languages, thesis/dissertation, 3 comprehensive exams, economics, quantitative and qualitative course, dissertation prospectus and defense. *Entrance requirements:* For master's, GMAT or GRE General Test, previous course work in economics, foreign language, undergraduate degree; for doctorate, GRE General Test, master's degree. Additional exam requirements/recommendations for international students: Required—TOEFL (minimum score 600 paper-based; 100 iBT) or IELTS (minimum score 7). Electronic applications accepted. *Expenses:* Contact institution. *Faculty research:* International economics; international relations/regional studies; international development; energy, resources, and environment; international security/strategic studies.

The New School, The New School for Social Research, Department of Economics, New York, NY 10003. Offers economics (MA, MS, PhD); global political economy and finance (MA). *Program availability:* Part-time. *Faculty:* 9 full-time (3 women), 2 part-time/adjunct (both women). *Students:* 80 full-time (22 women), 20 part-time (8 women); includes 17 minority (4 Black or African American, non-Hispanic/Latino; 6 Asian, non-Hispanic/Latino; 7 Hispanic/Latino), 53 international. Average age 32. 146 applicants, 66% accepted, 21 enrolled. In 2017, 23 master's, 8 doctorates awarded. Terminal master's awarded for partial completion of doctoral program. *Degree requirements:* For master's, comprehensive exam (for some programs), mentored research/internship; for doctorate, one foreign language, comprehensive exam, thesis/dissertation. *Entrance requirements:* For master's, GRE, letters of recommendation, writing sample, essays, transcript; for doctorate, letters of recommendation, writing sample, essays, transcript. Additional exam requirements/recommendations for international students: Required—TOEFL (minimum score 100 iBT), IELTS (minimum score 7), PTE (minimum score 68). *Application deadline:* For fall admission, 1/5 priority date for domestic and international students; for spring admission, 10/15 priority date for domestic and international students. Applications are processed on a rolling basis. Application fee: $50. Electronic applications accepted. *Expenses:* $2,180 per credit. *Financial support:* In 2017–18, 72 students received support, including 14 fellowships (averaging $16,694 per year), 7 research assistantships (averaging $13,681 per year), 23 teaching assistantships with full and partial tuition reimbursements available (averaging $7,340 per year); career-related internships or fieldwork, Federal Work-Study, scholarships/grants, tuition waivers (full and partial), and unspecified assistantships also available. Support available to part-time students. Financial award application deadline: 2/1; financial award applicants required to submit FAFSA. *Unit head:* Dr. William Milberg, Dean, The New School for Social Research, 212-229-5777, E-mail: milbergw@newschool.edu. *Application contact:* Dana Messinger, Director of Graduate Admission, 212-229-5150 Ext. 2300, E-mail: socialresearchadmit@newschool.edu.
Website: https://www.newschool.edu/nssr/economics/

Pace University, Lubin School of Business, Advanced Professional Certificate Program, New York, NY 10038. Offers business economics (APC); e-business (APC); financial management (APC); international business (APC); international economics (APC); investment management (APC); marketing (APC); public accounting (APC). *Program availability:* Part-time, evening/weekend. *Students:* 1 applicant, 100% accepted. *Entrance requirements:* For degree, MBA or MS in business discipline, relevant professional experience. Additional exam requirements/recommendations for international students: Required—TOEFL (minimum score 90 iBT), IELTS (minimum score 7) or PTE (minimum score 61). *Application deadline:* For fall admission, 8/1 priority date for domestic students, 6/1 for international students; for spring admission, 12/1 for domestic students, 10/1 for international students. Applications are processed on a rolling basis. Application fee: $70. Electronic applications accepted. *Unit head:* Dr. Jack Yurkiewicz, Director, 212-618-6567, E-mail: jyurkiewicz@pace.edu. *Application contact:* Susan Ford-Goldschein, Director of Graduate Admissions, 212-346-1531, Fax: 212-346-1585, E-mail: graduateadmission@pace.edu.
Website: http://www.pace.edu/lubin/agc

University of California, San Diego, Graduate Division, School of Global Policy and Strategy, Master of International Affairs Program, La Jolla, CA 92093. Offers international development and nonprofit management (MIA); international economics (MIA); international environmental policy (MIA); international management (MIA); international politics (MIA). Students will choose one of the following country/regional specializations: China, Japan, Korea, Latin America, or Southeast Asia. *Degree requirements:* For master's, one foreign language. *Entrance requirements:* For master's, GMAT or GRE General Test. Additional exam requirements/recommendations for international students: Required—TOEFL (minimum score 90 iBT), IELTS (minimum score 7). Electronic applications accepted.

University of New Mexico, Graduate Studies, College of Arts and Sciences, Program in Economics, Albuquerque, NM 87131-2039. Offers econometrics (MA); economic theory (MA); environmental/natural resource economics (MA, PhD); international/development and sustainability economics (MA, PhD); public economics (MA, PhD). *Program availability:* Part-time. *Faculty:* 12 full-time (5 women), 1 (woman) part-time/adjunct. *Students:* 28 full-time (6 women), 22 part-time (8 women); includes 5 minority (all Hispanic/Latino), 31 international. Average age 33. 49 applicants, 20% accepted, 10 enrolled. In 2017, 7 master's, 4 doctorates awarded. Terminal master's awarded for partial completion of doctoral program. *Degree requirements:* For master's, comprehensive exam, thesis (for some programs); for doctorate, comprehensive exam,

thesis/dissertation. *Entrance requirements:* For master's and doctorate, GRE General Test, 3 letters of recommendation, letter of intent, curriculum vitae. Additional exam requirements/recommendations for international students: Required—TOEFL (minimum score 520 paper-based; 68 iBT). *Application deadline:* For fall admission, 3/1 priority date for domestic students, 3/1 for international students. Applications are processed on a rolling basis. Application fee: $50. Electronic applications accepted. *Financial support:* Fellowships with tuition reimbursements, research assistantships with tuition reimbursements, teaching assistantships with tuition reimbursements, career-related internships or fieldwork, Federal Work-Study, scholarships/grants, health care benefits, and unspecified assistantships available. Support available to part-time students. Financial award application deadline: 3/1; financial award applicants required to submit FAFSA. *Faculty research:* Core theory, econometrics, public finance, international/development economics, labor/human resource economics, environmental/natural resource economics. *Total annual research expenditures:* $167,690. *Unit head:* Dr. Janie Chermak, Chair, 505-277-2037, Fax: 505-277-9445, E-mail: jchermak@unm.edu. *Application contact:* Jeff Newcomer Miller, Academic Advisor, 505-277-3056, Fax: 505-277-9445, E-mail: econgrad@unm.edu. Website: http://econ.unm.edu

Valparaiso University, Graduate School and Continuing Education, Program in International Economics and Finance, Valparaiso, IN 46383. Offers MS. *Program availability:* Part-time, evening/weekend. *Entrance requirements:* For master's, 1 semester of college-level calculus; 1 statistics or quantitative methods class; 2 semesters of introductory economics (course content in introductory economics must include both introductory microeconomics and macroeconomics); 1 introductory accounting course; minimum undergraduate GPA of 3.0; 2 letters of recommendation. Additional exam requirements/recommendations for international students: Required—TOEFL (minimum score 550 paper-based; 80 iBT), IELTS (minimum score 6). *Expenses: Tuition:* Full-time $11,340; part-time $630 per credit hour. *Required fees:* $520; $250 per year. $125 per semester. Tuition and fees vary according to program and reciprocity agreements.

Wayne State University, College of Liberal Arts and Sciences, Department of Economics, Detroit, MI 48202. Offers applied macroeconomics (MA, PhD); health economics (MA, PhD); industrial organization (MA, PhD); international economics (MA, PhD); labor and human resources (MA, PhD); JD/MA. *Faculty:* 11. *Students:* 34 full-time (8 women), 9 part-time (3 women); includes 5 minority (4 Black or African American, non-Hispanic/Latino; 1 Asian, non-Hispanic/Latino), 17 international. Average age 30. 90 applicants, 30% accepted, 13 enrolled. In 2017, 10 master's, 6 doctorates awarded. *Degree requirements:* For master's, comprehensive exam; for doctorate, comprehensive exam, thesis/dissertation, oral examination on research, completion of course work in quantitative methods, final lecture. *Entrance requirements:* For master's, minimum upper-division GPA of 3.0; prior coursework in intermediate microeconomic and macroeconomic theory, statistics, and elementary calculus; for doctorate, GRE, minimum upper-division GPA of 3.0, prior coursework in intermediate microeconomic and macroeconomic theory, statistics, two courses in calculus, three letters of recommendation from officials or teaching staff at institution(s) most recently attended, statement of purpose. Additional exam requirements/recommendations for international students: Required—TOEFL (minimum score 550 paper-based; 79 iBT), TWE (minimum score 5.5), Michigan English Language Assessment Battery (minimum score 85); Recommended—IELTS (minimum score 6.5). *Application deadline:* For fall admission, 5/1 for domestic and international students; for winter admission, 10/1 priority date for domestic students, 9/1 priority date for international students; for spring admission, 1/1 priority date for domestic and international students. Applications are processed on a rolling basis. Application fee: $50. Electronic applications accepted. *Expenses:* Tuition, state resident: full-time $10,224; part-time $638.98 per credit hour. Tuition, nonresident: full-time $22,145; part-time $1384.04 per credit hour. Tuition and fees vary according to course load and program. *Financial support:* In 2017–18, 25 students received support, including 2 fellowships with tuition reimbursements available (averaging $16,000 per year), 17 teaching assistantships with tuition reimbursements available (averaging $18,534 per year); research assistantships with tuition reimbursements available, scholarships/grants, health care benefits, and unspecified assistantships also available. Support available to part-time students. Financial award applicants required to submit FAFSA. *Faculty research:* Health economics, international economics, macroeconomics, urban and labor economics, econometrics. *Unit head:* Dr. Kevin Cotter, Interim Chair, 313-577-3345, E-mail: kevin.cotter@wayne.edu. *Application contact:* Dr. Li Way Lee, Professor and Director of Graduate Studies, 313-577-3345, E-mail: aa1313@wayne.edu. Website: http://clas.wayne.edu/economics/

Wichita State University, Graduate School, W. Frank Barton School of Business, Department of Economics, Wichita, KS 67260. Offers economic analysis (MA); financial economics (MA); international economics (MA). *Program availability:* Part-time, evening/weekend. *Unit head:* Dr. Jen-Chi Cheng, Chair, 316-978-3220, Fax: 316-978-3845, E-mail: jenchi.cheng@wichita.edu. *Application contact:* Jordan Oleson, Admissions Coordinator, 316-978-3095, Fax: 316-978-3253, E-mail: jordan.oleson@wichita.edu. Website: http://www.wichita.edu/econ

Wilfrid Laurier University, Faculty of Graduate and Postdoctoral Studies, School of International Policy and Governance, International Public Policy Program, Waterloo, ON N2L 3C5, Canada. Offers global governance (MIPP); human security (MIPP); international economic relations (MIPP); international environmental policy (MIPP). Offered jointly with University of Waterloo. *Entrance requirements:* For master's, honours BA with minimum B average. Additional exam requirements/recommendations for international students: Required—TOEFL (minimum score 89 iBT). Electronic applications accepted. *Faculty research:* International environmental policy, international economic relations, human security, global governance.

Yale University, Graduate School of Arts and Sciences, Department of Economics, Program in International and Development Economics, New Haven, CT 06520. Offers MA. *Entrance requirements:* For master's, GRE General Test.

Mineral Economics

Colorado School of Mines, Office of Graduate Studies, Department of Economics and Business, Golden, CO 80401. Offers engineering and technology management (MS); mineral and energy economics (MS, PhD); operations research and engineering (PhD); petroleum economics and management with mineral and energy economics (MS). *Program availability:* Part-time. *Faculty:* 17 full-time (5 women), 4 part-time/adjunct (1 woman). *Students:* 93 full-time (26 women), 20 part-time (2 women); includes 20 minority (3 Black or African American, non-Hispanic/Latino; 4 Asian, non-Hispanic/Latino; 8 Hispanic/Latino; 5 Two or more races, non-Hispanic/Latino), 30 international. Average age 28. 154 applicants, 82% accepted, 53 enrolled. In 2017, 50 master's, 5 doctorates awarded. *Degree requirements:* For master's, thesis (for some programs); for doctorate, comprehensive exam, thesis/dissertation. *Entrance requirements:* For master's and doctorate, GRE General Test. Additional exam requirements/recommendations for international students: Required—TOEFL (minimum score 550 paper-based; 79 iBT). *Application deadline:* For fall admission, 12/15 priority date for domestic and international students; for spring admission, 9/1 priority date for domestic and international students. Application fee: $60 ($80 for international students). Electronic applications accepted. *Expenses:* Tuition, state resident: full-time $16,170. Tuition, nonresident: full-time $35,220. *Required fees:* $2216. *Financial support:* In 2017–18, 7 research assistantships with full tuition reimbursements, 22 teaching assistantships with full tuition reimbursements were awarded; fellowships, scholarships/grants, health care benefits, and unspecified assistantships also available. Financial award application deadline: 12/15; financial award applicants required to submit FAFSA. *Faculty research:* International trade, resource and environmental economics, energy economics, operations research. *Unit head:* Dr. Roderick Eggert, Interim Director, 303-273-3981, E-mail: reggert@mines.edu. *Application contact:* Kathleen Martin, Program Assistant, 303-273-3482, Fax: 303-273-3416, E-mail: kmartin@mines.edu. Website: http://econbus.mines.edu

Michigan Technological University, Graduate School, School of Business and Economics, Houghton, MI 49931. Offers accounting (MS); applied natural resource economics (MS); business administration (MBA). *Accreditation:* AACSB. *Program availability:* Part-time, evening/weekend. *Faculty:* 24 full-time (6 women), 1 part-time/adjunct. *Students:* 25 full-time (12 women), 21 part-time (13 women); includes 1 minority (Two or more races, non-Hispanic/Latino), 14 international. Average age 27. 165 applicants, 23% accepted, 22 enrolled. In 2017, 24 master's awarded. *Degree requirements:* For master's, thesis (for some programs). *Entrance requirements:* For master's, GMAT/GRE (recommended minimum score in the 55th percentile), statement of purpose, personal statement, official transcripts, 2 letters of recommendation, resume/curriculum vitae. Additional exam requirements/recommendations for international students: Required—TOEFL (recommended minimum score 95 iBT) or IELTS (minimum score 7). *Application deadline:* For fall admission, 7/1 for domestic and international students; for spring admission, 12/1 for domestic and international students. Applications are processed on a rolling basis. Electronic applications accepted. *Expenses:* Tuition, state resident: full-time $17,100; part-time $950 per credit. Tuition, nonresident: full-time $17,100; part-time $950 per credit. *Required fees:* $248; $124 per term. Tuition and fees vary according to course load and program. *Financial support:* In 2017–18, 22 students received support. Health care benefits and unspecified assistantships available. Financial award application deadline: 2/1; financial award applicants required to submit FAFSA. *Faculty research:* Natural resource and mineral economics, entrepreneurship, management of technology and innovation, engineering management, management information systems. *Total annual research expenditures:* $5,749. *Unit head:* Dr. Dean Johnson, Dean, 906-487-2668, Fax: 906-487-1863, E-mail: dean@mtu.edu. *Application contact:* Carol T. Wingerson, Administrative Aide, 906-487-2328, Fax: 906-487-2284, E-mail: gradadms@mtu.edu. Website: http://www.mtu.edu/business/

The University of Texas at Austin, Graduate School, Cockrell School of Engineering, Department of Petroleum and Geosystems Engineering, Program in Energy and Earth Resources, Austin, TX 78712-1111. Offers MA. *Degree requirements:* For master's, thesis, seminar. *Entrance requirements:* For master's, GRE General Test. Additional exam requirements/recommendations for international students: Required—TOEFL. Electronic applications accepted.

UCLA
Master of Applied Economics

 For more information, visit http://petersons.to/uclaeconomics

Programs of Study

Designed by UCLA's world-class faculty, the Master of Applied Economics program (M.A.E.) will prepare its students to prosper in an increasingly complex and opportunity-rich global economy. Students will master rigorous economic analysis and develop techniques for accurately interpreting cutting-edge research for real-world application. Graduates of the program will be able to examine pressing global economic issues to help decision-makers strategize effective and successful policies in corporations and government institutions.

The M.A.E. provides students with meaningful interactions with renowned faculty, policy makers, and industry executives. This program will include classes on the forefront of economics and introduce the techniques of data analysis for both economics and finance. In addition, classes in writing and presentation skills will enable students to communicate economic arguments effectively to colleagues, board members, investors, and the public at large.

UCLA's Department of Economics is one of the highest-ranked in the world. The young and active faculty are shaping policy and informing critical issues with their world-renowned research. The Department's alumni also play key roles in banking, consulting, finance, accounting, management, business, technology, marketing, and human resources—to name a few.

The program was created in response to the increasingly high demand from students seeking a terminal master's degree in economics from UCLA and employers looking for candidates with advanced training. Its inaugural year was 2016–17. The MAE is designed to better prepare students with a baccalaureate in economics or a related field to serve the financial sector, federal and state governments, and private industry with sophisticated methods and rigorous models of analysis.

The M.A.E. program is designed specifically for the students who want to enter or re-enter the workforce. Graduates will be qualified for positions that require economical analysis or a quantitative background. Some employment opportunities include, but are not limited to, central banks, international organizations, government ministries, consulting firms, think tanks, hospitals, and banks. Recent graduates have been employed by AmTech, Bank of Hope, China Eastern Airlines, China Merchant Capital, Comunidad Mujer, CybEye, Geringer Capital, Global Genius Fund, Kayne Anderson, K2 Economics, Liferay, Protiviti, Resolution Economics, Sohu. com, Soochow Security, Uphonest Capital, Westlake Ventures, University of Zurich, and others.

This intensive, full-time, 9-month/3 quarter (fall, winter, and spring) program integrates theory and applications. The first quarter will consist of microeconomic theory, macroeconomic theory, and quantitative methods courses that cover the basic tools and models used in economics literature. These same courses will continue into the second quarter, but with greater emphasis on applying the tools and methods. In addition to the three economics courses, the first two quarters will also include courses on written and oral communication of economic ideas, which will focus on how to structure a presentation or paper and how to communicate effectively when presenting arguments. The third quarter will consist of a variety of elective courses on specific subfields within economics. Each student will prepare and present a final project based on the content of one of these courses.

Economics in Action

Students will learn how economic theory maps into policy-making. Renowned and influential policy makers from central banks, economics ministries, and international organizations will lecture on today's most compelling policy-relevant topics. Students will complete a capstone project that fully engages the economic theories explored in lecture.

Each spring, students will choose four elective courses and will prepare a final project based on the content of one of these courses. The final project will be designed by the student in concert with their faculty advisor and would enhance the student's portfolio when they enter, or re-enter the job market. They will submit and present the results of their project in the form of a research paper. This capstone paper serves as a student's "thesis" and is required for graduation.

Financial Aid

The Department of Economics does not cover any costs for the MAE program. The Financial Aid Office's website at financialaid.ucla.edu has information about financial aid specific to graduate students.

As a self-supporting program, the M.A.E. is billed to veterans at the in-state tuition rate, and thus is eligible for tuition coverage under the Post 9/11 GI Bill® up to the amount of the applicant's eligibility percentage from the VA. Prospective students must apply online for veteran's educational benefits.

Cost of Study

The total program fee for the 2017–18 academic year was $53,434.78. This includes health insurance, but excludes books and other costs of attendance. There is a nonrefundable admission enrollment deposit of $1,500. Estimated costs for books and supplies are $1,287, room and meals are $17,793, transportation is $1,371, and personal expenses are $2,217.

Living and Housing Costs

Because this is a full-time, on-campus program there are several housing options available for M.A.E. students.

Students can choose to apply for university apartments, which are assigned via a lottery system. In order to have a higher chance of being assigned university housing, students must apply to the lottery program by May.

The Community Housing Office provides non-university owned rental listings and rental resources to the entire UCLA community. Full-time UCLA students may search listings for free. In addition, the office also maintains additional resources to assist those searching for housing in the Los Angeles area. In order to use this service, students will need to have a my.ucla account registered.

More detailed information is available at https://master.econ.ucla.edu/admitted-mae-students/.

Student Group

One of the largest and most notable in the country, the Department of Economics at UCLA is home to over 3,300 undergraduates and 110 doctoral students, who represent over 60 countries across the world. There are approximately 50 students in the M.A.E. program.

Location

UCLA is located in Westwood, California, 6 miles east of the Pacific Ocean and 13 miles west of downtown. Bordered by iconic neighborhoods—Bel Air, Brentwood, Santa Monica, and Beverly Hills—UCLA is a crossroads of ideas, cultures, and limitless experiences and opportunities.

From an expansive medical complex, to more than 290 research centers, to libraries, museums, film and music archives, and art galleries, UCLA provides horizon-broadening, humanity-serving resources not only to its students but to every citizen of California.

The University

UCLA's primary purpose as a public research university is the creation, dissemination, preservation, and application of knowledge for the betterment of global society. Learning and teaching at UCLA are guided by the belief that undergraduate, graduate, and professional school students and their teachers belong to a community of scholars. Discovery, creativity, and innovation are hallmarks of UCLA.

Civic engagement is fundamental to UCLA's mission as a public university. Located on the Pacific Rim in one of the world's most diverse and vibrant cities, UCLA reaches beyond campus boundaries to establish partnerships locally and globally. We seek to serve society through both teaching and scholarship, to educate successive generations of leaders, and to pass on to students a renewable set of skills and commitment to social engagement.

The Faculty

The M.A.E. program features instruction from mostly tenured faculty, providing students with the opportunity to engage in critical discussion on a diversity of topics.

Program Director Aaron Tornell is a Professor of Economics at UCLA. He received his Ph.D. in Economics from the Massachusetts Institute of Technology in 1987, specializing in international finance and political economy. He taught economics at Columbia University and Harvard University prior to UCLA and served as the advisor to the Minister of Finance of Mexico from 1989 to 1991.

Dora Costa is Professor and Chair in the Department of Economics at UCLA where she teaches economic history. She is also an associate director of the California Population Research Center, a research associate in the National Bureau of Economic Research's (NBER) programs on the Development of the American Economy and on Aging, and the co-director of the NBER working group Cohort Studies.

The M.A.E. program also features a number of distinguished lecturers who come from central banks, government ministries, and international organizations to discuss economic policy and topics of current relevance. Guests will be announced in the early part of each year.

UCLA

Information regarding other members of the Department of Economics faculty is available online at https://economics.ucla.edu.

Applying

Applications for fall 2019 enrollment will be accepted starting in fall 2018. The application is online, except for academic records and test scores, which must also be sent directly to the Department of Economics. All applicants must apply online via the UCLA Application for Graduate Admission. The application deadline is March 15. Complete applications will be reviewed in the order in which they are received.

Applicants to the M.A.E. program should have a quantitative background including courses like linear algebra, multivariate calculus, probability, and statistics. Students will gain familiarity with computer assignments involving the use of statistical and econometric applications such as R, Matlab, Stata, and Python. Applicants should be adept at using quantitative concepts in order to complete the program. A combination of relevant undergraduate and graduate coursework and scores on the GRE quantitative sections are used to assess students' quantitative abilities. Documented work experience in research, business, or other professional environments is also valued.

The minimum requirement for admission for a U.S. applicant is a bachelor's degree from a regionally accredited institution, comparable in standard and content to a bachelor's degree from the University of California. A scholastic average of B (3.0 on a 4.0 scale) or better, or its equivalent if the letter grade system is not used, is required for the last 60 semester units or 90 quarter units of undergraduate study and in any post-baccalaureate study.

An international applicant whose post-secondary education is completed outside of the U.S. is expected to hold a degree representing completion of at least four years of study with above average scholarship from a university or university-level institution.

Applicants must complete the online application and submit official academic records, GRE scores, TOEFL or IELTS scores (if applicable), a statement of purpose, personal history statement, resume/CV, two letters of recommendation, and a $105 application fee.

Additional details regarding the application process can be found at https://master.econ.ucla.edu/admissions/#toggle-id-8.

Correspondence and Information

UCLA Economics
8283 Bunche Hall
Mail Code: 147703
Los Angeles, California 90095
Phone: 310-825-7155
Fax: 310-825-9528
E-mail: mae-office@econ.ucla.edu
Website: https://master.econ.ucla.edu

Section 20
Family and Consumer Sciences

This section contains a directory of institutions offering graduate work in family and consumer sciences. Additional information about programs listed in the directory but not augmented by an in-depth entry may be obtained by writing directly to the dean of a graduate school or chair of a department at the address given in the directory.

For programs offering related work, see also in this book *Economics, Psychology and Counseling,* and *Sociology, Anthropology, and Archaeology.* In another guide in this series:

Graduate Programs in Business, Education, Health, Information Studies, Law & Social Work

See *Social Work*

CONTENTS

Program Directories

Featured Schools: Displays and Close-Ups

Family and Consumer Sciences-General

Alabama Agricultural and Mechanical University, School of Graduate Studies, College of Agricultural, Life and Natural Sciences, Department of Family and Consumer Sciences, Huntsville, AL 35811. Offers apparel, merchandising and design (MS); family and consumer sciences (MS); human development and family studies (MS); nutrition and hospitality management (MS). *Program availability:* Part-time, evening/weekend. *Degree requirements:* For master's, comprehensive exam, thesis optional. *Entrance requirements:* For master's, GRE General Test. Additional exam requirements/recommendations for international students: Required—TOEFL (minimum score 500 paper-based; 61 iBT). Electronic applications accepted. *Faculty research:* Food biotechnology, nutrition, food microbiology, food engineering, food chemistry.

Ball State University, Graduate School, Teachers College, Department of Family, Consumer, and Technology Education, Muncie, IN 47306. Offers family and consumer science (MS), including apparel design (MA, MS), fashion merchandising (MA, MS), interior design (MA, MS), residential property management (MA, MS); family and consumer sciences (MA), including apparel design (MA, MS), fashion merchandising (MA, MS), interior design (MA, MS), residential property management (MA, MS); nutrition and dietetics (MA, MS). *Program availability:* Part-time, evening/weekend, 100% online. *Students:* 9 full-time (5 women), 54 part-time (20 women); includes 9 minority (5 Black or African American, non-Hispanic/Latino; 1 Asian, non-Hispanic/Latino; 3 Hispanic/Latino), 6 international. Average age 36. 63 applicants, 48% accepted, 26 enrolled. In 2017, 19 master's awarded. *Entrance requirements:* For master's, letter of intent, resume, two letters of recommendation, portfolio (for interior design option). Additional exam requirements/recommendations for international students: Required—TOEFL (minimum score 550 paper-based; 79 iBT), IELTS (minimum score 6.5). *Application deadline:* For fall admission, 2/15 for domestic students; for spring admission, 9/25 for domestic students. Applications are processed on a rolling basis. Application fee: $60. Electronic applications accepted. *Financial support:* Research assistantships with partial tuition reimbursements and unspecified assistantships available. Financial award application deadline: 3/1; financial award applicants required to submit FAFSA. *Unit head:* Dr. Scott Hall, Chairperson, 765-285-5943, Fax: 765-285-2314, E-mail: sshall@bsu.edu. *Application contact:* Dr. Scott Hall, Chairperson, 765-285-5943, Fax: 765-285-2314, E-mail: sshall@bsu.edu. Website: http://www.bsu.edu/fcs

California State University, Northridge, Graduate Studies, College of Health and Human Development, Department of Family and Consumer Sciences, Northridge, CA 91330. Offers MS. *Program availability:* Part-time, evening/weekend. *Students:* 23 full-time (20 women), 24 part-time (22 women); includes 24 minority (4 Black or African American, non-Hispanic/Latino; 5 Asian, non-Hispanic/Latino; 14 Hispanic/Latino; 1 Two or more races, non-Hispanic/Latino), 8 international. Average age 32. 52 applicants, 52% accepted, 18 enrolled. In 2017, 42 master's awarded. *Degree requirements:* For master's, thesis, project, or comprehensive exam. *Entrance requirements:* For master's, GRE General Test or minimum GPA of 3.0. Additional exam requirements/recommendations for international students: Required—TOEFL. *Application deadline:* For fall admission, 11/30 for domestic students. Application fee: $55. *Financial support:* Teaching assistantships, career-related internships or fieldwork, Federal Work-Study, and institutionally sponsored loans available. Financial award application deadline: 3/1. *Unit head:* Dr. Yi Cai, Chair, 818-677-3051, E-mail: yi.cai@csun.edu. Website: http://www.csun.edu/hhd/fcs/

Central Michigan University, College of Graduate Studies, College of Education and Human Services, Department of Human Environmental Studies, Mount Pleasant, MI 48859. Offers apparel product development and merchandising technology (MS); gerontology (Graduate Certificate); human development and family studies (MA); nutrition and dietetics (MS). *Program availability:* Part-time, evening/weekend. *Degree requirements:* For master's, thesis or alternative. Electronic applications accepted. *Faculty research:* Human growth and development, family studies and human sexuality, human nutrition and dietetics, apparel and textile retailing, computer-aided design for apparel.

Central Washington University, School of Graduate Studies and Research, College of Education and Professional Studies, Department of Family and Consumer Sciences, Ellensburg, WA 98926. Offers career and technical education (MS); family and child life (MS); family and consumer sciences education (MS). *Program availability:* Part-time. *Entrance requirements:* For master's, minimum GPA of 3.0. Additional exam requirements/recommendations for international students: Required—TOEFL (minimum score 550 paper-based; 79 iBT). *Application deadline:* For fall admission, 2/1 priority date for domestic students; for winter admission, 10/1 for domestic students; for spring admission, 1/1 for domestic students. Applications are processed on a rolling basis. Application fee: $50. Electronic applications accepted. *Financial support:* Application deadline: 3/1; applicants required to submit FAFSA. *Unit head:* Dr. Duane Dowd, Department Chair, 509-963-2740, E-mail: duane.dowd@cwu.edu. *Application contact:* Justine Eason, Admissions Program Coordinator, 509-963-3103, Fax: 509-963-1799, E-mail: masters@cwu.edu. Website: http://www.cwu.edu/~fandcs/

Clemson University, Graduate School, College of Behavioral, Social and Health Sciences, Department of Youth, Family and Community Studies, Clemson, SC 29634. Offers international family and community studies (PhD, Certificate). *Program availability:* Part-time-only, online only, blended/hybrid learning. *Faculty:* 6 full-time (4 women), 1 part-time/adjunct (0 women). *Students:* 13 full-time (12 women), 24 part-time (19 women), 15 international. Average age 40. 27 applicants, 52% accepted, 10 enrolled. In 2017, 5 doctorates awarded. *Degree requirements:* For doctorate, comprehensive exam, thesis/dissertation. *Entrance requirements:* For doctorate and Certificate, GRE General Test, unofficial transcripts, personal statement, writing sample, letters of recommendation. Additional exam requirements/recommendations for international students: Required—TOEFL (minimum score 80 iBT), IELTS (minimum score 6.5), PTE (minimum score 54). *Application deadline:* For fall admission, 2/1 priority date for domestic and international students. Application fee: $80 ($90 for international students). Electronic applications accepted. *Expenses:* $4,318 per semester full-time resident, $8,036 per semester full-time non-resident, $425 per credit hour part-time resident, $837 per credit hour part-time non-resident; $467 per credit hour online; other fees may apply per session. *Financial support:* In 2017–18, 11 students received support, including 1 fellowship with partial tuition reimbursement available (averaging $10,000 per year), 9 research assistantships with partial tuition reimbursements available (averaging $23,556 per year); career-related internships or fieldwork and unspecified assistantships also available. Financial award application deadline: 2/1. *Faculty research:* Community development and engagement, health and human rights, bullying prevention, suicidal behavior, dating violence. *Total annual research expenditures:* $1 million. *Unit head:* Dr. Mark Small, Department Chair, 864-656-6286, E-mail: msmall@clemson.edu. *Application contact:* Shelli Charles, Graduate

Studies Coordinator, 864-656-3410, E-mail: shellic@clemson.edu. Website: http://www.clemson.edu/cbshs/departments/family-community-studies/index.html

Florida State University, The Graduate School, College of Human Sciences, Tallahassee, FL 32306-1490. Offers MS, PhD. *Accreditation:* AAMFT/COAMFTE. *Program availability:* Part-time. *Faculty:* 40 full-time (20 women). *Students:* 117 full-time (80 women), 5 part-time (2 women); includes 26 minority (8 Black or African American, non-Hispanic/Latino; 3 Asian, non-Hispanic/Latino; 3 Hispanic/Latino; 12 Two or more races, non-Hispanic/Latino), 19 international. 137 applicants, 53% accepted, 34 enrolled. In 2017, 33 master's, 16 doctorates awarded. *Degree requirements:* For master's, comprehensive exam (for some programs), thesis optional; for doctorate, thesis/dissertation. *Entrance requirements:* For master's, GRE General Test, minimum upper-division GPA of 3.0; for doctorate, GRE General Test, minimum upper-division GPA of 3.0, master's degree. Additional exam requirements/recommendations for international students: Required—TOEFL (minimum score 550 paper-based; 80 iBT). *Application deadline:* For fall admission, 4/1 for domestic and international students; for spring admission, 10/1 for domestic and international students. Applications are processed on a rolling basis. Application fee: $30. Electronic applications accepted. *Expenses:* $480 per credit hour in-state; $1,111 per credit hour out-of-state. *Financial support:* In 2017–18, 89 students received support, including 36 research assistantships with full tuition reimbursements available (averaging $8,312 per year), 69 teaching assistantships with full tuition reimbursements available (averaging $15,247 per year); career-related internships or fieldwork, Federal Work-Study, scholarships/grants, and unspecified assistantships also available. Financial award application deadline: 1/15; financial award applicants required to submit FAFSA. *Faculty research:* Body composition, functional food, chronic disease and aging response; food safety, food allergy, and safety/quality detection methods; sports nutrition, energy balance and human performance; cardiovascular function, families at risk, relational interventions, parenting, martial process and family therapy; merchandising and product development. *Total annual research expenditures:* $1.3 million. *Unit head:* Dr. Michael D. Delp, Dean, 850-644-1281, Fax: 850-644-0700, E-mail: mdelp@fsu.edu. *Application contact:* Tara L. Hartman, Academic Program Specialist, 850-644-7221, Fax: 850-644-0700, E-mail: thartman@fsu.edu. Website: http://humansciences.fsu.edu

Fontbonne University, Graduate Programs, St. Louis, MO 63105-3098. Offers accounting (MBA, MS); art (MA); art (K-12) (MAT); business (MBA); computer science (MS); deaf education (MA); early intervention in deaf education (MA); education (MA), including autism spectrum disorders, curriculum and instruction, diverse learners, early childhood education, reading, special education; elementary education (MAT); family and consumer sciences (MA), including multidisciplinary health communication studies; fine arts (MFA); instructional design and technology (MS); management and leadership (MM); middle school education (MAT); secondary education (MAT); special education (MAT); speech-language pathology (MS); supply chain management (MS); theatre (MA). *Program availability:* Part-time, evening/weekend, online learning. *Degree requirements:* For master's, comprehensive exam (for some programs), thesis (for some programs). *Entrance requirements:* Additional exam requirements/recommendations for international students: Required—TOEFL (minimum score 500 paper-based; 65 iBT). Electronic applications accepted.

Hofstra University, School of Education, Programs in Teacher Education, Hempstead, NY 11549. Offers bilingual education (MA); bilingual extension (Advanced Certificate), including education/speech language pathology, intensive teacher institute; business education (MS Ed); curriculum studies (MS Ed); early childhood and childhood education (MS Ed); early childhood education (MA, MS Ed); educational technology (Advanced Certificate); elementary education (MA, MS Ed), including science, technology, engineering, and mathematics (STEM) (MA); English education (MS Ed); family and consumer science (MS Ed); fine arts and music education (Advanced Certificate); fine arts education (MS Ed); foreign language and TESOL (MS Ed); foreign language education (MA, MS Ed), including Arabic (MS Ed), biology, chemistry, Chinese (MS Ed), earth science, French, German, Italian (MS Ed), Mandarin (MS Ed), physics, Russian, Spanish; foundations of education (Advanced Certificate), including grades 5-6, grades 7-9; languages other than English and teaching English as a second language (MA); learning and teaching (Ed D), including applied linguistics, art education, arts and humanities, early childhood education, English education, human development, math education, math, science, and technology, multicultural education, physical education, science education, social studies education, special education; mathematics education (MA, MS Ed); music education (MA, MS Ed); science education (MA), including biology (MA, MS Ed), chemistry (MA, MS Ed), earth science (MA, MS Ed), physics (MA, MS Ed); secondary education (Advanced Certificate); social studies education (MA, MS Ed); teaching languages other than English and TESOL (MS Ed); technology for learning (MA); TESOL (MS Ed, Advanced Certificate); TESOL with specialization in STEM (MA); work based learning extension (Advanced Certificate). *Program availability:* Part-time, evening/weekend, blended/hybrid learning. *Students:* 119 full-time (83 women), 124 part-time (90 women); includes 54 minority (15 Black or African American, non-Hispanic/Latino; 9 Asian, non-Hispanic/Latino; 29 Hispanic/Latino; 1 Native Hawaiian or other Pacific Islander, non-Hispanic/Latino), 12 international. Average age 29. 205 applicants, 88% accepted, 93 enrolled. In 2017, 103 master's, 4 doctorates, 32 other advanced degrees awarded. *Degree requirements:* For master's, comprehensive exam, thesis (for some programs), exit project, student teaching, fieldwork, electronic portfolio, curriculum project, minimum GPA of 3.0; for doctorate, thesis/dissertation; for Advanced Certificate, 3 foreign languages, comprehensive exam (for some programs), thesis project. *Entrance requirements:* For master's, GRE, 2 letters of recommendation, portfolio, teacher certification (MA), interview, essay; for doctorate, GMAT, GRE, LSAT, or MAT; for Advanced Certificate, 2 letters of recommendation, essay, interview and/or portfolio, teaching certificate. Additional exam requirements/recommendations for international students: Required—TOEFL (minimum score 550 paper-based; 80 iBT). *Application deadline:* Applications are processed on a rolling basis. Application fee: $75. Electronic applications accepted. *Expenses:* Tuition: Full-time $1292. *Required fees:* $970. Tuition and fees vary according to program. *Financial support:* In 2017–18, 112 students received support, including 56 fellowships with full and partial tuition reimbursements available (averaging $4,998 per year), 2 research assistantships with full and partial tuition reimbursements available (averaging $8,753 per year); career-related internships or fieldwork, Federal Work-Study, institutionally sponsored loans, scholarships/grants, traineeships, tuition waivers (full and partial), and unspecified assistantships also available. Support available to part-time students. Financial award applicants required to submit FAFSA. *Faculty research:* Educational interventions that foster critical-thinking skills; teachers' attitudes about professional development; threats to teacher quality. *Unit head:* Dr. Eustace Thompson, Chairperson, 516-463-5749, Fax:

516-463-6275, E-mail: eustace.g.thompson@hofstra.edu. *Application contact:* Sunil Samuel, Assistant Vice President of Admissions, 516-463-4723, Fax: 516-463-4664, E-mail: graduateadmission@hofstra.edu.
Website: http://www.hofstra.edu/education/

Illinois State University, Graduate School, College of Applied Science and Technology, Department of Family and Consumer Sciences, Normal, IL 61790. Offers MA, MS. *Degree requirements:* For master's, thesis or alternative. *Entrance requirements:* For master's, GRE General Test, minimum GPA of 2.8 in last 60 hours of course work. *Faculty research:* Graduate practicum assistantships, startup for Jump Start of McLean County grant, providing low-income preschool children with early literacy experiences, generations of Hope-ICI replication.

Iowa State University of Science and Technology, Program in Family and Consumer Sciences, Ames, IA 50011. Offers MFCS. *Degree requirements:* For master's, thesis or alternative. *Entrance requirements:* For master's, GRE General Test. Additional exam requirements/recommendations for international students: Required—TOEFL (minimum score 550 paper-based; 79 iBT), IELTS (minimum score 6.5). Electronic applications accepted.

Kansas State University, Graduate School, College of Human Ecology, Manhattan, KS 66506. Offers MS, PhD, Graduate Certificate. *Program availability:* Part-time, online learning. *Degree requirements:* For master's, residency; for doctorate, thesis/dissertation, residency. Electronic applications accepted. *Faculty research:* Apparel and textiles, food service and hospitality management, life span human development, family life education and consultation, marriage and family therapy.

Lamar University, College of Graduate Studies, College of Education and Human Development, Department of Family and Consumer Sciences, Beaumont, TX 77701. Offers MS. *Program availability:* Part-time, evening/weekend. *Faculty:* 10 full-time (9 women), 4 part-time/adjunct (3 women). *Students:* 12 full-time (10 women), 16 part-time (15 women); includes 10 minority (7 Black or African American, non-Hispanic/Latino; 2 Asian, non-Hispanic/Latino; 1 Native Hawaiian or other Pacific Islander, non-Hispanic/Latino), 4 international. Average age 30. 17 applicants, 100% accepted, 6 enrolled. In 2017, 8 master's awarded. *Degree requirements:* For master's, thesis optional. *Entrance requirements:* For master's, GRE General Test. Additional exam requirements/recommendations for international students: Required—TOEFL (minimum score 550 paper-based; 79 iBT), IELTS (minimum score 6.5). *Application deadline:* For fall admission, 8/10 for domestic students, 7/1 for international students; for spring admission, 1/5 for domestic students, 12/1 for international students. Applications are processed on a rolling basis. Application fee: $25 ($50 for international students). Electronic applications accepted. *Expenses:* Contact institution. *Financial support:* In 2017–18, 3 teaching assistantships (averaging $5,000 per year) were awarded; fellowships, research assistantships, career-related internships or fieldwork, Federal Work-Study, and institutionally sponsored loans also available. Support available to part-time students. Financial award application deadline: 4/1; financial award applicants required to submit FAFSA. *Faculty research:* Maternal and infant nutrition, eating disorders, sports nutrition, human sexuality, family violence. *Unit head:* Dr. Tammy Henderson, Chair, 409-880-8668, Fax: 409-880-8666. *Application contact:* Deidre Mayer, Interim Director, Admissions and Academic Services, 409-880-8888, Fax: 409-880-7419, E-mail: gradmissions@lamar.edu.
Website: http://education.lamar.edu/family-and-consumer-sciences

Louisiana State University and Agricultural & Mechanical College, Graduate School, College of Agriculture, School of Human Ecology, Baton Rouge, LA 70803. Offers MS, PhD. *Faculty:* 11 full-time (8 women). *Students:* 10 full-time (6 women), 1 (woman) part-time; includes 2 minority (both Black or African American, non-Hispanic/Latino), 6 international. Average age 31. 28 applicants, 75% accepted, 2 enrolled. In 2017, 1 master's, 2 doctorates awarded. *Financial support:* In 2017–18, 1 research assistantship (averaging $17,547 per year), 7 teaching assistantships (averaging $19,425 per year) were awarded.

New Mexico State University, College of Agricultural, Consumer and Environmental Sciences, Department of Family and Consumer Sciences, Las Cruces, NM 88003. Offers clothing, textiles, and merchandising (MS); family and child science (MS); family and consumer science education (MS); family and consumer sciences (MS); food science and technology (MS); hotel, restaurant, and tourism management (MS); human nutrition and dietetic sciences (MS). *Program availability:* Part-time. *Faculty:* 9 full-time (6 women), 1 (woman) part-time/adjunct. *Students:* 38 full-time (30 women), 3 part-time (all women); includes 28 minority (3 Black or African American, non-Hispanic/Latino; 1 American Indian or Alaska Native, non-Hispanic/Latino; 1 Asian, non-Hispanic/Latino; 23 Hispanic/Latino). Average age 29. 26 applicants, 69% accepted, 17 enrolled. In 2017, 15 master's awarded. *Degree requirements:* For master's, comprehensive exam (for some programs), thesis (for some programs), oral exam. *Entrance requirements:* For master's, GRE, 3 letters of reference from faculty members or employers, resume, letter of interest. Additional exam requirements/recommendations for international students: Required—TOEFL (minimum score 550 paper-based; 79 iBT), IELTS (minimum score 6.5). *Application deadline:* For fall admission, 2/1 priority date for domestic and international students; for spring admission, 10/1 for domestic and international students. Applications are processed on a rolling basis. Application fee: $40 ($50 for international students). Electronic applications accepted. *Expenses:* Tuition, state resident: full-time $4390. Tuition, nonresident: full-time $15,309. *Required fees:* $853. *Financial support:* In 2017–18, 30 students received support, including 8 research assistantships (averaging $13,150 per year), 8 teaching assistantships (averaging $14,082 per year); career-related internships or fieldwork, Federal Work-Study, scholarships/grants, traineeships, health care benefits, and unspecified assistantships also available. Support available to part-time students. Financial award application deadline: 3/1. *Faculty research:* Food product analysis, childhood obesity, dietary decision-making, military families, equine assisted psychotherapy. *Total annual research expenditures:* $356,004. *Unit head:* Dr. Priscilla Bloomquist, Interim Department Head, 575-646-3936, Fax: 575-646-8100, E-mail: pbloomqu@nmsu.edu. *Application contact:* Dr. Kourtney Vaillancourt, Graduate Program Contact, 575-646-3383, Fax: 575-646-1889, E-mail: kvaillan@nmsu.edu.
Website: http://aces.nmsu.edu/academics/fcs

North Dakota State University, College of Graduate and Interdisciplinary Studies, College of Human Development and Education, School of Education, Program in Family and Consumer Sciences Education, Fargo, ND 58102. Offers M Ed, MS. *Accreditation:* NCATE. *Program availability:* Part-time. *Degree requirements:* For master's, comprehensive exam, thesis or alternative. *Entrance requirements:* For master's, MAT. Additional exam requirements/recommendations for international students: Required—TOEFL. *Faculty research:* Needs of beginning teachers, learning styles and achievement, school-level variables and curriculum change.

The Ohio State University, Graduate School, College of Education and Human Ecology, Department of Human Sciences, Columbus, OH 43210. Offers consumer sciences (MS, PhD); human development and family science (PhD); human nutrition (MS, PhD); kinesiology (MA, Ed D, PhD). *Program availability:* Part-time. *Faculty:* 55. *Students:* 127 full-time (71 women), 14 part-time (12 women). Average age 27. In 2017, 31 master's, 14 doctorates awarded. *Degree requirements:* For master's, thesis optional; for doctorate, thesis/dissertation. *Entrance requirements:* For master's and doctorate, GRE. Additional exam requirements/recommendations for international students: Required—TOEFL (minimum score 550 paper-based; 79 iBT), Michigan English Language Assessment Battery (minimum score 82); Recommended—IELTS (minimum score 7). *Application deadline:* For fall admission, 12/1 priority date for domestic and international students. Applications are processed on a rolling basis. Application fee: $60 ($70 for international students). Electronic applications accepted. *Financial support:* Fellowships with tuition reimbursements, research assistantships with tuition reimbursements, teaching assistantships with tuition reimbursements, Federal Work-Study, and institutionally sponsored loans available. Support available to part-time students. *Unit head:* Dr. Brian Focht, Associate Chair and Professor, E-mail: focht.10@osu.edu. *Application contact:* Graduate and Professional Admissions, 614-292-9444, Fax: 614-292-3895, E-mail: gpadmissions@osu.edu.
Website: http://ehe.osu.edu/human-sciences/

Oklahoma State University, College of Human Sciences, Department of Human Development and Family Science, Stillwater, OK 74078. Offers human development and family science (MS, PhD), including family financial planning (MS), human environmental sciences (PhD). *Accreditation:* AAMFT/COAMFTE (one or more programs are accredited). *Program availability:* Online learning. *Faculty:* 33 full-time (23 women), 13 part-time/adjunct (11 women). *Students:* 36 full-time (29 women), 49 part-time (43 women); includes 27 minority (12 Black or African American, non-Hispanic/Latino; 1 American Indian or Alaska Native, non-Hispanic/Latino; 1 Asian, non-Hispanic/Latino; 9 Hispanic/Latino; 4 Two or more races, non-Hispanic/Latino), 3 international. Average age 31. 54 applicants, 59% accepted, 30 enrolled. In 2017, 20 master's, 1 doctorate awarded. *Entrance requirements:* For master's and doctorate, GRE or GMAT. Additional exam requirements/recommendations for international students: Required—TOEFL (minimum score 550 paper-based; 79 iBT). *Application deadline:* For fall admission, 3/1 priority date for international students; for spring admission, 8/1 priority date for international students. Applications are processed on a rolling basis. Application fee: $40 ($75 for international students). Electronic applications accepted. *Expenses:* Tuition, state resident: full-time $4019; part-time $2679.60 per year. Tuition, nonresident: full-time $15,286; part-time $10,190.40 per year. *Required fees:* $2129; $1419 per unit. Tuition and fees vary according to program. *Financial support:* Research assistantships, teaching assistantships, career-related internships or fieldwork, Federal Work-Study, scholarships/grants, health care benefits, tuition waivers (partial), and unspecified assistantships available. Support available to part-time students. Financial award application deadline: 3/1; financial award applicants required to submit FAFSA. *Faculty research:* Family relations and child development, consequences of adolescent parenting, family stress and coping, impacts of sexual abuse on families, children's social cognition and self-competence, gerontology and health care. *Unit head:* Dr. Sissy Osteen, Department Head, 405-744-4741, Fax: 405-744-6344, E-mail: sissy.osteen@okstate.edu. *Application contact:* Dr. Michael Criss, Graduate Coordinator, 405-744-5057, Fax: 405-744-6344, E-mail: michael.criss@okstate.edu.
Website: https://humansciences.okstate.edu/hdfs/

Queens College of the City University of New York, Mathematics and Natural Sciences Division, Department of Family, Nutrition and Exercise Sciences, Queens, NY 11367-1597. Offers exercise science specialist (MS); family and consumer science (K-12) (AC); family and consumer science/teaching curriculum (K-12) (MS Ed); nutrition and exercise science (MS); nutrition specialist (MS); physical education (K-12) (AC); physical education/teaching curriculum (pre K-12) (MS Ed). *Program availability:* Part-time, evening/weekend. *Faculty:* 13 full-time (11 women), 7 part-time/adjunct (4 women). *Students:* 15 full-time (7 women), 136 part-time (75 women); includes 67 minority (19 Black or African American, non-Hispanic/Latino; 1 American Indian or Alaska Native, non-Hispanic/Latino; 21 Asian, non-Hispanic/Latino; 25 Hispanic/Latino; 1 Two or more races, non-Hispanic/Latino), 3 international. Average age 30. 95 applicants, 76% accepted, 45 enrolled. In 2017, 34 master's, 12 other advanced degrees awarded. *Degree requirements:* For master's, research project. *Entrance requirements:* For master's, minimum GPA of 3.0. Additional exam requirements/recommendations for international students: Required—TOEFL (minimum paper-based score of 600) or IELTS (for program in nutrition). *Application deadline:* For fall admission, 4/1 for domestic students; for spring admission, 11/1 for domestic students. Applications are processed on a rolling basis. Application fee: $125. Electronic applications accepted. *Financial support:* Career-related internships or fieldwork and unspecified assistantships available. Financial award application deadline: 4/1; financial award applicants required to submit FAFSA. *Faculty research:* Health disparities; correlates of taste acuity, structuring and implementation of competition and competitive activities in physical education; exercise and metabolic risk in people living with HIV/AIDS; biomechanics, motor learning and motor control. *Unit head:* Dr. Ashima K. Kant, Chair, 718-997-4156 Ext. 4475, Fax: 718-997-4163, E-mail: ashima.kant@qc.cuny.edu. *Application contact:* Elizabeth D'Amico-Ramirez, Assistant Director of Graduate Admissions, 718-997-5203, E-mail: elizabeth.damicoramirez@qc.cuny.edu.

Sam Houston State University, College of Health Sciences, Department of Family and Consumer Sciences, Huntsville, TX 77341. Offers dietetics (MS); family and consumer sciences (MS). *Program availability:* Part-time, evening/weekend. *Degree requirements:* For master's, comprehensive exam, thesis optional, internship. *Entrance requirements:* For master's, GRE General Test, letters of recommendation, personal statement, writing sample. Additional exam requirements/recommendations for international students: Required—TOEFL (minimum score 550 paper-based; 79 iBT), IELTS (minimum score 6.5). Electronic applications accepted.

San Francisco State University, Division of Graduate Studies, College of Health and Social Sciences, Department of Family Interiors Nutrition and Apparel, San Francisco, CA 94132-1722. Offers family and consumer sciences (MA). *Program availability:* Part-time. *Application deadline:* Applications are processed on a rolling basis. *Unit head:* Dr. Connie Ulasewicz, Chair, 415-338-2060, Fax: 415-338-0947, E-mail: cbu@sfsu.edu. *Application contact:* Kelly Vuong, Academic Office Coordinator, 415-338-1219, Fax: 415-338-0947, E-mail: kvuong@sfsu.edu.
Website: http://fina.sfsu.edu/

South Carolina State University, College of Graduate and Professional Studies, Department of Family and Consumer Sciences, Orangeburg, SC 29117-0001. Offers individual and family development (MS); nutritional sciences (MS). *Program availability:* Part-time, evening/weekend. *Faculty:* 4 full-time (3 women), 4 part-time/adjunct (all women). *Students:* 11 full-time (8 women), 6 part-time (4 women); all minorities (all Black or African American, non-Hispanic/Latino). Average age 35. 14 applicants, 93% accepted, 9 enrolled. In 2017, 2 master's awarded. *Degree requirements:* For master's, comprehensive exam, thesis optional, departmental qualifying exam. *Entrance requirements:* For master's, GRE, MAT, or NTE, minimum GPA of 2.7. *Application deadline:* For fall admission, 6/15 priority date for domestic students, 6/15 for international students; for spring admission, 11/1 for domestic and international students. Application fee: $25. Electronic applications accepted. *Expenses:* Tuition, state resident: full-time $9388; part-time $607 per credit hour. Tuition, nonresident: full-time $19,968; part-time $1194 per credit hour. *Required fees:* $766; $766 per credit hour. *Financial support:* Fellowships, Federal Work-Study, and scholarships/grants

available. Financial award application deadline: 6/1. *Unit head:* Dr. William H. Whitaker, Chair, Department of Family and Consumer Sciences, 803-536-8958, Fax: 803-533-3268, E-mail: wwhitak3@scsu.edu. *Application contact:* Curtis Foskey, Coordinator of Graduate Admission, 803-536-8419, Fax: 803-536-8812, E-mail: cfoskey@scsu.edu.

South Dakota State University, Graduate School, College of Education and Human Sciences, Department of Consumer Sciences, Brookings, SD 57007. Offers family financial planning (MS); merchandising (MS). *Entrance requirements:* For master's, resume. Additional exam requirements/recommendations for international students: Required—TOEFL (minimum score 525 paper-based).

Stephen F. Austin State University, Graduate School, College of Education, Department of Human Sciences, Nacogdoches, TX 75962. Offers MS. *Degree requirements:* For master's, comprehensive exam, thesis or alternative. *Entrance requirements:* For master's, GRE General Test. Additional exam requirements/recommendations for international students: Required—TOEFL. *Faculty research:* Consumer economics, nutrition education, clothing and textiles, family, interior design.

Tennessee State University, The School of Graduate Studies and Research, College of Agriculture, Human and Natural Sciences, Nashville, TN 37209-1561. Offers agricultural sciences (MS), including agribusiness, agricultural and extension education, animal science, plant and soil science; biological sciences (MS, PhD); biotechnology (PhD); chemistry (MS). *Program availability:* Part-time, evening/weekend. *Degree requirements:* For master's, thesis. *Entrance requirements:* For master's, GRE General Test, GRE Subject Test, MAT. *Faculty research:* Small farm economics, ornamental horticulture, beef cattle production, rural elderly.

Texas A&M University–Kingsville, College of Graduate Studies, Dick and Mary Lewis Kleberg College of Agriculture, Natural Resources and Human Sciences, Department of Human Sciences, Kingsville, TX 78363. Offers MS. *Degree requirements:* For master's, variable foreign language requirement, comprehensive exam, thesis (for some programs). *Entrance requirements:* For master's, GRE, MAT, GMAT. Additional exam requirements/recommendations for international students: Required—TOEFL (minimum score 550 paper-based; 79 iBT). Electronic applications accepted. *Faculty research:* Mexican-American families, abuse in families, nontraditional students.

Texas Southern University, College of Liberal Arts and Behavioral Sciences, Department of Human Services and Consumer Sciences, Houston, TX 77004-4584. Offers MS. *Program availability:* Part-time, evening/weekend. *Degree requirements:* For master's, comprehensive exam, thesis (for some programs). *Entrance requirements:* For master's, GRE General Test, minimum GPA of 2.5. Additional exam requirements/recommendations for international students: Required—TOEFL. Electronic applications accepted. *Faculty research:* Food radiation/food for space travel, adolescent parenting, gerontology/grandparenting.

Texas State University, The Graduate College, College of Applied Arts, Program in Merchandising and Consumer Studies, San Marcos, TX 78666. Offers MS. *Program availability:* Part-time. *Faculty:* 5 full-time (4 women), 1 (woman) part-time/adjunct. *Students:* 5 full-time (all women), 2 part-time (both women); includes 4 minority (1 Black or African American, non-Hispanic/Latino; 2 Hispanic/Latino; 1 Two or more races, non-Hispanic/Latino), 1 international. Average age 27. 7 applicants, 71% accepted, 2 enrolled. In 2017, 3 master's awarded. *Degree requirements:* For master's, comprehensive exam, thesis optional. *Entrance requirements:* For master's, GRE General Test (preferred minimum score of 300 verbal and quantitative sections combined) or GMAT (preferred minimum score of 500), baccalaureate degree from regionally-accredited institution with minimum GPA of 3.0 on last 60 hours of undergraduate coursework; two letters of recommendation; statement of purpose describing professional goals and rationale for pursuing graduate study; resume. Additional exam requirements/recommendations for international students: Required—TOEFL (minimum score 550 paper-based; 78 iBT), IELTS (minimum score 6.5). *Application deadline:* For fall admission, 6/15 for domestic students, 6/1 for international students; for spring admission, 10/15 for domestic students, 10/1 for international students; for summer admission, 4/15 for domestic students, 3/15 for international students. Applications are processed on a rolling basis. Application fee: $40 ($90 for international students). Electronic applications accepted. *Expenses:* Tuition, state resident: full-time $7868; part-time $3934 per semester. Tuition, nonresident: full-time $17,828; part-time $8914 per semester. *Required fees:* $2092; $1435 per semester. Tuition and fees vary according to course load. *Financial support:* In 2017–18, 4 students received support, including 3 research assistantships (averaging $10,031 per year), 2 teaching assistantships (averaging $12,308 per year); scholarships/grants and unspecified assistantships also available. Financial award application deadline: 3/1; financial award applicants required to submit FAFSA. *Faculty research:* Branding of destination marketing organizations; small business orientation theory development; climate change and STEM education in apparel and textile curriculums; sustainable household behavior and the drought; marketing of wool-based compost; animal welfare and fiber production; wool and pediatric sleep enhancement; mislabeling of rayon;. *Unit head:* Dr. Gwendolyn Hustvedt, Graduate Advisor, 512-245-4689, E-mail: gh21@txstate.edu. *Application contact:* Dr. Andrea Golato, Dean of the Graduate College, 512-245-2581, Fax: 512-245-8365, E-mail: gradcollege@txstate.edu.
Website: http://www.fcs.txstate.edu/graduate_programs/ms_fm.html

Tufts University, Graduate School of Arts and Sciences, Eliot-Pearson Department of Child Study and Human Development, Medford, MA 02155. Offers child study and human development (MA, PhD). *Program availability:* Part-time. *Students:* 78 full-time (66 women), 1 (woman) part-time; includes 19 minority (4 Black or African American, non-Hispanic/Latino; 8 Asian, non-Hispanic/Latino; 5 Hispanic/Latino; 2 Two or more races, non-Hispanic/Latino), 17 international. Average age 27. 129 applicants, 59% accepted, 37 enrolled. In 2017, 26 master's, 7 doctorates awarded. *Degree requirements:* For master's, thesis (for some programs); for doctorate, comprehensive exam, thesis/dissertation. *Entrance requirements:* For master's and doctorate, GRE General Test. Additional exam requirements/recommendations for international students: Required—TOEFL (minimum score 550 paper-based; 80 iBT), IELTS (minimum score 6.5). *Application deadline:* For fall admission, 12/1 priority date for domestic and international students. Applications are processed on a rolling basis. Application fee: $85. Electronic applications accepted. *Expenses:* Contact institution. *Financial support:* Fellowships, research assistantships, teaching assistantships, Federal Work-Study, scholarships/grants, tuition waivers (full and partial), and unspecified assistantships available. Support available to part-time students. Financial award application deadline: 1/15. *Unit head:* Dr. David Henry Feldman, Graduate Program Director, 617-627-3355. *Application contact:* Office of Graduate Admissions, 617-627-3395, E-mail: gradadmissions@tufts.edu.
Website: http://ase.tufts.edu/epcd

The University of Alabama, Graduate School, College of Human Environmental Sciences, Tuscaloosa, AL 35487. Offers MA, MS, MSHES, PhD. *Program availability:* Part-time, evening/weekend, online learning. *Faculty:* 57 full-time (40 women), 8 part-time/adjunct (6 women). *Students:* 209 full-time (139 women), 425 part-time (308 women); includes 147 minority (95 Black or African American, non-Hispanic/Latino; 3 American Indian or Alaska Native, non-Hispanic/Latino; 7 Asian, non-Hispanic/Latino; 21 Hispanic/Latino; 4 Native Hawaiian or other Pacific Islander, non-Hispanic/Latino; 17 Two or more races, non-Hispanic/Latino), 2 international. Average age 33. 147 applicants, 82% accepted, 112 enrolled. In 2017, 275 master's, 8 doctorates awarded. *Degree requirements:* For doctorate, thesis/dissertation. *Entrance requirements:* For master's, GRE General Test or MAT (minimum score: 50th percentile), minimum GPA of 3.0; for doctorate, GRE General Test or MAT, minimum GPA of 3.0. *Application deadline:* For fall admission, 7/6 for domestic students. Applications are processed on a rolling basis. Application fee: $50 ($60 for international students). Electronic applications accepted. *Financial support:* In 2017–18, 44 students received support, including research assistantships with full tuition reimbursements available (averaging $9,000 per year); fellowships with tuition reimbursements available, teaching assistantships with full tuition reimbursements available, career-related internships or fieldwork, Federal Work-Study, institutionally sponsored loans, and scholarships/grants also available. *Faculty research:* Students' use of credit, determinants of income differential: comparing Asians with blacks and whites, expenditure patterns of Chinese, racial and ethnic differences in the likelihood of charitable contributions, health insurance coverage and precautionary behavior savings. *Total annual research expenditures:* $168,243. *Unit head:* Dr. Milla D. Boschung, Dean, 205-348-6250, Fax: 205-348-1786, E-mail: mboschun@ches.ua.edu. *Application contact:* Patrick D. Fuller, Admissions Officer, 205-348-5923, Fax: 205-348-0400, E-mail: patrick.d.fuller@ua.edu.
Website: http://www.ches.ua.edu/

University of Alberta, Faculty of Graduate Studies and Research, Department of Human Ecology, Edmonton, AB T6G 2E1, Canada. Offers family ecology and practice (M Sc, PhD); textiles and clothing (M Sc, MA, PhD). *Program availability:* Online learning. *Degree requirements:* For master's, thesis (for some programs); for doctorate, comprehensive exam, thesis/dissertation. *Entrance requirements:* For master's and doctorate, minimum GPA of 7.0 on a 9.0 scale. Additional exam requirements/recommendations for international students: Required—TOEFL (minimum score 580 paper-based). *Faculty research:* Families and aging, family and child poverty, paid and unpaid work of families, textiles and clothing, parent-child relationships.

The University of Arizona, College of Agriculture and Life Sciences, School of Family and Consumer Sciences, Tucson, AZ 85721. Offers PhD. *Program availability:* Part-time. *Entrance requirements:* For doctorate, GRE General Test, minimum GPA of 3.0. Additional exam requirements/recommendations for international students: Required—TOEFL (minimum score 550 paper-based; 79 iBT). Electronic applications accepted. *Faculty research:* Interpersonal relationships, human development, retailing management, consumer behaviors.

University of Arkansas, Graduate School, Dale Bumpers College of Agricultural, Food and Life Sciences, School of Human Environmental Sciences, Fayetteville, AR 72701. Offers MS. *Program availability:* Part-time, online learning. In 2017, 8 master's awarded. *Degree requirements:* For master's, comprehensive exam, thesis (for some programs). *Application deadline:* For fall admission, 8/1 for domestic students, 4/1 for international students; for spring admission, 12/1 for domestic students, 10/1 for international students; for summer admission, 4/15 for domestic students, 3/1 for international students. Application fee: $60. Electronic applications accepted. *Expenses:* Tuition, state resident: full-time $3782. Tuition, nonresident: full-time $10,238. *Financial support:* In 2017–18, 14 research assistantships were awarded; fellowships, teaching assistantships, and Federal Work-Study also available. Support available to part-time students. Financial award application deadline: 4/1; financial award applicants required to submit FAFSA. *Unit head:* Dr. Betsy Garrison, Director, 479-575-4305, E-mail: megarris@uark.edu.
Website: https://human-environmental-sciences.uark.edu/index.php

University of Central Arkansas, Graduate School, College of Health and Behavioral Sciences, Department of Family and Consumer Sciences, Conway, AR 72035-0001. Offers MS. *Program availability:* Part-time, evening/weekend, online learning. *Degree requirements:* For master's, comprehensive exam, thesis optional. *Entrance requirements:* For master's, GRE General Test, minimum GPA of 2.7. Additional exam requirements/recommendations for international students: Required—TOEFL (minimum score 550 paper-based). Electronic applications accepted. *Expenses:* Contact institution. *Faculty research:* Neurology, developmental disabilities, diet consequences.

University of Central Oklahoma, The Jackson College of Graduate Studies, College of Education and Professional Studies, Department of Human Environmental Sciences, Edmond, OK 73034-5209. Offers family and child studies (MS), including family life education, infant/child specialist, marriage and family therapy; nutrition-food science (MS). *Program availability:* Part-time. *Faculty:* 5 full-time (4 women), 8 part-time/adjunct (6 women). *Students:* 46 full-time (38 women), 65 part-time (62 women); includes 48 minority (27 Black or African American, non-Hispanic/Latino; 3 American Indian or Alaska Native, non-Hispanic/Latino; 3 Asian, non-Hispanic/Latino; 7 Hispanic/Latino; 8 Two or more races, non-Hispanic/Latino), 13 international. Average age 29. 68 applicants, 93% accepted, 31 enrolled. In 2017, 37 master's awarded. *Degree requirements:* For master's, comprehensive exam (for some programs), thesis (for some programs). *Entrance requirements:* For master's, GRE, essay, physical, CPR and First Aid training. Additional exam requirements/recommendations for international students: Required—TOEFL (minimum score 550 paper-based; 79 iBT), IELTS (minimum score 6.5). *Application deadline:* For fall admission, 1/15 for domestic students, 7/15 for international students; for spring admission, 11/15 for international students. Applications are processed on a rolling basis. Application fee: $60. Electronic applications accepted. *Expenses:* Tuition, state resident: full-time $5375; part-time $268.75 per credit hour. Tuition, nonresident: full-time $13,295; part-time $664.75 per credit hour. *Required fees:* $626; $31.30 per credit hour. One-time fee: $50. Tuition and fees vary according to program. *Financial support:* In 2017–18, 11 students received support, including 8 research assistantships with partial tuition reimbursements available (averaging $4,436 per year); teaching assistantships, career-related internships or fieldwork, scholarships/grants, tuition waivers (partial), and unspecified assistantships also available. Financial award application deadline: 3/31; financial award applicants required to submit FAFSA. *Unit head:* Dr. Kaye Sears, Chair, 405-974-5551, Fax: 405-974-3850. *Application contact:* Carlie Wellington, Assistant Director, CEPS Graduate Enrollment, 405-974-5105, Fax: 405-974-3851, E-mail: gradcoll@uco.edu.
Website: http://sites.uco.edu/ceps/dept/Professional-Studies-Programs/hes/index.asp

University of Florida, Graduate School, College of Agricultural and Life Sciences, Department of Family, Youth, and Community Sciences, Gainesville, FL 32611. Offers community studies (MS); family and youth development (MS); family, youth and community sciences (MS); nonprofit organization development (MS). *Program availability:* Part-time, online learning. *Degree requirements:* For master's, comprehensive exam (for some programs), thesis (for some programs). *Entrance requirements:* For master's, GRE General Test, minimum GPA of 3.0. Additional exam requirements/recommendations for international students: Required—TOEFL (minimum score 550 paper-based; 80 iBT), IELTS (minimum score 6). Electronic applications accepted. *Faculty research:* Adolescent risk behaviors, family risk and resilience, family financial management, community-based organizations/interventions, nutrition and wellness.

University of Georgia, College of Family and Consumer Sciences, Athens, GA 30602. Offers MS, PhD. *Degree requirements:* For doctorate, thesis/dissertation. *Entrance*

requirements: For master's and doctorate, GRE General Test. Electronic applications accepted.

University of Houston, College of Technology, Department of Human Development and Consumer Science, Houston, TX 77204. Offers future studies in commerce (MS); human resources development (MS). *Program availability:* Part-time. *Degree requirements:* For master's, project or thesis. *Entrance requirements:* For master's, GMAT, MAT. Additional exam requirements/recommendations for international students: Required—TOEFL (minimum score 550 paper-based; 79 iBT). Electronic applications accepted.

University of Maryland, College Park, Academic Affairs, School of Public Health, Department of Family Science, College Park, MD 20742. Offers family studies (PhD); marriage and family therapy (MS); maternal and child health (PhD). *Accreditation:* AAMFT/COAMFTE. *Program availability:* Part-time, evening/weekend. *Degree requirements:* For master's, thesis or alternative; for doctorate, comprehensive exam, thesis/dissertation, oral defense. *Entrance requirements:* For master's, GRE General Test, minimum GPA of 3.0, 3 letters of recommendation; for doctorate, GRE General Test, minimum GPA of 3.0, 3 letters of recommendation, research sample. Electronic applications accepted. *Faculty research:* Family life quality, interracial couples, child support, homeless families, family and child well-being.

University of Missouri, Office of Research and Graduate Studies, College of Human Environmental Sciences, Columbia, MO 65211. Offers MA, MS, PhD, Certificate, Graduate Certificate. *Program availability:* Part-time. *Degree requirements:* For doctorate, thesis/dissertation. *Entrance requirements:* For master's and doctorate, GRE General Test, minimum GPA of 3.0. Additional exam requirements/recommendations for international students: Required—TOEFL (minimum score 550 paper-based; 80 iBT), IELTS (minimum score 6.5).

University of Nebraska–Lincoln, Graduate College, College of Education and Human Sciences, Department of Child, Youth and Family Studies, Lincoln, NE 68588. Offers child development/early childhood education (MS, PhD); child, youth and family studies (MS); family and consumer sciences education (MS, PhD); family financial planning (MS); family science (MS, PhD); gerontology (PhD); human sciences (PhD), including child, youth and family studies, gerontology, medical family therapy; marriage and family therapy (MS); medical family therapy (PhD); youth development (MS). *Accreditation:* AAMFT/COAMFTE (one or more programs are accredited). *Program availability:* Online learning. *Degree requirements:* For master's, thesis optional. *Entrance requirements:* For master's, GRE. Additional exam requirements/recommendations for international students: Required—TOEFL (minimum score 550 paper-based). Electronic applications accepted. *Faculty research:* Marriage and family therapy, child development/early childhood education, family financial management.

University of Puerto Rico–Río Piedras, College of Education, Program in Family Ecology and Nutrition, San Juan, PR 00931-3300. Offers M Ed. *Program availability:* Part-time. *Degree requirements:* For master's, thesis. *Entrance requirements:* For master's, PAEG or GRE, minimum GPA of 3.0, letter of recommendation.

University of South Africa, College of Agriculture and Environmental Sciences, Pretoria, South Africa. Offers agriculture (MS); consumer science (MCS); environmental management (MA, MS, PhD); environmental science (MA, MS, PhD); geography (MA, MS, PhD); horticulture (M Tech); human ecology (MHE); life sciences (MS); nature conservation (M Tech).

The University of Tennessee, Graduate School, College of Education, Health and Human Sciences, Program in Human Ecology, Knoxville, TN 37996. Offers child and family studies (PhD); community health (PhD); nutrition science (PhD); retailing and consumer sciences (PhD); textile science (PhD). *Degree requirements:* For doctorate, thesis/dissertation. *Entrance requirements:* For doctorate, GRE General Test, minimum GPA of 2.7. Additional exam requirements/recommendations for international students: Required—TOEFL. Electronic applications accepted.

The University of Tennessee at Martin, Graduate Programs, College of Agriculture and Applied Sciences, Department of Family and Consumer Sciences, Martin, TN 38238. Offers dietetics (MSFCS); general family and consumer sciences (MSFCS). *Program availability:* Part-time, 100% online. *Faculty:* 9. *Students:* 10 full-time (7 women), 31 part-time (27 women); includes 11 minority (9 Black or African American, non-Hispanic/Latino; 1 Hispanic/Latino; 1 Two or more races, non-Hispanic/Latino). Average age 30. 50 applicants, 86% accepted, 20 enrolled. In 2017, 12 master's

awarded. *Degree requirements:* For master's, comprehensive exam, thesis optional. *Entrance requirements:* For master's, GRE General Test, minimum GPA of 2.5. Additional exam requirements/recommendations for international students: Required—TOEFL (minimum score 525 paper-based; 71 iBT). *Application deadline:* For fall admission, 7/27 priority date for domestic and international students; for spring admission, 12/17 priority date for domestic and international students; for summer admission, 5/10 priority date for domestic and international students. Applications are processed on a rolling basis. Application fee: $30 ($130 for international students). Electronic applications accepted. *Expenses:* Tuition, state resident: full-time $8658; part-time $481 per credit hour. Tuition, nonresident: full-time $14,418; part-time $801 per credit hour. *International tuition:* $22,602 full-time. *Required fees:* $1404; $79 per credit hour. Part-time tuition and fees vary according to course load. *Financial support:* In 2017–18, 20 students received support, including 1 research assistantship with full tuition reimbursement available (averaging $7,540 per year), 7 teaching assistantships with full tuition reimbursements available (averaging $7,432 per year); scholarships/grants and tuition waivers (full and partial) also available. Financial award application deadline: 2/1; financial award applicants required to submit FAFSA. *Faculty research:* Children with developmental disabilities, regional food product development and marketing, parent education. *Unit head:* Dr. Lisa LeBleu, Coordinator, 731-881-7116, Fax: 731-881-7106, E-mail: llebleu@utm.edu. *Application contact:* Jolene L. Cunningham, Student Services Specialist, 731-881-7012, Fax: 731-881-7499, E-mail: jcunningham@utm.edu.
Website: http://www.utm.edu/departments/caas/fcs/index.php

The University of Texas at Austin, Graduate School, College of Natural Sciences, School of Human Ecology, Austin, TX 78712-1111. Offers human development and family sciences (MA, PhD); nutritional sciences (MA, MS, PhD), including nutrition (MA); nutritional sciences (PhD); textile and apparel technology (MS). *Degree requirements:* For master's, thesis; for doctorate, thesis/dissertation. *Entrance requirements:* For master's and doctorate, GRE General Test. Electronic applications accepted.

University of Wisconsin–Madison, Graduate School, School of Human Ecology, Madison, WI 53706. Offers consumer behavior and family economics (MS, PhD); design studies (MFA, MS, PhD); human development and family studies (MS, PhD). Terminal master's awarded for partial completion of doctoral program. *Degree requirements:* For master's, thesis (for some programs); for doctorate, comprehensive exam, thesis/dissertation. *Entrance requirements:* For master's, GRE General Test, portfolio (design studies), 3 letters of recommendation; for doctorate, GRE General Test. Additional exam requirements/recommendations for international students: Required—TOEFL (minimum score 580 paper-based; 92 iBT). Electronic applications accepted.

University of Wisconsin–Stevens Point, College of Professional Studies, School of Health Promotion and Human Development, Program in Human and Community Resources, Stevens Point, WI 54481-3897. Offers MS. *Program availability:* Part-time. *Degree requirements:* For master's, thesis or alternative. *Entrance requirements:* For master's, minimum GPA of 2.75.

Utah State University, School of Graduate Studies, Emma Eccles Jones College of Education and Human Services, Department of Family, Consumer, and Human Development, Logan, UT 84322. Offers family and human development (MFHD); family, consumer, and human development (MS, PhD), including adolescence/youth (MS); adult development/aging (MS); consumer science (MS); infancy/childhood (MS); marriage and family relations (MS), marriage and family therapy (MS). *Accreditation:* AAMFT/COAMFTE (one or more programs are accredited). *Program availability:* Part-time, evening/weekend, online learning. *Degree requirements:* For master's, thesis; for doctorate, comprehensive exam, thesis/dissertation, competencies. *Entrance requirements:* For master's, GRE General Test or MAT, minimum GPA of 3.0, 3 letters of recommendation; for doctorate, GRE, minimum GPA of 3.0, 3 letters of recommendation. Additional exam requirements/recommendations for international students: Required—TOEFL. Electronic applications accepted. *Faculty research:* Marriage and family relations, adolescent problem behavior, family financial management, early literacy, mental health in the elderly, parent child attachment.

Western Michigan University, Graduate College, College of Education and Human Development, Department of Family and Consumer Sciences, Kalamazoo, MI 49008. Offers career and technical education (MA); family and consumer sciences (MA).

Child and Family Studies

Alabama Agricultural and Mechanical University, School of Graduate Studies, College of Agricultural, Life and Natural Sciences, Department of Family and Consumer Sciences, Huntsville, AL 35811. Offers apparel, merchandising and design (MS); family and consumer sciences (MS); human development and family studies (MS); nutrition and hospitality management (MS). *Program availability:* Part-time, evening/weekend. *Degree requirements:* For master's, comprehensive exam, thesis optional. *Entrance requirements:* For master's, GRE General Test. Additional exam requirements/recommendations for international students: Required—TOEFL (minimum score 500 paper-based; 61 iBT). Electronic applications accepted. *Faculty research:* Food biotechnology, nutrition, food microbiology, food engineering, food chemistry.

Amberton University, Graduate School, Program in Family Studies, Garland, TX 75041-5595. Offers family studies (MS), including Christian counseling. Application fee: $0. *Expenses: Tuition:* Part-time $795 per course. *Unit head:* Academic Dean, 972-279-6511 Ext. 153, Fax: 972-279-9773. *Application contact:* Adviser, 972-279-6511 Ext. 180, Fax: 972-279-9773, E-mail: advisor@amberton.edu.
Website: http://www.amberton.edu/programs-and-courses/masters-degree-programs/family-studies/index.html

Arizona State University at the Tempe campus, College of Liberal Arts and Sciences, School of Social and Family Dynamics, Tempe, AZ 85287-3701. Offers family and human development (MS, PhD); infant-family practice (MAS); marriage and family therapy (MAS); sociology (MA, PhD). Terminal master's awarded for partial completion of doctoral program. *Degree requirements:* For master's, thesis or alternative, interactive Program of Study (iPOS) submitted before completing 50 percent of required credit hours; for doctorate, thesis/dissertation, interactive Program of Study (iPOS) submitted before completing 50 percent of required credit hours. *Entrance requirements:* For master's and doctorate, GRE, minimum GPA of 3.0 or equivalent in last 2 years of work leading to bachelor's degree. Additional exam requirements/recommendations for international students: Required—TOEFL, IELTS, or PTE. Electronic applications accepted. *Expenses:* Contact institution.

Asbury University, School of Graduate and Professional Studies, Master of Social Work Program, Wilmore, KY 40390-1198. Offers child and family services (MSW). *Accreditation:* CSWE. *Degree requirements:* For master's, comprehensive exam, 954 praticum hours completed in agency. *Entrance requirements:* For master's, prerequisite courses in psychology, sociology, and statistics. Additional exam requirements/recommendations for international students: Required—TOEFL. Electronic applications accepted. *Expenses:* Contact institution. *Faculty research:* Integration of faith and practice, survivors of family violence, program evaluation, cross-cultural counseling.

Assumption College, Clinical Counseling Psychology Program, Worcester, MA 01609-1296. Offers child and family interventions (MA); clinical counseling psychology (CAGS); cognitive-behavioral therapies (MA). *Program availability:* Part-time, evening/weekend. *Faculty:* 4 full-time (2 women), 7 part-time/adjunct (2 women). *Students:* 47 full-time (34 women), 19 part-time (all women); includes 9 minority (3 Black or African American, non-Hispanic/Latino; 2 Asian, non-Hispanic/Latino; 3 Hispanic/Latino; 1 Two or more races, non-Hispanic/Latino), 1 international. Average age 27. 59 applicants, 80% accepted, 19 enrolled. In 2017, 20 master's awarded. *Degree requirements:* For master's, comprehensive exam, internship, practicum; for CAGS, comprehensive exam. *Entrance requirements:* For master's, bachelor's degree and at least six psychology courses completed with minimum GPA of 3.0 both overall and in the psychology courses; three letters of recommendation; official transcripts; personal statement; current resume; for CAGS, master's degree in clinical counseling psychology or mental health counseling, or baccalaureate degree and at least six psychology courses with minimum GPA of 3.0 overall and in psychology courses; three letters of recommendation; official transcripts; personal statement; current resume; interview. Additional exam requirements/recommendations for international students: Required—TOEFL (minimum score 540 paper-based; 76 iBT), IELTS (minimum score 6). *Application deadline:* For fall admission, 3/1 priority date for domestic and international students; for spring admission, 10/5 for domestic and international students; for summer admission, 2/8 for domestic and international students. Application fee: $30. Electronic applications accepted. *Expenses: Tuition:* Full-time $11,952; part-time $664 per credit.

Required fees: $70 per term. *Financial support:* In 2017–18, 18 students received support, including 10 fellowships with full tuition reimbursements available; tuition waivers (full and partial), unspecified assistantships, and institutional discounts also available. Financial award application deadline: 3/1; financial award applicants required to submit FAFSA. *Faculty research:* Mood disorders, adjustment to life-threatening illness, perception of movement, socioemotional development of young children, discovery versus disclosure. *Unit head:* Dr. Leonard A. Doerfler, Director, 508-767-7549, Fax: 508-767-7263, E-mail: doerfler@assumption.edu. *Application contact:* Karen Stoyanoff, Director of Recruitment for Graduate Enrollment, 508-767-7442, Fax: 508-799-4412, E-mail: graduate@assumption.edu.
Website: http://graduate.assumption.edu/counseling-psychology/ma-clinical-counseling-psychology-overview

Auburn University, Graduate School, College of Human Sciences, Department of Human Development and Family Studies, Auburn University, AL 36849. Offers MS, PhD. *Accreditation:* AAMFT/COAMFTE (one or more programs are accredited). *Program availability:* Part-time. *Faculty:* 24 full-time (16 women). *Students:* 21 full-time (all women), 16 part-time (12 women); includes 12 minority (6 Black or African American, non-Hispanic/Latino; 1 Asian, non-Hispanic/Latino; 3 Hispanic/Latino; 1 Native Hawaiian or other Pacific Islander, non-Hispanic/Latino; 1 Two or more races, non-Hispanic/Latino). Average age 27. 50 applicants, 22% accepted, 11 enrolled. In 2017, 8 master's, 4 doctorates awarded. *Degree requirements:* For master's, thesis, oral exam; for doctorate, thesis/dissertation. *Entrance requirements:* For master's, GRE General Test; for doctorate, GRE General Test, master's degree. *Application deadline:* Applications are processed on a rolling basis. Application fee: $50 ($60 for international students). *Expenses:* Tuition, state resident: full-time $10,974; part-time $519 per credit hour. Tuition, nonresident: full-time $29,658; part-time $1557 per credit hour. *Required fees:* $816 per semester. Tuition and fees vary according to degree level and program. *Financial support:* Research assistantships, teaching assistantships, and Federal Work-Study available. Support available to part-time students. Financial award application deadline: 3/15; financial award applicants required to submit FAFSA. *Faculty research:* Family influences on personality and social development, parent-child relations, infancy, day care, parent education. *Unit head:* Dr. Joe F. Pittman, Jr., Head, 334-844-3242, E-mail: mbradbar@humsci.auburn.edu. *Application contact:* Dr. George Flowers, Dean of the Graduate School, 334-844-2125.
Website: http://www.humsci.auburn.edu/hdfs/

Bank Street College of Education, Graduate School, Program in Child Life, New York, NY 10025. Offers MS. *Degree requirements:* For master's, thesis. *Entrance requirements:* For master's, interview, essays, 100 hours of volunteer experience in a child life setting. Additional exam requirements/recommendations for international students: Required—TOEFL (minimum score 600 paper-based; 100 iBT), IELTS (minimum score 7). *Faculty research:* Therapeutic play in child life setting, child advocacy, psychosocial and educational intervention with care of sick children.

Bank Street College of Education, Graduate School, Program in Infant and Family Development and Early Intervention, New York, NY 10025. Offers infant and family development (MS Ed); infant and family early childhood special and general education (MS Ed); infant and family/early childhood special education (Ed M). *Degree requirements:* For master's, thesis. *Entrance requirements:* For master's, interview, essays. Additional exam requirements/recommendations for international students: Required—TOEFL (minimum score 600 paper-based; 100 iBT), IELTS (minimum score 7). Electronic applications accepted. *Faculty research:* Early intervention, early attachment practice in infant and toddler childcare, parenting skills in adolescents.

Brandeis University, The Heller School for Social Policy and Management, Program in Public Policy, Waltham, MA 02454-9110. Offers aging (MPP); behavioral health (MPP); children, youth and families (MPP); general social policy (MPP); health (MPP); poverty alleviation and development (MPP); MPP/MA. *Degree requirements:* For master's, thesis. *Entrance requirements:* For master's, GRE, 3 letters of recommendation, statement of purpose, 3 to 5 years of professional experience. Additional exam requirements/recommendations for international students: Required—TOEFL (minimum score 600 paper-based; 100 iBT). Electronic applications accepted. *Expenses: Tuition:* Full-time $48,720. *Required fees:* $88. Tuition and fees vary according to course load, degree level, program and student level. *Faculty research:* Health and behavioral health, children and families, disabilities, aging policy, substance abuse, work, inequality and social change, women/gender, poverty alleviation.

Brandeis University, The Heller School for Social Policy and Management, Program in Social Policy, Waltham, MA 02454-9110. Offers assets and inequalities (PhD); children, youth and families (PhD); global health and development (PhD); health and behavioral health (PhD). *Degree requirements:* For doctorate, comprehensive exam, thesis/dissertation, qualifying paper, 2-year residency. *Entrance requirements:* For doctorate, GRE General Test, 3 letters of recommendation, statement of purpose, writing sample, at least 3-5 years of professional experience. Additional exam requirements/recommendations for international students: Required—TOEFL (minimum score 600 paper-based; 100 iBT). Electronic applications accepted. *Expenses: Tuition:* Full-time $48,720. *Required fees:* $88. Tuition and fees vary according to course load, degree level, program and student level. *Faculty research:* Health; mental health; substance abuse; children, youth, and families; aging; international and community development; disabilities; work and inequality; hunger and poverty.

Brigham Young University, Graduate Studies, College of Family, Home, and Social Sciences, Program in Marriage, Family and Human Development, Provo, UT 84602. Offers MS, PhD. *Accreditation:* AAMFT/COAMFTE. *Faculty:* 21 full-time (4 women). *Students:* 22 full-time (16 women), 3 international. Average age 26. 26 applicants, 42% accepted, 11 enrolled. In 2017, 10 master's, 1 doctorate awarded. *Degree requirements:* For master's, thesis; for doctorate, comprehensive exam, thesis/dissertation. *Entrance requirements:* For master's and doctorate, GRE General Test, minimum GPA of 3.0 in last 60 semester hours, letters of recommendation. Additional exam requirements/recommendations for international students: Required—TOEFL (minimum score 580 paper-based; 85 iBT), IELTS (minimum score 7). *Application deadline:* For fall admission, 1/10 for domestic and international students. Application fee: $50. Electronic applications accepted. *Expenses:* Contact institution. *Financial support:* In 2017–18, 22 students received support, including 22 research assistantships with full and partial tuition reimbursements available (averaging $8,736 per year), 3 teaching assistantships with tuition reimbursements available (averaging $2,800 per year); scholarships/grants and unspecified assistantships also available. Financial award application deadline: 3/25. *Faculty research:* Family studies and family process, marriage, adolescence and emerging adulthood, adult development and aging, child development. *Unit head:* Dr. Dean M. Busby, Director, School of Life, 801-422-2069, Fax: 801-422-0230, E-mail: dean_busby@byu.edu. *Application contact:* Graduate Secretary, 801-422-2060, E-mail: mfhdgrad@byu.edu.
Website: http://mfhd.byu.edu

Brock University, Faculty of Graduate Studies, Faculty of Social Sciences, Program in Child and Youth Studies, St. Catharines, ON L2S 3A1, Canada. Offers MA. *Program availability:* Part-time. *Degree requirements:* For master's, thesis. *Entrance requirements:* For master's, honors BA. Additional exam requirements/recommendations for international students: Required—TOEFL (minimum score 550 paper-based; 80 iBT), IELTS (minimum score 6.5), TWE (minimum score 4). Electronic applications accepted. *Faculty research:* Cognitive mechanisms, youth resilience, developmental disabilities, parent-child interactions and communication.

California State University, East Bay, Office of Graduate Studies, College of Letters, Arts, and Social Sciences, Department of Social Work, Hayward, CA 94542-3000. Offers children, youth, and family services (MSW); community mental health services (MSW). *Accreditation:* CSWE. *Faculty:* 8 full-time (7 women), 10 part-time/adjunct (9 women). *Students:* 137 full-time (108 women), 1 (woman) part-time; includes 118 minority (34 Black or African American, non-Hispanic/Latino; 19 Asian, non-Hispanic/Latino; 58 Hispanic/Latino; 1 Native Hawaiian or other Pacific Islander, non-Hispanic/Latino; 6 Two or more races, non-Hispanic/Latino), 5 international. Average age 32. 334 applicants, 26% accepted, 71 enrolled. In 2017, 90 master's awarded. *Degree requirements:* For master's, comprehensive exam. *Entrance requirements:* For master's, minimum GPA of 2.8; courses in statistics and either human biology, physiology, or anatomy; liberal arts or social science baccalaureate degree; 3 letters of recommendation; personal statement; criminal background check; student professional liability insurance. Additional exam requirements/recommendations for international students: Required—TOEFL (minimum score 550 paper-based). *Application deadline:* For fall admission, 12/1 for domestic and international students. Applications are processed on a rolling basis. Application fee: $55. Electronic applications accepted. *Financial support:* Fellowships, career-related internships or fieldwork, Federal Work-Study, institutionally sponsored loans, and scholarships/grants available. Support available to part-time students. Financial award application deadline: 3/2; financial award applicants required to submit FAFSA. *Unit head:* Dr. Holly Vugia, Interim Chair, 510-885-2121, E-mail: holly.vugia@csueastbay.edu. *Application contact:* Philip Cole-Regis, Administrative Support Coordinator, 510-885-3286, E-mail: philip.coleregis@csueastbay.edu.
Website: http://www20.csueastbay.edu/class/departments/socialwork/

California State University, Los Angeles, Graduate Studies, College of Health and Human Services, Department of Child and Family Studies, Los Angeles, CA 90032-8530. Offers child development (MA). *Program availability:* Part-time, evening/weekend. *Degree requirements:* For master's, comprehensive exam, project or thesis. *Entrance requirements:* Additional exam requirements/recommendations for international students: Required—TOEFL (minimum score 500 paper-based). *Faculty research:* Nutrition education, laundry product and fabric durability, computer usage in public school home economics.

California State University, San Marcos, College of Education, Health and Human Services, Department of Social Work, San Marcos, CA 92096-0001. Offers behavioral health (MSW); children, youth and families (MSW). *Accreditation:* CSWE. *Degree requirements:* For master's, thesis, capstone project. *Expenses:* Contact institution. *Unit head:* Dr. Blake Beecher, Chair, 760-750-7373.
Website: http://www.csusm.edu/socialwork/

Capella University, Harold Abel School of Social and Behavioral Science, Master's Programs in Counseling, Minneapolis, MN 55402. Offers child and adolescent development (MS); general addiction counseling (MS); general marriage and family counseling/therapy (MS); general mental health counseling (MS); general school counseling (MS).

Central Michigan University, College of Graduate Studies, College of Education and Human Services, Department of Human Environmental Studies, Mount Pleasant, MI 48859. Offers apparel product development and merchandising technology (MS); gerontology (Graduate Certificate); human development and family studies (MA); nutrition and dietetics (MS). *Program availability:* Part-time, evening/weekend. *Degree requirements:* For master's, thesis or alternative. Electronic applications accepted. *Faculty research:* Human growth and development, family studies and human sexuality, human nutrition and dietetics, apparel and textile retailing, computer-aided design for apparel.

Central Washington University, School of Graduate Studies and Research, College of Education and Professional Studies, Department of Family and Consumer Sciences, Ellensburg, WA 98926. Offers career and technical education (MS); family and child life (MS); family and consumer sciences education (MS). *Program availability:* Part-time. *Entrance requirements:* For master's, minimum GPA of 3.0. Additional exam requirements/recommendations for international students: Required—TOEFL (minimum score 550 paper-based; 79 iBT). *Application deadline:* For fall admission, 2/1 priority date for domestic students; for winter admission, 10/1 for domestic students; for spring admission, 1/1 for domestic students. Applications are processed on a rolling basis. Application fee: $50. Electronic applications accepted. *Financial support:* Application deadline: 3/1; applicants required to submit FAFSA. *Unit head:* Dr. Duane Dowd, Department Chair, 509-963-2740, E-mail: duane.dowd@cwu.edu. *Application contact:* Justine Eason, Admissions Program Coordinator, 509-963-3103, Fax: 509-963-1799, E-mail: masters@cwu.edu.
Website: http://www.cwu.edu/~fandcs/

Colorado State University, College of Health and Human Sciences, Department of Human Development and Family Studies, Fort Collins, CO 80523-1570. Offers applied developmental science (PhD); family and developmental studies (MS); marriage and family therapy (MS). *Accreditation:* AAMFT/COAMFTE. *Faculty:* 18 full-time (15 women), 3 part-time/adjunct (1 woman). *Students:* 31 full-time (28 women), 3 part-time (all women); includes 6 minority (2 Asian, non-Hispanic/Latino; 4 Hispanic/Latino), 1 international. Average age 27. 95 applicants, 26% accepted, 14 enrolled. In 2017, 13 master's, 3 doctorates awarded. Terminal master's awarded for partial completion of doctoral program. *Degree requirements:* For master's, thesis; for doctorate, comprehensive exam, thesis/dissertation. *Entrance requirements:* For master's and doctorate, GRE General Test, 3 letters of recommendation; minimum GPA of 3.0; bachelor's degree; curriculum vitae/resume. Additional exam requirements/recommendations for international students: Required—TOEFL (minimum score 550 paper-based; 80 iBT), IELTS (minimum score 6.5), PTE (minimum score 58). *Application deadline:* For fall admission, 1/2 priority date for domestic and international students. Application fee: $60 ($70 for international students). Electronic applications accepted. *Expenses:* Tuition, state resident: full-time $9917. Tuition, nonresident: full-time $24,312. *Required fees:* $2284. Tuition and fees vary according to course load and program. *Financial support:* In 2017–18, 2 fellowships with full and partial tuition reimbursements (averaging $7,128 per year), 10 research assistantships with full and partial tuition reimbursements (averaging $12,830 per year), 17 teaching assistantships with full and partial tuition reimbursements (averaging $9,224 per year) were awarded; Federal Work-Study, scholarships/grants, health care benefits, and unspecified assistantships also available. *Faculty research:* Risk, resilience, and developmental psychopathology; treatment, intervention, and prevention science; emotion, regulation, and relational processes; adult development and aging; cultural context and diversity. *Total annual research expenditures:* $1.7 million. *Unit head:* Dr. Lise Youngblade, Department Head, 970-491-3581, Fax: 970-491-7975, E-mail: lise.youngblade@colostate.edu. *Application contact:* Mary Daughtrey, Administrative Assistant III, 970-491-2872, Fax: 970-491-7975, E-mail: mary.daughtrey@colostate.edu.
Website: http://www.hdfs.chhs.colostate.edu/

Concordia University, School of Graduate Studies, Faculty of Arts and Science, Department of Education, Program in Child Studies, Montréal, QC H3G 1M8, Canada. Offers MA. *Degree requirements:* For master's, one foreign language, thesis optional. *Entrance requirements:* For master's, minimum B average in undergraduate course work. *Faculty research:* Development and family relations, children and technology, cooperative learning strategies, exceptional children, second language acquisition.

Concordia University Wisconsin, Graduate Programs, Department of Education, Program in Family Studies, Mequon, WI 53097-2402. Offers MS Ed. *Degree requirements:* For master's, comprehensive exam, thesis or alternative. *Entrance requirements:* For master's, minimum GPA of 3.0. Additional exam requirements/recommendations for international students: Required—TOEFL.

Cornell University, Graduate School, Graduate Fields of Human Ecology, Field of Human Development, Ithaca, NY 14853. Offers developmental psychology (MA, PhD), including cognitive development, developmental psychopathology, ecology of human development, social and personality development; human development and family studies (MA, PhD), including ecology of human development, family studies and the life course. *Degree requirements:* For doctorate, comprehensive exam, thesis/dissertation, pre-doctoral research project, teaching experience. *Entrance requirements:* For doctorate, GRE General Test, 2 letters of recommendation. Additional exam requirements/recommendations for international students: Required—TOEFL (minimum score 550 paper-based; 77 iBT). Electronic applications accepted. *Faculty research:* Cognitive development, developmental psychopathology, ecology of human development, family studies and the life course, social and personality development.

Dallas Theological Seminary, Graduate Programs, Dallas, TX 75204-6499. Offers adult education (Th M); apologetics (Th M); Bible backgrounds (Th M); Bible translation (Th M); Biblical and theological studies (Certificate); biblical counseling (MA); biblical exegesis and linguistics (MA); biblical exposition (PhD); biblical studies (MA); Biblical theology (Th M); children's education (Th M); Christian education (MA, D Min); Christian leadership (MA); cross-cultural ministries (MA); educational administration (Th M); educational leadership (Th M); evangelism and discipleship (Th M); exposition of Biblical books (Th M); family life education (Th M); general studies (Th M); Hebrew and cognate studies (Th M); hermeneutics (Th M); historical theology (Th M); homiletics (Th M); intercultural ministries (Th M); Jesus studies (Th M); leadership studies (Th M); media and communication (MA); media arts (Th M); ministry (D Min); ministry with women (Th M); New Testament studies (Th M, PhD); Old Testament studies (Th M, PhD); parachurch ministries (Th M); pastoral care and counseling (Th M); pastoral theology and practice (Th M); philosophy (Th M); sacred theology (STM); spiritual formation (Th M); systematic theology (Th M); teaching in Christian institutions (Th M); theological studies (PhD); urban ministries (Th M); worship studies (Th M); youth education (Th M). *Program availability:* Part-time, online learning. *Degree requirements:* For master's, variable foreign language requirement, thesis (for some programs); for doctorate, 2 foreign languages, thesis/dissertation. *Entrance requirements:* For master's, GRE or MAT (if minimum undergraduate cumulative GPA is below 2.5 or undergraduate degree is unaccredited). Additional exam requirements/recommendations for international students: Required—TOEFL (minimum score 575 paper-based; 85 iBT), TWE. Electronic applications accepted.

East Carolina University, Graduate School, College of Health and Human Performance, Department of Human Development and Family Science, Greenville, NC 27858-4353. Offers birth through kindergarten education (MA Ed); human development and family science (MS); marriage and family therapy (MS); medical family therapy (PhD). *Accreditation:* AAMFT/COAMFTE. *Program availability:* Part-time. *Students:* 73 full-time (69 women), 24 part-time (21 women); includes 20 minority (14 Black or African American, non-Hispanic/Latino; 3 American Indian or Alaska Native, non-Hispanic/Latino; 2 Hispanic/Latino; 1 Native Hawaiian or other Pacific Islander, non-Hispanic/Latino; 2 international. Average age 28. 98 applicants, 50% accepted, 35 enrolled. In 2017, 26 master's, 3 doctorates awarded. *Degree requirements:* For master's, comprehensive exam, thesis optional. *Entrance requirements:* Additional exam requirements/recommendations for international students: Recommended—TOEFL (minimum score 78 iBT), IELTS (minimum score 6.5). *Application deadline:* For fall admission, 1/15 for domestic students; for spring admission, 10/15 for domestic students. Applications are processed on a rolling basis. Application fee: $75. *Expenses:* Tuition, state resident: full-time $4749; part-time $297 per credit hour. Tuition, nonresident: full-time $17,898; part-time $1119 per credit hour. *Required fees:* $2691; $224 per credit hour. Part-time tuition and fees vary according to course load and program. *Financial support:* Research assistantships, teaching assistantships, career-related internships or fieldwork, Federal Work-Study, institutionally sponsored loans, and scholarships/grants available. Support available to part-time students. Financial award application deadline: 6/1. *Faculty research:* Child care quality, mental health delivery systems for children, family violence. *Unit head:* Dr. Sharon Ballard, Interim Chair, 252-328-1356, E-mail: ballards@ecu.edu. Website: https://hhp.ecu.edu/hdfs/

Eastern University, Department of Marriage and Family Therapy, St. Davids, PA 19087-3696. Offers marriage and family therapy (PhD); marriage and family therapy studies (DA). *Program availability:* Evening/weekend, online learning. *Students:* 63 full-time (45 women); includes 42 minority (33 Black or African American, non-Hispanic/Latino; 2 Asian, non-Hispanic/Latino; 5 Hispanic/Latino; 2 Two or more races, non-Hispanic/Latino), 1 international. Average age 43. In 2017, 7 doctorates awarded. *Application deadline:* Applications are processed on a rolling basis. Application fee: $75. Electronic applications accepted. Application fee is waived when completed online. *Expenses:* Contact institution. *Unit head:* Michael Dziedziak, Executive Director of Enrollment, 800-452-0996, E-mail: gpsadmissions@eastern.edu. Website: https://www.eastern.edu/academics/programs/department-marriage-and-family-therapy

Fairfield University, Graduate School of Education and Allied Professions, Fairfield, CT 06824. Offers applied behavior analysis (ATC); applied psychology (MA); clinical mental health counseling (MA, CAS); educational technology (MA); elementary education (MA, CAS); family studies (MA); integration of spirituality and religion in counseling (ATC); marriage and family therapy (MA); reading and language development (Sixth Year Certificate); school counseling (MA, CAS); school psychology (MA, CAS); school-based marriage and family therapy (ATC); secondary education (MA); special education (MA, CAS); substance abuse counseling (ATC); teaching (Certificate); teaching and foundations (MA, CAS); TESOL, world languages, and bilingual education (MA, CAS). *Accreditation:* NCATE. *Program availability:* Part-time, evening/weekend. *Faculty:* 23 full-time (17 women), 39 part-time/adjunct (28 women). *Students:* 199 full-time (168 women), 251 part-time (206 women); includes 85 minority (21 Black or African American, non-Hispanic/Latino; 9 Asian, non-Hispanic/Latino; 49 Hispanic/Latino; 6 Two or more races, non-Hispanic/Latino), 4 international. Average age 32. 370 applicants, 56% accepted, 125 enrolled. In 2017, 136 master's, 28 other advanced degrees awarded. *Degree requirements:* For master's, comprehensive exam. *Entrance requirements:* For master's, minimum GPA of 3.0, 2 recommendations, resume. Additional exam requirements/recommendations for international students: Required—TOEFL (minimum score 550 paper-based; 84 iBT) or IELTS (minimum score 7.5). *Application deadline:* For fall admission, 2/15 for international students; for spring

admission, 10/1 for international students. Application fee: $60. Electronic applications accepted. *Expenses:* $750 per credit hour. *Financial support:* In 2017–18, 34 students received support. Career-related internships or fieldwork and unspecified assistantships available. Support available to part-time students. Financial award applicants required to submit FAFSA. *Faculty research:* Reading and literacy, writing, social justice and inequality in education, addictions and mental health issues, therapeutic relationships and clinical supervision. *Unit head:* Dr. Robert D. Hannafin, Dean, 203-254-4250, Fax: 203-254-4241, E-mail: rhannafin@fairfield.edu. *Application contact:* Marianne Gumpper, Director of Graduate Admission, 203-254-4184, Fax: 203-254-4073, E-mail: gradadmis@fairfield.edu. Website: http://www.fairfield.edu/gseap

Florida State University, The Graduate School, College of Human Sciences, Department of Family and Child Sciences, Tallahassee, FL 32306-1491. Offers family and child sciences (MS); human development and family sciences (PhD); marriage and family therapy (PhD). *Accreditation:* AAMFT/COAMFTE. *Program availability:* Part-time. *Faculty:* 14 full-time (8 women). *Students:* 28 full-time (21 women); includes 9 minority (6 Black or African American, non-Hispanic/Latino; 1 Asian, non-Hispanic/Latino; 1 Hispanic/Latino; 1 Two or more races, non-Hispanic/Latino), 2 international. 21 applicants, 33% accepted, 5 enrolled. In 2017, 6 master's, 7 doctorates awarded. Terminal master's awarded for partial completion of doctoral program. *Degree requirements:* For master's, thesis optional; for doctorate, thesis/dissertation, preliminary examination; clinical examination (for marriage and family therapy). *Entrance requirements:* For master's and doctorate, GRE General Test, writing assessment, minimum GPA of 3.0. Additional exam requirements/recommendations for international students: Required—TOEFL (minimum score 550 paper-based; 80 iBT). *Application deadline:* For fall admission, 12/1 for domestic and international students. Applications are processed on a rolling basis. Application fee: $30. Electronic applications accepted. *Expenses:* $480 per credit hour in-state; $1,111 per credit hour out-of-state. *Financial support:* In 2017–18, 33 students received support, including 12 research assistantships with full tuition reimbursements available (averaging $6,062 per year), 32 teaching assistantships with full tuition reimbursements available (averaging $16,142 per year); fellowships with partial tuition reimbursements available, career-related internships or fieldwork, Federal Work-Study, institutionally sponsored loans, scholarships/grants, health care benefits, and unspecified assistantships also available. Financial award application deadline: 1/5; financial award applicants required to submit FAFSA. *Faculty research:* Family therapy, parent-child relations, distressed families and foster care, marital processes, relational interventions, family structural complexity. *Total annual research expenditures:* $1.3 million. *Unit head:* Dr. Joseph Grzywacz, Department Chair, 850-644-3217, Fax: 850-644-3439, E-mail: jgrzywacz@fsu.edu. *Application contact:* Mary-Sue McLemore, Academic Support Assistant, 850-644-1117, E-mail: mmclemore@fsu.edu. Website: https://humansciences.fsu.edu/family-child-sciences/students/graduate-programs/

Iowa State University of Science and Technology, Department of Human Development and Family Studies, Ames, IA 50011. Offers human development and family studies (MFCS, MS, PhD). *Degree requirements:* For master's, thesis; for doctorate, thesis/dissertation. *Entrance requirements:* For master's and doctorate, GRE General Test. Additional exam requirements/recommendations for international students: Required—TOEFL (minimum score 550 paper-based; 79 iBT), IELTS (minimum score 6.5). Electronic applications accepted. *Faculty research:* Child development, early childhood education, family resource management and housing, life span studies.

Kansas State University, Graduate School, College of Human Ecology, Doctorate in Human Ecology Program, Manhattan, KS 66506-1407. Offers apparel and textiles (PhD); applied family sciences (PhD); couple and family therapy (PhD); hospitality administration (PhD); kinesiology (PhD); life-span human development (PhD). *Program availability:* Part-time. *Degree requirements:* For doctorate, thesis/dissertation. *Entrance requirements:* Additional exam requirements/recommendations for international students: Required—TOEFL. Electronic applications accepted.

Kansas State University, Graduate School, College of Human Ecology, School of Family Studies and Human Services, Manhattan, KS 66506-1403. Offers applied family sciences (MS); communication sciences and disorders (MS); conflict resolution (Graduate Certificate); couple and family therapy (MS); early childhood education (MS); family and community service (MS); life-span human development (MS); personal financial planning (MS, PhD, Graduate Certificate); youth development (MS, Graduate Certificate). *Accreditation:* AAMFT/COAMFTE; ASHA. *Program availability:* Part-time, online learning. *Degree requirements:* For master's, comprehensive exam (for some programs), thesis optional. *Entrance requirements:* For master's, GRE, minimum GPA of 3.0 in last 2 years (60 semester hours) of undergraduate study; for doctorate, GRE. Additional exam requirements/recommendations for international students: Required—TOEFL (minimum score 600 paper-based). Electronic applications accepted. *Faculty research:* Health and security of military families, training in and evaluation of professional human services (marriage and couple therapy, family life education, treatment of speech and swallowing disorders, financial therapy), disorders of communication and swallowing, family and relationship development and health, financial decision-making.

Kean University, College of Education, Program in Early Childhood Education, Union, NJ 07083. Offers administration in early childhood and family studies (MA); advanced curriculum and teaching (MA); classroom instruction - P-3 certification (MA). *Accreditation:* NCATE. *Program availability:* Part-time. *Faculty:* 13 full-time (7 women). *Students:* 4 full-time (2 women), 10 part-time (all women); includes 6 minority (3 Asian, non-Hispanic/Latino; 3 Hispanic/Latino). Average age 30. 4 applicants, 75% accepted, 3 enrolled. In 2017, 5 master's awarded. *Entrance requirements:* For master's, GRE General Test, PRAXIS Early Childhood Content Knowledge (for some programs), minimum GPA of 3.0, 2 letters of recommendation, teacher certification (for some programs), personal statement, official transcripts, resume. Additional exam requirements/recommendations for international students: Required—TOEFL (minimum score 550 paper-based; 79 iBT), IELTS (minimum score 6.5). *Application deadline:* For fall admission, 6/30 for domestic and international students; for spring admission, 12/1 for domestic and international students. Applications are processed on a rolling basis. Application fee: $75. Electronic applications accepted. *Expenses:* Tuition, state resident: full-time $13,419; part-time $653 per credit. Tuition, nonresident: full-time $18,188; part-time $801 per credit. *Required fees:* $3382; $154 per credit. Tuition and fees vary according to course level, course load, degree level and program. *Financial support:* Scholarships/grants and unspecified assistantships available. Financial award applicants required to submit FAFSA. *Unit head:* Dr. Jennifer Chen, Program Coordinator, 908-737-3809, E-mail: jchen@kean.edu. *Application contact:* Brittany Gerstenhaber, Admissions Counselor, 908-737-7100, E-mail: gradadmissions@kean.edu.

Kent State University, College of Education, Health and Human Services, School of Lifespan Development and Educational Sciences, Program in Human Development and Family Studies, Kent, OH 44242-0001. Offers MA. *Degree requirements:* For master's, thesis optional. *Entrance requirements:* For master's, minimum undergraduate GPA of

Child and Family Studies

3.0, 3 letters of reference, goals statement. Additional exam requirements/recommendations for international students: Required—TOEFL (minimum score 550 paper-based; 80 iBT). *Expenses:* Tuition, state resident: full-time $11,310; part-time $515 per credit hour. Tuition, nonresident: full-time $20,396; part-time $928 per credit hour. *International tuition:* $18,544 full-time.

Liberty University, School of Behavioral Sciences, Lynchburg, VA 24515. Offers applied psychology (MA), including developmental psychology (MA, MS), industrial/organizational psychology (MA, MS); clinical mental health counseling (MA); community care and counseling (Ed D), including marriage and family counseling, pastoral care and counseling, traumatology; counselor education and supervision (PhD); human services counseling (MA), including addictions and recovery, business, child and family law, Christian ministries, criminal justice, crisis response and trauma, executive leadership, health and wellness, life coaching, marriage and family, military resilience; marriage and family counseling (MA); marriage and family therapy (MA); military resilience (Certificate); pastoral counseling (MA), including addictions and recovery, community chaplaincy, crisis response and trauma, discipleship and church ministry, leadership, life coaching, marriage and family, marriage and family studies, military resilience, parenting and child/adolescent, pastoral counseling, theology; professional counseling (MA); psychology (MS), including developmental psychology (MA, MS), industrial/organizational psychology (MA, MS); school counseling (M Ed). *Program availability:* Part-time, online learning. *Students:* 2,649 full-time (2,085 women), 5,086 part-time (4,015 women); includes 2,275 minority (1,784 Black or African American, non-Hispanic/Latino; 44 American Indian or Alaska Native, non-Hispanic/Latino; 67 Asian, non-Hispanic/Latino; 200 Hispanic/Latino; 11 Native Hawaiian or other Pacific Islander, non-Hispanic/Latino; 169 Two or more races, non-Hispanic/Latino), 145 international. Average age 39. 5,839 applicants, 51% accepted, 1710 enrolled. In 2017, 1,626 master's, 7 doctorates, 61 other advanced degrees awarded. *Application deadline:* Applications are processed on a rolling basis. Application fee: $50. Electronic applications accepted. *Financial support:* Applicants required to submit FAFSA. *Unit head:* Dr. Ronald Hawkins, Founding Dean, School of Behavioral Sciences. *Application contact:* Jay Bridge, Director of Admissions, 800-424-9595, Fax: 800-628-7977, E-mail: gradadmissions@liberty.edu.

Loma Linda University, School of Behavioral Health, Department of Counseling and Family Sciences, Loma Linda, CA 92350. Offers child life specialist (MS); clinical mediation (Certificate); counseling (MS); drug and alcohol counseling (Certificate); family life education (Certificate); marital and family therapy (DMFT); school counseling (Certificate). *Degree requirements:* For master's, comprehensive exam, thesis optional; for doctorate, comprehensive exam, thesis/dissertation (for some programs). *Entrance requirements:* For master's, minimum GPA of 3.0; for doctorate, GRE. Additional exam requirements/recommendations for international students: Required—TOEFL (minimum score 550 paper-based). Electronic applications accepted.

London Metropolitan University, Graduate Programs, London, United Kingdom. Offers applied psychology (M Sc); architecture (MA); biomedical science (M Sc); blood science (M Sc); cancer pharmacology (M Sc); computer networking and cyber security (M Sc); computing and information systems (M Sc); conference interpreting (MA); counter-terrorism studies (M Sc); creative, digital and professional writing (MA); crime, violence and prevention (M Sc); criminology (M Sc); curating contemporary art (MA); data analytics (M Sc); digital media (MA); early childhood studies (MA); education (MA, Ed D); financial services law, regulation and compliance (LL M); food science (M Sc); forensic psychology (M Sc); health and social care management and policy (M Sc); human nutrition (M Sc); human resource management (MA); human rights and international conflict (MA); information technology (M Sc); intelligence and security studies (M Sc); international oil, gas and energy law (LL M); international relations (MA); interpreting (MA); learning and teaching in higher education (MA); legal practice (LL M); media and entertainment law (LL M); organizational and consumer psychology (M Sc); psychological therapy (M Sc); psychology of mental health (M Sc); public health (M Sc); public policy and management (MPA); security studies (M Sc); social work (M Sc); spatial planning and urban design (MA); sports therapy (M Sc); supporting older children and young people with dyslexia (MA); teaching languages (MA), including Arabic, English; translation (MA); woman and child abuse (MA).

Miami University, College of Education, Health and Society, Department of Family Studies and Social Work, Oxford, OH 45056. Offers MA. *Students:* 34 full-time (30 women), 6 part-time (4 women); includes 13 minority (8 Black or African American, non-Hispanic/Latino; 1 Asian, non-Hispanic/Latino; 2 Hispanic/Latino; 2 Two or more races, non-Hispanic/Latino), 1 international. Average age 30. In 2017, 18 master's awarded. *Expenses:* Tuition, state resident: full-time $13,812; part-time $575 per credit hour. Tuition, nonresident: full-time $30,860; part-time $1286 per credit hour. *Unit head:* Dr. Elise Radina, Professor and Chair, 513-529-3639, E-mail: radiname@miamioh.edu. *Application contact:* Kevin Bush, Associate Dean for Faculty Development and Graduate Studies, 513-529-0405, E-mail: bushkr@miamioh.edu.
Website: http://www.MiamiOH.edu/fsw

Michigan State University, The Graduate School, College of Social Science, Department of Family and Child Ecology, East Lansing, MI 48824. Offers child development (MA); community services (MS); family and child ecology (PhD); family studies (MA); marriage and family therapy (MA); youth development (MA). *Accreditation:* AAMFT/COAMFTE (one or more programs are accredited). *Entrance requirements:* For master's, GRE General Test, minimum GPA of 3.0 in last 2 years of undergraduate course work, 3 letters of recommendation; for doctorate, GRE General Test, minimum GPA of 3.0, 3 letters of recommendation, background in behavioral sciences. Additional exam requirements/recommendations for international students: Required—TOEFL. Electronic applications accepted.

Mississippi State University, College of Agriculture and Life Sciences, School of Human Sciences, Mississippi State, MS 39762. Offers agriculture and extension education (MS), including communication, leadership; agriculture science (PhD), including agriculture and extension education; fashion design and merchandising (MS), including design and product development, merchandising; human development and family studies (MS, PhD). *Accreditation:* NCATE (one or more programs are accredited). *Program availability:* Part-time. *Faculty:* 20 full-time (11 women). *Students:* 31 full-time (23 women), 54 part-time (38 women); includes 19 minority (15 Black or African American, non-Hispanic/Latino; 1 Hispanic/Latino; 3 Two or more races, non-Hispanic/Latino), 5 international. Average age 36. 26 applicants, 65% accepted, 15 enrolled. In 2017, 19 master's, 2 doctorates awarded. *Degree requirements:* For master's, thesis optional, comprehensive oral or written exam. *Entrance requirements:* For master's, GRE, minimum GPA of 2.75 in last 4 semesters of course work; for doctorate, minimum GPA of 3.0 on prior graduate work. Additional exam requirements/recommendations for international students: Required—TOEFL (minimum score 477 paper-based; 53 iBT); Recommended—IELTS (minimum score 4.5). *Application deadline:* For fall admission, 7/1 for domestic students, 5/1 for international students; for spring admission, 11/1 for domestic students, 9/1 for international students. Applications are processed on a rolling basis. Application fee: $60 ($80 for international students). Electronic applications accepted. *Expenses:* Tuition, state resident: full-time $8318; part-time $462.12 per credit hour. Tuition, nonresident: full-time $22,358; part-time $1242.12 per credit hour. *Required fees:* $110; $12.24 per credit hour. $6.12 per semester. *Financial support:* In

2017–18, 13 research assistantships (averaging $13,718 per year) were awarded; Federal Work-Study, institutionally sponsored loans, and unspecified assistantships also available. Financial award application deadline: 4/1; financial award applicants required to submit FAFSA. *Faculty research:* Animal welfare, agroscience, information technology, learning styles, problem solving. *Unit head:* Dr. Michael Newman, Professor and Director, 662-325-2950, E-mail: mnewman@humansci.msstate.edu. *Application contact:* Marina Hunt, Admissions and Enrollment Assistant, 662-325-5188, E-mail: mhunt@grad.msstate.edu.
Website: http://www.humansci.msstate.edu

Missouri State University, Graduate College, College of Education, Department of Childhood Education and Family Studies, Program in Early Childhood and Family Development, Springfield, MO 65897. Offers MS. *Program availability:* Part-time, 100% online, blended/hybrid learning. *Faculty:* 11 full-time (10 women), 11 part-time/adjunct (6 women). *Students:* 2 full-time (both women), 45 part-time (44 women); includes 6 minority (2 Black or African American, non-Hispanic/Latino; 1 Asian, non-Hispanic/Latino; 1 Hispanic/Latino; 2 Two or more races, non-Hispanic/Latino), 1 international. Average age 25. 25 applicants, 88% accepted, 19 enrolled. In 2017, 16 master's awarded. *Entrance requirements:* For master's, GRE, minimum GPA of 3.0. Additional exam requirements/recommendations for international students: Required—TOEFL (minimum score 550 paper-based; 79 iBT), IELTS (minimum score 6). *Application deadline:* For fall admission, 7/20 priority date for domestic students, 5/1 for international students; for spring admission, 12/20 priority date for domestic students, 9/1 for international students; for summer admission, 5/20 priority date for domestic students. Applications are processed on a rolling basis. Application fee: $35 ($50 for international students). Electronic applications accepted. *Expenses:* Tuition, state resident: full-time $2915; part-time $2021 per credit hour. Tuition, nonresident: full-time $5354; part-time $3647 per credit hour. *International tuition:* $11,992 full-time. *Required fees:* $173; $173 per credit hour. Tuition and fees vary according to class time, course level, course load, degree level, campus/location and program. *Financial support:* Federal Work-Study, institutionally sponsored loans, scholarships/grants, and unspecified assistantships available. Financial award application deadline: 3/31; financial award applicants required to submit FAFSA. *Unit head:* Dr. Denise Cunningham, Department Head, 417-836-8915, Fax: 417-836-8900, E-mail: cefs@missouristate.edu. *Application contact:* Stephanie Praschan, Director, Graduate Enrollment Management, 417-836-5300, Fax: 417-836-6200, E-mail: stephaniepraschan@missouristate.edu.
Website: http://education.missouristate.edu/ecfd/

Montclair State University, The Graduate School, College of Education and Human Services, Doctoral Program in Family Studies, Montclair, NJ 07043-1624. Offers PhD. *Program availability:* Part-time, evening/weekend. *Degree requirements:* For doctorate, comprehensive exam, thesis/dissertation. *Entrance requirements:* For doctorate, GRE General Test, interview, 3 letters of recommendation, essay. Additional exam requirements/recommendations for international students: Required—TOEFL (minimum score 83 iBT), IELTS (minimum score 6.5). Electronic applications accepted.

Montclair State University, The Graduate School, College of Education and Human Services, Program in Family and Child Studies, Montclair, NJ 07043-1624. Offers MA. *Program availability:* Part-time, evening/weekend. *Degree requirements:* For master's, comprehensive exam, thesis or alternative. *Entrance requirements:* For master's, GRE General Test, essay, 2 letters of recommendation. Additional exam requirements/recommendations for international students: Required—TOEFL (minimum score 83 iBT), IELTS (minimum score 6.5). Electronic applications accepted.

Montclair State University, The Graduate School, College of Humanities and Social Sciences, Adolescent Advocacy Certificate Program, Montclair, NJ 07043-1624. Offers Certificate.

Montclair State University, The Graduate School, College of Humanities and Social Sciences, Child Advocacy and Policy Certificate Program, Montclair, NJ 07043-1624. Offers Certificate.

Mount Saint Vincent University, Graduate Programs, Department of Child and Youth Study, Halifax, NS B3M 2J6, Canada. Offers MA. *Program availability:* Part-time, evening/weekend. *Degree requirements:* For master's, thesis. *Entrance requirements:* For master's, bachelor's degree in related field, minimum B+ average, professional experience. Electronic applications accepted.

Mount Saint Vincent University, Graduate Programs, Department of Family Studies and Gerontology, Halifax, NS B3M 2J6, Canada. Offers MA. *Program availability:* Part-time, online learning. *Degree requirements:* For master's, thesis. *Entrance requirements:* For master's, minimum GPA of 3.0; course work in statistics, research methods, family and social theories.

North Carolina Agricultural and Technical State University, School of Graduate Studies, School of Agriculture and Environmental Sciences, Department of Family and Consumer Sciences, Greensboro, NC 27411. Offers child development early education and family studies (MAT); family and consumer sciences (MAT); food and nutrition (MS). *Program availability:* Part-time, evening/weekend. *Degree requirements:* For master's, comprehensive exam, thesis or alternative, qualifying exam. *Entrance requirements:* For master's, GRE General Test, minimum GPA of 2.6.

★ **North Dakota State University,** College of Graduate and Interdisciplinary Studies, College of Human Development and Education, Department of Human Development and Family Science, Fargo, ND 58102. Offers couple and family therapy (PhD); developmental science (PhD); family financial planning (MS, Certificate); gerontology (MS, Certificate); youth development (MS). *Program availability:* Part-time, evening/weekend, online learning. *Degree requirements:* For master's, thesis or alternative; for doctorate, thesis/dissertation. *Entrance requirements:* Additional exam requirements/recommendations for international students: Required—TOEFL (minimum score 525 paper-based; 71 iBT). *Faculty research:* Family therapy, resilience, parenting, adolescent development, mental health.
See Display on the next page and Close-Up on page 875.

Northern Illinois University, Graduate School, College of Health and Human Sciences, School of Family and Consumer Sciences, De Kalb, IL 60115-2854. Offers applied human development and family sciences (MS). *Accreditation:* AAMFT/COAMFTE. *Program availability:* Part-time. *Faculty:* 16 full-time (14 women), 2 part-time/adjunct (1 woman). *Students:* 56 full-time (52 women), 16 part-time (15 women); includes 15 minority (2 Black or African American, non-Hispanic/Latino; 1 Asian, non-Hispanic/Latino; 10 Hispanic/Latino; 2 Two or more races, non-Hispanic/Latino). Average age 26. 65 applicants, 74% accepted, 28 enrolled. In 2017, 19 master's awarded. *Degree requirements:* For master's, comprehensive exam, internship, thesis (for nutrition and dietetics). *Entrance requirements:* For master's, GRE General Test, minimum GPA of 2.75. Additional exam requirements/recommendations for international students: Required—TOEFL (minimum score 550 paper-based). *Application deadline:* For fall admission, 6/1 for domestic students, 5/1 for international students; for spring admission, 11/1 for domestic students, 10/1 for international students. Applications are processed on a rolling basis. Application fee: $40. Electronic applications accepted. *Financial support:* In 2017–18, 12 research assistantships with full tuition reimbursements, 17 teaching assistantships with full tuition reimbursements were

awarded; fellowships with full tuition reimbursements, career-related internships or fieldwork, Federal Work-Study, scholarships/grants, tuition waivers (full), and staff assistantships also available. Support available to part-time students. Financial award applicants required to submit FAFSA. *Faculty research:* Preliminary child development, hospitality administration in Asia, sports nutrition, eating disorders. *Unit head:* Dr. Thomas Pavkov, Chair, 815-753-6342, Fax: 815-753-1321, E-mail: tpavkov@niu.edu. *Application contact:* Graduate School Office, 815-753-0395, E-mail: gradsch@niu.edu. Website: http://www.chhs.niu.edu/facs/

The Ohio State University, Graduate School, College of Education and Human Ecology, Department of Human Sciences, Columbus, OH 43210. Offers consumer sciences (MS, PhD); human development and family science (PhD); human nutrition (MS, PhD); kinesiology (MA, Ed D, PhD). *Program availability:* Part-time. *Faculty:* 55. *Students:* 127 full-time (71 women), 14 part-time (12 women). Average age 27. In 2017, 31 master's, 14 doctorates awarded. *Degree requirements:* For master's, thesis optional; for doctorate, thesis/dissertation. *Entrance requirements:* For master's and doctorate, GRE. Additional exam requirements/recommendations for international students: Required—TOEFL (minimum score 550 paper-based; 79 iBT), Michigan English Language Assessment Battery (minimum score 82); Recommended—IELTS (minimum score 7). *Application deadline:* For fall admission, 12/1 priority date for domestic and international students. Applications are processed on a rolling basis. Application fee: $60 ($70 for international students). Electronic applications accepted. *Financial support:* Fellowships with tuition reimbursements, research assistantships with tuition reimbursements, teaching assistantships with tuition reimbursements, Federal Work-Study, and institutionally sponsored loans available. Support available to part-time students. *Unit head:* Dr. Brian Focht, Associate Chair and Professor, E-mail: focht.10@osu.edu. *Application contact:* Graduate and Professional Admissions, 614-292-9444, Fax: 614-292-3895, E-mail: gpadmissions@osu.edu. Website: http://ehe.osu.edu/human-sciences/

Ohio University, Graduate College, College of Health Sciences and Professions, Department of Social and Public Health, Athens, OH 45701-2979. Offers early child development and family life (MS); family studies (MS); health administration (MHA); public health (MPH); social work (MSW). *Program availability:* Part-time, evening/weekend, online learning. *Degree requirements:* For master's, capstone (MPH). *Entrance requirements:* For master's, GMAT, GRE General Test, previous course work in accounting, management, and statistics; previous public health background (MHA, MPH). Additional exam requirements/recommendations for international students: Required—TOEFL (minimum score 550 paper-based; 80 iBT) or IELTS (minimum score 6.5). Electronic applications accepted. *Expenses:* Contact institution. *Faculty research:* Health care management, health policy, managed care, health behavior, disease prevention.

Oklahoma State University, College of Human Sciences, Department of Human Development and Family Science, Stillwater, OK 74078. Offers human development and family science (MS, PhD), including family financial planning (MS), human environmental sciences (PhD). *Accreditation:* AAMFT/COAMFTE (one or more programs are accredited). *Program availability:* Online learning. *Faculty:* 33 full-time (23 women), 13 part-time/adjunct (11 women). *Students:* 36 full-time (29 women), 49 part-time (43 women); includes 27 minority (12 Black or African American, non-Hispanic/Latino; 1 American Indian or Alaska Native, non-Hispanic/Latino; 1 Asian, non-Hispanic/Latino; 9 Hispanic/Latino; 4 Two or more races, non-Hispanic/Latino), 3 international. Average age 31. 54 applicants, 59% accepted, 30 enrolled. In 2017, 20 master's, 1 doctorate awarded. *Entrance requirements:* For master's and doctorate, GRE or GMAT. Additional exam requirements/recommendations for international students: Required—TOEFL (minimum score 550 paper-based; 79 iBT). *Application deadline:* For fall admission, 3/1 priority date for international students; for spring admission, 8/1 priority date for international students. Applications are processed on a rolling basis. Application fee: $40 ($75 for international

students). Electronic applications accepted. *Expenses:* Tuition, state resident: full-time $4019; part-time $2679.60 per year. Tuition, nonresident: full-time $15,286; part-time $10,190.40 per year. *Required fees:* $2129; $1419 per unit. Tuition and fees vary according to program. *Financial support:* Research assistantships, teaching assistantships, career-related internships or fieldwork, Federal Work-Study, scholarships/grants, health care benefits, tuition waivers (partial), and unspecified assistantships available. Support available to part-time students. Financial award application deadline: 3/1; financial award applicants required to submit FAFSA. *Faculty research:* Family relations and child development, consequences of adolescent parenting, family stress and coping, impacts of sexual abuse on families, children's social cognition and self-competence, gerontology and health care. *Unit head:* Dr. Sissy Osteen, Department Head, 405-744-4741, Fax: 405-744-6344, E-mail: sissy.osteen@okstate.edu. *Application contact:* Dr. Michael Criss, Graduate Coordinator, 405-744-5057, Fax: 405-744-6344, E-mail: michael.criss@okstate.edu. Website: https://humansciences.okstate.edu/hdfs/

Oregon State University, College of Public Health and Human Sciences, Program in Human Development and Family Studies, Corvallis, OR 97331. Offers MS, PhD. *Entrance requirements:* For master's, GRE; for doctorate, GRE, master's degree (including thesis). Additional exam requirements/recommendations for international students: Required—TOEFL (minimum score 80 iBT), IELTS (minimum score 6.5). *Application deadline:* For fall admission, 4/15 for domestic and international students. *Financial support:* Application deadline: 1/2. *Unit head:* Megan Ferris, Advisor, 541-737-0781, E-mail: megan.ferris@oregonstate.edu. *Application contact:* Megan Ferris, Doctoral Programs Manager, 541-737-0781, E-mail: megan.ferris@oregonstate.edu. Website: http://health.oregonstate.edu/degrees/graduate/hdfs

Oxford Graduate School, Graduate Programs, Dayton, TN 37321-6736. Offers family life education (M Litt); integration of religion and society (M Litt); organizational leadership (M Litt). *Entrance requirements:* For master's, official transcripts, three letters of recommendation, bachelor's degree or its equivalent, minimum undergraduate GPA of 3.0, minimum of 3 years of professional experience; for doctorate, official transcripts, three letters of recommendation, master's degree with minimum GPA of 3.0, minimum of 5 years of professional experience. *Expenses:* Contact institution.

Penn State University Park, Graduate School, College of Health and Human Development, Department of Human Development and Family Studies, University Park, PA 16802. Offers MS, PhD. *Unit head:* Dr. Ann C. Crouter, Dean, 814-865-1420, Fax: 814-865-3282. *Application contact:* Lori Hawn, Director, Graduate Student Services, 814-865-1795, Fax: 814-863-4627, E-mail: l-gswww@lists.psu.edu. Website: http://hhd.psu.edu/hdfs/

Purdue University, Graduate School, College of Health and Human Sciences, Department of Child Development and Family Studies, West Lafayette, IN 47907. Offers developmental studies (MS, PhD); family studies (MS, PhD); marriage and family therapy (MS, PhD). *Program availability:* Part-time. *Faculty:* 19 full-time (11 women), 1 (woman) part-time/adjunct. *Students:* 22 full-time (21 women), 1 (woman) part-time; includes 3 minority (1 Black or African American, non-Hispanic/Latino; 1 Hispanic/Latino; 1 Two or more races, non-Hispanic/Latino), 5 international. Average age 26. 41 applicants, 29% accepted, 8 enrolled. In 2017, 4 master's, 3 doctorates awarded. Terminal master's awarded for partial completion of doctoral program. *Degree requirements:* For master's, thesis; for doctorate, thesis/dissertation. *Entrance requirements:* For master's and doctorate, GRE General Test (minimum score 1000 combined verbal and quantitative), minimum undergraduate GPA of 3.0 or equivalent. Additional exam requirements/recommendations for international students: Required—TOEFL (minimum score 600 paper-based; 90 iBT), TWE (minimum score 4). *Application deadline:* For fall admission, 1/4 for domestic and international students. Applications

are processed on a rolling basis. Application fee: $60 ($75 for international students). Electronic applications accepted. *Financial support:* Fellowships with full tuition reimbursements, research assistantships with full tuition reimbursements, teaching assistantships with full tuition reimbursements, and career-related internships or fieldwork available. Support available to part-time students. Financial award application deadline: 1/15; financial award applicants required to submit FAFSA. *Faculty research:* Inclusion of children with special needs, families as learning environments, relationships in child care, work-family relations, AIDS prevention. *Unit head:* Dr. Doran C. French, Head, 765-494-9511, E-mail: dcfrench@purdue.edu. *Application contact:* Tina Putz, Graduate Contact, 765-496-3816, E-mail: tputz@purdue.edu.
Website: http://www.purdue.edu/hhs/hdfs/

Purdue University Northwest, Graduate Studies Office, School of Liberal Arts and Social Sciences, Department of Behavioral Sciences, Hammond, IN 46323-2094. Offers child development and family studies (MS); marriage and family therapy (MS). *Accreditation:* AAMFT/COAMFTE. *Program availability:* Part-time. *Degree requirements:* For master's, thesis. *Entrance requirements:* For master's, GRE, interview. Additional exam requirements/recommendations for international students: Required—TOEFL. *Faculty research:* Substance abuse, sexual abuse, couple therapy, professional issues, adolescent therapy.

Queens College of the City University of New York, Mathematics and Natural Sciences Division, Department of Family, Nutrition and Exercise Sciences, Queens, NY 11367-1597. Offers exercise science specialist (MS); family and consumer science (K-12) (AC); family and consumer science/teaching curriculum (K-12) (MS Ed); nutrition and exercise science (MS); nutrition specialist (MS); physical education (K-12) (AC); physical education/teaching curriculum (pre K-12) (MS Ed). *Program availability:* Part-time, evening/weekend. *Faculty:* 13 full-time (11 women), 7 part-time/adjunct (4 women). *Students:* 15 full-time (7 women), 136 part-time (75 women); includes 67 minority (19 Black or African American, non-Hispanic/Latino; 1 American Indian or Alaska Native, non-Hispanic/Latino; 21 Asian, non-Hispanic/Latino; 25 Hispanic/Latino; 1 Two or more races, non-Hispanic/Latino), 3 international. Average age 30. 95 applicants, 76% accepted, 45 enrolled. In 2017, 34 master's, 12 other advanced degrees awarded. *Degree requirements:* For master's, research project. *Entrance requirements:* For master's, minimum GPA of 3.0. Additional exam requirements/recommendations for international students: Required—TOEFL (minimum paper-based score of 600) or IELTS (for program in nutrition). *Application deadline:* For fall admission, 4/1 for domestic students; for spring admission, 11/1 for domestic students. Applications are processed on a rolling basis. Application fee: $125. Electronic applications accepted. *Financial support:* Career-related internships or fieldwork and unspecified assistantships available. Financial award application deadline: 4/1; financial award applicants required to submit FAFSA. *Faculty research:* Health disparities; correlates of taste acuity, structuring and implementation of competition and competitive activities in physical education; exercise and metabolic risk in people living with HIV/AIDS; biomechanics, motor learning and motor control. *Unit head:* Dr. Ashima K. Kant, Chair, 718-997-4156 Ext. 4475, Fax: 718-997-4163, E-mail: ashima.kant@qc.cuny.edu. *Application contact:* Elizabeth D'Amico-Ramirez, Assistant Director of Graduate Admissions, 718-997-5203, E-mail: elizabeth.damicoramirez@qc.cuny.edu.

Roberts Wesleyan College, Department of Social Work, Rochester, NY 14624-1997. Offers child and family practice (MSW); mental health practice (MSW). *Accreditation:* CSWE. *Entrance requirements:* For master's, minimum GPA of 2.75. *Faculty research:* Religion and social work, family studies, values and ethics.

St. Cloud State University, School of Graduate Studies, School of Education, Department of Child and Family Studies, St. Cloud, MN 56301-4498. Offers MS. *Degree requirements:* For master's, thesis or alternative. *Entrance requirements:* For master's, GRE General Test, minimum GPA of 2.75. Additional exam requirements/recommendations for international students: Required—Michigan English Language Assessment Battery; Recommended—TOEFL (minimum score 550 paper-based), IELTS (minimum score 6.5). Electronic applications accepted.

San Diego State University, Graduate and Research Affairs, College of Education, Department of Child and Family Development, San Diego, CA 92182. Offers child development (MS). *Program availability:* Part-time. *Degree requirements:* For master's, thesis. *Entrance requirements:* For master's, GRE General Test, 3 letters of recommendation, interview. Additional exam requirements/recommendations for international students: Required—TOEFL. Electronic applications accepted.

South Carolina State University, College of Graduate and Professional Studies, Department of Family and Consumer Sciences, Orangeburg, SC 29117-0001. Offers individual and family development (MS); nutritional sciences (MS). *Program availability:* Part-time, evening/weekend. *Faculty:* 4 full-time (3 women), 4 part-time/adjunct (all women). *Students:* 11 full-time (8 women), 6 part-time (4 women); all minorities (all Black or African American, non-Hispanic/Latino). Average age 35. 14 applicants, 93% accepted, 9 enrolled. In 2017, 2 master's awarded. *Degree requirements:* For master's, comprehensive exam, thesis optional, departmental qualifying exam. *Entrance requirements:* For master's, GRE, MAT, or NTE, minimum GPA of 2.7. *Application deadline:* For fall admission, 6/15 priority date for domestic students, 6/15 for international students; for spring admission, 11/1 for domestic and international students. Application fee: $25. Electronic applications accepted. *Expenses:* Tuition, state resident: full-time $9388; part-time $607 per credit hour. Tuition, nonresident: full-time $19,968; part-time $1194 per credit hour. *Required fees:* $766; $766 per credit hour. *Financial support:* Fellowships, Federal Work-Study, and scholarships/grants available. Financial award application deadline: 6/1. *Unit head:* Dr. William H. Whitaker, Chair, Department of Family and Consumer Sciences, 803-536-8958, Fax: 803-533-3268, E-mail: wwhitak3@scsu.edu. *Application contact:* Curtis Foskey, Coordinator of Graduate Admission, 803-536-8419, Fax: 803-536-8812, E-mail: cfoskey@scsu.edu.

Spring Arbor University, School of Human Services, Spring Arbor, MI 49283-9799. Offers counseling (MAC); family studies (MAFS); nursing (MSN). *Program availability:* Part-time, evening/weekend, online learning. *Entrance requirements:* For master's, bachelor's degree from regionally-accredited college or university, minimum GPA of 3.0 for at least the last two years of the bachelor's degree, at least two recommendations from professional/academic individuals. Additional exam requirements/recommendations for international students: Required—TOEFL (minimum score 600 paper-based). Electronic applications accepted.

State University of New York at Oswego, Graduate Studies, School of Education, Department of Vocational Teacher Preparation, Oswego, NY 13126. Offers agriculture (MS Ed); business and marketing (MS Ed); family and consumer sciences (MS Ed); health careers (MS Ed); technical education (MS Ed); trade education (MS Ed). *Accreditation:* NCATE. *Program availability:* Part-time, evening/weekend. *Degree requirements:* For master's, comprehensive exam, thesis or alternative. *Entrance requirements:* Additional exam requirements/recommendations for international students: Required—TOEFL (minimum score 560 paper-based).

Syracuse University, David B. Falk College of Sport and Human Dynamics, Programs in Human Development and Family Science, Syracuse, NY 13244. Offers MA, MS, PhD. *Accreditation:* AAMFT/COAMFTE (one or more programs are accredited). *Program availability:* Part-time. *Degree requirements:* For master's, comprehensive exam (for some programs), thesis; for doctorate, comprehensive exam, thesis/dissertation. *Entrance requirements:* For master's and doctorate, GRE General Test, personal statement, official transcripts, three letters of recommendation, resume. Additional exam requirements/recommendations for international students: Required—TOEFL (minimum score 100 iBT). *Application deadline:* For fall admission, 2/15 priority date for domestic and international students; for spring admission, 11/15 priority date for domestic and international students. Application fee: $75. Electronic applications accepted. *Financial support:* Fellowships with full tuition reimbursements, research assistantships with tuition reimbursements, teaching assistantships with tuition reimbursements, career-related internships or fieldwork, and tuition waivers available. Financial award application deadline: 1/1. *Faculty research:* Family and child theories, research methods, family dynamics, child development. *Unit head:* Dr. Rachel R. Razza, Associate Professor/Graduate Program Director, 315-443-7377, Fax: 315-443-9402, E-mail: rrazza@syr.edu. *Application contact:* Felicia Otero, Director of Admissions, 315-443-5555, E-mail: falk@syr.edu.
Website: http://falk.syr.edu/ChildFamilyStudies/Default.aspx

Texas State University, The Graduate College, College of Applied Arts, Program in Family and Child Studies, San Marcos, TX 78666. Offers MS. *Program availability:* Part-time. *Faculty:* 6 full-time (5 women), 4 part-time/adjunct (all women). *Students:* 13 full-time (all women), 13 part-time (all women); includes 9 minority (1 Asian, non-Hispanic/Latino; 8 Hispanic/Latino). Average age 25. 70 applicants, 54% accepted, 10 enrolled. In 2017, 20 master's awarded. *Degree requirements:* For master's, comprehensive exam, thesis (for some programs), competitive child life internship (for some programs). *Entrance requirements:* For master's, GRE General Test (preferred minimum score of 285 verbal and quantitative sections combined with no less than 145 in verbal section and 140 in quantitative section), baccalaureate degree from regionally-accredited university; copy of official transcript from each institution where course credit was granted; minimum GPA of 3.0 in last 60 hours of undergraduate course work (plus any completed graduate courses); resume/curriculum vitae; statement of purpose; three letters of recommendation. Additional exam requirements/recommendations for international students: Required—TOEFL (minimum score 550 paper-based; 78 iBT), IELTS (minimum score 6.5). *Application deadline:* For fall admission, 2/15 for domestic and international students. Applications are processed on a rolling basis. Application fee: $40 ($90 for international students). Electronic applications accepted. *Expenses:* Tuition, state resident: full-time $7868; part-time $3934 per semester. Tuition, nonresident: full-time $17,828; part-time $8914 per semester. *Required fees:* $2092; $1435 per semester. Tuition and fees vary according to course load. *Financial support:* In 2017–18, 10 students received support, including 9 research assistantships (averaging $11,525 per year), 3 teaching assistantships (averaging $12,360 per year); scholarships/grants and unspecified assistantships also available. Financial award application deadline: 3/1; financial award applicants required to submit FAFSA. *Faculty research:* Mexican-origin student success; academic identity and its role in predicting post-secondary achievement; strengthening relationships/strengthening families;. *Total annual research expenditures:* $1.1 million. *Unit head:* Dr. Christine Gray, Graduate Advisor, 512-245-2904, Fax: 512-245-3829, E-mail: msfamilyandchild@txstate.edu. *Application contact:* Dr. Andrea Golato, Dean of the Graduate College, 512-245-2581, Fax: 512-245-8365, E-mail: er15@txstate.edu.
Website: http://www.fcs.txstate.edu/degrees-programs/fcd/fcdgrad.html

Texas Tech University, Graduate School, College of Human Sciences, Department of Human Development and Family Studies, Lubbock, TX 79409-1230. Offers human development and family studies (MS, PhD), including gerontology (MS). *Accreditation:* AAMFT/COAMFTE (one or more programs are accredited). *Faculty:* 25 full-time (21 women), 7 part-time/adjunct (all women). *Students:* 23 full-time (20 women), 41 part-time (26 women); includes 15 minority (5 Black or African American, non-Hispanic/Latino; 9 Hispanic/Latino; 1 Two or more races, non-Hispanic/Latino), 9 international. Average age 33. 34 applicants, 29% accepted, 6 enrolled. In 2017, 5 master's, 8 doctorates awarded. *Degree requirements:* For master's, thesis; for doctorate, comprehensive exam, thesis/dissertation. *Entrance requirements:* For master's and doctorate, GRE General Test. Additional exam requirements/recommendations for international students: Required—TOEFL (minimum score 550 paper-based; 79 iBT). *Application deadline:* For fall admission, 6/1 priority date for domestic students, 1/15 priority date for international students; for spring admission, 9/1 priority date for domestic students, 6/15 priority date for international students. Applications are processed on a rolling basis. Application fee: $60. Electronic applications accepted. *Expenses:* Contact institution. *Financial support:* In 2017–18, 31 students received support, including 30 fellowships (averaging $5,499 per year), 15 research assistantships (averaging $11,129 per year), 19 teaching assistantships (averaging $10,544 per year); scholarships/grants and unspecified assistantships also available. Financial award application deadline: 12/1; financial award applicants required to submit FAFSA. *Faculty research:* Parenting (including family relationships and parent-child interactions), marital and premarital relationships, adolescence (risk and resilience), life span, child development (including factors that influence developmental outcomes: poverty, risk, genetic and environmental factors). *Total annual research expenditures:* $79,092. *Unit head:* Dr. Ann M. Mastergeorge, Chairperson/Professor, 806-834-7162, Fax: 806-742-3042, E-mail: ann.mastergeorge@ttu.edu. *Application contact:* Dr. Malinda Colwell, Graduate Program Director, 806-834-4179, Fax: 806-742-0285, E-mail: malinda.colwell@ttu.edu.
Website: http://www.depts.ttu.edu/hdfs

Texas Woman's University, Graduate School, College of Professional Education, Department of Family Sciences, Denton, TX 76204. Offers child development (MS); child life (MS); counseling and development (MS); early childhood development and education (PhD); early childhood education (M Ed); family studies (MS, PhD); family therapy (MS, PhD). *Accreditation:* ACA (one or more programs are accredited). *Program availability:* Part-time, evening/weekend. *Faculty:* 24 full-time (19 women), 17 part-time/adjunct (15 women). *Students:* 153 full-time (146 women), 237 part-time (220 women); includes 169 minority (81 Black or African American, non-Hispanic/Latino; 9 Asian, non-Hispanic/Latino; 68 Hispanic/Latino; 11 Two or more races, non-Hispanic/Latino), 10 international. Average age 32. 235 applicants, 55% accepted, 87 enrolled. In 2017, 77 master's, 15 doctorates awarded. Terminal master's awarded for partial completion of doctoral program. *Degree requirements:* For master's, comprehensive exam (for some programs), thesis, professional paper, or coursework; practicums (for some programs); for doctorate, comprehensive exam, thesis/dissertation. *Entrance requirements:* For master's, GRE with preferred minimum score 147 Verbal, 144 Quantitative, 4.0 Analytical (for MS in child development and M Ed), minimum GPA of 3.0 (3.25 for family therapy), 3 letters of recommendations (1 for child life), letter of intent, curriculum vitae/resume, interview, writing sample; for doctorate, GRE (preferred minimum score 147 Verbal, 144 Quantitative, 4.0 Analytical), minimum GPA of 3.5 (3.35 for family studies) on all prior graduate work, curriculum vitae/resume, letter of intent. Additional exam requirements/recommendations for international students: Required—TOEFL (minimum score 550 paper-based; 79 iBT); Recommended—IELTS (minimum score 6.5), TSE (minimum score 53). *Application deadline:* For fall admission, 3/1 priority date for domestic and international students; for spring admission, 11/1 priority date for domestic students, 7/1 priority date for international students. Applications are processed on a rolling basis. Application fee: $50 ($75 for international students). Electronic applications accepted. *Expenses:* $7,520 per year full-time in-state; $16,820 per year full-time out-of-

state. *Financial support:* In 2017–18, 104 students received support, including 12 teaching assistantships (averaging $22,972 per year); career-related internships or fieldwork, Federal Work-Study, institutionally sponsored loans, scholarships/grants, traineeships, health care benefits, and unspecified assistantships also available. Support available to part-time students. Financial award application deadline: 3/1; financial award applicants required to submit FAFSA. *Faculty research:* Parenting/parent education, play therapy, healthy relationships, child development, technology integration. *Unit head:* Dr. Jerry Whitworth, Interim Chair, 940-898-2685, Fax: 940-898-2676, E-mail: famsci@twu.edu. *Application contact:* Korie Hawkins, Associate Director of Admissions, Graduate Recruitment, 940-898-3188, Fax: 940-898-3081, E-mail: admissions@twu.edu.
Website: http://www.twu.edu/family-sciences/

Towson University, College of Liberal Arts, Program in Child Life, Administration and Family Collaboration, Towson, MD 21252-0001. Offers MS. *Students:* 24 full-time (all women), 2 part-time (both women); includes 4 minority (1 Black or African American, non-Hispanic/Latino; 3 Hispanic/Latino). *Entrance requirements:* For master's, bachelor's degree; minimum GPA of 3.0; minimum of 40 hours of volunteer or paid work experience with children with special health care needs in a child life department under the direct supervision of a Certified Child Life Specialist; essay; volunteer/work experience verification form. *Application deadline:* For fall admission, 1/17 for domestic students, 5/15 for international students; for spring admission, 10/15 for domestic students, 12/1 for international students. Applications are processed on a rolling basis. Application fee: $45. Electronic applications accepted. *Expenses:* Tuition, state resident: full-time $7960; part-time $398 per unit. Tuition, nonresident: full-time $16,480; part-time $824 per unit. *Required fees:* $2600; $130 per year. $390 per term. *Unit head:* Prof. Lisa Martinelli, Graduate Program Director, 410-704-3766, E-mail: lmartinelli@towson.edu. *Application contact:* Coverley Beidleman, Assistant Director of Graduate Admissions, 410-704-5630, Fax: 410-704-3030, E-mail: cbeidleman@towson.edu.
Website: http://www.towson.edu/cla/departments/familystudies/grad/childlife/

Towson University, College of Liberal Arts, Program in Family-Professional Collaboration, Towson, MD 21252-0001. Offers Postbaccalaureate Certificate. *Students:* 24 full-time (all women), 3 part-time (all women); includes 4 minority (1 Black or African American, non-Hispanic/Latino; 3 Hispanic/Latino). *Entrance requirements:* For degree, minimum GPA of 3.0; bachelor's degree; resume; interview with program director. *Application deadline:* For fall admission, 1/17 for domestic students, 5/15 for international students; for spring admission, 10/15 for domestic students, 12/1 for international students. Applications are processed on a rolling basis. Application fee: $45. Electronic applications accepted. *Expenses:* Tuition, state resident: full-time $7960; part-time $398 per unit. Tuition, nonresident: full-time $16,480; part-time $824 per unit. *Required fees:* $2600; $130 per year. $390 per term. *Unit head:* Dr. Catherine Breneman, Graduate Program Director, 410-704-4871, E-mail: cbreneman@towson.edu. *Application contact:* Coverley Beidleman, Assistant Director of Graduate Admissions, 410-704-5630, Fax: 410-704-3030, E-mail: cbeidleman@towson.edu.
Website: http://www.towson.edu/cla/departments/familystudies/grad/famprofessionalpbc/index.html

Tufts University, Graduate School of Arts and Sciences, Eliot-Pearson Department of Child Study and Human Development, Medford, MA 02155. Offers child study and human development (MA, PhD). *Program availability:* Part-time. *Students:* 78 full-time (66 women), 1 (woman) part-time; includes 19 minority (4 Black or African American, non-Hispanic/Latino; 8 Asian, non-Hispanic/Latino; 5 Hispanic/Latino; 2 Two or more races, non-Hispanic/Latino), 17 international. Average age 27. 129 applicants, 59% accepted, 37 enrolled. In 2017, 26 master's, 7 doctorates awarded. *Degree requirements:* For master's, thesis (for some programs); for doctorate, comprehensive exam, thesis/dissertation. *Entrance requirements:* For master's and doctorate, GRE General Test. Additional exam requirements/recommendations for international students: Required—TOEFL (minimum score 550 paper-based; 80 iBT), IELTS (minimum score 6.5). *Application deadline:* For fall admission, 12/1 priority date for domestic and international students. Applications are processed on a rolling basis. Application fee: $85. Electronic applications accepted. *Expenses:* Contact institution. *Financial support:* Fellowships, research assistantships, teaching assistantships, Federal Work-Study, scholarships/grants, tuition waivers (full and partial), and unspecified assistantships available. Support available to part-time students. Financial award application deadline: 1/15. *Unit head:* Dr. David Henry Feldman, Graduate Program Director, 617-627-3355. *Application contact:* Office of Graduate Admissions, 617-627-3395, E-mail: gradadmissions@tufts.edu.
Website: http://ase.tufts.edu/epcd

The University of Akron, Graduate School, Buchtel College of Arts and Sciences, Department of Child and Family Development, Akron, OH 44325. Offers child development (MA). *Faculty:* 5 full-time (4 women), 3 part-time/adjunct (2 women). *Students:* 1 (woman) full-time. Average age 39. 1 applicant, 100% accepted, 1 enrolled. *Degree requirements:* For master's, comprehensive exam, project or thesis. *Entrance requirements:* For master's, GRE, minimum GPA of 3.0, three letters of recommendation, statement of purpose, resume. Additional exam requirements/recommendations for international students: Required—TOEFL (minimum score 79 iBT), IELTS (minimum score 6.5). *Application deadline:* For fall admission, 3/1 priority date for domestic and international students; for spring admission, 10/1 priority date for domestic and international students. Application fee: $45 ($70 for international students). Electronic applications accepted. *Unit head:* Dr. Paul Levy, Department Chair, 330-972-8369, E-mail: plevy@uakron.edu. *Application contact:* Dr. Shannon Zentall, Graduate Director, 330-972-6049, E-mail: szentall@uakron.edu.
Website: http://www.uakron.edu/child-family/

The University of Alabama, Graduate School, College of Human Environmental Sciences, Department of Human Development and Family Studies, Tuscaloosa, AL 35487. Offers human development and family studies (MSHES); marriage and family therapy (MSHES); parent and family life education (MSHES). *Faculty:* 11 full-time (8 women), 2 part-time/adjunct (both women). *Students:* 25 full-time (19 women), 1 (woman) part-time; includes 6 minority (4 Black or African American, non-Hispanic/Latino; 1 Hispanic/Latino; 1 Two or more races, non-Hispanic/Latino). Average age 26. 24 applicants, 75% accepted, 14 enrolled. In 2017, 14 master's awarded. Terminal master's awarded for partial completion of doctoral program. *Degree requirements:* For master's, comprehensive exam (for some programs), thesis (for some programs). *Entrance requirements:* For master's, GRE General Test or MAT, minimum GPA of 3.0. Additional exam requirements/recommendations for international students: Required—TOEFL (minimum score 79 iBT), IELTS (minimum score 6.5). *Application deadline:* For fall admission, 12/15 priority date for domestic and international students. Applications are processed on a rolling basis. Application fee: $50 ($60 for international students). Electronic applications accepted. *Financial support:* In 2017–18, 15 students received support, including research assistantships with full tuition reimbursements available (averaging $13,140 per year), teaching assistantships (averaging $13,140 per year); fellowships, career-related internships or fieldwork, Federal Work-Study, scholarships/grants, health care benefits, and unspecified assistantships also available. Financial award application deadline: 3/15. *Faculty research:* Parent/child relationships, preschool

curricula and quality measures for child care programs, family strengths and adolescent behaviors, depression in mothers and infants, word association and word learning in young children, bullying behaviors in children, attachment parenting, medical play therapy, socialization of young children, impact of daily experiences on relationship quality, re-entry of service members into civilian roles. *Unit head:* Dr. Carroll M. Tingle, Chair, 205-348-6158, Fax: 205-348-8153, E-mail: ctingle@ches.ua.edu. *Application contact:* Dr. Maria Hernandez-Reif, Professor, 205-348-5894, Fax: 205-348-8153, E-mail: mhernandez-reif@ches.ua.edu.
Website: http://www.hdfs.ches.ua.edu/

The University of Arizona, College of Education, Department of Disability and Psychoeducational Studies, Tucson, AZ 85721. Offers counseling and mental health (MA), including rehabilitation counseling, school counseling; family studies and human development (M Ed); rehabilitation counseling (PhD); school counseling (MA); school psychology (PhD, Ed S); special education (MA, PhD), including cross-categorical special education (MA), deaf and hard of hearing (MA), learning disabilities (MA), severe and multiple disabilities (MA), special education (PhD), visual impairment (MA). *Accreditation:* CORE. *Program availability:* Part-time. Terminal master's awarded for partial completion of doctoral program. *Degree requirements:* For master's, comprehensive exam, thesis optional; for doctorate, comprehensive exam, thesis/dissertation. *Entrance requirements:* For master's, statement of purpose; for doctorate, GRE General Test (minimum score 1100) or MAT, 3 letters of recommendation. Additional exam requirements/recommendations for international students: Required—TOEFL (minimum score 550 paper-based; 79 iBT).

University of Central Oklahoma, The Jackson College of Graduate Studies, College of Education and Professional Studies, Department of Human Environmental Sciences, Edmond, OK 73034-5209. Offers family and child studies (MS), including family life education, infant/child specialist, marriage and family therapy; nutrition-food science (MS). *Program availability:* Part-time. *Faculty:* 5 full-time (4 women), 8 part-time/adjunct (6 women). *Students:* 46 full-time (38 women), 65 part-time (62 women); includes 48 minority (27 Black or African American, non-Hispanic/Latino; 3 American Indian or Alaska Native, non-Hispanic/Latino; 3 Asian, non-Hispanic/Latino; 7 Hispanic/Latino; 8 Two or more races, non-Hispanic/Latino), 13 international. Average age 29. 68 applicants, 93% accepted, 31 enrolled. In 2017, 37 master's awarded. *Degree requirements:* For master's, comprehensive exam (for some programs), thesis (for some programs). *Entrance requirements:* For master's, GRE, essay, physical, CPR and First Aid training. Additional exam requirements/recommendations for international students: Required—TOEFL (minimum score 550 paper-based; 79 iBT), IELTS (minimum score 6.5). *Application deadline:* For fall admission, 1/15 for domestic students, 7/15 for international students; for spring admission, 11/15 for international students. Applications are processed on a rolling basis. Application fee: $60. Electronic applications accepted. *Expenses:* Tuition, state resident: full-time $5375; part-time $268.75 per credit hour. Tuition, nonresident: full-time $13,295; part-time $664.75 per credit hour. *Required fees:* $626; $31.30 per credit hour. One-time fee: $50. Tuition and fees vary according to program. *Financial support:* In 2017–18, 11 students received support, including 8 research assistantships with partial tuition reimbursements available (averaging $4,436 per year); teaching assistantships, career-related internships or fieldwork, scholarships/grants, tuition waivers (partial), and unspecified assistantships also available. Financial award application deadline: 3/31; financial award applicants required to submit FAFSA. *Unit head:* Dr. Kaye Sears, Chair, 405-974-5551, Fax: 405-974-3850. *Application contact:* Carlie Wellington, Assistant Director, CEPS Graduate Enrollment, 405-974-5105, Fax: 405-974-3851, E-mail: gradcoll@uco.edu.
Website: http://sites.uco.edu/ceps/dept/Professional-Studies-Programs/hes/index.asp

University of Connecticut, Graduate School, College of Liberal Arts and Sciences, Department of Human Development and Family Studies, Storrs, CT 06269. Offers MA, PhD. *Accreditation:* AAMFT/COAMFTE (one or more programs are accredited). Terminal master's awarded for partial completion of doctoral program. *Degree requirements:* For master's, comprehensive exam; for doctorate, thesis/dissertation. *Entrance requirements:* For doctorate, GRE General Test. Additional exam requirements/recommendations for international students: Required—TOEFL (minimum score 550 paper-based). Electronic applications accepted.

University of Delaware, College of Education and Human Development, Department of Human Development and Family Studies, Newark, DE 19716. Offers MS, PhD. *Program availability:* Part-time. Terminal master's awarded for partial completion of doctoral program. *Degree requirements:* For master's, thesis or alternative; for doctorate, comprehensive exam, thesis/dissertation. *Entrance requirements:* For master's and doctorate, GRE General Test, 3 letters of recommendation. Additional exam requirements/recommendations for international students: Required—TOEFL. Electronic applications accepted. *Faculty research:* Early childhood inclusive education, relationships, family risk and resilience, disability issues, program development and evaluation.

University of Denver, Morgridge College of Education, Denver, CO 80208. Offers child, family and school psychology (MA, PhD, Ed S); counseling psychology (MA, PhD); curriculum and instruction (MA, Ed D, PhD); curriculum instruction and teaching (Certificate); early childhood special education (MA, Certificate); educational leadership and policy studies (MA, Ed D, PhD, Certificate); higher education (Ed D, PhD); library and information science (MLIS); research methods and statistics (MA, PhD). *Accreditation:* ALA; APA (one or more programs are accredited). *Program availability:* Part-time, evening/weekend, online learning. *Faculty:* 39 full-time (29 women), 60 part-time/adjunct (42 women). *Students:* 502 full-time (406 women), 361 part-time (267 women); includes 233 minority (54 Black or African American, non-Hispanic/Latino; 6 American Indian or Alaska Native, non-Hispanic/Latino; 25 Asian, non-Hispanic/Latino; 113 Hispanic/Latino; 35 Two or more races, non-Hispanic/Latino), 52 international. Average age 31. 1,167 applicants, 64% accepted, 415 enrolled. In 2017, 285 master's, 51 doctorates, 157 other advanced degrees awarded. Terminal master's awarded for partial completion of doctoral program. *Degree requirements:* For master's, comprehensive exam; for doctorate, 2 foreign languages, comprehensive exam, thesis/dissertation. *Entrance requirements:* For master's and doctorate, GRE General Test or GMAT. Additional exam requirements/recommendations for international students: Required—TOEFL (minimum score 550 paper-based; 80 iBT). *Application deadline:* Applications are processed on a rolling basis. Application fee: $65. Electronic applications accepted. *Expenses:* $31,935 per year full-time. *Financial support:* In 2017–18, 765 students received support, including 26 research assistantships with tuition reimbursements available (averaging $10,957 per year), 38 teaching assistantships with tuition reimbursements available (averaging $3,391 per year); career-related internships or fieldwork, Federal Work-Study, institutionally sponsored loans, scholarships/grants, and unspecified assistantships also available. Support available to part-time students. Financial award application deadline: 2/15; financial award applicants required to submit FAFSA. *Faculty research:* Early childhood education, educational leadership, access and opportunity to postsecondary education, marriage and family therapy, data management and archival research. *Unit head:* Dr. Karen Riley, Dean, 303-871-3665, Fax: 303-871-4456, E-mail: karen.riley@du.edu. *Application contact:* Jodi Dye, Director of Admissions, 303-871-2510, Fax: 303-871-4456, E-mail: jodi.dye@du.edu.
Website: http://morgridge.du.edu

Child and Family Studies

University of Georgia, College of Family and Consumer Sciences, Department of Human Development and Family Science, Athens, GA 30602. Offers child and family development (MS). *Accreditation:* AAMFT/COAMFTE. *Degree requirements:* For master's, thesis (MS). *Entrance requirements:* For master's, GRE General Test. Electronic applications accepted.

University of Guelph, Graduate Studies, College of Social and Applied Human Sciences, Department of Family Relations and Applied Nutrition, Guelph, ON N1G 2W1, Canada. Offers applied nutrition (MAN); family relations and human development (M Sc, PhD), including applied human nutrition, couple and family therapy (M Sc), family relations and human development. *Accreditation:* AAMFT/COAMFTE (one or more programs are accredited). *Program availability:* Part-time. *Degree requirements:* For master's, thesis (for some programs); for doctorate, comprehensive exam, thesis/dissertation. *Entrance requirements:* For master's, minimum B+ average; for doctorate, master's degree in family relations and human development or related field with a minimum B+ average or master's degree in applied human nutrition. Additional exam requirements/recommendations for international students: Required—TOEFL (minimum score 600 paper-based). Electronic applications accepted. *Faculty research:* Child and adolescent development, social gerontology, family roles and relations, couple and family therapy, applied human nutrition.

University of Illinois at Springfield, Graduate Programs, College of Education and Human Services, Program in Human Services, Springfield, IL 62703-5407. Offers alcohol and substance abuse (Graduate Certificate); alcoholism and substance abuse (MA); child and family services (MA); gerontology (MA); social services administration (MA). *Program availability:* Part-time, evening/weekend, 100% online, blended/hybrid learning. *Faculty:* 5 full-time (all women). *Students:* 8 full-time (7 women), 72 part-time (63 women); includes 38 minority (26 Black or African American, non-Hispanic/Latino; 9 Hispanic/Latino; 3 Two or more races, non-Hispanic/Latino). Average age 33. 49 applicants, 47% accepted, 20 enrolled. In 2017, 21 master's, 1 other advanced degree awarded. *Degree requirements:* For master's, internship; capstone project. *Entrance requirements:* For master's, minimum undergraduate GPA of 3.0, 2 letters of recommendation from professional or academic sources, statement of intent, interview. Additional exam requirements/recommendations for international students: Required—TOEFL (minimum score 500 paper-based; 61 iBT). *Application deadline:* Applications are processed on a rolling basis. Application fee: $60 ($75 for international students). Electronic applications accepted. *Expenses:* Tuition, state resident: full-time $7896; part-time $329 per credit hour. Tuition, nonresident: full-time $16,200; part-time $675 per credit hour. Tuition and fees vary according to program. *Financial support:* In 2017–18, research assistantships with full tuition reimbursements (averaging $10,249 per year), teaching assistantships with full tuition reimbursements (averaging $10,303 per year) were awarded; fellowships, career-related internships or fieldwork, Federal Work-Study, scholarships/grants, health care benefits, and unspecified assistantships also available. Support available to part-time students. Financial award application deadline: 11/15; financial award applicants required to submit FAFSA. *Unit head:* Dr. Carolyn Peck, Program Administrator, 217-206-7577, Fax: 217-206-6775, E-mail: peck.carolyn@uis.edu.
Website: http://www.uis.edu/humanservices

University of Kentucky, Graduate School, College of Agriculture, Food and Environment, Program in Family Studies, Human Development, and Resource Management, Lexington, KY 40506-0032. Offers MS, PhD. *Accreditation:* AAMFT/COAMFTE. *Degree requirements:* For master's, comprehensive exam, thesis optional. *Entrance requirements:* For master's, GRE General Test, minimum undergraduate GPA of 2.75; for doctorate, GRE General Test, minimum undergraduate GPA of 3.0. Additional exam requirements/recommendations for international students: Required—TOEFL (minimum score 550 paper-based). Electronic applications accepted. *Faculty research:* Early childhood education, family therapy, family resource management and consumer studies, human development.

University of La Verne, LaFetra College of Education, Programs in Child Development/Child Life, La Verne, CA 91750-4443. Offers child development (MS); child life (MS). *Program availability:* Part-time. *Students:* 28 full-time (26 women), 78 part-time (75 women); includes 60 minority (3 Black or African American, non-Hispanic/Latino; 7 Asian, non-Hispanic/Latino; 47 Hispanic/Latino; 3 Two or more races, non-Hispanic/Latino), 5 international. Average age 31. *Entrance requirements:* For master's, minimum GPA of 3.0, 3 letters of reference, writing sample. Additional exam requirements/recommendations for international students: Required—TOEFL (minimum score 550 paper-based). *Application deadline:* Applications are processed on a rolling basis. Application fee: $50. *Expenses:* Contact institution. *Financial support:* Scholarships/grants and traineeships available. Financial award application deadline: 3/2; financial award applicants required to submit FAFSA. *Unit head:* Dr. Lisa Looney, Associate Professor, Education, 909-448-4653, E-mail: llooney@laverne.edu. *Application contact:* Kristen Ahn, Assistant Director of Graduate Admission, 909-448-4480, Fax: 909-971-2295, E-mail: sahn@laverne.edu.
Website: https://education.laverne.edu/child-development/

University of Maryland, College Park, Academic Affairs, School of Public Health, Department of Family Science, College Park, MD 20742. Offers family studies (PhD); marriage and family therapy (MS); maternal and child health (PhD). *Accreditation:* AAMFT/COAMFTE. *Program availability:* Part-time, evening/weekend. *Degree requirements:* For master's, thesis or alternative; for doctorate, comprehensive exam, thesis/dissertation, oral defense. *Entrance requirements:* For master's, GRE General Test, minimum GPA of 3.0, 3 letters of recommendation; for doctorate, GRE General Test, minimum GPA of 3.0, 3 letters of recommendation, research sample. Electronic applications accepted. *Faculty research:* Family life quality, interracial couples, child support, homeless families, family and child well-being.

University of Massachusetts Amherst, Graduate School, College of Education, Program in Education, Amherst, MA 01003. Offers bilingual, English as a second language, and multicultural education (M Ed, Ed S); child study and early education (M Ed); children, families and schools (Ed D, Ed S); early childhood and elementary teacher education (M Ed); educational leadership (M Ed); educational policy and leadership (Ed D); higher education (M Ed); international education (M Ed); language, literacy and culture (Ed D); learning, media and technology (M Ed, Ed S); mathematics, science, and learning technologies (Ed D); reading and writing (M Ed); research, educational measurement and psychometrics (Ed D); school counselor education (M Ed, Ed S); school psychology (Ed S); science education (Ed S); secondary teacher education (M Ed); social justice education (M Ed, Ed D, Ed S); special education (M Ed, Ed D, Ed S); teacher education and school improvement (Ed D, Ed S). *Accreditation:* NCATE. *Program availability:* Part-time, online learning. Terminal master's awarded for partial completion of doctoral program. *Degree requirements:* For doctorate, comprehensive exam, thesis/dissertation. *Entrance requirements:* Additional exam requirements/recommendations for international students: Required—TOEFL (minimum score 550 paper-based; 80 iBT), IELTS (minimum score 6.5). Electronic applications accepted.

University of Minnesota, Twin Cities Campus, Graduate School, College of Education and Human Development, Department of Family Social Science, Minneapolis, MN 55455-0213. Offers family education (M Ed); marriage and family therapy (MA, PhD); prevention science (MA). *Accreditation:* AAMFT/COAMFTE (one or more programs are accredited).

Faculty: 19 full-time (13 women). *Students:* 60 full-time (53 women), 35 part-time (32 women); includes 17 minority (7 Black or African American, non-Hispanic/Latino; 5 Asian, non-Hispanic/Latino; 3 Hispanic/Latino; 2 Two or more races, non-Hispanic/Latino), 7 international. Average age 35. 57 applicants, 61% accepted, 33 enrolled. In 2017, 18 master's, 6 doctorates awarded. *Degree requirements:* For master's, thesis; for doctorate, thesis/dissertation. *Entrance requirements:* For master's and doctorate, GRE General Test, minimum undergraduate GPA of 3.0 (preferred). Additional exam requirements/recommendations for international students: Required—TOEFL. *Application deadline:* For fall admission, 12/15 for domestic students. Application fee: $75 ($95 for international students). *Financial support:* In 2017–18, 3 fellowships, 33 research assistantships (averaging $11,720 per year), 13 teaching assistantships (averaging $8,528 per year) were awarded; career-related internships or fieldwork, Federal Work-Study, institutionally sponsored loans, and tuition waivers (partial) also available. Financial award application deadline: 6/30; financial award applicants required to submit FAFSA. *Faculty research:* Ethnicity, culture and diverse families in social context; family stress, loss, and trauma; family finances; parenting; family transitions; and child adjustment in a family context. *Total annual research expenditures:* $2.5 million. *Unit head:* Dr. Lynne Borden, Head, 612-625-1900, Fax: 612-625-4227, E-mail: lmborden@umn.edu. *Application contact:* Dr. Jodi Dworkin, Director of Graduate Studies, 612-624-3732, Fax: 612-625-4227, E-mail: jdworkin@umn.edu.
Website: http://www.cehd.umn.edu/fsos/

University of Missouri, Office of Research and Graduate Studies, College of Human Environmental Sciences, Department of Human Development and Family Studies, Columbia, MO 65211. Offers MA, MS, PhD. *Entrance requirements:* For master's, GRE General Test, minimum GPA of 3.0. Additional exam requirements/recommendations for international students: Required—TOEFL (minimum score 550 paper-based; 80 iBT). Electronic applications accepted.

University of Montana, Graduate School, Phyllis J. Washington College of Education and Human Sciences, Department of Counselor Education, Missoula, MT 59812. Offers clinical mental health counseling (MA); counseling and supervision (Ed D); counselor education (Ed S); intercultural youth and family development (MA); school counseling (MA). *Accreditation:* ACA. *Degree requirements:* For doctorate, thesis/dissertation. *Entrance requirements:* For master's, doctorate, and Ed S, GRE General Test. Additional exam requirements/recommendations for international students: Required—TOEFL.

University of Nebraska–Lincoln, Graduate College, College of Education and Human Sciences, Department of Child, Youth and Family Studies, Lincoln, NE 68588. Offers child development/early childhood education (MS, PhD); child, youth and family studies (MS); family and consumer sciences education (MS, PhD); family financial planning (MS); family science (MS, PhD); gerontology (PhD); human sciences (PhD), including child, youth and family studies, gerontology, medical family therapy; marriage and family therapy (MS); medical family therapy (PhD); youth development (MS). *Accreditation:* AAMFT/COAMFTE (one or more programs are accredited). *Program availability:* Online learning. *Degree requirements:* For master's, thesis optional. *Entrance requirements:* For master's, GRE. Additional exam requirements/recommendations for international students: Required—TOEFL (minimum score 550 paper-based). Electronic applications accepted. *Faculty research:* Marriage and family therapy, child development/early childhood education, family financial management.

University of Nevada, Reno, Graduate School, College of Education, Department of Human Development and Family Studies, Reno, NV 89557. Offers MS. *Degree requirements:* For master's, thesis optional. *Entrance requirements:* For master's, GRE General Test, minimum GPA of 2.75. Additional exam requirements/recommendations for international students: Required—TOEFL (minimum score 500 paper-based; 61 iBT), IELTS (minimum score 6). Electronic applications accepted. *Faculty research:* Early childhood/adolescent development, family studies.

University of New Hampshire, Graduate School, College of Health and Human Services, Department of Human Development and Family Studies, Durham, NH 03824. Offers adolescent development (Postbaccalaureate Certificate); human development and family studies (MS); human development and family studies: marriage and family therapy (MS). *Accreditation:* AAMFT/COAMFTE. *Program availability:* Part-time. *Students:* 11 full-time (10 women), 7 part-time (6 women); includes 3 minority (1 Asian, non-Hispanic/Latino; 2 Hispanic/Latino), 1 international. Average age 29. 33 applicants, 39% accepted, 8 enrolled. In 2017, 8 master's awarded. *Entrance requirements:* Additional exam requirements/recommendations for international students: Required—TOEFL (minimum score 550 paper-based; 80 iBT). *Application deadline:* For fall admission, 1/15 priority date for domestic students, 4/1 for international students. Application fee: $65. Electronic applications accepted. *Financial support:* In 2017–18, 10 students received support, including 4 teaching assistantships; fellowships, research assistantships, career-related internships or fieldwork, Federal Work-Study, scholarships/grants, and tuition waivers (full and partial) also available. Support available to part-time students. Financial award application deadline: 2/15. *Unit head:* Kerry Kazura, Chair, 603-862-2135. *Application contact:* Corinna Tucker, Administrative Assistant, 603-862-2153, E-mail: cjtucker@unh.edu.
Website: http://www.chhs.unh.edu/hdfs

University of New Mexico, Graduate Studies, College of Education, Program in Family Studies, Albuquerque, NM 87131-2039. Offers family life education (MA); family relations (MA); family studies (PhD); human development in families (MA). *Program availability:* Part-time, evening/weekend. *Faculty:* 5 full-time (2 women). *Students:* 10 full-time (9 women), 14 part-time (12 women); includes 12 minority (3 American Indian or Alaska Native, non-Hispanic/Latino; 9 Hispanic/Latino), 3 international. Average age 38. 4 applicants, 50% accepted, 2 enrolled. In 2017, 2 master's, 1 doctorate awarded. *Degree requirements:* For master's, comprehensive exam, thesis (for some programs); for doctorate, comprehensive exam, thesis/dissertation. *Entrance requirements:* For master's, written paper, 3 letters of recommendation, personal statement; for doctorate, GRE General Test, written paper, 3 letters of recommendation, personal statement, interview. Additional exam requirements/recommendations for international students: Required—TOEFL (minimum score 550 paper-based). *Application deadline:* For fall admission, 3/15 priority date for domestic and international students; for spring admission, 10/15 priority date for domestic and international students. Applications are processed on a rolling basis. Application fee: $50. Electronic applications accepted. *Financial support:* Fellowships, teaching assistantships, and unspecified assistantships available. Financial award application deadline: 3/1; financial award applicants required to submit FAFSA. *Faculty research:* Home, community and school relations; multicultural issues; parent-child interactions; grandparents as primary caretakers for grandchildren; fathering; early childhood evaluation; early childhood development; globalization and indigenous cultures. *Unit head:* Dr. Ziarat Hossain, Program Coordinator, 505-277-4162, Fax: 505-277-8361, E-mail: zhossain@unm.edu. *Application contact:* Cynthia Salas, Department Administrator, 505-277-4535, Fax: 505-277-8361, E-mail: divbse@unm.edu.
Website: https://coe.unm.edu/departments-programs/ifce/family-studies/

University of North Alabama, College of Arts and Sciences, Department of Sociology and Family Studies, Florence, AL 35632-0001. Offers family studies (MS). *Program availability:* Part-time, online only, 100% online. *Faculty:* 2 full-time (both women). *Students:* 2 full-time (both women), 12 part-time (11 women); includes 4 minority (3

Black or African American, non-Hispanic/Latino; 1 Hispanic/Latino). Average age 32. 14 applicants, 93% accepted, 8 enrolled. In 2017, 5 master's awarded. *Degree requirements:* For master's, comprehensive exam (for some programs), thesis optional. *Entrance requirements:* For master's, GRE or MAT, three professional references; writing sample; essay; resume. Additional exam requirements/recommendations for international students: Required—TOEFL (minimum score 79 iBT), IELTS (minimum score 6), PTE (minimum score 54). *Application deadline:* For fall admission, 7/1 for domestic and international students; for spring admission, 11/1 for domestic and international students; for summer admission, 4/1 for domestic and international students. Applications are processed on a rolling basis. Application fee: $50 ($100 for international students). Electronic applications accepted. *Expenses:* Tuition, state resident: full-time $7824; part-time $5943 per year. Tuition, nonresident: full-time $15,648; part-time $11,736 per year. *Required fees:* $3064; $2298 per unit. Tuition and fees vary according to course load and reciprocity agreements. *Financial support:* In 2017–18, 4 students received support. Federal Work-Study, scholarships/grants, and unspecified assistantships available. Financial award application deadline: 2/1; financial award applicants required to submit FAFSA. *Unit head:* Dr. Yaschica Williams, Chair, 256-765-4200, E-mail: ywilliams@una.edu. *Application contact:* Hillary N. Coats, Graduate Admissions Coordinator, 256-765-4447, E-mail: graduate@una.edu.
Website: https://www.una.edu/sociology/

The University of North Carolina at Charlotte, Cato College of Education, Department of Special Education and Child Development, Charlotte, NC 28223-0001. Offers academically or intellectually gifted (Graduate Certificate); autism spectrum disorders (Graduate Certificate); child and family development: birth through kindergarten (Graduate Certificate); child and family studies: early education (M Ed); special education (M Ed, PhD, Graduate Certificate), including academically or intellectually gifted (M Ed). *Program availability:* Part-time, 100% online, blended/hybrid learning. *Faculty:* 22 full-time (16 women), 9 part-time/adjunct (6 women). *Students:* 19 full-time (16 women), 108 part-time (102 women); includes 16 minority (10 Black or African American, non-Hispanic/Latino; 2 Hispanic/Latino; 4 Two or more races, non-Hispanic/Latino), 5 international. Average age 38. 72 applicants, 94% accepted, 52 enrolled. In 2017, 23 master's, 2 doctorates, 43 other advanced degrees awarded. *Degree requirements:* For master's, thesis or alternative, research project; for doctorate, thesis/dissertation, portfolio; for Graduate Certificate, internship. *Entrance requirements:* For master's, GRE or MAT, personal statement, letters of recommendation; for doctorate, GRE or MAT, 2 official transcripts of all academic work attempted since high school indicating minimum GPA of 3.5 in graduate degree program; at least 3 references of someone who knows applicant's current work and/or academic achievements in previous degree work; two-page essay; current resume or curriculum vitae; writing sample; documentation of teaching; for Graduate Certificate, undergraduate degree from regionally-accredited four-year institution; minimum cumulative undergraduate GPA of 3.0; three recommendations from persons knowledgeable of applicant's interaction with children and families; statement of purpose; clear criminal background check. Additional exam requirements/recommendations for international students: Required—TOEFL (minimum score 523 paper-based, 70 iBT) or IELTS (6.5). *Application deadline:* For fall admission, 12/1 for domestic and international students; for spring admission, 10/1 priority date for domestic and international students; for summer admission, 4/1 priority date for domestic and international students. Applications are processed on a rolling basis. Application fee: $75. Electronic applications accepted. *Expenses:* Tuition, state resident: full-time $4337. Tuition, nonresident: full-time $17,771. *Required fees:* $3211. Tuition and fees vary according to course load and program. *Financial support:* In 2017–18, 8 students received support, including 7 research assistantships (averaging $10,112 per year), 1 teaching assistantship (averaging $3,500 per year); career-related internships or fieldwork, institutionally sponsored loans, scholarships/grants, and unspecified assistantships also available. Support available to part-time students. Financial award application deadline: 3/1; financial award applicants required to submit FAFSA. *Total annual research expenditures:* $3.9 million. *Unit head:* Dr. Belva Collins, Chair, 704-687-8828, E-mail: belva.collins@uncc.edu. *Application contact:* Kathy B. Giddings, Director of Graduate Admissions, 704-687-5503, Fax: 704-687-1668, E-mail: gradadm@uncc.edu.
Website: http://spcd.uncc.edu/

The University of North Carolina at Charlotte, Cato College of Education, Interdisciplinary Education Programs, Charlotte, NC 28223-0001. Offers art education (Graduate Certificate); child and family development: early childhood education (MAT); curriculum and instruction (PhD); elementary education (MAT); foreign language education (MAT); middle grades education (MAT); secondary education (MAT); special education (MAT); teaching (Graduate Certificate); teaching English as a second language (MAT); theatre education (Graduate Certificate). *Program availability:* Part-time, 100% online, blended/hybrid learning. *Students:* 86 full-time (63 women), 533 part-time (423 women); includes 229 minority (169 Black or African American, non-Hispanic/Latino; 1 American Indian or Alaska Native, non-Hispanic/Latino; 7 Asian, non-Hispanic/Latino; 39 Hispanic/Latino; 13 Two or more races, non-Hispanic/Latino), 13 international. Average age 32. 382 applicants, 91% accepted, 253 enrolled. In 2017, 182 master's, 10 doctorates, 172 other advanced degrees awarded. *Degree requirements:* For master's, thesis or alternative, research project/portfolio. *Entrance requirements:* For master's, GRE or MAT, bachelor's degree, or its U.S. equivalent, from regionally-accredited college or university; minimum overall GPA of 3.0 on all previous work beyond high school; statement of purpose (essay); at least three recommendation forms; for doctorate, GRE or MAT, bachelor's degree (or its U.S. equivalent) from regionally-accredited college or university; minimum overall GPA of 3.5 in master's degree program; for Graduate Certificate, bachelor's degree from regionally-accredited university; minimum GPA of 2.75 on all post-secondary work attempted; transcripts; personal statement outlining why the applicant seeks admission to the program. Additional exam requirements/recommendations for international students: Required—TOEFL (minimum score 523 paper-based, 70 iBT) or IELTS (6.5). *Application deadline:* For fall admission, 3/1 priority date for domestic and international students; for spring admission, 10/1 priority date for domestic and international students; for summer admission, 4/1 priority date for domestic and international students. Applications are processed on a rolling basis. Application fee: $75. Electronic applications accepted. *Expenses:* Tuition, state resident: full-time $4337. Tuition, nonresident: full-time $17,771. *Required fees:* $3211. Tuition and fees vary according to course load and program. *Financial support:* Career-related internships or fieldwork, institutionally sponsored loans, scholarships/grants, and unspecified assistantships available. Support available to part-time students. Financial award application deadline: 3/1; financial award applicants required to submit FAFSA. *Unit head:* Dr. Ellen McIntyre, Dean, 704-687-8722, E-mail: ellen.mcintyre@uncc.edu. *Application contact:* Kathy B. Giddings, Director of Graduate Admissions, 704-687-5503, Fax: 704-687-1668, E-mail: gradadm@uncc.edu.
Website: http://education.uncc.edu/academic-programs

The University of North Carolina at Greensboro, Graduate School, School of Health and Human Sciences, Department of Human Development and Family Studies, Greensboro, NC 27412-5001. Offers M Ed, MS, PhD. *Degree requirements:* For master's, one foreign language; for doctorate, one foreign language, thesis/dissertation. *Entrance requirements:* For master's and doctorate, GRE General Test. Additional exam requirements/recommendations for international students: Required—TOEFL. Electronic applications accepted. *Expenses:* Contact institution. *Faculty research:* Adolescent mothers, multi-handicapped, older adults.

University of North Texas, Robert B. Toulouse School of Graduate Studies, Denton, TX 76203-5459. Offers accounting (MS); applied anthropology (MA, MS); applied behavior analysis (Certificate); applied geography (MA); applied technology and performance improvement (M Ed, MS); art education (MA); art history (MA); art museum education (Certificate); arts leadership (Certificate); audiology (Au D); behavior analysis (MS); behavioral science (PhD); biochemistry and molecular biology (MS); biology (MA, MS); biomedical engineering (MS); business analysis (MS); chemistry (MS); clinical health psychology (PhD); communication studies (MA, MS); computer engineering (MS); computer science (MS); counseling (M Ed, MS), including clinical mental health counseling (MS), college and university counseling, elementary school counseling, secondary school counseling; creative writing (MA); criminal justice (MS); curriculum and instruction (M Ed); decision sciences (MBA); design (MA, MFA), including fashion design (MFA), innovation studies, interior design (MFA); early childhood studies (MS); economics (MS); educational leadership (M Ed, Ed D); educational psychology (MS, PhD), including family studies (MS), gifted and talented (MS), human development (MS), learning and cognition (MS), research, measurement and evaluation (MS); electrical engineering (MS); emergency management (MPA); engineering technology (MS); English (MA); English as a second language (MA); environmental science (MS); finance (MBA, MS); financial management (MPA); French (MA); health services management (MBA); higher education (M Ed, Ed D); history (MA, MS); hospitality management (MS); human resources management (MPA); information science (MS); information systems (PhD); information technologies (MBA); interdisciplinary studies (MA, MS); international studies (MA); international sustainable tourism (MS); jazz studies (MM); journalism (MA, MJ, Graduate Certificate), including interactive and virtual digital communication (Graduate Certificate), narrative journalism (Graduate Certificate), public relations (Graduate Certificate); kinesiology (MS); linguistics (MA); local government management (MPA); logistics (PhD); logistics and supply chain management (MBA); long-term care, senior housing, and aging services (MA); management (PhD); marketing (MBA); mathematics (MA, MS); mechanical and energy engineering (MS, PhD); music (MA), including ethnomusicology, music theory, musicology, performance; music composition (PhD); music education (MM Ed, PhD); nonprofit management (MPA); operations and supply chain management (MBA); performance (MM, DMA); philosophy (MA); political science (MA); professional and technical communication (MA); radio, television and film (MA, MFA); rehabilitation counseling (Certificate); sociology (MA); Spanish (MA); special education (M Ed); speech-language pathology (MA); strategic management (MBA); studio art (MFA); teaching (M Ed); MBA/MS. *Program availability:* Part-time, evening/weekend, online learning. Terminal master's awarded for partial completion of doctoral program. *Degree requirements:* For master's, variable foreign language requirement, comprehensive exam (for some programs), thesis (for some programs); for doctorate, variable foreign language requirement, comprehensive exam (for some programs), thesis/dissertation; for other advanced degree, variable foreign language requirement, comprehensive exam (for some programs). *Entrance requirements:* For master's and doctorate, GRE, GMAT. Additional exam requirements/recommendations for international students: Required—TOEFL (minimum score 550 paper-based; 79 iBT). Electronic applications accepted.

University of Rhode Island, Graduate School, College of Health Sciences, Department of Human Development and Family Studies, Kingston, RI 02881. Offers college student personnel (MS); human development and family studies (MS); marriage and family therapy (MS). *Accreditation:* AAMFT/COAMFTE. *Program availability:* Part-time. *Faculty:* 16 full-time (11 women). *Students:* 47 full-time (35 women), 12 part-time (10 women); includes 13 minority (4 Black or African American, non-Hispanic/Latino; 1 American Indian or Alaska Native, non-Hispanic/Latino; 4 Asian, non-Hispanic/Latino; 3 Hispanic/Latino; 1 Two or more races, non-Hispanic/Latino), 2 international. 91 applicants, 43% accepted, 29 enrolled. In 2017, 24 master's awarded. *Entrance requirements:* Additional exam requirements/recommendations for international students: Required—TOEFL. *Application deadline:* For fall admission, 1/15 for domestic and international students. Application fee: $65. Electronic applications accepted. *Expenses:* Tuition, state resident: full-time $12,706; part-time $786 per credit. Tuition, nonresident: full-time $25,216; part-time $1401 per credit. *Required fees:* $1598; $45 per credit. One-time fee: $30 part-time. *Financial support:* In 2017–18, 1 research assistantship (averaging $4,431 per year), 4 teaching assistantships (averaging $10,128 per year) were awarded. Financial award application deadline: 1/15; financial award applicants required to submit FAFSA. *Unit head:* Dr. Karen McCurdy, Chair, 401-874-5960, Fax: 401-874-4020, E-mail: kmccurdy@uri.edu.
Website: http://www.uri.edu/hss/hdf/

University of Southern California, Graduate School, School of Social Work, Los Angeles, CA 90089. Offers community organization, planning and administration (MSW); families and children (MSW); health (MSW); mental health (MSW); military social work and veterans services (MSW); older adults (MSW); public child welfare (MSW); school settings (MSW); social work (MSW, PhD); systems of mental illness recovery (MSW); work and life (MSW); JD/MSW; M Pl/MSW; MPA/MSW; MSW/MBA; MSW/MJCS; MSW/MS. *Accreditation:* CSWE (one or more programs are accredited). *Degree requirements:* For doctorate, comprehensive exam, thesis/dissertation, qualifying exam/publishable paper. *Entrance requirements:* For doctorate, GRE General Test. Additional exam requirements/recommendations for international students: Required—TOEFL (minimum score 600 paper-based; 100 iBT), ESL exam. Electronic applications accepted. *Faculty research:* Department of Defense Educational Activity, detection/treatment of depression among older adults, health/aging, psychosocial adaptation to extreme environments/man made disasters; mental health needs of older adults.

University of Southern Mississippi, College of Education and Psychology, Department of Child and Family Studies, Hattiesburg, MS 39406-0001. Offers M Ed, MS. *Accreditation:* AAMFT/COAMFTE (one or more programs are accredited). *Program availability:* Part-time, online learning. *Students:* 31 full-time (26 women). 71 applicants, 56% accepted, 31 enrolled. In 2017, 3 master's awarded. *Degree requirements:* For master's, comprehensive exam, thesis optional. *Entrance requirements:* For master's, GRE General Test, minimum GPA of 2.75 on last 60 hours. Additional exam requirements/recommendations for international students: Required—TOEFL. *Application deadline:* For fall admission, 3/1 priority date for domestic students, 3/1 for international students; for spring admission, 1/1 priority date for domestic and international students. Applications are processed on a rolling basis. Application fee: $60. Electronic applications accepted. *Expenses:* Tuition, state resident: full-time $3830. *Financial support:* Fellowships, research assistantships with full tuition reimbursements, career-related internships or fieldwork, Federal Work-Study, institutionally sponsored loans, scholarships/grants, health care benefits, and unspecified assistantships available. Financial award application deadline: 3/15; financial award applicants required to submit FAFSA. *Faculty research:* School food service, teen pregnancy, diet and cholesterol metabolism. *Unit head:* Pat Sims, Chair, 601-266-6990, Fax: 601-266-4680.
Website: https://www.usm.edu/family-studies-child-development

Child and Family Studies

University of South Florida, College of Behavioral and Community Sciences, Department of Child and Family Studies, Tampa, FL 33620-9951. Offers applied behavior analysis (MA, MS, PhD); behavioral and community sciences (PhD); child and adolescent behavioral health (MS), including developmental disabilities, leadership in child and adolescent health, translational research and evaluation, youth and behavioral health; rehabilitation and mental health counseling (MA), including addictions and substance abuse counseling, marriage and family therapy. *Accreditation:* ACA. *Faculty:* 18 full-time (12 women), 2 part-time/adjunct (1 woman). *Students:* 188 full-time (166 women), 115 part-time (92 women); includes 121 minority (40 Black or African American, non-Hispanic/Latino; 8 Asian, non-Hispanic/Latino; 61 Hispanic/Latino; 12 Two or more races, non-Hispanic/Latino), 6 international. Average age 28. 287 applicants, 53% accepted, 89 enrolled. In 2017, 45 master's, 1 doctorate awarded. *Degree requirements:* For master's, comprehensive exam, thesis (for some programs); for doctorate, comprehensive exam, thesis/dissertation, Behavior Analyst Board Certification Exam. *Entrance requirements:* For master's, GRE General Test, minimum GPA of 3.0 in last 60 hours of coursework; letters of recommendation; one-page narrative describing experience, interest, and career goals in applied behavior analysis; resume or curriculum vitae (varies by program); for doctorate, GRE General Test, master's degree in behavioral analysis or closely-related field; minimum GPA of 3.5 in graduate course work; three letters of recommendation; campus visit with faculty interview; personal statement; curriculum vitae; evidence of research experiences and expertise. Additional exam requirements/recommendations for international students: Required—TOEFL (minimum score 550 paper-based; 79 iBT) or IELTS (minimum score 6.5). *Application deadline:* For fall admission, 12/5 for domestic and international students. Application fee: $30. *Financial support:* In 2017–18, 30 students received support. Unspecified assistantships available. *Faculty research:* Applied behavior analysis, autism, behavior management, behavioral intervention, children, developmental disabilities, experimental analysis of behavior, functional assessment, positive behavior support. *Total annual research expenditures:* $17.6 million. *Application contact:* Dr. Raymond G. Miltenberger, Professor/Director of Master's Program, 813-974-5079, Fax: 813-974-6115, E-mail: miltenbe@usf.edu.
Website: http://cfs.cbcs.usf.edu/

University of South Florida, Innovative Education, Tampa, FL 33620-9951. Offers adult, career and higher education (Graduate Certificate), including college teaching, leadership in developing human resources, leadership in higher education; Africana studies (Graduate Certificate), including diasporas and health disparities, genocide and human rights; aging studies (Graduate Certificate), including gerontology; art research (Graduate Certificate), including museum studies; business foundations (Graduate Certificate); chemical and biomedical engineering (Graduate Certificate), including materials science and engineering, water, health and sustainability; child and family studies (Graduate Certificate), including positive behavior support; civil and industrial engineering (Graduate Certificate), including transportation systems analysis; community and family health (Graduate Certificate), including maternal and child health, social marketing and public health, violence and injury: prevention and intervention, women's health; criminology (Graduate Certificate), including criminal justice administration; data science for public administration (Graduate Certificate); digital humanities (Graduate Certificate); educational measurement and research (Graduate Certificate), including evaluation; English (Graduate Certificate), including comparative literary studies, creative writing, professional and technical communication; entrepreneurship (Graduate Certificate); environmental health (Graduate Certificate), including safety management; epidemiology and biostatistics (Graduate Certificate), including applied biostatistics, biostatistics, concepts and tools of epidemiology, epidemiology, epidemiology of infectious diseases; geography, environment and planning (Graduate Certificate), including community development, environmental policy and management, geographical information systems; geology (Graduate Certificate), including hydrogeology; global health (Graduate Certificate), including disaster management, global health and Latin American and Caribbean studies, global health practice, humanitarian assistance, infection control; government and international affairs (Graduate Certificate), including Cuban studies, globalization studies; health policy and management (Graduate Certificate), including health management and leadership, public health policy and programs; hearing specialist: early intervention (Graduate Certificate); industrial and management systems engineering (Graduate Certificate), including systems engineering, technology management; information studies (Graduate Certificate), including school library media specialist; information systems/decision sciences (Graduate Certificate), including analytics and business intelligence; instructional technology (Graduate Certificate), including distance education, Florida digital/virtual educator, instructional design, multimedia design, Web design; internal medicine, bioethics and medical humanities (Graduate Certificate), including biomedical ethics; Latin American and Caribbean studies (Graduate Certificate); leadership for coastal resiliency planning (Graduate Certificate); mass communications (Graduate Certificate), including multimedia journalism; mathematics and statistics (Graduate Certificate), including mathematics; medicine (Graduate Certificate), including aging and neuroscience, bioinformatics, biotechnology, brain fitness and memory management, clinical investigation, hand and upper limb rehabilitation, health informatics, health sciences, integrative weight management, intellectual property, medicine and gender, metabolic and nutritional medicine, metabolic cardiology, pharmacy sciences; national and competitive intelligence (Graduate Certificate); nursing (Graduate Certificate), including simulation based academic fellowship in advanced pain management; psychological and social foundations (Graduate Certificate), including career counseling, college teaching, diversity in education, mental health counseling, school counseling; public affairs (Graduate Certificate), including nonprofit management, public management, research administration; public health (Graduate Certificate), including assessing chemical toxicity and public health risks, health equity, pharmacoepidemiology, public health generalist, toxicology, translational research in adolescent behavioral health; public health practices (Graduate Certificate), including planning for healthy communities; rehabilitation and mental health counseling (Graduate Certificate), including integrative mental health care, marriage and family therapy, rehabilitation technology; secondary education (Graduate Certificate), including ESOL, foreign language education: culture and content, foreign language education: professional; social work (Graduate Certificate), including geriatric social work/clinical gerontology; special education (Graduate Certificate), including autism spectrum disorder, disabilities education: severe/profound; world languages (Graduate Certificate), including teaching English as a second language (TESL) or foreign language. *Unit head:* Dr. Cynthia DeLuca, Associate Vice President and Assistant Vice Provost, 813-974-3077, Fax: 813-974-7061, E-mail: deluca@usf.edu. *Application contact:* Owen Hooper, Director, Summer and Alternative Calendar Programs, 813-974-6917, E-mail: hooper@usf.edu.
Website: http://www.usf.edu/innovative-education/

The University of Tennessee, Graduate School, College of Education, Health and Human Sciences, Department of Child and Family Studies, Knoxville, TN 37996. Offers child and family studies (MS); early childhood education (MS). *Program availability:* Part-time. *Degree requirements:* For master's, thesis or alternative. *Entrance requirements:* For master's, GRE General Test, minimum GPA of 2.7. Additional exam requirements/recommendations for international students: Required—TOEFL. Electronic applications accepted.

The University of Tennessee, Graduate School, College of Education, Health and Human Sciences, Program in Human Ecology, Knoxville, TN 37996. Offers child and family studies (PhD); community health (PhD); nutrition science (PhD); retailing and consumer sciences (PhD); textile science (PhD). *Degree requirements:* For doctorate, thesis/dissertation. *Entrance requirements:* For doctorate, GRE General Test, minimum GPA of 2.7. Additional exam requirements/recommendations for international students: Required—TOEFL. Electronic applications accepted.

The University of Tennessee at Martin, Graduate Programs, College of Agriculture and Applied Sciences, Department of Family and Consumer Sciences, Martin, TN 38238. Offers dietetics (MSFCS); general family and consumer sciences (MSFCS). *Program availability:* Part-time, 100% online. *Faculty:* 9. *Students:* 10 full-time (7 women), 31 part-time (27 women); includes 11 minority (9 Black or African American, non-Hispanic/Latino; 1 Hispanic/Latino; 1 Two or more races, non-Hispanic/Latino). Average age 30. 50 applicants, 86% accepted, 20 enrolled. In 2017, 12 master's awarded. *Degree requirements:* For master's, comprehensive exam, thesis optional. *Entrance requirements:* For master's, GRE General Test, minimum GPA of 2.5. Additional exam requirements/recommendations for international students: Required—TOEFL (minimum score 525 paper-based; 71 iBT). *Application deadline:* For fall admission, 7/27 priority date for domestic and international students; for spring admission, 12/17 priority date for domestic and international students; for summer admission, 5/10 priority date for domestic and international students. Applications are processed on a rolling basis. Application fee: $30 ($130 for international students). Electronic applications accepted. *Expenses:* Tuition, state resident: full-time $8658; part-time $481 per credit hour. Tuition, nonresident: full-time $14,418; part-time $801 per credit hour. *International tuition:* $22,602 full-time. *Required fees:* $1404; $79 per credit hour. Part-time tuition and fees vary according to course load. *Financial support:* In 2017–18, 20 students received support, including 1 research assistantship with full tuition reimbursement available (averaging $7,540 per year), 7 teaching assistantships with full tuition reimbursements available (averaging $7,432 per year); scholarships/grants and tuition waivers (full and partial) also available. Financial award application deadline: 2/1; financial award applicants required to submit FAFSA. *Faculty research:* Children with developmental disabilities, regional food product development and marketing, parent education. *Unit head:* Dr. Lisa LeBleu, Coordinator, 731-881-7116, Fax: 731-881-7106, E-mail: llebleu@utm.edu. *Application contact:* Jolene L. Cunningham, Student Services Specialist, 731-881-7012, Fax: 731-881-7499, E-mail: jcunningham@utm.edu.
Website: http://www.utm.edu/departments/caas/fcs/index.php

The University of Texas at Austin, Graduate School, College of Natural Sciences, School of Human Ecology, Program in Human Development and Family Sciences, Austin, TX 78712-1111. Offers MA, PhD. *Degree requirements:* For master's, thesis; for doctorate, thesis/dissertation. *Entrance requirements:* For master's and doctorate, GRE General Test. Additional exam requirements/recommendations for international students: Required—TOEFL. Electronic applications accepted. *Faculty research:* Marriage and family relationships, parenting, impact of television on children, courtship, family policy.

The University of Texas at Dallas, School of Behavioral and Brain Sciences, Program in Psychological Sciences, Richardson, TX 75080. Offers early childhood disorders (MS); psychological sciences (MS, PhD). *Program availability:* Part-time, evening/weekend. *Faculty:* 12 full-time (9 women), 2 part-time/adjunct (both women). *Students:* 67 full-time (54 women), 10 part-time (9 women); includes 29 minority (7 Black or African American, non-Hispanic/Latino; 5 Asian, non-Hispanic/Latino; 15 Hispanic/Latino; 2 Two or more races, non-Hispanic/Latino), 4 international. Average age 26. 139 applicants, 40% accepted, 24 enrolled. In 2017, 24 master's, 1 doctorate awarded. *Degree requirements:* For master's, directed project or internship; for doctorate, thesis/dissertation. *Entrance requirements:* For master's and doctorate, GRE General Test, minimum GPA of 3.0 in upper-level course work. Additional exam requirements/recommendations for international students: Required—TOEFL (minimum score 550 paper-based). *Application deadline:* For fall admission, 7/15 for domestic students, 5/1 priority date for international students; for spring admission, 11/15 for domestic students, 9/1 priority date for international students. Applications are processed on a rolling basis. Application fee: $50 ($100 for international students). Electronic applications accepted. *Expenses:* Tuition, state resident: full-time $12,916; part-time $718 per credit hour. Tuition, nonresident: full-time $25,252; part-time $1403 per credit hour. *Financial support:* In 2017–18, 46 students received support, including 8 research assistantships with partial tuition reimbursements available (averaging $29,172 per year), 21 teaching assistantships with partial tuition reimbursements available (averaging $17,966 per year); fellowships, career-related internships or fieldwork, Federal Work-Study, scholarships/grants, and unspecified assistantships also available. Support available to part-time students. Financial award application deadline: 4/30; financial award applicants required to submit FAFSA. *Faculty research:* Neurocognitive development in young adulthood, infant learning, infant and toddler eye tracking, social aggression. *Unit head:* Dr. Shayla Holub, Program Head, Psychological Sciences, 972-883-4473, Fax: 972-883-3491, E-mail: sholub@utdallas.edu.
Website: http://www.utdallas.edu/bbs/degrees/psy-degrees/

University of Utah, Graduate School, College of Social and Behavioral Science, Department of Family and Consumer Studies, Salt Lake City, UT 84112-0080. Offers human development and social policy (MS). *Program availability:* Part-time. *Faculty:* 15 full-time (7 women), 7 part-time/adjunct (4 women). *Students:* 9 full-time (8 women), 1 (woman) part-time. Average age 26. 12 applicants, 67% accepted, 7 enrolled. In 2017, 7 master's awarded. *Degree requirements:* For master's, comprehensive exam (for some programs), thesis (for some programs), thesis or project. *Entrance requirements:* For master's, GRE General Test, minimum undergraduate GPA of 3.0, courses in research methods and statistics. Additional exam requirements/recommendations for international students: Required—TOEFL (minimum score 550 paper-based). *Application deadline:* For fall admission, 2/15 priority date for domestic and international students. Applications are processed on a rolling basis. Application fee: $55 ($65 for international students). Electronic applications accepted. *Financial support:* In 2017–18, 6 students received support, including 2 research assistantships with full tuition reimbursements available (averaging $15,000 per year), 4 teaching assistantships with full tuition reimbursements available (averaging $15,000 per year); scholarships/grants also available. Financial award application deadline: 2/15. *Faculty research:* Social, physical, educational and economic contexts of individuals, families and communities; autism spectrum disorder; play/flow; division of labor. *Unit head:* Prof. Lori Kowaleski-Jones, PhD, Chair, 801-585-0074, Fax: 801-581-5156, E-mail: lk2700@fcs.utah.edu. *Application contact:* Prof. Jessie Fan, PhD, Graduate Director, 801-581-4170, E-mail: jessie.fan@fcs.utah.edu.
Website: http://fcs.utah.edu/

University of Victoria, Faculty of Graduate Studies, Faculty of Human and Social Development, School of Child and Youth Care, Victoria, BC V8W 2Y2, Canada. Offers MA, PhD. *Program availability:* Part-time. *Degree requirements:* For master's, thesis. *Entrance requirements:* For master's, resume, professional references, sample of

academic writing. Additional exam requirements/recommendations for international students: Required—TOEFL (minimum score 575 paper-based), IELTS (minimum score 7). Electronic applications accepted.

University of Wisconsin–Madison, Graduate School, School of Human Ecology, Program in Human Development and Family Studies, Madison, WI 53706-1380. Offers MS, PhD. *Program availability:* Part-time. Terminal master's awarded for partial completion of doctoral program. *Degree requirements:* For master's, thesis; for doctorate, comprehensive exam, thesis/dissertation. *Entrance requirements:* For master's, GRE General Test, 3 letters of recommendation; for doctorate, GRE General Test, MS or MA, 3 letters of recommendation. Additional exam requirements/recommendations for international students: Required—TOEFL (minimum score 580 paper-based; 92 iBT). Electronic applications accepted. *Faculty research:* Human development, adolescence, adulthood, prevention, intervention.

Utah State University, School of Graduate Studies, Emma Eccles Jones College of Education and Human Services, Department of Family, Consumer, and Human Development, Logan, UT 84322. Offers family and human development (MFHD); family, consumer, and human development (MS, PhD), including adolescence/youth (MS); adult development/aging (MS), consumer science (MS), infancy/childhood (MS), marriage and family relations (MS), marriage and family therapy (MS). *Accreditation:* AAMFT/COAMFTE (one or more programs are accredited). *Program availability:* Part-time, evening/weekend, online learning. *Degree requirements:* For master's, thesis; for doctorate, comprehensive exam, thesis/dissertation, competencies. *Entrance requirements:* For master's, GRE General Test or MAT, minimum GPA of 3.0, 3 letters of recommendation; for doctorate, GRE, minimum GPA of 3.0, 3 letters of recommendation. Additional exam requirements/recommendations for international students: Required—TOEFL. Electronic applications accepted. *Faculty research:* Marriage and family relations, adolescent problem behavior, family financial management, early literacy, mental health in the elderly, parent child attachment.

Vanderbilt University, Peabody College, Department of Psychology and Human Development, Nashville, TN 37240-1001. Offers child studies (M Ed); clinical psychological assessment (M Ed); quantitative methods (M Ed). *Accreditation:* APA. *Program availability:* Part-time. *Faculty:* 36 full-time (22 women), 7 part-time/adjunct (3 women). *Students:* 38 full-time (35 women), 12 part-time (all women); includes 7 minority (1 Black or African American, non-Hispanic/Latino; 1 Asian, non-Hispanic/Latino; 5 Hispanic/Latino), 7 international. Average age 25. 140 applicants, 36% accepted, 19 enrolled. In 2017, 24 master's awarded. *Degree requirements:* For master's, comprehensive exam (for some programs), thesis optional. *Entrance requirements:* For master's, GRE General Test. Additional exam requirements/recommendations for international students: Required—TOEFL (minimum score 550 paper-based; 80 iBT). *Application deadline:* For fall admission, 12/31 for domestic and international students; for spring admission, 11/1 for domestic and international students. Applications are processed on a rolling basis. Application fee: $0. Electronic applications accepted. *Financial support:* Fellowships with partial tuition reimbursements, research assistantships with partial tuition reimbursements, teaching assistantships with partial tuition reimbursements, Federal Work-Study, institutionally sponsored loans, scholarships/grants, tuition waivers (partial), and unspecified assistantships available. Financial award application deadline: 1/15; financial award applicants required to submit FAFSA. *Faculty research:* Cognitive development, quantitative methods, educational neuroscience, depression in adolescence, educational psychology. *Unit head:* Dr. Amy Needham, Chair, 615-322-8141, Fax: 615-343-9494, E-mail: amy.needham@vanderbilt.edu. *Application contact:* Ally Armstead, Educational Coordinator, 615-343-4963, Fax: 615-343-9494, E-mail: ally.armstead@vanderbilt.edu.
Website: http://peabody.vanderbilt.edu/departments/psych/index.php

Walden University, Graduate Programs, School of Counseling, Minneapolis, MN 55401. Offers addiction counseling (MS), including addictions and public health, child and adolescent counseling, family studies and interventions, forensic counseling, general program, military families and culture, trauma and crisis counseling; clinical mental health counseling (MS), including addiction counseling, forensic counseling, military families and culture, trauma and crisis counseling; counselor education and supervision (PhD), including consultation, counseling and social change, forensic mental health counseling, leadership and program evaluation, trauma and crisis; marriage, couple, and family counseling (MS), including addiction counseling, career counseling, forensic counseling, military families and culture, trauma and crisis counseling; school counseling (MS), including addiction counseling, career counseling, crisis and trauma, military families and culture. *Accreditation:* ACA. *Program availability:* Part-time, evening/weekend, online only, 100% online. *Degree requirements:* For master's, residency, field experience, professional development plan, licensure plan; for doctorate, thesis/dissertation, residency, practicum, internship. *Entrance requirements:* For master's, bachelor's degree or higher; minimum GPA of 2.5; official transcripts; goal statement (for some programs); access to computer and Internet; for doctorate, master's degree or higher; three years of related professional or academic experience (preferred); minimum GPA of 3.0; goal statement and current resume (for select programs); official transcripts; access to computer and Internet. Additional exam requirements/recommendations for international students: Required—TOEFL (minimum score 550 paper-based, 79 iBT), IELTS (minimum score 6.5), Michigan English Language Assessment Battery (minimum score 82), or PTE (minimum score 53). Electronic applications accepted.

Walden University, Graduate Programs, School of Social Work and Human Services, Minneapolis, MN 55401. Offers addictions and social work (DSW); advanced clinical practice (MSW); clinical expertise (DSW); criminal justice (DSW); disaster, crisis, and intervention (DSW); family studies and interventions (DSW); human and social services (PhD), including advanced research, community and social services, community intervention and leadership, conflict management, criminal justice, disaster crisis and intervention, family studies and intervention, gerontology, global social services, higher education, human services and nonprofit administration, mental health facilitation; medical social work (DSW); military social work (MSW); policy practice (DSW); social work (PhD), including addictions and social work, clinical expertise, criminal justice, disaster, crisis and intervention, family studies and interventions, medical social work, policy practice, social work administration; social work administration (DSW); social work in healthcare (MSW); social work with children and families (MSW). *Accreditation:* CSWE. *Program availability:* Part-time, evening/weekend, online only, 100% online. *Degree requirements:* For master's, residency (for some programs); for doctorate, thesis/dissertation, residency. *Entrance requirements:* For master's, bachelor's degree or higher; minimum GPA of 2.5; official transcripts; goal statement (for some programs); access to computer and Internet; for doctorate, master's degree or higher; three years of related professional or academic experience (preferred); minimum GPA of 3.0; goal statement and current resume (for select programs); official transcripts; access to computer and Internet. Additional exam requirements/recommendations for international students: Required—TOEFL (minimum score 550 paper-based, 79 iBT), IELTS (minimum score 6.5), Michigan English Language Assessment Battery (minimum score 82), or PTE (minimum score 53). Electronic applications accepted.

Washington University in St. Louis, Brown School, St. Louis, MO 63110. Offers American Indian/Alaska native (MSW); children, youth and families (MSW); epidemiology/biostatistics (MPH); generalist (MPH); global health (MPH); health (MSW); health policy analysis (MPH); individualized (MSW), including health; mental health (MSW); older adults and aging societies (MSW); public health sciences (PhD); social and economic development (MSW), including domestic, international; social work (PhD); urban design (MPH); violence and injury prevention (MSW); JD/MSW; M Arch/MSW; MPH/MBA; MSW/M Div; MSW/M Ed; MSW/MAPS; MSW/MBA; MSW/MPH; MUD/MSW. MSW/M Div and MSW/MAPS offered in partnership with Eden Theological Seminary. *Accreditation:* CSWE (one or more programs are accredited). *Faculty:* 54 full-time (31 women), 87 part-time/adjunct (61 women). *Students:* 294 full-time (254 women); includes 114 minority (56 Black or African American, non-Hispanic/Latino; 8 American Indian or Alaska Native, non-Hispanic/Latino; 17 Asian, non-Hispanic/Latino; 10 Hispanic/Latino; 1 Native Hawaiian or other Pacific Islander, non-Hispanic/Latino; 22 Two or more races, non-Hispanic/Latino), 246 international. Average age 26. *Degree requirements:* For master's, 60 credit hours (for MSW); 52 credit hours (for MPH); practicum; for doctorate, comprehensive exam, thesis/dissertation. *Entrance requirements:* For master's, GRE (preferred), GMAT, LSAT, MCAT, PCAT, or United States Medical Licensing Exam (for MPH); for doctorate, GRE. Additional exam requirements/recommendations for international students: Required—TOEFL (minimum score 100 iBT), IELTS (minimum score 7). *Application deadline:* For fall admission, 12/15 priority date for domestic and international students; for winter admission, 3/1 priority date for domestic and international students. Applications are processed on a rolling basis. Electronic applications accepted. *Expenses:* Contact institution. *Financial support:* In 2017–18, 30 fellowships, 60 research assistantships were awarded; career-related internships or fieldwork, Federal Work-Study, scholarships/grants, and unspecified assistantships also available. Support available to part-time students. Financial award applicants required to submit FAFSA. *Faculty research:* Mental health, social policy, health policy, epidemiology, social and economic development. *Total annual research expenditures:* $14.5 million. *Unit head:* Jamie L. Adkisson-Hennessey, Director of Admissions and Recruitment, 314-935-3524, Fax: 314-935-4859, E-mail: jadkisson@wustl.edu. *Application contact:* Office of Admissions and Recruitment, 314-935-6676, Fax: 314-935-4859, E-mail: brownadmissions@wustl.edu.
Website: http://brownschool.wustl.edu

Child Development

California State University, Los Angeles, Graduate Studies, College of Health and Human Services, Department of Child and Family Studies, Los Angeles, CA 90032-8530. Offers child development (MA). *Program availability:* Part-time, evening/weekend. *Degree requirements:* For master's, comprehensive exam, project or thesis. *Entrance requirements:* Additional exam requirements/recommendations for international students: Required—TOEFL (minimum score 500 paper-based). *Faculty research:* Nutrition education, laundry product and fabric durability, computer usage in public school home economics.

California State University, Sacramento, College of Education, Graduate and Professional Studies in Education, Sacramento, CA 95819. Offers behavioral science and gender equity (MA); child development (MA); counseling (MS); curriculum and instruction (MA); education (Ed D), including K-12 and community college; education leadership and policy studies (MA), including higher education, PreK-12; education specialist (Ed S), including school psychology; educational technology (MA); language and literacy (MA); multicultural education (MA); school psychology (MA); special education (MA); workforce development advocacy (MA). *Program availability:* Part-time, evening/weekend, blended/hybrid learning. *Students:* 381 full-time (294 women), 135 part-time (101 women); includes 296 minority (44 Black or African American, non-Hispanic/Latino; 1 American Indian or Alaska Native, non-Hispanic/Latino; 94 Asian, non-Hispanic/Latino; 153 Hispanic/Latino; 4 Native Hawaiian or other Pacific Islander, non-Hispanic/Latino), 3 international. Average age 32. 553 applicants, 53% accepted, 292 enrolled. In 2017, 147 master's, 13 doctorates, 10 other advanced degrees awarded. *Degree requirements:* For master's, thesis or project; writing proficiency exam; for doctorate, thesis/dissertation. *Entrance requirements:* For master's and doctorate, GRE. Additional exam requirements/recommendations for international students: Required—TOEFL (minimum score 550 paper-based; 80 iBT); Recommended—IELTS (minimum score 7), TSE. *Application deadline:* For fall admission, 2/15 for domestic students, 1/15 for international students. Applications are processed on a rolling basis. Application fee: $55. Electronic applications accepted. *Expenses:* Contact institution. *Financial support:* Career-related internships or fieldwork, Federal Work-Study, and scholarships/grants available. Support available to part-time students. Financial award application deadline: 3/1; financial award applicants required to submit FAFSA. *Unit head:* Dr. Elizabeth Liles, Chair, 916-278-5942, E-mail: coe@csus.edu. *Application contact:* Jose Martinez, Graduate Admissions Supervisor, 916-278-7871, E-mail: martinj@skymail.csus.edu.
Website: http://www.csus.edu/coe/academics/graduate/index.html

California State University, San Bernardino, Graduate Studies, College of Social and Behavioral Sciences, Department of Psychology, San Bernardino, CA 92407. Offers child development (MA); clinical/counseling psychology (MS); industrial/organizational psychology (MS); psychological science (MA). *Faculty:* 13 full-time (4 women), 2 part-time/adjunct (both women). *Students:* 61 full-time (41 women), 17 part-time (14 women); includes 47 minority (2 Black or African American, non-Hispanic/Latino; 3 Asian, non-Hispanic/Latino; 33 Hispanic/Latino; 9 Two or more races, non-Hispanic/Latino), 3 international. Average age 28. 190 applicants, 19% accepted, 33 enrolled. In 2017, 28 master's awarded. *Degree requirements:* For master's, comprehensive exam, thesis (for some programs). *Entrance requirements:* Additional exam requirements/recommendations for international students: Required—TOEFL. Application fee: $55. *Financial support:* Fellowships, research assistantships, and teaching assistantships available. *Faculty research:* Perceptual development, human memory, psychopharmacology, psychology of women, language acquisition. *Unit head:* Dr.

Robert Ricco, Chair, 909-537-5485, Fax: 909-537-7003, E-mail: rricco@csusb.edu. *Application contact:* Dr. Dorota Huizinga, Dean of Graduate Studies, 909-537-3064, E-mail: dorota.huizinga@csusb.edu.
Website: https://csbs.csusb.edu/psychology

California State University, San Bernardino, Graduate Studies, College of Social and Behavioral Sciences, Program in Child Development, San Bernardino, CA 92407. Offers psychology-life span (MA). *Faculty:* 1. *Students:* 5 full-time (all women), 12 part-time (11 women). Average age 29. 12 applicants, 42% accepted, 4 enrolled. In 2017, 5 master's awarded. *Degree requirements:* For master's, comprehensive exam. *Entrance requirements:* Additional exam requirements/recommendations for international students: Required—TOEFL. *Application deadline:* For fall admission, 5/1 for domestic students. Application fee: $55. *Unit head:* Dr. Sharon Ward, Director, 909-537-7304, E-mail: sward@csusb.edu. *Application contact:* Dr. Dorota Huizinga, Dean of Graduate Studies, 909-537-3064, E-mail: dorota.huizinga@csusb.edu.

Chaminade University of Honolulu, Office of Professional and Continuing Education, Program in Education, Honolulu, HI 96816-1578. Offers child development (M Ed); early childhood education (Montessori) (MAT); early childhood education (PK-3) (MAT); educational leadership (M Ed); elementary education (MAT); instructional leadership (M Ed); Montessori (M Ed); secondary education (MAT); special education (MAT); teacher leader (M Ed). *Program availability:* Part-time, evening/weekend, 100% online, blended/hybrid learning. *Faculty:* 7 full-time (3 women), 8 part-time/adjunct (6 women). *Students:* 86 full-time (68 women), 88 part-time (64 women); includes 113 minority (7 Black or African American, non-Hispanic/Latino; 2 American Indian or Alaska Native, non-Hispanic/Latino; 46 Asian, non-Hispanic/Latino; 7 Hispanic/Latino; 51 Native Hawaiian or other Pacific Islander, non-Hispanic/Latino), 6 international. Average age 34. 61 applicants, 98% accepted, 49 enrolled. In 2017, 91 master's awarded. *Degree requirements:* For master's, thesis or alternative. *Entrance requirements:* For master's, PRAXIS (for MAT), minimum GPA of 2.75 (for M Ed), 3.0 (for MAT); 2 letters of recommendation, resume, writing sample (for MAT). Additional exam requirements/ recommendations for international students: Required—TOEFL (minimum score 550 paper-based; 79 iBT). *Application deadline:* Applications are processed on a rolling basis. Application fee: $40. Electronic applications accepted. *Expenses:* $780 per credit hour plus $93 fee per online class. *Financial support:* Applicants required to submit FAFSA. *Unit head:* Dr. Dale Fryxell, Dean, 808-739-4652, Fax: 808-739-4607, E-mail: edu-office@chaminade.edu. *Application contact:* 808-735-4755, E-mail: gradserv@chaminade.edu.
Website: https://education.chaminade.edu/

East Carolina University, Graduate School, College of Health and Human Performance, Department of Human Development and Family Science, Greenville, NC 27858-4353. Offers birth through kindergarten education (MA Ed); human development and family science (MS); marriage and family therapy (MS); medical family therapy (PhD). *Accreditation:* AAMFT/COAMFTE. *Program availability:* Part-time. *Students:* 73 full-time (69 women), 24 part-time (21 women); includes 20 minority (14 Black or African American, non-Hispanic/Latino; 3 American Indian or Alaska Native, non-Hispanic/ Latino; 2 Hispanic/Latino; 1 Native Hawaiian or other Pacific Islander, non-Hispanic/ Latino), 2 international. Average age 28. 98 applicants, 50% accepted, 35 enrolled. In 2017, 26 master's, 3 doctorates awarded. *Degree requirements:* For master's, comprehensive exam, thesis optional. *Entrance requirements:* Additional exam requirements/recommendations for international students: Recommended—TOEFL (minimum score 78 iBT), IELTS (minimum score 6.5). *Application deadline:* For fall admission, 1/15 for domestic students; for spring admission, 10/15 for domestic students. Applications are processed on a rolling basis. Application fee: $75. *Expenses:* Tuition, state resident: full-time $4749; part-time $297 per credit hour. Tuition, nonresident: full-time $17,898; part-time $1119 per credit hour. *Required fees:* $2691; $224 per credit hour. Part-time tuition and fees vary according to course load and program. *Financial support:* Research assistantships, teaching assistantships, career-related internships or fieldwork, Federal Work-Study, institutionally sponsored loans, and scholarships/grants available. Support available to part-time students. Financial award application deadline: 6/1. *Faculty research:* Child care quality, mental health delivery systems for children, family violence. *Unit head:* Dr. Sharon Ballard, Interim Chair, 252-328-1356, E-mail: ballards@ecu.edu.
Website: https://hhp.ecu.edu/hdfs/

Erikson Institute, Academic Programs, Program in Child Development, Chicago, IL 60654. Offers MS. *Degree requirements:* For master's, comprehensive exam, internship. *Entrance requirements:* For master's, 3 letters of recommendation, minimum GPA of 2.75. Additional exam requirements/recommendations for international students: Required—TOEFL.

Fielding Graduate University, Graduate Programs, School of Leadership Studies, Programs in Infant and Early Childhood Development, Santa Barbara, CA 93105-3814. Offers infant and early childhood development (MA, PhD, Graduate Certificate), including early childhood development: education, mental health, and disruptive behaviors (MA), infant mental health and neurodevelopment (MA), reflective practice and supervision (Graduate Certificate). *Program availability:* Part-time, evening/ weekend, 100% online, blended/hybrid learning. *Faculty:* 1 (woman) full-time, 28 part-time/adjunct (22 women). *Students:* 84 full-time (79 women), 1 (woman) part-time; includes 33 minority (12 Black or African American, non-Hispanic/Latino; 2 American Indian or Alaska Native, non-Hispanic/Latino; 3 Asian, non-Hispanic/Latino; 10 Hispanic/ Latino; 6 Two or more races, non-Hispanic/Latino), 1 international. Average age 45. 17 applicants, 94% accepted, 14 enrolled. In 2017, 9 doctorates awarded. Terminal master's awarded for partial completion of doctoral program. *Degree requirements:* For master's, thesis or alternative, capstone; for doctorate, comprehensive exam, thesis/ dissertation. *Entrance requirements:* For master's and Graduate Certificate, bachelor's degree from regionally-accredited U.S. institution or equivalent; for doctorate, bachelor's or master's degree from regionally-accredited U.S. institution or equivalent, curriculum vitae, statement of purpose, critical thinking writing sample, 2 letters of recommendation, official transcript. *Application deadline:* For fall admission, 7/16 for domestic and international students; for spring admission, 11/1 for domestic and international students; for summer admission, 3/1 for domestic and international students. Application fee: $75. Electronic applications accepted. *Expenses:* Contact institution. *Financial support:* Research assistantships, teaching assistantships, and scholarships/grants available. Support available to part-time students. Financial award applicants required to submit FAFSA. *Unit head:* Dr. Barbara Mink, Program Director, E-mail: bmink@fielding.edu. *Application contact:* Enrollment Coordinator, 800-340-1099 Ext. 4098, Fax: 805-687-9793, E-mail: hodadmission@fielding.edu.
Website: http://www.fielding.edu/our-programs/school-of-leadership-studies/phd-infant-early-childhood-development/

Kansas State University, Graduate School, College of Human Ecology, School of Family Studies and Human Services, Manhattan, KS 66506-1403. Offers applied family sciences (MS); communication sciences and disorders (MS); conflict resolution (Graduate Certificate); couple and family therapy (MS); early childhood education (MS); family and community service (MS); life-span human development (MS); personal financial planning (MS, PhD, Graduate Certificate); youth development (MS, Graduate Certificate). *Accreditation:* AAMFT/COAMFTE; ASHA. *Program availability:* Part-time, online learning. *Degree requirements:* For master's, comprehensive exam (for some programs), thesis optional. *Entrance requirements:* For master's, GRE, minimum GPA of 3.0 in last 2 years (60 semester hours) of undergraduate study; for doctorate, GRE. Additional exam requirements/recommendations for international students: Required—TOEFL (minimum score 600 paper-based). Electronic applications accepted. *Faculty research:* Health and security of military families, training in and evaluation of professional human services (marriage and couple therapy, family life education, treatment of speech and swallowing disorders, financial therapy), disorders of communication and swallowing, family and relationship development and health, financial decision-making.

Lee University, Graduate Studies in Counseling, Cleveland, TN 37320-3450. Offers holistic child development (MS); marriage and family studies (MS); marriage and family therapy (MS); school counseling (MS). *Program availability:* Part-time, 100% online. *Faculty:* 7 full-time (3 women), 3 part-time/adjunct (0 women). *Students:* 95 full-time (71 women), 24 part-time (18 women); includes 27 minority (5 Black or African American, non-Hispanic/Latino; 19 Hispanic/Latino; 3 Two or more races, non-Hispanic/Latino), 7 international. Average age 30. 47 applicants, 87% accepted, 33 enrolled. In 2017, 32 master's awarded. *Degree requirements:* For master's, variable foreign language requirement, comprehensive exam (for some programs), thesis (for some programs), internship. *Entrance requirements:* For master's, GRE General Test or MAT (waived if undergraduate GPA is greater than 3.0 or if applicant already has a graduate degree), minimum undergraduate GPA of 3.0, 3 letters of recommendation, interview, official transcripts, essay. Additional exam requirements/recommendations for international students: Required—TOEFL (minimum score 61 iBT). *Application deadline:* For fall admission, 4/1 priority date for domestic and international students; for spring admission, 11/1 priority date for domestic and international students. Applications are processed on a rolling basis. Application fee: $25. Electronic applications accepted. *Expenses: Tuition:* Full-time $12,780; part-time $710 per credit hour. *Required fees:* $60; $60 per term. Tuition and fees vary according to program. *Financial support:* In 2017–18, 36 students received support. Career-related internships or fieldwork, Federal Work-Study, institutionally sponsored loans, scholarships/grants, and unspecified assistantships available. Financial award application deadline: 3/1; financial award applicants required to submit FAFSA. *Unit head:* Dr. Trevor Milliron, Director, 423-614-8126, Fax: 423-614-8124, E-mail: tmilliron@leeuniversity.edu.
Website: http://www.leeuniversity.edu/academics/graduate/counseling/

Michigan State University, The Graduate School, College of Social Science, Department of Family and Child Ecology, East Lansing, MI 48824. Offers child development (MA); community services (MS); family and child ecology (PhD); family studies (MA); marriage and family therapy (MA); youth development (MA). *Accreditation:* AAMFT/COAMFTE (one or more programs are accredited). *Entrance requirements:* For master's, GRE General Test, minimum GPA of 3.0 in last 2 years of undergraduate course work, 3 letters of recommendation; for doctorate, GRE General Test, minimum GPA of 3.0, 3 letters of recommendation, background in behavioral sciences. Additional exam requirements/recommendations for international students: Required—TOEFL. Electronic applications accepted.

Montclair State University, The Graduate School, College of Education and Human Services, Infant and Early Childhood Mental Health Certificate Program, Montclair, NJ 07043-1624. Offers Certificate.

Montclair State University, The Graduate School, College of Humanities and Social Sciences, MA Program in Child Advocacy and Policy, Montclair, NJ 07043-1624. Offers MA. *Program availability:* Online learning. *Degree requirements:* For master's, seminar. *Entrance requirements:* For master's, minimum GPA of 3.0 in undergraduate major, interview, writing sample.

Mount Saint Mary College, Division of Education, Newburgh, NY 12550-3494. Offers adolescence and special education (MS Ed); childhood education (MS Ed); literacy education (MS Ed); middle school (7-9) (MS Ed). *Accreditation:* NCATE. *Program availability:* Part-time, evening/weekend. *Faculty:* 10 full-time (9 women), 3 part-time/ adjunct (all women). *Students:* 11 full-time (9 women), 83 part-time (62 women); includes 9 minority (1 American Indian or Alaska Native, non-Hispanic/Latino; 6 Hispanic/Latino; 2 Two or more races, non-Hispanic/Latino). Average age 28. 20 applicants, 100% accepted, 16 enrolled. In 2017, 57 master's awarded. *Entrance requirements:* Additional exam requirements/recommendations for international students: Required—TOEFL (minimum score 80 iBT). *Application deadline:* Applications are processed on a rolling basis. Application fee: $45. Electronic applications accepted. Application fee is waived when completed online. *Expenses: Tuition:* Full-time $14,454; part-time $803 per credit. *Required fees:* $172; $86 per semester. *Financial support:* In 2017–18, 15 students received support. Unspecified assistantships available. Financial award application deadline: 4/15; financial award applicants required to submit FAFSA. *Faculty research:* Learning and teaching styles, computers in special education, language development. *Unit head:* Dr. Monica Merritt, Graduate Coordinator, 845-569-3430, Fax: 845-569-3535, E-mail: monica.merritt@msmc.edu. *Application contact:* Lisa Alvarez, Director of Admissions for Graduate Programs and Adult Degree Completion, 845-569-3166, Fax: 845-569-3450, E-mail: lisa.gallina@msmc.edu.
Website: http://www.msmc.edu/Academics/Graduate_Programs/ Master_of_Science_in_Education

North Carolina Agricultural and Technical State University, School of Graduate Studies, School of Agriculture and Environmental Sciences, Department of Family and Consumer Sciences, Greensboro, NC 27411. Offers child development early education and family studies (MAT); family and consumer sciences (MAT); food and nutrition (MS). *Program availability:* Part-time, evening/weekend. *Degree requirements:* For master's, comprehensive exam, thesis or alternative, qualifying exam. *Entrance requirements:* For master's, GRE General Test, minimum GPA of 2.6.

North Dakota State University, College of Graduate and Interdisciplinary Studies, College of Human Development and Education, Department of Human Development and Family Science, Program in Youth Development, Fargo, ND 58102. Offers MS. *Degree requirements:* For master's, comprehensive exam, thesis. *Entrance requirements:* Additional exam requirements/recommendations for international students: Required—TOEFL (minimum score 525 paper-based; 71 iBT). *Faculty research:* Gerontology, wellness, counselor education.

Ohio University, Graduate College, College of Health Sciences and Professions, Department of Social and Public Health, Athens, OH 45701-2979. Offers early child development and family life (MS); family studies (MS); health administration (MHA); public health (MPH); social work (MSW). *Program availability:* Part-time, evening/ weekend, online learning. *Degree requirements:* For master's, capstone (MPH). *Entrance requirements:* For master's, GMAT, GRE General Test, previous course work in accounting, management, and statistics; previous public health background (MHA, MPH). Additional exam requirements/recommendations for international students: Required—TOEFL (minimum score 550 paper-based; 80 iBT) or IELTS (minimum score 6.5). Electronic applications accepted. *Expenses:* Contact institution. *Faculty research:* Health care management, health policy, managed care, health behavior, disease prevention.

Purdue University, Graduate School, College of Health and Human Sciences, Department of Child Development and Family Studies, West Lafayette, IN 47907. Offers developmental studies (MS, PhD); family studies (MS, PhD); marriage and family therapy (MS, PhD). *Program availability:* Part-time. *Faculty:* 19 full-time (11 women), 1 (woman) part-time/adjunct. *Students:* 22 full-time (21 women), 1 (woman) part-time; includes 3 minority (1 Black or African American, non-Hispanic/Latino; 1 Hispanic/Latino; 1 Two or more races, non-Hispanic/Latino), 5 international. Average age 26. 41 applicants, 29% accepted, 8 enrolled. In 2017, 4 master's, 3 doctorates awarded. Terminal master's awarded for partial completion of doctoral program. *Degree requirements:* For master's, thesis; for doctorate, thesis/dissertation. *Entrance requirements:* For master's and doctorate, GRE General Test (minimum score 1000 combined verbal and quantitative), minimum undergraduate GPA of 3.0 or equivalent. Additional exam requirements/recommendations for international students: Required—TOEFL (minimum score 600 paper-based; 90 iBT), TWE (minimum score 4). *Application deadline:* For fall admission, 1/4 for domestic and international students. Applications are processed on a rolling basis. Application fee: $60 ($75 for international students). Electronic applications accepted. *Financial support:* Fellowships with full tuition reimbursements, research assistantships with full tuition reimbursements, teaching assistantships with full tuition reimbursements, and career-related internships or fieldwork available. Support available to part-time students. Financial award application deadline: 1/15; financial award applicants required to submit FAFSA. *Faculty research:* Inclusion of children with special needs, families as learning environments, relationships in child care, work-family relations, AIDS prevention. *Unit head:* Dr. Doran C. French, Head, 765-494-9511, E-mail: dcfrench@purdue.edu. *Application contact:* Tina Putz, Graduate Contact, 765-496-3816, E-mail: tputz@purdue.edu.
Website: http://www.purdue.edu/hhs/hdfs/

Purdue University Northwest, Graduate Studies Office, School of Liberal Arts and Social Sciences, Department of Behavioral Sciences, Hammond, IN 46323-2094. Offers child development and family studies (MS); marriage and family therapy (MS). *Accreditation:* AAMFT/COAMFTE. *Program availability:* Part-time. *Degree requirements:* For master's, thesis. *Entrance requirements:* For master's, GRE, interview. Additional exam requirements/recommendations for international students: Required—TOEFL. *Faculty research:* Substance abuse, sexual abuse, couple therapy, professional issues, adolescent therapy.

Rutgers University–Camden, Graduate School of Arts and Sciences, Program in Childhood Studies, Camden, NJ 08102. Offers MA, PhD. *Program availability:* Part-time, evening/weekend. *Degree requirements:* For master's, comprehensive exam, thesis (for some programs), 30 credits; for doctorate, comprehensive exam, thesis/dissertation, 60 credits. *Entrance requirements:* For master's and doctorate, GRE, 3 letters of recommendation; statement of personal, professional and academic goals. Additional exam requirements/recommendations for international students: Required—TOEFL, IELTS. Electronic applications accepted. *Faculty research:* Children's consumer culture, moral development, development of personality and social relations, children's literature, commodification of childhood.

San Diego State University, Graduate and Research Affairs, College of Education, Department of Child and Family Development, San Diego, CA 92182. Offers child development (MS). *Program availability:* Part-time. *Degree requirements:* For master's, thesis. *Entrance requirements:* For master's, GRE General Test, 3 letters of recommendation, interview. Additional exam requirements/recommendations for international students: Required—TOEFL. Electronic applications accepted.

San Jose State University, Graduate Studies and Research, Connie L. Lurie College of Education, San Jose, CA 95192-0071. Offers child and adolescent development (MA); education (MA), including counseling and student personnel, curriculum and instruction, speech pathology; educational leadership (MA, Ed D), including administration and supervision (MA), educational leadership (MA); elementary education (MA), including curriculum and instruction. *Accreditation:* NCATE. *Program availability:* Part-time, evening/weekend. *Faculty:* 29 full-time (22 women), 47 part-time/adjunct (40 women). *Students:* 414 full-time (339 women), 115 part-time (93 women); includes 341 minority (14 Black or African American, non-Hispanic/Latino; 87 Asian, non-Hispanic/Latino; 176 Hispanic/Latino; 64 Two or more races, non-Hispanic/Latino), 9 international. Average age 30. 654 applicants, 34% accepted, 161 enrolled. In 2017, 286 master's, 7 doctorates awarded. Terminal master's awarded for partial completion of doctoral program. *Degree requirements:* For master's, project or theses, graduate writing assessment; for doctorate, thesis/dissertation. *Entrance requirements:* For master's, GRE General Test (for some programs). Additional exam requirements/recommendations for international students: Required—TOEFL (minimum score 550 paper-based; 80 iBT), IELTS (minimum score 6.5), PTE (minimum score 53). *Application deadline:* For fall admission, 2/1 for domestic and international students. Applications are processed on a rolling basis. Application fee: $55. Electronic applications accepted. *Expenses:* Tuition, state resident: full-time $7176. Tuition, nonresident: full-time $16,680. Tuition and fees vary according to course load and program. *Financial support:* In 2017–18, 4 research assistantships with partial tuition reimbursements (averaging $2,500 per year) were awarded; fellowships, career-related internships or fieldwork, Federal Work-Study, scholarships/grants, traineeships, and tuition waivers (full and partial) also available. Support available to part-time students. Financial award application deadline: 4/28; financial award applicants required to submit FAFSA. *Faculty research:* Equity and social justice in public education, interdisciplinary practices, teacher training, and effective pedagogy, clinical efficacy, typical and atypical development in children. *Unit head:* Dr. Paul Cascella, Interim Dean, 408-924-3600, Fax: 408-924-3713, E-mail: paul.cascella@sjsu.edu.
Website: http://www.sjsu.edu/education/

Sarah Lawrence College, Graduate Studies, Program in Child Development, Bronxville, NY 10708-5999. Offers MA. *Program availability:* Part-time. *Degree requirements:* For master's, thesis, fieldwork. *Entrance requirements:* For master's, minimum B average in undergraduate coursework. Additional exam requirements/recommendations for international students: Required—TOEFL. Electronic applications accepted.

Texas Woman's University, Graduate School, College of Professional Education, Department of Family Sciences, Denton, TX 76204. Offers child development (MS); child life (MS); counseling and development (MS); early childhood development and education (PhD); early childhood education (M Ed); family studies (MS, PhD); family therapy (MS, PhD). *Accreditation:* ACA (one or more programs are accredited). *Program availability:* Part-time, evening/weekend. *Faculty:* 24 full-time (19 women), 17 part-time/adjunct (15 women). *Students:* 153 full-time (146 women), 237 part-time (220 women); includes 169 minority (81 Black or African American, non-Hispanic/Latino; 9 Asian, non-Hispanic/Latino; 68 Hispanic/Latino; 11 Two or more races, non-Hispanic/Latino), 10 international. Average age 32. 235 applicants, 55% accepted, 87 enrolled. In 2017, 77 master's, 15 doctorates awarded. Terminal master's awarded for partial completion of doctoral program. *Degree requirements:* For master's, comprehensive exam (for some programs), thesis, professional paper, or coursework; practicums (for some programs); for doctorate, comprehensive exam, thesis/dissertation. *Entrance requirements:* For master's, GRE with preferred minimum score 147 Verbal, 144 Quantitative, 4.0 Analytical (for MS in child development and M Ed), minimum GPA of 3.0 (3.25 for family

therapy), 3 letters of recommendations (1 for child life), letter of intent, curriculum vitae/resume, interview, writing sample; for doctorate, GRE (preferred minimum score 147 Verbal, 144 Quantitative, 4.0 Analytical), minimum GPA of 3.5 (3.35 for family studies) on all prior graduate work, curriculum vitae/resume, letter of intent. Additional exam requirements/recommendations for international students: Required—TOEFL (minimum score 550 paper-based; 79 iBT); Recommended—IELTS (minimum score 6.5), TSE (minimum score 53). *Application deadline:* For fall admission, 3/1 priority date for domestic and international students; for spring admission, 11/1 priority date for domestic students, 7/1 priority date for international students. Applications are processed on a rolling basis. Application fee: $50 ($75 for international students). Electronic applications accepted. *Expenses:* $7,520 per year full-time in-state; $16,820 per year full-time out-of-state. *Financial support:* In 2017–18, 104 students received support, including 12 teaching assistantships (averaging $22,972 per year); career-related internships or fieldwork, Federal Work-Study, institutionally sponsored loans, scholarships/grants, traineeships, health care benefits, and unspecified assistantships also available. Support available to part-time students. Financial award application deadline: 3/1; financial award applicants required to submit FAFSA. *Faculty research:* Parenting/parent education, play therapy, healthy relationships, child development, technology integration. *Unit head:* Dr. Jerry Whitworth, Interim Chair, 940-898-2685, Fax: 940-898-2676, E-mail: famsci@twu.edu. *Application contact:* Korie Hawkins, Associate Director of Admissions, Graduate Recruitment, 940-898-3188, Fax: 940-898-3081, E-mail: admissions@twu.edu.
Website: http://www.twu.edu/family-sciences/

Tufts University, Graduate School of Arts and Sciences, Eliot-Pearson Department of Child Study and Human Development, Medford, MA 02155. Offers child study and human development (MA, PhD). *Program availability:* Part-time. *Students:* 78 full-time (66 women), 1 (woman) part-time; includes 19 minority (4 Black or African American, non-Hispanic/Latino; 8 Asian, non-Hispanic/Latino; 5 Hispanic/Latino; 2 Two or more races, non-Hispanic/Latino), 17 international. Average age 27. 129 applicants, 59% accepted, 37 enrolled. In 2017, 26 master's, 7 doctorates awarded. *Degree requirements:* For master's, thesis (for some programs); for doctorate, comprehensive exam, thesis/dissertation. *Entrance requirements:* For master's and doctorate, GRE General Test. Additional exam requirements/recommendations for international students: Required—TOEFL (minimum score 550 paper-based; 80 iBT), IELTS (minimum score 6.5). *Application deadline:* For fall admission, 12/1 priority date for domestic and international students. Applications are processed on a rolling basis. Application fee: $85. Electronic applications accepted. *Expenses:* Contact institution. *Financial support:* Fellowships, research assistantships, teaching assistantships, Federal Work-Study, scholarships/grants, tuition waivers (full and partial), and unspecified assistantships available. Support available to part-time students. Financial award application deadline: 1/15. *Unit head:* Dr. David Henry Feldman, Graduate Program Director, 617-627-3355. *Application contact:* Office of Graduate Admissions, 617-627-3395, E-mail: gradadmissions@tufts.edu.
Website: http://ase.tufts.edu/epcd

The University of Akron, Graduate School, Buchtel College of Arts and Sciences, Department of Child and Family Development, Akron, OH 44325. Offers child development (MA). *Faculty:* 5 full-time (4 women), 3 part-time/adjunct (2 women). *Students:* 1 (woman) full-time. Average age 39. 1 applicant, 100% accepted, 1 enrolled. *Degree requirements:* For master's, comprehensive exam, project or thesis. *Entrance requirements:* For master's, GRE, minimum GPA of 3.0, three letters of recommendation, statement of purpose, resume. Additional exam requirements/recommendations for international students: Required—TOEFL (minimum score 79 iBT), IELTS (minimum score 6.5). *Application deadline:* For fall admission, 3/1 priority date for domestic and international students; for spring admission, 10/1 priority date for domestic and international students. Application fee: $45 ($70 for international students). Electronic applications accepted. *Unit head:* Dr. Paul Levy, Department Chair, 330-972-8369, E-mail: plevy@uakron.edu. *Application contact:* Dr. Shannon Zentall, Graduate Director, 330-972-6049, E-mail: szentall@uakron.edu.
Website: http://www.uakron.edu/child-family/

University of California, Davis, Graduate Studies, Graduate Group in Child Development, Davis, CA 95616. Offers MS. *Degree requirements:* For master's, comprehensive exam (for some programs), thesis (for some programs). *Entrance requirements:* For master's, GRE General Test, minimum GPA of 3.0. Additional exam requirements/recommendations for international students: Required—TOEFL (minimum score 550 paper-based). Electronic applications accepted. *Faculty research:* Cognitive development, socio-emotional development, early childhood.

University of Florida, Graduate School, College of Agricultural and Life Sciences, Department of Family, Youth, and Community Sciences, Gainesville, FL 32611. Offers community studies (MS); family and youth development (MS); family, youth and community sciences (MS); nonprofit organization development (MS). *Program availability:* Part-time, online learning. *Degree requirements:* For master's, comprehensive exam (for some programs), thesis (for some programs). *Entrance requirements:* For master's, GRE General Test, minimum GPA of 3.0. Additional exam requirements/recommendations for international students: Required—TOEFL (minimum score 550 paper-based; 80 iBT), IELTS (minimum score 6). Electronic applications accepted. *Faculty research:* Adolescent risk behaviors, family risk and resilience, family financial management, community-based organizations/interventions, nutrition and wellness.

University of La Verne, LaFetra College of Education, Programs in Child Development/Child Life, La Verne, CA 91750-4443. Offers child development (MS); child life (MS). *Program availability:* Part-time. *Students:* 28 full-time (26 women), 78 part-time (75 women); includes 60 minority (3 Black or African American, non-Hispanic/Latino; 7 Asian, non-Hispanic/Latino; 47 Hispanic/Latino; 3 Two or more races, non-Hispanic/Latino), 5 international. Average age 31. *Entrance requirements:* For master's, minimum GPA of 3.0, 3 letters of reference, writing sample. Additional exam requirements/recommendations for international students: Required—TOEFL (minimum score 550 paper-based). *Application deadline:* Applications are processed on a rolling basis. Application fee: $50. *Expenses:* Contact institution. *Financial support:* Scholarships/grants and traineeships available. Financial award application deadline: 3/2; financial award applicants required to submit FAFSA. *Unit head:* Dr. Lisa Looney, Associate Professor, Education, 909-448-4653, E-mail: llooney@laverne.edu. *Application contact:* Kristen Ahn, Assistant Director of Graduate Admission, 909-448-4480, Fax: 909-971-2295, E-mail: sahn@laverne.edu.
Website: https://education.laverne.edu/child-development/

University of La Verne, Regional and Online Campuses, Graduate Program, ULV Online, La Verne, CA 91750-4443. Offers business administration for experienced professionals (MBA); child development (MS); leadership and management (MS). *Program availability:* Part-time, evening/weekend, online learning. *Students:* Average age 37. In 2017, 57 master's awarded. *Entrance requirements:* For master's, GMAT, MAT, or GRE, minimum undergraduate GPA of 3.0, 2 letters of recommendation, resume, statement of purpose. *Application deadline:* Applications are processed on a rolling basis. Application fee: $50. Tuition and fees vary according to program. *Financial support:* Application deadline: 3/2; applicants required to submit FAFSA. *Unit head:*

Barbara Colley, Coordinator, ULV Online, 909-448-4944, E-mail: bcolley@ulv.edu. *Application contact:* Jesse S. Martinez, Associate Director of Admission, 909-448-4961, E-mail: jmartinez@laverne.edu.
Website: http://laverne.edu/admission/online/

University of Minnesota, Twin Cities Campus, Graduate School, College of Education and Human Development, Institute of Child Development, Minneapolis, MN 55455-0213. Offers applied child and adolescent development (MA); child psychology (PhD); early childhood education (M Ed). *Program availability:* Online learning. *Faculty:* 15 full-time (8 women). *Students:* 55 full-time (49 women), 12 part-time (all women); includes 17 minority (5 Black or African American, non-Hispanic/Latino; 3 Asian, non-Hispanic/Latino; 6 Hispanic/Latino; 3 Two or more races, non-Hispanic/Latino), 2 international. Average age 27. 120 applicants, 25% accepted, 30 enrolled. In 2017, 41 master's, 9 doctorates awarded. Application fee: $75 ($95 for international students). *Financial support:* In 2017–18, 21 fellowships, 17 research assistantships with full tuition reimbursements (averaging $16,246 per year), 19 teaching assistantships with full tuition reimbursements (averaging $14,389 per year) were awarded. *Faculty research:* Developmental affective and cognitive neuroscience; developmental psychopathology; intervention and prevention science; social and emotional development; cognitive, language, and perceptual development. *Total annual research expenditures:* $7.5 million. *Unit head:* Dr. Megan Gunnar, Director, 612-624-2713, E-mail: gunnar@umn.edu. *Application contact:* Dr. Kathleen Thomas, Director of Graduate Studies, 612-625-3389, E-mail: thoma114@umn.edu.
Website: http://www.cehd.umn.edu/ICD

University of Nebraska–Lincoln, Graduate College, College of Education and Human Sciences, Department of Child, Youth and Family Studies, Lincoln, NE 68588. Offers child development/early childhood education (MS, PhD); child, youth and family studies (MS); family and consumer sciences education (MS, PhD); family financial planning (MS); family science (MS, PhD); gerontology (PhD); human sciences (PhD), including child, youth and family studies, gerontology, medical family therapy; marriage and family therapy (MS); medical family therapy (PhD); youth development (MS). *Accreditation:* AAMFT/COAMFTE (one or more programs are accredited). *Program availability:* Online learning. *Degree requirements:* For master's, thesis optional. *Entrance requirements:* For master's, GRE. Additional exam requirements/recommendations for international students: Required—TOEFL (minimum score 550 paper-based). Electronic applications accepted. *Faculty research:* Marriage and family therapy, child development/early childhood education, family financial management.

The University of North Carolina at Charlotte, Cato College of Education, Department of Special Education and Child Development, Charlotte, NC 28223-0001. Offers academically or intellectually gifted (Graduate Certificate); autism spectrum disorders (Graduate Certificate); child and family development: birth through kindergarten (Graduate Certificate); child and family studies: early education (M Ed); special education (M Ed, PhD, Graduate Certificate), including academically or intellectually gifted (M Ed). *Program availability:* Part-time, 100% online, blended/hybrid learning. *Faculty:* 22 full-time (16 women), 9 part-time/adjunct (6 women). *Students:* 19 full-time (16 women), 108 part-time (102 women); includes 16 minority (10 Black or African American, non-Hispanic/Latino; 2 Hispanic/Latino; 4 Two or more races, non-Hispanic/Latino), 5 international. Average age 38. 72 applicants, 94% accepted, 52 enrolled. In 2017, 23 master's, 2 doctorates, 43 other advanced degrees awarded. *Degree requirements:* For master's, thesis or alternative, research project; for doctorate, thesis/dissertation, portfolio; for Graduate Certificate, internship. *Entrance requirements:* For master's, GRE or MAT, personal statement, letters of recommendation; for doctorate, GRE or MAT, 2 official transcripts of all academic work attempted since high school indicating minimum GPA of 3.5 in graduate degree program; at least 3 references of someone who knows applicant's current work and/or academic achievements in previous degree work; two-page essay; current resume or curriculum vitae; writing sample; documentation of teaching; for Graduate Certificate, undergraduate degree from regionally-accredited four-year institution; minimum cumulative undergraduate GPA of 3.0; three recommendations from persons knowledgeable of applicant's interaction with children and families; statement of purpose; clear criminal background check. Additional exam requirements/recommendations for international students: Required—TOEFL (minimum score 523 paper-based, 70 iBT) or IELTS (6.5). *Application deadline:* For fall admission, 12/1 for domestic and international students; for spring admission, 10/1 priority date for domestic and international students; for summer admission, 4/1 priority date for domestic and international students. Applications are processed on a rolling basis. Application fee: $75. Electronic applications accepted. *Expenses:* Tuition, state resident: full-time $4337. Tuition, nonresident: full-time $17,771. *Required fees:* $3211. Tuition and fees vary according to course load and program. *Financial support:* In 2017–18, 8 students received support, including 7 research assistantships (averaging $10,112 per year), 1 teaching assistantship (averaging $3,500 per year); career-related internships or fieldwork, institutionally sponsored loans, scholarships/grants, and unspecified assistantships also available. Support available to part-time students. Financial award application deadline: 3/1; financial award applicants required to submit FAFSA. *Total annual research expenditures:* $3.9 million. *Unit head:* Dr. Belva Collins, Chair, 704-687-8828, E-mail: belva.collins@uncc.edu. *Application contact:* Kathy B. Giddings, Director of Graduate Admissions, 704-687-5503, Fax: 704-687-1668, E-mail: gradadm@uncc.edu.
Website: http://spcd.uncc.edu/

The University of Tennessee at Martin, Graduate Programs, College of Agriculture and Applied Sciences, Department of Family and Consumer Sciences, Martin, TN 38238. Offers dietetics (MSFCS); general family and consumer sciences (MSFCS). *Program availability:* Part-time, 100% online. *Faculty:* 9. *Students:* 10 full-time (7 women), 31 part-time (27 women); includes 11 minority (9 Black or African American, non-Hispanic/Latino; 1 Hispanic/Latino; 1 Two or more races, non-Hispanic/Latino). Average age 30. 50 applicants, 86% accepted, 20 enrolled. In 2017, 12 master's awarded. *Degree requirements:* For master's, comprehensive exam, thesis optional. *Entrance requirements:* For master's, GRE General Test, minimum GPA of 2.5. Additional exam requirements/recommendations for international students: Required—TOEFL (minimum score 525 paper-based; 71 iBT). *Application deadline:* For fall admission, 7/27 priority date for domestic and international students; for spring admission, 12/17 priority date for domestic and international students; for summer admission, 5/10 priority date for domestic and international students. Applications are processed on a rolling basis. Application fee: $30 ($130 for international students). Electronic applications accepted. *Expenses:* Tuition, state resident: full-time $8658; part-time $481 per credit hour. Tuition, nonresident: full-time $14,418; part-time $801 per credit hour. *International tuition:* $22,602 full-time. *Required fees:* $1404; $79 per credit hour. Part-time tuition and fees vary according to course load. *Financial support:* In 2017–18, 20 students received support, including 1 research assistantship with full tuition reimbursement available (averaging $7,540 per year), 7 teaching assistantships with full tuition reimbursements available (averaging $7,432 per year); scholarships/grants and tuition waivers (full and partial) also available. Financial award application deadline: 2/1; financial award applicants required to submit FAFSA. *Faculty research:* Children with developmental disabilities, regional food product development and marketing, parent education. *Unit head:* Dr. Lisa LeBleu, Coordinator, 731-881-7116, Fax: 731-881-7106, E-mail: llebleu@utm.edu. *Application contact:* Jolene L. Cunningham, Student Services Specialist, 731-881-7012, Fax: 731-881-7499, E-mail: jcunningham@utm.edu.
Website: http://www.utm.edu/departments/caas/fcs/index.php

The University of Texas at Austin, Graduate School, College of Natural Sciences, School of Human Ecology, Austin, TX 78712-1111. Offers human development and family sciences (MA, PhD); nutritional sciences (MA, MS, PhD), including nutrition (MA), nutritional sciences (PhD); textile and apparel technology (MS). *Degree requirements:* For master's, thesis; for doctorate, thesis/dissertation. *Entrance requirements:* For master's and doctorate, GRE General Test. Electronic applications accepted.

The University of West Alabama, School of Graduate Studies, College of Education, Program in Early Childhood Education, Livingston, AL 35470. Offers early childhood development (M Ed); early childhood education P-3 (M Ed, Ed S). *Accreditation:* NCATE. *Program availability:* Part-time, evening/weekend, 100% online. *Faculty:* 6 full-time (all women), 23 part-time/adjunct (18 women). *Students:* 102 (101 women); includes 37 minority (36 Black or African American, non-Hispanic/Latino; 1 Two or more races, non-Hispanic/Latino). Average age 33. 30 applicants, 93% accepted, 22 enrolled. In 2017, 11 master's, 13 Ed Ss awarded. *Degree requirements:* For master's, comprehensive exam, thesis optional; for Ed S, comprehensive exam. *Entrance requirements:* For master's, GRE, minimum GPA of 2.75, verification of background clearance/fingerprints, valid bachelor's-level Professional Educator Certificate in same teaching field. Additional exam requirements/recommendations for international students: Required—TOEFL (minimum score 500 paper-based; 61 iBT). *Application deadline:* Applications are processed on a rolling basis. Application fee: $40. Electronic applications accepted. *Expenses:* Tuition, state resident: part-time $371 per credit hour. Tuition, nonresident: part-time $742 per credit hour. *Required fees:* $130 per semester. *Financial support:* Teaching assistantships, Federal Work-Study, scholarships/grants, and unspecified assistantships available. Support available to part-time students. Financial award application deadline: 3/1; financial award applicants required to submit FAFSA. *Unit head:* Dr. Jodie Winship, Chair of Teaching and Learning, 205-652-5415, Fax: 205-652-3706, E-mail: jwinship@uwa.edu. *Application contact:* Dr. B. J. Kimbrough, Dean of Graduate Studies, 205-652-3647, Fax: 205-652-3670, E-mail: bkimbrough@uwa.edu.

University of Wyoming, College of Agriculture and Natural Resources, Department of Family and Consumer Sciences, Laramie, WY 82071. Offers early childhood development (MS); family and consumer sciences (MS); food science and human nutrition (MS). *Program availability:* Part-time. *Degree requirements:* For master's, thesis, project. *Entrance requirements:* For master's, GRE General Test or MCAT, minimum GPA of 3.0. Additional exam requirements/recommendations for international students: Required—TOEFL (minimum score 540 paper-based; 76 iBT). Electronic applications accepted. *Faculty research:* Asthma, obesity and healthy weights, nutrition concerns of children with special health care needs, food product development, food safety, postpartum health, exercise nutrition.

Whittier College, Graduate Programs, Department of Education and Child Development, Whittier, CA 90608-0634. Offers educational administration (MA Ed); elementary education (MA Ed); secondary education (MA Ed). *Program availability:* Part-time, evening/weekend. *Degree requirements:* For master's, thesis. *Entrance requirements:* For master's, GRE General Test, MAT, minimum GPA of 3.5, academic writing sample.

Clothing and Textiles

Alabama Agricultural and Mechanical University, School of Graduate Studies, College of Agricultural, Life and Natural Sciences, Department of Family and Consumer Sciences, Huntsville, AL 35811. Offers apparel, merchandising and design (MS); family and consumer sciences (MS); human development and family studies (MS); nutrition and hospitality management (MS). *Program availability:* Part-time, evening/weekend. *Degree requirements:* For master's, comprehensive exam, thesis optional. *Entrance requirements:* For master's, GRE General Test. Additional exam requirements/recommendations for international students: Required—TOEFL (minimum score 500 paper-based; 61 iBT). Electronic applications accepted. *Faculty research:* Food biotechnology, nutrition, food microbiology, food engineering, food chemistry.

Auburn University, Graduate School, College of Human Sciences, Department of Consumer Affairs, Auburn University, AL 36849. Offers MS, PhD. *Program availability:* Part-time. *Faculty:* 17 full-time (16 women). *Students:* 19 full-time (14 women), 12 part-time (all women); includes 3 minority (1 Black or African American, non-Hispanic/Latino; 1 Asian, non-Hispanic/Latino; 1 Two or more races, non-Hispanic/Latino), 13 international. Average age 31. 27 applicants, 52% accepted, 8 enrolled. In 2017, 4 master's, 5 doctorates awarded. *Degree requirements:* For master's, thesis (for some programs). *Entrance requirements:* For master's, GRE General Test. *Application deadline:* Applications are processed on a rolling basis. Application fee: $50 ($60 for international students). Electronic applications accepted. *Expenses:* Tuition, state resident: full-time $10,974; part-time $519 per credit hour. Tuition, nonresident: full-time $29,658; part-time $1557 per credit hour. *Required fees:* $816 per semester. Tuition and fees vary according to degree level and program. *Financial support:* Fellowships, research assistantships, teaching assistantships, career-related internships or fieldwork, and Federal Work-Study available. Support available to part-time students. Financial award application deadline: 3/15; financial award applicants required to submit FAFSA. *Faculty research:* Merchandising, consumer behavior, international marketing of textiles and apparel, apparel product development. *Unit head:* Dr. Pamela V. Ulrich, Head, 334-844-3266, E-mail: cwarfiel@humsci.auburn.edu. *Application contact:* Dr. George Flowers, Dean of the Graduate School, 334-844-2125.

Central Michigan University, College of Graduate Studies, College of Education and Human Services, Department of Human Environmental Studies, Mount Pleasant, MI

48859. Offers apparel product development and merchandising technology (MS); gerontology (Graduate Certificate); human development and family studies (MA); nutrition and dietetics (MS). *Program availability:* Part-time, evening/weekend. *Degree requirements:* For master's, thesis or alternative. Electronic applications accepted. *Faculty research:* Human growth and development, family studies and human sexuality, human nutrition and dietetics, apparel and textile retailing, computer-aided design for apparel.

Cornell University, Graduate School, Graduate Fields of Human Ecology, Field of Fiber Science and Apparel Design, Ithaca, NY 14853. Offers apparel design (MA, MPS); fiber science (MS, PhD); polymer science (MS, PhD); textile science (MS, PhD). *Degree requirements:* For master's, thesis (MA, MS), project paper (MPS); for doctorate, comprehensive exam, thesis/dissertation. *Entrance requirements:* For master's, GRE General Test, 2 letters of recommendation, portfolio (for functional apparel design); for doctorate, GRE General Test, 2 letters of recommendation. Additional exam requirements/recommendations for international students: Required—TOEFL (minimum score 600 paper-based; 77 iBT). Electronic applications accepted. *Faculty research:* Apparel design, consumption, mass customization, 3-D body scanning.

Drexel University, Westphal College of Media Arts and Design, Program in Retail and Merchandising, Philadelphia, PA 19104-2875. Offers MS. *Program availability:* Online learning.

Eastern Michigan University, Graduate School, College of Technology, School of Visual and Built Environments, Program in Apparel Textiles and Merchandising, Ypsilanti, MI 48197. Offers MS. *Program availability:* Part-time, evening/weekend, online learning. *Students:* 6 full-time (all women), 8 part-time (7 women); includes 5 minority (3 Black or African American, non-Hispanic/Latino; 1 American Indian or Alaska Native, non-Hispanic/Latino; 1 Hispanic/Latino), 5 international. Average age 33. 7 applicants, 71% accepted, 1 enrolled. In 2017, 2 master's awarded. *Entrance requirements:* Additional exam requirements/recommendations for international students: Required—TOEFL. *Application deadline:* Applications are processed on a rolling basis. Application fee: $45. *Financial support:* Fellowships, research assistantships with full tuition reimbursements, teaching assistantships with full tuition reimbursements, career-related internships or fieldwork, Federal Work-Study, institutionally sponsored loans, scholarships/grants, tuition waivers (partial), and unspecified assistantships available. Support available to part-time students. Financial award applicants required to submit FAFSA. *Application contact:* Dr. Subhas Ghosh, Program Coordinator, 734-487-2476, Fax: 734-487-7690, E-mail: sghosh@emich.edu.

Fashion Institute of Technology, School of Graduate Studies, Program in Fashion and Textile Studies: History, Theory, Museum Practice, New York, NY 10001-5992. Offers MA. *Accreditation:* NASAD. *Degree requirements:* For master's, one foreign language, thesis, internship. *Entrance requirements:* For master's, GRE General Test or GRE Subject Test, previous course work in art history and chemistry, 4 semesters of a foreign language. Additional exam requirements/recommendations for international students: Required—TOEFL (minimum score 550 paper-based). Electronic applications accepted.

Fashion Institute of Technology, School of Graduate Studies, Program in Fashion Design, New York, NY 10001-5992. Offers MFA. *Entrance requirements:* For master's, portfolio.

Georgia State University, Ernest G. Welch School of Art and Design, Program in Studio Art, Atlanta, GA 30302-3083. Offers ceramics (MFA); drawing and painting (MFA); graphic design (MFA); interior design (MFA); photography (MFA); printmaking (MFA); sculpture (MFA); textiles (MFA). *Accreditation:* NASAD. Application fee: $50. Electronic applications accepted. *Expenses:* Tuition, state resident: full-time $7020. Tuition, nonresident: full-time $22,518. *Required fees:* $2128. Tuition and fees vary according to degree level and program. *Financial support:* Fellowships, research assistantships, teaching assistantships, scholarships/grants, and unspecified assistantships available. Financial award application deadline: 4/15; financial award applicants required to submit FAFSA. *Faculty research:* Advertising and typography, new media, traditional media, three-dimensional art, architectural and environmental design. *Unit head:* Michael White, Director, Welch School of Art and Design, 404-413-5221, Fax: 404-413-5261, E-mail: mwhite@gsu.edu. *Application contact:* Hubert Stanley Anderson, Director of Graduate Studies, 404-413-5229, Fax: 404-413-5261, E-mail: artgrad@gsu.edu.
Website: http://artdesign.gsu.edu/graduate/admissions/masters-of-fine-arts-in-studio/

Iowa State University of Science and Technology, Department of Apparel, Events, and Hospitality Management, Ames, IA 50011-1078. Offers apparel, merchandising, and design (MS, PhD); hospitality management (MS, PhD). *Program availability:* Online learning. *Degree requirements:* For doctorate, thesis/dissertation. *Entrance requirements:* For master's and doctorate, GRE General Test. Additional exam requirements/recommendations for international students: Required—TOEFL (minimum score 550 paper-based; 79 iBT), IELTS (minimum score 6.5). Electronic applications accepted.

Iowa State University of Science and Technology, Program in Apparel, Merchandising, and Design, Ames, IA 50011. Offers MS, PhD. *Degree requirements:* For master's, thesis; for doctorate, thesis/dissertation. *Entrance requirements:* Additional exam requirements/recommendations for international students: Required—TOEFL (minimum score 550 paper-based; 79 iBT), IELTS (minimum score 6.5). Electronic applications accepted.

Kansas State University, Graduate School, College of Human Ecology, Department of Apparel, Textiles, and Interior Design, Manhattan, KS 66506. Offers apparel and textiles (MS), including general apparel and textiles, merchandising. Merchandising option offered online through the Great Plains Interactive Distance Education Alliance, including Oklahoma State University, North Dakota State University, and South Dakota State University. *Program availability:* Online learning. *Degree requirements:* For master's, comprehensive exam (for some programs), thesis (for some programs). *Entrance requirements:* For master's, GRE General Test (except for merchandising applicants), minimum undergraduate GPA of 3.0. Additional exam requirements/recommendations for international students: Required—TOEFL (minimum score 550 paper-based; 79 iBT), IELTS (minimum score 6.1). Electronic applications accepted. *Expenses:* Contact institution. *Faculty research:* Apparel marketing and consumer behavior, social and environmental responsibility, apparel design, new product development.

Kansas State University, Graduate School, College of Human Ecology, Doctorate in Human Ecology Program, Manhattan, KS 66506-1407. Offers apparel and textiles (PhD); applied family sciences (PhD); couple and family therapy (PhD); hospitality administration (PhD); kinesiology (PhD); life-span human development (PhD). *Program availability:* Part-time. *Degree requirements:* For doctorate, thesis/dissertation. *Entrance requirements:* Additional exam requirements/recommendations for international students: Required—TOEFL. Electronic applications accepted.

LIM College, MPS Program, New York, NY 10022-5268. Offers business of fashion (MPS); fashion marketing (MPS); fashion merchandising and retail management (MPS); global fashion supply chain management (MPS). *Accreditation:* ACBSP. *Program availability:* Part-time, 100% online. *Faculty:* 1 full-time, 28 part-time/adjunct. *Students:* 113 full-time (111 women), 48 part-time (44 women). Average age 24. 285 applicants, 71% accepted, 114 enrolled. *Entrance requirements:* Additional exam requirements/recommendations for international students: Required—TOEFL (minimum score 550 paper-based), IELTS (minimum score 6.5), PTE (minimum score 55). *Application deadline:* Applications are processed on a rolling basis. Application fee: $40. Electronic applications accepted. *Expenses: Tuition:* Full-time $27,750; part-time $925 per credit. *Required fees:* $100 per term. *Unit head:* Dr. Susan Baxter, Dean of Graduate Studies, E-mail: graduatestudies@limcollege.edu. *Application contact:* Haley Drogus, Assistant Director of Graduate Admissions, 212-310-0639, E-mail: graduateadmissions@limcollege.edu.
Website: http://www.limcollege.edu/academics/graduate

Mississippi State University, College of Agriculture and Life Sciences, School of Human Sciences, Mississippi State, MS 39762. Offers agriculture and extension education (MS), including communication, leadership; agriculture science (PhD), including agriculture and extension education; fashion design and merchandising (MS), including design and product development, merchandising; human development and family studies (MS, PhD). *Accreditation:* NCATE (one or more programs are accredited). *Program availability:* Part-time. *Faculty:* 20 full-time (11 women). *Students:* 31 full-time (23 women), 54 part-time (38 women); includes 19 minority (15 Black or African American, non-Hispanic/Latino; 1 Hispanic/Latino; 3 Two or more races, non-Hispanic/Latino), 5 international. Average age 36. 26 applicants, 65% accepted, 15 enrolled. In 2017, 19 master's, 2 doctorates awarded. *Degree requirements:* For master's, thesis optional, comprehensive oral or written exam. *Entrance requirements:* For master's, GRE, minimum GPA of 2.75 in last 4 semesters of course work; for doctorate, minimum GPA of 3.0 on prior graduate work. Additional exam requirements/recommendations for international students: Required—TOEFL (minimum score 477 paper-based; 53 iBT); Recommended—IELTS (minimum score 4.5). *Application deadline:* For fall admission, 7/1 for domestic students, 5/1 for international students; for spring admission, 11/1 for domestic students, 9/1 for international students. Applications are processed on a rolling basis. Application fee: $60 ($80 for international students). Electronic applications accepted. *Expenses:* Tuition, state resident: full-time $8318; part-time $462.12 per credit hour. Tuition, nonresident: full-time $22,358; part-time $1242.12 per credit hour. *Required fees:* $110; $12.24 per credit hour. $6.12 per semester. *Financial support:* In 2017–18, 13 research assistantships (averaging $13,718 per year) were awarded; Federal Work-Study, institutionally sponsored loans, and unspecified assistantships also available. Financial award application deadline: 4/1; financial award applicants required to submit FAFSA. *Faculty research:* Animal welfare, agroscience, information technology, learning styles, problem solving. *Unit head:* Dr. Michael Newman, Professor and Director, 662-325-2950, E-mail: mnewman@humansci.msstate.edu. *Application contact:* Marina Hunt, Admissions and Enrollment Assistant, 662-325-5188, E-mail: mhunt@grad.msstate.edu.
Website: http://www.humansci.msstate.edu

New Mexico State University, College of Agricultural, Consumer and Environmental Sciences, Department of Family and Consumer Sciences, Las Cruces, NM 88003. Offers clothing, textiles, and merchandising (MS); family and child science (MS); family and consumer science education (MS); family and consumer sciences (MS); food science and technology (MS); hotel, restaurant, and tourism management (MS); human nutrition and dietetic sciences (MS). *Program availability:* Part-time. *Faculty:* 9 full-time (6 women), 1 (woman) part-time/adjunct. *Students:* 38 full-time (30 women), 3 part-time (all women); includes 28 minority (3 Black or African American, non-Hispanic/Latino; 1 American Indian or Alaska Native, non-Hispanic/Latino; 1 Asian, non-Hispanic/Latino; 23 Hispanic/Latino). Average age 29. 26 applicants, 69% accepted, 17 enrolled. In 2017, 15 master's awarded. *Degree requirements:* For master's, comprehensive exam (for some programs), thesis (for some programs), oral exam. *Entrance requirements:* For master's, GRE, 3 letters of reference from faculty members or employers, resume, letter of interest. Additional exam requirements/recommendations for international students: Required—TOEFL (minimum score 550 paper-based; 79 iBT), IELTS (minimum score 6.5). *Application deadline:* For fall admission, 2/1 priority date for domestic and international students; for spring admission, 10/1 for domestic and international students. Applications are processed on a rolling basis. Application fee: $40 ($50 for international students). Electronic applications accepted. *Expenses:* Tuition, state resident: full-time $4390. Tuition, nonresident: full-time $15,309. *Required fees:* $853. *Financial support:* In 2017–18, 30 students received support, including 8 research assistantships (averaging $13,150 per year), 8 teaching assistantships (averaging $14,082 per year); career-related internships or fieldwork, Federal Work-Study, scholarships/grants, traineeships, health care benefits, and unspecified assistantships also available. Support available to part-time students. Financial award application deadline: 3/1. *Faculty research:* Food product analysis, childhood obesity, dietary decision-making, military families, equine assisted psychotherapy. *Total annual research expenditures:* $356,004. *Unit head:* Dr. Priscilla Bloomquist, Interim Department Head, 575-646-3936, Fax: 575-646-8100, E-mail: pbloomqu@nmsu.edu. *Application contact:* Dr. Kourtney Vaillancourt, Graduate Program Contact, 575-646-3383, Fax: 575-646-1889, E-mail: kvaillan@nmsu.edu.
Website: http://aces.nmsu.edu/academics/fcs

The New School, Parsons Paris, Program in Fashion Studies, New York, NY 10011. Offers MA. *Program availability:* Part-time. *Faculty:* 5 full-time (2 women), 46 part-time/adjunct (31 women). *Students:* 22 full-time (21 women), 3 part-time (2 women); includes 5 minority (2 Black or African American, non-Hispanic/Latino; 2 Asian, non-Hispanic/Latino; 1 Two or more races, non-Hispanic/Latino), 14 international. Average age 25. 18 applicants, 100% accepted, 18 enrolled. *Degree requirements:* For master's, thesis. *Entrance requirements:* For master's, transcripts, resume, statement of purpose, recommendation letters, interview. Additional exam requirements/recommendations for international students: Required—TOEFL (minimum score 100 iBT), IELTS (minimum score 7), PTE (minimum score 68). *Application deadline:* For fall admission, 1/1 priority date for domestic and international students. Applications are processed on a rolling basis. Application fee: $50. Electronic applications accepted. *Expenses:* $19,203 per term full-time, $1,339 per credit part-time; $100 fee per term for maintenance of status. *Financial support:* In 2017–18, 18 students received support. Career-related internships or fieldwork and scholarships/grants available. *Unit head:* Marco Pecorari, Coordinator, 33-176217661, E-mail: pecorarm@newschool.edu. *Application contact:* Mike Fakih, Director of Admissions, Parsons Paris, 33 176 21 76 67, E-mail: thinkparsonsparis@newschool.edu.

North Carolina State University, Graduate School, College of Textiles, Program in Textile Technology Management, Raleigh, NC 27695. Offers PhD. *Degree requirements:* For doctorate, one foreign language, thesis/dissertation, cumulative exams. *Entrance requirements:* For doctorate, GRE or GMAT. Electronic applications accepted. *Faculty research:* Niche markets, supply chain, globalization, logistics.

North Dakota State University, College of Graduate and Interdisciplinary Studies, College of Human Development and Education, Department of Apparel, Design, and Hospitality Management, Fargo, ND 58102. Offers merchandising (MS, Certificate). *Program availability:* Online learning. *Degree requirements:* For master's, practicum and/or thesis. Electronic applications accepted.

Oklahoma State University, College of Human Sciences, Department of Design, Housing and Merchandising, Stillwater, OK 74078. Offers MS, PhD. *Faculty:* 16 full-time

(12 women). *Students:* 10 part-time (7 women); includes 3 minority (1 Black or African American, non-Hispanic/Latino; 1 Hispanic/Latino; 1 Two or more races, non-Hispanic/Latino), 5 international. Average age 28. 11 applicants, 27% accepted, 3 enrolled. In 2017, 1 master's, 1 doctorate awarded. *Entrance requirements:* For master's and doctorate, GRE or GMAT. Additional exam requirements/recommendations for international students: Required—TOEFL (minimum score 550 paper-based; 79 iBT). *Application deadline:* For fall admission, 3/1 priority date for international students; for spring admission, 8/1 priority date for international students. Applications are processed on a rolling basis. Application fee: $40 ($75 for international students). Electronic applications accepted. *Expenses:* Tuition, state resident: full-time $4019; part-time $2679.60 per year. Tuition, nonresident: full-time $15,286; part-time $10,190.40 per year. *Required fees:* $2129; $1419 per unit. Tuition and fees vary according to program. *Financial support:* Research assistantships, teaching assistantships, career-related internships or fieldwork, Federal Work-Study, scholarships/grants, health care benefits, tuition waivers (partial), and unspecified assistantships available. Support available to part-time students. Financial award application deadline: 3/1; financial award applicants required to submit FAFSA. *Faculty research:* Environmental sciences design, housing and merchandising; creativity and physical environment; product development, production and evaluation; experimental learning and critical thinking; technology strategies and assessment; customer expectation and satisfaction. *Unit head:* Dr. Jane Swinney, Interim Department Head, 405-744-6552, Fax: 405-744-6910, E-mail: jane.swinney@okstate.edu. *Application contact:* Dr. Christine Johnson, Associate Dean for Research and Graduate Studies, 405-744-1744, E-mail: christine.johnson@okstate.edu.
Website: https://humansciences.okstate.edu/dhm/

Rutgers University–Newark, Rutgers Business School–Newark and New Brunswick, Program in Business of Fashion, Newark, NJ 07102. Offers MBA.

Savannah College of Art and Design, Program in Accessory Design, Savannah, GA 31402-3146. Offers MA, MFA. *Program availability:* Part-time. *Faculty:* 5 full-time (4 women). *Students:* 15 full-time (14 women), 4 part-time (all women); includes 5 minority (2 Asian, non-Hispanic/Latino; 3 Hispanic/Latino), 9 international. Average age 27. 11 applicants, 36% accepted, 3 enrolled. In 2017, 5 master's awarded. *Degree requirements:* For master's, final project (for MA); thesis (for MFA). *Entrance requirements:* For master's, GRE (recommended), portfolio (submitted in digital format), audition or writing submission, resume, statement of purpose, two letters of recommendation. Additional exam requirements/recommendations for international students: Recommended—TOEFL (minimum score 550 paper-based; 85 iBT), IELTS (minimum score 6.5). *Application deadline:* For fall admission, 4/1 for domestic and international students. Applications are processed on a rolling basis. Application fee: $40. Electronic applications accepted. *Expenses: Tuition:* Full-time $36,765; part-time $817 per credit hour. One-time fee: $500. *Financial support:* Career-related internships or fieldwork, Federal Work-Study, and scholarships/grants available. Financial award application deadline: 4/1; financial award applicants required to submit FAFSA. *Unit head:* Michael Fink, Dean, School of Fashion. *Application contact:* Jenny Jaquillard, Executive Director of Admissions, Recruitment and Events, 912-525-5100, Fax: 912-525-5985, E-mail: admission@scad.edu.
Website: http://www.scad.edu/academics/programs/accessory-design

Thomas Jefferson University, Kanbar College of Design, Engineering and Commerce, Program in Fashion Design Management, Philadelphia, PA 19107. Offers MS.

Thomas Jefferson University, Kanbar College of Design, Engineering and Commerce, Program in Global Fashion Enterprise, Philadelphia, PA 19107. Offers MS. *Program availability:* Part-time. *Entrance requirements:* For master's, GRE or GMAT, minimum GPA of 2.8, official transcripts, two letters of recommendation, essay. Additional exam requirements/recommendations for international students: Required—TOEFL (minimum score 550 paper-based; 79 iBT). Electronic applications accepted.

The University of Akron, Graduate School, Buchtel College of Arts and Sciences, Department of Fashion Merchandising, Akron, OH 44325. Offers clothing, textiles and interiors (MA). *Faculty:* 2 full-time (both women), 1 (woman) part-time/adjunct. *Students:* Average age 27. 8 applicants. In 2017, 1 master's awarded. *Degree requirements:* For master's, comprehensive exam, thesis or project. *Entrance requirements:* For master's, GRE, minimum GPA of 3.0, three letters of recommendation, statement of purpose, resume. Additional exam requirements/recommendations for international students: Required—TOEFL (minimum score 79 iBT), IELTS (minimum score 6.5). *Application deadline:* For fall admission, 3/1 priority date for domestic and international students; for spring admission, 10/1 priority date for domestic and international students. Application fee: $45 ($70 for international students). Electronic applications accepted. *Unit head:* Dr. Sandra Buckland, Professor, 330-972-8090, E-mail: skb@uakron.edu.
Website: http://www.uakron.edu/fashion/

The University of Alabama, Graduate School, College of Human Environmental Sciences, Department of Clothing, Textiles, and Interior Design, Tuscaloosa, AL 35487. Offers apparel and textiles (MSHES). *Faculty:* 6 full-time (all women). *Students:* 1 (woman) full-time. Average age 25. 2 applicants. *Degree requirements:* For master's, comprehensive exam (for some programs), thesis optional. *Entrance requirements:* For master's, GRE General Test or MAT, minimum GPA of 3.0. Additional exam requirements/recommendations for international students: Required—TOEFL. *Application deadline:* For fall admission, 7/1 for domestic students; for spring admission, 10/30 for domestic students; for summer admission, 4/30 for domestic students. Applications are processed on a rolling basis. Application fee: $50 ($60 for international students). Electronic applications accepted. *Financial support:* In 2017–18, research assistantships with full tuition reimbursements (averaging $12,000 per year), teaching assistantships with partial tuition reimbursements (averaging $6,000 per year) were awarded; fellowships, career-related internships or fieldwork, Federal Work-Study, scholarships/grants, and health care benefits also available. Financial award application deadline: 4/15. *Faculty research:* Archeological and historic textiles with material culture analysis, textile science sustainability issues and fibers, scholarship of engagement in higher education, international marketing and trade with soft goods branding management, apparel design with sustainability and zero-waste pattern development. *Unit head:* Dr. Shirley Foster, Chair and Assistant Professor, 205-348-6176, Fax: 205-348-0022, E-mail: sfoster@ches.ua.edu. *Application contact:* Patrick D. Fuller, Admissions Officer, 205-348-5923, Fax: 205-348-0400, E-mail: patrick.d.fuller@ua.edu.
Website: http://www.ctd.ches.ua.edu/

University of Alberta, Faculty of Graduate Studies and Research, Department of Human Ecology, Edmonton, AB T6G 2E1, Canada. Offers family ecology and practice (M Sc, PhD); textiles and clothing (M Sc, MA, PhD). *Program availability:* Online learning. *Degree requirements:* For master's, thesis (for some programs); for doctorate, comprehensive exam, thesis/dissertation. *Entrance requirements:* For master's and doctorate, minimum GPA of 7.0 on a 9.0 scale. Additional exam requirements/recommendations for international students: Required—TOEFL (minimum score 580 paper-based). *Faculty research:* Families and aging, family and child poverty, paid and unpaid work of families, textiles and clothing, parent-child relationships.

University of California, Davis, Graduate Studies, Graduate Group in Textiles, Davis, CA 95616. Offers MS. *Degree requirements:* For master's, comprehensive exam (for some programs), thesis (for some programs). *Entrance requirements:* For master's, GRE General Test, minimum GPA of 3.0. Additional exam requirements/recommendations for international students: Required—TOEFL (minimum score 550 paper-based). Electronic applications accepted. *Faculty research:* Fiber science, social psychology, consumer psychology, chemical and physical properties of fibrous and polymeric materials.

University of Delaware, College of Arts and Sciences, Department of Fashion and Apparel Studies, Newark, DE 19716. Offers MS.

University of Georgia, College of Family and Consumer Sciences, Department of Textiles, Merchandising, and Interiors, Athens, GA 30602. Offers historical and cultural aspects of dress and textiles (MS); interior environments (MS); international merchandising (PhD); merchandising and international trade (MS); polymer, fiber and textile science (MS); polymer, fiber, and textile sciences (PhD). *Accreditation:* NASAD. *Degree requirements:* For master's, thesis; for doctorate, thesis/dissertation. *Entrance requirements:* For master's and doctorate, GRE General Test. Electronic applications accepted.

The University of Manchester, School of Materials, Manchester, United Kingdom. Offers advanced aerospace materials engineering (M Sc); advanced metallic systems (PhD); biomedical materials (M Phil, M Sc, PhD); ceramics and glass (M Phil, M Sc, PhD); composite materials (M Sc, PhD); corrosion and protection (M Phil, M Sc, PhD); materials (M Phil, PhD); metallic materials (M Phil, M Sc, PhD); nanostructural materials (M Phil, M Sc, PhD); paper science (M Phil, M Sc, PhD); polymer science and engineering (M Phil, M Sc, PhD); technical textiles (M Sc); textile design, fashion and management (M Phil, M Sc, PhD); textile science and technology (M Phil, M Sc, PhD); textiles (M Phil, PhD); textiles and fashion (M Ent).

University of Minnesota, Twin Cities Campus, Graduate School, College of Design, Department of Design, Housing, and Apparel, Minneapolis, MN 55455-0213. Offers apparel (MA, MS, PhD); design communication (MA, MS, PhD); housing studies (MA, MS, PhD, Postbaccalaureate Certificate); interactive design (MFA); interior design (MA, MS, PhD). *Program availability:* Part-time. *Degree requirements:* For master's and Postbaccalaureate Certificate, comprehensive exam, thesis (for some programs); for doctorate, comprehensive exam, thesis/dissertation. *Entrance requirements:* For master's, GRE General Test, minimum GPA of 3.0 (preferred), portfolio, 3 letters of recommendation; for doctorate, GRE General Test, minimum GPA of 3.0 (preferred), portfolio, 3 letters of recommendation, writing sample; for Postbaccalaureate Certificate, GRE General Test, minimum GPA of 3.0 (preferred). Additional exam requirements/recommendations for international students: Required—TOEFL (minimum score 550 paper-based; 79 iBT). Electronic applications accepted. *Faculty research:* Housing policy and community development; consumer behavior; interactive design; design history; social, cultural, and behavioral issues related to designed environments.

University of Missouri, Office of Research and Graduate Studies, College of Human Environmental Sciences, Department of Textile and Apparel Management, Columbia, MO 65211. Offers MS, PhD. *Entrance requirements:* For master's, GRE General Test, minimum GPA of 3.0. Additional exam requirements/recommendations for international students: Required—TOEFL (minimum score 550 paper-based; 80 iBT). Electronic applications accepted.

University of Nebraska–Lincoln, Graduate College, College of Education and Human Sciences, Department of Textiles, Clothing and Design, Lincoln, NE 68588. Offers human sciences (PhD), including textiles, clothing and design (MS, PhD); merchandising (MS); textile history/quilt studies (MA); textile science (MS); textile-apparel (MA); textiles, clothing and design (MA, MS), including textiles, clothing and design (MS, PhD). *Program availability:* Part-time, online learning. *Degree requirements:* For master's, thesis optional. *Entrance requirements:* For master's, GRE General Test. Additional exam requirements/recommendations for international students: Required—TOEFL (minimum score 550 paper-based). Electronic applications accepted. *Faculty research:* Merchandising, textile science, fiber arts, textile history, quilt studies.

University of Rhode Island, Graduate School, College of Business, Program in Textiles, Fashion Merchandising and Design, Kingston, RI 02881. Offers fashion merchandising (Certificate); master seamstress (Certificate); textiles, fashion merchandising and design (MS), including fashion merchandising, historic fashion and textiles, textile conservation, and cultural analysis, textile science. *Program availability:* Part-time. *Faculty:* 8 full-time (6 women). *Students:* 8 full-time (all women), 3 part-time (2 women), 3 international. 9 applicants, 67% accepted, 2 enrolled. In 2017, 4 master's awarded. *Entrance requirements:* Additional exam requirements/recommendations for international students: Required—TOEFL. *Application deadline:* For fall admission, 7/1 for domestic students, 2/1 for international students; for spring admission, 11/1 for domestic students, 7/1 for international students. Application fee: $65. Electronic applications accepted. *Expenses:* Tuition, state resident: full-time $12,706; part-time $786 per credit. Tuition, nonresident: full-time $25,216; part-time $1401 per credit. *Required fees:* $1598; $45 per credit. One-time fee: $30 part-time. *Financial support:* Research assistantships and teaching assistantships available. Financial award application deadline: 2/1; financial award applicants required to submit FAFSA. *Unit head:* Dr. Susan Hannel, Chair, 401-874-2882, Fax: 401-874-2581, E-mail: susanhannel@uri.edu. *Application contact:* Dr. Linda Welters, Co-Chair, 401-874-4525, Fax: 401-874-2581, E-mail: lwelters@uri.edu.
Website: https://web.uri.edu/tmd/ms-textiles-fashion-merchandising-and-design/

The University of Tennessee, Graduate School, College of Education, Health and Human Sciences, Department of Consumer and Industry Services Management, Program in Consumer Services Management, Knoxville, TN 37996. Offers retail and consumer sciences (MS); textile science (MS). *Program availability:* Part-time. *Degree requirements:* For master's, thesis or alternative. *Entrance requirements:* For master's, GRE General Test, minimum GPA of 2.7. Additional exam requirements/recommendations for international students: Required—TOEFL. Electronic applications accepted.

The University of Tennessee, Graduate School, College of Education, Health and Human Sciences, Program in Human Ecology, Knoxville, TN 37996. Offers child and family studies (PhD); community health (PhD); nutrition science (PhD); retailing and consumer sciences (PhD); textile science (PhD). *Degree requirements:* For doctorate, thesis/dissertation. *Entrance requirements:* For doctorate, GRE General Test, minimum GPA of 2.7. Additional exam requirements/recommendations for international students: Required—TOEFL. Electronic applications accepted.

University of the Incarnate Word, School of Media and Design, San Antonio, TX 78209-6397. Offers communication arts (MA); fashion design (MA). *Program availability:* Part-time, evening/weekend. *Faculty:* 10 full-time (6 women). *Students:* 27 full-time (15 women), 9 part-time (5 women); includes 26 minority (4 Black or African American, non-Hispanic/Latino; 22 Hispanic/Latino), 3 international. In 2017, 15 master's awarded. *Degree requirements:* For master's, thesis or alternative, capstone. *Entrance requirements:* For master's, GRE, interview, writing sample. Additional exam requirements/recommendations for international students: Required—TOEFL (minimum score 560 paper-based; 83 iBT). *Application deadline:* Applications are processed on a rolling basis. Application fee: $20. Electronic applications accepted. *Expenses: Tuition:* Full-time $16,470; part-time $915 per credit hour. Tuition and fees vary according to

degree level, program and student level. *Financial support:* Federal Work-Study, scholarships/grants, tuition waivers (partial), and unspecified assistantships available. Financial award applicants required to submit FAFSA. *Faculty research:* Representation of minority groups on screen, communication effectiveness and human relationships, philosophy of communication and social theories, spirituality in higher education, examining the role of race, gender and sexuality in political cartoons. *Unit head:* Dr. Sharon Welkey, Dean, 210-829-6091, Fax: 210-829-3196, E-mail: welkey@uiwtx.edu. *Application contact:* Johnny Garcia, Graduate Admissions Counselor, 210-805-3554, Fax: 210-829-3921, E-mail: admis@uiwtx.edu.
Website: http://www.uiw.edu/simd/index.htm

Washington State University, College of Agricultural, Human, and Natural Resource Sciences, Department of Apparel, Merchandising, Design, and Textiles, Pullman, WA 99164-2020. Offers MA. Programs offered at the Pullman campus. *Program availability:* Part-time. *Degree requirements:* For master's, comprehensive exam (for some programs), thesis, oral exam. *Entrance requirements:* For master's, minimum GPA of 3.0, 2 writing samples, 2 letters of recommendation. Additional exam requirements/recommendations for international students: Required—TOEFL, IELTS. Electronic applications accepted. *Faculty research:* Product development, supply chain management, cultural diversity, consumer behavior, functional design.

Wayne State University, College of Fine, Performing and Communication Arts, James Pearson Duffy Department of Art and Art History, Detroit, MI 48202. Offers art (MA, MFA), including ceramics, drawing, fashion design and merchandising (MA), fibers, graphic design, industrial design (MA), interior design (MA), metalsmithing, painting, photography, printmaking, sculpture; art history (MA). *Students:* 13 full-time (8 women), 12 part-time (9 women); includes 5 minority (3 Black or African American, non-Hispanic/Latino; 1 Asian, non-Hispanic/Latino; 1 Hispanic/Latino), 2 international. Average age 34. 46 applicants, 24% accepted, 6 enrolled. In 2017, 5 master's awarded. *Degree requirements:* For master's, thesis (for some programs), essay or thesis. *Entrance requirements:* For master's, BFA or another degree and equivalent course work, portfolio, personal interview, reference letters, statement of intent (except for art history program). Additional exam requirements/recommendations for international students: Required—TOEFL (minimum score 550 paper-based; 79 iBT), TWE (minimum score 5.5), Michigan English Language Assessment Battery (minimum score 85); Recommended—IELTS (minimum score 6.5). *Application deadline:* For fall admission, 2/1 for domestic and international students; for winter admission, 10/1 for domestic and international students. Application fee: $50. Electronic applications accepted. *Expenses:* Contact institution. *Financial support:* In 2017–18, 18 students received support, including 1 research assistantship (averaging $22,241 per year), 6 teaching assistantships with tuition reimbursements available (averaging $18,534 per year); fellowships with tuition reimbursements available, scholarships/grants, and unspecified assistantships also available. Support available to part-time students. Financial award applicants required to submit FAFSA. *Unit head:* Dr. John Richardson, Chair, 313-577-2980, Fax: 313-577-3491, E-mail: af5343@wayne.edu. *Application contact:* 313-577-2980, E-mail: art@wayne.edu.
Website: http://art.wayne.edu/

Consumer Economics

Colorado State University, College of Health and Human Sciences, Department of Design and Merchandising, Fort Collins, CO 80523-1574. Offers apparel and merchandising (MS). *Program availability:* Part-time. *Faculty:* 8 full-time (all women). *Students:* 10 full-time (9 women), 10 part-time (8 women), 3 international. Average age 31. 25 applicants, 72% accepted, 5 enrolled. In 2017, 5 master's awarded. *Degree requirements:* For master's, thesis or alternative. *Entrance requirements:* For master's, minimum cumulative undergraduate GPA of 3.0; 4-year bachelor's degree from accredited university. Additional exam requirements/recommendations for international students: Required—TOEFL (minimum score 550 paper-based; 80 iBT), IELTS (minimum score 6.5). *Application deadline:* For fall admission, 2/15 priority date for domestic and international students; for spring admission, 10/15 priority date for domestic and international students. Applications are processed on a rolling basis. Application fee: $60 ($70 for international students). Electronic applications accepted. *Expenses:* Tuition, state resident: full-time $9917. Tuition, nonresident: full-time $24,312. *Required fees:* $2284. Tuition and fees vary according to course load and program. *Financial support:* In 2017–18, 8 students received support, including 1 research assistantship with full and partial tuition reimbursement available (averaging $14,256 per year), 6 teaching assistantships with full and partial tuition reimbursements available (averaging $14,256 per year); fellowships with full and partial tuition reimbursements available, Federal Work-Study, scholarships/grants, health care benefits, and unspecified assistantships also available. Financial award application deadline: 2/15. *Faculty research:* Design/product development, design communication/creativity, merchandising/consumer behavior, social responsibility, social/cultural/historical aspects of the near environment. *Total annual research expenditures:* $53,999. *Unit head:* Dr. Karen Hyllegard, Professor and Department Head, 970-491-4627, Fax: 970-491-4855, E-mail: karen.hyllegard@colostate.edu. *Application contact:* Dr. Jennifer Ogle, Professor and Graduate Coordinator, 970-491-3794, Fax: 970-491-4855, E-mail: jennifer.ogle@colostate.edu.
Website: http://www.dm.chhs.colostate.edu/

Cornell University, Graduate School, Graduate Fields of Human Ecology, Field of Policy Analysis and Management, Ithaca, NY 14853. Offers consumer policy (PhD); family and social welfare policy (PhD); health administration (MHA); health management and policy (PhD); public policy (PhD). *Degree requirements:* For master's, thesis; for doctorate, thesis/dissertation. *Entrance requirements:* For master's, GRE General Test or GMAT, 2 letters of recommendation; for doctorate, GRE General Test, 2 letters of recommendation. Additional exam requirements/recommendations for international students: Required—TOEFL (minimum score 550 paper-based; 77 iBT). Electronic applications accepted. *Faculty research:* Health policy, family policy, social welfare policy, program evaluation, consumer policy.

Kansas State University, Graduate School, College of Human Ecology, Department of Food, Nutrition, Dietetics and Health, Manhattan, KS 66506. Offers dietetics (MS); human nutrition (PhD); nutrition, dietetics and sensory sciences (MS); nutritional sciences (PhD); public health nutrition (PhD); public health physical activity (PhD); sensory analysis and consumer behavior (PhD). *Program availability:* Part-time. *Degree requirements:* For master's, thesis or alternative, residency; for doctorate, thesis/dissertation, residency. *Entrance requirements:* For master's, GRE General Test, minimum undergraduate GPA of 3.0; for doctorate, GRE General Test, minimum graduate GPA of 3.0. Additional exam requirements/recommendations for international students: Required—TOEFL (minimum score 550 paper-based; 79 iBT), IELTS (minimum score 6.5). Electronic applications accepted. *Faculty research:* Cancer and immunology, obesity, sensory analysis and consumer behavior, nutrient metabolism, clinical and community interventions.

Kansas State University, Graduate School, College of Human Ecology, School of Family Studies and Human Services, Manhattan, KS 66506-1403. Offers applied family sciences (MS); communication sciences and disorders (MS); conflict resolution (Graduate Certificate); couple and family therapy (MS); early childhood education (MS); family and community service (MS); life-span human development (MS); personal financial planning (MS, PhD, Graduate Certificate); youth development (MS, Graduate Certificate). *Accreditation:* AAMFT/COAMFTE; ASHA. *Program availability:* Part-time, online learning. *Degree requirements:* For master's, comprehensive exam (for some programs), thesis optional. *Entrance requirements:* For master's, GRE, minimum GPA of 3.0 in last 2 years (60 semester hours) of undergraduate study; for doctorate, GRE. Additional exam requirements/recommendations for international students: Required—TOEFL (minimum score 600 paper-based). Electronic applications accepted. *Faculty research:* Health and security of military families, training in and evaluation of professional human services (marriage and couple therapy, family life education, treatment of speech and swallowing disorders, financial therapy), disorders of communication and swallowing, family and relationship development and health, financial decision-making.

North Carolina Agricultural and Technical State University, School of Graduate Studies, School of Agriculture and Environmental Sciences, Department of Family and Consumer Sciences, Greensboro, NC 27411. Offers child development early education and family studies (MAT); family and consumer sciences (MAT); food and nutrition (MS). *Program availability:* Part-time, evening/weekend. *Degree requirements:* For master's, comprehensive exam, thesis or alternative, qualifying exam. *Entrance requirements:* For master's, GRE General Test, minimum GPA of 2.6.

North Dakota State University, College of Graduate and Interdisciplinary Studies, College of Human Development and Education, Department of Human Development and Family Science, Program in Family Financial Planning, Fargo, ND 58102. Offers MS, Certificate. Electronic applications accepted.

Ohio University, Graduate College, College of Health Sciences and Professions, School of Applied Health Sciences and Wellness, Program in Food and Nutrition, Athens, OH 45701-2979. Offers human and consumer sciences (MS).

Oklahoma State University, College of Human Sciences, Department of Human Development and Family Science, Stillwater, OK 74078. Offers human development and family science (MS, PhD), including family financial planning (MS), human environmental sciences (PhD). *Accreditation:* AAMFT/COAMFTE (one or more programs are accredited). *Program availability:* Online learning. *Faculty:* 33 full-time (23 women), 13 part-time/adjunct (11 women). *Students:* 36 full-time (29 women), 49 part-time (43 women); includes 27 minority (12 Black or African American, non-Hispanic/Latino; 1 American Indian or Alaska Native, non-Hispanic/Latino; 1 Asian, non-Hispanic/Latino; 9 Hispanic/Latino; 4 Two or more races, non-Hispanic/Latino), 3 international. Average age 31. 54 applicants, 59% accepted, 30 enrolled. In 2017, 20 master's, 1 doctorate awarded. *Entrance requirements:* For master's and doctorate, GRE or GMAT. Additional exam requirements/recommendations for international students: Required—TOEFL (minimum score 550 paper-based; 79 iBT). *Application deadline:* For fall admission, 3/1 priority date for international students; for spring admission, 8/1 priority date for international students. Applications are processed on a rolling basis. Application fee: $40 ($75 for international students). Electronic applications accepted. *Expenses:* Tuition, state resident: full-time $4019; part-time $2679.60 per year. Tuition, nonresident: full-time $15,286; part-time $10,190.40 per year. *Required fees:* $2129; $1419 per unit. Tuition and fees vary according to program. *Financial support:* Research assistantships, teaching assistantships, career-related internships or fieldwork, Federal Work-Study, scholarships/grants, health care benefits, tuition waivers (partial), and unspecified assistantships available. Support available to part-time students. Financial award application deadline: 3/1; financial award applicants required to submit FAFSA. *Faculty research:* Family relations and child development, consequences of adolescent parenting, family stress and coping, impacts of sexual abuse on families, children's social cognition and self-competence, gerontology and health care. *Unit head:* Dr. Sissy Osteen, Department Head, 405-744-4741, Fax: 405-744-6344, E-mail: sissy.osteen@okstate.edu. *Application contact:* Dr. Michael Criss, Graduate Coordinator, 405-744-5057, Fax: 405-744-6344, E-mail: michael.criss@okstate.edu.
Website: https://humansciences.okstate.edu/hdfs/

Purdue University, Graduate School, College of Health and Human Sciences, Department of Consumer Sciences and Retailing, West Lafayette, IN 47907. Offers consumer behavior (MS, PhD); family and consumer economics (MS, PhD). *Program availability:* Part-time. *Faculty:* 13 full-time (6 women). *Students:* 15 full-time (8 women), 6 part-time (2 women); includes 5 minority (1 Black or African American, non-Hispanic/Latino; 2 Asian, non-Hispanic/Latino; 2 Hispanic/Latino), 11 international. Average age 29. 28 applicants, 50% accepted, 7 enrolled. In 2017, 5 master's, 4 doctorates awarded. *Degree requirements:* For master's, thesis, oral presentation, final examination; for doctorate, comprehensive exam, thesis/dissertation, oral presentation, final examination. *Entrance requirements:* For master's, GMAT or GRE General Test (minimum 50th percentile), minimum undergraduate GPA of 3.0 or equivalent; for doctorate, GMAT or GRE General Test (minimum 50th percentile), minimum undergraduate GPA of 3.0 or equivalent; master's degree with minimum GPA of 3.25 or equivalent. Additional exam requirements/recommendations for international students: Required—TOEFL (minimum score 550 paper-based; 77 iBT). *Application deadline:* For fall admission, 2/15 priority date for domestic students, 2/15 for international students. Applications are processed on a rolling basis. Application fee: $60 ($75 for international students). Electronic applications accepted. *Financial support:* Fellowships, research assistantships with tuition reimbursements, teaching assistantships with tuition reimbursements, and career-related internships or fieldwork available. Support available to part-time students. Financial award applicants required to submit FAFSA. *Faculty research:* Family financial resources, retail management and patronage, chemical analysis of textile dyes and finishes. *Unit head:* Richard Ghiselli, Interim Head of the Graduate Program, 765-494-2683, E-mail: ghiselli@purdue.edu. *Application contact:* Graduate School Admissions, 765-494-2600, Fax: 765-494-0136, E-mail: gradinfo@purdue.edu.
Website: http://www.purdue.edu/hhs/csr/

Consumer Economics

South Dakota State University, Graduate School, College of Education and Human Sciences, Department of Consumer Sciences, Brookings, SD 57007. Offers family financial planning (MS); merchandising (MS). *Entrance requirements:* For master's, resume. Additional exam requirements/recommendations for international students: Required—TOEFL (minimum score 525 paper-based).

State University of New York at Oswego, Graduate Studies, School of Education, Department of Vocational Teacher Preparation, Oswego, NY 13126. Offers agriculture (MS Ed); business and marketing (MS Ed); family and consumer sciences (MS Ed); health careers (MS Ed); technical education (MS Ed); trade education (MS Ed). *Accreditation:* NCATE. *Program availability:* Part-time, evening/weekend. *Degree requirements:* For master's, comprehensive exam, thesis or alternative. *Entrance requirements:* Additional exam requirements/recommendations for international students: Required—TOEFL (minimum score 560 paper-based).

Texas Tech University, Graduate School, College of Human Sciences, Department of Personal Financial Planning, Lubbock, TX 79409-1210. Offers MS, PhD, JD/MS. *Program availability:* Part-time, blended/hybrid learning. *Faculty:* 11 full-time (5 women), 3 part-time/adjunct (2 women). *Students:* 96 full-time (37 women), 61 part-time (23 women); includes 50 minority (10 Black or African American, non-Hispanic/Latino; 2 Asian, non-Hispanic/Latino; 34 Hispanic/Latino; 4 Two or more races, non-Hispanic/Latino), 35 international. Average age 30. 113 applicants, 78% accepted, 67 enrolled. In 2017, 41 master's, 2 doctorates awarded. Terminal master's awarded for partial completion of doctoral program. *Degree requirements:* For master's, thesis or alternative; for doctorate, comprehensive exam, thesis/dissertation. *Entrance requirements:* For doctorate, GRE, GMAT, or LSAT. Additional exam requirements/recommendations for international students: Required—TOEFL (minimum score 550 paper-based; 79 iBT). *Application deadline:* For fall admission, 6/1 priority date for domestic students, 1/15 priority date for international students; for spring admission, 9/1 priority date for domestic students, 6/15 priority date for international students. Applications are processed on a rolling basis. Application fee: $60. Electronic applications accepted. *Expenses:* Contact institution. *Financial support:* In 2017–18, 91 students received support, including 90 fellowships (averaging $3,439 per year), 10 research assistantships (averaging $14,695 per year), 27 teaching assistantships (averaging $15,871 per year); Federal Work-Study, scholarships/grants, health care benefits, and unspecified assistantships also available. Financial award application deadline: 1/15; financial award applicants required to submit FAFSA. *Faculty research:* Financial literacy, retirement planning and living, financial risk tolerance, charitable financial planning, reverse mortgages. *Total annual research expenditures:* $284,827. *Unit head:* Dr. Vickie Hampton, Department Chair, 806-834-1824, Fax: 806-742-5033, E-mail: vickie.hampton@ttu.edu. *Application contact:* Dr. John Gilliam, MS Program Director, 806-834-8864, Fax: 806-742-5033, E-mail: john.gilliam@ttu.edu.
Website: http://www.pfp.ttu.edu

Université Laval, Faculty of Agricultural and Food Sciences, Department of Agricultural Economics and Consumer Sciences, Program in Consumer Sciences, Québec, QC G1K 7P4, Canada. Offers Diploma. *Program availability:* Part-time. *Entrance requirements:* For degree, knowledge of French and English. Electronic applications accepted.

The University of Alabama, Graduate School, College of Human Environmental Sciences, Department of Consumer Sciences, Tuscaloosa, AL 35487-0158. Offers MS. *Program availability:* Part-time, evening/weekend, online learning. *Faculty:* 12 full-time (6 women), 3 part-time/adjunct (2 women). *Students:* 19 full-time (10 women), 54 part-time (27 women); includes 17 minority (10 Black or African American, non-Hispanic/Latino; 1 Asian, non-Hispanic/Latino; 2 Hispanic/Latino; 4 Two or more races, non-Hispanic/Latino). Average age 35. 37 applicants, 84% accepted, 31 enrolled. In 2017, 24 master's awarded. *Degree requirements:* For master's, capstone. *Entrance requirements:* For master's, GRE or GMAT (50th percentile or higher), minimum GPA of 3.0. Additional exam requirements/recommendations for international students: Required—TOEFL. *Application deadline:* For fall admission, 7/1 priority date for domestic and international students; for winter admission, 1/1 priority date for domestic and international students. Applications are processed on a rolling basis. Application fee: $50 ($60 for international students). Electronic applications accepted. *Financial support:* In 2017–18, 4 students received support, including research assistantships with full tuition reimbursements available (averaging $13,000 per year), teaching assistantships with full tuition reimbursements available (averaging $13,000 per year). Financial award application deadline: 3/15. *Faculty research:* Consumer economics, financial planning, policy evaluation, retirement preparedness, financial wellness. *Unit head:* Dr. Milla D. Boschung, Chair, 205-348-6250, Fax: 205-348-3789, E-mail: mboschun@ches.ua.edu. *Application contact:* Lauren Creel, Departmental Assistant, 205-348-6178, Fax: 205-348-3789, E-mail: lcreel@ches.ua.edu.
Website: http://www.csm.ches.ua.edu/

University of Guelph, Graduate Studies, College of Management and Economics, Department of Marketing and Consumer Studies, Guelph, ON N1G 2W1, Canada. Offers M Sc. *Degree requirements:* For master's, thesis. *Entrance requirements:* For master's, GMAT or GRE General Test, minimum B average during previous 2 years of course work. Additional exam requirements/recommendations for international students: Required—TOEFL (minimum score 575 paper-based). Electronic applications accepted. *Faculty research:* Marketing, quality management, consumer economics, housing and real estate management, problem gambling.

University of Idaho, College of Graduate Studies, College of Agricultural and Life Sciences, Margaret Ritchie School of Family and Consumer Sciences, Moscow, ID 83844-3183. Offers MS. *Faculty:* 8 full-time. *Students:* 10 full-time, 6 part-time. Average age 32. In 2017, 11 master's awarded. *Entrance requirements:* For master's, minimum GPA of 3.0. Additional exam requirements/recommendations for international students: Required—TOEFL (minimum score 79 iBT). *Application deadline:* For fall admission, 8/1 for domestic students; for spring admission, 12/15 for domestic students. Application fee: $60. *Expenses:* Tuition, state resident: full-time $6722; part-time $430 per credit hour. Tuition, nonresident: full-time $23,046; part-time $1337 per credit hour. *Required fees:* $2142; $63 per credit hour. *Financial support:* Research assistantships and teaching assistantships available. *Faculty research:* Food and nutrition; clothing, textiles and design; child, family and consumer studies; early childhood education. *Unit head:* Dr. Sonya Sue Meyer, Interim Chair, 208-885-6546, E-mail: famcon@uidaho.edu. *Application contact:* Sean Scoggin, Graduate Recruitment Coordinator, 208-885-4001, Fax: 208-885-4406, E-mail: graduateadmissions@uidaho.edu.
Website: http://www.uidaho.edu/cals/family-and-consumer-sciences

University of Illinois at Urbana–Champaign, Graduate College, College of Agricultural, Consumer and Environmental Sciences, Department of Agricultural and Consumer Economics, Champaign, IL 61820. Offers agricultural and applied economics (MS, PhD).

University of Missouri, Office of Research and Graduate Studies, College of Human Environmental Sciences, Department of Personal Financial Planning, Columbia, MO 65211. Offers MS, PhD, Certificate, Graduate Certificate. *Entrance requirements:* For master's, GRE General Test, minimum GPA of 3.0. Additional exam requirements/recommendations for international students: Required—TOEFL (minimum score 550 paper-based; 80 iBT). Electronic applications accepted.

University of Nebraska–Lincoln, Graduate College, College of Education and Human Sciences, Department of Child, Youth and Family Studies, Lincoln, NE 68588. Offers child development/early childhood education (MS, PhD); child, youth and family studies (MS); family and consumer sciences education (MS, PhD); family financial planning (MS); family science (MS, PhD); gerontology (PhD); human sciences (PhD), including child, youth and family studies, gerontology, medical family therapy; marriage and family therapy (MS); medical family therapy (PhD); youth development (MS). *Accreditation:* AAMFT/COAMFTE (one or more programs are accredited). *Program availability:* Online learning. *Degree requirements:* For master's, thesis optional. *Entrance requirements:* For master's, GRE. Additional exam requirements/recommendations for international students: Required—TOEFL (minimum score 550 paper-based). Electronic applications accepted. *Faculty research:* Marriage and family therapy, child development/early childhood education, family financial management.

University of South Carolina, The Graduate School, College of Hospitality, Retail, and Sport Management, Department of Retailing, Columbia, SC 29208. Offers MR. *Program availability:* Part-time. *Degree requirements:* For master's, comprehensive exam, internship or thesis. *Entrance requirements:* For master's, GMAT or GRE General Test, minimum GPA of 3.0. Additional exam requirements/recommendations for international students: Required—TOEFL (minimum score 80 iBT). Electronic applications accepted. *Faculty research:* Retail technology, retail strategy, international retailing.

The University of Tennessee, Graduate School, College of Education, Health and Human Sciences, Department of Consumer and Industry Services Management, Program in Consumer Services Management, Knoxville, TN 37996. Offers retail and consumer sciences (MS); textile science (MS). *Program availability:* Part-time. *Degree requirements:* For master's, thesis or alternative. *Entrance requirements:* For master's, GRE General Test, minimum GPA of 2.7. Additional exam requirements/recommendations for international students: Required—TOEFL. Electronic applications accepted.

The University of Tennessee, Graduate School, College of Education, Health and Human Sciences, Program in Human Ecology, Knoxville, TN 37996. Offers child and family studies (PhD); community health (PhD); nutrition science (PhD); retailing and consumer sciences (PhD); textile science (PhD). *Degree requirements:* For doctorate, thesis/dissertation. *Entrance requirements:* For doctorate, GRE General Test, minimum GPA of 2.7. Additional exam requirements/recommendations for international students: Required—TOEFL. Electronic applications accepted.

University of Wisconsin–Madison, Graduate School, School of Human Ecology, Program in Consumer Behavior and Family Economics, Madison, WI 53706-1380. Offers MS, PhD. Terminal master's awarded for partial completion of doctoral program. *Degree requirements:* For master's, thesis optional; for doctorate, comprehensive exam, thesis/dissertation. *Entrance requirements:* For master's and doctorate, GRE General Test, 3 letters of recommendation. Additional exam requirements/recommendations for international students: Required—TOEFL (minimum score 580 paper-based; 92 iBT). Electronic applications accepted. *Faculty research:* Economic well-being of elderly, finance, financial planning, health care policy, consumer behavior.

University of Wyoming, College of Agriculture and Natural Resources, Department of Family and Consumer Sciences, Laramie, WY 82071. Offers early childhood development (MS); family and consumer sciences (MS); food science and human nutrition (MS). *Program availability:* Part-time. *Degree requirements:* For master's, thesis, project. *Entrance requirements:* For master's, GRE General Test or MCAT, minimum GPA of 3.0. Additional exam requirements/recommendations for international students: Required—TOEFL (minimum score 540 paper-based; 76 iBT). Electronic applications accepted. *Faculty research:* Asthma, obesity and healthy weights, nutrition concerns of children with special health care needs, food product development, food safety, postpartum health, exercise nutrition.

Utah State University, School of Graduate Studies, College of Agriculture and Applied Sciences, School of Applied Sciences, Technology and Education, Logan, UT 84322. Offers agricultural extension and education (MS); family and consumer sciences education and extension (MS); technology and engineering education (MS). *Program availability:* Part-time, online learning. *Degree requirements:* For master's, comprehensive exam (for some programs), thesis (for some programs). *Entrance requirements:* For master's, GRE General Test, MAT, BS in agricultural education, agricultural extension, or related agricultural or science discipline; minimum GPA of 3.0. Additional exam requirements/recommendations for international students: Required—TOEFL. *Faculty research:* Extension and adult education; structures and environment; low-input agriculture; farm safety, systems, and mechanizations.

Gerontology

Adelphi University, Ruth S. Ammon School of Education, Program in Physical Education and Human Performance Science, Garden City, NY 11530-0701. Offers aging (Certificate); physical/educational human performance science (MA). *Program availability:* Part-time, evening/weekend. *Students:* 84 full-time (32 women), 78 part-time (30 women); includes 56 minority (26 Black or African American, non-Hispanic/Latino; 1 American Indian or Alaska Native, non-Hispanic/Latino; 1 Asian, non-Hispanic/Latino; 25 Hispanic/Latino; 3 Two or more races, non-Hispanic/Latino), 8 international. Average age 27. 131 applicants, 69% accepted, 59 enrolled. In 2017, 45 master's awarded. *Degree requirements:* For master's, internship. *Entrance requirements:* For master's, 3 letters of recommendation, resume. Additional exam requirements/recommendations for international students: Required—TOEFL (minimum score 550 paper-based; 80 iBT), IELTS (minimum score 6.5). *Application deadline:* For fall admission, 4/1 for international students; for spring admission, 11/1 for international students. Applications are processed on a rolling basis. Application fee: $50. Electronic applications accepted. *Expenses:* Contact institution. *Financial support:* Research assistantships, teaching assistantships, career-related internships or fieldwork, institutionally sponsored loans,

scholarships/grants, traineeships, and unspecified assistantships available. Support available to part-time students. Financial award application deadline: 2/15; financial award applicants required to submit FAFSA. *Faculty research:* Physical education for the handicapped, sport sociology, sport pedagogy. *Unit head:* Dr. Ronald Feingold, Chair, 516-877-4764, E-mail: feingold@adelphi.edu. *Application contact:* E-mail: graduateadmissions@adelphi.edu.

Alliant International University–Los Angeles, California School of Professional Psychology, Program in Couple and Family Therapy, Alhambra, CA 91803. Offers chemical dependency (MA); gerontology (MA); Latin American family therapy (MA). *Accreditation:* AAMFT/COAMFTE. *Program availability:* Part-time, evening/weekend. Terminal master's awarded for partial completion of doctoral program. *Degree requirements:* For master's, comprehensive exam, 50 hours of professional development activities. *Entrance requirements:* Additional exam requirements/recommendations for international students: Required—TOEFL (minimum score 550 paper-based). Electronic applications accepted. *Faculty research:* Foster care, therapy with minority couples, parenting, marriage, trauma.

Arizona State University at the Tempe campus, College of Public Programs, School of Social Work, Phoenix, AZ 85004-0689. Offers advanced direct practice (MSW); assessment of integrative health modalities (Graduate Certificate); gerontology (Graduate Certificate); Latino cultural competency (Graduate Certificate); planning, administration and community practice (MSW); social work (PhD); trauma and bereavement (Graduate Certificate); MPA/MSW. *Accreditation:* CSWE (one or more programs are accredited). *Program availability:* Part-time. Terminal master's awarded for partial completion of doctoral program. *Degree requirements:* For master's, thesis or alternative, capstone project, interactive Program of Study (iPOS) submitted before completing 50 percent of required credit hours; for doctorate, comprehensive exam, thesis/dissertation, interactive Program of Study (iPOS) submitted before completing 50 percent of required credit hours. *Entrance requirements:* For master's, GRE or MAT, minimum GPA of 3.2 or equivalent in last 2 years of work leading to bachelor's degree; for doctorate, GRE, minimum GPA of 3.0 or equivalent in last 2 years of work leading to bachelor's degree, 3 letters of recommendation, resume, samples of professional writing, personal statement. Additional exam requirements/recommendations for international students: Required—TOEFL, IELTS, or PTE. Electronic applications accepted. *Expenses:* Contact institution.

Arkansas State University, Graduate School, College of Nursing and Health Professions, School of Nursing, State University, AR 72467. Offers aging studies (Graduate Certificate); health care management (Graduate Certificate); health sciences (MS); health sciences education (Graduate Certificate); nurse anesthesia (MSN); nursing (MSN); nursing practice (DNP). *Accreditation:* AANA/CANAEP (one or more programs are accredited); ACEN. *Program availability:* Part-time. *Degree requirements:* For master's and Graduate Certificate, comprehensive exam, thesis or alternative; for doctorate, comprehensive exam, thesis/dissertation. *Entrance requirements:* For master's, GRE General Test or MAT, appropriate bachelor's degree, current Arkansas nursing license, CPR certification, physical examination, professional liability insurance, critical care experience, ACLS Certification, PALS Certification, interview, immunization records, personal goal statement, health assessment; for doctorate, GRE or MAT, NCLEX-RN Exam, appropriate master's degree, current Arkansas nursing license, CPR certification, physical examination, professional liability insurance, critical care experience, ACLS Certification, PALS Certification, interview, immunization records, personal goal statement, health assessment, TB skin test, background check; for Graduate Certificate, GRE or MAT, appropriate bachelor's degree, official transcripts, immunization records, proof of employment in healthcare, TB Skin Test, TB Mask Fit Test, CPR Certification. Additional exam requirements/recommendations for international students: Required—TOEFL (minimum score 550 paper-based; 79 iBT), IELTS (minimum score 6), PTE (minimum score 56). Electronic applications accepted. *Expenses:* Contact institution.

California State University, Fullerton, Graduate Studies, College of Health and Human Development, Department of Public Health, Fullerton, CA 92831-3599. Offers environmental and occupational health and safety (MPH); gerontological health (MPH); health promotion and disease (MPH). *Accreditation:* CEPH. *Program availability:* Part-time. *Students:* 37 full-time (31 women), 29 part-time (21 women); includes 41 minority (2 Black or African American, non-Hispanic/Latino; 14 Asian, non-Hispanic/Latino; 23 Hispanic/Latino; 1 Native Hawaiian or other Pacific Islander, non-Hispanic/Latino; 1 Two or more races, non-Hispanic/Latino), 2 international. Average age 30. 105 applicants, 47% accepted, 21 enrolled. In 2017, 26 master's awarded. *Entrance requirements:* For master's, minimum GPA of 3.0 in last 60 units attempted. Application fee: $55. *Financial support:* Career-related internships or fieldwork, Federal Work-Study, institutionally sponsored loans, and scholarships/grants available. Support available to part-time students. Financial award application deadline: 3/1; financial award applicants required to submit FAFSA. *Unit head:* Head, 657-278-2620. *Application contact:* Admissions/Applications, 657-278-2371.
Website: http://hhd.fullerton.edu/hesc/

California State University, Fullerton, Graduate Studies, College of Humanities and Social Sciences, Program in Gerontology, Fullerton, CA 92831-3599. Offers MS. *Program availability:* Part-time. *Faculty:* 3 part-time/adjunct (all women). *Students:* 7 full-time (all women), 11 part-time (10 women); includes 9 minority (4 Asian, non-Hispanic/Latino; 4 Hispanic/Latino; 1 Two or more races, non-Hispanic/Latino). Average age 40. 10 applicants, 90% accepted, 7 enrolled. *Financial support:* Career-related internships or fieldwork, Federal Work-Study, institutionally sponsored loans, and scholarships/grants available. Financial award application deadline: 3/1; financial award applicants required to submit FAFSA. *Unit head:* Dr. Barbara Cherry, Coordinator, 657-278-3035. *Application contact:* Admissions/Applications, 657-278-2371.

California State University, Long Beach, Graduate Studies, College of Health and Human Services, Program in Gerontology, Long Beach, CA 90840. Offers MS. *Program availability:* Part-time. *Degree requirements:* For master's, thesis optional. Electronic applications accepted.

Capella University, School of Public Service Leadership, Master's Programs in Healthcare, Minneapolis, MN 55402. Offers criminal justice (MS); emergency management (MS); general public health (MPH); gerontology (MS); health administration (MHA); health care operations (MHA); health management policy (MPH); health policy (MHA); homeland security (MS); multidisciplinary human services (MS); public administration (MPA); public safety leadership (MS); social and community services (MS); social behavioral sciences (MPH); MS/MPA.

Central Michigan University, College of Graduate Studies, College of Education and Human Services, Department of Human Environmental Studies, Mount Pleasant, MI 48859. Offers apparel product development and merchandising technology (MS); gerontology (Graduate Certificate); human development and family studies (MA); nutrition and dietetics (MS). *Program availability:* Part-time, evening/weekend. *Degree requirements:* For master's, thesis or alternative. Electronic applications accepted. *Faculty research:* Human growth and development, family studies and human sexuality, human nutrition and dietetics, apparel and textile retailing, computer-aided design for apparel.

The College at Brockport, State University of New York, School of Education, Health, and Human Services, Greater Rochester Collaborative Master of Social Work Program, Brockport, NY 14420-2997. Offers family and community practice (MSW); gerontology (AGC); interdisciplinary health practice (MSW). Program offered jointly with Nazareth College of Rochester. *Accreditation:* CSWE. *Program availability:* Part-time. *Faculty:* 6 full-time (4 women), 6 part-time/adjunct (4 women). *Students:* 54 full-time (47 women), 144 part-time (128 women); includes 35 minority (19 Black or African American, non-Hispanic/Latino; 1 American Indian or Alaska Native, non-Hispanic/Latino; 2 Asian, non-Hispanic/Latino; 6 Hispanic/Latino; 1 Native Hawaiian or other Pacific Islander, non-Hispanic/Latino; 6 Two or more races, non-Hispanic/Latino). 143 applicants, 78% accepted, 78 enrolled. In 2017, 72 master's, 9 other advanced degrees awarded. *Degree requirements:* For master's, thesis or alternative. *Entrance requirements:* For master's, minimum GPA of 3.0, letters of recommendation, statement of objectives. Additional exam requirements/recommendations for international students: Required—TOEFL (minimum score 550 paper-based; 79 iBT), IELTS (minimum score 6.5). *Application deadline:* For fall admission, 1/15 priority date for domestic and international students; for summer admission, 1/15 priority date for domestic and international students. Application fee: $50. Electronic applications accepted. *Expenses:* Tuition, state resident: full-time $10,870; part-time $453 per credit hour. Tuition, nonresident: full-time $22,210. *Required fees:* $988; $246 per semester. *Financial support:* Federal Work-Study, scholarships/grants, and unspecified assistantships available. Support available to part-time students. Financial award application deadline: 3/15; financial award applicants required to submit FAFSA. *Faculty research:* Care giving, child welfare, gerontological social work, home-school-community partnerships, domestic violence. *Unit head:* Debra Fromm Faria, Co-Director, 585-395-8455, Fax: 585-395-8603, E-mail: grcmsw@brockport.edu. *Application contact:* Brad Snyder, Coordinator of Admissions, 585-395-3845, Fax: 585-395-8603, E-mail: bsynder@brockport.edu.
Website: https://www.brockport.edu/academics/social_work/graduate/masters.html

Concordia University Chicago, College of Graduate and Innovative Programs, Program in Gerontology, River Forest, IL 60305-1499. Offers MA. *Program availability:* Part-time, evening/weekend. *Degree requirements:* For master's, comprehensive exam, thesis. *Entrance requirements:* For master's, minimum GPA of 2.9. Additional exam requirements/recommendations for international students: Required—TOEFL (minimum score 550 paper-based). Electronic applications accepted.

DeSales University, Division of Healthcare, Center Valley, PA 18034-9568. Offers adult-gerontology acute care (Post Master's Certificate); adult-gerontology acute care nurse practitioner (MSN); adult-gerontology acute certified nurse practitioner (Post Master's Certificate); adult-gerontology clinical nurse specialist (MSN, Post Master's Certificate); clinical leadership (DNP); family nurse practitioner (MSN, Post Master's Certificate); general nursing practice (DNP); nurse anesthetist (MSN); nurse educator (Post Master's Certificate, Postbaccalaureate Certificate); nurse midwife (MSN); nurse practitioner (MSN); psychiatric-mental health nurse practitioner (MSN, Post Master's Certificate); DNP/MBA. *Accreditation:* ACEN. *Program availability:* Part-time. *Faculty:* 26 full-time (20 women), 30 part-time/adjunct (19 women). *Students:* 282 full-time (210 women), 101 part-time (85 women); includes 39 minority (12 Black or African American, non-Hispanic/Latino; 11 Asian, non-Hispanic/Latino; 12 Hispanic/Latino; 4 Two or more races, non-Hispanic/Latino), 1 international. Average age 29. 2,884 applicants, 5% accepted, 114 enrolled. In 2017, 76 master's, 6 doctorates awarded. *Degree requirements:* For master's, minimum GPA of 3.0, portfolio; for doctorate, minimum GPA of 3.0, scholarly capstone project. *Entrance requirements:* For master's, GRE or MAT (waived if applicant has an undergraduate GPA of 3.0 or higher), BSN from ACEN- or CCNE-accredited program, minimum undergraduate GPA of 3.0, active RN license or eligibility, two letters of recommendation, essay, health care experience, personal interview; for doctorate, BSN or MSN from ACEN- or CCNE-accredited institution, minimum GPA of 3.3 in graduate program, current licensure as an RN. Additional exam requirements/recommendations for international students: Required—TOEFL (minimum score 104 iBT). *Application deadline:* Applications are processed on a rolling basis. Application fee: $50. Electronic applications accepted. *Expenses:* Contact institution. *Financial support:* Applicants required to submit FAFSA. *Unit head:* Ronald Nordone, Dean of Graduate Education, 610-282-1100 Ext. 1289, E-mail: ronald.nordone@desales.edu. *Application contact:* Julia Ferraro, Director of Graduate Admissions, 610-282-1100 Ext. 1768, E-mail: gradadmissions@desales.edu.

Duke University, School of Nursing, Durham, NC 27708-0586. Offers acute care pediatric nurse practitioner (MSN, Post-Graduate Certificate); adult-gerontology nurse practitioner (MSN, Post-Graduate Certificate), including acute care, primary care; family nurse practitioner (MSN, Post-Graduate Certificate); neonatal nurse practitioner (MSN, Post-Graduate Certificate); nurse anesthesia (DNP); nurse practitioner (DNP); nursing (PhD); nursing and health care leadership (MSN, Post-Graduate Certificate); nursing education (MSN, Post-Graduate Certificate); nursing informatics (MSN, Post-Graduate Certificate); pediatric nurse practitioner (MSN, Post-Graduate Certificate), including primary care; psychiatric mental health nurse practitioner (MSN, Post-Graduate Certificate); women's health nurse practitioner (MSN, Post-Graduate Certificate). *Accreditation:* AACN; AANA/CANAEP. *Program availability:* Part-time, evening/weekend, online with on-campus intensives. *Faculty:* 72 full-time (61 women). *Students:* 155 full-time (137 women), 613 part-time (548 women); includes 177 minority (64 Black or African American, non-Hispanic/Latino; 2 American Indian or Alaska Native, non-Hispanic/Latino; 47 Asian, non-Hispanic/Latino; 34 Hispanic/Latino; 30 Two or more races, non-Hispanic/Latino), 10 international. Average age 34. 631 applicants, 47% accepted, 211 enrolled. In 2017, 221 master's, 71 doctorates, 26 other advanced degrees awarded. Terminal master's awarded for partial completion of doctoral program. *Degree requirements:* For master's, thesis optional; for doctorate, capstone project. *Entrance requirements:* For master's, GRE General Test (waived if undergraduate GPA of 3.4 or higher), 1 year of nursing experience (recommended), BSN, minimum GPA of 3.0, previous course work in statistics; for doctorate, GRE General Test (waived if undergraduate GPA of 3.4 or higher), BSN or MSN, minimum GPA of 3.0, resume, personal statement, undergraduate statistics course, current licensure as a registered nurse, transcripts from all post-secondary institutions; for Post-Graduate Certificate, MSN, licensure or eligibility as a professional nurse, transcripts from all post-secondary institutions, previous course work in statistics. Additional exam requirements/recommendations for international students: Required—TOEFL (minimum score 100 iBT), IELTS (minimum score 7). *Application deadline:* For fall admission, 12/1 for domestic and international students; for spring admission, 5/1 for domestic and international students. Application fee: $50. Electronic applications accepted. *Expenses:* Contact institution. *Financial support:* Institutionally sponsored loans, scholarships/grants, and traineeships available. Support available to part-time students. Financial award applicants required to submit FAFSA. *Faculty research:* Cardiovascular disease, caregiver skill training, data mining, prostate cancer, neonatal immune system. *Unit head:* Dr. Marion E. Broome, Dean/Vice Chancellor for Nursing Affairs/Associate Vice President for Academic Affairs for Nursing, 919-684-9446, Fax: 919-684-9414, E-mail: marion.broome@duke.edu. *Application contact:* Dr. Ernie Rushing, Director of Admissions and Recruitment, 919-668-6274, Fax: 919-668-4693, E-mail: ernie.rushing@dm.duke.edu.
Website: http://www.nursing.duke.edu/

Gerontology

East Carolina University, Graduate School, College of Health and Human Performance, School of Social Work, Greenville, NC 27858-4353. Offers gerontology (Certificate); social work (MSW); substance abuse (Certificate). *Accreditation:* CSWE. *Program availability:* Online learning. *Students:* 103 full-time (95 women), 23 part-time (22 women); includes 65 minority (52 Black or African American, non-Hispanic/Latino; 1 American Indian or Alaska Native, non-Hispanic/Latino; 3 Asian, non-Hispanic/Latino; 7 Hispanic/Latino; 2 Two or more races, non-Hispanic/Latino), 1 international. Average age 30. 107 applicants, 87% accepted, 62 enrolled. In 2017, 69 master's, 30 other advanced degrees awarded. *Degree requirements:* For master's, comprehensive exam. *Entrance requirements:* For master's, GRE or MAT. Additional exam requirements/recommendations for international students: Recommended—TOEFL (minimum score 78 iBT), IELTS (minimum score 6.5). *Application deadline:* For fall admission, 2/1 priority date for domestic and international students. Application fee: $75. *Expenses:* Tuition, state resident: full-time $4749; part-time $297 per credit hour. Tuition, nonresident: full-time $17,898; part-time $1119 per credit hour. *Required fees:* $2691; $224 per credit hour. Part-time tuition and fees vary according to course load and program. *Financial support:* Fellowships and research assistantships available. Financial award application deadline: 6/1. *Faculty research:* Social research, gerontology, women's issues, social services in schools, human behavior. *Unit head:* Dr. Shelia Bunch, Director, 252-328-4202, E-mail: bunchs@ecu.edu.
Website: https://hhp.ecu.edu/socw/

Eastern Illinois University, Graduate School, College of Health and Human Services, Program in Aging Studies, Charleston, IL 61920. Offers MA. *Program availability:* Part-time, evening/weekend. *Degree requirements:* For master's, comprehensive exam (for some programs), thesis (for some programs). *Entrance requirements:* For master's, GMAT or GRE. Additional exam requirements/recommendations for international students: Required—TOEFL (minimum score 500 paper-based; 61 iBT), IELTS (minimum score 6). *Application deadline:* For fall admission, 5/15 for domestic and international students; for spring admission, 10/15 for domestic and international students. Applications are processed on a rolling basis. Application fee: $30. Electronic applications accepted. *Financial support:* Teaching assistantships with full tuition reimbursements, career-related internships or fieldwork, Federal Work-Study, and unspecified assistantships available. Support available to part-time students. Financial award application deadline: 3/1; financial award applicants required to submit FAFSA. *Unit head:* Kathleen A. O'Rourke, Coordinator, 217-581-6350, Fax: 217-581-6090, E-mail: kaorourke@eiu.edu. *Application contact:* Jacquelyn Frank, Associate Professor, 217-581-7843, Fax: 217-581-6090, E-mail: jbfrank@eiu.edu.
Website: http://www.eiu.edu/ma_agingstudies/

Eastern Michigan University, Graduate School, College of Health and Human Services, School of Health Sciences, Programs in Gerontology and Dementia, Ypsilanti, MI 48197. Offers dementia (Graduate Certificate); gerontology (Graduate Certificate). *Students:* 6 part-time (all women); includes 2 minority (1 Black or African American, non-Hispanic/Latino; 1 Asian, non-Hispanic/Latino). Average age 39. 7 applicants, 100% accepted, 1 enrolled. In 2017, 12 Graduate Certificates awarded. Application fee: $45. *Application contact:* Dr. Andrea Gossett Zakrajsek, Director, Aging Studies Program, 734-487-3220, Fax: 734-487-4095, E-mail: azakrajs@emich.edu.

East Tennessee State University, School of Graduate Studies, College of Public Health, Program in Public Health, Johnson City, TN 37614. Offers biostatistics (MPH, Postbaccalaureate Certificate); community health (MPH, DPH); environmental health (MPH); epidemiology (MPH, DPH, Postbaccalaureate Certificate); gerontology (Postbaccalaureate Certificate); global health (Postbaccalaureate Certificate); health care management (Postbaccalaureate Certificate); health management and policy (DPH); public health (Postbaccalaureate Certificate); public health services administration (MPH); rural health (Postbaccalaureate Certificate). *Accreditation:* CEPH. *Program availability:* Part-time, online learning. *Degree requirements:* For master's, comprehensive exam, field experience; for doctorate, thesis/dissertation, practicum. *Entrance requirements:* For master's, GRE General Test, minimum GPA of 2.75, SOPHAS application, three letters of recommendation; for doctorate, GRE General Test, SOPHAS application, three letters of recommendation; for Postbaccalaureate Certificate, minimum GPA of 2.5, three letters of recommendation, resume. Additional exam requirements/recommendations for international students: Required—TOEFL (minimum score 550 paper-based; 79 iBT), IELTS (minimum score 6.5). *Application deadline:* For fall admission, 3/1 for domestic and international students. Application fee: $35 ($45 for international students). Electronic applications accepted. *Financial support:* Research assistantships with tuition reimbursements, teaching assistantships with full tuition reimbursements, career-related internships or fieldwork, institutionally sponsored loans, scholarships/grants, and unspecified assistantships available. Financial award application deadline: 7/1; financial award applicants required to submit FAFSA. *Unit head:* Dr. Randy Wykoff, Dean, 423-439-4243, Fax: 423-439-5238, E-mail: wykoff@etsu.edu. *Application contact:* Dr. Randy Wykoff, Dean, 423-439-4243, Fax: 423-439-5238, E-mail: wykoff@etsu.edu.
Website: http://www.etsu.edu/cph/

Georgia State University, College of Arts and Sciences, Gerontology Institute, Atlanta, GA 30302-3083. Offers MA, Certificate. *Program availability:* Part-time. *Faculty:* 4 full-time (all women). *Students:* 13 full-time (11 women), 17 part-time (15 women); includes 20 minority (14 Black or African American, non-Hispanic/Latino; 3 Asian, non-Hispanic/Latino; 1 Hispanic/Latino; 2 Two or more races, non-Hispanic/Latino), 4 international. Average age 45. 29 applicants, 93% accepted, 17 enrolled. In 2017, 10 master's, 6 other advanced degrees awarded. *Entrance requirements:* For master's, GRE. Additional exam requirements/recommendations for international students: Required—TOEFL. *Application deadline:* For fall admission, 4/15 for domestic and international students; for spring admission, 10/15 for domestic and international students. Applications are processed on a rolling basis. Application fee: $50. Electronic applications accepted. *Expenses:* Tuition, state resident: full-time $7020. Tuition, nonresident: full-time $22,518. *Required fees:* $2128. Tuition and fees vary according to degree level and program. *Financial support:* In 2017–18, research assistantships with full tuition reimbursements (averaging $6,000 per year) were awarded; career-related internships or fieldwork, scholarships/grants, and unspecified assistantships also available. Financial award application deadline: 4/15; financial award applicants required to submit FAFSA. *Faculty research:* Long term care and assisted living, aging workforce, health disparities and aging, sexuality and relationships over the life course, caregiving and social relationships with age. *Unit head:* Dr. Elizabeth O. Burgess, Director, 404-413-5210, Fax: 404-413-5219, E-mail: eburgess@gsu.edu. *Application contact:* Dr. Candace L. Kemp, Director of Graduate Studies, 404-413-5210, Fax: 404-413-5219, E-mail: ckemp@gsu.edu.
Website: http://gerontology.gsu.edu/students/graduate/

Kansas State University, Graduate School, College of Human Ecology, Center on Aging, Manhattan, KS 66506. Offers gerontology (MS, Graduate Certificate). *Program availability:* Part-time, online learning. *Degree requirements:* For master's, comprehensive exam. *Entrance requirements:* For master's, bachelor's degree with minimum GPA of 3.0 from college or university accredited by the cognizant regional accrediting agency. Electronic applications accepted. *Expenses:* Contact institution.

Faculty research: Long-term care, environments and aging, sexuality and aging, aging in rural America.

Kent State University, College of Arts and Sciences, Department of Psychological Sciences, Kent, OH 44242-0001. Offers clinical psychology (MA, PhD), including gerontology (MA), psychological sciences (MA); experimental psychology (MA, PhD), including gerontology (MA), psychological sciences (MA). *Accreditation:* APA (one or more programs are accredited). *Program availability:* Part-time. *Faculty:* 29 full-time (15 women), 5 part-time/adjunct (2 women). *Students:* 84 full-time (66 women); includes 15 minority (8 Black or African American, non-Hispanic/Latino; 4 Asian, non-Hispanic/Latino; 2 Hispanic/Latino; 1 Two or more races, non-Hispanic/Latino), 3 international. Average age 26. 217 applicants, 10% accepted, 14 enrolled. In 2017, 10 master's, 16 doctorates awarded. Terminal master's awarded for partial completion of doctoral program. *Degree requirements:* For master's, thesis; for doctorate, comprehensive exam, thesis/dissertation. *Entrance requirements:* For master's and doctorate, GRE General Test, statement of goals and motivations, transcripts, 3 letters of recommendation, minimum junior-senior GPA of 3.0, at least one course in statistics and a broad background in psychology. Additional exam requirements/recommendations for international students: Required—TOEFL (minimum score 550 paper-based, 79 iBT), Michigan English Language Assessment Battery (minimum score 77), IELTS (minimum score 6.5) or PTE (minimum score 58). *Application deadline:* For fall admission, 12/1 for domestic and international students. Applications are processed on a rolling basis. Application fee: $45 ($70 for international students). Electronic applications accepted. *Expenses:* Tuition, state resident: full-time $11,310; part-time $515 per credit hour. Tuition, nonresident: full-time $20,396; part-time $928 per credit hour. *International tuition:* $18,544 full-time. *Financial support:* Federal Work-Study, health care benefits, and unspecified assistantships available. Financial award application deadline: 12/1. *Unit head:* Dr. Maria S. Zaragoza, Professor and Chair, 330-672-2166, E-mail: mzaragoz@kent.edu. *Application contact:* Dr. John A. Updegraff, Professor and Graduate Coordinator, 330-672-2166, E-mail: jupdegr1@kent.edu.
Website: https://www.kent.edu/psychology

Lakehead University, Graduate Studies, Department of History, Thunder Bay, ON P7B 5E1, Canada. Offers gerontology (MA); history (MA); women's studies (MA). *Program availability:* Part-time. *Degree requirements:* For master's, one foreign language, thesis. *Entrance requirements:* For master's, minimum B average. Additional exam requirements/recommendations for international students: Required—TOEFL. *Faculty research:* Canadian history, British history, Russian/German history, women's studies.

Lakehead University, Graduate Studies, Faculty of Education, Thunder Bay, ON P7B 5E1, Canada. Offers educational studies (PhD); gerontology (M Ed); women's studies (M Ed). *Program availability:* Part-time, evening/weekend. *Degree requirements:* For master's, project or thesis. *Entrance requirements:* For master's, minimum B average. Additional exam requirements/recommendations for international students: Required—TOEFL. *Faculty research:* Art education, AIDS education, language arts education, gerontology, women's studies.

Lakehead University, Graduate Studies, Faculty of Social Sciences and Humanities, Department of Sociology, Thunder Bay, ON P7B 5E1, Canada. Offers gerontology (MA); health services and policy research (MA); sociology (MA); women's studies (MA). *Program availability:* Part-time, evening/weekend. *Degree requirements:* For master's, research project or thesis. *Entrance requirements:* For master's, minimum B average. Additional exam requirements/recommendations for international students: Required—TOEFL. *Faculty research:* Sociology of medicine, cultural and social change, health human resources, gerontology, women's studies.

Lakehead University, Graduate Studies, Gerontology Collaborative Program-Northern Educational Center for Aging and Health, Thunder Bay, ON P7B 5E1, Canada. Offers gerontology (M Ed, M Sc, MA, MSW). *Program availability:* Part-time. *Degree requirements:* For master's, thesis (for some programs). *Entrance requirements:* Additional exam requirements/recommendations for international students: Required—TOEFL. *Faculty research:* Integrated health information systems.

Lakehead University, Graduate Studies, School of Kinesiology, Thunder Bay, ON P7B 5E1, Canada. Offers kinesiology (M Sc); kinesiology and gerontology (M Sc). *Program availability:* Part-time. *Degree requirements:* For master's, thesis. *Entrance requirements:* For master's, minimum B average. Additional exam requirements/recommendations for international students: Required—TOEFL. *Faculty research:* Social psychology and physical education, sport history, sports medicine, exercise physiology, gerontology.

Lakehead University, Graduate Studies, School of Social Work, Thunder Bay, ON P7B 5E1, Canada. Offers gerontology (MSW); social work (MSW); women's studies (MSW). *Program availability:* Part-time. *Degree requirements:* For master's, thesis or project. *Entrance requirements:* For master's, minimum B average. Additional exam requirements/recommendations for international students: Required—TOEFL. *Faculty research:* Clinical psychology, social work and practice theory, long-term care, health care for frail elderly, women's studies.

La Salle University, School of Nursing and Health Sciences, Program in Nursing, Philadelphia, PA 19141-1199. Offers adult gerontology primary care nurse practitioner (MSN, Certificate); adult health and illness clinical nurse specialist (MSN); adult-gerontology clinical nurse specialist (MSN, Certificate); clinical nurse leader (MSN); family primary care nurse practitioner (MSN, Certificate); gerontology (Certificate); nurse anesthetist (MSN, Certificate); nursing (MSN, Certificate); nursing administration (MSN, Certificate); nursing education (Certificate); nursing practice (DNP); nursing service administration (MSN); public health nursing (MSN, Certificate); school nursing (Certificate); MSN/MBA; MSN/MPH. *Accreditation:* AACN. *Program availability:* Part-time, evening/weekend, 100% online. *Faculty:* 12 full-time (11 women), 14 part-time/adjunct (11 women). *Students:* 1 (woman) full-time, 277 part-time (220 women); includes 72 minority (36 Black or African American, non-Hispanic/Latino; 1 American Indian or Alaska Native, non-Hispanic/Latino; 18 Asian, non-Hispanic/Latino; 10 Hispanic/Latino; 1 Native Hawaiian or other Pacific Islander, non-Hispanic/Latino; 6 Two or more races, non-Hispanic/Latino), 1 international. Average age 36. 70 applicants, 56% accepted, 24 enrolled. In 2017, 81 master's, 4 doctorates, 13 other advanced degrees awarded. *Degree requirements:* For doctorate, minimum of 1,000 hours of post baccalaureate clinical practice supervised by preceptors. *Entrance requirements:* For master's, GRE, MAT, or GMAT (for students with BSN GPA of less than 3.2), baccalaureate degree in nursing from ACEN- or CCNE-accredited program or an MSN Bridge program; Pennsylvania RN license; 2 letters of reference; resume; statement of philosophy articulating professional values and future educational goal; 1 year of work experience as a registered nurse; for doctorate, GRE (waived for applicants with MSN cumulative GPA of 3.7 or above), MSN, master's degree, MBA or MHA from nationally-accredited program; resume or curriculum vitae; 2 letters of reference; interview; for Certificate, GRE, MAT, or GMAT (for students with BSN GPA of less than 3.2, baccalaureate degree in nursing from ACEN- or CCNE-accredited program or an MSN Bridge program; Pennsylvania RN license; 2 letters of reference; resume; statement of philosophy articulating professional values and future educational goal; 1 year of work experience as a registered nurse. Additional exam requirements/recommendations for international students: Required—TOEFL. *Application deadline:* For fall admission, 8/15 priority date

for domestic students, 7/15 for international students; for spring admission, 12/15 priority date for domestic students, 11/15 for international students; for summer admission, 4/15 priority date for domestic students, 3/15 for international students. Applications are processed on a rolling basis. Application fee: $35. Electronic applications accepted. Application fee is waived when completed online. *Expenses:* Contact institution. *Financial support:* In 2017–18, 7 students received support. Scholarships/grants and traineeships available. Support available to part-time students. Financial award application deadline: 8/31; financial award applicants required to submit FAFSA. *Unit head:* Dr. Patricia M. Dillon, Director, 215-951-1322, Fax: 215-951-1896, E-mail: msnapn@lasalle.edu. *Application contact:* Elizabeth Heenan, Director, Graduate and Adult Enrollment, 215-951-1100, Fax: 215-951-1462, E-mail: heenan@lasalle.edu. Website: http://www.lasalle.edu/nursing/program-options/

Loma Linda University, School of Behavioral Health, Department of Social Work and Social Ecology, Loma Linda, CA 92350. Offers criminal justice (MS); gerontology (MS); social policy and social research (PhD); social work (MSW). *Accreditation:* CSWE. *Degree requirements:* For master's, comprehensive exam, thesis optional; for doctorate, comprehensive exam, thesis/dissertation. *Entrance requirements:* For master's and doctorate, GRE General Test. Additional exam requirements/recommendations for international students: Required—TOEFL, Michigan English Language Assessment Battery. Electronic applications accepted.

Long Island University–LIU Brooklyn, School of Business, Public Administration and Information Sciences, Brooklyn, NY 11201-8423. Offers accounting (MBA); accounting (MS); business administration (MBA); computer science (MS); gerontology (Advanced Certificate); health administration (MPA); human resources management (MS); not-for-profit management (Advanced Certificate); public administration (MPA); taxation (MS). *Program availability:* Part-time, evening/weekend. *Faculty:* 18 full-time (7 women), 28 part-time/adjunct (8 women). *Students:* 226 full-time (140 women), 232 part-time (150 women); includes 272 minority (192 Black or African American, non-Hispanic/Latino; 2 American Indian or Alaska Native, non-Hispanic/Latino; 35 Asian, non-Hispanic/Latino; 40 Hispanic/Latino; 3 Two or more races, non-Hispanic/Latino), 88 international. Average age 32. 495 applicants, 64% accepted, 149 enrolled. In 2017, 189 master's, 13 other advanced degrees awarded. *Entrance requirements:* Additional exam requirements/recommendations for international students: Required—TOEFL (minimum score 550 paper-based; 75 iBT). *Application deadline:* Applications are processed on a rolling basis. Application fee: $50. Electronic applications accepted. *Expenses: Tuition:* Full-time $21,618; part-time $1201 per credit. *Required fees:* $1840; $920 per term. Tuition and fees vary according to course load. *Financial support:* In 2017–18, 78 students received support. Career-related internships or fieldwork, Federal Work-Study, scholarships/grants, and unspecified assistantships available. Support available to part-time students. Financial award application deadline: 2/15; financial award applicants required to submit FAFSA. *Faculty research:* Tax policy; public sector budgeting and gender inequities; technology and innovation; game theory; knowledge management. *Unit head:* Dr. Edward Rogoff, Dean, 718-488-1159, E-mail: edward.rogoff@liu.edu. *Application contact:* Luis Santiago, Dean of Enrollment, 718-488-1011, Fax: 718-780-6110, E-mail: bkln-admissions@liu.edu. Website: http://liu.edu/Brooklyn/Academics/School-of-Business-Public-Administration-and-Information-Sciences

Long Island University–LIU Post, School of Health Professions and Nursing, Brookville, NY 11548-1300. Offers biomedical science (MS); cardiovascular perfusion (MS); clinical lab sciences (MS); clinical laboratory management (MS); dietetic internship (Advanced Certificate); family nurse practitioner (MS, Advanced Certificate); forensic social work (Advanced Certificate); gerontology (Advanced Certificate); health administration (MPA); non-profit management (Advanced Certificate); nursing education (MS); nutrition (MS); public administration (MPA); social work (MSW). *Program availability:* Part-time, blended/hybrid learning. *Faculty:* 23 full-time (17 women), 33 part-time/adjunct (19 women). *Students:* 228 full-time (174 women), 227 part-time (185 women); includes 172 minority (76 Black or African American, non-Hispanic/Latino; 1 American Indian or Alaska Native, non-Hispanic/Latino; 44 Asian, non-Hispanic/Latino; 48 Hispanic/Latino; 3 Two or more races, non-Hispanic/Latino), 60 international. Average age 31. 392 applicants, 67% accepted, 138 enrolled. In 2017, 180 master's, 26 other advanced degrees awarded. *Degree requirements:* For master's, comprehensive exam (for some programs), thesis (for some programs). *Entrance requirements:* Additional exam requirements/recommendations for international students: Required—TOEFL (minimum score 85 iBT) or IELTS (7.5). *Application deadline:* Applications are processed on a rolling basis. Application fee: $50. Electronic applications accepted. *Expenses: Tuition:* Full-time $21,618; part-time $1201 per credit. *Required fees:* $1840; $920 per term. Tuition and fees vary according to course load. *Financial support:* In 2017–18, 102 students received support. Research assistantships, teaching assistantships, career-related internships or fieldwork, Federal Work-Study, scholarships/grants, and unspecified assistantships available. Support available to part-time students. Financial award application deadline: 2/15; financial award applicants required to submit FAFSA. *Faculty research:* Antibiotic resistance, evidence-based practice, family care, interprofessional learning, simulation learning. *Unit head:* Dr. Stacy Gropack, Dean, 516-299-2485, Fax: 516-299-2527, E-mail: post-shpn@liu.edu. *Application contact:* Kathy Riley, Associate Director of Graduate Admissions, 516-299-2900, Fax: 516-299-2137, E-mail: post-enroll@liu.edu. Website: http://liu.edu/post/health

Marywood University, Academic Affairs, College of Health and Human Services, School of Social Work, Program in Gerontology, Scranton, PA 18509-1598. Offers MS. *Program availability:* Part-time. Electronic applications accepted.

McDaniel College, Graduate and Professional Studies, Program in Gerontology, Westminster, MD 21157-4390. Offers MS, Postbaccalaureate Certificate. *Program availability:* Part-time, evening/weekend, online only, 100% online. *Faculty:* 1 (woman) full-time, 3 part-time/adjunct (2 women). *Students:* 6 full-time (4 women), 12 part-time (all women); includes 5 minority (3 Black or African American, non-Hispanic/Latino; 1 Asian, non-Hispanic/Latino; 1 Hispanic/Latino). Average age 36. 12 applicants, 75% accepted, 6 enrolled. In 2017, 7 master's, 3 other advanced degrees awarded. *Degree requirements:* For master's, portfolio. *Entrance requirements:* For master's, 3 recommendations. Additional exam requirements/recommendations for international students: Required—TOEFL (minimum score 79 iBT), IELTS (minimum score 6). *Application deadline:* For fall admission, 6/1 priority date for domestic students; for spring admission, 11/1 priority date for domestic students; for summer admission, 3/1 priority date for domestic students. Applications are processed on a rolling basis. Application fee: $75. Electronic applications accepted. *Expenses: Tuition:* Full-time $11,760; part-time $490 per credit hour. Tuition and fees vary according to course load and program. *Financial support:* Application deadline: 3/1; applicants required to submit FAFSA. *Unit head:* Fax: 410-857-2515, E-mail: gradadms@mcdaniel.edu. *Application contact:* Penny Pfeiffer, Senior Graduate Enrollment Management Specialist, 410-857-2513, Fax: 410-857-2515, E-mail: ppfeiffer@mcdaniel.edu.

Mercer University, Graduate Studies, Cecil B. Day Campus, Penfield College, Atlanta, GA 30341. Offers certified rehabilitation counseling (MS); clinical mental health (MS); counselor education and supervision (PhD); criminal justice and public safety leadership (MS); health informatics (MS); human services (MS), including child and adolescent services, gerontology services; organizational leadership (MS), including leadership for the health care professional, leadership for the nonprofit organization, organizational development and change; school counseling (MS). *Program availability:* Part-time, evening/weekend, 100% online, blended/hybrid learning. *Faculty:* 17 full-time (10 women), 27 part-time/adjunct (24 women). *Students:* 199 full-time (165 women), 266 part-time (218 women); includes 268 minority (226 Black or African American, non-Hispanic/Latino; 1 American Indian or Alaska Native, non-Hispanic/Latino; 19 Asian, non-Hispanic/Latino; 19 Hispanic/Latino; 3 Two or more races, non-Hispanic/Latino). Average age 32. 300 applicants, 45% accepted, 114 enrolled. In 2017, 101 master's, 5 doctorates awarded. *Degree requirements:* For master's, comprehensive exam (for some programs), thesis (for some programs); for doctorate, thesis/dissertation. *Entrance requirements:* For master's, GRE or MAT, Georgia Professional Standards Commission (GPSC) Certification at the SC-5 level; for doctorate, GRE or MAT. Additional exam requirements/recommendations for international students: Recommended—TOEFL (minimum score 550 paper-based; 80 iBT), IELTS (minimum score 6.5). *Application deadline:* For fall admission, 7/1 priority date for domestic and international students; for spring admission, 11/1 priority date for domestic and international students; for summer admission, 4/1 priority date for domestic and international students. Application fee: $35. Electronic applications accepted. Application fee is waived when completed online. *Expenses:* $637 per credit. *Financial support:* In 2017–18, 32 students received support. Federal Work-Study, scholarships/grants, and unspecified assistantships available. Financial award applicants required to submit FAFSA. *Faculty research:* Marriage and families issues, leadership and ethics, cyber-bullying, trauma, narrative counseling and theory. *Total annual research expenditures:* $85,000. *Unit head:* Dr. Priscilla R. Danheiser, Dean, 678-547-6028, Fax: 678-547-6008, E-mail: danheiser_p@mercer.edu. *Application contact:* Dr. Melissa McCants Cruz, Director of Graduate Admissions, 678-547-6024, E-mail: penfield.admissions@mercer.edu. Website: http://penfield.mercer.edu/programs/graduate-professional/

Miami University, College of Arts and Science, Department of Sociology and Gerontology, Oxford, OH 45056. Offers gerontology (MGS); population and social gerontology (MPSG); social gerontology (PhD). *Students:* 30 full-time (26 women), 8 part-time (7 women); includes 5 minority (1 Black or African American, non-Hispanic/Latino; 3 Asian, non-Hispanic/Latino; 1 Hispanic/Latino), 12 international. Average age 32. In 2017, 7 master's, 2 doctorates awarded. *Expenses:* Tuition, state resident: full-time $13,812; part-time $575 per credit hour. Tuition, nonresident: full-time $30,860; part-time $1286 per credit hour. *Unit head:* Dr. Stephen Lippman, Chair and Associate Professor, 513-529-8515, E-mail: lippmas@miamioh.edu. *Application contact:* Dr. Jennifer Kinney, Director of Graduate Studies, 513-529-2915, E-mail: kinneyjm@miamioh.edu. Website: http://www.MiamiOH.edu/sociology/

Middle Tennessee State University, College of Graduate Studies, College of Liberal Arts, Program in Gerontology, Murfreesboro, TN 37132. Offers Graduate Certificate. *Program availability:* Part-time, evening/weekend, online learning. *Entrance requirements:* Additional exam requirements/recommendations for international students: Required—TOEFL (minimum score 525 paper-based; 71 iBT) or IELTS (minimum score 6). Electronic applications accepted.

Minnesota State University Mankato, College of Graduate Studies and Research, College of Social and Behavioral Sciences, Program in Aging Studies, Mankato, MN 56001. Offers MS. *Degree requirements:* For master's, comprehensive exam, thesis optional. *Entrance requirements:* For master's, GRE, minimum GPA of 3.0 during previous 2 years, letters of recommendation. Additional exam requirements/recommendations for international students: Required—TOEFL. Electronic applications accepted.

Morehead State University, Graduate Programs, Caudill College of Arts, Humanities and Social Sciences, Department of Sociology, Social Work and Criminology, Morehead, KY 40351. Offers criminology (MA); general sociology (MA); gerontology (MA); sociology regional analysis (MA); sociology/chemical dependency (MA). *Program availability:* Part-time, evening/weekend. *Degree requirements:* For master's, comprehensive exam, thesis (for some programs). *Entrance requirements:* For master's, GRE General Test, minimum GPA of 3.0 in sociology, 2.75 overall; 18 hours of course work in sociology, writing sample. Additional exam requirements/recommendations for international students: Required—TOEFL (minimum score 500 paper-based). Electronic applications accepted. *Faculty research:* Death and dying; aging, drinking, and drugs; economic development; adult children of alcoholics.

Mount Saint Vincent University, Graduate Programs, Department of Family Studies and Gerontology, Halifax, NS B3M 2J6, Canada. Offers MA. *Program availability:* Part-time, online learning. *Degree requirements:* For master's, thesis. *Entrance requirements:* For master's, minimum GPA of 3.0; course work in statistics, research methods, family and social theories.

North Dakota State University, College of Graduate and Interdisciplinary Studies, College of Human Development and Education, Department of Human Development and Family Science, Program in Gerontology, Fargo, ND 58102. Offers MS, Certificate. Electronic applications accepted.

Northeastern Illinois University, College of Graduate Studies and Research, College of Arts and Sciences, Program in Gerontology, Chicago, IL 60625. Offers MA. *Program availability:* Part-time, evening/weekend. *Degree requirements:* For master's, comprehensive exam, paper and project or thesis, practicum. *Entrance requirements:* For master's, 15 hours in social sciences (3 hours in gerontology), course in research methods or statistics, minimum GPA of 2.75. Additional exam requirements/recommendations for international students: Required—TOEFL (minimum score 550 paper-based; 79 iBT). *Application deadline:* For fall admission, 4/1 priority date for domestic students; for spring admission, 8/15 for domestic students. Applications are processed on a rolling basis. Application fee: $30. Electronic applications accepted. *Expenses:* Tuition, state resident: full-time $7274; part-time $404.11 per credit hour. Tuition, nonresident: full-time $14,548; part-time $808.23 per credit hour. *Required fees:* $1284. *Financial support:* Applicants required to submit FAFSA. *Faculty research:* Later life development, cultural diversity, humanities and aging, elder abuse, AIDS and aging, computer training. *Unit head:* Dr. Lisa Hollis-Sawyer, Coordinator/Advisor, 773-442-5846, E-mail: l-hollissawyer@neiu.edu. *Application contact:* Martha Narvaez, Graduate Admission Representative, 773-442-6006, E-mail: m-narvaez@neiu.edu.

Oregon Health & Science University, School of Nursing, Program in Nursing Education, Portland, OR 97239-3098. Offers MN, Post Master's Certificate. *Program availability:* Part-time, online only, 100% online. *Entrance requirements:* For master's, minimum cumulative GPA of 3.0, 3 letters of recommendation, essay, RN license or eligibility, BS with major in nursing or BSN, statistics taken in last 5 years with minimum B- grade; for Post Master's Certificate, minimum cumulative GPA of 3.0, 3 letters of recommendation, essay, RN license or eligibility, master's degree in nursing, statistics taken in last 5 years with minimum B- grade. Additional exam requirements/recommendations for international students: Required—TOEFL (minimum score 83 iBT). Electronic applications accepted. *Expenses:* Contact institution. *Faculty research:* Quality of end-of-life care in long-term settings, ethical issues in studying dying people and their families, strategies for improving clinical judgement.

Gerontology

Sage Graduate School, School of Management, Program in Health Services Administration, Troy, NY 12180-4115. Offers gerontology (MS). *Program availability:* Part-time, evening/weekend. *Faculty:* 5 full-time (3 women), 5 part-time/adjunct (1 woman). *Students:* 8 full-time (6 women), 19 part-time (15 women); includes 4 minority (1 Black or African American, non-Hispanic/Latino; 2 Asian, non-Hispanic/Latino; 1 Hispanic/Latino). Average age 31. 26 applicants, 42% accepted, 5 enrolled. In 2017, 14 master's awarded. *Entrance requirements:* For master's, minimum GPA of 2.75, resume, 2 letters of recommendation. Additional exam requirements/recommendations for international students: Required—TOEFL (minimum score 550 paper-based). *Application deadline:* Applications are processed on a rolling basis. Application fee: $30. Electronic applications accepted. Tuition and fees vary according to degree level and program. *Financial support:* Fellowships, research assistantships, and unspecified assistantships available. Financial award application deadline: 3/1; financial award applicants required to submit FAFSA. *Unit head:* Dr. Kimberly Fredericks, Dean, School of Management, 518-292-1782, Fax: 518-292-1964, E-mail: fredek1@sage.edu. *Application contact:* Wendy D. Diefendorf, Director of Graduate and Adult Admission, 518-244-2443, Fax: 518-244-6880, E-mail: diefew@sage.edu.

St. Cloud State University, School of Graduate Studies, School of Health and Human Services, Program in Gerontology, St. Cloud, MN 56301-4498. Offers MS. *Program availability:* Part-time. *Degree requirements:* For master's, thesis or alternative. *Entrance requirements:* For master's, GRE General Test, minimum GPA of 2.75. Additional exam requirements/recommendations for international students: Required—Michigan English Language Assessment Battery; Recommended—TOEFL (minimum score 550 paper-based), IELTS (minimum score 6.5). Electronic applications accepted.

San Diego State University, Graduate and Research Affairs, College of Health and Human Services, Department of Gerontology, San Diego, CA 92182. Offers MS. *Program availability:* Part-time, evening/weekend. *Degree requirements:* For master's, thesis. *Entrance requirements:* For master's, GRE General Test. Additional exam requirements/recommendations for international students: Required—TOEFL. Electronic applications accepted.

San Francisco State University, Division of Graduate Studies, College of Health and Social Sciences, Gerontology Program, San Francisco, CA 94132-1722. Offers MA. *Program availability:* Part-time. *Application deadline:* Applications are processed on a rolling basis. *Financial support:* Career-related internships or fieldwork and unspecified assistantships available. *Unit head:* Dr. Darlene Yee-Melichar, Program Coordinator, 415-338-1684, Fax: 415-338-3556, E-mail: dyee@sfsu.edu.
Website: http://gerontology.sfsu.edu/

San Francisco State University, Division of Graduate Studies, College of Health and Social Sciences, Public Administration Program, San Francisco, CA 94132-1722. Offers criminal justice administration (MPA); environmental administration and policy (MPA); gerontology (MPA); nonprofit administration (MPA); public management (MPA); public policy (MPA); urban administration (MPA). *Accreditation:* NASPAA. *Unit head:* Dr. Jennifer Shea, Graduate Coordinator, 415-817-4462, Fax: 415-817-4464, E-mail: jshea@sfsu.edu.
Website: http://mpa.sfsu.edu/

Simon Fraser University, Office of Graduate Studies and Postdoctoral Fellows, Faculty of Arts and Social Sciences, Department of Gerontology, Vancouver, BC V6B 5K3, Canada. Offers MA, PhD. *Program availability:* Part-time. *Degree requirements:* For master's, thesis or alternative, internship; for doctorate, comprehensive exam, thesis/dissertation. *Entrance requirements:* For master's, minimum GPA of 3.0 (on scale of 4.33) or 3.33 based on last 60 credits of undergraduate courses; for doctorate, minimum GPA of 3.5 (on scale of 4.33). Additional exam requirements/recommendations for international students: Recommended—TOEFL (minimum score 580 paper-based; 93 iBT), IELTS (minimum score 7), TWE (minimum score 5). Electronic applications accepted. *Faculty research:* Aging and the built environment, changing demography and lifestyles, health promotion/population health and aging, prevention of victimization and exploitation of older persons, technology and aging.

Temple University, College of Public Health, Department of Nursing, Philadelphia, PA 19122. Offers adult-gerontology primary care (DNP); family-individual across the lifespan (DNP); nursing (DNP). *Accreditation:* AACN. *Program availability:* Part-time. *Faculty:* 12 full-time (all women). *Students:* 5 full-time (4 women), 53 part-time (46 women); includes 31 minority (13 Black or African American, non-Hispanic/Latino; 12 Asian, non-Hispanic/Latino; 5 Hispanic/Latino; 1 Two or more races, non-Hispanic/Latino). 11 applicants, 18% accepted. In 2017, 17 doctorates awarded. *Degree requirements:* For doctorate, evidence-based practice project. *Entrance requirements:* For doctorate, GRE General Test or MAT, 2 letters of reference, RN license, interview, statement of purpose, resume. Additional exam requirements/recommendations for international students: Required—TOEFL (minimum score 600 paper-based; 100 iBT). *Application deadline:* For fall admission, 2/15 priority date for domestic students, 1/15 for international students; for spring admission, 10/15 for domestic students, 9/15 for international students. Applications are processed on a rolling basis. Application fee: $60. Electronic applications accepted. *Expenses:* Contact institution. *Financial support:* Federal Work-Study, scholarships/grants, traineeships, and tuition waivers available. Support available to part-time students. Financial award application deadline: 1/15. *Faculty research:* Health promotion, chronic illness, family support systems, primary care, health policy, community health services, evidence-based practice. *Unit head:* Dolores Zygmont, Graduate Director, 215-707-3789, E-mail: zygmont@temple.edu. *Application contact:* Audrey Scriven, Academic Coordinator, Graduate Program, 215-707-4618, E-mail: tunurse@temple.edu.
Website: https://cph.temple.edu/nursing/home

Texas Christian University, Harris College of Nursing and Health Sciences, Doctor of Nursing Practice Program, Fort Worth, TX 76129. Offers clinical nurse specialist - adult/gerontology nursing (DNP); clinical nurse specialist - pediatrics (DNP); family nurse practitioner (DNP); general (DNP); nursing administration (DNP). *Accreditation:* AACN. *Program availability:* Part-time. *Faculty:* 29 full-time (26 women), 2 part-time/adjunct (both women). *Students:* 51 full-time (45 women), 10 part-time (9 women); includes 16 minority (6 Black or African American, non-Hispanic/Latino; 2 Asian, non-Hispanic/Latino; 6 Hispanic/Latino; 2 Two or more races, non-Hispanic/Latino). Average age 41. 59 applicants, 64% accepted, 24 enrolled. In 2017, 23 doctorates awarded. *Degree requirements:* For doctorate, thesis/dissertation or alternative, practicum. *Entrance requirements:* For doctorate, three reference letters, essay, resume, two official transcripts from each institution attended, APRN recognition or MSN with experience in nursing administration. Additional exam requirements/recommendations for international students: Required—TOEFL. *Application deadline:* For summer admission, 11/15 for domestic and international students. Application fee: $60. Electronic applications accepted. *Expenses:* $1,555 per credit hour, $125 per course fee, $500 lab fee. *Financial support:* In 2017–18, 14 students received support. Scholarships/grants available. Financial award application deadline: 2/15; financial award applicants required to submit FAFSA. *Faculty research:* Geriatrics, cancer survivorship, health literacy, endothelial cells, clinical simulation outcomes. *Unit head:* Dr. Kathy Ellis, Division Director, Graduate Nursing, 817-257-6726, Fax: 817-257-7944, E-mail: kathryn.ellis@tcu.edu. *Application contact:* Heather Lyon, Academic Program Specialist, 817-257-6726, Fax: 817-257-7944, E-mail: graduatenursing@tcu.edu.
Website: http://dnp.tcu.edu/

Texas State University, The Graduate College, College of Liberal Arts, Program in Dementia and Aging Studies, San Marcos, TX 78666. Offers MS. *Program availability:* Part-time, evening/weekend. *Faculty:* 7 full-time (3 women). *Students:* 12 full-time (10 women), 29 part-time (21 women); includes 17 minority (8 Black or African American, non-Hispanic/Latino; 2 Asian, non-Hispanic/Latino; 7 Hispanic/Latino). Average age 39. 28 applicants, 79% accepted, 13 enrolled. In 2017, 14 master's awarded. *Degree requirements:* For master's, comprehensive exam, thesis (for some programs). *Entrance requirements:* For master's, baccalaureate degree from regionally-accredited university with minimum GPA of 3.0 on last 60 undergraduate semester hours, background course work in social science or gerontology, resume, statement of purpose describing personal goals, 3 letters of recommendation. Additional exam requirements/recommendations for international students: Required—TOEFL (minimum score 550 paper-based; 78 iBT), IELTS (minimum score 6.5). *Application deadline:* For fall admission, 3/1 priority date for domestic and international students; for spring admission, 10/15 for domestic students, 10/1 for international students; for summer admission, 4/15 for domestic students, 3/15 for international students. Applications are processed on a rolling basis. Application fee: $40 ($90 for international students). Electronic applications accepted. *Expenses:* Tuition, state resident: full-time $7868; part-time $3934 per semester. Tuition, nonresident: full-time $17,828; part-time $8914 per semester. *Required fees:* $2092; $1435 per semester. Tuition and fees vary according to course load. *Financial support:* In 2017–18, 15 students received support, including 1 teaching assistantship (averaging $12,152 per year); research assistantships, career-related internships or fieldwork, Federal Work-Study, institutionally sponsored loans, scholarships/grants, health care benefits, and unspecified assistantships also available. Support available to part-time students. Financial award application deadline: 3/1; financial award applicants required to submit FAFSA. *Faculty research:* Evaluation of Harris Counties Protective Services, advancing peer support in integrated health care evaluation, evaluate early childhood mental health program. *Total annual research expenditures:* $37,358. *Unit head:* Dr. Patti Giuffre, Graduate Advisor, 512-245-8983, Fax: 512-245-8362, E-mail: pg07@txstate.edu. *Application contact:* Dr. Andrea Golato, Dean of Graduate School, 512-245-2581, Fax: 512-245-8365, E-mail: gradcollege@txstate.edu.
Website: http://www.soci.txstate.edu/Graduate-Degree/msda.html

Texas Tech University, Graduate School, College of Human Sciences, Department of Human Development and Family Studies, Lubbock, TX 79409-1230. Offers human development and family studies (MS, PhD), including gerontology (MS). *Accreditation:* AAMFT/COAMFTE (one or more programs are accredited). *Faculty:* 25 full-time (21 women), 7 part-time/adjunct (all women). *Students:* 23 full-time (20 women), 41 part-time (26 women); includes 15 minority (5 Black or African American, non-Hispanic/Latino; 9 Hispanic/Latino; 1 Two or more races, non-Hispanic/Latino), 9 international. Average age 33. 34 applicants, 29% accepted, 6 enrolled. In 2017, 5 master's, 8 doctorates awarded. *Degree requirements:* For master's, thesis; for doctorate, comprehensive exam, thesis/dissertation. *Entrance requirements:* For master's and doctorate, GRE General Test. Additional exam requirements/recommendations for international students: Required—TOEFL (minimum score 550 paper-based; 79 iBT). *Application deadline:* For fall admission, 6/1 priority date for domestic students, 1/15 priority date for international students; for spring admission, 9/1 priority date for domestic students, 6/15 priority date for international students. Applications are processed on a rolling basis. Application fee: $60. Electronic applications accepted. *Expenses:* Contact institution. *Financial support:* In 2017–18, 31 students received support, including 30 fellowships (averaging $5,499 per year), 15 research assistantships (averaging $11,129 per year), 19 teaching assistantships (averaging $10,544 per year); scholarships/grants and unspecified assistantships also available. Financial award application deadline: 12/1; financial award applicants required to submit FAFSA. *Faculty research:* Parenting (including family relationships and parent-child interactions), marital and premarital relationships, adolescence (risk and resilience), life span, child development (including factors that influence developmental outcomes: poverty, risk, genetic and environmental factors). *Total annual research expenditures:* $79,092. *Unit head:* Dr. Ann M. Mastergeorge, Chairperson/Professor, 806-834-7162, Fax: 806-742-3042, E-mail: ann.mastergeorge@ttu.edu. *Application contact:* Dr. Malinda Colwell, Graduate Program Director, 806-834-4179, Fax: 806-742-0285, E-mail: malinda.colwell@ttu.edu.
Website: http://www.depts.ttu.edu/hdfs

Université de Sherbrooke, Faculty of Letters and Human Sciences, Department of Psychology, Sherbrooke, QC J1K 2R1, Canada. Offers gerontology (MA). *Degree requirements:* For master's, thesis. *Faculty research:* Human relations.

Université Laval, Faculty of Medicine, Post-Professional Programs in Medical Studies, Québec, QC G1K 7P4, Canada. Offers anatomy–pathology (DESS); anesthesiology (DESS); cardiology (DESS); care of older people (Diploma); clinical research (DESS); community health (DESS); dermatology (DESS); diagnostic radiology (DESS); emergency medicine (Diploma); family medicine (DESS); general surgery (DESS); geriatrics (DESS); hematology (DESS); internal medicine (DESS); maternal and fetal medicine (Diploma); medical biochemistry (DESS); medical microbiology and infectious diseases (DESS); medical oncology (DESS); nephrology (DESS); neurology (DESS); neurosurgery (DESS); obstetrics and gynecology (DESS); ophthalmology (DESS); orthopedic surgery (DESS); oto-rhino-laryngology (DESS); palliative medicine (Diploma); pediatrics (DESS); plastic surgery (DESS); psychiatry (DESS); pulmonary medicine (DESS); radiology–oncology (DESS); thoracic surgery (DESS); urology (DESS). *Degree requirements:* For other advanced degree, comprehensive exam. *Entrance requirements:* For degree, knowledge of French. Electronic applications accepted.

The University of Akron, Graduate School, Buchtel College of Arts and Sciences, Department of Psychology, Program in Adult Development and Aging, Akron, OH 44325. Offers PhD. *Students:* 8 full-time (5 women), 2 part-time (both women); includes 2 minority (1 Hispanic/Latino; 1 Two or more races, non-Hispanic/Latino), 1 international. Average age 25. 11 applicants, 45% accepted, 3 enrolled. In 2017, 3 doctorates awarded. *Degree requirements:* For doctorate, one foreign language, comprehensive exam, thesis/dissertation. *Entrance requirements:* For doctorate, GRE, minimum graduate GPA of 3.25, three letters of recommendation, personal statement, resume. Additional exam requirements/recommendations for international students: Required—TOEFL (minimum score 79 iBT), IELTS (minimum score 6.5). *Application deadline:* For fall admission, 1/15 for domestic and international students. Application fee: $45 ($70 for international students). Electronic applications accepted. *Financial support:* Fellowships with full tuition reimbursements, research assistantships with full tuition reimbursements, and teaching assistantships with full tuition reimbursements available. *Faculty research:* Changes in memory and cognition with age, automaticity and effects of training, models of visual word recognition, experimental neuropsychology. *Unit head:* Dr. Paul Levy, Department Chair, 330-972-8369, E-mail: plevy@uakron.edu.
Website: http://www.uakron.edu/psychology/academics/adult-development-and-aging/

University of Arkansas at Little Rock, Graduate School, College of Education and Health Professions, School of Social Work, Program in Gerontology, Little Rock, AR 72204-1099. Offers Graduate Certificate.

University of Central Missouri, The Graduate School, Warrensburg, MO 64093. Offers accountancy (MA); accounting (MBA); applied mathematics (MS); aviation safety (MA); biology (MS); business administration (MBA); career and technical education leadership (MS); college student personnel administration (MS); communication (MA); computer science (MS); counseling (MS); criminal justice (MS); educational leadership (Ed D); educational technology (MS); elementary and early childhood education (MSE); English (MA); environmental studies (MA); finance (MBA); history (MA); human services/ educational technology (Ed S); human services/learning resources (Ed S); human services/professional counseling (Ed S); industrial hygiene (MS); industrial management (MS); information systems (MBA); information technology (MS); kinesiology (MS); library science and information services (MS); literacy education (MSE); marketing (MBA); mathematics (MS); music (MA); occupational safety management (MS); psychology (MS); rural family nursing (MS); school administration (MSE); social gerontology (MS); sociology (MA); special education (MSE); speech language pathology (MS); superintendency (Ed S); teaching (MAT); teaching English as a second language (MA); technology (MS); technology management (PhD); theatre (MA). *Program availability:* Part-time, 100% online, blended/hybrid learning. *Faculty:* 337 full-time (145 women), 41 part-time/adjunct (28 women). *Students:* 785 full-time (398 women), 1,633 part-time (1,063 women); includes 231 minority (102 Black or African American, non-Hispanic/ Latino; 4 American Indian or Alaska Native, non-Hispanic/Latino; 16 Asian, non-Hispanic/Latino; 52 Hispanic/Latino; 57 Two or more races, non-Hispanic/Latino), 692 international. Average age 30. In 2017, 2,605 master's, 122 other advanced degrees awarded. *Degree requirements:* For master's and Ed S, comprehensive exam (for some programs), thesis (for some programs). *Entrance requirements:* Additional exam requirements/recommendations for international students: Required—TOEFL (minimum score 550 paper-based; 79 iBT). *Application deadline:* For fall admission, 6/1 priority date for domestic and international students; for spring admission, 10/1 priority date for domestic and international students; for summer admission, 4/1 priority date for domestic and international students. Applications are processed on a rolling basis. Application fee: $30 ($75 for international students). Electronic applications accepted. *Expenses:* Tuition, state resident: full-time $8771; part-time $292.35 per credit hour. Tuition, nonresident: full-time $17,541; part-time $584.70 per credit hour. *Required fees:* $372; $24.78 per credit hour. *Financial support:* In 2017–18, 99 students received support. Research assistantships, teaching assistantships, career-related internships or fieldwork, Federal Work-Study, scholarships/grants, and administrative and laboratory assistantships available. Support available to part-time students. Financial award application deadline: 3/1; financial award applicants required to submit FAFSA. *Unit head:* Shellie Hewitt, Director of Graduate and International Student Services, 660-543-4621, Fax: 660-543-4778, E-mail: hewitt@ucmo.edu. *Application contact:* 660-543-4621, E-mail: admit_intl@ucmo.edu.
Website: http://www.ucmo.edu/graduate/

University of Central Oklahoma, The Jackson College of Graduate Studies, College of Liberal Arts, Department of Sociology, Gerontology, and Substance Abuse Studies, Edmond, OK 73034-5209. Offers gerontology (MA); substance abuse studies (MA), including substance abuse studies. *Program availability:* Part-time. *Faculty:* 8 full-time (6 women), 6 part-time/adjunct (3 women). *Students:* 31 full-time (25 women), 30 part-time (23 women); includes 25 minority (14 Black or African American, non-Hispanic/Latino; 1 American Indian or Alaska Native, non-Hispanic/Latino; 2 Asian, non-Hispanic/Latino; 3 Hispanic/Latino; 5 Two or more races, non-Hispanic/Latino), 3 international. Average age 39. 39 applicants, 92% accepted, 22 enrolled. In 2017, 21 master's awarded. *Degree requirements:* For master's, variable foreign language requirement, comprehensive exam (for some programs), thesis (for some programs). *Entrance requirements:* Additional exam requirements/recommendations for international students: Required—TOEFL (minimum score 550 paper-based; 79 iBT), IELTS (minimum score 6.5). *Application deadline:* For fall admission, 7/15 for international students; for spring admission, 11/15 for international students. Applications are processed on a rolling basis. Application fee: $60. Electronic applications accepted. *Expenses:* Tuition, state resident: full-time $5375; part-time $268.75 per credit hour. Tuition, nonresident: full-time $13,295; part-time $664.75 per credit hour. *Required fees:* $626; $31.30 per credit hour. One-time fee: $50. Tuition and fees vary according to program. *Financial support:* In 2017–18, 10 students received support, including 2 research assistantships with partial tuition reimbursements available (averaging $2,958 per year), 1 teaching assistantship with partial tuition reimbursement available (averaging $11,830 per year); career-related internships or fieldwork, scholarships/ grants, tuition waivers (partial), and unspecified assistantships also available. Financial award application deadline: 3/31; financial award applicants required to submit FAFSA. *Unit head:* Dr. Douglas Reed, Chair, 405-974-5540, Fax: 405-974-3823, E-mail: gradcoll@uco.edu.
Website: http://www.uco.edu/la/soc-gero-sas/index.asp

University of Georgia, College of Public Health, Institute of Gerontology, Athens, GA 30602. Offers Certificate.

University of Illinois at Springfield, Graduate Programs, College of Education and Human Services, Program in Human Services, Springfield, IL 62703-5407. Offers alcohol and substance abuse (Graduate Certificate); alcoholism and substance abuse (MA); child and family services (MA); gerontology (MA); social services administration (MA). *Program availability:* Part-time, evening/weekend, 100% online, blended/hybrid learning. *Faculty:* 5 full-time (all women). *Students:* 8 full-time (7 women), 72 part-time (63 women); includes 38 minority (26 Black or African American, non-Hispanic/Latino; 9 Hispanic/Latino; 3 Two or more races, non-Hispanic/Latino). Average age 33. 49 applicants, 47% accepted, 20 enrolled. In 2017, 21 master's, 1 other advanced degree awarded. *Degree requirements:* For master's, internship; capstone project. *Entrance requirements:* For master's, minimum undergraduate GPA of 3.0, 2 letters of recommendation from professional or academic sources, statement of intent, interview. Additional exam requirements/recommendations for international students: Required— TOEFL (minimum score 500 paper-based; 61 iBT). *Application deadline:* Applications are processed on a rolling basis. Application fee: $60 ($75 for international students). Electronic applications accepted. *Expenses:* Tuition, state resident: full-time $7896; part-time $329 per credit hour. Tuition, nonresident: full-time $16,200; part-time $675 per credit hour. Tuition and fees vary according to program. *Financial support:* In 2017– 18, research assistantships with full tuition reimbursements (averaging $10,249 per year), teaching assistantships with full tuition reimbursements (averaging $10,303 per year) were awarded; fellowships, career-related internships or fieldwork, Federal Work-Study, scholarships/grants, health care benefits, and unspecified assistantships also available. Support available to part-time students. Financial award application deadline: 11/15; financial award applicants required to submit FAFSA. *Unit head:* Dr. Carolyn Peck, Program Administrator, 217-206-7577, Fax: 217-206-6775, E-mail: peck.carolyn@uis.edu.
Website: http://www.uis.edu/humanservices

University of Indianapolis, Graduate Programs, Center for Aging and Community, Indianapolis, IN 46227-3697. Offers gerontology (MS, Certificate). *Program availability:* Part-time, evening/weekend, online learning. *Degree requirements:* For master's, capstone course. *Entrance requirements:* For master's, 3 letters of recommendation. Additional exam requirements/recommendations for international students: Required— TOEFL (minimum score 550 paper-based).

University of Indianapolis, Graduate Programs, School of Nursing, Indianapolis, IN 46227-3697. Offers advanced practice nursing (DNP); family nurse practitioner (MSN); gerontological nurse practitioner (MSN); neonatal nurse practitioner (MSN); nurse-midwifery (MSN); nursing (MSN); nursing and health systems leadership (MSN); nursing education (MSN); women's health nurse practitioner (MSN); MBA/MSN. *Accreditation:* AACN. *Entrance requirements:* For master's, minimum GPA of 3.0, interview, letters of recommendation, resume, IN nursing license, 1 year of professional practice; for doctorate, graduate of ACEN- or CCNE-accredited nursing program; MSN or MA with nursing major and minimum cumulative GPA of 3.25; unencumbered RN license with eligibility for licensure in Indiana; completion of graduate-level statistics course within last 5 years with minimum grade of B; resume; essay; official transcripts from all academic institutions. Additional exam requirements/recommendations for international students: Required—TOEFL (minimum score 550 paper-based). Electronic applications accepted.

The University of Kansas, Graduate Studies, College of Liberal Arts and Sciences, Program in Gerontology, Lawrence, KS 66045. Offers PhD. *Entrance requirements:* For doctorate, GRE, 3 letters of recommendation; resume; personal statement; transcripts; list of all courses taken in relevant areas such as sociology, psychology, human development, social welfare, biology, and health services. Additional exam requirements/recommendations for international students: Required—TOEFL. *Application deadline:* For fall admission, 12/1 for domestic and international students. Application fee: $65 ($85 for international students). Electronic applications accepted. *Financial support:* Fellowships, research assistantships, career-related internships or fieldwork, traineeships, and unspecified assistantships available. Financial award application deadline: 1/15. *Faculty research:* Communication and aging, work and retirement, cognitive aging, dementia, environmental gerontology. *Unit head:* Tamara Baker, Director, 785-864-6528, E-mail: tbakerthomas@ku.edu. *Application contact:* Graduate Admissions Contact, 785-864-4130, Fax: 785-864-2666, E-mail: gerontology@ku.edu.
Website: http://www.gerontology.ku.edu/

University of Kentucky, Graduate School, College of Public Health, Program in Gerontology, Lexington, KY 40506-0032. Offers PhD, Graduate Certificate. *Degree requirements:* For doctorate, comprehensive exam, thesis/dissertation. *Entrance requirements:* For doctorate, GRE General Test, minimum undergraduate GPA of 2.75, graduate 3.0. Additional exam requirements/recommendations for international students: Required—TOEFL (minimum score 550 paper-based). Electronic applications accepted.

University of La Verne, College of Business and Public Management, Master's Program in Public Administration, La Verne, CA 91750-4443. Offers gerontology (MPA); nonprofit (MPA); public health (MPA); urban management and affairs (MPA). *Accreditation:* NASPAA. *Program availability:* Part-time. *Faculty:* 11 full-time (5 women), 1 part-time/adjunct (0 women). *Students:* 33 full-time (18 women), 21 part-time (15 women); includes 40 minority (3 Black or African American, non-Hispanic/Latino; 2 Asian, non-Hispanic/Latino; 35 Hispanic/Latino), 1 international. Average age 33. *Entrance requirements:* For master's, minimum undergraduate GPA of 3.0, statement of purpose, 2 letters of recommendation, resume. Additional exam requirements/ recommendations for international students: Required—TOEFL (minimum score 550 paper-based). *Application deadline:* Applications are processed on a rolling basis. Application fee: $50. *Expenses:* Contact institution. *Financial support:* Institutionally sponsored loans and scholarships/grants available. Financial award application deadline: 3/2; financial award applicants required to submit FAFSA. *Unit head:* Marcia Godwin, Chairperson, 909-448-4103, E-mail: mgodwin@laverne.edu. *Application contact:* Cathy Cook, Associate Director of Graduate Admissions, 909-448-4719, Fax: 909-971-2295, E-mail: ccook2@laverne.edu.
Website: https://business.laverne.edu/mpa/

University of La Verne, College of Business and Public Management, Program in Gerontology, La Verne, CA 91750-4443. Offers MS, Certificate. *Program availability:* Part-time. *Faculty:* 1 (woman) full-time, 1 (woman) part-time/adjunct. *Students:* 9 full-time (8 women), 11 part-time (10 women); includes 12 minority (3 Black or African American, non-Hispanic/Latino; 9 Hispanic/Latino), 3 international. Average age 39. *Entrance requirements:* For master's, bachelor's degree, minimum preferred GPA of 2.75, 2 recommendations, personal statement. Additional exam requirements/ recommendations for international students: Required—TOEFL (minimum score 550 paper-based). *Application deadline:* Applications are processed on a rolling basis. Application fee: $50. *Expenses:* Contact institution. *Financial support:* Federal Work-Study, institutionally sponsored loans, and scholarships/grants available. Financial award application deadline: 3/2; financial award applicants required to submit FAFSA. *Unit head:* Kelly Niles-Yokum, Program Director, 909-448-1584, E-mail: knilesyokum@laverne.edu. *Application contact:* Barbara Cox, Program and Admissions Specialist, 909-448-4004, Fax: 909-971-2295, E-mail: bcox@laverne.edu.
Website: https://business.laverne.edu/gerontology/

University of Louisiana at Monroe, Graduate School, College of Health and Pharmaceutical Sciences, Department of Gerontology, Monroe, LA 71209-0001. Offers aging studies (MA); gerontology (CGS); grief care management (MA); long-term care administration (MA); mental health (MA); program administration (MA); small business management (MA). *Program availability:* Part-time. *Faculty:* 1 (woman) full-time, 5 part-time/adjunct (3 women). *Students:* 6 full-time (5 women), 8 part-time (all women); includes 5 minority (all Black or African American, non-Hispanic/Latino). Average age 36. 7 applicants, 43% accepted, 3 enrolled. In 2017, 3 master's awarded. *Degree requirements:* For master's, thesis (for some programs), internship. *Entrance requirements:* For master's, GRE General Test (waived for students with a 2.5 GPA or above); for CGS, GRE General Test. Additional exam requirements/recommendations for international students: Required—TOEFL (minimum score 500 paper-based; 61 iBT). *Application deadline:* For fall admission, 8/24 priority date for domestic students, 7/1 for international students; for winter admission, 12/14 priority date for domestic students; for spring admission, 1/19 for domestic students, 11/1 for international students. Applications are processed on a rolling basis. Application fee: $20 ($30 for international students). Electronic applications accepted. *Expenses:* Tuition, state resident: full-time $6489; part-time $479 per hour. Tuition, nonresident: full-time $12,100; part-time $479 per hour. *Required fees:* $8860; $802 per hour. $3273 per semester. *Financial support:* In 2017–18, 2 students received support. Career-related internships or fieldwork, Federal Work-Study, and unspecified assistantships available. Financial award application deadline: 4/1; financial award applicants required to submit FAFSA. *Unit head:* Dr. Anita Sharma, Director, 318-342-1467, E-mail: sharma@ulm.edu.
Website: http://www.ulm.edu/gerontology/

University of Louisville, Graduate School, Kent School of Social Work, Louisville, KY 40292-0001. Offers marriage and family therapy (PMC), including mental health; social work (MSSW, PhD), including alcohol and drug counseling (MSSW), gerontology (MSSW), marriage and family (PhD), school social work (MSSW). *Accreditation:* AAMFT/COAMFTE; CSWE (one or more programs are accredited). *Program availability:* Part-time, evening/weekend, 100% online, blended/hybrid learning. *Faculty:* 31 full-time (22 women), 44 part-time/adjunct (35 women). *Students:* 402 full-time (357 women), 103 part-time (88 women); includes 119 minority (68 Black or African

American, non-Hispanic/Latino; 1 American Indian or Alaska Native, non-Hispanic/Latino; 8 Asian, non-Hispanic/Latino; 16 Hispanic/Latino; 26 Two or more races, non-Hispanic/Latino), 5 international. Average age 31. 396 applicants, 78% accepted, 228 enrolled. In 2017, 179 master's awarded. *Degree requirements:* For doctorate, comprehensive exam, thesis/dissertation. *Entrance requirements:* For master's, GRE or minimum GPA of 2.75; for doctorate, GRE General Test, interview, writing sample. Additional exam requirements/recommendations for international students: Required—TOEFL (minimum score 550 paper-based; 79 iBT), IELTS (minimum score 6.5). *Application deadline:* For fall admission, 5/30 for domestic and international students; for spring admission, 9/30 for domestic and international students; for summer admission, 2/28 for domestic and international students. Applications are processed on a rolling basis. Application fee: $65. Electronic applications accepted. *Expenses:* Contact institution. *Financial support:* In 2017–18, 11 research assistantships with full tuition reimbursements (averaging $21,500 per year), 1 teaching assistantship with full tuition reimbursement (averaging $19,000 per year) were awarded; scholarships/grants, health care benefits, and unspecified assistantships also available. Financial award application deadline: 5/15; financial award applicants required to submit FAFSA. *Faculty research:* Equipping young children with skills, assisting abused or neglected children, helping juveniles with sexual behavioral problems, illuminating the contributions that men and women make to their families, managing chronic conditions, enhancing trauma-informed services, addressing social and health issues of older adults, palliative and end-of-life care. *Total annual research expenditures:* $6.1 million. *Unit head:* Dr. David Jenkins, Dean, 502-852-3944, Fax: 502-852-0422, E-mail: dajenk03@exchange.louisville.edu. *Application contact:* Misty Kupka, Program Manager for Admissions and Recruitment, 502-852-0414, Fax: 502-852-0422, E-mail: misty.kupka@louisville.edu.
Website: http://www.louisville.edu/kent

University of Maryland, Baltimore, Graduate School, Graduate Program in Life Sciences, Program in Gerontology, Baltimore, MD 21201. Offers PhD. *Students:* 8 full-time (all women), 2 part-time (both women); includes 3 minority (1 Black or African American, non-Hispanic/Latino; 1 Hispanic/Latino; 1 Two or more races, non-Hispanic/Latino), 4 international. Average age 32. 4 applicants, 50% accepted, 2 enrolled. In 2017, 1 doctorate awarded. *Degree requirements:* For doctorate, comprehensive exam, thesis/dissertation. *Entrance requirements:* For doctorate, GRE General Test, minimum GPA of 3.0, curriculum vitae, essay, 3 letters of recommendation. Additional exam requirements/recommendations for international students: Required—TOEFL (minimum score 80 iBT); Recommended—IELTS (minimum score 7). *Application deadline:* For fall admission, 1/15 for domestic and international students. Application fee: $75. Electronic applications accepted. *Expenses:* Tuition, state resident: full-time $13,990; part-time $661 per credit. Tuition, nonresident: full-time $30,484; part-time $1310 per credit. *Required fees:* $1894; $94 per credit. $415 per semester. Part-time tuition and fees vary according to course load, degree level and program. *Financial support:* Fellowships, research assistantships, and health care benefits available. Financial award application deadline: 3/1; financial award applicants required to submit FAFSA. *Faculty research:* Aging policy issues; epidemiology of aging; social, cultural, behavioral sciences. *Unit head:* Dr. Denise Orwig, Professor and Program Director, 410-706-4926, E-mail: dorwig@epi.umaryland.edu. *Application contact:* Justine Golden, Coordinator, 410-706-1733, E-mail: jgolden@epi.umaryland.edu.
Website: http://www.gerontologyphd.umaryland.edu/

University of Maryland, Baltimore, School of Medicine, Department of Epidemiology and Public Health, Baltimore, MD 21201. Offers biostatistics (MS); clinical research (MS); epidemiology and preventive medicine (MPH, MS, PhD); gerontology (PhD); human genetics and genomic medicine (MS, PhD); molecular epidemiology (MS, PhD); toxicology (MS, PhD); JD/MS; MD/PhD; MS/PhD. *Accreditation:* CEPH. *Program availability:* Part-time. *Students:* 88 full-time (72 women), 53 part-time (38 women); includes 51 minority (21 Black or African American, non-Hispanic/Latino; 20 Asian, non-Hispanic/Latino; 7 Hispanic/Latino; 3 Two or more races, non-Hispanic/Latino), 29 international. Average age 30. In 2017, 24 master's, 14 doctorates awarded. *Degree requirements:* For doctorate, comprehensive exam, thesis/dissertation. *Entrance requirements:* For master's and doctorate, GRE General Test. Additional exam requirements/recommendations for international students: Required—TOEFL (minimum score 550 paper-based; 80 iBT); Recommended—IELTS (minimum score 7). *Application deadline:* For fall admission, 1/15 for domestic and international students. Application fee: $75. Electronic applications accepted. *Expenses:* Contact institution. *Financial support:* In 2017–18, research assistantships with partial tuition reimbursements (averaging $26,000 per year) were awarded; fellowships, Federal Work-Study, scholarships/grants, and unspecified assistantships also available. Financial award application deadline: 3/1; financial award applicants required to submit FAFSA. *Unit head:* Dr. Laura Hungerford, Program Director, 410-706-8492, Fax: 410-706-4225. *Application contact:* Jessica Kelley, Program Coordinator, 410-706-8492, Fax: 410-706-4225, E-mail: jkelley@som.umaryland.edu.
Website: http://lifesciences.umaryland.edu/epidemiology/

University of Maryland, Baltimore County, The Graduate School, College of Arts, Humanities and Social Sciences, PhD Program in Gerontology at UMB/UMBC, Baltimore, MD 21201. Offers aging policy issues (PhD); epidemiology of aging (PhD); social, cultural, and behavioral sciences (PhD); MA/PhD; MS/PhD. Program offered with University of Maryland, Baltimore. *Program availability:* Part-time. *Faculty:* 15 part-time/adjunct (10 women). *Students:* 12 full-time (11 women), 8 part-time (7 women); includes 6 minority (3 Black or African American, non-Hispanic/Latino; 1 Asian, non-Hispanic/Latino; 2 Hispanic/Latino), 4 international. Average age 35. 10 applicants, 20% accepted, 2 enrolled. In 2017, 3 doctorates awarded. *Degree requirements:* For doctorate, comprehensive exam, thesis/dissertation. *Entrance requirements:* For doctorate, GRE General Test. Additional exam requirements/recommendations for international students: Required—TOEFL, TWE. *Application deadline:* For spring admission, 1/15 for domestic and international students. Application fee: $45. Electronic applications accepted. *Expenses: Required fees:* $132. *Financial support:* In 2017–18, 11 students received support, including 2 fellowships with full tuition reimbursements available (averaging $23,844 per year), 9 research assistantships with full tuition reimbursements available (averaging $20,000 per year); health care benefits and dissertation awards also available. Financial award application deadline: 2/1; financial award applicants required to submit FAFSA. *Faculty research:* Aging and health policy, behavioral aspects of aging, epidemiology of aging. *Total annual research expenditures:* $15.2 million. *Unit head:* Dr. John Schumacher, Co-Director, UMBC Campus, 410-455-3184, Fax: 410-455-2074, E-mail: jschuma@umbc.edu. *Application contact:* Justine Golden, Academic Coordinator, 410-706-4926, Fax: 410-706-4433, E-mail: jgold002@umaryland.edu.
Website: http://lifesciences.umaryland.edu/gerontologyphd/

University of Maryland, Baltimore County, The Graduate School, Erickson School of Aging Studies, Baltimore, MD 21228. Offers management of aging services (MA). *Program availability:* Part-time. *Faculty:* 4 full-time (1 woman), 7 part-time/adjunct (1 woman). *Students:* 18 full-time (11 women); includes 9 minority (8 Black or African American, non-Hispanic/Latino; 1 Hispanic/Latino). Average age 30. 23 applicants, 91% accepted, 18 enrolled. In 2017, 13 master's awarded. *Entrance requirements:* For master's, essays. *Application deadline:* For fall admission, 6/1 for domestic students; for spring admission, 12/1 for domestic students. Applications are processed on a rolling

basis. Application fee: $50. Electronic applications accepted. *Expenses:* Contact institution. *Financial support:* In 2017–18, 15 students received support, including 1 teaching assistantship with full tuition reimbursement available (averaging $21,600 per year). Financial award applicants required to submit FAFSA. *Faculty research:* Policy implications of entitlement programs, demographic impact of aging population, person-centered care for dementia, changing culture in long-term care. *Unit head:* Bill Holman, Graduate Program Director, 443-543-5603, E-mail: holman1@umbc.edu. *Application contact:* Michelle Howell, Administrative Assistant, 443-543-5607, E-mail: mhowell@umbc.edu.
Website: http://www.umbc.edu/erickson/

University of Massachusetts Boston, McCormack Graduate School of Policy and Global Studies, Program in Gerontology, Boston, MA 02125-3393. Offers gerontology (PhD). *Program availability:* Part-time. *Faculty:* 11 full-time (8 women), 1 (woman) part-time/adjunct. *Students:* 24 full-time (22 women), 98 part-time (79 women); includes 19 minority (10 Black or African American, non-Hispanic/Latino; 6 Asian, non-Hispanic/Latino; 1 Hispanic/Latino; 2 Two or more races, non-Hispanic/Latino), 17 international. Average age 39. 41 applicants, 66% accepted, 20 enrolled. In 2017, 40 master's, 7 doctorates, 5 other advanced degrees awarded. *Entrance requirements:* For doctorate, GRE General Test, minimum GPA of 3.0. *Application deadline:* For fall admission, 2/1 for domestic students. *Expenses:* Tuition, state resident: full-time $17,375. Tuition, nonresident: full-time $33,915. *Required fees:* $355. *Financial support:* Research assistantships, teaching assistantships, career-related internships or fieldwork, Federal Work-Study, and unspecified assistantships available. Support available to part-time students. Financial award application deadline: 3/1; financial award applicants required to submit FAFSA. *Faculty research:* Aging with a chronic disability, pension policy and social security system, elderly minorities, health services research, living arrangements. *Unit head:* Dr. Jeffrey Burr, Department Chair, 617-287-7318, E-mail: jeffrey.burr@umb.edu. *Application contact:* Graduate Admissions Coordinator, 617-287-6400, Fax: 617-287-6236, E-mail: bos.gadm@dpc.umassp.edu.

University of Michigan–Flint, School of Nursing, Flint, MI 48502-1950. Offers adult-gerontology acute care (DNP); adult-gerontology primary care (DNP); family nurse practitioner (DNP); nursing (MSN); psychiatric mental health (DNP); psychiatric mental health nurse practitioner (Certificate). *Accreditation:* AACN. *Program availability:* Part-time, evening/weekend, 100% online. *Faculty:* 36 full-time (35 women), 66 part-time/adjunct (61 women). *Students:* 159 full-time (143 women), 148 part-time (126 women); includes 80 minority (36 Black or African American, non-Hispanic/Latino; 5 American Indian or Alaska Native, non-Hispanic/Latino; 14 Asian, non-Hispanic/Latino; 14 Hispanic/Latino; 2 Native Hawaiian or other Pacific Islander, non-Hispanic/Latino; 9 Two or more races, non-Hispanic/Latino), 3 international. Average age 37. 86 applicants, 78% accepted, 41 enrolled. In 2017, 12 master's, 42 doctorates, 9 other advanced degrees awarded. *Entrance requirements:* For master's, BSN from regionally-accredited college; minimum GPA of 3.2; current unencumbered RN license in the United States; three or more credits in college-level chemistry or statistics with minimum C grade; for doctorate, BSN or MSN (with APRN certification) from regionally-accredited college or university with minimum overall undergraduate GPA of 3.2; college-level statistics with minimum C grade; for Certificate, completion of nurse practitioner program with MS from regionally-accredited college or university with minimum overall GPA of 3.2; current unencumbered RN license in the United States; current unencumbered license as nurse practitioner; current certification as nurse practitioner in specialty other than discipline of study. Additional exam requirements/recommendations for international students: Required—TOEFL (minimum score 84 iBT), IELTS (minimum score 6.5). *Application deadline:* For fall admission, 7/1 for domestic students, 5/1 for international students; for winter admission, 11/1 for domestic students, 9/1 for international students; for spring admission, 3/15 for domestic students, 1/1 for international students. Applications are processed on a rolling basis. Application fee: $55. Electronic applications accepted. *Expenses:* Contact institution. *Financial support:* Federal Work-Study, scholarships/grants, and unspecified assistantships available. Support available to part-time students. Financial award application deadline: 3/1; financial award applicants required to submit FAFSA. *Faculty research:* Family system stress, self breast exam, family roads evaluation, causal model testing for psycho social development, basic needs, nurse preparation training. *Unit head:* Dr. Constance J. Creech, Director, 810-762-3420, Fax: 810-766-6851, E-mail: ccreech@umflint.edu. *Application contact:* Bradley T. Maki, Director of Graduate Admissions, 810-762-3171, Fax: 810-766-6789, E-mail: bmaki@umflint.edu.
Website: https://www.umflint.edu/nursing/graduate-nursing-programs

University of Missouri, Office of Research and Graduate Studies, School of Social Work, Columbia, MO 65211. Offers gerontological social work (Certificate); military social work (Certificate); social work (MSW, PhD). *Accreditation:* CSWE. *Program availability:* Part-time. *Entrance requirements:* For master's, GRE General Test, minimum GPA of 3.0. Additional exam requirements/recommendations for international students: Required—TOEFL (minimum score 90 iBT), IELTS (minimum score 7). Electronic applications accepted.

University of Nebraska at Omaha, Graduate Studies, College of Public Affairs and Community Service, Department of Gerontology, Omaha, NE 68182. Offers gerontology (PhD, Certificate); social gerontology (MA). *Program availability:* Part-time, evening/weekend. *Degree requirements:* For master's, comprehensive exam, thesis. *Entrance requirements:* For master's, minimum GPA of 3.0, official transcripts, 2 letters of recommendation; for Certificate, minimum GPA of 3.0, official transcripts, 3 letters of recommendation. Additional exam requirements/recommendations for international students: Required—TOEFL (minimum score 550 paper-based), IELTS (minimum score 5.5), PTE (minimum score 44). Electronic applications accepted.

University of Nebraska–Lincoln, Graduate College, College of Education and Human Sciences, Department of Child, Youth and Family Studies, Lincoln, NE 68588. Offers child development/early childhood education (MS, PhD); child, youth and family studies (MS); family and consumer sciences education (MS, PhD); family financial planning (MS); family science (MS, PhD); gerontology (PhD); human sciences (PhD), including child, youth and family studies, gerontology, medical family therapy; marriage and family therapy (MS); medical family therapy (PhD); youth development (MS). *Accreditation:* AAMFT/COAMFTE (one or more programs are accredited). *Program availability:* Online learning. *Degree requirements:* For master's, thesis optional. *Entrance requirements:* For master's, GRE. Additional exam requirements/recommendations for international students: Required—TOEFL (minimum score 550 paper-based). Electronic applications accepted. *Faculty research:* Marriage and family therapy, child development/early childhood education, family financial management.

The University of North Carolina at Charlotte, College of Liberal Arts and Sciences, Interdisciplinary Liberal Arts and Sciences Programs, Charlotte, NC 28223-0001. Offers gender, sexuality, and women's studies (Graduate Certificate); gerontology (MA, Graduate Certificate); Latin American studies (MA); liberal studies (MA); organizational science (PhD); public policy (PhD). *Program availability:* Part-time, evening/weekend. *Faculty:* 1 full-time (0 women). *Students:* 66 full-time (48 women), 66 part-time (52 women); includes 41 minority (14 Black or African American, non-Hispanic/Latino; 2 Asian, non-Hispanic/Latino; 24 Hispanic/Latino; 1 Two or more races, non-Hispanic/Latino), 16 international. Average age 27. 129 applicants, 53% accepted, 43 enrolled. In

2017, 22 master's, 10 doctorates, 9 other advanced degrees awarded. *Degree requirements:* For master's, comprehensive exam (for some programs), thesis (for some programs), practicum, project; for doctorate, comprehensive exam, thesis/dissertation; for Graduate Certificate, practicum (for gerontology). *Entrance requirements:* For master's, GRE General Test or MAT, bachelor's degree from accredited college or university; official transcripts of all previous academic work attempted beyond high school with minimum overall GPA of 3.0; statement of purpose; recommendation letters; for doctorate, GRE or GMAT, statement of purpose discussing interest in program and objectives for pursuing degree, current resume or curriculum vitae, unofficial transcripts; for Graduate Certificate, bachelor's degree from accredited university and either enrolled and in good standing in a graduate degree program at UNC Charlotte or have a minimum undergraduate GPA of 3.0. Additional exam requirements/recommendations for international students: Required—TOEFL (minimum score 523 paper-based, 70 iBT) or IELTS (6.5). *Application deadline:* For fall admission, 2/15 for domestic and international students; for spring admission, 10/1 for domestic and international students; for summer admission, 4/1 for domestic and international students. Applications are processed on a rolling basis. Application fee: $75. Electronic applications accepted. *Expenses:* Tuition, state resident: full-time $4337. Tuition, nonresident: full-time $17,771. *Required fees:* $3211. Tuition and fees vary according to course load and program. *Financial support:* In 2017–18, 21 students received support, including 19 research assistantships (averaging $12,011 per year), 1 teaching assistantship (averaging $18,600 per year); career-related internships or fieldwork, institutionally sponsored loans, scholarships/grants, unspecified assistantships, and administrative assistantships also available. Support available to part-time students. Financial award application deadline: 3/1; financial award applicants required to submit FAFSA. *Unit head:* Dr. Nancy A. Gutierrez, Dean, 704-687-0081, E-mail: ngutierr@uncc.edu. *Application contact:* Kathy B. Giddings, Director of Graduate Admissions, 704-687-5503, Fax: 704-687-3279, E-mail: gradadm@uncc.edu.
Website: http://clas.uncc.edu/academics

The University of North Carolina at Greensboro, Graduate School, School of Health and Human Sciences, Program in Gerontology, Greensboro, NC 27412-5001. Offers MS, Certificate, MS/MBA. Electronic applications accepted.

The University of North Carolina Wilmington, School of Health and Applied Human Sciences, Wilmington, NC 28403-3297. Offers applied gerontology (MS). *Program availability:* Part-time. *Faculty:* 12 full-time (8 women). *Students:* 2 full-time (both women), 2 part-time (both women); includes 1 minority (Black or African American, non-Hispanic/Latino). Average age 41. 4 applicants, 100% accepted, 2 enrolled. In 2017, 4 master's awarded. *Degree requirements:* For master's, practicum, final project. *Entrance requirements:* For master's, 3 recommendations, essay. Additional exam requirements/recommendations for international students: Required—TOEFL (minimum score 550 paper-based; 79 iBT), IELTS (minimum score 6.5). *Application deadline:* For fall admission, 6/15 for domestic students; for spring admission, 11/15 for domestic students; for summer admission, 3/15 for domestic students. Applications are processed on a rolling basis. Application fee: $75. Electronic applications accepted. *Expenses:* Tuition, state resident: full-time $4626; part-time $226.76 per credit hour. Tuition, nonresident: full-time $17,834; part-time $874.22 per credit hour. *Required fees:* $2124. Tuition and fees vary according to program. *Financial support:* Scholarships/grants and unspecified assistantships available. Financial award application deadline: 1/1; financial award applicants required to submit FAFSA. *Unit head:* Dr. Steve Elliott, Interim Director, 910-962-2115, Fax: 910-962-7073, E-mail: elliotts@uncw.edu. *Application contact:* Dr. Anne Glass, Program Coordinator, 910-962-7509, E-mail: glassa@uncw.edu.
Website: http://www.uncw.edu/shahs/

University of Northern Colorado, Graduate School, College of Natural and Health Sciences, School of Human Sciences, Program in Gerontology, Greeley, CO 80639. Offers MA. *Program availability:* Part-time. *Degree requirements:* For master's, comprehensive exam. *Entrance requirements:* For master's, GRE General Test or MAT, 2 letters of recommendation. Electronic applications accepted.

University of Northern Colorado, Graduate School, College of Natural and Health Sciences, School of Nursing, Greeley, CO 80639. Offers adult-gerontology acute care nurse practitioner (MSN, DNP); family nurse practitioner (MSN, DNP); nursing education (PhD); nursing practice (DNP). *Accreditation:* AACN. *Program availability:* Online learning. *Degree requirements:* For master's, comprehensive exam, thesis or alternative; for doctorate, comprehensive exam, thesis/dissertation. *Entrance requirements:* For master's and doctorate, GRE General Test, minimum GPA of 3.0 in last 60 hours, BS in nursing, 2 letters of recommendation. Electronic applications accepted.

University of North Texas, Robert B. Toulouse School of Graduate Studies, Denton, TX 76203-5459. Offers accounting (MS); applied anthropology (MA, MS); applied behavior analysis (Certificate); applied geography (MA); applied technology and performance improvement (M Ed, MS); art education (MA); art history (MA); art museum education (Certificate); arts leadership (Certificate); audiology (Au D); behavior analysis (MS); behavioral science (PhD); biochemistry and molecular biology (MS); biology (MA, MS); biomedical engineering (MS); business analysis (MS); chemistry (MS); clinical health psychology (PhD); communication studies (MA, MS); computer engineering (MS); computer science (MS); counseling (M Ed, MS), including clinical mental health counseling (MS), college and university counseling, elementary school counseling, secondary school counseling; creative writing (MA); criminal justice (MS); curriculum and instruction (M Ed); decision sciences (MBA); design (MA, MFA), including fashion design (MFA), innovation studies, interior design (MFA); early childhood studies (MS); economics (MS); educational leadership (M Ed, Ed D); educational psychology (MS, PhD), including family studies (MS), gifted and talented (MS), human development (MS), learning and cognition (MS), research, measurement and evaluation (MS); electrical engineering (MS); emergency management (MPA); engineering technology (MS); English (MA); English as a second language (MA); environmental science (MS); finance (MBA, MS); financial management (MPA); French (MA); health services management (MBA); higher education (M Ed, Ed D); history (MA, MS); hospitality management (MS); human resources management (MPA); information science (MS); information systems (PhD); information technologies (MBA); interdisciplinary studies (MA, MS); international studies (MA); international sustainable tourism (MS); jazz studies (MM); journalism (MA, MJ, Graduate Certificate), including interactive and virtual digital communication (Graduate Certificate), narrative journalism (Graduate Certificate), public relations (Graduate Certificate); kinesiology (MS); linguistics (MA); local government management (MPA); logistics (PhD); logistics and supply chain management (MBA); long-term care, senior housing, and aging services (MA); management (PhD); marketing (MBA); mathematics (MA, MS); mechanical and energy engineering (MS, PhD); music (MA), including ethnomusicology, music theory, musicology, performance; music composition (PhD); music education (MM Ed, PhD); nonprofit management (MPA); operations and supply chain management (MBA); performance (MM, DMA); philosophy (MA); political science (MA); professional and technical communication (MA); radio, television and film (MA, MFA); rehabilitation counseling (Certificate); sociology (MA); Spanish (MA); special education (M Ed); speech-language pathology (MA); strategic management (MBA); studio art (MFA); teaching (M Ed); MBA/MS. *Program availability:* Part-time, evening/weekend, online learning. Terminal master's awarded for partial completion of doctoral program. *Degree requirements:* For master's, variable foreign language requirement, comprehensive exam (for some programs), thesis (for some programs); for doctorate, variable foreign language requirement, comprehensive exam (for some programs), thesis/dissertation; for other advanced degree, variable foreign language requirement, comprehensive exam (for some programs). *Entrance requirements:* For master's and doctorate, GRE, GMAT. Additional exam requirements/recommendations for international students: Required—TOEFL (minimum score 550 paper-based; 79 iBT). Electronic applications accepted.

University of Phoenix–Central Valley Campus, College of Nursing, Fresno, CA 93720-1552. Offers education (MHA); gerontology (MHA); health administration (MHA); nursing (MSN); MSN/MBA.

University of Phoenix–Hawaii Campus, College of Nursing, Honolulu, HI 96813-3800. Offers education (MHA); family nurse practitioner (MSN); gerontology (MHA); health administration (MHA); nursing (MSN); nursing/health care education (MSN); MSN/MBA. *Program availability:* Evening/weekend. *Degree requirements:* For master's, thesis (for some programs). *Entrance requirements:* For master's, minimum undergraduate GPA of 2.5, 3 years of work experience, RN license. Additional exam requirements/recommendations for international students: Required—TOEFL (minimum score 550 paper-based; 79 iBT). Electronic applications accepted.

University of Puerto Rico–Medical Sciences Campus, Graduate School of Public Health, Department of Human Development, Program in Gerontology, San Juan, PR 00936-5067. Offers MPH, Certificate. *Program availability:* Part-time, evening/weekend. *Entrance requirements:* For master's, GRE, previous course work in social sciences, biology, psychology, and algebra.

University of Regina, Faculty of Graduate Studies and Research, Faculty of Arts, Program in Gerontology, Regina, SK S4S 0A2, Canada. Offers M Sc, MA. *Program availability:* Part-time. *Students:* 2 full-time (both women). 1 applicant. *Degree requirements:* For master's, thesis. *Entrance requirements:* Additional exam requirements/recommendations for international students: Required—TOEFL (minimum score 580 paper-based; 80 iBT), IELTS (minimum score 6.5), PTE (minimum score 59). *Application deadline:* For fall admission, 3/31 for domestic and international students. Application fee: $100. Electronic applications accepted. *Expenses:* $10,681. *Financial support:* In 2017–18, 2 fellowships, 1 teaching assistantship (averaging $2,562 per year) were awarded; research assistantships and scholarships/grants also available. Financial award application deadline: 6/15. *Faculty research:* Health economics and policy; aging, society, and human service work; end-of-life issues for human service workers; physiology of aging; ethical decision-making in kinesiology and health care administration. *Unit head:* Dr. Abigail Wickson-Griffiths, Program Coordinator, 306-337-2132, E-mail: abigail.wickson-griffiths@uregina.ca.

University of South Carolina, The Graduate School, Program in Gerontology, Columbia, SC 29208. Offers Certificate. *Program availability:* Part-time. *Degree requirements:* For Certificate, practicum. Electronic applications accepted.

★ **University of Southern California,** Graduate School, Davis School of Gerontology, Los Angeles, CA 90089. Offers aging services management (MASM); biology of aging (PhD); gerontology (MA, MS, PhD, Graduate Certificate); long term care administration (MLTCA); JD/MS; M Pl/MS; MBA/MS; MHA/MS; MPA/MS; MS/MSW; Pharm D/MS. PhD in biology of aging offered jointly with Buck Institute for Research on Aging. *Program availability:* Part-time, online learning. Terminal master's awarded for partial completion of doctoral program. *Degree requirements:* For master's, thesis or alternative; for doctorate, comprehensive exam, thesis/dissertation. *Entrance requirements:* For doctorate, GRE. Electronic applications accepted. *Faculty research:* Sex steroids and Alzheimer's disease, memory, cognition and brain plasticity, environment and injury prevention, antioxidants, stress and aging, inflammation and aging, euthanasia, caloric restriction and chemotherapy, biodemographic of aging, health outcomes research, families and intergenerational relatives, care-giving of elderly, biology, psychology, sociology, policy.

See Display on the next page and Close-Up on page 877.

University of Southern California, Graduate School, School of Social Work, Los Angeles, CA 90089. Offers community organization, planning and administration (MSW); families and children (MSW); health (MSW); mental health (MSW); military social work and veterans services (MSW); older adults (MSW); public child welfare (MSW); school settings (MSW); social work (MSW, PhD); systems of mental illness recovery (MSW); work and life (MSW); JD/MSW; M Pl/MSW; MPA/MSW; MSW/MBA; MSW/MJCS; MSW/MS. *Accreditation:* CSWE (one or more programs are accredited). *Degree requirements:* For doctorate, comprehensive exam, thesis/dissertation, qualifying exam/publishable paper. *Entrance requirements:* For doctorate, GRE General Test. Additional exam requirements/recommendations for international students: Required—TOEFL (minimum score 600 paper-based; 100 iBT), ESL exam. Electronic applications accepted. *Faculty research:* Department of Defense Educational Activity, detection/treatment of depression among older adults, health/aging, psychosocial adaptation to extreme environments/man made disasters; mental health needs of older adults.

University of Southern Indiana, Graduate Studies, College of Nursing and Health Professions, Program in Nursing, Evansville, IN 47712-3590. Offers adult-gerontology acute care nurse practitioner (MSN, PMC); adult-gerontology clinical nurse specialist (MSN, PMC); adult-gerontology primary care nurse practitioner (MSN, PMC); advanced nursing practice (DNP); family nurse practiioner (MSN); family nurse practitioner (PMC); nursing education (MSN, PMC); nursing management and leadership (MSN, PMC); organizational and systems leadership (DNP); psychiatric mental health nurse practitioner (MSN, PMC). *Accreditation:* AACN. *Program availability:* Part-time, online learning. *Faculty:* 9 full-time (8 women), 2 part-time/adjunct (both women). *Students:* 73 full-time (59 women), 370 part-time (314 women); includes 47 minority (18 Black or African American, non-Hispanic/Latino; 2 American Indian or Alaska Native, non-Hispanic/Latino; 10 Asian, non-Hispanic/Latino; 12 Hispanic/Latino; 1 Native Hawaiian or other Pacific Islander, non-Hispanic/Latino; 4 Two or more races, non-Hispanic/Latino), 1 international. Average age 36. In 2017, 91 master's, 10 doctorates, 18 other advanced degrees awarded. *Entrance requirements:* For master's, BSN from nationally-accredited school; minimum cumulative GPA of 3.0; satisfactory completion of a course in undergraduate statistics (minimum grade C); one year of full-time experience or 2,000 hours of clinical practice as an RN (recommended); unencumbered U.S. RN license; for doctorate, minimum GPA of 3.0, completion of graduate research course with minimum B grade, unencumbered RN license, resume/curriculum vitae, three professional references, 1-2 page narrative of practice experience and professional goals, Capstone Project Information form. Additional exam requirements/recommendations for international students: Required—TOEFL (minimum score 550 paper-based; 79 iBT), IELTS (minimum score 6). *Application deadline:* For fall admission, 2/1 for domestic students, 1/1 priority date for international students. Applications are processed on a rolling basis. Application fee: $40. Electronic applications accepted. *Expenses:* Contact institution. *Financial support:* In 2017–18, 1 student received support. Federal Work-Study, scholarships/grants, tuition waivers (full and partial), and unspecified assistantships available. Financial award application deadline: 3/1; financial award applicants required to submit FAFSA. *Unit head:* Dr. Mellisa A. Hall, Chair of the Master of Science in Nursing Program, 812-465-1168, E-mail:

mhall@usi.edu. *Application contact:* Dr. Mayola Rowser, Director, Graduate Studies, 812-465-7015, Fax: 812-464-1956, E-mail: mrowser@usi.edu.
Website: https://www.usi.edu/health/nursing/

University of South Florida, College of Behavioral and Community Sciences, School of Aging Studies, Tampa, FL 33620-9951. Offers aging studies (PhD); gerontology (MA). *Program availability:* Part-time, evening/weekend. *Faculty:* 9 full-time (4 women). *Students:* 23 full-time (17 women), 6 part-time (5 women); includes 8 minority (4 Black or African American, non-Hispanic/Latino; 1 Asian, non-Hispanic/Latino; 1 Hispanic/Latino; 2 Two or more races, non-Hispanic/Latino), 1 international. Average age 29. 36 applicants, 36% accepted, 8 enrolled. In 2017, 7 master's, 5 doctorates awarded. *Degree requirements:* For master's, comprehensive exam, thesis optional; for doctorate, comprehensive exam, thesis/dissertation. *Entrance requirements:* For master's, GRE General Test, minimum GPA of 3.0; for doctorate, GRE General Test, minimum GPA of 3.25, three letters of recommendation, summary of career goals, single-authored writing sample. Additional exam requirements/recommendations for international students: Required—TOEFL (minimum score 79 iBT). *Application deadline:* For fall admission, 12/11 priority date for domestic and international students; for spring admission, 10/15 for domestic students, 9/15 for international students; for summer admission, 2/15 for domestic students, 1/15 for international students. Application fee: $30. Electronic applications accepted. *Financial support:* In 2017–18, 4 students received support, including 2 research assistantships with tuition reimbursements available (averaging $15,690 per year), 13 teaching assistantships with tuition reimbursements available (averaging $13,503 per year). Financial award application deadline: 2/3. *Faculty research:* Aging and mental health, public policy and long-term care, minority aging, care-giving, guardianship, cognitive aging, Alzheimer's disease. *Total annual research expenditures:* $288,030. *Unit head:* Dr. Cathy L. McEvoy, Director and Professor, 813-974-1940, Fax: 813-974-9754, E-mail: cmcevoy@usf.edu. *Application contact:* Brent Small, Professor, 813-974-9746, Fax: 813-974-9754, E-mail: bsmall@usf.edu.
Website: http://agingstudies.cbcs.usf.edu/aprog/

University of South Florida, Innovative Education, Tampa, FL 33620-9951. Offers adult, career and higher education (Graduate Certificate), including college teaching, leadership in developing human resources, leadership in higher education; Africana studies (Graduate Certificate), including diasporas and health disparities, genocide and human rights; aging studies (Graduate Certificate), including gerontology; art research (Graduate Certificate), including museum studies; business foundations (Graduate Certificate); chemical and biomedical engineering (Graduate Certificate), including materials science and engineering, water, health and sustainability; child and family studies (Graduate Certificate), including positive behavior support; civil and industrial engineering (Graduate Certificate), including transportation systems analysis; community and family health (Graduate Certificate), including maternal and child health, social marketing and public health, violence and injury: prevention and intervention, women's health; criminology (Graduate Certificate), including criminal justice administration; data science for public administration (Graduate Certificate); digital humanities (Graduate Certificate); educational measurement and research (Graduate Certificate), including evaluation; English (Graduate Certificate), including comparative literary studies, creative writing, professional and technical communication; entrepreneurship (Graduate Certificate); environmental health (Graduate Certificate), including safety management; epidemiology and biostatistics (Graduate Certificate), including applied biostatistics, biostatistics, concepts and tools of epidemiology, epidemiology, epidemiology of infectious diseases; geography, environment and planning (Graduate Certificate), including community development, environmental policy and management, geographical information systems; geology (Graduate Certificate), including hydrogeology; global health (Graduate Certificate), including disaster management, global health and Latin American and Caribbean studies, global health

practice, humanitarian assistance, infection control; government and international affairs (Graduate Certificate), including Cuban studies, globalization studies; health policy and management (Graduate Certificate), including health management and leadership, public health policy and programs; hearing specialist: early intervention (Graduate Certificate); industrial and management systems engineering (Graduate Certificate), including systems engineering, technology management; information studies (Graduate Certificate), including school library media specialist; information systems/decision sciences (Graduate Certificate), including analytics and business intelligence; instructional technology (Graduate Certificate), including distance education, Florida digital/virtual educator, instructional design, multimedia design, Web design; internal medicine, bioethics and medical humanities (Graduate Certificate), including biomedical ethics; Latin American and Caribbean studies (Graduate Certificate); leadership for coastal resiliency planning (Graduate Certificate); mass communications (Graduate Certificate), including multimedia journalism; mathematics and statistics (Graduate Certificate), including mathematics; medicine (Graduate Certificate), including aging and neuroscience, bioinformatics, biotechnology, brain fitness and memory management, clinical investigation, hand and upper limb rehabilitation, health informatics, health sciences, integrative weight management, intellectual property, medicine and gender, metabolic and nutritional medicine, metabolic cardiology, pharmacy sciences; national and competitive intelligence (Graduate Certificate); nursing (Graduate Certificate), including simulation based academic fellowship in advanced pain management; psychological and social foundations (Graduate Certificate), including career counseling, college teaching, diversity in education, mental health counseling, school counseling; public affairs (Graduate Certificate), including nonprofit management, public management, research administration; public health (Graduate Certificate), including assessing chemical toxicity and public health risks, health equity, pharmacoepidemiology, public health generalist, toxicology, translational research in adolescent behavioral health; public health practices (Graduate Certificate), including planning for healthy communities; rehabilitation and mental health counseling (Graduate Certificate), including integrative mental health care, marriage and family therapy, rehabilitation technology; secondary education (Graduate Certificate), including ESOL, foreign language education: culture and content, foreign language education: professional; social work (Graduate Certificate), including geriatric social work/clinical gerontology; special education (Graduate Certificate), including autism spectrum disorder, disabilities education: severe/profound; world languages (Graduate Certificate), including teaching English as a second language (TESL) or foreign language. *Unit head:* Dr. Cynthia DeLuca, Associate Vice President and Assistant Vice Provost, 813-974-3077, Fax: 813-974-7061, E-mail: deluca@usf.edu. *Application contact:* Owen Hooper, Director, Summer and Alternative Calendar Programs, 813-974-6917, E-mail: hooper@usf.edu.
Website: http://www.usf.edu/innovative-education/

University of South Florida, Morsani College of Medicine and College of Graduate Studies, Graduate Programs in Medical Sciences, Tampa, FL 33620-9951. Offers advanced athletic training (MS); athletic training (MS); bioinformatics and computational biology (MSBCB); biotechnology (MSB); health informatics (MSHI); medical sciences (MSMS, PhD), including aging and neuroscience (MSMS), allergy, immunology and infectious disease (PhD), anatomy, biochemistry and molecular biology, clinical and translational research, health science (MSMS), interdisciplinary medical sciences (MSMS), medical microbiology and immunology (MSMS), metabolic and nutritional medicine (MSMS), microbiology and immunology (PhD), molecular medicine, molecular pharmacology and physiology (PhD), neuroscience (PhD), pathology and cell biology (PhD), women's health (MSMS). *Students:* 372 full-time (212 women), 216 part-time (142 women); includes 257 minority (78 Black or African American, non-Hispanic/Latino; 1 American Indian or Alaska Native, non-Hispanic/Latino; 79 Asian, non-Hispanic/

Latino; 84 Hispanic/Latino; 15 Two or more races, non-Hispanic/Latino), 62 international. Average age 28. 1,048 applicants, 46% accepted, 309 enrolled. In 2017, 351 master's, 56 doctorates awarded. Terminal master's awarded for partial completion of doctoral program. *Degree requirements:* For master's, comprehensive exam, thesis; for doctorate, comprehensive exam, thesis/dissertation. *Entrance requirements:* For master's, GRE General Test or GMAT, bachelor's degree or equivalent from regionally-accredited university with minimum GPA of 3.0 in upper-division sciences coursework; prerequisites in general biology, general chemistry, general physics, organic chemistry, quantitative analysis, and integral and differential calculus; for doctorate, GRE General Test, bachelor's degree from regionally-accredited university with minimum GPA of 3.0 in upper-division sciences coursework; 3 letters of recommendation; personal interview; 1-2 page personal statement; prerequisites in biology, chemistry, physics, organic chemistry, quantitative analysis, and integral/differential calculus. Additional exam requirements/recommendations for international students: Required—TOEFL (minimum score 550 paper-based; 79 iBT) or IELTS (minimum score 6.5). *Application deadline:* For fall admission, 2/1 priority date for domestic students, 2/1 for international students. Application fee: $30. Electronic applications accepted. *Expenses:* Contact institution. *Financial support:* In 2017–18, 109 students received support. *Faculty research:* Anatomy, biochemistry, cancer biology, cardiovascular disease, cell biology, immunology, microbiology, molecular biology, neuroscience, pharmacology, physiology. *Total annual research expenditures:* $45.3 million. *Unit head:* Dr. Michael Barber, Professor/Associate Dean for Graduate and Postdoctoral Affairs, 813-974-9908, Fax: 813-974-4317, E-mail: mbarber@health.usf.edu. *Application contact:* Dr. Eric Bennett, Graduate Director, PhD Program in Medical Sciences, 813-974-1545, Fax: 813-974-4317, E-mail: esbennet@health.usf.edu.
Website: http://health.usf.edu/nocms/medicine/graduatestudies/

The University of Tennessee, Graduate School, College of Education, Health and Human Sciences, Program in Public Health, Knoxville, TN 37996. Offers community health education (MPH); gerontology (MPH); health planning/administration (MPH); MS/MPH. *Accreditation:* CEPH. *Degree requirements:* For master's, thesis optional. *Entrance requirements:* For master's, minimum GPA of 2.7. Additional exam requirements/recommendations for international students: Required—TOEFL. Electronic applications accepted.

The University of Toledo, College of Graduate Studies, College of Medicine and Life Sciences, Department of Public Health and Preventative Medicine, Toledo, OH 43606-3390. Offers biostatistics and epidemiology (Certificate); contemporary gerontological practice (Certificate); environmental and occupational health and safety (MPH); epidemiology (Certificate); global public health (Certificate); health promotion and education (MPH); industrial hygiene (MSOH); medical and health science teaching and learning (Certificate); occupational health (Certificate); public health administration (MPH); public health and emergency response (Certificate); public health epidemiology (MPH); public health nutrition (MPH); MD/MPH. *Program availability:* Part-time, evening/weekend. *Degree requirements:* For master's, thesis or alternative. *Entrance requirements:* For master's, GRE, minimum undergraduate GPA of 3.0, three letters of recommendation, statement of purpose, transcripts from all prior institutions attended, resume; for Certificate, minimum undergraduate GPA of 3.0, three letters of recommendation, statement of purpose, transcripts from all prior institutions attended, resume. Additional exam requirements/recommendations for international students: Required—TOEFL (minimum score 550 paper-based; 80 iBT), IELTS (minimum score 6.5). Electronic applications accepted.

University of Utah, Graduate School, College of Nursing, Gerontology Interdisciplinary Program, Salt Lake City, UT 84112. Offers MS, Certificate. *Program availability:* Part-time, evening/weekend, online only, 100% online, blended/hybrid learning. *Faculty:* 9 full-time (8 women). *Students:* 2 full-time (both women), 4 part-time (all women). Average age 34. 5 applicants, 100% accepted, 4 enrolled. In 2017, 3 master's awarded. *Degree requirements:* For master's, thesis or project. *Entrance requirements:* For master's, GRE General Test (if cumulative GPA is less than 3.2), minimum undergraduate GPA of 3.0. Additional exam requirements/recommendations for international students: Required—TOEFL (minimum score 500 paper-based; 85 iBT). *Application deadline:* For fall admission, 1/15 for domestic and international students. Application fee: $55 ($65 for international students). Electronic applications accepted. *Expenses:* $12,018.08. *Financial support:* In 2017–18, 8 students received support, including 4 fellowships with full tuition reimbursements available (averaging $7,500 per year); teaching assistantships, scholarships/grants, and health care benefits also available. Support available to part-time students. Financial award application deadline: 1/15; financial award applicants required to submit FAFSA. *Faculty research:* Spousal bereavement, family caregiving, health promotion and self-care, geriatric care management, technology and aging. *Unit head:* Dr. Jackie Eaton, Director, 801-587-9638, Fax: 801-587-7697, E-mail: jacqueline.eaton@nurs.utah.edu. *Application contact:* Arminka Zeljkovic, Program Manager, 801-581-8198, Fax: 801-585-9705, E-mail: arminka.zeljkovic@nurs.utah.edu.
Website: http://www.nursing.utah.edu/gerontology/

University of Wisconsin–Milwaukee, Graduate School, Helen Bader School of Social Welfare, Department of Social Work, Milwaukee, WI 53201-0413. Offers applied gerontology (Graduate Certificate); nonprofit management (Graduate Certificate); social welfare (PhD); social work (MSW, PhD). *Accreditation:* CSWE. *Program availability:* Part-time. *Students:* 194 full-time (169 women), 111 part-time (97 women); includes 83 minority (36 Black or African American, non-Hispanic/Latino; 1 American Indian or Alaska Native, non-Hispanic/Latino; 9 Asian, non-Hispanic/Latino; 1 Hispanic/Latino; 36 Two or more races, non-Hispanic/Latino), 3 international. Average age 31. 361 applicants, 61% accepted, 128 enrolled. In 2017, 156 master's, 68 other advanced degrees awarded. *Entrance requirements:* For doctorate, GRE, bachelor's degree. Additional exam requirements/recommendations for international students: Required—TOEFL (minimum score 550 paper-based; 79 iBT), IELTS (minimum score 6.5). *Application deadline:* For fall admission, 1/1 priority date for domestic students; for spring admission, 9/1 for domestic students. Application fee: $56 ($96 for international students). Electronic applications accepted. *Financial support:* Fellowships, research assistantships, teaching assistantships, career-related internships or fieldwork, health care benefits, unspecified assistantships, and project assistantships available. Support available to part-time students. Financial award application deadline: 4/15; financial award applicants required to submit FAFSA. *Application contact:* Deb Padgett, Associate Professor, Social Work, 414-229-6452, E-mail: dpadgett@uwm.edu.
Website: http://uwm.edu/socialwelfare/academics/

Virginia Commonwealth University, Graduate School, School of Allied Health Professions, Department of Gerontology, Richmond, VA 23284-9005. Offers gerontology (MS). *Program availability:* Part-time. *Entrance requirements:* For master's, GRE General Test or MAT. Additional exam requirements/recommendations for international students: Required—TOEFL (minimum score 600 paper-based; 100 iBT); Recommended—IELTS (minimum score 6.5). Electronic applications accepted. *Faculty research:* Alzheimer's disease, age-related alcoholism and suicide, pain perception, curriculum development and evaluation in gerontology/geriatrics.

Virginia Commonwealth University, Graduate School, School of Allied Health Professions, Doctoral Program in Health Related Sciences, Richmond, VA 23284-9005.

Offers clinical laboratory sciences (PhD); gerontology (PhD); health administration (PhD); nurse anesthesia (PhD); occupational therapy (PhD); physical therapy (PhD); radiation sciences (PhD); rehabilitation leadership (PhD). *Entrance requirements:* For doctorate, GRE General Test or MAT, minimum GPA of 3.3 in master's degree. Additional exam requirements/recommendations for international students: Required—TOEFL (minimum score 600 paper-based; 100 iBT); Recommended—IELTS (minimum score 6.5). Electronic applications accepted.

Walden University, Graduate Programs, School of Social Work and Human Services, Minneapolis, MN 55401. Offers addictions and social work (DSW); advanced clinical practice (MSW); clinical expertise (DSW); criminal justice (DSW); disaster, crisis, and intervention (DSW); family studies and interventions (DSW); human and social services (PhD), including advanced research, community and social services, community intervention and leadership, conflict management, criminal justice, disaster crisis and intervention, family studies and intervention, gerontology, global social services, higher education, human services and nonprofit administration, mental health facilitation; medical social work (DSW); military social work (MSW); policy practice (DSW); social work (PhD), including addictions and social work, clinical expertise, criminal justice, disaster, crisis and intervention, family studies and interventions, medical social work, policy practice, social work administration; social work administration (DSW); social work in healthcare (MSW); social work with children and families (MSW). *Accreditation:* CSWE. *Program availability:* Part-time, evening/weekend, online only, 100% online. *Degree requirements:* For master's, residency (for some programs); for doctorate, thesis/dissertation, residency. *Entrance requirements:* For master's, bachelor's degree or higher; minimum GPA of 2.5; official transcripts; goal statement (for some programs); access to computer and Internet; for doctorate, master's degree or higher; three years of related professional or academic experience (preferred); minimum GPA of 3.0; goal statement and current resume (for select programs); official transcripts; access to computer and Internet. Additional exam requirements/recommendations for international students: Required—TOEFL (minimum score 550 paper-based, 79 iBT), IELTS (minimum score 6.5), Michigan English Language Assessment Battery (minimum score 82), or PTE (minimum score 53). Electronic applications accepted.

Washington University in St. Louis, Brown School, St. Louis, MO 63110. Offers American Indian/Alaska native (MSW); children, youth and families (MSW); epidemiology/biostatistics (MPH); generalist (MPH); global health (MPH); health (MSW); health policy analysis (MPH); individualized (MSW), including health; mental health (MSW); older adults and aging societies (MSW); public health sciences (PhD); social and economic development (MSW), including domestic, international; social work (PhD); urban design (MPH); violence and injury prevention (MSW); JD/MSW; M Arch/MSW; MPH/MBA; MSW/M Div; MSW/M Ed; MSW/MAPS; MSW/MBA; MSW/MPH; MUD/MSW. MSW/M Div and MSW/MAPS offered in partnership with Eden Theological Seminary. *Accreditation:* CSWE (one or more programs are accredited). *Faculty:* 54 full-time (31 women), 87 part-time/adjunct (61 women). *Students:* 294 full-time (254 women); includes 114 minority (56 Black or African American, non-Hispanic/Latino; 8 American Indian or Alaska Native, non-Hispanic/Latino; 17 Asian, non-Hispanic/Latino; 10 Hispanic/Latino; 1 Native Hawaiian or other Pacific Islander, non-Hispanic/Latino; 22 Two or more races, non-Hispanic/Latino), 246 international. Average age 26. *Degree requirements:* For master's, 60 credit hours (for MSW); 52 credit hours (for MPH); practicum; for doctorate, comprehensive exam, thesis/dissertation. *Entrance requirements:* For master's, GRE (preferred), GMAT, LSAT, MCAT, PCAT, or United States Medical Licensing Exam (for MPH); for doctorate, GRE. Additional exam requirements/recommendations for international students: Required—TOEFL (minimum score 100 iBT), IELTS (minimum score 7). *Application deadline:* For fall admission, 12/15 priority date for domestic and international students; for winter admission, 3/1 priority date for domestic and international students. Applications are processed on a rolling basis. Electronic applications accepted. *Expenses:* Contact institution. *Financial support:* In 2017–18, 30 fellowships, 60 research assistantships were awarded; career-related internships or fieldwork, Federal Work-Study, scholarships/grants, and unspecified assistantships also available. Support available to part-time students. Financial award applicants required to submit FAFSA. *Faculty research:* Mental health, social policy, health policy, epidemiology, social and economic development. *Total annual research expenditures:* $14.5 million. *Unit head:* Jamie L. Adkisson-Hennessey, Director of Admissions and Recruitment, 314-935-3524, Fax: 314-935-4859, E-mail: jadkisson@wustl.edu. *Application contact:* Office of Admissions and Recruitment, 314-935-6676, Fax: 314-935-4859, E-mail: brownadmissions@wustl.edu.
Website: http://brownschool.wustl.edu

Washington University in St. Louis, The Graduate School, Department of Psychological and Brain Sciences, St. Louis, MO 63130-4899. Offers aging and development (PhD). Terminal master's awarded for partial completion of doctoral program. *Degree requirements:* For doctorate, thesis/dissertation. *Entrance requirements:* For doctorate, GRE General Test. Additional exam requirements/recommendations for international students: Required—TOEFL. Electronic applications accepted. *Faculty research:* Behavior/brain/cognition; clinical; aging/development; social/personality.

Wayne State University, School of Social Work, Detroit, MI 48202. Offers gerontology (Certificate); social work (MSW, PhD). Application deadlines: April 1 for MSW, December 19 for PhD. *Accreditation:* CSWE (one or more programs are accredited). *Program availability:* Part-time, evening/weekend. *Degree requirements:* For master's, filed work; for doctorate, variable foreign language requirement, comprehensive exam, thesis/dissertation. *Entrance requirements:* For master's, personal interest statement, resume, 3 references; for doctorate, GRE (minimum combined score of 1000 on Verbal and Quantitative components), minimum undergraduate GPA of 3.5, MSW from CSWE-accredited institution (or working towards one), resume, three letters of reference, personal statement, summary of relevant research and professional experience, writing sample, interview; for Certificate, MSW or actively enrolled in advanced portion of MSW program. Additional exam requirements/recommendations for international students: Required—TOEFL (minimum score 550 paper-based; 79 iBT), TWE (minimum score 5.5), Michigan English Language Assessment Battery (minimum score 85); Recommended—IELTS (minimum score 6.5). *Application deadline:* Applications are processed on a rolling basis. Application fee: $50. Electronic applications accepted. *Expenses:* Contact institution. *Financial support:* Fellowships with tuition reimbursements, research assistantships with tuition reimbursements, teaching assistantships with tuition reimbursements, scholarships/grants, and unspecified assistantships available. Financial award applicants required to submit FAFSA. *Faculty research:* Aging, child welfare, health and behavioral health, interpersonal violence, community development, policy and program development. *Unit head:* Dr. Jerrold Brandell, Interim Dean, 313-577-4409, E-mail: aa4537@wayne.edu. *Application contact:* Shantalea Johns, Interim Director of Admissions, 313-577-4409, E-mail: shantalea@wayne.edu.
Website: http://socialwork.wayne.edu/

Webster University, College of Arts and Sciences, Department of Psychology, St. Louis, MO 63119-3194. Offers counseling psychology (MS); gerontology (MS). *Program availability:* Part-time. *Entrance requirements:* Additional exam requirements/recommendations for international students: Required—TOEFL.

Gerontology

Webster University, George Herbert Walker School of Business and Technology, Department of Business, St. Louis, MO 63119-3194. Offers business and organizational security management (MBA); decision support systems (MBA); environmental management (MBA); finance (MBA, MS); forensic accounting (MS); gerontology (MBA); human resources development (MBA); human resources management (MBA); information technology management (MBA); international business (MA, MBA); international relations (MBA); management and leadership (MBA); marketing (MBA); media communications (MBA); procurement and acquisitions management (MBA); Web services (MBA). *Accreditation:* ACBSP. *Program availability:* Part-time, evening/weekend, online learning. *Degree requirements:* For master's, comprehensive exam (for some programs), thesis (for some programs). *Entrance requirements:* Additional exam requirements/recommendations for international students: Required—TOEFL.

West Chester University of Pennsylvania, College of Education and Social Work, Department of Social Work, West Chester, PA 19383. Offers gerontology (Certificate); social work (MSW). *Accreditation:* CSWE. *Program availability:* Part-time, evening/weekend. *Students:* 190 full-time (165 women), 100 part-time (83 women); includes 143 minority (111 Black or African American, non-Hispanic/Latino; 3 Asian, non-Hispanic/Latino; 17 Hispanic/Latino; 12 Two or more races, non-Hispanic/Latino). Average age 30. 275 applicants, 77% accepted, 137 enrolled. In 2017, 80 master's, 3 other advanced degrees awarded. *Degree requirements:* For master's, completion of foundation courses and field practicums. *Entrance requirements:* For master's, minimum GPA of 3.0, personal statement of 3 to 5 pages clearly articulating professional goals, two letters of recommendation. Additional exam requirements/recommendations for international students: Required—TOEFL or IELTS. *Application deadline:* For fall admission, 5/15 for international students; for spring admission, 10/15 for international students. Applications are processed on a rolling basis. Application fee: $50. Electronic applications accepted. *Expenses:* Tuition, state resident: full-time $9000; part-time $500 per credit. Tuition, nonresident: full-time $13,500; part-time $750 per credit. *Required fees:* $2959; $149.79 per credit. *Financial support:* Scholarships/grants and unspecified assistantships available. Financial award application deadline: 2/15; financial award applicants required to submit FAFSA. *Faculty research:* Recovery in mental health and substance abuse disorders, integrated health and interprofessional education, trauma and disaster intervention, multicultural resources, human rights including LGBTQA rights. *Unit head:* Dr. Christina M. Chiarelli-Helminiak, Chairperson, 610-436-3615, E-mail: cchiarelli-helminiak@wcupa.edu. *Application contact:* Dr. Stacie Metz, Graduate Coordinator, 610-436-2101, Fax: 610-436-2763, E-mail: smetz@wcupa.edu. Website: http://www.wcupa.edu/education-socialWork/gradSocialWork/

Wichita State University, Graduate School, College of Health Professions, Department of Public Health Sciences, Wichita, KS 67260. Offers aging studies (MA). *Program availability:* Part-time, 100% online, blended/hybrid learning. *Unit head:* Dr. Nicole Rogers, Chairperson, 316-978-3060, Fax: 316-978-3072, E-mail: nicole.rogers@wichita.edu. *Application contact:* Jordan Oleson, Admissions Coordinator, 316-978-3095, Fax: 316-978-3253, E-mail: jordan.oleson@wichita.edu. Website: http://www.wichita.edu/phs

Youngstown State University, Graduate School, College of Liberal Arts and Social Sciences, Program in Gerontology, Youngstown, OH 44555-0001. Offers MA. *Program availability:* Part-time, evening/weekend, online learning. *Degree requirements:* For master's, thesis optional. *Entrance requirements:* For master's, GRE, minimum GPA of 3.0, three letters of recommendation, letter of intent, resume or curriculum vitae, social statistics course at undergraduate or graduate level, minimum of 9 credit hours of aging-related coursework at undergraduate or graduate level.

NORTH DAKOTA STATE UNIVERSITY

College of Human Development and Education

 For more information, visit http://petersons.to/ndstatehumandevelopmenteducation

NDSU GRADUATE SCHOOL

Programs of Study

The College of Human Development and Education at North Dakota State University educates and trains students who want to make a difference in others' lives. Its rigorous programs and innovative research focus on people and how they interact in educational, living, and work environments.

The college's fifteen master's degree programs and seven doctoral degree programs are provided through four departments:

- Apparel, Design, and Hospitality Management
- School of Education
- Health, Nutrition, and Exercise Sciences
- Human Development and Family Science

The college provides a student-focused, friendly community where students are actively involved in the learning process. As a result, they acquire the knowledge and skills to improve the lives of individuals within communities, families, and the workplace.

Online Master of Science (M.S.) program in Human Development and Family Science: The M.S. in Human Development and Family Science is a 36-credit, online program with three options: youth development, gerontology, and family financial planning.

The youth development option trains individuals to develop and implement programs and services that promote the positive development of adolescents. The gerontology option provides in-depth knowledge of the social, physical, and mental changes associated with aging. The family financial planning option provides extensive knowledge of family and personal financial management and eligibility to take the CFP® Certification Examination.

Doctor of Philosophy (Ph.D.) programs in Human Development and Family Science: The College of Human Development and Education also offers Ph.D. programs in developmental science and in couple and family therapy.

The 60-credit Ph.D. in Developmental Science program focuses on human development across the lifespan. It integrates the biological, cognitive, and socio-emotional aspects of development and incorporates the cultural, familial, institutional, and social contexts in which development occurs.

The 81-credit Ph.D. in Couple and Family Therapy program focuses on feminist and social justice principles. This foundation prepares students for clinical, research, and supervisory work with diverse and marginalized populations and communities.

Graduate programs in Health, Nutrition, and Exercise Sciences: The Department of Health, Nutrition, and Exercise Sciences offers six graduate programs, including the M.S. in Health, Nutrition, and Exercise Sciences and the Ph.D. in Exercise Science and Nutrition.

M.S. programs in Health, Nutrition, and Exercise Sciences prepare students for advanced positions in exercise science, health promotion, nutrition/dietetics, physical activity, and physical education teaching and coaching. There are three options: the 31-credit exercise and nutrition option; the 30-credit, online

leadership in physical education and sport option; and the 36-credit, online dietetics option.

The 60-credit Ph.D. program in Exercise Science and Nutrition prepares students for leadership positions in community settings, government agencies, professional agencies and organizations, and universities.

Research

The College of Human Development and Education provides many resources and opportunities for students to engage in cutting-edge research, including state-of-the-art equipment, modern labs, and dedicated teachers.

Faculty members are dedicated to conducting research that improves people's lives and strengthens communities. Graduate students work closely with faculty members to investigate issues relevant to their field, develop academic and grant-writing skills, and publish articles in periodicals. They regularly coauthor refereed journal articles and give numerous presentations at professional conferences.

Financial Aid

Graduate students in the College of Human Development and Education may qualify for the following financial assistance programs: graduate assistantships (teaching or research), scholarships (from the University and private funders), grants, fellowships, loans (through federal programs or private lenders), military and veteran assistance, and employer tuition reimbursement programs.

Applicants should consult with their academic departments and the Office of Financial Aid and Scholarships to learn about their financial aid options.

Cost of Study

The most current information on tuition and fees can be found online at https://www.ndsu.edu/onestop/accounts/tuition/.

Living and Housing Costs

Information about on-campus housing for graduate students can be found at www.ndsu.edu/reslife/general_apartment_information. While there is no specific residence hall for graduate students, they are able to live in the University apartments. There are also numerous housing options in the Fargo community.

The Faculty

Faculty members like James Deal, Ph.D. are accomplished teachers, scholars, and leaders. They bring cutting-edge research to their classrooms, serve on editorial boards of scholarly journals, and serve as officers of professional organizations, among other endeavors.

Professor Deal joined the Department of Human Development and Family Science in 1993. He has received several grants and published numerous articles in his areas of interest: whole

North Dakota State University

family function, quantitative research methods, and personality development in children.

Student Life

Graduate students at North Dakota State University join a warm and opportunity-rich community where they can achieve their educational, personal, research, and social goals. Academic, wellness, and support resources include the Counseling Center, Center for Writers, Office of International Students and Study Abroad Services, Office of Multicultural Programs, Wallman Wellness Center, and more.

Additional amenities include banking services, childcare, on-campus housing, graphic services, and meeting rooms. Social resources include affinity groups, recreational programs, arts and culture, and student organizations.

Location

North Dakota State University is located on the eastern edge of North Dakota in Fargo, the state's largest community. With its sister city, Moorhead, Minnesota, directly across the Red River, Fargo is one of the largest metropolitan centers between Minneapolis and Seattle and offers a family-friendly environment with excellent schools, safe neighborhoods, and a low crime rate; an active arts and cultural scene, including a symphony, civic opera company, art museums, and community theater; and many places to shop and eat, including numerous restaurants, coffee shops, and a newly refurbished downtown district.

The University

Established in 1890, North Dakota State University is a student-focused, land-grant, research institution known nationally and internationally for excellence in education and research. Its vibrant campus community includes more than 14,300 students (approximately 2,000 of whom are graduate students), more than 1,000 faculty members and educators, and approximately 4,000 staff members. It offers students nearly 100 undergraduate majors, 86 master's programs, and 53 doctoral programs. The National Science Foundation ranks a number of North Dakota State University's programs among the top 100 in the country.

Applying

The North Dakota State University graduate school application procedure places responsibility on the applicant to gather all supporting credentials and verifying that the application file is complete. The deadline for submission is dependent upon the program. If no deadline is listed on the program's bulletin page, all application materials are due at least one month prior the start of the semester.

Prospective students must file their application online. There is a $35 nonrefundable application fee. A statement of purpose—covering reasons for pursuing graduate study, special interests within the chosen discipline, and preparation, skills, and experience in the proposed field of study—is required for admission consideration and

must be uploaded with the online application. Other requirements include three letters of recommendation; official transcripts from each college or university attended; and official GRE or GMAT scores if required. Some programs may have additional requirements, as stated on the individual program pages.

The online application and additional details regarding the application process are available at https://www.ndsu.edu/gradschool/prospective_students.

Correspondence and Information

College of Human Development and Education
Graduate School
North Dakota State University
Dept. 2820, P.O. Box 6050
Fargo, North Dakota 58108-6050
Phone: 701-231-7033
　　　800-608-6378 (toll-free)
E-mail: ndsu.grad.school@ndsu.edu
Website: www.ndsu.edu/gradschool
Facebook: facebook.com/ndsugradschool
Twitter: @NDSUGradSchool

The College of Human Development and Education offers graduate programs that focus on people. These nationally recognized programs conduct research and other scholarly activities that focus on individuals as they interact at work and in educational and living environments.

UNIVERSITY OF SOUTHERN CALIFORNIA

Leonard Davis School of Gerontology

USC Leonard Davis
School of Gerontology

 For more information, visit http://petersons.to/uscgerontology

The University of Southern California (USC) Leonard Davis School of Gerontology was established in 1975 and is the longest-running and largest school of its kind. It offers a complete collection of gerontology degree programs, a variety of exceptional research opportunities, and an academic environment which students will find challenging yet supportive. The Leonard Davis School of Gerontology is a unique school rooted in research. Its research and services division, the Ethel Percy Andrus Gerontology Center—is home to not only today's leaders in the field, but also tomorrow's.

USC's gerontology programs study the human lifespan by exploring the biological, psychological, sociological, political, medical, and business dimensions of adult life. The curriculum is aimed at preparing future professionals in the field of aging with the specific skills and knowledge necessary to effectively handle the needs of an aging population. Students have access to a wide range of scientific and professional gerontology courses and an outstanding faculty from a variety of disciplines.

The USC Leonard Davis School of Gerontology explores all aspects of human development and aging. Coursework and research opportunities in biology, psychology, sociology, policy, and aging services result in a unique, multidisciplinary curriculum. Students gain a broad theoretical understanding of lifespan development and experience in the field. Internship programs expose students to an array of industries: health, medicine, business, finance, direct services, program development, public policy, and counseling. Post-graduate career placement is also available.

USC offers many distance-learning programs. All of the USC Leonard Davis School of Gerontology master's programs and graduate certificate programs are available in their entirety online.

Graduate programs offered by USC Leonard Davis School of Gerontology include the following:

Master of Science in Gerontology (MSG): This degree program prepares graduates to take on major leadership roles in the private and public sectors, working in planning, evaluating, and administering programs. It is also designed for graduate students who want to assume executive positions that deliver direct services to older people and their families or teach older adults and service providers.

USC also offers dual-degree options in conjunction with the MSG program. It can be combined with a degree in business administration, health administration, planning, public administration, law, pharmacy, and social work. This program is also available online.

Master of Arts in Gerontology (MAG): This degree program offers current professionals in the field a chance to acquire skills and formal training in gerontology. The MAG program complements real-world experience, offers executive preparation, and helps graduates boost their career potential. This program can be completed online.

Master of Aging Services Management (MASM): This degree program is designed to give current and future aging services managers the knowledge and skill set to offer services, programs, and products to older adults. Students will be prepared to utilize their skills and respond effectively to changes in the economic, legal, and regulatory environments in which they are employed. Courses in the degree program are available online.

Master of Long-Term Care Administration (MLTCA): This is a multi-USC school program. It combines the multifaceted aspects of aging with training in the administration and management of long-term care organizations. Students will take classes offered by the USC Leonard Davis School of Gerontology, the USC Marshall School of Business, and the USC Sol Price School of Public Policy. Students have the option of taking these courses online.

Master of Science in Nutrition, Healthspan, and Longevity (MSNHL): This program is for those who want to pursue a career in nutrition and dietetics. The program promotes health and longevity based on scientific evidence and integrating academic study with professional practice experience. The program includes 46 units of coursework and 1,200 hours of supervised practice in hospital, community, and food service settings.

Before applying, prerequisite courses are required. Students must also complete 40 hours of paid or volunteer work experience with a registered dietitian. The program is a candidate for accreditation by the Accreditation Council for Education in Nutrition and Dietetics (ACEND).

Students are eligible to take the Commission of Dietetics Registration's national registration examination once they receive the master's degree diploma. Upon successful completion, students receive the Registered Dietitian Nutritionist (RDN) credential. This degree program may be completed online.

Graduate Certificate in Gerontology: This certificate program gives students the opportunity to obtain a greater understanding of gerontological theory and research, even if they completed a bachelor's degree in another field. The program consists of 16 units of study in gerontology designed to offer a broad range of knowledge relating to professional practice. This program is also available to students online.

Ph.D. in Gerontology: Students working towards a Ph.D. in Gerontology will learn about the physiology of human development and aging; examining social policies related to aging; and the psychological, behavioral, and sociological impact on lifespan development.

Working closely with a faculty mentor, students focus on a specific area of interest and begin the process of discovering and shaping their own academic specialization. Activities include: working on research and publications, participating in colloquia, attending and presenting at national organization meetings, and acquiring teaching experience. Students can develop a rich academic, personal, and professional network.

Ph.D. in Biology of Aging: The Biology of Aging doctoral program brings together the USC Leonard Davis School of Gerontology and the Buck Institute for Research on Aging in Northern California. Student academic research activities take place on both campuses.

Students work closely with a faculty mentor to concentrate on molecular, cellular, and regenerative medicine in addition to the integrative biology of aging. Students can take core courses on the molecular and cellular biology of aging as well as age-related diseases. They then can choose a specialty of neuroscience, molecular, and cellular biology; stem cell and regenerative sciences; or biomedical sciences.

Research Facilities

The USC Leonard Davis School of Gerontology faculty and students are constantly pushing the boundaries of their various disciplines both in and out of the lab. Several broad areas of focus spark curiosity and collaboration in researchers at all levels, and their goal is to discover and perfect new breakthroughs, technologies, and findings that benefit older adults around the world. Students have access to opportunities at a wide range of centers and laboratories related to gerontology at USC.

Financial Aid

A variety of options are available to help students fund their graduate education at USC. There is a variety of merit scholarships for students seeking to earn master's degrees. The Leonard Davis School also awards $500,000 to graduate students in scholarships annually. Loans, work-study, and student employment is also available.

The Graduate School works with doctoral programs at USC to support a vast majority of Ph.D. students with fellowships, teaching assistantships, and research assistantships, or some combination of these funding sources.

Graduate students are also encouraged to apply for external funding—funds from sources not affiliated with USC. Sponsors range from government agencies, corporations and private institutions. Funds may be limited to a single year of enrollment or may be renewable for multiple years and may be paid to the student or directly to the university.

Cost of Study

Tuition for the 2018–19 academic year for a master's degree program is $55,320 for 15–18 units per semester; $37,260 for 8–14 units per semester; $22,356 for 4–7 units per semester; and $7,452 for 2 units per semester. Mandatory fees range from $1,602 to $2,269; books and supplies are estimated to cost between $300 and $1,200. Doctoral programs are fully funded.

Living and Housing

USC Housing offers graduate students on-campus residences or off-campus apartments specially designed to give students and their families privacy and independence. Some 500 spaces have been set aside for graduate students in the North University Park area. Students also have easy access to public transportation if they choose to live away from campus. USC offers high-quality, accredited child care programs that serve children from six weeks to five years.

Location

USC's main campuses can be found in the heart of Los Angeles. A world leader in aerospace, entertainment, fashion, technology, telecommunications, biomedicine and trade, Los Angeles offers prime opportunities to expand learning outside the classroom, as well as an array of cultural experiences. The amazingly diverse terrain of the region provides students a remarkable climate and makes possible an enormous range of outdoor activities.

The University/School

The University of Southern California is one of the world's leading private research universities. It is home to over 25,000 top-caliber graduate and professional students—more than half the entire USC student population—who represent all 50 states and 135 countries around the world. USC hosts one of the largest numbers of international students in the United States and offers over 400 highly regarded graduate and professional programs in its liberal arts college and 19 professional schools.

Faculty

USC faculty has won hundreds of academic and professional honors. Its intellectual clout can also be measured by the amount of research funding they receive—more than $645 million annually.

Yet faculty remains accessible to their students. USC's learner-centered approach to graduate education fosters intellectual partnerships between faculty and students, and faculty members play active roles in helping students hone their skills in locating, assessing, applying and presenting information. Graduate students are taught by and pursue research with distinguished faculty, making groundbreaking discoveries that address critical issues facing our global society.

Applying

Applicants to the graduate-level gerontology programs at USC must complete an online application; submit an application fee of $90; upload any additional materials required by the program; mail official transcripts; and submit test scores.

Once the admission committee for your intended program of study has completed the review process, the Office of Graduate Admission will notify by e-mail that the admission decision is available. Most students seeking admission to the fall term receive admission decisions by June. Students seeking admission to the spring term usually receive admission decisions by December.

Correspondence and Information

The Leonard Davis School of Gerontology
3715 McClintock Avenue
Los Angeles, California 90089
Phone: 213-740-5156
Fax: 213-740-5150
E-mail: ldsgero@usc.edu
Website: http://gero.usc.edu

Cohen Laboratory

Stever Courtyard

Section 21
Geography

This section contains a directory of institutions offering graduate work in geography. Additional information about programs listed in the directory may be obtained by writing directly to the dean of a graduate school or chair of a department at the address given in the directory.

For programs offering related work, see also in this book *Area and Cultural Studies* and *Humanities.* In another guide in this series:

Graduate Programs in the Physical Sciences, Mathematics, Agricultural Sciences, the Environment & Natural Resources
See *Geosciences*

CONTENTS

Program Directories

Geographic Information Systems

Acadia University, Faculty of Pure and Applied Science, Program in Applied Geomatics, Wolfville, NS B4P 2R6, Canada. Offers M Sc. Program offered jointly with Nova Scotia Community College. *Entrance requirements:* Additional exam requirements/recommendations for international students: Required—TOEFL (minimum score 580 paper-based; 93 iBT), IELTS (minimum score 6.5). *Application deadline:* For fall admission, 2/1 for domestic and international students. Applications are processed on a rolling basis. Application fee: $50. *Financial support:* Application deadline: 2/1. *Unit head:* Dr. Ian Spooner, Department Head, 902-585-1312, E-mail: ian.spooner@acadiau.ca. *Application contact:* Theresa Starratt, Graduate Studies Officer, 902-585-1914, Fax: 902-585-1096, E-mail: gradadmissions@acadiau.ca. Website: http://gradstudies.acadiau.ca/AppliedGeomatics.html

Appalachian State University, Cratis D. Williams Graduate School, Department of Geography and Planning, Boone, NC 28608. Offers geography (MA), including geographic information science. *Program availability:* Part-time, online learning. *Degree requirements:* For master's, comprehensive exam, thesis or alternative. *Entrance requirements:* For master's, GRE General Test, 3 letters of recommendation. Additional exam requirements/recommendations for international students: Required—TOEFL (minimum score 570 paper-based; 79 iBT), IELTS (minimum score 6.5). Electronic applications accepted. *Faculty research:* Global change, climatology, production cartography, geographic information systems, North Carolina geography, Latin America.

Arizona State University at the Tempe campus, College of Liberal Arts and Sciences, School of Geographical Sciences and Urban Planning, Tempe, AZ 85287-5302. Offers geographic information systems (MAS); geographical information science (Graduate Certificate); geography (MA, PhD); transportation systems (Graduate Certificate); urban and environmental planning (MUEP); urban planning (PhD). *Accreditation:* ACSP. Terminal master's awarded for partial completion of doctoral program. *Degree requirements:* For master's, thesis, interactive Program of Study (iPOS) submitted before completing 50 percent of required credit hours; for doctorate, comprehensive exam, thesis/dissertation, interactive Program of Study (iPOS) submitted before completing 50 percent of required credit hours. *Entrance requirements:* For master's and doctorate, GRE, minimum GPA of 3.0 or equivalent in last 2 years of work leading to bachelor's degree. Additional exam requirements/recommendations for international students: Required—TOEFL, IELTS, or PTE. Electronic applications accepted. *Expenses:* Contact institution.

Auburn University at Montgomery, College of Public Policy and Justice, Department of Sociology, Anthropology and Geography, Montgomery, AL 36124-4023. Offers geographic information systems (MS). *Faculty:* 2 full-time (0 women). *Students:* 1 full-time (0 women), 10 part-time (5 women); includes 2 minority (1 Black or African American, non-Hispanic/Latino; 1 Two or more races, non-Hispanic/Latino). Average age 37. 4 applicants, 100% accepted, 3 enrolled. In 2017, 1 master's awarded. *Entrance requirements:* For master's, GRE or MAT. Additional exam requirements/recommendations for international students: Recommended—TOEFL (minimum score 500 paper-based; 61 iBT), IELTS (minimum score 5.5), TSE (minimum score 44). *Application deadline:* For fall admission, 7/15 for international students; for spring admission, 11/15 for international students; for summer admission, 4/15 for international students. Applications are processed on a rolling basis. Application fee: $25. Electronic applications accepted. *Expenses:* Tuition, state resident: full-time $6930; part-time $385 per credit hour. Tuition, nonresident: full-time $15,588; part-time $866 per credit hour. *Required fees:* $640. *Financial support:* Applicants required to submit FAFSA. *Unit head:* Dr. Annice Yarber-Allen, Chair, 334-244-3432, Fax: 334-244-3740, E-mail: ayarber@aum.edu.
Website: http://cppj.aum.edu/departments/sociology

Ball State University, Graduate School, College of Sciences and Humanities, Department of Geography, Muncie, IN 47306. Offers geographic information systems (Certificate); geography (MS); professional meteorology and climatology (Certificate). *Program availability:* Part-time. *Faculty:* 8 full-time (2 women). *Students:* 5 full-time (4 women), 4 part-time (1 woman); includes 1 minority (Hispanic/Latino), 1 international. Average age 24. 17 applicants, 71% accepted, 5 enrolled. In 2017, 3 master's awarded. *Entrance requirements:* For master's, minimum baccalaureate GPA of 2.75 or 3.0 in latter half of baccalaureate, letter of interest, three letters of recommendation, resume or curriculum vitae, official transcripts. Additional exam requirements/recommendations for international students: Required—TOEFL (minimum score 550 paper-based; 79 iBT), IELTS (minimum score 6.5). *Application deadline:* Applications are processed on a rolling basis. Application fee: $60. Electronic applications accepted. *Financial support:* In 2017–18, 5 students received support, including 5 teaching assistantships with partial tuition reimbursements available (averaging $9,800 per year). Financial award application deadline: 3/1; financial award applicants required to submit FAFSA. *Faculty research:* Remote sensing, tourism and recreation, Latin American urbanization. *Unit head:* Dr. Kevin Turcotte, Chairperson/Professor, 765-285-1776, Fax: 765-285-2351, E-mail: turk@bsu.edu. *Application contact:* Dr. Jason Yang, Associate Professor/Graduate Program Director, 765-285-1761, Fax: 765-285-2351, E-mail: jyang@bsu.edu.
Website: http://www.bsu.edu/geography/

Boston University, Graduate School of Arts and Sciences, Department of Earth and Environment, Boston, MA 02215. Offers earth and environment (MA, PhD); energy and environment (MA); remote sensing and geospatial sciences (MA). *Students:* 67 full-time (33 women), 7 part-time (5 women); includes 7 minority (2 Asian, non-Hispanic/Latino; 4 Hispanic/Latino; 1 Two or more races, non-Hispanic/Latino), 30 international. Average age 25. 252 applicants, 54% accepted, 41 enrolled. In 2017, 18 master's, 8 doctorates awarded. Terminal master's awarded for partial completion of doctoral program. *Degree requirements:* For master's, comprehensive exam (for some programs), thesis (for some programs); for doctorate, comprehensive exam, thesis/dissertation. *Entrance requirements:* For master's and doctorate, GRE General Test, 3 letters of recommendation, official transcripts, personal statement. Additional exam requirements/recommendations for international students: Required—TOEFL (minimum score 550 paper-based; 84 iBT). *Application deadline:* For fall admission, 12/19 for domestic and international students; for winter admission, 11/1 for domestic and international students. Application fee: $95. Electronic applications accepted. *Financial support:* In 2017–18, 43 students received support, including 6 fellowships with full tuition reimbursements available (averaging $22,000 per year), 21 research assistantships with full tuition reimbursements available (averaging $22,000 per year), 14 teaching assistantships with full tuition reimbursements available (averaging $22,000 per year); Federal Work-Study, scholarships/grants, traineeships, and health care benefits also available. Financial award application deadline: 12/19. *Faculty research:* Biogeosciences, climate and surface processes; energy, environment and society; geographical sciences; geology, geochemistry and geophysics. *Unit head:* Mark Friedl, Interim Chair, 617-353-5745, E-mail: friedl@bu.edu. *Application contact:* Alissa Beideck, Graduate Program Coordinator, 617-353-2529, Fax: 617-353-8399, E-mail:

abeideck@bu.edu.
Website: http://www.bu.edu/earth/

Central Michigan University, College of Graduate Studies, College of Science and Technology, Department of Geography, Mount Pleasant, MI 48859. Offers geographic information sciences (MS). *Degree requirements:* For master's, thesis optional. *Entrance requirements:* For master's, GRE.

Chicago State University, School of Graduate and Professional Studies, College of Arts and Sciences, Department of Geography, Sociology, History, African-American Studies and Anthropology, Chicago, IL 60628. Offers geographic information systems (MA); history (MA). *Entrance requirements:* For master's, minimum GPA of 3.0. *Application deadline:* For fall admission, 3/15 for domestic students; for spring admission, 10/15 for domestic students. Application fee: $30. *Unit head:* Dr. Arthur Redman, Chair, 773-995-2186, Fax: 773-995-2030. *Application contact:* Anika Miller, Graduate Studies Office, 773-995-2404, E-mail: g-studies1@csu.edu.
Website: http://www.csu.edu/gsea/

Claremont Graduate University, Graduate Programs, Center for Information Systems and Technology, Claremont, CA 91711-6160. Offers cybersecurity and networking (MS); data science and analytics (MS); electronic commerce (PhD); geographic information systems (MS); health informatics (MS); information systems (Certificate); IT strategy and innovation (MS); knowledge management (PhD); systems development (PhD); telecommunications and networking (PhD); MBA/MS. *Program availability:* Part-time. *Degree requirements:* For doctorate, comprehensive exam, thesis/dissertation, portfolio. *Entrance requirements:* For master's and doctorate, GMAT, GRE General Test. Additional exam requirements/recommendations for international students: Required—TOEFL (minimum score 75 iBT). Electronic applications accepted. *Faculty research:* Man-machine interaction, organizational aspects of computing, implementation of information systems, information systems practice.

Clark University, Graduate School, Department of International Development, Community, and Environment, Program in Geographic Information Science for Development and Environment, Worcester, MA 01610-1477. Offers MS. *Students:* 41 full-time (21 women); includes 7 minority (1 Black or African American, non-Hispanic/Latino; 2 Asian, non-Hispanic/Latino; 2 Hispanic/Latino; 2 Two or more races, non-Hispanic/Latino), 16 international. Average age 26. 158 applicants, 59% accepted, 37 enrolled. In 2017, 20 master's awarded. *Degree requirements:* For master's, thesis. *Entrance requirements:* For master's, 2 references, resume or curriculum vitae, personal statement. Additional exam requirements/recommendations for international students: Required—TOEFL (minimum score 575 paper-based; 90 iBT), IELTS (minimum score 6.5). *Application deadline:* For fall admission, 4/15 for domestic and international students. Application fee: $75. Electronic applications accepted. *Expenses:* $5,685 tuition per unit, $490 fees. *Financial support:* Fellowships, research assistantships, teaching assistantships, institutionally sponsored loans, and scholarships/grants available. *Faculty research:* Land-use change, the effects of environmental influences on child health and development, quantitative methods, watershed management, brownfields redevelopment, human/environment interactions, biodiversity conservation, climate change. *Unit head:* Dr. Ron Eastman, 508-839-2321, E-mail: reastman@clarku.edu. *Application contact:* Sawsan Berjawi, Manager of Academic and Student Affairs, 508-421-3846, Fax: 508-793-8820, E-mail: sberjawi@clarku.edu.
Website: http://www.clarku.edu/programs/masters-geographic-information-science-development-and-environment

Cleveland State University, College of Graduate Studies, Maxine Goodman Levin College of Urban Affairs, Program in Urban Planning and Development, Cleveland, OH 44115. Offers economic development (MUPD); environmental sustainability (MUPD); historic preservation (MUPD); housing and neighborhood development (MUPD); real estate development and finance (MUPD); urban economic development (Certificate); urban geographic information systems (MUPD); JD/MUPDD. *Accreditation:* ACSP. *Program availability:* Part-time, evening/weekend. *Faculty:* 16 full-time (8 women), 13 part-time/adjunct (5 women). *Students:* 20 full-time (7 women), 15 part-time (5 women); includes 1 minority (Black or African American, non-Hispanic/Latino), 2 international. Average age 28. 48 applicants, 56% accepted, 14 enrolled. In 2017, 24 master's awarded. *Degree requirements:* For master's, thesis or alternative, exit project. *Entrance requirements:* For master's, GRE General Test (minimum score: 50th percentile combined verbal and quantitative, 4.0 analytical writing), minimum GPA of 3.0. Additional exam requirements/recommendations for international students: Required—TOEFL (minimum score 550 paper-based; 78 iBT), IELTS (6.0), or International Test of English Proficiency (iTEP). *Application deadline:* For fall admission, 7/1 priority date for domestic students; 5/15 for international students; for spring admission, 11/15 for domestic students, 11/1 for international students; for summer admission, 4/1 for domestic students, 3/15 for international students. Applications are processed on a rolling basis. Application fee: $40. Electronic applications accepted. *Expenses:* Contact institution. *Financial support:* In 2017–18, 10 students received support, including 5 research assistantships with full tuition reimbursements available (averaging $7,200 per year), 3 teaching assistantships with partial tuition reimbursements available (averaging $2,400 per year); scholarships/grants, tuition waivers (full and partial), and unspecified assistantships also available. Support available to part-time students. Financial award application deadline: 3/1; financial award applicants required to submit FAFSA. *Faculty research:* Housing and neighborhood development, urban housing policy, environmental sustainability, economic development, GIS and planning decision support. *Unit head:* Dr. Stephanie Ryberg-Webster, Assistant Professor/Program Director, 216-802-3386, Fax: 216-687-2013, E-mail: s.ryberg@csuohio.edu. *Application contact:* David Arrighi, Graduate Academic Advisor, 216-523-7522, Fax: 216-687-5398, E-mail: d.arrighi@csuohio.edu.
Website: http://www.csuohio.edu/urban/mupd/mupd

The College of William and Mary, Faculty of Arts and Sciences, Department of Applied Science, Williamsburg, VA 23185. Offers accelerator science (PhD); applied mathematics (PhD); applied mechanics (PhD); applied robotics (PhD); applied science (MS); atmospheric and environmental science (PhD); computational neuroscience (PhD); interface, thin film and surface science (PhD); lasers and optics (PhD); magnetic resonance (PhD); materials science and engineering (PhD); mathematical and computational biology (PhD); medical imaging (PhD); nanotechnology (PhD); neuroscience (PhD); non-destructive evaluation (PhD); polymer chemistry (PhD); remote sensing (PhD). *Program availability:* Part-time. *Faculty:* 11 full-time (3 women). *Students:* 30 full-time (11 women), 3 part-time (0 women); includes 6 minority (2 Black or African American, non-Hispanic/Latino; 1 Asian, non-Hispanic/Latino; 2 Hispanic/Latino; 1 Two or more races, non-Hispanic/Latino), 13 international. Average age 27. 34 applicants, 47% accepted, 10 enrolled. In 2017, 5 doctorates awarded. Terminal master's awarded for partial completion of doctoral program. *Degree requirements:* For

master's, comprehensive exam, thesis; for doctorate, comprehensive exam, thesis/dissertation, 4 core courses. *Entrance requirements:* For master's and doctorate, GRE General Test, GRE Subject Test. Additional exam requirements/recommendations for international students: Required—TOEFL, IELTS. *Application deadline:* For fall admission, 2/1 priority date for domestic students, 2/1 for international students; for spring admission, 10/5 priority date for domestic students, 10/5 for international students. Applications are processed on a rolling basis. Application fee: $50. Electronic applications accepted. *Expenses:* Contact institution. *Financial support:* In 2017–18, 8 students received support, including 27 research assistantships (averaging $26,000 per year), 1 teaching assistantship (averaging $9,500 per year); fellowships, scholarships/grants, health care benefits, tuition waivers (full), and unspecified assistantships also available. Financial award application deadline: 4/15; financial award applicants required to submit FAFSA. *Faculty research:* Computational biology, non-destructive evaluation, neurophysiology, laser spectroscopy, nanotechnology. *Total annual research expenditures:* $536,220. *Unit head:* Dr. Christopher Del Negro, Chair, 757-221-7808, Fax: 757-221-2050, E-mail: cadeln@wm.edu. *Application contact:* Lianne Rios Ashburne, Graduate Program Coordinator, 757-221-2563, Fax: 757-221-2050, E-mail: lrashburne@wm.edu.
Website: http://www.wm.edu/as/appliedscience

East Carolina University, Graduate School, Thomas Harriot College of Arts and Sciences, Department of Geography, Planning, and Environment, Greenville, NC 27858-4353. Offers development and environmental planning (Certificate); economic development (Certificate); geographic information science and technology (Certificate); geography (MA), including geography, planning, rural development. *Program availability:* Part-time, evening/weekend, online learning. *Students:* 15 full-time (8 women), 6 part-time (2 women); includes 4 minority (3 Black or African American, non-Hispanic/Latino; 1 Hispanic/Latino). Average age 27. 14 applicants, 93% accepted, 8 enrolled. In 2017, 5 master's, 1 other advanced degree awarded. *Degree requirements:* For master's, comprehensive exam, thesis optional. *Entrance requirements:* For master's, GRE General Test. Additional exam requirements/recommendations for international students: Recommended—TOEFL (minimum score 78 iBT), IELTS (minimum score 6.5). *Application deadline:* For fall admission, 4/1 priority date for domestic and international students. Applications are processed on a rolling basis. Application fee: $75. Electronic applications accepted. *Expenses:* Tuition, state resident: full-time $4749; part-time $297 per credit hour. Tuition, nonresident: full-time $17,898; part-time $1119 per credit hour. *Required fees:* $2691; $224 per credit hour. Part-time tuition and fees vary according to course load and program. *Financial support:* Research assistantships with partial tuition reimbursements, teaching assistantships with partial tuition reimbursements, and Federal Work-Study available. Support available to part-time students. Financial award application deadline: 3/1. *Faculty research:* Coastal vulnerability and adaptation, emergency management, public understanding of risk, catastrophic events. *Unit head:* Dr. Thad Wasklewicz, Chair, 252-328-6230, E-mail: wasklewiczt@ecu.edu. *Application contact:* Dean of Graduate School, 252-328-6012, Fax: 252-328-6071, E-mail: gradschool@ecu.edu.
Website: http://www.ecu.edu/geog/

Eastern Illinois University, Graduate School, College of Liberal Arts and Sciences, Department of Geology and Geography, Charleston, IL 61920. Offers geographic information sciences (PSM). *Program availability:* Part-time, evening/weekend. *Entrance requirements:* For master's, GMAT or GRE. Additional exam requirements/recommendations for international students: Required—TOEFL (minimum score 500 paper-based; 61 iBT), IELTS (minimum score 6). *Application deadline:* For fall admission, 5/15 for domestic and international students; for spring admission, 10/15 for domestic and international students. Applications are processed on a rolling basis. Application fee: $30. Electronic applications accepted. *Financial support:* Teaching assistantships with full tuition reimbursements, career-related internships or fieldwork, Federal Work-Study, and unspecified assistantships available. Support available to part-time students. Financial award application deadline: 3/1; financial award applicants required to submit FAFSA. *Unit head:* Dr. Barry J. Kronenfeld, Vice Chair/Graduate Coordinator, 217-581-7014, Fax: 217-581-7141, E-mail: bjkronenfeld@eiu.edu. *Application contact:* Dr. Barry J. Kronenfeld, Vice Chair/Graduate Coordinator, 217-581-7014, Fax: 217-581-7141, E-mail: bjkronenfeld@eiu.edu.
Website: http://www.eiu.edu/psm/index.php

Eastern Illinois University, Graduate School, Lumpkin College of Business and Technology, Program in Business Administration, Charleston, IL 61920. Offers accountancy (MBA); applied management (MBA); geographic information systems (MBA); research (MBA). *Accreditation:* AACSB. *Program availability:* Part-time, evening/weekend. *Entrance requirements:* For master's, GMAT or GRE. Additional exam requirements/recommendations for international students: Required—TOEFL (minimum score 500 paper-based; 61 iBT), IELTS (minimum score 6). *Application deadline:* For fall admission, 5/15 for domestic and international students; for spring admission, 10/15 for domestic and international students. Applications are processed on a rolling basis. Application fee: $30. Electronic applications accepted. *Financial support:* Research assistantships with full tuition reimbursements, teaching assistantships with full tuition reimbursements, career-related internships or fieldwork, Federal Work-Study, and unspecified assistantships available. Support available to part-time students. Financial award application deadline: 3/1; financial award applicants required to submit FAFSA. *Unit head:* Dr. Melody L. Wollan, Coordinator, 217-581-3028, Fax: 217-581-6642, E-mail: mlwollan@eiu.edu. *Application contact:* Dr. Melody L. Wollan, Coordinator, 217-581-3028, Fax: 217-581-6642, E-mail: mlwollan@eiu.edu.
Website: http://www.eiu.edu/mba/index.php

Eastern Michigan University, Graduate School, College of Arts and Sciences, Department of Geography and Geology, Programs in Geographic Information Systems, Ypsilanti, MI 48197. Offers geographic information systems (MS); geographic information systems for educators (Graduate Certificate); geographic information systems for professionals (Graduate Certificate). *Students:* 10 full-time (4 women), 14 part-time (2 women), 12 international. Average age 27. 10 applicants, 90% accepted, 7 enrolled. In 2017, 10 master's, 2 other advanced degrees awarded. Application fee: $45. *Application contact:* Dr. Hugh Semple, Program Advisor, 734-487-8169, Fax: 734-487-6979, E-mail: hsemple@emich.edu.

East Tennessee State University, School of Graduate Studies, College of Arts and Sciences, Department of Geosciences, Johnson City, TN 37614-1709. Offers geographic information systems (Postbaccalaureate Certificate); geospatial analysis (MS); paleontology (MS). *Program availability:* Part-time. *Degree requirements:* For master's, thesis. *Entrance requirements:* For master's, bachelor's degree in geosciences or related discipline, minimum GPA of 3.0, three letters of recommendation, resume, two-page letter that discusses career goals and specific academic and research interests; for Postbaccalaureate Certificate, minimum undergraduate GPA of 2.5, personal essay. Additional exam requirements/recommendations for international students: Required—TOEFL (minimum score 550 paper-based; 79 iBT). *Application deadline:* For fall admission, 2/1 for domestic and international students. Application fee: $55 ($65 for international students). Electronic applications accepted. *Financial support:* Research assistantships with full tuition reimbursements, teaching assistantships with full tuition reimbursements, career-related

internships or fieldwork, institutionally sponsored loans, scholarships/grants, and unspecified assistantships available. Financial award application deadline: 7/1; financial award applicants required to submit FAFSA. *Faculty research:* Vertebrate paleontology; volcanology; soils and geological engineering; geological hazards stemming from volcanoes and tsunamis and the sociological responses; applications of geospatial analysis to meteorology, weather and climate, and geomorphology/watershed management; shallow surface geophysics, sedimentology, and stratigraphy. *Unit head:* Arpita Nandi, Chair, 423-439-6086, Fax: 423-439-7520, E-mail: nandi@etsu.edu. *Application contact:* Ingrid Luffman, Graduate Coordinator, 423-439-7551, Fax: 423-439-5624, E-mail: luffman@etsu.edu.
Website: http://www.etsu.edu/cas/geosciences/

Elizabeth City State University, Department of Mathematics and Computer Science, Master of Science in Mathematics Program, Elizabeth City, NC 27909-7806. Offers applied mathematics (MS); community college teaching (MS); mathematics education (MS); remote sensing (MS). *Program availability:* Part-time, evening/weekend. *Faculty:* 7 full-time (2 women). *Students:* 25 part-time (13 women); includes 19 minority (all Black or African American, non-Hispanic/Latino). Average age 25. 5 applicants, 80% accepted, 4 enrolled. In 2017, 18 master's awarded. *Degree requirements:* For master's, thesis. *Entrance requirements:* For master's, MAT and/or GRE, minimum GPA of 3.0, 3 letters of recommendation, two official transcripts from all undergraduate/graduate schools attended, typewritten one-page request for entry into program that includes description of student's educational preparation. Additional exam requirements/recommendations for international students: Required—TOEFL (minimum score 550 paper-based, 80 iBT) or IELTS (minimum score 6.5). *Application deadline:* For fall admission, 7/15 priority date for domestic and international students; for spring admission, 11/15 priority date for domestic and international students; for summer admission, 3/15 priority date for domestic and international students. Applications are processed on a rolling basis. Application fee: $30. Electronic applications accepted. Tuition and fees vary according to course load and program. *Financial support:* In 2017–18, 22 students received support, including 3 research assistantships (averaging $19,000 per year), 2 teaching assistantships (averaging $18,000 per year); scholarships/grants and tuition waivers also available. Financial award application deadline: 6/30; financial award applicants required to submit FAFSA. *Faculty research:* Oceanic temperature effects, mathematics strategies in elementary schools, multimedia, Antarctic temperature mapping, computer networks, water quality, remote sensing, polar ice, satellite imagery. *Total annual research expenditures:* $25,000. *Unit head:* Dr. Kenneth L. Jones, Chair, 252-335-3858, E-mail: kljones@ecsu.edu. *Application contact:* Dr. Sharon D. Raynor, Director, Graduate Education Program, 252-335-3945, E-mail: sdraynor@ecsu.edu.
Website: http://www.ecsu.edu/academics/mathsciencetechnology/

Elmhurst College, Graduate Programs, Program in Geographic Information Systems, Elmhurst, IL 60126-3296. Offers MS. *Program availability:* Part-time, evening/weekend, online only, 100% online. *Faculty:* 6 part-time/adjunct (2 women). *Students:* 16 part-time (10 women); includes 2 minority (1 American Indian or Alaska Native, non-Hispanic/Latino; 1 Hispanic/Latino). Average age 31. 28 applicants, 68% accepted, 16 enrolled. In 2017, 5 master's awarded. *Entrance requirements:* For master's, 3 recommendations, resume, statement of purpose. Additional exam requirements/recommendations for international students: Required—TOEFL (minimum score 550 paper-based; 79 iBT). *Application deadline:* Applications are processed on a rolling basis. Application fee: $0. Electronic applications accepted. *Expenses:* Contact institution. *Financial support:* In 2017–18, 6 students received support. Scholarships/grants available. Support available to part-time students. Financial award application deadline: 3/1; financial award applicants required to submit FAFSA. *Unit head:* Judy Bock, Director, 630-617-3128, E-mail: judith.bock@elmhurst.edu. *Application contact:* Timothy J. Panfil, Director of Enrollment Management, 630-617-3300 Ext. 3256, Fax: 630-617-6471, E-mail: panfilt@elmhurst.edu.
Website: http://www.elmhurst.edu/applied_geospatial_sciences

Florida State University, The Graduate School, College of Social Sciences and Public Policy, Department of Geography, Tallahassee, FL 32306. Offers geographic information science (MS); geography (MA, MS, PhD). *Program availability:* Part-time. *Faculty:* 12 full-time (3 women), 7 part-time/adjunct (5 women). *Students:* 47 full-time (21 women), 13 part-time (5 women); includes 16 minority (1 Black or African American, non-Hispanic/Latino; 1 Asian, non-Hispanic/Latino; 2 Hispanic/Latino; 12 Two or more races, non-Hispanic/Latino), 9 international. Average age 30. 70 applicants, 73% accepted, 30 enrolled. In 2017, 17 master's, 4 doctorates awarded. Terminal master's awarded for partial completion of doctoral program. *Degree requirements:* For master's, thesis (for some programs); for doctorate, comprehensive exam, thesis/dissertation. *Entrance requirements:* For master's and doctorate, GRE General Test, minimum GPA of 3.0. Additional exam requirements/recommendations for international students: Required—TOEFL (minimum score 80 iBT). *Application deadline:* For fall admission, 3/1 priority date for domestic and international students; for spring admission, 10/1 priority date for domestic and international students. Applications are processed on a rolling basis. Application fee: $30. Electronic applications accepted. *Financial support:* In 2017–18, 44 students received support, including 7 research assistantships with full tuition reimbursements available (averaging $17,687 per year), 37 teaching assistantships with full tuition reimbursements available (averaging $17,687 per year); career-related internships or fieldwork, Federal Work-Study, institutionally sponsored loans, scholarships/grants, health care benefits, tuition waivers (full and partial), and unspecified assistantships also available. Financial award application deadline: 3/1; financial award applicants required to submit FAFSA. *Faculty research:* Society-nature interactions, geographic information science, environmental studies, hurricanes, remote sensing, urban, transportation, race and indigenous populations. *Total annual research expenditures:* $159,022. *Unit head:* Prof. James Elsner, Chair, 850-644-1706, Fax: 850-644-5913, E-mail: jelsner@fsu.edu. *Application contact:* Prof. Victor Mesev, Graduate Director, 850-645-2498, Fax: 850-644-5193, E-mail: vmesev@fsu.edu.
Website: http://geography.fsu.edu/

George Mason University, College of Science, Department of Geography and Geoinformation Science, Fairfax, VA 22030. Offers earth system science (MS); earth systems and geoinformation sciences (PhD); environmental geoinformation science and biodiversity conservation (Certificate); geography and geoinformation science (Certificate). *Faculty:* 18 full-time (3 women), 4 part-time/adjunct (0 women). *Students:* 67 full-time (25 women), 91 part-time (31 women); includes 23 minority (4 Black or African American, non-Hispanic/Latino; 12 Asian, non-Hispanic/Latino; 5 Hispanic/Latino; 2 Two or more races, non-Hispanic/Latino), 35 international. Average age 34. 78 applicants, 82% accepted, 36 enrolled. In 2017, 25 master's, 14 doctorates, 14 other advanced degrees awarded. *Degree requirements:* For master's, comprehensive exam (for some programs), thesis (for some programs); for doctorate, comprehensive exam, thesis/dissertation. *Entrance requirements:* For master's, GRE, bachelor's degree with minimum GPA of 3.0; 2 copies of official transcripts; current resume; expanded goals statement; 3 letters of recommendation; for doctorate, GRE, bachelor's degree with minimum GPA of 3.0; 2 copies of official transcripts; 3 letters of recommendation; resume; expanded goals statement; for Certificate, GRE, baccalaureate degree with minimum GPA of 3.0; 2 official copies of transcripts; expanded goals statement; 3 letters of recommendation; resume. Additional exam requirements/recommendations for

international students: Required—TOEFL (minimum score 575 paper-based; 88 iBT), IELTS (minimum score 6.5), PTE (minimum score 59). *Application deadline:* For fall admission, 2/1 priority date for domestic and international students. Application fee: $75 ($80 for international students). Electronic applications accepted. *Expenses:* $895 per credit in-state tuition, $1,616 out-of-state. *Financial support:* In 2017–18, 34 students received support, including 1 fellowship, 22 research assistantships with tuition reimbursements available (averaging $16,785 per year), 12 teaching assistantships with tuition reimbursements available (averaging $10,352 per year); career-related internships or fieldwork, Federal Work-Study, scholarships/grants, unspecified assistantships, and health care benefits (for full-time research or teaching assistantship recipients) also available. Support available to part-time students. Financial award application deadline: 3/1; financial award applicants required to submit FAFSA. *Faculty research:* Urban geography; remote sensing; spatial databases; crowdsourcing geospatial data; spatial data mining. *Total annual research expenditures:* $1.2 million. *Unit head:* Anthony Stefanidis, Acting Chair, 703-993-9237, Fax: 703-993-9230, E-mail: astefani@gmu.edu. *Application contact:* Samantha Cooke, Department Manager, 703-993-1212, E-mail: scooke4@gmu.edu.
Website: http://ggs.gmu.edu/

Georgia Institute of Technology, Graduate Studies, College of Design, School of City and Regional Planning, Atlanta, GA 30332-0001. Offers city and regional planning (PhD); economic development (MCRP); environmental planning and management (MCRP); geographic information systems (MCRP); land and community development (MCRP); land use planning (MCRP); transportation (MCRP); urban design (MCRP); MCP/MSCE. *Accreditation:* ACSP. *Degree requirements:* For master's, thesis, internship. *Entrance requirements:* For master's, GRE General Test, minimum GPA of 2.7. Additional exam requirements/recommendations for international students: Required—TOEFL. Electronic applications accepted.

Georgia State University, College of Arts and Sciences, Department of Geosciences, Program in Geographic Information Systems, Atlanta, GA 30302-3083. Offers Certificate. *Program availability:* Part-time. *Entrance requirements:* For degree, GRE. Additional exam requirements/recommendations for international students: Required—TOEFL (minimum score 550 paper-based; 80 iBT). Electronic applications accepted. *Expenses:* Tuition, state resident: full-time $7020. Tuition, nonresident: full-time $22,518. *Required fees:* $2128. Tuition and fees vary according to degree level and program. *Financial support:* Career-related internships or fieldwork available. *Faculty research:* Geographic information science. *Unit head:* Dr. W. Crawford Elliott, Chair, 404-413-5756, E-mail: wcelliott@gsu.edu.
Website: http://geosciences.gsu.edu/grad-programs/

Hood College, Graduate School, Program in Environmental Biology, Frederick, MD 21701-8575. Offers environmental biology (MS); geographic information systems (Certificate). *Program availability:* Part-time, evening/weekend. *Faculty:* 2 full-time (1 woman), 3 part-time/adjunct (2 women). *Students:* 4 full-time (3 women), 35 part-time (25 women); includes 8 minority (2 Black or African American, non-Hispanic/Latino; 2 Asian, non-Hispanic/Latino; 2 Hispanic/Latino; 2 Two or more races, non-Hispanic/Latino), 2 international. Average age 30. 16 applicants, 81% accepted, 7 enrolled. In 2017, 12 master's, 7 other advanced degrees awarded. *Degree requirements:* For master's, thesis or alternative. *Entrance requirements:* For master's, minimum GPA of 2.75, 1 year of undergraduate biology and chemistry, 1 semester of mathematics, essay. Additional exam requirements/recommendations for international students: Required—TOEFL (minimum score 575 paper-based; 89 iBT), IELTS (minimum score 6.5). *Application deadline:* For fall admission, 8/15 priority date for domestic students, 8/5 for international students; for spring admission, 12/1 priority date for domestic students, 12/1 for international students; for summer admission, 5/1 for domestic students, 4/15 for international students. Applications are processed on a rolling basis. Application fee: $35. Electronic applications accepted. *Expenses:* $465 per credit plus $110 comprehensive fee per semester. *Financial support:* Research assistantships with full tuition reimbursements, tuition waivers (partial), and unspecified assistantships available. Financial award applicants required to submit FAFSA. *Unit head:* Dr. April M. Boulton, Dean of the Graduate School, 301-696-3600, E-mail: gofurther@hood.edu. *Application contact:* Jan Marcus, Assistant Director of Graduate Admissions, 301-696-3600, E-mail: gofurther@hood.edu.
Website: http://www.hood.edu/graduate

Hunter College of the City University of New York, Graduate School, School of Arts and Sciences, Department of Geography, New York, NY 10065-5085. Offers geographic information science (Certificate); geography (MA); geoinformatics (MS). *Program availability:* Part-time, evening/weekend. *Degree requirements:* For master's, comprehensive exam or thesis. *Entrance requirements:* For master's, GRE General Test, minimum B average in major, B- overall; 18 credits of course work in geography; 2 letters of recommendation; for Certificate, minimum B average in major, B- overall. Additional exam requirements/recommendations for international students: Required—TOEFL. *Faculty research:* Urban geography, economic geography, geographic information science, demographic methods, climate change.

Idaho State University, Office of Graduate Studies, College of Science and Engineering, Department of Geosciences, Pocatello, ID 83209-8072. Offers geographic information science (MS); geology (MNS, MS); geology with emphasis in environmental geoscience (MS); geophysics/hydrology/geology (MS); geotechnology (Postbaccalaureate Certificate). *Program availability:* Part-time. *Degree requirements:* For master's, comprehensive exam, thesis, oral colloquium; for Postbaccalaureate Certificate, thesis optional, minimum 19 credits. *Entrance requirements:* For master's, GRE General Test (minimum 50th percentile in 2 sections), 3 letters of recommendation; for Postbaccalaureate Certificate, GRE General Test, 3 letters of recommendation, bachelor's degree, statement of goals. Additional exam requirements/recommendations for international students: Required—TOEFL (minimum score 550 paper-based; 80 iBT). Electronic applications accepted. *Faculty research:* Quantitative field mapping and sampling: microscopic, geochemical, and isotopic analysis of rocks, minerals and water; remote sensing, geographic information systems, and global positioning systems: environmental and watershed management; surficial and fluvial processes: landscape change; regional tectonics, structural geology; planetary geology.

Indiana University of Pennsylvania, School of Graduate Studies and Research, College of Humanities and Social Sciences, Department of Geography and Regional Planning, Geographic Information Science/Cartography Track, Indiana, PA 15705. Offers MS. *Program availability:* Part-time. *Faculty:* 10 full-time (2 women). *Students:* 2 full-time (0 women). Average age 27. 1 applicant, 100% accepted, 1 enrolled. In 2017, 1 master's awarded. *Degree requirements:* For master's, thesis optional. *Entrance requirements:* Additional exam requirements/recommendations for international students: Required—TOEFL (minimum score 550 paper-based). *Application deadline:* Applications are processed on a rolling basis. Application fee: $50. Electronic applications accepted. *Expenses:* Tuition, state resident: full-time $12,000; part-time $500 per credit. Tuition, nonresident: full-time $18,000; part-time $750 per credit. *Required fees:* $4073; $165.55 per credit. $64 per term. *Financial support:* In 2017–18, 4 research assistantships with tuition reimbursements (averaging $5,198 per year) were awarded; career-related internships or fieldwork, Federal Work-Study, scholarships/grants, and unspecified assistantships also available. Financial award application deadline: 4/15; financial award applicants required to submit FAFSA. *Unit head:* Dr. Richard Hoch, Graduate Coordinator, 724-357-5990, E-mail: richard.hoch@iup.edu.
Website: http://www.iup.edu/georegionalplan/grad/default.aspx

Indiana University of Pennsylvania, School of Graduate Studies and Research, College of Humanities and Social Sciences, Department of Geography and Regional Planning, Program in Geographic Information Science and Geospatial Techniques, Indiana, PA 15705. Offers Certificate. *Faculty:* 10 full-time (2 women). *Students:* 3 applicants, 100% accepted. In 2017, 1 Certificate awarded. *Entrance requirements:* Additional exam requirements/recommendations for international students: Required—TOEFL (minimum score 550 paper-based). *Application deadline:* Applications are processed on a rolling basis. Application fee: $50. Electronic applications accepted. *Expenses:* Tuition, state resident: full-time $12,000; part-time $500 per credit. Tuition, nonresident: full-time $18,000; part-time $750 per credit. *Required fees:* $4073; $165.55 per credit. $64 per term. *Financial support:* Application deadline: 4/15; applicants required to submit FAFSA. *Unit head:* Dr. Richard Hoch, Graduate Coordinator, 724-357-5990, E-mail: richard.hoch@iup.edu.
Website: http://www.iup.edu/georegionalplan/grad/default.aspx

Indiana University–Purdue University Indianapolis, School of Liberal Arts, Department of Geography, Indianapolis, IN 46202. Offers geographic information systems (MS, Certificate). *Program availability:* Part-time. *Degree requirements:* For master's, variable foreign language requirement, thesis; for Certificate, variable foreign language requirement. *Entrance requirements:* For master's, GRE (minimum verbal or quantitative score of 600, with the other score above 500), minimum GPA of 3.0; for Certificate, minimum GPA of 3.0. Additional exam requirements/recommendations for international students: Required—TOEFL (minimum score 550 paper-based), IELTS. Electronic applications accepted. *Expenses:* Contact institution. *Faculty research:* Remote sensing, geographic information systems, epidemiology, public health, weather and climate, soils.

Johns Hopkins University, Zanvyl Krieger School of Arts and Sciences, Advanced Academic Programs, Program in Environmental Sciences and Policy, Washington, DC 20036. Offers energy policy and climate (MS); environmental sciences (MS); geographic information systems (MS, Certificate). *Program availability:* Part-time, evening/weekend, online learning. *Degree requirements:* For master's, thesis (for some programs). *Entrance requirements:* For master's, minimum GPA of 3.0, coursework in chemistry and calculus. Additional exam requirements/recommendations for international students: Required—TOEFL (minimum score 100 iBT). Electronic applications accepted.

Kansas State University, Graduate School, College of Arts and Sciences, Department of Geography, Manhattan, KS 66506. Offers geographic information science (Graduate Certificate); geography (MA, PhD). *Degree requirements:* For master's, thesis optional, oral exam; for doctorate, one foreign language, thesis/dissertation. *Entrance requirements:* For master's and doctorate, GRE General Test, minimum GPA of 3.0. Electronic applications accepted. *Faculty research:* Human environment interaction, health and population, culture and landscape, physical geography, geospatial analysis and applications.

Kent State University, College of Arts and Sciences, Department of Geography, Kent, OH 44242-0001. Offers geographic information science (MGIS), including cyber geographic information science, environmental geographic information science, geographic information science and health; geography (MA, PhD). *Program availability:* Part-time. *Faculty:* 13 full-time (5 women), 3 part-time/adjunct (1 woman). *Students:* 41 full-time (12 women), 39 part-time (14 women); includes 14 minority (7 Black or African American, non-Hispanic/Latino; 3 Asian, non-Hispanic/Latino; 4 Two or more races, non-Hispanic/Latino), 19 international. Average age 31. 47 applicants, 77% accepted, 26 enrolled. In 2017, 5 master's, 4 doctorates awarded. *Degree requirements:* For master's, thesis, practicum (MGIS); for doctorate, comprehensive exam, thesis/dissertation. *Entrance requirements:* For master's, GRE, minimum undergraduate GPA of 3.0, undergraduate degree in geography or a related field, transcripts, two letters of recommendation, goal statement; for doctorate, GRE, transcripts, three letters of recommendation, goal statement, resume. Additional exam requirements/recommendations for international students: Required—TOEFL (minimum score 550 paper-based, 79 iBT), Michigan English Language Assessment Battery (minimum score 77), IELTS (minimum score 6.5) or PTE (minimum score 58). *Application deadline:* For fall admission, 2/1 for domestic and international students; for spring admission, 11/1 for domestic and international students; for summer admission, 4/1 for domestic and international students. Applications are processed on a rolling basis. Application fee: $45 ($70 for international students). Electronic applications accepted. *Expenses:* Tuition, state resident: full-time $11,310; part-time $515 per credit hour. Tuition, nonresident: full-time $20,396; part-time $928 per credit hour. *International tuition:* $18,544 full-time. *Financial support:* Fellowships with full tuition reimbursements, research assistantships with full tuition reimbursements, teaching assistantships with full tuition reimbursements, Federal Work-Study, scholarships/grants, and unspecified assistantships available. Financial award application deadline: 2/1. *Unit head:* Dr. Scott Sheridan, Professor and Chair, 330-672-3224, Fax: 330-672-4304, E-mail: ssherid1@kent.edu. *Application contact:* Dr. David H. Kaplan, Professor and Graduate Coordinator, 330-672-3221, E-mail: dkaplan@kent.edu.
Website: https://www.kent.edu/geography

Michigan Technological University, Graduate School, School of Technology, Houghton, MI 49931. Offers integrated geospatial technology (MS); medical informatics (MS). *Program availability:* Part-time, 100% online, blended/hybrid learning. *Faculty:* 16 full-time, 4 part-time/adjunct. *Students:* 8 full-time (4 women), 18 part-time (11 women); includes 2 minority (1 American Indian or Alaska Native, non-Hispanic/Latino; 1 Hispanic/Latino), 8 international. Average age 36. 70 applicants, 33% accepted, 5 enrolled. In 2017, 7 master's awarded. *Degree requirements:* For master's, comprehensive exam (for some programs), thesis (for some programs), thesis or comprehensive exam. *Entrance requirements:* For master's, GRE (for some programs), statement of purpose, personal statement, official transcripts, 2-3 letters of recommendation, resume/curriculum vitae. Additional exam requirements/recommendations for international students: Required—TOEFL (recommended minimum score 79 iBT) or IELTS (recommended minimum score of 6.5). *Application deadline:* Applications are processed on a rolling basis. Electronic applications accepted. *Expenses:* Tuition, state resident: full-time $17,100; part-time $950 per credit. Tuition, nonresident: full-time $17,100; part-time $950 per credit. *Required fees:* $248; $124 per term. Tuition and fees vary according to course load and program. *Financial support:* In 2017–18, 7 students received support, including 1 fellowship (averaging $15,790 per year), 3 research assistantships (averaging $15,790 per year); career-related internships or fieldwork, Federal Work-Study, scholarships/grants, and health care benefits also available. Financial award applicants required to submit FAFSA. *Faculty research:* Cybersecurity, medical image processing, sensory data fusion, architectural and archaeological laser scanning, high resolution remote sensing. *Total annual research expenditures:* $232,742. *Unit head:* Dr. James O. Frendewey, Dean, 906-487-2260, Fax: 906-487-2583, E-mail: jimf@mtu.edu. *Application contact:* Peggy A. Gorton, Executive Assistant, 906-487-2260, Fax: 906-487-2583, E-mail:

pagorton@mtu.edu.
Website: http://www.mtu.edu/technology/

Millersville University of Pennsylvania, College of Graduate Studies and Adult Learning, College of Science and Technology, Department of Earth Sciences, Program in Integrated Scientific Applications: GeoInformatics Option, Millersville, PA 17551-0302. Offers MS. *Program availability:* Part-time, evening/weekend, blended/hybrid learning. *Faculty:* 4 full-time (1 woman), 4 part-time/adjunct (0 women). *Students:* 3 full-time (1 woman). Average age 28. In 2017, 3 master's awarded. *Degree requirements:* For master's, thesis optional, internship, applied research. *Entrance requirements:* For master's, GRE, MAT or GMAT (if cumulative GPA is lower than 3.0), official transcript, three professional letters of recommendation, academic and professional goals statement, current resume. Additional exam requirements/recommendations for international students: Required—TOEFL (minimum score 80 iBT), IELTS (minimum score 6.5), PTE (minimum score 60). *Application deadline:* Applications are processed on a rolling basis. Application fee: $40. Electronic applications accepted. *Expenses:* $500 per credit resident tuition and fees; $750 per credit non-resident tuition and fees; $114.75 per credit general fee (maximum of 12 credits); technology fee $27 per credit (resident), $39 per credit (non-resident). *Financial support:* In 2017–18, 1 student received support. Unspecified assistantships available. Financial award application deadline: 3/15; financial award applicants required to submit FAFSA. *Faculty research:* Climatology and meteorology, remote sensing, geoinformatics, environmental economics and policy, business management, business operations analysis, finance and accounting, statistical applications, satellite data analytics. *Unit head:* Dr. Richard D. Clark, Chairperson and Graduate Program Coordinator, 717-871-7434, Fax: 717-871-7918, E-mail: richard.clark@millersville.edu. *Application contact:* Dr. Victor S. DeSantis, Dean of College of Graduate Studies and Adult Learning/Associate Provost for Civic and Community Engagement, 717-871-7619, Fax: 717-871-7954, E-mail: victor.desantis@millersville.edu.
Website: http://www.millersville.edu/esci/msisa/geoinformatics.php

Montclair State University, The Graduate School, College of Science and Mathematics, Geographic Information Science Certificate Program, Montclair, NJ 07043-1624. Offers Certificate.

Naval Postgraduate School, Departments and Academic Groups, Department of Information Sciences, Monterey, CA 93943. Offers electronic warfare systems engineering (MS); information sciences (PhD); information systems and operations (MS); information technology management (MS); information warfare systems engineering (MS); knowledge superiority (Certificate); remote sensing intelligence (MS); system technology (command, control and communications) (MS). Program open only to commissioned officers of the United States and friendly nations and selected United States federal civilian employees. *Program availability:* Part-time. *Degree requirements:* For master's, thesis (for some programs); for doctorate, thesis/dissertation. *Faculty research:* Designing inter-organisational collectivities for dynamic fit: stability, manoeuvrability and application in disaster relief endeavours; system self-awareness and related methods for Improving the use and understanding of data within DoD; evaluating a macrocognition model of team collaboration using real-world data from the Haiti relief effort; cyber distortion in command and control; performance and QoS in service-based systems.

North Carolina Central University, College of Arts and Sciences, Department of Environmental, Earth and Geospatial Sciences, Durham, NC 27707-3129. Offers earth sciences (MS); environmental and geographic sciences (MS). *Degree requirements:* For master's, one foreign language, comprehensive exam. *Entrance requirements:* For master's, GRE, minimum GPA of 3.0 in major, 2.5 overall. Additional exam requirements/recommendations for international students: Required—TOEFL. *Application deadline:* For fall admission, 8/1 for domestic students. Application fee: $30. *Expenses:* Tuition, state resident: full-time $2770; part-time $692.50 per credit hour. Tuition, nonresident: full-time $9247; part-time $2311.75 per credit hour. *Financial support:* Application deadline: 5/1. *Unit head:* Gordana Vlahovic, Chair, 919-530-5172, E-mail: gvlahovic@nccu.edu. *Application contact:* Gordana Vlahovic, Chair, 919-530-5172, E-mail: gvlahovic@nccu.edu.

North Carolina State University, Graduate School, College of Natural Resources, Department of Parks, Recreation and Tourism Management, Raleigh, NC 27695. Offers natural resource management (MPRTM, MS); park and recreation management (MPRTM, MS); parks, recreation and tourism management (PhD); recreational sport management (MPRTM, MS); spatial information science (MPRTM, MS); tourism policy and development (MPRTM, MS). *Degree requirements:* For master's, thesis (for some programs); for doctorate, thesis/dissertation. *Entrance requirements:* For master's and doctorate, GRE General Test. Additional exam requirements/recommendations for international students: Required—TOEFL. Electronic applications accepted. *Faculty research:* Tourism policy and development, spatial information systems, natural resource management, recreational sports management, park and recreation management.

Northeastern Illinois University, College of Graduate Studies and Research, College of Arts and Sciences, Program in Geography and Environmental Studies, Chicago, IL 60625. Offers geographic information science (Graduate Certificate); geography and environmental studies (MA). *Program availability:* Part-time, evening/weekend. *Degree requirements:* For master's, comprehensive exam, thesis optional. *Entrance requirements:* For master's, undergraduate minor in geography or environmental studies, minimum GPA of 2.75. Additional exam requirements/recommendations for international students: Required—TOEFL (minimum score 550 paper-based; 79 iBT). *Application deadline:* For fall admission, 4/1 priority date for domestic students; for spring admission, 8/15 for domestic students. Applications are processed on a rolling basis. Application fee: $30. Electronic applications accepted. *Expenses:* Tuition, state resident: full-time $7274; part-time $404.11 per credit hour. Tuition, nonresident: full-time $14,548; part-time $808.23 per credit hour. *Required fees:* $1284. *Financial support:* Applicants required to submit FAFSA. *Faculty research:* Segregation and urbanization of minority groups in the Chicago area, scale dependence and parameterization in nonpoint source pollution modeling, ecological land classification and mapping, ecosystem restoration, soil-vegetation relationships. *Unit head:* Dr. Michael Wenz, Acting Chair, 772-442-5597, E-mail: m-wenz@neiu.edu. *Application contact:* Martha Narvaez, Graduate Admission Representative, 773-442-6006, E-mail: m-narvaez@neiu.edu.

Northeastern University, College of Professional Studies, Boston, MA 02115-5096. Offers applied nutrition (MS); college athletics administration (MSL); commerce and economic development (MS); corporate and organizational communication (MS); criminal justice (MS); digital media (MPS); elearning and instructional design (M Ed); elementary education (MAT); geographic information technology (MPS); global studies and international relations (MS); higher education administration (M Ed); homeland security (MA); human services (MS); informatics (MPS); leadership (MS); learning analytics (M Ed); learning and instruction (M Ed); nonprofit management (MS); professional sports administration (MSL); project management (MS); regulatory affairs for drugs, biologics, and medical devices (MS); respiratory care leadership (MS); special education (M Ed); technical communication (MS). *Program availability:* Part-time, evening/weekend, 100% online, blended/hybrid learning. *Faculty:* 82 full-time (51

women), 853 part-time/adjunct (366 women). *Students:* 5,278 part-time (3,230 women). In 2017, 1,586 master's awarded. *Application deadline:* Applications are processed on a rolling basis. Application fee: $0. Electronic applications accepted. *Expenses:* Contact institution. *Financial support:* Applicants required to submit FAFSA. *Unit head:* Dr. Mary Loeffelholz, Dean of the College of Professional Studies. *Application contact:* E-mail: cpsadmissions@northeastern.edu.
Website: https://cps.northeastern.edu/

Northern Arizona University, College of Social and Behavioral Sciences, Department of Geography, Planning, and Recreation, Flagstaff, AZ 86011. Offers applied geospatial sciences (MS); community planning (Certificate); geographic information systems (Certificate); parks and recreation management (MS). *Program availability:* Part-time, 100% online, blended/hybrid learning. *Faculty:* 18 full-time (9 women), 1 part-time/adjunct (0 women). *Students:* 22 full-time (16 women), 25 part-time (11 women); includes 7 minority (3 Black or African American, non-Hispanic/Latino; 2 Hispanic/Latino; 2 Two or more races, non-Hispanic/Latino), 2 international. Average age 33. 42 applicants, 86% accepted, 35 enrolled. In 2017, 14 master's, 7 other advanced degrees awarded. *Degree requirements:* For master's, variable foreign language requirement, comprehensive exam (for some programs), thesis (for some programs); for Certificate, comprehensive exam (for some programs). *Entrance requirements:* Additional exam requirements/recommendations for international students: Required—TOEFL (minimum score 80 iBT), IELTS (minimum score 6.5). *Application deadline:* For fall admission, 3/1 for domestic and international students; for spring admission, 10/1 for domestic and international students. Applications are processed on a rolling basis. Application fee: $65. Electronic applications accepted. *Expenses:* Tuition, state resident: full-time $9240; part-time $458 per credit hour. Tuition, nonresident: full-time $21,588; part-time $1199 per credit hour. *Required fees:* $1021; $14 per credit hour. $646 per semester. Tuition and fees vary according to course load, campus/location and program. *Financial support:* In 2017–18, 5 students received support, including 5 teaching assistantships with partial tuition reimbursements available (averaging $9,000 per year); institutionally sponsored loans, health care benefits, tuition waivers (partial), and unspecified assistantships also available. Financial award application deadline: 2/1; financial award applicants required to submit FAFSA. *Unit head:* Dr. Alan Lew, Chair, 928-523-6567, Fax: 928-523-2275. *Application contact:* Dana Mandino, Administrative Associate, 928-523-7988, Fax: 928-523-2275, E-mail: geog@nau.edu.
Website: https://nau.edu/SBS/GPR/

Northern Kentucky University, Office of Graduate Programs, College of Informatics, Department of Computer Science, Highland Heights, KY 41099. Offers computer science (MSCS); geographic information systems (Certificate); secure software engineering (Certificate). *Program availability:* Part-time, evening/weekend. *Degree requirements:* For master's, thesis optional. *Entrance requirements:* For master's, GRE, minimum GPA of 3.0, at least 4 semesters of undergraduate study in computer science including intermediate computer programming and data structures, one year of calculus, one course in discrete mathematics. Additional exam requirements/recommendations for international students: Required—TOEFL (minimum score 550 paper-based; 79 iBT); Recommended—IELTS (minimum score 6.5). Electronic applications accepted. *Faculty research:* Data privacy, data mining, wireless security, secure software engineering, secure networking.

Northwest Missouri State University, Graduate School, College of Arts and Sciences, Maryville, MO 64468-6001. Offers biology (MS); elementary mathematics specialist (MS Ed); English (MA); English education (MS Ed); English pedagogy (MA); geographic information science (MS, Certificate); history (MS Ed); mathematics (MS); mathematics education (MS Ed); teaching: science (MS Ed). *Program availability:* Part-time. *Faculty:* 67 full-time (21 women). *Students:* 11 full-time (5 women), 70 part-time (39 women); includes 9 minority (2 Black or African American, non-Hispanic/Latino; 1 American Indian or Alaska Native, non-Hispanic/Latino; 3 Hispanic/Latino; 3 Two or more races, non-Hispanic/Latino). Average age 34. 33 applicants, 42% accepted, 10 enrolled. In 2017, 19 master's, 7 other advanced degrees awarded. *Degree requirements:* For master's, comprehensive exam. *Entrance requirements:* For master's, GRE General Test, writing sample. Additional exam requirements/recommendations for international students: Required—TOEFL (minimum score 550 paper-based). *Application deadline:* For fall admission, 7/1 for domestic and international students; for spring admission, 11/15 for domestic and international students. Applications are processed on a rolling basis. Application fee: $0 ($50 for international students). Electronic applications accepted. *Expenses:* Tuition, state resident: full-time $4551; part-time $252.86 per credit hour. Tuition, nonresident: full-time $9103; part-time $505.72 per credit hour. *Required fees:* $2453; $136.25 per credit hour. Tuition and fees vary according to course load and program. *Financial support:* Research assistantships with full tuition reimbursements, teaching assistantships with full tuition reimbursements, and administrative assistantships, tutorial assistantships available. Financial award application deadline: 4/1; financial award applicants required to submit FAFSA. *Unit head:* Dr. Michael Steiner, Dean, 660-562-1197.
Website: https://www.nwmissouri.edu/academics/undergraduate/majors/liberal-arts-sciences.htm

Oregon State University, College of Forestry, Program in Natural Resources, Corvallis, OR 97331. Offers fisheries management (MNR); forests and climate change (MNR); geographic information science (MNR); sustainable natural resources (MNR); urban forestry (MNR); water conflict management and transformation (MNR); wildlife management (MNR). *Program availability:* Part-time, online only, 100% online. *Entrance requirements:* For master's, GRE. Additional exam requirements/recommendations for international students: Required—TOEFL (minimum score 80 iBT), IELTS (minimum score 6.5). Application fee: $75 ($85 for international students). *Expenses:* Contact institution. *Unit head:* Juliet Suttton, Online Program Coordinator, 541-737-6008, E-mail: juliet.sutton@oregonstate.edu. *Application contact:* Juliet Suttton, Online Program Coordinator, 541-737-6008, E-mail: juliet.sutton@oregonstate.edu.
Website: http://ecampus.oregonstate.edu/online-degrees/graduate/natural-resources/

Saint Mary's University of Minnesota, Schools of Graduate and Professional Programs, Graduate School of Business and Technology, Geographic Information Science Program, Winona, MN 55987-1399. Offers MS, Certificate. *Unit head:* John Ebert, Director, 507-457-6961, E-mail: jebert@smumn.edu. *Application contact:* Jami Spitzer, Information Contact, 507-457-7500, E-mail: jspitzer@smumn.edu.
Website: http://www.smumn.edu/graduate-home/areas-of-study/graduate-school-of-business-technology/ms-in-geographic-information-science

Salisbury University, Program in Geographic Information Systems Management, Salisbury, MD 21801-6837. Offers MS. *Program availability:* Part-time, evening/weekend, online only, 100% online. *Faculty:* 2 full-time (0 women). *Students:* 4 full-time (2 women), 13 part-time (4 women); includes 1 minority (Two or more races, non-Hispanic/Latino). Average age 29. 10 applicants, 70% accepted, 7 enrolled. In 2017, 5 master's awarded. *Entrance requirements:* For master's, three letters of recommendation; transcripts from colleges and universities attended; personal statement; resume. Additional exam requirements/recommendations for international students: Required—TOEFL (minimum score 550 paper-based; 79 iBT), IELTS (minimum score 6.5). *Application deadline:* For fall admission, 8/1 priority date for domestic and international students; for spring admission, 12/1 priority date for domestic

and international students; for summer admission, 5/1 priority date for domestic and international students. Applications are processed on a rolling basis. Application fee: $65. Electronic applications accepted. *Expenses:* $650 per credit hour online. *Financial support:* Career-related internships or fieldwork and scholarships/grants available. Support available to part-time students. Financial award application deadline: 3/1; financial award applicants required to submit FAFSA. *Faculty research:* GIS; parallel processing; LIDAR; environmental modeling; GIS management. *Unit head:* Dr. Stuart Hamilton, Graduate Program Director, Geographic Information Systems Management, 410-543-6456, E-mail: sehamilton@salisbury.edu. *Application contact:* Jennifer Horsman, Program Management Specialist, 410-543-6460, E-mail: jlgordy@salisbury.edu.
Website: http://www.salisbury.edu/gsr/gradstudies/GISpage.html

Sam Houston State University, College of Sciences, Department of Geography and Geology, Huntsville, TX 77341. Offers applied geographic information science (MS); geographic information science (Certificate). *Program availability:* Part-time. *Degree requirements:* For master's, comprehensive exam, thesis (for some programs). *Entrance requirements:* For master's, GRE General Test, letters of recommendation. Additional exam requirements/recommendations for international students: Required—TOEFL (minimum score 550 paper-based; 79 iBT), IELTS (minimum score 6.5). Electronic applications accepted.

San Francisco State University, Division of Graduate Studies, College of Science and Engineering, Department of Geography and Environment, San Francisco, CA 94132-1722. Offers geographic information science (MS); geography (MA); resource management and environmental planning (MA). *Unit head:* Dr. Jerry Davis, Chair, 415-338-2983, Fax: 415-338-6243, E-mail: jerry@sfsu.edu. *Application contact:* Dr. Nancy Wilkinson, Graduate Coordinator, 415-338-1439, Fax: 415-338-6243, E-mail: nancyw@sfsu.edu.
Website: http://geog.sfsu.edu/

State University of New York College of Environmental Science and Forestry, Department of Environmental Resources Engineering, Syracuse, NY 13210-2779. Offers ecological engineering (MPS, MS, PhD); environmental management (MPS); environmental resources engineering (MPS, MS, PhD); geospatial information science and engineering (MPS, MS, PhD); water resources engineering (MPS, MS, PhD). *Program availability:* Part-time. *Faculty:* 9 full-time (1 woman), 3 part-time/adjunct (0 women). *Students:* 30 full-time (9 women), 5 part-time (2 women); includes 3 minority (1 Asian, non-Hispanic/Latino; 1 Hispanic/Latino; 1 Two or more races, non-Hispanic/Latino), 18 international. Average age 28. 45 applicants, 62% accepted, 8 enrolled. In 2017, 8 master's, 3 doctorates awarded. Terminal master's awarded for partial completion of doctoral program. *Degree requirements:* For master's, thesis (for some programs); for doctorate, comprehensive exam, thesis/dissertation. *Entrance requirements:* For master's and doctorate, GRE General Test, minimum GPA of 3.0. Additional exam requirements/recommendations for international students: Required—TOEFL (minimum score 550 paper-based; 80 iBT), IELTS (minimum score 6). *Application deadline:* For fall admission, 1/15 priority date for domestic and international students; for spring admission, 11/1 priority date for domestic and international students. Applications are processed on a rolling basis. Application fee: $60. Electronic applications accepted. *Expenses:* Tuition, state resident: full-time $10,870; part-time $453 per credit. Tuition, nonresident: full-time $22,210; part-time $925 per credit. *Required fees:* $1435; $70.85 per credit. One-time fee: $25 full-time. Part-time tuition and fees vary according to course load. *Financial support:* In 2017–18, 11 students received support. Unspecified assistantships available. Financial award application deadline: 6/30; financial award applicants required to submit FAFSA. *Faculty research:* Ecological engineering, environmental resources engineering, geospatial information science and engineering, water resources engineering, environmental science. *Total annual research expenditures:* $781,517. *Unit head:* Dr. Theodore Endreny, Chair, 315-470-6565, Fax: 315-470-6958, E-mail: te@esf.edu. *Application contact:* Scott Shannon, Associate Provost for Instruction/Dean of the Graduate School, 315-470-6599, Fax: 315-470-6978, E-mail: esfgrad@esf.edu.
Website: http://www.esf.edu/ere

Stony Brook University, State University of New York, Graduate School, School of Marine and Atmospheric Sciences, Sustainability Studies Program, Stony Brook, NY 11794. Offers geospatial sciences (Graduate Certificate). *Faculty:* 9 full-time (5 women). *Students:* 1 full-time (0 women), 6 part-time (5 women); includes 1 minority (Hispanic/Latino). Average age 29. 3 applicants, 100% accepted, 3 enrolled. In 2017, 3 Graduate Certificates awarded. *Entrance requirements:* For degree, personal statement, letters of recommendation, official transcripts. Additional exam requirements/recommendations for international students: Required—TOEFL (minimum score 85 iBT). *Application deadline:* For fall admission, 1/15 for domestic students. Application fee: $100. *Expenses:* Contact institution. *Financial support:* Teaching assistantships available. *Unit head:* Dr. Kate Aubrecht, Director, 631-632-9404, Fax: 631-632-5375, E-mail: katherine.aubrecht@stonybrook.edu. *Application contact:* 631-632-9404, Fax: 631-632-5375, E-mail: katherine.aubrecht@stonybrook.edu.
Website: https://www.somas.stonybrook.edu/sustainability-studies/

Temple University, College of Liberal Arts, Department of Geography and Urban Studies, Philadelphia, PA 19122-6096. Offers geographic information systems (PSM, Graduate Certificate); geography and urban studies (MA, PhD). *Faculty:* 22 full-time (7 women), 2 part-time/adjunct (1 woman). *Students:* 27 full-time (16 women), 22 part-time (10 women); includes 14 minority (9 Black or African American, non-Hispanic/Latino; 2 Asian, non-Hispanic/Latino; 3 Hispanic/Latino), 7 international. 53 applicants, 45% accepted, 15 enrolled. In 2017, 4 master's, 2 doctorates, 3 other advanced degrees awarded. *Degree requirements:* For master's, comprehensive exam, thesis or alternative. *Entrance requirements:* For master's, GRE General Test, minimum GPA of 3.0, 3 letters of recommendation; for doctorate, GRE, minimum GPA of 3.0, 3 letters of recommendation. Additional exam requirements/recommendations for international students: Required—TOEFL (minimum score 575 paper-based; 88 iBT). *Application deadline:* For fall admission, 1/15 for domestic students, 12/15 for international students; for spring admission, 10/15 for domestic students, 8/1 for international students. Applications are processed on a rolling basis. Application fee: $60. Electronic applications accepted. *Expenses:* Tuition, state resident: full-time $16,164; part-time $898 per credit hour. Tuition, nonresident: full-time $22,158; part-time $1231 per credit hour. *Required fees:* $890; $445 per semester. Full-time tuition and fees vary according to course load, degree level, campus/location and program. *Financial support:* Fellowships, teaching assistantships, career-related internships or fieldwork, Federal Work-Study, and tuition waivers (partial) available. Financial award application deadline: 1/15; financial award applicants required to submit FAFSA. *Faculty research:* Social justice, sustainability, globalization, geographic methods, urban processes. *Unit head:* Dr. C. Hamil Pearsall, Graduate Director, 215-204-3074, Fax: 215-204-7833, E-mail: hamil.pearsall@temple.edu. *Application contact:* Julia Falcon, Student Services Coordinator, 215-204-3386, E-mail: julia.falcon@temple.edu.
Website: http://www.cla.temple.edu/gus/

Texas A&M University–Corpus Christi, College of Graduate Studies, College of Science and Engineering, Program in Geospatial Computing Sciences, Corpus Christi, TX 78412. Offers PhD. *Students:* 13 full-time (1 woman), 1 part-time (0 women); includes 2 minority (1 Black or African American, non-Hispanic/Latino; 1 Hispanic/Latino), 10 international. Average age 32. 22 applicants, 36% accepted, 7 enrolled. *Degree requirements:* For doctorate, thesis/dissertation. *Entrance requirements:* For doctorate, GRE, essay (500-1000 words in length), three letters of recommendation, curriculum vitae. Additional exam requirements/recommendations for international students: Required—TOEFL (minimum score 550 paper-based; 79 iBT), IELTS (minimum score 6.5). *Application deadline:* For fall admission, 7/15 for domestic and international students; for spring admission, 11/15 for domestic and international students. Applications are processed on a rolling basis. Application fee: $50 ($70 for international students). Electronic applications accepted. *Expenses:* Tuition, state resident: full-time $3568; part-time $198.24 per credit hour. Tuition, nonresident: full-time $11,038; part-time $613.24 per credit hour. *Required fees:* $2129; $1422.58 per semester. Tuition and fees vary according to program. *Financial support:* Research assistantships, teaching assistantships, institutionally sponsored loans, scholarships/grants, health care benefits, and unspecified assistantships available. Support available to part-time students. Financial award application deadline: 3/15; financial award applicants required to submit FAFSA. *Unit head:* Dr. Scott King, Department Chair, 361-825-6068, E-mail: scott.king@tamucc.edu. *Application contact:* Graduate Admissions Coordinator, 361-825-2177, Fax: 361-825-2755, E-mail: gradweb@tamucc.edu.
Website: http://sci.tamucc.edu/CSCI/GSCS/index.html

Texas A&M University–Corpus Christi, College of Graduate Studies, College of Science and Engineering, Program in Geospatial Surveying Engineering, Corpus Christi, TX 78412. Offers MS. *Students:* 10 full-time (3 women), 6 part-time (3 women); includes 5 minority (1 Asian, non-Hispanic/Latino; 4 Hispanic/Latino), 3 international. Average age 33. 13 applicants, 62% accepted, 7 enrolled. In 2017, 5 master's awarded. *Degree requirements:* For master's, thesis or creative project. *Entrance requirements:* For master's, GRE, essay, two letters of recommendation. Additional exam requirements/recommendations for international students: Required—TOEFL (minimum score 550 paper-based; 79 iBT), IELTS (minimum score 6.5). *Application deadline:* For fall admission, 8/1 for domestic students, 7/15 for international students; for spring admission, 11/1 for domestic students, 10/15 for international students. Applications are processed on a rolling basis. Application fee: $50 ($70 for international students). Electronic applications accepted. *Expenses:* Tuition, state resident: full-time $3568; part-time $198.24 per credit hour. Tuition, nonresident: full-time $11,038; part-time $613.24 per credit hour. *Required fees:* $2129; $1422.58 per semester. Tuition and fees vary according to program. *Financial support:* Research assistantships, teaching assistantships, institutionally sponsored loans, scholarships/grants, health care benefits, and unspecified assistantships available. Support available to part-time students. Financial award application deadline: 3/15; financial award applicants required to submit FAFSA. *Unit head:* Dr. Gary Jeffress, Director, Conrad Blucher Institute, 361-825-2720, E-mail: gary.jeffress@tamucc.edu. *Application contact:* Graduate Admissions Coordinator, 361-825-2177, Fax: 361-825-2755, E-mail: gradweb@tamucc.edu.
Website: http://sci.tamucc.edu/CSCI/GISC/graduate/graduate.html

Texas State University, The Graduate College, College of Liberal Arts, Doctoral Program in Geographic Information Science, San Marcos, TX 78666. Offers PhD. *Program availability:* Part-time, evening/weekend. *Faculty:* 6 full-time (2 women). *Students:* 10 full-time (5 women), 7 part-time (3 women); includes 4 minority (3 Asian, non-Hispanic/Latino; 1 Hispanic/Latino), 9 international. Average age 34. 16 applicants, 63% accepted, 2 enrolled. In 2017, 2 doctorates awarded. *Degree requirements:* For doctorate, comprehensive exam, thesis/dissertation. *Entrance requirements:* For doctorate, GRE (minimum preferred score of 303 verbal and quantitative), baccalaureate degree from regionally accredited university, master's degree in geography or related field with minimum GPA of 3.5, 3 letters of recommendation, statement of purpose, curriculum vitae, completion of master's thesis or demonstrated evidence of scholarly research. Additional exam requirements/recommendations for international students: Required—TOEFL (minimum score 550 paper-based; 78 iBT), IELTS (minimum score 6). *Application deadline:* For fall admission, 1/15 priority date for domestic and international students. Applications are processed on a rolling basis. Application fee: $40 ($90 for international students). Electronic applications accepted. *Expenses:* Tuition, state resident: full-time $7868; part-time $3934 per semester. Tuition, nonresident: full-time $17,828; part-time $8914 per semester. *Required fees:* $2092; $1435 per semester. Tuition and fees vary according to course load. *Financial support:* In 2017–18, 15 students received support, including 4 research assistantships (averaging $25,337 per year), 15 teaching assistantships (averaging $20,822 per year); career-related internships or fieldwork, Federal Work-Study, institutionally sponsored loans, and scholarships/grants also available. Support available to part-time students. Financial award application deadline: 3/1; financial award applicants required to submit FAFSA. *Faculty research:* Connecting geographic concepts and content, teaching best ideas and practices. *Total annual research expenditures:* $76,974. *Unit head:* Dr. Yongmei Lu, PhD Program Director, 512-245-1337, Fax: 512-245-8353, E-mail: yl10@txstate.edu. *Application contact:* Dr. Andrea Golato, Dean of Graduate School, 512-245-2581, Fax: 512-245-8365, E-mail: gradcollege@txstate.edu.
Website: http://www.gradcollege.txstate.edu/programs/gis-phd.html

Texas State University, The Graduate College, College of Liberal Arts, Master's Program in Geography, San Marcos, TX 78666. Offers environmental geography (MS); geographic education (MAG, MS); geographic information science (MAG); geography (MAG); resources and environmental studies (MAG). *Program availability:* Evening/weekend. *Faculty:* 29 full-time (10 women), 6 part-time/adjunct (1 woman). *Students:* 36 full-time (14 women), 23 part-time (12 women); includes 13 minority (2 Black or African American, non-Hispanic/Latino; 2 Asian, non-Hispanic/Latino; 9 Hispanic/Latino), 6 international. Average age 30. 64 applicants, 67% accepted, 13 enrolled. In 2017, 24 master's awarded. *Degree requirements:* For master's, comprehensive exam, thesis (for some programs). *Entrance requirements:* For master's, GRE General Test (minimum preferred score of 300 verbal and quantitative), baccalaureate degree from regionally-accredited institution with minimum GPA of 3.2 in last 60 hours of course work (for MAG), 3.4 (for MS); 2 letters of recommendation; statement of purpose; current resume. Additional exam requirements/recommendations for international students: Required—TOEFL (minimum score 550 paper-based; 78 iBT), IELTS (minimum score 6.5). *Application deadline:* For fall admission, 2/1 priority date for domestic and international students; for spring admission, 10/15 priority date for domestic students, 10/1 for international students. Applications are processed on a rolling basis. Application fee: $40 ($90 for international students). Electronic applications accepted. *Expenses:* Tuition, state resident: full-time $7868; part-time $3934 per semester. Tuition, nonresident: full-time $17,828; part-time $8914 per semester. *Required fees:* $2092; $1435 per semester. Tuition and fees vary according to course load. *Financial support:* In 2017–18, 32 students received support, including 7 research assistantships (averaging $13,647 per year), 14 teaching assistantships (averaging $13,293 per year); career-related internships or fieldwork, Federal Work-Study, institutionally sponsored loans, scholarships/grants, and unspecified assistantships also available. Support available to part-time students. Financial award application deadline: 3/1; financial award applicants required to submit FAFSA. *Unit head:* Dr. Yongmei Lu, Graduate Adviser, 512-245-1337, Fax: 512-245-8353, E-mail: yl10@txstate.edu. *Application contact:* Dr. Andrea Golato, Dean of Graduate School, 512-245-2581, Fax: 512-245-

8365, E-mail: gradcollege@txstate.edu.
Website: http://www.geo.txstate.edu/degrees-programs/graduate.html

Université du Québec à Montréal, Graduate Programs, Program in Geographical Information Systems, Montréal, QC H3C 3P8, Canada. Offers Diploma. *Program availability:* Part-time. *Entrance requirements:* For degree, appropriate bachelor's degree or equivalent, proficiency in French.

Université Laval, Faculty of Administrative Sciences, Programs in Business Administration, Québec, QC G1K 7P4, Canada. Offers accounting (MBA); agri-food management (MBA); electronic business (MBA, Diploma); factory management and logistics (MBA); finance (MBA); firm management (MBA); geomatic management (MBA); information technology management (MBA); international management (MBA); management (MBA); management accounting (MBA, Diploma); marketing (MBA); modeling and organizational decision (MBA); occupational health and safety management (MBA); pharmacy management (MBA); social and environmental responsibility (MBA); technological entrepreneurship (Diploma). *Accreditation:* AACSB. *Program availability:* Part-time, evening/weekend, online learning. *Entrance requirements:* For master's and Diploma, knowledge of French and English. Electronic applications accepted.

University at Albany, State University of New York, College of Arts and Sciences, Department of Geography and Planning, Albany, NY 12222-0001. Offers geographic information science (Certificate); geography (MA); regional planning (MRP); urban policy (Certificate). *Program availability:* Part-time. *Faculty:* 13 full-time (3 women). *Students:* 32 full-time (13 women), 18 part-time (5 women); includes 9 minority (5 Black or African American, non-Hispanic/Latino; 2 Asian, non-Hispanic/Latino; 1 Hispanic/Latino; 1 Two or more races, non-Hispanic/Latino), 6 international. 46 applicants, 83% accepted, 21 enrolled. In 2017, 13 master's, 9 other advanced degrees awarded. *Entrance requirements:* Additional exam requirements/recommendations for international students: Required—TOEFL (minimum score 550 paper-based). *Application deadline:* For fall admission, 3/1 for domestic students, 5/1 for international students; for spring admission, 11/1 for international students. Applications are processed on a rolling basis. Application fee: $75. Electronic applications accepted. *Expenses:* Tuition, state resident: full-time $10,870; part-time $453 per credit hour. Tuition, nonresident: full-time $22,210; part-time $925 per credit hour. *Required fees:* $84.68 per credit hour. $508.06 per semester. Part-time tuition and fees vary according to course load and program. *Financial support:* Fellowships, teaching assistantships, career-related internships or fieldwork, Federal Work-Study, and institutionally sponsored loans available. Financial award application deadline: 3/1. *Faculty research:* Urban geography, social/cultural geography, urban planning, remote sensing, spatial analysis/geographic information systems. *Unit head:* Catherine Lawson, Chair, 518-442-4636, Fax: 518-442-4742, E-mail: lawsonc@albany.edu. *Application contact:* Michael DeRensis, Director, Graduate Admissions, 518-442-3980, Fax: 518-442-3922, E-mail: graduate@albany.edu.
Website: http://www.albany.edu/gp/

University at Buffalo, the State University of New York, Graduate School, College of Arts and Sciences, Department of Geography, Buffalo, NY 14260. Offers earth systems science (MA, MS); economic geography and business geographics (MS); environmental modeling and analysis (MA); geographic information science (MA, MS); geography (MA, PhD); health geography (MS); international trade (MA); urban and regional analysis (MA). *Program availability:* Part-time. *Faculty:* 19 full-time (9 women), 1 part-time/adjunct (0 women). *Students:* 100 full-time (45 women); includes 66 minority (1 Black or African American, non-Hispanic/Latino; 64 Asian, non-Hispanic/Latino; 1 Hispanic/Latino). Average age 28. 140 applicants, 23% accepted, 29 enrolled. In 2017, 19 master's, 4 doctorates awarded. Terminal master's awarded for partial completion of doctoral program. *Degree requirements:* For master's, thesis (for some programs), project or portfolio; for doctorate, thesis/dissertation. *Entrance requirements:* For master's, GRE General Test, minimum GPA of 2.9; for doctorate, GRE General Test, minimum GPA of 3.0. Additional exam requirements/recommendations for international students: Required—TOEFL (minimum score 550 paper-based; 79 iBT). *Application deadline:* For fall admission, 5/1 priority date for domestic students, 3/10 priority date for international students; for spring admission, 11/1 priority date for domestic students, 9/1 priority date for international students. Applications are processed on a rolling basis. Application fee: $75. Electronic applications accepted. *Expenses:* Contact institution. *Financial support:* In 2017–18, 15 students received support, including 9 fellowships with full tuition reimbursements available (averaging $3,070 per year), 7 research assistantships with full tuition reimbursements available (averaging $14,000 per year), 15 teaching assistantships with full tuition reimbursements available (averaging $14,080 per year); career-related internships or fieldwork, Federal Work-Study, institutionally sponsored loans, traineeships, health care benefits, and unspecified assistantships also available. Financial award application deadline: 1/10. *Faculty research:* International business and world trade, geographic information systems and cartography, transportation, urban and regional analysis, physical and environmental geography. *Total annual research expenditures:* $2.6 million. *Unit head:* Dr. Sean Bennett, Chair, 716-645-0490, Fax: 716-645-2329, E-mail: seanb@buffalo.edu. *Application contact:* Wendy Zitzka, Graduate Secretary, 716-645-0471, Fax: 716-645-2329, E-mail: wzitzka@buffalo.edu.
Website: http://www.geog.buffalo.edu/

The University of Alabama, Graduate School, College of Arts and Sciences, Department of Geography, Tuscaloosa, AL 35487. Offers earth system science (MS, PhD); environment and natural resources (MS, PhD); environment and society (MS, PhD); geographic information science (MS, PhD). *Program availability:* Part-time. *Faculty:* 17 full-time (2 women). *Students:* 28 full-time (11 women), 4 part-time (1 woman); includes 2 minority (both Hispanic/Latino), 10 international. Average age 26. 32 applicants, 34% accepted, 10 enrolled. In 2017, 14 master's awarded. *Degree requirements:* For master's, comprehensive exam, thesis; for doctorate, comprehensive exam, thesis/dissertation. *Entrance requirements:* For master's, GRE, minimum GPA of 3.0. Additional exam requirements/recommendations for international students: Required—TOEFL (minimum score 550 paper-based; 79 iBT). *Application deadline:* For fall admission, 2/15 priority date for domestic and international students; for spring admission, 10/1 priority date for domestic and international students. Applications are processed on a rolling basis. Application fee: $50 ($60 for international students). Electronic applications accepted. *Financial support:* In 2017–18, 24 students received support, including fellowships with full tuition reimbursements available (averaging $15,000 per year), research assistantships with full tuition reimbursements available (averaging $14,013 per year), teaching assistantships with full tuition reimbursements available (averaging $14,013 per year); career-related internships or fieldwork, health care benefits, and unspecified assistantships also available. Financial award application deadline: 2/15. *Faculty research:* Earth system science; geographic information science; environment and natural resources; environment and society. *Total annual research expenditures:* $229,136. *Unit head:* Dr. Douglas Sherman, Chair, 205-348-5047, Fax: 205-348-2278, E-mail: douglas.j.sherman@ua.edu. *Application contact:* Dr. Justin Hart, Associate Professor, 205-348-5047, Fax: 205-348-2278, E-mail: hart013@ua.edu.
Website: http://geography.ua.edu

University of Alaska Fairbanks, College of Natural Sciences and Mathematics, Department of Geosciences, Fairbanks, AK 99775-5780. Offers geophysics (MS), including remote sensing geophysics, snow, ice, and permafrost geophysics, solid-earth geophysics. *Program availability:* Part-time. *Degree requirements:* For master's, comprehensive exam, thesis, oral defense of thesis. *Entrance requirements:* For master's, GRE General Test, bachelor's degree in geology, geophysics, or an appropriate physical science or engineering with minimum cumulative undergraduate and major GPA of 3.0. Additional exam requirements/recommendations for international students: Required—TOEFL (minimum score 550 paper-based; 79 iBT), IELTS (minimum score 6.5). Electronic applications accepted. *Faculty research:* Glacial surging, volcanology, geochronology, impact cratering, permafrost geophysics.

The University of Arizona, College of Social and Behavioral Sciences, School of Geography and Development, Tucson, AZ 85721. Offers geographic information systems technology (MA); geography (PhD). *Program availability:* Part-time. Terminal master's awarded for partial completion of doctoral program. *Degree requirements:* For master's, thesis or additional course work; for doctorate, variable foreign language requirement, thesis/dissertation. *Entrance requirements:* For master's, GRE General Test, 2 letters of recommendation; for doctorate, GRE General Test, statement of purpose, 2 letters of recommendation, master's degree. Additional exam requirements/recommendations for international students: Required—TOEFL (minimum score 550 paper-based; 79 iBT). Electronic applications accepted. *Faculty research:* Population, Latin America, Anglo-America, the former Soviet Union, the Middle East.

University of Central Arkansas, Graduate School, College of Liberal Arts, Department of Geography, Conway, AR 72035-0001. Offers community and economic development (MS); geographic information systems (MGIS, Certificate). *Program availability:* Part-time, online learning. *Entrance requirements:* Additional exam requirements/recommendations for international students: Required—TOEFL (minimum score 550 paper-based). Electronic applications accepted.

University of Central Arkansas, Graduate School, College of Liberal Arts, Program in Community and Economic Development, Conway, AR 72035-0001. Offers community and economic development (MS); geographic and information systems (MGIS, Graduate Certificate). *Program availability:* Part-time, online learning. *Degree requirements:* For master's, comprehensive exam, thesis. *Entrance requirements:* For master's, GRE General Test, minimum GPA of 2.7. Additional exam requirements/recommendations for international students: Required—TOEFL (minimum score 550 paper-based). Electronic applications accepted. *Expenses:* Contact institution.

University of Central Florida, College of Graduate Studies, Program in Interdisciplinary Studies, Orlando, FL 32816. Offers geographic information systems (Certificate); interdisciplinary studies (MA, MS). *Students:* 14 full-time (11 women), 36 part-time (24 women); includes 16 minority (5 Black or African American, non-Hispanic/Latino; 1 Asian, non-Hispanic/Latino; 9 Hispanic/Latino; 1 Two or more races, non-Hispanic/Latino), 2 international. Average age 30. 44 applicants, 84% accepted, 30 enrolled. In 2017, 3 master's, 1 other advanced degree awarded. *Degree requirements:* For master's, thesis or alternative. *Entrance requirements:* For master's, GRE, minimum GPA of 3.0 in last 60 hours, letters of recommendation, resume, personal statement. Additional exam requirements/recommendations for international students: Required—TOEFL. *Application deadline:* For fall admission, 7/15 for domestic students; for spring admission, 12/1 for domestic students. Application fee: $30. Electronic applications accepted. *Expenses:* Tuition, state resident: part-time $288.16 per credit hour. Tuition, nonresident: part-time $1073.31 per credit hour. Tuition and fees vary according to program. *Financial support:* Teaching assistantships available. Financial award application deadline: 3/1; financial award applicants required to submit FAFSA. *Unit head:* Dr. John Weishampel, Associate Dean, 407-823-6634, E-mail: john.weishampel@ucf.edu. *Application contact:* Associate Director, Graduate Admissions, 407-823-2766, Fax: 407-823-6442, E-mail: gradadmissions@ucf.edu.
Website: https://www.graduate.ucf.edu/IDS/

University of Colorado Denver, Business School, Program in Information Systems, Denver, CO 80217. Offers accounting and information systems audit and control (MS); business intelligence systems (MS); digital health entrepreneurship (MS); enterprise risk management (MS); enterprise technology management (MS); geographic information systems (MS); health information technology (MS); technology innovation and entrepreneurship (MS); Web and mobile computing (MS). *Program availability:* Part-time, evening/weekend, online learning. *Degree requirements:* For master's, 30 credit hours. *Entrance requirements:* For master's, GMAT, resume, essay, two letters of recommendation, financial statements (for international applicants). Additional exam requirements/recommendations for international students: Required—TOEFL (minimum score 525 paper-based; 71 iBT); Recommended—IELTS (minimum score 6.5). Electronic applications accepted. *Expenses:* Contact institution. *Faculty research:* Human-computer interaction, expert systems, database management, electronic commerce, object-oriented software development.

University of Colorado Denver, College of Engineering and Applied Science, Department of Civil Engineering, Denver, CO 80217. Offers civil engineering (EASPh D); civil engineering systems (PhD); environmental and sustainability engineering (MS, PhD); geographic information systems (MS); geotechnical engineering (MS, PhD); hydrology and hydraulics (MS, PhD); structural engineering (MS, PhD); transportation engineering (MS, PhD). *Program availability:* Part-time, evening/weekend. *Degree requirements:* For master's, comprehensive exam, 30 credit hours, project or thesis; for doctorate, comprehensive exam, thesis/dissertation, 60 credit hours (30 of which are dissertation research). *Entrance requirements:* For master's, GRE, statement of purpose, transcripts, three references; for doctorate, GRE, statement of purpose, transcripts, references, letter of support from faculty stating willingness to serve as dissertation advisor and outlining plan for financial support. Additional exam requirements/recommendations for international students: Required—TOEFL (minimum score 537 paper-based; 75 iBT); Recommended—IELTS (minimum score 6.5). Electronic applications accepted. *Expenses:* Contact institution. *Faculty research:* Earthquake source physics, environmental biotechnology, hydrologic and hydraulic engineering, sustainability assessments, transportation energy use and greenhouse gas emissions.

University of Colorado Denver, College of Engineering and Applied Science, Master of Engineering Program, Denver, CO 80217-3364. Offers civil engineering (M Eng), including civil engineering, geographic information systems, transportation systems; electrical engineering (M Eng); mechanical engineering (M Eng). *Program availability:* Part-time. *Degree requirements:* For master's, comprehensive exam, 27 credit hours of course work, 3 credit hours of report or thesis work. *Entrance requirements:* For master's, GRE (for those with GPA below 2.75), transcripts, references, statement of purpose. Additional exam requirements/recommendations for international students: Required—TOEFL (minimum score 537 paper-based; 75 iBT); Recommended—IELTS (minimum score 6.5). Electronic applications accepted. *Expenses:* Contact institution. *Faculty research:* Civil, electrical and mechanical engineering.

University of Colorado Denver, College of Liberal Arts and Sciences, Department of Geography and Environmental Sciences, Denver, CO 80217. Offers environmental sciences (MS), including air quality, ecosystems, environmental health, environmental

science education, geospatial analysis, urban agriculture, water quality. *Program availability:* Part-time, evening/weekend. *Degree requirements:* For master's, thesis or alternative, 30 credits including 21 of core requirements and 9 of environmental science electives. *Entrance requirements:* For master's, GRE General Test, BA in one of the natural/physical sciences or engineering (or equivalent background); prerequisite coursework in calculus and physics (one semester each); general chemistry with lab and general biology with lab (two semesters each); three letters of recommendation. Additional exam requirements/recommendations for international students: Required—TOEFL (minimum score 537 paper-based; 75 iBT); Recommended—IELTS (minimum score 6.5). Electronic applications accepted. *Faculty research:* Air quality, environmental health, ecosystems, hazardous waste, water quality, geospatial analysis and environmental science education.

University of Denver, Division of Natural Sciences and Mathematics, Department of Geography and the Environment, Denver, CO 80208. Offers geographic information science (MS); geography (MA, PhD). *Program availability:* Part-time. *Students:* Average age 33. 44 applicants, 66% accepted, 18 enrolled. In 2017, 22 master's awarded. Terminal master's awarded for partial completion of doctoral program. *Degree requirements:* For master's, comprehensive exam (for some programs), thesis or alternative; for doctorate, one foreign language, comprehensive exam, thesis/dissertation. *Entrance requirements:* For master's, GRE General Test, bachelor's degree, transcripts, personal statement, three letters of recommendation; for doctorate, GRE General Test, master's degree, transcripts, personal statement, three letters of recommendation. Additional exam requirements/recommendations for international students: Required—TOEFL (minimum score 570 paper-based; 88 iBT). *Application deadline:* For fall admission, 1/15 priority date for domestic and international students. Applications are processed on a rolling basis. Application fee: $65. Electronic applications accepted. *Expenses:* Contact institution. *Financial support:* In 2017–18, 54 students received support, including 14 teaching assistantships with tuition reimbursements available (averaging $17,262 per year); career-related internships or fieldwork, Federal Work-Study, institutionally sponsored loans, scholarships/grants, and unspecified assistantships also available. Support available to part-time students. Financial award application deadline: 2/15; financial award applicants required to submit FAFSA. *Faculty research:* Geographic information science, geomorphology, political ecology, transportation, urban studies. *Unit head:* Dr. Andrew Goetz, Professor and Chair, 303-871-2674, Fax: 303-871-2201, E-mail: agoetz@du.edu. *Application contact:* Nicole Chauvet, Assistant to the Chair, 303-871-2654, Fax: 303-871-2201, E-mail: nchauvet@du.edu.
Website: http://www.du.edu/nsm/departments/geography

University of Denver, University College, Denver, CO 80208. Offers arts and culture (MA, Certificate); communication management (MS, Certificate), including translation studies (Certificate), world history and culture (Certificate); environmental policy and management (MS); geographic information systems (MS); global affairs (MA, Certificate), including human capital in organizations (Certificate), philanthropic leadership (Certificate), project management (Certificate), strategic innovation and change (Certificate); healthcare leadership (MS); information communications and technology (MS); leadership and organizations (MS); professional creative writing (MA, Certificate), including emergency planning and response (Certificate), organizational security (Certificate); security management (MS, Certificate); strategic human resources (Certificate). *Program availability:* Part-time, evening/weekend, online learning. *Faculty:* 118 part-time/adjunct (62 women). *Students:* 56 full-time (32 women), 1,287 part-time (707 women); includes 330 minority (99 Black or African American, non-Hispanic/Latino; 7 American Indian or Alaska Native, non-Hispanic/Latino; 43 Asian, non-Hispanic/Latino; 141 Hispanic/Latino; 3 Native Hawaiian or other Pacific Islander, non-Hispanic/Latino; 37 Two or more races, non-Hispanic/Latino), 84 international. Average age 34. 783 applicants, 86% accepted, 420 enrolled. In 2017, 461 master's, 173 other advanced degrees awarded. *Degree requirements:* For master's, capstone project. *Entrance requirements:* For master's, transcripts, two letters of recommendation, personal statement, resume. Additional exam requirements/recommendations for international students: Required—TOEFL (minimum score 550 paper-based; 80 iBT). *Application deadline:* For fall admission, 6/21 priority date for domestic students, 5/1 priority date for international students; for winter admission, 9/14 priority date for domestic students, 9/19 priority date for international students; for spring admission, 1/11 priority date for domestic students, 12/12 priority date for international students; for summer admission, 3/29 priority date for domestic students, 3/6 priority date for international students. Applications are processed on a rolling basis. Application fee: $75. Electronic applications accepted. *Expenses:* $7,968 per year half-time. *Financial support:* In 2017–18, 29 students received support. Teaching assistantships available. Financial award applicants required to submit FAFSA. *Unit head:* Dr. Michael McGuire, Dean, 303-871-3518, Fax: 303-871-3303, E-mail: mmcguire@du.edu. *Application contact:* Information Contact, 303-871-2291, E-mail: ucoladm@du.edu.
Website: http://universitycollege.du.edu/

University of Florida, Graduate School, College of Liberal Arts and Sciences, Department of Geography, Gainesville, FL 32611. Offers applications of geographic technologies (MA, MS); geographic information systems (MA, MS, PhD); geography (MA, MS, PhD); hydrologic sciences (MS, PhD); tropical conservation and development (MA, MS, PhD); wetland sciences (MA, MS, PhD). *Degree requirements:* For master's, thesis; for doctorate, comprehensive exam, thesis/dissertation. *Entrance requirements:* For master's and doctorate, GRE General Test, minimum GPA of 3.0. Additional exam requirements/recommendations for international students: Required—TOEFL (minimum score 550 paper-based; 80 iBT), IELTS (minimum score 6). Electronic applications accepted. *Faculty research:* Economic development, physical geography, hydrology, climatology, tropical agriculture.

The University of Iowa, Graduate College, Program in Informatics, Iowa City, IA 52242-1316. Offers bioinformatics (MS, PhD); bioinformatics and computational biology (Certificate); geoinformatics (MS, PhD, Certificate); health informatics (MS, PhD, Certificate); information science (MS, PhD, Certificate). *Degree requirements:* For master's, thesis optional; for doctorate, comprehensive exam, thesis/dissertation. *Entrance requirements:* For master's and doctorate, GRE General Test, minimum GPA of 3.0. Additional exam requirements/recommendations for international students: Required—TOEFL (minimum score 550 paper-based; 81 iBT). Electronic applications accepted.

The University of Kansas, Graduate Studies, College of Liberal Arts and Sciences, Department of Geography, Lawrence, KS 66045-7613. Offers atmospheric science (MS); geographic information science (Graduate Certificate); geography (MA, PhD); MUP/MA. *Program availability:* Part-time. *Students:* 54 full-time (25 women), 6 part-time (2 women); includes 9 minority (7 American Indian or Alaska Native, non-Hispanic/Latino; 1 Asian, non-Hispanic/Latino; 1 Hispanic/Latino), 9 international. Average age 32. 36 applicants, 53% accepted, 13 enrolled. In 2017, 11 master's, 5 doctorates awarded. *Entrance requirements:* For master's and doctorate, GRE General Test, 3 letters of reference, transcripts, statement of interests, resume. Additional exam requirements/recommendations for international students: Required—TOEFL. *Application deadline:* For fall admission, 1/15 priority date for domestic and international students; for spring admission, 11/1 for domestic and international students; for summer admission, 4/1 for domestic and international students. Application fee: $65 ($85 for international students). Electronic applications accepted. *Financial support:* Fellowships, research assistantships, teaching assistantships, and unspecified assistantships available. Financial award application deadline: 1/15. *Faculty research:* Physical geography, human/cultural/regional geography, geographic information science, atmospheric science. *Unit head:* Nathaniel Brunsell, Chair, 785-864-2021, E-mail: brunsell@ku.edu. *Application contact:* Beverly Koerner, Graduate Admission Contact, 785-864-7706, E-mail: koerner@ku.edu.
Website: http://www.geog.ku.edu/

University of Lethbridge, School of Graduate Studies, Lethbridge, AB T1K 3M4, Canada. Offers addictions counseling (M Sc); agricultural biotechnology (M Sc); agricultural studies (M Sc, MA); anthropology (MA); archaeology (M Sc, MA); art (MA, MFA); biochemistry (M Sc); biological sciences (M Sc); biomolecular science (PhD); biosystems and biodiversity (PhD); Canadian studies (MA); chemistry (M Sc); computer science (M Sc); computer science and geographical information science (M Sc); counseling (MC); counseling psychology (M Ed); dramatic arts (MA); earth, space, and physical science (PhD); economics (MA); education (MA, PhD); educational leadership (M Ed); English (MA); environmental science (M Sc); evolution and behavior (PhD); exercise science (M Sc); French (MA); French/German (MA); French/Spanish (MA); general education (M Ed); geography (M Sc, MA); German (MA); health sciences (M Sc); individualized multidisciplinary (M Sc, MA); kinesiology (M Sc, MA); management (M Sc), including accounting, finance, human resource management and labor relations, information systems, international management, marketing, policy and strategy; mathematics (M Sc); music (M Mus, MA); Native American studies (MA); neuroscience (M Sc, PhD); new media (MA, MFA); nursing (M Sc, MN); philosophy (MA); physics (M Sc); political science (MA); psychology (M Sc, MA); religious studies (MA); sociology (MA); theatre and dramatic arts (MFA); theoretical and computational science (PhD); urban and regional studies (MA); women and gender studies (MA). *Program availability:* Part-time, evening/weekend. *Degree requirements:* For master's, thesis (for some programs); for doctorate, comprehensive exam, thesis/dissertation. *Entrance requirements:* For master's, GMAT (for M Sc in management), bachelor's degree in related field, minimum GPA of 3.0 during previous 20 graded semester courses, 2 years' teaching or related experience (M Ed); for doctorate, master's degree, minimum graduate GPA of 3.5. Additional exam requirements/recommendations for international students: Required—TOEFL (minimum score 580 paper-based; 93 iBT). Electronic applications accepted. *Faculty research:* Movement and brain plasticity, gibberellin physiology, photosynthesis, carbon cycling, molecular properties of main-group ring components.

University of Maryland, Baltimore County, The Graduate School, College of Arts, Humanities and Social Sciences, Department of Geography and Environmental Systems, Program in Geographic Information Systems, Rockville, MD 20850. Offers MPS, Certificate. *Program availability:* Part-time, evening/weekend. *Faculty:* 13 part-time/adjunct (3 women). *Students:* 5 full-time (2 women), 22 part-time (10 women); includes 8 minority (5 Black or African American, non-Hispanic/Latino; 1 Asian, non-Hispanic/Latino; 2 Hispanic/Latino), 10 international. Average age 33. 8 applicants, 100% accepted, 6 enrolled. In 2017, 3 master's, 3 Certificates awarded. *Entrance requirements:* Additional exam requirements/recommendations for international students: Required—TOEFL (minimum score 99 iBT), IELTS (minimum score 7). *Application deadline:* For fall admission, 8/1 for domestic students, 6/1 for international students; for spring admission, 12/1 for domestic students, 11/1 for international students. Applications are processed on a rolling basis. Application fee: $50. Electronic applications accepted. *Expenses:* Contact institution. *Faculty research:* Enterprise GIS. *Unit head:* Dr. Erwin Villiger, Program Director, 301-738-6087, E-mail: villiger@umbc.edu. *Application contact:* Rickeysha Jones, Program Coordinator, 301-738-6285, E-mail: rcjones@umbc.edu.
Website: http://www.umbc.edu/gis

University of Memphis, Graduate School, College of Arts and Sciences, Department of Earth Sciences, Memphis, TN 38152. Offers earth sciences (MA, MS, PhD), including archaeology (MS), geography (MS), geology (MS), geophysics (MS), interdisciplinary studies (MS); geographic information systems (Graduate Certificate), including geographic information systems, GIS educator, GIS planning, GIS professional. *Program availability:* Part-time, evening/weekend. *Faculty:* 18 full-time (3 women), 4 part-time/adjunct (0 women). *Students:* 55 full-time (23 women), 24 part-time (4 women); includes 5 minority (1 Black or African American, non-Hispanic/Latino; 4 Asian, non-Hispanic/Latino), 19 international. Average age 31. 17 applicants, 82% accepted, 11 enrolled. In 2017, 7 master's, 5 doctorates, 3 other advanced degrees awarded. Terminal master's awarded for partial completion of doctoral program. *Degree requirements:* For master's, comprehensive exam, thesis, seminar presentation; for doctorate, comprehensive exam, thesis/dissertation, qualifying exam, submission of two manuscripts for publication in peer-reviewed journal or books. *Entrance requirements:* For master's, GRE General Test, 3 letters of recommendation, statement of research interests; for doctorate, GRE General Test, 2 letters of recommendation, resume, personal statement. Additional exam requirements/recommendations for international students: Required—TOEFL (minimum score 550 paper-based; 79 iBT). *Application deadline:* For fall admission, 1/15 for domestic students; for spring admission, 11/1 for domestic students. Applications are processed on a rolling basis. Application fee: $35 ($60 for international students). Electronic applications accepted. *Expenses:* Contact institution. *Financial support:* In 2017–18, 18 students received support, including 2 research assistantships with full tuition reimbursements available (averaging $17,000 per year), 13 teaching assistantships with full tuition reimbursements available (averaging $16,692 per year); fellowships with full tuition reimbursements available, Federal Work-Study, scholarships/grants, and unspecified assistantships also available. Financial award application deadline: 2/1; financial award applicants required to submit FAFSA. *Faculty research:* Hazards, active tectonics, geophysics, hydrology and water resources, spatial analysis. *Unit head:* Dr. Daniel Larsen, Chair, 901-678-4538, Fax: 901-678-2178, E-mail: dlarsen@memphis.edu. *Application contact:* Dr. Randel T. Cox, Graduate Coordinator, 901-678-4361, Fax: 901-678-2178, E-mail: randycox@memphis.edu.
Website: http://www.memphis.edu/earthsciences/

University of Minnesota, Twin Cities Campus, Graduate School, College of Food, Agricultural and Natural Resource Sciences, Program in Natural Resources Science and Management, St. Paul, MN 55108. Offers assessment, monitoring, and geospatial analysis (MS, PhD); economics, policy, management, and society (MS, PhD); forest hydrology and watershed management (MS, PhD); forest products (MS, PhD); forests: biology, ecology, conservation, and management (MS, PhD); natural resources science and management (MS, PhD); paper science and engineering (MS, PhD); recreation resources, tourism, and environmental education (MS, PhD). *Program availability:* Part-time. *Faculty:* 72 full-time (29 women), 52 part-time/adjunct (8 women). *Students:* 88 full-time (49 women), 21 part-time (12 women); includes 11 minority (2 Black or African American, non-Hispanic/Latino; 2 American Indian or Alaska Native, non-Hispanic/Latino; 3 Asian, non-Hispanic/Latino; 4 Hispanic/Latino), 12 international. Average age 30. 69 applicants, 54% accepted, 30 enrolled. In 2017, 18 master's, 4 doctorates awarded. Terminal master's awarded for partial completion of doctoral program. *Degree requirements:* For master's, comprehensive exam, thesis (for some programs); for

doctorate, comprehensive exam, thesis/dissertation. *Entrance requirements:* For master's and doctorate, GRE General Test. Additional exam requirements/recommendations for international students: Required—TOEFL (minimum score 550 paper-based; 79 iBT); Recommended—IELTS (minimum score 6.5). *Application deadline:* For fall admission, 12/15 priority date for domestic and international students; for spring admission, 10/15 for domestic and international students. Applications are processed on a rolling basis. Application fee: $75 ($95 for international students). Electronic applications accepted. *Financial support:* In 2017–18, 6 students received support, including fellowships with full tuition reimbursements available (averaging $41,000 per year), research assistantships with full tuition reimbursements available (averaging $41,000 per year), teaching assistantships with full tuition reimbursements available (averaging $36,000 per year); scholarships/grants, health care benefits, and unspecified assistantships also available. *Faculty research:* Forest hydrology, biology, ecology, conservation, and management; recreation resources and environmental education; wildlife ecology; economics, policy, and society; geographic information systems (GIS); forest products and paper science. *Unit head:* Dr. Mae Davenport, Director of Graduate Studies, 612-624-2721, E-mail: mdaven@umn.edu. *Application contact:* Toni Abts, Graduate Program Coordinator, 612-624-7683, Fax: 612-625-5212, E-mail: twheeler@umn.edu.
Website: http://www.nrsm.umn.edu

University of Minnesota, Twin Cities Campus, Graduate School, College of Liberal Arts, Program in Geographic Information Science, Minneapolis, MN 55455-0213. Offers MGIS. *Program availability:* Part-time. *Degree requirements:* For master's, comprehensive exam, capstone project. *Entrance requirements:* For master's, minimum GPA of 3.0; course work in college-level math, statistics, and computer programming. Additional exam requirements/recommendations for international students: Required—TOEFL (minimum score 600 paper-based; 100 iBT). *Expenses:* Contact institution. *Faculty research:* Geographic information science and society, spatial analysis and modeling, spatial databases, remote sensing, geovisualization.

University of Missouri, Office of Research and Graduate Studies, College of Agriculture, Food and Natural Resources, School of Natural Resources, Columbia, MO 65211. Offers agroforestry (MS, Certificate); conservation biology (Certificate); fisheries and wildlife sciences (MS, PhD); forestry (MS, PhD); geographical information science (Certificate); human dimensions of natural resources (MS, PhD); parks, recreation and tourism (MS); society and ecosystems (Certificate); soil, environmental and atmospheric sciences (MS, PhD); water resources (MS, PhD). *Program availability:* Part-time. *Degree requirements:* For doctorate, thesis/dissertation. *Entrance requirements:* For master's and doctorate, GRE General Test (minimum score 1200 Verbal and Quantitative), minimum GPA of 3.2. Additional exam requirements/recommendations for international students: Required—TOEFL (minimum score 550 paper-based; 80 iBT), IELTS (minimum score 6.5). Electronic applications accepted.

University of Missouri, Office of Research and Graduate Studies, College of Arts and Science, Department of Geography, Columbia, MO 65211. Offers geographic information science (Graduate Certificate); geography (MA). *Degree requirements:* For master's, thesis or alternative. *Entrance requirements:* For master's, GRE General Test (minimum score 1000 verbal and quantitative), minimum GPA of 3.0. Additional exam requirements/recommendations for international students: Required—TOEFL (minimum score 500 paper-based; 61 iBT). Electronic applications accepted. *Faculty research:* Human geography, nature/society relationships, the physical environment, application of geographic information sciences.

University of Nebraska at Omaha, Graduate Studies, College of Arts and Sciences, Department of Geography and Geology, Omaha, NE 68182. Offers geographic information science (Certificate); geography (MA). *Program availability:* Part-time. *Degree requirements:* For master's, comprehensive exam, thesis (for some programs). *Entrance requirements:* For master's, GRE, minimum GPA of 3.0, 15 undergraduate geography hours, transcripts, resume, statement of purpose, 2 letters of recommendation; for Certificate, minimum GPA of 3.0, transcripts, resume, statement of purpose, 2 letters of recommendation. Additional exam requirements/recommendations for international students: Required—TOEFL, IELTS, PTE. Electronic applications accepted.

University of New Hampshire, Graduate School, Interdisciplinary Programs, Program in Geospatial Science, Durham, NH 03824. Offers Postbaccalaureate Certificate. *Students:* 1 (woman) full-time, 1 part-time (0 women). Average age 39. 1 applicant, 100% accepted, 1 enrolled. In 2017, 3 Postbaccalaureate Certificates awarded. *Entrance requirements:* Additional exam requirements/recommendations for international students: Required—TOEFL (minimum score 550 paper-based; 80 iBT). *Application deadline:* For fall admission, 7/1 for domestic students; for spring admission, 12/1 for domestic students; for summer admission, 4/1 for domestic students. Application fee: $25. Electronic applications accepted. *Financial support:* Fellowships, research assistantships, and teaching assistantships available. Financial award application deadline: 2/15. *Unit head:* Michael Routhier, Coordinator, 603-862-1754, E-mail: mike.routhier@unh.edu.
Website: http://gss.unh.edu/

University of New Haven, Graduate School, College of Arts and Sciences, Program in Environmental Science, West Haven, CT 06516. Offers environmental ecology (MS); environmental geoscience (MS); environmental health and management (MS); environmental science (MS); geographical information systems (MS). *Program availability:* Part-time, evening/weekend. *Students:* 27 full-time (17 women), 8 part-time (3 women); includes 3 minority (2 Black or African American, non-Hispanic/Latino; 1 Hispanic/Latino), 6 international. Average age 25. 46 applicants, 87% accepted, 19 enrolled. In 2017, 11 master's awarded. *Entrance requirements:* Additional exam requirements/recommendations for international students: Required—TOEFL (minimum score 80 iBT), IELTS, PTE. *Application deadline:* Applications are processed on a rolling basis. Application fee: $50. Electronic applications accepted. Application fee is waived when completed online. *Expenses:* Tuition: Full-time $16,020; part-time $890 per credit hour. *Required fees:* $220; $90 per term. *Financial support:* Research assistantships with partial tuition reimbursements, teaching assistantships with partial tuition reimbursements, Federal Work-Study, scholarships/grants, and unspecified assistantships available. Support available to part-time students. Financial award applicants required to submit FAFSA. *Unit head:* Dr. Roman Zajac, Coordinator, 203-932-7114, E-mail: rzajac@newhaven.edu. *Application contact:* Michelle Mason, Director of Graduate Enrollment, 203-932-7067, E-mail: mmason@newhaven.edu.
Website: http://www.newhaven.edu/4728/

University of North Alabama, College of Arts and Sciences, Department of Geography, Florence, AL 35632-0001. Offers geospatial science (MS). *Program availability:* Part-time, 100% online. *Faculty:* 7 full-time (1 woman). *Students:* 8 full-time (2 women), 8 part-time (3 women); includes 1 minority (Asian, non-Hispanic/Latino), 2 international. Average age 28. 8 applicants, 75% accepted, 2 enrolled. In 2017, 3 master's awarded. *Degree requirements:* For master's, comprehensive exam (for some programs), thesis optional. *Entrance requirements:* For master's, GRE, three letters of recommendation; personal statement; letter of intent. Additional exam requirements/recommendations for international students: Required—TOEFL (minimum score 550 paper-based; 79 iBT), IELTS (minimum score 6), PTE (minimum score 54). *Application deadline:* Applications are processed on a rolling basis. Application fee: $50 ($100 for international students). Electronic applications accepted. *Expenses:* Tuition, state resident: full-time $7824; part-time $5943 per year. Tuition, nonresident: full-time $15,648; part-time $11,736 per year. *Required fees:* $3064; $2298 per unit. Tuition and fees vary according to course load and reciprocity agreements. *Financial support:* In 2017–18, 10 students received support. Federal Work-Study, scholarships/grants, and unspecified assistantships available. Financial award application deadline: 2/1; financial award applicants required to submit FAFSA. *Total annual research expenditures:* $8,644. *Unit head:* Dr. Francis T. Koti, Chair, 256-765-4219, E-mail: ftkoti@una.edu. *Application contact:* Hillary N. Coats, Graduate Admissions Coordinator, 256-765-4447, E-mail: graduate@una.edu.
Website: http://www.una.edu/geography/

The University of North Carolina at Charlotte, College of Liberal Arts and Sciences, Department of Geography and Earth Sciences, Charlotte, NC 28223-0001. Offers earth sciences (MS); geography (MA), including community planning, geographic information science and technologies, location analysis, urban-regional analysis; geography and urban regional analysis (PhD). *Program availability:* Part-time, evening/weekend. *Faculty:* 32 full-time (13 women), 1 part-time/adjunct (0 women). *Students:* 42 full-time (17 women), 27 part-time (11 women); includes 14 minority (4 Black or African American, non-Hispanic/Latino; 2 Asian, non-Hispanic/Latino; 5 Hispanic/Latino; 3 Two or more races, non-Hispanic/Latino), 14 international. Average age 32. 34 applicants, 74% accepted, 10 enrolled. In 2017, 11 master's, 4 doctorates awarded. Terminal master's awarded for partial completion of doctoral program. *Degree requirements:* For master's, comprehensive exam, thesis or alternative, project; for doctorate, thesis/dissertation. *Entrance requirements:* For master's, GRE General Test or MAT, minimum GPA of 2.75, 3.0 for junior and senior years, transcripts, letters of recommendation, and personal essays (for MS); minimum GPA of 3.1 overall or for the last 2 years, 3.2 in major, three letters of reference, and personal essay (for MA); for doctorate, GRE, MA or MS in geography or a field related to the primary emphases of the program; minimum master's-level GPA of 3.5; GIS proficiency. Additional exam requirements/recommendations for international students: Required—TOEFL (minimum score 523 paper-based, 70 iBT) or IELTS (6.5). *Application deadline:* For fall admission, 2/1 for domestic and international students; for spring admission, 9/30 for domestic and international students. Applications are processed on a rolling basis. Application fee: $75. Electronic applications accepted. *Expenses:* Tuition, state resident: full-time $4337. Tuition, nonresident: full-time $17,771. *Required fees:* $3211. Tuition and fees vary according to course load and program. *Financial support:* In 2017–18, 37 students received support, including 5 research assistantships (averaging $7,350 per year), 32 teaching assistantships (averaging $8,594 per year); career-related internships or fieldwork, institutionally sponsored loans, scholarships/grants, and unspecified assistantships also available. Support available to part-time students. Financial award application deadline: 3/1; financial award applicants required to submit FAFSA. *Total annual research expenditures:* $321,902. *Unit head:* Dr. Craig Allan, Chair, 704-687-5999, E-mail: ges@uncc.edu. *Application contact:* Kathy B. Giddings, Director of Graduate Admissions, 704-687-5503, Fax: 704-687-1668, E-mail: gradadm@uncc.edu.
Website: https://geoearth.uncc.edu/

The University of North Carolina at Greensboro, Graduate School, College of Arts and Sciences, Department of Geography, Greensboro, NC 27412-5001. Offers applied geography (MA); geographic information science (Certificate); geography (PhD); urban and economic development (Certificate). *Degree requirements:* For master's, comprehensive exam, thesis or alternative. *Entrance requirements:* For master's, GRE General Test. Additional exam requirements/recommendations for international students: Required—TOEFL. Electronic applications accepted.

The University of North Carolina Wilmington, College of Arts and Sciences, Department of Earth and Ocean Sciences, Wilmington, NC 28403-3297. Offers geographic information science (Graduate Certificate); geoscience (MS). *Program availability:* Part-time. *Faculty:* 16 full-time (8 women). *Students:* 10 full-time (4 women), 33 part-time (13 women); includes 3 minority (1 Black or African American, non-Hispanic/Latino; 1 Hispanic/Latino; 1 Two or more races, non-Hispanic/Latino). Average age 26. 34 applicants, 74% accepted, 19 enrolled. In 2017, 23 master's awarded. *Degree requirements:* For master's, comprehensive exam, thesis (for some programs). *Entrance requirements:* For master's, GRE General Test, 3 recommendations, research essay. Additional exam requirements/recommendations for international students: Required—TOEFL (minimum score 550 paper-based; 79 iBT), IELTS (minimum score 6.5). *Application deadline:* For fall admission, 4/15 for domestic students; for spring admission, 11/30 for domestic students. Applications are processed on a rolling basis. Application fee: $75. Electronic applications accepted. *Expenses:* Tuition, state resident: full-time $4626; part-time $226.76 per credit hour. Tuition, nonresident: full-time $17,834; part-time $874.22 per credit hour. *Required fees:* $2124. Tuition and fees vary according to program. *Financial support:* Research assistantships, teaching assistantships, and scholarships/grants available. Financial award application deadline: 1/1; financial award applicants required to submit FAFSA. *Unit head:* Dr. Doug Gamble, Chair, 910-962-3778, Fax: 910-962-7077, E-mail: gambled@uncw.edu. *Application contact:* Dr. Joanne Halls, Graduate Coordinator, 910-962-7614, Fax: 910-962-7077, E-mail: hallsj@uncw.edu.
Website: http://uncw.edu/msgeoscience/index.html

University of North Dakota, Graduate School, College of Arts and Sciences, Department of Geography and Geographic Information Science, Grand Forks, ND 58202. Offers MA, MS. *Program availability:* Part-time. *Degree requirements:* For master's, comprehensive exam, thesis or alternative. *Entrance requirements:* For master's, minimum GPA of 3.0. Additional exam requirements/recommendations for international students: Required—TOEFL (minimum score 550 paper-based; 79 iBT), IELTS (minimum score 6.5). Electronic applications accepted. *Faculty research:* Regional and urban development, environmental geography, geographic education, geographic techniques.

University of North Texas Health Science Center at Fort Worth, School of Public Health, Fort Worth, TX 76107-2699. Offers biostatistics (MS); epidemiology (MPH, MS, PhD); food security and public health (Graduate Certificate); GIS in public health (Graduate Certificate); global health (Graduate Certificate); global health for medical professionals (Graduate Certificate); health administration (MHA); health behavior research (MS, PhD); maternal and child health (MPH); public health (Graduate Certificate); public health practice (MPH); DO/MPH; MS/MPH. *Accreditation:* CEPH. *Program availability:* Part-time, evening/weekend, 100% online. *Degree requirements:* For master's, thesis or alternative, supervised internship; for doctorate, thesis/dissertation, supervised internship. *Entrance requirements:* For master's, GRE General Test. Additional exam requirements/recommendations for international students: Required—TOEFL. Electronic applications accepted. *Expenses:* Contact institution.

University of Pennsylvania, School of Design, Department of City and Regional Planning, Philadelphia, PA 19104. Offers city and regional planning (PhD); city planning (MCP); GIS and spatial analysis (Certificate); land preservation (Certificate); urban design (Certificate); urban redevelopment (Certificate); urban spatial analytics (MUSA). *Accreditation:* ACSP (one or more programs are accredited). *Program availability:* Part-time. *Faculty:* 16 full-time (8 women), 3 part-time/adjunct (0 women). *Students:* 148 full-

time (83 women), 5 part-time (2 women); includes 22 minority (5 Black or African American, non-Hispanic/Latino; 8 Asian, non-Hispanic/Latino; 6 Hispanic/Latino; 1 Native Hawaiian or other Pacific Islander, non-Hispanic/Latino; 2 Two or more races, non-Hispanic/Latino), 56 international. Average age 27. 395 applicants, 62% accepted, 101 enrolled. In 2017, 65 master's, 5 doctorates, 7 other advanced degrees awarded. *Degree requirements:* For doctorate, thesis/dissertation. *Entrance requirements:* Additional exam requirements/recommendations for international students: Required—TOEFL (minimum score 100 iBT); Recommended—IELTS (minimum score 7), TSE (minimum score 68). *Application deadline:* For spring admission, 1/12 for domestic students. Application fee: $80. Electronic applications accepted. *Financial support:* In 2017–18, 39 teaching assistantships (averaging $2,000 per year) were awarded; fellowships, research assistantships, and Federal Work-Study also available. Financial award application deadline: 2/15; financial award applicants required to submit FAFSA. *Faculty research:* Transportation planning, community and economic development, public private development, land use and environmental planning, urban design. *Unit head:* Dr. John Landis, Department Chair, 215-746-2340, E-mail: jlan@design.upenn.edu. *Application contact:* Roslynne Carter, Administrative Assistant, 215-898-8330, Fax: 215-898-5730, E-mail: admissions@design.upenn.edu.
Website: https://www.design.upenn.edu/city-regional-planning

University of Pittsburgh, Kenneth P. Dietrich School of Arts and Sciences, Department of Geology and Environmental Science, Pittsburgh, PA 15260. Offers geographical information systems and remote sensing (Pro-MS); geology and environmental science (MS, PhD). *Program availability:* Part-time. *Faculty:* 10 full-time (3 women). *Students:* 12 full-time (4 women), 2 part-time (1 woman). Average age 30. 70 applicants, 33% accepted, 12 enrolled. In 2017, 5 master's, 2 doctorates awarded. *Degree requirements:* For master's, comprehensive exam, thesis; for doctorate, comprehensive exam, thesis/dissertation. *Entrance requirements:* For master's and doctorate, GRE. Additional exam requirements/recommendations for international students: Required—TOEFL (minimum score 100 iBT); Recommended—IELTS (minimum score 7). *Application deadline:* For fall admission, 1/15 for domestic and international students. Application fee: $50. Electronic applications accepted. *Expenses:* Contact institution. *Financial support:* In 2017–18, 25 students received support, including 9 fellowships (averaging $32,181 per year), 3 research assistantships with full tuition reimbursements available (averaging $14,933 per year), 12 teaching assistantships with full tuition reimbursements available (averaging $17,910 per year). Financial award application deadline: 1/15. *Faculty research:* Volcanology; sedimentary geology; geochemistry; hydrology; geophysics; geomorphology; remote sensing. *Total annual research expenditures:* $1.6 million. *Unit head:* Cindy Niznik, Administrative Officer, 412-624-9070, E-mail: niznik@pitt.edu. *Application contact:* Annemarie L. Vranesevic, Academic Coordinator, 412-624-8779, E-mail: gpsgrad@pitt.edu.
Website: http://geology.pitt.edu/

University of Redlands, College of Arts and Sciences, Program in Geographic Information Systems, Redlands, CA 92373-0999. Offers MS. *Entrance requirements:* For master's, 2 years of professional experience using GIS or 2 university-level GIS courses plus internship, minimum undergraduate GPA of 3.0, 2 letters of recommendation. Additional exam requirements/recommendations for international students: Required—TOEFL (minimum score 550 paper-based); Recommended—IELTS (minimum score 5.5). Electronic applications accepted. *Expenses:* Contact institution.

University of Southern California, Graduate School, Dana and David Dornsife College of Letters, Arts and Sciences, Spatial Sciences Institute, Los Angeles, CA 90089. Offers geographic information science and technology (MS, Graduate Certificate). *Program availability:* Part-time, evening/weekend, online learning. Terminal master's awarded for partial completion of doctoral program. *Degree requirements:* For master's, thesis. *Entrance requirements:* For master's, GRE. Additional exam requirements/recommendations for international students: Required—TOEFL. Electronic applications accepted. *Faculty research:* Geocoding, geocomputation, GIS, environmental exposure estimation, spatial data accuracy and uncertainty.

University of South Florida, College of Arts and Sciences, School of Geosciences, Tampa, FL 33620-9951. Offers environmental science and policy (MS); geography (MA), including environmental geography, geographic information science and spatial analysis, human geography; geography and environmental science and policy (PhD); geology (MS, PhD). *Program availability:* Part-time, evening/weekend. *Faculty:* 31 full-time (6 women). *Students:* 106 full-time (50 women), 41 part-time (21 women); includes 82 minority (67 Black or African American, non-Hispanic/Latino; 5 Asian, non-Hispanic/Latino; 6 Hispanic/Latino; 4 Two or more races, non-Hispanic/Latino), 41 international. Average age 29. 132 applicants, 57% accepted, 38 enrolled. In 2017, 32 master's, 10 doctorates awarded. *Degree requirements:* For master's, comprehensive exam, thesis (for some programs); for doctorate, comprehensive exam, thesis/dissertation. *Entrance requirements:* For master's, GRE General Test, minimum GPA of 3.0 for last 60 credits of undergraduate degree, letter of intent, letters of recommendation; for doctorate, GRE General Test, minimum GPA of 3.0 (for geology), 3.2 (for environmental science and policy and geography); letter of intent; letters of recommendation. Additional exam requirements/recommendations for international students: Required—TOEFL minimum score 550 paper-based; 79 iBT or IELTS minimum score 6.5 (for MA and MURP); TOEFL minimum score 600 paper-based (for MS and PhD). *Application deadline:* For fall admission, 2/15 priority date for domestic students, 2/15 for international students; for spring admission, 10/15 priority date for domestic students, 9/15 for international students; for summer admission, 2/15 priority date for domestic students, 1/15 for international students. Application fee: $30. Electronic applications accepted. *Financial support:* In 2017–18, 43 students received support, including 3 research assistantships (averaging $12,345 per year), 25 teaching assistantships with tuition reimbursements available (averaging $12,807 per year); unspecified assistantships also available. Financial award application deadline: 3/1. *Faculty research:* Geography: human geography, environmental geography, geographic information science and spatial analysis, urban geography, social theory; environmental science, policy, and planning: water resources, wildlife ecology, Karst and wetland environments, natural hazards, soil contamination, meteorology and climatology, environmental sustainability and policy, urban and regional planning. *Total annual research expenditures:* $2.9 million. *Unit head:* Dr. Mark Rains, Professor and Chair, 813-974-3310, Fax: 813-974-5911, E-mail: mrains@usf.edu. *Application contact:* Dr. Ruiliang Pu, Associate Professor and Graduate Program Coordinator, 813-974-1508, Fax: 813-974-5911, E-mail: rpu@usf.edu.
Website: http://hennarot.forest.usf.edu/main/depts/geosci/

University of South Florida, Innovative Education, Tampa, FL 33620-9951. Offers adult, career and higher education (Graduate Certificate), including college teaching, leadership in developing human resources, leadership in higher education; Africana studies (Graduate Certificate), including diasporas and health disparities, genocide and human rights; aging studies (Graduate Certificate), including gerontology; art research (Graduate Certificate), including museum studies; business foundations (Graduate Certificate); chemical and biomedical engineering (Graduate Certificate), including materials science and engineering, water, health and sustainability; child and family studies (Graduate Certificate), including positive behavior support; civil and industrial engineering (Graduate Certificate), including transportation systems analysis; community and family health (Graduate Certificate), including maternal and child health, social marketing and public health, violence and injury: prevention and intervention, women's health; criminology (Graduate Certificate), including criminal justice administration; data science for public administration (Graduate Certificate); digital humanities (Graduate Certificate); educational measurement and research (Graduate Certificate), including evaluation; English (Graduate Certificate), including comparative literary studies, creative writing, professional and technical communication; entrepreneurship (Graduate Certificate); environmental health (Graduate Certificate), including safety management; epidemiology and biostatistics (Graduate Certificate), including applied biostatistics, biostatistics, concepts and tools of epidemiology, epidemiology, epidemiology of infectious diseases; geography, environment and planning (Graduate Certificate), including community development, environmental policy and management, geographical information systems; geology (Graduate Certificate), including hydrogeology; global health (Graduate Certificate), including disaster management, global health and Latin American and Caribbean studies, global health practice, humanitarian assistance, infection control; government and international affairs (Graduate Certificate), including Cuban studies, globalization studies; health policy and management (Graduate Certificate), including health management and leadership, public health policy and programs; hearing specialist: early intervention (Graduate Certificate); industrial and management systems engineering (Graduate Certificate), including systems engineering, technology management; information studies (Graduate Certificate), including school library media specialist; information systems/decision sciences (Graduate Certificate), including analytics and business intelligence; instructional technology (Graduate Certificate), including distance education, Florida digital/virtual educator, instructional design, multimedia design, Web design; internal medicine, bioethics and medical humanities (Graduate Certificate), including biomedical ethics; Latin American and Caribbean studies (Graduate Certificate); leadership for coastal resiliency planning (Graduate Certificate); mass communications (Graduate Certificate), including multimedia journalism; mathematics and statistics (Graduate Certificate), including mathematics; medicine (Graduate Certificate), including aging and neuroscience, bioinformatics, biotechnology, brain fitness and memory management, clinical investigation, hand and upper limb rehabilitation, health informatics, health sciences, integrative weight management, intellectual property, medicine and gender, metabolic and nutritional medicine, metabolic cardiology, pharmacy sciences; national and competitive intelligence (Graduate Certificate); nursing (Graduate Certificate), including simulation based academic fellowship in advanced pain management; psychological and social foundations (Graduate Certificate), including career counseling, college teaching, diversity in education, mental health counseling, school counseling; public affairs (Graduate Certificate), including nonprofit management, public management, research administration; public health (Graduate Certificate), including assessing chemical toxicity and public health risks, health equity, pharmacoepidemiology, public health generalist, toxicology, translational research in adolescent behavioral health; public health practices (Graduate Certificate), including planning for healthy communities; rehabilitation and mental health counseling (Graduate Certificate), including integrative mental health care, marriage and family therapy, rehabilitation technology; secondary education (Graduate Certificate), including ESOL, foreign language education: culture and content, foreign language education: professional; social work (Graduate Certificate), including geriatric social work/clinical gerontology; special education (Graduate Certificate), including autism spectrum disorder, disabilities education: severe/profound; world languages (Graduate Certificate), including teaching English as a second language (TESL) or foreign language. *Unit head:* Dr. Cynthia DeLuca, Associate Vice President and Assistant Vice Provost, 813-974-3077, Fax: 813-974-7061, E-mail: deluca@usf.edu. *Application contact:* Owen Hooper, Director, Summer and Alternative Calendar Programs, 813-974-6917, E-mail: hooper@usf.edu.
Website: http://www.usf.edu/innovative-education/

The University of Texas at Dallas, School of Economic, Political and Policy Sciences, Program in Geospatial Information Sciences, Richardson, TX 75080. Offers MS, PhD. *Program availability:* Part-time, evening/weekend. *Faculty:* 8 full-time (1 woman). *Students:* 50 full-time (15 women), 33 part-time (13 women); includes 11 minority (3 Black or African American, non-Hispanic/Latino; 3 Asian, non-Hispanic/Latino; 4 Hispanic/Latino; 1 Two or more races, non-Hispanic/Latino), 39 international. Average age 31. 77 applicants, 40% accepted, 13 enrolled. In 2017, 10 master's, 2 doctorates awarded. *Degree requirements:* For master's, thesis (for some programs), project or thesis; internship; for doctorate, comprehensive exam, thesis/dissertation. *Entrance requirements:* For master's and doctorate, GRE General Test, minimum GPA of 3.0 in upper-level coursework in field. Additional exam requirements/recommendations for international students: Required—TOEFL (minimum score 550 paper-based). *Application deadline:* For fall admission, 7/15 for domestic students, 5/1 priority date for international students; for spring admission, 11/15 for domestic students, 9/1 priority date for international students. Applications are processed on a rolling basis. Application fee: $50 ($100 for international students). Electronic applications accepted. *Expenses:* Tuition, state resident: full-time $12,916; part-time $718 per credit hour. Tuition, nonresident: full-time $25,252; part-time $1403 per credit hour. *Financial support:* In 2017–18, 30 students received support, including 2 research assistantships with partial tuition reimbursements available (averaging $18,755 per year), 12 teaching assistantships with partial tuition reimbursements available (averaging $13,100 per year); fellowships, career-related internships or fieldwork, Federal Work-Study, institutionally sponsored loans, scholarships/grants, and unspecified assistantships also available. Support available to part-time students. Financial award application deadline: 4/30; financial award applicants required to submit FAFSA. *Faculty research:* Urban and regional development, artificial intelligence techniques for geospatial investigation, improvement of current spatial analysis and modeling techniques, demographic studies. *Unit head:* Dr. Fang Qiu, Program Head, 972-883-4134, Fax: 972-883-2735, E-mail: ffqiu@utdallas.edu. *Application contact:* Judy Du, Graduate Program Administrator, 972-883-4964, Fax: 972-883-6297, E-mail: judy.du@utdallas.edu.
Website: http://www.utdallas.edu/epps/geospatial-science/

The University of Toledo, College of Graduate Studies, College of Languages, Literature and Social Sciences, Department of Geography and Planning, Toledo, OH 43606-3390. Offers geographic information science and applied geographics (Certificate); geography and planning (MA); spatially-integrated social science (PhD). *Program availability:* Part-time. *Degree requirements:* For master's, comprehensive exam, thesis; for doctorate, thesis/dissertation. *Entrance requirements:* For master's and doctorate, GRE General Test, minimum cumulative point-hour ratio of 2.7 for all previous academic work, three letters of recommendation; for Certificate, minimum cumulative point-hour ratio of 2.7 for all previous academic work, three letters of recommendation. Additional exam requirements/recommendations for international students: Required—TOEFL (minimum score 550 paper-based; 80 iBT). Electronic applications accepted.

University of Utah, Graduate School, College of Social and Behavioral Science, Department of Geography, Salt Lake City, UT 84112-9155. Offers geographic information science (MS); geography (MS, PhD). *Program availability:* Part-time. *Faculty:* 14 full-time (4 women), 10 part-time/adjunct (4 women). *Students:* 33 full-time

(11 women), 17 part-time (11 women); includes 8 minority (2 Asian, non-Hispanic/Latino; 5 Hispanic/Latino; 1 Native Hawaiian or other Pacific Islander, non-Hispanic/Latino), 4 international. Average age 27. 66 applicants, 58% accepted, 16 enrolled. In 2017, 18 master's, 2 doctorates awarded. *Degree requirements:* For master's, thesis (for some programs), 6 research hours (for MS in geography); skills portfolio (for MS in geographic information science); for doctorate, comprehensive exam, thesis/dissertation, 14 research hours, 2 consecutive full-time semesters. *Entrance requirements:* For master's, GRE General Test (except for MS in geographic information science), minimum undergraduate GPA of 3.0; for doctorate, GRE General Test, minimum undergraduate GPA of 3.0. Additional exam requirements/recommendations for international students: Required—TOEFL (minimum score 550 paper-based; 80 iBT), IELTS (minimum score 6.5). *Application deadline:* For fall admission, 1/10 priority date for domestic and international students; for spring admission, 10/1 for domestic and international students. Application fee: $55 ($65 for international students). Electronic applications accepted. *Expenses:* $4420.93 per semester resident tuition; $14,208.67 per semester non-resident tuition. *Financial support:* In 2017–18, 6 students received support, including 3 fellowships (averaging $15,167 per year), 13 research assistantships (averaging $13,462 per year), 11 teaching assistantships (averaging $14,727 per year); scholarships/grants, health care benefits, tuition waivers (full), and unspecified assistantships also available. Financial award application deadline: 1/10. *Faculty research:* Urban-economic geography, earth system science, geographic information science and remote sensing, paleoenvironmental studies, hazards. *Total annual research expenditures:* $1 million. *Unit head:* Dr. Andrea R. Brunelle, Chair, 801-581-8218, Fax: 801-581-8219, E-mail: andrea.brunelle@geog.utah.edu. *Application contact:* Dr. Summer B. Rupper, Director of Graduate Studies, 801-581-8218, Fax: 801-581-8219, E-mail: summer.rupper@geog.utah.edu.
Website: http://www.geog.utah.edu

University of West Florida, Hal Marcus College of Science and Engineering, Department of Earth and Environmental Sciences, Pensacola, FL 32514-5750. Offers environmental science (MS); geographic information science administration (MS). *Program availability:* Part-time. *Entrance requirements:* For master's, GRE (minimum score: 50th percentile for verbal; 40th percentile for quantitative), official transcripts; formal letter of interest, background, and professional goals; three letters of recommendation by individuals in professionally-relevant fields (waived for graduates of UWF Department of Environmental Sciences); current curriculum vitae/resume. Additional exam requirements/recommendations for international students: Required—TOEFL (minimum score 550 paper-based).

University of West Georgia, College of Science and Mathematics, Carrollton, GA 30118. Offers biology (MS); computer science (MS); geographic information systems (Postbaccalaureate Certificate); mathematics (MS). *Program availability:* Part-time, evening/weekend, 100% online, blended/hybrid learning. *Faculty:* 47 full-time (16 women). *Students:* 19 full-time (9 women), 68 part-time (23 women); includes 24 minority (15 Black or African American, non-Hispanic/Latino; 1 American Indian or Alaska Native, non-Hispanic/Latino; 6 Asian, non-Hispanic/Latino; 2 Two or more races, non-Hispanic/Latino), 3 international. Average age 31. 72 applicants, 88% accepted, 54 enrolled. In 2017, 30 master's, 4 other advanced degrees awarded. *Entrance requirements:* Additional exam requirements/recommendations for international students: Required—TOEFL (minimum score 523 paper-based; 69 iBT); Recommended—IELTS (minimum score 6.5). *Application deadline:* For fall admission, 6/1 for domestic and international students; for spring admission, 11/15 for domestic students, 10/15 for international students; for summer admission, 4/1 for domestic students, 3/30 for international students. Applications are processed on a rolling basis. Application fee: $40. Electronic applications accepted. Tuition and fees vary according to degree level and program. *Financial support:* Fellowships, research assistantships, teaching assistantships, career-related internships or fieldwork, Federal Work-Study, institutionally sponsored loans, scholarships/grants, and unspecified assistantships available. Support available to part-time students. Financial award application deadline: 4/1; financial award applicants required to submit FAFSA. *Unit head:* Dr. Lok C. Lew Yan Voon, Dean of Science and Mathematics, 678-839-5190, Fax: 678-839-5191, E-mail: lokl@westga.edu. *Application contact:* Dr. Toby Ziglar, Assistant Dean of the Graduate School, 678-839-1394, Fax: 678-839-1395, E-mail: graduate@westga.edu.
Website: http://www.westga.edu/cosm

University of Wisconsin–Madison, Graduate School, College of Letters and Science, Department of Geography, Madison, WI 53706-1380. Offers cartography and geographic information systems (MS); geographic information systems (Certificate); geography (MS, PhD). *Program availability:* Part-time. *Degree requirements:* For master's, thesis; for doctorate, thesis/dissertation; for Certificate, internship. *Entrance requirements:* For master's and doctorate, GRE General Test, minimum GPA of 3.25. Electronic applications accepted. *Faculty research:* Physical geography, urban/historical geography, people-environment, history of cartography, GIS.

University of Wisconsin–Milwaukee, Graduate School, School of Architecture and Urban Planning, Department of Architecture, Milwaukee, WI 53201-0413. Offers architecture (M Arch, MS Arch, PhD); geographic information systems (Graduate Certificate). *Students:* 97 full-time (47 women), 13 part-time (4 women); includes 15 minority (2 Black or African American, non-Hispanic/Latino; 1 American Indian or Alaska Native, non-Hispanic/Latino; 4 Asian, non-Hispanic/Latino; 1 Hispanic/Latino; 7 Two or more races, non-Hispanic/Latino), 16 international. Average age 29. 145 applicants, 55% accepted, 35 enrolled. In 2017, 39 master's, 5 doctorates, 9 other advanced degrees awarded. *Degree requirements:* For master's, comprehensive exam, thesis; for doctorate, comprehensive exam, thesis/dissertation. *Entrance requirements:* For master's, GRE General Test, portfolio. Additional exam requirements/recommendations for international students: Required—TOEFL (minimum score 600 paper-based; 100 iBT), IELTS (minimum score 7). *Application deadline:* For fall admission, 1/1 priority date for domestic students; for spring admission, 9/1 for domestic students. Application fee: $56 ($96 for international students). Electronic applications accepted. *Financial support:* Fellowships, teaching assistantships, career-related internships or fieldwork, health care benefits, unspecified assistantships, and project assistantships available. Support available to part-time students. Financial award application deadline: 4/15; financial award applicants required to submit FAFSA. *Unit head:* Robert Greenstreet, Dean, 414-229-4016. *Application contact:* Student Advising Office, 414-229-4015, E-mail: sarup-grad@uwm.edu.
Website: https://uwm.edu/sarup/architecture/

Virginia Commonwealth University, Graduate School, L. Douglas Wilder School of Government and Public Affairs, Program in Geographic Information Systems, Richmond, VA 23284-9005. Offers Certificate. *Entrance requirements:* Additional exam requirements/recommendations for international students: Required—TOEFL (minimum score 600 paper-based; 100 iBT); Recommended—IELTS (minimum score 6.5). Electronic applications accepted.

West Chester University of Pennsylvania, College of Business and Public Management, Department of Geography and Planning, West Chester, PA 19383. Offers geographic information systems (Certificate); geography (MS); geography and planning (MURP); urban and regional planning (Certificate). *Program availability:* Part-time, evening/weekend. *Students:* 10 full-time (4 women), 10 part-time (5 women); includes 1 minority (Black or African American, non-Hispanic/Latino). Average age 29. 17 applicants, 94% accepted, 11 enrolled. In 2017, 10 master's, 11 other advanced degrees awarded. *Degree requirements:* For master's, 48 credits: 27 credits required, 21 credits electives (for MURP); 33 credits or 11 courses (for MS); thesis or independent research course; for Certificate, 12 credits or 4 courses (for geographic information systems); 18 credits or 6 courses (for urban and regional planning). *Entrance requirements:* For master's and Certificate, minimum GPA of 2.8, resume, two letters of recommendation. Additional exam requirements/recommendations for international students: Required—TOEFL or IELTS. *Application deadline:* For fall admission, 5/15 for international students; for spring admission, 10/15 for international students. Applications are processed on a rolling basis. Application fee: $50. Electronic applications accepted. *Expenses:* Tuition, state resident: full-time $9000; part-time $500 per credit. Tuition, nonresident: full-time $13,500; part-time $750 per credit. *Required fees:* $2959; $149.79 per credit. *Financial support:* Scholarships/grants and unspecified assistantships available. Financial award application deadline: 2/15; financial award applicants required to submit FAFSA. *Faculty research:* Sustainability and environmental conservation, land use/suburban planning, geographic information systems, transportation planning, housing, economic development. *Unit head:* Dr. Dottie Ives Dewey, Chair/Graduate Coordinator for Certificate Programs, 610-436-2746, Fax: 610-436-2889, E-mail: divesdewey@wcupa.edu. *Application contact:* Dr. Matin Katirai, Graduate Coordinator, 610-436-2392, Fax: 610-436-2889, E-mail: mkatirai@wcupa.edu.
Website: http://www.wcupa.edu/business-publicManagement/geographyPlanning/

Western Illinois University, School of Graduate Studies, College of Arts and Sciences, Department of Biological Sciences, Macomb, IL 61455-1390. Offers biology (MS); environmental GIS (Certificate); zoo and aquarium studies (Certificate). *Program availability:* Part-time. *Students:* 43 full-time (24 women), 24 part-time (14 women); includes 5 minority (1 Black or African American, non-Hispanic/Latino; 2 Hispanic/Latino; 2 Two or more races, non-Hispanic/Latino), 21 international. Average age 28. 20 applicants, 90% accepted, 12 enrolled. In 2017, 22 master's awarded. *Degree requirements:* For master's, thesis or alternative. *Entrance requirements:* Additional exam requirements/recommendations for international students: Required—TOEFL (minimum score 550 paper-based; 80 iBT); Recommended—IELTS. *Application deadline:* Applications are processed on a rolling basis. Application fee: $30. Electronic applications accepted. *Financial support:* In 2017–18, 13 research assistantships with full tuition reimbursements (averaging $7,544 per year), 19 teaching assistantships with full tuition reimbursements (averaging $8,688 per year) were awarded; unspecified assistantships also available. Financial award applicants required to submit FAFSA. *Unit head:* Dr. Richard Musser, Chairperson, 309-298-1546. *Application contact:* Dr. Nancy Parsons, Associate Provost and Director of Graduate Studies, 309-298-1806, Fax: 309-298-2345, E-mail: grad-office@wiu.edu.
Website: http://wiu.edu/biology

Western Illinois University, School of Graduate Studies, College of Arts and Sciences, Department of Geography, Macomb, IL 61455-1390. Offers geography (MA); GIS analysis: ecological GIS (Certificate); GIS analysis: GIS applications (Certificate). *Program availability:* Part-time. *Students:* 9 full-time (6 women), 2 part-time (1 woman), 1 international. Average age 26. 8 applicants, 100% accepted, 6 enrolled. In 2017, 3 master's awarded. *Degree requirements:* For master's, thesis or alternative. *Entrance requirements:* Additional exam requirements/recommendations for international students: Required—TOEFL (minimum score 550 paper-based; 80 iBT). *Application deadline:* Applications are processed on a rolling basis. Application fee: $30. Electronic applications accepted. *Financial support:* In 2017–18, 6 students received support, including research assistantships with full tuition reimbursements available (averaging $7,544 per year); unspecified assistantships also available. Financial award applicants required to submit FAFSA. *Unit head:* Dr. Sam Thompson, Chairperson, 309-298-1648. *Application contact:* Dr. Nancy Parsons, Associate Provost and Director of Graduate School, 309-298-1806, Fax: 309-298-2345, E-mail: grad-office@wiu.edu.
Website: http://www.wiu.edu/cas/geography/

Western Michigan University, Graduate College, College of Arts and Sciences, Department of Geography, Kalamazoo, MI 49008. Offers geographic information science (Graduate Certificate); geography (MA). *Degree requirements:* For master's, thesis.

Geography

Appalachian State University, Cratis D. Williams Graduate School, Department of Geography and Planning, Boone, NC 28608. Offers geography (MA), including geographic information science. *Program availability:* Part-time, online learning. *Degree requirements:* For master's, comprehensive exam, thesis or alternative. *Entrance requirements:* For master's, GRE General Test, 3 letters of recommendation. Additional exam requirements/recommendations for international students: Required—TOEFL (minimum score 570 paper-based; 79 iBT), IELTS (minimum score 6.5). Electronic applications accepted. *Faculty research:* Global change, climatology, production cartography, geographic information systems, North Carolina geography, Latin America.

Arizona State University at the Tempe campus, College of Liberal Arts and Sciences, School of Geographical Sciences and Urban Planning, Tempe, AZ 85287-5302. Offers geographic information systems (MAS); geographical information science (Graduate Certificate); geography (MA, PhD); transportation systems (Graduate Certificate); urban and environmental planning (MUEP); urban planning (PhD). *Accreditation:* ACSP. Terminal master's awarded for partial completion of doctoral program. *Degree requirements:* For master's, thesis, interactive Program of Study (iPOS) submitted before completing 50 percent of required credit hours; for doctorate, comprehensive exam, thesis/dissertation, interactive Program of Study (iPOS) submitted before completing 50 percent of required credit hours. *Entrance requirements:* For master's and

doctorate, GRE, minimum GPA of 3.0 or equivalent in last 2 years of work leading to bachelor's degree. Additional exam requirements/recommendations for international students: Required—TOEFL, IELTS, or PTE. Electronic applications accepted. *Expenses:* Contact institution.

Auburn University, Graduate School, College of Sciences and Mathematics, Department of Geology and Geography, Auburn University, AL 36849. Offers MS. *Program availability:* Part-time. *Faculty:* 18 full-time (5 women). *Students:* 24 full-time (11 women), 15 part-time (6 women); includes 3 minority (1 Asian, non-Hispanic/Latino; 2 Hispanic/Latino), 9 international. Average age 25. 38 applicants, 79% accepted, 20 enrolled. In 2017, 18 master's awarded. *Degree requirements:* For master's, computer language or geographic information systems, field camp. *Entrance requirements:* For master's, GRE General Test. *Application deadline:* Applications are processed on a rolling basis. Application fee: $50 ($60 for international students). Electronic applications accepted. *Expenses:* Tuition, state resident: full-time $10,974; part-time $519 per credit hour. Tuition, nonresident: full-time $29,658; part-time $1557 per credit hour. *Required fees:* $816 per semester. Tuition and fees vary according to degree level and program. *Financial support:* Research assistantships, teaching assistantships, and Federal Work-Study available. Support available to part-time students. Financial award application deadline: 3/15; financial award applicants required to submit FAFSA. *Faculty research:* Empirical magma dynamics and melt migration, ore mineralogy, role of terrestrial plant biomass in deposition, metamorphic petrology and isotope geochemistry, reef development, crinoid topology. *Unit head:* Dr. Mark Steltenpohl, Chair, 334-844-4893. *Application contact:* Dr. George Flowers, Dean of the Graduate School, 334-844-2125.

Ball State University, Graduate School, College of Sciences and Humanities, Department of Geography, Muncie, IN 47306. Offers geographic information systems (Certificate); geography (MS); professional meteorology and climatology (Certificate). *Program availability:* Part-time. *Faculty:* 8 full-time (2 women). *Students:* 5 full-time (4 women), 4 part-time (1 woman); includes 1 minority (Hispanic/Latino), 1 international. Average age 24. 17 applicants, 71% accepted, 5 enrolled. In 2017, 3 master's awarded. *Entrance requirements:* For master's, minimum baccalaureate GPA of 2.75 or 3.0 in latter half of baccalaureate, letter of interest, three letters of recommendation, resume or curriculum vitae, official transcripts. Additional exam requirements/recommendations for international students: Required—TOEFL (minimum score 550 paper-based; 79 iBT), IELTS (minimum score 6.5). *Application deadline:* Applications are processed on a rolling basis. Application fee: $60. Electronic applications accepted. *Financial support:* In 2017–18, 5 students received support, including 5 teaching assistantships with partial tuition reimbursements available (averaging $9,800 per year). Financial award application deadline: 3/1; financial award applicants required to submit FAFSA. *Faculty research:* Remote sensing, tourism and recreation, Latin American urbanization. *Unit head:* Dr. Kevin Turcotte, Chairperson/Professor, 765-285-1776, Fax: 765-285-2351, E-mail: turk@bsu.edu. *Application contact:* Dr. Jason Yang, Associate Professor/ Graduate Program Director, 765-285-1761, Fax: 765-285-2351, E-mail: jyang@bsu.edu. Website: http://www.bsu.edu/geography/

Binghamton University, State University of New York, Graduate School, Harpur College of Arts and Sciences, Department of Geography, Binghamton, NY 13902-6000. Offers MA. *Program availability:* Part-time. *Faculty:* 12 full-time (3 women). *Students:* 29 full-time (15 women), 1 part-time (0 women); includes 9 minority (5 Black or African American, non-Hispanic/Latino; 4 Hispanic/Latino), 12 international. Average age 26. 30 applicants, 93% accepted, 15 enrolled. In 2017, 22 master's awarded. *Degree requirements:* For master's, one foreign language, thesis (for some programs). *Entrance requirements:* For master's, GRE General Test. Additional exam requirements/ recommendations for international students: Required—TOEFL (minimum score 550 paper-based; 80 iBT). *Application deadline:* For fall admission, 5/15 priority date for domestic and international students; for spring admission, 1/15 priority date for domestic and international students. Application fee: $75. Electronic applications accepted. *Financial support:* In 2017–18, 18 students received support, including 8 teaching assistantships with full tuition reimbursements available (averaging $15,000 per year); career-related internships or fieldwork, Federal Work-Study, institutionally sponsored loans, scholarships/grants, health care benefits, tuition waivers (full and partial), and unspecified assistantships also available. Financial award application deadline: 1/15; financial award applicants required to submit FAFSA. *Unit head:* John Frazier, Director of Graduate Studies, 607-777-6179, E-mail: frazier@binghamton.edu. *Application contact:* Ben Balkaya, Assistant Dean and Director, 607-777-2151, Fax: 607-777-2501, E-mail: balkaya@binghamton.edu.

Brock University, Faculty of Graduate Studies, Faculty of Social Sciences, Program in Geography, St. Catharines, ON L2S 3A1, Canada. Offers MA. *Program availability:* Part-time. *Degree requirements:* For master's, thesis optional. *Entrance requirements:* For master's, honors degree. Additional exam requirements/recommendations for international students: Required—TOEFL (minimum score 550 paper-based; 80 iBT), IELTS (minimum score 6.5), TWE (minimum score 4).

California State University, East Bay, Office of Graduate Studies, College of Letters, Arts, and Social Sciences, Department of Anthropology, Geography and Environmental Studies, Hayward, CA 94542-3000. Offers anthropology (MA); geography (MA). *Program availability:* Part-time. *Faculty:* 7 full-time (1 woman), 10 part-time/adjunct (8 women). *Students:* 2 part-time (both women); includes 1 minority (Hispanic/Latino). Average age 61. In 2017, 5 master's awarded. *Degree requirements:* For master's, variable foreign language requirement, project or thesis. *Entrance requirements:* For master's, minimum GPA of 3.0 in field. Additional exam requirements/recommendations for international students: Required—TOEFL (minimum score 550 paper-based). *Application deadline:* For fall admission, 6/1 for domestic and international students. Applications are processed on a rolling basis. Application fee: $55. Electronic applications accepted. *Financial support:* Fellowships, teaching assistantships, career-related internships or fieldwork, Federal Work-Study, institutionally sponsored loans, and scholarships/grants available. Support available to part-time students. Financial award application deadline: 3/2; financial award applicants required to submit FAFSA. *Faculty research:* Sustainability, water resources, geographic information systems (GIS), mapping. *Unit head:* Dr. David Larson, Chair, 510-885-3192, E-mail: david.larson@csueastbay.edu. *Application contact:* Prof. David Woo, Graduate Advisor for Geography, 510-885-3160, Fax: 510-885-2353, E-mail: david.woo@csueastbay.edu. Website: http://www20.csueastbay.edu/class/departments/ages/index.html

California State University, Fullerton, Graduate Studies, College of Humanities and Social Sciences, Department of Geography, Fullerton, CA 92831-3599. Offers MA. *Program availability:* Part-time. *Faculty:* 5 full-time (1 woman). *Students:* 2 full-time (1 woman), 16 part-time (8 women); includes 5 minority (1 Black or African American, non-Hispanic/Latino; 4 Hispanic/Latino), 2 international. Average age 33. 4 applicants, 100% accepted, 3 enrolled. *Entrance requirements:* For master's, minimum GPA of 3.0, 18 undergraduate credits in field. Application fee: $55. *Financial support:* Career-related internships or fieldwork, Federal Work-Study, institutionally sponsored loans, and scholarships/grants available. Support available to part-time students. Financial award application deadline: 3/1; financial award applicants required to submit FAFSA. *Faculty research:* Human geography, physical geography. *Unit head:* Mark Drayse, Chair, 657-278-7593, E-mail: mdrayse@fullerton.edu. *Application contact:* Admissions/ Applications, 657-278-2371.

California State University, Long Beach, Graduate Studies, College of Liberal Arts, Department of Geography, Long Beach, CA 90840. Offers MA, MS. *Program availability:* Part-time. *Degree requirements:* For master's, thesis. Electronic applications accepted. *Faculty research:* Demography, geographic information systems, world landforms and societies.

California State University, Los Angeles, Graduate Studies, College of Natural and Social Sciences, Department of Geography and Urban Analysis, Los Angeles, CA 90032-8530. Offers geography (MA). *Program availability:* Part-time, evening/weekend. *Degree requirements:* For master's, one foreign language, comprehensive exam or thesis. *Entrance requirements:* Additional exam requirements/recommendations for international students: Required—TOEFL (minimum score 500 paper-based). Electronic applications accepted. *Faculty research:* Technique focus-air photography, cartography, location analysis.

California State University, Northridge, Graduate Studies, College of Social and Behavioral Sciences, Department of Geography, Northridge, CA 91330. Offers MA. *Program availability:* Part-time. *Students:* 13 full-time (6 women), 18 part-time (11 women); includes 19 minority (1 Black or African American, non-Hispanic/Latino; 8 Asian, non-Hispanic/Latino; 9 Hispanic/Latino; 1 Two or more races, non-Hispanic/ Latino). Average age 32. 32 applicants, 69% accepted, 16 enrolled. In 2017, 7 master's awarded. *Degree requirements:* For master's, one foreign language, thesis. *Entrance requirements:* For master's, GRE General Test or minimum GPA of 3.0. Additional exam requirements/recommendations for international students: Required—TOEFL. *Application deadline:* For fall admission, 11/30 for domestic students. Application fee: $55. *Financial support:* Teaching assistantships available. Financial award application deadline: 3/1. *Unit head:* Edward Jackiewicz, Chair, 818-677-3532. Website: http://www.csun.edu/csbs/departments/geography/index.html

Carleton University, Faculty of Graduate Studies, Faculty of Arts and Social Sciences, Department of Geography and Environmental Studies, Ottawa, ON K1S 5B6, Canada. Offers geography (M Sc, MA, PhD). *Degree requirements:* For master's, thesis, seminar; for doctorate, one foreign language, thesis/dissertation, 2 comprehensive exams. *Entrance requirements:* For master's, honors degree; for doctorate, master's degree in geography. Additional exam requirements/recommendations for international students: Required—TOEFL. *Faculty research:* Human dimensions of global environmental change, winter environments, population studies, historical geography, globalization.

Central Connecticut State University, School of Graduate Studies, College of Liberal Arts and Social Sciences, Department of Geography, New Britain, CT 06050-4010. Offers MS. *Program availability:* Part-time, evening/weekend. *Faculty:* 6 full-time (2 women). *Students:* 7 full-time (4 women), 23 part-time (13 women); includes 6 minority (3 Black or African American, non-Hispanic/Latino; 2 Hispanic/Latino; 1 Native Hawaiian or other Pacific Islander, non-Hispanic/Latino). Average age 35. 14 applicants, 93% accepted, 7 enrolled. In 2017, 10 master's awarded. *Degree requirements:* For master's, comprehensive exam, thesis or alternative, special project. *Entrance requirements:* For master's, minimum undergraduate GPA of 3.0, essay. Additional exam requirements/ recommendations for international students: Required—TOEFL (minimum score 550 paper-based; 79 iBT); Recommended—IELTS (minimum score 6.5). *Application deadline:* For fall admission, 8/1 for domestic students, 5/1 for international students; for spring admission, 11/1 for domestic and international students. Applications are processed on a rolling basis. Application fee: $50. Electronic applications accepted. *Expenses: Tuition, area resident:* Full-time $6757. Tuition, state resident: full-time $9750; part-time $374 per credit. Tuition, nonresident: full-time $18,102; part-time $374 per credit. *Required fees:* $4635; $255 per credit. *Financial support:* In 2017–18, 3 students received support. Career-related internships or fieldwork, Federal Work-Study, scholarships/grants, and unspecified assistantships available. Support available to part-time students. Financial award application deadline: 3/1; financial award applicants required to submit FAFSA. *Faculty research:* Regional planning, environmental protection, tourism, computer mapping and geographic information systems. *Unit head:* Dr. Richard Benfield, Chair, 860-832-2785, E-mail: benfieldr@ccsu.edu. *Application contact:* Patricia Gardner, Associate Director of Graduate Studies, 860-832-2350, Fax: 860-832-2362.
Website: http://www.ccsu.edu/geography/index.html

Central Washington University, School of Graduate Studies and Research, College of the Sciences, Program in Cultural and Environmental Resource Management, Ellensburg, WA 98926. Offers anthropology (MS); geography (MS). *Entrance requirements:* For master's, GRE, minimum GPA of 3.0. Additional exam requirements/ recommendations for international students: Required—TOEFL (minimum score 550 paper-based; 79 iBT). *Application deadline:* For fall admission, 2/1 priority date for domestic students; for spring admission, 1/1 for domestic students. Applications are processed on a rolling basis. Application fee: $50. Electronic applications accepted. *Financial support:* Application deadline: 3/1; applicants required to submit FAFSA. *Unit head:* Dr. Karl Lillquist, Co-Director, 509-963-1188, Fax: 509-963-3224, E-mail: lillquis@cwu.edu. *Application contact:* Justine Eason, Admissions Program Coordinator, 509-963-3103, Fax: 509-963-1799, E-mail: masters@cwu.edu.

Clark University, Graduate School, School of Geography, Worcester, MA 01610-1477. Offers geography (PhD). *Faculty:* 19 full-time (7 women), 3 part-time/adjunct (2 women). *Students:* 55 full-time (29 women); includes 8 minority (1 Black or African American, non-Hispanic/Latino; 3 Asian, non-Hispanic/Latino; 4 Hispanic/Latino), 21 international. Average age 32. 135 applicants, 13% accepted, 9 enrolled. In 2017, 11 doctorates awarded. *Degree requirements:* For doctorate, thesis/dissertation. *Entrance requirements:* For doctorate, GRE General Test. Additional exam requirements/ recommendations for international students: Required—TOEFL (minimum score 575 paper-based; 90 iBT), IELTS (minimum score 6.5). *Application deadline:* For fall admission, 12/31 priority date for domestic and international students. Application fee: $75. Electronic applications accepted. *Financial support:* Fellowships, research assistantships, teaching assistantships, career-related internships or fieldwork, and tuition waivers (full) available. *Faculty research:* Global environmental change, geographic information systems, natural and technological hazards, water resources, urbanization. *Unit head:* Dr. Deb Martin, Director, 508-793-7104, E-mail: dmartin@clarku.edu.
Website: http://www.clarku.edu/departments/geography/

Concordia University, School of Graduate Studies, Faculty of Arts and Science, Department of Geography, Planning and Environment, Montréal, QC H3G 1M8, Canada. Offers environmental assessment (M Env, Diploma); geography, urban and environmental studies (M Sc, PhD).

Concordia University, School of Graduate Studies, Faculty of Arts and Science, Department of Political Science, Montréal, QC H3G 1M8, Canada. Offers political science (PhD); public policy and public administration (MA), including geography. *Degree requirements:* For master's, one foreign language, comprehensive exam, thesis optional, internship. *Entrance requirements:* For master's, honors degree or equivalent. Additional exam requirements/recommendations for international students: Required—TOEFL. *Faculty research:* International public policy and administration, Quebec public

administration, public policy and social/political theory, geography and public policy, public administration and decision making.

East Carolina University, Graduate School, Thomas Harriot College of Arts and Sciences, Department of Geography, Planning, and Environment, Greenville, NC 27858-4353. Offers development and environmental planning (Certificate); economic development (Certificate); geographic information science and technology (Certificate); geography (MA), including geography, planning, rural development. *Program availability:* Part-time, evening/weekend, online learning. *Students:* 15 full-time (8 women), 6 part-time (2 women); includes 4 minority (3 Black or African American, non-Hispanic/Latino; 1 Hispanic/Latino). Average age 27. 14 applicants, 93% accepted, 8 enrolled. In 2017, 5 master's, 1 other advanced degree awarded. *Degree requirements:* For master's, comprehensive exam, thesis optional. *Entrance requirements:* For master's, GRE General Test. Additional exam requirements/recommendations for international students: Recommended—TOEFL (minimum score 78 iBT), IELTS (minimum score 6.5). *Application deadline:* For fall admission, 4/1 priority date for domestic and international students. Applications are processed on a rolling basis. Application fee: $75. Electronic applications accepted. *Expenses:* Tuition, state resident: full-time $4749; part-time $297 per credit hour. Tuition, nonresident: full-time $17,898; part-time $1119 per credit hour. *Required fees:* $2691; $224 per credit hour. Part-time tuition and fees vary according to course load and program. *Financial support:* Research assistantships with partial tuition reimbursements, teaching assistantships with partial tuition reimbursements, and Federal Work-Study available. Support available to part-time students. Financial award application deadline: 3/1. *Faculty research:* Coastal vulnerability and adaptation, emergency management, public understanding of risk, catastrophic events. *Unit head:* Dr. Thad Wasklewicz, Chair, 252-328-6230, E-mail: wasklewiczt@ecu.edu. *Application contact:* Dean of Graduate School, 252-328-6012, Fax: 252-328-6071, E-mail: gradschool@ecu.edu.
Website: http://www.ecu.edu/geog

East Stroudsburg University of Pennsylvania, Graduate and Extended Studies, College of Arts and Sciences, Department of History and Geography, East Stroudsburg, PA 18301-2999. Offers M Ed, MA. *Program availability:* Part-time, evening/weekend. *Faculty:* 6 full-time (4 women). *Students:* 13 full-time (4 women), 8 part-time (1 woman), 7 international. Average age 30. 15 applicants, 87% accepted, 10 enrolled. In 2017, 6 master's awarded. *Degree requirements:* For master's, comprehensive exam, thesis, thesis defense. *Entrance requirements:* For master's, Commonwealth of Pennsylvania Department of Education certification requirements (M Ed). Additional exam requirements/recommendations for international students: Recommended—TOEFL (minimum score 560 paper-based; 83 iBT), IELTS. *Application deadline:* For fall admission, 7/31 priority date for domestic students, 6/30 priority date for international students; for spring admission, 11/30 for domestic students, 10/31 for international students. Applications are processed on a rolling basis. Application fee: $50. Electronic applications accepted. *Expenses:* Tuition, state resident: full-time $4500; part-time $3000 per credit. Tuition, nonresident: full-time $6750; part-time $4500 per credit. *Required fees:* $2642; $1756 per credit. $878 per semester. Tuition and fees vary according to course load, campus/location and program. *Financial support:* Research assistantships with tuition reimbursements, Federal Work-Study, and unspecified assistantships available. Support available to part-time students. Financial award application deadline: 3/1; financial award applicants required to submit FAFSA. *Unit head:* Martin Wilson, Graduate Coordinator, 570-422-3536, Fax: 570-422-3937, E-mail: mwilson@esu.edu. *Application contact:* Kevin Quintero, Associate Director, Graduate and Extended Studies, 570-422-3890, Fax: 570-422-2711, E-mail: kquintero@esu.edu.

Florida State University, The Graduate School, College of Social Sciences and Public Policy, Department of Geography, Tallahassee, FL 32306. Offers geographic information science (MS); geography (MA, MS, PhD). *Program availability:* Part-time. *Faculty:* 12 full-time (3 women), 7 part-time/adjunct (5 women). *Students:* 47 full-time (21 women), 13 part-time (5 women); includes 16 minority (1 Black or African American, non-Hispanic/Latino; 1 Asian, non-Hispanic/Latino; 2 Hispanic/Latino; 12 Two or more races, non-Hispanic/Latino), 9 international. Average age 30. 70 applicants, 73% accepted, 30 enrolled. In 2017, 17 master's, 4 doctorates awarded. Terminal master's awarded for partial completion of doctoral program. *Degree requirements:* For master's, thesis (for some programs); for doctorate, comprehensive exam, thesis/dissertation. *Entrance requirements:* For master's and doctorate, GRE General Test, minimum GPA of 3.0. Additional exam requirements/recommendations for international students: Required—TOEFL (minimum score 80 iBT). *Application deadline:* For fall admission, 3/1 priority date for domestic and international students; for spring admission, 10/1 priority date for domestic and international students. Applications are processed on a rolling basis. Application fee: $30. Electronic applications accepted. *Financial support:* In 2017–18, 44 students received support, including 7 research assistantships with full tuition reimbursements available (averaging $17,687 per year), 37 teaching assistantships with full tuition reimbursements available (averaging $17,687 per year); career-related internships or fieldwork, Federal Work-Study, institutionally sponsored loans, scholarships/grants, health care benefits, tuition waivers (full and partial), and unspecified assistantships also available. Financial award application deadline: 3/1; financial award applicants required to submit FAFSA. *Faculty research:* Society-nature interactions, geographic information science, environmental studies, hurricanes, remote sensing, urban, transportation, race and indigenous populations. *Total annual research expenditures:* $159,022. *Unit head:* Prof. James Elsner, Chair, 850-644-1706, Fax: 850-644-5913, E-mail: jelsner@fsu.edu. *Application contact:* Prof. Victor Mesev, Graduate Director, 850-645-2498, Fax: 850-644-5193, E-mail: vmesev@fsu.edu.
Website: http://geography.fsu.edu/

Fort Hays State University, Graduate School, College of Science, Technology and Mathematics, Department of Geosciences, Program in Geosciences, Hays, KS 67601-4099. Offers geography (MS); geology (MS). *Degree requirements:* For master's, comprehensive exam, thesis. *Entrance requirements:* For master's, GRE General Test. Additional exam requirements/recommendations for international students: Required—TOEFL (minimum score 550 paper-based). Electronic applications accepted. *Faculty research:* Cretaceous and late Cenozoic stratigraphy, sedimentation, paleontology.

George Mason University, College of Science, Department of Geography and Geoinformation Science, Fairfax, VA 22030. Offers earth system science (MS); earth systems and geoinformation sciences (PhD); environmental geoinformation science and biodiversity conservation (Certificate); geography and geoinformation science (Certificate). *Faculty:* 18 full-time (3 women), 4 part-time/adjunct (0 women). *Students:* 67 full-time (25 women), 91 part-time (31 women); includes 23 minority (4 Black or African American, non-Hispanic/Latino; 12 Asian, non-Hispanic/Latino; 5 Hispanic/Latino; 2 Two or more races, non-Hispanic/Latino), 35 international. Average age 34. 78 applicants, 82% accepted, 36 enrolled. In 2017, 25 master's, 14 doctorates, 14 other advanced degrees awarded. *Degree requirements:* For master's, comprehensive exam (for some programs), thesis (for some programs); for doctorate, comprehensive exam, thesis/dissertation. *Entrance requirements:* For master's, GRE, bachelor's degree with minimum GPA of 3.0; 2 copies of official transcripts; current resume; expanded goals statement; 3 letters of recommendation; for doctorate, GRE, bachelor's degree with minimum GPA of 3.0; 2 copies of official transcripts; 3 letters of recommendation; resume; expanded goals statement; for Certificate, GRE, baccalaureate degree with

minimum GPA of 3.0; 2 official copies of transcripts; expanded goals statement; 3 letters of recommendation; resume. Additional exam requirements/recommendations for international students: Required—TOEFL (minimum score 575 paper-based; 88 iBT), IELTS (minimum score 6.5), PTE (minimum score 59). *Application deadline:* For fall admission, 2/1 priority date for domestic and international students. Application fee: $75 ($80 for international students). Electronic applications accepted. *Expenses:* $895 per credit in-state tuition, $1,616 out-of-state. *Financial support:* In 2017–18, 34 students received support, including 1 fellowship, 22 research assistantships with tuition reimbursements available (averaging $16,785 per year), 12 teaching assistantships with tuition reimbursements available (averaging $10,352 per year); career-related internships or fieldwork, Federal Work-Study, scholarships/grants, unspecified assistantships, and health care benefits (for full-time research or teaching assistantship recipients) also available. Support available to part-time students. Financial award application deadline: 3/1; financial award applicants required to submit FAFSA. *Faculty research:* Urban geography; remote sensing; spatial databases; crowdsourcing geospatial data; spatial data mining. *Total annual research expenditures:* $1.2 million. *Unit head:* Anthony Stefanidis, Acting Chair, 703-993-9237, Fax: 703-993-9230, E-mail: astefani@gmu.edu. *Application contact:* Samantha Cooke, Department Manager, 703-993-1212, E-mail: scooke4@gmu.edu.
Website: http://ggs.gmu.edu/

The George Washington University, Columbian College of Arts and Sciences, Department of Geography, Washington, DC 20052. Offers MA, Graduate Certificate. *Faculty:* 11 full-time (5 women), 15 part-time/adjunct (5 women). *Students:* 22 full-time (13 women), 16 part-time (7 women); includes 8 minority (6 Black or African American, non-Hispanic/Latino; 1 Asian, non-Hispanic/Latino; 1 Two or more races, non-Hispanic/Latino), 2 international. Average age 28. 48 applicants, 75% accepted, 20 enrolled. In 2017, 12 master's, 23 other advanced degrees awarded. *Degree requirements:* For master's, comprehensive exam, thesis or alternative. *Entrance requirements:* For master's, GRE General Test, BA in geography or related field, minimum GPA of 3.0. Additional exam requirements/recommendations for international students: Required—TOEFL (minimum score 550 paper-based; 80 iBT). *Application deadline:* For fall admission, 4/1 priority date for domestic students, 1/15 priority date for international students; for spring admission, 10/1 priority date for domestic students, 9/1 priority date for international students. Applications are processed on a rolling basis. Application fee: $75. Electronic applications accepted. *Expenses: Tuition:* Full-time $28,800; part-time $1655 per credit hour. *Required fees:* $45; $2.75 per credit hour. *Financial support:* In 2017–18, 10 students received support. Fellowships with tuition reimbursements available, teaching assistantships with tuition reimbursements available, Federal Work-Study, institutionally sponsored loans, and tuition waivers available. Financial award application deadline: 1/15. *Unit head:* Dr. Marie Price, Chair, 202-994-6187, E-mail: mprice@gwu.edu. *Application contact:* Information Contact, 202-994-6185, Fax: 202-994-2484.
Website: http://geography.columbian.gwu.edu/

Georgia State University, College of Arts and Sciences, Department of Geosciences, Program in Geography, Atlanta, GA 30302-3083. Offers MS. *Program availability:* Part-time. *Entrance requirements:* For master's, GRE General Test. Additional exam requirements/recommendations for international students: Required—TOEFL. *Application deadline:* Applications are processed on a rolling basis. Application fee: $50. Electronic applications accepted. *Expenses:* Tuition, state resident: full-time $7020. Tuition, nonresident: full-time $22,518. *Required fees:* $2128. Tuition and fees vary according to degree level and program. *Financial support:* Research assistantships and teaching assistantships available. *Faculty research:* Urban economics, biogeography, cartography, geographic information science. *Unit head:* Dr. W. Crawford Elliott, Chair, 404-413-5756, E-mail: wcelliott@gsu.edu.
Website: http://geosciences.gsu.edu/grad-programs/

Georgia State University, College of Education and Human Development, Department of Middle and Secondary Education, Atlanta, GA 30302-3083. Offers curriculum and instruction (Ed D); English education (MAT); mathematics education (M Ed, MAT); middle level education (MAT); reading, language and literacy education (M Ed, MAT), including reading instruction (M Ed); science education (M Ed, MAT), including biology (MAT), broad field science (MAT), chemistry (MAT), earth science (MAT), physics (MAT); social studies education (M Ed, MAT), including economics (MAT), geography (MAT), history (MAT), political science (MAT); teaching and learning (PhD), including language and literacy, mathematics education, music education, science education, social studies education, teaching and teacher education. *Accreditation:* NCATE. *Program availability:* Part-time, evening/weekend, online learning. *Faculty:* 24 full-time (18 women). *Students:* 179 full-time (110 women), 192 part-time (133 women); includes 193 minority (130 Black or African American, non-Hispanic/Latino; 1 American Indian or Alaska Native, non-Hispanic/Latino; 23 Asian, non-Hispanic/Latino; 25 Hispanic/Latino; 14 Two or more races, non-Hispanic/Latino), 6 international. Average age 33. 175 applicants, 58% accepted, 83 enrolled. In 2017, 81 master's, 17 doctorates awarded. *Entrance requirements:* For master's, GRE; GACE I (for initial teacher preparation programs), baccalaureate degree or equivalent, resume, goals statement, two letters of recommendation, minimum undergraduate GPA of 2.5; proof of initial teacher certification in the content area (for M Ed); for doctorate, GRE, resume, goals statement, writing sample, two letters of recommendation, minimum graduate GPA of 3.3, interview. *Application deadline:* For fall admission, 1/15 priority date for domestic and international students; for spring admission, 10/1 for domestic and international students. Application fee: $50. Electronic applications accepted. *Expenses:* Tuition, state resident: full-time $7020. Tuition, nonresident: full-time $22,518. *Required fees:* $2128. Tuition and fees vary according to degree level and program. *Financial support:* In 2017–18, fellowships with full tuition reimbursements (averaging $19,667 per year), research assistantships with full tuition reimbursements (averaging $5,436 per year), teaching assistantships with full tuition reimbursements (averaging $2,779 per year) were awarded; career-related internships or fieldwork, Federal Work-Study, scholarships/grants, health care benefits, tuition waivers (full and partial), and unspecified assistantships also available. Financial award application deadline: 3/15. *Faculty research:* Teacher education in language and literacy, mathematics, science, and social studies in urban middle and secondary school settings; learning technologies in school, community, and corporate settings; multicultural education and education for social justice; urban education; international education. *Unit head:* Dr. Dana L. Fox, Chair, 404-413-8060, Fax: 404-413-8063, E-mail: dfox@gsu.edu. *Application contact:* Bobbie Turner, Administrative Coordinator, 404-413-8405, Fax: 404-413-8063, E-mail: bnturner@gsu.edu.
Website: http://mse.education.gsu.edu/

Hunter College of the City University of New York, Graduate School, School of Arts and Sciences, Department of Geography, New York, NY 10065-5085. Offers geographic information science (Certificate); geography (MA); geoinformatics (MS). *Program availability:* Part-time, evening/weekend. *Degree requirements:* For master's, comprehensive exam or thesis. *Entrance requirements:* For master's, GRE General Test, minimum B average in major, B- overall; 18 credits of course work in geography; 2 letters of recommendation; for Certificate, minimum B average in major, B- overall. Additional exam requirements/recommendations for international students: Required—TOEFL. *Faculty research:* Urban geography, economic geography, geographic information science, demographic methods, climate change.

Geography

Indiana University Bloomington, University Graduate School, College of Arts and Sciences, Department of Geography, Bloomington, IN 47405. Offers PhD. *Degree requirements:* For doctorate, comprehensive exam, thesis/dissertation. *Entrance requirements:* For doctorate, GRE General Test, minimum GPA of 3.0. Additional exam requirements/recommendations for international students: Required—TOEFL (minimum score 620 paper-based; 105 iBT), IELTS (minimum score 7). Electronic applications accepted. *Faculty research:* Statistical climatology, dendrochronology, land-change science, cultural and political ecology, cultural geography, economic geography, geographic information science, spatial data analysis and modeling.

Indiana University of Pennsylvania, School of Graduate Studies and Research, College of Humanities and Social Sciences, Department of Geography and Regional Planning, MA Program in Geography, Indiana, PA 15705. Offers MA. *Program availability:* Part-time. *Faculty:* 10 full-time (2 women). *Degree requirements:* For master's, thesis optional. *Entrance requirements:* For master's, GRE, 2 letters of recommendation. Additional exam requirements/recommendations for international students: Required—TOEFL (minimum score 540 paper-based). *Application deadline:* Applications are processed on a rolling basis. Application fee: $50. Electronic applications accepted. *Expenses:* Tuition, state resident: full-time $12,000; part-time $500 per credit. Tuition, nonresident: full-time $18,000; part-time $750 per credit. *Required fees:* $4073; $165.55 per credit. $64 per term. *Financial support:* Federal Work-Study, scholarships/grants, and unspecified assistantships available. Support available to part-time students. Financial award application deadline: 4/15; financial award applicants required to submit FAFSA. *Unit head:* Dr. Richard Hoch, Graduate Coordinator, 724-357-5990, E-mail: richard.hoch@iup.edu. Website: http://www.iup.edu/georegionalplan/grad/default.aspx

Kansas State University, Graduate School, College of Arts and Sciences, Department of Geography, Manhattan, KS 66506. Offers geographic information science (Graduate Certificate); geography (MA, PhD). *Degree requirements:* For master's, thesis optional, oral exam; for doctorate, one foreign language, thesis/dissertation. *Entrance requirements:* For master's and doctorate, GRE General Test, minimum GPA of 3.0. Electronic applications accepted. *Faculty research:* Human environment interaction, health and population, culture and landscape, physical geography, geospatial analysis and applications.

Kent State University, College of Arts and Sciences, Department of Geography, Kent, OH 44242-0001. Offers geographic information science (MGIS), including cyber geographic information science, environmental geographic information science, geographic information science and health; geography (MA, PhD). *Program availability:* Part-time. *Faculty:* 13 full-time (5 women), 3 part-time/adjunct (1 woman). *Students:* 41 full-time (12 women), 39 part-time (14 women); includes 14 minority (7 Black or African American, non-Hispanic/Latino; 3 Asian, non-Hispanic/Latino; 4 Two or more races, non-Hispanic/Latino), 19 international. Average age 31. 47 applicants, 77% accepted, 26 enrolled. In 2017, 5 master's, 4 doctorates awarded. *Degree requirements:* For master's, thesis, practicum (MGIS); for doctorate, comprehensive exam, thesis/dissertation. *Entrance requirements:* For master's, GRE, minimum undergraduate GPA of 3.0, undergraduate degree in geography or a related field, transcripts, two letters of recommendation, goal statement; for doctorate, GRE, transcripts, three letters of recommendation, goal statement, resume. Additional exam requirements/recommendations for international students: Required—TOEFL (minimum score 550 paper-based, 79 iBT), Michigan English Language Assessment Battery (minimum score 77), IELTS (minimum score 6.5) or PTE (minimum score 58). *Application deadline:* For fall admission, 2/1 for domestic and international students; for spring admission, 11/1 for domestic and international students; for summer admission, 4/1 for domestic and international students. Applications are processed on a rolling basis. Application fee: $45 ($70 for international students). Electronic applications accepted. *Expenses:* Tuition, state resident: full-time $11,310; part-time $515 per credit hour. Tuition, nonresident: full-time $20,396; part-time $928 per credit hour. *International tuition:* $18,544 full-time. *Financial support:* Fellowships with full tuition reimbursements, research assistantships with full tuition reimbursements, teaching assistantships with full tuition reimbursements, Federal Work-Study, scholarships/grants, and unspecified assistantships available. Financial award application deadline: 2/1. *Unit head:* Dr. Scott Sheridan, Professor and Chair, 330-672-3224, Fax: 330-672-4304, E-mail: ssherid1@kent.edu. *Application contact:* Dr. David H. Kaplan, Professor and Graduate Coordinator, 330-672-3221, E-mail: dkaplan@kent.edu. Website: https://www.kent.edu/geography

Louisiana State University and Agricultural & Mechanical College, Graduate School, College of Humanities and Social Sciences, Department of Geography and Anthropology, Baton Rouge, LA 70803. Offers geography (MA, MS); geography and anthropology (PhD). *Faculty:* 27 full-time (13 women). *Students:* 59 full-time (36 women), 23 part-time (11 women); includes 14 minority (3 Black or African American, non-Hispanic/Latino; 1 American Indian or Alaska Native, non-Hispanic/Latino; 1 Asian, non-Hispanic/Latino; 8 Hispanic/Latino; 1 Two or more races, non-Hispanic/Latino), 22 international. Average age 30. 64 applicants, 55% accepted, 16 enrolled. In 2017, 16 master's, 6 doctorates awarded. *Financial support:* In 2017–18, 3 fellowships (averaging $22,799 per year), 26 research assistantships (averaging $19,473 per year), 28 teaching assistantships (averaging $17,412 per year) were awarded. *Total annual research expenditures:* $925,707.

Marshall University, Academic Affairs Division, College of Liberal Arts, Department of Geography, Huntington, WV 25755. Offers MA, MS, Certificate. *Students:* 7 full-time (2 women), 1 part-time (0 women). Average age 35. In 2017, 2 master's awarded. *Degree requirements:* For master's, thesis optional. *Entrance requirements:* For master's, GRE General Test (for MS). Application fee: $40. *Unit head:* Dr. Joshua Hagen, Chairperson, 304-696-2505, E-mail: hagenj@marshall.edu. *Application contact:* Information Contact, 304-746-1907, Fax: 304-746-1902, E-mail: services@marshall.edu.

McGill University, Faculty of Graduate and Postdoctoral Studies, Faculty of Science, Department of Geography, Montréal, QC H3A 2T5, Canada. Offers geography (M Sc, MA, PhD); neo-tropical environment (MA, PhD); social statistics (MA).

McMaster University, School of Graduate Studies, Faculty of Science, School of Geography and Earth Sciences, Hamilton, ON L8S 4M2, Canada. Offers geochemistry (PhD); geology (M Sc, PhD); human geography (MA, PhD); physical geography (M Sc, PhD). *Program availability:* Part-time. Terminal master's awarded for partial completion of doctoral program. *Degree requirements:* For master's, thesis; for doctorate, comprehensive exam, thesis/dissertation. *Entrance requirements:* For master's, minimum B+ average. Additional exam requirements/recommendations for international students: Required—TOEFL (minimum score 550 paper-based).

Memorial University of Newfoundland, School of Graduate Studies, Department of Geography, St. John's, NL A1C 5S7, Canada. Offers M Sc, MA, PhD. *Program availability:* Part-time. *Degree requirements:* For master's, thesis; for doctorate, comprehensive exam, thesis/dissertation, seminar, oral defense of thesis. *Entrance requirements:* For master's, 2nd class degree; for doctorate, master's degree. Electronic applications accepted. *Faculty research:* Cultural/historical geography, physical geography, economic geography, cartography, geographical information systems.

Miami University, College of Arts and Science, Department of Geography, Oxford, OH 45056. Offers MA. In 2017, 2 master's awarded. *Expenses:* Tuition, state resident: full-time $13,812; part-time $575 per credit hour. Tuition, nonresident: full-time $30,860; part-time $1286 per credit hour. *Unit head:* Dr. Bruce D'Arcus, Department Chair/Associate Professor of Geography, 513-529-1521, E-mail: darcusb@miamioh.edu. *Application contact:* Marcia England, Graduate Program Director, Department of Geography, 513-529-5010, E-mail: geography@miamioh.edu. Website: http://www.MiamiOH.edu/geography/

Michigan State University, The Graduate School, College of Social Science, Department of Geography, East Lansing, MI 48824. Offers geographic information science (MS); geography (MS, PhD). *Degree requirements:* For master's, comprehensive exam, thesis (for some programs), presentation of poster/paper or oral defense of thesis; for doctorate, comprehensive exam, thesis/dissertation, presentation of poster/paper, presentation and defense of dissertation proposal, oral exam in defense of dissertation. *Entrance requirements:* Additional exam requirements/recommendations for international students: Required—TOEFL (minimum score 600 paper-based). Electronic applications accepted.

Minnesota State University Mankato, College of Graduate Studies and Research, College of Social and Behavioral Sciences, Department of Geography, Mankato, MN 56001. Offers MS. *Program availability:* Part-time. *Degree requirements:* For master's, one foreign language, comprehensive exam, thesis optional. *Entrance requirements:* For master's, minimum GPA of 3.0. Electronic applications accepted.

Mississippi State University, College of Arts and Sciences, Department of Geosciences, Mississippi State, MS 39762. Offers applied meteorology (MS); broadcast meteorology (MS); earth and atmospheric science (PhD); environmental geosciences (MS); geography (MS); geology (MS); geospatial sciences (MS); professional meteorology/climatology (MS); teachers in geosciences (MS). *Program availability:* Blended/hybrid learning. *Faculty:* 21 full-time (6 women), 1 part-time/adjunct (0 women). *Students:* 68 full-time (20 women), 190 part-time (89 women); includes 44 minority (7 Black or African American, non-Hispanic/Latino; 2 American Indian or Alaska Native, non-Hispanic/Latino; 2 Asian, non-Hispanic/Latino; 25 Hispanic/Latino; 2 Native Hawaiian or other Pacific Islander, non-Hispanic/Latino; 6 Two or more races, non-Hispanic/Latino), 17 international. Average age 33. 161 applicants, 72% accepted, 96 enrolled. In 2017, 55 master's, 9 doctorates awarded. *Degree requirements:* For master's, thesis (for some programs), comprehensive oral or written exam; for doctorate, thesis/dissertation, comprehensive oral or written exam. *Entrance requirements:* For master's, GRE (for on-campus applicants), minimum undergraduate GPA of 2.75; for doctorate, thesis-based MS with background in one department emphasis area. Additional exam requirements/recommendations for international students: Required—TOEFL (minimum score 477 paper-based; 53 iBT); Recommended—IELTS (minimum score 4.5). *Application deadline:* For fall admission, 7/1 for domestic students, 5/1 for international students; for spring admission, 11/1 for domestic students, 9/1 for international students. Applications are processed on a rolling basis. Application fee: $60 ($80 for international students). Electronic applications accepted. *Expenses:* Tuition, state resident: full-time $8318; part-time $462.12 per credit hour. Tuition, nonresident: full-time $22,358; part-time $1242.12 per credit hour. *Required fees:* $110; $12.24 per credit hour. $6.12 per semester. *Financial support:* In 2017–18, 5 research assistantships with full tuition reimbursements (averaging $13,050 per year), 28 teaching assistantships with full tuition reimbursements (averaging $14,571 per year) were awarded; Federal Work-Study, institutionally sponsored loans, scholarships/grants, tuition waivers (partial), and unspecified assistantships also available. Financial award application deadline: 4/1; financial award applicants required to submit FAFSA. *Faculty research:* Climatology, hydrogeology, sedimentology, meteorology. *Total annual research expenditures:* $7.3 million. *Unit head:* Dr. John C. Rodgers, III, Professor and Interim Head, 662-325-1032, Fax: 662-325-9423, E-mail: jcr100@msstate.edu. *Application contact:* Nathan Drake, Admissions and Enrollment Assistant, 662-325-3804, E-mail: ndrake@grad.msstate.edu. Website: http://www.geosciences.msstate.edu

Missouri State University, Graduate College, College of Natural and Applied Sciences, Department of Geography, Geology, and Planning, Springfield, MO 65897. Offers geography, geology, and planning (Certificate); natural and applied science (MNAS), including geography, geology and planning; secondary education (MS Ed), including earth science, physical geography. *Program availability:* Part-time, evening/weekend. *Faculty:* 18 full-time (4 women), 1 part-time/adjunct (0 women). *Students:* 27 full-time (10 women), 7 part-time (6 women); includes 2 minority (both Two or more races, non-Hispanic/Latino), 3 international. Average age 29. 27 applicants, 48% accepted, 13 enrolled. In 2017, 32 master's awarded. *Degree requirements:* For master's, comprehensive exam, thesis (for some programs). *Entrance requirements:* For master's, GRE General Test (MS, MNAS), minimum undergraduate GPA of 3.0 (MS, MNAS), 9-12 teacher certification (MS Ed). Additional exam requirements/recommendations for international students: Required—TOEFL (minimum score 550 paper-based; 79 iBT), IELTS (minimum score 6). *Application deadline:* For fall admission, 7/20 priority date for domestic students, 5/1 for international students; for spring admission, 12/20 priority date for domestic students, 9/1 for international students. Applications are processed on a rolling basis. Application fee: $35 ($50 for international students). Electronic applications accepted. *Expenses:* Tuition, state resident: full-time $2915; part-time $2021 per credit hour. Tuition, nonresident: full-time $5354; part-time $3647 per credit hour. *International tuition:* $11,992 full-time. *Required fees:* $173; $173 per credit hour. Tuition and fees vary according to class time, course level, course load, degree level, campus/location and program. *Financial support:* In 2017–18, 3 research assistantships with full tuition reimbursements (averaging $11,574 per year), 15 teaching assistantships with full tuition reimbursements (averaging $9,365 per year) were awarded; career-related internships or fieldwork, Federal Work-Study, institutionally sponsored loans, scholarships/grants, and unspecified assistantships also available. Financial award application deadline: 3/31; financial award applicants required to submit FAFSA. *Faculty research:* Stratigraphy and ancient meteorite impacts, environmental geochemistry of karst, hyperspectral image processing, water quality, small town planning. *Unit head:* Dr. Toby Dogwiler, Department Head, 417-836-5800, Fax: 417-836-6934, E-mail: tobydogwiler@missouristate.edu. *Application contact:* Stephanie Praschan, Director, Graduate Enrollment Management, 417-836-5330, Fax: 417-836-6200, E-mail: stephaniepraschan@missouristate.edu. Website: http://geosciences.missouristate.edu/

New Mexico State University, College of Arts and Sciences, Department of Geography, Las Cruces, NM 88003. Offers applied geography (MAG). *Program availability:* Part-time. *Faculty:* 5 full-time (2 women), 1 part-time/adjunct (0 women). *Students:* 7 full-time (2 women), 16 part-time (7 women); includes 8 minority (all Hispanic/Latino). Average age 35. 9 applicants, 44% accepted, 2 enrolled. In 2017, 6 master's awarded. *Entrance requirements:* For master's, bachelor's degree in geography or related field. Additional exam requirements/recommendations for international students: Required—TOEFL (minimum score 550 paper-based; 79 iBT), IELTS (minimum score 6.5). *Application deadline:* For spring admission, 2/1 for domestic students, 2/1 priority date for international students. Applications are processed on a rolling basis. Application fee: $40 ($50 for international students).

Electronic applications accepted. *Expenses:* Tuition, state resident: full-time $4390. Tuition, nonresident: full-time $15,309. *Required fees:* $853. *Financial support:* In 2017–18, 10 students received support, including 2 fellowships (averaging $4,390 per year), 6 teaching assistantships (averaging $17,031 per year); career-related internships or fieldwork, Federal Work-Study, scholarships/grants, traineeships, health care benefits, and unspecified assistantships also available. Support available to part-time students. Financial award application deadline: 3/1. *Faculty research:* Landscape ecology, land use, geomorphology, Latin America and the U.S.-Mexico border, geographic information systems, geographic education, biogeography, water resources research. *Total annual research expenditures:* $30,510. *Unit head:* Dr. Carol Campbell, Department Head, 575-646-3509, Fax: 575-646-7430, E-mail: geobird@nmsu.edu. *Application contact:* Dr. Daniel P. Dugas, Graduate Advisor, 575-646-1045, Fax: 575-646-7430, E-mail: ddugas@nmsu.edu.
Website: http://geography.nmsu.edu

Northeastern Illinois University, College of Graduate Studies and Research, College of Arts and Sciences, Program in Geography and Environmental Studies, Chicago, IL 60625. Offers geographic information science (Graduate Certificate); geography and environmental studies (MA). *Program availability:* Part-time, evening/weekend. *Degree requirements:* For master's, comprehensive exam, thesis optional. *Entrance requirements:* For master's, undergraduate minor in geography or environmental studies, minimum GPA of 2.75. Additional exam requirements/recommendations for international students: Required—TOEFL (minimum score 550 paper-based; 79 iBT). *Application deadline:* For fall admission, 4/1 priority date for domestic students; for spring admission, 8/15 for domestic students. Applications are processed on a rolling basis. Application fee: $30. Electronic applications accepted. *Expenses:* Tuition, state resident: full-time $7274; part-time $404.11 per credit hour. Tuition, nonresident: full-time $14,548; part-time $808.23 per credit hour. *Required fees:* $1284. *Financial support:* Applicants required to submit FAFSA. *Faculty research:* Segregation and urbanization of minority groups in the Chicago area, scale dependence and parameterization in nonpoint source pollution modeling, ecological land classification and mapping, ecosystem restoration, soil-vegetation relationships. *Unit head:* Dr. Michael Wenz, Acting Chair, 772-442-5597, E-mail: m-wenz@neiu.edu. *Application contact:* Martha Narvaez, Graduate Admission Representative, 773-442-6006, E-mail: m-narvaez@neiu.edu.

Northern Arizona University, College of Social and Behavioral Sciences, Department of Geography, Planning, and Recreation, Flagstaff, AZ 86011. Offers applied geospatial sciences (MS); community planning (Certificate); geographic information systems (Certificate); parks and recreation management (MS). *Program availability:* Part-time, 100% online, blended/hybrid learning. *Faculty:* 18 full-time (9 women), 1 part-time/adjunct (0 women). *Students:* 22 full-time (16 women), 25 part-time (11 women); includes 7 minority (3 Black or African American, non-Hispanic/Latino; 2 Hispanic/Latino; 2 Two or more races, non-Hispanic/Latino), 2 international. Average age 33. 42 applicants, 86% accepted, 35 enrolled. In 2017, 14 master's, 7 other advanced degrees awarded. *Degree requirements:* For master's, variable foreign language requirement, comprehensive exam (for some programs), thesis (for some programs); for Certificate, comprehensive exam (for some programs). *Entrance requirements:* Additional exam requirements/recommendations for international students: Required—TOEFL (minimum score 80 iBT), IELTS (minimum score 6.5). *Application deadline:* For fall admission, 3/1 for domestic and international students; for spring admission, 10/1 for domestic and international students. Applications are processed on a rolling basis. Application fee: $65. Electronic applications accepted. *Expenses:* Tuition, state resident: full-time $9240; part-time $458 per credit hour. Tuition, nonresident: full-time $21,588; part-time $1199 per credit hour. *Required fees:* $1021; $14 per credit hour. $646 per semester. Tuition and fees vary according to course load, campus/location and program. *Financial support:* In 2017–18, 5 students received support, including 5 teaching assistantships with partial tuition reimbursements available (averaging $9,000 per year); institutionally sponsored loans, health care benefits, tuition waivers (partial), and unspecified assistantships also available. Financial award application deadline: 2/1; financial award applicants required to submit FAFSA. *Unit head:* Dr. Alan Lew, Chair, 928-523-6567, Fax: 928-523-2275. *Application contact:* Dana Mandino, Administrative Associate, 928-523-7988, Fax: 928-523-2275, E-mail: geog@nau.edu.
Website: https://nau.edu/SBS/GPR/

Northern Illinois University, Graduate School, College of Liberal Arts and Sciences, Department of Geography, De Kalb, IL 60115-2854. Offers MS, PhD. *Program availability:* Part-time. *Faculty:* 8 full-time (2 women). *Students:* 18 full-time (9 women), 7 part-time (1 woman); includes 7 minority (2 Asian, non-Hispanic/Latino; 2 Hispanic/Latino; 3 Two or more races, non-Hispanic/Latino), 5 international. Average age 32. 25 applicants, 48% accepted, 3 enrolled. In 2017, 7 master's, 2 doctorates awarded. *Degree requirements:* For master's, comprehensive exam, thesis optional, research seminar. *Entrance requirements:* For master's, GRE General Test, minimum GPA of 2.75; for doctorate, master's degree. Additional exam requirements/recommendations for international students: Required—TOEFL (minimum score 550 paper-based). *Application deadline:* For fall admission, 2/1 priority date for domestic students, 5/1 for international students; for spring admission, 10/1 priority date for domestic students, 10/1 for international students. Applications are processed on a rolling basis. Application fee: $40. Electronic applications accepted. *Financial support:* In 2017–18, 4 research assistantships with full tuition reimbursements, 17 teaching assistantships with full tuition reimbursements were awarded; fellowships with full tuition reimbursements, career-related internships or fieldwork, Federal Work-Study, scholarships/grants, tuition waivers (full), and unspecified assistantships also available. Support available to part-time students. Financial award applicants required to submit FAFSA. *Faculty research:* Synoptic meteorology, human impacts on soil properties, plant-soil relationships, hydrological cycle, climate variability. *Unit head:* Dr. David Changnon, Chair, 815-753-6826, Fax: 815-753-6872, E-mail: dchangnon@niu.edu. *Application contact:* Dr. Michael Konen, Coordinator of Graduate Studies, 815-753-0631, E-mail: mkonen@niu.edu.
Website: http://globe.geog.niu.edu/

The Ohio State University, Graduate School, College of Arts and Sciences, Division of Social and Behavioral Sciences, Department of Geography, Columbus, OH 43210. Offers atmospheric sciences (MS, PhD); geography (MA, PhD). *Faculty:* 23. *Students:* 48 full-time (26 women), 23 international. Average age 27. In 2017, 6 master's, 8 doctorates awarded. *Degree requirements:* For doctorate, variable foreign language requirement, thesis/dissertation. *Entrance requirements:* For master's and doctorate, GRE. Additional exam requirements/recommendations for international students: Required—Michigan English Language Assessment Battery (minimum score 86); Recommended—TOEFL (minimum score 600 paper-based; 100 iBT), IELTS (minimum score 8). *Application deadline:* For fall admission, 12/13 priority date for domestic students, 11/30 priority date for international students. Applications are processed on a rolling basis. Application fee: $60 ($70 for international students). Electronic applications accepted. *Financial support:* Fellowships, research assistantships, teaching assistantships, Federal Work-Study, and institutionally sponsored loans available. Support available to part-time students. *Unit head:* Dr. Morton O'Kelly, Professor and Chair, 614-292-8744, E-mail: okelly.1@osu.edu. *Application contact:* Graduate and Professional Admissions, 614-292-9444, Fax: 614-292-3895, E-mail: gpadmissions@osu.edu.
Website: http://geography.osu.edu/

Ohio University, Graduate College, College of Arts and Sciences, Department of Geography, Athens, OH 45701-2979. Offers MA, MS. *Program availability:* Part-time. *Degree requirements:* For master's, thesis or alternative. *Entrance requirements:* For master's, GRE General Test, minimum GPA of 3.0. Additional exam requirements/recommendations for international students: Required—TOEFL (minimum score 600 paper-based; 100 iBT) or IELTS (minimum score 8). Electronic applications accepted. *Faculty research:* Environmental geography, cartography and geographic information systems, cultural ecology, area studies, historical geography.

Oklahoma State University, College of Arts and Sciences, Department of Geography, Stillwater, OK 74078. Offers MS, PhD. *Faculty:* 14 full-time (4 women). *Students:* 2 full-time (1 woman), 30 part-time (15 women); includes 4 minority (2 Asian, non-Hispanic/Latino; 2 Two or more races, non-Hispanic/Latino), 7 international. Average age 31. 16 applicants, 50% accepted, 8 enrolled. In 2017, 2 master's, 1 doctorate awarded. *Entrance requirements:* For master's and doctorate, GRE. Additional exam requirements/recommendations for international students: Required—TOEFL (minimum score 550 paper-based; 79 iBT). *Application deadline:* For fall admission, 3/1 priority date for international students; for spring admission, 8/1 priority date for international students. Applications are processed on a rolling basis. Application fee: $40 ($75 for international students). Electronic applications accepted. *Expenses:* Tuition, state resident: full-time $4019; part-time $2679.60 per year. Tuition, nonresident: full-time $15,286; part-time $10,190.40 per year. *Required fees:* $2129; $1419 per unit. Tuition and fees vary according to program. *Financial support:* Research assistantships, teaching assistantships, career-related internships or fieldwork, Federal Work-Study, scholarships/grants, health care benefits, tuition waivers (partial), and unspecified assistantships available. Support available to part-time students. Financial award application deadline: 3/1; financial award applicants required to submit FAFSA. *Faculty research:* Cultural ecology, resource management, historical/cultural geography, central Asia, geographic information systems. *Unit head:* Dr. Dale Lightfoot, Department Head, 405-744-6250, Fax: 405-744-5620, E-mail: d.lightfoot@okstate.edu.
Website: http://geog.okstate.edu

Oregon State University, College of Earth, Ocean, and Atmospheric Sciences, Program in Geography, Corvallis, OR 97331. Offers geographic information science (MA, MS, PhD); physical geography (MA, MS, PhD); resource geography (MA, MS, PhD). Terminal master's awarded for partial completion of doctoral program. *Entrance requirements:* For master's and doctorate, GRE, minimum GPA of 3.0 in last 90 hours. Additional exam requirements/recommendations for international students: Required—TOEFL (minimum score 80 iBT), IELTS (minimum score 6.5). *Application deadline:* For fall admission, 1/5 for domestic students. Application fee: $75 ($85 for international students). *Financial support:* Application deadline: 1/5. *Faculty research:* Resources, physical geography, cartography, remote sensing. *Unit head:* Dr. Julia Jones, Director, 541-737-1224, E-mail: jonesj@geo.oregonstate.edu. *Application contact:* Lori Hartline, Geography Advisor, 541-737-5188, E-mail: hartline@coas.oregonstate.edu.
Website: http://ceoas.oregonstate.edu/academics/geography/

Penn State University Park, Graduate School, College of Earth and Mineral Sciences, Department of Geography, University Park, PA 16802. Offers geography (MS, PhD). *Unit head:* Dr. William E. Easterling, III, Dean, 814-865-7482, Fax: 814-863-7708. *Application contact:* Lori Hawn, Director, Graduate Student Services, 814-865-1795, Fax: 814-863-4627, E-mail: l-gswww@lists.psu.edu.
Website: http://geog.psu.edu/

Portland State University, Graduate Studies, College of Liberal Arts and Sciences, Department of Geography, Portland, OR 97207-0751. Offers geography (MA, MAT, MS, MST, PhD). *Program availability:* Part-time. *Faculty:* 8 full-time (1 woman), 10 part-time/adjunct (2 women). *Students:* 22 full-time (12 women), 29 part-time (9 women); includes 13 minority (1 Black or African American, non-Hispanic/Latino; 1 Asian, non-Hispanic/Latino; 6 Hispanic/Latino; 5 Two or more races, non-Hispanic/Latino). Average age 30. 40 applicants, 90% accepted, 25 enrolled. In 2017, 11 master's awarded. *Degree requirements:* For master's, thesis (for some programs). *Entrance requirements:* For master's, GRE General Test (minimum score of 297), geography degree with minimum GPA of 3.0 overall, 3 letters of recommendation. Additional exam requirements/recommendations for international students: Required—TOEFL (minimum score 550 paper-based; 80 iBT), IELTS (minimum score 6.5), PTE (minimum score 60). *Application deadline:* For fall admission, 1/15 priority date for domestic and international students. Applications are processed on a rolling basis. Application fee: $65. *Expenses:* Tuition, state resident: full-time $14,436; part-time $401 per credit. Tuition, nonresident: full-time $21,780; part-time $605 per credit. *Required fees:* $1380; $22 per credit. $119 per quarter. One-time fee: $325. Tuition and fees vary according to program. *Financial support:* In 2017–18, 17 students received support, including 8 research assistantships with full and partial tuition reimbursements available (averaging $14,541 per year), 9 teaching assistantships with full and partial tuition reimbursements available (averaging $16,580 per year); career-related internships or fieldwork, Federal Work-Study, scholarships/grants, and unspecified assistantships also available. Support available to part-time students. Financial award application deadline: 3/1; financial award applicants required to submit FAFSA. *Faculty research:* Geographic information systems, natural lands, Latin American subsistence farming, climatic change, urban perspectives. *Total annual research expenditures:* $328,804. *Unit head:* Dr. Heejun Chang, Chair, 503-725-3162, Fax: 503-725-3162, E-mail: changh@pdx.edu. *Application contact:* Dr. Martin Lafrenz, Graduate Committee Chair, 503-725-3163, E-mail: lafrenz@pdx.edu.
Website: http://www.pdx.edu/geography/

Queen's University at Kingston, School of Graduate Studies, Faculty of Arts and Sciences, Department of Geography, Kingston, ON K7L 3N6, Canada. Offers M Sc, MA, PhD. *Degree requirements:* For master's, thesis; for doctorate, comprehensive exam, thesis/dissertation. *Entrance requirements:* Additional exam requirements/recommendations for international students: Required—TOEFL. *Faculty research:* Urban and economic geography, historical-cultural geography, earth system science.

Rutgers University–New Brunswick, Graduate School-New Brunswick, Program in Geography, Piscataway, NJ 08854-8097. Offers MA, MS, PhD. Terminal master's awarded for partial completion of doctoral program. *Degree requirements:* For master's, thesis or alternative; for doctorate, comprehensive exam, thesis/dissertation. *Entrance requirements:* For master's and doctorate, GRE General Test. Additional exam requirements/recommendations for international students: Required—TOEFL. *Faculty research:* Urban social theory, climate, political biology, hazards, economic development.

St. Cloud State University, School of Graduate Studies, College of Social Sciences, Department of Geography and Planning, St. Cloud, MN 56301-4498. Offers MS. *Degree requirements:* For master's, comprehensive exam (for some programs), thesis or alternative. *Entrance requirements:* For master's, GRE General Test, minimum GPA of 2.75. Additional exam requirements/recommendations for international students: Required—Michigan English Language Assessment Battery; Recommended—TOEFL (minimum score 550 paper-based), IELTS (minimum score 6.5). Electronic applications accepted.

Geography

Salem State University, School of Graduate Studies, Program in Geo-Information Science, Salem, MA 01970-5353. Offers MS. *Program availability:* Part-time, evening/weekend. *Degree requirements:* For master's, thesis optional. *Entrance requirements:* For master's, GRE or MAT. Additional exam requirements/recommendations for international students: Required—TOEFL (minimum score 550 paper-based; 80 iBT) or IELTS (minimum score 5.5).

San Diego State University, Graduate and Research Affairs, College of Arts and Letters, Department of Geography, San Diego, CA 92182. Offers MA, PhD. PhD offered jointly with University of California, Santa Barbara. *Degree requirements:* For master's, thesis; for doctorate, thesis/dissertation. *Entrance requirements:* For master's, GRE General Test, bachelor's degree in related field, 3 letters of recommendation. Additional exam requirements/recommendations for international students: Required—TOEFL. Electronic applications accepted. *Faculty research:* Physical geography, human geography, biogeography, environmental resources, geographic analysis.

San Francisco State University, Division of Graduate Studies, College of Science and Engineering, Department of Geography and Environment, San Francisco, CA 94132-1722. Offers geographic information science (MS); geography (MA); resource management and environmental planning (MA). *Unit head:* Dr. Jerry Davis, Chair, 415-338-2983, Fax: 415-338-6243, E-mail: jerry@sfsu.edu. *Application contact:* Dr. Nancy Wilkinson, Graduate Coordinator, 415-338-1439, Fax: 415-338-6243, E-mail: nancyw@sfsu.edu.
Website: http://geog.sfsu.edu/

San Jose State University, Graduate Studies and Research, College of Social Sciences, San Jose, CA 95192-0107. Offers applied anthropology (MA); communication studies (MA); economics (MA), including applied economics, economics; environmental studies (MS); geography (MA); history (MA), including history, history education; Mexican American studies (MA); psychology (MA, MS), including clinical psychology (MS), industrial/organizational psychology (MS), research and experimental psychology (MA); public administration (MPA); social sciences (MS); sociology (MA). *Faculty:* 59 full-time (29 women), 18 part-time/adjunct (5 women). *Students:* 181 full-time (126 women), 221 part-time (127 women); includes 228 minority (15 Black or African American, non-Hispanic/Latino; 48 Asian, non-Hispanic/Latino; 112 Hispanic/Latino; 3 Native Hawaiian or other Pacific Islander, non-Hispanic/Latino; 50 Two or more races, non-Hispanic/Latino), 38 international. Average age 30. 532 applicants, 44% accepted, 156 enrolled. In 2017, 139 master's awarded. *Degree requirements:* For master's, one foreign language, comprehensive exam, thesis (for some programs), project, field work, professional work experience. *Entrance requirements:* Additional exam requirements/recommendations for international students: Required—TOEFL (minimum score 550 paper-based; 80 iBT), IELTS (minimum score 6.5), PTE (minimum score 53). *Application deadline:* For fall admission, 2/1 for domestic and international students. Applications are processed on a rolling basis. Application fee: $55. Electronic applications accepted. *Expenses:* Tuition, state resident: full-time $7176. Tuition, nonresident: full-time $16,680. Tuition and fees vary according to course load and program. *Financial support:* Fellowships, research assistantships, career-related internships or fieldwork, Federal Work-Study, scholarships/grants, tuition waivers (full and partial), and unspecified assistantships available. Support available to part-time students. Financial award application deadline: 4/28; financial award applicants required to submit FAFSA. *Unit head:* Dr. Walt Jacobs, Dean, 408-924-5300, Fax: 408-924-5303, E-mail: walter.jacobs@sjsu.edu.
Website: http://www.sjsu.edu/socialsciences/

Shippensburg University of Pennsylvania, School of Graduate Studies, College of Education and Human Services, Department of Teacher Education, Shippensburg, PA 17257-2299. Offers curriculum and instruction (M Ed), including biology, early childhood education, elementary education, geography/earth science, history, mathematics, middle school education, modern languages; reading (M Ed). *Accreditation:* NCATE. *Program availability:* Part-time, evening/weekend, 100% online, blended/hybrid learning. *Faculty:* 13 full-time (8 women), 1 (woman) part-time/adjunct. *Students:* 10 full-time (7 women), 94 part-time (81 women); includes 10 minority (3 Black or African American, non-Hispanic/Latino; 2 Asian, non-Hispanic/Latino; 5 Hispanic/Latino), 1 international. Average age 34. 71 applicants, 86% accepted, 35 enrolled. In 2017, 23 master's awarded. *Degree requirements:* For master's, comprehensive exam (for some programs), thesis optional, practicum or internship; capstone seminar (for some programs). *Entrance requirements:* For master's, MAT or GRE (if GPA less than 2.75), interview, 3 letters of reference, questionnaire of teaching background and future goals, resume. Additional exam requirements/recommendations for international students: Required—TOEFL (minimum score 550 paper-based, 68 iBT) or IELTS (minimum score 6). *Application deadline:* For fall admission, 4/1 priority date for domestic students, 4/30 for international students; for spring admission, 9/1 priority date for domestic students, 9/30 for international students; for summer admission, 2/1 priority date for domestic students. Applications are processed on a rolling basis. Application fee: $45. Electronic applications accepted. *Expenses:* Tuition, state resident: part-time $500 per credit. Tuition, nonresident: part-time $750 per credit. *Required fees:* $145 per credit. *Financial support:* In 2017–18, 1 student received support. Career-related internships or fieldwork, scholarships/grants, unspecified assistantships, and resident hall director and student payroll positions available. Support available to part-time students. Financial award application deadline: 3/1; financial award applicants required to submit FAFSA. *Unit head:* Dr. Christine A. Royce, Chairperson, 717-477-1688, Fax: 717-477-4046, E-mail: caroyc@ship.edu. *Application contact:* Maya T. Mapp, Director of Admissions, 717-477-1231, Fax: 717-477-4016, E-mail: mtmapp@ship.edu.
Website: http://www.ship.edu/teacher/

Simon Fraser University, Office of Graduate Studies and Postdoctoral Fellows, Faculty of Environment, Department of Geography, Burnaby, BC V5A 1S6, Canada. Offers M Sc, MA, PhD. *Degree requirements:* For master's, one foreign language, thesis; for doctorate, one foreign language, comprehensive exam, thesis/dissertation. *Entrance requirements:* For master's, minimum GPA of 3.0 (on scale of 4.33) or 3.33 based on last 60 credits of undergraduate courses; for doctorate, minimum GPA of 3.5 (on scale of 4.33). Additional exam requirements/recommendations for international students: Recommended—TOEFL (minimum score 580 paper-based; 93 iBT), IELTS (minimum score 7), TWE (minimum score 5). Electronic applications accepted. *Faculty research:* Theoretical and systematic aspects of geography, ginseng research, geographic information sciences, tourism and community planning, geomorphology.

South Dakota State University, Graduate School, College of Arts and Science, Department of Geography, Brookings, SD 57007. Offers MS. *Program availability:* Part-time. *Degree requirements:* For master's, thesis, oral exam. *Entrance requirements:* Additional exam requirements/recommendations for international students: Required—TOEFL (minimum score 525 paper-based; 71 iBT). *Faculty research:* Contemporary agriculture and rural land use, geography of Indian casino gambling, geography of illegal drug trade, geography of crop circles.

Southern Illinois University Carbondale, Graduate School, College of Liberal Arts, Department of Geography, Carbondale, IL 62901-4701. Offers MS, PhD. *Degree requirements:* For master's, thesis; for doctorate, thesis/dissertation. *Entrance requirements:* For master's, GRE (recommended), minimum GPA of 2.7; for doctorate, minimum GPA of 3.25. Additional exam requirements/recommendations for international

students: Required—TOEFL. *Faculty research:* Natural resources management emphasizing water resources and environmental quality of air, water, and land systems.

Southern Illinois University Edwardsville, Graduate School, College of Arts and Sciences, Department of Geography, Edwardsville, IL 62026. Offers MS. *Program availability:* Part-time, evening/weekend. *Degree requirements:* For master's, thesis optional, final exam. *Entrance requirements:* For master's, GRE (for applicants with a GPA less than 2.8). Additional exam requirements/recommendations for international students: Required—TOEFL (minimum score 550 paper-based; 79 iBT), IELTS (minimum score 6.5). Electronic applications accepted.

Syracuse University, Maxwell School of Citizenship and Public Affairs, Programs in Geography, Syracuse, NY 13207. Offers MA, PhD. *Program availability:* Part-time, evening/weekend. *Degree requirements:* For master's, thesis or alternative; for doctorate, comprehensive exam, thesis/dissertation. *Entrance requirements:* For master's and doctorate, GRE General Test, personal statement, three letters of recommendation, official transcripts, resume. Additional exam requirements/recommendations for international students: Required—TOEFL (minimum score 100 iBT). *Application deadline:* For fall admission, 1/5 priority date for domestic and international students. Application fee: $75. Electronic applications accepted. *Financial support:* Fellowships with full tuition reimbursements, research assistantships, and teaching assistantships available. Financial award application deadline: 1/1. *Faculty research:* Biogeography, geomorphology, human impacts on vegetation and land forms, geographic information systems, remote sensing. *Unit head:* Dr. Jamie Winders, Department Chair, 315-443-2607, E-mail: jwinders@maxwell.syr.edu. *Application contact:* Margie Johnson, Recruiting Contact, E-mail: mmjohnso@maxwell.syr.edu.
Website: http://www.maxwell.syr.edu/geo/

Temple University, College of Liberal Arts, Department of Geography and Urban Studies, Philadelphia, PA 19122-6096. Offers geographic information systems (PSM, Graduate Certificate); geography and urban studies (MA, PhD). *Faculty:* 22 full-time (7 women), 2 part-time/adjunct (1 woman). *Students:* 27 full-time (16 women), 22 part-time (10 women); includes 14 minority (9 Black or African American, non-Hispanic/Latino; 2 Asian, non-Hispanic/Latino; 3 Hispanic/Latino), 7 international. 53 applicants, 45% accepted, 15 enrolled. In 2017, 4 master's, 2 doctorates, 3 other advanced degrees awarded. *Degree requirements:* For master's, comprehensive exam, thesis or alternative. *Entrance requirements:* For master's, GRE General Test, minimum GPA of 3.0, 3 letters of recommendation; for doctorate, GRE, minimum GPA of 3.0, 3 letters of recommendation. Additional exam requirements/recommendations for international students: Required—TOEFL (minimum score 575 paper-based; 88 iBT). *Application deadline:* For fall admission, 1/15 for domestic students, 12/15 for international students; for spring admission, 10/15 for domestic students, 8/1 for international students. Applications are processed on a rolling basis. Application fee: $60. Electronic applications accepted. *Expenses:* Tuition, state resident: full-time $16,164; part-time $898 per credit hour. Tuition, nonresident: full-time $22,158; part-time $1231 per credit hour. *Required fees:* $890; $445 per semester. Full-time tuition and fees vary according to course load, degree level, campus/location and program. *Financial support:* Fellowships, teaching assistantships, career-related internships or fieldwork, Federal Work-Study, and tuition waivers (partial) available. Financial award application deadline: 1/15; financial award applicants required to submit FAFSA. *Faculty research:* Social justice, sustainability, globalization, geographic methods, urban processes. *Unit head:* Dr. C. Hamil Pearsall, Graduate Director, 215-204-3074, Fax: 215-204-7833, E-mail: hamil.pearsall@temple.edu. *Application contact:* Julia Falcon, Student Services Coordinator, 215-204-3386, E-mail: julia.falcon@temple.edu.
Website: http://www.cla.temple.edu/gus/

Texas A&M University, College of Geosciences, Department of Geography, College Station, TX 77843. Offers MS, PhD. *Program availability:* Part-time. *Faculty:* 18. *Students:* 71 full-time (33 women), 33 part-time (15 women); includes 21 minority (4 Black or African American, non-Hispanic/Latino; 3 Asian, non-Hispanic/Latino; 12 Hispanic/Latino; 2 Two or more races, non-Hispanic/Latino), 24 international. Average age 30. 109 applicants, 77% accepted, 51 enrolled. In 2017, 8 master's, 9 doctorates awarded. *Degree requirements:* For master's, thesis optional; for doctorate, thesis/dissertation. *Entrance requirements:* For master's and doctorate, GRE General Test. Additional exam requirements/recommendations for international students: Required—TOEFL (minimum score 550 paper-based; 80 iBT), IELTS (minimum score 6), PTE (minimum score 53). *Application deadline:* For fall admission, 1/1 priority date for domestic students. Applications are processed on a rolling basis. Application fee: $50 ($90 for international students). Electronic applications accepted. *Expenses:* Contact institution. *Financial support:* In 2017–18, 71 students received support, including 19 fellowships with tuition reimbursements available (averaging $14,102 per year), 26 research assistantships with tuition reimbursements available (averaging $9,813 per year), 26 teaching assistantships with tuition reimbursements available (averaging $10,642 per year); career-related internships or fieldwork, institutionally sponsored loans, scholarships/grants, traineeships, health care benefits, tuition waivers (full and partial), and unspecified assistantships also available. Support available to part-time students. Financial award application deadline: 3/15; financial award applicants required to submit FAFSA. *Faculty research:* Geomorphology, historical geography, urban-economic geography, geographic education and technology, human-environment interaction. *Unit head:* Dr. David M. Cairns, Department Head, 979-845-2783, E-mail: cairns@tamu.edu. *Application contact:* Dr. Steven M. Quiring, Associate Professor and Director of Graduate Programs, 979-458-1712, Fax: 979-862-4487, E-mail: squiring@tamu.edu.
Website: http://geography.tamu.edu

Texas State University, The Graduate College, College of Liberal Arts, Doctoral Program in Geographic Education, San Marcos, TX 78666. Offers PhD. *Program availability:* Part-time, evening/weekend. *Faculty:* 6 full-time (1 woman), 1 part-time/adjunct (0 women). *Students:* 3 full-time (2 women), 2 part-time (1 woman); includes 2 minority (1 Hispanic/Latino; 1 Two or more races, non-Hispanic/Latino), 1 international. Average age 37. 2 applicants, 50% accepted. In 2017, 1 doctorate awarded. *Degree requirements:* For doctorate, comprehensive exam, thesis/dissertation. *Entrance requirements:* For doctorate, GRE General Test (minimum preferred score of 303 verbal and quantitative), master's degree in geography or related field with minimum GPA of 3.5 on all graduate coursework, 3 letters of recommendation, statement of purpose, curriculum vitae, completion of master's thesis or demonstrated evidence of scholarly research. Additional exam requirements/recommendations for international students: Required—TOEFL (minimum score 550 paper-based; 78 iBT), IELTS (minimum score 6). *Application deadline:* For fall admission, 1/15 priority date for domestic and international students. Applications are processed on a rolling basis. Application fee: $40 ($90 for international students). Electronic applications accepted. *Expenses:* Tuition, state resident: full-time $7868; part-time $3934 per semester. Tuition, nonresident: full-time $17,828; part-time $8914 per semester. *Required fees:* $2092; $1435 per semester. Tuition and fees vary according to course load. *Financial support:* In 2017–18, 3 students received support, including 1 research assistantship (averaging $26,780 per year), 2 teaching assistantships (averaging $27,583 per year); career-related internships or fieldwork, Federal Work-Study, institutionally sponsored loans, and unspecified assistantships also available. Support available to part-time students.

Financial award application deadline: 3/1; financial award applicants required to submit FAFSA. *Faculty research:* Geography online educational delivery, transformative research in geography education, building capacity for learning progressions. *Total annual research expenditures:* $52,071. *Unit head:* Dr. Yongmei Lu, PhD Program Director, 512-245-1337, Fax: 512-245-8353, E-mail: yl10@txstate.edu. *Application contact:* Dr. Andrea Golato, Dean of Graduate School, 512-245-2581, Fax: 512-245-8365, E-mail: gradcollege@txstate.edu.
Website: http://www.gradcollege.txstate.edu/programs/geo-ed-phd.html

Texas State University, The Graduate College, College of Liberal Arts, Doctoral Program in Geography, San Marcos, TX 78666. Offers PhD. *Program availability:* Part-time. *Faculty:* 4 full-time (2 women), 1 part-time/adjunct (0 women). *Students:* 19 full-time (9 women), 4 part-time (3 women); includes 4 minority (1 Black or African American, non-Hispanic/Latino; 3 Hispanic/Latino), 8 international. Average age 34. 19 applicants, 53% accepted, 5 enrolled. In 2017, 2 doctorates awarded. *Degree requirements:* For doctorate, comprehensive exam, thesis/dissertation. *Entrance requirements:* For doctorate, GRE (minimum preferred score of 303 verbal and quantitative), baccalaureate and master's degrees in related field from regionally-accredited institution with minimum GPA of 3.5 in completed graduate course work, 3 letters of recommendation, statement of purpose, curriculum vitae, completion of master's thesis or demonstrated evidence of scholarly research and writing. Additional exam requirements/recommendations for international students: Required—TOEFL (minimum score 550 paper-based; 78 iBT), IELTS (minimum score 6). *Application deadline:* For fall admission, 1/15 priority date for domestic and international students. Applications are processed on a rolling basis. Application fee: $40 ($90 for international students). Electronic applications accepted. *Expenses:* Tuition, state resident: full-time $7868; part-time $3934 per semester. Tuition, nonresident: full-time $17,828; part-time $8914 per semester. *Required fees:* $2092; $1435 per semester. Tuition and fees vary according to course load. *Financial support:* In 2017–18, 4 students received support, including 1 research assistantship (averaging $27,583 per year); teaching assistantships, career-related internships or fieldwork, Federal Work-Study, and institutionally sponsored loans also available. Support available to part-time students. Financial award application deadline: 3/1; financial award applicants required to submit FAFSA. *Faculty research:* Texas Aquatic Connectivity Assessment, cross-scale interactions among climate, land use and river water quality, land management impact on water quality in New Zealand. *Total annual research expenditures:* $47,312. *Unit head:* Dr. Yongmei Lu, PhD Program Director, 512-245-1337, Fax: 512-245-8353, E-mail: yl10@txstate.edu. *Application contact:* Dr. Andrea Golato, Dean of Graduate School, 512-245-2581, Fax: 512-245-8365, E-mail: gradcollege@txstate.edu.
Website: http://www.gradcollege.txstate.edu/programs/geo-phd.html

Texas State University, The Graduate College, College of Liberal Arts, Master's Program in Geography, San Marcos, TX 78666. Offers environmental geography (MS); geographic education (MAG, MS); geographic information science (MAG); geography (MAG); resources and environmental studies (MAG). *Program availability:* Evening/weekend. *Faculty:* 29 full-time (10 women), 6 part-time/adjunct (1 woman). *Students:* 36 full-time (14 women), 23 part-time (12 women); includes 13 minority (2 Black or African American, non-Hispanic/Latino; 2 Asian, non-Hispanic/Latino; 9 Hispanic/Latino), 6 international. Average age 30. 64 applicants, 67% accepted, 13 enrolled. In 2017, 24 master's awarded. *Degree requirements:* For master's, comprehensive exam, thesis (for some programs). *Entrance requirements:* For master's, GRE General Test (minimum preferred score of 300 verbal and quantitative), baccalaureate degree from regionally-accredited institution with minimum GPA of 3.2 in last 60 hours of course work (for MAG), 3.4 (for MS); 2 letters of recommendation; statement of purpose; current resume. Additional exam requirements/recommendations for international students: Required—TOEFL (minimum score 550 paper-based; 78 iBT), IELTS (minimum score 6.5). *Application deadline:* For fall admission, 2/1 priority date for domestic and international students; for spring admission, 10/15 priority date for domestic students, 10/1 for international students. Applications are processed on a rolling basis. Application fee: $40 ($90 for international students). Electronic applications accepted. *Expenses:* Tuition, state resident: full-time $7868; part-time $3934 per semester. Tuition, nonresident: full-time $17,828; part-time $8914 per semester. *Required fees:* $2092; $1435 per semester. Tuition and fees vary according to course load. *Financial support:* In 2017–18, 32 students received support, including 7 research assistantships (averaging $13,647 per year), 14 teaching assistantships (averaging $13,293 per year); career-related internships or fieldwork, Federal Work-Study, institutionally sponsored loans, scholarships/grants, and unspecified assistantships also available. Support available to part-time students. Financial award application deadline: 3/1; financial award applicants required to submit FAFSA. *Unit head:* Dr. Yongmei Lu, Graduate Adviser, 512-245-1337, Fax: 512-245-8353, E-mail: yl10@txstate.edu. *Application contact:* Dr. Andrea Golato, Dean of Graduate School, 512-245-2581, Fax: 512-245-8365, E-mail: gradcollege@txstate.edu.
Website: http://www.geo.txstate.edu/degrees-programs/graduate.html

Texas Tech University, Graduate School, College of Arts and Sciences, Department of Geosciences, Lubbock, TX 79409. Offers atmospheric science (MS); geography (MS); geosciences (MS, PhD). *Program availability:* Part-time. *Faculty:* 29 full-time (4 women), 3 part-time/adjunct (1 woman). *Students:* 64 full-time (19 women), 9 part-time (5 women); includes 11 minority (1 Black or African American, non-Hispanic/Latino; 1 Asian, non-Hispanic/Latino; 7 Hispanic/Latino; 2 Two or more races, non-Hispanic/Latino), 17 international. Average age 28. 120 applicants, 22% accepted, 17 enrolled. In 2017, 28 master's, 5 doctorates awarded. Terminal master's awarded for partial completion of doctoral program. *Degree requirements:* For master's, thesis; for doctorate, comprehensive exam, thesis/dissertation. *Entrance requirements:* For master's and doctorate, GRE General Test. Additional exam requirements/recommendations for international students: Required—TOEFL (minimum score 550 paper-based; 79 iBT). *Application deadline:* For fall admission, 6/1 priority date for domestic students, 1/15 priority date for international students; for spring admission, 9/1 priority date for domestic students, 6/15 priority date for international students. Applications are processed on a rolling basis. Application fee: $60. Electronic applications accepted. *Expenses:* Contact institution. *Financial support:* In 2017–18, 73 students received support, including 53 fellowships (averaging $2,448 per year), 42 research assistantships (averaging $11,629 per year), 46 teaching assistantships (averaging $13,673 per year); Federal Work-Study, scholarships/grants, health care benefits, tuition waivers (partial), and unspecified assistantships also available. Financial award application deadline: 2/15; financial award applicants required to submit FAFSA. *Faculty research:* Geology, geophysics, geochemistry, geospatial technology, atmospheric sciences. *Total annual research expenditures:* $2.8 million. *Unit head:* Dr. Jeffrey A. Lee, Chairman, 806-834-8228, Fax: 806-742-0100, E-mail: jeff.lee@ttu.edu. *Application contact:* Dr. Callum Hetherington, Associate Professor, 806-834-3110, Fax: 806-724-0100, E-mail: callum.hetherington@ttu.edu.
Website: http://www.depts.ttu.edu/geosciences/

Thomas Jefferson University, College of Architecture and the Built Environment, Program in Geospatial Technology for Geodesign, Philadelphia, PA 19107. Offers MS. *Program availability:* Part-time.

Towson University, College of Liberal Arts, Program in Geography and Environmental Planning, Towson, MD 21252-0001. Offers MA. *Program availability:* Part-time, evening/weekend. *Students:* 5 full-time (0 women), 11 part-time (2 women); includes 5 minority (2 Black or African American, non-Hispanic/Latino; 2 Hispanic/Latino; 1 Two or more races, non-Hispanic/Latino). *Degree requirements:* For master's, thesis optional. *Entrance requirements:* For master's, bachelor's degree with minimum of 9 credits of course work in geography, minimum GPA of 3.0 overall and in all geography courses, 2 letters of recommendation, essay. *Application deadline:* For fall admission, 1/17 for domestic students, 5/15 for international students; for spring admission, 10/15 for domestic students, 12/1 for international students. Applications are processed on a rolling basis. Application fee: $45. Electronic applications accepted. *Expenses:* Tuition, state resident: full-time $7960; part-time $398 per unit. Tuition, nonresident: full-time $16,480; part-time $824 per unit. *Required fees:* $2600; $130 per year. $390 per term. *Financial support:* Application deadline: 4/1. *Unit head:* Dr. Charles Schmitz, Graduate Program Director, 410-704-2966, E-mail: cschmitz@towson.edu. *Application contact:* Coverley Beidleman, Assistant Director of Graduate Admissions, 410-704-5630, Fax: 410-704-3030, E-mail: cbeidleman@towson.edu.
Website: http://www.towson.edu/cla/departments/geography/gradgeography/

Trent University, Graduate Studies, Program in Applications of Modeling in the Natural and Social Sciences, Peterborough, ON K9J 7B8, Canada. Offers applications of modeling in the natural and social sciences (MA); biology (M Sc, PhD); chemistry (M Sc); computer studies (M Sc); geography (M Sc, PhD); physics (M Sc). *Program availability:* Part-time. *Degree requirements:* For master's, thesis. *Entrance requirements:* For master's, honours degree. *Faculty research:* Computation of heat transfer, atmospheric physics, statistical mechanics, stress and coping, evolutionary ecology.

Trent University, Graduate Studies, Program in Environmental and Life Sciences and Program in Applications of Modeling in the Natural and Social Sciences, Department of Geography, Peterborough, ON K9J 7B8, Canada. Offers M Sc, PhD. *Program availability:* Part-time. *Degree requirements:* For master's, thesis; for doctorate, thesis/dissertation. *Entrance requirements:* For master's, honors degree; for doctorate, master's degree. *Faculty research:* Hydrometeorology, snow and ice, urban hydrology, fluvial geomorphology.

Université de Montréal, Faculty of Arts and Sciences, Department of Geography, Montréal, QC H3C 3J7, Canada. Offers environment and durable development (DESS); geography (M Sc, PhD, DESS). *Degree requirements:* For master's, 2 foreign languages, thesis (for some programs); for doctorate, 3 foreign languages, thesis/dissertation, general exam. *Entrance requirements:* For master's, bachelor's degree in related field; for doctorate, MA in geography or related field. Electronic applications accepted. *Faculty research:* Cartography, palynology, geomorphology, economic geography, regional and urban development.

Université de Sherbrooke, Faculty of Letters and Human Sciences, Department of Geography and Remote Sensing, Sherbrooke, QC J1K 2R1, Canada. Offers M Sc, PhD. *Degree requirements:* For master's, one foreign language, thesis; for doctorate, thesis/dissertation. *Faculty research:* Cartography.

Université du Québec à Montréal, Graduate Programs, Program in Geography, Montréal, QC H3C 3P8, Canada. Offers M Sc. *Program availability:* Part-time. *Degree requirements:* For master's, thesis optional. *Entrance requirements:* For master's, appropriate bachelor's degree or equivalent and proficiency in French.

Université Laval, Faculty of Forestry, Geography and Geomatics, Department of Geography, Program in Geographical Sciences, Québec, QC G1K 7P4, Canada. Offers M Sc Geogr, PhD. Terminal master's awarded for partial completion of doctoral program. *Degree requirements:* For master's, thesis; for doctorate, comprehensive exam, thesis/dissertation. *Entrance requirements:* For master's, knowledge of French; for doctorate, knowledge of French, knowledge of a second language. Electronic applications accepted.

University at Albany, State University of New York, College of Arts and Sciences, Department of Geography and Planning, Albany, NY 12222-0001. Offers geographic information science (Certificate); geography (MA); regional planning (MRP); urban policy (Certificate). *Program availability:* Part-time. *Faculty:* 13 full-time (3 women). *Students:* 32 full-time (13 women), 18 part-time (5 women); includes 9 minority (5 Black or African American, non-Hispanic/Latino; 2 Asian, non-Hispanic/Latino; 1 Hispanic/Latino; 1 Two or more races, non-Hispanic/Latino), 6 international. 46 applicants, 83% accepted, 21 enrolled. In 2017, 13 master's, 9 other advanced degrees awarded. *Entrance requirements:* Additional exam requirements/recommendations for international students: Required—TOEFL (minimum score 550 paper-based). *Application deadline:* For fall admission, 3/1 for domestic students, 5/1 for international students; for spring admission, 11/1 for international students. Applications are processed on a rolling basis. Application fee: $75. Electronic applications accepted. *Expenses:* Tuition, state resident: full-time $10,870; part-time $453 per credit hour. Tuition, nonresident: full-time $22,210; part-time $925 per credit hour. *Required fees:* $84.68 per credit hour. $508.06 per semester. Part-time tuition and fees vary according to course load and program. *Financial support:* Fellowships, teaching assistantships, career-related internships or fieldwork, Federal Work-Study, and institutionally sponsored loans available. Financial award application deadline: 3/1. *Faculty research:* Urban geography, social/cultural geography, urban planning, remote sensing, spatial analysis/geographic information systems. *Unit head:* Catherine Lawson, Chair, 518-442-4636, Fax: 518-442-4742, E-mail: lawsonc@albany.edu. *Application contact:* Michael DeRensis, Director, Graduate Admissions, 518-442-3980, Fax: 518-442-3922, E-mail: graduate@albany.edu.
Website: http://www.albany.edu/gp/

University at Buffalo, the State University of New York, Graduate School, College of Arts and Sciences, Department of Geography, Buffalo, NY 14260. Offers earth systems science (MA, MS); economic geography and business geographics (MS); environmental modeling and analysis (MA); geographic information science (MA, MS); geography (MA, PhD); health geography (MS); international trade (MA); urban and regional analysis (MA). *Program availability:* Part-time. *Faculty:* 19 full-time (9 women), 1 part-time/adjunct (0 women). *Students:* 100 full-time (45 women); includes 66 minority (1 Black or African American, non-Hispanic/Latino; 64 Asian, non-Hispanic/Latino; 1 Hispanic/Latino). Average age 28. 140 applicants, 23% accepted, 29 enrolled. In 2017, 19 master's, 4 doctorates awarded. Terminal master's awarded for partial completion of doctoral program. *Degree requirements:* For master's, thesis (for some programs), project or portfolio; for doctorate, thesis/dissertation. *Entrance requirements:* For master's, GRE General Test, minimum GPA of 2.9; for doctorate, GRE General Test, minimum GPA of 3.0. Additional exam requirements/recommendations for international students: Required—TOEFL (minimum score 550 paper-based; 79 iBT). *Application deadline:* For fall admission, 5/1 priority date for domestic students, 3/10 priority date for international students; for spring admission, 11/1 priority date for domestic students, 9/1 priority date for international students. Applications are processed on a rolling basis. Application fee: $75. Electronic applications accepted. *Expenses:* Contact institution. *Financial support:* In 2017–18, 15 students received support, including 9 fellowships with full tuition reimbursements available (averaging $3,070 per year), 7 research

assistantships with full tuition reimbursements available (averaging $14,000 per year), 15 teaching assistantships with full tuition reimbursements available (averaging $14,080 per year); career-related internships or fieldwork, Federal Work-Study, institutionally sponsored loans, traineeships, health care benefits, and unspecified assistantships also available. Financial award application deadline: 1/10. *Faculty research:* International business and world trade, geographic information systems and cartography, transportation, urban and regional analysis, physical and environmental geography. *Total annual research expenditures:* $2.6 million. *Unit head:* Dr. Sean Bennett, Chair, 716-645-0490, Fax: 716-645-2329, E-mail: seanb@buffalo.edu. *Application contact:* Wendy Zitzka, Graduate Secretary, 716-645-0471, Fax: 716-645-2329, E-mail: wzitzka@buffalo.edu.
Website: http://www.geog.buffalo.edu/

The University of Alabama, Graduate School, College of Arts and Sciences, Department of Geography, Tuscaloosa, AL 35487. Offers earth system science (MS, PhD); environment and natural resources (MS, PhD); environment and society (MS, PhD); geographic information science (MS, PhD). *Program availability:* Part-time. *Faculty:* 17 full-time (2 women). *Students:* 28 full-time (11 women), 4 part-time (1 woman); includes 2 minority (both Hispanic/Latino), 10 international. Average age 26. 32 applicants, 34% accepted, 10 enrolled. In 2017, 14 master's awarded. *Degree requirements:* For master's, comprehensive exam, thesis; for doctorate, comprehensive exam, thesis/dissertation. *Entrance requirements:* For master's, GRE, minimum GPA of 3.0. Additional exam requirements/recommendations for international students: Required—TOEFL (minimum score 550 paper-based; 79 iBT). *Application deadline:* For fall admission, 2/15 priority date for domestic and international students; for spring admission, 10/1 priority date for domestic and international students. Applications are processed on a rolling basis. Application fee: $50 ($60 for international students). Electronic applications accepted. *Financial support:* In 2017–18, 24 students received support, including fellowships with full tuition reimbursements available (averaging $15,000 per year), research assistantships with full tuition reimbursements available (averaging $14,013 per year), teaching assistantships with full tuition reimbursements available (averaging $14,013 per year); career-related internships or fieldwork, health care benefits, and unspecified assistantships also available. Financial award application deadline: 2/15. *Faculty research:* Earth system science; geographic information science; environment and natural resources; environment and society. *Total annual research expenditures:* $229,136. *Unit head:* Dr. Douglas Sherman, Chair, 205-348-5047, Fax: 205-348-2278, E-mail: douglas.j.sherman@ua.edu. *Application contact:* Dr. Justin Hart, Associate Professor, 205-348-5047, Fax: 205-348-2278, E-mail: hart013@ua.edu.
Website: http://geography.ua.edu

The University of Arizona, College of Social and Behavioral Sciences, School of Geography and Development, Tucson, AZ 85721. Offers geographic information systems technology (MA); geography (PhD). *Program availability:* Part-time. Terminal master's awarded for partial completion of doctoral program. *Degree requirements:* For master's, thesis or additional course work; for doctorate, variable foreign language requirement, thesis/dissertation. *Entrance requirements:* For master's, GRE General Test, 2 letters of recommendation; for doctorate, GRE General Test, statement of purpose, 2 letters of recommendation, master's degree. Additional exam requirements/recommendations for international students: Required—TOEFL (minimum score 550 paper-based; 79 iBT). Electronic applications accepted. *Faculty research:* Population, Latin America, Anglo-America, the former Soviet Union, the Middle East.

University of Arkansas, Graduate School, J. William Fulbright College of Arts and Sciences, Department of Geosciences, Program in Geography, Fayetteville, AR 72701. Offers MA. *Program availability:* Part-time. In 2017, 6 master's awarded. *Degree requirements:* For master's, thesis. *Application deadline:* For fall admission, 8/1 for domestic students, 4/1 for international students; for spring admission, 12/1 for domestic students, 10/1 for international students; for summer admission, 4/15 for domestic students, 3/1 for international students. Applications are processed on a rolling basis. Application fee: $60. Electronic applications accepted. *Expenses:* Tuition, state resident: full-time $3782. Tuition, nonresident: full-time $10,238. *Financial support:* In 2017–18, 7 research assistantships, 5 teaching assistantships were awarded; fellowships, career-related internships or fieldwork, and Federal Work-Study also available. Support available to part-time students. Financial award application deadline: 4/1; financial award applicants required to submit FAFSA. *Unit head:* Dr. Christopher Liner, Department Chair, 479-575-3355, Fax: 479-575-3469, E-mail: lmilliga@uark.edu. *Application contact:* Dr. Fiona Davidson, Graduate Coordinator, 479-575-3879, E-mail: fdavidso@uark.edu.
Website: https://fulbright.uark.edu/departments/geosciences/

The University of British Columbia, Faculty of Arts and Faculty of Graduate Studies, Department of Geography, Vancouver, BC V6T 1Z2, Canada. Offers M Sc, MA, PhD. *Program availability:* Part-time. Terminal master's awarded for partial completion of doctoral program. *Degree requirements:* For master's, thesis; for doctorate, comprehensive exam, thesis/dissertation. *Entrance requirements:* For master's and doctorate, minimum B average, 2nd class honors, upper division (class II, division I). Additional exam requirements/recommendations for international students: Required—TOEFL. Electronic applications accepted. *Expenses:* Contact institution. *Faculty research:* Earth system science, environmental geography, historical geography, social geography, urban geography.

University of Calgary, Faculty of Graduate Studies, Faculty of Arts, Department of Geography, Calgary, AB T2N 1N4, Canada. Offers M Sc, MA, MGIS, PhD. *Program availability:* Part-time. *Degree requirements:* For master's, thesis, departmental conference; for doctorate, thesis/dissertation, candidacy exam, departmental conference. *Entrance requirements:* For master's, minimum undergraduate GPA of 3.0 during last 2 years; for doctorate, minimum GPA of 3.0 during previous 2 years, master's degree. Additional exam requirements/recommendations for international students: Required—TOEFL (minimum score 550 paper-based). Electronic applications accepted. *Faculty research:* Geographic information systems, remote sensing, geomorphology, earth system processes, urban and required environmental health research.

University of California, Berkeley, Graduate Division, College of Letters and Science, Department of Geography, Berkeley, CA 94720-1500. Offers PhD. *Degree requirements:* For doctorate, thesis/dissertation, qualifying exam. *Entrance requirements:* For doctorate, GRE General Test, minimum GPA of 3.0, 3 letters of recommendation. Additional exam requirements/recommendations for international students: Required—TOEFL (minimum score 570 paper-based; 90 iBT). Electronic applications accepted.

University of California, Davis, Graduate Studies, Graduate Group in Geography, Davis, CA 95616. Offers MA, PhD. Terminal master's awarded for partial completion of doctoral program. *Degree requirements:* For master's, comprehensive exam (for some programs), thesis (for some programs); for doctorate, thesis/dissertation. *Entrance requirements:* For master's, GRE General Test, minimum GPA of 3.0; for doctorate, GRE General Test, master's degree, minimum GPA of 3.0. Additional exam requirements/recommendations for international students: Required—TOEFL (minimum score 550 paper-based). Electronic applications accepted. *Faculty research:* Cultural agrosystems, mountain society habitat and South Asia.

University of California, Los Angeles, Graduate Division, College of Letters and Science, Department of Geography, Los Angeles, CA 90095. Offers MA, PhD. Terminal master's awarded for partial completion of doctoral program. *Degree requirements:* For master's, thesis; for doctorate, thesis/dissertation, oral and written qualifying exams. *Entrance requirements:* For doctorate, GRE General Test, bachelor's degree; minimum undergraduate GPA of 3.3, 3.5 in graduate work (or its equivalent if letter grade system not used); writing sample. Additional exam requirements/recommendations for international students: Required—TOEFL. Electronic applications accepted.

University of California, Santa Barbara, Graduate Division, College of Letters and Sciences, Division of Mathematics, Life, and Physical Sciences, Department of Geography, Santa Barbara, CA 93106-4060. Offers cognitive science (PhD); geography (MA, PhD); global studies (PhD); quantitative methods in the social sciences (PhD); technology and society (PhD); transportation (PhD); MA/PhD. Terminal master's awarded for partial completion of doctoral program. *Degree requirements:* For master's, comprehensive exam (for some programs), thesis or alternative; for doctorate, comprehensive exam, thesis/dissertation, 1 quarter of teaching assistantship. *Entrance requirements:* For master's and doctorate, GRE (minimum combined verbal and quantitative scores above 1100 in old scoring system or 301 in new scoring system). Additional exam requirements/recommendations for international students: Required—TOEFL (minimum score 550 paper-based; 80 iBT), IELTS (minimum score 7). Electronic applications accepted. *Faculty research:* Earth system science; human environment relations; modeling, measurement, and computation.

University of Central Arkansas, Graduate School, College of Liberal Arts, Department of Geography, Conway, AR 72035-0001. Offers community and economic development (MS); geographic information systems (MGIS, Certificate). *Program availability:* Part-time, online learning. *Entrance requirements:* Additional exam requirements/recommendations for international students: Required—TOEFL (minimum score 550 paper-based). Electronic applications accepted.

University of Cincinnati, Graduate School, McMicken College of Arts and Sciences, Department of Geography, Cincinnati, OH 45221. Offers MA, PhD. Terminal master's awarded for partial completion of doctoral program. *Degree requirements:* For master's, thesis optional; for doctorate, one foreign language, comprehensive exam, thesis/dissertation. *Entrance requirements:* For master's and doctorate, GRE General Test. Additional exam requirements/recommendations for international students: Required—TOEFL. Electronic applications accepted. *Expenses: Tuition, area resident:* Full-time $14,468. Tuition, state resident: full-time $14,968; part-time $754 per credit hour. Tuition, nonresident: full-time $24,210; part-time $1311 per credit hour. *International tuition:* $26,460 full-time. *Required fees:* $3958; $84 per credit hour. One-time fee: $85 full-time. Tuition and fees vary according to course load, degree level and program. *Faculty research:* Urban-economics, GIS, physical-environmental.

University of Colorado Boulder, Graduate School, College of Arts and Sciences, Department of Geography, Boulder, CO 80309. Offers MA, PhD. *Faculty:* 25 full-time (9 women). *Students:* 70 full-time (34 women), 1 (woman) part-time; includes 5 minority (1 Asian, non-Hispanic/Latino; 2 Hispanic/Latino; 2 Two or more races, non-Hispanic/Latino), 13 international. Average age 31. 109 applicants, 31% accepted, 17 enrolled. In 2017, 7 master's, 9 doctorates awarded. Terminal master's awarded for partial completion of doctoral program. *Degree requirements:* For master's, thesis; for doctorate, one foreign language, comprehensive exam, thesis/dissertation. *Entrance requirements:* For master's, GRE General Test, minimum undergraduate GPA of 3.0; for doctorate, GRE General Test. *Application deadline:* For fall admission, 12/1 for domestic students; for spring admission, 12/1 for domestic students. Application fee: $60 ($80 for international students). Electronic applications accepted. Application fee is waived when completed online. *Financial support:* In 2017–18, 167 students received support, including 23 fellowships (averaging $9,029 per year), 18 research assistantships with full and partial tuition reimbursements available (averaging $35,693 per year), 40 teaching assistantships with full and partial tuition reimbursements available (averaging $22,044 per year); institutionally sponsored loans, scholarships/grants, health care benefits, and unspecified assistantships also available. Financial award application deadline: 2/15; financial award applicants required to submit FAFSA. *Faculty research:* Physical geography; hydrology; cultural geography; earth sciences; ecology. *Total annual research expenditures:* $49.6 million. *Application contact:* E-mail: geoggrad@colorado.edu.
Website: http://geography.colorado.edu

University of Colorado Colorado Springs, College of Letters, Arts and Sciences, Department of Geography and Environmental Studies, Colorado Springs, CO 80918. Offers MA. *Program availability:* Part-time. *Faculty:* 14 full-time (4 women), 5 part-time/adjunct (3 women). *Students:* 3 full-time (1 woman), 14 part-time (8 women); includes 3 minority (1 Asian, non-Hispanic/Latino; 1 Hispanic/Latino; 1 Two or more races, non-Hispanic/Latino). Average age 35. 16 applicants, 75% accepted, 5 enrolled. In 2017, 4 master's awarded. *Degree requirements:* For master's, comprehensive exam (for some programs), thesis (for some programs). *Entrance requirements:* For master's, GRE (recommended minimum combined score for the verbal and quantitative tests of 1000), minimum undergraduate GPA of 3.0, statement of intent (essay). Additional exam requirements/recommendations for international students: Recommended—TOEFL (minimum score 550 paper-based; 80 iBT), IELTS (minimum score 6.5). *Application deadline:* For fall admission, 2/1 priority date for domestic and international students. Applications are processed on a rolling basis. Application fee: $60 ($100 for international students). Electronic applications accepted. *Expenses:* $10,350 per year resident tuition, $20,935 nonresident, $11,961 nonresidential online; annual costs vary depending on program, course-load, and residency status. *Financial support:* In 2017–18, 9 students received support. Federal Work-Study, scholarships/grants, health care benefits, and unspecified assistantships available. Support available to part-time students. Financial award application deadline: 3/1; financial award applicants required to submit FAFSA. *Faculty research:* Socio-ecological implications of conservation strategies, cultural geography, militarized spaces, geovisualization, geographic information systems, hydrology, biogeography, human-environment interactions, geomorphology, population. *Total annual research expenditures:* $142,630. *Unit head:* Dr. Kelli Klebe, Dean of the Graduate School, 719-255-3779, Fax: 719-255-3045, E-mail: kklebe@uccs.edu. *Application contact:* David Havlick, Associate Professor, 719-255-4906, E-mail: dhavlick@uccs.edu.
Website: http://www.uccs.edu/geography/

University of Connecticut, Graduate School, College of Liberal Arts and Sciences, Department of Geography, Storrs, CT 06269. Offers MA, PhD. *Degree requirements:* For master's, comprehensive exam; for doctorate, thesis/dissertation. *Entrance requirements:* For master's and doctorate, GRE General Test. Additional exam requirements/recommendations for international students: Required—TOEFL (minimum score 550 paper-based). Electronic applications accepted.

University of Delaware, College of Earth, Ocean, and Environment, Department of Geography, Newark, DE 19716. Offers MA, MS, PhD. *Degree requirements:* For master's, thesis; for doctorate, thesis/dissertation. *Entrance requirements:* For master's and doctorate, GRE General Test. Additional exam requirements/recommendations for international students: Required—TOEFL. Electronic applications accepted. *Faculty research:* Permafrost, glaciers, climatology, physical geography, human geography.

University of Denver, Division of Natural Sciences and Mathematics, Department of Geography and the Environment, Denver, CO 80208. Offers geographic information science (MS); geography (MA, PhD). *Program availability:* Part-time. *Students:* Average age 33. 44 applicants, 66% accepted, 18 enrolled. In 2017, 22 master's awarded. Terminal master's awarded for partial completion of doctoral program. *Degree requirements:* For master's, comprehensive exam (for some programs), thesis or alternative; for doctorate, one foreign language, comprehensive exam, thesis/dissertation. *Entrance requirements:* For master's, GRE General Test, bachelor's degree, transcripts, personal statement, three letters of recommendation; for doctorate, GRE General Test, master's degree, transcripts, personal statement, three letters of recommendation. Additional exam requirements/recommendations for international students: Required—TOEFL (minimum score 570 paper-based; 88 iBT). *Application deadline:* For fall admission, 1/15 priority date for domestic and international students. Applications are processed on a rolling basis. Application fee: $65. Electronic applications accepted. *Expenses:* Contact institution. *Financial support:* In 2017–18, 54 students received support, including 14 teaching assistantships with tuition reimbursements available (averaging $17,262 per year); career-related internships or fieldwork, Federal Work-Study, institutionally sponsored loans, scholarships/grants, and unspecified assistantships also available. Support available to part-time students. Financial award application deadline: 2/15; financial award applicants required to submit FAFSA. *Faculty research:* Geographic information science, geomorphology, political ecology, transportation, urban studies. *Unit head:* Dr. Andrew Goetz, Professor and Chair, 303-871-2674, Fax: 303-871-2201, E-mail: agoetz@du.edu. *Application contact:* Nicole Chauvet, Assistant to the Chair, 303-871-2654, Fax: 303-871-2201, E-mail: nchauvet@du.edu.
Website: http://www.du.edu/nsm/departments/geography

University of Florida, Graduate School, College of Liberal Arts and Sciences, Department of Geography, Gainesville, FL 32611. Offers applications of geographic technologies (MA, MS); geographic information systems (MA, MS, PhD); geography (MA, MS, PhD); hydrologic sciences (MS, PhD); tropical conservation and development (MA, MS, PhD); wetland sciences (MA, MS, PhD). *Degree requirements:* For master's, thesis; for doctorate, comprehensive exam, thesis/dissertation. *Entrance requirements:* For master's and doctorate, GRE General Test, minimum GPA of 3.0. Additional exam requirements/recommendations for international students: Required—TOEFL (minimum score 550 paper-based; 80 iBT), IELTS (minimum score 6). Electronic applications accepted. *Faculty research:* Economic development, physical geography, hydrology, climatology, tropical agriculture.

University of Georgia, Franklin College of Arts and Sciences, Department of Geography, Athens, GA 30602. Offers MA, MS, PhD. *Degree requirements:* For master's, one foreign language, thesis; for doctorate, one foreign language, thesis/dissertation. *Entrance requirements:* For master's and doctorate, GRE General Test. Electronic applications accepted.

University of Guelph, Graduate Studies, College of Social and Applied Human Sciences, Department of Geography, Guelph, ON N1G 2W1, Canada. Offers M Sc, MA, PhD. *Program availability:* Part-time. *Degree requirements:* For master's, thesis (for some programs); for doctorate, comprehensive exam, thesis/dissertation. *Entrance requirements:* For master's, minimum B average during previous 2 years of course work; for doctorate, minimum A- average. Additional exam requirements/recommendations for international students: Required—TOEFL (minimum score 550 paper-based). Electronic applications accepted. *Faculty research:* Rural resource evaluation, environmental analysis, biophysical process, rural settlement and land use, resource assessment.

University of Hawaii at Manoa, Office of Graduate Education, College of Social Sciences, Department of Geography, Honolulu, HI 96822. Offers geography (MA, PhD); ocean policy (Graduate Certificate). *Program availability:* Part-time. *Degree requirements:* For master's, one foreign language, comprehensive exam, thesis; for doctorate, one foreign language, comprehensive exam, thesis/dissertation. *Entrance requirements:* For master's, GRE General Test; for doctorate, GRE General Test, sample of written work. Additional exam requirements/recommendations for international students: Required—TOEFL (minimum score 500 paper-based; 61 iBT), IELTS (minimum score 5). *Faculty research:* Physical geography, human geography, methodology.

University of Idaho, College of Graduate Studies, College of Science, Department of Geography, Moscow, ID 83844. Offers MS, PhD. *Faculty:* 9 full-time. *Students:* 13. Average age 32. In 2017, 4 master's, 3 doctorates awarded. *Degree requirements:* For doctorate, thesis/dissertation. *Entrance requirements:* For master's and doctorate, GRE, minimum GPA of 3.0. Additional exam requirements/recommendations for international students: Required—TOEFL (minimum score 79 iBT). *Application deadline:* For fall admission, 8/1 for domestic students; for spring admission, 12/15 for domestic students. Applications are processed on a rolling basis. Application fee: $60. Electronic applications accepted. *Expenses:* Tuition, state resident: full-time $6722; part-time $430 per credit hour. Tuition, nonresident: full-time $23,046; part-time $1337 per credit hour. *Required fees:* $2142; $63 per credit hour. *Financial support:* Research assistantships and teaching assistantships available. Financial award applicants required to submit FAFSA. *Faculty research:* Land cover land use changes, rural development, geographic trade models, climate change. *Unit head:* Dr. Leslie Baker, Chair, 208-885-6216, E-mail: geography@uidaho.edu. *Application contact:* Sean Scoggin, Graduate Recruitment Coordinator, 208-885-4723, Fax: 208-885-4406, E-mail: graduateadmissions@uidaho.edu.
Website: https://www.uidaho.edu/sci/geography

University of Illinois at Chicago, College of Liberal Arts and Sciences, Department of Anthropology, Program in Environmental and Urban Geography, Chicago, IL 60607-7128. Offers MA. *Program availability:* Part-time. *Degree requirements:* For master's, thesis. *Entrance requirements:* For master's, GRE General Test, minimum GPA of 2.75. Additional exam requirements/recommendations for international students: Required—TOEFL. Electronic applications accepted.

University of Illinois at Urbana–Champaign, Graduate College, College of Liberal Arts and Sciences, School of Earth, Society and Environment, Department of Geography and Geographic Information Science, Champaign, IL 61820. Offers MA, MS, PhD.

The University of Iowa, Graduate College, College of Liberal Arts and Sciences, Department of Geographical and Sustainability Sciences, Iowa City, IA 52242-1316. Offers MA, PhD, Certificate. *Degree requirements:* For master's, thesis optional, exam; for doctorate, comprehensive exam, thesis/dissertation. *Entrance requirements:* For master's and doctorate, GRE General Test, minimum GPA of 3.0. Additional exam requirements/recommendations for international students: Required—TOEFL (minimum score 550 paper-based; 81 iBT). Electronic applications accepted.

The University of Kansas, Graduate Studies, College of Liberal Arts and Sciences, Department of Geography, Lawrence, KS 66045-7613. Offers atmospheric science (MS); geographic information science (Graduate Certificate); geography (MA, PhD); MUP/MA. *Program availability:* Part-time. *Students:* 54 full-time (25 women), 6 part-time (2 women); includes 9 minority (7 American Indian or Alaska Native, non-Hispanic/Latino; 1 Asian, non-Hispanic/Latino; 1 Hispanic/Latino), 9 international. Average age 32. 36 applicants, 53% accepted, 13 enrolled. In 2017, 11 master's, 5 doctorates awarded. *Entrance requirements:* For master's and doctorate, GRE General Test, 3 letters of reference, transcripts, statement of interests, resume. Additional exam requirements/recommendations for international students: Required—TOEFL. *Application deadline:* For fall admission, 1/15 priority date for domestic and international students; for spring admission, 11/1 for domestic and international students; for summer admission, 4/1 for domestic and international students. Application fee: $65 ($85 for international students). Electronic applications accepted. *Financial support:* Fellowships, research assistantships, teaching assistantships, and unspecified assistantships available. Financial award application deadline: 1/15. *Faculty research:* Physical geography, human/cultural/regional geography, geographic information science, atmospheric science. *Unit head:* Nathaniel Brunsell, Chair, 785-864-2021, E-mail: brunsell@ku.edu. *Application contact:* Beverly Koerner, Graduate Admission Contact, 785-864-7706, E-mail: koerner@ku.edu.
Website: http://www.geog.ku.edu/

University of Kentucky, Graduate School, College of Arts and Sciences, Program in Geography, Lexington, KY 40506-0032. Offers MA, PhD. *Degree requirements:* For master's, comprehensive exam, thesis optional; for doctorate, one foreign language, comprehensive exam, thesis/dissertation. *Entrance requirements:* For master's, GRE General Test, minimum undergraduate GPA of 2.75; for doctorate, GRE General Test, minimum graduate GPA of 3.0. Additional exam requirements/recommendations for international students: Required—TOEFL (minimum score 550 paper-based). Electronic applications accepted. *Faculty research:* Cultural, industrial, medical, political, social, population, and transportation geography; geographic analysis; Third World (especially Southeast Asia theory); Eastern Europe.

University of Lethbridge, School of Graduate Studies, Lethbridge, AB T1K 3M4, Canada. Offers addictions counseling (M Sc); agricultural biotechnology (M Sc); agricultural studies (M Sc, MA); anthropology (MA); archaeology (M Sc, MA); art (MA, MFA); biochemistry (M Sc); biological sciences (M Sc); biomolecular science (PhD); biosystems and biodiversity (PhD); Canadian studies (MA); chemistry (M Sc); computer science (M Sc); computer science and geographical information science (M Sc); counseling (MC); counseling psychology (M Ed); dramatic arts (MA); earth, space, and physical science (PhD); economics (MA); education (MA, PhD); educational leadership (M Ed); English (MA); environmental science (M Sc); evolution and behavior (PhD); exercise science (M Sc); French (MA); French/German (MA); French/Spanish (MA); general education (M Ed); geography (M Sc, MA); German (MA); health sciences (M Sc); individualized multidisciplinary (M Sc, MA); kinesiology (M Sc, MA); management (M Sc), including accounting, finance, human resource management and labor relations, information systems, international management, marketing, policy and strategy; mathematics (M Sc); music (M Mus, MA); Native American studies (MA); neuroscience (M Sc, PhD); new media (MA, MFA); nursing (M Sc, MN); philosophy (MA); physics (M Sc); political science (MA); psychology (M Sc, MA); religious studies (MA); sociology (MA); theatre and dramatic arts (MFA); theoretical and computational science (PhD); urban and regional studies (MA); women and gender studies (MA). *Program availability:* Part-time, evening/weekend. *Degree requirements:* For master's, thesis (for some programs); for doctorate, comprehensive exam, thesis/dissertation. *Entrance requirements:* For master's, GMAT (for M Sc in management), bachelor's degree in related field, minimum GPA of 3.0 during previous 20 graded semester courses, 2 years' teaching or related experience (M Ed); for doctorate, master's degree, minimum graduate GPA of 3.5. Additional exam requirements/recommendations for international students: Required—TOEFL (minimum score 580 paper-based; 93 iBT). Electronic applications accepted. *Faculty research:* Movement and brain plasticity, gibberellin physiology, photosynthesis, carbon cycling, molecular properties of main-group ring components.

University of Louisville, Graduate School, College of Arts and Sciences, Department of Geography and Geosciences, Louisville, KY 40292-0001. Offers applied geography (MS). *Program availability:* Part-time, blended/hybrid learning. *Faculty:* 11 full-time (3 women), 1 part-time/adjunct (0 women). *Students:* 7 full-time (1 woman), 4 part-time (0 women). Average age 28. 3 applicants, 100% accepted, 2 enrolled. In 2017, 5 master's awarded. *Degree requirements:* For master's, comprehensive exam (for some programs), thesis (for some programs). *Entrance requirements:* For master's, GRE (minimum combined score of 1000), BA/BS with minimum cumulative GPA of 3.0. Additional exam requirements/recommendations for international students: Required—TOEFL (minimum score 550 paper-based, 79 iBT) or IELTS. *Application deadline:* For fall admission, 3/15 priority date for domestic and international students; for spring admission, 11/15 priority date for domestic and international students; for summer admission, 3/15 for domestic and international students. Application fee: $65. Electronic applications accepted. *Expenses:* $12,560. *Financial support:* In 2017–18, 2 fellowships (averaging $5,000 per year), 2 research assistantships with full tuition reimbursements (averaging $14,000 per year) were awarded; teaching assistantships, scholarships/grants, and unspecified assistantships also available. Financial award application deadline: 3/15. *Faculty research:* Climate change, environmental health, population modeling, globalization, urban and food systems, geographic information systems, remote sensing, spatial modeling, qualitative analysis. *Total annual research expenditures:* $254,679. *Unit head:* Dr. David A. Howarth, Professor and Chair of Geography and Geosciences, 502-852-2693. *Application contact:* Dr. Margath Walker, Director, Graduate Studies, 502-852-2694, Fax: 502-852-4560, E-mail: margath.walker@louisville.edu.
Website: http://louisville.edu/geography/

The University of Manchester, School of Environment and Development, Manchester, United Kingdom. Offers architecture (M Phil, PhD); development policy and management (M Phil, PhD); human geography (M Phil, PhD); physical geography (M Phil, PhD); planning and landscape (M Phil, PhD).

The University of Manchester, School of Nursing, Midwifery and Social Work, Manchester, United Kingdom. Offers nursing (M Phil, PhD); social work (M Phil, PhD).

University of Manitoba, Faculty of Graduate Studies, Clayton H. Riddell Faculty of Environment, Earth, and Resources, Department of Environment and Geography, Winnipeg, MB R3T 2N2, Canada. Offers environment (M Env); environment and geography (M Sc); geography (MA, PhD). *Degree requirements:* For master's, thesis; for doctorate, one foreign language, thesis/dissertation.

University of Maryland, Baltimore County, The Graduate School, College of Arts, Humanities and Social Sciences, Department of Geography and Environmental Systems, Program in Geography and Environmental Systems, Baltimore, MD 21250. Offers MS, PhD. *Program availability:* Part-time. *Faculty:* 14 full-time (5 women), 11 part-time/adjunct (2 women). *Students:* 26 full-time (14 women), 40 part-time (16 women); includes 18 minority (7 Black or African American, non-Hispanic/Latino; 4 Asian, non-Hispanic/Latino; 6 Hispanic/Latino; 1 Two or more races, non-Hispanic/Latino). Average age 32. 38 applicants, 50% accepted, 13 enrolled. In 2017, 3 master's, 1 doctorate awarded. Terminal master's awarded for partial completion of doctoral program. *Degree requirements:* For master's, thesis optional, annual faculty evaluation, research paper; for doctorate, comprehensive exam, thesis/dissertation, annual faculty evaluation, qualifying exams, proposal and dissertation defense. *Entrance requirements:* For master's and doctorate, GRE, minimum GPA of 3.0 overall, 3.3 in major. Additional

exam requirements/recommendations for international students: Required—TOEFL (minimum score 550 paper-based; 80 iBT); Recommended—IELTS. *Application deadline:* For fall admission, 2/1 for domestic students, 1/1 for international students. Application fee: $50. Electronic applications accepted. *Expenses:* Contact institution. *Financial support:* In 2017–18, 18 students received support, including 1 fellowship with full tuition reimbursement available (averaging $19,700 per year), 5 research assistantships with full tuition reimbursements available (averaging $19,700 per year), 11 teaching assistantships with full tuition reimbursements available (averaging $19,700 per year); scholarships/grants, traineeships, health care benefits, and unspecified assistantships also available. Financial award application deadline: 2/1. *Faculty research:* Watershed processes; political ecology; land change and land use; conservation and development; urbanization; economic geography; climate and weather systems; ecology and biogeography; landscape ecology; urban sustainability; environmental health; environmental policy; geographic information science and remote sensing. *Total annual research expenditures:* $73,260. *Unit head:* Dr. David Lansing, Graduate Program Director, 410-455-2971, E-mail: dlansing@umbc.edu. *Application contact:* Kathryn Nee, Coordinator of Domestic Admissions, 410-455-2944, E-mail: nee@umbc.edu.
Website: http://ges.umbc.edu/graduate/

University of Maryland, College Park, Academic Affairs, College of Behavioral and Social Sciences, Department of Geography, College Park, MD 20742. Offers MA, PhD, MA/MLS. *Program availability:* Part-time, evening/weekend. Terminal master's awarded for partial completion of doctoral program. *Degree requirements:* For master's, thesis, oral exam; for doctorate, comprehensive exam, thesis/dissertation. *Entrance requirements:* For master's, GRE General Test, minimum GPA of 3.0, 3 letters of recommendation; for doctorate, GRE General Test. Additional exam requirements/recommendations for international students: Required—TOEFL, TWE. Electronic applications accepted. *Faculty research:* Cartography and automated mapping, environmental systems analysis, metropolitan analysis and planning, historical and human geography, coastal geomorphology.

University of Massachusetts Amherst, Graduate School, College of Natural Sciences, Department of Geosciences, Program in Geography, Amherst, MA 01003. Offers MS. *Program availability:* Part-time. *Degree requirements:* For master's, thesis or alternative. *Entrance requirements:* For master's, GRE General Test. Additional exam requirements/recommendations for international students: Required—TOEFL (minimum score 550 paper-based; 80 iBT), IELTS (minimum score 6.5). Electronic applications accepted.

University of Memphis, Graduate School, College of Arts and Sciences, Department of Earth Sciences, Memphis, TN 38152. Offers earth sciences (MA, MS, PhD), including archaeology (MS), geography (MS), geology (MS), geophysics (MS), interdisciplinary studies (MS); geographic information systems (Graduate Certificate), including geographic information systems, GIS educator, GIS planning, GIS professional. *Program availability:* Part-time, evening/weekend. *Faculty:* 18 full-time (3 women), 4 part-time/adjunct (0 women). *Students:* 55 full-time (23 women), 24 part-time (4 women); includes 5 minority (1 Black or African American, non-Hispanic/Latino; 4 Asian, non-Hispanic/Latino), 19 international. Average age 31. 17 applicants, 82% accepted, 11 enrolled. In 2017, 7 master's, 5 doctorates, 3 other advanced degrees awarded. Terminal master's awarded for partial completion of doctoral program. *Degree requirements:* For master's, comprehensive exam, thesis, seminar presentation; for doctorate, comprehensive exam, thesis/dissertation, qualifying exam, submission of two manuscripts for publication in peer-reviewed journal or books. *Entrance requirements:* For master's, GRE General Test, 3 letters of recommendation, statement of research interests; for doctorate, GRE General Test, 2 letters of recommendation, resume, personal statement. Additional exam requirements/recommendations for international students: Required—TOEFL (minimum score 550 paper-based; 79 iBT). *Application deadline:* For fall admission, 1/15 for domestic students; for spring admission, 11/1 for domestic students. Applications are processed on a rolling basis. Application fee: $35 ($60 for international students). Electronic applications accepted. *Expenses:* Contact institution. *Financial support:* In 2017–18, 18 students received support, including 2 research assistantships with full tuition reimbursements available (averaging $17,000 per year), 13 teaching assistantships with full tuition reimbursements available (averaging $16,692 per year); fellowships with full tuition reimbursements available, Federal Work-Study, scholarships/grants, and unspecified assistantships also available. Financial award application deadline: 2/1; financial award applicants required to submit FAFSA. *Faculty research:* Hazards, active tectonics, geophysics, hydrology and water resources, spatial analysis. *Unit head:* Dr. Daniel Larsen, Chair, 901-678-4538, Fax: 901-678-2178, E-mail: dlarsen@memphis.edu. *Application contact:* Dr. Randel T. Cox, Graduate Coordinator, 901-678-4361, Fax: 901-678-2178, E-mail: randycox@memphis.edu.
Website: http://www.memphis.edu/earthsciences/

University of Miami, Graduate School, College of Arts and Sciences, Department of Geography and Regional Studies, Coral Gables, FL 33124. Offers geography (MA). *Program availability:* Part-time. *Degree requirements:* For master's, thesis. *Entrance requirements:* For master's, GRE, 3 letters of recommendation, official transcripts. Additional exam requirements/recommendations for international students: Required—TOEFL. Electronic applications accepted. *Faculty research:* Urbanization, globalization, environmental change.

University of Minnesota, Twin Cities Campus, Graduate School, College of Liberal Arts, Department of Geography, Environment and Society, Minneapolis, MN 55455. Offers MA, PhD. *Faculty:* 16 full-time (5 women), 16 part-time/adjunct (8 women). *Students:* 50 full-time (26 women); includes 4 minority (2 Black or African American, non-Hispanic/Latino; 2 Asian, non-Hispanic/Latino), 13 international. Average age 27. 63 applicants, 25% accepted, 9 enrolled. In 2017, 2 master's, 3 doctorates awarded. Terminal master's awarded for partial completion of doctoral program. *Degree requirements:* For master's, comprehensive exam, thesis or 3 papers; for doctorate, comprehensive exam, thesis/dissertation. *Entrance requirements:* For master's and doctorate, GRE General Test, minimum GPA of 3.5. Additional exam requirements/recommendations for international students: Required—TOEFL (minimum score 600 paper-based; 100 iBT), IELTS (minimum score 7). *Application deadline:* For fall admission, 12/15 for domestic and international students. Application fee: $75 ($95 for international students). Electronic applications accepted. *Financial support:* In 2017–18, 37 students received support, including 7 fellowships with full tuition reimbursements available (averaging $22,500 per year), 5 research assistantships with full tuition reimbursements available (averaging $17,000 per year), 27 teaching assistantships with full and partial tuition reimbursements available (averaging $17,000 per year); career-related internships or fieldwork, scholarships/grants, traineeships, health care benefits, tuition waivers (full and partial), and unspecified assistantships also available. Financial award application deadline: 12/15. *Faculty research:* Geovisualization; geographic information systems; spatial analysis and modeling; spatial databases; remote sensing; biogeography; international labor migrations; political globalization and uneven development; governance, citizenship and justice; environmental change; culture, place and flow; nature and society; health geography; dendrochronology. *Total annual research expenditures:* $101,623. *Unit head:* Bruce Braun, Chair, 612-625-6080, Fax: 612-624-1044, E-mail: braun038@umn.edu. *Application contact:* Sara C. Braun, Graduate Program Coordinator, 612-625-6080, Fax: 612-624-1044, E-mail: geogdgs@umn.edu.
Website: http://www.geog.umn.edu/

University of Missouri, Office of Research and Graduate Studies, College of Arts and Science, Department of Geography, Columbia, MO 65211. Offers geographic information science (Graduate Certificate); geography (MA). *Degree requirements:* For master's, thesis or alternative. *Entrance requirements:* For master's, GRE General Test (minimum score 1000 verbal and quantitative), minimum GPA of 3.0. Additional exam requirements/recommendations for international students: Required—TOEFL (minimum score 500 paper-based; 61 iBT). Electronic applications accepted. *Faculty research:* Human geography, nature/society relationships, the physical environment, application of geographic information sciences.

University of Montana, Graduate School, College of Humanities and Sciences, Department of Geography, Missoula, MT 59812. Offers community and environmental planning (MA); geography (MA, MS). *Entrance requirements:* For master's, GRE General Test. Additional exam requirements/recommendations for international students: Required—TOEFL.

University of Nebraska at Omaha, Graduate Studies, College of Arts and Sciences, Department of Geography and Geology, Omaha, NE 68182. Offers geographic information science (Certificate); geography (MA). *Program availability:* Part-time. *Degree requirements:* For master's, comprehensive exam, thesis (for some programs). *Entrance requirements:* For master's, GRE, minimum GPA of 3.0, 15 undergraduate geography hours, transcripts, resume, statement of purpose, 2 letters of recommendation; for Certificate, minimum GPA of 3.0, transcripts, resume, statement of purpose, 2 letters of recommendation. Additional exam requirements/recommendations for international students: Required—TOEFL, IELTS, PTE. Electronic applications accepted.

University of Nebraska–Lincoln, Graduate College, College of Arts and Sciences, Department of Anthropology and Geography, Program in Geography, Lincoln, NE 68588. Offers MA, PhD. *Degree requirements:* For master's, thesis optional; for doctorate, comprehensive exam, thesis/dissertation. *Entrance requirements:* For master's and doctorate, GRE General Test. Additional exam requirements/recommendations for international students: Required—TOEFL (minimum score 550 paper-based). Electronic applications accepted. *Faculty research:* Climatology, historical-cultural geography, geographic information systems/cartography/remote sensing, human geography, Great Plains studies.

University of Nevada, Reno, Graduate School, College of Science, Mackay School of Earth Sciences and Engineering, Department of Geography, Program in Geography, Reno, NV 89557. Offers MS, PhD. Terminal master's awarded for partial completion of doctoral program. *Degree requirements:* For master's, comprehensive exam, thesis; for doctorate, comprehensive exam, thesis/dissertation. *Entrance requirements:* For master's and doctorate, GRE General Test, minimum GPA of 2.75. Additional exam requirements/recommendations for international students: Required—TOEFL (minimum score 500 paper-based; 61 iBT), IELTS (minimum score 6). Electronic applications accepted. *Faculty research:* Natural resources, education, climatology, biogeography, ethnic/cultural geography.

University of New Mexico, Graduate Studies, College of Arts and Sciences, Program in Geography and Environmental Studies, Albuquerque, NM 87131-2039. Offers MS. *Program availability:* Part-time. *Faculty:* 8 full-time (4 women), 1 (woman) part-time/adjunct. *Students:* 13 full-time (3 women), 12 part-time (8 women); includes 4 minority (1 Black or African American, non-Hispanic/Latino; 1 American Indian or Alaska Native, non-Hispanic/Latino; 2 Hispanic/Latino), 2 international. Average age 32. 20 applicants, 75% accepted, 11 enrolled. In 2017, 6 master's awarded. *Degree requirements:* For master's, comprehensive exam (for some programs), thesis (for some programs). *Entrance requirements:* For master's, GRE. Additional exam requirements/recommendations for international students: Required—TOEFL. *Application deadline:* For fall admission, 2/1 priority date for domestic students, 1/1 priority date for international students; for spring admission, 11/15 for domestic and international students. Application fee: $50. Electronic applications accepted. *Financial support:* Research assistantships with full tuition reimbursements, teaching assistantships with full tuition reimbursements, health care benefits, and tuition waivers (full and partial) available. Financial award applicants required to submit FAFSA. *Faculty research:* Geographic information science, environmental management. *Unit head:* Dr. Scott M. Freundschuh, Chair, 505-277-0058, Fax: 505-277-3614, E-mail: sfreunds@unm.edu. *Application contact:* Dr. Maria D. Lane, Director of Graduate Studies, 505-277-4075, Fax: 505-277-3614, E-mail: mdlane@unm.edu.
Website: http://geography.unm.edu

University of New Orleans, Graduate School, College of Liberal Arts, Department of Geography, New Orleans, LA 70148. Offers MA. *Entrance requirements:* For master's, GRE General Test. Additional exam requirements/recommendations for international students: Required—TOEFL (minimum score 550 paper-based; 79 iBT). Electronic applications accepted.

The University of North Carolina at Chapel Hill, Graduate School, College of Arts and Sciences, Department of Geography, Chapel Hill, NC 27599. Offers MA, PhD. *Degree requirements:* For master's, one foreign language, comprehensive exam, thesis; for doctorate, 2 foreign languages, comprehensive exam, thesis/dissertation. *Entrance requirements:* For master's and doctorate, GRE General Test, minimum GPA of 3.0. *Faculty research:* Geographic information systems, climatology, hydrology, population research, Latino immigration.

The University of North Carolina at Charlotte, College of Liberal Arts and Sciences, Department of Geography and Earth Sciences, Charlotte, NC 28223-0001. Offers earth sciences (MS); geography (MA), including community planning, geographic information science and technologies, location analysis, urban-regional analysis; geography and urban regional analysis (PhD). *Program availability:* Part-time, evening/weekend. *Faculty:* 32 full-time (13 women), 1 part-time/adjunct (0 women). *Students:* 42 full-time (17 women), 27 part-time (11 women); includes 14 minority (4 Black or African American, non-Hispanic/Latino; 2 Asian, non-Hispanic/Latino; 5 Hispanic/Latino; 3 Two or more races, non-Hispanic/Latino), 14 international. Average age 32. 34 applicants, 74% accepted, 10 enrolled. In 2017, 11 master's, 4 doctorates awarded. Terminal master's awarded for partial completion of doctoral program. *Degree requirements:* For master's, comprehensive exam, thesis or alternative, project; for doctorate, thesis/dissertation. *Entrance requirements:* For master's, GRE General Test or MAT, minimum GPA of 2.75, 3.0 for junior and senior years, transcripts, letters of recommendation, and personal essays (for MS); minimum GPA of 3.1 overall or for the last 2 years, 3.2 in major, three letters of reference, and personal essay (for MA); for doctorate, GRE, MA or MS in geography or a field related to the primary emphases of the program; minimum master's-level GPA of 3.5; GIS proficiency. Additional exam requirements/recommendations for international students: Required—TOEFL (minimum score 523 paper-based, 70 iBT) or IELTS (6.5). *Application deadline:* For fall admission, 2/1 for domestic and international students; for spring admission, 9/30 for domestic and international students. Applications are processed on a rolling basis. Application fee: $75. Electronic applications accepted. *Expenses:* Tuition, state resident: full-time

$4337. Tuition, nonresident: full-time $17,771. *Required fees:* $3211. Tuition and fees vary according to course load and program. *Financial support:* In 2017–18, 37 students received support, including 5 research assistantships (averaging $7,350 per year), 32 teaching assistantships (averaging $8,594 per year); career-related internships or fieldwork, institutionally sponsored loans, scholarships/grants, and unspecified assistantships also available. Support available to part-time students. Financial award application deadline: 3/1; financial award applicants required to submit FAFSA. *Total annual research expenditures:* $321,902. *Unit head:* Dr. Craig Allan, Chair, 704-687-5999, E-mail: ges@uncc.edu. *Application contact:* Kathy B. Giddings, Director of Graduate Admissions, 704-687-5503, Fax: 704-687-1668, E-mail: gradadm@uncc.edu.
Website: https://geoearth.uncc.edu/

The University of North Carolina at Greensboro, Graduate School, College of Arts and Sciences, Department of Geography, Greensboro, NC 27412-5001. Offers applied geography (MA); geographic information science (Certificate); geography (PhD); urban and economic development (Certificate). *Degree requirements:* For master's, comprehensive exam, thesis or alternative. *Entrance requirements:* For master's, GRE General Test. Additional exam requirements/recommendations for international students: Required—TOEFL. Electronic applications accepted.

University of North Dakota, Graduate School, College of Arts and Sciences, Department of Geography and Geographic Information Science, Grand Forks, ND 58202. Offers MA, MS. *Program availability:* Part-time. *Degree requirements:* For master's, comprehensive exam, thesis or alternative. *Entrance requirements:* For master's, minimum GPA of 3.0. Additional exam requirements/recommendations for international students: Required—TOEFL (minimum score 550 paper-based; 79 iBT), IELTS (minimum score 6.5). Electronic applications accepted. *Faculty research:* Regional and urban development, environmental geography, geographic education, geographic techniques.

University of Northern Iowa, Graduate College, College of Social and Behavioral Sciences, Department of Geography, Cedar Falls, IA 50614. Offers MA. *Program availability:* Part-time. *Degree requirements:* For master's, thesis or alternative. *Entrance requirements:* For master's, minimum GPA of 3.0; 2 letters of recommendation; brief statement about professional interests and career objectives. Additional exam requirements/recommendations for international students: Required—TOEFL (minimum score 500 paper-based; 61 iBT). Electronic applications accepted.

University of North Texas, Robert B. Toulouse School of Graduate Studies, Denton, TX 76203-5459. Offers accounting (MS); applied anthropology (MA, MS); applied behavior analysis (Certificate); applied geography (MA); applied technology and performance improvement (M Ed, MS); art education (MA); art history (MA); art museum education (Certificate); arts leadership (Certificate); audiology (Au D); behavior analysis (MS); behavioral science (PhD); biochemistry and molecular biology (MS); biology (MA, MS); biomedical engineering (MS); business analysis (MS); chemistry (MS); clinical health psychology (PhD); communication studies (MA, MS); computer engineering (MS); computer science (MS); counseling (M Ed, MS), including clinical mental health counseling (MS), college and university counseling, elementary school counseling, secondary school counseling; creative writing (MA); criminal justice (MS); curriculum and instruction (M Ed); decision sciences (MBA); design (MA, MFA), including fashion design (MFA), innovation studies, interior design (MFA); early childhood studies (MS); economics (MS); educational leadership (M Ed, Ed D); educational psychology (MS, PhD), including family studies (MS), gifted and talented (MS), human development (MS), learning and cognition (MS), research, measurement and evaluation (MS); electrical engineering (MS); emergency management (MPA); engineering technology (MS); English (MA); English as a second language (MA); environmental science (MS); finance (MBA, MS); financial management (MPA); French (MA); health services management (MBA); higher education (M Ed, Ed D); history (MA, MS); hospitality management (MS); human resources management (MPA); information science (MS); information systems (PhD); information technologies (MBA); interdisciplinary studies (MA, MS); international studies (MA); international sustainable tourism (MS); jazz studies (MM); journalism (MA, MJ, Graduate Certificate), including interactive and virtual digital communication (Graduate Certificate), narrative journalism (Graduate Certificate), public relations (Graduate Certificate); kinesiology (MS); linguistics (MA); local government management (MPA); logistics (PhD); logistics and supply chain management (MBA); long-term care, senior housing, and aging services (MA); management (PhD); marketing (MBA); mathematics (MA, MS); mechanical and energy engineering (MS, PhD); music (MA), including ethnomusicology, music theory, musicology, performance; music composition (PhD); music education (MM Ed, PhD); nonprofit management (MPA); operations and supply chain management (MBA); performance (MM, DMA); philosophy (MA); political science (MA); professional and technical communication (MA); radio, television and film (MA, MFA); rehabilitation counseling (Certificate); sociology (MA); Spanish (MA); special education (M Ed); speech-language pathology (MA); strategic management (MBA); studio art (MFA); teaching (M Ed); MBA/MS. *Program availability:* Part-time, evening/weekend, online learning. Terminal master's awarded for partial completion of doctoral program. *Degree requirements:* For master's, variable foreign language requirement, comprehensive exam (for some programs), thesis (for some programs); for doctorate, variable foreign language requirement, comprehensive exam (for some programs), thesis/dissertation; for other advanced degree, variable foreign language requirement, comprehensive exam (for some programs). *Entrance requirements:* For master's and doctorate, GRE, GMAT. Additional exam requirements/recommendations for international students: Required—TOEFL (minimum score 550 paper-based; 79 iBT). Electronic applications accepted.

University of Oklahoma, College of Atmospheric and Geographic Sciences, Department of Geography and Environmental Sustainability, Norman, OK 73019. Offers environmental sustainability (MS); geography (MA, MS, PhD), including geospatial technologies (MS), physical geography (MS). *Program availability:* Part-time. *Faculty:* 23 full-time (8 women). *Students:* 29 full-time (21 women), 10 part-time (5 women); includes 9 minority (2 Black or African American, non-Hispanic/Latino; 1 Asian, non-Hispanic/Latino; 4 Hispanic/Latino; 2 Two or more races, non-Hispanic/Latino), 9 international. Average age 29. 26 applicants, 69% accepted, 14 enrolled. In 2017, 8 master's, 4 doctorates awarded. *Degree requirements:* For master's, comprehensive exam (for some programs), thesis (for some programs); for doctorate, comprehensive exam (for some programs), thesis/dissertation (for some programs). *Entrance requirements:* For master's and doctorate, GRE, personal statement, transcripts, two letters of recommendation, writing sample. Additional exam requirements/recommendations for international students: Required—TOEFL (minimum score 79 iBT) or IELTS (minimum score 6.5). *Application deadline:* For fall admission, 1/15 for domestic and international students; for spring admission, 9/1 for domestic students, 11/1 for international students. Application fee: $50 ($100 for international students). Electronic applications accepted. *Expenses:* Tuition, state resident: full-time $5119; part-time $213.30 per credit hour. Tuition, nonresident: full-time $19,778; part-time $824.10 per credit hour. *Required fees:* $3458; $133.55 per credit hour. $126.50 per semester. *Financial support:* In 2017–18, 37 students received support, including 1 fellowship (averaging $5,000 per year), 14 research assistantships with full tuition reimbursements available (averaging $14,389 per year), 13 teaching assistantships with full tuition reimbursements available (averaging $14,024 per year); scholarships/grants and unspecified assistantships also available. Financial award application deadline: 6/1; financial award applicants required to submit FAFSA. *Faculty research:* Land cover land use change; economic geography; landscape ecology; environmental economics; renewable energy. *Total annual research expenditures:* $1.6 million. *Unit head:* Dr. Kirsten de Beurs, 405-325-5325, E-mail: kdebeurs@ou.edu. *Application contact:* Laurel Smith, Graduate Liaison, 405-325-5325, E-mail: laurel@ou.edu.
Website: http://geography.ou.edu

University of Oregon, Graduate School, College of Arts and Sciences, Department of Geography, Eugene, OR 97403. Offers MA, MS, PhD. *Degree requirements:* For master's, one foreign language, thesis; for doctorate, one foreign language, thesis/dissertation. *Entrance requirements:* For master's and doctorate, GRE General Test, minimum GPA of 3.0. Additional exam requirements/recommendations for international students: Required—TOEFL. *Faculty research:* Place-name research, past climates, quaternary environments, plant diffusions, population redistributions.

University of Ottawa, Faculty of Graduate and Postdoctoral Studies, Faculty of Arts, Department of Geography, Ottawa, ON K1N 6N5, Canada. Offers M Geog, M Sc, MA, PhD. *Degree requirements:* For master's, one foreign language, thesis; for doctorate, one foreign language, comprehensive exam, thesis/dissertation. *Entrance requirements:* For master's, honors degree or equivalent, minimum B average; for doctorate, master's degree, minimum B+ average. Electronic applications accepted. *Faculty research:* The physical geography of cold environment; space, place and society, environmental change.

University of Prince Edward Island, Faculty of Arts, Charlottetown, PE C1A 4P3, Canada. Offers island studies (MA). *Program availability:* Part-time. *Degree requirements:* For master's, thesis. *Entrance requirements:* Additional exam requirements/recommendations for international students: Required—TOEFL (minimum score 550 paper-based; 80 iBT), Canadian Academic English Language Assessment, Michigan English Language Assessment Battery, Canadian Test of English for Scholars and Trainees. *Faculty research:* International island studies.

University of Regina, Faculty of Graduate Studies and Research, Faculty of Arts, Department of Geography, Regina, SK S4S 0A2, Canada. Offers M Sc, MA, PhD. Offered as a special case program. *Program availability:* Part-time. *Faculty:* 9 full-time (4 women), 1 part-time/adjunct (0 women). *Students:* 2 full-time (1 woman). 1 applicant, 100% accepted. *Degree requirements:* For master's, thesis; for doctorate, thesis/dissertation. *Entrance requirements:* Additional exam requirements/recommendations for international students: Required—TOEFL (minimum score 580 paper-based; 80 iBT), IELTS (minimum score 6.5), PTE (minimum score 59). *Application deadline:* For fall admission, 3/1 for domestic and international students; for winter admission, 10/1 for domestic and international students. Applications are processed on a rolling basis. Application fee: $100. Electronic applications accepted. *Expenses:* $10,681. *Financial support:* In 2017–18, 1 fellowship (averaging $7,000 per year), 3 teaching assistantships (averaging $2,562 per year) were awarded; research assistantships and scholarships/grants also available. Financial award application deadline: 6/15. *Faculty research:* Cultural, historical, economic, rural, urban, population, and prairie geography; thematic and atlas cartography; climatology and meteorology; geomorphology; biogeography. *Unit head:* Dr. Kyle Hodder, Department Head, 306-585-5127, Fax: 306-585-4815, E-mail: kyle.hodder@uregina.ca.
Website: http://www.uregina.ca/arts/geography

University of Saskatchewan, College of Graduate Studies and Research, College of Arts and Science, Department of Geography, Saskatoon, SK S7N 5A2, Canada. Offers M Sc, MA, PhD. *Degree requirements:* For master's, thesis; for doctorate, comprehensive exam (for some programs), thesis/dissertation. *Entrance requirements:* Additional exam requirements/recommendations for international students: Required—TOEFL (minimum score 80 iBT); Recommended—IELTS (minimum score 6.5). Electronic applications accepted.

University of South Africa, College of Agriculture and Environmental Sciences, Pretoria, South Africa. Offers agriculture (MS); consumer science (MCS); environmental management (MA, MS, PhD); environmental science (MA, MS, PhD); geography (MA, MS, PhD); horticulture (M Tech); human ecology (MHE); life sciences (MS); nature conservation (M Tech).

University of South Carolina, The Graduate School, College of Arts and Sciences, Department of Geography, Columbia, SC 29208. Offers geography (MA, MS, PhD); geography education (IMA). IMA and MAT offered in cooperation with the College of Education. *Program availability:* Part-time. *Degree requirements:* For master's, comprehensive exam, thesis (for some programs); for doctorate, comprehensive exam, thesis/dissertation. *Entrance requirements:* For master's, GRE General Test; for doctorate, GRE General Test, master's degree. Electronic applications accepted. *Faculty research:* Geographic information processing; economic, cultural, physical, and environmental geography.

University of Southern California, Graduate School, Dana and David Dornsife College of Letters, Arts and Sciences, Spatial Sciences Institute, Los Angeles, CA 90089. Offers geographic information science and technology (MS, Graduate Certificate). *Program availability:* Part-time, evening/weekend, online learning. Terminal master's awarded for partial completion of doctoral program. *Degree requirements:* For master's, thesis. *Entrance requirements:* For master's, GRE. Additional exam requirements/recommendations for international students: Required—TOEFL. Electronic applications accepted. *Faculty research:* Geocoding, geocomputation, GIS, environmental exposure estimation, spatial data accuracy and uncertainty.

University of Southern Mississippi, College of Science and Technology, Department of Geography and Geology, Hattiesburg, MS 39406-0001. Offers geography (PhD); geography and geology (MS). *Program availability:* Part-time. *Students:* 7 full-time (3 women). 20 applicants, 50% accepted, 7 enrolled. *Degree requirements:* For master's, comprehensive exam, thesis (for some programs), internships; for doctorate, comprehensive exam, thesis/dissertation. *Entrance requirements:* For master's, GMAT, GRE General Test, minimum GPA of 3.0 for last 60 hours; for doctorate, GRE, minimum GPA of 3.5. Additional exam requirements/recommendations for international students: Required—TOEFL, IELTS. *Application deadline:* For fall admission, 3/15 for domestic and international students; for spring admission, 1/3 for domestic students. Applications are processed on a rolling basis. Application fee: $60. Electronic applications accepted. *Expenses:* Tuition, state resident: full-time $3830. *Financial support:* Fellowships with full tuition reimbursements, research assistantships with tuition reimbursements, teaching assistantships with full tuition reimbursements, career-related internships or fieldwork, Federal Work-Study, scholarships/grants, health care benefits, and unspecified assistantships available. Financial award application deadline: 3/15; financial award applicants required to submit FAFSA. *Faculty research:* City and regional planning, geographic techniques, physical geography, human geography. *Unit head:* Dr. David Cochran, Chair, 601-266-4728, Fax: 601-266-6219.
Website: https://www.usm.edu/geography-geology

University of South Florida, Innovative Education, Tampa, FL 33620-9951. Offers adult, career and higher education (Graduate Certificate), including college teaching, leadership in developing human resources, leadership in higher education; Africana studies (Graduate Certificate), including diasporas and health disparities, genocide and

human rights; aging studies (Graduate Certificate), including gerontology; art research (Graduate Certificate), including museum studies; business foundations (Graduate Certificate); chemical and biomedical engineering (Graduate Certificate), including materials science and engineering, water, health and sustainability; child and family studies (Graduate Certificate), including positive behavior support; civil and industrial engineering (Graduate Certificate), including transportation systems analysis; community and family health (Graduate Certificate), including maternal and child health, social marketing and public health, violence and injury: prevention and intervention, women's health; criminology (Graduate Certificate), including criminal justice administration; data science for public administration (Graduate Certificate); digital humanities (Graduate Certificate); educational measurement and research (Graduate Certificate), including evaluation; English (Graduate Certificate), including comparative literary studies, creative writing, professional and technical communication; entrepreneurship (Graduate Certificate); environmental health (Graduate Certificate), including safety management; epidemiology and biostatistics (Graduate Certificate), including applied biostatistics, biostatistics, concepts and tools of epidemiology, epidemiology, epidemiology of infectious diseases; geography, environment and planning (Graduate Certificate), including community development, environmental policy and management, geographical information systems; geology (Graduate Certificate), including hydrogeology; global health (Graduate Certificate), including disaster management, global health and Latin American and Caribbean studies, global health practice, humanitarian assistance, infection control; government and international affairs (Graduate Certificate), including Cuban studies, globalization studies; health policy and management (Graduate Certificate), including health management and leadership, public health policy and programs; hearing specialist: early intervention (Graduate Certificate); industrial and management systems engineering (Graduate Certificate), including systems engineering, technology management; information studies (Graduate Certificate), including school library media specialist; information systems/decision sciences (Graduate Certificate), including analytics and business intelligence; instructional technology (Graduate Certificate), including distance education, Florida digital/virtual educator, instructional design, multimedia design, Web design; internal medicine, bioethics and medical humanities (Graduate Certificate), including biomedical ethics; Latin American and Caribbean studies (Graduate Certificate); leadership for coastal resiliency planning (Graduate Certificate); mass communications (Graduate Certificate), including multimedia journalism; mathematics and statistics (Graduate Certificate), including mathematics; medicine (Graduate Certificate), including aging and neuroscience, bioinformatics, biotechnology, brain fitness and memory management, clinical investigation, hand and upper limb rehabilitation, health informatics, health sciences, integrative weight management, intellectual property, medicine and gender, metabolic and nutritional medicine, metabolic cardiology, pharmacy sciences; national and competitive intelligence (Graduate Certificate); nursing (Graduate Certificate), including simulation based academic fellowship in advanced pain management; psychological and social foundations (Graduate Certificate), including career counseling, college teaching, diversity in education, mental health counseling, school counseling; public affairs (Graduate Certificate), including nonprofit management, public management, research administration; public health (Graduate Certificate), including assessing chemical toxicity and public health risks, health equity, pharmacoepidemiology, public health generalist, toxicology, translational research in adolescent behavioral health; public health practices (Graduate Certificate), including planning for healthy communities; rehabilitation and mental health counseling (Graduate Certificate), including integrative mental health care, marriage and family therapy, rehabilitation technology; secondary education (Graduate Certificate), including ESOL, foreign language education: culture and content, foreign language education: professional; social work (Graduate Certificate), including geriatric social work/clinical gerontology; special education (Graduate Certificate), including autism spectrum disorder, disabilities education: severe/profound; world languages (Graduate Certificate), including teaching English as a second language (TESL) or foreign language. *Unit head:* Dr. Cynthia DeLuca, Associate Vice President and Assistant Vice Provost, 813-974-3077, Fax: 813-974-7061, E-mail: deluca@usf.edu. *Application contact:* Owen Hooper, Director, Summer and Alternative Calendar Programs, 813-974-6917, E-mail: hooper@usf.edu.
Website: http://www.usf.edu/innovative-education/

The University of Tennessee, Graduate School, College of Arts and Sciences, Department of Geography, Knoxville, TN 37996. Offers MS, PhD. *Degree requirements:* For master's, thesis or alternative; for doctorate, thesis/dissertation. *Entrance requirements:* For master's and doctorate, GRE General Test, minimum GPA of 2.7. Additional exam requirements/recommendations for international students: Required—TOEFL. Electronic applications accepted.

The University of Texas at Austin, Graduate School, College of Liberal Arts, Department of Geography and the Environment, Austin, TX 78712-1111. Offers MA, PhD. *Degree requirements:* For master's, thesis or alternative; for doctorate, thesis/dissertation. *Entrance requirements:* For master's and doctorate, GRE General Test. Additional exam requirements/recommendations for international students: Required—TOEFL. Electronic applications accepted. *Faculty research:* Cultural and historical geography, environmental and physical geography, human-environment interactions, electronic technology and hypermedia, international area studies.

The University of Texas at Dallas, School of Economic, Political and Policy Sciences, Program in Geospatial Information Sciences, Richardson, TX 75080. Offers MS, PhD. *Program availability:* Part-time, evening/weekend. *Faculty:* 8 full-time (1 woman). *Students:* 50 full-time (15 women), 33 part-time (13 women); includes 11 minority (3 Black or African American, non-Hispanic/Latino; 3 Asian, non-Hispanic/Latino; 4 Hispanic/Latino; 1 Two or more races, non-Hispanic/Latino), 39 international. Average age 31. 77 applicants, 40% accepted, 13 enrolled. In 2017, 10 master's, 2 doctorates awarded. *Degree requirements:* For master's, thesis (for some programs), project or thesis; internship; for doctorate, comprehensive exam, thesis/dissertation. *Entrance requirements:* For master's and doctorate, GRE General Test, minimum GPA of 3.0 in upper-level coursework in field. Additional exam requirements/recommendations for international students: Required—TOEFL (minimum score 550 paper-based). *Application deadline:* For fall admission, 7/15 for domestic students, 5/1 priority date for international students; for spring admission, 11/15 for domestic students, 9/1 priority date for international students. Applications are processed on a rolling basis. Application fee: $50 ($100 for international students). Electronic applications accepted. *Expenses:* Tuition, state resident: full-time $12,916; part-time $718 per credit hour. Tuition, nonresident: full-time $25,252; part-time $1403 per credit hour. *Financial support:* In 2017–18, 30 students received support, including 2 research assistantships with partial tuition reimbursements available (averaging $18,755 per year), 12 teaching assistantships with partial tuition reimbursements available (averaging $13,100 per year); fellowships, career-related internships or fieldwork, Federal Work-Study, institutionally sponsored loans, scholarships/grants, and unspecified assistantships also available. Support available to part-time students. Financial award application deadline: 4/30; financial award applicants required to submit FAFSA. *Faculty research:* Urban and regional development, artificial intelligence techniques for geospatial investigation, improvement of current spatial analysis and modeling techniques, demographic studies. *Unit head:* Dr. Fang Qiu, Program Head, 972-883-4134, Fax: 972-883-2735, E-mail: ffqiu@utdallas.edu. *Application contact:* Judy Du, Graduate Program Administrator, 972-883-4964, Fax: 972-883-6297, E-mail: judy.du@utdallas.edu.
Website: http://www.utdallas.edu/epps/geospatial-science/

The University of Toledo, College of Graduate Studies, College of Languages, Literature and Social Sciences, Department of Geography and Planning, Toledo, OH 43606-3390. Offers geographic information science and applied geographics (Certificate); geography and planning (MA); spatially-integrated social science (PhD). *Program availability:* Part-time. *Degree requirements:* For master's, comprehensive exam, thesis; for doctorate, thesis/dissertation. *Entrance requirements:* For master's and doctorate, GRE General Test, minimum cumulative point-hour ratio of 2.7 for all previous academic work, three letters of recommendation; for Certificate, minimum cumulative point-hour ratio of 2.7 for all previous academic work, three letters of recommendation. Additional exam requirements/recommendations for international students: Required—TOEFL (minimum score 550 paper-based; 80 iBT). Electronic applications accepted.

University of Toronto, School of Graduate Studies, Faculty of Arts and Science, Department of Geography, Toronto, ON M5S 1A1, Canada. Offers geography (M Sc, MA, PhD); planning (M Sc Pl, MUDS, PhD); urban design (MUD). *Program availability:* Part-time. *Degree requirements:* For master's, thesis optional; for doctorate, thesis/dissertation. *Entrance requirements:* For master's, bachelor's degree or equivalent in geography or a closely related field, minimum B+ average in each of 2 final years of degree, 3 letters of reference; for doctorate, master of geography degree, minimum A- average. Additional exam requirements/recommendations for international students: Required—TOEFL (minimum score 580 paper-based; 93 iBT), TWE (minimum score 5). Electronic applications accepted. *Faculty research:* Spatial statistics, computer cartography, climatology, hydrology, biogeography.

University of Utah, Graduate School, College of Social and Behavioral Science, Department of Geography, Salt Lake City, UT 84112-9155. Offers geographic information science (MS); geography (MS, PhD). *Program availability:* Part-time. *Faculty:* 14 full-time (4 women), 10 part-time/adjunct (4 women). *Students:* 33 full-time (11 women), 17 part-time (11 women); includes 8 minority (2 Asian, non-Hispanic/Latino; 5 Hispanic/Latino; 1 Native Hawaiian or other Pacific Islander, non-Hispanic/Latino), 4 international. Average age 27. 66 applicants, 58% accepted, 16 enrolled. In 2017, 18 master's, 2 doctorates awarded. *Degree requirements:* For master's, thesis (for some programs), 6 research hours (for MS in geography); skills portfolio (for MS in geographic information science); for doctorate, comprehensive exam, thesis/dissertation, 14 research hours, 2 consecutive full-time semesters. *Entrance requirements:* For master's, GRE General Test (except for MS in geographic information science), minimum undergraduate GPA of 3.0; for doctorate, GRE General Test, minimum undergraduate GPA of 3.0. Additional exam requirements/recommendations for international students: Required—TOEFL (minimum score 550 paper-based; 80 iBT), IELTS (minimum score 6.5). *Application deadline:* For fall admission, 1/10 priority date for domestic and international students; for spring admission, 10/1 for domestic and international students. Application fee: $55 ($65 for international students). Electronic applications accepted. *Expenses:* $4420.93 per semester resident tuition; $14,208.67 per semester non-resident tuition. *Financial support:* In 2017–18, 6 students received support, including 3 fellowships (averaging $15,167 per year), 13 research assistantships (averaging $13,462 per year), 11 teaching assistantships (averaging $14,727 per year); scholarships/grants, health care benefits, tuition waivers (full), and unspecified assistantships also available. Financial award application deadline: 1/10. *Faculty research:* Urban-economic geography, earth system science, geographic information science and remote sensing, paleoenvironmental studies, hazards. *Total annual research expenditures:* $1 million. *Unit head:* Dr. Andrea R. Brunelle, Chair, 801-581-8218, Fax: 801-581-8219, E-mail: andrea.brunelle@geog.utah.edu. *Application contact:* Dr. Summer B. Rupper, Director of Graduate Studies, 801-581-8218, Fax: 801-581-8219, E-mail: summer.rupper@geog.utah.edu.
Website: http://www.geog.utah.edu

University of Victoria, Faculty of Graduate Studies, Faculty of Social Sciences, Department of Geography, Victoria, BC V8W 2Y2, Canada. Offers M Sc, MA, PhD. *Program availability:* Part-time. *Degree requirements:* For master's, thesis; for doctorate, comprehensive exam, thesis/dissertation, candidacy exam. *Entrance requirements:* For master's, minimum B+ average in undergraduate course work; for doctorate, master's degree. Additional exam requirements/recommendations for international students: Required—TOEFL (minimum score 575 paper-based), IELTS (minimum score 7). Electronic applications accepted. *Faculty research:* Resources and protected areas, remote sensing and forestry, geographic information systems and cartography, urban regional planning, physical climatology.

University of Washington, Graduate School, College of Arts and Sciences, Department of Geography, Seattle, WA 98195. Offers MA, PhD. *Degree requirements:* For master's, thesis; for doctorate, thesis/dissertation. *Entrance requirements:* For master's and doctorate, GRE General Test. Additional exam requirements/recommendations for international students: Required—TOEFL. Electronic applications accepted. *Faculty research:* Globalization and social theory, nature and society, regional economic development, urban patterns and processes, geographic information systems.

University of Waterloo, Graduate Studies, Faculty of Environment, Department of Geography and Environmental Management, Waterloo, ON N2L 3G1, Canada. Offers MA, PhD. MA, PhD offered jointly with Wilfrid Laurier University. *Degree requirements:* For master's, thesis optional; for doctorate, one foreign language, comprehensive exam, thesis/dissertation. *Entrance requirements:* For master's, honors degree, minimum B average; for doctorate, master's degree, minimum A- average. Additional exam requirements/recommendations for international students: Required—TOEFL, IELTS, PTE. Electronic applications accepted. *Faculty research:* Urban economic geography; physical geography; resource management; cultural, regional, historical geography; spatial data.

The University of Western Ontario, Faculty of Graduate Studies, Social Sciences Division, Department of Geography, London, ON N6A 5B8, Canada. Offers M Sc, MA, PhD. *Degree requirements:* For master's, thesis; for doctorate, thesis/dissertation. *Entrance requirements:* For master's, GRE, honors degree, minimum B average; for doctorate, honors degree, minimum B average. Additional exam requirements/recommendations for international students: Required—TOEFL.

University of Wisconsin–Madison, Graduate School, College of Letters and Science, Department of Geography, Madison, WI 53706-1380. Offers cartography and geographic information systems (MS); geographic information systems (Certificate); geography (MS, PhD). *Program availability:* Part-time. *Degree requirements:* For master's, thesis; for doctorate, thesis/dissertation; for Certificate, internship. *Entrance requirements:* For master's and doctorate, GRE General Test, minimum GPA of 3.25. Electronic applications accepted. *Faculty research:* Physical geography, urban/historical geography, people-environment, history of cartography, GIS.

University of Wisconsin–Milwaukee, Graduate School, College of Letters and Science, Department of Geography, Milwaukee, WI 53201-0413. Offers international interests (MA, MS, PhD); physical geography and environmental studies (MA, MS, PhD); urban development (MA, MS, PhD). *Students:* 15 full-time (9 women), 4 part-time

(2 women); includes 3 minority (1 Black or African American, non-Hispanic/Latino; 2 Asian, non-Hispanic/Latino), 9 international. Average age 31. 18 applicants, 33% accepted, 5 enrolled. In 2017, 3 master's, 2 doctorates awarded. *Degree requirements:* For master's, comprehensive exam, thesis; for doctorate, thesis/dissertation. *Entrance requirements:* For master's and doctorate, GRE. Additional exam requirements/recommendations for international students: Required—TOEFL (minimum score 550 paper-based; 79 iBT), IELTS (minimum score 6.5). *Application deadline:* For fall admission, 1/1 priority date for domestic students; for spring admission, 9/1 for domestic students. Application fee: $56 ($96 for international students). Electronic applications accepted. *Financial support:* Fellowships, research assistantships, teaching assistantships, career-related internships or fieldwork, unspecified assistantships, and project assistantships available. Support available to part-time students. Financial award application deadline: 4/15; financial award applicants required to submit FAFSA. *Unit head:* Mark Schwartz, Department Chair, 414-229-3740, E-mail: mds@uwm.edu. *Application contact:* General Information Contact, 414-229-4982, Fax: 414-229-6967, E-mail: gradschool@uwm.edu.
Website: http://www4.uwm.edu/letsci/geography/

University of Wyoming, College of Arts and Sciences, Department of Geography, Laramie, WY 82071. Offers geography (MA, MP, MST); geography/water resources (MA); rural planning and natural resources (MP), including community and regional planning and natural resources. *Program availability:* Online learning. *Degree requirements:* For master's, thesis optional. *Entrance requirements:* For master's, GRE General Test, minimum GPA of 3.0. Additional exam requirements/recommendations for international students: Required—TOEFL. Electronic applications accepted. *Faculty research:* Landscape ecology, landscape change, public land management, rural and small town planning, GIS.

Utah State University, School of Graduate Studies, S.J. and Jessie E. Quinney College of Natural Resources, Department of Environment and Society, Logan, UT 84322. Offers bioregional planning (MS); geography (MA, MS); human dimensions of ecosystem science and management (MS, PhD); recreation resource management (MS, PhD). *Degree requirements:* For master's, comprehensive exam, thesis (for some programs). *Entrance requirements:* For master's and doctorate, GRE General Test, minimum GPA of 3.0. Additional exam requirements/recommendations for international students: Required—TOEFL. Electronic applications accepted. *Faculty research:* Geographic information systems/geographic and environmental education, bioregional planning, natural resource and environmental policy, outdoor recreation and tourism, natural resource and environmental management.

Virginia Polytechnic Institute and State University, Graduate School, College of Natural Resources and Environment, Blacksburg, VA 24061. Offers fisheries and wildlife (MS, PhD); forestry and forest products (PhD); geography (MS); geospatial and environmental analysis (PhD); natural resources (MNR); MS/MF. *Faculty:* 75 full-time (18 women). *Students:* 174 full-time (84 women), 79 part-time (39 women); includes 29 minority (6 Black or African American, non-Hispanic/Latino; 5 Asian, non-Hispanic/Latino; 15 Hispanic/Latino; 1 Native Hawaiian or other Pacific Islander, non-Hispanic/Latino; 2 Two or more races, non-Hispanic/Latino), 34 international. Average age 31. 118 applicants, 53% accepted, 46 enrolled. In 2017, 89 master's, 13 doctorates awarded. *Degree requirements:* For master's, comprehensive exam (for some programs), thesis (for some programs); for doctorate, comprehensive exam (for some programs), thesis/dissertation (for some programs). *Entrance requirements:* For master's and doctorate, GRE/GMAT. Additional exam requirements/recommendations for international students: Required—TOEFL (minimum score 80 iBT). *Application deadline:* For fall admission, 8/1 for domestic students, 4/1 for international students; for spring admission, 1/1 for domestic students, 9/1 for international students. Applications are processed on a rolling basis. Application fee: $75. Electronic applications accepted. *Expenses:* Tuition, state resident: full-time $15,072; part-time $718.50 per credit hour. Tuition, nonresident: full-time $28,810; part-time $1448.25 per credit hour. *Required fees:* $2741; $502 per semester. Tuition and fees vary according to course load, campus/location and program. *Financial support:* In 2017–18, 78 research assistantships with full tuition reimbursements (averaging $22,092 per year), 41 teaching assistantships with full tuition reimbursements (averaging $19,106 per year) were awarded. Financial award application deadline: 3/1; financial award applicants required to submit FAFSA. *Total annual research expenditures:* $16.5 million. *Unit head:* Dr. Paul M. Winistorfer, Dean, 540-231-5481, Fax: 540-231-7664, E-mail: pstorfer@vt.edu. *Application contact:* Arlice Banks, Executive Assistant, 540-231-7051, Fax: 540-231-7664, E-mail: arbanks@vt.edu.
Website: http://cnre.vt.edu/

West Chester University of Pennsylvania, College of Business and Public Management, Department of Geography and Planning, West Chester, PA 19383. Offers geographic information systems (Certificate); geography (MS); geography and planning (MURP); urban and regional planning (Certificate). *Program availability:* Part-time, evening/weekend. *Students:* 10 full-time (4 women), 10 part-time (5 women); includes 1 minority (Black or African American, non-Hispanic/Latino). Average age 29. 17 applicants, 94% accepted, 11 enrolled. In 2017, 10 master's, 11 other advanced degrees awarded. *Degree requirements:* For master's, 48 credits: 27 credits required, 21 credits electives (for MURP); 33 credits or 11 courses (for MS); thesis or independent research course; for Certificate, 12 credits or 4 courses (for geographic information systems); 18 credits or 6 courses (for urban and regional planning). *Entrance requirements:* For master's and Certificate, minimum GPA of 2.8, resume, two letters of recommendation. Additional exam requirements/recommendations for international students: Required—TOEFL or IELTS. *Application deadline:* For fall admission, 5/15 for international students; for spring admission, 10/15 for international students. Applications are processed on a rolling basis. Application fee: $50. Electronic applications accepted. *Expenses:* Tuition, state resident: full-time $9000; part-time $500 per credit. Tuition, nonresident: full-time $13,500; part-time $750 per credit. *Required fees:* $2959; $149.79 per credit. *Financial support:* Scholarships/grants and unspecified assistantships available. Financial award application deadline: 2/15; financial award applicants required to submit FAFSA. *Faculty research:* Sustainability and environmental conservation, land use/suburban planning, geographic information systems, transportation planning, housing, economic development. *Unit head:* Dr. Dottie Ives Dewey, Chair/Graduate Coordinator for Certificate Programs, 610-436-2746, Fax: 610-436-2889, E-mail: divesdewey@wcupa.edu. *Application contact:* Dr. Matin Katirai, Graduate Coordinator, 610-436-2392, Fax: 610-436-2889, E-mail: mkatirai@wcupa.edu.
Website: http://www.wcupa.edu/business-publicManagement/geographyPlanning/

Western Illinois University, School of Graduate Studies, College of Arts and Sciences, Department of Geography, Macomb, IL 61455-1390. Offers geography (MA); GIS analysis: ecological GIS (Certificate); GIS analysis: GIS applications (Certificate). *Program availability:* Part-time. *Students:* 9 full-time (6 women), 2 part-time (1 woman), 1 international. Average age 26. 8 applicants, 100% accepted, 6 enrolled. In 2017, 3 master's awarded. *Degree requirements:* For master's, thesis or alternative. *Entrance requirements:* Additional exam requirements/recommendations for international students: Required—TOEFL (minimum score 550 paper-based; 80 iBT). *Application deadline:* Applications are processed on a rolling basis. Application fee: $30. Electronic applications accepted. *Financial support:* In 2017–18, 6 students received support, including research assistantships with full tuition reimbursements available (averaging $7,544 per year); unspecified assistantships also available. Financial award applicants required to submit FAFSA. *Unit head:* Dr. Sam Thompson, Chairperson, 309-298-1648. *Application contact:* Dr. Nancy Parsons, Associate Provost and Director of Graduate School, 309-298-1806, Fax: 309-298-2345, E-mail: grad-office@wiu.edu.
Website: http://www.wiu.edu/cas/geography/

Western Michigan University, Graduate College, College of Arts and Sciences, Department of Geography, Kalamazoo, MI 49008. Offers geographic information science (Graduate Certificate); geography (MA). *Degree requirements:* For master's, thesis.

Western Michigan University, Graduate College, College of Arts and Sciences, Department of Interdisciplinary Arts and Sciences, Kalamazoo, MI 49008. Offers science education (MA, PhD), including biological sciences (PhD), chemistry (PhD), geosciences (PhD), physical geography (PhD), physics (PhD), science education (PhD). *Degree requirements:* For doctorate, thesis/dissertation.

Western Washington University, Graduate School, Huxley College of the Environment, Department of Environmental Studies, Program in Geography, Bellingham, WA 98225-5996. Offers MS. *Entrance requirements:* Additional exam requirements/recommendations for international students: Required—TOEFL (minimum score 567 paper-based). Electronic applications accepted.

West Virginia University, Eberly College of Arts and Sciences, Morgantown, WV 26506. Offers biology (MS, PhD); chemistry (MS, PhD); communication studies (MA, PhD); computational statistics (PhD); creative writing (MFA); English (MA, PhD); forensic and investigative science (MS); forensic science (PhD); geography (MA); geology (MA, PhD); history (MA, PhD); legal studies (MLS); math (MS); physics (MS, PhD); political science (MA, PhD); professional writing and editing (MA); psychology (MA); public administration (MPA); social work (MSW); sociology (MA, PhD); statistics (MS). *Program availability:* Part-time, evening/weekend, online learning. *Students:* 831 full-time (437 women), 236 part-time (142 women); includes 112 minority (35 Black or African American, non-Hispanic/Latino; 15 Asian, non-Hispanic/Latino; 29 Hispanic/Latino; 33 Two or more races, non-Hispanic/Latino), 235 international. Terminal master's awarded for partial completion of doctoral program. *Degree requirements:* For master's, thesis (for some programs); for doctorate, comprehensive exam, thesis/dissertation. *Entrance requirements:* For master's and doctorate, GRE. Additional exam requirements/recommendations for international students: Required—TOEFL (minimum score 600 paper-based); Recommended—TWE. *Application deadline:* For spring admission, 2/15 priority date for domestic and international students. Applications are processed on a rolling basis. Application fee: $45. Electronic applications accepted. *Expenses:* Tuition, state resident: full-time $9450. Tuition, nonresident: full-time $24,390. *Financial support:* Fellowships with full tuition reimbursements, research assistantships with full tuition reimbursements, teaching assistantships with full tuition reimbursements, career-related internships or fieldwork, Federal Work-Study, institutionally sponsored loans, scholarships/grants, health care benefits, tuition waivers (full and partial), unspecified assistantships, and administrative assistantships available. Financial award application deadline: 2/1; financial award applicants required to submit FAFSA. *Faculty research:* Humanities, social sciences, life science, physical sciences, mathematics. *Unit head:* Dr. Mary Ellen Mazey, Dean, 304-293-4611, Fax: 304-293-6858, E-mail: mary.mazey@mail.wvu.edu. *Application contact:* Dr. Fred L. King, Associate Dean for Graduate Studies, 304-293-4611 Ext. 5205, Fax: 304-293-6858, E-mail: fred.king@mail.wvu.edu.
Website: http://www.as.wvu.edu/

Wilfrid Laurier University, Faculty of Graduate and Postdoctoral Studies, Faculty of Arts, Department of Geography and Environmental Studies, Waterloo, ON N2L 3C5, Canada. Offers environmental and resource management (MA, MES, PhD); environmental science (M Sc, MES, PhD); geomatics (M Sc, MES, PhD); human geography (MES, PhD). *Program availability:* Part-time. *Degree requirements:* For master's, thesis optional; for doctorate, thesis/dissertation. *Entrance requirements:* For master's, honors BA in geography, minimum B average in undergraduate course work; honors BSc with minimum B+ or honors BES or BA in physical geography, environmental or earth sciences or the equivalent; for doctorate, MA in geography, minimum A- average. Additional exam requirements/recommendations for international students: Required—TOEFL (minimum score 89 iBT). Electronic applications accepted. *Faculty research:* Resources management, urban, economic, physical, cultural, earth surfaces, geomatics, historical, regional, spatial data handling.

York University, Faculty of Graduate Studies, Faculty of Liberal Arts and Professional Studies, Program in Geography, Toronto, ON M3J 1P3, Canada. Offers M Sc, MA, PhD. *Program availability:* Part-time. *Degree requirements:* For master's, thesis or alternative; for doctorate, comprehensive exam, thesis/dissertation. Electronic applications accepted.

Section 22
Military and Defense Studies

This section contains a directory of institutions offering graduate work in military and defense studies. Additional information about programs listed in the directory may be obtained by writing directly to the dean of a graduate school or chair of a department at the address given in the directory.

For programs offering related work, see also in this book *History* and *Political Science and International Affairs*.

CONTENTS

Program Directories

Featured School: Display and Close-Up

See:

Military and Defense Studies

Adler University, Graduate Programs, MA in Psychology Program: Specialization in Military Psychology, Chicago, IL 60602. Offers MA. *Program availability:* Online learning. *Degree requirements:* For master's, capstone project.

American Public University System, AMU/APU Graduate Programs, Charles Town, WV 25414. Offers accounting (MS); applied business analytics (MS); business administration (MBA); criminal justice (MA); cybersecurity studies (MS); educational leadership (M Ed); environmental policy and management (MS); global security (DGS); health information management (MS); history (MA), including American military history, American Revolution, civil war, war since 1945, World War II; information technology (MS); international relations and conflict resolution (MA), including American politics and government, comparative government and development, general, international relations, public policy; national security studies (MA); nursing (MSN); political science (MA); public policy (MPP); reverse logistics management (MA), including comparative and security issues, conflict resolution, international and transnational security issues, peacekeeping; space studies (MS); sports management (MS); strategic intelligence (DSI); teaching (M Ed), including secondary social studies; transportation and logistics management (MA). *Program availability:* Part-time, evening/weekend, online only, 100% online. *Students:* 455 full-time (227 women), 7,939 part-time (3,353 women); includes 2,793 minority (1,429 Black or African American, non-Hispanic/Latino; 48 American Indian or Alaska Native, non-Hispanic/Latino; 205 Asian, non-Hispanic/Latino; 766 Hispanic/Latino; 62 Native Hawaiian or other Pacific Islander, non-Hispanic/Latino; 283 Two or more races, non-Hispanic/Latino), 101 international. Average age 37. In 2017, 2,977 master's awarded. *Degree requirements:* For master's, comprehensive exam or practicum. *Entrance requirements:* For master's, official transcript showing earned bachelor's degree from institution accredited by recognized accrediting body. Additional exam requirements/recommendations for international students: Required—TOEFL (minimum score 550 paper-based), IELTS (minimum score 6.5). *Application deadline:* Applications are processed on a rolling basis. Application fee: $0. Electronic applications accepted. *Expenses: Tuition:* Full-time $6300; part-time $350 per credit. *Required fees:* $300; $50 per course. *Financial support:* Scholarships/grants available. Financial award applicants required to submit FAFSA. *Unit head:* Dr. Wallace Boston, President, 877-468-6268, Fax: 304-728-2348, E-mail: president@apus.edu. *Application contact:* Yoci Deal, Associate Vice President, Graduate and International Admissions, 877-468-6268, Fax: 304-724-3764, E-mail: info@apus.edu.
Website: http://www.apus.edu

Austin Peay State University, College of Graduate Studies, College of Arts and Letters, Department of History and Philosophy, Clarksville, TN 37044. Offers military history (MA). *Program availability:* Part-time, online learning. *Faculty:* 13 full-time (3 women). *Students:* 10 full-time (5 women), 24 part-time (5 women); includes 2 minority (both Black or African American, non-Hispanic/Latino). Average age 39. 15 applicants, 100% accepted, 11 enrolled. In 2017, 6 master's awarded. *Degree requirements:* For master's, comprehensive exam, thesis optional. *Entrance requirements:* For master's, GRE General Test, minimum undergraduate GPA of 2.75, 3 letters of recommendation. Additional exam requirements/recommendations for international students: Required—TOEFL (minimum score 500 paper-based). *Application deadline:* For fall admission, 8/8 priority date for domestic students. Applications are processed on a rolling basis. Application fee: $45 ($50 for international students). Electronic applications accepted. *Expenses:* Tuition, state resident: full-time $7686; part-time $427 per credit hour. Tuition, nonresident: full-time $20,268; part-time $1126 per credit hour. *Required fees:* $1529; $76.45 per credit hour. *Financial support:* Research assistantships with full tuition reimbursements, career-related internships or fieldwork, Federal Work-Study, institutionally sponsored loans, scholarships/grants, and unspecified assistantships available. Support available to part-time students. Financial award application deadline: 4/1; financial award applicants required to submit FAFSA. *Faculty research:* Russia, eastern Europe, diplomatic military history, the Gilded Age, foreign relations. *Unit head:* Dr. Cameron Sutt, Chair, 931-221-7919, Fax: 931-221-7917, E-mail: suttc@apsu.edu. *Application contact:* Megan Mitchell, Coordinator of Graduate Admissions, 931-221-6189, Fax: 931-221-7662, E-mail: mitchellm@apsu.edu.
Website: http://www.apsu.edu/history-and-philosophy/

Bellevue University, Graduate School, College of Arts and Sciences, Bellevue, NE 68005-3098. Offers clinical counseling (MS); healthcare administration (MHA); human services (MA); international security and intelligence studies (MS); managerial communication (MA). *Program availability:* Online learning.

The Citadel, The Military College of South Carolina, Citadel Graduate College, Department of Leadership Studies, Charleston, SC 29409. Offers MS, Graduate Certificate. *Program availability:* Part-time, evening/weekend, 100% online, blended/hybrid learning. *Entrance requirements:* For master's, GRE (minimum verbal and quantitative combination of 290) or MAT (minimum of 396), official transcript reflecting highest degree earned from regionally-accredited college or university; for Graduate Certificate, official transcript for baccalaureate degree from regionally-accredited college or university. Additional exam requirements/recommendations for international students: Required—TOEFL (minimum score 550 paper-based; 79 iBT). Electronic applications accepted. *Expenses:* Tuition, state resident: part-time $587 per credit hour. Tuition, nonresident: part-time $988 per credit hour. *Required fees:* $90 per term.

The Citadel, The Military College of South Carolina, Citadel Graduate College, School of Humanities and Social Sciences, Department of Criminal Justice, Charleston, SC 29409. Offers homeland security (Graduate Certificate); intelligence analysis (Graduate Certificate); intelligence and security studies (MA). *Program availability:* Part-time, evening/weekend, 100% online, blended/hybrid learning. *Entrance requirements:* For master's, GRE or MAT, writing sample that demonstrates strong critical thinking and communication skills. Additional exam requirements/recommendations for international students: Required—TOEFL (minimum score 550 paper-based; 79 iBT). Electronic applications accepted. *Expenses:* Tuition, state resident: part-time $587 per credit hour. Tuition, nonresident: part-time $988 per credit hour. *Required fees:* $90 per term.

East Carolina University, Graduate School, Thomas Harriot College of Arts and Sciences, Department of History, Greenville, NC 27858-4353. Offers American history (MA); Atlantic world (MA); European history (MA); maritime studies (MA); military history (MA); public history (MA). *Program availability:* Part-time. *Students:* 39 full-time (16 women), 49 part-time (21 women); includes 11 minority (2 Black or African American, non-Hispanic/Latino; 1 Asian, non-Hispanic/Latino; 5 Hispanic/Latino; 3 Two or more races, non-Hispanic/Latino), 1 international. Average age 29. 35 applicants, 83% accepted, 19 enrolled. In 2017, 15 master's awarded. *Degree requirements:* For master's, one foreign language, comprehensive exam, thesis. *Entrance requirements:* For master's, GRE General Test. Additional exam requirements/recommendations for international students: Recommended—TOEFL (minimum score 78 iBT), IELTS (minimum score 6.5). *Application deadline:* For fall admission, 4/1 priority date for

domestic and international students; for spring admission, 10/15 priority date for domestic and international students. Applications are processed on a rolling basis. Application fee: $75. Electronic applications accepted. *Expenses:* Tuition, state resident: full-time $4749; part-time $297 per credit hour. Tuition, nonresident: full-time $17,898; part-time $1119 per credit hour. *Required fees:* $2691; $224 per credit hour. Part-time tuition and fees vary according to course load and program. *Financial support:* Fellowships, research assistantships with partial tuition reimbursements, teaching assistantships with partial tuition reimbursements, and Federal Work-Study available. Support available to part-time students. Financial award application deadline: 1/15. *Unit head:* Dr. Christopher Oakley, Chair, 252-328-1025, E-mail: oakleyc@ecu.edu. *Application contact:* Dean of Graduate School, 252-328-6012, E-mail: gradschool@ecu.edu.
Website: http://www.ecu.edu/cs-cas/history/

Embry-Riddle Aeronautical University–Prescott, Security and Intelligence Program, Prescott, AZ 86301-3720. Offers security and intelligence studies (MSSIS). *Faculty:* 6 full-time (0 women), 1 part-time/adjunct (0 women). *Students:* 33 full-time (10 women), 4 part-time (3 women); includes 11 minority (1 Black or African American, non-Hispanic/Latino; 2 Asian, non-Hispanic/Latino; 3 Hispanic/Latino; 5 Two or more races, non-Hispanic/Latino), 1 international. Average age 29. 40 applicants, 70% accepted, 12 enrolled. In 2017, 12 master's awarded. *Degree requirements:* For master's, variable foreign language requirement, experimental research project, thesis, or comprehensive examination. *Entrance requirements:* For master's, transcripts, statement of goals, letters of recommendation, resume. Additional exam requirements/recommendations for international students: Required—TOEFL (minimum score 550 paper-based; 79 iBT), IELTS (minimum score 6). *Application deadline:* For fall admission, 1/15 priority date for domestic students; for spring admission, 11/1 priority date for domestic students; for summer admission, 4/1 priority date for domestic students. Applications are processed on a rolling basis. Application fee: $50. Electronic applications accepted. *Expenses: Tuition:* Full-time $16,704; part-time $1358 per credit hour. *Required fees:* $1254; $627 per semester. *Financial support:* Research assistantships, teaching assistantships, scholarships/grants, and unspecified assistantships available. Financial award application deadline: 3/15; financial award applicants required to submit FAFSA. *Unit head:* Philip Jones, PhD, Dean and Professor, College of Security and Intelligence, 928-777-6992, E-mail: philip.e.jones@erau.edu. *Application contact:* Graduate Admissions, 928-777-6600, E-mail: prescott@erau.edu.
Website: http://prescott.erau.edu/degrees/master/security-intelligence/

The George Washington University, Elliott School of International Affairs, Program in Security Policy Studies, Washington, DC 20052. Offers MA. *Program availability:* Part-time. *Students:* 128 full-time (50 women), 59 part-time (23 women); includes 45 minority (9 Black or African American, non-Hispanic/Latino; 11 Asian, non-Hispanic/Latino; 16 Hispanic/Latino; 9 Two or more races, non-Hispanic/Latino), 8 international. Average age 27. 291 applicants, 87% accepted, 72 enrolled. In 2017, 63 master's awarded. *Degree requirements:* For master's, one foreign language, capstone project. *Entrance requirements:* For master's, GRE General Test, 2 semesters of introductory economics, 2 years of a modern foreign language or 1 semester of statistics. Additional exam requirements/recommendations for international students: Required—TOEFL (minimum score 100 iBT), IELTS (minimum score 7). *Application deadline:* For fall admission, 1/15 priority date for domestic and international students; for spring admission, 10/1 for domestic and international students. Application fee: $75. Electronic applications accepted. *Expenses: Tuition:* Full-time $28,800; part-time $1655 per credit hour. *Required fees:* $45; $2.75 per credit hour. *Financial support:* In 2017–18, 22 students received support. Fellowships with partial tuition reimbursements available, Federal Work-Study, and scholarships/grants available. Financial award application deadline: 1/15; financial award applicants required to submit FAFSA. *Faculty research:* U.S. arms transfer policies, military balance in the Third World, U.S. foreign policy, technology and security policy. *Unit head:* Joanna Spear, Director, 202-994-1088, E-mail: jspear@gwu.edu. *Application contact:* Nicole A. Campbell, Director of Graduate Admissions, 202-994-7050, Fax: 202-994-9537, E-mail: esiagrad@gwu.edu.
Website: http://elliott.gwu.edu/academics/graduate/sps

Hawai'i Pacific University, College of Liberal Arts, Program in Diplomacy and Military Studies, Honolulu, HI 96813. Offers MA. *Program availability:* Part-time, evening/weekend. *Faculty:* 10 full-time (2 women), 2 part-time/adjunct (0 women). *Students:* 32 full-time (9 women), 29 part-time (10 women); includes 25 minority (2 Black or African American, non-Hispanic/Latino; 10 Asian, non-Hispanic/Latino; 6 Hispanic/Latino; 7 Two or more races, non-Hispanic/Latino), 4 international. Average age 35. 35 applicants, 91% accepted, 21 enrolled. In 2017, 20 master's awarded. *Entrance requirements:* Additional exam requirements/recommendations for international students: Recommended—TOEFL (minimum score 550 paper-based; 80 iBT), IELTS (minimum score 6), TWE (minimum score 5). *Application deadline:* For fall admission, 1/15 priority date for domestic students; for spring admission, 10/15 priority date for domestic students. Applications are processed on a rolling basis. Application fee: $50. Electronic applications accepted. *Expenses: Tuition:* Full-time $18,000; part-time $1000 per credit. *Required fees:* $200; $26 per credit. Tuition and fees vary according to course load and program. *Financial support:* In 2017–18, 4 students received support. Career-related internships or fieldwork, Federal Work-Study, scholarships/grants, tuition waivers (partial), and unspecified assistantships available. Financial award application deadline: 3/1; financial award applicants required to submit FAFSA. *Unit head:* Dr. Russell Hart, Director, 808-544-8043, E-mail: rhart@hpu.edu. *Application contact:* Danny Lam, Assistant Director of Graduate Admissions, 808-544-1135, E-mail: graduate@hpu.edu.
Website: https://www.hpu.edu/cla/history-intstudies/madms/index.html

Henley-Putnam School of Strategic Security, Master of Science Program in Intelligence Management, Rapid City, SD 57701. Offers MS. *Program availability:* Part-time, online learning. *Degree requirements:* For master's, thesis. *Entrance requirements:* For master's, bachelor's degree from an institution accredited by an agency recognized by the U.S. Department of Education and/or the Council for Higher Education Accreditation; background check. Additional exam requirements/recommendations for international students: Required—TOEFL (minimum score 650 paper-based; 79 iBT); Recommended—IELTS (minimum score 7). *Expenses:* Contact institution.

Henley-Putnam School of Strategic Security, Master of Science Program in Strategic Security and Protection Management, Rapid City, SD 57701. Offers extremist organizations (MS). *Program availability:* Part-time, online learning. *Degree requirements:* For master's, comprehensive exam, thesis. *Entrance requirements:* For master's, bachelor's degree from institution accredited by an agency recognized by the U.S. Department of Education and/or the Council for Higher Education Accreditation, background check. Additional exam requirements/recommendations for international

students: Required—TOEFL (minimum score 650 paper-based; 79 iBT); Recommended—IELTS. *Expenses:* Contact institution.

Henley-Putnam School of Strategic Security, Master of Science Program in Terrorism and Counterterrorism Studies, Rapid City, SD 57701. Offers intelligence operations (MS); protective intelligence (MS). *Program availability:* Part-time, online learning. *Degree requirements:* For master's, thesis. *Entrance requirements:* For master's, bachelor's degree from institution accredited by an agency recognized by the U.S. Department of Education and/or the Council for Higher Education Accreditation, background check. Additional exam requirements/recommendations for international students: Required—TOEFL (minimum score 650 paper-based; 79 iBT); Recommended—IELTS (minimum score 7). *Expenses:* Contact institution.

The Institute of World Politics, Graduate Programs in National Security, Intelligence, and International Affairs, Washington, DC 20036. Offers American foreign policy (Certificate); comparative political culture (Certificate); counterintelligence (Certificate); democracy building (Certificate); intelligence (Certificate); international politics (Certificate); national security affairs (Certificate); public diplomacy and political warfare (Certificate); statecraft and national security affairs (MA); statecraft and world politics (MA); strategic intelligence studies (MA). *Program availability:* Part-time, evening/weekend. *Degree requirements:* For master's, comprehensive exam, thesis optional. *Entrance requirements:* For master's, GRE General Test. Additional exam requirements/recommendations for international students: Required—TOEFL. Electronic applications accepted. *Faculty research:* Intelligence, national security, statecraft.

Johns Hopkins University, School of Education, Master's Programs in Education, Baltimore, MD 21218. Offers counseling (MS), including clinical mental health counseling, school counseling; education (MS), including educational studies, gifted education, reading, school administration and supervision, technology for educators; elementary education (MAT); health professions (M Ed); intelligence analysis (MS); organizational leadership (MS); secondary education (MAT), including biology, chemistry, earth/space science, English, physics, social studies; special education (MS), including early childhood special education, general special education studies, mild to moderate disabilities, severe disabilities. *Program availability:* Part-time, evening/weekend, 100% online, blended/hybrid learning. *Degree requirements:* For master's, comprehensive exam (for some programs), portfolio, capstone project and/or internship; PRAXIS II (subject area assessments) for initial teacher preparation programs that lead to licensure. *Entrance requirements:* For master's, GRE (for full-time programs only); PRAXIS I/core or state-approved alternative (for initial teacher preparation programs that lead to licensure), minimum of bachelor's degree from regionally- or nationally-accredited institution; minimum GPA of 3.0 in all previous programs of study; official transcripts from all post-secondary institutions attended; essay; curriculum vitae/resume; letters of recommendation (3 for full-time programs, 2 for part-time programs); dispositions survey. Additional exam requirements/recommendations for international students: Required—TOEFL (minimum score 600 paper-based; 100 iBT), IELTS (minimum score 7). Electronic applications accepted. *Expenses:* Contact institution.

The Judge Advocate General's School, U.S. Army, Graduate Programs, Charlottesville, VA 22903-1781. Offers LL M. Program available only to active duty military lawyers. *Accreditation:* ABA. *Degree requirements:* For master's, thesis optional. *Entrance requirements:* For master's, active duty military lawyer, international military officer, or DOD civilian attorney; JD or LL B. *Faculty research:* Criminal law, administrative and civil law, contract law, international law, legal research and writing.

Liberty University, School of Divinity, Lynchburg, VA 24515. Offers Biblical exposition (MA); Biblical languages (M Div); Biblical studies (M Div, MA, MAR, Th M, D Min); chaplaincy (M Div, D Min); Christian apologetics (M Div, MA, MAR, Th M); Christian leadership and church ministries (M Div); Christian ministries (M Div); Christian ministry (MA); Christian thought (M Div); church history (M Div, MAR, Th M); community chaplaincy (M Div, MAR); discipleship (D Min); discipleship and church ministry (M Div, MAR, MCM); evangelism and church planting (MAR, MCM, D Min); expository preaching (D Min); global ministry (MA); global studies (M Div, MAR, MCM, MGS, Th M); healthcare chaplaincy (M Div); homiletics (M Div, MAR, Th M); leadership (M Div, MAR); marketplace chaplaincy (M Div, MCM); ministry leadership (Ed D); pastoral counseling (M Div, MA, MAR, D Min), including addictions and recovery (MA), crisis response and trauma (MA), discipleship and church ministries (MA), leadership (MA), life coaching (MA), marketplace chaplaincy (MA), marriage and family (MA), military resilience (MA), pastoral counseling (MA); pastoral leadership (D Min); pastoral ministries (M Div, M Serv Soc, MCM); religious education (MRE); sports chaplaincy (MA); theology (M Div, MAR, MTS, Th M); theology and apologetics (D Min, PhD); worship (M Div, MAR, MCM, D Min); youth and family ministries (M Div). *Program availability:* Part-time, online learning. *Students:* 2,140 full-time (615 women), 3,020 part-time (906 women); includes 1,312 minority (1,016 Black or African American, non-Hispanic/Latino; 9 American Indian or Alaska Native, non-Hispanic/Latino; 100 Asian, non-Hispanic/Latino; 90 Hispanic/Latino; 7 Native Hawaiian or other Pacific Islander, non-Hispanic/Latino; 90 Two or more races, non-Hispanic/Latino), 158 international. Average age 42. 4,673 applicants, 33% accepted, 977 enrolled. In 2017, 904 master's, 54 doctorates awarded. *Degree requirements:* For master's, 2 foreign languages, thesis (for some programs); for doctorate, 2 foreign languages, thesis/dissertation. *Entrance requirements:* For master's, minimum undergraduate GPA of 2.0; for doctorate, GRE General Test or MAT, minimum graduate GPA of 3.0. Additional exam requirements/recommendations for international students: Required—TOEFL (minimum score 600 paper-based; 100 iBT). *Application deadline:* For fall admission, 6/1 for domestic students; for spring admission, 11/1 for domestic students. Applications are processed on a rolling basis. Application fee: $50. Electronic applications accepted. *Expenses:* Contact institution. *Financial support:* Teaching assistantships with tuition reimbursements, career-related internships or fieldwork, and Federal Work-Study available. Financial award applicants required to submit FAFSA. *Unit head:* Dr. Ed Hindson, Dean, 434-592-4140, Fax: 434-522-0415, E-mail: ehindson@liberty.edu. *Application contact:* Jay Bridge, Director of Graduate Admissions, 800-424-9595, Fax: 800-628-7977, E-mail: gradadmissions@liberty.edu.
Website: https://www.liberty.edu/divinity/

London Metropolitan University, Graduate Programs, London, United Kingdom. Offers applied psychology (M Sc); architecture (MA); biomedical science (M Sc); blood science (M Sc); cancer pharmacology (M Sc); computer networking and cyber security (M Sc); computing and information systems (M Sc); conference interpreting (MA); counter-terrorism studies (M Sc); creative, digital and professional writing (MA); crime, violence and prevention (M Sc); criminology (M Sc); curating contemporary art (MA); data analytics (M Sc); digital media (MA); early childhood studies (MA); education (MA, Ed D); financial services law, regulation and compliance (LL M); food science (M Sc); forensic psychology (M Sc); health and social care management and policy (M Sc); human nutrition (M Sc); human resource management (MA); human rights and international conflict (MA); information technology (M Sc); intelligence and security studies (M Sc); international oil, gas and energy law (LL M); international relations (MA); interpreting (MA); learning and teaching in higher education (MA); legal practice (LL M); media and entertainment law (LL M); organizational and consumer psychology (M Sc); psychological therapy (M Sc); psychology of mental health (M Sc); public health (M Sc); public policy and management (MPA); security studies (M Sc); social work (M Sc); spatial planning and urban design (MA); sports therapy (M Sc); supporting older children and young people with dyslexia (MA); teaching languages (MA), including Arabic, English; translation (MA); woman and child abuse (MA).

Missouri State University, Graduate College, College of Humanities and Public Affairs, Department of Defense and Strategic Studies, Fairfax, VA 22031. Offers defense and strategic studies (Certificate); general weapons of mass destruction (MS). *Program availability:* Part-time. *Faculty:* 2 full-time (0 women), 19 part-time/adjunct (5 women). *Students:* 24 full-time (5 women), 55 part-time (19 women); includes 17 minority (4 Black or African American, non-Hispanic/Latino; 3 Asian, non-Hispanic/Latino; 5 Hispanic/Latino; 5 Two or more races, non-Hispanic/Latino), 3 international. Average age 33. 46 applicants, 76% accepted, 34 enrolled. In 2017, 39 master's awarded. *Degree requirements:* For master's, comprehensive exam, thesis or alternative. *Entrance requirements:* For master's, GRE, minimum GPA of 2.75, 3 letters of recommendation. Additional exam requirements/recommendations for international students: Required—TOEFL (minimum score 550 paper-based; 79 iBT), IELTS (minimum score 6). *Application deadline:* For fall admission, 4/15 priority date for domestic students, 4/15 for international students. Applications are processed on a rolling basis. Application fee: $35 ($50 for international students). Electronic applications accepted. *Expenses:* Tuition, state resident: full-time $2915; part-time $2021 per credit hour. Tuition, nonresident: full-time $5354; part-time $3647 per credit hour. *International tuition:* $11,992 full-time. *Required fees:* $173; $173 per credit hour. Tuition and fees vary according to class time, course level, course load, degree level, campus/location and program. *Financial support:* Career-related internships or fieldwork, Federal Work-Study, institutionally sponsored loans, scholarships/grants, and unspecified assistantships available. Financial award application deadline: 3/31; financial award applicants required to submit FAFSA. *Faculty research:* Middle East, terrorism, arms control, U.S.-Soviet military balance, strategic defense initiative. *Unit head:* Dr. Keith Payne, Head, 703-218-3565, Fax: 703-218-3568, E-mail: kbpayne@missouristate.edu. *Application contact:* Stephanie Praschan, Director, Graduate Enrollment Management, 417-836-5330, Fax: 417-836-6200, E-mail: stephaniepraschan@missouristate.edu.
Website: http://dss.missouristate.edu

National Defense University, The Dwight D. Eisenhower School for National Security and Resource Strategy, Washington, DC 20319-5066. Offers national resource strategy (MS). Open only to Department of Defense employees and specific federal agencies. *Degree requirements:* For master's, comprehensive exam. *Entrance requirements:* Additional exam requirements/recommendations for international students: Required—TOEFL. *Faculty research:* Industrial base and relation to national security, acquisition and relation to national security, resourcing the national security strategy.

National Defense University, Joint Advanced Warfighting School, Norfolk, VA 23511. Offers joint campaign planning and strategy (MS). Open only to Department of Defense employees and specific federal agencies. *Degree requirements:* For master's, thesis. *Faculty research:* Irregular warfare, national policy and strategy, international organizations and policies, modern military history and applications of lessons learned, historical military leadership relating to present-day environments.

National Defense University, National War College, Washington, DC 20319-5066. Offers national security strategy (MS). Open only to Department of Defense employees and specific federal agencies. *Degree requirements:* For master's, comprehensive exam. *Entrance requirements:* Additional exam requirements/recommendations for international students: Required—TOEFL. *Faculty research:* National security policy, regional security, U.S. national security strategy, U.S. military, strategy.

National Intelligence University, Graduate Program, Washington, DC 20340-5100. Offers MSSI. Open only to federal government employees. *Program availability:* Part-time, evening/weekend. *Degree requirements:* For master's, thesis. *Entrance requirements:* For master's, MAT, authorized nomination. *Faculty research:* Law and intelligence, intelligence and higher education, low-intensity conflict, intelligence information systems.

Naval Postgraduate School, Departments and Academic Groups, Department of Computer Science, Monterey, CA 93943. Offers computer science (MS, PhD); identity management and cyber security (MA); modeling of virtual environments and simulations (MS, PhD); software engineering (MS, PhD). Program only open to commissioned officers of the United States and friendly nations and selected United States federal civilian employees. *Program availability:* Part-time, online learning. *Degree requirements:* For master's, thesis; for doctorate, thesis/dissertation.

Naval Postgraduate School, Departments and Academic Groups, Department of Defense Analysis, Monterey, CA 93943. Offers command and control (MS); communications (MS); defense analysis (MS), including astronautics; financial management (MS); information operations (MS); irregular warfare (MS); national security affairs (MS); operations analysis (MS); special operations (MA, MS), including command and control (MS), communications (MS), financial management (MS), information operations (MS), irregular warfare (MS), national security affairs, operations analysis (MS), tactile missiles (MS), terrorist operations and financing (MS); tactile missiles (MS); terrorist operations and financing (MS). Program only open to commissioned officers of the United States and friendly nations and selected United States federal civilian employees. *Program availability:* Part-time. *Degree requirements:* For master's, thesis. *Faculty research:* CTF Global Ecco Project, Afghanistan endgames, core lab Philippines project, Defense Manpower Data Center (DMDC) data vulnerability.

Naval Postgraduate School, Departments and Academic Groups, Department of National Security Affairs, Monterey, CA 93943. Offers national security affairs (MA); security studies (MA), including civil-military relations, combating terrorism: policy and strategy, defense decision-making and planning, Europe and Eurasia, Far East, Southeast Asia, the Pacific, homeland security and defense, Middle East, South Asia, Sub-Saharan Africa, stabilization and reconstruction, western hemisphere. Program only open to commissioned officers of the United States and friendly nations and selected United States federal civilian employees. *Program availability:* Part-time. *Degree requirements:* For master's, thesis (for some programs). *Faculty research:* Privatizing welfare in the Middle East; social construction of Russia's resurgence; institutions, ethnicity and political mobilization in South Africa; Hezbollah; China's strategic interests in Cambodia.

Naval Postgraduate School, Departments and Academic Groups, Graduate School of Business and Public Policy, Monterey, CA 93943. Offers acquisition and contract management (MBA); business administration (EMBA, MBA); contract management (MS); defense business management (MBA); defense systems analysis (MS), including management; defense systems management (international) (MBA); financial management (MBA); information management (MBA); manpower systems analysis (MS); material logistics support management (MBA); program management (MS); resource planning and management for international defense (MBA); supply chain management (MBA); systems acquisition management (MBA); transportation management (MBA). Program only open to commissioned officers of the United States and friendly nations and selected United States federal civilian employees. *Accreditation:* AACSB; NASPAA. *Program availability:* Part-time, online learning. *Degree requirements:* For master's, thesis (for some programs), terminal project/

capstone (for some programs). *Faculty research:* U.S. and European public procurement policies for small and medium-sized enterprises, examining external validity criticisms in the choice of students as subjects in accounting experiment studies, assurance of learning in contract management education, contracting for cloud computing: opportunities and risks, NPS, Apple App Store as a business model supporting U.S. Navy requirements.

Naval Postgraduate School, Departments and Academic Groups, Undersea Warfare Academic Group, Monterey, CA 93943. Offers applied mathematics (MS); applied physics (MS); applied science (MS), including acoustics, operations research, physical oceanography, signal processing; electrical engineering (MS); engineering acoustics (MS, PhD); engineering science (MS), including electrical engineering, mechanical engineering; mechanical engineer (ME); mechanical engineering (MS, MSME); meteorology (MS); operations research (MS); physical oceanography (MS). Program only open to commissioned officers of the United States and friendly nations and selected United States federal civilian employees. *Program availability:* Part-time. *Degree requirements:* For master's, thesis. *Faculty research:* Unmanned/autonomous vehicles, sea mines and countermeasures, submarine warfare in the twentieth and twenty-first centuries.

Norwich University, College of Graduate and Continuing Studies, Master of Arts in Military History Program, Northfield, VT 05663. Offers MA. *Program availability:* Evening/weekend, online only, mostly all online with a week-long residency requirement. *Degree requirements:* For master's, thesis optional, capstone. *Entrance requirements:* For master's, minimum undergraduate GPA of 2.75. Additional exam requirements/recommendations for international students: Required—TOEFL (minimum score 550 paper-based; 80 iBT), IELTS (minimum score 6.5). Electronic applications accepted. *Expenses:* Contact institution.

Royal Military College of Canada, Division of Graduate Studies and Research, Continuing Studies, Department of History, Kingston, ON K7K 7B4, Canada. Offers defense management and policy (MA); history (PhD); war studies (MA). *Degree requirements:* For master's, thesis. *Entrance requirements:* For master's, honours degree with second-class standing; for doctorate, master's degree. Electronic applications accepted.

School of Advanced Air and Space Studies, Program in Airpower Art and Science, Maxwell AFB, AL 36112-6424. Offers MA. Available to active duty military officers only. *Degree requirements:* For master's, comprehensive exam, thesis. *Entrance requirements:* For master's, less than 16 years total of active commissioned service; master's degree or undergraduate degree with a minimum GPA of 2.75. Additional exam requirements/recommendations for international students: Required—TOEFL. *Faculty research:* Military history, political science, international relations, social history, technology.

United States Army Command and General Staff College, Graduate Program, Fort Leavenworth, KS 66027-2301. Offers military art and science (MMAS). Only career military officers are selected to attend United States Army Command and General Staff College; Graduate Program is voluntary for first-year students, but mandatory for second-year students.

University of Calgary, Faculty of Graduate Studies, Centre for Military and Strategic Studies, Calgary, AB T2N 1N4, Canada. Offers MSS, PhD. PhD offered in special cases only. *Program availability:* Part-time. *Degree requirements:* For master's, thesis; for doctorate, comprehensive exam, thesis/dissertation. *Entrance requirements:* For master's, minimum GPA of 3.4. Additional exam requirements/recommendations for international students: Recommended—TOEFL (minimum score 550 paper-based). *Faculty research:* Military history, Israeli studies, strategic studies, int'l relations, Arctic security.

University of Colorado Denver, School of Public Affairs, Program in Public Affairs and Administration, Denver, CO 80127. Offers public administration (MPA), including domestic violence, emergency management and homeland security, environmental policy, management and law, homeland security and defense, local government, nonprofit management, public administration; public affairs (PhD). *Accreditation:* NASPAA. *Program availability:* Part-time, evening/weekend, online learning. *Degree requirements:* For master's, thesis or alternative, 36-39 credit hours; for doctorate, comprehensive exam, thesis/dissertation, minimum of 66 semester hours, including at least 30 hours of dissertation. *Entrance requirements:* For master's, GRE, GMAT or LSAT, resume, essay, transcripts, recommendations; for doctorate, GRE, resume, essay, transcripts, recommendations. Additional exam requirements/recommendations for international students: Required—TOEFL (minimum score 550 paper-based; 80 iBT); Recommended—IELTS (minimum score 6.5). Electronic applications accepted. *Expenses:* Contact institution. *Faculty research:* Housing, education and the social and economic issues of vulnerable populations; nonprofit governance and management; education finance, effectiveness and reform; P-20 education initiatives; municipal government accountability.

University of Pittsburgh, Graduate School of Public and International Affairs, Master of Public and International Affairs Program, Pittsburgh, PA 15260. Offers human security (MPIA); international political economy (MPIA); security and intelligence studies (MPIA); JD/MPIA; MBA/MPIA; MPH/MPIA; MPIA/MSW; MSIS/MPIA. *Program availability:* Part-time, evening/weekend. *Faculty:* 30 full-time (11 women), 14 part-time/adjunct (5 women). *Students:* 87 full-time (42 women), 14 part-time (7 women); includes 15 minority (6 Black or African American, non-Hispanic/Latino; 3 Asian, non-Hispanic/Latino; 6 Hispanic/Latino), 14 international. Average age 27. 173 applicants, 88% accepted, 37 enrolled. In 2017, 54 master's awarded. *Degree requirements:* For master's, thesis optional, capstone seminar. *Entrance requirements:* For master's, GRE General Test or GMAT, 2 letters of recommendation, resume, undergraduate transcripts, personal statement. Additional exam requirements/recommendations for international students: Required—TOEFL (minimum score 80 iBT); Recommended—IELTS (minimum score 7). *Application deadline:* For fall admission, 2/1 priority date for domestic students, 1/15 priority date for international students; for spring admission, 11/1 priority date for domestic students, 8/1 priority date for international students. Application fee: $50. Electronic applications accepted. *Expenses:* $23,140 per year in-state, $37,830 out-of-state. *Financial support:* In 2017–18, 47 students received support, including 7 fellowships with full tuition reimbursements available (averaging $37,000 per year), 8 research assistantships with full tuition reimbursements available (averaging $37,000 per year); scholarships/grants also available. Financial award application deadline: 2/1; financial award applicants required to submit FAFSA. *Faculty research:* International political economy, human security, security and intelligence studies. *Total annual research expenditures:* $1.6 million. *Unit head:* Dr. John Keeler, Dean, 412-648-7605, Fax: 412-648-7601, E-mail: gspia@pitt.edu. *Application contact:* Dr. Michael Rizzi, Director of Student Services, 412-648-7643, Fax: 412-648-7641, E-mail: rizzim@pitt.edu.
Website: http://www.gspia.pitt.edu/

National Security

American Public University System, AMU/APU Graduate Programs, Charles Town, WV 25414. Offers accounting (MS); applied business analytics (MS); business administration (MBA); criminal justice (MA); cybersecurity studies (MS); educational leadership (M Ed); environmental policy and management (MS); global security (DGS); health information management (MS); history (MA), including American military history, American Revolution, civil war, war since 1945, World War II; information technology (MS); international relations and conflict resolution (MA), including American politics and government, comparative government and development, general, international relations, public policy; national security studies (MA); nursing (MSN); political science (MA); public policy (MPP); reverse logistics management (MA), including comparative and security issues, conflict resolution, international and transnational security issues, peacekeeping; space studies (MS); sports management (MS); strategic intelligence (DSI); teaching (M Ed), including secondary social studies; transportation and logistics management (MA). *Program availability:* Part-time, evening/weekend, online only, 100% online. *Students:* 455 full-time (227 women), 7,939 part-time (3,353 women); includes 2,793 minority (1,429 Black or African American, non-Hispanic/Latino; 48 American Indian or Alaska Native, non-Hispanic/Latino; 205 Asian, non-Hispanic/Latino; 766 Hispanic/Latino; 62 Native Hawaiian or other Pacific Islander, non-Hispanic/Latino; 283 Two or more races, non-Hispanic/Latino), 101 international. Average age 37. In 2017, 2,977 master's awarded. *Degree requirements:* For master's, comprehensive exam or practicum. *Entrance requirements:* For master's, official transcript showing earned bachelor's degree from institution accredited by recognized accrediting body. Additional exam requirements/recommendations for international students: Required—TOEFL (minimum score 550 paper-based), IELTS (minimum score 6.5). *Application deadline:* Applications are processed on a rolling basis. Application fee: $0. Electronic applications accepted. *Expenses: Tuition:* Full-time $6300; part-time $350 per credit. *Required fees:* $300; $50 per course. *Financial support:* Scholarships/grants available. Financial award applicants required to submit FAFSA. *Unit head:* Dr. Wallace Boston, President, 877-468-6268, Fax: 304-728-2348, E-mail: president@apus.edu. *Application contact:* Yoci Deal, Associate Vice President, Graduate and International Admissions, 877-468-6268, Fax: 304-724-3764, E-mail: info@apus.edu.
Website: http://www.apus.edu

American University, School of International Service, Washington, DC 20016-8071. Offers comparative and regional studies (Certificate); cross-cultural communication (Certificate); development management (MS); ethics, peace, and global affairs (MA); European studies (Certificate); global environmental policy (MA, Certificate); global information technology (Certificate); global media (MA); international affairs (MA), including comparative and regional studies, global governance, politics, and security, international economic relations, natural resources and sustainable development, U.S. foreign policy and national security; international arts management (Certificate); international communication (MA, Certificate); international development (MA); international economic policy (Certificate); international economic relations (Certificate); international economics (MA); international peace and conflict resolution (MA, Certificate); international politics (Certificate); international relations (MA, PhD); international service (MIS); peacebuilding (Certificate); social enterprise (MA); the Americas (Certificate); United States foreign policy (Certificate); JD/MA. *Program availability:* Part-time, evening/weekend, 100% online. *Faculty:* 112 full-time (50 women), 46 part-time/adjunct (19 women). *Students:* 495 full-time (333 women), 518 part-time (276 women); includes 360 minority (95 Black or African American, non-Hispanic/Latino; 2 American Indian or Alaska Native, non-Hispanic/Latino; 60 Asian, non-Hispanic/Latino; 164 Hispanic/Latino; 39 Two or more races, non-Hispanic/Latino), 98 international. Average age 30. 1,559 applicants, 81% accepted, 356 enrolled. In 2017, 427 master's, 9 doctorates, 5 other advanced degrees awarded. Terminal master's awarded for partial completion of doctoral program. *Degree requirements:* For master's, one foreign language, comprehensive exam, thesis or alternative; for doctorate, one foreign language, comprehensive exam, thesis/dissertation. *Entrance requirements:* For master's, GRE; GMAT or GRE (for MA in social enterprise), transcripts, resume, 2 letters of recommendation, statement of purpose; for doctorate, GRE, transcripts, resume, 3 letters of recommendation, statement of purpose. Additional exam requirements/recommendations for international students: Required—TOEFL (minimum score 600 paper-based; 100 iBT). *Application deadline:* For fall admission, 1/15 for domestic students, 1/1 for international students; for spring admission, 10/1 for domestic students, 9/15 for international students. Application fee: $55. Electronic applications accepted. *Expenses:* Contact institution. *Financial support:* Research assistantships, teaching assistantships, institutionally sponsored loans, scholarships/grants, and unspecified assistantships available. Financial award application deadline: 1/15; financial award applicants required to submit FAFSA. *Application contact:* 202-885-1646, Fax: 202-885-1109, E-mail: sisgrad@american.edu.
Website: http://www.american.edu/sis/

Angelo State University, College of Graduate Studies and Research, College of Arts and Humanities, Department of Security Studies and Criminal Justice, San Angelo, TX 76909. Offers criminal justice (MS); homeland security (MS); intelligence, security studies, and analysis (MSS); security studies (MSS). *Program availability:* Part-time, evening/weekend, online learning. *Students:* 56 full-time (28 women), 146 part-time (44 women); includes 81 minority (27 Black or African American, non-Hispanic/Latino; 2 American Indian or Alaska Native, non-Hispanic/Latino; 10 Asian, non-Hispanic/Latino; 35 Hispanic/Latino; 7 Two or more races, non-Hispanic/Latino). Average age 32. *Degree requirements:* For master's, comprehensive exam. *Entrance requirements:* For master's, essay, letters of recommendation. Additional exam requirements/recommendations for international students: Required—TOEFL or IELTS. *Application deadline:* For fall admission, 7/15 priority date for domestic students, 6/10 for international students; for spring admission, 12/1 priority date for domestic students, 11/1 for international students. Applications are processed on a rolling basis. Application fee: $40 ($50 for international students). Electronic applications accepted. *Expenses:* Tuition, state resident: full-time $3856. Tuition, nonresident: full-time $11,324. *Required fees:* $2650. *Financial support:* Federal Work-Study and scholarships/grants available.

Support available to part-time students. Financial award application deadline: 3/1; financial award applicants required to submit FAFSA. *Unit head:* Dr. William A. Taylor, Chair, 325-486-6689, Fax: 325-942-2544, E-mail: william.taylor@angelo.edu. Website: http://www.angelo.edu/dept/security_studies_criminal_justice/

Bellevue University, Graduate School, College of Arts and Sciences, Bellevue, NE 68005-3098. Offers clinical counseling (MS); healthcare administration (MHA); human services (MA); international security and intelligence studies (MS); managerial communication (MA). *Program availability:* Online learning.

California State University, San Bernardino, Graduate Studies, College of Social and Behavioral Sciences, Program in National Security Studies, San Bernardino, CA 92407. Offers MA. *Program availability:* Part-time, evening/weekend. *Students:* 10 full-time (5 women), 31 part-time (14 women); includes 14 minority (1 Black or African American, non-Hispanic/Latino; 1 Asian, non-Hispanic/Latino; 11 Hispanic/Latino; 1 Two or more races, non-Hispanic/Latino), 2 international. Average age 26. 19 applicants, 89% accepted, 13 enrolled. In 2017, 10 master's awarded. *Degree requirements:* For master's, comprehensive exam. *Entrance requirements:* Additional exam requirements/recommendations for international students: Required—TOEFL. *Application deadline:* For fall admission, 4/15 for domestic students; for winter admission, 10/16 for domestic students; for spring admission, 1/22 for domestic students. Application fee: $55. *Unit head:* Dr. Mark Clark, Director, 909-537-5491, Fax: 909-537-7018, E-mail: mtclark@csusb.edu. *Application contact:* Dr. Dorota Huizinga, Dean of Graduate Studies, 909-537-3064, E-mail: dorota.huizinga@csusb.edu.

The Citadel, The Military College of South Carolina, Citadel Graduate College, School of Humanities and Social Sciences, Department of Criminal Justice, Charleston, SC 29409. Offers homeland security (Graduate Certificate); intelligence analysis (Graduate Certificate); intelligence and security studies (MA). *Program availability:* Part-time, evening/weekend, 100% online, blended/hybrid learning. *Entrance requirements:* For master's, GRE or MAT, writing sample that demonstrates strong critical thinking and communication skills. Additional exam requirements/recommendations for international students: Required—TOEFL (minimum score 550 paper-based; 79 iBT). Electronic applications accepted. *Expenses:* Tuition, state resident: part-time $587 per credit hour. Tuition, nonresident: part-time $988 per credit hour. *Required fees:* $90 per term.

Daniel Morgan Graduate School of National Security, Graduate Programs, Washington, DC 20036. Offers integrated risk value communications (MA); national security (MA).

George Mason University, Schar School of Policy and Government, Program in Biodefense, Arlington, VA 22201. Offers MS, PhD, Certificate. *Program availability:* Evening/weekend, 100% online. *Faculty:* 3 full-time (1 woman), 10 part-time/adjunct (4 women). *Students:* 21 full-time (14 women), 36 part-time (24 women); includes 12 minority (4 Asian, non-Hispanic/Latino; 6 Hispanic/Latino; 2 Two or more races, non-Hispanic/Latino), 1 international. Average age 30. 37 applicants, 59% accepted, 16 enrolled. In 2017, 15 master's, 3 doctorates, 4 other advanced degrees awarded. *Degree requirements:* For master's, thesis, project; for doctorate, comprehensive exam, thesis/dissertation. *Entrance requirements:* For master's, GRE (taken in the past five years), transcripts from all previous institutions attended in the U.S.; goals statement; two letters of recommendation; current resume; writing sample; for doctorate, GRE (taken in the past five years), official transcript from all colleges and universities attended; current resume; two letters of recommendation; statement of goals (not to exceed 500 words); writing sample (approximately 10-25 pages in length). Additional exam requirements/recommendations for international students: Required—TOEFL (minimum score 575 paper-based; 88 iBT), IELTS (minimum score 6.5), PTE (minimum score 59). *Application deadline:* For fall admission, 2/1 priority date for domestic and international students; for spring admission, 11/1 priority date for domestic and international students. Application fee: $75 ($80 for international students). Electronic applications accepted. *Expenses:* $795 per credit in-state tuition, $1,516 out-of-state. *Financial support:* In 2017–18, 6 students received support, including 1 fellowship, 5 research assistantships with tuition reimbursements available (averaging $15,009 per year); career-related internships or fieldwork, Federal Work-Study, scholarships/grants, unspecified assistantships, and health care benefits (for full-time research or teaching assistantship recipients) also available. Support available to part-time students. Financial award application deadline: 3/1; financial award applicants required to submit FAFSA. *Faculty research:* Weapons of mass destruction; global health security; homeland security; terrorism; genome editing and synthetic biology. *Unit head:* Gregory Koblentz, Director, 703-993-1266, Fax: 703-993-1399, E-mail: gkoblent@gmu.edu. *Application contact:* Stephanie Ellis, Graduate Admissions Coordinator, 703-993-4478, E-mail: sellis11@gmu.edu.

The George Washington University, Law School, Washington, DC 20052. Offers law (SJD); national security and U.S. foreign relations (LL M). *Accreditation:* ABA. *Program availability:* Part-time, evening/weekend. *Faculty:* 84 full-time (33 women), 233 part-time/adjunct (65 women). *Students:* 1,444 full-time (760 women), 249 part-time (118 women); includes 422 minority (157 Black or African American, non-Hispanic/Latino; 11 American Indian or Alaska Native, non-Hispanic/Latino; 198 Asian, non-Hispanic/Latino; 38 Hispanic/Latino; 4 Native Hawaiian or other Pacific Islander, non-Hispanic/Latino; 14 Two or more races, non-Hispanic/Latino), 190 international. Average age 27. 191 applicants, 100% accepted, 128 enrolled. In 2017, 167 master's, 4 doctorates awarded. *Entrance requirements:* For master's, JD or equivalent; for doctorate, LSAT (for JD), LL M or equivalent (for SJD). *Application deadline:* For fall admission, 3/1 for domestic students. Applications are processed on a rolling basis. Application fee: $75. *Expenses:* Contact institution. *Financial support:* Research assistantships, career-related internships or fieldwork, Federal Work-Study, institutionally sponsored loans, scholarships/grants, and tuition waivers (full and partial) available. Support available to part-time students. Financial award application deadline: 3/1; financial award applicants required to submit CSS PROFILE or FAFSA. *Unit head:* Blake D. Morant, Dean, E-mail: bmorant@law.gwu.edu. *Application contact:* Sophia Sim, Assistant Dean of Admissions and Financial Aid, 202-994-7235, Fax: 202-739-0624, E-mail: ssim@law.gwu.edu. Website: http://www.law.gwu.edu/

Henley-Putnam School of Strategic Security, Doctorate Program in Strategic Security, Rapid City, SD 57701. Offers DSS. *Program availability:* Part-time, online learning. *Degree requirements:* For doctorate, thesis/dissertation. *Entrance requirements:* For doctorate, 5 years of strategic security experience; background check; interview with dean; copy of master's thesis; master's or bachelor's degree with equivalent of 30 graduate-level semester hours in strategic security or related field from accredited institution. Additional exam requirements/recommendations for international students: Required—TOEFL (minimum score 650 paper-based; 79 iBT); Recommended—IELTS (minimum score 7). *Expenses:* Contact institution.

The Institute of World Politics, Graduate Programs in National Security, Intelligence, and International Affairs, Washington, DC 20036. Offers American foreign policy (Certificate); comparative political culture (Certificate); counterintelligence (Certificate); democracy building (Certificate); intelligence (Certificate); international politics (Certificate); national security affairs (Certificate); public diplomacy and political warfare (Certificate); statecraft and national security affairs (MA); statecraft and world politics (MA); strategic intelligence studies (MA). *Program availability:* Part-time, evening/

weekend. *Degree requirements:* For master's, comprehensive exam, thesis optional. *Entrance requirements:* For master's, GRE General Test. Additional exam requirements/recommendations for international students: Required—TOEFL. Electronic applications accepted. *Faculty research:* Intelligence, national security, statecraft.

Kansas State University, Graduate School, College of Arts and Sciences, Security Studies Program, Manhattan, KS 66506. Offers MA, PhD. *Program availability:* Part-time. Terminal master's awarded for partial completion of doctoral program. *Degree requirements:* For doctorate, comprehensive exam, thesis/dissertation. *Entrance requirements:* For doctorate, GRE. Additional exam requirements/recommendations for international students: Required—TOEFL (minimum score 550 paper-based; 79 iBT), IELTS (minimum score 6.5), PTE (minimum score 58). Electronic applications accepted. *Faculty research:* International conflict and security, military history.

National Defense University, College of International Security Affairs, Washington, DC 20319-5066. Offers strategic security studies (MA), including counterterrorism, homeland defense, international security studies. *Program availability:* Part-time, evening/weekend. *Degree requirements:* For master's, thesis. *Entrance requirements:* Additional exam requirements/recommendations for international students: Required—TOEFL.

National Defense University, National War College, Washington, DC 20319-5066. Offers national security strategy (MS). Open only to Department of Defense employees and specific federal agencies. *Degree requirements:* For master's, comprehensive exam. *Entrance requirements:* Additional exam requirements/recommendations for international students: Required—TOEFL. *Faculty research:* National security policy, regional security, U.S. national security strategy, U.S. military, strategy.

Naval Postgraduate School, Departments and Academic Groups, Department of Defense Analysis, Monterey, CA 93943. Offers command and control (MS); communications (MS); defense analysis (MS), including astronautics; financial management (MS); information operations (MS); irregular warfare (MS); national security affairs (MS); operations analysis (MS); special operations (MA, MS), including command and control (MS), communications (MS), financial management (MS), information operations (MS), irregular warfare (MS), national security affairs, operations analysis (MS), tactile missiles (MS), terrorist operations and financing (MS); tactile missiles (MS); terrorist operations and financing (MS). Program only open to commissioned officers of the United States and friendly nations and selected United States federal civilian employees. *Program availability:* Part-time. *Degree requirements:* For master's, thesis. *Faculty research:* CTF Global Ecco Project, Afghanistan endgames, core lab Philippines project, Defense Manpower Data Center (DMDC) data vulnerability.

Naval Postgraduate School, Departments and Academic Groups, Department of National Security Affairs, Monterey, CA 93943. Offers national security affairs (MA); security studies (MA), including civil-military relations, combating terrorism: policy and strategy, defense decision-making and planning, Europe and Eurasia, Far East, Southeast Asia, the Pacific, homeland security and defense, Middle East, South Asia, Sub-Saharan Africa, stabilization and reconstruction, western hemisphere. Program only open to commissioned officers of the United States and friendly nations and selected United States federal civilian employees. *Program availability:* Part-time. *Degree requirements:* For master's, thesis (for some programs). *Faculty research:* Privatizing welfare in the Middle East; social construction of Russia's resurgence; institutions, ethnicity and political mobilization in South Africa; Hezbollah; China's strategic interests in Cambodia.

Naval Postgraduate School, Departments and Academic Groups, Global Public Policy Academic Group, Monterey, CA 93943. Offers stability, security, and development in complex operations (Certificate). *Degree requirements:* For Certificate, certificate hybrid course (requiring short biographical essay and short introductory session with instructor during the distributed learning component). *Faculty research:* Implementing program budgeting in the Serbian Ministry of Defense, recognizing patterns of anomie that set the conditions for insurgency.

Naval War College, Program in National Security and Strategic Studies, Newport, RI 02841-1207. Offers MA. Program open only to full-time military personnel.

New Jersey City University, College of Professional Studies, Program in National Security Studies, Jersey City, NJ 07305-1597. Offers civil security leadership (D Sc); national security studies (MS, Certificate). *Program availability:* Part-time. *Entrance requirements:* Additional exam requirements/recommendations for international students: Required—TOEFL (minimum score 79 iBT).

Regent University, Graduate School, Robertson School of Government, Virginia Beach, VA 23464. Offers government (MA), including American government, healthcare policy and ethics (MA, MPA), international relations, law and public policy, national security studies, political communication, political theory, religion and politics; national security studies (MA), including cybersecurity, homeland security, international security, Middle East politics; public administration (MPA), including emergency management and homeland security, federal government, general public administration, healthcare policy and ethics (MA, MPA), law, nonprofit administration and faith-based organizations, public leadership and management, servant leadership. *Program availability:* Part-time, evening/weekend, 100% online, blended/hybrid learning. *Faculty:* 8 full-time (1 woman), 20 part-time/adjunct (3 women). *Students:* 39 full-time (23 women), 137 part-time (78 women); includes 83 minority (49 Black or African American, non-Hispanic/Latino; 1 American Indian or Alaska Native, non-Hispanic/Latino; 7 Asian, non-Hispanic/Latino; 15 Hispanic/Latino; 11 Two or more races, non-Hispanic/Latino). Average age 35. 345 applicants, 31% accepted, 57 enrolled. In 2017, 38 master's awarded. *Degree requirements:* For master's, thesis optional, internship. *Entrance requirements:* For master's, GRE General Test or LSAT, personal essay, writing sample, resume, college transcripts. Additional exam requirements/recommendations for international students: Required—TOEFL (minimum score 577 paper-based). *Application deadline:* For fall admission, 5/1 priority date for domestic students; for spring admission, 11/1 priority date for domestic students. Applications are processed on a rolling basis. Application fee: $50. Electronic applications accepted. *Expenses:* $650 per credit; $300 technology fee per semester. *Financial support:* In 2017–18, 116 students received support. Career-related internships or fieldwork, scholarships/grants, and unspecified assistantships available. Support available to part-time students. *Faculty research:* International relations and politics, public administration, leadership and ethics, Biblical law, Constitutional law and Supreme Court. *Unit head:* Dr. Eric Patterson, Dean, 757-352-4616, Fax: 757-352-4735, E-mail: epatterson@regent.edu. *Application contact:* Heidi Cece, Assistant Vice President of Enrollment Management, 800-373-5504, Fax: 757-352-4381, E-mail: admissions@regent.edu. Website: https://www.regent.edu/robertson-school-of-government/

Regent University, Graduate School, School of Law, Virginia Beach, VA 23464. Offers American legal studies (LL M); human rights (LL M); law (MA, JD), including advanced paralegal studies (MA), alternative dispute resolution (MA), business (MA), criminal justice (MA), general legal studies (MA), human resources management (MA), human rights and rule of law (MA), national security (MA), non-profit organizational law (MA), regulatory compliance (MA), wealth management and financial planning (MA); JD/MA; JD/MBA. *Accreditation:* ABA. *Program availability:* Part-time, 100% online, blended/

hybrid learning. *Faculty:* 16 full-time (5 women), 76 part-time/adjunct (22 women). *Students:* 313 full-time (181 women), 248 part-time (175 women); includes 240 minority (155 Black or African American, non-Hispanic/Latino; 3 American Indian or Alaska Native, non-Hispanic/Latino; 15 Asian, non-Hispanic/Latino; 45 Hispanic/Latino; 2 Native Hawaiian or other Pacific Islander, non-Hispanic/Latino; 20 Two or more races, non-Hispanic/Latino), 59 international. Average age 35. 923 applicants, 36% accepted, 188 enrolled. In 2017, 138 master's, 80 doctorates awarded. *Entrance requirements:* For master's, college transcripts, resume, personal statement; for doctorate, LSAT, minimum undergraduate GPA of 3.0, official transcripts, 2 letters of recommendation, resume, personal statement. Additional exam requirements/recommendations for international students: Required—TOEFL (minimum score 600 paper-based). *Application deadline:* For fall admission, 3/1 for domestic students. Applications are processed on a rolling basis. Application fee: $50. Electronic applications accepted. *Expenses:* $650 per credit (MA, LL M); $1,140 per credit (JD); $300 per semester technology fee. *Financial support:* In 2017–18, 459 students received support. Career-related internships or fieldwork, scholarships/grants, and unspecified assistantships available. Support available to part-time students. *Faculty research:* Family law, Constitutional law, law and culture, evidence and practice, intellectual property. *Unit head:* Michael Hernandez, Dean, 757-352-4040, Fax: 757-352-4595, E-mail: michher@regent.edu. *Application contact:* Ernie Walton, Assistant Dean of Admissions, 757-352-4315, E-mail: lawschool@regent.edu.
Website: https://www.regent.edu/school-of-law/

Texas A&M University, Bush School of Government and Public Service, College Station, TX 77845. Offers homeland security (Certificate); international affairs (MIA, Certificate); national security affairs (Certificate); non-profit management (Certificate); public service and administration (MPSA). *Accreditation:* NASPAA. *Faculty:* 66. *Students:* 332 full-time (182 women), 54 part-time (16 women); includes 94 minority (19 Black or African American, non-Hispanic/Latino; 10 Asian, non-Hispanic/Latino; 56 Hispanic/Latino; 9 Two or more races, non-Hispanic/Latino), 41 international. Average age 28. 297 applicants, 94% accepted, 164 enrolled. In 2017, 154 master's awarded. *Degree requirements:* For master's, summer internship. *Entrance requirements:* For master's, GRE (preferred) or GMAT. Additional exam requirements/recommendations for international students: Required—TOEFL (minimum score 550 paper-based; 80 iBT), IELTS (minimum score 6), PTE (minimum score 53). *Application deadline:* For fall admission, 1/15 for domestic and international students. Application fee: $50 ($90 for international students). Electronic applications accepted. *Expenses:* Contact institution. *Financial support:* In 2017–18, 417 students received support, including 29 fellowships with tuition reimbursements available (averaging $20,966 per year), 71 research assistantships with tuition reimbursements available (averaging $9,778 per year); teaching assistantships, career-related internships or fieldwork, institutionally sponsored loans, scholarships/grants, traineeships, health care benefits, tuition waivers (full and partial), and unspecified assistantships also available. Support available to part-time students. Financial award application deadline: 3/15; financial award applicants required to submit FAFSA. *Faculty research:* Public policy, Presidential studies, public leadership, economic policy, social policy. *Unit head:* Dr. Mark Welsh, Dean, 979-862-8007, E-mail: mwelsh@tamu.edu. *Application contact:* Kathryn Meyer, Director of Recruitment and Admissions, 979-458-4767, Fax: 979-845-4155, E-mail: bushschooladmissions@tamu.edu.
Website: http://bush.tamu.edu/

Trinity Washington University, School of Business and Graduate Studies, Washington, DC 20017-1094. Offers business administration (MBA); communication (MA); international security studies (MA); organizational management (MSA), including federal program management, human resource management, nonprofit management, organizational development, public and community health. *Program availability:* Part-time, evening/weekend. *Degree requirements:* For master's, thesis (for some programs), capstone project (MSA). *Entrance requirements:* For master's, minimum GPA of 2.5. Additional exam requirements/recommendations for international students: Required—TOEFL (minimum score 550 paper-based).

University of Central Florida, College of Sciences, Department of Political Science, Orlando, FL 32816. Offers intelligence and national security (Certificate); political science (MA); security studies (PhD). *Program availability:* Part-time, evening/weekend. *Students:* 48 full-time (18 women), 16 part-time (7 women); includes 17 minority (4 Black or African American, non-Hispanic/Latino; 1 Asian, non-Hispanic/Latino; 10 Hispanic/Latino; 2 Two or more races, non-Hispanic/Latino), 15 international. Average age 31. 43 applicants, 74% accepted, 25 enrolled. In 2017, 10 master's, 2 doctorates, 7 other advanced degrees awarded. *Degree requirements:* For master's, comprehensive exam, thesis; for doctorate, one foreign language, thesis/dissertation, oral qualifying examination, written candidacy exam. *Entrance requirements:* For master's, GRE General Test, letters of recommendation, personal statement; for doctorate, GRE General Test, master's degree or its equivalent in political science, international politics, international relations, or related discipline; letters of recommendation; personal statement; writing sample; resume. Additional exam requirements/recommendations for international students: Required—TOEFL. *Application deadline:* For fall admission, 7/15 for domestic students; for spring admission, 12/1 for domestic students. Application fee: $30. Electronic applications accepted. *Expenses:* Tuition, state resident: part-time $288.16 per credit hour. Tuition, nonresident: part-time $1073.31 per credit hour. Tuition and fees vary according to program. *Financial support:* In 2017–18, 25 students received support, including 8 fellowships with partial tuition reimbursements available (averaging $10,575 per year), 1 research assistantship with partial tuition reimbursement available (averaging $14,868 per year), 21 teaching assistantships with partial tuition reimbursements available (averaging $12,928 per year); career-related internships or fieldwork, Federal Work-Study, institutionally sponsored loans, health care benefits, tuition waivers (partial), and unspecified assistantships also available. Financial award application deadline: 3/1; financial award applicants required to submit FAFSA. *Faculty research:* Environment, international relations, security studies, comparative politics. *Unit head:* Dr. Kerstin Hamann, Chair, 407-823-2085, Fax: 407-823-0051, E-mail: kerstin.hamann@ucf.edu. *Application contact:* Associate Director, Graduate Admissions, 407-823-2766, Fax: 407-823-6442, E-mail: gradadmissions@ucf.edu.
Website: http://politicalscience.cos.ucf.edu/

University of Nebraska at Omaha, Graduate Studies, College of Arts and Sciences, Department of Political Science, Omaha, NE 68182. Offers American government (Certificate); global information operations (Certificate); intelligence and national security (Certificate); political science (MS). *Program availability:* Part-time, evening/weekend, online learning. *Degree requirements:* For master's, comprehensive exam, thesis (for some programs). *Entrance requirements:* For master's, 15 undergraduate political science hours, minimum undergraduate GPA of 3.0, 2 letters of recommendation, official transcripts. Additional exam requirements/recommendations for international students: Required—TOEFL, IELTS, PTE. Electronic applications accepted.

University of New Haven, Graduate School, Henry C. Lee College of Criminal Justice and Forensic Sciences, Program in National Security, West Haven, CT 06516. Offers national security (MS, Graduate Certificate); national security administration (Graduate Certificate). *Program availability:* Part-time, evening/weekend. *Students:* 31 full-time (14 women), 35 part-time (19 women); includes 14 minority (3 Black or African American, non-Hispanic/Latino; 8 Hispanic/Latino; 3 Two or more races, non-Hispanic/Latino), 4 international. Average age 32. 38 applicants, 97% accepted, 17 enrolled. In 2017, 38 master's, 3 other advanced degrees awarded. *Entrance requirements:* Additional exam requirements/recommendations for international students: Required—TOEFL (minimum score 70 iBT), IELTS, or PTE (minimum score of 53). *Application deadline:* Applications are processed on a rolling basis. Application fee: $50. Electronic applications accepted. Application fee is waived when completed online. *Expenses: Tuition:* Full-time $16,020; part-time $890 per credit hour. *Required fees:* $220; $90 per term. *Financial support:* Research assistantships with partial tuition reimbursements, teaching assistantships with partial tuition reimbursements, Federal Work-Study, scholarships/grants, and unspecified assistantships available. Support available to part-time students. Financial award applicants required to submit FAFSA. *Unit head:* Dr. Jibey Asthappan, Director, 203-479-4147, E-mail: jasthappan@newhaven.edu. *Application contact:* Michelle Mason, Director of Graduate Enrollment, 203-932-7067, E-mail: mmason@newhaven.edu.
Website: http://www.newhaven.edu/5924/

See Display on page 784 and Close-Up on page 799.

Virginia Polytechnic Institute and State University, VT Online, Blacksburg, VA 24061. Offers advanced transportation systems (Certificate); aerospace engineering (MS); agricultural and life sciences (MSLFS); business information systems (Graduate Certificate); career and technical education (MS); civil engineering (MS); computer engineering (M Eng, MS); decision support systems (Graduate Certificate); eLearning leadership (MA); electrical engineering (M Eng, MS); engineering administration (MEA); environmental engineering (Certificate); environmental politics and policy (Graduate Certificate); environmental sciences and engineering (MS); foundations of political analysis (Graduate Certificate); health product risk management (Graduate Certificate); industrial and systems engineering (MS); information policy and society (Graduate Certificate); information security (Graduate Certificate); information technology (MIT); instructional technology (MA); integrative STEM education (MA Ed); liberal arts (Graduate Certificate); life sciences: health product risk management (MS); natural resources (MNR, Graduate Certificate); networking (Graduate Certificate); nonprofit and nongovernmental organization management (Graduate Certificate); ocean engineering (MS); political science (MA); security studies (Graduate Certificate); software development (Graduate Certificate). *Expenses:* Tuition, state resident: full-time $15,072; part-time $718.50 per credit hour. Tuition, nonresident: full-time $28,810; part-time $1448.25 per credit hour. *Required fees:* $2741; $502 per semester. Tuition and fees vary according to course load, campus/location and program.

Western Michigan University Thomas M. Cooley Law School, Graduate Programs, Lansing, MI 48901-3038. Offers administrative law (public law) (JD); business transactions (JD); Canadian law practice (JD); corporate law and finance (LL M); environmental law (public law) (JD); general practice (JD), including solo and small firm; general studies (LL M); homeland and national security law (LL M); insurance law (LL M); intellectual property (JD); intellectual property law (LL M); international law (JD); litigation (JD); taxation (LL M); U.S. legal studies for foreign attorneys (LL M); JD/LL M; JD/MBA; JD/MHA; JD/MPA; JD/MSW. *Program availability:* Part-time, evening/weekend, 100% online, blended/hybrid learning. *Degree requirements:* For master's, thesis (for some programs); for doctorate, minimum of 3 credits of clinical experience. *Entrance requirements:* For master's, JD or LL B; for doctorate, LSAT. Additional exam requirements/recommendations for international students: Required—TOEFL (for U.S. legal studies for foreign attorneys LL M program); Recommended—TOEFL. Electronic applications accepted. *Expenses:* Contact institution. *Faculty research:* Wrongful convictions, civil rights, environmental law, litigation techniques, data mining, intellectual property, practical and skills-based legal education.

Section 23
Political Science and International Affairs

This section contains a directory of institutions offering graduate work in political science and international affairs. Additional information about programs listed in the directory but not augmented by an in-depth entry may be obtained by writing directly to the dean of a graduate school or chair of a department at the address given in the directory.

For programs offering related work, see also in this book *Area and Cultural Studies, History, Language and Literature,* and *Public, Regional, and Industrial Affairs.* In another guide in this series:

Graduate Programs in Business, Education, Information Studies, Law & Social Work

See *International Business*

CONTENTS

Program Directories

Featured Schools: Displays and Close-Ups

International Affairs

American Graduate School in Paris, Program in International Relations and Diplomacy, Paris, France. Offers MA, PhD.

American Public University System, AMU/APU Graduate Programs, Charles Town, WV 25414. Offers accounting (MS); applied business analytics (MS); business administration (MBA); criminal justice (MA); cybersecurity studies (MS); educational leadership (M Ed); environmental policy and management (MS); global security (DGS); health information management (MS); history (MA), including American military history, American Revolution, civil war, war since 1945, World War II; information technology (MS); international relations and conflict resolution (MA), including American politics and government, comparative government and development, general, international relations, public policy; national security studies (MA); nursing (MSN); political science (MA); public policy (MPP); reverse logistics management (MA), including comparative and security issues, conflict resolution, international and transnational security issues, peacekeeping; space studies (MS); sports management (MS); strategic intelligence (DSI); teaching (M Ed), including secondary social studies; transportation and logistics management (MA). *Program availability:* Part-time, evening/weekend, online only, 100% online. *Students:* 455 full-time (227 women), 7,939 part-time (3,353 women); includes 2,793 minority (1,429 Black or African American, non-Hispanic/Latino; 48 American Indian or Alaska Native, non-Hispanic/Latino; 205 Asian, non-Hispanic/Latino; 766 Hispanic/Latino; 62 Native Hawaiian or other Pacific Islander, non-Hispanic/Latino; 283 Two or more races, non-Hispanic/Latino), 101 international. Average age 37. In 2017, 2,977 master's awarded. *Degree requirements:* For master's, comprehensive exam or practicum. *Entrance requirements:* For master's, official transcript showing earned bachelor's degree from institution accredited by recognized accrediting body. Additional exam requirements/recommendations for international students: Required—TOEFL (minimum score 550 paper-based), IELTS (minimum score 6.5). *Application deadline:* Applications are processed on a rolling basis. Application fee: $0. Electronic applications accepted. *Expenses: Tuition:* Full-time $6300; part-time $350 per credit. *Required fees:* $300; $50 per course. *Financial support:* Scholarships/grants available. Financial award applicants required to submit FAFSA. *Unit head:* Dr. Wallace Boston, President, 877-468-6268, Fax: 304-728-2348, E-mail: president@apus.edu. *Application contact:* Yoci Deal, Associate Vice President, Graduate and International Admissions, 877-468-6268, Fax: 304-724-3764, E-mail: info@apus.edu.
Website: http://www.apus.edu

American University, School of International Service, Washington, DC 20016-8071. Offers comparative and regional studies (Certificate); cross-cultural communication (Certificate); development management (MS); ethics, peace, and global affairs (MA); European studies (Certificate); global environmental policy (MA, Certificate); global information technology (Certificate); global media (MA); international affairs (MA), including comparative and regional studies, global governance, politics, and security, international economic relations, natural resources and sustainable development, U.S. foreign policy and national security; international arts management (Certificate); international communication (MA, Certificate); international development (MA); international economic policy (Certificate); international economic relations (Certificate); international economics (MA); international peace and conflict resolution (MA, Certificate); international politics (Certificate); international relations (MA, PhD); international service (MIS); peacebuilding (Certificate); social enterprise (MA); the Americas (Certificate); United States foreign policy (Certificate); JD/MA. *Program availability:* Part-time, evening/weekend, 100% online. *Faculty:* 112 full-time (50 women), 46 part-time/adjunct (19 women). *Students:* 495 full-time (333 women), 518 part-time (276 women); includes 360 minority (95 Black or African American, non-Hispanic/Latino; 2 American Indian or Alaska Native, non-Hispanic/Latino; 60 Asian, non-Hispanic/Latino; 164 Hispanic/Latino; 39 Two or more races, non-Hispanic/Latino), 98 international. Average age 30. 1,559 applicants, 81% accepted, 356 enrolled. In 2017, 427 master's, 9 doctorates, 5 other advanced degrees awarded. Terminal master's awarded for partial completion of doctoral program. *Degree requirements:* For master's, one foreign language, comprehensive exam, thesis or alternative; for doctorate, one foreign language, comprehensive exam, thesis/dissertation. *Entrance requirements:* For master's, GRE; GMAT or GRE (for MA in social enterprise), transcripts, resume, 2 letters of recommendation, statement of purpose; for doctorate, GRE, transcripts, resume, 3 letters of recommendation, statement of purpose. Additional exam requirements/recommendations for international students: Required—TOEFL (minimum score 600 paper-based; 100 iBT). *Application deadline:* For fall admission, 1/15 for domestic students, 1/1 for international students; for spring admission, 10/1 for domestic students, 9/15 for international students. Application fee: $55. Electronic applications accepted. *Expenses:* Contact institution. *Financial support:* Research assistantships, teaching assistantships, institutionally sponsored loans, scholarships/grants, and unspecified assistantships available. Financial award application deadline: 1/15; financial award applicants required to submit FAFSA. *Application contact:* 202-885-1646, Fax: 202-885-1109, E-mail: sisgrad@american.edu.
Website: http://www.american.edu/sis/

The American University in Cairo, School of Global Affairs and Public Policy, Cairo, Egypt. Offers gender and women's studies (MA); global affairs (MGA); international and comparative law (LL M); international human rights law (MA); journalism and mass communication (MA); Middle East studies (MA); migration and refugee studies (MA, Diploma); public administration (MPA); public policy (MPP); television and digital journalism (MA). *Program availability:* Part-time, evening/weekend. *Faculty:* 26 full-time (11 women), 4 part-time/adjunct (3 women). *Students:* 65 full-time (50 women), 201 part-time (136 women), 39 international. Average age 29. 357 applicants, 51% accepted, 72 enrolled. In 2017, 94 master's awarded. *Degree requirements:* For master's, comprehensive exam (for some programs), thesis (for some programs). *Entrance requirements:* Additional exam requirements/recommendations for international students: Required—TOEFL (minimum score 450 paper-based; 45 iBT), IELTS (minimum score 5). *Application deadline:* For fall admission, 2/1 for domestic and international students; for spring admission, 10/15 for domestic and international students. Applications are processed on a rolling basis. Application fee: $85. Electronic applications accepted. *Expenses:* Contact institution. *Financial support:* Fellowships with partial tuition reimbursements, scholarships/grants, and unspecified assistantships available. Financial award application deadline: 3/10. *Faculty research:* Law, media and journalism; public policy and public administration; gender studies; Middle East Studies; global affairs; refugees studies. *Unit head:* Dr. Nabil Fahmy, Dean, 20-2-2615-2671, E-mail: nfahmy@aucegypt.edu. *Application contact:* Maha Hegazi, Director for Graduate Admissions, 20-2-2615-1462, E-mail: mahahegazi@aucegypt.edu.
Website: http://www.aucegypt.edu/GAPP/Pages/default.aspx

American University of Armenia, Graduate Programs, Yerevan, Armenia. Offers business administration (MBA); computer and information science (MS), including business management, design and manufacturing, energy (ME, MS), industrial engineering and systems management; economics (MS); industrial engineering and systems management (ME), including business, computer aided design/manufacturing, energy (ME, MS), information technology; law (LL M); political science and international affairs (MPSIA); public health (MPH); teaching English as a foreign language (MA). *Program availability:* Part-time, evening/weekend. *Degree requirements:* For master's, thesis (for some programs), capstone/project. *Entrance requirements:* For master's, GRE, GMAT, or LSAT. Additional exam requirements/recommendations for international students: Recommended—TOEFL (minimum score 79 iBT), IELTS (minimum score 6.5). *Faculty research:* Microfinance, finance (rural/development, international, corporate), firm life cycle theory, TESOL, language proficiency testing, public policy, administrative law, economic development, cryptography, artificial intelligence, energy efficiency/renewable energy, computer-aided design/manufacturing, health financing, tuberculosis control, mother/child health, preventive ophthalmology, post-earthquake psychopathological investigations, tobacco control, environmental health risk assessments.

American University of Beirut, Graduate Programs, Faculty of Arts and Sciences, 1107 2020, Lebanon. Offers anthropology (MA); Arab and Middle Eastern history (PhD); Arabic language and literature (MA, PhD); archaeology (MA); art history and curating (MA); biology (MS); cell and molecular biology (PhD); chemistry (MS); clinical psychology (MA); computational sciences (MS); computer science (MS); economics (MA); education (MA), including administration and policy studies, elementary education, mathematics education, psychology school guidance, psychology test and measurements, science education, teaching English as a foreign language; English language (MA); English literature (MA); environmental policy planning (MS); financial economics (MAFE); general psychology (MA); geology (MS); history (MA); Islamic studies (MA); mathematics (MS); media studies (MA); Middle East studies (MA); philosophy (MA); physics (MS); political studies (MA); public administration (MA); public policy and international affairs (MA); sociology (MA); theoretical physics (PhD). *Program availability:* Part-time. *Faculty:* 108 full-time (36 women), 5 part-time/adjunct (4 women). *Students:* 251 full-time (180 women), 233 part-time (172 women). Average age 26. 425 applicants, 65% accepted, 121 enrolled. In 2017, 47 master's, 2 doctorates awarded. *Degree requirements:* For master's, one foreign language, comprehensive exam, thesis (for some programs), project; for doctorate, one foreign language, comprehensive exam, thesis/dissertation. *Entrance requirements:* For master's, GRE General Test (for some programs); for doctorate, GRE General Test (GRE Subject Test for theoretical physics). Additional exam requirements/recommendations for international students: Required—TOEFL (minimum score 583 paper-based; 97 iBT), IELTS (minimum score 7). *Application deadline:* For fall admission, 2/8 for domestic students; for spring admission, 11/3 for domestic students. Application fee: $50. Electronic applications accepted. *Expenses:* Contact institution. *Financial support:* In 2017–18, 29 fellowships, 40 research assistantships were awarded; teaching assistantships, scholarships/grants, tuition waivers (full and partial), and unspecified assistantships also available. Financial award application deadline: 4/4. *Unit head:* Dr. Nadia Maria El Cheikh, Dean, Faculty of Arts and Sciences, 961-1-374374 Ext. 3800, Fax: 961-1-744461, E-mail: nmcheikh@aub.edu.lb. *Application contact:* Rima Rassi, Graduate Studies Officer, 961-1-350000 Ext. 3833, Fax: 961-1-744461, E-mail: rr46@aub.edu.lb.
Website: http://www.aub.edu.lb/fas/pages/default.aspx

The American University of Paris, Graduate Programs, Paris, France. Offers cross-cultural and sustainable business management (MA); cultural translation (MA); global communications (MA); global communications and civil society (MA); international affairs (MA); international affairs, conflict resolution and civil society development (MA); Middle East and Islamic studies (MA); Middle East and Islamic studies and international affairs (MA); public policy and international affairs (MA); public policy and international law (MA). *Degree requirements:* For master's, thesis (for some programs). *Entrance requirements:* For master's, minimum undergraduate GPA of 3.0. Additional exam requirements/recommendations for international students: Recommended—TOEFL, IELTS. Electronic applications accepted.

Anabaptist Mennonite Biblical Seminary, Graduate and Professional Programs, Elkhart, IN 46517-1999. Offers chaplaincy (M Div); Christian faith formation (M Div); Christian formation (MA); Christian spiritual formation (Certificate); divinity (M Div); pastoral ministry (M Div); pastoral theology for financial professionals (Certificate); peace studies (M Div), including environmental sustainability leadership (M Div, MA); theological studies (M Div, Certificate), including peace studies (M Div), theology and ethics (M Div); theology and peace studies (MA), including conflict transformation, environmental sustainability leadership (M Div, MA), international development administration; United Methodist leadership (M Div). Conflict transformation and environmental sustainability leadership concentrations offered in cooperation with Goshen College; international development administration offered in cooperation with Andrews University. *Accreditation:* ACIPE; ATS. *Program availability:* Part-time, 100% online, blended/hybrid learning. *Degree requirements:* For master's, variable foreign language requirement, comprehensive exam (for some programs), thesis optional, senior interview. *Entrance requirements:* For master's, undergraduate degree transcripts, 3 letters of reference, essay. Additional exam requirements/recommendations for international students: Required—TOEFL (minimum score 90 iBT); Recommended—IELTS (minimum score 7). Electronic applications accepted. *Faculty research:* Biblical studies, peace studies, theology, ethics, creation care or environmental ethics, church history, church leadership, mission, ministry, preaching, pastoral leadership, social justice, peacemaking, Jesus Christ, Christianity, Anabaptism, Mennonite, Scripture, Bible, Old Testament, New Testament, spirituality, clinical pastoral education, teaching, faith formation, pastoral care, Koine Greek, Hebrew, Aramaic, Syriac, Ugaritic.

Arcadia University, College of Arts and Sciences, Program in International Public Relations, Glenside, PA 19038-3295. Offers MA. *Degree requirements:* For master's, thesis, internship. *Expenses:* Contact institution.

★ **Baruch College of the City University of New York,** Austin W. Marxe School of Public and International Affairs, Program in International Affairs, New York, NY 10010-5585. Offers international nongovernmental organizations (MIA); trade policy and global economic governance (MIA); Western Hemisphere affairs (MIA). *Program availability:* Part-time.

See Display on page 912 and Close-Up on page 955.

Baylor University, Graduate School, College of Arts and Sciences, Department of Political Science, Waco, TX 76798. Offers international studies (MA); political science (MA, PhD); public policy and administration (MPPA); JD/MPPA. *Faculty:* 19 full-time (3 women), 1 part-time/adjunct (0 women). *Students:* 28 full-time (14 women); includes 1 minority (Hispanic/Latino). Average age 26. 27 applicants, 22% accepted, 4 enrolled. In 2017, 4 master's, 5 doctorates awarded. Terminal master's awarded for partial

completion of doctoral program. *Degree requirements:* For master's, variable foreign language requirement, comprehensive exam (for some programs), thesis (for some programs); for doctorate, variable foreign language requirement, comprehensive exam, thesis/dissertation. *Entrance requirements:* For master's and doctorate, GRE General Test. Additional exam requirements/recommendations for international students: Required—TOEFL. *Application deadline:* For fall admission, 12/20 for domestic and international students. Application fee: $50. Electronic applications accepted. *Financial support:* In 2017–18, 26 students received support, including 26 research assistantships with full tuition reimbursements available (averaging $16,000 per year); career-related internships or fieldwork, Federal Work-Study, and institutionally sponsored loans also available. Financial award application deadline: 12/20; financial award applicants required to submit FAFSA. *Unit head:* Dr. Timothy Burns, Graduate Program Director, 254-710-6237, Fax: 254-710-3122, E-mail: timothy_burns@baylor.edu. *Application contact:* Jenice Langston, Office Manager, 254-710-3161, Fax: 254-710-3122, E-mail: jenice_langston@baylor.edu. Website: http://www.baylor.edu/political_science/

Baylor University, Graduate School, Hankamer School of Business, Department of Economics, Waco, TX 76798. Offers MS Eco. *Students:* 12 full-time (7 women), 1 part-time (0 women); includes 1 minority (Asian, non-Hispanic/Latino), 5 international. In 2017, 7 master's awarded. *Entrance requirements:* For master's, GMAT or GRE General Test. Additional exam requirements/recommendations for international students: Required—TOEFL (minimum score 600 paper-based; 100 iBT), IELTS (minimum score 7). Application fee: $25. Electronic applications accepted. *Financial support:* In 2017–18, 12 students received support. Research assistantships, Federal Work-Study, and institutionally sponsored loans available. Financial award application deadline: 3/1. *Faculty research:* Econometrics, international economics, economic development, comparative economic systems, computational economics, health economics, economics of education, monetary economics, labor economics, experimental economics. *Unit head:* Dr. Van Pham, Graduate Program Director, 254-710-3521, Fax: 254-710-6142, E-mail: van_pham@baylor.edu. *Application contact:* Susan Armstrong, Office Manager, 254-710-6177, Fax: 254-710-6142, E-mail: susan_armstrong@baylor.edu. Website: http://www.baylor.edu/business/economics/

⭐ **Boston University,** Graduate School of Arts and Sciences, Frederick S. Pardee School of Global Studies, Boston, MA 02215. Offers global policy (MA); international affairs (MA); international relations (MA); Latin American studies (MA); MA/JD; MBA/MA. *Faculty:* 33 full-time (8 women), 10 part-time/adjunct (4 women). *Students:* 100 full-time (62 women), 10 part-time (4 women); includes 17 minority (5 Black or African American, non-Hispanic/Latino; 6 Asian, non-Hispanic/Latino; 5 Hispanic/Latino; 1 Two or more races, non-Hispanic/Latino), 45 international. Average age 25. 377 applicants, 79% accepted, 41 enrolled. In 2017, 31 master's awarded. *Degree requirements:* For master's, one foreign language, thesis (for some programs), capstone. *Entrance requirements:* For master's, GRE General Test, 3 letters of recommendation, transcript of all prior college coursework, personal statement, resume or curriculum vitae (recommended). Additional exam requirements/recommendations for international students: Required—TOEFL (minimum score 550 paper-based; 84 iBT). *Application deadline:* For fall admission, 1/15 priority date for domestic and international students; for spring admission, 12/15 for domestic and international students. Applications are processed on a rolling basis. Application fee: $95. Electronic applications accepted. *Financial support:* In 2017–18, 55 students received support. Federal Work-Study, scholarships/grants, and unspecified assistantships available. Financial award application deadline: 1/15. *Faculty research:* International relations, area studies, political economy, global development policy, global climate. *Unit head:* Adil Najam, Dean, 617-358-0988, Fax: 617-353-9290, E-mail:

anajam@bu.edu. *Application contact:* Holly Chase, Graduate Affairs Manager, 617-358-8625, Fax: 617-353-9290, E-mail: psgsgrad@bu.edu.
Website: http://www.bu.edu/PardeeSchool

See Display below and Close-Up on page 957.

Brandeis University, Graduate School of Arts and Sciences, Program in Global Studies, Waltham, MA 02454-9110. Offers MA. *Program availability:* Part-time. *Faculty:* 12 full-time (4 women), 2 part-time/adjunct (both women). *Students:* 8 full-time (6 women), 3 part-time (all women); includes 3 minority (1 Black or African American, non-Hispanic/Latino; 1 Hispanic/Latino; 1 Two or more races, non-Hispanic/Latino), 4 international. Average age 26. 19 applicants, 74% accepted, 6 enrolled. In 2017, 6 master's awarded. *Degree requirements:* For master's, one foreign language, thesis. *Entrance requirements:* For master's, GRE General Test, transcripts, recommendation letters, resume, statement of purpose, written work. Additional exam requirements/recommendations for international students: Required—PTE (minimum score 68), TOEFL (minimum score 600 paper-based, 100 iBT) or IELTS (7). *Application deadline:* For fall admission, 5/1 priority date for domestic students. Applications are processed on a rolling basis. Application fee: $75. Electronic applications accepted. *Expenses: Tuition:* Full-time $48,720. *Required fees:* $88. Tuition and fees vary according to course load, degree level, program and student level. *Financial support:* In 2017–18, 11 students received support, including 9 teaching assistantships with partial tuition reimbursements available (averaging $3,200 per year); Federal Work-Study, scholarships/grants, and tuition waivers (partial) also available. Support available to part-time students. Financial award application deadline: 4/15; financial award applicants required to submit FAFSA. *Faculty research:* Globalization; global service: preparing for work with non-profits; emerging powers; transnational security and migration. *Unit head:* Dr. Kristen Lucken, Director of Graduate Studies, 781-736-2743, E-mail: klucken@brandeis.edu. *Application contact:* Mangok Bol, Department Administrator, 781-736-5900, E-mail: mbol@brandeis.edu.
Website: http://www.brandeis.edu/gsas/programs/global_studies.html

Brigham Young University, Graduate Studies, BYU Marriott School of Business, MBA Program, Provo, UT 84602. Offers entrepreneurship (MBA); finance (MBA); global supply chain management (MBA); marketing (MBA); strategic human resources (MBA); JD/MBA; MBA/MS. *Accreditation:* AACSB. *Faculty:* 134 full-time (15 women), 65 part-time/adjunct (16 women). *Students:* 303 full-time (65 women); includes 26 minority (3 American Indian or Alaska Native, non-Hispanic/Latino; 8 Asian, non-Hispanic/Latino; 11 Hispanic/Latino; 4 Native Hawaiian or other Pacific Islander, non-Hispanic/Latino), 58 international. Average age 30. 339 applicants, 52% accepted, 136 enrolled. In 2017, 163 master's awarded. *Entrance requirements:* For master's, GMAT or GRE, commitment to BYU Honor Code, undergraduate degree. Additional exam requirements/recommendations for international students: Required—TOEFL (minimum score 590 paper-based; 100 iBT), IELTS (minimum score 7). *Application deadline:* For fall admission, 5/1 for domestic students, 3/1 for international students. Applications are processed on a rolling basis. Application fee: $50. Electronic applications accepted. *Expenses:* Contact institution. *Financial support:* Research assistantships, teaching assistantships, career-related internships or fieldwork, institutionally sponsored loans, and scholarships/grants available. Financial award application deadline: 3/1; financial award applicants required to submit FAFSA. *Faculty research:* Finance, marketing, supply chain management, entrepreneurship, strategic human resources. *Unit head:* Dr. Grant McQueen, Director, 801-422-3500, E-mail: mba@byu.edu. *Application contact:* Yvette Anderson, MBA Program Admissions Director, 801-422-3500, Fax: 801-422-0513, E-mail: mba@byu.edu.
Website: http://mba.byu.edu

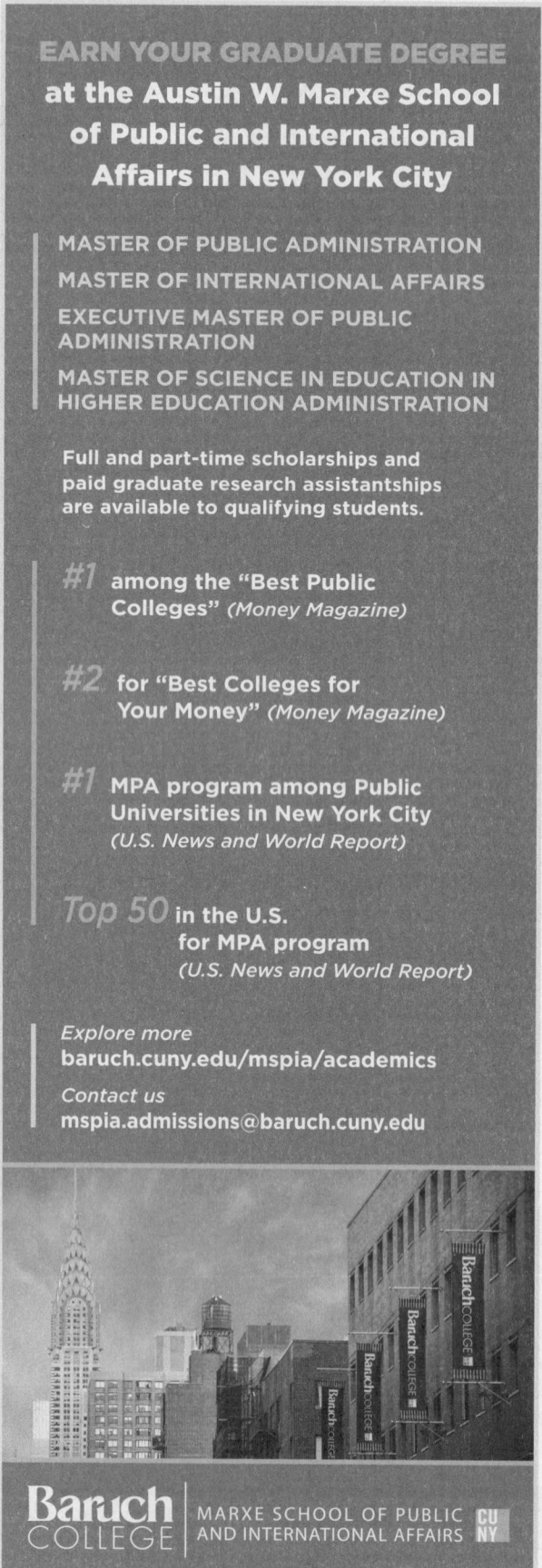

Brock University, Faculty of Graduate Studies, Faculty of Social Sciences, Program in Political Science, St. Catharines, ON L2S 3A1, Canada. Offers Canadian politics (MA); comparative politics (MA); international relations (MA); political theory or philosophy (MA); public policy (MA). *Program availability:* Part-time. *Degree requirements:* For master's, thesis optional. *Entrance requirements:* For master's, honors degree. Additional exam requirements/recommendations for international students: Required—TOEFL (minimum score 550 paper-based; 80 iBT), IELTS (minimum score 6.5), TWE (minimum score 4). Electronic applications accepted. *Faculty research:* Public administration reform, economic and social justice, politics of societies, Canadian politics, international relations.

Brooklyn College of the City University of New York, School of Humanities and Social Sciences, Department of Political Science, Brooklyn, NY 11210-2889. Offers international affairs (MA); political science (MA); urban policy and administration (MA). *Program availability:* Part-time, evening/weekend. *Degree requirements:* For master's, comprehensive exam (for some programs), thesis or alternative, foreign language exam (for international affairs program). *Entrance requirements:* For master's, 2 letters of recommendation, personal statement. Additional exam requirements/recommendations for international students: Required—TOEFL (minimum score 500 paper-based; 61 iBT). *Faculty research:* Ethics and politics, politics of criminal justice, Western Europe, international law and politics, labor politics.

Carleton University, Faculty of Graduate Studies, Faculty of Public Affairs and Management, Norman Paterson School of International Affairs, Ottawa, ON K1S 5B6, Canada. Offers MA, PhD. *Program availability:* Part-time. *Degree requirements:* For master's, one foreign language, comprehensive exam, thesis optional. *Entrance requirements:* For master's, honors degree. Additional exam requirements/recommendations for international students: Required—TOEFL. *Faculty research:* International conflict, development, political economy, conflict analysis.

The Catholic University of America, School of Arts and Sciences, Department of Politics, Washington, DC 20064. Offers American government (MA, PhD); Congressional and Presidential studies (MA); international affairs (MA); international political economics (MA); political theory (MA, PhD); world politics (MA, PhD); MA/JD. MA/JD offered jointly with Columbus School of Law. *Program availability:* Part-time. *Faculty:* 13 full-time (2 women), 6 part-time/adjunct (1 woman). *Students:* 18 full-time (5 women), 42 part-time (9 women); includes 12 minority (3 Black or African American, non-Hispanic/Latino; 2 Asian, non-Hispanic/Latino; 5 Hispanic/Latino; 2 Two or more races, non-Hispanic/Latino), 12 international. Average age 32. 50 applicants, 58% accepted, 8 enrolled. In 2017, 13 master's, 4 doctorates awarded. *Degree requirements:* For master's, one foreign language, comprehensive exam, thesis or alternative; for doctorate, variable foreign language requirement, comprehensive exam, thesis/dissertation. *Entrance requirements:* For master's, GRE General Test, statement of purpose, official copies of academic transcripts, three letters of recommendation, minimum GPA of 3.0; for doctorate, GRE General Test, statement of purpose, official copies of academic transcripts, three letters of recommendation. Additional exam requirements/recommendations for international students: Required—TOEFL (minimum score 550 paper-based; 80 iBT). *Application deadline:* For fall admission, 7/15 priority date for domestic students, 7/1 for international students; for spring admission, 11/15 priority date for domestic students, 11/1 for international students. Applications are processed on a rolling basis. Application fee: $55. Electronic applications accepted. *Expenses:* Contact institution. *Financial support:* Fellowships, research assistantships, teaching assistantships, Federal Work-Study, scholarships/grants, tuition waivers (full and partial), and unspecified assistantships available. Financial award application deadline: 2/1; financial award applicants required to submit FAFSA. *Faculty research:* Political philosophy, American political institutions and processes, political economy, international relations, U.S. political leadership since 1789. *Unit head:* Dr. Dennis Coyle, Chair, 202-319-5813, Fax: 202-319-6289, E-mail: coyle@cua.edu. *Application contact:* Dr. Steven Brown, Director of Graduate Admissions, 202-319-5057, Fax: 202-319-6533, E-mail: cua-admissions@cua.edu.
Website: http://politics.cua.edu/

Central Connecticut State University, School of Graduate Studies, College of Liberal Arts and Social Sciences, Program in International Studies, New Britain, CT 06050-4010. Offers MS. *Program availability:* Part-time, evening/weekend. *Faculty:* 6 full-time (3 women). *Students:* 12 full-time (4 women), 17 part-time (9 women); includes 7 minority (3 Black or African American, non-Hispanic/Latino; 4 Hispanic/Latino). Average age 34. 18 applicants, 83% accepted, 11 enrolled. In 2017, 9 master's awarded. *Degree requirements:* For master's, thesis or alternative, special project. *Entrance requirements:* For master's, minimum undergraduate GPA of 3.0, essay, resume. Additional exam requirements/recommendations for international students: Required—TOEFL (minimum score 550 paper-based; 79 iBT); Recommended—IELTS (minimum score 6.5). *Application deadline:* For fall admission, 5/1 for domestic and international students; for spring admission, 11/1 for domestic and international students. Applications are processed on a rolling basis. Application fee: $50. Electronic applications accepted. *Expenses: Tuition, area resident:* Full-time $6757. *Tuition, state resident:* full-time $9750; part-time $374 per credit. *Tuition, nonresident:* full-time $18,102; part-time $374 per credit. *Required fees:* $4635; $255 per credit. *Financial support:* In 2017–18, 6 students received support. Career-related internships or fieldwork, Federal Work-Study, scholarships/grants, and unspecified assistantships available. Support available to part-time students. Financial award application deadline: 3/1; financial award applicants required to submit FAFSA. *Unit head:* Dr. Paul Petterson, Program Director, 860-832-2969, E-mail: pettersonp@ccsu.edu. *Application contact:* Patricia Gardner, Associate Director of Graduate Studies, 860-832-2350, Fax: 860-832-2362.
Website: http://www.ccsu.edu/internationalstudies/

Central European University, Department of International Relations, 1051, Hungary. Offers global economic relations (MA); international relations (MA, PhD). *Faculty:* 10 full-time (2 women), 4 part-time/adjunct (2 women). *Students:* 96 full-time (49 women), 3 part-time (1 woman). Average age 27. 575 applicants, 23% accepted, 67 enrolled. In 2017, 31 master's, 6 doctorates awarded. *Degree requirements:* For master's, one foreign language, thesis; for doctorate, one foreign language, comprehensive exam, thesis/dissertation. *Entrance requirements:* For master's, 500-word essay, statement of purpose; for doctorate, interview. Additional exam requirements/recommendations for international students: Required—TOEFL (minimum score 570 paper-based); Recommended—IELTS (minimum score 6.5). *Application deadline:* For fall admission, 2/4 for domestic and international students. Application fee: $30. Electronic applications accepted. *Expenses: Tuition:* Full-time 12,000 euros. *Required fees:* 230 euros. One-time fee: 30 euros full-time. Tuition and fees vary according to course level, course load, degree level and program. *Financial support:* In 2017–18, 71 students received support. Fellowships, career-related internships or fieldwork, scholarships/grants, health care benefits, and tuition waivers (full and partial) available. *Faculty research:* International relations theory, in both its traditional and critical forms, and to the two major sub-disciplines of security studies and international political economy, forms the foundation of the program, complemented by a multi-disciplinary approach to the study of the EU and its role as a global actor. *Unit head:* Alexander Astrov, Head of Department, 36 1 327-3243 Ext. 2219, E-mail: ir@ceu.edu. *Application contact:* Zsuzsanna Jaszberenyi,

Admissions Officer, 361-324-3009, Fax: 367-327-3211, E-mail: admissions@ceu.edu.
Website: http://ir.ceu.edu/

Central Michigan University, Central Michigan University Global Campus, Program in Administration, Mount Pleasant, MI 48859. Offers acquisitions administration (MSA, Certificate); engineering management administration (MSA, Certificate); general administration (MSA, Certificate); health services administration (MSA, Certificate); human resources administration (MSA, Certificate); information resource management (MSA); information resource management administration (Certificate); international administration (MSA, Certificate); leadership (MSA, Certificate); philanthropy and fundraising administration (MSA, Certificate); public administration (MSA, Certificate); recreation and park administration (MSA); research administration (MSA, Certificate). *Program availability:* Part-time, evening/weekend, online learning. *Entrance requirements:* For master's, minimum GPA of 2.7 in major. Electronic applications accepted.

Chapman University, Wilkinson College of Arts, Humanities, and Social Sciences, International Studies Program, Orange, CA 92866. Offers MA. *Program availability:* Part-time, evening/weekend. *Faculty:* 3 full-time (1 woman). *Students:* 12 full-time (6 women), 1 (woman) part-time; includes 4 minority (1 Black or African American, non-Hispanic/Latino; 1 Asian, non-Hispanic/Latino; 2 Hispanic/Latino), 2 international. Average age 28. 14 applicants, 71% accepted, 4 enrolled. In 2017, 3 master's awarded. *Degree requirements:* For master's, thesis. *Entrance requirements:* For master's, GRE (if undergraduate GPA less than 3.0), minimum undergraduate GPA of 2.5. *Application deadline:* For fall admission, 2/1 priority date for domestic students. Applications are processed on a rolling basis. Application fee: $60. Electronic applications accepted. *Expenses:* Contact institution. *Financial support:* Fellowships, Federal Work-Study, scholarships/grants, and unspecified assistantships available. Financial award applicants required to submit FAFSA. *Unit head:* Dr. Lynn Horton, Director, 714-997-6976, E-mail: horton@chapman.edu.
Website: https://www.chapman.edu/wilkinson/graduate-studies/ma-international-studies/index.aspx

City College of the City University of New York, Graduate School, Colin Powell School for Civic and Global Leadership, Program in International Relations, New York, NY 10031-9198. Offers MA. *Program availability:* Part-time. *Degree requirements:* For master's, one foreign language, thesis. *Entrance requirements:* For master's, GRE, 3 letters of recommendation. Additional exam requirements/recommendations for international students: Required—TOEFL (minimum score 600 paper-based; 100 iBT). Electronic applications accepted. *Faculty research:* International finance, international economics, European diplomatic history, area studies, international politics and diplomacy.

Claremont Graduate University, Graduate Programs, School of Social Science, Policy and Evaluation, Department of Politics and Policy, Claremont, CA 91711-6160. Offers American politics (MA, PhD); comparative politics (PhD); international political economy (MA); international studies (MA); political philosophy (PhD); political science (PhD); politics, economics and business (MA); public policy (MA, PhD); world politics (PhD); MBA/PhD. *Program availability:* Part-time. Terminal master's awarded for partial completion of doctoral program. *Entrance requirements:* For master's and doctorate, GRE General Test. Additional exam requirements/recommendations for international students: Required—TOEFL (minimum score 75 iBT). Electronic applications accepted. *Faculty research:* Environmental policy, international debt, global democratization, Third World development, public sector discrimination.

Cleveland State University, College of Graduate Studies, College of Liberal Arts and Social Sciences, Department of Political Science, Cleveland, OH 44115. Offers global interactions (MA), including global business interactions, global political interactions. *Faculty:* 3 full-time (1 woman). *Students:* 15 full-time (10 women), 6 part-time (1 woman); includes 8 minority (5 Black or African American, non-Hispanic/Latino; 3 Two or more races, non-Hispanic/Latino), 4 international. Average age 26. 33 applicants, 100% accepted, 5 enrolled. In 2017, 11 master's awarded. *Entrance requirements:* For master's, minimum undergraduate GPA of 3.0 or GRE (50th percentile or above); two letters of recommendation; undergraduate degree in economics, political science, international relations, or a related discipline; completion of undergraduate macro and micro economics course. Additional exam requirements/recommendations for international students: Required—TOEFL (minimum score 550 paper-based; 78 iBT). *Application deadline:* Applications are processed on a rolling basis. Application fee: $40. Electronic applications accepted. *Expenses:* Contact institution. *Financial support:* Research assistantships, tuition waivers (full), and unspecified assistantships available. Financial award applicants required to submit FAFSA. *Faculty research:* International political economy, globalization, new regionalism, European integration, adaptation to climate change. *Unit head:* Dr. Rodger M. Govea, Associate Professor/Chairperson, 216-687-4554, E-mail: r.govea@csuohio.edu. *Application contact:* Janice McCowan, Public Inquiries Assistant, 216-523-7473, Fax: 216-687-9210, E-mail: j.c.mccowan@csuohio.edu.
Website: http://www.csuohio.edu/class/politicalscience/

Columbia University, Graduate School of Arts and Sciences, New York, NY 10027. Offers African-American studies (MA); American studies (MA); anthropology (MA, PhD); art history and archaeology (MA, PhD); astronomy (PhD); biological sciences (PhD); biotechnology (MA); chemical physics (PhD); chemistry (PhD); classical studies (MA, PhD); classics (MA, PhD); climate and society (MA); conservation biology (MA); earth and environmental sciences (PhD); East Asia: regional studies (MA); East Asian languages and cultures (MA, PhD); ecology, evolution and environmental biology (MA), including conservation biology; ecology, evolution, and environmental biology (PhD), including ecology and evolutionary biology, evolutionary primatology; economics (MA, PhD); English and comparative literature (MA, PhD); French and Romance philology (MA, PhD); Germanic languages (MA, PhD); global French studies (MA); global thought (MA); Hispanic cultural studies (MA); history (PhD); history and literature (MA); human rights studies (MA); Islamic studies (MA); Italian (MA, PhD); Japanese pedagogy (MA); Jewish studies (MA); Latin America and the Caribbean: regional studies (MA); Latin American and Iberian cultures (PhD); mathematics (MA, PhD), including finance (MA); medieval and Renaissance studies (MA); Middle Eastern, South Asian, and African studies (MA, PhD); modern art: critical and curatorial studies (MA); modern European studies (MA); museum anthropology (MA); music (DMA, PhD); oral history (MA); philosophical foundations of physics (MA); philosophy (MA, PhD); physics (PhD); political science (MA, PhD); psychology (PhD); quantitative methods in the social sciences (MA); religion (MA, PhD); Russia, Eurasia and East Europe: regional studies (MA); Russian translation (MA); Slavic cultures (MA); Slavic languages (MA, PhD); sociology (MA, PhD); South Asian studies (MA); statistics (MA, PhD); theatre (PhD). Dual-degree programs require admission to both Graduate School of Arts and Sciences and another Columbia school. *Program availability:* Part-time. Terminal master's awarded for partial completion of doctoral program. *Degree requirements:* For master's, variable foreign language requirement, comprehensive exam (for some programs), thesis (for some programs); for doctorate, variable foreign language requirement, comprehensive exam (for some programs), thesis/dissertation. *Entrance requirements:* For master's and doctorate, GRE General Test, GRE Subject Test (for some programs). Additional exam requirements/recommendations for international students: Required—TOEFL, IELTS. Electronic applications accepted. *Expenses: Tuition:* Full-time $44,864; part-time $1704 per credit. *Required fees:* $2370 per semester. One-time fee: $105.

Columbia University, School of International and Public Affairs, Program in International Affairs, New York, NY 10027. Offers MIA, JD/MIA, MBA/MIA, MIA/MS, MPH/MIA, MSJ/MIA. *Degree requirements:* For master's, one foreign language, comprehensive exam. *Entrance requirements:* For master's, GRE General Test. Additional exam requirements/recommendations for international students: Required—TOEFL (minimum score 600 paper-based; 100 iBT), IELTS (minimum score 7), PTE (minimum score 68). Electronic applications accepted. *Expenses: Tuition:* Full-time $44,864; part-time $1704 per credit. *Required fees:* $2370 per semester. One-time fee: $105.

★ **Concordia University Irvine,** School of Professional Studies, Irvine, CA 92612-3299. Offers healthcare administration (MHA); international studies (MAIS), including Africa, China; nursing (MSN).

See Display on the next page and Close-Up on page 959.

Cornell University, Graduate School, Graduate Fields of Arts and Sciences, Field of Government, Ithaca, NY 14853. Offers American politics (PhD); comparative politics (PhD); international relations (PhD); political methodology (PhD); political thought (PhD); public policy (PhD). *Degree requirements:* For doctorate, comprehensive exam, thesis/dissertation. *Entrance requirements:* For doctorate, GRE General Test, sample of written work, 3 letters of recommendation. Additional exam requirements/recommendations for international students: Required—TOEFL (minimum score 550 paper-based; 77 iBT). Electronic applications accepted. *Faculty research:* Political theory, American politics, comparative politics, international relations, methodology.

Dallas Baptist University, Gary Cook School of Leadership, Program in International Studies, Dallas, TX 75211-9299. Offers East Asian studies (MA); European studies (MA); general international studies (MA); global business (MA); international immersion (MA); international ministry (MA); international relations (MA). *Program availability:* Part-time, evening/weekend. *Application deadline:* Applications are processed on a rolling basis. Application fee: $25. Electronic applications accepted. Application fee is waived when completed online. *Expenses: Tuition:* Full-time $16,308; part-time $906 per credit hour. *Required fees:* $900; $450 per semester. Tuition and fees vary according to course load and degree level. *Unit head:* Dr. Jack Goodyear, Dean, 214-333-5595, Fax: 214-333-6809, E-mail: jackg@dbu.edu. *Application contact:* Lee Bratcher, Program Director, 214-333-5808, E-mail: leeb@dbu.edu.
Website: http://www4.dbu.edu/leadership/mainternational

DePaul University, College of Liberal Arts and Social Sciences, Chicago, IL 60614. Offers Arabic (MA); Chinese (MA); critical ethnic studies (MA); English (MA); French (MA); German (MA); history (MA); interdisciplinary studies (MA, MS); international public service (MS); international studies (MA); Italian (MA); Japanese (MA); liberal studies (MA); nonprofit management (MNM); public administration (MPA); public health (MPH); public policy (MPP); public service management (MS); refugee and forced migration studies (MS); social work (MSW); sociology (MA); Spanish (MA); sustainable urban development (MA); women's and gender studies (MA); writing and publishing (MA); writing, rhetoric and discourse (MA); MA/PhD. *Program availability:* Part-time, evening/weekend, online learning. Terminal master's awarded for partial completion of doctoral program. *Degree requirements:* For master's, variable foreign language requirement, comprehensive exam (for some programs), thesis (for some programs). *Application deadline:* Applications are processed on a rolling basis. Application fee: $40. Electronic applications accepted. *Financial support:* Applicants required to submit FAFSA. *Unit head:* Dr. Guillermo Vasquez de Velasco, Dean, 773-325-7305. *Application contact:* Ann Spittle, Director of Graduate Admission, 773-325-8369, Fax: 312-476-3244, E-mail: graddepaul@depaul.edu.
Website: http://las.depaul.edu/

East Carolina University, Graduate School, Thomas Harriot College of Arts and Sciences, Program in International Studies, Greenville, NC 27858-4353. Offers international studies (MA); international teaching (Certificate). *Program availability:* Part-time. *Students:* 13 full-time (9 women), 3 part-time (1 woman); includes 5 minority (3 Black or African American, non-Hispanic/Latino; 2 Hispanic/Latino), 2 international. Average age 27. 8 applicants, 100% accepted, 7 enrolled. In 2017, 5 master's, 2 other advanced degrees awarded. *Degree requirements:* For master's, comprehensive exam, thesis optional, international field experience. *Entrance requirements:* For master's, GRE General Test, MAT or GMAT. Additional exam requirements/recommendations for international students: Recommended—TOEFL (minimum score 78 iBT), IELTS (minimum score 6.5). *Application deadline:* For fall admission, 7/1 priority date for domestic and international students; for spring admission, 11/15 priority date for domestic and international students; for summer admission, 3/15 priority date for domestic and international students. Applications are processed on a rolling basis. Application fee: $75. Electronic applications accepted. *Expenses:* Tuition, state resident: full-time $4749; part-time $297 per credit hour. Tuition, nonresident: full-time $17,898; part-time $1119 per credit hour. *Required fees:* $2691; $224 per credit hour. Part-time tuition and fees vary according to course load and program. *Financial support:* Research assistantships with partial tuition reimbursements available. Financial award application deadline: 3/1. *Unit head:* Dr. David L. Smith, Director, 252-328-5524, E-mail: smithdav@ecu.edu. *Application contact:* Dean of Graduate School, 252-328-6012, Fax: 252-328-6071, E-mail: gradschool@ecu.edu.
Website: http://www.ecu.edu/cs-cas/international/maisindex.cfm

Eastern University, Department of Global Studies and Mission, St. Davids, PA 19087-3696. Offers international development (MA); theological and cultural anthropology (MA). *Students:* 23 full-time (11 women), 26 part-time (15 women); includes 11 minority (8 Black or African American, non-Hispanic/Latino; 1 Asian, non-Hispanic/Latino; 2 Hispanic/Latino), 1 international. Average age 35. In 2017, 19 master's awarded. *Application deadline:* Applications are processed on a rolling basis. Application fee: $35. Electronic applications accepted. Application fee is waived when completed online. *Expenses:* Contact institution. *Unit head:* Michael Dziedziak, Executive Director of Enrollment, 800-452-0996, E-mail: gpsadmissions@eastern.edu.
Website: https://www.eastern.edu/academics/global-studies-mission

Embry-Riddle Aeronautical University–Worldwide, Department of Security and Emergency Services, Daytona Beach, FL 32114-3900. Offers cybersecurity management and policy (MSCMP); human security and resilience (MSHSR). *Program availability:* Part-time, evening/weekend, EagleVision Classroom (between classrooms), EagleVision Home (faculty and students at home), and a blend of Classroom or Home. *Faculty:* 3 full-time (0 women), 12 part-time/adjunct (4 women). *Students:* 53 full-time (19 women), 66 part-time (23 women); includes 51 minority (16 Black or African American, non-Hispanic/Latino; 8 Asian, non-Hispanic/Latino; 12 Hispanic/Latino; 15 Two or more races, non-Hispanic/Latino), 2 international. Average age 36. 58 applicants, 66% accepted, 34 enrolled. In 2017, 6 master's awarded. *Degree requirements:* For master's, capstone project (for MSHSR). *Entrance requirements:* Additional exam requirements/recommendations for international students: Required—TOEFL (minimum score 550 paper-based; 79 iBT), IELTS (minimum score 6). *Application deadline:* Applications are processed on a rolling basis. Application fee: $50. Electronic applications accepted. *Expenses: Tuition:* Full-time $7680; part-time $640 per

credit hour. Tuition and fees vary according to program. *Financial support:* Career-related internships or fieldwork and scholarships/grants available. Financial award applicants required to submit FAFSA. *Unit head:* Dr. Ronald Wakeham, Department Chair, E-mail: ronald.wakeham@erau.edu. *Application contact:* Worldwide Campus, 800-522-6787, E-mail: worldwide@erau.edu.
Website: http://worldwide.erau.edu/colleges/arts-sciences/department-emergency-services

Fairleigh Dickinson University, Metropolitan Campus, University College: Arts, Sciences, and Professional Studies, School of History, Political and International Studies, Program in International Studies, Teaneck, NJ 07666-1914. Offers MA.

Florida International University, Steven J. Green School of International and Public Affairs, Department of Politics and International Relations, Miami, FL 33199. Offers international relations (MA, PhD), including international relations (PhD), international studies (MA); political science (MA, PhD). PhD program has fall admissions only. *Program availability:* Part-time, evening/weekend. *Faculty:* 28 full-time (10 women), 31 part-time/adjunct (7 women). *Students:* 166 full-time (86 women), 29 part-time (9 women); includes 107 minority (13 Black or African American, non-Hispanic/Latino; 4 Asian, non-Hispanic/Latino; 86 Hispanic/Latino; 4 Two or more races, non-Hispanic/Latino), 49 international. Average age 29. 172 applicants, 62% accepted, 68 enrolled. In 2017, 39 master's, 19 doctorates awarded. *Degree requirements:* For master's, one foreign language, thesis optional; for doctorate, one foreign language, comprehensive exam, thesis/dissertation. *Entrance requirements:* For master's and doctorate, GRE General Test, minimum GPA of 3.0, letters of recommendation. Additional exam requirements/recommendations for international students: Required—TOEFL (minimum score 550 paper-based; 80 iBT). *Application deadline:* For fall admission, 3/15 for domestic and international students; for spring admission, 8/15 for domestic and international students. Application fee: $30. Electronic applications accepted. *Expenses:* Tuition, state resident: full-time $8912; part-time $446 per credit hour. Tuition, nonresident: full-time $21,393; part-time $992 per credit hour. *Required fees:* $390; $195 per semester. *Financial support:* Institutionally sponsored loans, scholarships/grants, and unspecified assistantships available. Financial award application deadline: 3/1; financial award applicants required to submit FAFSA. *Unit head:* Dr. John Clark, Chair, 305-348-2227, Fax: 305-348-3765, E-mail: john.clark@fiu.edu. *Application contact:* Nanett Rojas, Manager, Admissions Operations, 305-348-7464, E-mail: nanett.rojas@fiu.edu.
Website: http://pir.fiu.edu

Florida State University, The Graduate School, College of Social Sciences and Public Policy, Program in International Affairs, Tallahassee, FL 32306. Offers MA, MS, JD/MA, JD/MS. *Program availability:* Part-time. *Faculty:* 4 full-time (all women), 4 part-time/adjunct (0 women). *Students:* 37 full-time (9 women), 24 part-time (12 women); includes 24 minority (6 Black or African American, non-Hispanic/Latino; 12 Hispanic/Latino; 6 Two or more races, non-Hispanic/Latino), 8 international. Average age 27. 32 applicants, 97% accepted, 19 enrolled. In 2017, 25 master's awarded. *Degree requirements:* For master's, one foreign language, comprehensive exam, thesis optional. *Entrance requirements:* For master's, GRE General Test, minimum GPA of 3.0. Additional exam requirements/recommendations for international students: Required—TOEFL (minimum score 550 paper-based, 80 iBT) or IELTS (6.5). *Application deadline:* For fall admission, 7/1 for domestic and international students; for spring admission, 11/1 for domestic and international students; for summer admission, 3/1 for domestic and international students. Applications are processed on a rolling basis. Application fee: $30. Electronic applications accepted. *Expenses:* $479.32 in-state per credit hour; $1,110.72 out-of-state per credit hour. *Financial support:* In 2017–18, 7 students received support, including 5 research assistantships with full tuition reimbursements available (averaging $6,000 per year), 2 teaching assistantships with full tuition reimbursements available (averaging $6,000 per year); career-related internships or fieldwork, Federal Work-Study, institutionally sponsored loans, scholarships/grants, and unspecified assistantships also available. Financial award application deadline: 2/1; financial award applicants required to submit FAFSA. *Faculty research:* Deception in World War II. *Unit head:* Dr. Lee K. Metcalf, Director, 850-644-4418, Fax: 850-645-4981, E-mail: lmetcalf@fsu.edu. *Application contact:* Sabrina Smith, Academic Program Specialist, 850-644-4418, Fax: 850-645-4981, E-mail: ssmith9@fsu.edu.
Website: http://coss.fsu.edu/inaprog/programs/graduate/g-IA

Fordham University, Graduate School of Arts and Sciences, Program in International Political Economy and Development, New York, NY 10458. Offers MA, Certificate. *Program availability:* Part-time, evening/weekend. *Students:* 38 full-time (18 women), 8 part-time (2 women); includes 3 minority (1 Asian, non-Hispanic/Latino; 2 Hispanic/Latino), 15 international. Average age 27. 89 applicants, 60% accepted, 24 enrolled. In 2017, 24 master's, 1 other advanced degree awarded. *Degree requirements:* For master's, comprehensive exam. *Entrance requirements:* For master's, GRE General Test. Additional exam requirements/recommendations for international students: Required—TOEFL (minimum score 600 paper-based). *Application deadline:* For fall admission, 1/4 priority date for domestic students; for spring admission, 11/1 for domestic students. Application fee: $70. Electronic applications accepted. *Financial support:* In 2017–18, 35 students received support, including 4 fellowships with tuition reimbursements available (averaging $17,014 per year); research assistantships with tuition reimbursements available, career-related internships or fieldwork, institutionally sponsored loans, tuition waivers (full and partial), and unspecified assistantships also available. Financial award application deadline: 1/4; financial award applicants required to submit FAFSA. *Faculty research:* International economics, comparative international politics, international banking and finance, international development, emerging markets and country risk analysis. *Unit head:* Dr. Henry Schwalbenberg, Chair, 718-817-3866, Fax: 718-817-3518. *Application contact:* Bernadette Valentino-Morrison, Director of Graduate Admissions, 718-817-4419, Fax: 718-817-3566, E-mail: valentinomor@fordham.edu.

George Mason University, College of Humanities and Social Sciences, Program in Global Affairs, Fairfax, VA 22030. Offers MA. *Faculty:* 18 full-time (8 women), 5 part-time/adjunct (3 women). *Students:* 22 full-time (13 women), 19 part-time (14 women); includes 9 minority (1 Black or African American, non-Hispanic/Latino; 1 American Indian or Alaska Native, non-Hispanic/Latino; 3 Asian, non-Hispanic/Latino; 4 Hispanic/Latino), 2 international. Average age 29. 51 applicants, 90% accepted, 21 enrolled. In 2017, 33 master's awarded. *Degree requirements:* For master's, residency abroad (two weeks); capstone seminar. *Entrance requirements:* For master's, expanded goals statement, 2 letters of recommendation, writing sample, resume, official transcripts, evidence of professional competency in a second language tested through Language Testing International or other means approved by the department. Additional exam requirements/recommendations for international students: Required—TOEFL (minimum score 575 paper-based; 88 iBT), IELTS (minimum score 6.5), PTE (minimum score 59). *Application deadline:* For fall admission, 3/15 for domestic and international students; for spring admission, 10/15 for domestic and international students. Application fee: $75 ($80 for international students). Electronic applications accepted. *Expenses:* Tuition, state resident: full-time $11,228; part-time $459.50 per credit. Tuition, nonresident: full-time $30,932; part-time $1280.50 per credit. *Required fees:* $3252; $135.50 per credit. Part-time tuition and fees vary according to course load and program. *Financial support:* Career-related internships or fieldwork, Federal Work-Study, and scholarships/grants available. Financial award application deadline: 3/1; financial award applicants required to submit FAFSA. *Faculty research:* Social movements, globalization, law and economics, comparative politics, global environmentalism and governance, international business and economic development. *Unit head:* Lisa Breglia, Director, 703-993-9184,

Fax: 703-993-1244, E-mail: lbreglia@gmu.edu. *Application contact:* Stephanie Lister, Graduate Coordinator, 703-993-5056, Fax: 703-993-1244, E-mail: slister1@gmu.edu. Website: http://globalaffairs.gmu.edu

George Mason University, Schar School of Policy and Government, Program in International Commerce and Policy, Arlington, VA 22201. Offers MA. *Faculty:* 11 full-time (3 women), 6 part-time/adjunct (1 woman). *Students:* 41 full-time (23 women), 72 part-time (37 women); includes 45 minority (16 Black or African American, non-Hispanic/Latino; 14 Asian, non-Hispanic/Latino; 14 Hispanic/Latino; 1 Two or more races, non-Hispanic/Latino), 14 international. Average age 29. 61 applicants, 85% accepted, 34 enrolled. In 2017, 33 master's awarded. *Degree requirements:* For master's, thesis or alternative. *Entrance requirements:* For master's, GRE/GMAT (for students seeking merit-based scholarships), bachelor's degree with minimum GPA of 3.0; expanded goals statement; current resume; 2 official copies of transcripts; 2 letters of recommendation. Additional exam requirements/recommendations for international students: Required—TOEFL (minimum score 575 paper-based; 88 iBT), IELTS (minimum score 6.5), PTE (minimum score 59). *Application deadline:* For fall admission, 2/1 priority date for domestic and international students; for spring admission, 11/1 priority date for domestic and international students. Application fee: $75 ($80 for international students). Electronic applications accepted. *Expenses:* $795 per credit in-state tuition, $1,516 out-of-state. *Financial support:* Career-related internships or fieldwork, Federal Work-Study, and scholarships/grants available. Financial award application deadline: 3/1; financial award applicants required to submit FAFSA. *Faculty research:* Globalization and development; applied trade policy analysis; open-economy macroeconomics; development policy; international negotiations. *Unit head:* Kenneth Reinert, Director, 703-993-8212, Fax: 703-993-8215, E-mail: kreinert@gmu.edu. *Application contact:* Stephanie Ellis, Graduate Admissions Coordinator, 703-993-4478, E-mail: sellis11@gmu.edu.
Website: http://spgia.gmu.edu/programs/graduate-degrees/international-commerce-and-policy-icp/

Georgetown University, Graduate School of Arts and Sciences, School of Continuing Studies, Washington, DC 20057. Offers American studies (MALS); applied intelligence (MPS); Catholic studies (MALS); classical civilizations (MALS); emergency and disaster management (MPS); ethics and the professions (MALS); global strategic communications (MPS); hospitality management (MPS); human resources management (MPS); humanities (MALS); individualized study (MALS); integrated marketing communications (MPS); international affairs (MALS); Islam and Muslim-Christian relations (MALS); journalism (MPS); liberal studies (DLS); literature and society (MALS); medieval and early modern European studies (MALS); public relations and corporate communications (MPS); real estate (MPS); religious studies (MALS); social and public policy (MALS); sports industry management (MPS); systems engineering management (MPS); technology management (MPS); the theory and practice of American democracy (MALS); urban and regional planning (MPS); visual culture (MALS). MPS in systems engineering management offered jointly with Stevens Institute of Technology. *Entrance requirements:* Additional exam requirements/recommendations for international students: Required—TOEFL.

Georgetown University, Graduate School of Arts and Sciences, Walsh School of Foreign Service, BMW Center for German and European Studies, Washington, DC 20057. Offers MA, MA/JD, MA/PhD. *Degree requirements:* For master's, 2 foreign languages, comprehensive exam. *Entrance requirements:* For master's, GRE General Test. Additional exam requirements/recommendations for international students: Required—TOEFL. Electronic applications accepted. *Faculty research:* Transatlantic relations, European Union, German and European Studies.

Georgetown University, Graduate School of Arts and Sciences, Walsh School of Foreign Service, Master of Science in Foreign Service Program, Washington, DC 20057. Offers global business and finance (MS); global politics and security (MS); international development (MS); self-designed studies (MS); JD/MS; MA/MS; MBA/MS; MPP/MS. *Faculty:* 28 full-time (7 women), 41 part-time/adjunct (6 women). *Students:* 203 full-time (105 women); includes 42 minority (9 Black or African American, non-Hispanic/Latino; 1 American Indian or Alaska Native, non-Hispanic/Latino; 14 Asian, non-Hispanic/Latino; 11 Hispanic/Latino; 7 Two or more races, non-Hispanic/Latino), 53 international. Average age 27. 729 applicants. In 2017, 105 master's awarded. *Degree requirements:* For master's, one foreign language, comprehensive exam, internship. *Entrance requirements:* For master's, GRE General Test or GMAT (for students with undergraduate degree from English-speaking institution), one semester each of micro and macroeconomics with minimum B- grade; two to three years of experience with a second language besides native tongue. Additional exam requirements/recommendations for international students: Required—TOEFL (minimum score 100 iBT) or IELTS (minimum score 7). *Application deadline:* For fall admission, 1/15 for domestic and international students. Application fee: $90. Electronic applications accepted. *Expenses:* Contact institution. *Financial support:* In 2017–18, 87 students received support, including 4 research assistantships (averaging $5,000 per year), 4 teaching assistantships (averaging $5,000 per year); career-related internships or fieldwork, scholarships/grants, tuition waivers (partial), and unspecified assistantships also available. Financial award application deadline: 1/15. *Faculty research:* International business diplomacy, political risk analysis, science and technology, intercultural perspectives on contemporary issues. *Unit head:* Nancy McEldowney, Director, 202-687-5763. *Application contact:* MSFS Admissions, 202-687-5763, E-mail: msfsinfo@georgetown.edu.
Website: http://msfs.georgetown.edu/

Georgetown University, Law Center, Washington, DC 20001. Offers environmental law (LL M); global health law (LL M); global health law and international institutions (LL M); individualized study (LL M); international business and economic law (LL M); law (JD, SJD); national security law (LL M); securities and financial regulation (LL M); taxation (LL M); JD/LL M; JD/MA; JD/MBA; JD/MPH; JD/PhD. *Accreditation:* ABA. *Program availability:* Part-time, evening/weekend. *Degree requirements:* For master's, thesis; for doctorate, thesis/dissertation (for some programs). *Entrance requirements:* For master's, JD, LL B, or first law degree earned in country of origin; for doctorate, LSAT (for JD). Additional exam requirements/recommendations for international students: Required—TOEFL. *Expenses:* Contact institution. *Faculty research:* Constitutional law, legal history, jurisprudence.

The George Washington University, Elliott School of International Affairs, Program in International Affairs, Washington, DC 20052. Offers MA. *Program availability:* Part-time. *Faculty:* 72 full-time (23 women). *Students:* 213 full-time (149 women), 74 part-time (49 women); includes 84 minority (23 Black or African American, non-Hispanic/Latino; 19 Asian, non-Hispanic/Latino; 33 Hispanic/Latino; 9 Two or more races, non-Hispanic/Latino), 36 international. Average age 26. 620 applicants, 79% accepted, 126 enrolled. In 2017, 132 master's awarded. *Degree requirements:* For master's, one foreign language, capstone project. *Entrance requirements:* For master's, GRE General Test, 2 years of a modern foreign language, 2 semesters of introductory economics. Additional exam requirements/recommendations for international students: Required—TOEFL (minimum score 100 iBT), IELTS (minimum score 7). *Application deadline:* For fall admission, 1/15 priority date for domestic and international students; for spring admission, 10/1 for domestic students. Application fee: $75. Electronic applications

accepted. *Expenses: Tuition:* Full-time $28,800; part-time $1655 per credit hour. *Required fees:* $45; $2.75 per credit hour. *Financial support:* In 2017–18, 61 students received support. Fellowships with partial tuition reimbursements available and Federal Work-Study available. Financial award application deadline: 1/15; financial award applicants required to submit FAFSA. *Faculty research:* Area studies, international economics, national security policy studies, international economic development, Sino-Soviet studies. *Unit head:* Dr. Marcus King, Director, 202-994-0216, E-mail: mdking@gwu.edu. *Application contact:* Nicole A. Campbell, Director of Graduate Admissions, 202-994-7050, Fax: 202-994-9537, E-mail: esiagrad@gwu.edu.
Website: http://elliott.gwu.edu/international-affairs-masters

The George Washington University, Elliott School of International Affairs, Program in International Policy and Practice, Washington, DC 20052. Offers MIPP. *Program availability:* Part-time. *Students:* 19 full-time (7 women), 20 part-time (9 women); includes 14 minority (4 Black or African American, non-Hispanic/Latino; 3 Asian, non-Hispanic/Latino; 4 Hispanic/Latino; 3 Two or more races, non-Hispanic/Latino), 7 international. Average age 38. 68 applicants, 71% accepted, 22 enrolled. In 2017, 22 master's awarded. *Degree requirements:* For master's, one foreign language. *Entrance requirements:* For master's, GRE (recommended), advanced degree or 8 years of experience plus BA, introductory microeconomics and macroeconomics. Additional exam requirements/recommendations for international students: Required—TOEFL (minimum score 100 iBT), IELTS (minimum score 7). *Application deadline:* For fall admission, 1/15 priority date for domestic and international students; for spring admission, 10/1 for domestic and international students. Application fee: $75. Electronic applications accepted. *Expenses: Tuition:* Full-time $28,800; part-time $1655 per credit hour. *Required fees:* $45; $2.75 per credit hour. *Financial support:* In 2017–18, 13 students received support. Fellowships with partial tuition reimbursements available, Federal Work-Study, and scholarships/grants available. Financial award application deadline: 1/15; financial award applicants required to submit FAFSA. *Unit head:* Prof. Matthew Levinger, Director, 202-994-9946, E-mail: mlevinger@gwu.edu. *Application contact:* Nicole A. Campbell, Director of Graduate Admissions, 202-994-7050, Fax: 202-994-9537, E-mail: esiagrad@gwu.edu.
Website: http://elliott.gwu.edu/international-policy-and-practice

The George Washington University, Elliott School of International Affairs, Program in International Studies, Washington, DC 20052. Offers MIS. *Program availability:* Part-time. *Students:* Average age 35. *Entrance requirements:* For master's, 2 years (or equivalent) of a modern, spoken foreign language; introductory microeconomics/macroeconomics coursework. Additional exam requirements/recommendations for international students: Required—TOEFL (minimum score 600 paper-based; 100 iBT), IELTS (minimum score 7). *Application deadline:* For fall admission, 1/15 priority date for domestic and international students; for spring admission, 10/1 for domestic students. Application fee: $75. Electronic applications accepted. *Expenses: Tuition:* Full-time $28,800; part-time $1655 per credit hour. *Required fees:* $45; $2.75 per credit hour. *Financial support:* Fellowships with partial tuition reimbursements, Federal Work-Study, and scholarships/grants available. Financial award application deadline: 1/15; financial award applicants required to submit FAFSA. *Unit head:* Lisa Stephenson, Associate Dean for Academic Programs, 202-994-6034, E-mail: lstephen@gwu.edu. *Application contact:* Nicole A. Campbell, Director of Graduate Admissions, 202-994-7050, Fax: 202-994-9537, E-mail: esiagrad@gwu.edu.
Website: http://elliott.gwu.edu/international-studies-masters

The George Washington University, Law School, Washington, DC 20052. Offers law (SJD); national security and U.S. foreign relations (LL M). *Accreditation:* ABA. *Program availability:* Part-time, evening/weekend. *Faculty:* 84 full-time (33 women), 233 part-time/adjunct (65 women). *Students:* 1,444 full-time (760 women), 249 part-time (118 women); includes 422 minority (157 Black or African American, non-Hispanic/Latino; 11 American Indian or Alaska Native, non-Hispanic/Latino; 198 Asian, non-Hispanic/Latino; 38 Hispanic/Latino; 4 Native Hawaiian or other Pacific Islander, non-Hispanic/Latino; 14 Two or more races, non-Hispanic/Latino), 190 international. Average age 27. 191 applicants, 100% accepted, 128 enrolled. In 2017, 167 master's, 4 doctorates awarded. *Entrance requirements:* For master's, JD or equivalent; for doctorate, LSAT (for JD), LL M or equivalent (for SJD). *Application deadline:* For fall admission, 3/1 for domestic students. Applications are processed on a rolling basis. Application fee: $75. *Expenses:* Contact institution. *Financial support:* Research assistantships, career-related internships or fieldwork, Federal Work-Study, institutionally sponsored loans, scholarships/grants, and tuition waivers (full and partial) available. Support available to part-time students. Financial award application deadline: 3/1; financial award applicants required to submit CSS PROFILE or FAFSA. *Unit head:* Blake D. Morant, Dean, E-mail: bmorant@law.gwu.edu. *Application contact:* Sophia Sim, Assistant Dean of Admissions and Financial Aid, 202-994-7235, Fax: 202-739-0624, E-mail: ssim@law.gwu.edu.
Website: http://www.law.gwu.edu/

Georgia Institute of Technology, Graduate Studies, Ivan Allen College of Liberal Arts, Sam Nunn School of International Affairs, Atlanta, GA 30332-0001. Offers MS. *Program availability:* Part-time. Terminal master's awarded for partial completion of doctoral program. *Degree requirements:* For master's, one foreign language, thesis optional, minimum GPA of 3.0, literacy in economics and technology. *Entrance requirements:* For master's, GRE. Additional exam requirements/recommendations for international students: Required—TOEFL (minimum score 600 paper-based; 100 iBT). Electronic applications accepted. *Faculty research:* International political economy, international security, Asian and European studies.

Harvard University, Graduate School of Arts and Sciences, Department of Government, Cambridge, MA 02138. Offers political science (PhD), including American politics, comparative politics, international relations, political thought, quantitative methods. *Degree requirements:* For doctorate, one foreign language, thesis/dissertation, general exams. *Entrance requirements:* For doctorate, GRE General Test. Additional exam requirements/recommendations for international students: Required—TOEFL.

Harvard University, Law School, Professional Programs in Law, Cambridge, MA 02138. Offers international and comparative law (JD); law and business (JD); law and government (JD); law and social change (JD); law, science and technology (JD); JD/MALD; JD/MBA; JD/MPH; JD/MPP; JD/PhD. *Accreditation:* ABA. *Degree requirements:* For doctorate, 3rd-year paper. *Entrance requirements:* For doctorate, LSAT. *Faculty research:* Constitutional law, voting rights law, cyber law.

Indiana University Bloomington, University Graduate School, College of Arts and Sciences, School of Global and International Studies, Program in International Studies, Bloomington, IN 47405-7000. Offers MA, MS.

Indiana University South Bend, College of Liberal Arts and Sciences, South Bend, IN 46615. Offers advanced computer programming (Graduate Certificate); applied informatics (Graduate Certificate); applied mathematics and computer science (MS); behavior modification (Graduate Certificate); computer applications (Graduate Certificate); computer programming (Graduate Certificate); correctional management and supervision (Graduate Certificate); English (MA); health systems management (Graduate Certificate); international studies (Graduate Certificate); liberal studies (MLS); nonprofit management (Graduate Certificate); paralegal studies (Graduate Certificate);

professional writing (Graduate Certificate); public affairs (MPA); public management (Graduate Certificate); social and cultural diversity (Graduate Certificate); strategic sustainability leadership (Graduate Certificate); technology for administration (Graduate Certificate). *Program availability:* Part-time, evening/weekend. *Degree requirements:* For master's, variable foreign language requirement, thesis (for some programs). *Entrance requirements:* For master's, minimum GPA of 3.0. Additional exam requirements/recommendations for international students: Required—TOEFL (minimum score 550 paper-based; 80 iBT). *Expenses:* Contact institution. *Faculty research:* Artificial intelligence, bioinformatics, English language and literature, creative writing, computer networks.

Instituto Tecnologico de Santo Domingo, Graduate School, Area of Humanities and Social Sciences, Santo Domingo, Dominican Republic. Offers accounting (Certificate); adult education (Certificate); applied linguistics (MA); economics (MA); education (M Ed); educational psychology (MA, Certificate); gender and development (MA, Certificate); humanistic studies (MA); international marketing management (Certificate); international relations in the Caribbean basin (Certificate); intervention systems in family therapy (MA); linguistic and literary communication (Certificate); pedagogical support (MA); social science education (M Ed); sustainable human development (MA); terminal illness and death psychology (Certificate); youth and adult education (M Ed).

Instituto Tecnológico y de Estudios Superiores de Monterrey, Campus Ciudad Obregón, Program in International Relations, Ciudad Obregón, Mexico. Offers MIR.

International University in Geneva, Leadership Programs, Geneva, Switzerland. Offers international relations and diplomacy (MIRD); media and communication (MA); public administration (DPA). *Degree requirements:* For master's, comprehensive exam. *Entrance requirements:* Additional exam requirements/recommendations for international students: Required—TOEFL. Electronic applications accepted.

Johns Hopkins University, School of Advanced International Studies, Washington, DC 20036. Offers global risk (MA); international development (MA, Certificate), including international economics (MA); international economics (Certificate); international economics and finance (MA); international public policy (MIPP); international relations (PhD); international studies (Certificate); Japan studies (MA), including international economics; Korea studies (MA), including international economics; South Asia studies (MA), including international economics; Southeast Asia studies (MA), including international economics; JD/MA; MBA/MA; MHS/MA. Terminal master's awarded for partial completion of doctoral program. *Degree requirements:* For master's, 4-6 international economics courses, 5-6 functional or regional concentration courses, 2 core examinations, proficiency in language other than native language, capstone project; for doctorate, 2 foreign languages, thesis/dissertation, 3 comprehensive exams, economics, quantitative and qualitative course, dissertation prospectus and defense. *Entrance requirements:* For master's, GMAT or GRE General Test, previous course work in economics, foreign language, undergraduate degree; for doctorate, GRE General Test, master's degree. Additional exam requirements/recommendations for international students: Required—TOEFL (minimum score 600 paper-based; 100 iBT) or IELTS (minimum score 7). Electronic applications accepted. *Expenses:* Contact institution. *Faculty research:* International economics; international relations/regional studies; international development; energy, resources, and environment; international security/strategic studies.

Kennesaw State University, College of Humanities and Social Sciences, Program in International Policy Management, Kennesaw, GA 30144. Offers MS. *Program availability:* Online learning. *Degree requirements:* For master's, practicum or thesis. *Entrance requirements:* For master's, GRE, resume, letters of recommendation, writing sample. Additional exam requirements/recommendations for international students: Required—TOEFL (minimum score 550 paper-based; 80 iBT), IELTS (minimum score 6.5). Electronic applications accepted.

Lebanese American University, School of Arts and Sciences, Beirut, Lebanon. Offers computer science (MS); international affairs (MA).

Lesley University, Graduate School of Arts and Social Sciences, Cambridge, MA 02138-2790. Offers clinical mental health counseling (MA), including holistic counseling, school and community counseling, trauma studies; counseling psychology (MA, CAGS), including professional counseling (MA), school counseling (MA); creative writing (MFA); expressive therapies (MA, PhD, CAGS), including art (MA), clinical mental health counseling (MA), dance (MA), expressive therapies (MA), music (MA); independent studies (CAGS); independent study (MA); intercultural relations (MA, CAGS); interdisciplinary studies (MA), including individualized studies, integrative holistic health, mindfulness studies, peace and conflict transformation, trauma sensitive assessment, intervention, and consultation, women's studies; urban environmental leadership (MA). *Program availability:* Part-time, online learning. *Degree requirements:* For master's, internship, practicum, thesis (for expressive therapies); for doctorate, thesis/dissertation, arts apprenticeship, field placement; for CAGS, thesis, internship (for counseling psychology, expressive therapies). *Entrance requirements:* For master's, MAT (counseling psychology), interview, writing samples, art portfolio; for doctorate, GRE or MAT, interview, master's degree; for CAGS, interview, master's degree. Additional exam requirements/recommendations for international students: Required—TOEFL (minimum score 550 paper-based; 80 iBT). Electronic applications accepted. *Faculty research:* Psychotherapy and culture; psychotherapy and psychological trauma; women's issues in art, teaching and psychotherapy; community-based art, psycho-spiritual inquiry.

Liberty University, Helms School of Government, Lynchburg, VA 24515. Offers criminal justice (MS), including forensic psychology, homeland security, public administration (MA, MS); international relations (MS); political science (MS); public administration (MPA), including business and government, healthcare, law and public policy, public and non-profit management; public policy (MA), including campaigns and elections, international affairs, Middle East affairs, public administration (MA, MS). *Program availability:* Part-time, online learning. *Students:* 287 full-time (148 women), 639 part-time (248 women); includes 231 minority (173 Black or African American, non-Hispanic/Latino; 4 American Indian or Alaska Native, non-Hispanic/Latino; 8 Asian, non-Hispanic/Latino; 20 Hispanic/Latino; 1 Native Hawaiian or other Pacific Islander, non-Hispanic/Latino; 25 Two or more races, non-Hispanic/Latino), 7 international. Average age 35. 876 applicants, 64% accepted, 277 enrolled. In 2017, 211 master's awarded. *Entrance requirements:* For master's, minimum undergraduate GPA of 3.0. Additional exam requirements/recommendations for international students: Required—TOEFL (minimum score 600 paper-based; 100 iBT). *Application deadline:* Applications are processed on a rolling basis. Application fee: $50. Electronic applications accepted. *Unit head:* Shawn D. Akers, Dean, 434-592-4986. *Application contact:* Jay Bridge, Director of Admissions, 800-424-9595, Fax: 800-628-7977, E-mail: gradadmissions@liberty.edu.

Liberty University, School of Divinity, Lynchburg, VA 24515. Offers Biblical exposition (MA); Biblical languages (M Div); Biblical studies (M Div, MA, MAR, Th M, D Min); chaplaincy (M Div, D Min); Christian apologetics (M Div, MA, MAR, Th M); Christian leadership and church ministries (M Div); Christian ministries (M Div); Christian ministry (MA); Christian thought (M Div); church history (M Div, MAR, Th M); community chaplaincy (M Div, MAR); discipleship (D Min); discipleship and church ministry (M Div, MAR, MCM); evangelism and church planting (MAR, MCM, D Min); expository preaching (D Min); global ministry (MA); global studies (M Div, MAR, MCM, MGS, Th M); healthcare chaplaincy (M Div); homiletics (M Div, MAR, Th M); leadership (M Div, MAR); marketplace chaplaincy (M Div, MCM); ministry leadership (Ed D); pastoral counseling (M Div, MA, MAR, D Min), including addictions and recovery (MA), crisis response and trauma (MA), discipleship and church ministries (MA), leadership (MA), life coaching (MA), marketplace chaplaincy (MA), marriage and family (MA), military resilience (MA), pastoral counseling (MA); pastoral leadership (D Min); pastoral ministries (M Div, M Serv Soc, MCM); religious education (MRE); sports chaplaincy (MA); theology (M Div, MAR, MTS, Th M); theology and apologetics (D Min, PhD); worship (M Div, MAR, MCM, D Min); youth and family ministries (M Div). *Program availability:* Part-time, online learning. *Students:* 2,140 full-time (615 women), 3,020 part-time (906 women); includes 1,312 minority (1,016 Black or African American, non-Hispanic/Latino; 9 American Indian or Alaska Native, non-Hispanic/Latino; 100 Asian, non-Hispanic/Latino; 90 Hispanic/Latino; 7 Native Hawaiian or other Pacific Islander, non-Hispanic/Latino; 90 Two or more races, non-Hispanic/Latino), 158 international. Average age 42. 4,673 applicants, 33% accepted, 977 enrolled. In 2017, 904 master's, 54 doctorates awarded. *Degree requirements:* For master's, 2 foreign languages, thesis (for some programs); for doctorate, 2 foreign languages, thesis/dissertation. *Entrance requirements:* For master's, minimum undergraduate GPA of 2.0; for doctorate, GRE General Test or MAT, minimum graduate GPA of 3.0. Additional exam requirements/recommendations for international students: Required—TOEFL (minimum score 600 paper-based; 100 iBT). *Application deadline:* For fall admission, 6/1 for domestic students; for spring admission, 11/1 for domestic students. Applications are processed on a rolling basis. Application fee: $50. Electronic applications accepted. *Expenses:* Contact institution. *Financial support:* Teaching assistantships with tuition reimbursements, career-related internships or fieldwork, and Federal Work-Study available. Financial award applicants required to submit FAFSA. *Unit head:* Dr. Ed Hindson, Dean, 434-592-4140, Fax: 434-522-0415, E-mail: ehindson@liberty.edu. *Application contact:* Jay Bridge, Director of Graduate Admissions, 800-424-9595, Fax: 800-628-7977, E-mail: gradadmissions@liberty.edu.
Website: https://www.liberty.edu/divinity/

Lipscomb University, Program in Organizational Leadership, Nashville, TN 37204-3951. Offers aging services leadership (Certificate); global leadership (Certificate); organizational leadership (MPS); performance coaching (Certificate); strategic leadership (Certificate). *Program availability:* Part-time, online only, blended/hybrid learning. *Faculty:* 1 (woman) full-time, 3 part-time/adjunct (1 woman). *Students:* 27 full-time (14 women), 6 part-time (4 women); includes 8 minority (4 Black or African American, non-Hispanic/Latino; 4 Hispanic/Latino), 1 international. Average age 43. 34 applicants, 68% accepted, 15 enrolled. In 2017, 7 master's, 17 Certificates awarded. *Entrance requirements:* For master's, GRE or GMAT, two references, resume, interview. Additional exam requirements/recommendations for international students: Required—TOEFL (minimum score 550 paper-based). *Application deadline:* For fall admission, 8/1 for domestic students. Applications are processed on a rolling basis. Application fee: $50 ($75 for international students). Electronic applications accepted. *Expenses:* Contact institution. *Unit head:* Dr. Hope Nordstrom, Director, 615-966-1107, E-mail: hope.nordstrom@lipscomb.edu. *Application contact:* Barbara Blackman, Coordinator of Graduate Studies, 615-966-6287, Fax: 615-966-7619, E-mail: graduatestudies@lipscomb.edu.

London Metropolitan University, Graduate Programs, London, United Kingdom. Offers applied psychology (M Sc); architecture (MA); biomedical science (M Sc); blood science (M Sc); cancer pharmacology (M Sc); computer networking and cyber security (M Sc); computing and information systems (M Sc); conference interpreting (MA); counter-terrorism studies (M Sc); creative, digital and professional writing (MA); crime, violence and prevention (M Sc); criminology (M Sc); curating contemporary art (MA); data analytics (M Sc); digital media (MA); early childhood studies (MA); education (MA, Ed D); financial services law, regulation and compliance (LL M); food science (M Sc); forensic psychology (M Sc); health and social care management and policy (M Sc); human nutrition (M Sc); human resource management (MA); human rights and international conflict (MA); information technology (M Sc); intelligence and security studies (M Sc); international oil, gas and energy law (LL M); international relations (MA); interpreting (MA); learning and teaching in higher education (MA); legal practice (LL M); media and entertainment law (LL M); organizational and consumer psychology (M Sc); psychological therapy (M Sc); psychology of mental health (M Sc); public health (M Sc); public policy and management (MPA); security studies (M Sc); social work (M Sc); spatial planning and urban design (MA); sports therapy (M Sc); supporting older children and young people with dyslexia (MA); teaching languages (MA), including Arabic, English; translation (MA); woman and child abuse (MA).

Marquette University, Graduate School, College of Arts and Sciences, Department of History, Milwaukee, WI 53201-1881. Offers European history (MA, PhD); global studies (MA); United States history (MA, PhD). *Program availability:* Part-time. *Degree requirements:* For master's, comprehensive exam, essay, 2 classes of research seminars (6 hours); for doctorate, one foreign language, comprehensive exam, thesis/dissertation, 2 research seminars, dissertation seminar. *Entrance requirements:* For master's, GRE General Test, official transcripts from all current and previous colleges/universities except Marquette, one-page statement of purpose, three letters of recommendation from former teachers; for doctorate, GRE General Test, official transcripts from all current and previous colleges/universities except Marquette, one-page statement of purpose, three letters of recommendation from former teachers, writing sample. Additional exam requirements/recommendations for international students: Required—TOEFL. Electronic applications accepted. *Faculty research:* Children's history, Soviet and post-Soviet history, modern Ireland and Britain, Japan and martial arts, American Catholicism.

Marquette University, Graduate School, College of Arts and Sciences, Department of Political Science, Milwaukee, WI 53201-1881. Offers international affairs (MA); political science (MA); public service (MA); JD/MA; MA/MBA. *Program availability:* Part-time. *Degree requirements:* For master's, comprehensive exam, thesis optional. *Entrance requirements:* For master's, GRE General Test, official transcripts from all current and previous colleges/universities except Marquette, three letters of recommendation, statement of purpose. Additional exam requirements/recommendations for international students: Required—TOEFL (minimum score 530 paper-based). Electronic applications accepted. *Faculty research:* Public opinion and electoral behavior, public policy analysis, Congress and the Presidency, judicial behavior, political system transitions.

McMaster University, School of Graduate Studies, Faculty of Humanities and Faculty of Social Sciences, Institute on Globalization and the Human Condition, Hamilton, ON L8S 4M2, Canada. Offers globalization studies (MA).

McMaster University, School of Graduate Studies, Faculty of Social Sciences, Department of Political Science, Hamilton, ON L8S 4M2, Canada. Offers international relations (PhD); political science (MA); public and the global economy (MA); public policy (PhD); public policy and administration (MA). MA program in public policy and administration offered jointly with University of Guelph. *Program availability:* Part-time. *Degree requirements:* For master's, thesis or alternative. *Entrance requirements:* For master's, minimum B+ average. Additional exam requirements/recommendations for international students: Required—TOEFL (minimum score 580 paper-based). *Faculty*

research: Organizational theory, internationalization of public policy, water resource policies, political interest intermediation, comparative politics.

Middlebury Institute of International Studies at Monterey, Graduate School of International Policy and Management, Program in International Policy and Development, Monterey, CA 93940-2691. Offers MA. *Degree requirements:* For master's, one foreign language. *Entrance requirements:* For master's, minimum GPA of 3.0, proficiency in a foreign language. Additional exam requirements/recommendations for international students: Required—TOEFL (minimum score 550 paper-based; 80 iBT). Electronic applications accepted.

Middle Tennessee State University, College of Graduate Studies, College of Liberal Arts, Department of Political Science, Murfreesboro, TN 37132. Offers international affairs (MA). *Program availability:* Part-time, evening/weekend, online learning. *Entrance requirements:* Additional exam requirements/recommendations for international students: Required—TOEFL (minimum score 525 paper-based; 71 iBT) or IELTS (minimum score 6). Electronic applications accepted.

Missouri State University, Graduate College, College of Humanities and Public Affairs, Department of Political Science, Program in Global Studies, Springfield, MO 65897. Offers MGS. *Program availability:* Part-time. *Faculty:* 6 full-time (2 women). *Students:* 18 full-time (9 women), 2 part-time (1 woman); includes 2 minority (1 Black or African American, non-Hispanic/Latino; 1 Two or more races, non-Hispanic/Latino), 5 international. Average age 26. 14 applicants, 29% accepted, 4 enrolled. In 2017, 8 master's awarded. *Degree requirements:* For master's, 2 foreign languages, comprehensive exam, thesis or alternative. *Entrance requirements:* For master's, GRE, minimum GPA of 3.0. Additional exam requirements/recommendations for international students: Required—TOEFL (minimum score 550 paper-based; 79 iBT), IELTS (minimum score 6). *Application deadline:* For fall admission, 7/20 priority date for domestic students, 5/1 for international students; for spring admission, 12/20 priority date for domestic students, 9/1 for international students; for summer admission, 5/20 priority date for domestic students. Applications are processed on a rolling basis. Application fee: $35 ($50 for international students). Electronic applications accepted. *Expenses:* Tuition, state resident: full-time $2915; part-time $2021 per credit hour. Tuition, nonresident: full-time $5354; part-time $3647 per credit hour. *International tuition:* $11,992 full-time. *Required fees:* $173; $173 per credit hour. Tuition and fees vary according to class time, course level, course load, degree level, campus/location and program. *Financial support:* Federal Work-Study, institutionally sponsored loans, scholarships/grants, and unspecified assistantships available. Support available to part-time students. Financial award application deadline: 3/31; financial award applicants required to submit FAFSA. *Faculty research:* U.S. China policy, Eastern European politics, South American political reform, landmine use policy. *Unit head:* Dr. George Connor, Department Head, 417-836-5630, Fax: 417-836-6655, E-mail: georgeconnor@missouristate.edu. *Application contact:* Stephanie Praschan, Director, Graduate Enrollment Management, 417-836-5330, Fax: 417-836-6200, E-mail: stephaniepraschan@missouristate.edu.
Website: http://polsci.missouristate.edu/mgs/

Morgan State University, School of Graduate Studies, College of Liberal Arts, Department of World Languages and International Studies, Baltimore, MD 21251. Offers international studies (MA). *Program availability:* Part-time, evening/weekend. *Degree requirements:* For master's, one foreign language, comprehensive exam, thesis. *Entrance requirements:* For master's, GRE. Additional exam requirements/recommendations for international students: Required—TOEFL (minimum score 550 paper-based). *Application deadline:* For fall admission, 2/1 priority date for domestic students; for spring admission, 10/1 priority date for domestic students. Applications are processed on a rolling basis. Application fee: $0. *Expenses:* Tuition, state resident: part-time $433 per credit. Tuition, nonresident: part-time $851 per credit. *Required fees:* $81.50 per credit. *Financial support:* Application deadline: 2/1. *Unit head:* Dr. Helen Harrison, Interim Department Chair, E-mail: helen.harrison@morgan.edu. *Application contact:* Dr. Dean Campbell, Graduate Recruitment Specialist, 443-885-3185, Fax: 443-885-8226, E-mail: dean.campbell@morgan.edu.

New England College, Program in Management, Henniker, NH 03242-3293. Offers accounting (MSA); healthcare administration (MS); international relations (MA); marketing management (MS); nonprofit leadership (MS); project management (MS); strategic leadership (MS). *Program availability:* Part-time, evening/weekend. *Degree requirements:* For master's, independent research project. Electronic applications accepted.

The New School, Schools of Public Engagement, Program in International Affairs, New York, NY 10011. Offers cities and social justice (MA); conflict and security (MA); development (MA); governance and rights (MA); international affairs (MS); media and culture (MA). *Program availability:* Part-time. *Faculty:* 23 full-time (12 women), 11 part-time/adjunct (2 women). *Students:* 116 full-time (84 women), 52 part-time (34 women); includes 74 minority (24 Black or African American, non-Hispanic/Latino; 11 Asian, non-Hispanic/Latino; 32 Hispanic/Latino; 7 Two or more races, non-Hispanic/Latino), 31 international. Average age 29. 166 applicants, 95% accepted, 56 enrolled. In 2017, 90 master's awarded. *Degree requirements:* For master's, thesis or alternative, capstone project. *Entrance requirements:* For master's, academic writing sample, two letters of recommendation, statement of purpose, resume, transcripts. Additional exam requirements/recommendations for international students: Required—TOEFL (minimum score 92 iBT), IELTS (minimum score 7), PTE (minimum score 68). *Application deadline:* For fall admission, 1/15 priority date for domestic and international students; for spring admission, 10/15 priority date for domestic and international students. Applications are processed on a rolling basis. Application fee: $50. Electronic applications accepted. *Expenses:* $1,650 per credit. *Financial support:* In 2017–18, 135 students received support, including 2 teaching assistantships (averaging $3,126 per year); career-related internships or fieldwork, Federal Work-Study, scholarships/grants, and unspecified assistantships also available. Support available to part-time students. Financial award application deadline: 2/1; financial award applicants required to submit FAFSA. *Application contact:* Gabriela Garcia Juarez, Assistant Director, Graduate Admission, 212-229-5150 Ext. 1666, E-mail: garciajg@newschool.edu.
Website: https://www.newschool.edu/public-engagement/ma-ms-international-affairs/

New York University, Graduate School of Arts and Science, Department of Politics, New York, NY 10012-1019. Offers political campaign management (MA); politics (MA, PhD); JD/MA; MBA/MA. *Program availability:* Part-time. *Students:* Average age 27. 670 applicants, 45% accepted, 80 enrolled. In 2017, 101 master's, 13 doctorates awarded. Terminal master's awarded for partial completion of doctoral program. *Degree requirements:* For master's, one foreign language, thesis or alternative; for doctorate, 2 foreign languages, comprehensive exam, thesis/dissertation. *Entrance requirements:* For master's and doctorate, GRE General Test. Additional exam requirements/recommendations for international students: Required—TOEFL. *Application deadline:* For fall admission, 12/18 priority date for domestic students, 12/18 for international students. Application fee: $100. *Expenses: Tuition:* Full-time $41,352; part-time $19,968 per year. *Required fees:* $2496; $1628 per unit. $814 per term. Tuition and fees vary according to course load and program. *Financial support:* Fellowships, teaching assistantships, career-related internships or fieldwork, Federal Work-Study, and institutionally sponsored loans available. Financial award application deadline: 12/18;

financial award applicants required to submit FAFSA. *Faculty research:* Comparative politics, democratic theory and practice, rational choice, political economy, international relations. *Unit head:* Sanford Gordon, Director of Graduate Studies, PhD Program, 212-998-8500, Fax: 212-995-4184, E-mail: politics.phd@nyu.edu. *Application contact:* Nicole Simonelli, Director of Graduate Studies, Master's Program, 212-998-8500, Fax: 212-995-4184, E-mail: politics.masters@nyu.edu.
Website: http://www.nyu.edu/gsas/dept/politics/

New York University, School of Professional Studies, Center for Global Affairs, New York, NY 10012-1019. Offers global affairs (MS), including environment/energy policy, global gender studies, human rights and international law, international development and humanitarian assistance, international relations/global futures, peace building, private sector, transnational security. *Program availability:* Part-time, evening/weekend. *Students:* 143 full-time (90 women), 115 part-time (65 women); includes 73 minority (18 Black or African American, non-Hispanic/Latino; 16 Asian, non-Hispanic/Latino; 32 Hispanic/Latino; 7 Two or more races, non-Hispanic/Latino), 82 international. Average age 28. 285 applicants, 73% accepted, 79 enrolled. In 2017, 238 master's awarded. *Degree requirements:* For master's, thesis. *Entrance requirements:* For master's, GRE or GMAT (only upon request), bachelor's degree, resume with relevant professional work, internship or volunteer experience, two letters of recommendation, statement of purpose. Additional exam requirements/recommendations for international students: Required—TOEFL (minimum score 600 paper-based; 100 iBT), IELTS (minimum score 7). *Application deadline:* For fall admission, 2/1 priority date for domestic and international students; for spring admission, 10/15 priority date for domestic students, 8/15 priority date for international students. Applications are processed on a rolling basis. Application fee: $150. Electronic applications accepted. *Expenses:* $20,244 per term. *Financial support:* Fellowships, career-related internships or fieldwork, Federal Work-Study, scholarships/grants, and health care benefits available. Support available to part-time students. Financial award application deadline: 6/30; financial award applicants required to submit FAFSA. *Unit head:* Vera Jelinek, Divisional Dean and Clinical Associate Professor, 212-992-8380. *Application contact:* Office of Admissions, 212-998-7100, E-mail: sps.gradadmissions@nyu.edu.
Website: http://www.sps.nyu.edu/academics/departments/global-affairs.html

North Carolina State University, Graduate School, College of Humanities and Social Sciences, School of Public and International Affairs, Program in International Studies, Raleigh, NC 27695. Offers MIS. *Degree requirements:* For master's, thesis optional. *Entrance requirements:* For master's, GRE General Test, minimum GPA of 3.0 during previous 2 years. Electronic applications accepted. *Faculty research:* Global environmental policy and climate change, drug policy and the Caribbean, U.S. national security politics, local responses to globalization, the political economy of the European Union.

Northeastern University, College of Professional Studies, Boston, MA 02115-5096. Offers applied nutrition (MS); college athletics administration (MSL); commerce and economic development (MS); corporate and organizational communication (MS); criminal justice (MS); digital media (MPS); elearning and instructional design (M Ed); elementary education (MAT); geographic information technology (MPS); global studies and international relations (MS); higher education administration (M Ed); homeland security (MA); human services (MS); informatics (MPS); leadership (MS); learning analytics (M Ed); learning and instruction (M Ed); nonprofit management (MS); professional sports administration (MSL); project management (MS); regulatory affairs for drugs, biologics, and medical devices (MS); respiratory care leadership (MS); special education (M Ed); technical communication (MS). *Program availability:* Part-time, evening/weekend, 100% online, blended/hybrid learning. *Faculty:* 82 full-time (51 women), 853 part-time/adjunct (366 women). *Students:* 5,278 part-time (3,230 women). In 2017, 1,586 master's awarded. *Application deadline:* Applications are processed on a rolling basis. Application fee: $0. Electronic applications accepted. *Expenses:* Contact institution. *Financial support:* Applicants required to submit FAFSA. *Unit head:* Dr. Mary Loeffelholz, Dean of the College of Professional Studies. *Application contact:* E-mail: cpsadmissions@northeastern.edu.
Website: https://cps.northeastern.edu/

Northeastern University, College of Social Sciences and Humanities, Boston, MA 02115. Offers criminology and criminal justice (MSCJ); criminology and justice policy (PhD); economics (MA, PhD); English (MA, PhD); international affairs (MA); law and public policy (PhD); political science (MA, PhD); public administration (MPA); public policy (MPP); security and resilience studies (MS); sociology (MA, PhD); urban and regional policy (MS); urban informatics (MS); world history (MA, PhD). *Program availability:* Online learning. *Faculty:* 242. *Students:* 491. In 2017, 143 master's, 38 doctorates awarded. *Degree requirements:* For doctorate, variable foreign language requirement, comprehensive exam, thesis/dissertation. *Entrance requirements:* For master's and doctorate, GRE. Additional exam requirements/recommendations for international students: Required—TOEFL, IELTS. Application fee: $75. Electronic applications accepted. *Expenses:* Contact institution. *Financial support:* Teaching assistantships, career-related internships or fieldwork, scholarships/grants, health care benefits, tuition waivers (full and partial), and unspecified assistantships available. Support available to part-time students. Financial award applicants required to submit FAFSA. *Unit head:* Dr. Uta Poiger, Dean, 617-373-5173, E-mail: college_of_social_sciences_and_humanities@neu.edu. *Application contact:* 617-373-5990, E-mail: gradcssh@northeastern.edu.
Website: http://www.northeastern.edu/cssh/

Northwestern University, The Graduate School, Center for International and Comparative Studies, Evanston, IL 60208. Offers Certificate.

Northwestern University, Pritzker School of Law, Chicago, IL 60611-3069. Offers international human rights (LL M); law (JD); law and business (LL M); science law (MSL); tax (LL M in Tax); JD/LL M; JD/MBA; JD/PhD; LL M/Certificate. Executive LL M programs offered in Madrid (Spain), Seoul (South Korea), and Tel Aviv (Israel). *Accreditation:* ABA. *Entrance requirements:* For master's, law degree or equivalent, letter of recommendation, resume; for doctorate, LSAT, 1 letter of recommendation, resume. Additional exam requirements/recommendations for international students: Required—TOEFL. Electronic applications accepted. *Expenses:* Contact institution. *Faculty research:* Constitutional law, corporate law, international law, law and social policy, ethical studies.

Norwich University, College of Graduate and Continuing Studies, Master of Arts in Diplomacy Program, Northfield, VT 05663. Offers diplomacy (MA), including cyber diplomacy - policy, cyber diplomacy - technical, international commerce, international conflict management, international terrorism. *Program availability:* Evening/weekend, online only, mostly all online with a week-long residency requirement. *Degree requirements:* For master's, comprehensive exam, thesis optional. *Entrance requirements:* For master's, minimum undergraduate GPA of 2.75. Additional exam requirements/recommendations for international students: Required—TOEFL (minimum score 550 paper-based; 80 iBT), IELTS (minimum score 6.5). Electronic applications accepted. *Expenses:* Contact institution.

Norwich University, College of Graduate and Continuing Studies, Master of Arts in International Relations Program, Northfield, VT 05663. Offers international relations

(MA), including cyber diplomacy-policy, cyber diplomacy-technical, international development, international security, national security, regions of the world. *Program availability:* Evening/weekend, online only, mostly all online with a week-long residency requirement. *Degree requirements:* For master's, research paper. *Entrance requirements:* For master's, minimum undergraduate GPA of 2.75. Additional exam requirements/recommendations for international students: Required—TOEFL (minimum score 550 paper-based; 80 iBT), IELTS (minimum score 6.5). Electronic applications accepted. *Expenses:* Contact institution.

Ohio University, Graduate College, Center for International Studies, Program in Communications and Development Studies, Athens, OH 45701-2979. Offers MA. *Program availability:* Part-time. *Degree requirements:* For master's, one foreign language, thesis optional, internship. *Entrance requirements:* For master's, minimum GPA of 3.0. Additional exam requirements/recommendations for international students: Required—TOEFL (minimum score 550 paper-based; 80 iBT), IELTS (minimum score 6.5). Electronic applications accepted. *Faculty research:* National development processes, public relations and participatory research, audio and video production, health communication, urban development.

Oklahoma State University, Graduate College, Stillwater, OK 74078. Offers aerospace security (Graduate Certificate); bioenergy and sustainable technology (Graduate Certificate); business data mining (Graduate Certificate); business sustainability (Graduate Certificate); environmental science (MS); international studies (MS); non-profit management (Graduate Certificate); teaching English to speakers of other languages (Graduate Certificate); telecommunications management (MS). Programs are interdisciplinary. *Students:* 31 full-time (21 women), 55 part-time (32 women); includes 15 minority (5 Black or African American, non-Hispanic/Latino; 3 Asian, non-Hispanic/Latino; 5 Hispanic/Latino; 2 Two or more races, non-Hispanic/Latino), 44 international. Average age 29. 334 applicants, 84% accepted, 73 enrolled. In 2017, 29 master's, 5 doctorates awarded. *Degree requirements:* For master's, thesis (for some programs); for doctorate, comprehensive exam, thesis/dissertation. *Entrance requirements:* For master's and doctorate, GRE or GMAT. Additional exam requirements/recommendations for international students: Required—TOEFL (minimum score 550 paper-based; 79 iBT). *Application deadline:* For fall admission, 3/1 priority date for domestic and international students; for spring admission, 8/1 priority date for domestic and international students. Applications are processed on a rolling basis. Application fee: $40 ($75 for international students). Electronic applications accepted. *Expenses:* Tuition, state resident: full-time $4019; part-time $2679.60 per year. Tuition, nonresident: full-time $15,286; part-time $10,190.40 per year. *Required fees:* $2129; $1419 per unit. Tuition and fees vary according to program. *Financial support:* Research assistantships, career-related internships or fieldwork, Federal Work-Study, scholarships/grants, health care benefits, tuition waivers (partial), and unspecified assistantships available. Support available to part-time students. Financial award application deadline: 3/1; financial award applicants required to submit FAFSA. *Unit head:* Dr. Sheryl Tucker, Dean, 405-744-6368, Fax: 405-744-0355, E-mail: gradi@okstate.edu. *Application contact:* Dr. Susan Mathew, Assistant Director of Graduate Admissions, 405-744-6368, Fax: 405-744-0355, E-mail: gradi@okstate.edu. Website: http://gradcollege.okstate.edu/

Old Dominion University, College of Arts and Letters, Graduate Program in International Studies, Norfolk, VA 23529. Offers conflict and cooperation (MA, PhD); interdependence and transnationalism (MA, PhD); international cultural studies (MA, PhD); international political economy and development (MA, PhD); modeling and simulation (MA, PhD); U.S. foreign policy and international relations (MA, PhD). *Program availability:* Part-time. *Faculty:* 15 full-time (4 women). *Students:* 32 full-time (13 women), 40 part-time (16 women); includes 11 minority (7 Black or African American, non-Hispanic/Latino; 2 Hispanic/Latino; 2 Two or more races, non-Hispanic/Latino), 16 international. Average age 37. 95 applicants, 58% accepted, 40 enrolled. In 2017, 2 master's, 7 doctorates awarded. Terminal master's awarded for partial completion of doctoral program. *Degree requirements:* For master's, one foreign language, comprehensive exam, thesis optional; for doctorate, one foreign language, comprehensive exam, thesis/dissertation. *Entrance requirements:* For master's, GRE General Test, sample of written work, 2 letters of recommendation; for doctorate, GRE General Test, sample of written work, 3 letters of recommendation. Additional exam requirements/recommendations for international students: Required—TOEFL (minimum score 570 paper-based). *Application deadline:* For fall admission, 1/15 for domestic and international students; for spring admission, 10/15 for domestic and international students. Application fee: $50. Electronic applications accepted. *Expenses:* Contact institution. *Financial support:* In 2017–18, 12 students received support, including 1 fellowship (averaging $15,000 per year), 5 research assistantships with tuition reimbursements available (averaging $15,000 per year), 4 teaching assistantships with tuition reimbursements available (averaging $15,000 per year); career-related internships or fieldwork, institutionally sponsored loans, and unspecified assistantships also available. Financial award application deadline: 1/15; financial award applicants required to submit FAFSA. *Faculty research:* U.S. foreign policy, international security, transatlantic and transpacific relations, transnational issues, international political economy and development. *Total annual research expenditures:* $330,391. *Unit head:* Dr. Regina Karp, Graduate Program Director, 757-683-5700, Fax: 757-683-5701, E-mail: rkarp@odu.edu. *Application contact:* Dr. Dale Miller, Associate Dean for Research and Graduate Studies, 757-683-3866, E-mail: demiller@odu.edu. Website: http://www.odu.edu/gpis

Penn State University Park, Graduate School, School of International Affairs, University Park, PA 16802. Offers MIA. *Program availability:* Part-time, evening/weekend. *Students:* 70 full-time (37 women), 4 part-time (1 woman). Average age 25. 236 applicants, 79% accepted, 74 enrolled. In 2017, 54 master's awarded. *Entrance requirements:* Additional exam requirements/recommendations for international students: Required—TOEFL (minimum score 550 paper-based; 80 iBT), IELTS. *Application deadline:* Applications are processed on a rolling basis. Application fee: $65. Electronic applications accepted. *Expenses:* Contact institution. *Financial support:* Fellowships, research assistantships, teaching assistantships, career-related internships or fieldwork, Federal Work-Study, scholarships/grants, traineeships, health care benefits, and unspecified assistantships available. Support available to part-time students. Financial award application deadline: 2/15; financial award applicants required to submit FAFSA. *Unit head:* Hari M. Osofsky, Dean, 814-863-1521, Fax: 814-863-7274. *Application contact:* Lori Hawn, Director, Graduate Student Services, 814-865-1795, Fax: 814-863-4627, E-mail: l-gswww@lists.psu.edu. Website: http://sia.psu.edu/

Pepperdine University, Graduate School of Education and Psychology, Division of Education, Los Angeles, CA 90263. Offers administration and preliminary administrative services (MS); education (MA); educational leadership, administration, and policy (Ed D); global leadership and change (PhD); learning technologies (MA, Ed D); organizational leadership (Ed D); social entrepreneurship and change (MA); teaching (MA); teaching: TESOL (MA). *Program availability:* Part-time, evening/weekend, blended/hybrid learning. *Students:* 214 full-time (139 women), 327 part-time (216 women); includes 248 minority (113 Black or African American, non-Hispanic/Latino; 2 American Indian or Alaska Native, non-Hispanic/Latino; 48 Asian, non-Hispanic/Latino;

61 Hispanic/Latino; 6 Native Hawaiian or other Pacific Islander, non-Hispanic/Latino; 18 Two or more races, non-Hispanic/Latino), 49 international. Average age 39. 410 applicants, 91% accepted, 160 enrolled. In 2017, 151 master's, 88 doctorates awarded. *Degree requirements:* For doctorate, thesis/dissertation. *Entrance requirements:* For master's, GRE General Test; for doctorate, GRE General Test, MAT. Additional exam requirements/recommendations for international students: Required—TOEFL. *Application deadline:* Applications are processed on a rolling basis. Application fee: $55. Electronic applications accepted. *Expenses:* Contact institution. *Financial support:* Research assistantships, teaching assistantships, career-related internships or fieldwork, institutionally sponsored loans, and scholarships/grants available. Support available to part-time students. Financial award application deadline: 7/1; financial award applicants required to submit FAFSA. *Unit head:* Dr. Martine Jago, Associate Dean, Education Division, 310-568-2828, E-mail: martine.jago@pepperdine.edu. *Application contact:* Chris Costa, Director of Enrollment, 310-568-2850, E-mail: chris.costa@pepperdine.edu. Website: http://gsep.pepperdine.edu/masters-education/

Pepperdine University, School of Public Policy, Malibu, CA 90263. Offers American politics (MPP); economics (MPP); international relations (MPP); state and local policy (MPP); JD/MPP; MBA/MPP; MDR/MPP. *Students:* Average age 25. 174 applicants, 55% accepted, 29 enrolled. In 2017, 34 master's awarded. *Entrance requirements:* For master's, GRE or GMAT, 2 letters of recommendation, resume, two essays. Additional exam requirements/recommendations for international students: Required—TOEFL. *Application deadline:* For fall admission, 6/15 for domestic students. Applications are processed on a rolling basis. Application fee: $50. Electronic applications accepted. *Expenses:* Contact institution. *Financial support:* Institutionally sponsored loans and scholarships/grants available. Financial award application deadline: 5/1; financial award applicants required to submit FAFSA. *Unit head:* Dr. Pete Peterson, Dean, School of Public Policy, 310-506-7490, Fax: 310-506-7494, E-mail: pete.n.peterson@pepperdine.edu. *Application contact:* Carson Bruno, Assistant Dean for Admission and Program Relations, 310-506-7493, E-mail: carson.bruno@pepperdine.edu. Website: http://publicpolicy.pepperdine.edu/

Pontificia Universidad Catolica Madre y Maestra, Graduate School, Faculty of Social and Administrative Sciences, Santiago, Dominican Republic. Offers business administration (MBA), including business development, finance, international business, management skills (M Mgmt, MBA), marketing, operations, strategic cost management, strategy, tourist destination planning and management; law (LL M), including civil law, corporate business law, criminal law, international relations, real estate law; management (M Mgmt), including higher financial management, insurance program administration, management skills (M Mgmt, MBA); psychology (MA), including clinical child and adolescent psychology, forensic psychology; strategic human resources (EMBA).

Portland State University, Graduate Studies, College of Urban and Public Affairs, Hatfield School of Government, Division of Political Science, Portland, OR 97207-0751. Offers political science (MA), including American politics, comparative politics, international relations, political theory. *Program availability:* Part-time. *Faculty:* 10 full-time (4 women), 8 part-time/adjunct (2 women). *Students:* 9 full-time (4 women), 11 part-time (3 women); includes 1 minority (Asian, non-Hispanic/Latino), 2 international. Average age 36. 13 applicants, 69% accepted, 8 enrolled. In 2017, 2 master's awarded. *Degree requirements:* For master's, variable foreign language requirement, comprehensive exam, thesis. *Entrance requirements:* For master's, GRE General Test, minimum undergraduate GPA of 3.0 or 3.1 in graduate-level coursework, 2 letters of recommendation, statement of intent. Additional exam requirements/recommendations for international students: Required—TOEFL (minimum score 550 paper-based; 90 iBT). *Application deadline:* For fall admission, 4/1 priority date for domestic students, 3/1 priority date for international students; for spring admission, 11/1 for domestic and international students. Application fee: $65. *Expenses:* Tuition, state resident: full-time $14,436; part-time $401 per credit. Tuition, nonresident: full-time $21,780; part-time $605 per credit. *Required fees:* $1380; $22 per credit. $119 per quarter. One-time fee: $325. Tuition and fees vary according to program. *Financial support:* In 2017–18, 6 students received support, including 8 research assistantships with full and partial tuition reimbursements available (averaging $3,572 per year), 2 teaching assistantships with full and partial tuition reimbursements available (averaging $7,443 per year); career-related internships or fieldwork, Federal Work-Study, and unspecified assistantships also available. Support available to part-time students. Financial award application deadline: 3/1; financial award applicants required to submit FAFSA. *Faculty research:* Congress, presidency, political reform, international environment, hate speech. *Unit head:* Christopher Shortell, Chair, 503-725-5139, Fax: 503-725-8444, E-mail: shortell@pdx.edu. Website: https://www.pdx.edu/hatfieldschool/political-science

Princeton University, Graduate School, Woodrow Wilson School of Public and International Affairs, Princeton, NJ 08544-1019. Offers public affairs (MPA, PhD); public policy (MPP); JD/MPA. JD/MPA offered jointly with Columbia University, New York University, Stanford University. Terminal master's awarded for partial completion of doctoral program. *Degree requirements:* For master's, internship; for doctorate, one foreign language, thesis/dissertation. *Entrance requirements:* For master's, GRE General Test, original policy memo; for doctorate, GRE General Test. Additional exam requirements/recommendations for international students: Required—TOEFL (minimum score 600 paper-based). Electronic applications accepted.

Queen's University at Kingston, School of Graduate Studies, Faculty of Arts and Sciences, Department of Political Studies, Kingston, ON K7L 3N6, Canada. Offers Canadian politics (PhD); comparative politics (PhD); gender and politics (PhD); international relations (PhD); political theory (PhD). *Degree requirements:* For master's, thesis or alternative; for doctorate, one foreign language, thesis/dissertation, qualifying exams. *Entrance requirements:* Additional exam requirements/recommendations for international students: Required—TOEFL (minimum score 600 paper-based). *Faculty research:* Canadian politics, comparative politics, political thought, international politics, women and politics.

Regent's University London, Webster Graduate School, London, United Kingdom. Offers business (MBA); finance (MS); human resources (MA); information technology management (MA); international business (MA); international non-governmental organizations (MA); international relations (MA); management and leadership (MA); marketing (MA). *Program availability:* Part-time.

Regent University, Graduate School, Robertson School of Government, Virginia Beach, VA 23464. Offers government (MA), including American government, healthcare policy and ethics (MA, MPA), international relations, law and public policy, national security studies, political communication, political theory, religion and politics; national security studies (MA), including cybersecurity, homeland security, international security, Middle East politics; public administration (MPA), including emergency management and homeland security, federal government, general public administration, healthcare policy and ethics (MA, MPA), law, nonprofit administration and faith-based organizations, public leadership and management, servant leadership. *Program availability:* Part-time, evening/weekend, 100% online, blended/hybrid learning. *Faculty:*

8 full-time (1 woman), 20 part-time/adjunct (3 women). *Students:* 39 full-time (23 women), 137 part-time (78 women); includes 83 minority (49 Black or African American, non-Hispanic/Latino; 1 American Indian or Alaska Native, non-Hispanic/Latino; 7 Asian, non-Hispanic/Latino; 15 Hispanic/Latino; 11 Two or more races, non-Hispanic/Latino). Average age 35. 345 applicants, 31% accepted, 57 enrolled. In 2017, 38 master's awarded. *Degree requirements:* For master's, thesis optional, internship. *Entrance requirements:* For master's, GRE General Test or LSAT, personal essay, writing sample, resume, college transcripts. Additional exam requirements/recommendations for international students: Required—TOEFL (minimum score 577 paper-based). *Application deadline:* For fall admission, 5/1 priority date for domestic students; for spring admission, 11/1 priority date for domestic students. Applications are processed on a rolling basis. Application fee: $50. Electronic applications accepted. *Expenses:* $650 per credit; $300 technology fee per semester. *Financial support:* In 2017–18, 116 students received support. Career-related internships or fieldwork, scholarships/grants, and unspecified assistantships available. Support available to part-time students. *Faculty research:* International relations and politics, public administration, leadership and ethics, Biblical law, Constitutional law and Supreme Court. *Unit head:* Dr. Eric Patterson, Dean, 757-352-4616, Fax: 757-352-4735, E-mail: epatterson@regent.edu. *Application contact:* Heidi Cece, Assistant Vice President of Enrollment Management, 800-373-5504, Fax: 757-352-4381, E-mail: admissions@regent.edu. Website: https://www.regent.edu/robertson-school-of-government/

Richmond, The American International University in London, MA in International Relations Program, Richmond, United Kingdom. Offers MA. *Program availability:* Part-time. *Entrance requirements:* Additional exam requirements/recommendations for international students: Required—TOEFL, IELTS. Electronic applications accepted.

Rutgers University–Camden, Graduate School of Arts and Sciences, Department of Public Policy and Administration, Camden, NJ 08102. Offers education policy and leadership (MPA); international public service and development (MPA); public management (MPA); JD/MPA; MPA/MA. *Accreditation:* NASPAA. *Program availability:* Part-time, evening/weekend. *Degree requirements:* For master's, directed study, research workshop, 42 credits. *Entrance requirements:* For master's, GRE General Test, GMAT or LSAT, 3 letters of recommendation; resume. Additional exam requirements/recommendations for international students: Required—TOEFL (minimum score 550 paper-based), IELTS. Electronic applications accepted. *Faculty research:* Nonprofit management, county and municipal administration, health and human services, government communication, administrative law, educational finance.

Rutgers University–Newark, Graduate School, Division of Global Affairs, Newark, NJ 07102. Offers MS, PhD. *Program availability:* Part-time, evening/weekend. *Degree requirements:* For master's, one foreign language, thesis optional. *Entrance requirements:* For master's and doctorate, GRE General Test, minimum B average. Electronic applications accepted. *Faculty research:* International organizations, diplomacy, world history, international political economy, global environment.

Rutgers University–Newark, Graduate School, Program in Political Science, Newark, NJ 07102. Offers American political system (MA); international relations (MA); JD/MA. *Program availability:* Part-time, evening/weekend. *Degree requirements:* For master's, comprehensive exam, thesis optional. *Entrance requirements:* For master's, GRE, minimum undergraduate B average. Electronic applications accepted. *Faculty research:* Policymaking and policy evaluation in the United States; government and politics in Europe, Middle East, Asia, Africa, and Latin America.

Rutgers University–New Brunswick, Graduate School-New Brunswick, Department of Political Science, Piscataway, NJ 08854-8097. Offers American politics (PhD); comparative politics (PhD); international relations (PhD); political theory (PhD); public law (PhD); United Nations and global policy studies (MA); women and politics (PhD). *Degree requirements:* For doctorate, one foreign language, comprehensive exam, thesis/dissertation. *Entrance requirements:* For master's, bachelor's degree from accredited U.S. college or university or a comparable institution in another country; for doctorate, GRE General Test. Additional exam requirements/recommendations for international students: Required—TOEFL.

Rutgers University–New Brunswick, Graduate School-New Brunswick, Program in Global and Comparative History, New Brunswick, NJ 08901. Offers MA. *Entrance requirements:* For master's, GRE, minimum GPA of 3.0, official transcripts, two letters of recommendation, 1-2 page personal statement, 10-15 page writing sample. Electronic applications accepted.

St. Mary's University, Graduate Studies, Program in International Relations, San Antonio, TX 78228. Offers conflict transformation (Certificate); international conflict resolution (MA); international development (MA); international relations (MA); security policy (MA); JD/MA. *Program availability:* Part-time, evening/weekend, 100% online. *Students:* 22 full-time (12 women), 48 part-time (16 women); includes 38 minority (5 Black or African American, non-Hispanic/Latino; 1 American Indian or Alaska Native, non-Hispanic/Latino; 1 Asian, non-Hispanic/Latino; 30 Hispanic/Latino; 1 Two or more races, non-Hispanic/Latino), 5 international. Average age 31. 89 applicants, 39% accepted, 19 enrolled. In 2017, 36 master's awarded. *Degree requirements:* For master's, one foreign language, comprehensive exam (for some programs), thesis (for some programs), thesis or comprehensive exam. *Entrance requirements:* For master's, minimum undergraduate cumulative GPA of 3.0. Additional exam requirements/recommendations for international students: Required—TOEFL (minimum score 550 paper-based; 80 iBT), IELTS (minimum score 6). *Application deadline:* For fall admission, 7/1 for domestic students; for spring admission, 11/15 for domestic students; for summer admission, 4/1 for domestic students. Applications are processed on a rolling basis. Application fee: $0. Electronic applications accepted. *Expenses: Tuition:* Full-time $16,200; part-time $900 per credit hour. *Required fees:* $810; $405 per semester. *Financial support:* Research assistantships, Federal Work-Study, tuition waivers (full), unspecified assistantships, and grants for active-duty and retired military, DOD employees, and their spouses available. Financial award application deadline: 3/31; financial award applicants required to submit FAFSA. *Faculty research:* Anthropology and ethics, states in crisis and socioeconomic development, politics and society of South Asia, political psychology, international relations theory. *Unit head:* Dr. Larry Hufford, Graduate International Relations, 210-431-6790, E-mail: lhufford@stmarytx.edu. *Application contact:* Kim Thornton, Director of Graduate Admission, 210-436-3101, E-mail: kthornton@stmarytx.edu. Website: https://www.stmarytx.edu/academics/programs/master-international-relations/

Salve Regina University, Program in International Relations, Newport, RI 02840-4192. Offers MA, CGS. *Program availability:* Part-time, evening/weekend, online learning. *Entrance requirements:* For master's, GMAT, GRE General Test, MAT or LSAT. Additional exam requirements/recommendations for international students: Required—TOEFL (minimum score 600 paper-based; 100 iBT) or IELTS. Electronic applications accepted.

San Francisco State University, Division of Graduate Studies, College of Liberal and Creative Arts, Department of International Relations, San Francisco, CA 94132-1722. Offers MA. *Unit head:* Dr. Mahmood Monshipouri, Chair, 415-338-2239, Fax: 415-338-6159, E-mail: mmonship@sfsu.edu. *Application contact:* Dr. Juanita Darling, Graduate

Coordinator, 415-405-3492, Fax: 415-338-6159, E-mail: juanitad@sfsu.edu. Website: http://internationalrelations.sfsu.edu/

Schiller International University, Program in International Relations and Diplomacy, Paris, France. Offers MA. *Program availability:* Part-time, evening/weekend. *Degree requirements:* For master's, one foreign language, final comprehensive exam or thesis. *Entrance requirements:* For master's, undergraduate mathematics (strongly advised). Additional exam requirements/recommendations for international students: Required—TOEFL (minimum score 550 paper-based).

Seton Hall University, School of Diplomacy and International Relations, South Orange, NJ 07079-2697. Offers diplomacy and international relations (MA); global health management (Graduate Certificate); post-conflict state reconstruction and sustainability (Graduate Certificate); United Nations studies (Graduate Certificate); JD/MA; MA/MA; MBA/MA; MPA/MA. *Program availability:* Part-time, evening/weekend, 100% online, blended/hybrid learning. *Degree requirements:* For master's, thesis (for some programs), 45 credits; for Graduate Certificate, 15 credits. *Entrance requirements:* For master's, GRE, GMAT, or LSAT. Additional exam requirements/recommendations for international students: Required—TOEFL. Electronic applications accepted. *Expenses:* Contact institution. *Faculty research:* International economics and development, global health, United Nations, conflict negotiation, foreign policy analysis, international security, energy politics, Eastern and Central Europe, Latin America, Africa, peacemaking, genocide prevention, international organizations, international political economy, U.S.-China relations, democratization, international law, research methods.

Simon Fraser University, Office of Graduate Studies and Postdoctoral Fellows, Faculty of Arts and Social Sciences, School for International Studies, Burnaby, BC V5A 1S6, Canada. Offers MA. *Entrance requirements:* Additional exam requirements/recommendations for international students: Required—TOEFL (minimum score 580 paper-based; 93 iBT), IELTS (minimum score 7), TWE (minimum score 5). Electronic applications accepted. *Faculty research:* Peace and security, international development, human rights and international law, governance and civil society.

SIT Graduate Institute, Graduate Programs, Master's Programs in Intercultural Service, Leadership, and Management, Brattleboro, VT 05302-0676. Offers intercultural service, leadership, and management (self-designed) (MA); international education (MA); peace and justice leadership (MA); sustainable development (MA). *Program availability:* Online learning. *Degree requirements:* For master's, one foreign language, thesis. *Entrance requirements:* For master's, 3 letters of reference. Additional exam requirements/recommendations for international students: Required—TOEFL, IELTS. *Faculty research:* Intercultural communication, conflict resolution, international education, world issues, international affairs.

Syracuse University, Maxwell School of Citizenship and Public Affairs, Dual MA Program in Economics and International Relations, Syracuse, NY 13244. Offers MA/MA. *Entrance requirements:* Additional exam requirements/recommendations for international students: Required—TOEFL (minimum score 100 iBT). *Application deadline:* For fall admission, 2/1 priority date for domestic and international students. Application fee: $75. Electronic applications accepted. *Financial support:* Fellowships with full tuition reimbursements, research assistantships, and teaching assistantships available. Financial award application deadline: 1/1. *Faculty research:* Economic concepts, urban and regional economics, policy-oriented settings, public and international affairs, comparative foreign policy. *Unit head:* Dr. Robert Bifulco, Associate Dean and Chair, Public Administration and International Affairs, 315-443-3232, E-mail: rbifulco@maxwell.syr.edu. *Application contact:* Christine Omolino, Associate Director, 315-443-4000, Fax: 315-443-3423, E-mail: comolino@syr.edu. Website: https://www.maxwell.syr.edu/paia/degrees/MAIR/Economics_Overview/

Syracuse University, Maxwell School of Citizenship and Public Affairs, Dual MPA/IR Program in Public Administration and International Relations, Syracuse, NY 13244. Offers MPA/MA. *Students:* Average age 27. *Entrance requirements:* Additional exam requirements/recommendations for international students: Required—TOEFL (minimum score 100 iBT). *Application deadline:* For fall admission, 2/1 priority date for domestic and international students. Application fee: $75. Electronic applications accepted. *Financial support:* Fellowships with full tuition reimbursements, research assistantships, and teaching assistantships available. Financial award application deadline: 1/1; financial award applicants required to submit FAFSA. *Faculty research:* Economics for public decisions, comparative foreign policy, international and development administration, public and nonprofit management, quantitative analysis. *Unit head:* Dr. Robert Bifulco, Associate Dean and Chair, Department of Public Administration and International Affairs, 315-443-3232, E-mail: rbifulco@maxwell.syr.edu. *Application contact:* Christine Omolino, Director, 315-443-4000, E-mail: comolino@syr.edu. Website: https://www.maxwell.syr.edu/paia.aspx?id=6442451202

Syracuse University, Maxwell School of Citizenship and Public Affairs, EMIR Program of International Relations, Syracuse, NY 13244. Offers EMIR. *Program availability:* Part-time. *Entrance requirements:* For master's, resume, personal statement, official transcripts, three letters of recommendation, proof of competence in a second language. Additional exam requirements/recommendations for international students: Required—TOEFL (minimum score 100 iBT). *Application deadline:* For fall admission, 2/1 priority date for domestic and international students; for spring admission, 8/1 priority date for domestic and international students. Applications are processed on a rolling basis. Application fee: $75. Electronic applications accepted. *Financial support:* Application deadline: 2/1. *Unit head:* Steven Lux, Director of Executive Education, 315-443-3759, E-mail: sjlux@maxwell.syr.edu. *Application contact:* Margaret Lane, Assistant Director, 315-443-8708, E-mail: melane02@maxwell.syr.edu. Website: https://www.maxwell.syr.edu/exed/Degree_Programs/EMIR/Overview/

Syracuse University, Maxwell School of Citizenship and Public Affairs, MA/MS Program in Public Diplomacy, Syracuse, NY 13244. Offers MS/MA. *Students:* Average age 26. *Entrance requirements:* Additional exam requirements/recommendations for international students: Required—TOEFL (minimum score 100 iBT). *Application deadline:* For fall admission, 2/1 for domestic students, 2/1 priority date for international students. Application fee: $75. Electronic applications accepted. *Financial support:* Fellowships with full tuition reimbursements, research assistantships, and teaching assistantships available. Financial award application deadline: 1/1. *Faculty research:* Public diplomacy and communications, economic dimensions of global power, comparative foreign policy, development and sustainability, culture in world affairs. *Unit head:* Dr. Dennis Kinsey, Director, Program in International Relations and Public Relations/Professor of Public Relations, S.I. Newhouse School of Public Communications, 315-443-3801, E-mail: dfkinsey@syr.edu. *Application contact:* Martha Coria, Program Contact, 315-443-5749, Fax: 315-443-1834, E-mail: pcgrad@syr.edu. Website: http://publicdiplomacy.syr.edu/

Syracuse University, Maxwell School of Citizenship and Public Affairs, MA Program in International Relations, Syracuse, NY 13244. Offers MA. *Program availability:* Part-time, evening/weekend. *Entrance requirements:* For master's, GRE General Test, resume, personal statement, three letters of recommendation, official transcripts. Additional exam requirements/recommendations for international students: Required—TOEFL (minimum score 100 iBT). *Application deadline:* For fall admission, 2/1 priority date for domestic and international students. Application fee: $75. Electronic applications

accepted. *Financial support:* Fellowships with full tuition reimbursements, research assistantships, and teaching assistantships available. Financial award application deadline: 1/1. *Faculty research:* International actors and issues, challenges of international management and leadership, comparative foreign policy, economic dimensions of global power, development and sustainability. *Unit head:* Dr. Robert Bifulco, Associate Dean and Chair, Public Administration and International Affairs, 315-443-3232, E-mail: rbifulco@maxwell.syr.edu. *Application contact:* Christine Omolino, Director, 315-443-4000, E-mail: comolino@syr.edu.
Website: https://www.maxwell.syr.edu/paia/degrees/MA_in_International_Relations/

Teachers College, Columbia University, Department of Arts and Humanities, New York, NY 10027. Offers applied linguistics (MA, Ed D); art and art education (Ed M, MA, Ed D, Ed DCT); arts administration (MA); bilingual and bicultural education (MA); global competence (Certificate); history and education (Ed D, PhD); music and music education (Ed DCT); philosophy and education (MA, Ed D, PhD); social studies education (Ed M, PhD); teaching English to speakers of other languages (Ed M); teaching of English and English education (Ed M, MA, Ed D, PhD), including English education (Ed M, Ed D, PhD), teaching of English (MA); teaching of social studies (MA); TESOL (MA, Ed D). *Program availability:* Part-time, evening/weekend. *Students:* 391 full-time (305 women), 418 part-time (283 women); includes 246 minority (62 Black or African American, non-Hispanic/Latino; 3 American Indian or Alaska Native, non-Hispanic/Latino; 94 Asian, non-Hispanic/Latino; 75 Hispanic/Latino; 12 Two or more races, non-Hispanic/Latino), 209 international. Average age 30. 1,053 applicants, 60% accepted, 334 enrolled. Terminal master's awarded for partial completion of doctoral program. *Financial support:* Fellowships, research assistantships, teaching assistantships, career-related internships or fieldwork, Federal Work-Study, institutionally sponsored loans, tuition waivers (full and partial), and unspecified assistantships available. Support available to part-time students. *Unit head:* Prof. William Gaudelli, Department Chair, E-mail: gaudelli@tc.columbia.edu. *Application contact:* David Estrella, Director of Admissions, 212-678-3305, Fax: 212-678-4171, E-mail: estrella@tc.columbia.edu.

Texas A&M University, Bush School of Government and Public Service, College Station, TX 77845. Offers homeland security (Certificate); international affairs (MIA, Certificate); national security affairs (Certificate); non-profit management (Certificate); public service and administration (MPSA). *Accreditation:* NASPAA. *Faculty:* 66. *Students:* 332 full-time (182 women), 54 part-time (16 women); includes 94 minority (19 Black or African American, non-Hispanic/Latino; 10 Asian, non-Hispanic/Latino; 56 Hispanic/Latino; 9 Two or more races, non-Hispanic/Latino), 41 international. Average age 28. 297 applicants, 94% accepted, 164 enrolled. In 2017, 154 master's awarded. *Degree requirements:* For master's, summer internship. *Entrance requirements:* For master's, GRE (preferred) or GMAT. Additional exam requirements/recommendations for international students: Required—TOEFL (minimum score 550 paper-based; 80 iBT), IELTS (minimum score 6), PTE (minimum score 53). *Application deadline:* For fall admission, 1/15 for domestic and international students. Application fee: $50 ($90 for international students). Electronic applications accepted. *Expenses:* Contact institution. *Financial support:* In 2017–18, 417 students received support, including 29 fellowships with tuition reimbursements available (averaging $20,966 per year), 71 research assistantships with tuition reimbursements available (averaging $9,778 per year); teaching assistantships, career-related internships or fieldwork, institutionally sponsored loans, scholarships/grants, traineeships, health care benefits, tuition waivers (full and partial), and unspecified assistantships also available. Support available to part-time students. Financial award application deadline: 3/15; financial award applicants required to submit FAFSA. *Faculty research:* Public policy, Presidential studies, public leadership, economic policy, social policy. *Unit head:* Dr. Mark Welsh, Dean, 979-862-8007, E-mail: mwelsh@tamu.edu. *Application contact:* Kathryn Meyer, Director of Recruitment and Admissions, 979-458-4767, Fax: 979-845-4155, E-mail: bushschooladmissions@tamu.edu.
Website: http://bush.tamu.edu/

Texas State University, The Graduate College, College of Liberal Arts, Program in International Studies, San Marcos, TX 78666. Offers MA. *Program availability:* Part-time. *Faculty:* 12 full-time (4 women). *Students:* 24 full-time (10 women), 11 part-time (5 women); includes 15 minority (7 Black or African American, non-Hispanic/Latino; 1 American Indian or Alaska Native, non-Hispanic/Latino; 1 Asian, non-Hispanic/Latino; 5 Hispanic/Latino; 1 Two or more races, non-Hispanic/Latino), 2 international. Average age 27. 30 applicants, 60% accepted, 10 enrolled. In 2017, 7 master's awarded. *Degree requirements:* For master's, comprehensive exam, thesis (for some programs). *Entrance requirements:* For master's, baccalaureate degree from regionally-accredited university, minimum GPA of 3.0 in last 60 hours leading to bachelor's degree, background courses including 6 hours of economics, proficiency in a language other than English (speaking, reading, and oral comprehension), resume, statement of purpose, 2 letters of recommendation. Additional exam requirements/recommendations for international students: Required—TOEFL (minimum score 550 paper-based; 78 iBT), IELTS (minimum score 6.5). *Application deadline:* For fall admission, 2/15 priority date for domestic and international students; for spring admission, 10/15 for domestic students, 10/1 for international students; for summer admission, 4/15 for domestic students, 3/15 for international students. Applications are processed on a rolling basis. Application fee: $40 ($90 for international students). Electronic applications accepted. *Expenses:* Tuition, state resident: full-time $7868; part-time $3934 per semester. Tuition, nonresident: full-time $17,828; part-time $8914 per semester. *Required fees:* $2092; $1435 per semester. Tuition and fees vary according to course load. *Financial support:* In 2017–18, 25 students received support, including 1 research assistantship (averaging $11,855 per year), 4 teaching assistantships (averaging $12,230 per year); Federal Work-Study, institutionally sponsored loans, scholarships/grants, health care benefits, and unspecified assistantships also available. Support available to part-time students. Financial award application deadline: 3/1; financial award applicants required to submit FAFSA. *Unit head:* Dr. Dennis Dunn, Graduate Advisor, 512-245-2107, E-mail: dd05@txstate.edu. *Application contact:* Dr. Andrea Golato, Dean of Graduate School, 512-245-2581, Fax: 512-245-8365, E-mail: gradcollege@txstate.edu.
Website: http://www.txstate.edu/internationalstudies

Texas State University, The Graduate College, College of Liberal Arts, Program in Public Administration, San Marcos, TX 78666. Offers international relations (MPA); legal and judicial administration (MPA). *Accreditation:* NASPAA. *Program availability:* Part-time, evening/weekend. *Faculty:* 7 full-time (3 women), 1 (woman) part-time/adjunct. *Students:* 31 full-time (14 women), 64 part-time (36 women); includes 45 minority (11 Black or African American, non-Hispanic/Latino; 4 Asian, non-Hispanic/Latino; 29 Hispanic/Latino; 1 Two or more races, non-Hispanic/Latino), 2 international. Average age 30. 89 applicants, 76% accepted, 31 enrolled. In 2017, 37 master's awarded. *Degree requirements:* For master's, comprehensive exam, applied research project. *Entrance requirements:* For master's, baccalaureate degree from regionally-accredited university with minimum GPA of 3.0 on last 60 undergraduate semester hours, statement of purpose, 2 letters of recommendation. Additional exam requirements/recommendations for international students: Required—TOEFL (minimum score 550 paper-based; 78 iBT), IELTS (minimum score 6.5). *Application deadline:* For fall admission, 2/1 priority date for domestic and international students; for spring admission, 10/15 for domestic students, 10/1 for international students; for summer

admission, 4/15 for domestic students, 3/15 for international students. Applications are processed on a rolling basis. Application fee: $40 ($90 for international students). Electronic applications accepted. *Expenses:* Tuition, state resident: full-time $7868; part-time $3934 per semester. Tuition, nonresident: full-time $17,828; part-time $8914 per semester. *Required fees:* $2092; $1435 per semester. Tuition and fees vary according to course load. *Financial support:* In 2017–18, 51 students received support, including 10 teaching assistantships (averaging $12,194 per year); research assistantships, career-related internships or fieldwork, Federal Work-Study, institutionally sponsored loans, scholarships/grants, and unspecified assistantships also available. Support available to part-time students. Financial award application deadline: 3/1; financial award applicants required to submit FAFSA. *Unit head:* Dr. Patricia Shields, Graduate Advisor, 512-245-3256, Fax: 512-245-7815, E-mail: ps07@txstate.edu. *Application contact:* Dr. Andrea Golato, Dean of Graduate School, 512-245-2581, Fax: 512-245-8365, E-mail: gradcollege@txstate.edu.
Website: http://mpa.polisci.txstate.edu/

Troy University, Graduate School, College of Arts and Sciences, Program in International Relations, Troy, AL 36082. Offers MS. *Program availability:* Part-time, evening/weekend, 100% online, blended/hybrid learning. *Faculty:* 15 full-time (1 woman), 6 part-time/adjunct (1 woman). *Students:* 51 full-time (20 women), 208 part-time (49 women); includes 31 minority (16 Black or African American, non-Hispanic/Latino; 1 American Indian or Alaska Native, non-Hispanic/Latino; 6 Asian, non-Hispanic/Latino; 8 Hispanic/Latino). Average age 39. 153 applicants, 97% accepted, 77 enrolled. In 2017, 66 master's awarded. *Degree requirements:* For master's, comprehensive exam (for some programs), thesis (for some programs), comprehensive exam or thesis, minimum GPA of 3.0, admission to candidacy, minimum B grade on research. *Entrance requirements:* For master's, GRE (minimum score of 920 on old exam or 294 on new exam), MAT (minimum score of 396) or GMAT (minimum score of 490), bachelor's degree; minimum undergraduate GPA of 2.5 or 3.0 on last 30 semester hours. Additional exam requirements/recommendations for international students: Required—TOEFL (minimum score 523 paper-based; 70 iBT), IELTS (minimum score 6). *Application deadline:* Applications are processed on a rolling basis. Application fee: $50. Electronic applications accepted. *Expenses:* Tuition, state resident: part-time $417 per credit hour. Tuition, nonresident: part-time $834 per credit hour. *Required fees:* $42 per credit hour. $50 per semester. Tuition and fees vary according to campus/location. *Financial support:* Fellowships, career-related internships or fieldwork, and scholarships/grants available. Support available to part-time students. Financial award applicants required to submit FAFSA. *Faculty research:* Elections, religion and world politics, terrorism. *Unit head:* Dr. Doug Davis, Director, International Relations, 334-670-5968, Fax: 334-670-5647, E-mail: gddavis@troy.edu. *Application contact:* Jessica A. Kimbro, Director of Graduate Admissions, 334-670-3178, Fax: 334-670-3733, E-mail: jacord@troy.edu.

Tufts University, The Fletcher School of Law and Diplomacy, Medford, MA 02155. Offers economics and public policy (PhD); international affairs (PhD); international business (MIB); international law (LL M); law and diplomacy (MA, MALD); transatlantic affairs (MA); DVM/MA; JD/MALD; MALD/MA; MALD/MBA; MALD/MS; MD/MA. MA in transatlantic affairs offered jointly with The College of Europe; PhD in economics and public policy with Tufts' Graduate School of Arts and Sciences. *Program availability:* Online learning. *Degree requirements:* For master's, one foreign language, thesis; for doctorate, one foreign language, comprehensive exam, thesis/dissertation, dissertation defense. *Entrance requirements:* For master's and doctorate, GMAT or GRE General Test. Additional exam requirements/recommendations for international students: Required—TOEFL (minimum score 600 paper-based; 100 iBT), IELTS (minimum score 7). Electronic applications accepted. *Expenses:* Contact institution. *Faculty research:* Negotiation and conflict resolution, international organizations, international business and economic law, security studies, development economics.

Tufts University, Graduate School of Arts and Sciences, Department of History, Medford, MA 02155. Offers history (MA, PhD), including global history (PhD); history and museum studies (MA). *Students:* 20 full-time (16 women); includes 4 minority (1 Black or African American, non-Hispanic/Latino; 3 Asian, non-Hispanic/Latino), 5 international. Average age 26. 57 applicants, 42% accepted, 7 enrolled. In 2017, 11 master's, 1 doctorate awarded. Terminal master's awarded for partial completion of doctoral program. *Degree requirements:* For master's, one foreign language, thesis optional; for doctorate, 2 foreign languages, comprehensive exam, thesis/dissertation. *Entrance requirements:* For master's and doctorate, GRE General Test, writing sample. Additional exam requirements/recommendations for international students: Required—TOEFL (minimum score 550 paper-based; 80 iBT), IELTS (minimum score 6.5). *Application deadline:* For fall admission, 1/15 for domestic and international students. Applications are processed on a rolling basis. Application fee: $85. Electronic applications accepted. *Expenses:* Contact institution. *Financial support:* Teaching assistantships, Federal Work-Study, scholarships/grants, tuition waivers (full and partial), and unspecified assistantships available. Financial award application deadline: 1/15. *Unit head:* Dr. Steven Marrone, Graduate Program Director, 617-627-2781. *Application contact:* Office of Graduate Admissions, 617-627-3395, E-mail: gradadmissions@tufts.edu.
Website: http://www.ase.tufts.edu/history/

United States International University–Africa, School of Arts and Sciences, Nairobi, Kenya. Offers counseling psychology (MA), including chemical dependency, health psychology; international relations (MA), including development studies, diplomacy and foreign policy, peace and conflict studies. *Program availability:* Part-time, evening/weekend. *Degree requirements:* For master's, thesis, practicum. *Entrance requirements:* For master's, GRE General Test, 2 letters of recommendation, resume. Additional exam requirements/recommendations for international students: Required—TOEFL. *Faculty research:* Trauma in children, African intellectualism, psychological assessment tools.

Universidad de las Americas, A.C., Program in International Organizations and Institutions, Mexico City, Mexico. Offers MA.

Universidad Nacional Pedro Henriquez Urena, Graduate School, Santo Domingo, Dominican Republic. Offers agricultural diversity (MS), including horticultural/fruit production, tropical animal production; conservation of monuments and cultural assets (M Arch); ecology and environment (MS); environmental engineering (MEE); international relations (MA); natural resource management (MS); political science (MA); project optimization (MPM); project feasibility (MPM); project management (MPM); sanitation engineering (ME); science for teachers (MS); tropical Caribbean architecture (M Arch).

Université de Montréal, Faculty of Arts and Sciences, Programs in International Studies, Montréal, QC H3C 3J7, Canada. Offers M Sc, DESS.

Université Laval, Québec Institute for Advanced International Studies, Program in International Relations, Québec, QC G1K 7P4, Canada. Offers MA, PhD. *Degree requirements:* For master's, thesis (for some programs). *Entrance requirements:* For master's, English exam, French exam. Electronic applications accepted.

University of Bridgeport, College of Public and International Affairs, Bridgeport, CT 06604. Offers East Asian and Pacific Rim studies (MA); global development and peace

(MA); global media and communication studies (MA). *Program availability:* Part-time, evening/weekend. *Degree requirements:* For master's, thesis. *Entrance requirements:* Additional exam requirements/recommendations for international students: Recommended—TOEFL (minimum score 550 paper-based; 80 iBT), IELTS (minimum score 6.5).

The University of British Columbia, Institute of Asian Research, Vancouver, BC V6T 1Z2, Canada. Offers Asia Pacific policy studies (MAAPPS); public policy and global affairs (MPPGA). *Degree requirements:* For master's, thesis optional. *Entrance requirements:* Additional exam requirements/recommendations for international students: Required—TOEFL. Electronic applications accepted. *Expenses:* Contact institution. *Faculty research:* Social cohesion, globalization, social safety nets, policy research, research and development alliances, knowledge-based workshops on Asia-Pacific studies.

University of California, Berkeley, Graduate Division, Program in Global Studies, Berkeley, CA 94720-1500. Offers MA. Electronic applications accepted.

University of California, San Diego, Graduate Division, Department of Political Science, La Jolla, CA 92093. Offers political science (PhD); political science and international affairs (PhD). *Students:* 75 full-time (24 women). 325 applicants, 13% accepted, 17 enrolled. In 2017, 9 doctorates awarded. *Degree requirements:* For doctorate, comprehensive exam, thesis/dissertation. *Entrance requirements:* For doctorate, GRE General Test, letters of recommendation. Additional exam requirements/recommendations for international students: Required—TOEFL (minimum score 600 paper-based; 100 iBT), IELTS. *Application deadline:* For fall admission, 12/13 for domestic students. Application fee: $105 ($125 for international students). Electronic applications accepted. *Financial support:* Fellowships, research assistantships, teaching assistantships, and scholarships/grants available. Financial award applicants required to submit FAFSA. *Faculty research:* American politics, comparative politics, international relations, methodology, political theory. *Unit head:* Thad Kousser, Chair, 858-534-3239, E-mail: tkousser@ucsd.edu. *Application contact:* Tyra Hawthorne, Graduate Coordinator, 858-534-2705, E-mail: psgradadmissions@ucsd.edu. Website: http://polisci.ucsd.edu/

University of California, San Diego, Graduate Division, School of Global Policy and Strategy, Master of International Affairs Program, La Jolla, CA 92093. Offers international development and nonprofit management (MIA); international economics (MIA); international environmental policy (MIA); international management (MIA); international politics (MIA). Students will choose one of the following country/regional specializations: China, Japan, Korea, Latin America, or Southeast Asia. *Degree requirements:* For master's, one foreign language. *Entrance requirements:* For master's, GMAT or GRE General Test. Additional exam requirements/recommendations for international students: Required—TOEFL (minimum score 90 iBT), IELTS (minimum score 7). Electronic applications accepted.

University of California, Santa Barbara, Graduate Division, College of Letters and Sciences, Division of Humanities and Fine Arts, Department of English, Santa Barbara, CA 93106-3170. Offers English (PhD), including environment and society, European medieval studies, feminist studies, global studies, technology and society, translation studies, writing studies; MA/PhD. Terminal master's awarded for partial completion of doctoral program. *Degree requirements:* For doctorate, one foreign language, comprehensive exam, thesis/dissertation. *Entrance requirements:* For doctorate, GRE General Test, GRE Subject Test (English literature). Additional exam requirements/recommendations for international students: Required—TOEFL (minimum score 550 paper-based; 80 iBT), IELTS (minimum score 7). Electronic applications accepted. *Faculty research:* Medieval, Romantic and Victorian studies; gender studies and feminist theory; literature and the mind; American literature; literature and new media/information culture.

University of California, Santa Barbara, Graduate Division, College of Letters and Sciences, Division of Humanities and Fine Arts, Department of History, Santa Barbara, CA 93106-9410. Offers European medieval studies (PhD); global studies (PhD); public historical studies (PhD); technology and society (PhD); women's studies (PhD); MA/PhD. *Degree requirements:* For doctorate, variable foreign language requirement, comprehensive exam, thesis/dissertation. *Entrance requirements:* For doctorate, GRE. Additional exam requirements/recommendations for international students: Required—TOEFL (minimum score 550 paper-based; 80 iBT), IELTS (minimum score 7). Electronic applications accepted. *Faculty research:* Europe, United States, Latin America, Africa, Middle East, East Asia.

University of California, Santa Barbara, Graduate Division, College of Letters and Sciences, Division of Humanities and Fine Arts, Department of Religious Studies, Santa Barbara, CA 93106-3130. Offers ancient Mediterranean studies (PhD); cognitive science (PhD); European medieval studies (PhD); feminist studies (PhD); global studies (PhD); religious studies (MA, PhD); translation studies (PhD); MA/PhD. Terminal master's awarded for partial completion of doctoral program. *Degree requirements:* For master's, one foreign language, comprehensive exam (for some programs), thesis (for some programs); for doctorate, 2 foreign languages, thesis/dissertation, methodology. *Entrance requirements:* For master's and doctorate, GRE General Test. Additional exam requirements/recommendations for international students: Required—TOEFL (minimum score 550 paper-based; 80 iBT), IELTS (minimum score 7). Electronic applications accepted. *Faculty research:* Area studies; religious traditions; theory and method in the study of religion; religion, culture, and politics; spirituality and religious experience.

University of California, Santa Barbara, Graduate Division, College of Letters and Sciences, Division of Humanities and Fine Arts, Program in Comparative Literature, Santa Barbara, CA 93106-4130. Offers comparative literature (PhD); East Asian literatures (PhD); feminist studies (PhD); French (PhD); global studies (PhD); translation studies (PhD); MA/PhD. *Degree requirements:* For doctorate, 2 foreign languages, comprehensive exam, thesis/dissertation. *Entrance requirements:* For doctorate, GRE. Additional exam requirements/recommendations for international students: Required—TOEFL (minimum score 550 paper-based; 80 iBT), IELTS (minimum score 7). Electronic applications accepted. *Faculty research:* Comparative literary studies in global context, critical theory, translation studies, media technological studies, trauma studies.

University of California, Santa Barbara, Graduate Division, College of Letters and Sciences, Division of Mathematics, Life, and Physical Sciences, Department of Geography, Santa Barbara, CA 93106-4060. Offers cognitive science (PhD); geography (MA, PhD); global studies (PhD); quantitative methods in the social sciences (PhD); technology and society (PhD); transportation (PhD); MA/PhD. Terminal master's awarded for partial completion of doctoral program. *Degree requirements:* For master's, comprehensive exam (for some programs), thesis or alternative; for doctorate, comprehensive exam, thesis/dissertation, 1 quarter of teaching assistantship. *Entrance requirements:* For master's and doctorate, GRE (minimum combined verbal and quantitative scores above 1100 in old scoring system or 301 in new scoring system). Additional exam requirements/recommendations for international students: Required—TOEFL (minimum score 550 paper-based; 80 iBT), IELTS (minimum score 7). Electronic applications accepted. *Faculty research:* Earth system science; human environment relations; modeling, measurement, and computation.

University of California, Santa Barbara, Graduate Division, College of Letters and Sciences, Division of Social Sciences, Department of Global Studies, Santa Barbara, CA 93106-7065. Offers global culture, ideology, and religion (MA, PhD); global government, human rights, and civil society (MA, PhD); political economy, sustainable development, and the environment (MA, PhD). *Degree requirements:* For master's, one foreign language, thesis, 2 years of a second language; for doctorate, one foreign language, thesis/dissertation, reading proficiency in at least one language other than English. *Entrance requirements:* For master's, GRE, 2 years of a second language with minimum B grade in the final term, statement of purpose, resume or curriculum vitae, 3 letters of recommendation, transcripts (from all post-secondary institutions attended), writing sample (15-20 pages); for doctorate, GRE, statement of purpose, personal achievements/contributions statement, resume or curriculum vitae, 3 letters of recommendation, transcripts from all post-secondary institutions attended, writing sample (15-20 pages). Additional exam requirements/recommendations for international students: Required—TOEFL (minimum score 600 paper-based; 94 iBT), IELTS (minimum score 7). Electronic applications accepted.

University of California, Santa Barbara, Graduate Division, College of Letters and Sciences, Division of Social Sciences, Department of Sociology, Santa Barbara, CA 93106-9430. Offers interdisciplinary emphasis: Black studies (PhD); interdisciplinary emphasis: environment and society (PhD); interdisciplinary emphasis: feminist studies (PhD); interdisciplinary emphasis: global studies (PhD); interdisciplinary emphasis: language, interaction and social organization (PhD); interdisciplinary emphasis: quantitative methods in the social sciences (PhD); interdisciplinary emphasis: technology and society (PhD); sociology (PhD); MA/PhD. Terminal master's awarded for partial completion of doctoral program. *Degree requirements:* For doctorate, comprehensive exam, thesis/dissertation. *Entrance requirements:* For doctorate, GRE General Test. Additional exam requirements/recommendations for international students: Required—TOEFL (minimum score 550 paper-based; 80 iBT), IELTS (minimum score 7). Electronic applications accepted. *Faculty research:* Gender and sexualities, race/ethnicity, social movements, conversation analysis, global sociology.

University of California, Santa Cruz, Division of Graduate Studies, Division of Social Sciences, Program in International Economics, Santa Cruz, CA 95064. Offers PhD. *Degree requirements:* For doctorate, thesis/dissertation, 4 field exams, field papers, econometrics project, qualifying exams. *Entrance requirements:* For doctorate, GRE General Test. Additional exam requirements/recommendations for international students: Required—TOEFL (minimum score 550 paper-based; 83 iBT); Recommended—IELTS (minimum score 8). Electronic applications accepted. *Faculty research:* Current and emerging issues in taxation, industrial policy, environmental regulation, market structure, labor economics focus on behavior and adjustment in an interdependent world economy.

University of Chicago, Division of the Social Sciences, Committee on International Relations, Chicago, IL 60637. Offers MA. *Faculty:* 38. *Students:* 61 full-time (25 women); includes 16 minority (4 Black or African American, non-Hispanic/Latino; 6 Asian, non-Hispanic/Latino; 4 Hispanic/Latino; 2 Two or more races, non-Hispanic/Latino), 18 international. Average age 25. 234 applicants, 75% accepted, 57 enrolled. In 2017, 41 master's awarded. *Degree requirements:* For master's, thesis. *Entrance requirements:* For master's, GRE General Test, 3 letters of recommendation, statement of purpose, transcripts, resume or curriculum vitae, writing sample (dependent on department). Additional exam requirements/recommendations for international students: Required—TOEFL (minimum score 104 iBT), IELTS (minimum score 7). *Application deadline:* For fall admission, 1/4 for domestic and international students. Application fee: $90. Electronic applications accepted. *Expenses:* $57,996 tuition. *Financial support:* In 2017–18, 42 students received support. Federal Work-Study, institutionally sponsored loans, and scholarships/grants available. Financial award application deadline: 1/4. *Unit head:* Prof. Paul Staniland, Chair, E-mail: ssd-admissions@uchicago.edu. *Application contact:* Office of the Dean of Students, 773-702-8415, E-mail: ssd-admissions@uchicago.edu.
Website: http://cir.uchicago.edu

University of Colorado Denver, College of Liberal Arts and Sciences, Program in Humanities, Denver, CO 80217. Offers community health science (MSS); humanities (MH); international studies (MSS); philosophy and theory (MH); social justice (MSS); society and the environment (MSS); visual studies (MH); women's and gender studies (MSS). *Program availability:* Part-time, evening/weekend. *Degree requirements:* For master's, 36 credit hours, project or thesis. *Entrance requirements:* For master's, writing sample, statement of purpose/letter of intent, three letters of recommendation. Additional exam requirements/recommendations for international students: Required—TOEFL (minimum score 537 paper-based; 75 iBT); Recommended—IELTS (minimum score 6.5). Electronic applications accepted. *Faculty research:* Women and gender in the classical Mediterranean, communication theory and democracy, relationship between psychology and philosophy.

University of Connecticut, Graduate School, College of Liberal Arts and Sciences, Field of International Studies, Program in International Studies, Storrs, CT 06269. Offers European studies (MA); Italian history and culture (MA); Latino and Latin American studies (MA). *Degree requirements:* For master's, comprehensive exam. *Entrance requirements:* For master's, GRE General Test. Additional exam requirements/recommendations for international students: Required—TOEFL (minimum score 550 paper-based). Electronic applications accepted.

University of Delaware, College of Arts and Sciences, Department of Political Science and International Relations, Newark, DE 19716. Offers MA, PhD. Terminal master's awarded for partial completion of doctoral program. *Degree requirements:* For master's, research paper; for doctorate, one foreign language, comprehensive exam, thesis/dissertation. *Entrance requirements:* For master's and doctorate, GRE General Test, minimum GPA of 3.2 in major, 3.0 overall. Additional exam requirements/recommendations for international students: Required—TOEFL (minimum score 600 paper-based). Electronic applications accepted. *Faculty research:* Social constructivism, international migration, international security, democratization, human rights.

University of Denver, Division of Arts, Humanities and Social Sciences, Department of Media, Film and Journalism Studies, Denver, CO 80208. Offers international and intercultural communication (MA); media and public communication (MA), including media and globalization, strategic communication. *Program availability:* Part-time. *Faculty:* 16 full-time (10 women), 5 part-time/adjunct (4 women). *Students:* 3 full-time (all women), 21 part-time (17 women); includes 5 minority (1 Asian, non-Hispanic/Latino; 4 Hispanic/Latino), 2 international. Average age 26. 34 applicants, 85% accepted, 8 enrolled. In 2017, 12 master's awarded. *Degree requirements:* For master's, thesis (for some programs). *Entrance requirements:* For master's, GRE General Test, bachelor's degree, transcripts, personal statement, three letters of recommendation. Additional exam requirements/recommendations for international students: Required—TOEFL (minimum score 620 paper-based; 105 iBT). *Application deadline:* For fall admission, 2/15 priority date for domestic students, 1/1 priority date for international students. Applications are processed on a rolling basis. Application fee: $65. Electronic applications accepted. *Expenses:* $31,935 per year full-time. *Financial support:* In 2017–18, 18 students received support. Teaching assistantships with tuition reimbursements available, career-related internships or fieldwork, Federal Work-Study,

institutionally sponsored loans, scholarships/grants, and unspecified assistantships available. Support available to part-time students. Financial award application deadline: 2/15; financial award applicants required to submit FAFSA. *Faculty research:* Branding; public relations; health communication; social media; international communication. *Unit head:* Dr. Lynn Schofield Clark, Professor and Chair, 303-871-3984, Fax: 303-871-4949, E-mail: lynn.clark@du.edu. *Application contact:* Information Contact, 303-871-2166, E-mail: mfjs@du.edu.
Website: http://www.du.edu/ahss/mfjs

University of Denver, Josef Korbel School of International Studies, Denver, CO 80208. Offers conflict resolution (MA); global business and corporate social responsibility (Certificate); global finance, trade and economic integration (MA); global health affairs (Certificate); homeland security (Certificate); humanitarian assistance (Certificate); international administration (MA); international development (MA); international human rights (MA); international security (MA); international studies (MA, PhD); public policy studies (MPP); religion and international affairs (Certificate). *Program availability:* Part-time. *Faculty:* 46 full-time (16 women), 28 part-time/adjunct (8 women). *Students:* 245 full-time (132 women), 40 part-time (21 women); includes 58 minority (8 Black or African American, non-Hispanic/Latino; 2 American Indian or Alaska Native, non-Hispanic/Latino; 11 Asian, non-Hispanic/Latino; 27 Hispanic/Latino; 10 Two or more races, non-Hispanic/Latino), 22 international. Average age 27. 627 applicants, 74% accepted, 106 enrolled. In 2017, 218 master's, 6 doctorates, 25 other advanced degrees awarded. *Degree requirements:* For master's, one foreign language, thesis (for some programs); for doctorate, one foreign language, comprehensive exam, thesis/dissertation, two extended research papers. *Entrance requirements:* For master's, GRE General Test, bachelor's degree, transcripts, two letters of recommendation, statement of purpose, resume or curriculum vitae; for doctorate, GRE General Test, master's degree, transcripts, three letters of recommendation, statement of purpose, resume or curriculum vitae, writing sample; for Certificate, bachelor's degree, transcripts, two letters of recommendation, statement of purpose, resume or curriculum vitae. Additional exam requirements/recommendations for international students: Required—TOEFL (minimum score 587 paper-based; 95 iBT). *Application deadline:* For fall admission, 1/15 priority date for domestic and international students; for winter admission, 11/1 for domestic and international students. Applications are processed on a rolling basis. Application fee: $65. Electronic applications accepted. *Expenses:* $47,823 per year full-time. *Financial support:* In 2017–18, 225 students received support, including 1 teaching assistantship with tuition reimbursement available (averaging $2,236 per year); research assistantships with tuition reimbursements available, career-related internships or fieldwork, Federal Work-Study, institutionally sponsored loans, scholarships/grants, and unspecified assistantships also available. Support available to part-time students. Financial award application deadline: 2/15; financial award applicants required to submit FAFSA. *Faculty research:* Human rights and international security, international politics and economics, economic-social and political development, international technology analysis and management. *Unit head:* Dr. Pardis Mahdavi, Dean, 303-871-6338, E-mail: pardis.mahdavi@du.edu. *Application contact:* Admissions Contact, E-mail: korbeladm@du.edu.
Website: http://www.du.edu/korbel

University of Denver, University College, Denver, CO 80208. Offers arts and culture (MA, Certificate); communication management (MS, Certificate), including translation studies (Certificate), world history and culture (Certificate); environmental policy and management (MS); geographic information systems (MS); global affairs (MA, Certificate), including human capital in organizations (Certificate), philanthropic leadership (Certificate), project management (Certificate), strategic innovation and change (Certificate); healthcare leadership (MS); information communications and technology (MS); leadership and organizations (MS); professional creative writing (MA, Certificate), including emergency planning and response (Certificate), organizational security (Certificate); security management (MS, Certificate); strategic human resources (Certificate). *Program availability:* Part-time, evening/weekend, online learning. *Faculty:* 118 part-time/adjunct (62 women). *Students:* 56 full-time (32 women), 1,287 part-time (707 women); includes 330 minority (99 Black or African American, non-Hispanic/Latino; 7 American Indian or Alaska Native, non-Hispanic/Latino; 43 Asian, non-Hispanic/Latino; 141 Hispanic/Latino; 3 Native Hawaiian or other Pacific Islander, non-Hispanic/Latino; 37 Two or more races, non-Hispanic/Latino), 84 international. Average age 34. 783 applicants, 86% accepted, 420 enrolled. In 2017, 461 master's, 173 other advanced degrees awarded. *Degree requirements:* For master's, capstone project. *Entrance requirements:* For master's, transcripts, two letters of recommendation, personal statement, resume. Additional exam requirements/recommendations for international students: Required—TOEFL (minimum score 550 paper-based; 80 iBT). *Application deadline:* For fall admission, 6/21 priority date for domestic students, 5/1 priority date for international students; for winter admission, 9/14 priority date for domestic students, 9/19 priority date for international students; for spring admission, 1/11 priority date for domestic students, 12/12 priority date for international students; for summer admission, 3/29 priority date for domestic students, 3/6 priority date for international students. Applications are processed on a rolling basis. Application fee: $75. Electronic applications accepted. *Expenses:* $7,968 per year half-time. *Financial support:* In 2017–18, 29 students received support. Teaching assistantships available. Financial award applicants required to submit FAFSA. *Unit head:* Dr. Michael McGuire, Dean, 303-871-3518, Fax: 303-871-3303, E-mail: mmcguire@du.edu. *Application contact:* Information Contact, 303-871-2291, E-mail: ucoladm@du.edu.
Website: http://universitycollege.du.edu/

University of Florida, Graduate School, College of Liberal Arts and Sciences, Department of Political Science, Program in International Relations, Gainesville, FL 32611. Offers MA, MAT. *Degree requirements:* For master's, comprehensive exam (for some programs), thesis optional. *Entrance requirements:* For master's, GRE General Test, minimum GPA of 3.0. Additional exam requirements/recommendations for international students: Required—TOEFL (minimum score 550 paper-based; 80 iBT), IELTS (minimum score 6). Electronic applications accepted. *Faculty research:* International relations theory, international political economy, feminist international relations, international security, international organization.

University of Georgia, School of Public and International Affairs, Department of International Affairs, Athens, GA 30602. Offers MA, MIP, PhD.

University of Georgia, School of Public and International Affairs, Program in Political Science/International Affairs, Athens, GA 30602. Offers MA, PhD. *Degree requirements:* For master's, one foreign language, thesis; for doctorate, one foreign language, thesis/dissertation. *Entrance requirements:* For master's and doctorate, GRE General Test. Electronic applications accepted.

University of Hawaii at Manoa, Office of Graduate Education, International Cultural Studies Graduate Certificate Program, Honolulu, HI 96822. Offers Graduate Certificate. *Program availability:* Part-time. *Entrance requirements:* For degree, GRE General Test. Additional exam requirements/recommendations for international students: Required—TOEFL (minimum score 540 paper-based; 76 iBT), IELTS (minimum score 5).

University of Indianapolis, Graduate Programs, College of Arts and Sciences, Department of History and Political Science, Indianapolis, IN 46227-3697. Offers history (MA); international relations (MA). *Program availability:* Part-time, evening/weekend. *Degree requirements:* For master's, thesis optional. *Entrance requirements:* For master's, GRE Subject Test, minimum GPA of 3.0, 3 letters of recommendation. Additional exam requirements/recommendations for international students: Required—TOEFL (minimum score 550 paper-based). Electronic applications accepted.

The University of Kansas, Graduate Studies, College of Liberal Arts and Sciences, Center for Global and International Studies, Lawrence, KS 66045. Offers MA. *Program availability:* Part-time, evening/weekend. *Students:* 24 full-time (5 women), 16 part-time (5 women); includes 8 minority (1 Black or African American, non-Hispanic/Latino; 1 Asian, non-Hispanic/Latino; 2 Hispanic/Latino; 4 Two or more races, non-Hispanic/Latino), 4 international. Average age 32. 33 applicants, 88% accepted, 21 enrolled. In 2017, 21 master's awarded. *Entrance requirements:* For master's, GRE, minimum GPA of 3.0, 2 letters of reference, curriculum vitae, reflective essay, 300-500 word statement of interest describing relevant aspects of background and addressing how program will help meet academic and professional goals. Additional exam requirements/recommendations for international students: Required—TOEFL (minimum score 80 iBT). *Application deadline:* For fall admission, 4/1 priority date for domestic and international students; for spring admission, 10/1 priority date for domestic and international students. Application fee: $65 ($85 for international students). Electronic applications accepted. *Financial support:* Research assistantships, teaching assistantships, scholarships/grants, health care benefits, and unspecified assistantships available. Support available to part-time students. *Faculty research:* Globalization, environmental sociology, economic development, comparative government, international relations. *Unit head:* Shannon O'Lear, Director, 785-864-2041, E-mail: olear@ku.edu. *Application contact:* Alyssa McDonald, Graduate Admissions Contact, 785-864-9814, E-mail: mcdonalda@ku.edu.
Website: http://global.ku.edu/

University of Kentucky, Graduate School, Patterson School of Diplomacy and International Commerce, Lexington, KY 40506-0027. Offers MA. *Degree requirements:* For master's, one foreign language, comprehensive exam, statistics. *Entrance requirements:* For master's, GRE General Test, minimum undergraduate GPA of 3.0. Additional exam requirements/recommendations for international students: Required—TOEFL (minimum score 550 paper-based; 79 iBT). Electronic applications accepted. *Faculty research:* International relations, foreign and defense policy, cross-cultural negotiation, international science and technology, diplomacy, international economics and development, geopolitical modeling.

University of Maine, Graduate School, College of Liberal Arts and Sciences, School of Policy and International Affairs, Orono, ME 04469. Offers global policy (MA). *Faculty:* 4 full-time (1 woman), 6 part-time/adjunct (0 women). *Students:* 19 full-time (10 women), 1 (woman) part-time, 5 international. Average age 25. 17 applicants, 94% accepted, 8 enrolled. In 2017, 11 master's awarded. *Entrance requirements:* For master's, GRE. Additional exam requirements/recommendations for international students: Required—TOEFL (minimum score 80 iBT), IELTS (minimum score 6.5). *Application deadline:* Applications are processed on a rolling basis. Application fee: $65. Electronic applications accepted. *Expenses:* Tuition, state resident: full-time $7722; part-time $429 per credit hour. Tuition, nonresident: full-time $25,146; part-time $1397 per credit hour. *Required fees:* $1162; $581 per credit hour. *Financial support:* In 2017–18, 10 students received support, including 3 fellowships (averaging $19,700 per year), 2 teaching assistantships (averaging $15,200 per year); career-related internships or fieldwork, Federal Work-Study, scholarships/grants, and unspecified assistantships also available. Financial award application deadline: 3/1. *Faculty research:* International political economy; international environmental policy; dynamics of political conflict; international development; foreign direct investment. *Unit head:* Capt. James Settele, Director, 207-581-3153, E-mail: james.settele@umit.maine.edu. *Application contact:* Scott G. Delcourt, Assistant Vice President for Graduate Studies and Senior Associate Dean, 207-581-3291, Fax: 207-581-3232, E-mail: graduate@maine.edu.
Website: http://spia.umaine.edu/

The University of Manchester, School of Arts, Histories and Cultures, Manchester, United Kingdom. Offers anthropology, media and performance (PhD); applied theatre professional (PhD); archaeology (PhD); art history and visual studies (PhD); arts management and cultural policy (PhD); classics and ancient history (PhD); composition (PhD); creative writing (PhD); drama (PhD); economic and social history (PhD); electroacoustic composition (PhD); English and American studies (PhD); history (PhD); humanitarianism and conflict response (PhD); museology (PhD); music (PhD); musicology (PhD); religions and theology (PhD).

University of Massachusetts Boston, McCormack Graduate School of Policy and Global Studies, Program in Global Governance and Human Security, Boston, MA 02125-3393. Offers MA. *Students:* 20 full-time (10 women), 31 part-time (19 women); includes 9 minority (2 Black or African American, non-Hispanic/Latino; 2 Asian, non-Hispanic/Latino; 3 Hispanic/Latino; 2 Two or more races, non-Hispanic/Latino), 22 international. Average age 35. 43 applicants, 33% accepted, 11 enrolled. In 2017, 7 master's awarded. *Expenses:* Tuition, state resident: full-time $17,375. Tuition, nonresident: full-time $33,915. *Required fees:* $355. *Unit head:* Dr. David Cash, Dean, 617-287-5000. *Application contact:* Graduate Admissions Coordinator, 617-287-6400, Fax: 617-287-6236, E-mail: bos.gadm@dpc.umassp.edu.

University of Massachusetts Boston, McCormack Graduate School of Policy and Global Studies, Program in International Relations, Boston, MA 02125-3393. Offers MA. *Students:* 14 full-time (5 women), 5 part-time (2 women); includes 1 minority (Black or African American, non-Hispanic/Latino), 5 international. Average age 30. 23 applicants, 43% accepted, 7 enrolled. *Expenses:* Tuition, state resident: full-time $17,375. Tuition, nonresident: full-time $33,915. *Required fees:* $355. *Unit head:* Dr. David Cash, Dean, 617-287-5551, E-mail: david.cash@umb.edu. *Application contact:* Graduate Admissions Coordinator, 617-287-6400, Fax: 617-287-6236, E-mail: bos.gadm@dpc.umassp.edu.
Website: https://mccormack.umb.edu/academics/crhsgg/programs/international-relations-ma

University of Miami, Graduate School, College of Arts and Sciences, Department of International Studies, Coral Gables, FL 33124. Offers MA, PhD. *Degree requirements:* For master's, one foreign language, comprehensive exam; for doctorate, one foreign language, comprehensive exam, thesis/dissertation. *Entrance requirements:* For master's, GRE General Test, minimum GPA of 3.0; for doctorate, GRE General Test. Additional exam requirements/recommendations for international students: Required—TOEFL. Electronic applications accepted. *Faculty research:* Latin American studies, international economics, international security and conflict, comparative development, international health policy.

University of Miami, Graduate School, Program in International Administration, Coral Gables, FL 33124. Offers MAIA. *Program availability:* Part-time, evening/weekend. *Degree requirements:* For master's, practicum. *Entrance requirements:* For master's, GRE General Test. Additional exam requirements/recommendations for international students: Required—TOEFL (minimum score 550 paper-based), IELTS (minimum score 6.5). Electronic applications accepted.

University of Michigan–Flint, College of Arts and Sciences, Program in Social Sciences, Flint, MI 48502-1950. Offers gender studies (MA); global studies (MA); U.S. history and politics (MA). *Program availability:* Part-time. *Faculty:* 12 full-time (7 women),

6 part-time/adjunct (4 women). *Students:* 2 full-time (1 woman), 12 part-time (6 women); includes 4 minority (3 Black or African American, non-Hispanic/Latino; 1 Hispanic/Latino). Average age 43. 8 applicants, 88% accepted, 6 enrolled. In 2017, 11 master's awarded. *Entrance requirements:* For master's, bachelor's degree from regionally-accredited institution, minimum overall undergraduate GPA of 3.0. Additional exam requirements/recommendations for international students: Required—TOEFL (minimum score 84 iBT), IELTS (minimum score 6.5). *Application deadline:* For fall admission, 8/1 for domestic students, 5/1 for international students; for winter admission, 11/15 for domestic students, 9/1 for international students; for spring admission, 3/15 for domestic students, 1/1 for international students; for summer admission, 5/15 for domestic students. Applications are processed on a rolling basis. Application fee: $55. Electronic applications accepted. *Expenses:* Contact institution. *Financial support:* Federal Work-Study, scholarships/grants, and unspecified assistantships available. Financial award application deadline: 3/1; financial award applicants required to submit FAFSA. *Unit head:* Dr. Adam Lutzker, Director, 810-762-3470, Fax: 810-762-3281, E-mail: alutzker@umflint.edu. *Application contact:* Bradley T. Maki, Director of Graduate Admissions, 810-762-3171, Fax: 810-766-6789, E-mail: bmaki@umflint.edu.
Website: http://www.umflint.edu/graduateprograms/social-sciences-ma

The University of North Carolina at Chapel Hill, Graduate School, College of Arts and Sciences, Center for Slavic, Eurasian and East European Studies, Chapel Hill, NC 27599. Offers global studies (MA). *Program availability:* Part-time. *Degree requirements:* For master's, one foreign language, thesis. *Entrance requirements:* For master's, GRE General Test. Additional exam requirements/recommendations for international students: Required—TOEFL. Electronic applications accepted. *Faculty research:* Language, area studies, social sciences, professional schools.

University of Northern British Columbia, Office of Graduate Studies, Prince George, BC V2N 4Z9, Canada. Offers business administration (Diploma); community health science (M Sc); disability management (MA); education (M Ed); first nations studies (MA); gender studies (MA); history (MA); interdisciplinary studies (MA); international studies (MA); mathematical, computer and physical sciences (M Sc); natural resources and environmental studies (M Sc, MA, MNRES, PhD); political science (MA); psychology (M Sc, PhD); social work (MSW). *Program availability:* Part-time, evening/weekend, online learning. *Degree requirements:* For master's, thesis; for doctorate, thesis/dissertation. *Entrance requirements:* For master's, GRE, minimum B average in undergraduate course work; for doctorate, candidacy exam, minimum A average in graduate course work.

University of North Georgia, Program in International Affairs, Dahlonega, GA 30597. Offers MAIA. *Program availability:* Part-time, evening/weekend, 100% online. *Faculty:* 5 full-time (1 woman). *Students:* 10 full-time (3 women), 31 part-time (12 women); includes 8 minority (5 Black or African American, non-Hispanic/Latino; 1 Hispanic/Latino; 2 Two or more races, non-Hispanic/Latino). Average age 33. 20 applicants, 80% accepted, 10 enrolled. In 2017, 12 master's awarded. *Degree requirements:* For master's, capstone. *Entrance requirements:* For master's, GRE, minimum undergraduate GPA of 2.75, 2 UNG recommendation forms, 600-word personal statement. Additional exam requirements/recommendations for international students: Required—TOEFL (minimum score 550 paper-based; 79 iBT), IELTS (minimum score 6.5). *Application deadline:* For fall admission, 8/1 priority date for domestic students; for spring admission, 12/1 priority date for domestic students; for summer admission, 5/1 priority date for domestic students. Applications are processed on a rolling basis. Application fee: $40. Electronic applications accepted. *Expenses:* Contact institution. *Financial support:* In 2017–18, 1 student received support. Unspecified assistantships available. Financial award application deadline: 3/17; financial award applicants required to submit CSS PROFILE or FAFSA. *Faculty research:* Strategic thought and strategic culture; comparative global development; U.S. foreign policy making; migration; social and political intolerance in Europe. *Unit head:* Dr. Cristian Harris, Program Coordinator, 706-867-3251, E-mail: cristian.harris@ung.edu. *Application contact:* Melinda Maxwell, Director of Graduate Admissions, 706-864-1543, E-mail: melinda.maxwell@ung.edu.
Website: http://ung.edu/political-science-international-affairs/

University of North Texas, Robert B. Toulouse School of Graduate Studies, Denton, TX 76203-5459. Offers accounting (MS); applied anthropology (MA, MS); applied behavior analysis (Certificate); applied geography (MA); applied technology and performance improvement (M Ed, MS); art education (MA); art history (MA); art museum education (Certificate); arts leadership (Certificate); audiology (Au D); behavior analysis (MS); behavioral science (PhD); biochemistry and molecular biology (MS); biology (MA, MS); biomedical engineering (MS); business analysis (MS); chemistry (MS); clinical health psychology (PhD); communication studies (MA, MS); computer engineering (MS); computer science (MS); counseling (M Ed, MS), including clinical mental health counseling (MS), college and university counseling, elementary school counseling, secondary school counseling; creative writing (MA); criminal justice (MS); curriculum and instruction (M Ed); decision sciences (MBA); design (MA, MFA), including fashion design (MFA), innovation studies, interior design (MFA); early childhood studies (MS); economics (MS); educational leadership (M Ed, Ed D); educational psychology (MS, PhD), including family studies (MS), gifted and talented (MS), human development (MS), learning and cognition (MS), research, measurement and evaluation (MS); electrical engineering (MS); emergency management (MPA); engineering technology (MS); English (MA); English as a second language (MA); environmental science (MS); finance (MBA, MS); financial management (MPA); French (MA); health services management (MBA); higher education (M Ed, Ed D); history (MA, MS); hospitality management (MS); human resources management (MPA); information science (MS); information systems (PhD); information technologies (MBA); interdisciplinary studies (MA, MS); international studies (MA); international sustainable tourism (MS); jazz studies (MM); journalism (MA, MJ, Graduate Certificate), including interactive and virtual digital communication (Graduate Certificate), narrative journalism (Graduate Certificate), public relations (Graduate Certificate); kinesiology (MS); linguistics (MA); local government management (MPA); logistics (PhD); logistics and supply chain management (MBA); long-term care, senior housing, and aging services (MA); management (PhD); marketing (MBA); mathematics (MA, MS); mechanical and energy engineering (MS, PhD); music (MA), including ethnomusicology, music theory, musicology, performance; music composition (PhD); music education (MM Ed, PhD); nonprofit management (MPA); operations and supply chain management (MBA); performance (MM, DMA); philosophy (MA); political science (MA); professional and technical communication (MA); radio, television and film (MA, MFA); rehabilitation counseling (Certificate); sociology (MA); Spanish (MA); special education (M Ed); speech-language pathology (MA); strategic management (MBA); studio art (MFA); teaching (M Ed); MBA/MS. *Program availability:* Part-time, evening/weekend, online learning. Terminal master's awarded for partial completion of doctoral program. *Degree requirements:* For master's, variable foreign language requirement, comprehensive exam (for some programs), thesis (for some programs); for doctorate, variable foreign language requirement, comprehensive exam (for some programs), thesis/dissertation; for other advanced degree, variable foreign language requirement, comprehensive exam (for some programs). *Entrance requirements:* For master's and doctorate, GRE, GMAT. Additional exam requirements/recommendations for international students: Required—TOEFL (minimum score 550 paper-based; 79 iBT). Electronic applications accepted.

University of Notre Dame, Graduate School, Keough School of Global Affairs, Notre Dame, IN 46556. Offers global affairs (MGA); international peace studies (MGA); sustainable development (MGA).

University of Oklahoma, College of International Studies, Norman, OK 73019. Offers economics and development (MAIS), including global economics and development, global security studies (MA, MAIS); global affairs (MA), including economics and development, global security studies (MA, MAIS); JD/MAIS; MAIS/MSW. *Program availability:* Part-time, online courses with an 8-10 day study abroad. *Faculty:* 20 full-time (7 women), 1 part-time/adjunct (0 women). *Students:* 80 full-time (35 women), 307 part-time (97 women); includes 118 minority (33 Black or African American, non-Hispanic/Latino; 2 American Indian or Alaska Native, non-Hispanic/Latino; 15 Asian, non-Hispanic/Latino; 45 Hispanic/Latino; 1 Native Hawaiian or other Pacific Islander, non-Hispanic/Latino; 22 Two or more races, non-Hispanic/Latino), 7 international. Average age 32. 121 applicants, 89% accepted, 68 enrolled. In 2017, 73 master's awarded. Terminal master's awarded for partial completion of doctoral program. *Degree requirements:* For master's, variable foreign language requirement, 36 credit hours (33 online); thesis, policy paper or internship project; faculty-led overseas travel program of 8-10 days that will vary in location (online). *Entrance requirements:* For master's, GRE. Additional exam requirements/recommendations for international students: Required—TOEFL (minimum score 79 iBT) or IELTS (minimum score 6.5). *Application deadline:* For fall admission, 2/15 for domestic and international students. Applications are processed on a rolling basis. Application fee: $50 ($100 for international students). Electronic applications accepted. *Expenses:* Tuition, state resident: full-time $5119; part-time $213.30 per credit hour. Tuition, nonresident: full-time $19,778; part-time $824.10 per credit hour. *Required fees:* $3458; $133.55 per credit hour. $126.50 per semester. *Financial support:* In 2017–18, 31 students received support, including 4 research assistantships with full tuition reimbursements available (averaging $13,500 per year), 4 teaching assistantships with full tuition reimbursements available (averaging $13,500 per year); fellowships with full tuition reimbursements available, career-related internships or fieldwork, scholarships/grants, health care benefits, and unspecified assistantships also available. Financial award application deadline: 6/1; financial award applicants required to submit FAFSA. *Faculty research:* Area studies, including the Middle East, China, East and South Asia, Latin America, and Europe; political economy and development; international security; identity and nationalism; global history and culture. *Total annual research expenditures:* $1,502. *Unit head:* Dr. Mitchell Smith, Professor/Associate Dean for Academic Affairs, 405-325-1584, Fax: 405-325-7738, E-mail: mps@ou.edu. *Application contact:* Katie Watkins, Academic Advisor, 405-325-2337, Fax: 405-325-7738, E-mail: kwatkins@ou.edu.
Website: http://www.ou.edu/dias

University of Oregon, Graduate School, College of Arts and Sciences, Program in International Studies, Eugene, OR 97403. Offers MA. *Program availability:* Part-time. *Degree requirements:* For master's, one foreign language, thesis, internship. *Entrance requirements:* For master's, minimum GPA of 3.0. Additional exam requirements/recommendations for international students: Required—TOEFL. *Faculty research:* International development studies; environmental studies; cross-cultural communications; planning, public policy, and management; several world regions.

University of Pennsylvania, School of Arts and Sciences, Graduate Group in International Studies, Philadelphia, PA 19104. Offers AM. *Faculty:* 7 full-time (1 woman), 6 part-time/adjunct (2 women). *Students:* 12 full-time (3 women); includes 1 minority (Hispanic/Latino), 6 international. Average age 32. In 2017, 77 master's awarded. Application fee: $70.
Website: http://www.sas.upenn.edu/graduate-division

University of Pittsburgh, Graduate School of Public and International Affairs, Master of Public Administration Program, Pittsburgh, PA 15260. Offers energy and environment (MPA); governance and international public management (MPA); policy research and analysis (MPA); public and nonprofit management (MPA); urban affairs and planning (MPA); JD/MPA; MPH/MPA; MSIS/MPA; MSW/MPA. *Accreditation:* NASPAA. *Program availability:* Part-time, evening/weekend. *Faculty:* 30 full-time (11 women), 14 part-time/adjunct (5 women). *Students:* 100 full-time (75 women), 18 part-time (12 women); includes 13 minority (6 Black or African American, non-Hispanic/Latino; 3 Asian, non-Hispanic/Latino; 4 Hispanic/Latino), 54 international. Average age 26. 220 applicants, 87% accepted, 44 enrolled. In 2017, 54 master's awarded. *Degree requirements:* For master's, thesis optional, capstone seminar. *Entrance requirements:* For master's, GRE General Test or GMAT, 2 letters of recommendation, resume, undergraduate transcripts, personal statement. Additional exam requirements/recommendations for international students: Required—TOEFL (minimum score 80 iBT); Recommended—IELTS (minimum score 7). *Application deadline:* For fall admission, 2/1 priority date for domestic students, 1/15 priority date for international students; for spring admission, 11/1 priority date for domestic students, 8/1 priority date for international students. Application fee: $50. Electronic applications accepted. *Expenses:* $23,140 per year in-state, $37,830 out-of-state. *Financial support:* In 2017–18, 23 students received support, including 1 fellowship with full tuition reimbursement available (averaging $37,000 per year), 1 research assistantship with full tuition reimbursement available (averaging $37,000 per year); career-related internships or fieldwork and scholarships/grants also available. Financial award application deadline: 2/1; financial award applicants required to submit FAFSA. *Faculty research:* Urban affairs and planning, governance and international public management, public and nonprofit management, policy research and analysis, energy and environment. *Total annual research expenditures:* $1.6 million. *Unit head:* Dr. John Keeler, Dean, 412-648-7605, Fax: 412-648-7601, E-mail: gspia@pitt.edu. *Application contact:* Dr. Michael Rizzi, Director of Student Services, 412-648-7643, Fax: 412-648-7641, E-mail: rizzim@pitt.edu.
Website: http://www.gspia.pitt.edu/

University of Pittsburgh, Graduate School of Public and International Affairs, Master of Public and International Affairs Program, Pittsburgh, PA 15260. Offers human security (MPIA); international political economy (MPIA); security and intelligence studies (MPIA); JD/MPIA; MBA/MPIA; MPH/MPIA; MPIA/MSW; MSIS/MPIA. *Program availability:* Part-time, evening/weekend. *Faculty:* 30 full-time (11 women), 14 part-time/adjunct (5 women). *Students:* 87 full-time (42 women), 14 part-time (7 women); includes 15 minority (6 Black or African American, non-Hispanic/Latino; 3 Asian, non-Hispanic/Latino; 6 Hispanic/Latino), 14 international. Average age 27. 173 applicants, 88% accepted, 37 enrolled. In 2017, 54 master's awarded. *Degree requirements:* For master's, thesis optional, capstone seminar. *Entrance requirements:* For master's, GRE General Test or GMAT, 2 letters of recommendation, resume, undergraduate transcripts, personal statement. Additional exam requirements/recommendations for international students: Required—TOEFL (minimum score 80 iBT); Recommended—IELTS (minimum score 7). *Application deadline:* For fall admission, 2/1 priority date for domestic students, 1/15 priority date for international students; for spring admission, 11/1 priority date for domestic students, 8/1 priority date for international students. Application fee: $50. Electronic applications accepted. *Expenses:* $23,140 per year in-state, $37,830 out-of-state. *Financial support:* In 2017–18, 47 students received support, including 7 fellowships with full tuition reimbursements available (averaging $37,000 per year), 8 research assistantships with full tuition reimbursements available (averaging $37,000 per year); scholarships/grants also available. Financial award

application deadline: 2/1; financial award applicants required to submit FAFSA. *Faculty research:* International political economy, human security, security and intelligence studies. *Total annual research expenditures:* $1.6 million. *Unit head:* Dr. John Keeler, Dean, 412-648-7605, Fax: 412-648-7601, E-mail: gspia@pitt.edu. *Application contact:* Dr. Michael Rizzi, Director of Student Services, 412-648-7643, Fax: 412-648-7641, E-mail: rizzim@pitt.edu.
Website: http://www.gspia.pitt.edu/

University of Pittsburgh, Graduate School of Public and International Affairs, PhD Program in Public and International Affairs, Pittsburgh, PA 15260. Offers international affairs (PhD); international development (PhD); public administration (PhD); public policy (PhD). *Program availability:* Part-time, online learning. *Faculty:* 30 full-time (11 women), 14 part-time/adjunct (5 women). *Students:* 31 full-time (11 women), 2 part-time (0 women); includes 5 minority (1 Black or African American, non-Hispanic/Latino; 2 Asian, non-Hispanic/Latino; 2 Hispanic/Latino), 12 international. Average age 37. 69 applicants, 13% accepted, 8 enrolled. In 2017, 2 doctorates awarded. *Degree requirements:* For doctorate, thesis/dissertation, mid-term evaluation, preliminary exam, annual review. *Entrance requirements:* For doctorate, GRE or GMAT, 2 letters of recommendation, resume, undergraduate transcripts, personal statement, writing sample. Additional exam requirements/recommendations for international students: Required—TOEFL (minimum score 80 iBT); Recommended—IELTS (minimum score 7). *Application deadline:* For fall admission, 1/15 for domestic and international students. Application fee: $50. Electronic applications accepted. *Expenses:* $23,140 per year in-state, $37,830 out-of-state. *Financial support:* In 2017–18, 19 students received support, including 19 research assistantships with full tuition reimbursements available (averaging $37,000 per year); fellowships, teaching assistantships, and unspecified assistantships also available. Financial award application deadline: 1/15; financial award applicants required to submit FAFSA. *Faculty research:* International development, international affairs, public policy, public administration. *Total annual research expenditures:* $1.6 million. *Unit head:* Dr. John Keeler, Dean, 412-648-7605, Fax: 412-648-7601, E-mail: gspia@pitt.edu. *Application contact:* Dr. Michael Rizzi, Director of Student Services, 412-648-7640, Fax: 412-648-7641, E-mail: rizzim@pitt.edu.
Website: http://www.gspia.pitt.edu/

University of Pittsburgh, Katz Graduate School of Business, MBA/Master of Public and International Affairs Dual-Degree Program, Pittsburgh, PA 15260. Offers MBA/MPIA. *Accreditation:* AACSB. *Program availability:* Part-time, evening/weekend. *Faculty:* 91 full-time (30 women), 14 part-time/adjunct (4 women). *Students:* 1 (woman) full-time. Average age 24. 3 applicants, 33% accepted, 1 enrolled. *Entrance requirements:* Additional exam requirements/recommendations for international students: Required—TOEFL (minimum score 100 iBT) or IELTS (minimum score 7.0). *Application deadline:* For fall admission, 4/1 priority date for domestic students, 2/1 priority date for international students. Application fee: $50. Electronic applications accepted. *Financial support:* Scholarships/grants available. Financial award application deadline: 6/1; financial award applicants required to submit FAFSA. *Faculty research:* Accounting systems/financial reporting, corporate finance, shopper marketing/consumer behavior, management information systems, organizational behavior and entrepreneurship. *Total annual research expenditures:* $475,077. *Unit head:* Dr. Arjang A. Assad, Dean, 412-648-1556, Fax: 412-648-1552, E-mail: aassad@katz.pitt.edu. *Application contact:* Thomas Keller, Director of MBA Admissions, 412-648-1700, Fax: 412-648-1659, E-mail: mba@katz.pitt.edu.
Website: https://www.katz.business.pitt.edu/mba/joint-and-dual/international-affairs#section-1

University of Pittsburgh, University Center for International Studies, Pittsburgh, PA 15260. Offers African studies (Certificate); Asian studies (Certificate); European Union studies (Certificate); global studies (Certificate); Latin American studies (Certificate); Russian and East European studies (Certificate); West European studies (Certificate). *Program availability:* Part-time, evening/weekend, online learning. *Students:* 183 full-time (108 women), 9 part-time (all women); includes 78 minority (6 Black or African American, non-Hispanic/Latino; 23 Asian, non-Hispanic/Latino; 47 Hispanic/Latino; 2 Two or more races, non-Hispanic/Latino). Average age 29. *Degree requirements:* For Certificate, one foreign language, comprehensive exam (for some programs). *Entrance requirements:* Additional exam requirements/recommendations for international students: Required—TOEFL. *Expenses:* No tuition and fees. *Financial support:* In 2017–18, 25 fellowships with full tuition reimbursements (averaging $26,117 per year) were awarded; scholarships/grants, traineeships, health care benefits, and unspecified assistantships also available. *Unit head:* Dr. Ariel Armony, Director, 412-648-7374, Fax: 412-624-4672, E-mail: armony@pitt.edu.
Website: http://www.ucis.pitt.edu

University of San Diego, College of Arts and Sciences, Master of Arts Program in International Relations, San Diego, CA 92110-2492. Offers MA, JD/MA. *Program availability:* Part-time, evening/weekend. *Faculty:* 4 full-time (1 woman), 2 part-time/adjunct (0 women). *Students:* 17 full-time (3 women), 17 part-time (9 women); includes 12 minority (1 Black or African American, non-Hispanic/Latino; 2 Asian, non-Hispanic/Latino; 8 Hispanic/Latino; 1 Two or more races, non-Hispanic/Latino), 2 international. Average age 30. 34 applicants, 82% accepted, 14 enrolled. In 2017, 13 master's awarded. *Degree requirements:* For master's, comprehensive exam. *Entrance requirements:* For master's, GRE General Test (minimum scores: 153 verbal/147 quantitative/4.5 analytical writing), minimum GPA of 3.2; 24 units in political science, history and/or economics. Additional exam requirements/recommendations for international students: Required—TOEFL (minimum score 580 paper-based; 83 iBT), TWE. *Application deadline:* For fall admission, 3/1 priority date for domestic and international students; for spring admission, 10/1 priority date for domestic and international students. Applications are processed on a rolling basis. Application fee: $45. Electronic applications accepted. *Financial support:* In 2017–18, 26 students received support. Institutionally sponsored loans and unspecified assistantships available. Support available to part-time students. Financial award application deadline: 4/1; financial award applicants required to submit FAFSA. *Faculty research:* Comparative politics, international relations, international security, foreign policy, and international development. *Unit head:* Dr. David Shirk, Graduate Program Director, 619-260-2315, Fax: 619-260-6840, E-mail: mair@sandiego.edu. *Application contact:* Monica Mahon, Associate Director of Graduate Admissions, 619-260-4524, Fax: 619-260-4158, E-mail: grads@sandiego.edu.
Website: http://www.sandiego.edu/cas/ma-international-relations/

University of San Francisco, College of Arts and Sciences, International Studies Program, San Francisco, CA 94117-1080. Offers MA. *Program availability:* Part-time. *Entrance requirements:* Additional exam requirements/recommendations for international students: Required—TOEFL, IELTS, PTE. Electronic applications accepted.

University of San Francisco, College of Arts and Sciences, Program in Migration Studies, San Francisco, CA 94117-1080. Offers MMS. *Entrance requirements:* For master's, statement of purpose. Additional exam requirements/recommendations for international students: Required—TOEFL, IELTS, PTE. Electronic applications accepted.

University of South Carolina, The Graduate School, College of Arts and Sciences, Department of Political Science, Program in International Studies, Columbia, SC 29208. Offers MA, PhD. *Program availability:* Part-time. Terminal master's awarded for partial completion of doctoral program. *Degree requirements:* For master's, one foreign language, thesis or alternative; for doctorate, one foreign language, comprehensive exam, thesis/dissertation. *Entrance requirements:* For master's, GRE General Test, minimum GPA of 3.3; for doctorate, GRE General Test, minimum GPA of 3.5. Additional exam requirements/recommendations for international students: Required—TOEFL. Electronic applications accepted. *Faculty research:* International relations, international organization, foreign policy, comparative politics.

University of Southern California, Graduate School, Annenberg School for Communication and Journalism, School of Communication, Program in Public Diplomacy, Los Angeles, CA 90089. Offers MPD. *Program availability:* Part-time. *Degree requirements:* For master's, thesis. *Entrance requirements:* For master's, GRE, resume, writing samples, statement of purpose, recommendation letters. Additional exam requirements/recommendations for international students: Required—TOEFL (minimum score 114 iBT), IELTS (minimum score 8). Electronic applications accepted.

University of Southern California, Graduate School, Dana and David Dornsife College of Letters, Arts and Sciences, Political Science and International Relations PhD Program, Los Angeles, CA 90089. Offers PhD. *Degree requirements:* For doctorate, variable foreign language requirement, comprehensive exam, thesis/dissertation. *Entrance requirements:* For doctorate, GRE (minimum score 1000). Additional exam requirements/recommendations for international students: Required—TOEFL (minimum score 600 paper-based; 100 iBT). Electronic applications accepted. *Faculty research:* American politics, foreign policy analysis, international political economy, race/ethics politics, security studies.

University of Southern California, Graduate School, Sol Price School of Public Policy, Master of International Public Policy and Management Program, Los Angeles, CA 90089. Offers MPPM. *Program availability:* Part-time. *Entrance requirements:* Additional exam requirements/recommendations for international students: Required—TOEFL (minimum score 71 iBT). Electronic applications accepted. *Expenses:* Contact institution. *Faculty research:* International development, economic development, social policy problems, issues of developing countries, international and comparative.

University of South Florida, Innovative Education, Tampa, FL 33620-9951. Offers adult, career and higher education (Graduate Certificate), including college teaching, leadership in developing human resources, leadership in higher education; Africana studies (Graduate Certificate), including diasporas and health disparities, genocide and human rights; aging studies (Graduate Certificate), including gerontology; art research (Graduate Certificate), including museum studies; business foundations (Graduate Certificate); chemical and biomedical engineering (Graduate Certificate), including materials science and engineering, water, health and sustainability; child and family studies (Graduate Certificate), including positive behavior support; civil and industrial engineering (Graduate Certificate), including transportation systems analysis; community and family health (Graduate Certificate), including maternal and child health, social marketing and public health, violence and injury: prevention and intervention, women's health; criminology (Graduate Certificate), including criminal justice administration; data science for public administration (Graduate Certificate); digital humanities (Graduate Certificate); educational measurement and research (Graduate Certificate), including evaluation; English (Graduate Certificate), including comparative literary studies, creative writing, professional and technical communication; entrepreneurship (Graduate Certificate); environmental health (Graduate Certificate), including safety management; epidemiology and biostatistics (Graduate Certificate), including applied biostatistics, biostatistics, concepts and tools of epidemiology, epidemiology, epidemiology of infectious diseases; geography, environment and planning (Graduate Certificate), including community development, environmental policy and management, geographical information systems; geology (Graduate Certificate), including hydrogeology; global health (Graduate Certificate), including disaster management, global health and Latin American and Caribbean studies, global health practice, humanitarian assistance, infection control; government and international affairs (Graduate Certificate), including Cuban studies, globalization studies; health policy and management (Graduate Certificate), including health management and leadership, public health policy and programs; hearing specialist: early intervention (Graduate Certificate); industrial and management systems engineering (Graduate Certificate), including systems engineering, technology management; information studies (Graduate Certificate), including school library media specialist; information systems/decision sciences (Graduate Certificate), including analytics and business intelligence; instructional technology (Graduate Certificate), including distance education, Florida digital/virtual educator, instructional design, multimedia design, Web design; internal medicine, bioethics and medical humanities (Graduate Certificate), including biomedical ethics; Latin American and Caribbean studies (Graduate Certificate); leadership for coastal resiliency planning (Graduate Certificate); mass communications (Graduate Certificate), including multimedia journalism; mathematics and statistics (Graduate Certificate), including mathematics; medicine (Graduate Certificate), including aging and neuroscience, bioinformatics, biotechnology, brain fitness and memory management, clinical investigation, hand and upper limb rehabilitation, health informatics, health sciences, integrative weight management, intellectual property, medicine and gender, metabolic and nutritional medicine, metabolic cardiology, pharmacy sciences; national and competitive intelligence (Graduate Certificate); nursing (Graduate Certificate), including simulation based academic fellowship in advanced pain management; psychological and social foundations (Graduate Certificate), including career counseling, college teaching, diversity in education, mental health counseling, school counseling; public affairs (Graduate Certificate), including nonprofit management, public management, research administration; public health (Graduate Certificate), including assessing chemical toxicity and public health risks, health equity, pharmacoepidemiology, public health generalist, toxicology, translational research in adolescent behavioral health; public health practices (Graduate Certificate), including planning for healthy communities; rehabilitation and mental health counseling (Graduate Certificate), including integrative mental health care, marriage and family therapy, rehabilitation technology; secondary education (Graduate Certificate), including ESOL, foreign language education: culture and content, foreign language education: professional; social work (Graduate Certificate), including geriatric social work/clinical gerontology; special education (Graduate Certificate), including autism spectrum disorder, disabilities education: severe/profound; world languages (Graduate Certificate), including teaching English as a second language (TESL) or foreign language. *Unit head:* Dr. Cynthia DeLuca, Associate Vice President and Assistant Vice Provost, 813-974-3077, Fax: 813-974-7061, E-mail: deluca@usf.edu. *Application contact:* Owen Hooper, Director, Summer and Alternative Calendar Programs, 813-974-6917, E-mail: hooper@usf.edu.
Website: http://www.usf.edu/innovative-education/

University of the Pacific, McGeorge School of Law, Sacramento, CA 95817. Offers advocacy (JD); international water resources law (JSD); public policy and law (LL M); JD/MBA; JD/MPPA. *Accreditation:* ABA. *Program availability:* Part-time, evening/weekend. *Faculty:* 39 full-time (18 women), 38 part-time/adjunct (14 women). *Students:*

376 full-time (200 women), 219 part-time (126 women); includes 199 minority (22 Black or African American, non-Hispanic/Latino; 4 American Indian or Alaska Native, non-Hispanic/Latino; 40 Asian, non-Hispanic/Latino; 119 Hispanic/Latino; 2 Native Hawaiian or other Pacific Islander, non-Hispanic/Latino; 12 Two or more races, non-Hispanic/Latino), 181 international. Average age 29. 1,063 applicants, 61% accepted, 201 enrolled. In 2017, 26 master's, 135 doctorates awarded. *Degree requirements:* For master's, thesis (for some programs); for doctorate, thesis/dissertation (for some programs). *Entrance requirements:* For master's, JD; for doctorate, LSAT (for JD), LL M (for JSD). Additional exam requirements/recommendations for international students: Required—TOEFL (minimum score 600 paper-based; 100 iBT). *Application deadline:* For fall admission, 3/15 priority date for domestic students. Applications are processed on a rolling basis. Application fee: $50. Electronic applications accepted. *Expenses:* Contact institution. *Financial support:* Fellowships, research assistantships, teaching assistantships, career-related internships or fieldwork, Federal Work-Study, institutionally sponsored loans, and scholarships/grants available. Support available to part-time students. Financial award applicants required to submit FAFSA. *Faculty research:* International legal studies, public policy and law, advocacy, intellectual property law, taxation, criminal law. *Unit head:* Michael Schwartz, Dean, 916-739-7151, E-mail: jmootz@pacific.edu. *Application contact:* 916-739-7105, Fax: 916-739-7301, E-mail: mcgeorge@pacific.edu.
Website: http://www.mcgeorge.edu/

University of Toronto, School of Graduate Studies, Munk School of Global Affairs, Toronto, ON M5S 1A1, Canada. Offers European, Russian and Eurasian studies (MA); global affairs (MGA); JD/MA. *Entrance requirements:* For master's, GRE General Test, GMAT, or LSAT, Honours (4-year) BA or equivalent, minimum cumulative and final year GPA of 3.5. Additional exam requirements/recommendations for international students: Required—TOEFL (minimum score 100 iBT), TWE (minimum score 5). Electronic applications accepted.

University of Utah, Graduate School, College of Social and Behavioral Science, Department of Political Science, Program in Political Science, Salt Lake City, UT 84112. Offers American politics (MA, MS, PhD); comparative politics (MA, MS, PhD); international relations (MA, MS, PhD); political theory (MA, MS, PhD); public administration (MA, MS, PhD). *Faculty:* 23 full-time (6 women), 10 part-time/adjunct (2 women). *Students:* 23 full-time (9 women), 28 part-time (8 women); includes 6 minority (2 Asian, non-Hispanic/Latino; 2 Hispanic/Latino; 2 Two or more races, non-Hispanic/Latino), 4 international. Average age 35. 44 applicants, 45% accepted, 11 enrolled. In 2017, 3 master's, 4 doctorates awarded. Terminal master's awarded for partial completion of doctoral program. *Degree requirements:* For master's, variable foreign language requirement, thesis or research paper; for doctorate, comprehensive exam, thesis/dissertation. *Entrance requirements:* For master's and doctorate, GRE General Test, minimum GPA of 3.2. Additional exam requirements/recommendations for international students: Required—TOEFL (minimum score 580 paper-based; 61 iBT), IELTS (minimum score 6). *Application deadline:* For fall admission, 1/15 priority date for domestic and international students. Application fee: $55 ($65 for international students). Electronic applications accepted. *Expenses:* $1,489 for 1 credit hour, $267 for each additional hour (resident); $4,233 for 1 credit hour, $908 for each additional hour (non-resident). *Financial support:* In 2017–18, 10 students received support, including 5 fellowships with full tuition reimbursements available (averaging $15,250 per year), 13 teaching assistantships with full tuition reimbursements available (averaging $15,000 per year); career-related internships or fieldwork, scholarships/grants, health care benefits, and unspecified assistantships also available. Financial award application deadline: 1/15; financial award applicants required to submit FAFSA. *Faculty research:* International politics, comparative politics, political theory, American politics, public administration. *Total annual research expenditures:* $15,000. *Unit head:* Mark Button, Chair, 801-585-7987, Fax: 801-585-6492, E-mail: mark.button@poli-sci.utah.edu. *Application contact:* Sandy Hiskey, Graduate Academic Advisor, 801-581-8608, Fax: 801-585-6492, E-mail: sandy.hiskey@utah.edu.
Website: http://www.poli-sci.utah.edu/

University of Utah, Graduate School, College of Social and Behavioral Science, Master of Science in International Affairs and Global Enterprise Program, Salt Lake City, UT 84112. Offers MS. *Program availability:* Part-time. *Students:* 26 full-time (13 women), 9 part-time (6 women); includes 11 minority (1 Black or African American, non-Hispanic/Latino; 2 Asian, non-Hispanic/Latino; 5 Hispanic/Latino; 3 Two or more races, non-Hispanic/Latino). Average age 30. 29 applicants, 76% accepted, 18 enrolled. In 2017, 15 master's awarded. *Entrance requirements:* For master's, GMAT, LSAT, or GRE, undergraduate coursework in statistics, microeconomics theory and macroeconomics theory. Additional exam requirements/recommendations for international students: Required—TOEFL (minimum score 600 paper-based; 100 iBT). Application fee: $55 ($65 for international students). Electronic applications accepted. *Expenses:* Contact institution. *Financial support:* In 2017–18, 5 students received support. Fellowships and unspecified assistantships available. Financial award application deadline: 2/15. *Unit head:* Dr. Stephen Reynolds, Director, 801-581-8620, Fax: 801-585-5081, E-mail: stephen.reynolds@csbs.utah.edu. *Application contact:* Elizabeth Henke, Program Manager, 801-585-7722, Fax: 801-587-7861, E-mail: elizabeth.henke@cppa.utah.edu.
Website: http://www.miage.utah.edu

University of Virginia, College and Graduate School of Arts and Sciences, Department of Politics, Program in Foreign Affairs, Charlottesville, VA 22903. Offers MA, PhD; JD/MA, MBA/MA. *Students:* 34 full-time (16 women); includes 2 minority (1 Asian, non-Hispanic/Latino; 1 Hispanic/Latino), 15 international. Average age 29. 126 applicants, 16% accepted, 10 enrolled. In 2017, 2 master's, 10 doctorates awarded. *Degree requirements:* For master's, one foreign language, 2 research/statistics courses or thesis; for doctorate, variable foreign language requirement, thesis/dissertation, 2 research/statistics courses. *Entrance requirements:* For master's and doctorate, GRE General Test, long writing sample; 2 letters of recommendation. Additional exam requirements/recommendations for international students: Required—TOEFL (minimum score 600 paper-based; 90 iBT), IELTS (minimum score 7). *Application deadline:* For fall admission, 12/4 for domestic and international students. Applications are processed on a rolling basis. Application fee: $60. Electronic applications accepted. *Financial support:* Fellowships and teaching assistantships available. Financial award application deadline: 12/4; financial award applicants required to submit FAFSA. *Unit head:* John Owen, Chair, 434-924-3523, Fax: 434-924-3359, E-mail: jmo4n@virginia.edu. *Application contact:* Philip Potter, Director of Graduate Studies, 434-982-1043, Fax: 434-924-3359, E-mail: pbp2s@virginia.edu.
Website: http://politics.virginia.edu/

University of Washington, Graduate School, College of Arts and Sciences, Henry M. Jackson School of International Studies, International Studies MA Program, Seattle, WA 98195. Offers MAIS, JD/MAIS, MBA/MAIS, MFR/MAIS, MMA/MAIS, MPA/MAIS, MPH/MAIS. *Degree requirements:* For master's, one foreign language, thesis optional. *Entrance requirements:* For master's, minimum GPA of 3.0 in last two years. Additional exam requirements/recommendations for international students: Required—TOEFL (minimum score 500 paper-based; 92 iBT), IELTS (minimum score 7). Electronic applications accepted.

University of Washington, Graduate School, College of Arts and Sciences, Henry M. Jackson School of International Studies, International Studies PhD Program, Seattle, WA 98195. Offers PhD. *Degree requirements:* For doctorate, variable foreign language requirement, comprehensive exam, thesis/dissertation, research tutorial with capstone presentation; dissertation prospectus defense; final examination. *Entrance requirements:* For doctorate, GRE General Test, master's degree. Additional exam requirements/recommendations for international students: Required—TOEFL (minimum score 500 paper-based; 92 iBT), IELTS (minimum score 7).

University of Waterloo, Graduate Studies, Faculty of Arts, Department of Political Science, Waterloo, ON N2L 3G1, Canada. Offers global governance (MA, PhD). *Program availability:* Part-time. *Degree requirements:* For master's, thesis (for some programs), research paper. *Entrance requirements:* For master's, honors degree, minimum B average, writing sample. Additional exam requirements/recommendations for international students: Required—TOEFL, IELTS, PTE. Electronic applications accepted. *Faculty research:* Conflict and conflict resolution, political economy, contemporary political theory, Canadian state and society.

University of Waterloo, Graduate Studies, Faculty of Arts, Global Governance Program, Waterloo, ON N2L 3G1, Canada. Offers MA, PhD. *Entrance requirements:* For doctorate, MA. Additional exam requirements/recommendations for international students: Required—TOEFL, IELTS, PTE. Electronic applications accepted. *Faculty research:* Global political economy, global environment, peace and security, global justice and human rights, multilateral institutions and diplomacy.

University of Wyoming, College of Arts and Sciences, Program in International Studies, Laramie, WY 82071. Offers international peace corps (MA); international studies (MA). *Program availability:* Part-time. *Degree requirements:* For master's, one foreign language, thesis. *Entrance requirements:* For master's, GRE General Test, minimum GPA of 3.0. Additional exam requirements/recommendations for international students: Required—TOEFL (minimum score 525 paper-based). Electronic applications accepted. *Faculty research:* International political economy, comparative social institutions, foreign policy, economic development.

Virginia International University, School of Public and International Affairs, Fairfax, VA 22030. Offers international relations (MS); public administration (MPA).

Virginia Polytechnic Institute and State University, Graduate School, College of Architecture and Urban Studies, Blacksburg, VA 24061. Offers architecture (M Arch, MS); architecture and design research (PhD); building construction science management (MS); creative technologies (MFA); environmental design and planning (PhD); government and international affairs (MPIA); landscape architecture (MLA, PhD); planning, governance, and globalization (PhD); public administration and public affairs (MPA, PhD); urban and regional planning (MURPL). *Accreditation:* ASLA (one or more programs are accredited). *Faculty:* 139 full-time (58 women), 1 (woman) part-time/adjunct. *Students:* 339 full-time (165 women), 210 part-time (97 women); includes 115 minority (49 Black or African American, non-Hispanic/Latino; 1 American Indian or Alaska Native, non-Hispanic/Latino; 30 Asian, non-Hispanic/Latino; 29 Hispanic/Latino; 6 Two or more races, non-Hispanic/Latino), 136 international. Average age 32. 649 applicants, 49% accepted, 105 enrolled. In 2017, 142 master's, 18 doctorates awarded. *Degree requirements:* For master's, comprehensive exam (for some programs), thesis (for some programs); for doctorate, comprehensive exam (for some programs), thesis/dissertation (for some programs). *Entrance requirements:* For master's and doctorate, GRE/GMAT. Additional exam requirements/recommendations for international students: Required—TOEFL (minimum score 80 iBT). *Application deadline:* For fall admission, 8/1 for domestic students, 4/1 for international students; for spring admission, 1/1 for domestic students, 9/1 for international students. Applications are processed on a rolling basis. Application fee: $75. Electronic applications accepted. *Expenses:* Tuition, state resident: full-time $15,072; part-time $718.50 per credit hour. Tuition, nonresident: full-time $28,810; part-time $1448.25 per credit hour. *Required fees:* $2741; $502 per semester. Tuition and fees vary according to course load, campus/location and program. *Financial support:* In 2017–18, 17 research assistantships with full tuition reimbursements (averaging $18,561 per year), 41 teaching assistantships with full tuition reimbursements (averaging $17,340 per year) were awarded. Financial award application deadline: 3/1; financial award applicants required to submit FAFSA. *Total annual research expenditures:* $3.1 million. *Unit head:* Dr. Richard Blythe, Dean, 540-231-6416, Fax: 540-231-6332, E-mail: richbl1@vt.edu. *Application contact:* Christine Mattsson-Coon, Executive Assistant, 540-231-6416, Fax: 540-231-6332, E-mail: cmattsso@vt.edu.
Website: http://www.caus.vt.edu/

Walden University, Graduate Programs, School of Public Policy and Administration, Minneapolis, MN 55401. Offers criminal justice (MPA, MPP, MS, Graduate Certificate), including emergency management (MS, PhD), general program (MS), global leadership (MS, PhD), homeland security and policy coordination (MS, PhD), law and public policy (MS, PhD), policy analysis (MS, PhD), public management and leadership (MS, PhD), self-designed (MS), terrorism, mediation, and peace (MS, PhD); criminal justice and executive management (MS), including global leadership (MS, PhD); criminal justice leadership and executive management (MS), including emergency management (MS, PhD), general program, homeland security and policy coordination (MS, PhD), law and public policy (MS, PhD), policy analysis (MS, PhD), public management and leadership (MS, PhD), self-designed, terrorism, mediation, and peace (MS, PhD); emergency management (MPA, MPP, MS), including criminal justice (MS, PhD), general program (MS), homeland security (MS), public management and leadership (MS, PhD), terrorism and emergency management (MS); general program (MPA, MPP); global leadership (MPA, MPP); government management (Graduate Certificate); health policy (MPA, MPP); homeland security (Graduate Certificate); homeland security and policy coordination (MPA, MPP); international nongovernmental organizations (MPA, MPP); law and public policy (MPA, MPP); local government management for sustainable communities (MPA, MPP); nonprofit management (Graduate Certificate); nonprofit management and leadership (MPA, MPP, MS), including global leadership (MS, PhD), international nongovernmental organization (MS), local government for sustainable communities (MS), self designed (MS); online teaching in higher education (Post-Master's Certificate); policy analysis (MPA); public management and leadership (MPA, MPP, Graduate Certificate); public policy (Graduate Certificate); public policy and administration (PhD), including criminal justice (MS, PhD), emergency management (MS, PhD), global leadership (MS, PhD), health policy, homeland security and policy coordination (MS, PhD), international nongovernmental organizations, law and public policy (MS, PhD), local government management for sustainable communities, nonprofit management and leadership, policy analysis (MS, PhD), public management and leadership (MS, PhD), terrorism, mediation, and peace (MS, PhD); strategic planning and public policy (Graduate Certificate); terrorism, mediation, and peace (MPA, MPP). *Program availability:* Part-time, evening/weekend, online only, 100% online. *Degree requirements:* For doctorate, thesis/dissertation, residency. *Entrance requirements:* For master's, bachelor's degree or higher; minimum GPA of 2.5; official transcripts; goal statement (for some programs); access to computer and Internet; for doctorate, master's degree or higher; three years of related professional or academic experience (preferred); minimum GPA of 3.0; goal statement and current resume (for select programs); official transcripts; access to computer and Internet; for other advanced

degree, relevant work experience; access to computer and Internet. Additional exam requirements/recommendations for international students: Required—TOEFL (minimum score 550 paper-based, 79 iBT), IELTS (minimum score 6.5), Michigan English Language Assessment Battery (minimum score 82), or PTE (minimum score 53). Electronic applications accepted.

Webster University, College of Arts and Sciences, Department of History, Politics and International Relations, Program in International Nongovernmental Organizations, St. Louis, MO 63119-3194. Offers MA. Program available only at the Geneva, Switzerland campus.

Webster University, College of Arts and Sciences, Department of History, Politics and International Relations, Program in International Relations, St. Louis, MO 63119-3194. Offers MA. *Program availability:* Part-time, evening/weekend. *Degree requirements:* For master's, thesis optional. *Faculty research:* International organizations, international political economy, politics of development, environmental law, Latin American law.

Webster University, College of Arts and Sciences, Institute for Human Rights and Humanitarian Studies, St. Louis, MO 63119-3194. Offers international human rights (MA).

Webster University, George Herbert Walker School of Business and Technology, Department of Business, St. Louis, MO 63119-3194. Offers business and organizational security management (MBA); decision support systems (MBA); environmental management (MBA); finance (MBA, MS); forensic accounting (MS); gerontology (MBA); human resources development (MBA); human resources management (MBA); information technology management (MBA); international business (MA, MBA); international relations (MBA); management and leadership (MBA); marketing (MBA); media communications (MBA); procurement and acquisitions management (MBA); Web services (MBA). *Accreditation:* ACBSP. *Program availability:* Part-time, evening/weekend, online learning. *Degree requirements:* For master's, comprehensive exam (for some programs), thesis (for some programs). *Entrance requirements:* Additional exam requirements/recommendations for international students: Required—TOEFL.

Western Michigan University, Graduate College, College of Arts and Sciences, Department of Political Science, Kalamazoo, MI 49008. Offers international development administration (MIDA), including Peace Corps; political science (MA, PhD). *Degree requirements:* For master's, thesis optional; for doctorate, thesis/dissertation.

Wilfrid Laurier University, Faculty of Graduate and Postdoctoral Studies, Faculty of Arts, Department of Political Science, Waterloo, ON N2L 3C5, Canada. Offers Canadian political studies (MA); comparative politics/international relations (MA). *Program availability:* Part-time. *Degree requirements:* For master's, thesis optional. *Entrance requirements:* For master's, honors bachelor's degree or the equivalent in political science, minimum B average in undergraduate course work. Additional exam requirements/recommendations for international students: Required—TOEFL (minimum score 89 iBT). Electronic applications accepted. *Faculty research:* Political behavior/political psychology, Canadian political studies, comparative, politics/relations, public opinion and electoral studies, international.

Wilfrid Laurier University, Faculty of Graduate and Postdoctoral Studies, School of International Policy and Governance, Global Governance Program, Waterloo, ON N2L 3C5, Canada. Offers conflict and security (PhD); global environment (PhD); global justice and human rights (PhD); global political economy (PhD); global social governance (PhD); multilateral institutions and diplomacy (PhD). Offered jointly with University of Waterloo. *Degree requirements:* For doctorate, thesis/dissertation. *Entrance requirements:* For doctorate, MA in political science, history, economics, international development studies, international peace studies, globalization studies, environmental studies or related field with minimum A-. Additional exam requirements/recommendations for international students: Required—TOEFL (minimum score 89 iBT). Electronic applications accepted. *Faculty research:* Global political economy, global environment, conflict and security, global justice and human rights, multilateral institutions and diplomacy.

Wilfrid Laurier University, Faculty of Graduate and Postdoctoral Studies, School of International Policy and Governance, International Public Policy Program, Waterloo, ON N2L 3C5, Canada. Offers global governance (MIPP); human security (MIPP); international economic relations (MIPP); international environmental policy (MIPP). Offered jointly with University of Waterloo. *Entrance requirements:* For master's, honours BA with minimum B average. Additional exam requirements/recommendations for international students: Required—TOEFL (minimum score 89 iBT). Electronic applications accepted. *Faculty research:* International environmental policy, international economic relations, human security, global governance.

Wilfrid Laurier University, Laurier Brantford, Brantford, ON N3T 2Y3, Canada. Offers criminology (MA), including culture, crime and policy, international crime and justice, media criminology. *Degree requirements:* For master's, thesis. *Entrance requirements:* For master's, honours bachelor's degree with major in criminology or equivalent degree; minimum B+ average in final year and in all criminology courses. Additional exam requirements/recommendations for international students: Required—TOEFL (minimum score 89 iBT). Electronic applications accepted.

Yale University, Graduate School of Arts and Sciences, Department of Economics, Program in International and Development Economics, New Haven, CT 06520. Offers MA. *Entrance requirements:* For master's, GRE General Test.

Yale University, Graduate School of Arts and Sciences, Graduate Program in Global Affairs, New Haven, CT 06501. Offers MA, JD/MA, MBA/MA, MEM/MA, MF/MA, MFS/MA, MPH/MA. *Faculty:* 241. *Students:* 53 full-time (29 women); includes 27 minority (7 Black or African American, non-Hispanic/Latino; 14 Asian, non-Hispanic/Latino; 6 Hispanic/Latino), 25 international. Average age 28. 378 applicants, 9% accepted, 23 enrolled. In 2017, 28 master's awarded. *Degree requirements:* For master's, one foreign language, summer internship or project. *Entrance requirements:* For master's, GRE General Test, professional experience and introductory coursework in microeconomics and macroeconomics (strongly preferred). Additional exam requirements/recommendations for international students: Required—TOEFL (minimum score 102 iBT) or IELTS (minimum score 7.5). *Application deadline:* For fall admission, 1/2 for domestic and international students. Application fee: $105. Electronic applications accepted. *Expenses:* Contact institution. *Financial support:* In 2017–18, 49 students received support, including 23 fellowships with full and partial tuition reimbursements available (averaging $18,091 per year), 37 teaching assistantships (averaging $6,595 per year); research assistantships, career-related internships or fieldwork, institutionally sponsored loans, scholarships/grants, tuition waivers (full and partial), unspecified assistantships, and competitive summer fellowships for unpaid internships and projects also available. Financial award application deadline: 1/2. *Faculty research:* International security studies, global health, international economic development, political economy, policy. *Unit head:* James Levinsohn, Director, Jackson Institute for Global Affairs, 203-432-6253, Fax: 203-432-9886, E-mail: jackson.institute@yale.edu. *Application contact:* Asha Rangappa, Director of Admissions, Jackson Institute for Global Affairs, 203-436-1316, Fax: 203-432-9886, E-mail: asha.rangappa@yale.edu.
Website: http://jackson.yale.edu/ma-degree

York University, Faculty of Graduate Studies, Glendon Campus, Program in Public and International Affairs, Toronto, ON M3J 1P3, Canada. Offers MA.

International Development

American University, School of International Service, Washington, DC 20016-8071. Offers comparative and regional studies (Certificate); cross-cultural communication (Certificate); development management (MS); ethics, peace, and global affairs (MA); European studies (Certificate); global environmental policy (MA, Certificate); global information technology (Certificate); global media (MA); international affairs (MA), including comparative and regional studies, global governance, politics, and security, international economic relations, natural resources and sustainable development, U.S. foreign policy and national security; international arts management (Certificate); international communication (MA, Certificate); international development (MA); international economic policy (Certificate); international economic relations (Certificate); international economics (MA); international peace and conflict resolution (MA, Certificate); international politics (Certificate); international relations (MA, PhD); international service (MIS); peacebuilding (Certificate); social enterprise (MA); the Americas (Certificate); United States foreign policy (Certificate); JD/MA. *Program availability:* Part-time, evening/weekend, 100% online. *Faculty:* 112 full-time (50 women), 46 part-time/adjunct (19 women). *Students:* 495 full-time (333 women), 518 part-time (276 women); includes 360 minority (95 Black or African American, non-Hispanic/Latino; 2 American Indian or Alaska Native, non-Hispanic/Latino; 60 Asian, non-Hispanic/Latino; 164 Hispanic/Latino; 39 Two or more races, non-Hispanic/Latino), 98 international. Average age 30. 1,559 applicants, 81% accepted, 356 enrolled. In 2017, 427 master's, 9 doctorates, 5 other advanced degrees awarded. Terminal master's awarded for partial completion of doctoral program. *Degree requirements:* For master's, one foreign language, comprehensive exam, thesis or alternative; for doctorate, one foreign language, comprehensive exam, thesis/dissertation. *Entrance requirements:* For master's, GRE; GMAT or GRE (for MA in social enterprise), transcripts, resume, 2 letters of recommendation, statement of purpose; for doctorate, GRE, transcripts, resume, 3 letters of recommendation, statement of purpose. Additional exam requirements/recommendations for international students: Required—TOEFL (minimum score 600 paper-based; 100 iBT). *Application deadline:* For fall admission, 1/15 for domestic students, 1/1 for international students; for spring admission, 10/1 for domestic students, 9/15 for international students. Application fee: $55. Electronic applications accepted. *Expenses:* Contact institution. *Financial support:* Research assistantships, teaching assistantships, institutionally sponsored loans, scholarships/grants, and unspecified assistantships available. Financial award application deadline: 1/15; financial award applicants required to submit FAFSA. *Application contact:* 202-885-1646, Fax: 202-885-1109, E-mail: sisgrad@american.edu.
Website: http://www.american.edu/sis/

Andrews University, School of Graduate Studies, College of Arts and Sciences, Department of Behavioral Science, Program in International Development, Berrien Springs, MI 49104. Offers community and international development (MSCID). *Program availability:* Online learning. *Faculty:* 10 full-time (2 women), 1 part-time/adjunct (0 women). *Students:* 18 full-time (13 women), 3 part-time (all women); includes 7 minority (3 Black or African American, non-Hispanic/Latino; 2 Asian, non-Hispanic/Latino; 2 Hispanic/Latino), 12 international. Average age 31. In 2017, 11 master's awarded. *Entrance requirements:* For master's, GRE General Test. Additional exam requirements/recommendations for international students: Required—TOEFL (minimum score 550 paper-based). Application fee: $40. *Unit head:* Dr. Duane C. McBride, Director, 269-471-3152. *Application contact:* Justina Clayburn, Supervisor of Graduate Admission, 800-253-2874, Fax: 269-471-6321, E-mail: graduate@andrews.edu.
Website: http://www.andrews.edu/grad/programs/community-and-international-development-off-campus.html

Athabasca University, Centre for Interdisciplinary Studies, Athabasca, AB T9S 3A3, Canada. Offers adult education (MA); community studies (MA); cultural studies (MA); educational studies (MA); global change (MA); heritage resource management (Postbaccalaureate Certificate); legislative drafting (Postbaccalaureate Certificate); work, organization, and leadership (MA). *Program availability:* Part-time, evening/weekend, online learning. *Degree requirements:* For master's, project. *Entrance requirements:* Additional exam requirements/recommendations for international students: Required—TOEFL (minimum score 560 paper-based). Electronic applications accepted. *Faculty research:* Women's history, literature and culture studies, sustainable development, labor and education.

Clark University, Graduate School, Department of International Development, Community, and Environment, Program in International Development and Social Change, Worcester, MA 01610-1477. Offers MA. *Students:* 40 full-time (22 women); includes 11 minority (8 Black or African American, non-Hispanic/Latino; 1 Asian, non-Hispanic/Latino; 2 Hispanic/Latino), 9 international. Average age 31. 142 applicants, 55% accepted, 23 enrolled. In 2017, 24 master's awarded. *Degree requirements:* For master's, thesis. *Entrance requirements:* For master's, 2 references, resume or curriculum vitae, personal statement. Additional exam requirements/recommendations for international students: Required—TOEFL (minimum score 575 paper-based; 90 iBT), IELTS (minimum score 6.5). *Application deadline:* For fall admission, 4/15 for domestic and international students. Application fee: $75. Electronic applications accepted. *Expenses:* $5,685 tuition per unit, $490 fees. *Financial support:* Fellowships, research assistantships, teaching assistantships, institutionally sponsored loans, and scholarships/grants available. *Faculty research:* Community action research, gender analysis, land-use planning, geographic information systems, HIV and AIDS, global health and social justice, environmental health, climate change and sustainability. *Unit head:* Dr. David Bell, 508-793-7568, Fax: 508-793-8820, E-mail: dbell@clarku.edu. *Application contact:* Sawsan Berjawi, Manager of Academic and Student Affairs, 508-421-3846, E-mail: sberjawi@clarku.edu.
Website: http://www.clarku.edu/programs/masters-international-development-and-social-change

The College of William and Mary, Faculty of Arts and Sciences, Public Policy Program, Williamsburg, VA 23187-8795. Offers international development and policy (MPP); public policy analysis (MPP); JD/MPP; MBA/MPP; MS/MPP. *Faculty:* 32 full-time (10 women), 5 part-time/adjunct (1 woman). *Students:* 31 full-time (18 women); includes 5 minority (1 Black or African American, non-Hispanic/Latino; 1 American Indian or Alaska Native, non-Hispanic/Latino; 2 Hispanic/Latino; 1 Two or more races, non-Hispanic/Latino), 2 international. Average age 24. 71 applicants, 65% accepted, 21 enrolled. In 2017, 18 master's awarded. *Entrance requirements:* For master's, GRE General Test. Additional exam requirements/recommendations for international students: Required—TOEFL (minimum score 600 paper-based; 100 iBT), IELTS (minimum score 7.5). *Application deadline:* For fall admission, 2/15 priority date for domestic and international students. Application fee: $50. Electronic applications accepted. *Financial support:* In 2017–18, 33 students received support, including 20 research assistantships with partial tuition reimbursements available (averaging $7,000 per year), 15 teaching assistantships with partial tuition reimbursements available (averaging $8,000 per year); career-related internships or fieldwork and unspecified assistantships also available. Financial award application deadline: 1/15; financial award applicants required to submit FAFSA. *Faculty research:* Social policy, international development, health care policy, environmental policy, state and local policy, education policy, regulatory policy. *Total annual research expenditures:* $225,421. *Unit head:* Dr. John Gilmour, Director, 757-221-2368, Fax: 757-221-1175, E-mail: jbgilm@wm.edu. *Application contact:* Sarah Fowkes, Director of Admissions, 757-221-2384, Fax: 757-221-2390, E-mail: sefowk@wm.edu.
Website: http://www.wm.edu/publicpolicy

Dalhousie University, Faculty of Arts and Social Science, Department of International Development Studies, Halifax, NS B3H 4R2, Canada. Offers MA. *Entrance requirements:* Additional exam requirements/recommendations for international students: Required—TOEFL, IELTS, CANTEST, CAEL, or Michigan English Language Assessment Battery. Electronic applications accepted.

Duke University, Sanford School of Public Policy, Master of International Development Policy Program, Durham, NC 27708-0237. Offers MIDP. *Faculty:* 12 full-time (5 women), 9 part-time/adjunct (2 women). *Students:* 75 full-time (37 women); includes 6 minority (5 Black or African American, non-Hispanic/Latino; 1 Two or more races, non-Hispanic/Latino), 63 international. Average age 33. 169 applicants, 76% accepted, 42 enrolled. In 2017, 43 master's awarded. *Degree requirements:* For master's, thesis, internship, project. *Entrance requirements:* For master's, minimum five years of professional experience in a development-related field. Additional exam requirements/recommendations for international students: Required—TOEFL (minimum score 577 paper-based; 90 iBT), IELTS (minimum score 7), PTE (minimum score 64). *Application deadline:* For fall admission, 1/5 priority date for domestic and international students. Applications are processed on a rolling basis. Application fee: $80. Electronic applications accepted. *Expenses:* Contact institution. *Financial support:* In 2017–18, 28 students received support. Scholarships/grants available. Financial award application deadline: 1/5. *Faculty research:* Economic development, social policy and development, peace and conflict resolution, public finance, international taxation. *Unit head:* Dr. Corinne Krupp, Director of Graduate Studies, 919-613-9221, Fax: 919-684-2861, E-mail: midpinfo@duke.edu. *Application contact:* Cheryl Bailey, Assistant Director, Admissions, 919-613-9281, Fax: 919-684-2861, E-mail: midinfo@duke.edu.
Website: http://dcid.sanford.duke.edu/academics/midp

Eastern University, Department of Global Studies and Mission, St. Davids, PA 19087-3696. Offers international development (MA); theological and cultural anthropology (MA). *Students:* 23 full-time (11 women), 26 part-time (15 women); includes 11 minority (8 Black or African American, non-Hispanic/Latino; 1 Asian, non-Hispanic/Latino; 2 Hispanic/Latino), 1 international. Average age 35. In 2017, 19 master's awarded. *Application deadline:* Applications are processed on a rolling basis. Application fee: $35. Electronic applications accepted. Application fee is waived when completed online. *Expenses:* Contact institution. *Unit head:* Michael Dziedziak, Executive Director of Enrollment, 800-452-0996, E-mail: gpsadmissions@eastern.edu.
Website: https://www.eastern.edu/academics/global-studies-mission

Fordham University, Graduate School of Arts and Sciences, Program in International Political Economy and Development, New York, NY 10458. Offers MA, Certificate. *Program availability:* Part-time, evening/weekend. *Students:* 38 full-time (18 women), 8 part-time (2 women); includes 3 minority (1 Asian, non-Hispanic/Latino; 2 Hispanic/Latino), 15 international. Average age 27. 89 applicants, 60% accepted, 24 enrolled. In 2017, 24 master's, 1 other advanced degree awarded. *Degree requirements:* For master's, comprehensive exam. *Entrance requirements:* For master's, GRE General Test. Additional exam requirements/recommendations for international students: Required—TOEFL (minimum score 600 paper-based). *Application deadline:* For fall admission, 1/4 priority date for domestic students; for spring admission, 11/1 for domestic students. Application fee: $70. Electronic applications accepted. *Financial support:* In 2017–18, 35 students received support, including 4 fellowships with tuition reimbursements available (averaging $17,014 per year); research assistantships with tuition reimbursements available, career-related internships or fieldwork, institutionally sponsored loans, tuition waivers (full and partial), and unspecified assistantships also available. Financial award application deadline: 1/4; financial award applicants required to submit FAFSA. *Faculty research:* International economics, comparative international politics, international banking and finance, international development, emerging markets and country risk analysis. *Unit head:* Dr. Henry Schwalbenberg, Chair, 718-817-3866, Fax: 718-817-3518. *Application contact:* Bernadette Valentino-Morrison, Director of Graduate Admissions, 718-817-4419, Fax: 718-817-3566, E-mail: valentinomor@fordham.edu.

Georgetown University, McCourt School of Public Policy, Washington, DC 20057. Offers data science for public policy (MDSPP); international development policy (MIDP); policy leadership (EMPL); policy management (MPM); public policy (MPP); MBA/MPP; MPP/JD; MPP/MA; MPP/MSFS; MPP/PhD. *Program availability:* Part-time. *Entrance requirements:* For master's, GRE General Test or GMAT, minimum B average. Additional exam requirements/recommendations for international students: Required—TOEFL (minimum score 100 iBT). *Application deadline:* For fall admission, 1/15 priority date for domestic students. Applications are processed on a rolling basis. Application fee: $90. Electronic applications accepted. *Financial support:* Research assistantships, teaching assistantships, career-related internships or fieldwork, scholarships/grants, and unspecified assistantships available. Financial award application deadline: 2/1; financial award applicants required to submit FAFSA. *Faculty research:* Analytic methods, data analysis, development policy, economic policy, education policy, environmental and energy policy, federalism, health and healthcare policy, international economic policy, leadership, policy analysis, politics and political strategy, poverty and social policy, public and nonprofit management, state and local government, urban policy. *Unit head:* Dr. Michael A. Bailey, Dean, McCourt School of Public Policy, 202-687-6163. *Application contact:* Dr. Adam Thomas, Director of Admissions, 202-687-9186, E-mail: mccourtadmissions@georgetown.edu.
Website: https://mccourt.georgetown.edu/

The George Washington University, Columbian College of Arts and Sciences, Department of Anthropology, Washington, DC 20052. Offers anthropology (MA, PhD); international development (MA); medical anthropology (MA); museum training (MA). *Program availability:* Part-time, evening/weekend. *Faculty:* 3 full-time (2 women), 18 part-time/adjunct (7 women). *Students:* 32 full-time (20 women), 16 part-time (13 women); includes 13 minority (1 Black or African American, non-Hispanic/Latino; 3 Asian, non-Hispanic/Latino; 5 Hispanic/Latino; 4 Two or more races, non-Hispanic/Latino), 9 international. Average age 28. 85 applicants, 42% accepted, 18 enrolled. In 2017, 14 master's awarded. *Degree requirements:* For master's, one foreign language, comprehensive exam, thesis or alternative. *Entrance requirements:* For master's, GRE General Test, minimum GPA of 3.0. Additional exam requirements/recommendations for international students: Required—TOEFL (minimum score 550 paper-based; 80 iBT). *Application deadline:* For fall admission, 1/15 priority date for international students; for spring admission, 9/15 priority date for domestic students, 9/1 priority date for international students. Applications are processed on a rolling basis. Application fee: $75. Electronic applications accepted. *Expenses: Tuition:* Full-time $28,800; part-time $1655 per credit hour. *Required fees:* $45; $2.75 per credit hour. *Financial support:* In 2017–18, 8 students received support. Fellowships, teaching assistantships, career-related internships or fieldwork, and Federal Work-Study available. Financial award application deadline: 1/15. *Unit head:* Richard Grinker, Chair, 202-994-6984, E-mail: rgrink@email.gwu.edu. *Application contact:* Information Contact, 202-994-6075, E-mail: anth@gwu.edu.
Website: http://anthropology.columbian.gwu.edu/

The George Washington University, Elliott School of International Affairs, Program in International Development Studies, Washington, DC 20052. Offers MA. *Program availability:* Part-time. *Students:* 51 full-time (42 women), 31 part-time (24 women); includes 29 minority (13 Black or African American, non-Hispanic/Latino; 7 Asian, non-Hispanic/Latino; 7 Hispanic/Latino; 2 Two or more races, non-Hispanic/Latino), 11 international. Average age 27. 205 applicants, 87% accepted, 37 enrolled. In 2017, 48 master's awarded. *Degree requirements:* For master's, one foreign language, capstone project. *Entrance requirements:* For master's, GRE General Test, 2 years (or the equivalent) of a modern foreign language, introductory courses in microeconomics and macroeconomics. Additional exam requirements/recommendations for international students: Required—TOEFL (minimum score 100 iBT), IELTS (minimum score 7). *Application deadline:* For fall admission, 1/15 priority date for domestic and international students; for spring admission, 10/1 for domestic students. Application fee: $75. Electronic applications accepted. *Expenses: Tuition:* Full-time $28,800; part-time $1655 per credit hour. *Required fees:* $45; $2.75 per credit hour. *Financial support:* In 2017–18, 27 students received support. Fellowships with partial tuition reimbursements available, Federal Work-Study, and scholarships/grants available. Financial award application deadline: 1/15; financial award applicants required to submit FAFSA. *Faculty research:* Development, anthropology, health and development, political science, education. *Unit head:* Prof. Sean Roberts, Director, 202-994-7739, Fax: 202-994-5477, E-mail: seanrr@gwu.edu. *Application contact:* Nicole A. Campbell, Director of Graduate Admissions, 202-994-7050, Fax: 202-994-9537, E-mail: esiagrad@gwu.edu.
Website: http://elliott.gwu.edu/international-development-studies

Harvard University, John F. Kennedy School of Government, Master in Public Administration in International Development Program, Cambridge, MA 02138. Offers MPAID. *Students:* 130 full-time (59 women); includes 15 minority (5 Black or African American, non-Hispanic/Latino; 5 Asian, non-Hispanic/Latino; 3 Hispanic/Latino; 2 Two or more races, non-Hispanic/Latino), 103 international. Average age 29. 251 applicants, 39% accepted, 61 enrolled. In 2017, 64 master's awarded. *Entrance requirements:* For master's, one course each in microeconomics and macroeconomics; two college-level calculus courses (one must contain multivariable calculus); bachelor's degree; 2-3 years of professional experience in development (strongly encouraged). Additional exam requirements/recommendations for international students: Required—TOEFL (minimum score 600 paper-based; 100 iBT). *Application deadline:* For fall admission, 12/1 for domestic students. Application fee: $100. Electronic applications accepted. *Financial support:* In 2017–18, 75 fellowships (averaging $45,739 per year) were awarded; career-related internships or fieldwork, Federal Work-Study, scholarships/grants, health care benefits, and unspecified assistantships also available. Financial award application deadline: 2/24; financial award applicants required to submit FAFSA. *Unit head:* Carol Finney, Director, 617-495-7799, E-mail: carol_finney@harvard.edu. *Application contact:* 617-495-2133, E-mail: mpaid_program@hks.harvard.edu.
Website: http://www.hks.harvard.edu/degrees/masters/mpa-id

Hope International University, School of Graduate and Professional Studies, Program in Business Administration, Fullerton, CA 92831-3138. Offers general management (MBA, MSM); international development (MBA, MSM); marketing management (MBA, MSM); non-profit management (MBA, MSM). *Program availability:* Part-time, online learning. *Degree requirements:* For master's, comprehensive exam (for some programs), thesis (for some programs), project. *Entrance requirements:* For master's, minimum GPA of 3.0; 2 references. Additional exam requirements/recommendations for international students: Required—TOEFL (minimum score 550 paper-based; 86 iBT); Recommended—IELTS (minimum score 6.5). Electronic applications accepted. *Expenses:* Contact institution.

Indiana University Bloomington, School of Public and Environmental Affairs, Public Affairs Programs, Bloomington, IN 47405. Offers economic development (MPA); energy (MPA); environmental policy (PhD); environmental policy and natural resource management (MPA); information systems (MPA); international development (MPA); local government management (MPA); nonprofit management (MPA, Certificate); policy analysis (MPA); public budgeting and financial management (Certificate); public finance (PhD); public financial administration (MPA); public management (MPA, PhD, Certificate); public policy analysis (PhD); social entrepreneurship (Certificate); specialized public affairs (MPA); sustainability and sustainable development (MPA); JD/MPA; MPA/MA; MPA/MIS; MPA/MLS; MSES/MPA. *Accreditation:* NASPAA (one or more programs are accredited). *Program availability:* Part-time. *Degree requirements:* For master's, capstone, internship; for doctorate, comprehensive exam, thesis/dissertation. *Entrance requirements:* For master's, GRE General Test or GMAT, official transcripts, 3 letters of recommendation, resume, personal statement; for doctorate, GRE General Test, official transcripts, 3 letters of recommendation, statement of purpose. Additional exam requirements/recommendations for international students: Required—TOEFL (minimum score 600 paper-based; 96 iBT); Recommended—IELTS (minimum score 7). Electronic applications accepted. *Faculty research:* International development, environmental policy and resource management, policy analysis, public finance, public management, urban management, nonprofit management, energy policy, social policy, public finance.

Johns Hopkins University, School of Advanced International Studies, Washington, DC 20036. Offers global risk (MA); international development (MA, Certificate), including international economics (MA); international economics (Certificate); international economics and finance (MA); international public policy (MIPP); international relations (PhD); international studies (Certificate); Japan studies (MA), including international economics; Korea studies (MA), including international economics; South Asia studies (MA), including international economics; Southeast Asia studies (MA), including international economics; JD/MA; MBA/MA; MHS/MA. Terminal master's awarded for partial completion of doctoral program. *Degree requirements:* For master's, 4-6

international economics courses, 5-6 functional or regional concentration courses, 2 core examinations, proficiency in language other than native language, capstone project; for doctorate, 2 foreign languages, thesis/dissertation, 3 comprehensive exams, economics, quantitative and qualitative course, dissertation prospectus and defense. *Entrance requirements:* For master's, GMAT or GRE General Test, previous course work in economics, foreign language, undergraduate degree; for doctorate, GRE General Test, master's degree. Additional exam requirements/recommendations for international students: Required—TOEFL (minimum score 600 paper-based; 100 iBT) or IELTS (minimum score 7). Electronic applications accepted. *Expenses:* Contact institution. *Faculty research:* International economics; international relations/regional studies; international development; energy, resources, and environment; international security/strategic studies.

Marymount California University, Program in Leadership and Global Development, Rancho Palos Verdes, CA 90275-6299. Offers MS.

McGill University, Faculty of Graduate and Postdoctoral Studies, Desautels Faculty of Management, Montréal, QC H3A 2T5, Canada. Offers administration (PhD); entrepreneurial studies (MBA); finance (MBA); general management (Post Master's Certificate); information systems (MBA); international business (MBA); international practicing management (MM); management (MBA); management for development (MBA); manufacturing management (MMM); marketing (MBA); operations management (MBA); public accountancy (Diploma); strategic management (MBA); MBA/LL B; MD/MBA. MMM offered jointly with Faculty of Engineering; PhD with Concordia University, HEC Montreal, Université de Montréal, Université du Québec à Montréal.

Middlebury Institute of International Studies at Monterey, Graduate School of International Policy and Management, Program in International Policy and Development, Monterey, CA 93940-2691. Offers MA. *Degree requirements:* For master's, one foreign language. *Entrance requirements:* For master's, minimum GPA of 3.0, proficiency in a foreign language. Additional exam requirements/recommendations for international students: Required—TOEFL (minimum score 550 paper-based; 80 iBT). Electronic applications accepted.

Norwich University, College of Graduate and Continuing Studies, Master of Arts in International Relations Program, Northfield, VT 05663. Offers international relations (MA), including cyber diplomacy-policy, cyber diplomacy-technical, international development, international security, national security, regions of the world. *Program availability:* Evening/weekend, online only, mostly all online with a week-long residency requirement. *Degree requirements:* For master's, research paper. *Entrance requirements:* For master's, minimum undergraduate GPA of 2.75. Additional exam requirements/recommendations for international students: Required—TOEFL (minimum score 550 paper-based; 80 iBT), IELTS (minimum score 6.5). Electronic applications accepted. *Expenses:* Contact institution.

Norwich University, College of Graduate and Continuing Studies, Master of Public Administration Program, Northfield, VT 05663. Offers criminal justice and public safety (MPA); fiscal management (MPA); international development and influence (MPA); municipal governance (MPA); nonprofit management (MPA); policy analysis and analytics (MPA); public administration leadership and crisis management (MPA); public works and sustainability (MPA). *Program availability:* Evening/weekend, online only, mostly all online with a week-long residency requirement. *Degree requirements:* For master's, capstone. *Entrance requirements:* For master's, minimum undergraduate GPA of 2.75. Additional exam requirements/recommendations for international students: Required—TOEFL (minimum score 550 paper-based; 80 iBT), IELTS (minimum score 6.5). Electronic applications accepted. *Expenses:* Contact institution.

Ohio University, Graduate College, Center for International Studies, Program in International Development Studies, Athens, OH 45701-2979. Offers MA. *Program availability:* Part-time. *Degree requirements:* For master's, one foreign language, thesis optional. *Entrance requirements:* For master's, minimum GPA of 3.0. Additional exam requirements/recommendations for international students: Required—TOEFL (minimum score 550 paper-based; 80 iBT), IELTS (minimum score 6.5). Electronic applications accepted. *Faculty research:* Problems and issues in social, economic, political, health and environmental development.

Old Dominion University, College of Arts and Letters, Graduate Program in International Studies, Norfolk, VA 23529. Offers conflict and cooperation (MA, PhD); interdependence and transnationalism (MA, PhD); international cultural studies (MA, PhD); international political economy and development (MA, PhD); modeling and simulation (MA, PhD); U.S. foreign policy and international relations (MA, PhD). *Program availability:* Part-time. *Faculty:* 15 full-time (4 women). *Students:* 32 full-time (13 women), 40 part-time (16 women); includes 11 minority (7 Black or African American, non-Hispanic/Latino; 2 Hispanic/Latino; 2 Two or more races, non-Hispanic/Latino), 16 international. Average age 37. 95 applicants, 58% accepted, 40 enrolled. In 2017, 2 master's, 7 doctorates awarded. Terminal master's awarded for partial completion of doctoral program. *Degree requirements:* For master's, one foreign language, comprehensive exam, thesis optional; for doctorate, one foreign language, comprehensive exam, thesis/dissertation. *Entrance requirements:* For master's, GRE General Test, sample of written work, 2 letters of recommendation; for doctorate, GRE General Test, sample of written work, 3 letters of recommendation. Additional exam requirements/recommendations for international students: Required—TOEFL (minimum score 570 paper-based). *Application deadline:* For fall admission, 1/15 for domestic and international students; for spring admission, 10/15 for domestic and international students. Application fee: $50. Electronic applications accepted. *Expenses:* Contact institution. *Financial support:* In 2017–18, 12 students received support, including 1 fellowship (averaging $15,000 per year), 5 research assistantships with tuition reimbursements available (averaging $15,000 per year), 4 teaching assistantships with tuition reimbursements available (averaging $15,000 per year); career-related internships or fieldwork, institutionally sponsored loans, and unspecified assistantships also available. Financial award application deadline: 1/15; financial award applicants required to submit FAFSA. *Faculty research:* U.S. foreign policy, international security, transatlantic and transpacific relations, transnational issues, international political economy and development. *Total annual research expenditures:* $330,391. *Unit head:* Dr. Regina Karp, Graduate Program Director, 757-683-5700, Fax: 757-683-5701, E-mail: rkarp@odu.edu. *Application contact:* Dr. Dale Miller, Associate Dean for Research and Graduate Studies, 757-683-3866, E-mail: demiller@odu.edu. Website: http://www.odu.edu/gpis

Rutgers University–Camden, Graduate School of Arts and Sciences, Department of Public Policy and Administration, Camden, NJ 08102. Offers education policy and leadership (MPA); international public service and development (MPA); public management (MPA); JD/MPA; MPA/MA. *Accreditation:* NASPAA. *Program availability:* Part-time, evening/weekend. *Degree requirements:* For master's, directed study, research workshop, 42 credits. *Entrance requirements:* For master's, GRE General Test, GMAT or LSAT, 3 letters of recommendation; resume. Additional exam requirements/recommendations for international students: Required—TOEFL (minimum score 550 paper-based), IELTS. Electronic applications accepted. *Faculty research:* Nonprofit management, county and municipal administration, health and human services, government communication, administrative law, educational finance.

Saint Mary's University, Faculty of Arts, International Development Studies Program, Halifax, NS B3H 3C3, Canada. Offers MA, Graduate Diploma. *Program availability:* Part-time. *Degree requirements:* For master's, thesis. *Entrance requirements:* For master's, honors degree. *Faculty research:* Dynamics of global development, gender and development, policy analysis, models and strategies for development, Latin American and Caribbean development.

St. Mary's University, Graduate Studies, Program in International Relations, San Antonio, TX 78228. Offers conflict transformation (Certificate); international conflict resolution (MA); international development (MA); international relations (MA); security policy (MA); JD/MA. *Program availability:* Part-time, evening/weekend, 100% online. *Students:* 22 full-time (12 women), 48 part-time (16 women); includes 38 minority (5 Black or African American, non-Hispanic/Latino; 1 American Indian or Alaska Native, non-Hispanic/Latino; 1 Asian, non-Hispanic/Latino; 30 Hispanic/Latino; 1 Two or more races, non-Hispanic/Latino), 5 international. Average age 31. 89 applicants, 39% accepted, 19 enrolled. In 2017, 36 master's awarded. *Degree requirements:* For master's, one foreign language, comprehensive exam (for some programs), thesis (for some programs), thesis or comprehensive exam. *Entrance requirements:* For master's, minimum undergraduate cumulative GPA of 3.0. Additional exam requirements/recommendations for international students: Required—TOEFL (minimum score 550 paper-based; 80 iBT), IELTS (minimum score 6). *Application deadline:* For fall admission, 7/1 for domestic students; for spring admission, 11/15 for domestic students; for summer admission, 4/1 for domestic students. Applications are processed on a rolling basis. Application fee: $0. Electronic applications accepted. *Expenses: Tuition:* Full-time $16,200; part-time $900 per credit hour. *Required fees:* $810; $405 per semester. *Financial support:* Research assistantships, Federal Work-Study, tuition waivers (full), unspecified assistantships, and grants for active-duty and retired military, DOD employees, and their spouses available. Financial award application deadline: 3/31; financial award applicants required to submit FAFSA. *Faculty research:* Anthropology and ethics, states in crisis and socioeconomic development, politics and society of South Asia, political psychology, international relations theory. *Unit head:* Dr. Larry Hufford, Graduate International Relations, 210-431-6790, E-mail: lhufford@stmarytx.edu. *Application contact:* Kim Thornton, Director of Graduate Admission, 210-436-3101, E-mail: kthornton@stmarytx.edu. Website: https://www.stmarytx.edu/academics/programs/master-international-relations/

Saint Mary's University of Minnesota, Schools of Graduate and Professional Programs, Graduate School of Business and Technology, International Development Program, Winona, MN 55987-1399. Offers MA. *Program availability:* Online learning. *Unit head:* Matt Bluem, Director, 612-238-4535, E-mail: mbluem@smumn.edu. *Application contact:* James Callinan, Director of Admissions for Graduate and Professional Programs, 612-728-5158, Fax: 612-728-5121, E-mail: jcallina@smumn.edu. Website: http://onlineprograms.smumn.edu/maid/master-of-arts-in-international-development

Tufts University, Graduate School of Arts and Sciences, Department of Urban and Environmental Policy and Planning, Medford, MA 02155. Offers community development (MA); environmental policy (MA); health and human welfare (MA); housing policy (MA); international environment/development policy (MA); public policy (MPP); MA/JD; MA/MBA; MA/MPH; MA/MS; MALD/MA. MALD/MA offered in connection with The Fletcher School of Law and Diplomacy; MA/MPH with School of Medicine; MA/MS with School of Nutrition Science and Policy or School of Engineering; MA/MBA with Boston College, Carroll School of Management; MA/JD with Boston College Law School. *Accreditation:* ACSP (one or more programs are accredited). *Program availability:* Part-time. *Students:* 95 full-time (68 women), 17 part-time (14 women); includes 34 minority (14 Black or African American, non-Hispanic/Latino; 10 Asian, non-Hispanic/Latino; 6 Hispanic/Latino; 4 Two or more races, non-Hispanic/Latino), 14 international. Average age 30. 153 applicants, 78% accepted, 51 enrolled. In 2017, 45 master's awarded. *Degree requirements:* For master's, thesis or alternative, internship. *Entrance requirements:* For master's, GRE General Test. Additional exam requirements/recommendations for international students: Required—TOEFL (minimum score 550 paper-based; 80 iBT), IELTS (minimum score 6.5). *Application deadline:* For fall admission, 1/15 for domestic and international students. Applications are processed on a rolling basis. Application fee: $85. Electronic applications accepted. *Expenses:* Contact institution. *Financial support:* Fellowships, research assistantships, teaching assistantships, career-related internships or fieldwork, Federal Work-Study, scholarships/grants, tuition waivers (full and partial), and unspecified assistantships available. Support available to part-time students. Financial award application deadline: 1/15. *Unit head:* Dr. Mary Davis, Graduate Program Director, 617-627-3394. *Application contact:* Office of Graduate Admissions, 617-627-3395, E-mail: gradadmissions@tufts.edu. Website: http://ase.tufts.edu/uep/

Tulane University, School of Law, The Payson Center for International Development, New Orleans, LA 70118. Offers international development (MS, PhD); law and development (LL M); JD/MS. *Program availability:* Part-time. Terminal master's awarded for partial completion of doctoral program. *Degree requirements:* For master's, comprehensive exam (for some programs), thesis optional; for doctorate, comprehensive exam, thesis/dissertation. *Entrance requirements:* For master's, GRE General Test, minimum 3.0 GPA in undergraduate course work; for doctorate, GRE. Additional exam requirements/recommendations for international students: Required—TOEFL (minimum score 600 paper-based; 90 iBT). Electronic applications accepted. *Expenses:* Contact institution. *Faculty research:* Poverty and inequality, sustainability, health and human development, GIS for development, monitoring and evaluation.

University of California, San Diego, Graduate Division, School of Global Policy and Strategy, Master of International Affairs Program, La Jolla, CA 92093. Offers international development and nonprofit management (MIA); international economics (MIA); international environmental policy (MIA); international management (MIA); international politics (MIA). Students will choose one of the following country/regional specializations: China, Japan, Korea, Latin America, or Southeast Asia. *Degree requirements:* For master's, one foreign language. *Entrance requirements:* For master's, GMAT or GRE General Test. Additional exam requirements/recommendations for international students: Required—TOEFL (minimum score 90 iBT), IELTS (minimum score 7). Electronic applications accepted.

University of Denver, Josef Korbel School of International Studies, Denver, CO 80208. Offers conflict resolution (MA); global business and corporate social responsibility (Certificate); global finance, trade and economic integration (MA); global health affairs (Certificate); homeland security (Certificate); humanitarian assistance (Certificate); international administration (MA); international development (MA); international human rights (MA); international security (MA); international studies (MA, PhD); public policy studies (MPP); religion and international affairs (Certificate). *Program availability:* Part-time. *Faculty:* 46 full-time (16 women), 28 part-time/adjunct (8 women). *Students:* 245 full-time (132 women), 40 part-time (21 women); includes 58 minority (8 Black or African American, non-Hispanic/Latino; 2 American Indian or Alaska Native, non-Hispanic/Latino; 11 Asian, non-Hispanic/Latino; 27 Hispanic/Latino; 10 Two or more races, non-Hispanic/Latino), 22 international. Average age 27. 627 applicants, 74% accepted, 106

enrolled. In 2017, 218 master's, 6 doctorates, 25 other advanced degrees awarded. *Degree requirements:* For master's, one foreign language, thesis (for some programs); for doctorate, one foreign language, comprehensive exam, thesis/dissertation, two extended research papers. *Entrance requirements:* For master's, GRE General Test, bachelor's degree, transcripts, two letters of recommendation, statement of purpose, resume or curriculum vitae; for doctorate, GRE General Test, master's degree, transcripts, three letters of recommendation, statement of purpose, resume or curriculum vitae, writing sample; for Certificate, bachelor's degree, transcripts, two letters of recommendation, statement of purpose, resume or curriculum vitae. Additional exam requirements/recommendations for international students: Required—TOEFL (minimum score 587 paper-based; 95 iBT). *Application deadline:* For fall admission, 1/15 priority date for domestic and international students; for winter admission, 11/1 for domestic and international students. Applications are processed on a rolling basis. Application fee: $65. Electronic applications accepted. *Expenses:* $47,823 per year full-time. *Financial support:* In 2017–18, 225 students received support, including 1 teaching assistantship with tuition reimbursement available (averaging $2,236 per year); research assistantships with tuition reimbursements available, career-related internships or fieldwork, Federal Work-Study, institutionally sponsored loans, scholarships/grants, and unspecified assistantships also available. Support available to part-time students. Financial award application deadline: 2/15; financial award applicants required to submit FAFSA. *Faculty research:* Human rights and international security, international politics and economics, economic-social and political development, international technology analysis and management. *Unit head:* Dr. Pardis Mahdavi, Dean, 303-871-6338, E-mail: pardis.mahdavi@du.edu. *Application contact:* Admissions Contact, E-mail: korbeladm@du.edu.
Website: http://www.du.edu/korbel

University of Florida, Graduate School, College of Liberal Arts and Sciences, Department of Political Science, Gainesville, FL 32611. Offers educational policy (PhD); international development policy and administration (MA, Certificate); international relations (MA, MAT); political campaigning (MA, Certificate); political science (MA, PhD); public affairs (MA, Certificate); tropical conservation and development (MA, PhD); JD/MA. Terminal master's awarded for partial completion of doctoral program. *Degree requirements:* For master's, variable foreign language requirement, comprehensive exam (for some programs), thesis or alternative, internship (for some programs); for doctorate, variable foreign language requirement, comprehensive exam, thesis/dissertation. *Entrance requirements:* For master's and doctorate, GRE General Test (minimum score: 308 combined verbal/quantitative), minimum GPA of 3.5. Additional exam requirements/recommendations for international students: Required—TOEFL (minimum score 550 paper-based; 80 iBT), IELTS (minimum score 6). Electronic applications accepted. *Faculty research:* American electoral politics and political institutions, comparative democratization and development, theories of international relation, and political theory.

University of Guelph, Graduate Studies, Collaborative International Development Studies, Guelph, ON N1G 2W1, Canada. Offers M Eng, M Sc, MA, MBA, PhD. *Program availability:* Part-time. *Degree requirements:* For master's, thesis (for some programs), seminar; for doctorate, comprehensive exam (for some programs), thesis/dissertation. *Entrance requirements:* For master's, honour's degree with courses in economics, social science, and empirical methods. *Faculty research:* Transformation of developing societies, regional differences, national and international processes of development, long-term change.

University of Hawaii at Manoa, Office of Graduate Education, College of Social Sciences, Department of Urban and Regional Planning, Honolulu, HI 96822. Offers community planning (MURP); disaster management and humanitarian assistance (Graduate Certificate); environmental planning and sustainability (MURP); international development planning (MURP); land use, transportation and infrastructure planning (MURP); planning studies (Graduate Certificate); urban and regional planning (PhD, Graduate Certificate). *Accreditation:* ACSP. *Program availability:* Part-time. *Entrance requirements:* For master's, GRE General Test, minimum GPA of 3.0; for doctorate, GRE General Test. Additional exam requirements/recommendations for international students: Required—TOEFL (minimum score 500 paper-based; 61 iBT), IELTS (minimum score 5).

The University of Manchester, School of Environment and Development, Manchester, United Kingdom. Offers architecture (M Phil, PhD); development policy and management (M Phil, PhD); human geography (M Phil, PhD); physical geography (M Phil, PhD); planning and landscape (M Phil, PhD).

University of Massachusetts Boston, Graduate School of Global Inclusion and Social Development, Program in Global Inclusion and Social Development, Boston, MA 02125-3393. Offers MA, PhD. *Students:* 20 full-time (18 women), 29 part-time (25 women); includes 11 minority (6 Black or African American, non-Hispanic/Latino; 2 Hispanic/Latino; 1 Native Hawaiian or other Pacific Islander, non-Hispanic/Latino; 2 Two or more races, non-Hispanic/Latino), 8 international. Average age 37. 48 applicants, 40% accepted, 7 enrolled. *Expenses:* Tuition, state resident: full-time $17,375. Tuition, nonresident: full-time $33,915. *Required fees:* $355. *Application contact:* Graduate Admissions Coordinator, 617-287-6400, Fax: 617-287-6236, E-mail: bos.gadm@dpc.umassp.edu.

University of Minnesota, Twin Cities Campus, Graduate School, Humphrey School of Public Affairs, Master of Development Practice Program, Minneapolis, MN 55455. Offers MDP. Program offered jointly with Interdisciplinary Center for the Study of Global Change. *Degree requirements:* For master's, thesis or alternative, international field experience. *Entrance requirements:* For master's, GRE. Additional exam requirements/recommendations for international students: Required—TOEFL (minimum score 600 paper-based; 100 iBT), IELTS (minimum score 7). Electronic applications accepted. *Expenses:* Contact institution. *Faculty research:* Policy analysis and management, health and education, natural sciences, social sciences, interdisciplinary research methods.

University of New Brunswick Fredericton, School of Graduate Studies, Policy Studies Program, Fredericton, NB E3B 5A3, Canada. Offers citizen engagement/dispute resolution (M Phil); community development (M Phil); international development (M Phil); leadership (M Phil); sustainability/environmental issues (M Phil); worldviews (M Phil). *Program availability:* Part-time. *Degree requirements:* For master's, thesis, report. *Entrance requirements:* For master's, minimum GPA of 3.5. Additional exam requirements/recommendations for international students: Required—TWE (minimum score 5.5), TOEFL (minimum score 600 paper-based; 100 iBT) or IELTS (minimum score 7). Electronic applications accepted. *Faculty research:* International development, worldviews, citizenship/dispute resolution, sustainability/environmental issues, leadership, community development.

University of New Mexico, Graduate Studies, College of Arts and Sciences, Program in Economics, Albuquerque, NM 87131-2039. Offers econometrics (MA); economic theory (MA); environmental/natural resource economics (MA, PhD); international/development and sustainability economics (MA, PhD); public economics (MA, PhD). *Program availability:* Part-time. *Faculty:* 12 full-time (5 women), 1 (woman) part-time/adjunct. *Students:* 28 full-time (6 women), 22 part-time (8 women); includes 5 minority

(all Hispanic/Latino), 31 international. Average age 33. 49 applicants, 20% accepted, 10 enrolled. In 2017, 7 master's, 4 doctorates awarded. Terminal master's awarded for partial completion of doctoral program. *Degree requirements:* For master's, comprehensive exam, thesis (for some programs); for doctorate, comprehensive exam, thesis/dissertation. *Entrance requirements:* For master's and doctorate, GRE General Test, 3 letters of recommendation, letter of intent, curriculum vitae. Additional exam requirements/recommendations for international students: Required—TOEFL (minimum score 520 paper-based; 68 iBT). *Application deadline:* For fall admission, 3/1 priority date for domestic students, 3/1 for international students. Applications are processed on a rolling basis. Application fee: $50. Electronic applications accepted. *Financial support:* Fellowships with tuition reimbursements, research assistantships with tuition reimbursements, teaching assistantships with tuition reimbursements, career-related internships or fieldwork, Federal Work-Study, scholarships/grants, health care benefits, and unspecified assistantships available. Support available to part-time students. Financial award application deadline: 3/1; financial award applicants required to submit FAFSA. *Faculty research:* Core theory, econometrics, public finance, international/development economics, labor/human resource economics, environmental/natural resource economics. *Total annual research expenditures:* $167,690. *Unit head:* Dr. Janie Chermak, Chair, 505-277-2037, Fax: 505-277-9445, E-mail: jchermak@unm.edu. *Application contact:* Jeff Newcomer Miller, Academic Advisor, 505-277-3056, Fax: 505-277-9445, E-mail: econgrad@unm.edu.
Website: http://econ.unm.edu

University of Ottawa, Faculty of Graduate and Postdoctoral Studies, Program in Globalization and International Development, Ottawa, ON K1N 6N5, Canada. Offers MA. *Degree requirements:* For master's, thesis or alternative. *Entrance requirements:* For master's, honours bachelor's degree or equivalent, minimum B average.

University of Pittsburgh, Graduate School of Public and International Affairs, Master of International Development Program, Pittsburgh, PA 15260. Offers energy and environment (MID); governance and international public management (MID); human security (MID); nongovernmental organizations and civil society (MID); urban affairs and planning (MID); MID/JD; MID/MBA; MID/MPH; MID/MSIS; MID/MSW. *Program availability:* Part-time, evening/weekend. *Faculty:* 30 full-time (11 women), 14 part-time/adjunct (5 women). *Students:* 55 full-time (45 women), 6 part-time (4 women); includes 11 minority (4 Black or African American, non-Hispanic/Latino; 4 Asian, non-Hispanic/Latino; 3 Hispanic/Latino), 9 international. Average age 28. 71 applicants, 90% accepted, 10 enrolled. In 2017, 30 master's awarded. *Degree requirements:* For master's, thesis optional, capstone seminar. *Entrance requirements:* For master's, GRE General Test or GMAT, 2 letters of recommendation; undergraduate transcripts; resume; personal statement. Additional exam requirements/recommendations for international students: Required—TOEFL (minimum score 80 iBT); Recommended—IELTS (minimum score 7). *Application deadline:* For fall admission, 2/1 priority date for domestic students, 1/15 for international students; for spring admission, 11/1 priority date for domestic students, 8/1 for international students. Application fee: $50. Electronic applications accepted. *Expenses:* $23,140 per year in-state, $37,830 out-of-state. *Financial support:* In 2017–18, 38 students received support, including 2 fellowships with full tuition reimbursements available (averaging $37,000 per year), 3 research assistantships with full tuition reimbursements available (averaging $37,000 per year); career-related internships or fieldwork and scholarships/grants also available. Financial award application deadline: 2/1; financial award applicants required to submit FAFSA. *Faculty research:* Nongovernmental organizations and civil society, energy and environment, human security, urban affairs and planning, governance and international public management. *Total annual research expenditures:* $1.6 million. *Unit head:* Dr. John Keeler, Dean, 412-648-7605, Fax: 412-648-7601, E-mail: gspia@pitt.edu. *Application contact:* Dr. Michael Rizzi, Director of Student Services, 412-648-7640, Fax: 412-648-7641, E-mail: rizzim@pitt.edu.
Website: http://www.gspia.pitt.edu/

University of Pittsburgh, Graduate School of Public and International Affairs, PhD Program in Public and International Affairs, Pittsburgh, PA 15260. Offers international affairs (PhD); international development (PhD); public administration (PhD); public policy (PhD). *Program availability:* Part-time, online learning. *Faculty:* 30 full-time (11 women), 14 part-time/adjunct (5 women). *Students:* 31 full-time (11 women), 2 part-time (0 women); includes 5 minority (1 Black or African American, non-Hispanic/Latino; 2 Asian, non-Hispanic/Latino; 2 Hispanic/Latino), 12 international. Average age 37. 69 applicants, 13% accepted, 8 enrolled. In 2017, 2 doctorates awarded. *Degree requirements:* For doctorate, thesis/dissertation, mid-term evaluation, preliminary exam, annual review. *Entrance requirements:* For doctorate, GRE or GMAT, 2 letters of recommendation, resume, undergraduate transcripts, personal statement, writing sample. Additional exam requirements/recommendations for international students: Required—TOEFL (minimum score 80 iBT); Recommended—IELTS (minimum score 7). *Application deadline:* For fall admission, 1/15 for domestic and international students. Application fee: $50. Electronic applications accepted. *Expenses:* $23,140 per year in-state, $37,830 out-of-state. *Financial support:* In 2017–18, 19 students received support, including 19 research assistantships with full tuition reimbursements available (averaging $37,000 per year); fellowships, teaching assistantships, and unspecified assistantships also available. Financial award application deadline: 1/15; financial award applicants required to submit FAFSA. *Faculty research:* International development, international affairs, public policy, public administration. *Total annual research expenditures:* $1.6 million. *Unit head:* Dr. John Keeler, Dean, 412-648-7605, Fax: 412-648-7601, E-mail: gspia@pitt.edu. *Application contact:* Dr. Michael Rizzi, Director of Student Services, 412-648-7640, Fax: 412-648-7641, E-mail: rizzim@pitt.edu.
Website: http://www.gspia.pitt.edu/

University of Pittsburgh, Katz Graduate School of Business, MBA/Master of International Development Joint Degree Program, Pittsburgh, PA 15260. Offers MID/MBA. *Accreditation:* AACSB. *Program availability:* Part-time, evening/weekend. *Faculty:* 91 full-time (30 women), 14 part-time/adjunct (4 women). *Students:* 1 (woman) full-time. Average age 26. 8 applicants, 50% accepted. *Entrance requirements:* Additional exam requirements/recommendations for international students: Required—TOEFL (minimum score 100 iBT) or IELTS (minimum score 7.0). *Application deadline:* For fall admission, 4/1 priority date for domestic students, 2/1 priority date for international students. Application fee: $50. Electronic applications accepted. *Financial support:* Scholarships/grants available. Financial award application deadline: 6/1; financial award applicants required to submit FAFSA. *Faculty research:* Accounting systems/financial reporting, corporate finance, shopper marketing/consumer behavior, management information systems, organizational behavior and entrepreneurship. *Total annual research expenditures:* $475,077. *Unit head:* Dr. Arjang A. Assad, Dean, 412-648-1556, Fax: 412-648-1552, E-mail: aassad@katz.pitt.edu. *Application contact:* Thomas Keller, Director of MBA Admissions, 412-648-1700, Fax: 412-648-1659, E-mail: mba@katz.pitt.edu.
Website: https://www.katz.business.pitt.edu/mba/joint-and-dual/international-development#section-1

University of San Francisco, College of Arts and Sciences, International and Development Economics Program, San Francisco, CA 94117-1080. Offers MA.

University of Southern Mississippi, College of Arts and Letters, Department of Political Science, International Development and International Affairs, Hattiesburg, MS

39406-0001. Offers MA, PhD. *Program availability:* Part-time, evening/weekend, online learning. *Students:* 5 full-time (2 women), 1 (woman) part-time. 16 applicants, 75% accepted, 6 enrolled. In 2017, 53 master's, 8 doctorates awarded. *Degree requirements:* For master's, comprehensive exam, thesis (for some programs); for doctorate, comprehensive exam, thesis/dissertation. *Entrance requirements:* For master's, GRE General Test, minimum GPA of 2.75 in last 2 years, 3.0 in field of study; for doctorate, GRE General Test, minimum GPA of 3.5. Additional exam requirements/recommendations for international students: Required—TOEFL, IELTS. *Application deadline:* For fall admission, 3/1 priority date for domestic students, 3/1 for international students. Applications are processed on a rolling basis. Application fee: $60. Electronic applications accepted. *Expenses:* Tuition, state resident: full-time $3830. *Financial support:* Research assistantships with full and partial tuition reimbursements, teaching assistantships with full tuition reimbursements, career-related internships or fieldwork, Federal Work-Study, scholarships/grants, health care benefits, and unspecified assistantships available. Financial award application deadline: 3/15; financial award applicants required to submit FAFSA. *Faculty research:* American politics, international politics, political theory, comparative politics, public law. *Unit head:* Edward Sayre, Chair, 601-266-4310. *Application contact:* Marek Steedman, Director, Graduate Studies, 601-266-4317, Fax: 601-266-4172.
Website: https://www.usm.edu/political-science-international-development-affairs

Walden University, Graduate Programs, School of Public Policy and Administration, Minneapolis, MN 55401. Offers criminal justice (MPA, MPP, MS, Graduate Certificate), including emergency management (MS, PhD), general program (MS), global leadership (MS, PhD), homeland security and policy coordination (MS, PhD), law and public policy (MS, PhD), policy analysis (MS, PhD), public management and leadership (MS, PhD), self-designed (MS); terrorism, mediation, and peace (MS, PhD); criminal justice and executive management (MS), including global leadership (MS, PhD); criminal justice leadership and executive management (MS), including emergency management (MS, PhD), general program, homeland security and policy coordination (MS, PhD), law and public policy (MS, PhD), policy analysis (MS, PhD), public management and leadership (MS, PhD), self-designed, terrorism, mediation, and peace (MS, PhD); emergency management (MPA, MPP, MS), including criminal justice (MS, PhD), general program (MS), homeland security (MS), public management and leadership (MS, PhD), terrorism and emergency management (MS); general program (MPA, MPP); global leadership (MPA, MPP); government management (Graduate Certificate); health policy (MPA, MPP); homeland security (Graduate Certificate); homeland security and policy coordination (MPA, MPP); international nongovernmental organizations (MPA, MPP); law and public policy (MPA, MPP); local government management for sustainable communities (MPA, MPP); nonprofit management (Graduate Certificate); nonprofit management and leadership (MPA, MPP, MS), including global leadership (MS, PhD), international nongovernmental organization (MS), local government for sustainable communities (MS), self designed (MS); online teaching in higher education (Post-Master's Certificate); policy analysis (MPA); public management and leadership (MPA, MPP, Graduate Certificate); public policy (Graduate Certificate); public policy and administration (PhD), including criminal justice (MS, PhD), emergency management (MS, PhD), global leadership (MS, PhD), health policy, homeland security and policy coordination (MS, PhD), international nongovernmental organizations, law and public policy (MS, PhD), local government management for sustainable communities, nonprofit management and leadership, policy analysis (MS, PhD), public management and leadership (MS, PhD), terrorism, mediation, and peace (MS, PhD); strategic planning and public policy (Graduate Certificate); terrorism, mediation, and peace (MPA, MPP). *Program availability:* Part-time, evening/weekend, online only, 100% online. *Degree requirements:* For doctorate, thesis/dissertation, residency. *Entrance requirements:* For master's, bachelor's degree or higher; minimum GPA of 2.5; official transcripts; goal statement (for some programs); access to computer and Internet; for doctorate, master's degree or higher; three years of related professional or academic experience (preferred); minimum GPA of 3.0; goal statement and current resume (for select programs); official transcripts; access to computer and Internet; for other advanced degree, relevant work experience; access to computer and Internet. Additional exam requirements/recommendations for international students: Required—TOEFL (minimum score 550 paper-based, 79 iBT), IELTS (minimum score 6.5), Michigan English Language Assessment Battery (minimum score 82), or PTE (minimum score 53). Electronic applications accepted.

International Trade Policy

★ **Baruch College of the City University of New York,** Austin W. Marxe School of Public and International Affairs, Program in International Affairs, New York, NY 10010-5585. Offers international nongovernmental organizations (MIA); trade policy and global economic governance (MIA); Western Hemisphere affairs (MIA). *Program availability:* Part-time.
See Display on page 910 and Close-Up on page 955.

The George Washington University, Elliott School of International Affairs, Program in International Trade and Investment Policy, Washington, DC 20052. Offers MA. *Program availability:* Part-time. *Students:* 27 full-time (10 women), 15 part-time (8 women); includes 14 minority (3 Black or African American, non-Hispanic/Latino; 2 Asian, non-Hispanic/Latino; 7 Hispanic/Latino; 2 Two or more races, non-Hispanic/Latino), 15 international. Average age 27. 57 applicants, 72% accepted, 13 enrolled. In 2017, 24 master's awarded. *Degree requirements:* For master's, one foreign language, capstone project. *Entrance requirements:* For master's, GRE General Test, 2 years of a modern foreign language, 2 semesters of introductory economics. Additional exam requirements/recommendations for international students: Required—TOEFL (minimum score 100 iBT), IELTS (minimum score 7). *Application deadline:* For fall admission, 1/15 priority date for domestic and international students; for spring admission, 10/1 for domestic students. Application fee: $75. Electronic applications accepted. *Expenses: Tuition:* Full-time $28,800; part-time $1655 per credit hour. *Required fees:* $45; $2.75 per credit hour. *Financial support:* In 2017–18, 11 students received support.

Fellowships with partial tuition reimbursements available, Federal Work-Study, and scholarships/grants available. Financial award application deadline: 1/15. *Unit head:* Prof. Michael Moore, Director, 202-994-5230, E-mail: itip@gwu.edu. *Application contact:* Nicole A. Campbell, Director of Graduate Admissions, 202-994-7050, Fax: 202-994-9537, E-mail: esiagrad@gwu.edu.
Website: http://elliott.gwu.edu/international-trade-investment-policy

Middlebury Institute of International Studies at Monterey, Graduate School of International Policy and Management, Program in International Trade and Economic Diplomacy, Monterey, CA 93940-2691. Offers MA. *Entrance requirements:* For master's, statement of purpose, resume or curriculum vitae, undergraduate transcripts, 2 letters of recommendation, interview. Additional exam requirements/recommendations for international students: Required—TOEFL or IELTS.

Valparaiso University, Graduate School and Continuing Education, Program in International Commerce and Policy, Valparaiso, IN 46383. Offers MS, JD/MS. *Program availability:* Part-time, evening/weekend. *Entrance requirements:* For master's, minimum GPA of 3.0. Additional exam requirements/recommendations for international students: Required—TOEFL (minimum score 550 paper-based; 80 iBT), IELTS (minimum score 6). Electronic applications accepted. *Expenses: Tuition:* Full-time $11,340; part-time $630 per credit hour. *Required fees:* $520; $250 per year. $125 per semester. Tuition and fees vary according to program and reciprocity agreements.

Political Science

Acadia University, Faculty of Arts, Department of Political Science, Wolfville, NS B4P 2R6, Canada. Offers MA. *Entrance requirements:* For master's, honors degree or equivalent. Additional exam requirements/recommendations for international students: Required—TOEFL (minimum score 580 paper-based; 93 iBT), IELTS (minimum score 6.5). *Application deadline:* For fall admission, 2/1 priority date for domestic and international students. Applications are processed on a rolling basis. Application fee: $50. *Financial support:* Application deadline: 2/1. *Faculty research:* Atlantic Canada, international relations and organization, human rights, Canadian politics, political thought, technology. *Unit head:* Dr. Can E. Mutlu, Graduate Coordinator, 902-585-1293, E-mail: can.mutlu@acadiau.ca. *Application contact:* Danielle Fraser, Administrative Secretary, 902-585-1506, Fax: 902-585-1070, E-mail: polisci@acadiau.ca.
Website: http://polisci.acadiau.ca/

American Public University System, AMU/APU Graduate Programs, Charles Town, WV 25414. Offers accounting (MS); applied business analytics (MS); business administration (MBA); criminal justice (MA); cybersecurity studies (MS); educational leadership (M Ed); environmental policy and management (MS); global security (DGS); health information management (MS); history (MA), including American military history, American Revolution, civil war, war since 1945, World War II; information technology (MS); international relations and conflict resolution (MA), including American politics and government, comparative government and development, general, international relations, public policy; national security studies (MA); nursing (MSN); political science (MA); public policy (MPP); reverse logistics management (MA), including comparative and security issues, conflict resolution, international and transnational security issues, peacekeeping; space studies (MS); sports management (MS); strategic intelligence (DSI); teaching (M Ed), including secondary social studies; transportation and logistics management (MA). *Program availability:* Part-time, evening/weekend, online only, 100% online. *Students:* 455 full-time (227 women), 7,939 part-time (3,353 women); includes 2,793 minority (1,429 Black or African American, non-Hispanic/Latino; 48 American Indian or Alaska Native, non-Hispanic/Latino; 205 Asian, non-Hispanic/Latino; 766 Hispanic/Latino; 62 Native Hawaiian or other Pacific Islander, non-Hispanic/Latino; 283 Two or more races, non-Hispanic/Latino), 101 international. Average age 37. In 2017, 2,977 master's awarded. *Degree requirements:* For master's, comprehensive exam or practicum. *Entrance requirements:* For master's, official transcript showing earned bachelor's degree from institution accredited by recognized accrediting body. Additional exam requirements/recommendations for international students: Required—TOEFL (minimum score 550 paper-based), IELTS (minimum score 6.5). *Application deadline:* Applications are processed on a rolling basis. Application fee: $0. Electronic applications accepted. *Expenses: Tuition:* Full-time $6300; part-time $350 per credit. *Required fees:* $300; $50 per course. *Financial support:* Scholarships/grants available. Financial award applicants required to submit FAFSA. *Unit head:* Dr. Wallace Boston, President, 877-468-6268, Fax: 304-728-2348, E-mail: president@apus.edu. *Application contact:* Yoci Deal, Associate Vice President, Graduate and International Admissions, 877-468-6268, Fax: 304-724-3764, E-mail: info@apus.edu.
Website: http://www.apus.edu

American University, School of International Service, Washington, DC 20016-8071. Offers comparative and regional studies (Certificate); cross-cultural communication (Certificate); development management (MS); ethics, peace, and global affairs (MA); European studies (Certificate); global environmental policy (MA, Certificate); global information technology (Certificate); global media (MA); international affairs (MA), including comparative and regional studies, global governance, politics, and security, international economic relations, natural resources and sustainable development, U.S. foreign policy and national security; international arts management (Certificate); international communication (MA, Certificate); international development (MA); international economic policy (Certificate); international economic relations (Certificate); international economics (MA); international peace and conflict resolution (MA, Certificate); international politics (Certificate); international relations (MA, PhD); international service (MIS); peacebuilding (Certificate); social enterprise (MA); the Americas (Certificate); United States foreign policy (Certificate); JD/MA. *Program availability:* Part-time, evening/weekend, 100% online. *Faculty:* 112 full-time (50 women), 46 part-time/adjunct (19 women). *Students:* 495 full-time (333 women), 518

part-time (276 women); includes 360 minority (95 Black or African American, non-Hispanic/Latino; 2 American Indian or Alaska Native, non-Hispanic/Latino; 60 Asian, non-Hispanic/Latino; 164 Hispanic/Latino; 39 Two or more races, non-Hispanic/Latino), 98 international. Average age 30. 1,559 applicants, 81% accepted, 356 enrolled. In 2017, 427 master's, 9 doctorates, 5 other advanced degrees awarded. Terminal master's awarded for partial completion of doctoral program. *Degree requirements:* For master's, one foreign language, comprehensive exam, thesis or alternative; for doctorate, one foreign language, comprehensive exam, thesis/dissertation. *Entrance requirements:* For master's, GRE; GMAT or GRE (for MA in social enterprise), transcripts, resume, 2 letters of recommendation, statement of purpose; for doctorate, GRE, transcripts, resume, 3 letters of recommendation, statement of purpose. Additional exam requirements/recommendations for international students: Required—TOEFL (minimum score 600 paper-based; 100 iBT). *Application deadline:* For fall admission, 1/15 for domestic students, 1/1 for international students; for spring admission, 10/1 for domestic students, 9/15 for international students. Application fee: $55. Electronic applications accepted. *Expenses:* Contact institution. *Financial support:* Research assistantships, teaching assistantships, institutionally sponsored loans, scholarships/grants, and unspecified assistantships available. Financial award application deadline: 1/15; financial award applicants required to submit FAFSA. *Application contact:* 202-885-1646, Fax: 202-885-1109, E-mail: sisgrad@american.edu.
Website: http://www.american.edu/sis/

American University, School of Public Affairs, Department of Government, Washington, DC 20016-8130. Offers political communication (MA); political science (MA, PhD), including American politics (MA), applied politics (MA); women, policy and political leadership (Certificate). *Program availability:* Part-time, evening/weekend. *Faculty:* 52 full-time (19 women), 15 part-time/adjunct (4 women). *Students:* 52 full-time (19 women), 15 part-time (4 women); includes 16 minority (5 Black or African American, non-Hispanic/Latino; 6 Asian, non-Hispanic/Latino; 4 Hispanic/Latino; 1 Two or more races, non-Hispanic/Latino), 10 international. Average age 28. 138 applicants, 58% accepted, 31 enrolled. In 2017, 24 master's, 3 doctorates, 1 other advanced degree awarded. Terminal master's awarded for partial completion of doctoral program. *Application deadline:* For fall admission, 2/15 for domestic students, 5/1 for international students; for spring admission, 9/15 for domestic students, 11/1 for international students. *Expenses:* Contact institution. *Financial support:* Research assistantships, teaching assistantships, and institutionally sponsored loans available. Financial award application deadline: 2/1; financial award applicants required to submit FAFSA. *Unit head:* Candice Nelson, Chair, Government, 202-885-2338, E-mail: cnelson@american.edu. *Application contact:* Jennifer Forney, Assistant Dean, Graduate Enrollment, E-mail: forney@american.edu.
Website: http://www.american.edu/spa/gov/

American University of Armenia, Graduate Programs, Yerevan, Armenia. Offers business administration (MBA); computer and information science (MS), including business management, design and manufacturing, energy (ME, MS), industrial engineering and systems management; economics (MS); industrial engineering and systems management (ME), including business, computer aided design/manufacturing, energy (ME, MS), information technology; law (LL M); political science and international affairs (MPSIA); public health (MPH); teaching English as a foreign language (MA). *Program availability:* Part-time, evening/weekend. *Degree requirements:* For master's, thesis (for some programs), capstone/project. *Entrance requirements:* For master's, GRE, GMAT, or LSAT. Additional exam requirements/recommendations for international students: Recommended—TOEFL (minimum score 79 iBT), IELTS (minimum score 6.5). *Faculty research:* Microfinance, finance (rural/development, international, corporate), firm life cycle theory, TESOL, language proficiency testing, public policy, administrative law, economic development, cryptography, artificial intelligence, energy efficiency/renewable energy, computer-aided design/manufacturing, health financing, tuberculosis control, mother/child health, preventive ophthalmology, post-earthquake psychopathological investigations, tobacco control, environmental health risk assessments.

American University of Beirut, Graduate Programs, Faculty of Arts and Sciences, 1107 2020, Lebanon. Offers anthropology (MA); Arab and Middle Eastern history (PhD); Arabic language and literature (MA, PhD); archaeology (MA); art history and curating (MA); biology (MS); cell and molecular biology (PhD); chemistry (MS); clinical psychology (MA); computational sciences (MS); computer science (MS); economics (MA); education (MA), including administration and policy studies, elementary education, mathematics education, psychology school guidance, psychology test and measurements, science education, teaching English as a foreign language; English language (MA); English literature (MA); environmental policy planning (MS); financial economics (MAFE); general psychology (MA); geology (MS); history (MA); Islamic studies (MA); mathematics (MS); media studies (MA); Middle East studies (MA); philosophy (MA); physics (MS); political studies (MA); public administration (MA); public policy and international affairs (MA); sociology (MA); theoretical physics (PhD). *Program availability:* Part-time. *Faculty:* 108 full-time (36 women), 5 part-time/adjunct (4 women). *Students:* 251 full-time (180 women), 233 part-time (172 women). Average age 26. 425 applicants, 65% accepted, 121 enrolled. In 2017, 47 master's, 2 doctorates awarded. *Degree requirements:* For master's, one foreign language, comprehensive exam, thesis (for some programs), project; for doctorate, one foreign language, comprehensive exam, thesis/dissertation. *Entrance requirements:* For master's, GRE General Test (for some programs); for doctorate, GRE General Test (GRE Subject Test for theoretical physics). Additional exam requirements/recommendations for international students: Required—TOEFL (minimum score 583 paper-based; 97 iBT), IELTS (minimum score 7). *Application deadline:* For fall admission, 2/8 for domestic students; for spring admission, 11/3 for domestic students. Application fee: $50. Electronic applications accepted. *Expenses:* Contact institution. *Financial support:* In 2017–18, 29 fellowships, 40 research assistantships were awarded; teaching assistantships, scholarships/grants, tuition waivers (full and partial), and unspecified assistantships also available. Financial award application deadline: 4/4. *Unit head:* Dr. Nadia Maria El Cheikh, Dean, Faculty of Arts and Sciences, 961-1-374374 Ext. 3800, Fax: 961-1-744461, E-mail: nmcheikh@aub.edu.lb. *Application contact:* Rima Rassi, Graduate Studies Officer, 961-1-350000 Ext. 3833, Fax: 961-1-744461, E-mail: rr46@aub.edu.lb.
Website: http://www.aub.edu.lb/fas/pages/default.aspx

Appalachian State University, Cratis D. Williams Graduate School, Department of Government and Justice Studies, Boone, NC 28608. Offers political science (MA), including American government; public administration (MPA), including public management. *Accreditation:* NASPAA. *Program availability:* Part-time, online learning. *Degree requirements:* For master's, variable foreign language requirement, comprehensive exam, thesis optional. *Entrance requirements:* For master's, GRE General Test, 3 letters of recommendation. Additional exam requirements/recommendations for international students: Required—TOEFL (minimum score 570 paper-based; 79 iBT), IELTS (minimum score 6.5). Electronic applications accepted. *Faculty research:* Campaign finance, emerging democracies, bureaucratic politics, judicial behavior, administration of justice.

Arizona State University at the Tempe campus, College of Liberal Arts and Sciences, School of Politics and Global Studies, Tempe, AZ 85287-3902. Offers political science (MA, PhD). *Program availability:* Part-time. Terminal master's awarded for partial completion of doctoral program. *Degree requirements:* For master's, thesis or alternative, interactive Program of Study (iPOS) submitted before completing 50 percent of required credit hours; for doctorate, comprehensive exam, thesis/dissertation, interactive Program of Study (iPOS) submitted before completing 50 percent of required credit hours. *Entrance requirements:* For master's and doctorate, GRE, minimum GPA of 3.0 or equivalent in last 2 years of work leading to bachelor's degree. Additional exam requirements/recommendations for international students: Required—TOEFL, IELTS, or PTE. Electronic applications accepted.

Arkansas State University, Graduate School, College of Humanities and Social Sciences, Department of Political Science, State University, AR 72467. Offers political science (MA); political science education (SCCT); public administration (MPA). *Accreditation:* NASPAA (one or more programs are accredited). *Program availability:* Part-time. *Degree requirements:* For master's, comprehensive exam, thesis or alternative; for SCCT, comprehensive exam. *Entrance requirements:* For master's, GRE General Test or MAT, GMAT, appropriate bachelor's degree, letters of recommendation, official transcripts, immunization records, statement of purpose; for SCCT, GRE General Test or MAT, GMAT, interview, master's degree, official transcript, letters of recommendation, immunization records. Additional exam requirements/recommendations for international students: Required—TOEFL (minimum score 550 paper-based; 79 iBT), IELTS (minimum score 6), PTE (minimum score 56). Electronic applications accepted.

Ashland University, College of Arts and Sciences, Program in American History and Government, Ashland, OH 44805-3702. Offers American history and government (MAHG). *Program availability:* Part-time, evening/weekend, 100% online, blended/hybrid learning. *Faculty:* 6 full-time (1 woman), 31 part-time/adjunct (4 women). *Students:* 16 full-time (4 women), 159 part-time (96 women); includes 15 minority (11 Black or African American, non-Hispanic/Latino; 1 American Indian or Alaska Native, non-Hispanic/Latino; 2 Hispanic/Latino; 1 Two or more races, non-Hispanic/Latino). Average age 39. 104 applicants, 87% accepted, 65 enrolled. In 2017, 54 master's awarded. *Degree requirements:* For master's, capstone project, thesis, or comprehensive exam. *Entrance requirements:* For master's, minimum undergraduate GPA of 2.75, 3.0 graduate. *Application deadline:* Applications are processed on a rolling basis. Application fee: $30. Electronic applications accepted. *Expenses:* $561 per semester hour tuition (on-campus), $412 per semester hour (online). *Financial support:* In 2017–18, 92 students received support. Scholarships/grants available. Financial award application deadline: 4/1. *Faculty research:* American founding, United States Civil War, Progressive Era, twentieth-century America, religion in America. *Unit head:* Dr. John E. Moser, Chair, 419-289-5411, Fax: 419-289-5425, E-mail: jmoser1@ashland.edu. *Application contact:* Christian A. Pascarella, Director, 419-289-5411, Fax: 419-289-5425, E-mail: cpascare@ashland.edu.
Website: http://mahg.ashland.edu

Auburn University, Graduate School, College of Liberal Arts, Department of Political Science, Auburn University, AL 36849. Offers public administration (MPA, PhD, Graduate Certificate); MPA/MCP. *Program availability:* Part-time. *Faculty:* 28 full-time (16 women), 4 part-time/adjunct (3 women). *Students:* 101 full-time (52 women), 40 part-time (15 women); includes 27 minority (24 Black or African American, non-Hispanic/Latino; 1 American Indian or Alaska Native, non-Hispanic/Latino; 1 Asian, non-Hispanic/Latino; 1 Hispanic/Latino), 55 international. Average age 31. 77 applicants, 88% accepted, 27 enrolled. In 2017, 14 master's, 3 doctorates, 7 other advanced degrees awarded. *Degree requirements:* For doctorate, thesis/dissertation. *Entrance requirements:* For master's, GRE General Test, minimum GPA of 3.0 in political science, 2.5 overall; for doctorate, GRE General Test. *Application deadline:* Applications are processed on a rolling basis. Application fee: $50 ($60 for international students). Electronic applications accepted. *Expenses:* Tuition, state resident: full-time $10,974; part-time $519 per credit hour. Tuition, nonresident: full-time $29,658; part-time $1557 per credit hour. *Required fees:* $816 per semester. Tuition and fees vary according to degree level and program. *Financial support:* Fellowships, research assistantships, teaching assistantships, career-related internships or fieldwork, and Federal Work-Study available. Support available to part-time students. Financial award application deadline: 3/15; financial award applicants required to submit FAFSA. *Faculty research:* Policy evaluation, political economy, privatization, participation, election administration. *Unit head:* Cynthia Bowling, Chair, 334-844-6152. *Application contact:* Dr. George Flowers, Dean of the Graduate School, 334-844-2125.
Website: http://cla.auburn.edu/polisci/

Auburn University at Montgomery, College of Public Policy and Justice, Department of Political Science and Public Administration, Montgomery, AL 36124-4023. Offers political science (MPS); public administration (MPA); public administration and public policy (PhD). PhD offered jointly with Auburn University. *Accreditation:* NASPAA (one or more programs are accredited). *Program availability:* Part-time, evening/weekend. *Faculty:* 4 full-time (1 woman). *Students:* 11 full-time (5 women), 22 part-time (15 women); includes 18 minority (all Black or African American, non-Hispanic/Latino), 4 international. Average age 31. 23 applicants, 78% accepted, 9 enrolled. In 2017, 5 master's awarded. *Degree requirements:* For master's, comprehensive exam; for doctorate, thesis/dissertation. *Entrance requirements:* For master's, GRE General Test or MAT; for doctorate, GRE General Test. Additional exam requirements/recommendations for international students: Recommended—TOEFL (minimum score 500 paper-based; 61 iBT), IELTS (minimum score 5.5), TSE (minimum score 44). *Application deadline:* For fall admission, 7/15 for international students; for spring admission, 11/15 for international students; for summer admission, 4/15 for international students. Applications are processed on a rolling basis. Application fee: $25. Electronic applications accepted. *Expenses:* Tuition, state resident: full-time $6930; part-time $385 per credit hour. Tuition, nonresident: full-time $15,588; part-time $866 per credit hour. *Required fees:* $640. *Financial support:* Research assistantships, teaching assistantships, career-related internships or fieldwork, and scholarships/grants available. Support available to part-time students. Financial award application deadline: 3/1; financial award applicants required to submit FAFSA. *Unit head:* Dr. Andrew Cortell, Head, 334-244-3622, E-mail: acortell@aum.edu.
Website: http://cppj.aum.edu/departments/political-science

Ball State University, Graduate School, College of Sciences and Humanities, Department of Political Science, Program in Political Science, Muncie, IN 47306. Offers MA. *Program availability:* Part-time. *Students:* 9 full-time (2 women), 5 part-time (2 women); includes 2 minority (both Hispanic/Latino), 3 international. Average age 28. 8 applicants, 75% accepted, 6 enrolled. In 2017, 1 master's awarded. *Degree requirements:* For master's, comprehensive exam. *Entrance requirements:* For master's, GRE General Test, minimum baccalaureate GPA of 2.8. Additional exam requirements/recommendations for international students: Required—TOEFL (minimum score 550 paper-based; 79 iBT), IELTS (minimum score 6.5). *Application deadline:* Applications are processed on a rolling basis. Application fee: $60. Electronic applications accepted. *Financial support:* Research assistantships with partial tuition reimbursements available. Financial award application deadline: 3/1; financial award applicants required to submit FAFSA. *Faculty research:* Survey research, public policy. *Unit head:* Dr. Daniel Reagan, Chairperson, 765-285-8789, Fax: 765-285-5345, E-mail:

dreagan@bsu.edu. *Application contact:* Dr. Charles Taylor, Associate Professor/ Graduate Advisor, 765-285-8794, Fax: 765-285-8780, E-mail: cdtaylor@bsu.edu. Website: http://www.bsu.edu/poli-sci

Baylor University, Graduate School, College of Arts and Sciences, Department of Political Science, Waco, TX 76798. Offers international studies (MA); political science (MA, PhD); public policy and administration (MPPA); JD/MPPA. *Faculty:* 19 full-time (3 women), 1 part-time/adjunct (0 women). *Students:* 28 full-time (14 women); includes 1 minority (Hispanic/Latino). Average age 26. 27 applicants, 22% accepted, 4 enrolled. In 2017, 4 master's, 5 doctorates awarded. Terminal master's awarded for partial completion of doctoral program. *Degree requirements:* For master's, variable foreign language requirement, comprehensive exam (for some programs), thesis (for some programs); for doctorate, variable foreign language requirement, comprehensive exam, thesis/dissertation. *Entrance requirements:* For master's and doctorate, GRE General Test. Additional exam requirements/recommendations for international students: Required—TOEFL. *Application deadline:* For fall admission, 12/20 for domestic and international students. Application fee: $50. Electronic applications accepted. *Financial support:* In 2017–18, 26 students received support, including 26 research assistantships with full tuition reimbursements available (averaging $16,000 per year); career-related internships or fieldwork, Federal Work-Study, and institutionally sponsored loans also available. Financial award application deadline: 12/20; financial award applicants required to submit FAFSA. *Unit head:* Dr. Timothy Burns, Graduate Program Director, 254-710-6237, Fax: 254-710-3122, E-mail: timothy_burns@baylor.edu. *Application contact:* Jenice Langston, Office Manager, 254-710-3161, Fax: 254-710-3122, E-mail: jenice_langston@baylor.edu. Website: http://www.baylor.edu/political_science/

Binghamton University, State University of New York, Graduate School, Harpur College of Arts and Sciences, Department of Political Science, Binghamton, NY 13902-6000. Offers MA, PhD. *Program availability:* Part-time. *Faculty:* 18 full-time (6 women), 3 part-time/adjunct (2 women). *Students:* 19 full-time (7 women), 19 part-time (5 women); includes 5 minority (1 Black or African American, non-Hispanic/Latino; 1 Asian, non-Hispanic/Latino; 2 Hispanic/Latino; 1 Two or more races, non-Hispanic/Latino), 16 international. Average age 30. 52 applicants, 65% accepted, 9 enrolled. In 2017, 8 master's, 6 doctorates awarded. Terminal master's awarded for partial completion of doctoral program. *Degree requirements:* For master's, comprehensive exam (for some programs), thesis (for some programs); for doctorate, variable foreign language requirement, comprehensive exam, thesis/dissertation. *Entrance requirements:* For master's and doctorate, GRE General Test. Additional exam requirements/ recommendations for international students: Required—TOEFL (minimum score 550 paper-based; 80 iBT). *Application deadline:* For fall admission, 1/15 priority date for domestic and international students. Application fee: $75. Electronic applications accepted. *Financial support:* In 2017–18, 25 students received support, including 4 research assistantships with full tuition reimbursements available (averaging $15,000 per year), 19 teaching assistantships with full tuition reimbursements available (averaging $15,000 per year); career-related internships or fieldwork, Federal Work-Study, institutionally sponsored loans, scholarships/grants, health care benefits, tuition waivers (full and partial), and unspecified assistantships also available. Financial award applicants required to submit FAFSA. *Unit head:* Dr. David H. Clark, Chairperson, 607-777-2675, E-mail: dclark@binghamton.edu. *Application contact:* Ben Balkaya, Assistant Dean and Director, 607-777-2151, Fax: 607-777-2501, E-mail: balkaya@binghamton.edu.

Boise State University, School of Public Service, Department of Political Science, Boise, ID 83725-0399. Offers MA. *Program availability:* Part-time. *Faculty:* 4. *Students:* 11 full-time (4 women), 4 part-time (1 woman); includes 2 minority (1 Hispanic/Latino; 1 Native Hawaiian or other Pacific Islander, non-Hispanic/Latino), 1 international. Average age 37. 18 applicants, 67% accepted, 10 enrolled. *Degree requirements:* For master's, comprehensive exam, thesis (for some programs), thesis or professional project. *Entrance requirements:* For master's, GRE General Test. Additional exam requirements/ recommendations for international students: Required—TOEFL (minimum score 550 paper-based; 80 iBT), IELTS (minimum score 6). *Application deadline:* For fall admission, 5/1 for domestic and international students. Application fee: $65 ($94 for international students). Electronic applications accepted. *Expenses:* Tuition, state resident: full-time $6471; part-time $390 per credit. Tuition, nonresident: full-time $21,787; part-time $685 per credit. *Required fees:* $2283; $100 per term. Part-time tuition and fees vary according to course load and program. *Financial support:* Research assistantships, scholarships/grants, and unspecified assistantships available. Financial award application deadline: 2/15; financial award applicants required to submit FAFSA. *Unit head:* Dr. Lori Hausegger, Chair, 208-426-5804, E-mail: lorihausegger@boisestate.edu. *Application contact:* Dr. Michael Allen, Graduate Program Coordinator, 208-426-2518, E-mail: michaelaallen@boisestate.edu. Website: https://sps.boisestate.edu/politicalscience/

Boston College, Graduate School of Arts and Sciences, Department of Political Science, Chestnut Hill, MA 02467-3800. Offers MA, PhD. Terminal master's awarded for partial completion of doctoral program. *Degree requirements:* For master's, thesis or alternative; for doctorate, one foreign language, thesis/dissertation. *Entrance requirements:* For master's and doctorate, GRE General Test. Additional exam requirements/recommendations for international students: Required—TOEFL (minimum score 600 paper-based; 100 iBT), IELTS (minimum score 8). Electronic applications accepted. *Faculty research:* Political theory, American politics, international politics, comparative politics.

Boston University, Graduate School of Arts and Sciences, Department of Political Science, Boston, MA 02215. Offers PhD. *Students:* 30 full-time (15 women), 5 part-time (3 women); includes 4 minority (2 Asian, non-Hispanic/Latino; 2 Hispanic/Latino), 21 international. Average age 28. 114 applicants, 15% accepted, 5 enrolled. In 2017, 6 doctorates awarded. Terminal master's awarded for partial completion of doctoral program. *Degree requirements:* For doctorate, comprehensive exam, thesis/ dissertation. *Entrance requirements:* For doctorate, GRE General Test, 3 letters of recommendation, transcripts, personal statement, curriculum vitae. Additional exam requirements/recommendations for international students: Required—TOEFL (minimum score 600 paper-based; 100 iBT). *Application deadline:* For fall admission, 12/1 for domestic and international students. Application fee: $95. Electronic applications accepted. *Financial support:* In 2017–18, 35 students received support, including 9 fellowships with full tuition reimbursements available (averaging $22,000 per year), 3 research assistantships with full tuition reimbursements available (averaging $22,000 per year), 12 teaching assistantships with full tuition reimbursements available (averaging $22,000 per year); career-related internships or fieldwork, Federal Work-Study, scholarships/grants, and health care benefits also available. Support available to part-time students. Financial award application deadline: 12/1. *Unit head:* David Mayers, Chair, 617-353-2540, Fax: 617-353-5508, E-mail: dmayers@bu.edu. *Application contact:* Cady Steinberg, Graduate Program Coordinator, 617-353-2540, Fax: 617-353-5508, E-mail: pograd@bu.edu. Website: http://www.bu.edu/polisci/

Brandeis University, Graduate School of Arts and Sciences, Department of Politics, Waltham, MA 02454-9110. Offers MA, PhD. *Faculty:* 13 full-time (3 women), 2 part-time/ adjunct (1 woman). *Students:* 11 full-time (7 women); includes 1 minority (Hispanic/ Latino), 4 international. Average age 27. 99 applicants, 3% accepted, 2 enrolled. In 2017, 5 master's, 3 doctorates awarded. Terminal master's awarded for partial completion of doctoral program. *Degree requirements:* For master's, thesis or alternative, proseminar; for doctorate, one foreign language, comprehensive exam, thesis/dissertation, proseminar; teaching requirement; research tools requirement; qualifying exams. *Entrance requirements:* For master's and doctorate, GRE General Test, critical writing sample, resume, letters of recommendation, statement of purpose, transcripts. Additional exam requirements/recommendations for international students: Required—PTE (minimum score 68), TOEFL (minimum score 600 paper-based, 100 iBT) or IELTS (7). *Application deadline:* For fall admission, 1/15 priority date for domestic students. Applications are processed on a rolling basis. Application fee: $75. Electronic applications accepted. *Expenses: Tuition:* Full-time $48,720. *Required fees:* $88. Tuition and fees vary according to course load, degree level, program and student level. *Financial support:* In 2017–18, 11 students received support, including 9 fellowships with full tuition reimbursements available (averaging $24,480 per year), 6 teaching assistantships with partial tuition reimbursements available (averaging $3,200 per year); Federal Work-Study, scholarships/grants, health care benefits, and tuition waivers (partial) also available. Financial award application deadline: 4/15; financial award applicants required to submit FAFSA. *Faculty research:* American political development and contemporary politics, international law and foreign policy, political theory, comparative politics, European politics. *Unit head:* Dr. Bernard Yack, Director of Graduate Studies, 781-736-2640, E-mail: yack@brandeis.edu. *Application contact:* Rosanne Colocouris, Department Administrator, 781-736-2755, E-mail: colocour@brandeis.edu. Website: http://www.brandeis.edu/gsas/programs/politics.html

Brigham Young University, Graduate Studies, BYU Marriott School of Business, Master of Public Administration Program, Provo, UT 84602. Offers healthcare (MPA); local government (MPA); nonprofit management (MPA); state and federal government (MPA); JD/MPA. *Accreditation:* NASPAA. *Faculty:* 134 full-time (15 women), 65 part-time/adjunct (16 women). *Students:* 105 full-time (50 women); includes 10 minority (3 Black or African American, non-Hispanic/Latino; 3 Asian, non-Hispanic/Latino; 3 Hispanic/Latino; 1 Native Hawaiian or other Pacific Islander, non-Hispanic/Latino), 14 international. Average age 27. 95 applicants, 73% accepted, 50 enrolled. In 2017, 41 master's awarded. *Entrance requirements:* For master's, GMAT or GRE, commitment to BYU Honor Code. Additional exam requirements/recommendations for international students: Required—TOEFL (minimum score 580 paper-based; 85 iBT). *Application deadline:* For fall admission, 1/15 for domestic and international students. Application fee: $50. Electronic applications accepted. *Expenses:* Contact institution. *Financial support:* Research assistantships, teaching assistantships, career-related internships or fieldwork, institutionally sponsored loans, and scholarships/grants available. Financial award application deadline: 4/15; financial award applicants required to submit FAFSA. *Faculty research:* Taxes, budgeting, nonprofit, ethics, decision modeling, work balance, organizational behavior. *Unit head:* Dr. Lori Wadsworth, Director, 801-422-5956, E-mail: mpa@byu.edu. *Application contact:* Catherine Cooper, Associate Director, 801-422-9173, E-mail: mpa@byu.edu. Website: https://marriottschool.byu.edu/mpa/

Brock University, Faculty of Graduate Studies, Faculty of Social Sciences, Program in Political Science, St. Catharines, ON L2S 3A1, Canada. Offers Canadian politics (MA); comparative politics (MA); international relations (MA); political theory or philosophy (MA); public policy (MA). *Program availability:* Part-time. *Degree requirements:* For master's, thesis optional. *Entrance requirements:* For master's, honors degree. Additional exam requirements/recommendations for international students: Required—TOEFL (minimum score 550 paper-based; 80 iBT), IELTS (minimum score 6.5), TWE (minimum score 4). Electronic applications accepted. *Faculty research:* Public administration reform, economic and social justice, politics of societies, Canadian politics, international relations.

Brooklyn College of the City University of New York, School of Humanities and Social Sciences, Department of Political Science, Brooklyn, NY 11210-2889. Offers international affairs (MA); political science (MA); urban policy and administration (MA). *Program availability:* Part-time, evening/weekend. *Degree requirements:* For master's, comprehensive exam (for some programs), thesis or alternative, foreign language exam (for international affairs program). *Entrance requirements:* For master's, 2 letters of recommendation, personal statement. Additional exam requirements/recommendations for international students: Required—TOEFL (minimum score 500 paper-based; 61 iBT). *Faculty research:* Ethics and politics, politics of criminal justice, Western Europe, international law and politics, labor politics.

Brown University, Graduate School, Department of Political Science, Providence, RI 02912. Offers PhD. *Degree requirements:* For doctorate, thesis/dissertation. *Entrance requirements:* For doctorate, GRE General Test.

California Polytechnic State University, San Luis Obispo, College of Liberal Arts, Department of Political Science, San Luis Obispo, CA 93407. Offers MPP. *Program availability:* Part-time. *Faculty:* 4 full-time (2 women). *Students:* 5 full-time (3 women), 16 part-time (11 women); includes 11 minority (1 Asian, non-Hispanic/Latino; 8 Hispanic/ Latino; 2 Two or more races, non-Hispanic/Latino). Average age 32. 23 applicants, 57% accepted, 9 enrolled. In 2017, 4 master's awarded. *Degree requirements:* For master's, comprehensive exam. *Entrance requirements:* For master's, GRE. Additional exam requirements/recommendations for international students: Required—TOEFL (minimum score 80 iBT). *Application deadline:* For fall admission, 4/1 for domestic students, 3/1 for international students. Application fee: $55. *Expenses:* Tuition, state resident: full-time $7176; part-time $4164 per year. *Required fees:* $3690; $3219 per year. $1073 per trimester. *Financial support:* Fellowships, research assistantships, career-related internships or fieldwork, Federal Work-Study, and scholarships/grants available. Support available to part-time students. Financial award application deadline: 3/2; financial award applicants required to submit FAFSA. *Faculty research:* Public policy analysis, public finance, policy internship. *Unit head:* Dr. Michael Latner, Graduate Coordinator, 805-756-6402, E-mail: mlatner@calpoly.edu. Website: http://mpp.calpoly.edu/

California State University, Chico, Office of Graduate Studies, College of Behavioral and Social Sciences, Department of Political Science and Criminal Justice, Program in Political Science, Chico, CA 95929-0722. Offers MA. *Program availability:* Part-time. *Degree requirements:* For master's, thesis or comprehensive examination. *Entrance requirements:* For master's, 2 letters of recommendation, statement of purpose. Additional exam requirements/recommendations for international students: Required—TOEFL (minimum score 550 paper-based; 80 iBT), IELTS (minimum score 6.5), PTE (minimum score 59). Electronic applications accepted.

California State University, Fullerton, Graduate Studies, College of Humanities and Social Sciences, Division of Politics, Administration, and Justice, Fullerton, CA 92831-3599. Offers political science (MA); public administration (MPA). *Accreditation:* NASPAA (one or more programs are accredited). *Program availability:* Part-time. *Faculty:* 12 full-time (6 women). *Students:* 20 full-time (8 women), 102 part-time (53 women); includes 84 minority (8 Black or African American, non-Hispanic/Latino; 11 Asian, non-Hispanic/ Latino; 61 Hispanic/Latino; 4 Two or more races, non-Hispanic/Latino), 4 international.

Average age 29. 99 applicants, 60% accepted, 30 enrolled. *Degree requirements:* For master's, comprehensive exam, project or thesis. *Entrance requirements:* For master's, minimum GPA of 2.5 in last 60 units of course work, 12 units of course work in social sciences. Application fee: $55. *Financial support:* Career-related internships or fieldwork, Federal Work-Study, institutionally sponsored loans, and scholarships/grants available. Support available to part-time students. Financial award application deadline: 3/1; financial award applicants required to submit FAFSA. *Faculty research:* Emergency management plans. *Unit head:* Dr. Stephen Stambough, Chair, 657-278-2933. *Application contact:* Admissions/Applications, 657-278-2371.

California State University, Long Beach, Graduate Studies, College of Liberal Arts, Department of Political Science, Long Beach, CA 90840. Offers MA. *Program availability:* Part-time. *Degree requirements:* For master's, one foreign language, comprehensive exam or thesis. *Entrance requirements:* For master's, GRE General Test, minimum GPA of 3.0 in field. Electronic applications accepted. *Faculty research:* Social welfare policy, international political economy, Marxism, voting behavior.

California State University, Los Angeles, Graduate Studies, College of Natural and Social Sciences, Department of Political Science, Los Angeles, CA 90032-8530. Offers political science (MA); public administration (MS). *Program availability:* Part-time, evening/weekend. *Degree requirements:* For master's, comprehensive exam or thesis. *Entrance requirements:* Additional exam requirements/recommendations for international students: Required—TOEFL (minimum score 500 paper-based). Electronic applications accepted. *Faculty research:* Government; public policy and law; international, political, and economic relations; comparative politics.

California State University, Northridge, Graduate Studies, College of Social and Behavioral Sciences, Department of Political Science, Northridge, CA 91330. Offers MA. *Students:* 12 full-time (4 women), 6 part-time (5 women); includes 10 minority (2 Asian, non-Hispanic/Latino; 8 Hispanic/Latino), 1 international. Average age 30. 471 applicants, 59% accepted, 9 enrolled. In 2017, 330 master's awarded. *Degree requirements:* For master's, comprehensive exam. *Entrance requirements:* For master's, GRE (if cumulative undergraduate GPA less than 3.0), 2 letters of recommendation. Additional exam requirements/recommendations for international students: Required—TOEFL. *Application deadline:* For fall admission, 11/30 for domestic students. Application fee: $55. *Financial support:* Application deadline: 3/1. *Unit head:* Dr. David Leitch, Chair, 818-677-3488.
Website: http://www.csun.edu/csbs/departments/political_science/index.html

California State University, Sacramento, College of Social Sciences and Interdisciplinary Studies, Department of Government, Sacramento, CA 95819. Offers MA. *Program availability:* Part-time. *Students:* 4 full-time (2 women), 25 part-time (11 women); includes 11 minority (4 Black or African American, non-Hispanic/Latino; 2 Asian, non-Hispanic/Latino; 5 Hispanic/Latino). Average age 28. 18 applicants, 89% accepted, 11 enrolled. In 2017, 8 master's awarded. *Degree requirements:* For master's, thesis, project or comprehensive exam; writing proficiency exam. *Entrance requirements:* For master's, GRE, minimum GPA of 3.0 during previous 2 years. Additional exam requirements/recommendations for international students: Required—TOEFL (minimum score 550 paper-based; 80 iBT); Recommended—IELTS, TSE. *Application deadline:* For fall admission, 3/1 for domestic and international students. Applications are processed on a rolling basis. Application fee: $55. Electronic applications accepted. *Expenses:* Contact institution. *Financial support:* Career-related internships or fieldwork, Federal Work-Study, and scholarships/grants available. Support available to part-time students. Financial award application deadline: 3/1; financial award applicants required to submit FAFSA. *Unit head:* Dr. Jim Cox, Professor and Graduate Coordinator, 916-278-6378, E-mail: jhcox@csus.edu. *Application contact:* Jose Martinez, Graduate Admissions Supervisor, 916-278-7871, E-mail: martinj@skymail.csus.edu.
Website: http://www.csus.edu/govt

Carleton University, Faculty of Graduate Studies, Faculty of Public Affairs and Management, Department of Political Science, Ottawa, ON K1S 5B6, Canada. Offers MA, PhD. *Degree requirements:* For master's, one foreign language, comprehensive exam, thesis optional; for doctorate, one foreign language, comprehensive exam, thesis/dissertation. *Entrance requirements:* For master's, honors degree in political science, minimum B average; for doctorate, master's degree in political science. Additional exam requirements/recommendations for international students: Required—TOEFL. *Faculty research:* Canadian politics, comparative politics, international relations, public administration and policy analysis, political theory.

Carleton University, Faculty of Graduate Studies, Faculty of Public Affairs and Management, Institute of Political Economy, Ottawa, ON K1S 5B6, Canada. Offers MA, PhD. *Degree requirements:* For master's, thesis optional. *Entrance requirements:* For master's, honors degree. Additional exam requirements/recommendations for international students: Required—TOEFL. *Faculty research:* Relationships between economy and politics as they affect the political, social and cultural life of societies; historical processes whereby social change is located in the interaction of the economic, political and cultural, and ideological moments of social life.

Case Western Reserve University, School of Graduate Studies, Department of Political Science, Cleveland, OH 44106. Offers MA, PhD. *Faculty:* 8 full-time (4 women), 6 part-time/adjunct (0 women). *Students:* 2 applicants. In 2017, 4 master's awarded. Terminal master's awarded for partial completion of doctoral program. *Degree requirements:* For master's, comprehensive exam (for some programs), thesis (for some programs); for doctorate, thesis/dissertation. *Entrance requirements:* For master's and doctorate, GRE General Test, undergraduate degree in political science, three letters of recommendation, statement of objectives. Additional exam requirements/recommendations for international students: Required—TOEFL (minimum score 577 paper-based; 90 iBT); Recommended—IELTS (minimum score 7). *Application deadline:* For fall admission, 6/1 priority date for domestic students; for spring admission, 11/1 for domestic students. Applications are processed on a rolling basis. Application fee: $50. Electronic applications accepted. *Expenses: Tuition:* Full-time $43,854; part-time $1827 per credit hour. *Required fees:* $50; $50 per credit hour. Tuition and fees vary according to course load and program. *Financial support:* Federal Work-Study and institutionally sponsored loans available. Financial award application deadline: 2/1; financial award applicants required to submit CSS PROFILE or FAFSA. *Faculty research:* American political institutions, elections and political parties both in the United States and abroad; legislative politics; international relations with an emphasis on international political economy; the development and decline of nation-states; the politics of gender; public policy and public organizations; research methods; comparative politics with regional concentrations including Western Europe, Africa, Central Asia and the Middle East. *Unit head:* Karen Beckwith, Professor and Chair, Department of Political Science, 216-368-4129, Fax: 216-368-4681, E-mail: karen.beckwith@case.edu. *Application contact:* Jessica Jurcak, Department Assistant, 216-368-2424, Fax: 216-368-4681, E-mail: jessica.jurcak@case.edu.
Website: http://politicalscience.case.edu/

The Catholic University of America, School of Arts and Sciences, Department of Politics, Washington, DC 20064. Offers American government (MA, PhD); Congressional and Presidential studies (MA); international affairs (MA); international political economics (MA); political theory (MA, PhD); world politics (MA, PhD); MA/JD. MA/JD offered jointly with Columbus School of Law. *Program availability:* Part-time. *Faculty:* 13 full-time (2 women), 6 part-time/adjunct (1 woman). *Students:* 18 full-time (5 women), 42 part-time (9 women); includes 12 minority (3 Black or African American, non-Hispanic/Latino; 2 Asian, non-Hispanic/Latino; 5 Hispanic/Latino; 2 Two or more races, non-Hispanic/Latino), 12 international. Average age 32. 50 applicants, 58% accepted, 8 enrolled. In 2017, 13 master's, 4 doctorates awarded. *Degree requirements:* For master's, one foreign language, comprehensive exam, thesis or alternative; for doctorate, variable foreign language requirement, comprehensive exam, thesis/dissertation. *Entrance requirements:* For master's, GRE General Test, statement of purpose, official copies of academic transcripts, three letters of recommendation, minimum GPA of 3.0; for doctorate, GRE General Test, statement of purpose, official copies of academic transcripts, three letters of recommendation. Additional exam requirements/recommendations for international students: Required—TOEFL (minimum score 550 paper-based; 80 iBT). *Application deadline:* For fall admission, 7/15 priority date for domestic students, 7/1 for international students; for spring admission, 11/15 priority date for domestic students, 11/1 for international students. Applications are processed on a rolling basis. Application fee: $55. Electronic applications accepted. *Expenses:* Contact institution. *Financial support:* Fellowships, research assistantships, teaching assistantships, Federal Work-Study, scholarships/grants, tuition waivers (full and partial), and unspecified assistantships available. Financial award application deadline: 2/1; financial award applicants required to submit FAFSA. *Faculty research:* Political philosophy, American political institutions and processes, political economy, international relations, U.S. political leadership since 1789. *Unit head:* Dr. Dennis Coyle, Chair, 202-319-5813, Fax: 202-319-6289, E-mail: coyle@cua.edu. *Application contact:* Dr. Steven Brown, Director of Graduate Admissions, 202-319-5057, Fax: 202-319-6533, E-mail: cua-admissions@cua.edu.
Website: http://politics.cua.edu/

Central European University, Department of Political Science, Budapest, Hungary. Offers MA, PhD. *Faculty:* 17 full-time (4 women), 8 part-time/adjunct (1 woman). *Students:* 112 full-time (41 women). Average age 27. 390 applicants, 27% accepted, 68 enrolled. In 2017, 35 master's, 9 doctorates awarded. *Degree requirements:* For master's, one foreign language, thesis; for doctorate, one foreign language, comprehensive exam, thesis/dissertation. *Entrance requirements:* For master's and doctorate, interview. Additional exam requirements/recommendations for international students: Required—TOEFL (minimum score 570 paper-based); Recommended—IELTS (minimum score 6.5). *Application deadline:* For fall admission, 2/4 for domestic and international students. Application fee: $30. Electronic applications accepted. *Expenses: Tuition:* Full-time 12,000 euros. *Required fees:* 230 euros. One-time fee: 30 euros full-time. Tuition and fees vary according to course level, course load, degree level and program. *Financial support:* Fellowships, teaching assistantships, career-related internships or fieldwork, scholarships/grants, health care benefits, and tuition waivers (full and partial) available. *Faculty research:* Comparative and international political economy, public policy analysis, public understanding of genetics, legislation on abortion and euthanasia, democratization and elite change, rational choice theory, experimental economics (behavioral game theory), Cold War history, gender and politics. *Unit head:* Dr. Zoltan Miklosi, Head of Department, 36 1 235-6164, E-mail: polsci@ceu.edu. *Application contact:* Zsuzsanna Jaszberenyi, Admissions Officer, 361-324-3009, Fax: 367-327-3211, E-mail: admissions@ceu.edu.
Website: http://politicalscience.ceu.edu

Central European University, Nationalism Studies Program, Budapest, Hungary. Offers MA. *Faculty:* 4 full-time (2 women), 4 part-time/adjunct (0 women). *Students:* 32 full-time (18 women). Average age 26. 114 applicants, 32% accepted, 23 enrolled. In 2017, 20 master's awarded. *Degree requirements:* For master's, one foreign language, thesis. *Entrance requirements:* For master's, interview. Additional exam requirements/recommendations for international students: Required—TOEFL (minimum score 570 paper-based); Recommended—IELTS (minimum score 6.5). *Application deadline:* For fall admission, 2/4 for domestic and international students. Application fee: $30. Electronic applications accepted. *Expenses: Tuition:* Full-time 12,000 euros. *Required fees:* 230 euros. One-time fee: 30 euros full-time. Tuition and fees vary according to course level, course load, degree level and program. *Financial support:* In 2017–18, 32 students received support. Fellowships, scholarships/grants, health care benefits, and tuition waivers (full and partial) available. *Faculty research:* Issues of territory, power, and identity; comparative welfare state studies; social history of social policy in Central and Eastern Europe; gender and ethnic aspects of old and new poverty; ethnic minorities, Jewish studies. *Unit head:* Dr. Michael Laurence Miller, Program Director, 36 1 327-3081, E-mail: nationalism@ceu.edu. *Application contact:* Zsuzsanna Jaszberenyi, Admissions Officer, 361-324-3009, Fax: 367-327-3211, E-mail: admissions@ceu.edu.
Website: http://nationalism.ceu.edu

Central Michigan University, Central Michigan University Global Campus, Program in Public Administration, Mount Pleasant, MI 48859. Offers general public administration (MPA); public management (MPA); state and local government (MPA). *Accreditation:* NASPAA. *Program availability:* Part-time, evening/weekend. *Entrance requirements:* For master's, minimum GPA of 2.8. Additional exam requirements/recommendations for international students: Required—TOEFL. Electronic applications accepted.

Central Michigan University, College of Graduate Studies, College of Humanities and Social and Behavioral Sciences, Department of Political Science and Public Administration, Program in Political Science, Mount Pleasant, MI 48859. Offers American politics (MA), including American politics, comparative/international politics. *Program availability:* Part-time. *Degree requirements:* For master's, thesis or alternative. Electronic applications accepted.

Central Michigan University, College of Graduate Studies, College of Humanities and Social and Behavioral Sciences, Department of Political Science and Public Administration, Program in Public Administration, Mount Pleasant, MI 48859. Offers professional development in public administration (Graduate Certificate); public administration (MPA); public management (MPA); state and local government (MPA). *Accreditation:* NASPAA. *Program availability:* Part-time. *Degree requirements:* For master's, thesis or alternative. Electronic applications accepted.

The Citadel, The Military College of South Carolina, Citadel Graduate College, School of Humanities and Social Sciences, Department of Political Science, Charleston, SC 29409. Offers international politics and military affairs (MA); social science (MA). *Program availability:* Part-time, evening/weekend, 100% online, blended/hybrid learning. *Entrance requirements:* For master's, GRE (minimum combined score of 290 verbal and quantitative), MAT (minimum raw score of 396), written statement of purpose setting forth intentions, goals, and preparation for graduate study; at least 2 academic letters of recommendation addressing ability to undertake coursework at graduate level. Additional exam requirements/recommendations for international students: Required—TOEFL (minimum score 550 paper-based; 79 iBT). Electronic applications accepted. *Expenses:* Tuition, state resident: part-time $587 per credit hour. Tuition, nonresident: part-time $988 per credit hour. *Required fees:* $90 per term.

Claremont Graduate University, Graduate Programs, School of Social Science, Policy and Evaluation, Department of Politics and Policy, Claremont, CA 91711-6160. Offers American politics (MA, PhD); comparative politics (PhD); international political economy

(MA); international studies (MA); political philosophy (PhD); political science (PhD); politics, economics and business (MA); public policy (MA, PhD); world politics (PhD); MBA/PhD. *Program availability:* Part-time. Terminal master's awarded for partial completion of doctoral program. *Entrance requirements:* For master's and doctorate, GRE General Test. Additional exam requirements/recommendations for international students: Required—TOEFL (minimum score 75 iBT). Electronic applications accepted. *Faculty research:* Environmental policy, international debt, global democratization, Third World development, public sector discrimination.

Claremont Graduate University, Graduate Programs, School of Social Science, Policy and Evaluation, Program in Politics, Economics, and Business, Claremont, CA 91711-6160. Offers MA. *Program availability:* Part-time. *Entrance requirements:* For master's, GRE General Test. Additional exam requirements/recommendations for international students: Required—TOEFL (minimum score 75 iBT). Electronic applications accepted.

Clark Atlanta University, School of Arts and Sciences, Department of Political Science, Atlanta, GA 30314. Offers MA, PhD. *Program availability:* Part-time. *Faculty:* 5 full-time (2 women), 9 part-time/adjunct (2 women). *Students:* 11 full-time (5 women), 23 part-time (14 women); includes 28 minority (all Black or African American, non-Hispanic/Latino). Average age 40. 14 applicants, 57% accepted, 3 enrolled. In 2017, 4 doctorates awarded. Terminal master's awarded for partial completion of doctoral program. *Degree requirements:* For master's, one foreign language, comprehensive exam, thesis; for doctorate, 2 foreign languages, comprehensive exam, thesis/dissertation. *Entrance requirements:* For master's, GRE General Test, minimum GPA of 2.5; for doctorate, GRE General Test, minimum graduate GPA of 3.0. Additional exam requirements/recommendations for international students: Required—TOEFL (minimum score 500 paper-based; 61 iBT). *Application deadline:* For fall admission, 4/1 for domestic and international students; for spring admission, 11/1 for domestic and international students. Applications are processed on a rolling basis. Application fee: $40 ($55 for international students). *Financial support:* Fellowships, scholarships/grants, and unspecified assistantships available. Financial award application deadline: 4/30; financial award applicants required to submit FAFSA. *Faculty research:* Public policy and education, rural politics, women and state economic programs, reconstruction after war in Africa, environmental policies. *Unit head:* Dr. Henry Elonge, Chairperson, 404-880-6653, Fax: 404-880-8717, E-mail: helonge@cau.edu.

Colorado State University, College of Liberal Arts, Department of Political Science, Fort Collins, CO 80523-1782. Offers environmental politics and policy (PhD); political science (MA). *Program availability:* Part-time. *Faculty:* 10 full-time (4 women), 1 (woman) part-time/adjunct. *Students:* 26 full-time (14 women), 17 part-time (10 women); includes 5 minority (2 Asian, non-Hispanic/Latino; 3 Hispanic/Latino), 2 international. Average age 29. 39 applicants, 77% accepted, 16 enrolled. In 2017, 8 master's, 1 doctorate awarded. Terminal master's awarded for partial completion of doctoral program. *Degree requirements:* For master's, thesis (for some programs), methods; for doctorate, comprehensive exam, thesis/dissertation, methods. *Entrance requirements:* For master's, GRE General Test (minimum verbal and quantitative scores of 301 [1080 on old scoring system] and analytical score of 5.0), bachelor's degree; for doctorate, GRE General Test (minimum verbal and quantitative scores of 308 [1200 on old scoring system] and analytical score of 5.0), minimum graduate-level GPA of 3.5; 15-page writing sample. Additional exam requirements/recommendations for international students: Required—TOEFL (minimum score 600 paper-based). *Application deadline:* For fall admission, 2/15 priority date for domestic and international students; for spring admission, 10/15 priority date for domestic students, 8/1 priority date for international students. Applications are processed on a rolling basis. Application fee: $60 ($70 for international students). Electronic applications accepted. *Expenses:* Tuition, state resident: full-time $9917. Tuition, nonresident: full-time $24,312. Required fees: $2284. Tuition and fees vary according to course load and program. *Financial support:* In 2017–18, 26 students received support, including 25 teaching assistantships with full tuition reimbursements available (averaging $16,573 per year); Federal Work-Study and health care benefits also available. Financial award application deadline: 2/15; financial award applicants required to submit FAFSA. *Faculty research:* Environmental politics and policy; political institutions; political behavior; democracy; political power. *Total annual research expenditures:* $9,178. *Unit head:* Dr. Michele Betsill, Professor and Chair, 970-491-5157, E-mail: m.betsill@colostate.edu. *Application contact:* April Lindgren, Program Assistant, 970-491-5157, E-mail: april.lindgren@colostate.edu. Website: http://polisci.colostate.edu/

Columbia University, Graduate School of Arts and Sciences, New York, NY 10027. Offers African-American studies (MA); American studies (MA); anthropology (MA, PhD); art history and archaeology (MA, PhD); astronomy (PhD); biological sciences (PhD); biotechnology (MA); chemical physics (PhD); chemistry (PhD); classical studies (MA, PhD); classics (MA, PhD); climate and society (MA); conservation biology (MA); earth and environmental sciences (PhD); East Asia: regional studies (MA); East Asian languages and cultures (MA, PhD); ecology, evolution and environmental biology (MA), including conservation biology; ecology, evolution, and environmental biology (PhD), including ecology and evolutionary biology, evolutionary primatology; economics (MA, PhD); English and comparative literature (MA, PhD); French and Romance philology (MA, PhD); Germanic languages (MA, PhD); global French studies (MA); global thought (MA); Hispanic cultural studies (MA); history (PhD); history and literature (MA); human rights studies (MA); Islamic studies (MA); Italian (MA, PhD); Japanese pedagogy (MA); Jewish studies (MA); Latin America and the Caribbean: regional studies (MA); Latin American and Iberian cultures (PhD); mathematics (MA, PhD), including finance (MA); medieval and Renaissance studies (MA); Middle Eastern, South Asian, and African studies (MA, PhD); modern art: critical and curatorial studies (MA); modern European studies (MA); museum anthropology (MA); music (DMA, PhD); oral history (MA); philosophical foundations of physics (MA); philosophy (MA, PhD); physics (PhD); political science (MA, PhD); psychology (PhD); quantitative methods in the social sciences (MA); religion (MA, PhD); Russia, Eurasia and East Europe: regional studies (MA); Russian translation (MA); Slavic cultures (MA); Slavic languages (MA, PhD); sociology (MA, PhD); South Asian studies (MA); statistics (MA, PhD); theatre (PhD). Dual-degree programs require admission to both Graduate School of Arts and Sciences and another Columbia school. *Program availability:* Part-time. Terminal master's awarded for partial completion of doctoral program. *Degree requirements:* For master's, variable foreign language requirement, comprehensive exam (for some programs), thesis (for some programs); for doctorate, variable foreign language requirement, comprehensive exam (for some programs), thesis/dissertation. *Entrance requirements:* For master's and doctorate, GRE General Test, GRE Subject Test (for some programs). Additional exam requirements/recommendations for international students: Required—TOEFL, IELTS. Electronic applications accepted. *Expenses:* Tuition: Full-time $44,864; part-time $1704 per credit. Required fees: $2370 per semester. One-time fee: $105.

Columbus State University, Graduate Studies, College of Letters and Sciences, Department of Political Science and Public Administration, Columbus, GA 31907-5645. Offers public administration (MPA), including criminal justice, environmental policy, government administration, health services administration, political campaigning, urban policy. *Program availability:* Part-time, evening/weekend, 100% online, blended/hybrid learning. *Faculty:* 15 full-time (6 women), 14 part-time/adjunct (0 women). *Students:* 34 full-time (21 women), 44 part-time (24 women); includes 40 minority (32 Black or African

American, non-Hispanic/Latino; 2 Asian, non-Hispanic/Latino; 3 Hispanic/Latino; 1 Native Hawaiian or other Pacific Islander, non-Hispanic/Latino; 2 Two or more races, non-Hispanic/Latino), 3 international. Average age 33. 68 applicants, 43% accepted, 21 enrolled. In 2017, 38 master's awarded. *Degree requirements:* For master's, comprehensive exam. *Entrance requirements:* For master's, GRE General Test, minimum GPA of 2.75, three letters of recommendation. Additional exam requirements/recommendations for international students: Required—TOEFL (minimum score 550 paper-based; 79 iBT). *Application deadline:* For fall admission, 6/30 for domestic students, 5/1 for international students; for spring admission, 11/1 for domestic and international students; for summer admission, 3/1 for domestic and international students. Applications are processed on a rolling basis. Application fee: $50. Electronic applications accepted. *Expenses:* Tuition, state resident: full-time $3708; part-time $2472 per year. Tuition, nonresident: full-time $14,418; part-time $9612 per year. *International tuition:* $19,218 full-time. *Required fees:* $1605. Tuition and fees vary according to program. *Financial support:* In 2017–18, 4 students received support, including 6 research assistantships with partial tuition reimbursements available (averaging $3,000 per year); career-related internships or fieldwork, Federal Work-Study, institutionally sponsored loans, scholarships/grants, tuition waivers (partial), and unspecified assistantships also available. Support available to part-time students. Financial award application deadline: 5/1; financial award applicants required to submit FAFSA. *Unit head:* Dr. Frederick Gordon, Director, 706-565-7875, E-mail: gordon_frederick@colstate.edu. *Application contact:* Catrina Smith-Edmond, Assistant Director for Graduate and Global Admission, 706-507-8824, Fax: 706-568-5091, E-mail: smithedmond_catrina@columbusstate.edu.
Website: http://politicalscience.columbusstate.edu/

Concordia University, School of Graduate Studies, Faculty of Arts and Science, Department of Political Science, Montréal, QC H3G 1M8, Canada. Offers political science (PhD); public policy and public administration (MA), including geography. *Degree requirements:* For master's, one foreign language, comprehensive exam, thesis optional, internship. *Entrance requirements:* For master's, honors degree or equivalent. Additional exam requirements/recommendations for international students: Required—TOEFL. *Faculty research:* International public policy and administration, Quebec public administration, public policy and social/political theory, geography and public policy, public administration and decision making.

Converse College, Program in Liberal Arts, Spartanburg, SC 29302. Offers English (MLA); history (MLA); political science (MLA). *Degree requirements:* For master's, capstone paper. *Entrance requirements:* For master's, minimum GPA of 3.0, 2 recommendations. *Application deadline:* For fall admission, 5/1 priority date for domestic students; for spring admission, 1/30 for domestic students. Application fee: $40. *Unit head:* Lienne Medford, Dean of Graduate Studies and Distance Education, 864-596-9082, E-mail: lienne.medford@converse.edu.

Cornell University, Graduate School, Graduate Fields of Arts and Sciences, Field of Government, Ithaca, NY 14853. Offers American politics (PhD); comparative politics (PhD); international relations (PhD); political methodology (PhD); political thought (PhD); public policy (PhD). *Degree requirements:* For doctorate, comprehensive exam, thesis/dissertation. *Entrance requirements:* For doctorate, GRE General Test, sample of written work, 3 letters of recommendation. Additional exam requirements/recommendations for international students: Required—TOEFL (minimum score 550 paper-based; 77 iBT). Electronic applications accepted. *Faculty research:* Political theory, American politics, comparative politics, international relations, methodology.

Dalhousie University, Faculty of Arts and Social Science, Department of Political Science, Halifax, NS B3H 4R2, Canada. Offers MA, PhD. *Entrance requirements:* Additional exam requirements/recommendations for international students: Required—TOEFL, IELTS, CANTEST, CAEL, or Michigan English Language Assessment Battery. Electronic applications accepted. *Faculty research:* Canadian political behavior and institutions, international politics, foreign policy, African politics, liberalism and modern political theory.

Dominican University of California, School of Liberal Arts and Education, Humanities Program, San Rafael, CA 94901-2298. Offers applied music (MA); art history (MA); creative writing (MA); gender studies (MA); history (MA); philosophy (MA); political theory (MA); religion (MA). *Program availability:* Part-time. *Faculty:* 7 full-time (4 women), 1 (woman) part-time/adjunct. *Students:* 6 full-time (5 women), 16 part-time (12 women); includes 8 minority (3 Black or African American, non-Hispanic/Latino; 4 Hispanic/Latino; 1 Two or more races, non-Hispanic/Latino), 2 international. Average age 45. 7 applicants, 100% accepted, 5 enrolled. In 2017, 14 master's awarded. *Degree requirements:* For master's, thesis or alternative. *Entrance requirements:* For master's, minimum GPA of 3.0, interview. Additional exam requirements/recommendations for international students: Required—TOEFL (minimum score 550 paper-based; 80 iBT), IELTS (minimum score 6.5). *Application deadline:* For fall admission, 5/15 priority date for domestic and international students; for spring admission, 11/15 priority date for domestic and international students. Applications are processed on a rolling basis. Application fee: $0. Electronic applications accepted. *Expenses:* Tuition: Full-time $17,370; part-time $965 per credit. Required fees: $150 per semester. Tuition and fees vary according to course load and program. *Financial support:* In 2017–18, 4 students received support. Scholarships/grants available. Support available to part-time students. Financial award application deadline: 3/2; financial award applicants required to submit FAFSA. *Unit head:* Joan Baranow, Program Director, 415-485-3264, E-mail: joan.baranow@dominican.edu. *Application contact:* Michael Lavigna, Assistant Director of Graduate Admissions, 415-485-3253, Fax: 415-485-3214, E-mail: gradmissions@dominican.edu.
Website: https://www.dominican.edu/academics/lae/graduate-programs/ma-in-humanities/index_html

Duke University, Graduate School, Department of Political Science, Durham, NC 27708. Offers AM, PhD, JD/AM. Terminal master's awarded for partial completion of doctoral program. *Degree requirements:* For doctorate, 2 foreign languages, thesis/dissertation. *Entrance requirements:* For master's and doctorate, GRE General Test. Additional exam requirements/recommendations for international students: Required—TOEFL (minimum score 577 paper-based; 90 iBT) or IELTS (minimum score 7). Electronic applications accepted.

East Carolina University, Graduate School, Thomas Harriot College of Arts and Sciences, Department of Political Science, Greenville, NC 27858-4353. Offers public administration (MPA); security studies (MS, Certificate). *Accreditation:* NASPAA. *Program availability:* Part-time, evening/weekend, online learning. *Students:* 29 full-time (13 women), 76 part-time (30 women); includes 27 minority (16 Black or African American, non-Hispanic/Latino; 1 American Indian or Alaska Native, non-Hispanic/Latino; 1 Asian, non-Hispanic/Latino; 9 Hispanic/Latino), 1 international. Average age 34. 28 applicants, 100% accepted, 18 enrolled. In 2017, 21 master's, 10 other advanced degrees awarded. *Degree requirements:* For master's, internship, professional paper. *Entrance requirements:* For master's, GRE General Test. Additional exam requirements/recommendations for international students: Recommended—TOEFL (minimum score 78 iBT), IELTS (minimum score 6.5). *Application deadline:* For fall admission, 6/1 priority date for domestic students; for spring admission, 10/15 for domestic students. Applications are processed on a rolling basis. Application fee: $75. Electronic

applications accepted. *Expenses:* Tuition, state resident: full-time $4749; part-time $297 per credit hour. Tuition, nonresident: full-time $17,898; part-time $1119 per credit hour. *Required fees:* $2691; $224 per credit hour. Part-time tuition and fees vary according to course load and program. *Financial support:* Research assistantships with partial tuition reimbursements, teaching assistantships with partial tuition reimbursements, and Federal Work-Study available. Support available to part-time students. Financial award application deadline: 3/1. *Unit head:* Dr. Alethia Cook, Chair, 252-328-5869, E-mail: cooka@ecu.edu. *Application contact:* Dean of Graduate School, 252-328-6012, Fax: 252-328-6071, E-mail: gradschool@ecu.edu.
Website: http://www.ecu.edu/polsci/

Eastern Illinois University, Graduate School, College of Liberal Arts and Sciences, Department of Political Science, Charleston, IL 61920. Offers MA. *Program availability:* Part-time, evening/weekend. *Degree requirements:* For master's, comprehensive exam (for some programs), thesis (for some programs). *Entrance requirements:* For master's, GMAT or GRE. Additional exam requirements/recommendations for international students: Required—TOEFL (minimum score 500 paper-based; 61 iBT), IELTS (minimum score 6). *Application deadline:* For fall admission, 5/15 for domestic and international students; for spring admission, 10/15 for domestic and international students. Applications are processed on a rolling basis. Application fee: $30. Electronic applications accepted. *Financial support:* Research assistantships with full tuition reimbursements, teaching assistantships with full tuition reimbursements, career-related internships or fieldwork, Federal Work-Study, and unspecified assistantships available. Support available to part-time students. Financial award application deadline: 3/1; financial award applicants required to submit FAFSA. *Unit head:* Melinda A. Mueller, Chair, 217-581-2523, Fax: 217-581-2926, E-mail: mamueller@eiu.edu. *Application contact:* Dr. Jeffrey Ashley, Graduate Coordinator, 217-581-8418, Fax: 217-581-2926, E-mail: jsashley@eiu.edu.
Website: http://www.eiu.edu/poliscigrad/

Eastern Kentucky University, The Graduate School, College of Arts and Sciences, Department of Government, Program in Political Science, Richmond, KY 40475-3102. Offers MA. *Entrance requirements:* For master's, GRE General Test, minimum GPA of 2.5.

East Stroudsburg University of Pennsylvania, Graduate and Extended Studies, College of Arts and Sciences, Department of Political Science and Economics, East Stroudsburg, PA 18301-2999. Offers management and leadership in public administration (MS); political science (MA). *Program availability:* Part-time, evening/weekend. *Faculty:* 5 full-time (1 woman), 1 (woman) part-time/adjunct. *Students:* 9 full-time (5 women), 10 part-time (6 women); includes 7 minority (1 Asian, non-Hispanic/Latino; 5 Hispanic/Latino; 1 Two or more races, non-Hispanic/Latino), 2 international. Average age 30. 17 applicants, 82% accepted, 8 enrolled. In 2017, 7 master's awarded. *Degree requirements:* For master's, variable foreign language requirement, comprehensive exam, thesis or alternative. *Entrance requirements:* Additional exam requirements/recommendations for international students: Recommended—TOEFL (minimum score 560 paper-based; 83 iBT), IELTS. *Application deadline:* For fall admission, 7/31 priority date for domestic students, 6/30 priority date for international students; for spring admission, 11/30 for domestic students, 10/31 for international students. Applications are processed on a rolling basis. Application fee: $50. Electronic applications accepted. *Expenses:* Tuition, state resident: full-time $4500; part-time $3000 per credit. Tuition, nonresident: full-time $6750; part-time $4500 per credit. *Required fees:* $2642; $1756 per credit. $878 per semester. Tuition and fees vary according to course load, campus/location and program. *Financial support:* Research assistantships with tuition reimbursements, Federal Work-Study, and unspecified assistantships available. Support available to part-time students. Financial award application deadline: 3/1; financial award applicants required to submit FAFSA. *Unit head:* Ko Mishima, Graduate Coordinator, 570-422-3248. *Application contact:* Kevin Quintero, Associate Director, Graduate and Extended Studies, 570-422-3890, Fax: 570-422-2711, E-mail: kquintero@esu.edu.
Website: http://www.esu.edu/academics/departments/polisci-econ/index.cfm

Edinboro University of Pennsylvania, Department of History, Politics, Languages and Cultures, Edinboro, PA 16444. Offers social sciences (MA), including anthropology, history. *Program availability:* Part-time, evening/weekend. *Degree requirements:* For master's, thesis or alternative, competency exam. *Entrance requirements:* For master's, GRE or MAT, minimum QPA of 2.5. Electronic applications accepted.

Emory University, Laney Graduate School, Department of Political Science, Atlanta, GA 30322-1100. Offers PhD. *Degree requirements:* For doctorate, comprehensive exam, thesis/dissertation. *Entrance requirements:* For doctorate, GRE General Test, minimum GPA of 3.0. Additional exam requirements/recommendations for international students: Required—TOEFL. Electronic applications accepted. *Faculty research:* Post-Soviet politics, comparative politics, international politics, judicial politics and methodology, American national political institutions.

Fairleigh Dickinson University, Metropolitan Campus, University College: Arts, Sciences, and Professional Studies, School of History, Political and International Studies, Program in Political Science, Teaneck, NJ 07666-1914. Offers MA.

Florida Agricultural and Mechanical University, Division of Graduate Studies, Research, and Continuing Education, College of Social Sciences, Arts and Humanities, Department of History and Political Science, Program in Applied Social Science, Tallahassee, FL 32307-3200. Offers criminal justice (MASS); history (MASS); political science (MASS); public administration (MASS). *Program availability:* Part-time. *Degree requirements:* For master's, thesis optional. *Entrance requirements:* For master's, GRE General Test, minimum GPA of 3.0. *Faculty research:* Southern history, black history, election trends, Presidential history.

Florida Atlantic University, Dorothy F. Schmidt College of Arts and Letters, Department of Political Science, Boca Raton, FL 33431-0991. Offers MA. *Program availability:* Part-time. *Faculty:* 15 full-time (3 women). *Students:* 19 full-time (10 women), 7 part-time (2 women); includes 15 minority (3 Black or African American, non-Hispanic/Latino; 3 Asian, non-Hispanic/Latino; 9 Hispanic/Latino). Average age 28. 17 applicants, 59% accepted, 8 enrolled. In 2017, 8 master's awarded. *Degree requirements:* For master's, one foreign language, thesis or alternative. *Entrance requirements:* For master's, GRE General Test, minimum GPA of 3.0 during last 60 hours of course work. Additional exam requirements/recommendations for international students: Required—TOEFL (minimum score 500 paper-based; 61 iBT), IELTS (minimum score 6). *Application deadline:* For fall admission, 7/1 for domestic students, 2/15 for international students; for spring admission, 11/1 for domestic students, 7/15 for international students. Applications are processed on a rolling basis. Application fee: $30. Electronic applications accepted. *Expenses:* Tuition, state resident: full-time $7400; part-time $369.82 per credit. Tuition, nonresident: full-time $20,496; part-time $1042.81 per credit. *Financial support:* Research assistantships, teaching assistantships with partial tuition reimbursements, career-related internships or fieldwork, Federal Work-Study, and institutionally sponsored loans available. Support available to part-time students. Financial award application deadline: 4/16. *Faculty research:* Public policy, comparative policy affecting women, Congress, international system, urban policy. *Unit head:* Dr. Kevin K. Wagner, Chair, 561-297-3211, E-mail: kwagne15@fau.edu. *Application contact:* Dr. Mehmet Gurses, Director of Graduate Studies, 561-297-3213, E-mail: gurses@fau.edu.
Website: http://www.fau.edu/politicalscience/

Florida International University, Steven J. Green School of International and Public Affairs, Department of Politics and International Relations, Miami, FL 33199. Offers international relations (MA, PhD), including international relations (PhD), international studies (MA); political science (MA, PhD). PhD program has fall admissions only. *Program availability:* Part-time, evening/weekend. *Faculty:* 28 full-time (10 women), 31 part-time/adjunct (7 women). *Students:* 166 full-time (86 women), 29 part-time (9 women); includes 107 minority (13 Black or African American, non-Hispanic/Latino; 4 Asian, non-Hispanic/Latino; 86 Hispanic/Latino; 4 Two or more races, non-Hispanic/Latino), 49 international. Average age 29. 172 applicants, 62% accepted, 68 enrolled. In 2017, 39 master's, 19 doctorates awarded. *Degree requirements:* For master's, one foreign language, thesis optional; for doctorate, one foreign language, comprehensive exam, thesis/dissertation. *Entrance requirements:* For master's and doctorate, GRE General Test, minimum GPA of 3.0, letters of recommendation. Additional exam requirements/recommendations for international students: Required—TOEFL (minimum score 550 paper-based; 80 iBT). *Application deadline:* For fall admission, 3/15 for domestic and international students; for spring admission, 8/15 for domestic and international students. Application fee: $30. Electronic applications accepted. *Expenses:* Tuition, state resident: full-time $8912; part-time $446 per credit hour. Tuition, nonresident: full-time $21,393; part-time $992 per credit hour. *Required fees:* $390; $195 per semester. *Financial support:* Institutionally sponsored loans, scholarships/grants, and unspecified assistantships available. Financial award application deadline: 3/1; financial award applicants required to submit FAFSA. *Unit head:* Dr. John Clark, Chair, 305-348-2227, Fax: 305-348-3765, E-mail: john.clark@fiu.edu. *Application contact:* Nanett Rojas, Manager, Admissions Operations, 305-348-7464, E-mail: nanett.rojas@fiu.edu.
Website: http://pir.fiu.edu

Florida State University, The Graduate School, College of Social Sciences and Public Policy, Department of Political Science, Tallahassee, FL 32306-2230. Offers applied American politics and policy (MS); political science (MS, PhD). *Program availability:* Part-time. *Faculty:* 22 full-time (4 women), 1 part-time/adjunct (0 women). *Students:* 42 full-time (15 women), 33 part-time (12 women); includes 24 minority (5 Black or African American, non-Hispanic/Latino; 5 Asian, non-Hispanic/Latino; 12 Hispanic/Latino; 2 Two or more races, non-Hispanic/Latino). Average age 25. 73 applicants, 70% accepted, 34 enrolled. In 2017, 28 master's, 5 doctorates awarded. Terminal master's awarded for partial completion of doctoral program. *Degree requirements:* For master's, thesis optional; for doctorate, comprehensive exam, thesis/dissertation. *Entrance requirements:* For master's, GRE General Test, minimum undergraduate GPA of 3.0; for doctorate, GRE General Test, minimum graduate GPA of 3.5, undergraduate 3.0. Additional exam requirements/recommendations for international students: Required—TOEFL (minimum score 600 paper-based; 100 iBT). *Application deadline:* For fall admission, 1/15 priority date for domestic and international students. Applications are processed on a rolling basis. Application fee: $30. Electronic applications accepted. *Financial support:* In 2017–18, 34 students received support, including 25 research assistantships with full tuition reimbursements available (averaging $17,500 per year), 9 teaching assistantships with full tuition reimbursements available (averaging $17,500 per year); Federal Work-Study, institutionally sponsored loans, scholarships/grants, and unspecified assistantships also available. Financial award application deadline: 1/15; financial award applicants required to submit FAFSA. *Faculty research:* American government, international relations, comparative government, public policy. *Total annual research expenditures:* $130,000. *Unit head:* Dr. Mark Souva, Director of Graduate Studies, 850-644-7315, Fax: 850-644-1367, E-mail: msouva@fsu.edu. *Application contact:* Jeremiah J. Fisher, Academic Coordinator, 850-644-7305, Fax: 850-644-1367, E-mail: jeremiah.fisher@fsu.edu.
Website: http://coss.fsu.edu/polisci/

Fordham University, Graduate School of Arts and Sciences, Program in Elections and Campaign Management, New York, NY 10458. Offers MA. *Students:* 10 full-time (4 women), 5 part-time (3 women); includes 5 minority (2 Black or African American, non-Hispanic/Latino; 3 Hispanic/Latino), 1 international. Average age 29. 18 applicants, 83% accepted, 8 enrolled. In 2017, 7 master's awarded. Application fee: $70. *Unit head:* Dr. Monika McDermott, Director, 718-817-3963, E-mail: mmcdermott@fordham.edu. *Application contact:* Travis Strattion, Interim Director of Graduate Admissions, 718-817-4417, Fax: 718-817-3566, E-mail: tstrattion@fordham.edu.
Website: http://www.fordham.edu/academics/programs_at_fordham_/elections__campaign_/

George Mason University, Schar School of Policy and Government, Program in Political Science, Arlington, VA 22201. Offers MA, PhD. *Faculty:* 20 full-time (6 women), 5 part-time/adjunct (1 woman). *Students:* 27 full-time (12 women), 37 part-time (14 women); includes 12 minority (3 Black or African American, non-Hispanic/Latino; 2 Asian, non-Hispanic/Latino; 5 Hispanic/Latino; 2 Two or more races, non-Hispanic/Latino), 4 international. Average age 31. 89 applicants, 48% accepted, 11 enrolled. In 2017, 13 master's, 4 doctorates awarded. *Degree requirements:* For master's, research project or thesis; for doctorate, comprehensive exam, thesis/dissertation. *Entrance requirements:* For master's, GRE (taken in the past five years), transcripts from all previous institutions attended in the U.S.; goals statement; two letters of recommendation; current resume; writing sample; for doctorate, GRE (taken in the past five years), official transcript from all colleges and universities attended; current resume; three letters of recommendation; statement of professional goals; writing sample (approximately 10-25 pages in length). Additional exam requirements/recommendations for international students: Required—TOEFL (minimum score 575 paper-based; 88 iBT), IELTS (minimum score 6.5), PTE (minimum score 59). *Application deadline:* For fall admission, 2/1 priority date for domestic and international students; for spring admission, 11/1 for domestic students, 11/1 priority date for international students. Application fee: $75 ($80 for international students). Electronic applications accepted. *Expenses:* Tuition, state resident: full-time $11,228; part-time $459.50 per credit. Tuition, nonresident: full-time $30,932; part-time $1280.50 per credit. *Required fees:* $3252; $135.50 per credit. Part-time tuition and fees vary according to course load and program. *Financial support:* In 2017–18, 15 students received support, including 1 fellowship, 1 research assistantship with tuition reimbursement available, 14 teaching assistantships with tuition reimbursements available (averaging $17,857 per year); career-related internships or fieldwork, Federal Work-Study, scholarships/grants, unspecified assistantships, and health care benefits (for full-time research or teaching assistantship recipients) also available. Support available to part-time students. Financial award application deadline: 3/1; financial award applicants required to submit FAFSA. *Unit head:* Ming Wan, Director, 703-993-2955, Fax: 703-993-1399, E-mail: mwan@gmu.edu. *Application contact:* Stephanie Ellis, Graduate Admissions Coordinator, 703-993-4478, E-mail: sellis11@gmu.edu.
Website: http://spgia.gmu.edu/programs/graduate-degrees/ma-in-political-science/

Georgetown University, Graduate School of Arts and Sciences, Department of Government, Program in Democracy and Governance, Washington, DC 20057. Offers MA.

Political Science

Georgetown University, Graduate School of Arts and Sciences, School of Continuing Studies, Washington, DC 20057. Offers American studies (MALS); applied intelligence (MPS); Catholic studies (MALS); classical civilizations (MALS); emergency and disaster management (MPS); ethics and the professions (MALS); global strategic communications (MPS); hospitality management (MPS); human resources management (MPS); humanities (MALS); individualized study (MALS); integrated marketing communications (MPS); international affairs (MALS); Islam and Muslim-Christian relations (MALS); journalism (MPS); liberal studies (DLS); literature and society (MALS); medieval and early modern European studies (MALS); public relations and corporate communications (MPS); real estate (MPS); religious studies (MALS); social and public policy (MALS); sports industry management (MPS); systems engineering management (MPS); technology management (MPS); the theory and practice of American democracy (MALS); urban and regional planning (MPS); visual culture (MALS). MPS in systems engineering management offered jointly with Stevens Institute of Technology. *Entrance requirements:* Additional exam requirements/recommendations for international students: Required—TOEFL.

The George Washington University, College of Professional Studies, Graduate School of Political Management, Program in Legislative Affairs, Washington, DC 20052. Offers MPS. *Program availability:* Part-time, evening/weekend. *Faculty:* 6 part-time/adjunct (0 women). *Students:* 37 full-time (10 women), 41 part-time (15 women); includes 15 minority (6 Black or African American, non-Hispanic/Latino; 8 Hispanic/Latino; 1 Two or more races, non-Hispanic/Latino). Average age 30. 77 applicants, 95% accepted, 52 enrolled. In 2017, 60 master's awarded. *Degree requirements:* For master's, comprehensive exam. *Entrance requirements:* For master's, GRE General Test, minimum GPA of 3.0. Additional exam requirements/recommendations for international students: Required—TOEFL (minimum score 550 paper-based). *Application deadline:* For fall admission, 4/1 priority date for domestic and international students; for spring admission, 10/1 priority date for domestic and international students. Applications are processed on a rolling basis. Application fee: $75. Electronic applications accepted. *Expenses: Tuition:* Full-time $28,800; part-time $1655 per credit hour. *Required fees:* $45; $2.75 per credit hour. *Financial support:* Application deadline: 2/1. *Unit head:* Dr. Steven E. Billet, Director, 202-994-1149, E-mail: sbillet@gwu.edu. *Application contact:* Information Contact, 202-994-6000, Fax: 202-994-6006, E-mail: gspmmail@gwu.edu.
Website: http://www.gwu.edu/~gspm/academics/mala.shtml

The George Washington University, Columbian College of Arts and Sciences, Department of Political Science, Washington, DC 20052. Offers legal institutions and theory (MA); political science (MA). *Program availability:* Part-time, evening/weekend. *Faculty:* 33 full-time (9 women), 35 part-time/adjunct (9 women). *Students:* 40 full-time (19 women), 47 part-time (16 women); includes 12 minority (3 Black or African American, non-Hispanic/Latino; 3 Asian, non-Hispanic/Latino; 5 Hispanic/Latino; 1 Two or more races, non-Hispanic/Latino), 17 international. Average age 30. 378 applicants, 16% accepted, 21 enrolled. In 2017, 13 master's, 14 doctorates awarded. Terminal master's awarded for partial completion of doctoral program. *Degree requirements:* For master's, one foreign language, comprehensive exam, thesis or alternative; for doctorate, 2 foreign languages, thesis/dissertation, general exam. *Entrance requirements:* For master's and doctorate, GRE General Test, minimum GPA of 3.0. Additional exam requirements/recommendations for international students: Required—TOEFL (minimum score 550 paper-based; 80 iBT). *Application deadline:* For fall admission, 1/15 priority date for domestic students; for spring admission, 10/1 priority date for domestic students. Applications are processed on a rolling basis. Application fee: $75. Electronic applications accepted. *Expenses: Tuition:* Full-time $28,800; part-time $1655 per credit hour. *Required fees:* $45; $2.75 per credit hour. *Financial support:* In 2017–18, 43 students received support. Fellowships with tuition reimbursements available, teaching assistantships with tuition reimbursements available, Federal Work-Study, and tuition waivers available. *Unit head:* Christopher J. Deering, Chair, 202-994-6564, E-mail: rocket@gwu.edu. *Application contact:* 202-994-6290, Fax: 202-994-6213, E-mail: askccas@gwu.edu.
Website: http://politicalscience.columbian.gwu.edu/

The George Washington University, Elliott School of International Affairs, Program in Security Policy Studies, Washington, DC 20052. Offers MA. *Program availability:* Part-time. *Students:* 128 full-time (50 women), 59 part-time (23 women); includes 45 minority (9 Black or African American, non-Hispanic/Latino; 11 Asian, non-Hispanic/Latino; 16 Hispanic/Latino; 9 Two or more races, non-Hispanic/Latino), 8 international. Average age 27. 291 applicants, 87% accepted, 72 enrolled. In 2017, 63 master's awarded. *Degree requirements:* For master's, one foreign language, capstone project. *Entrance requirements:* For master's, GRE General Test, 2 semesters of introductory economics, 2 years of a modern foreign language or 1 semester of statistics. Additional exam requirements/recommendations for international students: Required—TOEFL (minimum score 100 iBT), IELTS (minimum score 7). *Application deadline:* For fall admission, 1/15 priority date for domestic and international students; for spring admission, 10/1 for domestic and international students. Application fee: $75. Electronic applications accepted. *Expenses: Tuition:* Full-time $28,800; part-time $1655 per credit hour. *Required fees:* $45; $2.75 per credit hour. *Financial support:* In 2017–18, 22 students received support. Fellowships with partial tuition reimbursements available, Federal Work-Study, and scholarships/grants available. Financial award application deadline: 1/15; financial award applicants required to submit FAFSA. *Faculty research:* U.S. arms transfer policies, military balance in the Third World, U.S. foreign policy, technology and security policy. *Unit head:* Joanna Spear, Director, 202-994-1088, E-mail: jspear@gwu.edu. *Application contact:* Nicole A. Campbell, Director of Graduate Admissions, 202-994-7050, Fax: 202-994-9537, E-mail: esiagrad@gwu.edu.
Website: http://elliott.gwu.edu/academics/graduate/sps

Georgia State University, College of Arts and Sciences, Department of Communication, Atlanta, GA 30302-3083. Offers film, video, and digital imaging (MA), including critical studies, production, screenwriting; human communication and social influence (MA); mass communication (MA); media and society (PhD); moving image studies (PhD); public communication (PhD); rhetoric and politics (PhD). *Program availability:* Part-time. *Faculty:* 57 full-time (34 women). *Students:* 71 full-time (51 women), 17 part-time (9 women); includes 36 minority (28 Black or African American, non-Hispanic/Latino; 1 Asian, non-Hispanic/Latino; 4 Hispanic/Latino; 1 Native Hawaiian or other Pacific Islander, non-Hispanic/Latino; 2 Two or more races, non-Hispanic/Latino), 15 international. Average age 33. 63 applicants, 54% accepted, 17 enrolled. In 2017, 20 master's, 10 doctorates awarded. *Degree requirements:* For master's, variable foreign language requirement, thesis (for some programs); for doctorate, comprehensive exam, thesis/dissertation. *Entrance requirements:* For master's and doctorate, GRE. Additional exam requirements/recommendations for international students: Required—TOEFL (minimum score 550 paper-based; 80 iBT), IELTS (minimum score 6.5). *Application deadline:* For fall admission, 2/10 for domestic and international students; for spring admission, 10/15 for domestic and international students. Application fee: $50. Electronic applications accepted. *Expenses:* Tuition, state resident: full-time $7020. Tuition, nonresident: full-time $22,518. *Required fees:* $2128. Tuition and fees vary according to degree level and program. *Financial support:* In 2017–18, fellowships with tuition reimbursements (averaging $15,000 per year), teaching assistantships with tuition reimbursements (averaging $15,000 per year) were awarded; career-related internships or fieldwork and unspecified assistantships also available. Financial award applicants required to submit FAFSA. *Faculty research:* New media, mass media and journalism, rhetoric, film and media studies, film production. *Unit head:* Dr. Greg Lisby, Chair, 404-413-5639, Fax: 404-413-5634, E-mail: glisby@gsu.edu.
Website: http://communication.gsu.edu

Georgia State University, College of Arts and Sciences, Department of Political Science, Atlanta, GA 30302-3083. Offers MA, PhD. *Program availability:* Part-time, evening/weekend. *Faculty:* 26 full-time (8 women). *Students:* 69 full-time (36 women), 22 part-time (11 women); includes 21 minority (14 Black or African American, non-Hispanic/Latino; 3 Asian, non-Hispanic/Latino; 1 Hispanic/Latino; 3 Two or more races, non-Hispanic/Latino), 20 international. Average age 32. 88 applicants, 74% accepted, 28 enrolled. In 2017, 14 master's, 2 doctorates awarded. Terminal master's awarded for partial completion of doctoral program. *Entrance requirements:* For master's and doctorate, GRE. *Application deadline:* For fall admission, 2/1 priority date for domestic and international students; for spring admission, 10/15 for domestic and international students. Applications are processed on a rolling basis. Application fee: $50. Electronic applications accepted. *Expenses:* Tuition, state resident: full-time $7020. Tuition, nonresident: full-time $22,518. *Required fees:* $2128. Tuition and fees vary according to degree level and program. *Financial support:* In 2017–18, fellowships with full tuition reimbursements (averaging $19,000 per year), research assistantships with full tuition reimbursements (averaging $14,000 per year), teaching assistantships with full tuition reimbursements (averaging $4,000 per year) were awarded; career-related internships or fieldwork and health care benefits also available. Financial award application deadline: 2/1; financial award applicants required to submit FAFSA. *Faculty research:* Political behavior and attitudes, judicial politics and policymaking, comparative democratization, international governance, national and international political institutions and structures. *Unit head:* Dr. Carrie Manning, Chair, 404-413-6162, Fax: 404-413-6156, E-mail: cmanning2@gsu.edu. *Application contact:* Dr. Amy Steigerwalt, Director of Graduate Studies, 404-413-6162, Fax: 404-413-6156, E-mail: asteigerwalt@gsu.edu.
Website: http://politicalscience.gsu.edu/home/graduate/degree-requirements/

Georgia State University, College of Education and Human Development, Department of Middle and Secondary Education, Atlanta, GA 30302-3083. Offers curriculum and instruction (Ed D); English education (MAT); mathematics education (M Ed, MAT); middle level education (MAT); reading, language and literacy education (M Ed, MAT), including reading instruction (M Ed); science education (M Ed, MAT), including biology (MAT), broad field science (MAT), chemistry (MAT), earth science (MAT), physics (MAT); social studies education (M Ed, MAT), including economics (MAT), geography (MAT), history (MAT), political science (MAT); teaching and learning (PhD), including language and literacy, mathematics education, music education, science education, social studies education, teaching and teacher education. *Accreditation:* NCATE. *Program availability:* Part-time, evening/weekend, online learning. *Faculty:* 24 full-time (18 women). *Students:* 179 full-time (110 women), 192 part-time (133 women); includes 193 minority (130 Black or African American, non-Hispanic/Latino; 1 American Indian or Alaska Native, non-Hispanic/Latino; 23 Asian, non-Hispanic/Latino; 25 Hispanic/Latino; 14 Two or more races, non-Hispanic/Latino), 6 international. Average age 33. 175 applicants, 58% accepted, 83 enrolled. In 2017, 81 master's, 17 doctorates awarded. *Entrance requirements:* For master's, GRE; GACE I (for initial teacher preparation programs), baccalaureate degree or equivalent, resume, goals statement, two letters of recommendation, minimum undergraduate GPA of 2.5; proof of initial teacher certification in the content area (for M Ed); for doctorate, GRE, resume, goals statement, writing sample, two letters of recommendation, minimum graduate GPA of 3.3, interview. *Application deadline:* For fall admission, 1/15 priority date for domestic and international students; for spring admission, 10/1 for domestic and international students. Application fee: $50. Electronic applications accepted. *Expenses:* Tuition, state resident: full-time $7020. Tuition, nonresident: full-time $22,518. *Required fees:* $2128. Tuition and fees vary according to degree level and program. *Financial support:* In 2017–18, fellowships with full tuition reimbursements (averaging $19,667 per year), research assistantships with full tuition reimbursements (averaging $5,436 per year), teaching assistantships with full tuition reimbursements (averaging $2,779 per year) were awarded; career-related internships or fieldwork, Federal Work-Study, scholarships/grants, health care benefits, tuition waivers (full and partial), and unspecified assistantships also available. Financial award application deadline: 3/15. *Faculty research:* Teacher education in language and literacy, mathematics, science, and social studies in urban middle and secondary school settings; learning technologies in school, community, and corporate settings; multicultural education and education for social justice; urban education; international education. *Unit head:* Dr. Dana L. Fox, Chair, 404-413-8060, Fax: 404-413-8063, E-mail: dfox@gsu.edu. *Application contact:* Bobbie Turner, Administrative Coordinator, 404-413-8405, Fax: 404-413-8063, E-mail: bnturner@gsu.edu.
Website: http://mse.education.gsu.edu/

Governors State University, College of Arts and Sciences, Program in Political and Justice Studies, University Park, IL 60484. Offers MA. *Program availability:* Part-time. *Faculty:* 60 full-time (34 women), 115 part-time/adjunct (58 women). *Students:* 3 full-time (1 woman), 26 part-time (12 women); includes 16 minority (all Black or African American, non-Hispanic/Latino), 1 international. Average age 37. 2 applicants, 50% accepted. In 2017, 5 master's awarded. *Application deadline:* For fall admission, 4/1 for domestic students. Applications are processed on a rolling basis. Application fee: $50. Electronic applications accepted. *Expenses:* Tuition, state resident: full-time $8472; part-time $353 per credit hour. Tuition, nonresident: full-time $16,944; part-time $706 per credit hour. *Required fees:* $1824; $76 per credit hour. $38 per term. Tuition and fees vary according to course load, degree level and program. *Financial support:* Application deadline: 5/1; applicants required to submit FAFSA. *Unit head:* Lori Montalbano, Chair, Division of Arts and Letters, 708-534-5000 Ext. 2802, E-mail: lmontalbano@govst.edu.

The Graduate Center, City University of New York, Graduate Studies, Program in Political Science, New York, NY 10016-4039. Offers MA, PhD. *Faculty:* 56 full-time (10 women). *Students:* 90 full-time (41 women), 21 part-time (10 women); includes 22 minority (5 Black or African American, non-Hispanic/Latino; 5 Asian, non-Hispanic/Latino; 11 Hispanic/Latino; 1 Two or more races, non-Hispanic/Latino), 21 international. Average age 34. 194 applicants, 45% accepted, 36 enrolled. In 2017, 14 master's, 20 doctorates awarded. Terminal master's awarded for partial completion of doctoral program. *Degree requirements:* For master's, one foreign language, thesis; for doctorate, one foreign language, thesis/dissertation. *Entrance requirements:* For master's and doctorate, GRE General Test. Additional exam requirements/recommendations for international students: Required—TOEFL. *Application deadline:* For fall admission, 2/1 for domestic students. Application fee: $125. Electronic applications accepted. *Financial support:* In 2017–18, 90 students received support, including 82 fellowships, 6 research assistantships, 7 teaching assistantships; career-related internships or fieldwork, Federal Work-Study, institutionally sponsored loans, and tuition waivers (full and partial) also available. Financial award application deadline: 2/1; financial award applicants required to submit FAFSA. *Unit head:* Dr. Alyson Cole, Executive Officer, 212-817-8671, Fax: 212-817-1532. *Application contact:* Les Gribben, Director of Admissions, 212-817-7470, Fax: 212-817-1624, E-mail: lgribben@gc.cuny.edu.

Grambling State University, School of Graduate Studies and Research, College of Arts and Sciences, Department of Political Science and Public Administration, Grambling, LA 71270. Offers health services administration (MPA); human resource management (MPA); public management (MPA); state and local government (MPA). *Accreditation:* NASPAA. *Program availability:* Part-time. *Degree requirements:* For master's, comprehensive exam (for some programs), thesis optional. *Entrance requirements:* For master's, GRE, minimum GPA of 2.75 on last degree. Additional exam requirements/recommendations for international students: Required—TOEFL (minimum score 500 paper-based; 62 iBT). Electronic applications accepted.

Harvard University, Graduate School of Arts and Sciences, Committee on Political Economy and Government, Cambridge, MA 02138. Offers PhD. *Entrance requirements:* For doctorate, GRE General Test or GMAT. Additional exam requirements/recommendations for international students: Required—TOEFL.

Harvard University, Graduate School of Arts and Sciences, Department of Government, Cambridge, MA 02138. Offers political science (PhD), including American politics, comparative politics, international relations, political thought, quantitative methods. *Degree requirements:* For doctorate, one foreign language, thesis/dissertation, general exams. *Entrance requirements:* For doctorate, GRE General Test. Additional exam requirements/recommendations for international students: Required—TOEFL.

Harvard University, John F. Kennedy School of Government, Cambridge, MA 02138. Offers MPA, MPAID, MPP, PhD, JD/MPP, MBA/MPP, MD/MPP. *Students:* 927 full-time (512 women), 6 part-time (2 women); includes 159 minority (34 Black or African American, non-Hispanic/Latino; 1 American Indian or Alaska Native, non-Hispanic/Latino; 69 Asian, non-Hispanic/Latino; 37 Hispanic/Latino; 1 Native Hawaiian or other Pacific Islander, non-Hispanic/Latino; 17 Two or more races, non-Hispanic/Latino), 430 international. Average age 31. 2,722 applicants, 33% accepted, 628 enrolled. In 2017, 540 master's awarded. *Degree requirements:* For doctorate, thesis/dissertation. *Entrance requirements:* For master's, GMAT or GRE General Test; for doctorate, GRE General Test. Additional exam requirements/recommendations for international students: Required—TOEFL (minimum score 600 paper-based; 100 iBT), TWE. *Application deadline:* For fall admission, 12/1 for domestic students. Application fee: $100. Electronic applications accepted. *Financial support:* Fellowships, research assistantships, teaching assistantships, career-related internships or fieldwork, Federal Work-Study, institutionally sponsored loans, scholarships/grants, and unspecified assistantships available. Support available to part-time students. Financial award application deadline: 2/24; financial award applicants required to submit CSS PROFILE or FAFSA. *Unit head:* Douglas W. Elmendorf, Dean, 617-495-1122. *Application contact:* 617-495-1155, Fax: 617-496-1165, E-mail: hks_admissions@harvard.edu.
Website: http://www.hks.harvard.edu/

Hillsdale College, Van Andel Graduate School of Statesmanship, Hillsdale, MI 49242. Offers politics (MA, PhD). *Faculty:* 11 full-time, 1 part-time/adjunct. *Students:* 48 full-time. Average age 27. In 2017, 10 master's awarded. Terminal master's awarded for partial completion of doctoral program. *Degree requirements:* For master's, comprehensive exam (for some programs), thesis (for some programs); for doctorate, 2 foreign languages, comprehensive exam, thesis/dissertation. *Entrance requirements:* For master's and doctorate, GRE. Additional exam requirements/recommendations for international students: Required—TOEFL. *Application deadline:* For fall admission, 12/15 priority date for domestic and international students; for spring admission, 10/15 for domestic and international students. Application fee: $25. Electronic applications accepted. *Expenses: Tuition:* Full-time $23,420; part-time $1280 per credit hour. *Financial support:* In 2017–18, 48 students received support, including 23 fellowships with full tuition reimbursements available (averaging $20,000 per year), 28 research assistantships with full tuition reimbursements available (averaging $4,000 per year); institutionally sponsored loans, scholarships/grants, and unspecified assistantships also available. Financial award application deadline: 12/15. *Unit head:* Dr. Ronald J. Pestritto, Dean, 517-607-2483, E-mail: gradschool@hillsdale.edu. *Application contact:* Mariel Stauff, Graduate Program Coordinator, 517-607-2483, E-mail: gradschool@hillsdale.edu.
Website: http://gradschool.hillsdale.edu

Howard University, Graduate School, Department of Political Science, Program in Political Science, Washington, DC 20059-0002. Offers MA, PhD. *Degree requirements:* For master's, comprehensive exam. *Entrance requirements:* For master's, GRE General Test, minimum GPA of 3.0; for doctorate, GRE General Test, minimum GPA of 2.8.

Idaho State University, Office of Graduate Studies, College of Arts and Letters, Department of Political Science, Pocatello, ID 83209-8073. Offers political science (MA, DA); public administration (MPA). *Program availability:* Part-time. *Degree requirements:* For master's, comprehensive exam, thesis optional; for doctorate, comprehensive exam, thesis/dissertation, teaching internship. *Entrance requirements:* For master's, GRE General Test, minimum GPA of 3.0 in last 2 years of undergraduate study, 3 letters of recommendation; for doctorate, GRE General Test, major field of American politics, minimum GPA of 3.0 in last 2 years of undergraduate study, 3 letters of recommendation. Additional exam requirements/recommendations for international students: Required—TOEFL (minimum score 550 paper-based; 80 iBT). Electronic applications accepted. *Faculty research:* International affairs, environmental policy, decision making, Constitution, executive/legislative relations.

Illinois State University, Graduate School, College of Arts and Sciences, Department of Politics and Government, Normal, IL 61790. Offers MA, MS. *Degree requirements:* For master's, thesis or alternative. *Entrance requirements:* For master's, GRE General Test, minimum GPA of 3.0 in last 60 hours of course work, 15 hours of course work in political science. *Faculty research:* Political tolerance in a democracy under external threats: a survey of public opinion.

Indiana University Bloomington, University Graduate School, College of Arts and Sciences, Department of Political Science, Bloomington, IN 47405-7000. Offers MA, PhD. Terminal master's awarded for partial completion of doctoral program. *Degree requirements:* For master's, thesis, 30 credit hours; for doctorate, comprehensive exam, thesis/dissertation. *Entrance requirements:* For master's, GRE, personal statement, transcripts, 3 letters of recommendation; for doctorate, GRE, sample of written work, 3 letters of recommendation, personal statement. Additional exam requirements/recommendations for international students: Required—TOEFL (minimum score 640 paper-based; 112 iBT). Electronic applications accepted. *Faculty research:* American politics, international relations, public policy, political theory, comparative politics, theory and methodology.

Indiana University–Purdue University Indianapolis, School of Liberal Arts, Department of Political Science, Indianapolis, IN 46202. Offers MA.

Institute for Christian Studies, Graduate Programs, Toronto, ON M5T 1R4, Canada. Offers education (M Phil F, PhD); history of philosophy (M Phil F, PhD); philosophical aesthetics (M Phil F, PhD); philosophy of religion (M Phil F, PhD); political theory (M Phil F, PhD); systematic philosophy (M Phil F, PhD); theology (M Phil F, PhD); worldview studies (MWS). *Program availability:* Part-time, online learning. *Degree requirements:* For master's, one foreign language, thesis; for doctorate, 2 foreign languages, thesis/dissertation. *Entrance requirements:* For master's and doctorate, philosophy background. Additional exam requirements/recommendations for international students: Required—TOEFL (minimum score 600 paper-based). *Faculty research:* Human rights, anthropology of self, medieval discourse, gender and body, post-modern thought; biblical hermeneutics, creational aesthetics, ecumenism, epistemology, political theory and public policy, relational psychotherapy.

The Institute of World Politics, Graduate Programs in National Security, Intelligence, and International Affairs, Washington, DC 20036. Offers American foreign policy (Certificate); comparative political culture (Certificate); counterintelligence (Certificate); democracy building (Certificate); intelligence (Certificate); international politics (Certificate); national security affairs (Certificate); public diplomacy and political warfare (Certificate); statecraft and national security affairs (MA); statecraft and world politics (MA); strategic intelligence studies (MA). *Program availability:* Part-time, evening/weekend. *Degree requirements:* For master's, comprehensive exam, thesis optional. *Entrance requirements:* For master's, GRE General Test. Additional exam requirements/recommendations for international students: Required—TOEFL. Electronic applications accepted. *Faculty research:* Intelligence, national security, statecraft.

Iowa State University of Science and Technology, Department of Political Science, Ames, IA 50011. Offers political science (MA); public administration (MPA); JD/MA. JD/MA offered jointly with Drake University. *Degree requirements:* For master's, thesis (for some programs). *Entrance requirements:* For master's, GRE General Test, GMAT or LSAT. Additional exam requirements/recommendations for international students: Required—TOEFL (minimum score 570 paper-based; 80 iBT), IELTS (minimum score 6.5). Electronic applications accepted.

Jackson State University, Graduate School, College of Liberal Arts, Department of Political Science, Jackson, MS 39217. Offers MA. *Program availability:* Part-time, evening/weekend. *Degree requirements:* For master's, comprehensive exam, thesis or alternative. *Entrance requirements:* For master's, GRE General Test. Additional exam requirements/recommendations for international students: Required—TOEFL (minimum score 520 paper-based; 67 iBT).

Jacksonville State University, College of Graduate Studies and Continuing Education, College of Arts and Sciences, Department of Political Science, Jacksonville, AL 36265-1602. Offers MPA. *Program availability:* Part-time, evening/weekend. *Degree requirements:* For master's, comprehensive exam, thesis (for some programs). *Entrance requirements:* For master's, GRE General Test or MAT. Additional exam requirements/recommendations for international students: Required—TOEFL (minimum score 61 iBT). Electronic applications accepted.

James Madison University, The Graduate School, College of Arts and Letters, Program in Political Science, Harrisonburg, VA 22801. Offers political science (MA), including European Union policy studies. *Students:* 16 full-time (9 women); includes 3 minority (1 Black or African American, non-Hispanic/Latino; 1 Hispanic/Latino; 1 Two or more races, non-Hispanic/Latino), 1 international. Average age 30. In 2017, 12 master's awarded. Application fee: $55. Electronic applications accepted. *Expenses:* Tuition, state resident: full-time $10,512; part-time $438 per credit hour. Tuition, nonresident: full-time $28,358; part-time $1162 per credit hour. *Required fees:* $1128. *Financial support:* Application deadline: 3/1; applicants required to submit FAFSA. *Unit head:* Dr. Charles Blake, Academic Unit Head, 540-568-6344, Fax: 540-568-8021, E-mail: blakech@jmu.edu. *Application contact:* Lynette D. Michael, Director of Graduate Admissions, 540-568-6131 Ext. 6395, Fax: 540-568-7860, E-mail: michaeld@jmu.edu.
Website: http://www.jmu.edu/eurounionpolicy.shtml

Johns Hopkins University, Zanvyl Krieger School of Arts and Sciences, Advanced Academic Programs, Program in Government, Washington, DC 20036. Offers global security studies (MA); government (MA); national securities study (Certificate); nonprofit management (Certificate); public management (MA); research administration (MS); MA/MBA. *Program availability:* Part-time, evening/weekend, online learning. *Degree requirements:* For master's, thesis. *Entrance requirements:* For master's, minimum GPA of 3.0. Additional exam requirements/recommendations for international students: Required—TOEFL (minimum score 100 iBT). Electronic applications accepted.

Johns Hopkins University, Zanvyl Krieger School of Arts and Sciences, Department of Political Science, Baltimore, MD 21218. Offers MA, PhD. *Degree requirements:* For doctorate, one foreign language, comprehensive exam, thesis/dissertation. *Entrance requirements:* For doctorate, GRE General Test. Additional exam requirements/recommendations for international students: Required—TOEFL (minimum score 600 paper-based; 100 iBT), IELTS. Electronic applications accepted. *Faculty research:* American politics, comparative politics, international relations, political theory, urban politics.

Kansas State University, Graduate School, College of Arts and Sciences, Department of Political Science, Manhattan, KS 66506. Offers political science (MA); public administration (MPA). *Accreditation:* NASPAA. *Program availability:* Part-time. *Degree requirements:* For master's, comprehensive exam, thesis or alternative. *Entrance requirements:* For master's, GRE (recommended), minimum GPA of 3.0. Additional exam requirements/recommendations for international students: Required—TOEFL (minimum score 550 paper-based; 79 iBT); Recommended—IELTS (minimum score 6.5), TSE (minimum score 58). Electronic applications accepted. *Faculty research:* Armed conflict, civil military relations, comparative public administration and policy, electoral competition, legislative studies.

Kent State University, College of Arts and Sciences, Department of Political Science, Kent, OH 44242-0001. Offers political science (MA, PhD), including American politics and policy, conflict analysis and management, transnational and comparative politics and policy; public administration (MPA). *Accreditation:* NASPAA. *Program availability:* Part-time, online learning. *Faculty:* 16 full-time (4 women), 3 part-time/adjunct (2 women). *Students:* 28 full-time (11 women), 58 part-time (36 women); includes 13 minority (8 Black or African American, non-Hispanic/Latino; 1 American Indian or Alaska Native, non-Hispanic/Latino; 3 Asian, non-Hispanic/Latino; 1 Hispanic/Latino), 9 international. Average age 35. 46 applicants, 83% accepted, 24 enrolled. In 2017, 34 master's, 4 doctorates awarded. *Degree requirements:* For master's, thesis optional; for doctorate, comprehensive exam, thesis/dissertation. *Entrance requirements:* For master's, GRE, goal statement, transcripts, writing sample, 3 letters of recommendation, minimum GPA of 3.0, resume; for doctorate, GRE, goal statement, transcripts, writing sample, 3 letters of recommendation, minimum GPA of 3.0. Additional exam requirements/recommendations for international students: Required—TOEFL (minimum score 550 paper-based, 79 iBT), Michigan English Language Assessment Battery (minimum score 77), IELTS (minimum score 6.5) or PTE (minimum score 58). *Application deadline:* For fall admission, 1/31 for domestic and international students. Applications are processed on a rolling basis. Application fee: $45 ($70 for international students). Electronic applications accepted. *Expenses:* Tuition, state resident: full-time $11,310; part-time $515 per credit hour. Tuition, nonresident: full-time $20,396; part-time $928 per credit hour. *International tuition:* $18,544 full-time. *Financial support:* Research assistantships with full tuition reimbursements, teaching assistantships with full tuition reimbursements, and unspecified assistantships available. Financial award application deadline: 1/31. *Unit head:* Dr. Andrew Barnes, Associate Professor and Chair, 330-672-2060, E-mail: abarnes3@kent.edu. *Application contact:* Julie Mazzei, Associate Professor and Graduate Coordinator, 330-672-8934, E-mail: jmazzei@kent.edu.
Website: http://www.kent.edu/polisci

Political Science

Lamar University, College of Graduate Studies, College of Arts and Sciences, Department of Political Science, Beaumont, TX 77701. Offers public administration (MPA). *Program availability:* Part-time. *Faculty:* 8 full-time (3 women), 1 part-time/adjunct (0 women). *Students:* 10 part-time (6 women); includes 3 minority (all Black or African American, non-Hispanic/Latino), 1 international. Average age 28. 7 applicants, 100% accepted, 7 enrolled. In 2017, 3 master's awarded. *Entrance requirements:* For master's, GRE General Test. Additional exam requirements/recommendations for international students: Required—TOEFL (minimum score 550 paper-based; 79 iBT), IELTS (minimum score 6.5). *Application deadline:* For fall admission, 8/10 for domestic students, 7/1 for international students; for spring admission, 1/5 for domestic students, 12/1 for international students. Applications are processed on a rolling basis. Application fee: $25 ($50 for international students). Electronic applications accepted. *Expenses:* Contact institution. *Financial support:* Fellowships, research assistantships, teaching assistantships, career-related internships or fieldwork, Federal Work-Study, and institutionally sponsored loans available. Financial award application deadline: 4/1; financial award applicants required to submit FAFSA. *Faculty research:* Political activities of administrators, administrative response to Hurricane Rita, budgeting, environmental politics, urban planning. *Unit head:* Dr. Terri Davis, Chair, 409-880-8285, Fax: 409-880-8710. *Application contact:* Deidre Mayer, Interim Director, Admissions and Academic Services, 409-880-8888, Fax: 409-880-7419, E-mail: gradmissions@lamar.edu.
Website: http://artssciences.lamar.edu/political-science

Lehigh University, College of Arts and Sciences, Department of Political Science, Bethlehem, PA 18015. Offers politics and policy (MA), including political theory. *Program availability:* Part-time, evening/weekend. *Faculty:* 10 full-time (5 women). *Students:* 12 full-time (7 women), 2 part-time (both women); includes 3 minority (1 Black or African American, non-Hispanic/Latino; 1 Asian, non-Hispanic/Latino; 1 Hispanic/Latino), 4 international. Average age 27. 18 applicants, 83% accepted, 10 enrolled. In 2017, 7 master's awarded. *Degree requirements:* For master's, thesis optional, research project. *Entrance requirements:* For master's, transcripts, three letters of recommendation with at least two from academics, resume, statement of objectives. Additional exam requirements/recommendations for international students: Recommended—TOEFL (minimum score 85 iBT), IELTS (minimum score 6.5). *Application deadline:* For fall admission, 6/1 for domestic and international students. Applications are processed on a rolling basis. Application fee: $75. Electronic applications accepted. *Expenses:* $1,460 per credit. *Financial support:* In 2017–18, 8 students received support, including 2 teaching assistantships with full tuition reimbursements available; fellowships and scholarships/grants also available. Financial award application deadline: 3/15. *Faculty research:* American politics and institutions, comparative politics, public policy, political theory. *Unit head:* Dr. Laura Katz-Olson, Chairperson, 610-758-3346, Fax: 610-758-3348, E-mail: lko1@lehigh.edu. *Application contact:* Dr. Holona Ochs, Director, Graduate Studies, 610-758-6508, Fax: 610-758-3348, E-mail: hlo209@lehigh.edu.
Website: http://polisci.cas2.lehigh.edu/

Liberty University, Helms School of Government, Lynchburg, VA 24515. Offers criminal justice (MS), including forensic psychology, homeland security, public administration (MA, MS); international relations (MS); political science (MS); public administration (MPA), including business and government, healthcare, law and public policy, public and non-profit management; public policy (MA), including campaigns and elections, international affairs, Middle East affairs, public administration (MA, MS). *Program availability:* Part-time, online learning. *Students:* 287 full-time (148 women), 639 part-time (248 women); includes 231 minority (173 Black or African American, non-Hispanic/Latino; 4 American Indian or Alaska Native, non-Hispanic/Latino; 8 Asian, non-Hispanic/Latino; 20 Hispanic/Latino; 1 Native Hawaiian or other Pacific Islander, non-Hispanic/Latino; 25 Two or more races, non-Hispanic/Latino), 7 international. Average age 35. 876 applicants, 64% accepted, 277 enrolled. In 2017, 211 master's awarded. *Entrance requirements:* For master's, minimum undergraduate GPA of 3.0. Additional exam requirements/recommendations for international students: Required—TOEFL (minimum score 600 paper-based; 100 iBT). *Application deadline:* Applications are processed on a rolling basis. Application fee: $50. Electronic applications accepted. *Unit head:* Shawn D. Akers, Dean, 434-592-4986. *Application contact:* Jay Bridge, Director of Admissions, 800-424-9595, Fax: 800-628-7977, E-mail: gradadmissions@liberty.edu.

Long Island University–LIU Brooklyn, Richard L. Conolly College of Liberal Arts and Sciences, Brooklyn, NY 11201-8423. Offers biology (MS); chemistry (MS); clinical psychology (PhD); creative writing (MFA); English (MA); media arts (MA, MFA); political science (MA); psychology (MA); social science (MS); United Nations (Advanced Certificate); urban studies (MA); writing and production for television (MFA). *Program availability:* Part-time. *Faculty:* 32 full-time (13 women), 17 part-time/adjunct (6 women). *Students:* 178 full-time (123 women), 143 part-time (96 women); includes 128 minority (65 Black or African American, non-Hispanic/Latino; 22 Asian, non-Hispanic/Latino; 31 Hispanic/Latino; 10 Two or more races, non-Hispanic/Latino), 54 international. Average age 30. 629 applicants, 38% accepted, 74 enrolled. In 2017, 147 master's, 9 doctorates, 8 other advanced degrees awarded. Terminal master's awarded for partial completion of doctoral program. *Degree requirements:* For master's, comprehensive exam (for some programs), thesis (for some programs); for doctorate, thesis/dissertation. *Entrance requirements:* For doctorate, GRE. Additional exam requirements/recommendations for international students: Required—TOEFL (minimum score 550 paper-based, 79 iBT) or IELTS. *Application deadline:* Applications are processed on a rolling basis. Application fee: $50. Electronic applications accepted. *Expenses:* Tuition: Full-time $21,618; part-time $1201 per credit. *Required fees:* $1840; $920 per term. Tuition and fees vary according to course load. *Financial support:* In 2017–18, 214 students received support, including 120 fellowships with full and partial tuition reimbursements available (averaging $915 per year), 5 research assistantships with full and partial tuition reimbursements available (averaging $2,300 per year), 136 teaching assistantships with full and partial tuition reimbursements available (averaging $2,300 per year); career-related internships or fieldwork, Federal Work-Study, institutionally sponsored loans, scholarships/grants, and unspecified assistantships also available. Support available to part-time students. Financial award application deadline: 2/15; financial award applicants required to submit FAFSA. *Faculty research:* Quantum gravity and astrophysics; string theory; pharmaceutical biotechnology with a focus on molecular details of drug susceptibility/resistance mechanisms; entomology, population and community ecology, agroecology, and biodiversity; psychotherapy process-outcome, particularly therapeutic alliance development, the role of common factors, and the study of treatment failures; personality pathology, borderline personality disorder and pathological narcissism. *Unit head:* Dr. Scott Krawczyk, Dean, 718-488-1003, E-mail: scott.krawczyk@liu.edu. *Application contact:* Bayu Sutrisno, Graduate Admissions Counselor, 718-488-1564, Fax: 718-780-6110, E-mail: bayu.sutrisno@liu.edu.

Long Island University–LIU Post, College of Liberal Arts and Sciences, Brookville, NY 11548-1300. Offers applied mathematics (MS); behavior analysis (MA); biology (MS); criminal justice (MS); earth science (MS); English (MA); environmental sustainability (MS); genetic counseling (MS); history (MA); interdisciplinary studies (MA, MS); political science (MA); psychology (MA). *Program availability:* Part-time, evening/weekend, blended/hybrid learning. *Faculty:* 41 full-time (21 women), 24 part-time/adjunct (13 women). *Students:* 173 full-time (124 women), 62 part-time (35 women); includes 54 minority (11 Black or African American, non-Hispanic/Latino; 13 Asian, non-Hispanic/Latino; 23 Hispanic/Latino; 7 Two or more races, non-Hispanic/Latino), 12 international. Average age 28. 368 applicants, 54% accepted, 74 enrolled. In 2017, 89 master's, 15 other advanced degrees awarded. Terminal master's awarded for partial completion of doctoral program. *Degree requirements:* For master's, comprehensive exam (for some programs), thesis (for some programs). *Entrance requirements:* Additional exam requirements/recommendations for international students: Required—TOEFL, IELTS, or PTE. *Application deadline:* Applications are processed on a rolling basis. Application fee: $50. Electronic applications accepted. *Expenses:* Tuition: Full-time $21,618; part-time $1201 per credit. *Required fees:* $1840; $920 per term. Tuition and fees vary according to course load. *Financial support:* In 2017–18, 165 students received support. Fellowships, research assistantships, teaching assistantships, career-related internships or fieldwork, Federal Work-Study, scholarships/grants, tuition waivers (partial), and unspecified assistantships available. Support available to part-time students. Financial award application deadline: 2/15; financial award applicants required to submit FAFSA. *Faculty research:* Biology, environmental sustainability, mathematics, psychology, genetic counseling. *Unit head:* Dr. Nathaniel Bowditch, Dean, 516-299-2234, Fax: 516-299-4140, E-mail: nathaniel.bowditch@liu.edu. *Application contact:* Rita Langdon, Graduate Admissions, 516-299-2900, Fax: 516-299-2137, E-mail: post-enroll@liu.edu.
Website: http://liu.edu/CWPost/Academics/Schools/CLAS

Louisiana State University and Agricultural & Mechanical College, Graduate School, College of Humanities and Social Sciences, Department of Political Science, Baton Rouge, LA 70803. Offers MA, PhD. *Faculty:* 21 full-time (5 women). *Students:* 38 full-time (14 women), 8 part-time (4 women); includes 10 minority (3 Black or African American, non-Hispanic/Latino; 2 Asian, non-Hispanic/Latino; 5 Hispanic/Latino), 9 international. Average age 30. 28 applicants, 54% accepted, 7 enrolled. In 2017, 7 master's, 5 doctorates awarded. *Financial support:* In 2017–18, 2 fellowships (averaging $37,353 per year), 4 research assistantships (averaging $19,250 per year), 25 teaching assistantships (averaging $19,911 per year) were awarded. *Total annual research expenditures:* $105,656.

Loyola University Chicago, Graduate School, Department of Political Science, Chicago, IL 60660. Offers global politics (PhD); political science (MA). *Program availability:* Part-time, evening/weekend. *Faculty:* 19 full-time (5 women). *Students:* 20 full-time (8 women); includes 1 minority (Black or African American, non-Hispanic/Latino), 7 international. Average age 30. 32 applicants, 53% accepted, 5 enrolled. In 2017, 4 master's, 4 doctorates awarded. Terminal master's awarded for partial completion of doctoral program. *Degree requirements:* For master's, comprehensive exam, thesis or alternative; for doctorate, comprehensive exam, thesis/dissertation. *Entrance requirements:* For master's and doctorate, GRE General Test. Additional exam requirements/recommendations for international students: Required—TOEFL (minimum score 550 paper-based; 79 iBT). *Application deadline:* For fall admission, 6/1 for domestic and international students; for spring admission, 10/1 for domestic and international students. Applications are processed on a rolling basis. Application fee: $0. Electronic applications accepted. *Expenses:* $20,000. *Financial support:* In 2017–18, 9 students received support, including 9 fellowships with full tuition reimbursements available (averaging $19,000 per year), 9 research assistantships with full tuition reimbursements available (averaging $19,000 per year); Federal Work-Study, institutionally sponsored loans, scholarships/grants, tuition waivers (full and partial), and unspecified assistantships also available. Financial award application deadline: 2/15. *Faculty research:* American elections, parties and political institutions; comparative politics; foreign policy analysis; international relations theory; modern and contemporary political thought. *Unit head:* Prof. Peter Sanchez, Graduate Program Director, 773-508-8658, Fax: 773-508-3131, E-mail: psanche@luc.edu. *Application contact:* Jill Schur, Director, Graduate Enrollment Management, 312-915-8902, E-mail: gradinfo@luc.edu.
Website: http://www.luc.edu/politicalscience/

Marquette University, Graduate School, College of Arts and Sciences, Department of Political Science, Milwaukee, WI 53201-1881. Offers international affairs (MA); political science (MA); public service (MA); JD/MA; MA/MBA. *Program availability:* Part-time. *Degree requirements:* For master's, comprehensive exam, thesis optional. *Entrance requirements:* For master's, GRE General Test, official transcripts from all current and previous colleges/universities except Marquette, three letters of recommendation, statement of purpose. Additional exam requirements/recommendations for international students: Required—TOEFL (minimum score 530 paper-based). Electronic applications accepted. *Faculty research:* Public opinion and electoral behavior, public policy analysis, Congress and the Presidency, judicial behavior, political system transitions.

Marshall University, Academic Affairs Division, College of Liberal Arts, Department of Political Science, Huntington, WV 25755. Offers MA, MPA. *Students:* 19 full-time (12 women), 5 part-time (1 woman); includes 4 minority (1 Black or African American, non-Hispanic/Latino; 1 American Indian or Alaska Native, non-Hispanic/Latino; 2 Hispanic/Latino). Average age 27. In 2017, 8 master's awarded. *Degree requirements:* For master's, thesis optional. *Entrance requirements:* For master's, GRE General Test. Application fee: $40. *Unit head:* Dr. George Davis, Chair, 304-696-2766, Fax: 304-696-3245, E-mail: davg@marshall.edu. *Application contact:* Graduate Admissions, 304-746-1900, Fax: 304-746-1902, E-mail: services@marshall.edu.
Website: http://www.marshall.edu/polsci/

Massachusetts Institute of Technology, School of Humanities, Arts, and Social Sciences, Department of Political Science, Cambridge, MA 02139. Offers SM, PhD. Terminal master's awarded for partial completion of doctoral program. *Degree requirements:* For master's, thesis, minimum GPA of 3.5 in all subjects; for doctorate, one foreign language, comprehensive exam, thesis/dissertation. *Entrance requirements:* For master's and doctorate, GRE General Test. Additional exam requirements/recommendations for international students: Required—TOEFL, IELTS. Electronic applications accepted. *Faculty research:* International relations, security studies, American politics, comparative politics, political economy, models and methods.

McGill University, Faculty of Graduate and Postdoctoral Studies, Faculty of Arts, Department of Political Science, Montréal, QC H3A 2T5, Canada. Offers MA, PhD.

McMaster University, School of Graduate Studies, Faculty of Social Sciences, Department of Political Science, Hamilton, ON L8S 4M2, Canada. Offers international relations (PhD); political science (MA); public and the global economy (MA); public policy (PhD); public policy and administration (MA). MA program in public policy and administration offered jointly with University of Guelph. *Program availability:* Part-time. *Degree requirements:* For master's, thesis or alternative. *Entrance requirements:* For master's, minimum B+ average. Additional exam requirements/recommendations for international students: Required—TOEFL (minimum score 580 paper-based). *Faculty research:* Organizational theory, internationalization of public policy, water resource policies, political interest intermediation, comparative politics.

Memorial University of Newfoundland, School of Graduate Studies, Department of Political Science, St. John's, NL A1C 5S7, Canada. Offers MA. *Program availability:* Part-time, evening/weekend. *Degree requirements:* For master's, thesis optional. *Entrance requirements:* For master's, minimum 2nd class bachelor's degree. Electronic applications accepted. *Faculty research:* Comparative politics, Canadian government and politics, Newfoundland politics, and the politics of multi-level systems.

Miami University, College of Arts and Science, Department of Political Science, Oxford, OH 45056. Offers MA. *Students:* 8. In 2017, 13 master's awarded. *Expenses:* Tuition, state resident: full-time $13,812; part-time $575 per credit hour. Tuition, nonresident: full-time $30,860; part-time $1286 per credit hour. *Unit head:* Dr. Bryan Marshall, Chair, 513-529-0161, E-mail: marshabw@miamioh.edu. *Application contact:* Dr. Brian Dannoff, Associate Professor and Graduate Studies Director, 513-529-0160, E-mail: danoffbf@miamioh.edu.
Website: http://miamioh.edu/cas/academics/departments/political-science/academics/graduate-studies/

Michigan State University, The Graduate School, College of Social Science, Department of Political Science, East Lansing, MI 48824. Offers political science (MA, PhD); public policy (MPP). *Degree requirements:* For master's, practicum; for doctorate, comprehensive exam, presentation of dissertation. *Entrance requirements:* Additional exam requirements/recommendations for international students: Required—TOEFL. Electronic applications accepted.

Middle Tennessee State University, College of Graduate Studies, College of Liberal Arts, Department of Political Science, Murfreesboro, TN 37132. Offers international affairs (MA). *Program availability:* Part-time, evening/weekend, online learning. *Entrance requirements:* Additional exam requirements/recommendations for international students: Required—TOEFL (minimum score 525 paper-based; 71 iBT) or IELTS (minimum score 6). Electronic applications accepted.

Midwestern State University, Billie Doris McAda Graduate School, Prothro-Yeager College of Humanities and Social Sciences, Department of Political Science, Wichita Falls, TX 76308. Offers MA. *Degree requirements:* For master's, one foreign language, comprehensive exam, thesis optional. *Entrance requirements:* For master's, GRE General Test/GMAT/MAT, bachelor's degree from regionally-accredited institution, minimum GPA of 3.0 on last 60 hours of undergraduate work. Additional exam requirements/recommendations for international students: Required—TOEFL (minimum score 550 paper-based). Electronic applications accepted. *Faculty research:* American politics, political behavior, political research methods, conflict processes, Latin American politics.

Mississippi College, Graduate School, College of Arts and Sciences, School of Humanities and Social Sciences, Department of History, Political Science, Administration of Justice, and Paralegal Studies, Clinton, MS 39058. Offers administration of justice (MSS); history (M Ed, MA, MSS); paralegal studies (Certificate); political science (MSS); social sciences (M Ed, MSS). *Program availability:* Part-time. *Degree requirements:* For master's, one foreign language, comprehensive exam, thesis (for some programs). *Entrance requirements:* For master's, GRE or NTE, minimum GPA of 2.5. Additional exam requirements/recommendations for international students: Recommended—TOEFL, IELTS. Electronic applications accepted.

Mississippi State University, College of Arts and Sciences, Department of Political Science and Public Administration, Mississippi State, MS 39762. Offers political science (MA); public policy and administration (MPPA, PhD). *Accreditation:* NASPAA (one or more programs are accredited). *Program availability:* Evening/weekend, blended/hybrid learning. *Faculty:* 15 full-time (6 women). *Students:* 30 full-time (14 women), 31 part-time (18 women); includes 24 minority (21 Black or African American, non-Hispanic/Latino; 1 American Indian or Alaska Native, non-Hispanic/Latino; 2 Hispanic/Latino), 3 international. Average age 32. 54 applicants, 87% accepted, 33 enrolled. In 2017, 13 master's, 7 doctorates awarded. *Degree requirements:* For master's, thesis optional, comprehensive oral or written exam; for doctorate, thesis/dissertation, comprehensive oral and written exam. *Entrance requirements:* For master's, GRE, minimum GPA of 3.0 on the last two years of undergraduate courses or graduate work; for doctorate, GRE General Test, minimum graduate GPA of 3.35. Additional exam requirements/recommendations for international students: Required—TOEFL (minimum score 600 paper-based; 100 iBT); Recommended—IELTS (minimum score 7.5). *Application deadline:* For fall admission, 8/1 priority date for domestic students, 5/1 for international students; for spring admission, 12/1 priority date for domestic students, 9/1 for international students. Applications are processed on a rolling basis. Application fee: $60 ($80 for international students). Electronic applications accepted. *Expenses:* Tuition, state resident: full-time $8318; part-time $462.12 per credit hour. Tuition, nonresident: full-time $22,358; part-time $1242.12 per credit hour. *Required fees:* $110; $12.24 per credit hour. $6.12 per semester. *Financial support:* In 2017–18, 8 teaching assistantships with full tuition reimbursements (averaging $10,469 per year) were awarded; Federal Work-Study, institutionally sponsored loans, scholarships/grants, and unspecified assistantships also available. Financial award application deadline: 4/1; financial award applicants required to submit FAFSA. *Faculty research:* American politics, international relations, state and local government, comparative government, public administration. *Total annual research expenditures:* $811,000. *Unit head:* Dr. P. Edward French, Professor and Head, 662-325-2711, Fax: 662-325-2716, E-mail: efrench@pspa.msstate.edu. *Application contact:* Nathan Drake, Admissions and Enrollment Assistant, 662-325-3804, E-mail: ndrake@grad.msstate.edu.
Website: http://www.pspa.msstate.edu/

Missouri State University, Graduate College, College of Humanities and Public Affairs, Department of Political Science, Springfield, MO 65897. Offers global studies (MGS); public administration (MPA); public management (Certificate). *Program availability:* Part-time. *Faculty:* 14 full-time (2 women). *Students:* 25 full-time (13 women), 12 part-time (7 women); includes 2 minority (1 Black or African American, non-Hispanic/Latino; 1 Two or more races, non-Hispanic/Latino), 8 international. Average age 28. 24 applicants, 46% accepted, 11 enrolled. In 2017, 20 master's awarded. *Degree requirements:* For master's, variable foreign language requirement, comprehensive exam, thesis or alternative. *Entrance requirements:* For master's, GRE, minimum GPA of 3.0. Additional exam requirements/recommendations for international students: Required—TOEFL (minimum score 550 paper-based; 79 iBT), IELTS (minimum score 6). *Application deadline:* For fall admission, 7/20 priority date for domestic students, 5/1 for international students; for spring admission, 12/20 priority date for domestic students, 9/1 for international students. Applications are processed on a rolling basis. Application fee: $35 ($50 for international students). Electronic applications accepted. *Expenses:* Tuition, state resident: full-time $2915; part-time $2021 per credit hour. Tuition, nonresident: full-time $5354; part-time $3647 per credit hour. *International tuition:* $11,992 full-time. *Required fees:* $173; $173 per credit hour. Tuition and fees vary according to class time, course level, course load, degree level, campus/location and program. *Financial support:* Career-related internships or fieldwork, Federal Work-Study, scholarships/grants, and unspecified assistantships available. Support available to part-time students. Financial award application deadline: 3/31; financial award applicants required to submit FAFSA. *Faculty research:* Public procurement; Missouri politics; international relations of East Asia, law of church and state. *Unit head:* Dr. George Connor, Department Head, 417-836-5630, Fax: 417-836-6655, E-mail: georgeconnor@missouristate.edu. *Application contact:* Stephanie Praschan, Director, Graduate Enrollment Management, 417-836-5330, Fax: 417-836-6200, E-mail: stephaniepraschan@missouristate.edu.
Website: http://polsci.missouristate.edu

Montclair State University, The Graduate School, College of Humanities and Social Sciences, MA Program in Law and Governance, Montclair, NJ 07043-1624. Offers conflict management and peace studies (MA); governance, compliance and regulation (MA); intellectual property (MA); law and governance (MA); legal management (MA). *Program availability:* Part-time, evening/weekend. *Degree requirements:* For master's, thesis or comprehensive exam. *Entrance requirements:* For master's, GRE General Test, minimum cumulative GPA of 2.75 for undergraduate work, 2 letters of recommendation, essay. Additional exam requirements/recommendations for international students: Required—TOEFL (minimum score 83 iBT) or IELTS (minimum score 6.5). Electronic applications accepted.

Murray State University, College of Humanities and Fine Arts, Department of Political Science and Sociology, Murray, KY 42071. Offers MPA. *Program availability:* Part-time, evening/weekend. *Faculty:* 4 full-time (1 woman). *Students:* 28 full-time (18 women), 29 part-time (20 women); includes 18 minority (15 Black or African American, non-Hispanic/Latino; 1 Asian, non-Hispanic/Latino; 1 Hispanic/Latino; 1 Two or more races, non-Hispanic/Latino), 12 international. Average age 33. 102 applicants, 82% accepted, 25 enrolled. In 2017, 9 master's awarded. *Entrance requirements:* For master's, GRE or GMAT, minimum university GPA of 2.75. Additional exam requirements/recommendations for international students: Required—TOEFL (minimum score 527 paper-based; 71 iBT). *Application deadline:* Applications are processed on a rolling basis. Application fee: $40 ($50 for international students). Electronic applications accepted. *Expenses:* Tuition, state resident: full-time $9504. Tuition, nonresident: full-time $26,811. *International tuition:* $14,400 full-time. Tuition and fees vary according to course load, degree level and reciprocity agreements. *Financial support:* Federal Work-Study and unspecified assistantships available. Financial award applicants required to submit FAFSA. *Unit head:* Dr. Choong-Nam Kang, Chair, Department of Political Science and Sociology, 270-809-4213, Fax: 270-809-2688, E-mail: ckang1@murraystate.edu. *Application contact:* Kaitlyn Burzynski, Interim Assistant Director for Graduate Admission and Records, 270-809-5732, Fax: 270-809-3780, E-mail: msu.graduateadmissions@murraystate.edu.
Website: http://www.murraystate.edu/academics/CollegesDepartments/CollegeOfHumanitiesAndFineArts/politicalScienceandSociology/Programs/MastersPublicAdministrat

New Mexico Highlands University, Graduate Studies, College of Arts and Sciences, Department of History, Political Science, and Languages and Culture, Las Vegas, NM 87701. Offers public affairs (MA), including historical and cross-cultural perspectives, history/political science, political and governmental processes. *Degree requirements:* For master's, comprehensive exam, thesis or alternative. *Entrance requirements:* Additional exam requirements/recommendations for international students: Required—TOEFL (minimum score 540 paper-based).

New Mexico State University, College of Arts and Sciences, Department of Government, Las Cruces, NM 88003. Offers government (MA); public administration (MPA). *Accreditation:* NASPAA (one or more programs are accredited). *Program availability:* Part-time. *Faculty:* 8 full-time (3 women), 1 (woman) part-time/adjunct. *Students:* 22 full-time (9 women), 13 part-time (7 women); includes 22 minority (3 Black or African American, non-Hispanic/Latino; 18 Hispanic/Latino; 1 Two or more races, non-Hispanic/Latino), 1 international. Average age 31. 25 applicants, 76% accepted, 14 enrolled. In 2017, 6 master's awarded. *Degree requirements:* For master's, comprehensive exam (for some programs), thesis optional. *Entrance requirements:* For master's, GRE (if GPA less than 3.0), writing sample, 3 letters of recommendation, resume. Additional exam requirements/recommendations for international students: Required—TOEFL (minimum score 550 paper-based; 79 iBT), IELTS (minimum score 6.5). *Application deadline:* For fall admission, 10/1 for domestic and international students; for spring admission, 3/1 for domestic and international students; for summer admission, 3/1 for domestic and international students. Application fee: $40 ($50 for international students). Electronic applications accepted. *Expenses:* Tuition, state resident: full-time $4390. Tuition, nonresident: full-time $15,309. *Required fees:* $853. *Financial support:* In 2017–18, 19 students received support, including 11 teaching assistantships (averaging $12,723 per year); career-related internships or fieldwork, Federal Work-Study, scholarships/grants, health care benefits, and unspecified assistantships also available. Support available to part-time students. Financial award application deadline: 3/1. *Faculty research:* U.S.-Mexico border studies, public administration and policy, international relations, Latin America, American politics and theory, Native American policy. *Total annual research expenditures:* $6,901. *Unit head:* Dr. Neil Harvey, Department Head, 575-646-4935, Fax: 575-646-2052, E-mail: nharvey@nmsu.edu. *Application contact:* Dr. Neil Harvey, Director of Master of Arts in Government Program, 575-646-4935, Fax: 575-646-2052, E-mail: nharvey@nmsu.edu.
Website: http://deptofgov.nmsu.edu

The New School, The New School for Social Research, Department of Historical Studies, New York, NY 10011. Offers historical studies (MA); politics (PhD), including historical studies; sociology (PhD), including historical studies. *Program availability:* Part-time, evening/weekend. *Faculty:* 1 (woman) full-time. *Students:* 8 full-time (3 women), 3 part-time (2 women); includes 2 minority (1 Asian, non-Hispanic/Latino; 1 Hispanic/Latino), 1 international. Average age 28. 19 applicants, 95% accepted, 6 enrolled. In 2017, 3 master's awarded. *Degree requirements:* For master's, thesis. *Entrance requirements:* For master's, GRE, two letters of recommendation, writing sample, essays, transcripts. Additional exam requirements/recommendations for international students: Required—TOEFL (minimum score 100 iBT), IELTS (minimum score 7), PTE (minimum score 68). *Application deadline:* For fall admission, 1/15 priority date for domestic and international students; for spring admission, 10/15 priority date for domestic and international students. Applications are processed on a rolling basis. Application fee: $50. Electronic applications accepted. *Expenses:* $2,180 per credit. *Financial support:* In 2017–18, 8 students received support, including 5 teaching assistantships (averaging $5,520 per year); Federal Work-Study, scholarships/grants, health care benefits, and tuition waivers (full and partial) also available. Support available to part-time students. Financial award application deadline: 2/1; financial award applicants required to submit FAFSA. *Unit head:* Dr. William Milberg, Dean, The New School for Social Research, 212-229-5777, E-mail: milbergw@newschool.edu. *Application contact:* Dana Messinger, Director of Graduate Admission, 212-229-5150 Ext. 2300, E-mail: messingd@newschool.edu.
Website: http://www.newschool.edu/nssr/historical-studies/

The New School, The New School for Social Research, Department of Political Science, New York, NY 10003. Offers politics (M Phil, MA, PhD). *Program availability:* Part-time. *Faculty:* 13 full-time (9 women). *Students:* 88 full-time (40 women), 10 part-time (2 women); includes 11 minority (1 Black or African American, non-Hispanic/Latino; 1 Asian, non-Hispanic/Latino; 5 Hispanic/Latino; 4 Two or more races, non-Hispanic/Latino), 45 international. Average age 33. 107 applicants, 72% accepted, 11 enrolled. In 2017, 12 master's, 6 doctorates awarded. Terminal master's awarded for partial completion of doctoral program. *Degree requirements:* For master's, portfolio of two papers; for doctorate, one foreign language, comprehensive exam, thesis/dissertation. *Entrance requirements:* For master's, GRE, letters of recommendation, writing sample, essays, transcripts; for doctorate, letters of recommendation, writing sample, essays, transcripts. Additional exam requirements/recommendations for international students: Required—TOEFL (minimum score 100 iBT), IELTS (minimum score 7), PTE (minimum score 68). *Application deadline:* For fall admission, 1/5 priority date for domestic and

international students; for spring admission, 10/15 priority date for domestic and international students. Applications are processed on a rolling basis. Application fee: $50. Electronic applications accepted. *Expenses:* $2,180 per credit. *Financial support:* In 2017–18, 67 students received support, including 11 fellowships with full and partial tuition reimbursements available (averaging $19,043 per year), 19 teaching assistantships (averaging $9,486 per year); Federal Work-Study, scholarships/grants, and tuition waivers (full and partial) also available. Support available to part-time students. Financial award application deadline: 2/1; financial award applicants required to submit FAFSA. *Unit head:* Dr. William Milberg, Dean, The New School for Social Research, 212-229-5777, E-mail: milbergw@newschool.edu. *Application contact:* Dana Messinger, Director of Graduate Admission, 212-229-5150 Ext. 2300, E-mail: socialresearchadmit@newschool.edu.
Website: http://www.newschool.edu/nssr/politics/

New York University, Graduate School of Arts and Science, Department of Politics, New York, NY 10012-1019. Offers political campaign management (MA); politics (MA, PhD); JD/MA; MBA/MA. *Program availability:* Part-time. *Students:* Average age 27. 670 applicants, 45% accepted, 80 enrolled. In 2017, 101 master's, 13 doctorates awarded. Terminal master's awarded for partial completion of doctoral program. *Degree requirements:* For master's, one foreign language, thesis or alternative; for doctorate, 2 foreign languages, comprehensive exam, thesis/dissertation. *Entrance requirements:* For master's and doctorate, GRE General Test. Additional exam requirements/recommendations for international students: Required—TOEFL. *Application deadline:* For fall admission, 12/18 priority date for domestic students, 12/18 for international students. Application fee: $100. *Expenses: Tuition:* Full-time $41,352; part-time $19,968 per year. *Required fees:* $2496; $1628 per unit. $814 per term. Tuition and fees vary according to course load and program. *Financial support:* Fellowships, teaching assistantships, career-related internships or fieldwork, Federal Work-Study, and institutionally sponsored loans available. Financial award application deadline: 12/18; financial award applicants required to submit FAFSA. *Faculty research:* Comparative politics, democratic theory and practice, rational choice, political economy, international relations. *Unit head:* Sanford Gordon, Director of Graduate Studies, PhD Program, 212-998-8500, Fax: 212-995-4184, E-mail: politics.phd@nyu.edu. *Application contact:* Nicole Simonelli, Director of Graduate Studies, Master's Program, 212-998-8500, Fax: 212-995-4184, E-mail: politics.masters@nyu.edu.
Website: http://www.nyu.edu/gsas/dept/politics/

Northeastern Illinois University, College of Graduate Studies and Research, College of Arts and Sciences, Program in Political Science, Chicago, IL 60625. Offers MA. *Program availability:* Part-time, evening/weekend. *Degree requirements:* For master's, comprehensive exam, thesis optional. *Entrance requirements:* For master's, minimum GPA of 2.75. Additional exam requirements/recommendations for international students: Required—TOEFL (minimum score 550 paper-based; 79 iBT). *Application deadline:* For fall admission, 4/1 priority date for domestic students; for spring admission, 8/15 for domestic students. Applications are processed on a rolling basis. Application fee: $30. Electronic applications accepted. *Expenses:* Tuition, state resident: full-time $7274; part-time $404.11 per credit hour. Tuition, nonresident: full-time $14,548; part-time $808.23 per credit hour. *Required fees:* $1284. *Financial support:* Applicants required to submit FAFSA. *Faculty research:* Chinese politics, Latin American democratization, Jewish feminism, administration and delegation. *Unit head:* Dr. Jeffrey Hill, Acting Chair, 773-442-5659, E-mail: j-hill@neiu.edu. *Application contact:* Martha Narvaez, Graduate Admission Representative, 773-442-6006, E-mail: m-narvaez@neiu.edu.

Northeastern University, College of Social Sciences and Humanities, Boston, MA 02115. Offers criminology and criminal justice (MSCJ); criminology and justice policy (PhD); economics (MA, PhD); English (MA, PhD); international affairs (MA); law and public policy (PhD); political science (MA, PhD); public administration (MPA); public policy (MPP); security and resilience studies (MS); sociology (MA, PhD); urban and regional policy (MS); urban informatics (MS); world history (MA, PhD). *Program availability:* Online learning. *Faculty:* 242. *Students:* 491. In 2017, 143 master's, 38 doctorates awarded. *Degree requirements:* For doctorate, variable foreign language requirement, comprehensive exam, thesis/dissertation. *Entrance requirements:* For master's and doctorate, GRE. Additional exam requirements/recommendations for international students: Required—TOEFL, IELTS. Application fee: $75. Electronic applications accepted. *Expenses:* Contact institution. *Financial support:* Teaching assistantships, career-related internships or fieldwork, scholarships/grants, health care benefits, tuition waivers (full and partial), and unspecified assistantships available. Support available to part-time students. Financial award applicants required to submit FAFSA. *Unit head:* Dr. Uta Poiger, Dean, 617-373-5173, E-mail: college_of_social_sciences_and_humanities@neu.edu. *Application contact:* 617-373-5990, E-mail: gradcssh@northeastern.edu.
Website: http://www.northeastern.edu/cssh/

Northern Arizona University, College of Social and Behavioral Sciences, Department of Politics and International Affairs, Flagstaff, AZ 86011. Offers political science (MA, PhD, Graduate Certificate); public administration (MPA); public management (Graduate Certificate). *Program availability:* Part-time, 100% online, blended/hybrid learning. *Faculty:* 20 full-time (6 women), 1 (woman) part-time/adjunct. *Students:* 26 full-time (15 women), 18 part-time (10 women); includes 15 minority (1 Black or African American, non-Hispanic/Latino; 6 American Indian or Alaska Native, non-Hispanic/Latino; 2 Asian, non-Hispanic/Latino; 4 Hispanic/Latino; 2 Two or more races, non-Hispanic/Latino), 8 international. Average age 33. 36 applicants, 69% accepted, 23 enrolled. In 2017, 10 master's, 5 doctorates, 1 other advanced degree awarded. *Degree requirements:* For master's, variable foreign language requirement, comprehensive exam (for some programs), thesis (for some programs); for doctorate, variable foreign language requirement, comprehensive exam (for some programs), thesis/dissertation (for some programs); for Graduate Certificate, comprehensive exam (for some programs). *Entrance requirements:* For master's and doctorate, GRE General Test. Additional exam requirements/recommendations for international students: Required—TOEFL (minimum score 93 iBT), IELTS (minimum score 6.5). *Application deadline:* For fall admission, 2/1 for domestic and international students; for spring admission, 10/1 for domestic and international students. Applications are processed on a rolling basis. Application fee: $65. Electronic applications accepted. *Expenses:* Tuition, state resident: full-time $9240; part-time $458 per credit hour. Tuition, nonresident: full-time $21,588; part-time $1199 per credit hour. *Required fees:* $1021; $14 per credit hour. $646 per semester. Tuition and fees vary according to course load, campus/location and program. *Financial support:* In 2017–18, 12 students received support, including 12 teaching assistantships with full and partial tuition reimbursements available (averaging $13,500 per year); institutionally sponsored loans, health care benefits, tuition waivers (full and partial), and unspecified assistantships also available. Financial award application deadline: 2/1; financial award applicants required to submit FAFSA. *Unit head:* Dr. Lori Poloni-Staudinger, Chair, 928-523-6546, Fax: 928-523-6777, E-mail: lori.poloni-staudinger@nau.edu. *Application contact:* Pamela Ruth Bowen, Administrative Associate, 928-523-6544, Fax: 928-523-6777, E-mail: political.science@nau.edu.
Website: http://www.nau.edu/SBS/Politics

Northern Illinois University, Graduate School, College of Liberal Arts and Sciences, Department of Political Science, De Kalb, IL 60115-2854. Offers MA, PhD. *Program availability:* Part-time, evening/weekend. *Faculty:* 24 full-time (5 women), 8 part-time/adjunct (2 women). *Students:* 19 full-time (8 women), 20 part-time (6 women); includes 4 minority (1 Asian, non-Hispanic/Latino; 2 Hispanic/Latino; 1 Two or more races, non-Hispanic/Latino), 17 international. Average age 33. 26 applicants, 65% accepted, 8 enrolled. In 2017, 47 master's, 5 doctorates awarded. Terminal master's awarded for partial completion of doctoral program. *Degree requirements:* For master's, comprehensive exam, thesis optional; for doctorate, variable foreign language requirement, thesis/dissertation, candidacy exam, dissertation defense. *Entrance requirements:* For master's, GRE General Test, minimum GPA of 2.75, 9 hours of course work in political science; for doctorate, GRE General Test, minimum GPA of 2.75 (undergraduate), 3.2 (graduate); undergraduate major in related field. Additional exam requirements/recommendations for international students: Required—TOEFL (minimum score 550 paper-based). *Application deadline:* For fall admission, 3/1 priority date for domestic students, 5/1 for international students; for spring admission, 11/1 for domestic students, 10/1 for international students. Applications are processed on a rolling basis. Application fee: $40. Electronic applications accepted. *Financial support:* In 2017–18, 1 research assistantship with full tuition reimbursement, 21 teaching assistantships with full tuition reimbursements were awarded; fellowships with full tuition reimbursements, career-related internships or fieldwork, Federal Work-Study, scholarships/grants, tuition waivers (full), and unspecified assistantships also available. Support available to part-time students. Financial award applicants required to submit FAFSA. *Faculty research:* Terrorism and dynamics of trade, U.S. foreign policy, political economy of development, biopolitical theory, women and politics. *Unit head:* Dr. Scott Schraufnagel, Chair/Director, Graduate Studies, 815-753-7046, Fax: 815-753-6302, E-mail: sschrauf@niu.edu.
Website: http://polisci.niu.edu/

Northwestern University, The Graduate School, Judd A. and Marjorie Weinberg College of Arts and Sciences, Department of Political Science, Evanston, IL 60208. Offers PhD, JD/PhD. Admissions and degrees offered through The Graduate School. Terminal master's awarded for partial completion of doctoral program. *Degree requirements:* For doctorate, thesis/dissertation, qualifying exams. *Entrance requirements:* For doctorate, GRE General Test, sample of written work. Additional exam requirements/recommendations for international students: Required—TOEFL. *Faculty research:* Formal theory/formal political economy, political economy of development/state-business relations, labor market institutions and welfare policy, public opinion and political behavior, feminist political theory.

The Ohio State University, Graduate School, College of Arts and Sciences, Division of Social and Behavioral Sciences, Department of Political Science, Columbus, OH 43210. Offers PhD. *Faculty:* 32. *Students:* 78 full-time (21 women), 3 part-time (2 women), 20 international. Average age 28. In 2017, 9 doctorates awarded. Terminal master's awarded for partial completion of doctoral program. *Entrance requirements:* For doctorate, GRE General Test. Additional exam requirements/recommendations for international students: Recommended—TOEFL (minimum score 600 paper-based; 100 iBT), IELTS (minimum score 8). *Application deadline:* For fall admission, 12/15 priority date for domestic students, 11/30 priority date for international students. Applications are processed on a rolling basis. Application fee: $60 ($70 for international students). Electronic applications accepted. *Financial support:* Fellowships, research assistantships, teaching assistantships, Federal Work-Study, and institutionally sponsored loans available. Support available to part-time students. *Faculty research:* American, comparative, and international politics; political theory. *Unit head:* Dr. Richard Herrmann, Chair, 614-292-2880, Fax: 614-292-1146, E-mail: herrmann.1@osu.edu. *Application contact:* Graduate and Professional Admissions, 614-292-9444, Fax: 614-292-3895, E-mail: gpadmissions@osu.edu.
Website: http://polisci.osu.edu/

Ohio University, Graduate College, College of Arts and Sciences, Department of Political Science, Athens, OH 45701-2979. Offers MA. *Program availability:* Part-time, evening/weekend. *Degree requirements:* For master's, comprehensive exam, thesis or alternative. *Entrance requirements:* For master's, GRE General Test, minimum GPA of 3.0. Additional exam requirements/recommendations for international students: Required—TOEFL (minimum score 550 paper-based; 80 iBT) or IELTS (minimum score 6.5). Electronic applications accepted. *Faculty research:* International relations, Latin American politics, public policy, economic development, political theory.

Oklahoma State University, College of Arts and Sciences, Department of Political Science, Stillwater, OK 74078. Offers fire and emergency management administration (MS, PhD); political science (MA). *Faculty:* 21 full-time (7 women), 2 part-time/adjunct (0 women). *Students:* 29 full-time (7 women), 45 part-time (6 women); includes 13 minority (2 Black or African American, non-Hispanic/Latino; 2 Asian, non-Hispanic/Latino; 9 Hispanic/Latino), 13 international. Average age 36. 33 applicants, 52% accepted, 15 enrolled. In 2017, 11 master's, 5 doctorates awarded. *Entrance requirements:* For master's and doctorate, GRE. Additional exam requirements/recommendations for international students: Required—TOEFL (minimum score 550 paper-based; 79 iBT). *Application deadline:* For fall admission, 3/1 priority date for international students; for spring admission, 8/1 priority date for international students. Applications are processed on a rolling basis. Application fee: $40 ($75 for international students). Electronic applications accepted. *Expenses:* Tuition, state resident: full-time $4019; part-time $2679.60 per year. Tuition, nonresident: full-time $15,286; part-time $10,190.40 per year. *Required fees:* $2129; $1419 per unit. Tuition and fees vary according to program. *Financial support:* Research assistantships, teaching assistantships, career-related internships or fieldwork, Federal Work-Study, scholarships/grants, health care benefits, tuition waivers (partial), and unspecified assistantships available. Support available to part-time students. Financial award application deadline: 3/1; financial award applicants required to submit FAFSA. *Faculty research:* Fire and emergency management, environmental dispute resolution, voting and elections, women and politics, urban politics. *Unit head:* Dr. Jeanette Mendez, Department Head, 405-744-5607, E-mail: jeanette.mendez@okstate.edu.
Website: http://polsci.okstate.edu

Penn State University Park, Graduate School, College of the Liberal Arts, Department of Political Science, University Park, PA 16802. Offers MA, PhD. *Unit head:* Dr. Susan Welch, Dean, 814-865-7691, Fax: 814-863-2085. *Application contact:* Lori Hawn, Director, Graduate Student Services, 814-865-1795, Fax: 814-863-4627, E-mail: l-gswww@lists.psu.edu.
Website: http://polisci.la.psu.edu/

Pepperdine University, School of Public Policy, Malibu, CA 90263. Offers American politics (MPP); economics (MPP); international relations (MPP); state and local policy (MPP); JD/MPP; MBA/MPP; MDR/MPP. *Students:* Average age 25. 174 applicants, 55% accepted, 29 enrolled. In 2017, 34 master's awarded. *Entrance requirements:* For master's, GRE or GMAT, 2 letters of recommendation, resume, two essays. Additional exam requirements/recommendations for international students: Required—TOEFL. *Application deadline:* For fall admission, 6/15 for domestic students. Applications are processed on a rolling basis. Application fee: $50. Electronic applications accepted. *Expenses:* Contact institution. *Financial support:* Institutionally sponsored loans and scholarships/grants available. Financial award application deadline: 5/1; financial award applicants required to submit FAFSA. *Unit head:* Dr. Pete Peterson, Dean, School of Public Policy, 310-506-7490,

Fax: 310-506-7494, E-mail: pete.n.peterson@pepperdine.edu. *Application contact:* Carson Bruno, Assistant Dean for Admission and Program Relations, 310-506-7493, E-mail: carson.bruno@pepperdine.edu.
Website: http://publicpolicy.pepperdine.edu/

Portland State University, Graduate Studies, College of Urban and Public Affairs, Hatfield School of Government, Division of Political Science, Portland, OR 97207-0751. Offers political science (MA), including American politics, comparative politics, international relations, political theory. *Program availability:* Part-time. *Faculty:* 10 full-time (4 women), 8 part-time/adjunct (2 women). *Students:* 9 full-time (4 women), 11 part-time (3 women); includes 1 minority (Asian, non-Hispanic/Latino), 2 international. Average age 36. 13 applicants, 69% accepted, 8 enrolled. In 2017, 2 master's awarded. *Degree requirements:* For master's, variable foreign language requirement, comprehensive exam, thesis. *Entrance requirements:* For master's, GRE General Test, minimum undergraduate GPA of 3.0 or 3.1 in graduate-level coursework, 2 letters of recommendation, statement of intent. Additional exam requirements/recommendations for international students: Required—TOEFL (minimum score 550 paper-based; 90 iBT). *Application deadline:* For fall admission, 4/1 priority date for domestic students, 3/1 priority date for international students; for spring admission, 11/1 for domestic and international students. Application fee: $65. *Expenses:* Tuition, state resident: full-time $14,436; part-time $401 per credit. Tuition, nonresident: full-time $21,780; part-time $605 per credit. *Required fees:* $1380; $22 per credit. $119 per quarter. One-time fee: $325. Tuition and fees vary according to program. *Financial support:* In 2017–18, 6 students received support, including 8 research assistantships with full and partial tuition reimbursements available (averaging $3,572 per year), 2 teaching assistantships with full and partial tuition reimbursements available (averaging $7,443 per year); career-related internships or fieldwork, Federal Work-Study, and unspecified assistantships also available. Support available to part-time students. Financial award application deadline: 3/1; financial award applicants required to submit FAFSA. *Faculty research:* Congress, presidency, political reform, international environment, hate speech. *Unit head:* Christopher Shortell, Chair, 503-725-5139, Fax: 503-725-8444, E-mail: shortell@pdx.edu.
Website: https://www.pdx.edu/hatfieldschool/political-science

Princeton University, Graduate School, Department of Politics, Princeton, NJ 08544-1019. Offers political philosophy (PhD); politics (PhD). *Degree requirements:* For doctorate, comprehensive exam, thesis/dissertation, teaching experience. *Entrance requirements:* For doctorate, GRE General Test, sample of written work, letters of recommendation. Additional exam requirements/recommendations for international students: Required—TOEFL (minimum score 600 paper-based). Electronic applications accepted. *Faculty research:* American politics, comparative politics, formal and quantitative methods, international relations, public law, political theory.

Purdue University, Graduate School, College of Liberal Arts, Department of Political Science, West Lafayette, IN 47907. Offers MA, PhD. *Program availability:* Part-time, evening/weekend. *Faculty:* 21 full-time (9 women), 1 part-time/adjunct (0 women). *Students:* 32 full-time (12 women), 16 part-time (7 women); includes 4 minority (2 Black or African American, non-Hispanic/Latino; 2 Hispanic/Latino), 14 international. Average age 31. 19 applicants, 63% accepted, 9 enrolled. In 2017, 5 master's, 2 doctorates awarded. Terminal master's awarded for partial completion of doctoral program. *Degree requirements:* For master's, comprehensive exam; for doctorate, comprehensive exam, thesis/dissertation. *Entrance requirements:* For master's and doctorate, GRE General Test (minimum score of 160 verbal, 600 on old scoring), minimum undergraduate GPA of 3.0. Additional exam requirements/recommendations for international students: Required—TOEFL (minimum score 600 paper-based; 90 iBT). *Application deadline:* For fall admission, 12/15 priority date for domestic and international students; for spring admission, 10/15 for domestic and international students. Applications are processed on a rolling basis. Application fee: $60 ($75 for international students). Electronic applications accepted. *Financial support:* Fellowships, research assistantships, teaching assistantships, and career-related internships or fieldwork available. Support available to part-time students. Financial award application deadline: 2/1; financial award applicants required to submit FAFSA. *Faculty research:* International relations, political behavior and institutions, comparative politics, political theory, public policy. *Unit head:* Dr. Rosalee A. Clawson, Head, 765-494-4162, E-mail: clawsonr@purdue.edu. *Application contact:* Graduate School Admissions, 765-494-2600, Fax: 765-494-0136, E-mail: gradinfo@purdue.edu.
Website: http://www.polsci.purdue.edu/

Purdue University Global, School of Legal Studies, Davenport, IA 52807. Offers health care delivery (MS); pathway to paralegal (Postbaccalaureate Certificate); state and local government (MS). *Program availability:* Part-time, evening/weekend, online learning. *Entrance requirements:* Additional exam requirements/recommendations for international students: Required—TOEFL (minimum score 550 paper-based; 80 iBT).

Queen's University at Kingston, School of Graduate Studies, Faculty of Arts and Sciences, Department of Political Studies, Kingston, ON K7L 3N6, Canada. Offers Canadian politics (PhD); comparative politics (PhD); gender and politics (PhD); international relations (PhD); political theory (PhD). *Degree requirements:* For master's, thesis or alternative; for doctorate, one foreign language, thesis/dissertation, qualifying exams. *Entrance requirements:* Additional exam requirements/recommendations for international students: Required—TOEFL (minimum score 600 paper-based). *Faculty research:* Canadian politics, comparative politics, political thought, international politics, women and politics.

Regent University, Graduate School, Robertson School of Government, Virginia Beach, VA 23464. Offers government (MA), including American government, healthcare policy and ethics (MA, MPA), international relations, law and public policy, national security studies, political communication, political theory, religion and politics; national security studies (MA), including cybersecurity, homeland security, international security, Middle East politics; public administration (MPA), including emergency management and homeland security, federal government, general public administration, healthcare policy and ethics (MA, MPA), law, nonprofit administration and faith-based organizations, public leadership and management, servant leadership. *Program availability:* Part-time, evening/weekend, 100% online, blended/hybrid learning. *Faculty:* 8 full-time (1 woman), 20 part-time/adjunct (3 women). *Students:* 39 full-time (23 women), 137 part-time (78 women); includes 83 minority (49 Black or African American, non-Hispanic/Latino; 1 American Indian or Alaska Native, non-Hispanic/Latino; 7 Asian, non-Hispanic/Latino; 15 Hispanic/Latino; 11 Two or more races, non-Hispanic/Latino). Average age 35. 345 applicants, 31% accepted, 57 enrolled. In 2017, 38 master's awarded. *Degree requirements:* For master's, thesis optional, internship. *Entrance requirements:* For master's, GRE General Test or LSAT, personal essay, writing sample, resume, college transcripts. Additional exam requirements/recommendations for international students: Required—TOEFL (minimum score 577 paper-based). *Application deadline:* For fall admission, 5/1 priority date for domestic students; for spring admission, 11/1 priority date for domestic students. Applications are processed on a rolling basis. Application fee: $50. Electronic applications accepted. *Expenses:* $650 per credit; $300 technology fee per semester. *Financial support:* In 2017–18, 116 students received support. Career-related internships or fieldwork, scholarships/grants, and unspecified assistantships available. Support available to part-time students. *Faculty research:* International relations and politics, public administration, leadership

and ethics, Biblical law, Constitutional law and Supreme Court. *Unit head:* Dr. Eric Patterson, Dean, 757-352-4616, Fax: 757-352-4735, E-mail: epatterson@regent.edu. *Application contact:* Heidi Cece, Assistant Vice President of Enrollment Management, 800-373-5504, Fax: 757-352-4381, E-mail: admissions@regent.edu.
Website: https://www.regent.edu/robertson-school-of-government/

Rice University, Graduate Programs, School of Social Sciences, Department of Political Science, Houston, TX 77251-1892. Offers PhD. Terminal master's awarded for partial completion of doctoral program. *Degree requirements:* For doctorate, comprehensive exam, thesis/dissertation, 42 hours of coursework. *Entrance requirements:* For doctorate, GRE General Test. Additional exam requirements/recommendations for international students: Required—TOEFL (minimum score 600 paper-based; 90 iBT). Electronic applications accepted. *Faculty research:* Comparative government in Western Europe and the former Soviet Union, international relations, Congress and public policy in American government, minority politics.

Rutgers University–Newark, Graduate School, Program in Political Science, Newark, NJ 07102. Offers American political system (MA); international relations (MA); JD/MA. *Program availability:* Part-time, evening/weekend. *Degree requirements:* For master's, comprehensive exam, thesis optional. *Entrance requirements:* For master's, GRE, minimum undergraduate B average. Electronic applications accepted. *Faculty research:* Policymaking and policy evaluation in the United States; government and politics in Europe, Middle East, Asia, Africa, and Latin America.

Rutgers University–New Brunswick, Graduate School-New Brunswick, Department of Political Science, Piscataway, NJ 08854-8097. Offers American politics (PhD); comparative politics (PhD); international relations (PhD); political theory (PhD); public law (PhD); United Nations and global policy studies (MA); women and politics (PhD). *Degree requirements:* For doctorate, one foreign language, comprehensive exam, thesis/dissertation. *Entrance requirements:* For master's, bachelor's degree from accredited U.S. college or university or a comparable institution in another country; for doctorate, GRE General Test. Additional exam requirements/recommendations for international students: Required—TOEFL.

St. John's University, St. John's College of Liberal Arts and Sciences, Department of Government and Politics and Division of Library and Information Science, Program in Government and Library and Information Science, Queens, NY 11439. Offers MA/MS. *Program availability:* Part-time, evening/weekend. *Students:* 1 applicant, 100% accepted. *Entrance requirements:* Additional exam requirements/recommendations for international students: Required—TOEFL (minimum score 80 iBT), IELTS (minimum score 6.5). *Application deadline:* For fall admission, 5/1 for domestic students; for spring admission, 11/1 for domestic students. Applications are processed on a rolling basis. Application fee: $70. Electronic applications accepted. *Expenses:* Tuition: Full-time $44,280; part-time $1230 per credit. *Required fees:* $340; $340 per credit. Tuition and fees vary according to course load, degree level and program. *Financial support:* Fellowships, research assistantships, teaching assistantships, scholarships/grants, tuition waivers, and unspecified assistantships available. Support available to part-time students. Financial award application deadline: 2/1; financial award applicants required to submit FAFSA. *Faculty research:* Presidential leadership, morality and politics, U.S. foreign policy, U.S. national security policy, NY state and local government and politics, state building and social policy, public opinion, campaigns and elections, education politics, North African politics, energy and European Union politics. *Unit head:* Dr. Fred Pompeo Cocozzelli, Chair, 718-990-5267, E-mail: cocozzef@stjohns.edu. *Application contact:* Robert Medrano, Director of Graduate Admission, 718-990-1601, Fax: 718-990-5686, E-mail: gradhelp@stjohns.edu.

St. John's University, St. John's College of Liberal Arts and Sciences, Department of Government and Politics, Program in Government and Politics, Queens, NY 11439. Offers government and politics (MA); international law and diplomacy (Adv C); public administration (Adv C); JD/MA. *Program availability:* Part-time, evening/weekend. *Students:* 39 full-time (19 women), 18 part-time (15 women); includes 36 minority (17 Black or African American, non-Hispanic/Latino; 1 American Indian or Alaska Native, non-Hispanic/Latino; 1 Asian, non-Hispanic/Latino; 13 Hispanic/Latino; 4 Two or more races, non-Hispanic/Latino), 1 international. Average age 27. 85 applicants, 78% accepted, 28 enrolled. In 2017, 25 master's awarded. *Degree requirements:* For master's, comprehensive exam, thesis optional. *Entrance requirements:* For master's, letters of recommendation, transcripts, resume, personal statement. Additional exam requirements/recommendations for international students: Required—TOEFL (minimum score 80 iBT), IELTS (minimum score 6.5). *Application deadline:* For fall admission, 5/1 for domestic students; for spring admission, 11/1 for domestic students. Applications are processed on a rolling basis. Application fee: $70. Electronic applications accepted. *Expenses:* Tuition: Full-time $44,280; part-time $1230 per credit. *Required fees:* $340; $340 per credit. Tuition and fees vary according to course load, degree level and program. *Financial support:* Fellowships, research assistantships, teaching assistantships, scholarships/grants, tuition waivers, and unspecified assistantships available. Support available to part-time students. Financial award application deadline: 2/1; financial award applicants required to submit FAFSA. *Faculty research:* Presidential leadership, morality and politics, U.S. foreign policy, U.S. national security policy, NY state and local government and politics, state building and social policy, public opinion, campaigns and elections, education politics, North African politics, energy and European Union politics. *Unit head:* Dr. Fred Pompeo Cocozzelli, Chair, 718-990-5267, E-mail: cocozzef@stjohns.edu. *Application contact:* Robert Medrano, Director of Graduate Admissions, 718-990-1601, Fax: 718-990-5686, E-mail: gradhelp@stjohns.edu.
Website: https://www.stjohns.edu/academics/schools-and-colleges/st-johns-college-liberal-arts-and-sciences/programs-and-majors/government-and-politics-master-a

Saint Louis University, Graduate Programs, College of Arts and Sciences and Graduate Programs, Department of Political Science, St. Louis, MO 63103. Offers MA. *Program availability:* Part-time. *Entrance requirements:* For master's, GRE or LSAT, letters of recommendation, resume, writing sample. Additional exam requirements/recommendations for international students: Required—TOEFL (minimum score 525 paper-based). Electronic applications accepted. *Faculty research:* Part of Asia, Africa, Latin America, and Russia; international political economy; diplomacy and international organization; theories of democracy and justice; American political institutions.

Sam Houston State University, College of Humanities and Social Sciences, Department of Political Science, Huntsville, TX 77341. Offers political science (MA); public administration (MPA). *Program availability:* Part-time, online learning. *Degree requirements:* For master's, comprehensive exam, thesis optional, internship. *Entrance requirements:* For master's, GRE General Test, GMAT, writing sample of scholarly work, letters of recommendation, statement of purpose, resume. Additional exam requirements/recommendations for international students: Required—TOEFL (minimum score 550 paper-based; 79 iBT), IELTS (minimum score 6.5). Electronic applications accepted.

San Diego State University, Graduate and Research Affairs, College of Arts and Letters, Department of Political Science, San Diego, CA 92182. Offers MA. *Program availability:* Part-time. *Degree requirements:* For master's, thesis. *Entrance requirements:* For master's, GRE General Test, minimum GPA of 3.0, 2 letters of reference. Additional exam requirements/recommendations for international students: Required—TOEFL. Electronic applications accepted.

Political Science

San Francisco State University, Division of Graduate Studies, College of Liberal and Creative Arts, Department of Political Science, San Francisco, CA 94132-1722. Offers MA. *Financial support:* Research assistantships and teaching assistantships available. *Unit head:* Nicole Watts, Chair, 415-405-2470, Fax: 415-338-2391, E-mail: nfwatts@sfsu.edu. *Application contact:* Dr. Katherine Gordy, Graduate Coordinator, 415-338-7528, Fax: 415-338-2391, E-mail: kgordy@sfsu.edu. Website: http://politicalscience.sfsu.edu/

Simon Fraser University, Office of Graduate Studies and Postdoctoral Fellows, Faculty of Arts and Social Sciences, Department of Political Science, Burnaby, BC V5A 1S6, Canada. Offers MA, PhD. *Degree requirements:* For master's, thesis or alternative, field exams; for doctorate, one foreign language, comprehensive exam, thesis/dissertation. *Entrance requirements:* For master's, minimum GPA of 3.0 (on scale of 4.33) or 3.33 based on last 60 credits of undergraduate courses; for doctorate, minimum GPA of 3.5 (on scale of 4.33). Additional exam requirements/recommendations for international students: Recommended—TOEFL (minimum score 580 paper-based; 93 iBT), IELTS (minimum score 7), TWE (minimum score 5). Electronic applications accepted. *Faculty research:* Political theory and methodology, Canadian politics, comparative politics, international relations, urban politics, public policy, and public administration.

Sonoma State University, School of Social Sciences, Department of Political Science, Rohnert Park, CA 94928. Offers public administration (MPA). *Program availability:* Part-time, evening/weekend. *Entrance requirements:* For master's, GRE General Test, minimum GPA of 3.0. Additional exam requirements/recommendations for international students: Required—TOEFL (minimum score 500 paper-based). *Application deadline:* For fall admission, 11/30 for domestic students; for spring admission, 8/31 for domestic students. Application fee: $55. *Financial support:* Research assistantships, teaching assistantships, career-related internships or fieldwork, and Federal Work-Study available. Support available to part-time students. Financial award application deadline: 3/2; financial award applicants required to submit FAFSA. *Unit head:* David McCuan, Department Chair, 707-664-2179, E-mail: mccuan@sonoma.edu. *Application contact:* Emily Ray, Graduate Program Coordinator, 707-664-2731, Fax: 707-664-3920, E-mail: emily.ray@sonoma.edu. Website: http://www.sonoma.edu/polisci/

Southern Connecticut State University, School of Graduate Studies, School of Arts and Sciences, Department of Political Science, New Haven, CT 06515-1355. Offers MS. *Program availability:* Part-time, evening/weekend. *Degree requirements:* For master's, thesis or alternative. *Entrance requirements:* For master's, interview. Electronic applications accepted.

Southern Illinois University Carbondale, Graduate School, College of Liberal Arts, Department of Political Science, Program in Political Science, Carbondale, IL 62901-4701. Offers MA, PhD, JD/PhD. *Program availability:* Part-time. *Degree requirements:* For doctorate, thesis/dissertation. *Entrance requirements:* For master's, GRE General Test, minimum GPA of 2.7; for doctorate, GRE General Test, minimum GPA of 3.5. Additional exam requirements/recommendations for international students: Required—TOEFL. *Faculty research:* Public law, international relations, comparative government, American government.

Southern New Hampshire University, School of Arts and Sciences, Manchester, NH 03106-1045. Offers clinical mental health counseling (MS); creative writing (MA); criminal justice (MS); cyber security (MS); English (MA); fiction and nonfiction (MFA); history (MA); political science (MS); psychology (MS). *Program availability:* Part-time, evening/weekend. *Degree requirements:* For master's, one foreign language, thesis. *Entrance requirements:* For master's, minimum GPA of 2.75 (for MS in teaching English as a foreign language), 3.0 (for MFA). Additional exam requirements/recommendations for international students: Required—TOEFL (minimum score 550 paper-based; 79 iBT), IELTS (minimum score 6.5), TWE (minimum score 5). *Application deadline:* For fall admission, 7/1 priority date for domestic students; for winter admission, 11/1 priority date for domestic students; for spring admission, 6/1 priority date for domestic students. Applications are processed on a rolling basis. Application fee: $40. Electronic applications accepted. *Expenses:* Contact institution. *Financial support:* Research assistantships, career-related internships or fieldwork, and scholarships/grants available. Financial award applicants required to submit FAFSA. *Faculty research:* Action research, state of the art practice in behavioral health services, wraparound approaches to working with youth, learning styles. *Unit head:* Steven K. Johnson, Dean, 603-629-4626. *Application contact:* Office of Graduate Admission, 888-327-SNHU, Fax: 603-644-3144, E-mail: enroll@snhu.edu.

Southern University and Agricultural and Mechanical College, Graduate School, Nelson Mandela School of Public Policy and Urban Affairs, Department of Political Science and Geography, Baton Rouge, LA 70813. Offers social sciences (MA). *Degree requirements:* For master's, thesis. *Entrance requirements:* For master's, GMAT or GRE General Test, minimum GPA of 3.0. Additional exam requirements/recommendations for international students: Required—TOEFL. *Faculty research:* Redistricting, comparative studies, environmental politics, political geography, mayoral elections.

Stanford University, School of Humanities and Sciences, Department of Political Science, Stanford, CA 94305-2004. Offers MA, PhD. Terminal master's awarded for partial completion of doctoral program. *Degree requirements:* For doctorate, one foreign language, thesis/dissertation, oral exam. *Entrance requirements:* For master's and doctorate, GRE General Test. Additional exam requirements/recommendations for international students: Required—TOEFL. Electronic applications accepted. *Expenses:* Tuition: Full-time $48,987; part-time $10,620 per quarter. One-time fee: $400. Tuition and fees vary according to program.

Stony Brook University, State University of New York, Graduate School, College of Arts and Sciences, Department of Political Science, Stony Brook, NY 11794. Offers political science (MA, PhD); public policy (MAPP); public policy and urban development (MA). *Program availability:* Evening/weekend. *Faculty:* 19 full-time (6 women), 9 part-time/adjunct (3 women). *Students:* 59 full-time (27 women), 19 part-time (6 women); includes 12 minority (4 Black or African American, non-Hispanic/Latino; 5 Asian, non-Hispanic/Latino; 3 Hispanic/Latino), 17 international. Average age 28. 96 applicants, 66% accepted, 37 enrolled. In 2017, 45 master's, 3 doctorates awarded. *Degree requirements:* For doctorate, thesis/dissertation. *Entrance requirements:* For master's and doctorate, GRE General Test. Additional exam requirements/recommendations for international students: Required—TOEFL (minimum score 90 iBT). *Application deadline:* For fall admission, 1/15 for domestic students; for spring admission, 10/1 for domestic students. Application fee: $100. Electronic applications accepted. *Expenses:* Contact institution. *Financial support:* In 2017–18, 11 teaching assistantships were awarded; fellowships and research assistantships also available. *Faculty research:* Public opinion, political methodology, political science, political parties, political behavior. Total annual research expenditures: $22,173. *Unit head:* Dr. Matthew Lebo, Chair, 631-632-7554, Fax: 631-632-4116, E-mail: matthew.lebo@stonybrook.edu. *Application contact:* Carri Ann Horner, Coordinator, 631-632-7667, Fax: 631-632-4116, E-mail: carri.horner@stonybrook.edu. Website: http://www.sunysb.edu/polsci/

Suffolk University, College of Arts and Sciences, Department of Government, Boston, MA 02108-2770. Offers international relations (MSPS); political science (MSPS); professional politics (MSPS, CAGS); MPA/MSPS. *Program availability:* Part-time, evening/weekend. *Faculty:* 4 full-time (2 women), 2 part-time/adjunct (0 women). *Students:* 7 full-time (3 women), 7 part-time (5 women); includes 5 minority (3 Black or African American, non-Hispanic/Latino; 2 Asian, non-Hispanic/Latino), 1 international. Average age 26. 23 applicants, 74% accepted, 2 enrolled. In 2017, 5 master's awarded. *Degree requirements:* For master's, thesis optional. *Entrance requirements:* For master's, GRE General Test or MAT, 2 letters of recommendation, resume. Additional exam requirements/recommendations for international students: Required—TOEFL (minimum score 550 paper-based; 80 iBT). *Application deadline:* For fall admission, 3/15 priority date for domestic and international students; for spring admission, 10/15 priority date for domestic and international students. Applications are processed on a rolling basis. Application fee: $50. Electronic applications accepted. *Expenses:* $29,520 per year full-time tuition; $1,230 per credit part-time. *Financial support:* In 2017–18, 10 students received support, including 1 fellowship (averaging $6,200 per year); career-related internships or fieldwork, Federal Work-Study, and institutionally sponsored loans also available. Support available to part-time students. Financial award application deadline: 4/1; financial award applicants required to submit FAFSA. *Faculty research:* Political marketing, social movements and political parties, election administration, urban resilience, the regulatory state. *Unit head:* Rachel Cobb, Department Chair, 617-305-6380, E-mail: rcobb@suffolk.edu. *Application contact:* Mara Marzocchi, Associate Director of Graduate Admissions, 617-573-8302, Fax: 617-305-1733, E-mail: grad.admission@suffolk.edu. Website: http://www.suffolk.edu/government

Suffolk University, Sawyer Business School, Department of Public Administration, Boston, MA 02108-2770. Offers community health (MPA); information systems, performance management, and big data analytics (MPA); nonprofit management (MPA); state and local government (MPA); JD/MPA; MPA/MS; MPA/MSCJ; MPA/MSMHC; MPA/MSPS. *Accreditation:* NASPAA (one or more programs are accredited). *Program availability:* Part-time, evening/weekend. *Faculty:* 6 full-time (3 women), 8 part-time/adjunct (6 women). *Students:* 25 full-time (12 women), 90 part-time (56 women); includes 43 minority (20 Black or African American, non-Hispanic/Latino; 7 Asian, non-Hispanic/Latino; 14 Hispanic/Latino; 2 Two or more races, non-Hispanic/Latino), 2 international. Average age 34. 134 applicants, 38% accepted, 5 enrolled. In 2017, 44 master's awarded. *Entrance requirements:* Additional exam requirements/recommendations for international students: Required—TOEFL (minimum score 550 paper-based; 80 iBT). *Application deadline:* For fall admission, 3/15 priority date for domestic and international students; for spring admission, 10/15 priority date for domestic and international students. Applications are processed on a rolling basis. Application fee: $50. Electronic applications accepted. *Expenses:* $35,130 per year full-time tuition; $1,171 per credit part-time. *Financial support:* In 2017–18, 76 students received support, including 2 fellowships (averaging $4,650 per year); career-related internships or fieldwork, Federal Work-Study, institutionally sponsored loans, and scholarships/grants also available. Support available to part-time students. Financial award application deadline: 4/1; financial award applicants required to submit FAFSA. *Faculty research:* Local government, health care, federal policy, mental health, HIV/AIDS. *Unit head:* Brenda Bond, Director/Department Chair, 617-305-1768, E-mail: bbond@suffolk.edu. *Application contact:* Mara Marzocchi, Associate Director of Graduate Admissions, 617-573-8302, Fax: 617-305-1733, E-mail: grad.admission@suffolk.edu. Website: http://www.suffolk.edu/mpa

Sul Ross State University, College of Arts and Sciences, Department of Behavioral and Social Sciences, Program in Political Science, Alpine, TX 79832. Offers MA. *Program availability:* Part-time, evening/weekend. *Degree requirements:* For master's, thesis optional. *Entrance requirements:* For master's, GRE General Test, minimum undergraduate GPA of 2.5 in last 60 hours. *Faculty research:* Local government, state government, borderland studies, British studies.

Syracuse University, Maxwell School of Citizenship and Public Affairs, Programs in Political Science, Syracuse, NY 13244. Offers MA, PhD, JD/MA, JD/PhD, MAIR/PhD. *Students:* Average age 31. *Degree requirements:* For doctorate, comprehensive exam, thesis/dissertation. *Entrance requirements:* For master's and doctorate, GRE General Test, three letters of recommendation, personal statement, official transcripts, resume. Additional exam requirements/recommendations for international students: Required—TOEFL (minimum score 100 iBT). *Application deadline:* For fall admission, 1/15 priority date for domestic and international students. Application fee: $75. Electronic applications accepted. *Financial support:* Fellowships with full tuition reimbursements, research assistantships, and teaching assistantships available. Financial award application deadline: 1/1. *Faculty research:* Comparative politics, political theory and methods, international relations, public administration and policy. *Unit head:* Dr. Brian Taylor, Department Chair, 315-443-3713, E-mail: bdtaylor@maxwell.syr.edu. *Application contact:* Candy Brooks, Recruiting Contact, 315-443-2238, E-mail: cbrooks01@syr.edu. Website: http://www.maxwell.syr.edu/psc/

Syracuse University, School of Information Studies, CAS Program in E-Government Management and Leadership, Syracuse, NY 13244. Offers CAS. *Program availability:* Part-time. *Entrance requirements:* For degree, resume, personal statement, official transcripts, three letters of recommendation. Additional exam requirements/recommendations for international students: Required—TOEFL (minimum score 100 iBT). *Application deadline:* For fall admission, 2/1 priority date for domestic students; for spring admission, 8/15 priority date for domestic and international students. Applications are processed on a rolling basis. Application fee: $75. Electronic applications accepted. *Faculty research:* Information strategy and management in the public sector, enterprise technologies, policy analysis, networked governance. *Unit head:* Carsten Osterlund, Program Director, 315-443-8773, E-mail: costerlu@syr.edu. *Application contact:* Margaret Lane, Assistant Director, Executive Education, 315-443-8708, E-mail: melane02@maxwell.syr.edu. Website: https://ischool.syr.edu/academics/graduate/cas/cas-e-government-management-and-leadership/

Tarleton State University, College of Graduate Studies, College of Liberal and Fine Arts, Department of Social Sciences, Stephenville, TX 76402. Offers history (MA). *Program availability:* Part-time, evening/weekend. *Faculty:* 5 full-time (4 women), 1 part-time/adjunct (0 women). *Students:* 2 full-time (1 woman), 10 part-time (7 women); includes 1 minority (Hispanic/Latino). Average age 34. 7 applicants, 71% accepted, 2 enrolled. In 2017, 1 master's awarded. *Degree requirements:* For master's, comprehensive exam, thesis optional. *Entrance requirements:* For master's, GRE General Test, minimum GPA of 3.0. Additional exam requirements/recommendations for international students: Required—TOEFL (minimum score 550 paper-based; 80 iBT), IELTS (minimum score 6). *Application deadline:* For fall admission, 8/15 priority date for domestic students; for spring admission, 1/7 for domestic students. Applications are processed on a rolling basis. Application fee: $45 ($145 for international students). Electronic applications accepted. *Expenses:* Contact institution. *Financial support:* Research assistantships, teaching assistantships, career-related internships or fieldwork, and Federal Work-Study available. Support available to part-time students. Financial award application deadline: 5/1; financial award applicants required to submit

FAFSA. *Unit head:* Dr. Eric Morrow, Department Head, 254-968-9626, E-mail: morrow@tarleton.edu. *Application contact:* Information Contact, 254-968-9104, Fax: 254-968-9670, E-mail: gradoffice@tarleton.edu.

Teachers College, Columbia University, Department of Education Policy and Social Analysis, New York, NY 10027-6696. Offers economics and education (Ed M, MA, PhD); education policy (Ed M, MA, Ed D, PhD); politics and education (Ed M, MA, Ed D, PhD); sociology and education (Ed M, MA, Ed D, PhD). *Students:* 144 full-time (109 women), 107 part-time (85 women); includes 100 minority (43 Black or African American, non-Hispanic/Latino; 17 Asian, non-Hispanic/Latino; 33 Hispanic/Latino; 7 Two or more races, non-Hispanic/Latino), 69 international. Average age 29. 524 applicants, 53% accepted, 104 enrolled. *Unit head:* Dr. Aaron Pallas, Chair, E-mail: amp155@tc.columbia.edu. *Application contact:* David Estrella, Director of Admissions, 212-678-3305, E-mail: estrella@tc.columbia.edu.
Website: http://www.tc.columbia.edu/education-policy-and-social-analysis/

Temple University, College of Liberal Arts, Department of Political Science, Philadelphia, PA 19122-6096. Offers MA, PhD. *Program availability:* Part-time. *Faculty:* 21 full-time (8 women), 3 part-time/adjunct (0 women). *Students:* 63 full-time (31 women), 10 part-time (8 women); includes 17 minority (5 Black or African American, non-Hispanic/Latino; 3 Asian, non-Hispanic/Latino; 7 Hispanic/Latino; 2 Two or more races, non-Hispanic/Latino), 4 international. 64 applicants, 67% accepted, 23 enrolled. In 2017, 6 master's, 5 doctorates awarded. Terminal master's awarded for partial completion of doctoral program. *Degree requirements:* For master's, comprehensive exam; for doctorate, thesis/dissertation, preliminary and oral exams. *Entrance requirements:* For master's and doctorate, GRE General Test, minimum GPA of 3.0, 3 letters of recommendation. Additional exam requirements/recommendations for international students: Required—TOEFL (minimum score 600 paper-based; 100 iBT). *Application deadline:* For fall admission, 12/1 for domestic students, 12/15 for international students; for spring admission, 10/15 for domestic students, 8/1 for international students. Applications are processed on a rolling basis. Application fee: $60. Electronic applications accepted. *Expenses:* Tuition, state resident: full-time $16,164; part-time $898 per credit hour. Tuition, nonresident: full-time $22,158; part-time $1231 per credit hour. *Required fees:* $890; $445 per semester. Full-time tuition and fees vary according to course load, degree level, campus/location and program. *Financial support:* Fellowships, research assistantships, teaching assistantships with tuition reimbursements, career-related internships or fieldwork, Federal Work-Study, institutionally sponsored loans, scholarships/grants, and tuition waivers (partial) available. Financial award application deadline: 1/15; financial award applicants required to submit FAFSA. *Faculty research:* American politics, international relations, comparative politics, political theory, public policy. *Unit head:* Ryan Vander Wielen, Graduate Chair, 215-204-1469, Fax: 215-204-3770, E-mail: rwielen@temple.edu. *Application contact:* Tanya Taylor, Coordinator, 215-204-1469, Fax: 215-204-3770, E-mail: ttaylo01@temple.edu.
Website: http://www.cla.temple.edu/politicalscience/

Texas A&M International University, Office of Graduate Studies and Research, College of Arts and Sciences, Department of Humanities, Laredo, TX 78041. Offers English (MA); Hispanic studies (PhD); history and political thought (MA); language, literature and translation (MA). *Degree requirements:* For master's, comprehensive exam (for some programs), thesis (for some programs). *Entrance requirements:* For master's, GRE General Test. Additional exam requirements/recommendations for international students: Required—TOEFL (minimum score 550 paper-based; 79 iBT).

Texas A&M International University, Office of Graduate Studies and Research, College of Arts and Sciences, Department of Public Affairs and Social Research, Laredo, TX 78041. Offers criminal justice (MS); history and political thought (MA); political science (MA); public administration (MPA). *Degree requirements:* For master's, comprehensive exam (for some programs), thesis (for some programs). *Entrance requirements:* For master's, GRE General Test. Additional exam requirements/recommendations for international students: Required—TOEFL (minimum score 550 paper-based; 79 iBT).

Texas A&M University, College of Liberal Arts, Department of Political Science, College Station, TX 77843. Offers MA, PhD. *Faculty:* 28. *Students:* 48 full-time (20 women), 1 (woman) part-time; includes 4 minority (all Hispanic/Latino), 23 international. Average age 29. 55 applicants, 56% accepted, 12 enrolled. In 2017, 3 master's, 7 doctorates awarded. *Degree requirements:* For doctorate, comprehensive exam, thesis/dissertation. *Entrance requirements:* For doctorate, GRE General Test, minimum GPA of 3.4. Additional exam requirements/recommendations for international students: Required—TOEFL (minimum score 550 paper-based; 80 iBT), IELTS (minimum score 6), PTE (minimum score 53). *Application deadline:* For fall admission, 12/22 for domestic and international students. Application fee: $50 ($90 for international students). Electronic applications accepted. *Expenses:* Contact institution. *Financial support:* In 2017–18, 48 students received support, including 1 fellowship with tuition reimbursement available (averaging $27,000 per year), 39 research assistantships with tuition reimbursements available (averaging $11,703 per year), 22 teaching assistantships with tuition reimbursements available (averaging $8,852 per year); career-related internships or fieldwork, institutionally sponsored loans, scholarships/grants, traineeships, health care benefits, tuition waivers (full and partial), unspecified assistantships, and assistant lecturer positions also available. Support available to part-time students. Financial award application deadline: 3/15; financial award applicants required to submit FAFSA. *Faculty research:* American politics, international relations, comparative politics, political theory, public policy. *Unit head:* Dr. William Clark, Department Head, 979-845-2827, E-mail: wrclark@tamu.edu. *Application contact:* Dr. Alex C. Pacek, Director of Graduate Studies, 979-845-3229, Fax: 979-847-8924, E-mail: a-pacek@tamu.edu.
Website: http://pols.tamu.edu/

Texas A&M University–Central Texas, Graduate Studies and Research, Killeen, TX 76549. Offers accounting (MS); business administration (MBA); clinical mental health counseling (MS); criminal justice (MCJ); curriculum and instruction (M Ed); educational administration (M Ed); educational psychology - experimental psychology (MS); history (MA); human resource management (MS); information systems (MS); liberal studies (MS); management and leadership (MS); marriage and family therapy (MS); mathematics (MS); political science (MA); school counseling (M Ed); school psychology (Ed S).

Texas A&M University–Commerce, College of Humanities, Social Sciences and Arts, Commerce, TX 75429. Offers applied criminology (MS); applied linguistics (MA, MS); art (MA, MFA); computational linguistics (Graduate Certificate); creative writing (Graduate Certificate); criminal justice management (Graduate Certificate); criminal justice studies (Graduate Certificate); English (MA, MS, PhD); film studies (Graduate Certificate); history (MA, MS); history of Christianity (Graduate Certificate); Holocaust studies (Graduate Certificate); homeland security (Graduate Certificate); music education (MM); music performance (MM); political science (MA, MS); public history (Graduate Certificate); sociology (MS); Spanish (MA); studies in children's and adolescent literature and culture (Graduate Certificate); teaching English to speakers of other languages (Graduate Certificate); theater (MA, MS); world history (Graduate Certificate). *Program availability:* Part-time. *Faculty:* 56 full-time (26 women), 10 part-time/adjunct (5 women). *Students:* 133 full-time (85 women), 439 part-time (311 women); includes 204 minority (79 Black or African American, non-Hispanic/Latino; 4 American Indian or Alaska Native, non-Hispanic/Latino; 9 Asian, non-Hispanic/Latino; 98 Hispanic/Latino; 14 Two or more races, non-Hispanic/Latino), 26 international. Average age 36. 261 applicants, 50% accepted, 113 enrolled. In 2017, 105 master's, 5 doctorates awarded. *Degree requirements:* For master's, one foreign language, comprehensive exam, thesis (for some programs); for doctorate, one foreign language, comprehensive exam, thesis/dissertation, departmental qualifying exam. *Entrance requirements:* For master's and doctorate, GRE General Test. Additional exam requirements/recommendations for international students: Required—TOEFL (minimum score 550 paper-based; 79 iBT), IELTS (minimum score 6). *Application deadline:* Applications are processed on a rolling basis. Application fee: $50. Electronic applications accepted. *Expenses:* Contact institution. *Financial support:* In 2017–18, 43 students received support, including 9 research assistantships with partial tuition reimbursements available (averaging $9,000 per year), 68 teaching assistantships with partial tuition reimbursements available (averaging $9,000 per year); Federal Work-Study, institutionally sponsored loans, scholarships/grants, health care benefits, and unspecified assistantships also available. Financial award application deadline: 5/1; financial award applicants required to submit FAFSA. *Unit head:* Dr. William F. Kuracina, Interim Dean, 903-886-5166, Fax: 903-886-5774, E-mail: william.kuracina@tamuc.edu. *Application contact:* Vicky Turner, Doctoral Degree and Special Programs Coordinator, 903-886-5167, E-mail: vicky.turner@tamuc.edu.
Website: http://www.tamuc.edu/academics/graduateSchool/programs/humanitiesSocialScienceArts/default.aspx

Texas State University, The Graduate College, College of Liberal Arts, Program in Political Science, San Marcos, TX 78666. Offers MA. *Program availability:* Part-time, evening/weekend. *Faculty:* 19 full-time (4 women), 1 (woman) part-time/adjunct. *Students:* 12 full-time (5 women), 17 part-time (8 women); includes 11 minority (2 Black or African American, non-Hispanic/Latino; 8 Hispanic/Latino; 1 Two or more races, non-Hispanic/Latino). Average age 30. 35 applicants, 63% accepted, 10 enrolled. In 2017, 7 master's awarded. *Degree requirements:* For master's, comprehensive exam, thesis optional. *Entrance requirements:* For master's, baccalaureate degree in political science from regionally-accredited university; minimum GPA of 3.0 on last 60 undergraduate course work; at least 9 hours in upper-level political science or related field; resume; statement of purpose; 3 letters of recommendation; writing sample from political science/humanities courses. Additional exam requirements/recommendations for international students: Required—TOEFL (minimum score 550 paper-based; 78 iBT), IELTS (minimum score 6.5). *Application deadline:* For fall admission, 2/15 priority date for domestic and international students; for spring admission, 10/15 for domestic students, 10/1 for international students; for summer admission, 4/15 for domestic students, 3/15 for international students. Applications are processed on a rolling basis. Application fee: $40 ($90 for international students). Electronic applications accepted. *Expenses:* Tuition, state resident: full-time $7868; part-time $3934 per semester. Tuition, nonresident: full-time $17,828; part-time $8914 per semester. *Required fees:* $2092; $1435 per semester. Tuition and fees vary according to course load. *Financial support:* In 2017–18, 16 students received support, including 10 teaching assistantships (averaging $12,355 per year); research assistantships, career-related internships or fieldwork, Federal Work-Study, institutionally sponsored loans, scholarships/grants, health care benefits, and unspecified assistantships also available. Support available to part-time students. Financial award application deadline: 3/1; financial award applicants required to submit FAFSA. *Unit head:* Dr. Cecilia Castillio, Graduate Adviser, 512-245-2143, Fax: 512-345-7815, E-mail: cr09@txstate.edu. *Application contact:* Dr. Andrea Golato, Dean of Graduate School, 512-245-2581, Fax: 512-245-8365, E-mail: gradcollege@txstate.edu.
Website: http://ma.polisci.txstate.edu/

Texas Tech University, Graduate School, College of Arts and Sciences, Department of Political Science, Lubbock, TX 79409. Offers political science (MA, PhD); public administration (MPA); JD/MPA. *Accreditation:* NASPAA (one or more programs are accredited). *Program availability:* 100% online, blended/hybrid learning. *Faculty:* 33 full-time (7 women). *Students:* 50 full-time (22 women), 25 part-time (10 women); includes 15 minority (4 Black or African American, non-Hispanic/Latino; 2 Asian, non-Hispanic/Latino; 8 Hispanic/Latino; 1 Two or more races, non-Hispanic/Latino), 18 international. Average age 32. 58 applicants, 62% accepted, 17 enrolled. In 2017, 20 master's, 2 doctorates awarded. *Degree requirements:* For master's, thesis or alternative; for doctorate, thesis/dissertation. *Entrance requirements:* For master's and doctorate, GRE General Test, 3 letters of reference. Additional exam requirements/recommendations for international students: Required—TOEFL (minimum score 550 paper-based; 79 iBT). *Application deadline:* For fall admission, 6/1 priority date for domestic students, 1/15 priority date for international students; for spring admission, 9/1 priority date for domestic students, 6/15 priority date for international students. Applications are processed on a rolling basis. Application fee: $60. Electronic applications accepted. *Expenses:* Contact institution. *Financial support:* In 2017–18, 48 students received support, including 36 fellowships (averaging $2,419 per year), 42 teaching assistantships (averaging $11,039 per year); research assistantships, scholarships/grants, tuition waivers, and grader positions also available. Financial award application deadline: 4/15; financial award applicants required to submit FAFSA. *Faculty research:* State politics, American institutions and behavior, Asian politics, international and comparative political relations and economics, public administration and organizations. *Total annual research expenditures:* $76,298. *Unit head:* Dr. Timothy Nokken, Department Chairperson, 806-834-2988, Fax: 806-742-0850, E-mail: timothy.nokken@ttu.edu. *Application contact:* Dr. Toby Rider, Graduate Director, 806-834-8640, Fax: 806-742-0850, E-mail: toby.rider@ttu.edu.
Website: http://www.depts.ttu.edu/politicalscience/

Texas Woman's University, Graduate School, College of Arts and Sciences, Department of History and Government, Denton, TX 76204. Offers government (MA); history (MA). *Program availability:* Part-time, evening/weekend. *Faculty:* 8 full-time (4 women), 2 part-time/adjunct (0 women). *Students:* 4 full-time (0 women), 24 part-time (20 women); includes 9 minority (3 Black or African American, non-Hispanic/Latino; 2 Asian, non-Hispanic/Latino; 4 Hispanic/Latino), 2 international. Average age 33. 9 applicants, 67% accepted, 5 enrolled. In 2017, 4 master's awarded. *Degree requirements:* For master's, comprehensive exam, thesis (for some programs), professional paper or thesis. *Entrance requirements:* For master's, minimum GPA of 3.25, written statement of purpose, 2 letters of recommendation. Additional exam requirements/recommendations for international students: Required—TOEFL (minimum score 550 paper-based; 79 iBT); Recommended—IELTS (minimum score 6.5), TSE (minimum score 53). *Application deadline:* For fall admission, 3/1 priority date for domestic and international students; for spring admission, 11/1 priority date for domestic students, 7/1 priority date for international students. Applications are processed on a rolling basis. Application fee: $50 ($75 for international students). Electronic applications accepted. *Expenses:* $7,520 per year full-time in-state; $16,820 per year full-time out-of-state. *Financial support:* In 2017–18, 12 students received support, including 1 research assistantship (averaging $23,270 per year); teaching assistantships, career-related internships or fieldwork, Federal Work-Study, institutionally sponsored loans, scholarships/grants, traineeships, health care benefits, and unspecified assistantships

also available. Support available to part-time students. Financial award application deadline: 3/1; financial award applicants required to submit FAFSA. *Faculty research:* U.S. history politics and law, global history politics and law, Latin American and Caribbean history; legal studies. *Total annual research expenditures:* $219,734. *Unit head:* Dr. Jonathan Olsen, Chair, 940-898-2133, Fax: 940-898-2130, E-mail: historygov@twu.edu. *Application contact:* Korie Hawkins, Associate Director of Admissions, Graduate Recruitment, 940-898-3188, Fax: 940-898-3081, E-mail: admissions@twu.edu.
Website: http://www.twu.edu/history-government/

Tulane University, School of Liberal Arts, Department of Political Science, New Orleans, LA 70118-5669. Offers PhD. *Degree requirements:* For doctorate, 2 foreign languages, thesis/dissertation. *Entrance requirements:* For doctorate, GRE General Test. Additional exam requirements/recommendations for international students: Required—TOEFL. Electronic applications accepted. *Expenses: Tuition:* Full-time $50,920; part-time $2829 per credit hour. *Required fees:* $2040; $44.50 per credit hour. $580 per term. Tuition and fees vary according to course load, degree level and program.

Universidad Nacional Pedro Henriquez Urena, Graduate School, Santo Domingo, Dominican Republic. Offers agricultural diversity (MS), including horticultural/fruit production, tropical animal production; conservation of monuments and cultural assets (M Arch); ecology and environment (MS); environmental engineering (MEE); international relations (MA); natural resource management (MS); political science (MA); project optimization (MPM); project feasibility (MPM); project management (MPM); sanitation engineering (ME); science for teachers (MS); tropical Caribbean architecture (M Arch).

Université de Montréal, Faculty of Arts and Sciences, Department of Political Science, Montréal, QC H3C 3J7, Canada. Offers M Sc, PhD. *Degree requirements:* For master's, thesis; for doctorate, thesis/dissertation, general exam. *Entrance requirements:* For master's, minimum GPA of 2.8; for doctorate, master's degree, minimum GPA of 3.0. Electronic applications accepted.

Université du Québec à Montréal, Graduate Programs, Program in Political Science, Montréal, QC H3C 3P8, Canada. Offers MA, PhD. *Program availability:* Part-time. *Degree requirements:* For master's, thesis; for doctorate, thesis/dissertation. *Entrance requirements:* For master's, appropriate bachelor's degree or equivalent, proficiency in French; for doctorate, appropriate master's degree or equivalent, proficiency in French.

Université Laval, Faculty of Social Sciences, Department of Political Science, Program in Policy Analysis, Québec, QC G1K 7P4, Canada. Offers MA. *Degree requirements:* For master's, thesis (for some programs). *Entrance requirements:* For master's, knowledge of French, comprehension of written English. Electronic applications accepted.

Université Laval, Faculty of Social Sciences, Department of Political Science, Programs in Political Science, Québec, QC G1K 7P4, Canada. Offers MA, PhD. Terminal master's awarded for partial completion of doctoral program. *Degree requirements:* For master's, thesis (for some programs); for doctorate, comprehensive exam, thesis/dissertation. *Entrance requirements:* For master's, knowledge of French; for doctorate, knowledge of French, comprehension of written English. Electronic applications accepted.

University at Albany, State University of New York, Nelson A. Rockefeller College of Public Affairs and Policy, Department of Political Science, Albany, NY 12222-0001. Offers MA, PhD. *Faculty:* 20 full-time (7 women). *Students:* 23 full-time (10 women), 24 part-time (8 women); includes 3 minority (1 Asian, non-Hispanic/Latino; 1 Hispanic/Latino; 1 Two or more races, non-Hispanic/Latino), 9 international. Average age 34. 44 applicants, 59% accepted, 10 enrolled. In 2017, 5 master's, 3 doctorates awarded. *Degree requirements:* For doctorate, one foreign language, thesis/dissertation. *Entrance requirements:* For doctorate, GRE General Test. Additional exam requirements/recommendations for international students: Required—TOEFL (minimum score 550 paper-based). *Application deadline:* For fall admission, 2/1 priority date for domestic students, 5/1 for international students; for spring admission, 11/1 for international students. Applications are processed on a rolling basis. Application fee: $75. Electronic applications accepted. *Expenses:* Tuition, state resident: full-time $10,870; part-time $453 per credit hour. Tuition, nonresident: full-time $22,210; part-time $925 per credit hour. *Required fees:* $84.68 per credit hour. $508.06 per semester. Part-time tuition and fees vary according to course load and program. *Financial support:* Fellowships available. Financial award application deadline: 2/1. *Unit head:* Patricia Strach, Chair, 518-442-5256, E-mail: pstrach@albany.edu.
Website: http://www.albany.edu/rockefeller/pos/index.htm

University at Buffalo, the State University of New York, Graduate School, College of Arts and Sciences, Department of Political Science, Buffalo, NY 14260. Offers MA, PhD. *Faculty:* 14 full-time (4 women), 2 part-time/adjunct (0 women). *Students:* 20 full-time (8 women), 9 part-time (5 women); includes 3 minority (all Black or African American, non-Hispanic/Latino), 1 international. Average age 28. 31 applicants, 81% accepted, 9 enrolled. In 2017, 6 master's, 4 doctorates awarded. Terminal master's awarded for partial completion of doctoral program. *Degree requirements:* For master's, comprehensive exam, thesis or alternative, paper, project, portfolio; for doctorate, comprehensive exam, thesis/dissertation. *Entrance requirements:* For master's, GRE General Test, minimum GPA of 3.0; for doctorate, GRE General Test, minimum GPA of 3.3. Additional exam requirements/recommendations for international students: Required—TOEFL (minimum score 550 paper-based; 79 iBT), IELTS (minimum score 6.5), PTE (minimum score 55). *Application deadline:* For fall admission, 8/1 priority date for domestic students, 3/1 for international students; for spring admission, 11/1 priority date for domestic students, 10/1 for international students. Applications are processed on a rolling basis. Application fee: $75. Electronic applications accepted. *Financial support:* In 2017–18, 12 students received support, including 2 fellowships with full tuition reimbursements available (averaging $6,000 per year), 12 teaching assistantships with full tuition reimbursements available (averaging $13,500 per year); research assistantships, career-related internships or fieldwork, Federal Work-Study, health care benefits, tuition waivers (full), and unspecified assistantships also available. Financial award application deadline: 1/1; financial award applicants required to submit FAFSA. *Faculty research:* American politics, public law, comparative politics, international politics. *Unit head:* Dr. Harvey Palmer, Chairman, 716-645-8449, Fax: 716-645-2166, E-mail: hpalmer@buffalo.edu. *Application contact:* Mary E. O'Brien, Graduate Coordinator, 716-645-3441, Fax: 716-645-2166, E-mail: meobrien@buffalo.edu.
Website: http://www.polsci.buffalo.edu/graduate/

The University of Akron, Graduate School, Buchtel College of Arts and Sciences, Department of Political Science, Akron, OH 44325. Offers MA, MAP, JD/MAP. *Program availability:* Part-time. *Faculty:* 11 full-time (1 woman), 8 part-time/adjunct (3 women). *Students:* 21 full-time (5 women), 8 part-time (4 women); includes 4 minority (all Black or African American, non-Hispanic/Latino), 3 international. Average age 28. 25 applicants, 96% accepted, 10 enrolled. In 2017, 15 master's awarded. *Entrance requirements:* For master's, minimum GPA of 3.0, three letters of recommendation (two of which must be from faculty members), statement of purpose. Additional exam requirements/recommendations for international students: Required—TOEFL (minimum score 79 iBT), IELTS (minimum score 6.5). *Application deadline:* For fall admission, 4/1 for domestic and international students; for spring admission, 12/1 for domestic and international students. Applications are processed on a rolling basis. Application fee: $45 ($70 for international students). Electronic applications accepted. *Financial support:* In 2017–18, 9 teaching assistantships with full and partial tuition reimbursements were awarded. *Faculty research:* Public opinion and public policy, international/comparative politics, the politics of criminal justice, conflict management. *Total annual research expenditures:* $139,335. *Unit head:* Dr. Nancy Marion, Department Chair, 330-972-5551, E-mail: nmarion@uakron.edu. *Application contact:* Dr. Karl Kaltenthaler, Graduate Director, 330-972-8060, E-mail: kck@uakron.edu.
Website: http://www.uakron.edu/polisci/

The University of Alabama, Graduate School, College of Arts and Sciences, Department of Political Science, Tuscaloosa, AL 35487. Offers political science (MA, PhD); public administration (MPA). *Program availability:* Part-time. *Faculty:* 15 full-time (3 women). *Students:* 46 full-time (15 women), 19 part-time (7 women); includes 11 minority (7 Black or African American, non-Hispanic/Latino; 1 American Indian or Alaska Native, non-Hispanic/Latino; 2 Asian, non-Hispanic/Latino; 1 Two or more races, non-Hispanic/Latino), 6 international. Average age 30. 38 applicants, 66% accepted, 13 enrolled. In 2017, 16 master's, 3 doctorates awarded. Terminal master's awarded for partial completion of doctoral program. *Degree requirements:* For master's, comprehensive exam, thesis optional; for doctorate, comprehensive exam, thesis/dissertation. *Entrance requirements:* For master's and doctorate, GRE, minimum undergraduate GPA of 3.0. Additional exam requirements/recommendations for international students: Required—TOEFL. *Application deadline:* For fall admission, 6/30 for domestic and international students; for spring admission, 10/15 for domestic and international students. Applications are processed on a rolling basis. Application fee: $50 ($60 for international students). Electronic applications accepted. *Financial support:* In 2017–18, 19 students received support, including fellowships with full tuition reimbursements available (averaging $15,000 per year), teaching assistantships with full tuition reimbursements available (averaging $12,500 per year); career-related internships or fieldwork and Federal Work-Study also available. Financial award application deadline: 2/15. *Faculty research:* American politics, comparative politics, international relations, public policy and administration, political theory. *Total annual research expenditures:* $13,262. *Unit head:* Dr. Joseph Smith, Chair and Professor, 205-348-5981, E-mail: josmith@bama.ua.edu. *Application contact:* Dr. Douglas Gibler, Graduate Advisor, 205-348-5528, Fax: 205-348-5298, E-mail: dmgibler@bama.ua.edu.
Website: http://www.as.ua.edu/psc/

University of Alberta, Faculty of Graduate Studies and Research, Department of Political Science, Edmonton, AB T6G 2E1, Canada. Offers MA, PhD. *Program availability:* Part-time. *Degree requirements:* For master's, thesis (for some programs); for doctorate, one foreign language, thesis/dissertation. *Entrance requirements:* Additional exam requirements/recommendations for international students: Required—TOEFL. *Faculty research:* Canadian politics, international relations, globalization, classical and contemporary political theory, gender and politics.

The University of Arizona, College of Social and Behavioral Sciences, Department of Political Science, Tucson, AZ 85721. Offers MA, PhD. Terminal master's awarded for partial completion of doctoral program. *Degree requirements:* For master's, thesis or alternative; for doctorate, variable foreign language requirement, comprehensive exam, thesis/dissertation. *Entrance requirements:* For master's, GRE General Test, minimum GPA of 3.2, 3 letters of recommendation, writing sample; for doctorate, GRE General Test, minimum GPA of 3.2, 3 letters of recommendation, statement of purpose, writing sample. Additional exam requirements/recommendations for international students: Required—TOEFL (minimum score 550 paper-based; 79 iBT). Electronic applications accepted. *Faculty research:* Voting behavior, political participation, Soviet domestic and Sino-Soviet relations, presidential leadership and congressional behavior.

University of Arkansas, Graduate School, J. William Fulbright College of Arts and Sciences, Department of Political Science, Program in Political Science, Fayetteville, AR 72701. Offers MA. In 2017, 9 master's awarded. *Degree requirements:* For master's, thesis or alternative. *Entrance requirements:* For master's, GRE General Test. *Application deadline:* For fall admission, 8/1 for domestic students, 4/1 for international students; for spring admission, 12/1 for domestic students, 10/1 for international students; for summer admission, 4/15 for domestic students, 3/1 for international students. Applications are processed on a rolling basis. Application fee: $60. Electronic applications accepted. *Expenses:* Tuition, state resident: full-time $3782. Tuition, nonresident: full-time $10,238. *Financial support:* In 2017–18, 1 research assistantship, 6 teaching assistantships were awarded; fellowships, career-related internships or fieldwork, and Federal Work-Study also available. Support available to part-time students. Financial award application deadline: 4/1; financial award applicants required to submit FAFSA. *Unit head:* Dr. Pearl K. Dowe, Department Chair, 479-575-3356, Fax: 479-575-6432, E-mail: pkford@uark.edu. *Application contact:* Dr. Pearl Dowe, Graduate Coordinator, 479-575-6434, E-mail: pkford@uark.edu.
Website: https://fulbright.uark.edu/departments/political-science/

The University of British Columbia, Faculty of Arts, Department of Political Science, Vancouver, BC V6T 1Z1, Canada. Offers MA, PhD. *Program availability:* Part-time. *Degree requirements:* For master's, thesis; for doctorate, comprehensive exam, thesis/dissertation. *Entrance requirements:* For master's, BA in political science; for doctorate, GRE, BA and MA in political science. Additional exam requirements/recommendations for international students: Required—TOEFL, TWE. Electronic applications accepted. *Expenses:* Contact institution. *Faculty research:* Canadian politics, international relations, political theory, comparative politics, public policy.

University of Calgary, Faculty of Graduate Studies, Faculty of Arts, Department of Political Science, Calgary, AB T2N 1N4, Canada. Offers MA, PhD. *Degree requirements:* For master's, thesis; for doctorate, one foreign language, comprehensive exam, thesis/dissertation, prospectus, oral and written candidacy exams. *Entrance requirements:* For master's, minimum GPA of 3.4; for doctorate, minimum GPA of 3.7. Additional exam requirements/recommendations for international students: Required—TOEFL (minimum score 620 paper-based). Electronic applications accepted. *Faculty research:* Canadian politics, international relations, comparative politics, theory, public policy.

University of California, Berkeley, Graduate Division, College of Letters and Science, Charles and Louise Travers Department of Political Science, Berkeley, CA 94720-1500. Offers PhD. *Degree requirements:* For doctorate, thesis/dissertation, oral qualifying exams. *Entrance requirements:* For doctorate, GRE General Test, minimum GPA of 3.0, 3 letters of recommendation. Additional exam requirements/recommendations for international students: Required—TOEFL (minimum score 570 paper-based; 90 iBT). Electronic applications accepted.

University of California, Davis, Graduate Studies, Program in Political Science, Davis, CA 95616. Offers MA, PhD. Terminal master's awarded for partial completion of doctoral program. *Degree requirements:* For master's, thesis; for doctorate, thesis/dissertation. *Entrance requirements:* For master's and doctorate, GRE General Test, minimum GPA of 3.0, writing sample. Additional exam requirements/recommendations for international students: Required—TOEFL (minimum score 550 paper-based). Electronic applications

accepted. *Faculty research:* American government and politics, political theory, comparative politics, international relations, public law.

University of California, Irvine, School of Social Sciences, Department of Political Science, Irvine, CA 92697. Offers political psychology (PhD); political sciences (PhD); public choice (PhD). *Students:* 59 full-time (19 women), 1 part-time (0 women); includes 23 minority (3 Black or African American, non-Hispanic/Latino; 8 Asian, non-Hispanic/Latino; 7 Hispanic/Latino; 5 Two or more races, non-Hispanic/Latino), 11 international. Average age 29. 89 applicants, 40% accepted, 19 enrolled. In 2017, 10 doctorates awarded. *Degree requirements:* For doctorate, thesis/dissertation. *Entrance requirements:* For doctorate, GRE General Test, minimum GPA of 3.0. Additional exam requirements/recommendations for international students: Required—TOEFL (minimum score 550 paper-based). *Application deadline:* For fall admission, 1/15 priority date for domestic students, 1/15 for international students. Applications are processed on a rolling basis. Application fee: $105 ($125 for international students). Electronic applications accepted. *Financial support:* Fellowships, research assistantships with full tuition reimbursements, teaching assistantships, institutionally sponsored loans, traineeships, health care benefits, and unspecified assistantships available. Financial award application deadline: 3/1; financial award applicants required to submit FAFSA. *Faculty research:* Political behavior, political economy, international relations. *Unit head:* Jeffrey Kopstein, Chair, 949-824-4012, E-mail: kopstein@uci.edu. *Application contact:* Robert Uriu, Graduate Program Director, 949-824-1868, E-mail: rmuriu@uci.edu.
Website: http://www.polisci.uci.edu/

University of California, Los Angeles, Graduate Division, College of Letters and Science, Department of Political Science, Los Angeles, CA 90095. Offers MA, PhD. Terminal master's awarded for partial completion of doctoral program. *Degree requirements:* For master's, comprehensive exam; for doctorate, one foreign language, thesis/dissertation, oral and written qualifying exams. *Entrance requirements:* For doctorate, GRE General Test, bachelor's degree; minimum undergraduate GPA of 3.0 (or its equivalent if letter grade system not used); writing sample. Additional exam requirements/recommendations for international students: Required—TOEFL. Electronic applications accepted.

University of California, Riverside, Graduate Division, Department of Political Science, Riverside, CA 92521-0102. Offers MA, PhD. *Program availability:* Part-time. Terminal master's awarded for partial completion of doctoral program. *Degree requirements:* For master's, comprehensive exams or thesis; for doctorate, thesis/dissertation, qualifying exams. *Entrance requirements:* For master's and doctorate, GRE General Test, minimum GPA of 3.2. Additional exam requirements/recommendations for international students: Required—TOEFL (minimum score 550 paper-based; 80 iBT). Electronic applications accepted. *Expenses:* Tuition, state resident: full-time $5746. Tuition, nonresident: full-time $10,780. Tuition and fees vary according to campus/location and program. *Faculty research:* American politics, mass political behavior, comparative politics, international relations, political theory.

University of California, San Diego, Graduate Division, Department of Political Science, La Jolla, CA 92093. Offers political science (PhD); political science and international affairs (PhD). *Students:* 75 full-time (24 women). 325 applicants, 13% accepted, 17 enrolled. In 2017, 9 doctorates awarded. *Degree requirements:* For doctorate, comprehensive exam, thesis/dissertation. *Entrance requirements:* For doctorate, GRE General Test, letters of recommendation. Additional exam requirements/recommendations for international students: Required—TOEFL (minimum score 600 paper-based; 100 iBT), IELTS. *Application deadline:* For fall admission, 12/13 for domestic students. Application fee: $105 ($125 for international students). Electronic applications accepted. *Financial support:* Fellowships, research assistantships, teaching assistantships, and scholarships/grants available. Financial award applicants required to submit FAFSA. *Faculty research:* American politics, comparative politics, international relations, methodology, political theory. *Unit head:* Thad Kousser, Chair, 858-534-3239, E-mail: tkousser@ucsd.edu. *Application contact:* Tyra Hawthorne, Graduate Coordinator, 858-534-2705, E-mail: psgradadmissions@ucsd.edu.
Website: http://polisci.ucsd.edu/

University of California, San Diego, Graduate Division, School of Global Policy and Strategy, La Jolla, CA 92093. Offers Chinese economic and political affairs (MCEPA), including Chinese economy, Chinese environment, Chinese foreign relations and security, Chinese politics and public policy; international affairs (MAS, MIA), including international development and nonprofit management (MIA), international economics (MIA), international environmental policy (MIA), international management (MIA), international politics (MIA); political science and international affairs (PhD); public policy (MPP), including American policy in global context, business, government and regulation, energy and environmental policy, health policy, program design and evaluation, security policy. *Program availability:* Part-time. *Degree requirements:* For master's, language requirement (for MIA and MCEPA); for doctorate, thesis/dissertation. *Entrance requirements:* For master's, GMAT or GRE General Test; for doctorate, GRE General Test. Additional exam requirements/recommendations for international students: Required—TOEFL (minimum score 90 iBT), IELTS (minimum score 7). Electronic applications accepted. *Expenses:* Contact institution. *Faculty research:* Public policy; international management, finance and trade; international development; international politics in Latin America, China, Korea, Japan, and Southeast Asia; international environmental policy.

University of California, Santa Barbara, Graduate Division, College of Letters and Sciences, Division of Social Sciences, Department of Global Studies, Santa Barbara, CA 93106-7065. Offers global culture, ideology, and religion (MA, PhD); global government, human rights, and civil society (MA, PhD); political economy, sustainable development, and the environment (MA, PhD). *Degree requirements:* For master's, one foreign language, thesis, 2 years of a second language; for doctorate, one foreign language, thesis/dissertation, reading proficiency in at least one language other than English. *Entrance requirements:* For master's, GRE, 2 years of a second language with minimum B grade in the final term, statement of purpose, resume or curriculum vitae, 3 letters of recommendation, transcripts (from all post-secondary institutions attended), writing sample (15-20 pages); for doctorate, GRE, statement of purpose, personal achievements/contributions statement, resume or curriculum vitae, 3 letters of recommendation, transcripts from all post-secondary institutions attended, writing sample (15-20 pages). Additional exam requirements/recommendations for international students: Required—TOEFL (minimum score 600 paper-based; 94 iBT), IELTS (minimum score 7). Electronic applications accepted.

University of California, Santa Barbara, Graduate Division, College of Letters and Sciences, Division of Social Sciences, Department of Political Science, Santa Barbara, CA 93106-9420. Offers PhD, MA/PhD. Terminal master's awarded for partial completion of doctoral program. *Degree requirements:* For doctorate, one foreign language, thesis/dissertation, 2 comprehensive exams or 1 exam and field paper. *Entrance requirements:* For doctorate, GRE General Test. Additional exam requirements/recommendations for international students: Required—TOEFL (minimum score 600 paper-based; 100 iBT), IELTS. Electronic applications accepted. *Faculty research:* American politics, comparative politics, international relations, political theory.

University of California, Santa Cruz, Division of Graduate Studies, Division of Social Sciences, Politics Department, Santa Cruz, CA 95064. Offers PhD. *Degree requirements:* For doctorate, qualifying exam. *Entrance requirements:* For doctorate, GRE. Additional exam requirements/recommendations for international students: Required—TOEFL (minimum score 550 paper-based; 83 iBT); Recommended—IELTS (minimum score 8). Electronic applications accepted. *Faculty research:* Political and social thought, political institutions, political economy, political and social forces.

University of Central Florida, College of Sciences, Department of Political Science, Orlando, FL 32816. Offers intelligence and national security (Certificate); political science (MA); security studies (PhD). *Program availability:* Part-time, evening/weekend. *Students:* 48 full-time (18 women), 16 part-time (7 women); includes 17 minority (4 Black or African American, non-Hispanic/Latino; 1 Asian, non-Hispanic/Latino; 10 Hispanic/Latino; 2 Two or more races, non-Hispanic/Latino), 15 international. Average age 31. 43 applicants, 74% accepted, 25 enrolled. In 2017, 10 master's, 2 doctorates, 7 other advanced degrees awarded. *Degree requirements:* For master's, comprehensive exam, thesis; for doctorate, one foreign language, thesis/dissertation, oral qualifying examination, written candidacy exam. *Entrance requirements:* For master's, GRE General Test, letters of recommendation, personal statement; for doctorate, GRE General Test, master's degree or its equivalent in political science, international politics, international relations, or related discipline; letters of recommendation; personal statement; writing sample; resume. Additional exam requirements/recommendations for international students: Required—TOEFL. *Application deadline:* For fall admission, 7/15 for domestic students; for spring admission, 12/1 for domestic students. Application fee: $30. Electronic applications accepted. *Expenses:* Tuition, state resident: part-time $288.16 per credit hour. Tuition, nonresident: part-time $1073.31 per credit hour. Tuition and fees vary according to program. *Financial support:* In 2017–18, 25 students received support, including 8 fellowships with partial tuition reimbursements available (averaging $10,575 per year), 1 research assistantship with partial tuition reimbursement available (averaging $14,868 per year), 21 teaching assistantships with partial tuition reimbursements available (averaging $12,928 per year); career-related internships or fieldwork, Federal Work-Study, institutionally sponsored loans, health care benefits, tuition waivers (partial), and unspecified assistantships also available. Financial award application deadline: 3/1; financial award applicants required to submit FAFSA. *Faculty research:* Environment, international relations, security studies, comparative politics. *Unit head:* Dr. Kerstin Hamann, Chair, 407-823-2085, Fax: 407-823-0051, E-mail: kerstin.hamann@ucf.edu. *Application contact:* Associate Director, Graduate Admissions, 407-823-2766, Fax: 407-823-6442, E-mail: gradadmissions@ucf.edu.
Website: http://politicalscience.cos.ucf.edu/

University of Central Oklahoma, The Jackson College of Graduate Studies, College of Liberal Arts, Department of Political Science, Edmond, OK 73034-5209. Offers political science (MA), including international affairs; public administration (MPA), including public and nonprofit management, urban management. *Program availability:* Part-time. *Faculty:* 11 full-time (4 women), 1 part-time/adjunct (0 women). *Students:* 42 full-time (21 women), 58 part-time (26 women); includes 33 minority (14 Black or African American, non-Hispanic/Latino; 3 American Indian or Alaska Native, non-Hispanic/Latino; 10 Hispanic/Latino; 6 Two or more races, non-Hispanic/Latino), 18 international. Average age 32. 127 applicants, 84% accepted, 29 enrolled. In 2017, 32 master's awarded. *Degree requirements:* For master's, comprehensive exam (for some programs), thesis (for some programs). *Entrance requirements:* For master's, 18 undergraduate hours in political science. Additional exam requirements/recommendations for international students: Required—TOEFL (minimum score 550 paper-based; 79 iBT), IELTS (minimum score 6.5). *Application deadline:* For fall admission, 7/15 for international students; for spring admission, 11/15 for international students. Applications are processed on a rolling basis. Application fee: $60. Electronic applications accepted. *Expenses:* Tuition, state resident: full-time $5375; part-time $268.75 per credit hour. Tuition, nonresident: full-time $13,295; part-time $664.75 per credit hour. *Required fees:* $626; $31.30 per credit hour. One-time fee: $50. Tuition and fees vary according to program. *Financial support:* In 2017–18, 20 students received support, including 3 research assistantships with partial tuition reimbursements available (averaging $3,943 per year), 4 teaching assistantships with partial tuition reimbursements available (averaging $7,394 per year); career-related internships or fieldwork, scholarships/grants, tuition waivers (partial), and unspecified assistantships also available. Financial award application deadline: 3/31; financial award applicants required to submit FAFSA. *Unit head:* Dr. Lou Furmanski, Department Chair, 405-974-5540, Fax: 405-974-3823. *Application contact:* Dr. Jan Hardt, Graduate Advisor, 405-974-5840, Fax: 405-974-3823, E-mail: gradcoll@uco.edu.
Website: http://sites.uco.edu/la/political-science/index.asp

University of Chicago, Division of the Social Sciences, Department of Political Science, Chicago, IL 60637. Offers PhD. *Faculty:* 34. *Students:* 109 full-time (50 women); includes 36 minority (14 Black or African American, non-Hispanic/Latino; 6 Asian, non-Hispanic/Latino; 12 Hispanic/Latino; 4 Two or more races, non-Hispanic/Latino), 35 international. Average age 30. 458 applicants, 8% accepted, 13 enrolled. In 2017, 13 doctorates awarded. *Degree requirements:* For doctorate, one foreign language, thesis/dissertation, exam, qualifying paper. *Entrance requirements:* For doctorate, GRE General Test, 3 letters of recommendation, statement of purpose, transcripts, resume or curriculum vitae, writing sample (dependent on department). Additional exam requirements/recommendations for international students: Required—TOEFL (minimum score 104 iBT), IELTS (minimum score 7). *Application deadline:* For fall admission, 12/15 for domestic and international students. Application fee: $90. Electronic applications accepted. *Financial support:* In 2017–18, 14 students received support, including 14 fellowships with full tuition reimbursements available (averaging $27,000 per year); research assistantships, teaching assistantships, career-related internships or fieldwork, Federal Work-Study, institutionally sponsored loans, scholarships/grants, and health care benefits also available. Financial award application deadline: 12/15. *Faculty research:* Political philosophy, international political economy, strategic studies, public policy and race relations, comparative politics (China, Middle East, Soviet Union, Africa, India, Japan). *Unit head:* William Howell, 773-702 8058, E-mail: whowell@uchicago.edu. *Application contact:* Office of the Dean of Students, 773-702-8415, E-mail: ssd-admissions@uchicago.edu.
Website: http://political-science.uchicago.edu

University of Cincinnati, Graduate School, McMicken College of Arts and Sciences, Department of Political Science, Cincinnati, OH 45221. Offers MA, PhD. Terminal master's awarded for partial completion of doctoral program. *Degree requirements:* For master's, thesis (for some programs); for doctorate, thesis/dissertation. *Entrance requirements:* For master's and doctorate, GRE General Test, GRE Subject Test. Additional exam requirements/recommendations for international students: Required—TOEFL. Electronic applications accepted. *Expenses: Tuition, area resident:* Full-time $14,468. Tuition, state resident: full-time $14,968; part-time $754 per credit hour. Tuition, nonresident: full-time $24,210; part-time $1311 per credit hour. *International tuition:* $26,460 full-time. *Required fees:* $3958; $84 per credit hour. One-time fee: $85 full-time. Tuition and fees vary according to course load, degree level and program. *Faculty research:* International security, methodology, American politics, comparative politics.

Political Science

University of Colorado Boulder, Graduate School, College of Arts and Sciences, Department of Political Science, Boulder, CO 80309. Offers MA, PhD. *Faculty:* 26 full-time (8 women). *Students:* 48 full-time (22 women); includes 6 minority (1 Asian, non-Hispanic/Latino; 2 Hispanic/Latino; 3 Two or more races, non-Hispanic/Latino), 7 international. Average age 28. 81 applicants, 28% accepted, 10 enrolled. In 2017, 6 master's, 11 doctorates awarded. Terminal master's awarded for partial completion of doctoral program. *Degree requirements:* For master's, comprehensive exam, thesis; for doctorate, one foreign language, thesis/dissertation. *Entrance requirements:* For master's, GRE General Test, minimum undergraduate GPA of 3.0; for doctorate, GRE General Test, minimum GPA of 3.5 (undergraduate), 3.0 (graduate). *Application deadline:* For fall admission, 12/1 for domestic students; for spring admission, 12/1 for domestic students. Application fee: $60 ($80 for international students). Electronic applications accepted. Application fee is waived when completed online. *Financial support:* In 2017–18, 143 students received support, including 29 fellowships (averaging $730 per year), 2 research assistantships with full and partial tuition reimbursements available (averaging $24,890 per year), 44 teaching assistantships with full and partial tuition reimbursements available (averaging $23,894 per year); institutionally sponsored loans, scholarships/grants, health care benefits, and unspecified assistantships also available. Financial award application deadline: 2/15; financial award applicants required to submit FAFSA. *Faculty research:* Political science; comparative government; political economics/economy; democracy; international relations/diplomacy. *Total annual research expenditures:* $541,240. *Application contact:* E-mail: pscigrad@colorado.edu.
Website: http://polsci.colorado.edu/

University of Colorado Denver, College of Liberal Arts and Sciences, Department of Political Science, Denver, CO 80217. Offers MA. *Program availability:* Part-time, evening/weekend. *Degree requirements:* For master's, project or thesis, minimum of 30 credit hours. *Entrance requirements:* For master's, 18 hours of course work in political science; minimum GPA of 3.0 (3.2 preferred); statement of purpose; academic writing sample. Additional exam requirements/recommendations for international students: Required—TOEFL (minimum score 537 paper-based; 75 iBT); Recommended—IELTS (minimum score 6.5). Electronic applications accepted. *Faculty research:* Indigenous peoples in the international legal and political arena; political developments in Europe and the former Soviet Union; early Chinese industrialization, modern Chinese political and economic development, and human rights; Congressional oversight and Congressional-executive relations.

University of Colorado Denver, School of Public Affairs, Program in Public Affairs and Administration, Denver, CO 80127. Offers public administration (MPA), including domestic violence, emergency management and homeland security, environmental policy, management and law, homeland security and defense, local government, nonprofit management, public administration; public affairs (PhD). *Accreditation:* NASPAA. *Program availability:* Part-time, evening/weekend, online learning. *Degree requirements:* For master's, thesis or alternative, 36-39 credit hours; for doctorate, comprehensive exam, thesis/dissertation, minimum of 66 semester hours, including at least 30 hours of dissertation. *Entrance requirements:* For master's, GRE, GMAT or LSAT, resume, essay, transcripts, recommendations; for doctorate, GRE, resume, essay, transcripts, recommendations. Additional exam requirements/recommendations for international students: Required—TOEFL (minimum score 550 paper-based; 80 iBT); Recommended—IELTS (minimum score 6.5). Electronic applications accepted. *Expenses:* Contact institution. *Faculty research:* Housing, education and the social and economic issues of vulnerable populations; nonprofit governance and management; education finance, effectiveness and reform; P-20 education initiatives; municipal government accountability.

University of Connecticut, Graduate School, College of Liberal Arts and Sciences, Department of Political Science, Storrs, CT 06269. Offers MA, PhD. Terminal master's awarded for partial completion of doctoral program. *Degree requirements:* For master's, comprehensive exam; for doctorate, 2 foreign languages, thesis/dissertation. *Entrance requirements:* For master's and doctorate, GRE General Test. Additional exam requirements/recommendations for international students: Required—TOEFL (minimum score 550 paper-based). Electronic applications accepted.

University of Dallas, Braniff Graduate School of Liberal Arts, Institute of Philosophic Studies, Doctoral Program in Politics, Irving, TX 75062-4736. Offers PhD. *Degree requirements:* For doctorate, 2 foreign languages, comprehensive exam, thesis/dissertation. *Entrance requirements:* For doctorate, GRE General Test. Additional exam requirements/recommendations for international students: Required—TOEFL. *Application deadline:* For fall admission, 2/15 priority date for domestic students. Application fee: $50. *Expenses: Tuition:* Full-time $33,750; part-time $22,500 per year. Tuition and fees vary according to program. *Financial support:* Application deadline: 2/15. *Faculty research:* Classical, medieval, and modern political philosophy; American political thought and institutions; politics and literature. *Unit head:* Dr. Richard Dougherty, Graduate Director, 972-721-5043, Fax: 972-721-4007, E-mail: doughr@udallas.edu.

University of Dallas, Braniff Graduate School of Liberal Arts, Master's Program in Politics, Irving, TX 75062-4736. Offers M Pol, MA. *Program availability:* Part-time. *Degree requirements:* For master's, one foreign language, comprehensive exam, thesis. *Entrance requirements:* For master's, GRE General Test. Additional exam requirements/recommendations for international students: Required—TOEFL. *Application deadline:* For fall admission, 2/15 priority date for domestic students; for spring admission, 11/15 for domestic students. Applications are processed on a rolling basis. Application fee: $50. *Expenses: Tuition:* Full-time $33,750; part-time $22,500 per year. Tuition and fees vary according to program. *Financial support:* Application deadline: 2/15. *Faculty research:* Classical, medieval, and modern political philosophy; American political thought and institutions; politics and literature. *Unit head:* Dr. Richard Dougherty, Graduate Director, 972-721-5043, Fax: 972-721-4007, E-mail: doughr@udallas.edu.

University of Delaware, College of Arts and Sciences, Department of Political Science and International Relations, Newark, DE 19716. Offers MA, PhD. Terminal master's awarded for partial completion of doctoral program. *Degree requirements:* For master's, research paper; for doctorate, one foreign language, comprehensive exam, thesis/dissertation. *Entrance requirements:* For master's and doctorate, GRE General Test, minimum GPA of 3.2 in major, 3.0 overall. Additional exam requirements/recommendations for international students: Required—TOEFL (minimum score 600 paper-based). Electronic applications accepted. *Faculty research:* Social constructivism, international migration, international security, democratization, human rights.

University of Florida, Graduate School, College of Liberal Arts and Sciences, Department of Political Science, Gainesville, FL 32611. Offers educational policy (PhD); international development policy and administration (MA, Certificate); international relations (MA, MAT); political campaigning (MA, Certificate); political science (MA, PhD); public affairs (MA, Certificate); tropical conservation and development (MA, PhD); JD/MA. Terminal master's awarded for partial completion of doctoral program. *Degree requirements:* For master's, variable foreign language requirement, comprehensive exam (for some programs), thesis or alternative, internship (for some programs); for doctorate, variable foreign language requirement, comprehensive exam, thesis/dissertation. *Entrance requirements:* For master's and doctorate, GRE General Test (minimum score: 308 combined verbal/quantitative), minimum GPA of 3.5. Additional exam requirements/recommendations for international students: Required—TOEFL (minimum score 550 paper-based; 80 iBT), IELTS (minimum score 6). Electronic applications accepted. *Faculty research:* American electoral politics and political institutions, comparative democratization and development, theories of international relation, and political theory.

University of Georgia, School of Public and International Affairs, Program in Political Science/International Affairs, Athens, GA 30602. Offers MA, PhD. *Degree requirements:* For master's, one foreign language, thesis; for doctorate, one foreign language, thesis/dissertation. *Entrance requirements:* For master's and doctorate, GRE General Test. Electronic applications accepted.

University of Guelph, Graduate Studies, College of Social and Applied Human Sciences, Department of Political Science, Guelph, ON N1G 2W1, Canada. Offers comparative politics (MA); international development (MA); political science (MA); public policy and public administration (MA); the Americas (Canada emphasis) (MA). MA in public policy and public administration offered in collaboration with Department of Political Science of McMaster University. *Degree requirements:* For master's, thesis or paper. *Entrance requirements:* For master's, minimum B average during previous 2 years of course work, 4 year Honours Degree in Political Science. Additional exam requirements/recommendations for international students: Required—TOEFL. Electronic applications accepted. *Faculty research:* Political ethics, constitutional power.

University of Hawaii at Manoa, Office of Graduate Education, College of Social Sciences, Department of Political Science, Honolulu, HI 96822. Offers MA, PhD. *Program availability:* Part-time. Terminal master's awarded for partial completion of doctoral program. *Degree requirements:* For master's, thesis optional; for doctorate, comprehensive exam, thesis/dissertation. *Entrance requirements:* Additional exam requirements/recommendations for international students: Required—TOEFL (minimum score 540 paper-based; 76 iBT), IELTS (minimum score 5). *Faculty research:* Asia/Pacific, political economy, human rights, futures, postmodernism.

University of Houston, College of Liberal Arts and Social Sciences, Department of Political Science, Houston, TX 77204. Offers political science (MA, PhD); public administration (MA). *Program availability:* Part-time. Terminal master's awarded for partial completion of doctoral program. *Degree requirements:* For master's, thesis optional; for doctorate, thesis/dissertation. *Entrance requirements:* For master's and doctorate, GRE. Additional exam requirements/recommendations for international students: Required—TOEFL (minimum score 550 paper-based; 79 iBT). *Faculty research:* American politics, political theory, judicial process, public policy, comparative politics.

University of Idaho, College of Graduate Studies, College of Letters, Arts and Social Sciences, Department of Politics and Philosophy, Moscow, ID 83844. Offers political science (MA, PhD); public administration (MPA). *Faculty:* 5 full-time. *Students:* 7 full-time, 10 part-time. Average age 31. In 2017, 7 master's, 1 doctorate awarded. *Entrance requirements:* For master's, GRE, minimum GPA of 3.0. Additional exam requirements/recommendations for international students: Required—TOEFL (minimum score 96 iBT). *Expenses:* Tuition, state resident: full-time $6722; part-time $430 per credit hour. Tuition, nonresident: full-time $23,046; part-time $1337 per credit hour. *Required fees:* $2142; $63 per credit hour. *Faculty research:* Political socialization, international and domestic conflict processes, constitutional law. *Unit head:* Dr. Brian Ellison, Chair, 208-885-6328, E-mail: politicsphilosophy@uidaho.edu. *Application contact:* Sean Scoggin, Graduate Recruitment Coordinator, 208-885-4723, E-mail: graduateadmissions@uidaho.edu.
Website: https://www.uidaho.edu/class/politics-and-philosophy

University of Illinois at Chicago, College of Liberal Arts and Sciences, Department of Political Science, Chicago, IL 60607-7128. Offers MA, PhD. *Program availability:* Part-time. Terminal master's awarded for partial completion of doctoral program. *Degree requirements:* For master's, thesis or comprehensive exam. *Entrance requirements:* For master's, GRE General Test, minimum GPA of 3.0. Additional exam requirements/recommendations for international students: Required—TOEFL. Electronic applications accepted. *Faculty research:* Policy analysis/national urban politics and policy, electoral behavior.

University of Illinois at Springfield, Graduate Programs, College of Public Affairs and Administration, Department of Political Science, Springfield, IL 62703-5407. Offers MA. *Program availability:* Part-time, evening/weekend, 100% online, blended/hybrid learning. *Faculty:* 7 full-time (3 women), 2 part-time/adjunct (1 woman). *Students:* 20 full-time (12 women), 61 part-time (21 women); includes 11 minority (7 Black or African American, non-Hispanic/Latino; 4 Hispanic/Latino). Average age 33. 64 applicants, 48% accepted, 19 enrolled. In 2017, 7 master's awarded. *Degree requirements:* For master's, comprehensive exam, participant/observer case study, or thesis. *Entrance requirements:* For master's, minimum undergraduate GPA of 3.0. Additional exam requirements/recommendations for international students: Required—TOEFL (minimum score 500 paper-based; 61 iBT). *Application deadline:* Applications are processed on a rolling basis. Application fee: $60 ($75 for international students). Electronic applications accepted. *Expenses:* Tuition, state resident: full-time $7896; part-time $329 per credit hour. Tuition, nonresident: full-time $16,200; part-time $675 per credit hour. Tuition and fees vary according to program. *Financial support:* In 2017–18, research assistantships with full tuition reimbursements (averaging $10,249 per year), teaching assistantships with full tuition reimbursements (averaging $10,303 per year) were awarded; fellowships, career-related internships or fieldwork, Federal Work-Study, scholarships/grants, health care benefits, and unspecified assistantships also available. Support available to part-time students. Financial award application deadline: 11/15; financial award applicants required to submit FAFSA. *Unit head:* Dr. John Transue, Program Administrator, 217-206-6535, E-mail: jtran8@uis.edu.
Website: http://www.uis.edu/politicalstudies/

University of Illinois at Urbana–Champaign, Graduate College, College of Liberal Arts and Sciences, Department of Political Science, Champaign, IL 61820. Offers MA, PhD, PhD/JD.

The University of Iowa, Graduate College, College of Liberal Arts and Sciences, Department of Political Science, Iowa City, IA 52242-1316. Offers PhD. *Degree requirements:* For doctorate, comprehensive exam, thesis/dissertation. *Entrance requirements:* For doctorate, GRE General Test, minimum GPA of 3.0. Additional exam requirements/recommendations for international students: Required—TOEFL (minimum score 600 paper-based; 100 iBT). Electronic applications accepted.

The University of Kansas, Graduate Studies, College of Liberal Arts and Sciences, Department of Political Science, Lawrence, KS 66045. Offers MA, PhD, PhD/MA. *Program availability:* Part-time. *Students:* 37 full-time (16 women), 5 part-time (1 woman); includes 6 minority (1 Black or African American, non-Hispanic/Latino; 1 American Indian or Alaska Native, non-Hispanic/Latino; 2 Asian, non-Hispanic/Latino; 1 Hispanic/Latino; 1 Two or more races, non-Hispanic/Latino), 7 international. Average age 33. 33 applicants, 73% accepted, 7 enrolled. In 2017, 1 master's, 9 doctorates awarded. Terminal master's awarded for partial completion of doctoral program. *Entrance requirements:* For master's, GRE General Test, 3 letters of recommendation, curriculum vitae, transcripts, personal statement; for doctorate, GRE General Test, 3

letters of recommendation, transcripts, personal statement, curriculum vitae. Additional exam requirements/recommendations for international students: Required—TOEFL. *Application deadline:* For fall admission, 4/15 for domestic and international students. Application fee: $65 ($85 for international students). Electronic applications accepted. *Financial support:* Fellowships, research assistantships, teaching assistantships, scholarships/grants, health care benefits, and unspecified assistantships available. Financial award application deadline: 1/7. *Faculty research:* Latino politics, gender politics, Middle East and North African politics, American politics/voting behavior, environmental policy. *Unit head:* Don Haider-Markel, Chair, 785-864-9034, E-mail: dhmarkel@ku.edu. *Application contact:* Graduate Coordinator, 785-864-3523, E-mail: gradpols@ku.edu.
Website: https://kups.ku.edu/

University of Kentucky, Graduate School, College of Arts and Sciences, Program in Political Science, Lexington, KY 40506-0032. Offers MA, PhD. *Degree requirements:* For master's, comprehensive exam, thesis optional; for doctorate, comprehensive exam, thesis/dissertation. *Entrance requirements:* For master's, GRE General Test, minimum undergraduate GPA of 2.75; for doctorate, GRE General Test, minimum graduate GPA of 3.0. Additional exam requirements/recommendations for international students: Required—TOEFL (minimum score 550 paper-based). Electronic applications accepted. *Faculty research:* International political economy, critical policy studies, regional conflict and integration, race and American politics, media studies.

University of Lethbridge, School of Graduate Studies, Lethbridge, AB T1K 3M4, Canada. Offers addictions counseling (M Sc); agricultural biotechnology (M Sc); agricultural studies (M Sc, MA); anthropology (MA); archaeology (M Sc, MA); art (MA, MFA); biochemistry (M Sc); biological sciences (M Sc); biomolecular science (PhD); biosystems and biodiversity (PhD); Canadian studies (MA); chemistry (M Sc); computer science (M Sc); computer science and geographical information science (M Sc); counseling (MC); counseling psychology (M Ed); dramatic arts (MA); earth, space, and physical science (PhD); economics (MA); education (MA, PhD); educational leadership (M Ed); English (MA); environmental science (M Sc); evolution and behavior (PhD); exercise science (M Sc); French (MA); French/German (MA); French/Spanish (MA); general education (M Ed); geography (M Sc, MA); German (MA); health sciences (M Sc); individualized multidisciplinary (M Sc, MA); kinesiology (M Sc, MA); management (M Sc), including accounting, finance, human resource management and labor relations, information systems, international management, marketing, policy and strategy; mathematics (M Sc); music (M Mus, MA); Native American studies (MA); neuroscience (M Sc, PhD); new media (MA, MFA); nursing (M Sc, MN); philosophy (MA); physics (M Sc); political science (MA); psychology (M Sc, MA); religious studies (MA); sociology (MA); theatre and dramatic arts (MFA); theoretical and computational science (PhD); urban and regional studies (MA); women and gender studies (MA). *Program availability:* Part-time, evening/weekend. *Degree requirements:* For master's, thesis (for some programs); for doctorate, comprehensive exam, thesis/dissertation. *Entrance requirements:* For master's, GMAT (for M Sc in management), bachelor's degree in related field, minimum GPA of 3.0 during previous 20 graded semester courses, 2 years' teaching or related experience (M Ed); for doctorate, master's degree, minimum graduate GPA of 3.5. Additional exam requirements/recommendations for international students: Required—TOEFL (minimum score 580 paper-based; 93 iBT). Electronic applications accepted. *Faculty research:* Movement and brain plasticity, gibberellin physiology, photosynthesis, carbon cycling, molecular properties of main-group ring components.

University of Louisville, Graduate School, College of Arts and Sciences, Department of Political Science, Louisville, KY 40292-0001. Offers digital politics (MA); political science (MA). *Program availability:* Part-time, evening/weekend. *Faculty:* 20 full-time (8 women), 5 part-time/adjunct (2 women). *Students:* 11 full-time (3 women), 3 part-time (0 women); includes 3 minority (1 Black or African American, non-Hispanic/Latino; 2 Two or more races, non-Hispanic/Latino). Average age 26. 18 applicants, 83% accepted, 11 enrolled. In 2017, 5 master's awarded. *Degree requirements:* For master's, thesis optional. *Entrance requirements:* For master's, GRE, minimum overall undergraduate GPA of 3.0 or 3.2 in final two years of undergraduate study. Additional exam requirements/recommendations for international students: Required—TOEFL (minimum score 550 paper-based; 79 iBT), IELTS (minimum score 6.5). *Application deadline:* For fall admission, 7/15 for domestic and international students; for spring admission, 11/15 for domestic and international students. Applications are processed on a rolling basis. Application fee: $65. Electronic applications accepted. Application fee is waived when completed online. *Expenses:* Tuition, state resident: full-time $12,246; part-time $681 per credit hour. Tuition, nonresident: full-time $25,486; part-time $1417 per credit hour. *Required fees:* $196. Tuition and fees vary according to course load, program and reciprocity agreements. *Financial support:* In 2017–18, 3 research assistantships with full tuition reimbursements (averaging $12,000 per year) were awarded; health care benefits and unspecified assistantships also available. Financial award application deadline: 4/1. *Faculty research:* American politics, public policy, international relations, comparative politics, Internet and politics. *Total annual research expenditures:* $397,905. *Unit head:* Dr. Jasmine Farrier, Professor/Chair, 502-852-3310, Fax: 502-852-7923, E-mail: j.farrier@louisville.edu. *Application contact:* Amanda LeDuke, Senior Program Coordinator, 502-852-3303, Fax: 502-852-7923, E-mail: amanda.leduke@louisville.edu.
Website: http://louisville.edu/politicalscience

The University of Manchester, School of Social Sciences, Manchester, United Kingdom. Offers ethnographic documentary (M Phil); interdisciplinary study of culture (PhD); philosophy (PhD); politics (PhD); social anthropology (PhD); social anthropology with visual media (PhD); social change (PhD); social statistics (PhD); sociology (PhD); visual anthropology (M Phil).

University of Manitoba, Faculty of Graduate Studies, Faculty of Arts, Department of Political Studies, Winnipeg, MB R3T 2N2, Canada. Offers political studies (MA); public administration (MPA). *Degree requirements:* For master's, one foreign language, thesis or alternative.

University of Maryland, College Park, Academic Affairs, College of Behavioral and Social Sciences, Department of Government and Politics, College Park, MD 20742. Offers American politics (PhD); comparative politics (PhD); international relations (PhD); political economy (PhD); political theory (PhD). *Program availability:* Part-time, evening/weekend. *Degree requirements:* For doctorate, comprehensive exam, thesis/dissertation, written exams in 2 fields. *Entrance requirements:* For doctorate, GRE General Test, minimum GPA of 3.5, writing sample. Additional exam requirements/recommendations for international students: Required—TOEFL. Electronic applications accepted. *Faculty research:* International development/conflict, international security, post-communist society, public service, dynamics of conflict and conflict resolution.

University of Massachusetts Amherst, Graduate School, College of Social and Behavioral Sciences, Department of Political Science, Amherst, MA 01003. Offers MA, PhD. *Program availability:* Part-time. Terminal master's awarded for partial completion of doctoral program. *Degree requirements:* For master's, one foreign language, thesis or alternative; for doctorate, one foreign language, comprehensive exam, thesis/dissertation. *Entrance requirements:* For master's and doctorate, GRE General Test, writing sample, 3 letters of recommendation. Additional exam requirements/recommendations for international students: Required—TOEFL (minimum score 550 paper-based; 80 iBT), IELTS (minimum score 6.5). Electronic applications accepted.

University of Memphis, Graduate School, College of Arts and Sciences, Department of Political Science, Memphis, TN 38152. Offers MA. *Faculty:* 5 full-time (2 women). *Students:* 15 full-time (9 women), 4 part-time (3 women); includes 7 minority (all Black or African American, non-Hispanic/Latino), 1 international. Average age 26. 14 applicants, 100% accepted, 11 enrolled. In 2017, 6 master's awarded. *Degree requirements:* For master's, comprehensive exam (for some programs), thesis or alternative, internship. *Entrance requirements:* For master's, GRE General Test or LSAT, minimum GPA of 3.0, letters of recommendation, statement of career goals and interests. *Application deadline:* For fall admission, 8/1 for domestic students; for spring admission, 12/1 for domestic students. Applications are processed on a rolling basis. Application fee: $35 ($60 for international students). Electronic applications accepted. *Expenses:* Contact institution. *Financial support:* In 2017–18, 10 students received support, including 10 research assistantships with full tuition reimbursements available (averaging $15,300 per year); Federal Work-Study, scholarships/grants, and unspecified assistantships also available. Financial award application deadline: 2/1; financial award applicants required to submit FAFSA. *Faculty research:* Political philosophy, comparative judicial studies, conflict studies, legislative studies, foreign policy. *Unit head:* Dr. Matthias Kaelberer, Chair, 901-678-2395, Fax: 901-678-2983, E-mail: mkaelbrr@memphis.edu. *Application contact:* Dr. Nicole Detraz, Graduate Studies Coordinator, 901-678-2395, Fax: 901-678-2983, E-mail: ndetraz@memphis.edu.
Website: http://www.memphis.edu/polisci/

University of Miami, Graduate School, College of Arts and Sciences, Department of Political Science, Coral Gables, FL 33124. Offers MPA, MPA/JD, MPA/MPH. *Program availability:* Part-time, evening/weekend. *Degree requirements:* For master's, thesis optional. *Entrance requirements:* For master's, GRE General Test. Additional exam requirements/recommendations for international students: Required—TOEFL (minimum score 550 paper-based; 80 iBT). Electronic applications accepted. *Faculty research:* Financial management, non-profit management, human resource management, public service ethics, information technology management.

University of Michigan, Rackham Graduate School, College of Literature, Science, and the Arts, Department of Political Science, Ann Arbor, MI 48109-1045. Offers political science (PhD); political science and public policy (PhD); social work and political science (PhD). *Faculty:* 48 full-time (17 women), 6 part-time/adjunct (4 women). *Students:* 118 full-time (51 women); includes 17 minority (5 Black or African American, non-Hispanic/Latino; 4 Asian, non-Hispanic/Latino; 6 Hispanic/Latino; 2 Two or more races, non-Hispanic/Latino), 29 international. Average age 29. 442 applicants, 8% accepted, 21 enrolled. In 2017, 27 doctorates awarded. Terminal master's awarded for partial completion of doctoral program. *Degree requirements:* For doctorate, comprehensive exam, thesis/dissertation, oral defense of dissertation, preliminary exams. *Entrance requirements:* For doctorate, GRE General Test. Additional exam requirements/recommendations for international students: Required—TOEFL. *Application deadline:* For fall admission, 12/15 for domestic and international students. Application fee: $75 ($90 for international students). Electronic applications accepted. *Expenses:* $22,442 in-state, $44,230 out-of-state/international. *Financial support:* In 2017–18, 100 students received support, including 14 fellowships with full tuition reimbursements available (averaging $23,399 per year), 17 research assistantships with full tuition reimbursements available (averaging $23,399 per year), 46 teaching assistantships with full tuition reimbursements available (averaging $23,399 per year); scholarships/grants, health care benefits, tuition waivers (full), and unspecified assistantships also available. Financial award application deadline: 12/15. *Faculty research:* Political theory; American politics; world politics; comparative politics; research methods; law, courts, and politics. *Unit head:* Nancy Burns, Chair, 734-764-6313, Fax: 734-764-3522. *Application contact:* Kimberly Smith, Graduate Program Coordinator, 734-764-6313, Fax: 734-764-3522, E-mail: psgradinfo@umich.edu.
Website: http://www.lsa.umich.edu/polisci

University of Michigan, School of Social Work, Interdisciplinary PhD Program in Social Work and Social Science, Ann Arbor, MI 48109. Offers social work and anthropology (PhD); social work and economics (PhD); social work and political science (PhD); social work and psychology (PhD); social work and sociology (PhD). Programs offered through the Rackham Graduate School. *Faculty:* 57 full-time (36 women). *Students:* 53 full-time (38 women); includes 27 minority (10 Black or African American, non-Hispanic/Latino; 2 American Indian or Alaska Native, non-Hispanic/Latino; 9 Asian, non-Hispanic/Latino; 6 Hispanic/Latino). Average age 32. 124 applicants, 6% accepted, 7 enrolled. In 2017, 10 doctorates awarded. *Degree requirements:* For doctorate, thesis/dissertation, oral defense of dissertation, preliminary exam. *Entrance requirements:* For doctorate, GRE General Test. Additional exam requirements/recommendations for international students: Required—TOEFL (minimum score 620 paper-based, 88 iBT) or IELTS. *Application deadline:* For fall admission, 12/1 for domestic and international students. Application fee: $75 ($90 for international students). Electronic applications accepted. *Expenses:* Contact institution. *Financial support:* In 2017–18, 59 students received support, including 24 fellowships with full tuition reimbursements available (averaging $17,600 per year), 7 research assistantships with full tuition reimbursements available (averaging $20,399 per year), 21 teaching assistantships with full tuition reimbursements available (averaging $20,399 per year); career-related internships or fieldwork, scholarships/grants, traineeships, health care benefits, tuition waivers (full and partial), and unspecified assistantships also available. Financial award application deadline: 12/1; financial award applicants required to submit FAFSA. *Faculty research:* Children and family, aging, community organization, health and mental health, police and evaluation. *Total annual research expenditures:* $4.1 million. *Unit head:* Dr. William Elliott, III, Director, 734-763-5768, E-mail: willelli@umich.edu. *Application contact:* Todd Huynh, Graduate Coordinator, 734-647-2554, Fax: 734-615-3192, E-mail: ssw.phd.info@umich.edu.
Website: https://ssw.umich.edu/offices/phd

University of Michigan–Flint, College of Arts and Sciences, Program in Social Sciences, Flint, MI 48502-1950. Offers gender studies (MA); global studies (MA); U.S. history and politics (MA). *Program availability:* Part-time. *Faculty:* 12 full-time (7 women), 6 part-time/adjunct (4 women). *Students:* 2 full-time (1 woman), 12 part-time (6 women); includes 4 minority (3 Black or African American, non-Hispanic/Latino; 1 Hispanic/Latino). Average age 43. 8 applicants, 88% accepted, 6 enrolled. In 2017, 11 master's awarded. *Entrance requirements:* For master's, bachelor's degree from regionally-accredited institution, minimum overall undergraduate GPA of 3.0. Additional exam requirements/recommendations for international students: Required—TOEFL (minimum score 84 iBT), IELTS (minimum score 6.5). *Application deadline:* For fall admission, 8/1 for domestic students, 5/1 for international students; for winter admission, 11/15 for domestic students, 9/1 for international students; for spring admission, 3/15 for domestic students, 1/1 for international students; for summer admission, 5/15 for domestic students. Applications are processed on a rolling basis. Application fee: $55. Electronic applications accepted. *Expenses:* Contact institution. *Financial support:* Federal Work-Study, scholarships/grants, and unspecified assistantships available. Financial award application deadline: 3/1; financial award applicants required to submit FAFSA. *Unit head:* Dr. Adam Lutzker, Director, 810-762-3470, Fax: 810-762-3281, E-mail:

alutzker@umflint.edu. *Application contact:* Bradley T. Maki, Director of Graduate Admissions, 810-762-3171, Fax: 810-766-6789, E-mail: bmaki@umflint.edu.
Website: http://www.umflint.edu/graduateprograms/social-sciences-ma

University of Minnesota, Twin Cities Campus, Graduate School, College of Liberal Arts, Department of Political Science, Minneapolis, MN 55455. Offers PhD. *Degree requirements:* For doctorate, thesis/dissertation, 1 foreign language or statistics. *Entrance requirements:* For doctorate, GRE. Additional exam requirements/recommendations for international students: Required—TOEFL; Recommended—IELTS. Electronic applications accepted. *Faculty research:* American politics, comparative politics, international relations, political theory, research methodology.

University of Mississippi, Graduate School, College of Liberal Arts, University, MS 38677. Offers anthropology (MA); biology (MS, PhD); chemistry (MS, DA, PhD); creative writing (MFA); documentary expression (MFA); economics (MA, PhD); English (MA, PhD); experimental psychology (PhD); history (MA, PhD); mathematics (MS, PhD); modern languages (MA); music (MM); philosophy (MA); physics (MA, MS, PhD); political science (MA, PhD); Southern studies (MA); studio art (MFA). *Program availability:* Part-time. *Faculty:* 465 full-time (207 women), 82 part-time/adjunct (46 women). *Students:* 466 full-time (229 women), 72 part-time (34 women); includes 87 minority (38 Black or African American, non-Hispanic/Latino; 18 Asian, non-Hispanic/Latino; 24 Hispanic/Latino; 7 Two or more races, non-Hispanic/Latino), 121 international. Average age 29. *Degree requirements:* For doctorate, thesis/dissertation. *Entrance requirements:* For master's, GRE General Test, minimum GPA of 3.0; for doctorate, GRE General Test. Additional exam requirements/recommendations for international students: Required—TOEFL. *Application deadline:* For fall admission, 2/1 priority date for domestic students; for spring admission, 10/1 for domestic students. Applications are processed on a rolling basis. Application fee: $50. Electronic applications accepted. *Financial support:* Fellowships, research assistantships, teaching assistantships, career-related internships or fieldwork, Federal Work-Study, institutionally sponsored loans, scholarships/grants, and unspecified assistantships available. Financial award application deadline: 3/1; financial award applicants required to submit FAFSA. *Unit head:* Dr. Lee Michael Cohen, Dean, 662-915-7177, Fax: 662-915-5792, E-mail: libarts@olemiss.edu. *Application contact:* Dr. Christy M. Wyandt, Associate Dean of Graduate School, 662-915-7474, Fax: 662-915-7577, E-mail: cwyandt@olemiss.edu.

University of Missouri, Office of Research and Graduate Studies, College of Arts and Science, Department of Political Science, Columbia, MO 65211. Offers MA, PhD. Terminal master's awarded for partial completion of doctoral program. *Degree requirements:* For doctorate, one foreign language, comprehensive exam, thesis/dissertation. *Entrance requirements:* For master's, GRE General Test (minimum combined score 1000 Verbal and Quantitative), minimum GPA of 3.0 in last 60 hours and in political science courses; at least 12 hours of upper-level course work in political science; for doctorate, GRE General Test (minimum combined score 1200 Verbal and Quantitative), minimum GPA of 3.0 in last 60 hours and in political science courses; at least 12 hours of upper-level course work in political science. Additional exam requirements/recommendations for international students: Required—TOEFL (minimum score 570 paper-based; 88 iBT). Electronic applications accepted. *Faculty research:* American politics, comparative politics, international relations, public policy and administration.

University of Missouri–Kansas City, College of Arts and Sciences, Department of Political Science, Kansas City, MO 64110-2499. Offers MA. PhD (interdisciplinary) offered through the School of Graduate Studies. *Program availability:* Part-time, evening/weekend. Terminal master's awarded for partial completion of doctoral program. *Degree requirements:* For master's, thesis optional. *Entrance requirements:* For master's, GRE, minimum GPA of 3.0, course work in political science, 2 letters of recommendation. Additional exam requirements/recommendations for international students: Required—TOEFL (minimum score 550 paper-based; 80 iBT). Electronic applications accepted. *Faculty research:* Sex and gender, Chinese politics, voting behavior, politics of Presidency and social security, public law.

University of Missouri–St. Louis, College of Arts and Sciences, Department of Political Science, St. Louis, MO 63121. Offers American politics (MA); comparative politics (MA); international politics (MA); political process and behavior (MA); political science (PhD); public administration and public policy (MA); urban and regional politics (MA). *Program availability:* Part-time, evening/weekend. *Faculty:* 15 full-time (5 women), 9 part-time/adjunct (2 women). *Students:* 32 full-time (11 women), 21 part-time (9 women); includes 11 minority (10 Black or African American, non-Hispanic/Latino; 1 Hispanic/Latino), 4 international. 10 applicants, 80% accepted, 7 enrolled. Terminal master's awarded for partial completion of doctoral program. *Degree requirements:* For master's, thesis optional; for doctorate, thesis/dissertation. *Entrance requirements:* For master's, GRE General Test, 2 letters of recommendation, statement of purpose; for doctorate, GRE General Test, 3 letters of recommendation, statement of purpose. Additional exam requirements/recommendations for international students: Required—TOEFL (minimum score 550 paper-based; 79 iBT), IELTS (minimum score 6.5). *Application deadline:* For fall admission, 2/15 priority date for domestic and international students; for winter admission, 10/15 for domestic and international students; for spring admission, 10/15 priority date for domestic and international students. Applications are processed on a rolling basis. Application fee: $50 ($40 for international students). Electronic applications accepted. *Expenses:* Tuition, state resident: part-time $476.50 per credit hour. Tuition, nonresident: part-time $1169.70 per credit hour. *Financial support:* Fellowships, research assistantships with tuition reimbursements, teaching assistantships with tuition reimbursements, and career-related internships or fieldwork available. Support available to part-time students. Financial award application deadline: 3/15; financial award applicants required to submit FAFSA. *Faculty research:* Public policy, urban politics and administration, American government. *Unit head:* Dave Robertson, Chairperson, 314-516-5521, Fax: 314-516-7236. *Application contact:* 314-516-5458, Fax: 314-516-6996, E-mail: gradadm@umsl.edu.
Website: http://www.umsl.edu/~polisci/

University of Montana, Graduate School, College of Humanities and Sciences, Department of Political Science, Program in Political Science, Missoula, MT 59812. Offers MA. *Degree requirements:* For master's, thesis. *Entrance requirements:* For master's, GRE General Test.

University of Nebraska at Omaha, Graduate Studies, College of Arts and Sciences, Department of Political Science, Omaha, NE 68182. Offers American government (Certificate); global information operations (Certificate); intelligence and national security (Certificate); political science (MS). *Program availability:* Part-time, evening/weekend, online learning. *Degree requirements:* For master's, comprehensive exam, thesis (for some programs). *Entrance requirements:* For master's, 15 undergraduate political science hours, minimum undergraduate GPA of 3.0, 2 letters of recommendation, official transcripts. Additional exam requirements/recommendations for international students: Required—TOEFL, IELTS, PTE. Electronic applications accepted.

University of Nebraska–Lincoln, Graduate College, College of Arts and Sciences, Department of Political Science, Lincoln, NE 68588. Offers political science (MA, PhD); public policy analysis (Graduate Certificate). *Degree requirements:* For master's, thesis optional; for doctorate, variable foreign language requirement, comprehensive exam, thesis/dissertation. *Entrance requirements:* For master's and doctorate, GRE General Test, writing sample. Additional exam requirements/recommendations for international students: Required—TOEFL (minimum score 600 paper-based). Electronic applications accepted. *Faculty research:* Public policy; comparative politics; international relations; political theory, behavior, and methodology; American politics.

University of Nevada, Las Vegas, Graduate College, College of Liberal Arts, Department of Political Science, Las Vegas, NV 89154-5029. Offers MA, PhD. *Program availability:* Part-time. *Faculty:* 9 full-time (3 women). *Students:* 14 full-time (4 women), 17 part-time (6 women); includes 9 minority (4 Black or African American, non-Hispanic/Latino; 1 Asian, non-Hispanic/Latino; 1 Hispanic/Latino; 3 Two or more races, non-Hispanic/Latino). Average age 35. 14 applicants, 50% accepted, 3 enrolled. In 2017, 2 master's, 2 doctorates awarded. *Degree requirements:* For master's, thesis, professional paper; for doctorate, one foreign language, comprehensive exam, thesis/dissertation, oral examination. *Entrance requirements:* For master's, GRE General Test, 2 letters of recommendation; personal statement; bachelor's degree; minimum GPA of 3.0; for doctorate, GRE General Test, minimum GPA of 3.3 in BA, 3.5 in MA; 3 letters of recommendation; personal statement; writing sample. Additional exam requirements/recommendations for international students: Required—TOEFL (minimum score 550 paper-based; 80 iBT), IELTS (minimum score 7). *Application deadline:* For fall admission, 2/1 for domestic students. Application fee: $60 ($95 for international students). Electronic applications accepted. *Expenses:* $275 per credit, $850 per course, $7,969 per year resident, $22,157 per year non-resident, $7,094 non-resident fee (7 credits or more), $1,307 annual health insurance fee. *Financial support:* In 2017–18, 11 students received support, including 2 research assistantships with partial tuition reimbursements available (averaging $15,000 per year), 9 teaching assistantships with partial tuition reimbursements available (averaging $15,153 per year); institutionally sponsored loans, scholarships/grants, health care benefits, and unspecified assistantships also available. Financial award application deadline: 3/15; financial award applicants required to submit FAFSA. *Faculty research:* International political economy and security, religion and politics, democratization, demographic change and its consequences, international security and political violence, ancient political philosophy, political behavior, political institutions. *Total annual research expenditures:* $61,461. *Unit head:* Dr. John P. Tuman, Chair and Professor, 702-895-5258, Fax: 702-895-1065, E-mail: john.tuman@unlv.edu. *Application contact:* Dr. David Damore, Graduate Coordinator, 702-895-3217, Fax: 702-895-1065, E-mail: david.damore@unlv.edu.
Website: http://liberalarts.unlv.edu/Political_Science/

University of Nevada, Reno, Graduate School, College of Liberal Arts, Department of Political Science, Program in Political Science, Reno, NV 89557. Offers MA, PhD. Terminal master's awarded for partial completion of doctoral program. *Degree requirements:* For master's, comprehensive exam, oral exam/thesis or professional paper; for doctorate, thesis/dissertation, 2 field exams, oral exam. *Entrance requirements:* For master's, GRE General Test, GMAT, LSAT, minimum GPA of 2.75; for doctorate, GRE General Test, GMAT, LSAT, minimum GPA of 3.0. Additional exam requirements/recommendations for international students: Required—TOEFL (minimum score 500 paper-based; 61 iBT), IELTS (minimum score 6). Electronic applications accepted. *Faculty research:* Analysis of political processes, institutions, and policies.

University of New Brunswick Fredericton, School of Graduate Studies, Faculty of Arts, Department of Political Science, Fredericton, NB E3B 5A3, Canada. Offers MA. *Program availability:* Part-time. *Degree requirements:* For master's, thesis (for some programs). *Entrance requirements:* For master's, minimum cumulative GPA of 3.3; 4-year bachelor's degree, or equivalent, in political science. Additional exam requirements/recommendations for international students: Required—TOEFL. Electronic applications accepted. *Faculty research:* Political theory, public policy, gender and politics, global political economy and Canadian politics.

University of New Hampshire, Graduate School, College of Liberal Arts, Department of Political Science, Durham, NH 03824. Offers political science (MA, Postbaccalaureate Certificate), including political science (MA), sustainability politics and policy (Postbaccalaureate Certificate). *Program availability:* Part-time. *Students:* 12 full-time (7 women), 30 part-time (16 women); includes 5 minority (2 Black or African American, non-Hispanic/Latino; 1 Asian, non-Hispanic/Latino; 1 Hispanic/Latino; 1 Two or more races, non-Hispanic/Latino), 1 international. Average age 30. 27 applicants, 70% accepted, 13 enrolled. In 2017, 13 master's awarded. *Entrance requirements:* For master's, GRE General Test. Additional exam requirements/recommendations for international students: Required—TOEFL (minimum score 550 paper-based; 80 iBT). *Application deadline:* For fall admission, 4/1 for domestic and international students; for spring admission, 11/1 for domestic students. Application fee: $65. Electronic applications accepted. *Financial support:* In 2017–18, 4 students received support, including 3 teaching assistantships; fellowships, research assistantships, career-related internships or fieldwork, Federal Work-Study, scholarships/grants, and tuition waivers (full and partial) also available. Support available to part-time students. Financial award application deadline: 2/15. *Unit head:* Mary Malone, Chair, 603-862-1406. *Application contact:* Tama Andrews, Graduate Program Coordinator, 603-862-2321.
Website: http://cola.unh.edu/political-science

University of New Mexico, Graduate Studies, College of Arts and Sciences, Program in Political Science, Albuquerque, NM 87131-2039. Offers MA, PhD. *Program availability:* Part-time. *Faculty:* 8 full-time (4 women). *Students:* 21 full-time (12 women), 10 part-time (4 women); includes 12 minority (10 Hispanic/Latino; 2 Two or more races, non-Hispanic/Latino), 5 international. Average age 31. 20 applicants, 50% accepted, 5 enrolled. In 2017, 7 master's, 2 doctorates awarded. Terminal master's awarded for partial completion of doctoral program. *Degree requirements:* For master's, comprehensive exam, thesis optional; for doctorate, comprehensive exam, thesis/dissertation, field research paper, minimum cumulative GPA of 3.5. *Entrance requirements:* For master's and doctorate, GRE General Test, 3 letters of recommendation, writing sample, letter of intent. Additional exam requirements/recommendations for international students: Required—TOEFL. *Application deadline:* For fall admission, 1/15 priority date for domestic and international students. Application fee: $50. Electronic applications accepted. *Financial support:* Fellowships with full tuition reimbursements, research assistantships with full tuition reimbursements, teaching assistantships with full tuition reimbursements, scholarships/grants, health care benefits, and unspecified assistantships available. Financial award application deadline: 1/15; financial award applicants required to submit FAFSA. *Faculty research:* Latin American politics, American politics, comparative politics, public policy, international relations, methodology. *Unit head:* Dr. William Stanley, Chair, 505-277-5104, Fax: 505-277-2821, E-mail: wstanley@unm.edu. *Application contact:* Shoshana Handel, Graduate Program Assistant, 505-277-5104, Fax: 505-277-2821, E-mail: shandel@unm.edu.
Website: http://polisci.unm.edu/index.html

University of New Orleans, Graduate School, College of Liberal Arts, Department of Political Science, New Orleans, LA 70148. Offers political science (MA, PhD); public administration (MPA). *Program availability:* Evening/weekend. *Degree requirements:* For master's, one foreign language, thesis or alternative; for doctorate, one foreign language, thesis/dissertation. *Entrance requirements:* For master's, GRE General Test; for doctorate, GRE General Test, GRE Subject Test. Additional exam requirements/

recommendations for international students: Required—TOEFL (minimum score 550 paper-based; 79 iBT), IELTS (minimum score 6.5). Electronic applications accepted. *Faculty research:* Judicial politics, public policy, voting rights, Southern politics, presidential-congressional relations.

University of North Alabama, College of Arts and Sciences, Department of Politics, Justice, and Law, Florence, AL 35632-0001. Offers criminal justice (MSCJ). *Program availability:* Part-time, 100% online. *Faculty:* 4 full-time (0 women), 3 part-time/adjunct (1 woman). *Students:* 5 full-time (4 women), 17 part-time (11 women); includes 9 minority (6 Black or African American, non-Hispanic/Latino; 3 Hispanic/Latino). Average age 30. 18 applicants, 94% accepted, 9 enrolled. In 2017, 6 master's awarded. *Degree requirements:* For master's, comprehensive exam (for some programs), thesis optional. *Entrance requirements:* For master's, GRE General Test, MAT, three letters of recommendation; essay. Additional exam requirements/recommendations for international students: Required—TOEFL (minimum score 79 iBT), IELTS (minimum score 6), PTE (minimum score 54). *Application deadline:* Applications are processed on a rolling basis. Application fee: $50 ($100 for international students). Electronic applications accepted. *Expenses:* Tuition, state resident: full-time $7824; part-time $5943 per year. Tuition, nonresident: full-time $15,648; part-time $11,736 per year. *Required fees:* $3064; $2298 per unit. Tuition and fees vary according to course load and reciprocity agreements. *Financial support:* Federal Work-Study, scholarships/grants, and unspecified assistantships available. Financial award application deadline: 2/1; financial award applicants required to submit FAFSA. *Unit head:* Dr. Tim Collins, Chair, 256-765-5045, E-mail: jtcollins@una.edu. *Application contact:* Hillary N. Coats, Graduate Admissions Coordinator, 256-765-4447, E-mail: graduate@una.edu.
Website: http://www.una.edu/criminaljustice/

The University of North Carolina at Chapel Hill, Graduate School, College of Arts and Sciences, Department of Political Science, Chapel Hill, NC 27599. Offers Latin American studies (Certificate); political science (MA, PhD); trans-Atlantic studies (MA). *Degree requirements:* For master's, comprehensive exam; for doctorate, one foreign language, comprehensive exam, thesis/dissertation. *Entrance requirements:* For master's and doctorate, GRE General Test, minimum GPA of 3.0 recommended. Electronic applications accepted.

The University of North Carolina at Greensboro, Graduate School, College of Arts and Sciences, Department of Political Science, Greensboro, NC 27412-5001. Offers nonprofit management (Certificate); public affairs (MPA); urban and economic development (Certificate). *Accreditation:* NASPAA. *Degree requirements:* For master's, comprehensive exam. *Entrance requirements:* For master's, GRE General Test. Additional exam requirements/recommendations for international students: Required—TOEFL. Electronic applications accepted. *Faculty research:* U.S. Constitution, Canadian parliament, public management, ethical challenge of public service.

University of Northern British Columbia, Office of Graduate Studies, Prince George, BC V2N 4Z9, Canada. Offers business administration (Diploma); community health science (M Sc); disability management (MA); education (M Ed); first nations studies (MA); gender studies (MA); history (MA); interdisciplinary studies (MA); international studies (MA); mathematical, computer and physical sciences (M Sc); natural resources and environmental studies (M Sc, MA, MNRES, PhD); political science (MA); psychology (M Sc, PhD); social work (MSW). *Program availability:* Part-time, evening/weekend, online learning. *Degree requirements:* For master's, thesis; for doctorate, thesis/dissertation. *Entrance requirements:* For master's, GRE, minimum B average in undergraduate course work; for doctorate, candidacy exam, minimum A average in graduate course work.

University of North Texas, Robert B. Toulouse School of Graduate Studies, Denton, TX 76203-5459. Offers accounting (MS); applied anthropology (MA, MS); applied behavior analysis (Certificate); applied geography (MA); applied technology and performance improvement (M Ed, MS); art education (MA); art history (MA); art museum education (Certificate); arts leadership (Certificate); audiology (Au D); behavior analysis (MS); behavioral science (PhD); biochemistry and molecular biology (MS); biology (MA, MS); biomedical engineering (MS); business analysis (MS); chemistry (MS); clinical health psychology (PhD); communication studies (MA, MS); computer engineering (MS); computer science (MS); counseling (M Ed, MS), including clinical mental health counseling (MS), college and university counseling, elementary school counseling, secondary school counseling; creative writing (MA); criminal justice (MS); curriculum and instruction (M Ed); decision sciences (MBA); design (MA, MFA), including fashion design (MFA), innovation studies, interior design (MFA); early childhood studies (MS); economics (MS); educational leadership (M Ed, Ed D); educational psychology (MS, PhD), including family studies (MS), gifted and talented (MS), human development (MS), learning and cognition (MS), research, measurement and evaluation (MS); electrical engineering (MS); emergency management (MPA); engineering technology (MS); English (MA); English as a second language (MA); environmental science (MS); finance (MBA, MS); financial management (MPA); French (MA); health services management (MBA); higher education (M Ed, Ed D); history (MA, MS); hospitality management (MS); human resources management (MPA); information science (MS); information systems (PhD); information technologies (MBA); interdisciplinary studies (MA, MS); international studies (MA); international sustainable tourism (MS); jazz studies (MM); journalism (MA, MJ, Graduate Certificate), including interactive and virtual digital communication (Graduate Certificate), narrative journalism (Graduate Certificate), public relations (Graduate Certificate); kinesiology (MS); linguistics (MA); local government management (MPA); logistics (PhD); logistics and supply chain management (MBA); long-term care, senior housing, and aging services (MA); management (PhD); marketing (MBA); mathematics (MA, MS); mechanical and energy engineering (MS, PhD); music (MA), including ethnomusicology, music theory, musicology, performance; music composition (PhD); music education (MM Ed, PhD); nonprofit management (MPA); operations and supply chain management (MBA); performance (MM, DMA); philosophy (MA); political science (MA); professional and technical communication (MA); radio, television and film (MA, MFA); rehabilitation counseling (Certificate); sociology (MA); Spanish (MA); special education (M Ed); speech-language pathology (MA); strategic management (MBA); studio art (MFA); teaching (M Ed); MBA/MS. *Program availability:* Part-time, evening/weekend, online learning. Terminal master's awarded for partial completion of doctoral program. *Degree requirements:* For master's, variable foreign language requirement, comprehensive exam (for some programs), thesis (for some programs); for doctorate, variable foreign language requirement, comprehensive exam (for some programs), thesis/dissertation; for other advanced degree, variable foreign language requirement, comprehensive exam (for some programs). *Entrance requirements:* For master's and doctorate, GRE, GMAT. Additional exam requirements/recommendations for international students: Required—TOEFL (minimum score 550 paper-based; 79 iBT). Electronic applications accepted.

University of Notre Dame, Graduate School, College of Arts and Letters, Division of Social Science, Department of Political Science, Notre Dame, IN 46556. Offers PhD. *Degree requirements:* For doctorate, one foreign language, comprehensive exam, thesis/dissertation, candidacy exam. *Entrance requirements:* For doctorate, GRE General Test. Additional exam requirements/recommendations for international students: Required—TOEFL (minimum score 600 paper-based; 80 iBT). Electronic applications accepted. *Faculty research:* American government, comparative politics, international relations, political theory.

University of Oklahoma, College of Arts and Sciences, Department of Political Science, Program in Political Science, Norman, OK 73019. Offers MA, PhD. *Students:* 27 full-time (9 women), 18 part-time (7 women); includes 5 minority (1 Black or African American, non-Hispanic/Latino; 3 Hispanic/Latino; 1 Two or more races, non-Hispanic/Latino), 9 international. Average age 30. 21 applicants, 33% accepted, 4 enrolled. In 2017, 5 master's awarded. Terminal master's awarded for partial completion of doctoral program. *Degree requirements:* For master's, comprehensive exam, thesis optional, 36 hours; for doctorate, comprehensive exam, thesis/dissertation, 90 hours. *Entrance requirements:* For master's and doctorate, GRE, purpose statement, writing sample, three letters of recommendation. Additional exam requirements/recommendations for international students: Required—TOEFL (minimum score 100 iBT) or IELTS (minimum score 7.0). *Application deadline:* For fall admission, 2/1 priority date for domestic and international students. Application fee: $50 ($100 for international students). Electronic applications accepted. *Expenses:* Tuition, state resident: full-time $5119; part-time $213.30 per credit hour. Tuition, nonresident: full-time $19,778; part-time $824.10 per credit hour. *Required fees:* $3458; $133.55 per credit hour. $126.50 per semester. *Financial support:* In 2017–18, 30 students received support. Research assistantships with full tuition reimbursements available, teaching assistantships with full tuition reimbursements available, scholarships/grants, health care benefits, unspecified assistantships, and travel and conference attendance funding available. Financial award application deadline: 6/1; financial award applicants required to submit FAFSA. *Faculty research:* American and comparative politics, public administration and policy, international relations, political theory and research methods. *Unit head:* Prof. Scott Robinson, Chair, 405-325-2061, Fax: 405-325-0718, E-mail: pscgradprog@ou.edu. *Application contact:* Jeff Alexander, Graduate Programs Coordinator, 405-325-1845, Fax: 405-325-0718, E-mail: pscgradprog@ou.edu.
Website: http://www.ou.edu/content/cas/psc/graduate.html

University of Oregon, Graduate School, College of Arts and Sciences, Department of Political Science, Eugene, OR 97403. Offers MA, MS, PhD. Terminal master's awarded for partial completion of doctoral program. *Degree requirements:* For master's, thesis or alternative; for doctorate, thesis/dissertation. *Entrance requirements:* For master's and doctorate, GRE General Test, minimum GPA of 3.0. Additional exam requirements/recommendations for international students: Required—TOEFL. *Faculty research:* Public policy, public choice, comparative politics, political economy, international relations.

University of Ottawa, Faculty of Graduate and Postdoctoral Studies, Faculty of Social Sciences, Department of Political Studies, Ottawa, ON K1N 6N5, Canada. Offers MA, PhD. *Degree requirements:* For master's, thesis or alternative, fluency in English and French; for doctorate, comprehensive exam, thesis/dissertation. *Entrance requirements:* For master's, honors bachelor's degree or equivalent, minimum B average; for doctorate, master's degree, minimum B+ average. Electronic applications accepted. *Faculty research:* Political thought and analysis of ideologies, Canadian and Québécois policies, international and comparative policies.

University of Pennsylvania, School of Arts and Sciences, Fels Institute of Government, Philadelphia, PA 19104. Offers economic development and growth (Certificate); government administration (MGA); nonprofit administration (Certificate); organization dynamics (MS); politics (Certificate); public administration (MPA); public finance (Certificate). *Program availability:* Part-time, evening/weekend. *Students:* 44 full-time (27 women), 78 part-time (41 women); includes 30 minority (9 Black or African American, non-Hispanic/Latino; 8 Asian, non-Hispanic/Latino; 10 Hispanic/Latino; 3 Two or more races, non-Hispanic/Latino), 10 international. Average age 31. 333 applicants, 47% accepted, 88 enrolled. In 2017, 57 master's, 9 other advanced degrees awarded. *Financial support:* Application deadline: 1/1.
Website: http://www.fels.upenn.edu/

University of Pennsylvania, School of Arts and Sciences, Graduate Group in Political Science, Philadelphia, PA 19104. Offers AM, PhD, MGA/AM. *Faculty:* 36 full-time (12 women), 2 part-time/adjunct (1 woman). *Students:* 67 full-time (32 women), 1 (woman) part-time; includes 13 minority (2 Black or African American, non-Hispanic/Latino; 3 Asian, non-Hispanic/Latino; 5 Hispanic/Latino; 3 Two or more races, non-Hispanic/Latino), 19 international. Average age 29. 330 applicants, 8% accepted, 11 enrolled. In 2017, 6 master's, 9 doctorates awarded. Terminal master's awarded for partial completion of doctoral program. *Financial support:* Teaching assistantships available.
Website: http://www.sas.upenn.edu/polisci/content/graduate-program

University of Pittsburgh, Graduate School of Public and International Affairs, Master of Public and International Affairs Program, Pittsburgh, PA 15260. Offers human security (MPIA); international political economy (MPIA); security and intelligence studies (MPIA); JD/MPIA; MBA/MPIA; MPH/MPIA; MPIA/MSW; MSIS/MPIA. *Program availability:* Part-time, evening/weekend. *Faculty:* 30 full-time (11 women), 14 part-time/adjunct (5 women). *Students:* 87 full-time (42 women), 14 part-time (7 women); includes 15 minority (6 Black or African American, non-Hispanic/Latino; 3 Asian, non-Hispanic/Latino; 6 Hispanic/Latino), 14 international. Average age 27. 173 applicants, 88% accepted, 37 enrolled. In 2017, 54 master's awarded. *Degree requirements:* For master's, thesis optional, capstone seminar. *Entrance requirements:* For master's, GRE General Test or GMAT, 2 letters of recommendation, resume, undergraduate transcripts, personal statement. Additional exam requirements/recommendations for international students: Required—TOEFL (minimum score 80 iBT); Recommended—IELTS (minimum score 7). *Application deadline:* For fall admission, 2/1 priority date for domestic students, 1/15 priority date for international students; for spring admission, 11/1 priority date for domestic students, 8/1 priority date for international students. Application fee: $50. Electronic applications accepted. *Expenses:* $23,140 per year in-state, $37,830 out-of-state. *Financial support:* In 2017–18, 47 students received support, including 7 fellowships with full tuition reimbursements available (averaging $37,000 per year), 8 research assistantships with full tuition reimbursements available (averaging $37,000 per year); scholarships/grants also available. Financial award application deadline: 2/1; financial award applicants required to submit FAFSA. *Faculty research:* International political economy, human security, security and intelligence studies. *Total annual research expenditures:* $1.6 million. *Unit head:* Dr. John Keeler, Dean, 412-648-7605, Fax: 412-648-7601, E-mail: gspia@pitt.edu. *Application contact:* Dr. Michael Rizzi, Director of Student Services, 412-648-7643, Fax: 412-648-7641, E-mail: rizzim@pitt.edu.
Website: http://www.gspia.pitt.edu/

University of Pittsburgh, Kenneth P. Dietrich School of Arts and Sciences, Department of Political Science, Pittsburgh, PA 15260. Offers MA, PhD. *Faculty:* 21 full-time (8 women). *Students:* 54 full-time (19 women); includes 22 minority (12 Asian, non-Hispanic/Latino; 10 Hispanic/Latino). Average age 30. 101 applicants, 17% accepted, 11 enrolled. Terminal master's awarded for partial completion of doctoral program. *Degree requirements:* For master's and doctorate, comprehensive exam. *Entrance requirements:* For doctorate, GRE General Test, minimum QPA of 3.0. Additional exam requirements/recommendations for international students: Required—TOEFL (minimum score 90 iBT). *Application deadline:* For fall admission, 1/8 for domestic and international students. Application fee: $50. Electronic applications accepted. *Financial*

support: In 2017–18, 15 fellowships with full tuition reimbursements (averaging $21,000 per year), 14 research assistantships with full tuition reimbursements (averaging $18,815 per year), 13 teaching assistantships with full tuition reimbursements (averaging $18,815 per year) were awarded; health care benefits and tuition waivers (full) also available. *Total annual research expenditures:* $223,268. *Unit head:* Dr. Steven Finkel, Chair, 412-648-7290, E-mail: finkel@pitt.edu. *Application contact:* Brian Deutsch, Graduate Administrator, 412-648-7270, E-mail: brd51@pitt.edu.
Website: http://www.polisci.pitt.edu/

University of Regina, Faculty of Graduate Studies and Research, Faculty of Arts, Program in Social and Political Thought, Regina, SK S4S 0A2, Canada. Offers MA. *Program availability:* Part-time. *Faculty:* 11 full-time (4 women). *Students:* 7 full-time (3 women), 5 part-time (1 woman). 9 applicants, 11% accepted. In 2017, 2 master's awarded. *Degree requirements:* For master's, thesis. *Entrance requirements:* Additional exam requirements/recommendations for international students: Required—TOEFL (minimum score 580 paper-based; 80 iBT), IELTS (minimum score 6.5), PTE (minimum score 59). *Application deadline:* For fall admission, 3/30 for domestic and international students. Application fee: $100. Electronic applications accepted. *Expenses:* $10,681. *Financial support:* In 2017–18, fellowships (averaging $6,000 per year), 2 teaching assistantships (averaging $2,562 per year) were awarded; research assistantships and scholarships/grants also available. Financial award application deadline: 6/15. *Faculty research:* Liberalism and freedom, neo-conservatism, Aristotle's ethics, Kant's ethical theory and political philosophy, Hegel's philosophy of right. *Unit head:* Dr. Lee Ward, Graduate Coordinator, 306-359-1259, E-mail: lee.ward@uregina.ca. *Application contact:* Doreen Thompson, Administrative Assistant, 306-585-4332, E-mail: doreen.thompson@uregina.ca.

University of Rhode Island, Graduate School, College of Arts and Sciences, Department of Political Science, Kingston, RI 02881. Offers international relations (MA), including American politics; public policy and administration (MPA). *Program availability:* Part-time. *Faculty:* 13 full-time (6 women). *Students:* 17 full-time (10 women), 36 part-time (19 women); includes 7 minority (2 Black or African American, non-Hispanic/Latino; 2 Asian, non-Hispanic/Latino; 2 Hispanic/Latino; 1 Two or more races, non-Hispanic/Latino). 34 applicants, 94% accepted, 25 enrolled. In 2017, 21 master's awarded. *Entrance requirements:* For master's, GRE, GMAT, or MAT if undergraduate GPA below 3.0, 2 letters of recommendation. Additional exam requirements/recommendations for international students: Required—TOEFL. *Application deadline:* For fall admission, 11/15 for domestic students, 2/1 for international students; for spring admission, 7/15 for domestic students, 7/15 priority date for international students. Application fee: $65. Electronic applications accepted. *Expenses:* Tuition, state resident: full-time $12,706; part-time $786 per credit. Tuition, nonresident: full-time $25,216; part-time $1401 per credit. *Required fees:* $1598; $45 per credit. One-time fee: $30 part-time. *Financial support:* In 2017–18, 4 teaching assistantships with tuition reimbursements (averaging $10,761 per year) were awarded. Financial award application deadline: 2/1; financial award applicants required to submit FAFSA. *Unit head:* Dr. Brian Krueger, Department Chair, 401-874-4058, Fax: 401-874-4072, E-mail: bkrueger@uri.edu. *Application contact:* Dr. Marc Hutchison, Director/Associate Professor, 401-874-4054, Fax: 401-874-4072, E-mail: mlhutch@uri.edu.
Website: http://www.uri.edu/artsci/psc/

University of Rochester, School of Arts and Sciences, Department of Political Science, Rochester, NY 14627. Offers PhD. *Faculty:* 22 full-time (5 women). *Students:* 40 full-time (16 women), 3 part-time (2 women); includes 6 minority (3 Asian, non-Hispanic/Latino; 2 Hispanic/Latino; 1 Two or more races, non-Hispanic/Latino), 23 international. Average age 29. 112 applicants, 17% accepted, 5 enrolled. In 2017, 5 doctorates awarded. *Degree requirements:* For doctorate, comprehensive exam, thesis/dissertation, prospectus defense. *Entrance requirements:* For doctorate, GRE General Test, three letters of recommendation, personal statement, transcripts, writing sample. Additional exam requirements/recommendations for international students: Required—TOEFL. *Application deadline:* For fall admission, 1/7 for domestic and international students. Application fee: $60. Electronic applications accepted. *Expenses:* $1,596 per credit hour. *Financial support:* In 2017–18, 5 students received support, including 5 fellowships with full tuition reimbursements available (averaging $27,000 per year); research assistantships, teaching assistantships, and tuition waivers (full) also available. Financial award application deadline: 1/8; financial award applicants required to submit FAFSA. *Faculty research:* Democratic political institutions, positive political theory, comparative politics, political methodology, social choice theory. *Total annual research expenditures:* $86,777. *Unit head:* Gerald Gamm, Chair, 585-275-8573, E-mail: gerald.gamm@rochester.edu. *Application contact:* AnneMarie Tyll, Secretary, 585-275-8745, E-mail: atyll@ur.rochester.edu.
Website: http://www.sas.rochester.edu/psc/graduate/introduction.php

University of Saskatchewan, College of Graduate Studies and Research, College of Arts and Science, Department of Political Studies, Saskatoon, SK S7N 5A2, Canada. Offers MA. *Degree requirements:* For master's, thesis. *Entrance requirements:* Additional exam requirements/recommendations for international students: Required—TOEFL (minimum score 80 iBT); Recommended—IELTS (minimum score 6.5). Electronic applications accepted.

University of South Africa, College of Human Sciences, Pretoria, South Africa. Offers adult education (M Ed); African languages (MA, PhD); African politics (MA, PhD); Afrikaans (MA, PhD); ancient history (MA, PhD); ancient Near Eastern studies (MA, PhD); anthropology (MA, PhD); applied linguistics (MA); Arabic (MA, PhD); archaeology (MA); art history (MA); Biblical archaeology (MA); Biblical studies (M Th, D Th, PhD); Christian spirituality (M Th, D Th); church history (M Th, D Th); classical studies (MA, PhD); clinical psychology (MA); communication (MA, PhD); comparative education (M Ed, Ed D); consulting psychology (D Admin, D Com, PhD); curriculum studies (M Ed, Ed D); development studies (M Admin, MA, D Admin, PhD); didactics (M Ed, Ed D); education (M Tech); education management (M Ed, Ed D); educational psychology (M Ed); English (MA); environmental education (M Ed); French (MA, PhD); German (MA, PhD); Greek (MA); guidance and counseling (M Ed); health studies (MA, PhD), including health sciences education (MA), health services management (MA), medical and surgical nursing science (critical care general) (MA), midwifery and neonatal nursing science (MA), trauma and emergency care (MA); history (MA, PhD); history of education (Ed D); inclusive education (M Ed, Ed D); information and communications technology policy and regulation (MA); information science (MA, MIS, PhD); international politics (MA, PhD); Islamic studies (MA, PhD); Italian (MA, PhD); Judaica (MA, PhD); linguistics (MA, PhD); mathematical education (M Ed); mathematics education (MA); missiology (M Th, D Th); modern Hebrew (MA, PhD); musicology (MA, MMus, D Mus, PhD); natural science education (M Ed); New Testament (M Th, D Th); Old Testament (D Th); pastoral therapy (M Th, D Th); philosophy (MA); philosophy of education (M Ed, Ed D); politics (MA, PhD); Portuguese (MA, PhD); practical theology (M Th, D Th); psychology (MA, MS, PhD); psychology of education (M Ed, Ed D); public health (MA); religious studies (MA, D Th, PhD); Romance languages (MA); Russian (MA, PhD); Semitic languages (MA, PhD); social behavior studies in HIV/AIDS (MA); social science (mental health) (MA); social science in development studies (MA); social science in psychology (MA); social science in social work (MA); social science in sociology (MA); social work (MSW, DSW, PhD); socio-education (M Ed, Ed D); sociolinguistics (MA); sociology (MA, PhD); Spanish (MA, PhD); systematic theology (M Th, D Th); TESOL (teaching English to speakers of other languages) (MA); theological ethics (M Th, D Th); theory of literature (MA, PhD); urban ministries (D Th); urban ministry (M Th).

University of South Carolina, The Graduate School, College of Arts and Sciences, Department of Political Science, Program in Political Science, Columbia, SC 29208. Offers MA, PhD. *Program availability:* Part-time. Terminal master's awarded for partial completion of doctoral program. *Degree requirements:* For master's, one foreign language, thesis; for doctorate, one foreign language, comprehensive exam, thesis/dissertation. *Entrance requirements:* For master's and doctorate, GRE General Test, minimum GPA of 3.5. Additional exam requirements/recommendations for international students: Required—TOEFL. Electronic applications accepted. *Faculty research:* American government and politics, comparative politics, political theory, international politics, public administration and policy.

University of Southern California, Graduate School, Annenberg School for Communication and Journalism, School of Communication, Program in Public Diplomacy, Los Angeles, CA 90089. Offers MPD. *Program availability:* Part-time. *Degree requirements:* For master's, thesis. *Entrance requirements:* For master's, GRE, resume, writing samples, statement of purpose, recommendation letters. Additional exam requirements/recommendations for international students: Required—TOEFL (minimum score 114 iBT), IELTS (minimum score 8). Electronic applications accepted.

University of Southern California, Graduate School, Dana and David Dornsife College of Letters, Arts and Sciences, Political Science and International Relations PhD Program, Los Angeles, CA 90089. Offers PhD. *Degree requirements:* For doctorate, variable foreign language requirement, comprehensive exam, thesis/dissertation. *Entrance requirements:* For doctorate, GRE (minimum score 1000). Additional exam requirements/recommendations for international students: Required—TOEFL (minimum score 600 paper-based; 100 iBT). Electronic applications accepted. *Faculty research:* American politics, foreign policy analysis, international political economy, race/ethics politics, security studies.

University of Southern Mississippi, College of Arts and Letters, Department of Political Science, International Development and International Affairs, Hattiesburg, MS 39406-0001. Offers MA, PhD. *Program availability:* Part-time, evening/weekend, online learning. *Students:* 5 full-time (2 women), 1 (woman) part-time. 16 applicants, 75% accepted, 6 enrolled. In 2017, 53 master's, 8 doctorates awarded. *Degree requirements:* For master's, comprehensive exam, thesis (for some programs); for doctorate, comprehensive exam, thesis/dissertation. *Entrance requirements:* For master's, GRE General Test, minimum GPA of 2.75 in last 2 years, 3.0 in field of study; for doctorate, GRE General Test, minimum GPA of 3.5. Additional exam requirements/recommendations for international students: Required—TOEFL, IELTS. *Application deadline:* For fall admission, 3/1 priority date for domestic students, 3/1 for international students. Applications are processed on a rolling basis. Application fee: $60. Electronic applications accepted. *Expenses:* Tuition, state resident: full-time $3830. *Financial support:* Research assistantships with full and partial tuition reimbursements, teaching assistantships with full tuition reimbursements, career-related internships or fieldwork, Federal Work-Study, scholarships/grants, health care benefits, and unspecified assistantships available. Financial award application deadline: 3/15; financial award applicants required to submit FAFSA. *Faculty research:* American politics, international politics, political theory, comparative politics, public law. *Unit head:* Edward Sayre, Chair, 601-266-4310. *Application contact:* Marek Steedman, Director, Graduate Studies, 601-266-4317, Fax: 601-266-4172.
Website: https://www.usm.edu/political-science-international-development-affairs

University of South Florida, College of Arts and Sciences, School of Interdisciplinary Global Studies, Tampa, FL 33620-9951. Offers government (PhD); Latin American, Caribbean and Latino studies (MA); liberal arts (MA), including Africana studies; political science (MA), including comparative government and politics. *Accreditation:* NASPAA. *Program availability:* Part-time, evening/weekend. *Faculty:* 14 full-time (2 women). *Students:* 3 applicants. In 2017, 9 master's, 1 doctorate awarded. *Degree requirements:* For master's, comprehensive exam, thesis; for doctorate, comprehensive exam, thesis/dissertation. *Entrance requirements:* For master's, GRE General Test, minimum GPA of 3.0 in upper-division undergraduate course work; letters of recommendation (2 for MPA, 3 for MS); 500-word personal statement and undergraduate background in political science or related fields (for MS); one-page career statement (for MPA); for doctorate, GRE General Test, 500-word personal statement, three letters of recommendation, transcripts of MA/BA coursework, writing sample. Additional exam requirements/recommendations for international students: Required—TOEFL (minimum score 550 paper-based; 79 iBT) or IELTS (minimum score 6.5). *Application deadline:* For fall admission, 1/5 for domestic and international students; for spring admission, 10/15 for domestic students, 9/15 for international students. Applications are processed on a rolling basis. Application fee: $30. Electronic applications accepted. *Financial support:* In 2017–18, 3 students received support, including 18 teaching assistantships with tuition reimbursements available (averaging $12,390 per year); unspecified assistantships also available. Financial award application deadline: 4/1. *Faculty research:* Citizenship and identity, social movements, global governance, American politics, public policy. *Total annual research expenditures:* $195,426. *Unit head:* Dr. Steven Tauber, Associate Professor/Interim Chair, 813-974-2278, Fax: 813-974-0832, E-mail: stauber@usf.edu. *Application contact:* Dr. Bernd Reiter, Associate Professor and Director of Graduate Studies, 813-974-3583, Fax: 813-974-0832, E-mail: breiter@usf.edu.
Website: http://gia.usf.edu/

University of South Florida, Innovative Education, Tampa, FL 33620-9951. Offers adult, career and higher education (Graduate Certificate), including college teaching, leadership in developing human resources, leadership in higher education; Africana studies (Graduate Certificate), including diasporas and health disparities, genocide and human rights; aging studies (Graduate Certificate), including gerontology; art research (Graduate Certificate), including museum studies; business foundations (Graduate Certificate); chemical and biomedical engineering (Graduate Certificate), including materials science and engineering, water, health and sustainability; child and family studies (Graduate Certificate), including positive behavior support; civil and industrial engineering (Graduate Certificate), including transportation systems analysis; community and family health (Graduate Certificate), including maternal and child health, social marketing and public health, violence and injury: prevention and intervention, women's health; criminology (Graduate Certificate), including criminal justice administration; data science for public administration (Graduate Certificate); digital humanities (Graduate Certificate); educational measurement and research (Graduate Certificate), including evaluation; English (Graduate Certificate), including comparative literary studies, creative writing, professional and technical communication; entrepreneurship (Graduate Certificate); environmental health (Graduate Certificate), including safety management; epidemiology and biostatistics (Graduate Certificate), including applied biostatistics, biostatistics, concepts and tools of epidemiology, epidemiology, epidemiology of infectious diseases; geography, environment and planning (Graduate Certificate), including community development, environmental policy and management, geographical information systems; geology (Graduate Certificate), including hydrogeology; global health (Graduate Certificate), including disaster

management, global health and Latin American and Caribbean studies, global health practice, humanitarian assistance, infection control; government and international affairs (Graduate Certificate), including Cuban studies, globalization studies; health policy and management (Graduate Certificate), including health management and leadership, public health policy and programs; hearing specialist: early intervention (Graduate Certificate); industrial and management systems engineering (Graduate Certificate), including systems engineering, technology management; information studies (Graduate Certificate), including school library media specialist; information systems/decision sciences (Graduate Certificate), including analytics and business intelligence; instructional technology (Graduate Certificate), including distance education, Florida digital/virtual educator, instructional design, multimedia design, Web design; internal medicine, bioethics and medical humanities (Graduate Certificate), including biomedical ethics; Latin American and Caribbean studies (Graduate Certificate); leadership for coastal resiliency planning (Graduate Certificate); mass communications (Graduate Certificate), including multimedia journalism; mathematics and statistics (Graduate Certificate), including mathematics; medicine (Graduate Certificate), including aging and neuroscience, bioinformatics, biotechnology, brain fitness and memory management, clinical investigation, hand and upper limb rehabilitation, health informatics, health sciences, integrative weight management, intellectual property, medicine and gender, metabolic and nutritional medicine, metabolic cardiology, pharmacy sciences; national and competitive intelligence (Graduate Certificate); nursing (Graduate Certificate), including simulation based academic fellowship in advanced pain management; psychological and social foundations (Graduate Certificate), including career counseling, college teaching, diversity in education, mental health counseling, school counseling; public affairs (Graduate Certificate), including nonprofit management, public management, research administration; public health (Graduate Certificate), including assessing chemical toxicity and public health risks, health equity, pharmacoepidemiology, public health generalist, toxicology, translational research in adolescent behavioral health; public health practices (Graduate Certificate), including planning for healthy communities; rehabilitation and mental health counseling (Graduate Certificate), including integrative mental health care, marriage and family therapy, rehabilitation technology; secondary education (Graduate Certificate), including ESOL, foreign language education: culture and content, foreign language education: professional; social work (Graduate Certificate), including geriatric social work/clinical gerontology; special education (Graduate Certificate), including autism spectrum disorder, disabilities education: severe/profound; world languages (Graduate Certificate), including teaching English as a second language (TESL) or foreign language. *Unit head:* Dr. Cynthia DeLuca, Associate Vice President and Assistant Vice Provost, 813-974-3077, Fax: 813-974-7061, E-mail: deluca@usf.edu. *Application contact:* Owen Hooper, Director, Summer and Alternative Calendar Programs, 813-974-6917, E-mail: hooper@usf.edu.
Website: http://www.usf.edu/innovative-education/

The University of Tennessee, Graduate School, College of Arts and Sciences, Department of Political Science, Program in Political Science, Knoxville, TN 37996. Offers MA, PhD. *Program availability:* Part-time. *Degree requirements:* For master's, thesis or alternative; for doctorate, one foreign language, thesis/dissertation. *Entrance requirements:* For master's and doctorate, GRE General Test, minimum GPA of 2.7. Additional exam requirements/recommendations for international students: Required—TOEFL. Electronic applications accepted.

The University of Tennessee, Graduate School, College of Arts and Sciences, Department of Sociology, Knoxville, TN 37996. Offers criminology (MA, PhD); energy, environment, and resource policy (MA, PhD); political economy (MA, PhD). *Program availability:* Part-time. *Degree requirements:* For master's, thesis or alternative; for doctorate, thesis/dissertation. *Entrance requirements:* For master's, GRE General Test, minimum GPA of 3.0; for doctorate, GRE General Test, minimum GPA of 3.5. Additional exam requirements/recommendations for international students: Required—TOEFL. Electronic applications accepted.

The University of Texas at Arlington, Graduate School, College of Liberal Arts, Department of Political Science, Arlington, TX 76019. Offers MA. *Program availability:* Part-time, evening/weekend. *Degree requirements:* For master's, comprehensive exam, thesis optional. *Entrance requirements:* For master's, GRE, minimum GPA of 3.0 in last 60 hours of course work. Additional exam requirements/recommendations for international students: Required—TOEFL (minimum score 550 paper-based). Electronic applications accepted.

The University of Texas at Austin, Graduate School, College of Liberal Arts, Department of Government, Austin, TX 78712-1111. Offers MA, PhD, PhD/JD. *Degree requirements:* For master's, thesis; for doctorate, comprehensive exam, thesis/dissertation. *Entrance requirements:* For master's and doctorate, GRE General Test. Electronic applications accepted.

The University of Texas at Dallas, School of Economic, Political and Policy Sciences, Program in Political Science, Richardson, TX 75080. Offers Constitutional law (MA); legislative studies (MA); political science (MA, PhD). *Program availability:* Part-time, evening/weekend. *Faculty:* 11 full-time (2 women), 1 part-time/adjunct (0 women). *Students:* 29 full-time (7 women), 18 part-time (8 women); includes 10 minority (5 Black or African American, non-Hispanic/Latino; 1 Asian, non-Hispanic/Latino; 4 Hispanic/Latino), 10 international. Average age 34. 34 applicants, 53% accepted, 12 enrolled. In 2017, 7 master's, 3 doctorates awarded. Terminal master's awarded for partial completion of doctoral program. *Degree requirements:* For master's, thesis optional, independent study; for doctorate, thesis/dissertation, practicum research. *Entrance requirements:* For master's, GRE (minimum combined verbal and quantitative score of 1100), minimum undergraduate GPA of 3.0; for doctorate, GRE (minimum combined verbal and quantitative score of 1200, writing 4.5), minimum undergraduate GPA of 3.2. Additional exam requirements/recommendations for international students: Required—TOEFL (minimum score 550 paper-based). *Application deadline:* For fall admission, 7/15 for domestic students, 5/1 priority date for international students; for spring admission, 11/15 for domestic students, 9/1 priority date for international students. Applications are processed on a rolling basis. Application fee: $50 ($100 for international students). Electronic applications accepted. *Expenses:* Tuition, state resident: full-time $12,916; part-time $718 per credit hour. Tuition, nonresident: full-time $25,252; part-time $1403 per credit hour. *Financial support:* In 2017–18, 28 students received support, including 1 research assistantship with partial tuition reimbursement available (averaging $17,466 per year), 15 teaching assistantships with partial tuition reimbursements available (averaging $13,100 per year); career-related internships or fieldwork, Federal Work-Study, institutionally sponsored loans, and scholarships/grants also available. Support available to part-time students. Financial award application deadline: 4/30; financial award applicants required to submit FAFSA. *Faculty research:* Terrorism and democratic stability, redistricting and representation, trust and social exchange, how economic ideas impact political thought and public policy. *Unit head:* Dr. Jennifer Holmes, Program Head, 972-883-6843, Fax: 972-883-2735, E-mail: jholmes@utdallas.edu. *Application contact:* Victoria Diesing, Graduate Program Administrator, 972-883-2932, Fax: 972-883-2735, E-mail: psci@utdallas.edu.
Website: http://www.utdallas.edu/epps/political-science/

The University of Texas at Dallas, School of Economic, Political and Policy Sciences, Program in Public Policy and Political Economy, Richardson, TX 75080. Offers international political economy (MS); public policy (MPP); public policy and political economy (PhD); social data analytics and research (MS). *Program availability:* Part-time, evening/weekend. *Faculty:* 12 full-time (1 woman), 1 part-time/adjunct (0 women). *Students:* 46 full-time (22 women), 33 part-time (14 women); includes 27 minority (8 Black or African American, non-Hispanic/Latino; 8 Asian, non-Hispanic/Latino; 10 Hispanic/Latino; 1 Two or more races, non-Hispanic/Latino), 21 international. Average age 33. 69 applicants, 52% accepted, 22 enrolled. In 2017, 21 master's, 3 doctorates awarded. *Degree requirements:* For doctorate, thesis/dissertation. *Entrance requirements:* For master's and doctorate, GRE General Test, minimum GPA of 3.0 in upper-level course work in field. Additional exam requirements/recommendations for international students: Required—TOEFL (minimum score 550 paper-based). *Application deadline:* For fall admission, 7/15 for domestic students, 5/1 priority date for international students; for spring admission, 11/15 for domestic students, 9/1 priority date for international students. Applications are processed on a rolling basis. Application fee: $50 ($100 for international students). Electronic applications accepted. *Expenses:* Tuition, state resident: full-time $12,916; part-time $718 per credit hour. Tuition, nonresident: full-time $25,252; part-time $1403 per credit hour. *Financial support:* In 2017–18, 46 students received support, including 4 research assistantships with partial tuition reimbursements available (averaging $17,697 per year), 14 teaching assistantships with partial tuition reimbursements available (averaging $13,100 per year); career-related internships or fieldwork, Federal Work-Study, institutionally sponsored loans, scholarships/grants, and unspecified assistantships also available. Support available to part-time students. Financial award application deadline: 4/30; financial award applicants required to submit FAFSA. *Faculty research:* Ethnicity, community and local public good provision; community mental health policy; Texas Schools Project; biological and chemical arms control; cross-disciplinary applications of quantitative methodology. *Unit head:* Dr. Jennifer Holmes, Program Head, 972-883-6843, Fax: 972-883-6297, E-mail: jholmes@utdallas.edu. *Application contact:* Marjorie McDonald, Graduate Program Administrator, 972-883-6406, Fax: 972-883-6297, E-mail: pppe@utdallas.edu.
Website: http://www.utdallas.edu/epps/public-policy-and-political-economy/

The University of Texas at El Paso, Graduate School, College of Liberal Arts, Department of Political Science, El Paso, TX 79968-0001. Offers MA. *Program availability:* Part-time, evening/weekend. *Degree requirements:* For master's, thesis optional. *Entrance requirements:* For master's, GRE, letters of recommendation, personal statement, transcripts. Additional exam requirements/recommendations for international students: Required—TOEFL; Recommended—IELTS. Electronic applications accepted. *Faculty research:* Democracy and democratization, political institutions, regional integration, international security, presidential and legislative politics.

The University of Texas at San Antonio, College of Liberal and Fine Arts, Department of Political Science and Geography, San Antonio, TX 78249-0617. Offers geography (MA); political science (MA). *Program availability:* Part-time, evening/weekend. *Faculty:* 8 full-time (2 women), 1 part-time/adjunct (0 women). *Students:* 9 full-time (4 women), 14 part-time (9 women); includes 13 minority (1 Black or African American, non-Hispanic/Latino; 11 Hispanic/Latino; 1 Two or more races, non-Hispanic/Latino). Average age 33. 15 applicants, 87% accepted, 8 enrolled. In 2017, 15 master's awarded. *Degree requirements:* For master's, comprehensive exam (for some programs), thesis optional. *Entrance requirements:* For master's, GRE General Test or LSAT, 18 semester credit hours in upper-division undergraduate or graduate-level courses in political science or directly-related fields in the social or behavioral sciences; 3 letters of recommendation; statement of purpose. Additional exam requirements/recommendations for international students: Required—TOEFL (minimum score 550 paper-based; 79 iBT), IELTS (minimum score 6.5). *Application deadline:* For fall admission, 6/15 for domestic students, 3/1 for international students; for spring admission, 10/15 for domestic students, 9/15 for international students. Application fee: $50 ($90 for international students). Electronic applications accepted. *Expenses:* Tuition, state resident: full-time $5495. Tuition, nonresident: full-time $21,938. *Required fees:* $1915. Tuition and fees vary according to program. *Financial support:* Applicants required to submit FAFSA. *Faculty research:* Minority representation and legislation, comparative welfare policy, strategic conflict in India and Pakistan, homeland security, global governance, American political behavior. *Total annual research expenditures:* $4,181. *Unit head:* Dr. James D. Calder, Interim Chair, 210-458-5645, E-mail: james.calder@utsa.edu.
Website: http://colfa.utsa.edu/polisci-geography/

The University of Texas at Tyler, College of Arts and Sciences, Department of Political Science, Tyler, TX 75799-0001. Offers MA. *Program availability:* Part-time, evening/weekend. *Degree requirements:* For master's, comprehensive exam, thesis optional. *Entrance requirements:* Additional exam requirements/recommendations for international students: Required—TOEFL. *Faculty research:* American politics, comparative politics, international relations, political theory and philosophy.

The University of Texas of the Permian Basin, Office of Graduate Studies, College of Arts and Sciences, Department of Social Sciences, Odessa, TX 79762-0001. Offers criminal justice administration (MS); political science (MPA). *Program availability:* Part-time, evening/weekend. *Degree requirements:* For master's, comprehensive exam (for some programs), thesis (for some programs). *Entrance requirements:* For master's, GRE General Test. Additional exam requirements/recommendations for international students: Required—TOEFL (minimum score 550 paper-based).

The University of Toledo, College of Graduate Studies, College of Languages, Literature and Social Sciences, Department of Political Science and Public Administration, Toledo, OH 43606-3390. Offers health care policy and administration (Certificate); management of non-profit organizations (Certificate); municipal administration (Certificate); political science (MA); public administration (MPA); JD/MPA. *Program availability:* Part-time. *Degree requirements:* For master's, comprehensive exam (for some programs), thesis. *Entrance requirements:* For master's, GRE General Test, minimum cumulative point-hour ratio of 2.7 (3.0 for MPA) for all previous academic work, three letters of recommendation, statement of purpose, transcripts from all prior institutions attended; for Certificate, minimum cumulative point-hour ratio of 2.7 for all previous academic work, three letters of recommendation, statement of purpose, transcripts from all prior institutions attended. Additional exam requirements/recommendations for international students: Required—TOEFL (minimum score 550 paper-based; 80 iBT). Electronic applications accepted. *Faculty research:* Economic development, health care, Third World, criminal justice, Eastern Europe.

University of Toronto, School of Graduate Studies, Faculty of Arts and Science, Department of Political Science, Toronto, ON M5S 1A1, Canada. Offers MA, PhD, JD/MA, JD/PhD. *Program availability:* Part-time. *Degree requirements:* For master's, thesis optional; for doctorate, one foreign language, thesis/dissertation, reading competency in a language other than English. *Entrance requirements:* For master's, 3 letters of recommendation, writing sample, statement of scholarly intent, minimum cumulative GPA of B+ in a four-year bachelor's program including B+ average over five to eight suitably-distributed full-year political science courses; for doctorate, 4 letters of

recommendation, writing sample, minimum A- in most recent political science (or equivalent) degree. Additional exam requirements/recommendations for international students: Required—TOEFL (minimum score 580 paper-based; 93 iBT), TWE (minimum score 5). Electronic applications accepted.

University of Utah, Graduate School, College of Humanities, Program in Middle East Studies, Salt Lake City, UT 84112. Offers Arabic (MA, PhD); Hebrew (MA); history (MA, PhD); Persian (MA, PhD); political science (MA, PhD). *Students:* 2 part-time (1 woman); includes 1 minority (Asian, non-Hispanic/Latino). In 2017, 1 doctorate awarded. *Entrance requirements:* For master's, GRE General Test, minimum GPA of 3.2; for doctorate, GRE General Test, MA in Middle East studies or equivalent, minimum GPA of 3.2. Additional exam requirements/recommendations for international students: Required—TOEFL (minimum score 580 paper-based; 92 iBT); Recommended—IELTS (minimum score 7). Application fee: $55 ($65 for international students). Electronic applications accepted. *Financial support:* In 2017–18, 5 students received support, including 2 teaching assistantships with full tuition reimbursements available (averaging $13,500 per year); fellowships and unspecified assistantships also available. Financial award application deadline: 1/15. *Faculty research:* Islamic studies; Middle Eastern history; political science; Judaic studies; anthropology; Arabic, Persian, Hebrew, and Turkish language and literature. *Unit head:* Johanna Watzinger-Tharp, Director, 801-581-7148, Fax: 801-581-6105, E-mail: j.tharp@utah.edu. *Application contact:* Kellie Hubbard, Academic Advisor, 801-581-5362, Fax: 801-581-6105, E-mail: kellie.hubbard@utah.edu.
Website: http://www.mec.utah.edu

University of Utah, Graduate School, College of Social and Behavioral Science, Department of Political Science, Program in Political Science, Salt Lake City, UT 84112. Offers American politics (MA, MS, PhD); comparative politics (MA, MS, PhD); international relations (MA, MS, PhD); political theory (MA, MS, PhD); public administration (MA, MS, PhD). *Faculty:* 23 full-time (6 women), 10 part-time/adjunct (2 women). *Students:* 23 full-time (9 women), 28 part-time (8 women); includes 6 minority (2 Asian, non-Hispanic/Latino; 2 Hispanic/Latino; 2 Two or more races, non-Hispanic/Latino), 4 international. Average age 35. 44 applicants, 45% accepted, 11 enrolled. In 2017, 3 master's, 4 doctorates awarded. Terminal master's awarded for partial completion of doctoral program. *Degree requirements:* For master's, variable foreign language requirement, thesis or research paper; for doctorate, comprehensive exam, thesis/dissertation. *Entrance requirements:* For master's and doctorate, GRE General Test, minimum GPA of 3.2. Additional exam requirements/recommendations for international students: Required—TOEFL (minimum score 580 paper-based; 61 iBT), IELTS (minimum score 6). *Application deadline:* For fall admission, 1/15 priority date for domestic and international students. Application fee: $55 ($65 for international students). Electronic applications accepted. *Expenses:* $1,489 for 1 credit hour, $267 for each additional hour (resident); $4,233 for 1 credit hour, $908 for each additional hour (non-resident). *Financial support:* In 2017–18, 10 students received support, including 5 fellowships with full tuition reimbursements available (averaging $15,250 per year), 13 teaching assistantships with full tuition reimbursements available (averaging $15,000 per year); career-related internships or fieldwork, scholarships/grants, health care benefits, and unspecified assistantships also available. Financial award application deadline: 1/15; financial award applicants required to submit FAFSA. *Faculty research:* International politics, comparative politics, political theory, American politics, public administration. *Total annual research expenditures:* $15,000. *Unit head:* Mark Button, Chair, 801-585-7987, Fax: 801-585-6492, E-mail: mark.button@poli-sci.utah.edu. *Application contact:* Sandy Hiskey, Graduate Academic Advisor, 801-581-8608, Fax: 801-585-6492, E-mail: sandy.hiskey@utah.edu.
Website: http://www.poli-sci.utah.edu/

University of Victoria, Faculty of Graduate Studies, Faculty of Social Sciences, Department of Political Science, Victoria, BC V8W 2Y2, Canada. Offers MA, PhD. *Program availability:* Part-time. *Degree requirements:* For master's, thesis; for doctorate, thesis/dissertation, candidacy exam. *Entrance requirements:* For master's, minimum B+ average in last 2 years of undergraduate course work. Additional exam requirements/recommendations for international students: Required—TOEFL (minimum score 600 paper-based). Electronic applications accepted. *Faculty research:* Political theory, political parties, international political economy, comparative public policy, British Columbian politics.

University of Virginia, College and Graduate School of Arts and Sciences, Department of Politics, Program in Government, Charlottesville, VA 22903. Offers MA, PhD, JD/MA, MBA/MA. *Students:* 21 full-time (8 women); includes 3 minority (1 Black or African American, non-Hispanic/Latino; 1 Asian, non-Hispanic/Latino; 1 Two or more races, non-Hispanic/Latino), 2 international. Average age 28. 87 applicants, 24% accepted, 7 enrolled. In 2017, 6 master's, 4 doctorates awarded. *Degree requirements:* For master's, 2 research/statistics courses or thesis; for doctorate, variable foreign language requirement, thesis/dissertation, 2 research/statistics courses. *Entrance requirements:* For master's and doctorate, GRE General Test, long writing sample; 2 letters of recommendation. Additional exam requirements/recommendations for international students: Required—TOEFL (minimum score 600 paper-based; 90 iBT), IELTS (minimum score 7). *Application deadline:* For fall admission, 12/4 for domestic and international students. Applications are processed on a rolling basis. Application fee: $60. Electronic applications accepted. *Financial support:* Fellowships and teaching assistantships available. Financial award application deadline: 12/4; financial award applicants required to submit FAFSA. *Unit head:* John Owen, Chair, 434-924-3523, Fax: 434-924-3159, E-mail: jmo4n@virginia.edu. *Application contact:* Philip Potter, Director of Graduate Studies, 434-982-1043, Fax: 434-924-3159, E-mail: pbp2s@virginia.edu.
Website: http://politics.virginia.edu/

University of Washington, Graduate School, College of Arts and Sciences, Department of Political Science, Seattle, WA 98195. Offers MA, PhD. *Degree requirements:* For doctorate, thesis/dissertation. *Entrance requirements:* For master's and doctorate, GRE General Test, minimum GPA of 3.0. Additional exam requirements/recommendations for international students: Required—TOEFL. Electronic applications accepted. *Faculty research:* American politics, comparative politics, international relations, political theory, political economy.

University of Waterloo, Graduate Studies, Faculty of Arts, Department of Political Science, Waterloo, ON N2L 3G1, Canada. Offers global governance (MA, PhD). *Program availability:* Part-time. *Degree requirements:* For master's, thesis (for some programs), research paper. *Entrance requirements:* For master's, honors degree, minimum B average, writing sample. Additional exam requirements/recommendations for international students: Required—TOEFL, IELTS, PTE. Electronic applications accepted. *Faculty research:* Conflict and conflict resolution, political economy, contemporary political theory, Canadian state and society.

University of Waterloo, Graduate Studies, Faculty of Arts, Global Governance Program, Waterloo, ON N2L 3G1, Canada. Offers MA, PhD. *Entrance requirements:* For doctorate, MA. Additional exam requirements/recommendations for international students: Required—TOEFL, IELTS, PTE. Electronic applications accepted. *Faculty research:* Global political economy, global environment, peace and security, global justice and human rights, multilateral institutions and diplomacy.

The University of Western Ontario, Faculty of Graduate Studies, Social Sciences Division, Department of Political Science, London, ON N6A 5B8, Canada. Offers MA, MPA, PhD. *Program availability:* Part-time. *Degree requirements:* For master's, thesis; for doctorate, comprehensive exam, thesis/dissertation. *Entrance requirements:* For master's, minimum B average, honors BA in political science or equivalent, sample of written work; for doctorate, MA in political science or equivalent. *Faculty research:* Political theory, Canadian politics, local government, comparative politics, international relations.

University of West Florida, College of Arts, Social Sciences, and Humanities, Department of Government, Pensacola, FL 32514-5750. Offers political science (MA), including political science, security and diplomacy. *Program availability:* Part-time, evening/weekend. *Degree requirements:* For master's, thesis or alternative. *Entrance requirements:* For master's, GRE, official transcripts; minimum GPA of 3.0; 500-word writing sample in form of letter of intent; resume. Additional exam requirements/recommendations for international students: Required—TOEFL (minimum score 550 paper-based). *Faculty research:* Political campaigns, elections, law enforcement, growth management.

University of Windsor, Faculty of Graduate Studies, Faculty of Arts and Social Sciences, Department of Political Science, Windsor, ON N9B 3P4, Canada. Offers MA. *Program availability:* Part-time. *Entrance requirements:* For master's, minimum B+ average. Additional exam requirements/recommendations for international students: Required—TOEFL (minimum score 600 paper-based). Electronic applications accepted. *Faculty research:* Canadian politics and government, local government, comparative political Canadian public administration, public policy.

University of Wisconsin–Madison, Graduate School, College of Letters and Science, Department of Political Science, Madison, WI 53706-1380. Offers PhD. *Degree requirements:* For doctorate, thesis/dissertation. *Entrance requirements:* For doctorate, GRE General Test. Electronic applications accepted. *Faculty research:* Comparative politics, American politics, international relations, political theory, political methodology.

University of Wisconsin–Milwaukee, Graduate School, College of Letters and Science, Department of Political Science, Milwaukee, WI 53201-0413. Offers MA, PhD. *Students:* Average age 31. 30 applicants, 60% accepted, 6 enrolled. In 2017, 4 master's, 2 doctorates awarded. *Degree requirements:* For master's, thesis or alternative; for doctorate, one foreign language, thesis/dissertation. *Entrance requirements:* For master's and doctorate, GRE General Test, minimum GPA of 3.0. Additional exam requirements/recommendations for international students: Required—TOEFL (minimum score 550 paper-based; 79 iBT), IELTS (minimum score 6.5). *Application deadline:* For fall admission, 1/1 priority date for domestic students; for spring admission, 9/1 for domestic students. Applications are processed on a rolling basis. Application fee: $56 ($96 for international students). Electronic applications accepted. *Financial support:* Fellowships, research assistantships, teaching assistantships, career-related internships or fieldwork, unspecified assistantships, and project assistantships available. Support available to part-time students. Financial award application deadline: 4/15; financial award applicants required to submit FAFSA. *Unit head:* Thomas Holbrook, Department Chair, 414-229-4221, E-mail: holbroot@uwm.edu. *Application contact:* General Information Contact, 414-229-4982, Fax: 414-229-6967, E-mail: gradschool@uwm.edu.
Website: http://www.uwm.edu/dept/polsci/

University of Wyoming, College of Arts and Sciences, Department of Political Science, Program in Political Science, Laramie, WY 82071. Offers MA. *Program availability:* Part-time. *Degree requirements:* For master's, thesis or alternative. *Entrance requirements:* For master's, GRE General Test, bachelor's degree in political science, minimum GPA of 3.0. Additional exam requirements/recommendations for international students: Required—TOEFL (minimum score 525 paper-based). Electronic applications accepted. *Faculty research:* American government, public law, judicial politics, political theory, international relations.

Utah State University, School of Graduate Studies, College of Humanities and Social Sciences, Department of Political Science, Logan, UT 84322. Offers MA, MS. *Program availability:* Part-time. *Degree requirements:* For master's, one foreign language, thesis. *Entrance requirements:* For master's, GRE General Test, minimum GPA of 3.0. Additional exam requirements/recommendations for international students: Required—TOEFL. *Faculty research:* Political parties; social choice; international political economics; foreign policy; politics, markets, and public policy.

Vanderbilt University, Department of Political Science, Nashville, TN 37240-1001. Offers MA, MAT, PhD. *Faculty:* 25 full-time (8 women). *Students:* 34 full-time (14 women), 1 (woman) part-time; includes 2 minority (1 Black or African American, non-Hispanic/Latino; 1 Two or more races, non-Hispanic/Latino), 12 international. Average age 28. 176 applicants, 16% accepted, 8 enrolled. In 2017, 8 master's, 6 doctorates awarded. Terminal master's awarded for partial completion of doctoral program. *Degree requirements:* For master's, thesis; for doctorate, thesis/dissertation, final and qualifying exams. *Entrance requirements:* For master's and doctorate, GRE General Test, writing sample. Additional exam requirements/recommendations for international students: Required—TOEFL (minimum score 570 paper-based; 88 iBT). *Application deadline:* For fall admission, 1/15 for domestic and international students. Electronic applications accepted. *Financial support:* Fellowships with full tuition reimbursements, research assistantships with full tuition reimbursements, teaching assistantships with full tuition reimbursements, Federal Work-Study, institutionally sponsored loans, scholarships/grants, and health care benefits available. Financial award application deadline: 1/15; financial award applicants required to submit CSS PROFILE or FAFSA. *Faculty research:* American politics, comparative politics, international politics, political theory, political culture and life. *Unit head:* Dr. David Lewis, Chair, 615-322-6222, Fax: 615-343-6003, E-mail: david.lewis@vanderbilt.edu. *Application contact:* Jon Hiskey, Director of Graduate Studies, 615-322-6222, Fax: 615-343-6003, E-mail: j.hiskey@vanderbilt.edu.
Website: http://www.vanderbilt.edu/political-science/

Villanova University, Graduate School of Liberal Arts and Sciences, Department of Political Science, Villanova, PA 19085-1699. Offers MA. *Program availability:* Part-time, evening/weekend, online learning. *Faculty:* 6. *Students:* 22 full-time (10 women), 8 part-time (2 women); includes 3 minority (2 Hispanic/Latino; 1 Two or more races, non-Hispanic/Latino), 4 international. Average age 28. 18 applicants, 83% accepted, 12 enrolled. In 2017, 13 master's awarded. *Degree requirements:* For master's, comprehensive exam (for some programs). *Entrance requirements:* For master's, GRE, minimum GPA of 3.0. Additional exam requirements/recommendations for international students: Required—TOEFL. *Application deadline:* For fall admission, 5/1 priority date for international students; for spring admission, 10/15 for international students. Applications are processed on a rolling basis. Application fee: $50. Electronic applications accepted. *Financial support:* Research assistantships, scholarships/grants, and unspecified assistantships available. Financial award applicants required to submit FAFSA. *Unit head:* Dr. Markus Kreuzer, Director, 610-519-4710.
Website: http://www.psc.villanova.edu/gradwww.htm

Virginia Commonwealth University, Graduate School, L. Douglas Wilder School of Government and Public Affairs, Richmond, VA 23284-9005. Offers MA, MPA, MS, MURP, PhD, Certificate, Graduate Certificate, Postbaccalaureate Certificate.

Virginia Polytechnic Institute and State University, VT Online, Blacksburg, VA 24061. Offers advanced transportation systems (Certificate); aerospace engineering (MS); agricultural and life sciences (MSLFS); business information systems (Graduate Certificate); career and technical education (MS); civil engineering (MS); computer engineering (M Eng, MS); decision support systems (Graduate Certificate); eLearning leadership (MA); electrical engineering (M Eng, MS); engineering administration (MEA); environmental engineering (Certificate); environmental politics and policy (Graduate Certificate); environmental sciences and engineering (MS); foundations of political analysis (Graduate Certificate); health product risk management (Graduate Certificate); industrial and systems engineering (MS); information policy and society (Graduate Certificate); information security (Graduate Certificate); information technology (MIT); instructional technology (MA); integrative STEM education (MA Ed); liberal arts (Graduate Certificate); life sciences: health product risk management (MS); natural resources (MNR, Graduate Certificate); networking (Graduate Certificate); nonprofit and nongovernmental organization management (Graduate Certificate); ocean engineering (MS); political science (MA); security studies (Graduate Certificate); software development (Graduate Certificate). *Expenses:* Tuition, state resident: full-time $15,072; part-time $718.50 per credit hour. Tuition, nonresident: full-time $28,810; part-time $1448.25 per credit hour. *Required fees:* $2741; $502 per semester. Tuition and fees vary according to course load, campus/location and program.

Walden University, Graduate Programs, School of Public Policy and Administration, Minneapolis, MN 55401. Offers criminal justice (MPA, MPP, MS, Graduate Certificate), including emergency management (MS, PhD), general program (MS), global leadership (MS, PhD), homeland security and policy coordination (MS, PhD), law and public policy (MS, PhD), policy analysis (MS, PhD), public management and leadership (MS, PhD), self-designed (MS), terrorism, mediation, and peace (MS, PhD); criminal justice and executive management (MS), including global leadership (MS, PhD); criminal justice leadership and executive management (MS), including emergency management (MS, PhD), general program, homeland security and policy coordination (MS, PhD), law and public policy (MS, PhD), policy analysis (MS, PhD), public management and leadership (MS, PhD), self-designed, terrorism, mediation, and peace (MS, PhD); emergency management (MPA, MPP, MS), including criminal justice (MS, PhD), general program (MS), homeland security (MS), public management and leadership (MS, PhD), terrorism and emergency management (MS); general program (MPA, MPP); global leadership (MPA, MPP); government management (Graduate Certificate); health policy (MPA, MPP); homeland security (Graduate Certificate); homeland security and policy coordination (MPA, MPP); international nongovernmental organizations (MPA, MPP); law and public policy (MPA, MPP); local government management for sustainable communities (MPA, MPP); nonprofit management (Graduate Certificate); nonprofit management and leadership (MPA, MPP, MS), including global leadership (MS, PhD), international nongovernmental organization (MS), local government for sustainable communities (MS), self designed (MS); online teaching in higher education (Post-Master's Certificate); policy analysis (MPA); public management and leadership (MPA, MPP, Graduate Certificate); public policy (Graduate Certificate); public policy and administration (PhD), including criminal justice (MS, PhD), emergency management (MS, PhD), global leadership (MS, PhD), health policy, homeland security and policy coordination (MS, PhD), international nongovernmental organizations, law and public policy (MS, PhD), local government management for sustainable communities, nonprofit management and leadership, policy analysis (MS, PhD), public management and leadership (MS, PhD), terrorism, mediation, and peace (MS, PhD); strategic planning and public policy (Graduate Certificate); terrorism, mediation, and peace (MPA, MPP). *Program availability:* Part-time, evening/weekend, online only, 100% online. *Degree requirements:* For doctorate, thesis/dissertation, residency. *Entrance requirements:* For master's, bachelor's degree or higher; minimum GPA of 2.5; official transcripts; goal statement (for some programs); access to computer and Internet; for doctorate, master's degree or higher; three years of related professional or academic experience (preferred); minimum GPA of 3.0; goal statement and current resume (for select programs); official transcripts; access to computer and Internet; for other advanced degree, relevant work experience; access to computer and Internet. Additional exam requirements/recommendations for international students: Required—TOEFL (minimum score 550 paper-based, 79 iBT), IELTS (minimum score 6.5), Michigan English Language Assessment Battery (minimum score 82), or PTE (minimum score 53). Electronic applications accepted.

Washington State University, College of Arts and Sciences, School of Politics, Philosophy and Public Affairs, Pullman, WA 99164-4880. Offers bioethics (Graduate Certificate); political science (MA, PhD); public affairs (MPA). MPA, MA, and PhD programs also offered at the Vancouver campus; Graduate Certificate offered through Global (online) campus. *Accreditation:* NASPAA. *Program availability:* Online learning. Terminal master's awarded for partial completion of doctoral program. *Degree requirements:* For master's, comprehensive exam (for some programs), thesis, oral exam; for doctorate, comprehensive exam, thesis/dissertation, oral exam, written exam. *Entrance requirements:* For master's, GRE General Test, minimum GPA of 3.0; for doctorate, GRE General Test, minimum GPA of 3.5. Additional exam requirements/recommendations for international students: Required—TOEFL. Electronic applications accepted. *Faculty research:* Political psychology and image theory, grass roots environmental policy, federal juvenile policy.

Washington University in St. Louis, The Graduate School, Department of Political Science, St. Louis, MO 63130-4899. Offers PhD. *Degree requirements:* For doctorate, thesis/dissertation. *Entrance requirements:* For doctorate, GRE General Test. Additional exam requirements/recommendations for international students: Required—TOEFL. Electronic applications accepted. *Faculty research:* American politics (including law and courts); comparative politics; formal theory; international politics; normative theory; political methodology.

Wayne State University, College of Liberal Arts and Sciences, Department of Political Science, Detroit, MI 48202. Offers political science (MA, PhD); public administration (MPA), including economic development policy and management, health and human services policy and management, human and fiscal resource management, nonprofit policy and management, organizational behavior and management, urban and metropolitan policy and management; JD/MA. *Accreditation:* NASPAA. *Faculty:* 18. *Students:* 48 full-time (20 women), 68 part-time (36 women); includes 37 minority (26 Black or African American, non-Hispanic/Latino; 3 Asian, non-Hispanic/Latino; 2 Hispanic/Latino; 6 Two or more races, non-Hispanic/Latino), 6 international. Average age 32. 105 applicants, 39% accepted, 20 enrolled. In 2017, 17 master's, 3 doctorates awarded. *Degree requirements:* For master's, comprehensive exam (for some programs), thesis (for some programs); for doctorate, thesis/dissertation. *Entrance requirements:* For master's, GRE General Test, substantial undergraduate preparation in the social sciences, minimum upper-division undergraduate GPA of 3.0, two letters of recommendation, personal statement; for doctorate, GRE General Test, 3 letters of recommendation; personal statement; interview. Additional exam requirements/recommendations for international students: Required—TOEFL (minimum score 550 paper-based; 79 iBT), TWE (minimum score 5.5), Michigan English Language Assessment Battery (minimum score 85); Recommended—IELTS (minimum score 6.5). *Application deadline:* For fall admission, 5/15 for domestic students, 5/1 priority date for international students; for winter admission, 10/15 for domestic students, 9/1 priority date for international students. Applications are processed on a rolling basis. Application fee: $50. Electronic applications accepted. *Expenses:* Contact institution. *Financial support:* In 2017–18, 44 students received support, including 6 fellowships with tuition reimbursements available (averaging $11,698 per year), 12 teaching assistantships with tuition reimbursements available (averaging $18,534 per year); research assistantships with tuition reimbursements available, scholarships/grants, health care benefits, and unspecified assistantships also available. Financial award applicants required to submit FAFSA. *Faculty research:* American government and politics, comparative politics, political methodology, political theory, public administration, public law, public policy, world politics/international relations, formal theory/modeling, gender and politics, international law, peace research, political economy, political psychology, politics of developing countries, race, religion, and ethnicity, urban politics. *Unit head:* Dr. Daniel Geller, Professor and Chair, 313-577-6328, E-mail: dgeller@wayne.edu. *Application contact:* Dr. Sharon Lean, Graduate Director, 313-577-2630, E-mail: gradpolisci@wayne.edu.
Website: http://clas.wayne.edu/politicalscience/

Western Illinois University, School of Graduate Studies, College of Arts and Sciences, Department of Political Science, Macomb, IL 61455-1390. Offers MA. *Program availability:* Part-time. *Students:* 14 full-time (6 women), 5 part-time (3 women); includes 8 minority (5 Black or African American, non-Hispanic/Latino; 1 Asian, non-Hispanic/Latino; 2 Hispanic/Latino), 6 international. Average age 26. 13 applicants, 62% accepted, 5 enrolled. In 2017, 7 master's awarded. *Degree requirements:* For master's, comprehensive exam, thesis or alternative. *Entrance requirements:* Additional exam requirements/recommendations for international students: Required—TOEFL (minimum score 550 paper-based; 80 iBT). *Application deadline:* Applications are processed on a rolling basis. Application fee: $30. Electronic applications accepted. *Financial support:* In 2017–18, 12 students received support. Unspecified assistantships available. Financial award applicants required to submit FAFSA. *Unit head:* Dr. Keith Boeckelman, Chairperson, 309-298-1055. *Application contact:* Dr. Nancy Parsons, Associate Provost and Director of Graduate Studies, 309-298-1806, Fax: 309-298-2345, E-mail: grad-office@wiu.edu.
Website: http://www.wiu.edu/cas/Political_Science/

Western Kentucky University, Graduate Studies, Potter College of Arts and Letters, Department of Political Science, Bowling Green, KY 42101. Offers MPA. *Accreditation:* NASPAA. *Program availability:* Part-time, evening/weekend. *Degree requirements:* For master's, comprehensive exam, final exam. *Entrance requirements:* For master's, GRE General Test, minimum GPA of 2.75. Additional exam requirements/recommendations for international students: Required—TOEFL (minimum score 555 paper-based; 79 iBT). *Faculty research:* Role of non-profits, comparative policy analysis, social welfare policy, rural administration, ethics and bureaucracy.

Western Michigan University, Graduate College, College of Arts and Sciences, Department of Political Science, Kalamazoo, MI 49008. Offers international development administration (MIDA), including Peace Corps; political science (MA, PhD). *Degree requirements:* For master's, thesis optional; for doctorate, thesis/dissertation.

Western Washington University, Graduate School, College of Humanities and Social Sciences, Department of Political Science, Bellingham, WA 98225-5996. Offers MA. *Program availability:* Part-time. *Degree requirements:* For master's, comprehensive exam, thesis (for some programs). *Entrance requirements:* For master's, GRE General Test, minimum GPA of 3.0 in last 60 semester hours or last 90 quarter hours. Additional exam requirements/recommendations for international students: Required—TOEFL (minimum score 567 paper-based). Electronic applications accepted. *Faculty research:* Elections, environment, identity, international relations.

West Virginia University, Eberly College of Arts and Sciences, Morgantown, WV 26506. Offers biology (MS, PhD); chemistry (MS, PhD); communication studies (MA, PhD); computational statistics (PhD); creative writing (MFA); English (MA, PhD); forensic and investigative science (MS); forensic science (PhD); geography (MA); geology (MA, PhD); history (MA, PhD); legal studies (MLS); math (MS); physics (MS, PhD); political science (MA, PhD); professional writing and editing (MA); psychology (MA); public administration (MPA); social work (MSW); sociology (MA, PhD); statistics (MS). *Program availability:* Part-time, evening/weekend, online learning. *Students:* 831 full-time (437 women), 236 part-time (142 women); includes 112 minority (35 Black or African American, non-Hispanic/Latino; 15 Asian, non-Hispanic/Latino; 29 Hispanic/Latino; 33 Two or more races, non-Hispanic/Latino), 235 international. Terminal master's awarded for partial completion of doctoral program. *Degree requirements:* For master's, thesis (for some programs); for doctorate, comprehensive exam, thesis/dissertation. *Entrance requirements:* For master's and doctorate, GRE. Additional exam requirements/recommendations for international students: Required—TOEFL (minimum score 600 paper-based); Recommended—TWE. *Application deadline:* For spring admission, 2/15 priority date for domestic and international students. Applications are processed on a rolling basis. Application fee: $45. Electronic applications accepted. *Expenses:* Tuition, state resident: full-time $9450. Tuition, nonresident: full-time $24,390. *Financial support:* Fellowships with full tuition reimbursements, research assistantships with full tuition reimbursements, teaching assistantships with full tuition reimbursements, career-related internships or fieldwork, Federal Work-Study, institutionally sponsored loans, scholarships/grants, health care benefits, tuition waivers (full and partial), unspecified assistantships, and administrative assistantships available. Financial award application deadline: 2/1; financial award applicants required to submit FAFSA. *Faculty research:* Humanities, social sciences, life science, physical sciences, mathematics. *Unit head:* Dr. Mary Ellen Mazey, Dean, 304-293-4611, Fax: 304-293-6858, E-mail: mary.mazey@mail.wvu.edu. *Application contact:* Dr. Fred L. King, Associate Dean for Graduate Studies, 304-293-4611 Ext. 5205, Fax: 304-293-6858, E-mail: fred.king@mail.wvu.edu.
Website: http://www.as.wvu.edu/

Wilfrid Laurier University, Faculty of Graduate and Postdoctoral Studies, Faculty of Arts, Department of Political Science, Waterloo, ON N2L 3C5, Canada. Offers Canadian political studies (MA); comparative politics/international relations (MA). *Program availability:* Part-time. *Degree requirements:* For master's, thesis optional. *Entrance requirements:* For master's, honors bachelor's degree or the equivalent in political science, minimum B average in undergraduate course work. Additional exam requirements/recommendations for international students: Required—TOEFL (minimum score 89 iBT). Electronic applications accepted. *Faculty research:* Political behavior/political psychology, Canadian political studies, comparative, politics/relations, public opinion and electoral studies, international.

Wilfrid Laurier University, Faculty of Graduate and Postdoctoral Studies, School of International Policy and Governance, Global Governance Program, Waterloo, ON N2L 3C5, Canada. Offers conflict and security (PhD); global environment (PhD); global justice and human rights (PhD); global political economy (PhD); global social governance (PhD); multilateral institutions and diplomacy (PhD). Offered jointly with University of Waterloo. *Degree requirements:* For doctorate, thesis/dissertation. *Entrance requirements:* For doctorate, MA in political science, history, economics, international development studies, international peace studies, globalization studies, environmental studies or related field with minimum A-. Additional exam requirements/recommendations for international students: Required—TOEFL (minimum score 89

Political Science

iBT). Electronic applications accepted. *Faculty research:* Global political economy, global environment, conflict and security, global justice and human rights, multilateral institutions and diplomacy.

Wilfrid Laurier University, Faculty of Graduate and Postdoctoral Studies, School of International Policy and Governance, International Public Policy Program, Waterloo, ON N2L 3C5, Canada. Offers global governance (MIPP); human security (MIPP); international economic relations (MIPP); international environmental policy (MIPP). Offered jointly with University of Waterloo. *Entrance requirements:* For master's, honours BA with minimum B average. Additional exam requirements/recommendations for international students: Required—TOEFL (minimum score 89 iBT). Electronic applications accepted. *Faculty research:* International environmental policy, international economic relations, human security, global governance.

Yale University, Graduate School of Arts and Sciences, Department of Political Science, New Haven, CT 06520. Offers PhD. *Degree requirements:* For doctorate, one foreign language, thesis/dissertation. *Entrance requirements:* For doctorate, GRE General Test. *Faculty research:* U.N. and international security.

York University, Faculty of Graduate Studies, Faculty of Liberal Arts and Professional Studies, Program in Political Science, Toronto, ON M3J 1P3, Canada. Offers MA, PhD. *Program availability:* Part-time. *Degree requirements:* For master's, thesis or alternative; for doctorate, one foreign language, comprehensive exam, thesis/dissertation. Electronic applications accepted.

York University, Faculty of Graduate Studies, Program in Social and Political Thought, Toronto, ON M3J 1P3, Canada. Offers MA, PhD. *Program availability:* Part-time. *Degree requirements:* For master's, one foreign language, thesis or alternative, oral exams; for doctorate, one foreign language, comprehensive exam, thesis/dissertation. Electronic applications accepted.

AUSTIN W. MARXE SCHOOL OF PUBLIC AND INTERNATIONAL AFFAIRS AT BARUCH COLLEGE

School of International Affairs

 For more information, visit http://petersons.to/baruchaustinwmarxe

Programs of Study

Austin W. Marxe School of Public and International Affairs at Baruch College provides "education that makes a difference." It's the only public graduate school in New York City dedicated to public affairs. It provides a variety of programs including undergraduate and graduate programs in public policy and administration, master's programs in higher education administration and educational leadership, and certificate programs in several areas.

It draws from the largest public affairs faculty in the country. Faculty members include award-winning scholars and former New York City commissioners as well as a member of the National Academy of Public Administration and a presidential professor.

The school takes an interdisciplinary approach to professional development, research, and teaching and develops new programs to provide the most relevant education and training. In addition, it provides a forum to discuss public policy and maintains research centers to conduct innovative studies concerning matters of the public interest.

Master of Public Administration (M.P.A.): The M.P.A. program at Austin W. Marxe School of Public and International Affairs is one of the top programs in country. Its curriculum, which can be completed on a full-time or part-time basis, has a minimum of 42 credits for students with administrative experience. Students without this experience complete an additional three-credit internship. Specializations are offered in five areas: health care policy, nonprofit administration, policy analysis and evaluation, public management, and urban development and sustainability.

The M.P.A. has two nontraditional delivery models: Executive M.P.A. and National Urban Fellows M.P.A. The 42-credit Executive M.P.A. was created for mid-career professionals who want to develop analytical and leadership skills. The 33-credit National Urban Fellows M.P.A. is offered in collaboration with National Urban Fellows, Inc. It enables people from underrepresented communities to earn M.P.A. degrees through a combination of full-time study and internships.

Master of International Affairs (M.I.A.): The two-year Master of International Affairs program provides multidisciplinary analysis and understanding of global policy and governance in the international setting. Its curriculum has 42 credits of core and concentration courses. Concentrations include international nongovernmental organizations, western hemisphere affairs, trade policy and global economic governance, and special concentration.

Students also receive advanced training in key techniques of policy analysis, budgeting, assessment of political culture, global communication strategies, regionally specific issues, and comparative methods. The program offers opportunities for study in a variety of substantial social and public policy areas (e.g., welfare and social security, international development, housing, migration, health), across a range of national, regional (Latin America, Asia, Africa, and the European Union), and global settings. While the concentration in Western Hemisphere Affairs will focus on that region, the M.I.A. program is committed to analyzing problems in a global context. The School has relationships with educational institutions in Europe, Latin America, and Asia and students will have the opportunity to do internships or study abroad.

Master of Science in Higher Education Administration: This M.S.Ed. program was created for higher education professionals. It offers two programs: generalist and institutional research and assessment specialization.

The 36-credit generalist program provides skills and knowledge in higher education management with a focus on student services. It has 21 credits of core courses including a capstone course and 15 credits of electives. Students without administrative experience must also complete a three-credit internship.

The institutional research and assessment specialization also has 36 credits (27 credits of core and 9 credits of elective courses). It builds upon capstone and core courses in the generalist program. Its curriculum includes research and analysis requirements and electives in budgeting, institutional research, and program evaluation.

Research Opportunities

The Austin W. Marxe School of Public and International Affairs supports public policy through civic engagement and applied research. Its innovative policy and research programs promote public affairs education and social advocacy. It has seven centers:

- Baruch College Survey Research
- Center for Educational Leadership
- Center on Equality Pluralism and Policy
- Center for Nonprofit Strategy and Management
- CUNY Institute for Demographic Research
- International Comparative Policy Analysis Forum
- New York Federal Statistical Research Data Center

These centers provide in-depth knowledge about a wide array of policy topics as well as hands-on experience that can be applied to career pursuits and research projects.

Financial Aid

Baruch College offers graduate students who reside in New York State competitive tuition rates in comparison to many other universities and colleges in the New York City metropolitan area. Financial aid in the forms of federal loans, graduate research assistantships, and scholarships helps students fund their education. There are competitive fellowship and scholarship packages available to qualified incoming and continuing students. Some of the fellowship opportunities provide full tuition coverage.

Cost of Study

For the 2018–19 academic year, tuition for the M.P.A. and M.I.A. programs is $6,190 per semester for New York State residents and $980 per credit for out-of-state residents and international students. Tuition for the M.S.Ed. program is $5,385 per semester for New York State residents and $830 per credit for out-of-state residents and international students. Fees for all programs total $680 per semester.

Student Group

In fall 2016, there were 815 graduate students enrolled in programs through the Marxe School of Public and International Affairs. Of that

Austin W. Marxe School of Public and International Affairs at Baruch College

group, 550 were enrolled in the M.P.A. program, 115 in the M.S.Ed. program. The student body in the School is 36 percent male and 64 percent female. There are more than 8,000 alumni of the School.

Location

Baruch College is located in New York City, New York in the northeastern region of the United States. Its vibrant campus provides many academic and social resources, including easy access to Midtown; Wall Street; and the international headquarters of major companies, cultural institutions, and nonprofit organizations. This gives student numerous career, internship, and networking opportunities. Students also have access to New York City's diverse array of cultural, dining, entertainment, and outdoor recreational options.

The College

A member of the City University of New York, Baruch College was founded in 1847 as the Free Academy. It was the first free public college in the country. Today, it continues the tradition of providing academic excellence and opportunity for students in New York City, the metropolitan region, and the world.

The college educates one of the most diverse student bodies in the United States. It has over 18,000 students who speak more than 130 languages and trace their roots to 170-plus countries. It offers 29 undergraduate majors, 56 undergraduate minors, 53 graduate programs, and two doctoral programs. *U.S. News & World Report*, *Forbes*, and the Princeton Review rank Baruch College among the nation's top colleges.

Faculty

The faculty of the Marxe School of Public and International Affairs is among the largest and most globally diverse in the country. Accomplished and widely recognized in their fields, each member brings a wealth of experience in advising or leading cabinet-level agencies, political leaders, and major health, nonprofit, or government organizations around the world. Their goal is to help students grow both personally and professionally while addressing today's most pressing public policy challenges and providing guidance on course work, development opportunities, and careers.

Faculty members bring expertise and scholarship in numerous areas to the classroom. For example, Professor Cristina Balboa examines comparative policy, international relations, and organization theory to explain the relationship between organizations' internal characteristics and external accountability, effectiveness, and legitimacy. She's also an administrator for the Global Issues/Transnational Actors interest group, which is part of the Association for Research on Nonprofit Organizations and Voluntary Action. A complete staff listing is available online at http://www.baruch.cuny.edu/mspia/faculty-and-staff/index.html.

Applying

Graduate programs in the Austin W. Marxe School of Public and International Affairs attract students from all over the world, representing a wide range of backgrounds, cultures, and professions. They come to engage, interact, and be part of the School's interdisciplinary approach to learning and professional development.

Students interested in the M.P.A., Executive M.P.A., M.I.A., or M.S.Ed. program may apply online at https://app.applyyourself.com/AYApplicantLogin/fl_ApplicantConnectLogin.asp?id=baruch-spa.

Correspondence and Information

The Austin W. Marxe School of Public and International Affairs
Young Hah, Director of Graduate Admissions and Enrollment Services
Baruch College, CUNY
One Bernard Baruch Way, Box D-0901
New York, New York 10010-5585
Phone: 646-660-6750
E-mail: mspia.admissions@baruch.cuny.edu
Website: http://www.baruch.cuny.edu/mspia

Baruch College Newman Library

Neighborhood around Baruch College

BOSTON UNIVERSITY
The Frederick S. Pardee School of Global Studies

 For more information, visit http://petersons.to/bostonu_globalstudies

Boston University Frederick S. Pardee School of Global Studies

Programs of Study

The Frederick S. Pardee School of Global Studies at Boston University (www.bu.edu/pardeeschool) is dedicated to advancing human progress. Through rigorous and creative undergraduate, graduate, and professional education; path-breaking research; and active engagement in innovative initiatives, students apply their education and knowledge to make a real-world difference in the critical challenges humanity faces.

The School has one of the largest programs in international relations in the United States, as well as one of the largest graduate programs within the College of Arts and Sciences at Boston University (BU). It offers more courses on intelligence than any other civilian school in the nation. Other strengths include security, development, environment, religion, regional studies, and cross-cultural studies. Additional information can be found online at www.bu.edu/pardeeschool/academics/undergraduate/international-relations.

Each program is designed to educate and train students for a variety of international relations careers, including positions related to diplomacy, sustainable development, foreign policy analysis, intelligence, international communication, environmental policy, and the corporate sector.

Master of Arts Programs: The Pardee School offers six Master of Arts (M.A.) programs with eight functional specializations, two dual-degree programs, one regional degree, and two graduate certificates (www.bu.edu/pardeeschool/academics/graduate).

In addition to the flagship two-year M.A. in International Affairs program (MAIA), the Pardee School offers degrees in Global Policy (MGP), Latin American Studies (LAS M.A.), and a rigorous five-year B.A. in International Relations/M.A. in International Affairs program. An accelerated one-year International Relations program (MAIR) is available for both civilian professionals and military officers looking to advance their international affairs careers. Dual degrees are offered in International Relations and Master of Business Administration (IR/M.B.A. Dual Degree) and International Relations and Juris Doctor (IR/J.D. Dual Degree). Students can also choose to complete a graduate certificate in African Studies or Asian Studies in conjunction with their degree.

These programs provide students with dynamic opportunities to learn about global issues through course work not only in the Pardee School but also in related departments at BU, enabling students to tailor their program to fit their individual career goals and interests. By providing a wide-ranging and comprehensive set of analytical tools, the School's multidisciplinary approach gives students the skills they need to analyze diverse real-world situations.

Off-Campus Programs: The Pardee School offers a range of high-quality study-abroad options that provide M.A. students opportunities to study and intern in some of the most interesting and important places on the planet. All programs are conducted in English. Unless otherwise noted, programs are open to all Pardee students, including Geneva: Global Governance, Economic Development, and Human Rights; Brussels: The EU in the 21st Century; Geneva and London: International Conflict Resolution; London: Mass Communication; London: Journalism; Kenya: Field Practicum in Public Health and Environment; and Washington, D.C.: Journalism. More information is available at www.bu.edu/pardeeschool/academics/graduate ma-study-abroad-programs.

Related Programs and Centers

The Pardee School complements and enhances the BU educational experience by sponsoring a range of conferences and seminars, bringing dynamic, prominent guest speakers to the school. Regional and Thematic Studies Centers within the Pardee School include the African Studies Center, the Center for the Study of Asia, the Center for the Study of Europe, the Institute for the Study of Muslim Societies and Civilizations, the Center for Latin American Studies, the Global Development Policy Center, and the Institute on Culture, Religion & World Affairs. For more information, visit www.bu.edu/pardeeschool/research/centers-programs. BU's various schools and departments offer numerous opportunities to attend sponsored talks and participate in research related to a variety of international affairs issues.

Financial Aid

Boston University provides $26.2 million in financial aid annually through its comprehensive financial aid services. Students have access to a number of graduate scholarships, fellowships, and assistantships, including the Martin Luther King Jr. Fellowship for students committed to community involvement and social justice, the Whitney M. Young Jr. Fellowship for students studying race relations and urban problems, and graduate research assistantships. Over 50 percent of the 2016 incoming class was offered scholarship aid. Federal Work-Study and other funds are also available. Further details are available at schoohttp://www.bu.edu/cas/prospective-students/graduate-admissions/graduate-financial-aid.

Cost of Study

Most students attend full-time (16–18 credits per term) while completing course work, and pay full-time tuition accordingly. It is also possible to take course work on a part-time basis, in which case students pay by the class. Some students require an extra term after finishing their course work to write the capstone M.A. Paper, during which time they pay a modest continuing student fee, equivalent to the cost of a 2-credit class.

Boston University

The most up-to-date information on tuition and fees can be found online at http://www.bu.edu/cas/prospective-students/graduate-admissions/graduate-financial-aid.

Living and Housing Opportunities

The Boston University Real Estate office rents apartments owned by Boston University to full-time Boston University graduate students, current faculty, and staff only. Apartments are not to be rented to undergraduate students or those not affiliated with Boston University. Graduate students often choose BU on-campus apartments because of the wide selection of options in price, size, and location and convenience to campus and area amenities.

The University and The School

With a foundation dating back to 1839, Boston University remains one of the most dynamic universities in the world. Nearly one in seven students is classified as an international student, with students hailing from more than 139 nations. Boston University has satellite campuses and exchange programs in more than 30 cities on six continents.

The combination of cutting-edge research and instruction in global studies with the deep resources of BU is what gives Pardee School students their advantage in the workforce and on the world stage. From the class of 2014, 87 percent of graduates are working full time in government offices, NGOs, and the private sector.

Experienced, Dedicated Faculty

The Pardee School offers a world-class array of faculty members with backgrounds in diplomacy, intelligence, academia, the military, and more. Moreover, the Pardee School prides itself on being a teaching school, with students rating the accessibility and engagement of their professors at the highest levels.

Faculty members of BU have been recipients of a wide range of awards and honors, including the Nobel Prize, Presidential Citizens Medal, Pulitzer Prize, and Guggenheim Fellowships, as well as recognition from the American Academy of Arts and Sciences, American Academy of Arts and Letters, and National Academy of Sciences.

More information about the faculty is available on the School's website at http://www.bu.edu/pardeeschool/academics/faculty.

Applying

Applicants to the Pardee School M.A. programs apply through the Graduate School of Arts & Sciences. The application is online and all materials must be submitted electronically; no application materials should be sent directly to the Pardee School. Applicants interested in the IR/J.D. or IR/M.B.A. programs need to apply twice,

both to the Pardee School and partner school. For applications to the partner schools, applicants must follow all policies, procedures, and deadlines of those schools.

Applications should include the Application Form, transcripts of all prior university studies, three letters of recommendation, official GRE general scores, a personal statement, a resume or CV (recommended, not required), and official TOEFL Scores (for most international students).

Application deadlines are May 1 for fall enrollment and December 15 for spring enrollment. The application system opens to accept new applications in early September. Priority deadline for aid consideration is January 18.

Correspondence and Information
Graduate Office
Boston University
156 Bay State Road
Boston, Massachusetts 02215
United States
Phone: 617-358-8625
E-mail: psgsgrad@bu.edu
Website: bu.edu/pardeeschool

CONCORDIA UNIVERSITY IRVINE
International Studies

 For more information, visit http://petersons.to/concordiaintlstudies

Program of Study

The online Master of Arts in International Studies (M.A.I.S.) at Concordia University Irvine (CUI) prepares students to make a real impact on communities all over the world. This accelerated program provides in-depth knowledge about the integration of business and culture. It also allows students to develop ethical leadership abilities so they can serve people and communities with sensitivity and integrity.

The M.A.I.S. curriculum has 34 units of coursework that can be completed online in 16 to 18 months. Students can choose to begin in the fall or spring semester. Core courses equip students with a comprehensive understanding of the diverse aspects of international studies. Courses include:

- Intercultural Competency
- Global Politics and Leadership
- International Field Work
- International Social Research Methods
- International Development Theory and Practices
- Global Economics and Finance
- Global Religious Landscape
- Global Conflicts and Conflict Resolution
- Social Change and Project Management

The International Field Work course allows students to focus their studies on a particular region. It includes three weeks of international travel, which an M.A.I.S. faculty member coordinates and leads, to one of four regions: Africa, Central/South America, China, or Southeast Asia. This experience provides students with a rich setting for applying academic knowledge, a social laboratory for conducting research, and a setting for developing relationships with residents of regional communities.

Coursework culminates with a capstone project in which students apply both theoretical knowledge and practical observations and research gained from their international experiences. The capstone project intends for students to apply theory and principles in a situation that approximates some aspect of a professional practice in a global/multicultural environment. The main components of the project come from the signature assignments of the various courses in the program. The completed project needs to be reviewed and approved by the Capstone advisor and the course instructor. A total of two consecutive terms are allowed for the Capstone project. Students will be assigned a CUI-approved faculty advisor or mentor to complete this project. Students will be awarded their master's diploma when they have successfully completed both the core courses and the Capstone project.

Concordia University's online education ascribes to a model in which real time synchronous learning experiences comprise a certain percentage of every course, bringing students face-to-face with faculty.

M.A.I.S. students strengthen and develop analytical, speech, and writing skills and gain detailed knowledge about global relations. As a result, the graduates are prepared for careers in government, international affairs, international business, journalism, law, nongovernmental organizations (NGOs), nonprofit organizations (NPOs), research, and teaching. Alumni are working both in the U.S. and throughout the world in a wide range of industries and institutions such as universities, law offices, hospitals, the foreign services sector, advertising/marketing departments of various industries, business, and more.

Field Experiences

Concordia's M.A.I.S. program includes three weeks of international fieldwork in one of four chosen regions: Africa, Central and South America, China, or Southeast Asia. Once students have completed their coursework they will travel with a group to the region of their choice and learn by doing.

Africa: Students who select the Africa field experience have access to one of three countries: Cameroon, Ghana, or Sierra Leone. They focus on project research and evaluation, community-driven development, agribusiness and climate change, or advocacy and communication. Activities include business observation and visits, lectures/seminars/talks on regional critical issues by the local experts, and participatory service trips to existing NGO/NPO project sites.

Central/South America: Students who select the Central/South America field experience have access to one of three countries: Argentina, Brazil, and Costa Rica. They can focus on community-driven development, regional politics, international relations, or intra-/inter-continent migration. Activities include lectures/seminars/talks by local experts, participatory service trips to existing NGO/NPO project sites, and visits to cultural sites.

China: Students who select the China field experience have access to one or more of the following Chinese regions: Jiangsu, Yunnan, Chengdu, or Shanghai. They can focus on sustainable economic growth, regional conflict and resolution, community-driven development, internal human migration, or public policy. Student participate in lectures/seminars/talks by local experts, international business and company visits, government agency visits, participatory service learning trips, and visits to cultural sites.

Southeast Asia: Students who select the Southeast Asia field experience have access to one or more of the following four countries: Thailand, Laos, Cambodia, or Myanmar. They can focus on regional and global diplomacy, human security studies, or peace studies. Activities include lectures/seminars/talks by local experts, business observation and visits, intense learning of human security studies, NGO/NPO projects, service trips, and visits to cultural sites.

Financial Aid

Most graduate students are eligible for the Federal Direct Unsubsidized Stafford Loan Program of up to $20,500 per academic year. They may also qualify for federal loans or assistance through the Post 9/11 GI Bill and Yellow Ribbon programs.

Students will need to apply for financial aid by completing the FAFSA or FAFSA Renewal form.

Cost of Study

Tuition for the M.A. in International Studies program at Concordia University Irvine is $525 per unit for the 2018–19 academic year. There is a $50 application fee ($150 for international applicants). Students also incur travel costs associated with the international fieldwork experience. Tuition and fees are subject to change.

Location

Concordia University Irvine's campus is located in Orange County, California; however, the M.A.I.S. program is delivered online, with the exception of the field experience components.

The University

Concordia University Irvine is a *U.S. News* Top Tier Regional University and has been named by *The Chronicle of Higher Education* as one of

Concordia University Irvine

the fastest growing private nonprofit master's institutions. CUI prepares more than 4,000 students for their callings in life. It offers undergraduate, graduate, doctoral, and certificate programs at its Southern California location and online. Its high-quality distance learning programs provide relevant and marketable outcomes.

U.S. News & World Report ranked Concordia University Irvine as one of the Best Regional Universities, and the *Chronicle of Higher Education* ranked it among the top-20 fastest growing master's level universities in the nation.

Faculty

M.A.I.S. faculty members are multicultural educators who possess global mindsets. They are also scholars and practitioners who have a wealth of experience working in international and nonprofit organizations.

Professor of International Studies Elizabeth Childs Drury, Ph.D. is an experienced practitioner who works to create intercultural effectiveness in changing, diverse, or global settings. She has worked and lived in Costa Rica, Germany, and Hungary. She trained hundreds of teachers for international appointments, and she directed Central Europe programs for a Christian educational services organization. Her scholarly work includes numerous talks, presentations, and publications.

Professor of International Studies Paul Chambers, Ph.D. is a prolific researcher who investigates subjects related to Southeast Asia. His research focuses primarily on Thailand, but he has also conducted research concerning Cambodia, Laos, Myanmar, and the Philippines. He has authored and coauthored five books, numerous journal articles, and several book chapters about Southeast Asia's democratization, international politics, and military. His articles have been published in *Asian Survey*, *Contemporary Southeast Asia*, *Journal of Contemporary Asia*, and other scholarly publications.

Additional information regarding faculty members in the M.A.I.S. program can be found online at https://www.cui.edu/online/degrees/masters/international-studies/faculty-and-staff.

Applying

Applicants to Concordia University Irvine's online M.A.I.S. program must have a bachelor's degree from a regionally accredited institution with a minimum undergraduate cumulative GPA of 2.75 before cohort starts. Applicants need to submit an online application with a nonrefundable application fee of $50 ($150 for international applicants); a statement of intent including both short- and long-term career objectives; an official transcript from the institution where they earned their bachelor's degree; two recommendations from references such as a professor, employer, immediate supervisor, pastor, or colleague; and a complete and current resume.

In addition, international applicants must demonstrate adequate English language proficiency to the satisfaction of the M.A.I.S. program for course participation and completion; submit the Affidavit of Financial Support and Certificate of Bank Balance forms; and an official, detailed transcript evaluation from an approved international credential evaluation service International Education Research Foundation or Educational Credential Evaluators (www.ece.org) that shows the equivalent of a regionally accredited U.S. degree.

Correspondence and Information

Marsha Castillo, Program Coordinator
Concordia University Irvine
1530 Concordia West
Irvine, California 92612
Phone: 949-214-3485
Fax: 949-214-3485
E-mail: marsha.castillo@cui.edu
        gradadmissions@cui.edu
Website: https://www.cui.edu/online/degrees/masters/
    international-studies

Section 24
Psychology and Counseling

This section contains a directory of institutions offering graduate work in psychology and counseling, followed by in-depth entries submitted by institutions that chose to prepare detailed program descriptions. Additional information about programs listed in the directory but not augmented by an in-depth entry may be obtained by writing directly to the dean of a graduate school or chair of a department at the address given in the directory.

For programs offering related work, see also in this book *Criminology and Forensics, Family and Consumer Sciences,* and *Sociology, Anthropology, and Archaeology.* In the other guides in this series:

Graduate Programs in the Biological/Biomedical Sciences & Health-Related Medical Professions

See *Biological and Biomedical Sciences; Genetics, Developmental Biology, and Reproductive Biology; Neuroscience and Neurobiology; Nursing (Psychiatric Nursing); Pharmacy and Pharmaceutical Sciences; Pharmacology and Toxicology;* and *Public Health*

Graduate Programs in Business, Education, Information Studies, Law & Social Work

See *Education* and *Social Work*

CONTENTS

Program Directories

Featured Schools: Displays and Close-Ups

Psychology—General

Abilene Christian University, Graduate Programs, College of Arts and Sciences, Department of Psychology, Program in Psychology, Abilene, TX 79699. Offers MS. *Students:* 3 full-time (1 woman), 1 part-time (0 women); includes 1 minority (Hispanic/Latino). 6 applicants, 50% accepted. In 2017, 5 master's awarded. *Degree requirements:* For master's, comprehensive exam, thesis. *Entrance requirements:* Additional exam requirements/recommendations for international students: Required—TOEFL (minimum score 80 iBT), IELTS (minimum score 6), PTE. *Application deadline:* For fall admission, 3/30 priority date for domestic students; for spring admission, 11/1 for domestic students. Applications are processed on a rolling basis. Application fee: $50. Electronic applications accepted. *Expenses:* $1,148 per hour. *Financial support:* In 2017–18, 2 students received support. Federal Work-Study and scholarships/grants available. Support available to part-time students. Financial award application deadline: 4/1; financial award applicants required to submit FAFSA. *Unit head:* Dr. Cherisse Flangan, Graduate Director, 325-674-4826, Fax: 325-674-6968, E-mail: cherisse.flanagan@acu.edu. *Application contact:* Graduate Admissions, 325-674-6911, Fax: 325-674-6717, E-mail: gradinfo@acu.edu.
Website: http://www.acu.edu/graduate/academics/psychology.html

Acadia University, Faculty of Pure and Applied Science, Department of Psychology, Wolfville, NS B4P 2R6, Canada. Offers clinical psychology (M Sc). *Entrance requirements:* For master's, GRE General Test, GRE Subject Test, honors degree or equivalent. Additional exam requirements/recommendations for international students: Required—TOEFL (minimum score 580 paper-based; 93 iBT), IELTS (minimum score 6.5). *Application deadline:* For fall admission, 2/1 priority date for domestic and international students. Applications are processed on a rolling basis. Application fee: $50. *Financial support:* Application deadline: 2/1. *Faculty research:* Social psychology, job stress, psychotherapy, cognition perception, development. *Unit head:* Dr. Lisa Price, Graduate Advisor, 902-585-1196, E-mail: lisa.price@acadiau.ca. *Application contact:* Dr. Peter Horvath, Graduate Coordinator, 902-585-1200, Fax: 902-585-1078, E-mail: peter.horvath@acadiau.ca.
Website: http://psychology.acadiau.ca

Adelphi University, Gordon F. Derner School of Psychology, Program in General Psychology, Garden City, NY 11530-0701. Offers MA. *Students:* 59 full-time (47 women), 23 part-time (19 women); includes 28 minority (15 Black or African American, non-Hispanic/Latino; 4 Asian, non-Hispanic/Latino; 8 Hispanic/Latino; 1 Two or more races, non-Hispanic/Latino), 10 international. Average age 28. 110 applicants, 68% accepted, 36 enrolled. In 2017, 43 master's awarded. *Degree requirements:* For master's, comprehensive exam. *Entrance requirements:* For master's, 2 letters of recommendation; minimum GPA of 3.0; course work in psychology including developmental psychology, psychopathology, and research design or experimental psychology; personal essay; transcripts from all previously-attended schools. Additional exam requirements/recommendations for international students: Required—TOEFL (minimum score 550 paper-based; 80 iBT). *Application deadline:* For fall admission, 5/1 priority date for international students; for spring admission, 11/1 priority date for international students. Applications are processed on a rolling basis. Application fee: $50. Electronic applications accepted. *Expenses:* Contact institution. *Financial support:* Research assistantships with full and partial tuition reimbursements, teaching assistantships, career-related internships or fieldwork, institutionally sponsored loans, scholarships/grants, traineeships, and unspecified assistantships available. Support available to part-time students. Financial award application deadline: 2/15; financial award applicants required to submit FAFSA. *Unit head:* Dr. Errol Rodriguez, Assistant Dean, 516-237-8572, E-mail: erodriguez@adelphi.edu. *Application contact:* E-mail: graduateadmissions@adelphi.edu.
Website: http://derner.adelphi.edu/psychology/graduate/ma-general-psychology/

Alabama Agricultural and Mechanical University, School of Graduate Studies, College of Education, Humanities, and Behavioral Sciences, Department of Social Work, Psychology and Counseling, Huntsville, AL 35811. Offers psychology and counseling (MS, Ed S), including clinical psychology (MS), counseling psychology (MS), guidance and counseling, rehabilitation counseling (MS), school counseling (MS), school psychology (MS), school psychometry (MS); social work (MSW). *Accreditation:* CORE; NCATE. *Program availability:* Part-time, evening/weekend. *Degree requirements:* For master's, comprehensive exam. *Entrance requirements:* For master's, GRE General Test. Additional exam requirements/recommendations for international students: Required—TOEFL (minimum score 500 paper-based; 61 iBT). *Faculty research:* Increasing numbers of minorities in special education and speech-language pathology.

Alliant International University–Fresno, California School of Professional Psychology, Fresno, CA 93727. Offers MA, PhD, Psy D, MA/PhD, Psy D/MA. *Accreditation:* APA. *Degree requirements:* For doctorate, comprehensive exam, thesis/dissertation. *Entrance requirements:* For doctorate, minimum GPA of 3.0, letters of recommendation, essay, interview. Additional exam requirements/recommendations for international students: Required—TOEFL (minimum score 550 paper-based), TWE (minimum score 5). Electronic applications accepted. *Faculty research:* Parent-child relationships, LGBT families, social justice, women's health, neurocognitive functioning.

Alliant International University–Los Angeles, California School of Professional Psychology, Alhambra, CA 91803. Offers MA, PhD, Psy D. *Accreditation:* APA. *Degree requirements:* For doctorate, comprehensive exam, thesis/dissertation. *Entrance requirements:* For doctorate, interview, minimum GPA of 3.0 in psychology and overall, letters of recommendation. Additional exam requirements/recommendations for international students: Required—TOEFL (minimum score 600 paper-based), TWE (minimum score 5). Electronic applications accepted. *Faculty research:* Family therapy, multi-cultural psychology, post-traumatic stress, assessment, community mental health.

Alliant International University–Sacramento, California School of Professional Psychology, Sacramento, CA 95833. Offers MA, Psy D. *Program availability:* Part-time. *Degree requirements:* For doctorate, comprehensive exam, thesis/dissertation. *Entrance requirements:* For master's and doctorate, minimum GPA of 3.0, recommendations, essay. Additional exam requirements/recommendations for international students: Required—TOEFL (minimum score 600 paper-based), TWE (minimum score 5). Electronic applications accepted. *Faculty research:* International research testing a model of health behavior change for the developing world, immigration stress, addiction, issues facing LGBTQI community life.

Alliant International University–San Diego, California School of Professional Psychology, San Diego, CA 92131. Offers MA, MS, PhD, Psy D. *Accreditation:* APA. *Program availability:* Part-time. Terminal master's awarded for partial completion of doctoral program. *Degree requirements:* For master's, practicum; for doctorate, comprehensive exam, thesis/dissertation, internship or practicum. *Entrance requirements:* For master's and doctorate, minimum GPA of 3.0, essay, letters of recommendation, interview. Additional exam requirements/recommendations for international students: Required—TOEFL (minimum score 550 paper-based; 80 iBT), TWE (minimum score 5). *Faculty research:* Couples therapy, depression, multicultural and international issues, evidence-based practice, neuropsychology of autism, ADHD.

Alliant International University–San Francisco, California School of Professional Psychology, San Francisco, CA 94133. Offers MA, Post-Doctoral MS, PhD, Psy D, Certificate. *Accreditation:* APA (one or more programs are accredited). *Degree requirements:* For doctorate, comprehensive exam, thesis/dissertation, internship. *Entrance requirements:* For master's and doctorate, minimum GPA of 3.0, recommendations, essay, interview. Additional exam requirements/recommendations for international students: Required—TOEFL (minimum score 550 paper-based; 80 iBT), TWE (minimum score 5). Electronic applications accepted. *Faculty research:* Multicultural issues, lesbian/gay/bisexual/transgender issues, health psychology, family systems, substance abuse.

American International College, School of Business, Arts and Sciences, Springfield, MA 01109-3189. Offers accounting and taxation (MS); business administration (MBA); clinical psychology (MA); educational psychology (Ed D); forensic psychology (MS); general psychology (MA, CAGS); management (CAGS); resort and casino management (MBA, CAGS). *Program availability:* Part-time, evening/weekend. *Faculty:* 4 full-time (2 women), 25 part-time/adjunct (13 women). *Students:* 178 full-time (120 women), 24 part-time (20 women); includes 94 minority (42 Black or African American, non-Hispanic/Latino; 1 American Indian or Alaska Native, non-Hispanic/Latino; 4 Asian, non-Hispanic/Latino; 39 Hispanic/Latino; 8 Two or more races, non-Hispanic/Latino), 13 international. Average age 28. 155 applicants, 83% accepted, 71 enrolled. In 2017, 87 master's, 3 doctorates awarded. *Degree requirements:* For master's, practicum; for doctorate, comprehensive exam, thesis/dissertation, practicum. *Entrance requirements:* For master's, BS or BA, minimum undergraduate GPA of 2.75, 2 letters of recommendation, official transcripts, personal goal statement or essay; for doctorate, 3 letters of recommendation; BS or BA; minimum undergraduate GPA of 3.0 (3.25 recommended); official transcripts; personal goal statement or essay. Additional exam requirements/recommendations for international students: Required—TOEFL (minimum score 550 paper-based; 80 iBT). *Application deadline:* For fall admission, 8/15 for domestic and international students; for spring admission, 12/15 for domestic and international students. Applications are processed on a rolling basis. Application fee: $50. *Expenses:* Contact institution. *Financial support:* In 2017–18, 6 students received support, including 6 research assistantships with full tuition reimbursements available (averaging $1,500 per year). Financial award application deadline: 4/1; financial award applicants required to submit FAFSA. *Faculty research:* Substance abuse, forensic psychology, special education. *Unit head:* Dr. Susanne Swanker, Dean, 413-205-3216, Fax: 413-205-3943, E-mail: susanne.swanker@aic.edu. *Application contact:* Kerry Barnes, Dean of Graduate Admissions, 413-205-3703, Fax: 413-205-3051, E-mail: kerry.barnes@aic.edu.
Website: http://www.aic.edu/school-of-business-arts-and-sciences/

American University, College of Arts and Sciences, Department of Psychology, Washington, DC 22016-8062. Offers addiction and addictive behavior (Certificate); behavior, cognition, and neuroscience (PhD); clinical psychology (PhD); psychobiology of healing (Certificate); psychology (MA). *Accreditation:* APA. *Program availability:* Part-time. *Faculty:* 20 full-time (8 women), 9 part-time/adjunct (7 women). *Students:* 80 full-time (68 women), 8 part-time (7 women); includes 15 minority (5 Black or African American, non-Hispanic/Latino; 4 Asian, non-Hispanic/Latino; 5 Hispanic/Latino; 1 Two or more races, non-Hispanic/Latino), 6 international. Average age 28. 461 applicants, 12% accepted, 23 enrolled. In 2017, 24 master's, 11 doctorates awarded. *Degree requirements:* For master's, comprehensive exam, thesis or alternative; for doctorate, comprehensive exam, thesis/dissertation. *Entrance requirements:* For master's, GRE General Test, GRE Subject Test, statement of purpose, transcripts, 2 letters of recommendation; for doctorate, GRE General Test, GRE Subject Test, 3 letters of recommendation, statement of purpose, transcripts, resume. Additional exam requirements/recommendations for international students: Required—TOEFL (minimum score 600 paper-based; 100 iBT). *Application deadline:* For fall admission, 3/1 priority date for domestic students. Application fee: $55. *Expenses:* Contact institution. *Financial support:* Research assistantships, teaching assistantships, institutionally sponsored loans, scholarships/grants, and unspecified assistantships available. Financial award application deadline: 2/1; financial award applicants required to submit FAFSA. *Unit head:* Dr. David Haaga, Department Chair, 202-885-1718, Fax: 202-885-1023, E-mail: ahrens@american.edu. *Application contact:* Jonathan Harper, Associate Director, Graduate Recruitment, 202-885-3622, E-mail: jharper@american.edu.
Website: http://www.american.edu/CAS/Psychology/

The American University in Cairo, School of Humanities and Social Sciences, Cairo, Egypt. Offers Arab and Islamic civilizations (Graduate Diploma); Arabic studies (MA); comparative literary studies (Graduate Diploma); Egyptology and Coptology (MA); English and comparative literature (MA); humanities and social sciences (Graduate Diploma); philosophy (MA); psychology (MA); sociology and anthropology (MA); teaching Arabic as a foreign language (MA); teaching English to speakers of other languages (MA). *Program availability:* Part-time, evening/weekend. *Faculty:* 52 full-time (27 women), 7 part-time/adjunct (3 women). *Students:* 52 full-time (41 women), 159 part-time (119 women), 38 international. Average age 31. 209 applicants, 36% accepted, 39 enrolled. In 2017, 73 master's awarded. *Degree requirements:* For master's, comprehensive exam (for some programs), thesis (for some programs). *Entrance requirements:* Additional exam requirements/recommendations for international students: Required—TOEFL (minimum score 450 paper-based; 45 iBT), IELTS (minimum score 5). *Application deadline:* For fall admission, 2/1 priority date for domestic and international students; for spring admission, 10/15 priority date for domestic and international students. Applications are processed on a rolling basis. Application fee: $85. Electronic applications accepted. *Financial support:* Fellowships with partial tuition reimbursements, scholarships/grants, tuition waivers (partial), and unspecified assistantships available. Financial award application deadline: 3/10. *Faculty research:* English literature, political science, psychology, sociology, anthropology and Egyptology, philosophy, Arabic studies, history, teaching Arabic as a foreign language, teaching English to speakers of other languages. *Unit head:* Dr. Robert Switzer, Interim Dean, 20-2-2615-1068, E-mail: nbowditch@aucegypt.edu. *Application contact:* Maha Hegazi, Director for Graduate Admissions, 20-2-2615-1462, E-mail: mahahegazi@aucegypt.edu.
Website: http://www.aucegypt.edu/huss/Pages/default.aspx

American University of Beirut, Graduate Programs, Faculty of Arts and Sciences, 1107 2020, Lebanon. Offers anthropology (MA); Arab and Middle Eastern history (PhD); Arabic language and literature (MA, PhD); archaeology (MA); art history and curating (MA); biology (MS); cell and molecular biology (PhD); chemistry (MS); clinical

psychology (MA); computational sciences (MS); computer science (MS); economics (MA); education (MA), including administration and policy studies, elementary education, mathematics education, psychology school guidance, psychology test and measurements, science education, teaching English as a foreign language; English language (MA); English literature (MA); environmental policy planning (MS); financial economics (MAFE); general psychology (MA); geology (MS); history (MA); Islamic studies (MA); mathematics (MS); media studies (MA); Middle East studies (MA); philosophy (MA); physics (MS); political studies (MA); public administration (MA); public policy and international affairs (MA); sociology (MA); theoretical physics (PhD). *Program availability:* Part-time. *Faculty:* 108 full-time (36 women), 5 part-time/adjunct (4 women). *Students:* 251 full-time (180 women), 233 part-time (172 women). Average age 26. 425 applicants, 65% accepted, 121 enrolled. In 2017, 47 master's, 2 doctorates awarded. *Degree requirements:* For master's, one foreign language, comprehensive exam, thesis (for some programs), project; for doctorate, one foreign language, comprehensive exam, thesis/dissertation. *Entrance requirements:* For master's, GRE General Test (for some programs); for doctorate, GRE General Test (GRE Subject Test for theoretical physics). Additional exam requirements/recommendations for international students: Required—TOEFL (minimum score 583 paper-based; 97 iBT), IELTS (minimum score 7). *Application deadline:* For fall admission, 2/8 for domestic students; for spring admission, 11/3 for domestic students. Application fee: $50. Electronic applications accepted. *Expenses:* Contact institution. *Financial support:* In 2017–18, 29 fellowships, 40 research assistantships were awarded; teaching assistantships, scholarships/grants, tuition waivers (full and partial), and unspecified assistantships also available. Financial award application deadline: 4/4. *Unit head:* Dr. Nadia Maria El Cheikh, Dean, Faculty of Arts and Sciences, 961-1-374374 Ext. 3800, Fax: 961-1-744461, E-mail: nmcheikh@aub.edu.lb. *Application contact:* Rima Rassi, Graduate Studies Officer, 961-1-350000 Ext. 3833, Fax: 961-1-744461, E-mail: rr46@aub.edu.lb.
Website: http://www.aub.edu.lb/fas/pages/default.aspx

Andrews University, School of Graduate Studies, School of Education, Department of Graduate Psychology and Counseling, Berrien Springs, MI 49104. Offers community counseling (MA), including clinical mental health counseling, community counseling; counseling psychology (MA, PhD); educational and developmental psychology (MA, Ed D, PhD), including educational and developmental psychology (MA), educational psychology (Ed D, PhD); school counseling (MA); school psychology (Ed S); special education (MS). *Accreditation:* ACA (one or more programs are accredited). *Program availability:* Part-time. *Faculty:* 12 full-time (5 women), 4 part-time/adjunct (2 women). *Students:* 76 full-time (55 women), 8 part-time (7 women); includes 27 minority (17 Black or African American, non-Hispanic/Latino; 8 Hispanic/Latino; 2 Two or more races, non-Hispanic/Latino), 25 international. Average age 35. 79 applicants, 52% accepted, 23 enrolled. In 2017, 25 master's, 6 doctorates, 8 other advanced degrees awarded. Terminal master's awarded for partial completion of doctoral program. *Degree requirements:* For master's, thesis optional; for doctorate, thesis/dissertation. *Entrance requirements:* For master's, GRE Subject Test, minimum GPA of 2.6; for doctorate, GRE General Test, MA, minimum GPA of 3.5, sample of research. Additional exam requirements/recommendations for international students: Required—TOEFL (minimum score 550 paper-based). *Application deadline:* Applications are processed on a rolling basis. Application fee: $40. *Faculty research:* Testing methods, temperament, African-American studies, counseling process, multicultural issues. *Unit head:* Dr. Rudi Bailey, Chair, 269-471-3473. *Application contact:* Justina Clayburn, Supervisor of Graduate Admission, 800-253-2874, Fax: 269-471-6321, E-mail: graduate@andrews.edu.
Website: https://www.andrews.edu/sed/gpc/

Angelo State University, College of Graduate Studies and Research, Archer College of Health and Human Services, Department of Psychology and Sociology, San Angelo, TX 76909. Offers industrial-organizational psychology (MS). *Program availability:* Part-time, evening/weekend. *Students:* 83 full-time (55 women), 41 part-time (28 women); includes 39 minority (8 Black or African American, non-Hispanic/Latino; 1 Asian, non-Hispanic/Latino; 28 Hispanic/Latino; 2 Two or more races, non-Hispanic/Latino), 6 international. Average age 32. *Degree requirements:* For master's, comprehensive exam, thesis optional. *Entrance requirements:* For master's, GRE General Test (for industrial and organizational psychology only), essay, letters of recommendation (for industrial and organizational psychology only). Additional exam requirements/recommendations for international students: Required—TOEFL or IELTS. *Application deadline:* For fall admission, 7/15 priority date for domestic students, 6/10 for international students; for spring admission, 12/1 priority date for domestic students, 11/1 for international students. Applications are processed on a rolling basis. Application fee: $40 ($50 for international students). Electronic applications accepted. *Expenses:* Tuition, state resident: full-time $3856. Tuition, nonresident: full-time $11,324. *Required fees:* $2650. *Financial support:* Teaching assistantships, career-related internships or fieldwork, Federal Work-Study, scholarships/grants, and unspecified assistantships available. Support available to part-time students. Financial award application deadline: 3/1; financial award applicants required to submit FAFSA. *Unit head:* Dr. James N. Forbes, Chair, 325-486-6120, Fax: 325-942-2290, E-mail: james.forbes@angelo.edu.
Website: http://www.angelo.edu/dept/psychology_sociology/

Antioch University Los Angeles, Program in Psychology, Culver City, CA 90230. Offers clinical psychology (MA); psychology (MA). *Program availability:* Part-time. *Faculty:* 19. *Students:* 428 full-time (312 women), 35 part-time (27 women); includes 140 minority (25 Black or African American, non-Hispanic/Latino; 13 Asian, non-Hispanic/Latino; 81 Hispanic/Latino; 1 Native Hawaiian or other Pacific Islander, non-Hispanic/Latino; 20 Two or more races, non-Hispanic/Latino), 1 international. Average age 36. In 2017, 118 master's awarded. *Degree requirements:* For master's, thesis (for some programs), internship. *Entrance requirements:* For master's, interview. Additional exam requirements/recommendations for international students: Required—TOEFL. *Application deadline:* For fall admission, 8/4 priority date for domestic students; for winter admission, 11/3 priority date for domestic students; for spring admission, 2/4 priority date for domestic students. Applications are processed on a rolling basis. Application fee: $60. *Financial support:* In 2017–18, 167 students received support. Career-related internships or fieldwork, Federal Work-Study, scholarships/grants, and traineeships available. Support available to part-time students. Financial award application deadline: 3/24; financial award applicants required to submit FAFSA. *Faculty research:* Creativity and humor, ethnic humor, adult development, Jungian theory, psychoanalytic theory. *Unit head:* Joy Turek, Chair, 310-578-1080 Ext. 306, Fax: 310-822-4824, E-mail: joy_turek@antiochla.edu. *Application contact:* Information Contact, 310-578-1090, Fax: 310-822-4824, E-mail: admissions@antiochla.edu.

Appalachian State University, Cratis D. Williams Graduate School, Department of Psychology, Boone, NC 28608. Offers clinical health psychology (MA). *Program availability:* Part-time. *Degree requirements:* For master's, comprehensive exam, thesis optional, exit exam. *Entrance requirements:* For master's, GRE General Test, 3 letters of recommendation. Additional exam requirements/recommendations for international students: Required—TOEFL (minimum score 550 paper-based; 79 iBT) or IELTS (minimum score 6.5). Electronic applications accepted. *Faculty research:* Eating disorders, school-based consultations, organizational behavior management, brain mechanisms of sound localization, parenting styles.

Arcadia University, College of Arts and Sciences, Department of Psychology, Glenside, PA 19038-3295. Offers applied behavior analysis (MAC); autism (MAC); child/family therapy (MAC); community public health (MAC); counseling/international peace and conflict resolution dual degree (MAC); mental health counseling (MAC); trauma (MAC). *Program availability:* Part-time. *Degree requirements:* For master's, practicum. *Entrance requirements:* For master's, GRE General Test or MAT. *Expenses:* Contact institution.

Arcadia University, School of Education, Glenside, PA 19038-3295. Offers art education (M Ed); computer education (CAS); curriculum (CAS); curriculum studies (M Ed); early childhood education (M Ed), including individualized, master teacher, research in child development; educational leadership (M Ed, Ed D, CAS); elementary education (M Ed); English education (MA Ed); environmental education (MA Ed); instructional technology (M Ed); language arts (M Ed); library science (M Ed); mathematics education (M Ed, MA Ed); music education (MA Ed); psychology (MA Ed); reading (M Ed, CAS); science education (M Ed, CAS); secondary education (M Ed, CAS); special education (M Ed, Ed D, CAS); theater arts (MA Ed); written communication (MA Ed). *Accreditation:* NASAD. *Program availability:* Part-time, evening/weekend, online learning. Electronic applications accepted. *Expenses:* Contact institution.

Argosy University, Atlanta, Georgia School of Professional Psychology, Atlanta, GA 30328. Offers clinical psychology (MA, Psy D, Postdoctoral Respecialization Certificate), including child and family psychology (Psy D), general adult clinical (Psy D), health psychology (Psy D), neuropsychology/geropsychology (Psy D); community counseling (MA), including marriage and family therapy; counselor education and supervision (Ed D); forensic psychology (MA); industrial organizational psychology (MA); marriage and family therapy (Certificate); sport-exercise psychology (MA). *Accreditation:* APA.

Argosy University, Chicago, Illinois School of Professional Psychology, Chicago, IL 60601. Offers clinical psychology (MA, Psy D), including child and adolescent psychology (Psy D), client-centered and experiential psychotherapies (Psy D), diversity and multicultural psychology (Psy D), family psychology (Psy D), forensic psychology (Psy D), health psychology (Psy D), neuropsychology (Psy D), organizational consulting (Psy D), psychoanalytic psychology (Psy D), psychology and spirituality (Psy D); community counseling (MA); counseling psychology (Ed D), including counselor education and supervision; counselor education and supervision (Ed D); industrial organizational psychology (MA). *Accreditation:* APA (one or more programs are accredited). *Program availability:* Online learning.

Argosy University, Hawai`i, Hawai'i School of Professional Psychology, Honolulu, HI 96813. Offers MA, MS, Ed D, Psy D, Certificate, Postdoctoral Respecialization Certificate. *Accreditation:* APA.

Argosy University, Los Angeles, College of Psychology and Behavioral Sciences, Los Angeles, CA 90045. Offers clinical psychology/marriage and family therapy (MA); counseling psychology (Ed D); counseling psychology/marriage and family therapy (MA); forensic psychology (MA).

Argosy University, Northern Virginia, American School of Professional Psychology, Arlington, VA 22209. Offers clinical psychology (MA, Psy D), including child and family psychology (Psy D), diversity and multicultural psychology (Psy D), forensic psychology (Psy D), health and neuropsychology (Psy D); community counseling (MA); counseling psychology (Ed D), including counselor education and supervision; counselor education and supervision (Ed D); forensic psychology (MA).

Argosy University, Orange County, American School of Professional Psychology, Orange, CA 92868. Offers MA, Ed D, Psy D. *Accreditation:* APA. *Program availability:* Part-time, evening/weekend. *Degree requirements:* For master's, comprehensive exam; for doctorate, comprehensive exam, thesis/dissertation. *Entrance requirements:* For master's and doctorate, 3 letters of recommendation, interview, resume. Additional exam requirements/recommendations for international students: Required—TOEFL. Electronic applications accepted. *Faculty research:* The psychological aspects of infertility medicine, depression, psychoanalytic therapy, experiential approaches to teaching.

Argosy University, Phoenix, Arizona School of Professional Psychology, Phoenix, AZ 85021. Offers MA, Psy D.

Argosy University, Seattle, College of Psychology and Behavioral Sciences, Seattle, WA 98121. Offers MA, Ed D, Psy D, Postdoctoral Respecialization Certificate.

Argosy University, Tampa, Florida School of Professional Psychology, Tampa, FL 33607. Offers clinical psychology (MA, Psy D), including clinical psychology; counselor education and supervision (Ed D); industrial organizational psychology (MA); marriage and family therapy (MA); mental health counseling (MA).

Argosy University, Twin Cities, Minnesota School of Professional Psychology, Eagan, MN 55121. Offers clinical psychology (MA, Psy D), including child and family psychology (Psy D), forensic psychology (Psy D), health and neuropsychology (Psy D), trauma (Psy D); forensic counseling (Post-Graduate Certificate); forensic psychology (MA); industrial organizational psychology (MA); marriage and family therapy (MA, DMFT), including forensic counseling (MA). *Accreditation:* AAMFT; AAMFT/COAMFTE; APA.

Arizona State University at the Tempe campus, College of Liberal Arts and Sciences, Department of Psychology, Tempe, AZ 85287-1104. Offers applied behavior analysis (MS); behavioral neuroscience (PhD); clinical psychology (PhD); cognitive science (PhD); developmental psychology (PhD); quantitative psychology (PhD); social psychology (PhD). *Accreditation:* APA. *Degree requirements:* For doctorate, comprehensive exam, thesis/dissertation, interactive Program of Study (iPOS) submitted before completing 50 percent of required credit hours. *Entrance requirements:* For doctorate, GRE General Test, GRE Subject Test, minimum GPA of 3.0 or equivalent in last 2 years of work leading to bachelor's degree. Additional exam requirements/recommendations for international students: Required—TOEFL, IELTS, or PTE. Electronic applications accepted.

Arizona State University at the Tempe campus, New College of Interdisciplinary Arts and Sciences, Program in Psychology, Phoenix, AZ 85069-7100. Offers MS. *Program availability:* Part-time, evening/weekend. *Degree requirements:* For master's, thesis or applied project, interactive Program of Study (iPOS) submitted before completing 50 percent of required credit hours. *Entrance requirements:* For master's, GRE, bachelor's degree in psychology or related field; minimum cumulative GPA of 3.0; successful completion of undergraduate statistics and research methods courses; three letters of recommendation from faculty; personal statement of research interests and goals. Additional exam requirements/recommendations for international students: Required—TOEFL, IELTS, or PTE. Electronic applications accepted. *Faculty research:* Emotion; stress; social identity, intergroup relations and prejudice; psychology and the legal system; discursive psychology; cognitive neuroscience, bilingualism and cognition; social psychology and bullying; health related decision-making; psychophysiology; attention, eye-tracking and natural behavior.

Arkansas Tech University, College of Arts and Humanities, Russellville, AR 72801. Offers applied sociology (MS); English (M Ed, MA); history (MA); liberal arts (MLA); multi-media journalism (MA); psychology (MS); teaching English as a second language

(MA). *Program availability:* Part-time, 100% online, blended/hybrid learning. *Students:* 35 full-time (22 women), 122 part-time (94 women); includes 34 minority (11 Black or African American, non-Hispanic/Latino; 2 Asian, non-Hispanic/Latino; 19 Hispanic/Latino; 2 Two or more races, non-Hispanic/Latino), 19 international. Average age 34. In 2017, 85 master's awarded. *Degree requirements:* For master's, comprehensive exam (for some programs), thesis (for some programs), project. *Entrance requirements:* Additional exam requirements/recommendations for international students: Required—TOEFL (minimum score 550 paper-based; 79 iBT), IELTS (minimum score 6.5), PTE (minimum score 58). *Application deadline:* For fall admission, 3/1 priority date for domestic students, 5/1 priority date for international students; for spring admission, 10/1 priority date for domestic and international students. Applications are processed on a rolling basis. Application fee: $40 ($90 for international students). Electronic applications accepted. *Expenses:* Tuition, state resident: full-time $6816; part-time $284 per credit hour. Tuition, nonresident: full-time $13,632; part-time $568 per credit hour. *Required fees:* $420 per semester. Tuition and fees vary according to course load. *Financial support:* In 2017–18, research assistantships with full and partial tuition reimbursements (averaging $4,800 per year), teaching assistantships with full and partial tuition reimbursements (averaging $4,800 per year) were awarded; career-related internships or fieldwork, Federal Work-Study, scholarships/grants, health care benefits, and unspecified assistantships also available. Support available to part-time students. Financial award application deadline: 4/15; financial award applicants required to submit FAFSA. *Unit head:* Dr. Jeffrey Woods, Dean, 479-968-0274, Fax: 479-964-0812, E-mail: jwoods@atu.edu. *Application contact:* Dr. Mary B. Gunter, Dean of Graduate College, 479-968-0398, Fax: 479-964-0542, E-mail: gradcollege@atu.edu.
Website: http://www.atu.edu/humanities/

Auburn University, Graduate School, College of Liberal Arts, Department of Psychology, Auburn University, AL 36849. Offers MS, PhD. *Accreditation:* APA (one or more programs are accredited). *Program availability:* Part-time. *Faculty:* 22 full-time (7 women), 3 part-time/adjunct (all women). *Students:* 43 full-time (31 women), 32 part-time (20 women); includes 13 minority (2 Black or African American, non-Hispanic/Latino; 3 Asian, non-Hispanic/Latino; 5 Hispanic/Latino; 3 Two or more races, non-Hispanic/Latino), 5 international. Average age 27. 365 applicants, 6% accepted, 16 enrolled. In 2017, 18 master's, 15 doctorates awarded. *Degree requirements:* For doctorate, thesis/dissertation. *Entrance requirements:* For master's, GRE General Test, GRE Subject Test, minimum GPA of 3.25 in psychology, 3.0 overall; for doctorate, GRE General Test, GRE Subject Test. *Application deadline:* Applications are processed on a rolling basis. Application fee: $50 ($60 for international students). Electronic applications accepted. *Expenses:* Tuition, state resident: full-time $10,974; part-time $519 per credit hour. Tuition, nonresident: full-time $29,658; part-time $1557 per credit hour. *Required fees:* $816 per semester. Tuition and fees vary according to degree level and program. *Financial support:* Research assistantships, teaching assistantships, and Federal Work-Study available. Support available to part-time students. Financial award application deadline: 3/15; financial award applicants required to submit FAFSA. *Faculty research:* Clinical psychology, learning, industrial psychology, organizational psychology. *Unit head:* Dr. Ana Franco-Watkins, Head, 334-844-6492. *Application contact:* Dr. George Flowers, Dean of the Graduate School, 334-844-2125.

Auburn University at Montgomery, College of Arts and Sciences, Department of Psychology, Montgomery, AL 36124-4023. Offers clinical psychology (MS). *Program availability:* Part-time, evening/weekend. *Faculty:* 7 full-time (4 women), 1 (woman) part-time/adjunct. *Students:* 15 full-time (9 women), 6 part-time (5 women); includes 11 minority (10 Black or African American, non-Hispanic/Latino; 1 Asian, non-Hispanic/Latino). Average age 27. 12 applicants, 75% accepted, 8 enrolled. In 2017, 8 master's awarded. *Degree requirements:* For master's, comprehensive exam, thesis optional. *Entrance requirements:* For master's, GRE General Test or MAT. Additional exam requirements/recommendations for international students: Recommended—TOEFL (minimum score 500 paper-based; 61 iBT), IELTS (minimum score 5.5), TSE (minimum score 44). *Application deadline:* For fall admission, 4/15 for domestic students, 7/15 for international students; for spring admission, 11/15 for international students; for summer admission, 4/15 for international students. Applications are processed on a rolling basis. Application fee: $25. Electronic applications accepted. *Expenses:* Tuition, state resident: full-time $6930; part-time $385 per credit hour. Tuition, nonresident: full-time $15,588; part-time $866 per credit hour. *Required fees:* $640. *Financial support:* In 2017–18, 1 teaching assistantship was awarded; career-related internships or fieldwork and scholarships/grants also available. Support available to part-time students. Financial award application deadline: 3/1; financial award applicants required to submit FAFSA. *Faculty research:* Community service, diagnosis, behavior modification. *Unit head:* Dr. Glen Ray, Acting Head, 334-244-3690, Fax: 334-244-3826, E-mail: gray@aum.edu. *Application contact:* Tonya Sexton, Administrative Associate, 334-244-3306, Fax: 334-244-3826, E-mail: tsexton1@aum.edu.
Website: http://www.cas.aum.edu/departments/psychology

Augusta University, College of Science and Mathematics, Department of Psychological Sciences, Augusta, GA 30912. Offers MS. *Degree requirements:* For master's, thesis optional, written/oral exam. *Entrance requirements:* For master's, GRE General Test, minimum GPA of 3.0, bachelor's degree in psychology or equivalent course work, three letters of recommendation. Additional exam requirements/recommendations for international students: Required—TOEFL. Electronic applications accepted. *Faculty research:* Developmental, cognitive, gender and aging issues, consumer behavior, conditioned taste aversions, circadian rhythms, use of slang and offensive language.

Austin Peay State University, College of Graduate Studies, College of Behavioral and Health Sciences, Department of Psychological Science and Counseling, Clarksville, TN 37044. Offers industrial-organizational psychology (MS); mental health counseling (MS), including clinical mental health, school counseling; school counseling (MS). *Program availability:* Part-time, online learning. *Faculty:* 11 full-time (6 women), 1 (woman) part-time/adjunct. *Students:* 60 full-time (46 women), 12 part-time (10 women); includes 16 minority (11 Black or African American, non-Hispanic/Latino; 4 Hispanic/Latino; 1 Two or more races, non-Hispanic/Latino). Average age 29. 59 applicants, 69% accepted, 31 enrolled. In 2017, 30 master's awarded. *Degree requirements:* For master's, comprehensive exam, thesis (for some programs). *Entrance requirements:* For master's, GRE General Test, minimum undergraduate GPA of 2.5, 3 letters of recommendation, bachelor's degree. Additional exam requirements/recommendations for international students: Required—TOEFL (minimum score 500 paper-based). *Application deadline:* For fall admission, 8/8 priority date for domestic students. Applications are processed on a rolling basis. Application fee: $45 ($55 for international students). Electronic applications accepted. *Expenses:* Tuition, state resident: full-time $7686; part-time $427 per credit hour. Tuition, nonresident: full-time $20,268; part-time $1126 per credit hour. *Required fees:* $1529; $76.45 per credit hour. *Financial support:* Research assistantships with full tuition reimbursements, career-related internships or fieldwork, Federal Work-Study, institutionally sponsored loans, scholarships/grants, and unspecified assistantships available. Support available to part-time students. Financial award application deadline: 4/1; financial award applicants required to submit FAFSA. *Unit head:* Dr. Nicole Knickmeyer, Chair, 931-221-7232, Fax: 931-221-6267, E-mail: knickmeyer@apsu.edu. *Application contact:* Brad Averitt, Coordinator of Graduate Admissions, 800-859-4723, Fax: 931-221-7641, E-mail: gradadmissions@apsu.edu.
Website: http://www.apsu.edu/psychology/index.php

Avila University, Department of Psychology, Kansas City, MO 64145-1698. Offers counseling psychology (MS); psychology (MS). *Program availability:* Part-time. *Faculty:* 7 full-time (6 women), 4 part-time/adjunct (1 woman). *Students:* 104 full-time (88 women), 17 part-time (12 women); includes 39 minority (25 Black or African American, non-Hispanic/Latino; 2 American Indian or Alaska Native, non-Hispanic/Latino; 2 Asian, non-Hispanic/Latino; 6 Hispanic/Latino; 4 Two or more races, non-Hispanic/Latino), 3 international. Average age 33. 69 applicants, 65% accepted, 34 enrolled. In 2017, 24 master's awarded. *Degree requirements:* For master's, thesis optional, capstone project. *Entrance requirements:* For master's, bachelor's degree, minimum GPA of 3.0 in all previous undergraduate and graduate coursework, 2 letters of recommendation, letter of intent, resume. Additional exam requirements/recommendations for international students: Required—TOEFL (minimum score 80 iBT). *Application deadline:* Applications are processed on a rolling basis. Application fee: $0. Electronic applications accepted. *Expenses:* Contact institution. *Financial support:* In 2017–18, 17 students received support, including 5 research assistantships with partial tuition reimbursements available; career-related internships or fieldwork, scholarships/grants, and unspecified assistantships also available. Support available to part-time students. Financial award applicants required to submit FAFSA. *Faculty research:* Emotional regulation, embodied cognition, trauma and restorative justice, psychophysiology of public speaking anxiety. *Unit head:* Phil Gebauer, Director of Graduate Psychology Enrollment Management, 816-501-0419, Fax: 816-501-2455, E-mail: philip.gebauer@avila.edu. *Application contact:* Tamika Doolin, Graduate Admissions Advisor, 816-501-3661, Fax: 816-501-2455, E-mail: gradpsych@avila.edu.
Website: https://www.avila.edu/psychology/

Azusa Pacific University, School of Behavioral and Applied Sciences, Department of Psychology, Azusa, CA 91702-7000. Offers child life (MS); research psychology and data analytics (MS).

Ball State University, Graduate School, College of Sciences and Humanities, Department of Psychological Science, Muncie, IN 47306. Offers clinical psychology (MA); cognitive and social processes (MA). *Program availability:* Part-time. *Faculty:* 9 full-time (6 women). *Students:* 28 full-time (22 women), 4 part-time (3 women); includes 8 minority (4 Black or African American, non-Hispanic/Latino; 3 Hispanic/Latino; 1 Two or more races, non-Hispanic/Latino), 4 international. Average age 24. 90 applicants, 18% accepted, 15 enrolled. In 2017, 13 master's awarded. *Entrance requirements:* For master's, GRE General Test, minimum baccalaureate GPA of 2.75 or 3.0 in latter half of baccalaureate, goals statements, curriculum vitae, letters of recommendation. Additional exam requirements/recommendations for international students: Required—TOEFL (minimum score 550 paper-based; 79 iBT), IELTS (minimum score 6.5). *Application deadline:* For fall admission, 2/1 for domestic students. Applications are processed on a rolling basis. Application fee: $60. Electronic applications accepted. *Financial support:* In 2017–18, 19 students received support, including 15 research assistantships with partial tuition reimbursements available (averaging $10,175 per year), 4 teaching assistantships with partial tuition reimbursements available (averaging $9,575 per year); unspecified assistantships also available. Financial award application deadline: 3/1; financial award applicants required to submit FAFSA. *Unit head:* Dr. Guy Mittleman, Chairperson, 765-285-1960, Fax: 765-285-1702, E-mail: gmittleman@bsu.edu.
Website: http://www.bsu.edu/psychology

Barry University, College of Arts and Sciences, Department of Psychology, Miami Shores, FL 33161-6695. Offers clinical psychology (MS); school psychology (MS, SSP). *Program availability:* Part-time, evening/weekend. *Degree requirements:* For master's, thesis, practicum. *Entrance requirements:* For master's, GRE General Test, minimum GPA of 3.0, course work in psychology. Electronic applications accepted. *Faculty research:* Closed head injury, memory and aging, infant/mother interaction, evolutionary aspects of behavior, gender roles.

Baylor University, Graduate School, College of Arts and Sciences, Department of Psychology and Neuroscience, Program in Psychology, Waco, TX 76798. Offers MA, PhD. *Faculty:* 18 full-time (6 women). *Students:* 21 full-time (14 women); includes 4 minority (1 Asian, non-Hispanic/Latino; 1 Hispanic/Latino; 2 Two or more races, non-Hispanic/Latino), 1 international. Average age 27. 60 applicants, 5% accepted, 3 enrolled. In 2017, 2 master's, 2 doctorates awarded. Terminal master's awarded for partial completion of doctoral program. *Degree requirements:* For master's, thesis; for doctorate, comprehensive exam, thesis/dissertation. *Entrance requirements:* For master's and doctorate, GRE General Test. Additional exam requirements/recommendations for international students: Required—TOEFL, IELTS. *Application deadline:* For fall admission, 12/1 for domestic and international students. Application fee: $50. Electronic applications accepted. *Expenses:* $1,237 per hour; $174 per hour student fees. *Financial support:* In 2017–18, 21 students received support, including 1 research assistantship with full tuition reimbursement available (averaging $23,000 per year), 20 teaching assistantships with full tuition reimbursements available (averaging $23,000 per year); health care benefits and travel to professional conference (limited) also available. Financial award application deadline: 12/1; financial award applicants required to submit FAFSA. *Faculty research:* Animal learning/behavior, psychopharmacology, memory and cognition, health psychology, psychology of religion. *Unit head:* Dr. Jim H. Patton, Graduate Program Director, 254-710-2237, Fax: 254-710-3033, E-mail: jim_patton@baylor.edu. *Application contact:* Laura Sumrall, Graduate Studies Coordinator, 254-710-2961, Fax: 254-710-3033, E-mail: laura_sumrall@baylor.edu.
Website: http://www.baylor.edu/psychologyneuroscience/

Binghamton University, State University of New York, Graduate School, Harpur College of Arts and Sciences, Department of Psychology, Binghamton, NY 13902-6000. Offers psychology - behavioral neuroscience (PhD); psychology - clinical psychology (PhD); psychology - cognitive and behavioral science (PhD). *Accreditation:* APA. *Program availability:* Part-time. *Faculty:* 33 full-time (16 women). *Students:* 50 full-time (29 women), 34 part-time (24 women); includes 19 minority (2 Black or African American, non-Hispanic/Latino; 8 Asian, non-Hispanic/Latino; 4 Hispanic/Latino; 5 Two or more races, non-Hispanic/Latino), 3 international. Average age 28. 162 applicants, 21% accepted, 19 enrolled. In 2017, 15 doctorates awarded. Terminal master's awarded for partial completion of doctoral program. *Degree requirements:* For doctorate, comprehensive exam (for some programs), thesis/dissertation. *Entrance requirements:* For doctorate, GRE General Test. Additional exam requirements/recommendations for international students: Required—TOEFL (minimum score 550 paper-based; 80 iBT). Application fee: $75. Electronic applications accepted. *Financial support:* In 2017–18, 69 students received support, including 15 research assistantships with full tuition reimbursements available (averaging $17,500 per year), 40 teaching assistantships with full tuition reimbursements available (averaging $17,500 per year); career-related internships or fieldwork, Federal Work-Study, institutionally sponsored loans, scholarships/grants, health care benefits, tuition waivers (full and partial), and unspecified assistantships also available. Financial award applicants required to submit FAFSA. *Unit head:* Dr. Matthew D. Johnson, Chair, 607-777-2370, E-mail: mjohnson@binghamton.edu. *Application contact:* Ben Balkaya, Assistant Dean and Director, 607-777-2151, Fax: 607-777-2501, E-mail: balkaya@binghamton.edu.

Biola University, Rosemead School of Psychology, La Mirada, CA 90639-0001. Offers clinical psychology (PhD, Psy D). *Accreditation:* APA. *Faculty:* 24. *Students:* 122 full-time (92 women), 46 part-time (39 women); includes 69 minority (7 Black or African American, non-Hispanic/Latino; 1 American Indian or Alaska Native, non-Hispanic/Latino; 31 Asian, non-Hispanic/Latino; 23 Hispanic/Latino; 7 Two or more races, non-Hispanic/Latino), 3 international. 96 applicants, 41% accepted, 21 enrolled. In 2017, 19 doctorates awarded. *Degree requirements:* For doctorate, comprehensive exam, thesis/dissertation. *Entrance requirements:* For doctorate, GRE General Test, interview, 30 undergraduate semester hours of credits in psychology, minimum GPA of 3.0. Additional exam requirements/recommendations for international students: Required—TOEFL (minimum score 600 paper-based; 100 iBT). *Application deadline:* For fall admission, 12/1 priority date for domestic students, 12/1 for international students. Application fee: $65. Electronic applications accepted. *Expenses:* Contact institution. *Financial support:* Scholarships/grants and unspecified assistantships available. Financial award applicants required to submit FAFSA. *Faculty research:* Integration of psychology and theology, psychology of child/adolescent, psychology of marriage, psychology of gender, psychology of trauma, psychology of forensics, multi-cultural studies and mental health. *Unit head:* Dr. Clark Campbell, Dean, 562-903-4867, Fax: 562-903-4864. *Application contact:* Jon Garcia, Graduate Admissions Counselor, 562-903-4752, E-mail: graduate.admissions@biola.edu.
Website: http://www.rosemead.edu/

Boston College, Graduate School of Arts and Sciences, Department of Psychology, Chestnut Hill, MA 02467-3800. Offers PhD. *Degree requirements:* For doctorate, thesis/dissertation, fieldwork. *Entrance requirements:* For doctorate, GRE General Test, GRE Subject Test. Additional exam requirements/recommendations for international students: Required—TOEFL (minimum score 600 paper-based; 100 iBT), IELTS (minimum score 8). Electronic applications accepted. *Faculty research:* Behavioral neuroscience, cognitive neuroscience, developmental psychology, quantitative psychology and social psychology.

Boston Graduate School of Psychoanalysis, BGSP-New Jersey, Brookline, MA 02446-4602. Offers psychoanalysis (MA); psychoanalytic counseling (MA). Programs offered in conjunction with Academic of Clinical and Applied Psychoanalysis in Livingston, NJ.

Boston Graduate School of Psychoanalysis, New York Graduate School of Psychoanalysis, New York, NY 10011. Offers MA. *Program availability:* Part-time. *Degree requirements:* For master's, thesis. *Entrance requirements:* For master's, interview, BA, writing sample, letters of recommendation. Additional exam requirements/recommendations for international students: Required—TOEFL.

Boston University, Graduate School of Arts and Sciences, Department of Psychological and Brain Sciences, Boston, MA 02215. Offers MA, PhD. *Accreditation:* APA (one or more programs are accredited). *Students:* 94 full-time (71 women), 6 part-time (5 women); includes 20 minority (3 Black or African American, non-Hispanic/Latino; 5 Asian, non-Hispanic/Latino; 10 Hispanic/Latino; 2 Two or more races, non-Hispanic/Latino), 17 international. Average age 25. 986 applicants, 12% accepted, 34 enrolled. In 2017, 32 master's, 10 doctorates awarded. Terminal master's awarded for partial completion of doctoral program. *Degree requirements:* For master's, thesis or alternative, research apprenticeship; for doctorate, comprehensive exam, thesis/dissertation. *Entrance requirements:* For master's and doctorate, GRE General Test, GRE Subject Test (recommended), three letters of recommendation, transcripts, personal statement, curriculum vitae. Additional exam requirements/recommendations for international students: Required—TOEFL (minimum score 550 paper-based; 84 iBT). *Application deadline:* For fall admission, 12/1 for domestic and international students. Application fee: $95. Electronic applications accepted. *Financial support:* In 2017–18, 75 students received support, including 3 fellowships with full tuition reimbursements available (averaging $22,000 per year), 28 research assistantships with full tuition reimbursements available (averaging $22,000 per year), 32 teaching assistantships with full tuition reimbursements available (averaging $22,000 per year); career-related internships or fieldwork, Federal Work-Study, scholarships/grants, traineeships, and health care benefits also available. Financial award application deadline: 12/1. *Unit head:* David Somers, Chairman, 617-358-1372, Fax: 617-353-6933, E-mail: somers@bu.edu. *Application contact:* Martin Gastmann, Assistant Director of Admissions and Financial Aid, 617-353-2696, Fax: 617-358-5492, E-mail: grs@bu.edu.
Website: http://www.bu.edu/psych/

Boston University, School of Medicine, Division of Graduate Medical Sciences, Program in Mental Health Counseling and Behavioral Medicine, Boston, MA 02215. Offers MA. *Faculty research:* HIV/AIDS, trauma, behavioral medicine (obesity, breast cancer), neurosciences, autism, serious mental illness, sports psychology. *Unit head:* Dr. Stephen Brady, Director, 617-414-2320, Fax: 617-414-2323, E-mail: sbrady@bu.edu. *Application contact:* GMS Admissions Office, 617-638-5255, E-mail: askgms@bu.edu.
Website: http://www.bumc.bu.edu/mhbm/

Bowling Green State University, Graduate College, College of Arts and Sciences, Department of Psychology, Bowling Green, OH 43403. Offers clinical psychology (MA, PhD); developmental psychology (MA, PhD); experimental psychology (MA, PhD); industrial/organizational psychology (MA, PhD); quantitative psychology (MA, PhD). *Accreditation:* APA (one or more programs are accredited). *Degree requirements:* For doctorate, thesis/dissertation. *Entrance requirements:* For doctorate, GRE General Test, GRE Subject Test. Additional exam requirements/recommendations for international students: Required—TOEFL. Electronic applications accepted. *Faculty research:* Personnel psychology, developmental-mathematical models, behavioral medication, brain process, child/adolescent social cognition.

Brandeis University, Graduate School of Arts and Sciences, Department of Psychology, Waltham, MA 02454-9110. Offers brain, body and behavior (PhD); cognitive neuroscience (PhD); general psychology (MA); social/developmental psychology (PhD). *Program availability:* Part-time. *Faculty:* 14 full-time (7 women), 4 part-time/adjunct (3 women). *Students:* 34 full-time (26 women), 4 part-time (2 women); includes 8 minority (5 Asian, non-Hispanic/Latino; 3 Hispanic/Latino), 10 international. Average age 27. 124 applicants, 31% accepted, 15 enrolled. In 2017, 13 master's, 7 doctorates awarded. Terminal master's awarded for partial completion of doctoral program. *Degree requirements:* For master's, thesis or alternative; for doctorate, thesis/dissertation, research reports. *Entrance requirements:* For master's and doctorate, GRE General Test; GRE Subject Test (recommended), letters of recommendation, statement of purpose, transcripts, resume. Additional exam requirements/recommendations for international students: Required—PTE (minimum score 68), TOEFL (minimum score 600 paper-based, 100 iBT) or IELTS (7). *Application deadline:* For fall admission, 12/1 priority date for domestic students. Applications are processed on a rolling basis. Application fee: $75. Electronic applications accepted. *Expenses: Tuition:* Full-time $48,720. *Required fees:* $88. Tuition and fees vary according to course load, degree level, program and student level. *Financial support:* In 2017–18, 40 students received support, including 20 fellowships with full tuition reimbursements available (averaging $24,480 per year), 26 teaching assistantships with partial tuition reimbursements available (averaging $3,200 per year); Federal Work-Study, scholarships/grants, health care benefits, and tuition waivers (partial) also available. Support available to part-time students. Financial award application deadline: 4/15; financial award applicants required to submit FAFSA. *Faculty research:* Brain, body, and behavior across the lifespan; face perception and nonverbal communication; learning and memory; motor control and spatial orientation; neurophysiology of learning and decision making; personality and cognition in adulthood and old age; social, cultural and affective neuroscience; social relations and health physiology; speech comprehension and memory; taste physiology and psychophysics; visual perception. *Unit head:* Dr. Angela Gutchess, Department Chair, 781-736-3303, E-mail: gutchess@brandeis.edu. *Application contact:* Dr. Sarah Lupis, Department Administrator, 781-736-3303, E-mail: slupis@brandeis.edu.
Website: http://www.brandeis.edu/gsas/programs/psychology.html

Brandman University, School of Arts and Sciences, Irvine, CA 92618. Offers psychology (MA), including counseling, marriage and family therapy, professional clinical counseling; social work (MSW). *Expenses: Tuition:* Part-time $640 per credit hour. Tuition and fees vary according to degree level and program. *Unit head:* Dr. Jeremy Korr, Dean, 949-341-9831. *Application contact:* Dr. Jeremy Korr, Dean, 949-341-9831.
Website: https://www.brandman.edu/academic-programs/arts-and-sciences

Brenau University, Sydney O. Smith Graduate School, College of Health Sciences, Gainesville, GA 30501. Offers family nurse practitioner (MSN); nurse educator (MSN); nursing management (MSN); occupational therapy (MS); psychology (MS). *Accreditation:* AOTA. *Program availability:* Part-time, evening/weekend. *Degree requirements:* For master's, comprehensive exam (for some programs), thesis (for some programs), clinical practicum hours. *Entrance requirements:* For master's, GRE General Test or MAT (for some programs), interview, writing sample, references (for some programs). Additional exam requirements/recommendations for international students: Required—TOEFL (minimum score 500 paper-based; 61 iBT); Recommended—IELTS (minimum score 5). Electronic applications accepted. *Expenses:* Contact institution.

Bridgewater State University, College of Graduate Studies, College of Humanities and Social Sciences, Department of Psychology, Bridgewater, MA 02325. Offers MA. *Program availability:* Part-time, evening/weekend. *Entrance requirements:* For master's, GRE General Test.

Brigham Young University, Graduate Studies, College of Family, Home, and Social Sciences, Department of Psychology, Provo, UT 84602. Offers clinical psychology (PhD); cognitive and behavioral neuroscience (PhD). *Accreditation:* APA. *Faculty:* 31 full-time (8 women), 16 part-time/adjunct (7 women). *Students:* 59 full-time (33 women); includes 7 minority (2 Black or African American, non-Hispanic/Latino; 3 Asian, non-Hispanic/Latino; 1 Hispanic/Latino; 1 Native Hawaiian or other Pacific Islander, non-Hispanic/Latino), 4 international. Average age 29. 49 applicants, 33% accepted, 10 enrolled. In 2017, 11 doctorates awarded. *Degree requirements:* For doctorate, comprehensive exam (for some programs), thesis/dissertation, publishable paper. *Entrance requirements:* For doctorate, GRE General Test, minimum GPA of 3.0. Additional exam requirements/recommendations for international students: Required—TOEFL (minimum score 580 paper-based; 85 iBT). *Application deadline:* For fall admission, 12/1 for domestic and international students. Application fee: $50. Electronic applications accepted. *Expenses:* $10,320 per academic year for members of the Church of Jesus Christ of Latter-day Saints; $20,640 for those who are not members of the Church. *Financial support:* In 2017–18, 41 students received support, including 39 research assistantships with partial tuition reimbursements available (averaging $12,000 per year), 5 teaching assistantships with partial tuition reimbursements available (averaging $12,000 per year); career-related internships or fieldwork, scholarships/grants, tuition waivers (partial), and unspecified assistantships also available. Financial award application deadline: 5/31. *Faculty research:* Psychotherapy process, Alzheimer's disease/dementia, psychology and law, health, psychology, addiction. *Total annual research expenditures:* $711,243. *Unit head:* Dr. Dawson Hedges, Chair, 801-422-6357, Fax: 801-422-0602, E-mail: dawson_hedges@byu.edu. *Application contact:* Leesa D. Scott, Coordinator of Student Programs, 801-422-4560, Fax: 801-422-0602, E-mail: leesa_scott@byu.edu.
Website: http://psychology.byu.edu/

Brock University, Faculty of Graduate Studies, Faculty of Social Sciences, Program in Psychology, St. Catharines, ON L2S 3A1, Canada. Offers behavioral neuroscience (MA, PhD); life span development (MA, PhD); social personality (MA, PhD). *Program availability:* Part-time. *Degree requirements:* For master's, thesis; for doctorate, thesis/dissertation. *Entrance requirements:* For master's, GRE, honors degree; for doctorate, GRE, master's degree. Additional exam requirements/recommendations for international students: Required—TOEFL (minimum score 550 paper-based; 80 iBT), IELTS (minimum score 6.5), TWE (minimum score 4). Electronic applications accepted. *Faculty research:* Social personality, behavioral neuroscience, life-span development.

Brooklyn College of the City University of New York, School of Natural and Behavioral Sciences, Department of Psychology, Brooklyn, NY 11210-2889. Offers experimental psychology (MA); industrial and organizational psychology (MA), including human relations, organizational behavior; mental health counseling (MA); psychology (PhD). *Program availability:* Part-time. *Degree requirements:* For master's, comprehensive exam, thesis (for some programs). *Entrance requirements:* For master's, minimum GPA of 3.0, 2 letters of recommendation, essay; for doctorate, GRE. Additional exam requirements/recommendations for international students: Required—TOEFL (minimum score 520 paper-based; 69 iBT). Electronic applications accepted.

Brown University, Graduate School, Department of Cognitive, Linguistic and Psychological Sciences, Providence, RI 02912. Offers cognitive science (Sc M, PhD); linguistics (AM, PhD); psychology (PhD). *Degree requirements:* For master's, one foreign language, thesis or alternative; for doctorate, 2 foreign languages, thesis/dissertation.

Bucknell University, Graduate Studies, College of Arts and Sciences, Department of Psychology, Lewisburg, PA 17837. Offers MS. *Degree requirements:* For master's, thesis. *Entrance requirements:* For master's, GRE General Test, GRE Subject Test, minimum GPA of 3.0. Additional exam requirements/recommendations for international students: Required—TOEFL (minimum score 600 paper-based).

California Coast University, School of Behavioral Science, Santa Ana, CA 92701. Offers psychology (MS). *Program availability:* Online learning.

California Institute of Integral Studies, School of Consciousness and Transformation, San Francisco, CA 94103. Offers anthropology and social change (MA, PhD); Asian philosophies and cultures (MA); creative inquiry/interdisciplinary arts (MFA); East-West psychology (MA, PhD); integral and transpersonal psychology (PhD); philosophy and religion (PhD), including ecology, spirituality, and religion, philosophy, cosmology, and consciousness, women's spirituality; philosophy, cosmology, and consciousness (Certificate); transformative leadership (MA); transformative studies (PhD); women, gender, spirituality and social justice (MA); writing and consciousness (MFA). *Program availability:* Part-time, evening/weekend, 100% online, blended/hybrid learning. *Students:* 392 full-time (265 women), 141 part-time (98 women); includes 145 minority (40 Black or African American, non-Hispanic/Latino; 1 American Indian or Alaska Native, non-Hispanic/Latino; 19 Asian, non-Hispanic/Latino; 54 Hispanic/Latino; 31 Two or more races, non-Hispanic/Latino), 61 international. Average age 43. 212 applicants, 96% accepted, 153 enrolled. In 2017, 49 master's, 36 doctorates awarded. Terminal master's

awarded for partial completion of doctoral program. *Degree requirements:* For master's, thesis optional; for doctorate, comprehensive exam, thesis/dissertation, 1 foreign language (for Asian philosophies and cultures). *Entrance requirements:* For master's, minimum GPA of 3.0, letters of recommendation, writing sample; for doctorate, master's degree, minimum GPA of 3.0, letters of recommendation, writing sample. Additional exam requirements/recommendations for international students: Required—TOEFL. *Application deadline:* For fall admission, 2/1 priority date for domestic and international students; for spring admission, 10/15 priority date for domestic and international students. Applications are processed on a rolling basis. Application fee: $65. Electronic applications accepted. *Expenses:* $21,400 tuition and fees (for MA); $28,390 (for MFA); $24,658 (for PhD). *Financial support:* Fellowships, research assistantships, teaching assistantships, career-related internships or fieldwork, Federal Work-Study, and scholarships/grants available. Support available to part-time students. Financial award application deadline: 4/15; financial award applicants required to submit FAFSA. *Faculty research:* Ecology and sustainability, philosophy and religion, East-West psychology, integrative health, social and cultural anthropology, transformative leadership. *Unit head:* Kathy Littles, Academic Dean, 415-575-6100, E-mail: klittles@ciis.edu. *Application contact:* Ellen Durst, Director of Admissions, 415-575-6100, Fax: 415-575-1268, E-mail: admissions@ciis.edu.
Website: http://www.ciis.edu/

California Institute of Integral Studies, School of Professional Psychology and Health, San Francisco, CA 94103. Offers clinical psychology (Psy D); community mental health (MA); drama therapy (MA); expressive arts therapy (MA); integral counseling psychology (MA); integrative health studies (MA); psychological studies (MA); somatic psychology (MA). *Program availability:* Part-time, evening/weekend, 100% online, blended/hybrid learning. *Students:* 507 full-time (401 women), 96 part-time (77 women); includes 167 minority (29 Black or African American, non-Hispanic/Latino; 3 American Indian or Alaska Native, non-Hispanic/Latino; 32 Asian, non-Hispanic/Latino; 62 Hispanic/Latino; 2 Native Hawaiian or other Pacific Islander, non-Hispanic/Latino; 39 Two or more races, non-Hispanic/Latino), 60 international. Average age 34. 302 applicants, 89% accepted, 171 enrolled. In 2017, 194 master's, 18 doctorates awarded. *Degree requirements:* For doctorate, comprehensive exam, thesis/dissertation. *Entrance requirements:* For master's, minimum GPA of 3.0, letters of recommendation, writing sample; for doctorate, GRE, MA in psychology or social work with appropriate practical experience for advanced standing, or BA with a minimum GPA of 3.1; letters of recommendation; writing sample. Additional exam requirements/recommendations for international students: Required—TOEFL. *Application deadline:* For fall admission, 2/1 priority date for domestic and international students; for spring admission, 10/15 priority date for domestic and international students. Applications are processed on a rolling basis. Application fee: $65. Electronic applications accepted. *Expenses:* $21,400 (for MA); $32,734 (for PsyD). *Financial support:* Research assistantships with tuition reimbursements, teaching assistantships with tuition reimbursements, career-related internships or fieldwork, Federal Work-Study, and scholarships/grants available. Support available to part-time students. Financial award application deadline: 4/15; financial award applicants required to submit FAFSA. *Faculty research:* Transpersonal psychology, somatic psychology, expressive arts therapy, drama therapy, community mental health, ecopsychology, integrative health, human sexuality. *Unit head:* Nicolle Zapien, Academic Dean, 415-575-5577, E-mail: nzapien@ciis.edu. *Application contact:* Ellen Durst, Director of Admissions, 415-575-6100, Fax: 415-575-1268, E-mail: admissions@ciis.edu.

California Lutheran University, Graduate Studies, Department of Psychology, Thousand Oaks, CA 91360-2787. Offers clinical psychology (MS, Psy D); marital and family therapy (MS). *Accreditation:* APA. *Program availability:* Part-time. *Faculty:* 10 full-time (6 women), 19 part-time/adjunct (15 women). *Students:* 155 full-time (122 women), 35 part-time (10 women); includes 72 minority (4 Black or African American, non-Hispanic/Latino; 3 American Indian or Alaska Native, non-Hispanic/Latino; 4 Asian, non-Hispanic/Latino; 57 Hispanic/Latino; 4 Two or more races, non-Hispanic/Latino), 6 international. Average age 30. 261 applicants, 46% accepted, 66 enrolled. In 2017, 37 master's, 7 doctorates awarded. *Degree requirements:* For master's, thesis or comprehensive exams; for doctorate, thesis/dissertation, internship. *Entrance requirements:* For master's, GRE General Test, interview, minimum GPA of 3.0; for doctorate, GRE General Test. *Application deadline:* For fall admission, 12/1 priority date for domestic and international students. Applications are processed on a rolling basis. Application fee: $50. Electronic applications accepted. *Expenses: Tuition:* Full-time $15,000. Full-time tuition and fees vary according to degree level and program. *Unit head:* Dr. Richard Holigrock, Dean, 805-493-3723. *Application contact:* 805-493-3325, Fax: 805-493-3861, E-mail: clugrad@callutheran.edu.

California Polytechnic State University, San Luis Obispo, College of Liberal Arts, Department of Psychology and Child Development, San Luis Obispo, CA 93407. Offers psychology (MS). *Program availability:* Part-time. *Faculty:* 4 full-time (1 woman), 1 (woman) part-time/adjunct. *Students:* 27 full-time (24 women), 6 part-time (4 women); includes 8 minority (6 Hispanic/Latino; 2 Two or more races, non-Hispanic/Latino). Average age 25. 60 applicants, 47% accepted, 13 enrolled. In 2017, 11 master's awarded. *Degree requirements:* For master's, comprehensive exam (for some programs), thesis (for some programs). *Entrance requirements:* For master's, GRE. Additional exam requirements/recommendations for international students: Required—TOEFL (minimum score 80 iBT). *Application deadline:* For fall admission, 1/1 for domestic and international students. Application fee: $55. Electronic applications accepted. *Expenses:* Tuition, state resident: full-time $7176; part-time $4164 per year. *Required fees:* $3690; $3219 per year. $1073 per trimester. *Financial support:* Fellowships, research assistantships, career-related internships or fieldwork, Federal Work-Study, and institutionally sponsored loans available. Support available to part-time students. Financial award application deadline: 3/2; financial award applicants required to submit FAFSA. *Faculty research:* Eating disorders, mood disorders, neuropsychology, forensic psychology, group therapy. *Unit head:* Dr. Lisa Sweatt, Graduate Coordinator, 805-756-6123, E-mail: lsweatt@calpoly.edu.
Website: http://psycd.calpoly.edu/graduate/?pid-3

California State Polytechnic University, Pomona, Program in Psychology, Pomona, CA 91768-2557. Offers MS. *Program availability:* Part-time, evening/weekend. *Students:* 30 full-time (23 women), 1 (woman) part-time; includes 23 minority (4 Asian, non-Hispanic/Latino; 16 Hispanic/Latino; 3 Two or more races, non-Hispanic/Latino), 1 international. Average age 26. 96 applicants, 16% accepted, 15 enrolled. In 2017, 15 master's awarded. *Entrance requirements:* Additional exam requirements/recommendations for international students: Required—TOEFL (minimum score 550 paper-based). *Application deadline:* Applications are processed on a rolling basis. Application fee: $55. Electronic applications accepted. *Expenses:* Contact institution. *Financial support:* Application deadline: 3/2; applicants required to submit FAFSA. *Unit head:* Dr. Jeffery Mio, Director of Graduate Studies, 909-869-3899, Fax: 909-869-4930, E-mail: jsmio@cpp.edu. *Application contact:* Deborah L. Brandon, Executive Director of Admissions and Enrollment Planning, 909-869-3427, Fax: 909-869-5315, E-mail: dlbrandon@cpp.edu.
Website: http://www.cpp.edu/~class/psychology-sociology/psychology/masters-program.shtml

California State University, Chico, Office of Graduate Studies, College of Behavioral and Social Sciences, Department of Psychology, Program in Psychological Science, Chico, CA 95929-0722. Offers MA. *Degree requirements:* For master's, thesis. *Entrance requirements:* For master's, GRE General Test or MAT, 3 letters of recommendation, statement of purpose. Additional exam requirements/recommendations for international students: Required—TOEFL (minimum score 550 paper-based; 80 iBT), IELTS (minimum score 6.5), PTE (minimum score 59). Electronic applications accepted.

California State University, Dominguez Hills, College of Natural and Behavioral Sciences, Department of Psychology, Carson, CA 90747-0001. Offers clinical psychology (MA); health psychology (MA). *Program availability:* Part-time, evening/weekend. Terminal master's awarded for partial completion of doctoral program. *Degree requirements:* For master's, comprehensive exam, thesis optional. *Entrance requirements:* For master's, GRE General Test or MAT, interview, minimum GPA of 3.0, prerequisite psychology courses. Additional exam requirements/recommendations for international students: Required—TOEFL (minimum score 550 paper-based). Electronic applications accepted. *Faculty research:* Culture and health, neuropsychology and HIV, psychohistory of the Holocaust, community and adolescents, malingering.

California State University, Fresno, Division of Research and Graduate Studies, College of Science and Mathematics, Department of Psychology, Fresno, CA 93740-8027. Offers applied behavior analysis (MA); general/experimental psychology (MA); school psychology (Ed S). *Degree requirements:* For master's, thesis. *Entrance requirements:* For master's, GRE General Test, GRE Subject Test, minimum GPA of 3.0. Additional exam requirements/recommendations for international students: Required—TOEFL. Electronic applications accepted. *Faculty research:* Oncology prediction, parenting stress, wellness, aging and memory, retrieval inhibition, anger, minority mental health.

California State University, Fullerton, Graduate Studies, College of Humanities and Social Sciences, Department of Psychology, Fullerton, CA 92831-3599. Offers clinical psychology (MS); psychology (MA). *Program availability:* Part-time. *Faculty:* 20 full-time (14 women), 2 part-time/adjunct (both women). *Students:* 65 full-time (48 women), 11 part-time (8 women); includes 35 minority (3 Black or African American, non-Hispanic/Latino; 7 Asian, non-Hispanic/Latino; 22 Hispanic/Latino; 3 Two or more races, non-Hispanic/Latino), 3 international. Average age 26. 155 applicants, 19% accepted, 27 enrolled. *Entrance requirements:* For master's, GRE General Test, GRE Subject Test, undergraduate major in psychology or related field. Application fee: $55. *Financial support:* Career-related internships or fieldwork, Federal Work-Study, institutionally sponsored loans, and scholarships/grants available. Support available to part-time students. Financial award application deadline: 3/1; financial award applicants required to submit FAFSA. *Unit head:* Eriko Self, Chair, 657-278-3514, Fax: 657-278-7134. *Application contact:* Admissions/Applications, 657-278-2371.

California State University, Long Beach, Graduate Studies, College of Liberal Arts, Department of Psychology, Long Beach, CA 90840. Offers human factors (MS); industrial/organizational psychology (MS); psychology (MA). *Program availability:* Part-time, evening/weekend. *Degree requirements:* For master's, comprehensive exam, thesis. *Entrance requirements:* For master's, GRE General Test, GRE Subject Test. Electronic applications accepted. *Faculty research:* Physiological psychology, social and personality psychology, community-clinical psychology, industrial-organizational psychology, developmental psychology.

California State University, Los Angeles, Graduate Studies, College of Natural and Social Sciences, Department of Psychology, Los Angeles, CA 90032-8530. Offers MA, MS. *Program availability:* Part-time, evening/weekend. *Degree requirements:* For master's, comprehensive exam or thesis. *Entrance requirements:* Additional exam requirements/recommendations for international students: Required—TOEFL (minimum score 500 paper-based). Electronic applications accepted. *Faculty research:* Binaural resolution of the size of an acoustic array, response and generalization of matching to sample in children.

California State University, Northridge, Graduate Studies, College of Social and Behavioral Sciences, Department of Psychology, Northridge, CA 91330. Offers clinical psychology (MA); general experimental psychology (MA). *Students:* 46 full-time (36 women), 7 part-time (4 women); includes 25 minority (2 Black or African American, non-Hispanic/Latino; 4 Asian, non-Hispanic/Latino; 18 Hispanic/Latino; 1 Two or more races, non-Hispanic/Latino), 1 international. Average age 25. 263 applicants, 27% accepted, 23 enrolled. In 2017, 55 master's awarded. *Degree requirements:* For master's, thesis. *Entrance requirements:* For master's, GRE General Test, GRE Subject Test, minimum GPA of 3.0, letters of recommendation. Additional exam requirements/recommendations for international students: Required—TOEFL. *Application deadline:* For fall admission, 11/30 for domestic students. Application fee: $55. *Financial support:* Application deadline: 3/1. *Unit head:* Jill Razani, Chair, 818-677-3506.
Website: http://www.csun.edu/csbs/departments/psychology/index.html

California State University, Sacramento, College of Social Sciences and Interdisciplinary Studies, Department of Psychology, Sacramento, CA 95819. Offers applied behavior analysis (MA); industrial/organizational psychology (MA). *Program availability:* Part-time. *Students:* 19 full-time (11 women), 29 part-time (21 women); includes 17 minority (4 Asian, non-Hispanic/Latino; 11 Hispanic/Latino; 2 Native Hawaiian or other Pacific Islander, non-Hispanic/Latino), 1 international. Average age 27. 77 applicants, 32% accepted, 17 enrolled. In 2017, 9 master's awarded. *Degree requirements:* For master's, thesis, project; writing proficiency exam. *Entrance requirements:* For master's, GRE, minimum GPA of 3.0 during previous 2 years. Additional exam requirements/recommendations for international students: Required—TOEFL (minimum score 550 paper-based; 80 iBT); Recommended—IELTS, TSE. *Application deadline:* For fall admission, 3/1 for domestic and international students. Applications are processed on a rolling basis. Application fee: $55. Electronic applications accepted. *Expenses:* Contact institution. *Financial support:* Teaching assistantships, career-related internships or fieldwork, Federal Work-Study, and scholarships/grants available. Support available to part-time students. Financial award application deadline: 3/1; financial award applicants required to submit FAFSA. *Unit head:* Dr. Rebecca Cameron, Interim Department Chair, 916-278-6254, E-mail: cameron@csus.edu. *Application contact:* Jose Martinez, Graduate Admissions Supervisor, 916-278-7871, E-mail: martinj@skymail.csus.edu.
Website: http://www.csus.edu/psyc

California State University, San Bernardino, Graduate Studies, College of Social and Behavioral Sciences, Department of Psychology, San Bernardino, CA 92407. Offers child development (MA); clinical/counseling psychology (MS); industrial/organizational psychology (MS); psychological science (MA). *Faculty:* 13 full-time (4 women), 2 part-time/adjunct (both women). *Students:* 61 full-time (41 women), 17 part-time (14 women); includes 47 minority (2 Black or African American, non-Hispanic/Latino; 3 Asian, non-Hispanic/Latino; 33 Hispanic/Latino; 9 Two or more races, non-Hispanic/Latino), 3 international. Average age 28. 190 applicants, 19% accepted, 33 enrolled. In 2017, 28 master's awarded. *Degree requirements:* For master's, comprehensive exam, thesis (for some programs). *Entrance requirements:* Additional exam requirements/recommendations for international students: Required—TOEFL. Application fee: $55. *Financial support:* Fellowships, research assistantships, and teaching assistantships

available. *Faculty research:* Perceptual development, human memory, psychopharmacology, psychology of women, language acquisition. *Unit head:* Dr. Robert Ricco, Chair, 909-537-5485, Fax: 909-537-7003, E-mail: rricco@csusb.edu. *Application contact:* Dr. Dorota Huizinga, Dean of Graduate Studies, 909-537-3064, E-mail: dorota.huizinga@csusb.edu.
Website: https://csbs.csusb.edu/psychology

California State University, San Marcos, College of Humanities, Arts, Behavioral and Social Sciences, Program in Psychological Science, San Marcos, CA 92096-0001. Offers psychological science (MA). *Entrance requirements:* For master's, GRE General Test, GRE Subject Test in psychology (recommended), 3 letters of recommendation. Additional exam requirements/recommendations for international students: Required—TOEFL (minimum score 550 paper-based). *Application deadline:* For fall admission, 2/1 for domestic students. Application fee: $55. Electronic applications accepted. *Expenses:* Tuition, state resident: full-time $7176. Tuition, nonresident: full-time $9504. *Faculty research:* Psychopharmacology, recovery from major surgery, computer literacy in children, neuropsychology of hemispheric differences, conservation psychology. *Unit head:* Dr. Nancy Caine, Graduate Program Coordinator, 760-750-4145, E-mail: ncaine@csusm.edu.
Website: http://www.csusm.edu/psychology/maprogram/

California State University, Stanislaus, College of Science, Programs in Psychology, Turlock, CA 95382. Offers behavior analysis (MA, MS); counseling psychology (MS); general psychology (MA). *Program availability:* Part-time. *Degree requirements:* For master's, thesis. *Entrance requirements:* For master's, GRE, minimum GPA of 3.0, 3 letters of reference, 16 psychology prerequisites, personal statement. Additional exam requirements/recommendations for international students: Required—TOEFL (minimum score 550 paper-based). Electronic applications accepted. *Faculty research:* Hedonic tone judgment, syntax and autism, early literacy assessment and native and non-native languages.

Cambridge College, School of Psychology and Counseling, Boston, MA 02129. Offers addiction counseling (M Ed); alcohol and drug counseling (Certificate); counseling psychology (M Ed, CAGS); counseling psychology: forensic counseling (M Ed); marriage and family therapy (M Ed); mental health and addiction counseling (M Ed); mental health counseling (M Ed); mental health counseling for school guidance counselors (Post Master's Certificate); psychological studies (M Ed); school adjustment and mental health counseling (M Ed); school adjustment, mental health and addiction counseling (M Ed); school guidance counselor (M Ed); trauma studies (Certificate). *Program availability:* Part-time, evening/weekend. *Degree requirements:* For master's and other advanced degree, thesis, practicum/internship. *Entrance requirements:* For master's, resume, 2 professional references; for other advanced degree, official transcripts, documents for transfer credit evaluation, resume, written personal statement/essay, 2 professional references, health insurance, immunizations form. Additional exam requirements/recommendations for international students: Required—TOEFL (minimum score 550 paper-based; 79 iBT), Michigan English Language Assessment Battery (minimum score 85); Recommended—IELTS (minimum score 6). Electronic applications accepted. *Expenses:* Contact institution. *Faculty research:* Trauma, drug and alcohol counseling, cross-cultural issues, school counseling, trauma in schools.

Cameron University, Office of Graduate Studies, Program in Behavioral Sciences, Lawton, OK 73505-6377. Offers MS. *Program availability:* Part-time, evening/weekend. *Degree requirements:* For master's, comprehensive exam, thesis optional. *Entrance requirements:* Additional exam requirements/recommendations for international students: Required—TOEFL (minimum score 550 paper-based). Electronic applications accepted. *Faculty research:* Student burnout, attention deficit hyperactivity disorder, group decision making, counseling outcomes, smoking cessation.

Capella University, Harold Abel School of Social and Behavioral Science, Doctoral Programs in Psychology, Minneapolis, MN 55402. Offers addiction psychology (PhD); clinical psychology (Psy D); educational psychology (PhD); general advanced studies in human behavior (PhD); general psychology (PhD); industrial/organizational psychology (PhD); school psychology (Psy D).

Capella University, Harold Abel School of Social and Behavioral Science, Master's Programs in Psychology, Minneapolis, MN 55402. Offers applied behavior analysis (MS); clinical psychology (MS); counseling psychology (MS); educational psychology (MS); evaluation, research, and measurement (MS); general advanced studies in human behavior (MS); general psychology (MS); industrial/organizational psychology (MS); leadership coaching psychology (MS); school psychology (MS); sport psychology (MS).

Cardinal Stritch University, College of Arts and Sciences, Department of Psychology, Milwaukee, WI 53217-3985. Offers clinical psychology (MA). *Program availability:* Part-time, evening/weekend. *Students:* 23 full-time (17 women), 13 part-time (12 women); includes 9 minority (3 Black or African American, non-Hispanic/Latino; 2 American Indian or Alaska Native, non-Hispanic/Latino; 1 Asian, non-Hispanic/Latino; 2 Hispanic/Latino; 1 Two or more races, non-Hispanic/Latino), 10 international. Average age 26. 70 applicants, 100% accepted, 14 enrolled. In 2017, 12 master's awarded. *Degree requirements:* For master's, thesis, portfolio, clinical practicum. *Entrance requirements:* For master's, interview, minimum GPA of 3.0, 3 letters of recommendation. Additional exam requirements/recommendations for international students: Required—TOEFL (minimum score 79 iBT), IELTS (minimum score 6.5). *Application deadline:* For fall admission, 7/15 priority date for domestic students; for spring admission, 12/15 priority date for domestic students. Applications are processed on a rolling basis. Electronic applications accepted. *Expenses:* $782 per credit. *Financial support:* Research assistantships with partial tuition reimbursements, career-related internships or fieldwork, Federal Work-Study, and scholarships/grants available. Financial award applicants required to submit FAFSA. *Unit head:* Dr. Trevor Hyde, Chair, 414-410-4489, E-mail: tfhyde@stritch.edu. *Application contact:* Graduate Admissions, 800-347-8822 Ext. 4042, E-mail: admissions@stritch.edu.

Carleton University, Faculty of Graduate Studies, Faculty of Arts and Social Sciences, Department of Psychology, Ottawa, ON K1S 5B6, Canada. Offers neuroscience (M Sc); psychology (MA, PhD). *Program availability:* Part-time. *Degree requirements:* For master's, thesis; for doctorate, comprehensive exam, thesis/dissertation. *Entrance requirements:* For master's, honors degree; for doctorate, GRE, master's degree. Additional exam requirements/recommendations for international students: Required—TOEFL. *Faculty research:* Behavioral neuroscience, social and personality psychology, cognitive/perception, developmental psychology, computer user research and evaluation, forensic psychology, health psychology.

Carlos Albizu University, Graduate Programs, San Juan, PR 00901. Offers clinical psychology (MS, PhD, Psy D); general psychology (PhD); industrial/organizational psychology (MS, PhD); speech and language pathology (MS). *Accreditation:* APA (one or more programs are accredited). *Program availability:* Part-time, evening/weekend. Terminal master's awarded for partial completion of doctoral program. *Degree requirements:* For master's, one foreign language, comprehensive exam, thesis; for doctorate, one foreign language, comprehensive exam, thesis/dissertation, written qualifying exams. *Entrance requirements:* For master's, GRE General Test or EXADEP, interview; minimum GPA of 2.8 (industrial/organizational psychology); for doctorate, GRE General Test or EXADEP, interview; minimum GPA of 3.0 (PhD in industrial/organizational psychology and clinical psychology), 3.25 (Psy D). *Faculty research:* Psychotherapeutic techniques for Hispanics, psychology of the aged, school dropouts, stress, violence.

Carlos Albizu University, Miami Campus, Graduate Programs, Miami, FL 33172-2209. Offers clinical psychology (PhD, Psy D); entrepreneurship (MBA); exceptional student education (MS); human services (PhD); industrial/organizational psychology (MS); marriage and family therapy (MS); mental health counseling (MS); nonprofit management (MBA); organizational management (MBA); psychology (MS); speech and language pathology (MS); teaching English for speakers of other languages (MS). *Accreditation:* APA. *Program availability:* Part-time, evening/weekend, 100% online, blended/hybrid learning. *Faculty:* 32 full-time (24 women), 27 part-time/adjunct (15 women). *Students:* 411 full-time (345 women), 248 part-time (215 women); includes 562 minority (53 Black or African American, non-Hispanic/Latino; 4 Asian, non-Hispanic/Latino; 498 Hispanic/Latino; 7 Two or more races, non-Hispanic/Latino), 23 international. Average age 34. 391 applicants, 42% accepted, 154 enrolled. In 2017, 96 master's, 54 doctorates awarded. Terminal master's awarded for partial completion of doctoral program. *Degree requirements:* For master's, comprehensive exam (for some programs), integrative project (for MBA); research project (for exceptional student education, teaching English as a second language); for doctorate, comprehensive examinations, internship, project/dissertation. *Entrance requirements:* For master's, GRE/EXADEP, bachelor's degree from accredited institution, minimum GPA of 3.0, 3 letters of recommendation, interview, resume, statement of purpose, official transcripts; for doctorate, GRE (for Psy D), 3 letters of recommendation, resume, interview, statement of purpose, official transcripts; bachelor's degree and minimum GPA of 3.25 (for Psy D); master's degree and minimum GPA of 3.0 (for PhD). Additional exam requirements/recommendations for international students: Required—Michigan Test of English Language Proficiency. *Application deadline:* For fall admission, 4/1 priority date for domestic students, 5/1 priority date for international students; for spring admission, 11/1 priority date for domestic students, 9/1 priority date for international students. Applications are processed on a rolling basis. Application fee: $50. Electronic applications accepted. Application fee is waived when completed online. *Expenses:* Contact institution. *Financial support:* In 2017–18, 145 students received support. Federal Work-Study, scholarships/grants, unspecified assistantships, and tuition discounts available. Financial award application deadline: 6/1; financial award applicants required to submit FAFSA. *Faculty research:* Psychotherapy, forensic psychology, neuropsychology, special education, speech-language pathology, criminal justice. *Unit head:* Dr. Etiony Aldarondo, Provost, 305-593-1223 Ext. 3138, Fax: 305-592-7930, E-mail: ealdarondo@albizu.edu. *Application contact:* Sonia Feliciano, Institutional Director of Student Recruitment, 305-593-1223 Ext. 3108, Fax: 305-477-8983, E-mail: sfeliciano@albizu.edu.

Carlow University, College of Leadership and Social Change, Program in Psychology, Pittsburgh, PA 15213-3165. Offers MA. *Program availability:* Part-time, evening/weekend. *Entrance requirements:* For master's, personal essay; resume or curriculum vitae; two recommendations; official transcripts; interview; minimum undergraduate GPA of 3.0. Additional exam requirements/recommendations for international students: Required—TOEFL (minimum score 550 paper-based). *Application deadline:* Applications are processed on a rolling basis. *Expenses: Tuition:* Full-time $12,103; part-time $825 per credit hour. Tuition and fees vary according to program. *Financial support:* Application deadline: 4/1; applicants required to submit FAFSA. *Unit head:* Dr. Allyson M. Lowe, Dean, 412-578-6663, Fax: 412-578-6357, E-mail: amlowe@carlow.edu. *Application contact:* 412-578-6059, Fax: 412-578-6321, E-mail: gradstudies@carlow.edu.
Website: http://www.carlow.edu/MA_in_psychology.aspx

Carnegie Mellon University, Dietrich College of Humanities and Social Sciences, Department of Psychology, Pittsburgh, PA 15213-3891. Offers cognitive neuroscience (PhD); cognitive psychology (PhD); developmental psychology (PhD); social/personality/health psychology (PhD). *Degree requirements:* For doctorate, comprehensive exam, thesis/dissertation. *Entrance requirements:* For doctorate, GRE General Test. Additional exam requirements/recommendations for international students: Required—TOEFL. *Faculty research:* Artificial intelligence, stress and the immune system, children's learning strategies, neural basis of cognition.

Case Western Reserve University, School of Graduate Studies, Psychological Sciences Department, Cleveland, OH 44106. Offers clinical psychology (PhD); communication sciences (MA, PhD), including speech-language pathology; experimental psychology (PhD). *Accreditation:* APA (one or more programs are accredited). *Program availability:* Part-time. *Faculty:* 17 full-time (13 women), 10 part-time/adjunct (8 women). *Students:* 50 full-time (39 women), 7 part-time (all women); includes 4 minority (1 Black or African American, non-Hispanic/Latino; 1 Asian, non-Hispanic/Latino; 2 Hispanic/Latino), 1 international. Average age 27. 368 applicants, 5% accepted, 15 enrolled. In 2017, 17 master's, 6 doctorates awarded. Terminal master's awarded for partial completion of doctoral program. *Degree requirements:* For master's, comprehensive exam, thesis optional; for doctorate, thesis/dissertation, internship. *Entrance requirements:* For doctorate, GRE General Test, GRE Subject Test, personal statement; curriculum vitae. Additional exam requirements/recommendations for international students: Required—TOEFL (minimum score 577 paper-based; 90 iBT); Recommended—IELTS (minimum score 7). *Application deadline:* For fall admission, 12/1 priority date for domestic students. Application fee: $50. Electronic applications accepted. *Expenses: Tuition:* Full-time $43,854; part-time $1827 per credit hour. *Required fees:* $50; $50 per credit hour. Tuition and fees vary according to course load and program. *Financial support:* Fellowships, research assistantships, teaching assistantships, and tuition waivers (full and partial) available. Financial award application deadline: 12/1. *Faculty research:* Adolescent suicide, cognitive processing, repressive responses, visual perception, impact of HIV infection, neuropsychology; traumatic brain injury, phonological disorders, child language disorders, communication problems in the aged and Alzheimer's patients, cleft palate, voice disorders. *Unit head:* Dr. Heath Demaree, Professor and Chair, 216-368-6468, E-mail: psychsciences@case.edu. *Application contact:* Dr. Norah Feeny, Director of Clinical Training, 216-368-2695, E-mail: psychsciences@case.edu.
Website: http://psychsciences.case.edu/

Castleton University, Division of Graduate Studies, Department of Psychology, Castleton, VT 05735. Offers forensic psychology (MA). *Degree requirements:* For master's, thesis. *Entrance requirements:* For master's, GRE General Test, minimum undergraduate GPA of 3.5, previous course work in research methodology and statistics. Additional exam requirements/recommendations for international students: Required—TOEFL. *Faculty research:* Psychology and law, juvenile delinquency, criminal psychology, correctional psychology, police psychology.

The Catholic University of America, School of Arts and Sciences, Department of Psychology, Washington, DC 20064. Offers applied experimental psychology (PhD); clinical psychology (PhD); general psychology (MA); human development psychology (PhD); human factors (MA); MA/JD. MA/JD offered jointly with Columbus School of Law. *Accreditation:* APA (one or more programs are accredited). *Program availability:* Part-

time. *Faculty:* 11 full-time (6 women), 9 part-time/adjunct (3 women). *Students:* 38 full-time (27 women), 33 part-time (25 women); includes 22 minority (4 Black or African American, non-Hispanic/Latino; 4 Asian, non-Hispanic/Latino; 5 Hispanic/Latino; 9 Two or more races, non-Hispanic/Latino), 6 international. Average age 29. 183 applicants, 26% accepted, 21 enrolled. In 2017, 18 master's, 9 doctorates awarded. *Degree requirements:* For master's, comprehensive exam, thesis (for some programs); for doctorate, comprehensive exam, thesis/dissertation. *Entrance requirements:* For master's, GRE General Test, statement of purpose, official copies of academic transcripts, three letters of recommendation; for doctorate, GRE General Test, GRE Subject Test, statement of purpose, official copies of academic transcripts, three letters of recommendation. Additional exam requirements/recommendations for international students: Required—TOEFL (minimum score 550 paper-based; 80 iBT). *Application deadline:* For fall admission, 7/15 priority date for domestic students, 7/1 for international students; for spring admission, 11/15 priority date for domestic students, 11/1 for international students. Applications are processed on a rolling basis. Application fee: $55. Electronic applications accepted. *Expenses:* Contact institution. *Financial support:* Fellowships, research assistantships, teaching assistantships, Federal Work-Study, scholarships/grants, tuition waivers (full and partial), and unspecified assistantships available. Financial award application deadline: 2/1; financial award applicants required to submit FAFSA. *Faculty research:* Clinical psychology, applied cognitive science, psychopathology, cognitive neuroscience, psychotherapy. *Total annual research expenditures:* $243,144. *Unit head:* Dr. Marc M. Sebrechts, Chair, 202-319-5750, Fax: 202-319-6263, E-mail: sebrechts@cua.edu. *Application contact:* Dr. Steven Brown, Director of Graduate Admissions, 202-319-5057, Fax: 202-319-6533, E-mail: cua-admissions@cua.edu.
Website: http://psychology.cua.edu/

Central Connecticut State University, School of Graduate Studies, College of Liberal Arts and Social Sciences, Department of Psychological Science, New Britain, CT 06050-4010. Offers MA. *Program availability:* Part-time, evening/weekend. *Faculty:* 12 full-time (9 women). *Students:* 17 full-time (14 women), 10 part-time (9 women); includes 11 minority (4 Black or African American, non-Hispanic/Latino; 4 Asian, non-Hispanic/Latino; 2 Hispanic/Latino; 1 Two or more races, non-Hispanic/Latino). Average age 30. 43 applicants, 51% accepted, 13 enrolled. In 2017, 7 master's awarded. *Degree requirements:* For master's, thesis or alternative. *Entrance requirements:* For master's, minimum undergraduate GPA of 2.7, letters of recommendation, personal statement. Additional exam requirements/recommendations for international students: Required—TOEFL (minimum score 550 paper-based; 79 iBT); Recommended—IELTS (minimum score 6.5). *Application deadline:* For fall admission, 4/1 for domestic and international students; for spring admission, 11/1 for domestic and international students. Applications are processed on a rolling basis. Application fee: $50. Electronic applications accepted. *Expenses:* Tuition, area resident: Full-time $6757. Tuition, state resident: full-time $9750; part-time $374 per credit. Tuition, nonresident: full-time $18,102; part-time $374 per credit. *Required fees:* $4635; $255 per credit. *Financial support:* In 2017–18, 10 students received support. Career-related internships or fieldwork, Federal Work-Study, scholarships/grants, and unspecified assistantships available. Support available to part-time students. Financial award application deadline: 3/1; financial award applicants required to submit FAFSA. *Faculty research:* Clinical psychology, general psychology, child development, cognitive development, drugs/behavior. *Unit head:* Dr. Carolyn Fallahi, Chair, 860-832-3100, E-mail: fallahic@ccsu.edu. *Application contact:* Patricia Gardner, Associate Director of Graduate Studies, 860-832-2350, Fax: 860-832-2362.
Website: http://www.ccsu.edu/psychology/index.html

Central Michigan University, College of Graduate Studies, College of Humanities and Social and Behavioral Sciences, Department of Psychology, Mount Pleasant, MI 48859. Offers clinical psychology (PhD); experimental psychology (MS, PhD), including applied experimental psychology (PhD), experimental psychology (MS); industrial and organizational psychology (MA, PhD), including industrial and organizational psychology, occupational health psychology (PhD); neuroscience (MS, PhD); school psychology (PhD, S Psy S), including psychological services (S Psy S), school psychology (PhD). *Accreditation:* APA (one or more programs are accredited). Terminal master's awarded for partial completion of doctoral program. *Degree requirements:* For master's, thesis or alternative; for doctorate, thesis/dissertation; for S Psy S, thesis. *Entrance requirements:* For doctorate, GRE. Electronic applications accepted. *Faculty research:* Experimental psychology, clinical psychology, industrial/organizational psychology, school psychology, neuroscience.

Central Washington University, School of Graduate Studies and Research, College of the Sciences, Department of Psychology, Ellensburg, WA 98926. Offers experimental psychology (MS); mental health counseling (MS); school psychology (Ed S). *Program availability:* Evening/weekend. *Entrance requirements:* For master's, GRE General Test, minimum GPA of 3.0. Additional exam requirements/recommendations for international students: Required—TOEFL (minimum score 550 paper-based; 79 iBT). *Application deadline:* For fall admission, 2/1 for domestic students. Applications are processed on a rolling basis. Application fee: $50. Electronic applications accepted. *Financial support:* Application deadline: 3/1; applicants required to submit FAFSA. *Unit head:* Dr. Stephanie Stein, Chairperson, 509-963-2381, E-mail: steins@cwu.edu. *Application contact:* Justine Eason, Admissions Program Coordinator, 509-963-3103, Fax: 509-963-1799, E-mail: masters@cwu.edu.

Chestnut Hill College, School of Graduate Studies, Division of Psychology, Philadelphia, PA 19118-2693. Offers clinical and counseling psychology (MS, CAS), including clinical and counseling psychology; clinical psychology (Psy D), including clinical psychology. *Program availability:* Part-time, evening/weekend. *Degree requirements:* For master's, thesis optional, practica; for doctorate, comprehensive exam, thesis/dissertation, internship, practica, clinical competency exam. *Entrance requirements:* For master's, GRE General Test, writing sample, letters of recommendation; for doctorate, GRE General Test, master's degree in counseling/clinical psychology or closely-related field, official transcripts, letters of recommendation, statement of professional goals, writing sample; for CAS, GRE General Test, official transcripts, letters of recommendation, statement of professional goals, writing sample. Additional exam requirements/recommendations for international students: Required—TOEFL (minimum score 500 paper-based), IELTS (minimum score 6.0), or TWE (minimum score 22). *Expenses:* Contact institution. *Faculty research:* Lifespan development, trauma and sexual abuse, cultural diversity, family psychology and family therapy, psychodynamic therapy.

The Chicago School of Professional Psychology, Program in Business Psychology, Chicago, IL 60610. Offers business psychology (PhD); industrial and organizational business psychology (Psy D); industrial and organizational psychology (MA); organizational leadership (MA, PhD). *Degree requirements:* For doctorate, thesis/dissertation optional. *Entrance requirements:* For doctorate, GRE. Additional exam requirements/recommendations for international students: Required—TOEFL.

The Chicago School of Professional Psychology at Irvine, Program in Psychology, Irvine, CA 92612. Offers generalist (Psy D); psychodynamic psychotherapy (Psy D).

The Chicago School of Professional Psychology: Online, Program in International Psychology, Chicago, IL 60654. Offers PhD.

The Chicago School of Professional Psychology: Online, Program in Psychology, Chicago, IL 60654. Offers child and adolescent psychology (MA); generalist (MA); gerontology (MA); international psychology (MA); organizational leadership (MA); sport and exercise psychology (MA).

The Citadel, The Military College of South Carolina, Citadel Graduate College, School of Humanities and Social Sciences, Department of Psychology, Charleston, SC 29409. Offers psychology (MA), including clinical counseling; school psychology (Ed S). *Program availability:* Part-time, evening/weekend. *Degree requirements:* For master's, comprehensive exam, practicum; internship (written and oral presentation of a case study as part of internship); for Ed S, comprehensive exam, thesis (for some programs), practicum, internship. *Entrance requirements:* For master's, GRE (minimum combined score of 297, 150 on verbal reasoning and 141 on quantitative reasoning) or MAT (minimum score of 410), minimum undergraduate GPA of 3.0; 12 credit hours in psychology or minimum score on GRE Subject Test in psychology of 600; 2 letters of recommendation; for Ed S, GRE (minimum combined score of 297, 150 on verbal reasoning and 147 on quantitative reasoning) or MAT (minimum score of 410), minimum undergraduate or graduate GPA of 3.0; 2 letters of recommendation. Additional exam requirements/recommendations for international students: Required—TOEFL (minimum score 550 paper-based; 79 iBT). Electronic applications accepted. *Expenses:* Tuition, state resident: part-time $587 per credit hour. Tuition, nonresident: part-time $988 per credit hour. *Required fees:* $90 per term.

City College of the City University of New York, Graduate School, Colin Powell School for Civic and Global Leadership, Department of Psychology, New York, NY 10031-9198. Offers clinical psychology (PhD); general psychology (MA); mental health counseling (MA). PhD program offered jointly with Graduate School and University Center of the City University of New York. *Accreditation:* APA (one or more programs are accredited). *Program availability:* Part-time. *Degree requirements:* For master's, one foreign language, comprehensive exam, thesis. *Entrance requirements:* For master's, GRE. Additional exam requirements/recommendations for international students: Required—TOEFL (minimum score 550 paper-based; 79 iBT). Electronic applications accepted. *Faculty research:* Social/personality psychology, physiological psychology, cognition and development.

Claremont Graduate University, Graduate Programs, School of Social Science, Policy and Evaluation, Department of Psychology, Claremont, CA 91711-6160. Offers advanced study in evaluation (Certificate); cognitive psychology (MA, PhD); developmental psychology (MA, PhD); evaluation and applied research methods (MA, PhD); health behavior research and evaluation (MA, PhD); human resource development and evaluation (MA); industrial/organizational psychology (MA, PhD); organizational behavior (MA, PhD); organizational psychology (MA, PhD); social psychology (MA, PhD); MBA/PhD. *Program availability:* Part-time. Terminal master's awarded for partial completion of doctoral program. *Entrance requirements:* For master's and doctorate, GRE General Test. Additional exam requirements/recommendations for international students: Required—TOEFL (minimum score 75 iBT). Electronic applications accepted. *Faculty research:* Social intervention, diversity in organizations, eyewitness memory, aging and cognition, drug policy.

Clayton State University, School of Graduate Studies, College of Arts and Sciences, Program in Psychology, Morrow, GA 30260-0285. Offers applied developmental psychology (MS); clinical/counseling psychology (MS). *Entrance requirements:* For master's, GRE, 2 official transcripts; 3 letters of recommendation; statement of purpose; on-campus interview; background check. Additional exam requirements/recommendations for international students: Required—TOEFL (minimum score 550 paper-based). Electronic applications accepted.

Cleveland State University, College of Graduate Studies, College of Sciences and Health Professions, Department of Psychology, Cleveland, OH 44115. Offers MA, PhD, Psy S. *Accreditation:* APA. *Faculty:* 9 full-time (3 women), 14 part-time/adjunct (5 women). *Students:* 77 full-time (62 women), 28 part-time (15 women); includes 24 minority (14 Black or African American, non-Hispanic/Latino; 2 Asian, non-Hispanic/Latino; 5 Hispanic/Latino; 3 Two or more races, non-Hispanic/Latino), 8 international. Average age 27. 167 applicants, 44% accepted, 36 enrolled. In 2017, 28 master's, 10 other advanced degrees awarded. Terminal master's awarded for partial completion of doctoral program. *Entrance requirements:* For master's and doctorate, GRE General Test. Additional exam requirements/recommendations for international students: Required—TOEFL (minimum score 550 paper-based; 78 iBT). Application fee: $40. Electronic applications accepted. *Financial support:* In 2017–18, 40 students received support, including 21 research assistantships with full tuition reimbursements available (averaging $7,200 per year), 28 teaching assistantships with full tuition reimbursements available (averaging $7,200 per year); career-related internships or fieldwork, Federal Work-Study, scholarships/grants, tuition waivers (partial), and unspecified assistantships also available. Financial award application deadline: 3/1; financial award applicants required to submit FAFSA. *Faculty research:* Cognition and language, neuropsychological functioning and assessment, academic and behavioral interventions for schoolchildren, dementia care giving, emotional regulation. *Total annual research expenditures:* $68,057. *Unit head:* Dr. Kathleen M. McNamara, Chairperson, 216-687-2545, Fax: 216-687-9294, E-mail: k.mcnamara@csuohio.edu. *Application contact:* Barbara E. Durfey, Administrative Secretary, 216-687-2544, Fax: 216-687-9294, E-mail: b.durfey@csuohio.edu.
Website: http://www.csuohio.edu/sciences/dept/psychology/

The College at Brockport, State University of New York, School of Arts and Sciences, Department of Psychology, Brockport, NY 14420-2997. Offers clinical psychology (with applied emphasis) (MA); clinical psychology (with research emphasis) (MA); general psychology (MA). *Program availability:* Part-time. *Faculty:* 10 full-time (7 women), 1 (woman) part-time/adjunct. *Students:* 11 full-time (7 women), 7 part-time (all women); includes 3 minority (1 Black or African American, non-Hispanic/Latino; 2 Two or more races, non-Hispanic/Latino). 28 applicants, 43% accepted, 8 enrolled. In 2017, 8 master's awarded. *Degree requirements:* For master's, thesis optional. *Entrance requirements:* For master's, GRE General Test, letters of recommendation, interview, minimum GPA of 3.0. Additional exam requirements/recommendations for international students: Required—TOEFL (minimum score 550 paper-based; 79 iBT), IELTS (minimum score 6.5). *Application deadline:* For fall admission, 4/1 priority date for domestic and international students. Application fee: $50. Electronic applications accepted. *Expenses:* Tuition, state resident: full-time $10,870; part-time $453 per credit hour. Tuition, nonresident: full-time $22,210. *Required fees:* $988; $246 per semester. *Financial support:* In 2017–18, 3 teaching assistantships with full tuition reimbursements (averaging $6,000 per year) were awarded; Federal Work-Study, scholarships/grants, and unspecified assistantships also available. Support available to part-time students. Financial award application deadline: 3/15; financial award applicants required to submit FAFSA. *Faculty research:* Positive psychology, decision-making and applied behavior analysis, family processes and close relationships, cognition and neuropsychology, social/personality and industrial/organizational psychology. *Unit head:* Dr. Sara Margolin, 585-395-2908, Fax: 585-395-2116, E-mail: smargoli@brockport.edu. *Application contact:* Danielle A. Welch, Graduate Counselor, 585-295-5430, Fax: 585-395-2115, E-mail: dwelch@brockport.edu.
Website: https://www.brockport.edu/academics/psychology/graduate/masters.html

College of Saint Elizabeth, Department of Psychology, Morristown, NJ 07960-6989. Offers counseling psychology (MA, Psy D), including mental health counseling (MA), school counseling (MA). *Program availability:* Part-time. *Faculty:* 4 full-time (3 women), 7 part-time/adjunct (all women). *Students:* 37 full-time (32 women), 40 part-time (37 women); includes 30 minority (12 Black or African American, non-Hispanic/Latino; 1 Asian, non-Hispanic/Latino; 16 Hispanic/Latino; 1 Two or more races, non-Hispanic/Latino). Average age 31. 37 applicants, 81% accepted, 24 enrolled. In 2017, 17 master's, 3 doctorates awarded. *Degree requirements:* For master's, thesis or alternative; for doctorate, thesis/dissertation. *Entrance requirements:* For master's, minimum GPA of 3.0, BA in psychology (preferred), 12 credits of course work in psychology; for doctorate, GRE, 3 letters of recommendation from professionals who can comment on the applicant's qualifications for doctoral study; master's degree in counseling psychology, forensic psychology and counseling, or its equivalent. Additional exam requirements/recommendations for international students: Required—TOEFL (minimum score 550 paper-based; 79 iBT), IELTS (minimum score 6.5). *Application deadline:* For fall admission, 5/1 for international students. Applications are processed on a rolling basis. Application fee: $35. Electronic applications accepted. Application fee is waived when completed online. *Expenses:* Contact institution. *Financial support:* Career-related internships or fieldwork, scholarships/grants, tuition waivers (partial), and unspecified assistantships available. Support available to part-time students. Financial award applicants required to submit FAFSA. *Unit head:* Dr. Michelle M. Barrett, Director, Graduate and Doctoral Programs in Psychology, 973-290-4027, Fax: 973-290-4676, E-mail: mbarrett01@cse.edu. *Application contact:* Lori J. Fragoso, Director of Graduate and Continuing Studies Admissions, 973-290-4413, Fax: 973-290-4710, E-mail: apply@cse.edu.
Website: https://www.cse.edu/academics/prof-studies/psychology/

College of St. Joseph, Graduate Programs, Division of Psychology and Human Services, Rutland, VT 05701-3899. Offers alcohol and substance abuse counseling (MS); clinical mental health counseling (MS); clinical psychology (MS); community counseling (MS); school guidance counseling (MS). *Program availability:* Part-time, evening/weekend. *Degree requirements:* For master's, comprehensive exam, thesis optional. *Entrance requirements:* For master's, official college transcripts; 2 letters of reference. Additional exam requirements/recommendations for international students: Required—TOEFL (minimum score 550 paper-based). Electronic applications accepted.

The College of William and Mary, Faculty of Arts and Sciences, Department of Psychological Sciences, Williamsburg, VA 23185. Offers MS. *Faculty:* 24 full-time (12 women), 4 part-time/adjunct (1 woman). *Students:* 15 full-time (12 women); includes 3 minority (2 Black or African American, non-Hispanic/Latino; 1 Two or more races, non-Hispanic/Latino), 2 international. Average age 23. 76 applicants, 11% accepted, 8 enrolled. In 2017, 8 master's awarded. *Degree requirements:* For master's, thesis. *Entrance requirements:* For master's, GRE, course in statistics and research methods. Additional exam requirements/recommendations for international students: Required—TOEFL, IELTS. *Application deadline:* For fall admission, 2/1 for domestic and international students. Application fee: $50. Electronic applications accepted. *Expenses:* Contact institution. *Financial support:* In 2017–18, 17 students received support, including 1 research assistantship with full tuition reimbursement available (averaging $13,995 per year), 16 teaching assistantships with full tuition reimbursements available (averaging $13,995 per year). *Faculty research:* Personality, developmental, clinical and neuroscience, social psychology. *Total annual research expenditures:* $249,023. *Unit head:* Dr. Josh Burk, Chair, 757-221-3870, E-mail: jabur2@wm.edu. *Application contact:* Danielle Dallaire, Director of Graduate Studies, 757-221-3870, Fax: 757-221-3896, E-mail: dhdall@wm.edu.
Website: http://www.wm.edu/as/psychology

Colorado State University, College of Natural Sciences, Department of Psychology, Fort Collins, CO 80523-1876. Offers psychology (PhD). *Accreditation:* APA. *Program availability:* 100% online. *Faculty:* 30 full-time (18 women), 5 part-time/adjunct (3 women). *Students:* 58 full-time (40 women), 95 part-time (59 women); includes 28 minority (4 Black or African American, non-Hispanic/Latino; 1 American Indian or Alaska Native, non-Hispanic/Latino; 3 Asian, non-Hispanic/Latino; 13 Hispanic/Latino; 7 Two or more races, non-Hispanic/Latino), 3 international. Average age 28. 117 applicants, 44% accepted, 49 enrolled. In 2017, 26 master's, 14 doctorates awarded. *Degree requirements:* For master's, comprehensive exam, thesis; for doctorate, comprehensive exam, thesis/dissertation. *Entrance requirements:* For master's, GRE General Test, GRE Subject Test in psychology (for some programs; minimum scores within 50th percentile), minimum GPA of 3.0, 3 letters of recommendation, resume/curriculum vitae; for doctorate, GRE, minimum GPA of 3.0, 3 letters of recommendation, resume/curriculum vitae, transcripts. Additional exam requirements/recommendations for international students: Required—TOEFL (minimum score 550 paper-based; 80 iBT); Recommended—IELTS (minimum score 6.5), TSE (minimum score 58). *Application deadline:* For fall admission, 12/1 for domestic and international students. Application fee: $60 ($70 for international students). Electronic applications accepted. *Expenses:* $2,000 per semester (for master's in addiction counseling). *Financial support:* In 2017–18, 6 fellowships with full tuition reimbursements (averaging $12,010 per year), 7 research assistantships with full tuition reimbursements (averaging $16,241 per year), 49 teaching assistantships with full tuition reimbursements (averaging $14,127 per year) were awarded; scholarships/grants and traineeships also available. Financial award applicants required to submit FAFSA. *Faculty research:* Occupational health psychology; developmental disabilities; memory and aging; understanding well-being and meaning of life; embodied perception and cognition. *Total annual research expenditures:* $2.8 million. *Unit head:* Dr. Don Rojas, Department Chair, 970-491-5213, E-mail: don.rojas@colostate.edu. *Application contact:* Linda Thornton, Administrative Assistant II, 970-491-5212, E-mail: linda.thornton@colostate.edu.
Website: http://www.colostate.edu/Depts/Psychology/

Columbia University, Graduate School of Arts and Sciences, New York, NY 10027. Offers African-American studies (MA); American studies (MA); anthropology (MA, PhD); art history and archaeology (MA, PhD); astronomy (PhD); biological sciences (PhD); biotechnology (MA); chemical physics (PhD); chemistry (PhD); classical studies (MA, PhD); classics (MA, PhD); climate and society (MA); conservation biology (MA); earth and environmental sciences (PhD); East Asia: regional studies (MA); East Asian languages and cultures (MA, PhD); ecology, evolution and environmental biology (MA), including conservation biology; ecology, evolution, and environmental biology (PhD), including ecology and evolutionary biology, evolutionary primatology; economics (MA, PhD); English and comparative literature (MA, PhD); French and Romance philology (MA, PhD); Germanic languages (MA, PhD); global French studies (MA); global thought (MA); Hispanic cultural studies (MA); history (PhD); history and literature (MA); human rights studies (MA); Islamic studies (MA); Italian (MA, PhD); Japanese pedagogy (MA); Jewish studies (MA); Latin America and the Caribbean: regional studies (MA); Latin American and Iberian cultures (PhD); mathematics (MA, PhD), including finance (MA); medieval and Renaissance studies (MA); Middle Eastern, South Asian, and African studies (MA, PhD); modern art: critical and curatorial studies (MA); modern European studies (MA); museum anthropology (MA); music (DMA, PhD); oral history (MA); philosophical foundations of physics (MA); philosophy (MA, PhD); physics (PhD); political science (MA, PhD); psychology (PhD); quantitative methods in the social sciences (MA); religion (MA, PhD); Russia, Eurasia and East Europe: regional studies (MA); Russian translation (MA); Slavic cultures (MA); Slavic languages (MA, PhD); sociology (MA, PhD); South Asian studies (MA); statistics (MA, PhD); theatre (PhD). Dual-degree programs require admission to both Graduate School of Arts and Sciences and another Columbia school. *Program availability:* Part-time. Terminal master's awarded for partial completion of doctoral program. *Degree requirements:* For master's, variable foreign language requirement, comprehensive exam (for some programs), thesis (for some programs); for doctorate, variable foreign language requirement, comprehensive exam (for some programs), thesis/dissertation. *Entrance requirements:* For master's and doctorate, GRE General Test, GRE Subject Test (for some programs). Additional exam requirements/recommendations for international students: Required—TOEFL, IELTS. Electronic applications accepted. *Expenses: Tuition:* Full-time $44,864; part-time $1704 per credit. *Required fees:* $2370 per semester. One-time fee: $105.

Concordia University, School of Graduate Studies, Faculty of Arts and Science, Department of Psychology, MA Program in Psychology, Montréal, QC H3G 1M8, Canada. Offers MA. *Degree requirements:* For master's, comprehensive exam, thesis. *Entrance requirements:* For master's, GRE General Test, GRE Subject Test, honors degree in psychology or equivalent. *Faculty research:* Appetitive motivation and drug dependence, human information processing, psychology of physical activity.

Concordia University Chicago, College of Graduate and Innovative Programs, Program in Psychology, River Forest, IL 60305-1499. Offers MA. *Program availability:* Part-time, evening/weekend. *Degree requirements:* For master's, comprehensive exam, thesis optional. *Entrance requirements:* For master's, minimum GPA of 2.9. Additional exam requirements/recommendations for international students: Required—TOEFL (minimum score 550 paper-based). Electronic applications accepted. *Faculty research:* Lutheran high school counseling research.

Cornell University, Graduate School, Graduate Fields of Arts and Sciences, Field of Psychology, Ithaca, NY 14853. Offers biopsychology (PhD); human experimental psychology (PhD); personality and social psychology (PhD). *Degree requirements:* For doctorate, comprehensive exam, thesis/dissertation, 2 semesters of teaching experience. *Entrance requirements:* For doctorate, GRE General Test, 3 letters of recommendation. Additional exam requirements/recommendations for international students: Required—TOEFL (minimum score 550 paper-based; 77 iBT). Electronic applications accepted. *Faculty research:* Sensory and perceptual systems, social cognition, cognitive development, quantitative and computational modeling, behavioral neuroscience.

Dalhousie University, Faculty of Science, Department of Psychology, Halifax, NS B3H 4R2, Canada. Offers clinical psychology (PhD); psychology (M Sc, PhD); psychology/neuroscience (M Sc, PhD). *Degree requirements:* For master's, thesis; for doctorate, thesis/dissertation. *Entrance requirements:* For doctorate, GRE General Test. Additional exam requirements/recommendations for international students: Required—TOEFL, IELTS, CANTEST, CAEL, or Michigan English Language Assessment Battery. Electronic applications accepted. *Faculty research:* Physiological psychology, psychology of learning, learning and behavior, forensic clinical health psychology, development perception and cognition.

Dartmouth College, School of Graduate and Advanced Studies, Department of Psychological and Brain Sciences, Hanover, NH 03755. Offers cognitive neuroscience (PhD); psychology (PhD). *Faculty:* 28 full-time (8 women), 7 part-time/adjunct (5 women). *Students:* 39 full-time (18 women); includes 5 minority (1 American Indian or Alaska Native, non-Hispanic/Latino; 1 Asian, non-Hispanic/Latino; 3 Hispanic/Latino), 15 international. Average age 28. 94 applicants, 11% accepted, 5 enrolled. In 2017, 3 doctorates awarded. *Degree requirements:* For doctorate, thesis/dissertation. *Entrance requirements:* For doctorate, GRE General Test, GRE Subject Test. Additional exam requirements/recommendations for international students: Required—TOEFL. *Application deadline:* For fall admission, 12/1 for domestic students. Application fee: $50. Electronic applications accepted. *Faculty research:* Behavioral neuroscience, cognitive neuroscience, cognitive science, social/personality psychology. *Unit head:* Dr. David Bucci, Chair, 603-646-3439. *Application contact:* Julia Abraham, Department Administrator, 603-646-2744, E-mail: julia.s.abraham@dartmouth.edu.
Website: http://www.dartmouth.edu/~psych/graduate/

DePaul University, College of Science and Health, Chicago, IL 60604. Offers applied mathematics (MS); applied statistics (MS); biological sciences (MA, MS); chemistry (MS); environmental science (MS); mathematics education (MA); mathematics for teaching (MS); nursing (MS); nursing practice (DNP); physics (MS); polymer and coatings science (MS); psychology (MS); pure mathematics (MS); science education (MS); MA/PhD. *Accreditation:* AACN. *Application deadline:* Applications are processed on a rolling basis. Application fee: $40. Electronic applications accepted. *Financial support:* Applicants required to submit FAFSA. *Unit head:* Dr. Gerald P. Koocher, Dean, 773-325-8300. *Application contact:* Ann Spittle, Director of Graduate Admission, 773-325-7315, Fax: 312-476-3244, E-mail: graddepaul@depaul.edu.
Website: http://csh.depaul.edu/

Divine Mercy University, School of Counseling, Arlington, VA 30327. Offers clinical mental health counseling (MS); psychology (MS). *Program availability:* Online learning.

Drexel University, College of Arts and Sciences, Department of Psychology, Philadelphia, PA 19104-2875. Offers clinical psychology (PhD), including clinical psychology, forensic psychology, health psychology, neuropsychology; psychology (MS); JD/PhD. *Accreditation:* APA (one or more programs are accredited). *Degree requirements:* For doctorate, thesis/dissertation, internship. *Entrance requirements:* For doctorate, GRE General Test. Additional exam requirements/recommendations for international students: Required—TOEFL. Electronic applications accepted. *Expenses:* Contact institution. *Faculty research:* Neurosciences, rehabilitation psychology, cognitive science, neurological assessment.

Duke University, Graduate School, Department of Psychology and Neuroscience, Durham, NC 27708. Offers biological psychology (PhD); clinical psychology (PhD); cognitive psychology (PhD); developmental psychology (PhD); experimental psychology (PhD); health psychology (PhD); human social development (PhD); JD/MA. *Accreditation:* APA (one or more programs are accredited). *Degree requirements:* For doctorate, thesis/dissertation. *Entrance requirements:* For doctorate, GRE General Test. Additional exam requirements/recommendations for international students: Required—TOEFL (minimum score 577 paper-based; 90 iBT) or IELTS (minimum score 7). Electronic applications accepted.

Duquesne University, Graduate School of Liberal Arts, Department of Psychology, Pittsburgh, PA 15282-0001. Offers clinical psychology (PhD). *Accreditation:* APA. *Faculty:* 13 full-time (7 women). *Students:* 48 full-time (29 women); includes 9 minority (2 Black or African American, non-Hispanic/Latino; 1 Asian, non-Hispanic/Latino; 5 Hispanic/Latino; 1 Two or more races, non-Hispanic/Latino), 7 international. Average age 32. 121 applicants, 7% accepted, 8 enrolled. In 2017, 6 doctorates awarded. *Degree requirements:* For doctorate, comprehensive exam, thesis/dissertation. *Entrance requirements:* For doctorate, GRE General Test, MA in psychology. Additional exam requirements/recommendations for international students: Required—TOEFL. *Application deadline:* For fall admission, 12/15 for domestic and international students. Application fee: $0. Electronic applications accepted. *Expenses:* $1,259 per credit. *Financial support:* In 2017–18, 38 students received support, including 28 teaching assistantships with full tuition reimbursements available (averaging $17,000 per year);

career-related internships or fieldwork, scholarships/grants, tuition waivers (partial), and unspecified assistantships also available. Financial award application deadline: 5/1. *Faculty research:* Emotion, language motivation, imagination, development. *Unit head:* Dr. Leswin Laubscher, Chair, 412-396-1843, E-mail: laubscherl@duq.edu. *Application contact:* Linda Rendulic, Assistant to the Dean, 412-396-6400, Fax: 412-396-5265, E-mail: rendulic@duq.edu.
Website: http://www.duq.edu/academics/schools/liberal-arts/graduate-school/programs/clinical-psychology

East Central University, School of Graduate Studies, Department of Psychology, Ada, OK 74820. Offers MSPS. *Program availability:* Part-time, evening/weekend. *Entrance requirements:* For master's, GRE General Test, MAT. *Application deadline:* Applications are processed on a rolling basis. Application fee: $0 ($50 for international students). Electronic applications accepted. *Financial support:* Teaching assistantships, career-related internships or fieldwork, Federal Work-Study, institutionally sponsored loans, and tuition waivers (partial) available. *Unit head:* Marc Klippenstine, Chair, 580-559-5342, E-mail: mklippen@ecok.edu. *Application contact:* Marc Klippenstine, Chair, 580-559-5342, E-mail: mklippen@ecok.edu.
Website: http://www.ecok.edu/academics/colleges-and-schools/college-education-and-psychology/department-psychology

Eastern Illinois University, Graduate School, College of Liberal Arts and Sciences, Department of Psychology, Charleston, IL 61920. Offers clinical psychology (MA); school psychology (SSP). *Program availability:* Part-time, evening/weekend. *Degree requirements:* For master's, comprehensive exam, thesis; for SSP, thesis. *Entrance requirements:* For master's and SSP, GMAT or GRE. Additional exam requirements/recommendations for international students: Required—TOEFL (minimum score 500 paper-based; 61 iBT), IELTS (minimum score 6). *Application deadline:* For fall admission, 5/15 for domestic and international students; for spring admission, 10/15 for domestic and international students. Applications are processed on a rolling basis. Application fee: $30. Electronic applications accepted. *Financial support:* Research assistantships with full tuition reimbursements, teaching assistantships with full tuition reimbursements, career-related internships or fieldwork, Federal Work-Study, and unspecified assistantships available. Support available to part-time students. Financial award application deadline: 3/1; financial award applicants required to submit FAFSA. *Unit head:* John H. Mace, Chair, 217-581-2127, Fax: 217-581-6764, E-mail: jhmace@eiu.edu. *Application contact:* John H. Mace, Chair, 217-581-2127, Fax: 217-581-6764, E-mail: jhmace@eiu.edu.
Website: http://www.eiu.edu/psych/index.php

Eastern Kentucky University, The Graduate School, College of Arts and Sciences, Department of Psychology, Richmond, KY 40475-3102. Offers clinical psychology (MS); industrial/organizational psychology (MS); school psychology (Psy S). *Program availability:* Part-time. *Entrance requirements:* For master's and Psy S, GRE General Test, minimum GPA of 2.5. *Faculty research:* Autism, social psychology, parenting, assessment of depression/anxiety, reading.

Eastern Michigan University, Graduate School, College of Arts and Sciences, Department of Psychology, Ypsilanti, MI 48197. Offers clinical behavioral psychology (MS); clinical psychology (PhD); general clinical psychology (MS); general experimental psychology (MS). *Accreditation:* APA. *Faculty:* 24 full-time (14 women). *Students:* 46 full-time (38 women), 50 part-time (40 women); includes 21 minority (6 Black or African American, non-Hispanic/Latino; 1 American Indian or Alaska Native, non-Hispanic/Latino; 5 Asian, non-Hispanic/Latino; 4 Hispanic/Latino; 5 Two or more races, non-Hispanic/Latino), 2 international. Average age 27. 223 applicants, 18% accepted, 33 enrolled. In 2017, 14 master's, 9 doctorates awarded. *Degree requirements:* For master's, 600-hour practicum; for doctorate, 1500-hour practicum; 2000-hour internship. *Entrance requirements:* For master's and doctorate, GRE. *Application deadline:* For fall admission, 2/15 for domestic students. Application fee: $45. *Financial support:* Fellowships available. *Unit head:* Dr. Carol Freedman-Doan, Department Head, 734-487-1155, Fax: 734-487-6553, E-mail: cfreedman@emich.edu.

Eastern Washington University, Graduate Studies, College of Social Sciences, Department of Psychology, Cheney, WA 99004-2431. Offers clinical psychology (MS); experimental psychology (MS); mental health counseling (MS), including applied psychology, mental health counseling; school counseling (MS), including applied psychology, school counseling; school psychology respecialization (Ed S). *Faculty:* 24. *Students:* 95 full-time (69 women), 37 part-time (29 women); includes 7 minority (2 Black or African American, non-Hispanic/Latino; 1 American Indian or Alaska Native, non-Hispanic/Latino; 1 Asian, non-Hispanic/Latino; 3 Hispanic/Latino), 3 international. Average age 32. 156 applicants, 29% accepted, 35 enrolled. In 2017, 44 master's awarded. *Degree requirements:* For master's, comprehensive exam, thesis or alternative. *Entrance requirements:* For master's, GRE General Test, minimum GPA of 3.0. Additional exam requirements/recommendations for international students: Required—TOEFL (minimum score 580 paper-based; 92 iBT), IELTS (minimum score 7), PTE (minimum score 63). *Application deadline:* For fall admission, 3/1 for domestic students. Applications are processed on a rolling basis. Application fee: $75. Electronic applications accepted. *Expenses:* Tuition, state resident: full-time $11,191; part-time $373.06 per credit. Tuition, nonresident: full-time $25,995; part-time $866.52 per credit. *Financial support:* Teaching assistantships with partial tuition reimbursements, career-related internships or fieldwork, Federal Work-Study, institutionally sponsored loans, scholarships/grants, health care benefits, tuition waivers (partial), and unspecified assistantships available. Support available to part-time students. Financial award application deadline: 2/1; financial award applicants required to submit FAFSA. *Unit head:* Dennis Anderson, 509-359-2087, E-mail: danderson2@ewu.edu. *Application contact:* Kathy White, Advisor/Recruiter for Graduate Studies, 509-359-6297, Fax: 509-359-6044, E-mail: gradprograms@ewu.edu.

East Tennessee State University, School of Graduate Studies, College of Arts and Sciences, Department of Psychology, Johnson City, TN 37614. Offers clinical psychology (PhD); experimental psychology (PhD). *Accreditation:* APA. Terminal master's awarded for partial completion of doctoral program. *Degree requirements:* For doctorate, thesis/dissertation, externship. *Entrance requirements:* For doctorate, GRE General Test, minimum GPA of 3.0, three letters of recommendation, interview, minimum of 18 semester hours in undergraduate psychology. Additional exam requirements/recommendations for international students: Required—TOEFL (minimum score 550 paper-based; 79 iBT). *Application deadline:* For fall admission, 12/1 for domestic and international students. Application fee: $55 ($65 for international students). Electronic applications accepted. *Financial support:* Research assistantships with full tuition reimbursements, teaching assistantships with full tuition reimbursements, career-related internships or fieldwork, institutionally sponsored loans, scholarships/grants, and unspecified assistantships available. Financial award application deadline: 7/1; financial award applicants required to submit FAFSA. *Faculty research:* Women's issues, prenatal stress, childhood obesity, suicide prevention, behavioral pediatrics, self-control, substance dependence, violence. *Unit head:* Dr. Wallace E. Dixon, Jr., Chair, 423-439-6656, Fax: 423-439-5695, E-mail: dixonw@etsu.edu. *Application contact:* Dr. Wallace E. Dixon, Jr., Chair, 423-439-6656, Fax: 423-439-5695, E-mail: dixonw@etsu.edu.
Website: http://www.etsu.edu/cas/psychology/

Elizabeth City State University, Department of Education, Psychology and Health, Elizabeth City, NC 27909-7806. Offers M Ed, MSA. *Program availability:* Part-time, evening/weekend. *Faculty:* 7 full-time (4 women), 1 (woman) part-time/adjunct. *Students:* 3 full-time (2 women), 42 part-time (33 women); includes 21 minority (20 Black or African American, non-Hispanic/Latino; 1 Two or more races, non-Hispanic/Latino). Average age 37. 3 applicants, 100% accepted, 2 enrolled. In 2017, 51 master's awarded. *Degree requirements:* For master's, comprehensive exam (for some programs), thesis. *Application deadline:* For fall admission, 11/1 priority date for domestic students; for spring admission, 3/15 priority date for domestic students. Applications are processed on a rolling basis. Application fee: $30. Electronic applications accepted. Tuition and fees vary according to course load and program. *Financial support:* In 2017–18, 25 students received support. Scholarships/grants and tuition waivers (partial) available. *Unit head:* Dr. Sharon D. Raynor, Director, Graduate Education Program, 252-335-3945, E-mail: sdraynor@ecsu.edu.
Website: http://www.ecsu.edu/academics/educationpsychology/index.cfm

Emory University, Laney Graduate School, Department of Psychology, Atlanta, GA 30322-1100. Offers clinical psychology (PhD); cognition and development (PhD); neuroscience and animal behavior (PhD). *Accreditation:* APA. *Degree requirements:* For doctorate, comprehensive exam, thesis/dissertation. *Entrance requirements:* For doctorate, GRE General Test, minimum GPA of 3.25. Additional exam requirements/recommendations for international students: Required—TOEFL. Electronic applications accepted. *Faculty research:* Neuroscience and animal behavior; adult and child psychopathology, cognition development assessment.

Emporia State University, Program in Psychology, Emporia, KS 66801-5415. Offers general psychology (MS); industrial/organizational psychology (MS). *Program availability:* Part-time. *Faculty:* 8 full-time (4 women). *Students:* 9 full-time (5 women), 4 part-time (2 women); includes 1 minority (Black or African American, non-Hispanic/Latino), 2 international. 20 applicants, 75% accepted, 5 enrolled. In 2017, 3 master's awarded. *Degree requirements:* For master's, comprehensive exam or thesis, internship. *Entrance requirements:* For master's, GRE General Test or MAT, essay exam, appropriate bachelor's degree, letters of recommendation. Additional exam requirements/recommendations for international students: Required—TOEFL (minimum score 520 paper-based; 68 iBT). *Application deadline:* For fall admission, 6/1 priority date for domestic students; for spring admission, 10/1 for domestic students. Applications are processed on a rolling basis. Application fee: $30 ($75 for international students). Electronic applications accepted. *Expenses:* Tuition, state resident: full-time $6084; part-time $253.50 per credit hour. Tuition, nonresident: full-time $18,924; part-time $788.50 per credit hour. *Required fees:* $1943; $80.95 per credit hour. Tuition and fees vary according to campus/location. *Financial support:* In 2017–18, 11 teaching assistantships with full tuition reimbursements (averaging $7,344 per year) were awarded; career-related internships or fieldwork, Federal Work-Study, institutionally sponsored loans, health care benefits, and unspecified assistantships also available. Financial award application deadline: 3/15; financial award applicants required to submit FAFSA. *Faculty research:* Driving under the influence (DUI) personality, lifestyles and imposter phenomenon. *Unit head:* Dr. Jim Persinger, Chair, 620-341-5317, E-mail: jpersing@emporia.edu. *Application contact:* Mary Sewell, Admissions Coordinator, 800-950-GRAD, Fax: 620-341-5909, E-mail: msewell@emporia.edu.

Fairleigh Dickinson University, Florham Campus, Maxwell Becton College of Arts and Sciences, Department of Psychology, Madison, NJ 07940-1099. Offers clinical mental health counseling (MA); counseling (MA); industrial/organizational psychology (MA); organizational behavior (MA, Certificate), including organizational behavior (MA), organizational leadership (Certificate); MA/MBA.

Fairleigh Dickinson University, Metropolitan Campus, University College: Arts, Sciences, and Professional Studies, School of Psychology, Teaneck, NJ 07666-1914. Offers clinical psychology (MA, PhD); clinical psychopharmacology (MA); forensic psychology (MA); general-theoretical psychology (MA, Certificate); school psychology (MA, Psy D). *Accreditation:* APA (one or more programs are accredited).

Fayetteville State University, Graduate School, Program in Psychology, Fayetteville, NC 28301-4298. Offers MA. *Program availability:* Part-time, evening/weekend. *Faculty:* 6 full-time (4 women), 1 (woman) part-time/adjunct. *Students:* 15 full-time (13 women), 5 part-time (4 women); includes 9 minority (6 Black or African American, non-Hispanic/Latino; 3 Asian, non-Hispanic/Latino). Average age 32. 7 applicants, 29% accepted. In 2017, 4 master's awarded. *Degree requirements:* For master's, comprehensive exam, internship. *Entrance requirements:* For master's, GRE. Additional exam requirements/recommendations for international students: Required—TOEFL. *Application deadline:* For fall admission, 4/15 for domestic students. Applications are processed on a rolling basis. Application fee: $40. Electronic applications accepted. *Expenses:* Tuition, state resident: full-time $8604. Tuition, nonresident: full-time $19,669. *Financial support:* Application deadline: 3/1; applicants required to submit FAFSA. *Faculty research:* Psychopathology and psychotherapy, psychological assessment, psychological disorders and behaviors, cognitive, psychophysiology, social epidemiology. *Unit head:* Dr. Timothy O. Moore, Interim Chair, 910-672-1413, Fax: 910-672-1043, E-mail: tmoore40@uncfsu.edu. *Application contact:* Dr. David Wallace, Graduate Coordinator for Experimental Track, 910-672-1419, Fax: 910-672-1043, E-mail: dwallace@uncfsu.edu.

Fielding Graduate University, Graduate Programs, School of Psychology, Santa Barbara, CA 93105-3814. Offers MA, PhD, Graduate Certificate, Post-Doctoral Certificate, Postbaccalaureate Certificate. *Accreditation:* APA. *Program availability:* Part-time, evening/weekend, 100% online, blended/hybrid learning. *Faculty:* 33 full-time (22 women), 44 part-time/adjunct (23 women). *Students:* 474 full-time (365 women), 70 part-time (48 women); includes 204 minority (72 Black or African American, non-Hispanic/Latino; 2 American Indian or Alaska Native, non-Hispanic/Latino; 19 Asian, non-Hispanic/Latino; 78 Hispanic/Latino; 33 Two or more races, non-Hispanic/Latino), 4 international. Average age 41. 347 applicants, 57% accepted, 118 enrolled. In 2017, 19 master's, 56 doctorates, 50 other advanced degrees awarded. Terminal master's awarded for partial completion of doctoral program. *Degree requirements:* For master's, thesis or alternative, capstone project; for doctorate, comprehensive exam, thesis/dissertation. *Entrance requirements:* For master's, BA from regionally-accredited institution or equivalent, minimum GPA of 2.5; for doctorate, BA or MA from regionally-accredited institution or equivalent; for other advanced degree, BA from regionally-accredited institution or equivalent. *Application deadline:* For fall admission, 1/24 for domestic and international students; for spring admission, 11/1 for domestic and international students; for summer admission, 3/1 for domestic and international students. Application fee: $75. Electronic applications accepted. *Expenses:* Contact institution. *Financial support:* In 2017–18, 104 students received support, including 1 research assistantship (averaging $400 per year), 9 teaching assistantships (averaging $1,900 per year); scholarships/grants also available. Support available to part-time students. Financial award applicants required to submit FAFSA. *Unit head:* Dr. Gerald Porter, Provost and Senior Vice President, 805-898-2940, E-mail: gporter@fielding.edu. *Application contact:* Enrollment Coordinator, 800-340-1099 Ext. 4098, Fax: 805-687-9793, E-mail: psyadmission@fielding.edu.
Website: http://www.fielding.edu/our-programs/school-of-psychology/

Fisk University, Division of Graduate Studies, Department of Psychology, Nashville, TN 37208-3051. Offers clinical psychology (MA); psychology (MA). *Degree requirements:* For master's, thesis. *Entrance requirements:* For master's, GRE General Test, GRE Subject Test, minimum GPA of 3.0. Electronic applications accepted. *Faculty research:* Ethnic and gender identity, development, female adolescent development, juvenile delinquency prevention.

Fitchburg State University, Division of Graduate and Continuing Education, Program in Interdisciplinary Studies, Fitchburg, MA 01420-2697. Offers applied communications (CAGS); counseling/psychology (CAGS); individualized track (CAGS); reading specialist (CAGS). *Program availability:* Part-time, evening/weekend. *Students:* 11 full-time (all women), 14 part-time (13 women); includes 3 minority (all Hispanic/Latino). Average age 36. 5 applicants, 100% accepted, 5 enrolled. In 2017, 14 CAGSs awarded. *Entrance requirements:* Additional exam requirements/recommendations for international students: Required—TOEFL (minimum score 550 paper-based; 79 iBT). *Application deadline:* For fall admission, 7/15 for international students; for spring admission, 12/1 for international students. Applications are processed on a rolling basis. Application fee: $50. Electronic applications accepted. *Expenses:* Contact institution. *Financial support:* In 2017–18, research assistantships with partial tuition reimbursements (averaging $5,500 per year) were awarded; Federal Work-Study, scholarships/grants, and unspecified assistantships also available. Support available to part-time students. Financial award application deadline: 3/1; financial award applicants required to submit FAFSA. *Unit head:* Dr. Jessica Robey, Chair, 978-665-3386, Fax: 978-665-3658, E-mail: gce@fitchburgstate.edu. *Application contact:* Jinawa McNeil, Director of Admissions, 978-665-3140, Fax: 978-665-4540, E-mail: admissions@fitchburgstate.edu.

Florida Agricultural and Mechanical University, Division of Graduate Studies, Research, and Continuing Education, College of Social Sciences, Arts and Humanities, Department of Psychology, Tallahassee, FL 32307-3200. Offers community psychology (MS). *Degree requirements:* For master's, thesis. *Entrance requirements:* For master's, GRE General Test, minimum GPA of 3.0. Additional exam requirements/recommendations for international students: Required—TOEFL.

Florida Atlantic University, Charles E. Schmidt College of Science, Department of Psychology, Boca Raton, FL 33431-0991. Offers MA. *Faculty:* 21 full-time (7 women). *Students:* 39 full-time (22 women), 15 part-time (6 women); includes 14 minority (3 Black or African American, non-Hispanic/Latino; 3 Asian, non-Hispanic/Latino; 8 Hispanic/Latino), 7 international. Average age 28. 82 applicants, 26% accepted, 19 enrolled. In 2017, 13 master's awarded. Terminal master's awarded for partial completion of doctoral program. *Degree requirements:* For master's, one foreign language, thesis or alternative. *Entrance requirements:* For master's, GRE General Test, minimum GPA of 3.0 during previous 2 years. Additional exam requirements/recommendations for international students: Required—TOEFL (minimum score 500 paper-based; 61 iBT), IELTS (minimum score 6). *Application deadline:* For fall admission, 5/1 for domestic students, 5/15 for international students. Application fee: $30. Electronic applications accepted. *Expenses:* Tuition, state resident: full-time $7400; part-time $369.82 per credit. Tuition, nonresident: full-time $20,496; part-time $1042.81 per credit. *Financial support:* Research assistantships with partial tuition reimbursements, teaching assistantships with partial tuition reimbursements, Federal Work-Study, institutionally sponsored loans, scholarships/grants, and unspecified assistantships available. Financial award application deadline: 3/1; financial award applicants required to submit FAFSA. *Faculty research:* Cognition, psychobiology, developmental psychology, social psychology, neuroscience. *Unit head:* E-mail: psychology@fau.edu. Website: http://psy.fau.edu.

Florida Institute of Technology, College of Psychology and Liberal Arts, Melbourne, FL 32901-6975. Offers MA, MS, PhD, Psy D. *Program availability:* Part-time, evening/weekend, 100% online. *Faculty:* 34 full-time (17 women), 9 part-time/adjunct (4 women). *Students:* Average age 29. 735 applicants, 36% accepted, 138 enrolled. In 2017, 144 master's, 28 doctorates awarded. Terminal master's awarded for partial completion of doctoral program. *Degree requirements:* For master's, comprehensive exam (for some programs), thesis or final exam; for doctorate, comprehensive exam, thesis/dissertation optional, internship. *Entrance requirements:* For master's, GRE General Test, minimum GPA of 3.0, 2 letters of recommendation, resume, statement of objectives; for doctorate, GRE General Test, GRE Subject Test, 3 letters of recommendation, minimum GPA of 3.2, resume, statement of objectives. Additional exam requirements/recommendations for international students: Required—TOEFL (minimum score 550 paper-based; 79 iBT). *Application deadline:* For fall admission, 4/1 for international students; for spring admission, 9/30 for international students. Applications are processed on a rolling basis. Electronic applications accepted. *Expenses:* Tuition: Part-time $1241 per credit hour. Part-time tuition and fees vary according to campus/location. *Financial support:* In 2017–18, 68 research assistantships with partial tuition reimbursements, 31 teaching assistantships with partial tuition reimbursements (averaging $8,002 per year) were awarded; fellowships, career-related internships or fieldwork, institutionally sponsored loans, tuition waivers (partial), unspecified assistantships, and tuition remissions also available. Support available to part-time students. Financial award application deadline: 3/1; financial award applicants required to submit FAFSA. *Unit head:* Dr. Mary Beth Kenkel, Dean, 321-674-8142, Fax: 321-674-7105, E-mail: mkenkel@fit.edu. *Application contact:* Cheryl A. Brown, Associate Director of Graduate Admissions, 321-674-7581, Fax: 321-723-9468, E-mail: cbrown@fit.edu. Website: http://cpla.fit.edu

Florida International University, College of Arts, Sciences, and Education, Department of Psychology, Miami, FL 33199. Offers behavioral analysis (MS); clinical science (PhD); cognitive neuroscience (PhD); counseling psychology (MS); developmental science (MS, PhD); legal psychology (MS, PhD); organizational psychology (MS, PhD). Program has fall admissions only. *Accreditation:* APA. *Program availability:* Part-time, evening/weekend. *Faculty:* 45 full-time (28 women), 48 part-time/adjunct (31 women). *Students:* 162 full-time (122 women), 13 part-time (5 women); includes 94 minority (11 Black or African American, non-Hispanic/Latino; 5 Asian, non-Hispanic/Latino; 75 Hispanic/Latino; 3 Two or more races, non-Hispanic/Latino), 12 international. Average age 27. 290 applicants, 21% accepted, 50 enrolled. In 2017, 43 master's, 13 doctorates awarded. Terminal master's awarded for partial completion of doctoral program. *Degree requirements:* For master's, thesis; for doctorate, comprehensive exam, thesis/dissertation. *Entrance requirements:* For master's, GRE General Test, minimum GPA of 3.0, resume, 3 letters of recommendation; for doctorate, GRE General Test, 3 letters of recommendation, resume, letter of intent, two writing samples, minimum GPA of 3.0. Additional exam requirements/recommendations for international students: Required—TOEFL (minimum score 550 paper-based; 80 iBT). *Application deadline:* For fall admission, 12/15 for domestic and international students. Application fee: $30. Electronic applications accepted. *Expenses:* Tuition, state resident: full-time $8912; part-time $446 per credit hour. Tuition, nonresident: full-time $21,393; part-time $992 per credit hour. Required fees: $390; $195 per semester. *Financial support:* Institutionally sponsored loans and scholarships/grants available. Financial award application deadline: 3/1. *Faculty research:* Legal psychology, organizational and industrial psychology, child behavior psychology. *Unit head:* Dr. Jeremy Pettit, Interim Chair, 305-348-1671, Fax: 305-348-3646, E-mail: jeremy.pettit@fiu.edu. *Application contact:* Nanett Rojas, Assistant Director, Graduate Admissions, 305-348-7464, Fax: 305-348-7441, E-mail: gradadm@fiu.edu.

Florida State University, The Graduate School, College of Arts and Sciences, Department of Psychology, Tallahassee, FL 32306-4301. Offers applied behavior analysis (MS); clinical psychology (PhD); cognitive psychology (PhD); developmental psychology (PhD); social psychology (PhD). *Accreditation:* APA (one or more programs are accredited). *Faculty:* 46 full-time (18 women). *Students:* 157 full-time (120 women), 10 part-time (9 women); includes 40 minority (4 Black or African American, non-Hispanic/Latino; 10 Asian, non-Hispanic/Latino; 16 Hispanic/Latino; 10 Two or more races, non-Hispanic/Latino), 4 international. Average age 28. 328 applicants, 17% accepted, 37 enrolled. In 2017, 32 master's, 15 doctorates awarded. Terminal master's awarded for partial completion of doctoral program. *Degree requirements:* For master's, comprehensive exam (for some programs), thesis (for some programs); for doctorate, comprehensive exam, thesis/dissertation. *Entrance requirements:* For master's, GRE General Test, minimum GPA of 3.0; for doctorate, GRE General Test. Additional exam requirements/recommendations for international students: Required—TOEFL (minimum score 80 iBT). Application fee: $30. Electronic applications accepted. *Financial support:* In 2017–18, 133 students received support, including 14 fellowships with full tuition reimbursements available (averaging $23,330 per year), 32 research assistantships with full tuition reimbursements available (averaging $23,815 per year), 89 teaching assistantships with full tuition reimbursements available (averaging $19,000 per year); career-related internships or fieldwork and health care benefits also available. Financial award applicants required to submit FAFSA. *Total annual research expenditures:* $9.3 million. *Unit head:* Dr. Jeanette Taylor, Chairman, 850-644-2040, Fax: 850-644-7739, E-mail: taylor@psy.fsu.edu. *Application contact:* Lynda L. Gibson, Graduate Program Associate, 850-644-2499, Fax: 850-644-7739, E-mail: grad-info@psy.fsu.edu. Website: http://www.psy.fsu.edu/

Fordham University, Graduate School of Arts and Sciences, Department of Psychology, New York, NY 10458. Offers applied developmental psychology (PhD); applied psychological methods (MS); clinical psychology (PhD); clinical research methods (MS); psychometrics and quantitative psychology (PhD). *Faculty:* 25 full-time (8 women), 3 part-time/adjunct (2 women). *Students:* 108 full-time (86 women), 10 part-time (8 women); includes 31 minority (8 Black or African American, non-Hispanic/Latino; 1 American Indian or Alaska Native, non-Hispanic/Latino; 7 Asian, non-Hispanic/Latino; 15 Hispanic/Latino), 19 international. Average age 31. 958 applicants, 14% accepted, 26 enrolled. In 2017, 15 master's, 15 doctorates awarded. Terminal master's awarded for partial completion of doctoral program. *Degree requirements:* For master's, comprehensive exam; for doctorate, comprehensive exam, thesis/dissertation. *Entrance requirements:* For doctorate, GRE General Test, GRE Subject Test. Additional exam requirements/recommendations for international students: Required—TOEFL (minimum score 600 paper-based). *Application deadline:* For fall admission, 12/14 for domestic students. Application fee: $70. Electronic applications accepted. *Financial support:* In 2017–18, 73 students received support, including 16 fellowships with tuition reimbursements available (averaging $24,561 per year), 12 research assistantships with tuition reimbursements available (averaging $15,170 per year), 11 teaching assistantships with tuition reimbursements available (averaging $12,286 per year); career-related internships or fieldwork, institutionally sponsored loans, tuition waivers (full and partial), and unspecified assistantships also available. Financial award application deadline: 12/14; financial award applicants required to submit FAFSA. *Total annual research expenditures:* $2.8 million. *Unit head:* Dr. Barry Rosenfeld, Chair, 718-817-3794, Fax: 718-817-3699, E-mail: rosenfeld@fordham.edu. *Application contact:* Bernadette Valentino-Morrison, Director of Graduate Admissions, 718-817-4419, Fax: 718-817-3566, E-mail: valentinomor@fordham.edu.

Fort Hays State University, Graduate School, College of Arts and Sciences, Department of Psychology, Hays, KS 67601-4099. Offers psychology (MS); school psychology (Ed S). *Degree requirements:* For master's and Ed S, comprehensive exam, thesis. *Entrance requirements:* For master's, GRE General Test. Additional exam requirements/recommendations for international students: Required—TOEFL (minimum score 550 paper-based). Electronic applications accepted. *Faculty research:* Memory, learning, motivation, clinical and experimental psychology, history and systems of psychological stressors in rural environments.

Francis Marion University, Graduate Programs, Department of Psychology, Florence, SC 29502-0547. Offers applied psychology (MS), including clinical/counseling psychology, school psychology; school psychology (SSP). *Program availability:* Part-time, evening/weekend. *Degree requirements:* For master's, internship. *Entrance requirements:* For master's, GRE General Test, official transcripts, two letters of recommendation. Additional exam requirements/recommendations for international students: Required—TOEFL (minimum score 550 paper-based; 79 iBT). *Faculty research:* Parenting and family relationships, child development, applied behavioral analysis, post-traumatic stress disorder, clinical psychology in adults.

Frostburg State University, College of Liberal Arts and Sciences, Department of Psychology, Frostburg, MD 21532. Offers counseling psychology (MS). *Program availability:* Part-time, evening/weekend. *Faculty:* 6 full-time (4 women). *Students:* 24 full-time (17 women), 5 part-time (all women); includes 2 minority (1 Black or African American, non-Hispanic/Latino; 1 Hispanic/Latino), 1 international. Average age 27. 34 applicants, 38% accepted, 11 enrolled. In 2017, 7 master's awarded. *Degree requirements:* For master's, internship. *Entrance requirements:* For master's, GRE General Test or MAT, interview, minimum GPA of 3.0, resume. Additional exam requirements/recommendations for international students: Required—TOEFL. *Application deadline:* For fall admission, 2/1 for domestic students. Applications are processed on a rolling basis. Application fee: $45. Electronic applications accepted. *Expenses:* Tuition, state resident: part-time $433 per credit hour. Tuition, nonresident: part-time $557 per credit hour. Required fees: $121 per credit hour; $27 per term. *Financial support:* In 2017–18, 7 research assistantships with full tuition reimbursements (averaging $5,000 per year) were awarded; career-related internships or fieldwork and Federal Work-Study also available. Financial award application deadline: 4/1; financial award applicants required to submit FAFSA. *Unit head:* Dr. Jennifer Flinn, Chair, 301-687-4491, E-mail: jaflinn@frostburg.edu. *Application contact:* Vickie Mazer, Director, Graduate Services, 301-687-7053, Fax: 301-687-4597, E-mail: vmmazer@frostburg.edu.

Gardner-Webb University, Graduate School, School of Psychology, Boiling Springs, NC 28017. Offers mental health counseling (MA); school counseling (MA). *Program availability:* Part-time, evening/weekend. *Faculty:* 5 full-time (4 women), 4 part-time/adjunct (2 women). *Students:* 1 full-time (0 women), 88 part-time (76 women); includes 19 minority (13 Black or African American, non-Hispanic/Latino; 1 American Indian or Alaska Native, non-Hispanic/Latino; 3 Hispanic/Latino; 2 Two or more races, non-Hispanic/Latino). Average age 31. *Degree requirements:* For master's, comprehensive exam. *Entrance requirements:* For master's, GRE General Test, MAT, minimum GPA of 2.7. *Application deadline:* For fall admission, 7/1 priority date for domestic students. Applications are processed on a rolling basis. Electronic applications accepted. *Expenses:* Contact institution. *Financial support:* Unspecified assistantships available. *Unit head:* Dr. David Carscaddon, Chair, 704-406-4437, Fax: 704-406-4329, E-mail: dcarscaddon@gardner-webb.edu. *Application contact:* Office of Graduate Admissions, 877-498-4723, Fax: 704-406-3895, E-mail: gradinfo@gardner-webb.edu.

Geneva College, Master of Arts in Counseling Program, Beaver Falls, PA 15010-3599. Offers clinical mental health counseling (MA); marriage and family counseling (MA); school counseling (MA). *Accreditation:* ACA. *Program availability:* Part-time, evening/weekend. *Faculty:* 6 full-time (3 women), 3 part-time/adjunct (1 woman). *Students:* 34 full-time (26 women), 20 part-time (16 women); includes 12 minority (11 Black or African American, non-Hispanic/Latino; 1 Hispanic/Latino), 1 international. Average age 33. In 2017, 34 master's awarded. *Degree requirements:* For master's, comprehensive exam, 60 credits including practicum and internship. *Entrance requirements:* For master's, minimum GPA of 3.0 (preferred), 3 letters of recommendation, essay on career goals, resume of educational and professional experiences. Additional exam requirements/recommendations for international students: Required—TOEFL. *Application deadline:* For fall admission, 9/1 for domestic students; for spring admission, 1/10 for domestic students. Applications are processed on a rolling basis. Electronic applications accepted. *Expenses:* $670 per credit. *Financial support:* Research assistantships, teaching assistantships, career-related internships or fieldwork, and unspecified assistantships available. Financial award application deadline: 8/1; financial award applicants required to submit FAFSA. *Faculty research:* Blended family counseling; premarital and newlywed couples; religion in clinical supervision; conceptual mapping in research, supervision, and clinical work. *Unit head:* Dr. Shannan Shiderly, Program Director, 724-847-6649, Fax: 724-847-6101, E-mail: slshider@geneva.edu. *Application contact:* Marina Frazier, Graduate Program Manager, 724-847-6697, E-mail: counseling@geneva.edu.
Website: http://www.geneva.edu/page/grad_counseling

George Mason University, College of Humanities and Social Sciences, Department of Psychology, Fairfax, VA 22030. Offers applied developmental psychology (MA, PhD); clinical psychology (PhD); cognitive and behavioral neuroscience (MA, PhD); cognitive neuroscience (Certificate); human factors/applied cognition (MA, PhD, Certificate), including transportation human factors (Certificate), usability (Certificate); industrial/organizational psychology (MA, PhD). *Accreditation:* APA. *Faculty:* 41 full-time (20 women), 5 part-time/adjunct (all women). *Students:* 152 full-time (101 women), 56 part-time (39 women); includes 47 minority (15 Black or African American, non-Hispanic/Latino; 13 Asian, non-Hispanic/Latino; 13 Hispanic/Latino; 1 Native Hawaiian or other Pacific Islander, non-Hispanic/Latino; 5 Two or more races, non-Hispanic/Latino), 12 international. Average age 27. 719 applicants, 19% accepted, 61 enrolled. In 2017, 55 master's, 18 doctorates, 8 other advanced degrees awarded. *Degree requirements:* For master's, comprehensive exam, thesis or practicum research; for doctorate, comprehensive exam, thesis/dissertation, 2nd-year project. *Entrance requirements:* For master's, GRE, 2 official transcripts; goals statement; 15 undergraduate credits in concentration for which the applicant is applying; for doctorate, GRE, 3 letters of recommendation; resume; goals statement; minimum GPA of 3.0 overall for last 60 undergraduate credits, 3.25 in psychology courses; 15 undergraduate credits in concentration for which the applicant is applying; 2 official transcripts; for Certificate, GRE, 2 official transcripts; expanded goals statement; 3 letters of recommendation. Additional exam requirements/recommendations for international students: Required—TOEFL (minimum score 575 paper-based; 88 iBT), IELTS (minimum score 6.5), PTE (minimum score 59). Application fee: $75 ($80 for international students). Electronic applications accepted. *Expenses:* Tuition, state resident: full-time $11,228; part-time $459.50 per credit. Tuition, nonresident: full-time $30,932; part-time $1280.50 per credit. *Required fees:* $3252; $135.50 per credit. Part-time tuition and fees vary according to course load and program. *Financial support:* In 2017–18, 110 students received support, including 6 fellowships (averaging $4,829 per year), 52 research assistantships with tuition reimbursements available (averaging $10,933 per year), 70 teaching assistantships with tuition reimbursements available (averaging $7,703 per year); career-related internships or fieldwork, Federal Work-Study, scholarships/grants, tuition waivers (partial), unspecified assistantships, and health care benefits (for full-time research or teaching assistantship recipients) also available. Support available to part-time students. Financial award application deadline: 3/1; financial award applicants required to submit FAFSA. *Faculty research:* Applied developmental psychology, biopsychology, clinical psychology, human factors/applied cognition psychology, industrial/organizational psychology, school psychology. *Total annual research expenditures:* $2.6 million. *Unit head:* Reeshad Dalal, Department Chair, 703-993-9487, Fax: 703-993-1359, E-mail: rdalal@gmu.edu. *Application contact:* Michael Hock, Graduate Program Coordinator, 703-993-1548, Fax: 703-993-1359, E-mail: mhock2@gmu.edu.
Website: http://psychology.gmu.edu

Georgetown University, Graduate School of Arts and Sciences, Department of Psychology, Washington, DC 20057. Offers human development and public policy (PhD); lifespan cognitive neuroscience (PhD); PhD/MPP. PhD/MPP offered jointly with McCourt School of Public Policy. *Faculty:* 13 full-time (9 women). *Students:* 17 full-time (11 women), 3 international. 105 applicants, 5 enrolled. *Degree requirements:* For doctorate, thesis/dissertation, area paper. *Entrance requirements:* For doctorate, GRE General Test, GRE Subject Test. Additional exam requirements/recommendations for international students: Required—TOEFL. *Application deadline:* For fall admission, 12/1 for domestic and international students. Application fee: $50 ($55 for international students). Electronic applications accepted. *Financial support:* In 2017–18, 16 students received support, including 16 teaching assistantships with full tuition reimbursements available (averaging $28,000 per year); research assistantships also available. Financial award application deadline: 2/1; financial award applicants required to submit FAFSA. *Unit head:* Dr. Chandan Vaidya, Chair, 202-687-4274, Fax: 202-687-6050, E-mail: cjv2@georgetown.edu. *Application contact:* Graduate School Admissions Office, 202-687-5568, E-mail: gradmail@georgetown.edu.
Website: https://psychology.georgetown.edu

The George Washington University, Columbian College of Arts and Sciences, Department of Psychology, Washington, DC 20052. Offers applied social psychology (PhD); clinical psychology (PhD); cognitive neuroscience (PhD). *Accreditation:* APA. *Program availability:* Part-time, evening/weekend. *Faculty:* 26 full-time (15 women), 10 part-time/adjunct (7 women). *Students:* 41 full-time (27 women), 25 part-time (17 women); includes 24 minority (10 Black or African American, non-Hispanic/Latino; 8 Asian, non-Hispanic/Latino; 4 Hispanic/Latino; 2 Two or more races, non-Hispanic/Latino), 6 international. Average age 28. 452 applicants, 35% accepted, 87 enrolled. In 2017, 10 doctorates awarded. *Degree requirements:* For doctorate, thesis/dissertation or alternative, general exam. *Entrance requirements:* For doctorate, GRE General Test, minimum GPA of 3.0. Additional exam requirements/recommendations for international students: Required—TOEFL (minimum score 550 paper-based; 80 iBT). *Application deadline:* For fall admission, 1/15 for domestic and international students. Application fee: $75. *Expenses: Tuition:* Full-time $28,800; part-time $1655 per credit hour. *Required fees:* $45; $2.75 per credit hour. *Financial support:* In 2017–18, 62 students received support. Fellowships with tuition reimbursements available, teaching assistantships with tuition reimbursements available, career-related internships or fieldwork, Federal Work-Study, and tuition waivers available. *Unit head:* Dr. Carol Sigelman, Chair, 202-994-8422, E-mail: carol@gwu.edu. *Application contact:* Information Contact, 202-994-6320, Fax: 202-994-1602, E-mail: psych@gwu.edu.
Website: http://psychology.columbian.gwu.edu/

The George Washington University, Columbian College of Arts and Sciences, Program in Professional Psychology, Washington, DC 20052. Offers MA, Psy D, Graduate Certificate. *Accreditation:* APA. *Faculty:* 13 full-time (5 women), 7 part-time/adjunct (5 women). *Students:* 127 full-time (110 women), 116 part-time (91 women); includes 60 minority (17 Black or African American, non-Hispanic/Latino; 10 Asian, non-Hispanic/Latino; 24 Hispanic/Latino; 9 Two or more races, non-Hispanic/Latino), 8 international. Average age 28. 452 applicants, 35% accepted, 87 enrolled. In 2017, 77 master's, 24 doctorates, 11 other advanced degrees awarded. *Entrance requirements:* For doctorate, GRE General Test, interview, minimum GPA of 3.0. Additional exam requirements/recommendations for international students: Required—TOEFL (minimum score 550 paper-based; 80 iBT). *Application deadline:* For fall admission, 12/1 priority date for domestic students. Applications are processed on a rolling basis. Application fee: $75. Electronic applications accepted. *Expenses: Tuition:* Full-time $28,800; part-time $1655 per credit hour. *Required fees:* $45; $2.75 per credit hour. *Financial support:* Fellowships with partial tuition reimbursements available. *Unit head:* Dr. Loring Ingraham, Director, 202-994-4929, Fax: 202-496-6263, E-mail: ingraham@gwu.edu. *Application contact:* 202-994-4929, Fax: 202-994-4800, E-mail: psyd@gwu.edu.
Website: http://psyd.columbian.gwu.edu/

Georgia Institute of Technology, Graduate Studies, College of Sciences, School of Psychology, Atlanta, GA 30332-0001. Offers MS, PhD. *Program availability:* Part-time. Terminal master's awarded for partial completion of doctoral program. *Degree requirements:* For master's, thesis; for doctorate, thesis/dissertation. *Entrance requirements:* For master's and doctorate, GRE General Test, GRE Subject Test. Additional exam requirements/recommendations for international students: Required—TOEFL (minimum score 550 paper-based; 79 iBT). Electronic applications accepted. *Faculty research:* Experimental, industrial-organizational, and engineering psychology; cognitive aging and processes; leadership; human factors.

Georgia Southern University, Jack N. Averitt College of Graduate Studies, College of Liberal Arts and Social Sciences, Program in Psychology, Statesboro, GA 30460. Offers clinical psychology (Psy D); psychology (MS). *Faculty:* 19 full-time (9 women), 1 (woman) part-time/adjunct. *Students:* 51 full-time (36 women), 10 part-time (7 women); includes 15 minority (2 Black or African American, non-Hispanic/Latino; 2 Asian, non-Hispanic/Latino; 7 Hispanic/Latino; 4 Two or more races, non-Hispanic/Latino). Average age 26. 135 applicants, 23% accepted, 18 enrolled. In 2017, 24 master's, 9 doctorates awarded. Terminal master's awarded for partial completion of doctoral program. *Degree requirements:* For master's, comprehensive exam, thesis (for some programs), terminal exam; for doctorate, comprehensive exam, thesis/dissertation, clinical qualifying exam, practicum, internship. *Entrance requirements:* For master's, GRE General Test, minimum GPA of 3.0, introductory courses in psychology and statistics, letters of recommendation; for doctorate, GRE General Test; GRE Subject Test (if no undergraduate degree in psychology), minimum undergraduate GPA of 3.25; 3 letters of reference; statement of purpose. Additional exam requirements/recommendations for international students: Required—TOEFL (minimum score 550 paper-based; 80 iBT), IELTS (minimum score 6). *Application deadline:* For fall admission, 1/15 priority date for domestic students, 1/15 for international students. Application fee: $50. Electronic applications accepted. *Expenses:* Tuition, state resident: full-time $4986; part-time $3324 per year. Tuition, nonresident: full-time $21,982; part-time $15,352 per year. *Required fees:* $2092; $1802 per credit hour. $901 per semester. Tuition and fees vary according to course load, campus/location and program. *Financial support:* In 2017–18, 45 students received support, including 4 fellowships with full tuition reimbursements available (averaging $7,750 per year), 6 research assistantships with full tuition reimbursements available (averaging $7,750 per year), 17 teaching assistantships with full tuition reimbursements available (averaging $7,750 per year); career-related internships or fieldwork, Federal Work-Study, scholarships/grants, tuition waivers (full), and unspecified assistantships also available. Support available to part-time students. Financial award application deadline: 4/15; financial award applicants required to submit FAFSA. *Faculty research:* Clinical psychology, cognitive psychology, social psychology, developmental psychology, teaching and psychology, social judgment and behavior, psychology of religion. *Unit head:* Dr. Michael Nielsen, Graduate Director, 912-478-5539, Fax: 912-478-0751, E-mail: mnielsen@georgiasouthern.edu.
Website: http://class.georgiasouthern.edu/psychology/

Georgia State University, College of Arts and Sciences, Department of Psychology, Atlanta, GA 30302-3083. Offers clinical psychology (PhD); cognitive sciences (PhD); community psychology (PhD); developmental psychology (PhD); neuropsychology and behavioral neuroscience (PhD). *Accreditation:* APA. *Faculty:* 40 full-time (26 women). *Students:* 102 full-time (80 women), 4 part-time (all women); includes 26 minority (7 Black or African American, non-Hispanic/Latino; 10 Asian, non-Hispanic/Latino; 4 Hispanic/Latino; 5 Two or more races, non-Hispanic/Latino), 8 international. Average age 27. 450 applicants, 7% accepted, 16 enrolled. In 2017, 21 doctorates awarded. *Entrance requirements:* For doctorate, GRE. Additional exam requirements/recommendations for international students: Required—TOEFL (minimum score 550 paper-based; 80 iBT). *Application deadline:* For fall admission, 12/1 for domestic and international students. Application fee: $50. Electronic applications accepted. *Expenses:* Tuition, state resident: full-time $7020. Tuition, nonresident: full-time $22,518. *Required fees:* $2128. Tuition and fees vary according to degree level and program. *Financial support:* In 2017–18, fellowships with full tuition reimbursements (averaging $19,282 per year), research assistantships with full tuition reimbursements (averaging $5,173 per year), teaching assistantships with full tuition reimbursements (averaging $6,389 per year) were awarded; scholarships/grants, traineeships, health care benefits, and unspecified assistantships also available. Financial award applicants required to submit FAFSA. *Faculty research:* Clinical psychology, developmental psychology, community psychology, neuropsychology and behavioral neuroscience, cognitive sciences. *Unit head:* Dr. Lisa Armistead, Chair, 404-413-6205, Fax: 404-413-6207, E-mail: lparmistead@gsu.edu. *Application contact:* Dr. Lindsey Cohen, Director of Graduate Studies, 404-413-6263, Fax: 404-413-6207, E-mail: llcohen@gsu.edu.

Goddard College, Graduate Division, Master of Arts in Psychology Program, Plainfield, VT 05667-9432. Offers expressive arts therapy (MA); psychology (MA); sexual orientation (MA). *Program availability:* Part-time, online learning. *Degree requirements:* For master's, thesis or alternative, clinical internship. *Entrance requirements:* For master's, eight specific undergraduate prerequisite courses taken within previous five years (or preparatory semester at Goddard), statement of purpose, 3 letters of recommendation, interview. Electronic applications accepted.

Golden Gate University, Ageno School of Business, San Francisco, CA 94105-2968. Offers accounting (MBA); adaptive leadership (MBA); advanced financial planning (MS); business administration (EMBA, MBA, DBA); business analytics (MBA, MS); entrepreneurship (MBA); finance (MBA, MS, Certificate); financial life planning (Certificate); financial planning (MS, Certificate); global supply chain management (MBA, Certificate); human resource management (MBA, MS, Certificate); information technology management (MBA, MS, Certificate); international business (MBA); marketing (MBA, MS, Certificate); project management (MBA, MS, Certificate); psychology (MA, Certificate); public administration (EMPA, MBA); public administration leadership (Certificate); JD/MBA. *Program availability:* Part-time, evening/weekend. *Faculty:* 17 full-time (7 women), 280 part-time/adjunct (95 women). *Students:* 309 full-

time (147 women), 527 part-time (266 women); includes 286 minority (56 Black or African American, non-Hispanic/Latino; 1 American Indian or Alaska Native, non-Hispanic/Latino; 131 Asian, non-Hispanic/Latino; 83 Hispanic/Latino; 4 Native Hawaiian or other Pacific Islander, non-Hispanic/Latino; 11 Two or more races, non-Hispanic/Latino), 209 international. Average age 35. 549 applicants, 66% accepted, 185 enrolled. *Degree requirements:* For doctorate, thesis/dissertation, qualifying examination. *Entrance requirements:* For master's, GMAT (for MBA), minimum GPA of 2.5 (MS). Additional exam requirements/recommendations for international students: Required—TOEFL (minimum score 550 paper-based; 79 iBT). *Application deadline:* For fall admission, 5/15 for domestic and international students; for winter admission, 1/15 for domestic and international students; for spring admission, 9/15 for domestic and international students. Applications are processed on a rolling basis. Application fee: $65 ($105 for international students). Electronic applications accepted. *Expenses:* $3,150 per 3-unit course. *Financial support:* Career-related internships or fieldwork, Federal Work-Study, institutionally sponsored loans, and scholarships/grants available. Support available to part-time students. Financial award applicants required to submit FAFSA. *Unit head:* Marianne Koch, Associate Dean, 415-442-6542, Fax: 415-442-6579, E-mail: mkoch@ggu.edu. *Application contact:* Angela Melero, Enrollment Services, 415-442-7800, Fax: 415-442-7807, E-mail: info@ggu.edu.
Website: http://www.ggu.edu/programs/business-and-management

Governors State University, College of Education, Program in Psychology, University Park, IL 60484. Offers MA. *Program availability:* Part-time. *Faculty:* 28 full-time (21 women), 29 part-time/adjunct (23 women). *Students:* 27 full-time (24 women), 46 part-time (40 women); includes 35 minority (23 Black or African American, non-Hispanic/Latino; 10 Hispanic/Latino; 2 Two or more races, non-Hispanic/Latino), 2 international. Average age 33. 67 applicants, 33% accepted, 19 enrolled. In 2017, 14 master's awarded. *Application deadline:* For fall admission, 4/1 for domestic students. Applications are processed on a rolling basis. Application fee: $50. Electronic applications accepted. *Expenses:* Contact institution. *Financial support:* Application deadline: 5/1; applicants required to submit FAFSA. *Unit head:* Patricia Robey, Interim Chair, Division of Psychology and Counseling, 708-534-5000 Ext. 4975, E-mail: sdermer@govst.edu.

The Graduate Center, City University of New York, Graduate Studies, Program in Psychology, New York, NY 10016-4039. Offers basic applied neurocognition (PhD); biopsychology (PhD); clinical psychology (PhD); developmental psychology (PhD); environmental psychology (PhD); experimental psychology (PhD); industrial psychology (PhD); learning processes (PhD); neuropsychology (PhD); psychology (PhD); social personality (PhD). *Faculty:* 119 full-time (40 women). *Students:* 428 full-time (308 women); includes 118 minority (31 Black or African American, non-Hispanic/Latino; 31 Asian, non-Hispanic/Latino; 47 Hispanic/Latino; 1 Native Hawaiian or other Pacific Islander, non-Hispanic/Latino; 8 Two or more races, non-Hispanic/Latino), 53 international. Average age 33. 795 applicants, 12% accepted, 56 enrolled. In 2017, 46 doctorates awarded. *Degree requirements:* For doctorate, one foreign language, thesis/dissertation. *Entrance requirements:* For doctorate, GRE General Test. Additional exam requirements/recommendations for international students: Required—TOEFL. *Application deadline:* For fall admission, 12/1 priority date for domestic students. Application fee: $125. Electronic applications accepted. *Financial support:* In 2017–18, 371 students received support, including 340 fellowships, 34 research assistantships, 33 teaching assistantships; career-related internships or fieldwork, Federal Work-Study, institutionally sponsored loans, and tuition waivers (full and partial) also available. Financial award application deadline: 2/1; financial award applicants required to submit FAFSA. *Unit head:* Richard Bodnar, Executive Officer, 212-817-8706, Fax: 212-817-1533, E-mail: rbodnar@gc.cuny.edu. *Application contact:* Les Gribben, Director of Admissions, 212-817-7470, Fax: 212-817-1624, E-mail: lgribben@gc.cuny.edu.

Grand Canyon University, College of Doctoral Studies, Phoenix, AZ 85017-1097. Offers data analytics (DBA); general psychology (PhD), including cognition and instruction, industrial and organizational psychology, integrating technology, learning, and psychology, performance psychology; management (DBA); marketing (DBA); organizational leadership (Ed D), including behavioral health, Christian ministry, health care administration, organizational development. *Degree requirements:* For doctorate, comprehensive exam, thesis/dissertation. *Entrance requirements:* For doctorate, minimum GPA of 3.4 on earned advanced degree from regionally-accredited institution; transcripts; goals statement.

Hampton University, School of Liberal Arts and Education, Program in Psychology, Hampton, VA 23668. Offers marriage and family studies (MS); psychology (MS). *Program availability:* Part-time. *Students:* 1 (woman) full-time, 6 part-time (5 women); all minorities (all Black or African American, non-Hispanic/Latino). Average age 24. 13 applicants, 8% accepted. *Degree requirements:* For master's, thesis. *Entrance requirements:* For master's, GRE. Additional exam requirements/recommendations for international students: Required—TOEFL (minimum score 525 paper-based) or IELTS (6.5). *Application deadline:* For fall admission, 6/1 priority date for domestic students, 4/1 priority date for international students; for spring admission, 11/1 priority date for domestic students, 9/1 priority date for international students; for summer admission, 4/1 priority date for domestic and international students. Application fee: $35. Electronic applications accepted. *Expenses:* Contact institution. *Financial support:* Unspecified assistantships available. Financial award application deadline: 6/30; financial award applicants required to submit FAFSA. *Faculty research:* Marriage and family studies, violence prevention, racial identity and race relations, learning styles, psychosocial factors influencing health. *Unit head:* Dr. Tamara Williams, Interim Chairperson, 757-727-5301.

Hardin-Simmons University, Graduate School, Cynthia Ann Parker College of Liberal Arts, Department of Psychology, Abilene, TX 79698-0001. Offers clinical counseling and marriage and family therapy (MA). *Program availability:* Part-time. *Faculty:* 9 full-time (7 women). *Students:* 25 full-time (19 women), 2 part-time (both women); includes 3 minority (1 Black or African American, non-Hispanic/Latino; 1 Hispanic/Latino; 1 Two or more races, non-Hispanic/Latino), 1 international. Average age 31. 20 applicants, 85% accepted, 15 enrolled. In 2017, 11 master's awarded. *Degree requirements:* For master's, comprehensive exam, clinical experience, project. *Entrance requirements:* For master's, 21 semester hours of course work in psychology (18 in upper-division classes); minimum undergraduate GPA of 3.0 in major, 2.7 overall; writing sample; letters of recommendation. Additional exam requirements/recommendations for international students: Required—TOEFL (minimum score 550 paper-based; 79 iBT). *Application deadline:* For fall admission, 8/15 priority date for domestic students, 4/1 for international students; for spring admission, 1/5 priority date for domestic students, 9/1 for international students. Applications are processed on a rolling basis. Application fee: $50 ($150 for international students). Electronic applications accepted. *Expenses: Tuition:* Full-time $13,500; part-time $750 per semester hour. *Required fees:* $220 per term. One-time fee: $50. Tuition and fees vary according to course load, campus/location and program. *Financial support:* In 2017–18, 21 students received support, including 17 fellowships (averaging $1,047 per year); career-related internships or fieldwork and scholarships/grants also available. Support available to part-time students. Financial award application deadline: 6/30; financial award applicants required to submit FAFSA. *Faculty research:* Spirituality in marriage, intimacy and sexuality in marriage, sex education in the church, role of faith in marital satisfaction, family stress management. *Unit head:* Dr. Sherry Rosenblad, Program Director, 325-671-2271, Fax: 325-670-1458, E-mail: sherry.rosenblad@hsutx.edu. *Application contact:* Dr. Nancy Kucinski, Dean of Graduate Studies, 325-670-1298, Fax: 325-670-1564, E-mail: gradoff@hsutx.edu.
Website: http://www.hsutx.edu/academics/cap/psychology/

Harvard University, Graduate School of Arts and Sciences, Department of Psychology, Cambridge, MA 02138. Offers psychology (PhD), including behavior and decision analysis, cognition, developmental psychology, experimental psychology, personality, psychobiology, psychopathology; social psychology (PhD). *Accreditation:* APA. *Degree requirements:* For doctorate, thesis/dissertation, general exams. *Entrance requirements:* For doctorate, GRE General Test. Additional exam requirements/recommendations for international students: Required—TOEFL.

Hofstra University, College of Liberal Arts and Sciences, Programs in Psychology, Hempstead, NY 11549. Offers applied organizational psychology (PhD); clinical psychology (PhD); industrial/organizational psychology (MA); school-community psychology (Psy D). *Accreditation:* APA. *Program availability:* Part-time, evening/weekend. *Students:* 199 full-time (130 women), 24 part-time (20 women); includes 44 minority (5 Black or African American, non-Hispanic/Latino; 12 Asian, non-Hispanic/Latino; 25 Hispanic/Latino; 1 Native Hawaiian or other Pacific Islander, non-Hispanic/Latino; 1 Two or more races, non-Hispanic/Latino), 19 international. Average age 27. 314 applicants, 45% accepted, 60 enrolled. In 2017, 47 master's, 25 doctorates awarded. *Degree requirements:* For master's, comprehensive exam, thesis optional, internship, minimum GPA of 3.0; for doctorate, comprehensive exam, thesis/dissertation, 1st year qualifying examination, 2nd year research project, successful practicum/externship placements, written presentation and successful oral defense of dissertation, completion of full-time internship. *Entrance requirements:* For master's, GRE General Test, minimum GPA of 3.0, essay, interview; for doctorate, GRE General Test, GRE Subject Test (psychology), 3 letters of recommendation, interview, essay, curriculum vitae. Additional exam requirements/recommendations for international students: Required—TOEFL (minimum score 550 paper-based; 80 iBT). *Application deadline:* For fall admission, 12/31 for domestic and international students. Application fee: $75. Electronic applications accepted. *Expenses: Tuition:* Full-time $1292. *Required fees:* $970. Tuition and fees vary according to program. *Financial support:* In 2017–18, 131 students received support, including 126 fellowships with full and partial tuition reimbursements available (averaging $7,840 per year), 4 research assistantships with full and partial tuition reimbursements available (averaging $5,974 per year); career-related internships or fieldwork, Federal Work-Study, institutionally sponsored loans, scholarships/grants, traineeships, tuition waivers (full and partial), and unspecified assistantships also available. Support available to part-time students. Financial award applicants required to submit FAFSA. *Faculty research:* Coping with job stress; schizophrenia; positive clinical psychology; treatments (including virtual reality based) for phobias, trauma, and PTSD; scientific reasoning in children and adults. *Unit head:* Dr. Craig Johnson, Chairperson, 516-463-5636, E-mail: craig.a.johnson@hofstra.edu. *Application contact:* Sunil Samuel, Assistant Vice President of Admissions, 516-463-4723, Fax: 516-463-4664, E-mail: graduateadmission@hofstra.edu.
Website: http://www.hofstra.edu/hclas

Hood College, Graduate School, Programs in Human Behavior, Frederick, MD 21701-8575. Offers interdisciplinary studies in human behavior (MA), including psychology; thanatology (Certificate). *Program availability:* Part-time, evening/weekend. *Faculty:* 1 (woman) full-time, 2 part-time/adjunct (0 women). *Students:* 9 full-time (6 women), 22 part-time (16 women); includes 4 minority (2 Black or African American, non-Hispanic/Latino; 2 Two or more races, non-Hispanic/Latino), 2 international. Average age 37. 7 applicants, 100% accepted, 2 enrolled. In 2017, 9 master's, 11 other advanced degrees awarded. *Degree requirements:* For master's, comprehensive exam, thesis optional, capstone/research project. *Entrance requirements:* For master's, minimum GPA of 2.75, essay; for Certificate, minimum GPA of 2.75, essay, resume. Additional exam requirements/recommendations for international students: Required—TOEFL (minimum score 575 paper-based; 89 iBT), IELTS (minimum score 6.5). *Application deadline:* For fall admission, 8/15 priority date for domestic students, 8/5 for international students; for spring admission, 12/1 priority date for domestic students, 12/1 for international students; for summer admission, 5/1 priority date for domestic students, 4/15 for international students. Applications are processed on a rolling basis. Application fee: $35. Electronic applications accepted. *Expenses:* $465 per credit hour plus $110 comprehensive fee per semester. *Financial support:* Research assistantships with full tuition reimbursements, tuition waivers (partial), and unspecified assistantships available. Financial award applicants required to submit FAFSA. *Faculty research:* Mind-body medicine and multicultural healing, the New Orleans jazz funeral, death practices in African-American culture, bereavement theories and gender differences, Piaget's theory of cognitive development as a formal mathematical model. *Unit head:* Dr. April M. Boulton, Dean of the Graduate School, 301-696-3600, E-mail: gofurther@hood.edu. *Application contact:* Jan Marcus, Assistant Director of Graduate Admissions, 301-696-3600, E-mail: gofurther@hood.edu.
Website: http://www.hood.edu/graduate

Houston Baptist University, College of Education and Behavioral Sciences, Program in Psychology, Houston, TX 77074-3298. Offers school psychology (MAP). *Program availability:* Part-time, evening/weekend. *Students:* 47 full-time (42 women), 53 part-time (46 women); includes 70 minority (36 Black or African American, non-Hispanic/Latino; 10 Asian, non-Hispanic/Latino; 23 Hispanic/Latino; 1 Two or more races, non-Hispanic/Latino), 4 international. Average age 32. 129 applicants, 25% accepted, 16 enrolled. In 2017, 23 master's awarded. *Degree requirements:* For master's, comprehensive exam, thesis. *Entrance requirements:* For master's, GRE (waived with a cumulative GPA of 3.0 or higher), minimum GPA of 2.5, two recommendations, resume, bachelor's degree conferred transcript. Additional exam requirements/recommendations for international students: Required—TOEFL (minimum score 80 iBT), IELTS (minimum score 6.5). *Application deadline:* For fall admission, 8/1 for domestic students, 6/1 for international students; for spring admission, 1/1 for domestic students, 11/1 for international students; for summer admission, 5/1 for domestic students, 3/1 for international students. Applications are processed on a rolling basis. Application fee: $0 ($100 for international students). Electronic applications accepted. Application fee is waived when completed online. *Expenses:* $20,350 tuition; $4,500 fees (general, technology and parking). *Financial support:* In 2017–18, 11 students received support. Federal Work-Study and scholarships/grants available. Support available to part-time students. Financial award application deadline: 4/1; financial award applicants required to submit FAFSA. *Faculty research:* Drug and alcohol abuse in relation to delinquency, mental health and school factors, chronic stress, coping strategies. *Unit head:* Dr. Renata Nero, Chair, 281-649-3171, Fax: 281-649-3361, E-mail: rnero@hbu.edu. *Application contact:* Victoria Humphreys, Administrative Assistant to the Dean, 281-649-3131, E-mail: vhumphreys@hbu.edu.
Website: http://www.hbu.edu/MAP

Howard University, Graduate School, Department of Psychology, Washington, DC 20059-0002. Offers clinical psychology (PhD); developmental psychology (PhD); experimental psychology (PhD); neuropsychology (PhD); personality psychology (PhD);

psychology (MS); social psychology (PhD). *Accreditation:* APA (one or more programs are accredited). *Program availability:* Part-time. *Degree requirements:* For master's, thesis; for doctorate, comprehensive exam, thesis/dissertation, qualifying exam. *Entrance requirements:* For master's, GRE General Test, minimum GPA of 2.5, bachelor's degree in psychology or related field; for doctorate, GRE General Test, minimum GPA of 3.0. *Faculty research:* Personality and psychophysiology, educational and social development of African-American children, child and adult psychopathology.

Humboldt State University, Academic Programs, College of Professional Studies, Department of Psychology, Arcata, CA 95521-8299. Offers psychology (MA), including biological psychology, counseling, developmental psychopathology, school psychology, social and environmental psychology. *Degree requirements:* For master's, thesis. *Entrance requirements:* For master's, appropriate bachelor's degree, minimum GPA of 2.5. Additional exam requirements/recommendations for international students: Required—TOEFL (minimum score 500 paper-based). *Faculty research:* School psychology, counseling, eating disorders, mood induction, depression.

Hunter College of the City University of New York, Graduate School, School of Arts and Sciences, Department of Psychology, New York, NY 10065-5085. Offers animal behavior and conservation (MA, Certificate); general psychology (MA). *Program availability:* Part-time, evening/weekend. *Degree requirements:* For master's, comprehensive exam, thesis. *Entrance requirements:* For master's, GRE General Test, minimum 12 credits of course work in psychology, including statistics and experimental psychology; 2 letters of recommendation. Additional exam requirements/recommendations for international students: Required—TOEFL. *Faculty research:* Personality, cognitive and linguistic development, hormonal and neural control of behavior, gender and culture, social cognition of health and attitudes.

Idaho State University, Office of Graduate Studies, College of Arts and Letters, Department of Psychology, Pocatello, ID 83209-8112. Offers clinical psychology (PhD); experimental psychology (PhD). *Accreditation:* APA. *Program availability:* Part-time. *Degree requirements:* For doctorate, comprehensive exam, thesis/dissertation, 1 year full-time clinical internship. *Entrance requirements:* For doctorate, GRE General Test, GRE Subject Test, MS in psychology, recommendation from Clinical Admissions Committee. Additional exam requirements/recommendations for international students: Required—TOEFL (minimum score 550 paper-based; 80 iBT). Electronic applications accepted. *Faculty research:* Substance abuse, sexual decision making, trauma, behavioral pharmacology, developmental psychopathology, working memory and strategies, goal setting, person perception, developmental psychobiology, parent-child interactions.

Illinois Institute of Technology, Graduate College, Lewis College of Human Sciences, Department of Psychology, Chicago, IL 60616. Offers clinical psychology (PhD); industrial and organizational psychology (PhD); personnel and human resource development (MS); rehabilitation and mental health counseling (MS); rehabilitation counseling education (PhD). *Accreditation:* APA (one or more programs are accredited); CORE. *Program availability:* Part-time, evening/weekend. Terminal master's awarded for partial completion of doctoral program. *Degree requirements:* For master's, thesis (for some programs); for doctorate, comprehensive exam, thesis/dissertation, minimum of 107 credit hours, 1-year full-time internship. *Entrance requirements:* For master's, GRE General Test (minimum score 298 Quantitative and Verbal, 3.0 Analytical Writing), minimum GPA of 3.0; 3 letters of recommendation; bachelor's degree from accredited institution (for personnel and human resource development); for doctorate, GRE General Test (minimum score 298 Quantitative and Verbal, 3.0 Analytical Writing), bachelor's or master's degree from accredited institution, recommendations. Additional exam requirements/recommendations for international students: Required—TOEFL (minimum score 550 paper-based; 80 iBT). Electronic applications accepted. *Faculty research:* Clinical psychology, rehabilitation and mental health counseling, industrial organizational psychology.

Illinois State University, Graduate School, College of Arts and Sciences, Department of Psychology, Normal, IL 61790. Offers psychology (MA, MS), including clinical-counseling psychology, cognitive and behavioral sciences, developmental psychology, industrial/organizational-social psychology; school psychology (PhD, SSP). *Accreditation:* APA. *Degree requirements:* For master's, thesis or alternative; for doctorate, variable foreign language requirement, thesis/dissertation, 2 terms of residency, internship, practicum. *Entrance requirements:* For master's, GRE General Test, GRE Subject Test, minimum GPA of 3.0 in last 60 hours of course work; for doctorate, GRE General Test. *Faculty research:* Comprehensive evaluation system for the central region professional development grant, Illinois school psychology internship consortium, for children's sake.

Immaculata University, College of Graduate Studies, Department of Psychology, Immaculata, PA 19345. Offers clinical mental health counseling (MA); clinical psychology (Psy D); forensic psychology (Graduate Certificate); integrative psychotherapy (Graduate Certificate); neuropsychology (Graduate Certificate); psychodynamic psychotherapy (Graduate Certificate); psychological testing (Graduate Certificate); school counseling (MA, Graduate Certificate); school psychology (MA). *Accreditation:* APA. *Program availability:* Part-time, evening/weekend. Terminal master's awarded for partial completion of doctoral program. *Degree requirements:* For master's, comprehensive exam, thesis optional; for doctorate, comprehensive exam, thesis/dissertation. *Entrance requirements:* For master's, GRE General Test or MAT, minimum GPA of 3.0; for doctorate, GRE General Test or MAT, minimum GPA of 3.5. Additional exam requirements/recommendations for international students: Required—TOEFL, IELTS. Electronic applications accepted. *Faculty research:* Supervision ethics, psychology of teaching, gender.

Indiana State University, College of Graduate and Professional Studies, College of Arts and Sciences, Department of Psychology, Terre Haute, IN 47809. Offers clinical psychology (Psy D); general psychology (MA, MS). *Accreditation:* APA (one or more programs are accredited). Terminal master's awarded for partial completion of doctoral program. *Degree requirements:* For master's, thesis (for some programs); for doctorate, comprehensive exam, thesis/dissertation, internship, professional research project. *Entrance requirements:* For master's, GRE General Test, 12 semester hours of course work in psychology, minimum GPA of 2.75; for doctorate, GRE General Test, minimum GPA of 3.0. Additional exam requirements/recommendations for international students: Required—TOEFL (minimum score 550 paper-based). Electronic applications accepted.

Indiana Tech, Program in Psychology, Fort Wayne, IN 46803-1297. Offers MS.

Indiana University Bloomington, University Graduate School, College of Arts and Sciences, Department of Psychological and Brain Sciences, Bloomington, IN 47405. Offers clinical science (PhD); cognitive neuroscience (PhD); cognitive psychology (PhD); developmental psychology (PhD); methods of behavior (PhD); molecular systems neuroscience (PhD); social psychology (PhD). *Accreditation:* APA. *Degree requirements:* For doctorate, comprehensive exam, 90 credit hours, 2 advanced statistics/methods courses, 2 written research projects, the teaching of psychology course, teaching 1 semester of undergraduate methods course, qualifying examination, minor or a second major, first-year research seminar course, dissertation defense, written dissertation. *Entrance requirements:* For doctorate, GRE. Additional exam requirements/recommendations for international students: Required—TOEFL (minimum score 550 paper-based; 79 iBT). Electronic applications accepted. *Faculty research:* Clinical science, cognitive neuroscience, cognitive psychology, developmental psychology, mechanisms of behavior, molecular and systems neuroscience, social psychology.

Indiana University of Pennsylvania, School of Graduate Studies and Research, College of Natural Sciences and Mathematics, Department of Psychology, Indiana, PA 15705. Offers clinical psychology (Psy D); psychology (MA). *Accreditation:* APA (one or more programs are accredited). *Program availability:* Part-time. *Faculty:* 13 full-time (7 women). *Students:* 48 full-time (35 women), 20 part-time (11 women); includes 13 minority (1 Black or African American, non-Hispanic/Latino; 5 Asian, non-Hispanic/Latino; 6 Hispanic/Latino; 1 Two or more races, non-Hispanic/Latino), 3 international. Average age 26. 245 applicants, 18% accepted, 15 enrolled. In 2017, 20 master's, 15 doctorates awarded. Terminal master's awarded for partial completion of doctoral program. *Entrance requirements:* For doctorate, GRE General Test, minimum GPA of 3.0, interview, 3 letters of recommendation. Additional exam requirements/recommendations for international students: Required—TOEFL (minimum score 540 paper-based). *Application deadline:* Applications are processed on a rolling basis. Application fee: $50. Electronic applications accepted. *Expenses:* Tuition, state resident: full-time $12,000; part-time $500 per credit. Tuition, nonresident: full-time $18,000; part-time $750 per credit. *Required fees:* $4073; $165.55 per credit. $64 per term. *Financial support:* In 2017–18, 13 fellowships with full tuition reimbursements (averaging $522 per year), 45 research assistantships with tuition reimbursements (averaging $2,625 per year), 2 teaching assistantships with partial tuition reimbursements (averaging $23,305 per year) were awarded; career-related internships or fieldwork, Federal Work-Study, scholarships/grants, and unspecified assistantships also available. Support available to part-time students. Financial award application deadline: 4/15; financial award applicants required to submit FAFSA. *Unit head:* Dr. Pearl S. Berman, Chairperson, 724-357-2426, E-mail: psberman@iup.edu. *Application contact:* Dr. David LaPorte, Graduate Coordinator, 724-357-2426, E-mail: laporte@iup.edu.
Website: http://www.iup.edu/psychology

Indiana University–Purdue University Indianapolis, School of Science, Department of Psychology, Indianapolis, IN 46202-3275. Offers addiction neuroscience (PhD); applied social and organizational psychology (PhD); clinical psychology (PhD); industrial/organizational psychology (MS). *Accreditation:* APA (one or more programs are accredited). Terminal master's awarded for partial completion of doctoral program. *Degree requirements:* For master's, thesis; for doctorate, thesis/dissertation. *Entrance requirements:* For master's, GRE General Test, minimum undergraduate GPA of 3.0; for doctorate, GRE General Test, GRE Subject Test (clinical psychology), minimum undergraduate GPA of 3.2. Additional exam requirements/recommendations for international students: Required—TOEFL (minimum score 567 paper-based; 86 iBT), IELTS (minimum score 6.5). Electronic applications accepted. *Faculty research:* Severe mental illness, health psychology, neurological research, alcoholism and psychopathology, functional activities within organizations.

Inter American University of Puerto Rico, Metropolitan Campus, Graduate Programs, Program in Psychology, San Juan, PR 00919-1293. Offers counseling psychology (MA, PhD); industrial/organizational psychology (MA, PhD); labor relations (MA); school psychology (MA, PhD). *Degree requirements:* For master's, comprehensive exam. *Entrance requirements:* For master's, GRE or EXADEP, interview. Electronic applications accepted.

Inter American University of Puerto Rico, San Germán Campus, Graduate Studies Center, Program in Psychology, San Germán, PR 00683-5008. Offers counseling psychology (MA, PhD); school psychology (MA, PhD). *Program availability:* Part-time, evening/weekend. *Degree requirements:* For master's, comprehensive exam, thesis; for doctorate, comprehensive exam, thesis/dissertation. *Entrance requirements:* For master's, GRE General Test or EXADEP, minimum GPA of 3.0; for doctorate, GRE, EXADEP or MAT, minimum GPA of 3.0.

Iona College, School of Arts and Science, Department of Psychology, New Rochelle, NY 10801-1890. Offers general-experimental psychology (MA); human resources (Certificate); industrial-organizational psychology (MA); mental health counseling (MA); organizational behavior (Certificate); psychology (MA); school psychology (MA). *Program availability:* Part-time. *Faculty:* 9 full-time (5 women), 7 part-time/adjunct (5 women). *Students:* 75 full-time (55 women), 37 part-time (24 women); includes 46 minority (9 Black or African American, non-Hispanic/Latino; 2 Asian, non-Hispanic/Latino; 34 Hispanic/Latino; 1 Two or more races, non-Hispanic/Latino), 1 international. Average age 25. 88 applicants, 88% accepted, 40 enrolled. In 2017, 23 master's awarded. *Degree requirements:* For master's, thesis (for some programs), literature review (for some programs). *Entrance requirements:* For master's, BA in psychology including 3 credits each in psychology statistics and experimental research methods, or 9 credits in psychology including 3 credits each in psychology statistics, psychology research methods and upper-level coursework. Additional exam requirements/recommendations for international students: Required—TOEFL (minimum score 550 paper-based), IELTS (minimum score 6.5). *Application deadline:* For fall admission, 8/15 for domestic students, 5/1 for international students; for spring admission, 1/15 for domestic students, 9/1 for international students. Applications are processed on a rolling basis. Electronic applications accepted. Tuition and fees vary according to program. *Financial support:* In 2017–18, 27 students received support. Research assistantships with partial tuition reimbursements available, tuition waivers (partial), and unspecified assistantships available. Support available to part-time students. Financial award application deadline: 4/15; financial award applicants required to submit FAFSA. *Faculty research:* Non-suicidal self-injury, trauma response, performance appraisal and evaluation, diversity infusion, assessment and treatment of sexual offenders. *Unit head:* Patricia Oswald, PhD, Chair, 914-633-2374, E-mail: poswald@iona.edu. *Application contact:* Katelyn Brunck, Assistant Director, Graduate Admissions, 914-633-2451, Fax: 914-633-2277, E-mail: kbrunck@iona.edu.
Website: http://www.iona.edu/Academics/School-of-Arts-Science/Departments/Psychology/Graduate-Programs.aspx

Iowa State University of Science and Technology, Department of Psychology, Ames, IA 50011. Offers cognitive psychology (PhD); counseling psychology (PhD); psychology (MS, PhD); social psychology (PhD). *Accreditation:* APA (one or more programs are accredited). *Entrance requirements:* For doctorate, GRE General Test, GRE Subject Test (psychology), 3 letters of recommendation. Additional exam requirements/recommendations for international students: Required—TOEFL (minimum score 560 paper-based; 79 iBT), IELTS (minimum score 6.5). Electronic applications accepted. *Faculty research:* Counseling psychology, cognitive psychology, social psychology, health psychology, psychology and public policy.

Jackson State University, Graduate School, College of Liberal Arts, Department of Psychology, Jackson, MS 39217. Offers clinical psychology (PhD). *Accreditation:* APA. *Degree requirements:* For doctorate, comprehensive exam, thesis/dissertation. *Entrance requirements:* For doctorate, MAT, GRE. Additional exam requirements/recommendations for international students: Required—TOEFL (minimum score 520 paper-based; 67 iBT).

Jacksonville State University, College of Graduate Studies and Continuing Education, College of Arts and Sciences, Department of Psychology, Jacksonville, AL 36265-1602. Offers MS. *Program availability:* Part-time, evening/weekend. *Degree requirements:* For master's, comprehensive exam, thesis (for some programs). *Entrance requirements:* For master's, GRE General Test or MAT. Additional exam requirements/recommendations for international students: Required—TOEFL (minimum score 500 paper-based; 61 iBT). Electronic applications accepted.

James Madison University, The Graduate School, College of Health and Behavioral Studies, Program in Psychological Sciences, Harrisonburg, VA 22801. Offers applied research (MA); behavior analysis (MA); experimental psychology (MA); quantitative psychology (MA). *Program availability:* Part-time, evening/weekend. *Students:* 18 full-time (10 women), 2 part-time (1 woman); includes 3 minority (1 American Indian or Alaska Native, non-Hispanic/Latino; 1 Asian, non-Hispanic/Latino; 1 Two or more races, non-Hispanic/Latino), 1 international. Average age 30. In 2017, 9 master's awarded. Application fee: $55. Electronic applications accepted. *Expenses:* Tuition, state resident: full-time $10,512; part-time $438 per credit hour. Tuition, nonresident: full-time $28,358; part-time $1162 per credit hour. *Required fees:* $1128. *Financial support:* In 2017–18, 18 students received support, including 1 teaching assistantship with full tuition reimbursement available (averaging $9,284 per year); career-related internships or fieldwork, Federal Work-Study, and 16 assistantships (averaging $7911) also available. Financial award application deadline: 3/1; financial award applicants required to submit FAFSA. *Unit head:* Dr. Jeff S. Dyche, Graduate Program Director, 540-568-4965, E-mail: dychejs@jmu.edu. *Application contact:* Lynette D. Michael, Director of Graduate Admissions, 540-568-6131 Ext. 6395, Fax: 540-568-7860, E-mail: michaeld@jmu.edu.
Website: http://www.psyc.jmu.edu/psycsciences/

John F. Kennedy University, Graduate School of Holistic Studies, Department of Integral Studies, Program in Integral Psychology, Pleasant Hill, CA 94523-4817. Offers dream studies (Certificate); integral psychology (MA); life coaching (Certificate). *Program availability:* Part-time, evening/weekend.

John F. Kennedy University, Graduate School of Professional Psychology, Pleasant Hill, CA 94523-4817. Offers MA, Psy D, Certificate. *Accreditation:* APA. *Program availability:* Part-time, evening/weekend. *Degree requirements:* For master's, thesis or alternative. *Entrance requirements:* For master's, interview. Additional exam requirements/recommendations for international students: Required—TOEFL.

Johns Hopkins University, Zanvyl Krieger School of Arts and Sciences, Department of Psychological and Brain Sciences, Baltimore, MD 21218. Offers PhD. *Faculty:* 13 full-time (4 women), 9 part-time/adjunct (2 women). *Students:* 36 full-time (27 women). Average age 26. 122 applicants, 7% accepted, 6 enrolled. In 2017, 2 doctorates awarded. *Degree requirements:* For doctorate, thesis/dissertation, research project, teaching experience. *Entrance requirements:* For doctorate, GRE General Test. Additional exam requirements/recommendations for international students: Required—TOEFL (minimum score 600 paper-based; 100 iBT), IELTS (minimum score 7). *Application deadline:* For fall admission, 12/15 for domestic and international students. Application fee: $75. Electronic applications accepted. *Expenses:* Contact institution. *Financial support:* In 2017–18, 36 students received support, including 36 research assistantships with full tuition reimbursements available (averaging $33,333 per year); scholarships/grants, health care benefits, tuition waivers (full), and unspecified assistantships also available. Financial award application deadline: 4/15; financial award applicants required to submit FAFSA. *Faculty research:* Biopsychology, cognitive psychology, cognitive neuroscience, developmental psychology, neurobiology. *Total annual research expenditures:* $2.5 million. *Unit head:* Dr. Peter Holland, Chair, 410-516-6396, Fax: 410-516-4478, E-mail: pbs@jhu.edu. *Application contact:* Tracy Cottrell, Academic Program Coordinator, 410-516-6175, Fax: 410-516-4478, E-mail: tcottrell@jhu.edu.
Website: http://pbs.jhu.edu/

Kansas State University, Graduate School, College of Arts and Sciences, Department of Psychological Sciences, Manhattan, KS 66506. Offers MS, PhD. *Program availability:* Part-time. *Degree requirements:* For master's, thesis or alternative; for doctorate, thesis/dissertation, preliminary exam. *Entrance requirements:* For master's, GRE General Test, minimum undergraduate GPA of 3.0; for doctorate, GRE General Test, minimum GPA of 3.0. Additional exam requirements/recommendations for international students: Required—TOEFL (minimum score 600 paper-based). Electronic applications accepted. *Faculty research:* Personal and occupational health, neurological bases of drug use and abuse, measurement and reduction of prejudice, judgment and decision-making, visual perception.

Kean University, College of Liberal Arts, Program in Psychology, Union, NJ 07083. Offers human behavior and organizational psychology (MA); psychological services (MA). *Program availability:* Part-time. *Faculty:* 18 full-time (14 women). *Students:* 65 full-time (46 women), 49 part-time (34 women); includes 74 minority (26 Black or African American, non-Hispanic/Latino; 13 Asian, non-Hispanic/Latino; 31 Hispanic/Latino; 1 Native Hawaiian or other Pacific Islander, non-Hispanic/Latino; 3 Two or more races, non-Hispanic/Latino), 2 international. Average age 28. 82 applicants, 89% accepted, 48 enrolled. In 2017, 25 master's awarded. *Degree requirements:* For master's, comprehensive exam, research component, two semesters of advanced seminar. *Entrance requirements:* For master's, GRE General Test, minimum GPA of 3.0; official transcripts from all institutions attended; two letters of recommendation; professional resume/curriculum vitae; 12 credits in behavioral sciences on the undergraduate level. Additional exam requirements/recommendations for international students: Required—TOEFL (minimum score 550 paper-based; 79 iBT), IELTS (minimum score 6.5). *Application deadline:* For fall admission, 6/30 for domestic and international students; for spring admission, 12/1 for domestic and international students. Applications are processed on a rolling basis. Application fee: $75. Electronic applications accepted. *Expenses:* Tuition, state resident: full-time $13,419; part-time $653 per credit. Tuition, nonresident: full-time $18,188; part-time $801 per credit. *Required fees:* $3382; $154 per credit. Tuition and fees vary according to course level, course load, degree level and program. *Financial support:* Scholarships/grants and unspecified assistantships available. Financial award applicants required to submit FAFSA. *Unit head:* Dr. Zandra Gratz, Program Coordinator, 908-737-5881, E-mail: zgratz@kean.edu. *Application contact:* Amy Clark, Program Assistant, 908-737-7100, E-mail: gradadmissions@kean.edu.
Website: http://grad.kean.edu/masters-programs/psychological-services

Keiser University, MS in Psychology Program, Fort Lauderdale, FL 33309. Offers MS.
Website: http://www.keiseruniversity.edu/graduateschool/psychology-ms.php

Keiser University, PhD in Psychology Program, Fort Lauderdale, FL 33309. Offers PhD.
Website: http://www.keiseruniversity.edu/graduateschool/phd-psychology.php

Kent State University, College of Arts and Sciences, Department of Psychological Sciences, Kent, OH 44242-0001. Offers clinical psychology (MA, PhD), including gerontology (MA), psychological sciences (MA); experimental psychology (MA, PhD), including gerontology (MA), psychological sciences (MA). *Accreditation:* APA (one or more programs are accredited). *Program availability:* Part-time. *Faculty:* 29 full-time (15

women), 5 part-time/adjunct (2 women). *Students:* 84 full-time (66 women); includes 15 minority (8 Black or African American, non-Hispanic/Latino; 4 Asian, non-Hispanic/Latino; 2 Hispanic/Latino; 1 Two or more races, non-Hispanic/Latino), 3 international. Average age 26. 217 applicants, 10% accepted, 14 enrolled. In 2017, 10 master's, 16 doctorates awarded. Terminal master's awarded for partial completion of doctoral program. *Degree requirements:* For master's, thesis; for doctorate, comprehensive exam, thesis/dissertation. *Entrance requirements:* For master's and doctorate, GRE General Test, statement of goals and motivations, transcripts, 3 letters of recommendation, minimum junior-senior GPA of 3.0, at least one course in statistics and a broad background in psychology. Additional exam requirements/recommendations for international students: Required—TOEFL (minimum score 550 paper-based, 79 iBT), Michigan English Language Assessment Battery (minimum score 77), IELTS (minimum score 6.5) or PTE (minimum score 58). *Application deadline:* For fall admission, 12/1 for domestic and international students. Applications are processed on a rolling basis. Application fee: $45 ($70 for international students). Electronic applications accepted. *Expenses:* Tuition, state resident: full-time $11,310; part-time $515 per credit hour. Tuition, nonresident: full-time $20,396; part-time $928 per credit hour. *International tuition:* $18,544 full-time. *Financial support:* Federal Work-Study, health care benefits, and unspecified assistantships available. Financial award application deadline: 12/1. *Unit head:* Dr. Maria S. Zaragoza, Professor and Chair, 330-672-2166, E-mail: mzaragoz@kent.edu. *Application contact:* Dr. John A. Updegraff, Professor and Graduate Coordinator, 330-672-2166, E-mail: jupdegr1@kent.edu.
Website: https://www.kent.edu/psychology

Kent State University, College of Public Health, Kent, OH 44242-0001. Offers public health (MPH, PhD), including biostatistics (MPH), environmental health sciences (MPH), epidemiology, health policy and management, prevention science (PhD), social and behavioral sciences (MPH). *Accreditation:* CEPH. *Program availability:* Part-time, online learning. *Faculty:* 23 full-time (14 women), 12 part-time/adjunct (3 women). *Students:* 123 full-time (87 women), 152 part-time (120 women); includes 57 minority (37 Black or African American, non-Hispanic/Latino; 1 American Indian or Alaska Native, non-Hispanic/Latino; 8 Asian, non-Hispanic/Latino; 6 Hispanic/Latino; 5 Two or more races, non-Hispanic/Latino), 40 international. Average age 31. 176 applicants, 76% accepted, 81 enrolled. In 2017, 79 master's, 5 doctorates awarded. *Degree requirements:* For master's, comprehensive exam, 300 hours' placement at public health agency, final portfolio and presentation; for doctorate, comprehensive exam, thesis/dissertation. *Entrance requirements:* For master's, GRE, minimum GPA of 3.0, transcripts, goal statement, 3 letters of recommendation; for doctorate, GRE, minimum GPA of 3.0, personal statement, resume, interview, 3 letters of recommendation. Additional exam requirements/recommendations for international students: Required—TOEFL (minimum score 550 paper-based; 79 iBT), IELTS (minimum score 6.5), PTE (minimum score 58), Michigan English Language Assessment Battery. *Application deadline:* For fall admission, 6/15 for domestic and international students; for spring admission, 10/15 for domestic and international students; for summer admission, 3/15 for domestic and international students. Applications are processed on a rolling basis. Application fee: $45 ($70 for international students). Electronic applications accepted. *Expenses:* Tuition, state resident: full-time $11,310; part-time $515 per credit hour. Tuition, nonresident: full-time $20,396; part-time $928 per credit hour. *International tuition:* $18,544 full-time. *Financial support:* Unspecified assistantships available. *Unit head:* Dr. Sonia Alemagno, Dean and Professor of Health Policy and Management, 330-672-6500, E-mail: salemagn@kent.edu. *Application contact:* Dr. Mark A. James, Professor/Chair/Graduate Advisor, 330-672-6506, E-mail: mjames22@kent.edu.
Website: http://www.kent.edu/publichealth/

Kentucky State University, College of Arts and Sciences, Frankfort, KY 40601. Offers interdisciplinary behavioral sciences (MA). *Program availability:* Part-time, evening/weekend. *Faculty:* 3 full-time (2 women). *Students:* 6 full-time (3 women), 3 part-time (1 woman); includes 7 minority (all Black or African American, non-Hispanic/Latino). Average age 31. 8 applicants, 75% accepted, 5 enrolled. In 2017, 4 master's awarded. *Degree requirements:* For master's, comprehensive exam, thesis optional. *Entrance requirements:* For master's, GRE, statement of educational goals and career objectives, essay, resume, 3 letters of reference. Additional exam requirements/recommendations for international students: Required—TOEFL (minimum score 500 paper-based, 61 iBT) or IELTS (minimum score 6). *Application deadline:* For fall admission, 7/1 for domestic students, 4/1 for international students; for spring admission, 11/15 for domestic students, 8/15 for international students; for summer admission, 5/1 for domestic students, 2/1 for international students. Applications are processed on a rolling basis. Application fee: $30 ($100 for international students). Electronic applications accepted. *Expenses:* Contact institution. *Financial support:* In 2017–18, 9 students received support, including 1 research assistantship (averaging $12,955 per year); scholarships/grants, tuition waivers (partial), and unspecified assistantships also available. Financial award application deadline: 4/15; financial award applicants required to submit FAFSA. *Faculty research:* Validity and reliability of forensic science; cognitive human factors in forensic science; judicial decision-making; education, training, and certification of forensic science practitioners; sex and race effects on offender sentence; job satisfaction; policing; victimology; perceptions versus realities; cultural capital; educational deficits; community-based participatory research; American race relations; race and fear; social media and political awareness. *Total annual research expenditures:* $486,144. *Unit head:* Dr. Arthur Hayden, Acting Chair of Behavioral and Social Sciences, 502-597-6893, E-mail: arthur.hayden@kysu.edu. *Application contact:* Dr. James Obielodan, Director of Graduate Studies, 502-597-4723, E-mail: james.obielodan@kysu.edu.

Lakehead University, Graduate Studies, Department of Psychology, Thunder Bay, ON P7B 5E1, Canada. Offers clinical psychology (PhD); experimental psychology (MA). *Program availability:* Part-time, evening/weekend. *Degree requirements:* For master's, thesis optional; for doctorate, thesis/dissertation, 2 comprehensive exams, internship. *Entrance requirements:* For master's, GRE, honors degree in psychology, advanced course work in statistics, minimum B average; for doctorate, GRE, minimum B average. Additional exam requirements/recommendations for international students: Required—TOEFL. *Faculty research:* Chaos theory, health psychology, counseling psychology, gerontology, women's studies.

Lamar University, College of Graduate Studies, College of Arts and Sciences, Department of Psychology, Beaumont, TX 77701. Offers clinical psychology (MS); industrial/organizational psychology (MS). *Program availability:* Part-time. *Faculty:* 9 full-time (5 women), 4 part-time/adjunct (1 woman). *Students:* 9 full-time (7 women), 6 part-time (4 women); includes 7 minority (2 Black or African American, non-Hispanic/Latino; 4 Hispanic/Latino; 1 Two or more races, non-Hispanic/Latino), 1 international. Average age 28. 24 applicants, 75% accepted, 7 enrolled. In 2017, 5 master's awarded. *Degree requirements:* For master's, thesis, practicum. *Entrance requirements:* For master's, GRE General Test, minimum GPA of 2.75 in last 60 hours of undergraduate course work. Additional exam requirements/recommendations for international students: Required—TOEFL (minimum score 550 paper-based; 79 iBT), IELTS (minimum score 6.5). *Application deadline:* For fall admission, 8/10 for domestic students, 7/1 for international students; for spring admission, 1/5 for domestic students, 12/1 for international students. Application fee: $25 ($50 for international students). *Expenses:* Contact institution. *Financial support:* In 2017–18, 12 students received support,

including 3 teaching assistantships (averaging $4,500 per year); fellowships, research assistantships, career-related internships or fieldwork, Federal Work-Study, scholarships/grants, and tuition waivers (partial) also available. Support available to part-time students. Financial award application deadline: 4/1. *Faculty research:* Group think, health psychology, school psychology, behavioral neuroscience. *Unit head:* Dr. Edythe E. Kirk, Chair, 409-880-8285, Fax: 409-880-1710. *Application contact:* Deidre Mayer, Interim Director, Admissions and Academic Services, 409-880-8888, Fax: 409-880-7419, E-mail: gradmissions@lamar.edu.
Website: http://artssciences.lamar.edu/psychology

La Salle University, School of Arts and Sciences, Program in Clinical Psychology, Philadelphia, PA 19141-1199. Offers child clinical psychology (Psy D); clinical health psychology (Psy D); clinical psychology (MA); general practice psychology (Psy D). *Accreditation:* AAMFT/COAMFTE. *Program availability:* Part-time, evening/weekend. *Faculty:* 9 full-time (7 women), 7 part-time/adjunct (4 women). *Students:* 82 full-time (69 women), 27 part-time (20 women); includes 12 minority (2 Black or African American, non-Hispanic/Latino; 4 Asian, non-Hispanic/Latino; 4 Hispanic/Latino; 2 Two or more races, non-Hispanic/Latino), 2 international. Average age 27. 400 applicants, 16% accepted, 23 enrolled. In 2017, 19 master's, 24 doctorates awarded. Terminal master's awarded for partial completion of doctoral program. *Degree requirements:* For doctorate, comprehensive exam, thesis/dissertation. *Entrance requirements:* For doctorate, GRE (minimum scores of 148 on both the Verbal Reasoning and Quantitative Reasoning sections strongly recommended); GRE Subject Test in psychology (for those entering with bachelor's degree), baccalaureate degree from accredited institution with major in psychology or related discipline; minimum undergraduate GPA of 3.0, 3.2 graduate; three letters of recommendation; statement of interest and intent; curriculum vitae or resume; personal interview. Additional exam requirements/recommendations for international students: Required—TOEFL. *Application deadline:* For fall admission, 1/15 for domestic students, 1/1 for international students. Application fee: $35. Electronic applications accepted. Application fee is waived when completed online. *Expenses:* Contact institution. *Financial support:* In 2017–18, 31 students received support. Scholarships/grants and unspecified assistantships available. Financial award application deadline: 8/31; financial award applicants required to submit FAFSA. *Unit head:* Dr. Randy Fingerhut, Director, 215-951-1284, Fax: 215-951-5140, E-mail: psyd@lasalle.edu. *Application contact:* Elizabeth Heenan, Director, Graduate and Adult Enrollment, 215-951-1100, Fax: 215-951-1462, E-mail: heenan@lasalle.edu.
Website: http://www.lasalle.edu/doctor-of-psychology/

Laurentian University, School of Graduate Studies and Research, Programme in Psychology, Sudbury, ON P3E 2C6, Canada. Offers applied psychology (MA); experimental psychology (MA).

Lehigh University, College of Arts and Sciences, Department of Psychology, Bethlehem, PA 18015. Offers MS, PhD. *Faculty:* 15 full-time (10 women). *Students:* 18 full-time (12 women), 1 (woman) part-time; includes 4 minority (2 Black or African American, non-Hispanic/Latino; 1 Asian, non-Hispanic/Latino; 1 Hispanic/Latino), 5 international. Average age 26. 76 applicants, 13% accepted, 4 enrolled. In 2017, 2 master's awarded. Terminal master's awarded for partial completion of doctoral program. *Degree requirements:* For master's, thesis; for doctorate, comprehensive exam, thesis/dissertation. *Entrance requirements:* For master's and doctorate, GRE General Test. Additional exam requirements/recommendations for international students: Required—TOEFL. *Application deadline:* For fall admission, 1/1 for domestic and international students. Application fee: $75. Electronic applications accepted. *Expenses:* $1,460 per credit. *Financial support:* In 2017–18, 13 students received support, including 1 research assistantship with full tuition reimbursement available (averaging $21,000 per year), 12 teaching assistantships with full tuition reimbursements available (averaging $21,000 per year). Financial award application deadline: 1/1. *Faculty research:* Cognition, memory, language, and their development; prosocial cognition, emotion, and action; conflict and cooperation between and within groups; self-control of cognition and emotion; optimizing developmental and relational outcomes. *Total annual research expenditures:* $355,274. *Unit head:* Dr. Gordon Moskowitz, Chairperson, 610-758-3624, Fax: 610-758-6277, E-mail: gbm4@lehigh.edu. *Application contact:* Dr. Almut Hupbach, Program Director, 610-758-6762, Fax: 610-758-6277, E-mail: alh309@lehigh.edu.
Website: http://psychology.cas2.lehigh.edu/

Lesley University, Graduate School of Arts and Social Sciences, Cambridge, MA 02138-2790. Offers clinical mental health counseling (MA), including holistic counseling, school and community counseling, trauma studies; counseling psychology (MA, CAGS), including professional counseling (MA), school counseling (MA); creative writing (MFA); expressive therapies (MA, PhD, CAGS), including art (MA), clinical mental health counseling (MA), dance (MA), expressive therapies (MA), music (MA); independent studies (CAGS); independent study (MA); intercultural relations (MA, CAGS); interdisciplinary studies (MA), including individualized studies, integrative holistic health, mindfulness studies, peace and conflict transformation, trauma sensitive assessment, intervention, and consultation, women's studies; urban environmental leadership (MA). *Program availability:* Part-time, online learning. *Degree requirements:* For master's, internship, practicum, thesis (for expressive therapies); for doctorate, thesis/dissertation, arts apprenticeship, field placement; for CAGS, thesis, internship (for counseling psychology, expressive therapies). *Entrance requirements:* For master's, MAT (counseling psychology), interview, writing samples, art portfolio; for doctorate, GRE or MAT, interview, master's degree; for CAGS, interview, master's degree. Additional exam requirements/recommendations for international students: Required—TOEFL (minimum score 550 paper-based; 80 iBT). Electronic applications accepted. *Faculty research:* Psychotherapy and culture; psychotherapy and psychological trauma; women's issues in art, teaching and psychotherapy; community-based art, psycho-spiritual inquiry.

LeTourneau University, Graduate Programs, Longview, TX 75607-7001. Offers business (MBA); counseling (MA), including licensed professional counselor, marriage and family therapy, school counseling; curriculum and instruction (M Ed); educational administration (M Ed); engineering (ME, MS); engineering management (MEM); health care administration (MS); marriage and family therapy (MA); psychology (MA); strategic leadership (MSL); teacher leadership (M Ed); teaching and learning (M Ed). *Program availability:* Part-time, 100% online, blended/hybrid learning. *Students:* 55 full-time (35 women), 337 part-time (266 women); includes 218 minority (140 Black or African American, non-Hispanic/Latino; 2 American Indian or Alaska Native, non-Hispanic/Latino; 5 Asian, non-Hispanic/Latino; 32 Hispanic/Latino; 39 Two or more races, non-Hispanic/Latino), 3 international. Average age 37. *Entrance requirements:* Additional exam requirements/recommendations for international students: Required—TOEFL. *Application deadline:* For fall admission, 8/22 for domestic students, 8/29 for international students; for winter admission, 10/10 for domestic students; for spring admission, 1/2 for domestic students, 1/10 for international students; for summer admission, 5/1 for domestic and international students. Applications are processed on a rolling basis. Electronic applications accepted. *Expenses:* Contact institution. *Financial support:* Research assistantships, institutionally sponsored loans, and unspecified assistantships available. Financial award applicants required to submit FAFSA.
Website: http://www.letu.edu

Liberty University, School of Behavioral Sciences, Lynchburg, VA 24515. Offers applied psychology (MA), including developmental psychology (MA, MS), industrial/organizational psychology (MA, MS); clinical mental health counseling (MA); community care and counseling (Ed D), including marriage and family counseling, pastoral care and counseling, traumatology; counselor education and supervision (PhD); human services counseling (MA), including addictions and recovery, business, child and family law, Christian ministries, criminal justice, crisis response and trauma, executive leadership, health and wellness, life coaching, marriage and family, military resilience; marriage and family counseling (MA); marriage and family therapy (MA); military resilience (Certificate); pastoral counseling (MA), including addictions and recovery, community chaplaincy, crisis response and trauma, discipleship and church ministry, leadership, life coaching, marriage and family, marriage and family studies, military resilience, parenting and child/adolescent, pastoral counseling, theology; professional counseling (MA); psychology (MS), including developmental psychology (MA, MS), industrial/organizational psychology (MA, MS); school counseling (M Ed). *Program availability:* Part-time, online learning. *Students:* 2,649 full-time (2,085 women), 5,086 part-time (4,015 women); includes 2,275 minority (1,784 Black or African American, non-Hispanic/Latino; 44 American Indian or Alaska Native, non-Hispanic/Latino; 67 Asian, non-Hispanic/Latino; 200 Hispanic/Latino; 11 Native Hawaiian or other Pacific Islander, non-Hispanic/Latino; 169 Two or more races, non-Hispanic/Latino), 145 international. Average age 39. 5,839 applicants, 51% accepted, 1710 enrolled. In 2017, 1,626 master's, 7 doctorates, 61 other advanced degrees awarded. *Application deadline:* Applications are processed on a rolling basis. Application fee: $50. Electronic applications accepted. *Financial support:* Applicants required to submit FAFSA. *Unit head:* Dr. Ronald Hawkins, Founding Dean, School of Behavioral Sciences. *Application contact:* Jay Bridge, Director of Admissions, 800-424-9595, Fax: 800-628-7977, E-mail: gradadmissions@liberty.edu.

Lipscomb University, Department of Psychology, Counseling, and Family Science, Nashville, TN 37204-3951. Offers clinical mental health counseling (MS); counseling psychology (Certificate); marriage and family therapy (MMFT); psychology (MS). *Program availability:* Part-time, evening/weekend. *Faculty:* 10 full-time (3 women), 10 part-time/adjunct (4 women). *Students:* 120 full-time (92 women), 30 part-time (27 women); includes 38 minority (22 Black or African American, non-Hispanic/Latino; 1 American Indian or Alaska Native, non-Hispanic/Latino; 1 Asian, non-Hispanic/Latino; 11 Hispanic/Latino; 3 Two or more races, non-Hispanic/Latino), 2 international. Average age 28. 144 applicants, 44% accepted, 42 enrolled. In 2017, 68 master's, 1 other advanced degree awarded. *Degree requirements:* For master's, thesis (for some programs), practicum, internship, capstone. *Entrance requirements:* For master's, GRE, resume, 3 reference letters, transcripts, goals statement. Additional exam requirements/recommendations for international students: Required—TOEFL (minimum score 570 paper-based; 80 iBT). *Application deadline:* For fall admission, 7/1 for domestic students; for spring admission, 11/1 for domestic students. Applications are processed on a rolling basis. Application fee: $50 ($75 for international students). Electronic applications accepted. *Expenses:* Contact institution. *Financial support:* Scholarships/grants and unspecified assistantships available. Financial award applicants required to submit FAFSA. *Faculty research:* Cognitive psychology, neuroscience, health psychology, grief issues. *Unit head:* Dr. Shanna Ray, Director/Professor of Psychology, 615-966-5833, E-mail: shanna.ray@lipscomb.edu. *Application contact:* Kathi Johnson, Recruiting and Marketing Coordinator, 615-966-5237, E-mail: kathi.johnson@lipscomb.edu.
Website: http://www.lipscomb.edu/psychology/graduate-programs

Loma Linda University, School of Behavioral Health, Department of Psychology, Loma Linda, CA 92350. Offers clinical psychology (PhD, Psy D). *Accreditation:* APA. *Degree requirements:* For doctorate, comprehensive exam, thesis/dissertation. *Entrance requirements:* For doctorate, GRE General Test, three letters of recommendation. Additional exam requirements/recommendations for international students: Required—TOEFL (minimum score 550 paper-based; 80 iBT). Electronic applications accepted.

Long Island University–LIU Brooklyn, Richard L. Conolly College of Liberal Arts and Sciences, Brooklyn, NY 11201-8423. Offers biology (MS); chemistry (MS); clinical psychology (PhD); creative writing (MFA); English (MA); media arts (MA, MFA); political science (MA); psychology (MA); social science (MS); United Nations (Advanced Certificate); urban studies (MA); writing and production for television (MFA). *Program availability:* Part-time. *Faculty:* 32 full-time (13 women), 17 part-time/adjunct (6 women). *Students:* 178 full-time (123 women), 143 part-time (96 women); includes 128 minority (65 Black or African American, non-Hispanic/Latino; 22 Asian, non-Hispanic/Latino; 31 Hispanic/Latino; 10 Two or more races, non-Hispanic/Latino), 54 international. Average age 30. 629 applicants, 38% accepted, 74 enrolled. In 2017, 147 master's, 9 doctorates, 8 other advanced degrees awarded. Terminal master's awarded for partial completion of doctoral program. *Degree requirements:* For master's, comprehensive exam (for some programs), thesis (for some programs); for doctorate, thesis/dissertation. *Entrance requirements:* For doctorate, GRE. Additional exam requirements/recommendations for international students: Required—TOEFL (minimum score 550 paper-based, 79 iBT) or IELTS. *Application deadline:* Applications are processed on a rolling basis. Application fee: $50. Electronic applications accepted. *Expenses: Tuition:* Full-time $21,618; part-time $1201 per credit. *Required fees:* $1840; $920 per term. Tuition and fees vary according to course load. *Financial support:* In 2017–18, 214 students received support, including 120 fellowships with full and partial tuition reimbursements available (averaging $915 per year), 5 research assistantships with full and partial tuition reimbursements available (averaging $2,300 per year), 136 teaching assistantships with full and partial tuition reimbursements available (averaging $2,300 per year); career-related internships or fieldwork, Federal Work-Study, institutionally sponsored loans, scholarships/grants, and unspecified assistantships also available. Support available to part-time students. Financial award application deadline: 2/15; financial award applicants required to submit FAFSA. *Faculty research:* Quantum gravity and astrophysics; string theory; pharmaceutical biotechnology with a focus on molecular details of drug susceptibility/resistance mechanisms; entomology, population and community ecology, agroecology, and biodiversity; psychotherapy process-outcome, particularly therapeutic alliance development, the role of common factors, and the study of treatment failures; personality pathology, borderline personality disorder and pathological narcissism. *Unit head:* Dr. Scott Krawczyk, Dean, 718-488-1003, E-mail: scott.krawczyk@liu.edu. *Application contact:* Bayu Sutrisno, Graduate Admissions Counselor, 718-488-1564, Fax: 718-780-6110, E-mail: bayu.sutrisno@liu.edu.

Long Island University–LIU Post, College of Liberal Arts and Sciences, Brookville, NY 11548-1300. Offers applied mathematics (MS); behavior analysis (MA); biology (MS); criminal justice (MS); earth science (MS); English (MA); environmental sustainability (MS); genetic counseling (MS); history (MA); interdisciplinary studies (MA, MS); political science (MA); psychology (MA). *Program availability:* Part-time, evening/weekend, blended/hybrid learning. *Faculty:* 41 full-time (21 women), 24 part-time/adjunct (13 women). *Students:* 173 full-time (124 women), 62 part-time (35 women); includes 54 minority (11 Black or African American, non-Hispanic/Latino; 13 Asian, non-Hispanic/Latino; 23 Hispanic/Latino; 7 Two or more races, non-Hispanic/Latino), 12 international. Average age 28. 368 applicants, 54% accepted, 74 enrolled. In 2017, 89 master's, 15 other advanced degrees awarded. Terminal master's awarded for partial completion of doctoral program. *Degree requirements:* For master's, comprehensive exam (for some

programs), thesis (for some programs). *Entrance requirements:* Additional exam requirements/recommendations for international students: Required—TOEFL, IELTS, or PTE. *Application deadline:* Applications are processed on a rolling basis. Application fee: $50. Electronic applications accepted. *Expenses: Tuition:* Full-time $21,618; part-time $1201 per credit. *Required fees:* $1840; $920 per term. Tuition and fees vary according to course load. *Financial support:* In 2017–18, 165 students received support. Fellowships, research assistantships, teaching assistantships, career-related internships or fieldwork, Federal Work-Study, scholarships/grants, tuition waivers (partial), and unspecified assistantships available. Support available to part-time students. Financial award application deadline: 2/15; financial award applicants required to submit FAFSA. *Faculty research:* Biology, environmental sustainability, mathematics, psychology, genetic counseling. *Unit head:* Dr. Nathaniel Bowditch, Dean, 516-299-2234, Fax: 516-299-4140, E-mail: nathaniel.bowditch@liu.edu. *Application contact:* Rita Langdon, Graduate Admissions, 516-299-2900, Fax: 516-299-2137, E-mail: post-enroll@liu.edu.
Website: http://liu.edu/CWPost/Academics/Schools/CLAS

Louisiana State University and Agricultural & Mechanical College, Graduate School, College of Humanities and Social Sciences, Department of Psychology, Baton Rouge, LA 70803. Offers biological psychology (MA, PhD); clinical psychology (MA, PhD); cognitive psychology (MA, PhD); developmental psychology (MA, PhD); school psychology (MA, PhD). *Accreditation:* APA (one or more programs are accredited). *Faculty:* 29 full-time (11 women). *Students:* 78 full-time (57 women), 18 part-time (14 women); includes 25 minority (8 Black or African American, non-Hispanic/Latino; 5 Asian, non-Hispanic/Latino; 5 Hispanic/Latino; 1 Native Hawaiian or other Pacific Islander, non-Hispanic/Latino; 6 Two or more races, non-Hispanic/Latino), 4 international. Average age 27. 239 applicants, 8% accepted, 18 enrolled. In 2017, 15 master's, 12 doctorates awarded. *Financial support:* In 2017–18, 7 fellowships (averaging $41,483 per year), 9 research assistantships (averaging $19,441 per year), 58 teaching assistantships (averaging $19,688 per year) were awarded. *Total annual research expenditures:* $326,871.

Loyola University Chicago, Graduate School, Programs in Non-Clinical Psychology, Chicago, IL 60660. Offers developmental psychology (PhD). *Faculty:* 7 full-time (2 women), 1 (woman) part-time/adjunct. *Students:* 44 full-time (38 women), 5 part-time (all women); includes 16 minority (6 Black or African American, non-Hispanic/Latino; 2 Asian, non-Hispanic/Latino; 5 Hispanic/Latino; 3 Two or more races, non-Hispanic/Latino), 3 international. Average age 28. 108 applicants, 11% accepted, 6 enrolled. In 2017, 5 master's, 5 doctorates awarded. Terminal master's awarded for partial completion of doctoral program. *Entrance requirements:* For master's and doctorate, GRE General Test, sample of written work. Additional exam requirements/recommendations for international students: Required—TOEFL. *Application deadline:* For fall admission, 1/15 for domestic and international students. Application fee: $50. Electronic applications accepted. Application fee is waived when completed online. *Expenses:* $1,033 per credit hour tuition, $432 pere semester mandatory fees. *Financial support:* In 2017–18, 1 fellowship with tuition reimbursement (averaging $16,000 per year), 5 research assistantships with tuition reimbursements (averaging $16,000 per year), 1 teaching assistantship with tuition reimbursement (averaging $16,000 per year) were awarded; career-related internships or fieldwork, Federal Work-Study, and scholarships/grants also available. Financial award application deadline: 12/15; financial award applicants required to submit FAFSA. *Faculty research:* Program evaluation, attitudes and prejudice, psychological well-being, self esteem and relationships, groups and organizations. *Total annual research expenditures:* $150,000. *Unit head:* Dr. Christine Li-Grine, Graduate Department Head, 773-508-8225, Fax: 773-508-8713, E-mail: cligrining@luc.edu. *Application contact:* Jill Schur, Director, Graduate Enrollment Management, 312-915-8902, E-mail: gradinfo@luc.edu.

Loyola University Maryland, Graduate Programs, Loyola College of Arts and Sciences, Department of Psychology, Baltimore, MD 21210-2699. Offers clinical psychology (MS, Psy D, CAS); counseling psychology (MS, CAS). *Accreditation:* APA. *Program availability:* Part-time, evening/weekend. *Faculty:* 64 full-time (37 women), 31 part-time/adjunct (20 women). *Students:* 137 full-time (111 women), 58 part-time (46 women); includes 50 minority (18 Black or African American, non-Hispanic/Latino; 1 American Indian or Alaska Native, non-Hispanic/Latino; 13 Asian, non-Hispanic/Latino; 10 Hispanic/Latino; 8 Two or more races, non-Hispanic/Latino), 6 international. Average age 27. In 2017, 52 master's, 13 doctorates awarded. *Degree requirements:* For doctorate, thesis/dissertation. *Entrance requirements:* For master's, GRE, essay, 3 letters of recommendation, transcript. Additional exam requirements/recommendations for international students: Required—TOEFL (minimum score 550 paper-based), IELTS (minimum score 7). *Application deadline:* For fall admission, 12/1 for domestic students, 3/1 for international students. Application fee: $60. Electronic applications accepted. *Expenses:* Contact institution. *Financial support:* Scholarships/grants and unspecified assistantships available. Financial award application deadline: 4/15; financial award applicants required to submit FAFSA. *Unit head:* Carolyn M. Barry, Chair, 410-617-5325, E-mail: cbarry@loyola.edu. *Application contact:* Office of Graduate Admission, 410-617-5020, E-mail: graduate@loyola.edu.

Lynn University, College of Arts and Sciences, Boca Raton, FL 33431-5598. Offers criminal justice (MS); mental health counseling (MS); psychology (MS), including general psychology, industrial/organizational psychology. *Program availability:* Part-time, evening/weekend, 100% online, blended/hybrid learning. *Faculty:* 59 full-time (26 women), 22 part-time/adjunct (16 women). *Students:* 60 full-time (47 women), 38 part-time (24 women); includes 32 minority (15 Black or African American, non-Hispanic/Latino; 2 Asian, non-Hispanic/Latino; 15 Hispanic/Latino), 6 international. Average age 30. 73 applicants, 82% accepted, 47 enrolled. In 2017, 64 master's awarded. *Degree requirements:* For master's, comprehensive exam (for some programs), thesis (for some programs). *Entrance requirements:* For master's, bachelor's degree from accredited institution, minimum undergraduate GPA of 3.0, official undergraduate transcripts, two letters of recommendation from academic or professional sources, writing sample demonstrating capacity to perform at graduate level. Additional exam requirements/recommendations for international students: Required—TOEFL (minimum score 550 paper-based; 80 iBT), IELTS (minimum score 6.5). *Application deadline:* For fall admission, 8/18 for domestic students, 8/4 for international students; for spring admission, 12/15 for domestic students, 12/1 for international students; for summer admission, 4/17 for domestic students, 4/3 for international students. Applications are processed on a rolling basis. Application fee: $45. Electronic applications accepted. *Expenses:* $740 per credit. *Financial support:* Career-related internships or fieldwork, Federal Work-Study, scholarships/grants, tuition waivers (full and partial), and unspecified assistantships available. Support available to part-time students. Financial award application deadline: 3/1; financial award applicants required to submit FAFSA. *Faculty research:* Personality and social media, learning strategies, personal health behaviors and compliance, using drums in substance abuse groups, interpersonal behaviors with individuals with autism, case conceptualization, teaching case conceptualization across the curriculum. *Unit head:* Dr. Katrina Carter-Tellison, Dean, 561-237-7412, E-mail: kcartertellison@lynn.edu. *Application contact:* Steven Pruitt, Director of Graduate Admission, 561-237-7834, Fax: 561-237-7100, E-mail: admissionpm@lynn.edu.
Website: https://www.lynn.edu/academics/colleges-schools/arts-and-sciences

Madonna University, Department of Psychology, Livonia, MI 48150-1173. Offers clinical psychology (MSCP). *Program availability:* Part-time, evening/weekend. *Degree requirements:* For master's, thesis or alternative. *Entrance requirements:* Additional exam requirements/recommendations for international students: Required—TOEFL. Electronic applications accepted.

Mansfield University of Pennsylvania, Graduate Studies, Program in Organizational Leadership, Mansfield, PA 16933. Offers MA. *Program availability:* Online learning.

Marietta College, Program in Psychology, Marietta, OH 45750-4000. Offers MAP. *Program availability:* Part-time. *Faculty:* 5 full-time (2 women). *Students:* 7 full-time (4 women), 1 part-time (0 women); includes 1 minority (Two or more races, non-Hispanic/Latino). Average age 24. 12 applicants, 83% accepted, 7 enrolled. In 2017, 5 master's awarded. *Degree requirements:* For master's, thesis. *Entrance requirements:* For master's, GRE, transcripts, essay, two letters of recommendation. Additional exam requirements/recommendations for international students: Required—TOEFL. *Application deadline:* Applications are processed on a rolling basis. Application fee: $25. *Expenses:* $775 per credit hour. *Financial support:* Unspecified assistantships available. *Unit head:* Dr. Chris Klein, Director, 740-376-4795, E-mail: clk002@marietta.edu.

Marist College, Graduate Programs, School of Social and Behavioral Sciences, Poughkeepsie, NY 12601-1387. Offers education (M Ed, MA); mental health counseling (MA); school psychology (MA, Adv C). *Program availability:* Part-time, evening/weekend. *Degree requirements:* For master's, thesis optional. *Entrance requirements:* For master's, GRE General Test, letters of recommendation, minimum undergraduate GPA of 3.0, interview. Additional exam requirements/recommendations for international students: Required—TOEFL (minimum score 550 paper-based; 80 iBT); Recommended—IELTS (minimum score 6.5). Electronic applications accepted. *Faculty research:* AIDS prevention, educational intervention, humanistic counseling research, aging and development, neuroimaging.

Marquette University, Graduate School, College of Arts and Sciences, Department of Psychology, Milwaukee, WI 53201-1881. Offers PhD. *Accreditation:* APA. Terminal master's awarded for partial completion of doctoral program. *Degree requirements:* For doctorate, thesis/dissertation, internship, qualifying exam. *Entrance requirements:* For doctorate, GRE General Test, sample of scholarly writing, official transcripts from all current and previous colleges/universities except Marquette, personal statement, three letters of reference. Additional exam requirements/recommendations for international students: Required—TOEFL (minimum score 530 paper-based). Electronic applications accepted. *Faculty research:* Mental imagery, moral development, organizational behavior, depression, psychotherapy outcomes.

Marshall University, Academic Affairs Division, College of Liberal Arts, Department of Psychology, Huntington, WV 25755. Offers clinical psychology (Certificate); psychology (MA, Psy D). *Accreditation:* APA. *Students:* 74 full-time (56 women), 9 part-time (6 women); includes 6 minority (3 Black or African American, non-Hispanic/Latino; 1 Hispanic/Latino; 1 Native Hawaiian or other Pacific Islander, non-Hispanic/Latino; 1 Two or more races, non-Hispanic/Latino). Average age 27. In 2017, 42 master's, 13 doctorates awarded. *Degree requirements:* For master's, thesis optional. *Entrance requirements:* For master's, GRE General Test or MAT. *Application deadline:* For fall admission, 3/1 for domestic students; for spring admission, 11/1 for domestic students. Application fee: $40. *Financial support:* Teaching assistantships with tuition reimbursements available. *Unit head:* Dr. Marianna Linz, Chair, 304-696-2774, E-mail: linz@marshall.edu. *Application contact:* Graduate Admissions, 304-746-1900, Fax: 304-746-1902, E-mail: services@marshall.edu.

Martin University, Division of Psychology, Indianapolis, IN 46218-3867. Offers community psychology (MS). *Program availability:* Part-time, evening/weekend. *Degree requirements:* For master's, thesis. *Entrance requirements:* For master's, GRE General Test, GRE Subject Test.

Marywood University, Academic Affairs, Reap College of Education and Human Development, Department of Psychology and Counseling, Program in Psychology, Scranton, PA 18509-1598. Offers clinical services (MA); general theoretical psychology (MA). *Program availability:* Part-time. Electronic applications accepted.

McGill University, Faculty of Graduate and Postdoctoral Studies, Faculty of Medicine, Department of Psychiatry, Montréal, QC H3A 2T5, Canada. Offers M Sc.

McGill University, Faculty of Graduate and Postdoctoral Studies, Faculty of Science, Department of Psychology, Montréal, QC H3A 2T5, Canada. Offers clinical psychology (PhD); experimental psychology (M Sc, MA, PhD).

McMaster University, School of Graduate Studies, Faculty of Science, Department of Psychology, Hamilton, ON L8S 4M2, Canada. Offers M Sc, PhD. *Degree requirements:* For doctorate, comprehensive exam, thesis/dissertation. *Entrance requirements:* For doctorate, GRE General Test, honors degree, minimum B+ average. Additional exam requirements/recommendations for international students: Required—TOEFL (minimum score 550 paper-based).

McNeese State University, Doré School of Graduate Studies, Burton College of Education, Department of Psychology, Lake Charles, LA 70609. Offers applied behavior analysis (MA, Graduate Certificate); counseling psychology (MA); general/experimental psychology (MA). *Program availability:* Evening/weekend. *Entrance requirements:* For master's, GRE. *Application deadline:* For fall admission, 5/15 priority date for domestic and international students; for spring admission, 10/15 priority date for domestic and international students. Applications are processed on a rolling basis. Application fee: $20 ($30 for international students). *Financial support:* Application deadline: 5/1. *Unit head:* Dr. Dena L. Matzenbacher, Head, 337-475-5434, Fax: 337-562-4115, E-mail: dena@mcneese.edu. *Application contact:* Dr. Dustin M. Hebert, Director of Dore' School of Graduate Studies, 337-475-5396, Fax: 337-475-5397, E-mail: admissions@mcneese.edu.

Medaille College, Programs in Psychology, Buffalo, NY 14214-2695. Offers clinical psychology (Psy D); marriage and family therapy (MA); mental health counseling (MA); psychology (MA). *Accreditation:* ACA. *Program availability:* Part-time, evening/weekend. *Degree requirements:* For master's, comprehensive exam (for some programs), thesis (for some programs). *Entrance requirements:* For master's, GRE General Test (psychology), minimum GPA of 2.75 (psychology). Additional exam requirements/recommendations for international students: Required—TOEFL (minimum score 550 paper-based). Electronic applications accepted. *Faculty research:* Schizophrenia, Parkinson's Disease, eyewitness testimony, methodology.

Memorial University of Newfoundland, School of Graduate Studies, Department of Psychology, St. John's, NL A1C 5S7, Canada. Offers applied psychological sciences (MAPS); clinical psychology (Psy D); experimental psychology (M Sc, PhD). *Program availability:* Part-time. *Degree requirements:* For master's, workterms (MASP), thesis (M Sc); for doctorate, comprehensive exam, thesis/dissertation, oral thesis defense. *Entrance requirements:* For master's, GRE, honors bachelor's degree of high second class standing or equivalent; for doctorate, GRE, master's or honors degree. Electronic applications accepted. *Faculty research:* Behavioral neuroscience, cognition, theory and research on abnormal behavior.

Psychology—General

Mercy College, School of Social and Behavioral Sciences, Program in Psychology, Dobbs Ferry, NY 10522-1189. Offers MS. *Program availability:* Part-time, evening/weekend, 100% online, blended/hybrid learning. *Students:* 23 full-time (20 women), 29 part-time (22 women); includes 35 minority (15 Black or African American, non-Hispanic/Latino; 3 Asian, non-Hispanic/Latino; 17 Hispanic/Latino), 1 international. Average age 34. 40 applicants, 48% accepted, 12 enrolled. In 2017, 12 master's awarded. *Degree requirements:* For master's, thesis (for some programs), written comprehensive exam or 6-credit thesis. *Entrance requirements:* For master's, essay, interview, resume, letter of recommendation, undergraduate transcript with minimum GPA of 3.0. Additional exam requirements/recommendations for international students: Required—TOEFL (minimum score 600 paper-based; 100 iBT), IELTS (minimum score 8). *Application deadline:* For fall admission, 8/1 for international students. Applications are processed on a rolling basis. Application fee: $40. Electronic applications accepted. *Expenses: Tuition:* Full-time $15,426; part-time $857 per credit hour. *Required fees:* $630; $158 per term. Tuition and fees vary according to course load, degree level and program. *Financial support:* Career-related internships or fieldwork, Federal Work-Study, scholarships/grants, and unspecified assistantships available. Support available to part-time students. Financial award applicants required to submit FAFSA. *Unit head:* Dr. Karol Dean, Dean, School of Social and Behavioral Sciences, 914-674-7517, E-mail: kdean@mercy.edu. *Application contact:* Allison Gurdineer, Senior Director of Admissions, 877-637-2946, Fax: 914-674-7382, E-mail: admissions@mercy.edu.
Website: https://www.mercy.edu/degrees-programs/ms-psychology

Meredith College, School of Education, Health and Human Sciences, Master of Arts in Psychology Program, Raleigh, NC 27607-5298. Offers industrial/organizational psychology (MA). *Degree requirements:* For master's, internship. *Entrance requirements:* For master's, GRE, official transcripts, two recommendation forms, resume or curriculum vitae, essay. *Application deadline:* Applications are processed on a rolling basis. Application fee: $60. Tuition and fees vary according to course load and program. *Unit head:* Lori Kelley, Program Manager/Admissions Counselor, 919-760-8723, E-mail: lrkelley@meredith.edu.
Website: https://www.meredith.edu/master-of-psychology

Miami University, College of Arts and Science, Department of Psychology, Oxford, OH 45056. Offers MA, PhD. *Accreditation:* APA (one or more programs are accredited). *Students:* 66 full-time (48 women), 1 (woman) part-time; includes 15 minority (1 Black or African American, non-Hispanic/Latino; 4 Asian, non-Hispanic/Latino; 10 Hispanic/Latino), 8 international. Average age 27. In 2017, 6 master's, 10 doctorates awarded. *Expenses:* Tuition, state resident: full-time $13,812; part-time $575 per credit hour. Tuition, nonresident: full-time $30,860; part-time $1286 per credit hour. *Unit head:* Dr. Joe Johnson, Department Chair, 513-529-2400, E-mail: johnsojg@miamioh.edu. *Application contact:* 513-529-2400, E-mail: psychology@miamioh.edu.
Website: http://www.MiamiOH.edu/psychology/

Michigan School of Professional Psychology, MA and Psy D Programs in Clinical Psychology, Farmington Hills, MI 48334. Offers MA, Psy D. *Accreditation:* APA. *Program availability:* Part-time, evening/weekend. *Faculty:* 11 full-time (7 women), 21 part-time/adjunct (17 women). *Students:* 109 full-time (85 women), 64 part-time (51 women); includes 46 minority (30 Black or African American, non-Hispanic/Latino; 3 Asian, non-Hispanic/Latino; 2 Hispanic/Latino; 11 Two or more races, non-Hispanic/Latino), 1 international. Average age 31. 194 applicants, 47% accepted, 80 enrolled. In 2017, 37 master's, 16 doctorates awarded. *Degree requirements:* For master's, practicum; for doctorate, comprehensive exam, thesis/dissertation, internship, practicum. *Entrance requirements:* For master's, undergraduate degree from accredited institution with minimum GPA of 2.5; major in psychology, social work, or counseling; for doctorate, GRE General Test, undergraduate degree from accredited institution with minimum GPA of 2.5; graduate degree in psychology, social work, or counseling from accredited institution with minimum GPA of 3.25; graduate-level practicum. Additional exam requirements/recommendations for international students: Required—TOEFL (minimum score 550 paper-based; 79 iBT). *Application deadline:* For fall admission, 8/15 for domestic students. Applications are processed on a rolling basis. Application fee: $75. Electronic applications accepted. *Expenses:* $35,871 per academic year full-time tuition and fees (doctoral); $32,518 per academic year full-time tuition and fees (for master's). *Financial support:* In 2017–18, 12 students received support, including 1 research assistantship (averaging $8,566 per year), 5 teaching assistantships (averaging $14,436 per year); institutionally sponsored loans, scholarships/grants, and unspecified assistantships also available. Financial award application deadline: 8/30; financial award applicants required to submit FAFSA. *Faculty research:* Health psychology, trauma, multicultural, humanistic, applied behavior analysis. *Unit head:* Dr. Frances Brown, Program Director, 248-476-1122, Fax: 248-476-1125. *Application contact:* Carrie Hauser, Coordinator of Admissions and Student Engagement, 248-476-1122 Ext. 117, Fax: 248-476-1125, E-mail: chauser@mispp.edu.
Website: http://www.mispp.edu

Michigan State University, The Graduate School, College of Social Science, Department of Psychology, East Lansing, MI 48824. Offers MA, PhD. *Accreditation:* APA (one or more programs are accredited). *Entrance requirements:* Additional exam requirements/recommendations for international students: Required—TOEFL (minimum score 550 paper-based), Michigan State University ELT (minimum score 85), Michigan English Language Assessment Battery (minimum score 83). Electronic applications accepted.

Middle Tennessee State University, College of Graduate Studies, College of Behavioral and Health Sciences, Department of Psychology, Murfreesboro, TN 37132. Offers clinical psychology (MA); experimental psychology (MA); industrial/organizational psychology (MA); psychology (MA, Ed S); quantitative psychology (MA); school psychology (MA). *Program availability:* Part-time, evening/weekend, online learning. *Degree requirements:* For master's, comprehensive exam, thesis. *Entrance requirements:* For master's, GRE. Additional exam requirements/recommendations for international students: Required—TOEFL (minimum score 525 paper-based; 71 iBT) or IELTS (minimum score 6). Electronic applications accepted. *Faculty research:* Health psychology, industrial/organizational psychology, experimental psychology.

Millersville University of Pennsylvania, College of Graduate Studies and Adult Learning, College of Education and Human Services, Department of Psychology, Millersville, PA 17551-0302. Offers clinical psychology (MS); school counseling (M Ed); school psychology (MS). *Program availability:* Part-time, evening/weekend. *Faculty:* 12 full-time (8 women), 1 part-time/adjunct (0 women). *Students:* 67 full-time (55 women), 55 part-time (47 women); includes 19 minority (8 Black or African American, non-Hispanic/Latino; 1 American Indian or Alaska Native, non-Hispanic/Latino; 8 Hispanic/Latino; 2 Two or more races, non-Hispanic/Latino), 2 international. Average age 28. 110 applicants, 72% accepted, 43 enrolled. In 2017, 36 master's awarded. *Degree requirements:* For master's, comprehensive exam (for some programs), thesis optional, internship, practicum, portfolio, candidacy project. *Entrance requirements:* For master's, GRE or MAT (if cumulative GPA is lower than 3.0), at least 1 academic reference. Additional exam requirements/recommendations for international students: Required—TOEFL (minimum score 80 iBT), IELTS (minimum score 6.5), PTE (minimum score 60). *Application deadline:* For fall admission, 1/15 for domestic students; for winter admission, 6/1 for domestic students; for spring admission, 10/1 for domestic students.

Application fee: $40. Electronic applications accepted. *Expenses:* $500 per credit resident tuition and fees; $750 per credit non-resident tuition and fees; $114.75 per credit general fee (maximum of 12 credits); technology fee $27 per credit (resident), $39 per credit (non-resident). *Financial support:* In 2017–18, 43 students received support. Unspecified assistantships available. Financial award application deadline: 3/15; financial award applicants required to submit FAFSA. *Unit head:* Dr. Frederick S. Foster-Clark, Chair, 717-871-7265, Fax: 717-871-7946, E-mail: frederick.foster-clark@millersville.edu. *Application contact:* Dr. Victor S. DeSantis, Dean of College of Graduate Studies and Adult Learning/Associate Provost for Civic and Community Engagement, 717-871-7619, Fax: 717-871-7954, E-mail: victor.desantis@millersville.edu.
Website: http://www.millersville.edu/psychology/

Minnesota State University Mankato, College of Graduate Studies and Research, College of Social and Behavioral Sciences, Department of Psychology, Mankato, MN 56001. Offers clinical psychology (MA); industrial/organizational psychology (MA); school psychology (Psy D). *Program availability:* Part-time. *Degree requirements:* For master's, one foreign language, comprehensive exam, thesis (for some programs). *Entrance requirements:* For master's, GRE General Test, GRE Subject Test (clinical psychology), minimum GPA of 3.0 during previous 2 years, 3 letters of reference. Additional exam requirements/recommendations for international students: Required—TOEFL. Electronic applications accepted.

Mississippi State University, College of Arts and Sciences, Department of Psychology, Mississippi State, MS 39762. Offers applied psychology (PhD), including clinical, cognitive science; psychology (MS). *Accreditation:* APA. *Faculty:* 18 full-time (6 women). *Students:* 33 full-time (18 women), 7 part-time (all women); includes 8 minority (4 Black or African American, non-Hispanic/Latino; 3 Asian, non-Hispanic/Latino; 1 Two or more races, non-Hispanic/Latino), 1 international. Average age 27. 46 applicants, 26% accepted, 10 enrolled. In 2017, 7 master's, 6 doctorates awarded. Terminal master's awarded for partial completion of doctoral program. *Degree requirements:* For master's, comprehensive exam, thesis; for doctorate, thesis/dissertation, qualifying exam, comprehensive written and oral exam. *Entrance requirements:* For master's, GRE General Test, minimum GPA of 2.75 on last two years of undergraduate courses; for doctorate, GRE General Test, proficiency in at least 1 computer language, minimum GPA of 3.0. Additional exam requirements/recommendations for international students: Required—TOEFL (minimum score 477 paper-based; 53 iBT); Recommended—IELTS (minimum score 4.5). *Application deadline:* For fall admission, 4/1 priority date for domestic students, 5/1 for international students; for spring admission, 11/1 priority date for domestic students, 9/1 for international students. Applications are processed on a rolling basis. Application fee: $60 ($80 for international students). Electronic applications accepted. *Expenses:* Tuition, state resident: full-time $8318; part-time $462.12 per credit hour. Tuition, nonresident: full-time $22,358; part-time $1242.12 per credit hour. *Required fees:* $110; $12.24 per credit hour. $6.12 per semester. *Financial support:* In 2017–18, 6 research assistantships with full tuition reimbursements (averaging $14,703 per year), 22 teaching assistantships with full tuition reimbursements (averaging $12,157 per year) were awarded; career-related internships or fieldwork, Federal Work-Study, institutionally sponsored loans, scholarships/grants, and unspecified assistantships also available. Financial award application deadline: 4/1; financial award applicants required to submit FAFSA. *Faculty research:* Personality type, alcoholism, blindness and low vision, mental retardation, language comprehension. *Total annual research expenditures:* $1.4 million. *Unit head:* Dr. Mitchell E. Berman, Professor and Head, 662-325-3202, Fax: 662-325-7212, E-mail: mberman@psychology.msstate.edu. *Application contact:* Lakan Drinker, Admissions and Enrollment Assistant, 662-325-8951, E-mail: ldrinker@grad.msstate.edu.
Website: http://www.psychology.msstate.edu/

Missouri State University, Graduate College, College of Health and Human Services, Department of Psychology, Springfield, MO 65897. Offers applied behavior analysis (MS); clinical psychology (MS); experimental psychology (MS); forensic child psychology (Certificate); industrial/organizational psychology (MS). *Faculty:* 25 full-time (11 women), 4 part-time/adjunct (0 women). *Students:* 54 full-time (41 women), 12 part-time (9 women); includes 9 minority (2 Black or African American, non-Hispanic/Latino; 2 Hispanic/Latino; 5 Two or more races, non-Hispanic/Latino), 5 international. Average age 23. 127 applicants, 17% accepted, 21 enrolled. In 2017, 41 master's awarded. *Degree requirements:* For master's, comprehensive exam, thesis. *Entrance requirements:* For master's, GRE General Test, GRE Subject Test, minimum GPA of 3.25 in major, 3.0 overall; 20 hours of course work in psychology. Additional exam requirements/recommendations for international students: Required—TOEFL (minimum score 550 paper-based; 79 iBT), IELTS (minimum score 6). *Application deadline:* For fall admission, 2/15 priority date for domestic and international students. Application fee: $35 ($50 for international students). Electronic applications accepted. *Expenses:* Tuition, state resident: full-time $2915; part-time $2021 per credit hour. Tuition, nonresident: full-time $5354; part-time $3647 per credit hour. *International tuition:* $11,992 full-time. *Required fees:* $173; $173 per credit hour. Tuition and fees vary according to class time, course level, course load, degree level, campus/location and program. *Financial support:* In 2017–18, 9 research assistantships with full tuition reimbursements (averaging $8,772 per year), 8 teaching assistantships with full tuition reimbursements (averaging $8,772 per year) were awarded; career-related internships or fieldwork, Federal Work-Study, institutionally sponsored loans, scholarships/grants, and unspecified assistantships also available. Financial award application deadline: 3/31; financial award applicants required to submit FAFSA. *Faculty research:* Work-family conflict, child forensic psychology, sports psychology, body image assessment, visual learning. *Unit head:* Dr. Paul Deal, Department Head, 417-836-5797, Fax: 417-836-8330, E-mail: psychology@missouristate.edu. *Application contact:* Stephanie Praschan, Director, Graduate Enrollment Management, 417-836-5330, Fax: 417-836-6200, E-mail: stephaniepraschan@missouristate.edu.
Website: http://psychology.missouristate.edu/

Monmouth University, Graduate Studies, Department of Professional Counseling, West Long Branch, NJ 07764-1898. Offers addiction studies (MA); clinical mental health counseling (MS); professional counseling (PMC). *Accreditation:* ACA. *Program availability:* Part-time, evening/weekend. *Faculty:* 11 full-time (5 women), 5 part-time/adjunct (4 women). *Students:* 106 full-time (97 women), 68 part-time (55 women); includes 42 minority (14 Black or African American, non-Hispanic/Latino; 5 Asian, non-Hispanic/Latino; 18 Hispanic/Latino; 5 Two or more races, non-Hispanic/Latino), 3 international. Average age 30. In 2017, 67 master's, 16 other advanced degrees awarded. *Degree requirements:* For master's, comprehensive exam (for some programs), thesis optional, fieldwork. *Entrance requirements:* For master's, GRE, minimum GPA of 3.0 overall, 12 credits in psychology or closely-related field, two Monmouth University psychological counseling recommendation forms, narrative essay; for PMC, degree or current enrollment in CACREP-accredited master's program in counseling with minimum cumulative GPA of 3.0. Additional exam requirements/recommendations for international students: Required—TOEFL (minimum score 550 paper-based; 79 iBT), IELTS (minimum score 6), Michigan English Language Assessment Battery (minimum score 77) or Certificate of Advanced English (minimum score 160). *Application deadline:* For fall admission, 7/15 priority date for domestic students, 6/1 for international students; for spring admission, 12/1 priority date for

domestic students, 11/1 for international students; for summer admission, 5/1 for domestic students. Applications are processed on a rolling basis. Application fee: $50. Electronic applications accepted. *Expenses: Tuition:* Full-time $21,366; part-time $7122 per credit. *Required fees:* $700; $175 per term. *Financial support:* In 2017–18, 82 students received support. Institutionally sponsored loans, scholarships/grants, and unspecified assistantships available. Support available to part-time students. Financial award applicants required to submit FAFSA. *Faculty research:* Violent crime, single parenting, the African-American male, counseling older women, successful behavior for under-achieving youth. *Unit head:* Dr. David Burkholder, Program Director, 732-923-4621, Fax: 732-923-4661, E-mail: dburkhol@monmouth.edu. *Application contact:* Andrea Thompson, Graduate Admission Counselor, 732-571-3452, Fax: 732-263-5123, E-mail: gradadm@monmouth.edu.
Website: https://www.monmouth.edu/school-of-humanities-social-sciences/professional-counseling.aspx

Montana State University, The Graduate School, College of Letters and Science, Department of Psychology, Bozeman, MT 59717. Offers MS. *Program availability:* Part-time. *Degree requirements:* For master's, comprehensive exam, thesis (for some programs). *Entrance requirements:* For master's, GRE General Test. Additional exam requirements/recommendations for international students: Required—TOEFL (minimum score 550 paper-based). Electronic applications accepted. *Faculty research:* Psychological study of social cognitive, neuro and eating behaviors.

Montana State University Billings, College of Arts and Sciences, Department of Psychology, Billings, MT 59101. Offers MS. *Program availability:* Part-time. *Degree requirements:* For master's, thesis optional. *Entrance requirements:* For master's, GRE General Test, 3 letters of recommendation, resume. Additional exam requirements/recommendations for international students: Required—TOEFL (minimum score 79 iBT), IELTS (minimum score 6.5). *Application deadline:* For fall admission, 3/15 for domestic students, 7/15 for international students; for spring admission, 12/1 for international students. Applications are processed on a rolling basis. Application fee: $40. Electronic applications accepted. *Expenses:* Tuition, state resident: full-time $11,740; part-time $7880 per year. Tuition, nonresident: full-time $32,200; part-time $24,140 per year. *Financial support:* Research assistantships with partial tuition reimbursements, teaching assistantships with partial tuition reimbursements, career-related internships or fieldwork, Federal Work-Study, institutionally sponsored loans, scholarships/grants, tuition waivers (partial), and unspecified assistantships available. Support available to part-time students. Financial award application deadline: 5/1; financial award applicants required to submit FAFSA. *Unit head:* Dr. Matthew McMullen, Chair, 406-657-2958, E-mail: mmcmullen@msubillings.edu. *Application contact:* Dr. Matthew McMullen, Chair, 406-657-2958, E-mail: mmcmullen@msubillings.edu.
Website: http://www.msubillings.edu/cas/psych/

Montclair State University, The Graduate School, College of Humanities and Social Sciences, Program in Psychology, Montclair, NJ 07043-1624. Offers MA. *Program availability:* Part-time, evening/weekend. *Degree requirements:* For master's, thesis. *Entrance requirements:* For master's, GRE General Test, 2 letters of recommendation, essay. Additional exam requirements/recommendations for international students: Required—TOEFL (minimum score 83 iBT), IELTS (minimum score 6.5). Electronic applications accepted. *Faculty research:* Information processing, cerebral lateralization, hedonics.

Morehead State University, Graduate Programs, College of Science and Technology, Department of Psychology, Morehead, KY 40351. Offers clinical/counseling psychology (MS); general/experimental psychology (MS). *Program availability:* Part-time, evening/weekend. *Degree requirements:* For master's, comprehensive exam, thesis optional. *Entrance requirements:* For master's, GRE General Test, 18 undergraduate hours in psychology, minimum GPA of 3.0, 3 letters of recommendation. Additional exam requirements/recommendations for international students: Required—TOEFL (minimum score 500 paper-based). Electronic applications accepted. *Faculty research:* Mood induction effects, serotonin receptor activity, stress, perceptual processes.

Morgan State University, School of Graduate Studies, College of Liberal Arts, Department of Psychology, Baltimore, MD 21251. Offers psychometrics (MS, PhD). *Entrance requirements:* For master's and doctorate, GRE. Application fee: $0. *Expenses:* Tuition, state resident: part-time $433 per credit. Tuition, nonresident: part-time $851 per credit. *Required fees:* $81.50 per credit. *Financial support:* Application deadline: 2/1. *Unit head:* Dr. R. Trent Haines, Program Coordinator, 443-885-3291, E-mail: trent.haines@morgan.edu. *Application contact:* Dr. Dean Campbell, Graduate Recruitment Specialist, 443-885-3185, Fax: 443-885-8226, E-mail: dean.campbell@morgan.edu.

Murray State University, College of Humanities and Fine Arts, Department of Psychology, Murray, KY 42071. Offers clinical psychology (MA, MS); general experimental psychology (MA, MS); research design and analysis (Certificate). *Program availability:* Part-time. *Faculty:* 9 full-time (5 women). *Students:* 21 full-time (16 women), 1 part-time (0 women); includes 2 minority (1 Hispanic/Latino; 1 Two or more races, non-Hispanic/Latino), 1 international. Average age 25. 44 applicants, 68% accepted, 11 enrolled. In 2017, 9 master's awarded. *Entrance requirements:* For master's and Certificate, GRE or GMAT, minimum university GPA of 2.75. Additional exam requirements/recommendations for international students: Required—TOEFL (minimum score 527 paper-based; 71 iBT). *Application deadline:* Applications are processed on a rolling basis. Application fee: $40 ($50 for international students). Electronic applications accepted. *Expenses:* Tuition, state resident: full-time $9504. Tuition, nonresident: full-time $26,811. *International tuition:* $14,400 full-time. Tuition and fees vary according to course load, degree level and reciprocity agreements. *Financial support:* In 2017–18, 5 research assistantships were awarded; Federal Work-Study and unspecified assistantships also available. Financial award applicants required to submit FAFSA. *Unit head:* Dr. Paula Waddill, Chair, Department of Psychology, 270-809-2851, Fax: 270-809-2991, E-mail: pwaddill@murraystate.edu. *Application contact:* Kaitlyn Burzynski, Interim Assistant Director for Graduate Admission and Records, 270-809-5732, Fax: 270-809-3780, E-mail: msu.graduateadmissions@murraystate.edu.
Website: https://www.murraystate.edu/academics/CollegesDepartments/CollegeOfHumanitiesAndFineArts/Psychology/

Naropa University, Graduate Programs, Program in Ecopsychology, Boulder, CO 80302-6697. Offers MA. *Program availability:* Part-time, blended/hybrid learning. *Faculty:* 2 full-time (1 woman). *Students:* 9 full-time (7 women), 11 part-time (7 women); includes 2 minority (both Hispanic/Latino), 3 international. Average age 36. 14 applicants, 86% accepted, 9 enrolled. In 2017, 8 master's awarded. *Degree requirements:* For master's, thesis, service learning. *Entrance requirements:* For master's, curriculum vitae/resume with pertinent academic, employment and volunteer activities; 2 letters of recommendation; transcripts; letter of interest. Additional exam requirements/recommendations for international students: Required—TOEFL (minimum score 550 paper-based; 80 iBT). *Application deadline:* For fall admission, 1/15 priority date for domestic and international students. Applications are processed on a rolling basis. Application fee: $60. Electronic applications accepted. *Expenses:* $995 per credit. *Financial support:* In 2017–18, 11 students received support. Career-related internships or fieldwork, Federal Work-Study, scholarships/grants, tuition waivers (partial), and unspecified assistantships available. Support available to part-time students. Financial

award application deadline: 3/1; financial award applicants required to submit FAFSA. *Unit head:* Dr. Tina Fields, Chair, Ecopsychology, 303-245-4654, E-mail: tfields@naropa.edu. *Application contact:* Office of Admissions, 303-546-3572, Fax: 303-546-3583, E-mail: admissions@naropa.edu.
Website: http://www.naropa.edu/academics/masters/ecopsychology/index.php

National Louis University, College of Arts and Sciences, Chicago, IL 60603. Offers adult education (Ed D); counseling and human services (MS); language and academic development (M Ed, Certificate); psychology (MA, PhD, Certificate); public policy (MA); written communication (MS, Certificate). *Program availability:* Part-time, evening/weekend, online learning. *Degree requirements:* For master's and Certificate, comprehensive exam (for some programs), thesis (for some programs); for doctorate, thesis/dissertation. *Entrance requirements:* For master's, MAT or GRE, 3 professional or academic references, interview, minimum GPA of 3.0; for doctorate, GRE General Test, MAT, or Watson-Glaser Critical Thinking Appraisal, three professional or academic references, statement of academic and professional goals, 3 years of experience in field, interview, master's degree, resume, writing sample; for Certificate, GRE, MAT, or Watson-Glaser Critical Thinking Appraisal, three professional or academic references, statement of academic and professional goals, interview, minimum GPA of 3.0. Additional exam requirements/recommendations for international students: Required—Department of Language Studies Assessment or TOEFL (minimum score 550 paper-based; 79 iBT). Electronic applications accepted.

New Mexico Highlands University, Graduate Studies, College of Arts and Sciences, Department of Social and Behavioral Sciences, Las Vegas, NM 87701. Offers psychology (MS), including clinical psychology/counseling, general psychology; public affairs (MA), including applied sociology; Southwest studies (MA), including anthropology. *Program availability:* Part-time. *Degree requirements:* For master's, comprehensive exam, thesis or alternative. *Entrance requirements:* For master's, minimum undergraduate GPA of 3.0. Additional exam requirements/recommendations for international students: Required—TOEFL (minimum score 540 paper-based). *Faculty research:* Southwest Native American resettlement development, community-level interventions, neurochemistry of personality, comparative criminal justice, social theory and activism.

New Mexico State University, College of Arts and Sciences, Department of Psychology, Las Cruces, NM 88003. Offers engineering psychology (PhD); psychology (MA). *Faculty:* 11 full-time (3 women). *Students:* 24 full-time (14 women), 6 part-time (3 women); includes 9 minority (2 Asian, non-Hispanic/Latino; 5 Hispanic/Latino; 2 Two or more races, non-Hispanic/Latino), 2 international. Average age 30. 24 applicants, 38% accepted, 4 enrolled. In 2017, 5 master's, 1 doctorate awarded. *Degree requirements:* For master's, thesis; for doctorate, comprehensive exam, thesis/dissertation, work-related experience (teaching or internship). *Entrance requirements:* For master's, GRE General Test, letters of recommendation, curriculum vitae, personal statement, writing sample; for doctorate, GRE General Test, letters of recommendation, master's thesis, curriculum vitae, personal statement, writing sample. Additional exam requirements/recommendations for international students: Required—TOEFL (minimum score 550 paper-based; 79 iBT), IELTS (minimum score 6.5). *Application deadline:* For fall admission, 1/15 priority date for domestic students, 1/15 for international students. Applications are processed on a rolling basis. Application fee: $40 ($50 for international students). Electronic applications accepted. *Expenses:* Tuition, state resident: full-time $4390. Tuition, nonresident: full-time $15,309. *Required fees:* $853. *Financial support:* In 2017–18, 26 students received support, including 2 fellowships (averaging $4,390 per year), 2 research assistantships (averaging $13,127 per year), 14 teaching assistantships (averaging $15,173 per year); career-related internships or fieldwork, Federal Work-Study, scholarships/grants, traineeships, health care benefits, and unspecified assistantships also available. Support available to part-time students. Financial award application deadline: 3/1. *Faculty research:* Engineering, cognitive, and social psychology; applied cognitive science. *Total annual research expenditures:* $204,371. *Unit head:* Dr. Dominic A. Simon, Department Head, 575-646-2502, Fax: 575-646-6212, E-mail: domsimon@nmsu.edu. *Application contact:* Dr. Laura J. Madson, Chair of Graduate Committee, 575-646-6207, Fax: 575-646-6212, E-mail: lmadson@nmsu.edu.
Website: http://psych.nmsu.edu

The New School, The New School for Social Research, Department of Psychology, New York, NY 10011. Offers clinical psychology (PhD); cognitive, social, and developmental psychology (PhD); psychology (MA). *Accreditation:* APA (one or more programs are accredited). *Program availability:* Part-time. *Faculty:* 14 full-time (8 women), 4 part-time/adjunct (0 women). *Students:* 154 full-time (121 women), 77 part-time (58 women); includes 42 minority (8 Black or African American, non-Hispanic/Latino; 12 Asian, non-Hispanic/Latino; 17 Hispanic/Latino; 5 Two or more races, non-Hispanic/Latino), 39 international. Average age 29. 250 applicants, 83% accepted, 71 enrolled. In 2017, 45 master's, 18 doctorates awarded. Terminal master's awarded for partial completion of doctoral program. *Degree requirements:* For master's, comprehensive exam, thesis (for some programs); for doctorate, comprehensive exam, thesis/dissertation. *Entrance requirements:* For master's, GRE, letters of recommendation, writing sample, essays, transcripts; for doctorate, letters of recommendation, writing sample, essays, transcripts. Additional exam requirements/recommendations for international students: Required—TOEFL (minimum score 100 iBT), IELTS (minimum score 7), PTE (minimum score 68). *Application deadline:* For fall admission, 1/5 priority date for domestic and international students; for spring admission, 10/15 priority date for domestic and international students. Applications are processed on a rolling basis. Application fee: $50. Electronic applications accepted. *Expenses:* $2,180 per credit. *Financial support:* In 2017–18, 191 students received support, including 21 fellowships with full and partial tuition reimbursements available (averaging $19,453 per year), 45 teaching assistantships with full and partial tuition reimbursements available (averaging $9,505 per year); career-related internships or fieldwork, Federal Work-Study, scholarships/grants, and tuition waivers (full and partial) also available. Support available to part-time students. Financial award application deadline: 2/1; financial award applicants required to submit FAFSA. *Unit head:* Dr. William Milberg, Dean, The New School for Social Research, 212-229-5777, E-mail: milbergw@newschool.edu. *Application contact:* Dana Messinger, Director of Graduate Admission, 212-229-5150 Ext. 2300, E-mail: socialresearchadmit@newschool.edu.

New York Medical College, School of Health Sciences and Practice, Valhalla, NY 10595. Offers behavioral sciences and health promotion (MPH); biostatistics (MS); children with special health care (Graduate Certificate); emergency preparedness (Graduate Certificate); environmental health science (MPH); epidemiology (MPH, MS); global health (Graduate Certificate); health education (Graduate Certificate); health policy and management (MPH, Dr PH); industrial hygiene (Graduate Certificate); pediatric dysphagia (Post-Graduate Certificate); physical therapy (DPT); public health (Graduate Certificate); speech-language pathology (MS). *Accreditation:* CEPH. *Program availability:* Part-time, evening/weekend, 100% online, blended/hybrid learning. *Faculty:* 48 full-time (33 women), 235 part-time/adjunct (141 women). *Students:* 221 full-time (153 women), 270 part-time (194 women); includes 202 minority (83 Black or African American, non-Hispanic/Latino; 2 American Indian or Alaska Native, non-Hispanic/Latino; 64 Asian, non-Hispanic/Latino; 47 Hispanic/Latino; 1 Native Hawaiian or other

Pacific Islander, non-Hispanic/Latino; 5 Two or more races, non-Hispanic/Latino), 19 international. Average age 29. 1,118 applicants, 38% accepted, 169 enrolled. In 2017, 110 master's, 41 doctorates awarded. *Degree requirements:* For master's, comprehensive exam (for some programs), thesis (for some programs); for doctorate, thesis/dissertation. *Entrance requirements:* For master's, GRE (for MS in speech-language pathology); for doctorate, GRE. Additional exam requirements/recommendations for international students: Required—TOEFL, IELTS. *Application deadline:* For fall admission, 8/1 for domestic students, 4/15 for international students; for spring admission, 12/1 for domestic students; for summer admission, 5/1 for domestic students, 4/15 for international students. Application fee: $125. Electronic applications accepted. *Expenses:* $1,125 per credit, $245 fees. *Financial support:* In 2017–18, 10,000 students received support. Scholarships/grants and unspecified assistantships available. Financial award application deadline: 4/30; financial award applicants required to submit FAFSA. *Unit head:* Ben Watson, PhD, Vice Dean, 914-594-4531, E-mail: ben_watson@nymc.edu. *Application contact:* Irene Bundziak, Assistant to Director of Admissions, 914-594-4905, E-mail: irene_bundziak@nymc.edu.
Website: http://www.nymc.edu/school-of-health-sciences-and-practice-shsp/

New York University, Graduate School of Arts and Science, Department of Psychology, New York, NY 10012-1019. Offers cognition and perception (PhD); general psychology (MA); industrial/organizational psychology (MA); psychotherapy and psychoanalysis (Advanced Certificate); social psychology (PhD). *Program availability:* Part-time. *Students:* Average age 31. 874 applicants, 46% accepted, 153 enrolled. In 2017, 102 master's, 9 doctorates, 10 other advanced degrees awarded. Terminal master's awarded for partial completion of doctoral program. *Degree requirements:* For master's, comprehensive exam, thesis or alternative; for doctorate, thesis/dissertation. *Entrance requirements:* For master's and doctorate, GRE General Test. Additional exam requirements/recommendations for international students: Required—TOEFL. *Application deadline:* For fall admission, 12/12 for domestic and international students. Application fee: $100. *Expenses: Tuition:* Full-time $41,352; part-time $19,968 per year. *Required fees:* $2496; $1628 per unit. $814 per term. Tuition and fees vary according to course load and program. *Financial support:* Fellowships, research assistantships, teaching assistantships, career-related internships or fieldwork, Federal Work-Study, institutionally sponsored loans, scholarships/grants, traineeships, health care benefits, and unspecified assistantships available. Financial award application deadline: 12/12; financial award applicants required to submit FAFSA. *Faculty research:* Vision, memory, social cognition, social and cognitive development, relationships. *Unit head:* Gabriele Oettingen, Director of Graduate Studies, PhD Program, 212-998-7900, Fax: 212-995-4018, E-mail: psychq@psych.nyu.edu. *Application contact:* Adrienne Gans, Director of Graduate Studies, MA Program, 212-998-7900, Fax: 212-995-4018, E-mail: psychq@psych.nyu.edu.
Website: http://www.psych.nyu.edu/

New York University, Steinhardt School of Culture, Education, and Human Development, Department of Applied Psychology, Programs in Educational and Developmental Psychology, New York, NY 10012. Offers developmental psychology (PhD); human development and social intervention (MA); psychology and social intervention (PhD). *Accreditation:* APA (one or more programs are accredited). *Program availability:* Part-time. *Students:* Average age 27. 137 applicants, 26% accepted, 13 enrolled. In 2017, 16 master's, 4 doctorates awarded. *Entrance requirements:* For doctorate, GRE General Test, interview. Additional exam requirements/recommendations for international students: Required—TOEFL. *Application deadline:* For fall admission, 12/1 priority date for domestic and international students. Applications are processed on a rolling basis. Application fee: $75. Electronic applications accepted. *Expenses: Tuition:* Full-time $41,352; part-time $19,968 per year. *Required fees:* $2496; $1628 per unit. $814 per term. Tuition and fees vary according to course load and program. *Financial support:* Teaching assistantships with partial tuition reimbursements, career-related internships or fieldwork, Federal Work-Study, institutionally sponsored loans, and tuition waivers (partial) available. Support available to part-time students. Financial award application deadline: 2/1; financial award applicants required to submit FAFSA. *Faculty research:* Schools and communities, self-regulation and academic achievement, intervention and social change, trauma and resilience, cognition. *Unit head:* Prof. Clancy Blair, Director, 212-998-5853, Fax: 212-995-4358, E-mail: clancy.blair@nyu.edu. *Application contact:* 212-998-5030, Fax: 212-995-4328, E-mail: steinhardt.gradadmissions@nyu.edu.
Website: http://steinhardt.nyu.edu/appsych

Norfolk State University, School of Graduate Studies, School of Liberal Arts, Department of Psychology, Norfolk, VA 23504. Offers community/clinical psychology (MA); psychology (Psy D). Psy D offered through the Virginia Consortium for Professional Psychology. *Program availability:* Part-time. *Degree requirements:* For master's, comprehensive exam, thesis or alternative; for doctorate, comprehensive exam, thesis/dissertation. *Entrance requirements:* For master's, minimum GPA of 2.7.

North Carolina Central University, College of Behavioral and Social Sciences, Department of Psychology, Durham, NC 27707-3129. Offers clinical psychology (MA); general psychology (MA). *Program availability:* Part-time, evening/weekend. *Degree requirements:* For master's, one foreign language, comprehensive exam, thesis. *Entrance requirements:* For master's, GRE, minimum GPA of 3.0 in major, 2.5 overall. Additional exam requirements/recommendations for international students: Required—TOEFL. *Application deadline:* For fall admission, 8/1 for domestic students. Application fee: $30. *Expenses:* Tuition, state resident: full-time $2770; part-time $692.50 per credit hour. Tuition, nonresident: full-time $9247; part-time $2311.75 per credit hour. *Financial support:* Application deadline: 5/1; applicants required to submit FAFSA. *Unit head:* Vinston J. Goldman, Graduate Coordinator, 919-530-6471, Fax: 919-530-5380, E-mail: vgoldman@nccu.edu. *Application contact:* Vinston J. Goldman, Graduate Coordinator, 919-530-6471, Fax: 919-530-5380, E-mail: vgoldman@nccu.edu.

North Carolina State University, Graduate School, College of Humanities and Social Sciences, Department of Psychology, Raleigh, NC 27695. Offers developmental psychology (PhD); ergonomics and experimental psychology (PhD); industrial/organizational psychology (PhD); psychology in the public interest (PhD); school psychology (PhD). *Accreditation:* APA. *Degree requirements:* For doctorate, comprehensive exam, thesis/dissertation. *Entrance requirements:* For doctorate, GRE General Test, GRE Subject Test (industrial/organizational psychology), MAT (recommended), minimum GPA of 3.0 in major. Electronic applications accepted. *Faculty research:* Cognitive and social development (human factors, families, the workplace, community issues and health, aging).

Northcentral University, Graduate Studies, San Diego, CA 92106. Offers business (MBA, DBA, PhD, Postbaccalaureate Certificate); education (M Ed, Ed D, PhD, Ed S, Post-Master's Certificate, Postbaccalaureate Certificate); marriage and family therapy (MA, DMFT, PhD, Post-Master's Certificate, Postbaccalaureate Certificate); psychology (MA, PhD, Post-Master's Certificate, Postbaccalaureate Certificate); technology (MS, PhD), including computer science, cybersecurity (MS), data science, technology and innovation management (PhD). *Program availability:* Part-time, evening/weekend, online only, 100% online. *Faculty:* 98 full-time (63 women), 385 part-time/adjunct (203 women). *Students:* 5,036 full-time (3,291 women), 5,747 part-time (3,977 women); includes 3,777 minority (2,550 Black or African American, non-Hispanic/Latino; 76 American Indian or Alaska Native, non-Hispanic/Latino; 192 Asian, non-Hispanic/Latino; 603 Hispanic/Latino; 39 Native Hawaiian or other Pacific Islander, non-Hispanic/Latino; 317 Two or more races, non-Hispanic/Latino). Average age 45. In 2017, 929 master's, 782 doctorates, 278 other advanced degrees awarded. *Degree requirements:* For doctorate, comprehensive exam, thesis/dissertation. *Entrance requirements:* For master's, bachelor's degree from regionally- or nationally-accredited institution, current resume or curriculum vitae, statement of intent, interview, and background check (for marriage and family therapy); for doctorate, post-baccalaureate master's degree and/or doctoral degree from nationally- or regionally-accredited academic institution; for other advanced degree, bachelor's-level or higher degree from accredited institution or university (for Post-Baccalaureate Certificate); master's and/or doctoral degree from regionally- or nationally-accredited academic institution (for Post-Master's Certificate). Additional exam requirements/recommendations for international students: Required—TOEFL (minimum score 550 paper-based; 79 iBT), IELTS (minimum score 6.5), PTE (minimum score 53). *Application deadline:* Applications are processed on a rolling basis. Application fee: $0. Electronic applications accepted. Tuition and fees vary according to program. *Financial support:* Scholarships/grants available. *Faculty research:* Business management, curriculum and instruction, educational leadership, health psychology, organizational behavior. *Unit head:* Dr. David Harpool, Acting Provost, 888-327-2877 Ext. 8181, E-mail: provost@ncu.edu. *Application contact:* Ken Boutelle, Vice President, Enrollment Services, 888-628-4979, E-mail: enrollmentservices@ncu.edu.

North Dakota State University, College of Graduate and Interdisciplinary Studies, College of Science and Mathematics, Department of Psychology, Fargo, ND 58102. Offers clinical psychology (MS); health and social psychology (PhD); psychological clinical science (PhD); psychology (MS); visual and cognitive neuroscience (PhD). *Degree requirements:* For master's, thesis; for doctorate, thesis/dissertation. *Entrance requirements:* For master's and doctorate, GRE General Test, GRE Subject Test. Additional exam requirements/recommendations for international students: Required—TOEFL (minimum score 525 paper-based; 71 iBT). Electronic applications accepted. *Faculty research:* Cognition science, neuropsychology, group behavior, applied behavior analysis, behavior therapy.

Northeastern State University, College of Education, Department of Psychology and Counseling, Tahlequah, OK 74464-2399. Offers counseling (MS). *Program availability:* Part-time, evening/weekend. *Faculty:* 12 full-time (4 women), 4 part-time/adjunct (3 women). *Students:* 86 full-time (71 women), 54 part-time (39 women); includes 58 minority (6 Black or African American, non-Hispanic/Latino; 23 American Indian or Alaska Native, non-Hispanic/Latino; 2 Asian, non-Hispanic/Latino; 2 Hispanic/Latino; 25 Two or more races, non-Hispanic/Latino). Average age 32. In 2017, 60 master's awarded. *Degree requirements:* For master's, thesis (for some programs), written and oral examinations. *Entrance requirements:* For master's, GRE, minimum GPA of 2.5. *Application deadline:* Applications are processed on a rolling basis. Application fee: $25. Electronic applications accepted. *Expenses:* Tuition, state resident: part-time $222 per credit hour. Tuition, nonresident: part-time $501.75 per credit hour. *Required fees:* $37.40 per credit hour. Tuition and fees vary according to degree level. *Financial support:* Teaching assistantships, career-related internships or fieldwork, and Federal Work-Study available. Financial award application deadline: 3/1. *Unit head:* Dr. Elizabeth Keller-Dupree, Program Chair, 918-449-6534, E-mail: kellere@nsuok.edu. *Application contact:* Josh McCollum, Graduate Coordinator, 918-444-2093, E-mail: mccolluj@nsuok.edu.
Website: https://academics.nsuok.edu/education/EducationHome/COEDepartments/PsychologyCounseling.aspx

Northeastern University, College of Science, Boston, MA 02115-5096. Offers applied mathematics (MS); bioinformatics (MS); biology (PhD); biotechnology (MS); chemistry and chemical biology (MS, PhD); environmental science and policy (MS); marine and environmental sciences (PhD); marine biology (MS); mathematics (MS, PhD); operations research (MSOR); physics (MS, PhD); psychology (PhD). *Program availability:* Part-time. Terminal master's awarded for partial completion of doctoral program. *Degree requirements:* For master's, comprehensive exam (for some programs), thesis; for doctorate, comprehensive exam (for some programs), thesis/dissertation. *Entrance requirements:* For master's, GRE General Test. *Application deadline:* Applications are processed on a rolling basis. Application fee: $75. Electronic applications accepted. *Expenses:* Contact institution. *Financial support:* Fellowships with tuition reimbursements, research assistantships with tuition reimbursements, teaching assistantships with tuition reimbursements, career-related internships or fieldwork, scholarships/grants, health care benefits, tuition waivers (full and partial), and unspecified assistantships available. Support available to part-time students. Financial award applicants required to submit FAFSA. *Unit head:* Dr. Kenneth Henderson, Dean, 617-373-5089, E-mail: k.henderson@northeastern.edu. *Application contact:* Graduate Student Services, 617-373-4275, E-mail: gradcos@northeastern.edu.
Website: https://cos.northeastern.edu/

Northern Arizona University, College of Social and Behavioral Sciences, Department of Psychological Sciences, Flagstaff, AZ 86011. Offers psychological sciences (MA). *Program availability:* Part-time. *Faculty:* 30 full-time (16 women). *Students:* 25 full-time (18 women), 1 part-time (0 women); includes 9 minority (1 Black or African American, non-Hispanic/Latino; 6 Hispanic/Latino; 2 Two or more races, non-Hispanic/Latino). Average age 25. 33 applicants, 58% accepted, 17 enrolled. In 2017, 12 master's awarded. *Degree requirements:* For master's, variable foreign language requirement, comprehensive exam (for some programs), thesis (for some programs). *Entrance requirements:* For master's, GRE General Test. Additional exam requirements/recommendations for international students: Required—TOEFL (minimum score 80 iBT), IELTS (minimum score 6.5). *Application deadline:* For fall admission, 3/1 for domestic and international students; for spring admission, 10/1 for domestic and international students. Applications are processed on a rolling basis. Application fee: $65. Electronic applications accepted. *Expenses:* Tuition, state resident: full-time $9240; part-time $458 per credit hour. Tuition, nonresident: full-time $21,588; part-time $1199 per credit hour. *Required fees:* $1021; $14 per credit hour. $646 per semester. Tuition and fees vary according to course load, campus/location and program. *Financial support:* In 2017–18, 26 students received support, including 1 research assistantship with partial tuition reimbursement available (averaging $9,000 per year), 19 teaching assistantships with partial tuition reimbursements available (averaging $9,000 per year); institutionally sponsored loans, health care benefits, tuition waivers (partial), and unspecified assistantships also available. Financial award application deadline: 2/1; financial award applicants required to submit FAFSA. *Unit head:* Dr. Robert E. Till, Chair, 928-523-0713, Fax: 928-523-6777, E-mail: robert.till@nau.edu. *Application contact:* M. Delfina Rodriguez, Administrative Associate, 928-523-0654, Fax: 928-523-6777.
Website: http://nau.edu/sbs/psych/

Northern Illinois University, Graduate School, College of Liberal Arts and Sciences, Department of Psychology, De Kalb, IL 60115-2854. Offers MA, PhD. *Accreditation:* APA (one or more programs are accredited). *Faculty:* 26 full-time (11 women), 5 part-time/adjunct (1 woman). *Students:* 84 full-time (63 women), 23 part-time (19 women); includes 20 minority (8 Black or African American, non-Hispanic/Latino; 3 Asian, non-Hispanic/Latino; 8 Hispanic/Latino; 1 Two or more races, non-Hispanic/Latino), 7

international. Average age 27. 415 applicants, 10% accepted, 22 enrolled. In 2017, 14 master's, 23 doctorates awarded. *Degree requirements:* For master's, comprehensive exam, thesis optional; for doctorate, thesis/dissertation, candidacy exam, dissertation defense. *Entrance requirements:* For master's, GRE General Test, minimum GPA of 3.0 for last 2 years of undergraduate work; for doctorate, GRE General Test, minimum undergraduate GPA of 2.75, graduate 3.2; master's degree with research thesis. Additional exam requirements/recommendations for international students: Required—TOEFL (minimum score 550 paper-based). *Application deadline:* For fall admission, 3/1 for domestic students, 5/1 for international students; for spring admission, 11/1 for domestic students, 10/1 for international students. Applications are processed on a rolling basis. Application fee: $40. Electronic applications accepted. *Financial support:* In 2017–18, 22 research assistantships with full tuition reimbursements, 65 teaching assistantships with full tuition reimbursements were awarded; fellowships with full tuition reimbursements, career-related internships or fieldwork, Federal Work-Study, scholarships/grants, tuition waivers (full), and staff assistantships also available. Support available to part-time students. Financial award applicants required to submit FAFSA. *Faculty research:* Neglect syndrome, ADHD, workplace discrimination, adolescent suicide, social dilemmas. *Unit head:* Dr. Leslie Matuszewich, Chair, 815-753-7065, E-mail: lmatekaitis@niu.edu. *Application contact:* Dr. James V. Corwin, Director, Graduate Studies, 815-753-7088, E-mail: jcorwin@niu.edu.
Website: http://www.niu.edu/psyc/

Northern Michigan University, Office of Graduate Education and Research, College of Arts and Sciences, Department of Psychological Science, Marquette, MI 49855-5301. Offers applied behavior analysis (MS); psychological science (MS). *Program availability:* Part-time. *Degree requirements:* For master's, thesis (for some programs). *Entrance requirements:* For master's, minimum GPA of 3.0; bachelor's degree (preferably in psychology); undergraduate courses in introduction to psychology and statistics; personal statement; 3 letters of recommendation. Additional exam requirements/recommendations for international students: Required—TOEFL (minimum score 550 paper-based; 79 iBT), IELTS (minimum score 6.5). *Application deadline:* For fall admission, 7/1 for domestic students; for winter admission, 11/15 for domestic students; for spring admission, 3/17 for domestic students. Applications are processed on a rolling basis. Application fee: $50. Electronic applications accepted. *Expenses:* Tuition, state resident: full-time $9417; part-time $542 per credit hour. Tuition, nonresident: full-time $12,873; part-time $758 per credit hour. Tuition and fees vary according to course load, degree level and program. *Financial support:* Teaching assistantships with full tuition reimbursements, Federal Work-Study, institutionally sponsored loans, scholarships/grants, and unspecified assistantships available. Support available to part-time students. Financial award application deadline: 3/1; financial award applicants required to submit FAFSA. *Faculty research:* Emotion and cognition, neuropsychopharmacology, sensation and perception, behavior analysis, developmental psychology. *Unit head:* Dr. Adam Prus, Head, 906-227-2935. *Application contact:* Dr. Adam Prus, Head, 906-227-2935.
Website: http://www.nmu.edu/psychology/

Northwestern State University of Louisiana, Graduate Studies and Research, Department of Psychology, Natchitoches, LA 71497. Offers clinical psychology (MS). *Degree requirements:* For master's, comprehensive exam, thesis or alternative. *Entrance requirements:* For master's, GRE General Test, GRE Subject Test, minimum undergraduate GPA of 2.5. Additional exam requirements/recommendations for international students: Required—TOEFL. Electronic applications accepted.

Northwestern University, The Graduate School, Judd A. and Marjorie Weinberg College of Arts and Sciences, Department of Psychology, Evanston, IL 60208. Offers brain, behavior and cognition (PhD); clinical psychology (PhD); cognitive psychology (PhD); personality psychology (PhD); social psychology (PhD); JD/PhD. Admissions and degrees offered through The Graduate School. *Accreditation:* APA (one or more programs are accredited). *Program availability:* Part-time. *Degree requirements:* For doctorate, thesis/dissertation. *Entrance requirements:* For doctorate, GRE General Test, GRE Subject Test. Additional exam requirements/recommendations for international students: Required—TOEFL. Electronic applications accepted. *Faculty research:* Memory and higher order cognition, anxiety and depression, effectiveness of psychotherapy, social cognition, molecular basis of memory.

Northwest University, College of Social and Behavioral Sciences, Kirkland, WA 98033. Offers counseling psychology (MA, Psy D); international community development (MA). *Program availability:* Evening/weekend. *Entrance requirements:* For master's, 3 character references. Additional exam requirements/recommendations for international students: Required—TOEFL (minimum score 580 paper-based). *Expenses:* Contact institution.

Nova Southeastern University, College of Psychology, Fort Lauderdale, FL 33314-7796. Offers clinical mental health counseling (MS); clinical psychology (PhD, Psy D); counseling (MS); experimental psychology (MS); forensic psychology (MS); general psychology (MS); school counseling (MS); school psychology (Psy D, Psy S); substance abuse counseling (MS); substance abuse counseling and education (MS). *Accreditation:* APA (one or more programs are accredited). *Program availability:* 100% online, blended/hybrid learning. *Faculty:* 51 full-time (21 women), 120 part-time/adjunct (70 women). *Students:* 751 full-time (618 women), 821 part-time (709 women); includes 787 minority (268 Black or African American, non-Hispanic/Latino; 2 American Indian or Alaska Native, non-Hispanic/Latino; 38 Asian, non-Hispanic/Latino; 431 Hispanic/Latino; 2 Native Hawaiian or other Pacific Islander, non-Hispanic/Latino; 46 Two or more races, non-Hispanic/Latino), 45 international. Average age 31. 1,117 applicants, 38% accepted, 294 enrolled. In 2017, 459 master's, 100 doctorates, 10 other advanced degrees awarded. Terminal master's awarded for partial completion of doctoral program. *Degree requirements:* For master's, comprehensive exam, 3 practica; for doctorate, thesis/dissertation, clinical internship, competency exam; for Psy S, comprehensive exam, internship. *Entrance requirements:* For master's and Psy S, GRE General Test, letters of recommendation, research/personal statement, interview; for doctorate, GRE General Test, GRE Subject Test (recommended), minimum undergraduate GPA of 3.0, letters of recommendation, research/personal statement, interview, curriculum vitae/resume. Additional exam requirements/recommendations for international students: Required—TOEFL (minimum score 550 paper-based). *Application deadline:* Applications are processed on a rolling basis. Application fee: $50. Electronic applications accepted. *Expenses:* Contact institution. *Financial support:* In 2017–18, 197 students received support, including 15 research assistantships (averaging $5,600 per year), 68 teaching assistantships (averaging $2,000 per year); career-related internships or fieldwork, Federal Work-Study, institutionally sponsored loans, scholarships/grants, and unspecified assistantships also available. Support available to part-time students. Financial award application deadline: 4/15; financial award applicants required to submit FAFSA. *Faculty research:* Clinical health psychology, multicultural/diversity psychology, clinical neuropsychology, clinical child psychology, family violence. *Unit head:* Dr. Karen Grosby, Dean, 954-262-5712, Fax: 954-262-3859, E-mail: grosby@nova.edu. *Application contact:* Carlos Perez, Senior Manager of Outreach, 954-262-5702, Fax: 954-262-3893, E-mail: gradschool@nova.edu.
Website: http://psychology.nova.edu/

The Ohio State University, Graduate School, College of Arts and Sciences, Division of Social and Behavioral Sciences, Department of Psychology, Columbus, OH 43210. Offers behavioral neuroscience (PhD); clinical psychology (PhD); cognitive psychology (PhD); developmental psychology (PhD); intellectual and developmental disabilities psychology (PhD); quantitative psychology (PhD); social psychology (PhD). *Accreditation:* APA. *Faculty:* 52. *Students:* 144 full-time (86 women); includes 18 minority (8 Asian, non-Hispanic/Latino; 10 Hispanic/Latino), 28 international. Average age 26. In 2017, 21 doctorates awarded. *Entrance requirements:* For doctorate, GRE General Test. Additional exam requirements/recommendations for international students: Required—TOEFL (minimum score 600 paper-based; 100 iBT); Recommended—IELTS (minimum score 8). *Application deadline:* For fall admission, 12/1 for domestic and international students. Applications are processed on a rolling basis. Application fee: $60 ($70 for international students). Electronic applications accepted. *Financial support:* Fellowships, research assistantships, and teaching assistantships available. *Unit head:* Dr. John Bruno, Chair, 614-292-3038, E-mail: bruno.1@osu.edu. *Application contact:* Graduate and Professional Admissions, 614-292-9444, Fax: 614-292-3895, E-mail: gpadmissions@osu.edu.
Website: http://psychology.osu.edu/

Ohio University, Graduate College, College of Arts and Sciences, Department of Psychology, Athens, OH 45701-2979. Offers clinical psychology (PhD); experimental psychology (PhD); organizational psychology (PhD). *Accreditation:* APA. *Degree requirements:* For doctorate, one foreign language, comprehensive exam, thesis/dissertation. *Entrance requirements:* For doctorate, GRE General Test, GRE Subject Test. Additional exam requirements/recommendations for international students: Required—TOEFL (minimum score 550 paper-based; 80 iBT) or IELTS (minimum score 6.5). Electronic applications accepted. *Faculty research:* Health, cognitive, child clinical, and social psychology.

Oklahoma State University, College of Arts and Sciences, Department of Psychology, Stillwater, OK 74078. Offers clinical psychology (PhD); general psychology (MS). *Accreditation:* APA (one or more programs are accredited). *Faculty:* 33 full-time (20 women), 1 part-time/adjunct (0 women). *Students:* 31 full-time (25 women), 26 part-time (22 women); includes 13 minority (4 American Indian or Alaska Native, non-Hispanic/Latino; 1 Asian, non-Hispanic/Latino; 4 Hispanic/Latino; 1 Native Hawaiian or other Pacific Islander, non-Hispanic/Latino; 3 Two or more races, non-Hispanic/Latino), 2 international. Average age 27. 142 applicants, 7% accepted, 10 enrolled. In 2017, 8 master's, 13 doctorates awarded. *Entrance requirements:* For master's and doctorate, GRE General Test. Additional exam requirements/recommendations for international students: Required—TOEFL (minimum score 550 paper-based; 79 iBT). *Application deadline:* For fall admission, 3/1 priority date for international students; for spring admission, 8/1 priority date for international students. Applications are processed on a rolling basis. Application fee: $40 ($75 for international students). Electronic applications accepted. *Expenses:* Tuition, state resident: full-time $4019; part-time $2679.60 per year. Tuition, nonresident: full-time $15,286; part-time $10,190.40 per year. *Required fees:* $2129; $1419 per unit. Tuition and fees vary according to program. *Financial support:* Research assistantships, teaching assistantships, career-related internships or fieldwork, Federal Work-Study, scholarships/grants, health care benefits, tuition waivers (partial), and unspecified assistantships available. Support available to part-time students. Financial award application deadline: 3/1; financial award applicants required to submit FAFSA. *Unit head:* Dr. Thad Leffingwell, Department Head, 405-744-7494, Fax: 405-744-8067, E-mail: thad.leffingwell@okstate.edu. *Application contact:* Patricia Alexander, Graduate Advisor, 405-744-7591, Fax: 405-744-8967, E-mail: patricia.alexander@okstate.edu.
Website: http://psychology.okstate.edu

Old Dominion University, College of Sciences, Doctoral Program in Psychology, Norfolk, VA 23529. Offers applied psychological sciences (PhD); human factors psychology (PhD); industrial/organizational psychology (PhD). *Faculty:* 21 full-time (8 women). *Students:* 14 full-time (9 women), 14 part-time (8 women); includes 4 minority (1 Black or African American, non-Hispanic/Latino; 3 Hispanic/Latino). Average age 29. 99 applicants, 11% accepted, 6 enrolled. In 2017, 9 doctorates awarded. *Degree requirements:* For doctorate, comprehensive exam, thesis/dissertation, candidacy exam. *Entrance requirements:* For doctorate, GRE General Test, GRE Subject Test, 3 recommendation letters. Additional exam requirements/recommendations for international students: Required—TOEFL. *Application deadline:* For fall and winter admission, 1/5 for domestic and international students. Application fee: $50. Electronic applications accepted. *Expenses:* Contact institution. *Financial support:* In 2017–18, 26 students received support, including 4 research assistantships with full tuition reimbursements available (averaging $15,000 per year), 22 teaching assistantships with full tuition reimbursements available (averaging $15,000 per year); scholarships/grants also available. Financial award application deadline: 1/15. *Faculty research:* Human factors, industrial psychology, organizational psychology, applied psychological sciences (health, developmental, community, quantitative). *Total annual research expenditures:* $1.2 million. *Unit head:* Dr. Debra A. Major, Graduate Program Director, 757-683-4235, Fax: 757-683-5087, E-mail: dmajor@odu.edu. *Application contact:* William Heffelfinger, Director of Graduate Admissions, 757-683-5554, Fax: 757-683-3255, E-mail: gradadmit@odu.edu.
Website: http://www.odu.edu/psychology/

Old Dominion University, College of Sciences, Master of Science in Psychology Program, Norfolk, VA 23529. Offers MS. *Program availability:* Part-time. *Faculty:* 21 full-time (8 women). *Students:* 26 full-time (14 women), 2 part-time (both women); includes 7 minority (1 Black or African American, non-Hispanic/Latino; 3 Asian, non-Hispanic/Latino; 1 Hispanic/Latino; 2 Two or more races, non-Hispanic/Latino). Average age 26. 44 applicants, 23% accepted, 8 enrolled. In 2017, 11 master's awarded. Terminal master's awarded for partial completion of doctoral program. *Degree requirements:* For master's, thesis. *Entrance requirements:* For master's, GRE General Test, minimum GPA of 3.0 in major, previous course work in psychology. Additional exam requirements/recommendations for international students: Required—TOEFL (minimum score 550 paper-based; 79 iBT), GRE. *Application deadline:* For fall admission, 5/15 for domestic and international students. Applications are processed on a rolling basis. Application fee: $50. Electronic applications accepted. *Expenses:* Contact institution. *Financial support:* In 2017–18, 2 students received support, including 2 teaching assistantships with full tuition reimbursements available (averaging $12,000 per year); research assistantships also available. Financial award application deadline: 2/15; financial award applicants required to submit FAFSA. *Faculty research:* Social psychology, developmental psychology, human factors psychology, community psychology, physiopsychology, clinical psychology, industrial/organizational psychology, health psychology. *Total annual research expenditures:* $978,563. *Unit head:* Dr. James M. Henson, Graduate Program Director, 757-683-5761, Fax: 757-683-5087, E-mail: jhenson@odu.edu. *Application contact:* William Heffelfinger, Director of Graduate Admissions, 757-683-5554, Fax: 757-683-3255, E-mail: gradadmit@odu.edu.

Oregon State University, College of Liberal Arts, Program in Psychology, Corvallis, OR 97331. Offers applied cognition (MS, PhD); engineering psychology (MS, PhD); health psychology (MS, PhD). *Application deadline:* For fall admission, 12/15 for domestic and international students. Application fee: $75 ($85 for international students). *Unit head:*

Psychology—General

Jason McCarley, Graduate Education Chair, E-mail: jason.mccarley@oregonstate.edu. *Application contact:* Aurora Sherman, Associate Professor and Graduate Education Chair, 541-737-1361, E-mail: aurora.sherman@oregonstate.edu. Website: http://liberalarts.oregonstate.edu/school-psychological-science/psychology/graduate-psychology

Our Lady of the Lake University, College of Professional Studies, Program in Psychology, San Antonio, TX 78207-4689. Offers marriage and family therapy (MS); school psychology (MS). *Accreditation:* APA. *Program availability:* Part-time. *Faculty:* 2 full-time (both women), 2 part-time/adjunct (1 woman). *Students:* 101 full-time (87 women), 14 part-time (13 women); includes 78 minority (12 Black or African American, non-Hispanic/Latino; 66 Hispanic/Latino). Average age 30. 81 applicants, 78% accepted, 37 enrolled. In 2017, 40 master's awarded. *Degree requirements:* For master's, comprehensive exam, practicum. *Entrance requirements:* For master's, GRE General Test or MAT, bachelor's degree with at least 12 undergraduate semester hours in psychology including one course in statistics and minimum cumulative GPA of 3.0; criminal background check; personal statement addressing background in psychology, expectations of the MS program, and professional goals; statement of purpose; 2 letters of recommendation. Additional exam requirements/recommendations for international students: Required—TOEFL. *Application deadline:* For fall admission, 3/1 priority date for domestic and international students. Application fee: $40 ($50 for international students). Electronic applications accepted. Application fee is waived when completed online. *Expenses: Tuition:* Full-time $10,668; part-time $5334 per year. *Required fees:* $816; $816 per year. $408 per semester. *Financial support:* In 2017–18, 2 students received support. Federal Work-Study, scholarships/grants, unspecified assistantships, and tuition discounts available. Support available to part-time students. Financial award application deadline: 5/1; financial award applicants required to submit FAFSA. *Faculty research:* Providing competent services to diverse client populations. *Unit head:* Dr. Deborah Healy, Psychology Department, 210-431-7118, E-mail: dahealy@ollusa.edu. *Application contact:* Office of Graduate Admissions, 210-431-3995, Fax: 210-431-3945, E-mail: gradadm@lake.ollusa.edu.
Website: http://www.ollusa.edu/s/1190/hybrid/default-hybrid-ollu.aspx?sid-1190&gid-1&pgid-7908

Pace University, Dyson College of Arts and Sciences, Department of Psychology, Program in Psychology, New York, NY 10038. Offers MA. *Program availability:* Part-time, evening/weekend. *Students:* 31 full-time (24 women), 9 part-time (8 women); includes 22 minority (11 Black or African American, non-Hispanic/Latino; 2 Asian, non-Hispanic/Latino; 9 Hispanic/Latino), 4 international. Average age 26. In 2017, 8 master's awarded. *Entrance requirements:* For master's, GRE, two letters of recommendation, resume, statement of purpose, all official transcripts, bachelor's degree from accredited institution, at least 9 hours of undergraduate psychology course prerequisites. Additional exam requirements/recommendations for international students: Required—TOEFL (minimum score 88 iBT), IELTS (minimum score 7) or PTE (minimum score 60). *Application deadline:* For fall admission, 8/1 priority date for domestic students, 6/1 for international students; for spring admission, 12/1 for domestic students, 10/1 for international students. Applications are processed on a rolling basis. Application fee: $70. Electronic applications accepted. *Financial support:* Scholarships/grants available. Financial award application deadline: 2/15; financial award applicants required to submit FAFSA. *Unit head:* Dr. Barbara Mowder, Director of Graduate Psychology Programs, 212-346-1556, E-mail: bmowder@pace.edu. *Application contact:* Susan Ford-Goldschein, Director of Graduate Admissions, 212-346-1531, Fax: 212-346-1585, E-mail: graduateadmission@pace.edu.
Website: http://www.pace.edu/dyson/academic-departments-and-programs/psychology---nyc/graduate-programs

Pacifica Graduate Institute, Graduate Programs, Carpinteria, CA 93013. Offers clinical psychology (PhD); counseling psychology (MA); depth psychology (MA, PhD); mythological studies (MA, PhD). Terminal master's awarded for partial completion of doctoral program. *Degree requirements:* For master's, thesis (for some programs), practicum; for doctorate, comprehensive exam, thesis/dissertation, internship. *Entrance requirements:* For master's, resume, 3 letters of recommendation, writing sample, interview; for doctorate, resumé, 4 letters of recommendation, writing sample, interview. Additional exam requirements/recommendations for international students: Required—TOEFL. *Faculty research:* Imaginal and archetypal theory; post-Colonial psychoanalytic and Jungian theory; myth literature as it applies to the theory and practice of psychology.

Pacific University, School of Professional Psychology, Forest Grove, OR 97116-1797. Offers applied psychological science (MA, MS); clinical psychology (PhD, Psy D). *Accreditation:* APA (one or more programs are accredited). *Program availability:* Part-time. *Degree requirements:* For master's, comprehensive exam (for some programs), thesis (for some programs); for doctorate, comprehensive exam, thesis/dissertation. *Entrance requirements:* For master's, course work in introductory psychology, statistics, and abnormal psychology; minimum GPA of 3.0; for doctorate, GRE General Test, minimum GPA of 3.0, undergraduate course work in psychology, minimum GPA of 3.1 in last 2 years. Additional exam requirements/recommendations for international students: Required—TOEFL (minimum score 600 paper-based). Electronic applications accepted. *Expenses:* Contact institution. *Faculty research:* Neuropsychological assessment, assessment and treatment of anxiety, forensic psychology, cross-cultural psychology, child and adolescent psychopathology.

Palo Alto University, MS in Psychology (PhD Prep) Program, Palo Alto, CA 94304. Offers MS. *Program availability:* Part-time, online only, online program with 1-week on-campus intensive. *Faculty:* 6 full-time (5 women), 4 part-time/adjunct (3 women). *Students:* 2 full-time (both women), 36 part-time (25 women); includes 14 minority (1 Black or African American, non-Hispanic/Latino; 1 Asian, non-Hispanic/Latino; 7 Hispanic/Latino; 5 Two or more races, non-Hispanic/Latino). Average age 28. 51 applicants, 80% accepted, 19 enrolled. In 2017, 13 master's awarded. *Degree requirements:* For master's, online program with a 1-week on-campus intensive. *Entrance requirements:* For master's, undergraduate degree in psychology with minimum GPA of 3.3. Additional exam requirements/recommendations for international students: Required—TOEFL. *Application deadline:* For fall admission, 6/30 priority date for domestic and international students. Applications are processed on a rolling basis. Application fee: $50. Electronic applications accepted. *Expenses:* Contact institution. *Financial support:* In 2017–18, 1 student received support. Federal Work-Study available. Financial award applicants required to submit FAFSA. *Unit head:* Dr. Olga Rosito, Director of MS in Psychology Program/Adjunct Professor, E-mail: orosito@paloaltou.edu. *Application contact:* Yukti Singh, Director of Admissions Marketing and Master's Enrollment, E-mail: ysingh@paloaltou.edu.
Website: http://www.paloaltou.edu/graduate-programs/masters-degree-programs/ms-psychology-phd-prep

Palo Alto University, PhD in Clinical Psychology Program, Palo Alto, CA 94304. Offers PhD. *Accreditation:* APA. *Faculty:* 33 full-time (19 women), 37 part-time/adjunct (24 women). *Students:* 435 full-time (344 women), 18 part-time (14 women); includes 168 minority (24 Black or African American, non-Hispanic/Latino; 1 American Indian or Alaska Native, non-Hispanic/Latino; 45 Asian, non-Hispanic/Latino; 57 Hispanic/Latino; 2 Native Hawaiian or other Pacific Islander, non-Hispanic/Latino; 39 Two or more races, non-Hispanic/Latino). Average age 26. 346 applicants, 73% accepted, 82 enrolled. In

2017, 64 doctorates awarded. *Degree requirements:* For doctorate, comprehensive exam, thesis/dissertation, 2000-hour clinical internship. *Entrance requirements:* For doctorate, GRE General Test, undergraduate or graduate degree in psychology or related area; 4 course prerequisites: biopsychology, abnormal psychology, developmental psychology, and statistics. Additional exam requirements/recommendations for international students: Required—TOEFL, IELTS. *Application deadline:* For fall admission, 12/4 priority date for domestic and international students. Applications are processed on a rolling basis. Application fee: $50. Electronic applications accepted. *Expenses:* Contact institution. *Financial support:* In 2017–18, 115 students received support, including fellowships (averaging $7,500 per year), research assistantships (averaging $4,000 per year), teaching assistantships (averaging $3,000 per year); Federal Work-Study and scholarships/grants also available. Financial award applicants required to submit FAFSA. *Faculty research:* Forensic psychology, LGBT psychology, trauma, diversity and community mental health, neuropsychology. *Unit head:* Dr. Rowena Gomez, Director of Clinical Training, 650-433-3823, E-mail: rgomez@paloaltou.edu. *Application contact:* Eirian Williams, Vice President of Enrollment Management, 800-818-6136, E-mail: admissions@paloaltou.edu.
Website: http://www.paloaltou.edu/graduate-programs/phd-programs/phd-clinical-psychology

Penn State Harrisburg, Graduate School, School of Behavioral Sciences and Education, Middletown, PA 17057. Offers adult education in the health and medical professions (Certificate); applied behavior analysis (MA); applied clinical psychology (MA); applied psychological research (MA); community psychology and social change (MA); English as a second language (ESL) program specialist and leadership (Certificate); health education (M Ed); lifelong learning and adult education (M Ed, D Ed); literacy education (M Ed); literacy leadership (Certificate); psychology: applications in clinical psychology (Certificate); psychology: health psychology (Certificate); teaching and curriculum (M Ed); training and development (M Ed, Certificate). *Program availability:* Part-time, evening/weekend. *Unit head:* Dr. Mukund S. Kulkarni, Chancellor, 717-948-6105, Fax: 717-948-6452. *Application contact:* Robert W. Coffman, Jr., Director of Enrollment Management, Recruitment and Admissions, 717-948-6250, Fax: 717-948-6325, E-mail: hbgadmit@psu.edu.
Website: https://harrisburg.psu.edu/behavioral-sciences-and-education/

Penn State University Park, Graduate School, College of the Liberal Arts, Department of Psychology, University Park, PA 16802. Offers psychology (MS, PhD). *Accreditation:* APA (one or more programs are accredited). *Unit head:* Dr. Susan Welch, Dean, 814-865-7691, Fax: 814-863-2085. *Application contact:* Lori Hawn, Director, Graduate Student Services, 814-865-1795, Fax: 814-863-4627, E-mail: l-gswww@lists.psu.edu.
Website: http://psych.la.psu.edu/

Pepperdine University, Graduate School of Education and Psychology, Division of Psychology, Los Angeles, CA 90263. Offers behavioral psychology (MS); clinical psychology (Psy D); clinical psychology (MA), including marriage and family therapy; clinical psychology with Latinos (MA); psychology (MA). *Program availability:* Part-time, evening/weekend. *Students:* 499 full-time (417 women), 416 part-time (343 women); includes 401 minority (90 Black or African American, non-Hispanic/Latino; 4 American Indian or Alaska Native, non-Hispanic/Latino; 68 Asian, non-Hispanic/Latino; 205 Hispanic/Latino; 5 Native Hawaiian or other Pacific Islander, non-Hispanic/Latino; 29 Two or more races, non-Hispanic/Latino), 68 international. Average age 31. 574 applicants, 75% accepted, 254 enrolled. In 2017, 253 master's, 34 doctorates awarded. *Entrance requirements:* For master's and doctorate, GRE General Test. Additional exam requirements/recommendations for international students: Required—TOEFL. *Application deadline:* For fall admission, 2/1 for domestic students. Applications are processed on a rolling basis. Application fee: $55. Electronic applications accepted. *Expenses:* Contact institution. *Financial support:* Research assistantships, teaching assistantships, career-related internships or fieldwork, and scholarships/grants available. Support available to part-time students. Financial award application deadline: 7/1; financial award applicants required to submit FAFSA. *Unit head:* Dr. Robert A. deMayo, Associate Dean, Psychology Division, 310-568-5747, E-mail: robert.demayo@pepperdine.edu. *Application contact:* Chris Costa, Director of Enrollment, 310-568-2850, E-mail: chris.costa@pepperdine.edu.
Website: http://gsep.pepperdine.edu/masters-psychology/

Philadelphia College of Osteopathic Medicine, Graduate and Professional Programs, Department of Psychology, Philadelphia, PA 19131-1694. Offers applied behavior analysis (Certificate); clinical health psychology (Post-Doctoral Certificate); clinical neuropsychology (Post-Doctoral Certificate); clinical psychology (Psy D); educational psychology (PhD); mental health counseling (MS); organizational development and leadership (MS); psychology (Certificate); public health management and administration (MS); school psychology (MS, Psy D, Ed S). *Accreditation:* APA. *Faculty:* 19 full-time (11 women), 122 part-time/adjunct (58 women). *Students:* 487 (335 women); includes 138 minority (89 Black or African American, non-Hispanic/Latino; 4 American Indian or Alaska Native, non-Hispanic/Latino; 11 Asian, non-Hispanic/Latino; 12 Hispanic/Latino; 22 Two or more races, non-Hispanic/Latino). 298 applicants, 44% accepted, 100 enrolled. In 2017, 50 master's, 43 doctorates, 10 other advanced degrees awarded. Terminal master's awarded for partial completion of doctoral program. *Degree requirements:* For master's, comprehensive exam (for some programs), thesis (for some programs); for doctorate, comprehensive exam, thesis/dissertation. *Entrance requirements:* For master's, GRE or MAT, minimum GPA of 3.0; bachelor's degree from regionally-accredited college or university; for doctorate, PRAXIS II (for Psy D in school psychology), minimum undergraduate GPA of 3.0; for other advanced degree, GRE (for Ed S). Additional exam requirements/recommendations for international students: Required—TOEFL (minimum score 79 iBT). *Application deadline:* Applications are processed on a rolling basis. Application fee: $50. Electronic applications accepted. *Financial support:* In 2017–18, 28 teaching assistantships were awarded; Federal Work-Study, institutionally sponsored loans, and scholarships/grants also available. Financial award application deadline: 3/15; financial award applicants required to submit FAFSA. *Faculty research:* Adult and childhood anxiety and ADHD; coping with chronic illness; primary care psychology/integrated health care; applied behavior analysis; psychological, educational, and neuropsychological assessment. *Total annual research expenditures:* $533,489. *Unit head:* Dr. Robert DiTomasso, Chairman, 215-871-6442, Fax: 215-871-6458, E-mail: robertd@pcom.edu. *Application contact:* Johnathan Cox, Associate Director of Admissions, 215-871-6700, Fax: 215-871-6719, E-mail: johnathancox@pcom.edu.

See Display on the next page and Close-Up on page 1203.

Phillips Graduate University, Master's Program in Psychology, Chatsworth, CA 91311. Offers art therapy (MA); marriage and family therapy (MA); school counseling (MA); school psychology (MA). *Program availability:* Evening/weekend. *Degree requirements:* For master's, comprehensive exam, thesis. *Entrance requirements:* For master's, minimum GPA of 2.5. *Application deadline:* For fall admission, 4/16 priority date for domestic students; for spring admission, 11/15 for domestic students. Applications are processed on a rolling basis. Application fee: $80. Electronic applications accepted. *Expenses: Tuition:* Part-time $897 per unit. *Required fees:* $375 per semester. Part-time tuition and fees vary according to degree level and program. *Financial support:* Federal Work-Study and tuition waivers (full and partial) available.

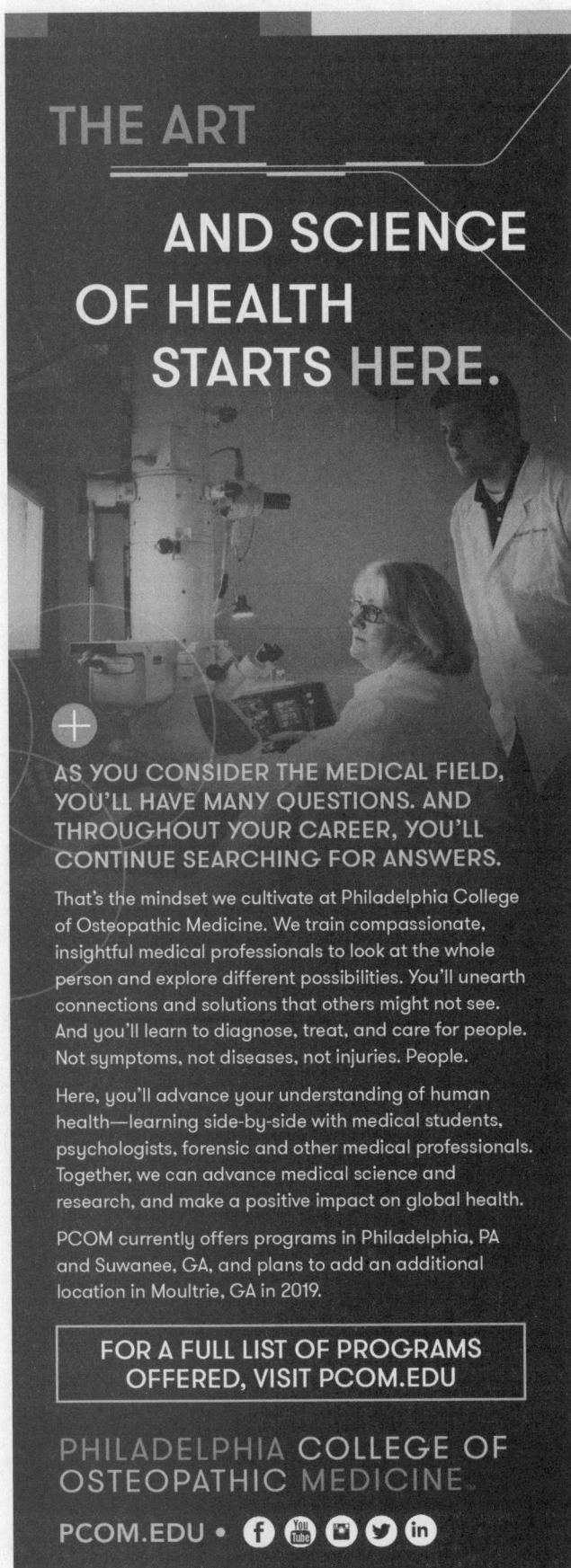
Financial award application deadline: 8/15; financial award applicants required to submit FAFSA. *Faculty research:* Integration of interpersonal psychological theory, systems approach, firsthand experiential learning. *Application contact:* Christine Montagna, Admissions Advisor, 818-600-4945, Fax: 818-386-5699, E-mail: cmontagna@pgu.edu.

Pittsburg State University, Graduate School, College of Education, Department of Psychology and Counseling, Program in Psychology, Pittsburg, KS 66762. Offers psychology (MS), including clinical psychology, general psychology. *Students:* 30. In 2017, 10 master's awarded. *Degree requirements:* For master's, thesis or alternative. *Entrance requirements:* For master's, GRE General Test, minimum GPA of 2.8. Additional exam requirements/recommendations for international students: Required— TOEFL (minimum score 550 paper-based; 79 iBT), IELTS (minimum score 6.5), PTE (minimum score 53). *Application deadline:* Applications are processed on a rolling basis. Application fee: $35 ($60 for international students). Electronic applications accepted. *Expenses:* Contact institution. *Financial support:* Teaching assistantships, career-related internships or fieldwork, and Federal Work-Study available. Financial award application deadline: 2/1; financial award applicants required to submit FAFSA. *Unit head:* Dr. David Hurford, Chairperson, 620-235-4521. *Application contact:* Lisa Allen, Assistant Director of Graduate and Continuing Studies, 620-235-4218, Fax: 620-235-4219, E-mail: lallen@pittstate.edu.

Pontifical Catholic University of Puerto Rico, College of Graduate Studies in Behavioral Science and Community Affairs, Ponce, PR 00717-0777. Offers clinical psychology (PhD, Psy D); clinical social work (MSW); criminology (MA); industrial psychology (PhD); psychology (PhD); public administration (MSS); rehabilitation counseling (MA). *Program availability:* Part-time, evening/weekend. *Degree requirements:* For master's, thesis; for doctorate, comprehensive exam, thesis/ dissertation. *Entrance requirements:* For master's, EXADEP, GRE General Test, 3 letters of recommendation, interview, minimum GPA of 2.75.

Pontificia Universidad Catolica Madre y Maestra, Graduate School, Faculty of Social and Administrative Sciences, Santiago, Dominican Republic. Offers business administration (MBA), including business development, finance, international business, management skills (M Mgmt, MBA), marketing, operations, strategic cost management, strategy, tourist destination planning and management; law (LL M), including civil law, corporate business law, criminal law, international relations, real estate law; management (M Mgmt), including higher financial management, insurance program administration, management skills (M Mgmt, MBA); psychology (MA), including clinical child and adolescent psychology, forensic psychology; strategic human resources (EMBA).

Portland State University, Graduate Studies, College of Liberal Arts and Sciences, Department of Psychology, Portland, OR 97207-0751. Offers MA, MS, PhD. *Faculty:* 23 full-time (11 women), 20 part-time/adjunct (14 women). *Students:* 45 full-time (34 women), 16 part-time (15 women); includes 12 minority (1 Black or African American, non-Hispanic/Latino; 1 American Indian or Alaska Native, non-Hispanic/Latino; 3 Asian, non-Hispanic/Latino; 4 Hispanic/Latino; 3 Two or more races, non-Hispanic/Latino). Average age 31. 186 applicants, 10% accepted, 18 enrolled. In 2017, 13 master's, 2 doctorates awarded. *Degree requirements:* For master's, variable foreign language requirement, thesis; for doctorate, variable foreign language requirement, comprehensive exam, thesis/dissertation. *Entrance requirements:* For master's, GRE General Test, personal statement, 3 letters of reference. Additional exam requirements/ recommendations for international students: Required—TOEFL (minimum score 550 paper-based). *Application deadline:* For fall admission, 12/15 for domestic and international students. Application fee: $65. *Expenses:* Tuition, state resident: full-time $14,436; part-time $401 per credit. Tuition, nonresident: full-time $21,780; part-time $605 per credit. *Required fees:* $1380; $22 per credit. $119 per quarter. One-time fee: $325. Tuition and fees vary according to program. *Financial support:* In 2017–18, 34 students received support, including 10 research assistantships with full and partial tuition reimbursements available (averaging $11,181 per year), 26 teaching assistantships with full and partial tuition reimbursements available (averaging $12,589 per year); career-related internships or fieldwork, Federal Work-Study, scholarships/ grants, and unspecified assistantships also available. Support available to part-time students. Financial award application deadline: 3/1; financial award applicants required to submit FAFSA. *Faculty research:* Organizational psychology, work and the family, quantitative psychology, decision-making, psychosocial factors affecting health. *Total annual research expenditures:* $1.4 million. *Unit head:* Dr. Ellen Skinner, Chair, 503-725-3966, Fax: 503-725-3904, E-mail: skinnere@pdx.edu. *Application contact:* Dr. Thomas Kindermann, 503-725-3970, E-mail: kindermannt@pdx.edu. Website: http://www.pdx.edu/psy/

Portland State University, Graduate Studies, College of Liberal Arts and Sciences, Systems Science Program, Portland, OR 97207-0751. Offers computational intelligence (Certificate); computer modeling and simulation (Certificate); systems science (MS); systems science/anthropology (PhD); systems science/business administration (PhD); systems science/civil engineering (PhD); systems science/economics (PhD); systems science/engineering management (PhD); systems science/general (PhD); systems science/mathematical sciences (PhD); systems science/mechanical engineering (PhD); systems science/psychology (PhD); systems science/sociology (PhD). *Faculty:* 2 full-time (0 women), 4 part-time/adjunct (0 women). *Students:* 12 full-time (4 women), 22 part-time (6 women); includes 6 minority (4 Hispanic/Latino; 2 Two or more races, non-Hispanic/Latino). Average age 37. 18 applicants, 94% accepted, 16 enrolled. In 2017, 6 master's awarded. *Degree requirements:* For master's, comprehensive exam (for some programs), thesis optional; for doctorate, variable foreign language requirement, comprehensive exam (for some programs), thesis/dissertation. *Entrance requirements:* For master's, GRE/GMAT (recommended), minimum GPA of 3.0 on undergraduate or graduate work, 2 letters of recommendation, statement of interest; for doctorate, GMAT, GRE General Test, minimum GPA of 3.0 undergraduate, 3.25 graduate; 3 letters of recommendation; statement of interest. Additional exam requirements/ recommendations for international students: Required—TOEFL (minimum score 550 paper-based; 80 iBT). *Application deadline:* For fall admission, 1/15 for domestic and international students; for spring admission, 11/1 for domestic students. Application fee: $65. Electronic applications accepted. *Expenses:* Tuition, state resident: full-time $14,436; part-time $401 per credit. Tuition, nonresident: full-time $21,780; part-time $605 per credit. *Required fees:* $1380; $22 per credit. $119 per quarter. One-time fee: $325. Tuition and fees vary according to program. *Financial support:* In 2017–18, 1 teaching assistantship with full and partial tuition reimbursement (averaging $7,830 per year) was awarded; research assistantships, career-related internships or fieldwork, Federal Work-Study, scholarships/grants, and unspecified assistantships also available. Support available to part-time students. Financial award application deadline: 3/1; financial award applicants required to submit FAFSA. *Faculty research:* Systems theory and methodology, artificial intelligence neural networks, information theory, nonlinear dynamics/chaos, modeling and simulation. *Total annual research expenditures:* $169,034. *Unit head:* Dr. Wayne Wakeland, Chair, 503-725-4975, E-mail: wakeland@pdx.edu. Website: http://www.pdx.edu/sysc/

Princeton University, Graduate School, Department of Psychology, Princeton, NJ 08544-1019. Offers neuroscience (PhD); psychology (PhD). *Degree requirements:* For

doctorate, thesis/dissertation. *Entrance requirements:* For doctorate, GRE General Test, GRE Subject Test. Additional exam requirements/recommendations for international students: Required—TOEFL (minimum score 550 paper-based). Electronic applications accepted.

Purdue University, Graduate School, College of Health and Human Sciences, Department of Psychological Sciences, West Lafayette, IN 47907. Offers behavioral neuroscience (PhD); clinical psychology (PhD); cognitive psychology (PhD); industrial/organizational psychology (PhD); mathematical and computational cognitive science (PhD). *Accreditation:* APA. *Faculty:* 46 full-time (18 women), 1 part-time/adjunct (0 women). *Students:* 64 full-time (41 women), 4 part-time (3 women); includes 13 minority (1 Black or African American, non-Hispanic/Latino; 4 Asian, non-Hispanic/Latino; 6 Hispanic/Latino; 2 Two or more races, non-Hispanic/Latino), 12 international. Average age 27. 288 applicants, 8% accepted, 16 enrolled. In 2017, 9 doctorates awarded. Terminal master's awarded for partial completion of doctoral program. *Degree requirements:* For doctorate, thesis/dissertation. *Entrance requirements:* For doctorate, GRE General Test, minimum undergraduate GPA of 3.0 or equivalent. Additional exam requirements/recommendations for international students: Required—TOEFL (minimum score 550 paper-based; 77 iBT); Recommended—TWE. *Application deadline:* For fall admission, 12/3 for domestic and international students. Applications are processed on a rolling basis. Application fee: $60 ($75 for international students). Electronic applications accepted. *Financial support:* Fellowships with partial tuition reimbursements, research assistantships with partial tuition reimbursements, teaching assistantships with partial tuition reimbursements, and career-related internships or fieldwork available. Support available to part-time students. Financial award applicants required to submit FAFSA. *Faculty research:* Career development of women in science, development of friendships during childhood and adolescence, social competence, human information processing. *Unit head:* Dr. David Rollock, Head, 765-494-6061, E-mail: rollock@purdue.edu. *Application contact:* Nancy A. O'Brien, Graduate Contact, 765-494-6067, E-mail: nobrien@psych.pardue.edu.
Website: http://www.psych.purdue.edu/

Queens College of the City University of New York, Mathematics and Natural Sciences Division, Department of Psychology, Queens, NY 11367-1597. Offers applied behavior analysis (MA); behavioral neuroscience (MA); general psychology (MA). *Program availability:* Part-time. *Students:* 2 full-time (1 woman), 99 part-time (78 women); includes 55 minority (10 Black or African American, non-Hispanic/Latino; 1 American Indian or Alaska Native, non-Hispanic/Latino; 11 Asian, non-Hispanic/Latino; 31 Hispanic/Latino; 2 Two or more races, non-Hispanic/Latino), 3 international. Average age 27. *Degree requirements:* For master's, comprehensive exam (for some programs), thesis. *Entrance requirements:* For master's, minimum GPA of 3.0. Additional exam requirements/recommendations for international students: Required—TOEFL, IELTS. *Application deadline:* For fall admission, 4/1 for domestic students; for spring admission, 11/1 for domestic students. Applications are processed on a rolling basis. Application fee: $125. Electronic applications accepted. *Financial support:* Career-related internships or fieldwork, institutionally sponsored loans, and unspecified assistantships available. Financial award application deadline: 4/1; financial award applicants required to submit FAFSA. *Unit head:* Robert Lanson, Chair, 718-997-3200, E-mail: robert.lanson@qc.cuny.edu. *Application contact:* Elizabeth D'Amico-Ramirez, Assistant Director of Graduate Admissions, 718-997-5203, E-mail: elizabeth.damicoramirez@qc.cuny.edu.
Website: http://psychology.qc.cuny.edu/

Queen's University at Kingston, School of Graduate Studies, Faculty of Arts and Sciences, Department of Psychology, Kingston, ON K7L 3N6, Canada. Offers brain behavior and cognitive science (MA, PhD); clinical psychology (MA, PhD); developmental psychology (MA, PhD); social personality psychology (MA, PhD). *Degree requirements:* For master's, thesis; for doctorate, comprehensive exam, thesis/dissertation. *Entrance requirements:* For master's and doctorate, GRE General Test. Additional exam requirements/recommendations for international students: Required—TOEFL. *Faculty research:* Human development, social, personality, behavioral neuroscience, forensic.

Radford University, College of Graduate Studies and Research, Program in Psychology, Radford, VA 24142. Offers clinical-counseling psychology (MA, MS); experimental psychology (MA); industrial-organizational psychology (MA, MS). *Program availability:* Part-time. *Faculty:* 21 full-time (14 women). *Students:* 39 full-time (30 women); includes 5 minority (2 Black or African American, non-Hispanic/Latino; 1 Asian, non-Hispanic/Latino; 2 Hispanic/Latino). Average age 23. 87 applicants, 51% accepted, 22 enrolled. In 2017, 28 master's awarded. *Degree requirements:* For master's, comprehensive exam, thesis (for some programs). *Entrance requirements:* For master's, GRE, minimum GPA of 3.0, 3 letters of reference, essay, resume, official transcripts. Additional exam requirements/recommendations for international students: Required—TOEFL (minimum score 550 paper-based; 79 iBT), IELTS (minimum score 6.5). *Application deadline:* For fall admission, 2/15 priority date for domestic students, 12/1 for international students; for spring admission, 7/1 for international students. Applications are processed on a rolling basis. Application fee: $50. Electronic applications accepted. *Expenses:* Tuition, state resident: full-time $8336; part-time $347 per credit hour. Tuition, nonresident: full-time $16,862; part-time $702 per credit hour. *Required fees:* $3220; $135 per credit hour. Tuition and fees vary according to course load and program. *Financial support:* In 2017–18, 19 students received support, including 2 research assistantships (averaging $7,500 per year), 14 teaching assistantships (averaging $10,500 per year); career-related internships or fieldwork, scholarships/grants, and unspecified assistantships also available. Support available to part-time students. Financial award application deadline: 3/1; financial award applicants required to submit FAFSA. *Faculty research:* Social cognition and interpersonal relationships, relationship between one's self-concept and social interactions, creativity and innovation, organizational politics and ethical decision-making, victimization in childhood. *Unit head:* Dr. Jeffery Aspelmeier, Chair, 540-831-5361, Fax: 540-831-6113, E-mail: jaspelme@radford.edu.
Website: http://www.radford.edu/content/chbs/home/psychology.html

Rhode Island College, School of Graduate Studies, Faculty of Arts and Sciences, Department of Psychology, Providence, RI 02908-1991. Offers health psychology (CGS); psychology (MA). *Program availability:* Part-time, evening/weekend. *Faculty:* 2. *Students:* 3 full-time (all women), 10 part-time (9 women); includes 2 minority (1 Black or African American, non-Hispanic/Latino; 1 American Indian or Alaska Native, non-Hispanic/Latino). Average age 28. In 2017, 2 master's awarded. *Degree requirements:* For master's, comprehensive exam. *Entrance requirements:* For master's, GRE, 3 letters of recommendation. Additional exam requirements/recommendations for international students: Recommended—TOEFL (minimum score 550 paper-based; 79 iBT). *Application deadline:* For fall admission, 3/1 for domestic students; for spring admission, 11/1 for domestic students. Applications are processed on a rolling basis. Application fee: $50. Electronic applications accepted. *Expenses:* Tuition, state resident: full-time $9768; part-time $407 per credit. Tuition, nonresident: full-time $19,008; part-time $792 per credit. *Required fees:* $696; $29 per credit. One-time fee: $200 full-time; $100 part-time. Tuition and fees vary according to course load. *Financial support:* In 2017–18, 3 teaching assistantships with full tuition reimbursements (averaging $3,500 per year) were awarded; Federal Work-Study, scholarships/grants, health care benefits, and unspecified assistantships also available. Support available to part-time students. Financial award application deadline: 5/15; financial award applicants required to submit FAFSA. *Unit head:* Dr. Randi Kim, Chair, 401-456-8015. *Application contact:* Graduate Studies, 401-456-8700.
Website: http://www.ric.edu/psychology/index.php

Rice University, Graduate Programs, School of Humanities, Department of Religious Studies, Houston, TX 77251-1892. Offers African religions (PhD); African-American religions (PhD); contemplative studies (PhD); ghosticism, esotericism, mysticism (PhD); Islam (PhD); Jewish thought and philosophy (PhD); modern Christianity in thought and popular culture (PhD); psychology of religion (PhD); the Bible and beyond (PhD). *Degree requirements:* For doctorate, 2 foreign languages, comprehensive exam, thesis/dissertation. *Entrance requirements:* For doctorate, GRE, letters of recommendation, writing sample. Additional exam requirements/recommendations for international students: Required—TOEFL (minimum score 600 paper-based; 90 iBT). Electronic applications accepted. *Faculty research:* Origins and historical development of Islam, history of Christianity, the study of comparative religion, African-American religion, religion and culture.

Rice University, Graduate Programs, School of Social Sciences, Department of Psychology, Houston, TX 77251-1892. Offers cognitive sciences (MA, PhD); industrial-organizational/social psychology (MA, PhD); psychology (MA, PhD). Terminal master's awarded for partial completion of doctoral program. *Degree requirements:* For master's, thesis; for doctorate, thesis/dissertation. *Entrance requirements:* For doctorate, GRE General Test, minimum GPA of 3.0. Additional exam requirements/recommendations for international students: Required—TOEFL. Electronic applications accepted. *Faculty research:* Cognitive, cognitive neuropsychology, human factors, human-computer interaction, industrial-organizational psychology.

Rivier University, School of Graduate Studies, Department of Psychology, Nashua, NH 03060. Offers clinical psychology (MS); experimental psychology (MS).

Roberts Wesleyan College, Graduate Psychology Programs, Rochester, NY 14624-1997. Offers clinical/school psychology (Psy D); school counseling (MS); school psychology (MS). *Program availability:* Part-time, evening/weekend. *Degree requirements:* For master's, comprehensive exam, PRAXIS II (for school psychology). *Entrance requirements:* For master's, GRE. Electronic applications accepted. Application fee is waived when completed online. *Faculty research:* Counselor supervision, forgiveness, community health psychology, applied research in group process.

Rochester Institute of Technology, Graduate Enrollment Services, College of Liberal Arts, Psychology Department, Rochester, NY 14623. Offers engineering psychology (Advanced Certificate); experimental psychology (MS); school psychology (MS, Advanced Certificate). *Program availability:* Part-time. *Students:* 30 full-time (25 women), 4 part-time (2 women); includes 3 minority (2 Black or African American, non-Hispanic/Latino; 1 Two or more races, non-Hispanic/Latino). Average age 25. 53 applicants, 51% accepted, 14 enrolled. In 2017, 10 master's, 9 other advanced degrees awarded. *Entrance requirements:* For master's, GRE, minimum GPA of 3.0 (recommended). *Application deadline:* For fall admission, 2/15 priority date for domestic and international students; for spring admission, 12/15 priority date for domestic and international students. Applications are processed on a rolling basis. Application fee: $65. Electronic applications accepted. *Expenses:* $1,815 per credit hour. *Financial support:* In 2017–18, 22 students received support. Research assistantships with partial tuition reimbursements available, teaching assistantships with partial tuition reimbursements available, career-related internships or fieldwork, scholarships/grants, and unspecified assistantships available. Support available to part-time students. Financial award applicants required to submit FAFSA. *Faculty research:* Human factors, human performance measurement and modeling; cognitive neuroscience, brain and behavior relationships; human development and personality assessment; curriculum-based measurement, multi-tier system of supports; psychophysiological and neuropsychological assessment. *Unit head:* Dr. Joseph Baschnagel, Chair, 585-475-4187, E-mail: jsbgsh@rit.edu. *Application contact:* Diane Ellison, Senior Associate Vice President, Graduate Enrollment Services, 585-475-2229, Fax: 585-475-7164, E-mail: gradinfo@rit.edu.
Website: http://www.rit.edu/cla/psychology/

Roosevelt University, Graduate Division, College of Arts and Sciences, Department of Psychology, Program in Clinical Psychology, Chicago, IL 60605. Offers MA, Psy D. *Students:* 83 full-time (66 women), 38 part-time (30 women); includes 30 minority (7 Black or African American, non-Hispanic/Latino; 14 Asian, non-Hispanic/Latino; 6 Hispanic/Latino; 3 Two or more races, non-Hispanic/Latino), 4 international. Average age 27. 247 applicants, 23% accepted, 28 enrolled. In 2017, 27 master's, 15 doctorates awarded. Application fee: $40. Electronic applications accepted. *Financial support:* Scholarships/grants and unspecified assistantships available. *Application contact:* Sivling Lam, Graduate Admission Counselor, 312-281-3252, E-mail: slam02@roosevelt.edu.

Rosalind Franklin University of Medicine and Science, College of Health Professions, Department of Psychology, North Chicago, IL 60064-3095. Offers clinical psychology (MS, PhD). *Accreditation:* APA. Terminal master's awarded for partial completion of doctoral program. *Degree requirements:* For master's, capstone experience. *Entrance requirements:* For master's, minimum GPA of 3.0, bachelor's degree (preferably in related subject); for doctorate, GRE, minimum GPA of 3.0, bachelor's or master's degree. Additional exam requirements/recommendations for international students: Required—TOEFL. *Faculty research:* Anxiety, pain, psychopathy, epilepsy, neuropsychology.

Rowan University, Graduate School, College of Science and Mathematics, Department of Psychology, Glassboro, NJ 08028-1701. Offers MA, CAGS. Electronic applications accepted. *Expenses:* Tuition, state resident: full-time $15,020; part-time $751 per semester hour. Tuition, nonresident: full-time $15,020; part-time $751 per semester hour. *Required fees:* $3158; $157.90 per semester hour. Tuition and fees vary according to course load, campus/location and program.

Rutgers University–Camden, Graduate School of Arts and Sciences, Program in Psychology, Camden, NJ 08102. Offers MA. *Program availability:* Part-time, evening/weekend. *Degree requirements:* For master's, thesis, 30 credits. *Entrance requirements:* For master's, GRE, 3 letters of recommendation; statement of personal, professional, and academic goals; prerequisite course work in introductory psychology, statistics and experimental psychology. Additional exam requirements/recommendations for international students: Required—TOEFL, IELTS. Electronic applications accepted. *Faculty research:* Cognitive psychology, sexuality, health psychology, personality psychology, clinical psychology.

Rutgers University–Newark, Graduate School, Program in Psychology, Newark, NJ 07102. Offers cognitive neuroscience (PhD); cognitive science (PhD); perception (PhD); psychobiology (PhD); social cognition (PhD). *Degree requirements:* For doctorate, comprehensive exam, thesis/dissertation. *Entrance requirements:* For doctorate, GRE General Test, GRE Subject Test, minimum undergraduate B average. Electronic applications accepted. *Faculty research:* Visual perception (luminance, motion), neuroendocrine mechanisms in behavior (reproduction, pain), attachment theory, connectionist modeling of cognition.

Rutgers University–New Brunswick, Graduate School-New Brunswick, Program in Psychology, Piscataway, NJ 08854-8097. Offers behavioral neuroscience (PhD); clinical psychology (PhD); cognitive psychology (PhD); interdisciplinary health psychology (PhD); social psychology (PhD). *Accreditation:* APA. *Degree requirements:* For doctorate, comprehensive exam, thesis/dissertation. *Entrance requirements:* For doctorate, GRE General Test, 3 letters of recommendation. Additional exam requirements/recommendations for international students: Required—TOEFL (minimum score 577 paper-based). Electronic applications accepted. *Faculty research:* Learning and memory, behavioral ecology, hormones and behavior, psychopharmacology, anxiety disorders.

Sage Graduate School, School of Health Sciences, Department of Psychology, Troy, NY 12180-4115. Offers MA, Certificate. *Program availability:* Part-time, evening/weekend. *Faculty:* 6 full-time (all women), 2 part-time/adjunct (both women). *Students:* 32 full-time (28 women), 33 part-time (27 women); includes 13 minority (4 Black or African American, non-Hispanic/Latino; 1 Asian, non-Hispanic/Latino; 4 Hispanic/Latino; 4 Two or more races, non-Hispanic/Latino). Average age 28. 72 applicants, 56% accepted, 22 enrolled. In 2017, 26 master's awarded. *Degree requirements:* For master's, thesis or alternative. *Entrance requirements:* Additional exam requirements/recommendations for international students: Required—TOEFL (minimum score 550 paper-based). *Application deadline:* Applications are processed on a rolling basis. Application fee: $30. Electronic applications accepted. Tuition and fees vary according to degree level and program. *Financial support:* Fellowships, research assistantships, scholarships/grants, and unspecified assistantships available. Financial award application deadline: 3/1; financial award applicants required to submit FAFSA. *Faculty research:* Effectiveness of arts integration programs in elementary and secondary schools, literacy-based substance abuse program, outcome evaluation of program to increase college entry among urban youth. *Unit head:* Dr. Theresa Hand, Dean, School of Health Sciences, 518-244-2264, Fax: 518-244-4571, E-mail: handt@sage.edu. *Application contact:* Dr. Gayle Morse, Graduate Program Director, 518-292-1819, E-mail: morseg@sage.edu.

St. Cloud State University, School of Graduate Studies, School of Education, Department of Educational Leadership and Higher Education, St. Cloud, MN 56301. Offers college counseling and student development (MS); higher education administration (MS, Ed D); rehabilitation counseling (MS); school counseling (MS). *Degree requirements:* For master's, thesis or alternative; for doctorate, comprehensive exam, thesis/dissertation. *Entrance requirements:* For master's, GRE General Test (for some programs), minimum GPA of 2.75; for doctorate, GRE General Test. Additional exam requirements/recommendations for international students: Required—Michigan English Language Assessment Battery; Recommended—TOEFL (minimum score 550 paper-based), IELTS (minimum score 6.5). Electronic applications accepted.

St. John's University, St. John's College of Liberal Arts and Sciences, Department of Psychology, Psychology Program, Queens, NY 11439. Offers MA. *Program availability:* Part-time, evening/weekend. *Students:* 10 full-time (8 women), 3 part-time (2 women); includes 7 minority (4 Black or African American, non-Hispanic/Latino; 3 Hispanic/Latino), 1 international. Average age 25. 36 applicants, 58% accepted, 5 enrolled. In 2017, 9 master's awarded. Terminal master's awarded for partial completion of doctoral program. *Degree requirements:* For master's, comprehensive exam (for some programs), thesis (for some programs), core courses in history and systems of psychology, inferential statistics, research methods, and psychological measurement. *Entrance requirements:* For master's, GRE General Test, letters of recommendation, transcripts, resume, personal statement, 24 credits of psychology prerequisites, lab paper, term paper. Additional exam requirements/recommendations for international students: Required—TOEFL (minimum score 80 iBT), IELTS (minimum score 6.5). *Application deadline:* For fall admission, 5/1 for domestic students. Applications are processed on a rolling basis. Application fee: $70. Electronic applications accepted. *Expenses: Tuition:* Full-time $44,280; part-time $1230 per credit. *Required fees:* $340; $340 per credit. Tuition and fees vary according to course load, degree level and program. *Financial support:* Fellowships, research assistantships, teaching assistantships, scholarships/grants, tuition waivers, and unspecified assistantships available. Support available to part-time students. Financial award application deadline: 2/1; financial award applicants required to submit FAFSA. *Faculty research:* Psychological factors in cardiovascular disease, numerical literacy, Post-Traumatic Stress Disorder, personality, anger and aggression. *Unit head:* Dr. Wilson McDermut, Coordinator, 718-990-5560, Fax: 718-990-5926, E-mail: mcdermuw@stjohns.edu. *Application contact:* Robert Medrano, Director of Graduate Admission, 718-990-1601, Fax: 718-990-5686, E-mail: gradhelp@stjohns.edu.
Website: https://www.stjohns.edu/academics/schools-and-colleges/st-johns-college-liberal-arts-and-sciences/programs-and-majors/psychology-master-arts

Saint Joseph's University, College of Arts and Sciences, Department of Criminal Justice, Philadelphia, PA 19131-1395. Offers behavior analysis (MS, Post-Master's Certificate); behavior management (MS); criminal justice (MS); federal law enforcement (MS); intelligence and crime analysis (MS). *Program availability:* Part-time, evening/weekend, 100% online, blended/hybrid learning. *Faculty:* 4 full-time (3 women), 33 part-time/adjunct (16 women). *Students:* 18 full-time (13 women), 371 part-time (272 women); includes 105 minority (83 Black or African American, non-Hispanic/Latino; 2 American Indian or Alaska Native, non-Hispanic/Latino; 4 Asian, non-Hispanic/Latino; 16 Hispanic/Latino). Average age 32. 189 applicants, 66% accepted, 94 enrolled. In 2017, 142 master's, 26 other advanced degrees awarded. *Degree requirements:* For master's, thesis optional. *Entrance requirements:* For master's, 2 letters of recommendation, personal statement, resume, official transcripts, minimum GPA of 3.0. Additional exam requirements/recommendations for international students: Required—TOEFL (minimum score 550 paper-based; 80 iBT). *Application deadline:* For fall admission, 7/15 for international students; for spring admission, 11/1 for international students. Applications are processed on a rolling basis. Application fee: $35. Electronic applications accepted. *Expenses:* Contact institution. *Financial support:* In 2017–18, 5 students received support. Federal Work-Study and unspecified assistantships available. Financial award application deadline: 5/1; financial award applicants required to submit FAFSA. *Faculty research:* Ethics in policing, multiculturalism, behavior analysis. *Total annual research expenditures:* $17,309. *Unit head:* Sylvia M. DeSantis, Director, 610-660-3131, E-mail: gradcas@sju.edu. *Application contact:* Lauren Weiss, Graduate Admissions, College of Arts and Sciences, 610-660-3131, E-mail: gradcas@sju.edu.
Website: http://www.sju.edu/majors-programs/graduate-arts-sciences/masters/criminal-justice-ms

Saint Joseph's University, College of Arts and Sciences, Department of Psychology, Philadelphia, PA 19131-1395. Offers MS. *Program availability:* Evening/weekend. *Faculty:* 6 full-time (4 women), 3 part-time/adjunct (2 women). *Students:* 22 full-time (14 women), 1 (woman) part-time; includes 4 minority (3 Black or African American, non-Hispanic/Latino; 1 Hispanic/Latino). Average age 26. 49 applicants, 43% accepted, 11 enrolled. In 2017, 14 master's awarded. *Entrance requirements:* For master's, GRE General Test, 2 letters of recommendation, official transcripts, personal statement. Additional exam requirements/recommendations for international students: Required—TOEFL (minimum score 550 paper-based; 80 iBT). *Application deadline:* For fall admission, 3/1 priority date for domestic and international students. Electronic applications accepted. *Expenses:* Contact institution. *Financial support:* Scholarships/grants and unspecified assistantships available. Financial award application deadline: 5/1; financial award applicants required to submit FAFSA. *Faculty research:* Causes and consequences of psychological entitlement, neural and hormonal mechanisms of social behavior, risk factors of depression, mild traumatic brain injury, social and moral development in children. *Unit head:* Dr. Jodi Mindell, Director, 610-660-3131, E-mail: gradcas@sju.edu. *Application contact:* Graduate Admissions, College of Arts and Sciences, 610-660-3131, E-mail: gradcas@sju.edu.
Website: http://www.sju.edu/academics/cas/grad/psychology

Saint Louis University, Graduate Programs, College of Arts and Sciences and Graduate Programs, Department of Psychology, St. Louis, MO 63103. Offers clinical psychology (MS-R, PhD); experimental psychology (MS-R, PhD); industrial-organizational psychology (PhD); psychology (PhD). *Accreditation:* APA (one or more programs are accredited). *Program availability:* Part-time. *Degree requirements:* For master's, comprehensive exam, thesis; for doctorate, thesis/dissertation, clinical internship (for clinical psychology PhD). *Entrance requirements:* For master's, GRE General Test, interview, letters of recommendation, resume; for doctorate, GRE General Test, interview, letters of recommendation, resumé, transcripts, goal statement. Additional exam requirements/recommendations for international students: Required—TOEFL (minimum score 550 paper-based). Electronic applications accepted. *Faculty research:* Violence and trauma; neural basis of learning and memory function; eating disorders; body image and health behavior; prejudice, stereotyping, and victimization; memory, cognitive aging and language processing.

Saint Mary's University, Faculty of Science, Department of Psychology, Halifax, NS B3H 3C3, Canada. Offers applied psychology (M Sc, PhD), including industrial/organizational psychology (M Sc). *Program availability:* Part-time. *Degree requirements:* For master's, thesis, 500-hour internship; for doctorate, comprehensive exam, thesis/dissertation, research project. *Entrance requirements:* For master's and doctorate, GRE General Test. *Faculty research:* Assessment, health psychology, social psychology, cognition.

Salem State University, School of Graduate Studies, Program in Counseling and Psychological Services, Salem, MA 01970-5353. Offers MS, Graduate Certificate. *Program availability:* Part-time, evening/weekend. *Entrance requirements:* For master's, GRE or MAT. Additional exam requirements/recommendations for international students: Required—TOEFL (minimum score 550 paper-based; 80 iBT) or IELTS (minimum score 5.5).

Sam Houston State University, College of Humanities and Social Sciences, Department of Psychology and Philosophy, Huntsville, TX 77341. Offers psychology (MA, PhD, SSP), including clinical psychology (MA, PhD), psychology (MA), school psychology (SSP). *Accreditation:* APA. *Program availability:* Part-time. Terminal master's awarded for partial completion of doctoral program. *Degree requirements:* For master's, comprehensive exam, thesis optional; for doctorate, comprehensive exam, thesis/dissertation. *Entrance requirements:* For master's, GRE General Test, personal statement, letters of recommendation; for doctorate, GRE General Test, GRE Subject Test (advanced psychology), personal essay, letters of recommendation, resume. Additional exam requirements/recommendations for international students: Required—TOEFL (minimum score 550 paper-based; 79 iBT), IELTS (minimum score 6.5). Electronic applications accepted.

San Diego State University, Graduate and Research Affairs, College of Sciences, Department of Psychology, San Diego, CA 92182. Offers clinical psychology (MS, PhD); industrial and organizational psychology (MS); program evaluation (MS); psychology (MA). PhD offered jointly with University of California, San Diego. *Accreditation:* APA (one or more programs are accredited). Terminal master's awarded for partial completion of doctoral program. *Degree requirements:* For master's, thesis, oral exam; for doctorate, thesis/dissertation. *Entrance requirements:* For master's, GRE General Test, GRE Subject Test, 3 letters of recommendation; for doctorate, GRE General Test, GRE Subject Test, minimum GPA of 3.0, 3 letters of recommendation. Additional exam requirements/recommendations for international students: Required—TOEFL. Electronic applications accepted.

San Francisco State University, Division of Graduate Studies, College of Science and Engineering, Department of Psychology, San Francisco, CA 94132-1722. Offers clinical psychology (MS); developmental psychology (MA); industrial/organizational psychology (MS); mind, brain, and behavior (MA); school psychology (MS, Credential); social psychology (MA). *Financial support:* Teaching assistantships available. Financial award application deadline: 3/1. *Unit head:* Dr. Dawn Terrell, Chair, 415-338-7555, Fax: 415-338-2398, E-mail: schen9@sfsu.edu. *Application contact:* Dr. Diane Harris, Graduate Program Coordinator, 415-338-7064, Fax: 415-338-2398, E-mail: dharris@sfsu.edu.
Website: http://psychology.sfsu.edu/graduate/application.html

San Jose State University, Graduate Studies and Research, College of Social Sciences, San Jose, CA 95192-0107. Offers applied anthropology (MA); communication studies (MA); economics (MA), including applied economics, economics; environmental studies (MS); geography (MA); history (MA), including history, history education; Mexican American studies (MA); psychology (MA, MS), including clinical psychology (MS), industrial/organizational psychology (MS), research and experimental psychology (MA); public administration (MPA); social sciences (MS); sociology (MA). *Faculty:* 59 full-time (29 women), 18 part-time/adjunct (5 women). *Students:* 181 full-time (126 women), 221 part-time (127 women); includes 228 minority (15 Black or African American, non-Hispanic/Latino; 48 Asian, non-Hispanic/Latino; 112 Hispanic/Latino; 3 Native Hawaiian or other Pacific Islander, non-Hispanic/Latino; 50 Two or more races, non-Hispanic/Latino), 38 international. Average age 30. 532 applicants, 44% accepted, 156 enrolled. In 2017, 139 master's awarded. *Degree requirements:* For master's, one foreign language, comprehensive exam, thesis (for some programs), project, field work, professional work experience. *Entrance requirements:* Additional exam requirements/recommendations for international students: Required—TOEFL (minimum score 550 paper-based; 80 iBT), IELTS (minimum score 6.5), PTE (minimum score 53). *Application deadline:* For fall admission, 2/1 for domestic and international students. Applications are processed on a rolling basis. Application fee: $55. Electronic applications accepted. *Expenses:* Tuition, state resident: full-time $7176. Tuition, nonresident: full-time $16,680. Tuition and fees vary according to course load and program. *Financial support:* Fellowships, research assistantships, career-related internships or fieldwork, Federal Work-Study, scholarships/grants, tuition waivers (full and partial), and unspecified assistantships available. Support available to part-time students. Financial award application deadline: 4/28; financial award applicants required to submit FAFSA. *Unit head:* Dr. Walt Jacobs, Dean, 408-924-5300, Fax: 408-924-5303, E-mail: walter.jacobs@sjsu.edu.
Website: http://www.sjsu.edu/socialsciences/

Saybrook University, LIOS MA Residential Programs, Kirkland, WA 98033. Offers leadership and organization development (MA); psychology counseling (MA). *Degree requirements:* For master's, thesis (for some programs), oral exams. *Entrance requirements:* For master's, bachelor's degree from an accredited university or college. Additional exam requirements/recommendations for international students: Recommended—TOEFL, IELTS, TWE.

Psychology—General

Saybrook University, School of Psychology and Interdisciplinary Inquiry, San Francisco, CA 94612. Offers human science (MA, PhD), including consciousness and spirituality, humanistic and transpersonal psychology, integrative health studies, organizational systems, social transformation; organizational systems (MA, PhD), including consciousness and spirituality, humanistic and transpersonal psychology, integrative health studies, leadership of sustainable systems (MA), organizational systems, social transformation; psychology (MA, PhD), including consciousness and spirituality, creativity studies (MA), humanistic and transpersonal psychology, integrative health studies, Jungian studies, marriage and family therapy (MA), organizational systems, social transformation. *Program availability:* Online learning. Terminal master's awarded for partial completion of doctoral program. *Degree requirements:* For master's, thesis or alternative; for doctorate, thesis/dissertation. *Entrance requirements:* Additional exam requirements/recommendations for international students: Required—TOEFL (minimum score 580 paper-based; 93 iBT). Electronic applications accepted. *Faculty research:* Humanistic theory, health studies, organizational systems, consciousness and spirituality, social transformation.

The Seattle School of Theology and Psychology, Graduate Programs, Seattle, WA 98121. Offers Christian studies (MA); counseling psychology (MA); divinity (M Div). *Program availability:* Part-time. *Entrance requirements:* For master's, MAT.

Seattle University, College of Arts and Sciences, Department of Psychology, Seattle, WA 98122-1090. Offers existential and phenomenological therapeutic psychology (MA Psych). *Faculty:* 7 full-time (4 women), 5 part-time/adjunct (3 women). *Students:* 31 full-time (22 women), 1 (woman) part-time; includes 3 minority (all Hispanic/Latino), 1 international. Average age 32. 57 applicants, 47% accepted, 20 enrolled. In 2017, 19 master's awarded. *Degree requirements:* For master's, thesis optional. *Entrance requirements:* For master's, interview, minimum GPA of 3.0, previous undergraduate course work in psychology, experience (paid or volunteer) in counseling or human services. *Application deadline:* For fall admission, 1/15 for domestic and international students. Application fee: $55. Electronic applications accepted. *Expenses: Tuition:* Full-time $12,960. *Required fees:* $570. Tuition and fees vary according to program. *Financial support:* In 2017–18, 23 students received support. Career-related internships or fieldwork and Federal Work-Study available. Support available to part-time students. Financial award applicants required to submit FAFSA. *Faculty research:* Interpersonal relations, psychotherapy, qualitative research, trauma, philosophy and psychology. *Unit head:* Dr. Kevin Krycka, Director of Graduate Programs, 206-296-5398, Fax: 206-296-2141, E-mail: krycka@seattleu.edu. *Application contact:* Janet Shandley, Associate Dean of Graduate Admissions, 206-296-5900, Fax: 206-298-5656, E-mail: grad_admissions@seattleu.edu.
Website: http://www.seattleu.edu/artsci/departments/psychology/

Seton Hall University, College of Arts and Sciences, Department of Psychology, South Orange, NJ 07079-2697. Offers experimental psychology (MS). *Program availability:* Part-time, evening/weekend. *Degree requirements:* For master's, thesis optional. *Entrance requirements:* For master's, GRE, minimum of 18 credits in psychology with minimum GPA of 3.0. Additional exam requirements/recommendations for international students: Required—TOEFL. Electronic applications accepted. *Faculty research:* Behavioral neuroscience, cognitive psychology, social psychology, perception/motor skills, memory, depression, anxiety.

Seton Hall University, College of Education and Human Services, Department of Professional Psychology and Family Therapy, South Orange, NJ 07079-2697. Offers counseling psychology (MA, PhD), including counseling psychology (PhD), school counseling (MA); psychological studies (MA), including individualized, marriage and family therapy, sport and exercise psychology; school psychology (MA). *Accreditation:* APA. *Program availability:* Part-time, evening/weekend, blended/hybrid learning. Terminal master's awarded for partial completion of doctoral program. *Degree requirements:* For master's, comprehensive exam, case study; for doctorate, comprehensive exam, thesis/dissertation, internship. *Entrance requirements:* For master's, GRE or MAT; for doctorate, GRE, interview. *Faculty research:* Counseling process, ethics, family systems, child pathology.

Shippensburg University of Pennsylvania, School of Graduate Studies, College of Arts and Sciences, Department of Psychology, Shippensburg, PA 17257-2299. Offers psychological science (MS). *Program availability:* Part-time, evening/weekend. *Faculty:* 8 full-time (5 women). *Students:* 10 full-time (6 women), 12 part-time (5 women); includes 1 minority (Two or more races, non-Hispanic/Latino). Average age 25. 29 applicants, 86% accepted, 10 enrolled. In 2017, 14 master's awarded. *Degree requirements:* For master's, comprehensive exam (for some programs), thesis (for some programs), thesis, field experience, or competency exam. *Entrance requirements:* For master's, minimum GPA of 2.75, course in statistics, 9 undergraduate credit hours in psychology, supplemental form with personal goals statement. Additional exam requirements/recommendations for international students: Required—TOEFL (minimum score 550 paper-based, 68 iBT) or IELTS (minimum score 6). *Application deadline:* For fall admission, 3/1 priority date for domestic students, 3/1 for international students; for spring admission, 11/1 priority date for domestic students, 11/1 for international students; for summer admission, 3/1 for domestic students. Applications are processed on a rolling basis. Application fee: $45. Electronic applications accepted. *Expenses:* Tuition, state resident: part-time $500 per credit. Tuition, nonresident: part-time $750 per credit. *Required fees:* $145 per credit. *Financial support:* In 2017–18, 10 students received support. Career-related internships or fieldwork, scholarships/grants, unspecified assistantships, and resident hall director and student payroll positions available. Support available to part-time students. Financial award application deadline: 3/1; financial award applicants required to submit FAFSA. *Unit head:* Dr. Kathryn M. Potoczak, Associate Professor and Program Coordinator, 717-477-1657, Fax: 717-477-4057, E-mail: kmpoto@ship.edu. *Application contact:* Maya T. Mapp, Director of Admissions, 717-477-1231, Fax: 717-477-4016, E-mail: mtmapp@ship.edu.
Website: http://www.ship.edu/psychology/

Simon Fraser University, Office of Graduate Studies and Postdoctoral Fellows, Faculty of Arts and Social Sciences, Department of Psychology, Burnaby, BC V5A 1S6, Canada. Offers MA, PhD. *Degree requirements:* For master's, thesis; for doctorate, comprehensive exam, thesis/dissertation, clinical training (for some programs). *Entrance requirements:* For master's, GRE General Test, GRE Subject Test (psychology), minimum GPA of 3.0 (on scale of 4.33) or 3.33 based on last 60 credits of undergraduate courses; for doctorate, GRE General Test, GRE Subject Test (psychology), minimum GPA of 3.5 (on scale of 4.33). Additional exam requirements/recommendations for international students: Recommended—TOEFL (minimum score 580 paper-based; 93 iBT), IELTS (minimum score 7), TWE (minimum score 5). Electronic applications accepted. *Expenses:* Contact institution. *Faculty research:* Cognitive and neural sciences; developmental, law and forensic psychology; social history; quantitative and theoretical psychology; clinical sciences.

Sofia University, Hybrid: Face-to-Face/Online Programs, Palo Alto, CA 94303. Offers transpersonal psychology (MA, PhD), including transpersonal psychology (PhD). *Program availability:* Online learning. *Entrance requirements:* For master's, bachelor's degree; for doctorate, bachelor's degree; master's degree. Electronic applications accepted.

Sofia University, Residential Programs, Palo Alto, CA 94303. Offers clinical psychology (Psy D); computer science (MS); counseling psychology (MA); transpersonal psychology (MA, PhD). *Program availability:* Part-time, evening/weekend. Terminal master's awarded for partial completion of doctoral program. *Degree requirements:* For doctorate, thesis/dissertation. *Entrance requirements:* For master's, bachelor's degree; for doctorate, bachelor's degree; master's degree (for some programs). Electronic applications accepted.

Southeastern Baptist Theological Seminary, Graduate and Professional Programs, Wake Forest, NC 27587. Offers advanced biblical studies (M Div); Christian education (M Div, MACE); Christian ethics (PhD); Christian ministry (M Div); Christian planting (M Div); church music (MACM); counseling (MACO); evangelism (PhD); language (M Div); ministry (D Min); New Testament (PhD); Old Testament (PhD); philosophy (PhD); theology (Th M, PhD); women's studies (M Div). *Accreditation:* ACIPE; ATS (one or more programs are accredited). *Degree requirements:* For master's, thesis (for some programs), oral exam; for doctorate, thesis/dissertation, fieldwork. *Entrance requirements:* For master's, Cooperative English Test, minimum GPA of 2.0, M Div or equivalent (Th M); for doctorate, GRE General Test or MAT, Cooperative English Test, M Div or equivalent, 3 years of professional experience.

Southeastern Louisiana University, College of Arts, Humanities and Social Sciences, Department of Psychology, Hammond, LA 70402. Offers industrial/organizational psychology (MA). *Program availability:* Part-time. *Faculty:* 7 full-time (5 women). *Students:* 23 full-time (14 women), 15 part-time (11 women); includes 8 minority (1 Black or African American, non-Hispanic/Latino; 1 Asian, non-Hispanic/Latino; 3 Hispanic/Latino; 3 Two or more races, non-Hispanic/Latino). Average age 26. 38 applicants, 61% accepted, 12 enrolled. In 2017, 10 master's awarded. *Degree requirements:* For master's, comprehensive exam, thesis, 38 hours of psychology course work including core courses in statistics, social psychology, cognition, and physiological psychology. *Entrance requirements:* For master's, GRE (minimum combined score of 294 on Verbal and Quantitative sections). Additional exam requirements/recommendations for international students: Required—TOEFL (minimum score 500 paper-based; 61 iBT). *Application deadline:* For fall admission, 7/15 priority date for domestic students, 6/1 priority date for international students; for spring admission, 12/1 priority date for domestic students, 10/1 priority date for international students. Applications are processed on a rolling basis. Application fee: $20 ($30 for international students). Electronic applications accepted. *Expenses:* Tuition, state resident: full-time $6684. Tuition, nonresident: full-time $19,162. *Required fees:* $2088. *Financial support:* In 2017–18, 17 students received support, including 15 research assistantships (averaging $8,624 per year); career-related internships or fieldwork, Federal Work-Study, institutionally sponsored loans, scholarships/grants, and traineeships also available. Support available to part-time students. Financial award application deadline: 5/1; financial award applicants required to submit FAFSA. *Faculty research:* Eating disorders, evolutionary psychology, violence exposure effects on children, parental behavior, neurobiology of mental disorders and addiction. *Unit head:* Dr. Susan Coats, Department Head, 985-549-2154, Fax: 985-549-6892, E-mail: scoats@southeastern.edu. *Application contact:* Amanda Harper, Graduate Admissions Analyst, 985-549-5620, Fax: 985-549-5632, E-mail: admissions@southeastern.edu.
Website: http://www.southeastern.edu/acad_research/depts/psyc/index.html

Southern Adventist University, School of Education and Psychology, Collegedale, TN 37315-0370. Offers clinical mental health counseling (MS); instructional leadership (MS Ed); literacy education (MS Ed); outdoor education (MS Ed); professional school counseling (MS). *Accreditation:* NCATE. *Program availability:* Part-time, evening/weekend. *Degree requirements:* For master's, comprehensive exam (for some programs), thesis optional, position paper (MS), portfolio (MS Ed in outdoor education). *Entrance requirements:* For master's, interview (MS); 9 semester hours of upper-division course work in psychology or related field, including 1 course in psychology research or statistics; 9 semester hours of education (MS Ed). Additional exam requirements/recommendations for international students: Required—TOEFL (minimum score 600 paper-based; 100 iBT). *Application deadline:* For fall admission, 7/1 priority date for domestic students, 6/1 priority date for international students; for winter admission, 11/1 priority date for domestic students, 10/1 priority date for international students; for spring admission, 4/1 priority date for domestic students, 3/1 priority date for international students. Applications are processed on a rolling basis. Application fee: $40. Electronic applications accepted. *Expenses: Tuition:* Full-time $11,430; part-time $635 per credit hour. Tuition and fees vary according to degree level and program. *Financial support:* Research assistantships with full tuition reimbursements, teaching assistantships with full tuition reimbursements, career-related internships or fieldwork, scholarships/grants, tuition waivers (partial), and unspecified assistantships available. Support available to part-time students. Financial award application deadline: 4/1; financial award applicants required to submit FAFSA. *Unit head:* Bonnie Eder, Interim Dean, 423-236-2759, Fax: 423-236-1765, E-mail: beder@southern.edu. *Application contact:* Mikhaile Spence, Graduate Enrollment Counselor, 423-236-2496, Fax: 423-236-1765, E-mail: maspence@southern.edu.
Website: https://www.southern.edu/academics/edpsych.html

Southern California Seminary, Graduate and Professional Programs, El Cajon, CA 92019. Offers Biblical studies (MABS); counseling psychology (MACP); marriage and family therapy (MAMFT); psychology (Psy D); religious studies (MRS); theology (M Div). *Program availability:* Part-time, evening/weekend, online learning. *Degree requirements:* For master's, thesis (for some programs); for doctorate, thesis/dissertation. *Entrance requirements:* For doctorate, master's degree in psychology. Additional exam requirements/recommendations for international students: Required—TOEFL (minimum score 550 paper-based). Electronic applications accepted.

Southern Connecticut State University, School of Graduate Studies, School of Arts and Sciences, Department of Psychology, New Haven, CT 06515-1355. Offers MA. *Program availability:* Part-time, evening/weekend. *Degree requirements:* For master's, thesis or alternative. *Entrance requirements:* For master's, interview, previous course work in psychology. Electronic applications accepted.

Southern Illinois University Carbondale, Graduate School, College of Education and Human Services, Program in Behavior Analysis and Therapy, Carbondale, IL 62901-4701. Offers MS. *Entrance requirements:* Additional exam requirements/recommendations for international students: Required—TOEFL.

Southern Illinois University Carbondale, Graduate School, College of Liberal Arts, Department of Psychology, Carbondale, IL 62901-4701. Offers clinical psychology (PhD); counseling psychology (PhD); experimental psychology (MA, MS). *Accreditation:* APA (one or more programs are accredited). *Degree requirements:* For master's, thesis; for doctorate, thesis/dissertation. *Entrance requirements:* For master's, GRE General Test, GRE Subject Test, minimum GPA of 2.7; for doctorate, GRE General Test, GRE Subject Test, minimum GPA of 3.25. Additional exam requirements/recommendations for international students: Required—TOEFL. *Faculty research:* Developmental neuropsychology; smoking, affect, and cognition; personality measurement; vocational psychology; program evaluation.

Southern Illinois University Edwardsville, Graduate School, School of Education, Health, and Human Behavior, Department of Psychology, Edwardsville, IL 62026. Offers

clinical child and school psychology (MS); clinical psychology (MA); industrial-organizational psychology (MA); school psychology (SD). *Program availability:* Part-time, evening/weekend. *Degree requirements:* For master's, thesis (for some programs), research paper; for SD, thesis. *Entrance requirements:* For master's, GRE. Additional exam requirements/recommendations for international students: Required—TOEFL (minimum score 550 paper-based; 79 iBT), IELTS (minimum score 6.5). Electronic applications accepted.

Southern Methodist University, Dedman College of Humanities and Sciences, Department of Psychology, Dallas, TX 75275. Offers clinical psychology (PhD). *Accreditation:* APA. Terminal master's awarded for partial completion of doctoral program. *Degree requirements:* For doctorate, comprehensive exam, thesis/dissertation, oral exam, practicum, research presentation and publication. *Entrance requirements:* For doctorate, GRE General Test, minimum GPA of 3.4. Additional exam requirements/recommendations for international students: Required—TOEFL (minimum score 550 paper-based). Electronic applications accepted. *Faculty research:* Experimental, social, developmental, and cognitive psychology; anger/violence; mood disorders; depression and anxiety; family assessment and development; chronic pain and mental health.

Southern Nazarene University, College of Professional and Graduate Studies, Department of Psychology and Counseling, Bethany, OK 73008. Offers counseling psychology (MA, MSCP); marital and family therapy (MA). *Degree requirements:* For master's, thesis optional. *Entrance requirements:* For master's, English proficiency exam, minimum GPA of 3.0 in last 60 hours/major, 2.7 overall.

Southern New Hampshire University, School of Arts and Sciences, Manchester, NH 03106-1045. Offers clinical mental health counseling (MS); creative writing (MA); criminal justice (MS); cyber security (MS); English (MA); fiction and nonfiction (MFA); history (MA); political science (MS); psychology (MS). *Program availability:* Part-time, evening/weekend. *Degree requirements:* For master's, one foreign language, thesis. *Entrance requirements:* For master's, minimum GPA of 2.75 (for MS in teaching English as a foreign language), 3.0 (for MFA). Additional exam requirements/recommendations for international students: Required—TOEFL (minimum score 550 paper-based; 79 iBT), IELTS (minimum score 6.5), TWE (minimum score 5). *Application deadline:* For fall admission, 7/1 priority date for domestic students; for winter admission, 11/1 priority date for domestic students; for spring admission, 6/1 priority date for domestic students. Applications are processed on a rolling basis. Application fee: $40. Electronic applications accepted. *Expenses:* Contact institution. *Financial support:* Research assistantships, career-related internships or fieldwork, and scholarships/grants available. Financial award applicants required to submit FAFSA. *Faculty research:* Action research, state of the art practice in behavioral health services, wraparound approaches to working with youth, learning styles. *Unit head:* Steven K. Johnson, Dean, 603-629-4626. *Application contact:* Office of Graduate Admission, 888-327-SNHU, Fax: 603-644-3144, E-mail: enroll@snhu.edu.

Southern Oregon University, Graduate Studies, Department of Psychology, Ashland, OR 97520. Offers MHC. *Accreditation:* ACA. *Program availability:* Part-time, online learning. *Degree requirements:* For master's, thesis, portfolio, oral defense. *Entrance requirements:* For master's, GRE General Test, minimum cumulative GPA of 3.0 in the last 90 quarter credits (60 semester credits) of undergraduate coursework. Additional exam requirements/recommendations for international students: Required—TOEFL (minimum score 540 paper-based; 76 iBT), IELTS (minimum score 6), ELPT (minimum score 964) or ELS (minimum score 112). Electronic applications accepted.

Southern University and Agricultural and Mechanical College, Graduate School, College of Sciences, Department of Psychology, Baton Rouge, LA 70813. Offers rehabilitation counseling (MS). *Degree requirements:* For master's, comprehensive exam, thesis optional. *Entrance requirements:* For master's, GMAT or GRE General Test. Additional exam requirements/recommendations for international students: Required—TOEFL (minimum score 525 paper-based). *Faculty research:* Cultural diversity, professional preparation and participation of minorities, needs and satisfaction of students with disabilities, prediction model for rehabilitation outcome, diabetes.

Southwestern College, Program in Psychodrama and Action Methods, Santa Fe, NM 87502-4788. Offers Certificate. *Entrance requirements:* For degree, 3 letters of reference.

Spalding University, Graduate Studies, Kosair College of Health and Natural Sciences, School of Professional Psychology, Louisville, KY 40203-2188. Offers clinical psychology (MA, Psy D). *Accreditation:* APA (one or more programs are accredited). *Program availability:* Part-time. Terminal master's awarded for partial completion of doctoral program. *Degree requirements:* For master's, comprehensive exam; for doctorate, thesis/dissertation. *Entrance requirements:* For master's and doctorate, GRE General Test, 18 hours of undergraduate course work in psychology, interview, letters of recommendation, writing sample, autobiographical statement. Additional exam requirements/recommendations for international students: Required—TOEFL (minimum score 535 paper-based). *Faculty research:* Substance abuse, prayer research, end-of-life issues, complementary and alternative medicine, research methodology and statistical inference.

Stanford University, School of Humanities and Sciences, Department of Psychology, Stanford, CA 94305-2004. Offers PhD. *Degree requirements:* For doctorate, thesis/dissertation, oral exam. *Entrance requirements:* For doctorate, GRE General Test, GRE Subject Test. Additional exam requirements/recommendations for international students: Required—TOEFL. Electronic applications accepted. *Expenses: Tuition:* Full-time $48,987; part-time $10,620 per quarter. One-time fee: $400. Tuition and fees vary according to program.

State University of New York at New Paltz, Graduate and Extended Learning School, School of Liberal Arts and Sciences, Department of Psychology, New Paltz, NY 12561. Offers clinical mental health counseling (MS); mental health counseling (AC); psychological science (MS); school counseling (MS); trauma and disaster mental health (AC). *Program availability:* Part-time, evening/weekend. *Faculty:* 12 full-time (9 women), 1 (woman) part-time/adjunct. *Students:* 61 full-time (44 women), 19 part-time (15 women); includes 18 minority (2 Black or African American, non-Hispanic/Latino; 1 Asian, non-Hispanic/Latino; 12 Hispanic/Latino; 1 Native Hawaiian or other Pacific Islander, non-Hispanic/Latino; 2 Two or more races, non-Hispanic/Latino). 109 applicants, 57% accepted, 40 enrolled. In 2017, 16 master's awarded. *Degree requirements:* For master's, comprehensive exam, thesis. *Entrance requirements:* For master's, GRE General Test, minimum GPA of 3.0. Additional exam requirements/recommendations for international students: Required—TOEFL (minimum score 550 paper-based; 80 iBT), IELTS (minimum score 6.5). *Application deadline:* For fall admission, 2/1 priority date for domestic and international students; for spring admission, 11/15 priority date for domestic and international students. Application fee: $50. Electronic applications accepted. *Financial support:* In 2017–18, 6 teaching assistantships with partial tuition reimbursements (averaging $5,000 per year) were awarded. Financial award application deadline: 8/1. *Faculty research:* Disaster mental health, women's objectification, mate selection, cultural psychology, achievement motivation. *Unit head:* Dr. Glenn Geher, Chair, 845-257-3091, E-mail: geherg@newpaltz.edu. *Application contact:* Dr. Tabitha Holmes, Program Coordinator, 845-257-3955, E-mail: holmest@newpaltz.edu.
Website: http://www.newpaltz.edu/psychology/

State University of New York at Plattsburgh, School of Arts and Sciences, Department of Psychology, Plattsburgh, NY 12901-2681. Offers school psychology (MA, CAS). *Program availability:* Part-time. *Entrance requirements:* For master's, GRE General Test, minimum GPA of 3.0. Additional exam requirements/recommendations for international students: Required—TOEFL. *Faculty research:* Alzheimer's disease, adolescent behavior, intellectual assessment, learning disabilities, reading skill acquisition.

Stephen F. Austin State University, Graduate School, College of Liberal Arts, Department of Psychology, Nacogdoches, TX 75962. Offers MA. *Degree requirements:* For master's, comprehensive exam, thesis. *Entrance requirements:* For master's, GRE General Test. Additional exam requirements/recommendations for international students: Required—TOEFL.

Stony Brook University, State University of New York, Graduate School, College of Arts and Sciences, Department of Psychology, Stony Brook, NY 11794. Offers clinical psychology (PhD); cognitive psychology (PhD); integrative neuroscience (PhD); psychology (MA); social and health psychology (PhD). *Accreditation:* APA (one or more programs are accredited). *Faculty:* 30 full-time (17 women), 1 part-time/adjunct (0 women). *Students:* 100 full-time (77 women); includes 22 minority (5 Black or African American, non-Hispanic/Latino; 7 Asian, non-Hispanic/Latino; 7 Hispanic/Latino; 3 Two or more races, non-Hispanic/Latino), 15 international. Average age 27. 477 applicants, 6% accepted, 14 enrolled. In 2017, 33 master's, 12 doctorates awarded. *Degree requirements:* For doctorate, thesis/dissertation. *Entrance requirements:* For doctorate, GRE General Test, GRE Subject Test. Additional exam requirements/recommendations for international students: Required—TOEFL (minimum score 90 iBT). *Application deadline:* For fall admission, 1/15 for domestic students; for spring admission, 10/1 for domestic students. Application fee: $100. *Expenses:* Contact institution. *Financial support:* In 2017–18, 10 fellowships, 11 research assistantships, 37 teaching assistantships were awarded; career-related internships or fieldwork also available. *Faculty research:* Clinical psychology, cognitive development or processes, cognitive neuropsychology, developmental psychopathology, emotions. *Total annual research expenditures:* $3.6 million. *Unit head:* Dr. Sheri Levy, Chair, 631-632-4355, E-mail: sheri.levy@stonybrook.edu. *Application contact:* Marilynn Wollmuth, Coordinator, 631-632-7855, Fax: 631-632-7876, E-mail: marilyn.wollmuth@stonybrook.edu.
Website: http://www.psychology.sunysb.edu/psychology/

Suffolk University, College of Arts and Sciences, Department of Psychology, Boston, MA 02108-2770. Offers clinical psychology (PhD); college admission counseling (Certificate); mental health counseling (MS); school counseling (MS). *Accreditation:* APA. *Faculty:* 14 full-time (7 women), 3 part-time/adjunct (all women). *Students:* 52 full-time (47 women), 35 part-time (28 women); includes 17 minority (4 Black or African American, non-Hispanic/Latino; 1 Asian, non-Hispanic/Latino; 11 Hispanic/Latino; 1 Two or more races, non-Hispanic/Latino), 7 international. Average age 27. 266 applicants, 23% accepted, 19 enrolled. In 2017, 23 master's, 7 doctorates, 11 other advanced degrees awarded. Terminal master's awarded for partial completion of doctoral program. *Degree requirements:* For master's, practicum, internship; for doctorate, thesis/dissertation, practicum. *Entrance requirements:* For doctorate, GRE General Test or MAT, 2 letters of recommendation, resume. Additional exam requirements/recommendations for international students: Required—TOEFL (minimum score 550 paper-based; 80 iBT). *Application deadline:* For fall admission, 12/1 for domestic and international students. Applications are processed on a rolling basis. Application fee: $50. Electronic applications accepted. *Expenses:* $36,936 per year full-time, $1,539 per credit part-time (for PhD); $15,675 per year full-time, $1,045 per credit part-time (for MS). *Financial support:* In 2017–18, 57 students received support, including 21 fellowships (averaging $17,193 per year); career-related internships or fieldwork, Federal Work-Study, institutionally sponsored loans, scholarships/grants, and unspecified assistantships also available. Support available to part-time students. Financial award application deadline: 4/1; financial award applicants required to submit FAFSA. *Faculty research:* Assessing exposure in the context of a family-based cognitive behavioral treatment for pediatric OCD, a mindfulness approach to designing and testing the efficacy of a new sexual revictimization prevention program for college women, olfaction and decision-making in substance-dependent individuals, the role of experiential avoidance in Generalized Anxiety Disorder, ego development as a predictor of dogmatism and intolerance in the political right and left. *Unit head:* Dr. Amy Marks, Chairperson, 617-573-8017, E-mail: akmarks@suffolk.edu. *Application contact:* Mara Marzocchi, Associate Director of Graduate Admissions, 617-573-8302, Fax: 617-305-1733, E-mail: grad.admission@suffolk.edu.
Website: http://www.suffolk.edu/college/graduate/69299.php

Sul Ross State University, College of Arts and Sciences, Department of Behavioral and Social Sciences, Program in Psychology, Alpine, TX 79832. Offers MA. *Entrance requirements:* For master's, GRE General Test, minimum GPA of 2.5 in last 60 hours of undergraduate work.

Syracuse University, College of Arts and Sciences, Department of Psychology, Syracuse, NY 13244. Offers clinical psychology (PhD); cognition, brain, and behavior (PhD); school psychology (PhD); social psychology (PhD). *Accreditation:* APA. In 2017, 1 doctorate awarded. Terminal master's awarded for partial completion of doctoral program. *Degree requirements:* For doctorate, comprehensive exam, thesis/dissertation. *Entrance requirements:* For doctorate, GRE General Test, GRE Subject Test, resume, personal statement, three letters of recommendation. Additional exam requirements/recommendations for international students: Required—TOEFL (minimum score 100 iBT). *Application deadline:* For fall admission, 12/1 priority date for domestic and international students. Application fee: $75. Electronic applications accepted. *Financial support:* Fellowships with full tuition reimbursements, research assistantships with tuition reimbursements, teaching assistantships with tuition reimbursements, and scholarships/grants available. Financial award application deadline: 1/1. *Faculty research:* Clinical psychology; cognition, brain, and behavior; school psychology; social psychology. *Unit head:* Dr. Amy Criss, Professor and Department Chair, Psychology, 315-443-1210, E-mail: acriss@syr.edu. *Application contact:* Alecia Zema, Curriculum Coordinator, 315-443-2760, E-mail: azema@syr.edu.
Website: http://psychology.syr.edu/graduate/overview.html

Teachers College, Columbia University, Department of Counseling and Clinical Psychology, New York, NY 10027-6696. Offers clinical psychology (PhD); counseling psychology (Ed M, Ed D, PhD); mental health counseling (ME); psychological counseling (ME, ND); psychology in education (MA, ND); school counselor (ME). *Accreditation:* APA (one or more programs are accredited). *Program availability:* Part-time. *Students:* 430 full-time (364 women), 237 part-time (201 women); includes 243 minority (65 Black or African American, non-Hispanic/Latino; 73 Asian, non-Hispanic/Latino; 83 Hispanic/Latino; 22 Two or more races, non-Hispanic/Latino), 142 international. Average age 28. 1,568 applicants, 38% accepted, 292 enrolled. *Unit head:* Prof. George Bonanno, Head, E-mail: gab38@tc.columbia.edu. *Application contact:* David Estrella, Director of Admission, 212-678-3305, E-mail: estrella@tc.columbia.edu.

Psychology—General

Temple University, College of Liberal Arts, Department of Psychology, Philadelphia, PA 19122-6096. Offers MA, MS, PhD. *Accreditation:* APA. *Faculty:* 39 full-time (21 women), 23 part-time/adjunct (14 women). *Students:* 101 full-time (86 women), 9 part-time (5 women); includes 22 minority (8 Black or African American, non-Hispanic/Latino; 3 Asian, non-Hispanic/Latino; 7 Hispanic/Latino; 4 Two or more races, non-Hispanic/Latino), 6 international. 537 applicants, 7% accepted, 24 enrolled. In 2017, 6 master's, 20 doctorates awarded. *Degree requirements:* For doctorate, thesis/dissertation. *Entrance requirements:* For doctorate, GRE General Test, minimum GPA of 3.0, 2 letters of recommendation. Additional exam requirements/recommendations for international students: Required—TOEFL (minimum score 620 paper-based; 105 iBT). *Application deadline:* For fall admission, 12/1 for domestic students, 12/15 for international students. Application fee: $60. Electronic applications accepted. *Expenses:* Tuition, state resident: full-time $16,164; part-time $898 per credit hour. Tuition, nonresident: full-time $22,158; part-time $1231 per credit hour. *Required fees:* $890; $445 per semester. Full-time tuition and fees vary according to course load, degree level, campus/location and program. *Financial support:* Fellowships, research assistantships, teaching assistantships, career-related internships or fieldwork, Federal Work-Study, institutionally sponsored loans, and unspecified assistantships available. Financial award application deadline: 12/15; financial award applicants required to submit FAFSA. *Faculty research:* Behavioral and cognitive neuroscience, cognitive and social development, psychopathology: study and treatment, social cognition and decision-making. *Unit head:* Deborah Drabick, Director of Graduate Studies, 215-204-5129, Fax: 215-204-5539, E-mail: deborah.drabick@temple.edu. *Application contact:* Vanessa Allen-Smith, Graduate Coordinator, 215-204-7667, Fax: 215-204-5539, E-mail: vallens@temple.edu.
Website: http://www.cla.temple.edu/psychology/

Tennessee State University, The School of Graduate Studies and Research, College of Education, Department of Psychology, Nashville, TN 37209-1561. Offers counseling psychology (MS). *Entrance requirements:* For master's, GRE General Test or MAT. Electronic applications accepted.

Texas A&M International University, Office of Graduate Studies and Research, College of Arts and Sciences, Department of Psychology and Communication, Laredo, TX 78041. Offers counseling psychology (MACP); psychology (MS). *Degree requirements:* For master's, thesis (for some programs). *Entrance requirements:* For master's, GRE General Test. Additional exam requirements/recommendations for international students: Required—TOEFL (minimum score 550 paper-based; 79 iBT).

Texas A&M University, College of Liberal Arts, Department of Psychology, College Station, TX 77843. Offers clinical psychology (PhD); industrial/organizational psychology (PhD); psychology (MS, PhD), including clinical psychology (PhD). *Accreditation:* APA (one or more programs are accredited). *Faculty:* 50. *Students:* 84 full-time (42 women), 15 part-time (9 women); includes 41 minority (8 Black or African American, non-Hispanic/Latino; 7 Asian, non-Hispanic/Latino; 23 Hispanic/Latino; 3 Two or more races, non-Hispanic/Latino), 12 international. Average age 28. 292 applicants, 12% accepted, 22 enrolled. In 2017, 10 master's, 18 doctorates awarded. *Degree requirements:* For doctorate, comprehensive exam (for some programs), thesis/dissertation. *Entrance requirements:* For doctorate, GRE General Test. Additional exam requirements/recommendations for international students: Required—TOEFL (minimum score 550 paper-based; 80 iBT), IELTS (minimum score 6), PTE (minimum score 53). *Application deadline:* For fall admission, 12/1 for domestic and international students. Application fee: $50 ($90 for international students). Electronic applications accepted. *Expenses:* Contact institution. *Financial support:* In 2017–18, 83 students received support, including 19 fellowships with tuition reimbursements available (averaging $37,600 per year), 30 research assistantships with tuition reimbursements available (averaging $11,994 per year), 58 teaching assistantships with tuition reimbursements available (averaging $11,425 per year); career-related internships or fieldwork, institutionally sponsored loans, scholarships/grants, traineeships, health care benefits, tuition waivers (full and partial), and unspecified assistantships also available. Support available to part-time students. Financial award application deadline: 3/15; financial award applicants required to submit FAFSA. *Unit head:* Dr. Heather Lench, Department Head, 979-845-0377, E-mail: hlench@tamu.edu. *Application contact:* Dr. Charles D. Samuelson, Director of Graduate Studies, 979-845-0880, Fax: 979-845-4727, E-mail: c-samuelson@tamu.edu.
Website: http://psychology.tamu.edu/

Texas A&M University–Commerce, College of Education and Human Services, Commerce, TX 75429. Offers counseling (M Ed, MS, PhD); early childhood education (M Ed, MS); educational administration (M Ed, MS, Ed D); educational psychology (PhD); educational technology leadership (M Ed, MS); educational technology library science (M Ed, MS); elementary education (M Ed); health, kinesiology and sports studies (MS); higher education (MS, Ed D); psychology (MS); reading (M Ed, MS); secondary education (M Ed, MS); social work (MSW); special education (M Ed, MS); supervision, curriculum and instruction-elementary education (Ed D); training and development (MS). *Program availability:* Part-time, evening/weekend, 100% online, blended/hybrid learning. *Faculty:* 91 full-time (51 women), 38 part-time/adjunct (31 women). *Students:* 400 full-time (310 women), 1,400 part-time (1,117 women); includes 724 minority (412 Black or African American, non-Hispanic/Latino; 8 American Indian or Alaska Native, non-Hispanic/Latino; 24 Asian, non-Hispanic/Latino; 220 Hispanic/Latino; 60 Two or more races, non-Hispanic/Latino), 18 international. Average age 37. 951 applicants, 46% accepted, 331 enrolled. In 2017, 564 master's, 24 doctorates awarded. *Degree requirements:* For master's, comprehensive exam, thesis optional, departmental qualifying exams (for some programs); for doctorate, comprehensive exam, thesis/dissertation, departmental qualifying exam; for SSP, comprehensive exam, thesis optional. *Entrance requirements:* For master's and doctorate, GRE General Test. Additional exam requirements/recommendations for international students: Required—TOEFL (minimum score 550 paper-based; 79 iBT), IELTS (minimum score 6). *Application deadline:* For fall admission, 6/1 priority date for international students; for spring admission, 10/15 priority date for international students; for summer admission, 3/15 priority date for international students. Applications are processed on a rolling basis. Application fee: $50. Electronic applications accepted. *Expenses:* Tuition, state resident: full-time $3630. Tuition, nonresident: full-time $11,100. *Required fees:* $2564. Tuition and fees vary according to course load, degree level and program. *Financial support:* In 2017–18, 84 students received support, including 40 research assistantships with partial tuition reimbursements available (averaging $10,800 per year), 12 teaching assistantships with partial tuition reimbursements available (averaging $13,000 per year); career-related internships or fieldwork, Federal Work-Study, institutionally sponsored loans, scholarships/grants, health care benefits, and unspecified assistantships also available. Financial award application deadline: 6/15; financial award applicants required to submit FAFSA. *Faculty research:* Cognitive and bilingual education, positive behavioral intervention, literacy, math readiness. *Total annual research expenditures:* $1.1 million. *Unit head:* Dr. Timothy Letzring, Dean, 903-886-5181, Fax: 903-886-5905, E-mail: tim.letzring@tamuc.edu. *Application contact:* Vicky Turner, Doctoral Degree and Special Programs Coordinator, 903-886-5167, E-mail: vicky.turner@tamuc.edu.
Website: http://www.tamuc.edu/academics/graduateSchool/programs/education/default.aspx

Texas A&M University–Corpus Christi, College of Graduate Studies, College of Liberal Arts, Program in Psychology, Corpus Christi, TX 78412. Offers clinical psychology (MA); general psychology (MA). *Program availability:* Part-time, evening/weekend. *Students:* 28 full-time (22 women), 10 part-time (all women); includes 25 minority (all Hispanic/Latino). Average age 28. 35 applicants, 74% accepted, 19 enrolled. In 2017, 12 master's awarded. *Degree requirements:* For master's, comprehensive exam. *Entrance requirements:* For master's, GRE (taken within 5 years; waived if candidate already has master's degree), minimum GPA of 3.0 in last 60 hours, essay (500-1000 words), 2 letters of recommendation. Additional exam requirements/recommendations for international students: Required—TOEFL (minimum score 550 paper-based; 79 iBT), IELTS (minimum score 6.5). *Application deadline:* For fall admission, 8/1 for domestic students, 5/1 for international students. Applications are processed on a rolling basis. Application fee: $50 ($70 for international students). Electronic applications accepted. *Expenses:* Tuition, state resident: full-time $3568; part-time $198.24 per credit hour. Tuition, nonresident: full-time $11,038; part-time $613.24 per credit hour. *Required fees:* $2129; $1422.58 per semester. Tuition and fees vary according to program. *Financial support:* Research assistantships, teaching assistantships, career-related internships or fieldwork, Federal Work-Study, institutionally sponsored loans, scholarships/grants, health care benefits, and unspecified assistantships available. Support available to part-time students. Financial award application deadline: 3/15; financial award applicants required to submit FAFSA. *Unit head:* Dr. Amy Houlihan, Chair, 361-825-2971, E-mail: amy.houlihan@tamucc.edu. *Application contact:* Graduate Admissions Coordinator, 361-825-2177, Fax: 361-825-2755, E-mail: gradweb@tamucc.edu.
Website: http://cla.tamucc.edu/psychology/pages/graduate.html

Texas A&M University–Kingsville, College of Graduate Studies, College of Arts and Sciences, Department of Psychology and Sociology, Program in Psychology, Kingsville, TX 78363. Offers MA, MS. *Entrance requirements:* Additional exam requirements/recommendations for international students: Required—TOEFL (minimum score 550 paper-based; 79 iBT); Recommended—IELTS. Electronic applications accepted.

Texas A&M University–Texarkana, Graduate Studies and Research, College of Health and Behavioral Sciences, Texarkana, TX 75503. Offers counseling psychology (MS). *Program availability:* Part-time, evening/weekend. *Degree requirements:* For master's, comprehensive exam (for some programs), thesis or alternative. *Entrance requirements:* For master's, minimum GPA of 3.0 in last 60 hours of bachelor's degree. Additional exam requirements/recommendations for international students: Required—TOEFL. Electronic applications accepted.

Texas Christian University, College of Science and Engineering, Department of Psychology, Fort Worth, TX 76129. Offers developmental trauma (MS); experimental psychology (PhD), including cognition/developmental, learning, neuroscience, social. *Faculty:* 13 full-time (6 women), 2 part-time/adjunct (both women). *Students:* 32 full-time (25 women); includes 5 minority (1 Asian, non-Hispanic/Latino; 2 Hispanic/Latino; 2 Two or more races, non-Hispanic/Latino), 2 international. Average age 26. 50 applicants, 34% accepted, 16 enrolled. In 2017, 8 master's, 2 doctorates awarded. Terminal master's awarded for partial completion of doctoral program. *Degree requirements:* For master's, thesis; for doctorate, thesis/dissertation. *Entrance requirements:* For doctorate, GRE General Test. Additional exam requirements/recommendations for international students: Required—TOEFL. *Application deadline:* For fall admission, 2/1 for domestic and international students. Application fee: $60 ($0 for international students). Electronic applications accepted. *Expenses:* Contact institution. *Financial support:* In 2017–18, 23 students received support, including 23 teaching assistantships with full tuition reimbursements available (averaging $19,750 per year); scholarships/grants also available. Financial award application deadline: 2/1; financial award applicants required to submit FAFSA. *Faculty research:* Neuroscience, human and animal learning, cognition, development, experimental social psychology. *Unit head:* Dr. Mauricio R. Papini, Chair, 817-257-7410, Fax: 817-257-7681, E-mail: m.papini@tcu.edu. *Application contact:* Cindy Hayes, Administrative Assistant, 817-257-7410, Fax: 817-257-7681, E-mail: c.hayes@tcu.edu.
Website: https://psychology.tcu.edu/current-graduate-students/

Texas Southern University, College of Liberal Arts and Behavioral Sciences, Department of Psychology, Houston, TX 77004-4584. Offers MA. Electronic applications accepted.

Texas State University, The Graduate College, College of Liberal Arts, Program in Psychological Research, San Marcos, TX 78666. Offers MA. *Program availability:* Part-time. *Faculty:* 28 full-time (18 women), 6 part-time/adjunct (4 women). *Students:* 30 full-time (20 women), 2 part-time (both women); includes 7 minority (1 Black or African American, non-Hispanic/Latino; 4 Hispanic/Latino; 2 Two or more races, non-Hispanic/Latino), 2 international. Average age 26. 41 applicants, 63% accepted, 12 enrolled. In 2017, 15 master's awarded. *Degree requirements:* For master's, comprehensive exam, thesis optional. *Entrance requirements:* For master's, GRE General Test, baccalaureate degree from regionally-accredited university with minimum GPA of 3.0 on last 60 undergraduate semester hours and in psychology, statistics, and experimental and research methods courses; statement of research interest; resume; statement of purpose; 3 letters of recommendation. Additional exam requirements/recommendations for international students: Required—TOEFL (minimum score 550 paper-based; 78 iBT), IELTS (minimum score 6.5). *Application deadline:* For fall admission, 2/3 priority date for domestic and international students. Applications are processed on a rolling basis. Application fee: $40 ($90 for international students). Electronic applications accepted. *Expenses:* Tuition, state resident: full-time $7868; part-time $3934 per semester. Tuition, nonresident: full-time $17,828; part-time $8914 per semester. *Required fees:* $2092; $1435 per semester. Tuition and fees vary according to course load. *Financial support:* In 2017–18, 28 students received support, including 2 research assistantships (averaging $12,445 per year), 23 teaching assistantships (averaging $12,041 per year); Federal Work-Study, institutionally sponsored loans, scholarships/grants, health care benefits, and unspecified assistantships also available. Support available to part-time students. Financial award application deadline: 3/1; financial award applicants required to submit FAFSA. *Faculty research:* Prescription drug misuse characteristics in adolescents and young adults, ecological momentary assessment of mechanisms related to college student prescriptions,. *Total annual research expenditures:* $47,219. *Unit head:* Dr. Ty Schepis, Graduate Advisor, 512-245-2526, Fax: 512-245-3153, E-mail: schepis@txstate.edu. *Application contact:* Dr. Andrea Golato, Dean of Graduate College, 512-245-2581, Fax: 512-245-8365, E-mail: gradcollege@txstate.edu.
Website: http://www.psych.txstate.edu/graduate/mapr.html

Texas Tech University, Graduate School, College of Arts and Sciences, Department of Psychological Sciences, Lubbock, TX 79409-2051. Offers clinical psychology (PhD); counseling psychology (MA, PhD); general experimental psychology (MA, PhD); psychology (MA). *Accreditation:* APA (one or more programs are accredited). *Faculty:* 31 full-time (14 women), 2 part-time/adjunct (both women). *Students:* 126 full-time (75 women), 10 part-time (5 women); includes 33 minority (4 Black or African American, non-Hispanic/Latino; 1 American Indian or Alaska Native, non-Hispanic/Latino; 10 Asian, non-Hispanic/Latino; 17 Hispanic/Latino; 1 Two or more races, non-Hispanic/Latino), 11 international. Average age 27. 278 applicants, 15% accepted, 28 enrolled. In 2017, 17 master's, 7 doctorates awarded. *Degree requirements:* For doctorate,

comprehensive exam, thesis/dissertation, 100 credit hours of organized courses, research credits, and practica. *Entrance requirements:* For master's, GRE General Test, GRE Subject Test, essays, letters of recommendation; for doctorate, GRE General Test, essays, letters of recommendation. *Additional exam requirements/recommendations for international students:* Required—TOEFL (minimum score 550 paper-based; 79 iBT). *Application deadline:* For fall admission, 6/1 priority date for domestic students, 1/15 priority date for international students; for spring admission, 9/1 priority date for domestic students, 6/15 priority date for international students. Applications are processed on a rolling basis. Application fee: $60. Electronic applications accepted. *Expenses:* Contact institution. *Financial support:* In 2017–18, 132 students received support, including 127 fellowships (averaging $2,830 per year), 58 research assistantships (averaging $8,094 per year), 105 teaching assistantships (averaging $11,486 per year); Federal Work-Study, institutionally sponsored loans, health care benefits, and unspecified assistantships also available. Financial award application deadline: 4/15; financial award applicants required to submit FAFSA. *Faculty research:* Health psychology, addictive behaviors, depression and suicide risk, sexuality/sexual risk behaviors/HIV, neuroscience/neuroimaging, forensic and correctional psychology. *Total annual research expenditures:* $647,634. *Unit head:* Dr. Robert Morgan, Professor and Chair, 806-834-7117, Fax: 806-742-0818, E-mail: robert.morgan@ttu.edu. *Application contact:* Kay Hill, Admissions Coordinator, 806-834-1350, Fax: 806-742-0818, E-mail: kay.hill@ttu.edu.
Website: http://www.depts.ttu.edu/psy/

Texas Woman's University, Graduate School, College of Arts and Sciences, Department of Psychology and Philosophy, Denton, TX 76204. Offers counseling psychology (MA, PhD); psychological science (MS); school psychology (PhD, SSP). *Accreditation:* APA (one or more programs are accredited). *Faculty:* 15 full-time (10 women), 3 part-time/adjunct (2 women). *Students:* 77 full-time (70 women), 41 part-time (37 women); includes 52 minority (13 Black or African American, non-Hispanic/Latino; 11 Asian, non-Hispanic/Latino; 23 Hispanic/Latino; 5 Two or more races, non-Hispanic/ Latino). Average age 28. 120 applicants, 21% accepted, 24 enrolled. In 2017, 4 master's, 13 doctorates, 4 other advanced degrees awarded. Terminal master's awarded for partial completion of doctoral program. *Degree requirements:* For master's, comprehensive exam (for some programs), thesis (for some programs), practica (for MA); for doctorate, comprehensive exam, thesis/dissertation, internship, residency; for SSP, comprehensive exam, internship, capstone evaluation. *Entrance requirements:* For master's, GRE (preferred minimum score 153 [500 old version] Verbal, 144 [500 old version] Quantitative, 4.0 Analytical Writing), BA/BS or 18 hours in psychology; minimum GPA of 3.0, 3.5 in psychology classes; 3 letters of reference; curriculum vitae; essay; for doctorate, GRE (preferred minimum score 153 [500 old version] Verbal, 144 [500 old version] Quantitative, 4 Analytical), 3 letters of reference, minimum GPA of 3.0 overall and 3.5 in psychology classes, MA in psychology or related discipline with thesis, curriculum vitae, essays; for SSP, GRE (preferred minimum score 153 [500 old version] Verbal, 144 [500 old version] Quantitative, 4 Analytical), BA/BS or 18 hours in psychology; minimum GPA of 3.0, 3.5 in psychology classes; 3 letters of reference; curriculum vitae; personal essay. *Additional exam requirements/recommendations for international students:* Required—TOEFL (minimum score 550 paper-based; 79 iBT); Recommended—IELTS (minimum score 6.5), TSE (minimum score 53). *Application deadline:* For fall admission, 2/1 for domestic and international students; for summer admission, 2/1 for domestic and international students. Applications are processed on a rolling basis. Application fee: $50 ($75 for international students). Electronic applications accepted. *Expenses:* $7,520 per year full-time in-state; $16,820 per year full-time out-of-state. *Financial support:* In 2017–18, 74 students received support, including 11 teaching assistantships (averaging $13,010 per year); research assistantships, career-related internships or fieldwork, Federal Work-Study, institutionally sponsored loans, scholarships/grants, traineeships, health care benefits, and unspecified assistantships also available. Support available to part-time students. Financial award application deadline: 3/1; financial award applicants required to submit FAFSA. *Faculty research:* Victimization, body image, moral and political philosophy, neuropsychology and assessment in children, neurobiology of memory and learning. *Total annual research expenditures:* $51,748. *Unit head:* Dr. Shannon Scott, Chair, 940-898-2303, Fax: 940-898-2301, E-mail: psychology@twu.edu. *Application contact:* Korie Hawkins, Associate Director of Admissions, Graduate Recruitment, 940-898-3188, Fax: 940-898-3081, E-mail: admissions@twu.edu.
Website: http://www.twu.edu/psychology-philosophy/

Tiffin University, Program in Psychology, Tiffin, OH 44883-2161. Offers MS. *Program availability:* Part-time, evening/weekend, online only, 100% online. *Entrance requirements:* Additional exam requirements/recommendations for international students: Recommended—TOEFL. Electronic applications accepted. *Expenses:* Contact institution.

Towson University, College of Liberal Arts, Program in Psychology, Towson, MD 21252-0001. Offers clinical psychology (MA); counseling psychology (MA); experimental psychology (MA); school psychology (MA). *Program availability:* Part-time, evening/weekend. *Students:* 98 full-time (75 women), 21 part-time (13 women); includes 32 minority (15 Black or African American, non-Hispanic/Latino; 4 Asian, non-Hispanic/Latino; 8 Hispanic/Latino; 5 Two or more races, non-Hispanic/Latino). *Degree requirements:* For master's, thesis (for some programs). *Entrance requirements:* For master's, GRE, minimum GPA of 3.0, letters of recommendation. *Application deadline:* For fall admission, 1/17 for domestic students, 5/15 for international students; for spring admission, 10/15 for domestic students, 12/1 for international students. Applications are processed on a rolling basis. Application fee: $45. Electronic applications accepted. *Expenses:* Tuition, state resident: full-time $7960; part-time $398 per unit. Tuition, nonresident: full-time $16,480; part-time $824 per unit. *Required fees:* $2600; $130 per year. $390 per term. *Financial support:* Application deadline: 4/1. *Unit head:* Dr. Geoffrey Munro, Department Chair, 410-704-2634, E-mail: psycdept@towson.edu. *Application contact:* Coverley Beidleman, Assistant Director of Graduate Admissions, 410-704-5630, Fax: 410-704-3030, E-mail: cbeidleman@towson.edu.
Website: https://www.towson.edu/cla/departments/psychology/grad/

Tufts University, Graduate School of Arts and Sciences, Department of Psychology, Medford, MA 02155. Offers cognitive science (PhD); psychology (MS, PhD). *Students:* 39 full-time (30 women); includes 7 minority (1 Black or African American, non-Hispanic/Latino; 4 Asian, non-Hispanic/Latino; 2 Hispanic/Latino), 4 international. Average age 27. 154 applicants, 8% accepted, 7 enrolled. In 2017, 4 master's, 8 doctorates awarded. Terminal master's awarded for partial completion of doctoral program. *Degree requirements:* For master's, thesis; for doctorate, thesis/dissertation. *Entrance requirements:* For master's and doctorate, GRE General Test, GRE Subject Test. Additional exam requirements/recommendations for international students: Required—TOEFL (minimum score 550 paper-based; 80 iBT), IELTS (minimum score 6.5). *Application deadline:* For fall admission, 12/15 for domestic and international students. Applications are processed on a rolling basis. Application fee: $85. Electronic applications accepted. *Expenses:* Contact institution. *Financial support:* Fellowships, research assistantships, teaching assistantships, Federal Work-Study, scholarships/grants, tuition waivers (full and partial), and unspecified assistantships available. Support available to part-time students. Financial award application deadline: 1/15. *Unit head:* Dr. Ayanna Thomas, Graduate Program Director, 617-627-4559. *Application*

contact: Office of Graduate Admissions, 617-627-3395, E-mail: gradadmissions@tufts.edu.
Website: http://ase.tufts.edu/psychology

Tulane University, School of Science and Engineering, Department of Psychology, New Orleans, LA 70118-5669. Offers MS, PhD. *Accreditation:* APA (one or more programs are accredited). Terminal master's awarded for partial completion of doctoral program. *Degree requirements:* For master's, variable foreign language requirement, thesis; for doctorate, thesis/dissertation. *Entrance requirements:* For master's, GRE General Test, minimum B average in undergraduate course work; for doctorate, GRE General Test. Additional exam requirements/recommendations for international students: Required—TOEFL. Electronic applications accepted. *Expenses: Tuition:* Full-time $50,920; part-time $2829 per credit hour. *Required fees:* $2040; $44.50 per credit hour. $580 per term. Tuition and fees vary according to course load, degree level and program. *Faculty research:* Hormones and behavior, aggression, personnel selection, cognitive development, stereotyping, diabetes.

Uniformed Services University of the Health Sciences, F. Edward Hebert School of Medicine, Graduate Programs in the Biomedical Sciences and Public Health, Department of Medical and Clinical Psychology, Bethesda, MD 20814. Offers clinical psychology (PhD); medical psychology (PhD). PhD in clinical psychology available to active duty military only. *Accreditation:* APA. Terminal master's awarded for partial completion of doctoral program. *Degree requirements:* For doctorate, comprehensive exam, thesis/dissertation, qualifying exam. *Entrance requirements:* For doctorate, GRE General Test, minimum GPA of 3.0, U.S. citizenship. Additional exam requirements/ recommendations for international students: Required—TOEFL. Electronic applications accepted. *Faculty research:* Addictive and appetitive behavior, psychopharmacology, stress and eating, obesity, health.

Union College, Graduate Programs, Department of Psychology, Barbourville, KY 40906-1499. Offers clinical psychology (MA); counseling psychology (MA); school psychology (MA).

Universidad de las Americas, A.C., Program in Psychology, Mexico City, Mexico. Offers family therapy (MA).

Universidad de las Américas Puebla, Division of Graduate Studies, School of Social Sciences, Program in Psychology, Puebla, Mexico. Offers MA. *Program availability:* Part-time, evening/weekend. *Degree requirements:* For master's, one foreign language, thesis. *Entrance requirements:* For master's, minimum B+ average. *Faculty research:* Testing, social hemispheric specialization, clinical psychology.

Université de Montréal, Faculty of Arts and Sciences, Department of Psychology, Montréal, QC H3C 3J7, Canada. Offers M Sc, PhD. Terminal master's awarded for partial completion of doctoral program. *Degree requirements:* For master's, one foreign language, thesis; for doctorate, one foreign language, thesis/dissertation, general exam. Electronic applications accepted. *Faculty research:* Vision, marital counseling, memory.

Université de Sherbrooke, Faculty of Letters and Human Sciences, Department of Psychology, Sherbrooke, QC J1K 2R1, Canada. Offers gerontology (MA). *Degree requirements:* For master's, thesis. *Faculty research:* Human relations.

Université du Québec à Montréal, Graduate Programs, Program in Psychology, Montréal, QC H3C 3P8, Canada. Offers D Ps, PhD. Programs offered jointly with Université du Québec à Trois-Rivières. *Program availability:* Part-time. *Degree requirements:* For doctorate, thesis/dissertation. *Entrance requirements:* For doctorate, appropriate master's degree or equivalent, proficiency in French.

Université du Québec à Trois-Rivières, Graduate Programs, Program in Psychology, Trois-Rivières, QC G9A 5H7, Canada. Offers PhD, Certificate. *Program availability:* Part-time. *Degree requirements:* For doctorate, thesis/dissertation. *Entrance requirements:* For doctorate, appropriate master's degree, proficiency in French. *Faculty research:* Child and family development, gerontology, mental health.

Université Laval, Faculty of Social Sciences, School of Psychology, Programs in Psychology, Québec, QC G1K 7P4, Canada. Offers clinical psychology (PhD); community psychology (PhD); psychology (PhD, Psy D). *Degree requirements:* For doctorate, comprehensive exam, thesis/dissertation. *Entrance requirements:* For doctorate, comprehension of written English, knowledge of French, interview. Electronic applications accepted.

University at Albany, State University of New York, College of Arts and Sciences, Department of Psychology, Albany, NY 12222-0001. Offers behavioral neuroscience (PhD); clinical psychology (PhD); cognitive psychology (PhD); industrial/organizational psychology (MA, PhD); social-personality psychology (PhD). *Accreditation:* APA (one or more programs are accredited). *Faculty:* 31 full-time (13 women). *Students:* 63 full-time (42 women), 49 part-time (33 women); includes 25 minority (4 Black or African American, non-Hispanic/Latino; 8 Asian, non-Hispanic/Latino; 4 Hispanic/Latino; 9 Two or more races, non-Hispanic/Latino), 11 international. 295 applicants, 14% accepted, 28 enrolled. In 2017, 13 master's, 5 doctorates awarded. *Degree requirements:* For doctorate, thesis/dissertation. *Entrance requirements:* For doctorate, GRE General Test, GRE Subject Test. Additional exam requirements/recommendations for international students: Required—TOEFL (minimum score 550 paper-based). *Application deadline:* For fall admission, 1/15 for domestic and international students. Application fee: $75. Electronic applications accepted. *Expenses:* Tuition, state resident: full-time $10,870; part-time $453 per credit hour. Tuition, nonresident: full-time $22,210; part-time $925 per credit hour. *Required fees:* $84.68 per credit hour. $508.06 per semester. Part-time tuition and fees vary according to course load and program. *Financial support:* Fellowships, research assistantships, teaching assistantships, and career-related internships or fieldwork available. Financial award application deadline: 2/1. *Unit head:* Christine K. Wagner, Chair, 518-442-4820, Fax: 518-442-4867, E-mail: cwagner@albany.edu. *Application contact:* Michael DeRensis, Director, Graduate Admissions, 518-442-3980, Fax: 518-442-3922, E-mail: graduate@albany.edu.
Website: http://www.albany.edu/psychology/

University at Buffalo, the State University of New York, Graduate School, College of Arts and Sciences, Department of Psychology, Buffalo, NY 14260. Offers MA, PhD. *Accreditation:* APA (one or more programs are accredited). *Faculty:* 30 full-time (14 women), 12 part-time/adjunct (6 women). *Students:* 76 full-time (56 women), 14 part-time (8 women); includes 20 minority (1 Black or African American, non-Hispanic/Latino; 11 Asian, non-Hispanic/Latino; 8 Hispanic/Latino), 10 international. Average age 27. 328 applicants, 16% accepted, 28 enrolled. In 2017, 18 master's, 10 doctorates awarded. Terminal master's awarded for partial completion of doctoral program. *Degree requirements:* For master's, project; for doctorate, thesis/dissertation. *Entrance requirements:* For master's and doctorate, GRE General Test. Additional exam requirements/recommendations for international students: Required—TOEFL (minimum score 550 paper-based; 79 iBT). *Application deadline:* For fall admission, 12/1 for domestic and international students. Application fee: $75. Electronic applications accepted. *Financial support:* In 2017–18, 80 students received support, including 5 fellowships with full tuition reimbursements available (averaging $14,280 per year), 14 research assistantships with full tuition reimbursements available (averaging $14,280 per year), 40 teaching assistantships with full tuition reimbursements available (averaging $14,280 per year); career-related internships or fieldwork, scholarships/

grants, health care benefits, tuition waivers (full and partial), and unspecified assistantships also available. Financial award application deadline: 12/1; financial award applicants required to submit FAFSA. *Faculty research:* Neural, endocrine, and molecular bases of behavior; adult mood and anxiety disorders; relationship dysfunction; attention deficit/hyperactivity disorder; psycho-linguistics. *Total annual research expenditures:* $528,527. *Unit head:* Dr. Stephen T. Tiffany, Chair, 716-645-0244, Fax: 716-645-3801, E-mail: chairpsych@buffalo.edu. *Application contact:* Mary Wlodarczyk, Admissions Officer, 716-645-8617, Fax: 716-645-3801, E-mail: psych@buffalo.edu.
Website: http://www.psychology.buffalo.edu/

The University of Akron, Graduate School, Buchtel College of Arts and Sciences, Department of Psychology, Akron, OH 44325. Offers adult development and aging (PhD); counseling psychology (MA, PhD); industrial/organizational psychology (MA, PhD); psychology (MA). *Accreditation:* APA (one or more programs are accredited). *Faculty:* 20 full-time (10 women), 5 part-time/adjunct (4 women). *Students:* 63 full-time (39 women), 28 part-time (15 women); includes 23 minority (8 Black or African American, non-Hispanic/Latino; 6 Asian, non-Hispanic/Latino; 6 Hispanic/Latino; 3 Two or more races, non-Hispanic/Latino), 7 international. Average age 26. 164 applicants, 18% accepted, 20 enrolled. In 2017, 16 master's, 13 doctorates awarded. Terminal master's awarded for partial completion of doctoral program. *Degree requirements:* For master's, thesis or specialty exam; for doctorate, one foreign language, comprehensive exam, thesis/dissertation. *Entrance requirements:* For master's, GRE, baccalaureate degree in psychology or extensive background in psychology; minimum cumulative undergraduate GPA of 3.0; three letters of recommendation; for doctorate, GRE, baccalaureate degree in psychology or 30 credits of psychology coursework; minimum cumulative undergraduate GPA of 3.0, 3.25 on all psychology coursework; current vita; declaration of intent; three letters of recommendation. Additional exam requirements/recommendations for international students: Required—TOEFL (minimum score 79 iBT), IELTS (minimum score 6.5). *Application deadline:* For fall admission, 12/1 for domestic and international students. Application fee: $45 ($70 for international students). Electronic applications accepted. *Financial support:* In 2017–18, 9 research assistantships with full tuition reimbursements, 46 teaching assistantships with full tuition reimbursements were awarded; administrative assistantships also available. *Faculty research:* Social cognitive determinants of behavior, the application of psychological principles to the workplace and career planning/development, the psychological processes of aging. *Total annual research expenditures:* $834,259. *Unit head:* Dr. Paul Levy, Department Chair, 330-972-8367, E-mail: plevy@uakron.edu.
Website: http://www.uakron.edu/psychology/

The University of Alabama, Graduate School, College of Arts and Sciences, Department of Psychology, Tuscaloosa, AL 35487. Offers clinical psychology (PhD); experimental psychology (PhD). *Faculty:* 29 full-time (17 women), 4 part-time/adjunct (3 women). *Students:* 84 full-time (65 women), 13 part-time (9 women); includes 14 minority (5 Black or African American, non-Hispanic/Latino; 3 Asian, non-Hispanic/Latino; 4 Hispanic/Latino; 2 Two or more races, non-Hispanic/Latino), 8 international. Average age 27. 309 applicants, 8% accepted, 15 enrolled. In 2017, 13 doctorates awarded. *Degree requirements:* For doctorate, thesis/dissertation, internship (for clinical psychology). *Entrance requirements:* For doctorate, GRE. Additional exam requirements/recommendations for international students: Required—TOEFL (minimum score 550 paper-based). *Application deadline:* For fall admission, 11/16 for domestic and international students. Application fee: $50 ($60 for international students). Electronic applications accepted. *Financial support:* In 2017–18, 65 students received support, including fellowships with full tuition reimbursements available (averaging $17,000 per year), research assistantships with tuition reimbursements available (averaging $12,744 per year), teaching assistantships with tuition reimbursements available (averaging $13,824 per year); career-related internships or fieldwork, institutionally sponsored loans, scholarships/grants, health care benefits, and unspecified assistantships also available. Financial award application deadline: 11/16. *Faculty research:* Cognitive development/disability, child clinical, psychology and law, health/aging, social psychology. *Total annual research expenditures:* $1.2 million. *Unit head:* Dr. Frances A. Conners, Chair, 205-348-1913, Fax: 205-348-8648, E-mail: fconners@ua.edu. *Application contact:* Mary Beth Hubbard, Information Contact, 205-348-1919, Fax: 205-348-8648, E-mail: mary.b.hubbard@ua.edu.
Website: http://www.psychology.ua.edu

The University of Alabama at Birmingham, College of Arts and Sciences, Program in Psychology, Birmingham, AL 35294. Offers behavioral neuroscience (PhD); lifespan developmental psychology (PhD); medical/clinical psychology (PhD); psychology (MA). *Accreditation:* APA (one or more programs are accredited). *Entrance requirements:* For master's and doctorate, GRE General Test, letters of recommendation. Electronic applications accepted. *Faculty research:* Biological basis of behavior structure, function of the nervous system.

The University of Alabama in Huntsville, School of Graduate Studies, College of Arts, Humanities, and Social Sciences, Department of Psychology, Huntsville, AL 35899. Offers industrial/organizational psychology (MA); psychology (MA). *Program availability:* Part-time, evening/weekend. *Degree requirements:* For master's, comprehensive exam, thesis or alternative, oral and written exams. *Entrance requirements:* For master's, GRE General Test, 15 hours of course work in psychology, minimum GPA of 3.25, sample of written work. Additional exam requirements/recommendations for international students: Required—TOEFL (minimum score 500 paper-based; 80 iBT), IELTS (minimum score 6.5). Electronic applications accepted. *Faculty research:* Virtual teams and teamwork, eyewitness identification, aging and memory, psychology of natural disasters and emergency preparedness, pain and pain management research.

University of Alaska Anchorage, College of Arts and Sciences, Department of Psychology, Anchorage, AK 99508. Offers clinical psychology (MS); clinical-community psychology with rural-indigenous emphasis (PhD). *Accreditation:* APA. *Program availability:* Part-time. *Degree requirements:* For master's, thesis. *Entrance requirements:* For master's, GRE General Test, GRE Subject Test, interview, references; for doctorate, interview, bachelor's or master's degree in psychology. Additional exam requirements/recommendations for international students: Required—TOEFL (minimum score 550 paper-based). *Faculty research:* Substance abuse, childhood autism, biofeedback, psychological assessment, mental health in Native Alaskans.

University of Alaska Fairbanks, College of Liberal Arts, Department of Psychology, Fairbanks, AK 99775-6480. Offers clinical-community psychology (PhD). Program offered jointly with University of Alaska Anchorage. *Degree requirements:* For doctorate, comprehensive exam, thesis/dissertation, oral defense of dissertation. *Entrance requirements:* For doctorate, bachelor's degree from accredited institution with minimum cumulative undergraduate and major GPA of 3.0; criminal background check; interview; course work in abnormal psychology, statistics, and research methods. Additional exam requirements/recommendations for international students: Required—TOEFL (minimum score 550 paper-based; 80 iBT), IELTS (minimum score 6.5). Electronic applications accepted. *Faculty research:* Clinical and community psychology; rural, indigenous, and cultural psychology.

University of Alberta, Faculty of Graduate Studies and Research, Department of Psychology, Edmonton, AB T6G 2E1, Canada. Offers M Sc, MA, PhD. Terminal master's awarded for partial completion of doctoral program. *Degree requirements:* For master's, thesis (for some programs); for doctorate, thesis/dissertation. *Entrance requirements:* For master's and doctorate, GRE. Additional exam requirements/recommendations for international students: Required—TOEFL (minimum score 550 paper-based). Electronic applications accepted. *Faculty research:* Animal behavior processes; cognitive, social and perceptual processes; development and aging; neuroscience.

The University of Arizona, College of Science, Department of Psychology, Tucson, AZ 85721. Offers MA, PhD. *Accreditation:* APA (one or more programs are accredited). *Degree requirements:* For doctorate, comprehensive exam, thesis/dissertation. *Entrance requirements:* For master's, GRE General Test, 3 letters of recommendation, statement of purpose; for doctorate, GRE General Test, 3 letters of recommendation. Additional exam requirements/recommendations for international students: Required—TOEFL (minimum score 550 paper-based; 79 iBT). Electronic applications accepted. *Faculty research:* Cognitive neuroscience, aging, law and psychology, psycholinguistics, family psychology.

University of Arkansas, Graduate School, J. William Fulbright College of Arts and Sciences, Department of Psychology, Fayetteville, AR 72701. Offers MA, PhD. *Accreditation:* APA (one or more programs are accredited). In 2017, 9 master's, 4 doctorates awarded. *Degree requirements:* For master's, thesis; for doctorate, variable foreign language requirement, thesis/dissertation. *Entrance requirements:* For doctorate, GRE General Test, GRE Subject Test. *Application deadline:* For fall admission, 8/1 for domestic students, 4/1 for international students; for spring admission, 12/1 for domestic students, 10/1 for international students; for summer admission, 4/15 for domestic students, 3/1 for international students. Applications are processed on a rolling basis. Application fee: $60. Electronic applications accepted. *Expenses:* Tuition, state resident: full-time $3782. Tuition, nonresident: full-time $10,238. *Financial support:* In 2017–18, 24 research assistantships, 8 teaching assistantships were awarded; fellowships with tuition reimbursements, career-related internships or fieldwork, Federal Work-Study, and traineeships also available. Support available to part-time students. Financial award application deadline: 4/1; financial award applicants required to submit FAFSA. *Unit head:* Dr. Douglas A. Behrend, Department Chair, 479-575-4256, Fax: 479-575-3219, E-mail: dbehrend@uark.edu. *Application contact:* Dr. Bill Levine, Associate Professor, 479-575-4256, E-mail: psycapp@uark.edu.
Website: https://fulbright.uark.edu/departments/psychological-science/

University of Arkansas at Little Rock, Graduate School, College of Social Sciences and Communication, Department of Psychology, Little Rock, AR 72204-1099. Offers applied psychology (MAP). *Program availability:* Part-time, evening/weekend. *Entrance requirements:* For master's, GRE General Test, minimum GPA of 2.7. *Faculty research:* Psychological methods and theories in business industry, government, and organizations; personnel program evaluation; training; affirmative action; organizational analysis and development.

The University of British Columbia, Faculty of Arts and Faculty of Graduate Studies, Department of Psychology, Vancouver, BC V6T 1Z4, Canada. Offers behavioral neuroscience (MA, PhD); clinical psychology (MA, PhD); cognitive science (MA, PhD); developmental psychology (MA, PhD); health psychology (MA, PhD); quantitative methods (MA, PhD); social/personality psychology (MA, PhD). *Accreditation:* APA (one or more programs are accredited). Terminal master's awarded for partial completion of doctoral program. *Degree requirements:* For master's, thesis; for doctorate, comprehensive exam, thesis/dissertation. *Entrance requirements:* For master's and doctorate, GRE General Test. Additional exam requirements/recommendations for international students: Required—TOEFL. Electronic applications accepted. *Expenses:* Contact institution. *Faculty research:* Clinical, developmental, social/personality, cognition, behavioral neuroscience.

University of Calgary, Faculty of Graduate Studies, Faculty of Arts, Department of Psychology, Calgary, AB T2N 1N4, Canada. Offers clinical psychology (M Sc, PhD); psychology (M Sc, PhD). *Degree requirements:* For master's, thesis; for doctorate, thesis/dissertation. *Entrance requirements:* For master's, GRE General Test, bachelor's degree in psychology, minimum GPA of 3.4. Additional exam requirements/recommendations for international students: Required—TOEFL (minimum score 550 paper-based). Electronic applications accepted. *Faculty research:* Cognition and cognitive development, social psychology, theoretical psychology, perception, aging.

University of California, Berkeley, Graduate Division, College of Letters and Science, Department of Psychology, Berkeley, CA 94720-1500. Offers PhD. *Accreditation:* APA. *Degree requirements:* For doctorate, thesis/dissertation, qualifying exam. *Entrance requirements:* For doctorate, GRE General Test, GRE Subject Test, minimum GPA of 3.0, 3 letters of recommendation. Electronic applications accepted.

University of California, Davis, Graduate Studies, Program in Psychology, Davis, CA 95616. Offers PhD. *Degree requirements:* For doctorate, thesis/dissertation. *Entrance requirements:* For doctorate, GRE General Test, GRE Subject Test, minimum GPA of 3.0. Additional exam requirements/recommendations for international students: Required—TOEFL (minimum score 550 paper-based). Electronic applications accepted. *Faculty research:* Social personality, perception, cognition, psychobiology.

University of California, Irvine, School of Social Ecology, Department of Psychology and Social Behavior, Irvine, CA 92697. Offers PhD. *Students:* 70 full-time (46 women), 1 (woman) part-time; includes 27 minority (2 Black or African American, non-Hispanic/Latino; 10 Asian, non-Hispanic/Latino; 9 Hispanic/Latino; 6 Two or more races, non-Hispanic/Latino), 7 international. Average age 27. 227 applicants, 11% accepted, 17 enrolled. In 2017, 10 doctorates awarded. *Degree requirements:* For doctorate, thesis/dissertation, research project. *Entrance requirements:* For doctorate, GRE General Test, minimum GPA of 3.0. Additional exam requirements/recommendations for international students: Required—TOEFL (minimum score 550 paper-based). *Application deadline:* For fall admission, 12/15 priority date for domestic and international students. Applications are processed on a rolling basis. Application fee: $105 ($125 for international students). Electronic applications accepted. *Financial support:* Fellowships, research assistantships with full tuition reimbursements, teaching assistantships, institutionally sponsored loans, traineeships, health care benefits, and unspecified assistantships available. Financial award application deadline: 3/1; financial award applicants required to submit FAFSA. *Faculty research:* Psychosocial development in children, adolescents, and adults; gerontology, childhood behavior disorders, and developmental psychopathology; sex differences; attitude change; social psychology. *Unit head:* Karen Rooks, Chair, 949-824-7069, Fax: 949-824-3002, E-mail: ksrook@uci.edu. *Application contact:* Roxane C. Silver, Professor, 949-824-2192, Fax: 949-824-3002, E-mail: rsilver@uci.edu.
Website: http://psb.soceco.uci.edu/

University of California, Irvine, School of Social Sciences, Department of Cognitive Sciences, Irvine, CA 92697. Offers psychology (PhD). *Students:* 51 full-time (22 women); includes 15 minority (11 Asian, non-Hispanic/Latino; 3 Hispanic/Latino; 1 Two or more races, non-Hispanic/Latino), 5 international. Average age 27. 89 applicants, 20% accepted, 10 enrolled. In 2017, 7 doctorates awarded. *Degree requirements:* For doctorate, thesis/dissertation. *Entrance requirements:* For doctorate, GRE General Test,

minimum GPA of 3.0. Additional exam requirements/recommendations for international students: Required—TOEFL (minimum score 550 paper-based). *Application deadline:* For fall admission, 1/15 priority date for domestic and international students. Applications are processed on a rolling basis. Application fee: $105 ($125 for international students). Electronic applications accepted. *Financial support:* Fellowships, research assistantships with full tuition reimbursements, teaching assistantships, institutionally sponsored loans, traineeships, health care benefits, and unspecified assistantships available. Financial award application deadline: 3/1; financial award applicants required to submit FAFSA. *Faculty research:* Mathematical psychology, visual and auditory perception, cognitive development, problem solving, experimental psychology. *Unit head:* Prof. Ramesh Srinivasan, Department Chair, 949-824-2969, E-mail: r.srinivasan@uci.edu. *Application contact:* Emily Grossman, Graduate Director, 949-824-1530, E-mail: grossman@uci.edu.
Website: http://www.cogsci.uci.edu/cs_graduates

University of California, Los Angeles, Graduate Division, College of Letters and Science, Department of Psychology, Los Angeles, CA 90034. Offers MA, PhD. *Accreditation:* APA (one or more programs are accredited). Terminal master's awarded for partial completion of doctoral program. *Degree requirements:* For master's, comprehensive exam; for doctorate, thesis/dissertation, oral and written qualifying exams, teaching experience. *Entrance requirements:* For doctorate, GRE General Test, GRE Subject Test (psychology), bachelor's degree; minimum undergraduate GPA of 3.0 (or its equivalent if letter grade system not used); interview. Additional exam requirements/recommendations for international students: Required—TOEFL. Electronic applications accepted.

University of California, Merced, Graduate Division, School of Social Sciences, Humanities and Arts, Merced, CA 95343. Offers cognitive and information sciences (PhD); interdisciplinary humanities (MA, PhD); psychological sciences (MA, PhD); social sciences (MA, PhD); sociology (MA, PhD). *Faculty:* 101 full-time (49 women), 3 part-time/adjunct (1 woman). *Students:* 197 full-time (131 women), 2 part-time (1 woman); includes 86 minority (7 Black or African American, non-Hispanic/Latino; 17 Asian, non-Hispanic/Latino; 55 Hispanic/Latino; 1 Native Hawaiian or other Pacific Islander, non-Hispanic/Latino; 6 Two or more races, non-Hispanic/Latino), 33 international. Average age 31. 190 applicants, 41% accepted, 49 enrolled. In 2017, 7 master's, 10 doctorates awarded. Terminal master's awarded for partial completion of doctoral program. *Degree requirements:* For master's, variable foreign language requirement, comprehensive exam, thesis or alternative; for doctorate, variable foreign language requirement, comprehensive exam, thesis/dissertation. *Entrance requirements:* For master's and doctorate, GRE. Additional exam requirements/recommendations for international students: Required—TOEFL (minimum score 550 paper-based; 80 iBT); Recommended—IELTS (minimum score 7). *Application deadline:* For fall admission, 1/15 for domestic and international students. Application fee: $90 ($110 for international students). Electronic applications accepted. *Expenses:* Tuition, state resident: full-time $11,502; part-time $5751 per semester. Tuition, nonresident: full-time $26,604; part-time $13,302 per semester. *Required fees:* $564 per semester. *Financial support:* In 2017–18, 167 students received support, including 17 fellowships with full tuition reimbursements available (averaging $23,250 per year), 13 research assistantships with full tuition reimbursements available (averaging $15,387 per year), 162 teaching assistantships with full tuition reimbursements available (averaging $16,103 per year); scholarships/grants, traineeships, and health care benefits also available. Financial award application deadline: 1/15. *Faculty research:* Social inequality, critical race and ethnic studies, public health and health sciences, cognitive science and language acquisition, political institutions, literature, cultural studies, anthropology, art history, ethnomusicology, history. *Total annual research expenditures:* $1.2 million. *Unit head:* Dr. Jill Robbins, Dean, 209-228-7843, E-mail: jillrobbins@ucmerced.edu. *Application contact:* Tsu Ya, Director of Admissions and Academic Services, 209-228-4521, Fax: 209-228-6906, E-mail: tya@ucmerced.edu.

University of California, Riverside, Graduate Division, Department of Psychology, Riverside, CA 92521-0102. Offers PhD. *Accreditation:* APA. *Degree requirements:* For doctorate, comprehensive exam, thesis/dissertation, 3 quarters of teaching experience, qualifying exams. *Entrance requirements:* For doctorate, GRE General Test, minimum GPA of 3.2. Additional exam requirements/recommendations for international students: Required—TOEFL (minimum score 550 paper-based; 80 iBT). Electronic applications accepted. *Expenses:* Tuition, state resident: full-time $5746. Tuition, nonresident: full-time $10,780. Tuition and fees vary according to campus/location and program. *Faculty research:* Neuroscience, personality and social psychology, developmental psychology, cognition, health psychology, quantitative psychology.

University of California, San Diego, Graduate Division, Department of Psychology, La Jolla, CA 92093. Offers PhD. *Students:* 41 full-time (20 women). 277 applicants, 8% accepted, 10 enrolled. In 2017, 12 doctorates awarded. *Degree requirements:* For doctorate, comprehensive exam, thesis/dissertation, 4 quarters of teaching assistantship. *Entrance requirements:* For doctorate, GRE General Test, minimum GPA of 3.0. Additional exam requirements/recommendations for international students: Required—TOEFL (minimum score 550 paper-based; 80 iBT), IELTS (minimum score 7). *Application deadline:* For fall admission, 12/1 for domestic students. Application fee: $105 ($125 for international students). Electronic applications accepted. *Financial support:* Fellowships, research assistantships, teaching assistantships, scholarships/grants, and unspecified assistantships available. Financial award applicants required to submit FAFSA. *Faculty research:* Cognitive and behavioral neuroscience, cognitive psychology, developmental psychology, sensation and perception, social psychology. *Unit head:* Victor Ferreira, Chair, 858-534-6303. *Application contact:* Samantha Llanos, Graduate Coordinator, 858-534-4416, E-mail: psycphdinfo@ucsd.edu.
Website: http://psychology.ucsd.edu/

University of California, Santa Barbara, Graduate Division, College of Letters and Sciences, Division of Mathematics, Life, and Physical Sciences, Department of Psychological and Brain Sciences, Santa Barbara, CA 93106-9660. Offers cognitive science (PhD); psychology (PhD); quantitative methods in the social sciences (PhD); technology and society (PhD). Terminal master's awarded for partial completion of doctoral program. *Degree requirements:* For doctorate, comprehensive exam, thesis/dissertation, teaching assistant training, progress report, papers, mini-convention presentation, 1 quarter of student teaching or teaching assistant class with section lab, continued participation in research and weekly area meetings. *Entrance requirements:* For doctorate, GRE General Test. Additional exam requirements/recommendations for international students: Required—TOEFL (minimum score 550 paper-based; 80 iBT) or IELTS (minimum score 7). Electronic applications accepted. *Faculty research:* Social psychology; developmental and evolutionary psychology; neuroscience and behavior; cognition, perception and cognitive neuroscience.

University of California, Santa Cruz, Division of Graduate Studies, Division of Social Sciences, Department of Psychology, Santa Cruz, CA 95064. Offers PhD. *Degree requirements:* For doctorate, thesis/dissertation, qualifying exam, seminars. *Entrance requirements:* For doctorate, GRE General Test. Additional exam requirements/recommendations for international students: Required—TOEFL (minimum score 550 paper-based; 83 iBT); Recommended—IELTS (minimum score 8). Electronic applications accepted. *Faculty research:* Cognitive psychology, developmental psychology, social psychology.

University of Central Arkansas, Graduate School, College of Health and Behavioral Sciences, Department of Counseling and Psychology, Conway, AR 72035-0001. Offers community counseling (MS); counseling psychology (MS); school psychology (MS, PhD, PMC). *Accreditation:* APA. Terminal master's awarded for partial completion of doctoral program. *Degree requirements:* For master's, comprehensive exam, thesis optional, internship; for doctorate, comprehensive exam, thesis/dissertation, internship. *Entrance requirements:* For master's, GRE General Test, minimum GPA of 2.75; for doctorate, GRE General Test, minimum GPA of 3.25. Additional exam requirements/recommendations for international students: Required—TOEFL (minimum score 550 paper-based). Electronic applications accepted.

University of Central Florida, College of Sciences, Department of Psychology, Orlando, FL 32816. Offers clinical psychology (MA, PhD); human factors and cognitive psychology (PhD), including human factors and cognitive psychology; industrial/organizational psychology (MS, PhD). *Accreditation:* APA. *Program availability:* Part-time. *Students:* 147 full-time (104 women), 8 part-time (4 women); includes 48 minority (9 Black or African American, non-Hispanic/Latino; 15 Asian, non-Hispanic/Latino; 20 Hispanic/Latino; 4 Two or more races, non-Hispanic/Latino), 9 international. Average age 27. 464 applicants, 19% accepted, 41 enrolled. In 2017, 38 master's, 14 doctorates awarded. *Degree requirements:* For master's, thesis; for doctorate, thesis/dissertation, candidacy exam. *Entrance requirements:* For master's, GRE General Test, minimum GPA of 3.0 in last 60 hours, resume or curriculum vitae, personal statement, letters of recommendation; for doctorate, GRE General Test, curriculum vitae, personal statement, letters of recommendation. Additional exam requirements/recommendations for international students: Required—TOEFL. *Application deadline:* For fall admission, 1/1 for domestic students. Application fee: $30. Electronic applications accepted. *Expenses:* Tuition, state resident: part-time $288.16 per credit hour. Tuition, nonresident: part-time $1073.31 per credit hour. Tuition and fees vary according to program. *Financial support:* In 2017–18, 102 students received support, including 47 fellowships with partial tuition reimbursements available (averaging $8,201 per year), 40 research assistantships with partial tuition reimbursements available (averaging $8,533 per year), 65 teaching assistantships with partial tuition reimbursements available (averaging $15,274 per year); career-related internships or fieldwork, Federal Work-Study, institutionally sponsored loans, health care benefits, tuition waivers (partial), and unspecified assistantships also available. Financial award application deadline: 3/1; financial award applicants required to submit FAFSA. *Unit head:* Dr. Clint Bowers, Interim Chair, 407-823-3576, E-mail: clint.bowers@ucf.edu. *Application contact:* Associate Director, Graduate Admissions, 407-823-2766, Fax: 407-823-6442, E-mail: gradadmissions@ucf.edu.
Website: http://sciences.ucf.edu/psychology/

University of Central Missouri, The Graduate School, Warrensburg, MO 64093. Offers accountancy (MA); accounting (MBA); applied mathematics (MS); aviation safety (MA); biology (MS); business administration (MBA); career and technical education leadership (MS); college student personnel administration (MS); communication (MA); computer science (MS); counseling (MS); criminal justice (MS); educational leadership (Ed D); educational technology (MS); elementary and early childhood education (MSE); English (MA); environmental studies (MA); finance (MBA); history (MA); human services/educational technology (Ed S); human services/learning resources (Ed S); human services/professional counseling (Ed S); industrial hygiene (MS); industrial management (MS); information systems (MBA); information technology (MS); kinesiology (MS); library science and information services (MS); literacy education (MSE); marketing (MBA); mathematics (MS); music (MA); occupational safety management (MS); psychology (MS); rural family nursing (MS); school administration (MSE); social gerontology (MS); sociology (MA); special education (MSE); speech language pathology (MS); superintendency (Ed S); teaching (MAT); teaching English as a second language (MA); technology (MS); technology management (PhD); theatre (MA). *Program availability:* Part-time, 100% online, blended/hybrid learning. *Faculty:* 337 full-time (145 women), 41 part-time/adjunct (28 women). *Students:* 785 full-time (398 women), 1,633 part-time (1,063 women); includes 231 minority (102 Black or African American, non-Hispanic/Latino; 4 American Indian or Alaska Native, non-Hispanic/Latino; 16 Asian, non-Hispanic/Latino; 52 Hispanic/Latino; 57 Two or more races, non-Hispanic/Latino), 692 international. Average age 30. In 2017, 2,605 master's, 122 other advanced degrees awarded. *Degree requirements:* For master's and Ed S, comprehensive exam (for some programs), thesis (for some programs). *Entrance requirements:* Additional exam requirements/recommendations for international students: Required—TOEFL (minimum score 550 paper-based; 79 iBT). *Application deadline:* For fall admission, 6/1 priority date for domestic and international students; for spring admission, 10/1 priority date for domestic and international students; for summer admission, 4/1 priority date for domestic and international students. Applications are processed on a rolling basis. Application fee: $30 ($75 for international students). Electronic applications accepted. *Expenses:* Tuition, state resident: full-time $8771; part-time $292.35 per credit hour. Tuition, nonresident: full-time $17,541; part-time $584.70 per credit hour. *Required fees:* $372; $24.78 per credit hour. *Financial support:* In 2017–18, 99 students received support. Research assistantships, teaching assistantships, career-related internships or fieldwork, Federal Work-Study, scholarships/grants, and administrative and laboratory assistantships available. Support available to part-time students. Financial award application deadline: 3/1; financial award applicants required to submit FAFSA. *Unit head:* Shellie Hewitt, Director of Graduate and International Student Services, 660-543-4621, Fax: 660-543-4778, E-mail: hewitt@ucmo.edu. *Application contact:* 660-543-4621, E-mail: admit_intl@ucmo.edu.
Website: http://www.ucmo.edu/graduate/

University of Central Oklahoma, The Jackson College of Graduate Studies, College of Education and Professional Studies, Department of Psychology, Edmond, OK 73034-5209. Offers psychology (MA), including counseling psychology, experimental psychology, forensic psychology, general psychology, school psychology. *Faculty:* 13 full-time (7 women), 1 part-time/adjunct (0 women). *Students:* 74 full-time (59 women), 35 part-time (29 women); includes 30 minority (4 Black or African American, non-Hispanic/Latino; 4 American Indian or Alaska Native, non-Hispanic/Latino; 3 Asian, non-Hispanic/Latino; 12 Hispanic/Latino; 7 Two or more races, non-Hispanic/Latino), 5 international. Average age 27. 109 applicants, 71% accepted, 51 enrolled. In 2017, 33 master's awarded. *Degree requirements:* For master's, thesis (for some programs). *Entrance requirements:* For master's, GRE. Additional exam requirements/recommendations for international students: Required—TOEFL (minimum score 550 paper-based; 79 iBT), IELTS (minimum score 6.5). *Application deadline:* For fall admission, 1/15 for domestic and international students; for spring admission, 11/15 for international students. Application fee: $60. Electronic applications accepted. *Expenses:* Tuition, state resident: full-time $5375; part-time $268.75 per credit hour. Tuition, nonresident: full-time $13,295; part-time $664.75 per credit hour. *Required fees:* $626; $31.30 per credit hour. One-time fee: $50. Tuition and fees vary according to program. *Financial support:* In 2017–18, 18 students received support, including 6 research assistantships with partial tuition reimbursements available (averaging $3,943 per year); teaching assistantships, career-related internships or fieldwork, scholarships/grants, tuition waivers (partial), and unspecified assistantships also available. Financial award

application deadline: 3/31; financial award applicants required to submit FAFSA. *Unit head:* Dr. Thomas Hancock, Chair, 405-974-5707, Fax: 405-974-3865. *Application contact:* Carlie Wellington, Assistant Director, CEPS Graduate Enrollment, 405-974-5105, Fax: 405-974-3851, E-mail: gradcoll@uco.edu.
Website: http://sites.uco.edu/ceps/dept/Professional-Studies-Programs/psy/index.asp

University of Chicago, Division of the Social Sciences, Department of Psychology, Chicago, IL 60637. Offers PhD. *Faculty:* 25. *Students:* 66 full-time (45 women); includes 17 minority (1 Black or African American, non-Hispanic/Latino; 1 American Indian or Alaska Native, non-Hispanic/Latino; 9 Asian, non-Hispanic/Latino; 6 Hispanic/Latino), 14 international. Average age 27. 218 applicants, 9% accepted, 13 enrolled. In 2017, 8 doctorates awarded. *Degree requirements:* For doctorate, one foreign language, thesis/dissertation. *Entrance requirements:* For doctorate, GRE General Test, 3 letters of recommendation, statement of purpose, transcripts, resume or curriculum vitae, writing sample (dependent on department). Additional exam requirements/recommendations for international students: Required—TOEFL (minimum score 104 iBT), IELTS (minimum score 7). *Application deadline:* For fall admission, 12/1 for domestic and international students. Application fee: $90. Electronic applications accepted. *Financial support:* In 2017–18, 8 students received support, including 8 fellowships with full tuition reimbursements available (averaging $27,000 per year); career-related internships or fieldwork, Federal Work-Study, institutionally sponsored loans, scholarships/grants, and health care benefits also available. Financial award application deadline: 12/1. *Unit head:* Prof. Susan C. Levine, Chair, 773-702-8844, Fax: 773-702-0886, E-mail: s-levine@uchicago.edu. *Application contact:* Office of the Dean of Students, 773-702-8415, E-mail: ssd-admissions@uchicago.edu.
Website: http://psychology.uchicago.edu

University of Cincinnati, Graduate School, McMicken College of Arts and Sciences, Department of Psychology, Cincinnati, OH 45221. Offers clinical psychology (PhD); experimental psychology (PhD). *Accreditation:* APA. *Degree requirements:* For doctorate, comprehensive exam, thesis/dissertation. *Entrance requirements:* For doctorate, GRE General Test. Additional exam requirements/recommendations for international students: Required—TOEFL. *Expenses: Tuition, area resident:* Full-time $14,468. Tuition, state resident: full-time $14,968; part-time $754 per credit hour. Tuition, nonresident: full-time $24,210; part-time $1311 per credit hour. *International tuition:* $26,460 full-time. *Required fees:* $3958; $84 per credit hour. One-time fee: $85 full-time. Tuition and fees vary according to course load, degree level and program. *Faculty research:* Neuropsychology, human factors, health.

University of Colorado Boulder, Graduate School, College of Arts and Sciences, Department of Psychology and Neuroscience, Boulder, CO 80309. Offers MA, PhD. *Accreditation:* APA (one or more programs are accredited). *Faculty:* 44 full-time (16 women). *Students:* 115 full-time (64 women), 2 part-time (1 woman); includes 10 minority (2 Asian, non-Hispanic/Latino; 6 Hispanic/Latino; 2 Two or more races, non-Hispanic/Latino), 4 international. Average age 29. 507 applicants, 4% accepted, 15 enrolled. In 2017, 9 master's, 26 doctorates awarded. Terminal master's awarded for partial completion of doctoral program. *Degree requirements:* For master's, comprehensive exam; for doctorate, thesis/dissertation. *Entrance requirements:* For master's, GRE General Test, minimum undergraduate GPA of 2.75; for doctorate, GRE General Test. *Application deadline:* For fall admission, 12/1 for domestic students; for spring admission, 12/1 for domestic students. Application fee: $60 ($80 for international students). Electronic applications accepted. Application fee is waived when completed online. *Financial support:* In 2017–18, 287 students received support, including 104 fellowships (averaging $6,076 per year), 27 research assistantships with full and partial tuition reimbursements available (averaging $31,518 per year), 63 teaching assistantships with full and partial tuition reimbursements available (averaging $19,338 per year); institutionally sponsored loans, scholarships/grants, health care benefits, and unspecified assistantships also available. Financial award application deadline: 2/15; financial award applicants required to submit FAFSA. *Faculty research:* Psychology; behavioral/experimental psychology; cognitive development/processes; neuroscience; social psychology. *Total annual research expenditures:* $17 million. *Application contact:* E-mail: grad-admissions@psych.colorado.edu.
Website: http://psych.colorado.edu/

University of Colorado Colorado Springs, College of Letters, Arts and Sciences, Department of Psychology, Colorado Springs, CO 80918. Offers MA, PhD. *Accreditation:* APA. *Program availability:* Part-time. *Faculty:* 18 full-time (8 women), 10 part-time/adjunct (6 women). *Students:* 32 full-time (27 women), 17 part-time (10 women); includes 6 minority (2 Black or African American, non-Hispanic/Latino; 1 Asian, non-Hispanic/Latino; 1 Hispanic/Latino; 2 Two or more races, non-Hispanic/Latino), 1 international. Average age 28. 330 applicants, 25% accepted, 15 enrolled. In 2017, 18 master's, 2 doctorates awarded. *Degree requirements:* For master's, thesis; for doctorate, comprehensive exam, thesis/dissertation. *Entrance requirements:* For master's, GRE, BA in psychology or equivalent background; minimum GPA of 3.0; for doctorate, GRE (minimum score of 1200 cumulative on the Verbal and Quantitative sections, or above the 50th percentile using the new scoring), minimum overall GPA of 3.0 in all undergraduate courses, 3.5 graduate. Additional exam requirements/recommendations for international students: Required—TOEFL (minimum score 550 paper-based; 80 iBT), IELTS (minimum score 6.5). *Application deadline:* For fall admission, 1/1 for domestic and international students. Applications are processed on a rolling basis. Application fee: $60 ($100 for international students). Electronic applications accepted. *Expenses:* $12,691 per year resident tuition, $22,339 nonresident, $15,003 nonresidential online; annual costs vary depending on program, course-load, and residency status. *Financial support:* In 2017–18, 38 students received support. Career-related internships or fieldwork, Federal Work-Study, scholarships/grants, and unspecified assistantships available. Support available to part-time students. Financial award application deadline: 3/1; financial award applicants required to submit FAFSA. *Faculty research:* Attention, emotion, neuroscience, adult development, relationship attachment style, attraction, event-related brain potentials, human adaptation from trauma, behavioral genetics, personality disorders, adolescent development, memory and executive function across the life span, early detection of Alzheimer's disease, psychometrics, differential attitudes toward and etiology of sexual abusers, clinical psychology, behavioral gerontology, forensic neuropsychology. *Total annual research expenditures:* $593,416. *Unit head:* Dr. Mary Coussons-Read, Department Chair, 719-255-3107, Fax: 719-255-4166, E-mail: mcousson@uccs.edu. *Application contact:* David Dubois, Graduate Student Advisor, 719-255-4500, Fax: 719-255-4166, E-mail: ddubois@uccs.edu.
Website: http://www.uccs.edu/~psych/

University of Connecticut, Graduate School, College of Liberal Arts and Sciences, Department of Psychology, Storrs, CT 06269. Offers behavioral neuroscience (PhD); biopsychology (PhD); clinical psychology (MA, PhD); cognition and instruction (PhD); developmental psychology (MA, PhD); ecological psychology (PhD); experimental psychology (PhD); general psychology (MA, PhD); industrial/organizational psychology (PhD); language and cognition (PhD); neuroscience (PhD); social psychology (MA, PhD). *Accreditation:* APA. Terminal master's awarded for partial completion of doctoral program. *Degree requirements:* For master's, comprehensive exam; for doctorate, thesis/dissertation. *Entrance requirements:* For master's and doctorate, GRE General Test, GRE Subject Test. Additional exam requirements/recommendations for international students: Required—TOEFL (minimum score 550 paper-based). Electronic applications accepted.

University of Dallas, Braniff Graduate School of Liberal Arts, Program in Psychology, Irving, TX 75062-4736. Offers clinical psychology (M Psych); psychology (M Psych, MA). *Program availability:* Part-time. *Degree requirements:* For master's, one foreign language, comprehensive exam (for some programs), thesis (for some programs). *Entrance requirements:* Additional exam requirements/recommendations for international students: Required—TOEFL. *Application deadline:* For fall admission, 2/15 priority date for domestic students; for spring admission, 11/15 for domestic students. Application fee: $50. *Expenses: Tuition:* Full-time $33,750; part-time $22,500 per year. Tuition and fees vary according to program. *Unit head:* Dr. Scott Churchill, Chairman, 972-721-5106, Fax: 972-721-4034.

University of Dayton, Program in General Psychology, Dayton, OH 45469. Offers MA. *Faculty:* 11 full-time (5 women). *Students:* 5 full-time (0 women), 1 (woman) part-time. Average age 26. 62 applicants, 8% accepted. In 2017, 2 master's awarded. *Degree requirements:* For master's, thesis. *Entrance requirements:* For master's, GRE General Test, GRE Subject Test (recommended), minimum undergraduate GPA of 2.7, 15 undergraduate course credits in psychology, psychology statistics, research methods. Additional exam requirements/recommendations for international students: Required—TOEFL (minimum score 550 paper-based; 80 iBT); Recommended—IELTS. *Application deadline:* For fall admission, 3/1 for domestic and international students. Application fee: $0 ($50 for international students). Electronic applications accepted. Tuition and fees vary according to degree level and program. *Financial support:* In 2017–18, 5 students received support, including 3 fellowships with full tuition reimbursements available (averaging $11,675 per year), 6 research assistantships with full tuition reimbursements available (averaging $11,675 per year), 6 teaching assistantships with full tuition reimbursements available (averaging $11,675 per year); institutionally sponsored loans, traineeships, and tuition waivers (partial) also available. Financial award application deadline: 3/1; financial award applicants required to submit FAFSA. *Faculty research:* Biopsychology, cognition and perception, social psychology and personality, neuropsychology, health psychology, child developmental psychology, cognition/perception. *Unit head:* Dr. Erin M. O'Mara, Graduate Program Director, 937-229-2161, E-mail: eomara1@udayton.edu.
Website: https://www.udayton.edu/artssciences/learn/graduate/psychology-ma.php

University of Delaware, College of Arts and Sciences, Department of Psychology, Newark, DE 19716. Offers behavioral neuroscience (PhD); clinical psychology (PhD); cognitive psychology (PhD); social psychology (PhD). *Accreditation:* APA. *Degree requirements:* For doctorate, thesis/dissertation. *Entrance requirements:* For doctorate, GRE General Test. Additional exam requirements/recommendations for international students: Required—TOEFL (minimum score 600 paper-based). Electronic applications accepted. *Faculty research:* Emotion development, neural and cognitive aspects of memory, neural control of feeding, intergroup relations, social cognition and communication.

University of Denver, Division of Arts, Humanities and Social Sciences, Department of Psychology, Denver, CO 80208. Offers affective/cognitive/social psychology (PhD); clinical child psychology (PhD); developmental psychology (PhD). *Accreditation:* APA. *Students:* Average age 28. 294 applicants, 4% accepted, 8 enrolled. In 2017, 8 doctorates awarded. Terminal master's awarded for partial completion of doctoral program. *Degree requirements:* For doctorate, variable foreign language requirement, comprehensive exam (for some programs), thesis/dissertation. *Entrance requirements:* For doctorate, GRE General Test, master's degree, transcripts, biographical statement, three letters of recommendation. Additional exam requirements/recommendations for international students: Required—TOEFL (minimum score 550 paper-based; 80 iBT). *Application deadline:* For fall admission, 12/1 priority date for domestic and international students. Application fee: $65. Electronic applications accepted. *Expenses:* Contact institution. *Financial support:* In 2017–18, 24 students received support, including 5 research assistantships with tuition reimbursements available (averaging $16,000 per year), 12 teaching assistantships with tuition reimbursements available (averaging $17,778 per year); Federal Work-Study, institutionally sponsored loans, scholarships/grants, and unspecified assistantships also available. Support available to part-time students. Financial award application deadline: 2/15; financial award applicants required to submit FAFSA. *Faculty research:* Stress and trauma, developmental science, affect science, clinical science, child psychopathology. *Unit head:* Dr. Anne DePrince, Professor and Chair, 303-871-2939, Fax: 303-871-4747, E-mail: adeprinc@du.edu. *Application contact:* Paula Houghtaling, Graduate Program Administrator, 303-871-3803, Fax: 303-871-4747, E-mail: phoughta@du.edu.
Website: http://www.du.edu/ahss/psychology

University of Denver, Graduate School of Professional Psychology, Denver, CO 80208. Offers clinical psychology (Psy D); forensic psychology (MA); international disaster psychology (MA); sport and performance psychology (MA); sport coaching (MA); strength and conditioning and fitness coaching (Certificate). *Accreditation:* APA. *Faculty:* 23 full-time (13 women), 25 part-time/adjunct (14 women). *Students:* 233 full-time (180 women), 79 part-time (46 women); includes 81 minority (22 Black or African American, non-Hispanic/Latino; 9 Asian, non-Hispanic/Latino; 31 Hispanic/Latino; 1 Native Hawaiian or other Pacific Islander, non-Hispanic/Latino; 18 Two or more races, non-Hispanic/Latino), 7 international. Average age 26. 866 applicants, 30% accepted, 135 enrolled. In 2017, 106 master's, 23 doctorates awarded. *Degree requirements:* For master's, comprehensive exam (for some programs); for doctorate, comprehensive exam (for some programs), paper, clinical internship. *Entrance requirements:* For master's and doctorate, GRE General Test, transcripts, resume, two letters of recommendation, essay. Additional exam requirements/recommendations for international students: Required—TOEFL (minimum score 550 paper-based; 80 iBT). *Application deadline:* For fall admission, 1/5 for domestic and international students. Application fee: $65. Electronic applications accepted. *Expenses:* $47,823 per year full-time. *Financial support:* In 2017–18, 235 students received support, including 2 teaching assistantships with tuition reimbursements available (averaging $1,976 per year); career-related internships or fieldwork, Federal Work-Study, institutionally sponsored loans, scholarships/grants, unspecified assistantships, and clinical assistantships also available. Support available to part-time students. Financial award application deadline: 2/15; financial award applicants required to submit FAFSA. *Unit head:* Dr. Shelly Smith-Acuna, Dean, 303-871-3880, Fax: 303-871-4220, E-mail: shelly.smith-acuna@du.edu. *Application contact:* Admissions Counselor, 303-871-3736, Fax: 303-871-4220, E-mail: gsppinfo@du.edu.
Website: http://www.du.edu/gspp

University of Florida, Graduate School, College of Liberal Arts and Sciences, Department of Psychology, Gainesville, FL 32611. Offers counseling psychology (PhD); psychology (MA, MS, PhD), including psychology (PhD), women's and gender studies (PhD); JD/PhD. *Degree requirements:* For master's, comprehensive exam, thesis or alternative; for doctorate, comprehensive exam, thesis/dissertation. *Entrance requirements:* For master's and doctorate, GRE General Test, minimum GPA of 3.0. Additional exam requirements/recommendations for international students: Required—TOEFL (minimum score 550 paper-based; 80 iBT), IELTS (minimum score 6). Electronic

applications accepted. *Faculty research:* Behavior analysis, behavioral and cognitive neuroscience, counseling, developmental psychology, social psychology.

University of Florida, Graduate School, College of Public Health and Health Professions, Department of Clinical and Health Psychology, Gainesville, FL 32611. Offers clinical and translational science (PhD); psychology (MS). *Accreditation:* APA (one or more programs are accredited). *Degree requirements:* For doctorate, comprehensive exam, thesis/dissertation, pre-doctoral internship. *Entrance requirements:* For master's and doctorate, GRE General Test, minimum GPA of 3.0. Additional exam requirements/recommendations for international students: Required—TOEFL (minimum score 550 paper-based; 80 iBT), IELTS (minimum score 6). Electronic applications accepted. *Faculty research:* Clinical child and pediatric psychology, medical psychology, neuropsychology, health promotion and aging.

University of Georgia, Franklin College of Arts and Sciences, Department of Psychology, Athens, GA 30602. Offers PhD. *Accreditation:* APA. *Degree requirements:* For doctorate, one foreign language, thesis/dissertation. *Entrance requirements:* For doctorate, GRE General Test. Additional exam requirements/recommendations for international students: Required—TOEFL. Electronic applications accepted.

University of Guelph, Graduate Studies, College of Social and Applied Human Sciences, Department of Psychology, Guelph, ON N1G 2W1, Canada. Offers applied social psychology (MA, PhD); clinical psychology: applied development emphasis (PhD); clinical psychology: applied developmental emphasis (MA); industrial/organizational psychology (MA, PhD); neuroscience and applied cognitive science (MA, PhD). *Degree requirements:* For master's, thesis; for doctorate, comprehensive exam, thesis/dissertation. *Entrance requirements:* For master's, GRE General Test, GRE Subject Test, minimum B+ average during previous 2 years of course work; for doctorate, GRE General Test, GRE Subject Test, minimum A- average. Additional exam requirements/recommendations for international students: Required—TOEFL (minimum score 89 iBT). Electronic applications accepted. *Faculty research:* Organizational psychology, reading comprehension and mathematical ability, drug addiction and relapse, gender issues and culture, memory, clinical psychology.

University of Hartford, College of Arts and Sciences, Department of Psychology, West Hartford, CT 06117-1599. Offers clinical practices (MA, Psy D), including clinical practices (Psy D); psychology (MA); general experimental psychology (MA); organizational behavior (MS); school psychology (MS). *Accreditation:* APA. *Program availability:* Part-time. *Degree requirements:* For master's, comprehensive exam, thesis (for some programs). *Entrance requirements:* For master's, GRE General Test, GRE Subject Test, minimum GPA of 3.0; for doctorate, GRE General Test, GRE Subject Test. Additional exam requirements/recommendations for international students: Required—TOEFL (minimum score 550 paper-based). Electronic applications accepted. *Expenses:* Contact institution.

University of Hawaii at Manoa, Office of Graduate Education, College of Social Sciences, Department of Psychology, Honolulu, HI 96822. Offers clinical psychology (PhD); community and cultural psychology (PhD); community and culture (MA); psychology (MA, PhD, Graduate Certificate). *Accreditation:* APA (one or more programs are accredited). *Program availability:* Part-time. Terminal master's awarded for partial completion of doctoral program. *Degree requirements:* For master's, comprehensive exam, thesis; for doctorate, comprehensive exam, thesis/dissertation. *Entrance requirements:* For master's and doctorate, GRE General Test, GRE Subject Test. Additional exam requirements/recommendations for international students: Required—TOEFL (minimum score 600 paper-based; 100 iBT), IELTS (minimum score 7). *Faculty research:* Cross-cultural psychology, health psychology, marine mammals, child/adult psychopathology.

University of Houston, College of Liberal Arts and Social Sciences, Department of Psychology, Houston, TX 77204. Offers clinical psychology (PhD); developmental psychology (PhD); industrial/organizational psychology (PhD); psychology (MA); social psychology (PhD). *Accreditation:* APA (one or more programs are accredited). *Degree requirements:* For master's, comprehensive exam, thesis; for doctorate, comprehensive exam, thesis/dissertation. *Entrance requirements:* For master's, GRE General Test, career statement, 3 letters of recommendation; for doctorate, GRE General Test, 3 letters of recommendation. Additional exam requirements/recommendations for international students: Required—TOEFL (minimum score 550 paper-based; 79 iBT). Electronic applications accepted. *Faculty research:* Health psychology, depression, child/family process, organizational effectiveness, close relationships.

University of Houston–Clear Lake, School of Human Sciences and Humanities, Programs in Human Sciences, Houston, TX 77058-1002. Offers behavioral sciences (MA), including criminology, cross cultural studies, general psychology, sociology; clinical psychology (MA); criminology (MA); cross cultural studies (MA); family therapy (MA); fitness and human performance (MA); school psychology (MA). *Accreditation:* AAMFT/COAMFTE. *Program availability:* Part-time, evening/weekend, online learning. *Degree requirements:* For master's, thesis or alternative. *Entrance requirements:* For master's, GRE General Test. Additional exam requirements/recommendations for international students: Required—TOEFL (minimum score 550 paper-based). Electronic applications accepted. *Faculty research:* Smoking cessation, adolescent sexuality, white collar crime, serial murder, human factors/human computer interaction.

University of Houston–Victoria, School of Arts and Sciences, Program in Psychology, Victoria, TX 77901-4450. Offers counseling psychology (MA); forensic psychology (MA); school psychology (MA). *Program availability:* Part-time, evening/weekend, online learning. *Degree requirements:* For master's, project or thesis. *Entrance requirements:* For master's, GRE General Test. Additional exam requirements/recommendations for international students: Required—TOEFL (minimum score 550 paper-based). Electronic applications accepted.

University of Idaho, College of Graduate Studies, College of Letters, Arts and Social Sciences, Department of Psychology and Communication Studies, Moscow, ID 83844. Offers experimental psychology (PhD); psychology and communication studies (MS). *Faculty:* 8. *Students:* 18 full-time (5 women), 11 part-time (5 women). Average age 30. In 2017, 11 master's awarded. *Entrance requirements:* For master's, GRE, minimum GPA of 3.0. Additional exam requirements/recommendations for international students: Required—TOEFL (minimum score 79 iBT). *Application deadline:* For fall admission, 8/1 for domestic students; for spring admission, 12/15 for domestic students. Applications are processed on a rolling basis. Application fee: $60. Electronic applications accepted. *Expenses:* Tuition, state resident: full-time $6722; part-time $430 per credit hour. Tuition, nonresident: full-time $23,046; part-time $1337 per credit hour. *Required fees:* $2142; $63 per credit hour. *Financial support:* Fellowships, research assistantships, and teaching assistantships available. Financial award applicants required to submit FAFSA. *Faculty research:* Instructional communication, visual and spatial cognition. *Unit head:* Dr. Todd Thorsteinson, Chair, 208-885-6324, E-mail: psyc-comm@uidaho.edu. *Application contact:* Sean Scoggin, Graduate Recruitment Coordinator, 208-885-4723, Fax: 208-885-4406, E-mail: graduateadmissions@uidaho.edu. Website: https://www.uidaho.edu/class/psychcomm

University of Illinois at Chicago, College of Liberal Arts and Sciences, Department of Psychology, Chicago, IL 60607-7128. Offers MA, PhD. *Accreditation:* APA. *Degree requirements:* For doctorate, thesis/dissertation, departmental qualifying exam.

Entrance requirements: For doctorate, GRE General Test, minimum GPA of 2.75. Additional exam requirements/recommendations for international students: Required—TOEFL. Electronic applications accepted. *Expenses:* Contact institution. *Faculty research:* Cognition, behavioral neuroscience, community and prevention research, social and personality.

University of Illinois at Urbana–Champaign, Graduate College, College of Liberal Arts and Sciences, Department of Psychology, Champaign, IL 61820. Offers MA, MS, PhD. *Accreditation:* APA (one or more programs are accredited).

University of Indianapolis, Graduate Programs, School of Psychological Sciences, Indianapolis, IN 46227-3697. Offers clinical psychology (Psy D); clinical psychology/mental health counseling (MA). *Accreditation:* APA. *Degree requirements:* For master's, practicum; for doctorate, comprehensive exam, thesis/dissertation, 1200 hours of clinical practicum, 2000-hour internship. *Entrance requirements:* For master's, GRE, 3 letters of recommendation; for doctorate, GRE, minimum GPA of 3.0, 18 hours of course work in psychology, 3 letters of recommendation. Additional exam requirements/recommendations for international students: Required—TOEFL (minimum score 550 paper-based).

The University of Iowa, Graduate College, College of Education, Department of Psychological and Quantitative Foundations, Iowa City, IA 52242-1316. Offers counseling psychology (PhD); educational measurement and statistics (MA, PhD); educational psychology (MA, PhD); school psychology (PhD, Ed S). *Accreditation:* APA. *Degree requirements:* For master's, thesis optional, exam; for doctorate, comprehensive exam, thesis/dissertation; for Ed S, exam. *Entrance requirements:* For master's, doctorate, and Ed S, GRE General Test, minimum GPA of 3.0. Additional exam requirements/recommendations for international students: Required—TOEFL (minimum score 550 paper-based; 81 iBT). Electronic applications accepted.

The University of Iowa, Graduate College, College of Liberal Arts and Sciences, Department of Psychology, Iowa City, IA 52242-1316. Offers MA, PhD. *Degree requirements:* For master's, thesis optional, exam; for doctorate, comprehensive exam, thesis/dissertation. *Entrance requirements:* For master's and doctorate, GRE General Test, minimum GPA of 3.0. Additional exam requirements/recommendations for international students: Required—TOEFL (minimum score 550 paper-based; 81 iBT). Electronic applications accepted.

The University of Kansas, Graduate Studies, College of Liberal Arts and Sciences, Department of Applied Behavioral Science, Lawrence, KS 66045. Offers applied behavioral science (MA); behavioral psychology (PhD); community health and development (Graduate Certificate); PhD/MPH. *Program availability:* Part-time. *Students:* 46 full-time (33 women), 15 part-time (12 women); includes 5 minority (3 Black or African American, non-Hispanic/Latino; 1 Asian, non-Hispanic/Latino; 1 Two or more races, non-Hispanic/Latino), 3 international. Average age 29. 79 applicants, 43% accepted, 30 enrolled. In 2017, 8 master's, 5 doctorates awarded. Terminal master's awarded for partial completion of doctoral program. *Entrance requirements:* For master's, curriculum vitae; 3 letters of recommendation; personal statement; all academic transcripts; copies of pertinent written work, published or not, as well as presented papers; for doctorate, curriculum vitae; 3 letters of recommendation; personal statement; copies of pertinent written work, published or not, as well as presented papers. Additional exam requirements/recommendations for international students: Required—TOEFL. *Application deadline:* For fall admission, 12/15 priority date for domestic students, 12/15 for international students. Application fee: $65 ($85 for international students). Electronic applications accepted. *Financial support:* Fellowships, research assistantships, teaching assistantships, career-related internships or fieldwork, traineeships, tuition waivers (full), and unspecified assistantships available. Financial award application deadline: 12/15; financial award applicants required to submit CSS PROFILE or FAFSA. *Faculty research:* Organizational behavioral management, community health and development, early childhood education and intervention, developmental disabilities, behavioral economics of choice. *Unit head:* Dr. Florence DiGennaro Reed, Chairperson, 785-864-0521, E-mail: fdreed@ku.edu. *Application contact:* Andrea Noltner, Office Manager, 785-864-0503, E-mail: anoltner@ku.edu. Website: http://absc.ku.edu

The University of Kansas, Graduate Studies, College of Liberal Arts and Sciences, Department of Psychology, Lawrence, KS 66045. Offers clinical psychology (MA, PhD); cognitive and brain sciences (MA, PhD); developmental psychology (MA, PhD); quantitative psychology (PhD); social psychology (MA, PhD). *Accreditation:* APA (one or more programs are accredited). *Program availability:* Part-time. *Students:* 92 full-time (63 women), 3 part-time (all women); includes 19 minority (7 Black or African American, non-Hispanic/Latino; 4 Asian, non-Hispanic/Latino; 4 Hispanic/Latino; 4 Two or more races, non-Hispanic/Latino), 10 international. Average age 28. 361 applicants, 7% accepted, 16 enrolled. In 2017, 9 master's, 17 doctorates awarded. Terminal master's awarded for partial completion of doctoral program. *Entrance requirements:* For doctorate, GRE General Test, three letters of recommendation, resume/curriculum vitae, statement of purpose/personal statement, writing sample. Additional exam requirements/recommendations for international students: Required—TOEFL. *Application deadline:* For fall admission, 12/1 for domestic and international students. Application fee: $65 ($85 for international students). Electronic applications accepted. *Financial support:* Fellowships, research assistantships, teaching assistantships, career-related internships or fieldwork, Federal Work-Study, scholarships/grants, health care benefits, and unspecified assistantships available. Financial award application deadline: 12/1; financial award applicants required to submit FAFSA. *Faculty research:* Origins, correlates and treatment of depression; health and emotion; concentration on topics related to prejudice, stereotyping, and intergroup relations; memory, cognitive development, language, perception, attention, aging; psychometric methods, item response theory, structural equation modeling. *Unit head:* Ruth Anne Atchley, Chair, 785-864-4131. *Application contact:* Graduate Officer, 785-864-4195, E-mail: psycgrad@ku.edu. Website: http://www.psych.ku.edu/

University of Kentucky, Graduate School, College of Arts and Sciences, Program in Psychology, Lexington, KY 40506-0032. Offers MA, PhD. *Accreditation:* APA (one or more programs are accredited). *Degree requirements:* For master's, comprehensive exam, thesis; for doctorate, comprehensive exam, thesis/dissertation. *Entrance requirements:* For master's, GRE General Test, minimum undergraduate GPA of 2.75; for doctorate, GRE General Test, minimum graduate GPA of 3.0. Additional exam requirements/recommendations for international students: Required—TOEFL (minimum score 550 paper-based). Electronic applications accepted. *Faculty research:* Psychopharmacology and teratology, behavioral neuroscience, social psychology, cognitive psychology, development and developmental psychobiology.

University of La Verne, College of Arts and Sciences, Department of Psychology, La Verne, CA 91750-4443. Offers clinical psychology (Psy D); marriage and family therapy (MFT, MS). *Accreditation:* APA (one or more programs are accredited). *Program availability:* Part-time. *Faculty:* 9 full-time (4 women), 17 part-time/adjunct (11 women). *Students:* 60 full-time (55 women), 48 part-time (40 women); includes 57 minority (7 Black or African American, non-Hispanic/Latino; 1 Asian, non-Hispanic/Latino; 48

Hispanic/Latino; 1 Two or more races, non-Hispanic/Latino), 1 international. Average age 27. *Degree requirements:* For master's, thesis, competency exam, fieldwork, culminating project; for doctorate, thesis/dissertation, clinical practica, clinical internship, competency exams, personal psychotherapy. *Entrance requirements:* For master's, minimum undergraduate GPA of 3.0, 5- to 7-page statement of purpose and autobiography, 3 letters of recommendation, interview, curriculum vitae; for doctorate, GRE, minimum GPA of 3.1, statement of professional goals and aspirations, 3 recommendations, interview, curriculum vitae. Additional exam requirements/recommendations for international students: Required—TOEFL (minimum score 600 paper-based; 100 iBT); Recommended—IELTS (minimum score 6.5). *Application deadline:* Applications are processed on a rolling basis. *Expenses:* Contact institution. *Financial support:* Career-related internships or fieldwork, scholarships/grants, and unspecified assistantships available. Financial award application deadline: 3/2; financial award applicants required to submit FAFSA. *Unit head:* Dr. Glenn Gamst, Department Chair, 909-448-4176, E-mail: ggamst@laverne.edu. *Application contact:* Christy Ranells, Associate Director of Graduate Admissions, 909-448-4644, Fax: 909-971-2295, E-mail: cranells@laverne.edu.
Website: http://laverne.edu/psychology/

University of Lethbridge, School of Graduate Studies, Lethbridge, AB T1K 3M4, Canada. Offers addictions counseling (M Sc); agricultural biotechnology (M Sc); agricultural studies (M Sc, MA); anthropology (MA); archaeology (M Sc, MA); art (MA, MFA); biochemistry (M Sc); biological sciences (M Sc); biomolecular science (PhD); biosystems and biodiversity (PhD); Canadian studies (MA); chemistry (M Sc); computer science (M Sc); computer science and geographical information science (M Sc); counseling (MC); counseling psychology (M Ed); dramatic arts (MA); earth, space, and physical science (PhD); economics (MA); education (MA, PhD); educational leadership (M Ed); English (MA); environmental science (M Sc); evolution and behavior (PhD); exercise science (M Sc); French (MA); French/German (MA); French/Spanish (MA); general education (M Ed); geography (M Sc, MA); German (MA); health sciences (M Sc); individualized multidisciplinary (M Sc, MA); kinesiology (M Sc, MA); management (M Sc), including accounting, finance, human resource management and labor relations, information systems, international management, marketing, policy and strategy; mathematics (M Sc); music (M Mus, MA); Native American studies (MA); neuroscience (M Sc, PhD); new media (MA, MFA); nursing (M Sc, MN); philosophy (MA); physics (M Sc); political science (MA); psychology (M Sc, MA); religious studies (MA); sociology (MA); theatre and dramatic arts (MFA); theoretical and computational science (PhD); urban and regional studies (MA); women and gender studies (MA). *Program availability:* Part-time, evening/weekend. *Degree requirements:* For master's, thesis (for some programs); for doctorate, comprehensive exam, thesis/dissertation. *Entrance requirements:* For master's, GMAT (for M Sc in management), bachelor's degree in related field, minimum GPA of 3.0 during previous 20 graded semester courses, 2 years' teaching or related experience (M Ed); for doctorate, master's degree, minimum graduate GPA of 3.5. Additional exam requirements/recommendations for international students: Required—TOEFL (minimum score 580 paper-based; 93 iBT). Electronic applications accepted. *Faculty research:* Movement and brain plasticity, gibberellin physiology, photosynthesis, carbon cycling, molecular properties of main-group ring components.

University of Louisiana at Lafayette, College of Liberal Arts, Department of Psychology, Program in Psychology, Lafayette, LA 70504. Offers MS. *Degree requirements:* For master's, comprehensive exam, thesis (for some programs). *Entrance requirements:* For master's, GRE General Test. Additional exam requirements/recommendations for international students: Required—TOEFL (minimum score 550 paper-based).

University of Louisiana at Monroe, Graduate School, College of Business and Social Sciences, Department of Psychology, Monroe, LA 71209-0001. Offers forensic psychology (MS); general psychology (MS); psychometrics (MS). *Program availability:* Part-time, evening/weekend, online learning. *Faculty:* 6 full-time (2 women). *Students:* 35 full-time (30 women), 19 part-time (14 women); includes 19 minority (12 Black or African American, non-Hispanic/Latino; 1 Asian, non-Hispanic/Latino; 3 Hispanic/Latino; 3 Two or more races, non-Hispanic/Latino), 7 international. Average age 26. 53 applicants, 58% accepted, 18 enrolled. In 2017, 18 master's awarded. *Degree requirements:* For master's, comprehensive exam, thesis optional. *Entrance requirements:* For master's, GRE General Test, minimum GPA of 2.75. Additional exam requirements/recommendations for international students: Required—TOEFL (minimum score 500 paper-based; 61 iBT). *Application deadline:* For fall admission, 7/1 for domestic and international students; for winter admission, 12/14 for domestic students; for spring admission, 12/1 for domestic and international students. Applications are processed on a rolling basis. Application fee: $20 ($30 for international students). Electronic applications accepted. *Expenses:* Tuition, state resident: full-time $6489; part-time $479 per hour. Tuition, nonresident: full-time $12,100; part-time $479 per hour. *Required fees:* $8860; $802 per hour. $3273 per semester. *Financial support:* In 2017–18, 19 students received support. Research assistantships, career-related internships or fieldwork, Federal Work-Study, and unspecified assistantships available. Financial award application deadline: 4/1; financial award applicants required to submit FAFSA. *Unit head:* Dr. Ashworth Burton, Director, 318-342-1439, E-mail: ashworth@ulm.edu. *Application contact:* Dr. Jack Palmer, Graduate Coordinator, 318-342-1345, E-mail: palmer@ulm.edu.
Website: http://www.ulm.edu/psychology

University of Louisville, Graduate School, College of Arts and Sciences, Department of Psychological and Brain Sciences, Louisville, KY 40292-0001. Offers clinical psychology (PhD); experimental psychology (PhD), including cognition and development, vision and hearing. *Accreditation:* APA. *Students:* 55 full-time (44 women), 1 (woman) part-time; includes 7 minority (1 Black or African American, non-Hispanic/Latino; 2 Asian, non-Hispanic/Latino; 2 Hispanic/Latino; 2 Two or more races, non-Hispanic/Latino), 4 international. Average age 29. 9 applicants, 78% accepted. In 2017, 1 doctorate awarded. *Degree requirements:* For doctorate, comprehensive exam, thesis/dissertation, internship (for clinical psychology). *Entrance requirements:* For doctorate, GRE General Test, GRE Subject Test. Additional exam requirements/recommendations for international students: Required—TOEFL. *Application deadline:* For fall and winter admission, 12/1 for domestic and international students. Application fee: $65. *Expenses:* Tuition, state resident: full-time $12,246; part-time $681 per credit hour. Tuition, nonresident: full-time $25,486; part-time $1417 per credit hour. *Required fees:* $196. Tuition and fees vary according to course load, program and reciprocity agreements. *Financial support:* In 2017–18, 8 fellowships with full tuition reimbursements (averaging $22,000 per year), 3 research assistantships with full tuition reimbursements (averaging $22,000 per year), 30 teaching assistantships with full tuition reimbursements (averaging $22,000 per year) were awarded; health care benefits and unspecified assistantships also available. Financial award application deadline: 12/1. *Faculty research:* Cognitive development, hearing/visual science, cognitive neuroscience/imaging, health psychology/mindfulness/stress and trauma, child/adult psychopathology, geropsychology. *Total annual research expenditures:* $923,340. *Unit head:* Dr. Suzanne Meeks, Chair, 502-852-6068, Fax: 502-852-8904, E-mail: smeeks@louisville.edu. *Application contact:* Maggie Leahy, Administrative Assistant, 502-852-4364, Fax: 502-852-8904, E-mail: maggie.leahy@louisville.edu.
Website: http://louisville.edu/psychology

University of Maine, Graduate School, College of Liberal Arts and Sciences, Department of Psychology, Orono, ME 04469. Offers psychological sciences (PhD). *Accreditation:* APA (one or more programs are accredited). *Faculty:* 13 full-time (7 women), 7 part-time/adjunct (5 women). *Students:* 24 full-time (20 women), 2 part-time (0 women); includes 5 minority (1 Asian, non-Hispanic/Latino; 4 Hispanic/Latino). Average age 27. 120 applicants, 8% accepted, 7 enrolled. In 2017, 6 master's, 6 doctorates awarded. Terminal master's awarded for partial completion of doctoral program. *Degree requirements:* For master's, thesis; for doctorate, comprehensive exam, thesis/dissertation. *Entrance requirements:* For master's and doctorate, GRE General Test, GRE Subject Test. Additional exam requirements/recommendations for international students: Required—TOEFL. *Application deadline:* For fall admission, 12/1 for domestic and international students. Applications are processed on a rolling basis. Application fee: $65. Electronic applications accepted. *Expenses:* Tuition, state resident: full-time $7722; part-time $429 per credit hour. Tuition, nonresident: full-time $25,146; part-time $1397 per credit hour. *Required fees:* $1162; $581 per credit hour. *Financial support:* In 2017–18, 27 students received support, including 1 fellowship with full tuition reimbursement available (averaging $25,000 per year), 4 research assistantships with full tuition reimbursements available (averaging $15,200 per year), 20 teaching assistantships with full tuition reimbursements available (averaging $15,200 per year); Federal Work-Study, institutionally sponsored loans, tuition waivers (full and partial), and unspecified assistantships also available. Financial award application deadline: 3/1. *Faculty research:* Cognitive aging; child and adolescent peer relations; neurobiology of learning and memory; self, social identification and social stigma; social cognition. *Total annual research expenditures:* $248,532. *Unit head:* Dr. Michael Robbins, Chair, 207-581-2051, Fax: 207-581-6128. *Application contact:* Scott G. Delcourt, Assistant Vice President for Graduate Studies and Senior Associate Dean, 207-581-3291, Fax: 207-581-3232, E-mail: graduate@maine.edu.
Website: http://www.umaine.edu/psychology/

The University of Manchester, School of Psychological Sciences, Manchester, United Kingdom. Offers audiology (M Phil, PhD); clinical psychology (M Phil, PhD, Psy D); psychology (M Phil, PhD).

University of Manitoba, Faculty of Graduate Studies, Faculty of Arts, Department of Psychology, Winnipeg, MB R3T 2N2, Canada. Offers clinical psychology (PhD); psychology (MA, PhD); school psychology (MA). *Degree requirements:* For master's, thesis; for doctorate, one foreign language, thesis/dissertation. *Entrance requirements:* For master's and doctorate, GRE General Test.

University of Maryland, Baltimore County, The Graduate School, College of Arts, Humanities and Social Sciences, Department of Psychology, Baltimore, MD 21250. Offers applied developmental psychology (PhD); human services psychology (MA, PhD), including applied behavioral analysis (MA), human services psychology (PhD); industrial/organizational psychology (MPS). *Accreditation:* APA (one or more programs are accredited). *Faculty:* 25 full-time (14 women), 22 part-time/adjunct (8 women). *Students:* 107 full-time (89 women), 31 part-time (3 women); includes 35 minority (11 Black or African American, non-Hispanic/Latino; 11 Asian, non-Hispanic/Latino; 11 Hispanic/Latino; 2 Two or more races, non-Hispanic/Latino). Average age 28. 160 applicants, 19% accepted, 20 enrolled. In 2017, 18 master's, 12 doctorates awarded. Terminal master's awarded for partial completion of doctoral program. *Degree requirements:* For master's, thesis or alternative; for doctorate, comprehensive exam, thesis/dissertation. *Entrance requirements:* For master's, GRE General Test; for doctorate, GRE General Test, GRE Subject Test, minimum GPA of 3.0. Additional exam requirements/recommendations for international students: Required—TOEFL. *Application deadline:* For fall admission, 12/1 for domestic and international students. Application fee: $50. Electronic applications accepted. *Expenses:* Contact institution. *Financial support:* In 2017–18, 60 students received support, including 3 fellowships with full tuition reimbursements available (averaging $22,000 per year), 30 research assistantships with full tuition reimbursements available (averaging $20,400 per year); teaching assistantships with full tuition reimbursements available, career-related internships or fieldwork, Federal Work-Study, health care benefits, and unspecified assistantships also available. Financial award application deadline: 3/1; financial award applicants required to submit FAFSA. *Faculty research:* Prevention and treatment of behavior problems, early intervention, cultural contexts, applications to education, behavioral medicine. *Unit head:* Dr. Christopher Murphy, Chair, 410-455-2415, Fax: 410-455-1055, E-mail: chmurphy@umbc.edu. *Application contact:* Beverly McDougall, Program Management Specialist, 410-455-2567, Fax: 410-455-1055, E-mail: psycdept@umbc.edu.
Website: http://psychology.umbc.edu/

University of Maryland, College Park, Academic Affairs, College of Behavioral and Social Sciences, Department of Psychology, College Park, MD 20742. Offers clinical psychology (PhD); developmental psychology (PhD); experimental psychology (PhD); industrial psychology (MA, MS, PhD); social psychology (PhD). *Accreditation:* APA (one or more programs are accredited). *Degree requirements:* For master's, thesis; for doctorate, variable foreign language requirement, comprehensive exam, thesis/dissertation. *Entrance requirements:* For master's and doctorate, GRE General Test, GRE Subject Test, minimum GPA of 3.5, research and/or work experience, 3 letters of recommendation. Electronic applications accepted. *Faculty research:* Social stereotyping and prejudice, anxiety disorders, auditory neuroethology, counseling and social psychology.

University of Massachusetts Amherst, Graduate School, College of Natural Sciences, Department of Psychological and Brain Sciences, Amherst, MA 01003. Offers clinical psychology (MS, PhD); cognitive psychology (MS, PhD); developmental science (MS, PhD); psychology of peace and violence (MS, PhD); social psychology (MS, PhD). *Accreditation:* APA (one or more programs are accredited). Terminal master's awarded for partial completion of doctoral program. *Degree requirements:* For master's, thesis; for doctorate, comprehensive exam, thesis/dissertation. *Entrance requirements:* For master's and doctorate, GRE General Test, 3 letters of recommendation. Additional exam requirements/recommendations for international students: Required—TOEFL (minimum score 550 paper-based; 80 iBT), IELTS (minimum score 6.5). Electronic applications accepted.

University of Massachusetts Dartmouth, Graduate School, College of Arts and Sciences, Department of Psychology, North Dartmouth, MA 02747-2300. Offers autism studies (Graduate Certificate); psychology - applied behavioral analysis (MA, Post-Master's Certificate); psychology - clinical (MA); psychology - research (MA). *Program availability:* Part-time. *Faculty:* 20 full-time (12 women), 8 part-time/adjunct (2 women). *Students:* 40 full-time (31 women), 57 part-time (52 women); includes 19 minority (4 Black or African American, non-Hispanic/Latino; 3 Asian, non-Hispanic/Latino; 7 Hispanic/Latino; 5 Two or more races, non-Hispanic/Latino), 1 international. Average age 29. 96 applicants, 54% accepted, 39 enrolled. In 2017, 21 master's awarded. *Degree requirements:* For master's, comprehensive exam (for some programs), thesis or comprehensive exam (for psychology - clinical); thesis (for psychology - research). *Entrance requirements:* For master's and other advanced degree, statement of purpose (minimum of 300 words), resume, 3 letters of recommendation, official transcripts.

Additional exam requirements/recommendations for international students: Required—TOEFL (minimum score 533 paper-based; 72 iBT), IELTS (minimum score 6). *Application deadline:* For fall admission, 3/1 priority date for domestic students, 2/1 priority date for international students. Application fee: $60. Electronic applications accepted. *Expenses:* Tuition, state resident: full-time $15,449; part-time $643.71 per credit. Tuition, nonresident: full-time $27,880; part-time $1161.67 per credit. *Required fees:* $405; $25.88 per credit. Tuition and fees vary according to course load and reciprocity agreements. *Financial support:* In 2017–18, 1 research assistantship (averaging $12,000 per year), 2 teaching assistantships (averaging $14,000 per year) were awarded; tuition waivers (full and partial) and unspecified assistantships also available. Support available to part-time students. Financial award application deadline: 3/1; financial award applicants required to submit FAFSA. *Faculty research:* Health inequities, language and cognitive development, interethnic dating and marriage, executive function and implicit learning in deaf children, behavioral medicine. *Total annual research expenditures:* $344,000. *Unit head:* Mahzad Hojjat, Graduate Program Director, Research Psychology, 508-999-8951, E-mail: mhojjat@umassd.edu. *Application contact:* Steven Briggs, Director of Marketing and Recruitment for Graduate Studies, 508-999-8604, Fax: 508-999-8183, E-mail: graduate@umassd.edu.
Website: http://www.umassd.edu/cas/psychology

University of Massachusetts Lowell, College of Fine Arts, Humanities and Social Sciences, Department of Psychology, Lowell, MA 01854. Offers community social psychology (MA). *Program availability:* Part-time. *Degree requirements:* For master's, thesis optional. *Entrance requirements:* For master's, GRE General Test or MAT. Electronic applications accepted. *Faculty research:* Domestic violence, youth sports, teen pregnancy, substance abuse, family and work roles.

University of Memphis, Graduate School, College of Arts and Sciences, Department of Psychology, Memphis, TN 38152-3230. Offers clinical psychology (PhD); experimental psychology (PhD); general psychology (MS); school psychology (MA, PhD, Ed S). *Accreditation:* APA. *Faculty:* 26 full-time (11 women), 3 part-time/adjunct (0 women). *Students:* 94 full-time (69 women), 17 part-time (12 women); includes 25 minority (10 Black or African American, non-Hispanic/Latino; 6 Asian, non-Hispanic/Latino; 6 Hispanic/Latino; 3 Two or more races, non-Hispanic/Latino), 6 international. Average age 27. 291 applicants, 16% accepted, 32 enrolled. In 2017, 23 master's, 13 doctorates, 8 other advanced degrees awarded. *Degree requirements:* For master's, comprehensive exam (for some programs), thesis (for some programs), 37 credit hours (for MA); 33 credit hours with thesis or 36 with exam (for MS); for doctorate, comprehensive exam, thesis/dissertation, 80 semester hours, major area paper; 1-year placement and 1-year internship (for clinical psychology); internship (for school psychology); for Ed S, 30 credit hours. *Entrance requirements:* For master's, GRE, 3 letters of recommendation, 18 undergraduate hours in psychology; for doctorate, GRE, minimum GPA of 2.75, 18 hours of undergraduate psychology courses, transcripts, personal statement, 3 letters of recommendation, interview; for Ed S, GRE, minimum GPA of 2.75, 18 hours of undergraduate psychology courses, 3 letters of recommendation. Additional exam requirements/recommendations for international students: Required—TOEFL (minimum score 550 paper-based; 79 iBT). *Application deadline:* For fall admission, 12/5 for domestic students. Applications are processed on a rolling basis. Application fee: $35 ($60 for international students). Electronic applications accepted. *Expenses:* Contact institution. *Financial support:* In 2017–18, 66 students received support, including 60 research assistantships with full tuition reimbursements available (averaging $11,846 per year), 25 teaching assistantships with full tuition reimbursements available (averaging $6,794 per year); fellowships with full tuition reimbursements available, Federal Work-Study, scholarships/grants, tuition waivers (partial), and unspecified assistantships also available. Financial award application deadline: 2/1; financial award applicants required to submit FAFSA. *Faculty research:* Clinical health; school, child and family psychology; psychotherapy; cognitive and behavioral neuroscience; industrial-organizational psychology. *Unit head:* Dr. Frank Andrasik, Chair, 901-678-2145, Fax: 901-678-2579, E-mail: rcohen@memphis.edu. *Application contact:* Dr. Robert Cohen, Coordinator of Graduate Studies, 901-678-4679, Fax: 901-678-2579, E-mail: rcohen@memphis.edu.
Website: http://www.memphis.edu/psychology

University of Miami, Graduate School, College of Arts and Sciences, Department of Psychology, Coral Gables, FL 33124. Offers adult clinical (PhD); behavioral neuroscience (PhD); child clinical (PhD); developmental psychology (PhD); health clinical (PhD); psychology (MS). *Accreditation:* APA (one or more programs are accredited). *Degree requirements:* For doctorate, comprehensive exam, thesis/dissertation. *Entrance requirements:* For doctorate, GRE General Test, minimum GPA of 3.5. Additional exam requirements/recommendations for international students: Required—TOEFL. Electronic applications accepted. *Faculty research:* Behavioral factors in cardiovascular disease and cancer adult psychopathology, developmental disabilities, social and emotional development, mechanisms of coping.

University of Michigan, Rackham Graduate School, College of Literature, Science, and the Arts, Department of Psychology, Ann Arbor, MI 48109. Offers biopsychology (PhD); clinical science (PhD); cognition and cognitive neuroscience (PhD); developmental psychology (PhD); personality and social contexts (PhD); social psychology (PhD). *Accreditation:* APA. *Faculty:* 66 full-time (31 women), 28 part-time/adjunct (17 women). *Students:* 148 full-time (113 women); includes 61 minority (13 Black or African American, non-Hispanic/Latino; 1 American Indian or Alaska Native, non-Hispanic/Latino; 12 Asian, non-Hispanic/Latino; 28 Hispanic/Latino; 7 Two or more races, non-Hispanic/Latino), 24 international. Average age 27. 691 applicants, 7% accepted, 35 enrolled. In 2017, 34 doctorates awarded. Terminal master's awarded for partial completion of doctoral program. *Degree requirements:* For doctorate, comprehensive exam, thesis/dissertation, oral defense of dissertation, preliminary exam. *Entrance requirements:* For doctorate, GRE General Test. Additional exam requirements/recommendations for international students: Required—TOEFL. *Application deadline:* For fall admission, 12/1 for domestic and international students. Application fee: $75 ($90 for international students). Electronic applications accepted. *Expenses:* $11,184 in-state, $22,578 out-of-state. *Financial support:* In 2017–18, 90 students received support, including 61 fellowships with full tuition reimbursements available (averaging $26,400 per year), 10 research assistantships with full tuition reimbursements available (averaging $26,400 per year), 89 teaching assistantships with full tuition reimbursements available (averaging $26,400 per year); career-related internships or fieldwork, traineeships, and health care benefits also available. Financial award application deadline: 4/15. *Unit head:* Prof. Patricia Reuter-Lorenz, Department Chair, 734-764-7429. *Application contact:* Sheri M. Circele, Psychology Student Academic Affairs, 734-764-2580, Fax: 734-764-3520, E-mail: psych.saa@umich.edu.
Website: http://www.lsa.umich.edu/psych/

University of Michigan, Rackham Graduate School, College of Literature, Science, and the Arts, Department of Women's Studies, Ann Arbor, MI 48109. Offers English and women's studies (PhD); history and women's studies (PhD); LGBTQ studies (Certificate); psychology and women's studies (PhD); women's studies (Certificate). *Degree requirements:* For doctorate, variable foreign language requirement, comprehensive exam (for some programs), thesis/dissertation. *Entrance requirements:* For doctorate, GRE General Test, previous undergraduate coursework in women's

studies. Electronic applications accepted. *Expenses:* Tuition, state resident: full-time $22,368; part-time $1201 per credit hour. Tuition, nonresident: full-time $45,156; part-time $2467 per credit hour. *Required fees:* $376 per term. Tuition and fees vary according to course load, degree level and program. *Faculty research:* LGBTQ studies, sexuality studies, feminist science studies, global feminism, health studies, international studies, cultural studies.

University of Michigan, Rackham Graduate School, Combined Program in Education and Psychology, Ann Arbor, MI 48109. Offers PhD. *Accreditation:* TEAC. *Degree requirements:* For doctorate, thesis/dissertation, independent research project, preliminary exam, oral defense of dissertation. *Entrance requirements:* For doctorate, GRE General Test with Analytical Writing Test. Additional exam requirements/recommendations for international students: Required—TOEFL (minimum score 600 paper-based; 100 iBT). Electronic applications accepted. *Expenses:* Contact institution. *Faculty research:* Human development in context of schools, families, communities; cognitive and learning sciences; motivation and self-regulated learning; culture, ethnicity, social and class influences on learning and motivation.

University of Michigan, School of Social Work, Interdisciplinary PhD Program in Social Work and Social Science, Ann Arbor, MI 48109. Offers social work and anthropology (PhD); social work and economics (PhD); social work and political science (PhD); social work and psychology (PhD); social work and sociology (PhD). Programs offered through the Rackham Graduate School. *Faculty:* 57 full-time (36 women). *Students:* 53 full-time (38 women); includes 27 minority (10 Black or African American, non-Hispanic/Latino; 2 American Indian or Alaska Native, non-Hispanic/Latino; 9 Asian, non-Hispanic/Latino; 6 Hispanic/Latino). Average age 32. 124 applicants, 6% accepted, 7 enrolled. In 2017, 10 doctorates awarded. *Degree requirements:* For doctorate, thesis/dissertation, oral defense of dissertation, preliminary exam. *Entrance requirements:* For doctorate, GRE General Test. Additional exam requirements/recommendations for international students: Required—TOEFL (minimum score 620 paper-based, 88 iBT) or IELTS. *Application deadline:* For fall admission, 12/1 for domestic and international students. Application fee: $75 ($90 for international students). Electronic applications accepted. *Expenses:* Contact institution. *Financial support:* In 2017–18, 59 students received support, including 24 fellowships with full tuition reimbursements available (averaging $17,600 per year), 7 research assistantships with full tuition reimbursements available (averaging $20,399 per year), 21 teaching assistantships with full tuition reimbursements available (averaging $20,399 per year); career-related internships or fieldwork, scholarships/grants, traineeships, health care benefits, tuition waivers (full and partial), and unspecified assistantships also available. Financial award application deadline: 12/1; financial award applicants required to submit FAFSA. *Faculty research:* Children and family, aging, community organization, health and mental health, police and evaluation. *Total annual research expenditures:* $4.1 million. *Unit head:* Dr. William Elliott, III, Director, 734-763-5768, E-mail: willelli@umich.edu. *Application contact:* Todd Huynh, Graduate Coordinator, 734-647-2554, Fax: 734-615-3192, E-mail: ssw.phd.info@umich.edu.
Website: https://ssw.umich.edu/offices/phd

University of Minnesota, Twin Cities Campus, Graduate School, College of Liberal Arts, Department of Psychology, Minneapolis, MN 55455-0213. Offers biological psychopathology (PhD); clinical psychology (PhD); cognitive and biological psychology (PhD); counseling psychology (PhD); industrial/organizational psychology (PhD); personality, individual differences, and behavior genetics (PhD); quantitative/psychometric methods (PhD); school psychology (PhD); social psychology (PhD). *Accreditation:* APA. *Degree requirements:* For doctorate, comprehensive exam, thesis/dissertation. *Entrance requirements:* For doctorate, GRE General Test, GRE Subject Test (recommended), 12 credits of upper-level psychology courses, including a course in statistics or psychological measurement. Additional exam requirements/recommendations for international students: Required—TOEFL (minimum score 79 iBT).

University of Missouri, Office of Research and Graduate Studies, College of Arts and Science, Department of Psychological Sciences, Columbia, MO 65211. Offers MA, MS, PhD. *Accreditation:* APA (one or more programs are accredited). Terminal master's awarded for partial completion of doctoral program. *Degree requirements:* For doctorate, comprehensive exam, thesis/dissertation. *Entrance requirements:* For master's, GRE General Test, minimum GPA of 3.0; for doctorate, GRE General Test; GRE Subject Test (strongly recommended), minimum GPA of 3.0. Additional exam requirements/recommendations for international students: Required—TOEFL (minimum score 500 paper-based; 61 iBT). Electronic applications accepted.

University of Missouri–Kansas City, College of Arts and Sciences, Department of Psychology, Kansas City, MO 64110-2499. Offers community psychology (PhD). PhD (interdisciplinary) offered through the School of Graduate Studies. *Accreditation:* APA. Terminal master's awarded for partial completion of doctoral program. *Degree requirements:* For master's, thesis; for doctorate, comprehensive exam, thesis/dissertation, residency. *Entrance requirements:* For master's, GRE, minimum GPA of 3.5, letter of recommendation; for doctorate, GRE, minimum GPA of 3.25. Additional exam requirements/recommendations for international students: Required—TOEFL (minimum score 550 paper-based; 80 iBT). Electronic applications accepted. *Faculty research:* HIV/AIDS research group, psycho-oncology, sensory and cognitive neuroscience, cognitive psychophysiology, obesity and related metabolic disorders.

University of Missouri–St. Louis, College of Arts and Sciences, Department of Psychological Sciences, St. Louis, MO 63121. Offers behavioral neuroscience (MA, PhD); clinical psychology (PhD); trauma studies (Certificate). *Accreditation:* APA (one or more programs are accredited). *Program availability:* Evening/weekend. *Students:* 58 full-time (41 women), 17 part-time (11 women); includes 12 minority (4 Black or African American, non-Hispanic/Latino; 4 Asian, non-Hispanic/Latino; 3 Hispanic/Latino; 1 Two or more races, non-Hispanic/Latino), 3 international. 242 applicants, 8% accepted, 16 enrolled. Terminal master's awarded for partial completion of doctoral program. *Degree requirements:* For master's, thesis; for doctorate, thesis/dissertation. *Entrance requirements:* For master's, GRE General Test, 3 letters of recommendation; for doctorate, GRE General Test, GRE Subject Test, 3 letters of recommendation. Additional exam requirements/recommendations for international students: Required—TOEFL (minimum score 550 paper-based; 79 iBT), IELTS (minimum score 6.5). *Application deadline:* For fall admission, 12/15 for domestic and international students. Application fee: $50 ($40 for international students). Electronic applications accepted. *Expenses:* Tuition, state resident: part-time $476.50 per credit hour. Tuition, nonresident: part-time $1169.70 per credit hour. *Financial support:* Fellowships with full tuition reimbursements, research assistantships with tuition reimbursements, teaching assistantships with tuition reimbursements, and scholarships/grants available. Financial award applicants required to submit FAFSA. *Faculty research:* Bereavement and loss, neuroscience, post-traumatic stress disorder, conflict and negotiation, social psychology. *Unit head:* Michael G. Griffin, Chair, 314-516-5391, Fax: 314-516-5392, E-mail: michael_griffin@umsl.edu. *Application contact:* 314-516-5458, Fax: 314-516-6996, E-mail: gradadm@umsl.edu.
Website: http://www.umsl.edu/divisions/artscience/psychology/

University of Montana, Graduate School, College of Humanities and Sciences, Department of Psychology, Missoula, MT 59812. Offers clinical psychology (PhD);

experimental psychology (PhD), including animal behavior psychology, developmental psychology; school psychology (MA, PhD, Ed S). *Accreditation:* APA (one or more programs are accredited). Terminal master's awarded for partial completion of doctoral program. *Degree requirements:* For master's, thesis; for doctorate, thesis/dissertation. *Entrance requirements:* For master's, doctorate, and Ed S, GRE General Test. Additional exam requirements/recommendations for international students: Required—TOEFL.

University of Nebraska at Omaha, Graduate Studies, College of Arts and Sciences, Department of Psychology, Omaha, NE 68182. Offers applied behavior analysis (Certificate); human resources and training (Certificate); industrial/organizational psychology (MS); psychology (MA, PhD); school psychology (MS, Ed S). *Program availability:* Part-time. *Degree requirements:* For master's, comprehensive exam, thesis (for some programs); for doctorate, comprehensive exam, thesis/dissertation. *Entrance requirements:* For master's and doctorate, GRE, minimum GPA of 3.0, official transcripts, 3 letters of recommendation, statement of purpose, writing sample, resume. Additional exam requirements/recommendations for international students: Required—TOEFL, IELTS, PTE. Electronic applications accepted.

University of Nebraska–Lincoln, Graduate College, College of Arts and Sciences, Department of Psychology, Lincoln, NE 68588. Offers biopsychology (PhD); clinical psychology (PhD); cognitive psychology (PhD); developmental psychology (PhD); psychology (MA); social/personality psychology (PhD); JD/MA; JD/PhD. *Accreditation:* APA (one or more programs are accredited). *Degree requirements:* For master's, thesis optional; for doctorate, comprehensive exam, thesis/dissertation. *Entrance requirements:* For master's and doctorate, GRE General Test. Additional exam requirements/recommendations for international students: Required—TOEFL (minimum score 550 paper-based). Electronic applications accepted. *Faculty research:* Law and psychology, rural mental health, chronic mental illness, neuropsychology, child clinical psychology.

University of Nevada, Las Vegas, Graduate College, College of Liberal Arts, Department of Psychology, Las Vegas, NV 89154-5030. Offers MA, PhD, Certificate. *Program availability:* Part-time. *Faculty:* 16 full-time (5 women), 3 part-time/adjunct (2 women). *Students:* 63 full-time (45 women), 11 part-time (8 women); includes 15 minority (2 Asian, non-Hispanic/Latino; 10 Hispanic/Latino; 3 Two or more races, non-Hispanic/Latino), 5 international. Average age 29. 125 applicants, 21% accepted, 12 enrolled. In 2017, 9 master's, 8 doctorates, 1 other advanced degree awarded. *Degree requirements:* For doctorate, comprehensive exam, thesis/dissertation, oral defense of dissertation. *Entrance requirements:* For doctorate, GRE General and Subject Tests, bachelor's degree with minimum GPA of 3.2 or master's degree with minimum GPA of 3.5; 3 recommendation letters; statement of purpose; interview. Additional exam requirements/recommendations for international students: Required—TOEFL (minimum score 550 paper-based; 80 iBT), IELTS (minimum score 7). *Application deadline:* For fall admission, 12/1 for domestic students. Application fee: $60 ($95 for international students). Electronic applications accepted. *Expenses:* $275 per credit, $850 per course, $7,969 per year resident, $22,157 per year non-resident, $7,094 non-resident fee (7 credits or more), $1,307 annual health insurance fee. *Financial support:* In 2017–18, 60 students received support, including 4 fellowships with partial tuition reimbursements available (averaging $18,750 per year), 33 research assistantships with full and partial tuition reimbursements available (averaging $15,500 per year), 27 teaching assistantships with full and partial tuition reimbursements available (averaging $15,500 per year); institutionally sponsored loans, scholarships/grants, health care benefits, and unspecified assistantships also available. Financial award application deadline: 3/15; financial award applicants required to submit FAFSA. *Faculty research:* School absenteeism and selective autism, schizophrenia and bipolar disorders, biomarkers for dementia and mental disorders, infant cognition and development, affective and cognitive neuroscience. *Total annual research expenditures:* $1.3 million. *Unit head:* Dr. Christopher Kearney, Chair/Professor, 702-895-0183, Fax: 702-895-0195, E-mail: chris.kearney@unlv.edu. *Application contact:* Dr. Jennifer Rennels, Graduate Coordinator, 702-895-0648, Fax: 702-895-0195, E-mail: jennifer.rennels@unlv.edu.
Website: http://psychology.unlv.edu/

University of Nevada, Reno, Graduate School, College of Liberal Arts, Department of Psychology, Reno, NV 89557. Offers behavior analysis (MA, PhD); clinical psychology (MA, PhD); cognitive brain science (MA, PhD). *Accreditation:* APA (one or more programs are accredited). Terminal master's awarded for partial completion of doctoral program. *Degree requirements:* For master's, thesis optional; for doctorate, thesis/dissertation. *Entrance requirements:* For master's, GRE General Test, GRE Subject Test, minimum GPA of 2.75; for doctorate, GRE General Test, GRE Subject Test, minimum GPA of 3.0. Additional exam requirements/recommendations for international students: Required—TOEFL (minimum score 500 paper-based; 61 iBT), IELTS (minimum score 6). Electronic applications accepted. *Faculty research:* Cognitive psychology, social psychological theory, animal and human intelligence, psychotherapy outcome, perception.

University of New Brunswick Fredericton, School of Graduate Studies, Faculty of Arts, Department of Psychology, Fredericton, NB E3B 5A3, Canada. Offers MA, PhD. *Program availability:* Part-time. *Degree requirements:* For doctorate, comprehensive exam, thesis/dissertation. *Entrance requirements:* For master's, BA (honors) in psychology or equivalent research experience; for doctorate, minimum GPA of 3.7. Additional exam requirements/recommendations for international students: Required—TOEFL (minimum score 600 paper-based). Electronic applications accepted. *Faculty research:* Brain-behavior relationships, cognitive science, social psychology, marginalized groups, human sexuality, sport and exercise psychology, child and adolescent development, health psychology.

University of New Brunswick Saint John, Department of Psychology, Saint John, NB E2L 4L5, Canada. Offers clinical psychology (PhD); experimental psychology (MA, PhD). *Program availability:* Part-time. *Degree requirements:* For master's, thesis. *Entrance requirements:* For master's, GRE General and Subject Tests, honors thesis; minimum GPA of 3.7. Additional exam requirements/recommendations for international students: Required—TOEFL (minimum score 550 paper-based), TWE. Electronic applications accepted. *Faculty research:* Forensic psychology, peer relationships and social skills, polygraph techniques, addictions, attachment and social adjustment, neuroscience, optical illusions, graphical perception, associative learning in animals, bio-psychology.

University of New Hampshire, Graduate School, College of Liberal Arts, Department of Psychology, Durham, NH 03824. Offers PhD. *Students:* 22 full-time (12 women), 2 part-time (1 woman); includes 3 minority (1 Asian, non-Hispanic/Latino; 2 Hispanic/Latino). Average age 29. 62 applicants, 11% accepted, 5 enrolled. In 2017, 3 doctorates awarded. *Entrance requirements:* For doctorate, GRE General Test, GRE Subject Test. Additional exam requirements/recommendations for international students: Required—TOEFL (minimum score 550 paper-based; 80 iBT). *Application deadline:* For fall admission, 1/15 for domestic and international students. Application fee: $65. Electronic applications accepted. *Financial support:* In 2017–18, 24 students received support, including 2 fellowships, 22 teaching assistantships; research assistantships, career-related internships or fieldwork, Federal Work-Study, scholarships/grants, and tuition waivers (full and partial) also available. Support available to part-time students. Financial award application deadline: 2/15. *Unit head:* Dr. William Stine, Chair, 603-862-2823. *Application contact:* Robin Scholefield, Administrative Assistant, 603-862-2369, E-mail: psychology.ph.d@unh.edu.
Website: http://cola.unh.edu/psychology

University of New Mexico, Graduate Studies, College of Arts and Sciences, Program in Psychology, Albuquerque, NM 87131-2039. Offers behavioral neuroscience (PhD); clinical psychology (PhD); cognitive neuroimaging (PhD); developmental psychology (PhD); evolution (PhD); health psychology (PhD); quantitative methodology (PhD). *Accreditation:* APA. *Students:* Average age 30. 227 applicants, 11% accepted, 16 enrolled. In 2017, 10 doctorates awarded. *Degree requirements:* For doctorate, comprehensive exam, thesis/dissertation. *Entrance requirements:* For doctorate, GRE General Test, GRE Subject Test (psychology), minimum GPA of 3.0. Additional exam requirements/recommendations for international students: Required—TOEFL (minimum score 550 paper-based; 79 iBT), IELTS (minimum score 6.5). *Application deadline:* For fall admission, 12/15 priority date for domestic and international students. Applications are processed on a rolling basis. Application fee: $50. Electronic applications accepted. *Financial support:* Fellowships, research assistantships, teaching assistantships, career-related internships or fieldwork, Federal Work-Study, institutionally sponsored loans, scholarships/grants, health care benefits, tuition waivers (partial), and unspecified assistantships available. Financial award application deadline: 3/1; financial award applicants required to submit FAFSA. *Faculty research:* Addiction, cognition, brain and behavior, developmental, evolutionary, functioning neuroimaging, health psychology, learning and memory, neuroscience. *Total annual research expenditures:* $727,970. *Unit head:* Dr. Jane Ellen Smith, Department Chair, 505-277-4121, Fax: 505-277-1394. *Application contact:* Rikk Murphy, Graduate Program Coordinator, 505-277-5009, Fax: 505-277-1394, E-mail: advising@unm.edu.
Website: http://psych.unm.edu

University of New Orleans, Graduate School, College of Sciences, Department of Psychology, New Orleans, LA 70148. Offers MS, PhD. *Degree requirements:* For doctorate, thesis/dissertation. *Entrance requirements:* For doctorate, GRE General Test, minimum GPA of 3.0, 21 hours of course work in psychology. Additional exam requirements/recommendations for international students: Required—TOEFL (minimum score 550 paper-based; 79 iBT), IELTS. Electronic applications accepted. *Faculty research:* Biofeedback, visual and auditory perception, psychopharmacology, neuropeptides.

The University of North Carolina at Chapel Hill, Graduate School, College of Arts and Sciences, Department of Psychology, Chapel Hill, NC 27599-3270. Offers behavioral neuroscience psychology (PhD); clinical psychology (PhD); cognitive psychology (PhD); developmental psychology (PhD); quantitative psychology (PhD); social psychology (PhD). *Accreditation:* APA. *Degree requirements:* For doctorate, comprehensive exam, thesis/dissertation. *Entrance requirements:* For doctorate, GRE General Test, minimum GPA of 3.0. Additional exam requirements/recommendations for international students: Required—TOEFL (minimum score 550 paper-based; 79 iBT), IELTS (minimum score 7). Electronic applications accepted. *Faculty research:* Expressed emotion, cognitive development, social cognitive neuroscience, human memory personality.

The University of North Carolina at Charlotte, College of Liberal Arts and Sciences, Department of Psychology, Charlotte, NC 28223-0001. Offers cognitive science (Graduate Certificate); health psychology (PhD); industrial/organizational psychology (MA); psychology (MA). *Accreditation:* APA. *Program availability:* Part-time. *Faculty:* 29 full-time (19 women), 2 part-time/adjunct (both women). *Students:* 42 full-time (38 women), 32 part-time (21 women); includes 22 minority (11 Black or African American, non-Hispanic/Latino; 8 Hispanic/Latino; 3 Two or more races, non-Hispanic/Latino), 1 international. Average age 28. 196 applicants, 12% accepted, 16 enrolled. In 2017, 13 master's, 9 doctorates, 1 other advanced degree awarded. *Degree requirements:* For master's, thesis (for some programs); for doctorate, comprehensive exam, thesis/dissertation, internship (clinical health students only). *Entrance requirements:* For master's, GRE, GMAT, MAT; for doctorate, GRE, at least 18 hours of coursework in psychology including introductory psychology and research methods, undergraduate course in statistics, transcripts of all academic work attempted since high school including evidence of the completion of a bachelor's degree, at least three references, personal statement, resume or curriculum vitae; for Graduate Certificate, enrolled and in good standing in a graduate degree program at UNC Charlotte, or have minimum GPA of 3.0 for undergraduate courses. Additional exam requirements/recommendations for international students: Required—TOEFL (minimum score 523 paper-based, 70 iBT) or IELTS (6.5). *Application deadline:* For fall admission, 11/15 for domestic and international students. Applications are processed on a rolling basis. Application fee: $75. Electronic applications accepted. *Expenses:* Contact institution. *Financial support:* In 2017–18, 32 students received support, including 1 fellowship (averaging $47,476 per year), 13 research assistantships (averaging $14,282 per year), 18 teaching assistantships (averaging $14,405 per year); career-related internships or fieldwork, Federal Work-Study, institutionally sponsored loans, scholarships/grants, and unspecified assistantships also available. Support available to part-time students. Financial award application deadline: 3/1; financial award applicants required to submit FAFSA. *Total annual research expenditures:* $440,921. *Unit head:* Dr. Eric Heggestad, Interim Chair, 704-687-1315. *Application contact:* Kathy B. Giddings, Director of Graduate Admissions, 704-687-5503, Fax: 704-687-1668, E-mail: gradadm@uncc.edu.
Website: http://psych.uncc.edu

The University of North Carolina at Greensboro, Graduate School, College of Arts and Sciences, Department of Psychology, Greensboro, NC 27412-5001. Offers clinical psychology (MA, PhD); cognitive psychology (MA, PhD); developmental psychology (MA, PhD); social psychology (MA, PhD). *Accreditation:* APA (one or more programs are accredited). Terminal master's awarded for partial completion of doctoral program. *Degree requirements:* For master's, comprehensive exam, thesis; for doctorate, one foreign language, thesis/dissertation, preliminary exam. *Entrance requirements:* For master's and doctorate, GRE General Test. Additional exam requirements/recommendations for international students: Required—TOEFL. Electronic applications accepted. *Faculty research:* Sensory and perceptual determinants; evoked potential: disorders, deafness, and development.

The University of North Carolina Wilmington, College of Arts and Sciences, Department of Psychology, Wilmington, NC 28403-3297. Offers clinical psychology (PhD); psychology (MA), including applied behavior analysis, psychological science. *Faculty:* 22 full-time (14 women). *Students:* 27 full-time (22 women), 39 part-time (33 women); includes 8 minority (1 Asian, non-Hispanic/Latino; 5 Hispanic/Latino; 2 Two or more races, non-Hispanic/Latino). Average age 24. 110 applicants, 21% accepted, 23 enrolled. In 2017, 26 master's awarded. *Degree requirements:* For master's, comprehensive exam, thesis; for doctorate, thesis/dissertation, 1-year external APA-accredited or APPIC-member internship. *Entrance requirements:* For master's, GRE General Test, GRE Subject Test (psychology) only if bachelor's degree was not in the area of psychology, 3 letters of recommendation, psychology research interest form, resume, essay; for doctorate, GRE General Test, GRE Subject Test (psychology) only if bachelor's degree was not in the area of psychology, 3 letters of recommendation, resume, statement of interest. Additional exam requirements/recommendations for

international students: Required—TOEFL (minimum score 550 paper-based; 79 iBT), IELTS (minimum score 6.5). *Application deadline:* For fall admission, 1/15 for domestic students. Applications are processed on a rolling basis. Application fee: $75. Electronic applications accepted. *Expenses:* Tuition, state resident: full-time $4626; part-time $226.76 per credit hour. Tuition, nonresident: full-time $17,834; part-time $874.22 per credit hour. *Required fees:* $2124. Tuition and fees vary according to program. *Financial support:* Research assistantships, teaching assistantships, Federal Work-Study, scholarships/grants, unspecified assistantships, and out-of-state tuition remission available. Financial award application deadline: 1/1; financial award applicants required to submit FAFSA. *Unit head:* Dr. Julian Keith, Chair, 910-962-3378, Fax: 910-962-7010, E-mail: keithj@uncw.edu. *Application contact:* Dr. Christine Hughes, Graduate Coordinator, 910-962-7795, Fax: 910-962-7010, E-mail: hughesc@uncw.edu.
Website: http://www.uncw.edu/psy/grad/

University of North Dakota, Graduate School, College of Arts and Sciences, Department of Psychology, Grand Forks, ND 58202. Offers clinical psychology (PhD); forensic psychology (MA, MS). *Accreditation:* APA (one or more programs are accredited). *Degree requirements:* For master's, thesis, final exam; for doctorate, comprehensive exam, thesis/dissertation, internship, final exam. *Entrance requirements:* For master's, GRE General Test, GRE Subject Test, minimum GPA of 3.0; for doctorate, GRE General Test, GRE Subject Test, minimum GPA of 3.5. Additional exam requirements/recommendations for international students: Required—TOEFL (minimum score 550 paper-based; 79 iBT), IELTS (minimum score 6.5). Electronic applications accepted. *Faculty research:* Developmental psychology, clinical social psychology, educational psychology, personality disorders.

University of Northern British Columbia, Office of Graduate Studies, Prince George, BC V2N 4Z9, Canada. Offers business administration (Diploma); community health science (M Sc); disability management (MA); education (M Ed); first nations studies (MA); gender studies (MA); history (MA); interdisciplinary studies (MA); international studies (MA); mathematical, computer and physical sciences (M Sc); natural resources and environmental studies (M Sc, MA, MNRES, PhD); political science (MA); psychology (M Sc, PhD); social work (MSW). *Program availability:* Part-time, evening/weekend, online learning. *Degree requirements:* For master's, thesis; for doctorate, thesis/dissertation. *Entrance requirements:* For master's, GRE, minimum B average in undergraduate course work; for doctorate, candidacy exam, minimum A average in graduate course work.

University of Northern Iowa, Graduate College, College of Social and Behavioral Sciences, Department of Psychology, Cedar Falls, IA 50614. Offers MA. *Program availability:* Part-time. *Degree requirements:* For master's, comprehensive exam, thesis. *Entrance requirements:* For master's, GRE, minimum GPA of 3.0, 3 letters of recommendation. Additional exam requirements/recommendations for international students: Required—TOEFL (minimum score 500 paper-based; 61 iBT). Electronic applications accepted.

University of North Florida, College of Arts and Sciences, Department of Psychology, Jacksonville, FL 32224. Offers counseling psychology (MAC); general psychology (MA). *Program availability:* Part-time, evening/weekend. *Degree requirements:* For master's, comprehensive exam, thesis optional, practicum. *Entrance requirements:* For master's, GRE General Test, 2 letters of recommendation, minimum GPA of 3.0 in last 60 hours of course work. Additional exam requirements/recommendations for international students: Required—TOEFL (minimum score 500 paper-based; 61 iBT). Electronic applications accepted. *Faculty research:* Sensory perception, social cognition, sexual behavior, evolutionary psychology, psychology and law.

University of North Texas, Robert B. Toulouse School of Graduate Studies, Denton, TX 76203-5459. Offers accounting (MS); applied anthropology (MA, MS); applied behavior analysis (Certificate); applied geography (MA); applied technology and performance improvement (M Ed, MS); art education (MA); art history (MA); art museum education (Certificate); arts leadership (Certificate); audiology (Au D); behavior analysis (MS); behavioral science (PhD); biochemistry and molecular biology (MS); biology (MA, MS); biomedical engineering (MS); business analysis (MS); chemistry (MS); clinical health psychology (PhD); communication studies (MA, MS); computer engineering (MS); computer science (MS); counseling (M Ed, MS), including clinical mental health counseling (MS), college and university counseling, elementary school counseling, secondary school counseling; creative writing (MA); criminal justice (MS); curriculum and instruction (M Ed); decision sciences (MBA); design (MA, MFA), including fashion design (MFA), innovation studies, interior design (MFA); early childhood studies (MS); economics (MS); educational leadership (M Ed, Ed D); educational psychology (MS, PhD), including family studies (MS), gifted and talented (MS), human development (MS), learning and cognition (MS), research, measurement and evaluation (MS); electrical engineering (MS); emergency management (MPA); engineering technology (MS); English (MA); English as a second language (MA); environmental science (MS); finance (MBA, MS); financial management (MPA); French (MA); health services management (MBA); higher education (M Ed, Ed D); history (MA, MS); hospitality management (MS); human resources management (MPA); information science (MS); information systems (PhD); information technologies (MBA); interdisciplinary studies (MA, MS); international studies (MA); international sustainable tourism (MS); jazz studies (MM); journalism (MA, MJ, Graduate Certificate), including interactive and virtual digital communication (Graduate Certificate), narrative journalism (Graduate Certificate), public relations (Graduate Certificate); kinesiology (MS); linguistics (MA); local government management (MPA); logistics (PhD); logistics and supply chain management (MBA); long-term care, senior housing, and aging services (MA); management (PhD); marketing (MBA); mathematics (MA, MS); mechanical and energy engineering (MS, PhD); music (MA), including ethnomusicology, music theory, musicology, performance; music composition (PhD); music education (MM Ed, PhD); nonprofit management (MPA); operations and supply chain management (MBA); performance (MM, DMA); philosophy (MA); political science (MA); professional and technical communication (MA); radio, television and film (MA, MFA); rehabilitation counseling (Certificate); sociology (MA); Spanish (MA); special education (M Ed); speech-language pathology (MA); strategic management (MBA); studio art (MFA); teaching (M Ed); MBA/MS. *Program availability:* Part-time, evening/weekend, online learning. Terminal master's awarded for partial completion of doctoral program. *Degree requirements:* For master's, variable foreign language requirement, comprehensive exam (for some programs), thesis (for some programs); for doctorate, variable foreign language requirement, comprehensive exam (for some programs), thesis/dissertation; for other advanced degree, variable foreign language requirement, comprehensive exam (for some programs). *Entrance requirements:* For master's and doctorate, GRE, GMAT. Additional exam requirements/recommendations for international students: Required—TOEFL (minimum score 550 paper-based; 79 iBT). Electronic applications accepted.

University of Notre Dame, Graduate School, College of Arts and Letters, Division of Social Science, Department of Psychology, Notre Dame, IN 46556. Offers cognitive psychology (PhD); counseling psychology (PhD); developmental psychology (PhD); quantitative psychology (PhD). *Accreditation:* APA. *Degree requirements:* For doctorate, comprehensive exam, thesis/dissertation, candidacy exam. *Entrance requirements:* For doctorate, GRE General Test, GRE Subject Test (strongly recommended). Additional exam requirements/recommendations for international students: Required—TOEFL (minimum score 600 paper-based; 80 iBT). Electronic applications accepted. *Faculty research:* Cognitive and socio-emotional development, statistical methods and quantitative models applicable to psychology, interpersonal relations, life span development and developmental delay, childhood depression, structural equation and dynamical systems.

University of Oklahoma, College of Arts and Sciences, Department of Psychology, Norman, OK 73019. Offers organizational dynamics (MA, Graduate Certificate), including human resource management (Graduate Certificate), organizational dynamics (MA), project management (Graduate Certificate); psychology (MS, PhD), including psychology. *Faculty:* 22 full-time (11 women). *Students:* 59 full-time (34 women), 44 part-time (29 women); includes 23 minority (4 Black or African American, non-Hispanic/Latino; 5 American Indian or Alaska Native, non-Hispanic/Latino; 4 Asian, non-Hispanic/Latino; 7 Hispanic/Latino; 3 Two or more races, non-Hispanic/Latino), 7 international. Average age 29. 110 applicants, 22% accepted, 22 enrolled. In 2017, 18 master's, 7 doctorates, 8 other advanced degrees awarded. Terminal master's awarded for partial completion of doctoral program. *Degree requirements:* For master's, comprehensive exam, thesis; for doctorate, comprehensive exam, thesis/dissertation. *Entrance requirements:* For master's and doctorate, GRE. Additional exam requirements/recommendations for international students: Required—TOEFL (minimum score 79 iBT) or IELTS (minimum score 6.5). *Application deadline:* For fall admission, 1/1 for domestic and international students. Application fee: $50 ($100 for international students). Electronic applications accepted. *Expenses:* Tuition, state resident: full-time $5119; part-time $213.30 per credit hour. Tuition, nonresident: full-time $19,778; part-time $824.10 per credit hour. *Required fees:* $3458; $133.55 per credit hour. $126.50 per semester. *Financial support:* In 2017–18, 69 students received support, including 15 fellowships with full tuition reimbursements available (averaging $2,156 per year), 6 research assistantships with full tuition reimbursements available (averaging $14,071 per year), 39 teaching assistantships with full tuition reimbursements available (averaging $14,853 per year). Financial award application deadline: 6/1; financial award applicants required to submit FAFSA. *Faculty research:* Behavioral statistics; leadership for innovation; eyewitness testimony; risk assessment and literacy; theory of mind. *Total annual research expenditures:* $480,281. *Unit head:* Dr. Eric Day, Chair, 405-325-4511, Fax: 405-325-4737, E-mail: eday@ou.edu. *Application contact:* Dr. Shane Connelly, Professor/Chair, 405-325-4580, Fax: 405-325-4737, E-mail: sconnelly@ou.edu.
Website: http://www.ou.edu/cas/psychology

University of Oregon, Graduate School, College of Arts and Sciences, Department of Psychology, Eugene, OR 97403. Offers clinical psychology (PhD); cognitive psychology (MA, MS, PhD); developmental psychology (MA, MS, PhD); physiological psychology (MA, MS, PhD); psychology (MA, MS, PhD); social/personality psychology (MA, MS, PhD). *Accreditation:* APA (one or more programs are accredited). Terminal master's awarded for partial completion of doctoral program. *Degree requirements:* For doctorate, thesis/dissertation. *Entrance requirements:* For master's, GRE General Test, minimum GPA of 3.0; for doctorate, GRE General Test. Additional exam requirements/recommendations for international students: Required—TOEFL.

University of Ottawa, Faculty of Graduate and Postdoctoral Studies, Faculty of Social Sciences, School of Psychology, Ottawa, ON K1N 6N5, Canada. Offers PhD. *Degree requirements:* For doctorate, thesis/dissertation. *Entrance requirements:* For doctorate, minimum B+ average. Electronic applications accepted. *Faculty research:* Behavioral neuroscience, social psychology, developmental psychology, cognition.

University of Pennsylvania, School of Arts and Sciences, Graduate Group in Psychology, Philadelphia, PA 19104. Offers PhD. *Accreditation:* APA. *Faculty:* 43 full-time (16 women), 19 part-time/adjunct (6 women). *Students:* 52 full-time (31 women); includes 10 minority (1 Black or African American, non-Hispanic/Latino; 4 Asian, non-Hispanic/Latino; 2 Hispanic/Latino; 3 Two or more races, non-Hispanic/Latino), 11 international. Average age 28. 622 applicants, 3% accepted, 8 enrolled. In 2017, 12 doctorates awarded.
Website: http://psychology.sas.upenn.edu/graduate-program

University of Philosophical Research, Master's in Transformational Psychology Program, Los Angeles, CA 90027. Offers MA. *Degree requirements:* For master's, thesis. Electronic applications accepted.

University of Phoenix–Online Campus, College of Social Science, Phoenix, AZ 85034-7209. Offers mediation (Certificate); psychology (MS), including behavioral health, industrial-organizational, psychology. *Program availability:* Evening/weekend, online learning. *Entrance requirements:* Additional exam requirements/recommendations for international students: Required—TOEFL, TOEIC (Test of English as an International Communication), Berlitz Online English Proficiency Exam, PTE, or IELTS. Electronic applications accepted. *Expenses:* Contact institution.

University of Phoenix–Phoenix Campus, College of Social Sciences, Tempe, AZ 85282-2371. Offers counseling (MS), including clinical mental health counseling, community counseling, counseling, marriage, family and child therapy; psychology (MS). *Program availability:* Evening/weekend, online learning. *Entrance requirements:* Additional exam requirements/recommendations for international students: Required—TOEFL, TOEIC (Test of English as an International Communication), Berlitz Online English Proficiency Exam, PTE, or IELTS. Electronic applications accepted. *Expenses:* Contact institution.

University of Pittsburgh, Kenneth P. Dietrich School of Arts and Sciences, Department of Psychology, Pittsburgh, PA 15260. Offers biological and health psychology (PhD); clinical psychology (PhD); cognitive psychology (PhD); developmental psychology (PhD); social psychology (PhD). *Accreditation:* APA. *Faculty:* 58 full-time (26 women). *Students:* 90 full-time (72 women); includes 25 minority (5 Black or African American, non-Hispanic/Latino; 11 Asian, non-Hispanic/Latino; 9 Hispanic/Latino), 9 international. Average age 26. 485 applicants, 6% accepted, 14 enrolled. In 2017, 6 doctorates awarded. Terminal master's awarded for partial completion of doctoral program. *Degree requirements:* For doctorate, comprehensive exam, thesis/dissertation. *Entrance requirements:* For doctorate, GRE General Test, minimum GPA of 3.0. Additional exam requirements/recommendations for international students: Required—TOEFL (minimum score 90 iBT) or IELTS (minimum score 7). *Application deadline:* For fall admission, 12/1 for domestic and international students. Application fee: $50. Electronic applications accepted. *Financial support:* In 2017–18, 76 students received support, including 20 fellowships with full tuition reimbursements available (averaging $22,000 per year), 28 research assistantships with full tuition reimbursements available (averaging $18,060 per year), 29 teaching assistantships with full tuition reimbursements available (averaging $19,180 per year); scholarships/grants, traineeships, and health care benefits also available. Financial award application deadline: 12/1. *Faculty research:* Developmental psychopathology; autism spectrum disorder; cardiovascular medicine; STEM research. *Total annual research expenditures:* $20 million. *Unit head:* Dr. Julie Fiez, Chair, 412-624-4500, E-mail: fiez@pitt.edu. *Application contact:* Stacy McLinden, Graduate Administrator, 412-624-4502, E-mail: psygrad@pitt.edu.
Website: http://www.psychology.pitt.edu/

University of Puerto Rico–Río Piedras, College of Social Sciences, Department of Psychology, San Juan, PR 00931-3300. Offers clinical psychology (MA); industrial organizational psychology (MA); investigative academic psychology (MA); psychology

(PhD); social-community psychology (MA). *Program availability:* Part-time. *Degree requirements:* For master's, comprehensive exam, thesis; for doctorate, comprehensive exam, thesis/dissertation, internship. *Entrance requirements:* For master's, GRE or PAEG, interview, minimum GPA of 3.0; for doctorate, GRE or PAEG, interview, master's degree, minimum GPA of 3.0. *Faculty research:* Intervention on depressed Latino youth, biosychosocial training.

University of Regina, Faculty of Graduate Studies and Research, Faculty of Arts, Department of Psychology, Regina, SK S4S 0A2, Canada. Offers clinical psychology (MA, PhD); experimental and applied psychology (MA, PhD). *Faculty:* 19 full-time (9 women), 5 part-time/adjunct (2 women). *Students:* 18 full-time (13 women), 2 part-time (0 women). 52 applicants, 19% accepted. In 2017, 4 master's, 4 doctorates awarded. *Degree requirements:* For master's, thesis; for doctorate, comprehensive exam, thesis/dissertation. *Entrance requirements:* For master's, GRE General Test; for doctorate, GRE General Test and GRE Subject Test (optional for those with a master's degree from a Canadian university). Additional exam requirements/recommendations for international students: Required—TOEFL (minimum score 580 paper-based; 80 iBT), IELTS (minimum score 6.5), PTE (minimum score 59). *Application deadline:* For fall admission, 1/15 for domestic and international students. Application fee: $100. Electronic applications accepted. *Expenses:* $10,681. *Financial support:* In 2017–18, 7 fellowships (averaging $6,714 per year), 17 teaching assistantships (averaging $2,562 per year) were awarded; research assistantships, career-related internships or fieldwork, and scholarships/grants also available. Financial award application deadline: 6/15. *Faculty research:* Clinical, experimental, cognitive, and applied psychology; post-traumatic stress disorder, anxiety, and panic disorder; traumatic brain injury; chronic pain; perception and memory. *Unit head:* Dr. Richard MacLennan, Department Head, 306-585-4458, Fax: 306-585-5429, E-mail: richard.maclennan@uregina.ca.
Website: http://www.uregina.ca/arts/psychology

University of Rhode Island, Graduate School, College of Health Sciences, Department of Psychology, Kingston, RI 02881. Offers behavioral science (PhD); clinical psychology (PhD); school psychology (MS, PhD). *Accreditation:* APA (one or more programs are accredited). *Program availability:* Part-time. *Faculty:* 17 full-time (11 women), 1 part-time/adjunct (0 women). *Students:* 63 full-time (49 women), 11 part-time (9 women); includes 12 minority (6 Black or African American, non-Hispanic/Latino; 1 American Indian or Alaska Native, non-Hispanic/Latino; 3 Asian, non-Hispanic/Latino; 2 Hispanic/Latino), 5 international. 253 applicants, 4% accepted, 7 enrolled. In 2017, 8 master's, 21 doctorates awarded. *Entrance requirements:* Additional exam requirements/recommendations for international students: Required—TOEFL. *Application deadline:* For fall admission, 12/1 for domestic and international students. Application fee: $65. Electronic applications accepted. *Expenses:* Tuition, state resident: full-time $12,706; part-time $786 per credit. Tuition, nonresident: full-time $25,216; part-time $1401 per credit. *Required fees:* $1598; $45 per credit. One-time fee: $30 part-time. *Financial support:* In 2017–18, 10 research assistantships with tuition reimbursements (averaging $17,979 per year), 24 teaching assistantships with tuition reimbursements (averaging $13,572 per year) were awarded. Financial award application deadline: 12/1; financial award applicants required to submit FAFSA. *Faculty research:* Health psychology, multicultural psychology, research methodology, child/family/developmental neuropsychology. *Unit head:* Dr. Mark Robbins, Chair, 401-874-5082, E-mail: markrobb@uri.edu.
Website: http://www.uri.edu/artsci/psy/

University of Rochester, School of Arts and Sciences, Department of Clinical and Social Sciences in Psychology, Rochester, NY 14627. Offers clinical psychology (PhD); developmental psychology (PhD); social-personality psychology (PhD). *Accreditation:* APA. *Faculty:* 14 full-time (7 women). *Students:* 46 full-time (39 women), 1 (woman) part-time; includes 9 minority (1 Black or African American, non-Hispanic/Latino; 4 Asian, non-Hispanic/Latino; 3 Hispanic/Latino; 1 Two or more races, non-Hispanic/Latino), 4 international. Average age 28. 246 applicants, 4% accepted, 8 enrolled. In 2017, 6 doctorates awarded. Terminal master's awarded for partial completion of doctoral program. *Degree requirements:* For doctorate, thesis/dissertation. *Entrance requirements:* For doctorate, GRE General Test; GRE Subject Test (required for clinical psychology, recommended for others), personal statement, official transcripts, three letters of recommendation, curriculum vitae, resume. Additional exam requirements/recommendations for international students: Required—TOEFL. *Application deadline:* For fall admission, 12/1 for domestic and international students. Application fee: $60. Electronic applications accepted. *Expenses:* $1,596 per credit hour. *Financial support:* In 2017–18, 37 students received support, including 2 fellowships, 37 research assistantships (averaging $22,000 per year); teaching assistantships, career-related internships or fieldwork, scholarships/grants, and tuition waivers (full) also available. Financial award application deadline: 4/15. *Faculty research:* Multisensory processing in social-communication difficulties, child emotion regulation, interpersonal relationships, social stress, understanding romantic relationships. *Total annual research expenditures:* $4.3 million. *Unit head:* Loisa Bennetto, Chair, 585-275-8712, E-mail: loisa.bennetto@rochester.edu. *Application contact:* April Engram, Academic Coordinator, 585-275-8704, E-mail: april.engram@rochester.edu.
Website: http://www.sas.rochester.edu/psy/graduate/index.html

University of Saint Mary, Graduate Programs, Program in Psychology, Leavenworth, KS 66048-5082. Offers MA. *Program availability:* Part-time, evening/weekend. *Degree requirements:* For master's, thesis. *Entrance requirements:* For master's, minimum undergraduate GPA of 2.75. Electronic applications accepted. *Expenses:* Contact institution.

University of Saskatchewan, College of Graduate Studies and Research, College of Arts and Science, Department of Psychology, Saskatoon, SK S7N 5A2, Canada. Offers MA, PhD. *Degree requirements:* For master's, thesis; for doctorate, comprehensive exam (for some programs), thesis/dissertation. *Entrance requirements:* Additional exam requirements/recommendations for international students: Required—TOEFL (minimum score 80 iBT); Recommended—IELTS (minimum score 6.5). Electronic applications accepted.

University of South Africa, College of Human Sciences, Pretoria, South Africa. Offers adult education (M Ed); African languages (MA, PhD); African politics (MA, PhD); Afrikaans (MA, PhD); ancient history (MA, PhD); ancient Near Eastern studies (MA, PhD); anthropology (MA, PhD); applied linguistics (MA); Arabic (MA, PhD); archaeology (MA); art history (MA); Biblical archaeology (MA); Biblical studies (M Th, D Th, PhD); Christian spirituality (M Th, D Th); church history (M Th, D Th); classical studies (MA, PhD); clinical psychology (MA); communication (MA, PhD); comparative education (M Ed, Ed D); consulting psychology (D Admin, D Com, PhD); curriculum studies (M Ed, Ed D); development studies (M Admin, MA, D Admin, PhD); didactics (M Ed, Ed D); education (M Tech); education management (M Ed, Ed D); educational psychology (M Ed); English (MA); environmental education (M Ed); French (MA, PhD); German (MA, PhD); Greek (MA); guidance and counseling (M Ed); health studies (MA, PhD), including health sciences education (MA), health services management (MA), medical and surgical nursing science (critical care general) (MA), midwifery and neonatal nursing science (MA), trauma and emergency care (MA); history (MA, PhD); history of education (Ed D); inclusive education (M Ed, Ed D); information and communications technology policy and regulation (MA); information science (MA, MIS, PhD); international politics (MA, PhD); Islamic studies (MA, PhD); Italian (MA, PhD); Judaica (MA, PhD); linguistics (MA, PhD); mathematical education (M Ed); mathematics education (MA); missiology (M Th, D Th); modern Hebrew (MA, PhD); musicology (MA, MMus, D Mus, PhD); natural science education (M Ed); New Testament (M Th, D Th); Old Testament (D Th); pastoral therapy (M Th, D Th); philosophy (MA); philosophy of education (M Ed, Ed D); politics (MA, PhD); Portuguese (MA, PhD); practical theology (M Th, D Th); psychology (MA, MS, PhD); psychology of education (M Ed, Ed D); public health (MA); religious studies (MA, D Th, PhD); Romance languages (MA); Russian (MA, PhD); Semitic languages (MA, PhD); social behavior studies in HIV/AIDS (MA); social science (mental health) (MA); social science in development studies (MA); social science in psychology (MA); social science in social work (MA); social science in sociology (MA); social work (MSW, DSW, PhD); socio-education (M Ed, Ed D); sociolinguistics (MA); sociology (MA, PhD); Spanish (MA, PhD); systematic theology (M Th, D Th); TESOL (teaching English to speakers of other languages) (MA); theological ethics (M Th, D Th); theory of literature (MA, PhD); urban ministries (D Th); urban ministry (M Th).

University of South Alabama, College of Arts and Sciences, Department of Psychology, Mobile, AL 36688. Offers MS. *Accreditation:* APA. *Program availability:* Part-time, evening/weekend. *Faculty:* 11 full-time (3 women). *Students:* 16 full-time (9 women); includes 4 minority (3 Black or African American, non-Hispanic/Latino; 1 Two or more races, non-Hispanic/Latino), 1 international. Average age 28. 14 applicants, 50% accepted, 5 enrolled. In 2017, 7 master's awarded. *Degree requirements:* For master's, comprehensive exam, thesis optional. *Entrance requirements:* For master's, GRE General Test, GRE Subject Test (recommended), minimum GPA of 3.0, major in psychology or equivalent. Additional exam requirements/recommendations for international students: Required—TOEFL. *Application deadline:* For fall admission, 2/15 for domestic students, 6/15 for international students. Application fee: $35. Electronic applications accepted. *Expenses:* Tuition, state resident: full-time $10,104; part-time $421 per semester hour. Tuition, nonresident: full-time $20,208; part-time $842 per semester hour. *Financial support:* Fellowships, research assistantships, teaching assistantships, career-related internships or fieldwork, Federal Work-Study, institutionally sponsored loans, scholarships/grants, and unspecified assistantships available. Support available to part-time students. Financial award application deadline: 3/31; financial award applicants required to submit FAFSA. *Faculty research:* Language acquisition and development, mechanics of sound production, clinical psychology, behavioral genetics, behavioral genetics. *Unit head:* Dr. Lisa A. Turner, Interim Chair, Psychology, 251-460-6013, Fax: 251-460-6320, E-mail: laturner@southalabama.edu. *Application contact:* Lisa Nash, Department Secretary, 251-460-6371, E-mail: lnash@southalabama.edu.
Website: http://www.southalabama.edu/colleges/artsandsci/psychology/index.html

University of South Carolina, The Graduate School, College of Arts and Sciences, Department of Psychology, Columbia, SC 29208. Offers clinical/community psychology (MA, PhD), including clinical/community psychology (PhD), general psychology (MA); experimental psychology (MA, PhD); school psychology (PhD). *Accreditation:* APA (one or more programs are accredited). Terminal master's awarded for partial completion of doctoral program. *Degree requirements:* For master's, thesis; for doctorate, comprehensive exam, thesis/dissertation. *Entrance requirements:* For master's and doctorate, GRE General Test. Additional exam requirements/recommendations for international students: Required—TOEFL. Electronic applications accepted. *Faculty research:* Developmental cognitive neuroscience, alcohol and drug addictions, reading and language processing, child and family, prevention.

University of South Dakota, Graduate School, College of Arts and Sciences, Department of Psychology, Vermillion, SD 57069. Offers clinical psychology (MA, PhD); human factors (MA, PhD). *Accreditation:* APA (one or more programs are accredited). *Degree requirements:* For master's, comprehensive exam, thesis; for doctorate, comprehensive exam, thesis/dissertation. *Entrance requirements:* For master's, GRE, minimum GPA of 3.0; for doctorate, GRE General Test, GRE Subject Test, minimum GPA of 3.0. Additional exam requirements/recommendations for international students: Required—TOEFL (minimum score 550 paper-based; 79 iBT). *Application deadline:* For fall admission, 2/1 for domestic students. Application fee: $35. Electronic applications accepted. *Financial support:* Fellowships, research assistantships with partial tuition reimbursements, teaching assistantships with partial tuition reimbursements, and unspecified assistantships available. Financial award applicants required to submit FAFSA. *Faculty research:* Human-computer interactions, perceptual-cognitive processing, medical psychology, depression, moral psychology. *Application contact:* Graduate School, 605-658-6140, Fax: 605-677-6118, E-mail: grad@usd.edu.
Website: http://http://www.usd.edu/psychology

University of Southern California, Graduate School, Dana and David Dornsife College of Letters, Arts and Sciences, Department of Psychology, Los Angeles, CA 90089. Offers brain and cognitive science (PhD); clinical science (PhD); developmental psychology (PhD); human behavior (MHB); quantitative methods (PhD); social psychology (PhD). *Accreditation:* APA. *Degree requirements:* For doctorate, comprehensive exam, thesis/dissertation, one-year internship (for clinical science students). *Entrance requirements:* For doctorate, GRE. Additional exam requirements/recommendations for international students: Recommended—TOEFL (minimum score 600 paper-based; 100 iBT). Electronic applications accepted. *Faculty research:* Affective neuroscience; children and families; vision, culture and ethnicity; intergroup relations; aggression and violence; language and reading development; substance abuse.

University of Southern Mississippi, College of Education and Psychology, Department of Psychology, Hattiesburg, MS 39406-0001. Offers MS, PhD. *Accreditation:* APA (one or more programs are accredited). *Students:* 33 full-time (25 women). 218 applicants, 19% accepted, 33 enrolled. Terminal master's awarded for partial completion of doctoral program. *Degree requirements:* For master's, comprehensive exam, thesis; for doctorate, comprehensive exam, thesis/dissertation. *Entrance requirements:* For master's, GRE General Test, minimum GPA of 3.0; for doctorate, GRE General Test, interview, minimum GPA of 3.5. Additional exam requirements/recommendations for international students: Required—TOEFL, IELTS. *Application deadline:* Applications are processed on a rolling basis. Application fee: $60. *Expenses:* Tuition, state resident: full-time $3830. *Financial support:* Research assistantships with full tuition reimbursements, teaching assistantships with full tuition reimbursements, career-related internships or fieldwork, Federal Work-Study, institutionally sponsored loans, scholarships/grants, health care benefits, and unspecified assistantships available. Financial award application deadline: 3/15; financial award applicants required to submit FAFSA. *Faculty research:* Psychopathology, alcohol and drug abuse, child clinical psychology, parenting, suicide, career/vocational, marine mammal, cognition, psychological psychology, behavioral interventions, positive psychology, anger/aggression, diversity issues. *Unit head:* Dr. Joe Olmi, Chair, 601-266-5693, Fax: 601-266-5580, E-mail: d.olmi@usm.edu. *Application contact:* Angela Pam, Administrative Assistant, 601-266-4592, Fax: 601-266-5580.
Website: https://www.usm.edu/psychology

University of South Florida, College of Arts and Sciences, Department of Psychology, Tampa, FL 33620-9951. Offers psychology (PhD), including clinical psychology, cognition, neuroscience and social psychology, industrial-organizational psychology.

Accreditation: APA. *Faculty:* 30 full-time (11 women). *Students:* 79 full-time (53 women), 11 part-time (8 women); includes 12 minority (1 Black or African American, non-Hispanic/Latino; 5 Asian, non-Hispanic/Latino; 4 Hispanic/Latino; 2 Two or more races, non-Hispanic/Latino), 7 international. Average age 28. 393 applicants, 3% accepted, 11 enrolled. In 2017, 17 doctorates awarded. *Degree requirements:* For doctorate, comprehensive exam, thesis/dissertation, internship. *Entrance requirements:* For doctorate, GRE General Test, minimum upper-division GPA of 3.4, three letters of recommendation, personal goals statement. Additional exam requirements/recommendations for international students: Required—TOEFL (minimum score 550 paper-based; 79 iBT) or IELTS (minimum score 6.5). *Application deadline:* For fall admission, 12/1 priority date for domestic and international students. Application fee: $30. Electronic applications accepted. *Expenses:* Contact institution. *Financial support:* In 2017–18, 43 students received support, including 18 research assistantships with tuition reimbursements available (averaging $14,727 per year), 57 teaching assistantships with tuition reimbursements available (averaging $14,543 per year); tuition waivers (partial) and unspecified assistantships also available. Financial award applicants required to submit FAFSA. *Faculty research:* Clinical, cognitive, neuroscience, social, and industrial/organizational. *Total annual research expenditures:* $2 million. *Unit head:* Dr. Toru Shimizu, Chairperson, 813-974-0352, Fax: 813-974-4617, E-mail: shimizu@usf.edu. *Application contact:* Dr. Sandra Schneider, Professor and Graduate Program Director, 813-974-0928, E-mail: sandra@usf.edu.
Website: http://psychology.usf.edu/

University of South Florida, St. Petersburg, College of Arts and Sciences, St. Petersburg, FL 33701. Offers digital journalism and design (MA); environmental science and policy (MA, MS); Florida studies (MLA); journalism and media studies (MA); liberal studies (MLA); psychology (MA). *Program availability:* Part-time, online learning. *Degree requirements:* For master's, comprehensive exam, thesis or project. *Entrance requirements:* For master's, GRE, LSAT, MCAT (varies by program), letter of intent, 3 letters of recommendation, writing samples, bachelor's degree from regionally-accredited institution with minimum GPA of 3.0 overall or in upper two years. Additional exam requirements/recommendations for international students: Required—TOEFL (minimum score 550 paper-based; 79 iBT); Recommended—IELTS. Electronic applications accepted.

The University of Tennessee, Graduate School, College of Arts and Sciences, Department of Psychology, Knoxville, TN 37996. Offers clinical psychology (PhD); experimental psychology (MA, PhD); psychology (MA). *Accreditation:* APA (one or more programs are accredited). Terminal master's awarded for partial completion of doctoral program. *Degree requirements:* For master's, thesis; for doctorate, thesis/dissertation. *Entrance requirements:* For master's and doctorate, GRE General Test, GRE Subject Test, minimum GPA of 2.7. Additional exam requirements/recommendations for international students: Required—TOEFL. Electronic applications accepted.

The University of Tennessee at Chattanooga, Program in Psychology, Chattanooga, TN 37403. Offers industrial/organizational psychology (MS); research psychology (MS). *Program availability:* Part-time. *Students:* 46 full-time (28 women), 4 part-time (3 women); includes 5 minority (2 Black or African American, non-Hispanic/Latino; 1 Asian, non-Hispanic/Latino; 2 Hispanic/Latino). Average age 25. 85 applicants, 38% accepted, 25 enrolled. In 2017, 20 master's awarded. *Degree requirements:* For master's, comprehensive exam (for some programs), thesis (for some programs), comprehensive exam or thesis. *Entrance requirements:* For master's, GRE General Test, minimum GPA of 2.5 on all undergraduate coursework or 3.0 in senior year. Additional exam requirements/recommendations for international students: Required—TOEFL (minimum score 550 paper-based; 79 iBT), IELTS (minimum score 6). *Application deadline:* For fall admission, 6/15 priority date for domestic students, 7/1 for international students; for spring admission, 11/1 priority date for domestic students, 11/1 for international students. Applications are processed on a rolling basis. Application fee: $35 ($40 for international students). Electronic applications accepted. *Expenses:* Contact institution. *Financial support:* Research assistantships, teaching assistantships, career-related internships or fieldwork, scholarships/grants, and unspecified assistantships available. Support available to part-time students. Financial award application deadline: 7/1; financial award applicants required to submit FAFSA. *Faculty research:* Decision processes, philosophical psychology, memory, social cognition, employee selection. *Total annual research expenditures:* $44,854. *Unit head:* Dr. Brian O'Leary, Department Head, 423-425-4283, Fax: 423-425-4284, E-mail: brian-o'leary@utc.edu. *Application contact:* Dr. Joanne Romagni, Dean of the Graduate School, 423-425-4478, Fax: 423-425-5223, E-mail: joanne-romagni@utc.edu.
Website: http://www.utc.edu/psychology/

The University of Texas at Arlington, Graduate School, College of Science, Department of Psychology, Arlington, TX 76019. Offers experimental health psychology (PhD); experimental psychology (MS, PhD); health/neuroscience psychology (MS, PhD); industrial and organizational psychology (MS). *Program availability:* Part-time. Terminal master's awarded for partial completion of doctoral program. *Degree requirements:* For master's, comprehensive exam or thesis; for doctorate, thesis/dissertation (for some programs). *Entrance requirements:* For master's and doctorate, GRE General Test, minimum GPA of 3.0 in last 60 hours of course work. Additional exam requirements/recommendations for international students: Required—TOEFL (minimum score 550 paper-based).

The University of Texas at Austin, Graduate School, College of Liberal Arts, Department of Psychology, Austin, TX 78712-1111. Offers behavioral neuroscience (PhD); clinical psychology (PhD); cognitive systems (PhD); developmental psychology (PhD); individual differences and evolutionary psychology (PhD); perceptual systems (PhD); social psychology (PhD). *Accreditation:* APA. *Degree requirements:* For doctorate, thesis/dissertation. *Entrance requirements:* For doctorate, GRE General Test. Electronic applications accepted. *Faculty research:* Behavioral neuroscience, sensory neuroscience, evolutionary psychology, cognitive processes in psychopathology, cognitive processes and their development.

The University of Texas at Dallas, School of Behavioral and Brain Sciences, Program in Psychological Sciences, Richardson, TX 75080. Offers early childhood disorders (MS); psychological sciences (MS, PhD). *Program availability:* Part-time, evening/weekend. *Faculty:* 12 full-time (9 women), 2 part-time/adjunct (both women). *Students:* 67 full-time (54 women), 10 part-time (9 women); includes 29 minority (7 Black or African American, non-Hispanic/Latino; 5 Asian, non-Hispanic/Latino; 15 Hispanic/Latino; 2 Two or more races, non-Hispanic/Latino), 4 international. Average age 26. 139 applicants, 40% accepted, 24 enrolled. In 2017, 24 master's, 1 doctorate awarded. *Degree requirements:* For master's, directed project or internship; for doctorate, thesis/dissertation. *Entrance requirements:* For master's and doctorate, GRE General Test, minimum GPA of 3.0 in upper-level course work. Additional exam requirements/recommendations for international students: Required—TOEFL (minimum score 550 paper-based). *Application deadline:* For fall admission, 7/15 for domestic students, 5/1 priority date for international students; for spring admission, 11/15 for domestic students, 9/1 priority date for international students. Applications are processed on a rolling basis. Application fee: $50 ($100 for international students). Electronic applications accepted. *Expenses:* Tuition, state resident: full-time $12,916; part-time $718 per credit hour. Tuition, nonresident: full-time $25,252; part-time $1403 per credit hour. *Financial*

support: In 2017–18, 46 students received support, including 8 research assistantships with partial tuition reimbursements available (averaging $29,172 per year), 21 teaching assistantships with partial tuition reimbursements available (averaging $17,966 per year); fellowships, career-related internships or fieldwork, Federal Work-Study, scholarships/grants, and unspecified assistantships also available. Support available to part-time students. Financial award application deadline: 4/30; financial award applicants required to submit FAFSA. *Faculty research:* Neurocognitive development in young adulthood, infant learning, infant and toddler eye tracking, social aggression. *Unit head:* Dr. Shayla Holub, Program Head, Psychological Sciences, 972-883-4473, Fax: 972-883-3491, E-mail: sholub@utdallas.edu.
Website: http://www.utdallas.edu/bbs/degrees/psy-degrees/

The University of Texas at El Paso, Graduate School, College of Liberal Arts, Department of Psychology, El Paso, TX 79968-0001. Offers clinical psychology (MA); experimental psychology (MA); psychology (PhD). *Program availability:* Part-time, evening/weekend. *Degree requirements:* For master's, thesis; for doctorate, thesis/dissertation. *Entrance requirements:* For master's, GRE, letters of recommendation; for doctorate, GRE, statement of purpose, letters of recommendation. Additional exam requirements/recommendations for international students: Required—TOEFL; Recommended—IELTS. Electronic applications accepted.

The University of Texas at San Antonio, College of Liberal and Fine Arts, Department of Psychology, San Antonio, TX 78249-0617. Offers MS, PhD. *Program availability:* Part-time. *Faculty:* 15 full-time (5 women). *Students:* 31 full-time (19 women), 18 part-time (10 women); includes 22 minority (2 Black or African American, non-Hispanic/Latino; 2 Asian, non-Hispanic/Latino; 17 Hispanic/Latino; 1 Two or more races, non-Hispanic/Latino). Average age 29. 60 applicants, 37% accepted, 16 enrolled. In 2017, 14 master's, 1 doctorate awarded. *Degree requirements:* For master's, comprehensive exam, thesis or alternative; for doctorate, comprehensive exam, thesis/dissertation. *Entrance requirements:* For master's, GRE, minimum GPA of 3.2 in last 60 hours and in all psychology courses; 18 hours of psychology courses including inferential statistics and research methods; two letters of recommendation; statement of purpose; for doctorate, GRE, master's degree with minimum GPA of 3.5, three letters of recommendation, statement of purpose. Additional exam requirements/recommendations for international students: Required—TOEFL (minimum score 550 paper-based; 79 iBT), IELTS (minimum score 6.5). *Application deadline:* For fall admission, 6/15 for domestic students, 3/1 for international students; for spring admission, 10/15 for domestic students, 9/15 for international students. Application fee: $50 ($90 for international students). Electronic applications accepted. *Expenses:* Contact institution. *Financial support:* Research assistantships, teaching assistantships, and tuition waivers (partial) available. *Faculty research:* Social psychology, cognitive psychology, developmental psychology, industrial/organizational psychology, biopsychology. *Total annual research expenditures:* $408,150. *Unit head:* Dr. James H Bray, Department Chair, 210-458-7352, E-mail: james.bray@utsa.edu.
Website: http://colfa.utsa.edu/psychology

The University of Texas at Tyler, College of Education and Psychology, Department of Psychology and Counseling, Tyler, TX 75799-0001. Offers clinical psychology (MS), including neuropsychology, school psychology; counseling psychology (MA), including general, marriage and family; interdisciplinary studies (MSIS); school counseling (MA). *Program availability:* Part-time, evening/weekend. *Degree requirements:* For master's, comprehensive exam, thesis optional. *Entrance requirements:* For master's, GRE General Test, minimum GPA of 3.0. Additional exam requirements/recommendations for international students: Required—TOEFL. Electronic applications accepted. *Faculty research:* Neuropsychology, child abuse, psychometric properties of psychological instruments, maternal behavior, clinical practice issues, victimization of women, post-traumatic stress disorder.

The University of Texas of the Permian Basin, Office of Graduate Studies, College of Arts and Sciences, Department of Psychology, Odessa, TX 79762-0001. Offers applied research psychology (MA); clinical psychology (MA). *Program availability:* Part-time, evening/weekend. *Degree requirements:* For master's, comprehensive exam, thesis, practicum. *Entrance requirements:* For master's, GRE General Test, 3 letters of recommendation. Additional exam requirements/recommendations for international students: Required—TOEFL (minimum score 550 paper-based).

The University of Texas Rio Grande Valley, College of Liberal Arts, Department of Psychological Science, Edinburg, TX 78539. Offers psychology (MA), including clinical psychology, experimental psychology. *Program availability:* Part-time, evening/weekend. *Faculty:* 12 full-time (1 woman), 3 part-time/adjunct (1 woman). *Students:* 32 full-time (25 women), 20 part-time (15 women); includes 50 minority (all Hispanic/Latino), 2 international. Average age 27. 29 applicants, 69% accepted, 15 enrolled. In 2017, 15 master's awarded. *Degree requirements:* For master's, comprehensive exam, thesis optional, internship. *Entrance requirements:* For master's, GRE, letters of recommendation. Additional exam requirements/recommendations for international students: Required—TOEFL or IELTS. *Application deadline:* For fall admission, 7/1 priority date for domestic and international students; for spring admission, 11/1 priority date for domestic and international students. Application fee: $50 ($100 for international students). *Expenses:* Tuition, state resident: full-time $5550; part-time $417 per credit hour. Tuition, nonresident: full-time $13,020; part-time $832 per credit hour. *Required fees:* $1169. *Faculty research:* Biofeedback, acculturation, health, stress/trauma, neuropsychological assessment, false memories, children's theory of mind. *Unit head:* Pamela Anderson-Mejias, Interim Chair, E-mail: pamela.andersonmejias@utrgv.edu.

University of the Pacific, College of the Pacific, Department of Psychology, Stockton, CA 95211-0197. Offers MA. *Faculty:* 7 full-time (4 women). *Students:* 15 part-time (9 women); includes 7 minority (1 Black or African American, non-Hispanic/Latino; 3 Asian, non-Hispanic/Latino; 2 Hispanic/Latino; 1 Two or more races, non-Hispanic/Latino), 1 international. Average age 24. 32 applicants, 44% accepted, 8 enrolled. In 2017, 5 master's awarded. *Degree requirements:* For master's, thesis. *Entrance requirements:* For master's, GRE General Test. Additional exam requirements/recommendations for international students: Required—TOEFL. *Application deadline:* For fall admission, 3/1 priority date for domestic students. Applications are processed on a rolling basis. Application fee: $75. *Financial support:* Teaching assistantships and institutionally sponsored loans available. Support available to part-time students. Financial award application deadline: 3/1; financial award applicants required to submit FAFSA. *Unit head:* Dr. Scott Jensen, Chairperson, 209-946-7320, E-mail: sjensen@pacific.edu. *Application contact:* Information Contact, 209-946-2133.
Website: http://www.pacific.edu/Documents/school-graduate/acrobat/Pacific-MA-Behavioral-Psychology-Fact-Sheet-17-18.pdf

University of the Rockies, Graduate Programs, Colorado Springs, CO 80903. Offers MA, Psy D.

University of the West, Department of Psychology, Rosemead, CA 91770. Offers Buddhist psychology (MA); multicultural counseling (MA). *Program availability:* Part-time, evening/weekend. *Degree requirements:* For master's, fieldwork; comprehensive exam or thesis.

The University of Toledo, College of Graduate Studies, College of Languages, Literature and Social Sciences, Department of Psychology, Toledo, OH 43606-3390.

Offers clinical psychology (MA, PhD); experimental psychology (MA, PhD). *Accreditation:* APA. *Degree requirements:* For master's, comprehensive exam, thesis; for doctorate, comprehensive exam, thesis/dissertation. *Entrance requirements:* For master's and doctorate, GRE General Test, GRE Subject Test, minimum cumulative point-hour ratio of 2.7 for all previous academic work, three letters of recommendation, statement of purpose, transcripts from all prior institutions attended. Additional exam requirements/recommendations for international students: Required—TOEFL (minimum score 550 paper-based; 80 iBT). Electronic applications accepted. *Faculty research:* Neural taste response.

University of Toronto, School of Graduate Studies, Faculty of Arts and Science, Department of Psychology, Toronto, ON M5S 1A1, Canada. Offers MA, PhD. *Degree requirements:* For master's, thesis; for doctorate, thesis/dissertation, oral exam. *Entrance requirements:* For master's, minimum A- average in last two years, 6 full courses in psychology, laboratory experience; for doctorate, minimum A- average, research experience. Additional exam requirements/recommendations for international students: Required—TOEFL (minimum score 580 paper-based; 93 iBT), TWE (minimum score 5). Electronic applications accepted.

The University of Tulsa, Graduate School, Kendall College of Arts and Sciences, Department of Psychology, Tulsa, OK 74104-3189. Offers clinical psychology (MA, PhD); industrial/organizational psychology (MA, PhD); JD/MA. *Accreditation:* APA (one or more programs are accredited). *Program availability:* Part-time. *Faculty:* 13 full-time (5 women). *Students:* 51 full-time (34 women), 6 part-time (5 women); includes 14 minority (7 Asian, non-Hispanic/Latino; 5 Hispanic/Latino; 2 Two or more races, non-Hispanic/Latino), 2 international. Average age 26. 235 applicants, 10% accepted, 13 enrolled. In 2017, 16 master's, 10 doctorates awarded. Terminal master's awarded for partial completion of doctoral program. *Degree requirements:* For doctorate, comprehensive exam, thesis/dissertation. *Entrance requirements:* For master's and doctorate, GRE General Test. Additional exam requirements/recommendations for international students: Required—TOEFL (minimum score 577 paper-based; 91 iBT), IELTS (minimum score 6.5). Application fee: $55. Electronic applications accepted. *Expenses: Tuition:* Full-time $22,230. *Required fees:* $2000. Tuition and fees vary according to course load and program. *Financial support:* In 2017–18, 70 students received support. Fellowships with full tuition reimbursements available, research assistantships with full tuition reimbursements available, teaching assistantships with full tuition reimbursements available, career-related internships or fieldwork, Federal Work-Study, scholarships/grants, health care benefits, tuition waivers (full and partial), and unspecified assistantships available. Support available to part-time students. Financial award application deadline: 2/1; financial award applicants required to submit FAFSA. *Faculty research:* Traumatic stress studies, randomized control trials of exposure treatments, pain modulation, neuropsychological assessment of health/mental health, psychological assessment, psychometrics, ethics, longitudinal assessment of child development, trauma and journalism, MMPI studies, personnel testing and selection, training, performance appraisal, organizational development, job attitudes and motivation, leadership. *Unit head:* Dr. John McNulty, Chairperson, 918-631-2835, Fax: 918-631-2833, E-mail: john-mcnulty@utulsa.edu. *Application contact:* Graduate School, 918-631-2336, Fax: 918-631-2156, E-mail: grad@utulsa.edu.
Website: http://artsandsciences.utulsa.edu/academics/departments-schools/psychology/

University of Utah, Graduate School, College of Social and Behavioral Science, Department of Psychology, Salt Lake City, UT 84112. Offers clinical psychology (PhD); psychology (PhD), including cognitive neuroscience, developmental psychology, social psychology. *Accreditation:* APA. *Faculty:* 32 full-time (15 women), 11 part-time/adjunct (7 women). *Students:* 53 full-time (36 women), 10 part-time (7 women); includes 10 minority (2 Black or African American, non-Hispanic/Latino; 1 Asian, non-Hispanic/Latino; 4 Hispanic/Latino; 3 Two or more races, non-Hispanic/Latino), 5 international. Average age 26. 295 applicants, 8% accepted, 13 enrolled. In 2017, 11 doctorates awarded. *Entrance requirements:* For doctorate, GRE General Test. Additional exam requirements/recommendations for international students: Required—TOEFL (minimum score 500 paper-based). Application fee: $55 ($65 for international students). Electronic applications accepted. *Expenses:* All admitted students are guaranteed funding and full tuition benefit for four years. *Financial support:* In 2017–18, 51 students received support, including 2 fellowships with full tuition reimbursements available (averaging $17,000 per year), 16 research assistantships with full tuition reimbursements available (averaging $16,800 per year), 30 teaching assistantships with full tuition reimbursements available (averaging $16,800 per year); career-related internships or fieldwork, health care benefits, and unspecified assistantships also available. Financial award application deadline: 4/15; financial award applicants required to submit FAFSA. *Faculty research:* Cognitive neuroscience, health, social cognition, psychopathology, cognitive and social development. *Total annual research expenditures:* $1.9 million. *Unit head:* Dr. Lisa G. Aspinwall, Chair, 801-581-8925, Fax: 801-581-5841, E-mail: lisa.aspinwall@utah.edu. *Application contact:* Nancy Seegmiller, Program Manager, 801-581-8925, Fax: 801-581-5841, E-mail: nancy.seegmiller@psych.utah.edu.
Website: http://www.psych.utah.edu/

University of Vermont, Graduate College, College of Arts and Sciences, Program in General/Experimental Psychology, Burlington, VT 05405-0134. Offers psychology (PhD), including biobehavioral psychology, developmental psychology, human behavioral pharmacology, social psychology. *Accreditation:* APA. *Students:* 15 (11 women). 22 applicants, 9% accepted, 2 enrolled. In 2017, 2 doctorates awarded. *Degree requirements:* For doctorate, thesis/dissertation. *Entrance requirements:* For doctorate, GRE General Test. Additional exam requirements/recommendations for international students: Required—TOEFL (minimum score 550 paper-based, 100 iBT) or IELTS (7). *Application deadline:* For fall admission, 12/1 for domestic and international students. Application fee: $65. Electronic applications accepted. *Expenses:* Tuition, state resident: full-time $11,628; part-time $646 per credit. Tuition, nonresident: full-time $29,340; part-time $1630 per credit. *Required fees:* $1994; $10 per credit. Tuition and fees vary according to course load and program. *Financial support:* In 2017–18, 15 students received support, including 15 teaching assistantships with full tuition reimbursements available (averaging $20,000 per year); fellowships and research assistantships also available. Financial award application deadline: 12/1. *Unit head:* Dr. Dianna Murray-Close, Coordinator, 802-656-2670, E-mail: dianna.murray-close@uvm.edu.
Website: https://www.uvm.edu/cas/psychology/general/experimental-psychology-phd-program

University of Victoria, Faculty of Graduate Studies, Faculty of Social Sciences, Department of Psychology, Victoria, BC V8W 2Y2, Canada. Offers clinical psychology (PhD); clinical psychology (neuropsychology) (M Sc); cognition and brain science (M Sc, PhD); experimental neuropsychology (M Sc, PhD); individualized study (M Sc, PhD); life span development psychology (PhD); life span developmental psychology (M Sc); social psychology (M Sc, PhD). *Degree requirements:* For master's, thesis; for doctorate, thesis/dissertation, candidacy exam. *Entrance requirements:* For master's and doctorate, GRE General Test. Additional exam requirements/recommendations for international students: Required—TOEFL (minimum score 600 paper-based). Electronic applications accepted. *Faculty research:* Life span development psychology and aging, behavioral neuroscience, cognitive psychology, behavioral psychology, environmental psychology.

University of Virginia, College and Graduate School of Arts and Sciences, Department of Psychology, Charlottesville, VA 22903. Offers MA, PhD. *Accreditation:* APA (one or more programs are accredited). *Faculty:* 29 full-time (11 women), 2 part-time/adjunct (0 women). *Students:* 71 full-time (44 women); includes 11 minority (2 Black or African American, non-Hispanic/Latino; 3 Asian, non-Hispanic/Latino; 4 Hispanic/Latino; 2 Two or more races, non-Hispanic/Latino), 7 international. Average age 27. 416 applicants, 6% accepted, 17 enrolled. In 2017, 15 master's, 14 doctorates awarded. *Degree requirements:* For master's, pre-dissertation research project; for doctorate, comprehensive exam, thesis/dissertation. *Entrance requirements:* For master's and doctorate, GRE General Test, 3 or more letters of recommendation. Additional exam requirements/recommendations for international students: Required—TOEFL (minimum score 600 paper-based; 90 iBT), IELTS (minimum score 7). *Application deadline:* For fall admission, 12/1 for domestic and international students. Applications are processed on a rolling basis. Application fee: $60. Electronic applications accepted. *Financial support:* Fellowships, research assistantships, and teaching assistantships available. Financial award applicants required to submit FAFSA. *Unit head:* Alev Erisir, Chair, 434-982-4750, Fax: 434-982-4766, E-mail: psy-dept@virginia.edu. *Application contact:* Daniel Willingham, Director of Graduate Studies, 434-982-4750, Fax: 434-982-4766, E-mail: psy-dept@virginia.edu.
Website: http://cacsprd.web.virginia.edu/Psych/Graduates

University of Washington, Graduate School, College of Arts and Sciences, Department of Psychology, Seattle, WA 98195. Offers animal behavior (PhD); applied child and adolescent psychology: prevention and treatment (MA); behavioral neuroscience (PhD); clinical psychology (PhD); cognition and perception (PhD); developmental psychology (PhD); quantitative psychology (PhD); social psychology and personality (PhD). *Accreditation:* APA (one or more programs are accredited). *Degree requirements:* For doctorate, thesis/dissertation. *Entrance requirements:* For doctorate, GRE General Test, minimum GPA of 3.0. Electronic applications accepted. *Faculty research:* Addictive behaviors, artificial intelligence, child psychopathology, mechanisms and development of vision, physiology of ingestive behaviors.

University of Waterloo, Graduate Studies, Faculty of Arts, Department of Psychology, Waterloo, ON N2L 3G1, Canada. Offers MA, MA Sc, PhD. Terminal master's awarded for partial completion of doctoral program. *Degree requirements:* For master's, thesis (for some programs); for doctorate, thesis/dissertation. *Entrance requirements:* For master's, GRE, honors degree in psychology, minimum B average; for doctorate, GRE, master's degree in psychology, minimum B average. Additional exam requirements/recommendations for international students: Required—TOEFL, IELTS, PTE. Electronic applications accepted. *Faculty research:* Memory and attention, attitudes and behavior in the workplace, object recognition, judgment and decision making, communication and knowledge in toddlers.

The University of Western Ontario, Faculty of Graduate Studies, Biosciences Division, Department of Psychology, London, ON N6A 5B8, Canada. Offers MA, PhD. *Degree requirements:* For master's, thesis; for doctorate, thesis/dissertation. *Entrance requirements:* For master's, minimum B average during last 2 years; for doctorate, MA in psychology. Additional exam requirements/recommendations for international students: Required—TOEFL. *Faculty research:* Clinical, applied and social/personality psychology; psychobiology; cognitive processes.

University of West Florida, Usha Kundu, MD College of Health, Department of Psychology, Pensacola, FL 32514-5750. Offers applied experimental (MA); counseling (MA); industrial-organizational (MA). *Program availability:* Part-time. *Degree requirements:* For master's, thesis (for some programs). *Entrance requirements:* For master's, GRE, official transcripts; minimum GPA of 3.0; writing sample; three letters of reference; field experience or skill sets; oral interview (for counseling specialization). Additional exam requirements/recommendations for international students: Required—TOEFL (minimum score 550 paper-based). *Faculty research:* Prose recall, brain imaging, peak performance, biofeedback and pain control, comparable worth.

University of West Georgia, College of Social Sciences, Carrollton, GA 30118. Offers criminology (MA); data analysis and evaluation methods (Postbaccalaureate Certificate); European Union studies (Postbaccalaureate Certificate); integrative health systems (Postbaccalaureate Certificate); nonprofit management and community development (Postbaccalaureate Certificate); psychology (MA, PhD), including consciousness and society (PhD); public administration (MPA); public management (Postbaccalaureate Certificate); sociology (MA). *Program availability:* Part-time, evening/weekend, 100% online, blended/hybrid learning. *Faculty:* 48 full-time (22 women). *Students:* 124 full-time (84 women), 73 part-time (46 women); includes 69 minority (56 Black or African American, non-Hispanic/Latino; 4 Asian, non-Hispanic/Latino; 6 Hispanic/Latino; 3 Two or more races, non-Hispanic/Latino), 10 international. Average age 32. 95 applicants, 89% accepted, 63 enrolled. In 2017, 44 master's, 2 doctorates, 4 other advanced degrees awarded. *Entrance requirements:* Additional exam requirements/recommendations for international students: Required—TOEFL (minimum score 523 paper-based; 69 iBT); Recommended—IELTS (minimum score 6.5). *Application deadline:* For fall admission, 7/15 for domestic students, 6/1 for international students; for spring admission, 11/30 for domestic students, 10/15 for international students; for summer admission, 5/15 for domestic students, 3/30 for international students. Applications are processed on a rolling basis. Application fee: $40. Electronic applications accepted. Tuition and fees vary according to degree level and program. *Financial support:* Fellowships, research assistantships, teaching assistantships, career-related internships or fieldwork, Federal Work-Study, institutionally sponsored loans, scholarships/grants, and unspecified assistantships available. Support available to part-time students. Financial award application deadline: 4/1; financial award applicants required to submit FAFSA. *Unit head:* Dr. N. Jane McCandless, Dean of Social Sciences, 678-839-5170, Fax: 678-839-5171, E-mail: jmccandl@westga.edu. *Application contact:* Dr. Toby Ziglar, Assistant Dean of the Graduate School, 678-839-1394, Fax: 678-839-1395, E-mail: graduate@westga.edu.
Website: https://www.westga.edu/coss

University of Windsor, Faculty of Graduate Studies, Faculty of Arts and Social Sciences, Department of Psychology, Windsor, ON N9B 3P4, Canada. Offers adult clinical (MA, PhD); applied social psychology (MA, PhD); child clinical (MA, PhD); clinical neuropsychology (MA, PhD). *Degree requirements:* For master's, thesis; for doctorate, comprehensive exam, thesis/dissertation. *Entrance requirements:* For master's, GRE General Test, GRE Subject Test in psychology, minimum B average; for doctorate, GRE General Test, GRE Subject Test in psychology, master's degree. Additional exam requirements/recommendations for international students: Required—TOEFL (minimum score 600 paper-based). Electronic applications accepted. *Faculty research:* Gambling, suicidology, emotional competence, psychotherapy and trauma.

University of Wisconsin–Eau Claire, College of Arts and Sciences, Department of Psychology, Eau Claire, WI 54702-4004. Offers school psychology (MSE, Ed S). *Program availability:* Part-time. *Degree requirements:* For master's, comprehensive exam, thesis, National Certified School Psychologist Professional Exam, written exam, externship. *Entrance requirements:* For master's, GRE, minimum undergraduate GPA of

3.0; courses in exceptional children and youth, statistics, psychopathology, and theories of counseling. Additional exam requirements/recommendations for international students: Required—TOEFL (minimum score 79 iBT).

University of Wisconsin–La Crosse, College of Liberal Studies, Department of Psychology, La Crosse, WI 54601-3742. Offers school psychology (MS Ed, Ed S). *Students:* 24 full-time (22 women), 12 part-time (10 women). Average age 24. 45 applicants, 42% accepted, 12 enrolled. In 2017, 11 master's, 11 Ed Ss awarded. *Degree requirements:* For master's, thesis, seminar, or comprehensive exams. *Entrance requirements:* For master's and Ed S, GRE. Additional exam requirements/ recommendations for international students: Required—TOEFL (minimum score 550 paper-based; 79 iBT). *Application deadline:* For fall admission, 1/31 for domestic and international students. Electronic applications accepted. *Financial support:* Research assistantships, Federal Work-Study, scholarships/grants, and health care benefits available. Support available to part-time students. *Unit head:* Dr. Robert Dixon, Director of the School Psychology Program, 608-785-6893, E-mail: rdixon@uwlax.edu. *Application contact:* Brandon Schaller, Senior Graduate Student Status Examiner, 608-785-8941, E-mail: admissions@uwlax.edu.
Website: https://www.uwlax.edu/Psychology/Graduate-program/

University of Wisconsin–Madison, Graduate School, College of Letters and Science, Department of Psychology, Madison, WI 53706-1380. Offers biology of brain and behavior (PhD); clinical psychology (PhD); cognitive neurosciences (PhD); developmental psychology (PhD); perception (PhD); psychology (PhD); social and personality psychology (PhD). *Accreditation:* APA. *Degree requirements:* For doctorate, comprehensive exam, thesis/dissertation. *Entrance requirements:* For doctorate, GRE General Test, minimum undergraduate GPA of 3.0. Additional exam requirements/ recommendations for international students: Required—TOEFL. Electronic applications accepted.

University of Wisconsin–Milwaukee, Graduate School, College of Letters and Science, Department of Psychology, Milwaukee, WI 53201-0413. Offers psychology (MS, PhD). *Accreditation:* APA (one or more programs are accredited). *Students:* 70 full-time (53 women), 17 part-time (10 women); includes 8 minority (1 Black or African American, non-Hispanic/Latino; 3 Asian, non-Hispanic/Latino; 4 Two or more races, non-Hispanic/Latino), 10 international. Average age 29. 243 applicants, 9% accepted, 21 enrolled. In 2017, 12 master's, 15 doctorates awarded. *Degree requirements:* For master's, thesis; for doctorate, variable foreign language requirement, thesis/ dissertation. *Entrance requirements:* For master's and doctorate, GRE General Test, GRE Subject Test. Additional exam requirements/recommendations for international students: Required—TOEFL (minimum score 550 paper-based; 79 iBT), IELTS (minimum score 6.5). *Application deadline:* For fall admission, 1/1 priority date for domestic students; for spring admission, 9/1 for domestic students. Application fee: $56 ($96 for international students). Electronic applications accepted. *Financial support:* Fellowships, research assistantships, teaching assistantships, career-related internships or fieldwork, unspecified assistantships, and project assistantships available. Support available to part-time students. Financial award application deadline: 4/15; financial award applicants required to submit FAFSA. *Unit head:* Douglas Woods, Department Chair, 414-229-6636, E-mail: dwoods@uwm.edu. *Application contact:* General Information Contact, 414-229-4982, Fax: 414-229-6967, E-mail: gradschool@uwm.edu.
Website: http://www.uwm.edu/dept/psychology/

University of Wisconsin–Oshkosh, Graduate Studies, College of Letters and Science, Department of Psychology, Oshkosh, WI 54901. Offers experimental psychology (MS); industrial/organizational psychology (MS). *Degree requirements:* For master's, thesis. *Entrance requirements:* For master's, GRE, 10 semester hours of undergraduate course work in psychology. Additional exam requirements/recommendations for international students: Required—TOEFL (minimum score 550 paper-based; 79 iBT). Electronic applications accepted. *Faculty research:* Performance evaluation, training, biological bases of behavior, tactile perception, aging.

University of Wisconsin–Whitewater, School of Graduate Studies, College of Letters and Sciences, Department of Psychology, Whitewater, WI 53190-1790. Offers school psychology (MSE, Ed S). *Program availability:* Part-time, evening/weekend, online learning. *Degree requirements:* For master's, comprehensive exam or thesis. *Entrance requirements:* For master's, MAT or GRE, interview, minimum GPA of 3.0, 3 letters of recommendation. Additional exam requirements/recommendations for international students: Required—TOEFL (minimum score 550 paper-based; 80 iBT), IELTS (minimum score 6). Electronic applications accepted. *Faculty research:* School violence/ youth violence; anger/aggression interventions; women's mental health; pedagogy of empathy, social psychology, and personality.

University of Wyoming, College of Arts and Sciences, Department of Psychology, Laramie, WY 82071. Offers MA, MS, PhD. *Accreditation:* APA (one or more programs are accredited). Terminal master's awarded for partial completion of doctoral program. *Degree requirements:* For master's, thesis; for doctorate, comprehensive exam, thesis/ dissertation. *Entrance requirements:* For master's and doctorate, GRE General Test, GRE Subject Test, minimum GPA of 3.0. Additional exam requirements/ recommendations for international students: Required—TOEFL. *Faculty research:* Child development, health psychology, psychology and law, social psychology, mood/anxiety disorders.

Utah State University, School of Graduate Studies, Emma Eccles Jones College of Education and Human Services, Department of Psychology, Logan, UT 84322. Offers clinical/counseling/school psychology (PhD); research and evaluation methodology (PhD); school counseling (MS); school psychology (MS). *Accreditation:* APA (one or more programs are accredited). *Program availability:* Part-time, evening/weekend, online learning. Terminal master's awarded for partial completion of doctoral program. *Degree requirements:* For master's, thesis (for some programs); for doctorate, thesis/ dissertation. *Entrance requirements:* For master's, GRE General Test (school psychology), MAT (school counseling), minimum GPA of 3.5; for doctorate, GRE General Test, minimum GPA of 3.5. Additional exam requirements/recommendations for international students: Required—TOEFL. *Faculty research:* Hearing loss detection in infancy, ADHD, eating disorders, domestic violence, neuropsychology, bilingual/Spanish speaking students/parents.

Valdosta State University, Department of Psychology, Counseling, and Family Therapy, Valdosta, GA 31698. Offers industrial/organizational psychology (MS); marriage and family therapy (MS); school counseling (M Ed, Ed S). *Accreditation:* AAMFT/COAMFTE. *Program availability:* Part-time, evening/weekend, 100% online, blended/hybrid learning. *Degree requirements:* For master's, thesis or alternative, comprehensive written and/or oral exams; for Ed S, thesis. *Entrance requirements:* For master's, GRE General Test or MAT, GACE; for Ed S, GRE General Test or MAT. Additional exam requirements/recommendations for international students: Required— TOEFL (minimum score 523 paper-based); Recommended—IELTS. *Application deadline:* For fall admission, 7/1 for domestic and international students; for spring admission, 11/15 for domestic and international students. Applications are processed on a rolling basis. Application fee: $45. Electronic applications accepted. *Expenses:* Contact institution. *Financial support:* Research assistantships with full tuition reimbursements, institutionally sponsored loans, and unspecified assistantships available. Support available to part-time students. Financial award application deadline: 7/1; financial award applicants required to submit FAFSA. *Unit head:* Dr. Kate Warner, Head, 229-293-6264, Fax: 229-259-5576, E-mail: kwarner@valdosta.edu. *Application contact:* Jessica Powers, Admission Specialist, 229-333-5694, Fax: 229-245-3853, E-mail: jldevane@valdosta.edu.
Website: https://www.valdosta.edu/colleges/education/pcft/

Vanderbilt University, Program in Psychological Sciences, Nashville, TN 37240-1001. Offers PhD. *Accreditation:* APA. *Faculty:* 49 full-time (20 women). *Students:* 74 full-time (49 women), 1 (woman) part-time; includes 6 minority (1 Black or African American, non-Hispanic/Latino; 1 Asian, non-Hispanic/Latino; 2 Hispanic/Latino; 2 Two or more races, non-Hispanic/Latino), 20 international. Average age 27. 486 applicants, 4% accepted, 8 enrolled. In 2017, 16 doctorates awarded. *Degree requirements:* For doctorate, comprehensive exam, thesis/dissertation, final and qualifying exams. *Entrance requirements:* For doctorate, GRE General Test, GRE Subject Test. Additional exam requirements/recommendations for international students: Required—TOEFL (minimum score 570 paper-based; 88 iBT). *Application deadline:* For fall admission, 12/1 for domestic and international students. Application fee: $0. Electronic applications accepted. *Expenses:* Contact institution. *Financial support:* Fellowships with full tuition reimbursements, research assistantships with full tuition reimbursements, teaching assistantships with full tuition reimbursements, career-related internships or fieldwork, Federal Work-Study, institutionally sponsored loans, scholarships/grants, traineeships, and health care benefits available. Financial award application deadline: 1/15; financial award applicants required to submit CSS PROFILE or FAFSA. *Faculty research:* Clinical, cognitive, developmental, and social psychology; neuroscience; vision; behavior. *Unit head:* Dr. Daniel T. Levin, Director of Graduate Studies for the Psychology of Human Development in Peabody College, 615-322-1518, Fax: 615-343-9494, E-mail: daniel.t.levin@vanderbilt.edu. *Application contact:* Dr. Rene Marois, Director of Graduate Studies for Psychological Studies in the College of Arts and Science, 615-322-1779, Fax: 615-343-5027, E-mail: r.marois@vanderbilt.edu.
Website: http://peabody.vanderbilt.edu/departments/psych/

Villanova University, Graduate School of Liberal Arts and Sciences, Department of Psychology, Villanova, PA 19085-1699. Offers MA, MS. *Program availability:* Part-time, evening/weekend. *Faculty:* 13. *Students:* 51 full-time (39 women); includes 8 minority (3 Black or African American, non-Hispanic/Latino; 1 Asian, non-Hispanic/Latino; 3 Hispanic/Latino; 1 Two or more races, non-Hispanic/Latino), 3 international. Average age 25. 94 applicants, 27% accepted, 20 enrolled. In 2017, 21 master's awarded. *Degree requirements:* For master's, thesis. *Entrance requirements:* For master's, GRE General Test, minimum GPA of 3.0, statement of goals. Additional exam requirements/ recommendations for international students: Required—TOEFL. *Application deadline:* For fall admission, 3/1 for domestic students, 5/1 priority date for international students; for spring admission, 11/15 for domestic students, 10/15 priority date for international students; for summer admission, 5/1 for domestic students. Applications are processed on a rolling basis. Application fee: $50. Electronic applications accepted. *Financial support:* Research assistantships, scholarships/grants, and unspecified assistantships available. Financial award applicants required to submit FAFSA. *Unit head:* Dr. Michael Brown, Director, 610-519-4720.
Website: http://www1.villanova.edu/villanova/artsci/psychology/graduate.html

Virginia Polytechnic Institute and State University, Graduate School, College of Science, Blacksburg, VA 24061. Offers biological sciences (MS, PhD); biomedical technology development and management (MS); chemistry (MS, PhD); data analysis and applied statistics (MA); economics (PhD); geosciences (MS, PhD); mathematics (MS, PhD); physics (MS, PhD); psychology (MS, PhD); statistics (MS, PhD). *Faculty:* 321 full-time (103 women). *Students:* 557 full-time (205 women), 39 part-time (18 women); includes 68 minority (13 Black or African American, non-Hispanic/Latino; 1 American Indian or Alaska Native, non-Hispanic/Latino; 14 Asian, non-Hispanic/Latino; 32 Hispanic/Latino; 8 Two or more races, non-Hispanic/Latino), 238 international. Average age 27. 1,060 applicants, 15% accepted, 121 enrolled. In 2017, 75 master's, 89 doctorates awarded. *Degree requirements:* For master's, comprehensive exam (for some programs), thesis (for some programs); for doctorate, comprehensive exam (for some programs), thesis/dissertation (for some programs). *Entrance requirements:* For master's and doctorate, GRE/GMAT. Additional exam requirements/recommendations for international students: Required—TOEFL (minimum score 80 iBT). *Application deadline:* For fall admission, 8/1 for domestic students, 4/1 for international students; for spring admission, 1/1 for domestic students, 9/1 for international students. Applications are processed on a rolling basis. Application fee: $75. Electronic applications accepted. *Expenses:* Tuition, state resident: full-time $15,072; part-time $718.50 per credit hour. Tuition, nonresident: full-time $28,810; part-time $1448.25 per credit hour. *Required fees:* $2741; $502 per semester. Tuition and fees vary according to course load, campus/location and program. *Financial support:* In 2017–18, 2 fellowships with full tuition reimbursements (averaging $12,267 per year), 140 research assistantships with full tuition reimbursements (averaging $23,004 per year), 351 teaching assistantships with full tuition reimbursements (averaging $20,157 per year) were awarded. Financial award application deadline: 3/1; financial award applicants required to submit FAFSA. *Total annual research expenditures:* $24.3 million. *Unit head:* Dr. Sally C. Morton, Dean, 540-231-5422, Fax: 540-231-3380, E-mail: scmorton@vt.edu. *Application contact:* Allison Craft, Executive Assistant, 540-231-6394, Fax: 540-231-3380, E-mail: crafta@vt.edu.
Website: http://www.science.vt.edu/

Virginia State University, College of Graduate Studies, College of Natural and Health Sciences, Department of Psychology, Petersburg, VA 23806-0001. Offers behavioral and community health sciences (PhD); clinical health psychology (PhD); clinical psychology (MS); general psychology (MS). *Degree requirements:* For master's, one foreign language, thesis. *Entrance requirements:* For master's, GRE General Test.

Wake Forest University, Graduate School of Arts and Sciences, Department of Psychology, Winston-Salem, NC 27109. Offers MA. *Degree requirements:* For master's, one foreign language, comprehensive exam, thesis. *Entrance requirements:* For master's, GRE General Test. Additional exam requirements/recommendations for international students: Required—TOEFL (minimum score 79 iBT). Electronic applications accepted. *Faculty research:* Developmental, social, personality, experimental, and physiological psychology.

Walden University, Graduate Programs, School of Psychology, Minneapolis, MN 55401. Offers clinical psychology (MS), including counseling, general program; forensic psychology (MS), including forensic psychology in the community, general program, mental health applications, program planning and evaluation in forensic settings, psychology and legal systems; industrial organizational (MS, PhD), including consulting psychology, forensic (MS), forensic psychology (PhD), general practice, leadership development and coaching (MS), organizational diversity and social change, research evaluation (PhD); online teaching in psychology (Post-Master's Certificate); organizational psychology and development (Postbaccalaureate Certificate); psychology (MS, PhD), including applied psychology (MS), clinical psychology (PhD), crisis management and response (MS), educational psychology, forensic psychology (PhD), general psychology (MS), general psychology research (PhD), general

psychology teaching (PhD), health psychology, leadership development and coaching (MS), psychology of culture (MS), psychology, public administration, and social change (MS), social psychology, terrorism and security (MS); psychology respecialization (Post-Doctoral Certificate). *Program availability:* Part-time, evening/weekend, online only, 100% online. Terminal master's awarded for partial completion of doctoral program. *Degree requirements:* For master's, thesis optional; for doctorate, thesis/dissertation, residency. *Entrance requirements:* For master's, bachelor's degree or higher; minimum GPA of 2.5; official transcripts; goal statement (for some programs); access to computer and Internet; for doctorate, master's degree or higher; three years of related professional or academic experience (preferred); minimum GPA of 3.0; goal statement and current resume (for select programs); official transcripts; access to computer and Internet; for other advanced degree, relevant work experience; access to computer and Internet. Additional exam requirements/recommendations for international students: Required—TOEFL (minimum score 550 paper-based, 79 iBT), IELTS (minimum score 6.5), Michigan English Language Assessment Battery (minimum score 82), or PTE (minimum score 53). Electronic applications accepted.

Washburn University, College of Arts and Sciences, Department of Psychology, Topeka, KS 66621. Offers clinical psychology (MA). *Program availability:* Part-time. *Degree requirements:* For master's, comprehensive exam (for some programs), thesis or alternative. *Entrance requirements:* For master's, GRE General Test, 15 hours of undergraduate course work in psychology. Additional exam requirements/recommendations for international students: Required—TOEFL (minimum score 80 iBT). Electronic applications accepted. *Faculty research:* Metacognition, anxiety disorders, auditory perception, sports performance psychology, ADHD.

Washington State University, College of Arts and Sciences, Department of Psychology, Pullman, WA 99164. Offers clinical psychology (PhD); experimental psychology (PhD). Program applications must be made through the Pullman campus. *Accreditation:* APA (one or more programs are accredited). *Degree requirements:* For doctorate, comprehensive exam, thesis/dissertation, oral exam, written exam. *Entrance requirements:* For doctorate, GRE General Test, three letters of reference; summary data form; at least 18 credits of study in psychology; at least one course in statistics and research methodology; official transcripts; minimum cumulative undergraduate GPA of 3.0 or master's degree in psychology. Additional exam requirements/recommendations for international students: Required—TOEFL, IELTS. Electronic applications accepted. *Faculty research:* Adult psychopathology and therapy, child psychopathology, neuropsychology, health psychology.

Washington University in St. Louis, The Graduate School, Department of Philosophy, Program in Philosophy-Neuroscience-Psychology, St. Louis, MO 63130-4899. Offers PhD. *Degree requirements:* For doctorate, thesis/dissertation. *Entrance requirements:* For doctorate, GRE General Test, sample of written work. Additional exam requirements/recommendations for international students: Required—TOEFL. Electronic applications accepted. *Faculty research:* Philosophy of mind and language with a special emphasis on the philosophical dimensions of psychology, neuroscience, and linguistics.

Washington University in St. Louis, The Graduate School, Department of Psychological and Brain Sciences, St. Louis, MO 63130-4899. Offers aging and development (PhD). Terminal master's awarded for partial completion of doctoral program. *Degree requirements:* For doctorate, thesis/dissertation. *Entrance requirements:* For doctorate, GRE General Test. Additional exam requirements/recommendations for international students: Required—TOEFL. Electronic applications accepted. *Faculty research:* Behavior/brain/cognition; clinical; aging/development; social/personality.

Wayne State University, College of Liberal Arts and Sciences, Department of Psychology, Detroit, MI 48202. Offers behavioral and cognitive neuroscience (PhD); clinical psychology (PhD); developmental science (PhD); industrial/organizational psychology (MA, PhD); social personality (PhD). Doctoral program admits for fall only. *Accreditation:* APA (one or more programs are accredited). *Faculty:* 38. *Students:* 94 full-time (63 women), 43 part-time (29 women); includes 23 minority (6 Black or African American, non-Hispanic/Latino; 3 Asian, non-Hispanic/Latino; 10 Hispanic/Latino; 4 Two or more races, non-Hispanic/Latino), 12 international. Average age 27. 478 applicants, 11% accepted, 39 enrolled. In 2017, 29 master's, 27 doctorates awarded. Terminal master's awarded for partial completion of doctoral program. *Degree requirements:* For master's, thesis (for some programs); for doctorate, thesis/dissertation, training assignments. *Entrance requirements:* For master's, GRE General Test, minimum undergraduate upper-division cumulative GPA of 3.0, courses in psychology and statistics; for doctorate, GRE General Test, bachelor's, master's, or other advanced degree; at least twelve credits in psychology with minimum GPA of 3.0; courses in laboratory psychology and statistical methods in psychology; at least three letters of recommendation; statement of purpose. Additional exam requirements/recommendations for international students: Required—TOEFL (minimum score 550 paper-based; 79 iBT), TWE (minimum score 5.5), Michigan English Language Assessment Battery (minimum score 85); Recommended—IELTS (minimum score 6.5). Application fee: $50. Electronic applications accepted. *Expenses:* Tuition, state resident: full-time $10,224; part-time $638.98 per credit hour. Tuition, nonresident: full-time $22,145; part-time $1384.04 per credit hour. Tuition and fees vary according to course load and program. *Financial support:* In 2017–18, 90 students received support, including 13 fellowships with tuition reimbursements available (averaging $11,212 per year), 8 research assistantships with tuition reimbursements available (averaging $18,534 per year), 50 teaching assistantships with tuition reimbursements available (averaging $18,534 per year); scholarships/grants, health care benefits, and unspecified assistantships also available. Financial award applicants required to submit FAFSA. *Faculty research:* Behavioral neuroscience, cognitive/neuroscience of development and aging research, children, adolescents, and family research, cognition research, emotion research, health psychology research, homelessness and poverty research, memory research, neuropsychology research, personality/cognition, relationships research, substance use and abuse research, workplace adaptation, well-being and evaluation research. *Unit head:* Boris Baltes, PhD, Chair/Professor, 313-577-2803, E-mail: b.baltes@wayne.edu. *Application contact:* Alia Allen, Academic Services Officer, 313-577-2823, E-mail: aallen@wayne.edu.
Website: http://clas.wayne.edu/psychology/

Webster University, College of Arts and Sciences, Department of Psychology, St. Louis, MO 63119-3194. Offers counseling psychology (MS); gerontology (MS). *Program availability:* Part-time. *Entrance requirements:* Additional exam requirements/recommendations for international students: Required—TOEFL.

West Chester University of Pennsylvania, College of the Sciences and Mathematics, Department of Psychology, West Chester, PA 19383. Offers clinical psychology (Psy D); industrial/organizational psychology (Certificate); psychology (MA), including general psychology, industrial/organizational psychology. *Program availability:* Part-time, evening/weekend, 100% online. *Students:* 56 full-time (37 women), 28 part-time (20 women); includes 18 minority (9 Black or African American, non-Hispanic/Latino; 2 Asian, non-Hispanic/Latino; 4 Hispanic/Latino; 3 Two or more races, non-Hispanic/Latino). Average age 26. 125 applicants, 62% accepted, 42 enrolled. In 2017, 47 master's awarded. Terminal master's awarded for partial completion of doctoral

program. *Degree requirements:* For master's, comprehensive exam (for some programs), thesis optional; for doctorate, comprehensive exam, thesis/dissertation, year-long pre-doctoral internship. *Entrance requirements:* For master's, GRE General Test, minimum GPA of 3.0 overall, psychology 3.25; three letters of reference; for doctorate, GRE General Test, minimum undergraduate GPA of 3.0 or graduate 3.3; three letters of reference; curriculum vitae; completion of courses (at the undergraduate level) in abnormal/clinical psychology, personality, research methods, and statistics; professional goals statement. Additional exam requirements/recommendations for international students: Required—TOEFL or IELTS. *Application deadline:* For fall admission, 5/15 for international students; for spring admission, 10/15 for international students. Applications are processed on a rolling basis. Application fee: $50. Electronic applications accepted. *Expenses:* Tuition, state resident: full-time $9000; part-time $500 per credit. Tuition, nonresident: full-time $13,500; part-time $750 per credit. *Required fees:* $2959; $149.79 per credit. *Financial support:* Scholarships/grants and unspecified assistantships available. Financial award application deadline: 2/15; financial award applicants required to submit FAFSA. *Faculty research:* Child and adolescent mental health, trauma, stress, coping and resilience, preventative interventions workplace stress, organizational leadership, eating disorders, several other areas including diversity, cognition, and animal behavior. *Unit head:* Dr. Sandra Kerr, Chairperson, 610-436-2945, E-mail: skerr@wcupa.edu. *Application contact:* Dr. Angela Clarke, Director of Clinical Training, Clinical Psychology PsyD Program, 610-436-3136, E-mail: aclarke@wcupa.edu.
Website: http://www.wcupa.edu/sciences-mathematics/psychology/

Western Carolina University, Graduate School, College of Education and Allied Professions, Department of Psychology, Cullowhee, NC 28723. Offers general psychology (MA). *Program availability:* Part-time. *Degree requirements:* For master's, comprehensive exam, thesis. *Entrance requirements:* For master's, GRE General Test, appropriate undergraduate degree, interview, 3 letters of recommendation. Additional exam requirements/recommendations for international students: Required—TOEFL (minimum score 550 paper-based; 79 iBT). *Expenses:* Tuition, state resident: full-time $4436. Tuition, nonresident: full-time $14,842. *Required fees:* $2926. *Faculty research:* Five-factor model of personality, evolutionary psychology, stress and worry, body image and physical attractiveness, moral decision-making, memory, learning styles.

Western Illinois University, School of Graduate Studies, College of Arts and Sciences, Department of Psychology, Macomb, IL 61455-1390. Offers clinical/community mental health (MS); general experimental psychology (MS); school psychology (SSP). *Program availability:* Part-time. *Students:* 39 full-time (28 women), 15 part-time (8 women); includes 6 minority (1 Black or African American, non-Hispanic/Latino; 2 Asian, non-Hispanic/Latino; 1 Hispanic/Latino; 2 Two or more races, non-Hispanic/Latino), 2 international. Average age 26. 77 applicants, 77% accepted, 30 enrolled. In 2017, 8 master's, 6 other advanced degrees awarded. *Degree requirements:* For master's, comprehensive exam (for some programs), thesis or alternative. *Entrance requirements:* For master's and SSP, GRE General Test. Additional exam requirements/recommendations for international students: Required—TOEFL (minimum score 550 paper-based; 80 iBT). Application fee: $30. Electronic applications accepted. *Financial support:* In 2017–18, 6 research assistantships with full tuition reimbursements (averaging $7,544 per year) were awarded; unspecified assistantships also available. Financial award applicants required to submit FAFSA. *Unit head:* Dr. Karen Sears, Chairperson, 309-298-1593. *Application contact:* Dr. Nancy Parsons, Associate Provost and Director of Graduate Studies, 309-298-1806, Fax: 309-298-2345, E-mail: grad-office@wiu.edu.
Website: http://wiu.edu/psychology

Western Kentucky University, Graduate Studies, College of Education and Behavioral Sciences, Department of Psychology, Bowling Green, KY 42101. Offers clinical psychology (MA); experimental psychology (MA); general psychology (MA); industrial/organizational psychology (MA); school psychology (Ed S). *Degree requirements:* For master's, comprehensive exam, thesis (for some programs); for Ed S, thesis, oral exam. *Entrance requirements:* For master's, GRE General Test; for Ed S, GRE General Test, minimum GPA of 3.5. Additional exam requirements/recommendations for international students: Required—TOEFL (minimum score 555 paper-based; 79 iBT). *Faculty research:* Neural regeneration, enhancing mobility in the elderly, improvement in visual processing in older adults, lifespan development.

Western Michigan University, Graduate College, College of Arts and Sciences, Department of Psychology, Kalamazoo, MI 49008. Offers behavior analysis (MA, PhD); clinical psychology (PhD); industrial/organizational behavior management (MA). *Accreditation:* APA (one or more programs are accredited). *Degree requirements:* For master's, variable foreign language requirement, thesis; for doctorate, 2 foreign languages, comprehensive exam, thesis/dissertation.

Western Washington University, Graduate School, College of Humanities and Social Sciences, Department of Psychology, Bellingham, WA 98225-5996. Offers experimental psychology (MS); mental health counseling (MS); school counseling (M Ed). *Accreditation:* ACA (one or more programs are accredited). *Degree requirements:* For master's, comprehensive exam, thesis (for some programs). *Entrance requirements:* For master's, GRE General Test, minimum GPA of 3.0 in last 60 semester hours or last 90 quarter hours. Additional exam requirements/recommendations for international students: Required—TOEFL (minimum score 567 paper-based). *Faculty research:* Social, cognitive, behavioral neuroscience, counseling/clinical, developmental.

Westfield State University, College of Graduate and Continuing Education, Department of Psychology, Westfield, MA 01086. Offers applied behavior analysis (MA); counseling (MA), including forensic mental health counseling, mental health counseling, school adjustment counseling, school guidance counseling. *Program availability:* Part-time, evening/weekend. *Faculty:* 8 full-time (3 women), 8 part-time/adjunct (5 women). *Students:* 53 full-time (40 women), 27 part-time (19 women); includes 12 minority (1 Black or African American, non-Hispanic/Latino; 2 Asian, non-Hispanic/Latino; 6 Hispanic/Latino; 3 Two or more races, non-Hispanic/Latino). Average age 29. 44 applicants, 84% accepted, 28 enrolled. In 2017, 22 master's awarded. *Degree requirements:* For master's, comprehensive exam, practicum. *Entrance requirements:* For master's, GRE General Test, MAT, minimum undergraduate GPA of 3.0. Additional exam requirements/recommendations for international students: Recommended—TOEFL (minimum score 550 paper-based; 79 iBT). *Application deadline:* For fall admission, 2/1 for domestic students. Applications are processed on a rolling basis. Application fee: $50. *Expenses:* Tuition, state resident: part-time $332 per credit. Tuition, nonresident: part-time $332 per credit. *Required fees:* $75 per semester. Tuition and fees vary according to program. *Financial support:* Unspecified assistantships available. Financial award application deadline: 3/1; financial award applicants required to submit FAFSA. *Unit head:* Dr. Ricki Kantrowitz, Director, 413-572-5378. *Application contact:* Shelly Henrichon, Coordinator of College of Graduate and Continuing Education Admissions, 413-572-8022, Fax: 413-572-5227, E-mail: mhenrichon@westfield.ma.edu.

West Texas A&M University, College of Education and Social Sciences, Department of Psychology, Sociology and Social Work, Canyon, TX 79015. Offers psychology (MA); social work (MS). *Program availability:* Part-time, evening/weekend. *Degree requirements:* For master's, comprehensive exam, thesis optional. *Entrance*

requirements: For master's, GRE General Test, 3 letters of recommendation; interview; minimum GPA of 3.25 in psychology, 3.0 overall. Additional exam requirements/recommendations for international students: Required—TOEFL. Electronic applications accepted.

West Virginia University, Eberly College of Arts and Sciences, Morgantown, WV 26506. Offers biology (MS, PhD); chemistry (MS, PhD); communication studies (MA, PhD); computational statistics (PhD); creative writing (MFA); English (MA, PhD); forensic and investigative science (MS); forensic science (PhD); geography (MA); geology (MA, PhD); history (MA, PhD); legal studies (MLS); math (MS); physics (MS, PhD); political science (MA, PhD); professional writing and editing (MA); psychology (MA); public administration (MPA); social work (MSW); sociology (MA, PhD); statistics (MS). *Program availability:* Part-time, evening/weekend, online learning. *Students:* 831 full-time (437 women), 236 part-time (142 women); includes 112 minority (35 Black or African American, non-Hispanic/Latino; 15 Asian, non-Hispanic/Latino; 29 Hispanic/Latino; 33 Two or more races, non-Hispanic/Latino), 235 international. Terminal master's awarded for partial completion of doctoral program. *Degree requirements:* For master's, thesis (for some programs); for doctorate, comprehensive exam, thesis/dissertation. *Entrance requirements:* For master's and doctorate, GRE. Additional exam requirements/recommendations for international students: Required—TOEFL (minimum score 600 paper-based); Recommended—TWE. *Application deadline:* For spring admission, 2/15 priority date for domestic and international students. Applications are processed on a rolling basis. Application fee: $45. Electronic applications accepted. *Expenses:* Tuition, state resident: full-time $9450. Tuition, nonresident: full-time $24,390. *Financial support:* Fellowships with full tuition reimbursements, research assistantships with full tuition reimbursements, teaching assistantships with full tuition reimbursements, career-related internships or fieldwork, Federal Work-Study, institutionally sponsored loans, scholarships/grants, health care benefits, tuition waivers (full and partial), unspecified assistantships, and administrative assistantships available. Financial award application deadline: 2/1; financial award applicants required to submit FAFSA. *Faculty research:* Humanities, social sciences, life science, physical sciences, mathematics. *Unit head:* Dr. Mary Ellen Mazey, Dean, 304-293-4611, Fax: 304-293-6858, E-mail: mary.mazey@mail.wvu.edu. *Application contact:* Dr. Fred L. King, Associate Dean for Graduate Studies, 304-293-4611 Ext. 5205, Fax: 304-293-6858, E-mail: fred.king@mail.wvu.edu.
Website: http://www.as.wvu.edu/

Wheaton College, Graduate School, Department of Psychology, Wheaton, IL 60187-5593. Offers clinical mental health counseling (MA); clinical psychology (Psy D); marriage and family therapy (MA). *Accreditation:* APA (one or more programs are accredited). *Faculty:* 15 full-time (7 women), 12 part-time/adjunct (9 women). *Students:* 132 full-time (99 women), 26 part-time (13 women); includes 40 minority (12 Black or African American, non-Hispanic/Latino; 2 American Indian or Alaska Native, non-Hispanic/Latino; 12 Asian, non-Hispanic/Latino; 7 Hispanic/Latino; 7 Two or more races, non-Hispanic/Latino), 28 international. Average age 28. 139 applicants, 74% accepted, 69 enrolled. In 2017, 62 master's, 20 doctorates awarded. Terminal master's awarded for partial completion of doctoral program. *Degree requirements:* For master's, thesis or alternative; for doctorate, thesis/dissertation, internship. *Entrance requirements:* For master's, GRE General Test, 18 hours of course work in psychology; for doctorate, GRE General Test. Additional exam requirements/recommendations for international students: Required—TOEFL (minimum score 550 paper-based; 80 iBT), IELTS (minimum score 6.5). *Application deadline:* For fall admission, 3/1 priority date for domestic students, 1/1 for international students. Applications are processed on a rolling basis. Application fee: $30. *Expenses: Tuition:* Full-time $19,800; part-time $825 per credit hour. Tuition and fees vary according to degree level and program. *Financial support:* In 2017–18, 3 research assistantships (averaging $4,800 per year) were awarded; career-related internships or fieldwork, Federal Work-Study, scholarships/grants, and unspecified assistantships also available. Financial award application deadline: 3/1; financial award applicants required to submit FAFSA. *Unit head:* Dr. Terri Watson, Associate Dean of Psychology, 630-752-5104, E-mail: psychology@wheaton.edu. *Application contact:* Director of Graduate Admissions, 630-752-5195, Fax: 630-752-7047, E-mail: graduate.admissions@wheaton.edu.
Website: https://www.wheaton.edu/academics/programs/psychology/graduate-programs/

Wichita State University, Graduate School, Fairmount College of Liberal Arts and Sciences, Department of Psychology, Wichita, KS 67260. Offers clinical (PhD); community (PhD); human factors (PhD). *Accreditation:* APA. *Program availability:* Part-time. *Application deadline:* For fall admission, 12/1 for domestic and international students. Application fee: $50 ($65 for international students). *Unit head:* Dr. Rhonda K. Lewis, Chair, 316-978-3170, Fax: 316-978-3006, E-mail: rhonda.lewis@wichita.edu. *Application contact:* Jordan Oleson, Admissions Coordinator, 316-978-3095, Fax: 316-978-3253, E-mail: jordan.oleson@wichita.edu.
Website: http://www.wichita.edu/psychology

Widener University, School of Human Service Professions, Institute for Graduate Clinical Psychology, Law-Psychology Program, Chester, PA 19013-5792. Offers JD/Psy D. *Faculty:* 15 full-time (6 women), 18 part-time/adjunct (10 women). *Students:* 2 full-time (both women). Average age 28. 21 applicants, 19% accepted. *Application deadline:* For fall admission, 2/1 for domestic students. Applications are processed on a rolling basis. Application fee: $60. Electronic applications accepted. *Financial support:* Research assistantships, career-related internships or fieldwork, Federal Work-Study, institutionally sponsored loans, and scholarships/grants available. Financial award application deadline: 5/31.

Wilfrid Laurier University, Faculty of Graduate and Postdoctoral Studies, Faculty of Science, Department of Psychology, Waterloo, ON N2L 3C5, Canada. Offers behavioral neuroscience (M Sc, PhD); cognitive neuroscience (M Sc, PhD); community psychology (MA, PhD); social and developmental psychology (MA, PhD). *Program availability:* Part-time. *Degree requirements:* For master's, thesis; for doctorate, thesis/dissertation. *Entrance requirements:* For master's, GRE General Test, honors BA or the equivalent in psychology, minimum B average in undergraduate course work; for doctorate, GRE General Test, master's degree, minimum A- average. Additional exam requirements/recommendations for international students: Required—TOEFL (minimum score 89 iBT). Electronic applications accepted. *Faculty research:* Brain and cognition, community psychology, social and developmental psychology.

William Carey University, Department of Psychology and Graduate Counseling, Hattiesburg, MS 39401. Offers counseling psychology (MS). *Program availability:* Part-time. *Entrance requirements:* For master's, GRE, PRAXIS, MAT, minimum GPA of 2.5. Additional exam requirements/recommendations for international students: Required—

TOEFL (minimum score 550 paper-based). *Expenses:* Contact institution. *Faculty research:* Addiction prevention, psychometric measurement, crisis counseling, gerontology.

William James College, Graduate Programs, Newton, MA 02459. Offers applied psychology in higher education student personnel administration (MA); clinical psychology (Psy D); counseling psychology (MA); counseling psychology and community mental health (MA); counseling psychology and global mental health (MA); executive coaching (Graduate Certificate); forensic and counseling psychology (MA); leadership psychology (Psy D); organizational psychology (MA); primary care psychology (MA); respecialization in clinical psychology (Certificate); school psychology (Psy D); MA/CAGS. *Accreditation:* APA. *Degree requirements:* For master's, comprehensive exam (for some programs); for doctorate, thesis/dissertation (for some programs). Electronic applications accepted.

Winthrop University, College of Arts and Sciences, Department of Psychology, Rock Hill, SC 29733. Offers MS, SSP. *Students:* 32 full-time (25 women); includes 3 minority (1 Black or African American, non-Hispanic/Latino; 2 Hispanic/Latino). Average age 25. In 2017, 9 master's, 8 other advanced degrees awarded. *Degree requirements:* For master's, comprehensive exam; for SSP, thesis or alternative, portfolio. *Entrance requirements:* For master's, GRE General Test, interview, minimum GPA of 3.0, 3 letters of recommendation, 15 hours of psychology courses in specified subject areas. Additional exam requirements/recommendations for international students: Required—TOEFL (minimum score 550 paper-based; 79 iBT), IELTS (minimum score 6). *Application deadline:* For fall admission, 2/15 priority date for domestic students. Application fee: $50. Electronic applications accepted. *Financial support:* Research assistantships with full tuition reimbursements, career-related internships or fieldwork, Federal Work-Study, scholarships/grants, and unspecified assistantships available. Support available to part-time students. Financial award application deadline: 2/1; financial award applicants required to submit FAFSA. *Unit head:* Dr. Joe Prus, Chair, 803-323-2117, E-mail: prusj@winthrop.edu. *Application contact:* 800-411-7041, Fax: 803-323-2292, E-mail: gradschool@winthrop.edu.
Website: http://www.winthrop.edu/graduateschool/schoolpsychology

Wisconsin School of Professional Psychology, Program in Clinical Psychology, Milwaukee, WI 53225-4960. Offers MA, Psy D. *Accreditation:* APA. *Program availability:* Part-time, evening/weekend. Terminal master's awarded for partial completion of doctoral program. *Degree requirements:* For master's, candidacy exam, 500 hours of supervised clinical practica; for doctorate, thesis/dissertation, 1 year clinical intern and practicum experience (2000 hrs), candidacy and clinical exams. *Entrance requirements:* For master's, GRE General Test, GRE Subject Test, bachelor's degree in psychology, writing sample; for doctorate, GRE General Test, GRE Subject Test, master's degree in clinical psychology or equivalent, writing sample. *Faculty research:* Violence prevention, psychology of women, forensic psychology, custody evaluation, aging, harm reduction in AODA.

The Wright Institute, Doctoral Program in Clinical Psychology, Berkeley, CA 94704-1796. Offers Psy D. *Degree requirements:* For doctorate, comprehensive exam, thesis/dissertation. *Entrance requirements:* For doctorate, GRE General Test, statistics, human development, theories of personality and/or abnormal psychology. Additional exam requirements/recommendations for international students: Required—TOEFL (minimum score 600 paper-based). Electronic applications accepted.

Wright State University, Graduate School, College of Science and Mathematics, Department of Psychology, Dayton, OH 45435. Offers human factors and industrial/organizational psychology (MS, PhD). *Degree requirements:* For master's, thesis; for doctorate, thesis/dissertation. *Entrance requirements:* For master's, GRE General Test. Additional exam requirements/recommendations for international students: Required—TOEFL.

Wright State University, School of Professional Psychology, Dayton, OH 45435. Offers clinical psychology (Psy D). *Accreditation:* APA. *Degree requirements:* For doctorate, thesis/dissertation. *Entrance requirements:* For doctorate, GRE General Test, GRE Subject Test. Additional exam requirements/recommendations for international students: Required—TOEFL. *Expenses:* Contact institution.

Xavier University, College of Social Sciences, Health and Education, Department of Psychology, Cincinnati, OH 45207. Offers clinical psychology (Psy D); industrial-organizational psychology (MA). *Accreditation:* APA (one or more programs are accredited). *Degree requirements:* For master's, one foreign language, comprehensive exam, thesis, internship; for doctorate, one foreign language, comprehensive exam, thesis/dissertation, internship. *Entrance requirements:* For master's, GRE, official transcript; 3 letters of recommendation; for doctorate, GRE General Test; GRE Subject Test in psychology (if no undergraduate degree in psychology), bachelor's or master's degree; 18 semester hours of psychology coursework; minimum GPA of 3.0; work and research experience; official transcript; 3 letters of recommendation; statement of purpose. Additional exam requirements/recommendations for international students: Required—TOEFL (minimum score 550 paper-based; 79 iBT), IELTS (minimum score 6.5). Electronic applications accepted. *Expenses:* Contact institution. *Faculty research:* Older adults, clinical child and adolescent issues, personnel selection and employee behavior, at-risk youth, sexual abuse.

Yale University, Graduate School of Arts and Sciences, Department of Psychology, New Haven, CT 06520. Offers behavioral neuroscience (PhD); clinical psychology (PhD); cognitive psychology (PhD); developmental psychology (PhD); social/personality psychology (PhD). *Accreditation:* APA. *Degree requirements:* For doctorate, thesis/dissertation. *Entrance requirements:* For doctorate, GRE General Test.

Yeshiva University, Ferkauf Graduate School of Psychology, New York, NY 10033-3201. Offers MA, PhD, Psy D. *Accreditation:* APA (one or more programs are accredited). *Program availability:* Part-time. *Degree requirements:* For doctorate, comprehensive exam, thesis/dissertation. *Entrance requirements:* For master's and doctorate, GRE General Test.

York University, Faculty of Graduate Studies, Faculty of Health, Program in Psychology, Toronto, ON M3J 1P3, Canada. Offers MA, PhD. *Program availability:* Part-time. *Degree requirements:* For master's, thesis, practicum; for doctorate, thesis/dissertation, practicum. *Entrance requirements:* For master's, GRE. Electronic applications accepted.

Youngstown State University, Graduate School, College of Liberal Arts and Social Sciences, Department of Psychology, Youngstown, OH 44555-0001. Offers applied behavior analysis (MS).

Addictions/Substance Abuse Counseling

Adler Graduate School, Program in Adlerian Counseling and Psychotherapy, Richfield, MN 55423. Offers Adlerian studies (MA); art therapy (MA); clinical mental health counseling (MA); co-occurring substance use and mental health disorders (MA); marriage and family therapy (MA); school counseling (MA). *Program availability:* Part-time, evening/weekend. *Faculty:* 71 part-time/adjunct (55 women). *Students:* 317 part-time (259 women); includes 51 minority (40 Black or African American, non-Hispanic/Latino; 6 American Indian or Alaska Native, non-Hispanic/Latino; 5 Hispanic/Latino). *Degree requirements:* For master's, thesis or alternative, 500-700 hour internship (depending on license choice). *Entrance requirements:* For master's, interview, official transcripts, minimum cumulative GPA of 3.0. *Application deadline:* Applications are processed on a rolling basis. Application fee: $50. Electronic applications accepted. *Expenses:* $575 per credit tuition. *Financial support:* Career-related internships or fieldwork and tuition waivers available. Support available to part-time students. Financial award applicants required to submit FAFSA. *Unit head:* Dr. Jeffrey Allen, President, 612-767-7048, Fax: 612-861-7559, E-mail: jeffrey.allen@alfredadler.edu. *Application contact:* Christina Hilpipre-Frischman, Director of Admissions, 612-767-7055, Fax: 612-861-7559, E-mail: christina@alfredadler.edu.
Website: http://alfredadler.edu/programs/masters-level-programs

Adler University, Graduate Programs, Certificate Programs, Chicago, IL 60602. Offers couple and family therapy (Certificate); substance abuse counseling (Certificate). *Entrance requirements:* For degree, baccalaureate degree, minimum GPA of 3.0.

Alliant International University–Los Angeles, California School of Professional Psychology, Program in Couple and Family Therapy, Alhambra, CA 91803. Offers chemical dependency (MA); gerontology (MA); Latin American family therapy (MA). *Accreditation:* AAMFT/COAMFTE. *Program availability:* Part-time, evening/weekend. Terminal master's awarded for partial completion of doctoral program. *Degree requirements:* For master's, comprehensive exam, 50 hours of professional development activities. *Entrance requirements:* Additional exam requirements/recommendations for international students: Required—TOEFL (minimum score 550 paper-based). Electronic applications accepted. *Faculty research:* Foster care, therapy with minority couples, parenting, marriage, trauma.

Antioch University New England, Graduate School, Department of Applied Psychology, Program in Clinical Mental Health Counseling, Keene, NH 03431-3552. Offers clinical mental health counseling (MA); substance abuse counseling (MA). *Accreditation:* ACA. *Degree requirements:* For master's, internship, practicum. *Entrance requirements:* For master's, previous course work and work experience in psychology. Additional exam requirements/recommendations for international students: Required—TOEFL (minimum score 550 paper-based). Electronic applications accepted. *Expenses:* Contact institution. *Faculty research:* Multicultural issues in field supervision.

Argosy University, Hawai`i, Hawai'i School of Professional Psychology, Program in Substance Abuse Counseling, Honolulu, HI 96813. Offers Certificate.

Arkansas State University, Graduate School, College of Nursing and Health Professions, Department of Social Work, State University, AR 72467. Offers addiction studies (Graduate Certificate); social work (MSW). *Accreditation:* CSWE. *Program availability:* Part-time. *Degree requirements:* For master's and Graduate Certificate, comprehensive exam, thesis (for some programs). *Entrance requirements:* For master's and Graduate Certificate, GRE or MAT, appropriate bachelor's degree, letters of reference, personal statement, resume, official transcript, immunization records. Additional exam requirements/recommendations for international students: Required—TOEFL (minimum score 550 paper-based; 79 iBT), IELTS (minimum score 6), PTE (minimum score 56). Electronic applications accepted. *Expenses:* Contact institution.

Assumption College, Addiction Counseling Program, Worcester, MA 01609-1296. Offers CGS. *Program availability:* Part-time, evening/weekend. *Entrance requirements:* For degree, bachelor's degree, three letters of recommendation, official transcripts, personal statement, current resume. Additional exam requirements/recommendations for international students: Required—TOEFL (minimum score 540 paper-based; 76 iBT), IELTS (minimum score 6). *Application deadline:* Applications are processed on a rolling basis. Application fee: $30. Electronic applications accepted. *Expenses: Tuition:* Full-time $11,952; part-time $664 per credit. *Required fees:* $70 per term. *Unit head:* Dr. Leonard A. Doerfler, Director, 508-767-7549, Fax: 508-767-7263, E-mail: doerfler@assumption.edu. *Application contact:* Karen Stoyanoff, Director of Recruitment for Graduate Enrollment, 508-767-7442, Fax: 508-799-4412, E-mail: graduate@assumption.edu.
Website: http://graduate.assumption.edu/addiction-counseling

Bay Path University, Program in Clinical Mental Health Counseling, Longmeadow, MA 01106-2292. Offers clinical mental health counseling (MS), including alcohol and drug abuse counseling, early intervention. Program also offered in Sturbridge and Burlington, MA. *Program availability:* Part-time, blended/hybrid learning. *Students:* 68 full-time (59 women), 82 part-time (75 women); includes 42 minority (21 Black or African American, non-Hispanic/Latino; 19 Hispanic/Latino; 2 Two or more races, non-Hispanic/Latino), 11 international. Average age 32. In 2017, 21 master's awarded. *Degree requirements:* For master's, 48 course credits plus 12 credit practicum, internship. *Application deadline:* Applications are processed on a rolling basis. Application fee: $45. Electronic applications accepted. Application fee is waived when completed online. *Expenses:* $815 per credit. *Financial support:* Unspecified assistantships available. Financial award applicants required to submit FAFSA. *Unit head:* Dr. Mark Benander, Director, 413-565-1332, E-mail: mbenander@baypath.edu. *Application contact:* Diane Ranaldi, Dean of Graduate Admissions, 413-565-1332, Fax: 413-565-1250, E-mail: dranaldi@baypath.edu.
Website: http://graduate.baypath.edu/graduate-programs/programs-on-campus/ms-programs/clinical-mental-health

Cambridge College, School of Psychology and Counseling, Boston, MA 02129. Offers addiction counseling (M Ed); alcohol and drug counseling (Certificate); counseling psychology (M Ed, CAGS); counseling psychology: forensic counseling (M Ed); marriage and family therapy (M Ed); mental health and addiction counseling (M Ed); mental health counseling (M Ed); mental health counseling for school guidance counselors (Post Master's Certificate); psychological studies (M Ed); school adjustment and mental health counseling (M Ed); school adjustment, mental health and addiction counseling (M Ed); school guidance counselor (M Ed); trauma studies (Certificate). *Program availability:* Part-time, evening/weekend. *Degree requirements:* For master's and other advanced degree, thesis, practicum/internship. *Entrance requirements:* For master's, resume, 2 professional references; for other advanced degree, official transcripts, documents for transfer credit evaluation, resume, written personal statement/essay, 2 professional references, health insurance, immunizations form. Additional exam requirements/recommendations for international students: Required—TOEFL (minimum score 550 paper-based; 79 iBT), Michigan English Language Assessment Battery (minimum score 85); Recommended—IELTS (minimum score 6). Electronic applications accepted. *Expenses:* Contact institution. *Faculty research:* Trauma, drug and alcohol counseling, cross-cultural issues, school counseling, trauma in schools.

Capella University, Harold Abel School of Social and Behavioral Science, Doctoral Programs in Psychology, Minneapolis, MN 55402. Offers addiction psychology (PhD); clinical psychology (Psy D); educational psychology (PhD); general advanced studies in human behavior (PhD); general psychology (PhD); industrial/organizational psychology (PhD); school psychology (Psy D).

Capella University, Harold Abel School of Social and Behavioral Science, Master's Programs in Counseling, Minneapolis, MN 55402. Offers child and adolescent development (MS); general addiction counseling (MS); general marriage and family counseling/therapy (MS); general mental health counseling (MS); general school counseling (MS).

The College of New Jersey, Office of Graduate and Advancing Education, School of Education, Department of Counselor Education, Program in Community Counseling: Substance Abuse and Addiction Specialization, Ewing, NJ 08628. Offers MA, Certificate. *Program availability:* Part-time. *Degree requirements:* For master's, comprehensive exam. *Entrance requirements:* For master's, GRE, minimum GPA of 3.0 in field or 2.75 overall; for Certificate, previous master's degree or higher. Additional exam requirements/recommendations for international students: Required—TOEFL. Electronic applications accepted.

College of St. Joseph, Graduate Programs, Division of Psychology and Human Services, Program in Alcohol and Substance Abuse Counseling, Rutland, VT 05701-3899. Offers MS. *Program availability:* Part-time. *Degree requirements:* For master's, comprehensive exam. *Entrance requirements:* For master's, official college transcripts; 2 letters of reference. Additional exam requirements/recommendations for international students: Required—TOEFL (minimum score 550 paper-based). Electronic applications accepted.

The College of William and Mary, School of Education, Program in Counselor Education, Williamsburg, VA 23187-8795. Offers addictions counseling (M Ed); community counseling (M Ed); counselor education (PhD); family counseling (M Ed); school counseling (M Ed). *Accreditation:* ACA; NCATE. *Program availability:* Part-time, evening/weekend, 100% online with required residency. *Faculty:* 12 full-time (4 women), 6 part-time/adjunct (5 women). *Students:* 64 full-time (50 women), 3 part-time (2 women); includes 14 minority (1 Black or African American, non-Hispanic/Latino; 2 Asian, non-Hispanic/Latino; 6 Hispanic/Latino; 5 Two or more races, non-Hispanic/Latino), 2 international. Average age 28. 163 applicants, 43% accepted, 32 enrolled. In 2017, 33 master's, 8 doctorates awarded. *Degree requirements:* For doctorate, comprehensive exam, thesis/dissertation. *Entrance requirements:* For master's, GRE, minimum GPA of 3.0; for doctorate, GRE, minimum GPA of 3.5. Additional exam requirements/recommendations for international students: Required—TOEFL (minimum score 100 iBT), IELTS (minimum score 7). *Application deadline:* For fall admission, 1/15 for domestic and international students. Application fee: $50. Electronic applications accepted. *Expenses:* $9,630 resident full-time, $535 resident part-time per credit hour; $25,920 nonresident full-time, $1,265 nonresident part-time per credit hour; $5,944 full-time fees. *Financial support:* In 2017–18, 34 students received support, including 26 research assistantships (averaging $18,723 per year); scholarships/grants also available. Financial award application deadline: 1/15; financial award applicants required to submit FAFSA. *Faculty research:* Sexuality, multicultural education, addiction counseling, transpersonal psychology, measurement and evaluation in counseling. *Unit head:* Dr. Charles F. Gressard, Department Chair, 757-221-2352, E-mail: cfgres@wm.edu. *Application contact:* Dorothy Smith Osborne, Assistant Dean for Academic Programs and Student Services, 757-221-2317, E-mail: dsosbo@wm.edu.
Website: http://education.wm.edu

Coppin State University, Division of Graduate Studies, Division of Arts and Sciences, Department of Applied Psychology and Rehabilitation Counseling, Program in Alcohol and Substance Abuse Counseling, Baltimore, MD 21216-3698. Offers MS. *Program availability:* Part-time. *Degree requirements:* For master's, comprehensive exam (for some programs), thesis optional, internship, clinical requirement. *Entrance requirements:* For master's, GRE General Test, interview, minimum GPA of 3.0.

East Carolina University, Graduate School, College of Allied Health Sciences, Department of Addictions and Rehabilitation Studies, Greenville, NC 27858-4353. Offers clinical counseling (MS); military and trauma counseling (Certificate); rehabilitation and career counseling (MS); rehabilitation counseling (Certificate); rehabilitation counseling and administration (PhD); substance abuse counseling (Certificate); vocational evaluation (Certificate). *Accreditation:* CORE. *Program availability:* Part-time, evening/weekend. *Students:* 82 full-time (64 women), 55 part-time (43 women); includes 39 minority (28 Black or African American, non-Hispanic/Latino; 1 American Indian or Alaska Native, non-Hispanic/Latino; 2 Asian, non-Hispanic/Latino; 5 Hispanic/Latino; 3 Two or more races, non-Hispanic/Latino). Average age 33. 51 applicants, 73% accepted, 31 enrolled. In 2017, 19 master's, 5 doctorates, 34 other advanced degrees awarded. *Degree requirements:* For master's, comprehensive exam, thesis or alternative, internship; for doctorate, thesis/dissertation, internship. *Entrance requirements:* For master's and doctorate, GRE General Test or MAT. Additional exam requirements/recommendations for international students: Recommended—TOEFL (minimum score 78 iBT), IELTS (minimum score 6.5). *Application deadline:* For fall admission, 3/1 priority date for domestic students; for spring admission, 10/1 priority date for domestic students. Applications are processed on a rolling basis. Application fee: $75. Electronic applications accepted. *Expenses:* Tuition, state resident: full-time $4749; part-time $297 per credit hour. Tuition, nonresident: full-time $17,898; part-time $1119 per credit hour. *Required fees:* $2691; $224 per credit hour. Part-time tuition and fees vary according to course load and program. *Financial support:* Research assistantships with partial tuition reimbursements, teaching assistantships with partial tuition reimbursements, Federal Work-Study, scholarships/grants, and unspecified assistantships available. Support available to part-time students. Financial award application deadline: 3/1; financial award applicants required to submit FAFSA. *Unit head:* Dr. Paul Toriello, Chair, 252-744-6292, E-mail: toriellop@ecu.edu.
Website: http://www.ecu.edu/rehb/

East Carolina University, Graduate School, College of Health and Human Performance, School of Social Work, Greenville, NC 27858-4353. Offers gerontology (Certificate); social work (MSW); substance abuse (Certificate). *Accreditation:* CSWE. *Program availability:* Online learning. *Students:* 103 full-time (95 women), 23 part-time (22 women); includes 65 minority (52 Black or African American, non-Hispanic/Latino; 1 American Indian or Alaska Native, non-Hispanic/Latino; 3 Asian, non-Hispanic/Latino; 7 Hispanic/Latino; 2 Two or more races, non-Hispanic/Latino), 1 international. Average

age 30. 107 applicants, 87% accepted, 62 enrolled. In 2017, 69 master's, 30 other advanced degrees awarded. *Degree requirements:* For master's, comprehensive exam. *Entrance requirements:* For master's, GRE or MAT. Additional exam requirements/recommendations for international students: Recommended—TOEFL (minimum score 78 iBT), IELTS (minimum score 6.5). *Application deadline:* For fall admission, 2/1 priority date for domestic and international students. Application fee: $75. *Expenses:* Tuition, state resident: full-time $4749; part-time $297 per credit hour. Tuition, nonresident: full-time $17,898; part-time $1119 per credit hour. *Required fees:* $2691; $224 per credit hour. Part-time tuition and fees vary according to course load and program. *Financial support:* Fellowships and research assistantships available. Financial award application deadline: 6/1. *Faculty research:* Social research, gerontology, women's issues, social services in schools, human behavior. *Unit head:* Dr. Shelia Bunch, Director, 252-328-4202, E-mail: bunchs@ecu.edu.
Website: https://hhp.ecu.edu/socw/

Fairfield University, Graduate School of Education and Allied Professions, Fairfield, CT 06824. Offers applied behavior analysis (ATC); applied psychology (MA); clinical mental health counseling (MA, CAS); educational technology (MA); elementary education (MA, CAS); family studies (MA); integration of spirituality and religion in counseling (ATC); marriage and family therapy (MA); reading and language development (Sixth Year Certificate); school counseling (MA, CAS); school psychology (MA, CAS); school-based marriage and family therapy (ATC); secondary education (MA); special education (MA, CAS); substance abuse counseling (ATC); teaching (Certificate); teaching and foundations (MA, CAS); TESOL, world languages, and bilingual education (MA, CAS). *Accreditation:* NCATE. *Program availability:* Part-time, evening/weekend. *Faculty:* 23 full-time (17 women), 39 part-time/adjunct (28 women). *Students:* 199 full-time (168 women), 251 part-time (206 women); includes 85 minority (21 Black or African American, non-Hispanic/Latino; 9 Asian, non-Hispanic/Latino; 49 Hispanic/Latino; 6 Two or more races, non-Hispanic/Latino), 4 international. Average age 32. 370 applicants, 56% accepted, 125 enrolled. In 2017, 136 master's, 28 other advanced degrees awarded. *Degree requirements:* For master's, comprehensive exam. *Entrance requirements:* For master's, minimum GPA of 3.0, 2 recommendations, resume. Additional exam requirements/recommendations for international students: Required—TOEFL (minimum score 550 paper-based; 84 iBT) or IELTS (minimum score 7.5). *Application deadline:* For fall admission, 2/15 for international students; for spring admission, 10/1 for international students. Application fee: $60. Electronic applications accepted. *Expenses:* $750 per credit hour. *Financial support:* In 2017–18, 34 students received support. Career-related internships or fieldwork and unspecified assistantships available. Support available to part-time students. Financial award applicants required to submit FAFSA. *Faculty research:* Reading and literacy, writing, social justice and inequality in education, addictions and mental health issues, therapeutic relationships and clinical supervision. *Unit head:* Dr. Robert D. Hannafin, Dean, 203-254-4250, Fax: 203-254-4241, E-mail: rhannafin@fairfield.edu. *Application contact:* Marianne Gumpper, Director of Graduate Admission, 203-254-4184, Fax: 203-254-4073, E-mail: gradadmis@fairfield.edu.
Website: http://www.fairfield.edu/gseap

The George Washington University, Graduate School of Education and Human Development, Department of Counseling and Human Development, Program in Rehabilitation Counseling, Washington, DC 20052. Offers autism spectrum disorder (MA Ed/HD); substance abuse and psychiatric disabilities (MA Ed/HD); traumatic brain injury (MA Ed/HD). *Accreditation:* CORE. *Program availability:* Online learning. *Students:* 30 full-time (17 women), 19 part-time (17 women); includes 17 minority (5 Black or African American, non-Hispanic/Latino; 1 American Indian or Alaska Native, non-Hispanic/Latino; 2 Asian, non-Hispanic/Latino; 7 Hispanic/Latino; 2 Two or more races, non-Hispanic/Latino), 8 international. Average age 35. 39 applicants, 74% accepted, 14 enrolled. In 2017, 22 master's awarded. *Entrance requirements:* For master's, GRE or MAT, two letters of recommendation, 1- to 2-page statement of purpose, official transcripts from all institutions attended, resume. Additional exam requirements/recommendations for international students: Required—TOEFL or IELTS. Electronic applications accepted. *Expenses: Tuition:* Full-time $28,800; part-time $1655 per credit hour. *Required fees:* $45; $2.75 per credit hour. *Unit head:* Dr. Kenneth C. Hergenrather, Director, 202-994-1334, E-mail: hergenkc@gwu.edu. *Application contact:* Sarah Lang, Director of Graduate Admissions, 202-994-1447, Fax: 202-994-7207, E-mail: slang@gwu.edu.
Website: http://gsehd.gwu.edu/rehabilitation-counseling-masters

Governors State University, College of Health and Human Services, Program in Addiction Studies and Behavioral Health, University Park, IL 60484. Offers MHS. *Program availability:* Part-time. *Faculty:* 9 full-time (6 women), 6 part-time/adjunct (4 women). *Students:* 31 full-time (26 women), 97 part-time (76 women); includes 90 minority (86 Black or African American, non-Hispanic/Latino; 2 Hispanic/Latino; 2 Two or more races, non-Hispanic/Latino). Average age 41. 32 applicants, 50% accepted, 12 enrolled. In 2017, 19 master's awarded. *Application deadline:* For fall admission, 4/1 for domestic students. Applications are processed on a rolling basis. Application fee: $50. Electronic applications accepted. *Expenses:* Tuition, state resident: full-time $8472; part-time $353 per credit hour. Tuition, nonresident: full-time $16,944; part-time $706 per credit hour. *Required fees:* $1824; $76 per credit hour. $38 per term. Tuition and fees vary according to course load, degree level and program. *Financial support:* Application deadline: 5/1; applicants required to submit FAFSA. *Unit head:* Cheryl Mejta, Chair, Department of Addictions Studies and Behavioral Health, 708-534-5000 Ext. 4911, E-mail: cmejta@govst.edu.

Hazelden Betty Ford Graduate School of Addiction Studies, Graduate Programs, Center City, MN 55012. Offers addiction counseling (MA, Certificate). *Program availability:* Part-time. *Entrance requirements:* Additional exam requirements/recommendations for international students: Required—TOEFL.

Hofstra University, School of Health Professions and Human Services, Programs in Counseling, Hempstead, NY 11549. Offers counseling (MS Ed, PD); creative arts therapy (MA); interdisciplinary transition specialist (Advanced Certificate); marriage and family therapy (MA); mental health counseling (MA, Advanced Certificate), including alcohol and substance abuse (Advanced Certificate); rehabilitation administration (PD); rehabilitation counseling (MS Ed, Advanced Certificate); rehabilitation counseling in mental health (MS Ed, Advanced Certificate). *Accreditation:* ACA. *Program availability:* Part-time, evening/weekend. *Students:* 103 full-time (87 women), 67 part-time (60 women); includes 50 minority (21 Black or African American, non-Hispanic/Latino; 11 Asian, non-Hispanic/Latino; 15 Hispanic/Latino; 1 Native Hawaiian or other Pacific Islander, non-Hispanic/Latino; 2 Two or more races, non-Hispanic/Latino), 6 international. Average age 30. 131 applicants, 79% accepted, 52 enrolled. In 2017, 66 master's, 4 other advanced degrees awarded. *Degree requirements:* For master's, comprehensive exam (for some programs), thesis (for some programs), internship, practicum, student teaching, seminars, minimum GPA of 3.0. *Entrance requirements:* For master's, GRE, interview, letters of recommendation, portfolio, essay, professional experience, certification; for other advanced degree, GRE, interview, letters of recommendation, essay, professional experience, resume, master's degree. Additional exam requirements/recommendations for international students: Required—TOEFL (minimum score 550 paper-based; 80 iBT). *Application deadline:* Applications are processed on a rolling basis. Application fee: $75. Electronic applications accepted. *Expenses: Tuition:* Full-time $1292. *Required fees:* $970. Tuition and fees vary according to program. *Financial support:* In 2017–18, 78 students received support, including 47 fellowships with full and partial tuition reimbursements available (averaging $3,138 per year), 5 research assistantships with full and partial tuition reimbursements available (averaging $5,702 per year); career-related internships or fieldwork, Federal Work-Study, institutionally sponsored loans, scholarships/grants, traineeships, tuition waivers (full and partial), and unspecified assistantships also available. Support available to part-time students. Financial award applicants required to submit FAFSA. *Faculty research:* Couple and family therapy infidelity; creative arts impact on Parkinson's disease; LGBTQ inclusion; substance abuse/heroin addiction's racial identity, multicultural issues, white privilege, Latinos, school counseling and the intensity of the high school curriculum. *Unit head:* Dr. Jamie Mitus, Chairperson, 516-463-5759, E-mail: jamie.s.mitus@hofstra.edu. *Application contact:* Sunil Samuel, Assistant Vice President of Admissions, 516-463-4723, Fax: 516-463-4664, E-mail: graduateadmission@hofstra.edu.
Website: http://www.hofstra.edu/academics/colleges/healthscienceshumanservices/

Houston Baptist University, College of Education and Behavioral Sciences, Program in Counseling, Houston, TX 77074-3298. Offers Christian counseling (MACC); counseling (MAC); marriage and family therapy (MA); pastoral counseling (MA), including addiction and recovery, crisis response, human sexuality, marriage and family therapy, military and veteran care and counseling, professional life coaching. *Program availability:* Part-time, evening/weekend, 100% online. *Students:* 42 full-time (35 women), 103 part-time (91 women); includes 80 minority (31 Black or African American, non-Hispanic/Latino; 10 Asian, non-Hispanic/Latino; 36 Hispanic/Latino; 3 Two or more races, non-Hispanic/Latino), 4 international. Average age 29. 178 applicants, 16% accepted, 16 enrolled. In 2017, 22 master's awarded. *Degree requirements:* For master's, comprehensive exam, practicum. *Entrance requirements:* For master's, GRE (waived if GPA is 3.0 or higher), two academic or professional recommendations, bachelor's degree conferred transcript, resume, interview. Additional exam requirements/recommendations for international students: Required—TOEFL (minimum score 80 iBT), IELTS (minimum score 6.5). *Application deadline:* For fall admission, 8/1 for domestic students, 6/1 for international students; for spring admission, 1/1 for domestic students, 11/1 for international students; for summer admission, 5/1 for domestic students, 3/1 for international students. Applications are processed on a rolling basis. Application fee: $0 ($100 for international students). Electronic applications accepted. Application fee is waived when completed online. *Expenses:* $33,000 tuition; $4,500 fees (general, technology and parking). *Financial support:* In 2017–18, 9 students received support. Career-related internships or fieldwork, Federal Work-Study, and scholarships/grants available. Support available to part-time students. Financial award application deadline: 4/1; financial award applicants required to submit FAFSA. *Faculty research:* Multicultural psychology, counseling: technology integration. *Unit head:* Dr. Maria Soto-Leggett, Program Coordinator, 281-649-3310, E-mail: msotoleggett@hbu.edu. *Application contact:* Victoria Humphreys, Administrative Assistant to the Dean, 281-649-3131, E-mail: vhumphreys@hbu.edu.
Website: http://www.hbu.edu/mac

Indiana University Northwest, College of Arts and Sciences, Gary, IN 46408. Offers clinical counseling (MS), including drug and alcohol counseling; community development/urban studies (Graduate Certificate); computer information systems (Graduate Certificate); liberal studies (MLS); race-ethnic studies (Graduate Certificate); women's and gender studies (Graduate Certificate). *Program availability:* Part-time, evening/weekend. *Entrance requirements:* For master's, GRE (recommended for MS), minimum undergraduate GPA of 3.0, bachelor's degree from accredited university (for MS). Electronic applications accepted. *Expenses:* Contact institution.

Indiana University Northwest, School of Social Work, Gary, IN 46408-1197. Offers health (MSW); mental health and addictions (MSW). *Program availability:* Part-time, evening/weekend. *Degree requirements:* For master's, practicum. *Entrance requirements:* For master's, minimum GPA of 3.0; bachelor's degree from accredited university including the successful completion of 6 courses in social or behavioral sciences and 1 course in statistics; 3 professional references. Electronic applications accepted. *Expenses:* Contact institution. *Faculty research:* Educational outcomes, generalist practice, homelessness.

Indiana University South Bend, School of Education, South Bend, IN 46615. Offers addiction counseling (MS Ed); alcohol and drug counseling (Graduate Certificate); clinical mental health counseling (MS Ed); educational leadership (MS Ed); elementary education (MS Ed); marriage, couple, and family counseling (MS Ed); school counseling (MS Ed); secondary education (MS Ed); special education (MAT, MS Ed), including intense intervention (MS Ed), mild intervention (MS Ed). *Accreditation:* NCATE. *Program availability:* Part-time, evening/weekend. *Degree requirements:* For master's, thesis or alternative, exit project. *Entrance requirements:* For master's, letters of recommendation, GRE or minimum GPA of 3.0. Additional exam requirements/recommendations for international students: Required—TOEFL. Electronic applications accepted. *Expenses:* Contact institution. *Faculty research:* Professional dispositions, early childhood literacy, online learning, program assessments, problem-based learning.

Indiana Wesleyan University, Graduate School, College of Arts and Sciences, Marion, IN 46953. Offers addictions counseling (MS); clinical mental health counseling (MS); community counseling (MS); marriage and family therapy (MS); school counseling (MS); student development counseling and administration (MS). *Accreditation:* ACA. *Program availability:* Part-time. *Degree requirements:* For master's, thesis or alternative. *Entrance requirements:* For master's, GRE General Test. Additional exam requirements/recommendations for international students: Required—TOEFL. Electronic applications accepted. *Expenses:* Contact institution. *Faculty research:* Community counseling, multicultural counseling, addictions.

Johnson & Wales University, Graduate Studies, MS Program in Counseling, Providence, RI 02903-3703. Offers addiction counseling (MS); clinical mental health counseling (MS). *Program availability:* Part-time. *Expenses: Tuition:* Full-time $12,636; part-time $702 per credit hour. *Application contact:* Graduate School Admissions, 401-598-1015, Fax: 401-598-1286, E-mail: pvdgrad@admissions.jwu.edu.

Kean University, Nathan Weiss Graduate College, Program in Counselor Education, Union, NJ 07083. Offers alcohol and drug abuse counseling (MA); clinical mental health counseling (MA); school counseling (MA). *Accreditation:* ACA; NCATE. *Program availability:* Part-time. *Faculty:* 9 full-time (5 women). *Students:* 146 full-time (115 women), 138 part-time (111 women); includes 123 minority (56 Black or African American, non-Hispanic/Latino; 1 American Indian or Alaska Native, non-Hispanic/Latino; 7 Asian, non-Hispanic/Latino; 53 Hispanic/Latino; 6 Two or more races, non-Hispanic/Latino), 3 international. Average age 32. 197 applicants, 45% accepted, 55 enrolled. In 2017, 80 master's awarded. *Degree requirements:* For master's, practicum, internship, portfolio. *Entrance requirements:* For master's, minimum GPA of 3.0, 2 letters of recommendation, personal statement, resume. Additional exam requirements/recommendations for international students: Required—TOEFL (minimum score 550 paper-based; 79 iBT), IELTS (minimum score 6.5). *Application deadline:* For fall admission, 3/1 for domestic and international students; for spring admission, 11/1 for domestic and international students. Applications are processed on a rolling basis.

Application fee: $75. Electronic applications accepted. *Expenses:* Tuition, state resident: full-time $13,419; part-time $653 per credit. Tuition, nonresident: full-time $18,188; part-time $801 per credit. *Required fees:* $3382; $154 per credit. Tuition and fees vary according to course level, course load, degree level and program. *Financial support:* Scholarships/grants and unspecified assistantships available. Financial award applicants required to submit FAFSA. *Unit head:* Dr. J. Barry Mascari, Program Coordinator, 908-737-5954, E-mail: jmascari@kean.edu. *Application contact:* Pedro Lopes, Admissions Counselor, 908-737-7100, E-mail: gradadmissions@kean.edu.
Website: http://grad.kean.edu/counseling

Lenoir-Rhyne University, Graduate Programs, School of Education, Program in Human Services, Hickory, NC 28601. Offers management (MA); substance abuse (MA); vocational strategies (MA). *Program availability:* Part-time, online only, 100% online. *Degree requirements:* For master's, comprehensive exam. *Entrance requirements:* For master's, GRE General Test or MAT, essay; minimum GPA of 2.7 undergraduate, 3.0 graduate. Additional exam requirements/recommendations for international students: Required—TOEFL (minimum score 600 paper-based). Electronic applications accepted. *Expenses:* Contact institution.

Lewis & Clark College, Graduate School of Education and Counseling, Department of Counseling Psychology, Program in Professional Mental Health Counseling - Addictions, Portland, OR 97219-7899. Offers MA, MS. *Program availability:* Part-time, evening/weekend. *Degree requirements:* For master's, thesis (MS). *Entrance requirements:* For master's, GRE General Test, minimum undergraduate GPA of 2.75. Additional exam requirements/recommendations for international students: Required—TOEFL (minimum score 575 paper-based). Electronic applications accepted.

Liberty University, School of Behavioral Sciences, Lynchburg, VA 24515. Offers applied psychology (MA), including developmental psychology (MA, MS), industrial/organizational psychology (MA, MS); clinical mental health counseling (MA); community care and counseling (Ed D), including marriage and family counseling, pastoral care and counseling, traumatology; counselor education and supervision (PhD); human services counseling (MA), including addictions and recovery, business, child and family law, Christian ministries, criminal justice, crisis response and trauma, executive leadership, health and wellness, life coaching, marriage and family, military resilience; marriage and family counseling (MA); marriage and family therapy (MA); military resilience (Certificate); pastoral counseling (MA), including addictions and recovery, community chaplaincy, crisis response and trauma, discipleship and church ministry, leadership, life coaching, marriage and family, marriage and family studies, military resilience, parenting and child/adolescent, pastoral counseling, theology; professional counseling (MA); psychology (MS), including developmental psychology (MA, MS), industrial/organizational psychology (MA, MS); school counseling (M Ed). *Program availability:* Part-time, online learning. *Students:* 2,649 full-time (2,085 women), 5,086 part-time (4,015 women); includes 2,275 minority (1,784 Black or African American, non-Hispanic/Latino; 44 American Indian or Alaska Native, non-Hispanic/Latino; 67 Asian, non-Hispanic/Latino; 200 Hispanic/Latino; 11 Native Hawaiian or other Pacific Islander, non-Hispanic/Latino; 169 Two or more races, non-Hispanic/Latino), 145 international. Average age 39. 5,839 applicants, 51% accepted, 1710 enrolled. In 2017, 1,626 master's, 7 doctorates, 61 other advanced degrees awarded. *Application deadline:* Applications are processed on a rolling basis. Application fee: $50. Electronic applications accepted. *Financial support:* Applicants required to submit FAFSA. *Unit head:* Dr. Ronald Hawkins, Founding Dean, School of Behavioral Sciences. *Application contact:* Jay Bridge, Director of Admissions, 800-424-9595, Fax: 800-628-7977, E-mail: gradadmissions@liberty.edu.

Liberty University, School of Divinity, Lynchburg, VA 24515. Offers Biblical exposition (MA); Biblical languages (M Div); Biblical studies (M Div, MA, MAR, Th M, D Min); chaplaincy (M Div, D Min); Christian apologetics (M Div, MA, MAR, Th M); Christian leadership and church ministries (M Div); Christian ministries (M Div); Christian ministry (MA); Christian thought (M Div); church history (M Div, MAR, Th M); community chaplaincy (M Div, MAR); discipleship (D Min); discipleship and church ministry (M Div, MAR, MCM); evangelism and church planting (MAR, MCM, D Min); expository preaching (D Min); global ministry (MA); global studies (M Div, MAR, MCM, MGS, Th M); healthcare chaplaincy (M Div); homiletics (M Div, MAR, Th M); leadership (M Div, MAR); marketplace chaplaincy (M Div, MCM); ministry leadership (Ed D); pastoral counseling (M Div, MA, MAR, D Min), including addictions and recovery (MA), crisis response and trauma (MA), discipleship and church ministries (MA), leadership (MA), life coaching (MA), marketplace chaplaincy (MA), marriage and family (MA), military resilience (MA), pastoral counseling (MA); pastoral leadership (D Min); pastoral ministries (M Div, M Serv Soc, MCM); religious education (MRE); sports chaplaincy (MA); theology (M Div, MAR, MTS, Th M); theology and apologetics (D Min, PhD); worship (M Div, MAR, MCM, D Min); youth and family ministries (M Div). *Program availability:* Part-time, online learning. *Students:* 2,140 full-time (615 women), 3,020 part-time (906 women); includes 1,312 minority (1,016 Black or African American, non-Hispanic/Latino; 9 American Indian or Alaska Native, non-Hispanic/Latino; 100 Asian, non-Hispanic/Latino; 90 Hispanic/Latino; 7 Native Hawaiian or other Pacific Islander, non-Hispanic/Latino; 90 Two or more races, non-Hispanic/Latino), 158 international. Average age 42. 4,673 applicants, 33% accepted, 977 enrolled. In 2017, 904 master's, 54 doctorates awarded. *Degree requirements:* For master's, 2 foreign languages, thesis (for some programs); for doctorate, 2 foreign languages, thesis/dissertation. *Entrance requirements:* For master's, minimum undergraduate GPA of 2.0; for doctorate, GRE General Test or MAT, minimum graduate GPA of 3.0. Additional exam requirements/recommendations for international students: Required—TOEFL (minimum score 600 paper-based; 100 iBT). *Application deadline:* For fall admission, 6/1 for domestic students; for spring admission, 11/1 for domestic students. Applications are processed on a rolling basis. Application fee: $50. Electronic applications accepted. *Expenses:* Contact institution. *Financial support:* Teaching assistantships with tuition reimbursements, career-related internships or fieldwork, and Federal Work-Study available. Financial award applicants required to submit FAFSA. *Unit head:* Dr. Ed Hindson, Dean, 434-592-4140, Fax: 434-522-0415, E-mail: ehindson@liberty.edu. *Application contact:* Jay Bridge, Director of Graduate Admissions, 800-424-9595, Fax: 800-628-7977, E-mail: gradadmissions@liberty.edu.
Website: https://www.liberty.edu/divinity/

Loma Linda University, School of Behavioral Health, Department of Counseling and Family Sciences, Loma Linda, CA 92350. Offers child life specialist (MS); clinical mediation (Certificate); counseling (MS); drug and alcohol counseling (Certificate); family life education (Certificate); marital and family therapy (DMFT); school counseling (Certificate). *Degree requirements:* For master's, comprehensive exam, thesis optional; for doctorate, comprehensive exam, thesis/dissertation (for some programs). *Entrance requirements:* For master's, minimum GPA of 3.0; for doctorate, GRE. Additional exam requirements/recommendations for international students: Required—TOEFL (minimum score 550 paper-based). Electronic applications accepted.

Long Island University–Hudson, Graduate School, Purchase, NY 10577. Offers autism (Advanced Certificate); bilingual education (Advanced Certificate); childhood education (MS Ed); crisis management (Advanced Certificate); early childhood education (MS Ed); educational leadership (MS Ed); health administration (MPA); literacy (MS Ed); marriage and family therapy (MS); mental health counseling (MS, Advanced Certificate), including credentialed alcoholism and substance abuse counselor (MS); middle childhood and adolescence education (MS Ed); pharmaceutics (MS), including cosmetic science, industrial pharmacy; public administration (MPA); school counseling (MS Ed, Advanced Certificate); school psychology (MS Ed); special education (MS Ed); TESOL (MS Ed); TESOL (all grades) (Advanced Certificate). *Program availability:* Part-time, evening/weekend. *Faculty:* 8 full-time (6 women), 41 part-time/adjunct (24 women). *Students:* 69 full-time (54 women), 249 part-time (200 women); includes 102 minority (29 Black or African American, non-Hispanic/Latino; 1 American Indian or Alaska Native, non-Hispanic/Latino; 9 Asian, non-Hispanic/Latino; 62 Hispanic/Latino; 1 Native Hawaiian or other Pacific Islander, non-Hispanic/Latino). Average age 33. 153 applicants, 96% accepted, 103 enrolled. In 2017, 138 master's, 36 other advanced degrees awarded. *Entrance requirements:* Additional exam requirements/recommendations for international students: Required—TOEFL. *Application deadline:* Applications are processed on a rolling basis. Application fee: $50. Electronic applications accepted. *Expenses:* Contact institution. *Financial support:* In 2017–18, 32 students received support. Scholarships/grants available. Support available to part-time students. Financial award application deadline: 2/15; financial award applicants required to submit FAFSA. *Unit head:* Dr. Sylvia Blake, Dean and Chief Operating Officer, 914-831-2700, E-mail: westchester@liu.edu. *Application contact:* Dr. Sylvia Blake, Dean and Chief Operating Officer, 914-831-2700, E-mail: westchester@liu.edu.

Maryville University of Saint Louis, Myrtle E. and Earl E. Walker College of Health Professions, Program in Rehabilitation Counseling, St. Louis, MO 63141-7299. Offers marriage and family therapy (MARC); music therapy (MARC); substance abuse (MARC). *Accreditation:* CORE. *Program availability:* Part-time. *Faculty:* 3 full-time (1 woman), 1 (woman) part-time/adjunct. *Students:* 17 full-time (all women), 15 part-time (10 women); includes 7 minority (6 Black or African American, non-Hispanic/Latino; 1 Hispanic/Latino). Average age 32. In 2017, 18 master's awarded. *Degree requirements:* For master's, internship, seminar. *Entrance requirements:* For master's, minimum cumulative GPA of 3.0, 2 letters of recommendation, interview, essay, transcripts, resume. Additional exam requirements/recommendations for international students: Required—TOEFL (minimum score 563 paper-based). *Application deadline:* For fall admission, 1/15 for domestic students; for spring admission, 10/1 for domestic students. Applications are processed on a rolling basis. Electronic applications accepted. *Expenses:* $663 per credit hour; $350 per semester fees. *Financial support:* Career-related internships or fieldwork, Federal Work-Study, and campus employment available. Financial award application deadline: 4/1; financial award applicants required to submit FAFSA. *Unit head:* Dr. Michael Kiener, Director, 314-529-9443, Fax: 314-529-9495, E-mail: mkiener@maryville.edu. *Application contact:* Jeannie DeLuca, Director, Admissions and Advising, 314-529-9355, Fax: 314-529-9927, E-mail: jdeluca@maryville.edu.
Website: http://www.maryville.edu/hp/rehabilitation-counseling/

Monmouth University, Graduate Studies, Department of Professional Counseling, West Long Branch, NJ 07764-1898. Offers addiction studies (MA); clinical mental health counseling (MS); professional counseling (PMC). *Accreditation:* ACA. *Program availability:* Part-time, evening/weekend. *Faculty:* 11 full-time (5 women), 5 part-time/adjunct (4 women). *Students:* 106 full-time (97 women), 68 part-time (55 women); includes 42 minority (14 Black or African American, non-Hispanic/Latino; 5 Asian, non-Hispanic/Latino; 18 Hispanic/Latino; 5 Two or more races, non-Hispanic/Latino), 3 international. Average age 30. In 2017, 67 master's, 16 other advanced degrees awarded. *Degree requirements:* For master's, comprehensive exam (for some programs), thesis optional, fieldwork. *Entrance requirements:* For master's, GRE, minimum GPA of 3.0 overall, 12 credits in psychology or closely-related field, two Monmouth University psychological counseling recommendation forms, narrative essay; for PMC, degree or current enrollment in CACREP-accredited master's program in counseling with minimum cumulative GPA of 3.0. Additional exam requirements/recommendations for international students: Required—TOEFL (minimum score 550 paper-based; 79 iBT), IELTS (minimum score 6), Michigan English Language Assessment Battery (minimum score 77) or Certificate of Advanced English (minimum score 160). *Application deadline:* For fall admission, 7/15 priority date for domestic students, 6/1 for international students; for spring admission, 12/1 priority date for domestic students, 11/1 for international students; for summer admission, 5/1 for domestic students. Applications are processed on a rolling basis. Application fee: $50. Electronic applications accepted. *Expenses: Tuition:* Full-time $21,366; part-time $7122 per credit. *Required fees:* $700; $175 per term. *Financial support:* In 2017–18, 82 students received support. Institutionally sponsored loans, scholarships/grants, and unspecified assistantships available. Support available to part-time students. Financial award applicants required to submit FAFSA. *Faculty research:* Violent crime, single parenting, the African-American male, counseling older women, successful behavior for under-achieving youth. *Unit head:* Dr. David Burkholder, Program Director, 732-923-4621, Fax: 732-923-4661, E-mail: dburkhol@monmouth.edu. *Application contact:* Andrea Thompson, Graduate Admission Counselor, 732-571-3452, Fax: 732-263-5123, E-mail: gradadm@monmouth.edu.
Website: https://www.monmouth.edu/school-of-humanities-social-sciences/professional-counseling.aspx

Montclair State University, The Graduate School, College of Education and Human Services, Certified Alcohol and Drug Counselor Certificate Program, Montclair, NJ 07043-1624. Offers Certificate.

Northern Vermont University–Johnson, Program in Counseling, Johnson, VT 05656. Offers addictions counseling (MA); clinical mental health counseling (MA); general counseling (MA); school counseling (MA). *Program availability:* Part-time. *Faculty:* 2 full-time (1 woman), 11 part-time/adjunct (6 women). *Students:* 2 full-time (1 woman), 15 part-time (9 women). In 2017, 50 master's awarded. *Degree requirements:* For master's, comprehensive exam. *Entrance requirements:* For master's, interview. Additional exam requirements/recommendations for international students: Required—TOEFL. *Application deadline:* For fall admission, 7/1 for domestic students, 2/1 for international students; for spring admission, 11/1 for domestic students, 7/1 for international students; for summer admission, 4/1 for domestic students. Applications are processed on a rolling basis. Electronic applications accepted. *Expenses:* Tuition, state resident: part-time $572 per credit hour. Tuition, nonresident: part-time $832 per credit hour. *Financial support:* Career-related internships or fieldwork and unspecified assistantships available. Support available to part-time students. Financial award application deadline: 3/1; financial award applicants required to submit FAFSA. *Unit head:* Dr. Kimberly Donovan, Coordinator, 802-635-1453, Fax: 802-635-1465, E-mail: kimberly.donovan@northernvermont.edu. *Application contact:* Catherine H. Higley, Administrative Assistant, 800-635-2356 Ext. 1244, Fax: 802-635-1248, E-mail: catherine.higley@jsc.edu.

Northwest Nazarene University, Program in Social Work, Nampa, ID 83686-5897. Offers clinical mental health and addictions practice (MSW). *Accreditation:* CSWE. *Program availability:* Part-time-only, evening/weekend. *Students:* Average age 27. 152 applicants, 54% accepted, 73 enrolled. In 2017, 54 master's awarded. *Degree requirements:* For master's, comprehensive exam, thesis or alternative. *Entrance requirements:* For master's, interview, letters of reference, degree from regionally-

accredited college/university, written personal statement. *Application deadline:* Applications are processed on a rolling basis. Application fee: $50. Electronic applications accepted. *Faculty research:* Test anxiety, trauma, statistics. *Unit head:* Dr. Lawanna Lancaster, Director/Department Chair, 208-467-8372, Fax: 208-467-8879, E-mail: mswinfo@nnu.edu. *Application contact:* Jodie Rodriguez-Engel, Program Coordinator, 208-467-8679, Fax: 208-467-8879, E-mail: jrodriguez-engel@nnu.edu. Website: http://msw.nnu.edu

Nova Southeastern University, College of Psychology, Fort Lauderdale, FL 33314-7796. Offers clinical mental health counseling (MS); clinical psychology (PhD, Psy D); counseling (MS); experimental psychology (MS); forensic psychology (MS); general psychology (MS); school counseling (MS); school psychology (Psy D, Psy S); substance abuse counseling (MS); substance abuse counseling and education (MS). *Accreditation:* APA (one or more programs are accredited). *Program availability:* 100% online, blended/hybrid learning. *Faculty:* 51 full-time (21 women), 120 part-time/adjunct (70 women). *Students:* 751 full-time (618 women), 821 part-time (709 women); includes 787 minority (268 Black or African American, non-Hispanic/Latino; 2 American Indian or Alaska Native, non-Hispanic/Latino; 38 Asian, non-Hispanic/Latino; 431 Hispanic/Latino; 2 Native Hawaiian or other Pacific Islander, non-Hispanic/Latino; 46 Two or more races, non-Hispanic/Latino), 45 international. Average age 31. 1,117 applicants, 38% accepted, 294 enrolled. In 2017, 459 master's, 100 doctorates, 10 other advanced degrees awarded. Terminal master's awarded for partial completion of doctoral program. *Degree requirements:* For master's, comprehensive exam, 3 practica; for doctorate, thesis/dissertation, clinical internship, competency exam; for Psy S, comprehensive exam, internship. *Entrance requirements:* For master's and Psy S, GRE General Test, letters of recommendation, research/personal statement, interview; for doctorate, GRE General Test, GRE Subject Test (recommended), minimum undergraduate GPA of 3.0, letters of recommendation, research/personal statement, interview, curriculum vitae/resume. Additional exam requirements/recommendations for international students: Required—TOEFL (minimum score 550 paper-based). *Application deadline:* Applications are processed on a rolling basis. Application fee: $50. Electronic applications accepted. *Expenses:* Contact institution. *Financial support:* In 2017–18, 197 students received support, including 15 research assistantships (averaging $5,600 per year), 68 teaching assistantships (averaging $2,000 per year); career-related internships or fieldwork, Federal Work-Study, institutionally sponsored loans, scholarships/grants, and unspecified assistantships also available. Support available to part-time students. Financial award application deadline: 4/15; financial award applicants required to submit FAFSA. *Faculty research:* Clinical health psychology, multicultural/diversity psychology, clinical neuropsychology, clinical child psychology, family violence. *Unit head:* Dr. Karen Grosby, Dean, 954-262-5712, Fax: 954-262-3859, E-mail: grosby@nova.edu. *Application contact:* Carlos Perez, Senior Manager of Outreach, 954-262-5702, Fax: 954-262-3893, E-mail: gradschool@nova.edu. Website: http://psychology.nova.edu/

Oral Roberts University, School of Theology and Missions, Tulsa, OK 74171. Offers biblical literature (MA), including advanced languages, Judaic-Christian studies; church ministries and leadership (D Min); clinical pastoral education (M Div); missions (MA); pastoral care and chaplaincy (M Div, D Min); practical theology (MA), including teaching ministries, urban ministries; professional counseling (MA), including addiction studies, marriage and family therapy; theological/historical studies (MA). *Accreditation:* ATS. *Program availability:* Part-time, online learning. *Faculty:* 17 full-time (2 women). *Students:* 371 full-time (156 women), 110 part-time (65 women); includes 177 minority (127 Black or African American, non-Hispanic/Latino; 5 American Indian or Alaska Native, non-Hispanic/Latino; 20 Asian, non-Hispanic/Latino; 25 Hispanic/Latino), 82 international. Average age 36. 159 applicants, 95% accepted, 124 enrolled. In 2017, 52 master's, 10 doctorates awarded. *Degree requirements:* For master's, thesis (for some programs), practicum/internship; for doctorate, thesis/dissertation, applied research project. *Entrance requirements:* For master's, GRE General Test or MAT (waived for those with undergraduate degree from regionally accredited institution and 3.0 or higher GPA), minimum GPA of 2.5 (professional) or 3.0 (academic); for doctorate, M Div, minimum GPA of 3.0, 3 years of full-time ministry experience. Additional exam requirements/recommendations for international students: Recommended—TOEFL (minimum score 550 paper-based; 79 iBT), IELTS (minimum score 7). *Application deadline:* Applications are processed on a rolling basis. Application fee: $35. Electronic applications accepted. Application fee is waived when completed online. *Financial support:* Fellowships and scholarships/grants available. Financial award application deadline: 6/1. *Unit head:* Dr. Bill Buker, Chair, 918-495-6493, E-mail: bbuker@oru.edu. *Application contact:* Michael Thomas, Enrollment Counselor, 918-495-6618, E-mail: mthomas@oru.edu. Website: http://www.gradtheology.oru.edu/

Pace University, Dyson College of Arts and Sciences, Department of Psychology, Program in Mental Health Counseling, New York, NY 10038. Offers grief and loss (MS); mental health counseling (MS, PhD); substance abuse (MS). Program offered at Pleasantville, NY location only. *Program availability:* Part-time, evening/weekend. *Students:* 72 full-time (57 women), 57 part-time (50 women); includes 42 minority (9 Black or African American, non-Hispanic/Latino; 1 American Indian or Alaska Native, non-Hispanic/Latino; 8 Asian, non-Hispanic/Latino; 24 Hispanic/Latino), 2 international. Average age 30. In 2017, 49 master's awarded. Terminal master's awarded for partial completion of doctoral program. *Degree requirements:* For master's, comprehensive exam, qualifying exams, internship; for doctorate, comprehensive exam, thesis/dissertation, internships. *Entrance requirements:* For master's, GRE, resume, personal statement, two letters of reference, official transcripts, interview; for doctorate, three letters of recommendation (two of which are academic in nature); personal statement; official transcripts; internship(s); interview; master's degree in mental health counseling or program with curriculum equivalent to that of Pace's graduate program in mental health counseling. Additional exam requirements/recommendations for international students: Required—TOEFL (minimum score 88 iBT), IELTS (minimum score 7) or PTE (minimum score 60). *Application deadline:* For fall admission, 8/1 priority date for domestic students, 6/1 for international students; for spring admission, 12/1 priority date for domestic students, 10/1 for international students. Applications are processed on a rolling basis. Application fee: $70. Electronic applications accepted. *Financial support:* Research assistantships, teaching assistantships, career-related internships or fieldwork, Federal Work-Study, and tuition waivers (partial) available. Financial award application deadline: 2/15; financial award applicants required to submit FAFSA. *Unit head:* Dr. Ross Robak, Psychology Department Chair/Director, Graduate Program in Counseling, 914-773-3786, E-mail: rrobak@pace.edu. *Application contact:* Susan Ford-Goldschein, Director of Graduate Admissions, 914-422-4283, Fax: 212-346-1585, E-mail: graduateadmission@pace.edu. Website: http://www.pace.edu/academics/graduate-students/degrees/mental-health-counseling-ms

Palm Beach Atlantic University, School of Education and Behavioral Studies, West Palm Beach, FL 33416-4708. Offers counseling psychology (MS), including addictions/mental health, general counseling, marriage and family therapy, mental health counseling, school guidance counseling. *Program availability:* Part-time, evening/weekend. *Entrance requirements:* For master's, GRE or MAT, minimum GPA of 3.0;

essay. Additional exam requirements/recommendations for international students: Required—TOEFL (minimum score 550 paper-based; 79 iBT). Electronic applications accepted. *Faculty research:* Group dynamics, phenomenology, spirituality, multicultural psychology.

Post University, Program in Counseling and Human Services, Waterbury, CT 06723-2540. Offers counseling and human services (MS); counseling and human services/alcohol and drug counseling (MS); counseling and human services/clinical mental health counseling (MS); counseling and human services/forensic mental health counseling (MS); counseling and human services/non-profit management (MS). *Program availability:* Part-time, evening/weekend, online learning. *Entrance requirements:* For master's, resume. *Expenses:* Tuition: Part-time $730 per credit hour. Part-time tuition and fees vary according to degree level and program. *Application contact:* Veronica Montalvo, Vice President, Online Education Enrollment Management and Admissions, 203-596-6164, E-mail: vmontalvo@post.edu. Website: https://post.edu/academics/online-master-of-science-in-counseling-and-human-services

Regent University, Graduate School, School of Psychology and Counseling, Virginia Beach, VA 23464-9800. Offers clinical mental health counseling (MA); clinical psychology (Psy D); counseling and psychological studies - clinical (PhD); counseling and psychological studies - research (PhD); counseling studies (CAGS); counselor education and supervision (PhD); general psychology (MS); human services (MA), including addictions counseling, Biblical counseling, Christian counseling, conflict and mediation ministry, criminal justice and ministry, grief counseling, human services counseling, human services for student affairs, life coaching, marriage and family ministry, trauma and crisis counseling; marriage, couple, and family counseling (MA); pastoral counseling (MA); school counseling (MA); M Div/MA; M Ed/MA; MBA/MA. *Accreditation:* ACA; APA (one or more programs are accredited). *Program availability:* Part-time, evening/weekend, 100% online, blended/hybrid learning. *Faculty:* 28 full-time (16 women), 51 part-time/adjunct (30 women). *Students:* 294 full-time (236 women), 404 part-time (317 women); includes 286 minority (218 Black or African American, non-Hispanic/Latino; 4 American Indian or Alaska Native, non-Hispanic/Latino; 17 Asian, non-Hispanic/Latino; 30 Hispanic/Latino; 17 Two or more races, non-Hispanic/Latino), 13 international. Average age 37. 2,109 applicants, 18% accepted, 233 enrolled. In 2017, 158 master's, 28 doctorates awarded. *Degree requirements:* For master's, thesis or alternative, internship, practicum, written competency exam; for doctorate, thesis/dissertation or alternative. *Entrance requirements:* For master's, GRE General Test (including writing exam) or MAT, minimum undergraduate GPA of 3.0, resume, transcripts, writing sample, personal goals statement; for doctorate, GRE General Test (including writing exam), minimum undergraduate GPA of 3.0, graduate 3.5; writing sample; 3 recommendations; resume; college transcripts; personal goals statement. Additional exam requirements/recommendations for international students: Required—TOEFL (minimum score 577 paper-based). *Application deadline:* For fall admission, 4/1 priority date for domestic students; for spring admission, 11/1 priority date for domestic students. Applications are processed on a rolling basis. Application fee: $50. Electronic applications accepted. *Expenses:* Contact institution. *Financial support:* In 2017–18, 557 students received support, including 5 fellowships (averaging $10,000 per year), 11 research assistantships (averaging $3,200 per year); career-related internships or fieldwork, scholarships/grants, and unspecified assistantships also available. Support available to part-time students. *Faculty research:* Marriage enrichment, clinical psychology, troubled youth, faith and learning, trauma. *Unit head:* Dr. William Hathaway, Dean, 757-352-4294, Fax: 757-352-4282, E-mail: willhat@regent.edu. *Application contact:* Heidi Cece, Assistant Vice President of Enrollment Management, 800-373-5504, Fax: 757-352-4381, E-mail: admissions@regent.edu. Website: https://www.regent.edu/school-of-psychology-and-counseling/

Rider University, College of Education and Human Services, Program in Counseling Services, Lawrenceville, NJ 08648-3001. Offers clinical mental health counseling (MA); counseling services (MA, Ed S); director of school counseling services (Certificate); life and career coaching (Certificate); school counseling (Certificate); student assistance coordinator (Certificate); substance awareness coordinator (Certificate). *Accreditation:* ACA; NCATE. *Program availability:* Part-time, evening/weekend. *Degree requirements:* For master's, comprehensive exam, research project; for other advanced degree, specialty seminar. *Entrance requirements:* For master's, GRE or MAT, interview, resume, 2 letters of recommendation; for other advanced degree, GRE or MAT, interview, professional experience, 2 letters of recommendation. Additional exam requirements/recommendations for international students: Required—TOEFL (minimum score 550 paper-based). Electronic applications accepted. *Faculty research:* Diversity in counseling.

Saint Mary's University of Minnesota, Schools of Graduate and Professional Programs, Graduate School of Health and Human Services, Counseling and Psychological Services Program, Winona, MN 55987-1399. Offers addiction studies (Certificate); counseling and psychological services (MA). *Unit head:* Dr. Mary Louise Wise, Associate Program Director, 612-728-5104, Fax: 612-728-5121, E-mail: mlwise@smumn.edu. *Application contact:* James Callinan, Director of Admissions for Graduate and Professional Programs, 612-728-5158, Fax: 612-728-5121, E-mail: jcallina@smumn.edu. Website: http://www.smumn.edu/graduate-home/areas-of-study/graduate-school-of-health-human-services/ma-in-counseling-psychological-services

Salve Regina University, Program in Rehabilitation Counseling, Newport, RI 02840-4192. Offers clinical rehabilitation and mental health counseling (MA); mental health (CAGS), including rehabilitation counseling; rehabilitation (CAGS), including substance abuse counseling; rehabilitation counseling (MA); substance abuse and treatment (CAGS). *Accreditation:* CORE. *Program availability:* Part-time, evening/weekend. *Entrance requirements:* For master's, GMAT, GRE General Test or MAT. Additional exam requirements/recommendations for international students: Required—TOEFL (minimum score 600 paper-based; 100 iBT) or IELTS. Electronic applications accepted.

Stephens College, Division of Graduate and Continuing Studies, Columbia, MO 65215-0002. Offers counseling (M Ed), including addictions counseling, clinical mental health counseling, school counseling; health information administration (Postbaccalaureate Certificate); physician assistant studies (MPAS); TV and screenwriting (MFA). *Program availability:* Part-time, evening/weekend, online learning. *Entrance requirements:* For master's, minimum GPA of 3.0 in last 60 hours. Additional exam requirements/recommendations for international students: Required—TOEFL (minimum score 79 iBT). Electronic applications accepted. *Faculty research:* Educational psychology, outcomes assessment.

Stony Brook University, State University of New York, Stony Brook Medicine, School of Medicine, Program in Public Health, Stony Brook, NY 11794. Offers community health (MPH); evaluation sciences (MPH); family violence (MPH); health communication (Certificate); health economics (MPH); health education and promotion (Certificate); population health (MPH); substance abuse (MPH). *Accreditation:* CEPH. *Program availability:* Part-time, evening/weekend. *Students:* 32 full-time (24 women), 11 part-time (10 women); includes 18 minority (4 Black or African American, non-Hispanic/Latino; 10 Asian, non-Hispanic/Latino; 4 Hispanic/Latino), 2 international. Average age 29. 128 applicants, 71% accepted, 29 enrolled. In 2017, 25 master's, 1 other advanced degree

awarded. *Entrance requirements:* For master's, GRE, 3 references, bachelor's degree from accredited college or university with minimum GPA of 3.0, essays, interview. Additional exam requirements/recommendations for international students: Required—TOEFL (minimum score 90 iBT). *Application deadline:* For fall admission, 7/15 for domestic students, 3/15 for international students. Application fee: $100. Electronic applications accepted. *Expenses:* Contact institution. *Financial support:* Fellowships available. *Faculty research:* Abnormal psychology, academic achievement, broadcast media, communications, communications systems, public health. *Total annual research expenditures:* $422,408. *Unit head:* Dr. Lisa A. Benz Scott, Director, 631-444-8811, E-mail: lisa.benzscott@stonybrook.edu. *Application contact:* Joanie Maniaci, Assistant Director for Student Affairs, 631-444-2074, Fax: 631-444-6035, E-mail: joanmarie.maniaci@stonybrook.edu.
Website: http://publichealth.stonybrookmedicine.edu/

Syracuse University, David B. Falk College of Sport and Human Dynamics, Programs in Addiction Studies, Syracuse, NY 13244. Offers MA, CAS. *Program availability:* Part-time. In 2017, 10 other advanced degrees awarded. *Entrance requirements:* For master's, GRE, personal statement, official transcripts, three letters of recommendation, resume; for CAS, personal statement, official transcripts, three letters of recommendation, resume. Additional exam requirements/recommendations for international students: Required—TOEFL (minimum score 100 iBT). *Application deadline:* For fall admission, 2/15 priority date for domestic and international students; for spring admission, 11/15 priority date for domestic and international students. Application fee: $75. Electronic applications accepted. *Financial support:* Fellowships, research assistantships, teaching assistantships, and scholarships/grants available. Financial award application deadline: 1/1. *Faculty research:* Alcohol, other drugs and behavioral (process) addictions, public health perspective of substance use and addictive behaviors, prevention and counseling. *Unit head:* Dr. Dessa Bergen-Cico, Coordinator, Addiction Studies Program in Public Health, 315-443-0250, E-mail: dkbergen@syr.edu. *Application contact:* Felicia Otero, Director of College Admissions, 315-443-5555, Fax: 315-443-2562, E-mail: falk@syr.edu.
Website: https://falk.syr.edu/public-health/academic-programs/#maas

Texas Tech University Health Sciences Center, School of Health Professions, Program in Addiction Counseling, Lubbock, TX 79430. Offers MS. *Program availability:* Part-time, online learning. *Faculty:* 5 full-time (2 women). *Students:* 1 (woman) full-time, 4 part-time (3 women); includes 3 minority (2 Hispanic/Latino; 1 Native Hawaiian or other Pacific Islander, non-Hispanic/Latino). Average age 37. 5 applicants, 100% accepted, 5 enrolled. *Degree requirements:* For master's, internship. *Entrance requirements:* Additional exam requirements/recommendations for international students: Required—TOEFL (minimum score 550 paper-based; 79 iBT). *Application deadline:* For fall admission, 8/1 for domestic students; for spring admission, 11/1 for domestic students. Applications are processed on a rolling basis. Application fee: $75. Electronic applications accepted. *Financial support:* Application deadline: 9/1; applicants required to submit FAFSA. *Unit head:* Dr. Zach Sneed, Program Director, 806-743-2590, Fax: 806-743-3244, E-mail: zach.sneed@ttuhsc.edu. *Application contact:* Lindsay Johnson, Associate Dean for Admissions and Student Affairs, 806-743-3220, Fax: 806-743-2994, E-mail: lindsay.johnson@ttuhsc.edu.
Website: http://www.ttuhsc.edu/health-professions/master-of-science-addiction-counseling/

United States International University–Africa, School of Arts and Sciences, Nairobi, Kenya. Offers counseling psychology (MA), including chemical dependency, health psychology; international relations (MA), including development studies, diplomacy and foreign policy, peace and conflict studies. *Program availability:* Part-time, evening/weekend. *Degree requirements:* For master's, thesis, practicum. *Entrance requirements:* For master's, GRE General Test, 2 letters of recommendation, resume. Additional exam requirements/recommendations for international students: Required—TOEFL. *Faculty research:* Trauma in children, African intellectualism, psychological assessment tools.

Universidad Central del Caribe, Program in Substance Abuse Counseling, Bayamón, PR 00960-6032. Offers MHS.

University of California, Berkeley, UC Berkeley Extension, Certificate Programs in Behavioral and Health Sciences, Berkeley, CA 94720-1500. Offers alcohol and drug abuse studies (Certificate). *Accreditation:* APA.

University of Central Oklahoma, The Jackson College of Graduate Studies, College of Liberal Arts, Department of Sociology, Gerontology, and Substance Abuse Studies, Edmond, OK 73034-5209. Offers gerontology (MA); substance abuse studies (MA), including substance abuse studies. *Program availability:* Part-time. *Faculty:* 8 full-time (6 women), 6 part-time/adjunct (3 women). *Students:* 31 full-time (25 women), 30 part-time (23 women); includes 25 minority (14 Black or African American, non-Hispanic/Latino; 1 American Indian or Alaska Native, non-Hispanic/Latino; 2 Asian, non-Hispanic/Latino; 3 Hispanic/Latino; 5 Two or more races, non-Hispanic/Latino), 3 international. Average age 39. 39 applicants, 92% accepted, 22 enrolled. In 2017, 21 master's awarded. *Degree requirements:* For master's, variable foreign language requirement, comprehensive exam (for some programs), thesis (for some programs). *Entrance requirements:* Additional exam requirements/recommendations for international students: Required—TOEFL (minimum score 550 paper-based; 79 iBT), IELTS (minimum score 6.5). *Application deadline:* For fall admission, 7/15 for international students; for spring admission, 11/15 for international students. Applications are processed on a rolling basis. Application fee: $60. Electronic applications accepted. *Expenses:* Tuition, state resident: full-time $5375; part-time $268.75 per credit hour. Tuition, nonresident: full-time $13,295; part-time $664.75 per credit hour. *Required fees:* $626; $31.30 per credit hour. One-time fee: $50. Tuition and fees vary according to program. *Financial support:* In 2017–18, 10 students received support, including 2 research assistantships with partial tuition reimbursements available (averaging $2,958 per year), 1 teaching assistantship with partial tuition reimbursement available (averaging $11,830 per year); career-related internships or fieldwork, scholarships/grants, tuition waivers (partial), and unspecified assistantships also available. Financial award application deadline: 3/31; financial award applicants required to submit FAFSA. *Unit head:* Dr. Douglas Reed, Chair, 405-974-5540, Fax: 405-974-3823, E-mail: gradcoll@uco.edu.
Website: http://www.uco.edu/la/soc-gero-sas/index.asp

University of Cincinnati, Graduate School, College of Education, Criminal Justice, and Human Services, School of Human Services, Counseling Program, Cincinnati, OH 45221. Offers counselor education (Ed D); mental health (MA); school counseling (M Ed); substance abuse prevention (Graduate Certificate). *Accreditation:* ACA (one or more programs are accredited); NCATE. *Program availability:* Part-time. Terminal master's awarded for partial completion of doctoral program. *Degree requirements:* For master's, comprehensive exam, thesis or alternative; for doctorate, comprehensive exam, thesis/dissertation. *Entrance requirements:* For master's and doctorate, GRE General Test, interview. Additional exam requirements/recommendations for international students: Required—TOEFL (minimum score 620 paper-based). Electronic applications accepted. *Expenses: Tuition, area resident:* Full-time $14,468. Tuition, state resident: full-time $14,968; part-time $754 per credit hour. Tuition, nonresident: full-time $24,210; part-time $1311 per credit hour. *International tuition:* $26,460 full-time. *Required fees:* $3958; $84 per credit hour. One-time fee: $85 full-time. Tuition and fees vary according to course load, degree level and program. *Faculty research:* Group work, career development, ecology, prevention, multicultural.

University of Detroit Mercy, College of Liberal Arts and Education, Detroit, MI 48221. Offers addiction counseling (MA); addiction studies (Certificate); clinical mental health counseling (MA); clinical psychology (MA, PhD); computer and information systems (MS); criminal justice (MA); curriculum and instruction (MA); economics (MA); educational administration (MA); financial economics (MA); industrial/organizational psychology (MA); information assurance (MS); intelligence analysis (MA); liberal studies (MALS); religious studies (MA); school counseling (MA, Certificate); school psychology (Spec); security administration (MS); special education: emotionally impaired/behaviorally disordered (MA); special education: learning disabilities (MA). *Program availability:* Part-time, evening/weekend. *Degree requirements:* For doctorate, departmental qualifying exam. *Faculty research:* Psychology of aging, history of technology, Renaissance humanism, U.S. and Japanese economic relations.

University of Illinois at Springfield, Graduate Programs, College of Education and Human Services, Program in Human Services, Springfield, IL 62703-5407. Offers alcohol and substance abuse (Graduate Certificate); alcoholism and substance abuse (MA); child and family services (MA); gerontology (MA); social services administration (MA). *Program availability:* Part-time, evening/weekend, 100% online, blended/hybrid learning. *Faculty:* 5 full-time (all women). *Students:* 8 full-time (7 women), 72 part-time (63 women); includes 38 minority (26 Black or African American, non-Hispanic/Latino; 9 Hispanic/Latino; 3 Two or more races, non-Hispanic/Latino). Average age 33. 49 applicants, 47% accepted, 20 enrolled. In 2017, 21 master's, 1 other advanced degree awarded. *Degree requirements:* For master's, internship; capstone project. *Entrance requirements:* For master's, minimum undergraduate GPA of 3.0, 2 letters of recommendation from professional or academic sources, statement of intent, interview. Additional exam requirements/recommendations for international students: Required—TOEFL (minimum score 500 paper-based; 61 iBT). *Application deadline:* Applications are processed on a rolling basis. Application fee: $60 ($75 for international students). Electronic applications accepted. *Expenses:* Tuition, state resident: full-time $7896; part-time $329 per credit hour. Tuition, nonresident: full-time $16,200; part-time $675 per credit hour. Tuition and fees vary according to program. *Financial support:* In 2017–18, research assistantships with full tuition reimbursements (averaging $10,249 per year), teaching assistantships with full tuition reimbursements (averaging $10,303 per year) were awarded; fellowships, career-related internships or fieldwork, Federal Work-Study, scholarships/grants, health care benefits, and unspecified assistantships also available. Support available to part-time students. Financial award application deadline: 11/15; financial award applicants required to submit FAFSA. *Unit head:* Dr. Carolyn Peck, Program Administrator, 217-206-7577, Fax: 217-206-6775, E-mail: peck.carolyn@uis.edu.
Website: http://www.uis.edu/humanservices

University of Lethbridge, School of Graduate Studies, Lethbridge, AB T1K 3M4, Canada. Offers addictions counseling (M Sc); agricultural biotechnology (M Sc); agricultural studies (M Sc, MA); anthropology (MA); archaeology (M Sc, MA); art (MA, MFA); biochemistry (M Sc); biological sciences (M Sc); biomolecular science (PhD); biosystems and biodiversity (PhD); Canadian studies (MA); chemistry (M Sc); computer science (M Sc); computer science and geographical information science (M Sc); counseling (MC); counseling psychology (M Ed); dramatic arts (MA); earth, space, and physical science (PhD); economics (MA); education (MA, PhD); educational leadership (M Ed); English (MA); environmental science (M Sc); evolution and behavior (PhD); exercise science (M Sc); French (MA); French/German (MA); French/Spanish (MA); general education (M Ed); geography (M Sc, MA); German (MA); health sciences (M Sc); individualized multidisciplinary (M Sc, MA); kinesiology (M Sc, MA); management (M Sc), including accounting, finance, human resource management and labor relations, information systems, international management, marketing, policy and strategy; mathematics (M Sc); music (M Mus, MA); Native American studies (MA); neuroscience (M Sc, PhD); new media (MA, MFA); nursing (M Sc, MN); philosophy (MA); physics (M Sc); political science (MA); psychology (M Sc, MA); religious studies (MA); sociology (MA); theatre and dramatic arts (MFA); theoretical and computational science (PhD); urban and regional studies (MA); women and gender studies (MA). *Program availability:* Part-time, evening/weekend. *Degree requirements:* For master's, thesis (for some programs); for doctorate, comprehensive exam, thesis/dissertation. *Entrance requirements:* For master's, GMAT (for M Sc in management), bachelor's degree in related field, minimum GPA of 3.0 during previous 20 graded semester courses, 2 years' teaching or related experience (M Ed); for doctorate, master's degree, minimum graduate GPA of 3.5. Additional exam requirements/recommendations for international students: Required—TOEFL (minimum score 580 paper-based; 93 iBT). Electronic applications accepted. *Faculty research:* Movement and brain plasticity, gibberellin physiology, photosynthesis, carbon cycling, molecular properties of main-group ring components.

University of Louisville, Graduate School, Kent School of Social Work, Louisville, KY 40292-0001. Offers marriage and family therapy (PMC), including mental health; social work (MSSW, PhD), including alcohol and drug counseling (MSSW), gerontology (MSSW), marriage and family (PhD), school social work (MSSW). *Accreditation:* AAMFT/COAMFTE; CSWE (one or more programs are accredited). *Program availability:* Part-time, evening/weekend, 100% online, blended/hybrid learning. *Faculty:* 31 full-time (22 women), 44 part-time/adjunct (35 women). *Students:* 402 full-time (357 women), 103 part-time (88 women); includes 119 minority (68 Black or African American, non-Hispanic/Latino; 1 American Indian or Alaska Native, non-Hispanic/Latino; 8 Asian, non-Hispanic/Latino; 16 Hispanic/Latino; 26 Two or more races, non-Hispanic/Latino), 5 international. Average age 31. 396 applicants, 78% accepted, 228 enrolled. In 2017, 179 master's awarded. *Degree requirements:* For doctorate, comprehensive exam, thesis/dissertation. *Entrance requirements:* For master's, GRE or minimum GPA of 2.75; for doctorate, GRE General Test, interview, writing sample. Additional exam requirements/recommendations for international students: Required—TOEFL (minimum score 550 paper-based; 79 iBT), IELTS (minimum score 6.5). *Application deadline:* For fall admission, 5/30 for domestic and international students; for spring admission, 9/30 for domestic and international students; for summer admission, 2/28 for domestic and international students. Applications are processed on a rolling basis. Application fee: $65. Electronic applications accepted. *Expenses:* Contact institution. *Financial support:* In 2017–18, 11 research assistantships with full tuition reimbursements (averaging $21,500 per year), 1 teaching assistantship with full tuition reimbursement (averaging $19,000 per year) were awarded; scholarships/grants, health care benefits, and unspecified assistantships also available. Financial award application deadline: 5/15; financial award applicants required to submit FAFSA. *Faculty research:* Equipping young children with skills, assisting abused or neglected children, helping juveniles with sexual behavioral problems, illuminating the contributions that men and women make to their families, managing chronic conditions, enhancing trauma-informed services, addressing social and health issues of older adults, palliative and end-of-life care. *Total annual research expenditures:* $6.1 million. *Unit head:* Dr. David Jenkins, Dean, 502-852-3944, Fax: 502-852-0422, E-mail: dajenk03@exchange.louisville.edu. *Application contact:* Misty Kupka, Program Manager for Admissions and Recruitment,

502-852-0414, Fax: 502-852-0422, E-mail: misty.kupka@louisville.edu. Website: http://www.louisville.edu/kent

University of Nevada, Las Vegas, Graduate College, College of Education, Department of Educational and Clinical Studies, Las Vegas, NV 89154-3066. Offers addiction studies (Advanced Certificate); counselor education (M Ed, MS), including clinical mental health (MS), school counseling (M Ed); early childhood education (M Ed); early childhood special education (Certificate), including infancy, preschool; English language learning (M Ed); mental health counseling (Advanced Certificate); special education (M Ed, PhD); PhD/JD. *Program availability:* Part-time. *Faculty:* 18 full-time (9 women), 28 part-time/adjunct (22 women). *Students:* 281 full-time (230 women), 193 part-time (148 women); includes 211 minority (54 Black or African American, non-Hispanic/Latino; 2 American Indian or Alaska Native, non-Hispanic/Latino; 28 Asian, non-Hispanic/Latino; 95 Hispanic/Latino; 4 Native Hawaiian or other Pacific Islander, non-Hispanic/Latino; 28 Two or more races, non-Hispanic/Latino), 13 international. Average age 34. 262 applicants, 76% accepted, 161 enrolled. In 2017, 204 master's, 8 doctorates, 1 other advanced degree awarded. *Degree requirements:* For master's, comprehensive exam (for some programs); for doctorate, comprehensive exam, thesis/dissertation; for other advanced degree, final project. *Entrance requirements:* For master's, bachelor's degree; letter of recommendation; statement of purpose; for doctorate, GRE General Test, statement of purpose; writing sample; 3 letters of recommendation. Additional exam requirements/recommendations for international students: Required—TOEFL (minimum score 550 paper-based; 80 iBT), IELTS (minimum score 7). Application fee: $60 ($95 for international students). Electronic applications accepted. *Expenses:* $275 per credit, $850 per course, $7,969 per year resident, $22,157 per year non-resident, $7,094 non-resident fee (7 credits or more), $1,307 annual health insurance fee. *Financial support:* In 2017–18, 35 students received support, including 10 research assistantships with full tuition reimbursements available (averaging $13,775 per year), 25 teaching assistantships with full tuition reimbursements available (averaging $17,140 per year); institutionally sponsored loans, scholarships/grants, health care benefits, and unspecified assistantships also available. Financial award application deadline: 3/15; financial award applicants required to submit FAFSA. *Faculty research:* Multicultural issues in counseling, academic interventions for students with disabilities, establishment of pro-social skills in young children with severe disabilities, inclusive strategies for students with disabilities, language and literacy for English language learners. *Total annual research expenditures:* $1.1 million. *Unit head:* Dr. Monica Brown, Interim Department Chair/Professor, 702-895-3167, Fax: 702-895-3205, E-mail: monica.brown@unlv.edu. *Application contact:* Dr. Joseph Morgan, Graduate Coordinator, 702-895-3329, Fax: 702-895-3205, E-mail: joseph.morgan@unlv.edu.
Website: http://education.unlv.edu/ecs/

University of New Hampshire, Graduate School, College of Health and Human Services, Department of Social Work, Durham, NH 03824. Offers child welfare (Postbaccalaureate Certificate); intellectual and development disabilities (Postbaccalaureate Certificate); social work (MSW); substance use disorders (Postbaccalaureate Certificate); MSW/JD; MSW/MS. *Accreditation:* CSWE. *Program availability:* Part-time, online learning. *Students:* 186 full-time (155 women), 36 part-time (31 women); includes 23 minority (3 Black or African American, non-Hispanic/Latino; 15 Hispanic/Latino; 5 Two or more races, non-Hispanic/Latino), 1 international. Average age 31. 182 applicants, 67% accepted, 72 enrolled. In 2017, 71 master's, 2 other advanced degrees awarded. *Entrance requirements:* Additional exam requirements/recommendations for international students: Required—TOEFL (minimum score 550 paper-based; 80 iBT). *Application deadline:* For fall admission, 2/1 for domestic and international students. Application fee: $65. Electronic applications accepted. *Financial support:* In 2017–18, 20 students received support, including 8 teaching assistantships; fellowships, research assistantships, career-related internships or fieldwork, Federal Work-Study, and scholarships/grants also available. Support available to part-time students. Financial award application deadline: 2/15. *Unit head:* Vernon Carter, Chair, 603-862-0199. *Application contact:* Emilie Cilley, Administrative Assistant, 603-862-0215, E-mail: emilie.cilley@unh.edu.
Website: https://chhs.unh.edu/sw/master-social-work-msw

University of New Hampshire, Graduate School Manchester Campus, Manchester, NH 03101. Offers business administration (MBA); cybersecurity policy and risk management (MS); educational administration and supervision (Ed S); educational studies (M Ed); elementary education (M Ed); information technology (MS); public administration (MPA); public health (MPH, Certificate); secondary education (M Ed, MAT); social work (MSW); substance use disorders (Certificate). *Program availability:* Part-time, evening/weekend. *Students:* 13 full-time (6 women), 17 part-time (0 women); includes 7 minority (1 Black or African American, non-Hispanic/Latino; 4 Asian, non-Hispanic/Latino; 1 Hispanic/Latino; 1 Two or more races, non-Hispanic/Latino), 10 international. Average age 33. 42 applicants, 71% accepted, 8 enrolled. In 2017, 4 master's awarded. *Entrance requirements:* Additional exam requirements/recommendations for international students: Required—TOEFL (minimum score 550 paper-based; 80 iBT). *Application deadline:* For fall admission, 6/1 for domestic students, 4/1 for international students; for spring admission, 12/1 for domestic students. Application fee: $65. Electronic applications accepted. *Financial support:* Fellowships, research assistantships, teaching assistantships, Federal Work-Study, scholarships/grants, health care benefits, and unspecified assistantships available. Support available to part-time students. Financial award application deadline: 2/15; financial award applicants required to submit FAFSA. *Unit head:* Candice Morey, Educational Programs Coordinator, 603-641-4313, E-mail: unhm.gradcenter@unh.edu.
Website: http://www.gradschool.unh.edu/manchester/

The University of North Carolina at Charlotte, Cato College of Education, Department of Counseling, Charlotte, NC 28223-0001. Offers counseling (MA); counselor education and supervision (PhD); play therapy (Postbaccalaureate Certificate); school counseling (Post-Master's Certificate); substance abuse counseling (Postbaccalaureate Certificate). *Accreditation:* ACA. *Program availability:* Part-time, evening/weekend. *Faculty:* 11 full-time (7 women), 9 part-time/adjunct (7 women). *Students:* 144 full-time (120 women), 83 part-time (72 women); includes 72 minority (46 Black or African American, non-Hispanic/Latino; 5 Asian, non-Hispanic/Latino; 18 Hispanic/Latino; 3 Two or more races, non-Hispanic/Latino), 2 international. Average age 30. 260 applicants, 49% accepted, 80 enrolled. In 2017, 59 master's, 6 doctorates, 23 other advanced degrees awarded. Terminal master's awarded for partial completion of doctoral program. *Degree requirements:* For master's, thesis or alternative, practicum, internship; for doctorate, thesis/dissertation; for other advanced degree, internship. *Entrance requirements:* For master's, GRE or MAT, bachelor's degree from regionally-accredited university, minimum overall GPA of 3.0, brief statement of purpose, professional references, official transcripts; for doctorate, GRE or MAT, master's degree in counseling from a CACREP-accredited program with minimum cumulative GPA of 3.5; one year of experience as a professional counselor (preferred); letters of reference; essay; interview; for other advanced degree, statement of purpose, three reference letters. Additional exam requirements/recommendations for international students: Required—TOEFL (minimum score 523 paper-based; 70 iBT) or IELTS (6.5). *Application deadline:* For fall admission, 12/1 for domestic and international students; for summer admission, 12/1 for domestic and international students. Applications are

processed on a rolling basis. Application fee: $75. Electronic applications accepted. *Expenses:* Tuition, state resident: full-time $4337. Tuition, nonresident: full-time $17,771. *Required fees:* $3211. Tuition and fees vary according to course load and program. *Financial support:* In 2017–18, 5 students received support, including 3 research assistantships (averaging $7,000 per year), 2 teaching assistantships (averaging $3,500 per year); career-related internships or fieldwork, institutionally sponsored loans, scholarships/grants, and unspecified assistantships also available. Support available to part-time students. Financial award application deadline: 3/1; financial award applicants required to submit FAFSA. *Total annual research expenditures:* $10,000. *Unit head:* Dr. Henry L. Harris, Chair, 704-687-8960, E-mail: hharris2@uncc.edu. *Application contact:* Kathy B. Giddings, Director of Graduate Admissions, 704-687-5503, Fax: 704-687-1668, E-mail: gradadm@uncc.edu.
Website: http://counseling.uncc.edu/

University of Oklahoma, Jeannine Rainbolt College of Education, Department of Educational Psychology, Program in Professional Counseling, Norman, OK 73019. Offers professional counseling (M Ed), including drug and alcohol counseling, Oklahoma licensed professional counseling, school counseling. *Students:* 32 full-time (23 women), 2 part-time (1 woman); includes 13 minority (2 Black or African American, non-Hispanic/Latino; 1 American Indian or Alaska Native, non-Hispanic/Latino; 6 Hispanic/Latino; 4 Two or more races, non-Hispanic/Latino). Average age 31. 43 applicants, 51% accepted, 17 enrolled. In 2017, 16 master's awarded. *Degree requirements:* For master's, comprehensive exam. *Entrance requirements:* For master's, GRE. Additional exam requirements/recommendations for international students: Required—TOEFL (minimum score 79 iBT) or IELTS (minimum score 6.5). *Application deadline:* For fall admission, 1/10 for domestic and international students. Application fee: $50 ($100 for international students). Electronic applications accepted. *Expenses:* Tuition, state resident: full-time $5119; part-time $213.30 per credit hour. Tuition, nonresident: full-time $19,778; part-time $824.10 per credit hour. *Required fees:* $3458; $133.55 per credit hour. $126.50 per semester. *Financial support:* In 2017–18, 12 students received support. Research assistantships with full and partial tuition reimbursements available, teaching assistantships with full and partial tuition reimbursements available, and scholarships/grants available. Financial award application deadline: 6/1; financial award applicants required to submit FAFSA. *Faculty research:* Group therapy interventions; family/child counseling; American Indian psychological issues; diversity issues in counseling; drug and alcohol (addictions) counseling/therapy. *Unit head:* Dr. Nancy E. Marchand-Martella, Chair, Department of Educational Psychology, 405-325-0624, Fax: 405-325-6655, E-mail: nmarchand-martella@ou.edu. *Application contact:* Anna Steele, Graduate Programs Specialist, 405-325-4525, Fax: 405-325-7390, E-mail: jrcoe_gps@ou.edu.
Website: http://www.ou.edu/education/edpy.html

University of South Dakota, Graduate School, College of Arts and Sciences, Program in Administrative Studies, Vermillion, SD 57069. Offers addiction studies (MSA); criminal justice studies (MSA); health services administration (MSA); human resources (MSA); interdisciplinary studies (MSA); long term care administration (MSA); organizational leadership (MSA). *Program availability:* Part-time, evening/weekend, 100% online. *Degree requirements:* For master's, thesis or alternative. *Entrance requirements:* For master's, 3 years of work or experience, minimum GPA of 2.7, resume. Additional exam requirements/recommendations for international students: Required—TOEFL (minimum score 550 paper-based; 79 iBT). *Application deadline:* Applications are processed on a rolling basis. Application fee: $35. Electronic applications accepted. *Financial support:* Teaching assistantships with partial tuition reimbursements available. Financial award applicants required to submit FAFSA. *Application contact:* Graduate School, 605-658-6140, Fax: 605-677-6118, E-mail: grad@usd.edu.
Website: http://www.usd.edu/onlinemsa

University of Southern Maine, College of Management and Human Service, School of Education and Human Development, Program in Counselor Education, Portland, ME 04103. Offers clinical mental health counseling (MS); counseling (CAS); culturally responsive practices in education and human development (CGS); mental health rehabilitation technician/community (CGS); rehabilitation counseling (MS); school counseling (MS); substance abuse counseling (CGS). *Accreditation:* ACA (one or more programs are accredited); CORE; TEAC. *Program availability:* Part-time, evening/weekend. *Degree requirements:* For master's, comprehensive exam, thesis or alternative; for other advanced degree, thesis or alternative. *Entrance requirements:* For master's, GRE General Test or MAT, interview; for other advanced degree, master's degree. Additional exam requirements/recommendations for international students: Required—TOEFL (minimum score 550 paper-based; 79 iBT). Electronic applications accepted. *Faculty research:* Counselor licensure, group dynamics, counseling theories, healthy adaptation, counselor educator well-being.

University of South Florida, College of Behavioral and Community Sciences, Department of Child and Family Studies, Tampa, FL 33620-9951. Offers applied behavior analysis (MA, MS, PhD); behavioral and community sciences (PhD); child and adolescent behavioral health (MS), including developmental disabilities, leadership in child and adolescent health, translational research and evaluation, youth and behavioral health; rehabilitation and mental health counseling (MA), including addictions and substance abuse counseling, marriage and family therapy. *Accreditation:* ACA. *Faculty:* 18 full-time (12 women), 2 part-time/adjunct (1 woman). *Students:* 188 full-time (166 women), 115 part-time (92 women); includes 121 minority (40 Black or African American, non-Hispanic/Latino; 8 Asian, non-Hispanic/Latino; 61 Hispanic/Latino; 12 Two or more races, non-Hispanic/Latino), 6 international. Average age 28. 287 applicants, 53% accepted, 89 enrolled. In 2017, 45 master's, 1 doctorate awarded. *Degree requirements:* For master's, comprehensive exam, thesis (for some programs); for doctorate, comprehensive exam, thesis/dissertation, Behavior Analyst Board Certification Exam. *Entrance requirements:* For master's, GRE General Test, minimum GPA of 3.0 in last 60 hours of coursework; letters of recommendation; one-page narrative describing experience, interest, and career goals in applied behavior analysis; resume or curriculum vitae (varies by program); for doctorate, GRE General Test, master's degree in behavioral analysis or closely-related field; minimum GPA of 3.5 in graduate course work; three letters of recommendation; campus visit with faculty interview; personal statement; curriculum vitae; evidence of research experiences and expertise. Additional exam requirements/recommendations for international students: Required—TOEFL (minimum score 550 paper-based; 79 iBT) or IELTS (minimum score 6.5). *Application deadline:* For fall admission, 12/5 for domestic and international students. Application fee: $30. *Financial support:* In 2017–18, 30 students received support. Unspecified assistantships available. *Faculty research:* Applied behavior analysis, autism, behavior management, behavioral intervention, children, developmental disabilities, experimental analysis of behavior, functional assessment, positive behavior support. *Total annual research expenditures:* $17.6 million. *Application contact:* Dr. Raymond G. Miltenberger, Professor/Director of Master's Program, 813-974-5079, Fax: 813-974-6115, E-mail: miltenbe@usf.edu.
Website: http://cfs.cbcs.usf.edu/

The University of Tennessee at Martin, Graduate Programs, College of Education, Health and Behavioral Sciences, Program in Counseling, Martin, TN 38238. Offers addictions counseling (MS Ed); community counseling (MS Ed); school counseling

(MS Ed); student affairs and college counseling (MS Ed). *Accreditation:* NCATE. *Program availability:* Part-time, online only, 100% online. *Students:* 17 full-time (15 women), 54 part-time (51 women); includes 7 minority (6 Black or African American, non-Hispanic/Latino; 1 Two or more races, non-Hispanic/Latino). Average age 34. 35 applicants, 54% accepted, 12 enrolled. In 2017, 14 master's awarded. *Degree requirements:* For master's, comprehensive exam. *Entrance requirements:* For master's, GRE General Test, minimum GPA of 2.5, resume, letters of reference. Additional exam requirements/recommendations for international students: Required—TOEFL (minimum score 525 paper-based; 71 iBT). *Application deadline:* For fall admission, 7/27 priority date for domestic and international students; for spring admission, 12/17 priority date for domestic and international students; for summer admission, 5/10 priority date for domestic and international students. Applications are processed on a rolling basis. Application fee: $30 ($130 for international students). Electronic applications accepted. *Expenses:* Tuition, state resident: full-time $8658; part-time $481 per credit hour. Tuition, nonresident: full-time $14,418; part-time $801 per credit hour. *International tuition:* $22,602 full-time. *Required fees:* $1404; $79 per credit hour. Part-time tuition and fees vary according to course load. *Financial support:* In 2017–18, 14 students received support, including 1 research assistantship with full tuition reimbursement available (averaging $7,540 per year), 2 teaching assistantships with full tuition reimbursements available (averaging $6,283 per year); scholarships/grants and tuition waivers (full and partial) also available. Financial award application deadline: 2/1; financial award applicants required to submit FAFSA. *Unit head:* Cynthia West, Dean, 731-881-7125, Fax: 731-881-7975, E-mail: cwest@utm.edu. *Application contact:* Jolene L. Cunningham, Student Services Specialist, 731-881-7012, Fax: 731-881-7499, E-mail: jcunningham@utm.edu.

Viterbo University, Master of Science in Mental Health Counseling Program, La Crosse, WI 54601-4797. Offers addiction counseling (MS); child and adolescent counseling (MS); complementary health and wellness counseling (MS). *Accreditation:* ACA. *Program availability:* Part-time, evening/weekend. *Degree requirements:* For master's, comprehensive exam, thesis, 54 credits of core program courses; 6 elective credits; minimum GPA of 3.0; action research project; practicum/internship experience. *Entrance requirements:* For master's, MAT, BS in a human service or social science discipline; prerequisite coursework in general psychology, behavior disorders/abnormal psychology, and research methods/statistics; minimum undergraduate cumulative GPA of 3.0; background check; personal statement; undergraduate transcripts; interview. Additional exam requirements/recommendations for international students: Required—TOEFL (minimum score 525 paper-based). Electronic applications accepted. Application fee is waived when completed online. *Expenses:* Contact institution. *Faculty research:* Supervision, recovery substance abuse, culture, counseling theory, health and wellness.

Walden University, Graduate Programs, School of Counseling, Minneapolis, MN 55401. Offers addiction counseling (MS), including addictions and public health, child and adolescent counseling, family studies and interventions, forensic counseling, general program, military families and culture, trauma and crisis counseling; clinical mental health counseling (MS), including addiction counseling, forensic counseling, military families and culture, trauma and crisis counseling; counselor education and supervision (PhD), including consultation, counseling and social change, forensic mental health counseling, leadership and program evaluation, trauma and crisis; marriage, couple, and family counseling (MS), including addiction counseling, career counseling, forensic counseling, military families and culture, trauma and crisis counseling; school counseling (MS), including addiction counseling, career counseling, crisis and trauma, military families and culture. *Accreditation:* ACA. *Program availability:* Part-time, evening/weekend, online only, 100% online. *Degree requirements:* For master's, residency, field experience, professional development plan, licensure plan; for doctorate, thesis/dissertation, residency, practicum, internship. *Entrance requirements:* For master's, bachelor's degree or higher; minimum GPA of 2.5; official transcripts; goal statement (for some programs); access to computer and Internet; for doctorate, master's degree or higher; three years of related professional or academic experience (preferred); minimum GPA of 3.0; goal statement and current resume (for select programs); official transcripts; access to computer and Internet. Additional exam requirements/recommendations for international students: Required—TOEFL (minimum score 550 paper-based, 79 iBT), IELTS (minimum score 6.5), Michigan English Language Assessment Battery (minimum score 82), or PTE (minimum score 53). Electronic applications accepted.

Walden University, Graduate Programs, School of Social Work and Human Services, Minneapolis, MN 55401. Offers addictions and social work (DSW); advanced clinical practice (MSW); clinical expertise (DSW); criminal justice (DSW); disaster, crisis, and intervention (DSW); family studies and interventions (DSW); human and social services (PhD), including advanced research, community and social services, community intervention and leadership, conflict management, criminal justice, disaster crisis and intervention, family studies and intervention, gerontology, global social services, higher education, human services and nonprofit administration, mental health facilitation; medical social work (DSW); military social work (MSW); policy practice (DSW); social work (PhD), including addictions and social work, clinical expertise, criminal justice, disaster, crisis and intervention, family studies and interventions, medical social work, policy practice, social work administration; social work administration (DSW); social work in healthcare (MSW); social work with children and families (MSW). *Accreditation:* CSWE. *Program availability:* Part-time, evening/weekend, online only, 100% online. *Degree requirements:* For master's, residency (for some programs); for doctorate, thesis/dissertation, residency. *Entrance requirements:* For master's, bachelor's degree or higher; minimum GPA of 2.5; official transcripts; goal statement (for some programs); access to computer and Internet; for doctorate, master's degree or higher; three years of related professional or academic experience (preferred); minimum GPA of 3.0; goal statement and current resume (for select programs); official transcripts; access to computer and Internet. Additional exam requirements/recommendations for international students: Required—TOEFL (minimum score 550 paper-based, 79 iBT), IELTS (minimum score 6.5), Michigan English Language Assessment Battery (minimum score 82), or PTE (minimum score 53). Electronic applications accepted.

Washburn University, School of Applied Studies, Department of Human Services, Topeka, KS 66621. Offers addiction counseling (MA). *Program availability:* Evening/weekend. *Entrance requirements:* For master's, minimum GPA of 3.0 in last 60 hours of coursework. Additional exam requirements/recommendations for international students: Required—TOEFL (minimum score 80 iBT). *Faculty research:* Professional identity development in students, expressive therapeutic writing, prevention, community mental health, agency professional development, behavioral analysis, group living among the elderly, ethical identity development, higher education pedagogy, Morita therapy/anxiety disorders, ecological/contextual healing, post-trauma.

Waynesburg University, Graduate and Professional Studies, Canonsburg, PA 15370. Offers business (MBA), including energy management, finance, health systems, human resources, leadership, market development; counseling (MA), including addictions counseling, clinical mental health; counselor education and supervision (PhD); criminal investigation (MA); education (M Ed), including autism, curriculum and instruction, educational leadership, online teaching; nursing (MSN), including administration, education, informatics; nursing practice (DNP); special education (M Ed); technology (M Ed); MSN/MBA. *Accreditation:* AACN. *Program availability:* Part-time, evening/weekend. *Degree requirements:* For doctorate, thesis/dissertation. *Entrance requirements:* Additional exam requirements/recommendations for international students: Required—TOEFL. Electronic applications accepted.

Winona State University, College of Education, Department of Counselor Education, Winona, MN 55987. Offers addiction counseling (Certificate); clinical mental health counseling (MS); human services (MS); school counseling (MS). *Accreditation:* ACA (one or more programs are accredited); NCATE. *Program availability:* Part-time, evening/weekend. *Degree requirements:* For master's, thesis or alternative. *Entrance requirements:* For master's, letters of reference, interview, group activity, on-site writing. Electronic applications accepted.

Applied Behavior Analysis

Antioch University New England, Graduate School, Department of Applied Psychology, Program in Autism Spectrum Disorders, Keene, NH 03431-3552. Offers applied behavior analysis (Certificate); applied behavior analysis internship (Certificate); autism spectrum disorders (Certificate). *Entrance requirements:* Additional exam requirements/recommendations for international students: Required—TOEFL (minimum score 550 paper-based).

Antioch University New England, Graduate School, Department of Education, Experienced Educators Program, Keene, NH 03431-3552. Offers foundations of education (M Ed), including applied behavioral analysis, autism spectrum disorders, educating for sustainability, next-generation learning using technology, problem-based learning using critical skills, teacher leadership; principal certification (PMC). *Degree requirements:* For master's, thesis, practicum. *Entrance requirements:* For master's, previous course work and work experience in education. Additional exam requirements/recommendations for international students: Required—TOEFL (minimum score 550 paper-based). Electronic applications accepted. *Expenses:* Contact institution. *Faculty research:* Classroom action research, school restructuring, problem-based learning, brain-based learning.

Arcadia University, College of Arts and Sciences, Department of Psychology, Glenside, PA 19038-3295. Offers applied behavior analysis (MAC); autism (MAC); child/family therapy (MAC); community public health (MAC); counseling/international peace and conflict resolution dual degree (MAC); mental health counseling (MAC); trauma (MAC). *Program availability:* Part-time. *Degree requirements:* For master's, practicum. *Entrance requirements:* For master's, GRE General Test or MAT. *Expenses:* Contact institution.

Arizona State University at the Tempe campus, College of Liberal Arts and Sciences, Department of Psychology, Tempe, AZ 85287-1104. Offers applied behavior analysis (MS); behavioral neuroscience (PhD); clinical psychology (PhD); cognitive science (PhD); developmental psychology (PhD); quantitative psychology (PhD); social psychology (PhD). *Accreditation:* APA. *Degree requirements:* For doctorate, comprehensive exam, thesis/dissertation, interactive Program of Study (iPOS) submitted before completing 50 percent of required credit hours. *Entrance requirements:* For doctorate, GRE General Test, GRE Subject Test, minimum GPA of 3.0 or equivalent in last 2 years of work leading to bachelor's degree. Additional exam requirements/recommendations for international students: Required—TOEFL, IELTS, or PTE. Electronic applications accepted.

Assumption College, Applied Behavior Analysis Program, Worcester, MA 01609-1296. Offers MA, CAGS. *Program availability:* Part-time, evening/weekend. *Faculty:* 1 (woman) full-time, 3 part-time/adjunct (2 women). *Students:* 7 full-time (6 women), 15 part-time (11 women); includes 3 minority (1 Black or African American, non-Hispanic/Latino; 1 Asian, non-Hispanic/Latino; 1 Hispanic/Latino), 1 international. Average age 32. 27 applicants, 81% accepted, 15 enrolled. *Degree requirements:* For master's, thesis optional, practicum; for CAGS, practicum. *Entrance requirements:* For master's, BA with minimum GPA of 3.0, three letters of recommendation, official transcripts, personal statement, current resume; for CAGS, MA/MS in related field, three letters of recommendation, official transcripts, personal statement, current resume. Additional exam requirements/recommendations for international students: Required—TOEFL (minimum score 540 paper-based; 76 iBT), IELTS (minimum score 6). *Application deadline:* For fall admission, 6/15 for domestic and international students. Application fee: $30. Electronic applications accepted. *Expenses: Tuition:* Full-time $11,952; part-time $664 per credit. *Required fees:* $70 per term. *Financial support:* In 2017–18, 8 students received support. Tuition waivers (full and partial) and institutional discounts available. Financial award application deadline: 6/15; financial award applicants required to submit FAFSA. *Unit head:* Dr. Karen Lionello-DeNolf, Director, 508-767-7498, E-mail: k.lionellodenolf@assumption.edu. *Application contact:* Karen Stoyanoff, Director of Recruitment for Graduate Enrollment, 508-767-7442, Fax: 508-799-4412, E-mail: graduate@assumption.edu.
Website: http://graduate.assumption.edu/applied-behavior/applied-behavior-analysis

Aurora University, School of Education and Human Performance, Aurora, IL 60506-4892. Offers applied behavioral analysis (MS); bilingual-ESL education (MA); educational leadership with principal endorsement (MA); educational technology (MA); leadership in adult learning higher education (Ed D); leadership in curriculum and instruction (Ed D); leadership in educational administration (Ed D); reading instruction (MA); special education (MA). *Accreditation:* NCATE. *Program availability:* Part-time, evening/weekend. *Faculty:* 15 full-time (8 women), 39 part-time/adjunct (20 women). *Students:* 421 full-time (299 women), 142 part-time (89 women); includes 90 minority (25 Black or African American, non-Hispanic/Latino; 7 Asian, non-Hispanic/Latino; 50 Hispanic/Latino; 2 Native Hawaiian or other Pacific Islander, non-Hispanic/Latino; 6 Two or more races, non-Hispanic/Latino). Average age 37. 169 applicants, 95% accepted, 59 enrolled. In 2017, 175 master's, 36 doctorates awarded. *Degree requirements:* For master's, student teaching; for doctorate, comprehensive exam, thesis/dissertation. *Entrance requirements:* For master's, 2 years of teaching experience, valid teaching

certificate, resume; for doctorate, appropriate master's degree, two references, curriculum vitae, personal statement, professional project, reflective essay. Additional exam requirements/recommendations for international students: Required—TOEFL (minimum score 550 paper-based; 79 iBT). *Application deadline:* For fall admission, 6/1 for international students; for spring admission, 10/1 for international students. Applications are processed on a rolling basis. Application fee: $0. Electronic applications accepted. *Expenses:* Contact institution. *Financial support:* In 2017–18, 34 students received support. Federal Work-Study, scholarships/grants, and unspecified assistantships available. Support available to part-time students. Financial award applicants required to submit FAFSA. *Unit head:* Dr. Jen Buckley, Dean, School of Education and Human Performance, 630-844-1542, Fax: 630-844-6155, E-mail: jbuckley@aurora.edu. *Application contact:* Elizabeth Botica, Graduate Education Recruiter, 630-947-8918, E-mail: ebotica@aurora.edu.
Website: http://aurora.edu/education

Ball State University, Graduate School, Teachers College, Department of Special Education, Program in Applied Behavior Analysis, Muncie, IN 47306. Offers applied behavior analysis (MA), including autism. *Program availability:* Part-time, online only, 100% online. *Students:* 158 full-time (144 women), 1,911 part-time (1,762 women); includes 454 minority (144 Black or African American, non-Hispanic/Latino; 72 Asian, non-Hispanic/Latino; 197 Hispanic/Latino; 3 Native Hawaiian or other Pacific Islander, non-Hispanic/Latino; 38 Two or more races, non-Hispanic/Latino), 18 international. Average age 29. 858 applicants, 76% accepted, 485 enrolled. In 2017, 615 master's awarded. *Entrance requirements:* For master's, minimum baccalaureate GPA of 2.75 or 3.0 in latter half of baccalaureate. Additional exam requirements/recommendations for international students: Required—TOEFL (minimum score 550 paper-based; 79 iBT), IELTS (minimum score 6.5). *Application deadline:* For fall admission, 7/10 for domestic students; for spring admission, 11/15 for domestic students; for summer admission, 4/15 for domestic students. Applications are processed on a rolling basis. Application fee: $60. Electronic applications accepted. *Financial support:* Research assistantships with partial tuition reimbursements available. Financial award application deadline: 3/1; financial award applicants required to submit FAFSA. *Unit head:* Dr. David McIntosh, Chairperson, 765-285-5700, Fax: 765-285-4280, E-mail: demcintosh@bsu.edu.
Website: http://www.bsu.edu/specialeducation

Baylor University, Graduate School, School of Education, Department of Educational Psychology, Waco, TX 76798. Offers applied behavior analysis (MS Ed); educational psychology (MA, MS Ed, PhD); exceptionalities (PhD); gifted and talented studies (MS Ed); learning and development (PhD); quantitative methods (MA); school psychology (Ed S). *Accreditation:* NCATE. *Faculty:* 11 full-time (6 women). *Students:* 45 full-time (41 women), 11 part-time (10 women); includes 16 minority (1 Black or African American, non-Hispanic/Latino; 3 Asian, non-Hispanic/Latino; 10 Hispanic/Latino; 2 Two or more races, non-Hispanic/Latino), 4 international. Average age 29. 90 applicants, 33% accepted, 30 enrolled. In 2017, 24 master's, 1 doctorate, 7 other advanced degrees awarded. Terminal master's awarded for partial completion of doctoral program. *Degree requirements:* For master's, thesis optional; for doctorate, comprehensive exam, thesis/dissertation; for Ed S, comprehensive exam, thesis or alternative. *Entrance requirements:* For master's, GRE, minimum GPA of 3.0; for doctorate, GRE General Test, master's degree; for Ed S, GRE General Test. Additional exam requirements/recommendations for international students: Required—TOEFL (minimum score 550 paper-based; 80 iBT), IELTS (minimum score 6.5). *Application deadline:* For fall admission, 2/1 priority date for domestic and international students. Application fee: $80. Electronic applications accepted. *Financial support:* In 2017–18, 42 students received support, including 20 fellowships with full and partial tuition reimbursements available, 22 research assistantships with full and partial tuition reimbursements available; career-related internships or fieldwork, Federal Work-Study, institutionally sponsored loans, scholarships/grants, health care benefits, tuition waivers (full and partial), unspecified assistantships, and stipends also available. Financial award application deadline: 2/1; financial award applicants required to submit FAFSA. *Faculty research:* Individual differences, quantitative methods, gifted and talented, special education, school psychology, autism, applied behavior analysis, learning, human development. *Total annual research expenditures:* $300,000. *Unit head:* Dr. Susan K. Johnsen, Professor and Interim Chair, 254-710-6116, E-mail: susan_johnsen@baylor.edu. *Application contact:* Heather Tindle, Office Manager, 254-710-3112, E-mail: heather_tindle@baylor.edu.
Website: http://www.baylor.edu/soe/EDP/

Bay Path University, Program in Applied Behavior Analysis, Longmeadow, MA 01106-2292. Offers applied behavior analysis (MS); autism spectrum disorders (MS). *Program availability:* Part-time, online learning. *Faculty:* 39 full-time (34 women), 155 part-time/adjunct (118 women). *Students:* 2 full-time (both women), 159 part-time (139 women); includes 27 minority (9 Black or African American, non-Hispanic/Latino; 2 Asian, non-Hispanic/Latino; 12 Hispanic/Latino; 4 Two or more races, non-Hispanic/Latino), 1 international. Average age 31. In 2017, 18 master's awarded. *Application deadline:* Applications are processed on a rolling basis. Application fee: $45. Electronic applications accepted. Application fee is waived when completed online. *Expenses:* $675 per credit. *Financial support:* Unspecified assistantships available. Financial award applicants required to submit FAFSA. *Unit head:* Susan Ainsleigh, Director, E-mail: sainsleigh@baypath.edu. *Application contact:* Diane Ranaldi, Dean of Graduate Admissions, 413-565-1332, Fax: 413-565-1250, E-mail: dranaldi@baypath.edu.

Cairn University, School of Education, Langhorne, PA 19047-2990. Offers applied behavior analysis (MS Sp Ed, Certificate); educational leadership and administration (MS El); instruction (MS Sp Ed); teacher education (MS Ed). *Program availability:* Part-time, evening/weekend, 100% online, blended/hybrid learning. *Entrance requirements:* Additional exam requirements/recommendations for international students: Required—TOEFL (minimum score 550 paper-based). Electronic applications accepted. Application fee is waived when completed online. *Expenses:* Contact institution.

Caldwell University, Department of Applied Behavior Analysis, Caldwell, NJ 07006-6195. Offers MA, PhD, Post-Master's Certificate. *Program availability:* Part-time. *Faculty:* 6 full-time (4 women). *Students:* 18 full-time (17 women), 66 part-time (59 women); includes 18 minority (3 Black or African American, non-Hispanic/Latino; 3 Asian, non-Hispanic/Latino; 11 Hispanic/Latino; 1 Two or more races, non-Hispanic/Latino). Average age 31. 57 applicants, 67% accepted, 17 enrolled. In 2017, 12 master's, 1 doctorate awarded. Terminal master's awarded for partial completion of doctoral program. *Degree requirements:* For master's, comprehensive exam, thesis; for doctorate, comprehensive exam, thesis/dissertation. *Entrance requirements:* For master's, GRE, MAT; for doctorate, GRE, MAT, ABA Certification. Additional exam requirements/recommendations for international students: Required—TOEFL (minimum score 580 paper-based). *Application deadline:* For fall admission, 6/1 for domestic students; for spring admission, 12/1 for domestic students; for summer admission, 4/1 for domestic students. Applications are processed on a rolling basis. Application fee: $50. Electronic applications accepted. *Expenses:* $975 per credit; $225 comprehensive fee per semester. *Financial support:* In 2017–18, 4 fellowships (averaging $35,000 per year) were awarded; 10 clinical assistantships (averaging $23,000 annually) also available. Financial award applicants required to submit FAFSA. *Faculty research:* Autism research. *Unit head:* Dr. Sharon Reeve, Department Chair and Co-Coordinator, 973-618-3315, Fax: 973-615-3580, E-mail: sreeve@caldwell.edu. *Application contact:* Tom Disch, Senior Graduate Admissions Counselor, 973-618-3544, E-mail: graduate@caldwell.edu.

California State University, Fresno, Division of Research and Graduate Studies, College of Science and Mathematics, Department of Psychology, Fresno, CA 93740-8027. Offers applied behavior analysis (MA); general/experimental psychology (MA); school psychology (Ed S). *Degree requirements:* For master's, thesis. *Entrance requirements:* For master's, GRE General Test, GRE Subject Test, minimum GPA of 3.0. Additional exam requirements/recommendations for international students: Required—TOEFL. Electronic applications accepted. *Faculty research:* Oncology prediction, parenting stress, wellness, aging and memory, retrieval inhibition, anger, minority mental health.

California State University, Sacramento, College of Social Sciences and Interdisciplinary Studies, Department of Psychology, Sacramento, CA 95819. Offers applied behavior analysis (MA); industrial/organizational psychology (MA). *Program availability:* Part-time. *Students:* 19 full-time (11 women), 29 part-time (21 women); includes 17 minority (4 Asian, non-Hispanic/Latino; 11 Hispanic/Latino; 2 Native Hawaiian or other Pacific Islander, non-Hispanic/Latino), 1 international. Average age 27. 77 applicants, 32% accepted, 17 enrolled. In 2017, 9 master's awarded. *Degree requirements:* For master's, thesis, project; writing proficiency exam. *Entrance requirements:* For master's, GRE, minimum GPA of 3.0 during previous 2 years. Additional exam requirements/recommendations for international students: Required—TOEFL (minimum score 550 paper-based; 80 iBT); Recommended—IELTS, TSE. *Application deadline:* For fall admission, 3/1 for domestic and international students. Applications are processed on a rolling basis. Application fee: $55. Electronic applications accepted. *Expenses:* Contact institution. *Financial support:* Teaching assistantships, career-related internships or fieldwork, Federal Work-Study, and scholarships/grants available. Support available to part-time students. Financial award application deadline: 3/1; financial award applicants required to submit FAFSA. *Unit head:* Dr. Rebecca Cameron, Interim Department Chair, 916-278-6254, E-mail: cameron@csus.edu. *Application contact:* Jose Martinez, Graduate Admissions Supervisor, 916-278-7871, E-mail: martinj@skymail.csus.edu.
Website: http://www.csus.edu/psyc

California State University, Stanislaus, College of Science, Programs in Psychology, Turlock, CA 95382. Offers behavior analysis (MA, MS); counseling psychology (MS); general psychology (MA). *Program availability:* Part-time. *Degree requirements:* For master's, thesis. *Entrance requirements:* For master's, GRE, minimum GPA of 3.0, 3 letters of reference, 16 psychology prerequisites, personal statement. Additional exam requirements/recommendations for international students: Required—TOEFL (minimum score 550 paper-based). Electronic applications accepted. *Faculty research:* Hedonic tone judgment, syntax and autism, early literacy assessment and native and non-native languages.

Capella University, Harold Abel School of Social and Behavioral Science, Master's Programs in Psychology, Minneapolis, MN 55402. Offers applied behavior analysis (MS); clinical psychology (MS); counseling psychology (MS); educational psychology (MS); evaluation, research, and measurement (MS); general advanced studies in human behavior (MS); general psychology (MS); industrial/organizational psychology (MS); leadership coaching psychology (MS); school psychology (MS); sport psychology (MS).

The Chicago School of Professional Psychology, Program in Applied Behavior Analysis, Chicago, IL 60610. Offers MS, PhD. *Degree requirements:* For master's, thesis, practicum; for doctorate, thesis/dissertation, practicum. *Entrance requirements:* For doctorate, GRE. Additional exam requirements/recommendations for international students: Required—TOEFL.

The Chicago School of Professional Psychology at Downtown Los Angeles, Program in Applied Behavior Analysis, Los Angeles, CA 90017. Offers Psy D.

The Chicago School of Professional Psychology at Downtown Los Angeles, Program in Clinical Psychology, Los Angeles, CA 90017. Offers applied behavior analysis (MA); clinical psychology (Psy D); marital and family therapy (MA).

College of Saint Elizabeth, Program in Applied Behavior Analysis, Morristown, NJ 07960-6989. Offers MA, Certificate. *Program availability:* Part-time. *Faculty:* 1 part-time/adjunct (0 women). *Students:* 1 (woman) full-time, 1 (woman) part-time. Average age 35. 4 applicants, 75% accepted, 2 enrolled. *Degree requirements:* For master's, thesis. *Entrance requirements:* Additional exam requirements/recommendations for international students: Required—TOEFL (minimum score 550 paper-based; 79 iBT), IELTS (minimum score 6.5). *Application deadline:* For fall admission, 5/1 for international students. Applications are processed on a rolling basis. Application fee: $35. Electronic applications accepted. Application fee is waived when completed online. *Financial support:* Career-related internships or fieldwork, scholarships/grants, and unspecified assistantships available. Financial award applicants required to submit FAFSA. *Unit head:* Dr. Brian S. Friedlander, Coordinator, 973-290-4386, E-mail: bfriedlander@cse.edu. *Application contact:* Lori J. Fragoso, Director of Graduate and Continuing Studies Admissions, 973-290-4413, Fax: 973-290-4710, E-mail: apply@cse.edu.
Website: http://www.cse.edu/academics/prof-studies/applied-behavior-analysis/ma-in-applied-behavior-analysis

Drake University, School of Education, Des Moines, IA 50311-4516. Offers applied behavior analysis (MS); counseling (MS); education (PhD); education administration (Ed D); educational leadership (MSE, Ed D); effective teaching (MSE); leadership development (MS); literacy (Ed S); literacy education (MSE); rehabilitation administration (MS); rehabilitation placement (MS); special education (MSE); STEM education (MSE); teacher education (5-12) (MAT); teacher education (K-8) (MST); teacher effectiveness and professional development (MSE). *Program availability:* Part-time, evening/weekend. *Degree requirements:* For master's and Ed S, comprehensive exam, internships (for some programs); for doctorate, comprehensive exam, thesis/dissertation, internships (for some programs). *Entrance requirements:* For master's, GRE General Test, MAT, or Drake Writing Assessment, resume, 2 letters of recommendation; for doctorate, GRE General Test or MAT, master's degree, 3 letters of recommendation; for Ed S, GRE General Test or MAT. Additional exam requirements/recommendations for international students: Required—TOEFL (minimum score 550 paper-based). *Application deadline:* For fall admission, 7/1 priority date for domestic students, 6/1 priority date for international students; for spring admission, 11/1 priority date for domestic students, 10/1 priority date for international students. Applications are processed on a rolling basis. Application fee: $25. Electronic applications accepted. *Expenses:* Contact institution. *Financial support:* Research assistantships, career-related internships or fieldwork, and unspecified assistantships available. Support available to part-time students. *Faculty research:* Counseling and rehabilitation, behavioral supports, inquiry-based science methods, teacher quality enhancement. *Unit head:* Dr. Janet McMahill, Dean, 515-271-3829, E-mail: janet.mcmahill@drake.edu.
Website: http://www.drake.edu/soe/

Drexel University, Goodwin College of Professional Studies, School of Education, Philadelphia, PA 19104-2875. Offers applied behavior analysis (MS); creativity and

innovation (MS); education improvement and transformation (MS); educational administration (MS); educational leadership and management (Ed D); educational leadership development and learning technologies (PhD); global and international education (MS); higher education (MS); human resources development (MS); learning technologies (MS); mathematics, learning and teaching (MS); special education (MS); teaching, learning and curriculum (MS). *Program availability:* Part-time, evening/weekend, online learning. *Degree requirements:* For doctorate, thesis/dissertation. *Entrance requirements:* For doctorate, GRE or GMAT. Additional exam requirements/recommendations for international students: Required—TOEFL, IELTS. Electronic applications accepted. Application fee is waived when completed online. *Expenses:* Contact institution. *Faculty research:* Leadership development, mathematics education, literacy, autism, educational technology.

Elms College, Division of Social Sciences, Chicopee, MA 01013-2839. Offers applied behavior analysis (MS); autism spectrum disorders (MS, CAGS); communication sciences and disorders (CAGS). *Program availability:* Part-time. *Faculty:* 2 full-time (1 woman), 3 part-time/adjunct (1 woman). *Students:* 3 full-time (all women), 22 part-time (19 women); includes 1 minority (Black or African American, non-Hispanic/Latino). Average age 31. 24 applicants, 75% accepted, 15 enrolled. In 2017, 6 master's, 3 other advanced degrees awarded. *Entrance requirements:* For degree, minimum GPA of 3.0. Additional exam requirements/recommendations for international students: Required—TOEFL. *Application deadline:* Applications are processed on a rolling basis. Application fee: $30. Electronic applications accepted. *Expenses: Tuition:* Full-time $13,860; part-time $770 per credit hour. *Required fees:* $200. Tuition and fees vary according to degree level and program. *Financial support:* Applicants required to submit FAFSA. *Unit head:* Dr. John Lambdin, Chair, Division of Social Sciences, 413-265-2442, E-mail: lambdinj@elms.edu. *Application contact:* School of Graduate and Professional Studies, 413-265-2445, E-mail: graduateeducation@elms.edu.

Endicott College, Van Loan School of Graduate and Professional Studies, Program in Autism and Applied Behavior Analysis, Beverly, MA 01915-2096. Offers applied behavior analysis (M Ed, PhD); autism (Certificate); autism and applied behavior analysis (M Ed). *Program availability:* Part-time, evening/weekend, 100% online, blended/hybrid learning. *Faculty:* 5 full-time (3 women), 23 part-time/adjunct (18 women). *Students:* 21 full-time (19 women), 178 part-time (149 women); includes 39 minority (12 Black or African American, non-Hispanic/Latino; 9 Asian, non-Hispanic/Latino; 17 Hispanic/Latino; 1 Two or more races, non-Hispanic/Latino), 1 international. Average age 31. 66 applicants, 95% accepted, 54 enrolled. In 2017, 59 master's awarded. *Degree requirements:* For master's, thesis; for doctorate, thesis/dissertation, qualifying examination. *Entrance requirements:* For master's, MAT or GRE, undergraduate transcript, two recommendations, personal statement. Additional exam requirements/recommendations for international students: Required—TOEFL. *Application deadline:* Applications are processed on a rolling basis. Application fee: $50. Electronic applications accepted. *Expenses:* Contact institution. *Financial support:* Applicants required to submit FAFSA. *Faculty research:* ABA intervention for autism, behavioral assessment, evidence-based treatments. *Unit head:* Dr. Mary Jane Weiss, Director of Autism and Applied Behavior Analysis, 978-232-2199, E-mail: mweiss@endicott.edu. *Application contact:* Ian Menchini, Director, Graduate Enrollment and Advising, 978-232-5292, Fax: 978-232-3000, E-mail: imenchin@endicott.edu.
Website: http://www.endicott.edu/VanLoan/Institute-Behavioral-Studies/Degree-Programs/Master-Ed-Autism-ABA.aspx

Fairfield University, Graduate School of Education and Allied Professions, Fairfield, CT 06824. Offers applied behavior analysis (ATC); applied psychology (MA); clinical mental health counseling (MA, CAS); educational technology (MA); elementary education (MA, CAS); family studies (MA); integration of spirituality and religion in counseling (ATC); marriage and family therapy (MA); reading and language development (Sixth Year Certificate); school counseling (MA, CAS); school psychology (MA, CAS); school-based marriage and family therapy (ATC); secondary education (MA); special education (MA, CAS); substance abuse counseling (ATC); teaching (Certificate); teaching and foundations (MA, CAS); TESOL, world languages, and bilingual education (MA, CAS). *Accreditation:* NCATE. *Program availability:* Part-time, evening/weekend. *Faculty:* 23 full-time (17 women), 39 part-time/adjunct (28 women). *Students:* 199 full-time (168 women), 251 part-time (206 women); includes 85 minority (21 Black or African American, non-Hispanic/Latino; 9 Asian, non-Hispanic/Latino; 49 Hispanic/Latino; 6 Two or more races, non-Hispanic/Latino), 4 international. Average age 32. 370 applicants, 56% accepted, 125 enrolled. In 2017, 136 master's, 28 other advanced degrees awarded. *Degree requirements:* For master's, comprehensive exam. *Entrance requirements:* For master's, minimum GPA of 3.0, 2 recommendations, resume. Additional exam requirements/recommendations for international students: Required—TOEFL (minimum score 550 paper-based; 84 iBT) or IELTS (minimum score 7.5). *Application deadline:* For fall admission, 2/15 for international students; for spring admission, 10/1 for international students. Application fee: $60. Electronic applications accepted. *Expenses:* $750 per credit hour. *Financial support:* In 2017–18, 34 students received support. Career-related internships or fieldwork and unspecified assistantships available. Support available to part-time students. Financial award applicants required to submit FAFSA. *Faculty research:* Reading and literacy, writing, social justice and inequality in education, addictions and mental health issues, therapeutic relationships and clinical supervision. *Unit head:* Dr. Robert D. Hannafin, Dean, 203-254-4250, Fax: 203-254-4241, E-mail: rhannafin@fairfield.edu. *Application contact:* Marianne Gumpper, Director of Graduate Admission, 203-254-4184, Fax: 203-254-4073, E-mail: gradadmis@fairfield.edu.
Website: http://www.fairfield.edu/gseap

Florida Institute of Technology, College of Psychology and Liberal Arts, Program in Applied Behavior Analysis, Melbourne, FL 32901-6975. Offers MS. *Program availability:* Part-time. *Students:* Average age 30. 146 applicants, 36% accepted, 27 enrolled. In 2017, 19 master's awarded. *Degree requirements:* For master's, comprehensive exam, thesis optional, minimum of 44 credit hours, all courses at least grade of B or better. *Entrance requirements:* For master's, GRE General Test, minimum GPA of 3.0, 3 letters of recommendation, resume, statement of objectives. Additional exam requirements/recommendations for international students: Required—TOEFL (minimum score 550 paper-based; 79 iBT). *Application deadline:* Applications are processed on a rolling basis. Application fee: $50. Electronic applications accepted. *Expenses: Tuition:* Part-time $1241 per credit hour. Part-time tuition and fees vary according to campus/location. *Financial support:* Research assistantships with partial tuition reimbursements, teaching assistantships with partial tuition reimbursements, career-related internships or fieldwork, and tuition waivers (partial) available. *Faculty research:* In-home behavioral programs for children, teaching language to autistic children, anticipated strategies in behavioral changes. *Unit head:* Dr. David Wilder, Program Chair, 321-674-7516, E-mail: dawilder@fit.edu. *Application contact:* Cheryl A. Brown, Associate Director of Graduate Admissions, 321-674-7581, Fax: 321-723-9468, E-mail: cbrown@fit.edu.
Website: http://cpla.fit.edu/aba/

Florida Institute of Technology, College of Psychology and Liberal Arts, Program in Applied Behavior Analysis and Organizational Behavior Management, Melbourne, FL 32901-6975. Offers MS. *Program availability:* Part-time. *Students:* Average age 25. 36 applicants, 39% accepted, 7 enrolled. In 2017, 5 master's awarded. *Degree requirements:* For master's, comprehensive exam, thesis or alternative, minimum of 50 credits, all course grades of B or higher. *Entrance requirements:* For master's, GRE General Test, 3 letters of recommendation, resume, statement of objectives. Additional exam requirements/recommendations for international students: Required—TOEFL (minimum score 550 paper-based; 79 iBT). *Application deadline:* Applications are processed on a rolling basis. Electronic applications accepted. *Expenses: Tuition:* Part-time $1241 per credit hour. Part-time tuition and fees vary according to campus/location. *Unit head:* Dr. David Wilder, Program Chair, 321-674-7516, E-mail: dawilder@fit.edu. *Application contact:* Cheryl A. Brown, Associate Director of Graduate Admissions, 321-674-7581, Fax: 321-723-9468, E-mail: cbrown@fit.edu.
Website: http://cpla.fit.edu/programs.php

Florida Institute of Technology, College of Psychology and Liberal Arts, Program in Behavior Analysis, Melbourne, FL 32901-6975. Offers PhD. *Program availability:* Evening/weekend. *Students:* Average age 30. 12 applicants, 33% accepted, 4 enrolled. In 2017, 2 doctorates awarded. *Degree requirements:* For doctorate, comprehensive exam, thesis/dissertation, minimum of 87 credit hours beyond bachelor's degree (44 credit hours at Florida Tech), all course grades of B or higher. *Entrance requirements:* For doctorate, GRE General Test, 3 letters of recommendation, resume, statement of objectives, minimum graduate GPA of 3.6 (undergraduate 3.0), interviews. Additional exam requirements/recommendations for international students: Required—TOEFL (minimum score 550 paper-based; 79 iBT). *Expenses: Tuition:* Part-time $1241 per credit hour. Part-time tuition and fees vary according to campus/location. *Unit head:* Dr. Jose Martinez-Diaz, Associate Dean, 321-674-8360, E-mail: jmartine@fit.edu. *Application contact:* Cheryl A. Brown, Associate Director of Graduate Admissions, 321-674-7581, Fax: 321-723-9468, E-mail: cbrown@fit.edu.
Website: http://www.fit.edu/programs/

Florida Institute of Technology, College of Psychology and Liberal Arts, Program in Professional Behavior Analysis, Melbourne, FL 32901-6975. Offers MA. *Accreditation:* APA. *Program availability:* Part-time, 100% online. *Students:* Average age 30. 122 applicants, 74% accepted, 57 enrolled. In 2017, 85 master's awarded. Terminal master's awarded for partial completion of doctoral program. *Degree requirements:* For master's, comprehensive exam, minimum of 45 credit hours. *Entrance requirements:* For master's, resume; statement of objectives; minimum undergraduate GPA of 3.0, 3.5 after taking 12 credit hours at graduate-level institution in behavior analysis; transcripts; 3 letters of recommendation. Additional exam requirements/recommendations for international students: Required—TOEFL (minimum score 550 paper-based; 79 iBT). *Application deadline:* For fall admission, 4/1 for international students; for spring admission, 9/30 for international students. Applications are processed on a rolling basis. Application fee: $0. Electronic applications accepted. *Expenses: Tuition:* Part-time $1241 per credit hour. Part-time tuition and fees vary according to campus/location. *Financial support:* Career-related internships or fieldwork, institutionally sponsored loans, tuition waivers (partial), unspecified assistantships, and tuition remissions available. Support available to part-time students. Financial award application deadline: 3/1; financial award applicants required to submit FAFSA. *Faculty research:* Addictions, neuropsychology, child abuse, assessment, psychological trauma. *Unit head:* Dr. Jose Martinez-Diaz, Head of School of Behavioral Analysis, 321-674-8359, Fax: 321-674-7105, E-mail: jmartine@fit.edu. *Application contact:* Cheryl A. Brown, Associate Director of Graduate Admissions, 321-674-7581, Fax: 321-723-9468, E-mail: cbrown@fit.edu.
Website: http://www.fit.edu/programs/

Florida International University, College of Arts, Sciences, and Education, Department of Psychology, Miami, FL 33199. Offers behavioral analysis (MS); clinical science (PhD); cognitive neuroscience (PhD); counseling psychology (MS); developmental science (MS, PhD); legal psychology (MS, PhD); organizational psychology (MS, PhD). Program has fall admissions only. *Accreditation:* APA. *Program availability:* Part-time, evening/weekend. *Faculty:* 45 full-time (28 women), 48 part-time/adjunct (31 women). *Students:* 162 full-time (122 women), 13 part-time (5 women); includes 94 minority (11 Black or African American, non-Hispanic/Latino; 5 Asian, non-Hispanic/Latino; 75 Hispanic/Latino; 3 Two or more races, non-Hispanic/Latino), 12 international. Average age 27. 290 applicants, 21% accepted, 50 enrolled. In 2017, 43 master's, 13 doctorates awarded. Terminal master's awarded for partial completion of doctoral program. *Degree requirements:* For master's, thesis; for doctorate, comprehensive exam, thesis/dissertation. *Entrance requirements:* For master's, GRE General Test, minimum GPA of 3.0, resume, 3 letters of recommendation; for doctorate, GRE General Test, 3 letters of recommendation, resume, letter of intent, two writing samples, minimum GPA of 3.0. Additional exam requirements/recommendations for international students: Required—TOEFL (minimum score 550 paper-based; 80 iBT). *Application deadline:* For fall admission, 12/15 for domestic and international students. Application fee: $30. Electronic applications accepted. *Expenses:* Tuition, state resident: full-time $8912; part-time $446 per credit hour. Tuition, nonresident: full-time $21,393; part-time $992 per credit hour. *Required fees:* $390; $195 per semester. *Financial support:* Institutionally sponsored loans and scholarships/grants available. Financial award application deadline: 3/1. *Faculty research:* Legal psychology, organizational and industrial psychology, child behavior psychology. *Unit head:* Dr. Jeremy Pettit, Interim Chair, 305-348-1671, Fax: 305-348-3646, E-mail: jeremy.pettit@fiu.edu. *Application contact:* Nanett Rojas, Assistant Director, Graduate Admissions, 305-348-7464, Fax: 305-348-7441, E-mail: gradadm@fiu.edu.

Florida State University, The Graduate School, College of Arts and Sciences, Department of Psychology, Program in Applied Behavior Analysis, Tallahassee, FL 32306. Offers MS. *Faculty:* 3 full-time (1 woman). *Students:* 37 full-time (35 women); includes 8 minority (1 Black or African American, non-Hispanic/Latino; 1 Asian, non-Hispanic/Latino; 3 Hispanic/Latino; 3 Two or more races, non-Hispanic/Latino). Average age 25. 59 applicants, 37% accepted, 16 enrolled. In 2017, 16 master's awarded. *Degree requirements:* For master's, comprehensive exam. *Entrance requirements:* For master's, GRE General Test, minimum GPA of 3.0. *Application deadline:* For fall admission, 1/15 for domestic and international students. Application fee: $30. Electronic applications accepted. *Financial support:* In 2017–18, 37 students received support, including 37 teaching assistantships with full tuition reimbursements available (averaging $17,000 per year); career-related internships or fieldwork and health care benefits also available. Financial award application deadline: 1/15; financial award applicants required to submit FAFSA. *Unit head:* Dr. Jon Bailey, Head, 850-644-1877, Fax: 850-645-7518, E-mail: bailey@psy.fsu.edu. *Application contact:* Lynda L. Gibson, Graduate Program Associate, 850-644-2499, Fax: 850-644-7739, E-mail: grad-info@psy.fsu.edu.
Website: http://www.psy.fsu.edu/

Georgian Court University, School of Arts and Sciences, Lakewood, NJ 08701-2697. Offers applied behavior analysis (MA); autism spectrum disorders (Certificate); clinical mental health counseling (MA); criminal justice and human rights (MS); holistic health studies (MA, Certificate); homeland security (Certificate); instructional technology (CPC); mercy spirituality (Certificate); parish business management (Certificate); professional counselor (Certificate); school psychology (MA, Certificate); theology (MA, Certificate). *Program availability:* Part-time, evening/weekend. *Faculty:* 18 full-time (11 women), 8 part-time/adjunct (4 women). *Students:* 100 full-time (86 women), 92 part-time (67 women); includes 34 minority (9 Black or African American, non-Hispanic/

Latino; 1 Asian, non-Hispanic/Latino; 20 Hispanic/Latino; 4 Two or more races, non-Hispanic/Latino), 2 international. Average age 34. 187 applicants, 56% accepted, 78 enrolled. In 2017, 58 master's, 20 other advanced degrees awarded. *Degree requirements:* For master's, comprehensive exam (for some programs), thesis (for some programs). *Entrance requirements:* For master's, GRE, GMAT, or NTE/PRAXIS, 3 letters of recommendation. Additional exam requirements/recommendations for international students: Required—TOEFL (minimum score 550 paper-based). *Application deadline:* For fall admission, 8/15 for domestic students, 5/1 for international students; for spring admission, 1/15 for domestic students, 10/1 for international students. Applications are processed on a rolling basis. Application fee: $40. Electronic applications accepted. *Expenses: Tuition:* Part-time $839 per credit. *Required fees:* $248 per semester. Tuition and fees vary according to campus/location and program. *Financial support:* Scholarships/grants, health care benefits, and unspecified assistantships available. Financial award application deadline: 4/15; financial award applicants required to submit FAFSA. *Unit head:* Dr. Mary Chinery, Dean, 732-987-2493, Fax: 732-987-2007, E-mail: mchinery@georgian.edu. *Application contact:* Patrick Givens, Director of Graduate and Professional Studies Admissions, 732-987-2736, Fax: 732-987-2000, E-mail: gps@georgian.edu.
Website: https://georgian.edu/academics/school-of-arts-sciences/

Hofstra University, School of Education, Specialized Programs in Education, Hempstead, NY 11549. Offers applied behavior analysis (Advanced Certificate); childhood special education (MS Ed); early childhood special education (MS Ed, Advanced Certificate); educational and policy leadership (Ed D); educational leadership (Advanced Certificate), including school building leader/school district business leader; educational leadership and policy studies (MS Ed), including K-12; elementary special education (MS Ed); gifted education (Advanced Certificate), including school building leader/school district business leader; health education (MS); health professions pedagogy and leadership (MS); higher education leadership and policy studies (MS Ed); inclusive early childhood special education (MS Ed); inclusive elementary special education (MS Ed); inclusive secondary special education (MS Ed); literacy studies (MA, MS Ed, Ed D, Advanced Certificate), including birth-grade 6 (MS Ed, Advanced Certificate), grades 5-12 (MS Ed, Advanced Certificate), literacy studies (Ed D); pedagogy for health professions (Advanced Certificate); physical education (MS); school district business leader (Advanced Certificate); secondary education generalist - students with disabilities 7-12 (MS Ed), including students with disabilities 7-12; secondary special education generalist (MS Ed), including extension in secondary education; special education (MS Ed, Advanced Certificate); special education assessment and diagnosis (Advanced Certificate); special education early childhood intervention (MS Ed); special education: international perspectives (MS Ed); teaching students with severe or multiple disabilities (Advanced Certificate). *Program availability:* Part-time, evening/weekend, blended/hybrid learning. *Students:* 148 full-time (110 women), 249 part-time (188 women); includes 105 minority (54 Black or African American, non-Hispanic/Latino; 1 American Indian or Alaska Native, non-Hispanic/Latino; 13 Asian, non-Hispanic/Latino; 35 Hispanic/Latino; 1 Native Hawaiian or other Pacific Islander, non-Hispanic/Latino; 1 Two or more races, non-Hispanic/Latino), 1 international. Average age 32. 228 applicants, 93% accepted, 132 enrolled. In 2017, 97 master's, 22 doctorates, 31 other advanced degrees awarded. *Degree requirements:* For master's, one foreign language, comprehensive exam (for some programs), thesis (for some programs), electronic portfolio, capstone course, internship, practicum, student teaching, seminars, minimum GPA of 3.0; for doctorate, one foreign language, comprehensive exam, thesis/dissertation, qualifying hearing. *Entrance requirements:* For master's, GRE, interview, letters of recommendation, portfolio, essay, certification; for doctorate, GRE or MAT, interview, resume, essay, master's degree, 3 letters of recommendation, writing sample; for Advanced Certificate, GRE, interview, letters of recommendation, essay, professional experience, resume, master's degree. Additional exam requirements/recommendations for international students: Required—TOEFL (minimum score 550 paper-based; 80 iBT). *Application deadline:* Applications are processed on a rolling basis. Application fee: $75. Electronic applications accepted. *Expenses: Tuition:* Full-time $1292. *Required fees:* $970. Tuition and fees vary according to program. *Financial support:* In 2017–18, 225 students received support, including 118 fellowships with full and partial tuition reimbursements available (averaging $3,887 per year), 12 research assistantships with full and partial tuition reimbursements available (averaging $7,215 per year); career-related internships or fieldwork, Federal Work-Study, institutionally sponsored loans, scholarships/grants, traineeships, tuition waivers (full and partial), and unspecified assistantships also available. Support available to part-time students. Financial award applicants required to submit FAFSA. *Faculty research:* Collaborative teaching and learning; language and culture; new media literacies; applied behavior analysis; K-12 leadership development. *Unit head:* Dr. Elfreda Blue, Chairperson, 516-463-5762, Fax: 516-463-6184, E-mail: elfreda.blue@hofstra.edu. *Application contact:* Sunil Samuel, Assistant Vice President of Admissions, 516-463-4723, Fax: 516-463-4664, E-mail: graduateadmission@hofstra.edu.
Website: http://www.hofstra.edu/education/

James Madison University, The Graduate School, College of Health and Behavioral Studies, Program in Psychological Sciences, Harrisonburg, VA 22801. Offers applied research (MA); behavior analysis (MA); experimental psychology (MA); quantitative psychology (MA). *Program availability:* Part-time, evening/weekend. *Students:* 18 full-time (10 women), 2 part-time (1 woman); includes 3 minority (1 American Indian or Alaska Native, non-Hispanic/Latino; 1 Asian, non-Hispanic/Latino; 1 Two or more races, non-Hispanic/Latino), 1 international. Average age 30. In 2017, 9 master's awarded. Application fee: $55. Electronic applications accepted. *Expenses:* Tuition, state resident: full-time $10,512; part-time $438 per credit hour. Tuition, nonresident: full-time $28,358; part-time $1162 per credit hour. *Required fees:* $1128. *Financial support:* In 2017–18, 18 students received support, including 1 teaching assistantship with full tuition reimbursement available (averaging $9,284 per year); career-related internships or fieldwork, Federal Work-Study, and 16 assistantships (averaging $7911) also available. Financial award application deadline: 3/1; financial award applicants required to submit FAFSA. *Unit head:* Dr. Jeff S. Dyche, Graduate Program Director, 540-568-4965, E-mail: dychejs@jmu.edu. *Application contact:* Lynette D. Michael, Director of Graduate Admissions, 540-568-6131 Ext. 6395, Fax: 540-568-7860, E-mail: michaeld@jmu.edu.
Website: http://www.psyc.jmu.edu/psycsciences/

Johns Hopkins University, School of Education, Certificate Programs in Education, Baltimore, MD 21218. Offers advanced methods for differentiated instruction and inclusive education (Graduate Certificate); applied behavior analysis (Post-Master's Certificate); clinical mental health counseling (Post-Master's Certificate); counseling (Advanced Certificate); data-based decision making and organizational improvement (Graduate Certificate); early intervention/preschool special education specialist (Graduate Certificate); education of students with autism and other pervasive developmental disorders (Graduate Certificate); educational leadership for independent schools (Graduate Certificate); evidence-based teaching in the health professions (Post-Master's Certificate); gifted education (Graduate Certificate); leadership in technology integration (Graduate Certificate); mind, brain and teaching (Graduate Certificate); school administration and supervision (Graduate Certificate); urban education (Graduate Certificate). *Program availability:* Part-time-only, evening/weekend, 100% online, blended/hybrid learning. *Entrance requirements:* For degree, minimum of bachelor's degree from regionally- or nationally-accredited institution (master's degree for some programs); minimum GPA of 3.0 in all previous programs of study; official transcripts from all post-secondary institutions attended; essay; curriculum vitae/resume; two letters of recommendation; dispositions survey. Electronic applications accepted. *Expenses:* Contact institution.

Lindenwood University, Graduate Programs, School of Education, St. Charles, MO 63301-1695. Offers behavioral analysis (MA); education (MA), including autism spectrum disorders, character education, early intervention in autism and sensory impairment, gifted, technology; educational administration (MA, Ed D, Ed S); English to speakers of other languages (MA); instructional leadership (Ed D, Ed S); library media (MA); professional counseling (MA); school administration (MA, Ed S); school counseling (MA); teaching (MA). *Program availability:* Part-time, evening/weekend, 100% online, blended/hybrid learning. *Faculty:* 47 full-time (31 women), 213 part-time/adjunct (135 women). *Students:* 434 full-time (319 women), 1,292 part-time (989 women); includes 387 minority (313 Black or African American, non-Hispanic/Latino; 9 American Indian or Alaska Native, non-Hispanic/Latino; 13 Asian, non-Hispanic/Latino; 37 Hispanic/Latino; 1 Native Hawaiian or other Pacific Islander, non-Hispanic/Latino; 14 Two or more races, non-Hispanic/Latino), 20 international. Average age 36. 828 applicants, 61% accepted, 378 enrolled. In 2017, 431 master's, 63 doctorates, 94 other advanced degrees awarded. *Degree requirements:* For master's, thesis (for some programs), minimum GPA of 3.0; for doctorate, thesis/dissertation, minimum GPA of 3.0; for Ed S, comprehensive exam, project, minimum GPA of 3.0. *Entrance requirements:* For master's, interview, minimum undergraduate cumulative GPA of 3.0, writing sample, letter of recommendation; for doctorate, GRE, minimum graduate GPA of 3.4, resume, interview, writing sample, 4 letters of recommendation; for Ed S, master's degree in education, relevant work experience. Additional exam requirements/recommendations for international students: Required—TOEFL (minimum score 550 paper-based; 80 iBT); Recommended—IELTS (minimum score 6.5). *Application deadline:* For fall admission, 8/27 priority date for domestic and international students; for spring admission, 1/14 priority date for domestic and international students; for summer admission, 6/4 priority date for domestic and international students. Applications are processed on a rolling basis. Application fee: $30 ($100 for international students). Electronic applications accepted. *Expenses: Tuition:* Full-time $16,300; part-time $460 per credit. *Required fees:* $660; $330 per credit. Tuition and fees vary according to degree level and program. *Financial support:* In 2017–18, 1,615 students received support. Career-related internships or fieldwork, Federal Work-Study, institutionally sponsored loans, scholarships/grants, tuition waivers (partial), and unspecified assistantships available. Financial award application deadline: 6/30; financial award applicants required to submit FAFSA. *Unit head:* Dr. Anthony Scheffler, Dean, School of Education, 636-949-4618, Fax: 636-949-4197, E-mail: ascheffler@lindenwood.edu. *Application contact:* Kara Schilli, Director, Evening and Graduate Admissions, 636-949-4349, Fax: 636-949-4109, E-mail: adultadmissions@lindenwood.edu.
Website: http://www.lindenwood.edu/academics/academic-schools/school-of-education/

Lipscomb University, College of Education, Nashville, TN 37204-3951. Offers applied behavior analysis (MS, Certificate); coaching for learning (M Ed, Certificate, Ed S); educational leadership (M Ed, Ed S); English language learning (M Ed, Ed S); instructional coaching (M Ed, Certificate, Ed S); instructional practice (M Ed); learning organizations and strategic change (Ed D); literacy coaching (Certificate, Ed S); reading specialty (M Ed, Ed S); school counseling (M Ed, Ed S); special education (M Ed); teaching, learning, and leading (M Ed); technology integration (M Ed, Ed S); technology integration specialist (Certificate). *Accreditation:* NCATE. *Program availability:* Part-time, evening/weekend, 100% online. *Faculty:* 21 full-time (14 women), 42 part-time/adjunct (29 women). *Students:* 565 full-time (452 women), 59 part-time (45 women); includes 154 minority (102 Black or African American, non-Hispanic/Latino; 2 American Indian or Alaska Native, non-Hispanic/Latino; 8 Asian, non-Hispanic/Latino; 26 Hispanic/Latino; 16 Two or more races, non-Hispanic/Latino). Average age 32. 395 applicants, 54% accepted, 196 enrolled. In 2017, 162 master's, 30 doctorates, 54 other advanced degrees awarded. *Degree requirements:* For master's, comprehensive exam, portfolio, research project and presentation; for doctorate, practical capstone project in experiential setting. *Entrance requirements:* For master's, MAT (minimum score 31) or GRE General Test (minimum score 294), 2 reference letters, goals statement, writing sample, interview; for doctorate, MAT or GRE General Test, 3 reference letters, artifact of demonstrated academic excellence, written personal statements, interview. Additional exam requirements/recommendations for international students: Required—TOEFL (minimum score 570 paper-based; 80 iBT). *Application deadline:* For fall admission, 8/29 priority date for domestic students; for spring admission, 1/15 priority date for domestic students. Applications are processed on a rolling basis. Application fee: $50 ($75 for international students). Electronic applications accepted. *Expenses:* Contact institution. *Financial support:* Scholarships/grants, unspecified assistantships, and partnerships with local school districts available. Financial award applicants required to submit FAFSA. *Faculty research:* Facilitative learning styles, leadership, student assessment, interactive multimedia inclusion, learning organizations and strategic change. *Unit head:* Dr. Deborah Boyd, Director of Graduate Studies, 615-966-6263, E-mail: deborah.boyd@lipscomb.edu. *Application contact:* Amanda Logsdon, Director of Enrollment and Outreach, 615-966-7199, E-mail: amanda.logsdon@lipscomb.edu.
Website: http://www.lipscomb.edu/education/graduate-programs

Long Island University–LIU Brooklyn, School of Education, Brooklyn, NY 11201-8423. Offers adolescence urban education (MS Ed); applied behavior analysis (Advanced Certificate); bilingual education (Advanced Certificate); bilingual education in urban setting (MS Ed); bilingual school counselor (MS Ed, Advanced Certificate); childhood urban education (MS Ed); childhood/early childhood education (MS Ed); childhood/early childhood urban education (MS Ed); early childhood urban education (MS Ed, Advanced Certificate); educational leadership (Advanced Certificate); marriage and family therapy (MS, Advanced Certificate); mental health counseling (MS, Advanced Certificate); school building district leader (Advanced Certificate); school counselor (MS Ed, Advanced Certificate); school psychologist (MS Ed); teaching students with disabilities (MS Ed); teaching urban children with disabilities (MS Ed); TESOL (MS Ed, Advanced Certificate). *Accreditation:* TEAC. *Program availability:* Part-time, evening/weekend, 100% online. *Faculty:* 14 full-time (12 women), 42 part-time/adjunct (32 women). *Students:* 140 full-time (130 women), 563 part-time (414 women); includes 417 minority (183 Black or African American, non-Hispanic/Latino; 1 American Indian or Alaska Native, non-Hispanic/Latino; 32 Asian, non-Hispanic/Latino; 187 Hispanic/Latino; 14 Two or more races, non-Hispanic/Latino), 10 international. Average age 31. 449 applicants, 82% accepted, 264 enrolled. In 2017, 408 master's, 31 other advanced degrees awarded. *Entrance requirements:* For master's, GRE. Additional exam requirements/recommendations for international students: Required—TOEFL (minimum score 527 paper-based, 75 iBT), IELTS, or PTE. *Application deadline:* Applications are processed on a rolling basis. Application fee: $50. Electronic applications accepted. *Expenses: Tuition:* Full-time $21,618; part-time $1201 per credit. *Required fees:* $1840; $920 per term. Tuition and fees vary according to course load. *Financial support:* In 2017–18, 58 students received support. Career-related internships or fieldwork, Federal Work-Study, scholarships/grants, and unspecified assistantships

available. Support available to part-time students. Financial award application deadline: 2/15; financial award applicants required to submit FAFSA. *Faculty research:* Diversity issues in education and mental health care, inclusion - disability studies, sustainability, teacher professional development. *Unit head:* Dean, 718-488-1055, E-mail: bkln-admissions@liu.edu. *Application contact:* Bayu Sutrisno, Graduate Admissions Counselor, 718-488-1011, Fax: 718-780-6110, E-mail: bkln-admissions@liu.edu.
Website: http://www.liu.edu/Brooklyn/Academics/School-of-Education

Long Island University–LIU Post, College of Liberal Arts and Sciences, Brookville, NY 11548-1300. Offers applied mathematics (MS); behavior analysis (MA); biology (MS); criminal justice (MS); earth science (MS); English (MA); environmental sustainability (MS); genetic counseling (MS); history (MA); interdisciplinary studies (MA, MS); political science (MA); psychology (MA). *Program availability:* Part-time, evening/weekend, blended/hybrid learning. *Faculty:* 41 full-time (21 women), 24 part-time/adjunct (13 women). *Students:* 173 full-time (124 women), 62 part-time (35 women); includes 54 minority (11 Black or African American, non-Hispanic/Latino; 13 Asian, non-Hispanic/Latino; 23 Hispanic/Latino; 7 Two or more races, non-Hispanic/Latino), 12 international. Average age 28. 368 applicants, 54% accepted, 74 enrolled. In 2017, 89 master's, 15 other advanced degrees awarded. Terminal master's awarded for partial completion of doctoral program. *Degree requirements:* For master's, comprehensive exam (for some programs), thesis (for some programs). *Entrance requirements:* Additional exam requirements/recommendations for international students: Required—TOEFL, IELTS, or PTE. *Application deadline:* Applications are processed on a rolling basis. Application fee: $50. Electronic applications accepted. *Expenses: Tuition:* Full-time $21,618; part-time $1201 per credit. *Required fees:* $1840; $920 per term. Tuition and fees vary according to course load. *Financial support:* In 2017–18, 165 students received support. Fellowships, research assistantships, teaching assistantships, career-related internships or fieldwork, Federal Work-Study, scholarships/grants, tuition waivers (partial), and unspecified assistantships available. Support available to part-time students. Financial award application deadline: 2/15; financial award applicants required to submit FAFSA. *Faculty research:* Biology, environmental sustainability, mathematics, psychology, genetic counseling. *Unit head:* Dr. Nathaniel Bowditch, Dean, 516-299-2234, Fax: 516-299-4140, E-mail: nathaniel.bowditch@liu.edu. *Application contact:* Rita Langdon, Graduate Admissions, 516-299-2900, Fax: 516-299-2137, E-mail: post-enroll@liu.edu.
Website: http://liu.edu/CWPost/Academics/Schools/CLAS

Long Island University–Riverhead, Graduate Programs, Riverhead, NY 11901. Offers applied behavior analysis (Advanced Certificate); childhood education (MS), including grades 1-6; cybersecurity policy (Advanced Certificate); homeland security management (MS, Advanced Certificate); literacy education (MS); literacy education B-6 (MS); teaching students with disabilities (MS), including grades 1-6; TESOL (Advanced Certificate). *Accreditation:* TEAC. *Program availability:* Part-time. *Faculty:* 4 full-time (1 woman), 11 part-time/adjunct (5 women). *Students:* 17 full-time (14 women), 58 part-time (36 women); includes 14 minority (4 Black or African American, non-Hispanic/Latino; 1 American Indian or Alaska Native, non-Hispanic/Latino; 1 Asian, non-Hispanic/Latino; 6 Hispanic/Latino; 2 Two or more races, non-Hispanic/Latino). Average age 32. 68 applicants, 79% accepted, 26 enrolled. In 2017, 30 master's, 7 other advanced degrees awarded. *Entrance requirements:* Additional exam requirements/recommendations for international students: Required—TOEFL or IELTS. *Application deadline:* Applications are processed on a rolling basis. Application fee: $50. Electronic applications accepted. *Expenses:* Contact institution. *Financial support:* In 2017–18, 53 students received support. Scholarships/grants available. Support available to part-time students. Financial award application deadline: 2/15; financial award applicants required to submit FAFSA. *Unit head:* Dr. Abagail VanVlerah, Dean and Chief Operating Officer, 631-299-3831, E-mail: abagail.vanvlerah@liu.edu. *Application contact:* Jean Conroy, Associate Dean, 631-287-8301, E-mail: jean.conroy@liu.edu.

McNeese State University, Doré School of Graduate Studies, Burton College of Education, Department of Psychology, Lake Charles, LA 70609. Offers applied behavior analysis (MA, Graduate Certificate); counseling psychology (MA); general/experimental psychology (MA). *Program availability:* Evening/weekend. *Entrance requirements:* For master's, GRE. *Application deadline:* For fall admission, 5/15 priority date for domestic and international students; for spring admission, 10/15 priority date for domestic and international students. Applications are processed on a rolling basis. Application fee: $20 ($30 for international students). *Financial support:* Application deadline: 5/1. *Unit head:* Dr. Dena L. Matzenbacher, Head, 337-475-5434, Fax: 337-562-4115, E-mail: dena@mcneese.edu. *Application contact:* Dr. Dustin M. Hebert, Director of Dore' School of Graduate Studies, 337-475-5396, Fax: 337-475-5397, E-mail: admissions@mcneese.edu.

Mercyhurst University, Graduate Studies, Program in Applied Behavior Analysis, Erie, PA 16546. Offers MABA. *Degree requirements:* For master's, thesis, project.

Mercyhurst University, Graduate Studies, Program in Special Education, Erie, PA 16546. Offers applied behavior analysis (MS); autism (MS); generalist (MS); higher education leadership and disabilities (MS). *Program availability:* Part-time, evening/weekend. *Degree requirements:* For master's, thesis optional. *Entrance requirements:* For master's, GRE or PRAXIS I, interview, resume, essay, three professional references, transcripts. Additional exam requirements/recommendations for international students: Required—TOEFL. Electronic applications accepted. *Faculty research:* College-age learning disabled program, teacher preparation/collaboration, applied behavior analysis, special education policy issues.

Missouri State University, Graduate College, College of Health and Human Services, Department of Psychology, Springfield, MO 65897. Offers applied behavior analysis (MS); clinical psychology (MS); experimental psychology (MS); forensic child psychology (Certificate); industrial/organizational psychology (MS). *Faculty:* 25 full-time (11 women), 4 part-time/adjunct (0 women). *Students:* 54 full-time (41 women), 12 part-time (9 women); includes 9 minority (2 Black or African American, non-Hispanic/Latino; 2 Hispanic/Latino; 5 Two or more races, non-Hispanic/Latino), 5 international. Average age 23. 127 applicants, 17% accepted, 21 enrolled. In 2017, 41 master's awarded. *Degree requirements:* For master's, comprehensive exam, thesis. *Entrance requirements:* For master's, GRE General Test, GRE Subject Test, minimum GPA of 3.25 in major, 3.0 overall; 20 hours of course work in psychology. Additional exam requirements/recommendations for international students: Required—TOEFL (minimum score 550 paper-based; 79 iBT), IELTS (minimum score 6). *Application deadline:* For fall admission, 2/15 priority date for domestic and international students. Application fee: $35 ($50 for international students). Electronic applications accepted. *Expenses:* Tuition, state resident: full-time $2915; part-time $2021 per credit hour. Tuition, nonresident: full-time $5354; part-time $3647 per credit hour. *International tuition:* $11,992 full-time. *Required fees:* $173; $173 per credit hour. Tuition and fees vary according to class time, course level, course load, degree level, campus/location and program. *Financial support:* In 2017–18, 9 research assistantships with full tuition reimbursements (averaging $8,772 per year), 8 teaching assistantships with full tuition reimbursements (averaging $8,772 per year) were awarded; career-related internships or fieldwork, Federal Work-Study, institutionally sponsored loans, scholarships/grants, and unspecified assistantships also available. Financial award application deadline: 3/31; financial award applicants required to submit FAFSA. *Faculty research:* Work-family conflict, child forensic psychology, sports psychology, body image assessment, visual learning. *Unit head:* Dr. Paul Deal, Department Head, 417-836-5797, Fax: 417-836-8330, E-mail: psychology@missouristate.edu. *Application contact:* Stephanie Praschan, Director, Graduate Enrollment Management, 417-836-5330, Fax: 417-836-6200, E-mail: stephaniepraschan@missouristate.edu.
Website: http://psychology.missouristate.edu/

Monmouth University, Graduate Studies, School of Education, West Long Branch, NJ 07764-1898. Offers applied behavior analysis (Certificate); autism (Certificate); director of school counseling services (Post-Master's Certificate); early childhood (M Ed); educational leadership (Ed D); elementary education (MAT), including elementary level, secondary level; English as a second language (M Ed); learning disabilities teacher-consultant (Post-Master's Certificate); literacy (MS Ed); school counseling (MS Ed); special education (MS Ed), including autism, learning disabilities teacher-consultant, teacher of students with disabilities, teaching in inclusive settings; speech-language pathology (MS Ed); student affairs and college counseling (MS Ed); supervisor (Post-Master's Certificate); teaching English to speakers of other languages (Certificate). *Accreditation:* NCATE. *Program availability:* Part-time, evening/weekend, 100% online, blended/hybrid learning. *Faculty:* 23 full-time (19 women), 33 part-time/adjunct (25 women). *Students:* 175 full-time (163 women), 168 part-time (142 women); includes 54 minority (10 Black or African American, non-Hispanic/Latino; 4 Asian, non-Hispanic/Latino; 32 Hispanic/Latino; 8 Two or more races, non-Hispanic/Latino). Average age 27. In 2017, 160 master's, 3 other advanced degrees awarded. *Entrance requirements:* For master's, GRE taken within last 5 years (for MS Ed in speech-language pathology); SAT (minimum combined score of 1660 in 3 sections), ACT (23), GRE (minimum score of 4.0 on analytical writing section and minimum combined score of 310 on quantitative and verbal sections), or passing scores on 3 parts of Core Academic Skills Educators, minimum GPA of 3.0 in major; 2 letters of recommendation (for some programs); resume, personal statement or essay (depending on program). Additional exam requirements/recommendations for international students: Required—TOEFL (minimum score 550 paper-based; 79 iBT), IELTS (minimum score 6), Michigan English Language Assessment Battery (minimum score 77) or Certificate of Advanced English (minimum score 160). *Application deadline:* For fall admission, 7/15 priority date for domestic students, 7/1 for international students; for spring admission, 12/1 priority date for domestic students, 11/1 for international students; for summer admission, 5/1 for domestic students. Applications are processed on a rolling basis. Application fee: $50. Electronic applications accepted. *Expenses: Tuition:* Full-time $21,366; part-time $7122 per credit. *Required fees:* $700; $175 per term. *Financial support:* In 2017–18, 125 students received support. Institutionally sponsored loans, scholarships/grants, and unspecified assistantships available. Support available to part-time students. Financial award applicants required to submit FAFSA. *Faculty research:* Multicultural literacy, science and mathematics teaching strategies, teacher as reflective practitioner, children with disabilities. *Unit head:* Dr. John E. Henning, Dean, 732-263-5513, Fax: 732-263-5277. *Application contact:* Laurie Kuhn, Associate Director of Graduate Admission, 732-571-3452, Fax: 732-263-5123, E-mail: gradadm@monmouth.edu.
Website: http://www.monmouth.edu/academics/schools/education/default.asp

Montana State University Billings, College of Education, Department of Educational Theory and Practice, Program in Special Education, Billings, MT 59101. Offers advanced studies (MS Sp Ed); applied behavior analysis (MS Sp Ed); generalist (MS Sp Ed). *Accreditation:* NCATE. *Program availability:* Part-time. *Degree requirements:* For master's, thesis or professional paper and/or field experience. *Entrance requirements:* For master's, GRE General Test or MAT, minimum GPA of 3.0. Additional exam requirements/recommendations for international students: Required—TOEFL (minimum score 79 iBT), IELTS (minimum score 6.5). *Application deadline:* Applications are processed on a rolling basis. Application fee: $40. Electronic applications accepted. *Expenses:* Tuition, state resident: full-time $11,740; part-time $7880 per year. Tuition, nonresident: full-time $32,200; part-time $24,140 per year. *Financial support:* Research assistantships with partial tuition reimbursements, teaching assistantships with partial tuition reimbursements, career-related internships or fieldwork, Federal Work-Study, institutionally sponsored loans, scholarships/grants, tuition waivers (partial), and unspecified assistantships available. Support available to part-time students. Financial award application deadline: 5/1; financial award applicants required to submit FAFSA. *Unit head:* Dr. Cindy Dell, Chair, Educational Theory and Practice, 406-657-1614, E-mail: cdell@msubillings.edu. *Application contact:* Dr. Cindy Dell, Chair, Educational Theory and Practice, 406-657-1614, E-mail: cdell@msubillings.edu.

National University, Academic Affairs, Sanford College of Education, La Jolla, CA 92037-1011. Offers advanced teaching practices (MS); applied behavior analysis (MS); applied school leadership (MS); e-teaching and learning (Certificate); education (MA); educational administration (MS); educational and instructional technology (MS); educational counseling (MS); higher education administration (MS); inspired teaching and learning (M Ed); school psychology (MS); special education (MA, MS). *Program availability:* Part-time, evening/weekend, 100% online, blended/hybrid learning. *Degree requirements:* For master's, thesis (for some programs). *Entrance requirements:* For master's, interview, minimum GPA of 2.5. Additional exam requirements/recommendations for international students: Required—TOEFL (minimum score 550 paper-based; 79 iBT), IELTS (minimum score 6). *Application deadline:* Applications are processed on a rolling basis. Application fee: $60 ($65 for international students). Electronic applications accepted. *Expenses: Tuition:* Part-time $430 per quarter hour. *Financial support:* Career-related internships or fieldwork, institutionally sponsored loans, scholarships/grants, and tuition waivers (partial) available. Support available to part-time students. Financial award application deadline: 6/30. *Faculty research:* Teacher education, special education, educational effectiveness, teaching abroad, school counseling. *Unit head:* Dr. Judy Mantle, Dean, 858-642-8320, E-mail: soe@nu.edu. *Application contact:* Brandon Jouganatos, Vice President for Enrollment Services, 800-628-8648, E-mail: advisor@nu.edu.
Website: http://www.nu.edu/OurPrograms/SchoolOfEducation.html

Niagara University, Graduate Division of Education, Niagara University, NY 14109. Offers applied behavior analysis (Certificate); educational leadership (MS Ed, PhD, Certificate), including leadership and policy (PhD), school building leader (MS Ed), school district business leader (Certificate), school district leader (MS Ed, Certificate); literacy instruction (MS Ed); mental health counseling (MS, Certificate); school counseling (MS Ed, Certificate); school psychology (MS); teacher education (MS, MS Ed, Certificate), including early childhood and childhood education (MS Ed, Certificate), early childhood special education (MS), middle and adolescence education (Certificate), special education (MS Ed), special education (grades 1-6) (Certificate), special education (grades 7-12) (Certificate), teaching English to speakers of other languages (TESOL) (Certificate). *Accreditation:* NCATE (one or more programs are accredited). *Program availability:* Part-time, evening/weekend. *Faculty:* 24 full-time, 49 part-time/adjunct. *Students:* 260 full-time (203 women), 311 part-time (239 women); includes 67 minority (35 Black or African American, non-Hispanic/Latino; 3 American Indian or Alaska Native, non-Hispanic/Latino; 3 Asian, non-Hispanic/Latino; 18 Hispanic/Latino; 8 Two or more races, non-Hispanic/Latino), 102 international. Average age 31. In 2017, 202 master's, 10 doctorates, 59 other advanced degrees awarded. *Entrance requirements:* For master's, GRE General Test or MAT. Additional exam requirements/

recommendations for international students: Required—TOEFL (minimum score 550 paper-based; 79 iBT), IELTS (minimum score 6). *Application deadline:* For fall admission, 8/1 for domestic students. Applications are processed on a rolling basis. Application fee: $30. *Expenses:* Contact institution. *Financial support:* Research assistantships with tuition reimbursements, teaching assistantships with tuition reimbursements, career-related internships or fieldwork, Federal Work-Study, scholarships/grants, and unspecified assistantships available. Financial award application deadline: 4/15; financial award applicants required to submit FAFSA. *Faculty research:* Instructional supervision, appraisal and evaluation, career opportunities. *Unit head:* Dr. Chandra Foote, Dean, College of Education, 716-286-8549, Fax: 716-286-8561, E-mail: cjf@niagara.edu. *Application contact:* Evan Pierce, Associate Director for Graduate Recruitment, 716-286-8769, Fax: 716-286-8170, E-mail: epierce@niagara.edu.
Website: http://www.niagara.edu/advance/

Northeastern University, Bouvé College of Health Sciences, Boston, MA 02115-5096. Offers applied behavior analysis (MS); audiology (Au D); counseling psychology (MS, PhD, CAGS); exercise science (MS); nursing (MS, PhD, CAGS), including administration (MS), adult-gerontology acute care nurse practitioner (MS, CAGS), adult-gerontology primary care nurse practitioner (MS, CAGS), anesthesia (MS), family nurse practitioner (MS, CAGS), neonatal nurse practitioner (MS, CAGS), pediatric nurse practitioner (MS, CAGS), psychiatric mental health nurse practitioner (MS, CAGS); nursing practice (DNP); pharmaceutical sciences (MS, PhD), including interdisciplinary concentration, pharmaceutics and drug delivery systems; pharmacology (MS); pharmacy (Pharm D); school psychology (PhD); speech-language pathology (MS); urban health (MPH); MS/MBA. *Accreditation:* ACPE (one or more programs are accredited). *Program availability:* Part-time, evening/weekend, online learning. *Faculty:* 192 full-time. *Students:* 1,685. In 2017, 352 master's, 312 doctorates, 25 other advanced degrees awarded. *Degree requirements:* For doctorate, thesis/dissertation (for some programs); for CAGS, comprehensive exam. Application fee: $75. Electronic applications accepted. *Expenses:* Contact institution. *Financial support:* Fellowships, research assistantships, teaching assistantships, career-related internships or fieldwork, scholarships/grants, health care benefits, tuition waivers, and unspecified assistantships available. Support available to part-time students. Financial award applicants required to submit FAFSA. *Unit head:* Susan L. Parish, Dean, Bouve College of Health Sciences, 617-373-3321, Fax: 617-373-3030, E-mail: s.parish@northeastern.edu. *Application contact:* 617-373-2708, Fax: 617-373-4701, E-mail: bouvegrad@northeastern.edu.
Website: https://www.northeastern.edu/bouve/

Northern Michigan University, Office of Graduate Education and Research, College of Arts and Sciences, Department of Psychological Science, Marquette, MI 49855-5301. Offers applied behavior analysis (MS); psychological science (MS). *Program availability:* Part-time. *Degree requirements:* For master's, thesis (for some programs). *Entrance requirements:* For master's, minimum GPA of 3.0; bachelor's degree (preferably in psychology); undergraduate courses in introduction to psychology and statistics; personal statement; 3 letters of recommendation. Additional exam requirements/recommendations for international students: Required—TOEFL (minimum score 550 paper-based; 79 iBT), IELTS (minimum score 6.5). *Application deadline:* For fall admission, 7/1 for domestic students; for winter admission, 11/15 for domestic students; for spring admission, 3/17 for domestic students. Applications are processed on a rolling basis. Application fee: $50. Electronic applications accepted. *Expenses:* Tuition, state resident: full-time $9417; part-time $542 per credit hour. Tuition, nonresident: full-time $12,873; part-time $758 per credit hour. Tuition and fees vary according to course load, degree level and program. *Financial support:* Teaching assistantships with full tuition reimbursements, Federal Work-Study, institutionally sponsored loans, scholarships/grants, and unspecified assistantships available. Support available to part-time students. Financial award application deadline: 3/1; financial award applicants required to submit FAFSA. *Faculty research:* Emotion and cognition, neuropsychopharmacology, sensation and perception, behavior analysis, developmental psychology. *Unit head:* Dr. Adam Prus, Head, 906-227-2935. *Application contact:* Dr. Adam Prus, Head, 906-227-2935.
Website: http://www.nmu.edu/psychology/

Northern Vermont University–Johnson, Program in Education, Johnson, VT 05656. Offers applied behavior analysis (MA Ed); curriculum and instruction (MA Ed); foundations of education (MA Ed); special education (MA Ed). *Program availability:* Part-time. *Faculty:* 5 full-time (3 women), 4 part-time/adjunct (3 women). *Students:* 3 full-time (all women), 36 part-time (30 women). In 2017, 23 master's awarded. *Degree requirements:* For master's, thesis or alternative, exit interview. *Entrance requirements:* For master's, interview. Additional exam requirements/recommendations for international students: Required—TOEFL. *Application deadline:* For fall admission, 5/1 for domestic students, 2/1 for international students. Applications are processed on a rolling basis. Electronic applications accepted. *Expenses:* Tuition, state resident: part-time $572 per credit hour. Tuition, nonresident: part-time $832 per credit hour. *Financial support:* Scholarships/grants and unspecified assistantships available. Financial award application deadline: 3/1; financial award applicants required to submit FAFSA. *Unit head:* Dr. Kathleen Brinegar, Chair, Department of Education, 802-635-1472, Fax: 802-635-1465, E-mail: kathleen.brinegar@jsc.edu. *Application contact:* Catherine H. Higley, Administrative Assistant, 800-635-2356 Ext. 1244, Fax: 802-635-1248, E-mail: catherine.higley@jsc.edu.
Website: http://www.jsc.edu/academics/education/majors-and-minors/master-of-arts-in-education/

Oakland University, Graduate Study and Lifelong Learning, School of Education and Human Services, Department of Human Development and Child Studies, Program in Special Education, Rochester, MI 48309-4401. Offers applied behavior analysis (Graduate Certificate); autism spectrum disorder (Graduate Certificate); emotional impairment (Graduate Certificate); special education (M Ed), including applied behavior analysis, autism spectrum disorder, emotional impairment, specific learning disabilities; specific learning disabilities (Graduate Certificate). *Accreditation:* TEAC. *Entrance requirements:* For master's, minimum GPA of 3.0, interview. Additional exam requirements/recommendations for international students: Required—TOEFL (minimum score 550 paper-based). Electronic applications accepted. *Expenses:* Tuition, state resident: full-time $16,950; part-time $706.25 per credit. Tuition, nonresident: full-time $24,648; part-time $1027 per credit.

Oklahoma City University, Petree College of Arts and Sciences, Oklahoma City, OK 73106-1402. Offers applied behavioral studies (M Ed); applied sociology: nonprofit leadership (MA); creative writing (MFA); criminology (MS); early childhood education (M Ed); elementary education (M Ed); general studies (MLA); leadership/management (MLA); moving image arts (MFA); professional counseling (M Ed); teaching (MA); teaching English to speakers of other languages (MA). *Program availability:* Part-time, evening/weekend. *Faculty:* 6 full-time (2 women), 16 part-time/adjunct (10 women). *Students:* 84 full-time (61 women), 32 part-time (23 women); includes 31 minority (13 Black or African American, non-Hispanic/Latino; 3 American Indian or Alaska Native, non-Hispanic/Latino; 1 Asian, non-Hispanic/Latino; 9 Hispanic/Latino; 5 Two or more races, non-Hispanic/Latino), 30 international. Average age 34. 192 applicants, 67% accepted, 57 enrolled. In 2017, 65 master's awarded. *Degree requirements:* For master's, capstone/practicum. *Entrance requirements:* For master's, bachelor's degree from accredited institution with minimum GPA of 3.0, essay, recommendation letters. Additional exam requirements/recommendations for international students: Required—TOEFL (minimum score 550 paper-based; 80 iBT). *Application deadline:* Applications are processed on a rolling basis. Application fee: $50. Electronic applications accepted. *Expenses:* $8,580. *Financial support:* In 2017–18, 19 students received support. Federal Work-Study, institutionally sponsored loans, scholarships/grants, and tuition waivers (full and partial) available. Support available to part-time students. Financial award application deadline: 6/1; financial award applicants required to submit FAFSA. *Unit head:* Dr. Amy Cataldi, Dean, 405-208-5446, Fax: 405-208-5447, E-mail: acataldi@okcu.edu. *Application contact:* Michael Harrington, Director of Graduate Admissions, 800-633-7242, Fax: 405-208-5356, E-mail: gadmissions@okcu.edu.
Website: https://www.okcu.edu/artsci/home

Oklahoma State University, College of Education, Health and Aviation, School of Applied Health and Educational Psychology, Stillwater, OK 74078. Offers applied behavioral studies (Ed D); applied health and educational psychology (MS, PhD, Ed S). *Accreditation:* APA (one or more programs are accredited). *Program availability:* Part-time. *Faculty:* 31 full-time (20 women), 9 part-time/adjunct (7 women). *Students:* 169 full-time (119 women), 158 part-time (102 women); includes 98 minority (29 Black or African American, non-Hispanic/Latino; 15 American Indian or Alaska Native, non-Hispanic/Latino; 5 Asian, non-Hispanic/Latino; 24 Hispanic/Latino; 25 Two or more races, non-Hispanic/Latino), 22 international. Average age 30. 140 applicants, 56% accepted, 69 enrolled. In 2017, 71 master's, 24 doctorates awarded. *Entrance requirements:* For master's and doctorate, GRE or GMAT. Additional exam requirements/recommendations for international students: Required—TOEFL (minimum score 550 paper-based; 79 iBT). *Application deadline:* For fall admission, 3/1 priority date for international students; for spring admission, 8/1 priority date for international students. Applications are processed on a rolling basis. Application fee: $40 ($75 for international students). Electronic applications accepted. *Expenses:* Tuition, state resident: full-time $4019; part-time $2679.60 per year. Tuition, nonresident: full-time $15,286; part-time $10,190.40 per year. *Required fees:* $2129; $1419 per unit. Tuition and fees vary according to program. *Financial support:* Research assistantships, teaching assistantships, career-related internships or fieldwork, Federal Work-Study, scholarships/grants, health care benefits, tuition waivers (partial), and unspecified assistantships available. Support available to part-time students. Financial award application deadline: 3/1; financial award applicants required to submit FAFSA. *Unit head:* Dr. Aric Warren, Head, 405-744-6040, Fax: 405-744-6779, E-mail: aric.warren@okstate.edu.
Website: http://education.okstate.edu/

Penn State Harrisburg, Graduate School, School of Behavioral Sciences and Education, Middletown, PA 17057. Offers adult education in the health and medical professions (Certificate); applied behavior analysis (MA); applied clinical psychology (MA); applied psychological research (MA); community psychology and social change (MA); English as a second language (ESL) program specialist and leadership (Certificate); health education (M Ed); lifelong learning and adult education (M Ed, D Ed); literacy education (M Ed); literacy leadership (Certificate); psychology: applications in clinical psychology (Certificate); psychology: health psychology (Certificate); teaching and curriculum (M Ed); training and development (M Ed, Certificate). *Program availability:* Part-time, evening/weekend. *Unit head:* Dr. Mukund S. Kulkarni, Chancellor, 717-948-6105, Fax: 717-948-6452. *Application contact:* Robert W. Coffman, Jr., Director of Enrollment Management, Recruitment and Admissions, 717-948-6250, Fax: 717-948-6325, E-mail: hbgadmit@psu.edu.
Website: https://harrisburg.psu.edu/behavioral-sciences-and-education/

Philadelphia College of Osteopathic Medicine, Graduate and Professional Programs, Department of Psychology, Philadelphia, PA 19131-1694. Offers applied behavior analysis (Certificate); clinical health psychology (Post-Doctoral Certificate); clinical neuropsychology (Post-Doctoral Certificate); clinical psychology (Psy D); educational psychology (PhD); mental health counseling (MS); organizational development and leadership (MS); psychology (Certificate); public health management and administration (MS); school psychology (MS, Psy D, Ed S). *Accreditation:* APA. *Faculty:* 19 full-time (11 women), 122 part-time/adjunct (58 women). *Students:* 487 (335 women); includes 138 minority (89 Black or African American, non-Hispanic/Latino; 4 American Indian or Alaska Native, non-Hispanic/Latino; 11 Asian, non-Hispanic/Latino; 12 Hispanic/Latino; 22 Two or more races, non-Hispanic/Latino). 298 applicants, 44% accepted, 100 enrolled. In 2017, 50 master's, 43 doctorates, 10 other advanced degrees awarded. Terminal master's awarded for partial completion of doctoral program. *Degree requirements:* For master's, comprehensive exam (for some programs), thesis (for some programs); for doctorate, comprehensive exam, thesis/dissertation. *Entrance requirements:* For master's, GRE or MAT, minimum GPA of 3.0; bachelor's degree from regionally-accredited college or university; for doctorate, PRAXIS II (for Psy D in school psychology), minimum undergraduate GPA of 3.0; for other advanced degree, GRE (for Ed S). Additional exam requirements/recommendations for international students: Required—TOEFL (minimum score 79 iBT). *Application deadline:* Applications are processed on a rolling basis. Application fee: $50. Electronic applications accepted. *Financial support:* In 2017–18, 28 teaching assistantships were awarded; Federal Work-Study, institutionally sponsored loans, and scholarships/grants also available. Financial award application deadline: 3/15; financial award applicants required to submit FAFSA. *Faculty research:* Adult and childhood anxiety and ADHD; coping with chronic illness; primary care psychology/integrated health care; applied behavior analysis; psychological, educational, and neuropsychological assessment. *Total annual research expenditures:* $533,489. *Unit head:* Dr. Robert DiTomasso, Chairman, 215-871-6442, Fax: 215-871-6458, E-mail: robertd@pcom.edu. *Application contact:* Johnathan Cox, Associate Director of Admissions, 215-871-6700, Fax: 215-871-6719, E-mail: johnathancox@pcom.edu.

See Display on page 982 and Close-Up on page 1203.

Queens College of the City University of New York, Mathematics and Natural Sciences Division, Department of Psychology, Queens, NY 11367-1597. Offers applied behavior analysis (MA); behavioral neuroscience (MA); general psychology (MA). *Program availability:* Part-time. *Students:* 2 full-time (1 woman), 99 part-time (78 women); includes 55 minority (10 Black or African American, non-Hispanic/Latino; 1 American Indian or Alaska Native, non-Hispanic/Latino; 11 Asian, non-Hispanic/Latino; 31 Hispanic/Latino; 2 Two or more races, non-Hispanic/Latino), 3 international. Average age 27. *Degree requirements:* For master's, comprehensive exam (for some programs), thesis. *Entrance requirements:* For master's, minimum GPA of 3.0. Additional exam requirements/recommendations for international students: Required—TOEFL, IELTS. *Application deadline:* For fall admission, 4/1 for domestic students; for spring admission, 11/1 for domestic students. Applications are processed on a rolling basis. Application fee: $125. Electronic applications accepted. *Financial support:* Career-related internships or fieldwork, institutionally sponsored loans, and unspecified assistantships available. Financial award application deadline: 4/1; financial award applicants required to submit FAFSA. *Unit head:* Robert Lanson, Chair, 718-997-3200, E-mail: robert.lanson@qc.cuny.edu. *Application contact:* Elizabeth D'Amico-Ramirez, Assistant Director of Graduate Admissions, 718-997-5203, E-mail: elizabeth.damicoramirez@qc.cuny.edu.
Website: http://psychology.qc.cuny.edu/

Applied Behavior Analysis

Regis College, Nursing and Health Sciences School, Weston, MA 02493. Offers applied behavior analysis (MS); counseling psychology (MA); health administration (MS); nurse practitioner (Certificate); nursing (MS, DNP); nursing education (Certificate); occupational therapy (MS). *Accreditation:* ACEN. *Program availability:* Part-time, evening/weekend, 100% online, blended/hybrid learning. *Degree requirements:* For doctorate, thesis/dissertation. *Entrance requirements:* For master's, GRE General Test or MAT, minimum GPA of 3.0, official transcripts, recommendations, personal statement, resume/curriculum vitae, interview; for doctorate, MAT or GRE if GPA from master's lower than 3.5. Additional exam requirements/recommendations for international students: Required—TOEFL (minimum score 560 paper-based; 79 iBT); Recommended—IELTS (minimum score 6.5). *Application deadline:* Applications are processed on a rolling basis. Application fee: $75. Electronic applications accepted. *Financial support:* Federal Work-Study, scholarships/grants, traineeships, and unspecified assistantships available. Support available to part-time students. Financial award applicants required to submit FAFSA. *Faculty research:* Global public health, health policy, education, aging, job satisfaction, psychiatric nursing, critical thinking. *Application contact:* Hillary Lyons, Graduate Admission Counselor, 781-768-7746, E-mail: hillary.lyons@regiscollege.edu.

Rollins College, Hamilton Holt School, Master of Arts in Applied Behavior Analysis and Clinical Science Program, Winter Park, FL 32789. Offers MA. *Program availability:* Part-time, evening/weekend. *Faculty:* 3 full-time (all women). *Students:* 22 full-time (21 women), 10 part-time (7 women); includes 11 minority (2 Black or African American, non-Hispanic/Latino; 1 Asian, non-Hispanic/Latino; 7 Hispanic/Latino; 1 Two or more races, non-Hispanic/Latino). Average age 28. In 2017, 4 master's awarded. *Degree requirements:* For master's, thesis, Board Certified Behavior Analyst Examination; intensive practicum. *Entrance requirements:* For master's, GRE, official transcripts, three letters of recommendation, essay, resume. Additional exam requirements/recommendations for international students: Required—TOEFL (minimum score 550 paper-based). *Application deadline:* For fall admission, 3/1 priority date for domestic students. Applications are processed on a rolling basis. Application fee: $50. Electronic applications accepted. *Expenses:* $2,388 per course. *Financial support:* In 2017–18, 1 student received support. Scholarships/grants and unspecified assistantships available. Support available to part-time students. Financial award applicants required to submit FAFSA. *Unit head:* Dr. Michele Williams, Director, Health Professions, 407-646-2036, E-mail: amwilliams2@rollins.edu. *Application contact:* Graduate Program Admission, 407-646-2232, Fax: 407-646-1551.

Rowan University, Graduate School, College of Science and Mathematics, Program in Applied Behavioral Analysis, Glassboro, NJ 08028-1701. Offers MA, CAGS. *Entrance requirements:* For master's, GRE General Test. Additional exam requirements/recommendations for international students: Required—TOEFL. *Expenses:* Tuition, state resident: full-time $15,020; part-time $751 per semester hour. Tuition, nonresident: full-time $15,020; part-time $751 per semester hour. *Required fees:* $3158; $157.90 per semester hour. Tuition and fees vary according to course load, campus/location and program.

Sage Graduate School, Esteves School of Education, Program in Applied Behavior Analysis and Autism, Troy, NY 12180-4115. Offers MS, Post Master's Certificate. *Program availability:* Part-time, evening/weekend, online only, 100% online. *Faculty:* 6 full-time (5 women), 8 part-time/adjunct (2 women). *Students:* 29 full-time (27 women), 166 part-time (142 women); includes 44 minority (14 Black or African American, non-Hispanic/Latino; 12 Asian, non-Hispanic/Latino; 16 Hispanic/Latino; 2 Two or more races, non-Hispanic/Latino). Average age 29. 202 applicants, 50% accepted, 66 enrolled. In 2017, 86 master's, 1 other advanced degree awarded. *Entrance requirements:* For master's, undergraduate degree with minimum GPA of 2.75. Additional exam requirements/recommendations for international students: Required—TOEFL (minimum score 550 paper-based). *Application deadline:* Applications are processed on a rolling basis. Application fee: $30. Electronic applications accepted. Tuition and fees vary according to degree level and program. *Financial support:* Scholarships/grants and unspecified assistantships available. Financial award applicants required to submit FAFSA. *Unit head:* Dr. John Pelizza, Interim Dean, Esteves School of Education, 518-244-2051, Fax: 518-244-2334, E-mail: pelizj@sage.edu. *Application contact:* Dr. Lori Finn, Department Chair, Center for Applied Behavior Analysis, 518-244-6873, Fax: 518-244-6880, E-mail: caba@sage.edu. Website: http://www.sage.edu/academics/education/programs/aba_autism/

St. Cloud State University, School of Graduate Studies, School of Health and Human Services, Department of Counseling and Community Psychology, Program in Applied Behavior Analysis, St. Cloud, MN 56301-4498. Offers MS. *Program availability:* Part-time, online learning. *Degree requirements:* For master's, comprehensive exam (for some programs), thesis or alternative. *Entrance requirements:* For master's, GRE General Test, minimum GPA of 2.75. Additional exam requirements/recommendations for international students: Required—Michigan English Language Assessment Battery; Recommended—TOEFL (minimum score 550 paper-based), IELTS (minimum score 6.5).

Saint Louis University, Graduate Programs, College for Public Health and Social Justice, School of Social Work, St. Louis, MO 63103. Offers applied behavior analysis (MS); social work (MSW, PhD). *Accreditation:* CSWE. *Program availability:* Part-time. *Entrance requirements:* For master's, minimum GPA of 3.0, letters of recommendation. Additional exam requirements/recommendations for international students: Required—TOEFL (minimum score 550 paper-based). *Expenses:* Contact institution. *Faculty research:* Gerontology, mental health issues, child welfare (especially abuse and neglect), social justice, and peace making, homelessness.

Saint Peter's University, Graduate Programs in Education, Jersey City, NJ 07306-5997. Offers director of school counseling services (Certificate); educational leadership (MA Ed, Ed D); higher education (Ed D); middle school mathematics (Certificate); professional/associate counselor (Certificate); reading (MA Ed); school business administrator (Certificate); school counseling (MA, Certificate); special education (MA Ed, Certificate), including applied behavioral analysis (MA Ed), literacy (MA Ed), teacher of students with disabilities (Certificate); teaching (MA Ed, Certificate), including 6-8 middle school education, K-12 secondary education, K-5 elementary education. *Accreditation:* TEAC. *Program availability:* Part-time, evening/weekend. *Degree requirements:* For master's, comprehensive exam; for doctorate, comprehensive exam, thesis/dissertation. *Entrance requirements:* For master's and doctorate, GRE or MAT. Additional exam requirements/recommendations for international students: Required—TOEFL. Electronic applications accepted.

Salve Regina University, Program in Applied Behavior Analysis, Newport, RI 02840-4192. Offers MA, CAGS.

Shenandoah University, College of Arts and Sciences, Winchester, VA 22601-5195. Offers applied behavior analysis (MS). *Program availability:* Part-time, evening/weekend. *Faculty:* 1 full-time (0 women), 2 part-time/adjunct (1 woman). *Students:* 19 full-time (14 women), 1 (woman) part-time; includes 4 minority (3 Black or African American, non-Hispanic/Latino; 1 Asian, non-Hispanic/Latino). Average age 27. 19 applicants, 89% accepted, 12 enrolled. In 2017, 7 master's awarded. *Degree requirements:* For master's, thesis or alternative, minimum of 37 credit hours, including

21 in coursework, 12 of supervised practical experience, and 4 for capstone project. *Entrance requirements:* Additional exam requirements/recommendations for international students: Required—TOEFL (minimum score 550 paper-based, 79 iBT) or IELTS (6.5). *Application deadline:* For fall admission, 7/15 for domestic and international students. Application fee: $30. Electronic applications accepted. *Expenses:* $19,245 tuition, $1,285 fees (technology fee and student services fee). *Financial support:* In 2017–18, 1 student received support. Scholarships/grants and unspecified assistantships available. Financial award applicants required to submit FAFSA. *Faculty research:* Psychology, applied behavioral analysis. *Unit head:* Jeff W. Coker, PhD, Dean, 540-665-4587, Fax: 540-665-4644, E-mail: jcoker2@su.edu. *Application contact:* Andrew Woodall, Executive Director of Recruitment and Admissions, 540-665-4581, Fax: 540-665-4627, E-mail: admit@su.edu.

Simmons College, School of Social Work, Boston, MA 02115. Offers behavior analysis (MS, PhD, Ed S); education (MS Ed); social work (MSW, PhD); special education (MS Ed), including moderate and severe disabilities; teaching (MAT), including elementary education; MSW/MBA. *Accreditation:* CSWE (one or more programs are accredited). *Program availability:* Part-time, 100% online, blended/hybrid learning. *Faculty:* 57 full-time (47 women), 48 part-time/adjunct (36 women). *Students:* 878 full-time (757 women), 979 part-time (869 women); includes 468 minority (213 Black or African American, non-Hispanic/Latino; 1 American Indian or Alaska Native, non-Hispanic/Latino; 45 Asian, non-Hispanic/Latino; 152 Hispanic/Latino; 3 Native Hawaiian or other Pacific Islander, non-Hispanic/Latino; 54 Two or more races, non-Hispanic/Latino), 12 international. Average age 30. 1,521 applicants, 74% accepted, 545 enrolled. In 2017, 611 master's, 7 doctorates, 1 other advanced degree awarded. Terminal master's awarded for partial completion of doctoral program. *Degree requirements:* For master's, thesis (for some programs); for doctorate, comprehensive exam (for some programs), thesis/dissertation (for some programs). *Entrance requirements:* For master's, GRE, MAT, Massachusetts Tests for Education Licensure (for different programs), minimum grade of B in introductory statistics course within five years prior to entering program, resume, transcripts, three letters of recommendation, personal statement; for doctorate, GRE, BCBA Analyst Exam. Additional exam requirements/recommendations for international students: Required—TOEFL (minimum score 600 paper-based; 100 iBT). *Application deadline:* For fall admission, 8/1 for domestic students; for spring admission, 12/15 for domestic students; for summer admission, 5/1 for domestic students. Applications are processed on a rolling basis. Application fee: $35. Electronic applications accepted. *Expenses:* $1,001 per credit hour, $3,003 per course, $55 activity fee per semester. *Financial support:* In 2017–18, 12 fellowships with partial tuition reimbursements were awarded; scholarships/grants and unspecified assistantships also available. Support available to part-time students. Financial award applicants required to submit FAFSA. *Unit head:* Dr. Cheryl Parks, Dean, 617-521-3293, E-mail: cheryl.parks@simmons.edu. *Application contact:* Carlos D. Frontado, Director of Admissions, 617-521-3920, Fax: 617-521-3980, E-mail: ssw@simmons.edu. Website: http://www.simmons.edu/ssw/

Teachers College, Columbia University, Department of Health and Behavior Studies, New York, NY 10027-6696. Offers applied behavior analysis (MA, PhD); applied educational psychology: school psychology (Ed M, PhD); behavioral nutrition (PhD), including nutrition (Ed D, PhD); community health education (MS); community nutrition education (Ed M), including community nutrition education; education of deaf and hard of hearing (MA, PhD); health education (MA, Ed D); hearing impairment (Ed D); intellectual disability/autism (MA, Ed D, PhD); nursing education (Ed D, Advanced Certificate); nutrition and education (MS); nutrition and exercise physiology (MS); nutrition and public health (MS); nutrition education (Ed D), including nutrition (Ed D, PhD); physical disabilities (Ed D); reading specialist (MA); severe or multiple disabilities (MA); special education (Ed M, MA, Ed D); teaching of sign language (MA). *Program availability:* Part-time, evening/weekend. *Students:* 245 full-time (226 women), 242 part-time (219 women); includes 167 minority (52 Black or African American, non-Hispanic/Latino; 2 American Indian or Alaska Native, non-Hispanic/Latino; 55 Asian, non-Hispanic/Latino; 48 Hispanic/Latino; 1 Native Hawaiian or other Pacific Islander, non-Hispanic/Latino; 9 Two or more races, non-Hispanic/Latino), 60 international. Average age 30. 480 applicants, 59% accepted, 157 enrolled. Terminal master's awarded for partial completion of doctoral program. *Unit head:* Prof. Dolores Perin, Chair, E-mail: dp111@tc.columbia.edu. *Application contact:* David Estrella, Director of Admission, 212-678-3305, E-mail: estrella@tc.columbia.edu. Website: http://www.tc.columbia.edu/health-and-behavior-studies/

Temple University, College of Education, Department of Psychological Studies in Education, Philadelphia, PA 19122-6096. Offers applied behavior analysis (MS Ed); counseling psychology (Ed M), including agency counseling, school counseling; educational psychology (Ed M); school psychology (PhD, Ed S). *Accreditation:* APA (one or more programs are accredited). *Program availability:* Part-time, evening/weekend. *Faculty:* 25 full-time (12 women), 23 part-time/adjunct (11 women). *Students:* 255 full-time (191 women), 188 part-time (137 women); includes 136 minority (90 Black or African American, non-Hispanic/Latino; 1 American Indian or Alaska Native, non-Hispanic/Latino; 18 Asian, non-Hispanic/Latino; 14 Hispanic/Latino; 13 Two or more races, non-Hispanic/Latino), 28 international. 376 applicants, 51% accepted, 109 enrolled. In 2017, 129 master's, 27 doctorates, 21 other advanced degrees awarded. Terminal master's awarded for partial completion of doctoral program. *Degree requirements:* For master's, thesis or alternative; for doctorate, thesis/dissertation. *Entrance requirements:* Additional exam requirements/recommendations for international students: Required—TOEFL (minimum score 550 paper-based; 79 iBT). *Application deadline:* For fall admission, 12/15 for international students; for spring admission, 8/1 for international students. Application fee: $60. *Expenses:* Tuition, state resident: full-time $16,164; part-time $898 per credit hour. Tuition, nonresident: full-time $22,158; part-time $1231 per credit hour. *Required fees:* $890; $445 per semester. Full-time tuition and fees vary according to course load, degree level, campus/location and program. *Financial support:* Fellowships, research assistantships with full tuition reimbursements, and teaching assistantships with full tuition reimbursements available. Financial award application deadline: 1/15; financial award applicants required to submit FAFSA. *Unit head:* Dr. Catherine Fiorello, Chair, 215-204-6254, E-mail: catherine.fiorello@temple.edu. Website: http://education.temple.edu/pse

Tennessee Technological University, College of Graduate Studies, College of Education, Department of Curriculum and Instruction, Program in Exceptional Learning, Cookeville, TN 38505. Offers applied behavior analysis (PhD); literacy (PhD); program planning and evaluation (PhD); STEM education (PhD). *Program availability:* Part-time, evening/weekend. *Students:* 9 full-time (4 women), 32 part-time (24 women); includes 2 minority (1 Black or African American, non-Hispanic/Latino; 1 Two or more races, non-Hispanic/Latino), 4 international. 24 applicants, 54% accepted, 11 enrolled. In 2017, 10 doctorates awarded. *Degree requirements:* For doctorate, comprehensive exam, thesis/dissertation. *Entrance requirements:* For doctorate, GRE, minimum GPA of 3.0. Additional exam requirements/recommendations for international students: Required—TOEFL (minimum score 550 paper-based; 79 iBT), IELTS (minimum score 5.5), PTE (minimum score 53), or TOEIC (Test of English as an International Communication). *Application deadline:* For fall admission, 8/1 for domestic students, 5/1 for international students; for spring admission, 12/1 for domestic students, 10/1 for international students; for summer admission, 5/1 for domestic students, 2/1 for international

students. Applications are processed on a rolling basis. Application fee: $35 ($40 for international students). Electronic applications accepted. *Expenses:* Tuition, state resident: full-time $9925; part-time $565 per credit hour. Tuition, nonresident: full-time $22,993; part-time $1291 per credit hour. *Financial support:* Fellowships, research assistantships, and teaching assistantships available. Financial award application deadline: 4/1. *Unit head:* Dr. Lisa Zagumny, Director, 931-372-3078, Fax: 931-372-3517, E-mail: lzagumny@tntech.edu. *Application contact:* Shelia K. Kendrick, Coordinator of Graduate Studies, 931-372-3808, Fax: 931-372-3497, E-mail: skendrick@tntech.edu.
Website: https://www.tntech.edu/education/elphd/

University of California, Riverside, Graduate Division, Graduate School of Education, Riverside, CA 92521. Offers applied behavior analysis (M Ed); diversity and equity (M Ed); education policy analysis and leadership (PhD); education specialist (Credential); education, society, and culture (MA, PhD); educational psychology (MA, PhD); general education (M Ed); higher education administration and policy (M Ed, PhD); multiple subject (Credential); research, evaluation, measurement and statistics (MA); school psychology (PhD); single subject (Credential); special education (M Ed, PhD); special education and autism (MA); TESOL (M Ed). *Faculty:* 29 full-time (16 women), 2 part-time/adjunct (1 woman). *Students:* 241 full-time (188 women). 396 applicants, 42% accepted, 166 enrolled. In 2017, 130 master's, 15 doctorates, 14 other advanced degrees awarded. Terminal master's awarded for partial completion of doctoral program. *Degree requirements:* For master's, comprehensive exams or thesis (MA), case study or analytical report (M Ed); for doctorate, comprehensive exam, thesis/dissertation, written and oral qualifying exams, college teaching practicum. *Entrance requirements:* For master's, GRE General Test (for MA); CBEST and CSET (for M Ed in general education only), UCR Extension TESOL certificate (for M Ed with TESOL emphasis only); for doctorate, GRE General Test, writing sample; for Credential, CBEST, CSET. Additional exam requirements/recommendations for international students: Required—TOEFL (minimum score 550 paper-based; 80 iBT), IELTS (minimum score 7). *Application deadline:* For fall admission, 9/1 for domestic students, 6/1 for international students; for winter admission, 11/15 for domestic students, 9/1 for international students; for spring admission, 3/1 for domestic students, 12/1 for international students. Applications are processed on a rolling basis. Application fee: $80 ($100 for international students). Electronic applications accepted. *Expenses:* Tuition, state resident: full-time $5746. Tuition, nonresident: full-time $10,780. Tuition and fees vary according to campus/location and program. *Financial support:* In 2017–18, 105 students received support, including 16 fellowships with full tuition reimbursements available (averaging $31,000 per year), 25 research assistantships with full tuition reimbursements available (averaging $31,000 per year), 10 teaching assistantships with full tuition reimbursements available (averaging $31,000 per year); career-related internships or fieldwork, Federal Work-Study, institutionally sponsored loans, scholarships/grants, and unspecified assistantships also available. Financial award application deadline: 12/15. *Faculty research:* Responsiveness to intervention, faculty core, response to intervention of English language learners, advanced modeling techniques, study on social capital, trust, and motivation. *Total annual research expenditures:* $1.7 million. *Unit head:* Thomas Smith, Dean, 951-827-4633, E-mail: thomas.smith@ucr.edu. *Application contact:* Heather Killeen, Graduate Program Coordinator, 951-827-6362, E-mail: heather.killeen@ucr.edu.
Website: http://www.education.ucr.edu/

The University of Kansas, Graduate Studies, College of Liberal Arts and Sciences, Department of Applied Behavioral Science, Lawrence, KS 66045. Offers applied behavioral science (MA); behavioral psychology (PhD); community health and development (Graduate Certificate); PhD/MPH. *Program availability:* Part-time. *Students:* 46 full-time (33 women), 15 part-time (12 women); includes 5 minority (3 Black or African American, non-Hispanic/Latino; 1 Asian, non-Hispanic/Latino; 1 Two or more races, non-Hispanic/Latino), 3 international. Average age 29. 79 applicants, 43% accepted, 30 enrolled. In 2017, 8 master's, 5 doctorates awarded. Terminal master's awarded for partial completion of doctoral program. *Entrance requirements:* For master's, curriculum vitae; 3 letters of recommendation; personal statement; all academic transcripts; copies of pertinent written work, published or not, as well as presented papers; for doctorate, curriculum vitae; 3 letters of recommendation; personal statement; copies of pertinent written work, published or not, as well as presented papers. Additional exam requirements/recommendations for international students: Required—TOEFL. *Application deadline:* For fall admission, 12/15 priority date for domestic students, 12/15 for international students. Application fee: $65 ($85 for international students). Electronic applications accepted. *Financial support:* Fellowships, research assistantships, teaching assistantships, career-related internships or fieldwork, traineeships, tuition waivers (full), and unspecified assistantships available. Financial award application deadline: 12/15; financial award applicants required to submit CSS PROFILE or FAFSA. *Faculty research:* Organizational behavioral management, community health and development, early childhood education and intervention, developmental disabilities, behavioral economics of choice. *Unit head:* Dr. Florence DiGennaro Reed, Chairperson, 785-864-0521, E-mail: fdreed@ku.edu. *Application contact:* Andrea Noltner, Office Manager, 785-864-0503, E-mail: anoltner@ku.edu.
Website: http://absc.ku.edu

University of Louisville, Graduate School, College of Education and Human Development, Departments of Early Childhood and Elementary Education, Middle and Secondary Education, and Special Education, Louisville, KY 40292-0001. Offers art education (MAT); autism and applied behavior analysis (Certificate); curriculum and instruction (PhD); early elementary education (MAT); exercise physiology (MS); health and physical education (MAT); health professions education (Certificate); higher education (MA); human resources and organization development (MS); instructional technology (M Ed); interdisciplinary early childhood education (MAT); middle school education (MAT); music education (MAT); secondary education (MAT); special education (MAT); sport administration (MS); teacher leadership (M Ed). *Program availability:* Part-time, evening/weekend. *Students:* 114 full-time (73 women), 173 part-time (114 women); includes 49 minority (19 Black or African American, non-Hispanic/Latino; 5 Asian, non-Hispanic/Latino; 13 Hispanic/Latino; 12 Two or more races, non-Hispanic/Latino), 7 international. Average age 29. 132 applicants, 73% accepted, 57 enrolled. In 2017, 70 master's, 2 doctorates, 2 other advanced degrees awarded. *Application deadline:* For spring admission, 1/1 priority date for international students. Application fee: $65. *Expenses:* Tuition, state resident: full-time $12,246; part-time $681 per credit hour. Tuition, nonresident: full-time $25,486; part-time $1417 per credit hour. *Required fees:* $196. Tuition and fees vary according to course load, program and reciprocity agreements. *Financial support:* Application deadline: 6/1; applicants required to submit FAFSA. *Faculty research:* STEM teaching and learning; content literacy for English language learners; social justice in teacher education; adolescent literacy; mathematics teacher development. *Total annual research expenditures:* $1.7 million. *Unit head:* Dr. Ann E. Larson, Dean, College of Education and Human Development, 502-852-6411, Fax: 502-852-1464, E-mail: ann@louisville.edu. *Application contact:* Betty Hampton, Director of Graduate Student Services, 502-852-5597, Fax: 502-852-1465, E-mail: edadvise@louisville.edu.
Website: http://louisville.edu/delphi

University of Massachusetts Dartmouth, Graduate School, College of Arts and Sciences, Department of Psychology, North Dartmouth, MA 02747-2300. Offers autism studies (Graduate Certificate); psychology - applied behavioral analysis (MA, Post-Master's Certificate); psychology - clinical (MA); psychology - research (MA). *Program availability:* Part-time. *Faculty:* 20 full-time (12 women), 8 part-time/adjunct (2 women). *Students:* 40 full-time (31 women), 57 part-time (52 women); includes 19 minority (4 Black or African American, non-Hispanic/Latino; 3 Asian, non-Hispanic/Latino; 7 Hispanic/Latino; 5 Two or more races, non-Hispanic/Latino), 1 international. Average age 29. 96 applicants, 54% accepted, 39 enrolled. In 2017, 21 master's awarded. *Degree requirements:* For master's, comprehensive exam (for some programs), thesis or comprehensive exam (for psychology - clinical); thesis (for psychology - research). *Entrance requirements:* For master's and other advanced degree, statement of purpose (minimum of 300 words), resume, 3 letters of recommendation, official transcripts. Additional exam requirements/recommendations for international students: Required—TOEFL (minimum score 533 paper-based; 72 iBT), IELTS (minimum score 6). *Application deadline:* For fall admission, 3/1 priority date for domestic students, 2/1 priority date for international students. Application fee: $60. Electronic applications accepted. *Expenses:* Tuition, state resident: full-time $15,449; part-time $643.71 per credit. Tuition, nonresident: full-time $27,880; part-time $1161.67 per credit. *Required fees:* $405; $25.88 per credit. Tuition and fees vary according to course load and reciprocity agreements. *Financial support:* In 2017–18, 1 research assistantship (averaging $12,000 per year), 2 teaching assistantships (averaging $14,000 per year) were awarded; tuition waivers (full and partial) and unspecified assistantships also available. Support available to part-time students. Financial award application deadline: 3/1; financial award applicants required to submit FAFSA. *Faculty research:* Health inequities, language and cognitive development, interethnic dating and marriage, executive function and implicit learning in deaf children, behavioral medicine. *Total annual research expenditures:* $344,000. *Unit head:* Mahzad Hojjat, Graduate Program Director, Research Psychology, 508-999-8951, E-mail: mhojjat@umassd.edu. *Application contact:* Steven Briggs, Director of Marketing and Recruitment for Graduate Studies, 508-999-8604, Fax: 508-999-8183, E-mail: graduate@umassd.edu.
Website: http://www.umassd.edu/cas/psychology

University of Memphis, Graduate School, College of Education, Department of Instruction and Curriculum Leadership, Memphis, TN 38152. Offers advanced studies in teaching and learning (M Ed); applied behavior analysis (Graduate Certificate); autism studies (Graduate Certificate); early childhood education (MAT, MS, Ed D); elementary education (MAT); instruction and curriculum (MS, Ed D); instruction design and technology (MS, Ed D); instructional design and technology (Graduate Certificate); literacy, leadership, and coaching (Graduate Certificate); reading (MS, Ed D); school library information specialist (Graduate Certificate); secondary education (MAT); special education (MAT, MS, Ed D); STEM teacher leadership (Graduate Certificate); urban education (Graduate Certificate). *Accreditation:* NCATE (one or more programs are accredited). *Program availability:* Part-time. *Faculty:* 22 full-time (14 women), 14 part-time/adjunct (10 women). *Students:* 36 full-time (27 women), 351 part-time (271 women); includes 159 minority (132 Black or African American, non-Hispanic/Latino; 1 American Indian or Alaska Native, non-Hispanic/Latino; 7 Asian, non-Hispanic/Latino; 10 Hispanic/Latino; 9 Two or more races, non-Hispanic/Latino), 4 international. Average age 35. 170 applicants, 85% accepted, 111 enrolled. In 2017, 84 master's, 14 doctorates, 32 other advanced degrees awarded. Terminal master's awarded for partial completion of doctoral program. *Degree requirements:* For master's, comprehensive exam, thesis or alternative; for doctorate, comprehensive exam, thesis/dissertation. *Entrance requirements:* For master's, GRE General Test, PRAXIS, minimum GPA of 2.5, letters of reference; for doctorate, GRE General Test, GRE Subject Test, 2 years of teaching experience, letters of reference, statement of purpose, interview. Additional exam requirements/recommendations for international students: Required—TOEFL (minimum score 550 paper-based; 79 iBT). *Application deadline:* For fall admission, 4/1 priority date for domestic students; for spring admission, 10/1 priority date for domestic students; for summer admission, 2/1 priority date for domestic students. Applications are processed on a rolling basis. Application fee: $35 ($60 for international students). Electronic applications accepted. *Expenses:* Contact institution. *Financial support:* In 2017–18, 2 research assistantships with full tuition reimbursements (averaging $10,000 per year), 3 teaching assistantships with full tuition reimbursements (averaging $10,666 per year) were awarded; career-related internships or fieldwork, Federal Work-Study, institutionally sponsored loans, scholarships/grants, traineeships, and unspecified assistantships also available. Support available to part-time students. Financial award application deadline: 2/1; financial award applicants required to submit FAFSA. *Faculty research:* Effective urban teachers, preparation and retention of urban teachers, technology utilization in schools, field-based teacher preparation programs, effective use of online instruction. *Unit head:* Dr. Angiline Powell, Interim Chair, 901-678-3310, E-mail: apowell3@memphis.edu. *Application contact:* Dr. James Meindl, Coordinator of Graduate Studies, 901-678-3310, E-mail: jnmeindl@memphis.edu.
Website: http://www.memphis.edu/icl/

University of Michigan–Dearborn, College of Education, Health, and Human Services, Master of Science Program in Applied Behavior Analysis, Dearborn, MI 48126. Offers MS. *Program availability:* Part-time, evening/weekend. *Faculty:* 2 full-time (1 woman), 1 (woman) part-time/adjunct. *Entrance requirements:* For master's, bachelor's degree from accredited institution, official transcripts from all post-secondary institutions attended, minimum GPA of 3.0, three professional letters of recommendation, personal statement. Additional exam requirements/recommendations for international students: Required—TOEFL (minimum score 560 paper-based; 84 iBT), IELTS (minimum score 6.5). *Application deadline:* For fall admission, 8/1 for domestic students, 5/1 for international students; for winter admission, 12/1 for domestic students, 9/1 for international students; for spring admission, 4/1 for domestic students, 1/1 for international students. Applications are processed on a rolling basis. Application fee: $60. Electronic applications accepted. *Expenses:* $683 per credit hour in-state; $1,176 per credit hour out-state. *Financial support:* Scholarships/grants available. Financial award application deadline: 3/1; financial award applicants required to submit FAFSA. *Faculty research:* Technology and teaching, pedagogy and interventions, education policy, learning disabilities, literacy. *Unit head:* Dr. Stein Brunvand, Director, Master's Programs, 313-583-6415, E-mail: sbrunvan@umich.edu. *Application contact:* Office of Graduate Studies, 313-583-6321, E-mail: umd-graduatestudies@umich.edu.
Website: https://umdearborn.edu/cehhs/graduate-programs/areas-study/ms-applied-behavior-analysis

University of Nebraska at Omaha, Graduate Studies, College of Arts and Sciences, Department of Psychology, Omaha, NE 68182. Offers applied behavior analysis (Certificate); human resources and training (Certificate); industrial/organizational psychology (MS); psychology (MA, PhD); school psychology (MS, Ed S). *Program availability:* Part-time. *Degree requirements:* For master's, comprehensive exam, thesis (for some programs); for doctorate, comprehensive exam, thesis/dissertation. *Entrance requirements:* For master's and doctorate, GRE, minimum GPA of 3.0, official transcripts, 3 letters of recommendation, statement of purpose, writing sample, resume. Additional exam requirements/recommendations for international students: Required—TOEFL, IELTS, PTE. Electronic applications accepted.

Applied Behavior Analysis

University of Nebraska Medical Center, Medical Sciences Interdepartmental Area, Omaha, NE 68198-4000. Offers applied behavior analysis (PhD); clinical translational research (MS, PhD); health practice and medical education research (MS); oral biology (MS, PhD). *Program availability:* Part-time. *Faculty:* 170 full-time, 20 part-time/adjunct. *Students:* 48 full-time (31 women), 59 part-time (37 women); includes 34 minority (1 Black or African American, non-Hispanic/Latino; 30 Asian, non-Hispanic/Latino; 3 Hispanic/Latino). Average age 32. 68 applicants, 34% accepted, 23 enrolled. In 2017, 26 master's, 915 doctorates awarded. Terminal master's awarded for partial completion of doctoral program. *Degree requirements:* For master's, comprehensive exam, thesis; for doctorate, comprehensive exam, thesis/dissertation. *Entrance requirements:* For master's, GRE General Test; for doctorate, GRE General Test, MCAT, DAT, LSAT. Additional exam requirements/recommendations for international students: Required—TOEFL (minimum score 550 paper-based; 80 iBT). *Application deadline:* For fall admission, 6/1 for domestic students, 4/1 for international students; for spring admission, 10/1 for domestic students, 9/1 for international students. Applications are processed on a rolling basis. Application fee: $60. Electronic applications accepted. *Expenses:* Contact institution. *Financial support:* In 2017–18, 72 students received support, including 1 fellowship with full tuition reimbursement available (averaging $23,400 per year), 37 research assistantships with full tuition reimbursements available (averaging $23,400 per year), 2 teaching assistantships with full tuition reimbursements available (averaging $23,400 per year); scholarships/grants and health care benefits also available. Financial award application deadline: 2/15; financial award applicants required to submit FAFSA. *Faculty research:* Molecular genetics, oral biology, veterinary pathology, newborn medicine, immunology, clinical research. *Unit head:* Dr. Laura Bilek, Graduate Committee Chair, 402-559-6923, E-mail: lbilek@unmc.edu. *Application contact:* Rhonda Sheibal-Carver, Interdisciplinary Programs Coordinator, 402-559-5141, E-mail: rhonda.sheibalcarver@unmc.edu.
Website: https://www.unmc.edu/msia/index.html

The University of North Carolina Wilmington, College of Arts and Sciences, Department of Psychology, Wilmington, NC 28403-3297. Offers clinical psychology (PhD); psychology (MA), including applied behavior analysis, psychological science. *Faculty:* 22 full-time (14 women). *Students:* 27 full-time (22 women), 39 part-time (33 women); includes 8 minority (1 Asian, non-Hispanic/Latino; 5 Hispanic/Latino; 2 Two or more races, non-Hispanic/Latino). Average age 24. 110 applicants, 21% accepted, 23 enrolled. In 2017, 26 master's awarded. *Degree requirements:* For master's, comprehensive exam, thesis; for doctorate, thesis/dissertation, 1-year external APA-accredited or APPIC-member internship. *Entrance requirements:* For master's, GRE General Test, GRE Subject Test (psychology) only if bachelor's degree was not in the area of psychology, 3 letters of recommendation, psychology research interest form, resume, essay; for doctorate, GRE General Test, GRE Subject Test (psychology) only if bachelor's degree was not in the area of psychology, 3 letters of recommendation, resume, statement of interest. Additional exam requirements/recommendations for international students: Required—TOEFL (minimum score 550 paper-based; 79 iBT), IELTS (minimum score 6.5). *Application deadline:* For fall admission, 1/15 for domestic students. Applications are processed on a rolling basis. Application fee: $75. Electronic applications accepted. *Expenses:* Tuition, state resident: full-time $4626; part-time $226.76 per credit hour. Tuition, nonresident: full-time $17,834; part-time $874.22 per credit hour. *Required fees:* $2124. Tuition and fees vary according to program. *Financial support:* Research assistantships, teaching assistantships, Federal Work-Study, scholarships/grants, unspecified assistantships, and out-of-state tuition remission available. Financial award application deadline: 1/1; financial award applicants required to submit FAFSA. *Unit head:* Dr. Julian Keith, Chair, 910-962-3378, Fax: 910-962-7010, E-mail: keithj@uncw.edu. *Application contact:* Dr. Christine Hughes, Graduate Coordinator, 910-962-7795, Fax: 910-962-7010, E-mail: hughesc@uncw.edu.
Website: http://www.uncw.edu/psy/grad/

University of North Florida, College of Education and Human Services, Department of Exceptional, Deaf, and Interpreter Education, Jacksonville, FL 32224. Offers American Sign Language (MS); American Sign Language/English interpreting (M Ed); applied behavior analysis (M Ed); autism (M Ed); deaf education (M Ed); disability services (M Ed); exceptional student education (M Ed). *Accreditation:* NCATE. *Program availability:* Part-time, evening/weekend. *Entrance requirements:* For master's, GRE General Test, minimum GPA of 3.0 in last 60 hours, interview, 3 letters of recommendation. Additional exam requirements/recommendations for international students: Required—TOEFL (minimum score 500 paper-based). Electronic applications accepted. *Faculty research:* Transportation, energy, communications, healthcare, nano-science and engineering, unmanned aircraft systems, biomedical applications.

University of North Texas, Robert B. Toulouse School of Graduate Studies, Denton, TX 76203-5459. Offers accounting (MS); applied anthropology (MA, MS); applied behavior analysis (Certificate); applied geography (MA); applied technology and performance improvement (M Ed, MS); art education (MA); art history (MA); art museum education (Certificate); arts leadership (Certificate); audiology (Au D); behavior analysis (MS); behavioral science (PhD); biochemistry and molecular biology (MS); biology (MA, MS); biomedical engineering (MS); business analysis (MS); chemistry (MS); clinical health psychology (PhD); communication studies (MA, MS); computer engineering (MS); computer science (MS); counseling (M Ed, MS), including clinical mental health counseling (MS), college and university counseling, elementary school counseling, secondary school counseling; creative writing (MA); criminal justice (MS); curriculum and instruction (M Ed); decision sciences (MBA); design (MA, MFA), including fashion design (MFA), innovation studies, interior design (MFA); early childhood studies (MS); economics (MS); educational leadership (M Ed, Ed D); educational psychology (MS, PhD), including family studies (MS), gifted and talented (MS), human development (MS), learning and cognition (MS), research, measurement and evaluation (MS); electrical engineering (MS); emergency management (MPA); engineering technology (MS); English (MA); English as a second language (MA); environmental science (MS); finance (MBA, MS); financial management (MPA); French (MA); health services management (MBA); higher education (M Ed, Ed D); history (MA, MS); hospitality management (MS); human resources management (MPA); information science (MS); information systems (PhD); information technologies (MBA); interdisciplinary studies (MA, MS); international studies (MA); international sustainable tourism (MS); jazz studies (MM); journalism (MA, MJ, Graduate Certificate), including interactive and virtual digital communication (Graduate Certificate), narrative journalism (Graduate Certificate), public relations (Graduate Certificate); kinesiology (MS); linguistics (MA); local government management (MPA); logistics (PhD); logistics and supply chain management (MBA); long-term care, senior housing, and aging services (MA); management (PhD); marketing (MBA); mathematics (MA, MS); mechanical and energy engineering (MS, PhD); music (MA), including ethnomusicology, music theory, musicology, performance; music composition (PhD); music education (MM Ed, PhD); nonprofit management (MPA); operations and supply chain management (MBA); performance (MM, DMA); philosophy (MA); political science (MA); professional and technical communication (MA); radio, television and film (MA, MFA); rehabilitation counseling (Certificate); sociology (MA); Spanish (MA); special education (M Ed); speech-language pathology (MA); strategic management (MBA); studio art (MFA); teaching (M Ed); MBA/MS. *Program availability:* Part-time, evening/weekend, online learning. Terminal master's awarded for partial completion of doctoral program. *Degree requirements:* For master's, variable foreign language requirement, comprehensive exam (for some programs), thesis (for some programs); for doctorate, variable foreign language requirement, comprehensive exam (for some programs), thesis/dissertation; for other advanced degree, variable foreign language requirement, comprehensive exam (for some programs). *Entrance requirements:* For master's and doctorate, GRE, GMAT. Additional exam requirements/recommendations for international students: Required—TOEFL (minimum score 550 paper-based; 79 iBT). Electronic applications accepted.

University of Oklahoma, Jeannine Rainbolt College of Education, Department of Educational Psychology, Program in Special Education, Norman, OK 73019. Offers applied behavior analysis (M Ed); higher education and community support (PhD); higher education professor (PhD); school instruction and leadership (PhD); secondary transition education (M Ed). *Accreditation:* NCATE. *Program availability:* Part-time, 100% online, blended/hybrid learning. *Students:* 25 full-time (21 women), 81 part-time (72 women); includes 20 minority (4 Black or African American, non-Hispanic/Latino; 5 American Indian or Alaska Native, non-Hispanic/Latino; 1 Asian, non-Hispanic/Latino; 5 Hispanic/Latino; 5 Two or more races, non-Hispanic/Latino), 4 international. Average age 36. 49 applicants, 59% accepted, 23 enrolled. In 2017, 11 master's, 1 doctorate awarded. Terminal master's awarded for partial completion of doctoral program. *Degree requirements:* For master's, thesis optional; for doctorate, comprehensive exam, thesis/dissertation. *Entrance requirements:* For doctorate, GRE. Additional exam requirements/recommendations for international students: Required—TOEFL (minimum score 79 iBT) or IELTS (minimum score 6.5). *Application deadline:* For fall admission, 2/1 for domestic and international students. Application fee: $50 ($100 for international students). Electronic applications accepted. *Expenses:* Tuition, state resident: full-time $5119; part-time $213.30 per credit hour. Tuition, nonresident: full-time $19,778; part-time $824.10 per credit hour. *Required fees:* $3458; $133.55 per credit hour. $126.50 per semester. *Financial support:* In 2017–18, 60 students received support. Research assistantships with full and partial tuition reimbursements available, teaching assistantships with full and partial tuition reimbursements available, and scholarships/grants available. Financial award application deadline: 6/1; financial award applicants required to submit FAFSA. *Faculty research:* K-12 literacy instruction for struggling readers; reading, writing, spelling, and mathematics interventions; applied behavioral analysis; secondary transition; self-determination and post-secondary outcomes. *Unit head:* Dr. Nancy E. Marchand-Martella, Chair, Department of Educational Psychology, 405-325-0624, Fax: 405-325-6655, E-mail: nmarchand-martella@ou.edu. *Application contact:* Anna Steele, Graduate Programs Specialist, 405-325-4525, Fax: 405-325-7390, E-mail: jrcoe_gps@ou.edu.
Website: http://www.ou.edu/education/edpy.html

University of Pittsburgh, School of Education, Department of Instruction and Learning, Program in Special Education, Pittsburgh, PA 15260. Offers applied behavior analysis (M Ed); early intervention (M Ed, PhD); general special education (M Ed, Ed D); special education teacher preparation (M Ed); vision studies (M Ed, PhD). *Program availability:* Part-time, evening/weekend. *Degree requirements:* For master's, thesis; for doctorate, thesis/dissertation. *Entrance requirements:* For master's, PRAXIS I; for doctorate, GRE General Test. Additional exam requirements/recommendations for international students: Required—TOEFL.

University of San Francisco, School of Nursing and Health Professions, Program in Behavioral Health, San Francisco, CA 94117-1080. Offers MS.

University of Southern Maine, College of Management and Human Service, School of Education and Human Development, Program in Educational Psychology, Portland, ME 04103. Offers applied behavior analysis (MS, CGS). *Program availability:* Part-time, evening/weekend. *Entrance requirements:* For master's, GRE or MAT. Additional exam requirements/recommendations for international students: Required—TOEFL (minimum score 550 paper-based; 79 iBT). Electronic applications accepted. *Faculty research:* Applied behavior analysis, functional behavioral analysis, positive behavioral interventions and supports.

University of South Florida, College of Behavioral and Community Sciences, Department of Child and Family Studies, Tampa, FL 33620-9951. Offers applied behavior analysis (MA, MS, PhD); behavioral and community sciences (PhD); child and adolescent behavioral health (MS), including developmental disabilities, leadership in child and adolescent health, translational research and evaluation, youth and behavioral health; rehabilitation and mental health counseling (MA), including addictions and substance abuse counseling, marriage and family therapy. *Accreditation:* ACA. *Faculty:* 18 full-time (12 women), 2 part-time/adjunct (1 woman). *Students:* 188 full-time (166 women), 115 part-time (92 women); includes 121 minority (40 Black or African American, non-Hispanic/Latino; 8 Asian, non-Hispanic/Latino; 61 Hispanic/Latino; 12 Two or more races, non-Hispanic/Latino), 6 international. Average age 28. 287 applicants, 53% accepted, 89 enrolled. In 2017, 45 master's, 1 doctorate awarded. *Degree requirements:* For master's, comprehensive exam, thesis (for some programs); for doctorate, comprehensive exam, thesis/dissertation, Behavior Analyst Board Certification Exam. *Entrance requirements:* For master's, GRE General Test, minimum GPA of 3.0 in last 60 hours of coursework; letters of recommendation; one-page narrative describing experience, interest, and career goals in applied behavior analysis; resume or curriculum vitae (varies by program); for doctorate, GRE General Test, master's degree in behavioral analysis or closely-related field; minimum GPA of 3.5 in graduate course work; three letters of recommendation; campus visit with faculty interview; personal statement; curriculum vitae; evidence of research experiences and expertise. Additional exam requirements/recommendations for international students: Required—TOEFL (minimum score 550 paper-based; 79 iBT) or IELTS (minimum score 6.5). *Application deadline:* For fall admission, 12/5 for domestic and international students. Application fee: $30. *Financial support:* In 2017–18, 30 students received support. Unspecified assistantships available. *Faculty research:* Applied behavior analysis, autism, behavior management, behavioral intervention, children, developmental disabilities, experimental analysis of behavior, functional assessment, positive behavior support. *Total annual research expenditures:* $17.6 million. *Application contact:* Dr. Raymond G. Miltenberger, Professor/Director of Master's Program, 813-974-5079, Fax: 813-974-6115, E-mail: miltenbe@usf.edu.
Website: http://cfs.cbcs.usf.edu/

The University of Texas at San Antonio, College of Education and Human Development, Department of Educational Psychology, San Antonio, TX 78207. Offers applied behavior analysis (Certificate); educational psychology (MA), including applied educational psychology, behavior assessment and intervention, general educational psychology, program evaluation; language acquisition and bilingual psychoeducational assessment (Certificate); school psychology (MA). *Program availability:* Part-time. *Faculty:* 9 full-time (5 women), 1 (woman) part-time/adjunct. *Students:* 34 full-time (27 women), 40 part-time (35 women); includes 52 minority (5 Black or African American, non-Hispanic/Latino; 1 Asian, non-Hispanic/Latino; 43 Hispanic/Latino; 3 Two or more races, non-Hispanic/Latino). Average age 28. 46 applicants, 72% accepted, 23 enrolled. In 2017, 16 master's, 23 other advanced degrees awarded. *Degree requirements:* For master's, comprehensive exam, thesis (for some programs). *Entrance requirements:* For master's, GRE, bachelor's degree with 18 credit hours in field of study or in another appropriate field of study, two letters of recommendation, statement of purpose; for Certificate, 18 hours in psychology, sociology, education, or anything related (for applied

behavioral analysis); minimum GPA of 2.7 in last 30 hours (for language acquisition and bilingual psychoeducational assessment). Additional exam requirements/recommendations for international students: Required—TOEFL (minimum score 550 paper-based; 79 iBT), IELTS (minimum score 6.5). *Application deadline:* For fall admission, 6/15 for domestic students, 3/1 for international students; for spring admission, 10/15 for domestic students, 9/15 for international students; for summer admission, 3/1 for international students. Applications are processed on a rolling basis. Application fee: $50 ($90 for international students). Electronic applications accepted. *Expenses:* Tuition, state resident: full-time $5495. Tuition, nonresident: full-time $21,938. *Required fees:* $1915. Tuition and fees vary according to program. *Financial support:* Research assistantships available. Financial award applicants required to submit FAFSA. *Faculty research:* Teacher consultation and culturally responsive school psychology practices, youth mentoring, cross-age peer mentoring, adolescent connectedness, pair counseling. *Total annual research expenditures:* $168,976. *Unit head:* Dr. Jeremy Sullivan, Department Chair, 210-458-2650, Fax: 210-458-2019, E-mail: jeremy.sullivan@utsa.edu.
Website: http://education.utsa.edu/educational_psychology

University of Utah, Graduate School, College of Education, Department of Special Education, Salt Lake City, UT 84112. Offers board certified behavior analyst (M Ed, MS, PhD); deaf and hard of hearing (M Ed); deaf/blind (M Ed, MS); early childhood deaf and hard of hearing (MS); early childhood special education (M Ed, MS, PhD); early childhood vision impairments (M Ed); mild/moderate disabilities (M Ed, MS, PhD); severe disabilities (M Ed, MS, PhD); visual impairment (M Ed, MS). *Program availability:* Part-time, evening/weekend, 100% online, blended/hybrid learning. *Faculty:* 9 full-time (6 women), 8 part-time/adjunct (7 women). *Students:* 45 full-time (41 women), 26 part-time (24 women); includes 6 minority (4 Asian, non-Hispanic/Latino; 2 Hispanic/Latino). Average age 31. 30 applicants, 97% accepted, 28 enrolled. In 2017, 29 master's awarded. Terminal master's awarded for partial completion of doctoral program. *Degree requirements:* For master's, comprehensive exam, thesis (for some programs), qualifying exam; for doctorate, thesis/dissertation, qualifying exam. *Entrance requirements:* For master's, GRE, minimum GPA of 3.0; for doctorate, GRE General Test, minimum GPA of 3.5. Additional exam requirements/recommendations for international students: Required—TOEFL (minimum score 600 paper-based; 100 iBT); Recommended—IELTS (minimum score 7). *Application deadline:* For fall admission, 3/1 for domestic and international students; for spring admission, 11/1 for domestic and international students; for summer admission, 5/16 for domestic and international students. Application fee: $55 ($65 for international students). Electronic applications accepted. *Financial support:* In 2017–18, 22 students received support, including 33 fellowships with partial tuition reimbursements available (averaging $4,350 per year), 3 teaching assistantships with tuition reimbursements available (averaging $10,000 per year); career-related internships or fieldwork and health care benefits also available. Support available to part-time students. Financial award application deadline: 3/1; financial award applicants required to submit FAFSA. *Faculty research:* Inclusive education, positive behavior support, reading, instruction and intervention strategies. *Total annual research expenditures:* $139,750. *Unit head:* Dr. Robert E. O'Neill, Chair, 801-581-8121, Fax: 801-585-6476, E-mail: rob.oneill@utah.edu. *Application contact:* Patty Davis, Academic Advisor, 801-581-4764, Fax: 801-585-6476, E-mail: patty.davis@utah.edu.
Website: http://special-ed.utah.edu/

University of West Florida, College of Education and Professional Studies, Department of Teacher Education and Educational Leadership, Program in Exceptional Student Education, Pensacola, FL 32514-5750. Offers applied behavior analysis (MA); special and alternative education (MA). *Accreditation:* NCATE. *Program availability:* Part-time, evening/weekend, online learning. *Entrance requirements:* For master's, GRE (minimum score 450 verbal) or MAT (minimum score 396) if bachelor's GPA less than 3.0, state teaching certification; letter of intent; two professional references. Additional exam requirements/recommendations for international students: Required—TOEFL (minimum score 550 paper-based). *Faculty research:* Memory, semantic structure, remedial programming.

Wayne State University, College of Education, Division of Theoretical and Behavioral Foundations, Detroit, MI 48202. Offers applied behavior analysis (Certificate); counseling (M Ed, MA, Ed D, Ed S); counseling psychology (MA, PhD); education evaluation and research (M Ed, Ed D); educational psychology (M Ed, PhD), including learning and instruction sciences (PhD); rehabilitation counseling and community inclusion (MA); school and community psychology (MA, Certificate). *Accreditation:* ACA (one or more programs are accredited); CORE (one or more programs are accredited). *Program availability:* Evening/weekend. *Students:* Average age 32. 294 applicants, 34% accepted, 72 enrolled. In 2017, 87 master's, 12 doctorates, 14 other advanced degrees awarded. *Entrance requirements:* For master's, GRE, interview, personal statement, portfolio (art therapy); for doctorate, GRE, department-written exam, interview, curriculum vitae, references, master's degree in closely-related field with minimum GPA of 3.5, demonstration of counseling skills (for Ed D in counseling); for other advanced degree, master's degree in counseling and counseling license (for Ed S); good standing

in school and community psychology MA program (for Certificate). Additional exam requirements/recommendations for international students: Required—TOEFL (minimum score 550 paper-based; 79 iBT), Michigan English Language Assessment Battery (minimum score 85); Recommended—IELTS (minimum score 6.5), TWE (minimum score 5.5). *Application deadline:* For fall admission, 6/1 priority date for domestic students, 5/1 priority date for international students; for winter admission, 10/1 priority date for domestic students, 9/1 priority date for international students; for spring admission, 2/1 priority date for domestic students, 1/1 priority date for international students. Applications are processed on a rolling basis. Application fee: $50. Electronic applications accepted. *Expenses:* Contact institution. *Financial support:* In 2017–18, 92 students received support, including 2 research assistantships with tuition reimbursements available (averaging $17,994 per year); fellowships, teaching assistantships, Federal Work-Study, scholarships/grants, health care benefits, and unspecified assistantships also available. Support available to part-time students. Financial award applicants required to submit FAFSA. *Faculty research:* Adolescents at risk, supervision of counseling. *Unit head:* Dr. Cheryl Somers, Assistant Dean, 313-577-1670, E-mail: c.somers@wayne.edu. *Application contact:* Janice Green, Assistant Dean, 313-577-1605, E-mail: jwgreen@wayne.edu.
Website: http://coe.wayne.edu/tbf/index.php

Western New England University, College of Arts and Sciences, Program in Behavior Analysis, Springfield, MA 01119. Offers applied behavior analysis (MS); behavior analysis (PhD). *Program availability:* Part-time, evening/weekend. *Faculty:* 11 full-time (5 women). *Students:* 163 part-time (134 women); includes 23 minority (6 Black or African American, non-Hispanic/Latino; 1 American Indian or Alaska Native, non-Hispanic/Latino; 9 Asian, non-Hispanic/Latino; 6 Hispanic/Latino; 1 Two or more races, non-Hispanic/Latino), 11 international. Average age 27. 86 applicants, 55% accepted, 44 enrolled. In 2017, 30 master's, 2 doctorates awarded. *Degree requirements:* For doctorate, thesis/dissertation. *Entrance requirements:* For master's, GRE, official transcript, personal statement, resume, three letters of recommendation; for doctorate, GRE, master's degree in behavior analysis with minimum GPA of 3.6, official transcript, personal statement, resume, three letters of recommendation. Additional exam requirements/recommendations for international students: Required—TOEFL (minimum score 79 iBT). *Application deadline:* For fall admission, 1/15 for domestic and international students. Application fee: $30. Electronic applications accepted. *Expenses:* Contact institution. *Financial support:* In 2017–18, 6 fellowships with tuition reimbursements were awarded. Support available to part-time students. Financial award application deadline: 4/15; financial award applicants required to submit FAFSA. *Unit head:* Dr. Gregory Hanley, Director of the PhD Program in Behavioral Analysis/Professor, 413-796-2367, E-mail: ghanley@wne.edu. *Application contact:* Matthew Fox, Director of Admissions for Graduate Students and Adult Learners, 413-782-1410, Fax: 413-782-1777, E-mail: study@wne.edu.
Website: http://www1.wne.edu/academics/graduate/index.cfm#?category-1

Westfield State University, College of Graduate and Continuing Education, Department of Psychology, Program in Applied Behavior Analysis, Westfield, MA 01086. Offers MA. *Program availability:* Part-time, evening/weekend. *Faculty:* 4 full-time (1 woman), 2 part-time/adjunct (1 woman). *Students:* 17 full-time (13 women), 11 part-time (8 women); includes 3 minority (1 Asian, non-Hispanic/Latino; 2 Hispanic/Latino). Average age 29. 15 applicants, 93% accepted, 12 enrolled. In 2017, 7 master's awarded. *Degree requirements:* For master's, comprehensive exam, thesis (for some programs). *Entrance requirements:* For master's, GRE General Test or MAT, minimum undergraduate GPA of 2.8. Additional exam requirements/recommendations for international students: Recommended—TOEFL (minimum score 550 paper-based; 79 iBT). *Application deadline:* For fall admission, 2/1 for domestic students. Applications are processed on a rolling basis. Application fee: $50. *Expenses:* Tuition, state resident: part-time $332 per credit. Tuition, nonresident: part-time $332 per credit. *Required fees:* $75 per semester. Tuition and fees vary according to program. *Financial support:* Unspecified assistantships available. Financial award application deadline: 3/1; financial award applicants required to submit FAFSA. *Unit head:* Dr. Jorge Reyes, Advisor, 413-572-8902, E-mail: jreyes@westfield.ma.edu. *Application contact:* Shelly Henrichon, Admissions Coordinator, 413-572-8022, Fax: 413-572-5227, E-mail: mhenrichon@westfield.ma.edu.

Wright State University, Graduate School, College of Liberal Arts, Program in Applied Behavioral Science, Criminal Justice and Social Problems, Dayton, OH 45435. Offers criminal justice and social problems (MA). *Degree requirements:* For master's, thesis optional. *Entrance requirements:* Additional exam requirements/recommendations for international students: Required—TOEFL. *Faculty research:* Training and development, criminal justice and social problems, community systems, human factors, industrial/organizational psychology.

Youngstown State University, Graduate School, College of Liberal Arts and Social Sciences, Department of Psychology, Youngstown, OH 44555-0001. Offers applied behavior analysis (MS).

Applied Psychology

Adler University, Graduate Programs, MA in Applied Psychology Program, Chicago, IL 60602. Offers gender and sexuality studies (MA). *Program availability:* Online learning. *Degree requirements:* For master's, thesis or capstone.

Antioch University New England, Graduate School, Department of Applied Psychology, Keene, NH 03431-3552. Offers autism spectrum disorders (Certificate), including applied behavioral analysis internship, autism spectrum disorders; clinical mental health counseling (MA), including clinical mental health counseling, substance abuse counseling; dance/movement therapy and counseling (M Ed, MA, PMC); marriage and family therapy (MA, PhD, Certificate). *Degree requirements:* For master's, internship, practicum. *Entrance requirements:* For master's, previous course work and work experience in psychology. Additional exam requirements/recommendations for international students: Required—TOEFL (minimum score 550 paper-based). Electronic applications accepted. *Expenses:* Contact institution. *Faculty research:* Diversity, descendents of survivors of the Holocaust and American slavery.

Arizona State University at the Tempe campus, Ira A. Fulton Schools of Engineering, The Polytechnic School, Applied Psychology Program, Mesa, AZ 85212. Offers MS. *Program availability:* Part-time. Terminal master's awarded for partial completion of doctoral program. *Degree requirements:* For master's, thesis or applied project with oral defense and exam; interactive Program of Study (iPOS) submitted before completing 50 percent of required credit hours. *Entrance requirements:* For master's, GRE, minimum

GPA of 3.0 or equivalent in last 2 years of work leading to bachelor's degree. Additional exam requirements/recommendations for international students: Required—TOEFL, IELTS, or PTE. Electronic applications accepted.

Athabasca University, Program in Counseling, Athabasca, AB T9S 3A3, Canada. Offers applied psychology (Post Master's Certificate); art therapy (MC); career counseling (MC); counseling (Advanced Certificate); counseling psychology (MC); school counseling (MC).

Boston College, Lynch School of Education, Program in Applied Developmental and Educational Psychology, Chestnut Hill, MA 02467-3800. Offers MA, PhD. *Program availability:* Part-time, evening/weekend. *Students:* 34 full-time (32 women), 9 part-time (8 women); includes 9 minority (2 Black or African American, non-Hispanic/Latino; 2 Asian, non-Hispanic/Latino; 4 Hispanic/Latino; 1 Two or more races, non-Hispanic/Latino), 10 international. Average age 27. 97 applicants, 61% accepted, 20 enrolled. In 2017, 13 master's, 3 doctorates awarded. Terminal master's awarded for partial completion of doctoral program. *Degree requirements:* For master's, comprehensive exam; for doctorate, comprehensive exam, thesis/dissertation. *Entrance requirements:* For master's and doctorate, GRE General Test. Additional exam requirements/recommendations for international students: Required—TOEFL (minimum score 100 iBT). *Application deadline:* For fall admission, 12/1 priority date for domestic and international students; for spring admission, 11/1 for domestic and international

students. Application fee: $65. Electronic applications accepted. *Financial support:* Fellowships with tuition reimbursements, research assistantships with tuition reimbursements, teaching assistantships with tuition reimbursements, career-related internships or fieldwork, Federal Work-Study, scholarships/grants, traineeships, health care benefits, tuition waivers (full and partial), and unspecified assistantships available. Support available to part-time students. Financial award applicants required to submit FAFSA. *Faculty research:* Cognitive learning and culture, effects of social policy reform on children and families, psychosocial trauma, human rights and international justice, positive youth development, children and adolescents living in poverty. *Unit head:* Dr. Rebekah Levine Coley, Chairperson, 617-552-6018, Fax: 617-552-4710. *Application contact:* Kimberly Rose, Graduate Admission Assistant, 617-552-4214, Fax: 617-552-0398, E-mail: roseki@bc.edu.

California State University, Chico, Office of Graduate Studies, College of Behavioral and Social Sciences, Department of Psychology, Program in Applied/School Psychology, Chico, CA 95929-0722. Offers MA. *Degree requirements:* For master's, thesis or comprehensive exam. *Entrance requirements:* For master's, GRE General Test or MAT, 3 letters of recommendation, statement of purpose. Additional exam requirements/recommendations for international students: Required—TOEFL (minimum score 550 paper-based; 80 iBT), IELTS (minimum score 6.5), PTE. Electronic applications accepted.

The Catholic University of America, School of Arts and Sciences, Department of Psychology, Washington, DC 20064. Offers applied experimental psychology (PhD); clinical psychology (PhD); general psychology (MA); human development psychology (PhD); human factors (MA); MA/JD. MA/JD offered jointly with Columbus School of Law. *Accreditation:* APA (one or more programs are accredited). *Program availability:* Part-time. *Faculty:* 11 full-time (6 women), 9 part-time/adjunct (3 women). *Students:* 38 full-time (27 women), 33 part-time (25 women); includes 22 minority (4 Black or African American, non-Hispanic/Latino; 4 Asian, non-Hispanic/Latino; 5 Hispanic/Latino; 9 Two or more races, non-Hispanic/Latino), 6 international. Average age 29. 183 applicants, 26% accepted, 21 enrolled. In 2017, 18 master's, 9 doctorates awarded. *Degree requirements:* For master's, comprehensive exam, thesis (for some programs); for doctorate, comprehensive exam, thesis/dissertation. *Entrance requirements:* For master's, GRE General Test, statement of purpose, official copies of academic transcripts, three letters of recommendation; for doctorate, GRE General Test, GRE Subject Test, statement of purpose, official copies of academic transcripts, three letters of recommendation. Additional exam requirements/recommendations for international students: Required—TOEFL (minimum score 550 paper-based; 80 iBT). *Application deadline:* For fall admission, 7/15 priority date for domestic students, 7/1 for international students; for spring admission, 11/15 priority date for domestic students, 11/1 for international students. Applications are processed on a rolling basis. Application fee: $55. Electronic applications accepted. *Expenses:* Contact institution. *Financial support:* Fellowships, research assistantships, teaching assistantships, Federal Work-Study, scholarships/grants, tuition waivers (full and partial), and unspecified assistantships available. Financial award application deadline: 2/1; financial award applicants required to submit FAFSA. *Faculty research:* Clinical psychology, applied cognitive science, psychopathology, cognitive neuroscience, psychotherapy. *Total annual research expenditures:* $243,144. *Unit head:* Dr. Marc M. Sebrechts, Chair, 202-319-5750, Fax: 202-319-6263, E-mail: sebrechts@cua.edu. *Application contact:* Dr. Steven Brown, Director of Graduate Admissions, 202-319-5057, Fax: 202-319-6533, E-mail: cua-admissions@cua.edu.
Website: http://psychology.cua.edu/

Central Michigan University, College of Graduate Studies, College of Humanities and Social and Behavioral Sciences, Department of Psychology, Program in Experimental Psychology, Mount Pleasant, MI 48859. Offers applied experimental psychology (PhD); experimental psychology (MS). *Program availability:* Part-time. *Degree requirements:* For master's, thesis or alternative; for doctorate, thesis/dissertation. Electronic applications accepted. *Faculty research:* Behavioral neuroscience, human development, perception and cognition, social/personal problem solving, psychophysiology.

The Chicago School of Professional Psychology: Online, Program in Applied Industrial and Organizational Psychology, Chicago, IL 60654. Offers MA, Certificate.

Clayton State University, School of Graduate Studies, College of Arts and Sciences, Program in Psychology, Morrow, GA 30260-0285. Offers applied developmental psychology (MS); clinical/counseling psychology (MS). *Entrance requirements:* For master's, GRE, 2 official transcripts; 3 letters of recommendation; statement of purpose; on-campus interview; background check. Additional exam requirements/recommendations for international students: Required—TOEFL (minimum score 550 paper-based). Electronic applications accepted.

Clemson University, Graduate School, College of Behavioral, Social and Health Sciences, Department of Psychology, Clemson, SC 29634. Offers applied psychology (MS); human factors psychology (PhD); industrial-organizational psychology (PhD). *Faculty:* 30 full-time (13 women), 1 (woman) part-time/adjunct. *Students:* 39 full-time (23 women), 4 part-time (3 women); includes 4 minority (1 Black or African American, non-Hispanic/Latino; 3 Hispanic/Latino). Average age 27. 214 applicants, 8% accepted, 10 enrolled. In 2017, 7 master's, 6 doctorates awarded. *Degree requirements:* For master's, thesis; for doctorate, comprehensive exam, thesis/dissertation. *Entrance requirements:* For master's and doctorate, GRE General Test, unofficial transcripts, letters of recommendation, statement of intent. Additional exam requirements/recommendations for international students: Required—TOEFL (minimum score 80 iBT), IELTS (minimum score 7), PTE (minimum score 54). *Application deadline:* For fall admission, 1/15 priority date for domestic and international students. Application fee: $80 ($90 for international students). Electronic applications accepted. *Expenses:* $6,564 per semester full-time resident, $12,538 per semester full-time non-resident, $743 per credit hour part-time resident, $1,486 per credit hour part-time non-resident, $1,203 per credit hour online, other fees may apply per session. *Financial support:* In 2017–18, 18 students received support, including 4 fellowships with partial tuition reimbursements available (averaging $8,750 per year), 2 research assistantships with partial tuition reimbursements available (averaging $12,000 per year), 11 teaching assistantships with partial tuition reimbursements available (averaging $13,386 per year); career-related internships or fieldwork and unspecified assistantships also available. Financial award application deadline: 1/15. *Faculty research:* Occupational health and organizational psychology; transportation safety; human factors in health care; ergonomics and human-computer interaction; aging, retirement, and return to work. *Total annual research expenditures:* $436,382. *Unit head:* Dr. Patrick Raymark, Chair, 864-656-4715, E-mail: praymar@clemson.edu. *Application contact:* Dr. Robert Sinclair, Graduate Program Coordinator, 864-656-3931, E-mail: rsincla@clemson.edu.
Website: http://www.clemson.edu/cbshs/departments/psychology/index.html

DEREE - The American College of Greece, Graduate Programs, Athens, Greece. Offers applied psychology (MS); communication (MA); leadership (MS); marketing (MS).

Eastern Washington University, Graduate Studies, College of Social Sciences, Department of Psychology, Program in Mental Health Counseling, Cheney, WA 99004-2431. Offers applied psychology (MS); mental health counseling (MS). *Students:* 16 full-time (11 women); includes 2 minority (1 Black or African American, non-Hispanic/Latino;

1 Hispanic/Latino). Average age 30. 48 applicants, 17% accepted, 7 enrolled. In 2017, 11 master's awarded. *Degree requirements:* For master's, comprehensive exam, thesis. *Entrance requirements:* For master's, GRE, minimum GPA of 3.0. Additional exam requirements/recommendations for international students: Required—TOEFL (minimum score 580 paper-based; 92 iBT), IELTS (minimum score 7), PTE (minimum score 63). Application fee: $75. Electronic applications accepted. *Expenses:* Tuition, state resident: full-time $11,191; part-time $373.06 per credit. Tuition, nonresident: full-time $25,995; part-time $866.52 per credit. *Financial support:* Application deadline: 2/1; applicants required to submit FAFSA. *Unit head:* Dr. Keely Hope, Associate Professor/Director, Counselor Education, 509-359-2439, E-mail: khope@ewu.edu. *Application contact:* Kathy White, Advisor/Recruiter for Graduate Studies, 509-359-6297, Fax: 509-359-6044, E-mail: gradprograms@ewu.edu.

Eastern Washington University, Graduate Studies, College of Social Sciences, Department of Psychology, Program in School Counseling, Cheney, WA 99004-2431. Offers applied psychology (MS); school counseling (MS). *Accreditation:* ACA. *Students:* 21 full-time (14 women). Average age 27. 22 applicants, 55% accepted, 10 enrolled. In 2017, 8 master's awarded. *Entrance requirements:* Additional exam requirements/recommendations for international students: Required—TOEFL (minimum score 580 paper-based; 92 iBT), IELTS (minimum score 7). *Expenses:* Tuition, state resident: full-time $11,191; part-time $373.06 per credit. Tuition, nonresident: full-time $25,995; part-time $866.52 per credit.

Fairfield University, Graduate School of Education and Allied Professions, Fairfield, CT 06824. Offers applied behavior analysis (ATC); applied psychology (MA); clinical mental health counseling (MA, CAS); educational technology (MA); elementary education (MA, CAS); family studies (MA); integration of spirituality and religion in counseling (ATC); marriage and family therapy (MA); reading and language development (Sixth Year Certificate); school counseling (MA, CAS); school psychology (MA, CAS); school-based marriage and family therapy (ATC); secondary education (MA); special education (MA, CAS); substance abuse counseling (ATC); teaching (Certificate); teaching and foundations (MA, CAS); TESOL, world languages, and bilingual education (MA, CAS). *Accreditation:* NCATE. *Program availability:* Part-time, evening/weekend. *Faculty:* 23 full-time (17 women), 39 part-time/adjunct (28 women). *Students:* 199 full-time (168 women), 251 part-time (206 women); includes 85 minority (21 Black or African American, non-Hispanic/Latino; 9 Asian, non-Hispanic/Latino; 49 Hispanic/Latino; 6 Two or more races, non-Hispanic/Latino), 4 international. Average age 32. 370 applicants, 56% accepted, 125 enrolled. In 2017, 136 master's, 28 other advanced degrees awarded. *Degree requirements:* For master's, comprehensive exam. *Entrance requirements:* For master's, minimum GPA of 3.0, 2 recommendations, resume. Additional exam requirements/recommendations for international students: Required—TOEFL (minimum score 550 paper-based; 84 iBT) or IELTS (minimum score 7.5). *Application deadline:* For fall admission, 2/15 for international students; for spring admission, 10/1 for international students. Application fee: $60. Electronic applications accepted. *Expenses:* $750 per credit hour. *Financial support:* In 2017–18, 34 students received support. Career-related internships or fieldwork and unspecified assistantships available. Support available to part-time students. Financial award applicants required to submit FAFSA. *Faculty research:* Reading and literacy, writing, social justice and inequality in education, addictions and mental health issues, therapeutic relationships and clinical supervision. *Unit head:* Dr. Robert D. Hannafin, Dean, 203-254-4250, Fax: 203-254-4241, E-mail: rhannafin@fairfield.edu. *Application contact:* Marianne Gumpper, Director of Graduate Admission, 203-254-4184, Fax: 203-254-4073, E-mail: gradadmis@fairfield.edu.
Website: http://www.fairfield.edu/gseap

Fordham University, Graduate School of Arts and Sciences, Department of Psychology, Program in Applied Developmental Psychology, New York, NY 10458. Offers PhD. *Accreditation:* APA. *Students:* 15 full-time (13 women), 3 part-time (all women); includes 4 minority (2 Black or African American, non-Hispanic/Latino; 1 Asian, non-Hispanic/Latino; 1 Hispanic/Latino), 4 international. Average age 31. 36 applicants, 33% accepted, 4 enrolled. In 2017, 5 doctorates awarded. *Degree requirements:* For doctorate, comprehensive exam, thesis/dissertation. *Entrance requirements:* For doctorate, GRE General Test, GRE Subject Test. Additional exam requirements/recommendations for international students: Required—TOEFL (minimum score 600 paper-based). *Application deadline:* For fall admission, 12/14 for domestic students. Application fee: $70. Electronic applications accepted. *Financial support:* In 2017–18, 15 students received support, including 4 fellowships with tuition reimbursements available (averaging $26,065 per year), 2 research assistantships with tuition reimbursements available (averaging $17,529 per year), 2 teaching assistantships with tuition reimbursements available (averaging $10,600 per year); career-related internships or fieldwork, institutionally sponsored loans, tuition waivers (full and partial), and unspecified assistantships also available. Financial award application deadline: 12/14. *Faculty research:* Development of citizenship, impact of participation in community service, impact of poverty on children, development of moral reasoning and behavior. *Unit head:* Dr. Tiffany Yip, Program Director, 718-817-3797, Fax: 718-817-3785, E-mail: tyip@fordham.edu. *Application contact:* Bernadette Valentino-Morrison, Director of Graduate Admissions, 718-817-4419, Fax: 718-817-3566, E-mail: valentinomor@fordham.edu.

Fordham University, Graduate School of Arts and Sciences, Department of Psychology, Program in Applied Psychological Methods, New York, NY 10458. Offers MS. *Students:* 5 full-time (4 women); includes 2 minority (both Hispanic/Latino), 3 international. Average age 27. 27 applicants, 56% accepted, 2 enrolled. In 2017, 7 master's awarded. *Degree requirements:* For master's, three-credit one-semester internship. *Entrance requirements:* For master's, GRE General Test. Additional exam requirements/recommendations for international students: Required—TOEFL. *Application deadline:* For fall admission, 1/4 priority date for domestic students, 1/4 for international students; for spring admission, 10/31 for domestic and international students. Application fee: $70. *Unit head:* Dr. Andrew Rasmussen, Program Director, 718-817-3775, E-mail: arasmussen@fordham.edu. *Application contact:* Bernadette Valentino-Morrison, Director of Graduate Admissions, 718-817-4419, Fax: 718-817-3566, E-mail: valentinomor@fordham.edu.

Francis Marion University, Graduate Programs, Department of Psychology, Florence, SC 29502-0547. Offers applied psychology (MS), including clinical/counseling psychology, school psychology; school psychology (SSP). *Program availability:* Part-time, evening/weekend. *Degree requirements:* For master's, internship. *Entrance requirements:* For master's, GRE General Test, official transcripts, two letters of recommendation. Additional exam requirements/recommendations for international students: Required—TOEFL (minimum score 550 paper-based; 79 iBT). *Faculty research:* Parenting and family relationships, child development, applied behavioral analysis, post-traumatic stress disorder, clinical psychology in adults.

The George Washington University, Columbian College of Arts and Sciences, Department of Psychology, Washington, DC 20052. Offers applied social psychology (PhD); clinical psychology (PhD); cognitive neuroscience (PhD). *Accreditation:* APA. *Program availability:* Part-time, evening/weekend. *Faculty:* 26 full-time (15 women), 10 part-time/adjunct (7 women). *Students:* 41 full-time (27 women), 25 part-time (17 women); includes 24 minority (10 Black or African American, non-Hispanic/Latino; 8

Asian, non-Hispanic/Latino; 4 Hispanic/Latino; 2 Two or more races, non-Hispanic/Latino), 6 international. Average age 28. 452 applicants, 35% accepted, 87 enrolled. In 2017, 10 doctorates awarded. *Degree requirements:* For doctorate, thesis/dissertation or alternative, general exam. *Entrance requirements:* For doctorate, GRE General Test, minimum GPA of 3.0. Additional exam requirements/recommendations for international students: Required—TOEFL (minimum score 550 paper-based; 80 iBT). *Application deadline:* For fall admission, 1/15 for domestic and international students. Application fee: $75. *Expenses: Tuition:* Full-time $28,800; part-time $1655 per credit hour. *Required fees:* $45; $2.75 per credit hour. *Financial support:* In 2017–18, 62 students received support. Fellowships with tuition reimbursements available, teaching assistantships with tuition reimbursements available, career-related internships or fieldwork, Federal Work-Study, and tuition waivers available. *Unit head:* Dr. Carol Sigelman, Chair, 202-994-8422, E-mail: carol@gwu.edu. *Application contact:* Information Contact, 202-994-6320, Fax: 202-994-1602, E-mail: psych@gwu.edu.
Website: http://psychology.columbian.gwu.edu/

Laurentian University, School of Graduate Studies and Research, Programme in Psychology, Sudbury, ON P3E 2C6, Canada. Offers applied psychology (MA); experimental psychology (MA).

Liberty University, School of Behavioral Sciences, Lynchburg, VA 24515. Offers applied psychology (MA), including developmental psychology (MA, MS), industrial/organizational psychology (MA, MS); clinical mental health counseling (MA); community care and counseling (Ed D), including marriage and family counseling, pastoral care and counseling, traumatology; counselor education and supervision (PhD); human services counseling (MA), including addictions and recovery, business, child and family law, Christian ministries, criminal justice, crisis response and trauma, executive leadership, health and wellness, life coaching, marriage and family, military resilience; marriage and family counseling (MA); marriage and family therapy (MA); military resilience (Certificate); pastoral counseling (MA), including addictions and recovery, community chaplaincy, crisis response and trauma, discipleship and church ministry, leadership, life coaching, marriage and family, marriage and family studies, military resilience, parenting and child/adolescent, pastoral counseling, theology; professional counseling (MA); psychology (MS), including developmental psychology (MA, MS), industrial/organizational psychology (MA, MS); school counseling (M Ed). *Program availability:* Part-time, online learning. *Students:* 2,649 full-time (2,085 women), 5,086 part-time (4,015 women); includes 2,275 minority (1,784 Black or African American, non-Hispanic/Latino; 44 American Indian or Alaska Native, non-Hispanic/Latino; 67 Asian, non-Hispanic/Latino; 200 Hispanic/Latino; 11 Native Hawaiian or other Pacific Islander, non-Hispanic/Latino; 169 Two or more races, non-Hispanic/Latino), 145 international. Average age 39. 5,839 applicants, 51% accepted, 1710 enrolled. In 2017, 1,626 master's, 7 doctorates, 61 other advanced degrees awarded. *Application deadline:* Applications are processed on a rolling basis. Application fee: $50. Electronic applications accepted. *Financial support:* Applicants required to submit FAFSA. *Unit head:* Dr. Ronald Hawkins, Founding Dean, School of Behavioral Sciences. *Application contact:* Jay Bridge, Director of Admissions, 800-424-9595, Fax: 800-628-7977, E-mail: gradadmissions@liberty.edu.

London Metropolitan University, Graduate Programs, London, United Kingdom. Offers applied psychology (M Sc); architecture (MA); biomedical science (M Sc); blood science (M Sc); cancer pharmacology (M Sc); computer networking and cyber security (M Sc); computing and information systems (M Sc); conference interpreting (MA); counter-terrorism studies (M Sc); creative, digital and professional writing (MA); crime, violence and prevention (M Sc); criminology (M Sc); curating contemporary art (MA); data analytics (M Sc); digital media (MA); early childhood studies (MA); education (MA, Ed D); financial services law, regulation and compliance (LL M); food science (M Sc); forensic psychology (M Sc); health and social care management and policy (M Sc); human nutrition (M Sc); human resource management (MA); human rights and international conflict (MA); information technology (M Sc); intelligence and security studies (M Sc); international oil, gas and energy law (LL M); international relations (MA); interpreting (MA); learning and teaching in higher education (MA); legal practice (LL M); media and entertainment law (LL M); organizational and consumer psychology (M Sc); psychological therapy (M Sc); psychology of mental health (M Sc); public health (M Sc); public policy and management (MPA); security studies (M Sc); social work (M Sc); spatial planning and urban design (MA); sports therapy (M Sc); supporting older children and young people with dyslexia (MA); teaching languages (MA), including Arabic, English; translation (MA); woman and child abuse (MA).

Loras College, Graduate Division, Program in Applied Psychology, Dubuque, IA 52004-0178. Offers MA. *Program availability:* Part-time, evening/weekend. *Degree requirements:* For master's, comprehensive exam, thesis (for some programs). *Entrance requirements:* For master's, Ohio State University Psychological Test or GRE General Test, minimum undergraduate GPA of 2.75.

Lynn University, College of Arts and Sciences, Boca Raton, FL 33431-5598. Offers criminal justice (MS); mental health counseling (MS); psychology (MS), including general psychology, industrial/organizational psychology. *Program availability:* Part-time, evening/weekend, 100% online, blended/hybrid learning. *Faculty:* 59 full-time (26 women), 22 part-time/adjunct (16 women). *Students:* 60 full-time (47 women), 38 part-time (24 women); includes 32 minority (15 Black or African American, non-Hispanic/Latino; 2 Asian, non-Hispanic/Latino; 15 Hispanic/Latino), 6 international. Average age 30. 73 applicants, 82% accepted, 47 enrolled. In 2017, 64 master's awarded. *Degree requirements:* For master's, comprehensive exam (for some programs), thesis (for some programs). *Entrance requirements:* For master's, bachelor's degree from accrediated institution, minimum undergraduate GPA of 3.0, official undergraduate transcripts, two letters of recommendation from academic or professional sources, writing sample demonstrating capacity to perform at graduate level. Additional exam requirements/recommendations for international students: Required—TOEFL (minimum score 550 paper-based; 80 iBT), IELTS (minimum score 6.5). *Application deadline:* For fall admission, 8/18 for domestic students, 8/4 for international students; for spring admission, 12/15 for domestic students, 12/1 for international students; for summer admission, 4/17 for domestic students, 4/3 for international students. Applications are processed on a rolling basis. Application fee: $45. Electronic applications accepted. *Expenses:* $740 per credit. *Financial support:* Career-related internships or fieldwork, Federal Work-Study, scholarships/grants, tuition waivers (full and partial), and unspecified assistantships available. Support available to part-time students. Financial award application deadline: 3/1; financial award applicants required to submit FAFSA. *Faculty research:* Personality and social media, learning strategies, personal health behaviors and compliance, using drums in substance abuse groups, interpersonal behaviors with individuals with autism, case conceptualization, teaching case conceptualization across the curriculum. *Unit head:* Dr. Katrina Carter-Tellison, Dean, 561-237-7412, E-mail: kcartertellison@lynn.edu. *Application contact:* Steven Pruitt, Director of Graduate Admission, 561-237-7834, Fax: 561-237-7100, E-mail: admissionpm@lynn.edu.
Website: https://www.lynn.edu/academics/colleges-schools/arts-and-sciences

Mississippi State University, College of Arts and Sciences, Department of Psychology, Mississippi State, MS 39762. Offers applied psychology (PhD), including clinical, cognitive science; psychology (MS). *Accreditation:* APA. *Faculty:* 18 full-time (6 women). *Students:* 33 full-time (18 women), 7 part-time (all women); includes 8 minority (4 Black or African American, non-Hispanic/Latino; 3 Asian, non-Hispanic/Latino; 1 Two or more races, non-Hispanic/Latino), 1 international. Average age 27. 46 applicants, 26% accepted, 10 enrolled. In 2017, 7 master's, 6 doctorates awarded. Terminal master's awarded for partial completion of doctoral program. *Degree requirements:* For master's, comprehensive exam, thesis; for doctorate, thesis/dissertation, qualifying exam, comprehensive written and oral exam. *Entrance requirements:* For master's, GRE General Test, minimum GPA of 2.75 on last two years of undergraduate courses; for doctorate, GRE General Test, proficiency in at least 1 computer language, minimum GPA of 3.0. Additional exam requirements/recommendations for international students: Required—TOEFL (minimum score 477 paper-based; 53 iBT); Recommended—IELTS (minimum score 4.5). *Application deadline:* For fall admission, 4/1 priority date for domestic students, 5/1 for international students; for spring admission, 11/1 priority date for domestic students, 9/1 for international students. Applications are processed on a rolling basis. Application fee: $60 ($80 for international students). Electronic applications accepted. *Expenses:* Tuition, state resident: full-time $8318; part-time $462.12 per credit hour. Tuition, nonresident: full-time $22,358; part-time $1242.12 per credit hour. *Required fees:* $110; $12.24 per credit hour. $6.12 per semester. *Financial support:* In 2017–18, 6 research assistantships with full tuition reimbursements (averaging $14,703 per year), 22 teaching assistantships with full tuition reimbursements (averaging $12,157 per year) were awarded; career-related internships or fieldwork, Federal Work-Study, institutionally sponsored loans, scholarships/grants, and unspecified assistantships also available. Financial award application deadline: 4/1; financial award applicants required to submit FAFSA. *Faculty research:* Personality type, alcoholism, blindness and low vision, mental retardation, language comprehension. *Total annual research expenditures:* $1.4 million. *Unit head:* Dr. Mitchell E. Berman, Professor and Head, 662-325-3202, Fax: 662-325-7212, E-mail: mberman@psychology.msstate.edu. *Application contact:* Lakan Drinker, Admissions and Enrollment Assistant, 662-325-8951, E-mail: ldrinker@grad.msstate.edu.
Website: http://www.psychology.msstate.edu/

New York University, Steinhardt School of Culture, Education, and Human Development, Department of Applied Psychology, New York, NY 10012. Offers counseling (MA, PhD, Advanced Certificate), including counseling and guidance (MA, Advanced Certificate), counseling for mental health and wellness (MA), counseling psychology (PhD), LGBT health, education, and social services (Advanced Certificate); educational and developmental psychology (MA, PhD), including developmental psychology (PhD), human development and social intervention (MA), psychology and social intervention (PhD); Advanced Certificate/MPH; MA/Advanced Certificate. *Accreditation:* APA (one or more programs are accredited). *Program availability:* Part-time. *Students:* Average age 28. 800 applicants, 32% accepted, 87 enrolled. In 2017, 103 master's, 11 doctorates awarded. Terminal master's awarded for partial completion of doctoral program. *Entrance requirements:* For doctorate, GRE General Test, interview. Additional exam requirements/recommendations for international students: Required—TOEFL (minimum score 100 iBT). *Application deadline:* For fall admission, 12/1 priority date for domestic and international students. Applications are processed on a rolling basis. Application fee: $75. Electronic applications accepted. *Expenses: Tuition:* Full-time $41,352; part-time $19,968 per year. *Required fees:* $2496; $1628 per unit. $814 per term. Tuition and fees vary according to course load and program. *Financial support:* Fellowships with full and partial tuition reimbursements, research assistantships with full and partial tuition reimbursements, teaching assistantships with full and partial tuition reimbursements, career-related internships or fieldwork, Federal Work-Study, institutionally sponsored loans, scholarships/grants, tuition waivers (partial), and unspecified assistantships available. Support available to part-time students. Financial award application deadline: 2/1; financial award applicants required to submit FAFSA. *Faculty research:* Applied measurement and research methods, health and human development, social and emotional development, cultural contexts and immigration. *Unit head:* Dr. LaRue Allen, Chairperson, 212-998-5076, Fax: 212-995-4358, E-mail: larue.allen@nyu.edu. *Application contact:* 212-998-5030, Fax: 212-995-4328, E-mail: steinhardt.gradadmissions@nyu.edu.
Website: http://steinhardt.nyu.edu/appsych/

Oklahoma State University, College of Education, Health and Aviation, School of Applied Health and Educational Psychology, Stillwater, OK 74078. Offers applied behavioral studies (Ed D); applied health and educational psychology (MS, PhD, Ed S). *Accreditation:* APA (one or more programs are accredited). *Program availability:* Part-time. *Faculty:* 31 full-time (20 women), 9 part-time/adjunct (7 women). *Students:* 169 full-time (119 women), 158 part-time (102 women); includes 98 minority (29 Black or African American, non-Hispanic/Latino; 15 American Indian or Alaska Native, non-Hispanic/Latino; 5 Asian, non-Hispanic/Latino; 24 Hispanic/Latino; 25 Two or more races, non-Hispanic/Latino), 22 international. Average age 30. 140 applicants, 56% accepted, 69 enrolled. In 2017, 71 master's, 24 doctorates awarded. *Entrance requirements:* For master's and doctorate, GRE or GMAT. Additional exam requirements/recommendations for international students: Required—TOEFL (minimum score 550 paper-based; 79 iBT). *Application deadline:* For fall admission, 3/1 priority date for international students; for spring admission, 8/1 priority date for international students. Applications are processed on a rolling basis. Application fee: $40 ($75 for international students). Electronic applications accepted. *Expenses:* Tuition, state resident: full-time $4019; part-time $2679.60 per year. Tuition, nonresident: full-time $15,286; part-time $10,190.40 per year. *Required fees:* $2129; $1419 per unit. Tuition and fees vary according to program. *Financial support:* Research assistantships, teaching assistantships, career-related internships or fieldwork, Federal Work-Study, scholarships/grants, health care benefits, tuition waivers (partial), and unspecified assistantships available. Support available to part-time students. Financial award application deadline: 3/1; financial award applicants required to submit FAFSA. *Unit head:* Dr. Aric Warren, Head, 405-744-6040, Fax: 405-744-6779, E-mail: aric.warren@okstate.edu.
Website: http://education.okstate.edu/

Old Dominion University, College of Sciences, Doctoral Program in Psychology, Norfolk, VA 23529. Offers applied psychological sciences (PhD); human factors psychology (PhD); industrial/organizational psychology (PhD). *Faculty:* 21 full-time (8 women). *Students:* 14 full-time (9 women), 14 part-time (8 women); includes 4 minority (1 Black or African American, non-Hispanic/Latino; 3 Hispanic/Latino). Average age 29. 99 applicants, 11% accepted, 6 enrolled. In 2017, 9 doctorates awarded. *Degree requirements:* For doctorate, comprehensive exam, thesis/dissertation, candidacy exam. *Entrance requirements:* For doctorate, GRE General Test, GRE Subject Test, 3 recommendation letters. Additional exam requirements/recommendations for international students: Required—TOEFL. *Application deadline:* For fall and winter admission, 1/5 for domestic and international students. Application fee: $50. Electronic applications accepted. *Expenses:* Contact institution. *Financial support:* In 2017–18, 26 students received support, including 4 research assistantships with full tuition reimbursements available (averaging $15,000 per year), 22 teaching assistantships with full tuition reimbursements available (averaging $15,000 per year); scholarships/grants also available. Financial award application deadline: 1/15. *Faculty research:* Human factors, industrial psychology, organizational psychology, applied psychological sciences (health, developmental, community, quantitative). *Total annual research*

expenditures: $1.2 million. *Unit head:* Dr. Debra A. Major, Graduate Program Director, 757-683-4235, Fax: 757-683-5087, E-mail: dmajor@odu.edu. *Application contact:* William Heffelfinger, Director of Graduate Admissions, 757-683-5554, Fax: 757-683-3255, E-mail: gradadmit@odu.edu.
Website: http://www.odu.edu/psychology/

Penn State Erie, The Behrend College, Graduate School, Erie, PA 16563. Offers accounting (MPAC); applied clinical psychology (MA); business administration (MBA); quality and manufacturing management (MMM). *Accreditation:* AACSB. *Program availability:* Part-time. *Students:* 31 full-time (15 women), 126 part-time (39 women); includes 10 minority (4 Black or African American, non-Hispanic/Latino; 1 Hispanic/Latino; 5 Two or more races, non-Hispanic/Latino). Average age 31. 104 applicants, 75% accepted, 75 enrolled. In 2017, 72 master's awarded. *Entrance requirements:* Additional exam requirements/recommendations for international students: Required—TOEFL (minimum score 550 paper-based; 80 iBT), IELTS. *Application deadline:* Applications are processed on a rolling basis. Application fee: $65. Electronic applications accepted. *Financial support:* Federal Work-Study available. Financial award application deadline: 2/15; financial award applicants required to submit FAFSA. *Unit head:* Dr. Ralph M. Ford, Chancellor, 814-898-6160, Fax: 814-898-6461. *Application contact:* Ann M. Burbules, Assistant Director, Graduate Admissions, 866-374-3378, Fax: 814-898-6044, E-mail: behrend.admissions@psu.edu.
Website: http://behrend.psu.edu/

Penn State Harrisburg, Graduate School, School of Behavioral Sciences and Education, Middletown, PA 17057. Offers adult education in the health and medical professions (Certificate); applied behavior analysis (MA); applied clinical psychology (MA); applied psychological research (MA); community psychology and social change (MA); English as a second language (ESL) program specialist and leadership (Certificate); health education (M Ed); lifelong learning and adult education (M Ed, D Ed); literacy education (M Ed); literacy leadership (Certificate); psychology: applications in clinical psychology (Certificate); psychology: health psychology (Certificate); teaching and curriculum (M Ed); training and development (M Ed, Certificate). *Program availability:* Part-time, evening/weekend. *Unit head:* Dr. Mukund S. Kulkarni, Chancellor, 717-948-6105, Fax: 717-948-6452. *Application contact:* Robert W. Coffman, Jr., Director of Enrollment Management, Recruitment and Admissions, 717-948-6250, Fax: 717-948-6325, E-mail: hbgadmit@psu.edu.
Website: https://harrisburg.psu.edu/behavioral-sciences-and-education/

Rutgers University–New Brunswick, Graduate School of Applied and Professional Psychology, Piscataway, NJ 08854. Offers Psy M, Psy D. *Accreditation:* APA (one or more programs are accredited). *Degree requirements:* For doctorate, comprehensive exam, thesis/dissertation, 1 year internship. *Entrance requirements:* For doctorate, GRE General Test, GRE Subject Test, bachelor's degree in psychology or equivalent. Additional exam requirements/recommendations for international students: Required—TOEFL. Electronic applications accepted. *Expenses:* Contact institution. *Faculty research:* Organizational psychology, behavior modification, long- and short-term dynamic therapy, school psychology, addictive behaviors.

Sacred Heart University, Graduate Programs, College of Arts and Sciences, Department of Psychology, Fairfield, CT 06825. Offers applied psychology (MS), including community psychology, general applied psychology, industrial-organizational psychology. *Program availability:* Part-time, evening/weekend, online learning. *Faculty:* 9 full-time (7 women). *Students:* 17 full-time (15 women), 76 part-time (58 women); includes 18 minority (6 Black or African American, non-Hispanic/Latino; 1 Asian, non-Hispanic/Latino; 8 Hispanic/Latino; 3 Two or more races, non-Hispanic/Latino), 2 international. Average age 31. 50 applicants, 54% accepted, 16 enrolled. In 2017, 42 master's awarded. *Degree requirements:* For master's, comprehensive exam, thesis optional. *Entrance requirements:* For master's, minimum overall GPA of 3.0, bachelor's degree from accredited college or university. Additional exam requirements/recommendations for international students: Required—TOEFL (minimum score 570 paper-based, 80 iBT), TWE, or IELTS (6.5). *Application deadline:* Applications are processed on a rolling basis. Application fee: $75. Electronic applications accepted. *Expenses:* Contact institution. *Financial support:* Unspecified assistantships available. Financial award applicants required to submit FAFSA. *Unit head:* Rachel Bowman, Interim Chair/Associate Professor, 203-396-8243, E-mail: bowmanr@sacredheart.edu. *Application contact:* Pam Pillo, Executive Director of Graduate Admissions, 203-365-7916, Fax: 203-365-4732, E-mail: gradstudies@sacredheart.edu.
Website: http://www.sacredheart.edu/academics/collegeofartssciences/academicdepartments/psychology/mastersinappliedpsychology/

Saint Mary's University, Faculty of Science, Department of Psychology, Halifax, NS B3H 3C3, Canada. Offers applied psychology (M Sc, PhD), including industrial/organizational psychology (M Sc). *Program availability:* Part-time. *Degree requirements:* For master's, thesis, 500-hour internship; for doctorate, comprehensive exam, thesis/dissertation, research project. *Entrance requirements:* For master's and doctorate, GRE General Test. *Faculty research:* Assessment, health psychology, social psychology, cognition.

Tarleton State University, College of Graduate Studies, College of Education, Department of Psychological Sciences, Stephenville, TX 76402. Offers applied psychology (MS). *Program availability:* Part-time, evening/weekend. *Faculty:* 4 full-time (2 women). *Students:* 5 full-time (3 women), 8 part-time (all women); includes 4 minority (2 Black or African American, non-Hispanic/Latino; 2 Hispanic/Latino), 1 international. Average age 28. 11 applicants, 82% accepted, 7 enrolled. *Degree requirements:* For master's, comprehensive exam, thesis optional. *Entrance requirements:* For master's, GRE General Test, minimum GPA of 3.0. Additional exam requirements/recommendations for international students: Required—TOEFL (minimum score 550 paper-based; 80 iBT), IELTS (minimum score 6). *Application deadline:* For fall admission, 8/15 priority date for domestic students; for spring admission, 1/7 for domestic students. Applications are processed on a rolling basis. Application fee: $45 ($145 for international students). Electronic applications accepted. *Expenses:* Contact institution. *Financial support:* Research assistantships, teaching assistantships, career-related internships or fieldwork, Federal Work-Study, institutionally sponsored loans, and tuition waivers (partial) available. Support available to part-time students. Financial award application deadline: 5/1; financial award applicants required to submit FAFSA. *Unit head:* Dr. Kimberly Rynearson, Department Head, 254-968-9916, E-mail: rynearson@tarleton.edu. *Application contact:* Information Contact, 254-968-9104, Fax: 254-968-9670, E-mail: gradoffice@tarleton.edu.

Teachers College, Columbia University, Department of Human Development, New York, NY 10027-6696. Offers applied statistics (MS); cognitive studies in education (MA, Ed D, PhD); developmental psychology (MA, Ed D, PhD); educational psychology-human cognition and learning (Ed M, MA, Ed D, PhD); learning analytics (MS); measurement and evaluation (ME, Ed D, PhD); measurement, evaluation, and statistics (MA, MS, Ed D, PhD). *Program availability:* Part-time. *Students:* 155 full-time (105 women), 135 part-time (106 women); includes 93 minority (26 Black or African American, non-Hispanic/Latino; 44 Asian, non-Hispanic/Latino; 21 Hispanic/Latino; 2 Two or more races, non-Hispanic/Latino), 118 international. Average age 29. 459 applicants, 53% accepted, 100 enrolled. *Unit head:* Jim Corter, Chair, E-mail: jec34@tc.columbia.edu. *Application contact:* David Estrella, Director of Admission, 212-678-3305, E-mail: estrella@tc.columbia.edu.
Website: http://www.tc.columbia.edu/human-development/

University of Arkansas at Little Rock, Graduate School, College of Social Sciences and Communication, Department of Psychology, Little Rock, AR 72204-1099. Offers applied psychology (MAP). *Program availability:* Part-time, evening/weekend. *Entrance requirements:* For master's, GRE General Test, minimum GPA of 2.7. *Faculty research:* Psychological methods and theories in business industry, government, and organizations; personnel program evaluation; training; affirmative action; organizational analysis and development.

University of Baltimore, Graduate School, Yale Gordon College of Arts and Sciences, Program in Applied Psychology, Baltimore, MD 21201-5779. Offers counseling psychology (MS). *Program availability:* Part-time, evening/weekend. *Degree requirements:* For master's, thesis optional. *Entrance requirements:* For master's, GRE, minimum GPA of 3.0. Additional exam requirements/recommendations for international students: Required—TOEFL (minimum score 550 paper-based). Electronic applications accepted. *Expenses:* Contact institution. *Faculty research:* Participatory decision-making, counter-productive workplace behavior, organizational consulting, substance abuse treatment, cognitive functioning in head injured.

University of Calgary, Faculty of Graduate Studies, Werklund School of Education, Division of Applied Psychology, Calgary, AB T2N 1N4, Canada. Offers counseling psychology (M Sc, MC, PhD); school and applied child psychology (M Ed, M Sc, PhD). *Program availability:* Part-time. *Degree requirements:* For master's, thesis (for some programs), final oral exam; for doctorate, thesis/dissertation, candidacy exam, final oral exam. *Entrance requirements:* For master's, minimum GPA of 3.0, 3 letters of reference; for doctorate, minimum GPA of 3.5, 3 letters of reference. *Faculty research:* Counselor education, family life studies, learning and cognition.

University of Guelph, Graduate Studies, College of Social and Applied Human Sciences, Department of Psychology, Guelph, ON N1G 2W1, Canada. Offers applied social psychology (MA, PhD); clinical psychology: applied development emphasis (PhD); clinical psychology: applied developmental emphasis (MA); industrial/organizational psychology (MA, PhD); neuroscience and applied cognitive science (MA, PhD). *Degree requirements:* For master's, thesis; for doctorate, comprehensive exam, thesis/dissertation. *Entrance requirements:* For master's, GRE General Test, GRE Subject Test, minimum B+ average during previous 2 years of course work; for doctorate, GRE General Test, GRE Subject Test, minimum A- average. Additional exam requirements/recommendations for international students: Required—TOEFL (minimum score 89 iBT). Electronic applications accepted. *Faculty research:* Organizational psychology, reading comprehension and mathematical ability, drug addiction and relapse, gender issues and culture, memory, clinical psychology.

University of Maryland, Baltimore County, The Graduate School, College of Arts, Humanities and Social Sciences, Department of Psychology, Program in Applied Developmental Psychology, Baltimore, MD 21250. Offers PhD. *Faculty:* 8 full-time (6 women), 11 part-time/adjunct (4 women). *Students:* 22 full-time (all women); includes 8 minority (2 Black or African American, non-Hispanic/Latino; 6 Asian, non-Hispanic/Latino), 4 international. Average age 25. 24 applicants, 21% accepted, 3 enrolled. In 2017, 1 doctorate awarded. *Degree requirements:* For doctorate, comprehensive exam, thesis/dissertation. *Entrance requirements:* For doctorate, GRE General Test, minimum GPA of 3.0. Additional exam requirements/recommendations for international students: Required—TOEFL. *Application deadline:* For fall admission, 12/1 for domestic and international students. Application fee: $50. Electronic applications accepted. *Expenses:* Contact institution. *Financial support:* In 2017–18, 17 students received support, including 4 fellowships with partial tuition reimbursements available (averaging $17,250 per year), 5 research assistantships with full tuition reimbursements available (averaging $20,400 per year), 8 teaching assistantships with full tuition reimbursements available (averaging $17,250 per year); career-related internships or fieldwork, Federal Work-Study, health care benefits, and unspecified assistantships also available. Financial award application deadline: 3/1; financial award applicants required to submit FAFSA. *Faculty research:* Early intervention and development, schooling and development, cultural aspects of development, development in high risk children, social-emotional development. *Unit head:* Dr. Susan Sonnenschein, Director, 410-455-2361, Fax: 410-455-1055, E-mail: sonnenschein@umbc.edu. *Application contact:* Beverly McDougall, Program Management Specialist, 410-455-2567, Fax: 410-455-1055, E-mail: psycdept@umbc.edu.
Website: http://psychology.umbc.edu/

University of Pennsylvania, School of Arts and Sciences, College of Liberal and Professional Studies, Philadelphia, PA 19104. Offers applied geosciences (MSAG); applied positive psychology (MAP); chemical sciences (MCS); environmental studies (MES); individualized study (MLA); liberal arts (M Phil); medical physics (MMP); organization dynamics (M Phil). *Students:* 191 full-time (112 women), 311 part-time (178 women); includes 99 minority (34 Black or African American, non-Hispanic/Latino; 2 American Indian or Alaska Native, non-Hispanic/Latino; 28 Asian, non-Hispanic/Latino; 24 Hispanic/Latino; 11 Two or more races, non-Hispanic/Latino), 83 international. Average age 34. 633 applicants, 52% accepted, 249 enrolled. In 2017, 141 master's awarded. *Unit head:* Nora Lewis, Vice Dean, Professional and Liberal Education, 215-898-7326, E-mail: nlewis@sas.upenn.edu.
Website: http://www.sas.upenn.edu/lps/graduate

University of Pittsburgh, School of Education, Department of Psychology in Education, Program in Applied Developmental Psychology, Pittsburgh, PA 15260. Offers M Ed, MS, PhD. *Program availability:* Part-time, evening/weekend. *Degree requirements:* For master's, thesis. *Entrance requirements:* For doctorate, GRE. Additional exam requirements/recommendations for international students: Required—TOEFL. Electronic applications accepted.

University of Regina, Faculty of Graduate Studies and Research, Faculty of Arts, Department of Psychology, Regina, SK S4S 0A2, Canada. Offers clinical psychology (MA, PhD); experimental and applied psychology (MA, PhD). *Faculty:* 19 full-time (9 women), 5 part-time/adjunct (2 women). *Students:* 18 full-time (13 women), 2 part-time (0 women). 52 applicants, 19% accepted. In 2017, 4 master's, 4 doctorates awarded. *Degree requirements:* For master's, thesis; for doctorate, comprehensive exam, thesis/dissertation. *Entrance requirements:* For master's, GRE General Test; for doctorate, GRE General Test and GRE Subject Test (optional for those with a master's degree from a Canadian university). Additional exam requirements/recommendations for international students: Required—TOEFL (minimum score 580 paper-based; 80 iBT), IELTS (minimum score 6.5), PTE (minimum score 59). *Application deadline:* For fall admission, 1/15 for domestic and international students. Application fee: $100. Electronic applications accepted. *Expenses:* $10,681. *Financial support:* In 2017–18, 7 fellowships (averaging $6,714 per year), 17 teaching assistantships (averaging $2,562 per year) were awarded; research assistantships, career-related internships or fieldwork, and scholarships/grants also available. Financial award application deadline: 6/15. *Faculty research:* Clinical, experimental, cognitive, and applied psychology; post-traumatic stress disorder, anxiety, and panic disorder; traumatic brain injury; chronic pain; perception and memory. *Unit head:* Dr. Richard MacLennan, Department Head,

306-585-4458, Fax: 306-585-5429, E-mail: richard.maclennan@uregina.ca.
Website: http://www.uregina.ca/arts/psychology

University of South Carolina Aiken, Program in Applied Clinical Psychology, Aiken, SC 29801. Offers MS. *Program availability:* Part-time. *Faculty:* 9 full-time (7 women). *Students:* 18 full-time (15 women), 13 part-time (11 women); includes 7 minority (3 Black or African American, non-Hispanic/Latino; 1 Asian, non-Hispanic/Latino; 1 Native Hawaiian or other Pacific Islander, non-Hispanic/Latino; 2 Two or more races, non-Hispanic/Latino). Average age 25. 36 applicants, 42% accepted, 8 enrolled. In 2017, 10 master's awarded. *Degree requirements:* For master's, thesis. *Entrance requirements:* For master's, GRE. Additional exam requirements/recommendations for international students: Required—TOEFL (minimum score 551 paper-based, 80 iBT), IELTS (6), or PTE (53). *Application deadline:* For fall admission, 5/1 priority date for domestic and international students. Applications are processed on a rolling basis. Application fee: $45 ($100 for international students). Electronic applications accepted. *Expenses:* Tuition, state resident: full-time $13,254; part-time $552.25 per credit hour. Tuition, nonresident: full-time $28,368; part-time $1182.70 per credit hour. *Required fees:* $12 per credit hour. $25 per semester. Full-time tuition and fees vary according to course load. *Financial support:* In 2017–18, 27 students received support, including 19 research assistantships with partial tuition reimbursements available (averaging $2,887 per year), 4 teaching assistantships with partial tuition reimbursements available (averaging $2,604 per year); career-related internships or fieldwork, Federal Work-Study, scholarships/grants, tuition waivers (partial), and unspecified assistantships also available. Financial award application deadline: 3/1; financial award applicants required to submit FAFSA. *Faculty research:* Addictive behaviors, interpersonal attraction, impression formation in zero-acquaintance situations, the influence of emotions on visual perception, executive function, cognitive control, inhibitory control, working memory, episodic memory, emotion regulation, anxiety, stress, cognitive functioning and development, social and personality psychology, ADHD, development of cognition and academic skills, teen pregnancy/parenting. *Total annual research expenditures:* $1,307. *Unit head:* Dr. Jane Stafford, Director, 803-641-3358, Fax: 803-641-3720, E-mail: jstafford@usca.edu. *Application contact:* Dan Robb, Associate Vice Chancellor for Enrollment Management, 803-641-3487, Fax: 803-641-3727, E-mail: danr@usca.edu.
Website: http://www.usca.edu/psychology/academics/ms-psychology/

The University of Tennessee, Graduate School, College of Education, Health and Human Sciences, Department of Educational Psychology and Counseling, Knoxville, TN 37996. Offers adult education (MS); applied educational psychology (MS); collaborative learning (Ed D); college student personnel (MS); mental health counseling (MS); rehabilitation counseling (MS); school counseling (MS). *Accreditation:* ACA (one or more programs are accredited); CORE (one or more programs are accredited); NCATE. *Program availability:* Part-time, evening/weekend. *Degree requirements:* For master's, thesis optional. *Entrance requirements:* For master's, GRE General Test, minimum GPA of 2.7. Additional exam requirements/recommendations for international students: Required—TOEFL. Electronic applications accepted.

The University of Texas at El Paso, Graduate School, College of Liberal Arts, Department of Sociology and Anthropology, El Paso, TX 79968-0001. Offers applied anthropology (Certificate); applied social sciences (Certificate); sociology (MA). *Program availability:* Part-time, evening/weekend. *Degree requirements:* For master's, thesis. *Entrance requirements:* For master's, GRE General Test, minimum GPA of 3.0. Additional exam requirements/recommendations for international students: Required—TOEFL. Electronic applications accepted. *Faculty research:* U.S.-Mexico border, social inequality, immigration, Chicano culture, Mexico.

The University of Texas of the Permian Basin, Office of Graduate Studies, College of Arts and Sciences, Department of Psychology, Odessa, TX 79762-0001. Offers applied research psychology (MA); clinical psychology (MA). *Program availability:* Part-time, evening/weekend. *Degree requirements:* For master's, comprehensive exam, thesis, practicum. *Entrance requirements:* For master's, GRE General Test, 3 letters of recommendation. Additional exam requirements/recommendations for international students: Required—TOEFL (minimum score 550 paper-based).

University of West Florida, Usha Kundu, MD College of Health, Department of Psychology, Pensacola, FL 32514-5750. Offers applied experimental (MA); counseling (MA); industrial-organizational (MA). *Program availability:* Part-time. *Degree requirements:* For master's, thesis (for some programs). *Entrance requirements:* For master's, GRE, official transcripts; minimum GPA of 3.0; writing sample; three letters of reference; field experience or skill sets; oral interview (for counseling specialization). Additional exam requirements/recommendations for international students: Required—TOEFL (minimum score 550 paper-based). *Faculty research:* Prose recall, brain imaging, peak performance, biofeedback and pain control, comparable worth.

University of Windsor, Faculty of Graduate Studies, Faculty of Arts and Social Sciences, Department of Psychology, Windsor, ON N9B 3P4, Canada. Offers adult clinical (MA, PhD); applied social psychology (MA, PhD); child clinical (MA, PhD); clinical neuropsychology (MA, PhD). *Degree requirements:* For master's, thesis; for doctorate, comprehensive exam, thesis/dissertation. *Entrance requirements:* For master's, GRE General Test, GRE Subject Test in psychology, minimum B average; for doctorate, GRE General Test, GRE Subject Test in psychology, master's degree. Additional exam requirements/recommendations for international students: Required—TOEFL (minimum score 600 paper-based). Electronic applications accepted. *Faculty research:* Gambling, suicidology, emotional competence, psychotherapy and trauma.

University of Wisconsin–Stout, Graduate School, College of Education, Health and Human Sciences, Program in Applied Psychology, Menomonie, WI 54751. Offers MS. *Program availability:* Part-time. *Degree requirements:* For master's, thesis. *Entrance requirements:* For master's, GRE General Test, GRE Subject Test, minimum GPA of 3.0, 15 semester credits of undergraduate course work in psychology, 8 semester credits in research methods and statistics. Additional exam requirements/recommendations for international students: Required—TOEFL (minimum score 500 paper-based; 61 iBT). Electronic applications accepted. *Faculty research:* Health complementary therapies, motivation, group dynamics, social reasoning, stress.

Walden University, Graduate Programs, School of Psychology, Minneapolis, MN 55401. Offers clinical psychology (MS), including counseling, general program; forensic psychology (MS), including forensic psychology in the community, general program, mental health applications, program planning and evaluation in forensic settings, psychology and legal systems; industrial organizational (MS, PhD), including consulting psychology, forensic (MS), forensic psychology (PhD), general practice, leadership development and coaching (MS), organizational diversity and social change, research evaluation (PhD); online teaching in psychology (Post-Master's Certificate); organizational psychology and development (Postbaccalaureate Certificate); psychology (MS, PhD), including applied psychology (MS), clinical psychology (PhD), crisis management and response (MS), educational psychology, forensic psychology (PhD), general psychology (MS), general psychology research (PhD), general psychology teaching (PhD), health psychology, leadership development and coaching (MS), psychology of culture (MS), psychology, public administration, and social change (MS), social psychology, terrorism and security (MS); psychology respecialization (Post-Doctoral Certificate). *Program availability:* Part-time, evening/weekend, online only, 100% online. Terminal master's awarded for partial completion of doctoral program. *Degree requirements:* For master's, thesis optional; for doctorate, thesis/dissertation, residency. *Entrance requirements:* For master's, bachelor's degree or higher; minimum GPA of 2.5; official transcripts; goal statement (for some programs); access to computer and Internet; for doctorate, master's degree or higher; three years of related professional or academic experience (preferred); minimum GPA of 3.0; goal statement and current resume (for select programs); official transcripts; access to computer and Internet; for other advanced degree, relevant work experience; access to computer and Internet. Additional exam requirements/recommendations for international students: Required—TOEFL (minimum score 550 paper-based, 79 iBT), IELTS (minimum score 6.5), Michigan English Language Assessment Battery (minimum score 82), or PTE (minimum score 53). Electronic applications accepted.

William James College, Graduate Programs, Newton, MA 02459. Offers applied psychology in higher education student personnel administration (MA); clinical psychology (Psy D); counseling psychology (MA); counseling psychology and community mental health (MA); counseling psychology and global mental health (MA); executive coaching (Graduate Certificate); forensic and counseling psychology (MA); leadership psychology (Psy D); organizational psychology (MA); primary care psychology (MA); respecialization in clinical psychology (Certificate); school psychology (Psy D); MA/CAGS. *Accreditation:* APA. *Degree requirements:* For master's, comprehensive exam (for some programs); for doctorate, thesis/dissertation (for some programs). Electronic applications accepted.

Clinical Psychology

Abilene Christian University, Graduate Programs, College of Arts and Sciences, Department of Psychology, Program in Clinical Psychology, Abilene, TX 79699. Offers MS. *Program availability:* Part-time. *Students:* 10 full-time (8 women), 2 international. 33 applicants, 36% accepted, 6 enrolled. In 2017, 6 master's awarded. *Degree requirements:* For master's, thesis, practicum. *Entrance requirements:* Additional exam requirements/recommendations for international students: Required—TOEFL (minimum score 80 iBT), IELTS (minimum score 6), PTE. *Application deadline:* For fall admission, 3/30 priority date for domestic students; for spring admission, 11/1 for domestic students. Applications are processed on a rolling basis. Application fee: $50. Electronic applications accepted. *Expenses:* $1,148 per hour. *Financial support:* In 2017–18, 6 students received support. Career-related internships or fieldwork, Federal Work-Study, scholarships/grants, and unspecified assistantships available. Support available to part-time students. Financial award application deadline: 4/1; financial award applicants required to submit FAFSA. *Unit head:* Dr. Cherisse Flanagan, Graduate Director, 325-674-4826, Fax: 325-674-6968, E-mail: cherisse.flanagan@acu.edu. *Application contact:* Graduate Admissions, 325-674-6911, Fax: 325-674-6717, E-mail: gradinfo@acu.edu.
Website: http://www.acu.edu/graduate/academics/clinical-psychology.html

Acadia University, Faculty of Pure and Applied Science, Department of Psychology, Wolfville, NS B4P 2R6, Canada. Offers clinical psychology (M Sc). *Entrance requirements:* For master's, GRE General Test, GRE Subject Test, honors degree or equivalent. Additional exam requirements/recommendations for international students: Required—TOEFL (minimum score 580 paper-based; 93 iBT), IELTS (minimum score 6.5). *Application deadline:* For fall admission, 2/1 priority date for domestic and international students. Applications are processed on a rolling basis. Application fee: $50. *Financial support:* Application deadline: 2/1. *Faculty research:* Social psychology, job stress, psychotherapy, cognition perception, development. *Unit head:* Dr. Lisa Price, Graduate Advisor, 902-585-1196, E-mail: lisa.price@acadiau.ca. *Application contact:* Dr. Peter Horvath, Graduate Coordinator, 902-585-1200, Fax: 902-585-1078, E-mail: peter.horvath@acadiau.ca.
Website: http://psychology.acadiau.ca

Adams State University, Office of Graduate Studies, Department of Counselor Education, Alamosa, CO 81101. Offers counselor education (MA), including clinical mental health counseling, school counseling; counselor education and supervision (PhD). *Accreditation:* ACA (one or more programs are accredited). *Program availability:* Part-time. *Degree requirements:* For master's, internship, qualifying exam. *Entrance requirements:* For master's, GRE General Test or MAT, minimum undergraduate GPA of 2.75. *Application deadline:* For fall admission, 5/15 priority date for domestic students; for spring admission, 10/15 for domestic students. Applications are processed on a rolling basis. Application fee: $30. *Expenses:* Tuition, state resident: full-time $4800; part-time $2400 per credit. Tuition, nonresident: full-time $7100; part-time $3550 per credit. *Required fees:* $213; $106 per credit. One-time fee: $100. Tuition and fees vary according to campus/location and program. *Financial support:* In 2017–18, fellowships with partial tuition reimbursements (averaging $4,000 per year), teaching assistantships with partial tuition reimbursements (averaging $4,000 per year) were awarded; career-related internships or fieldwork, Federal Work-Study, institutionally sponsored loans, and unspecified assistantships also available. Support available to part-time students. Financial award application deadline: 4/15; financial award applicants required to submit FAFSA. *Unit head:* Dr. Mark Manzanares, Chair, 719-587-7626, Fax: 719-587-7522, E-mail: ceonline@adams.edu. *Application contact:* Nate Pacheco, Assistant Coordinator, 719-587-8138, Fax: 719-587-7522, E-mail: ceonline@adams.edu.
Website: http://counselored.adams.edu/

Adelphi University, Gordon F. Derner School of Psychology, Program in Clinical Psychology, Garden City, NY 11530-0701. Offers PhD. *Students:* 79 full-time (59 women), 25 part-time (21 women); includes 31 minority (5 Black or African American, non-Hispanic/Latino; 9 Asian, non-Hispanic/Latino; 12 Hispanic/Latino; 5 Two or more races, non-Hispanic/Latino), 7 international. Average age 30. 152 applicants, 34% accepted, 22 enrolled. In 2017, 20 doctorates awarded. *Degree requirements:* For doctorate, thesis/dissertation, research component (second-year), 1-year internship. *Entrance requirements:* For doctorate, GRE General Test, GRE Subject Test, interview; resume; undergraduate course work in psychology, experimental psychology, statistics, developmental psychology, and abnormal psychology. Additional exam requirements/

recommendations for international students: Required—TOEFL (minimum score 550 paper-based; 80 iBT), IELTS (minimum score 6.5). *Application deadline:* For fall admission, 1/15 priority date for domestic and international students. Application fee: $50. Electronic applications accepted. *Expenses:* Contact institution. *Financial support:* Research assistantships with full and partial tuition reimbursements, teaching assistantships, career-related internships or fieldwork, institutionally sponsored loans, scholarships/grants, traineeships, and unspecified assistantships available. Support available to part-time students. Financial award application deadline: 2/15; financial award applicants required to submit FAFSA. *Unit head:* Dr. J. Christopher Muran, Associate Dean, 516-877-4803, E-mail: jcmuran@adelphi.edu. *Application contact:* E-mail: graduateadmissions@adelphi.edu.
Website: http://derner.adelphi.edu/psychology/doctoral-program/

Adler Graduate School, Program in Adlerian Counseling and Psychotherapy, Richfield, MN 55423. Offers Adlerian studies (MA); art therapy (MA); clinical mental health counseling (MA); co-occurring substance use and mental health disorders (MA); marriage and family therapy (MA); school counseling (MA). *Program availability:* Part-time, evening/weekend. *Faculty:* 71 part-time/adjunct (55 women). *Students:* 317 part-time (259 women); includes 51 minority (40 Black or African American, non-Hispanic/Latino; 6 American Indian or Alaska Native, non-Hispanic/Latino; 5 Hispanic/Latino). *Degree requirements:* For master's, thesis or alternative, 500-700 hour internship (depending on license choice). *Entrance requirements:* For master's, interview, official transcripts, minimum cumulative GPA of 3.0. *Application deadline:* Applications are processed on a rolling basis. Application fee: $50. Electronic applications accepted. *Expenses:* $575 per credit tuition. *Financial support:* Career-related internships or fieldwork and tuition waivers available. Support available to part-time students. Financial award applicants required to submit FAFSA. *Unit head:* Dr. Jeffrey Allen, President, 612-767-7048, Fax: 612-861-7559, E-mail: jeffrey.allen@alfredadler.edu. *Application contact:* Christina Hilpipre-Frischman, Director of Admissions, 612-767-7055, Fax: 612-861-7559, E-mail: christina@alfredadler.edu.
Website: http://alfredadler.edu/programs/masters-level-programs

Adler University, Graduate Programs, MA in Counseling Program: Specialization in Clinical Mental Health Counseling, Chicago, IL 60602. Offers MAC. *Program availability:* Part-time, evening/weekend, online learning. *Entrance requirements:* For master's, baccalaureate degree, minimum GPA of 3.0 (recommended), interview.

Adler University, Graduate Programs, Psy D in Clinical Psychology Program, Chicago, IL 60602. Offers advanced Adlerian psychotherapy (Psy D); child and adolescent clinical psychology (Psy D); military clinical psychology (Psy D); primary care psychology and behavioral medicine (Psy D); substance abuse treatment (Psy D); traumatic stress psychology (Psy D). Program also offered at Vancouver campus. *Degree requirements:* For doctorate, internship.

Alabama Agricultural and Mechanical University, School of Graduate Studies, College of Education, Humanities, and Behavioral Sciences, Department of Social Work, Psychology and Counseling, Huntsville, AL 35811. Offers psychology and counseling (MS, Ed S), including clinical psychology (MS), counseling psychology (MS), guidance and counseling, rehabilitation counseling (MS), school counseling (MS), school psychology (MS), school psychometry (MS); social work (MSW). *Accreditation:* CORE; NCATE. *Program availability:* Part-time, evening/weekend. *Degree requirements:* For master's, comprehensive exam. *Entrance requirements:* For master's, GRE General Test. Additional exam requirements/recommendations for international students: Required—TOEFL (minimum score 500 paper-based; 61 iBT). *Faculty research:* Increasing numbers of minorities in special education and speech-language pathology.

Alliant International University–Fresno, California School of Professional Psychology, PhD Program in Clinical Psychology, Fresno, CA 93727. Offers PhD. *Degree requirements:* For doctorate, comprehensive exam, thesis/dissertation. *Entrance requirements:* For doctorate, minimum GPA of 3.0 in both psychology and overall, letters of recommendation, interview. Additional exam requirements/recommendations for international students: Required—TOEFL (minimum score 550 paper-based; 80 iBT), TWE (minimum score 5). Electronic applications accepted. *Faculty research:* Teaching of psychology, ecosystemic child psychology, cultural competence, neuro-cognitive processes.

Alliant International University–Fresno, California School of Professional Psychology, Psy D Program in Clinical Psychology, Fresno, CA 93727. Offers Psy D. *Accreditation:* APA. *Degree requirements:* For doctorate, comprehensive exam, thesis/dissertation. *Entrance requirements:* For doctorate, minimum GPA of 3.0 in both psychology and overall, letters of recommendation, interview. Additional exam requirements/recommendations for international students: Required—TOEFL (minimum score 550 paper-based; 80 iBT), TWE (minimum score 5). Electronic applications accepted. *Faculty research:* Psychodynamic correlates of self-care behavior, women's health and development, gay and lesbian issues, child development and abuse, trauma.

Alliant International University–Los Angeles, California School of Professional Psychology, PhD Program in Clinical Psychology, Alhambra, CA 91803. Offers PhD. *Accreditation:* APA. *Degree requirements:* For doctorate, comprehensive exam, thesis/dissertation. *Entrance requirements:* For doctorate, interview, minimum GPA of 3.0 in both psychology and overall. Additional exam requirements/recommendations for international students: Required—TOEFL (minimum score 600 paper-based), TWE (minimum score 5). Electronic applications accepted. *Faculty research:* Multicultural and community clinical psychology, health and chronic disease, individual and family psychology, pediatric neuropsychology.

Alliant International University–Los Angeles, California School of Professional Psychology, Psy D Program in Clinical Psychology, Alhambra, CA 91803. Offers clinical health psychology (Psy D); family/child and couple clinical psychology (Psy D); multi-interest option (Psy D); multicultural community-clinical psychology (Psy D). *Accreditation:* APA. *Degree requirements:* For doctorate, comprehensive exam, thesis/dissertation. *Entrance requirements:* For doctorate, interview, minimum GPA of 3.0 in both psychology and overall. Additional exam requirements/recommendations for international students: Required—TOEFL (minimum score 600 paper-based), TWE. Electronic applications accepted. *Faculty research:* Child and family psychology, multicultural and community psychology, acculturation, lesbian and gay issues, women's health.

Alliant International University–Sacramento, California School of Professional Psychology, Program in Clinical Psychology, Sacramento, CA 95833. Offers Psy D. *Degree requirements:* For doctorate, comprehensive exam, thesis/dissertation, internship. *Entrance requirements:* For doctorate, minimum GPA of 3.0, letters of recommendation, interview. Additional exam requirements/recommendations for international students: Required—TOEFL (minimum score 600 paper-based; 80 iBT), TWE (minimum score 5). Electronic applications accepted. *Faculty research:* Creating and testing evidence-based interventions for underserved minority populations with cardiovascular disease and cancer, substance abuse treatment and relapse prediction, cultural diversity, personality disorders, trauma.

Alliant International University–San Diego, California School of Professional Psychology, Organizational Psychology Division, San Diego, CA 92131. Offers clinical/industrial organizational psychology (PhD); consulting psychology (PhD); industrial/organizational psychology (MA, MS, PhD); leadership (PhD). *Program availability:* Part-time, evening/weekend. Terminal master's awarded for partial completion of doctoral program. *Degree requirements:* For doctorate, comprehensive exam, thesis/dissertation, internship/practicum. *Entrance requirements:* For master's and doctorate, minimum GPA of 3.0, recommendations, essay, interview. Additional exam requirements/recommendations for international students: Required—TOEFL (minimum score 550 paper-based; 80 iBT), TWE (minimum score 5). Electronic applications accepted. *Faculty research:* Cultural diversity in the workplace, work motivation, personnel and performance management, organizational diagnosis.

Alliant International University–San Diego, California School of Professional Psychology, PhD Program in Clinical Psychology, San Diego, CA 92131. Offers PhD. *Accreditation:* APA. *Degree requirements:* For doctorate, comprehensive exam, thesis/dissertation, internship. *Entrance requirements:* For doctorate, interview, minimum GPA of 3.0, recommendations, essay, interview. Additional exam requirements/recommendations for international students: Required—TOEFL (minimum score 600 paper-based; 80 iBT), TWE (minimum score 5). Electronic applications accepted. *Faculty research:* Pediatric child clinical psychology, neuro-psychological assessment, ADHD, effect of alcohol and abstinence on the central nervous system.

Alliant International University–San Diego, California School of Professional Psychology, Psy D Program in Clinical Psychology, San Diego, CA 92131. Offers Psy D. *Accreditation:* APA. *Degree requirements:* For doctorate, comprehensive exam, thesis/dissertation, internship. *Entrance requirements:* For doctorate, minimum GPA of 3.0, recommendations, essay, interview. Additional exam requirements/recommendations for international students: Required—TOEFL (minimum score 550 paper-based; 80 iBT), TWE (minimum score 5). Electronic applications accepted. *Faculty research:* Forensic psychology, health psychology, family and child psychology, cultural competency in mental health services, women's health.

Alliant International University–San Francisco, California School of Forensic Studies, San Francisco, CA 94133. Offers applied criminology (MS), including victimology; clinical forensic psychology (PhD, Psy D). *Degree requirements:* For doctorate, comprehensive exam, thesis/dissertation, internship. *Entrance requirements:* For master's, minimum GPA of 3.0, recommendations, essay; for doctorate, minimum GPA of 3.0, recommendations, essay, interview. Additional exam requirements/recommendations for international students: Required—TOEFL (minimum score 550 paper-based; 80 iBT), TWE (minimum score 5). *Faculty research:* Post-traumatic stress disorder, correctional mental health.

Alliant International University–San Francisco, California School of Professional Psychology, PhD Program in Clinical Psychology, San Francisco, CA 94133. Offers PhD. *Degree requirements:* For doctorate, comprehensive exam, thesis/dissertation, internship. *Entrance requirements:* For doctorate, minimum GPA of 3.0, recommendations, essay, interview. Additional exam requirements/recommendations for international students: Required—TOEFL (minimum score 550 paper-based; 80 iBT), TWE (minimum score 5). Electronic applications accepted. *Faculty research:* Social model of disability, feminist models of clinical training, post-traumatic stress disorder, gay and lesbian parents and their children, psychology of women.

Alliant International University–San Francisco, California School of Professional Psychology, Psy D Program in Clinical Psychology, San Francisco, CA 94133. Offers Psy D, Certificate. *Accreditation:* APA (one or more programs are accredited). *Degree requirements:* For doctorate, comprehensive exam, thesis/dissertation, internship. *Entrance requirements:* For doctorate, minimum GPA of 3.0, recommendations, essay, interview. Additional exam requirements/recommendations for international students: Required—TOEFL (minimum score 550 paper-based; 80 iBT), TWE (minimum score 5). Electronic applications accepted. *Faculty research:* Health psychology, family and child psychology, social justice, multicultural and community psychology, gender issues.

American International College, School of Business, Arts and Sciences, Springfield, MA 01109-3189. Offers accounting and taxation (MS); business administration (MBA); clinical psychology (MA); educational psychology (Ed D); forensic psychology (MS); general psychology (MA, CAGS); management (CAGS); resort and casino management (MBA, CAGS). *Program availability:* Part-time, evening/weekend. *Faculty:* 4 full-time (2 women), 25 part-time/adjunct (13 women). *Students:* 178 full-time (120 women), 24 part-time (20 women); includes 94 minority (42 Black or African American, non-Hispanic/Latino; 1 American Indian or Alaska Native, non-Hispanic/Latino; 4 Asian, non-Hispanic/Latino; 39 Hispanic/Latino; 8 Two or more races, non-Hispanic/Latino), 13 international. Average age 28. 155 applicants, 83% accepted, 71 enrolled. In 2017, 87 master's, 3 doctorates awarded. *Degree requirements:* For master's, practicum; for doctorate, comprehensive exam, thesis/dissertation, practicum. *Entrance requirements:* For master's, BS or BA, minimum undergraduate GPA of 2.75, 2 letters of recommendation, official transcripts, personal goal statement or essay; for doctorate, 3 letters of recommendation; BS or BA; minimum undergraduate GPA of 3.0 (3.25 recommended); official transcripts; personal goal statement or essay. Additional exam requirements/recommendations for international students: Required—TOEFL (minimum score 550 paper-based; 80 iBT). *Application deadline:* For fall admission, 8/15 for domestic and international students; for spring admission, 12/15 for domestic and international students. Applications are processed on a rolling basis. Application fee: $50. *Expenses:* Contact institution. *Financial support:* In 2017–18, 6 students received support, including 6 research assistantships with full tuition reimbursements available (averaging $1,500 per year). Financial award application deadline: 4/1; financial award applicants required to submit FAFSA. *Faculty research:* Substance abuse, forensic psychology, special education. *Unit head:* Dr. Susanne Swanker, Dean, 413-205-3216, Fax: 413-205-3943, E-mail: susanne.swanker@aic.edu. *Application contact:* Kerry Barnes, Dean of Graduate Admissions, 413-205-3703, Fax: 413-205-3051, E-mail: kerry.barnes@aic.edu.
Website: http://www.aic.edu/school-of-business-arts-and-sciences/

American International College, School of Education, Low Residency Programs, Springfield, MA 01109-3189. Offers counseling psychology (MA); educational leadership and supervision (Ed D); professional counseling and supervision (Ed D); teaching and learning (Ed D). *Program availability:* Evening/weekend. *Faculty:* 2 full-time (1 woman), 4 part-time/adjunct (all women). *Students:* 117 full-time (90 women); includes 32 minority (22 Black or African American, non-Hispanic/Latino; 1 Asian, non-Hispanic/Latino; 7 Hispanic/Latino; 2 Two or more races, non-Hispanic/Latino). Average age 40. 35 applicants, 86% accepted, 20 enrolled. In 2017, 8 master's, 12 doctorates awarded. *Degree requirements:* For doctorate, thesis/dissertation. *Entrance requirements:* For master's, minimum undergraduate GPA of 3.0, 2 letters of recommendation, personal goal statement, official transcript of all academic work (graduate and undergraduate); for doctorate, minimum master's GPA of 3.0, 3 letters of recommendation, personal goal statement/essay (6-8 pages), official transcript of all academic work (graduate and undergraduate). Additional exam requirements/recommendations for international students: Required—TOEFL. *Application deadline:* For fall admission, 8/15 for domestic and international students; for spring admission, 1/3 for domestic and international students; for summer admission, 5/15 for domestic and international students. Applications are processed on a rolling basis. Application fee: $50. *Expenses:* $6,515 per trimester (for EdD); $505 per credit (for MA); $30 per term registration fee; $100 one-time graduation fee. *Faculty research:* Educational leadership, curriculum, program

evaluation, educational policy. *Unit head:* Dr. Nicholas Young, Dean, Low Residency Programs, 413-205-1726, E-mail: nicholas.young@aic.edu. *Application contact:* Kerry Barnes, Director of Graduate Admissions, 413-205-3703, Fax: 413-205-3051, E-mail: kerry.barnes@aic.edu.

American University, College of Arts and Sciences, Department of Psychology, Washington, DC 22016-8062. Offers addiction and addictive behavior (Certificate); behavior, cognition, and neuroscience (PhD); clinical psychology (PhD); psychobiology of healing (Certificate); psychology (MA). *Accreditation:* APA. *Program availability:* Part-time. *Faculty:* 20 full-time (8 women), 9 part-time/adjunct (7 women). *Students:* 80 full-time (68 women), 8 part-time (7 women); includes 15 minority (5 Black or African American, non-Hispanic/Latino; 4 Asian, non-Hispanic/Latino; 5 Hispanic/Latino; 1 Two or more races, non-Hispanic/Latino), 6 international. Average age 28. 461 applicants, 12% accepted, 23 enrolled. In 2017, 24 master's, 11 doctorates awarded. *Degree requirements:* For master's, comprehensive exam, thesis or alternative; for doctorate, comprehensive exam, thesis/dissertation. *Entrance requirements:* For master's, GRE General Test, GRE Subject Test, statement of purpose, transcripts, 2 letters of recommendation; for doctorate, GRE General Test, GRE Subject Test, 3 letters of recommendation, statement of purpose, transcripts, resume. Additional exam requirements/recommendations for international students: Required—TOEFL (minimum score 600 paper-based; 100 iBT). *Application deadline:* For fall admission, 3/1 priority date for domestic students. Application fee: $55. *Expenses:* Contact institution. *Financial support:* Research assistantships, teaching assistantships, institutionally sponsored loans, scholarships/grants, and unspecified assistantships available. Financial award application deadline: 2/1; financial award applicants required to submit FAFSA. *Unit head:* Dr. David Haaga, Department Chair, 202-885-1718, Fax: 202-885-1023, E-mail: ahrens@american.edu. *Application contact:* Jonathan Harper, Associate Director, Graduate Recruitment, 202-885-3622, E-mail: jharper@american.edu.
Website: http://www.american.edu/CAS/Psychology/

American University of Beirut, Graduate Programs, Faculty of Arts and Sciences, 1107 2020, Lebanon. Offers anthropology (MA); Arab and Middle Eastern history (PhD); Arabic language and literature (MA, PhD); archaeology (MA); art history and curating (MA); biology (MS); cell and molecular biology (PhD); chemistry (MS); clinical psychology (MA); computational sciences (MS); computer science (MS); economics (MA); education (MA), including administration and policy studies, elementary education, mathematics education, psychology school guidance, psychology test and measurements, science education, teaching English as a foreign language; English language (MA); English literature (MA); environmental policy planning (MS); financial economics (MAFE); general psychology (MA); geology (MS); history (MA); Islamic studies (MA); mathematics (MS); media studies (MA); Middle East studies (MA); philosophy (MA); physics (MS); political studies (MA); public administration (MA); public policy and international affairs (MA); sociology (MA); theoretical physics (PhD). *Program availability:* Part-time. *Faculty:* 108 full-time (36 women), 5 part-time/adjunct (4 women). *Students:* 251 full-time (180 women), 233 part-time (172 women). Average age 26. 425 applicants, 65% accepted, 121 enrolled. In 2017, 47 master's, 2 doctorates awarded. *Degree requirements:* For master's, one foreign language, comprehensive exam, thesis (for some programs), project; for doctorate, one foreign language, comprehensive exam, thesis/dissertation. *Entrance requirements:* For master's, GRE General Test (for some programs); for doctorate, GRE General Test (GRE Subject Test for theoretical physics). Additional exam requirements/recommendations for international students: Required—TOEFL (minimum score 583 paper-based; 97 iBT), IELTS (minimum score 7). *Application deadline:* For fall admission, 2/8 for domestic students; for spring admission, 11/3 for domestic students. Application fee: $50. Electronic applications accepted. *Expenses:* Contact institution. *Financial support:* In 2017–18, 29 fellowships, 40 research assistantships were awarded; teaching assistantships, scholarships/grants, tuition waivers (full and partial), and unspecified assistantships also available. Financial award application deadline: 4/4. *Unit head:* Dr. Nadia Maria El Cheikh, Dean, Faculty of Arts and Sciences, 961-1-374374 Ext. 3800, Fax: 961-1-744461, E-mail: nmcheikh@aub.edu.lb. *Application contact:* Rima Rassi, Graduate Studies Officer, 961-1-350000 Ext. 3833, Fax: 961-1-744461, E-mail: rr46@aub.edu.lb.
Website: http://www.aub.edu.lb/fas/pages/default.aspx

Andrews University, School of Graduate Studies, School of Education, Department of Graduate Psychology and Counseling, Program in Community Counseling, Berrien Springs, MI 49104. Offers clinical mental health counseling (MA); community counseling (MA). *Students:* 23 full-time (13 women), 3 part-time (all women); includes 7 minority (3 Black or African American, non-Hispanic/Latino; 4 Hispanic/Latino), 9 international. Average age 30. 25 applicants, 76% accepted, 7 enrolled. In 2017, 12 master's awarded. *Degree requirements:* For master's, thesis optional. *Entrance requirements:* For master's, GRE. Additional exam requirements/recommendations for international students: Required—TOEFL (minimum score 550 paper-based). Application fee: $40. *Unit head:* Dr. Nancy Carbonell, Coordinator, 269-471-3472. *Application contact:* Justina Clayburn, Supervisor of Graduate Admission, 800-253-2874, Fax: 269-471-6321, E-mail: graduate@andrews.edu.

Antioch University Los Angeles, Program in Psychology, Culver City, CA 90230. Offers clinical psychology (MA); psychology (MA). *Program availability:* Part-time. *Faculty:* 19. *Students:* 428 full-time (312 women), 35 part-time (27 women); includes 140 minority (25 Black or African American, non-Hispanic/Latino; 13 Asian, non-Hispanic/Latino; 81 Hispanic/Latino; 1 Native Hawaiian or other Pacific Islander, non-Hispanic/Latino; 20 Two or more races, non-Hispanic/Latino), 1 international. Average age 36. In 2017, 118 master's awarded. *Degree requirements:* For master's, thesis (for some programs), internship. *Entrance requirements:* For master's, interview. Additional exam requirements/recommendations for international students: Required—TOEFL. *Application deadline:* For fall admission, 8/4 priority date for domestic students; for winter admission, 11/3 priority date for domestic students; for spring admission, 2/4 priority date for domestic students. Applications are processed on a rolling basis. Application fee: $60. *Financial support:* In 2017–18, 167 students received support. Career-related internships or fieldwork, Federal Work-Study, scholarships/grants, and traineeships available. Support available to part-time students. Financial award application deadline: 3/24; financial award applicants required to submit FAFSA. *Faculty research:* Creativity and humor, ethnic humor, adult development, Jungian theory, psychoanalytic theory. *Unit head:* Joy Turek, Chair, 310-578-1080 Ext. 306, Fax: 310-822-4824, E-mail: joy_turek@antiochla.edu. *Application contact:* Information Contact, 310-578-1090, Fax: 310-822-4824, E-mail: admissions@antiochla.edu.

Antioch University New England, Graduate School, Department of Applied Psychology, Program in Clinical Mental Health Counseling, Keene, NH 03431-3552. Offers clinical mental health counseling (MA); substance abuse counseling (MA). *Accreditation:* ACA. *Degree requirements:* For master's, internship, practicum. *Entrance requirements:* For master's, previous course work and work experience in psychology. Additional exam requirements/recommendations for international students: Required—TOEFL (minimum score 550 paper-based). Electronic applications accepted. *Expenses:* Contact institution. *Faculty research:* Multicultural issues in field supervision.

Antioch University New England, Graduate School, Department of Clinical Psychology, Keene, NH 03431-3552. Offers Psy D. *Accreditation:* APA. *Degree requirements:* For doctorate, thesis/dissertation, internship, practicum. *Entrance*

requirements: For doctorate, GRE General Test, GRE Subject Test, previous course work in psychology, work sample. Additional exam requirements/recommendations for international students: Required—TOEFL (minimum score 550 paper-based). *Expenses:* Contact institution. *Faculty research:* Psychotherapy outcome and process in private practice, neuropsychiatric evaluations, effects of trauma on adults, supervision, clinical training evaluation.

Antioch University Santa Barbara, Program in Clinical Psychology, Santa Barbara, CA 93101-1581. Offers MA, Psy D. *Entrance requirements:* Additional exam requirements/recommendations for international students: Required—TOEFL (minimum score 550 paper-based). Electronic applications accepted.

Antioch University Seattle, Program in Clinical Psychology, Seattle, WA 98121. Offers psychology (Psy D). *Program availability:* Part-time, evening/weekend. *Students:* 66 full-time (51 women), 12 part-time (11 women). Average age 40. *Degree requirements:* For doctorate, thesis/dissertation. *Application deadline:* Applications are processed on a rolling basis. Electronic applications accepted. *Financial support:* Fellowships, research assistantships with tuition reimbursements, Federal Work-Study, scholarships/grants, and unspecified assistantships available. *Faculty research:* Trauma and post-traumatic stress disorders, workplace harassment and violence, multicultural issues and diversity. *Unit head:* Dana Waters, Associate Chair, 206-268-4865, E-mail: dwaters@antioch.edu. *Application contact:* Eileen Knight, Recruitment and Admissions Director, 206-268-4200, E-mail: eknight@antioch.edu.
Website: http://www.antiochseattle.edu/academics/psychology/

Antioch University Seattle, Program in Counseling, Therapy and Wellness, Seattle, WA 98121. Offers clinical mental health counseling (MA); counselor education and supervision (PhD); couple and family therapy (MA). *Students:* 258 full-time (220 women), 100 part-time (84 women); includes 81 minority (9 Black or African American, non-Hispanic/Latino; 3 American Indian or Alaska Native, non-Hispanic/Latino; 19 Asian, non-Hispanic/Latino; 30 Hispanic/Latino; 20 Two or more races, non-Hispanic/Latino), 1 international. Average age 35. *Unit head:* Peter Rojcewicz, Vice President of Academic Affairs, 206-268-4108, E-mail: projcewicz@antioch.edu. *Application contact:* Eileen Knight, Recruitment and Admissions Director, 206-268-4200, E-mail: psmith-mentz@antiochsea.edu.

Appalachian State University, Cratis D. Williams Graduate School, Department of Human Development and Psychological Counseling, Boone, NC 28608. Offers clinical mental health counseling (MA); college student development (MA); marriage and family therapy (MA); school counseling (MA). *Accreditation:* AAMFT/COAMFTE; ACA; NCATE. *Program availability:* Part-time. *Degree requirements:* For master's, comprehensive exam (for some programs), thesis optional, internships. *Entrance requirements:* For master's, GRE General Test, 3 letters of recommendation. Additional exam requirements/recommendations for international students: Required—TOEFL (minimum score 570 paper-based; 79 iBT), IELTS (minimum score 6.5). Electronic applications accepted. *Faculty research:* Multicultural counseling, addictions counseling, play therapy, expressive arts, child and adolescent therapy, sexual abuse counseling.

Appalachian State University, Cratis D. Williams Graduate School, Department of Psychology, Boone, NC 28608. Offers clinical health psychology (MA). *Program availability:* Part-time. *Degree requirements:* For master's, comprehensive exam, thesis optional, exit exam. *Entrance requirements:* For master's, GRE General Test, 3 letters of recommendation. Additional exam requirements/recommendations for international students: Required—TOEFL (minimum score 550 paper-based; 79 iBT) or IELTS (minimum score 6.5). Electronic applications accepted. *Faculty research:* Eating disorders, school-based consultations, organizational behavior management, brain mechanisms of sound localization, parenting styles.

Argosy University, Atlanta, Georgia School of Professional Psychology, Atlanta, GA 30328. Offers clinical psychology (MA, Psy D, Postdoctoral Respecialization Certificate), including child and family psychology (Psy D), general adult clinical (Psy D), health psychology (Psy D), neuropsychology/geropsychology (Psy D); community counseling (MA), including marriage and family therapy; counselor education and supervision (Ed D); forensic psychology (MA); industrial organizational psychology (MA); marriage and family therapy (Certificate); sport-exercise psychology (MA). *Accreditation:* APA.

Argosy University, Chicago, Illinois School of Professional Psychology, Doctoral Program in Clinical Psychology, Chicago, IL 60601. Offers child and adolescent psychology (Psy D); client-centered and experiential psychotherapies (Psy D); diversity and multicultural psychology (Psy D); family psychology (Psy D); forensic psychology (Psy D); health psychology (Psy D); neuropsychology (Psy D); organizational consulting (Psy D); psychoanalytic psychology (Psy D); psychology and spirituality (Psy D). *Accreditation:* APA.

Argosy University, Chicago, Illinois School of Professional Psychology, Master's Program in Clinical Psychology, Chicago, IL 60601. Offers MA.

Argosy University, Hawai`i, Hawai'i School of Professional Psychology, Program in Clinical Psychology, Honolulu, HI 96813. Offers clinical psychology (MA, Psy D, Postdoctoral Respecialization Certificate), including child and family clinical practice (Psy D), diversity in clinical practice (Psy D). *Accreditation:* APA.

Argosy University, Los Angeles, College of Psychology and Behavioral Sciences, Los Angeles, CA 90045. Offers clinical psychology/marriage and family therapy (MA); counseling psychology (Ed D); counseling psychology/marriage and family therapy (MA); forensic psychology (MA).

Argosy University, Northern Virginia, American School of Professional Psychology, Arlington, VA 22209. Offers clinical psychology (MA, Psy D), including child and family psychology (Psy D), diversity and multicultural psychology (Psy D), forensic psychology (Psy D), health and neuropsychology (Psy D); community counseling (MA); counseling psychology (Ed D), including counselor education and supervision; counselor education and supervision (Ed D); forensic psychology (MA).

Argosy University, Orange County, American School of Professional Psychology, Program in Clinical Psychology, Orange, CA 92868. Offers child and adolescent psychology (Psy D); forensic psychology (Psy D); marriage and family therapy (MA).

Argosy University, Phoenix, Arizona School of Professional Psychology, Program in Clinical Psychology, Phoenix, AZ 85021. Offers clinical psychology (MA); neuropsychology (Psy D); sports-exercise psychology (Psy D).

Argosy University, Seattle, College of Psychology and Behavioral Sciences, Program in Clinical Psychology, Seattle, WA 98121. Offers MA, Psy D, Postdoctoral Respecialization Certificate.

Argosy University, Tampa, Florida School of Professional Psychology, Program in Clinical Psychology, Tampa, FL 33607. Offers clinical psychology (MA, Psy D), including child and adolescent psychology (Psy D), geropsychology (Psy D), marriage/couples and family therapy (Psy D), neuropsychology (Psy D). *Accreditation:* APA.

Argosy University, Twin Cities, Minnesota School of Professional Psychology, Eagan, MN 55121. Offers clinical psychology (MA, Psy D), including child and family psychology (Psy D), forensic psychology (Psy D), health and neuropsychology (Psy D), trauma (Psy D); forensic counseling (Post-Graduate Certificate); forensic psychology (MA); industrial organizational psychology (MA); marriage and family therapy (MA, DMFT), including forensic counseling (MA). *Accreditation:* AAMFT; AAMFT/COAMFTE; APA.

Clinical Psychology

Arizona State University at the Tempe campus, College of Liberal Arts and Sciences, Department of Psychology, Tempe, AZ 85287-1104. Offers applied behavior analysis (MS); behavioral neuroscience (PhD); clinical psychology (PhD); cognitive science (PhD); developmental psychology (PhD); quantitative psychology (PhD); social psychology (PhD). *Accreditation:* APA. *Degree requirements:* For doctorate, comprehensive exam, thesis/dissertation, interactive Program of Study (iPOS) submitted before completing 50 percent of required credit hours. *Entrance requirements:* For doctorate, GRE General Test, GRE Subject Test, minimum GPA of 3.0 or equivalent in last 2 years of work leading to bachelor's degree. Additional exam requirements/ recommendations for international students: Required—TOEFL, IELTS, or PTE. Electronic applications accepted.

Arkansas State University, Graduate School, College of Education and Behavioral Science, Department of Psychology and Counseling, State University, AR 72467. Offers clinical mental health counseling (Graduate Certificate); college student personnel services (MS); dyslexia therapy (Graduate Certificate); psychological science (MS); psychology and counseling (Ed S); rehabilitation counseling (MRC); school counseling (MSE); student affairs (Graduate Certificate). *Accreditation:* ACA (one or more programs are accredited); CORE (one or more programs are accredited); NCATE. *Program availability:* Part-time. *Degree requirements:* For master's and other advanced degree, comprehensive exam, thesis or alternative. *Entrance requirements:* For master's, GRE General Test or MAT (for MSE), appropriate bachelor's degree, interview, letters of reference, official transcripts, immunization records, written statement, 2-3 page autobiography; for other advanced degree, GRE General Test, interview, master's degree, letters of reference, official transcript, personal statement, immunization records. Additional exam requirements/recommendations for international students: Required—TOEFL (minimum score 550 paper-based; 79 iBT), IELTS (minimum score 6), PTE (minimum score 56). Electronic applications accepted.

Ashland Theological Seminary, Graduate Programs, Ashland, OH 44805. Offers Biblical studies (MA); Christian ministries (MACM), including Black church studies (MACM, D Min), general Christian ministries, leadership, spiritual formation (MACM, D Min); clinical mental health counseling (MA); counseling (MAC); historical and theological studies (MA), including Anabaptism and Pietism, Christian theology, church history, New Testament, Old Testament; ministry (D Min), including Black church studies (MACM, D Min), chaplaincy (M Div, D Min), independent design, spiritual formation (MACM, D Min), transformational leadership; pastoral ministry (M Div), including chaplaincy (M Div, D Min), general ministry. MAC program offered in Detroit, MI. *Accreditation:* ATS. *Program availability:* Part-time. *Degree requirements:* For master's, 2 foreign languages, comprehensive exam (for some programs), thesis (for some programs); for doctorate, thesis/dissertation. *Entrance requirements:* For master's, bachelor's degree from accredited institution with minimum undergraduate GPA of 2.75; for doctorate, M Div, minimum undergraduate GPA of 3.0. Additional exam requirements/recommendations for international students: Required—TOEFL (minimum score 500 paper-based; 65 iBT). Electronic applications accepted. *Faculty research:* Semitic languages and linguistics, rhetorical and social-scientific criticism, Anabaptist studies, inner spiritual healing, African-American clergy in film and literature.

Auburn University at Montgomery, College of Arts and Sciences, Department of Psychology, Montgomery, AL 36124-4023. Offers clinical psychology (MS). *Program availability:* Part-time, evening/weekend. *Faculty:* 7 full-time (4 women), 1 (woman) part-time/adjunct. *Students:* 15 full-time (9 women), 6 part-time (5 women); includes 11 minority (10 Black or African American, non-Hispanic/Latino; 1 Asian, non-Hispanic/Latino). Average age 27. 12 applicants, 75% accepted, 8 enrolled. In 2017, 8 master's awarded. *Degree requirements:* For master's, comprehensive exam, thesis optional. *Entrance requirements:* For master's, GRE General Test or MAT. Additional exam requirements/recommendations for international students: Recommended—TOEFL (minimum score 500 paper-based; 61 iBT), IELTS (minimum score 5.5), TSE (minimum score 44). *Application deadline:* For fall admission, 4/15 for domestic students, 7/15 for international students; for spring admission, 11/15 for international students; for summer admission, 4/15 for international students. Applications are processed on a rolling basis. Application fee: $25. Electronic applications accepted. *Expenses:* Tuition, state resident: full-time $6930; part-time $385 per credit hour. Tuition, nonresident: full-time $15,588; part-time $866 per credit hour. *Required fees:* $640. *Financial support:* In 2017–18, 1 teaching assistantship was awarded; career-related internships or fieldwork and scholarships/grants also available. Support available to part-time students. Financial award application deadline: 3/1; financial award applicants required to submit FAFSA. *Faculty research:* Community service, diagnosis, behavior modification. *Unit head:* Dr. Glen Ray, Acting Head, 334-244-3690, Fax: 334-244-3826, E-mail: gray@aum.edu. *Application contact:* Tonya Sexton, Administrative Associate, 334-244-3306, Fax: 334-244-3826, E-mail: tsexton1@aum.edu.
Website: http://www.cas.aum.edu/departments/psychology

Auburn University at Montgomery, College of Education, Department of Counselor, Leadership, and Special Education, Montgomery, AL 36124-4023. Offers counselor education (M Ed, Ed S), including clinical mental health counseling, school counseling; early childhood special education (M Ed); instructional leadership (M Ed, Ed S); special education/collaborative teacher (M Ed, Ed S). *Accreditation:* ACA; NCATE. *Program availability:* Part-time, evening/weekend. *Faculty:* 7 full-time (4 women), 2 part-time/adjunct (both women). *Students:* 27 full-time (23 women), 57 part-time (51 women); includes 40 minority (38 Black or African American, non-Hispanic/Latino; 2 Hispanic/Latino). Average age 34. 76 applicants, 72% accepted, 26 enrolled. In 2017, 37 master's awarded. *Degree requirements:* For master's and Ed S, comprehensive exam. *Entrance requirements:* For master's, GRE General Test or MAT, certification, BS in teaching; for Ed S, GRE General Test or MAT, certification. Additional exam requirements/recommendations for international students: Recommended—TOEFL (minimum score 500 paper-based; 61 iBT), IELTS (minimum score 5.5), TSE (minimum score 44). *Application deadline:* For fall admission, 7/15 for international students; for spring admission, 11/15 for international students; for summer admission, 4/15 for international students. Applications are processed on a rolling basis. Electronic applications accepted. *Expenses:* Tuition, state resident: full-time $6930; part-time $385 per credit hour. Tuition, nonresident: full-time $15,588; part-time $866 per credit hour. *Required fees:* $640. *Financial support:* Career-related internships or fieldwork and scholarships/grants available. Support available to part-time students. Financial award application deadline: 3/1; financial award applicants required to submit FAFSA. *Unit head:* Dr. Samuel Flynt, Head, 334-244-3835, Fax: 334-244-3101, E-mail: sflynt@aum.edu. *Application contact:* Dr. Rhonda Morton, Associate Dean/Graduate Coordinator, 334-244-3287, Fax: 334-244-3978, E-mail: rmorton@aum.edu.
Website: http://education.aum.edu/academic-departments/counselor-leadership-and-special-education

Augusta University, College of Education, Department of Counselor Education, Leadership, and Research, Augusta, GA 30912. Offers counselor education (M Ed, Ed S), including clinical mental health counseling (M Ed), school counselor (M Ed). *Accreditation:* ACA; NCATE. *Program availability:* Part-time, evening/weekend. *Degree requirements:* For master's, comprehensive exam; for Ed S, comprehensive exam, thesis. *Entrance requirements:* For master's, GRE, MAT, minimum GPA of 2.5; for Ed S,

GRE, MAT. *Faculty research:* Restructuring schools, financing education, student transition.

Austin Peay State University, College of Graduate Studies, College of Behavioral and Health Sciences, Department of Psychological Science and Counseling, Clarksville, TN 37044. Offers industrial-organizational psychology (MS); mental health counseling (MS), including clinical mental health, school counseling; school counseling (MS). *Program availability:* Part-time, online learning. *Faculty:* 11 full-time (6 women), 1 (woman) part-time/adjunct. *Students:* 60 full-time (46 women), 12 part-time (10 women); includes 16 minority (11 Black or African American, non-Hispanic/Latino; 4 Hispanic/Latino; 1 Two or more races, non-Hispanic/Latino). Average age 29. 59 applicants, 69% accepted, 31 enrolled. In 2017, 30 master's awarded. *Degree requirements:* For master's, comprehensive exam, thesis (for some programs). *Entrance requirements:* For master's, GRE General Test, minimum undergraduate GPA of 2.5, 3 letters of recommendation, bachelor's degree. Additional exam requirements/recommendations for international students: Required—TOEFL (minimum score 500 paper-based). *Application deadline:* For fall admission, 8/8 priority date for domestic students. Applications are processed on a rolling basis. Application fee: $45 ($55 for international students). Electronic applications accepted. *Expenses:* Tuition, state resident: full-time $7686; part-time $427 per credit hour. Tuition, nonresident: full-time $20,268; part-time $1126 per credit hour. *Required fees:* $1529; $76.45 per credit hour. *Financial support:* Research assistantships with full tuition reimbursements, career-related internships or fieldwork, Federal Work-Study, institutionally sponsored loans, scholarships/grants, and unspecified assistantships available. Support available to part-time students. Financial award application deadline: 4/1; financial award applicants required to submit FAFSA. *Unit head:* Dr. Nicole Knickmeyer, Chair, 931-221-7232, Fax: 931-221-6267, E-mail: knickmeyer@apsu.edu. *Application contact:* Brad Averitt, Coordinator of Graduate Admissions, 800-859-4723, Fax: 931-221-7641, E-mail: gradadmissions@apsu.edu. Website: http://www.apsu.edu/psychology/index.php

Azusa Pacific University, School of Behavioral and Applied Sciences, Department of Clinical Psychology, Azusa, CA 91702-7000. Offers family psychology (Psy D). *Accreditation:* APA. *Program availability:* Part-time, evening/weekend. *Degree requirements:* For doctorate, comprehensive exam. *Entrance requirements:* Additional exam requirements/recommendations for international students: Required—TOEFL (minimum score 600 paper-based). *Expenses:* Contact institution.

Ball State University, Graduate School, College of Health, Department of Counseling Psychology, Social Psychology, and Counseling, Program in Counseling Psychology, Muncie, IN 47306. Offers counseling (MA), including clinical mental health counseling, mental health counseling, rehabilitation counseling, school counseling; counseling psychology (PhD). *Accreditation:* ACA; APA. *Program availability:* Part-time. *Students:* 88 full-time (57 women), 29 part-time (24 women); includes 18 minority (3 Black or African American, non-Hispanic/Latino; 1 Asian, non-Hispanic/Latino; 7 Hispanic/Latino; 7 Two or more races, non-Hispanic/Latino), 4 international. Average age 26. 133 applicants, 29% accepted, 39 enrolled. In 2017, 29 master's, 9 doctorates awarded. *Degree requirements:* For doctorate, thesis/dissertation. *Entrance requirements:* For master's, GRE General Test (minimum scores 144 quantitative, 153 verbal), minimum baccalaureate GPA of 2.75 or 3.0 in latter half of baccalaureate, minimum GPA of 3.0 in psychology coursework, three letters of recommendation; for doctorate, GRE General Test, interview, minimum graduate GPA of 3.2, resume. Additional exam requirements/recommendations for international students: Required—TOEFL (minimum score 550 paper-based; 79 iBT), IELTS (minimum score 6.5). *Application deadline:* For fall admission, 3/1 priority date for domestic students, 1/1 for international students. Applications are processed on a rolling basis. Application fee: $60. Electronic applications accepted. *Financial support:* Research assistantships with partial tuition reimbursements, teaching assistantships with partial tuition reimbursements, and unspecified assistantships available. Financial award application deadline: 3/1; financial award applicants required to submit FAFSA. *Unit head:* Dr. Sharon Bowman, Chairperson, 765-285-8040, Fax: 765-285-2067, E-mail: sbowman@bsu.edu. Website: http://www.bsu.edu/teachers/counseling/cpsy/

Ball State University, Graduate School, College of Health, Department of Counseling Psychology, Social Psychology, and Counseling, Program in Social Psychology, Muncie, IN 47306. Offers social psychology (MA); social psychology and clinical mental health counseling (MA). *Students:* 4 full-time (2 women), 4 part-time (all women); includes 2 minority (1 Black or African American, non-Hispanic/Latino; 1 Asian, non-Hispanic/Latino). Average age 27. 20 applicants, 15% accepted, 2 enrolled. In 2017, 4 master's awarded. *Entrance requirements:* For master's, GRE General Test (minimum scores 144 quantitative, 153 verbal), minimum baccalaureate GPA of 2.75 or 3.0 in latter half of baccalaureate, minimum GPA of 3.0 in psychology coursework, three letters of recommendation. Additional exam requirements/recommendations for international students: Required—TOEFL (minimum score 550 paper-based; 79 iBT), IELTS (minimum score 6.5). *Application deadline:* For fall admission, 3/1 priority date for domestic students, 1/1 priority date for international students. Applications are processed on a rolling basis. Application fee: $60. Electronic applications accepted. *Financial support:* Teaching assistantships with partial tuition reimbursements and unspecified assistantships available. Financial award application deadline: 3/1; financial award applicants required to submit FAFSA. *Unit head:* Dr. Sharon Bowman, Head, 765-285-8040, Fax: 765-285-2067, E-mail: sbowman@bsu.edu.

Ball State University, Graduate School, College of Sciences and Humanities, Department of Psychological Science, Program in Clinical Psychology, Muncie, IN 47306. Offers MA. *Students:* 15 full-time (13 women), 3 part-time (all women); includes 5 minority (3 Black or African American, non-Hispanic/Latino; 2 Hispanic/Latino), 1 international. Average age 24. 69 applicants, 14% accepted, 10 enrolled. In 2017, 9 master's awarded. *Entrance requirements:* For master's, GRE General Test, minimum baccalaureate GPA of 2.75 or 3.0 in latter half of baccalaureate, goals statements, curriculum vitae, letters of recommendation. Additional exam requirements/recommendations for international students: Required—TOEFL (minimum score 550 paper-based; 79 iBT), IELTS (minimum score 6.5). *Application deadline:* For fall admission, 2/1 for domestic students. Applications are processed on a rolling basis. Application fee: $60. Electronic applications accepted. *Financial support:* Research assistantships with partial tuition reimbursements and teaching assistantships with partial tuition reimbursements available. Financial award application deadline: 3/1; financial award applicants required to submit FAFSA. *Unit head:* Dr. Guy Mittleman, Chairperson, 765-285-1960, Fax: 765-285-1690, E-mail: gmittleman@bsu.edu. Website: http://www.bsu.edu/psysc/

Barry University, College of Arts and Sciences, Department of Psychology, Miami Shores, FL 33161-6695. Offers clinical psychology (MS); school psychology (MS, SSP). *Program availability:* Part-time, evening/weekend. *Degree requirements:* For master's, thesis, practicum. *Entrance requirements:* For master's, GRE General Test, minimum GPA of 3.0, course work in psychology. Electronic applications accepted. *Faculty research:* Closed head injury, memory and aging, infant/mother interaction, evolutionary aspects of behavior, gender roles.

Baylor University, Graduate School, College of Arts and Sciences, Department of Psychology and Neuroscience, Program in Clinical Psychology, Waco, TX 76798. Offers Psy D. *Accreditation:* APA. *Faculty:* 8 full-time (5 women), 5 part-time/adjunct (2

women). *Students:* 35 full-time (32 women); includes 10 minority (5 Asian, non-Hispanic/Latino; 1 Hispanic/Latino; 4 Two or more races, non-Hispanic/Latino), 1 international. Average age 28. 230 applicants, 3% accepted, 6 enrolled. In 2017, 5 doctorates awarded. *Degree requirements:* For doctorate, comprehensive exam, thesis/dissertation, year-long internship at APA-accredited internship site. *Entrance requirements:* For doctorate, GRE General Test, in-person interview. Additional exam requirements/recommendations for international students: Required—TOEFL, IELTS. *Application deadline:* For fall admission, 12/1 for domestic and international students. Application fee: $50. Electronic applications accepted. *Expenses:* $1,237 per hour; $174 per hour student fees. *Financial support:* In 2017–18, 32 students received support, including 6 research assistantships with full tuition reimbursements available (averaging $19,000 per year); career-related internships or fieldwork, institutionally sponsored loans, tuition waivers (full), and practicum stipends also available. Financial award application deadline: 12/1; financial award applicants required to submit FAFSA. *Faculty research:* Drug and alcohol, pediatric psychology, marital communication, religion and mental health, hypnosis/behavioral medicine. *Total annual research expenditures:* $700,000. *Unit head:* Dr. Sara Dolan, Graduate Program Director, 254-710-2573, Fax: 254-710-3033, E-mail: sara_dolan@baylor.edu. *Application contact:* Laura Sumrall, Graduate Studies Coordinator, 254-710-2961, Fax: 254-710-3033, E-mail: laura_sumrall@baylor.edu.
Website: http://www.baylor.edu/psychologyneuroscience/index.php?id=72649

Bay Path University, Program in Clinical Mental Health Counseling, Longmeadow, MA 01106-2292. Offers clinical mental health counseling (MS), including alcohol and drug abuse counseling, early intervention. Program also offered in Sturbridge and Burlington, MA. *Program availability:* Part-time, blended/hybrid learning. *Students:* 68 full-time (59 women), 82 part-time (75 women); includes 42 minority (21 Black or African American, non-Hispanic/Latino; 19 Hispanic/Latino; 2 Two or more races, non-Hispanic/Latino), 11 international. Average age 32. In 2017, 21 master's awarded. *Degree requirements:* For master's, 48 course credits plus 12 credit practicum, internship. *Application deadline:* Applications are processed on a rolling basis. Application fee: $45. Electronic applications accepted. Application fee is waived when completed online. *Expenses:* $815 per credit. *Financial support:* Unspecified assistantships available. Financial award applicants required to submit FAFSA. *Unit head:* Dr. Mark Benander, Director, 413-565-1332, E-mail: mbenander@baypath.edu. *Application contact:* Diane Ranaldi, Dean of Graduate Admissions, 413-565-1332, Fax: 413-565-1250, E-mail: dranaldi@baypath.edu.
Website: http://graduate.baypath.edu/graduate-programs/programs-on-campus/ms-programs/clinical-mental-health

Benedictine University, Graduate Programs, Program in Clinical Psychology, Lisle, IL 60532. Offers MS. *Program availability:* Part-time. *Degree requirements:* For master's, comprehensive exam, internship. *Entrance requirements:* For master's, MAT. Additional exam requirements/recommendations for international students: Required—TOEFL (minimum score 550 paper-based). Electronic applications accepted.

Bethel Seminary, Graduate and Professional Programs, St. Paul, MN 55112-6998. Offers Anglican studies (Certificate); children's and family ministry (MA); Christian studies (Certificate); Christian thought (MA); church planting (Certificate); Greek and Hebrew language (M Div); Greek language (M Div); Hebrew language (M Div); marriage and family therapy (MA, Certificate); mental health counseling (MA); ministry (MA, D Min); ministry practice (Certificate); theological studies (MA, Certificate); transformational leadership (MA); young life youth ministry (Certificate). *Accreditation:* ACIPE. *Program availability:* Part-time, evening/weekend, 100% online, blended/hybrid learning. *Faculty:* 16 full-time (4 women), 31 part-time/adjunct (15 women). *Students:* 380 full-time (170 women), 167 part-time (55 women); includes 161 minority (65 Black or African American, non-Hispanic/Latino; 52 Asian, non-Hispanic/Latino; 31 Hispanic/Latino; 1 Native Hawaiian or other Pacific Islander, non-Hispanic/Latino; 12 Two or more races, non-Hispanic/Latino), 5 international. Average age 38. 356 applicants, 62% accepted, 156 enrolled. In 2017, 120 master's, 15 doctorates, 4 other advanced degrees awarded. *Degree requirements:* For master's, variable foreign language requirement, thesis (for some programs); for doctorate, thesis/dissertation. *Entrance requirements:* For master's, letters of reference, transcripts, personal statement; for doctorate, M Div, letters of reference, organizational support; for Certificate, letters of reference, family essay, personal statement, and family of origin paper (for marriage and family therapy). Additional exam requirements/recommendations for international students: Required—TOEFL (minimum score 550 paper-based; 87 iBT). *Application deadline:* For fall admission, 8/1 priority date for domestic students, 8/1 for international students; for winter admission, 12/1 priority date for domestic students; for spring admission, 1/1 priority date for domestic students. Applications are processed on a rolling basis. Application fee: $0. Electronic applications accepted. *Expenses:* Contact institution. *Financial support:* Teaching assistantships, career-related internships or fieldwork, Federal Work-Study, and scholarships/grants available. Financial award applicants required to submit FAFSA. *Faculty research:* Nature of theology, ethics, Biblical commentaries, nature of God, science and theology. *Unit head:* Dr. Randy Bergen, Associate Provost, 651-635-8000, E-mail: r-bergen@bethel.edu. *Application contact:* Director of Admissions, 651-638-8000, Fax: 651-638-6002, E-mail: seminary-admissions@bethel.edu.
Website: https://www.bethel.edu/seminary

Binghamton University, State University of New York, Graduate School, Harpur College of Arts and Sciences, Department of Psychology, Program in Psychology - Clinical Psychology, Binghamton, NY 13902-6000. Offers PhD. *Accreditation:* APA. *Program availability:* Part-time. *Students:* 21 full-time (16 women), 13 part-time (11 women); includes 5 minority (1 Black or African American, non-Hispanic/Latino; 1 Asian, non-Hispanic/Latino; 1 Hispanic/Latino; 2 Two or more races, non-Hispanic/Latino), 2 international. Average age 27. 97 applicants, 13% accepted, 7 enrolled. In 2017, 8 doctorates awarded. Terminal master's awarded for partial completion of doctoral program. *Degree requirements:* For doctorate, comprehensive exam, thesis/dissertation. *Entrance requirements:* For doctorate, GRE General Test. Additional exam requirements/recommendations for international students: Required—TOEFL (minimum score 550 paper-based; 80 iBT). *Application deadline:* For fall admission, 12/1 priority date for domestic and international students. Application fee: $75. Electronic applications accepted. *Financial support:* In 2017–18, 27 students received support, including 9 research assistantships with full tuition reimbursements available (averaging $17,500 per year), 13 teaching assistantships with full tuition reimbursements available (averaging $17,500 per year); career-related internships or fieldwork, Federal Work-Study, institutionally sponsored loans, scholarships/grants, traineeships, health care benefits, tuition waivers (full and partial), and unspecified assistantships also available. Financial award applicants required to submit FAFSA. *Unit head:* Dr. Brandon E. Gibb, Program Coordinator, 607-777-2511, E-mail: bgibb@binghamton.edu. *Application contact:* Ben Balkaya, Assistant Dean and Director, 607-777-2151, Fax: 607-777-2501, E-mail: balkaya@binghamton.edu.

Biola University, Rosemead School of Psychology, La Mirada, CA 90639-0001. Offers clinical psychology (PhD, Psy D). *Accreditation:* APA. *Faculty:* 24. *Students:* 122 full-time (92 women), 46 part-time (39 women); includes 69 minority (7 Black or African American, non-Hispanic/Latino; 1 American Indian or Alaska Native, non-Hispanic/Latino; 31 Asian, non-Hispanic/Latino; 23 Hispanic/Latino; 7 Two or more races, non-Hispanic/Latino), 3 international. 96 applicants, 41% accepted, 21 enrolled. In 2017, 19 doctorates awarded. *Degree requirements:* For doctorate, comprehensive exam, thesis/dissertation. *Entrance requirements:* For doctorate, GRE General Test, interview, 30 undergraduate semester hours of credits in psychology, minimum GPA of 3.0. Additional exam requirements/recommendations for international students: Required—TOEFL (minimum score 600 paper-based; 100 iBT). *Application deadline:* For fall admission, 12/1 priority date for domestic students, 12/1 for international students. Application fee: $65. Electronic applications accepted. *Expenses:* Contact institution. *Financial support:* Scholarships/grants and unspecified assistantships available. Financial award applicants required to submit FAFSA. *Faculty research:* Integration of psychology and theology, psychology of child/adolescent, psychology of marriage, psychology of gender, psychology of trauma, psychology of forensics, multi-cultural studies and mental health. *Unit head:* Dr. Clark Campbell, Dean, 562-903-4867, Fax: 562-903-4864. *Application contact:* Jon Garcia, Graduate Admissions Counselor, 562-903-4752, E-mail: graduate.admissions@biola.edu.
Website: http://www.rosemead.edu/

Bowling Green State University, Graduate College, College of Arts and Sciences, Department of Psychology, Bowling Green, OH 43403. Offers clinical psychology (MA, PhD); developmental psychology (MA, PhD); experimental psychology (MA, PhD); industrial/organizational psychology (MA, PhD); quantitative psychology (MA, PhD). *Accreditation:* APA (one or more programs are accredited). *Degree requirements:* For doctorate, thesis/dissertation. *Entrance requirements:* For doctorate, GRE General Test, GRE Subject Test. Additional exam requirements/recommendations for international students: Required—TOEFL. Electronic applications accepted. *Faculty research:* Personnel psychology, developmental-mathematical models, behavioral medication, brain process, child/adolescent social cognition.

Bowling Green State University, Graduate College, College of Education and Human Development, School of Intervention Services, Program in Clinical Mental Health Counseling, Bowling Green, OH 43403. Offers clinical mental health counseling (MA); school counseling (M Ed). *Accreditation:* ACA; NCATE. *Program availability:* Part-time. *Degree requirements:* For master's, thesis or alternative. *Entrance requirements:* For master's, GRE General Test. Additional exam requirements/recommendations for international students: Required—TOEFL. Electronic applications accepted. *Faculty research:* Perfectionism, multicultural counseling, suicide, ethics and legal issues related to counseling, play therapy.

Bradley University, The Graduate School, College of Education and Health Sciences, Department of Leadership in Education, Nonprofits and Counseling, Peoria, IL 61625-0002. Offers counseling (MA), including clinical mental health counseling, professional school counseling; leadership in educational administration (MA); nonprofit leadership (MA). *Accreditation:* ACA; NCATE. *Program availability:* Part-time, evening/weekend. *Degree requirements:* For master's, comprehensive exam, thesis optional. *Entrance requirements:* For master's, GRE General Test or MAT, interview, 3 letters of recommendation. Additional exam requirements/recommendations for international students: Required—TOEFL (minimum score 550 paper-based; 79 iBT), IELTS (minimum score 6.5). Electronic applications accepted.

Brigham Young University, Graduate Studies, College of Family, Home, and Social Sciences, Department of Psychology, Provo, UT 84602. Offers clinical psychology (PhD); cognitive and behavioral neuroscience (PhD). *Accreditation:* APA. *Faculty:* 31 full-time (8 women), 16 part-time/adjunct (7 women). *Students:* 59 full-time (33 women); includes 7 minority (2 Black or African American, non-Hispanic/Latino; 3 Asian, non-Hispanic/Latino; 1 Hispanic/Latino; 1 Native Hawaiian or other Pacific Islander, non-Hispanic/Latino), 4 international. Average age 29. 49 applicants, 33% accepted, 10 enrolled. In 2017, 11 doctorates awarded. *Degree requirements:* For doctorate, comprehensive exam (for some programs), thesis/dissertation, publishable paper. *Entrance requirements:* For doctorate, GRE General Test, minimum GPA of 3.0. Additional exam requirements/recommendations for international students: Required—TOEFL (minimum score 580 paper-based; 85 iBT). *Application deadline:* For fall admission, 12/1 for domestic and international students. Application fee: $50. Electronic applications accepted. *Expenses:* $10,320 per academic year for members of the Church of Jesus Christ of Latter-day Saints; $20,640 for those who are not members of the Church. *Financial support:* In 2017–18, 41 students received support, including 39 research assistantships with partial tuition reimbursements available (averaging $12,000 per year), 5 teaching assistantships with partial tuition reimbursements available (averaging $12,000 per year); career-related internships or fieldwork, scholarships/grants, tuition waivers (partial), and unspecified assistantships also available. Financial award application deadline: 5/31. *Faculty research:* Psychotherapy process, Alzheimer's disease/dementia, psychology and law, health, psychology, addiction. *Total annual research expenditures:* $711,243. *Unit head:* Dr. Dawson Hedges, Chair, 801-422-6357, Fax: 801-422-0602, E-mail: dawson_hedges@byu.edu. *Application contact:* Leesa D. Scott, Coordinator of Student Programs, 801-422-4560, Fax: 801-422-0602, E-mail: leesa_scott@byu.edu.
Website: http://psychology.byu.edu/

Butler University, College of Education, Indianapolis, IN 46208-3485. Offers applied educational neuroscience (Certificate); educational administration (MS); effective teaching and leadership (MS); licensed mental health counselor (Certificate); school counseling (MS); wellness and sport leadership (Certificate). *Accreditation:* ACA; NCATE. *Program availability:* Part-time. *Faculty:* 12 full-time (8 women), 10 part-time/adjunct (7 women). *Students:* 3 full-time (2 women), 131 part-time (102 women); includes 13 minority (7 Black or African American, non-Hispanic/Latino; 2 Asian, non-Hispanic/Latino; 2 Hispanic/Latino; 2 Two or more races, non-Hispanic/Latino). Average age 31. 65 applicants, 75% accepted, 41 enrolled. In 2017, 45 master's, 10 other advanced degrees awarded. *Degree requirements:* For master's, thesis. *Entrance requirements:* For master's, GRE (minimum score 291) or MAT (minimum score 396) unless undergraduate GPA is a 3.0 or higher, two letters of recommendation, transcripts, interview, professional resume. Additional exam requirements/recommendations for international students: Required—TOEFL (minimum score 550 paper-based; 79 iBT), IELTS (minimum score 6). *Application deadline:* For fall admission, 2/1 for domestic and international students; for spring admission, 11/1 for domestic and international students; for summer admission, 4/1 for domestic and international students. Applications are processed on a rolling basis. Application fee: $0. Electronic applications accepted. *Expenses:* $560 per credit. *Financial support:* In 2017–18, 64 students received support. Scholarships/grants, tuition waivers (full and partial), and unspecified assistantships available. Financial award application deadline: 7/15; financial award applicants required to submit FAFSA. *Faculty research:* Principals role in school improvement, leadership and school climate, retention of teachers in special education, the neuro-diversity brain, school counseling intervention. *Unit head:* Dr. Ena Shelley, Dean, 317-940-9752, Fax: 317-940-6481. *Application contact:* Diane Dubord, Graduate Student Services Specialist, 317-940-8100, Fax: 317-940-8250, E-mail: ddubord@butler.edu.
Website: https://www.butler.edu/coe/graduate-programs

California Institute of Integral Studies, School of Professional Psychology and Health, San Francisco, CA 94103. Offers clinical psychology (Psy D); community mental health

(MA); drama therapy (MA); expressive arts therapy (MA); integral counseling psychology (MA); integrative health studies (MA); psychological studies (MA); somatic psychology (MA). *Program availability:* Part-time, evening/weekend, 100% online, blended/hybrid learning. *Students:* 507 full-time (401 women), 96 part-time (77 women); includes 167 minority (29 Black or African American, non-Hispanic/Latino; 3 American Indian or Alaska Native, non-Hispanic/Latino; 32 Asian, non-Hispanic/Latino; 62 Hispanic/Latino; 2 Native Hawaiian or other Pacific Islander, non-Hispanic/Latino; 39 Two or more races, non-Hispanic/Latino), 60 international. Average age 34. 302 applicants, 89% accepted, 171 enrolled. In 2017, 194 master's, 18 doctorates awarded. *Degree requirements:* For doctorate, comprehensive exam, thesis/dissertation. *Entrance requirements:* For master's, minimum GPA of 3.0, letters of recommendation, writing sample; for doctorate, GRE, MA in psychology or social work with appropriate practical experience for advanced standing, or BA with a minimum GPA of 3.1; letters of recommendation; writing sample. Additional exam requirements/recommendations for international students: Required—TOEFL. *Application deadline:* For fall admission, 2/1 priority date for domestic and international students; for spring admission, 10/15 priority date for domestic and international students. Applications are processed on a rolling basis. Application fee: $65. Electronic applications accepted. *Expenses:* $21,400 (for MA); $32,734 (for PsyD). *Financial support:* Research assistantships with tuition reimbursements, teaching assistantships with tuition reimbursements, career-related internships or fieldwork, Federal Work-Study, and scholarships/grants available. Support available to part-time students. Financial award application deadline: 4/15; financial award applicants required to submit FAFSA. *Faculty research:* Transpersonal psychology, somatic psychology, expressive arts therapy, drama therapy, community mental health, ecopsychology, integrative health, human sexuality. *Unit head:* Nicolle Zapien, Academic Dean, 415-575-5577, E-mail: nzapien@ciis.edu. *Application contact:* Ellen Durst, Director of Admissions, 415-575-6100, Fax: 415-575-1268, E-mail: admissions@ciis.edu.

California Lutheran University, Graduate Studies, Department of Psychology, Thousand Oaks, CA 91360-2787. Offers clinical psychology (MS, Psy D); marital and family therapy (MS). *Accreditation:* APA. *Program availability:* Part-time. *Faculty:* 10 full-time (6 women), 19 part-time/adjunct (15 women). *Students:* 155 full-time (122 women), 35 part-time (10 women); includes 72 minority (4 Black or African American, non-Hispanic/Latino; 3 American Indian or Alaska Native, non-Hispanic/Latino; 4 Asian, non-Hispanic/Latino; 57 Hispanic/Latino; 4 Two or more races, non-Hispanic/Latino), 6 international. Average age 30. 261 applicants, 46% accepted, 66 enrolled. In 2017, 37 master's, 7 doctorates awarded. *Degree requirements:* For master's, thesis or comprehensive exams; for doctorate, thesis/dissertation, internship. *Entrance requirements:* For master's, GRE General Test, interview, minimum GPA of 3.0; for doctorate, GRE General Test. *Application deadline:* For fall admission, 12/1 priority date for domestic and international students. Applications are processed on a rolling basis. Application fee: $50. Electronic applications accepted. *Expenses:* *Tuition:* Full-time $15,000. Full-time tuition and fees vary according to degree level and program. *Unit head:* Dr. Richard Holigrock, Dean, 805-493-3723. *Application contact:* 805-493-3325, Fax: 805-493-3861, E-mail: clugrad@callutheran.edu.

California State University, Dominguez Hills, College of Natural and Behavioral Sciences, Department of Psychology, Carson, CA 90747-0001. Offers clinical psychology (MA); health psychology (MA). *Program availability:* Part-time, evening/weekend. Terminal master's awarded for partial completion of doctoral program. *Degree requirements:* For master's, comprehensive exam, thesis optional. *Entrance requirements:* For master's, GRE General Test or MAT, interview, minimum GPA of 3.0, prerequisite psychology courses. Additional exam requirements/recommendations for international students: Required—TOEFL (minimum score 550 paper-based). Electronic applications accepted. *Faculty research:* Culture and health, neuropsychology and HIV, psychohistory of the Holocaust, community and adolescents, malingering.

California State University, Fullerton, Graduate Studies, College of Humanities and Social Sciences, Department of Psychology, Fullerton, CA 92831-3599. Offers clinical psychology (MS); psychology (MA). *Program availability:* Part-time. *Faculty:* 20 full-time (14 women), 2 part-time/adjunct (both women). *Students:* 65 full-time (48 women), 11 part-time (8 women); includes 35 minority (3 Black or African American, non-Hispanic/Latino; 7 Asian, non-Hispanic/Latino; 22 Hispanic/Latino; 3 Two or more races, non-Hispanic/Latino), 3 international. Average age 26. 155 applicants, 19% accepted, 27 enrolled. *Entrance requirements:* For master's, GRE General Test, GRE Subject Test, undergraduate major in psychology or related field. Application fee: $55. *Financial support:* Career-related internships or fieldwork, Federal Work-Study, institutionally sponsored loans, and scholarships/grants available. Support available to part-time students. Financial award application deadline: 3/1; financial award applicants required to submit FAFSA. *Unit head:* Eriko Self, Chair, 657-278-3514, Fax: 657-278-7134. *Application contact:* Admissions/Applications, 657-278-2371.

California State University, Northridge, Graduate Studies, College of Social and Behavioral Sciences, Department of Psychology, Northridge, CA 91330. Offers clinical psychology (MA); general experimental psychology (MA). *Students:* 46 full-time (36 women), 7 part-time (4 women); includes 25 minority (2 Black or African American, non-Hispanic/Latino; 4 Asian, non-Hispanic/Latino; 18 Hispanic/Latino; 1 Two or more races, non-Hispanic/Latino), 1 international. Average age 25. 263 applicants, 27% accepted, 23 enrolled. In 2017, 55 master's awarded. *Degree requirements:* For master's, thesis. *Entrance requirements:* For master's, GRE General Test, GRE Subject Test, minimum GPA of 3.0, letters of recommendation. Additional exam requirements/recommendations for international students: Required—TOEFL. *Application deadline:* For fall admission, 11/30 for domestic students. Application fee: $55. *Financial support:* Application deadline: 3/1. *Unit head:* Jill Razani, Chair, 818-677-3506.
Website: http://www.csun.edu/csbs/departments/psychology/index.html

California State University, San Bernardino, Graduate Studies, College of Social and Behavioral Sciences, Department of Psychology, San Bernardino, CA 92407. Offers child development (MA); clinical/counseling psychology (MS); industrial/organizational psychology (MS); psychological science (MA). *Faculty:* 13 full-time (4 women), 2 part-time/adjunct (both women). *Students:* 61 full-time (41 women), 17 part-time (14 women); includes 47 minority (2 Black or African American, non-Hispanic/Latino; 3 Asian, non-Hispanic/Latino; 33 Hispanic/Latino; 9 Two or more races, non-Hispanic/Latino), 3 international. Average age 28. 190 applicants, 19% accepted, 33 enrolled. In 2017, 28 master's awarded. *Degree requirements:* For master's, comprehensive exam, thesis (for some programs). *Entrance requirements:* Additional exam requirements/recommendations for international students: Required—TOEFL. Application fee: $55. *Financial support:* Fellowships, research assistantships, and teaching assistantships available. *Faculty research:* Perceptual development, human memory, psychopharmacology, psychology of women, language acquisition. *Unit head:* Dr. Robert Ricco, Chair, 909-537-5485, Fax: 909-537-7003, E-mail: rricco@csusb.edu. *Application contact:* Dr. Dorota Huizinga, Dean of Graduate Studies, 909-537-3064, E-mail: dorota.huizinga@csusb.edu.
Website: https://csbs.csusb.edu/psychology

California University of Pennsylvania, School of Graduate Studies and Research, College of Education and Human Services, Department of Counselor Education, California, PA 15419-1394. Offers clinical mental health counseling (MS); school counseling (M Ed). *Accreditation:* ACA; NCATE. *Program availability:* Part-time, evening/weekend. *Degree requirements:* For master's, comprehensive exam, thesis optional. *Entrance requirements:* For master's, MAT, minimum GPA of 3.0, resume, letters of reference. Additional exam requirements/recommendations for international students: Required—TOEFL (minimum score 550 paper-based; 80 iBT). *Application deadline:* For fall admission, 8/1 priority date for domestic and international students. Applications are processed on a rolling basis. Application fee: $25. Electronic applications accepted. *Financial support:* Applicants required to submit FAFSA. *Faculty research:* Mind-body theories and practice, grief issues, career development, supervision, sports counseling. *Unit head:* Dr. Grafton Eliason, Program Coordinator, 724-938-4464, E-mail: eliason@calu.edu. *Application contact:* Suzanne C. Powers, Director of Graduate Admissions and Recruitment, 724-938-4029, Fax: 724-938-5712, E-mail: powers_s@cup.edu.
Website: http://www.calu.edu/academics/colleges/education/counselor-education/

Capella University, Harold Abel School of Social and Behavioral Science, Doctoral Programs in Psychology, Minneapolis, MN 55402. Offers addiction psychology (PhD); clinical psychology (Psy D); educational psychology (PhD); general advanced studies in human behavior (PhD); general psychology (PhD); industrial/organizational psychology (PhD); school psychology (Psy D).

Capella University, Harold Abel School of Social and Behavioral Science, Master's Programs in Psychology, Minneapolis, MN 55402. Offers applied behavior analysis (MS); clinical psychology (MS); counseling psychology (MS); educational psychology (MS); evaluation, research, and measurement (MS); general advanced studies in human behavior (MS); general psychology (MS); industrial/organizational psychology (MS); leadership coaching psychology (MS); school psychology (MS); sport psychology (MS).

Cardinal Stritch University, College of Arts and Sciences, Department of Psychology, Milwaukee, WI 53217-3985. Offers clinical psychology (MA). *Program availability:* Part-time, evening/weekend. *Students:* 23 full-time (17 women), 13 part-time (12 women); includes 9 minority (3 Black or African American, non-Hispanic/Latino; 2 American Indian or Alaska Native, non-Hispanic/Latino; 1 Asian, non-Hispanic/Latino; 2 Hispanic/Latino; 1 Two or more races, non-Hispanic/Latino), 10 international. Average age 26. 70 applicants, 100% accepted, 14 enrolled. In 2017, 12 master's awarded. *Degree requirements:* For master's, thesis, portfolio, clinical practicum. *Entrance requirements:* For master's, interview, minimum GPA of 3.0, 3 letters of recommendation. Additional exam requirements/recommendations for international students: Required—TOEFL (minimum score 79 iBT), IELTS (minimum score 6.5). *Application deadline:* For fall admission, 7/15 priority date for domestic students; for spring admission, 12/15 priority date for domestic students. Applications are processed on a rolling basis. Electronic applications accepted. *Expenses:* $782 per credit. *Financial support:* Research assistantships with partial tuition reimbursements, career-related internships or fieldwork, Federal Work-Study, and scholarships/grants available. Financial award applicants required to submit FAFSA. *Unit head:* Dr. Trevor Hyde, Chair, 414-410-4489, E-mail: tfhyde@stritch.edu. *Application contact:* Graduate Admissions, 800-347-8822 Ext. 4042, E-mail: admissions@stritch.edu.

Carlos Albizu University, Graduate Programs, San Juan, PR 00901. Offers clinical psychology (MS, PhD, Psy D); general psychology (PhD); industrial/organizational psychology (MS, PhD); speech and language pathology (MS). *Accreditation:* APA (one or more programs are accredited). *Program availability:* Part-time, evening/weekend. Terminal master's awarded for partial completion of doctoral program. *Degree requirements:* For master's, one foreign language, comprehensive exam, thesis; for doctorate, one foreign language, comprehensive exam, thesis/dissertation, written qualifying exams. *Entrance requirements:* For master's, GRE General Test or EXADEP, interview; minimum GPA of 2.8 (industrial/organizational psychology); for doctorate, GRE General Test or EXADEP, interview; minimum GPA of 3.0 (PhD in industrial/organizational psychology and clinical psychology), 3.25 (Psy D). *Faculty research:* Psychotherapeutic techniques for Hispanics, psychology of the aged, school dropouts, stress, violence.

Carlos Albizu University, Miami Campus, Graduate Programs, Miami, FL 33172-2209. Offers clinical psychology (PhD, Psy D); entrepreneurship (MBA); exceptional student education (MS); human services (PhD); industrial/organizational psychology (MS); marriage and family therapy (MS); mental health counseling (MS); nonprofit management (MBA); organizational management (MBA); psychology (MS); speech and language pathology (MS); teaching English for speakers of other languages (MS). *Accreditation:* APA. *Program availability:* Part-time, evening/weekend, 100% online, blended/hybrid learning. *Faculty:* 32 full-time (24 women), 27 part-time/adjunct (15 women). *Students:* 411 full-time (345 women), 248 part-time (215 women); includes 562 minority (53 Black or African American, non-Hispanic/Latino; 4 Asian, non-Hispanic/Latino; 498 Hispanic/Latino; 7 Two or more races, non-Hispanic/Latino), 23 international. Average age 34. 391 applicants, 42% accepted, 154 enrolled. In 2017, 96 master's, 54 doctorates awarded. Terminal master's awarded for partial completion of doctoral program. *Degree requirements:* For master's, comprehensive exam (for some programs), integrative project (for MBA); research project (for exceptional student education, teaching English as a second language); for doctorate, comprehensive examinations, internship, project/dissertation. *Entrance requirements:* For master's, GRE/EXADEP, bachelor's degree from accredited institution, minimum GPA of 3.0, 3 letters of recommendation, interview, resume, statement of purpose, official transcripts; for doctorate, GRE (for Psy D), 3 letters of recommendation, resume, interview, statement of purpose, official transcripts; bachelor's degree and minimum GPA of 3.25 (for Psy D); master's degree and minimum GPA of 3.0 (for PhD). Additional exam requirements/recommendations for international students: Required—Michigan Test of English Language Proficiency. *Application deadline:* For fall admission, 4/1 priority date for domestic students, 5/1 priority date for international students; for spring admission, 11/1 priority date for domestic students, 9/1 priority date for international students. Applications are processed on a rolling basis. Application fee: $50. Electronic applications accepted. Application fee is waived when completed online. *Expenses:* Contact institution. *Financial support:* In 2017–18, 145 students received support. Federal Work-Study, scholarships/grants, unspecified assistantships, and tuition discounts available. Financial award application deadline: 6/1; financial award applicants required to submit FAFSA. *Faculty research:* Psychotherapy, forensic psychology, neuropsychology, special education, speech-language pathology, criminal justice. *Unit head:* Dr. Etiony Aldarondo, Provost, 305-593-1223 Ext. 3138, Fax: 305-592-7930, E-mail: ealdarondo@albizu.edu. *Application contact:* Sonia Feliciano, Institutional Director of Student Recruitment, 305-593-1223 Ext. 3108, Fax: 305-477-8983, E-mail: sfeliciano@albizu.edu.

Case Western Reserve University, School of Graduate Studies, Psychological Sciences Department, Program in Clinical Psychology, Cleveland, OH 44106. Offers PhD. *Accreditation:* APA. *Program availability:* Part-time. *Faculty:* 7 full-time (4 women). *Students:* 28 full-time (21 women); includes 4 minority (1 Black or African American, non-Hispanic/Latino; 1 Asian, non-Hispanic/Latino; 2 Hispanic/Latino). Average age 28. 165 applicants, 4% accepted, 5 enrolled. In 2017, 6 doctorates awarded. *Degree requirements:* For doctorate, thesis/dissertation, internship. *Entrance requirements:* For doctorate, GRE General Test, GRE Subject Test, personal statement; curriculum vitae;

three letters of recommendation. Additional exam requirements/recommendations for international students: Required—TOEFL (minimum score 577 paper-based; 90 iBT); Recommended—IELTS (minimum score 7). *Application deadline:* For fall admission, 12/1 priority date for domestic students. Application fee: $50. Electronic applications accepted. *Expenses: Tuition:* Full-time $43,854; part-time $1827 per credit hour. *Required fees:* $50; $50 per credit hour. Tuition and fees vary according to course load and program. *Financial support:* Fellowships, research assistantships, and teaching assistantships available. Financial award application deadline: 12/1; financial award applicants required to submit FAFSA. *Faculty research:* Pediatric psychology, family functioning, depression, geriatric psychopathology, creativity and play. *Unit head:* Dr. Heath Demaree, Professor and Chair, 216-368-6468, E-mail: psychsciences@case.edu. *Application contact:* Dr. Norah Feeny, Director of Clinical Training, 216-368-2695, E-mail: psychsciences@case.edu.
Website: http://psychsciences.case.edu/graduate/

The Catholic University of America, School of Arts and Sciences, Department of Psychology, Washington, DC 20064. Offers applied experimental psychology (PhD); clinical psychology (PhD); general psychology (MA); human development psychology (PhD); human factors (MA); MA/JD. MA/JD offered jointly with Columbus School of Law. *Accreditation:* APA (one or more programs are accredited). *Program availability:* Part-time. *Faculty:* 11 full-time (6 women), 9 part-time/adjunct (3 women). *Students:* 38 full-time (27 women), 33 part-time (25 women); includes 22 minority (4 Black or African American, non-Hispanic/Latino; 4 Asian, non-Hispanic/Latino; 5 Hispanic/Latino; 9 Two or more races, non-Hispanic/Latino), 6 international. Average age 29. 183 applicants, 26% accepted, 21 enrolled. In 2017, 18 master's, 9 doctorates awarded. *Degree requirements:* For master's, comprehensive exam, thesis (for some programs); for doctorate, comprehensive exam, thesis/dissertation. *Entrance requirements:* For master's, GRE General Test, statement of purpose, official copies of academic transcripts, three letters of recommendation; for doctorate, GRE General Test, GRE Subject Test, statement of purpose, official copies of academic transcripts, three letters of recommendation. Additional exam requirements/recommendations for international students: Required—TOEFL (minimum score 550 paper-based; 80 iBT). *Application deadline:* For fall admission, 7/15 priority date for domestic students, 7/1 for international students; for spring admission, 11/15 priority date for domestic students, 11/1 for international students. Applications are processed on a rolling basis. Application fee: $55. Electronic applications accepted. *Expenses:* Contact institution. *Financial support:* Fellowships, research assistantships, teaching assistantships, Federal Work-Study, scholarships/grants, tuition waivers (full and partial), and unspecified assistantships available. Financial award application deadline: 2/1; financial award applicants required to submit FAFSA. *Faculty research:* Clinical psychology, applied cognitive science, psychopathology, cognitive neuroscience, psychotherapy. *Total annual research expenditures:* $243,144. *Unit head:* Dr. Marc M. Sebrechts, Chair, 202-319-5750, Fax: 202-319-6263, E-mail: sebrechts@cua.edu. *Application contact:* Dr. Steven Brown, Director of Graduate Admissions, 202-319-5057, Fax: 202-319-6533, E-mail: cua-admissions@cua.edu.
Website: http://psychology.cua.edu/

Central Michigan University, College of Graduate Studies, College of Humanities and Social and Behavioral Sciences, Department of Psychology, Program in Clinical Psychology, Mount Pleasant, MI 48859. Offers PhD. *Accreditation:* APA. *Degree requirements:* For doctorate, thesis/dissertation. *Entrance requirements:* For doctorate, GRE. Electronic applications accepted. *Faculty research:* Applied youth development; emotional processes, personality disorders, and assessment; influence of affective variables on cognitive performance; post-traumatic stress disorder and panic disorder; validation of clinical inferences from psychological tests.

Chestnut Hill College, School of Graduate Studies, Division of Psychology, Program in Clinical and Counseling Psychology, Philadelphia, PA 19118-2693. Offers clinical and counseling psychology (MS, CAS), including child and adolescent therapy, child and adolescent therapy with autism spectrum disorders, co-occurring disorders, couple and family therapy, diverse and underserved communities, generalist (MS), trauma studies. *Program availability:* Part-time, evening/weekend. *Degree requirements:* For master's, thesis optional, practica. *Entrance requirements:* For master's, GRE General Test, writing sample, letters of recommendation. Additional exam requirements/recommendations for international students: Required—TOEFL (minimum score 500 paper-based), IELTS (minimum score 6.0), or TWE (minimum score 22). Electronic applications accepted. *Expenses:* Contact institution. *Faculty research:* Play therapy, eating disorders, addictions, group psychology and group therapy, health psychology.

Chestnut Hill College, School of Graduate Studies, Division of Psychology, Program in Clinical Psychology, Philadelphia, PA 19118-2693. Offers clinical psychology (Psy D), including clinical psychology, couple and family therapy, psychological assessment. *Accreditation:* APA. *Program availability:* Part-time, evening/weekend. *Degree requirements:* For doctorate, comprehensive exam, thesis/dissertation, internship, practica, clinical competency exam. *Entrance requirements:* For doctorate, GRE General Test, letters of recommendation, writing sample, master's degree in clinical/counseling psychology or closely-related field. Additional exam requirements/recommendations for international students: Required—TOEFL (minimum score 500 paper-based), IELTS (minimum score 6.0), or TWE (minimum score 22). Electronic applications accepted. *Expenses:* Contact institution. *Faculty research:* Psychological testing and assessment, LGBT issues, autism and developmental disorders, stepfamilies, gender issues.

The Chicago School of Professional Psychology, Program in Clinical Forensic Psychology, Chicago, IL 60610. Offers Psy D. *Degree requirements:* For doctorate, thesis/dissertation. *Entrance requirements:* For doctorate, GRE. Additional exam requirements/recommendations for international students: Required—TOEFL, IELTS.

The Chicago School of Professional Psychology, Program in Clinical Mental Health Counseling, Chicago, IL 60610. Offers MA. *Program availability:* Part-time.

The Chicago School of Professional Psychology, Program in Clinical Psychology, Chicago, IL 60610. Offers Psy D. *Accreditation:* APA. *Degree requirements:* For doctorate, comprehensive exam, thesis/dissertation. *Entrance requirements:* For doctorate, GRE, 18 hours of psychology credit (including courses in statistics, normal psychology and human development); minimum GPA of 3.2. Additional exam requirements/recommendations for international students: Required—TOEFL. Electronic applications accepted.

The Chicago School of Professional Psychology at Downtown Los Angeles, Program in Clinical Forensic Psychology, Los Angeles, CA 90017. Offers Psy D.

The Chicago School of Professional Psychology at Downtown Los Angeles, Program in Clinical Psychology, Los Angeles, CA 90017. Offers applied behavior analysis (MA); clinical psychology (Psy D); marital and family therapy (MA).

The Chicago School of Professional Psychology at Irvine, Program in Clinical Forensic Psychology, Irvine, CA 92612. Offers Psy D.

The Chicago School of Professional Psychology: Online, Program in Clinical Psychopharmacology, Chicago, IL 60654. Offers MS. *Program availability:* Online learning.

Chicago State University, School of Graduate and Professional Studies, College of Arts and Sciences, Department of Psychology, Chicago, IL 60628. Offers counseling (MA), including bilingual specialization, clinical mental health counseling, school counseling. *Accreditation:* ACA; NCATE. *Degree requirements:* For master's, comprehensive exam, thesis optional. *Entrance requirements:* For master's, minimum GPA of 3.0 for last 60 semester hours of course work or essay; interview. *Application deadline:* For fall admission, 3/1 for domestic students; for spring admission, 10/15 for domestic students. Application fee: $30. *Unit head:* Karen McCurtis-Witherspoon, Director of Counseling Graduate Program, 773-995-2359, Fax: 773-995-3513, E-mail: kmccurti@csu.edu. *Application contact:* Anika Miller, Graduate Studies Office, 773-995-2404, E-mail: g-studies1@csu.edu.
Website: http://www.csu.edu/cas/psychology/

City College of the City University of New York, Graduate School, Colin Powell School for Civic and Global Leadership, Department of Psychology, New York, NY 10031-9198. Offers clinical psychology (PhD); general psychology (MA); mental health counseling (MA). PhD program offered jointly with Graduate School and University Center of the City University of New York. *Accreditation:* APA (one or more programs are accredited). *Program availability:* Part-time. *Degree requirements:* For master's, one foreign language, comprehensive exam, thesis. *Entrance requirements:* For master's, GRE. Additional exam requirements/recommendations for international students: Required—TOEFL (minimum score 550 paper-based; 79 iBT). Electronic applications accepted. *Faculty research:* Social/personality psychology, physiological psychology, cognition and development.

Clark University, Graduate School, Hiatt School of Psychology, Program in Clinical Psychology, Worcester, MA 01610-1477. Offers PhD. *Accreditation:* APA. *Students:* 22 full-time (17 women), 1 (woman) part-time; includes 6 minority (1 Black or African American, non-Hispanic/Latino; 1 Asian, non-Hispanic/Latino; 4 Hispanic/Latino). Average age 28. *Entrance requirements:* For doctorate, GRE General Test. Additional exam requirements/recommendations for international students: Required—TOEFL. *Application deadline:* For fall admission, 12/15 priority date for domestic and international students. Applications are processed on a rolling basis. Application fee: $75. *Financial support:* Fellowships, research assistantships, teaching assistantships, and tuition waivers (full) available. *Faculty research:* Marital relations and interventions, adult emotional development, Latino men and depression, violence prevention. *Unit head:* Dr. Wendy Grolnick, 508-793-7276, E-mail: wgrolnick@clarku.edu.
Website: http://www.clarku.edu/departments/psychology/grad/clinical/index.cfm

Clayton State University, School of Graduate Studies, College of Arts and Sciences, Program in Psychology, Morrow, GA 30260-0285. Offers applied developmental psychology (MS); clinical/counseling psychology (MS). *Entrance requirements:* For master's, GRE, 2 official transcripts; 3 letters of recommendation; statement of purpose; on-campus interview; background check. Additional exam requirements/recommendations for international students: Required—TOEFL (minimum score 550 paper-based). Electronic applications accepted.

Clemson University, Graduate School, College of Education, Department of Education and Human Development, Clemson, SC 29634. Offers counselor education (M Ed, Ed S), including mental health counseling, school counseling, student affairs (M Ed); learning sciences (PhD); literacy (M Ed); literacy, language and culture (PhD); special education (M Ed, MAT, PhD). *Program availability:* Part-time, evening/weekend, 100% online. *Faculty:* 32 full-time (22 women). *Students:* 445 full-time (355 women), 169 part-time (159 women); includes 126 minority (52 Black or African American, non-Hispanic/Latino; 16 Asian, non-Hispanic/Latino; 34 Hispanic/Latino; 24 Two or more races, non-Hispanic/Latino), 5 international. Average age 28. 401 applicants, 60% accepted, 135 enrolled. In 2017, 212 master's, 1 doctorate, 117 other advanced degrees awarded. *Degree requirements:* For master's, thesis (for some programs); for doctorate, comprehensive exam (for some programs), thesis/dissertation. *Entrance requirements:* For master's and doctorate, GRE General Test, unofficial transcripts, letters of recommendation. Additional exam requirements/recommendations for international students: Required—TOEFL (minimum score 80 iBT), IELTS (minimum score 7), PTE (minimum score 54). *Application deadline:* For fall admission, 3/1 priority date for domestic and international students; for spring admission, 10/1 priority date for domestic and international students. Applications are processed on a rolling basis. Application fee: $80 ($90 for international students). Electronic applications accepted. *Expenses:* $5,174 per semester full-time resident, $9,714 per semester full-time non-resident, $511 per credit hour part-time resident, $1,017 per credit hour part-time non-resident; $741 per credit hour online; other fees may apply per session. *Financial support:* In 2017–18, 84 students received support, including 9 fellowships with partial tuition reimbursements available (averaging $8,148 per year), 18 teaching assistantships with partial tuition reimbursements available (averaging $13,707 per year); career-related internships or fieldwork and unspecified assistantships also available. Financial award application deadline: 3/1. *Total annual research expenditures:* $1.2 million. *Unit head:* Dr. Debi Switzer, Department Chair, 864-656-5098, E-mail: debi@clemson.edu. *Application contact:* Julie Jones, Student Services Program Coordinator, 864-656-5096, E-mail: jgambre@clemson.edu.
Website: http://www.clemson.edu/education/departments/education-human-development/index.html

College of St. Joseph, Graduate Programs, Division of Psychology and Human Services, Program in Clinical Mental Health Counseling, Rutland, VT 05701-3899. Offers MS. *Program availability:* Part-time. *Degree requirements:* For master's, comprehensive exam. *Entrance requirements:* For master's, official college transcripts; 2 letters of reference. Additional exam requirements/recommendations for international students: Required—TOEFL (minimum score 550 paper-based). Electronic applications accepted.

College of St. Joseph, Graduate Programs, Division of Psychology and Human Services, Program in Clinical Psychology, Rutland, VT 05701-3899. Offers MS. *Program availability:* Part-time, evening/weekend. *Degree requirements:* For master's, comprehensive exam, thesis optional. *Entrance requirements:* For master's, official college transcripts; 2 letters of reference. Additional exam requirements/recommendations for international students: Required—TOEFL (minimum score 550 paper-based). Electronic applications accepted.

College of Staten Island of the City University of New York, Graduate Programs, Division of Humanities and Social Sciences, Program in Clinical Mental Health Counseling, Staten Island, NY 10314-6600. Offers clinical mental health counseling (MA). *Faculty:* 5 full-time, 5 part-time/adjunct. *Students:* 64. 89 applicants, 34% accepted, 24 enrolled. In 2017, 16 master's awarded. *Degree requirements:* For master's, 16 required courses, practicum, three internship courses. *Entrance requirements:* For master's, BA/BS with minimum GPA of 3.0 and 15-19 credits in certain areas of psychology; 2 letters of recommendation; 1-2 page statement of experience and interest in the field. Additional exam requirements/recommendations for international students: Required—TOEFL (minimum score 600 paper-based; 100 iBT), IELTS (minimum score 7). *Application deadline:* For fall admission, 3/10 for domestic and international students. Applications are processed on a rolling basis. Application fee: $125. Electronic applications accepted. *Expenses:* Tuition, state resident: full-time $10,450; part-time $440 per credit. Tuition, nonresident: full-time $19,320; part-time

$440 per credit. *Required fees:* $181.10 per semester. Tuition and fees vary according to program. *Faculty research:* Child psychopathology, HIV/AIDS counseling, elder care and cognition, psychosocial burn rehabilitation, autism spectrum disorders. *Unit head:* Dr. Frances Melendez, Graduate Program Coordinator, 718-982-3960, E-mail: frances.melendez@csi.cuny.edu. *Application contact:* Sasha Spence, Associate Director for Graduate Admissions, 718-982-2019, Fax: 718-982-2500, E-mail: sasha.spence@csi.cuny.edu.
Website: https://www.csi.cuny.edu/sites/default/files/pdf/admissions/grad/pdf/Clinical%20Mental%20Health%20Counseling%20Fact%20Sheet.pdf

Columbus State University, Graduate Studies, College of Education and Health Professions, Department of Counseling, Foundations, and Leadership, Columbus, GA 31907-5645. Offers clinical mental health counseling (MS); curriculum and leadership (Ed D), including curriculum, educational leadership, higher education (M Ed, Ed D); educational leadership (M Ed, Ed S), including higher education (M Ed, Ed D); school counseling (M Ed, Ed S). *Accreditation:* ACA; NCATE. *Program availability:* Part-time, evening/weekend, 100% online, blended/hybrid learning. *Faculty:* 18 full-time (8 women), 20 part-time/adjunct (10 women). *Students:* 248 full-time (166 women), 308 part-time (236 women); includes 315 minority (278 Black or African American, non-Hispanic/Latino; 11 Asian, non-Hispanic/Latino; 15 Hispanic/Latino; 1 Native Hawaiian or other Pacific Islander, non-Hispanic/Latino; 10 Two or more races, non-Hispanic/Latino), 2 international. Average age 39. 155 applicants, 38% accepted, 40 enrolled. In 2017, 41 master's, 18 doctorates, 110 other advanced degrees awarded. *Degree requirements:* For master's, thesis, exit exam; for doctorate, comprehensive exam, thesis/dissertation; for Ed S, thesis or alternative. *Entrance requirements:* For master's, GRE General Test, minimum undergraduate GPA of 2.75; for doctorate, GRE General Test, minimum graduate GPA of 3.5, four years of professional service; for Ed S, GRE General Test, minimum undergraduate GPA of 2.75, graduate 3.0. Additional exam requirements/recommendations for international students: Required—TOEFL (minimum score 550 paper-based; 79 iBT). *Application deadline:* For fall admission, 6/30 for domestic and international students; for spring admission, 11/1 for domestic and international students; for summer admission, 3/1 for domestic and international students. Applications are processed on a rolling basis. Application fee: $50. Electronic applications accepted. *Expenses:* Tuition, state resident: full-time $3708; part-time $2472 per year. Tuition, nonresident: full-time $14,418; part-time $9612 per year. *International tuition:* $19,218 full-time. *Required fees:* $1605. Tuition and fees vary according to program. *Financial support:* In 2017–18, 34 students received support, including 14 research assistantships with partial tuition reimbursements available (averaging $3,000 per year); career-related internships or fieldwork, Federal Work-Study, institutionally sponsored loans, scholarships/grants, tuition waivers (partial), and unspecified assistantships also available. Support available to part-time students. Financial award application deadline: 5/1; financial award applicants required to submit FAFSA. *Unit head:* Dr. Tom Hackett, Department Chair, 706-507-8968, Fax: 706-569-3134, E-mail: hackett_paul@columbusstate.edu. *Application contact:* Catrina Smith-Edmond, Assistant Director for Graduate and Global Admission, 706-507-8824, Fax: 706-568-5091, E-mail: smithedmond_catrina@columbusstate.edu.
Website: http://cfl.columbusstate.edu/

Concordia University, School of Graduate Studies, Faculty of Arts and Science, Department of Psychology, PhD Program in Psychology, Montréal, QC H3G 1M8, Canada. Offers PhD, Certificate. *Degree requirements:* For doctorate, comprehensive exam, thesis/dissertation. *Entrance requirements:* For doctorate, master's degree in psychology. *Faculty research:* Developmental-clinical psychology, sensory deficits, sexual dysfunction.

Dalhousie University, Faculty of Science, Department of Psychology, Halifax, NS B3H 4R2, Canada. Offers clinical psychology (PhD); psychology (M Sc, PhD); psychology/neuroscience (M Sc, PhD). *Degree requirements:* For master's, thesis; for doctorate, thesis/dissertation. *Entrance requirements:* For doctorate, GRE General Test. Additional exam requirements/recommendations for international students: Required—TOEFL, IELTS, CANTEST, CAEL, or Michigan English Language Assessment Battery. Electronic applications accepted. *Faculty research:* Physiological psychology, psychology of learning, learning and behavior, forensic clinical health psychology, development perception and cognition.

DePaul University, College of Education, Chicago, IL 60614. Offers bilingual-bicultural education (M Ed, MA); counseling (M Ed, MA), including clinical mental health counseling, college student development, school counseling; curriculum studies (M Ed, MA, Ed D); early childhood education (M Ed, MA, Ed D); educational leadership (M Ed, MA, Ed D), including Catholic leadership (M Ed, MA), general (M Ed, MA), higher education (M Ed, MA), physical education (M Ed, MA), principal preparation (M Ed), teacher preparation (M Ed); elementary education (M Ed, MA); middle grades education (M Ed); middle school mathematics education (MS); reading specialist (M Ed, MA); secondary education (M Ed, MA); social and cultural foundations in education (M Ed, MA); special education (M Ed); sport, fitness and recreation leadership (MS); value-creating education for global citizenship (M Ed); world languages education (M Ed, MA). *Program availability:* Part-time, evening/weekend, online learning. *Degree requirements:* For doctorate, thesis/dissertation. *Application deadline:* Applications are processed on a rolling basis. Application fee: $40. Electronic applications accepted. *Financial support:* Application deadline: 12/31; applicants required to submit FAFSA. *Unit head:* Dr. Paul Zionts, Dean, 773-325-7581, Fax: 773-325-7713, E-mail: pzionts@depaul.edu. *Application contact:* Dr. Paul Zionts, Dean, 773-325-7581, Fax: 773-325-7713, E-mail: pzionts@depaul.edu.
Website: http://education.depaul.edu

Divine Mercy University, Institute for the Psychological Sciences, Arlington, VA 30327. Offers clinical psychology (Psy D). *Program availability:* Part-time. *Degree requirements:* For doctorate, comprehensive exam, thesis/dissertation. *Entrance requirements:* For doctorate, GRE. Additional exam requirements/recommendations for international students: Required—TOEFL.

Divine Mercy University, School of Counseling, Arlington, VA 30327. Offers clinical mental health counseling (MS); psychology (MS). *Program availability:* Online learning.

Drexel University, College of Arts and Sciences, Department of Psychology, Clinical Psychology Program, Philadelphia, PA 19104-2875. Offers clinical psychology (PhD); forensic psychology (PhD); health psychology (PhD); neuropsychology (PhD). *Accreditation:* APA. Terminal master's awarded for partial completion of doctoral program. *Degree requirements:* For doctorate, thesis/dissertation, qualifying exam. *Entrance requirements:* For doctorate, GRE General Test, GRE Subject Test, minimum GPA of 3.0. Electronic applications accepted. *Expenses:* Contact institution. *Faculty research:* Cognitive behavioral therapy, stress and coping, eating disorders, substance abuse, developmental disabilities.

Drexel University, College of Arts and Sciences, Department of Psychology, Program in Law-Psychology, Philadelphia, PA 19104-2875. Offers JD/PhD. Electronic applications accepted. *Expenses:* Contact institution. *Faculty research:* Mental health law issues, professional ethics, social science applications to law.

Duke University, Graduate School, Department of Psychology and Neuroscience, Durham, NC 27708. Offers biological psychology (PhD); clinical psychology (PhD); cognitive psychology (PhD); developmental psychology (PhD); experimental psychology (PhD); health psychology (PhD); human social development (PhD); JD/MA. *Accreditation:* APA (one or more programs are accredited). *Degree requirements:* For doctorate, thesis/dissertation. *Entrance requirements:* For doctorate, GRE General Test. Additional exam requirements/recommendations for international students: Required—TOEFL (minimum score 577 paper-based; 90 iBT) or IELTS (minimum score 7). Electronic applications accepted.

Duquesne University, Graduate School of Liberal Arts, Department of Psychology, Pittsburgh, PA 15282-0001. Offers clinical psychology (PhD). *Accreditation:* APA. *Faculty:* 13 full-time (7 women). *Students:* 48 full-time (29 women); includes 9 minority (2 Black or African American, non-Hispanic/Latino; 1 Asian, non-Hispanic/Latino; 5 Hispanic/Latino; 1 Two or more races, non-Hispanic/Latino), 7 international. Average age 32. 121 applicants, 7% accepted, 8 enrolled. In 2017, 6 doctorates awarded. *Degree requirements:* For doctorate, comprehensive exam, thesis/dissertation. *Entrance requirements:* For doctorate, GRE General Test, MA in psychology. Additional exam requirements/recommendations for international students: Required—TOEFL. *Application deadline:* For fall admission, 12/15 for domestic and international students. Application fee: $0. Electronic applications accepted. *Expenses:* $1,259 per credit. *Financial support:* In 2017–18, 38 students received support, including 28 teaching assistantships with full tuition reimbursements available (averaging $17,000 per year); career-related internships or fieldwork, scholarships/grants, tuition waivers (partial), and unspecified assistantships also available. Financial award application deadline: 5/1. *Faculty research:* Emotion, language motivation, imagination, development. *Unit head:* Dr. Leswin Laubscher, Chair, 412-396-1843, E-mail: laubscherl@duq.edu. *Application contact:* Linda Rendulic, Assistant to the Dean, 412-396-6400, Fax: 412-396-5265, E-mail: rendulic@duq.edu.
Website: http://www.duq.edu/academics/schools/liberal-arts/graduate-school/programs/clinical-psychology

Duquesne University, School of Education, Department of Counseling, Psychology, and Special Education, Program in Counselor Education, Pittsburgh, PA 15282-0001. Offers clinical mental health counseling (MS Ed, Post-Master's Certificate); counselor education and supervision (Ed D); counselor licensure (Post-Master's Certificate); marriage and family counseling (MS Ed); school counseling (MS Ed). *Accreditation:* ACA (one or more programs are accredited). *Program availability:* Part-time, evening/weekend. *Faculty:* 8 full-time (3 women). *Students:* 194 full-time (140 women), 10 part-time (6 women); includes 41 minority (21 Black or African American, non-Hispanic/Latino; 1 American Indian or Alaska Native, non-Hispanic/Latino; 5 Asian, non-Hispanic/Latino; 6 Hispanic/Latino; 8 Two or more races, non-Hispanic/Latino), 8 international. Average age 28. 149 applicants, 78% accepted, 66 enrolled. In 2017, 53 master's, 6 doctorates awarded. *Degree requirements:* For master's, thesis optional; for doctorate, thesis/dissertation. *Entrance requirements:* For master's, letters of recommendation, essay, interview, bachelor's degree; for doctorate, GRE, letters of recommendation, essay, interview, master's degree; for Post-Master's Certificate, GRE, letters of recommendation, essay, interview, bachelor's/master's degree. Additional exam requirements/recommendations for international students: Required—TOEFL (minimum score 550 paper-based), IELTS (minimum score 6.5). *Application deadline:* For fall admission, 4/2 for domestic students; for spring admission, 9/1 for domestic students. Applications are processed on a rolling basis. Application fee: $0. Electronic applications accepted. *Expenses:* $1,259 per credit. *Financial support:* Research assistantships, teaching assistantships, and Federal Work-Study available. Support available to part-time students. *Faculty research:* Trauma counseling, counseling supervision, purpose and meaning, Internet addictions, bullying and relational aggression. *Unit head:* Dr. Jered Kolbert, Professor/Director, 412-396-4471, Fax: 412-396-1340, E-mail: kolbertj@duq.edu. *Application contact:* Kelly McGinley, Graduate Admissions Assistant, 412-396-1559, Fax: 412-396-5585, E-mail: mcginleyk@duq.edu.

East Carolina University, Graduate School, College of Allied Health Sciences, Department of Addictions and Rehabilitation Studies, Greenville, NC 27858-4353. Offers clinical counseling (MS); military and trauma counseling (Certificate); rehabilitation and career counseling (MS); rehabilitation counseling (Certificate); rehabilitation counseling and administration (PhD); substance abuse counseling (Certificate); vocational evaluation (Certificate). *Accreditation:* CORE. *Program availability:* Part-time, evening/weekend. *Students:* 82 full-time (64 women), 55 part-time (43 women); includes 39 minority (28 Black or African American, non-Hispanic/Latino; 1 American Indian or Alaska Native, non-Hispanic/Latino; 2 Asian, non-Hispanic/Latino; 5 Hispanic/Latino; 3 Two or more races, non-Hispanic/Latino). Average age 33. 51 applicants, 73% accepted, 31 enrolled. In 2017, 19 master's, 5 doctorates, 34 other advanced degrees awarded. *Degree requirements:* For master's, comprehensive exam, thesis or alternative, internship; for doctorate, thesis/dissertation, internship. *Entrance requirements:* For master's and doctorate, GRE General Test or MAT. Additional exam requirements/recommendations for international students: Recommended—TOEFL (minimum score 78 iBT), IELTS (minimum score 6.5). *Application deadline:* For fall admission, 3/1 priority date for domestic students; for spring admission, 10/1 priority date for domestic students. Applications are processed on a rolling basis. Application fee: $75. Electronic applications accepted. *Expenses:* Tuition, state resident: full-time $4749; part-time $297 per credit hour. Tuition, nonresident: full-time $17,898; part-time $1119 per credit hour. *Required fees:* $2691; $224 per credit hour. Part-time tuition and fees vary according to course load and program. *Financial support:* Research assistantships with partial tuition reimbursements, teaching assistantships with partial tuition reimbursements, Federal Work-Study, scholarships/grants, and unspecified assistantships available. Support available to part-time students. Financial award application deadline: 3/1; financial award applicants required to submit FAFSA. *Unit head:* Dr. Paul Toriello, Chair, 252-744-6292, E-mail: toriellop@ecu.edu.
Website: http://www.ecu.edu/rehb/

East Carolina University, Graduate School, Thomas Harriot College of Arts and Sciences, Department of Psychology, Greenville, NC 27858-4353. Offers health psychology (PhD), including clinical health psychology, occupational health psychology, pediatric school psychology; industrial and organizational psychology (MA); quantitative methods for the social and behavioral sciences (Certificate); MA/CAS. *Program availability:* Part-time, evening/weekend. *Students:* 77 full-time (52 women), 17 part-time (15 women); includes 12 minority (8 Black or African American, non-Hispanic/Latino; 3 Hispanic/Latino; 1 Two or more races, non-Hispanic/Latino). Average age 26. 221 applicants, 31% accepted, 22 enrolled. In 2017, 31 master's, 7 doctorates, 21 other advanced degrees awarded. *Degree requirements:* For doctorate, comprehensive exam, thesis/dissertation or alternative. *Entrance requirements:* For master's and doctorate, GRE General Test. Additional exam requirements/recommendations for international students: Recommended—TOEFL (minimum score 78 iBT), IELTS (minimum score 6.5). *Application deadline:* For fall admission, 12/1 priority date for domestic and international students. Applications are processed on a rolling basis. Application fee: $75. Electronic applications accepted. *Expenses:* Tuition, state resident: full-time $4749; part-time $297 per credit hour. Tuition, nonresident: full-time $17,898; part-time $1119 per credit hour. *Required fees:* $2691; $224 per credit hour. Part-time tuition and fees vary according to course load and program. *Financial support:* Research assistantships with partial tuition reimbursements, teaching assistantships with partial tuition reimbursements, Federal Work-Study, and traineeships available.

Support available to part-time students. Financial award application deadline: 6/1. *Unit head:* Dr. Susan L. McCammon, Chair, 252-328-6357, E-mail: mccammons@ecu.edu. *Application contact:* Dean of Graduate School, 252-328-6012, Fax: 252-328-6071, E-mail: gradschool@ecu.edu. Website: http://www.ecu.edu/psyc/

East Central University, School of Graduate Studies, Department of Professional Programs in Human Services, Ada, OK 74820. Offers clinical rehabilitation and clinical mental health counseling (MSHR); criminal justice (MSHR); human resources (MSHR). *Accreditation:* CORE. *Program availability:* Part-time, evening/weekend. *Degree requirements:* For master's, thesis optional. *Entrance requirements:* For master's, GRE General Test, MAT, minimum GPA of 2.5. *Application deadline:* Applications are processed on a rolling basis. Application fee: $0 ($50 for international students). Electronic applications accepted. *Unit head:* Regina Robertson, Chair, 580-559-5647, E-mail: rrobrtsn@ecok.edu. *Application contact:* Regina Robertson, Chair, 580-559-5647, E-mail: rrobrtsn@ecok.edu. Website: http://www.ecok.edu/academics/colleges-and-schools/college-liberal-arts-and-social-sciences/department-human-resources

Eastern Illinois University, Graduate School, College of Liberal Arts and Sciences, Department of Psychology, Charleston, IL 61920. Offers clinical psychology (MA); school psychology (SSP). *Program availability:* Part-time, evening/weekend. *Degree requirements:* For master's, comprehensive exam, thesis; for SSP, thesis. *Entrance requirements:* For master's and SSP, GMAT or GRE. Additional exam requirements/recommendations for international students: Required—TOEFL (minimum score 500 paper-based; 61 iBT), IELTS (minimum score 6). *Application deadline:* For fall admission, 5/15 for domestic and international students; for spring admission, 10/15 for domestic and international students. Applications are processed on a rolling basis. Application fee: $30. Electronic applications accepted. *Financial support:* Research assistantships with full tuition reimbursements, teaching assistantships with full tuition reimbursements, career-related internships or fieldwork, Federal Work-Study, and unspecified assistantships available. Support available to part-time students. Financial award application deadline: 3/1; financial award applicants required to submit FAFSA. *Unit head:* John H. Mace, Chair, 217-581-2127, Fax: 217-581-6764, E-mail: jhmace@eiu.edu. *Application contact:* John H. Mace, Chair, 217-581-2127, Fax: 217-581-6764, E-mail: jhmace@eiu.edu. Website: http://www.eiu.edu/psych/index.php

Eastern Kentucky University, The Graduate School, College of Arts and Sciences, Department of Psychology, Richmond, KY 40475-3102. Offers clinical psychology (MS); industrial/organizational psychology (MS); school psychology (Psy S). *Program availability:* Part-time. *Entrance requirements:* For master's and Psy S, GRE General Test, minimum GPA of 2.5. *Faculty research:* Autism, social psychology, parenting, assessment of depression/anxiety, reading.

Eastern Michigan University, Graduate School, College of Arts and Sciences, Department of Psychology, Ypsilanti, MI 48197. Offers clinical behavioral psychology (MS); clinical psychology (PhD); general clinical psychology (MS); general experimental psychology (MS). *Accreditation:* APA. *Faculty:* 24 full-time (14 women). *Students:* 46 full-time (38 women), 50 part-time (40 women); includes 21 minority (6 Black or African American, non-Hispanic/Latino; 1 American Indian or Alaska Native, non-Hispanic/Latino; 5 Asian, non-Hispanic/Latino; 4 Hispanic/Latino; 5 Two or more races, non-Hispanic/Latino), 2 international. Average age 27. 223 applicants, 18% accepted, 33 enrolled. In 2017, 14 master's, 9 doctorates awarded. *Degree requirements:* For master's, 600-hour practicum; for doctorate, 1500-hour practicum; 2000-hour internship. *Entrance requirements:* For master's and doctorate, GRE. *Application deadline:* For fall admission, 2/15 for domestic students. Application fee: $45. *Financial support:* Fellowships available. *Unit head:* Dr. Carol Freedman-Doan, Department Head, 734-487-1155, Fax: 734-487-6553, E-mail: cfreedman@emich.edu.

Eastern Virginia Medical School, The Virginia Consortium Program in Clinical Psychology, Norfolk, VA 23501-1980. Offers Psy D. Program offered jointly with The College of William and Mary, Norfolk State University, and Old Dominion University. *Entrance requirements:* For doctorate, GRE, BS in behavioral sciences or equivalent. Additional exam requirements/recommendations for international students: Required—TOEFL. *Expenses:* Contact institution.

Eastern Washington University, Graduate Studies, College of Social Sciences, Department of Psychology, Program in Clinical Psychology, Cheney, WA 99004-2431. Offers MS. *Students:* 14 full-time (9 women), 3 part-time (2 women); includes 2 minority (1 Asian, non-Hispanic/Latino; 1 Hispanic/Latino), 2 international. Average age 32. 44 applicants, 20% accepted, 6 enrolled. In 2017, 5 master's awarded. *Degree requirements:* For master's, comprehensive exam (for some programs), thesis or research report; practicum. *Entrance requirements:* For master's, GRE General Test, minimum GPA of 3.0 in last 90 quarter or 60 semester graded credits; curriculum vitae; three letters of recommendation; bachelor's degree in psychology or its equivalent; background check. Additional exam requirements/recommendations for international students: Required—TOEFL (minimum score 580 paper-based; 92 iBT), IELTS (minimum score 7), PTE (minimum score 63). *Application deadline:* For fall admission, 1/15 priority date for domestic students. Application fee: $75. Electronic applications accepted. *Expenses:* Tuition, state resident: full-time $11,191; part-time $373.06 per credit. Tuition, nonresident: full-time $25,995; part-time $866.52 per credit. *Financial support:* Application deadline: 2/15; applicants required to submit FAFSA. *Unit head:* Dennis Anderson, Director, 509-359-2087, E-mail: danderson2@ewu.edu. *Application contact:* Kathy White, Advisor/Recruiter for Graduate Studies, 509-359-2491, Fax: 509-359-6044, E-mail: gradprograms@ewu.edu.

East Tennessee State University, School of Graduate Studies, College of Arts and Sciences, Department of Psychology, Johnson City, TN 37614. Offers clinical psychology (PhD); experimental psychology (PhD). *Accreditation:* APA. Terminal master's awarded for partial completion of doctoral program. *Degree requirements:* For doctorate, thesis/dissertation, externship. *Entrance requirements:* For doctorate, GRE General Test, minimum GPA of 3.0, three letters of recommendation, interview, minimum of 18 semester hours in undergraduate psychology. Additional exam requirements/recommendations for international students: Required—TOEFL (minimum score 550 paper-based; 79 iBT). *Application deadline:* For fall admission, 12/1 for domestic and international students. Application fee: $55 ($65 for international students). Electronic applications accepted. *Financial support:* Research assistantships with full tuition reimbursements, teaching assistantships with full tuition reimbursements, career-related internships or fieldwork, institutionally sponsored loans, scholarships/grants, and unspecified assistantships available. Financial award application deadline: 7/1; financial award applicants required to submit FAFSA. *Faculty research:* Women's issues, prenatal stress, childhood obesity, suicide prevention, behavioral pediatrics, self-control, substance dependence, violence. *Unit head:* Dr. Wallace E. Dixon, Jr., Chair, 423-439-6656, Fax: 423-439-5695, E-mail: dixonw@etsu.edu. *Application contact:* Dr. Wallace E. Dixon, Jr., Chair, 423-439-6656, Fax: 423-439-5695, E-mail: dixonw@etsu.edu. Website: http://www.etsu.edu/cas/psychology/

East Tennessee State University, School of Graduate Studies, College of Education, Department of Counseling and Human Services, Johnson City, TN 37614. Offers clinical mental health counseling (MA); college counseling/student affairs higher education (MA); couples and family therapy (MA); human services (MS); school counseling (MA). *Accreditation:* ACA; NCATE. *Program availability:* Part-time. *Degree requirements:* For master's, comprehensive exam, thesis optional, internship, student teaching, culminating experience. *Entrance requirements:* For master's, GRE General Test, minimum GPA of 3.0, three letters of recommendation, interview, 2-3 page essay detailing experiences that have shaped pursuit of degree, resume. Additional exam requirements/recommendations for international students: Required—TOEFL (minimum score 550 paper-based; 79 iBT). *Application deadline:* For fall admission, 1/31 priority date for domestic and international students. Application fee: $55 ($65 for international students). Electronic applications accepted. *Financial support:* Research assistantships with full tuition reimbursements, teaching assistantships with full tuition reimbursements, career-related internships or fieldwork, institutionally sponsored loans, scholarships/grants, traineeships, and unspecified assistantships available. Financial award application deadline: 7/1; financial award applicants required to submit FAFSA. *Faculty research:* Intervention and assistance with at-risk and under-served youth and high conflict families; service and social justice; women and girls' issues in counseling; counseling competence with LGBTQ individuals; counselor education and supervision. *Unit head:* Dr. Janna Scarborough, Chair, 423-439-4191, Fax: 423-439-7790, E-mail: scarboro@etsu.edu. *Application contact:* Dr. Janna Scarborough, Chair, 423-439-4191, Fax: 423-439-7790, E-mail: scarboro@etsu.edu. Website: http://www.etsu.edu/coe/chs/

Edinboro University of Pennsylvania, Department of Counseling, School Psychology and Special Education, Edinboro, PA 16444. Offers counseling (MA), including art therapy, clinical mental health counseling, college counseling, rehabilitation counseling, school counseling; educational psychology (M Ed); school psychology (Ed S); special education (M Ed), including autism, behavior management. *Accreditation:* ACA. *Program availability:* Part-time, evening/weekend. *Degree requirements:* For master's, thesis or alternative, competency exam; for Ed S, thesis or alternative. *Entrance requirements:* For master's and Ed S, GRE or MAT, minimum QPA of 2.5. Electronic applications accepted.

Emory University, Laney Graduate School, Department of Psychology, Atlanta, GA 30322-1100. Offers clinical psychology (PhD); cognition and development (PhD); neuroscience and animal behavior (PhD). *Accreditation:* APA. *Degree requirements:* For doctorate, comprehensive exam, thesis/dissertation. *Entrance requirements:* For doctorate, GRE General Test, minimum GPA of 3.25. Additional exam requirements/recommendations for international students: Required—TOEFL. Electronic applications accepted. *Faculty research:* Neuroscience and animal behavior; adult and child psychopathology, cognition development assessment.

Emporia State University, Program in Clinical Psychology, Emporia, KS 66801-5415. Offers MS. *Program availability:* Part-time. *Faculty:* 8 full-time (4 women). *Students:* 29 full-time (21 women), 4 part-time (3 women); includes 5 minority (3 Black or African American, non-Hispanic/Latino; 1 Hispanic/Latino; 1 Two or more races, non-Hispanic/Latino), 3 international. 34 applicants, 62% accepted, 5 enrolled. In 2017, 7 master's awarded. *Degree requirements:* For master's, comprehensive exam, clinical internship. *Entrance requirements:* For master's, GRE or MAT, 24 hours of course work in undergraduate psychology, 3 letters of recommendation. Additional exam requirements/recommendations for international students: Required—TOEFL (minimum score 520 paper-based; 68 iBT). *Application deadline:* For fall admission, 8/15 for domestic students. Applications are processed on a rolling basis. Application fee: $30 ($75 for international students). Electronic applications accepted. *Expenses:* Tuition, state resident: full-time $6084; part-time $253.50 per credit hour. Tuition, nonresident: full-time $18,924; part-time $788.50 per credit hour. *Required fees:* $1943; $80.95 per credit hour. Tuition and fees vary according to campus/location. *Financial support:* In 2017–18, 11 teaching assistantships with full tuition reimbursements (averaging $7,344 per year) were awarded; research assistantships with full tuition reimbursements, career-related internships or fieldwork, Federal Work-Study, institutionally sponsored loans, health care benefits, and unspecified assistantships also available. Support available to part-time students. Financial award application deadline: 3/15; financial award applicants required to submit FAFSA. *Unit head:* Dr. Jim Persinger, Chair, 620-341-5317, E-mail: jpersing@emporia.edu. *Application contact:* Mary Sewell, Admissions Coordinator, 800-950-GRAD, Fax: 620-341-5909, E-mail: msewell@emporia.edu.

Evangel University, Department of Behavioral and Social Sciences, Springfield, MO 65802. Offers clinical mental health counseling (MS). *Program availability:* Part-time. *Faculty:* 6 full-time (4 women), 2 part-time/adjunct (1 woman). *Students:* 33 full-time (27 women), 6 part-time (5 women); includes 3 minority (all Hispanic/Latino). Average age 31. 30 applicants, 70% accepted, 16 enrolled. In 2017, 14 master's awarded. *Degree requirements:* For master's, comprehensive exam. *Entrance requirements:* For master's, GRE General Test, minimum undergraduate GPA of 3.0. Additional exam requirements/recommendations for international students: Required—TOEFL (minimum score 550 paper-based). *Application deadline:* For fall admission, 7/15 priority date for domestic students, 8/1 for international students; for spring admission, 11/15 priority date for domestic students, 12/1 for international students. Applications are processed on a rolling basis. Application fee: $25. Electronic applications accepted. Application fee is waived when completed online. *Expenses: Tuition:* Full-time $7200; part-time $4800 per credit hour. *Required fees:* $210; $155 per semester. *Financial support:* In 2017–18, 12 students received support. Unspecified assistantships available. Financial award application deadline: 4/1; financial award applicants required to submit FAFSA. *Unit head:* Dr. Christine Arnzen, Program Coordinator, 417-865-2815 Ext. 8618, E-mail: arnzenc@evangel.edu. *Application contact:* Michael Mann, Enrollment Coordinator, Graduate Studies, 417-865-2815 Ext. 8276, Fax: 417-575-5484, E-mail: mannm@evangel.edu. Website: https://www.evangel.edu/departments/behavioral-social-sciences/about-the-department/

Fairfield University, Graduate School of Education and Allied Professions, Fairfield, CT 06824. Offers applied behavior analysis (ATC); applied psychology (MA); clinical mental health counseling (MA, CAS); educational technology (MA); elementary education (MA, CAS); family studies (MA); integration of spirituality and religion in counseling (ATC); marriage and family therapy (MA); reading and language development (Sixth Year Certificate); school counseling (MA, CAS); school psychology (MA, CAS); school-based marriage and family therapy (ATC); secondary education (MA); special education (MA, CAS); substance abuse counseling (ATC); teaching (Certificate); teaching and foundations (MA, CAS); TESOL, world languages, and bilingual education (MA, CAS). *Accreditation:* NCATE. *Program availability:* Part-time, evening/weekend. *Faculty:* 23 full-time (17 women), 39 part-time/adjunct (28 women). *Students:* 199 full-time (168 women), 251 part-time (206 women); includes 85 minority (21 Black or African American, non-Hispanic/Latino; 9 Asian, non-Hispanic/Latino; 49 Hispanic/Latino; 6 Two or more races, non-Hispanic/Latino), 4 international. Average age 32. 370 applicants, 56% accepted, 125 enrolled. In 2017, 136 master's, 28 other advanced degrees awarded. *Degree requirements:* For master's, comprehensive exam. *Entrance requirements:* For master's, minimum GPA of 3.0, 2 recommendations, resume.

Clinical Psychology

Additional exam requirements/recommendations for international students: Required— TOEFL (minimum score 550 paper-based; 84 iBT) or IELTS (minimum score 7.5). *Application deadline:* For fall admission, 2/15 for international students; for spring admission, 10/1 for international students. Application fee: $60. Electronic applications accepted. *Expenses:* $750 per credit hour. *Financial support:* In 2017–18, 34 students received support. Career-related internships or fieldwork and unspecified assistantships available. Support available to part-time students. Financial award applicants required to submit FAFSA. *Faculty research:* Reading and literacy, writing, social justice and inequality in education, addictions and mental health issues, therapeutic relationships and clinical supervision. *Unit head:* Dr. Robert D. Hannafin, Dean, 203-254-4250, Fax: 203-254-4241, E-mail: rhannafin@fairfield.edu. *Application contact:* Marianne Gumpper, Director of Graduate Admission, 203-254-4184, Fax: 203-254-4073, E-mail: gradadmis@fairfield.edu.
Website: http://www.fairfield.edu/gseap

Fairleigh Dickinson University, Florham Campus, Maxwell Becton College of Arts and Sciences, Department of Psychology, Program in Clinical Mental Health Counseling, Madison, NJ 07940-1099. Offers MA. *Accreditation:* ACA.

Fairleigh Dickinson University, Metropolitan Campus, University College: Arts, Sciences, and Professional Studies, School of Psychology, Program in Clinical Psychology, Teaneck, NJ 07666-1914. Offers MA, PhD. *Accreditation:* APA.

Fairleigh Dickinson University, Metropolitan Campus, University College: Arts, Sciences, and Professional Studies, School of Psychology, Program in Clinical Psychopharmacology, Teaneck, NJ 07666-1914. Offers MA.

Fielding Graduate University, Graduate Programs, School of Leadership Studies, Program in Clinical Mental Health Counseling, Santa Barbara, CA 93105-3814. Offers MA. *Degree requirements:* For master's, internship, seminar. *Entrance requirements:* For master's, bachelor's degree, minimum GPA of 3.0, resume, statement of purpose, 2 letters of recommendation, official transcripts, interview. *Application deadline:* For fall admission, 7/26 for domestic students. Tuition and fees vary according to course load, degree level and program. *Unit head:* Dr. Colleen Logan, Director. *Application contact:* Enrollment Coordinator, 800-340-1099 Ext. 4098, Fax: 805-687-9793, E-mail: hodadmission@fielding.edu.
Website: http://www.fielding.edu/our-programs/school-of-leadership-studies/ma-clinical-mental-health-counseling/

Fielding Graduate University, Graduate Programs, School of Psychology, Programs in Clinical Psychology, Santa Barbara, CA 93105-3814. Offers clinical psychology (PhD, Postbaccalaureate Certificate); respecialization in clinical psychology (Post-Doctoral Certificate). *Program availability:* Part-time, evening/weekend, 100% online, blended/hybrid learning. *Faculty:* 29 full-time (19 women), 24 part-time/adjunct (14 women). *Students:* 391 full-time (307 women), 14 part-time (11 women); includes 163 minority (59 Black or African American, non-Hispanic/Latino; 2 American Indian or Alaska Native, non-Hispanic/Latino; 15 Asian, non-Hispanic/Latino; 62 Hispanic/Latino; 25 Two or more races, non-Hispanic/Latino), 4 international. Average age 40. 287 applicants, 48% accepted, 83 enrolled. In 2017, 40 doctorates, 35 other advanced degrees awarded. *Degree requirements:* For doctorate, comprehensive exam, thesis/dissertation. *Entrance requirements:* For doctorate, bachelor's degree, minimum GPA of 3.0, curriculum vitae, statement of purpose, critical thinking writing sample, 3 letters of recommendation, official transcript; for other advanced degree, bachelor's degree (for Postbaccalaureate Certificate); doctoral degree in psychology (for Post-Doctoral Certificate); minimum GPA of 3.0, curriculum vitae, statement of purpose, 3 letters of recommendation, official transcript. *Application deadline:* For fall admission, 2/4 for domestic students, 2/1 for international students; for spring admission, 11/1 for domestic and international students; for summer admission, 3/1 for domestic and international students. Application fee: $75. Electronic applications accepted. *Expenses:* Contact institution. *Financial support:* In 2017–18, 69 students received support, including 1 research assistantship (averaging $400 per year), 8 teaching assistantships (averaging $1,900 per year); scholarships/grants also available. Financial award applicants required to submit FAFSA. *Unit head:* Dr. Marilyn Freimuth, Director. *Application contact:* Enrollment Coordinator, 800-898-4026 Ext. 4098, Fax: 805-687-9793, E-mail: psyadmission@fielding.edu.
Website: http://www.fielding.edu/our-programs/school-of-psychology/

Fisk University, Division of Graduate Studies, Department of Psychology, Nashville, TN 37208-3051. Offers clinical psychology (MA); psychology (MA). *Degree requirements:* For master's, thesis. *Entrance requirements:* For master's, GRE General Test, GRE Subject Test, minimum GPA of 3.0. Electronic applications accepted. *Faculty research:* Ethnic and gender identity, development, female adolescent development, juvenile delinquency prevention.

Florida Gulf Coast University, Elaine Nicpon Marieb College of Health and Human Services, Program in School Counseling, Fort Myers, FL 33965-6565. Offers clinical mental health counseling (MA); school counseling (MA). *Accreditation:* ACA. *Program availability:* Part-time, evening/weekend. *Faculty:* 71 full-time (49 women), 49 part-time/adjunct (32 women). *Students:* 12 full-time (9 women), 27 part-time (21 women); includes 6 minority (3 Black or African American, non-Hispanic/Latino; 3 Hispanic/Latino). Average age 30. 27 applicants, 89% accepted, 21 enrolled. In 2017, 12 master's awarded. *Degree requirements:* For master's, thesis or alternative. *Entrance requirements:* For master's, GRE General Test, MAT, minimum GPA of 3.0. Additional exam requirements/recommendations for international students: Required—TOEFL (minimum score 550 paper-based). *Application deadline:* For fall admission, 2/15 priority date for domestic students; for summer admission, 2/15 priority date for domestic students. Applications are processed on a rolling basis. Application fee: $30. Electronic applications accepted. *Expenses:* Tuition, state resident: part-time $290 per credit hour. Tuition, nonresident: part-time $1173 per credit hour. *Required fees:* $127 per credit hour. Tuition and fees vary according to course load. *Financial support:* In 2017–18, 9 students received support. Application deadline: 6/30; applicants required to submit FAFSA. *Faculty research:* Sexuality, confidentiality, school counselor roles, distance learning, exceptional students. *Unit head:* Dr. Madelyn Isaacs, Department Chair, 239-590-7785, Fax: 239-590-7801, E-mail: misaacs@fgcu.edu. *Application contact:* Ana Hill, Graduate Studies Admissions, 239-590-7408, Fax: 239-590-7843, E-mail: graduate@fgcu.edu.

Florida Institute of Technology, College of Psychology and Liberal Arts, Program in Clinical Psychology, Melbourne, FL 32901-6975. Offers Psy D. *Accreditation:* APA. *Program availability:* Part-time. *Students:* Average age 27. 175 applicants, 26% accepted, 21 enrolled. In 2017, 22 doctorates awarded. *Degree requirements:* For doctorate, comprehensive exam, thesis/dissertation or alternative, minimum of 4 years residency on campus (full-time status), minimum 124 credit hours beyond bachelor's degree, CPE exam, 2nd-year student review, minimum GPA of 3.2, research project, accredited internship of at least 2,000 hours. *Entrance requirements:* For doctorate, GRE General Test, GRE Subject Test (psychology), resume, 3 letters of recommendation, statement of objectives, 18 hours of psychology coursework (statistics, personality theory, abnormal psychology, learning, physiological psychology, and social psychology). Additional exam requirements/recommendations for international students: Required—TOEFL (minimum score 550 paper-based; 79 iBT).

Application deadline: For fall admission, 3/15 for domestic students, 4/1 for international students; for spring admission, 9/30 for international students. Applications are processed on a rolling basis. Electronic applications accepted. *Expenses: Tuition:* Part-time $1241 per credit hour. Part-time tuition and fees vary according to campus/location. *Financial support:* Fellowships, research assistantships, teaching assistantships, career-related internships or fieldwork, institutionally sponsored loans, tuition waivers (partial), unspecified assistantships, and tuition remissions available. Support available to part-time students. Financial award application deadline: 3/1; financial award applicants required to submit FAFSA. *Faculty research:* Addictions, neuropsychology, child abuse, gender issues, personality assessment, eating disorders, psychological trauma. *Unit head:* Dr. Linda Garcia-Shelton, Program Chair, 321-674-7121, Fax: 321-674-7105, E-mail: lgarciashelton@fit.edu. *Application contact:* Cheryl A. Brown, Associate Director of Graduate Admissions, 321-674-7581, Fax: 321-723-9468, E-mail: cbrown@fit.edu.
Website: http://cpla.fit.edu/clinical/

Florida International University, College of Arts, Sciences, and Education, Department of Leadership and Professional Studies, Miami, FL 33199. Offers adult education and human resource development (MS, Ed D); counseling (MS), including rehabilitation counseling, school counseling; counselor education (MS), including clinical mental health counseling; educational administration and supervision (Ed D); educational leadership (MS, Certificate, Ed S); higher education (Ed D); higher education administration (MS); international and comparative education (MS); recreation and sport management (MS), including recreation and sport management, recreational therapy; school psychology (Ed S); urban education (MS), including instruction in urban settings, learning technologies, multicultural/bilingual, multicultural/TESOL, urban education. *Program availability:* Part-time, evening/weekend. *Faculty:* 60 full-time (41 women), 112 part-time/adjunct (77 women). *Students:* 221 full-time (162 women), 301 part-time (239 women); includes 418 minority (127 Black or African American, non-Hispanic/Latino; 9 Asian, non-Hispanic/Latino; 271 Hispanic/Latino; 11 Two or more races, non-Hispanic/Latino), 10 international. Average age 31. 330 applicants, 55% accepted, 100 enrolled. In 2017, 181 master's, 6 doctorates awarded. *Degree requirements:* For doctorate, thesis/dissertation. *Entrance requirements:* For master's, minimum GPA of 3.0; for doctorate and other advanced degree, GRE General Test. Additional exam requirements/recommendations for international students: Required—TOEFL (minimum score 550 paper-based; 80 iBT), IELTS (minimum score 6.3). *Application deadline:* For fall admission, 6/1 priority date for domestic students, 4/1 for international students; for winter admission, 10/1 priority date for domestic students, 9/1 for international students; for spring admission, 3/1 priority date for domestic students, 2/1 for international students. Applications are processed on a rolling basis. Application fee: $30. Electronic applications accepted. *Expenses:* Tuition, state resident: full-time $8912; part-time $446 per credit hour. Tuition, nonresident: full-time $21,393; part-time $992 per credit hour. *Required fees:* $390; $195 per semester. *Financial support:* Fellowships, research assistantships with tuition reimbursements, teaching assistantships with tuition reimbursements, Federal Work-Study, and tuition waivers (full and partial) available. Support available to part-time students. Financial award applicants required to submit FAFSA. *Unit head:* Dr. Benjamin Baez, Chair, 305-348-3214, Fax: 305-348-1515, E-mail: benjamin.baez@fiu.edu. *Application contact:* Nanett Rojas, Assistant Director, Graduate Admissions, 305-348-7464, Fax: 305-348-7441, E-mail: gradadm@fiu.edu.
Website: http://education.fiu.edu

Florida International University, College of Arts, Sciences, and Education, Department of Psychology, Miami, FL 33199. Offers behavioral analysis (MS); clinical science (PhD); cognitive neuroscience (PhD); counseling psychology (MS); developmental science (MS, PhD); legal psychology (MS, PhD); organizational psychology (MS, PhD). Program has fall admissions only. *Accreditation:* APA. *Program availability:* Part-time, evening/weekend. *Faculty:* 45 full-time (28 women), 48 part-time/adjunct (31 women). *Students:* 162 full-time (122 women), 13 part-time (5 women); includes 94 minority (11 Black or African American, non-Hispanic/Latino; 5 Asian, non-Hispanic/Latino; 75 Hispanic/Latino; 3 Two or more races, non-Hispanic/Latino), 12 international. Average age 27. 290 applicants, 21% accepted, 50 enrolled. In 2017, 43 master's, 13 doctorates awarded. Terminal master's awarded for partial completion of doctoral program. *Degree requirements:* For master's, thesis; for doctorate, comprehensive exam, thesis/dissertation. *Entrance requirements:* For master's, GRE General Test, minimum GPA of 3.0, resume, 3 letters of recommendation; for doctorate, GRE General Test, 3 letters of recommendation, resume, letter of intent, two writing samples, minimum GPA of 3.0. Additional exam requirements/recommendations for international students: Required—TOEFL (minimum score 550 paper-based; 80 iBT). *Application deadline:* For fall admission, 12/15 for domestic and international students. Application fee: $30. Electronic applications accepted. *Expenses:* Tuition, state resident: full-time $8912; part-time $446 per credit hour. Tuition, nonresident: full-time $21,393; part-time $992 per credit hour. *Required fees:* $390; $195 per semester. *Financial support:* Institutionally sponsored loans and scholarships/grants available. Financial award application deadline: 3/1. *Faculty research:* Legal psychology, organizational and industrial psychology, child behavior psychology. *Unit head:* Dr. Jeremy Pettit, Interim Chair, 305-348-1671, Fax: 305-348-3646, E-mail: jeremy.pettit@fiu.edu. *Application contact:* Nanett Rojas, Assistant Director, Graduate Admissions, 305-348-7464, Fax: 305-348-7441, E-mail: gradadm@fiu.edu.

Florida State University, The Graduate School, College of Arts and Sciences, Department of Psychology, Program in Clinical Psychology, Tallahassee, FL 32306. Offers PhD. *Accreditation:* APA. *Faculty:* 15 full-time (7 women). *Students:* 58 full-time (41 women), 8 part-time (7 women); includes 13 minority (1 Black or African American, non-Hispanic/Latino; 3 Asian, non-Hispanic/Latino; 5 Hispanic/Latino; 4 Two or more races, non-Hispanic/Latino). Average age 28. 274 applicants, 8% accepted, 14 enrolled. In 2017, 8 doctorates awarded. Terminal master's awarded for partial completion of doctoral program. *Degree requirements:* For doctorate, comprehensive exam, thesis/dissertation. *Entrance requirements:* For doctorate, GRE General Test, minimum GPA of 3.3, research experience, letters of recommendation. Additional exam requirements/recommendations for international students: Required—TOEFL (minimum score 80 iBT). *Application deadline:* For fall admission, 12/1 for domestic and international students. Application fee: $30. Electronic applications accepted. *Financial support:* In 2017–18, 54 students received support, including 9 fellowships with full tuition reimbursements available (averaging $23,844 per year), 17 research assistantships with full tuition reimbursements available (averaging $23,815 per year), 28 teaching assistantships with full tuition reimbursements available (averaging $19,000 per year); career-related internships or fieldwork, traineeships, and health care benefits also available. Financial award application deadline: 12/1; financial award applicants required to submit FAFSA. *Faculty research:* Antisocial behavior, depression, addictive behavior, developmental psychopathology, anxiety. *Total annual research expenditures:* $6.6 million. *Unit head:* Dr. Jesse Cougle, Director, 850-645-8729, Fax: 850-644-7739, E-mail: cougle@psy.fsu.edu. *Application contact:* Lynda L. Gibson, Graduate Program Associate, 850-644-2499, Fax: 850-644-7739, E-mail: grad-info@psy.fsu.edu.
Website: http://www.psy.fsu.edu/

Fordham University, Graduate School of Arts and Sciences, Department of Psychology, Program in Clinical Psychology, New York, NY 10458. Offers PhD.

Students: 59 full-time (46 women), 4 part-time (3 women); includes 17 minority (6 Black or African American, non-Hispanic/Latino; 1 American Indian or Alaska Native, non-Hispanic/Latino; 3 Asian, non-Hispanic/Latino; 7 Hispanic/Latino), 4 international. Average age 30. 606 applicants, 2% accepted, 10 enrolled. In 2017, 7 doctorates awarded. Terminal master's awarded for partial completion of doctoral program. *Degree requirements:* For doctorate, comprehensive exam, thesis/dissertation, clinical internship. *Entrance requirements:* For doctorate, GRE General Test, GRE Subject Test. Additional exam requirements/recommendations for international students: Required—TOEFL (minimum score 600 paper-based). *Application deadline:* For fall admission, 12/14 for domestic students. Application fee: $70. Electronic applications accepted. *Financial support:* In 2017–18, 55 students received support, including 8 fellowships with tuition reimbursements available (averaging $26,390 per year), 10 research assistantships with tuition reimbursements available (averaging $12,285 per year), 7 teaching assistantships with tuition reimbursements available (averaging $12,871 per year); career-related internships or fieldwork, institutionally sponsored loans, tuition waivers (full and partial), and unspecified assistantships also available. Financial award application deadline: 12/14. *Total annual research expenditures:* $1.9 million. *Unit head:* Dr. Monica Rivera-Mindt, Program Director, 212-636-7453, E-mail: riveramindt@fordham.edu. *Application contact:* Bernadette Valentino-Morrison, Director of Graduate Admissions, 718-817-4419, Fax: 718-817-3566, E-mail: valentinomor@fordham.edu.

Franciscan University of Steubenville, Graduate Programs, Department of Clinical Mental Health Counseling, Steubenville, OH 43952-1763. Offers MA. *Accreditation:* ACA. *Program availability:* Part-time. *Faculty:* 4 full-time (1 woman), 2 part-time/adjunct (1 woman). *Students:* 41 full-time (28 women), 7 part-time (3 women); includes 5 minority (1 Black or African American, non-Hispanic/Latino; 2 Asian, non-Hispanic/Latino; 2 Hispanic/Latino). Average age 28. 44 applicants, 75% accepted, 24 enrolled. In 2017, 17 master's awarded. *Degree requirements:* For master's, case presentation, integrative paper. *Entrance requirements:* For master's, GRE General Test or MAT for those with a GPA below 3.0, minimum undergraduate GPA of 2.5. Additional exam requirements/recommendations for international students: Required—TOEFL. *Application deadline:* For fall admission, 8/1 for domestic students, 5/31 for international students; for spring admission, 1/10 for domestic students, 9/30 for international students. Applications are processed on a rolling basis. Application fee: $0. Electronic applications accepted. *Expenses:* $685 per semester hour. *Financial support:* Federal Work-Study and scholarships/grants available. Support available to part-time students. Financial award application deadline: 8/1; financial award applicants required to submit FAFSA. *Unit head:* Dr. Christin Jungers, Program Director, 740-284-7220, E-mail: cjungers@franciscan.edu. *Application contact:* Ryan Welch, Online Enrollment Counselor, 740-284-5239, Fax: 740-284-5456, E-mail: rwelch@franciscan.edu.
Website: http://www.franciscan.edu/cmhc/

Francis Marion University, Graduate Programs, Department of Psychology, Florence, SC 29502-0547. Offers applied psychology (MS), including clinical/counseling psychology, school psychology; school psychology (SSP). *Program availability:* Part-time, evening/weekend. *Degree requirements:* For master's, internship. *Entrance requirements:* For master's, GRE General Test, official transcripts, two letters of recommendation. Additional exam requirements/recommendations for international students: Required—TOEFL (minimum score 550 paper-based; 79 iBT). *Faculty research:* Parenting and family relationships, child development, applied behavioral analysis, post-traumatic stress disorder, clinical psychology in adults.

Fuller Theological Seminary, Graduate Programs, Pasadena, CA 91182. Offers Christian leadership (MACL); clinical psychology (PhD, Psy D); family studies (MA); global leadership (MA); global ministries (D Min); global ministries (Korean language) (D Min); intercultural studies (MA, Th M, PhD); intercultural studies (Korean language) (MA); marital and family therapy (MS); marriage and family enrichment (Certificate); ministry (M Div, D Min); missiology (D Miss); missiology (Korean language) (Th M); theology (MA, Th M, PhD), including evangelism (MA), family life education (MA), pastoral ministry (MA), recovery ministry (MA), worship music ministry (MA), worship, theology, and the arts (MA), youth, family, and culture (MA); theology and ministry (MA).

Gallaudet University, The Graduate School, Washington, DC 20002-3625. Offers American Sign Language/English bilingual early childhood deaf education: birth to 5 (Certificate); audiology (Au D); clinical psychology (PhD); deaf and hard of hearing infants, toddlers, and their families (Certificate); deaf education (MA, Ed S); deaf history (Certificate); deaf studies (Certificate); educating deaf students with disabilities (Certificate); education: teacher preparation (MA), including deaf education, early childhood education and deaf education, elementary education and deaf education, secondary education and deaf education; educational neuroscience (PhD); hearing, speech and language sciences (MS, PhD); international development (MA); interpretation (MA, PhD), including combined interpreting practice and research (MA), interpreting research (MA); linguistics (MA, PhD); mental health counseling (MA); peer mentoring (Certificate); public administration (MPA); school counseling (MA); school psychology (Psy S); sign language teaching (MA); social work (MSW); speech-language pathology (MS). *Program availability:* Part-time. Terminal master's awarded for partial completion of doctoral program. *Degree requirements:* For master's, comprehensive exam (for some programs), thesis optional; for doctorate, comprehensive exam, thesis/dissertation. *Entrance requirements:* For master's and doctorate, GRE General Test or MAT, letters of recommendation, interviews, goals statement, American Sign Language proficiency interview, written English competency. Additional exam requirements/recommendations for international students: Required—TOEFL. Electronic applications accepted. *Faculty research:* Signing math dictionaries, telecommunications access, cancer genetics, linguistics, visual language and visual learning, integrated quantum materials, deaf legal discourse, advance recruitment and retention in geosciences.

Gannon University, School of Graduate Studies, College of Humanities, Education, and Social Sciences, School of Humanities, Program in Clinical Mental Health Counseling, Erie, PA 16541-0001. Offers MS. *Accreditation:* ACA. *Program availability:* Part-time, evening/weekend. *Degree requirements:* For master's, thesis, internship. *Entrance requirements:* For master's, bachelor's degree from approved institution, resume, 3 letters of recommendation, essay, interview, minimum GPA of 2.8, PA child abuse clearances and PA State Police criminal record check dated within a year of application. Additional exam requirements/recommendations for international students: Required—TOEFL (minimum score 79 iBT). Electronic applications accepted. Application fee is waived when completed online.

Geneva College, Master of Arts in Counseling Program, Beaver Falls, PA 15010-3599. Offers clinical mental health counseling (MA); marriage and family counseling (MA); school counseling (MA). *Accreditation:* ACA. *Program availability:* Part-time, evening/weekend. *Faculty:* 6 full-time (3 women), 3 part-time/adjunct (1 woman). *Students:* 34 full-time (26 women), 20 part-time (16 women); includes 12 minority (11 Black or African American, non-Hispanic/Latino; 1 Hispanic/Latino), 1 international. Average age 33. In 2017, 34 master's awarded. *Degree requirements:* For master's, comprehensive exam, 60 credits including practicum and internship. *Entrance requirements:* For master's, minimum GPA of 3.0 (preferred), 3 letters of recommendation, essay on career goals, resume of educational and professional experiences. Additional exam requirements/recommendations for international students: Required—TOEFL. *Application deadline:* For fall admission, 9/1 for domestic students; for spring admission, 1/10 for domestic students. Applications are processed on a rolling basis. Electronic applications accepted. *Expenses:* $670 per credit. *Financial support:* Research assistantships, teaching assistantships, career-related internships or fieldwork, and unspecified assistantships available. Financial award application deadline: 8/1; financial award applicants required to submit FAFSA. *Faculty research:* Blended family counseling; premarital and newlywed couples; religion in clinical supervision; conceptual mapping in research, supervision, and clinical work. *Unit head:* Dr. Shannan Shiderly, Program Director, 724-847-6649, Fax: 724-847-6101, E-mail: slshider@geneva.edu. *Application contact:* Marina Frazier, Graduate Program Manager, 724-847-6697, E-mail: counseling@geneva.edu.
Website: http://www.geneva.edu/page/grad_counseling

George Fox University, College of Education, Graduate Department of Counseling, Newberg, OR 97132-2697. Offers clinical mental health counseling (MA); marriage, couple and family counseling (MA, Certificate); school counseling (MA, Certificate); school psychology (Ed S). *Program availability:* Part-time. *Degree requirements:* For master's, clinical project. *Entrance requirements:* For master's, MAT or GRE, bachelor's degree from regionally-accredited college or university, minimum cumulative GPA of 3.0, 1 professional and 1 academic reference, resume, on-campus interview, official transcripts. Additional exam requirements/recommendations for international students: Required—TOEFL (minimum score 577 paper-based; 90 iBT), IELTS (minimum score 7). Electronic applications accepted. *Expenses:* Contact institution.

George Fox University, Program in Clinical Psychology, Newberg, OR 97132-2697. Offers Psy D. *Accreditation:* APA. *Degree requirements:* For doctorate, thesis/dissertation, internship. *Entrance requirements:* For doctorate, GRE General Test, bachelor's degree from regionally-accredited university or college, minimum undergraduate GPA of 3.0 during previous 2 years, interview, official transcripts. Additional exam requirements/recommendations for international students: Required—TOEFL (minimum score 80 iBT), IELTS (minimum score 6.5). Electronic applications accepted. *Expenses:* Contact institution. *Faculty research:* Psychological assessment, impact of psychological services on medical outcome, spirituality and wellness, effectiveness of clinical training and supervision, shame.

George Mason University, College of Humanities and Social Sciences, Department of Psychology, Fairfax, VA 22030. Offers applied developmental psychology (MA, PhD); clinical psychology (PhD); cognitive and behavioral neuroscience (MA, PhD); cognitive neuroscience (Certificate); human factors/applied cognition (MA, PhD, Certificate), including transportation human factors (Certificate), usability (Certificate); industrial/organizational psychology (MA, PhD). *Accreditation:* APA. *Faculty:* 41 full-time (20 women), 5 part-time/adjunct (all women). *Students:* 152 full-time (101 women), 56 part-time (39 women); includes 47 minority (15 Black or African American, non-Hispanic/Latino; 13 Asian, non-Hispanic/Latino; 13 Hispanic/Latino; 1 Native Hawaiian or other Pacific Islander, non-Hispanic/Latino; 5 Two or more races, non-Hispanic/Latino), 12 international. Average age 27. 719 applicants, 19% accepted, 61 enrolled. In 2017, 55 master's, 18 doctorates, 8 other advanced degrees awarded. *Degree requirements:* For master's, comprehensive exam, thesis or practicum research; for doctorate, comprehensive exam, thesis/dissertation, 2nd-year project. *Entrance requirements:* For master's, GRE, 2 official transcripts; goals statement; 15 undergraduate credits in concentration for which the applicant is applying; for doctorate, GRE, 3 letters of recommendation; resume; goals statement; minimum GPA of 3.0 overall for last 60 undergraduate credits, 3.25 in psychology courses; 15 undergraduate credits in concentration for which the applicant is applying; 2 official transcripts; for Certificate, GRE, 2 official transcripts; expanded goals statement; 3 letters of recommendation. Additional exam requirements/recommendations for international students: Required—TOEFL (minimum score 575 paper-based; 88 iBT), IELTS (minimum score 6.5), PTE (minimum score 59). Application fee: $75 ($80 for international students). Electronic applications accepted. *Expenses:* Tuition, state resident: full-time $11,228; part-time $459.50 per credit. Tuition, nonresident: full-time $30,932; part-time $1280.50 per credit. *Required fees:* $3252; $135.50 per credit. Part-time tuition and fees vary according to course load and program. *Financial support:* In 2017–18, 110 students received support, including 6 fellowships (averaging $4,829 per year), 52 research assistantships with tuition reimbursements available (averaging $10,933 per year), 70 teaching assistantships with tuition reimbursements available (averaging $7,703 per year); career-related internships or fieldwork, Federal Work-Study, scholarships/grants, tuition waivers (partial), unspecified assistantships, and health care benefits (for full-time research or teaching assistantship recipients) also available. Support available to part-time students. Financial award application deadline: 3/1; financial award applicants required to submit FAFSA. *Faculty research:* Applied developmental psychology, biopsychology, clinical psychology, human factors/applied cognition psychology, industrial/organizational psychology, school psychology. *Total annual research expenditures:* $2.6 million. *Unit head:* Reeshad Dalal, Department Chair, 703-993-9487, Fax: 703-993-1359, E-mail: rdalal@gmu.edu. *Application contact:* Michael Hock, Graduate Program Coordinator, 703-993-1548, Fax: 703-993-1359, E-mail: mhock2@gmu.edu.
Website: http://psychology.gmu.edu

The George Washington University, Columbian College of Arts and Sciences, Department of Psychology, Washington, DC 20052. Offers applied social psychology (PhD); clinical psychology (PhD); cognitive neuroscience (PhD). *Accreditation:* APA. *Program availability:* Part-time, evening/weekend. *Faculty:* 26 full-time (15 women), 10 part-time/adjunct (7 women). *Students:* 41 full-time (27 women), 25 part-time (17 women); includes 24 minority (10 Black or African American, non-Hispanic/Latino; 8 Asian, non-Hispanic/Latino; 4 Hispanic/Latino; 2 Two or more races, non-Hispanic/Latino), 6 international. Average age 28. 452 applicants, 35% accepted, 87 enrolled. In 2017, 10 doctorates awarded. *Degree requirements:* For doctorate, thesis/dissertation or alternative, general exam. *Entrance requirements:* For doctorate, GRE General Test, minimum GPA of 3.0. Additional exam requirements/recommendations for international students: Required—TOEFL (minimum score 550 paper-based; 80 iBT). *Application deadline:* For fall admission, 1/15 for domestic and international students. Application fee: $75. *Expenses: Tuition:* Full-time $28,800; part-time $1655 per credit hour. *Required fees:* $45; $2.75 per credit hour. *Financial support:* In 2017–18, 62 students received support. Fellowships with tuition reimbursements available, teaching assistantships with tuition reimbursements available, career-related internships or fieldwork, Federal Work-Study, and tuition waivers available. *Unit head:* Dr. Carol Sigelman, Chair, 202-994-8422, E-mail: carol@gwu.edu. *Application contact:* Information Contact, 202-994-6320, Fax: 202-994-1602, E-mail: psych@gwu.edu.
Website: http://psychology.columbian.gwu.edu/

The George Washington University, Graduate School of Education and Human Development, Department of Counseling and Human Development, Program in Clinical Mental Health Counseling, Washington, DC 20052. Offers MA. *Students:* 36 full-time (30 women), 9 part-time (8 women); includes 19 minority (6 Black or African American, non-Hispanic/Latino; 5 Asian, non-Hispanic/Latino; 7 Hispanic/Latino; 1 Two or more races, non-Hispanic/Latino), 1 international. Average age 29. 161 applicants, 42% accepted, 25 enrolled. In 2017, 15 master's awarded. *Degree requirements:* For master's, internship. *Entrance requirements:* For master's, GRE or MAT, two letters of

recommendation, 1- to 2-page statement of purpose, official transcripts from all institutions attended, resume. Additional exam requirements/recommendations for international students: Required—TOEFL or IELTS. *Expenses: Tuition:* Full-time $28,800; part-time $1655 per credit hour. *Required fees:* $45; $2.75 per credit hour. *Financial support:* Fellowships available. *Unit head:* Dr. Kenneth C. Hergenrather, Chair, 202-994-1334, E-mail: hergenkc@gwu.edu. *Application contact:* Sarah Lang, Director of Graduate Admissions, 202-994-1447, Fax: 202-994-7207, E-mail: slang@gwu.edu.
Website: http://gsehd.gwu.edu/clinical-mental-health-counseling-masters

Georgian Court University, School of Arts and Sciences, Lakewood, NJ 08701-2697. Offers applied behavior analysis (MA); autism spectrum disorders (Certificate); clinical mental health counseling (MA); criminal justice and human rights (MS); holistic health studies (MA, Certificate); homeland security (Certificate); instructional technology (CPC); mercy spirituality (Certificate); parish business management (Certificate); professional counselor (Certificate); school psychology (MA, Certificate); theology (MA, Certificate). *Program availability:* Part-time, evening/weekend. *Faculty:* 18 full-time (11 women), 8 part-time/adjunct (4 women). *Students:* 100 full-time (86 women), 92 part-time (67 women); includes 34 minority (9 Black or African American, non-Hispanic/Latino; 1 Asian, non-Hispanic/Latino; 20 Hispanic/Latino; 4 Two or more races, non-Hispanic/Latino), 2 international. Average age 34. 187 applicants, 56% accepted, 78 enrolled. In 2017, 58 master's, 20 other advanced degrees awarded. *Degree requirements:* For master's, comprehensive exam (for some programs), thesis (for some programs). *Entrance requirements:* For master's, GRE, GMAT, or NTE/PRAXIS, 3 letters of recommendation. Additional exam requirements/recommendations for international students: Required—TOEFL (minimum score 550 paper-based). *Application deadline:* For fall admission, 8/15 for domestic students, 5/1 for international students; for spring admission, 1/15 for domestic students, 10/1 for international students. Applications are processed on a rolling basis. Application fee: $40. Electronic applications accepted. *Expenses: Tuition:* Part-time $839 per credit. *Required fees:* $248 per semester. Tuition and fees vary according to campus/location and program. *Financial support:* Scholarships/grants, health care benefits, and unspecified assistantships available. Financial award application deadline: 4/15; financial award applicants required to submit FAFSA. *Unit head:* Dr. Mary Chinery, Dean, 732-987-2493, Fax: 732-987-2007, E-mail: mchinery@georgian.edu. *Application contact:* Patrick Givens, Director of Graduate and Professional Studies Admissions, 732-987-2736, Fax: 732-987-2000, E-mail: gps@georgian.edu.
Website: https://georgian.edu/academics/school-of-arts-sciences/

Georgia Southern University, Jack N. Averitt College of Graduate Studies, College of Liberal Arts and Social Sciences, Program in Psychology, Statesboro, GA 30460. Offers clinical psychology (Psy D); psychology (MS). *Faculty:* 19 full-time (9 women), 1 (woman) part-time/adjunct. *Students:* 51 full-time (36 women), 10 part-time (7 women); includes 15 minority (2 Black or African American, non-Hispanic/Latino; 2 Asian, non-Hispanic/Latino; 7 Hispanic/Latino; 4 Two or more races, non-Hispanic/Latino). Average age 26. 135 applicants, 23% accepted, 18 enrolled. In 2017, 24 master's, 9 doctorates awarded. Terminal master's awarded for partial completion of doctoral program. *Degree requirements:* For master's, comprehensive exam, thesis (for some programs), terminal exam; for doctorate, comprehensive exam, thesis/dissertation, clinical qualifying exam, practicum, internship. *Entrance requirements:* For master's, GRE General Test, minimum GPA of 3.0, introductory courses in psychology and statistics, letters of recommendation; for doctorate, GRE General Test; GRE Subject Test (if no undergraduate degree in psychology), minimum undergraduate GPA of 3.25; 3 letters of reference; statement of purpose. Additional exam requirements/recommendations for international students: Required—TOEFL (minimum score 550 paper-based; 80 iBT), IELTS (minimum score 6). *Application deadline:* For fall admission, 1/15 priority date for domestic students, 1/15 for international students. Application fee: $50. Electronic applications accepted. *Expenses:* Tuition, state resident: full-time $4986; part-time $3324 per year. Tuition, nonresident: full-time $21,982; part-time $15,352 per year. *Required fees:* $2092; $1802 per credit hour. $901 per semester. Tuition and fees vary according to course load, campus/location and program. *Financial support:* In 2017–18, 45 students received support, including 4 fellowships with full tuition reimbursements available (averaging $7,750 per year), 6 research assistantships with full tuition reimbursements available (averaging $7,750 per year), 17 teaching assistantships with full tuition reimbursements available (averaging $7,750 per year); career-related internships or fieldwork, Federal Work-Study, scholarships/grants, tuition waivers (full), and unspecified assistantships also available. Support available to part-time students. Financial award application deadline: 4/15; financial award applicants required to submit FAFSA. *Faculty research:* Clinical psychology, cognitive psychology, social psychology, developmental psychology, teaching and psychology, social judgment and behavior, psychology of religion. *Unit head:* Dr. Michael Nielsen, Graduate Director, 912-478-5539, Fax: 912-478-0751, E-mail: mnielsen@georgiasouthern.edu.
Website: http://class.georgiasouthern.edu/psychology/

Georgia State University, College of Arts and Sciences, Department of Psychology, Atlanta, GA 30302-3083. Offers clinical psychology (PhD); cognitive sciences (PhD); community psychology (PhD); developmental psychology (PhD); neuropsychology and behavioral neuroscience (PhD). *Accreditation:* APA. *Faculty:* 40 full-time (26 women). *Students:* 102 full-time (80 women), 4 part-time (all women); includes 26 minority (7 Black or African American, non-Hispanic/Latino; 10 Asian, non-Hispanic/Latino; 4 Hispanic/Latino; 5 Two or more races, non-Hispanic/Latino), 8 international. Average age 27. 450 applicants, 7% accepted, 16 enrolled. In 2017, 21 doctorates awarded. *Entrance requirements:* For doctorate, GRE. Additional exam requirements/recommendations for international students: Required—TOEFL (minimum score 550 paper-based; 80 iBT). *Application deadline:* For fall admission, 12/1 for domestic and international students. Application fee: $50. Electronic applications accepted. *Expenses:* Tuition, state resident: full-time $7020. Tuition, nonresident: full-time $22,518. *Required fees:* $2128. Tuition and fees vary according to degree level and program. *Financial support:* In 2017–18, fellowships with full tuition reimbursements (averaging $19,282 per year), research assistantships with full tuition reimbursements (averaging $5,173 per year), teaching assistantships with full tuition reimbursements (averaging $6,389 per year) were awarded; scholarships/grants, traineeships, health care benefits, and unspecified assistantships also available. Financial award applicants required to submit FAFSA. *Faculty research:* Clinical psychology, developmental psychology, community psychology, neuropsychology and behavioral neuroscience, cognitive sciences. *Unit head:* Dr. Lisa Armistead, Chair, 404-413-6205, Fax: 404-413-6207, E-mail: lparmistead@gsu.edu. *Application contact:* Dr. Lindsey Cohen, Director of Graduate Studies, 404-413-6263, Fax: 404-413-6207, E-mail: llcohen@gsu.edu.

Goddard College, Graduate Division, Master of Arts in Clinical Mental Health Counseling Program, Plainfield, VT 05667-9432. Offers MA.

Grace College, Department of Graduate Counseling, Winona Lake, IN 46590-1294. Offers clinical mental health counseling (MA). *Accreditation:* ACA. *Program availability:* Part-time. *Faculty:* 5 full-time (2 women), 5 part-time/adjunct (1 woman). *Students:* 68 full-time (46 women), 23 part-time (16 women); includes 9 minority (6 Black or African American, non-Hispanic/Latino; 2 Hispanic/Latino; 1 Native Hawaiian or other Pacific Islander, non-Hispanic/Latino). Average age 32. In 2017, 23 master's awarded. *Degree requirements:* For master's, comprehensive exam, portfolio, internships. *Entrance requirements:* For master's, GRE, references, background check, interview, minimum GPA of 3.0. Additional exam requirements/recommendations for international students: Required—TOEFL. *Application deadline:* For fall admission, 8/1 priority date for domestic students; for spring admission, 12/1 priority date for domestic students. Applications are processed on a rolling basis. Application fee: $250. Electronic applications accepted. Application fee is waived when completed online. *Financial support:* Teaching assistantships with partial tuition reimbursements, career-related internships or fieldwork, and unspecified assistantships available. Financial award application deadline: 3/10; financial award applicants required to submit FAFSA. *Faculty research:* Trauma and sexual abuse. *Unit head:* Amy Gilbert, Chair, Department of Graduate Counseling, 574-322-5100 Ext. 6064, Fax: 574-372-5143, E-mail: gilberal@grace.edu. *Application contact:* Zachary Parrott, Graduate Admissions Counselor, 800-823.8533, E-mail: graceonline@grace.edu.

The Graduate Center, City University of New York, Graduate Studies, Program in Psychology, New York, NY 10016-4039. Offers basic applied neurocognition (PhD); biopsychology (PhD); clinical psychology (PhD); developmental psychology (PhD); environmental psychology (PhD); experimental psychology (PhD); industrial psychology (PhD); learning processes (PhD); neuropsychology (PhD); psychology (PhD); social personality (PhD). *Faculty:* 119 full-time (40 women). *Students:* 428 full-time (308 women); includes 118 minority (31 Black or African American, non-Hispanic/Latino; 31 Asian, non-Hispanic/Latino; 47 Hispanic/Latino; 1 Native Hawaiian or other Pacific Islander, non-Hispanic/Latino; 8 Two or more races, non-Hispanic/Latino), 53 international. Average age 33. 795 applicants, 12% accepted, 56 enrolled. In 2017, 46 doctorates awarded. *Degree requirements:* For doctorate, one foreign language, thesis/dissertation. *Entrance requirements:* For doctorate, GRE General Test. Additional exam requirements/recommendations for international students: Required—TOEFL. *Application deadline:* For fall admission, 12/1 priority date for domestic students. Application fee: $125. Electronic applications accepted. *Financial support:* In 2017–18, 371 students received support, including 340 fellowships, 34 research assistantships, 33 teaching assistantships; career-related internships or fieldwork, Federal Work-Study, institutionally sponsored loans, and tuition waivers (full and partial) also available. Financial award application deadline: 2/1; financial award applicants required to submit FAFSA. *Unit head:* Richard Bodnar, Executive Officer, 212-817-8706, Fax: 212-817-1533, E-mail: rbodnar@gc.cuny.edu. *Application contact:* Les Gribben, Director of Admissions, 212-817-7470, Fax: 212-817-1624, E-mail: lgribben@gc.cuny.edu.

Hawai`i Pacific University, College of Liberal Arts, Program in Clinical Mental Health Counseling, Honolulu, HI 96813. Offers MA. *Program availability:* Part-time, evening/weekend. *Faculty:* 6 full-time (3 women), 2 part-time/adjunct (1 woman). *Students:* 20 full-time (17 women), 16 part-time (12 women); includes 23 minority (4 Black or African American, non-Hispanic/Latino; 6 Asian, non-Hispanic/Latino; 2 Hispanic/Latino; 11 Two or more races, non-Hispanic/Latino), 1 international. Average age 29. 27 applicants, 85% accepted, 16 enrolled. In 2017, 9 master's awarded. *Entrance requirements:* For master's, GRE, transcripts, two letters of recommendation, statement of purpose, resume. Additional exam requirements/recommendations for international students: Recommended—TOEFL (minimum score 550 paper-based; 80 iBT), IELTS (minimum score 6), TWE (minimum score 5). *Application deadline:* For fall admission, 2/15 priority date for domestic students. Applications are processed on a rolling basis. Application fee: $50. Electronic applications accepted. *Expenses: Tuition:* Full-time $18,000; part-time $1000 per credit. *Required fees:* $200; $26 per credit. Tuition and fees vary according to course load and program. *Financial support:* In 2017–18, 5 students received support. Career-related internships or fieldwork, Federal Work-Study, scholarships/grants, tuition waivers (partial), and unspecified assistantships available. Financial award application deadline: 3/1; financial award applicants required to submit FAFSA. *Unit head:* Dr. Michael Erickson, Department Chair, 808-356-5211, E-mail: merickson@hpu.edu. *Application contact:* Danny Lam, Assistant Director of Graduate Admissions, 808-544-1135, E-mail: graduate@hpu.edu.
Website: https://www.hpu.edu/cla/psychology/ma-cmhc.html

Heidelberg University, Master of Arts in Counseling Program, Tiffin, OH 44883-2462. Offers clinical mental health counseling (MA); school counseling (MA). *Accreditation:* ACA. *Program availability:* Part-time, evening/weekend. *Students:* 19 full-time (15 women), 25 part-time (19 women). In 2017, 10 master's awarded. *Degree requirements:* For master's, counseling practicum, internship. *Entrance requirements:* For master's, bachelor's degree with minimum GPA of 2.9; 12 hours of coursework in behavioral sciences; 3 letters of recommendation; 2-3 page goal statement. Additional exam requirements/recommendations for international students: Required—TOEFL (minimum score 550 paper-based, 79 iBT) or IELTS (minimum score 6.5). *Application deadline:* Applications are processed on a rolling basis. Application fee: $0. Electronic applications accepted. *Expenses:* $525 per hour. *Financial support:* Scholarships/grants and unspecified assistantships available. Financial award applicants required to submit FAFSA. *Unit head:* Dr. Marjorie Shavers, Director of Graduate Studies in Counseling, 419-448-2308, E-mail: mshavers@heidelberg.edu. *Application contact:* Katie Zeyen, Graduate Admissions Coordinator, 419-448-2602, Fax: 419-448-2565, E-mail: kzeyen@heidelberg.edu.
Website: https://www.heidelberg.edu/academics/programs/master-of-counseling

Hodges University, Graduate Programs, Naples, FL 34119. Offers accounting (M Acc); business administration (MBA); clinical mental health counseling (MS); health services administration (MS); information systems management (MIS); legal studies (MS); management (MSM). *Program availability:* Part-time, evening/weekend, 100% online, blended/hybrid learning. *Degree requirements:* For master's, comprehensive exam (for some programs), thesis (for some programs). *Entrance requirements:* For master's, essay. Additional exam requirements/recommendations for international students: Recommended—TOEFL. Electronic applications accepted.

Hofstra University, College of Liberal Arts and Sciences, Programs in Psychology, Hempstead, NY 11549. Offers applied organizational psychology (PhD); clinical psychology (PhD); industrial/organizational psychology (MA); school-community psychology (Psy D). *Accreditation:* APA. *Program availability:* Part-time, evening/weekend. *Students:* 199 full-time (130 women), 24 part-time (20 women); includes 44 minority (5 Black or African American, non-Hispanic/Latino; 12 Asian, non-Hispanic/Latino; 25 Hispanic/Latino; 1 Native Hawaiian or other Pacific Islander, non-Hispanic/Latino; 1 Two or more races, non-Hispanic/Latino), 19 international. Average age 27. 314 applicants, 45% accepted, 60 enrolled. In 2017, 47 master's, 25 doctorates awarded. *Degree requirements:* For master's, comprehensive exam, thesis optional, internship, minimum GPA of 3.0; for doctorate, comprehensive exam, thesis/dissertation, 1st year qualifying examination, 2nd year research project, successful practicum/externship placements, written presentation and successful oral defense of dissertation, completion of full-time internship. *Entrance requirements:* For master's, GRE General Test, minimum GPA of 3.0, essay, interview; for doctorate, GRE General Test, GRE Subject Test (psychology), 3 letters of recommendation, interview, essay, curriculum vitae. Additional exam requirements/recommendations for international students: Required—TOEFL (minimum score 550 paper-based; 80 iBT). *Application deadline:* For fall admission, 12/31 for domestic and international students. Application fee: $75. Electronic applications accepted. *Expenses: Tuition:* Full-time $1292. *Required*

fees: $970. Tuition and fees vary according to program. *Financial support:* In 2017–18, 131 students received support, including 126 fellowships with full and partial tuition reimbursements available (averaging $7,840 per year), 4 research assistantships with full and partial tuition reimbursements available (averaging $5,974 per year); career-related internships or fieldwork, Federal Work-Study, institutionally sponsored loans, scholarships/grants, traineeships, tuition waivers (full and partial), and unspecified assistantships also available. Support available to part-time students. Financial award applicants required to submit FAFSA. *Faculty research:* Coping with job stress; schizophrenia; positive clinical psychology; treatments (including virtual reality based) for phobias, trauma, and PTSD; scientific reasoning in children and adults. *Unit head:* Dr. Craig Johnson, Chairperson, 516-463-5636, E-mail: craig.a.johnson@hofstra.edu. *Application contact:* Sunil Samuel, Assistant Vice President of Admissions, 516-463-4723, Fax: 516-463-4664, E-mail: graduateadmission@hofstra.edu. Website: http://www.hofstra.edu/hclas

Hood College, Graduate School, Program in Counseling, Frederick, MD 21701-8575. Offers clinical mental health counseling (MS); school counseling (MS). *Program availability:* Part-time, evening/weekend. *Faculty:* 2 full-time (1 woman), 2 part-time/adjunct (both women). *Students:* 36 full-time (32 women), 26 part-time (24 women); includes 12 minority (4 Black or African American, non-Hispanic/Latino; 1 American Indian or Alaska Native, non-Hispanic/Latino; 4 Hispanic/Latino; 3 Two or more races, non-Hispanic/Latino), 1 international. Average age 31. 27 applicants, 85% accepted, 18 enrolled. In 2017, 3 master's awarded. *Degree requirements:* For master's, practicum, internship. *Entrance requirements:* For master's, minimum GPA of 3.0, personal statement, resume, two letters of recommendation. Additional exam requirements/recommendations for international students: Required—TOEFL (minimum score 575 paper-based; 89 iBT), IELTS (minimum score 6.5). *Application deadline:* For fall admission, 6/15 for domestic and international students; for winter admission, 11/15 for domestic and international students. Application fee: $35. Electronic applications accepted. *Expenses:* $660 per credit plus $110 comprehensive fee per semester. *Financial support:* Research assistantships with full tuition reimbursements, tuition waivers (partial), and unspecified assistantships available. Financial award applicants required to submit FAFSA. *Unit head:* Dr. April M. Boulton, Dean of the Graduate School, 301-696-3600, E-mail: gofurther@hood.edu. *Application contact:* Jan Marcus, Assistant Director of Graduate Admissions, 301-696-3600, E-mail: gofurther@hood.edu.

Howard University, Graduate School, Department of Psychology, Washington, DC 20059-0002. Offers clinical psychology (PhD); developmental psychology (PhD); experimental psychology (PhD); neuropsychology (PhD); personality psychology (PhD); psychology (MS); social psychology (PhD). *Accreditation:* APA (one or more programs are accredited). *Program availability:* Part-time. *Degree requirements:* For master's, thesis; for doctorate, comprehensive exam, thesis/dissertation, qualifying exam. *Entrance requirements:* For master's, GRE General Test, minimum GPA of 2.5, bachelor's degree in psychology or related field; for doctorate, GRE General Test, minimum GPA of 3.0. *Faculty research:* Personality and psychophysiology, educational and social development of African-American children, child and adult psychopathology.

Husson University, Graduate Programs in Counseling and Human Relations, Bangor, ME 04401-2999. Offers clinical mental health counseling (MS); human relations (MS); school counseling (MS). *Accreditation:* ACA. *Program availability:* Part-time, evening/weekend. *Faculty:* 3 full-time (2 women), 5 part-time/adjunct (all women). *Students:* 21 full-time (18 women), 44 part-time (39 women); includes 2 minority (1 Black or African American, non-Hispanic/Latino; 1 Hispanic/Latino), 1 international. Average age 31. 49 applicants, 41% accepted, 13 enrolled. In 2017, 17 master's awarded. *Degree requirements:* For master's, comprehensive exam (for some programs), thesis optional. *Entrance requirements:* For master's, BS with minimum GPA of 3.0, letters of recommendation, interview. Additional exam requirements/recommendations for international students: Required—TOEFL (minimum score 550 paper-based; 80 iBT), IELTS (minimum score 6.5). *Application deadline:* For fall admission, 2/1 for domestic students. Application fee: $50. Electronic applications accepted. *Expenses:* $577 per credit; fees depend on number of credits. *Financial support:* In 2017–18, 2 students received support. Federal Work-Study, scholarships/grants, and unspecified assistantships available. Financial award application deadline: 4/15; financial award applicants required to submit FAFSA. *Faculty research:* Challenges and rewards of counseling practice in rural, small town and neighborhood settings. *Unit head:* Dr. Deborah Drew, Director, Graduate Counseling Programs, 207-992-4912, Fax: 207-992-4952, E-mail: drewd@husson.edu. *Application contact:* Kristen Card, Director of Graduate Admissions, 207-404-5660, Fax: 207-941-7935, E-mail: cardk@husson.edu. Website: http://www.husson.edu/college-of-health-and-education/school-of-education/graduate-programs/

Idaho State University, Office of Graduate Studies, College of Arts and Letters, Department of Psychology, Program in Clinical Psychology, Pocatello, ID 83209-8112. Offers PhD. *Degree requirements:* For doctorate, comprehensive exam, thesis/dissertation, 1 year full-time clinical internship. *Entrance requirements:* For doctorate, GRE General Test, GRE Subject Test, MS in psychology. Additional exam requirements/recommendations for international students: Required—TOEFL (minimum score 550 paper-based; 80 iBT). Electronic applications accepted. *Faculty research:* Pre-adolescent behavior, substance abuse training, trauma related problems.

Illinois Institute of Technology, Graduate College, Lewis College of Human Sciences, Department of Psychology, Chicago, IL 60616. Offers clinical psychology (PhD); industrial and organizational psychology (PhD); personnel and human resource development (MS); rehabilitation and mental health counseling (MS); rehabilitation counseling education (PhD). *Accreditation:* APA (one or more programs are accredited); CORE. *Program availability:* Part-time, evening/weekend. Terminal master's awarded for partial completion of doctoral program. *Degree requirements:* For master's, thesis (for some programs); for doctorate, comprehensive exam, thesis/dissertation, minimum of 107 credit hours, 1-year full-time internship. *Entrance requirements:* For master's, GRE General Test (minimum score 298 Quantitative and Verbal, 3.0 Analytical Writing), minimum GPA of 3.0; 3 letters of recommendation; bachelor's degree from accredited institution (for personnel and human resource development); for doctorate, GRE General Test (minimum score 298 Quantitative and Verbal, 3.0 Analytical Writing), bachelor's or master's degree from accredited institution, recommendations. Additional exam requirements/recommendations for international students: Required—TOEFL (minimum score 550 paper-based; 80 iBT). Electronic applications accepted. *Faculty research:* Clinical psychology, rehabilitation and mental health counseling, industrial organizational psychology.

Illinois State University, Graduate School, College of Arts and Sciences, Department of Psychology, Normal, IL 61790. Offers psychology (MA, MS), including clinical-counseling psychology, cognitive and behavioral sciences, developmental psychology, industrial/organizational-social psychology; school psychology (PhD, SSP). *Accreditation:* APA. *Degree requirements:* For master's, thesis or alternative; for doctorate, variable foreign language requirement, thesis/dissertation, 2 terms of residency, internship, practicum. *Entrance requirements:* For master's, GRE General Test, GRE Subject Test, minimum GPA of 3.0 in last 60 hours of course work; for doctorate, GRE General Test. *Faculty research:* Comprehensive evaluation system for

the central region professional development grant, Illinois school psychology internship consortium, for children's sake.

Immaculata University, College of Graduate Studies, Department of Psychology, Immaculata, PA 19345. Offers clinical mental health counseling (MA); clinical psychology (Psy D); forensic psychology (Graduate Certificate); integrative psychotherapy (Graduate Certificate); neuropsychology (Graduate Certificate); psychodynamic psychotherapy (Graduate Certificate); psychological testing (Graduate Certificate); school counseling (MA, Graduate Certificate); school psychology (MA). *Accreditation:* APA. *Program availability:* Part-time, evening/weekend. Terminal master's awarded for partial completion of doctoral program. *Degree requirements:* For master's, comprehensive exam, thesis optional; for doctorate, comprehensive exam, thesis/dissertation. *Entrance requirements:* For master's, GRE General Test or MAT, minimum GPA of 3.0; for doctorate, GRE General Test or MAT, minimum GPA of 3.5. Additional exam requirements/recommendations for international students: Required—TOEFL, IELTS. Electronic applications accepted. *Faculty research:* Supervision ethics, psychology of teaching, gender.

Indiana State University, College of Graduate and Professional Studies, Bayh College of Education, Department of Communication Disorders and Counseling, School, and Educational Psychology, Terre Haute, IN 47809. Offers clinical mental health counseling (MS); communication disorders (MS); school counseling (M Ed); school psychology (PhD, Ed S); MA/MS. *Accreditation:* ACA; ASHA; NCATE. *Program availability:* Part-time, evening/weekend. *Degree requirements:* For master's, thesis optional; for doctorate, thesis/dissertation, research tools proficiency tests. *Entrance requirements:* For master's, GRE General Test or MAT, minimum undergraduate GPA of 2.75; for doctorate, GRE General Test, master's degree, minimum undergraduate GPA of 3.5. Electronic applications accepted. *Faculty research:* Vocational development supervision.

Indiana State University, College of Graduate and Professional Studies, College of Arts and Sciences, Department of Psychology, Terre Haute, IN 47809. Offers clinical psychology (Psy D); general psychology (MA, MS). *Accreditation:* APA (one or more programs are accredited). Terminal master's awarded for partial completion of doctoral program. *Degree requirements:* For master's, thesis (for some programs); for doctorate, comprehensive exam, thesis/dissertation, internship, professional research project. *Entrance requirements:* For master's, GRE General Test, 12 semester hours of course work in psychology, minimum GPA of 2.75; for doctorate, GRE General Test, minimum GPA of 3.0. Additional exam requirements/recommendations for international students: Required—TOEFL (minimum score 550 paper-based). Electronic applications accepted.

Indiana University of Pennsylvania, School of Graduate Studies and Research, College of Education and Communications, Department of Counseling, Program in Clinical Mental Health Counseling, Indiana, PA 15705. Offers MA. *Program availability:* Part-time, evening/weekend. *Faculty:* 11 full-time (10 women), 5 part-time/adjunct (4 women). *Students:* 62 full-time (46 women), 42 part-time (35 women); includes 12 minority (7 Black or African American, non-Hispanic/Latino; 1 American Indian or Alaska Native, non-Hispanic/Latino; 1 Hispanic/Latino; 3 Two or more races, non-Hispanic/Latino), 1 international. Average age 31. 95 applicants, 59% accepted, 37 enrolled. In 2017, 32 master's awarded. *Entrance requirements:* For master's, minimum undergraduate GPA of 2.8. Additional exam requirements/recommendations for international students: Required—TOEFL (minimum score 540 paper-based). *Application deadline:* For fall admission, 3/17 priority date for domestic students. Electronic applications accepted. *Expenses:* Tuition, state resident: full-time $12,000; part-time $500 per credit. Tuition, nonresident: full-time $18,000; part-time $750 per credit. Required fees: $4073; $165.55 per credit. $64 per term. *Financial support:* In 2017–18, 13 research assistantships with tuition reimbursements (averaging $2,609 per year) were awarded; fellowships with full tuition reimbursements, career-related internships or fieldwork, Federal Work-Study, scholarships/grants, and unspecified assistantships also available. Financial award application deadline: 4/15; financial award applicants required to submit FAFSA. *Unit head:* Dr. Robert Witchel, Program Coordinator, 724-357-2306, E-mail: bwitchel@iup.edu. *Application contact:* Claire Dandeneau, Program Coordinator, 724-357-4534, E-mail: claire.dandeneau@iup.edu.

Indiana University of Pennsylvania, School of Graduate Studies and Research, College of Natural Sciences and Mathematics, Department of Psychology, Program in Clinical Psychology, Indiana, PA 15705. Offers Psy D. *Accreditation:* APA. *Program availability:* Part-time. *Faculty:* 13 full-time (7 women). *Students:* 48 full-time (35 women), 20 part-time (11 women); includes 13 minority (1 Black or African American, non-Hispanic/Latino; 5 Asian, non-Hispanic/Latino; 6 Hispanic/Latino; 1 Two or more races, non-Hispanic/Latino), 3 international. Average age 26. 245 applicants, 18% accepted, 15 enrolled. In 2017, 15 doctorates awarded. *Entrance requirements:* For doctorate, GRE General Test, minimum GPA of 3.0, 3 letters of recommendation, interview. Additional exam requirements/recommendations for international students: Required—TOEFL (minimum score 540 paper-based). *Application deadline:* For fall admission, 12/15 priority date for domestic students. Application fee: $50. Electronic applications accepted. *Expenses:* Contact institution. *Financial support:* Fellowships, research assistantships, teaching assistantships, career-related internships or fieldwork, Federal Work-Study, scholarships/grants, and unspecified assistantships available. Financial award application deadline: 4/15; financial award applicants required to submit FAFSA. *Unit head:* Dr. David LaPorte, Graduate Coordinator, 724-357-2426, E-mail: laporte@iup.edu. Website: http://www.iup.edu/psychology/grad/clinical-psychology-psyd/default.aspx

Indiana University–Purdue University Indianapolis, School of Science, Department of Psychology, Indianapolis, IN 46202-3275. Offers addiction neuroscience (PhD); applied social and organizational psychology (PhD); clinical psychology (PhD); industrial/organizational psychology (MS). *Accreditation:* APA (one or more programs are accredited). Terminal master's awarded for partial completion of doctoral program. *Degree requirements:* For master's, thesis; for doctorate, thesis/dissertation. *Entrance requirements:* For master's, GRE General Test, minimum undergraduate GPA of 3.0; for doctorate, GRE General Test, GRE Subject Test (clinical psychology), minimum undergraduate GPA of 3.2. Additional exam requirements/recommendations for international students: Required—TOEFL (minimum score 567 paper-based; 86 iBT), IELTS (minimum score 6.5). Electronic applications accepted. *Faculty research:* Severe mental illness, health psychology, neurological research, alcoholism and psychopathology, functional activities within organizations.

Indiana University South Bend, School of Education, South Bend, IN 46615. Offers addiction counseling (MS Ed); alcohol and drug counseling (Graduate Certificate); clinical mental health counseling (MS Ed); educational leadership (MS Ed); elementary education (MS Ed); marriage, couple, and family counseling (MS Ed); school counseling (MS Ed); secondary education (MS Ed); special education (MAT, MS Ed), including intense intervention (MS Ed), mild intervention (MS Ed). *Accreditation:* NCATE. *Program availability:* Part-time, evening/weekend. *Degree requirements:* For master's, thesis or alternative, exit project. *Entrance requirements:* For master's, letters of recommendation, GRE or minimum GPA of 3.0. Additional exam requirements/recommendations for international students: Required—TOEFL. Electronic applications accepted. *Expenses:* Contact institution. *Faculty research:* Professional dispositions, early childhood literacy, online learning, program assessments, problem-based learning.

Clinical Psychology

Jackson State University, Graduate School, College of Education and Human Development, Department of Counseling, Rehabilitation and Psychometric Services, Jackson, MS 39217. Offers clinical mental health (MS); rehabilitation counseling (MS); school counseling (MS Ed). *Accreditation:* ACA; CORE (one or more programs are accredited); NCATE. *Program availability:* Part-time, evening/weekend, 100% online, blended/hybrid learning. *Degree requirements:* For master's, comprehensive exam, thesis. *Entrance requirements:* For master's, GRE General Test. Additional exam requirements/recommendations for international students: Required—TOEFL (minimum score 520 paper-based; 67 iBT). Electronic applications accepted. *Expenses:* Contact institution.

Jackson State University, Graduate School, College of Liberal Arts, Department of Psychology, Jackson, MS 39217. Offers clinical psychology (PhD). *Accreditation:* APA. *Degree requirements:* For doctorate, comprehensive exam, thesis/dissertation. *Entrance requirements:* For doctorate, MAT, GRE. Additional exam requirements/ recommendations for international students: Required—TOEFL (minimum score 520 paper-based; 67 iBT).

James Madison University, The Graduate School, College of Health and Behavioral Studies, Clinical Mental Health Counseling Program, Harrisonburg, VA 22807. Offers MA/Ed S. *Accreditation:* ACA. *Program availability:* Part-time, evening/weekend. *Students:* 51 full-time (42 women), 22 part-time (16 women); includes 14 minority (7 Black or African American, non-Hispanic/Latino; 1 Asian, non-Hispanic/Latino; 5 Hispanic/Latino; 1 Two or more races, non-Hispanic/Latino). Average age 30. *Expenses:* Tuition, state resident: full-time $10,512; part-time $438 per credit hour. Tuition, nonresident: full-time $28,358; part-time $1162 per credit hour. *Required fees:* $1128. *Financial support:* In 2017–18, 46 students received support. Career-related internships or fieldwork, Federal Work-Study, and assistantships (averaging $7911) available. Financial award application deadline: 3/1; financial award applicants required to submit FAFSA.

James Madison University, The Graduate School, College of Health and Behavioral Studies, Program in Combined-Integrated Clinical and School Psychology, Harrisonburg, VA 22801. Offers Psy D. *Program availability:* Part-time, evening/ weekend. *Students:* 22 full-time (18 women), 3 part-time (1 woman); includes 4 minority (2 Black or African American, non-Hispanic/Latino; 2 Hispanic/Latino), 1 international. Average age 30. In 2017, 5 doctorates awarded. Application fee: $55. Electronic applications accepted. *Expenses:* Tuition, state resident: full-time $10,512; part-time $438 per credit hour. Tuition, nonresident: full-time $28,358; part-time $1162 per credit hour. *Required fees:* $1128. *Financial support:* In 2017–18, 17 students received support. Fellowships, teaching assistantships, Federal Work-Study, unspecified assistantships, and 17 doctoral assistantships (stipend varies) available. Financial award application deadline: 3/1; financial award applicants required to submit FAFSA. *Unit head:* Dr. Gregg R. Henriques, Graduate Program Director, 540-568-7857, E-mail: henrigg@jmu.edu. *Application contact:* Lynette D. Michael, Director of Graduate Admissions, 540-568-6131 Ext. 6395, Fax: 540-568-7860, E-mail: michaeld@jmu.edu. Website: http://www.psyc.jmu.edu/cipsyd/

John Brown University, Graduate Counseling Programs, Siloam Springs, AR 72761-2121. Offers clinical mental health counseling (MS); marriage and family therapy (MS); play therapy (Graduate Certificate); school counseling (MS). *Accreditation:* NCATE. *Program availability:* Part-time, evening/weekend. *Degree requirements:* For master's, practica or internships. *Entrance requirements:* For master's, GRE (minimum score of 300), recommendation forms from three people, 200-word essay describing professional plans and reason for seeking acceptance. Additional exam requirements/ recommendations for international students: Required—TOEFL (minimum score 550 paper-based; 79 iBT). Electronic applications accepted. *Expenses:* Contact institution.

Johns Hopkins University, Bloomberg School of Public Health, Department of Mental Health, Baltimore, MD 21218. Offers children's mental health services (PhD); mental health (MHS). *Degree requirements:* For master's, thesis (for some programs); for doctorate, thesis/dissertation, 1-year full-time residency, oral and written exams. *Entrance requirements:* For master's, GRE General Test, MCAT, 3 letters of recommendation, curriculum vitae; for doctorate, GRE General Test, MCAT or GMAT, 3 letters of recommendation, curriculum vitae. Additional exam requirements/ recommendations for international students: Required—TOEFL (minimum score 600 paper-based; 100 iBT). Electronic applications accepted. *Faculty research:* Etiology, development and prevention of aggressive and antisocial behavior; epidemiology of mental disorders; genetic epidemiology of mental disorders; brain and behavior.

Johnson & Wales University, Graduate Studies, MS Program in Counseling, Providence, RI 02903-3703. Offers addiction counseling (MS); clinical mental health counseling (MS). *Program availability:* Part-time. *Expenses: Tuition:* Full-time $12,636; part-time $702 per credit hour. *Application contact:* Graduate School Admissions, 401-598-1015, Fax: 401-598-1286, E-mail: pvdgrad@admissions.jwu.edu.

Johnson University, Graduate and Professional Programs, Knoxville, TN 37998-1001. Offers biblical interpretation (Graduate Certificate); business administration (MBA); Christian ministries (Graduate Certificate); clinical mental health counseling (MA); educational technology (MA); intercultural studies (MA); leadership (MBA); leadership studies (PhD); New Testament (MA); nonprofit management (MBA); school counseling (MA); spiritual formation and leadership (Graduate Certificate); strategic ministry (MA); teacher education (MA). *Program availability:* Part-time, evening/weekend, 100% online, blended/hybrid learning. *Degree requirements:* For master's, variable foreign language requirement, comprehensive exam, thesis (for some programs), internships; for doctorate, variable foreign language requirement, comprehensive exam, thesis/ dissertation, internships. *Entrance requirements:* For master's, PRAXIS (for MA in teacher education); MAT (for counseling); GRE or GMAT (for MBA), interview, 3 references, transcripts, essay, minimum GPA of 2.5 or 3.0 (depending on program); for doctorate, GRE or MAT (taken not less than 5 years prior), interview, 3 references, transcripts, essay, minimum GPA of 3.0; for Graduate Certificate, interview, 3 references, transcripts, essay, minimum GPA of 3.0. Additional exam requirements/ recommendations for international students: Required—TOEFL (minimum score 527 paper-based; 71 iBT). Electronic applications accepted. *Expenses:* Contact institution.

Judson University, Master of Arts in Clinical Mental Health Counseling Program, Elgin, IL 60123-1498. Offers MA. *Program availability:* Evening/weekend. *Faculty:* 2 full-time (1 woman), 7 part-time/adjunct (5 women). *Students:* 26 full-time (24 women), 3 part-time (1 woman); includes 7 minority (6 Black or African American, non-Hispanic/Latino; 1 Asian, non-Hispanic/Latino). Average age 44. 16 applicants, 100% accepted, 15 enrolled. *Application deadline:* Applications are processed on a rolling basis. Application fee: $35. Electronic applications accepted. Tuition and fees vary according to course load, degree level and program. *Financial support:* Unspecified assistantships available. *Faculty research:* Gerontological counseling, grief and loss counseling, spirituality and holistic wellness, clinical training for counselors and crisis intervention and trauma. *Unit head:* Dr. Amber Randolph, Program Director, 847-628-1544, E-mail: amber.randolph@judsonu.edu. *Application contact:* Maria Aguirre, Student Academic Advisor, 847-628-1160, E-mail: maguirre@judsonu.edu.

Kean University, Nathan Weiss Graduate College, Doctorate Program in Combined School and Clinical Psychology, Union, NJ 07083. Offers Psy D. *Program availability:* Part-time. *Faculty:* 7 full-time (4 women). *Students:* 42 full-time (33 women), 9 part-time (7 women); includes 18 minority (2 Black or African American, non-Hispanic/Latino; 5 Asian, non-Hispanic/Latino; 10 Hispanic/Latino; 1 Two or more races, non-Hispanic/ Latino). Average age 27. 66 applicants, 50% accepted, 12 enrolled. In 2017, 9 doctorates awarded. *Degree requirements:* For doctorate, comprehensive exam, thesis/ dissertation, externship. *Entrance requirements:* For doctorate, GRE General Test, GRE Subject Test in psychology (taken within last 5 years), minimum undergraduate GPA of 3.3, graduate 3.5; 3 letters of recommendation; personal interview; prerequisite coursework in theories of personality, abnormal psychology, tests and measurements, statistics, and experimental psychology; personal statement. Additional exam requirements/recommendations for international students: Required—TOEFL (minimum score 550 paper-based; 79 iBT), IELTS (minimum score 6.5). *Application deadline:* For fall admission, 1/1 for domestic and international students. Applications are processed on a rolling basis. Application fee: $75. Electronic applications accepted. *Expenses:* Contact institution. *Financial support:* Scholarships/grants and unspecified assistantships available. Financial award applicants required to submit FAFSA. *Unit head:* Dr. Jennifer Block-Lerner, Program Coordinator, 908-737-5864, E-mail: jlerner@kean.edu. *Application contact:* Pedro Lopes, Admissions Counselor, 908-737-7100, E-mail: gradadmissions@kean.edu.
Website: http://grad.kean.edu/doctoral-programs/combined-school-and-clinical-psychology

Kean University, Nathan Weiss Graduate College, Program in Counselor Education, Union, NJ 07083. Offers alcohol and drug abuse counseling (MA); clinical mental health counseling (MA); school counseling (MA). *Accreditation:* ACA; NCATE. *Program availability:* Part-time. *Faculty:* 9 full-time (5 women). *Students:* 146 full-time (115 women), 138 part-time (111 women); includes 123 minority (56 Black or African American, non-Hispanic/Latino; 1 American Indian or Alaska Native, non-Hispanic/ Latino; 7 Asian, non-Hispanic/Latino; 53 Hispanic/Latino; 6 Two or more races, non-Hispanic/Latino), 3 international. Average age 32. 197 applicants, 45% accepted, 55 enrolled. In 2017, 80 master's awarded. *Degree requirements:* For master's, practicum, internship, portfolio. *Entrance requirements:* For master's, minimum GPA of 3.0, 2 letters of recommendation, personal statement, resume. Additional exam requirements/ recommendations for international students: Required—TOEFL (minimum score 550 paper-based; 79 iBT), IELTS (minimum score 6.5). *Application deadline:* For fall admission, 3/1 for domestic and international students; for spring admission, 11/1 for domestic and international students. Applications are processed on a rolling basis. Application fee: $75. Electronic applications accepted. *Expenses:* Tuition, state resident: full-time $13,419; part-time $653 per credit. Tuition, nonresident: full-time $18,188; part-time $801 per credit. *Required fees:* $3382; $154 per credit. Tuition and fees vary according to course level, course load, degree level and program. *Financial support:* Scholarships/grants and unspecified assistantships available. Financial award applicants required to submit FAFSA. *Unit head:* Dr. J. Barry Mascari, Program Coordinator, 908-737-5954, E-mail: jmascari@kean.edu. *Application contact:* Pedro Lopes, Admissions Counselor, 908-737-7100, E-mail: gradadmissions@kean.edu.
Website: http://grad.kean.edu/counseling

Kent State University, College of Arts and Sciences, Department of Psychological Sciences, Kent, OH 44242-0001. Offers clinical psychology (MA, PhD), including gerontology (MA), psychological sciences (MA); experimental psychology (MA, PhD), including gerontology (MA), psychological sciences (MA). *Accreditation:* APA (one or more programs are accredited). *Program availability:* Part-time. *Faculty:* 29 full-time (15 women), 5 part-time/adjunct (2 women). *Students:* 84 full-time (66 women); includes 15 minority (8 Black or African American, non-Hispanic/Latino; 4 Asian, non-Hispanic/ Latino; 2 Hispanic/Latino; 1 Two or more races, non-Hispanic/Latino), 3 international. Average age 26. 217 applicants, 10% accepted, 14 enrolled. In 2017, 10 master's, 16 doctorates awarded. Terminal master's awarded for partial completion of doctoral program. *Degree requirements:* For master's, thesis; for doctorate, comprehensive exam, thesis/dissertation. *Entrance requirements:* For master's and doctorate, GRE General Test, statement of goals and motivations, transcripts, 3 letters of recommendation, minimum junior-senior GPA of 3.0, at least one course in statistics and a broad background in psychology. Additional exam requirements/recommendations for international students: Required—TOEFL (minimum score 550 paper-based, 79 iBT), Michigan English Language Assessment Battery (minimum score 77), IELTS (minimum score 6.5) or PTE (minimum score 58). *Application deadline:* For fall admission, 12/1 for domestic and international students. Applications are processed on a rolling basis. Application fee: $45 ($70 for international students). Electronic applications accepted. *Expenses:* Tuition, state resident: full-time $11,310; part-time $515 per credit hour. Tuition, nonresident: full-time $20,396; part-time $928 per credit hour. *International tuition:* $18,544 full-time. *Financial support:* Federal Work-Study, health care benefits, and unspecified assistantships available. Financial award application deadline: 12/1. *Unit head:* Dr. Maria S. Zaragoza, Professor and Chair, 330-672-2166, E-mail: mzaragoz@kent.edu. *Application contact:* Dr. John A. Updegraff, Professor and Graduate Coordinator, 330-672-2166, E-mail: jupdegr1@kent.edu.
Website: https://www.kent.edu/psychology

Kutztown University of Pennsylvania, College of Education, Program in Counseling Psychology, Kutztown, PA 19530-0730. Offers clinical mental health counseling (MA); marriage, couple and family counseling (MA). *Program availability:* Part-time, evening/ weekend. *Faculty:* 4 full-time (3 women), 1 part-time/adjunct (0 women). *Students:* 75 full-time (68 women), 54 part-time (45 women); includes 31 minority (14 Black or African American, non-Hispanic/Latino; 1 Asian, non-Hispanic/Latino; 14 Hispanic/Latino; 2 Two or more races, non-Hispanic/Latino), 1 international. Average age 29. 73 applicants, 67% accepted, 27 enrolled. In 2017, 36 master's awarded. *Degree requirements:* For master's, comprehensive exam, thesis optional. *Entrance requirements:* For master's, GRE General Test, 3 letters of recommendation, minimum undergraduate GPA of 3.0, psychobiographical statement, resume. Additional exam requirements/ recommendations for international students: Required—TOEFL (minimum score 550 paper-based, 79 iBT), IELTS (minimum score 6.5), or PTE (minimum score 53). *Application deadline:* For fall admission, 3/1 for domestic and international students; for spring admission, 10/1 for domestic and international students. Application fee: $35. Electronic applications accepted. *Expenses:* Tuition, state resident: part-time $500 per credit. Tuition, nonresident: part-time $750 per credit. *Required fees:* $115 per credit. One-time fee: $50 part-time. Tuition and fees vary according to degree level. *Financial support:* Career-related internships or fieldwork, Federal Work-Study, and unspecified assistantships available. Financial award application deadline: 3/1; financial award applicants required to submit FAFSA. *Faculty research:* Family addictions. *Unit head:* Dr. Helen S Hamlet, Department Chair, 610-683-4204, Fax: 610-683-1585, E-mail: hamlet@kutztown.edu.
Website: https://www.kutztown.edu/academics/graduate-programs/counseling.htm

LaGrange College, Graduate Programs, Program in Clinical Mental Health Counseling, LaGrange, GA 30240-2999. Offers MS. *Entrance requirements:* For master's, GRE or MAT, bachelor's degree, 3 letters of reference, essay, background check.

Lakehead University, Graduate Studies, Department of Psychology, Thunder Bay, ON P7B 5E1, Canada. Offers clinical psychology (PhD); experimental psychology (MA). *Program availability:* Part-time, evening/weekend. *Degree requirements:* For master's,

thesis optional; for doctorate, thesis/dissertation, 2 comprehensive exams, internship. *Entrance requirements:* For master's, GRE, honors degree in psychology, advanced course work in statistics, minimum B average; for doctorate, GRE, minimum B average. Additional exam requirements/recommendations for international students: Required—TOEFL. *Faculty research:* Chaos theory, health psychology, counseling psychology, gerontology, women's studies.

Lamar University, College of Graduate Studies, College of Arts and Sciences, Department of Psychology, Beaumont, TX 77701. Offers clinical psychology (MS); industrial/organizational psychology (MS). *Program availability:* Part-time. *Faculty:* 9 full-time (5 women), 4 part-time/adjunct (1 woman). *Students:* 9 full-time (7 women), 6 part-time (4 women); includes 7 minority (2 Black or African American, non-Hispanic/Latino; 4 Hispanic/Latino; 1 Two or more races, non-Hispanic/Latino), 1 international. Average age 28. 24 applicants, 75% accepted, 7 enrolled. In 2017, 5 master's awarded. *Degree requirements:* For master's, thesis, practicum. *Entrance requirements:* For master's, GRE General Test, minimum GPA of 2.75 in last 60 hours of undergraduate course work. Additional exam requirements/recommendations for international students: Required—TOEFL (minimum score 550 paper-based; 79 iBT), IELTS (minimum score 6.5). *Application deadline:* For fall admission, 8/10 for domestic students, 7/1 for international students; for spring admission, 1/5 for domestic students, 12/1 for international students. Application fee: $25 ($50 for international students). *Expenses:* Contact institution. *Financial support:* In 2017–18, 12 students received support, including 3 teaching assistantships (averaging $4,500 per year); fellowships, research assistantships, career-related internships or fieldwork, Federal Work-Study, scholarships/grants, and tuition waivers (partial) also available. Support available to part-time students. Financial award application deadline: 4/1. *Faculty research:* Group think, health psychology, school psychology, behavioral neuroscience. *Unit head:* Dr. Edythe E. Kirk, Chair, 409-880-8285, Fax: 409-880-1710. *Application contact:* Deidre Mayer, Interim Director, Admissions and Academic Services, 409-880-8888, Fax: 409-880-7419, E-mail: gradmissions@lamar.edu.
Website: http://artssciences.lamar.edu/psychology

Lamar University, College of Graduate Studies, College of Education and Human Development, Department of Counseling and Special Populations, Beaumont, TX 77701. Offers clinical mental health counseling (M Ed); school counseling (M Ed); special education (M Ed), including special education. *Accreditation:* ACA. *Faculty:* 15 full-time (12 women), 22 part-time/adjunct (18 women). *Students:* 27 full-time (22 women), 1,362 part-time (1,200 women); includes 700 minority (359 Black or African American, non-Hispanic/Latino; 6 American Indian or Alaska Native, non-Hispanic/Latino; 18 Asian, non-Hispanic/Latino; 305 Hispanic/Latino; 1 Native Hawaiian or other Pacific Islander, non-Hispanic/Latino; 11 Two or more races, non-Hispanic/Latino), 2 international. Average age 37. 1,317 applicants, 66% accepted, 234 enrolled. In 2017, 645 master's awarded. *Entrance requirements:* Additional exam requirements/recommendations for international students: Required—TOEFL (minimum score 550 paper-based; 79 iBT), IELTS (minimum score 6.5). *Application deadline:* For fall admission, 8/10 for domestic students, 7/1 for international students; for spring admission, 1/5 for domestic students, 12/1 for international students. Applications are processed on a rolling basis. Application fee: $25 ($50 for international students). Electronic applications accepted. *Expenses:* Contact institution. *Financial support:* Applicants required to submit FAFSA. *Unit head:* Dr. Rebecca Weinbaum, Interim Chair, 409-880-8978, Fax: 409-880-2263. *Application contact:* Deidre Mayer, Interim Director, Admissions and Academic Services, 409-880-8888, Fax: 409-880-7419, E-mail: gradmissions@lamar.edu.
Website: http://education.lamar.edu/counseling-and-special-populations

La Salle University, School of Arts and Sciences, Program in Clinical Psychology, Philadelphia, PA 19141-1199. Offers child clinical psychology (Psy D); clinical health psychology (Psy D); clinical psychology (MA); general practice psychology (Psy D). *Accreditation:* AAMFT/COAMFTE. *Program availability:* Part-time, evening/weekend. *Faculty:* 9 full-time (7 women), 7 part-time/adjunct (4 women). *Students:* 82 full-time (69 women), 27 part-time (20 women); includes 12 minority (2 Black or African American, non-Hispanic/Latino; 4 Asian, non-Hispanic/Latino; 4 Hispanic/Latino; 2 Two or more races, non-Hispanic/Latino), 2 international. Average age 27. 400 applicants, 16% accepted, 23 enrolled. In 2017, 19 master's, 24 doctorates awarded. Terminal master's awarded for partial completion of doctoral program. *Degree requirements:* For doctorate, comprehensive exam, thesis/dissertation. *Entrance requirements:* For doctorate, GRE (minimum scores of 148 on both the Verbal Reasoning and Quantitative Reasoning sections strongly recommended); GRE Subject Test in psychology (for those entering with bachelor's degree), baccalaureate degree from accredited institution with major in psychology or related discipline; minimum undergraduate GPA of 3.0, 3.2 graduate; three letters of recommendation; statement of interest and intent; curriculum vitae or resume; personal interview. Additional exam requirements/recommendations for international students: Required—TOEFL. *Application deadline:* For fall admission, 1/15 for domestic students, 1/1 for international students. Application fee: $35. Electronic applications accepted. Application fee is waived when completed online. *Expenses:* Contact institution. *Financial support:* In 2017–18, 31 students received support. Scholarships/grants and unspecified assistantships available. Financial award application deadline: 8/31; financial award applicants required to submit FAFSA. *Unit head:* Dr. Randy Fingerhut, Director, 215-951-1284, Fax: 215-951-5140, E-mail: psyd@lasalle.edu. *Application contact:* Elizabeth Heenan, Director, Graduate and Adult Enrollment, 215-951-1100, Fax: 215-951-1462, E-mail: heenan@lasalle.edu.
Website: http://www.lasalle.edu/doctor-of-psychology/

La Salle University, School of Arts and Sciences, Program in Counseling and Family Therapy, Philadelphia, PA 19141-1199. Offers industrial/organizational psychology (MA); marriage and family therapy (MA); professional clinical counseling (MA). *Accreditation:* ACA; APA. *Program availability:* Part-time, evening/weekend. *Faculty:* 7 full-time (2 women), 18 part-time/adjunct (10 women). *Students:* 47 full-time (38 women), 159 part-time (123 women); includes 63 minority (29 Black or African American, non-Hispanic/Latino; 4 Asian, non-Hispanic/Latino; 26 Hispanic/Latino; 4 Two or more races, non-Hispanic/Latino), 5 international. Average age 30. 125 applicants, 78% accepted, 42 enrolled. In 2017, 73 master's awarded. *Degree requirements:* For master's, comprehensive exam. *Entrance requirements:* For master's, GRE or MAT (waived for applicants that already possess a master's degree in any field or for applicants that have a cumulative GPA of 3.5 or higher), minimum of 15 hours in psychology, counseling, or marriage and family studies; minimum GPA of 3.0; three letters of recommendation; personal statement; work experience (paid or volunteer). Additional exam requirements/recommendations for international students: Required—TOEFL. *Application deadline:* For fall admission, 8/15 priority date for domestic students, 7/15 for international students; for spring admission, 12/15 priority date for domestic students, 11/15 for international students; for summer admission, 4/15 priority date for domestic students, 3/15 for international students. Applications are processed on a rolling basis. Application fee: $35. Electronic applications accepted. Application fee is waived when completed online. *Expenses:* Contact institution. *Financial support:* In 2017–18, 34 students received support. Scholarships/grants and unspecified assistantships available. Support available to part-time students. Financial award application deadline: 8/31; financial award applicants required to submit FAFSA. *Faculty research:* Cognitive therapy, attribution theory, work habits, single parent families, treatment of addictions. *Unit head:* Dr. Donna A. Tonrey, Director, 215-951-1767, Fax: 215-951-1843, E-mail: psyma@lasalle.edu. *Application contact:* Elizabeth Heenan, Director, Graduate and Adult Enrollment, 215-951-1100, Fax: 215-951-1462, E-mail: heenan@lasalle.edu.
Website: http://www.lasalle.edu/counseling-family-therapy/

Lenoir-Rhyne University, Graduate Programs, School of Counseling and Human Services, Program in Clinical Mental Health Counseling, Hickory, NC 28601. Offers MA. *Accreditation:* ACA. *Program availability:* Part-time, evening/weekend. *Degree requirements:* For master's, comprehensive exam, thesis optional. *Entrance requirements:* For master's, GRE General Test or MAT, writing sample; minimum undergraduate GPA of 2.7, graduate 3.0. Additional exam requirements/recommendations for international students: Required—TOEFL (minimum score 600 paper-based). Electronic applications accepted. *Expenses:* Contact institution.

Lesley University, Graduate School of Arts and Social Sciences, Cambridge, MA 02138-2790. Offers clinical mental health counseling (MA), including holistic counseling, school and community counseling, trauma studies; counseling psychology (MA, CAGS), including professional counseling (MA), school counseling (MA); creative writing (MFA); expressive therapies (MA, PhD, CAGS), including art (MA), clinical mental health counseling (MA), dance (MA), expressive therapies (MA), music (MA); independent studies (CAGS); independent study (MA); intercultural relations (MA, CAGS); interdisciplinary studies (MA), including individualized studies, integrative holistic health, mindfulness studies, peace and conflict transformation, trauma sensitive assessment, intervention, and consultation, women's studies; urban environmental leadership (MA). *Program availability:* Part-time, online learning. *Degree requirements:* For master's, internship, practicum, thesis (for expressive therapies); for doctorate, thesis/dissertation, arts apprenticeship, field placement; for CAGS, thesis, internship (for counseling psychology, expressive therapies). *Entrance requirements:* For master's, MAT (counseling psychology), interview, writing samples, art portfolio; for doctorate, GRE or MAT, interview, master's degree; for CAGS, interview, master's degree. Additional exam requirements/recommendations for international students: Required—TOEFL (minimum score 550 paper-based; 80 iBT). Electronic applications accepted. *Faculty research:* Psychotherapy and culture; psychotherapy and psychological trauma; women's issues in art, teaching and psychotherapy; community-based art, psycho-spiritual inquiry.

Lewis University, College of Arts and Sciences, Program in Clinical Mental Health Counseling, Romeoville, IL 60446. Offers adult mental health counseling (MA); child and adolescent counseling (MA). *Program availability:* Part-time, evening/weekend. *Students:* 58 full-time (49 women), 60 part-time (53 women); includes 33 minority (10 Black or African American, non-Hispanic/Latino; 2 Asian, non-Hispanic/Latino; 17 Hispanic/Latino; 1 Native Hawaiian or other Pacific Islander, non-Hispanic/Latino; 3 Two or more races, non-Hispanic/Latino). Average age 28. In 2017, 27 master's awarded. *Degree requirements:* For master's, comprehensive exam, thesis optional, practicum, internship. *Entrance requirements:* For master's, bachelor's degree, 15 hours of undergraduate psychology, including statistics or research; 2 letters of recommendation; minimum GPA of 3.0 in last 60 hours; interview, personal statement. Additional exam requirements/recommendations for international students: Required—TOEFL (minimum score 550 paper-based; 79 iBT), IELTS (minimum score 6). *Application deadline:* For fall admission, 5/1 priority date for international students; for spring admission, 11/15 priority date for international students. Applications are processed on a rolling basis. Application fee: $40. Electronic applications accepted. Tuition and fees vary according to program. *Financial support:* Federal Work-Study, scholarships/grants, tuition waivers, and unspecified assistantships available. Financial award application deadline: 5/1; financial award applicants required to submit FAFSA. *Faculty research:* Cognitive development, attitude formation, juvenile delinquency, gender issues, work-family conflict. *Unit head:* Dr. Katherine Helm-Lewis, Director, 815-838-0500 Ext. 5604, Fax: 815-836-5032, E-mail: helmka@lewisu.edu. *Application contact:* Linda Campbell, Graduate Admissions Counselor, 815-836-5610, Fax: 815-836-5578, E-mail: grad@lewisu.edu.
Website: http://www.lewisu.edu/academics/grad.htm/

Liberty University, School of Behavioral Sciences, Lynchburg, VA 24515. Offers applied psychology (MA), including developmental psychology (MA, MS), industrial/organizational psychology (MA, MS); clinical mental health counseling (MA); community care and counseling (Ed D), including marriage and family counseling, pastoral care and counseling, traumatology; counselor education and supervision (PhD); human services counseling (MA), including addictions and recovery, business, child and family law, Christian ministries, criminal justice, crisis response and trauma, executive leadership, health and wellness, life coaching, marriage and family, military resilience; marriage and family counseling (MA); marriage and family therapy (MA); military resilience (Certificate); pastoral counseling (MA), including addictions and recovery, community chaplaincy, crisis response and trauma, discipleship and church ministry, leadership, life coaching, marriage and family, marriage and family studies, military resilience, parenting and child/adolescent, pastoral counseling, theology; professional counseling (MA); psychology (MS), including developmental psychology (MA, MS), industrial/organizational psychology (MA, MS); school counseling (M Ed). *Program availability:* Part-time, online learning. *Students:* 2,649 full-time (2,085 women), 5,086 part-time (4,015 women); includes 2,275 minority (1,784 Black or African American, non-Hispanic/Latino; 44 American Indian or Alaska Native, non-Hispanic/Latino; 67 Asian, non-Hispanic/Latino; 200 Hispanic/Latino; 11 Native Hawaiian or other Pacific Islander, non-Hispanic/Latino; 169 Two or more races, non-Hispanic/Latino), 145 international. Average age 39. 5,839 applicants, 51% accepted, 1710 enrolled. In 2017, 1,626 master's, 7 doctorates, 61 other advanced degrees awarded. *Application deadline:* Applications are processed on a rolling basis. Application fee: $50. Electronic applications accepted. *Financial support:* Applicants required to submit FAFSA. *Unit head:* Dr. Ronald Hawkins, Founding Dean, School of Behavioral Sciences. *Application contact:* Jay Bridge, Director of Admissions, 800-424-9595, Fax: 800-628-7977, E-mail: gradadmissions@liberty.edu.

Lipscomb University, Department of Psychology, Counseling, and Family Science, Nashville, TN 37204-3951. Offers clinical mental health counseling (MS); counseling psychology (Certificate); marriage and family therapy (MMFT); psychology (MS). *Program availability:* Part-time, evening/weekend. *Faculty:* 10 full-time (3 women), 10 part-time/adjunct (4 women). *Students:* 120 full-time (92 women), 30 part-time (27 women); includes 38 minority (22 Black or African American, non-Hispanic/Latino; 1 American Indian or Alaska Native, non-Hispanic/Latino; 1 Asian, non-Hispanic/Latino; 11 Hispanic/Latino; 3 Two or more races, non-Hispanic/Latino), 2 international. Average age 28. 144 applicants, 44% accepted, 42 enrolled. In 2017, 68 master's, 1 other advanced degree awarded. *Degree requirements:* For master's, thesis (for some programs), practicum, internship, capstone. *Entrance requirements:* For master's, GRE, resume, 3 reference letters, transcripts, goals statement. Additional exam requirements/recommendations for international students: Required—TOEFL (minimum score 570 paper-based; 80 iBT). *Application deadline:* For fall admission, 7/1 for domestic students; for spring admission, 11/1 for domestic students. Applications are processed on a rolling basis. Application fee: $50 ($75 for international students). Electronic applications accepted. *Expenses:* Contact institution. *Financial support:* Scholarships/grants and unspecified assistantships available. Financial award applicants required to submit FAFSA. *Faculty research:* Cognitive psychology, neuroscience, health

psychology, grief issues. *Unit head:* Dr. Shanna Ray, Director/Professor of Psychology, 615-966-5833, E-mail: shanna.ray@lipscomb.edu. *Application contact:* Kathi Johnson, Recruiting and Marketing Coordinator, 615-966-5237, E-mail: kathi.johnson@lipscomb.edu.
Website: http://www.lipscomb.edu/psychology/graduate-programs

Lock Haven University of Pennsylvania, The Stephen Poorman College of Business, Information Systems, and Human Services, Lock Haven, PA 17745-2390. Offers clinical mental health counseling (MS); sport science (MS). *Program availability:* Online learning. *Degree requirements:* For master's, thesis. *Entrance requirements:* For master's, minimum undergraduate GPA of 3.0. Additional exam requirements/recommendations for international students: Required—TOEFL. Electronic applications accepted.

Loma Linda University, School of Behavioral Health, Department of Psychology, Loma Linda, CA 92350. Offers clinical psychology (PhD, Psy D). *Accreditation:* APA. *Degree requirements:* For doctorate, comprehensive exam, thesis/dissertation. *Entrance requirements:* For doctorate, GRE General Test, three letters of recommendation. Additional exam requirements/recommendations for international students: Required—TOEFL (minimum score 550 paper-based; 80 iBT). Electronic applications accepted.

London Metropolitan University, Graduate Programs, London, United Kingdom. Offers applied psychology (M Sc); architecture (MA); biomedical science (M Sc); blood science (M Sc); cancer pharmacology (M Sc); computer networking and cyber security (M Sc); computing and information systems (M Sc); conference interpreting (MA); counter-terrorism studies (M Sc); creative, digital and professional writing (MA); crime, violence and prevention (M Sc); criminology (M Sc); curating contemporary art (MA); data analytics (M Sc); digital media (MA); early childhood studies (MA); education (MA, Ed D); financial services law, regulation and compliance (LL M); food science (M Sc); forensic psychology (M Sc); health and social care management and policy (M Sc); human nutrition (M Sc); human resource management (MA); human rights and international conflict (MA); information technology (M Sc); intelligence and security studies (M Sc); international oil, gas and energy law (LL M); international relations (MA); interpreting (MA); learning and teaching in higher education (MA); legal practice (LL M); media and entertainment law (LL M); organizational and consumer psychology (M Sc); psychological therapy (M Sc); psychology of mental health (M Sc); public health (M Sc); public policy and management (MPA); security studies (M Sc); social work (M Sc); spatial planning and urban design (MA); sports therapy (M Sc); supporting older children and young people with dyslexia (MA); teaching languages (MA), including Arabic, English; translation (MA); woman and child abuse (MA).

Long Island University–Brentwood Campus, Graduate Programs, Brentwood, NY 11717. Offers childhood education (MS), including grades 1-6; childhood education/literacy B-6 (MS); childhood education/special education (grades 1-6) (MS); clinical mental health counseling (MS, Advanced Certificate); criminal justice (MS); early childhood education (MS); educational leadership (MS Ed); family nurse practitioner (MS, Advanced Certificate); health administration (MPA); library and information science (MS); literacy (B-6) (MS Ed); school counselor (MS, Advanced Certificate); social work (MSW); special education (MS Ed); students with disabilities generalist (grades 7-12) (Advanced Certificate). *Program availability:* Part-time. *Faculty:* 14 full-time (9 women), 22 part-time/adjunct (11 women). *Students:* 111 full-time (89 women), 47 part-time (34 women); includes 35 minority (8 Black or African American, non-Hispanic/Latino; 1 American Indian or Alaska Native, non-Hispanic/Latino; 3 Asian, non-Hispanic/Latino; 22 Hispanic/Latino; 1 Two or more races, non-Hispanic/Latino), 1 international. Average age 30. 110 applicants, 82% accepted, 63 enrolled. In 2017, 58 master's, 5 other advanced degrees awarded. *Entrance requirements:* For master's and Advanced Certificate, GRE. Additional exam requirements/recommendations for international students: Required—TOEFL or IELTS. *Application deadline:* Applications are processed on a rolling basis. Application fee: $50. Electronic applications accepted. *Expenses: Tuition:* Full-time $21,168; part-time $1201 per credit. *Required fees:* $1840; $920 per term. Tuition and fees vary according to course load. *Financial support:* In 2017–18, 121 students received support. Scholarships/grants available. Support available to part-time students. Financial award application deadline: 2/15; financial award applicants required to submit FAFSA. *Unit head:* Dr. Abby Van Vlerah, Dean and Chief Operating Officer, 631-299-3831, E-mail: abagail.vanvlerah@liu.edu. *Application contact:* Scott Aug, Associate Director of Enrollment Management, 631-287-8506, E-mail: scott.aug@liu.edu.
Website: http://liu.edu/brentwood

Long Island University–LIU Brooklyn, Richard L. Conolly College of Liberal Arts and Sciences, Brooklyn, NY 11201-8423. Offers biology (MS); chemistry (MS); clinical psychology (PhD); creative writing (MFA); English (MA); media arts (MA, MFA); political science (MA); psychology (MA); social science (MS); United Nations (Advanced Certificate); urban studies (MA); writing and production for television (MFA). *Program availability:* Part-time. *Faculty:* 32 full-time (13 women), 17 part-time/adjunct (6 women). *Students:* 178 full-time (123 women), 143 part-time (96 women); includes 128 minority (65 Black or African American, non-Hispanic/Latino; 22 Asian, non-Hispanic/Latino; 31 Hispanic/Latino; 10 Two or more races, non-Hispanic/Latino), 54 international. Average age 30. 629 applicants, 38% accepted, 74 enrolled. In 2017, 147 master's, 9 doctorates, 8 other advanced degrees awarded. Terminal master's awarded for partial completion of doctoral program. *Degree requirements:* For master's, comprehensive exam (for some programs), thesis (for some programs); for doctorate, thesis/dissertation. *Entrance requirements:* For doctorate, GRE. Additional exam requirements/recommendations for international students: Required—TOEFL (minimum score 550 paper-based, 79 iBT) or IELTS. *Application deadline:* Applications are processed on a rolling basis. Application fee: $50. Electronic applications accepted. *Expenses: Tuition:* Full-time $21,618; part-time $1201 per credit. *Required fees:* $1840; $920 per term. Tuition and fees vary according to course load. *Financial support:* In 2017–18, 214 students received support, including 120 fellowships with full and partial tuition reimbursements available (averaging $915 per year), 5 research assistantships with full and partial tuition reimbursements available (averaging $2,300 per year), 136 teaching assistantships with full and partial tuition reimbursements available (averaging $2,300 per year); career-related internships or fieldwork, Federal Work-Study, institutionally sponsored loans, scholarships/grants, and unspecified assistantships also available. Support available to part-time students. Financial award application deadline: 2/15; financial award applicants required to submit FAFSA. *Faculty research:* Quantum gravity and astrophysics; string theory; pharmaceutical biotechnology with a focus on molecular details of drug susceptibility/resistance mechanisms; entomology, population and community ecology, agroecology, and biodiversity; psychotherapy process-outcome, particularly therapeutic alliance development, the role of common factors, and the study of treatment failures; personality pathology, borderline personality disorder and pathological narcissism. *Unit head:* Dr. Scott Krawczyk, Dean, 718-488-1003, E-mail: scott.krawczyk@liu.edu. *Application contact:* Bayu Sutrisno, Graduate Admissions Counselor, 718-488-1564, Fax: 718-780-6110, E-mail: bayu.sutrisno@liu.edu.

Long Island University–LIU Post, College of Education, Information and Technology, Brookville, NY 11548-1300. Offers adolescence education (MS); adolescence education 7-12 (MS); archives and records management (AC); art education (MS); childhood education (MS); childhood education/literacy B-6 (MS); childhood education/special education (MS); clinical mental health counseling (MS, AC); early childhood education (MS); early childhood education/childhood education (MS); educational leadership (AC); educational technology (MS); information studies (PhD); interdisciplinary educational studies (Ed D); middle childhood education (MS); music education (MS); public library administration (AC); school counselor (MS); special education (MS Ed); speech-language pathology (MA); students with disabilities, 7-12 generalist (AC); TESOL (MA). *Accreditation:* TEAC. *Program availability:* Part-time, 100% online, blended/hybrid learning. *Faculty:* 40 full-time (26 women), 73 part-time/adjunct (38 women). *Students:* 472 full-time (400 women), 696 part-time (543 women); includes 254 minority (93 Black or African American, non-Hispanic/Latino; 46 Asian, non-Hispanic/Latino; 105 Hispanic/Latino; 10 Two or more races, non-Hispanic/Latino), 33 international. Average age 33. 917 applicants, 82% accepted, 357 enrolled. In 2017, 408 master's, 31 other advanced degrees awarded. Terminal master's awarded for partial completion of doctoral program. *Degree requirements:* For master's, variable foreign language requirement, comprehensive exam (for some programs), thesis optional; for doctorate, comprehensive exam, thesis/dissertation. *Entrance requirements:* For master's and AC, GRE (for some programs). Additional exam requirements/recommendations for international students: Required—TOEFL (minimum score 550 paper-based, 75 iBT), IELTS, or PTE. *Application deadline:* Applications are processed on a rolling basis. Application fee: $50. Electronic applications accepted. *Expenses: Tuition:* Full-time $21,618; part-time $1201 per credit. *Required fees:* $1840; $920 per term. Tuition and fees vary according to course load. *Financial support:* In 2017–18, 376 students received support. Career-related internships or fieldwork, Federal Work-Study, institutionally sponsored loans, scholarships/grants, tuition waivers (partial), and unspecified assistantships available. Support available to part-time students. Financial award application deadline: 2/15; financial award applicants required to submit FAFSA. *Faculty research:* Sleep; use of technology to develop executive function by students with disabilities; early childhood literacy development through play; social justice through education; using a structured protocol to discuss Bad News. *Unit head:* Dr. Albert Inserra, Dean, 516-299-2210, E-mail: albert.inserra@liu.edu. *Application contact:* Rita Langdon, Graduate Admissions, 516-299-2900, Fax: 516-299-2137, E-mail: post-enroll@liu.edu.
Website: http://liu.edu/CWPost/Academics/College-of-Education-Information-and-Technology

Louisiana State University and Agricultural & Mechanical College, Graduate School, College of Humanities and Social Sciences, Department of Psychology, Baton Rouge, LA 70803. Offers biological psychology (MA, PhD); clinical psychology (MA, PhD); cognitive psychology (MA, PhD); developmental psychology (MA, PhD); school psychology (MA, PhD). *Accreditation:* APA (one or more programs are accredited). *Faculty:* 29 full-time (11 women). *Students:* 78 full-time (57 women), 18 part-time (14 women); includes 25 minority (8 Black or African American, non-Hispanic/Latino; 5 Asian, non-Hispanic/Latino; 5 Hispanic/Latino; 1 Native Hawaiian or other Pacific Islander, non-Hispanic/Latino; 6 Two or more races, non-Hispanic/Latino), 4 international. Average age 27. 239 applicants, 8% accepted, 18 enrolled. In 2017, 15 master's, 12 doctorates awarded. *Financial support:* In 2017–18, 7 fellowships (averaging $41,483 per year), 9 research assistantships (averaging $19,441 per year), 58 teaching assistantships (averaging $19,688 per year) were awarded. *Total annual research expenditures:* $326,871.

Louisiana Tech University, Graduate School, College of Education, Ruston, LA 71272. Offers counseling and guidance (MA), including clinical mental health counseling, human services, orientation and mobility; counseling psychology (PhD); curriculum and instruction (M Ed); cyber education (Graduate Certificate); dynamics of domestic and family violence (Graduate Certificate); early childhood education - PreK-3 (MAT); educational leadership (M Ed, Ed D); elementary education and special education mild/moderate grades 1-5 (MAT); higher education administration (Graduate Certificate); industrial/organizational psychology (MA, PhD); kinesiology (MS); middle school education (MAT), including mathematics; orientation and mobility (Graduate Certificate); rehabilitation teaching for the blind (Graduate Certificate); secondary education (MAT), including agriculture, biology, business, chemistry, English; special education: visually impaired (MAT); teacher leader education (Graduate Certificate); visual impairments - blind education (Graduate Certificate). *Accreditation:* NCATE. *Program availability:* Part-time. *Faculty:* 28 full-time (16 women), 23 part-time/adjunct (22 women). *Students:* 269 full-time (192 women), 194 part-time (150 women); includes 127 minority (94 Black or African American, non-Hispanic/Latino; 2 American Indian or Alaska Native, non-Hispanic/Latino; 6 Asian, non-Hispanic/Latino; 16 Hispanic/Latino; 1 Native Hawaiian or other Pacific Islander, non-Hispanic/Latino; 8 Two or more races, non-Hispanic/Latino), 8 international. Average age 34. 226 applicants, 74% accepted, 60 enrolled. In 2017, 5 master's, 2 doctorates, 1 other advanced degree awarded. *Degree requirements:* For master's, thesis; for doctorate, thesis/dissertation. *Entrance requirements:* For master's and doctorate, GRE General Test. Additional exam requirements/recommendations for international students: Required—TOEFL (minimum score 550 paper-based; 80 iBT), IELTS (minimum score 6.5). *Application deadline:* For fall admission, 9/1 priority date for domestic students, 6/1 for international students; for winter admission, 11/1 priority date for domestic students, 9/1 for international students; for spring admission, 2/1 priority date for domestic students, 12/1 for international students; for summer admission, 5/1 priority date for domestic students, 3/1 for international students. Application fee: $40. Electronic applications accepted. *Expenses:* Tuition, state resident: full-time $5146. Tuition, nonresident: full-time $10,147. *International tuition:* $10,267 full-time. *Required fees:* $2273. *Financial support:* In 2017–18, 40 students received support, including 23 research assistantships (averaging $10,346 per year), 15 teaching assistantships (averaging $6,887 per year); fellowships and career-related internships or fieldwork also available. Financial award application deadline: 2/1. *Faculty research:* Blindness and the best methods for increasing independence for individuals who are blind or visually impaired; educating and investigating factors contributing to improvements in human performance across the lifespan and a reduction in injury rates during training. *Total annual research expenditures:* $2.1 million. *Unit head:* Dr. Don Schillinger, Dean, 318-257-3712, E-mail: dschill@latech.edu. *Application contact:* Dr. Dawn Basinger, Associate Dean of Academic Affairs, 318-257-2977, Fax: 318-257-2379, E-mail: dbasing@latech.edu.
Website: http://education.latech.edu/

Loyola University Chicago, Graduate School, Program in Clinical Psychology, Chicago, IL 60660. Offers MA, PhD. *Accreditation:* APA. *Faculty:* 9 full-time (7 women). *Students:* 37 full-time (32 women); includes 10 minority (4 Black or African American, non-Hispanic/Latino; 3 Asian, non-Hispanic/Latino; 3 Hispanic/Latino). Average age 26. 189 applicants, 3% accepted, 6 enrolled. In 2017, 6 master's, 6 doctorates awarded. Terminal master's awarded for partial completion of doctoral program. *Degree requirements:* For master's, thesis; for doctorate, comprehensive exam, thesis/dissertation, clinical internship. *Entrance requirements:* For doctorate, GRE General Test, GRE Subject Test, letters of recommendation, personal statement, curriculum vitae, transcript. Additional exam requirements/recommendations for international students: Recommended—TOEFL. *Application deadline:* For fall admission, 12/1 for domestic students. Application fee: $0. Electronic applications accepted. Tuition and fees vary according to course load, degree level and program. *Financial support:* In 2017–18, 22 students received support, including 2 fellowships with full tuition

reimbursements available (averaging $18,000 per year), 20 research assistantships with full tuition reimbursements available (averaging $18,000 per year), 5 teaching assistantships with full tuition reimbursements available (averaging $18,000 per year); career-related internships or fieldwork, scholarships/grants, and unspecified assistantships also available. Financial award application deadline: 12/1. *Faculty research:* Child and family, AIDS, ethics and professional practice, psychotherapy, stress and coping, positive youth development, pediatric psychology, adolescence, inner city youth, emerging adulthood, mental health services, exposure to violence, obesity, spina bifida, asthma, neuroscience of depression. *Unit head:* Dr. Grayson Holmbeck, Director of Clinical Training, 773-508-2967, Fax: 773-508-8713, E-mail: gholmbe@luc.edu. *Application contact:* Megan Daly, Senior Secretary, 773-508-3011, Fax: 773-508-8713, E-mail: mdaly3@luc.edu.
Website: https://luc.edu/psychology/graduate/clinicalpsychologyprogram/

Loyola University Chicago, School of Education, Program in Community Counseling, Chicago, IL 60660. Offers clinical mental health counseling (Ed S); community counseling (M Ed, MA). MA offered through the Graduate School. *Program availability:* Part-time. *Faculty:* 5 full-time (2 women), 5 part-time/adjunct (4 women). *Students:* 26 full-time (22 women), 1 (woman) part-time; includes 10 minority (3 Black or African American, non-Hispanic/Latino; 2 Asian, non-Hispanic/Latino; 5 Hispanic/Latino), 2 international. Average age 26. 56 applicants, 77% accepted, 13 enrolled. In 2017, 15 master's awarded. *Degree requirements:* For master's and Ed S, comprehensive exam. *Entrance requirements:* For master's, GRE General Test, minimum GPA of 3.0, letters of recommendation, resume. Additional exam requirements/recommendations for international students: Required—TOEFL (minimum score 550 paper-based; 79 iBT). *Application deadline:* For fall admission, 1/1 for domestic and international students. Application fee: $50. Electronic applications accepted. Application fee is waived when completed online. *Expenses:* $949 per semester hour, $2,847 per course, $8,541-$11,388 full-time semester tuition; $432 per semester fees, $225 additional fees (first semester only). *Financial support:* Career-related internships or fieldwork, institutionally sponsored loans, scholarships/grants, and unspecified assistantships available. Support available to part-time students. Financial award application deadline: 2/1; financial award applicants required to submit FAFSA. *Faculty research:* Career development, prevention, group counseling, family therapy, multicultural counseling. *Unit head:* Dr. Eunju Yoon, Director, 312-915-6461, E-mail: eyoon@luc.edu. *Application contact:* Mirtza Campbell, Information Contact, 312-915-8907, E-mail: mcampbell11@luc.edu.

Loyola University Maryland, Graduate Programs, Loyola College of Arts and Sciences, Department of Psychology, Baltimore, MD 21210-2699. Offers clinical psychology (MS, Psy D, CAS); counseling psychology (MS, CAS). *Accreditation:* APA. *Program availability:* Part-time, evening/weekend. *Faculty:* 64 full-time (37 women), 31 part-time/adjunct (20 women). *Students:* 137 full-time (111 women), 58 part-time (46 women); includes 50 minority (18 Black or African American, non-Hispanic/Latino; 1 American Indian or Alaska Native, non-Hispanic/Latino; 13 Asian, non-Hispanic/Latino; 10 Hispanic/Latino; 8 Two or more races, non-Hispanic/Latino), 6 international. Average age 27. In 2017, 52 master's, 13 doctorates awarded. *Degree requirements:* For doctorate, thesis/dissertation. *Entrance requirements:* For master's, GRE, essay, 3 letters of recommendation, transcript. Additional exam requirements/recommendations for international students: Required—TOEFL (minimum score 550 paper-based), IELTS (minimum score 7). *Application deadline:* For fall admission, 12/1 for domestic students, 3/1 for international students. Application fee: $60. Electronic applications accepted. *Expenses:* Contact institution. *Financial support:* Scholarships/grants and unspecified assistantships available. Financial award application deadline: 4/15; financial award applicants required to submit FAFSA. *Unit head:* Carolyn M. Barry, Chair, 410-617-5325, E-mail: cbarry@loyola.edu. *Application contact:* Office of Graduate Admission, 410-617-5020, E-mail: graduate@loyola.edu.

Loyola University New Orleans, College of Nursing and Health, Department of Counseling, New Orleans, LA 70118-6195. Offers counseling (MS), including marriage and family. *Program availability:* Part-time, evening/weekend. *Faculty:* 5 full-time (2 women). *Students:* 25 full-time (23 women), 42 part-time (40 women); includes 11 minority (6 Black or African American, non-Hispanic/Latino; 5 Hispanic/Latino), 2 international. Average age 29. 50 applicants, 84% accepted, 24 enrolled. In 2017, 17 master's awarded. *Degree requirements:* For master's, comprehensive exam, minimum GPA of 3.0 in counseling coursework. *Entrance requirements:* For master's, GRE, resume, transcripts, letters of recommendation, statement of objectives, degree from regionally-accredited institution, interview, writing sample. Additional exam requirements/recommendations for international students: Required—TOEFL (minimum score 550 paper-based; 79 iBT). *Application deadline:* For fall admission, 12/1 priority date for domestic and international students. Applications are processed on a rolling basis. Application fee: $0. Electronic applications accepted. *Expenses:* $818 per hour tuition; $738 per semester full-time fees, $376.50 part-time. *Financial support:* Research assistantships, career-related internships or fieldwork, and tuition waivers (partial) available. Support available to part-time students. Financial award application deadline: 5/1; financial award applicants required to submit FAFSA. *Faculty research:* Counseling theory, spirituality issues, group counseling, multicultural applications. *Unit head:* Dr. Thomas Foster, Chair, 504-864-7867, Fax: 504-864-7844, E-mail: counselingdept@loyno.edu. *Application contact:* Dianna Whitfield, Department Assistant, 504-864-7848, Fax: 504-864-7844, E-mail: counselingdept@loyno.edu.
Website: http://css.loyno.edu/counseling

Madonna University, Department of Psychology, Livonia, MI 48150-1173. Offers clinical psychology (MSCP). *Program availability:* Part-time, evening/weekend. *Degree requirements:* For master's, thesis or alternative. *Entrance requirements:* Additional exam requirements/recommendations for international students: Required—TOEFL. Electronic applications accepted.

Marquette University, Graduate School, College of Education, Department of Counselor Education and Counseling Psychology, Milwaukee, WI 53201-1881. Offers clinical mental health counseling (MS); community counseling (MA); counseling psychology (PhD); school counseling (MA). *Accreditation:* ACA. *Program availability:* Part-time. Terminal master's awarded for partial completion of doctoral program. *Degree requirements:* For master's, comprehensive exam, thesis (for some programs); for doctorate, thesis/dissertation, qualifying exam. *Entrance requirements:* For master's, GRE General Test or MAT, official transcripts from all current and previous colleges/universities except Marquette, three letters of recommendation, statement of purpose; for doctorate, GRE General Test, MAT, sample of written work, official transcripts from all current and previous colleges/universities except Marquette, three letters of recommendation, statement of purpose, resume/curriculum vitae. Additional exam requirements/recommendations for international students: Required—TOEFL (minimum score 530 paper-based). *Faculty research:* Ethical and legal issues in education, anxiety disorders, multicultural counseling, child psychopathology, group counseling and dynamics.

Marshall University, Academic Affairs Division, College of Liberal Arts, Department of Psychology, Huntington, WV 25755. Offers clinical psychology (Certificate); psychology (MA, Psy D). *Accreditation:* APA. *Students:* 74 full-time (56 women), 9 part-time (6 women); includes 6 minority (3 Black or African American, non-Hispanic/Latino; 1 Hispanic/Latino; 1 Native Hawaiian or other Pacific Islander, non-Hispanic/Latino; 1 Two

or more races, non-Hispanic/Latino). Average age 27. In 2017, 42 master's, 13 doctorates awarded. *Degree requirements:* For master's, thesis optional. *Entrance requirements:* For master's, GRE General Test or MAT. *Application deadline:* For fall admission, 3/1 for domestic students; for spring admission, 11/1 for domestic students. Application fee: $40. *Financial support:* Teaching assistantships with tuition reimbursements available. *Unit head:* Dr. Marianna Linz, Chair, 304-696-2774, E-mail: linz@marshall.edu. *Application contact:* Graduate Admissions, 304-746-1900, Fax: 304-746-1902, E-mail: services@marshall.edu.

Marymount University, School of Education and Human Services, Program in Counseling, Arlington, VA 22207-4299. Offers clinical mental health counseling (MA); pastoral counseling (MA); school counseling (MA); MA/MA. *Accreditation:* ACA (one or more programs are accredited). *Program availability:* Part-time, evening/weekend. *Faculty:* 9 full-time (7 women), 5 part-time/adjunct (all women). *Students:* 108 full-time (97 women), 38 part-time (32 women); includes 61 minority (28 Black or African American, non-Hispanic/Latino; 1 American Indian or Alaska Native, non-Hispanic/Latino; 5 Asian, non-Hispanic/Latino; 20 Hispanic/Latino; 7 Two or more races, non-Hispanic/Latino). Average age 29. 74 applicants, 92% accepted, 59 enrolled. In 2017, 40 master's awarded. *Degree requirements:* For master's, thesis or alternative, capstone/internship. *Entrance requirements:* For master's, GRE, 2 letters of recommendation, interview, resume, personal statement. Additional exam requirements/recommendations for international students: Required—TOEFL (minimum score 600 paper-based; 96 iBT), IELTS (minimum score 6.5). *Application deadline:* For fall admission, 1/15 priority date for domestic and international students. Applications are processed on a rolling basis. Application fee: $40. Electronic applications accepted. *Expenses:* Tuition: Full-time $17,550; part-time $975 per credit hour. *Required fees:* $198; $11 per credit hour. One-time fee: $250. Tuition and fees vary according to program. *Financial support:* In 2017–18, 19 students received support, including 4 research assistantships with full and partial tuition reimbursements available (averaging $8,325 per year), 8 teaching assistantships with full and partial tuition reimbursements available (averaging $8,016 per year); career-related internships or fieldwork, Federal Work-Study, scholarships/grants, and unspecified assistantships also available. Support available to part-time students. Financial award application deadline: 3/1; financial award applicants required to submit FAFSA. *Unit head:* Dr. Lisa Jackson-Cherry, Chair, Counseling, 703-284-1633, Fax: 703-284-5708, E-mail: lisa.jackson-cherry@marymount.edu. *Application contact:* Francesca Reed, Director, Graduate Admissions, 703-284-5901, Fax: 703-527-3815, E-mail: grad.admissions@marymount.edu.
Website: http://www.marymount.edu/Academics/School-of-Education-Human-Services/Graduate-Programs/Counseling-(M-A)

Marywood University, Academic Affairs, Reap College of Education and Human Development, Department of Psychology and Counseling, Program in Clinical Psychology, Scranton, PA 18509-1598. Offers Psy D. *Accreditation:* APA. *Program availability:* Part-time. Electronic applications accepted. *Expenses:* Contact institution.

Marywood University, Academic Affairs, Reap College of Education and Human Development, Department of Psychology and Counseling, Program in Psychology, Scranton, PA 18509-1598. Offers clinical services (MA); general theoretical psychology (MA). *Program availability:* Part-time. Electronic applications accepted.

McGill University, Faculty of Graduate and Postdoctoral Studies, Faculty of Science, Department of Psychology, Montréal, QC H3A 2T5, Canada. Offers clinical psychology (PhD); experimental psychology (M Sc, MA, PhD).

McKendree University, Graduate Programs, Master of Arts Program in Clinical Mental Health Counseling, Lebanon, IL 62254-1299. Offers MA. *Program availability:* Part-time, evening/weekend. *Degree requirements:* For master's, comprehensive exam, internship. *Entrance requirements:* For master's, official transcripts from each college or university attended, minimum undergraduate GPA of 3.0, three letters of recommendation, personal statement, completion of six undergraduate credit hours in a behavior science, curriculum vitae or resume. Electronic applications accepted.

Medaille College, Programs in Psychology, Buffalo, NY 14214-2695. Offers clinical psychology (Psy D); marriage and family therapy (MA); mental health counseling (MA); psychology (MA). *Accreditation:* ACA. *Program availability:* Part-time, evening/weekend. *Degree requirements:* For master's, comprehensive exam (for some programs), thesis (for some programs). *Entrance requirements:* For master's, GRE General Test (psychology), minimum GPA of 2.75 (psychology). Additional exam requirements/recommendations for international students: Required—TOEFL (minimum score 550 paper-based). Electronic applications accepted. *Faculty research:* Schizophrenia, Parkinson's Disease, eyewitness testimony, methodology.

Memorial University of Newfoundland, School of Graduate Studies, Department of Psychology, St. John's, NL A1C 5S7, Canada. Offers applied psychological sciences (MAPS); clinical psychology (Psy D); experimental psychology (M Sc, PhD). *Program availability:* Part-time. *Degree requirements:* For master's, workterms (MASP), thesis (M Sc); for doctorate, comprehensive exam, thesis/dissertation, oral thesis defense. *Entrance requirements:* For master's, GRE, honors bachelor's degree of high second class standing or equivalent; for doctorate, GRE, master's or honors degree. Electronic applications accepted. *Faculty research:* Behavioral neuroscience, cognition, theory and research on abnormal behavior.

Mercer University, Graduate Studies, Cecil B. Day Campus, Penfield College, Atlanta, GA 30341. Offers certified rehabilitation counseling (MS); clinical mental health (MS); counselor education and supervision (PhD); criminal justice and public safety leadership (MS); health informatics (MS); human services (MS), including child and adolescent services, gerontology services; organizational leadership (MS), including leadership for the health care professional, leadership for the nonprofit organization, organizational development and change; school counseling (MS). *Program availability:* Part-time, evening/weekend, 100% online, blended/hybrid learning. *Faculty:* 17 full-time (10 women), 27 part-time/adjunct (24 women). *Students:* 199 full-time (165 women), 266 part-time (218 women); includes 268 minority (226 Black or African American, non-Hispanic/Latino; 1 American Indian or Alaska Native, non-Hispanic/Latino; 19 Asian, non-Hispanic/Latino; 19 Hispanic/Latino; 3 Two or more races, non-Hispanic/Latino). Average age 32. 300 applicants, 45% accepted, 114 enrolled. In 2017, 101 master's, 5 doctorates awarded. *Degree requirements:* For master's, comprehensive exam (for some programs), thesis (for some programs); for doctorate, thesis/dissertation. *Entrance requirements:* For master's, GRE or MAT, Georgia Professional Standards Commission (GPSC) Certification at the SC-5 level; for doctorate, GRE or MAT. Additional exam requirements/recommendations for international students: Recommended—TOEFL (minimum score 550 paper-based; 80 iBT), IELTS (minimum score 6.5). *Application deadline:* For fall admission, 7/1 priority date for domestic and international students; for spring admission, 11/1 priority date for domestic and international students; for summer admission, 4/1 priority date for domestic and international students. Application fee: $35. Electronic applications accepted. Application fee is waived when completed online. *Expenses:* $637 per credit. *Financial support:* In 2017–18, 32 students received support. Federal Work-Study, scholarships/grants, and unspecified assistantships available. Financial award applicants required to submit FAFSA. *Faculty research:* Marriage and families issues, leadership and ethics, cyber-bullying, trauma, narrative

counseling and theory. *Total annual research expenditures:* $85,000. *Unit head:* Dr. Priscilla R. Danheiser, Dean, 678-547-6028, Fax: 678-547-6008, E-mail: danheiser_p@mercer.edu. *Application contact:* Dr. Melissa McCants Cruz, Director of Graduate Admissions, 678-547-6024, E-mail: penfield.admissions@mercer.edu. Website: http://penfield.mercer.edu/programs/graduate-professional/

Merrimack College, School of Liberal Arts, North Andover, MA 01845-5800. Offers clinical mental health counseling (MS); interfaith spirituality (Certificate); public affairs (MPA); spiritual direction (MA, Certificate); spirituality (MA). *Program availability:* Part-time, evening/weekend. *Faculty:* 7 full-time, 4 part-time/adjunct. *Students:* 30 full-time (23 women), 3 part-time (2 women); includes 3 minority (2 Black or African American, non-Hispanic/Latino; 1 Hispanic/Latino), 1 international. Average age 30. 40 applicants, 88% accepted, 20 enrolled. In 2017, 9 master's awarded. *Degree requirements:* For master's, internship/strategic capstone (for MPA); 700-hour fieldwork placement (for MS); practicum (for MA in spiritual direction); for Certificate, practicum (for spiritual direction). *Entrance requirements:* For master's, official college transcripts, resume, personal statement, 2 recommendations (3 for MS in clinical mental health counseling); interview (for MA in spirituality). Additional exam requirements/recommendations for international students: Required—TOEFL (minimum score 84 iBT), IELTS (minimum score 6.5), PTE (minimum score 56). *Application deadline:* For fall admission, 8/24 for domestic students, 7/30 for international students; for spring admission, 1/10 for domestic students, 12/10 for international students; for summer admission, 5/10 for domestic students, 4/10 for international students. Applications are processed on a rolling basis. Electronic applications accepted. *Expenses:* $865 per credit hour tuition; comprehensive fees are $165 for 1-8 credit hours per semester, $320 for 9+ credit hours per semester. *Financial support:* Career-related internships or fieldwork, scholarships/grants, and health care benefits available. Support available to part-time students. Financial award application deadline: 5/1; financial award applicants required to submit FAFSA. *Application contact:* Jennifer Greenwood, Graduate Admissions Counselor, 978-837-3563, E-mail: greenwoodjl@merrimack.edu.

Messiah College, Program in Counseling, Mechanicsburg, PA 17055. Offers clinical mental health counseling (MAC); counseling (CAGS); marriage, couple, and family counseling (MAC); school counseling (MAC). *Accreditation:* ACA. *Program availability:* Part-time, online learning. *Entrance requirements:* For master's, minimum undergraduate cumulative GPA of 3.0, 2 recommendations, resume or curriculum vitae, interview; for CAGS, bachelor's degree, minimum undergraduate cumulative GPA of 3.0, essay, two recommendations, resume or curriculum vitae, interview. Electronic applications accepted.

Michigan School of Professional Psychology, MA and Psy D Programs in Clinical Psychology, Farmington Hills, MI 48334. Offers MA, Psy D. *Accreditation:* APA. *Program availability:* Part-time, evening/weekend. *Faculty:* 11 full-time (7 women), 21 part-time/adjunct (17 women). *Students:* 109 full-time (85 women), 64 part-time (51 women); includes 46 minority (30 Black or African American, non-Hispanic/Latino; 3 Asian, non-Hispanic/Latino; 2 Hispanic/Latino; 11 Two or more races, non-Hispanic/Latino), 1 international. Average age 31. 194 applicants, 47% accepted, 80 enrolled. In 2017, 37 master's, 16 doctorates awarded. *Degree requirements:* For master's, practicum; for doctorate, comprehensive exam, thesis/dissertation, internship, practicum. *Entrance requirements:* For master's, undergraduate degree from accredited institution with minimum GPA of 2.5; major in psychology, social work, or counseling; for doctorate, GRE General Test, undergraduate degree from accredited institution with minimum GPA of 2.5; graduate degree in psychology, social work, or counseling from accredited institution with minimum GPA of 3.25; graduate-level practicum. Additional exam requirements/recommendations for international students: Required—TOEFL (minimum score 550 paper-based; 79 iBT). *Application deadline:* For fall admission, 8/15 for domestic students. Applications are processed on a rolling basis. Application fee: $75. Electronic applications accepted. *Expenses:* $35,871 per academic year full-time tuition and fees (doctoral); $32,518 per academic year full-time tuition and fees (for master's). *Financial support:* In 2017–18, 12 students received support, including 1 research assistantship (averaging $8,566 per year), 5 teaching assistantships (averaging $14,436 per year); institutionally sponsored loans, scholarships/grants, and unspecified assistantships also available. Financial award application deadline: 8/30; financial award applicants required to submit FAFSA. *Faculty research:* Health psychology, trauma, multicultural, humanistic, applied behavior analysis. *Unit head:* Dr. Frances Brown, Program Director, 248-476-1122, Fax: 248-476-1125. *Application contact:* Carrie Hauser, Coordinator of Admissions and Student Engagement, 248-476-1122 Ext. 117, Fax: 248-476-1125, E-mail: chauser@mispp.edu. Website: http://www.mispp.edu

MidAmerica Nazarene University, School of Behavioral Sciences and Counseling, Olathe, KS 66062-1899. Offers counseling (MA), including clinical mental health, marriage, couple and family, school counseling, spiritual formation in counseling. *Accreditation:* ACA. *Program availability:* Evening/weekend. *Degree requirements:* For master's, comprehensive exam. *Entrance requirements:* For master's, on-site writing assessment, official transcript, three recommendations, personal interview. Additional exam requirements/recommendations for international students: Required—TOEFL (minimum score 81 iBT). Electronic applications accepted. *Expenses:* Contact institution. *Faculty research:* Technology and intimacy, play therapy, interpersonal neurobiology, sexual addiction.

Middle Tennessee State University, College of Graduate Studies, College of Behavioral and Health Sciences, Department of Psychology, Murfreesboro, TN 37132. Offers clinical psychology (MA); experimental psychology (MA); industrial/organizational psychology (MA); psychology (MA, Ed S); quantitative psychology (MA); school psychology (MA). *Program availability:* Part-time, evening/weekend, online learning. *Degree requirements:* For master's, comprehensive exam, thesis. *Entrance requirements:* For master's, GRE. Additional exam requirements/recommendations for international students: Required—TOEFL (minimum score 525 paper-based; 71 iBT) or IELTS (minimum score 6). Electronic applications accepted. *Faculty research:* Health psychology, industrial/organizational psychology, experimental psychology.

Midwestern State University, Billie Doris McAda Graduate School, Prothro-Yeager College of Humanities and Social Sciences, Department of Psychology, Wichita Falls, TX 76308. Offers clinical/counseling psychology (MA). *Program availability:* Part-time, evening/weekend. *Degree requirements:* For master's, one foreign language, comprehensive exam, thesis optional. *Entrance requirements:* For master's, GRE General Test, 3 recommendation forms. Additional exam requirements/recommendations for international students: Required—TOEFL (minimum score 550 paper-based). Electronic applications accepted. *Faculty research:* Child assessment and treatment outcomes, Christianity as it relates to psychology, treatment of behavioral/emotional problems in childhood, people struggling with HIV/AIDS, educational psychology.

Midwestern University, Downers Grove Campus, College of Health Sciences, Illinois Campus, Program in Clinical Psychology, Downers Grove, IL 60515-1235. Offers MA, Psy D. *Accreditation:* APA. *Degree requirements:* For doctorate, thesis/dissertation, qualifying examination. *Entrance requirements:* For master's and doctorate, GRE, minimum overall GPA of 2.75, 3 letters of recommendation. Additional exam requirements/recommendations for international students: Required—TOEFL.

Midwestern University, Glendale Campus, College of Health Sciences, Arizona Campus, Program in Clinical Psychology, Glendale, AZ 85308. Offers Psy D. *Accreditation:* APA.

Millersville University of Pennsylvania, College of Graduate Studies and Adult Learning, College of Education and Human Services, Department of Psychology, Program in Clinical Psychology, Millersville, PA 17551-0302. Offers MS. *Program availability:* Part-time, evening/weekend. *Faculty:* 12 full-time (8 women), 1 part-time/adjunct (0 women). *Students:* 27 full-time (21 women), 20 part-time (16 women); includes 6 minority (3 Black or African American, non-Hispanic/Latino; 1 American Indian or Alaska Native, non-Hispanic/Latino; 2 Hispanic/Latino), 2 international. Average age 27. 55 applicants, 49% accepted, 12 enrolled. In 2017, 17 master's awarded. *Degree requirements:* For master's, comprehensive exam, thesis optional, internship. *Entrance requirements:* For master's, GRE or MAT (if cumulative GPA is lower than 3.0), at least 1 academic reference; interview; 18 undergraduate credits in psychology. Additional exam requirements/recommendations for international students: Required—TOEFL (minimum score 80 iBT), IELTS (minimum score 6.5), PTE (minimum score 60). *Application deadline:* For fall admission, 1/15 for domestic students; for winter admission, 6/1 for domestic students; for spring admission, 10/1 for domestic students. Application fee: $40. Electronic applications accepted. *Expenses:* $500 per credit resident tuition and fees; $750 per credit non-resident tuition and fees; $114.75 per credit general fee (maximum of 12 credits); technology fee $27 per credit (resident), $39 per credit (non-resident). *Financial support:* In 2017–18, 21 students received support. Unspecified assistantships available. Financial award application deadline: 3/15; financial award applicants required to submit FAFSA. *Faculty research:* Cognitive behavioral treatments, child social-emotional development, empirically supported treatments and evidence-based practices, humanistic/existential therapy, animal assisted therapy. *Unit head:* Dr. Claudia J. Haferkamp, Coordinator, 717-871-7273, Fax: 717-871-7946, E-mail: claudia.haferkamp@millersville.edu. *Application contact:* Dr. Victor S. DeSantis, Dean of College of Graduate Studies and Adult Learning/Associate Provost for Civic and Community Engagement, 717-871-7619, Fax: 717-871-7954, E-mail: victor.desantis@millersville.edu. Website: http://www.millersville.edu/psychology/Graduate%20Programs%20Webpages/Clinical%20Psychology/index.php

Milligan College, Area of Counselor Education Programs, Milligan College, TN 37682. Offers clinical mental health counseling (MSC); counseling ministry (Graduate Certificate); school counseling (MSC). *Program availability:* Part-time. *Faculty:* 4 full-time (all women), 2 part-time/adjunct (0 women). *Students:* 24 full-time (17 women), 7 part-time (6 women); includes 4 minority (3 Black or African American, non-Hispanic/Latino; 1 Two or more races, non-Hispanic/Latino), 1 international. Average age 32. 30 applicants, 70% accepted, 13 enrolled. In 2017, 9 master's awarded. *Degree requirements:* For master's, thesis or alternative. *Entrance requirements:* For master's, GRE General Test if undergraduate GPA is less than 3.0, undergraduate degree and supporting transcripts, essay/personal statement, professional recommendations, interview. Additional exam requirements/recommendations for international students: Required—TOEFL (minimum score 550 paper-based, 79 iBT) or IELTS (6.5). *Application deadline:* For fall admission, 8/1 for domestic students, 6/1 for international students. Applications are processed on a rolling basis. Application fee: $30. Electronic applications accepted. *Expenses:* $440 per hour tuition; $325 per semester tech/activity fees. *Financial support:* Scholarships/grants available. Financial award application deadline: 12/1; financial award applicants required to submit FAFSA. *Faculty research:* Parent-child interaction therapy/autism; childhood developmental trauma/childhood sexual abuse; poverty and homelessness; social justice advocacy and multicultural competencies; school based mental health. *Unit head:* Dr. Christine Browning, Director of Master of Science in Counseling Program, 423-461-3513, Fax: 423-461-8777, E-mail: cmbrowning@milligan.edu. *Application contact:* Jenni Duran, Graduate Admissions Recruiter, Healthcare Programs, 423-461-8424, Fax: 423-461-8789, E-mail: jduran@milligan.edu.

Minnesota State University Mankato, College of Graduate Studies and Research, College of Social and Behavioral Sciences, Department of Psychology, Mankato, MN 56001. Offers clinical psychology (MA); industrial/organizational psychology (MA); school psychology (Psy D). *Program availability:* Part-time. *Degree requirements:* For master's, one foreign language, comprehensive exam, thesis (for some programs). *Entrance requirements:* For master's, GRE General Test, GRE Subject Test (clinical psychology), minimum GPA of 3.0 during previous 2 years, 3 letters of reference. Additional exam requirements/recommendations for international students: Required—TOEFL. Electronic applications accepted.

Mississippi State University, College of Arts and Sciences, Department of Psychology, Mississippi State, MS 39762. Offers applied psychology (PhD), including clinical, cognitive science; psychology (MS). *Accreditation:* APA. *Faculty:* 18 full-time (6 women). *Students:* 33 full-time (18 women), 7 part-time (all women); includes 8 minority (4 Black or African American, non-Hispanic/Latino; 3 Asian, non-Hispanic/Latino; 1 Two or more races, non-Hispanic/Latino), 1 international. Average age 27. 46 applicants, 26% accepted, 10 enrolled. In 2017, 7 master's, 6 doctorates awarded. Terminal master's awarded for partial completion of doctoral program. *Degree requirements:* For master's, comprehensive exam, thesis; for doctorate, thesis/dissertation, qualifying exam, comprehensive written and oral exam. *Entrance requirements:* For master's, GRE General Test, minimum GPA of 2.75 on last two years of undergraduate courses; for doctorate, GRE General Test, proficiency in at least 1 computer language, minimum GPA of 3.0. Additional exam requirements/recommendations for international students: Required—TOEFL (minimum score 477 paper-based; 53 iBT); Recommended—IELTS (minimum score 4.5). *Application deadline:* For fall admission, 4/1 priority date for domestic students, 5/1 for international students; for spring admission, 11/1 priority date for domestic students, 9/1 for international students. Applications are processed on a rolling basis. Application fee: $60 ($80 for international students). Electronic applications accepted. *Expenses:* Tuition, state resident: full-time $8318; part-time $462.12 per credit hour. Tuition, nonresident: full-time $22,358; part-time $1242.12 per credit hour. *Required fees:* $110; $12.24 per credit hour. $6.12 per semester. *Financial support:* In 2017–18, 6 research assistantships with full tuition reimbursements (averaging $14,703 per year), 22 teaching assistantships with full tuition reimbursements (averaging $12,157 per year) were awarded; career-related internships or fieldwork, Federal Work-Study, institutionally sponsored loans, scholarships/grants, and unspecified assistantships also available. Financial award application deadline: 4/1; financial award applicants required to submit FAFSA. *Faculty research:* Personality type, alcoholism, blindness and low vision, mental retardation, language comprehension. *Total annual research expenditures:* $1.4 million. *Unit head:* Dr. Mitchell E. Berman, Professor and Head, 662-325-3202, Fax: 662-325-7212, E-mail: mberman@psychology.msstate.edu. *Application contact:* Lakan Drinker, Admissions and Enrollment Assistant, 662-325-8951, E-mail: ldrinker@grad.msstate.edu. Website: http://www.psychology.msstate.edu/

Mississippi State University, College of Education, Department of Counseling, Educational Psychology, and Foundations, Mississippi State, MS 39762. Offers clinical mental health (MS); college counseling (MS); counseling/mental health (PhD); counseling/school psychology (PhD); counselor education (Ed S); educational

psychology/general educational psychology (PhD); educational psychology/school psychology (PhD); general educational psychology (MS); psychometry (MS); rehabilitation counseling (MS); school counseling (MS); school psychology (Ed S); student affairs (MS). *Accreditation:* ACA (one or more programs are accredited); APA; CORE (one or more programs are accredited); NCATE. *Program availability:* Part-time, blended/hybrid learning. *Faculty:* 21 full-time (14 women), 3 part-time/adjunct (2 women). *Students:* 106 full-time (85 women), 51 part-time (43 women); includes 55 minority (44 Black or African American, non-Hispanic/Latino; 1 American Indian or Alaska Native, non-Hispanic/Latino; 1 Asian, non-Hispanic/Latino; 5 Hispanic/Latino; 4 Two or more races, non-Hispanic/Latino), 5 international. Average age 29. 136 applicants, 55% accepted, 54 enrolled. In 2017, 50 master's, 7 doctorates, 10 other advanced degrees awarded. Terminal master's awarded for partial completion of doctoral program. *Degree requirements:* For master's, comprehensive exam, thesis optional; for doctorate, thesis/dissertation, comprehensive oral and written exam. *Entrance requirements:* For master's, GRE (taken within the last five years), BS with minimum GPA of 2.75 on last 60 hours; for doctorate, GRE, MS from CACREP- or CORE-accredited program in counseling; for Ed S, GRE, MS in counseling or related field, minimum GPA of 3.3 on all graduate work. Additional exam requirements/recommendations for international students: Required—TOEFL (minimum score 550 paper-based; 79 iBT); Recommended—IELTS (minimum score 6.5). *Application deadline:* For fall admission, 2/1 priority date for domestic and international students. Applications are processed on a rolling basis. Application fee: $60 ($80 for international students). Electronic applications accepted. *Expenses:* Tuition, state resident: full-time $8318; part-time $462.12 per credit hour. Tuition, nonresident: full-time $22,358; part-time $1242.12 per credit hour. *Required fees:* $110; $12.24 per credit hour. $6.12 per semester. *Financial support:* In 2017–18, 4 research assistantships (averaging $9,000 per year), 10 teaching assistantships with full tuition reimbursements (averaging $8,401 per year) were awarded; career-related internships or fieldwork, Federal Work-Study, institutionally sponsored loans, and unspecified assistantships also available. Financial award application deadline: 2/1; financial award applicants required to submit FAFSA. *Faculty research:* HIV/AIDS in college population, substance abuse in youth and college students, ADHD and conduct disorders in youth, assessment and identification of early childhood disabilities, assessment and vocational transition of the disabled. *Unit head:* Dr. David Morse, Professor and Head, 662-325-3426, Fax: 662-325-3263, E-mail: dmorse@colled.msstate.edu. *Application contact:* Marina Hunt, Admissions and Enrollment Assistant, 662-325-3363, E-mail: mhunt@grad.msstate.edu. Website: http://www.cep.msstate.edu/

Missouri State University, Graduate College, College of Health and Human Services, Department of Psychology, Springfield, MO 65897. Offers applied behavior analysis (MS); clinical psychology (MS); experimental psychology (MS); forensic child psychology (Certificate); industrial/organizational psychology (MS). *Faculty:* 25 full-time (11 women), 4 part-time/adjunct (0 women). *Students:* 54 full-time (41 women), 12 part-time (9 women); includes 9 minority (2 Black or African American, non-Hispanic/Latino; 2 Hispanic/Latino; 5 Two or more races, non-Hispanic/Latino), 5 international. Average age 23. 127 applicants, 17% accepted, 21 enrolled. In 2017, 41 master's awarded. *Degree requirements:* For master's, comprehensive exam, thesis. *Entrance requirements:* For master's, GRE General Test, GRE Subject Test, minimum GPA of 3.25 in major, 3.0 overall; 20 hours of course work in psychology. Additional exam requirements/recommendations for international students: Required—TOEFL (minimum score 550 paper-based; 79 iBT), IELTS (minimum score 6). *Application deadline:* For fall admission, 2/15 priority date for domestic and international students. Application fee: $35 ($50 for international students). Electronic applications accepted. *Expenses:* Tuition, state resident: full-time $2915; part-time $2021 per credit hour. Tuition, nonresident: full-time $5354; part-time $3647 per credit hour. *International tuition:* $11,992 full-time. *Required fees:* $173; $173 per credit hour. Tuition and fees vary according to class time, course level, course load, degree level, campus/location and program. *Financial support:* In 2017–18, 9 research assistantships with full tuition reimbursements (averaging $8,772 per year), 8 teaching assistantships with full tuition reimbursements (averaging $8,772 per year) were awarded; career-related internships or fieldwork, Federal Work-Study, institutionally sponsored loans, scholarships/grants, and unspecified assistantships also available. Financial award application deadline: 3/31; financial award applicants required to submit FAFSA. *Faculty research:* Work-family conflict, child forensic psychology, sports psychology, body image assessment, visual learning. *Unit head:* Dr. Paul Deal, Department Head, 417-836-5797, Fax: 417-836-8330, E-mail: psychology@missouristate.edu. *Application contact:* Stephanie Praschan, Director, Graduate Enrollment Management, 417-836-5330, Fax: 417-836-6200, E-mail: stephaniepraschan@missouristate.edu.
Website: http://psychology.missouristate.edu/

Molloy College, Program in Clinical Mental Health Counseling, Rockville Centre, NY 11571-5002. Offers MS. *Program availability:* Part-time-only, evening/weekend. *Faculty:* 2 full-time (both women). *Students:* 13 full-time (11 women), 27 part-time (24 women); includes 13 minority (7 Black or African American, non-Hispanic/Latino; 1 American Indian or Alaska Native, non-Hispanic/Latino; 1 Asian, non-Hispanic/Latino; 3 Hispanic/Latino; 1 Two or more races, non-Hispanic/Latino). Average age 38. 40 applicants, 53% accepted, 16 enrolled. *Degree requirements:* For master's, comprehensive exam. *Entrance requirements:* Additional exam requirements/recommendations for international students: Required—TOEFL (minimum score 550 paper-based; 79 iBT). *Application deadline:* Applications are processed on a rolling basis. Application fee: $60. Electronic applications accepted. *Expenses: Tuition:* Full-time $19,980; part-time $1110 per credit. *Required fees:* $1040. Tuition and fees vary according to course load and degree level. *Financial support:* Application deadline: 3/1; applicants required to submit FAFSA. *Faculty research:* Mindfulness and stress reduction for counseling students and mental health professionals; multiculturalism in counseling; social justice and advocacy; eating disorders and body image; drama therapy and embodied counselor education. *Unit head:* Dr. Laura B. Kestemberg, Associate Dean and Director for Department of Clinical Mental Health Counseling, 516-323-3842, E-mail: lkestemberg@molloy.edu. *Application contact:* Jaclyn Machowicz, Assistant Director for Admissions, 516-323-4010, E-mail: jmachowicz@molloy.edu.
Website: http://www.molloy.edu/academics/graduate-programs/master-of-science-in-clinical-mental-health-counseling

Montclair State University, The Graduate School, College of Humanities and Social Sciences, Program in Clinical Psychology, Montclair, NJ 07043-1624. Offers MA. *Program availability:* Part-time, evening/weekend. *Entrance requirements:* For master's, GRE General Test, 2 letters of recommendation, essay. Additional exam requirements/recommendations for international students: Required—TOEFL (minimum score 83 iBT), IELTS (minimum score 6.5). Electronic applications accepted. *Faculty research:* Community psychology, infant cognitive development.

Morehead State University, Graduate Programs, College of Science and Technology, Department of Psychology, Morehead, KY 40351. Offers clinical/counseling psychology (MS); general/experimental psychology (MS). *Program availability:* Part-time, evening/weekend. *Degree requirements:* For master's, comprehensive exam, thesis optional. *Entrance requirements:* For master's, GRE General Test, 18 undergraduate hours in psychology, minimum GPA of 3.0, 3 letters of recommendation. Additional exam requirements/recommendations for international students: Required—TOEFL (minimum

score 500 paper-based). Electronic applications accepted. *Faculty research:* Mood induction effects, serotonin receptor activity, stress, perceptual processes.

Mount Mary University, Graduate Programs, Program in Counseling, Milwaukee, WI 53222-4597. Offers clinical mental health counseling (MS, Certificate); clinical rehabilitation counseling (MS, Certificate); school counseling (MS, Certificate); vocational rehabilitation counseling (MS, Certificate). *Accreditation:* ACA. *Program availability:* Part-time, evening/weekend. *Degree requirements:* For master's, comprehensive exam, thesis or alternative. *Entrance requirements:* For master's, minimum GPA of 3.0. Additional exam requirements/recommendations for international students: Required—TOEFL (minimum score 550 paper-based; 80 iBT); Recommended—IELTS (minimum score 6.5). Electronic applications accepted. *Expenses:* Contact institution. *Faculty research:* Cognitive behavioral interventions for depression, eating disorders and compliance, trauma-informed care.

Murray State University, College of Humanities and Fine Arts, Department of Psychology, Murray, KY 42071. Offers clinical psychology (MA, MS); general experimental psychology (MA, MS); research design and analysis (Certificate). *Program availability:* Part-time. *Faculty:* 9 full-time (5 women). *Students:* 21 full-time (16 women), 1 part-time (0 women); includes 2 minority (1 Hispanic/Latino; 1 Two or more races, non-Hispanic/Latino), 1 international. Average age 25. 44 applicants, 68% accepted, 11 enrolled. In 2017, 9 master's awarded. *Entrance requirements:* For master's and Certificate, GRE or GMAT, minimum university GPA of 2.75. Additional exam requirements/recommendations for international students: Required—TOEFL (minimum score 527 paper-based; 71 iBT). *Application deadline:* Applications are processed on a rolling basis. Application fee: $40 ($50 for international students). Electronic applications accepted. *Expenses:* Tuition, state resident: full-time $9504. Tuition, nonresident: full-time $26,811. *International tuition:* $14,400 full-time. Tuition and fees vary according to course load, degree level and reciprocity agreements. *Financial support:* In 2017–18, 5 research assistantships were awarded; Federal Work-Study and unspecified assistantships also available. Financial award applicants required to submit FAFSA. *Unit head:* Dr. Paula Waddill, Chair, Department of Psychology, 270-809-2851, Fax: 270-809-2991, E-mail: pwaddill@murraystate.edu. *Application contact:* Kaitlyn Burzynski, Interim Assistant Director for Graduate Admission and Records, 270-809-5732, Fax: 270-809-3780, E-mail: msu.graduateadmissions@murraystate.edu.
Website: https://www.murraystate.edu/academics/CollegesDepartments/CollegeOfHumanitiesAndFineArts/Psychology/

National University, Academic Affairs, College of Letters and Sciences, La Jolla, CA 92037-1011. Offers biology (MS); counseling psychology (MA), including licensed professional clinical counseling, marriage and family therapy; creative writing (MFA); english (MA); film studies (MA); forensic and crime scene investigations (Certificate); forensic sciences (MFS); human behavior (MA); mathematics for educators (MS); performance psychology (MA); strategic communications (MA). *Program availability:* Part-time, evening/weekend, 100% online, blended/hybrid learning. *Degree requirements:* For master's, thesis (for some programs). *Entrance requirements:* For master's, interview, minimum GPA of 2.5. Additional exam requirements/recommendations for international students: Required—TOEFL (minimum score 550 paper-based; 79 iBT), IELTS (minimum score 6). *Application deadline:* Applications are processed on a rolling basis. Application fee: $60 ($65 for international students). Electronic applications accepted. *Expenses: Tuition:* Part-time $430 per quarter hour. *Financial support:* Career-related internships or fieldwork, institutionally sponsored loans, scholarships/grants, and tuition waivers (partial) available. Support available to part-time students. Financial award application deadline: 6/30; financial award applicants required to submit FAFSA. *Unit head:* Dr. Carol Richardson, Dean, 858-642-8450, E-mail: cols@nu.edu. *Application contact:* Brandon Jouganatos, Interim Vice President for Enrollment Services, 800-628-8648, E-mail: advisor@nu.edu.
Website: http://www.nu.edu/OurPrograms/CollegeOfLettersAndSciences.html

Neumann University, Program in Pastoral Clinical Mental Health Counseling, Aston, PA 19014-1298. Offers pastoral care specialist (Certificate); pastoral clinical mental health counseling (MS); pastoral clinical mental health counseling certificate of advanced study (Certificate); pastoral counseling (PhD); spiritual formation and direction (CSD); spiritual formation and direction supervision certificate of advanced study (Certificate). *Program availability:* Part-time, evening/weekend. *Faculty:* 8 full-time (5 women), 1 (woman) part-time/adjunct. *Students:* 9 full-time (all women), 58 part-time (40 women); includes 17 minority (13 Black or African American, non-Hispanic/Latino; 1 Hispanic/Latino; 3 Two or more races, non-Hispanic/Latino), 1 international. Average age 47. 35 applicants, 40% accepted, 14 enrolled. In 2017, 22 master's, 2 doctorates awarded. *Degree requirements:* For doctorate, comprehensive exam, thesis/dissertation. *Entrance requirements:* For master's and other advanced degree, official transcripts from all institutions attended, letter of intent, three letters of recommendation; for doctorate, MAT, master's degree, official transcripts from all institutions attended, resume or curriculum vitae, letter of intent, two official letters of recommendation. Additional exam requirements/recommendations for international students: Required—TOEFL (minimum score 70 iBT). *Application deadline:* For fall admission, 8/1 for domestic students; for spring admission, 12/1 for domestic students. Applications are processed on a rolling basis. Application fee: $0. Electronic applications accepted. *Expenses:* $670 per credit hour (for master's degree); $830 per credit hour (for PhD). *Financial support:* Scholarships/grants and health care benefits available. Support available to part-time students. Financial award application deadline: 3/15; financial award applicants required to submit FAFSA. *Unit head:* Sr. Suzanne Mayer, Director of Pastoral Clinical Mental Health Counseling Program, 610-361-2292, Fax: 610-358-4525, E-mail: mayers@neumann.edu. *Application contact:* Dr. Erika K. Davis, Director of Adult and Graduate Admissions, 800-9-NEUMANN Ext. 5208, Fax: 610-361-2548, E-mail: gradadultadmiss@neumann.edu.

New Mexico Highlands University, Graduate Studies, College of Arts and Sciences, Department of Social and Behavioral Sciences, Las Vegas, NM 87701. Offers psychology (MS), including clinical psychology/counseling, general psychology; public affairs (MA), including applied sociology; Southwest studies (MA), including anthropology. *Program availability:* Part-time. *Degree requirements:* For master's, comprehensive exam, thesis or alternative. *Entrance requirements:* For master's, minimum undergraduate GPA of 3.0. Additional exam requirements/recommendations for international students: Required—TOEFL (minimum score 540 paper-based). *Faculty research:* Southwest Native American resettlement development, community-level interventions, neurochemistry of personality, comparative criminal justice, social theory and activism.

The New School, The New School for Social Research, Department of Psychology, New York, NY 10011. Offers clinical psychology (PhD); cognitive, social, and developmental psychology (PhD); psychology (MA). *Accreditation:* APA (one or more programs are accredited). *Program availability:* Part-time. *Faculty:* 14 full-time (8 women), 4 part-time/adjunct (0 women). *Students:* 154 full-time (121 women), 77 part-time (58 women); includes 42 minority (8 Black or African American, non-Hispanic/Latino; 12 Asian, non-Hispanic/Latino; 17 Hispanic/Latino; 5 Two or more races, non-Hispanic/Latino), 39 international. Average age 29. 250 applicants, 83% accepted, 71 enrolled. In 2017, 45 master's, 18 doctorates awarded. Terminal master's awarded for partial completion of doctoral program. *Degree requirements:* For master's,

comprehensive exam, thesis (for some programs); for doctorate, comprehensive exam, thesis/dissertation. *Entrance requirements:* For master's, GRE, letters of recommendation, writing sample, essays, transcripts; for doctorate, letters of recommendation, writing sample, essays, transcripts. Additional exam requirements/recommendations for international students: Required—TOEFL (minimum score 100 iBT), IELTS (minimum score 7), PTE (minimum score 68). *Application deadline:* For fall admission, 1/5 priority date for domestic and international students; for spring admission, 10/15 priority date for domestic and international students. Applications are processed on a rolling basis. Application fee: $50. Electronic applications accepted. *Expenses:* $2,180 per credit. *Financial support:* In 2017–18, 191 students received support, including 21 fellowships with full and partial tuition reimbursements available (averaging $19,453 per year), 45 teaching assistantships with full and partial tuition reimbursements available (averaging $9,505 per year); career-related internships or fieldwork, Federal Work-Study, scholarships/grants, and tuition waivers (full and partial) also available. Support available to part-time students. Financial award application deadline: 2/1; financial award applicants required to submit FAFSA. *Unit head:* Dr. William Milberg, Dean, The New School for Social Research, 212-229-5777, E-mail: milbergw@newschool.edu. *Application contact:* Dana Messinger, Director of Graduate Admission, 212-229-5150 Ext. 2300, E-mail: socialresearchadmit@newschool.edu.

Nicholls State University, Graduate Studies, College of Education, Department of Psychology, Counseling and Family Studies, Thibodaux, LA 70310. Offers clinical mental health counseling (MA); school counseling (M Ed); school psychology (SSP). *Accreditation:* NCATE. *Program availability:* Part-time, evening/weekend. *Degree requirements:* For master's, comprehensive exam; for SSP, comprehensive exam, internship. *Entrance requirements:* For master's, GRE General Test. Electronic applications accepted.

Norfolk State University, School of Graduate Studies, School of Liberal Arts, Department of Psychology, Program in Community/Clinical Psychology, Norfolk, VA 23504. Offers MA. *Degree requirements:* For master's, comprehensive exam, thesis or alternative. *Entrance requirements:* For master's, minimum GPA of 2.7.

North Carolina Central University, College of Behavioral and Social Sciences, Department of Psychology, Durham, NC 27707-3129. Offers clinical psychology (MA); general psychology (MA). *Program availability:* Part-time, evening/weekend. *Degree requirements:* For master's, one foreign language, comprehensive exam, thesis. *Entrance requirements:* For master's, GRE, minimum GPA of 3.0 in major, 2.5 overall. Additional exam requirements/recommendations for international students: Required—TOEFL. *Application deadline:* For fall admission, 8/1 for domestic students. Application fee: $30. *Expenses:* Tuition, state resident: full-time $2770; part-time $692.50 per credit hour. Tuition, nonresident: full-time $9247; part-time $2311.75 per credit hour. *Financial support:* Application deadline: 5/1; applicants required to submit FAFSA. *Unit head:* Vinston J. Goldman, Graduate Coordinator, 919-530-6471, Fax: 919-530-5380, E-mail: vgoldman@nccu.edu. *Application contact:* Vinston J. Goldman, Graduate Coordinator, 919-530-6471, Fax: 919-530-5380, E-mail: vgoldman@nccu.edu.

North Carolina Central University, School of Education, Program in Counselor Education, Durham, NC 27707-3129. Offers career counseling (MA); clinical mental health counseling (MA); school counseling (MA). *Accreditation:* ACA; NCATE. *Program availability:* Part-time, evening/weekend. *Degree requirements:* For master's, comprehensive exam, thesis or alternative. *Entrance requirements:* For master's, GRE, minimum GPA of 3.0 in major, 2.5 overall. Additional exam requirements/recommendations for international students: Required—TOEFL. *Application deadline:* For fall admission, 8/1 for domestic students. Application fee: $30. *Expenses:* Tuition, state resident: full-time $2770; part-time $692.50 per credit hour. Tuition, nonresident: full-time $9247; part-time $2311.75 per credit hour. *Financial support:* Application deadline: 5/1; applicants required to submit FAFSA. *Unit head:* Peggy Whiting, Coordinator, 919-530-6182, Fax: 919-530-7522, E-mail: pwhiting@nccu.edu. *Application contact:* Peggy Whiting, Coordinator, 919-530-6182, Fax: 919-530-7522, E-mail: pwhiting@nccu.edu.

North Dakota State University, College of Graduate and Interdisciplinary Studies, College of Science and Mathematics, Department of Psychology, Fargo, ND 58102. Offers clinical psychology (MS); health and social psychology (PhD); psychological clinical science (PhD); psychology (MS); visual and cognitive neuroscience (PhD). *Degree requirements:* For master's, thesis; for doctorate, thesis/dissertation. *Entrance requirements:* For master's and doctorate, GRE General Test, GRE Subject Test. Additional exam requirements/recommendations for international students: Required—TOEFL (minimum score 525 paper-based; 71 iBT). Electronic applications accepted. *Faculty research:* Cognition science, neuropsychology, group behavior, applied behavior analysis, behavior therapy.

Northern Kentucky University, Office of Graduate Programs, College of Education and Human Services, Clinical Mental Health Counseling Program, Highland Heights, KY 41099. Offers MS. *Accreditation:* ACA. *Program availability:* Part-time, evening/weekend. *Degree requirements:* For master's, comprehensive exam. *Entrance requirements:* For master's, GRE or MAT. Additional exam requirements/recommendations for international students: Required—TOEFL (minimum score 550 paper-based; 79 iBT); Recommended—IELTS (minimum score 6.5). Electronic applications accepted. *Faculty research:* Preferences for college counseling, accreditation, partner violence prevention, data-based school counseling, creativity in counseling.

Northern State University, MS Ed Program in Counseling, Aberdeen, SD 57401-7198. Offers clinical mental health counseling (MS Ed); school counseling (MS Ed). *Accreditation:* ACA; NCATE. *Program availability:* Part-time, online learning. *Degree requirements:* For master's, comprehensive exam, thesis optional. *Entrance requirements:* For master's, minimum GPA of 2.75. Additional exam requirements/recommendations for international students: Required—TOEFL (minimum score 550 paper-based; 78 iBT), IELTS (minimum score 6). Electronic applications accepted.

Northwestern State University of Louisiana, Graduate Studies and Research, Department of Psychology, Natchitoches, LA 71497. Offers clinical psychology (MS). *Degree requirements:* For master's, comprehensive exam, thesis or alternative. *Entrance requirements:* For master's, GRE General Test, GRE Subject Test, minimum undergraduate GPA of 2.5. Additional exam requirements/recommendations for international students: Required—TOEFL. Electronic applications accepted.

Northwestern University, The Graduate School, Judd A. and Marjorie Weinberg College of Arts and Sciences, Department of Psychology, Evanston, IL 60208. Offers brain, behavior and cognition (PhD); clinical psychology (PhD); cognitive psychology (PhD); personality psychology (PhD); social psychology (PhD); JD/PhD. Admissions and degrees offered through The Graduate School. *Accreditation:* APA (one or more programs are accredited). *Program availability:* Part-time. *Degree requirements:* For doctorate, thesis/dissertation. *Entrance requirements:* For doctorate, GRE General Test, GRE Subject Test. Additional exam requirements/recommendations for international students: Required—TOEFL. Electronic applications accepted. *Faculty research:* Memory and higher order cognition, anxiety and depression, effectiveness of psychotherapy, social cognition, molecular basis of memory.

Northwestern University, The Graduate School and Feinberg School of Medicine, Program in Clinical Psychology, Evanston, IL 60208. Offers clinical psychology (PhD), including clinical neuropsychology. Admissions and degree offered through The Graduate School. *Accreditation:* APA. *Degree requirements:* For doctorate, thesis/dissertation, clinical internship. *Entrance requirements:* For doctorate, GRE General Test, GRE Subject Test, minimum GPA of 3.2, course work in psychology. Additional exam requirements/recommendations for international students: Required—TOEFL. *Faculty research:* Cancer and cardiovascular risk reduction, evaluation of mental health services and policy, neuropsychological assessment, outcome of psychotherapy, cognitive therapy, pediatric and clinical child psychology.

Northwest Nazarene University, Program in Social Work, Nampa, ID 83686-5897. Offers clinical mental health and addictions practice (MSW). *Accreditation:* CSWE. *Program availability:* Part-time-only, evening/weekend. *Students:* Average age 27. 152 applicants, 54% accepted, 73 enrolled. In 2017, 54 master's awarded. *Degree requirements:* For master's, comprehensive exam, thesis or alternative. *Entrance requirements:* For master's, interview, letters of reference, degree from regionally-accredited college/university, written personal statement. *Application deadline:* Applications are processed on a rolling basis. Application fee: $50. Electronic applications accepted. *Faculty research:* Test anxiety, trauma, statistics. *Unit head:* Dr. Lawanna Lancaster, Director/Department Chair, 208-467-8372, Fax: 208-467-8879, E-mail: mswinfo@nnu.edu. *Application contact:* Jodie Rodriguez-Engel, Program Coordinator, 208-467-8679, Fax: 208-467-8879, E-mail: jrodriguez-engel@nnu.edu.
Website: http://msw.nnu.edu

Notre Dame de Namur University, Division of Academic Affairs, School of Education and Psychology, Program in Clinical Psychology, Belmont, CA 94002-1908. Offers MS. *Program availability:* Part-time. *Students:* 58 full-time (45 women), 48 part-time (42 women). Average age 33. *Degree requirements:* For master's, thesis. *Entrance requirements:* Additional exam requirements/recommendations for international students: Required—TOEFL (minimum score 550 paper-based; 79 iBT). *Application deadline:* For fall admission, 8/1 for domestic students; for spring admission, 12/1 for domestic students. Applications are processed on a rolling basis. Application fee: $60. Electronic applications accepted. *Expenses: Tuition:* Full-time $16,128; part-time $8064 per credit hour. *Required fees:* $80; $80 per credit hour. $40 per semester. *Financial support:* Career-related internships or fieldwork available. Support available to part-time students. Financial award applicants required to submit FAFSA. *Unit head:* Helen Marlo, Chair, Clinical Psychology Department, 650-508-3723, E-mail: hmarlo@ndnu.edu.

Nova Southeastern University, College of Psychology, Fort Lauderdale, FL 33314-7796. Offers clinical mental health counseling (MS); clinical psychology (PhD, Psy D); counseling (MS); experimental psychology (MS); forensic psychology (MS); general psychology (MS); school counseling (MS); school psychology (Psy D, Psy S); substance abuse counseling (MS); substance abuse counseling and education (MS). *Accreditation:* APA (one or more programs are accredited). *Program availability:* 100% online, blended/hybrid learning. *Faculty:* 51 full-time (21 women), 120 part-time/adjunct (70 women). *Students:* 751 full-time (618 women), 821 part-time (709 women); includes 787 minority (268 Black or African American, non-Hispanic/Latino; 2 American Indian or Alaska Native, non-Hispanic/Latino; 38 Asian, non-Hispanic/Latino; 431 Hispanic/Latino; 2 Native Hawaiian or other Pacific Islander, non-Hispanic/Latino; 46 Two or more races, non-Hispanic/Latino), 45 international. Average age 31. 1,117 applicants, 38% accepted, 294 enrolled. In 2017, 459 master's, 100 doctorates, 10 other advanced degrees awarded. Terminal master's awarded for partial completion of doctoral program. *Degree requirements:* For master's, comprehensive exam, 3 practica; for doctorate, thesis/dissertation, clinical internship, competency exam; for Psy S, comprehensive exam, internship. *Entrance requirements:* For master's and Psy S, GRE General Test, letters of recommendation, research/personal statement, interview; for doctorate, GRE General Test, GRE Subject Test (recommended), minimum undergraduate GPA of 3.0, letters of recommendation, research/personal statement, interview, curriculum vitae/resume. Additional exam requirements/recommendations for international students: Required—TOEFL (minimum score 550 paper-based). *Application deadline:* Applications are processed on a rolling basis. Application fee: $50. Electronic applications accepted. *Expenses:* Contact institution. *Financial support:* In 2017–18, 197 students received support, including 15 research assistantships (averaging $5,600 per year), 68 teaching assistantships (averaging $2,000 per year); career-related internships or fieldwork, Federal Work-Study, institutionally sponsored loans, scholarships/grants, and unspecified assistantships also available. Support available to part-time students. Financial award application deadline: 4/15; financial award applicants required to submit FAFSA. *Faculty research:* Clinical health psychology, multicultural/diversity psychology, clinical neuropsychology, clinical child psychology, family violence. *Unit head:* Dr. Karen Grosby, Dean, 954-262-5712, Fax: 954-262-3859, E-mail: grosby@nova.edu. *Application contact:* Carlos Perez, Senior Manager of Outreach, 954-262-5702, Fax: 954-262-3893, E-mail: gradschool@nova.edu.
Website: http://psychology.nova.edu/

The Ohio State University, Graduate School, College of Arts and Sciences, Division of Social and Behavioral Sciences, Department of Psychology, Columbus, OH 43210. Offers behavioral neuroscience (PhD); clinical psychology (PhD); cognitive psychology (PhD); developmental psychology (PhD); intellectual and developmental disabilities psychology (PhD); quantitative psychology (PhD); social psychology (PhD). *Accreditation:* APA. *Faculty:* 52. *Students:* 144 full-time (86 women); includes 18 minority (8 Asian, non-Hispanic/Latino; 10 Hispanic/Latino), 28 international. Average age 26. In 2017, 21 doctorates awarded. *Entrance requirements:* For doctorate, GRE General Test. Additional exam requirements/recommendations for international students: Required—TOEFL (minimum score 600 paper-based; 100 iBT); Recommended—IELTS (minimum score 8). *Application deadline:* For fall admission, 12/1 for domestic and international students. Applications are processed on a rolling basis. Application fee: $60 ($70 for international students). Electronic applications accepted. *Financial support:* Fellowships, research assistantships, and teaching assistantships available. *Unit head:* Dr. John Bruno, Chair, 614-292-3038, E-mail: bruno.1@osu.edu. *Application contact:* Graduate and Professional Admissions, 614-292-9444, Fax: 614-292-3895, E-mail: gpadmissions@osu.edu.
Website: http://psychology.osu.edu/

Ohio University, Graduate College, College of Arts and Sciences, Department of Psychology, Program in Clinical Psychology, Athens, OH 45701-2979. Offers PhD. *Accreditation:* APA. *Degree requirements:* For doctorate, one foreign language, comprehensive exam, thesis/dissertation. *Entrance requirements:* For doctorate, GRE General Test, GRE Subject Test, minimum graduate GPA of 3.4. Additional exam requirements/recommendations for international students: Required—TOEFL. *Faculty research:* Health psychology, child clinical psychology, psychotherapy outcomes.

Oklahoma State University, College of Arts and Sciences, Department of Psychology, Stillwater, OK 74078. Offers clinical psychology (PhD); general psychology (MS). *Accreditation:* APA (one or more programs are accredited). *Faculty:* 33 full-time (20 women), 1 part-time/adjunct (0 women). *Students:* 31 full-time (25 women), 26 part-time (22 women); includes 13 minority (4 American Indian or Alaska Native, non-Hispanic/Latino; 1 Asian, non-Hispanic/Latino; 4 Hispanic/Latino; 1 Native Hawaiian or other Pacific Islander, non-Hispanic/Latino; 3 Two or more races, non-Hispanic/Latino), 2 international. Average age 27. 142 applicants, 7% accepted, 10 enrolled. In 2017, 8

master's, 13 doctorates awarded. *Entrance requirements:* For master's and doctorate, GRE General Test. Additional exam requirements/recommendations for international students: Required—TOEFL (minimum score 550 paper-based; 79 iBT). *Application deadline:* For fall admission, 3/1 priority date for international students; for spring admission, 8/1 priority date for international students. Applications are processed on a rolling basis. Application fee: $40 ($75 for international students). Electronic applications accepted. *Expenses:* Tuition, state resident: full-time $4019; part-time $2679.60 per year. Tuition, nonresident: full-time $15,286; part-time $10,190.40 per year. *Required fees:* $2129; $1419 per unit. Tuition and fees vary according to program. *Financial support:* Research assistantships, teaching assistantships, career-related internships or fieldwork, Federal Work-Study, scholarships/grants, health care benefits, tuition waivers (partial), and unspecified assistantships available. Support available to part-time students. Financial award application deadline: 3/1; financial award applicants required to submit FAFSA. *Unit head:* Dr. Thad Leffingwell, Department Head, 405-744-7494, Fax: 405-744-8067, E-mail: thad.leffingwell@okstate.edu. *Application contact:* Patricia Alexander, Graduate Advisor, 405-744-7591, Fax: 405-744-8967, E-mail: patricia.alexander@okstate.edu.
Website: http://psychology.okstate.edu

Old Dominion University, College of Sciences, Virginia Consortium Program in Clinical Psychology, Norfolk, VA 23529. Offers PhD. Program offered jointly with Eastern Virginia Medical School and Norfolk State University. *Faculty:* 27 full-time (16 women). *Students:* 32 full-time (21 women); includes 11 minority (6 Black or African American, non-Hispanic/Latino; 3 Asian, non-Hispanic/Latino; 1 Hispanic/Latino; 1 Two or more races, non-Hispanic/Latino). Average age 28. 92 applicants, 17% accepted, 6 enrolled. In 2017, 5 doctorates awarded. *Degree requirements:* For doctorate, comprehensive exam, thesis/dissertation, internship. *Entrance requirements:* For doctorate, GRE General Test. Additional exam requirements/recommendations for international students: Required—TOEFL. *Application deadline:* For fall admission, 12/1 for domestic and international students. Application fee: $65. Electronic applications accepted. *Expenses:* Contact institution. *Financial support:* In 2017–18, 26 students received support, including 7 research assistantships with partial tuition reimbursements available (averaging $5,821 per year), 19 teaching assistantships with partial tuition reimbursements available (averaging $12,079 per year); scholarships/grants, traineeships, health care benefits, and unspecified assistantships also available. Financial award application deadline: 12/1; financial award applicants required to submit FAFSA. *Faculty research:* Health psychology, minority and women's issues, neuropsychology, assessment, substance abuse. *Unit head:* Dr. Robin Lewis, Director of Clinical Training, 757-451-7733, Fax: 757-823-8919, E-mail: rlewis@odu.edu. *Application contact:* Elaine Ross, Administrator, 757-451-7733, Fax: 757-823-8919, E-mail: emross@odu.edu.
Website: http://odu.edu/vcpcp/

Oregon State University, College of Education, Program in Counseling, Corvallis, OR 97331. Offers clinical mental health counseling (M Coun); counseling (PhD); school counseling (M Coun). *Accreditation:* ACA (one or more programs are accredited); NCATE. *Program availability:* Part-time, blended/hybrid learning. *Degree requirements:* For master's, thesis or alternative; for doctorate, one foreign language, thesis/dissertation. *Entrance requirements:* For master's, minimum GPA of 3.0 in last 90 hours; for doctorate, GRE or MAT, master's degree, minimum GPA of 3.0 in last 90 hours of course work, 2 years of teaching experience. Additional exam requirements/recommendations for international students: Required—TOEFL (minimum score 575 paper-based). *Application deadline:* For fall admission, 1/31 for domestic students. Application fee: $75 ($85 for international students). *Financial support:* Application deadline: 3/1. *Faculty research:* Counseling and guidance improvement in social services agencies, elementary and secondary schools. *Unit head:* Lisa Schulz, Counseling Lead, 541-737-5959, E-mail: lisa.schulz@oregonstate.edu. *Application contact:* Mary Aguilera, Advisor, 541-737-2232, E-mail: mary.aguilera@oregonstate.edu.
Website: http://education.oregonstate.edu/counseling

Pace University, Dyson College of Arts and Sciences, Department of Psychology, Program in School-Clinical Child Psychology, New York, NY 10038. Offers school psychology (MS Ed); school-clinical child psychology (Psy D). *Accreditation:* APA (one or more programs are accredited). *Students:* 68 full-time (60 women), 30 part-time (23 women); includes 23 minority (3 Black or African American, non-Hispanic/Latino; 9 Asian, non-Hispanic/Latino; 7 Hispanic/Latino; 1 Native Hawaiian or other Pacific Islander, non-Hispanic/Latino; 3 Two or more races, non-Hispanic/Latino), 5 international. Average age 27. In 2017, 15 master's, 22 doctorates awarded. Terminal master's awarded for partial completion of doctoral program. *Degree requirements:* For master's, qualifying exams, internship; for doctorate, comprehensive exam, thesis/dissertation, qualifying exams, externship, internship. *Entrance requirements:* For master's, GRE General Test, GRE Subject Test in psychology (recommended), interview, 3 letters of recommendation, resume, personal statement; for doctorate, GRE General Test, GRE Subject Test in psychology (recommended), interview, transcripts, 3 letters of recommendation. Additional exam requirements/recommendations for international students: Required—TOEFL (minimum score 88 iBT), IELTS (minimum score 7) or PTE (minimum score 60). *Application deadline:* For fall admission, 1/15 priority date for domestic students. Application fee: $70. Electronic applications accepted. *Financial support:* Scholarships/grants and unspecified assistantships available. Financial award application deadline: 1/15; financial award applicants required to submit FAFSA. *Unit head:* Dr. Barbara Mowder, Director of Graduate Psychology Programs, 212-346-1556, E-mail: bmowder@pace.edu. *Application contact:* Susan Ford-Goldschein, Director of Graduate Admissions, 212-346-1531, Fax: 212-346-1585, E-mail: graduateadmission@pace.edu.
Website: http://www.pace.edu/dyson/academic-departments-and-programs/psychology---nyc/graduate-programs

Pacifica Graduate Institute, Graduate Programs, Carpinteria, CA 93013. Offers clinical psychology (PhD); counseling psychology (MA); depth psychology (MA, PhD); mythological studies (MA, PhD). Terminal master's awarded for partial completion of doctoral program. *Degree requirements:* For master's, thesis (for some programs), practicum; for doctorate, comprehensive exam, thesis/dissertation, internship. *Entrance requirements:* For master's, resume, 3 letters of recommendation, writing sample, interview; for doctorate, resumé, 4 letters of recommendation, writing sample, interview. Additional exam requirements/recommendations for international students: Required—TOEFL. *Faculty research:* Imaginal and archetypal theory; post-Colonial psychoanalytic and Jungian theory; myth literature as it applies to the theory and practice of psychology.

Pacific University, School of Professional Psychology, Forest Grove, OR 97116-1797. Offers applied psychological science (MA, MS); clinical psychology (PhD, Psy D). *Accreditation:* APA (one or more programs are accredited). *Program availability:* Part-time. *Degree requirements:* For master's, comprehensive exam (for some programs), thesis (for some programs); for doctorate, comprehensive exam, thesis/dissertation. *Entrance requirements:* For master's, course work in introductory psychology, statistics, and abnormal psychology; minimum GPA of 3.0; for doctorate, GRE General Test, minimum GPA of 3.0, undergraduate course work in psychology, minimum GPA of 3.1 in last 2 years. Additional exam requirements/recommendations for international students: Required—TOEFL (minimum score 600 paper-based). Electronic applications accepted. *Expenses:* Contact institution. *Faculty research:* Neuropsychological assessment,

assessment and treatment of anxiety, forensic psychology, cross-cultural psychology, child and adolescent psychopathology.

Palo Alto University, MA in Counseling Program, Palo Alto, CA 94304. Offers clinical mental health (MA); marriage, family and child (MA). *Program availability:* Part-time, 100% online, blended/hybrid learning. *Faculty:* 6 full-time (4 women), 5 part-time/adjunct (4 women). *Students:* 158 full-time (130 women), 131 part-time (113 women); includes 138 minority (9 Black or African American, non-Hispanic/Latino; 35 Asian, non-Hispanic/Latino; 43 Hispanic/Latino; 51 Two or more races, non-Hispanic/Latino). Average age 34. 167 applicants, 74% accepted, 80 enrolled. In 2017, 110 master's awarded. *Degree requirements:* For master's, capstone project. *Entrance requirements:* For master's, undergraduate degree in psychology with minimum GPA of 3.3. Additional exam requirements/recommendations for international students: Required—TOEFL. *Application deadline:* For fall admission, 6/30 priority date for domestic and international students; for spring admission, 3/21 for domestic and international students. Applications are processed on a rolling basis. Application fee: $50. Electronic applications accepted. *Expenses:* Contact institution. *Financial support:* In 2017–18, 12 students received support. Federal Work-Study available. Financial award applicants required to submit FAFSA. *Unit head:* Dr. William Snow, Director of Counseling, 831-246-2440, E-mail: wsnow@paloaltou.edu. *Application contact:* Yukti Singh, Director of Admissions, 650-417-2055, E-mail: ysingh@paloaltou.edu.
Website: http://www.paloaltou.edu/graduate-programs/masters-programs/ma-counseling

Palo Alto University, PGSP-Stanford Psy D Consortium Program, Palo Alto, CA 94304. Offers Psy D. Program offered jointly with Stanford University. *Accreditation:* APA. *Faculty:* 14 full-time (12 women), 61 part-time/adjunct (42 women). *Students:* 167 full-time (140 women), 1 (woman) part-time; includes 56 minority (7 Black or African American, non-Hispanic/Latino; 1 American Indian or Alaska Native, non-Hispanic/Latino; 14 Asian, non-Hispanic/Latino; 15 Hispanic/Latino; 19 Two or more races, non-Hispanic/Latino). Average age 26. 417 applicants, 11% accepted, 30 enrolled. In 2017, 28 doctorates awarded. *Degree requirements:* For doctorate, comprehensive exam, thesis/dissertation, 2000-hour clinical internship. *Entrance requirements:* For doctorate, GRE General Test (minimum overall score 1200); GRE Subject Test in psychology (highly recommended), undergraduate degree in psychology or related area with minimum GPA of 3.3. Additional exam requirements/recommendations for international students: Required—TOEFL, IELTS. *Application deadline:* For fall admission, 12/2 priority date for domestic and international students. Applications are processed on a rolling basis. Application fee: $50. Electronic applications accepted. *Expenses:* Contact institution. *Financial support:* In 2017–18, 95 students received support, including fellowships (averaging $4,000 per year), research assistantships (averaging $1,000 per year), teaching assistantships (averaging $3,000 per year); Federal Work-Study and scholarships/grants also available. Financial award applicants required to submit FAFSA. *Unit head:* Dr. Steve Smith, Co-Director of Clinical Training, PGSP-Stanford Psy D Consortium, E-mail: stevesmith@paloaltou.edu. *Application contact:* Dr. Kimberly Hill, Co-Director of Clinical Training, PGSP-Stanford Psy D Consortium, 650-725-5582, E-mail: khill@paloaltou.edu.
Website: http://www.paloaltou.edu/graduate-programs/pgsp-psyd-stanford-consortium

Palo Alto University, PhD in Clinical Psychology Program, Palo Alto, CA 94304. Offers PhD. *Accreditation:* APA. *Faculty:* 33 full-time (19 women), 37 part-time/adjunct (24 women). *Students:* 435 full-time (344 women), 18 part-time (14 women); includes 168 minority (24 Black or African American, non-Hispanic/Latino; 1 American Indian or Alaska Native, non-Hispanic/Latino; 45 Asian, non-Hispanic/Latino; 57 Hispanic/Latino; 2 Native Hawaiian or other Pacific Islander, non-Hispanic/Latino; 39 Two or more races, non-Hispanic/Latino). Average age 26. 346 applicants, 73% accepted, 82 enrolled. In 2017, 64 doctorates awarded. *Degree requirements:* For doctorate, comprehensive exam, thesis/dissertation, 2000-hour clinical internship. *Entrance requirements:* For doctorate, GRE General Test, undergraduate or graduate degree in psychology or related area; 4 course prerequisites: biopsychology, abnormal psychology, developmental psychology, and statistics. Additional exam requirements/recommendations for international students: Required—TOEFL, IELTS. *Application deadline:* For fall admission, 12/4 priority date for domestic and international students. Applications are processed on a rolling basis. Application fee: $50. Electronic applications accepted. *Expenses:* Contact institution. *Financial support:* In 2017–18, 115 students received support, including fellowships (averaging $7,500 per year), research assistantships (averaging $4,000 per year), teaching assistantships (averaging $3,000 per year); Federal Work-Study and scholarships/grants also available. Financial award applicants required to submit FAFSA. *Faculty research:* Forensic psychology, LGBT psychology, trauma, diversity and community mental health, neuropsychology. *Unit head:* Dr. Rowena Gomez, Director of Clinical Training, 650-433-3823, E-mail: rgomez@paloaltou.edu. *Application contact:* Eirian Williams, Vice President of Enrollment Management, 800-818-6136, E-mail: admissions@paloaltou.edu.
Website: http://www.paloaltou.edu/graduate-programs/phd-programs/phd-clinical-psychology

Penn State Erie, The Behrend College, Graduate School, Erie, PA 16563. Offers accounting (MPAC); applied clinical psychology (MA); business administration (MBA); quality and manufacturing management (MMM). *Accreditation:* AACSB. *Program availability:* Part-time. *Students:* 31 full-time (15 women), 126 part-time (39 women); includes 10 minority (4 Black or African American, non-Hispanic/Latino; 1 Hispanic/Latino; 5 Two or more races, non-Hispanic/Latino). Average age 31. 104 applicants, 75% accepted, 75 enrolled. In 2017, 72 master's awarded. *Entrance requirements:* Additional exam requirements/recommendations for international students: Required—TOEFL (minimum score 550 paper-based; 80 iBT), IELTS. *Application deadline:* Applications are processed on a rolling basis. Application fee: $65. Electronic applications accepted. *Financial support:* Federal Work-Study available. Financial award application deadline: 2/15; financial award applicants required to submit FAFSA. *Unit head:* Dr. Ralph M. Ford, Chancellor, 814-898-6160, Fax: 814-898-6461. *Application contact:* Ann M. Burbules, Assistant Director, Graduate Admissions, 866-374-3378, Fax: 814-898-6044, E-mail: behrend.admissions@psu.edu.
Website: http://behrend.psu.edu/

Penn State Harrisburg, Graduate School, School of Behavioral Sciences and Education, Middletown, PA 17057. Offers adult education in the health and medical professions (Certificate); applied behavior analysis (MA); applied clinical psychology (MA); applied psychological research (MA); community psychology and social change (MA); English as a second language (ESL) program specialist and leadership (Certificate); health education (M Ed); lifelong learning and adult education (M Ed, D Ed); literacy education (M Ed); literacy leadership (Certificate); psychology: applications in clinical psychology (Certificate); psychology: health psychology (Certificate); teaching and curriculum (M Ed); training and development (M Ed, Certificate). *Program availability:* Part-time, evening/weekend. *Unit head:* Dr. Mukund S. Kulkarni, Chancellor, 717-948-6105, Fax: 717-948-6452. *Application contact:* Robert W. Coffman, Jr., Director of Enrollment Management, Recruitment and Admissions, 717-948-6250, Fax: 717-948-6325, E-mail: hbgadmit@psu.edu.
Website: https://harrisburg.psu.edu/behavioral-sciences-and-education/

Clinical Psychology

Pepperdine University, Graduate School of Education and Psychology, Division of Psychology, Los Angeles, CA 90263. Offers behavioral psychology (MS); clinical psychology (Psy D); clinical psychology (MA), including marriage and family therapy; clinical psychology with Latinos (MA); psychology (MA). *Program availability:* Part-time, evening/weekend. *Students:* 499 full-time (417 women), 416 part-time (343 women); includes 401 minority (90 Black or African American, non-Hispanic/Latino; 4 American Indian or Alaska Native, non-Hispanic/Latino; 68 Asian, non-Hispanic/Latino; 205 Hispanic/Latino; 5 Native Hawaiian or other Pacific Islander, non-Hispanic/Latino; 29 Two or more races, non-Hispanic/Latino), 68 international. Average age 31. 574 applicants, 75% accepted, 254 enrolled. In 2017, 253 master's, 34 doctorates awarded. *Entrance requirements:* For master's and doctorate, GRE General Test. Additional exam requirements/recommendations for international students: Required—TOEFL. *Application deadline:* For fall admission, 2/1 for domestic students. Applications are processed on a rolling basis. Application fee: $55. Electronic applications accepted. *Expenses:* Contact institution. *Financial support:* Research assistantships, teaching assistantships, career-related internships or fieldwork, and scholarships/grants available. Support available to part-time students. Financial award application deadline: 7/1; financial award applicants required to submit FAFSA. *Unit head:* Dr. Robert A. deMayo, Associate Dean, Psychology Division, 310-568-5747, E-mail: robert.demayo@pepperdine.edu. *Application contact:* Chris Costa, Director of Enrollment, 310-568-2850, E-mail: chris.costa@pepperdine.edu. Website: http://gsep.pepperdine.edu/masters-psychology/

Philadelphia College of Osteopathic Medicine, Graduate and Professional Programs, Department of Psychology, Philadelphia, PA 19131-1694. Offers applied behavior analysis (Certificate); clinical health psychology (Post-Doctoral Certificate); clinical neuropsychology (Post-Doctoral Certificate); clinical psychology (Psy D); educational psychology (PhD); mental health counseling (MS); organizational development and leadership (MS); psychology (Certificate); public health management and administration (MS); school psychology (MS, Psy D, Ed S). *Accreditation:* APA. *Faculty:* 19 full-time (11 women), 122 part-time/adjunct (58 women). *Students:* 487 (335 women); includes 138 minority (89 Black or African American, non-Hispanic/Latino; 4 American Indian or Alaska Native, non-Hispanic/Latino; 11 Asian, non-Hispanic/Latino; 12 Hispanic/Latino; 22 Two or more races, non-Hispanic/Latino). 298 applicants, 44% accepted, 100 enrolled. In 2017, 50 master's, 43 doctorates, 10 other advanced degrees awarded. Terminal master's awarded for partial completion of doctoral program. *Degree requirements:* For master's, comprehensive exam (for some programs), thesis (for some programs); for doctorate, comprehensive exam, thesis/dissertation. *Entrance requirements:* For master's, GRE or MAT, minimum GPA of 3.0; bachelor's degree from regionally-accredited college or university; for doctorate, PRAXIS II (for Psy D in school psychology), minimum undergraduate GPA of 3.0; for other advanced degree, GRE (for Ed S). Additional exam requirements/recommendations for international students: Required—TOEFL (minimum score 79 iBT). *Application deadline:* Applications are processed on a rolling basis. Application fee: $50. Electronic applications accepted. *Financial support:* In 2017–18, 28 teaching assistantships were awarded; Federal Work-Study, institutionally sponsored loans, and scholarships/grants also available. Financial award application deadline: 3/15; financial award applicants required to submit FAFSA. *Faculty research:* Adult and childhood anxiety and ADHD; coping with chronic illness; primary care psychology/integrated health care; applied behavior analysis; psychological, educational, and neuropsychological assessment. *Total annual research expenditures:* $533,489. *Unit head:* Dr. Robert DiTomasso, Chairman, 215-871-6442, Fax: 215-871-6458, E-mail: robertd@pcom.edu. *Application contact:* Johnathan Cox, Associate Director of Admissions, 215-871-6700, Fax: 215-871-6719, E-mail: johnathancox@pcom.edu.

See Display on page 982 and Close-Up on page 1203.

Pillar College, Program in Counseling, Newark, NJ 07102. Offers MA.

Pittsburg State University, Graduate School, College of Education, Department of Psychology and Counseling, Program in Psychology, Pittsburg, KS 66762. Offers psychology (MS), including clinical psychology, general psychology. *Students:* 30. In 2017, 10 master's awarded. *Degree requirements:* For master's, thesis or alternative. *Entrance requirements:* For master's, GRE General Test, minimum GPA of 2.8. Additional exam requirements/recommendations for international students: Required—TOEFL (minimum score 550 paper-based; 79 iBT), IELTS (minimum score 6.5), PTE (minimum score 53). *Application deadline:* Applications are processed on a rolling basis. Application fee: $35 ($60 for international students). Electronic applications accepted. *Expenses:* Contact institution. *Financial support:* Teaching assistantships, career-related internships or fieldwork, and Federal Work-Study available. Financial award application deadline: 2/1; financial award applicants required to submit FAFSA. *Unit head:* Dr. David Hurford, Chairperson, 620-235-4521. *Application contact:* Lisa Allen, Assistant Director of Graduate and Continuing Studies, 620-235-4218, Fax: 620-235-4219, E-mail: lallen@pittstate.edu.

Plymouth State University, College of Graduate Studies, Graduate Studies in Education, Certificate of Advanced Graduate Studies Programs, Plymouth, NH 03264-1595. Offers clinical mental health counseling (CAGS); educational leadership (CAGS); higher education (CAGS); school psychology (CAGS). *Program availability:* Part-time, evening/weekend.

Plymouth State University, College of Graduate Studies, Graduate Studies in Education, Program in Science, Plymouth, NH 03264-1595. Offers applied meteorology (MS); biology (MS); clinical mental health counseling (MS); environmental science and policy (MS); science education (MS).

Point Loma Nazarene University, College of Extended Learning, Program in Clinical Counseling, San Diego, CA 92108. Offers marriage and family therapy (MA); professional clinical counselor (MA). *Faculty:* 2 full-time (0 women), 12 part-time/adjunct (6 women). *Students:* 43 full-time (33 women), 4 part-time (all women); includes 23 minority (3 Black or African American, non-Hispanic/Latino; 3 Asian, non-Hispanic/Latino; 16 Hispanic/Latino; 1 Two or more races, non-Hispanic/Latino), 1 international. Average age 28. 33 applicants, 100% accepted, 25 enrolled. *Degree requirements:* For master's, comprehensive exam. *Expenses:* Contact institution. *Financial support:* Scholarships/grants available. Financial award applicants required to submit FAFSA. *Unit head:* Dr. Daniel Lee Jenkins, Program Director, 619-849-2282, E-mail: danieljenkins@pointloma.edu. *Application contact:* Joanie Joy, Senior Director of Enrollment Management, 619-329-6785, E-mail: gradinfo@pointloma.edu. Website: https://www.pointloma.edu/graduate-studies/programs/clinical-counseling-ma

Point Park University, School of Arts and Sciences, Department of Humanities and Human Sciences, Pittsburgh, PA 15222-1984. Offers clinical-community psychology (MA, Psy D).

Ponce Health Sciences University, Program in Clinical Psychology, Ponce, PR 00732-7004. Offers PhD, Psy D. *Accreditation:* APA. *Degree requirements:* For doctorate, one foreign language, comprehensive exam, thesis/dissertation, internship. *Entrance requirements:* For doctorate, GRE General Test or EXADEP, proficiency in Spanish and English; 2 letters of recommendation; minimum undergraduate GPA of 2.7, graduate 3.0; criminal background check.

Pontifical Catholic University of Puerto Rico, College of Graduate Studies in Behavioral Science and Community Affairs, Program in Clinical Psychology, Ponce, PR 00717-0777. Offers PhD, Psy D. *Program availability:* Part-time, evening/weekend. *Degree requirements:* For doctorate, comprehensive exam, thesis/dissertation. *Entrance requirements:* For doctorate, EXADEP, minimum GPA of 2.75.

Pontificia Universidad Catolica Madre y Maestra, Graduate School, Faculty of Social and Administrative Sciences, Santiago, Dominican Republic. Offers business administration (MBA), including business development, finance, international business, management skills (M Mgmt, MBA), marketing, operations, strategic cost management, strategy, tourist destination planning and management; law (LL M), including civil law, corporate business law, criminal law, international relations, real estate law; management (M Mgmt), including higher financial management, insurance program administration, management skills (M Mgmt, MBA); psychology (MA), including clinical child and adolescent psychology, forensic psychology; strategic human resources (EMBA).

Post University, Program in Counseling and Human Services, Waterbury, CT 06723-2540. Offers counseling and human services (MS); counseling and human services/alcohol and drug counseling (MS); counseling and human services/clinical mental health counseling (MS); counseling and human services/forensic mental health counseling (MS); counseling and human services/non-profit management (MS). *Program availability:* Part-time, evening/weekend, online learning. *Entrance requirements:* For master's, resume. *Expenses:* Tuition: Part-time $730 per credit hour. Part-time tuition and fees vary according to degree level and program. *Application contact:* Veronica Montalvo, Vice President, Online Education Enrollment Management and Admissions, 203-596-6164, E-mail: vmontalvo@post.edu. Website: https://post.edu/academics/online-master-of-science-in-counseling-and-human-services

Prairie View A&M University, College of Juvenile Justice and Psychology, Prairie View, TX 77446. Offers clinical adolescent psychology (PhD); juvenile forensic psychology (MSJFP); juvenile justice (MSJJ, PhD). *Program availability:* Part-time, evening/weekend, online only, 100% online. *Faculty:* 7 full-time (5 women), 3 part-time/adjunct (1 woman). *Students:* 23 full-time (18 women), 30 part-time (25 women); includes 50 minority (41 Black or African American, non-Hispanic/Latino; 8 Hispanic/Latino; 1 Two or more races, non-Hispanic/Latino), 2 international. Average age 31. 39 applicants, 82% accepted, 24 enrolled. In 2017, 19 master's, 3 doctorates awarded. *Degree requirements:* For master's, comprehensive exam; for doctorate, thesis/dissertation. *Entrance requirements:* For master's, GRE, minimum GPA of 2.75; for doctorate, GRE, previous course work in clinical adolescent psychology, minimum GPA of 3.5. Additional exam requirements/recommendations for international students: Required—TOEFL (minimum score 550 paper-based; 79 iBT). *Application deadline:* For fall admission, 5/1 priority date for domestic and international students; for spring admission, 10/1 priority date for domestic students, 9/1 priority date for international students; for summer admission, 3/1 priority date for domestic students, 2/1 priority date for international students. Applications are processed on a rolling basis. Application fee: $50. Electronic applications accepted. *Expenses:* Tuition, state resident: part-time $242 per credit. Tuition, nonresident: part-time $695 per credit. *Required fees:* $149 per credit. *Financial support:* Research assistantships, teaching assistantships, scholarships/grants, and unspecified assistantships available. Financial award application deadline: 4/1; financial award applicants required to submit FAFSA. *Faculty research:* Juvenile justice, community policing, adolescent substance use, reducing mental illness stigma and promoting positive psychological well-being in diverse communities, promoting prosocial behavior among at-risk youth. *Unit head:* Dr. Tamara L. Brown, Dean, 936-261-5206, Fax: 936-261-5253, E-mail: tlbrown@pvamu.edu. *Application contact:* Pauline Walker, Executive Secretary, Graduate Program, 936-261-3521, Fax: 936-261-3529, E-mail: gradadmissions@pvamu.edu.

Purdue University, Graduate School, College of Health and Human Sciences, Department of Psychological Sciences, West Lafayette, IN 47907. Offers behavioral neuroscience (PhD); clinical psychology (PhD); cognitive psychology (PhD); industrial/organizational psychology (PhD); mathematical and computational cognitive science (PhD). *Accreditation:* APA. *Faculty:* 46 full-time (18 women), 1 part-time/adjunct (0 women). *Students:* 64 full-time (41 women), 4 part-time (3 women); includes 13 minority (1 Black or African American, non-Hispanic/Latino; 4 Asian, non-Hispanic/Latino; 6 Hispanic/Latino; 2 Two or more races, non-Hispanic/Latino), 12 international. Average age 27. 288 applicants, 8% accepted, 16 enrolled. In 2017, 9 doctorates awarded. Terminal master's awarded for partial completion of doctoral program. *Degree requirements:* For doctorate, thesis/dissertation. *Entrance requirements:* For doctorate, GRE General Test, minimum undergraduate GPA of 3.0 or equivalent. Additional exam requirements/recommendations for international students: Required—TOEFL (minimum score 550 paper-based; 77 iBT); Recommended—TWE. *Application deadline:* For fall admission, 12/3 for domestic and international students. Applications are processed on a rolling basis. Application fee: $60 ($75 for international students). Electronic applications accepted. *Financial support:* Fellowships with partial tuition reimbursements, research assistantships with partial tuition reimbursements, teaching assistantships with partial tuition reimbursements, and career-related internships or fieldwork available. Support available to part-time students. Financial award applicants required to submit FAFSA. *Faculty research:* Career development of women in science, development of friendships during childhood and adolescence, social competence, human information processing. *Unit head:* Dr. David Rollock, Head, 765-494-6061, E-mail: rollock@purdue.edu. *Application contact:* Nancy A. O'Brien, Graduate Contact, 765-494-6067, E-mail: nobrien@psych.pardue.edu. Website: http://www.psych.purdue.edu/

Queen's University at Kingston, School of Graduate Studies, Faculty of Arts and Sciences, Department of Psychology, Kingston, ON K7L 3N6, Canada. Offers brain behavior and cognitive science (MA, PhD); clinical psychology (MA, PhD); developmental psychology (MA, PhD); social personality psychology (MA, PhD). *Degree requirements:* For master's, thesis; for doctorate, comprehensive exam, thesis/dissertation. *Entrance requirements:* For master's and doctorate, GRE General Test. Additional exam requirements/recommendations for international students: Required—TOEFL. *Faculty research:* Human development, social, personality, behavioral neuroscience, forensic.

Quincy University, Master of Science in Education Counseling Program, Quincy, IL 62301-2699. Offers clinical mental health counseling (MS Ed); college student personnel (MS Ed); school counseling (MS Ed). *Program availability:* Part-time, evening/weekend. *Degree requirements:* For master's, comprehensive exam, practicum, internship. *Entrance requirements:* For master's, MAT or GRE. Additional exam requirements/recommendations for international students: Required—TOEFL (minimum score 550 paper-based; 79 iBT). *Application deadline:* Applications are processed on a rolling basis. Application fee: $25. Electronic applications accepted. *Expenses:* Tuition: Part-time $450 per credit hour. *Financial support:* Applicants required to submit FAFSA. *Unit head:* Dr. Kenneth Oliver, Director, 217-228-5432 Ext. 3113, E-mail: oliveke@quincy.edu. *Application contact:* Office of Admissions, 217-228-5210, Fax: 217-228-5479, E-mail: admissions@quincy.edu. Website: http://www.quincy.edu/academics/graduate-programs/counseling/

Radford University, College of Graduate Studies and Research, Program in Psychology, Radford, VA 24142. Offers clinical-counseling psychology (MA, MS); experimental psychology (MA); industrial-organizational psychology (MA, MS). *Program availability:* Part-time. *Faculty:* 21 full-time (14 women). *Students:* 39 full-time (30 women); includes 5 minority (2 Black or African American, non-Hispanic/Latino; 1 Asian, non-Hispanic/Latino; 2 Hispanic/Latino). Average age 23. 87 applicants, 51% accepted, 22 enrolled. In 2017, 28 master's awarded. *Degree requirements:* For master's, comprehensive exam, thesis (for some programs). *Entrance requirements:* For master's, GRE, minimum GPA of 3.0, 3 letters of reference, essay, resume, official transcripts. Additional exam requirements/recommendations for international students: Required—TOEFL (minimum score 550 paper-based; 79 iBT), IELTS (minimum score 6.5). *Application deadline:* For fall admission, 2/15 priority date for domestic students, 12/1 for international students; for spring admission, 7/1 for international students. Applications are processed on a rolling basis. Application fee: $50. Electronic applications accepted. *Expenses:* Tuition, state resident: full-time $8336; part-time $347 per credit hour. Tuition, nonresident: full-time $16,862; part-time $702 per credit hour. *Required fees:* $3220; $135 per credit hour. Tuition and fees vary according to course load and program. *Financial support:* In 2017–18, 19 students received support, including 2 research assistantships (averaging $7,500 per year), 14 teaching assistantships (averaging $10,500 per year); career-related internships or fieldwork, scholarships/grants, and unspecified assistantships also available. Support available to part-time students. Financial award application deadline: 3/1; financial award applicants required to submit FAFSA. *Faculty research:* Social cognition and interpersonal relationships, relationship between one's self-concept and social interactions, creativity and innovation, organizational politics and ethical decision-making, victimization in childhood. *Unit head:* Dr. Jeffery Aspelmeier, Chair, 540-831-5361, Fax: 540-831-6113, E-mail: jaspelme@radford.edu.
Website: http://www.radford.edu/content/chbs/home/psychology.html

Regent University, Graduate School, School of Psychology and Counseling, Virginia Beach, VA 23464-9800. Offers clinical mental health counseling (MA); clinical psychology (Psy D); counseling and psychological studies - clinical (PhD); counseling and psychological studies - research (PhD); counseling studies (CAGS); counselor education and supervision (PhD); general psychology (MS); human services (MA), including addictions counseling, Biblical counseling, Christian counseling, conflict and mediation ministry, criminal justice and ministry, grief counseling, human services counseling, human services for student affairs, life coaching, marriage and family ministry, trauma and crisis counseling; marriage, couple, and family counseling (MA); pastoral counseling (MA); school counseling (MA); M Div/MA; M Ed/MA; MBA/MA. *Accreditation:* ACA; APA (one or more programs are accredited). *Program availability:* Part-time, evening/weekend, 100% online, blended/hybrid learning. *Faculty:* 28 full-time (16 women), 51 part-time/adjunct (30 women). *Students:* 294 full-time (236 women), 404 part-time (317 women); includes 286 minority (218 Black or African American, non-Hispanic/Latino; 4 American Indian or Alaska Native, non-Hispanic/Latino; 17 Asian, non-Hispanic/Latino; 30 Hispanic/Latino; 17 Two or more races, non-Hispanic/Latino), 13 international. Average age 37. 2,109 applicants, 18% accepted, 233 enrolled. In 2017, 158 master's, 28 doctorates awarded. *Degree requirements:* For master's, thesis or alternative, internship, practicum, written competency exam; for doctorate, thesis/dissertation or alternative. *Entrance requirements:* For master's, GRE General Test (including writing exam) or MAT, minimum undergraduate GPA of 3.0, resume, transcripts, writing sample, personal goals statement; for doctorate, GRE General Test (including writing exam), minimum undergraduate GPA of 3.0, graduate 3.5; writing sample; 3 recommendations; resume; college transcripts; personal goals statement. Additional exam requirements/recommendations for international students: Required—TOEFL (minimum score 577 paper-based). *Application deadline:* For fall admission, 4/1 priority date for domestic students; for spring admission, 11/1 priority date for domestic students. Applications are processed on a rolling basis. Application fee: $50. Electronic applications accepted. *Expenses:* Contact institution. *Financial support:* In 2017–18, 557 students received support, including 5 fellowships (averaging $10,000 per year), 11 research assistantships (averaging $3,200 per year); career-related internships or fieldwork, scholarships/grants, and unspecified assistantships also available. Support available to part-time students. *Faculty research:* Marriage enrichment, clinical psychology, troubled youth, faith and learning, trauma. *Unit head:* Dr. William Hathaway, Dean, 757-352-4294, Fax: 757-352-4282, E-mail: willhat@regent.edu. *Application contact:* Heidi Cece, Assistant Vice President of Enrollment Management, 800-373-5504, Fax: 757-352-4381, E-mail: admissions@regent.edu.
Website: https://www.regent.edu/school-of-psychology-and-counseling/

Richmont Graduate University, School of Counseling, Atlanta, GA 30339. Offers clinical mental health counseling (MA); marriage and family therapy (MA). *Accreditation:* ACA. *Program availability:* Part-time, evening/weekend. *Degree requirements:* For master's, comprehensive exam, thesis optional. *Entrance requirements:* For master's, GRE or MAT. Electronic applications accepted.

Rider University, College of Education and Human Services, Program in Counseling Services, Lawrenceville, NJ 08648-3001. Offers clinical mental health counseling (MA); counseling services (MA, Ed S); director of school counseling services (Certificate); life and career coaching (Certificate); school counseling (Certificate); student assistance coordinator (Certificate); substance awareness coordinator (Certificate). *Accreditation:* ACA; NCATE. *Program availability:* Part-time, evening/weekend. *Degree requirements:* For master's, comprehensive exam, research project; for other advanced degree, specialty seminar. *Entrance requirements:* For master's, GRE or MAT, interview, resume, 2 letters of recommendation; for other advanced degree, GRE or MAT, interview, professional experience, 2 letters of recommendation. Additional exam requirements/recommendations for international students: Required—TOEFL (minimum score 550 paper-based). Electronic applications accepted. *Faculty research:* Diversity in counseling.

Rivier University, School of Graduate Studies, Department of Psychology, Nashua, NH 03060. Offers clinical psychology (MS); experimental psychology (MS).

Roberts Wesleyan College, Graduate Psychology Programs, Rochester, NY 14624-1997. Offers clinical/school psychology (Psy D); school counseling (MS); school psychology (MS). *Program availability:* Part-time, evening/weekend. *Degree requirements:* For master's, comprehensive exam, PRAXIS II (for school psychology). *Entrance requirements:* For master's, GRE. Electronic applications accepted. Application fee is waived when completed online. *Faculty research:* Counselor supervision, forgiveness, community health psychology, applied research in group process.

Roger Williams University, Feinstein School of Social and Natural Sciences, Forensic Mental Health Counseling, Bristol, RI 02809. Offers clinical psychology (MA). *Expenses:* Contact institution.

Roosevelt University, Graduate Division, College of Arts and Sciences, Department of Psychology, Program in Clinical Psychology - Counseling Practice, Chicago, IL 60605. Offers MA. *Accreditation:* APA. *Students:* 113 full-time (86 women), 41 part-time (33 women); includes 58 minority (25 Black or African American, non-Hispanic/Latino; 8 Asian, non-Hispanic/Latino; 15 Hispanic/Latino; 10 Two or more races, non-Hispanic/Latino), 5 international. Average age 35. 138 applicants, 78% accepted, 55 enrolled. In 2017, 60 master's awarded. Application fee: $40. Electronic applications accepted. *Financial support:* Scholarships/grants and unspecified assistantships available. *Application contact:* Sivling Lam, Graduate Admission Counselor, 312-281-3252, E-mail: slam02@roosevelt.edu.

Roosevelt University, Graduate Division, College of Education, Program in Clinical Mental Health Counseling and School Counseling, Chicago, IL 60605. Offers clinical mental health counseling (MA); school counseling (MA). *Accreditation:* ACA. *Students:* 64 full-time (52 women), 33 part-time (25 women); includes 45 minority (25 Black or African American, non-Hispanic/Latino; 1 Asian, non-Hispanic/Latino; 15 Hispanic/Latino; 4 Two or more races, non-Hispanic/Latino), 2 international. Average age 28. 65 applicants, 98% accepted, 36 enrolled. In 2017, 35 master's awarded. Application fee: $40. *Financial support:* Scholarships/grants and unspecified assistantships available. *Application contact:* Laura Lag, Associate Dean for Graduate Admission, 312-853-4753, E-mail: llag@roosevelt.edu.

Rosalind Franklin University of Medicine and Science, College of Health Professions, Department of Psychology, North Chicago, IL 60064-3095. Offers clinical psychology (MS, PhD). *Accreditation:* APA. Terminal master's awarded for partial completion of doctoral program. *Degree requirements:* For master's, capstone experience. *Entrance requirements:* For master's, minimum GPA of 3.0, bachelor's degree (preferably in related subject); for doctorate, GRE, minimum GPA of 3.0, bachelor's or master's degree. Additional exam requirements/recommendations for international students: Required—TOEFL. *Faculty research:* Anxiety, pain, psychopathy, epilepsy, neuropsychology.

Rowan University, Graduate School, College of Science and Mathematics, Program in Clinical Mental Health Counseling, Glassboro, NJ 08028-1701. Offers MA, CAGS. *Program availability:* Part-time, evening/weekend. *Entrance requirements:* For master's, GRE General Test. Additional exam requirements/recommendations for international students: Required—TOEFL. *Expenses:* Tuition, state resident: full-time $15,020; part-time $751 per semester hour. Tuition, nonresident: full-time $15,020; part-time $751 per semester hour. *Required fees:* $3158; $157.90 per semester hour. Tuition and fees vary according to course load, campus/location and program.

Rutgers University–New Brunswick, Graduate School-New Brunswick, Program in Psychology, Piscataway, NJ 08854-8097. Offers behavioral neuroscience (PhD); clinical psychology (PhD); cognitive psychology (PhD); interdisciplinary health psychology (PhD); social psychology (PhD). *Accreditation:* APA. *Degree requirements:* For doctorate, comprehensive exam, thesis/dissertation. *Entrance requirements:* For doctorate, GRE General Test, 3 letters of recommendation. Additional exam requirements/recommendations for international students: Required—TOEFL (minimum score 577 paper-based). Electronic applications accepted. *Faculty research:* Learning and memory, behavioral ecology, hormones and behavior, psychopharmacology, anxiety disorders.

Rutgers University–New Brunswick, Graduate School of Applied and Professional Psychology, Department of Clinical Psychology, Piscataway, NJ 08854-8097. Offers Psy M, Psy D. *Accreditation:* APA (one or more programs are accredited). *Degree requirements:* For doctorate, comprehensive exam, thesis/dissertation, 1 year internship. *Entrance requirements:* For doctorate, GRE General Test, GRE Subject Test, bachelor's degree in psychology or equivalent. Additional exam requirements/recommendations for international students: Required—TOEFL. Electronic applications accepted. *Expenses:* Contact institution. *Faculty research:* Long- and short-term dynamic therapy, community psychology, cognitive-behavioral therapy: anxiety and depressive disorders, addictive behaviors: eating disorders and alcoholism.

St. John's University, St. John's College of Liberal Arts and Sciences, Department of Psychology, Program in Clinical Psychology, Queens, NY 11439. Offers clinical psychology-child (PhD); clinical psychology-general (PhD). *Accreditation:* APA. *Students:* 35 full-time (25 women), 20 part-time (16 women); includes 18 minority (4 Black or African American, non-Hispanic/Latino; 7 Asian, non-Hispanic/Latino; 5 Hispanic/Latino; 2 Two or more races, non-Hispanic/Latino). Average age 29. 283 applicants, 5% accepted, 10 enrolled. In 2017, 12 doctorates awarded. *Degree requirements:* For doctorate, comprehensive exam, thesis/dissertation. *Entrance requirements:* For doctorate, GRE General Test, GRE Subject Test, letters of recommendation, transcripts, resume, personal statement, 24 credits of psychology prerequisites, lab paper, term paper. Additional exam requirements/recommendations for international students: Required—TOEFL (minimum score 80 iBT), IELTS (minimum score 6.5). *Application deadline:* For fall admission, 12/31 priority date for domestic students. Application fee: $70. Electronic applications accepted. *Expenses:* $26,550 per year. *Financial support:* Fellowships, research assistantships, teaching assistantships, scholarships/grants, tuition waivers, and unspecified assistantships available. Support available to part-time students. Financial award application deadline: 2/1; financial award applicants required to submit FAFSA. *Faculty research:* Depression, parenting, Post-Traumatic Stress Disorder, personality, nondiscriminatory assessment. *Unit head:* Dr. Jeffrey S. Nevid, Director of Clinical Psychology, 718-990-1548, Fax: 718-990-6705, E-mail: nevidj@stjohns.edu. *Application contact:* Robert Medrano, Director of Graduate Admission, 718-990-1601, Fax: 718-990-5686, E-mail: gradhelp@stjohns.edu.
Website: https://www.stjohns.edu/academics/schools-and-colleges/st-johns-college-liberal-arts-and-sciences/psychology/clinical-psychology-phd

St. John's University, The School of Education, Department of Counselor Education, Program in Clinical Mental Health Counseling, Queens, NY 11439. Offers MS Ed, Adv C. Master's program admits in fall only; Advanced Certificate in spring only. *Students:* 45 full-time (34 women), 27 part-time (19 women); includes 40 minority (16 Black or African American, non-Hispanic/Latino; 3 Asian, non-Hispanic/Latino; 20 Hispanic/Latino; 1 Two or more races, non-Hispanic/Latino), 2 international. Average age 27. 67 applicants, 72% accepted, 22 enrolled. In 2017, 27 master's, 1 Adv C awarded. *Entrance requirements:* For master's, 2 letters of recommendation, interview; for Adv C, official master's transcripts, statement of purpose. *Application deadline:* For fall admission, 8/17 for domestic and international students; for summer admission, 5/15 for domestic and international students. Application fee: $70. Electronic applications accepted. *Expenses: Tuition:* Full-time $44,280; part-time $1230 per credit. *Required fees:* $340; $340 per credit. Tuition and fees vary according to course load, degree level and program. *Financial support:* Fellowships, research assistantships, scholarships/grants, and unspecified assistantships available. Support available to part-time students. Financial award application deadline: 2/1; financial award applicants required to submit FAFSA. *Faculty research:* Psychological issues of veterans as they return to civilian life, career issues of same populations, role of spirituality in recovery from substance abuse, issues around resilience, issues surrounding happiness, effective practice and supervision in on-line format, diversity issues in the presentation of pathology and special requirements for effective treatment. *Unit head:* Dr. Robert K. Eschenauer, Chair, 718-990-2120, E-mail: eschenar@stjohns.edu. *Application contact:* Dr. Robert K. Eschenauer, Chair, 718-990-2120, E-mail: eschenar@stjohns.edu.
Website: https://www.stjohns.edu/academics/schools-and-colleges/school-education/programs-and-majors/clinical-mental-health-counseling-master-science-education

Saint Louis University, Graduate Programs, College of Arts and Sciences and Graduate Programs, Department of Psychology, St. Louis, MO 63103. Offers clinical

psychology (MS-R, PhD); experimental psychology (MS-R, PhD); industrial-organizational psychology (PhD); psychology (PhD). *Accreditation:* APA (one or more programs are accredited). *Program availability:* Part-time. *Degree requirements:* For master's, comprehensive exam, thesis; for doctorate, thesis/dissertation, clinical internship (for clinical psychology PhD). *Entrance requirements:* For master's, GRE General Test, interview, letters of recommendation, resume; for doctorate, GRE General Test, interview, letters of recommendation, resumé, transcripts, goal statement. Additional exam requirements/recommendations for international students: Required—TOEFL (minimum score 550 paper-based). Electronic applications accepted. *Faculty research:* Violence and trauma; neural basis of learning and memory function; eating disorders; body image and health behavior; prejudice, stereotyping, and victimization; memory, cognitive aging and language processing.

Saint Michael's College, Graduate Programs, Program in Clinical Psychology, Colchester, VT 05439. Offers MA. *Program availability:* Part-time, evening/weekend. *Faculty:* 5 full-time (3 women), 11 part-time/adjunct (9 women). *Students:* 20 full-time (15 women), 17 part-time (14 women); includes 6 minority (2 Black or African American, non-Hispanic/Latino; 2 Asian, non-Hispanic/Latino; 2 Two or more races, non-Hispanic/Latino), 2 international. Average age 30. 14 applicants, 79% accepted, 10 enrolled. In 2017, 15 master's awarded. *Degree requirements:* For master's, thesis or alternative, internship, practicum, research seminar. *Entrance requirements:* For master's, GRE General Test, GRE Subject Test, undergraduate major in psychology or related area, minimum 12 credits in psychology, minimum GPA of 3.0, official transcripts, 2 references, resume. Additional exam requirements/recommendations for international students: Required—TOEFL (minimum score 79 iBT). *Application deadline:* For fall admission, 6/1 priority date for domestic students. Applications are processed on a rolling basis. Application fee: $50. Electronic applications accepted. *Expenses: Tuition:* Part-time $590 per credit. *Financial support:* Teaching assistantships with partial tuition reimbursements, career-related internships or fieldwork, Federal Work-Study, scholarships/grants, tuition waivers (partial), and unspecified assistantships available. Financial award application deadline: 5/1; financial award applicants required to submit FAFSA. *Faculty research:* Psychodynamic psychotherapy, family therapy, philosophical foundations of clinical psychology. *Unit head:* Dr. Ronald B. Miller, Director, 802-654-2206, Fax: 802-654-2664, E-mail: rmiller@smcvt.edu. *Application contact:* Lindsay A. Damici, Marketing Communications Manager, 802-654-2556, Fax: 802-654-2732.
Website: http://www.smcvt.edu/graduate-programs/academic-programs/clinical-psychology.aspx

Sam Houston State University, College of Humanities and Social Sciences, Department of Psychology and Philosophy, Huntsville, TX 77341. Offers psychology (MA, PhD, SSP), including clinical psychology (MA, PhD), psychology (MA), school psychology (SSP). *Accreditation:* APA. *Program availability:* Part-time. Terminal master's awarded for partial completion of doctoral program. *Degree requirements:* For master's, comprehensive exam, thesis optional; for doctorate, comprehensive exam, thesis/dissertation. *Entrance requirements:* For master's, GRE General Test, personal statement, letters of recommendation; for doctorate, GRE General Test, GRE Subject Test (advanced psychology), personal essay, letters of recommendation, resume. Additional exam requirements/recommendations for international students: Required—TOEFL (minimum score 550 paper-based; 79 iBT), IELTS (minimum score 6.5). Electronic applications accepted.

San Diego State University, Graduate and Research Affairs, College of Sciences, Department of Psychology, San Diego, CA 92182. Offers clinical psychology (MS, PhD); industrial and organizational psychology (MS); program evaluation (MS); psychology (MA). PhD offered jointly with University of California, San Diego. *Accreditation:* APA (one or more programs are accredited). Terminal master's awarded for partial completion of doctoral program. *Degree requirements:* For master's, thesis, oral exam; for doctorate, thesis/dissertation. *Entrance requirements:* For master's, GRE General Test, GRE Subject Test, 3 letters of recommendation; for doctorate, GRE General Test, GRE Subject Test, minimum GPA of 3.0, 3 letters of recommendation. Additional exam requirements/recommendations for international students: Required—TOEFL. Electronic applications accepted.

San Francisco State University, Division of Graduate Studies, College of Health and Social Sciences, Department of Counseling, San Francisco, CA 94132-1722. Offers clinical mental health counseling (MS); marriage, family and child counseling (MS). *Accreditation:* ACA. *Program availability:* Part-time. *Application deadline:* Applications are processed on a rolling basis. *Unit head:* Dr. Graciela Orozco, Chair, 415-338-2005, Fax: 415-338-0594, E-mail: counsel@sfsu.edu. *Application contact:* Dr. Alison Cerezo, College Counseling Coordinator, 415-338-1064, Fax: 415-338-0594, E-mail: acerezo@sfsu.edu.
Website: http://counseling.sfsu.edu

San Francisco State University, Division of Graduate Studies, College of Science and Engineering, Department of Psychology, San Francisco, CA 94132-1722. Offers clinical psychology (MS); developmental psychology (MA); industrial/organizational psychology (MS); mind, brain, and behavior (MA); school psychology (MS, Credential); social psychology (MA). *Financial support:* Teaching assistantships available. Financial award application deadline: 3/1. *Unit head:* Dr. Dawn Terrell, Chair, 415-338-7555, Fax: 415-338-2398, E-mail: schen9@sfsu.edu. *Application contact:* Dr. Diane Harris, Graduate Program Coordinator, 415-338-7064, Fax: 415-338-2398, E-mail: dharris@sfsu.edu.
Website: http://psychology.sfsu.edu/graduate/application.html

San Jose State University, Graduate Studies and Research, College of Social Sciences, San Jose, CA 95192-0107. Offers applied anthropology (MA); communication studies (MA); economics (MA), including applied economics, economics; environmental studies (MS); geography (MA); history (MA), including history, history education; Mexican American studies (MA); psychology (MA, MS), including clinical psychology (MS), industrial/organizational psychology (MS), research and experimental psychology (MA); public administration (MPA); social sciences (MS); sociology (MA). *Faculty:* 59 full-time (29 women), 18 part-time/adjunct (5 women). *Students:* 181 full-time (126 women), 221 part-time (127 women); includes 228 minority (15 Black or African American, non-Hispanic/Latino; 48 Asian, non-Hispanic/Latino; 112 Hispanic/Latino; 3 Native Hawaiian or other Pacific Islander, non-Hispanic/Latino; 50 Two or more races, non-Hispanic/Latino), 38 international. Average age 30. 532 applicants, 44% accepted, 156 enrolled. In 2017, 139 master's awarded. *Degree requirements:* For master's, one foreign language, comprehensive exam, thesis (for some programs), project, field work, professional work experience. *Entrance requirements:* Additional exam requirements/recommendations for international students: Required—TOEFL (minimum score 550 paper-based; 80 iBT), IELTS (minimum score 6.5), PTE (minimum score 53). *Application deadline:* For fall admission, 2/1 for domestic and international students. Applications are processed on a rolling basis. Application fee: $55. Electronic applications accepted. *Expenses:* Tuition, state resident: full-time $7176. Tuition, nonresident: full-time $16,680. Tuition and fees vary according to course load and program. *Financial support:* Fellowships, research assistantships, career-related internships or fieldwork, Federal Work-Study, scholarships/grants, tuition waivers (full and partial), and unspecified assistantships available. Support available to part-time students. Financial award application deadline: 4/28; financial award applicants required to submit FAFSA. *Unit head:* Dr. Walt Jacobs, Dean, 408-924-5300, Fax: 408-924-5303, E-mail: walter.jacobs@sjsu.edu.
Website: http://www.sjsu.edu/socialsciences/

Saybrook University, School of Clinical Psychology, San Francisco, CA 94612. Offers MA. Program offered jointly with Bastyr University. *Degree requirements:* For master's, thesis (for some programs), oral exams. *Entrance requirements:* For master's, bachelor's degree from an accredited university or college. *Faculty research:* Family systems theory, marriage and family therapy, systems consultation, family and culture of origin, personal authority.

Seattle Pacific University, PhD in Clinical Psychology Program, Seattle, WA 98119-1997. Offers PhD. *Accreditation:* APA. *Students:* 47 full-time (37 women), 21 part-time (19 women); includes 8 minority (1 Black or African American, non-Hispanic/Latino; 4 Asian, non-Hispanic/Latino; 2 Hispanic/Latino; 1 Two or more races, non-Hispanic/Latino), 3 international. Average age 28. 95 applicants, 19% accepted, 15 enrolled. In 2017, 13 doctorates awarded. *Degree requirements:* For doctorate, thesis/dissertation, clinical internship, practicum. *Entrance requirements:* For doctorate, GRE (preferred minimum score 1100 verbal and quantitative, taken within the last five years), BA, personal statement. Additional exam requirements/recommendations for international students: Required—TOEFL (minimum score 600 paper-based). *Application deadline:* For fall admission, 12/15 for domestic and international students. Electronic applications accepted. *Expenses:* Contact institution. *Financial support:* Fellowships and scholarships/grants available. Financial award applicants required to submit FAFSA. *Faculty research:* Social network support, attachment, integration of faith and family psychology, developmental psychology. *Unit head:* Dr. Lynette Bikos, Acting Chair, 206-281-2017, E-mail: lhbikos@spu.edu. *Application contact:* 206-281-2091.
Website: http://spu.edu/academics/school-of-psychology-family-community/graduate-programs/clinical-psychology-phd

Seminary of the Southwest, Graduate and Professional Programs, Austin, TX 78768-2247. Offers Anglican studies (Advanced Diploma); chaplaincy and pastoral care (MA); clinical mental health counseling (MA); Latino/Hispanic studies (M Div); ministry (M Div); religion (MAR); spiritual formation (MA). *Accreditation:* ACIPE; ATS (one or more programs are accredited). *Program availability:* Part-time, evening/weekend. *Faculty:* 10 full-time (5 women), 12 part-time/adjunct (5 women). *Students:* 60 full-time (31 women), 56 part-time (42 women); includes 22 minority (10 Black or African American, non-Hispanic/Latino; 1 American Indian or Alaska Native, non-Hispanic/Latino; 2 Asian, non-Hispanic/Latino; 6 Hispanic/Latino; 3 Two or more races, non-Hispanic/Latino). Average age 38. 49 applicants, 98% accepted, 31 enrolled. In 2017, 27 master's, 3 other advanced degrees awarded. *Degree requirements:* For master's, comprehensive exam (for some programs), thesis (for some programs). *Entrance requirements:* For master's, GRE, MAT, interview; for Advanced Diploma, interview. Additional exam requirements/recommendations for international students: Recommended—TOEFL. *Application deadline:* For fall admission, 6/30 priority date for domestic and international students; for spring admission, 12/1 for domestic and international students. Applications are processed on a rolling basis. Application fee: $50. Electronic applications accepted. *Expenses:* Contact institution. *Financial support:* In 2017–18, 92 students received support. Career-related internships or fieldwork and scholarships/grants available. Support available to part-time students. Financial award application deadline: 6/15; financial award applicants required to submit FAFSA. *Unit head:* Rev. Dr. Cynthia Briggs Kittredge, Dean and President, 512-472-4133 Ext. 332, Fax: 512-472-3098, E-mail: cynthia.kittredge@ssw.edu. *Application contact:* Hope Benko, Director of Enrollment Management, 512-472-4133 Ext. 375, Fax: 512-472-3098, E-mail: hope.benko@ssw.edu.

Shippensburg University of Pennsylvania, School of Graduate Studies, College of Education and Human Services, Department of Counseling, Shippensburg, PA 17257-2299. Offers college counseling (MS); college student personnel (MS); counselor education and supervision (Ed D); mental health counseling (MS); school counseling (M Ed). *Accreditation:* ACA (one or more programs are accredited); NCATE. *Program availability:* Part-time, evening/weekend, blended/hybrid learning. *Faculty:* 9 full-time (3 women), 1 part-time/adjunct (0 women). *Students:* 75 full-time (64 women), 49 part-time (40 women); includes 28 minority (17 Black or African American, non-Hispanic/Latino; 1 Asian, non-Hispanic/Latino; 7 Hispanic/Latino; 3 Two or more races, non-Hispanic/Latino), 3 international. Average age 29. 94 applicants, 54% accepted, 41 enrolled. In 2017, 56 master's awarded. *Degree requirements:* For master's, fieldwork, research project, internship, candidacy; for doctorate, thesis/dissertation, practicum, internship. *Entrance requirements:* For master's, GRE or MAT (for MS if GPA is less than 2.75), minimum GPA of 2.75 (3.0 for M Ed), resume, 3 letter of recommendation forms, one year of relevant work experience, on-campus interview, autobiographical statement; for doctorate, master's degree in counseling or related discipline; resume; three recommendation letters (1 each from employer, clinical supervisor, and prior graduate school faculty member); personal essay; interview with department chair. Additional exam requirements/recommendations for international students: Required—TOEFL (minimum score 550 paper-based, 68 iBT) or IELTS (minimum score 6). *Application deadline:* Applications are processed on a rolling basis. Application fee: $45. Electronic applications accepted. *Expenses:* Tuition, state resident: part-time $500 per credit. Tuition, nonresident: part-time $750 per credit. *Required fees:* $145 per credit. *Financial support:* In 2017–18, 54 students received support. Career-related internships or fieldwork, scholarships/grants, unspecified assistantships, and resident hall director and student payroll positions available. Support available to part-time students. Financial award application deadline: 3/1; financial award applicants required to submit FAFSA. *Unit head:* Dr. Kurt L. Kraus, Departmental Chair and Program Coordinator, 717-477-1603, Fax: 717-477-4056, E-mail: klkrau@ship.edu. *Application contact:* Maya T. Mapp, Director of Admissions, 717-477-1231, Fax: 717-477-4016, E-mail: mtmapp@ship.edu.
Website: http://www.ship.edu/counsel/

Siena Heights University, Graduate College, Adrian, MI 49221-1796. Offers clinical mental health counseling (MA); educational leadership (Specialist); leadership (MA), including health care leadership, organizational leadership; teacher education (MA), including early childhood education, early childhood education: Montessori, education leadership: principal, elementary education: reading K-12, leadership: higher education, secondary education: reading K-12, special education: cognitive impairment, special education: learning disabilities. *Program availability:* Part-time, evening/weekend. *Degree requirements:* For master's, thesis, presentation. *Entrance requirements:* For master's, minimum GPA of 3.0, current resume, essay, all post-secondary transcripts, 3 letters of reference, conviction disclosure form; copy of teaching certificate (for some education programs); for Specialist, master's degree, minimum GPA of 3.0, current resume, essay, all post-secondary transcripts, 3 letters of reference, conviction disclosure form; copy of teaching certificate (for some education programs). Electronic applications accepted.

Slippery Rock University of Pennsylvania, Graduate Studies (Recruitment), College of Education, Department of Counseling and Development, Slippery Rock, PA 16057-1383. Offers clinical mental health (MA); school counseling (M Ed); student affairs in higher education (MA); student affairs in higher education with college counseling (MA). *Accreditation:* ACA (one or more programs are accredited); NCATE. *Program availability:* Part-time, evening/weekend. *Degree requirements:* For master's, comprehensive exam, thesis (for some programs). *Entrance requirements:* For master's,

GRE General Test or MAT, official transcripts, personal statement, three letters of recommendation, interview. Additional exam requirements/recommendations for international students: Required—TOEFL (minimum score 550 paper-based; 80 iBT). Electronic applications accepted. *Expenses:* Contact institution.

Sofia University, Residential Programs, Palo Alto, CA 94303. Offers clinical psychology (Psy D); computer science (MS); counseling psychology (MA); transpersonal psychology (MA, PhD). *Program availability:* Part-time, evening/weekend. Terminal master's awarded for partial completion of doctoral program. *Degree requirements:* For doctorate, thesis/dissertation. *Entrance requirements:* For master's, bachelor's degree; for doctorate, bachelor's degree; master's degree (for some programs). Electronic applications accepted.

Sonoma State University, School of Social Sciences, Department of Counseling, Rohnert Park, CA 94928. Offers clinical mental health counseling (MA); school counseling (MA). *Accreditation:* ACA. *Program availability:* Part-time. *Entrance requirements:* For master's, minimum GPA of 3.0. Additional exam requirements/recommendations for international students: Required—TOEFL (minimum score 500 paper-based). *Application deadline:* For fall admission, 11/30 for domestic students. Application fee: $55. *Financial support:* Fellowships and career-related internships or fieldwork available. Financial award application deadline: 3/2; financial award applicants required to submit FAFSA. *Unit head:* Dr. Adam Zagelbaum, Chair, 707-664-2544, E-mail: adam.zagelbaum@sonoma.edu.
Website: http://www.sonoma.edu/counseling

Southeastern Oklahoma State University, School of Behavioral Sciences, Durant, OK 74701-0609. Offers clinical mental health counseling (MS). *Accreditation:* ACA. *Program availability:* Part-time, evening/weekend. *Degree requirements:* For master's, comprehensive exam, thesis optional. *Entrance requirements:* For master's, GRE General Test, minimum GPA of 3.0 in last 60 hours or 2.75 overall. Additional exam requirements/recommendations for international students: Required—TOEFL (minimum score 550 paper-based; 79 iBT). Electronic applications accepted.

Southern Illinois University Carbondale, Graduate School, College of Liberal Arts, Department of Psychology, Carbondale, IL 62901-4701. Offers clinical psychology (PhD); counseling psychology (PhD); experimental psychology (MA, MS). *Accreditation:* APA (one or more programs are accredited). *Degree requirements:* For master's, thesis; for doctorate, thesis/dissertation. *Entrance requirements:* For master's, GRE General Test, GRE Subject Test, minimum GPA of 2.7; for doctorate, GRE General Test, GRE Subject Test, minimum GPA of 3.25. Additional exam requirements/recommendations for international students: Required—TOEFL. *Faculty research:* Developmental neuropsychology; smoking, affect, and cognition; personality measurement; vocational psychology; program evaluation.

Southern Illinois University Edwardsville, Graduate School, School of Education, Health, and Human Behavior, Department of Psychology, Program in Clinical Child and School Psychology, Edwardsville, IL 62026. Offers MS. *Program availability:* Part-time. *Degree requirements:* For master's, thesis (for some programs), research project. *Entrance requirements:* For master's, GRE. Additional exam requirements/recommendations for international students: Required—TOEFL (minimum score 550 paper-based, 79 iBT), IELTS (minimum score 6.5), Michigan Test of English Language Proficiency or PTE. Electronic applications accepted.

Southern Illinois University Edwardsville, Graduate School, School of Education, Health, and Human Behavior, Department of Psychology, Program in Clinical Psychology, Edwardsville, IL 62026. Offers MA. *Program availability:* Part-time, evening/weekend. *Degree requirements:* For master's, comprehensive exam (for some programs), thesis (for some programs). *Entrance requirements:* For master's, GRE. Additional exam requirements/recommendations for international students: Required—TOEFL (minimum score 550 paper-based; 79 iBT), IELTS (minimum score 6.5). Electronic applications accepted.

Southern Methodist University, Dedman College of Humanities and Sciences, Department of Psychology, Program in Clinical Psychology, Dallas, TX 75275. Offers PhD. *Accreditation:* APA. *Degree requirements:* For doctorate, comprehensive exam, thesis/dissertation, research presentation and publication. *Entrance requirements:* For doctorate, GRE General Test, minimum GPA of 3.0, 3 letters of recommendation. Additional exam requirements/recommendations for international students: Required—TOEFL (minimum score 550 paper-based). Electronic applications accepted. *Faculty research:* Family violence, family assessment, anxiety disorders, personality disorders.

Southern New Hampshire University, School of Arts and Sciences, Manchester, NH 03106-1045. Offers clinical mental health counseling (MS); creative writing (MA); criminal justice (MS); cyber security (MS); English (MA); fiction and nonfiction (MFA); history (MA); political science (MS); psychology (MS). *Program availability:* Part-time, evening/weekend. *Degree requirements:* For master's, one foreign language, thesis. *Entrance requirements:* For master's, minimum GPA of 2.75 (for MS in teaching English as a foreign language), 3.0 (for MFA). Additional exam requirements/recommendations for international students: Required—TOEFL (minimum score 550 paper-based; 79 iBT), IELTS (minimum score 6.5), TWE (minimum score 5). *Application deadline:* For fall admission, 7/1 priority date for domestic students; for winter admission, 11/1 priority date for domestic students; for spring admission, 6/1 priority date for domestic students. Applications are processed on a rolling basis. Application fee: $40. Electronic applications accepted. *Expenses:* Contact institution. *Financial support:* Research assistantships, career-related internships or fieldwork, and scholarships/grants available. Financial award applicants required to submit FAFSA. *Faculty research:* Action research, state of the art practice in behavioral health services, wraparound approaches to working with youth, learning styles. *Unit head:* Steven K. Johnson, Dean, 603-629-4626. *Application contact:* Office of Graduate Admission, 888-327-SNHU, Fax: 603-644-3144, E-mail: enroll@snhu.edu.

Spalding University, Graduate Studies, Kosair College of Health and Natural Sciences, School of Professional Psychology, Louisville, KY 40203-2188. Offers clinical psychology (MA, Psy D). *Accreditation:* APA (one or more programs are accredited). *Program availability:* Part-time. Terminal master's awarded for partial completion of doctoral program. *Degree requirements:* For master's, comprehensive exam; for doctorate, thesis/dissertation. *Entrance requirements:* For master's and doctorate, GRE General Test, 18 hours of undergraduate course work in psychology, interview, letters of recommendation, writing sample, autobiographical statement. Additional exam requirements/recommendations for international students: Required—TOEFL (minimum score 535 paper-based). *Faculty research:* Substance abuse, prayer research, end-of-life issues, complementary and alternative medicine, research methodology and statistical inference.

Springfield College, Graduate Programs, Program in Human Services, Springfield, MA 01109-3797. Offers mental health counseling (MS); organizational management and leadership (MS). *Program availability:* Part-time, evening/weekend, blended/hybrid learning. *Degree requirements:* For master's, comprehensive exam, thesis (for some programs), Community Action Research Project. *Entrance requirements:* Additional exam requirements/recommendations for international students: Required—TOEFL (minimum score 550 paper-based). *Application deadline:* For fall admission, 8/31 for domestic and international students; for winter admission, 11/1 for domestic and

international students; for spring admission, 12/31 for domestic and international students; for summer admission, 4/30 for domestic and international students. Applications are processed on a rolling basis. Application fee: $40. Electronic applications accepted. *Expenses:* Contact institution. *Financial support:* Application deadline: 3/1; applicants required to submit FAFSA. *Unit head:* Dr. John Eisler, Dean, 413-748-3982, E-mail: jeisler@springfieldcollege.edu. *Application contact:* Marisol Guevara, Assistant Director of Recruitment and Outreach, 413-748-3624, E-mail: mguevara@springfieldcollege.edu.
Website: https://springfield.edu/school-of-professional-and-continuing-studies/degrees-and-programs/master-of-science

Springfield College, Graduate Programs, Programs in Psychology, Springfield, MA 01109-3797. Offers athletic counseling (MS, CAGS); clinical mental health counseling (M Ed, CAGS); counseling psychology (Psy D); general counseling (M Ed); industrial/organizational psychology (M Ed, CAGS); school counseling (M Ed, CAGS); student personnel administration in higher education (M Ed, CAGS). *Accreditation:* APA. *Program availability:* Part-time. *Students:* 192 applicants, 65% accepted, 64 enrolled. In 2017, 56 master's, 5 doctorates awarded. *Degree requirements:* For master's, research project, portfolio; for doctorate, dissertation project, 1500 hours of counseling psychology practicum, full-year internship. *Entrance requirements:* For doctorate, GRE. Additional exam requirements/recommendations for international students: Required—TOEFL (minimum score 550 paper-based); Recommended—IELTS (minimum score 7). *Application deadline:* For fall admission, 1/15 priority date for domestic students, 1/15 for international students; for winter admission, 11/1 for domestic and international students; for spring admission, 11/1 for domestic and international students. Applications are processed on a rolling basis. Application fee: $50. Electronic applications accepted. *Financial support:* Fellowships with partial tuition reimbursements, teaching assistantships with partial tuition reimbursements, career-related internships or fieldwork, Federal Work-Study, institutionally sponsored loans, scholarships/grants, and unspecified assistantships available. Financial award application deadline: 3/1; financial award applicants required to submit FAFSA. *Unit head:* Dr. Allison Cumming-McCann, Chair, 413-748-3025, Fax: 413-748-3854, E-mail: acumming@springfield.edu. *Application contact:* Anne Griffin, Director of Graduate Admissions, 413-748-3225, E-mail: agriffin2@springfield.edu.
Website: http://springfield.edu/programs

State University of New York at New Paltz, Graduate and Extended Learning School, School of Liberal Arts and Sciences, Department of Psychology, New Paltz, NY 12561. Offers clinical mental health counseling (MS); mental health counseling (AC); psychological science (MS); school counseling (MS); trauma and disaster mental health (AC). *Program availability:* Part-time, evening/weekend. *Faculty:* 12 full-time (9 women), 1 (woman) part-time/adjunct. *Students:* 61 full-time (44 women), 19 part-time (15 women); includes 18 minority (2 Black or African American, non-Hispanic/Latino; 1 Asian, non-Hispanic/Latino; 12 Hispanic/Latino; 1 Native Hawaiian or other Pacific Islander, non-Hispanic/Latino; 2 Two or more races, non-Hispanic/Latino). 109 applicants, 57% accepted, 40 enrolled. In 2017, 16 master's awarded. *Degree requirements:* For master's, comprehensive exam, thesis. *Entrance requirements:* For master's, GRE General Test, minimum GPA of 3.0. Additional exam requirements/recommendations for international students: Required—TOEFL (minimum score 550 paper-based; 80 iBT), IELTS (minimum score 6.5). *Application deadline:* For fall admission, 2/1 priority date for domestic and international students; for spring admission, 11/15 priority date for domestic and international students. Application fee: $50. Electronic applications accepted. *Financial support:* In 2017–18, 6 teaching assistantships with partial tuition reimbursements (averaging $5,000 per year) were awarded. Financial award application deadline: 8/1. *Faculty research:* Disaster mental health, women's objectification, mate selection, cultural psychology, achievement motivation. *Unit head:* Dr. Glenn Geher, Chair, 845-257-3091, E-mail: geherg@newpaltz.edu. *Application contact:* Dr. Tabitha Holmes, Program Coordinator, 845-257-3955, E-mail: holmest@newpaltz.edu.
Website: http://www.newpaltz.edu/psychology/

State University of New York at Plattsburgh, School of Education, Health, and Human Services, Department of Counselor Education, Plattsburgh, NY 12901-2681. Offers clinical mental health counseling (MS, Advanced Certificate); school counselor (MS Ed, CAS); student affairs counseling (MS). *Accreditation:* ACA (one or more programs are accredited); TEAC. *Program availability:* Part-time. *Entrance requirements:* For master's, GRE General Test or MAT, minimum GPA of 2.8. Additional exam requirements/recommendations for international students: Required—TOEFL. *Faculty research:* Campus violence, program accreditation, substance abuse, vocational assessment, group counseling, divorce.

Stephens College, Division of Graduate and Continuing Studies, Columbia, MO 65215-0002. Offers counseling (M Ed), including addictions counseling, clinical mental health counseling, school counseling; health information administration (Postbaccalaureate Certificate); physician assistant studies (MPAS); TV and screenwriting (MFA). *Program availability:* Part-time, evening/weekend, online learning. *Entrance requirements:* For master's, minimum GPA of 3.0 in last 60 hours. Additional exam requirements/recommendations for international students: Required—TOEFL (minimum score 79 iBT). Electronic applications accepted. *Faculty research:* Educational psychology, outcomes assessment.

Stony Brook University, State University of New York, Graduate School, College of Arts and Sciences, Department of Psychology, Program in Clinical Psychology, Stony Brook, NY 11794. Offers PhD. *Accreditation:* APA. *Students:* 34 full-time (29 women); includes 6 minority (1 Black or African American, non-Hispanic/Latino; 2 Asian, non-Hispanic/Latino; 3 Hispanic/Latino), 6 international. Average age 27. 353 applicants, 4% accepted, 8 enrolled. In 2017, 4 doctorates awarded. *Degree requirements:* For doctorate, thesis/dissertation. *Entrance requirements:* For doctorate, GRE General Test, GRE Subject Test. Additional exam requirements/recommendations for international students: Required—TOEFL (minimum score 90 iBT). *Application deadline:* For fall admission, 1/15 for domestic students; for spring admission, 10/1 for domestic students. Application fee: $100. *Expenses:* Contact institution. *Financial support:* In 2017–18, 6 fellowships, 4 research assistantships, 12 teaching assistantships were awarded. *Unit head:* Dr. Sheri Levy, Chair, 631-632-4355, E-mail: sheri.levy@stonybrook.edu. *Application contact:* Marilynn Wollmuth, Coordinator, 631-632-7855, Fax: 631-632-7876, E-mail: marilyn.wollmuth@stonybrook.edu.
Website: https://www.stonybrook.edu/commcms/psychology/clinical/overview.html

Suffolk University, College of Arts and Sciences, Department of Psychology, Boston, MA 02108-2770. Offers clinical psychology (PhD); college admission counseling (Certificate); mental health counseling (MS); school counseling (MS). *Accreditation:* APA. *Faculty:* 14 full-time (7 women), 3 part-time/adjunct (all women). *Students:* 52 full-time (47 women), 35 part-time (28 women); includes 17 minority (4 Black or African American, non-Hispanic/Latino; 1 Asian, non-Hispanic/Latino; 11 Hispanic/Latino; 1 Two or more races, non-Hispanic/Latino), 7 international. Average age 27. 266 applicants, 23% accepted, 19 enrolled. In 2017, 23 master's, 7 doctorates, 11 other advanced degrees awarded. Terminal master's awarded for partial completion of doctoral program. *Degree requirements:* For master's, practicum, internship; for doctorate, thesis/dissertation, practicum. *Entrance requirements:* For doctorate, GRE General Test

or MAT, 2 letters of recommendation, resume. Additional exam requirements/recommendations for international students: Required—TOEFL (minimum score 550 paper-based; 80 iBT). *Application deadline:* For fall admission, 12/1 for domestic and international students. Applications are processed on a rolling basis. Application fee: $50. Electronic applications accepted. *Expenses:* $36,936 per year full-time, $1,539 per credit part-time (for PhD); $15,675 per year full-time, $1,045 per credit part-time (for MS). *Financial support:* In 2017–18, 57 students received support, including 21 fellowships (averaging $17,193 per year); career-related internships or fieldwork, Federal Work-Study, institutionally sponsored loans, scholarships/grants, and unspecified assistantships also available. Support available to part-time students. Financial award application deadline: 4/1; financial award applicants required to submit FAFSA. *Faculty research:* Assessing exposure in the context of a family-based cognitive behavioral treatment for pediatric OCD, a mindfulness approach to designing and testing the efficacy of a new sexual revictimization prevention program for college women, olfaction and decision-making in substance-dependent individuals, the role of experiential avoidance in Generalized Anxiety Disorder, ego development as a predictor of dogmatism and intolerance in the political right and left. *Unit head:* Dr. Amy Marks, Chairperson, 617-573-8017, E-mail: akmarks@suffolk.edu. *Application contact:* Mara Marzocchi, Associate Director of Graduate Admissions, 617-573-8302, Fax: 617-305-1733, E-mail: grad.admission@suffolk.edu.
Website: http://www.suffolk.edu/college/graduate/69299.php

Syracuse University, College of Arts and Sciences, Department of Psychology, Syracuse, NY 13244. Offers clinical psychology (PhD); cognition, brain, and behavior (PhD); school psychology (PhD); social psychology (PhD). *Accreditation:* APA. In 2017, 1 doctorate awarded. Terminal master's awarded for partial completion of doctoral program. *Degree requirements:* For doctorate, comprehensive exam, thesis/dissertation. *Entrance requirements:* For doctorate, GRE General Test, GRE Subject Test, resume, personal statement, three letters of recommendation. Additional exam requirements/recommendations for international students: Required—TOEFL (minimum score 100 iBT). *Application deadline:* For fall admission, 12/1 priority date for domestic and international students. Application fee: $75. Electronic applications accepted. *Financial support:* Fellowships with full tuition reimbursements, research assistantships with tuition reimbursements, teaching assistantships with tuition reimbursements, and scholarships/grants available. Financial award application deadline: 1/1. *Faculty research:* Clinical psychology; cognition, brain, and behavior; school psychology; social psychology. *Unit head:* Dr. Amy Criss, Professor and Department Chair, Psychology, 315-443-1210, E-mail: acriss@syr.edu. *Application contact:* Alecia Zema, Curriculum Coordinator, 315-443-2760, E-mail: azema@syr.edu.
Website: http://psychology.syr.edu/graduate/overview.html

Syracuse University, School of Education, MS Program in Clinical Mental Health Counseling, Syracuse, NY 13207. Offers MS. *Program availability:* Part-time. *Entrance requirements:* For master's, GRE or MAT, baccalaureate degree from regionally-accredited college/university, relevant work experience, three letters of recommendation, personal statement, interview, transcripts. Additional exam requirements/recommendations for international students: Required—TOEFL (minimum score 100 iBT). *Application deadline:* For fall admission, 1/15 priority date for domestic and international students; for spring admission, 10/1 priority date for domestic and international students; for summer admission, 1/15 priority date for domestic and international students. Applications are processed on a rolling basis. Application fee: $75. Electronic applications accepted. *Financial support:* Fellowships with full tuition reimbursements, research assistantships, teaching assistantships, career-related internships or fieldwork, and scholarships/grants available. Financial award application deadline: 1/15. *Faculty research:* Community mental health counseling, counseling people with disabilities, substance abuse services, counseling with youth, crisis counseling. *Unit head:* Dr. Derek Seward, Department Chair, 315-443-2266, E-mail: dxseward@syr.edu. *Application contact:* Speranza Migliore, Graduate Admissions Recruiter, 315-443-2505, E-mail: gradrcrt@syr.edu.
Website: http://soeweb.syr.edu/academic/counseling_and_human_services/graduate/masters/clinical_mental_health_counseling/default.aspx

Tarleton State University, College of Graduate Studies, College of Health Sciences and Human Services, Stephenville, TX 76402. Offers clinical mental health counseling (Certificate); medical laboratory sciences and public health (MS), including medical laboratory sciences; nursing (MSN), including nursing administration, nursing education; social work (MSW). *Program availability:* Part-time. *Faculty:* 26 full-time (21 women), 11 part-time/adjunct (all women). *Students:* 72 full-time (60 women), 153 part-time (133 women); includes 89 minority (36 Black or African American, non-Hispanic/Latino; 2 American Indian or Alaska Native, non-Hispanic/Latino; 3 Asian, non-Hispanic/Latino; 43 Hispanic/Latino; 5 Two or more races, non-Hispanic/Latino), 4 international. Average age 32. 193 applicants, 90% accepted, 124 enrolled. In 2017, 14 master's awarded. *Degree requirements:* For master's, comprehensive exam, thesis (for some programs). *Entrance requirements:* Additional exam requirements/recommendations for international students: Required—TOEFL (minimum score 550 paper-based; 80 iBT), IELTS (minimum score 6). *Application deadline:* For fall admission, 8/15 for domestic students, 6/15 for international students; for spring admission, 1/5 for domestic students, 11/15 for international students; for summer admission, 5/1 for domestic students, 4/15 for international students. Applications are processed on a rolling basis. Application fee: $45 ($145 for international students). Electronic applications accepted. *Expenses:* Tuition, state resident: full-time $3775. Tuition, nonresident: full-time $11,245. *Required fees:* $2920. *Financial support:* Research assistantships, teaching assistantships, career-related internships or fieldwork, Federal Work-Study, scholarships/grants, and unspecified assistantships available. Financial award application deadline: 2/15; financial award applicants required to submit FAFSA. *Unit head:* Sally Lewis, Associate Dean, 254-968-1692. *Application contact:* Wendy Weiss, Graduate Admissions Coordinator, 254-968-9104, Fax: 254-968-9670, E-mail: weiss@tarleton.edu.
Website: http://www.tarleton.edu/chshs/

Teachers College, Columbia University, Department of Counseling and Clinical Psychology, New York, NY 10027-6696. Offers clinical psychology (PhD); counseling psychology (Ed M, Ed D, PhD); mental health counseling (ME); psychological counseling (ME, ND); psychology in education (MA, ND); school counselor (ME). *Accreditation:* APA (one or more programs are accredited). *Program availability:* Part-time. *Students:* 430 full-time (364 women), 237 part-time (201 women); includes 243 minority (65 Black or African American, non-Hispanic/Latino; 73 Asian, non-Hispanic/Latino; 83 Hispanic/Latino; 22 Two or more races, non-Hispanic/Latino), 142 international. Average age 28. 1,568 applicants, 38% accepted, 292 enrolled. *Unit head:* Prof. George Bonanno, Head, E-mail: gab38@tc.columbia.edu. *Application contact:* David Estrella, Director of Admission, 212-678-3305, E-mail: estrella@tc.columbia.edu.

Texas A&M University, College of Liberal Arts, Department of Psychology, College Station, TX 77843. Offers clinical psychology (PhD); industrial/organizational psychology (PhD); psychology (MS, PhD), including clinical psychology (PhD). *Accreditation:* APA (one or more programs are accredited). *Faculty:* 50. *Students:* 84 full-time (42 women), 15 part-time (9 women); includes 41 minority (8 Black or African American, non-Hispanic/Latino; 7 Asian, non-Hispanic/Latino; 23 Hispanic/Latino; 3 Two or more races, non-Hispanic/Latino), 12 international. Average age 28. 292 applicants, 12% accepted, 22 enrolled. In 2017, 10 master's, 18 doctorates awarded. *Degree requirements:* For doctorate, comprehensive exam (for some programs), thesis/dissertation. *Entrance requirements:* For doctorate, GRE General Test. Additional exam requirements/recommendations for international students: Required—TOEFL (minimum score 550 paper-based; 80 iBT), IELTS (minimum score 6), PTE (minimum score 53). *Application deadline:* For fall admission, 12/1 for domestic and international students. Application fee: $50 ($90 for international students). Electronic applications accepted. *Expenses:* Contact institution. *Financial support:* In 2017–18, 83 students received support, including 19 fellowships with tuition reimbursements available (averaging $37,600 per year), 30 research assistantships with tuition reimbursements available (averaging $11,994 per year), 58 teaching assistantships with tuition reimbursements available (averaging $11,425 per year); career-related internships or fieldwork, institutionally sponsored loans, scholarships/grants, traineeships, health care benefits, tuition waivers (full and partial), and unspecified assistantships also available. Support available to part-time students. Financial award application deadline: 3/15; financial award applicants required to submit FAFSA. *Unit head:* Dr. Heather Lench, Department Head, 979-845-0377, E-mail: hlench@tamu.edu. *Application contact:* Dr. Charles D. Samuelson, Director of Graduate Studies, 979-845-0880, Fax: 979-845-4727, E-mail: c-samuelson@tamu.edu.
Website: http://psychology.tamu.edu/

Texas A&M University–Central Texas, Graduate Studies and Research, Killeen, TX 76549. Offers accounting (MS); business administration (MBA); clinical mental health counseling (MS); criminal justice (MCJ); curriculum and instruction (M Ed); educational administration (M Ed); educational psychology - experimental psychology (MS); history (MA); human resource management (MS); information systems (MS); liberal studies (MS); management and leadership (MS); marriage and family therapy (MS); mathematics (MS); political science (MA); school counseling (M Ed); school psychology (Ed S).

Texas A&M University–Corpus Christi, College of Graduate Studies, College of Liberal Arts, Program in Psychology, Corpus Christi, TX 78412. Offers clinical psychology (MA); general psychology (MA). *Program availability:* Part-time, evening/weekend. *Students:* 28 full-time (22 women), 10 part-time (all women); includes 25 minority (all Hispanic/Latino). Average age 28. 35 applicants, 74% accepted, 19 enrolled. In 2017, 12 master's awarded. *Degree requirements:* For master's, comprehensive exam. *Entrance requirements:* For master's, GRE (taken within 5 years; waived if candidate already has master's degree), minimum GPA of 3.0 in last 60 hours, essay (500-1000 words), 2 letters of recommendation. Additional exam requirements/recommendations for international students: Required—TOEFL (minimum score 550 paper-based; 79 iBT), IELTS (minimum score 6.5). *Application deadline:* For fall admission, 8/1 for domestic students, 5/1 for international students. Applications are processed on a rolling basis. Application fee: $50 ($70 for international students). Electronic applications accepted. *Expenses:* Tuition, state resident: full-time $3568; part-time $198.24 per credit hour. Tuition, nonresident: full-time $11,038; part-time $613.24 per credit hour. *Required fees:* $2129; $1422.58 per semester. Tuition and fees vary according to program. *Financial support:* Research assistantships, teaching assistantships, career-related internships or fieldwork, Federal Work-Study, institutionally sponsored loans, scholarships/grants, health care benefits, and unspecified assistantships available. Support available to part-time students. Financial award application deadline: 3/15; financial award applicants required to submit FAFSA. *Unit head:* Dr. Amy Houlihan, Chair, 361-825-2971, E-mail: amy.houlihan@tamucc.edu. *Application contact:* Graduate Admissions Coordinator, 361-825-2177, Fax: 361-825-2755, E-mail: gradweb@tamucc.edu.
Website: http://cla.tamucc.edu/psychology/pages/graduate.html

Texas A&M University–San Antonio, Department of Counseling, Health and Kinesiology, San Antonio, TX 78224. Offers clinical mental health counseling (MA); counseling and guidance (MA); kinesiology (MS); marriage and family counseling (MA). *Program availability:* Part-time, evening/weekend, online learning. *Faculty:* 12 full-time (5 women), 6 part-time/adjunct (4 women). *Students:* 48 full-time (35 women), 146 part-time (118 women); includes 135 minority (24 Black or African American, non-Hispanic/Latino; 3 Asian, non-Hispanic/Latino; 103 Hispanic/Latino; 5 Two or more races, non-Hispanic/Latino), 2 international. Average age 34. 201 applicants, 56% accepted, 62 enrolled. In 2017, 68 master's awarded. *Degree requirements:* For master's, comprehensive exam, thesis or alternative. *Entrance requirements:* For master's, MAT or GRE (composite quantitative and verbal). Additional exam requirements/recommendations for international students: Required—TOEFL (minimum score 550 paper-based; 79 iBT), IELTS (minimum score 6). *Application deadline:* For fall admission, 3/15 priority date for domestic and international students; for spring admission, 11/1 priority date for domestic and international students; for summer admission, 4/1 priority date for domestic and international students. Applications are processed on a rolling basis. Application fee: $35 ($50 for international students). Electronic applications accepted. *Expenses:* Tuition, state resident: full-time $3475; part-time $1930 per semester. Tuition, nonresident: full-time $10,945; part-time $6080 per semester. *Required fees:* $2148; $1412 per year. $706 per semester. Tuition and fees vary according to course load. *Financial support:* In 2017–18, 10 students received support. Federal Work-Study, scholarships/grants, and tuition waivers available. Financial award application deadline: 3/15; financial award applicants required to submit FAFSA. *Unit head:* Dr. Suzanne Mudge, Department Chair. *Application contact:* Caitie Garza, Graduate Admissions Coordinator, 210-784-1300, E-mail: beajaguar@tamusa.edu.
Website: http://www.tamusa.edu/collegeofeducationandhumandevelopment/counselinghealthkinesiology/index.html

Texas State University, The Graduate College, College of Education, Program in Professional Counseling, San Marcos, TX 78666. Offers clinical mental health counseling (MA); marriage and family counseling (MA); school counseling (MA). *Accreditation:* ACA. *Program availability:* Part-time. *Faculty:* 12 full-time (11 women), 12 part-time/adjunct (9 women). *Students:* 87 full-time (71 women), 99 part-time (80 women); includes 49 minority (6 Black or African American, non-Hispanic/Latino; 6 Asian, non-Hispanic/Latino; 30 Hispanic/Latino; 7 Two or more races, non-Hispanic/Latino). Average age 31. 144 applicants, 46% accepted, 23 enrolled. In 2017, 57 master's awarded. *Degree requirements:* For master's, comprehensive exam, thesis optional, internship. *Entrance requirements:* For master's, GRE General Test (minimum preferred score of 291 [150 verbal, 141 quantitative]), baccalaureate degree from regionally-accredited institution with minimum GPA of 3.0 in last 60 hours of undergraduate work; resume; statement of purpose addressing professional goals, reasoning for specified emphasis (i.e., community, school, marital), strengths and weaknesses, and perspective on diversity; 3 references. Additional exam requirements/recommendations for international students: Required—TOEFL (minimum iBT scores: 22 listening, 22 reading, 24 speaking, 21 writing). *Application deadline:* For fall admission, 2/15 for domestic and international students; for spring admission, 10/1 for domestic and international students; for summer admission, 2/15 for domestic and international students. Applications are processed on a rolling basis. Application fee: $40 ($90 for international students). Electronic applications accepted. *Expenses:* Tuition, state resident: full-time $7868; part-time $3934 per semester. Tuition, nonresident: full-time $17,828; part-time $8914 per semester. *Required fees:* $2092;

$1435 per semester. Tuition and fees vary according to course load. *Financial support:* In 2017–18, 97 students received support, including 11 research assistantships (averaging $7,298 per year); teaching assistantships, Federal Work-Study, institutionally sponsored loans, and scholarships/grants also available. Support available to part-time students. Financial award application deadline: 3/1; financial award applicants required to submit FAFSA. *Unit head:* Dr. Kevin Fall, Graduate Advisor, 512-245-2081, Fax: 512-245-8872, E-mail: kf22@txstate.edu. *Application contact:* Dr. Andrea Golato, Dean of Graduate School, 512-245-2581, Fax: 512-245-8365, E-mail: gradcollege@txstate.edu. Website: http://www.gradcollege.txstate.edu/programs/counseling.html

Texas Tech University, Graduate School, College of Arts and Sciences, Department of Psychological Sciences, Lubbock, TX 79409-2051. Offers clinical psychology (PhD); counseling psychology (MA, PhD); general experimental psychology (MA, PhD); psychology (MA). *Accreditation:* APA (one or more programs are accredited). *Faculty:* 31 full-time (14 women), 2 part-time/adjunct (both women). *Students:* 126 full-time (75 women), 10 part-time (5 women); includes 33 minority (4 Black or African American, non-Hispanic/Latino; 1 American Indian or Alaska Native, non-Hispanic/Latino; 10 Asian, non-Hispanic/Latino; 17 Hispanic/Latino; 1 Two or more races, non-Hispanic/Latino), 11 international. Average age 27. 278 applicants, 15% accepted, 28 enrolled. In 2017, 17 master's, 7 doctorates awarded. *Degree requirements:* For doctorate, comprehensive exam, thesis/dissertation, 100 credit hours of organized courses, research credits, and practica. *Entrance requirements:* For master's, GRE General Test, GRE Subject Test, essays, letters of recommendation; for doctorate, GRE General Test, essays, letters of recommendation. Additional exam requirements/recommendations for international students: Required—TOEFL (minimum score 550 paper-based; 79 iBT). *Application deadline:* For fall admission, 6/1 priority date for domestic students, 1/15 priority date for international students; for spring admission, 9/1 priority date for domestic students, 6/15 priority date for international students. Applications are processed on a rolling basis. Application fee: $60. Electronic applications accepted. *Expenses:* Contact institution. *Financial support:* In 2017–18, 132 students received support, including 127 fellowships (averaging $2,830 per year), 58 research assistantships (averaging $8,094 per year), 105 teaching assistantships (averaging $11,486 per year); Federal Work-Study, institutionally sponsored loans, health care benefits, and unspecified assistantships also available. Financial award application deadline: 4/15; financial award applicants required to submit FAFSA. *Faculty research:* Health psychology, addictive behaviors, depression and suicide risk, sexuality/sexual risk behaviors/HIV, neuroscience/neuroimaging, forensic and correctional psychology. *Total annual research expenditures:* $647,634. *Unit head:* Dr. Robert Morgan, Professor and Chair, 806-834-7117, Fax: 806-742-0818, E-mail: robert.morgan@ttu.edu. *Application contact:* Kay Hill, Admissions Coordinator, 806-834-1350, Fax: 806-742-0818, E-mail: kay.hill@ttu.edu. Website: http://www.depts.ttu.edu/psy/

Texas Tech University Health Sciences Center, School of Health Professions, Program in Clinical Mental Health Counseling, Lubbock, TX 79430. Offers MS. *Program availability:* Part-time, online only. *Faculty:* 5 full-time (2 women). *Students:* 7 full-time (all women), 4 part-time (all women); includes 4 minority (2 Black or African American, non-Hispanic/Latino; 2 Hispanic/Latino). Average age 37. 12 applicants, 92% accepted, 11 enrolled. *Entrance requirements:* Additional exam requirements/recommendations for international students: Required—TOEFL (minimum score 550 paper-based; 79 iBT). *Application deadline:* For fall admission, 8/1 for domestic students; for spring admission, 11/1 for domestic students. Applications are processed on a rolling basis. Application fee: $75. Electronic applications accepted. *Financial support:* Application deadline: 9/1; applicants required to submit FAFSA. *Unit head:* Dr. Dave Schroeder, Director, 806-743-2590, Fax: 806-743-3244, E-mail: dave.schroeder@ttuhsc.edu. *Application contact:* Lindsay Johnson, Associate Dean for Admissions and Student Affairs, 806-743-3220, Fax: 806-743-2994, E-mail: lindsay.johnson@ttuhsc.edu. Website: http://www.ttuhsc.edu/health-professions/master-of-science-clinical-mental-health-counseling/

Trinity Washington University, School of Education, Washington, DC 20017-1094. Offers clinical mental health counseling (MA); early childhood education (MAT); educating for change (M Ed); educational administration (MSA); elementary education (MAT); reading (M Ed); school counseling (MA); secondary education (MAT), including English, social studies; special education (MAT). *Accreditation:* NCATE. *Program availability:* Part-time, evening/weekend. *Degree requirements:* For master's, thesis (for some programs), capstone project(s). *Entrance requirements:* For master's, PRAXIS I, minimum GPA of 2.8. Additional exam requirements/recommendations for international students: Required—TOEFL (minimum score 550 paper-based). *Faculty research:* Technology, literacy, special education, organizations, inclusion models.

Uniformed Services University of the Health Sciences, F. Edward Hebert School of Medicine, Graduate Programs in the Biomedical Sciences and Public Health, Department of Medical and Clinical Psychology, Bethesda, MD 20814. Offers clinical psychology (PhD); medical psychology (PhD). PhD in clinical psychology available to active duty military only. *Accreditation:* APA. Terminal master's awarded for partial completion of doctoral program. *Degree requirements:* For doctorate, comprehensive exam, thesis/dissertation, qualifying exam. *Entrance requirements:* For doctorate, GRE General Test, minimum GPA of 3.0, U.S. citizenship. Additional exam requirements/recommendations for international students: Required—TOEFL. Electronic applications accepted. *Faculty research:* Addictive and appetitive behavior, psychopharmacology, stress and eating, obesity, health.

Union College, Graduate Programs, Department of Psychology, Barbourville, KY 40906-1499. Offers clinical psychology (MA); counseling psychology (MA); school psychology (MA).

Union Institute & University, Master of Arts Program in Clinical Mental Health Counseling, Cincinnati, OH 45206-1925. Offers MA. *Program availability:* Part-time, online only, blended/hybrid learning. Terminal master's awarded for partial completion of doctoral program. *Degree requirements:* For master's, thesis, internship. *Entrance requirements:* For master's, transcripts, letters of recommendation, essay. Additional exam requirements/recommendations for international students: Recommended—TOEFL. *Application deadline:* Applications are processed on a rolling basis. Application fee: $50. Electronic applications accepted. *Expenses:* Contact institution. *Financial support:* Federal Work-Study available. Financial award applicants required to submit FAFSA. *Unit head:* Dr. Rosalyn Y. Brown Beatty, Director, 802-254-0152. *Application contact:* Director of Admissions, 888-828-8575. Website: https://myunion.edu/academics/masters/clinical-mental-health-counseling/

Universidad de Iberoamerica, Graduate School, San Jose, Costa Rica. Offers clinical neuropsychology (PhD); clinical psychology (M Psych); educational psychology (M Psych); forensic psychology (M Psych); hospital management (MHA); intensive care nursing (MN); medicine (MD).

Université Laval, Faculty of Social Sciences, School of Psychology, Programs in Psychology, Québec, QC G1K 7P4, Canada. Offers clinical psychology (PhD); community psychology (PhD); psychology (PhD, Psy D). *Degree requirements:* For doctorate, comprehensive exam, thesis/dissertation. *Entrance requirements:* For

doctorate, comprehension of written English, knowledge of French, interview. Electronic applications accepted.

University at Albany, State University of New York, College of Arts and Sciences, Department of Psychology, Albany, NY 12222-0001. Offers behavioral neuroscience (PhD); clinical psychology (PhD); cognitive psychology (PhD); industrial/organizational psychology (MA, PhD); social-personality psychology (PhD). *Accreditation:* APA (one or more programs are accredited). *Faculty:* 31 full-time (13 women). *Students:* 63 full-time (42 women), 49 part-time (33 women); includes 25 minority (4 Black or African American, non-Hispanic/Latino; 8 Asian, non-Hispanic/Latino; 4 Hispanic/Latino; 9 Two or more races, non-Hispanic/Latino), 11 international. 295 applicants, 14% accepted, 28 enrolled. In 2017, 13 master's, 5 doctorates awarded. *Degree requirements:* For doctorate, thesis/dissertation. *Entrance requirements:* For doctorate, GRE General Test, GRE Subject Test. Additional exam requirements/recommendations for international students: Required—TOEFL (minimum score 550 paper-based). *Application deadline:* For fall admission, 1/15 for domestic and international students. Application fee: $75. Electronic applications accepted. *Expenses:* Tuition, state resident: full-time $10,870; part-time $453 per credit hour. Tuition, nonresident: full-time $22,210; part-time $925 per credit hour. Required fees: $84.68 per credit hour. $508.06 per semester. Part-time tuition and fees vary according to course load and program. *Financial support:* Fellowships, research assistantships, teaching assistantships, and career-related internships or fieldwork available. Financial award application deadline: 2/1. *Unit head:* Christine K. Wagner, Chair, 518-442-4820, Fax: 518-442-4867, E-mail: cwagner@albany.edu. *Application contact:* Michael DeRensis, Director, Graduate Admissions, 518-442-3980, Fax: 518-442-3922, E-mail: graduate@albany.edu. Website: http://www.albany.edu/psychology/

The University of Akron, Graduate School, College of Health Professions, School of Counseling, Program in Clinical Mental Health Counseling, Akron, OH 44325. Offers MA. *Accreditation:* ACA; NCATE. *Students:* 41 full-time (33 women), 44 part-time (37 women); includes 17 minority (8 Black or African American, non-Hispanic/Latino; 2 Asian, non-Hispanic/Latino; 4 Hispanic/Latino; 3 Two or more races, non-Hispanic/Latino). Average age 29. 44 applicants, 45% accepted, 9 enrolled. In 2017, 20 master's awarded. *Degree requirements:* For master's, comprehensive exam. *Entrance requirements:* For master's, minimum GPA of 2.75, letters of recommendation, interview. Additional exam requirements/recommendations for international students: Required—TOEFL (minimum score 79 iBT), IELTS (minimum score 6.5). *Application deadline:* Applications are processed on a rolling basis. Application fee: $45 ($70 for international students). Electronic applications accepted. *Application contact:* Dr. Robert Schwartz, Program Coordinator, 330-972-8155, E-mail: rcs@uakron.edu. Website: http://www.uakron.edu/soc/masters/cmhc/index.dot

The University of Alabama, Graduate School, College of Arts and Sciences, Department of Psychology, Tuscaloosa, AL 35487. Offers clinical psychology (PhD); experimental psychology (PhD). *Faculty:* 29 full-time (17 women), 4 part-time/adjunct (3 women). *Students:* 84 full-time (65 women), 13 part-time (9 women); includes 14 minority (5 Black or African American, non-Hispanic/Latino; 3 Asian, non-Hispanic/Latino; 4 Hispanic/Latino; 2 Two or more races, non-Hispanic/Latino), 8 international. Average age 27. 309 applicants, 8% accepted, 15 enrolled. In 2017, 13 doctorates awarded. *Degree requirements:* For doctorate, thesis/dissertation, internship (for clinical psychology). *Entrance requirements:* For doctorate, GRE. Additional exam requirements/recommendations for international students: Required—TOEFL (minimum score 550 paper-based). *Application deadline:* For fall admission, 11/16 for domestic and international students. Application fee: $50 ($60 for international students). Electronic applications accepted. *Financial support:* In 2017–18, 65 students received support, including fellowships with full tuition reimbursements available (averaging $17,000 per year), research assistantships with tuition reimbursements available (averaging $12,744 per year), teaching assistantships with tuition reimbursements available (averaging $13,824 per year); career-related internships or fieldwork, institutionally sponsored loans, scholarships/grants, health care benefits, and unspecified assistantships also available. Financial award application deadline: 11/16. *Faculty research:* Cognitive development/disability, child clinical, psychology and law, health/aging, social psychology. *Total annual research expenditures:* $1.2 million. *Unit head:* Dr. Frances A. Conners, Chair, 205-348-1913, Fax: 205-348-8648, E-mail: fconners@ua.edu. *Application contact:* Mary Beth Hubbard, Information Contact, 205-348-1919, Fax: 205-348-8648, E-mail: mary.b.hubbard@ua.edu. Website: http://www.psychology.ua.edu

The University of Alabama at Birmingham, College of Arts and Sciences, Program in Psychology, Birmingham, AL 35294. Offers behavioral neuroscience (PhD); lifespan developmental psychology (PhD); medical/clinical psychology (PhD); psychology (MA). *Accreditation:* APA (one or more programs are accredited). *Entrance requirements:* For master's and doctorate, GRE General Test, letters of recommendation. Electronic applications accepted. *Faculty research:* Biological basis of behavior structure, function of the nervous system.

University of Alaska Anchorage, College of Arts and Sciences, Department of Psychology, Anchorage, AK 99508. Offers clinical psychology (MS); clinical-community psychology with rural-indigenous emphasis (PhD). *Accreditation:* APA. *Program availability:* Part-time. *Degree requirements:* For master's, thesis. *Entrance requirements:* For master's, GRE General Test, GRE Subject Test, interview, references; for doctorate, interview, bachelor's or master's degree in psychology. Additional exam requirements/recommendations for international students: Required—TOEFL (minimum score 550 paper-based). *Faculty research:* Substance abuse, childhood autism, biofeedback, psychological assessment, mental health in Native Alaskans.

University of Alaska Fairbanks, College of Liberal Arts, Department of Psychology, Fairbanks, AK 99775-6480. Offers clinical-community psychology (PhD). Program offered jointly with University of Alaska Anchorage. *Degree requirements:* For doctorate, comprehensive exam, thesis/dissertation, oral defense of dissertation. *Entrance requirements:* For doctorate, bachelor's degree from accredited institution with minimum cumulative undergraduate and major GPA of 3.0; criminal background check; interview; course work in abnormal psychology, statistics, and research methods. Additional exam requirements/recommendations for international students: Required—TOEFL (minimum score 550 paper-based; 80 iBT), IELTS (minimum score 6.5). Electronic applications accepted. *Faculty research:* Clinical and community psychology; rural, indigenous, and cultural psychology.

University of Bridgeport, School of Arts and Sciences, Department of Counseling, Bridgeport, CT 06604. Offers clinical mental health counseling (MS); college student personnel (MS); community counseling (MS); human resource development (MS); human service (MS). *Program availability:* Part-time, evening/weekend. *Degree requirements:* For master's, thesis, project. *Entrance requirements:* Additional exam requirements/recommendations for international students: Recommended—TOEFL (minimum score 550 paper-based; 80 iBT), IELTS (minimum score 6.5). Electronic applications accepted. *Expenses:* Contact institution.

The University of British Columbia, Faculty of Arts and Faculty of Graduate Studies, Department of Psychology, Vancouver, BC V6T 1Z4, Canada. Offers behavioral

neuroscience (MA, PhD); clinical psychology (MA, PhD); cognitive science (MA, PhD); developmental psychology (MA, PhD); health psychology (MA, PhD); quantitative methods (MA, PhD); social/personality psychology (MA, PhD). *Accreditation:* APA (one or more programs are accredited). Terminal master's awarded for partial completion of doctoral program. *Degree requirements:* For master's, thesis; for doctorate, comprehensive exam, thesis/dissertation. *Entrance requirements:* For master's and doctorate, GRE General Test. Additional exam requirements/recommendations for international students: Required—TOEFL. Electronic applications accepted. *Expenses:* Contact institution. *Faculty research:* Clinical, developmental, social/personality, cognition, behavioral neuroscience.

University of Calgary, Faculty of Graduate Studies, Faculty of Arts, Department of Psychology, Calgary, AB T2N 1N4, Canada. Offers clinical psychology (M Sc, PhD); psychology (M Sc, PhD). *Degree requirements:* For master's, thesis; for doctorate, thesis/dissertation. *Entrance requirements:* For master's, GRE General Test, bachelor's degree in psychology, minimum GPA of 3.4. Additional exam requirements/recommendations for international students: Required—TOEFL (minimum score 550 paper-based). Electronic applications accepted. *Faculty research:* Cognition and cognitive development, social psychology, theoretical psychology, perception, aging.

University of California, San Diego, Graduate Division, Program in Clinical Psychology, San Diego, CA 92120. Offers PhD. Program offered jointly with San Diego State University. *Students:* 60 part-time (53 women). In 2017, 12 doctorates awarded. *Degree requirements:* For doctorate, comprehensive exam, thesis/dissertation, 1-year full-time internship. *Entrance requirements:* For doctorate, GRE General Test, GRE Subject Test, minimum GPA of 3.25. Additional exam requirements/recommendations for international students: Required—TOEFL (minimum score 550 paper-based; 80 iBT), IELTS (minimum score 7). Electronic applications accepted. *Financial support:* Fellowships, research assistantships, teaching assistantships, scholarships/grants, and unspecified assistantships available. Financial award applicants required to submit FAFSA. *Faculty research:* Behavioral medicine, experimental psychopathology, neuropsychology. *Unit head:* Igor Grant, Director, 858-534-3684, E-mail: igrant@ucsd.edu. *Application contact:* Kristin Deveraux, Program Coordinator, 858-534-7653, E-mail: kdeveraux@ucsd.edu.
Website: http://clinpsyc.sdsu.edu/

University of California, Santa Barbara, Graduate Division, Gevirtz Graduate School of Education, Santa Barbara, CA 93106-9490. Offers counseling, clinical and school psychology (MA, PhD, Credential), including clinical psychology (PhD), counseling psychology (MA, PhD), pupil personnel services (Credential), school psychology (PhD); education (MA, PhD); teacher education (M Ed, Credential), including multiple subject teaching (Credential), single subject teaching (Credential), special education (Credential), teaching (M Ed); MA/PhD. *Accreditation:* APA (one or more programs are accredited). Terminal master's awarded for partial completion of doctoral program. *Degree requirements:* For master's, comprehensive exam (for some programs), thesis (for some programs); for doctorate, comprehensive exam (for some programs), thesis/dissertation. *Entrance requirements:* For master's and doctorate, GRE; for Credential, GRE or MAT, CSET, CBEST. Additional exam requirements/recommendations for international students: Required—TOEFL (minimum score 550 paper-based; 80 iBT), IELTS (minimum score 7). Electronic applications accepted. *Faculty research:* Needs of diverse students, school accountability and leadership, school violence, language learning and literacy, science/math education.

University of Central Florida, College of Sciences, Department of Psychology, Program in Clinical Psychology, Orlando, FL 32816. Offers MA, PhD. *Accreditation:* APA. *Students:* 64 full-time (49 women), 4 part-time (3 women); includes 26 minority (4 Black or African American, non-Hispanic/Latino; 9 Asian, non-Hispanic/Latino; 9 Hispanic/Latino; 4 Two or more races, non-Hispanic/Latino), 4 international. Average age 27. 287 applicants, 12% accepted, 21 enrolled. In 2017, 18 master's, 7 doctorates awarded. *Degree requirements:* For master's, thesis or alternative, clinical internship; for doctorate, thesis/dissertation, candidacy exam, internship. *Entrance requirements:* For master's, GRE General Test, minimum GPA of 3.0 in last 60 hours, resume, personal statement, letters of recommendation; for doctorate, GRE General Test, minimum GPA of 3.0 in last 60 hours, curriculum vitae, personal statement, letters of recommendation. Additional exam requirements/recommendations for international students: Required—TOEFL. *Application deadline:* For fall admission, 1/1 for domestic students. Application fee: $30. Electronic applications accepted. *Expenses:* Tuition, state resident: part-time $288.16 per credit hour. Tuition, nonresident: part-time $1073.31 per credit hour. Tuition and fees vary according to program. *Financial support:* In 2017–18, 38 students received support, including 15 fellowships with partial tuition reimbursements available (averaging $7,973 per year), 18 research assistantships with partial tuition reimbursements available (averaging $6,958 per year), 25 teaching assistantships with partial tuition reimbursements available (averaging $15,621 per year); career-related internships or fieldwork, Federal Work-Study, institutionally sponsored loans, health care benefits, tuition waivers (partial), and unspecified assistantships also available. Financial award application deadline: 3/1; financial award applicants required to submit FAFSA. *Unit head:* Dr. Brian Fisak, Program Director, 407-823-2822, E-mail: brian.fisak@ucf.edu. *Application contact:* Associate Director, Graduate Admissions, 407-823-2766, Fax: 407-823-6442, E-mail: gradadmissions@ucf.edu.
Website: http://psychology.cos.ucf.edu/graduate/

University of Cincinnati, Graduate School, McMicken College of Arts and Sciences, Department of Psychology, Cincinnati, OH 45221. Offers clinical psychology (PhD); experimental psychology (PhD). *Accreditation:* APA. *Degree requirements:* For doctorate, comprehensive exam, thesis/dissertation. *Entrance requirements:* For doctorate, GRE General Test. Additional exam requirements/recommendations for international students: Required—TOEFL. *Expenses: Tuition, area resident:* Full-time $14,468. Tuition, state resident: full-time $14,968; part-time $754 per credit hour. Tuition, nonresident: full-time $24,210; part-time $1311 per credit hour. *International tuition:* $26,460 full-time. *Required fees:* $3958; $84 per credit hour. One-time fee: $85 full-time. Tuition and fees vary according to course load, degree level and program. *Faculty research:* Neuropsychology, human factors, health.

University of Colorado Denver, College of Liberal Arts and Sciences, Department of Psychology, Denver, CO 80217. Offers clinical health (PhD); psychology (MA). *Program availability:* Part-time, evening/weekend. *Degree requirements:* For master's, 31-33 semester hours, thesis or internship, minimum GPA of 3.0; for doctorate, comprehensive exam, thesis/dissertation, 69 credits of coursework, minimum of 12 clinical practicum hours, 30 dissertation hours, three credits of pre-doctoral internship. *Entrance requirements:* For master's, GRE General Test; GRE Subject Test (recommended), undergraduate courses in psychological statistics, abnormal psychology and introductory psychology; minimum GPA of 3.0; three letters of recommendation; personal statement; resume; for doctorate, GRE General Test; GRE Subject Test (recommended), minimum GPA of 3.5; undergraduate courses in introductory psychology, psychological statistics, research methods and abnormal psychology; letters of recommendation; personal statement; resume. Additional exam requirements/recommendations for international students: Required—TOEFL (minimum score 537 paper-based; 75 iBT); Recommended—IELTS (minimum score 6.5). Electronic applications accepted. *Faculty research:* Organizational behavior, body image perception, professional ethics, infant perception and cognition, charismatic leadership.

University of Colorado Denver, School of Education and Human Development, Program in Counseling Psychology and Counselor Education, Denver, CO 80217. Offers counseling (MA), including clinical mental health counseling, couple and family counseling, multicultural counseling, school counseling; school counseling (MA). *Accreditation:* ACA; NCATE. *Program availability:* Part-time, evening/weekend. *Degree requirements:* For master's, comprehensive exam (for some programs), thesis or alternative, 63-66 hours. *Entrance requirements:* For master's, GRE or MAT (unless applicant already holds a graduate degree), letters of recommendation, interview, resume, transcripts from all colleges/universities attended. Additional exam requirements/recommendations for international students: Required—TOEFL (minimum score 525 paper-based; 71 iBT); Recommended—IELTS (minimum score 6.3). Electronic applications accepted. *Expenses:* Contact institution. *Faculty research:* Spiritual issues in counseling, multicultural and diversity issues in counseling, adolescent suicide, career development.

University of Connecticut, Graduate School, College of Liberal Arts and Sciences, Department of Psychology, Storrs, CT 06269. Offers behavioral neuroscience (PhD); biopsychology (PhD); clinical psychology (MA, PhD); cognition and instruction (PhD); developmental psychology (MA, PhD); ecological psychology (PhD); experimental psychology (PhD); general psychology (MA, PhD); industrial/organizational psychology (PhD); language and cognition (PhD); neuroscience (PhD); social psychology (MA, PhD). *Accreditation:* APA. Terminal master's awarded for partial completion of doctoral program. *Degree requirements:* For master's, comprehensive exam; for doctorate, thesis/dissertation. *Entrance requirements:* For master's and doctorate, GRE General Test, GRE Subject Test. Additional exam requirements/recommendations for international students: Required—TOEFL (minimum score 550 paper-based). Electronic applications accepted.

University of Dallas, Braniff Graduate School of Liberal Arts, Program in Psychology, Irving, TX 75062-4736. Offers clinical psychology (M Psych); psychology (M Psych, MA). *Program availability:* Part-time. *Degree requirements:* For master's, one foreign language, comprehensive exam (for some programs), thesis (for some programs). *Entrance requirements:* Additional exam requirements/recommendations for international students: Required—TOEFL. *Application deadline:* For fall admission, 2/15 priority date for domestic students; for spring admission, 11/15 for domestic students. Application fee: $50. *Expenses: Tuition:* Full-time $33,750; part-time $22,500 per year. Tuition and fees vary according to program. *Unit head:* Dr. Scott Churchill, Chairman, 972-721-5106, Fax: 972-721-4034.

University of Dayton, Department of Counselor Education and Human Services, Dayton, OH 45469. Offers clinical mental health counseling (MS Ed); college student personnel (MS Ed); higher education administration (MS Ed); human services (MS Ed); school counseling (MS Ed); school psychology (MS Ed, Ed S). *Accreditation:* ACA; NCATE. *Program availability:* Part-time. *Faculty:* 11 full-time (6 women), 34 part-time/adjunct (24 women). *Students:* 194 full-time (153 women), 83 part-time (68 women); includes 58 minority (37 Black or African American, non-Hispanic/Latino; 2 Asian, non-Hispanic/Latino; 9 Hispanic/Latino; 10 Two or more races, non-Hispanic/Latino), 3 international. Average age 30. 426 applicants, 28% accepted. In 2017, 107 master's, 6 Ed Ss awarded. *Degree requirements:* For master's, thesis (for some programs); for Ed S, thesis (for some programs), professional portfolio. *Entrance requirements:* For master's, MAT or GRE (if GPA less than 2.75), essays (for some programs). Additional exam requirements/recommendations for international students: Required—TOEFL (minimum score 550 paper-based; 80 iBT). *Application deadline:* For fall admission, 1/10 priority date for domestic and international students; for spring admission, 9/10 priority date for domestic and international students; for summer admission, 11/10 priority date for domestic and international students. Application fee: $0 ($50 for international students). Electronic applications accepted. *Expenses:* Contact institution. *Financial support:* In 2017–18, 5 research assistantships with partial tuition reimbursements (averaging $9,950 per year) were awarded; career-related internships or fieldwork, institutionally sponsored loans, and unspecified assistantships also available. Financial award application deadline: 3/1; financial award applicants required to submit FAFSA. *Faculty research:* Student school bonding, traumatic brain injuries, wellness and counseling, creativity in education. *Unit head:* Dr. Alan Demmitt, Chair, 937-229-3644, Fax: 937-229-1055, E-mail: ademmitt1@udayton.edu. *Application contact:* Kathleen Brown, Administrative Assistant, 937-229-3644, Fax: 937-229-1055, E-mail: kbrown1@udayton.edu.
Website: https://www.udayton.edu/education/departments_and_programs/edc/

University of Dayton, Program in Clinical Psychology, Dayton, OH 45469. Offers MA. *Faculty:* 6 full-time (3 women), 1 part-time/adjunct (0 women). *Students:* 12 full-time (8 women). Average age 24. 84 applicants, 7% accepted. In 2017, 4 master's awarded. *Degree requirements:* For master's, thesis, clinical practicum. *Entrance requirements:* For master's, GRE (minimum combined Verbal and Quantitative score 300; neither subtest below 148), minimum undergraduate GPA of 3.2. Additional exam requirements/recommendations for international students: Required—TOEFL (minimum score 550 paper-based; 80 iBT). *Application deadline:* For fall admission, 2/15 priority date for domestic and international students. Application fee: $0 ($50 for international students). Electronic applications accepted. Tuition and fees vary according to degree level and program. *Financial support:* In 2017–18, 6 research assistantships with full tuition reimbursements (averaging $11,645 per year) were awarded; fellowships, teaching assistantships, institutionally sponsored loans, and tuition waivers (full and partial) also available. Financial award application deadline: 3/1; financial award applicants required to submit FAFSA. *Faculty research:* Neural processing of emotion, interpersonal attraction, intimate partner violence, pediatric psychology, youth conduct problems. *Unit head:* Dr. Catherine L. Zois, Graduate Program Director, 937-229-2164, Fax: 937-229-2164, E-mail: czois1@udayton.edu. *Application contact:* Dr. Catherine L. Zois, Graduate Program Director, 937-229-2164, E-mail: czois1@udayton.edu.
Website: https://www.udayton.edu/artssciences/academics/psychology/grad/clinical_psych/index.php

University of Delaware, College of Arts and Sciences, Department of Psychology, Newark, DE 19716. Offers behavioral neuroscience (PhD); clinical psychology (PhD); cognitive psychology (PhD); social psychology (PhD). *Accreditation:* APA. *Degree requirements:* For doctorate, thesis/dissertation. *Entrance requirements:* For doctorate, GRE General Test. Additional exam requirements/recommendations for international students: Required—TOEFL (minimum score 600 paper-based). Electronic applications accepted. *Faculty research:* Emotion development, neural and cognitive aspects of memory, neural control of feeding, intergroup relations, social cognition and communication.

University of Denver, Division of Arts, Humanities and Social Sciences, Department of Psychology, Denver, CO 80208. Offers affective/cognitive/social psychology (PhD); clinical child psychology (PhD); developmental psychology (PhD). *Accreditation:* APA. *Students:* Average age 28. 294 applicants, 4% accepted, 8 enrolled. In 2017, 8 doctorates awarded. Terminal master's awarded for partial completion of doctoral program. *Degree requirements:* For doctorate, variable foreign language requirement, comprehensive exam (for some programs), thesis/dissertation. *Entrance requirements:*

For doctorate, GRE General Test, master's degree, transcripts, biographical statement, three letters of recommendation. Additional exam requirements/recommendations for international students: Required—TOEFL (minimum score 550 paper-based; 80 iBT). *Application deadline:* For fall admission, 12/1 priority date for domestic and international students. Application fee: $65. Electronic applications accepted. *Expenses:* Contact institution. *Financial support:* In 2017–18, 24 students received support, including 5 research assistantships with tuition reimbursements available (averaging $16,000 per year), 12 teaching assistantships with tuition reimbursements available (averaging $17,778 per year); Federal Work-Study, institutionally sponsored loans, scholarships/grants, and unspecified assistantships also available. Support available to part-time students. Financial award application deadline: 2/15; financial award applicants required to submit FAFSA. *Faculty research:* Stress and trauma, developmental science, affect science, clinical science, child psychopathology. *Unit head:* Dr. Anne DePrince, Professor and Chair, 303-871-2939, Fax: 303-871-4747, E-mail: adeprinc@du.edu. *Application contact:* Paula Houghtaling, Graduate Program Administrator, 303-871-3803, Fax: 303-871-4747, E-mail: phoughta@du.edu.
Website: http://www.du.edu/ahss/psychology

University of Denver, Graduate School of Professional Psychology, Denver, CO 80208. Offers clinical psychology (Psy D); forensic psychology (MA); international disaster psychology (MA); sport and performance psychology (MA); sport coaching (MA); strength and conditioning and fitness coaching (Certificate). *Accreditation:* APA. *Faculty:* 23 full-time (13 women), 25 part-time/adjunct (14 women). *Students:* 233 full-time (180 women), 79 part-time (46 women); includes 81 minority (22 Black or African American, non-Hispanic/Latino; 9 Asian, non-Hispanic/Latino; 31 Hispanic/Latino; 1 Native Hawaiian or other Pacific Islander, non-Hispanic/Latino; 18 Two or more races, non-Hispanic/Latino), 7 international. Average age 26. 866 applicants, 30% accepted, 135 enrolled. In 2017, 106 master's, 23 doctorates awarded. *Degree requirements:* For master's, comprehensive exam (for some programs); for doctorate, comprehensive exam (for some programs), paper, clinical internship. *Entrance requirements:* For master's and doctorate, GRE General Test, transcripts, resume, two letters of recommendation, essay. Additional exam requirements/recommendations for international students: Required—TOEFL (minimum score 550 paper-based; 80 iBT). *Application deadline:* For fall admission, 1/5 for domestic and international students. Application fee: $65. Electronic applications accepted. *Expenses:* $47,823 per year full-time. *Financial support:* In 2017–18, 235 students received support, including 2 teaching assistantships with tuition reimbursements available (averaging $1,976 per year); career-related internships or fieldwork, Federal Work-Study, institutionally sponsored loans, scholarships/grants, unspecified assistantships, and clinical assistantships also available. Support available to part-time students. Financial award application deadline: 2/15; financial award applicants required to submit FAFSA. *Unit head:* Dr. Shelly Smith-Acuna, Dean, 303-871-3880, Fax: 303-871-4220, E-mail: shelly.smith-acuna@du.edu. *Application contact:* Admissions Counselor, 303-871-3736, Fax: 303-871-4220, E-mail: gsppinfo@du.edu.
Website: http://www.du.edu/gspp

University of Detroit Mercy, College of Liberal Arts and Education, Detroit, MI 48221. Offers addiction counseling (MA); addiction studies (Certificate); clinical mental health counseling (MA); clinical psychology (MA, PhD); computer and information systems (MS); criminal justice (MA); curriculum and instruction (MA); economics (MA); educational administration (MA); financial economics (MA); industrial/organizational psychology (MA); information assurance (MS); intelligence analysis (MA); liberal studies (MALS); religious studies (MA); school counseling (MA, Certificate); school psychology (Spec); security administration (MS); special education: emotionally impaired/behaviorally disordered (MA); special education: learning disabilities (MA). *Program availability:* Part-time, evening/weekend. *Degree requirements:* For doctorate, departmental qualifying exam. *Faculty research:* Psychology of aging, history of technology, Renaissance humanism, U.S. and Japanese economic relations.

University of Florida, Graduate School, College of Public Health and Health Professions, Department of Clinical and Health Psychology, Gainesville, FL 32611. Offers clinical and translational science (PhD); psychology (MS). *Accreditation:* APA (one or more programs are accredited). *Degree requirements:* For doctorate, comprehensive exam, thesis/dissertation, pre-doctoral internship. *Entrance requirements:* For master's and doctorate, GRE General Test, minimum GPA of 3.0. Additional exam requirements/recommendations for international students: Required—TOEFL (minimum score 550 paper-based; 80 iBT), IELTS (minimum score 6). Electronic applications accepted. *Faculty research:* Clinical child and pediatric psychology, medical psychology, neuropsychology, health promotion and aging.

University of Guelph, Graduate Studies, College of Social and Applied Human Sciences, Department of Psychology, Guelph, ON N1G 2W1, Canada. Offers applied social psychology (MA, PhD); clinical psychology: applied development emphasis (PhD); clinical psychology: applied developmental emphasis (MA); industrial/organizational psychology (MA, PhD); neuroscience and applied cognitive science (MA, PhD). *Degree requirements:* For master's, thesis; for doctorate, comprehensive exam, thesis/dissertation. *Entrance requirements:* For master's, GRE General Test, GRE Subject Test, minimum B+ average during previous 2 years of course work; for doctorate, GRE General Test, GRE Subject Test, minimum A- average. Additional exam requirements/recommendations for international students: Required—TOEFL (minimum score 89 iBT). Electronic applications accepted. *Faculty research:* Organizational psychology, reading comprehension and mathematical ability, drug addiction and relapse, gender issues and culture, memory, clinical psychology.

University of Hartford, College of Arts and Sciences, Department of Psychology, Program in Clinical Practices, West Hartford, CT 06117-1599. Offers clinical practices (Psy D); psychology (MA). *Accreditation:* APA. *Degree requirements:* For master's, comprehensive exam, thesis optional. *Entrance requirements:* For master's, GRE General Test, GRE Subject Test, minimum GPA of 3.0, 3 letters of recommendation. Additional exam requirements/recommendations for international students: Required—TOEFL (minimum score 550 paper-based). Electronic applications accepted. *Faculty research:* Attachment issues, child abuse prevention, master's psychologist issues, neuropsychology.

University of Hawaii at Manoa, Office of Graduate Education, College of Social Sciences, Department of Psychology, Honolulu, HI 96822. Offers clinical psychology (PhD); community and cultural psychology (PhD); community and culture (MA); psychology (MA, PhD, Graduate Certificate). *Accreditation:* APA (one or more programs are accredited). *Program availability:* Part-time. Terminal master's awarded for partial completion of doctoral program. *Degree requirements:* For master's, comprehensive exam, thesis; for doctorate, comprehensive exam, thesis/dissertation. *Entrance requirements:* For master's and doctorate, GRE General Test, GRE Subject Test. Additional exam requirements/recommendations for international students: Required—TOEFL (minimum score 600 paper-based; 100 iBT), IELTS (minimum score 7). *Faculty research:* Cross-cultural psychology, health psychology, marine mammals, child/adult psychopathology.

University of Houston, College of Liberal Arts and Social Sciences, Department of Psychology, Houston, TX 77204. Offers clinical psychology (PhD); developmental psychology (PhD); industrial/organizational psychology (PhD); psychology (MA); social psychology (PhD). *Accreditation:* APA (one or more programs are accredited). *Degree requirements:* For master's, comprehensive exam, thesis; for doctorate, comprehensive exam, thesis/dissertation. *Entrance requirements:* For master's, GRE General Test, career statement, 3 letters of recommendation; for doctorate, GRE General Test, 3 letters of recommendation. Additional exam requirements/recommendations for international students: Required—TOEFL (minimum score 550 paper-based; 79 iBT). Electronic applications accepted. *Faculty research:* Health psychology, depression, child/family process, organizational effectiveness, close relationships.

University of Houston–Clear Lake, School of Human Sciences and Humanities, Programs in Human Sciences, Houston, TX 77058-1002. Offers behavioral sciences (MA), including criminology, cross cultural studies, general psychology, sociology; clinical psychology (MA); criminology (MA); cross cultural studies (MA); family therapy (MA); fitness and human performance (MA); school psychology (MA). *Accreditation:* AAMFT/COAMFTE. *Program availability:* Part-time, evening/weekend, online learning. *Degree requirements:* For master's, thesis or alternative. *Entrance requirements:* For master's, GRE General Test. Additional exam requirements/recommendations for international students: Required—TOEFL (minimum score 550 paper-based). Electronic applications accepted. *Faculty research:* Smoking cessation, adolescent sexuality, white collar crime, serial murder, human factors/human computer interaction.

University of Indianapolis, Graduate Programs, School of Psychological Sciences, Indianapolis, IN 46227-3697. Offers clinical psychology (Psy D); clinical psychology/mental health counseling (MA). *Accreditation:* APA. *Degree requirements:* For master's, practicum; for doctorate, comprehensive exam, thesis/dissertation, 1200 hours of clinical practicum, 2000-hour internship. *Entrance requirements:* For master's, GRE, 3 letters of recommendation; for doctorate, GRE, minimum GPA of 3.0, 18 hours of course work in psychology, 3 letters of recommendation. Additional exam requirements/recommendations for international students: Required—TOEFL (minimum score 550 paper-based).

The University of Kansas, Graduate Studies, College of Liberal Arts and Sciences, Department of Psychology, Lawrence, KS 66045. Offers clinical psychology (MA, PhD); cognitive and brain sciences (MA, PhD); developmental psychology (MA, PhD); quantitative psychology (PhD); social psychology (MA, PhD). *Accreditation:* APA (one or more programs are accredited). *Program availability:* Part-time. *Students:* 92 full-time (63 women), 3 part-time (all women); includes 19 minority (7 Black or African American, non-Hispanic/Latino; 4 Asian, non-Hispanic/Latino; 4 Hispanic/Latino; 4 Two or more races, non-Hispanic/Latino), 10 international. Average age 28. 361 applicants, 7% accepted, 16 enrolled. In 2017, 9 master's, 17 doctorates awarded. Terminal master's awarded for partial completion of doctoral program. *Entrance requirements:* For doctorate, GRE General Test, three letters of recommendation, resume/curriculum vitae, statement of purpose/personal statement, writing sample. Additional exam requirements/recommendations for international students: Required—TOEFL. *Application deadline:* For fall admission, 12/1 for domestic and international students. Application fee: $65 ($85 for international students). Electronic applications accepted. *Financial support:* Fellowships, research assistantships, teaching assistantships, career-related internships or fieldwork, Federal Work-Study, scholarships/grants, health care benefits, and unspecified assistantships available. Financial award application deadline: 12/1; financial award applicants required to submit FAFSA. *Faculty research:* Origins, correlates and treatment of depression; health and emotion; concentration on topics related to prejudice, stereotyping, and intergroup relations; memory, cognitive development, language, perception, attention, aging; psychometric methods, item response theory, structural equation modeling. *Unit head:* Ruth Anne Atchley, Chair, 785-864-4131. *Application contact:* Graduate Officer, 785-864-4195, E-mail: psycgrad@ku.edu.
Website: http://www.psych.ku.edu/

University of La Verne, College of Arts and Sciences, Department of Psychology, Program in Clinical Psychology, La Verne, CA 91750-4443. Offers Psy D. *Faculty:* 6 full-time (2 women), 5 part-time/adjunct (2 women). *Students:* 33 full-time (29 women), 28 part-time (22 women); includes 23 minority (4 Black or African American, non-Hispanic/Latino; 1 Asian, non-Hispanic/Latino; 17 Hispanic/Latino; 1 Two or more races, non-Hispanic/Latino), 1 international. Average age 28. *Degree requirements:* For doctorate, thesis/dissertation, clinical practica, clinical internship, competency exams, personal psychotherapy. *Entrance requirements:* For doctorate, GRE, minimum undergraduate GPA of 3.1, statement of professional goals and aspirations, 3 recommendations, interview, curriculum vitae. Additional exam requirements/recommendations for international students: Required—TOEFL (minimum score 600 paper-based; 100 iBT), IELTS (minimum score 6.5). *Application deadline:* For fall admission, 12/15 for domestic and international students. Application fee: $75. Electronic applications accepted. *Expenses:* Contact institution. *Financial support:* Career-related internships or fieldwork, institutionally sponsored loans, scholarships/grants, and unspecified assistantships available. Financial award application deadline: 3/2; financial award applicants required to submit FAFSA. *Unit head:* Dr. Jerry Kernes, Program Chairperson, 909-448-4414, E-mail: jkernes@laverne.edu. *Application contact:* Christy Ranells, Associate Director of Graduate Admissions, 909-448-4644, Fax: 909-971-2295, E-mail: cranells@laverne.edu.
Website: http://www.laverne.edu/psychology/psyd-program/

University of Louisiana at Monroe, Graduate School, College of Health and Pharmaceutical Sciences, Programs in Counseling Studies, Monroe, LA 71209-0001. Offers clinical mental health counseling (MS); school counseling (MS). *Accreditation:* ACA; NCATE. *Program availability:* Part-time, evening/weekend, online learning. *Faculty:* 3 full-time (all women). *Students:* 34 full-time (28 women), 8 part-time (7 women); includes 14 minority (12 Black or African American, non-Hispanic/Latino; 1 Asian, non-Hispanic/Latino; 1 Hispanic/Latino). Average age 32. 18 applicants, 94% accepted, 13 enrolled. In 2017, 19 master's awarded. *Degree requirements:* For master's, comprehensive exam, thesis. *Entrance requirements:* For master's, GRE General Test, minimum GPA of 2.8 in last 60 hours. Additional exam requirements/recommendations for international students: Required—TOEFL (minimum score 500 paper-based; 61 iBT). *Application deadline:* For fall admission, 8/24 priority date for domestic students, 7/1 for international students; for winter admission, 12/14 priority date for domestic students; for spring admission, 1/19 for domestic students, 11/1 for international students. Applications are processed on a rolling basis. Application fee: $20 ($30 for international students). Electronic applications accepted. *Expenses:* Tuition, state resident: full-time $6489; part-time $479 per hour. Tuition, nonresident: full-time $12,100; part-time $479 per hour. Required fees: $8860; $802 per hour. $3273 per semester. *Financial support:* In 2017–18, 9 students received support. Career-related internships or fieldwork, Federal Work-Study, and unspecified assistantships available. Financial award application deadline: 4/1; financial award applicants required to submit FAFSA. *Unit head:* Dr. David Hale, Director, 318-342-1349, E-mail: dhale@ulm.edu.
Website: http://www.ulm.edu/counseling/

University of Louisville, Graduate School, College of Arts and Sciences, Department of Psychological and Brain Sciences, Louisville, KY 40292-0001. Offers clinical psychology (PhD); experimental psychology (PhD), including cognition and development, vision and hearing. *Accreditation:* APA. *Students:* 55 full-time (44 women),

1 (woman) part-time; includes 7 minority (1 Black or African American, non-Hispanic/Latino; 2 Asian, non-Hispanic/Latino; 2 Hispanic/Latino; 2 Two or more races, non-Hispanic/Latino), 4 international. Average age 29. 9 applicants, 78% accepted. In 2017, 1 doctorate awarded. *Degree requirements:* For doctorate, comprehensive exam, thesis/dissertation, internship (for clinical psychology). *Entrance requirements:* For doctorate, GRE General Test, GRE Subject Test. Additional exam requirements/recommendations for international students: Required—TOEFL. *Application deadline:* For fall and winter admission, 12/1 for domestic and international students. Application fee: $65. *Expenses:* Tuition, state resident: full-time $12,246; part-time $681 per credit hour. Tuition, nonresident: full-time $25,486; part-time $1417 per credit hour. *Required fees:* $196. Tuition and fees vary according to course load, program and reciprocity agreements. *Financial support:* In 2017–18, 8 fellowships with full tuition reimbursements (averaging $22,000 per year), 3 research assistantships with full tuition reimbursements (averaging $22,000 per year), 30 teaching assistantships with full tuition reimbursements (averaging $22,000 per year) were awarded; health care benefits and unspecified assistantships also available. Financial award application deadline: 12/1. *Faculty research:* Cognitive development, hearing/visual science, cognitive neuroscience/imaging, health psychology/mindfulness/stress and trauma, child/adult psychopathology, geropsychology. *Total annual research expenditures:* $923,340. *Unit head:* Dr. Suzanne Meeks, Chair, 502-852-6068, Fax: 502-852-8904, E-mail: smeeks@louisville.edu. *Application contact:* Maggie Leahy, Administrative Assistant, 502-852-4364, Fax: 502-852-8904, E-mail: maggie.leahy@louisville.edu.
Website: http://louisville.edu/psychology

University of Lynchburg, Graduate Studies, M Ed Program in Clinical Mental Health Counseling, Lynchburg, VA 24501-3199. Offers M Ed. *Accreditation:* ACA. *Program availability:* Part-time, evening/weekend. *Faculty:* 17 full-time (10 women). *Students:* 31 full-time (27 women), 15 part-time (12 women); includes 6 minority (3 Black or African American, non-Hispanic/Latino; 1 Asian, non-Hispanic/Latino; 1 Hispanic/Latino; 1 Two or more races, non-Hispanic/Latino), 2 international. Average age 27. 24 applicants, 100% accepted, 10 enrolled. In 2017, 7 master's awarded. *Degree requirements:* For master's, counseling internship. *Entrance requirements:* For master's, GRE, minimum GPA of 3.0 (preferred), official transcripts (bachelor's, others as relevant), three letters of recommendation, career goals statement, personal interview. Additional exam requirements/recommendations for international students: Required—TOEFL (minimum score 550 paper-based; 80 iBT), IELTS (minimum score 6). *Application deadline:* For fall admission, 7/31 for domestic students, 6/1 for international students; for spring admission, 11/30 for domestic students, 10/15 for international students. Applications are processed on a rolling basis. Application fee: $30. Electronic applications accepted. Application fee is waived when completed online. *Expenses:* $510 per credit hour tuition, $100 fees. *Financial support:* Federal Work-Study, scholarships/grants, health care benefits, and unspecified assistantships available. Support available to part-time students. Financial award application deadline: 7/31; financial award applicants required to submit FAFSA. *Unit head:* Dr. Karena Heyward, Assistant Professor and Program Director, 434-544-8067, E-mail: heyward.k@lynchburg.edu. *Application contact:* Ellen Thompson, Graduate Admissions Counselor, 434-544-8841, E-mail: thompson_e@lynchburg.edu.
Website: http://www.lynchburg.edu/graduate/master-of-education-in-counselor-education/clinical-mental-health-counseling/

The University of Manchester, School of Psychological Sciences, Manchester, United Kingdom. Offers audiology (M Phil, PhD); clinical psychology (M Phil, PhD, Psy D); psychology (M Phil, PhD).

University of Manitoba, Faculty of Graduate Studies, Faculty of Arts, Department of Psychology, Winnipeg, MB R3T 2N2, Canada. Offers clinical psychology (PhD); psychology (MA, PhD); school psychology (MA). *Degree requirements:* For master's, thesis; for doctorate, one foreign language, thesis/dissertation. *Entrance requirements:* For master's and doctorate, GRE General Test.

University of Mary Hardin-Baylor, Graduate Studies in Counseling, Belton, TX 76513. Offers clinical and mental health counseling (MA); marriage, family and child counseling (MA); non-clinical professional studies (MA). *Accreditation:* ACA. *Program availability:* Part-time, evening/weekend. *Faculty:* 7 full-time (4 women), 1 part-time/adjunct (0 women). *Students:* 74 full-time (58 women), 13 part-time (8 women); includes 44 minority (23 Black or African American, non-Hispanic/Latino; 18 Hispanic/Latino; 3 Two or more races, non-Hispanic/Latino). Average age 32. 54 applicants, 65% accepted, 29 enrolled. In 2017, 27 master's awarded. *Degree requirements:* For master's, comprehensive exam. *Entrance requirements:* For master's, GRE General Test with minimum cumulative score of 300 on verbal and quantitative portions and 3.0 on analytical section (if overall undergraduate GPA is below a 3.0), minimum cumulative undergraduate GPA of 2.75 or 3.0 on last 60 hours of course work; three letters of recommendation; interview with departmental graduate admissions committee. Additional exam requirements/recommendations for international students: Required—TOEFL (minimum score 60 iBT), IELTS (minimum score 4.5). *Application deadline:* For fall admission, 6/1 for domestic students, 4/30 priority date for international students; for spring admission, 11/1 for domestic students, 9/30 priority date for international students. Applications are processed on a rolling basis. Application fee: $35 ($135 for international students). Electronic applications accepted. *Expenses: Tuition:* Full-time $15,570; part-time $10,380 per credit hour. *Required fees:* $1350; $75 per credit hour. $50 per term. Tuition and fees vary according to course load and degree level. *Financial support:* In 2017–18, 55 students received support. Federal Work-Study, unspecified assistantships, and scholarships for some active duty military personnel available. Support available to part-time students. Financial award applicants required to submit FAFSA. *Faculty research:* Teaching mindfulness skills as part of an interdisciplinary training protocol for doctor of physical therapy students; using symbolic art cards and oracle cards in supervision as a method for teaching appropriate self-disclosure, clinical reflection and counselor development reflection; understanding integral breath therapy. *Unit head:* Dr. Dan Williamson, Director, Graduate Counseling, 254-295-5018, E-mail: dwilliamson@umhb.edu. *Application contact:* Sharon Aguilera, Assistant Director, Graduate Admissions, 254-295-4835, E-mail: saguilera@umhb.edu.
Website: https://go.umhb.edu/graduate/counseling/home

University of Maryland, Baltimore County, The Graduate School, College of Arts, Humanities and Social Sciences, Department of Psychology, Program in Human Services Psychology, Baltimore, MD 21250. Offers applied behavioral analysis (MA); human services psychology (PhD), including behavioral medicine, clinical psychology, community psychology. *Faculty:* 17 full-time (9 women), 11 part-time/adjunct (4 women). *Students:* 82 full-time (65 women), 1 (woman) part-time; includes 26 minority (10 Black or African American, non-Hispanic/Latino; 6 Asian, non-Hispanic/Latino; 9 Hispanic/Latino; 1 Two or more races, non-Hispanic/Latino). Average age 25. 136 applicants, 21% accepted, 18 enrolled. In 2017, 25 master's, 7 doctorates awarded. *Degree requirements:* For master's, thesis; for doctorate, comprehensive exam, thesis/dissertation. *Entrance requirements:* For master's, GRE General Test, minimum GPA of 3.0; for doctorate, GRE General Test, GRE Subject Test, minimum GPA of 3.0. Additional exam requirements/recommendations for international students: Required—TOEFL. *Application deadline:* For fall admission, 12/1 for domestic and international students. Application fee: $50. Electronic applications accepted. *Expenses:* Contact institution. *Financial support:* In 2017–18, 43 students received support, including 3 fellowships with full tuition reimbursements available (averaging $26,000 per year), 27 research assistantships with full tuition reimbursements available (averaging $20,400 per year), 8 teaching assistantships with full tuition reimbursements available (averaging $17,250 per year); career-related internships or fieldwork, Federal Work-Study, scholarships/grants, health care benefits, tuition waivers, and unspecified assistantships also available. Financial award application deadline: 3/1; financial award applicants required to submit FAFSA. *Faculty research:* Addictive behaviors, cardiovascular and cerebrovascular disease, family violence, pediatric psychology, community prevention. *Unit head:* Dr. Lynnda Dahlquist, Director, 410-455-2567, Fax: 410-455-1055, E-mail: dahlquis@umbc.edu. *Application contact:* Beverly McDougall, Program Management Specialist, 410-455-2567, Fax: 410-455-1055, E-mail: psycdept@umbc.edu.
Website: http://psychology.umbc.edu/

University of Maryland, College Park, Academic Affairs, College of Behavioral and Social Sciences, Department of Psychology, College Park, MD 20742. Offers clinical psychology (PhD); developmental psychology (PhD); experimental psychology (PhD); industrial psychology (MA, MS, PhD); social psychology (PhD). *Accreditation:* APA (one or more programs are accredited). *Degree requirements:* For master's, thesis; for doctorate, variable foreign language requirement, comprehensive exam, thesis/dissertation. *Entrance requirements:* For master's and doctorate, GRE General Test, GRE Subject Test, minimum GPA of 3.5, research and/or work experience, 3 letters of recommendation. Electronic applications accepted. *Faculty research:* Social stereotyping and prejudice, anxiety disorders, auditory neuroethology, counseling and social psychology.

University of Massachusetts Amherst, Graduate School, College of Natural Sciences, Department of Psychological and Brain Sciences, Amherst, MA 01003. Offers clinical psychology (MS, PhD); cognitive psychology (MS, PhD); developmental science (MS, PhD); psychology of peace and violence (MS, PhD); social psychology (MS, PhD). *Accreditation:* APA (one or more programs are accredited). Terminal master's awarded for partial completion of doctoral program. *Degree requirements:* For master's, thesis; for doctorate, comprehensive exam, thesis/dissertation. *Entrance requirements:* For master's and doctorate, GRE General Test, 3 letters of recommendation. Additional exam requirements/recommendations for international students: Required—TOEFL (minimum score 550 paper-based; 80 iBT), IELTS (minimum score 6.5). Electronic applications accepted.

University of Massachusetts Boston, College of Liberal Arts, Program in Clinical Psychology, Boston, MA 02125-3393. Offers PhD. *Accreditation:* APA. *Faculty:* 31 full-time (23 women), 21 part-time/adjunct (14 women). *Students:* 48 full-time (39 women), 5 part-time (all women); includes 26 minority (7 Black or African American, non-Hispanic/Latino; 7 Asian, non-Hispanic/Latino; 8 Hispanic/Latino; 4 Two or more races, non-Hispanic/Latino), 1 international. Average age 29. 359 applicants, 2% accepted, 7 enrolled. In 2017, 6 doctorates awarded. *Entrance requirements:* For doctorate, GRE General Test, GRE Subject Test, minimum GPA of 2.75. *Application deadline:* For fall admission, 1/2 for domestic students. *Expenses:* Tuition, state resident: full-time $17,375. Tuition, nonresident: full-time $33,915. *Required fees:* $355. *Financial support:* Research assistantships, teaching assistantships, career-related internships or fieldwork, Federal Work-Study, and unspecified assistantships available. Support available to part-time students. Financial award application deadline: 3/1; financial award applicants required to submit FAFSA. *Faculty research:* Community psychology, psychology, racism and mental health, gender and culture, post-traumatic stress disorder. *Unit head:* Dr. Jane Adams, Department Chair, 617-287-6346. *Application contact:* Graduate Admissions Coordinator, 617-287-6400, Fax: 617-287-6236, E-mail: bos.gadm@dpc.umassp.edu.

University of Massachusetts Dartmouth, Graduate School, College of Arts and Sciences, Department of Psychology, North Dartmouth, MA 02747-2300. Offers autism studies (Graduate Certificate); psychology - applied behavioral analysis (MA, Post-Master's Certificate); psychology - clinical (MA); psychology - research (MA). *Program availability:* Part-time. *Faculty:* 20 full-time (12 women), 8 part-time/adjunct (2 women). *Students:* 40 full-time (31 women), 57 part-time (52 women); includes 19 minority (4 Black or African American, non-Hispanic/Latino; 3 Asian, non-Hispanic/Latino; 7 Hispanic/Latino; 5 Two or more races, non-Hispanic/Latino), 1 international. Average age 29. 96 applicants, 54% accepted, 39 enrolled. In 2017, 21 master's awarded. *Degree requirements:* For master's, comprehensive exam (for some programs), thesis or comprehensive exam (for psychology - clinical); thesis (for psychology - research). *Entrance requirements:* For master's and other advanced degree, statement of purpose (minimum of 300 words), resume, 3 letters of recommendation, official transcripts. Additional exam requirements/recommendations for international students: Required—TOEFL (minimum score 533 paper-based; 72 iBT), IELTS (minimum score 6). *Application deadline:* For fall admission, 3/1 priority date for domestic students, 2/1 priority date for international students. Application fee: $60. Electronic applications accepted. *Expenses:* Tuition, state resident: full-time $15,449; part-time $643.71 per credit. Tuition, nonresident: full-time $27,880; part-time $1161.67 per credit. *Required fees:* $405; $25.88 per credit. Tuition and fees vary according to course load and reciprocity agreements. *Financial support:* In 2017–18, 1 research assistantship (averaging $12,000 per year), 2 teaching assistantships (averaging $14,000 per year) were awarded; tuition waivers (full and partial) and unspecified assistantships also available. Support available to part-time students. Financial award application deadline: 3/1; financial award applicants required to submit FAFSA. *Faculty research:* Health inequities, language and cognitive development, interethnic dating and marriage, executive function and implicit learning in deaf children, behavioral medicine. *Total annual research expenditures:* $344,000. *Unit head:* Mahzad Hojjat, Graduate Program Director, Research Psychology, 508-999-8951, E-mail: mhojjat@umassd.edu. *Application contact:* Steven Briggs, Director of Marketing and Recruitment for Graduate Studies, 508-999-8604, Fax: 508-999-8183, E-mail: graduate@umassd.edu.
Website: http://www.umassd.edu/cas/psychology

University of Memphis, Graduate School, College of Arts and Sciences, Department of Psychology, Memphis, TN 38152-3230. Offers clinical psychology (PhD); experimental psychology (PhD); general psychology (MS); school psychology (MA, PhD, Ed S). *Accreditation:* APA. *Faculty:* 26 full-time (11 women), 3 part-time/adjunct (0 women). *Students:* 94 full-time (69 women), 17 part-time (12 women); includes 25 minority (10 Black or African American, non-Hispanic/Latino; 6 Asian, non-Hispanic/Latino; 6 Hispanic/Latino; 3 Two or more races, non-Hispanic/Latino), 6 international. Average age 27. 291 applicants, 16% accepted, 32 enrolled. In 2017, 23 master's, 13 doctorates, 8 other advanced degrees awarded. *Degree requirements:* For master's, comprehensive exam (for some programs), thesis (for some programs), 37 credit hours (for MA); 33 credit hours with thesis or 36 with exam (for MS); for doctorate, comprehensive exam, thesis/dissertation, 80 semester hours, major area paper; 1-year placement and 1-year internship (for clinical psychology); internship (for school psychology); for Ed S, 30 credit hours. *Entrance requirements:* For master's, GRE, 3 letters of recommendation, 18 undergraduate hours in psychology; for doctorate, GRE, minimum GPA of 2.75, 18 hours of undergraduate psychology courses, transcripts, personal statement, 3 letters of recommendation, interview; for Ed S, GRE, minimum GPA of 2.75, 18 hours of undergraduate psychology courses, 3 letters of

recommendation. Additional exam requirements/recommendations for international students: Required—TOEFL (minimum score 550 paper-based; 79 iBT). *Application deadline:* For fall admission, 12/5 for domestic students. Applications are processed on a rolling basis. Application fee: $35 ($60 for international students). Electronic applications accepted. *Expenses:* Contact institution. *Financial support:* In 2017–18, 66 students received support, including 60 research assistantships with full tuition reimbursements available (averaging $11,846 per year), 25 teaching assistantships with full tuition reimbursements available (averaging $6,794 per year); fellowships with full tuition reimbursements available, Federal Work-Study, scholarships/grants, tuition waivers (partial), and unspecified assistantships also available. Financial award application deadline: 2/1; financial award applicants required to submit FAFSA. *Faculty research:* Clinical health; school, child and family psychology; psychotherapy; cognitive and behavioral neuroscience; industrial-organizational psychology. *Unit head:* Dr. Frank Andrasik, Chair, 901-678-2145, Fax: 901-678-2579, E-mail: rcohen@memphis.edu. *Application contact:* Dr. Robert Cohen, Coordinator of Graduate Studies, 901-678-4679, Fax: 901-678-2579, E-mail: rcohen@memphis.edu.
Website: http://www.memphis.edu/psychology

University of Memphis, Graduate School, College of Education, Department of Counseling, Educational Psychology and Research, Memphis, TN 38152. Offers counseling (MS, Ed D), including clinical mental health counseling (MS), clinical rehabilitation counseling (MS), rehabilitation counseling (MS), school counseling (MS); counseling psychology (PhD); educational psychology and research (MS, PhD), including educational psychology, educational research. *Accreditation:* ACA (one or more programs are accredited); APA (one or more programs are accredited); CORE (one or more programs are accredited); NCATE. *Program availability:* Blended/hybrid learning. *Faculty:* 26 full-time (17 women), 8 part-time/adjunct (5 women). *Students:* 132 full-time (111 women), 87 part-time (66 women); includes 71 minority (51 Black or African American, non-Hispanic/Latino; 4 Asian, non-Hispanic/Latino; 10 Hispanic/Latino; 6 Two or more races, non-Hispanic/Latino), 5 international. Average age 31. 146 applicants, 49% accepted, 49 enrolled. In 2017, 39 master's, 13 doctorates awarded. *Degree requirements:* For master's, comprehensive exam, thesis or alternative, internship; for doctorate, comprehensive exam, thesis/dissertation, practicum, internship, residency, scholarly work. *Entrance requirements:* For master's, GRE General Test or MAT, minimum GPA of 2.5, letters of reference, interview; for doctorate, GRE General Test, master's degree or equivalent, letters of reference, interview, curriculum vitae, personal statement. Additional exam requirements/recommendations for international students: Required—TOEFL (minimum score 550 paper-based; 79 iBT). *Application deadline:* For fall admission, 10/1 priority date for domestic students; for spring admission, 4/1 priority date for domestic students. Applications are processed on a rolling basis. Application fee: $35 ($60 for international students). Electronic applications accepted. *Expenses:* Contact institution. *Financial support:* In 2017–18, 130 students received support, including 15 research assistantships with full tuition reimbursements available (averaging $13,426 per year), 12 teaching assistantships with full tuition reimbursements available (averaging $11,976 per year); fellowships with full tuition reimbursements available, career-related internships or fieldwork, Federal Work-Study, scholarships/grants, and unspecified assistantships also available. Financial award application deadline: 2/1; financial award applicants required to submit FAFSA. *Faculty research:* Anger management, aging and disability, supervision, multicultural counseling. *Unit head:* Dr. Steve West, Chair, 901-678-2841, Fax: 901-678-5114, E-mail: slwest@memphis.edu. *Application contact:* Dr. Suzanne Lease, Interim Assistant Dean of Education and Graduate Programs, 901-678-4476, Fax: 901-678-4778, E-mail: slease@memphis.edu.
Website: http://www.memphis.edu/cepr/

University of Miami, Graduate School, College of Arts and Sciences, Department of Psychology, Coral Gables, FL 33124. Offers adult clinical (PhD); behavioral neuroscience (PhD); child clinical (PhD); developmental psychology (PhD); health clinical (PhD); psychology (MS). *Accreditation:* APA (one or more programs are accredited). *Degree requirements:* For doctorate, comprehensive exam, thesis/dissertation. *Entrance requirements:* For doctorate, GRE General Test, minimum GPA of 3.5. Additional exam requirements/recommendations for international students: Required—TOEFL. Electronic applications accepted. *Faculty research:* Behavioral factors in cardiovascular disease and cancer adult psychopathology, developmental disabilities, social and emotional development, mechanisms of coping.

University of Michigan, Rackham Graduate School, College of Literature, Science, and the Arts, Department of Psychology, Ann Arbor, MI 48109. Offers biopsychology (PhD); clinical science (PhD); cognition and cognitive neuroscience (PhD); developmental psychology (PhD); personality and social contexts (PhD); social psychology (PhD). *Accreditation:* APA. *Faculty:* 66 full-time (31 women), 28 part-time/adjunct (17 women). *Students:* 148 full-time (113 women); includes 61 minority (13 Black or African American, non-Hispanic/Latino; 1 American Indian or Alaska Native, non-Hispanic/Latino; 12 Asian, non-Hispanic/Latino; 28 Hispanic/Latino; 7 Two or more races, non-Hispanic/Latino), 24 international. Average age 27. 691 applicants, 7% accepted, 35 enrolled. In 2017, 34 doctorates awarded. Terminal master's awarded for partial completion of doctoral program. *Degree requirements:* For doctorate, comprehensive exam, thesis/dissertation, oral defense of dissertation, preliminary exam. *Entrance requirements:* For doctorate, GRE General Test. Additional exam requirements/recommendations for international students: Required—TOEFL. *Application deadline:* For fall admission, 12/1 for domestic and international students. Application fee: $75 ($90 for international students). Electronic applications accepted. *Expenses:* $11,184 in-state, $22,578 out-of-state. *Financial support:* In 2017–18, 90 students received support, including 61 fellowships with full tuition reimbursements available (averaging $26,400 per year), 10 research assistantships with full tuition reimbursements available (averaging $26,400 per year), 89 teaching assistantships with full tuition reimbursements available (averaging $26,400 per year); career-related internships or fieldwork, traineeships, and health care benefits also available. Financial award application deadline: 4/15. *Unit head:* Prof. Patricia Reuter-Lorenz, Department Chair, 734-764-7429. *Application contact:* Sheri M. Circele, Psychology Student Academic Affairs, 734-764-2580, Fax: 734-764-3520, E-mail: psych.saa@umich.edu.
Website: http://www.lsa.umich.edu/psych/

University of Michigan–Dearborn, College of Arts, Sciences, and Letters, Master of Science in Psychology Program, Dearborn, MI 48128. Offers clinical health psychology (MS); health psychology (MS). *Program availability:* Part-time. *Faculty:* 17 full-time (10 women). *Students:* 21 full-time (15 women), 8 part-time (6 women); includes 5 minority (2 Black or African American, non-Hispanic/Latino; 1 Asian, non-Hispanic/Latino; 2 Hispanic/Latino), 2 international. Average age 27. 44 applicants, 55% accepted, 13 enrolled. In 2017, 18 master's awarded. *Degree requirements:* For master's, thesis optional. *Entrance requirements:* For master's, GRE, 3 letters of recommendation. Additional exam requirements/recommendations for international students: Required—TOEFL (minimum score 560 paper-based; 84 iBT), IELTS (minimum score 6.5). *Application deadline:* For fall admission, 3/15 for domestic and international students. Application fee: $60. Electronic applications accepted. *Expenses:* $683 per credit hour in-state; $1,176 per credit hour out-state. *Financial support:* In 2017–18, 15 students received support. Career-related internships or fieldwork, scholarships/grants, and non-resident tuition scholarships available. Financial award application deadline: 3/1;

financial award applicants required to submit FAFSA. *Faculty research:* Stress and health, adjustment to and coping with chronic illness, interpersonal relationships, personality and multicultural assessment, physiology and behavioral health. *Unit head:* Dr. Michelle Leonard, Program Director, 313-593-5608, E-mail: mtleon@umich.edu. *Application contact:* Office of Graduate Studies, 313-583-6321, E-mail: umd-graduatestudies@umich.edu.
Website: http://umdearborn.edu/casl/psychology/

University of Minnesota, Twin Cities Campus, Graduate School, College of Liberal Arts, Department of Psychology, Program in Clinical Psychology, Minneapolis, MN 55455-0213. Offers PhD. *Accreditation:* APA. *Degree requirements:* For doctorate, comprehensive exam, thesis/dissertation, internship. *Entrance requirements:* For doctorate, GRE General Test, minimum GPA of 3.5; 12 credits of upper-level psychology courses, including statistics or psychological measurement; previous course work in abnormal psychology. Additional exam requirements/recommendations for international students: Required—TOEFL (minimum score 550 paper-based; 79 iBT).

University of Missouri–St. Louis, College of Arts and Sciences, Department of Psychological Sciences, St. Louis, MO 63121. Offers behavioral neuroscience (MA, PhD); clinical psychology (PhD); trauma studies (Certificate). *Accreditation:* APA (one or more programs are accredited). *Program availability:* Evening/weekend. *Students:* 58 full-time (41 women), 17 part-time (11 women); includes 12 minority (4 Black or African American, non-Hispanic/Latino; 4 Asian, non-Hispanic/Latino; 3 Hispanic/Latino; 1 Two or more races, non-Hispanic/Latino), 3 international. 242 applicants, 8% accepted, 16 enrolled. Terminal master's awarded for partial completion of doctoral program. *Degree requirements:* For master's, thesis; for doctorate, thesis/dissertation. *Entrance requirements:* For master's, GRE General Test, 3 letters of recommendation; for doctorate, GRE General Test, GRE Subject Test, 3 letters of recommendation. Additional exam requirements/recommendations for international students: Required—TOEFL (minimum score 550 paper-based; 79 iBT), IELTS (minimum score 6.5). *Application deadline:* For fall admission, 12/15 for domestic and international students. Application fee: $50 ($40 for international students). Electronic applications accepted. *Expenses:* Tuition, state resident: part-time $476.50 per credit hour. Tuition, nonresident: part-time $1169.70 per credit hour. *Financial support:* Fellowships with full tuition reimbursements, research assistantships with tuition reimbursements, teaching assistantships with tuition reimbursements, and scholarships/grants available. Financial award applicants required to submit FAFSA. *Faculty research:* Bereavement and loss, neuroscience, post-traumatic stress disorder, conflict and negotiation, social psychology. *Unit head:* Michael G. Griffin, Chair, 314-516-5391, Fax: 314-516-5392, E-mail: michael_griffin@umsl.edu. *Application contact:* 314-516-5458, Fax: 314-516-6996, E-mail: gradadm@umsl.edu.
Website: http://www.umsl.edu/divisions/artscience/psychology/

University of Montana, Graduate School, College of Humanities and Sciences, Department of Psychology, Missoula, MT 59812. Offers clinical psychology (PhD); experimental psychology (PhD), including animal behavior psychology, developmental psychology; school psychology (MA, PhD, Ed S). *Accreditation:* APA (one or more programs are accredited). Terminal master's awarded for partial completion of doctoral program. *Degree requirements:* For master's, thesis; for doctorate, thesis/dissertation. *Entrance requirements:* For master's, doctorate, and Ed S, GRE General Test. Additional exam requirements/recommendations for international students: Required—TOEFL.

University of Montana, Graduate School, Phyllis J. Washington College of Education and Human Sciences, Department of Counselor Education, Missoula, MT 59812. Offers clinical mental health counseling (MA); counseling and supervision (Ed D); counselor education (Ed S); intercultural youth and family development (MA); school counseling (MA). *Accreditation:* ACA. *Degree requirements:* For doctorate, thesis/dissertation. *Entrance requirements:* For master's, doctorate, and Ed S, GRE General Test. Additional exam requirements/recommendations for international students: Required—TOEFL.

University of Nebraska–Lincoln, Graduate College, College of Arts and Sciences, Department of Psychology, Lincoln, NE 68588. Offers biopsychology (PhD); clinical psychology (PhD); cognitive psychology (PhD); developmental psychology (PhD); psychology (MA); social/personality psychology (PhD); JD/MA; JD/PhD. *Accreditation:* APA (one or more programs are accredited). *Degree requirements:* For master's, thesis optional; for doctorate, comprehensive exam, thesis/dissertation. *Entrance requirements:* For master's and doctorate, GRE General Test. Additional exam requirements/recommendations for international students: Required—TOEFL (minimum score 550 paper-based). Electronic applications accepted. *Faculty research:* Law and psychology, rural mental health, chronic mental illness, neuropsychology, child clinical psychology.

University of Nevada, Las Vegas, Graduate College, College of Education, Department of Educational and Clinical Studies, Las Vegas, NV 89154-3066. Offers addiction studies (Advanced Certificate); counselor education (M Ed, MS), including clinical mental health (MS), school counseling (M Ed); early childhood education (M Ed); early childhood special education (Certificate), including infancy, preschool; English language learning (M Ed); mental health counseling (Advanced Certificate); special education (M Ed, PhD); PhD/JD. *Program availability:* Part-time. *Faculty:* 18 full-time (9 women), 28 part-time/adjunct (22 women). *Students:* 281 full-time (230 women), 193 part-time (148 women); includes 211 minority (54 Black or African American, non-Hispanic/Latino; 2 American Indian or Alaska Native, non-Hispanic/Latino; 28 Asian, non-Hispanic/Latino; 95 Hispanic/Latino; 4 Native Hawaiian or other Pacific Islander, non-Hispanic/Latino; 28 Two or more races, non-Hispanic/Latino), 13 international. Average age 34. 262 applicants, 76% accepted, 161 enrolled. In 2017, 204 master's, 8 doctorates, 1 other advanced degree awarded. *Degree requirements:* For master's, comprehensive exam (for some programs); for doctorate, comprehensive exam, thesis/dissertation; for other advanced degree, final project. *Entrance requirements:* For master's, bachelor's degree; letter of recommendation; statement of purpose; for doctorate, GRE General Test, statement of purpose; writing sample; 3 letters of recommendation. Additional exam requirements/recommendations for international students: Required—TOEFL (minimum score 550 paper-based; 80 iBT), IELTS (minimum score 7). Application fee: $60 ($95 for international students). Electronic applications accepted. *Expenses:* $275 per credit, $850 per course, $7,969 per year resident, $22,157 per year non-resident, $7,094 non-resident fee (7 credits or more), $1,307 annual health insurance fee. *Financial support:* In 2017–18, 35 students received support, including 10 research assistantships with full tuition reimbursements available (averaging $13,775 per year), 25 teaching assistantships with full tuition reimbursements available (averaging $17,140 per year); institutionally sponsored loans, scholarships/grants, health care benefits, and unspecified assistantships also available. Financial award application deadline: 3/15; financial award applicants required to submit FAFSA. *Faculty research:* Multicultural issues in counseling, academic interventions for students with disabilities, establishment of pro-social skills in young children with severe disabilities, inclusive strategies for students with disabilities, language and literacy for English language learners. *Total annual research expenditures:* $1.1 million. *Unit head:* Dr. Monica Brown, Interim Department Chair/Professor, 702-895-3167, Fax: 702-895-3205, E-mail: monica.brown@unlv.edu. *Application contact:* Dr. Joseph Morgan, Graduate Coordinator, 702-895-3329, Fax: 702-895-3205, E-mail: joseph.morgan@unlv.edu.
Website: http://education.unlv.edu/ecs/

Clinical Psychology

University of Nevada, Reno, Graduate School, College of Liberal Arts, Department of Psychology, Program in Clinical Psychology, Reno, NV 89557. Offers PhD. Terminal master's awarded for partial completion of doctoral program. *Degree requirements:* For doctorate, comprehensive exam, thesis/dissertation. *Entrance requirements:* For doctorate, GRE Subject Test (psychology), minimum GPA of 3.0. Additional exam requirements/recommendations for international students: Required—TOEFL (minimum score 500 paper-based; 61 iBT), IELTS (minimum score 6). Electronic applications accepted. *Faculty research:* Health behavior, domestic violence, verbal relations, anxiety.

University of New Brunswick Saint John, Department of Psychology, Saint John, NB E2L 4L5, Canada. Offers clinical psychology (PhD); experimental psychology (MA, PhD). *Program availability:* Part-time. *Degree requirements:* For master's, thesis. *Entrance requirements:* For master's, GRE General and Subject Tests, honors thesis; minimum GPA of 3.7. Additional exam requirements/recommendations for international students: Required—TOEFL (minimum score 550 paper-based), TWE. Electronic applications accepted. *Faculty research:* Forensic psychology, peer relationships and social skills, polygraph techniques, addictions, attachment and social adjustment, neuroscience, optical illusions, graphical perception, associative learning in animals, bio-psychology.

University of New Mexico, Graduate Studies, College of Arts and Sciences, Program in Psychology, Albuquerque, NM 87131-2039. Offers behavioral neuroscience (PhD); clinical psychology (PhD); cognitive neuroimaging (PhD); developmental psychology (PhD); evolution (PhD); health psychology (PhD); quantitative methodology (PhD). *Accreditation:* APA. *Students:* Average age 30. 227 applicants, 11% accepted, 16 enrolled. In 2017, 10 doctorates awarded. *Degree requirements:* For doctorate, comprehensive exam, thesis/dissertation. *Entrance requirements:* For doctorate, GRE General Test, GRE Subject Test (psychology), minimum GPA of 3.0. Additional exam requirements/recommendations for international students: Required—TOEFL (minimum score 550 paper-based; 79 iBT), IELTS (minimum score 6.5). *Application deadline:* For fall admission, 12/15 priority date for domestic and international students. Applications are processed on a rolling basis. Application fee: $50. Electronic applications accepted. *Financial support:* Fellowships, research assistantships, teaching assistantships, career-related internships or fieldwork, Federal Work-Study, institutionally sponsored loans, scholarships/grants, health care benefits, tuition waivers (partial), and unspecified assistantships available. Financial award application deadline: 3/1; financial award applicants required to submit FAFSA. *Faculty research:* Addiction, cognition, brain and behavior, developmental, evolutionary, functioning neuroimaging, health psychology, learning and memory, neuroscience. *Total annual research expenditures:* $727,970. *Unit head:* Dr. Jane Ellen Smith, Department Chair, 505-277-4121, Fax: 505-277-1394. *Application contact:* Rikk Murphy, Graduate Program Coordinator, 505-277-5009, Fax: 505-277-1394, E-mail: advising@unm.edu.
Website: http://psych.unm.edu

University of North Alabama, College of Education, Department of Counselor Education, Florence, AL 35632-0001. Offers clinical mental health counseling (MA); counseling (MA Ed). *Accreditation:* ACA; NCATE. *Program availability:* Part-time. *Faculty:* 3 full-time (all women), 2 part-time/adjunct (1 woman). *Students:* 13 full-time (12 women), 40 part-time (34 women); includes 7 minority (3 Black or African American, non-Hispanic/Latino; 1 American Indian or Alaska Native, non-Hispanic/Latino; 1 Hispanic/Latino; 2 Two or more races, non-Hispanic/Latino). Average age 30. 34 applicants, 44% accepted, 14 enrolled. In 2017, 11 master's awarded. *Degree requirements:* For master's, comprehensive exam. *Entrance requirements:* For master's, GRE, MAT, or NTE, minimum GPA of 2.5, Alabama Class B Certificate or equivalent, teaching experience. Additional exam requirements/recommendations for international students: Required—TOEFL (minimum score 79 iBT), IELTS (minimum score 6), PTE (minimum score 54). *Application deadline:* Applications are processed on a rolling basis. Application fee: $50 ($100 for international students). Electronic applications accepted. *Expenses:* Tuition, state resident: full-time $7824; part-time $5943 per year. Tuition, nonresident: full-time $15,648; part-time $11,736 per year. *Required fees:* $3064; $2298 per unit. Tuition and fees vary according to course load and reciprocity agreements. *Financial support:* In 2017–18, 2 students received support. Federal Work-Study, scholarships/grants, and unspecified assistantships available. Financial award application deadline: 2/1; financial award applicants required to submit FAFSA. *Unit head:* Dr. Quinn Pearson, Chair, 256-765-4763, Fax: 256-765-4159, E-mail: qmpearson@una.edu. *Application contact:* Hillary N. Coats, Graduate Admissions Coordinator, 256-765-4447, E-mail: graduate@una.edu.
Website: http://www.una.edu/education/departments/counselor-education.html

The University of North Carolina at Chapel Hill, Graduate School, College of Arts and Sciences, Department of Psychology, Chapel Hill, NC 27599-3270. Offers behavioral neuroscience psychology (PhD); clinical psychology (PhD); cognitive psychology (PhD); developmental psychology (PhD); quantitative psychology (PhD); social psychology (PhD). *Accreditation:* APA. *Degree requirements:* For doctorate, comprehensive exam, thesis/dissertation. *Entrance requirements:* For doctorate, GRE General Test, minimum GPA of 3.0. Additional exam requirements/recommendations for international students: Required—TOEFL (minimum score 550 paper-based; 79 iBT), IELTS (minimum score 7). Electronic applications accepted. *Faculty research:* Expressed emotion, cognitive development, social cognitive neuroscience, human memory personality.

The University of North Carolina at Greensboro, Graduate School, College of Arts and Sciences, Department of Psychology, Greensboro, NC 27412-5001. Offers clinical psychology (MA, PhD); cognitive psychology (MA, PhD); developmental psychology (MA, PhD); social psychology (MA, PhD). *Accreditation:* APA (one or more programs are accredited). Terminal master's awarded for partial completion of doctoral program. *Degree requirements:* For master's, comprehensive exam, thesis; for doctorate, one foreign language, thesis/dissertation, preliminary exam. *Entrance requirements:* For master's and doctorate, GRE General Test. Additional exam requirements/recommendations for international students: Required—TOEFL. Electronic applications accepted. *Faculty research:* Sensory and perceptual determinants; evoked potential; disorders, deafness, and development.

The University of North Carolina Wilmington, College of Arts and Sciences, Department of Psychology, Wilmington, NC 28403-3297. Offers clinical psychology (PhD); psychology (MA), including applied behavior analysis, psychological science. *Faculty:* 22 full-time (14 women). *Students:* 27 full-time (22 women), 39 part-time (33 women); includes 8 minority (1 Asian, non-Hispanic/Latino; 5 Hispanic/Latino; 2 Two or more races, non-Hispanic/Latino). Average age 24. 110 applicants, 21% accepted, 23 enrolled. In 2017, 26 master's awarded. *Degree requirements:* For master's, comprehensive exam, thesis; for doctorate, thesis/dissertation, 1-year external APA-accredited or APPIC-member internship. *Entrance requirements:* For master's, GRE General Test, GRE Subject Test (psychology) only if bachelor's degree was not in the area of psychology, 3 letters of recommendation, psychology research interest form, resume, essay; for doctorate, GRE General Test, GRE Subject Test (psychology) only if bachelor's degree was not in the area of psychology, 3 letters of recommendation, resume, statement of interest. Additional exam requirements/recommendations for international students: Required—TOEFL (minimum score 550 paper-based; 79 iBT), IELTS (minimum score 6.5). *Application deadline:* For fall admission, 1/15 for domestic

students. Applications are processed on a rolling basis. Application fee: $75. Electronic applications accepted. *Expenses:* Tuition, state resident: full-time $4626; part-time $226.76 per credit hour. Tuition, nonresident: full-time $17,834; part-time $874.22 per credit hour. *Required fees:* $2124. Tuition and fees vary according to program. *Financial support:* Research assistantships, teaching assistantships, Federal Work-Study, scholarships/grants, unspecified assistantships, and out-of-state tuition remission available. Financial award application deadline: 1/1; financial award applicants required to submit FAFSA. *Unit head:* Dr. Julian Keith, Chair, 910-962-3378, Fax: 910-962-7010, E-mail: keithj@uncw.edu. *Application contact:* Dr. Christine Hughes, Graduate Coordinator, 910-962-7795, Fax: 910-962-7010, E-mail: hughesc@uncw.edu.
Website: http://www.uncw.edu/psy/grad/

University of North Dakota, Graduate School, College of Arts and Sciences, Department of Psychology, Grand Forks, ND 58202. Offers clinical psychology (PhD); forensic psychology (MA, MS). *Accreditation:* APA (one or more programs are accredited). *Degree requirements:* For master's, thesis, final exam; for doctorate, comprehensive exam, thesis/dissertation, internship, final exam. *Entrance requirements:* For master's, GRE General Test, GRE Subject Test, minimum GPA of 3.0; for doctorate, GRE General Test, GRE Subject Test, minimum GPA of 3.5. Additional exam requirements/recommendations for international students: Required—TOEFL (minimum score 550 paper-based; 79 iBT), IELTS (minimum score 6.5). Electronic applications accepted. *Faculty research:* Developmental psychology, clinical social psychology, educational psychology, personality disorders.

University of Northern Colorado, Graduate School, College of Education and Behavioral Sciences, Department of Applied Psychology and Counselor Education, Program in Clinical Counseling, Greeley, CO 80639. Offers MA. *Program availability:* Part-time. Electronic applications accepted.

University of North Texas, Robert B. Toulouse School of Graduate Studies, Denton, TX 76203-5459. Offers accounting (MS); applied anthropology (MA, MS); applied behavior analysis (Certificate); applied geography (MA); applied technology and performance improvement (M Ed, MS); art education (MA); art history (MA); art museum education (Certificate); arts leadership (Certificate); audiology (Au D); behavior analysis (MS); behavioral science (PhD); biochemistry and molecular biology (MS); biology (MA, MS); biomedical engineering (MS); business analysis (MS); chemistry (MS); clinical health psychology (PhD); communication studies (MA, MS); computer engineering (MS); computer science (MS); counseling (M Ed, MS), including clinical mental health counseling (MS), college and university counseling, elementary school counseling, secondary school counseling; creative writing (MA); criminal justice (MS); curriculum and instruction (M Ed); decision sciences (MBA); design (MA, MFA), including fashion design (MFA), innovation studies, interior design (MFA); early childhood studies (MS); economics (MS); educational leadership (M Ed, Ed D); educational psychology (MS, PhD), including family studies (MS), gifted and talented (MS), human development (MS), learning and cognition (MS), research, measurement and evaluation (MS); electrical engineering (MS); emergency management (MPA); engineering technology (MS); English (MA); English as a second language (MA); environmental science (MS); finance (MBA, MS); financial management (MPA); French (MA); health services management (MBA); higher education (M Ed, Ed D); history (MA, MS); hospitality management (MS); human resources management (MPA); information science (MS); information systems (PhD); information technologies (MBA); interdisciplinary studies (MA, MS); international studies (MA); international sustainable tourism (MS); jazz studies (MM); journalism (MA, MJ, Graduate Certificate), including interactive and virtual digital communication (Graduate Certificate), narrative journalism (Graduate Certificate), public relations (Graduate Certificate); kinesiology (MS); linguistics (MA); local government management (MPA); logistics (PhD); logistics and supply chain management (MBA); long-term care, senior housing, and aging services (MA); management (PhD); marketing (MBA); mathematics (MA, MS); mechanical and energy engineering (MS, PhD); music (MA), including ethnomusicology, music theory, musicology, performance; music composition (PhD); music education (MM Ed, PhD); nonprofit management (MPA); operations and supply chain management (MBA); performance (MM, DMA); philosophy (MA); political science (MA); professional and technical communication (MA); radio, television and film (MA, MFA); rehabilitation counseling (Certificate); sociology (MA); Spanish (MA); special education (M Ed); speech-language pathology (MA); strategic management (MBA); studio art (MFA); teaching (M Ed); MBA/MS. *Program availability:* Part-time, evening/weekend, online learning. Terminal master's awarded for partial completion of doctoral program. *Degree requirements:* For master's, variable foreign language requirement, comprehensive exam (for some programs), thesis (for some programs); for doctorate, variable foreign language requirement, comprehensive exam (for some programs), thesis/dissertation; for other advanced degree, variable foreign language requirement, comprehensive exam (for some programs). *Entrance requirements:* For master's and doctorate, GRE, GMAT. Additional exam requirements/recommendations for international students: Required—TOEFL (minimum score 550 paper-based; 79 iBT). Electronic applications accepted.

University of North Texas at Dallas, Graduate School, Dallas, TX 75241. Offers accounting (MBA); counseling (M Ed, MS); criminal justice (MS); curriculum and instruction (M Ed); educational administration (M Ed); human resources and organizational behavior (MBA); public leadership (MS); strategic management (MBA).

University of Oklahoma, College of Arts and Sciences, Department of Human Relations, Norman, OK 73019. Offers clinical mental health (MHR); helping skills in human relations (Graduate Certificate); human relations (MHR); human resource diversity and development (Graduate Certificate); human resources (MHR); licensed professional counselor (MHR). *Program availability:* Part-time, evening/weekend. *Faculty:* 20 full-time (12 women), 9 part-time/adjunct (4 women). *Students:* 297 full-time (221 women), 335 part-time (227 women); includes 316 minority (159 Black or African American, non-Hispanic/Latino; 25 American Indian or Alaska Native, non-Hispanic/Latino; 21 Asian, non-Hispanic/Latino; 68 Hispanic/Latino; 3 Native Hawaiian or other Pacific Islander, non-Hispanic/Latino; 40 Two or more races, non-Hispanic/Latino), 13 international. Average age 35. 152 applicants, 89% accepted, 97 enrolled. In 2017, 255 master's, 95 other advanced degrees awarded. *Degree requirements:* For master's, comprehensive exam or thesis. *Entrance requirements:* For degree, minimum GPA of 3.0. Additional exam requirements/recommendations for international students: Required—TOEFL (minimum score 79 iBT) or IELTS (minimum score 6.5). *Application deadline:* For fall admission, 8/21 for domestic and international students; for spring admission, 1/23 for domestic and international students; for summer admission, 6/5 for domestic and international students. Application fee: $50 ($100 for international students). Electronic applications accepted. *Expenses:* Tuition, state resident: full-time $5119; part-time $213.30 per credit hour. Tuition, nonresident: full-time $19,778; part-time $824.10 per credit hour. *Required fees:* $3458; $133.55 per credit hour. $126.50 per semester. *Financial support:* In 2017–18, 101 students received support, including 6 research assistantships with full tuition reimbursements available (averaging $11,124 per year), 4 teaching assistantships with full tuition reimbursements available (averaging $12,468 per year); scholarships/grants also available. Financial award application deadline: 6/1; financial award applicants required to submit FAFSA. *Faculty research:* At-risk youth, strength model, women's health, adolescent addiction and recovery, group psychotherapy. *Unit head:* Dr. Wesley Long, Chair of Department of Human Relations,

405-325-1756, Fax: 405-325-4402, E-mail: wlong@ou.edu. *Application contact:* Lawana Miller, Admissions Coordinator, 405-325-1756, Fax: 405-325-4402, E-mail: lmiller@ou.edu.
Website: http://www.ou.edu/cas/humanrelations

University of Oregon, Graduate School, College of Arts and Sciences, Department of Psychology, Program in Clinical Psychology, Eugene, OR 97403. Offers PhD. *Accreditation:* APA. *Degree requirements:* For doctorate, thesis/dissertation. *Entrance requirements:* For doctorate, GRE General Test. Additional exam requirements/recommendations for international students: Required—TOEFL.

University of Phoenix–Phoenix Campus, College of Social Sciences, Tempe, AZ 85282-2371. Offers counseling (MS), including clinical mental health counseling, community counseling, counseling, marriage, family and child therapy; psychology (MS). *Program availability:* Evening/weekend, online learning. *Entrance requirements:* Additional exam requirements/recommendations for international students: Required—TOEFL, TOEIC (Test of English as an International Communication), Berlitz Online English Proficiency Exam, PTE, or IELTS. Electronic applications accepted. *Expenses:* Contact institution.

University of Pittsburgh, Kenneth P. Dietrich School of Arts and Sciences, Department of Psychology, Pittsburgh, PA 15260. Offers biological and health psychology (PhD); clinical psychology (PhD); cognitive psychology (PhD); developmental psychology (PhD); social psychology (PhD). *Accreditation:* APA. *Faculty:* 58 full-time (26 women). *Students:* 90 full-time (72 women); includes 25 minority (5 Black or African American, non-Hispanic/Latino; 11 Asian, non-Hispanic/Latino; 9 Hispanic/Latino), 9 international. Average age 26. 485 applicants, 6% accepted, 14 enrolled. In 2017, 6 doctorates awarded. Terminal master's awarded for partial completion of doctoral program. *Degree requirements:* For doctorate, comprehensive exam, thesis/dissertation. *Entrance requirements:* For doctorate, GRE General Test, minimum GPA of 3.0. Additional exam requirements/recommendations for international students: Required—TOEFL (minimum score 90 iBT) or IELTS (minimum score 7). *Application deadline:* For fall admission, 12/1 for domestic and international students. Application fee: $50. Electronic applications accepted. *Financial support:* In 2017–18, 76 students received support, including 20 fellowships with full tuition reimbursements available (averaging $22,000 per year), 28 research assistantships with full tuition reimbursements available (averaging $18,060 per year), 29 teaching assistantships with full tuition reimbursements available (averaging $19,180 per year); scholarships/grants, traineeships, and health care benefits also available. Financial award application deadline: 12/1. *Faculty research:* Developmental psychopathology; autism spectrum disorder; cardiovascular medicine; STEM research. *Total annual research expenditures:* $20 million. *Unit head:* Dr. Julie Fiez, Chair, 412-624-4500, E-mail: fiez@pitt.edu. *Application contact:* Stacy McLinden, Graduate Administrator, 412-624-4502, E-mail: psygrad@pitt.edu.
Website: http://www.psychology.pitt.edu/

University of Pittsburgh, School of Health and Rehabilitation Sciences, Department of Rehabilitation Science and Technology, Pittsburgh, PA 15260. Offers clinical rehabilitation and mental health counseling (MS); physician assistant studies (MS); prosthetics and orthotics (DPT); rehabilitation technology (MS). *Program availability:* Online learning. *Faculty:* 27 full-time (14 women), 7 part-time/adjunct (3 women). *Students:* 177 full-time (118 women), 9 part-time (8 women); includes 26 minority (6 Black or African American, non-Hispanic/Latino; 5 Asian, non-Hispanic/Latino; 9 Hispanic/Latino; 6 Two or more races, non-Hispanic/Latino), 12 international. Average age 25. 611 applicants, 25% accepted, 101 enrolled. In 2017, 72 master's awarded. *Degree requirements:* For master's, comprehensive exam (for some programs). *Entrance requirements:* For master's, GRE General Test, hands-on patient care experience, CPR certification. Additional exam requirements/recommendations for international students: Required—TOEFL (minimum score 550 paper-based; 80 iBT), IELTS (minimum score 6.5). *Application deadline:* For fall admission, 12/31 for domestic and international students; for spring admission, 11/1 for domestic students, 9/1 for international students. Application fee: $177. Electronic applications accepted. *Financial support:* In 2017–18, 14 research assistantships (averaging $23,650 per year) were awarded; career-related internships or fieldwork, Federal Work-Study, scholarships/grants, traineeships, and unspecified assistantships also available. *Faculty research:* Assistive and rehabilitation technology development; prevention and management of chronic conditions; universal design and accessibility; environmental optimization; rehabilitation outcomes measurement. *Total annual research expenditures:* $9.2 million. *Unit head:* Dr. Rory Cooper, Associate Dean for Inclusion/Chair/Professor, 412-822-3700, E-mail: rcooper@pitt.edu. *Application contact:* Jessica Maguire, Director of Admissions, 412-383-6557, Fax: 412-383-6535, E-mail: maguire@pitt.edu.
Website: http://www.shrs.pitt.edu/rst

University of Puerto Rico–Río Piedras, College of Social Sciences, Department of Psychology, San Juan, PR 00931-3300. Offers clinical psychology (MA); industrial organizational psychology (MA); investigative academic psychology (MA); psychology (PhD); social-community psychology (MA). *Program availability:* Part-time. *Degree requirements:* For master's, comprehensive exam, thesis; for doctorate, comprehensive exam, thesis/dissertation, internship. *Entrance requirements:* For master's, GRE or PAEG, interview, minimum GPA of 3.0; for doctorate, GRE or PAEG, interview, master's degree, minimum GPA of 3.0. *Faculty research:* Intervention on depressed Latino youth, biosychosocial training.

University of Regina, Faculty of Graduate Studies and Research, Faculty of Arts, Department of Psychology, Regina, SK S4S 0A2, Canada. Offers clinical psychology (MA, PhD); experimental and applied psychology (MA, PhD). *Faculty:* 19 full-time (9 women), 5 part-time/adjunct (2 women). *Students:* 18 full-time (13 women), 2 part-time (0 women). 52 applicants, 19% accepted. In 2017, 4 master's, 4 doctorates awarded. *Degree requirements:* For master's, thesis; for doctorate, comprehensive exam, thesis/dissertation. *Entrance requirements:* For master's, GRE General Test; for doctorate, GRE General Test and GRE Subject Test (optional for those with a master's degree from a Canadian university). Additional exam requirements/recommendations for international students: Required—TOEFL (minimum score 580 paper-based; 80 iBT), IELTS (minimum score 6.5), PTE (minimum score 59). *Application deadline:* For fall admission, 1/15 for domestic and international students. Application fee: $100. Electronic applications accepted. *Expenses:* $10,681. *Financial support:* In 2017–18, 7 fellowships (averaging $6,714 per year), 17 teaching assistantships (averaging $2,562 per year) were awarded; research assistantships, career-related internships or fieldwork, and scholarships/grants also available. Financial award application deadline: 6/15. *Faculty research:* Clinical, experimental, cognitive, and applied psychology; post-traumatic stress disorder, anxiety, and panic disorder; traumatic brain injury; chronic pain; perception and memory. *Unit head:* Dr. Richard MacLennan, Department Head, 306-585-4458, Fax: 306-585-5429, E-mail: richard.maclennan@uregina.ca.
Website: http://www.uregina.ca/arts/psychology

University of Rhode Island, Graduate School, College of Health Sciences, Department of Psychology, Kingston, RI 02881. Offers behavioral science (PhD); clinical psychology (PhD); school psychology (MS, PhD). *Accreditation:* APA (one or more programs are accredited). *Program availability:* Part-time. *Faculty:* 17 full-time (11 women), 1 part-time/adjunct (0 women). *Students:* 63 full-time (49 women), 11 part-time (9 women); includes 12 minority (6 Black or African American, non-Hispanic/Latino; 1 American Indian or Alaska Native, non-Hispanic/Latino; 3 Asian, non-Hispanic/Latino; 2 Hispanic/Latino), 5 international. 253 applicants, 4% accepted, 7 enrolled. In 2017, 8 master's, 21 doctorates awarded. *Entrance requirements:* Additional exam requirements/recommendations for international students: Required—TOEFL. *Application deadline:* For fall admission, 12/1 for domestic and international students. Application fee: $65. Electronic applications accepted. *Expenses:* Tuition, state resident: full-time $12,706; part-time $786 per credit. Tuition, nonresident: full-time $25,216; part-time $1401 per credit. *Required fees:* $1598; $45 per credit. One-time fee: $30 part-time. *Financial support:* In 2017–18, 10 research assistantships with tuition reimbursements (averaging $17,979 per year), 24 teaching assistantships with tuition reimbursements (averaging $13,572 per year) were awarded. Financial award application deadline: 12/1; financial award applicants required to submit FAFSA. *Faculty research:* Health psychology, multicultural psychology, research methodology, child/family/developmental neuropsychology. *Unit head:* Dr. Mark Robbins, Chair, 401-874-5082, E-mail: markrobb@uri.edu.
Website: http://www.uri.edu/artsci/psy/

University of Rochester, School of Arts and Sciences, Department of Clinical and Social Sciences in Psychology, Rochester, NY 14627. Offers clinical psychology (PhD); developmental psychology (PhD); social-personality psychology (PhD). *Accreditation:* APA. *Faculty:* 14 full-time (7 women). *Students:* 46 full-time (39 women), 1 (woman) part-time; includes 9 minority (1 Black or African American, non-Hispanic/Latino; 4 Asian, non-Hispanic/Latino; 3 Hispanic/Latino; 1 Two or more races, non-Hispanic/Latino), 4 international. Average age 28. 246 applicants, 4% accepted, 8 enrolled. In 2017, 6 doctorates awarded. Terminal master's awarded for partial completion of doctoral program. *Degree requirements:* For doctorate, thesis/dissertation. *Entrance requirements:* For doctorate, GRE General Test; GRE Subject Test (required for clinical psychology, recommended for others), personal statement, official transcripts, three letters of recommendation, curriculum vitae, resume. Additional exam requirements/recommendations for international students: Required—TOEFL. *Application deadline:* For fall admission, 12/1 for domestic and international students. Application fee: $60. Electronic applications accepted. *Expenses:* $1,596 per credit hour. *Financial support:* In 2017–18, 37 students received support, including 2 fellowships, 37 research assistantships (averaging $22,000 per year); teaching assistantships, career-related internships or fieldwork, scholarships/grants, and tuition waivers (full) also available. Financial award application deadline: 4/15. *Faculty research:* Multisensory processing in social-communication difficulties, child emotion regulation, interpersonal relationships, social stress, understanding romantic relationships. *Total annual research expenditures:* $4.3 million. *Unit head:* Loisa Bennetto, Chair, 585-275-8712, E-mail: loisa.bennetto@rochester.edu. *Application contact:* April Engram, Academic Coordinator, 585-275-8704, E-mail: april.engram@rochester.edu.
Website: http://www.sas.rochester.edu/psy/graduate/index.html

University of Saint Francis, Graduate School, Department of Behavioral and Social Sciences, Fort Wayne, IN 46808-3994. Offers clinical mental health counseling (MS, Post Master's Certificate); psychology (MS); school counseling (MS Ed). *Program availability:* Part-time, evening/weekend. *Faculty:* 4 full-time (0 women). *Students:* 23 full-time (18 women), 7 part-time (6 women); includes 8 minority (7 Black or African American, non-Hispanic/Latino; 1 Asian, non-Hispanic/Latino), 1 international. Average age 30. 18 applicants, 83% accepted, 12 enrolled. In 2017, 23 master's awarded. *Entrance requirements:* For master's, GRE with minimum score of 150 if undergraduate GPA is below 3.0 (for MS Ed in school counseling), minimum undergraduate GPA of 3.0; undergraduate coursework in psychology; statement of professional goals (for MS); 2 professional recommendations; interview (for mental health counseling and school counseling). Additional exam requirements/recommendations for international students: Required—TOEFL (minimum score 550 paper-based) or IELTS (minimum score 6.5). *Application deadline:* For fall admission, 7/1 for international students; for spring admission, 11/1 for international students; for summer admission, 3/1 for international students. Applications are processed on a rolling basis. Application fee: $0. Electronic applications accepted. *Expenses:* $905 per credit. *Financial support:* In 2017–18, 3 students received support. Federal Work-Study, scholarships/grants, and unspecified assistantships available. Financial award application deadline: 4/15; financial award applicants required to submit FAFSA. *Unit head:* Dr. John Brinkman, Chair of Department of Behavioral and Social Sciences, 260-399-7700 Ext. 8425, E-mail: jbrinkman@sf.edu. *Application contact:* Kyle Richardson, Associate Director of Enrollment Services for Adult Learning, 260-399-7700 Ext. 6310, Fax: 260-399-8152, E-mail: krichardson@sf.edu.
Website: https://bhvscience.sf.edu/

University of Saint Joseph, Department of Counseling and Applied Behavioral Studies, West Hartford, CT 06117-2700. Offers clinical mental health counseling (MA); school counseling (MA). *Accreditation:* ACA. *Program availability:* Part-time, evening/weekend. *Degree requirements:* For master's, comprehensive exam, thesis optional. *Entrance requirements:* For master's, 2 letters of recommendation. *Application deadline:* Applications are processed on a rolling basis. Application fee: $50. Electronic applications accepted. Application fee is waived when completed online. *Financial support:* Career-related internships or fieldwork and unspecified assistantships available. Support available to part-time students. Financial award applicants required to submit FAFSA.
Website: https://www.usj.edu/academics/schools/sihs/counseling-and-applied-behavioral-studies/

University of San Francisco, School of Nursing and Health Professions, Program in Clinical Psychology, San Francisco, CA 94117-1080. Offers Psy D. *Entrance requirements:* For doctorate, GRE General Test and GRE Subject Test in psychology (taken within five years of application), bachelor's degree from accredited institution; official transcripts; personal statement of interest; professional resume or curriculum vitae; three letters of recommendation; minimum undergraduate GPA of 3.0 in major and overall. Additional exam requirements/recommendations for international students: Required—TOEFL or IELTS.

The University of Scranton, Panuska College of Professional Studies, Department of Counseling and Human Services, Program in Clinical Mental Health Counseling, Scranton, PA 18510. Offers MS. *Accreditation:* ACA. *Program availability:* Part-time, evening/weekend. *Degree requirements:* For master's, comprehensive exam (for some programs), thesis (for some programs), capstone experience. *Entrance requirements:* For master's, minimum GPA of 3.0, three letters of reference. Additional exam requirements/recommendations for international students: Required—TOEFL (minimum score 500 paper-based; 80 iBT), IELTS (minimum score 6.5). Electronic applications accepted. *Faculty research:* Play therapy, expressive arts, identity development, counseling supervision.

University of South Africa, College of Human Sciences, Pretoria, South Africa. Offers adult education (M Ed); African languages (MA, PhD); African politics (MA, PhD); Afrikaans (MA, PhD); ancient history (MA, PhD); ancient Near Eastern studies (MA, PhD); anthropology (MA, PhD); applied linguistics (MA); Arabic (MA, PhD); archaeology (MA); art history (MA); Biblical archaeology (MA); Biblical studies (M Th, D Th, PhD); Christian spirituality (M Th, D Th); church history (M Th, D Th); classical studies (MA, PhD); clinical psychology (MA); communication (MA, PhD); comparative education

(M Ed, Ed D); consulting psychology (D Admin, D Com, PhD); curriculum studies (M Ed, Ed D); development studies (M Admin, MA, D Admin, PhD); didactics (M Ed, Ed D); education (M Tech); education management (M Ed, Ed D); educational psychology (M Ed); English (MA); environmental education (M Ed); French (MA, PhD); German (MA, PhD); Greek (MA); guidance and counseling (M Ed); health studies (MA, PhD), including health sciences education (MA), health services management (MA), medical and surgical nursing science (critical care general) (MA), midwifery and neonatal nursing science (MA), trauma and emergency care (MA); history (MA, PhD); history of education (Ed D); inclusive education (M Ed, Ed D); information and communications technology policy and regulation (MA); information science (MA, MIS, PhD); international politics (MA, PhD); Islamic studies (MA, PhD); Italian (MA, PhD); Judaica (MA, PhD); linguistics (MA, PhD); mathematical education (M Ed); mathematics education (MA); missiology (M Th, D Th); modern Hebrew (MA, PhD); musicology (MA, MMus, D Mus, PhD); natural science education (M Ed); New Testament (M Th, D Th); Old Testament (D Th); pastoral therapy (M Th, D Th); philosophy (MA); philosophy of education (M Ed, Ed D); politics (MA, PhD); Portuguese (MA, PhD); practical theology (M Th, D Th); psychology (MA, MS, PhD); psychology of education (M Ed, Ed D); public health (MA); religious studies (MA, D Th, PhD); Romance languages (MA); Russian (MA, PhD); Semitic languages (MA, PhD); social behavior studies in HIV/AIDS (MA); social science (mental health) (MA); social science in development studies (MA); social science in psychology (MA); social science in social work (MA); social science in sociology (MA); social work (MSW, DSW, PhD); socio-education (M Ed, Ed D); sociolinguistics (MA); sociology (MA, PhD); Spanish (MA, PhD); systematic theology (M Th, D Th); TESOL (teaching English to speakers of other languages) (MA); theological ethics (M Th, D Th); theory of literature (MA, PhD); urban ministries (D Th); urban ministry (M Th).

University of South Alabama, College of Education and Professional Studies, Department of Counseling and Instructional Sciences, Mobile, AL 36688. Offers clinical mental health counseling (MS); educational media (M Ed); educational media and technology (MS); instructional design and development (MS, PhD); instructional leadership (Ed S); school counseling (M Ed). *Accreditation:* NCATE. *Program availability:* Part-time. *Faculty:* 12 full-time (7 women), 10 part-time/adjunct (9 women). *Students:* 110 full-time (85 women), 39 part-time (32 women); includes 43 minority (33 Black or African American, non-Hispanic/Latino; 4 Asian, non-Hispanic/Latino; 5 Hispanic/Latino; 1 Two or more races, non-Hispanic/Latino), 5 international. Average age 34. 68 applicants, 53% accepted, 31 enrolled. In 2017, 32 master's, 9 doctorates, 10 other advanced degrees awarded. *Degree requirements:* For master's, comprehensive exam; for doctorate, comprehensive exam, thesis/dissertation. *Entrance requirements:* For master's, GRE General Test or MAT, minimum GPA of 3.0, three letters of recommendation; for doctorate, GRE, three letters of recommendation, master's degree in field or completion of prerequisites, resume. Additional exam requirements/recommendations for international students: Required—TOEFL (minimum score 525 paper-based; 71 iBT). *Application deadline:* For fall admission, 6/15 for domestic and international students; for spring admission, 12/1 for domestic students, 11/1 for international students; for summer admission, 4/1 for domestic and international students. Applications are processed on a rolling basis. Application fee: $35. Electronic applications accepted. *Expenses:* Tuition, state resident: full-time $10,104; part-time $421 per semester hour. Tuition, nonresident: full-time $20,208; part-time $842 per semester hour. *Financial support:* Fellowships, research assistantships, teaching assistantships, career-related internships or fieldwork, Federal Work-Study, institutionally sponsored loans, scholarships/grants, and unspecified assistantships available. Support available to part-time students. Financial award application deadline: 3/31; financial award applicants required to submit FAFSA. *Faculty research:* Agency counseling, rehabilitation counseling, school psychometry, juvenile delinquency, mixed methods research. *Unit head:* Dr. Tres Stefurak, Department Chair, 251-380-2734, Fax: 251-380-2713, E-mail: jstefurak@southalabama.edu. *Application contact:* Dr. James Van Haneghan, Graduate Coordinator, 251-380-2760, Fax: 251-380-2713, E-mail: jvanhane@southalabama.edu.
Website: http://www.southalabama.edu/colleges/ceps/cins/

University of South Alabama, Graduate School, Program in Clinical and Counseling Psychology, Mobile, AL 36688. Offers PhD. *Accreditation:* ACA. *Faculty:* 7 full-time (2 women). *Students:* 24 full-time (13 women), 6 part-time (5 women); includes 4 minority (2 Black or African American, non-Hispanic/Latino; 1 Hispanic/Latino; 1 Two or more races, non-Hispanic/Latino). Average age 28. 101 applicants, 7% accepted, 7 enrolled. In 2017, 10 doctorates awarded. *Degree requirements:* For doctorate, thesis/dissertation, capstone internship. *Entrance requirements:* For doctorate, GRE, three letters of recommendation, statement of purpose, curriculum vitae. Additional exam requirements/recommendations for international students: Required—TOEFL (minimum score 525 paper-based; 71 iBT). *Application deadline:* For fall admission, 12/15 for domestic students. Application fee: $50. Electronic applications accepted. *Expenses:* Tuition, state resident: full-time $10,104; part-time $421 per semester hour. Tuition, nonresident: full-time $20,208; part-time $842 per semester hour. *Financial support:* Fellowships, research assistantships, teaching assistantships, career-related internships or fieldwork, institutionally sponsored loans, scholarships/grants, and unspecified assistantships available. Support available to part-time students. Financial award application deadline: 3/31; financial award applicants required to submit FAFSA. *Faculty research:* Suicidal behaviors, healthy youth and families, integrated healthcare and undeserved communities following disasters. *Unit head:* Dr. Elise Labbe-coldsmih, Chair, 251-460-6622, E-mail: elabbe@southalabama.edu. *Application contact:* Dr. Joe Currier, Director of Clinical Training, 251-460-6622, E-mail: jcurrier@southalabama.edu.
Website: http://www.southalabama.edu/ccp/

University of South Carolina, The Graduate School, College of Arts and Sciences, Department of Psychology, Program in Clinical/Community Psychology, Columbia, SC 29208. Offers clinical/community psychology (PhD); general psychology (MA). *Accreditation:* APA. *Degree requirements:* For master's, comprehensive exam, thesis; for doctorate, comprehensive exam, thesis/dissertation. *Entrance requirements:* For doctorate, GRE General Test, minimum GPA of 3.2. Additional exam requirements/recommendations for international students: Required—TOEFL. Electronic applications accepted. *Faculty research:* Developmental psychopathology, health disparities, community-level interventions for psychological well being.

University of South Carolina Aiken, Program in Applied Clinical Psychology, Aiken, SC 29801. Offers MS. *Program availability:* Part-time. *Faculty:* 9 full-time (7 women). *Students:* 18 full-time (15 women), 13 part-time (11 women); includes 7 minority (3 Black or African American, non-Hispanic/Latino; 1 Asian, non-Hispanic/Latino; 1 Native Hawaiian or other Pacific Islander, non-Hispanic/Latino; 2 Two or more races, non-Hispanic/Latino). Average age 25. 36 applicants, 42% accepted, 8 enrolled. In 2017, 10 master's awarded. *Degree requirements:* For master's, thesis. *Entrance requirements:* For master's, GRE. Additional exam requirements/recommendations for international students: Required—TOEFL (minimum score 551 paper-based, 80 iBT), IELTS (6), or PTE (53). *Application deadline:* For fall admission, 5/1 priority date for domestic and international students. Applications are processed on a rolling basis. Application fee: $45 ($100 for international students). Electronic applications accepted. *Expenses:* Tuition, state resident: full-time $13,254; part-time $552.25 per credit hour. Tuition, nonresident: full-time $28,368; part-time $1182.70 per credit hour. *Required fees:* $12 per credit hour. $25 per semester. Full-time tuition and fees vary according to course load. *Financial support:* In 2017–18, 27 students received support, including 19 research assistantships with partial tuition reimbursements available (averaging $2,887 per year), 4 teaching assistantships with partial tuition reimbursements available (averaging $2,604 per year); career-related internships or fieldwork, Federal Work-Study, scholarships/grants, tuition waivers (partial), and unspecified assistantships also available. Financial award application deadline: 3/1; financial award applicants required to submit FAFSA. *Faculty research:* Addictive behaviors, interpersonal attraction, impression formation in zero-acquaintance situations, the influence of emotions on visual perception, executive function, cognitive control, inhibitory control, working memory, episodic memory, emotion regulation, anxiety, stress, cognitive functioning and development, social and personality psychology, ADHD, development of cognition and academic skills, teen pregnancy/parenting. *Total annual research expenditures:* $1,307. *Unit head:* Dr. Jane Stafford, Director, 803-641-3358, Fax: 803-641-3720, E-mail: jstafford@usca.edu. *Application contact:* Dan Robb, Associate Vice Chancellor for Enrollment Management, 803-641-3487, Fax: 803-641-3727, E-mail: danr@usca.edu.
Website: http://www.usca.edu/psychology/academics/ms-psychology/

University of South Dakota, Graduate School, College of Arts and Sciences, Department of Psychology, Vermillion, SD 57069. Offers clinical psychology (MA, PhD); human factors (MA, PhD). *Accreditation:* APA (one or more programs are accredited). *Degree requirements:* For master's, comprehensive exam, thesis; for doctorate, comprehensive exam, thesis/dissertation. *Entrance requirements:* For master's, GRE, minimum GPA of 3.0; for doctorate, GRE General Test, GRE Subject Test, minimum GPA of 3.0. Additional exam requirements/recommendations for international students: Required—TOEFL (minimum score 550 paper-based; 79 iBT). *Application deadline:* For fall admission, 2/1 for domestic students. Application fee: $35. Electronic applications accepted. *Financial support:* Fellowships, research assistantships with partial tuition reimbursements, teaching assistantships with partial tuition reimbursements, and unspecified assistantships available. Financial award applicants required to submit FAFSA. *Faculty research:* Human-computer interactions, perceptual-cognitive processing, medical psychology, depression, moral psychology. *Application contact:* Graduate School, 605-658-6140, Fax: 605-677-6118, E-mail: grad@usd.edu.
Website: http://http://www.usd.edu/psychology

University of Southern California, Graduate School, Dana and David Dornsife College of Letters, Arts and Sciences, Department of Psychology, Los Angeles, CA 90089. Offers brain and cognitive science (PhD); clinical science (PhD); developmental psychology (PhD); human behavior (MHB); quantitative methods (PhD); social psychology (PhD). *Accreditation:* APA. *Degree requirements:* For doctorate, comprehensive exam, thesis/dissertation, one-year internship (for clinical science students). *Entrance requirements:* For doctorate, GRE. Additional exam requirements/recommendations for international students: Recommended—TOEFL (minimum score 600 paper-based; 100 iBT). Electronic applications accepted. *Faculty research:* Affective neuroscience; children and families; vision, culture and ethnicity; intergroup relations; aggression and violence; language and reading development; substance abuse.

University of South Florida, College of Arts and Sciences, Department of Psychology, Tampa, FL 33620-9951. Offers psychology (PhD), including clinical psychology, cognition, neuroscience and social psychology, industrial-organizational psychology. *Accreditation:* APA. *Faculty:* 30 full-time (11 women). *Students:* 79 full-time (53 women), 11 part-time (8 women); includes 12 minority (1 Black or African American, non-Hispanic/Latino; 5 Asian, non-Hispanic/Latino; 4 Hispanic/Latino; 2 Two or more races, non-Hispanic/Latino), 7 international. Average age 28. 393 applicants, 3% accepted, 11 enrolled. In 2017, 17 doctorates awarded. *Degree requirements:* For doctorate, comprehensive exam, thesis/dissertation, internship. *Entrance requirements:* For doctorate, GRE General Test, minimum upper-division GPA of 3.4, three letters of recommendation, personal goals statement. Additional exam requirements/recommendations for international students: Required—TOEFL (minimum score 550 paper-based; 79 iBT) or IELTS (minimum score 6.5). *Application deadline:* For fall admission, 12/1 priority date for domestic and international students. Application fee: $30. Electronic applications accepted. *Expenses:* Contact institution. *Financial support:* In 2017–18, 43 students received support, including 18 research assistantships with tuition reimbursements available (averaging $14,727 per year), 57 teaching assistantships with tuition reimbursements available (averaging $14,543 per year); tuition waivers (partial) and unspecified assistantships also available. Financial award applicants required to submit FAFSA. *Faculty research:* Clinical, cognitive, neuroscience, social, and industrial/organizational. *Total annual research expenditures:* $2 million. *Unit head:* Dr. Toru Shimizu, Chairperson, 813-974-0352, Fax: 813-974-4617, E-mail: shimizu@usf.edu. *Application contact:* Dr. Sandra Schneider, Professor and Graduate Program Director, 813-974-0928, E-mail: sandra@usf.edu.
Website: http://psychology.usf.edu/

The University of Tennessee, Graduate School, College of Arts and Sciences, Department of Psychology, Knoxville, TN 37996. Offers clinical psychology (PhD); experimental psychology (MA, PhD); psychology (MA). *Accreditation:* APA (one or more programs are accredited). Terminal master's awarded for partial completion of doctoral program. *Degree requirements:* For master's, thesis; for doctorate, thesis/dissertation. *Entrance requirements:* For master's and doctorate, GRE General Test, GRE Subject Test, minimum GPA of 2.7. Additional exam requirements/recommendations for international students: Required—TOEFL. Electronic applications accepted.

The University of Texas at Austin, Graduate School, College of Liberal Arts, Department of Psychology, Austin, TX 78712-1111. Offers behavioral neuroscience (PhD); clinical psychology (PhD); cognitive systems (PhD); developmental psychology (PhD); individual differences and evolutionary psychology (PhD); perceptual systems (PhD); social psychology (PhD). *Accreditation:* APA. *Degree requirements:* For doctorate, thesis/dissertation. *Entrance requirements:* For doctorate, GRE General Test. Electronic applications accepted. *Faculty research:* Behavioral neuroscience, sensory neuroscience, evolutionary psychology, cognitive processes in psychopathology, cognitive processes and their development.

The University of Texas at El Paso, Graduate School, College of Liberal Arts, Department of Psychology, El Paso, TX 79968-0001. Offers clinical psychology (MA); experimental psychology (MA); psychology (PhD). *Program availability:* Part-time, evening/weekend. *Degree requirements:* For master's, thesis; for doctorate, thesis/dissertation. *Entrance requirements:* For master's, GRE, letters of recommendation; for doctorate, GRE, statement of purpose, letters of recommendation. Additional exam requirements/recommendations for international students: Required—TOEFL; Recommended—IELTS. Electronic applications accepted.

The University of Texas at Tyler, College of Education and Psychology, Department of Psychology and Counseling, Tyler, TX 75799-0001. Offers clinical psychology (MS), including neuropsychology, school psychology; counseling psychology (MA), including general, marriage and family; interdisciplinary studies (MSIS); school counseling (MA). *Program availability:* Part-time, evening/weekend. *Degree requirements:* For master's, comprehensive exam, thesis optional. *Entrance requirements:* For master's, GRE General Test, minimum GPA of 3.0. Additional exam requirements/recommendations for international students: Required—TOEFL. Electronic applications accepted. *Faculty research:* Neuropsychology, child abuse, psychometric properties of psychological

instruments, maternal behavior, clinical practice issues, victimization of women, post-traumatic stress disorder.

The University of Texas of the Permian Basin, Office of Graduate Studies, College of Arts and Sciences, Department of Psychology, Odessa, TX 79762-0001. Offers applied research psychology (MA); clinical psychology (MA). *Program availability:* Part-time, evening/weekend. *Degree requirements:* For master's, comprehensive exam, thesis, practicum. *Entrance requirements:* For master's, GRE General Test, 3 letters of recommendation. Additional exam requirements/recommendations for international students: Required—TOEFL (minimum score 550 paper-based).

The University of Texas Rio Grande Valley, College of Education and P-16 Integration, Department of Counseling, Edinburg, TX 78539. Offers clinical mental health counseling (M Ed); school counseling (M Ed). *Program availability:* Part-time. *Faculty:* 12. *Students:* 157. In 2017, 61 master's awarded. *Entrance requirements:* For master's, minimum GPA of 3.0 on undergraduate coursework. Additional exam requirements/recommendations for international students: Required—TOEFL (minimum score 550 paper-based; 79 iBT), IELTS (minimum score 6.5). *Application deadline:* For fall admission, 4/15 for domestic students; for spring admission, 11/1 for domestic students. Applications are processed on a rolling basis. Application fee: $50 ($75 for international students). Electronic applications accepted. *Expenses:* Tuition, state resident: full-time $5550; part-time $417 per credit hour. Tuition, nonresident: full-time $13,020; part-time $832 per credit hour. *Required fees:* $1169. *Financial support:* Research assistantships, institutionally sponsored loans, scholarships/grants, and unspecified assistantships available. Financial award application deadline: 4/15; financial award applicants required to submit FAFSA. *Faculty research:* Counseling, mental health. *Unit head:* Dr. Cynthia Wimberly, Chair, 956-665-2816, E-mail: cynthia.wimberly@utrgv.edu. *Application contact:* Stephanie Ozuna, Graduate Student Recruiter, 956-665-3558, E-mail: stephanie.ozuna@utrgv.edu.
Website: http://www.utrgv.edu/cg/

The University of Texas Rio Grande Valley, College of Liberal Arts, Department of Psychological Science, Edinburg, TX 78539. Offers psychology (MA), including clinical psychology, experimental psychology. *Program availability:* Part-time, evening/weekend. *Faculty:* 12 full-time (1 woman), 3 part-time/adjunct (1 woman). *Students:* 32 full-time (25 women), 20 part-time (15 women); includes 50 minority (all Hispanic/Latino), 2 international. Average age 27. 29 applicants, 69% accepted, 15 enrolled. In 2017, 15 master's awarded. *Degree requirements:* For master's, comprehensive exam, thesis optional, internship. *Entrance requirements:* For master's, GRE, letters of recommendation. Additional exam requirements/recommendations for international students: Required—TOEFL or IELTS. *Application deadline:* For fall admission, 7/1 priority date for domestic and international students; for spring admission, 11/1 priority date for domestic and international students. Application fee: $50 ($100 for international students). *Expenses:* Tuition, state resident: full-time $5550; part-time $417 per credit hour. Tuition, nonresident: full-time $13,020; part-time $832 per credit hour. *Required fees:* $1169. *Faculty research:* Biofeedback, acculturation, health, stress/trauma, neuropsychological assessment, false memories, children's theory of mind. *Unit head:* Pamela Anderson-Mejias, Interim Chair, E-mail: pamela.andersonmejias@utrgv.edu.

The University of Texas Southwestern Medical Center, Southwestern Graduate School of Biomedical Sciences, Clinical Psychology Program, Dallas, TX 75390. Offers PhD. *Accreditation:* APA. *Degree requirements:* For doctorate, thesis/dissertation, clinical and qualifying exams. *Entrance requirements:* For doctorate, GRE General Test, minimum undergraduate GPA of 3.0. Electronic applications accepted. *Faculty research:* Health psychology, depression, cross-cultural research, neuropsychology, sequelae children's illness.

University of the Cumberlands, Program in Clinical Psychology, Williamsburg, KY 40769-1372. Offers PhD. *Program availability:* Part-time, evening/weekend, online learning.

The University of Toledo, College of Graduate Studies, College of Languages, Literature and Social Sciences, Department of Psychology, Toledo, OH 43606-3390. Offers clinical psychology (MA, PhD); experimental psychology (MA, PhD). *Accreditation:* APA. *Degree requirements:* For master's, comprehensive exam, thesis; for doctorate, comprehensive exam, thesis/dissertation. *Entrance requirements:* For master's and doctorate, GRE General Test, GRE Subject Test, minimum cumulative point-hour ratio of 2.7 for all previous academic work, three letters of recommendation, statement of purpose, transcripts from all prior institutions attended. Additional exam requirements/recommendations for international students: Required—TOEFL (minimum score 550 paper-based; 80 iBT). Electronic applications accepted. *Faculty research:* Neural taste response.

The University of Tulsa, Graduate School, Kendall College of Arts and Sciences, Department of Psychology, Program in Clinical Psychology, Tulsa, OK 74104-3189. Offers MA, PhD, JD/MA. *Accreditation:* APA (one or more programs are accredited). *Program availability:* Part-time. *Faculty:* 9 full-time (4 women). *Students:* 33 full-time (24 women), 5 part-time (4 women); includes 8 minority (5 Asian, non-Hispanic/Latino; 3 Hispanic/Latino), 1 international. Average age 26. 145 applicants, 7% accepted, 8 enrolled. In 2017, 9 master's, 9 doctorates awarded. Terminal master's awarded for partial completion of doctoral program. *Degree requirements:* For master's, thesis (for some programs), 6 credit hours of practicum training; for doctorate, comprehensive exam, thesis/dissertation, 1-year pre-doctoral internship. *Entrance requirements:* For master's and doctorate, GRE General Test, interview, resume. Additional exam requirements/recommendations for international students: Required—TOEFL (minimum score 577 paper-based; 91 iBT), IELTS (minimum score 6.5). *Application deadline:* For fall admission, 12/1 for domestic and international students. Application fee: $55. Electronic applications accepted. *Expenses: Tuition:* Full-time $22,230. *Required fees:* $2000. Tuition and fees vary according to course load and program. *Financial support:* In 2017–18, 45 students received support, including 8 fellowships with full tuition reimbursements available (averaging $11,720 per year), 43 research assistantships with full tuition reimbursements available (averaging $9,000 per year), 16 teaching assistantships with full tuition reimbursements available (averaging $13,908 per year); career-related internships or fieldwork, Federal Work-Study, health care benefits, tuition waivers (full and partial), and unspecified assistantships also available. Support available to part-time students. Financial award application deadline: 2/1; financial award applicants required to submit FAFSA. *Faculty research:* Traumatic stress studies, randomized control trials of exposure treatments, pain modulation, neuropsychological assessment of health/mental health, psychological assessment, psychometrics, ethics, longitudinal assessment of child development, trauma and journalism, MMPI studies. *Unit head:* Dr. Michael Basso, Director, 918-631-3151, Fax: 918-631-2836, E-mail: michael-basso@utulsa.edu. *Application contact:* Information Contact, 800-882-4723, E-mail: grad@utulsa.edu.

University of Utah, Graduate School, College of Education, Department of Educational Psychology, Salt Lake City, UT 84112. Offers clinical mental health counseling (M Ed); counseling psychology (PhD); elementary education (M Ed); instructional design and educational technology (M Ed); instructional design and technology (MS); learning and cognition (MS, PhD); reading and literacy (M Ed, PhD); school counseling (M Ed); school psychology (M Ed, PhD, Ed S); statistics (M Stat). *Accreditation:* APA (one or more programs are accredited). *Faculty:* 19 full-time (9 women), 12 part-time/adjunct (8 women). *Students:* 122 full-time (95 women), 97 part-time (68 women); includes 26 minority (4 Asian, non-Hispanic/Latino; 16 Hispanic/Latino; 6 Two or more races, non-Hispanic/Latino), 7 international. Average age 31. 296 applicants, 27% accepted, 73 enrolled. In 2017, 65 master's, 15 doctorates awarded. Terminal master's awarded for partial completion of doctoral program. *Entrance requirements:* For master's and doctorate, GRE General Test, minimum GPA of 3.0. Additional exam requirements/recommendations for international students: Required—TOEFL (minimum score 80 iBT). *Application deadline:* For fall admission, 12/15 for domestic and international students; for winter admission, 11/1 for domestic and international students; for spring admission, 3/15 for domestic and international students. Application fee: $55 ($65 for international students). Electronic applications accepted. *Expenses:* Contact institution. *Financial support:* In 2017–18, 84 students received support, including 12 fellowships with full and partial tuition reimbursements available (averaging $17,000 per year), 16 research assistantships with full and partial tuition reimbursements available (averaging $15,500 per year), 39 teaching assistantships with full and partial tuition reimbursements available (averaging $15,500 per year); career-related internships or fieldwork, scholarships/grants, traineeships, health care benefits, and unspecified assistantships also available. Financial award application deadline: 4/1; financial award applicants required to submit FAFSA. *Faculty research:* Autism, computer technology and instruction, cognitive behavior, aging, group counseling. *Total annual research expenditures:* $620,935. *Unit head:* Dr. Anne E. Cook, Chair, 801-581-7148, Fax: 801-581-5566, E-mail: anne.cook@utah.edu. *Application contact:* JoLynn N. Yates, Academic Coordinator, 801-581-7148, Fax: 801-581-5566, E-mail: jo.yates@utah.edu.
Website: http://www.ed.utah.edu/edps/

University of Utah, Graduate School, College of Social and Behavioral Science, Department of Psychology, Salt Lake City, UT 84112. Offers clinical psychology (PhD); psychology (PhD), including cognitive neuroscience, developmental psychology, social psychology. *Accreditation:* APA. *Faculty:* 32 full-time (15 women), 11 part-time/adjunct (7 women). *Students:* 53 full-time (36 women), 10 part-time (7 women); includes 10 minority (2 Black or African American, non-Hispanic/Latino; 1 Asian, non-Hispanic/Latino; 4 Hispanic/Latino; 3 Two or more races, non-Hispanic/Latino), 5 international. Average age 26. 295 applicants, 8% accepted, 13 enrolled. In 2017, 11 doctorates awarded. *Entrance requirements:* For doctorate, GRE General Test. Additional exam requirements/recommendations for international students: Required—TOEFL (minimum score 500 paper-based). Application fee: $55 ($65 for international students). Electronic applications accepted. *Expenses:* All admitted students are guaranteed funding and full tuition benefit for four years. *Financial support:* In 2017–18, 51 students received support, including 2 fellowships with full tuition reimbursements available (averaging $17,000 per year), 16 research assistantships with full tuition reimbursements available (averaging $16,800 per year), 30 teaching assistantships with full tuition reimbursements available (averaging $16,800 per year); career-related internships or fieldwork, health care benefits, and unspecified assistantships also available. Financial award application deadline: 4/15; financial award applicants required to submit FAFSA. *Faculty research:* Cognitive neuroscience, health, social cognition, psychopathology, cognitive and social development. *Total annual research expenditures:* $1.9 million. *Unit head:* Dr. Lisa G. Aspinwall, Chair, 801-581-8925, Fax: 801-581-5841, E-mail: lisa.aspinwall@utah.edu. *Application contact:* Nancy Seegmiller, Program Manager, 801-581-8925, Fax: 801-581-5841, E-mail: nancy.seegmiller@psych.utah.edu.
Website: http://www.psych.utah.edu/

University of Vermont, Graduate College, College of Arts and Sciences, Program in Clinical Psychology, Burlington, VT 05405. Offers clinical developmental psychology (PhD); clinical psychology (PhD). *Students:* 23 (18 women). 173 applicants, 3% accepted, 4 enrolled. In 2017, 3 doctorates awarded. *Degree requirements:* For doctorate, thesis/dissertation. *Entrance requirements:* For doctorate, GRE General Test, writing sample, resume. Additional exam requirements/recommendations for international students: Required—TOEFL (minimum iBT score of 100) or IELTS (7). *Application deadline:* For fall admission, 12/1 for domestic and international students. Application fee: $65. Electronic applications accepted. *Expenses:* Tuition, state resident: full-time $11,628; part-time $646 per credit. Tuition, nonresident: full-time $29,340; part-time $1630 per credit. *Required fees:* $1994; $10 per credit. Tuition and fees vary according to course load and program. *Financial support:* In 2017–18, 23 students received support, including 23 teaching assistantships with full tuition reimbursements available (averaging $20,000 per year); research assistantships and health care benefits also available. Financial award application deadline: 12/1. *Unit head:* Dr. Kelly Rohan, Coordinator, 802-656-2670, E-mail: kelly.rohan@uvm.edu.
Website: https://www.uvm.edu/cas/psychology/clinical-psychology-phd-program

University of Vermont, Graduate College, College of Education and Social Services, Counseling Program, Burlington, VT 05405. Offers counseling (MS), including clinical mental health, school counseling. *Accreditation:* ACA; NCATE. *Students:* 68 (54 women); includes 4 minority (1 American Indian or Alaska Native, non-Hispanic/Latino; 1 Hispanic/Latino; 2 Two or more races, non-Hispanic/Latino). 99 applicants, 64% accepted, 35 enrolled. In 2017, 11 master's awarded. *Entrance requirements:* For master's, resume. Additional exam requirements/recommendations for international students: Required—TOEFL (minimum score 550 paper-based, 90 iBT) or IELTS (6.5). *Application deadline:* For fall admission, 2/1 for domestic and international students. Application fee: $65. Electronic applications accepted. *Expenses:* Tuition, state resident: full-time $11,628; part-time $646 per credit. Tuition, nonresident: full-time $29,340; part-time $1630 per credit. *Required fees:* $1994; $10 per credit. Tuition and fees vary according to course load and program. *Financial support:* In 2017–18, 1 student received support, including 1 teaching assistantship with partial tuition reimbursement available (averaging $8,000 per year); fellowships and research assistantships also available. Financial award application deadline: 2/1. *Faculty research:* Women and tenure, counseling children and adolescents. *Unit head:* Dr. Aaron Kindsvatter, Program Coordinator, 802-656-3888, E-mail: cslgprog@uvm.edu.
Website: https://www.uvm.edu/cess/dlds/counseling

University of Victoria, Faculty of Graduate Studies, Faculty of Social Sciences, Department of Psychology, Victoria, BC V8W 2Y2, Canada. Offers clinical psychology (PhD); clinical psychology (neuropsychology) (M Sc); cognition and brain science (M Sc, PhD); experimental neuropsychology (M Sc, PhD); individualized study (M Sc, PhD); life span development psychology (PhD); life span developmental psychology (M Sc); social psychology (M Sc, PhD). *Degree requirements:* For master's, thesis; for doctorate, thesis/dissertation, candidacy exam. *Entrance requirements:* For master's and doctorate, GRE General Test. Additional exam requirements/recommendations for international students: Required—TOEFL (minimum score 600 paper-based). Electronic applications accepted. *Faculty research:* Life span development psychology and aging, behavioral neuroscience, cognitive psychology, behavioral psychology, environmental psychology.

University of Virginia, Curry School of Education, Department of Human Services, Program in Clinical and School Psychology, Charlottesville, VA 22903. Offers PhD. *Students:* 23 full-time (22 women); includes 4 minority (2 Black or African American, non-Hispanic/Latino; 1 Hispanic/Latino; 1 Two or more races, non-Hispanic/Latino). Average age 26. 179 applicants, 4% accepted, 7 enrolled. In 2017, 5 doctorates

awarded. *Unit head:* Peter Sheras, Chair, 434-924-0795, E-mail: pls@virginia.edu. *Application contact:* E-mail: curry-admissions@virginia.edu.
Website: http://curry.virginia.edu/academics/areas-of-study/clinical-school-psychology

University of Washington, Graduate School, College of Arts and Sciences, Department of Psychology, Seattle, WA 98195. Offers animal behavior (PhD); applied child and adolescent psychology: prevention and treatment (MA); behavioral neuroscience (PhD); clinical psychology (PhD); cognition and perception (PhD); developmental psychology (PhD); quantitative psychology (PhD); social psychology and personality (PhD). *Accreditation:* APA (one or more programs are accredited). *Degree requirements:* For doctorate, thesis/dissertation. *Entrance requirements:* For doctorate, GRE General Test, minimum GPA of 3.0. Electronic applications accepted. *Faculty research:* Addictive behaviors, artificial intelligence, child psychopathology, mechanisms and development of vision, physiology of ingestive behaviors.

The University of West Alabama, School of Graduate Studies, College of Education, Program in Clinical Mental Health Counseling, Livingston, AL 35470. Offers MS. *Program availability:* Part-time, evening/weekend, 100% online. *Faculty:* 8 full-time (6 women), 17 part-time/adjunct (12 women). *Students:* 32 (27 women); includes 19 minority (all Black or African American, non-Hispanic/Latino). Average age 33. 19 applicants, 95% accepted, 16 enrolled. *Degree requirements:* For master's, comprehensive exam. *Entrance requirements:* For master's, GRE, minimum GPA of 2.75, verification of background clearance/fingerprints, essay, three academic references, resume. Additional exam requirements/recommendations for international students: Required—TOEFL (minimum score 500 paper-based; 61 iBT). *Application deadline:* Applications are processed on a rolling basis. Application fee: $40. Electronic applications accepted. *Expenses:* Tuition, state resident: part-time $371 per credit hour. Tuition, nonresident: part-time $742 per credit hour. *Required fees:* $130 per semester. *Financial support:* Teaching assistantships, Federal Work-Study, scholarships/grants, and unspecified assistantships available. Support available to part-time students. Financial award application deadline: 3/1; financial award applicants required to submit FAFSA. *Unit head:* Dr. Reenay Rogers, Chair of Instructional Leadership and Support, 205-652-5423, E-mail: rrogers@uwa.edu. *Application contact:* Dr. B.J. Kimbrough, Dean of Graduate Studies, 205-652-3647, Fax: 205-652-3670, E-mail: bkimbrough@uwa.edu.

University of Windsor, Faculty of Graduate Studies, Faculty of Arts and Social Sciences, Department of Psychology, Windsor, ON N9B 3P4, Canada. Offers adult clinical (MA, PhD); applied social psychology (MA, PhD); child clinical (MA, PhD); clinical neuropsychology (MA, PhD). *Degree requirements:* For master's, thesis; for doctorate, comprehensive exam, thesis/dissertation. *Entrance requirements:* For master's, GRE General Test, GRE Subject Test in psychology, minimum B average; for doctorate, GRE General Test, GRE Subject Test in psychology, master's degree. Additional exam requirements/recommendations for international students: Required—TOEFL (minimum score 600 paper-based). Electronic applications accepted. *Faculty research:* Gambling, suicidology, emotional competence, psychotherapy and trauma.

University of Wisconsin–Madison, Graduate School, College of Letters and Science, Department of Psychology, Program in Clinical Psychology, Madison, WI 53706-1380. Offers PhD. *Accreditation:* APA. *Degree requirements:* For doctorate, comprehensive exam, thesis/dissertation. *Entrance requirements:* For doctorate, GRE General Test, minimum undergraduate GPA of 3.0. Additional exam requirements/recommendations for international students: Required—TOEFL. Electronic applications accepted.

University of Wisconsin–Parkside, College of Natural and Health Sciences, Program in Clinical Mental Health Counseling, Kenosha, WI 53141-2000. Offers MS.

University of Wisconsin–Stout, Graduate School, College of Education, Health and Human Sciences, Program in Clinical Mental Health Counseling, Menomonie, WI 54751. Offers MS. *Accreditation:* ACA. *Program availability:* Part-time. *Degree requirements:* For master's, comprehensive exam or thesis. *Entrance requirements:* For master's, minimum GPA of 2.75. Additional exam requirements/recommendations for international students: Required—TOEFL (minimum score 500 paper-based; 61 iBT). Electronic applications accepted. *Faculty research:* Body image, gender issues, eating disorders, cognitive behavioral therapy.

Utah State University, School of Graduate Studies, Emma Eccles Jones College of Education and Human Services, Department of Psychology, Logan, UT 84322. Offers clinical/counseling/school psychology (PhD); research and evaluation methodology (PhD); school counseling (MS); school psychology (MS). *Accreditation:* APA (one or more programs are accredited). *Program availability:* Part-time, evening/weekend, online learning. Terminal master's awarded for partial completion of doctoral program. *Degree requirements:* For master's, thesis (for some programs); for doctorate, thesis/dissertation. *Entrance requirements:* For master's, GRE General Test (school psychology), MAT (school counseling), minimum GPA of 3.5; for doctorate, GRE General Test, minimum GPA of 3.5. Additional exam requirements/recommendations for international students: Required—TOEFL. *Faculty research:* Hearing loss detection in infancy, ADHD, eating disorders, domestic violence, neuropsychology, bilingual/Spanish speaking students/parents.

Valparaiso University, Graduate School and Continuing Education, Program in Clinical Mental Health Counseling, Valparaiso, IN 46383. Offers clinical mental health counseling (MA); JD/MA. *Program availability:* Part-time, evening/weekend. *Degree requirements:* For master's, thesis or alternative, internship. *Entrance requirements:* For master's, minimum GPA of 3.0; 15 credits in the social/behavioral sciences (psychology, sociology, human development, etc.) with minimum GPA of 3.0; course in introductory psychology; recent statistics course with minimum B average. Additional exam requirements/recommendations for international students: Required—TOEFL (minimum score 550 paper-based; 80 iBT), IELTS (minimum score 6). Electronic applications accepted. *Expenses: Tuition:* Full-time $11,340; part-time $630 per credit hour. *Required fees:* $520; $250 per year. $125 per semester. Tuition and fees vary according to program and reciprocity agreements. *Faculty research:* Environmental psychology, human sexuality, developmental psychopathology, social psychology.

Vanguard University of Southern California, Graduate Program in Clinical Psychology, Costa Mesa, CA 92626. Offers MS. *Program availability:* Part-time, evening/weekend. *Degree requirements:* For master's, thesis or alternative, completion of personal therapy. *Entrance requirements:* For master's, minimum GPA of 3.0. Additional exam requirements/recommendations for international students: Required—TOEFL (minimum score 550 paper-based; 79 iBT). Electronic applications accepted. *Expenses:* Contact institution.

Virginia Commonwealth University, Graduate School, College of Humanities and Sciences, Department of Psychology, Program in Clinical Psychology, Richmond, VA 23284-9005. Offers behavioral medicine (PhD); clinical child psychology (PhD). *Accreditation:* APA. *Degree requirements:* For doctorate, thesis/dissertation. *Entrance requirements:* For doctorate, GRE General Test. Additional exam requirements/recommendations for international students: Required—TOEFL (minimum score 600 paper-based; 100 iBT); Recommended—IELTS (minimum score 6.5). Electronic applications accepted. *Faculty research:* Clinical child/adolescent and behavioral medicine.

Virginia State University, College of Graduate Studies, College of Natural and Health Sciences, Department of Psychology, Petersburg, VA 23806-0001. Offers behavioral and community health sciences (PhD); clinical health psychology (PhD); clinical psychology (MS); general psychology (MS). *Degree requirements:* For master's, one foreign language, thesis. *Entrance requirements:* For master's, GRE General Test.

Walden University, Graduate Programs, School of Psychology, Minneapolis, MN 55401. Offers clinical psychology (MS), including counseling, general program; forensic psychology (MS), including forensic psychology in the community, general program, mental health applications, program planning and evaluation in forensic settings, psychology and legal systems; industrial organizational (MS, PhD), including consulting psychology, forensic (MS), forensic psychology (PhD), general practice, leadership development and coaching (MS), organizational diversity and social change, research evaluation (PhD); online teaching in psychology (Post-Master's Certificate); organizational psychology and development (Postbaccalaureate Certificate); psychology (MS, PhD), including applied psychology (MS), clinical psychology (PhD), crisis management and response (MS), educational psychology, forensic psychology (PhD), general psychology (MS), general psychology research (PhD), general psychology teaching (PhD), health psychology, leadership development and coaching (MS), psychology of culture (MS), psychology, public administration, and social change (MS), social psychology, terrorism and security (MS); psychology respecialization (Post-Doctoral Certificate). *Program availability:* Part-time, evening/weekend, online only, 100% online. Terminal master's awarded for partial completion of doctoral program. *Degree requirements:* For master's, thesis optional; for doctorate, thesis/dissertation, residency. *Entrance requirements:* For master's, bachelor's degree or higher; minimum GPA of 2.5; official transcripts; goal statement (for some programs); access to computer and Internet; for doctorate, master's degree or higher; three years of related professional or academic experience (preferred); minimum GPA of 3.0; goal statement and current resume (for select programs); official transcripts; access to computer and Internet; for other advanced degree, relevant work experience; access to computer and Internet. Additional exam requirements/recommendations for international students: Required—TOEFL (minimum score 550 paper-based, 79 iBT), IELTS (minimum score 6.5), Michigan English Language Assessment Battery (minimum score 82), or PTE (minimum score 53). Electronic applications accepted.

Washburn University, College of Arts and Sciences, Department of Psychology, Topeka, KS 66621. Offers clinical psychology (MA). *Program availability:* Part-time. *Degree requirements:* For master's, comprehensive exam (for some programs), thesis or alternative. *Entrance requirements:* For master's, GRE General Test, 15 hours of undergraduate course work in psychology. Additional exam requirements/recommendations for international students: Required—TOEFL (minimum score 80 iBT). Electronic applications accepted. *Faculty research:* Metacognition, anxiety disorders, auditory perception, sports performance psychology, ADHD.

Washington State University, College of Arts and Sciences, Department of Psychology, Pullman, WA 99164. Offers clinical psychology (PhD); experimental psychology (PhD). Program applications must be made through the Pullman campus. *Accreditation:* APA (one or more programs are accredited). *Degree requirements:* For doctorate, comprehensive exam, thesis/dissertation, oral exam, written exam. *Entrance requirements:* For doctorate, GRE General Test, three letters of reference; summary data form; at least 18 credits of study in psychology; at least one course in statistics and research methodology; official transcripts; minimum cumulative undergraduate GPA of 3.0 or master's degree in psychology. Additional exam requirements/recommendations for international students: Required—TOEFL, IELTS. Electronic applications accepted. *Faculty research:* Adult psychopathology and therapy, child psychopathology, neuropsychology, health psychology.

Waynesburg University, Graduate and Professional Studies, Canonsburg, PA 15370. Offers business (MBA), including energy management, finance, health systems, human resources, leadership, market development; counseling (MA), including addictions counseling, clinical mental health; counselor education and supervision (PhD); criminal investigation (MA); education (M Ed), including autism, curriculum and instruction, educational leadership, online teaching; nursing (MSN), including administration, education, informatics; nursing practice (DNP); special education (M Ed); technology (M Ed); MSN/MBA. *Accreditation:* AACN. *Program availability:* Part-time, evening/weekend. *Degree requirements:* For doctorate, thesis/dissertation. *Entrance requirements:* Additional exam requirements/recommendations for international students: Required—TOEFL. Electronic applications accepted.

Wayne State University, College of Liberal Arts and Sciences, Department of Psychology, Detroit, MI 48202. Offers behavioral and cognitive neuroscience (PhD); clinical psychology (PhD); developmental science (PhD); industrial/organizational psychology (MA, PhD); social personality (PhD). Doctoral program admits for fall only. *Accreditation:* APA (one or more programs are accredited). *Faculty:* 38. *Students:* 94 full-time (63 women), 43 part-time (29 women); includes 23 minority (6 Black or African American, non-Hispanic/Latino; 3 Asian, non-Hispanic/Latino; 10 Hispanic/Latino; 4 Two or more races, non-Hispanic/Latino), 12 international. Average age 27. 478 applicants, 11% accepted, 39 enrolled. In 2017, 29 master's, 27 doctorates awarded. Terminal master's awarded for partial completion of doctoral program. *Degree requirements:* For master's, thesis (for some programs); for doctorate, thesis/dissertation, training assignments. *Entrance requirements:* For master's, GRE General Test, minimum undergraduate upper-division cumulative GPA of 3.0, courses in psychology and statistics; for doctorate, GRE General Test, bachelor's, master's, or other advanced degree; at least twelve credits in psychology with minimum GPA of 3.0; courses in laboratory psychology and statistical methods in psychology; at least three letters of recommendation; statement of purpose. Additional exam requirements/recommendations for international students: Required—TOEFL (minimum score 550 paper-based; 79 iBT), TWE (minimum score 5.5), Michigan English Language Assessment Battery (minimum score 85); Recommended—IELTS (minimum score 6.5). Application fee: $50. Electronic applications accepted. *Expenses:* Tuition, state resident: full-time $10,224; part-time $638.98 per credit hour. Tuition, nonresident: full-time $22,145; part-time $1384.04 per credit hour. Tuition and fees vary according to course load and program. *Financial support:* In 2017–18, 90 students received support, including 13 fellowships with tuition reimbursements available (averaging $11,212 per year), 8 research assistantships with tuition reimbursements available (averaging $18,534 per year), 50 teaching assistantships with tuition reimbursements available (averaging $18,534 per year); scholarships/grants, health care benefits, and unspecified assistantships also available. Financial award applicants required to submit FAFSA. *Faculty research:* Behavioral neuroscience, cognitive/neuroscience of development and aging research, children, adolescents, and family research, cognition research, emotion research, health psychology research, homelessness and poverty research, memory research, neuropsychology research, personality/cognition, relationships research, substance use and abuse research, workplace adaptation, well-being and evaluation research. *Unit head:* Boris Baltes, PhD, Chair/Professor, 313-577-2803, E-mail: b.baltes@wayne.edu. *Application contact:* Alia Allen, Academic Services Officer, 313-577-2823, E-mail: aallen@wayne.edu.
Website: http://clas.wayne.edu/psychology/

West Chester University of Pennsylvania, College of Education and Social Work, Department of Counselor Education, West Chester, PA 19383. Offers clinical mental health counseling (MS); counseling (Certificate); higher education counseling (Post Master's Certificate); higher education counseling/student affairs (MS, Certificate); school counseling (M Ed). *Accreditation:* ACA; NCATE. *Program availability:* Part-time, evening/weekend. *Students:* 134 full-time (110 women), 40 part-time (32 women); includes 38 minority (17 Black or African American, non-Hispanic/Latino; 2 Asian, non-Hispanic/Latino; 11 Hispanic/Latino; 8 Two or more races, non-Hispanic/Latino), 1 international. Average age 27. 177 applicants, 58% accepted, 58 enrolled. In 2017, 79 master's, 1 other advanced degree awarded. *Degree requirements:* For master's, comprehensive exam. *Entrance requirements:* For master's, minimum GPA of 3.0, three letters of reference. Additional exam requirements/recommendations for international students: Required—TOEFL or IELTS. *Application deadline:* For fall admission, 5/15 for international students; for spring admission, 10/15 for international students. Applications are processed on a rolling basis. Application fee: $50. Electronic applications accepted. *Expenses:* Tuition, state resident: full-time $9000; part-time $500 per credit. Tuition, nonresident: full-time $13,500; part-time $750 per credit. *Required fees:* $2959; $149.79 per credit. *Financial support:* Scholarships/grants and unspecified assistantships available. Financial award application deadline: 2/15; financial award applicants required to submit FAFSA. *Faculty research:* Bullying in the schools, adolescent cognitive development, counseling pedagogy, motivational interviewing. *Unit head:* Dr. Eric Owens, Chair, 610-436-2559, Fax: 610-425-7432, E-mail: eowens@wcupa.edu. *Application contact:* Dr. Cheryl Neale-McFall, Graduate Coordinator, 610-436-2559, Fax: 610-425-7432, E-mail: cneale-mcfall@wcupa.edu.
Website: http://www.wcupa.edu/education-socialWork/counselorEducation/

West Chester University of Pennsylvania, College of the Sciences and Mathematics, Department of Psychology, West Chester, PA 19383. Offers clinical psychology (Psy D); industrial/organizational psychology (Certificate); psychology (MA), including general psychology, industrial/organizational psychology. *Program availability:* Part-time, evening/weekend, 100% online. *Students:* 56 full-time (37 women), 28 part-time (20 women); includes 18 minority (9 Black or African American, non-Hispanic/Latino; 2 Asian, non-Hispanic/Latino; 4 Hispanic/Latino; 3 Two or more races, non-Hispanic/Latino). Average age 26. 125 applicants, 62% accepted, 42 enrolled. In 2017, 47 master's awarded. Terminal master's awarded for partial completion of doctoral program. *Degree requirements:* For master's, comprehensive exam (for some programs), thesis optional; for doctorate, comprehensive exam, thesis/dissertation, year-long pre-doctoral internship. *Entrance requirements:* For master's, GRE General Test, minimum GPA of 3.0 overall, psychology 3.25; three letters of reference; for doctorate, GRE General Test, minimum undergraduate GPA of 3.0 or graduate 3.3; three letters of reference; curriculum vitae; completion of courses (at the undergraduate level) in abnormal/clinical psychology, personality, research methods, and statistics; professional goals statement. Additional exam requirements/recommendations for international students: Required—TOEFL or IELTS. *Application deadline:* For fall admission, 5/15 for international students; for spring admission, 10/15 for international students. Applications are processed on a rolling basis. Application fee: $50. Electronic applications accepted. *Expenses:* Tuition, state resident: full-time $9000; part-time $500 per credit. Tuition, nonresident: full-time $13,500; part-time $750 per credit. *Required fees:* $2959; $149.79 per credit. *Financial support:* Scholarships/grants and unspecified assistantships available. Financial award application deadline: 2/15; financial award applicants required to submit FAFSA. *Faculty research:* Child and adolescent mental health, trauma, stress, coping and resilience, preventative interventions workplace stress, organizational leadership, eating disorders, several other areas including diversity, cognition, and animal behavior. *Unit head:* Dr. Sandra Kerr, Chairperson, 610-436-2945, E-mail: skerr@wcupa.edu. *Application contact:* Dr. Angela Clarke, Director of Clinical Training, Clinical Psychology PsyD Program, 610-436-3136, E-mail: aclarke@wcupa.edu.
Website: http://www.wcupa.edu/sciences-mathematics/psychology/

Western Connecticut State University, Division of Graduate Studies, School of Professional Studies, Department of Education and Educational Psychology, Program in Clinical Mental Health Counseling, Danbury, CT 06810-6885. Offers MS. *Accreditation:* ACA. *Program availability:* Part-time. *Degree requirements:* For master's, practicum, internship, completion of program in 6 years. *Entrance requirements:* For master's, minimum GPA of 2.8, 3 letters of reference, interview, 9 hours of psychology. Additional exam requirements/recommendations for international students: Recommended—TOEFL (minimum score 550 paper-based; 79 iBT), IELTS (minimum score 6). *Expenses:* Tuition, state resident: full-time $6757; part-time $374 per credit hour. Tuition, nonresident: full-time $18,102; part-time $374 per credit hour. *Required fees:* $4994; $190 per credit hour. $60 per term. Tuition and fees vary according to degree level and program.

Western Illinois University, School of Graduate Studies, College of Arts and Sciences, Department of Psychology, Macomb, IL 61455-1390. Offers clinical/community mental health (MS); general experimental psychology (MS); school psychology (SSP). *Program availability:* Part-time. *Students:* 39 full-time (28 women), 15 part-time (8 women); includes 6 minority (1 Black or African American, non-Hispanic/Latino; 2 Asian, non-Hispanic/Latino; 1 Hispanic/Latino; 2 Two or more races, non-Hispanic/Latino), 2 international. Average age 26. 77 applicants, 77% accepted, 30 enrolled. In 2017, 8 master's, 6 other advanced degrees awarded. *Degree requirements:* For master's, comprehensive exam (for some programs), thesis or alternative. *Entrance requirements:* For master's and SSP, GRE General Test. Additional exam requirements/recommendations for international students: Required—TOEFL (minimum score 550 paper-based; 80 iBT). Application fee: $30. Electronic applications accepted. *Financial support:* In 2017–18, 6 research assistantships with full tuition reimbursements (averaging $7,544 per year) were awarded; unspecified assistantships also available. Financial award applicants required to submit FAFSA. *Unit head:* Dr. Karen Sears, Chairperson, 309-298-1593. *Application contact:* Dr. Nancy Parsons, Associate Provost and Director of Graduate Studies, 309-298-1806, Fax: 309-298-2345, E-mail: grad-office@wiu.edu.
Website: http://wiu.edu/psychology

Western Kentucky University, Graduate Studies, College of Education and Behavioral Sciences, Department of Psychology, Bowling Green, KY 42101. Offers clinical psychology (MA); experimental psychology (MA); general psychology (MA); industrial/organizational psychology (MA); school psychology (Ed S). *Degree requirements:* For master's, comprehensive exam, thesis (for some programs); for Ed S, thesis, oral exam. *Entrance requirements:* For master's, GRE General Test; for Ed S, GRE General Test, minimum GPA of 3.5. Additional exam requirements/recommendations for international students: Required—TOEFL (minimum score 555 paper-based; 79 iBT). *Faculty research:* Neural regeneration, enhancing mobility in the elderly, improvement in visual processing in older adults, lifespan development.

Western Michigan University, Graduate College, College of Arts and Sciences, Department of Psychology, Kalamazoo, MI 49008. Offers behavior analysis (MA, PhD); clinical psychology (PhD); industrial/organizational behavior management (MA). *Accreditation:* APA (one or more programs are accredited). *Degree requirements:* For master's, variable foreign language requirement, thesis; for doctorate, 2 foreign languages, comprehensive exam, thesis/dissertation.

Westminster College, Graduate School, Program in School Counseling, New Wilmington, PA 16172-0001. Offers clinical mental health counseling (MA); school counselor (M Ed). *Program availability:* Part-time, evening/weekend. *Degree requirements:* For master's, comprehensive exam (for M Ed). *Entrance requirements:* For master's, minimum GPA of 3.0, two recommendations. *Application deadline:* For fall admission, 8/15 priority date for domestic students; for spring admission, 1/8 priority date for domestic students. Applications are processed on a rolling basis. Application fee: $35. *Expenses: Tuition:* Part-time $454 per semester hour. *Required fees:* $235.50 per course. Tuition and fees vary according to course load. *Financial support:* Career-related internships or fieldwork and scholarships/grants available. *Unit head:* Coordinator, 724-946-7874, Fax: 724-946-6158. *Application contact:* Coordinator, 724-946-7874, Fax: 724-946-6158.

West Virginia University, College of Education and Human Services, Morgantown, WV 26506. Offers audiology (Au D); autism spectrum disorder (MA); clinical rehabilitation and mental health counseling (MS); communication science and disorders (PhD); counseling (MA); counseling psychology (PhD); curriculum and instruction (Ed D); early childhood education (MA); early intervention (MA); education (PhD); educational leadership (MA, Ed D); educational leadership/public school administration (MA); educational psychology (MA, Ed D); elementary education (MA); gifted education (MA); higher education administration (MA, Ed D); higher education curriculum and teaching (MA); institutional design and technology (MA); instructional design and technology (Ed D); literacy education (MA); secondary education (MA); secondary education/English (MA); special education (Ed D); speech pathology (MS). *Accreditation:* NCATE. *Program availability:* Part-time, evening/weekend, online learning. *Students:* 423 full-time (347 women), 367 part-time (316 women); includes 57 minority (14 Black or African American, non-Hispanic/Latino; 7 Asian, non-Hispanic/Latino; 20 Hispanic/Latino; 16 Two or more races, non-Hispanic/Latino), 13 international. *Degree requirements:* For master's, content exams; for doctorate, comprehensive exam, thesis/dissertation. *Entrance requirements:* Additional exam requirements/recommendations for international students: Required—TOEFL (minimum score 500 paper-based; 61 iBT). *Application deadline:* For fall admission, 8/1 for domestic students; for spring admission, 1/1 for domestic students; for summer admission, 5/1 for domestic students. Application fee: $60. Electronic applications accepted. *Expenses:* Tuition, state resident: full-time $9450. Tuition, nonresident: full-time $24,390. *Financial support:* Fellowships, research assistantships, teaching assistantships, career-related internships or fieldwork, Federal Work-Study, institutionally sponsored loans, health care benefits, tuition waivers (full and partial), and administrative assistantships available. Financial award applicants required to submit FAFSA. *Faculty research:* Internet training and integration for teachers, rural education, teacher preparation, organization of schools, evaluation of personnel. *Unit head:* Dr. Gypsy Denzine, Dean, 304-293-5703, Fax: 304-293-7565, E-mail: gypsy.denzine@mail.wvu.edu. *Application contact:* Dr. M. Cecil Smith, Associate Dean for Research and Graduate Education, 304-293-2174, Fax: 304-293-3802, E-mail: mcecil.smith@mail.wvu.edu.
Website: http://cehs.wvu.edu/

Wheaton College, Graduate School, Department of Psychology, Wheaton, IL 60187-5593. Offers clinical mental health counseling (MA); clinical psychology (Psy D); marriage and family therapy (MA). *Accreditation:* APA (one or more programs are accredited). *Faculty:* 15 full-time (7 women), 12 part-time/adjunct (9 women). *Students:* 132 full-time (99 women), 26 part-time (13 women); includes 40 minority (12 Black or African American, non-Hispanic/Latino; 2 American Indian or Alaska Native, non-Hispanic/Latino; 12 Asian, non-Hispanic/Latino; 7 Hispanic/Latino; 7 Two or more races, non-Hispanic/Latino), 28 international. Average age 28. 139 applicants, 74% accepted, 69 enrolled. In 2017, 62 master's, 20 doctorates awarded. Terminal master's awarded for partial completion of doctoral program. *Degree requirements:* For master's, thesis or alternative; for doctorate, thesis/dissertation, internship. *Entrance requirements:* For master's, GRE General Test, 18 hours of course work in psychology; for doctorate, GRE General Test. Additional exam requirements/recommendations for international students: Required—TOEFL (minimum score 550 paper-based; 80 iBT), IELTS (minimum score 6.5). *Application deadline:* For fall admission, 3/1 priority date for domestic students, 1/1 for international students. Applications are processed on a rolling basis. Application fee: $30. *Expenses: Tuition:* Full-time $19,800; part-time $825 per credit hour. Tuition and fees vary according to degree level and program. *Financial support:* In 2017–18, 3 research assistantships (averaging $4,800 per year) were awarded; career-related internships or fieldwork, Federal Work-Study, scholarships/grants, and unspecified assistantships also available. Financial award application deadline: 3/1; financial award applicants required to submit FAFSA. *Unit head:* Dr. Terri Watson, Associate Dean of Psychology, 630-752-5104, E-mail: psychology@wheaton.edu. *Application contact:* Director of Graduate Admissions, 630-752-5195, Fax: 630-752-7047, E-mail: graduate.admissions@wheaton.edu.
Website: https://www.wheaton.edu/academics/programs/psychology/graduate-programs/

Wichita State University, Graduate School, Fairmount College of Liberal Arts and Sciences, Department of Psychology, Wichita, KS 67260. Offers clinical (PhD); community (PhD); human factors (PhD). *Accreditation:* APA. *Program availability:* Part-time. *Application deadline:* For fall admission, 12/1 for domestic and international students. Application fee: $50 ($65 for international students). *Unit head:* Dr. Rhonda K. Lewis, Chair, 316-978-3170, Fax: 316-978-3006, E-mail: rhonda.lewis@wichita.edu. *Application contact:* Jordan Oleson, Admissions Coordinator, 316-978-3095, Fax: 316-978-3253, E-mail: jordan.oleson@wichita.edu.
Website: http://www.wichita.edu/psychology

Widener University, School of Human Service Professions, Institute for Graduate Clinical Psychology, Program in Clinical Psychology, Chester, PA 19013-5792. Offers Psy D, Psy D/M Ed, Psy D/MA, Psy D/MBA, Psy D/MHA, Psy D/MPA. *Accreditation:* APA. *Students:* 159 full-time (131 women), 5 part-time (4 women); includes 28 minority (9 Black or African American, non-Hispanic/Latino; 10 Asian, non-Hispanic/Latino; 5 Hispanic/Latino; 4 Two or more races, non-Hispanic/Latino), 3 international. Average age 27. 343 applicants, 17% accepted, 34 enrolled. In 2017, 26 doctorates awarded. *Degree requirements:* For doctorate, thesis/dissertation, final oral and written qualifying exams. *Entrance requirements:* For doctorate, GRE General Test or MAT. *Application deadline:* For fall admission, 12/31 for domestic students. Application fee: $75. Electronic applications accepted. *Expenses:* Contact institution. *Financial support:* Career-related internships or fieldwork, Federal Work-Study, institutionally sponsored loans, scholarships/grants, and stipends available. Financial award application deadline: 4/15. *Faculty research:* Cognitive and personality diagnostic testing, depression, child and adolescent competencies, learning disabilities, family therapy. *Unit head:* Dr. Sanjay Nath, Associate Dean/Director, 610-499-1208, Fax: 610-499-4625, E-mail: graduate.psychology@widener.edu. *Application contact:* Ellen Madison, Admissions Coordinator, 611-499-1206, Fax: 610-499-4625, E-mail: etmadison@widener.edu.
Website: http://www.widener.edu/academics/schools/shsp/psyd/default.aspx

Widener University, School of Human Service Professions, Institute for Graduate Clinical Psychology, Program in Clinical Psychology and Health and Medical Services

Administration, Chester, PA 19013-5792. Offers Psy D/MBA, Psy D/MHA. *Accreditation:* APA (one or more programs are accredited); CAHME. *Faculty:* 15 full-time (6 women), 18 part-time/adjunct (10 women). *Students:* 7 full-time (5 women); includes 1 minority (Black or African American, non-Hispanic/Latino). Average age 28. *Application deadline:* For fall admission, 12/31 for domestic students. Application fee: $75. Electronic applications accepted. *Financial support:* Career-related internships or fieldwork, Federal Work-Study, and institutionally sponsored loans available. Financial award application deadline: 5/31. *Faculty research:* Psychosocial competence, family systems, medical care systems and financing. *Unit head:* Dr. Hal Shorey, Director, 610-499-4598, Fax: 610-499-4625.

William James College, Graduate Programs, Newton, MA 02459. Offers applied psychology in higher education student personnel administration (MA); clinical psychology (Psy D); counseling psychology (MA); counseling psychology and community mental health (MA); counseling psychology and global mental health (MA); executive coaching (Graduate Certificate); forensic and counseling psychology (MA); leadership psychology (Psy D); organizational psychology (MA); primary care psychology (MA); respecialization in clinical psychology (Certificate); school psychology (Psy D); MA/CAGS. *Accreditation:* APA. *Degree requirements:* For master's, comprehensive exam (for some programs); for doctorate, thesis/dissertation (for some programs). Electronic applications accepted.

William Paterson University of New Jersey, College of Humanities and Social Sciences, Wayne, NJ 07470-8420. Offers applied sociology (MA); assessment and evaluation research (Certificate); bilingual education (Certificate); clinical and counseling psychology (MA); clinical psychology (Psy D); creative and professional writing (MFA); English (MA); history (MA); public policy and international affairs (MA); teaching English as a second language (Certificate). *Program availability:* Part-time. *Faculty:* 36 full-time (21 women), 10 part-time/adjunct (5 women). *Students:* 62 full-time (44 women), 102 part-time (71 women); includes 76 minority (12 Black or African American, non-Hispanic/Latino; 8 Asian, non-Hispanic/Latino; 50 Hispanic/Latino; 6 Two or more races, non-Hispanic/Latino), 6 international. Average age 33. 156 applicants, 51% accepted, 52 enrolled. In 2017, 39 master's awarded. *Degree requirements:* For master's, thesis (for some programs), internship (for some programs). *Entrance requirements:* For master's, GRE/MAT, minimum GPA of 3.0; 2 letters of recommendation; writing sample/personal statement. Additional exam requirements/recommendations for international students: Required—TOEFL (minimum score 550 paper-based; 79 iBT), IELTS (minimum score 6). *Application deadline:* For fall admission, 6/1 for domestic students, 3/1 for international students; for spring admission, 11/1 for domestic students, 10/1 for international students. Applications are processed on a rolling basis. Application fee: $50. Electronic applications accepted. *Expenses:* Tuition, state resident: full-time $13,920; part-time $6264 per year. Tuition, nonresident: full-time $21,700; part-time $9765 per year. *Required fees:* $80; $36 per year. Tuition and fees vary according to course load, degree level and program. *Financial support:* In 2017–18, 3,480 students received support. Career-related internships or fieldwork, Federal Work-Study, scholarships/grants, and unspecified assistantships available. Support available to part-time students. Financial award application deadline: 3/15; financial award applicants required to submit FAFSA. *Faculty research:* Relationship violence, work-family balance, social development of Japan, theories justifying war, reactions to trauma. *Total annual research expenditures:* $32,300. *Unit head:* Dr. Kara Rabbitt, Dean, 973-720-2180, Fax: 973-720-2955, E-mail: rabbittk@wpunj.edu. *Application contact:* Tinu Adeniran, Associate Director, Graduate Admissions, 973-720-2764, Fax: 973-720-2035, E-mail: adenirant@wpunj.edu.
Website: http://www.wpunj.edu/cohss

Wilmington University, College of Social and Behavioral Sciences, New Castle, DE 19720-6491. Offers administration of human services (MS); administration of justice (MS); clinical mental health counseling (MS); homeland security (MS). *Accreditation:* ACA. *Program availability:* Part-time, evening/weekend. *Faculty:* 11 full-time (6 women), 74 part-time/adjunct (34 women). *Students:* 174 full-time (132 women), 428 part-time (334 women); includes 269 minority (229 Black or African American, non-Hispanic/Latino; 5 American Indian or Alaska Native, non-Hispanic/Latino; 7 Asian, non-Hispanic/Latino; 17 Hispanic/Latino; 11 Two or more races, non-Hispanic/Latino), 11 international. Average age 35. 541 applicants, 81% accepted, 292 enrolled. In 2017, 271 master's awarded. *Entrance requirements:* Additional exam requirements/recommendations for international students: Required—TOEFL (minimum score 500 paper-based). *Application deadline:* Applications are processed on a rolling basis. Application fee: $35. Electronic applications accepted. *Expenses: Tuition:* Part-time $466 per credit. *Required fees:* $25 per semester. Tuition and fees vary according to degree level and campus/location. *Financial support:* Applicants required to submit FAFSA. *Unit head:* Dr. Edward L. Guthrie, Dean, 302-356-6870. *Application contact:* Laura Morris, Director of Admissions, 877-967-5464, E-mail: inquire@wilmcoll.edu.
Website: http://www.wilmu.edu/behavioralscience/

Winona State University, College of Education, Department of Counselor Education, Winona, MN 55987. Offers addiction counseling (Certificate); clinical mental health counseling (MS); human services (MS); school counseling (MS). *Accreditation:* ACA (one or more programs are accredited); NCATE. *Program availability:* Part-time, evening/weekend. *Degree requirements:* For master's, thesis or alternative. *Entrance requirements:* For master's, letters of reference, interview, group activity, on-site writing. Electronic applications accepted.

Wisconsin School of Professional Psychology, Program in Clinical Psychology, Milwaukee, WI 53225-4960. Offers MA, Psy D. *Accreditation:* APA. *Program availability:* Part-time, evening/weekend. Terminal master's awarded for partial completion of doctoral program. *Degree requirements:* For master's, candidacy exam, 500 hours of supervised clinical practica; for doctorate, thesis/dissertation, 1 year clinical intern and practicum experience (2000 hrs), candidacy and clinical exams. *Entrance requirements:* For master's, GRE General Test, GRE Subject Test, bachelor's degree in psychology, writing sample; for doctorate, GRE General Test, GRE Subject Test, master's degree in clinical psychology or equivalent, writing sample. *Faculty research:* Violence prevention, psychology of women, forensic psychology, custody evaluation, aging, harm reduction in AODA.

The Wright Institute, Doctoral Program in Clinical Psychology, Berkeley, CA 94704-1796. Offers Psy D. *Degree requirements:* For doctorate, comprehensive exam, thesis/dissertation. *Entrance requirements:* For doctorate, GRE General Test, statistics, human development, theories of personality and/or abnormal psychology. Additional exam requirements/recommendations for international students: Required—TOEFL (minimum score 600 paper-based). Electronic applications accepted.

Wright State University, School of Professional Psychology, Dayton, OH 45435. Offers clinical psychology (Psy D). *Accreditation:* APA. *Degree requirements:* For doctorate, thesis/dissertation. *Entrance requirements:* For doctorate, GRE General Test, GRE Subject Test. Additional exam requirements/recommendations for international students: Required—TOEFL. *Expenses:* Contact institution.

Xavier University, College of Social Sciences, Health and Education, Department of Psychology, Cincinnati, OH 45207. Offers clinical psychology (Psy D); industrial-organizational psychology (MA). *Accreditation:* APA (one or more programs are accredited). *Degree requirements:* For master's, one foreign language, comprehensive exam, thesis, internship; for doctorate, one foreign language, comprehensive exam, thesis/dissertation, internship. *Entrance requirements:* For master's, GRE, official transcript; 3 letters of recommendation; for doctorate, GRE General Test; GRE Subject Test in psychology (if no undergraduate degree in psychology), bachelor's or master's degree; 18 semester hours of psychology coursework; minimum GPA of 3.0; work and research experience; official transcript; 3 letters of recommendation; statement of purpose. Additional exam requirements/recommendations for international students: Required—TOEFL (minimum score 550 paper-based; 79 iBT), IELTS (minimum score 6.5). Electronic applications accepted. *Expenses:* Contact institution. *Faculty research:* Older adults, clinical child and adolescent issues, personnel selection and employee behavior, at-risk youth, sexual abuse.

Xavier University, College of Social Sciences, Health and Education, School of Education, Department of Counseling, Cincinnati, OH 45207. Offers clinical mental health counseling (MA); school counseling (MA). *Program availability:* Part-time, evening/weekend. *Degree requirements:* For master's, internship. *Entrance requirements:* For master's, GRE or MAT, minimum GPA of 3.0; 2 letters of recommendation; resume; official transcript; statement of purpose. Additional exam requirements/recommendations for international students: Required—TOEFL (minimum score 550 paper-based; 79 iBT). Electronic applications accepted. Application fee is waived when completed online. *Expenses:* Contact institution. *Faculty research:* Supervision, ethics, consultation, self-injury, bullying.

Yale University, Graduate School of Arts and Sciences, Department of Psychology, New Haven, CT 06520. Offers behavioral neuroscience (PhD); clinical psychology (PhD); cognitive psychology (PhD); developmental psychology (PhD); social/personality psychology (PhD). *Accreditation:* APA. *Degree requirements:* For doctorate, thesis/dissertation. *Entrance requirements:* For doctorate, GRE General Test.

Yeshiva University, Ferkauf Graduate School of Psychology, Program in Clinical Psychology, New York, NY 10033-3201. Offers Psy D. *Accreditation:* APA. *Program availability:* Part-time. *Degree requirements:* For doctorate, comprehensive exam, thesis/dissertation. *Entrance requirements:* For doctorate, GRE General Test. *Faculty research:* Psychotherapy, family therapy, psychoanalysis, cognitive behavior therapy.

Yeshiva University, Ferkauf Graduate School of Psychology, Program in School/Clinical-Child Psychology, New York, NY 10033-3201. Offers Psy D. *Accreditation:* APA. *Program availability:* Part-time. *Degree requirements:* For doctorate, comprehensive exam, thesis/dissertation. *Entrance requirements:* For doctorate, GRE General Test. *Faculty research:* Testing, early childhood intervention, child and adolescent psychotherapy, clinical child psychology.

Cognitive Sciences

American University, College of Arts and Sciences, Department of Psychology, Washington, DC 22016-8062. Offers addiction and addictive behavior (Certificate); behavior, cognition, and neuroscience (PhD); clinical psychology (PhD); psychobiology of healing (Certificate); psychology (MA). *Accreditation:* APA. *Program availability:* Part-time. *Faculty:* 20 full-time (8 women), 9 part-time/adjunct (7 women). *Students:* 80 full-time (68 women), 8 part-time (7 women); includes 15 minority (5 Black or African American, non-Hispanic/Latino; 4 Asian, non-Hispanic/Latino; 5 Hispanic/Latino; 1 Two or more races, non-Hispanic/Latino), 6 international. Average age 28. 461 applicants, 12% accepted, 23 enrolled. In 2017, 24 master's, 11 doctorates awarded. *Degree requirements:* For master's, comprehensive exam, thesis or alternative; for doctorate, comprehensive exam, thesis/dissertation. *Entrance requirements:* For master's, GRE General Test, GRE Subject Test, statement of purpose, transcripts, 2 letters of recommendation; for doctorate, GRE General Test, GRE Subject Test, 3 letters of recommendation, statement of purpose, transcripts, resume. Additional exam requirements/recommendations for international students: Required—TOEFL (minimum score 600 paper-based; 100 iBT). *Application deadline:* For fall admission, 3/1 priority date for domestic students. Application fee: $55. *Expenses:* Contact institution. *Financial support:* Research assistantships, teaching assistantships, institutionally sponsored loans, scholarships/grants, and unspecified assistantships available. Financial award application deadline: 2/1; financial award applicants required to submit FAFSA. *Unit head:* Dr. David Haaga, Department Chair, 202-885-1718, Fax: 202-885-1023, E-mail: ahrens@american.edu. *Application contact:* Jonathan Harper, Associate Director, Graduate Recruitment, 202-885-3622, E-mail: jharper@american.edu.
Website: http://www.american.edu/CAS/Psychology/

Arizona State University at the Tempe campus, College of Liberal Arts and Sciences, Department of Psychology, Tempe, AZ 85287-1104. Offers applied behavior analysis (MS); behavioral neuroscience (PhD); clinical psychology (PhD); cognitive science (PhD); developmental psychology (PhD); quantitative psychology (PhD); social psychology (PhD). *Accreditation:* APA. *Degree requirements:* For doctorate, comprehensive exam, thesis/dissertation, interactive Program of Study (iPOS) submitted before completing 50 percent of required credit hours. *Entrance requirements:* For doctorate, GRE General Test, GRE Subject Test, minimum GPA of 3.0 or equivalent in last 2 years of work leading to bachelor's degree. Additional exam requirements/recommendations for international students: Required—TOEFL, IELTS, or PTE. Electronic applications accepted.

Arizona State University at the Tempe campus, Ira A. Fulton Schools of Engineering, The Polytechnic School, Department of Engineering, Mesa, AZ 85212. Offers simulation, modeling, and applied cognitive science (PhD). *Program availability:* Part-time. *Degree requirements:* For doctorate, comprehensive exam, thesis/dissertation, interactive Program of Study (iPOS) submitted before completing 50 percent of required credit hours. *Entrance requirements:* For doctorate, GRE, master's degree in psychology, engineering, cognitive science, or computer science; 3 letters of recommendation; statement of research interests. Additional exam requirements/

recommendations for international students: Required—TOEFL, IELTS, or PTE. Electronic applications accepted. *Faculty research:* Software process and automated workflow, software architecture, dotal technologies, relational database systems, embedded systems.

Ball State University, Graduate School, College of Sciences and Humanities, Department of Psychological Science, Program in Cognitive and Social Processes, Muncie, IN 47306. Offers MA. *Students:* 13 full-time (9 women), 1 part-time (0 women); includes 3 minority (1 Black or African American, non-Hispanic/Latino; 1 Hispanic/Latino; 1 Two or more races, non-Hispanic/Latino), 3 international. Average age 24. 22 applicants, 27% accepted, 5 enrolled. In 2017, 4 master's awarded. *Entrance requirements:* For master's, GRE General Test, minimum baccalaureate GPA of 2.75 or 3.0 in latter half of baccalaureate, goals statements, curriculum vitae, letters of recommendation. Additional exam requirements/recommendations for international students: Required—TOEFL (minimum score 550 paper-based; 79 iBT), IELTS (minimum score 6.5). *Application deadline:* For fall admission, 2/1 for domestic students. Applications are processed on a rolling basis. Application fee: $60. Electronic applications accepted. *Financial support:* Research assistantships with partial tuition reimbursements, teaching assistantships with partial tuition reimbursements, and unspecified assistantships available. Financial award application deadline: 3/1; financial award applicants required to submit FAFSA. *Unit head:* Dr. Guy Mittleman, Chairperson, 765-285-1960, Fax: 765-285-1702, E-mail: gmittleman@bsu.edu.
Website: http://www.bsu.edu/psychology

Binghamton University, State University of New York, Graduate School, Harpur College of Arts and Sciences, Department of Psychology, Program in Psychology - Cognitive and Behavioral Science, Binghamton, NY 13902-6000. Offers PhD. *Program availability:* Part-time. *Students:* 13 full-time (5 women), 8 part-time (5 women); includes 5 minority (2 Asian, non-Hispanic/Latino; 1 Hispanic/Latino; 2 Two or more races, non-Hispanic/Latino), 1 international. Average age 28. 35 applicants, 23% accepted, 6 enrolled. In 2017, 4 doctorates awarded. Terminal master's awarded for partial completion of doctoral program. *Degree requirements:* For doctorate, thesis/dissertation. *Entrance requirements:* For doctorate, GRE General Test. Additional exam requirements/recommendations for international students: Required—TOEFL (minimum score 550 paper-based; 80 iBT). *Application deadline:* For fall admission, 12/31 priority date for domestic and international students. Application fee: $75. Electronic applications accepted. *Financial support:* In 2017–18, 18 students received support, including 3 research assistantships with full tuition reimbursements available (averaging $16,500 per year), 12 teaching assistantships with full tuition reimbursements available (averaging $16,500 per year); career-related internships or fieldwork, Federal Work-Study, institutionally sponsored loans, scholarships/grants, traineeships, health care benefits, tuition waivers (full and partial), and unspecified assistantships also available. Financial award applicants required to submit FAFSA. *Unit head:* Dr. Sarah Laszlo, Program Coordinator, 607-777-3380, E-mail: slaszlo@binghamton.edu. *Application contact:* Ben Balkaya, Assistant Dean and Director, 607-777-2151, Fax: 607-777-2501, E-mail: balkaya@binghamton.edu.

Brandeis University, Graduate School of Arts and Sciences, Department of Psychology, Waltham, MA 02454-9110. Offers brain, body and behavior (PhD); cognitive neuroscience (PhD); general psychology (MA); social/developmental psychology (PhD). *Program availability:* Part-time. *Faculty:* 14 full-time (7 women), 4 part-time/adjunct (3 women). *Students:* 34 full-time (26 women), 4 part-time (2 women); includes 8 minority (5 Asian, non-Hispanic/Latino; 3 Hispanic/Latino), 10 international. Average age 27. 124 applicants, 31% accepted, 15 enrolled. In 2017, 13 master's, 7 doctorates awarded. Terminal master's awarded for partial completion of doctoral program. *Degree requirements:* For master's, thesis or alternative; for doctorate, thesis/dissertation, research reports. *Entrance requirements:* For master's and doctorate, GRE General Test; GRE Subject Test (recommended), letters of recommendation, statement of purpose, transcripts, resume. Additional exam requirements/recommendations for international students: Required—PTE (minimum score 68), TOEFL (minimum score 600 paper-based, 100 iBT) or IELTS (7). *Application deadline:* For fall admission, 12/1 priority date for domestic students. Applications are processed on a rolling basis. Application fee: $75. Electronic applications accepted. *Expenses: Tuition:* Full-time $48,720. *Required fees:* $88. Tuition and fees vary according to course load, degree level, program and student level. *Financial support:* In 2017–18, 40 students received support, including 20 fellowships with full tuition reimbursements available (averaging $24,480 per year), 26 teaching assistantships with partial tuition reimbursements available (averaging $3,200 per year); Federal Work-Study, scholarships/grants, health care benefits, and tuition waivers (partial) also available. Support available to part-time students. Financial award application deadline: 4/15; financial award applicants required to submit FAFSA. *Faculty research:* Brain, body, and behavior across the lifespan; face perception and nonverbal communication; learning and memory; motor control and spatial orientation; neurophysiology of learning and decision making; personality and cognition in adulthood and old age; social, cultural and affective neuroscience; social relations and health physiology; speech comprehension and memory; taste physiology and psychophysics; visual perception. *Unit head:* Dr. Angela Gutchess, Department Chair, 781-736-3303, E-mail: gutchess@brandeis.edu. *Application contact:* Dr. Sarah Lupis, Department Administrator, 781-736-3303, E-mail: slupis@brandeis.edu.
Website: http://www.brandeis.edu/gsas/programs/psychology.html

Brigham Young University, Graduate Studies, College of Family, Home, and Social Sciences, Department of Psychology, Provo, UT 84602. Offers clinical psychology (PhD); cognitive and behavioral neuroscience (PhD). *Accreditation:* APA. *Faculty:* 31 full-time (8 women), 16 part-time/adjunct (7 women). *Students:* 59 full-time (33 women); includes 7 minority (2 Black or African American, non-Hispanic/Latino; 3 Asian, non-Hispanic/Latino; 1 Hispanic/Latino; 1 Native Hawaiian or other Pacific Islander, non-Hispanic/Latino), 4 international. Average age 29. 49 applicants, 33% accepted, 10 enrolled. In 2017, 11 doctorates awarded. *Degree requirements:* For doctorate, comprehensive exam (for some programs), thesis/dissertation, publishable paper. *Entrance requirements:* For doctorate, GRE General Test, minimum GPA of 3.0. Additional exam requirements/recommendations for international students: Required—TOEFL (minimum score 580 paper-based; 85 iBT). *Application deadline:* For fall admission, 12/1 for domestic and international students. Application fee: $50. Electronic applications accepted. *Expenses:* $10,320 per academic year for members of the Church of Jesus Christ of Latter-day Saints; $20,640 for those who are not members of the Church. *Financial support:* In 2017–18, 41 students received support, including 39 research assistantships with partial tuition reimbursements available (averaging $12,000 per year), 5 teaching assistantships with partial tuition reimbursements available (averaging $12,000 per year); career-related internships or fieldwork, scholarships/grants, tuition waivers (partial), and unspecified assistantships also available. Financial award application deadline: 5/31. *Faculty research:* Psychotherapy process, Alzheimer's disease/dementia, psychology and law, health, psychology, addiction. *Total annual research expenditures:* $711,243. *Unit head:* Dr. Dawson Hedges, Chair, 801-422-6357, Fax: 801-422-0602, E-mail: dawson_hedges@byu.edu. *Application contact:* Leesa D. Scott, Coordinator of Student Programs, 801-422-4560, Fax: 801-422-0602, E-mail: leesa_scott@byu.edu.
Website: http://psychology.byu.edu/

Brown University, Graduate School, Department of Cognitive, Linguistic and Psychological Sciences, Providence, RI 02912. Offers cognitive science (Sc M, PhD); linguistics (AM, PhD); psychology (PhD). *Degree requirements:* For master's, one foreign language, thesis or alternative; for doctorate, 2 foreign languages, thesis/dissertation.

Carleton University, Faculty of Graduate Studies, Faculty of Arts and Social Sciences, Program in Cognitive Science, Ottawa, ON K1S 5B6, Canada. Offers PhD. *Degree requirements:* For doctorate, thesis/dissertation. *Entrance requirements:* For doctorate, master's degree. *Faculty research:* Language, attention, artificial intelligence, symbol recognition, consciousness.

Carnegie Mellon University, Dietrich College of Humanities and Social Sciences, Department of Psychology, Area of Cognitive Neuroscience, Pittsburgh, PA 15213-3891. Offers PhD. *Degree requirements:* For doctorate, comprehensive exam, thesis/dissertation. *Entrance requirements:* For doctorate, GRE General Test. Additional exam requirements/recommendations for international students: Required—TOEFL.

Carnegie Mellon University, Dietrich College of Humanities and Social Sciences, Department of Psychology, Area of Cognitive Psychology, Pittsburgh, PA 15213-3891. Offers PhD. *Degree requirements:* For doctorate, comprehensive exam, thesis/dissertation. *Entrance requirements:* For doctorate, GRE General Test. Additional exam requirements/recommendations for international students: Required—TOEFL.

Case Western Reserve University, School of Graduate Studies, Department of Cognitive Science, Cleveland, OH 44106. Offers cognitive linguistics (MA). *Program availability:* Part-time. *Faculty:* 4 full-time (2 women), 4 part-time/adjunct (0 women). *Students:* 7 full-time (2 women), 1 part-time (0 women), 1 international. Average age 29. 5 applicants, 60% accepted, 2 enrolled. In 2017, 1 master's awarded. *Degree requirements:* For master's, thesis. *Entrance requirements:* For master's, GRE, statement of purpose, three letters of recommendation, writing sample. Additional exam requirements/recommendations for international students: Required—TOEFL (minimum score 577 paper-based; 90 iBT); Recommended—IELTS (minimum score 7). *Application deadline:* For fall admission, 5/1 priority date for domestic students. Application fee: $50. Electronic applications accepted. *Expenses: Tuition:* Full-time $43,854; part-time $1827 per credit hour. *Required fees:* $50; $50 per credit hour. Tuition and fees vary according to course load and program. *Faculty research:* Workings of the human mind in design, art, and technology; interaction of brain and culture in development and evolution; origins of human higher-order cognition; the role of the body and social interaction in shaping human cognition; operation of systems that human beings have invented to guide their thought and action individually and culturally. *Unit head:* Dr. William Deal, Chair, 216-368-2205, E-mail: william.deal@case.edu.
Website: http://cognitivescience.case.edu/

Central European University, Department of Cognitive Science, 1051, Hungary. Offers PhD. *Faculty:* 24 full-time (8 women), 5 part-time/adjunct (2 women). *Students:* 32 full-time (19 women). Average age 29. 62 applicants, 13% accepted, 6 enrolled. In 2017, 3 doctorates awarded. *Degree requirements:* For doctorate, one foreign language, comprehensive exam, thesis/dissertation. *Entrance requirements:* For doctorate, essay, interview. Additional exam requirements/recommendations for international students: Required—TOEFL (minimum score 570 paper-based); Recommended—IELTS (minimum score 6.5). *Application deadline:* For fall admission, 2/4 priority date for domestic and international students. Application fee: $30. Electronic applications accepted. *Expenses: Tuition:* Full-time 12,000 euros. *Required fees:* 230 euros. One-time fee: 30 euros full-time. Tuition and fees vary according to course level, course load, degree level and program. *Financial support:* In 2017–18, 6 students received support. Fellowships, career-related internships or fieldwork, scholarships/grants, and health care benefits available. *Faculty research:* Cognitive anthropology, developmental psychology, language and cognition, mathematical modeling of cognition, economics and cognition, social cognition. *Unit head:* Dr. Christophe Heintz, Head of Department, 36 1 887-5137, E-mail: heintzc@ceu.edu. *Application contact:* Zsuzsanna Jaszberenyi, Admissions Officer, 361-324-3009, Fax: 367-327-3211, E-mail: admissions@ceu.edu.
Website: http://cognitivescience.ceu.edu/

Claremont Graduate University, Graduate Programs, School of Social Science, Policy and Evaluation, Department of Psychology, Claremont, CA 91711-6160. Offers advanced study in evaluation (Certificate); cognitive psychology (MA, PhD); developmental psychology (MA, PhD); evaluation and applied research methods (MA, PhD); health behavior research and evaluation (MA, PhD); human resource development and evaluation (MA); industrial/organizational psychology (MA, PhD); organizational behavior (MA, PhD); organizational psychology (MA, PhD); social psychology (MA, PhD); MBA/PhD. *Program availability:* Part-time. Terminal master's awarded for partial completion of doctoral program. *Entrance requirements:* For master's and doctorate, GRE General Test. Additional exam requirements/recommendations for international students: Required—TOEFL (minimum score 75 iBT). Electronic applications accepted. *Faculty research:* Social intervention, diversity in organizations, eyewitness memory, aging and cognition, drug policy.

Cornell University, Graduate School, Graduate Fields of Arts and Sciences, Field of Information Science, Ithaca, NY 14853. Offers cognition (PhD); human computer interaction (PhD); information science (PhD); information systems (PhD); social aspects of information (PhD). *Degree requirements:* For doctorate, comprehensive exam, thesis/dissertation. *Entrance requirements:* For doctorate, GRE General Test, 3 letters of recommendation. Additional exam requirements/recommendations for international students: Required—TOEFL (minimum score 550 paper-based; 77 iBT). Electronic applications accepted. *Faculty research:* Digital libraries, game theory, data mining, human-computer interaction, computational linguistics.

Dartmouth College, School of Graduate and Advanced Studies, Department of Psychological and Brain Sciences, Program in Cognitive Neuroscience, Hanover, NH 03755. Offers PhD. *Students:* 6 full-time (4 women); includes 2 minority (both Two or more races, non-Hispanic/Latino), 3 international. Average age 28. 10 applicants, 10% accepted, 1 enrolled. In 2017, 2 doctorates awarded. *Entrance requirements:* Additional exam requirements/recommendations for international students: Required—TOEFL. *Application deadline:* For fall admission, 12/1 for domestic students. Application fee: $50. Electronic applications accepted. *Unit head:* Dr. Adina Roskies, Chair, 603-646-2112. *Application contact:* Elizabeth Cassell, Department Administrator, 603-646-0470, E-mail: liz.cassell@dartmouth.edu.

Duke University, Graduate School, Department of Psychology and Neuroscience, Durham, NC 27708. Offers biological psychology (PhD); clinical psychology (PhD); cognitive psychology (PhD); developmental psychology (PhD); experimental psychology (PhD); health psychology (PhD); human social development (PhD); JD/MA. *Accreditation:* APA (one or more programs are accredited). *Degree requirements:* For doctorate, thesis/dissertation. *Entrance requirements:* For doctorate, GRE General Test. Additional exam requirements/recommendations for international students: Required—TOEFL (minimum score 577 paper-based; 90 iBT) or IELTS (minimum score 7). Electronic applications accepted.

Emory University, Laney Graduate School, Department of Psychology, Atlanta, GA 30322-1100. Offers clinical psychology (PhD); cognition and development (PhD); neuroscience and animal behavior (PhD). *Accreditation:* APA. *Degree requirements:* For

doctorate, comprehensive exam, thesis/dissertation. *Entrance requirements:* For doctorate, GRE General Test, minimum GPA of 3.25. Additional exam requirements/recommendations for international students: Required—TOEFL. Electronic applications accepted. *Faculty research:* Neuroscience and animal behavior; adult and child psychopathology, cognition development assessment.

Florida International University, College of Arts, Sciences, and Education, Department of Psychology, Miami, FL 33199. Offers behavioral analysis (MS); clinical science (PhD); cognitive neuroscience (PhD); counseling psychology (MS); developmental science (MS, PhD); legal psychology (MS, PhD); organizational psychology (MS, PhD). Program has fall admissions only. *Accreditation:* APA. *Program availability:* Part-time, evening/weekend. *Faculty:* 45 full-time (28 women), 48 part-time/adjunct (31 women). *Students:* 162 full-time (122 women), 13 part-time (5 women); includes 94 minority (11 Black or African American, non-Hispanic/Latino; 5 Asian, non-Hispanic/Latino; 75 Hispanic/Latino; 3 Two or more races, non-Hispanic/Latino), 12 international. Average age 27. 290 applicants, 21% accepted, 50 enrolled. In 2017, 43 master's, 13 doctorates awarded. Terminal master's awarded for partial completion of doctoral program. *Degree requirements:* For master's, thesis; for doctorate, comprehensive exam, thesis/dissertation. *Entrance requirements:* For master's, GRE General Test, minimum GPA of 3.0, resume, 3 letters of recommendation; for doctorate, GRE General Test, 3 letters of recommendation, resume, letter of intent, two writing samples, minimum GPA of 3.0. Additional exam requirements/recommendations for international students: Required—TOEFL (minimum score 550 paper-based; 80 iBT). *Application deadline:* For fall admission, 12/15 for domestic and international students. Application fee: $30. Electronic applications accepted. *Expenses:* Tuition, state resident: full-time $8912; part-time $446 per credit hour. Tuition, nonresident: full-time $21,393; part-time $992 per credit hour. *Required fees:* $390; $195 per semester. *Financial support:* Institutionally sponsored loans and scholarships/grants available. Financial award application deadline: 3/1. *Faculty research:* Legal psychology, organizational and industrial psychology, child behavior psychology. *Unit head:* Dr. Jeremy Pettit, Interim Chair, 305-348-1671, Fax: 305-348-3646, E-mail: jeremy.pettit@fiu.edu. *Application contact:* Nanett Rojas, Assistant Director, Graduate Admissions, 305-348-7464, Fax: 305-348-7441, E-mail: gradadm@fiu.edu.

Florida State University, The Graduate School, College of Arts and Sciences, Department of Psychology, Program in Cognitive Psychology, Tallahassee, FL 32306. Offers PhD. *Faculty:* 8 full-time (2 women). *Students:* 19 full-time (10 women), 2 part-time (both women); includes 8 minority (1 Black or African American, non-Hispanic/Latino; 4 Asian, non-Hispanic/Latino; 2 Hispanic/Latino; 1 Two or more races, non-Hispanic/Latino), 1 international. Average age 30. 38 applicants, 16% accepted, 3 enrolled. In 2017, 2 doctorates awarded. Terminal master's awarded for partial completion of doctoral program. *Degree requirements:* For doctorate, comprehensive exam, thesis/dissertation. *Entrance requirements:* For doctorate, GRE General Test, minimum GPA of 3.0, research experience, letters of recommendation. Additional exam requirements/recommendations for international students: Required—TOEFL (minimum score 80 iBT). *Application deadline:* For fall admission, 12/1 for domestic and international students. Application fee: $30. Electronic applications accepted. *Financial support:* In 2017–18, 20 students received support, including 1 fellowship with full tuition reimbursement available (averaging $22,815 per year), 10 research assistantships with full tuition reimbursements available (averaging $23,815 per year), 9 teaching assistantships with full tuition reimbursements available (averaging $19,000 per year); health care benefits also available. Financial award application deadline: 12/1; financial award applicants required to submit FAFSA. *Faculty research:* Memory, learning and reading disabilities; expert performance; aging. *Total annual research expenditures:* $856,154. *Unit head:* Dr. Walter Boot, Director, 850-645-8734, Fax: 850-644-7739, E-mail: boot@psy.fsu.edu. *Application contact:* Lynda L. Gibson, Graduate Program Associate, 850-644-2499, Fax: 850-644-7739, E-mail: grad-info@psy.fsu.edu.
Website: http://www.psy.fsu.edu/

George Mason University, College of Humanities and Social Sciences, Department of Psychology, Fairfax, VA 22030. Offers applied developmental psychology (MA, PhD); clinical psychology (PhD); cognitive and behavioral neuroscience (MA, PhD); cognitive neuroscience (Certificate); human factors/applied cognition (MA, PhD, Certificate), including transportation human factors (Certificate), usability (Certificate); industrial/organizational psychology (MA, PhD). *Accreditation:* APA. *Faculty:* 41 full-time (20 women), 5 part-time/adjunct (all women). *Students:* 152 full-time (101 women), 56 part-time (39 women); includes 47 minority (15 Black or African American, non-Hispanic/Latino; 13 Asian, non-Hispanic/Latino; 13 Hispanic/Latino; 1 Native Hawaiian or other Pacific Islander, non-Hispanic/Latino; 5 Two or more races, non-Hispanic/Latino), 12 international. Average age 27. 719 applicants, 19% accepted, 61 enrolled. In 2017, 55 master's, 18 doctorates, 8 other advanced degrees awarded. *Degree requirements:* For master's, comprehensive exam, thesis or practicum research; for doctorate, comprehensive exam, thesis/dissertation, 2nd-year project. *Entrance requirements:* For master's, GRE, 2 official transcripts; goals statement; 15 undergraduate credits in concentration for which the applicant is applying; for doctorate, GRE, 3 letters of recommendation; resume; goals statement; minimum GPA of 3.0 overall for last 60 undergraduate credits, 3.25 in psychology courses; 15 undergraduate credits in concentration for which the applicant is applying; 2 official transcripts; for Certificate, GRE, 2 official transcripts; expanded goals statement; 3 letters of recommendation. Additional exam requirements/recommendations for international students: Required—TOEFL (minimum score 575 paper-based; 88 iBT), IELTS (minimum score 6.5), PTE (minimum score 59). Application fee: $75 ($80 for international students). Electronic applications accepted. *Expenses:* Tuition, state resident: full-time $11,228; part-time $459.50 per credit. Tuition, nonresident: full-time $30,932; part-time $1280.50 per credit. *Required fees:* $3252; $135.50 per credit. Part-time tuition and fees vary according to course load and program. *Financial support:* In 2017–18, 110 students received support, including 6 fellowships (averaging $4,829 per year), 52 research assistantships with tuition reimbursements available (averaging $10,933 per year), 70 teaching assistantships with tuition reimbursements available (averaging $7,703 per year); career-related internships or fieldwork, Federal Work-Study, scholarships/grants, tuition waivers (partial), unspecified assistantships, and health care benefits (for full-time research or teaching assistantship recipients) also available. Support available to part-time students. Financial award application deadline: 3/1; financial award applicants required to submit FAFSA. *Faculty research:* Applied developmental psychology, biopsychology, clinical psychology, human factors/applied cognition psychology, industrial/organizational psychology, school psychology. *Total annual research expenditures:* $2.6 million. *Unit head:* Reeshad Dalal, Department Chair, 703-993-9487, Fax: 703-993-1359, E-mail: rdalal@gmu.edu. *Application contact:* Michael Hock, Graduate Program Coordinator, 703-993-1548, Fax: 703-993-1359, E-mail: mhock2@gmu.edu.
Website: http://psychology.gmu.edu

The George Washington University, Columbian College of Arts and Sciences, Department of Psychology, Washington, DC 20052. Offers applied social psychology (PhD); clinical psychology (PhD); cognitive neuroscience (PhD). *Accreditation:* APA. *Program availability:* Part-time, evening/weekend. *Faculty:* 26 full-time (15 women), 10 part-time/adjunct (7 women). *Students:* 41 full-time (27 women), 25 part-time (17 women); includes 24 minority (10 Black or African American, non-Hispanic/Latino; 8 Asian, non-Hispanic/Latino; 4 Hispanic/Latino; 2 Two or more races, non-Hispanic/Latino), 6 international. Average age 28. 452 applicants, 35% accepted, 87 enrolled. In 2017, 10 doctorates awarded. *Degree requirements:* For doctorate, thesis/dissertation or alternative, general exam. *Entrance requirements:* For doctorate, GRE General Test, minimum GPA of 3.0. Additional exam requirements/recommendations for international students: Required—TOEFL (minimum score 550 paper-based; 80 iBT). *Application deadline:* For fall admission, 1/15 for domestic and international students. Application fee: $75. *Expenses: Tuition:* Full-time $28,800; part-time $1655 per credit hour. *Required fees:* $45; $2.75 per credit hour. *Financial support:* In 2017–18, 62 students received support. Fellowships with tuition reimbursements available, teaching assistantships with tuition reimbursements available, career-related internships or fieldwork, Federal Work-Study, and tuition waivers available. *Unit head:* Dr. Carol Sigelman, Chair, 202-994-8422, E-mail: carol@gwu.edu. *Application contact:* Information Contact, 202-994-6320, Fax: 202-994-1602, E-mail: psych@gwu.edu.
Website: http://psychology.columbian.gwu.edu/

Georgia State University, College of Arts and Sciences, Department of Psychology, Atlanta, GA 30302-3083. Offers clinical psychology (PhD); cognitive sciences (PhD); community psychology (PhD); developmental psychology (PhD); neuropsychology and behavioral neuroscience (PhD). *Accreditation:* APA. *Faculty:* 40 full-time (26 women). *Students:* 102 full-time (80 women), 4 part-time (all women); includes 26 minority (7 Black or African American, non-Hispanic/Latino; 10 Asian, non-Hispanic/Latino; 4 Hispanic/Latino; 5 Two or more races, non-Hispanic/Latino), 8 international. Average age 27. 450 applicants, 7% accepted, 16 enrolled. In 2017, 21 doctorates awarded. *Entrance requirements:* For doctorate, GRE. Additional exam requirements/recommendations for international students: Required—TOEFL (minimum score 550 paper-based; 80 iBT). *Application deadline:* For fall admission, 12/1 for domestic and international students. Application fee: $50. Electronic applications accepted. *Expenses:* Tuition, state resident: full-time $7020. Tuition, nonresident: full-time $22,518. *Required fees:* $2128. Tuition and fees vary according to degree level and program. *Financial support:* In 2017–18, fellowships with full tuition reimbursements (averaging $19,282 per year), research assistantships with full tuition reimbursements (averaging $5,173 per year), teaching assistantships with full tuition reimbursements (averaging $6,389 per year) were awarded; scholarships/grants, traineeships, health care benefits, and unspecified assistantships also available. Financial award applicants required to submit FAFSA. *Faculty research:* Clinical psychology, developmental psychology, community psychology, neuropsychology and behavioral neuroscience, cognitive sciences. *Unit head:* Dr. Lisa Armistead, Chair, 404-413-6205, Fax: 404-413-6207, E-mail: lparmistead@gsu.edu. *Application contact:* Dr. Lindsey Cohen, Director of Graduate Studies, 404-413-6263, Fax: 404-413-6207, E-mail: llcohen@gsu.edu.

The Graduate Center, City University of New York, Graduate Studies, Program in Psychology, New York, NY 10016-4039. Offers basic applied neurocognition (PhD); biopsychology (PhD); clinical psychology (PhD); developmental psychology (PhD); environmental psychology (PhD); experimental psychology (PhD); industrial psychology (PhD); learning processes (PhD); neuropsychology (PhD); psychology (PhD); social personality (PhD). *Faculty:* 119 full-time (40 women). *Students:* 428 full-time (308 women); includes 118 minority (31 Black or African American, non-Hispanic/Latino; 31 Asian, non-Hispanic/Latino; 47 Hispanic/Latino; 1 Native Hawaiian or other Pacific Islander, non-Hispanic/Latino; 8 Two or more races, non-Hispanic/Latino), 53 international. Average age 33. 795 applicants, 12% accepted, 56 enrolled. In 2017, 46 doctorates awarded. *Degree requirements:* For doctorate, one foreign language, thesis/dissertation. *Entrance requirements:* For doctorate, GRE General Test. Additional exam requirements/recommendations for international students: Required—TOEFL. *Application deadline:* For fall admission, 12/1 priority date for domestic students. Application fee: $125. Electronic applications accepted. *Financial support:* In 2017–18, 371 students received support, including 340 fellowships, 34 research assistantships, 33 teaching assistantships; career-related internships or fieldwork, Federal Work-Study, institutionally sponsored loans, and tuition waivers (full and partial) also available. Financial award application deadline: 2/1; financial award applicants required to submit FAFSA. *Unit head:* Richard Bodnar, Executive Officer, 212-817-8706, Fax: 212-817-1533, E-mail: rbodnar@gc.cuny.edu. *Application contact:* Les Gribben, Director of Admissions, 212-817-7470, Fax: 212-817-1624, E-mail: lgribben@gc.cuny.edu.

Grand Canyon University, College of Doctoral Studies, Phoenix, AZ 85017-1097. Offers data analytics (DBA); general psychology (PhD), including cognition and instruction, industrial and organizational psychology, integrating technology, learning, and psychology, performance psychology; management (DBA); marketing (DBA); organizational leadership (Ed D), including behavioral health, Christian ministry, health care administration, organizational development. *Degree requirements:* For doctorate, comprehensive exam, thesis/dissertation. *Entrance requirements:* For doctorate, minimum GPA of 3.4 on earned advanced degree from regionally-accredited institution; transcripts; goals statement.

Harvard University, Graduate School of Arts and Sciences, Department of Psychology, Cambridge, MA 02138. Offers psychology (PhD), including behavior and decision analysis, cognition, developmental psychology, experimental psychology, personality, psychobiology, psychopathology; social psychology (PhD). *Accreditation:* APA. *Degree requirements:* For doctorate, thesis/dissertation, general exams. *Entrance requirements:* For doctorate, GRE General Test. Additional exam requirements/recommendations for international students: Required—TOEFL.

Harvard University, Harvard Graduate School of Education, Master's Programs in Education, Cambridge, MA 02138. Offers arts in education (Ed M); education policy and management (Ed M); higher education (Ed M); human development and psychology (Ed M); international education policy (Ed M); language and literacy (Ed M); learning and teaching (Ed M); mind, brain, and education (Ed M); prevention science and practice (Ed M); school leadership (Ed M); special studies (Ed M); teacher education (Ed M); technology, innovation, and education (Ed M). *Program availability:* Part-time. *Entrance requirements:* For master's, GRE General Test, statement of purpose, 3 letters of recommendation, resume, official transcripts. Additional exam requirements/recommendations for international students: Required—TOEFL (minimum score 613 paper-based; 104 iBT), TWE (minimum score 5). Electronic applications accepted. *Faculty research:* Learning and development, educational leadership and organizations, education policy analysis.

Illinois State University, Graduate School, College of Arts and Sciences, Department of Psychology, Normal, IL 61790. Offers psychology (MA, MS), including clinical-counseling psychology, cognitive and behavioral sciences, developmental psychology, industrial/organizational-social psychology; school psychology (PhD, SSP). *Accreditation:* APA. *Degree requirements:* For master's, thesis or alternative; for doctorate, variable foreign language requirement, thesis/dissertation, 2 terms of residency, internship, practicum. *Entrance requirements:* For master's, GRE General Test, GRE Subject Test, minimum GPA of 3.0 in last 60 hours of course work; for doctorate, GRE General Test. *Faculty research:* Comprehensive evaluation system for the central region professional development grant, Illinois school psychology internship consortium, for children's sake.

Indiana University Bloomington, University Graduate School, College of Arts and Sciences, Cognitive Science Program, Bloomington, IN 47406-7512. Offers PhD.

Degree requirements: For doctorate, comprehensive exam, thesis/dissertation, research project; colloquia course. *Entrance requirements:* For doctorate, GRE, 3 letters of reference. Additional exam requirements/recommendations for international students: Required—TOEFL (minimum score 600 paper-based; 94 iBT), IELTS (minimum score 6.5). Electronic applications accepted. *Expenses:* Contact institution. *Faculty research:* Learning concepts, neural network models, language, animal cognition, dynamic and robotics systems approaches to behavior and cognition.

Indiana University Bloomington, University Graduate School, College of Arts and Sciences, Department of Psychological and Brain Sciences, Bloomington, IN 47405. Offers clinical science (PhD); cognitive neuroscience (PhD); cognitive psychology (PhD); developmental psychology (PhD); methods of behavior (PhD); molecular systems neuroscience (PhD); social psychology (PhD). *Accreditation:* APA. *Degree requirements:* For doctorate, comprehensive exam, 90 credit hours, 2 advanced statistics/methods courses, 2 written research projects, the teaching of psychology course, teaching 1 semester of undergraduate methods course, qualifying examination, minor or a second major, first-year research seminar course, dissertation defense, written dissertation. *Entrance requirements:* For doctorate, GRE. Additional exam requirements/recommendations for international students: Required—TOEFL (minimum score 550 paper-based; 79 iBT). Electronic applications accepted. *Faculty research:* Clinical science, cognitive neuroscience, cognitive psychology, developmental psychology, mechanisms of behavior, molecular and systems neuroscience, social psychology.

Iowa State University of Science and Technology, Department of Psychology, Ames, IA 50011. Offers cognitive psychology (PhD); counseling psychology (PhD); psychology (MS, PhD); social psychology (PhD). *Accreditation:* APA (one or more programs are accredited). *Entrance requirements:* For doctorate, GRE General Test, GRE Subject Test (psychology), 3 letters of recommendation. Additional exam requirements/recommendations for international students: Required—TOEFL (minimum score 560 paper-based; 79 iBT), IELTS (minimum score 6.5). Electronic applications accepted. *Faculty research:* Counseling psychology, cognitive psychology, social psychology, health psychology, psychology and public policy.

Johns Hopkins University, Zanvyl Krieger School of Arts and Sciences, Department of Cognitive Science, Baltimore, MD 21218. Offers MA, PhD. *Faculty:* 9 full-time (3 women), 1 (woman) part-time/adjunct. *Students:* 22 full-time (15 women); includes 3 minority (1 Black or African American, non-Hispanic/Latino; 2 Two or more races, non-Hispanic/Latino), 11 international. Average age 27. 65 applicants, 14% accepted, 8 enrolled. In 2017, 4 master's, 1 doctorate awarded. Terminal master's awarded for partial completion of doctoral program. *Degree requirements:* For master's, thesis, portfolio, or 1st research paper (depending on track); for doctorate, thesis/dissertation, 2 research papers. *Entrance requirements:* For master's, GRE, minimum GPA of 3.0, undergraduate degree relevant to cognitive science, resume or curriculum vitae, statement of purpose, transcripts from previous post-secondary institutions, 2 recommendation letters, research or course proposal; for doctorate, GRE General Test, 3 letters of recommendation, sample of work, statement of purpose, original transcripts from all previous post-secondary institutions. Additional exam requirements/recommendations for international students: Required—TOEFL (minimum score 600 paper-based; 100 iBT), IELTS (minimum score 7). *Application deadline:* For fall admission, 12/15 for domestic and international students; for spring admission, 10/15 for domestic and international students. Application fee: $75. Electronic applications accepted. *Expenses:* $52,170 per year resident; $2,687 per semester non-resident. *Financial support:* In 2017–18, 21 students received support, including 6 fellowships (averaging $29,000 per year), 3 research assistantships (averaging $29,000 per year), 11 teaching assistantships (averaging $29,000 per year); scholarships/grants, health care benefits, and tuition waivers (partial) also available. *Faculty research:* Language acquisition and development, cognitive neuropsychology and neuroscience, computational studies, psycholinguistics and cognitive psychology, theoretical linguistics. *Unit head:* Dr. Geraldine Legendre, Professor/Chair, E-mail: legendre@cogsci.jhu.edu. *Application contact:* Sarah Ciotola, Academic Program Coordinator, 410-516-6844, Fax: 410-516-8020, E-mail: sciotol3@jhu.edu. Website: http://cogsci.jhu.edu/

Louisiana State University and Agricultural & Mechanical College, Graduate School, College of Humanities and Social Sciences, Department of Psychology, Baton Rouge, LA 70803. Offers biological psychology (MA, PhD); clinical psychology (MA, PhD); cognitive psychology (MA, PhD); developmental psychology (MA, PhD); school psychology (MA, PhD). *Accreditation:* APA (one or more programs are accredited). *Faculty:* 29 full-time (11 women). *Students:* 78 full-time (57 women), 18 part-time (14 women); includes 25 minority (8 Black or African American, non-Hispanic/Latino; 5 Asian, non-Hispanic/Latino; 5 Hispanic/Latino; 1 Native Hawaiian or other Pacific Islander, non-Hispanic/Latino; 6 Two or more races, non-Hispanic/Latino), 4 international. Average age 27. 239 applicants, 8% accepted, 18 enrolled. In 2017, 15 master's, 12 doctorates awarded. *Financial support:* In 2017–18, 7 fellowships (averaging $41,483 per year), 9 research assistantships (averaging $19,441 per year), 58 teaching assistantships (averaging $19,688 per year) were awarded. *Total annual research expenditures:* $326,871.

Massachusetts Institute of Technology, School of Science, Department of Brain and Cognitive Sciences, Cambridge, MA 02139. Offers cognitive science (PhD); neuroscience (PhD). *Degree requirements:* For doctorate, comprehensive exam, thesis/dissertation. *Entrance requirements:* For doctorate, GRE General Test. Additional exam requirements/recommendations for international students: Required—TOEFL, IELTS. Electronic applications accepted. *Faculty research:* Vision, audition, and other perceptual systems: physiology and computation; learning, memory, and executive control: molecular and systems approaches; sensorimotor systems: physiology and computation; neural and cognitive development and plasticity; language and high-level cognition: learning, acquisition, and computation.

Michigan Technological University, Graduate School, College of Sciences and Arts, Department of Cognitive and Learning Sciences, Houghton, MI 49931. Offers applied cognitive science and human factors (MS, PhD); applied science education (MS); post-secondary STEM education (Graduate Certificate). *Program availability:* Part-time, blended/hybrid learning. *Faculty:* 23 full-time (9 women), 7 part-time/adjunct. *Students:* 12 full-time (7 women), 17 part-time (9 women); includes 2 minority (1 Black or African American, non-Hispanic/Latino; 1 Two or more races, non-Hispanic/Latino), 2 international. Average age 37. 37 applicants, 32% accepted, 3 enrolled. In 2017, 7 master's, 1 doctorate awarded. Terminal master's awarded for partial completion of doctoral program. *Degree requirements:* For master's, comprehensive exam (for some programs), thesis (for some programs); for doctorate, comprehensive exam, thesis/dissertation, applied internship experience. *Entrance requirements:* For master's, GRE (for applied cognitive science and human factors program only), statement of purpose, personal statement, official transcripts, 3 letters of recommendation, resume/curriculum vitae; for doctorate, GRE, statement of purpose, personal statement, official transcripts, 3 letters of recommendation, resume/curriculum vitae. Additional exam requirements/recommendations for international students: Required—TOEFL (recommended minimum score 90 iBT) or IELTS. *Application deadline:* For fall admission, 2/1 priority date for domestic and international students. Applications are processed on a rolling

basis. Electronic applications accepted. *Expenses:* Tuition, state resident: full-time $17,100; part-time $950 per credit. Tuition, nonresident: full-time $17,100; part-time $950 per credit. *Required fees:* $248; $124 per term. Tuition and fees vary according to course load and program. *Financial support:* In 2017–18, 14 students received support, including 5 fellowships (averaging $15,790 per year), 5 research assistantships with tuition reimbursements available (averaging $15,790 per year), 1 teaching assistantship (averaging $15,790 per year); career-related internships or fieldwork, Federal Work-Study, scholarships/grants, health care benefits, unspecified assistantships, and adjunct instructor positions also available. Financial award application deadline: 12/15; financial award applicants required to submit FAFSA. *Faculty research:* Applied science education, applied cognitive science, human factors, STEM education, human-computer interaction. *Total annual research expenditures:* $410,074. *Unit head:* Dr. Susan L. Amato-Henderson, Chair, 906-487-2536, Fax: 906-487-2468, E-mail: slamato@mtu.edu. *Application contact:* Kelly S. Steelman, Graduate Program Director, 906-487-2792, Fax: 906-487-2468, E-mail: steelman@mtu.edu. Website: http://www.mtu.edu/cls/

Mississippi State University, College of Arts and Sciences, Department of Psychology, Mississippi State, MS 39762. Offers applied psychology (PhD), including clinical, cognitive science; psychology (MS). *Accreditation:* APA. *Faculty:* 18 full-time (6 women). *Students:* 33 full-time (18 women), 7 part-time (all women); includes 8 minority (4 Black or African American, non-Hispanic/Latino; 3 Asian, non-Hispanic/Latino; 1 Two or more races, non-Hispanic/Latino), 1 international. Average age 27. 46 applicants, 26% accepted, 10 enrolled. In 2017, 7 master's, 6 doctorates awarded. Terminal master's awarded for partial completion of doctoral program. *Degree requirements:* For master's, comprehensive exam, thesis; for doctorate, thesis/dissertation, qualifying exam, comprehensive written and oral exam. *Entrance requirements:* For master's, GRE General Test, minimum GPA of 2.75 on last two years of undergraduate courses; for doctorate, GRE General Test, proficiency in at least 1 computer language, minimum GPA of 3.0. Additional exam requirements/recommendations for international students: Required—TOEFL (minimum score 477 paper-based; 53 iBT); Recommended—IELTS (minimum score 4.5). *Application deadline:* For fall admission, 4/1 priority date for domestic students, 5/1 for international students; for spring admission, 11/1 priority date for domestic students, 9/1 for international students. Applications are processed on a rolling basis. Application fee: $60 ($80 for international students). Electronic applications accepted. *Expenses:* Tuition, state resident: full-time $8318; part-time $462.12 per credit hour. Tuition, nonresident: full-time $22,358; part-time $1242.12 per credit hour. *Required fees:* $110; $12.24 per credit hour. $6.12 per semester. *Financial support:* In 2017–18, 6 research assistantships with full tuition reimbursements (averaging $14,703 per year), 22 teaching assistantships with full tuition reimbursements (averaging $12,157 per year) were awarded; career-related internships or fieldwork, Federal Work-Study, institutionally sponsored loans, scholarships/grants, and unspecified assistantships also available. Financial award application deadline: 4/1; financial award applicants required to submit FAFSA. *Faculty research:* Personality type, alcoholism, blindness and low vision, mental retardation, language comprehension. *Total annual research expenditures:* $1.4 million. *Unit head:* Dr. Mitchell E. Berman, Professor and Head, 662-325-3202, Fax: 662-325-7212, E-mail: mberman@psychology.msstate.edu. *Application contact:* Lakan Drinker, Admissions and Enrollment Assistant, 662-325-8951, E-mail: ldrinker@grad.msstate.edu. Website: http://www.psychology.msstate.edu/

The New School, The New School for Social Research, Department of Psychology, New York, NY 10011. Offers clinical psychology (PhD); cognitive, social, and developmental psychology (PhD); psychology (MA). *Accreditation:* APA (one or more programs are accredited). *Program availability:* Part-time. *Faculty:* 14 full-time (8 women), 4 part-time/adjunct (0 women). *Students:* 154 full-time (121 women), 77 part-time (58 women); includes 42 minority (8 Black or African American, non-Hispanic/Latino; 12 Asian, non-Hispanic/Latino; 17 Hispanic/Latino; 5 Two or more races, non-Hispanic/Latino), 39 international. Average age 29. 250 applicants, 83% accepted, 71 enrolled. In 2017, 45 master's, 18 doctorates awarded. Terminal master's awarded for partial completion of doctoral program. *Degree requirements:* For master's, comprehensive exam, thesis (for some programs); for doctorate, comprehensive exam, thesis/dissertation. *Entrance requirements:* For master's, GRE, letters of recommendation, writing sample, essays, transcripts; for doctorate, letters of recommendation, writing sample, essays, transcripts. Additional exam requirements/recommendations for international students: Required—TOEFL (minimum score 100 iBT), IELTS (minimum score 7), PTE (minimum score 68). *Application deadline:* For fall admission, 1/5 priority date for domestic and international students; for spring admission, 10/15 priority date for domestic and international students. Applications are processed on a rolling basis. Application fee: $50. Electronic applications accepted. *Expenses:* $2,180 per credit. *Financial support:* In 2017–18, 191 students received support, including 21 fellowships with full and partial tuition reimbursements available (averaging $19,453 per year), 45 teaching assistantships with full and partial tuition reimbursements available (averaging $9,505 per year); career-related internships or fieldwork, Federal Work-Study, scholarships/grants, and tuition waivers (full and partial) also available. Support available to part-time students. Financial award application deadline: 2/1; financial award applicants required to submit FAFSA. *Unit head:* Dr. William Milberg, Dean, The New School for Social Research, 212-229-5777, E-mail: milbergw@newschool.edu. *Application contact:* Dana Messinger, Director of Graduate Admission, 212-229-5150 Ext. 2300, E-mail: socialresearchadmit@newschool.edu.

New York University, Graduate School of Arts and Science, Department of Psychology, New York, NY 10012-1019. Offers cognition and perception (PhD); general psychology (MA); industrial/organizational psychology (MA); psychotherapy and psychoanalysis (Advanced Certificate); social psychology (PhD). *Program availability:* Part-time. *Students:* Average age 31. 874 applicants, 46% accepted, 153 enrolled. In 2017, 102 master's, 9 doctorates, 10 other advanced degrees awarded. Terminal master's awarded for partial completion of doctoral program. *Degree requirements:* For master's, comprehensive exam, thesis or alternative; for doctorate, thesis/dissertation. *Entrance requirements:* For master's and doctorate, GRE General Test. Additional exam requirements/recommendations for international students: Required—TOEFL. *Application deadline:* For fall admission, 12/12 for domestic and international students. Application fee: $100. *Expenses:* Tuition: full-time $41,352; part-time $19,968 per year. *Required fees:* $2496; $1628 per unit. $814 per term. Tuition and fees vary according to course load and program. *Financial support:* Fellowships, research assistantships, teaching assistantships, career-related internships or fieldwork, Federal Work-Study, institutionally sponsored loans, scholarships/grants, traineeships, health care benefits, and unspecified assistantships available. Financial award application deadline: 12/12; financial award applicants required to submit FAFSA. *Faculty research:* Vision, memory, social cognition, social and cognitive development, relationships. *Unit head:* Gabriele Oettingen, Director of Graduate Studies, PhD Program, 212-998-7900, Fax: 212-995-4018, E-mail: psychq@psych.nyu.edu. *Application contact:* Adrienne Gans, Director of Graduate Studies, MA Program, 212-998-7900, Fax: 212-995-4018, E-mail: psychq@psych.nyu.edu. Website: http://www.psych.nyu.edu/

North Dakota State University, College of Graduate and Interdisciplinary Studies, College of Science and Mathematics, Department of Psychology, Fargo, ND 58102.

Offers clinical psychology (MS); health and social psychology (PhD); psychological clinical science (PhD); psychology (MS); visual and cognitive neuroscience (PhD). *Degree requirements:* For master's, thesis; for doctorate, thesis/dissertation. *Entrance requirements:* For master's and doctorate, GRE General Test, GRE Subject Test. Additional exam requirements/recommendations for international students: Required—TOEFL (minimum score 525 paper-based; 71 iBT). Electronic applications accepted. *Faculty research:* Cognition science, neuropsychology, group behavior, applied behavior analysis, behavior therapy.

Northwestern University, The Graduate School, Judd A. and Marjorie Weinberg College of Arts and Sciences, Department of Psychology, Evanston, IL 60208. Offers brain, behavior and cognition (PhD); clinical psychology (PhD); cognitive psychology (PhD); personality psychology (PhD); social psychology (PhD); JD/PhD. Admissions and degrees offered through The Graduate School. *Accreditation:* APA (one or more programs are accredited). *Program availability:* Part-time. *Degree requirements:* For doctorate, thesis/dissertation. *Entrance requirements:* For doctorate, GRE General Test, GRE Subject Test. Additional exam requirements/recommendations for international students: Required—TOEFL. Electronic applications accepted. *Faculty research:* Memory and higher order cognition, anxiety and depression, effectiveness of psychotherapy, social cognition, molecular basis of memory.

The Ohio State University, Graduate School, College of Arts and Sciences, Division of Social and Behavioral Sciences, Department of Psychology, Columbus, OH 43210. Offers behavioral neuroscience (PhD); clinical psychology (PhD); cognitive psychology (PhD); developmental psychology (PhD); intellectual and developmental disabilities psychology (PhD); quantitative psychology (PhD); social psychology (PhD). *Accreditation:* APA. *Faculty:* 52. *Students:* 144 full-time (86 women); includes 18 minority (8 Asian, non-Hispanic/Latino; 10 Hispanic/Latino), 28 international. Average age 26. In 2017, 21 doctorates awarded. *Entrance requirements:* For doctorate, GRE General Test. Additional exam requirements/recommendations for international students: Required—TOEFL (minimum score 600 paper-based; 100 iBT); Recommended—IELTS (minimum score 8). *Application deadline:* For fall admission, 12/1 for domestic and international students. Applications are processed on a rolling basis. Application fee: $60 ($70 for international students). Electronic applications accepted. *Financial support:* Fellowships, research assistantships, and teaching assistantships available. *Unit head:* Dr. John Bruno, Chair, 614-292-3038, E-mail: bruno.1@osu.edu. *Application contact:* Graduate and Professional Admissions, 614-292-9444, Fax: 614-292-3895, E-mail: gpadmissions@osu.edu.
Website: http://psychology.osu.edu/

Oregon State University, College of Liberal Arts, Program in Psychology, Corvallis, OR 97331. Offers applied cognition (MS, PhD); engineering psychology (MS, PhD); health psychology (MS, PhD). *Application deadline:* For fall admission, 12/15 for domestic and international students. Application fee: $75 ($85 for international students). *Unit head:* Jason McCarley, Graduate Education Chair, E-mail: jason.mccarley@oregonstate.edu. *Application contact:* Aurora Sherman, Associate Professor and Graduate Education Chair, 541-737-1361, E-mail: aurora.sherman@oregonstate.edu.
Website: http://liberalarts.oregonstate.edu/school-psychological-science/psychology/graduate-psychology

Purdue University, Graduate School, College of Health and Human Sciences, Department of Psychological Sciences, West Lafayette, IN 47907. Offers behavioral neuroscience (PhD); clinical psychology (PhD); cognitive psychology (PhD); industrial/organizational psychology (PhD); mathematical and computational cognitive science (PhD). *Accreditation:* APA. *Faculty:* 46 full-time (18 women), 1 part-time/adjunct (0 women). *Students:* 64 full-time (41 women), 4 part-time (3 women); includes 13 minority (1 Black or African American, non-Hispanic/Latino; 4 Asian, non-Hispanic/Latino; 6 Hispanic/Latino; 2 Two or more races, non-Hispanic/Latino), 12 international. Average age 27. 288 applicants, 8% accepted, 16 enrolled. In 2017, 9 doctorates awarded. Terminal master's awarded for partial completion of doctoral program. *Degree requirements:* For doctorate, thesis/dissertation. *Entrance requirements:* For doctorate, GRE General Test, minimum undergraduate GPA of 3.0 or equivalent. Additional exam requirements/recommendations for international students: Required—TOEFL (minimum score 550 paper-based; 77 iBT); Recommended—TWE. *Application deadline:* For fall admission, 12/3 for domestic and international students. Applications are processed on a rolling basis. Application fee: $60 ($75 for international students). Electronic applications accepted. *Financial support:* Fellowships with partial tuition reimbursements, research assistantships with partial tuition reimbursements, teaching assistantships with partial tuition reimbursements, and career-related internships or fieldwork available. Support available to part-time students. Financial award applicants required to submit FAFSA. *Faculty research:* Career development of women in science, development of friendships during childhood and adolescence, social competence, human information processing. *Unit head:* Dr. David Rollock, Head, 765-494-6061, E-mail: rollock@purdue.edu. *Application contact:* Nancy A. O'Brien, Graduate Contact, 765-494-6067, E-mail: nobrien@psych.pardue.edu.
Website: http://www.psych.purdue.edu/

Queen's University at Kingston, School of Graduate Studies, Faculty of Arts and Sciences, Department of Psychology, Kingston, ON K7L 3N6, Canada. Offers brain behavior and cognitive science (MA, PhD); clinical psychology (MA, PhD); developmental psychology (MA, PhD); social personality psychology (MA, PhD). *Degree requirements:* For master's, thesis; for doctorate, comprehensive exam, thesis/dissertation. *Entrance requirements:* For master's and doctorate, GRE General Test. Additional exam requirements/recommendations for international students: Required—TOEFL. *Faculty research:* Human development, social, personality, behavioral neuroscience, forensic.

Rensselaer Polytechnic Institute, Graduate School, School of Humanities, Arts, and Social Sciences, Program in Cognitive Science, Troy, NY 12180-3590. Offers PhD. *Faculty:* 21 full-time (5 women), 2 part-time/adjunct (0 women). *Students:* 13 full-time (5 women), 2 part-time (0 women); includes 3 minority (1 Asian, non-Hispanic/Latino; 1 Hispanic/Latino; 1 Two or more races, non-Hispanic/Latino), 5 international. Average age 29. 13 applicants, 46% accepted, 3 enrolled. In 2017, 1 doctorate awarded. *Degree requirements:* For doctorate, thesis/dissertation. *Entrance requirements:* For doctorate, GRE. Additional exam requirements/recommendations for international students: Required—TOEFL (minimum score 600 paper-based; 100 iBT), IELTS (minimum score 7), PTE (minimum score 68). *Application deadline:* For fall admission, 1/1 priority date for domestic and international students. Applications are processed on a rolling basis. Application fee: $75. Electronic applications accepted. *Expenses: Tuition:* Full-time $52,550; part-time $2125 per credit hour. *Required fees:* $2890. *Financial support:* In 2017–18, research assistantships (averaging $23,000 per year), teaching assistantships (averaging $23,000 per year) were awarded; fellowships also available. Financial award application deadline: 1/1. *Faculty research:* Artificial intelligence, cognitive engineering, computational cognitive modeling, computational linguistics, human factors, perception and action, social interaction, social simulation and multi-agent modeling, theoretical neuroscience, vision science. *Unit head:* Dr. Wayne Gray, Graduate Program Director, 518-276-3315, E-mail: grayw@rpi.edu.
Website: http://www.cogsci.rpi.edu/pl/phd-cognitive-science

Rice University, Graduate Programs, School of Social Sciences, Department of Psychology, Houston, TX 77251-1892. Offers cognitive sciences (MA, PhD); industrial-organizational/social psychology (MA, PhD); psychology (MA, PhD). Terminal master's awarded for partial completion of doctoral program. *Degree requirements:* For master's, thesis; for doctorate, thesis/dissertation. *Entrance requirements:* For doctorate, GRE General Test, minimum GPA of 3.0. Additional exam requirements/recommendations for international students: Required—TOEFL. Electronic applications accepted. *Faculty research:* Cognitive, cognitive neuropsychology, human factors, human-computer interaction, industrial-organizational psychology.

Rochester Institute of Technology, Graduate Enrollment Services, College of Liberal Arts, Psychology Department, Advanced Certificate Program in Engineering Psychology, Rochester, NY 14623. Offers Advanced Certificate. *Program availability:* Part-time. *Students:* 1 (woman) full-time. Average age 22. 2 applicants, 100% accepted, 1 enrolled. In 2017, 1 Advanced Certificate awarded. *Entrance requirements:* For degree, minimum GPA of 3.0 (recommended). Additional exam requirements/recommendations for international students: Required—TOEFL (minimum score 550 paper-based; 79 iBT), IELTS (minimum score 6.5), PTE (minimum score 58). *Application deadline:* For fall admission, 2/15 priority date for domestic and international students; for spring admission, 12/15 priority date for domestic and international students. Applications are processed on a rolling basis. Application fee: $65. Electronic applications accepted. *Expenses:* $1,815 per credit hour. *Financial support:* In 2017–18, 1 student received support. Scholarships/grants available. Support available to part-time students. Financial award applicants required to submit FAFSA. *Unit head:* Dr. Suzanne Bamonto, Graduate Program Director, 585-475-2765, E-mail: sbggsp@rit.edu. *Application contact:* Diane Ellison, Senior Associate Vice President, Graduate Enrollment Services, 585-475-2229, Fax: 585-475-7164, E-mail: gradinfo@rit.edu.
Website: http://www.rit.edu/cla/psychology/advanced-certificates/engineering-psychology

Rutgers University–Newark, Graduate School, Program in Psychology, Newark, NJ 07102. Offers cognitive neuroscience (PhD); cognitive science (PhD); perception (PhD); psychobiology (PhD); social cognition (PhD). *Degree requirements:* For doctorate, comprehensive exam, thesis/dissertation. *Entrance requirements:* For doctorate, GRE General Test, GRE Subject Test, minimum undergraduate B average. Electronic applications accepted. *Faculty research:* Visual perception (luminance, motion), neuroendocrine mechanisms in behavior (reproduction, pain), attachment theory, connectionist modeling of cognition.

Rutgers University–New Brunswick, Graduate School-New Brunswick, Program in Psychology, Piscataway, NJ 08854-8097. Offers behavioral neuroscience (PhD); clinical psychology (PhD); cognitive psychology (PhD); interdisciplinary health psychology (PhD); social psychology (PhD). *Accreditation:* APA. *Degree requirements:* For doctorate, comprehensive exam, thesis/dissertation. *Entrance requirements:* For doctorate, GRE General Test, 3 letters of recommendation. Additional exam requirements/recommendations for international students: Required—TOEFL (minimum score 577 paper-based). Electronic applications accepted. *Faculty research:* Learning and memory, behavioral ecology, hormones and behavior, psychopharmacology, anxiety disorders.

Stony Brook University, State University of New York, Graduate School, College of Arts and Sciences, Department of Psychology, Program in Cognitive Psychology, Stony Brook, NY 11794. Offers PhD. *Students:* 16 full-time (9 women); includes 3 minority (1 Asian, non-Hispanic/Latino; 1 Hispanic/Latino; 1 Two or more races, non-Hispanic/Latino), 4 international. Average age 28. 33 applicants, 3% accepted. In 2017, 1 doctorate awarded. *Degree requirements:* For doctorate, thesis/dissertation. *Entrance requirements:* For doctorate, GRE General Test, GRE Subject Test. Additional exam requirements/recommendations for international students: Required—TOEFL (minimum score 90 iBT). *Application deadline:* For fall admission, 1/15 for domestic students; for spring admission, 10/1 for domestic students. Application fee: $100. Electronic applications accepted. *Expenses:* Contact institution. *Financial support:* In 2017–18, 1 fellowship, 4 research assistantships, 7 teaching assistantships were awarded. *Unit head:* Dr. Sheri Levy, Chair, 631-632-4355, E-mail: sheri.levy@stonybrook.edu. *Application contact:* Marilynn Wollmuth, Graduate Director, 631-632-7855, Fax: 631-632-7876, E-mail: marilyn.wollmuth@stonybrook.edu.
Website: http://www.stonybrook.edu/commcms/psychology/cognitive/overview.html

Syracuse University, College of Arts and Sciences, Department of Psychology, Syracuse, NY 13244. Offers clinical psychology (PhD); cognition, brain, and behavior (PhD); school psychology (PhD); social psychology (PhD). *Accreditation:* APA. In 2017, 1 doctorate awarded. Terminal master's awarded for partial completion of doctoral program. *Degree requirements:* For doctorate, comprehensive exam, thesis/dissertation. *Entrance requirements:* For doctorate, GRE General Test, GRE Subject Test, resume, personal statement, three letters of recommendation. Additional exam requirements/recommendations for international students: Required—TOEFL (minimum score 100 iBT). *Application deadline:* For fall admission, 12/1 priority date for domestic and international students. Application fee: $75. Electronic applications accepted. *Financial support:* Fellowships with full tuition reimbursements, research assistantships with tuition reimbursements, teaching assistantships with tuition reimbursements, and scholarships/grants available. Financial award application deadline: 1/1. *Faculty research:* Clinical psychology; cognition, brain, and behavior; school psychology; social psychology. *Unit head:* Dr. Amy Criss, Professor and Department Chair, Psychology, 315-443-1210, E-mail: acriss@syr.edu. *Application contact:* Alecia Zema, Curriculum Coordinator, 315-443-2760, E-mail: azema@syr.edu.
Website: http://psychology.syr.edu/graduate/overview.html

Texas Christian University, College of Science and Engineering, Department of Psychology, Fort Worth, TX 76129. Offers developmental trauma (MS); experimental psychology (PhD), including cognition/developmental, learning, neuroscience, social. *Faculty:* 13 full-time (6 women), 2 part-time/adjunct (both women). *Students:* 32 full-time (25 women); includes 5 minority (1 Asian, non-Hispanic/Latino; 2 Hispanic/Latino; 2 Two or more races, non-Hispanic/Latino), 2 international. Average age 26. 50 applicants, 34% accepted, 16 enrolled. In 2017, 8 master's, 2 doctorates awarded. Terminal master's awarded for partial completion of doctoral program. *Degree requirements:* For master's, thesis; for doctorate, thesis/dissertation. *Entrance requirements:* For doctorate, GRE General Test. Additional exam requirements/recommendations for international students: Required—TOEFL. *Application deadline:* For fall admission, 2/1 for domestic and international students. Application fee: $60 ($0 for international students). Electronic applications accepted. *Expenses:* Contact institution. *Financial support:* In 2017–18, 23 students received support, including 23 teaching assistantships with full tuition reimbursements available (averaging $19,750 per year); scholarships/grants also available. Financial award application deadline: 2/1; financial award applicants required to submit FAFSA. *Faculty research:* Neuroscience, human and animal learning, cognition, development, experimental social psychology. *Unit head:* Dr. Mauricio R. Papini, Chair, 817-257-7410, Fax: 817-257-7681, E-mail: m.papini@tcu.edu. *Application contact:* Cindy Hayes, Administrative Assistant, 817-257-7410, Fax: 817-257-7681, E-mail: c.hayes@tcu.edu.
Website: https://psychology.tcu.edu/current-graduate-students/

Tufts University, Graduate School of Arts and Sciences, Department of Psychology, Medford, MA 02155. Offers cognitive science (PhD); psychology (MS, PhD). *Students:* 39 full-time (30 women); includes 7 minority (1 Black or African American, non-Hispanic/Latino; 4 Asian, non-Hispanic/Latino; 2 Hispanic/Latino), 4 international. Average age 27. 154 applicants, 8% accepted, 7 enrolled. In 2017, 4 master's, 8 doctorates awarded. Terminal master's awarded for partial completion of doctoral program. *Degree requirements:* For master's, thesis; for doctorate, thesis/dissertation. *Entrance requirements:* For master's and doctorate, GRE General Test, GRE Subject Test. Additional exam requirements/recommendations for international students: Required—TOEFL (minimum score 550 paper-based; 80 iBT), IELTS (minimum score 6.5). *Application deadline:* For fall admission, 12/15 for domestic and international students. Applications are processed on a rolling basis. Application fee: $85. Electronic applications accepted. *Expenses:* Contact institution. *Financial support:* Fellowships, research assistantships, teaching assistantships, Federal Work-Study, scholarships/grants, tuition waivers (full and partial), and unspecified assistantships available. Support available to part-time students. Financial award application deadline: 1/15. *Unit head:* Dr. Ayanna Thomas, Graduate Program Director, 617-627-4559. *Application contact:* Office of Graduate Admissions, 617-627-3395, E-mail: gradadmissions@tufts.edu.
Website: http://ase.tufts.edu/psychology

Tufts University, School of Engineering, Department of Computer Science, Medford, MA 02155. Offers bioengineering (MS), including bioinformatics; cognitive science/computer science (PhD); computer science (MS, PhD); soft material robotics (PhD). *Program availability:* Part-time. *Faculty:* 20 full-time, 6 part-time/adjunct. *Students:* 89 full-time (24 women), 36 part-time (15 women); includes 16 minority (1 Black or African American, non-Hispanic/Latino; 10 Asian, non-Hispanic/Latino; 3 Hispanic/Latino; 2 Two or more races, non-Hispanic/Latino), 41 international. Average age 28. 218 applicants, 24% accepted, 23 enrolled. In 2017, 18 master's, 4 doctorates awarded. Terminal master's awarded for partial completion of doctoral program. *Entrance requirements:* For master's and doctorate, GRE General Test. Additional exam requirements/recommendations for international students: Required—TOEFL (minimum score 550 paper-based; 80 iBT), IELTS (minimum score 6.5). *Application deadline:* For fall admission, 1/15 for domestic and international students; for spring admission, 9/15 for domestic and international students. Applications are processed on a rolling basis. Application fee: $85. Electronic applications accepted. *Expenses: Tuition:* Full-time $49,892. *Required fees:* $874. Full-time tuition and fees vary according to degree level, program and student level. Part-time tuition and fees vary according to course load. *Financial support:* Fellowships with full tuition reimbursements, research assistantships with full and partial tuition reimbursements, teaching assistantships with full and partial tuition reimbursements, Federal Work-Study, scholarships/grants, tuition waivers (partial), and unspecified assistantships available. Financial award application deadline: 4/15; financial award applicants required to submit FAFSA. *Faculty research:* Computational biology, computational geometry, and computational systems biology; cognitive sciences, human-computer interaction, and human-robotic interaction; visualization and graphics, educational technologies; machine learning and data mining; programming languages and systems. *Unit head:* Dr. Samuel Guyer, Graduate Program Chair. *Application contact:* Office of Graduate Admissions, 617-623-3395, E-mail: gradadmissions@cs.tufts.edu.
Website: https://engineering.tufts.edu/cs/

University at Albany, State University of New York, College of Arts and Sciences, Department of Psychology, Albany, NY 12222-0001. Offers behavioral neuroscience (PhD); clinical psychology (PhD); cognitive psychology (PhD); industrial/organizational psychology (MA, PhD); social-personality psychology (PhD). *Accreditation:* APA (one or more programs are accredited). *Faculty:* 31 full-time (13 women). *Students:* 63 full-time (42 women), 49 part-time (33 women); includes 25 minority (4 Black or African American, non-Hispanic/Latino; 8 Asian, non-Hispanic/Latino; 4 Hispanic/Latino; 9 Two or more races, non-Hispanic/Latino), 11 international. 295 applicants, 14% accepted, 28 enrolled. In 2017, 13 master's, 5 doctorates awarded. *Degree requirements:* For doctorate, thesis/dissertation. *Entrance requirements:* For doctorate, GRE General Test, GRE Subject Test. Additional exam requirements/recommendations for international students: Required—TOEFL (minimum score 550 paper-based). *Application deadline:* For fall admission, 1/15 for domestic and international students. Application fee: $75. Electronic applications accepted. *Expenses:* Tuition, state resident: full-time $10,870; part-time $453 per credit hour. Tuition, nonresident: full-time $22,210; part-time $925 per credit hour. *Required fees:* $84.68 per credit hour. $508.06 per semester. Part-time tuition and fees vary according to course load and program. *Financial support:* Fellowships, research assistantships, teaching assistantships, and career-related internships or fieldwork available. Financial award application deadline: 2/1. *Unit head:* Christine K. Wagner, Chair, 518-442-4820, Fax: 518-442-4867, E-mail: cwagner@albany.edu. *Application contact:* Michael DeRensis, Director, Graduate Admissions, 518-442-3980, Fax: 518-442-3922, E-mail: graduate@albany.edu.
Website: http://www.albany.edu/psychology/

The University of British Columbia, Faculty of Arts and Faculty of Graduate Studies, Department of Psychology, Vancouver, BC V6T 1Z4, Canada. Offers behavioral neuroscience (MA, PhD); clinical psychology (MA, PhD); cognitive science (MA, PhD); developmental psychology (MA, PhD); health psychology (MA, PhD); quantitative methods (MA, PhD); social/personality psychology (MA, PhD). *Accreditation:* APA (one or more programs are accredited). Terminal master's awarded for partial completion of doctoral program. *Degree requirements:* For master's, thesis; for doctorate, comprehensive exam, thesis/dissertation. *Entrance requirements:* For master's and doctorate, GRE General Test. Additional exam requirements/recommendations for international students: Required—TOEFL. Electronic applications accepted. *Expenses:* Contact institution. *Faculty research:* Clinical, developmental, social/personality, cognition, behavioral neuroscience.

University of California, Merced, Graduate Division, School of Social Sciences, Humanities and Arts, Merced, CA 95343. Offers cognitive and information sciences (PhD); interdisciplinary humanities (MA, PhD); psychological sciences (MA, PhD); social sciences (MA, PhD); sociology (MA, PhD). *Faculty:* 101 full-time (49 women), 3 part-time/adjunct (1 woman). *Students:* 197 full-time (131 women), 2 part-time (1 woman); includes 86 minority (7 Black or African American, non-Hispanic/Latino; 17 Asian, non-Hispanic/Latino; 55 Hispanic/Latino; 1 Native Hawaiian or other Pacific Islander, non-Hispanic/Latino; 6 Two or more races, non-Hispanic/Latino), 33 international. Average age 31. 190 applicants, 41% accepted, 49 enrolled. In 2017, 7 master's, 10 doctorates awarded. Terminal master's awarded for partial completion of doctoral program. *Degree requirements:* For master's, variable foreign language requirement, comprehensive exam, thesis or alternative; for doctorate, variable foreign language requirement, comprehensive exam, thesis/dissertation. *Entrance requirements:* For master's and doctorate, GRE. Additional exam requirements/recommendations for international students: Required—TOEFL (minimum score 550 paper-based; 80 iBT); Recommended—IELTS (minimum score 7). *Application deadline:* For fall admission, 1/15 for domestic and international students. Application fee: $90 ($110 for international students). Electronic applications accepted. *Expenses:* Tuition, state resident: full-time $11,502; part-time $5751 per semester. Tuition, nonresident: full-time $26,604; part-time $13,302 per semester. *Required fees:* $564 per semester. *Financial support:* In

2017–18, 167 students received support, including 17 fellowships with full tuition reimbursements available (averaging $23,250 per year), 13 research assistantships with full tuition reimbursements available (averaging $15,387 per year), 162 teaching assistantships with full tuition reimbursements available (averaging $16,103 per year); scholarships/grants, traineeships, and health care benefits also available. Financial award application deadline: 1/15. *Faculty research:* Social inequality, critical race and ethnic studies, public health and health sciences, cognitive science and language acquisition, political institutions, literature, cultural studies, anthropology, art history, ethnomusicology, history. *Total annual research expenditures:* $1.2 million. *Unit head:* Dr. Jill Robbins, Dean, 209-228-7843, E-mail: jillrobbins@ucmerced.edu. *Application contact:* Tsu Ya, Director of Admissions and Academic Services, 209-228-4521, Fax: 209-228-6906, E-mail: tya@ucmerced.edu.

University of California, San Diego, Graduate Division, Department of Cognitive Science, La Jolla, CA 92093. Offers cognitive science (PhD). *Students:* 46 full-time (22 women). 146 applicants, 21% accepted, 12 enrolled. In 2017, 9 doctorates awarded. *Degree requirements:* For doctorate, one foreign language, thesis/dissertation, 1-quarter teaching assistantship for each academic year in residence. *Entrance requirements:* For doctorate, GRE General Test, minimum GPA of 3.0, letters of recommendation, statement of purpose. Additional exam requirements/recommendations for international students: Required—TOEFL (minimum score 550 paper-based; 80 iBT), IELTS (minimum score 7), PTE. *Application deadline:* For fall admission, 3/6 for domestic students. Application fee: $105 ($125 for international students). Electronic applications accepted. *Financial support:* Fellowships, research assistantships, teaching assistantships, scholarships/grants, and unspecified assistantships available. Financial award applicants required to submit FAFSA. *Faculty research:* Normal development of spatial analytic processing, flexible problem solving, specific language impairment, empirical analysis of change in scientific culture, co-evolutionary analysis of drug resistance in HIV. *Unit head:* Marta Kutas, Chair, 858-534-7141, E-mail: mkutas@ucsd.edu. *Application contact:* Oura Neak, Graduate Coordinator, 858-534-7141, E-mail: gradinfo@cogsci.ucsd.edu.
Website: http://www.cogsci.ucsd.edu

University of California, Santa Barbara, Graduate Division, College of Engineering, Department of Computer Science, Santa Barbara, CA 93106-5110. Offers computer science (MS, PhD), including cognitive science (PhD), computational science and engineering (PhD), technology and society (PhD). Terminal master's awarded for partial completion of doctoral program. *Degree requirements:* For master's, comprehensive exam (for some programs), thesis (for some programs); project (for some programs); for doctorate, thesis/dissertation. *Entrance requirements:* For master's and doctorate, GRE. Additional exam requirements/recommendations for international students: Required—TOEFL (minimum score 600 paper-based; 100 iBT), IELTS (minimum score 7). Electronic applications accepted. *Faculty research:* Algorithms and theory, computational science and engineering, computer architecture, database and information systems, machine learning and data mining, networking, operating systems and distributed systems, programming languages and software engineering, security and cryptography, social computing, visual computing and interaction.

University of California, Santa Barbara, Graduate Division, College of Letters and Sciences, Division of Humanities and Fine Arts, Department of Religious Studies, Santa Barbara, CA 93106-3130. Offers ancient Mediterranean studies (PhD); cognitive science (PhD); European medieval studies (PhD); feminist studies (PhD); global studies (PhD); religious studies (MA, PhD); translation studies (PhD); MA/PhD. Terminal master's awarded for partial completion of doctoral program. *Degree requirements:* For master's, one foreign language, comprehensive exam (for some programs), thesis (for some programs); for doctorate, 2 foreign languages, thesis/dissertation, methodology. *Entrance requirements:* For master's and doctorate, GRE General Test. Additional exam requirements/recommendations for international students: Required—TOEFL (minimum score 550 paper-based; 80 iBT), IELTS (minimum score 7). Electronic applications accepted. *Faculty research:* Area studies; religious traditions; theory and method in the study of religion; religion, culture, and politics; spirituality and religious experience.

University of California, Santa Barbara, Graduate Division, College of Letters and Sciences, Division of Mathematics, Life, and Physical Sciences, Department of Geography, Santa Barbara, CA 93106-4060. Offers cognitive science (PhD); geography (MA, PhD); global studies (PhD); quantitative methods in the social sciences (PhD); technology and society (PhD); transportation (PhD); MA/PhD. Terminal master's awarded for partial completion of doctoral program. *Degree requirements:* For master's, comprehensive exam (for some programs), thesis or alternative; for doctorate, comprehensive exam, thesis/dissertation, 1 quarter of teaching assistantship. *Entrance requirements:* For master's and doctorate, GRE (minimum combined verbal and quantitative scores above 1100 in old scoring system or 301 in new scoring system). Additional exam requirements/recommendations for international students: Required—TOEFL (minimum score 550 paper-based; 80 iBT), IELTS (minimum score 7). Electronic applications accepted. *Faculty research:* Earth system science; human environment relations; modeling, measurement, and computation.

University of California, Santa Barbara, Graduate Division, College of Letters and Sciences, Division of Mathematics, Life, and Physical Sciences, Department of Psychological and Brain Sciences, Santa Barbara, CA 93106-9660. Offers cognitive science (PhD); psychology (PhD); quantitative methods in the social sciences (PhD); technology and society (PhD). Terminal master's awarded for partial completion of doctoral program. *Degree requirements:* For doctorate, comprehensive exam, thesis/dissertation, teaching assistant training, progress report, papers, mini-convention presentation, 1 quarter of student teaching or teaching assistant class with section lab, continued participation in research and weekly area meetings. *Entrance requirements:* For doctorate, GRE General Test. Additional exam requirements/recommendations for international students: Required—TOEFL (minimum score 550 paper-based; 80 iBT) or IELTS (minimum score 7). Electronic applications accepted. *Faculty research:* Social psychology; developmental and evolutionary psychology; neuroscience and behavior; cognition, perception and cognitive neuroscience.

University of California, Santa Barbara, Graduate Division, College of Letters and Sciences, Division of Social Sciences, Department of Communication, Santa Barbara, CA 93106-4020. Offers cognitive science (PhD); communication (PhD); feminist studies (PhD); language, interaction and social organization (PhD); quantitative methods in the social sciences (PhD); society and technology (PhD); MA/PhD. Terminal master's awarded for partial completion of doctoral program. *Degree requirements:* For doctorate, comprehensive exam, thesis/dissertation. *Entrance requirements:* For doctorate, GRE. Additional exam requirements/recommendations for international students: Required—TOEFL (minimum score 80 iBT), IELTS (minimum score 7). Electronic applications accepted. *Faculty research:* Interpersonal, intergroup, intercultural, organizational, health, media.

University of Central Florida, College of Sciences, Department of Psychology, Program in Human Factors and Cognitive Psychology, Orlando, FL 32816. Offers human factors and cognitive psychology (PhD). *Students:* 36 full-time (24 women), 1 part-time (0 women); includes 8 minority (2 Asian, non-Hispanic/Latino; 6 Hispanic/Latino), 1 international. Average age 29. 48 applicants, 21% accepted, 6 enrolled. In 2017, 7 doctorates awarded. *Degree requirements:* For doctorate, thesis/dissertation,

departmental candidacy exam. *Entrance requirements:* For doctorate, GRE General Test, degree in psychology or allied area, resume or curriculum vitae, personal statement, letters of recommendation, evidence of successful completion of undergraduate courses in statistics and general areas of experimental psychology. Additional exam requirements/recommendations for international students: Required—TOEFL. *Application deadline:* For fall admission, 1/1 for domestic students. Application fee: $30. Electronic applications accepted. *Expenses:* Tuition, state resident: part-time $288.16 per credit hour. Tuition, nonresident: part-time $1073.31 per credit hour. Tuition and fees vary according to program. *Financial support:* In 2017–18, 35 students received support, including 24 fellowships with partial tuition reimbursements available (averaging $6,830 per year), 12 research assistantships with partial tuition reimbursements available (averaging $11,973 per year), 22 teaching assistantships with partial tuition reimbursements available (averaging $15,644 per year); career-related internships or fieldwork, Federal Work-Study, institutionally sponsored loans, health care benefits, tuition waivers (partial), and unspecified assistantships also available. Financial award application deadline: 3/1; financial award applicants required to submit FAFSA. *Unit head:* Dr. James Szalma, Program Director, 407-823-0920, E-mail: james.szalma@ucf.edu. *Application contact:* Associate Director, Graduate Admissions, 407-823-2766, Fax: 407-823-6442, E-mail: gradadmissions@ucf.edu.
Website: http://psychology.cos.ucf.edu/graduate/

University of Connecticut, Graduate School, College of Liberal Arts and Sciences, Department of Psychology, Storrs, CT 06269. Offers behavioral neuroscience (PhD); biopsychology (PhD); clinical psychology (MA, PhD); cognition and instruction (PhD); developmental psychology (MA, PhD); ecological psychology (PhD); experimental psychology (PhD); general psychology (MA, PhD); industrial/organizational psychology (PhD); language and cognition (PhD); neuroscience (PhD); social psychology (MA, PhD). *Accreditation:* APA. Terminal master's awarded for partial completion of doctoral program. *Degree requirements:* For master's, comprehensive exam; for doctorate, thesis/dissertation. *Entrance requirements:* For master's and doctorate, GRE General Test, GRE Subject Test. Additional exam requirements/recommendations for international students: Required—TOEFL (minimum score 550 paper-based). Electronic applications accepted.

University of Connecticut, Graduate School, Neag School of Education, Department of Educational Psychology, Cognition, Instruction, and Learning Technology Program, Storrs, CT 06269. Offers MA, PhD. *Degree requirements:* For master's, comprehensive exam; for doctorate, thesis/dissertation. *Entrance requirements:* For doctorate, GRE General Test. Additional exam requirements/recommendations for international students: Required—TOEFL (minimum score 550 paper-based). Electronic applications accepted.

University of Delaware, College of Arts and Sciences, Department of Linguistics and Cognitive Science, Newark, DE 19716. Offers linguistics (PhD); linguistics and cognitive science (MA). *Degree requirements:* For doctorate, one foreign language, comprehensive exam, thesis/dissertation, publishable research papers. *Entrance requirements:* For master's, GRE General Test; for doctorate, GRE General Test, writing sample. Additional exam requirements/recommendations for international students: Required—TOEFL (minimum score 600 paper-based). Electronic applications accepted. *Faculty research:* East Asian, Austronesian and Romance languages, phonology, phonetics, syntax, cognitive science, semantics, psycholinguistics, language acquisition, endangered languages.

University of Delaware, College of Arts and Sciences, Department of Psychology, Newark, DE 19716. Offers behavioral neuroscience (PhD); clinical psychology (PhD); cognitive psychology (PhD); social psychology (PhD). *Accreditation:* APA. *Degree requirements:* For doctorate, thesis/dissertation. *Entrance requirements:* For doctorate, GRE General Test. Additional exam requirements/recommendations for international students: Required—TOEFL (minimum score 600 paper-based). Electronic applications accepted. *Faculty research:* Emotion development, neural and cognitive aspects of memory, neural control of feeding, intergroup relations, social cognition and communication.

University of Guelph, Graduate Studies, College of Social and Applied Human Sciences, Department of Psychology, Guelph, ON N1G 2W1, Canada. Offers applied social psychology (MA, PhD); clinical psychology: applied development emphasis (PhD); clinical psychology: applied developmental emphasis (MA); industrial/organizational psychology (MA, PhD); neuroscience and applied cognitive science (MA, PhD). *Degree requirements:* For master's, thesis; for doctorate, comprehensive exam, thesis/dissertation. *Entrance requirements:* For master's, GRE General Test, GRE Subject Test, minimum B+ average during previous 2 years of course work; for doctorate, GRE General Test, GRE Subject Test, minimum A- average. Additional exam requirements/recommendations for international students: Required—TOEFL (minimum score 89 iBT). Electronic applications accepted. *Faculty research:* Organizational psychology, reading comprehension and mathematical ability, drug addiction and relapse, gender issues and culture, memory, clinical psychology.

The University of Kansas, Graduate Studies, College of Liberal Arts and Sciences, Department of Psychology, Lawrence, KS 66045. Offers clinical psychology (MA, PhD); cognitive and brain sciences (MA, PhD); developmental psychology (MA, PhD); quantitative psychology (PhD); social psychology (MA, PhD). *Accreditation:* APA (one or more programs are accredited). *Program availability:* Part-time. *Students:* 92 full-time (63 women), 3 part-time (all women); includes 19 minority (7 Black or African American, non-Hispanic/Latino; 4 Asian, non-Hispanic/Latino; 4 Hispanic/Latino; 4 Two or more races, non-Hispanic/Latino), 10 international. Average age 28. 361 applicants, 7% accepted, 16 enrolled. In 2017, 9 master's, 17 doctorates awarded. Terminal master's awarded for partial completion of doctoral program. *Entrance requirements:* For doctorate, GRE General Test, three letters of recommendation, resume/curriculum vitae, statement of purpose/personal statement, writing sample. Additional exam requirements/recommendations for international students: Required—TOEFL. *Application deadline:* For fall admission, 12/1 for domestic and international students. Application fee: $65 ($85 for international students). Electronic applications accepted. *Financial support:* Fellowships, research assistantships, teaching assistantships, career-related internships or fieldwork, Federal Work-Study, scholarships/grants, health care benefits, and unspecified assistantships available. Financial award application deadline: 12/1; financial award applicants required to submit FAFSA. *Faculty research:* Origins, correlates and treatment of depression; health and emotion; concentration on topics related to prejudice, stereotyping, and intergroup relations; memory, cognitive development, language, perception, attention, aging; psychometric methods, item response theory, structural equation modeling. *Unit head:* Ruth Anne Atchley, Chair, 785-864-4131. *Application contact:* Graduate Officer, 785-864-4195, E-mail: psycgrad@ku.edu.
Website: http://www.psych.ku.edu/

University of Louisiana at Lafayette, College of Sciences, Institute of Cognitive Science, Lafayette, LA 70504. Offers PhD. *Degree requirements:* For doctorate, comprehensive exam, thesis/dissertation. *Entrance requirements:* For doctorate, GRE General Test, minimum GPA of 3.25. Additional exam requirements/recommendations for international students: Required—TOEFL (minimum score 550 paper-based). Electronic applications accepted. *Faculty research:* Computational models of cognition, comparative cognition, cognitive development, computational cognitive neuroscience, memory.

University of Louisville, Graduate School, College of Arts and Sciences, Department of Psychological and Brain Sciences, Louisville, KY 40292-0001. Offers clinical psychology (PhD); experimental psychology (PhD), including cognition and development, vision and hearing. *Accreditation:* APA. *Students:* 55 full-time (44 women), 1 (woman) part-time; includes 7 minority (1 Black or African American, non-Hispanic/Latino; 2 Asian, non-Hispanic/Latino; 2 Hispanic/Latino; 2 Two or more races, non-Hispanic/Latino), 4 international. Average age 29. 9 applicants, 78% accepted. In 2017, 1 doctorate awarded. *Degree requirements:* For doctorate, comprehensive exam, thesis/dissertation, internship (for clinical psychology). *Entrance requirements:* For doctorate, GRE General Test, GRE Subject Test. Additional exam requirements/recommendations for international students: Required—TOEFL. *Application deadline:* For fall and winter admission, 12/1 for domestic and international students. Application fee: $65. *Expenses:* Tuition, state resident: full-time $12,246; part-time $681 per credit hour. Tuition, nonresident: full-time $25,486; part-time $1417 per credit hour. *Required fees:* $196. Tuition and fees vary according to course load, program and reciprocity agreements. *Financial support:* In 2017–18, 8 fellowships with full tuition reimbursements (averaging $22,000 per year), 3 research assistantships with full tuition reimbursements (averaging $22,000 per year), 30 teaching assistantships with full tuition reimbursements (averaging $22,000 per year) were awarded; health care benefits and unspecified assistantships also available. Financial award application deadline: 12/1. *Faculty research:* Cognitive development, hearing/visual science, cognitive neuroscience/imaging, health psychology/mindfulness/stress and trauma, child/adult psychopathology, geropsychology. *Total annual research expenditures:* $923,340. *Unit head:* Dr. Suzanne Meeks, Chair, 502-852-6068, Fax: 502-852-8904, E-mail: smeeks@louisville.edu. *Application contact:* Maggie Leahy, Administrative Assistant, 502-852-4364, Fax: 502-852-8904, E-mail: maggie.leahy@louisville.edu.
Website: http://louisville.edu/psychology

University of Maryland, Baltimore County, The Graduate School, College of Natural and Mathematical Sciences, Department of Biological Sciences, Program in Neuroscience and Cognitive Sciences, Baltimore, MD 21250. Offers PhD. *Faculty:* 6 full-time (3 women). *Students:* 3 full-time (2 women); includes 2 minority (1 Black or African American, non-Hispanic/Latino; 1 Asian, non-Hispanic/Latino). Average age 24. 11 applicants, 27% accepted, 3 enrolled. *Degree requirements:* For doctorate, thesis/dissertation. *Entrance requirements:* For doctorate, GRE General Test, minimum GPA of 3.0. Additional exam requirements/recommendations for international students: Required—TOEFL (minimum score 80 iBT), IELTS (minimum score 6.5). *Application deadline:* For fall admission, 4/15 priority date for domestic and international students. Application fee: $50. Electronic applications accepted. *Expenses: Required fees:* $132. *Financial support:* In 2017–18, 3 students received support, including 1 research assistantship with full tuition reimbursement available (averaging $24,600 per year), 2 teaching assistantships with full tuition reimbursements available (averaging $23,518 per year); health care benefits and unspecified assistantships also available. *Faculty research:* Developmental biology and neural tube defects, vision science, olfactory systems, neurobiological adaptations of animals, conversion of light into a biological signal in vision. *Unit head:* Dr. Michelle Starz-Gaiano, Director, 410-455-2217, Fax: 410-455-3875, E-mail: biograd@umbc.edu. *Application contact:* Brandy Darcey, Graduate Program Coordinator, 410-455-3669, E-mail: bdarcey@umbc.edu.
Website: http://biology.umbc.edu

University of Maryland, College Park, Academic Affairs, College of Behavioral and Social Sciences, Program in Neurosciences and Cognitive Sciences, College Park, MD 20742. Offers PhD. *Degree requirements:* For doctorate, comprehensive exam, thesis/dissertation. *Entrance requirements:* For doctorate, GRE General Test, 3 letters of recommendation. Additional exam requirements/recommendations for international students: Required—TOEFL. Electronic applications accepted. *Faculty research:* Molecular neurobiology, cognition, neural and behavioral systems language, memory, human development.

University of Massachusetts Amherst, Graduate School, College of Natural Sciences, Department of Psychological and Brain Sciences, Amherst, MA 01003. Offers clinical psychology (MS, PhD); cognitive psychology (MS, PhD); developmental science (MS, PhD); psychology of peace and violence (MS, PhD); social psychology (MS, PhD). *Accreditation:* APA (one or more programs are accredited). Terminal master's awarded for partial completion of doctoral program. *Degree requirements:* For master's, thesis; for doctorate, comprehensive exam, thesis/dissertation. *Entrance requirements:* For master's and doctorate, GRE General Test, 3 letters of recommendation. Additional exam requirements/recommendations for international students: Required—TOEFL (minimum score 550 paper-based; 80 iBT), IELTS (minimum score 6.5). Electronic applications accepted.

University of Massachusetts Amherst, Graduate School, Interdisciplinary Programs, Program in Neuroscience and Behavior, Amherst, MA 01003. Offers animal behavior and learning (PhD); molecular and cellular neuroscience (PhD); neural and behavioral development (PhD); neuroendocrinology (PhD); neuroscience and behavior (MS); sensorimotor, cognitive, and computational neuroscience (PhD). Terminal master's awarded for partial completion of doctoral program. *Degree requirements:* For master's, thesis or alternative; for doctorate, comprehensive exam, thesis/dissertation. *Entrance requirements:* For master's, GRE General Test; for doctorate, GRE General Test; GRE Subject Test in psychology, biology, or mathematics (recommended). Additional exam requirements/recommendations for international students: Required—TOEFL (minimum score 550 paper-based; 80 iBT), IELTS (minimum score 6.5). Electronic applications accepted.

University of Massachusetts Boston, College of Liberal Arts, Program in Developmental and Brain Sciences, Boston, MA 02125-3393. Offers MA. *Students:* 11 full-time (9 women), 9 part-time (7 women); includes 5 minority (1 Black or African American, non-Hispanic/Latino; 1 Hispanic/Latino; 3 Two or more races, non-Hispanic/Latino), 5 international. Average age 28. 2 applicants. *Entrance requirements:* Additional exam requirements/recommendations for international students: Required—TOEFL; Recommended—IELTS. *Expenses:* Tuition, state resident: full-time $17,375. Tuition, nonresident: full-time $33,915. *Required fees:* $355. *Application contact:* Graduate Admissions Coordinator, 617-287-6400, Fax: 617-287-6236, E-mail: bos.gadm@dpc.umassp.edu.
Website: http://www.umb.edu/academics/cla/psychology/grad/dbs

University of Michigan, Rackham Graduate School, College of Literature, Science, and the Arts, Department of Psychology, Ann Arbor, MI 48109. Offers biopsychology (PhD); clinical science (PhD); cognition and cognitive neuroscience (PhD); developmental psychology (PhD); personality and social contexts (PhD); social psychology (PhD). *Accreditation:* APA. *Faculty:* 66 full-time (31 women), 28 part-time/adjunct (17 women). *Students:* 148 full-time (113 women); includes 61 minority (13 Black or African American, non-Hispanic/Latino; 1 American Indian or Alaska Native, non-Hispanic/Latino; 12 Asian, non-Hispanic/Latino; 28 Hispanic/Latino; 7 Two or more races, non-Hispanic/Latino), 24 international. Average age 27. 691 applicants, 7% accepted, 35 enrolled. In 2017, 34 doctorates awarded. Terminal master's awarded for partial completion of doctoral program. *Degree requirements:* For doctorate,

comprehensive exam, thesis/dissertation, oral defense of dissertation, preliminary exam. *Entrance requirements:* For doctorate, GRE General Test. Additional exam requirements/recommendations for international students: Required—TOEFL. *Application deadline:* For fall admission, 12/1 for domestic and international students. Application fee: $75 ($90 for international students). Electronic applications accepted. *Expenses:* $11,184 in-state, $22,578 out-of-state. *Financial support:* In 2017–18, 90 students received support, including 61 fellowships with full tuition reimbursements available (averaging $26,400 per year), 10 research assistantships with full tuition reimbursements available (averaging $26,400 per year), 89 teaching assistantships with full tuition reimbursements available (averaging $26,400 per year); career-related internships or fieldwork, traineeships, and health care benefits also available. Financial award application deadline: 4/15. *Unit head:* Prof. Patricia Reuter-Lorenz, Department Chair, 734-764-7429. *Application contact:* Sheri M. Circele, Psychology Student Academic Affairs, 734-764-2580, Fax: 734-764-3520, E-mail: psych.saa@umich.edu.
Website: http://www.lsa.umich.edu/psych/

University of Minnesota, Twin Cities Campus, Graduate School, College of Liberal Arts, Department of Psychology, Program in Cognitive and Biological Psychology, Minneapolis, MN 55455-0213. Offers PhD. *Degree requirements:* For doctorate, comprehensive exam, thesis/dissertation. *Entrance requirements:* For doctorate, GRE General Test, GRE Subject Test (recommended), 12 credits of upper-level psychology courses, including a course in statistics or psychological measurement. Additional exam requirements/recommendations for international students: Required—TOEFL (minimum score 550 paper-based; 79 iBT).

University of Nebraska–Lincoln, Graduate College, College of Arts and Sciences, Department of Psychology, Lincoln, NE 68588. Offers biopsychology (PhD); clinical psychology (PhD); cognitive psychology (PhD); developmental psychology (PhD); psychology (MA); social/personality psychology (PhD); JD/MA; JD/PhD. *Accreditation:* APA (one or more programs are accredited). *Degree requirements:* For master's, thesis optional; for doctorate, comprehensive exam, thesis/dissertation. *Entrance requirements:* For master's and doctorate, GRE General Test. Additional exam requirements/recommendations for international students: Required—TOEFL (minimum score 550 paper-based). Electronic applications accepted. *Faculty research:* Law and psychology, rural mental health, chronic mental illness, neuropsychology, child clinical psychology.

University of Nebraska–Lincoln, Graduate College, College of Education and Human Sciences, Department of Educational Psychology, Lincoln, NE 68588. Offers cognition, learning and development (MA); counseling psychology (MA); educational psychology (MA, Ed S); psychological studies in education (PhD), including cognition, learning and development, counseling psychology, quantitative, qualitative, and psychometric methods, school psychology; quantitative, qualitative, and psychometric methods (MA); school psychology (MA, Ed S). *Accreditation:* APA (one or more programs are accredited); NCATE. *Degree requirements:* For master's, thesis optional. *Entrance requirements:* For master's, GRE General Test. Additional exam requirements/recommendations for international students: Required—TOEFL (minimum score 500 paper-based). Electronic applications accepted. *Faculty research:* Measurement and assessment, metacognition, academic skills, child development, multicultural education and counseling.

University of Nevada, Reno, Graduate School, College of Liberal Arts, Department of Psychology, Program in Cognitive Brain Science, Reno, NV 89557. Offers MA, PhD. Terminal master's awarded for partial completion of doctoral program. *Degree requirements:* For master's, thesis optional; for doctorate, comprehensive exam, thesis/dissertation. *Entrance requirements:* For master's, GRE General Test, minimum GPA of 2.75; for doctorate, GRE General Test, minimum GPA of 3.0. Additional exam requirements/recommendations for international students: Required—TOEFL (minimum score 500 paper-based; 61 iBT), IELTS (minimum score 6). Electronic applications accepted. *Faculty research:* Comparative psychology, cognition, perception.

University of New Mexico, Graduate Studies, College of Arts and Sciences, Program in Psychology, Albuquerque, NM 87131-2039. Offers behavioral neuroscience (PhD); clinical psychology (PhD); cognitive neuroimaging (PhD); developmental psychology (PhD); evolution (PhD); health psychology (PhD); quantitative methodology (PhD). *Accreditation:* APA. *Students:* Average age 30. 227 applicants, 11% accepted, 16 enrolled. In 2017, 10 doctorates awarded. *Degree requirements:* For doctorate, comprehensive exam, thesis/dissertation. *Entrance requirements:* For doctorate, GRE General Test, GRE Subject Test (psychology), minimum GPA of 3.0. Additional exam requirements/recommendations for international students: Required—TOEFL (minimum score 550 paper-based; 79 iBT), IELTS (minimum score 6.5). *Application deadline:* For fall admission, 12/15 priority date for domestic and international students. Applications are processed on a rolling basis. Application fee: $50. Electronic applications accepted. *Financial support:* Fellowships, research assistantships, teaching assistantships, career-related internships or fieldwork, Federal Work-Study, institutionally sponsored loans, scholarships/grants, health care benefits, tuition waivers (partial), and unspecified assistantships available. Financial award application deadline: 3/1; financial award applicants required to submit FAFSA. *Faculty research:* Addiction, cognition, brain and behavior, developmental, evolutionary, functioning neuroimaging, health psychology, learning and memory, neuroscience. *Total annual research expenditures:* $727,970. *Unit head:* Dr. Jane Ellen Smith, Department Chair, 505-277-4121, Fax: 505-277-1394. *Application contact:* Rikk Murphy, Graduate Program Coordinator, 505-277-5009, Fax: 505-277-1394, E-mail: advising@unm.edu.
Website: http://psych.unm.edu

The University of North Carolina at Chapel Hill, Graduate School, College of Arts and Sciences, Department of Psychology, Chapel Hill, NC 27599-3270. Offers behavioral neuroscience psychology (PhD); clinical psychology (PhD); cognitive psychology (PhD); developmental psychology (PhD); quantitative psychology (PhD); social psychology (PhD). *Accreditation:* APA. *Degree requirements:* For doctorate, comprehensive exam, thesis/dissertation. *Entrance requirements:* For doctorate, GRE General Test, minimum GPA of 3.0. Additional exam requirements/recommendations for international students: Required—TOEFL (minimum score 550 paper-based; 79 iBT), IELTS (minimum score 7). Electronic applications accepted. *Faculty research:* Expressed emotion, cognitive development, social cognitive neuroscience, human memory personality.

The University of North Carolina at Charlotte, College of Liberal Arts and Sciences, Department of Psychology, Charlotte, NC 28223-0001. Offers cognitive science (Graduate Certificate); health psychology (PhD); industrial/organizational psychology (MA); psychology (MA). *Accreditation:* APA. *Program availability:* Part-time. *Faculty:* 29 full-time (19 women), 2 part-time/adjunct (both women). *Students:* 42 full-time (38 women), 32 part-time (21 women); includes 22 minority (11 Black or African American, non-Hispanic/Latino; 8 Hispanic/Latino; 3 Two or more races, non-Hispanic/Latino), 1 international. Average age 28. 196 applicants, 12% accepted, 16 enrolled. In 2017, 13 master's, 9 doctorates, 1 other advanced degree awarded. *Degree requirements:* For master's, thesis (for some programs); for doctorate, comprehensive exam, thesis/dissertation, internship (clinical health students only). *Entrance requirements:* For master's, GRE, GMAT, MAT; for doctorate, GRE, at least 18 hours of coursework in psychology including introductory psychology and research methods, undergraduate course in statistics, transcripts of all academic work attempted since high school including evidence of the completion of a bachelor's degree, at least three references, personal statement, resume or curriculum vitae; for Graduate Certificate, enrolled and in good standing in a graduate degree program at UNC Charlotte, or have minimum GPA of 3.0 for undergraduate courses. Additional exam requirements/recommendations for international students: Required—TOEFL (minimum score 523 paper-based, 70 iBT) or IELTS (6.5). *Application deadline:* For fall admission, 11/15 for domestic and international students. Applications are processed on a rolling basis. Application fee: $75. Electronic applications accepted. *Expenses:* Contact institution. *Financial support:* In 2017–18, 32 students received support, including 1 fellowship (averaging $47,476 per year), 13 research assistantships (averaging $14,282 per year), 18 teaching assistantships (averaging $14,405 per year); career-related internships or fieldwork, Federal Work-Study, institutionally sponsored loans, scholarships/grants, and unspecified assistantships also available. Support available to part-time students. Financial award application deadline: 3/1; financial award applicants required to submit FAFSA. *Total annual research expenditures:* $440,921. *Unit head:* Dr. Eric Heggestad, Interim Chair, 704-687-1315. *Application contact:* Kathy B. Giddings, Director of Graduate Admissions, 704-687-5503, Fax: 704-687-1668, E-mail: gradadm@uncc.edu.
Website: http://psych.uncc.edu

The University of North Carolina at Greensboro, Graduate School, College of Arts and Sciences, Department of Psychology, Greensboro, NC 27412-5001. Offers clinical psychology (MA, PhD); cognitive psychology (MA, PhD); developmental psychology (MA, PhD); social psychology (MA, PhD). *Accreditation:* APA (one or more programs are accredited). Terminal master's awarded for partial completion of doctoral program. *Degree requirements:* For master's, comprehensive exam, thesis; for doctorate, one foreign language, thesis/dissertation, preliminary exam. *Entrance requirements:* For master's and doctorate, GRE General Test. Additional exam requirements/recommendations for international students: Required—TOEFL. Electronic applications accepted. *Faculty research:* Sensory and perceptual determinants; evoked potential: disorders, deafness, and development.

University of Notre Dame, Graduate School, College of Arts and Letters, Division of Social Science, Department of Psychology, Notre Dame, IN 46556. Offers cognitive psychology (PhD); counseling psychology (PhD); developmental psychology (PhD); quantitative psychology (PhD). *Accreditation:* APA. *Degree requirements:* For doctorate, comprehensive exam, thesis/dissertation, candidacy exam. *Entrance requirements:* For doctorate, GRE General Test, GRE Subject Test (strongly recommended). Additional exam requirements/recommendations for international students: Required—TOEFL (minimum score 600 paper-based; 80 iBT). Electronic applications accepted. *Faculty research:* Cognitive and socio-emotional development, statistical methods and quantitative models applicable to psychology, interpersonal relations, life span development and developmental delay, childhood depression, structural equation and dynamical systems.

University of Oregon, Graduate School, College of Arts and Sciences, Department of Psychology, Eugene, OR 97403. Offers clinical psychology (PhD); cognitive psychology (MA, MS, PhD); developmental psychology (MA, MS, PhD); physiological psychology (MA, MS, PhD); psychology (MA, MS, PhD); social/personality psychology (MA, MS, PhD). *Accreditation:* APA (one or more programs are accredited). Terminal master's awarded for partial completion of doctoral program. *Degree requirements:* For doctorate, thesis/dissertation. *Entrance requirements:* For master's, GRE General Test, minimum GPA of 3.0; for doctorate, GRE General Test. Additional exam requirements/recommendations for international students: Required—TOEFL.

University of Rochester, School of Arts and Sciences, Department of Brain and Cognitive Sciences, Rochester, NY 14627-0268. Offers PhD. *Faculty:* 16 full-time (4 women). *Students:* 38 full-time (18 women); includes 8 minority (2 Asian, non-Hispanic/Latino; 4 Hispanic/Latino; 2 Two or more races, non-Hispanic/Latino), 13 international. Average age 27. 109 applicants, 12% accepted, 4 enrolled. In 2017, 5 doctorates awarded. Terminal master's awarded for partial completion of doctoral program. *Degree requirements:* For doctorate, thesis/dissertation, qualifying exam. *Entrance requirements:* For doctorate, GRE, two letters of recommendation, personal statement, official transcripts. Additional exam requirements/recommendations for international students: Required—TOEFL. *Application deadline:* For fall admission, 12/1 for domestic and international students. Application fee: $60. Electronic applications accepted. *Expenses:* $1,596 per credit hour. *Financial support:* In 2017–18, 312 students received support, including 2 fellowships (averaging $32,000 per year), 29 research assistantships (averaging $27,750 per year); scholarships/grants, traineeships, health care benefits, and tuition waivers (full) also available. Financial award application deadline: 12/1. *Faculty research:* Perception and action, language, development and learning, control and decision making, concepts and categories. *Total annual research expenditures:* $5.1 million. *Unit head:* Greg DeAngelis, Professor/Chair, 585-275-1844, E-mail: gdeangelis@ur.rochester.edu. *Application contact:* Kathleen Corser, Graduate Program Coordinator, 585-275-1844, E-mail: kcorser@ur.rochester.edu.
Website: http://www.sas.rochester.edu/bcs/graduate/index.html

University of Southern California, Graduate School, Dana and David Dornsife College of Letters, Arts and Sciences, Department of Psychology, Los Angeles, CA 90089. Offers brain and cognitive science (PhD); clinical science (PhD); developmental psychology (PhD); human behavior (MHB); quantitative methods (PhD); social psychology (PhD). *Accreditation:* APA. *Degree requirements:* For doctorate, comprehensive exam, thesis/dissertation, one-year internship (for clinical science students). *Entrance requirements:* For doctorate, GRE. Additional exam requirements/recommendations for international students: Recommended—TOEFL (minimum score 600 paper-based; 100 iBT). Electronic applications accepted. *Faculty research:* Affective neuroscience; children and families; vision, culture and ethnicity; intergroup relations; aggression and violence; language and reading development; substance abuse.

University of South Florida, College of Arts and Sciences, Department of Psychology, Tampa, FL 33620-9951. Offers psychology (PhD), including clinical psychology, cognition, neuroscience and social psychology, industrial-organizational psychology. *Accreditation:* APA. *Faculty:* 30 full-time (11 women). *Students:* 79 full-time (53 women), 11 part-time (8 women); includes 12 minority (1 Black or African American, non-Hispanic/Latino; 5 Asian, non-Hispanic/Latino; 4 Hispanic/Latino; 2 Two or more races, non-Hispanic/Latino), 7 international. Average age 28. 393 applicants, 3% accepted, 11 enrolled. In 2017, 17 doctorates awarded. *Degree requirements:* For doctorate, comprehensive exam, thesis/dissertation, internship. *Entrance requirements:* For doctorate, GRE General Test, minimum upper-division GPA of 3.4, three letters of recommendation, personal goals statement. Additional exam requirements/recommendations for international students: Required—TOEFL (minimum score 550 paper-based; 79 iBT) or IELTS (minimum score 6.5). *Application deadline:* For fall admission, 12/1 priority date for domestic and international students. Application fee: $30. Electronic applications accepted. *Expenses:* Contact institution. *Financial support:* In 2017–18, 43 students received support, including 18 research assistantships with tuition reimbursements available (averaging $14,727 per year), 57 teaching assistantships with tuition reimbursements available (averaging $14,543 per year); tuition waivers (partial) and unspecified assistantships also available. Financial award applicants required to submit FAFSA. *Faculty research:* Clinical, cognitive, neuroscience, social, and industrial/organizational. *Total annual research expenditures:*

$2 million. *Unit head:* Dr. Toru Shimizu, Chairperson, 813-974-0352, Fax: 813-974-4617, E-mail: shimizu@usf.edu. *Application contact:* Dr. Sandra Schneider, Professor and Graduate Program Director, 813-974-0928, E-mail: sandra@usf.edu.
Website: http://psychology.usf.edu/

The University of Texas at Dallas, School of Behavioral and Brain Sciences, Program in Cognition and Neuroscience, Richardson, TX 75080. Offers applied cognition and neuroscience (MS); cognition and neuroscience (PhD). *Program availability:* Part-time, evening/weekend. *Faculty:* 31 full-time (11 women), 1 part-time/adjunct (0 women). *Students:* 186 full-time (101 women), 31 part-time (21 women); includes 65 minority (10 Black or African American, non-Hispanic/Latino; 2 American Indian or Alaska Native, non-Hispanic/Latino; 26 Asian, non-Hispanic/Latino; 19 Hispanic/Latino; 8 Two or more races, non-Hispanic/Latino), 50 international. Average age 27. 193 applicants, 51% accepted, 70 enrolled. In 2017, 76 master's, 15 doctorates awarded. *Degree requirements:* For master's, internship; for doctorate, thesis/dissertation. *Entrance requirements:* For master's and doctorate, GRE General Test, minimum GPA of 3.0 in upper-level coursework in field. Additional exam requirements/recommendations for international students: Required—TOEFL (minimum score 550 paper-based). *Application deadline:* For fall admission, 7/15 for domestic students, 5/1 priority date for international students; for spring admission, 11/15 for domestic students, 9/1 priority date for international students. Applications are processed on a rolling basis. Application fee: $50 ($100 for international students). Electronic applications accepted. *Expenses:* Tuition, state resident: full-time $12,916; part-time $718 per credit hour. Tuition, nonresident: full-time $25,252; part-time $1403 per credit hour. *Financial support:* In 2017–18, 116 students received support, including 32 research assistantships with partial tuition reimbursements available (averaging $29,711 per year), 52 teaching assistantships with partial tuition reimbursements available (averaging $18,873 per year); fellowships, career-related internships or fieldwork, Federal Work-Study, institutionally sponsored loans, scholarships/grants, and unspecified assistantships also available. Support available to part-time students. Financial award application deadline: 4/30; financial award applicants required to submit FAFSA. *Faculty research:* Neural plasticity, neuroimaging, face recognition, cognitive and neurobiological mechanisms of human memory, treatment interventions for semantic memory retrieval problems. *Unit head:* Dr. Francesca Filbey, Area Head, 972-883-3311, Fax: 972-883-3491, E-mail: francesca.filbey@utdallas.edu.
Website: http://www.utdallas.edu/bbs/degrees/cn-degrees/

University of Washington, Graduate School, College of Arts and Sciences, Department of Psychology, Seattle, WA 98195. Offers animal behavior (PhD); applied child and adolescent psychology: prevention and treatment (MA); behavioral neuroscience (PhD); clinical psychology (PhD); cognition and perception (PhD); developmental psychology (PhD); quantitative psychology (PhD); social psychology and personality (PhD). *Accreditation:* APA (one or more programs are accredited). *Degree requirements:* For doctorate, thesis/dissertation. *Entrance requirements:* For doctorate, GRE General Test, minimum GPA of 3.0. Electronic applications accepted. *Faculty research:* Addictive behaviors, artificial intelligence, child psychopathology, mechanisms and development of vision, physiology of ingestive behaviors.

University of Wisconsin–Madison, Graduate School, College of Letters and Science, Department of Psychology, Program in Cognitive Neurosciences, Madison, WI 53706-1380. Offers PhD. *Degree requirements:* For doctorate, comprehensive exam, thesis/dissertation. *Entrance requirements:* For doctorate, GRE General Test, minimum undergraduate GPA of 3.0. Additional exam requirements/recommendations for international students: Required—TOEFL. Electronic applications accepted.

University of Wisconsin–Madison, Graduate School, College of Letters and Science, Department of Psychology, Program in Perception, Madison, WI 53706-1380. Offers PhD. *Degree requirements:* For doctorate, comprehensive exam, thesis/dissertation. *Entrance requirements:* For doctorate, GRE General Test, minimum GPA of 3.0. Electronic applications accepted.

Wayne State University, College of Liberal Arts and Sciences, Department of Psychology, Detroit, MI 48202. Offers behavioral and cognitive neuroscience (PhD); clinical psychology (PhD); developmental science (PhD); industrial/organizational psychology (MA, PhD); social personality (PhD). Doctoral program admits for fall only. *Accreditation:* APA (one or more programs are accredited). *Faculty:* 38. *Students:* 94 full-time (63 women), 43 part-time (29 women); includes 23 minority (6 Black or African American, non-Hispanic/Latino; 3 Asian, non-Hispanic/Latino; 10 Hispanic/Latino; 4 Two or more races, non-Hispanic/Latino), 12 international. Average age 27. 478 applicants, 11% accepted, 39 enrolled. In 2017, 29 master's, 27 doctorates awarded. Terminal master's awarded for partial completion of doctoral program. *Degree requirements:* For master's, thesis (for some programs); for doctorate, thesis/dissertation, training assignments. *Entrance requirements:* For master's, GRE General Test, minimum undergraduate upper-division cumulative GPA of 3.0, courses in psychology and statistics; for doctorate, GRE General Test, bachelor's, master's, or other advanced degree; at least twelve credits in psychology with minimum GPA of 3.0; courses in laboratory psychology and statistical methods in psychology; at least three letters of recommendation; statement of purpose. Additional exam requirements/recommendations for international students: Required—TOEFL (minimum score 550 paper-based; 79 iBT), TWE (minimum score 5.5), Michigan English Language Assessment Battery (minimum score 85); Recommended—IELTS (minimum score 6.5). Application fee: $50. Electronic applications accepted. *Expenses:* Tuition, state resident: full-time $10,224; part-time $638.98 per credit hour. Tuition, nonresident: full-time $22,145; part-time $1384.04 per credit hour. Tuition and fees vary according to course load and program. *Financial support:* In 2017–18, 90 students received support, including 13 fellowships with tuition reimbursements available (averaging $11,212 per year), 8 research assistantships with tuition reimbursements available (averaging $18,534 per year), 50 teaching assistantships with tuition reimbursements available (averaging $18,534 per year); scholarships/grants, health care benefits, and unspecified assistantships also available. Financial award applicants required to submit FAFSA. *Faculty research:* Behavioral neuroscience, cognitive/neuroscience of development and aging research, children, adolescents, and family research, cognition research, emotion research, health psychology research, homelessness and poverty research, memory research, neuropsychology research, personality/cognition, relationships research, substance use and abuse research, workplace adaptation, well-being and evaluation research. *Unit head:* Boris Baltes, PhD, Chair/Professor, 313-577-2803, E-mail: b.baltes@wayne.edu. *Application contact:* Alia Allen, Academic Services Officer, 313-577-2823, E-mail: aallen@wayne.edu.
Website: http://clas.wayne.edu/psychology/

Wilfrid Laurier University, Faculty of Graduate and Postdoctoral Studies, Faculty of Science, Department of Psychology, Waterloo, ON N2L 3C5, Canada. Offers behavioral neuroscience (M Sc, PhD); cognitive neuroscience (M Sc, PhD); community psychology (MA, PhD); social and developmental psychology (MA, PhD). *Program availability:* Part-time. *Degree requirements:* For master's, thesis; for doctorate, thesis/dissertation. *Entrance requirements:* For master's, GRE General Test, honors BA or the equivalent in psychology, minimum B average in undergraduate course work; for doctorate, GRE General Test, master's degree, minimum A- average. Additional exam requirements/recommendations for international students: Required—TOEFL (minimum score 89 iBT). Electronic applications accepted. *Faculty research:* Brain and cognition, community psychology, social and developmental psychology.

Yale University, Graduate School of Arts and Sciences, Department of Psychology, New Haven, CT 06520. Offers behavioral neuroscience (PhD); clinical psychology (PhD); cognitive psychology (PhD); developmental psychology (PhD); social/personality psychology (PhD). *Accreditation:* APA. *Degree requirements:* For doctorate, thesis/dissertation. *Entrance requirements:* For doctorate, GRE General Test.

Counseling Psychology

Abilene Christian University, Graduate Programs, College of Arts and Sciences, Department of Psychology, Program in Counseling Psychology, Abilene, TX 79699. Offers MS. *Program availability:* Part-time. *Students:* 13 full-time (10 women); includes 2 minority (1 Black or African American, non-Hispanic/Latino; 1 Hispanic/Latino), 2 international. 31 applicants, 35% accepted, 7 enrolled. In 2017, 5 master's awarded. *Degree requirements:* For master's, comprehensive exam, thesis, practicum. *Entrance requirements:* Additional exam requirements/recommendations for international students: Required—TOEFL (minimum score 80 iBT), IELTS (minimum score 6), PTE. *Application deadline:* For fall admission, 3/30 priority date for domestic students; for spring admission, 11/1 for domestic students. Applications are processed on a rolling basis. Application fee: $50. Electronic applications accepted. *Expenses:* $1,148 per hour. *Financial support:* In 2017–18, 11 students received support. Scholarships/grants and unspecified assistantships available. Financial award application deadline: 4/1; financial award applicants required to submit FAFSA. *Unit head:* Dr. Cherisse Flanagan, Graduate Director, 325-674-4826, Fax: 325-674-6968, E-mail: cherisse.flanagan@acu.edu. *Application contact:* Graduate Admissions, 325-674-6911, Fax: 325-674-6717, E-mail: gradinfo@acu.edu.
Website: http://www.acu.edu/graduate/academics/counseling-psychology.html

Adelphi University, Gordon F. Derner School of Psychology, Program in Mental Health Counseling, Garden City, NY 11530-0701. Offers MA. *Students:* 47 full-time (40 women), 2 part-time (both women); includes 17 minority (3 Black or African American, non-Hispanic/Latino; 2 Asian, non-Hispanic/Latino; 12 Hispanic/Latino), 2 international. Average age 25. 88 applicants, 41% accepted, 25 enrolled. In 2017, 12 master's awarded. *Degree requirements:* For master's, comprehensive exam. *Entrance requirements:* For master's, GRE General Test, GRE Subject Test, minimum cumulative GPA of 3.1; interview; course work in developmental psychology, research methods, and psycho-pathology; 2 letters of recommendation. Additional exam requirements/recommendations for international students: Required—TOEFL (minimum score 550 paper-based; 80 iBT), IELTS (minimum score 6.5). *Application deadline:* For fall admission, 4/1 priority date for domestic students, 5/1 priority date for international students. Application fee: $50. Electronic applications accepted. *Expenses:* Contact institution. *Financial support:* Research assistantships with full and partial tuition reimbursements, teaching assistantships, career-related internships or fieldwork, institutionally sponsored loans, scholarships/grants, traineeships, and unspecified assistantships available. Support available to part-time students. *Unit head:* Dr. Errol Rodriguez, Assistant Dean, 516-237-8572, E-mail: erodriguez@adelphi.edu. *Application contact:* E-mail: graduateadmissions@adelphi.edu.
Website: http://derner.adelphi.edu/psychology/graduate/ma-mental-health-counseling/

Adler Graduate School, Program in Adlerian Counseling and Psychotherapy, Richfield, MN 55423. Offers Adlerian studies (MA); art therapy (MA); clinical mental health counseling (MA); co-occurring substance use and mental health disorders (MA); marriage and family therapy (MA); school counseling (MA). *Program availability:* Part-time, evening/weekend. *Faculty:* 71 part-time/adjunct (55 women). *Students:* 317 part-time (259 women); includes 51 minority (40 Black or African American, non-Hispanic/Latino; 6 American Indian or Alaska Native, non-Hispanic/Latino; 5 Hispanic/Latino). *Degree requirements:* For master's, thesis or alternative, 500-700 hour internship (depending on license choice). *Entrance requirements:* For master's, interview, official transcripts, minimum cumulative GPA of 3.0. *Application deadline:* Applications are processed on a rolling basis. Application fee: $50. Electronic applications accepted. *Expenses:* $575 per credit tuition. *Financial support:* Career-related internships or fieldwork and tuition waivers available. Support available to part-time students. Financial award applicants required to submit FAFSA. *Unit head:* Dr. Jeffrey Allen, President, 612-767-7048, Fax: 612-861-7559, E-mail: jeffrey.allen@alfredadler.edu. *Application contact:* Christina Hilpipre-Frischman, Director of Admissions, 612-767-7055, Fax: 612-861-7559, E-mail: christina@alfredadler.edu.
Website: http://alfredadler.edu/programs/masters-level-programs

Adler University, Graduate Programs, MA in Counseling Psychology Program, Chicago, IL 60602. Offers MACP. Program offered at Vancouver campus. *Program availability:* Evening/weekend.

Adler University, Graduate Programs, Master of Counseling Psychology Program, Chicago, IL 60602. Offers MCP. Program offered at Vancouver campus. *Program availability:* Part-time.

Alabama Agricultural and Mechanical University, School of Graduate Studies, College of Education, Humanities, and Behavioral Sciences, Department of Social Work, Psychology and Counseling, Huntsville, AL 35811. Offers psychology and counseling (MS, Ed S), including clinical psychology (MS), counseling psychology (MS), guidance and counseling, rehabilitation counseling (MS), school counseling (MS), school psychology (MS), school psychometry (MS); social work (MSW). *Accreditation:* CORE; NCATE. *Program availability:* Part-time, evening/weekend. *Degree requirements:* For master's, comprehensive exam. *Entrance requirements:* For master's, GRE General Test. Additional exam requirements/recommendations for international students: Required—TOEFL (minimum score 500 paper-based; 61 iBT).

Faculty research: Increasing numbers of minorities in special education and speech-language pathology.

Alaska Pacific University, Graduate Programs, Department of Counseling, Psychological Studies, and Human Services, Program in Counseling Psychology, Anchorage, AK 99508-4672. Offers MSCP.

Alfred University, Graduate School, Counseling and School Psychology Program, Alfred, NY 14802-1205. Offers mental health counseling (MS Ed); school counseling (MS Ed, CAS); school psychology (MA, Psy D, CAS). *Accreditation:* APA. *Degree requirements:* For master's, internship; for doctorate, thesis/dissertation, internship. *Entrance requirements:* For master's and doctorate, GRE General Test. Additional exam requirements/recommendations for international students: Required—TOEFL (minimum score 590 paper-based; 90 iBT), IELTS (minimum score 6.5). Electronic applications accepted. *Faculty research:* Family processes, alternative assessment approaches, behavior disorders in children, parent involvement, school psychology training issues.

Amberton University, Graduate School, Programs in Counseling, Garland, TX 75041-5595. Offers marriage and family therapy (MA); professional counseling (MA); school counseling (MA). *Entrance requirements:* For master's, minimum GPA of 3.0. *Application deadline:* Applications are processed on a rolling basis. Application fee: $0. *Expenses:* Tuition: Part-time $795 per course. *Unit head:* Dr. Don Hebbard, Academic Dean, 972-635-8641 Ext. 157, Fax: 972-279-9773, E-mail: dhebbard@amberton.edu. *Application contact:* Adviser, 972-279-6511 Ext. 180, Fax: 972-279-9773, E-mail: advisor@amberton.edu.

American International College, School of Education, Low Residency Programs, Springfield, MA 01109-3189. Offers counseling psychology (MA); educational leadership and supervision (Ed D); professional counseling and supervision (Ed D); teaching and learning (Ed D). *Program availability:* Evening/weekend. *Faculty:* 2 full-time (1 woman), 4 part-time/adjunct (all women). *Students:* 117 full-time (90 women); includes 32 minority (22 Black or African American, non-Hispanic/Latino; 1 Asian, non-Hispanic/Latino; 7 Hispanic/Latino; 2 Two or more races, non-Hispanic/Latino). Average age 40. 35 applicants, 86% accepted, 20 enrolled. In 2017, 8 master's, 12 doctorates awarded. *Degree requirements:* For doctorate, thesis/dissertation. *Entrance requirements:* For master's, minimum undergraduate GPA of 3.0, 2 letters of recommendation, personal goal statement, official transcript of all academic work (graduate and undergraduate); for doctorate, minimum master's GPA of 3.0, 3 letters of recommendation, personal goal statement/essay (6-8 pages), official transcript of all academic work (graduate and undergraduate). Additional exam requirements/recommendations for international students: Required—TOEFL. *Application deadline:* For fall admission, 8/15 for domestic and international students; for spring admission, 1/3 for domestic and international students; for summer admission, 5/15 for domestic and international students. Applications are processed on a rolling basis. Application fee: $50. *Expenses:* $6,515 per trimester (for EdD); $505 per credit (for MA); $30 per term registration fee; $100 one-time graduation fee. *Faculty research:* Educational leadership, curriculum, program evaluation, educational policy. *Unit head:* Dr. Nicholas Young, Dean, Low Residency Programs, 413-205-1726, E-mail: nicholas.young@aic.edu. *Application contact:* Kerry Barnes, Director of Graduate Admissions, 413-205-3703, Fax: 413-205-3051, E-mail: kerry.barnes@aic.edu.

Amridge University, Graduate and Professional Programs, Montgomery, AL 36117. Offers Biblical studies (MA, PhD); Christian ministry (MS); family therapy (D Min); human services (MS); leadership and management (MS); marriage and family therapy (M Div, MA, PhD); ministerial leadership (M Div, MS); New Testament studies (MA); Old Testament studies (MA); professional counseling (M Div, MA, PhD); theology (M Div, D Min). *Program availability:* Part-time, evening/weekend, online learning. *Faculty:* 23 full-time (3 women), 9 part-time/adjunct (5 women). *Students:* 105 full-time (55 women), 250 part-time (152 women); includes 217 minority (167 Black or African American, non-Hispanic/Latino; 4 Asian, non-Hispanic/Latino; 42 Hispanic/Latino; 4 Native Hawaiian or other Pacific Islander, non-Hispanic/Latino). Average age 42. 160 applicants, 100% accepted, 110 enrolled. *Degree requirements:* For master's, one foreign language, comprehensive exam (for some programs), thesis (for some programs); for doctorate, one foreign language, comprehensive exam (for some programs), thesis/dissertation (for some programs). *Entrance requirements:* For master's, official transcript showing an earned 4-year BA or BS from regionally- or nationally-accredited institution; for doctorate, official transcript showing earned graduate degree from regionally- or nationally-accredited institution; writing sample (e.g. career monograph, published journal article, term paper from master's degree or doctoral dissertation); interview. Additional exam requirements/recommendations for international students: Required—TOEFL (minimum score 79 iBT). *Application deadline:* Applications are processed on a rolling basis. Application fee: $50. Electronic applications accepted. *Financial support:* In 2017–18, 33 students received support. Federal Work-Study and scholarships/grants available. Support available to part-time students. Financial award applicants required to submit FAFSA. *Faculty research:* Technology and mental healthcare, resilience in black families, theology and congregational ministry. *Unit head:* Laina Costanza, Vice President, Student Affairs, 888-790-8080 Ext. 1, Fax: 334-387-3878, E-mail: cc@amridgeuniversity.edu. *Application contact:* Brooks Housley, Student Affairs Coordinator, 888-790-8080 Ext. 1, Fax: 334-387-3878, E-mail: admissions@amridgeuniversity.edu.

Andrews University, School of Graduate Studies, School of Education, Department of Graduate Psychology and Counseling, Program in Community Counseling, Berrien Springs, MI 49104. Offers clinical mental health counseling (MA); community counseling (MA). *Students:* 23 full-time (13 women), 3 part-time (all women); includes 7 minority (3 Black or African American, non-Hispanic/Latino; 4 Hispanic/Latino), 9 international. Average age 30. 25 applicants, 76% accepted, 7 enrolled. In 2017, 12 master's awarded. *Degree requirements:* For master's, thesis optional. *Entrance requirements:* For master's, GRE. Additional exam requirements/recommendations for international students: Required—TOEFL (minimum score 550 paper-based). Application fee: $40. *Unit head:* Dr. Nancy Carbonell, Coordinator, 269-471-3472. *Application contact:* Justina Clayburn, Supervisor of Graduate Admission, 800-253-2874, Fax: 269-471-6321, E-mail: graduate@andrews.edu.

Andrews University, School of Graduate Studies, School of Education, Department of Graduate Psychology and Counseling, Program in Counseling Psychology, Berrien Springs, MI 49104. Offers MA, PhD. *Students:* 26 full-time (21 women); includes 11 minority (8 Black or African American, non-Hispanic/Latino; 1 Hispanic/Latino; 2 Two or more races, non-Hispanic/Latino), 3 international. Average age 39. 23 applicants, 30% accepted, 6 enrolled. In 2017, 3 master's, 2 doctorates awarded. *Degree requirements:* For doctorate, thesis/dissertation. *Entrance requirements:* For master's, GRE. Additional exam requirements/recommendations for international students: Required—TOEFL (minimum score 550 paper-based). Application fee: $40. *Unit head:* Dr. Carole Woolford, Coordinator, 269-471-6074. *Application contact:* Justina Clayburn, Supervisor of Graduate Admission, 800-253-2874, Fax: 269-471-6321, E-mail: graduate@andrews.edu.

Anna Maria College, Graduate Division, Program in Counseling Psychology, Paxton, MA 01612. Offers counseling psychology (MA). *Program availability:* Part-time, evening/weekend. *Degree requirements:* For master's, comprehensive exam, practicum.

Entrance requirements: Additional exam requirements/recommendations for international students: Required—TOEFL (minimum score 500 paper-based). Electronic applications accepted.

Antioch University New England, Graduate School, Department of Applied Psychology, Program in Clinical Mental Health Counseling, Keene, NH 03431-3552. Offers clinical mental health counseling (MA); substance abuse counseling (MA). *Accreditation:* ACA. *Degree requirements:* For master's, internship, practicum. *Entrance requirements:* For master's, previous course work and work experience in psychology. Additional exam requirements/recommendations for international students: Required—TOEFL (minimum score 550 paper-based). Electronic applications accepted. *Expenses:* Contact institution. *Faculty research:* Multicultural issues in field supervision.

Appalachian State University, Cratis D. Williams Graduate School, Department of Human Development and Psychological Counseling, Boone, NC 28608. Offers clinical mental health counseling (MA); college student development (MA); marriage and family therapy (MA); school counseling (MA). *Accreditation:* AAMFT/COAMFTE; ACA; NCATE. *Program availability:* Part-time. *Degree requirements:* For master's, comprehensive exam (for some programs), thesis optional, internships. *Entrance requirements:* For master's, GRE General Test, 3 letters of recommendation. Additional exam requirements/recommendations for international students: Required—TOEFL (minimum score 570 paper-based; 79 iBT), IELTS (minimum score 6.5). Electronic applications accepted. *Faculty research:* Multicultural counseling, addictions counseling, play therapy, expressive arts, child and adolescent therapy, sexual abuse counseling.

Arcadia University, College of Arts and Sciences, Department of Psychology, Glenside, PA 19038-3295. Offers applied behavior analysis (MAC); autism (MAC); child/family therapy (MAC); community public health (MAC); counseling/international peace and conflict resolution dual degree (MAC); mental health counseling (MAC); trauma (MAC). *Program availability:* Part-time. *Degree requirements:* For master's, practicum. *Entrance requirements:* For master's, GRE General Test or MAT. *Expenses:* Contact institution.

Argosy University, Chicago, Illinois School of Professional Psychology, Doctoral Program in Clinical Psychology, Chicago, IL 60601. Offers child and adolescent psychology (Psy D); client-centered and experiential psychotherapies (Psy D); diversity and multicultural psychology (Psy D); family psychology (Psy D); forensic psychology (Psy D); health psychology (Psy D); neuropsychology (Psy D); organizational consulting (Psy D); psychoanalytic psychology (Psy D); psychology and spirituality (Psy D). *Accreditation:* APA.

Argosy University, Chicago, Illinois School of Professional Psychology, Program in Counseling Psychology, Chicago, IL 60601. Offers counselor education and supervision (Ed D). *Accreditation:* ACA. *Program availability:* Online learning.

Argosy University, Hawai'i, Hawai'i School of Professional Psychology, Program in Counseling Psychology, Honolulu, HI 96813. Offers Ed D.

Argosy University, Los Angeles, College of Psychology and Behavioral Sciences, Los Angeles, CA 90045. Offers clinical psychology/marriage and family therapy (MA); counseling psychology (Ed D); counseling psychology/marriage and family therapy (MA); forensic psychology (MA).

Argosy University, Northern Virginia, American School of Professional Psychology, Arlington, VA 22209. Offers clinical psychology (MA, Psy D), including child and family psychology (Psy D), diversity and multicultural psychology (Psy D), forensic psychology (Psy D), health and neuropsychology (Psy D); community counseling (MA); counseling psychology (Ed D), including counselor education and supervision; counselor education and supervision (Ed D); forensic psychology (MA).

Argosy University, Orange County, American School of Professional Psychology, Program in Counseling Psychology, Orange, CA 92868. Offers counseling psychology (Ed D); marriage and family therapy (MA).

Argosy University, Phoenix, Arizona School of Professional Psychology, Program in Mental Health Counseling, Phoenix, AZ 85021. Offers MA.

Argosy University, Seattle, College of Psychology and Behavioral Sciences, Program in Counseling Psychology, Seattle, WA 98121. Offers MA, Ed D.

Argosy University, Tampa, Florida School of Professional Psychology, Tampa, FL 33607. Offers clinical psychology (MA, Psy D), including clinical psychology; counselor education and supervision (Ed D); industrial organizational psychology (MA); marriage and family therapy (MA); mental health counseling (MA).

Arizona State University at the Tempe campus, School of Letters and Sciences, Program in Counseling Psychology, Tempe, AZ 85287-0811. Offers PhD. *Accreditation:* APA. *Degree requirements:* For doctorate, comprehensive exam, thesis/dissertation, internship/practica, interactive Program of Study (iPOS) submitted before completing 50 percent of required credit hours. *Entrance requirements:* For doctorate, GRE, minimum GPA of 3.0 or equivalent in last 2 years of work leading to bachelor's degree, 3 letters of recommendation, personal statement describing history and academic/professional goals, completed Biographical Information form, 7-page sample of expository writing. Additional exam requirements/recommendations for international students: Required—TOEFL, IELTS, or PTE. Electronic applications accepted.

Assumption College, Clinical Counseling Psychology Program, Worcester, MA 01609-1296. Offers child and family interventions (MA); clinical counseling psychology (CAGS); cognitive-behavioral therapies (MA). *Program availability:* Part-time, evening/weekend. *Faculty:* 4 full-time (2 women), 7 part-time/adjunct (2 women). *Students:* 47 full-time (34 women), 19 part-time (all women); includes 9 minority (3 Black or African American, non-Hispanic/Latino; 2 Asian, non-Hispanic/Latino; 3 Hispanic/Latino; 1 Two or more races, non-Hispanic/Latino), 1 international. Average age 27. 59 applicants, 80% accepted, 19 enrolled. In 2017, 20 master's awarded. *Degree requirements:* For master's, comprehensive exam, internship, practicum; for CAGS, comprehensive exam. *Entrance requirements:* For master's, bachelor's degree and at least six psychology courses completed with minimum GPA of 3.0 both overall and in the psychology courses; three letters of recommendation; official transcripts; personal statement; current resume; for CAGS, master's degree in clinical counseling psychology or mental health counseling, or baccalaureate degree and at least six psychology courses with minimum GPA of 3.0 overall and in psychology courses; three letters of recommendation; official transcripts; personal statement; current resume; interview. Additional exam requirements/recommendations for international students: Required—TOEFL (minimum score 540 paper-based; 76 iBT), IELTS (minimum score 6). *Application deadline:* For fall admission, 3/1 priority date for domestic and international students; for spring admission, 10/5 for domestic and international students; for summer admission, 2/8 for domestic and international students. Application fee: $30. Electronic applications accepted. *Expenses:* Tuition: Full-time $11,952; part-time $664 per credit. *Required fees:* $70 per term. *Financial support:* In 2017–18, 18 students received support, including 10 fellowships with full tuition reimbursements available; tuition waivers (full and partial), unspecified assistantships, and institutional discounts also available. Financial award application deadline: 3/1; financial award applicants required to submit FAFSA. *Faculty research:* Mood disorders, adjustment to life-threatening illness, perception of movement, socioemotional development of young children,

discovery versus disclosure. *Unit head:* Dr. Leonard A. Doerfler, Director, 508-767-7549, Fax: 508-767-7263, E-mail: doerfler@assumption.edu. *Application contact:* Karen Stoyanoff, Director of Recruitment for Graduate Enrollment, 508-767-7442, Fax: 508-799-4412, E-mail: graduate@assumption.edu.
Website: http://graduate.assumption.edu/counseling-psychology/ma-clinical-counseling-psychology-overview

Athabasca University, Program in Counseling, Athabasca, AB T9S 3A3, Canada. Offers applied psychology (Post Master's Certificate); art therapy (MC); career counseling (MC); counseling (Advanced Certificate); counseling psychology (MC); school counseling (MC).

Austin Peay State University, College of Graduate Studies, College of Behavioral and Health Sciences, Department of Psychological Science and Counseling, Clarksville, TN 37044. Offers industrial-organizational psychology (MS); mental health counseling (MS), including clinical mental health, school counseling; school counseling (MS). *Program availability:* Part-time, online learning. *Faculty:* 11 full-time (6 women), 1 (woman) part-time/adjunct. *Students:* 60 full-time (46 women), 12 part-time (10 women); includes 16 minority (11 Black or African American, non-Hispanic/Latino; 4 Hispanic/Latino; 1 Two or more races, non-Hispanic/Latino). Average age 29. 59 applicants, 69% accepted, 31 enrolled. In 2017, 30 master's awarded. *Degree requirements:* For master's, comprehensive exam, thesis (for some programs). *Entrance requirements:* For master's, GRE General Test, minimum undergraduate GPA of 2.5, 3 letters of recommendation, bachelor's degree. Additional exam requirements/recommendations for international students: Required—TOEFL (minimum score 500 paper-based). *Application deadline:* For fall admission, 8/8 priority date for domestic students. Applications are processed on a rolling basis. Application fee: $45 ($55 for international students). Electronic applications accepted. *Expenses:* Tuition, state resident: full-time $7686; part-time $427 per credit hour. Tuition, nonresident: full-time $20,268; part-time $1126 per credit hour. *Required fees:* $1529; $76.45 per credit hour. *Financial support:* Research assistantships with full tuition reimbursements, career-related internships or fieldwork, Federal Work-Study, institutionally sponsored loans, scholarships/grants, and unspecified assistantships available. Support available to part-time students. Financial award application deadline: 4/1; financial award applicants required to submit FAFSA. *Unit head:* Dr. Nicole Knickmeyer, Chair, 931-221-7232, Fax: 931-221-6267, E-mail: knickmeyer@apsu.edu. *Application contact:* Brad Averitt, Coordinator of Graduate Admissions, 800-859-4723, Fax: 931-221-7641, E-mail: gradadmissions@apsu.edu.
Website: http://www.apsu.edu/psychology/index.php

Avila University, Department of Psychology, Kansas City, MO 64145-1698. Offers counseling psychology (MS); psychology (MS). *Program availability:* Part-time. *Faculty:* 7 full-time (6 women), 4 part-time/adjunct (1 woman). *Students:* 104 full-time (88 women), 17 part-time (12 women); includes 39 minority (25 Black or African American, non-Hispanic/Latino; 2 American Indian or Alaska Native, non-Hispanic/Latino; 2 Asian, non-Hispanic/Latino; 6 Hispanic/Latino; 4 Two or more races, non-Hispanic/Latino), 3 international. Average age 33. 69 applicants, 65% accepted, 34 enrolled. In 2017, 24 master's awarded. *Degree requirements:* For master's, thesis optional, capstone project. *Entrance requirements:* For master's, bachelor's degree, minimum GPA of 3.0 in all previous undergraduate and graduate coursework, 2 letters of recommendation, letter of intent, resume. Additional exam requirements/recommendations for international students: Required—TOEFL (minimum score 80 iBT). *Application deadline:* Applications are processed on a rolling basis. Application fee: $0. Electronic applications accepted. *Expenses:* Contact institution. *Financial support:* In 2017–18, 17 students received support, including 5 research assistantships with partial tuition reimbursements available; career-related internships or fieldwork, scholarships/grants, and unspecified assistantships also available. Support available to part-time students. Financial award applicants required to submit FAFSA. *Faculty research:* Emotional regulation, embodied cognition, trauma and restorative justice, psychophysiology of public speaking anxiety. *Unit head:* Phil Gebauer, Director of Graduate Psychology Enrollment Management, 816-501-0419, Fax: 816-501-2455, E-mail: philip.gebauer@avila.edu. *Application contact:* Tamika Doolin, Graduate Admissions Advisor, 816-501-3661, Fax: 816-501-2455, E-mail: gradpsych@avila.edu.
Website: https://www.avila.edu/psychology/

Ball State University, Graduate School, College of Health, Department of Counseling Psychology, Social Psychology, and Counseling, Program in Counseling Psychology, Muncie, IN 47306. Offers counseling (MA), including clinical mental health counseling, mental health counseling, rehabilitation counseling, school counseling; counseling psychology (PhD). *Accreditation:* ACA; APA. *Program availability:* Part-time. *Students:* 88 full-time (57 women), 29 part-time (24 women); includes 18 minority (3 Black or African American, non-Hispanic/Latino; 1 Asian, non-Hispanic/Latino; 7 Hispanic/Latino; 7 Two or more races, non-Hispanic/Latino), 4 international. Average age 26. 133 applicants, 29% accepted, 39 enrolled. In 2017, 29 master's, 9 doctorates awarded. *Degree requirements:* For doctorate, thesis/dissertation. *Entrance requirements:* For master's, GRE General Test (minimum scores 144 quantitative, 153 verbal), minimum baccalaureate GPA of 2.75 or 3.0 in latter half of baccalaureate, minimum GPA of 3.0 in psychology coursework, three letters of recommendation; for doctorate, GRE General Test, interview, minimum graduate GPA of 3.2, resume. Additional exam requirements/recommendations for international students: Required—TOEFL (minimum score 550 paper-based; 79 iBT), IELTS (minimum score 6.5). *Application deadline:* For fall admission, 3/1 priority date for domestic students, 1/1 for international students. Applications are processed on a rolling basis. Application fee: $60. Electronic applications accepted. *Financial support:* Research assistantships with partial tuition reimbursements, teaching assistantships with partial tuition reimbursements, and unspecified assistantships available. Financial award application deadline: 3/1; financial award applicants required to submit FAFSA. *Unit head:* Dr. Sharon Bowman, Chairperson, 765-285-8040, Fax: 765-285-2067, E-mail: sbowman@bsu.edu.
Website: http://www.bsu.edu/teachers/counseling/cpsy/

Baruch College of the City University of New York, Weissman School of Arts and Sciences, Program in Mental Health Counseling, New York, NY 10010-5585. Offers MA. *Entrance requirements:* For master's, bachelor's degree from accredited institution, minimum undergraduate GPA of 3.2, relevant professional or volunteer experience, minimum of 15 credits in psychology, personal statement, three letters of recommendation, official transcript. Additional exam requirements/recommendations for international students: Required—TOEFL. Electronic applications accepted. *Faculty research:* Character analysis; shame and guilt; self-perceptions and moral affect; pedagogical development; self-efficacy and cognitive performance; sleep loss, fatigue and effort; environmental sustainability; cultural competence; behavioral obesity treatment; ADHD.

Bastyr University, School of Natural Health Arts and Sciences, Kenmore, WA 98028-4966. Offers counseling psychology (MA); maternal-child health systems (MA); midwifery (MS); nutrition (Certificate); nutrition and clinical health psychology (MS); nutrition and wellness (MS). *Accreditation:* AND. *Program availability:* Part-time. *Degree requirements:* For master's, thesis optional. *Entrance requirements:* For master's, 1-2 years' basic sciences course work (depending on program). Additional exam requirements/recommendations for international students: Required—TOEFL (minimum score 550 paper-based; 79 iBT). *Application deadline:* For fall admission, 3/15 priority date for domestic and international students. Applications are processed on a rolling basis. Application fee: $75. *Expenses: Tuition:* Part-time $714 per credit hour. *Required fees:* $75. *Financial support:* Career-related internships or fieldwork, Federal Work-Study, and scholarships/grants available. Support available to part-time students. Financial award application deadline: 4/15; financial award applicants required to submit FAFSA. *Faculty research:* Whole-food nutrition for type 2 diabetes; meditation in end-of-life care; stress management; Qi Gong, Tai Chi and yoga for older adults; Echinacea and immunology. *Unit head:* Dr. Lynelle Golden, Dean, 425-602-3110, Fax: 425-823-6222, E-mail: lgolden@bastyr.edu. *Application contact:* Admissions Office, 425-602-3330, Fax: 425-602-3090, E-mail: admissions@bastyr.edu.
Website: http://www.bastyr.edu/academics/schools-departments/school-natural-health-arts-sciences

Becker College, Program in Mental Health Counseling, Worcester, MA 01609. Offers community mental health (MA); school consultation (MA). *Entrance requirements:* For master's, GRE, interview, official transcript, three letters of recommendation, essay. Electronic applications accepted.

Bethel University, Graduate School, St. Paul, MN 55112-6999. Offers business administration (MBA); classroom management (Certificate); counseling (MA); K-12 education (MA); leadership (Ed D); leadership foundations (Certificate); nurse educator (MS, Certificate); nurse-midwifery (MS); physician assistant (MS); special education (MA); strategic leadership (MA); teaching (MA); teaching and learning (Certificate). *Program availability:* Part-time, evening/weekend, 100% online, blended/hybrid learning. *Faculty:* 22 full-time (16 women), 70 part-time/adjunct (44 women). *Students:* 611 full-time (431 women), 393 part-time (249 women); includes 176 minority (82 Black or African American, non-Hispanic/Latino; 4 American Indian or Alaska Native, non-Hispanic/Latino; 31 Asian, non-Hispanic/Latino; 39 Hispanic/Latino; 2 Native Hawaiian or other Pacific Islander, non-Hispanic/Latino; 18 Two or more races, non-Hispanic/Latino), 9 international. Average age 36. 668 applicants, 42% accepted, 223 enrolled. In 2017, 287 master's, 30 doctorates, 172 other advanced degrees awarded. *Degree requirements:* For master's, comprehensive exam (for some programs), thesis (for some programs); for doctorate, comprehensive exam, thesis/dissertation. *Entrance requirements:* Additional exam requirements/recommendations for international students: Required—TOEFL (minimum score 550 paper-based, 80 iBT) or IELTS. *Application deadline:* Applications are processed on a rolling basis. Application fee: $0. Electronic applications accepted. *Expenses:* Contact institution. *Financial support:* Teaching assistantships, career-related internships or fieldwork, and scholarships/grants available. Support available to part-time students. Financial award applicants required to submit FAFSA. *Unit head:* Dr. Randy Bergen, Associate Provost, 651-635-8000, Fax: 651-635-8004, E-mail: r-bergen@bethel.edu. *Application contact:* Director of Admissions, 651-635-8000, Fax: 651-635-8004, E-mail: gs@bethel.edu.
Website: https://www.bethel.edu/graduate/

Boston College, Lynch School of Education, Program in Mental Health Counseling, Chestnut Hill, MA 02467-3800. Offers counseling psychology (PhD); mental health counseling (MA); MA/MA. *Accreditation:* APA (one or more programs are accredited). *Students:* 122 full-time (93 women), 3 part-time (all women); includes 24 minority (5 Black or African American, non-Hispanic/Latino; 4 Asian, non-Hispanic/Latino; 11 Hispanic/Latino; 4 Two or more races, non-Hispanic/Latino), 25 international. Average age 24. 184 applicants, 75% accepted, 62 enrolled. In 2017, 55 master's awarded. Terminal master's awarded for partial completion of doctoral program. *Degree requirements:* For master's, comprehensive exam; for doctorate, comprehensive exam, thesis/dissertation. *Entrance requirements:* For master's and doctorate, GRE General Test. Additional exam requirements/recommendations for international students: Required—TOEFL (minimum score 550 paper-based; 100 iBT). *Application deadline:* For fall admission, 12/1 priority date for domestic and international students; for spring admission, 11/1 priority date for domestic and international students. Application fee: $65. Electronic applications accepted. *Financial support:* Fellowships with partial tuition reimbursements, research assistantships with partial tuition reimbursements, Federal Work-Study, tuition waivers (partial), and unspecified assistantships available. Support available to part-time students. *Unit head:* Dr. Penny Hauser-Cram, Chairperson, 617-552-4214, Fax: 617-552-4710. *Application contact:* Kimberly Rose, Graduate Admission Assistant, 617-552-4214, Fax: 617-552-0398, E-mail: roseki@bc.edu.

Boston Graduate School of Psychoanalysis, Master's Programs, Brookline, MA 02446-4602. Offers mental health counseling (MA); psychoanalysis (MA); psychoanalysis, society and culture (MA). *Program availability:* Part-time. Terminal master's awarded for partial completion of doctoral program. *Degree requirements:* For master's, thesis. *Entrance requirements:* For master's, interview, BA, personal statement, writing sample, 3 letters of recommendation. Additional exam requirements/recommendations for international students: Required—TOEFL (minimum score 550 paper-based; 79 iBT). *Faculty research:* Qualitative and narrative research methodologies, ethical conflicts and dual loyalties in health professionals, psychodynamics of social processes, treatment approaches for intractable patients, psychoanalytic research methodologies.

Boston University, School of Medicine, Division of Graduate Medical Sciences, Program in Mental Health Counseling and Behavioral Medicine, Boston, MA 02215. Offers MA. *Faculty research:* HIV/AIDS, trauma, behavioral medicine (obesity, breast cancer), neurosciences, autism, serious mental illness, sports psychology. *Unit head:* Dr. Stephen Brady, Director, 617-414-2320, Fax: 617-414-2323, E-mail: sbrady@bu.edu. *Application contact:* GMS Admissions Office, 617-638-5255, E-mail: askgms@bu.edu.
Website: http://www.bumc.bu.edu/mhbm/

Bowie State University, Graduate Programs, Program in Counseling Psychology, Bowie, MD 20715-9465. Offers MA. *Program availability:* Part-time, evening/weekend. *Degree requirements:* For master's, comprehensive exam, thesis optional, research paper, practicum. *Entrance requirements:* For master's, minimum GPA of 2.5, 3 recommendations. Electronic applications accepted.

Bowie State University, Graduate Programs, Program in Mental Health Counseling, Bowie, MD 20715-9465. Offers MA. *Accreditation:* ACA. *Program availability:* Part-time, evening/weekend. *Degree requirements:* For master's, comprehensive exam. *Entrance requirements:* For master's, 3 letters of recommendation, minimum GPA of 3.0, 12 undergraduate credit hours in counseling or psychology. Electronic applications accepted.

Bradley University, The Graduate School, College of Education and Health Sciences, Department of Leadership in Education, Nonprofits and Counseling, Peoria, IL 61625-0002. Offers counseling (MA), including clinical mental health counseling, professional school counseling; leadership in educational administration (MA); nonprofit leadership (MA). *Accreditation:* ACA; NCATE. *Program availability:* Part-time, evening/weekend. *Degree requirements:* For master's, comprehensive exam, thesis optional. *Entrance requirements:* For master's, GRE General Test or MAT, interview, 3 letters of recommendation. Additional exam requirements/recommendations for international students: Required—TOEFL (minimum score 550 paper-based; 79 iBT), IELTS (minimum score 6.5). Electronic applications accepted.

Brandman University, School of Arts and Sciences, Irvine, CA 92618. Offers psychology (MA), including counseling, marriage and family therapy, professional clinical counseling; social work (MSW). *Expenses: Tuition:* Part-time $640 per credit hour. Tuition and fees vary according to degree level and program. *Unit head:* Dr. Jeremy Korr, Dean, 949-341-9831. *Application contact:* Dr. Jeremy Korr, Dean, 949-341-9831.
Website: https://www.brandman.edu/academic-programs/arts-and-sciences

Brigham Young University, Graduate Studies, David O. McKay School of Education, Department of Counseling Psychology and Special Education, Provo, UT 84602. Offers counseling psychology (PhD); school psychology (Ed S); special education (MS). *Program availability:* Part-time. *Faculty:* 14 full-time (4 women), 9 part-time/adjunct (4 women). *Students:* 70 full-time (47 women), 20 part-time (18 women); includes 11 minority (1 Black or African American, non-Hispanic/Latino; 2 American Indian or Alaska Native, non-Hispanic/Latino; 1 Asian, non-Hispanic/Latino; 4 Hispanic/Latino; 3 Native Hawaiian or other Pacific Islander, non-Hispanic/Latino), 4 international. Average age 29. 76 applicants, 38% accepted, 28 enrolled. In 2017, 1 master's, 6 doctorates, 10 other advanced degrees awarded. *Degree requirements:* For master's and Ed S, comprehensive exam, thesis; for doctorate, comprehensive exam, thesis/dissertation. *Entrance requirements:* For master's, GRE General Test, minimum cumulative GPA of 3.0 in undergraduate coursework; for doctorate and Ed S, GRE General Test, minimum cumulative GPA of 3.0 in undergraduate coursework. Additional exam requirements/recommendations for international students: Required—TOEFL (minimum score 580 paper-based; 85 iBT), IELTS (minimum score 7). *Application deadline:* For fall admission, 1/15 for domestic and international students. Application fee: $50. Electronic applications accepted. *Expenses: Tuition:* Full-time $6880; part-time $405 per credit hour. Tuition and fees vary according to course load, program and student's religious affiliation. *Financial support:* In 2017–18, 64 students received support, including 64 research assistantships (averaging $9,270 per year); institutionally sponsored loans and tuition waivers (partial) also available. Financial award application deadline: 3/31. *Faculty research:* Autism, religious and spiritual values in counseling, school-based crisis intervention, behavior interventions in MTSS framework, counseling and psychotherapy process and outcomes. *Unit head:* Dr. Lane Fischer, Department Chair, 801-422-3857, E-mail: lane_fischer@byu.edu. *Application contact:* Diane E. Hancock, Executive Secretary, 801-422-3859, E-mail: diane_hancock@byu.edu.
Website: http://education.byu.edu/cpse/

Brooklyn College of the City University of New York, School of Natural and Behavioral Sciences, Department of Health and Nutrition Sciences, Brooklyn, NY 11210-2889. Offers community health (MA), including community health education, thanatology; grief counseling (CAS); nutrition (MS); public health (MPH), including general public health, health care policy and administration. *Program availability:* Part-time, evening/weekend. *Degree requirements:* For master's, thesis or alternative. *Entrance requirements:* For master's, GRE, essay, 2 letters of recommendation. Additional exam requirements/recommendations for international students: Required—TOEFL. Electronic applications accepted. *Faculty research:* Medical ethics, relocation stress, risk reduction, disease prevention, history of public health, computer applications.

Brooklyn College of the City University of New York, School of Natural and Behavioral Sciences, Department of Psychology, Brooklyn, NY 11210-2889. Offers experimental psychology (MA); industrial and organizational psychology (MA), including human relations, organizational behavior; mental health counseling (MA); psychology (PhD). *Program availability:* Part-time. *Degree requirements:* For master's, comprehensive exam, thesis (for some programs). *Entrance requirements:* For master's, minimum GPA of 3.0, 2 letters of recommendation, essay; for doctorate, GRE. Additional exam requirements/recommendations for international students: Required—TOEFL (minimum score 520 paper-based; 69 iBT). Electronic applications accepted.

Caldwell University, School of Psychology and Counseling, Caldwell, NJ 07006-6195. Offers art therapy (MA); counseling (MA), including art therapy, mental health, school counseling; director of school counseling (Post-Master's Certificate); professional counselor (Post-Master's Certificate); school counselor (Post-Master's Certificate). *Accreditation:* ACA. *Program availability:* Part-time. *Faculty:* 16 full-time (13 women), 13 part-time/adjunct (7 women). *Students:* 88 full-time (79 women), 84 part-time (82 women); includes 33 minority (12 Black or African American, non-Hispanic/Latino; 6 Asian, non-Hispanic/Latino; 15 Hispanic/Latino). Average age 30. 104 applicants, 100% accepted, 44 enrolled. In 2017, 31 master's awarded. *Degree requirements:* For master's, comprehensive exam, practicum, internship; for Post-Master's Certificate, comprehensive exam. *Entrance requirements:* For master's, minimum GPA of 3.2; two letters of recommendation; interview; writing sample. Additional exam requirements/recommendations for international students: Required—TOEFL (minimum score 580 paper-based, 92 iBT) or IELTS (7.5). *Application deadline:* For fall admission, 6/1 for domestic students, 7/1 for international students; for spring admission, 12/1 for domestic and international students; for summer admission, 4/1 for domestic and international students. Applications are processed on a rolling basis. Application fee: $50. Electronic applications accepted. *Expenses:* $975 per credit. *Financial support:* 2 general assistantships available. Financial award applicants required to submit FAFSA. *Faculty research:* Mental health counseling, school counseling, art therapy. *Unit head:* Dr. Thomson Ling, Associate Dean, 973-618-3596, E-mail: tling@caldwell.edu. *Application contact:* Tom Disch, Senior Graduate Admissions Counselor, 973-618-3544, E-mail: graduate@caldwell.edu.

California Baptist University, Program in Counseling Ministry and Counseling Psychology (Dual Master's), Riverside, CA 92504-3206. Offers MA/MS. *Program availability:* Part-time, evening/weekend. *Faculty:* 18 full-time (11 women), 10 part-time/adjunct (7 women). *Students:* 12 full-time (9 women), 1 part-time (0 women); includes 8 minority (2 Black or African American, non-Hispanic/Latino; 1 Asian, non-Hispanic/Latino; 5 Hispanic/Latino). Average age 29. 7 applicants, 57% accepted, 3 enrolled. *Entrance requirements:* Additional exam requirements/recommendations for international students: Required—TOEFL (minimum score 80 iBT). *Application deadline:* For fall admission, 8/1 priority date for domestic students, 7/1 for international students; for spring admission, 12/1 priority date for domestic students, 11/1 for international students. Applications are processed on a rolling basis. Application fee: $45. Electronic applications accepted. *Expenses:* Contact institution. *Financial support:* In 2017–18, 2 students received support. Federal Work-Study and scholarships/grants available. Financial award applicants required to submit CSS PROFILE or FAFSA. *Faculty research:* Law enforcement psychology, neuroethology, organizational neuroscience, integration of theology and behavioral science, cognitive development/cross-cultural psychology. *Unit head:* Dr. Jacqueline Gustafson, Dean, School of Behavioral Sciences, 951-343-4487, E-mail: jcraig@calbaptist.edu. *Application contact:* Mischa Routon, Director of Counseling Psychology Program, 951-343-4206, Fax: 877-228-8877, E-mail: mrouton@calbaptist.edu.
Website: http://www.calbaptist.edu/mft

California Baptist University, Program in Counseling Psychology, Riverside, CA 92504-3206. Offers counseling psychology (MS); forensic psychology (MS); professional clinical counseling (MS). *Program availability:* Part-time, evening/weekend. *Faculty:* 15 full-time (8 women), 17 part-time/adjunct (12 women). *Students:* 249 full-time (211 women), 91 part-time (76 women); includes 234 minority (58 Black or African American, non-Hispanic/Latino; 2 American Indian or Alaska Native, non-Hispanic/Latino; 11 Asian, non-Hispanic/Latino; 149 Hispanic/Latino; 1 Native Hawaiian or other Pacific Islander, non-Hispanic/Latino; 13 Two or more races, non-Hispanic/Latino), 2 international. Average age 31. 136 applicants, 69% accepted, 77 enrolled. In 2017, 114 master's awarded. *Degree requirements:* For master's, comprehensive exam, 24 (individual) or 50 hours (group) of psychotherapy, practicum. *Entrance requirements:* For master's, minimum undergraduate GPA of 2.75; official transcripts; three recommendations; 500-word essay; interview; 3 prerequisite courses completed with minimum C grade. Additional exam requirements/recommendations for international students: Required—TOEFL (minimum score 80 iBT). *Application deadline:* For fall admission, 8/1 priority date for domestic students, 7/1 for international students; for spring admission, 12/1 priority date for domestic students, 11/1 for international students. Applications are processed on a rolling basis. Application fee: $45. Electronic applications accepted. *Expenses:* Contact institution. *Financial support:* In 2017–18, 79 students received support. Federal Work-Study and scholarships/grants available. Financial award applicants required to submit CSS PROFILE or FAFSA. *Faculty research:* Identify formation, faith integration, psychological assessment, child abuse and child welfare, clinical psychology and crisis intervention techniques. *Unit head:* Dr. Jacqueline Gustafson, Dean, School of Behavioral Sciences, 951-343-4487, E-mail: jcraig@calbaptist.edu. *Application contact:* Deanna Meyer, Graduate Admission Counselor, 951-343-4463, E-mail: dmeyer@calbaptist.edu.
Website: http://www.calbaptist.edu/mft/

California Institute of Integral Studies, School of Professional Psychology and Health, San Francisco, CA 94103. Offers clinical psychology (Psy D); community mental health (MA); drama therapy (MA); expressive arts therapy (MA); integral counseling psychology (MA); integrative health studies (MA); psychological studies (MA); somatic psychology (MA). *Program availability:* Part-time, evening/weekend, 100% online, blended/hybrid learning. *Students:* 507 full-time (401 women), 96 part-time (77 women); includes 167 minority (29 Black or African American, non-Hispanic/Latino; 3 American Indian or Alaska Native, non-Hispanic/Latino; 32 Asian, non-Hispanic/Latino; 62 Hispanic/Latino; 2 Native Hawaiian or other Pacific Islander, non-Hispanic/Latino; 39 Two or more races, non-Hispanic/Latino), 60 international. Average age 34. 302 applicants, 89% accepted, 171 enrolled. In 2017, 194 master's, 18 doctorates awarded. *Degree requirements:* For doctorate, comprehensive exam, thesis/dissertation. *Entrance requirements:* For master's, minimum GPA of 3.0, letters of recommendation, writing sample; for doctorate, GRE, MA in psychology or social work with appropriate practical experience for advanced standing, or BA with a minimum GPA of 3.1; letters of recommendation; writing sample. Additional exam requirements/recommendations for international students: Required—TOEFL. *Application deadline:* For fall admission, 2/1 priority date for domestic and international students; for spring admission, 10/15 priority date for domestic and international students. Applications are processed on a rolling basis. Application fee: $65. Electronic applications accepted. *Expenses:* $21,400 (for MA); $32,734 (for PsyD). *Financial support:* Research assistantships with tuition reimbursements, teaching assistantships with tuition reimbursements, career-related internships or fieldwork, Federal Work-Study, and scholarships/grants available. Support available to part-time students. Financial award application deadline: 4/15; financial award applicants required to submit FAFSA. *Faculty research:* Transpersonal psychology, somatic psychology, expressive arts therapy, drama therapy, community mental health, ecopsychology, integrative health, human sexuality. *Unit head:* Nicolle Zapien, Academic Dean, 415-575-5577, E-mail: nzapien@ciis.edu. *Application contact:* Ellen Durst, Director of Admissions, 415-575-6100, Fax: 415-575-1268, E-mail: admissions@ciis.edu.

California State University, Bakersfield, Division of Graduate Studies, School of Social Sciences and Education, Program in Counseling Psychology, Bakersfield, CA 93311. Offers MS. *Faculty:* 11 part-time/adjunct (7 women). *Students:* 55 full-time (45 women); includes 34 minority (3 Black or African American, non-Hispanic/Latino; 4 Asian, non-Hispanic/Latino; 25 Hispanic/Latino; 2 Two or more races, non-Hispanic/Latino). Average age 28. 48 applicants, 50% accepted, 20 enrolled. In 2017, 18 master's awarded. *Degree requirements:* For master's, comprehensive exam. Application fee: $55. *Expenses:* Tuition, state resident: full-time $7176; part-time $4164 per year. *Financial support:* In 2017–18, fellowships (averaging $1,850 per year) were awarded; Federal Work-Study, scholarships/grants, and tuition waivers (full and partial) also available. Financial award application deadline: 3/2; financial award applicants required to submit FAFSA. *Unit head:* Liam Kelly, Program Director, 661-654-2363, Fax: 661-654-6955. *Application contact:* Debbie Blowers, Assistant Director of Admissions and Evaluations, 661-654-3381, E-mail: dblowers@csub.edu.
Website: https://www.csub.edu/psychology/mscounselingpsych/index.html

California State University, Fresno, Division of Research and Graduate Studies, Kremen School of Education and Human Development, Department of Counselor Education and Rehabilitation, Program in Clinical Rehabilitation and Mental Health Counseling, Fresno, CA 93740-8027. Offers MS. *Accreditation:* ACA; CORE. *Program availability:* Part-time, evening/weekend. *Degree requirements:* For master's, internship; project, thesis, or comprehensive exam. *Entrance requirements:* For master's, GRE General Test, MAT, minimum GPA of 3.0, official transcripts. Additional exam requirements/recommendations for international students: Required—TOEFL. Electronic applications accepted. *Faculty research:* Aging, career development, job retention, rehabilitation administration.

California State University, San Bernardino, Graduate Studies, College of Social and Behavioral Sciences, Department of Psychology, San Bernardino, CA 92407. Offers child development (MA); clinical/counseling psychology (MS); industrial/organizational psychology (MS); psychological science (MA). *Faculty:* 13 full-time (4 women), 2 part-time/adjunct (both women). *Students:* 61 full-time (41 women), 17 part-time (14 women); includes 47 minority (2 Black or African American, non-Hispanic/Latino; 3 Asian, non-Hispanic/Latino; 33 Hispanic/Latino; 9 Two or more races, non-Hispanic/Latino), 3 international. Average age 28. 190 applicants, 19% accepted, 33 enrolled. In 2017, 28 master's awarded. *Degree requirements:* For master's, comprehensive exam, thesis (for some programs). *Entrance requirements:* Additional exam requirements/recommendations for international students: Required—TOEFL. Application fee: $55. *Financial support:* Fellowships, research assistantships, and teaching assistantships available. *Faculty research:* Perceptual development, human memory, psychopharmacology, psychology of women, language acquisition. *Unit head:* Dr. Robert Ricco, Chair, 909-537-5485, Fax: 909-537-7003, E-mail: rricco@csusb.edu. *Application contact:* Dr. Dorota Huizinga, Dean of Graduate Studies, 909-537-3064, E-mail: dorota.huizinga@csusb.edu.
Website: https://csbs.csusb.edu/psychology

California State University, Stanislaus, College of Science, Programs in Psychology, Turlock, CA 95382. Offers behavior analysis (MA, MS); counseling psychology (MS); general psychology (MA). *Program availability:* Part-time. *Degree requirements:* For master's, thesis. *Entrance requirements:* For master's, GRE, minimum GPA of 3.0, 3 letters of reference, 16 psychology prerequisites, personal statement. Additional exam requirements/recommendations for international students: Required—TOEFL (minimum score 550 paper-based). Electronic applications accepted. *Faculty research:* Hedonic tone judgment, syntax and autism, early literacy assessment and native and non-native languages.

Counseling Psychology

California University of Pennsylvania, School of Graduate Studies and Research, College of Education and Human Services, Department of Counselor Education, California, PA 15419-1394. Offers clinical mental health counseling (MS); school counseling (M Ed). *Accreditation:* ACA; NCATE. *Program availability:* Part-time, evening/weekend. *Degree requirements:* For master's, comprehensive exam, thesis optional. *Entrance requirements:* For master's, MAT, minimum GPA of 3.0, resume, letters of reference. Additional exam requirements/recommendations for international students: Required—TOEFL (minimum score 550 paper-based; 80 iBT). *Application deadline:* For fall admission, 8/1 priority date for domestic and international students. Applications are processed on a rolling basis. Application fee: $25. Electronic applications accepted. *Financial support:* Applicants required to submit FAFSA. *Faculty research:* Mind-body theories and practice, grief issues, career development, supervision, sports counseling. *Unit head:* Dr. Grafton Eliason, Program Coordinator, 724-938-4464, E-mail: eliason@calu.edu. *Application contact:* Suzanne C. Powers, Director of Graduate Admissions and Recruitment, 724-938-4029, Fax: 724-938-5712, E-mail: powers_s@cup.edu.
Website: http://www.calu.edu/academics/colleges/education/counselor-education/

Cambridge College, School of Psychology and Counseling, Boston, MA 02129. Offers addiction counseling (M Ed); alcohol and drug counseling (Certificate); counseling psychology (M Ed, CAGS); counseling psychology: forensic counseling (M Ed); marriage and family therapy (M Ed); mental health and addiction counseling (M Ed); mental health counseling (M Ed); mental health counseling for school guidance counselors (Post Master's Certificate); psychological studies (M Ed); school adjustment and mental health counseling (M Ed); school adjustment, mental health and addiction counseling (M Ed); school guidance counselor (M Ed); trauma studies (Certificate). *Program availability:* Part-time, evening/weekend. *Degree requirements:* For master's and other advanced degree, thesis, practicum/internship. *Entrance requirements:* For master's, resume, 2 professional references; for other advanced degree, official transcripts, documents for transfer credit evaluation, resume, written personal statement/essay, 2 professional references, health insurance, immunizations form. Additional exam requirements/recommendations for international students: Required—TOEFL (minimum score 550 paper-based; 79 iBT), Michigan English Language Assessment Battery (minimum score 85); Recommended—IELTS (minimum score 6). Electronic applications accepted. *Expenses:* Contact institution. *Faculty research:* Trauma, drug and alcohol counseling, cross-cultural issues, school counseling, trauma in schools.

Capella University, Harold Abel School of Social and Behavioral Science, Master's Programs in Counseling, Minneapolis, MN 55402. Offers child and adolescent development (MS); general addiction counseling (MS); general marriage and family counseling/therapy (MS); general mental health counseling (MS); general school counseling (MS).

Capella University, Harold Abel School of Social and Behavioral Science, Master's Programs in Psychology, Minneapolis, MN 55402. Offers applied behavior analysis (MS); clinical psychology (MS); counseling psychology (MS); educational psychology (MS); evaluation, research, and measurement (MS); general advanced studies in human behavior (MS); general psychology (MS); industrial/organizational psychology (MS); leadership coaching psychology (MS); school psychology (MS); sport psychology (MS).

Carlos Albizu University, Miami Campus, Graduate Programs, Miami, FL 33172-2209. Offers clinical psychology (PhD, Psy D); entrepreneurship (MBA); exceptional student education (MS); human services (PhD); industrial/organizational psychology (MS); marriage and family therapy (MS); mental health counseling (MS); nonprofit management (MBA); organizational management (MBA); psychology (MS); speech and language pathology (MS); teaching English for speakers of other languages (MS). *Accreditation:* APA. *Program availability:* Part-time, evening/weekend, 100% online, blended/hybrid learning. *Faculty:* 32 full-time (24 women), 27 part-time/adjunct (15 women). *Students:* 411 full-time (345 women), 248 part-time (215 women); includes 562 minority (53 Black or African American, non-Hispanic/Latino; 4 Asian, non-Hispanic/Latino; 498 Hispanic/Latino; 7 Two or more races, non-Hispanic/Latino), 23 international. Average age 34. 391 applicants, 42% accepted, 154 enrolled. In 2017, 96 master's, 54 doctorates awarded. Terminal master's awarded for partial completion of doctoral program. *Degree requirements:* For master's, comprehensive exam (for some programs), integrative project (for MBA); research project (for exceptional student education, teaching English as a second language); for doctorate, comprehensive examinations, internship, project/dissertation. *Entrance requirements:* For master's, GRE/EXADEP, bachelor's degree from accredited institution, minimum GPA of 3.0, 3 letters of recommendation, interview, resume, statement of purpose, official transcripts; for doctorate, GRE (for Psy D), 3 letters of recommendation, resume, interview, statement of purpose, official transcripts; bachelor's degree and minimum GPA of 3.25 (for Psy D); master's degree and minimum GPA of 3.0 (for PhD). Additional exam requirements/recommendations for international students: Required—Michigan Test of English Language Proficiency. *Application deadline:* For fall admission, 4/1 priority date for domestic students, 5/1 priority date for international students; for spring admission, 11/1 priority date for domestic students, 9/1 priority date for international students. Applications are processed on a rolling basis. Application fee: $50. Electronic applications accepted. Application fee is waived when completed online. *Expenses:* Contact institution. *Financial support:* In 2017–18, 145 students received support. Federal Work-Study, scholarships/grants, unspecified assistantships, and tuition discounts available. Financial award application deadline: 6/1; financial award applicants required to submit FAFSA. *Faculty research:* Psychotherapy, forensic psychology, neuropsychology, special education, speech-language pathology, criminal justice. *Unit head:* Dr. Etiony Aldarondo, Provost, 305-593-1223 Ext. 3138, Fax: 305-592-7930, E-mail: ealdarondo@albizu.edu. *Application contact:* Sonia Feliciano, Institutional Director of Student Recruitment, 305-593-1223 Ext. 3108, Fax: 305-477-8983, E-mail: sfeliciano@albizu.edu.

Carlow University, College of Leadership and Social Change, Program in Counseling Psychology, Pittsburgh, PA 15213-3165. Offers Psy D. *Accreditation:* APA. *Program availability:* Part-time, evening/weekend. *Students:* 26 full-time (20 women), 11 part-time (8 women); includes 6 minority (2 Black or African American, non-Hispanic/Latino; 2 Asian, non-Hispanic/Latino; 1 Hispanic/Latino; 1 Two or more races, non-Hispanic/Latino). Average age 31. 29 applicants, 41% accepted, 11 enrolled. In 2017, 6 doctorates awarded. *Degree requirements:* For doctorate, thesis/dissertation, internship. *Entrance requirements:* For doctorate, GRE, resume or curriculum vitae; personal essay; reflective essay; official transcripts from all previous undergraduate and graduate institutions; three letters of recommendation; master's degree in closely-related field; interview. Additional exam requirements/recommendations for international students: Required—TOEFL (minimum score 550 paper-based). *Application deadline:* Applications are processed on a rolling basis. Electronic applications accepted. *Expenses:* Contact institution. *Financial support:* Unspecified assistantships available. Financial award application deadline: 4/1; financial award applicants required to submit FAFSA. *Unit head:* Dr. Joseph M. Roberts, Chair, Psy D Program, 412-575-6331, Fax: 412-578-6357, E-mail: jmroberts@carlow.edu. *Application contact:* 412-578-6059, Fax:

412-578-6321, E-mail: gradstudies@carlow.edu.
Website: http://www.carlow.edu/PsyD_Counseling_Psychology.aspx

Carlow University, College of Leadership and Social Change, Program in Professional Counseling, Pittsburgh, PA 15213-3165. Offers child and family (MS). *Program availability:* Part-time, evening/weekend. *Students:* 112 full-time (98 women), 18 part-time (13 women); includes 38 minority (29 Black or African American, non-Hispanic/Latino; 1 American Indian or Alaska Native, non-Hispanic/Latino; 2 Asian, non-Hispanic/Latino; 4 Hispanic/Latino; 2 Two or more races, non-Hispanic/Latino), 1 international. Average age 30. 75 applicants, 93% accepted, 30 enrolled. In 2017, 33 master's awarded. *Entrance requirements:* For master's, personal essay; resume or curriculum vitae; three recommendations; official transcripts; interview; minimum undergraduate GPA of 3.0. Additional exam requirements/recommendations for international students: Required—TOEFL (minimum score 550 paper-based). *Application deadline:* Applications are processed on a rolling basis. Electronic applications accepted. *Expenses:* Tuition: Full-time $12,103; part-time $825 per credit hour. Tuition and fees vary according to program. *Financial support:* Application deadline: 4/1; applicants required to submit FAFSA. *Unit head:* Dr. Travis W. Schermer, Director, 412-575-6650, Fax: 412-575-6357, E-mail: twschermer@carlow.edu.
Website: http://www.carlow.edu/Master_of_Science_in_Professional_Counseling.aspx

Carlow University, College of Leadership and Social Change, Program in Student Affairs/Professional Counseling, Pittsburgh, PA 15213-3165. Offers MA/MS. *Program availability:* Part-time, evening/weekend. *Students:* 14 full-time (12 women), 2 part-time (1 woman); includes 8 minority (6 Black or African American, non-Hispanic/Latino; 1 Hispanic/Latino; 1 Two or more races, non-Hispanic/Latino). Average age 33. 11 applicants, 82% accepted, 6 enrolled. *Entrance requirements:* Additional exam requirements/recommendations for international students: Required—TOEFL (minimum score 550 paper-based). *Application deadline:* Applications are processed on a rolling basis. Electronic applications accepted. *Expenses:* Tuition: Full-time $12,103; part-time $825 per credit hour. Tuition and fees vary according to program. *Financial support:* Application deadline: 4/1; applicants required to submit FAFSA. *Unit head:* Dr. Harriet Schwartz, Chair, 412-578-8720, E-mail: hlschwartz@carlow.edu. *Application contact:* 412-578-6059, Fax: 412-578-6321, E-mail: gradstudies@carlow.edu.

Centenary University, Program in Counseling Psychology, Hackettstown, NJ 07840-2100. Offers counseling (MA); counseling psychology (MA). *Program availability:* Part-time, evening/weekend, online learning. *Degree requirements:* For master's, thesis, fieldwork.

Central Michigan University, Central Michigan University Global Campus, Program in Counseling, Mount Pleasant, MI 48859. Offers professional counseling (MA); school counseling (MA). *Accreditation:* TEAC. *Program availability:* Part-time, evening/weekend. *Entrance requirements:* For master's, MAT, minimum GPA of 2.7. Additional exam requirements/recommendations for international students: Required—TOEFL. Electronic applications accepted.

Central Michigan University, College of Graduate Studies, College of Humanities and Social and Behavioral Sciences, Department of Psychology, Mount Pleasant, MI 48859. Offers clinical psychology (PhD); experimental psychology (MS, PhD), including applied experimental psychology (PhD), experimental psychology (MS); industrial and organizational psychology (MA, PhD), including industrial and organizational psychology, occupational health psychology (PhD); neuroscience (MS, PhD); school psychology (PhD, S Psy S), including psychological services (S Psy S), school psychology (PhD). *Accreditation:* APA (one or more programs are accredited). Terminal master's awarded for partial completion of doctoral program. *Degree requirements:* For master's, thesis or alternative; for doctorate, thesis/dissertation; for S Psy S, thesis. *Entrance requirements:* For doctorate, GRE. Electronic applications accepted. *Faculty research:* Experimental psychology, clinical psychology, industrial/organizational psychology, school psychology, neuroscience.

Central Washington University, School of Graduate Studies and Research, College of the Sciences, Department of Psychology, Program in Mental Health Counseling, Ellensburg, WA 98926. Offers MS. *Accreditation:* ACA. *Degree requirements:* For master's, thesis or alternative, internship. *Entrance requirements:* For master's, GRE General Test, minimum GPA of 3.0. Additional exam requirements/recommendations for international students: Required—TOEFL (minimum score 550 paper-based; 79 iBT). *Application deadline:* For fall admission, 2/1 for domestic students. Applications are processed on a rolling basis. Application fee: $50. Electronic applications accepted. *Financial support:* Application deadline: 3/1; applicants required to submit FAFSA. *Unit head:* Dr. Elizabeth Haviland, Program Director, 509-963-2371, E-mail: haviland@cwu.edu. *Application contact:* Justine Eason, Admissions Program Coordinator, 509-963-3103, Fax: 509-963-1799, E-mail: masters@cwu.edu.

Chaminade University of Honolulu, Office of Professional and Continuing Education, Program in Counseling Psychology, Honolulu, HI 96816-1578. Offers marriage and family counseling (MSCP); mental health counseling (MSCP); school counseling (MSCP). *Program availability:* Part-time, evening/weekend, blended/hybrid learning. *Faculty:* 6 full-time (3 women), 16 part-time/adjunct (7 women). *Students:* 158 full-time (118 women), 34 part-time (26 women); includes 131 minority (13 Black or African American, non-Hispanic/Latino; 2 American Indian or Alaska Native, non-Hispanic/Latino; 61 Asian, non-Hispanic/Latino; 14 Hispanic/Latino; 39 Native Hawaiian or other Pacific Islander, non-Hispanic/Latino; 2 Two or more races, non-Hispanic/Latino), 3 international. Average age 31. 53 applicants, 96% accepted, 37 enrolled. In 2017, 78 master's awarded. *Degree requirements:* For master's, comprehensive exam, internship/practicum. *Entrance requirements:* For master's, minimum undergraduate GPA of 3.0, 3 letters of recommendation, resume. Additional exam requirements/recommendations for international students: Required—TOEFL (minimum score 550 paper-based; 79 iBT). *Application deadline:* Applications are processed on a rolling basis. Application fee: $40. Electronic applications accepted. *Expenses:* $860 per credit hour plus $93 fee per online course. *Financial support:* Applicants required to submit FAFSA. *Unit head:* Dr. Robert G. Santee, Dean, 808-735-4751, Fax: 808-739-4670, E-mail: mscp@chaminade.edu. *Application contact:* 808-735-4755, E-mail: gradserv@chaminade.edu.
Website: https://pace.chaminade.edu/graduate-programs/mscp-program/

Chatham University, Program in Counseling Psychology, Pittsburgh, PA 15232-2826. Offers child, adolescent and family (MSCP); counseling psychology (Psy D); health and holistic (MSCP); organization and supervision (MSCP); sport and exercise (MSCP). *Accreditation:* APA. *Program availability:* Part-time, evening/weekend. *Faculty:* 11 full-time (10 women). *Students:* 61 full-time (46 women), 25 part-time (22 women); includes 12 minority (9 Black or African American, non-Hispanic/Latino; 2 Hispanic/Latino; 1 Two or more races, non-Hispanic/Latino), 3 international. Average age 30. 124 applicants, 62% accepted, 45 enrolled. In 2017, 38 master's awarded. *Degree requirements:* For master's, thesis optional, supervised internship; for doctorate, thesis/dissertation, internship. *Entrance requirements:* For master's, minimum GPA of 3.0; 2 letters of recommendation; resume; prerequisite coursework in statistics, biology, and psychology; for doctorate, GRE. Additional exam requirements/recommendations for international students: Required—TOEFL (minimum score 600 paper-based; 100 iBT), IELTS (minimum score 7), TWE. *Application deadline:* For fall admission, 4/1 priority

date for domestic and international students; for spring admission, 11/1 for domestic students, 10/1 for international students. Applications are processed on a rolling basis. Application fee: $45. Electronic applications accepted. Application fee is waived when completed online. *Expenses: Tuition:* Full-time $16,740; part-time $930 per credit. *Required fees:* $486; $27 per credit. $243 per semester. *Financial support:* Career-related internships or fieldwork available. Financial award applicants required to submit FAFSA. *Faculty research:* Trauma and recovery, hypnosis, psychospiritual dimensions of healing, psychotherapy of schizophrenia. *Unit head:* Dr. Mary Beth Mannarino, Director, 412-365-1196, Fax: 412-365-1505, E-mail: mmannarino@chatham.edu. *Application contact:* Katie Noel, Assistant Director of Graduate Admission, 412-365-2758, Fax: 412-365-1609, E-mail: gradadmissions@chatham.edu.
Website: http://www.chatham.edu/mscp

Chestnut Hill College, School of Graduate Studies, Division of Psychology, Program in Clinical and Counseling Psychology, Philadelphia, PA 19118-2693. Offers clinical and counseling psychology (MS, CAS), including child and adolescent therapy, child and adolescent therapy with autism spectrum disorders, co-occurring disorders, couple and family therapy, diverse and underserved communities, generalist (MS), trauma studies. *Program availability:* Part-time, evening/weekend. *Degree requirements:* For master's, thesis optional, practica. *Entrance requirements:* For master's, GRE General Test, writing sample, letters of recommendation. Additional exam requirements/recommendations for international students: Required—TOEFL (minimum score 500 paper-based), IELTS (minimum score 6.0), or TWE (minimum score 22). Electronic applications accepted. *Expenses:* Contact institution. *Faculty research:* Play therapy, eating disorders, addictions, group psychology and group therapy, health psychology.

City University of Seattle, Graduate Division, Division of Arts and Sciences, Seattle, WA 98121. Offers counseling psychology (MA). *Accreditation:* ACA. *Program availability:* Part-time, evening/weekend, online learning. *Degree requirements:* For master's, comprehensive exam (for some programs), thesis (for some programs). *Entrance requirements:* For master's, baccalaureate degree or equivalent from an accredited or otherwise recognized institution. Additional exam requirements/recommendations for international students: Recommended—TOEFL (minimum score 567 paper-based; 87 iBT), IELTS, TWE. Electronic applications accepted. *Expenses:* Contact institution.

Cleveland State University, College of Graduate Studies, College of Education and Human Services, Department of Counseling, Administration, Supervision and Adult Learning (CASAL), Cleveland, OH 44115. Offers adult learning and development (M Ed); counselor education (PhD); early childhood mental health counseling (Certificate); educational administration and supervision (M Ed). *Accreditation:* ACA (one or more programs are accredited). *Program availability:* Part-time, evening/weekend. *Faculty:* 15 full-time (8 women), 19 part-time/adjunct (10 women). *Students:* 121 full-time (98 women), 272 part-time (198 women); includes 127 minority (106 Black or African American, non-Hispanic/Latino; 1 American Indian or Alaska Native, non-Hispanic/Latino; 4 Asian, non-Hispanic/Latino; 11 Hispanic/Latino; 5 Two or more races, non-Hispanic/Latino), 8 international. Average age 33. 57 applicants, 93% accepted, 51 enrolled. In 2017, 99 master's awarded. *Degree requirements:* For master's, comprehensive exam (for some programs), thesis optional, internship. *Entrance requirements:* For master's, GRE General Test or MAT, letter of recommendation and minimum GPA of 2.75 (for counseling); 2 letters of recommendation and interviews (for organizational leadership). Additional exam requirements/recommendations for international students: Required—TOEFL (minimum score 550 paper-based; 78 iBT), IELTS (minimum score 6). *Application deadline:* For fall admission, 6/21 for domestic students, 5/15 for international students; for spring admission, 8/31 for domestic students, 11/1 for international students. Application fee: $40. Electronic applications accepted. *Financial support:* In 2017–18, 19 students received support, including 10 research assistantships with tuition reimbursements available (averaging $11,882 per year), 5 teaching assistantships with tuition reimbursements available (averaging $11,882 per year); scholarships/grants and unspecified assistantships also available. Support available to part-time students. *Faculty research:* Education law, career development, bullying, psychopharmacology, counseling and spirituality. *Total annual research expenditures:* $225,821. *Unit head:* Dr. R. Elliott Ingersoll, Chair/Professor, 216-687-4582, Fax: 216-687-5378, E-mail: r.ingersoll@csuohio.edu. *Application contact:* Deborah L. Brown, Interim Assistant Director, Graduate Admissions, 216-523-7572, Fax: 216-687-5400, E-mail: d.l.brown@csuohio.edu.
Website: http://www.csuohio.edu/cehs/departments/CASAL/casal_dept.html

Cleveland State University, College of Graduate Studies, College of Education and Human Services, Program in Urban Education, Specialization in Counseling Psychology, Cleveland, OH 44115. Offers PhD. *Faculty:* 5 full-time (3 women), 1 part-time/adjunct (0 women). *Students:* 19 full-time (15 women), 6 part-time (3 women); includes 5 minority (2 Black or African American, non-Hispanic/Latino; 2 Hispanic/Latino; 1 Two or more races, non-Hispanic/Latino), 2 international. Average age 30. 36 applicants, 31% accepted, 3 enrolled. In 2017, 5 doctorates awarded. *Entrance requirements:* For doctorate, GRE (Verbal, Quantitative, and Writing), minimum undergraduate GPA of 2.75, graduate 3.0); 3 letters of recommendation; personal statement; curriculum vitae; interview. Additional exam requirements/recommendations for international students: Required—TOEFL (minimum score 550 paper-based; 78 iBT), IELTS (minimum score 6). Application fee: $40. Electronic applications accepted. *Financial support:* In 2017–18, 14 students received support. Research assistantships, teaching assistantships, tuition waivers (partial), and unspecified assistantships available. Financial award application deadline: 1/15. *Faculty research:* Vocational psychology, low SES urban youth, women's identity and work, work and family integration, professional issues in psychology, clinical supervision and training, research productivity of psychologists and psychology trainees, leadership training in professional organizations, college students' development and adjustment, diversity issues with a focus on gender and sexual minorities, social constructionism, childhood career development, multicultural issues in mental health. *Unit head:* Dr. Graham Stead, Director of Doctoral Studies, 216-687-4697, Fax: 216-687-5378, E-mail: g.b.stead@csuohio.edu. *Application contact:* Rita M. Grabowski, Administrative Assistant, 216-687-4697, Fax: 216-687-5378, E-mail: r.grabowski@csuohio.edu.
Website: http://www.csuohio.edu/cehs/departments/DOC/cp_doc.html

The College at Brockport, State University of New York, School of Education, Health, and Human Services, Department of Counselor Education, Brockport, NY 14420-2997. Offers college counseling (MS Ed, CAS); mental health counseling (MS, CAS); school counseling (MS Ed, CAS); school counselor supervision (CAS). *Accreditation:* ACA (one or more programs are accredited). *Program availability:* Part-time. *Faculty:* 5 full-time (3 women), 6 part-time/adjunct (4 women). *Students:* 32 full-time (23 women), 74 part-time (63 women); includes 24 minority (13 Black or African American, non-Hispanic/Latino; 1 Asian, non-Hispanic/Latino; 4 Hispanic/Latino; 6 Two or more races, non-Hispanic/Latino). 94 applicants, 60% accepted, 24 enrolled. In 2017, 31 master's, 6 other advanced degrees awarded. *Degree requirements:* For master's, thesis, internship. *Entrance requirements:* For master's, group interview, letters of recommendation, written objectives, audio response; for CAS, master's degree, New York state school counselor certificate. Additional exam requirements/recommendations for international students: Required—TOEFL (minimum score 550 paper-based; 79 iBT),

IELTS (minimum score 6.5). *Application deadline:* For fall admission, 2/1 priority date for domestic and international students; for spring admission, 9/1 priority date for domestic and international students; for summer admission, 2/1 priority date for domestic and international students. Application fee: $80. Electronic applications accepted. *Expenses:* Tuition, state resident: full-time $10,870; part-time $453 per credit hour. Tuition, nonresident: full-time $22,210. *Required fees:* $988; $246 per semester. *Financial support:* In 2017–18, 1 fellowship with full tuition reimbursement (averaging $7,500 per year), 1 teaching assistantship with full tuition reimbursement (averaging $6,000 per year) were awarded; Federal Work-Study, scholarships/grants, and unspecified assistantships also available. Support available to part-time students. Financial award application deadline: 3/15; financial award applicants required to submit FAFSA. *Faculty research:* Gender and diversity issues; counseling outcomes; spirituality; school, college and mental health counseling; obesity. *Unit head:* Dr. Susan Seem, Chair, 585-395-5492, Fax: 585-395-2366, E-mail: sseem@brockport.edu. *Application contact:* Danielle A. Welch, Graduate Admissions Counselor, 585-395-5465, Fax: 585-395-2515.
Website: https://www.brockport.edu/academics/counselor_education/

The College of New Rochelle, Graduate School, Division of Human Services, Program in Guidance and Counseling, New Rochelle, NY 10805-2308. Offers MS, Advanced Certificate. *Program availability:* Part-time. *Degree requirements:* For master's, internship. *Entrance requirements:* For master's, interview. *Expenses: Tuition:* Full-time $17,406. *Required fees:* $1120.

The College of New Rochelle, Graduate School, Division of Human Services, Program in Mental Health Counseling, New Rochelle, NY 10805-2308. Offers mental health counseling (MS); thanatology (Certificate). *Degree requirements:* For Certificate, internship. *Expenses: Tuition:* Full-time $17,406. *Required fees:* $1120.

College of Saint Elizabeth, Department of Psychology, Morristown, NJ 07960-6989. Offers counseling psychology (MA, Psy D), including mental health counseling (MA), school counseling (MA). *Program availability:* Part-time. *Faculty:* 4 full-time (3 women), 7 part-time/adjunct (all women). *Students:* 37 full-time (32 women), 40 part-time (37 women); includes 30 minority (12 Black or African American, non-Hispanic/Latino; 1 Asian, non-Hispanic/Latino; 16 Hispanic/Latino; 1 Two or more races, non-Hispanic/Latino). Average age 31. 37 applicants, 81% accepted, 24 enrolled. In 2017, 17 master's, 3 doctorates awarded. *Degree requirements:* For master's, thesis or alternative; for doctorate, thesis/dissertation. *Entrance requirements:* For master's, minimum GPA of 3.0, BA in psychology (preferred), 12 credits of course work in psychology; for doctorate, GRE, 3 letters of recommendation from professionals who can comment on the applicant's qualifications for doctoral study; master's degree in counseling psychology, forensic psychology and counseling, or its equivalent. Additional exam requirements/recommendations for international students: Required—TOEFL (minimum score 550 paper-based; 79 iBT), IELTS (minimum score 6.5). *Application deadline:* For fall admission, 5/1 for international students. Applications are processed on a rolling basis. Application fee: $35. Electronic applications accepted. Application fee is waived when completed online. *Expenses:* Contact institution. *Financial support:* Career-related internships or fieldwork, scholarships/grants, tuition waivers (partial), and unspecified assistantships available. Support available to part-time students. Financial award applicants required to submit FAFSA. *Unit head:* Dr. Michelle M. Barrett, Director, Graduate and Doctoral Programs in Psychology, 973-290-4027, Fax: 973-290-4676, E-mail: mbarrett01@cse.edu. *Application contact:* Lori J. Fragoso, Director of Graduate and Continuing Studies Admissions, 973-290-4413, Fax: 973-290-4710, E-mail: apply@cse.edu.
Website: https://www.cse.edu/academics/prof-studies/psychology/

College of St. Joseph, Graduate Programs, Division of Psychology and Human Services, Program in Clinical Mental Health Counseling, Rutland, VT 05701-3899. Offers MS. *Program availability:* Part-time. *Degree requirements:* For master's, comprehensive exam. *Entrance requirements:* For master's, official college transcripts; 2 letters of reference. Additional exam requirements/recommendations for international students: Required—TOEFL (minimum score 550 paper-based). Electronic applications accepted.

The College of Saint Rose, Graduate Studies, Thelma P. Lally School of Education, Programs in Clinical Mental Health Counseling, Albany, NY 12203-1419. Offers clinical mental health counseling (Certificate); school counseling (MS Ed, Certificate), including mental health counseling (MS Ed). *Students:* 44 full-time (39 women), 20 part-time (17 women); includes 11 minority (6 Black or African American, non-Hispanic/Latino; 2 Asian, non-Hispanic/Latino; 2 Hispanic/Latino; 1 Two or more races, non-Hispanic/Latino), 2 international. Average age 28. 32 applicants, 63% accepted, 12 enrolled. In 2017, 23 master's awarded. *Entrance requirements:* For master's, minimum undergraduate GPA of 3.0. Additional exam requirements/recommendations for international students: Required—TOEFL (minimum score 550 paper-based; 80 iBT), IELTS (minimum score 6), PTE (minimum score 56). *Application deadline:* For fall admission, 4/1 for domestic and international students; for spring admission, 10/15 priority date for domestic and international students; for summer admission, 3/15 for domestic and international students. Applications are processed on a rolling basis. Application fee: $40. Electronic applications accepted. *Expenses: Tuition:* Full-time $7191; part-time $799 per credit hour. *Required fees:* $924; $462 per credit hour. Tuition and fees vary according to course load. *Financial support:* Career-related internships or fieldwork, scholarships/grants, tuition waivers (partial), and unspecified assistantships available. Support available to part-time students. Financial award application deadline: 4/15. *Unit head:* Claudia Lingertat-Putnam, Chair, 518-337-4311, E-mail: lingertc@strose.edu. *Application contact:* Cris Murray, Assistant Vice President for Graduate Recruitment and Enrollment, 518-485-3390, Fax: 518-458-5479, E-mail: grad@strose.edu.
Website: https://www.strose.edu/counseling/

College of Staten Island of the City University of New York, Graduate Programs, Division of Humanities and Social Sciences, Staten Island, NY 10314-6600. Offers autism spectrum disorders (Advanced Certificate); cinema and media studies (MA); clinical mental health counseling (MA), including clinical mental health counseling; English (MA), including English; history (MA), including history; liberal studies (MA); public history (Advanced Certificate). *Faculty:* 21 full-time, 16 part-time/adjunct. *Students:* 162. 307 applicants, 47% accepted, 91 enrolled. In 2017, 49 master's, 3 other advanced degrees awarded. *Expenses:* Tuition, state resident: full-time $10,450; part-time $440 per credit. Tuition, nonresident: full-time $19,320; part-time $440 per credit. *Required fees:* $181.10 per semester. Tuition and fees vary according to program. *Unit head:* Dr. Gerry Milligan, Dean of Humanities and Social Sciences, 718-982-2315, Fax: 718-982-2316, E-mail: gerry.milligan@csi.cuny.edu. *Application contact:* Sasha Spence, Associate Director for Graduate Admissions, 718-982-2019, Fax: 718-982-2500, E-mail: sasha.spence@csi.cuny.edu.
Website: http://www.csi.cuny.edu/academicsresearch/deanhumanities/

Colorado Christian University, Program in Counseling, Lakewood, CO 80226. Offers MAC. *Accreditation:* ACA. *Program availability:* Part-time, evening/weekend. *Degree requirements:* For master's, thesis optional. *Entrance requirements:* For master's, GRE General Test, 3 letters of recommendation. Additional exam requirements/recommendations for international students: Required—TOEFL. Electronic applications accepted. *Expenses:* Contact institution.

Counseling Psychology

Concordia University Chicago, College of Graduate and Innovative Programs, Program in Community Counseling, River Forest, IL 60305-1499. Offers MA. *Accreditation:* ACA. *Degree requirements:* For master's, final project. *Entrance requirements:* For master's, minimum GPA of 2.9. Additional exam requirements/recommendations for international students: Required—TOEFL (minimum score 550 paper-based). Electronic applications accepted.

Delaware Valley University, Program in Counseling Psychology, Doylestown, PA 18901-2697. Offers child and adolescent therapy (MA); social justice community counseling (MA).

DePaul University, College of Education, Chicago, IL 60614. Offers bilingual-bicultural education (M Ed, MA); counseling (M Ed, MA), including clinical mental health counseling, college student development, school counseling; curriculum studies (M Ed, MA, Ed D); early childhood education (M Ed, MA, Ed D); educational leadership (M Ed, MA, Ed D), including Catholic leadership (M Ed, MA), general (M Ed, MA), higher education (M Ed, MA), physical education (M Ed, MA), principal preparation (M Ed), teacher preparation (M Ed); elementary education (M Ed, MA); middle grades education (M Ed); middle school mathematics education (MS); reading specialist (M Ed, MA); secondary education (M Ed, MA); social and cultural foundations in education (M Ed, MA); special education (M Ed); sport, fitness and recreation leadership (MS); value-creating education for global citizenship (M Ed); world languages education (M Ed, MA). *Program availability:* Part-time, evening/weekend, online learning. *Degree requirements:* For doctorate, thesis/dissertation. *Application deadline:* Applications are processed on a rolling basis. Application fee: $40. Electronic applications accepted. *Financial support:* Application deadline: 12/31; applicants required to submit FAFSA. *Unit head:* Dr. Paul Zionts, Dean, 773-325-7581, Fax: 773-325-7713, E-mail: pzionts@depaul.edu. *Application contact:* Dr. Paul Zionts, Dean, 773-325-7581, Fax: 773-325-7713, E-mail: pzionts@depaul.edu.
Website: http://education.depaul.edu

Dominican University of California, School of Health and Natural Sciences, Counseling Psychology Department, San Rafael, CA 94901-2298. Offers general (MS); marriage and family therapy (MS). *Program availability:* Part-time, evening/weekend. *Faculty:* 4 full-time (2 women), 7 part-time/adjunct (5 women). *Students:* 48 full-time (40 women), 28 part-time (25 women); includes 21 minority (2 Black or African American, non-Hispanic/Latino; 1 Asian, non-Hispanic/Latino; 14 Hispanic/Latino; 1 Native Hawaiian or other Pacific Islander, non-Hispanic/Latino; 3 Two or more races, non-Hispanic/Latino), 1 international. Average age 38. 28 applicants, 100% accepted, 17 enrolled. In 2017, 12 master's awarded. *Degree requirements:* For master's, comprehensive exam (for some programs), thesis (for some programs). *Entrance requirements:* For master's, minimum GPA of 3.0 for last 60 units, autobiography, response to scenario. Additional exam requirements/recommendations for international students: Required—TOEFL (minimum score 550 paper-based; 80 iBT), IELTS (minimum score 6.5). *Application deadline:* For fall admission, 4/1 priority date for domestic and international students; for spring admission, 11/15 priority date for domestic and international students. Applications are processed on a rolling basis. Application fee: $0. Electronic applications accepted. *Expenses:* $1,100 per unit. *Financial support:* In 2017–18, 15 students received support. Career-related internships or fieldwork, scholarships/grants, and health care benefits available. Support available to part-time students. Financial award application deadline: 3/2; financial award applicants required to submit FAFSA. *Unit head:* Dr. Robin R. Gayle, Chair, 415-485-3263. *Application contact:* Michael Lavigna, Assistant Director, Graduate Admissions, 415-485-3253, Fax: 415-485-3214, E-mail: gradmissions@dominican.edu.
Website: https://www.dominican.edu/academics/hns2/counpsych

Duquesne University, School of Education, Department of Counseling, Psychology, and Special Education, Program in Counselor Education, Pittsburgh, PA 15282-0001. Offers clinical mental health counseling (MS Ed, Post-Master's Certificate); counselor education and supervision (Ed D); counselor licensure (Post-Master's Certificate); marriage and family counseling (MS Ed); school counseling (MS Ed). *Accreditation:* ACA (one or more programs are accredited). *Program availability:* Part-time, evening/weekend. *Faculty:* 8 full-time (3 women). *Students:* 194 full-time (140 women), 10 part-time (6 women); includes 41 minority (21 Black or African American, non-Hispanic/Latino; 1 American Indian or Alaska Native, non-Hispanic/Latino; 5 Asian, non-Hispanic/Latino; 6 Hispanic/Latino; 8 Two or more races, non-Hispanic/Latino), 8 international. Average age 28. 149 applicants, 78% accepted, 66 enrolled. In 2017, 53 master's, 6 doctorates awarded. *Degree requirements:* For master's, thesis optional; for doctorate, thesis/dissertation. *Entrance requirements:* For master's, letters of recommendation, essay, interview, bachelor's degree; for doctorate, GRE, letters of recommendation, essay, interview, master's degree; for Post-Master's Certificate, GRE, letters of recommendation, essay, interview, bachelor's/master's degree. Additional exam requirements/recommendations for international students: Required—TOEFL (minimum score 550 paper-based), IELTS (minimum score 6.5). *Application deadline:* For fall admission, 4/2 for domestic students; for spring admission, 9/1 for domestic students. Applications are processed on a rolling basis. Application fee: $0. Electronic applications accepted. *Expenses:* $1,259 per credit. *Financial support:* Research assistantships, teaching assistantships, and Federal Work-Study available. Support available to part-time students. *Faculty research:* Trauma counseling, counseling supervision, purpose and meaning, Internet addictions, bullying and relational aggression. *Unit head:* Dr. Jered Kolbert, Professor/Director, 412-396-4471, Fax: 412-396-1340, E-mail: kolbertj@duq.edu. *Application contact:* Kelly McGinley, Graduate Admissions Assistant, 412-396-1559, Fax: 412-396-5585, E-mail: mcginleyk@duq.edu.

Eastern Nazarene College, Adult and Graduate Studies, Program in Marriage and Family Therapy, Quincy, MA 02170. Offers MS. *Program availability:* Part-time, evening/weekend. *Entrance requirements:* For master's, 3 letters of recommendation, resume. Additional exam requirements/recommendations for international students: Required—TOEFL (minimum score 550 paper-based).

Eastern University, Department of Counseling Psychology, St. Davids, PA 19087-3696. Offers applied behavior analysis (Certificate); counseling (MA); professional counseling (Certificate). *Program availability:* Part-time. *Students:* 66 full-time (58 women), 64 part-time (50 women); includes 56 minority (43 Black or African American, non-Hispanic/Latino; 1 Asian, non-Hispanic/Latino; 9 Hispanic/Latino; 3 Two or more races, non-Hispanic/Latino), 2 international. Average age 29. In 2017, 26 master's, 9 other advanced degrees awarded. *Entrance requirements:* Additional exam requirements/recommendations for international students: Required—TOEFL (minimum score 550 paper-based; 79 iBT). *Application deadline:* Applications are processed on a rolling basis. Application fee: $35. Electronic applications accepted. Application fee is waived when completed online. *Expenses:* Contact institution. *Unit head:* Michael Dziedziak, Executive Director of Enrollment, 800-452-0996, E-mail: gpsadmissions@eastern.edu.
Website: https://www.eastern.edu/academics/programs/counseling-psychology-department

Eastern Washington University, Graduate Studies, College of Social Sciences, Department of Psychology, Program in Mental Health Counseling, Cheney, WA 99004-2431. Offers applied psychology (MS); mental health counseling (MS). *Students:* 16 full-time (11 women); includes 2 minority (1 Black or African American, non-Hispanic/Latino; 1 Hispanic/Latino). Average age 30. 48 applicants, 17% accepted, 7 enrolled. In 2017, 11 master's awarded. *Degree requirements:* For master's, comprehensive exam, thesis. *Entrance requirements:* For master's, GRE, minimum GPA of 3.0. Additional exam requirements/recommendations for international students: Required—TOEFL (minimum score 580 paper-based; 92 iBT), IELTS (minimum score 7), PTE (minimum score 63). Application fee: $75. Electronic applications accepted. *Expenses:* Tuition, state resident: full-time $11,191; part-time $373.06 per credit. Tuition, nonresident: full-time $25,995; part-time $866.52 per credit. *Financial support:* Application deadline: 2/1; applicants required to submit FAFSA. *Unit head:* Dr. Keely Hope, Associate Professor/Director, Counselor Education, 509-359-2439, E-mail: khope@ewu.edu. *Application contact:* Kathy White, Advisor/Recruiter for Graduate Studies, 509-359-6297, Fax: 509-359-6044, E-mail: gradprograms@ewu.edu.

East Texas Baptist University, Master of Arts in Counseling Program, Marshall, TX 75670-1498. Offers MA. *Program availability:* Part-time, evening/weekend. *Faculty:* 4 full-time (3 women), 1 (woman) part-time/adjunct. *Students:* 14 full-time (11 women), 19 part-time (16 women); includes 22 minority (20 Black or African American, non-Hispanic/Latino; 2 Hispanic/Latino). Average age 34. 20 applicants, 55% accepted, 8 enrolled. In 2017, 9 master's awarded. *Entrance requirements:* Additional exam requirements/recommendations for international students: Recommended—TOEFL (minimum score 550 paper-based; 79 iBT). *Application deadline:* For fall admission, 8/13 for domestic students; for spring admission, 1/7 for domestic students; for summer admission, 5/10 for domestic students. Applications are processed on a rolling basis. Application fee: $50. Electronic applications accepted. *Expenses:* $735 per credit hour tuition, $150 per semester fees ($75 per semester if less than 6 hours). *Financial support:* In 2017–18, 7 students received support. Scholarships/grants, unspecified assistantships, and staff grants available. Financial award applicants required to submit FAFSA. *Unit head:* Dr. LaShondra Manning, Director, 903-923-2088, E-mail: macounsel@etbu.edu. *Application contact:* Den Murley, Director of Graduate Admissions, 903-923-2079, Fax: 903-934-8115, E-mail: gradadmissions@etbu.edu.
Website: https://www.etbu.edu/sciences/master-arts-counseling/

Edinboro University of Pennsylvania, Department of Counseling, School Psychology and Special Education, Edinboro, PA 16444. Offers counseling (MA), including art therapy, clinical mental health counseling, college counseling, rehabilitation counseling, school counseling; educational psychology (M Ed); school psychology (Ed S); special education (M Ed), including autism, behavior management. *Accreditation:* ACA. *Program availability:* Part-time, evening/weekend. *Degree requirements:* For master's, thesis or alternative, competency exam; for Ed S, thesis or alternative. *Entrance requirements:* For master's and Ed S, GRE or MAT, minimum QPA of 2.5. Electronic applications accepted.

Emporia State University, Program in Clinical Counseling, Emporia, KS 66801-5415. Offers MS. *Accreditation:* ACA. *Program availability:* Part-time. *Faculty:* 13 full-time (9 women). *Students:* 25 full-time (21 women), 5 part-time (3 women); includes 6 minority (2 Black or African American, non-Hispanic/Latino; 2 Asian, non-Hispanic/Latino; 1 Hispanic/Latino; 1 Two or more races, non-Hispanic/Latino), 1 international. 24 applicants, 58% accepted, 6 enrolled. In 2017, 18 master's awarded. *Degree requirements:* For master's, comprehensive exam, internship. *Entrance requirements:* For master's, GRE or MAT. Additional exam requirements/recommendations for international students: Required—TOEFL (minimum score 520 paper-based; 68 iBT). *Application deadline:* For fall admission, 8/15 for domestic students. Applications are processed on a rolling basis. Application fee: $30 ($75 for international students). Electronic applications accepted. *Expenses:* Tuition, state resident: full-time $6084; part-time $253.50 per credit hour. Tuition, nonresident: full-time $18,924; part-time $788.50 per credit hour. *Required fees:* $1943; $80.95 per credit hour. Tuition and fees vary according to campus/location. *Financial support:* In 2017–18, 4 research assistantships with full tuition reimbursements (averaging $7,344 per year) were awarded; Federal Work-Study, institutionally sponsored loans, health care benefits, and unspecified assistantships also available. Financial award application deadline: 3/15; financial award applicants required to submit FAFSA. *Unit head:* Dr. Katrina Miller, Chair, 620-341-5791, E-mail: kmille12@emporia.edu. *Application contact:* Mary Sewell, Admissions Coordinator, 800-950-GRAD, Fax: 620-341-5909, E-mail: msewell@emporia.edu.

Evangel University, Department of Behavioral and Social Sciences, Springfield, MO 65802. Offers clinical mental health counseling (MS). *Program availability:* Part-time. *Faculty:* 6 full-time (4 women), 2 part-time/adjunct (1 woman). *Students:* 33 full-time (27 women), 6 part-time (5 women); includes 3 minority (all Hispanic/Latino). Average age 31. 30 applicants, 70% accepted, 16 enrolled. In 2017, 14 master's awarded. *Degree requirements:* For master's, comprehensive exam. *Entrance requirements:* For master's, GRE General Test, minimum undergraduate GPA of 3.0. Additional exam requirements/recommendations for international students: Required—TOEFL (minimum score 550 paper-based). *Application deadline:* For fall admission, 7/15 priority date for domestic students, 8/1 for international students; for spring admission, 11/15 priority date for domestic students, 12/1 for international students. Applications are processed on a rolling basis. Application fee: $25. Electronic applications accepted. Application fee is waived when completed online. *Expenses:* *Tuition:* Full-time $7200; part-time $4800 per credit hour. *Required fees:* $210; $155 per semester. *Financial support:* In 2017–18, 12 students received support. Unspecified assistantships available. Financial award application deadline: 4/1; financial award applicants required to submit FAFSA. *Unit head:* Dr. Christine Arnzen, Program Coordinator, 417-865-2815 Ext. 8618, E-mail: arnzenc@evangel.edu. *Application contact:* Michael Mann, Enrollment Coordinator, Graduate Studies, 417-865-2815 Ext. 8276, Fax: 417-575-5484, E-mail: mannm@evangel.edu.
Website: https://www.evangel.edu/departments/behavioral-social-sciences/about-the-department/

Fairfield University, Graduate School of Education and Allied Professions, Fairfield, CT 06824. Offers applied behavior analysis (ATC); applied psychology (MA); clinical mental health counseling (MA, CAS); educational technology (MA); elementary education (MA, CAS); family studies (MA); integration of spirituality and religion in counseling (ATC); marriage and family therapy (MA); reading and language development (Sixth Year Certificate); school counseling (MA, CAS); school psychology (MA, CAS); school-based marriage and family therapy (ATC); secondary education (MA); special education (MA, CAS); substance abuse counseling (ATC); teaching (Certificate); teaching and foundations (MA, CAS); TESOL, world languages, and bilingual education (MA, CAS). *Accreditation:* NCATE. *Program availability:* Part-time, evening/weekend. *Faculty:* 23 full-time (17 women), 39 part-time/adjunct (28 women). *Students:* 199 full-time (168 women), 251 part-time (206 women); includes 85 minority (21 Black or African American, non-Hispanic/Latino; 9 Asian, non-Hispanic/Latino; 49 Hispanic/Latino; 6 Two or more races, non-Hispanic/Latino), 4 international. Average age 32. 370 applicants, 56% accepted, 125 enrolled. In 2017, 136 master's, 28 other advanced degrees awarded. *Degree requirements:* For master's, comprehensive exam. *Entrance requirements:* For master's, minimum GPA of 3.0, 2 recommendations, resume. Additional exam requirements/recommendations for international students: Required—TOEFL (minimum score 550 paper-based; 84 iBT) or IELTS (minimum score 7.5). *Application deadline:* For fall admission, 2/15 for international students; for spring

admission, 10/1 for international students. Application fee: $60. Electronic applications accepted. *Expenses:* $750 per credit hour. *Financial support:* In 2017–18, 34 students received support. Career-related internships or fieldwork and unspecified assistantships available. Support available to part-time students. Financial award applicants required to submit FAFSA. *Faculty research:* Reading and literacy, writing, social justice and inequality in education, addictions and mental health issues, therapeutic relationships and clinical supervision. *Unit head:* Dr. Robert D. Hannafin, Dean, 203-254-4250, Fax: 203-254-4241, E-mail: rhannafin@fairfield.edu. *Application contact:* Marianne Gumpper, Director of Graduate Admission, 203-254-4184, Fax: 203-254-4073, E-mail: gradadmis@fairfield.edu.
Website: http://www.fairfield.edu/gseap

Fairleigh Dickinson University, Florham Campus, Maxwell Becton College of Arts and Sciences, Department of Psychology, Program in Clinical Mental Health Counseling, Madison, NJ 07940-1099. Offers MA. *Accreditation:* ACA.

Fairleigh Dickinson University, Florham Campus, Maxwell Becton College of Arts and Sciences, Department of Psychology, Program in Counseling, Madison, NJ 07940-1099. Offers MA. *Accreditation:* ACA.

Felician University, Program in Counseling Psychology, Lodi, NJ 07644-2117. Offers MA, Psy D. *Program availability:* Part-time, evening/weekend. *Faculty:* 4 full-time (1 woman), 8 part-time/adjunct (7 women). *Students:* 58 full-time (45 women), 18 part-time (13 women); includes 46 minority (11 Black or African American, non-Hispanic/Latino; 3 Asian, non-Hispanic/Latino; 30 Hispanic/Latino; 1 Native Hawaiian or other Pacific Islander, non-Hispanic/Latino; 1 Two or more races, non-Hispanic/Latino), 3 international. Average age 31. 39 applicants, 82% accepted, 20 enrolled. In 2017, 12 master's awarded. Terminal master's awarded for partial completion of doctoral program. *Degree requirements:* For master's, comprehensive exam, thesis, presentation; for doctorate, thesis/dissertation, scholarly project. *Entrance requirements:* For master's, two letters of recommendation, interview, resume, personal statement, graduation from accredited baccalaureate program. Additional exam requirements/recommendations for international students: Required—TOEFL (minimum score 550 paper-based; 79 iBT), IELTS (minimum score 6.5), PTE (minimum score 56). *Application deadline:* Applications are processed on a rolling basis. Application fee: $40. Electronic applications accepted. Application fee is waived when completed online. *Expenses:* Contact institution. *Financial support:* Federal Work-Study and scholarships/grants available. Financial award applicants required to submit FAFSA. *Faculty research:* Evidence-based practice, mindfulness of multi cultures, sports psychology, performance enhancement. *Unit head:* Dr. Daniel Mahoney, Director of the Master's in Counseling Program, 201-559-6161, E-mail: mahoneyd@felician.edu. *Application contact:* Michael Szarek, Assistant Vice-President of Graduate Admissions, 201-355-1450, E-mail: szarekm@felician.edu.

Fitchburg State University, Division of Graduate and Continuing Education, Programs in Counseling, Fitchburg, MA 01420-2697. Offers clinical mental health counseling (MS); school guidance counseling (MS). *Accreditation:* NCATE. *Program availability:* Part-time, evening/weekend. *Faculty:* 3 full-time (2 women), 10 part-time/adjunct (6 women). *Students:* 60 full-time (54 women), 6 part-time (5 women); includes 7 minority (2 Black or African American, non-Hispanic/Latino; 1 Asian, non-Hispanic/Latino; 4 Hispanic/Latino). Average age 32. 19 applicants, 100% accepted, 14 enrolled. In 2017, 13 master's awarded. *Entrance requirements:* Additional exam requirements/recommendations for international students: Required—TOEFL (minimum score 550 paper-based; 79 iBT). *Application deadline:* For fall admission, 7/15 for international students; for spring admission, 12/1 for international students. Applications are processed on a rolling basis. Application fee: $50. Electronic applications accepted. *Expenses:* Contact institution. *Financial support:* In 2017–18, research assistantships with partial tuition reimbursements (averaging $5,500 per year) were awarded; Federal Work-Study, scholarships/grants, and unspecified assistantships also available. Support available to part-time students. Financial award application deadline: 3/1; financial award applicants required to submit FAFSA. *Unit head:* Dr. Daneen Deptula, Chair, 978-665-3604, Fax: 978-665-3658, E-mail: gce@fitchburgstate.edu. *Application contact:* Jinawa McNeil, Director of Admissions, 978-665-3140, Fax: 978-665-4540, E-mail: admissions@fitchburgstate.edu.
Website: http://www.fitchburgstate.edu

Florida International University, College of Arts, Sciences, and Education, Department of Leadership and Professional Studies, Miami, FL 33199. Offers adult education and human resource development (MS, Ed D); counseling (MS), including rehabilitation counseling, school counseling; counselor education (MS), including clinical mental health counseling; educational administration and supervision (Ed D); educational leadership (MS, Certificate, Ed S); higher education (Ed D); higher education administration (MS); international and comparative education (MS); recreation and sport management (MS), including recreation and sport management, recreational therapy; school psychology (Ed S); urban education (MS), including instruction in urban settings, learning technologies, multicultural/bilingual, multicultural/TESOL, urban education. *Program availability:* Part-time, evening/weekend. *Faculty:* 60 full-time (41 women), 112 part-time/adjunct (77 women). *Students:* 221 full-time (162 women), 301 part-time (239 women); includes 418 minority (127 Black or African American, non-Hispanic/Latino; 9 Asian, non-Hispanic/Latino; 271 Hispanic/Latino; 11 Two or more races, non-Hispanic/Latino), 10 international. Average age 31. 330 applicants, 55% accepted, 100 enrolled. In 2017, 181 master's, 6 doctorates awarded. *Degree requirements:* For doctorate, thesis/dissertation. *Entrance requirements:* For master's, minimum GPA of 3.0; for doctorate and other advanced degree, GRE General Test. Additional exam requirements/recommendations for international students: Required—TOEFL (minimum score 550 paper-based; 80 iBT), IELTS (minimum score 6.3). *Application deadline:* For fall admission, 6/1 priority date for domestic students, 4/1 for international students; for winter admission, 10/1 priority date for domestic students, 9/1 for international students; for spring admission, 3/1 priority date for domestic students, 2/1 for international students. Applications are processed on a rolling basis. Application fee: $30. Electronic applications accepted. *Expenses:* Tuition, state resident: full-time $8912; part-time $446 per credit hour. Tuition, nonresident: full-time $21,393; part-time $992 per credit hour. *Required fees:* $390; $195 per semester. *Financial support:* Fellowships, research assistantships with tuition reimbursements, teaching assistantships with tuition reimbursements, Federal Work-Study, and tuition waivers (full and partial) available. Support available to part-time students. Financial award applicants required to submit FAFSA. *Unit head:* Dr. Benjamin Baez, Chair, 305-348-3214, Fax: 305-348-1515, E-mail: benjamin.baez@fiu.edu. *Application contact:* Nanett Rojas, Assistant Director, Graduate Admissions, 305-348-7464, Fax: 305-348-7441, E-mail: gradadm@fiu.edu.
Website: http://education.fiu.edu

Florida International University, College of Arts, Sciences, and Education, Department of Psychology, Miami, FL 33199. Offers behavioral analysis (MS); clinical science (PhD); cognitive neuroscience (PhD); counseling psychology (MS); developmental science (MS, PhD); legal psychology (MS, PhD); organizational psychology (MS, PhD). Program has fall admissions only. *Accreditation:* APA. *Program availability:* Part-time, evening/weekend. *Faculty:* 45 full-time (28 women), 48 part-time/adjunct (31 women). *Students:* 162 full-time (122 women), 13 part-time (5 women); includes 94 minority (11 Black or African American, non-Hispanic/Latino; 5 Asian, non-Hispanic/Latino; 75 Hispanic/Latino; 3 Two or more races, non-Hispanic/Latino), 12 international. Average age 27. 290 applicants, 21% accepted, 50 enrolled. In 2017, 43 master's, 13 doctorates awarded. Terminal master's awarded for partial completion of doctoral program. *Degree requirements:* For master's, thesis; for doctorate, comprehensive exam, thesis/dissertation. *Entrance requirements:* For master's, GRE General Test, minimum GPA of 3.0, resume, 3 letters of recommendation; for doctorate, GRE General Test, 3 letters of recommendation, resume, letter of intent, two writing samples, minimum GPA of 3.0. Additional exam requirements/recommendations for international students: Required—TOEFL (minimum score 550 paper-based; 80 iBT). *Application deadline:* For fall admission, 12/15 for domestic and international students. Application fee: $30. Electronic applications accepted. *Expenses:* Tuition, state resident: full-time $8912; part-time $446 per credit hour. Tuition, nonresident: full-time $21,393; part-time $992 per credit hour. *Required fees:* $390; $195 per semester. *Financial support:* Institutionally sponsored loans and scholarships/grants available. Financial award application deadline: 3/1. *Faculty research:* Legal psychology, organizational and industrial psychology, child behavior psychology. *Unit head:* Dr. Jeremy Pettit, Interim Chair, 305-348-1671, Fax: 305-348-3646, E-mail: jeremy.pettit@fiu.edu. *Application contact:* Nanett Rojas, Assistant Director, Graduate Admissions, 305-348-7464, Fax: 305-348-7441, E-mail: gradadm@fiu.edu.

Fordham University, Graduate School of Education, Division of Psychological and Educational Services, New York, NY 10023. Offers counseling and personnel services (MSE); counseling psychology (PhD); school psychology (PhD). *Accreditation:* APA (one or more programs are accredited); NCATE. *Program availability:* Part-time, evening/weekend. Terminal master's awarded for partial completion of doctoral program. *Degree requirements:* For master's, comprehensive exam (for some programs); for doctorate, comprehensive exam (for some programs), thesis/dissertation. *Entrance requirements:* For doctorate, GRE General Test. Additional exam requirements/recommendations for international students: Required—TOEFL (minimum score 577 paper-based; 90 iBT), IELTS (minimum score 7). Electronic applications accepted.

Fort Valley State University, College of Graduate Studies and Extended Education, Department of Counseling Psychology, Program in Mental Health Counseling, Fort Valley, GA 31030. Offers MS. *Accreditation:* ACA. *Program availability:* Part-time. *Degree requirements:* For master's, comprehensive exam (for some programs), thesis optional. *Entrance requirements:* For master's, GRE General Test or MAT. Additional exam requirements/recommendations for international students: Recommended—TOEFL.

Framingham State University, Graduate Studies, Program in Counseling Psychology, Framingham, MA 01701-9101. Offers MA. *Program availability:* Part-time, evening/weekend. *Unit head:* Deborah McMakin, Program Coordinator, E-mail: dmcmakin@framingham.edu. *Application contact:* Graduate Office, 508-626-4550, Fax: 508-626-4030, E-mail: dgce@frc.mass.edu.

Franciscan University of Steubenville, Graduate Programs, Department of Clinical Mental Health Counseling, Steubenville, OH 43952-1763. Offers MA. *Accreditation:* ACA. *Program availability:* Part-time. *Faculty:* 4 full-time (1 woman), 2 part-time/adjunct (1 woman). *Students:* 41 full-time (28 women), 7 part-time (3 women); includes 5 minority (1 Black or African American, non-Hispanic/Latino; 2 Asian, non-Hispanic/Latino; 2 Hispanic/Latino). Average age 28. 44 applicants, 75% accepted, 24 enrolled. In 2017, 17 master's awarded. *Degree requirements:* For master's, case presentation, integrative paper. *Entrance requirements:* For master's, GRE General Test or MAT for those with a GPA below 3.0, minimum undergraduate GPA of 2.5. Additional exam requirements/recommendations for international students: Required—TOEFL. *Application deadline:* For fall admission, 8/1 for domestic students, 5/31 for international students; for spring admission, 1/10 for domestic students, 9/30 for international students. Applications are processed on a rolling basis. Application fee: $0. Electronic applications accepted. *Expenses:* $685 per semester hour. *Financial support:* Federal Work-Study and scholarships/grants available. Support available to part-time students. Financial award application deadline: 8/1; financial award applicants required to submit FAFSA. *Unit head:* Dr. Christin Jungers, Program Director, 740-284-7220, E-mail: cjungers@franciscan.edu. *Application contact:* Ryan Welch, Online Enrollment Counselor, 740-284-5239, Fax: 740-284-5456, E-mail: rwelch@franciscan.edu.
Website: http://www.franciscan.edu/cmhc/

Francis Marion University, Graduate Programs, Department of Psychology, Florence, SC 29502-0547. Offers applied psychology (MS), including clinical/counseling psychology, school psychology; school psychology (SSP). *Program availability:* Part-time, evening/weekend. *Degree requirements:* For master's, internship. *Entrance requirements:* For master's, GRE General Test, official transcripts, two letters of recommendation. Additional exam requirements/recommendations for international students: Required—TOEFL (minimum score 550 paper-based; 79 iBT). *Faculty research:* Parenting and family relationships, child development, applied behavioral analysis, post-traumatic stress disorder, clinical psychology in adults.

Frostburg State University, College of Liberal Arts and Sciences, Department of Psychology, Program in Counseling Psychology, Frostburg, MD 21532. Offers MS. *Program availability:* Part-time, evening/weekend. *Faculty:* 6 full-time (4 women). *Students:* 24 full-time (17 women), 5 part-time (all women); includes 2 minority (1 Black or African American, non-Hispanic/Latino; 1 Hispanic/Latino), 1 international. Average age 27. 34 applicants, 38% accepted, 11 enrolled. In 2017, 7 master's awarded. *Degree requirements:* For master's, internship. *Entrance requirements:* For master's, GRE General Test or MAT, interview, minimum GPA of 3.0, resume. Additional exam requirements/recommendations for international students: Required—TOEFL. *Application deadline:* For fall admission, 2/1 for domestic students. Applications are processed on a rolling basis. Application fee: $45. Electronic applications accepted. *Expenses:* Tuition, state resident: part-time $433 per credit hour. Tuition, nonresident: part-time $557 per credit hour. *Required fees:* $121 per credit hour. $27 per term. *Financial support:* In 2017–18, 7 research assistantships with full tuition reimbursements (averaging $5,000 per year) were awarded; career-related internships or fieldwork and Federal Work-Study also available. Financial award application deadline: 4/1; financial award applicants required to submit FAFSA. *Unit head:* Dr. Mike Murtagh, Coordinator, 301-687-4193, E-mail: mpmurtagh@frostburg.edu. *Application contact:* Vickie Mazer, Director, Graduate Services, 301-687-7053, Fax: 301-687-4597, E-mail: vmmazer@frostburg.edu.

Gallaudet University, The Graduate School, Washington, DC 20002-3625. Offers American Sign Language/English bilingual early childhood deaf education: birth to 5 (Certificate); audiology (Au D); clinical psychology (PhD); deaf and hard of hearing infants, toddlers, and their families (Certificate); deaf education (MA, Ed S); deaf history (Certificate); deaf studies (Certificate); educating deaf students with disabilities (Certificate); education: teacher preparation (MA), including deaf education, early childhood education and deaf education, elementary education and deaf education, secondary education and deaf education; educational neuroscience (PhD); hearing, speech and language sciences (MS, PhD); international development (MA); interpretation (MA, PhD), including combined interpreting practice and research (MA), interpreting research (MA); linguistics (MA, PhD); mental health counseling (MA); peer

mentoring (Certificate); public administration (MPA); school counseling (MA); school psychology (Psy S); sign language teaching (MA); social work (MSW); speech-language pathology (MS). *Program availability:* Part-time. Terminal master's awarded for partial completion of doctoral program. *Degree requirements:* For master's, comprehensive exam (for some programs), thesis optional; for doctorate, comprehensive exam, thesis/dissertation. *Entrance requirements:* For master's and doctorate, GRE General Test or MAT, letters of recommendation, interviews, goals statement, American Sign Language proficiency interview, written English competency. Additional exam requirements/recommendations for international students: Required—TOEFL. Electronic applications accepted. *Faculty research:* Signing math dictionaries, telecommunications access, cancer genetics, linguistics, visual language and visual learning, integrated quantum materials, deaf legal discourse, advance recruitment and retention in geosciences.

Gannon University, School of Graduate Studies, College of Humanities, Education, and Social Sciences, School of Humanities, Program in Clinical Mental Health Counseling, Erie, PA 16541-0001. Offers MS. *Accreditation:* ACA. *Program availability:* Part-time, evening/weekend. *Degree requirements:* For master's, thesis, internship. *Entrance requirements:* For master's, bachelor's degree from approved institution, resume, 3 letters of recommendation, essay, interview, minimum GPA of 2.8, PA child abuse clearances and PA State Police criminal record check dated within a year of application. Additional exam requirements/recommendations for international students: Required—TOEFL (minimum score 79 iBT). Electronic applications accepted. Application fee is waived when completed online.

Gardner-Webb University, Graduate School, School of Psychology, Boiling Springs, NC 28017. Offers mental health counseling (MA); school counseling (MA). *Program availability:* Part-time, evening/weekend. *Faculty:* 5 full-time (4 women), 4 part-time/adjunct (2 women). *Students:* 1 full-time (0 women), 88 part-time (76 women); includes 19 minority (13 Black or African American, non-Hispanic/Latino; 1 American Indian or Alaska Native, non-Hispanic/Latino; 3 Hispanic/Latino; 2 Two or more races, non-Hispanic/Latino). Average age 31. *Degree requirements:* For master's, comprehensive exam. *Entrance requirements:* For master's, GRE General Test, MAT, minimum GPA of 2.7. *Application deadline:* For fall admission, 7/1 priority date for domestic students. Applications are processed on a rolling basis. Electronic applications accepted. *Expenses:* Contact institution. *Financial support:* Unspecified assistantships available. *Unit head:* Dr. David Carscaddon, Chair, 704-406-4437, Fax: 704-406-4329, E-mail: dcarscaddon@gardner-webb.edu. *Application contact:* Office of Graduate Admissions, 877-498-4723, Fax: 704-406-3895, E-mail: gradinfo@gardner-webb.edu.

Geneva College, Master of Arts in Counseling Program, Beaver Falls, PA 15010-3599. Offers clinical mental health counseling (MA); marriage and family counseling (MA); school counseling (MA). *Accreditation:* ACA. *Program availability:* Part-time, evening/weekend. *Faculty:* 6 full-time (3 women), 3 part-time/adjunct (1 woman). *Students:* 34 full-time (26 women), 20 part-time (16 women); includes 12 minority (11 Black or African American, non-Hispanic/Latino; 1 Hispanic/Latino), 1 international. Average age 33. In 2017, 34 master's awarded. *Degree requirements:* For master's, comprehensive exam, 60 credits including practicum and internship. *Entrance requirements:* For master's, minimum GPA of 3.0 (preferred), 3 letters of recommendation, essay on career goals, resume of educational and professional experiences. Additional exam requirements/recommendations for international students: Required—TOEFL. *Application deadline:* For fall admission, 9/1 for domestic students; for spring admission, 1/10 for domestic students. Applications are processed on a rolling basis. Electronic applications accepted. *Expenses:* $670 per credit. *Financial support:* Research assistantships, teaching assistantships, career-related internships or fieldwork, and unspecified assistantships available. Financial award application deadline: 8/1; financial award applicants required to submit FAFSA. *Faculty research:* Blended family counseling; premarital and newlywed couples; religion in clinical supervision; conceptual mapping in research, supervision, and clinical work. *Unit head:* Dr. Shannan Shiderly, Program Director, 724-847-6649, Fax: 724-847-6101, E-mail: slshider@geneva.edu. *Application contact:* Marina Frazier, Graduate Program Manager, 724-847-6697, E-mail: counseling@geneva.edu.
Website: http://www.geneva.edu/page/grad_counseling

George Fox University, College of Education, Graduate Department of Counseling, Newberg, OR 97132-2697. Offers clinical mental health counseling (MA); marriage, couple and family counseling (MA, Certificate); school counseling (MA, Certificate); school psychology (Ed S). *Program availability:* Part-time. *Degree requirements:* For master's, clinical project. *Entrance requirements:* For master's, MAT or GRE, bachelor's degree from regionally-accredited college or university, minimum cumulative GPA of 3.0, 1 professional and 1 academic reference, resume, on-campus interview, official transcripts. Additional exam requirements/recommendations for international students: Required—TOEFL (minimum score 577 paper-based; 90 iBT), IELTS (minimum score 7). Electronic applications accepted. *Expenses:* Contact institution.

Georgian Court University, School of Arts and Sciences, Lakewood, NJ 08701-2697. Offers applied behavior analysis (MA); autism spectrum disorders (Certificate); clinical mental health counseling (MA); criminal justice and human rights (MS); holistic health studies (MA, Certificate); homeland security (Certificate); instructional technology (CPC); mercy spirituality (Certificate); parish business management (Certificate); professional counselor (Certificate); school psychology (MA, Certificate); theology (MA, Certificate). *Program availability:* Part-time, evening/weekend. *Faculty:* 18 full-time (11 women), 8 part-time/adjunct (4 women). *Students:* 100 full-time (86 women), 92 part-time (67 women); includes 34 minority (9 Black or African American, non-Hispanic/Latino; 1 Asian, non-Hispanic/Latino; 20 Hispanic/Latino; 4 Two or more races, non-Hispanic/Latino), 2 international. Average age 34. 187 applicants, 56% accepted, 78 enrolled. In 2017, 58 master's, 20 other advanced degrees awarded. *Degree requirements:* For master's, comprehensive exam (for some programs), thesis (for some programs). *Entrance requirements:* For master's, GRE, GMAT, or NTE/PRAXIS, 3 letters of recommendation. Additional exam requirements/recommendations for international students: Required—TOEFL (minimum score 550 paper-based). *Application deadline:* For fall admission, 8/15 for domestic students, 5/1 for international students; for spring admission, 1/15 for domestic students, 10/1 for international students. Applications are processed on a rolling basis. Application fee: $40. Electronic applications accepted. *Expenses: Tuition:* Part-time $839 per credit. *Required fees:* $248 per semester. Tuition and fees vary according to campus/location and program. *Financial support:* Scholarships/grants, health care benefits, and unspecified assistantships available. Financial award application deadline: 4/15; financial award applicants required to submit FAFSA. *Unit head:* Dr. Mary Chinery, Dean, 732-987-2493, Fax: 732-987-2007, E-mail: mchinery@georgian.edu. *Application contact:* Patrick Givens, Director of Graduate and Professional Studies Admissions, 732-987-2736, Fax: 732-987-2000, E-mail: gps@georgian.edu.
Website: https://georgian.edu/academics/school-of-arts-sciences/

Georgia Southern University, Jack N. Averitt College of Graduate Studies, College of Education, Department of Leadership, Technology, and Human Development, Program in Counselor Education, Statesboro, GA 30460. Offers mental health counseling (M Ed); school counseling (M Ed). *Accreditation:* ACA; NCATE. *Program availability:* Part-time, evening/weekend. *Students:* 39 full-time (30 women), 9 part-time (6 women); includes 21 minority (20 Black or African American, non-Hispanic/Latino; 1 Asian, non-Hispanic/Latino). Average age 28. 34 applicants, 53% accepted, 11 enrolled. In 2017, 22 master's awarded. *Degree requirements:* For master's, comprehensive exam, transition point assessments. *Entrance requirements:* For master's, minimum GPA of 2.5, letters of recommendation, interview. Additional exam requirements/recommendations for international students: Required—TOEFL (minimum score 550 paper-based; 80 iBT), IELTS (minimum score 6). *Application deadline:* For fall admission, 3/2 for domestic students, 3/15 for international students; for spring admission, 3/2 for domestic students, 10/1 for international students. Application fee: $50. Electronic applications accepted. *Expenses:* Tuition, state resident: full-time $4986; part-time $3324 per year. Tuition, nonresident: full-time $21,982; part-time $15,352 per year. *Required fees:* $2092; $1802 per credit hour. $901 per semester. Tuition and fees vary according to course load, campus/location and program. *Financial support:* In 2017–18, 25 students received support, including 3 research assistantships with full tuition reimbursements available (averaging $7,750 per year); career-related internships or fieldwork, scholarships/grants, and unspecified assistantships also available. Financial award application deadline: 4/15; financial award applicants required to submit FAFSA. *Faculty research:* School counseling, test development, gender equity, career counseling, mental health counseling, best practices for preparing counselors. *Unit head:* Dr. Brandon Hunt, Program Director, 912-478-0502, Fax: 912-478-7104, E-mail: bhunt@georgiasouthern.edu. *Application contact:* Dr. Lydia Cross, Graduate Academic Services Center, 912-478-8664, E-mail: lcross@georgiasouthern.edu.
Website: http://coe.georgiasouthern.edu/coun/

Georgia State University, College of Education and Human Development, Department of Counseling and Psychological Services, Program in Mental Health Counseling, Atlanta, GA 30302-3083. Offers MS, Ed S. *Accreditation:* ACA (one or more programs are accredited); APA (one or more programs are accredited). *Entrance requirements:* For master's, GRE, goal statement, resume, 3 letters of recommendation, transcripts. Additional exam requirements/recommendations for international students: Required—TOEFL. Application fee: $50. Electronic applications accepted. *Expenses:* Tuition, state resident: full-time $7020. Tuition, nonresident: full-time $22,518. *Required fees:* $2128. Tuition and fees vary according to degree level and program. *Financial support:* Research assistantships, teaching assistantships, career-related internships or fieldwork, scholarships/grants, health care benefits, and unspecified assistantships available. Financial award application deadline: 4/1. *Faculty research:* Motivational interviewing, basic counseling skills, group counseling, addictions, spirituality. *Unit head:* Dr. Brian Dew, Chairperson, 404-413-8168, Fax: 404-413-8013, E-mail: bdew@gsu.edu.
Website: http://cps.education.gsu.edu/programs/mental-health-counseling/

Governors State University, College of Education, Program in Counseling, University Park, IL 60484. Offers MA. *Accreditation:* ACA. *Program availability:* Part-time. *Faculty:* 28 full-time (21 women), 29 part-time/adjunct (23 women). *Students:* 68 full-time (64 women), 130 part-time (110 women); includes 116 minority (91 Black or African American, non-Hispanic/Latino; 4 Asian, non-Hispanic/Latino; 16 Hispanic/Latino; 5 Two or more races, non-Hispanic/Latino). Average age 37. 70 applicants, 20% accepted, 11 enrolled. In 2017, 32 master's awarded. *Application deadline:* For fall admission, 4/1 for domestic students. Applications are processed on a rolling basis. Application fee: $50. Electronic applications accepted. *Expenses:* Contact institution. *Financial support:* Application deadline: 5/1; applicants required to submit FAFSA. *Unit head:* Patricia Robey, Interim Chair, Division of Psychology and Counseling, 708-534-5000 Ext. 4975, E-mail: probey@govst.edu.

Hardin-Simmons University, Graduate School, Cynthia Ann Parker College of Liberal Arts, Department of Psychology, Abilene, TX 79698-0001. Offers clinical counseling and marriage and family therapy (MA). *Program availability:* Part-time. *Faculty:* 9 full-time (7 women). *Students:* 25 full-time (19 women), 2 part-time (both women); includes 3 minority (1 Black or African American, non-Hispanic/Latino; 1 Hispanic/Latino; 1 Two or more races, non-Hispanic/Latino), 1 international. Average age 31. 20 applicants, 85% accepted, 15 enrolled. In 2017, 11 master's awarded. *Degree requirements:* For master's, comprehensive exam, clinical experience, project. *Entrance requirements:* For master's, 21 semester hours of course work in psychology (18 in upper-division classes); minimum undergraduate GPA of 3.0 in major, 2.7 overall; writing sample; letters of recommendation. Additional exam requirements/recommendations for international students: Required—TOEFL (minimum score 550 paper-based; 79 iBT). *Application deadline:* For fall admission, 8/15 priority date for domestic students, 4/1 for international students; for spring admission, 1/5 priority date for domestic students, 9/1 for international students. Applications are processed on a rolling basis. Application fee: $50 ($150 for international students). Electronic applications accepted. *Expenses: Tuition:* Full-time $13,500; part-time $750 per semester hour. *Required fees:* $220 per term. One-time fee: $50. Tuition and fees vary according to course load, campus/location and program. *Financial support:* In 2017–18, 21 students received support, including 17 fellowships (averaging $1,047 per year); career-related internships or fieldwork and scholarships/grants also available. Support available to part-time students. Financial award application deadline: 6/30; financial award applicants required to submit FAFSA. *Faculty research:* Spirituality in marriage, intimacy and sexuality in marriage, sex education in the church, role of faith in marital satisfaction, family stress management. *Unit head:* Dr. Sherry Rosenblad, Program Director, 325-671-2271, Fax: 325-670-1458, E-mail: sherry.rosenblad@hsutx.edu. *Application contact:* Dr. Nancy Kucinski, Dean of Graduate Studies, 325-670-1298, Fax: 325-670-1564, E-mail: gradoff@hsutx.edu.
Website: http://www.hsutx.edu/academics/cap/psychology/

Heidelberg University, Master of Arts in Counseling Program, Tiffin, OH 44883-2462. Offers clinical mental health counseling (MA); school counseling (MA). *Accreditation:* ACA. *Program availability:* Part-time, evening/weekend. *Students:* 19 full-time (15 women), 25 part-time (19 women). In 2017, 10 master's awarded. *Degree requirements:* For master's, counseling practicum, internship. *Entrance requirements:* For master's, bachelor's degree with minimum GPA of 2.9; 12 hours of coursework in behavioral sciences; 3 letters of recommendation; 2-3 page goal statement. Additional exam requirements/recommendations for international students: Required—TOEFL (minimum score 550 paper-based, 79 iBT) or IELTS (minimum score 6.5). *Application deadline:* Applications are processed on a rolling basis. Application fee: $0. Electronic applications accepted. *Expenses:* $525 per hour. *Financial support:* Scholarships/grants and unspecified assistantships available. Financial award applicants required to submit FAFSA. *Unit head:* Dr. Marjorie Shavers, Director of Graduate Studies in Counseling, 419-448-2308, E-mail: mshavers@heidelberg.edu. *Application contact:* Katie Zeyen, Graduate Admissions Coordinator, 419-448-2602, Fax: 419-448-2565, E-mail: kzeyen@heidelberg.edu.
Website: https://www.heidelberg.edu/academics/programs/master-of-counseling

Henderson State University, Graduate Studies, Teachers College, Department of Counselor Education, Arkadelphia, AR 71999-0001. Offers clinical mental health counseling (MS); developmental therapy (MS, Graduate Certificate); secondary school counseling (MSE). *Accreditation:* NCATE. *Program availability:* Part-time. *Entrance requirements:* For master's, GRE General Test or MAT, letters of recommendation, minimum GPA of 2.7, teacher certification. Additional exam requirements/

recommendations for international students: Required—TOEFL (minimum score 600 paper-based); Recommended—IELTS (minimum score 6.5).

Hodges University, Graduate Programs, Naples, FL 34119. Offers accounting (M Acc); business administration (MBA); clinical mental health counseling (MS); health services administration (MS); information systems management (MIS); legal studies (MS); management (MSM). *Program availability:* Part-time, evening/weekend, 100% online, blended/hybrid learning. *Degree requirements:* For master's, comprehensive exam (for some programs), thesis (for some programs). *Entrance requirements:* For master's, essay. Additional exam requirements/recommendations for international students: Recommended—TOEFL. Electronic applications accepted.

Hofstra University, School of Health Professions and Human Services, Programs in Counseling, Hempstead, NY 11549. Offers counseling (MS Ed, PD); creative arts therapy (MA); interdisciplinary transition specialist (Advanced Certificate); marriage and family therapy (MA); mental health counseling (MA, Advanced Certificate), including alcohol and substance abuse (Advanced Certificate); rehabilitation administration (PD); rehabilitation counseling (MS Ed, Advanced Certificate); rehabilitation counseling in mental health (MS Ed, Advanced Certificate). *Accreditation:* ACA. *Program availability:* Part-time, evening/weekend. *Students:* 103 full-time (87 women), 67 part-time (60 women); includes 50 minority (21 Black or African American, non-Hispanic/Latino; 11 Asian, non-Hispanic/Latino; 15 Hispanic/Latino; 1 Native Hawaiian or other Pacific Islander, non-Hispanic/Latino; 2 Two or more races, non-Hispanic/Latino), 6 international. Average age 30. 131 applicants, 79% accepted, 52 enrolled. In 2017, 66 master's, 4 other advanced degrees awarded. *Degree requirements:* For master's, comprehensive exam (for some programs), thesis (for some programs), internship, practicum, student teaching, seminars, minimum GPA of 3.0. *Entrance requirements:* For master's, GRE, interview, letters of recommendation, portfolio, essay, professional experience, certification; for other advanced degree, GRE, interview, letters of recommendation, essay, professional experience, resume, master's degree. Additional exam requirements/recommendations for international students: Required—TOEFL (minimum score 550 paper-based; 80 iBT). *Application deadline:* Applications are processed on a rolling basis. Application fee: $75. Electronic applications accepted. *Expenses: Tuition:* Full-time $1292. *Required fees:* $970. Tuition and fees vary according to program. *Financial support:* In 2017–18, 78 students received support, including 47 fellowships with full and partial tuition reimbursements available (averaging $3,138 per year), 5 research assistantships with full and partial tuition reimbursements available (averaging $5,702 per year); career-related internships or fieldwork, Federal Work-Study, institutionally sponsored loans, scholarships/grants, traineeships, tuition waivers (full and partial), and unspecified assistantships also available. Support available to part-time students. Financial award applicants required to submit FAFSA. *Faculty research:* Couple and family therapy infidelity; creative arts impact on Parkinson's disease; LGBTQ inclusion; substance abuse/heroin addiction's racial identity, multicultural issues, white privilege, Latinos, school counseling and the intensity of the high school curriculum. *Unit head:* Dr. Jamie Mitus, Chairperson, 516-463-5759, E-mail: jamie.s.mitus@hofstra.edu. *Application contact:* Sunil Samuel, Assistant Vice President of Admissions, 516-463-4723, Fax: 516-463-4664, E-mail: graduateadmission@hofstra.edu.
Website: http://www.hofstra.edu/academics/colleges/healthscienceshumanservices/

Holy Family University, Graduate and Professional Programs, School of Arts and Sciences, Program in Counseling Psychology, Philadelphia, PA 19114. Offers MS. *Program availability:* Part-time, evening/weekend. *Degree requirements:* For master's, comprehensive exam, thesis optional. *Entrance requirements:* For master's, GRE or MAT (if GPA is below 3.0), baccalaureate degree from accredited college or university; minimum undergraduate cumulative GPA of 3.0; 2 letters of recommendation; personal statement; official transcripts; interview. Additional exam requirements/recommendations for international students: Required—TOEFL (minimum score 550 paper-based; 79 iBT), IELTS (minimum score 6), PTE (minimum score 54). Electronic applications accepted. *Expenses: Tuition:* Full-time $13,518; part-time $9012 per credit hour. Tuition and fees vary according to degree level and program.

Holy Names University, Graduate Division, Department of Counseling Psychology, Oakland, CA 94619-1699. Offers counseling and forensic counseling (MA); counseling psychology (MA); forensic psychology (MA). *Program availability:* Part-time, evening/weekend. *Degree requirements:* For master's, comprehensive paper, seminars. *Entrance requirements:* For master's, minimum undergraduate GPA of 2.6 overall, 3.0 in major. Additional exam requirements/recommendations for international students: Required—TOEFL (minimum score 550 paper-based; 79 iBT). Electronic applications accepted. Application fee is waived when completed online. *Expenses:* Contact institution. *Faculty research:* Cognitive psychology, anger management, grief and grief counseling, post-modernism and psychotherapy, spirituality and psychology.

Houston Baptist University, College of Education and Behavioral Sciences, Program in Counseling, Houston, TX 77074-3298. Offers Christian counseling (MACC); counseling (MAC); marriage and family therapy (MA); pastoral counseling (MA), including addiction and recovery, crisis response, human sexuality, marriage and family therapy, military and veteran care and counseling, professional life coaching. *Program availability:* Part-time, evening/weekend, 100% online. *Students:* 42 full-time (35 women), 103 part-time (91 women); includes 80 minority (31 Black or African American, non-Hispanic/Latino; 10 Asian, non-Hispanic/Latino; 36 Hispanic/Latino; 3 Two or more races, non-Hispanic/Latino), 4 international. Average age 29. 178 applicants, 16% accepted, 16 enrolled. In 2017, 22 master's awarded. *Degree requirements:* For master's, comprehensive exam, practicum. *Entrance requirements:* For master's, GRE (waived if GPA is 3.0 or higher), two academic or professional recommendations, bachelor's degree conferred transcript, resume, interview. Additional exam requirements/recommendations for international students: Required—TOEFL (minimum score 80 iBT), IELTS (minimum score 6.5). *Application deadline:* For fall admission, 8/1 for domestic students, 6/1 for international students; for spring admission, 1/1 for domestic students, 11/1 for international students; for summer admission, 5/1 for domestic students, 3/1 for international students. Applications are processed on a rolling basis. Application fee: $0 ($100 for international students). Electronic applications accepted. Application fee is waived when completed online. *Expenses:* $33,000 tuition; $4,500 fees (general, technology and parking). *Financial support:* In 2017–18, 9 students received support. Career-related internships or fieldwork, Federal Work-Study, and scholarships/grants available. Support available to part-time students. Financial award application deadline: 4/1; financial award applicants required to submit FAFSA. *Faculty research:* Multicultural psychology, counseling: technology integration. *Unit head:* Dr. Maria Soto-Leggett, Program Coordinator, 281-649-3310, E-mail: msotoleggett@hbu.edu. *Application contact:* Victoria Humphreys, Administrative Assistant to the Dean, 281-649-3131, E-mail: vhumphreys@hbu.edu.
Website: http://www.hbu.edu/mac

Howard University, School of Education, Department of Human Development and Psychoeducational Studies, Program in Counseling Psychology, Washington, DC 20059-0002. Offers PhD. *Accreditation:* APA. *Program availability:* Part-time. *Degree requirements:* For doctorate, one foreign language, comprehensive exam, thesis/dissertation, expository writing exam, internship. *Entrance requirements:* For doctorate, GRE General Test, minimum GPA of 3.4. Additional exam requirements/

recommendations for international students: Required—TOEFL (minimum score 550 paper-based; 79 iBT). Electronic applications accepted. *Faculty research:* Cultural issues in counseling and psychotherapy, counseling theory construction, self-actualization black psychology.

Humboldt State University, Academic Programs, College of Professional Studies, Department of Psychology, Arcata, CA 95521-8299. Offers psychology (MA), including biological psychology, counseling, developmental psychopathology, school psychology, social and environmental psychology. *Degree requirements:* For master's, thesis. *Entrance requirements:* For master's, appropriate bachelor's degree, minimum GPA of 2.5. Additional exam requirements/recommendations for international students: Required—TOEFL (minimum score 500 paper-based). *Faculty research:* School psychology, counseling, eating disorders, mood induction, depression.

Husson University, Graduate Programs in Counseling and Human Relations, Bangor, ME 04401-2999. Offers clinical mental health counseling (MS); human relations (MS); school counseling (MS). *Accreditation:* ACA. *Program availability:* Part-time, evening/weekend. *Faculty:* 3 full-time (2 women), 5 part-time/adjunct (all women). *Students:* 21 full-time (18 women), 44 part-time (39 women); includes 2 minority (1 Black or African American, non-Hispanic/Latino; 1 Hispanic/Latino), 1 international. Average age 31. 49 applicants, 41% accepted, 13 enrolled. In 2017, 17 master's awarded. *Degree requirements:* For master's, comprehensive exam (for some programs), thesis optional. *Entrance requirements:* For master's, BS with minimum GPA of 3.0, letters of recommendation, interview. Additional exam requirements/recommendations for international students: Required—TOEFL (minimum score 550 paper-based; 80 iBT), IELTS (minimum score 6.5). *Application deadline:* For fall admission, 2/1 for domestic students. Application fee: $50. Electronic applications accepted. *Expenses:* $577 per credit; fees depend on number of credits. *Financial support:* In 2017–18, 2 students received support. Federal Work-Study, scholarships/grants, and unspecified assistantships available. Financial award application deadline: 4/15; financial award applicants required to submit FAFSA. *Faculty research:* Challenges and rewards of counseling practice in rural, small town and neighborhood settings. *Unit head:* Dr. Deborah Drew, Director, Graduate Counseling Programs, 207-992-4912, Fax: 207-992-4952, E-mail: drewd@husson.edu. *Application contact:* Kristen Card, Director of Graduate Admissions, 207-404-5660, Fax: 207-941-7935, E-mail: cardk@husson.edu. Website: http://www.husson.edu/college-of-health-and-education/school-of-education/graduate-programs/

Idaho State University, Office of Graduate Studies, School of Health Professions, Department of Counseling, Pocatello, ID 83209-8120. Offers counseling (M Coun, Ed S), including marriage and family counseling (M Coun), mental health counseling (M Coun), school counseling (M Coun), student affairs and college counseling (M Coun); counselor education and counseling (PhD). *Accreditation:* ACA (one or more programs are accredited). *Program availability:* Part-time. *Degree requirements:* For master's, comprehensive exam, thesis, 4 semesters resident graduate study, practicum/internship; for doctorate, comprehensive exam, thesis/dissertation, 3 semesters internship, 4 consecutive semesters doctoral-level study on campus; for Ed S, comprehensive exam, thesis, case studies, oral exam. *Entrance requirements:* For master's, GRE General Test, MAT, minimum GPA of 3.0, bachelors degree, interview, 3 letters of recommendation; for doctorate, GRE General Test, MAT, minimum graduate GPA of 3.0, resume, interview, counseling license, master's degree; for Ed S, GRE General Test, minimum graduate GPA of 3.0, master's degree in counseling, 3 letters of recommendation, 2 years work experience. Additional exam requirements/recommendations for international students: Required—TOEFL (minimum score 600 paper-based; 80 iBT). Electronic applications accepted. *Faculty research:* Group counseling, multicultural counseling, family counseling, child therapy, supervision.

Illinois State University, Graduate School, College of Arts and Sciences, Department of Psychology, Normal, IL 61790. Offers psychology (MA, MS), including clinical-counseling psychology, cognitive and behavioral sciences, developmental psychology, industrial/organizational-social psychology; school psychology (PhD, SSP). *Accreditation:* APA. *Degree requirements:* For master's, thesis or alternative; for doctorate, variable foreign language requirement, thesis/dissertation, 2 terms of residency, internship, practicum. *Entrance requirements:* For master's, GRE General Test, GRE Subject Test, minimum GPA of 3.0 in last 60 hours of course work; for doctorate, GRE General Test. *Faculty research:* Comprehensive evaluation system for the central region professional development grant, Illinois school psychology internship consortium, for children's sake.

Immaculata University, College of Graduate Studies, Department of Psychology, Immaculata, PA 19345. Offers clinical mental health counseling (MA); clinical psychology (Psy D); forensic psychology (Graduate Certificate); integrative psychotherapy (Graduate Certificate); neuropsychology (Graduate Certificate); psychodynamic psychotherapy (Graduate Certificate); psychological testing (Graduate Certificate); school counseling (MA, Graduate Certificate); school psychology (MA). *Accreditation:* APA. *Program availability:* Part-time, evening/weekend. Terminal master's awarded for partial completion of doctoral program. *Degree requirements:* For master's, comprehensive exam, thesis optional; for doctorate, comprehensive exam, thesis/dissertation. *Entrance requirements:* For master's, GRE General Test or MAT, minimum GPA of 3.0; for doctorate, GRE General Test or MAT, minimum GPA of 3.5. Additional exam requirements/recommendations for international students: Required—TOEFL, IELTS. Electronic applications accepted. *Faculty research:* Supervision ethics, psychology of teaching, gender.

Indiana University Northwest, College of Arts and Sciences, Gary, IN 46408. Offers clinical counseling (MS), including drug and alcohol counseling; community development/urban studies (Graduate Certificate); computer information systems (Graduate Certificate); liberal studies (MLS); race-ethnic studies (Graduate Certificate); women's and gender studies (Graduate Certificate). *Program availability:* Part-time, evening/weekend. *Entrance requirements:* For master's, GRE (recommended for MS), minimum undergraduate GPA of 3.0, bachelor's degree from accredited university (for MS). Electronic applications accepted. *Expenses:* Contact institution.

Indiana University South Bend, School of Education, South Bend, IN 46615. Offers addiction counseling (MS Ed); alcohol and drug counseling (Graduate Certificate); clinical mental health counseling (MS Ed); educational leadership (MS Ed); elementary education (MS Ed); marriage, couple, and family counseling (MS Ed); school counseling (MS Ed); secondary education (MS Ed); special education (MAT, MS Ed), including intense intervention (MS Ed), mild intervention (MS Ed). *Accreditation:* NCATE. *Program availability:* Part-time, evening/weekend. *Degree requirements:* For master's, thesis or alternative, exit project. *Entrance requirements:* For master's, letters of recommendation, GRE or minimum GPA of 3.0. Additional exam requirements/recommendations for international students: Required—TOEFL. Electronic applications accepted. *Expenses:* Contact institution. *Faculty research:* Professional dispositions, early childhood literacy, online learning, program assessments, problem-based learning.

Indiana Wesleyan University, Graduate School, College of Arts and Sciences, Marion, IN 46953. Offers addictions counseling (MS); clinical mental health counseling (MS); community counseling (MS); marriage and family therapy (MS); school counseling (MS); student development counseling and administration (MS). *Accreditation:* ACA. *Program*

availability: Part-time. *Degree requirements:* For master's, thesis or alternative. *Entrance requirements:* For master's, GRE General Test. Additional exam requirements/ recommendations for international students: Required—TOEFL. Electronic applications accepted. *Expenses:* Contact institution. *Faculty research:* Community counseling, multicultural counseling, addictions.

Instituto Tecnologico de Santo Domingo, Graduate School, Area of Humanities and Social Sciences, Santo Domingo, Dominican Republic. Offers accounting (Certificate); adult education (Certificate); applied linguistics (MA); economics (MA); education (M Ed); educational psychology (MA, Certificate); gender and development (MA, Certificate); humanistic studies (MA); international marketing management (Certificate); international relations in the Caribbean basin (Certificate); intervention systems in family therapy (MA); linguistic and literary communication (Certificate); pedagogical support (MA); social science education (M Ed); sustainable human development (MA); terminal illness and death psychology (Certificate); youth and adult education (M Ed).

Inter American University of Puerto Rico, Aguadilla Campus, Graduate School, Aguadilla, PR 00605. Offers accounting (MBA); counseling psychology specializing in family (MS); criminal justice (MA); educative management and leadership (MA); elementary education (M Ed); finance (MBA); human resources (MBA); industrial management (MBA); management information systems (MBA); marketing (MBA). *Program availability:* Part-time, evening/weekend. *Degree requirements:* For master's, comprehensive exam. *Entrance requirements:* For master's, EXADEP, 2 letters of recommendation, minimum GPA of 2.5. Electronic applications accepted.

Inter American University of Puerto Rico, Metropolitan Campus, Graduate Programs, Program in Psychology, San Juan, PR 00919-1293. Offers counseling psychology (MA, PhD); industrial/organizational psychology (MA, PhD); labor relations (MA); school psychology (MA, PhD). *Degree requirements:* For master's, comprehensive exam. *Entrance requirements:* For master's, GRE or EXADEP, interview. Electronic applications accepted.

Inter American University of Puerto Rico, San Germán Campus, Graduate Studies Center, Program in Psychology, San Germán, PR 00683-5008. Offers counseling psychology (MA, PhD); school psychology (MA, PhD). *Program availability:* Part-time, evening/weekend. *Degree requirements:* For master's, comprehensive exam, thesis; for doctorate, comprehensive exam, thesis/dissertation. *Entrance requirements:* For master's, GRE General Test or EXADEP, minimum GPA of 3.0; for doctorate, GRE, EXADEP or MAT, minimum GPA of 3.0.

Iona College, School of Arts and Science, Department of Psychology, New Rochelle, NY 10801-1890. Offers general-experimental psychology (MA); human resources (Certificate); industrial-organizational psychology (MA); mental health counseling (MA); organizational behavior (Certificate); psychology (MA); school psychology (MA). *Program availability:* Part-time. *Faculty:* 9 full-time (5 women), 7 part-time/adjunct (5 women). *Students:* 75 full-time (55 women), 37 part-time (24 women); includes 46 minority (9 Black or African American, non-Hispanic/Latino; 2 Asian, non-Hispanic/ Latino; 34 Hispanic/Latino; 1 Two or more races, non-Hispanic/Latino), 1 international. Average age 25. 88 applicants, 88% accepted, 40 enrolled. In 2017, 23 master's awarded. *Degree requirements:* For master's, thesis (for some programs), literature review (for some programs). *Entrance requirements:* For master's, BA in psychology including 3 credits each in psychology statistics and experimental research methods, or 9 credits in psychology including 3 credits each in psychology statistics, psychology research methods and upper-level coursework. Additional exam requirements/ recommendations for international students: Required—TOEFL (minimum score 550 paper-based), IELTS (minimum score 6.5). *Application deadline:* For fall admission, 8/15 for domestic students, 5/1 for international students; for spring admission, 1/15 for domestic students, 9/1 for international students. Applications are processed on a rolling basis. Electronic applications accepted. Tuition and fees vary according to program. *Financial support:* In 2017–18, 27 students received support. Research assistantships with partial tuition reimbursements available, tuition waivers (partial), and unspecified assistantships available. Support available to part-time students. Financial award application deadline: 4/15; financial award applicants required to submit FAFSA. *Faculty research:* Non-suicidal self-injury, trauma response, performance appraisal and evaluation, diversity infusion, assessment and treatment of sexual offenders. *Unit head:* Patricia Oswald, PhD, Chair, 914-633-2374, E-mail: poswald@iona.edu. *Application contact:* Katelyn Brunck, Assistant Director, Graduate Admissions, 914-633-2451, Fax: 914-633-2277, E-mail: kbrunck@iona.edu.
Website: http://www.iona.edu/Academics/School-of-Arts-Science/Departments/ Psychology/Graduate-Programs.aspx

Iowa State University of Science and Technology, Department of Psychology, Ames, IA 50011. Offers cognitive psychology (PhD); counseling psychology (PhD); psychology (MS, PhD); social psychology (PhD). *Accreditation:* APA (one or more programs are accredited). *Entrance requirements:* For doctorate, GRE General Test, GRE Subject Test (psychology), 3 letters of recommendation. Additional exam requirements/ recommendations for international students: Required—TOEFL (minimum score 560 paper-based; 79 iBT), IELTS (minimum score 6.5). Electronic applications accepted. *Faculty research:* Counseling psychology, cognitive psychology, social psychology, health psychology, psychology and public policy.

Jacksonville University, Brooks Rehabilitation College of Healthcare Sciences, School of Applied Health Sciences, Program in Clinical Mental Health Counseling, Jacksonville, FL 32211. Offers clinical mental health counseling (MS), including marriage and family therapy. *Program availability:* Part-time, blended/hybrid learning. *Faculty:* 3 full-time (2 women), 3 part-time/adjunct (0 women). *Students:* 53 full-time (41 women); includes 24 minority (20 Black or African American, non-Hispanic/Latino; 4 Hispanic/Latino). Average age 35. 39 applicants, 72% accepted, 24 enrolled. *Degree requirements:* For master's, 1,000-hour community-based clinical field experience. *Entrance requirements:* For master's, baccalaureate degree from accredited college or university with minimum GPA of 3.0; background check; 1-2 page essay stating intent; resume (education, work experience); 3 letters of recommendation; interview. Additional exam requirements/ recommendations for international students: Required—TOEFL (minimum score 650 paper-based; 114 iBT), IELTS (minimum score 8). *Application deadline:* For fall admission, 2/1 for domestic and international students. Applications are processed on a rolling basis. Application fee: $50. Electronic applications accepted. *Expenses:* $680 per credit hour. *Financial support:* Federal Work-Study, institutionally sponsored loans, scholarships/grants, and health care benefits available. Support available to part-time students. Financial award application deadline: 3/15; financial award applicants required to submit FAFSA. *Unit head:* Dr. Whitney George, Department Chair, Clinical Mental Health Counseling, 904-256-7620, E-mail: wgeorge@ju.edu. *Application contact:* Pamela Adrian, Assistant Director, Graduate Admissions, 904-256-7245, E-mail: padrian@ju.edu.
Website: https://www.ju.edu/mentalhealth/

James Madison University, The Graduate School, College of Health and Behavioral Studies, Clinical Mental Health Counseling Program, Harrisonburg, VA 22807. Offers MA/Ed S. *Accreditation:* ACA. *Program availability:* Part-time, evening/weekend. *Students:* 51 full-time (42 women), 22 part-time (16 women); includes 14 minority (7 Black or African American, non-Hispanic/Latino; 1 Asian, non-Hispanic/Latino; 5 Hispanic/Latino; 1 Two or more races, non-Hispanic/Latino). Average age 30. *Expenses:* Tuition, state resident: full-time $10,512; part-time $438 per credit hour. Tuition, nonresident: full-time $28,358; part-time $1162 per credit hour. *Required fees:* $1128. *Financial support:* In 2017–18, 46 students received support. Career-related internships or fieldwork, Federal Work-Study, and assistantships (averaging $7911) available. Financial award application deadline: 3/1; financial award applicants required to submit FAFSA.

James Madison University, The Graduate School, College of Health and Behavioral Studies, Program in Counseling and Supervision, Harrisonburg, VA 22801. Offers PhD. *Program availability:* Part-time, evening/weekend. *Students:* 8 full-time (4 women), 10 part-time (6 women); includes 5 minority (4 Black or African American, non-Hispanic/ Latino; 1 Hispanic/Latino), 1 international. Average age 30. In 2017, 1 doctorate awarded. Application fee: $55. Electronic applications accepted. *Expenses:* Tuition, state resident: full-time $10,512; part-time $438 per credit hour. Tuition, nonresident: full-time $28,358; part-time $1162 per credit hour. *Required fees:* $1128. *Financial support:* In 2017–18, 8 students received support. Fellowships, Federal Work-Study, and 8 assistantships (averaging $7911) available. Financial award application deadline: 3/1; financial award applicants required to submit FAFSA. *Unit head:* Dr. Robin Anderson, Department Head, 540-568-3293, E-mail: ander2rd@jmu.edu. *Application contact:* Lynette D. Michael, Director of Graduate Admissions, 540-568-6131 Ext. 6395, Fax: 540-568-7860, E-mail: michaeld@jmu.edu.
Website: http://psyc.jmu.edu/counseling/supervision/

John Brown University, Graduate Counseling Programs, Siloam Springs, AR 72761-2121. Offers clinical mental health counseling (MS); marriage and family therapy (MS); play therapy (Graduate Certificate); school counseling (MS). *Accreditation:* NCATE. *Program availability:* Part-time, evening/weekend. *Degree requirements:* For master's, practica or internships. *Entrance requirements:* For master's, GRE (minimum score of 300), recommendation forms from three people, 200-word essay describing professional plans and reason for seeking acceptance. Additional exam requirements/ recommendations for international students: Required—TOEFL (minimum score 550 paper-based; 79 iBT). Electronic applications accepted. *Expenses:* Contact institution.

John Carroll University, Graduate Studies, Program in Clinical Mental Health Counseling, University Heights, OH 44118. Offers clinical counseling (Certificate); community counseling (MA). *Accreditation:* ACA. *Program availability:* Part-time, evening/weekend. *Faculty:* 5 full-time (4 women), 11 part-time/adjunct (4 women). *Students:* 54 full-time (42 women), 37 part-time (30 women); includes 13 minority (6 Black or African American, non-Hispanic/Latino; 2 Asian, non-Hispanic/Latino; 3 Hispanic/Latino; 2 Two or more races, non-Hispanic/Latino), 2 international. Average age 31. In 2017, 42 master's awarded. *Degree requirements:* For master's, comprehensive exam, internship, practicum. *Entrance requirements:* For master's, MAT or GRE, minimum GPA of 2.75, statement of volunteer experience, interview, 12-18 hours of social science course work. Additional exam requirements/recommendations for international students: Required—TOEFL. *Application deadline:* For fall admission, 8/ 15 priority date for domestic students; for spring admission, 1/3 for domestic students. Applications are processed on a rolling basis. Application fee: $25 ($35 for international students). Electronic applications accepted. *Expenses: Tuition:* Full-time $16,238; part-time $788 per credit hour. One-time fee: $200. Part-time tuition and fees vary according to course load and program. *Financial support:* In 2017–18, 20 students received support, including 1 teaching assistantship with full tuition reimbursement available (averaging $8,000 per year); career-related internships or fieldwork, institutionally sponsored loans, and unspecified assistantships also available. Financial award application deadline: 3/1; financial award applicants required to submit FAFSA. *Faculty research:* Child and adolescent development, HIV, hypnosis, wellness, women's issues. *Unit head:* Dr. Cecile Brennan, Coordinator, 216-397-1987, Fax: 216-397-3045, E-mail: counseladmin@jcu.edu. *Application contact:* Jennifer L. Tucker, Records Management Assistant, 216-397-1925, Fax: 216-397-1835, E-mail: jtucker@jcu.edu.

John F. Kennedy University, Graduate School of Holistic Studies, Department of Counseling Psychology, Program in Counseling Psychology, Pleasant Hill, CA 94523-4817. Offers holistic studies (MA); somatic psychology (MA); transpersonal psychology (MA). *Program availability:* Part-time, evening/weekend. *Degree requirements:* For master's, thesis or alternative. *Entrance requirements:* For master's, interview. Additional exam requirements/recommendations for international students: Required—TOEFL.

John F. Kennedy University, Graduate School of Professional Psychology, Program in Counseling Psychology, Pleasant Hill, CA 94523-4817. Offers MA. *Program availability:* Part-time, evening/weekend. *Degree requirements:* For master's, thesis or alternative. *Entrance requirements:* For master's, interview. Additional exam requirements/ recommendations for international students: Required—TOEFL.

Johns Hopkins University, School of Education, Certificate Programs in Education, Baltimore, MD 21218. Offers advanced methods for differentiated instruction and inclusive education (Graduate Certificate); applied behavior analysis (Post-Master's Certificate); clinical mental health counseling (Post-Master's Certificate); counseling (Advanced Certificate); data-based decision making and organizational improvement (Graduate Certificate); early intervention/preschool special education specialist (Graduate Certificate); education of students with autism and other pervasive developmental disorders (Graduate Certificate); educational leadership for independent schools (Graduate Certificate); evidence-based teaching in the health professions (Post-Master's Certificate); gifted education (Graduate Certificate); leadership in technology integration (Graduate Certificate); mind, brain and teaching (Graduate Certificate); school administration and supervision (Graduate Certificate); urban education (Graduate Certificate). *Program availability:* Part-time-only, evening/weekend, 100% online, blended/hybrid learning. *Entrance requirements:* For degree, minimum of bachelor's degree from regionally- or nationally-accredited institution (master's degree for some programs); minimum GPA of 3.0 in all previous programs of study; official transcripts from all post-secondary institutions attended; essay; curriculum vitae/ resume; two letters of recommendation; dispositions survey. Electronic applications accepted. *Expenses:* Contact institution.

Johns Hopkins University, School of Education, Master's Programs in Education, Baltimore, MD 21218. Offers counseling (MS), including clinical mental health counseling, school counseling; education (MS), including educational studies, gifted education, reading, school administration and supervision, technology for educators; elementary education (MAT); health professions (M Ed); intelligence analysis (MS); organizational leadership (MS); secondary education (MAT), including biology, chemistry, earth/space science, English, physics, social studies; special education (MS), including early childhood special education, general special education studies, mild to moderate disabilities, severe disabilities. *Program availability:* Part-time, evening/ weekend, 100% online, blended/hybrid learning. *Degree requirements:* For master's, comprehensive exam (for some programs), portfolio, capstone project and/or internship; PRAXIS II (subject area assessments) for initial teacher preparation programs that lead to licensure. *Entrance requirements:* For master's, GRE (for full-time programs only); PRAXIS I/core or state-approved alternative (for initial teacher preparation programs that lead to licensure), minimum of bachelor's degree from regionally- or nationally-accredited institution; minimum GPA of 3.0 in all previous programs of study; official

transcripts from all post-secondary institutions attended; essay; curriculum vitae/resume; letters of recommendation (3 for full-time programs, 2 for part-time programs); dispositions survey. Additional exam requirements/recommendations for international students: Required—TOEFL (minimum score 600 paper-based; 100 iBT), IELTS (minimum score 7). Electronic applications accepted. *Expenses:* Contact institution.

Kean University, College of Liberal Arts, Program in Psychology, Union, NJ 07083. Offers human behavior and organizational psychology (MA); psychological services (MA). *Program availability:* Part-time. *Faculty:* 18 full-time (14 women). *Students:* 65 full-time (46 women), 49 part-time (34 women); includes 74 minority (26 Black or African American, non-Hispanic/Latino; 13 Asian, non-Hispanic/Latino; 31 Hispanic/Latino; 1 Native Hawaiian or other Pacific Islander, non-Hispanic/Latino; 3 Two or more races, non-Hispanic/Latino), 2 international. Average age 28. 82 applicants, 89% accepted, 48 enrolled. In 2017, 25 master's awarded. *Degree requirements:* For master's, comprehensive exam, research component, two semesters of advanced seminar. *Entrance requirements:* For master's, GRE General Test, minimum GPA of 3.0; official transcripts from all institutions attended; two letters of recommendation; professional resume/curriculum vitae; 12 credits in behavioral sciences on the undergraduate level. Additional exam requirements/recommendations for international students: Required—TOEFL (minimum score 550 paper-based; 79 iBT), IELTS (minimum score 6.5). *Application deadline:* For fall admission, 6/30 for domestic and international students; for spring admission, 12/1 for domestic and international students. Applications are processed on a rolling basis. Application fee: $75. Electronic applications accepted. *Expenses:* Tuition, state resident: full-time $13,419; part-time $653 per credit. Tuition, nonresident: full-time $18,188; part-time $801 per credit. *Required fees:* $3382; $154 per credit. Tuition and fees vary according to course level, course load, degree level and program. *Financial support:* Scholarships/grants and unspecified assistantships available. Financial award applicants required to submit FAFSA. *Unit head:* Dr. Zandra Gratz, Program Coordinator, 908-737-5881, E-mail: zgratz@kean.edu. *Application contact:* Amy Clark, Program Assistant, 908-737-7100, E-mail: gradadmissions@kean.edu.
Website: http://grad.kean.edu/masters-programs/psychological-services

Kean University, Nathan Weiss Graduate College, Program in Counselor Education, Union, NJ 07083. Offers alcohol and drug abuse counseling (MA); clinical mental health counseling (MA); school counseling (MA). *Accreditation:* ACA; NCATE. *Program availability:* Part-time. *Faculty:* 9 full-time (5 women). *Students:* 146 full-time (115 women), 138 part-time (111 women); includes 123 minority (56 Black or African American, non-Hispanic/Latino; 1 American Indian or Alaska Native, non-Hispanic/Latino; 7 Asian, non-Hispanic/Latino; 53 Hispanic/Latino; 6 Two or more races, non-Hispanic/Latino), 3 international. Average age 32. 197 applicants, 45% accepted, 55 enrolled. In 2017, 80 master's awarded. *Degree requirements:* For master's, practicum, internship, portfolio. *Entrance requirements:* For master's, minimum GPA of 3.0, 2 letters of recommendation, personal statement, resume. Additional exam requirements/recommendations for international students: Required—TOEFL (minimum score 550 paper-based; 79 iBT), IELTS (minimum score 6.5). *Application deadline:* For fall admission, 3/1 for domestic and international students; for spring admission, 11/1 for domestic and international students. Applications are processed on a rolling basis. Application fee: $75. Electronic applications accepted. *Expenses:* Tuition, state resident: full-time $13,419; part-time $653 per credit. Tuition, nonresident: full-time $18,188; part-time $801 per credit. *Required fees:* $3382; $154 per credit. Tuition and fees vary according to course level, course load, degree level and program. *Financial support:* Scholarships/grants and unspecified assistantships available. Financial award applicants required to submit FAFSA. *Unit head:* Dr. J. Barry Mascari, Program Coordinator, 908-737-5954, E-mail: jmascari@kean.edu. *Application contact:* Pedro Lopes, Admissions Counselor, 908-737-7100, E-mail: gradadmissions@kean.edu.
Website: http://grad.kean.edu/counseling

Kent State University, College of Education, Health and Human Services, School of Lifespan Development and Educational Sciences, Program in Clinical Mental Health Counseling, Kent, OH 44242-0001. Offers M Ed. *Accreditation:* ACA; NCATE. *Entrance requirements:* For master's, minimum GPA of 2.75, 2 letters of reference, goals statement, moral character form, interview. Additional exam requirements/recommendations for international students: Required—TOEFL (minimum score 550 paper-based; 80 iBT). Electronic applications accepted. *Expenses:* Tuition, state resident: full-time $11,310; part-time $515 per credit hour. Tuition, nonresident: full-time $20,396; part-time $928 per credit hour. *International tuition:* $18,544 full-time. *Faculty research:* Group work, personality assessment, family/child therapy, substance abuse counseling, clinical supervision.

Kutztown University of Pennsylvania, College of Education, Program in Counseling Psychology, Kutztown, PA 19530-0730. Offers clinical mental health counseling (MA); marriage, couple and family counseling (MA). *Program availability:* Part-time, evening/weekend. *Faculty:* 4 full-time (3 women), 1 part-time/adjunct (0 women). *Students:* 75 full-time (68 women), 54 part-time (45 women); includes 31 minority (14 Black or African American, non-Hispanic/Latino; 1 Asian, non-Hispanic/Latino; 14 Hispanic/Latino; 2 Two or more races, non-Hispanic/Latino), 1 international. Average age 29. 73 applicants, 67% accepted, 27 enrolled. In 2017, 36 master's awarded. *Degree requirements:* For master's, comprehensive exam, thesis optional. *Entrance requirements:* For master's, GRE General Test, 3 letters of recommendation, minimum undergraduate GPA of 3.0, psychobiographical statement, resume. Additional exam requirements/recommendations for international students: Required—TOEFL (minimum score 550 paper-based; 79 iBT), IELTS (minimum score 6.5), or PTE (minimum score 53). *Application deadline:* For fall admission, 3/1 for domestic and international students; for spring admission, 10/1 for domestic and international students. Application fee: $35. Electronic applications accepted. *Expenses:* Tuition, state resident: part-time $500 per credit. Tuition, nonresident: part-time $750 per credit. *Required fees:* $115 per credit. One-time fee: $50 part-time. Tuition and fees vary according to degree level. *Financial support:* Career-related internships or fieldwork, Federal Work-Study, and unspecified assistantships available. Financial award application deadline: 3/1; financial award applicants required to submit FAFSA. *Faculty research:* Family addictions. *Unit head:* Dr. Helen S Hamlet, Department Chair, 610-683-4204, Fax: 610-683-1585, E-mail: hamlet@kutztown.edu.
Website: https://www.kutztown.edu/academics/graduate-programs/counseling.htm

Lamar University, College of Graduate Studies, College of Education and Human Development, Department of Counseling and Special Populations, Beaumont, TX 77701. Offers clinical mental health counseling (M Ed); school counseling (M Ed); special education (M Ed), including special education. *Accreditation:* ACA. *Faculty:* 15 full-time (12 women), 22 part-time/adjunct (18 women). *Students:* 27 full-time (22 women), 1,362 part-time (1,200 women); includes 700 minority (359 Black or African American, non-Hispanic/Latino; 6 American Indian or Alaska Native, non-Hispanic/Latino; 18 Asian, non-Hispanic/Latino; 305 Hispanic/Latino; 1 Native Hawaiian or other Pacific Islander, non-Hispanic/Latino; 11 Two or more races, non-Hispanic/Latino), 2 international. Average age 37. 1,317 applicants, 66% accepted, 234 enrolled. In 2017, 645 master's awarded. *Entrance requirements:* Additional exam requirements/recommendations for international students: Required—TOEFL (minimum score 550 paper-based; 79 iBT), IELTS (minimum score 6.5). *Application deadline:* For fall admission, 8/10 for domestic students, 7/1 for international students; for spring

admission, 1/5 for domestic students, 12/1 for international students. Applications are processed on a rolling basis. Application fee: $25 ($50 for international students). Electronic applications accepted. *Expenses:* Contact institution. *Financial support:* Applicants required to submit FAFSA. *Unit head:* Dr. Rebecca Weinbaum, Interim Chair, 409-880-8978, Fax: 409-880-2263. *Application contact:* Deidre Mayer, Interim Director, Admissions and Academic Services, 409-880-8888, Fax: 409-880-7419, E-mail: gradmissions@lamar.edu.
Website: http://education.lamar.edu/counseling-and-special-populations

Lancaster Bible College, Graduate School, Lancaster, PA 17601-5036. Offers adult ministries (MA); Bible (MA); children and family ministry (MA); church planting (MA); consulting resource teacher (M Ed); elementary school counseling (M Ed); leadership (PhD); leadership studies (MA); marriage and family counseling (MA); mental health counseling (MA); pastoral studies (MA); secondary school counseling (M Ed); sports ministry (MA); student ministry (MA); town and country ministry (MA). *Program availability:* Part-time, evening/weekend. *Degree requirements:* For master's, comprehensive exam (for some programs), thesis (for some programs). *Entrance requirements:* For master's, bachelor's degree with a minimum of 30 credits of course work in Bible, minimum undergraduate GPA of 3.0, interview. Additional exam requirements/recommendations for international students: Required—TOEFL.

La Salle University, School of Arts and Sciences, Program in Counseling and Family Therapy, Philadelphia, PA 19141-1199. Offers industrial/organizational psychology (MA); marriage and family therapy (MA); professional clinical counseling (MA). *Accreditation:* ACA; APA. *Program availability:* Part-time, evening/weekend. *Faculty:* 7 full-time (2 women), 18 part-time/adjunct (10 women). *Students:* 47 full-time (38 women), 159 part-time (123 women); includes 63 minority (29 Black or African American, non-Hispanic/Latino; 4 Asian, non-Hispanic/Latino; 26 Hispanic/Latino; 4 Two or more races, non-Hispanic/Latino), 5 international. Average age 30. 125 applicants, 78% accepted, 42 enrolled. In 2017, 73 master's awarded. *Degree requirements:* For master's, comprehensive exam. *Entrance requirements:* For master's, GRE or MAT (waived for applicants that already possess a master's degree in any field or for applicants that have a cumulative GPA of 3.5 or higher), minimum of 15 hours in psychology, counseling, or marriage and family studies; minimum GPA of 3.0; three letters of recommendation; personal statement; work experience (paid or volunteer). Additional exam requirements/recommendations for international students: Required—TOEFL. *Application deadline:* For fall admission, 8/15 priority date for domestic students, 7/15 for international students; for spring admission, 12/15 priority date for domestic students, 11/15 for international students; for summer admission, 4/15 priority date for domestic students, 3/15 for international students. Applications are processed on a rolling basis. Application fee: $35. Electronic applications accepted. Application fee is waived when completed online. *Expenses:* Contact institution. *Financial support:* In 2017–18, 34 students received support. Scholarships/grants and unspecified assistantships available. Support available to part-time students. Financial award application deadline: 8/31; financial award applicants required to submit FAFSA. *Faculty research:* Cognitive therapy, attribution theory, work habits, single parent families, treatment of addictions. *Unit head:* Dr. Donna A. Tonrey, Director, 215-951-1767, Fax: 215-951-1843, E-mail: psyma@lasalle.edu. *Application contact:* Elizabeth Heenan, Director, Graduate and Adult Enrollment, 215-951-1100, Fax: 215-951-1462, E-mail: heenan@lasalle.edu.
Website: http://www.lasalle.edu/counseling-family-therapy/

Lee University, Graduate Studies in Counseling, Cleveland, TN 37320-3450. Offers holistic child development (MS); marriage and family studies (MS); marriage and family therapy (MS); school counseling (MS). *Program availability:* Part-time, 100% online. *Faculty:* 7 full-time (3 women), 3 part-time/adjunct (0 women). *Students:* 95 full-time (71 women), 24 part-time (18 women); includes 27 minority (5 Black or African American, non-Hispanic/Latino; 19 Hispanic/Latino; 3 Two or more races, non-Hispanic/Latino), 7 international. Average age 30. 47 applicants, 87% accepted, 33 enrolled. In 2017, 32 master's awarded. *Degree requirements:* For master's, variable foreign language requirement, comprehensive exam (for some programs), thesis (for some programs), internship. *Entrance requirements:* For master's, GRE General Test or MAT (waived if undergraduate GPA is greater than 3.0 or if applicant already has a graduate degree), minimum undergraduate GPA of 3.0, 3 letters of recommendation, interview, official transcripts, essay. Additional exam requirements/recommendations for international students: Required—TOEFL (minimum score 61 iBT). *Application deadline:* For fall admission, 4/1 priority date for domestic and international students; for spring admission, 11/1 priority date for domestic and international students. Applications are processed on a rolling basis. Application fee: $25. Electronic applications accepted. *Expenses:* Tuition: Full-time $12,780; part-time $710 per credit hour. *Required fees:* $60; $60 per term. Tuition and fees vary according to program. *Financial support:* In 2017–18, 36 students received support. Career-related internships or fieldwork, Federal Work-Study, institutionally sponsored loans, scholarships/grants, and unspecified assistantships available. Financial award application deadline: 3/1; financial award applicants required to submit FAFSA. *Unit head:* Dr. Trevor Milliron, Director, 423-614-8126, Fax: 423-614-8124, E-mail: tmilliron@leeuniversity.edu.
Website: http://www.leeuniversity.edu/academics/graduate/counseling/

Lehigh University, College of Education, Program in Counseling Psychology, Bethlehem, PA 18015. Offers counseling and human services (M Ed); counseling psychology (PhD); international counseling (M Ed, Certificate); school counseling (M Ed). *Accreditation:* APA (one or more programs are accredited). *Faculty:* 7 full-time (5 women), 10 part-time/adjunct (8 women). *Students:* 69 full-time (62 women), 28 part-time (22 women); includes 22 minority (6 Black or African American, non-Hispanic/Latino; 6 Asian, non-Hispanic/Latino; 10 Hispanic/Latino), 13 international. Average age 29. 181 applicants, 30% accepted, 22 enrolled. In 2017, 27 master's, 4 doctorates awarded. *Degree requirements:* For master's, thesis (for some programs); for doctorate, comprehensive exam, thesis/dissertation. *Entrance requirements:* For master's, minimum GPA of 3.0, 2 letters of recommendation, essay, transcript; for doctorate, GRE General Test, 2 letters of recommendation, transcript, essay; for Certificate, minimum GPA of 3.0 (undergraduate), 3.5 (graduate). Additional exam requirements/recommendations for international students: Required—TOEFL (minimum score 600 paper-based, 93 iBT) or IELTS. *Application deadline:* For fall admission, 2/1 for domestic and international students. Application fee: $65. Electronic applications accepted. *Financial support:* In 2017–18, 31 students received support, including 7 research assistantships with full and partial tuition reimbursements available (averaging $15,249 per year); fellowships and unspecified assistantships also available. Financial award application deadline: 2/15. *Faculty research:* Maternal/infant attachment, multicultural training and counseling, career development and health interventions, intersection of identities, community based participatory research, cognitive development, gerontology, multicultural competence, south Asian-Asian American concerns, sexual assault prevention, LGBTQ, intimate partner violence, feminist theory and therapy, sexual and reproductive health, women's health, culture and health, prevention, minority student development, educational access an. *Total annual research expenditures:* $423,020. *Unit head:* Dr. Christopher Liang, Director, 610-758-3253, Fax: 610-758-3227, E-mail: ctl212@lehigh.edu. *Application contact:* Kristi Ball, Coordinator, Counseling Psychology, 610-758-3250, Fax: 610-758-6223, E-mail: kmb618@lehigh.edu.
Website: https://ed.lehigh.edu/academics/programs/counseling-psychology

Counseling Psychology

Lenoir-Rhyne University, Graduate Programs, School of Counseling and Human Services, Program in Clinical Mental Health Counseling, Hickory, NC 28601. Offers MA. *Accreditation:* ACA. *Program availability:* Part-time, evening/weekend. *Degree requirements:* For master's, comprehensive exam, thesis optional. *Entrance requirements:* For master's, GRE General Test or MAT, writing sample; minimum undergraduate GPA of 2.7, graduate 3.0. Additional exam requirements/recommendations for international students: Required—TOEFL (minimum score 600 paper-based). Electronic applications accepted. *Expenses:* Contact institution.

Lesley University, Graduate School of Arts and Social Sciences, Cambridge, MA 02138-2790. Offers clinical mental health counseling (MA), including holistic counseling, school and community counseling, trauma studies; counseling psychology (MA, CAGS), including professional counseling (MA), school counseling (MA); creative writing (MFA); expressive therapies (MA, PhD, CAGS), including art (MA), clinical mental health counseling (MA), dance (MA), expressive therapies (MA), music (MA); independent studies (CAGS); independent study (MA); intercultural relations (MA, CAGS); interdisciplinary studies (MA), including individualized studies, integrative holistic health, mindfulness studies, peace and conflict transformation, trauma sensitive assessment, intervention, and consultation, women's studies; urban environmental leadership (MA). *Program availability:* Part-time, online learning. *Degree requirements:* For master's, internship, practicum, thesis (for expressive therapies); for doctorate, thesis/dissertation, arts apprenticeship, field placement; for CAGS, thesis, internship (for counseling psychology, expressive therapies). *Entrance requirements:* For master's, MAT (counseling psychology), interview, writing samples, art portfolio; for doctorate, GRE or MAT, interview, master's degree; for CAGS, interview, master's degree. Additional exam requirements/recommendations for international students: Required—TOEFL (minimum score 550 paper-based; 80 iBT). Electronic applications accepted. *Faculty research:* Psychotherapy and culture; psychotherapy and psychological trauma; women's issues in art, teaching and psychotherapy; community-based art, psycho-spiritual inquiry.

LeTourneau University, Graduate Programs, Longview, TX 75607-7001. Offers business (MBA); counseling (MA), including licensed professional counselor, marriage and family therapy, school counseling; curriculum and instruction (M Ed); educational administration (M Ed); engineering (ME, MS); engineering management (MEM); health care administration (MS); marriage and family therapy (MA); psychology (MA); strategic leadership (MSL); teacher leadership (M Ed); teaching and learning (M Ed). *Program availability:* Part-time, 100% online, blended/hybrid learning. *Students:* 55 full-time (35 women), 337 part-time (266 women); includes 218 minority (140 Black or African American, non-Hispanic/Latino; 2 American Indian or Alaska Native, non-Hispanic/Latino; 5 Asian, non-Hispanic/Latino; 32 Hispanic/Latino; 39 Two or more races, non-Hispanic/Latino), 3 international. Average age 37. *Entrance requirements:* Additional exam requirements/recommendations for international students: Required—TOEFL. *Application deadline:* For fall admission, 8/22 for domestic students, 8/29 for international students; for winter admission, 10/10 for domestic students; for spring admission, 1/2 for domestic students, 1/10 for international students; for summer admission, 5/1 for domestic and international students. Applications are processed on a rolling basis. Electronic applications accepted. *Expenses:* Contact institution. *Financial support:* Research assistantships, institutionally sponsored loans, and unspecified assistantships available. Financial award applicants required to submit FAFSA.
Website: http://www.letu.edu

Lewis & Clark College, Graduate School of Education and Counseling, Department of Counseling Psychology, Program in Professional Mental Health Counseling, Portland, OR 97219-7899. Offers MA, MS. *Accreditation:* ACA. *Program availability:* Part-time, evening/weekend. *Degree requirements:* For master's, thesis (MS). *Entrance requirements:* For master's, GRE General Test, minimum undergraduate GPA of 2.75. Additional exam requirements/recommendations for international students: Required—TOEFL (minimum score 575 paper-based). Electronic applications accepted.

Lewis University, College of Arts and Sciences, Program in Clinical Mental Health Counseling, Romeoville, IL 60446. Offers adult mental health counseling (MA); child and adolescent counseling (MA). *Program availability:* Part-time, evening/weekend. *Students:* 58 full-time (49 women), 60 part-time (53 women); includes 33 minority (10 Black or African American, non-Hispanic/Latino; 2 Asian, non-Hispanic/Latino; 17 Hispanic/Latino; 1 Native Hawaiian or other Pacific Islander, non-Hispanic/Latino; 3 Two or more races, non-Hispanic/Latino). Average age 28. In 2017, 27 master's awarded. *Degree requirements:* For master's, comprehensive exam, thesis optional, practicum, internship. *Entrance requirements:* For master's, bachelor's degree, 15 hours of undergraduate psychology, including statistics or research; 2 letters of recommendation; minimum GPA of 3.0 in last 60 hours; interview, personal statement. Additional exam requirements/recommendations for international students: Required—TOEFL (minimum score 550 paper-based; 79 iBT), IELTS (minimum score 6). *Application deadline:* For fall admission, 5/1 priority date for international students; for spring admission, 11/15 priority date for international students. Applications are processed on a rolling basis. Application fee: $40. Electronic applications accepted. Tuition and fees vary according to program. *Financial support:* Federal Work-Study, scholarships/grants, tuition waivers, and unspecified assistantships available. Financial award application deadline: 5/1; financial award applicants required to submit FAFSA. *Faculty research:* Cognitive development, attitude formation, juvenile delinquency, gender issues, work-family conflict. *Unit head:* Dr. Katherine Helm-Lewis, Director, 815-838-0500 Ext. 5604, Fax: 815-836-5032, E-mail: helmka@lewisu.edu. *Application contact:* Linda Campbell, Graduate Admissions Counselor, 815-836-5610, Fax: 815-836-5578, E-mail: grad@lewisu.edu.
Website: http://www.lewisu.edu/academics/grad.htm/

Liberty University, School of Behavioral Sciences, Lynchburg, VA 24515. Offers applied psychology (MA), including developmental psychology (MA, MS), industrial/organizational psychology (MA, MS); clinical mental health counseling (MA); community care and counseling (Ed D), including marriage and family counseling, pastoral care and counseling, traumatology; counselor education and supervision (PhD); human services counseling (MA), including addictions and recovery, business, child and family law, Christian ministries, criminal justice, crisis response and trauma, executive leadership, health and wellness, life coaching, marriage and family, military resilience; marriage and family counseling (MA); marriage and family therapy (MA); military resilience (Certificate); pastoral counseling (MA), including addictions and recovery, community chaplaincy, crisis response and trauma, discipleship and church ministry, leadership, life coaching, marriage and family, marriage and family studies, military resilience, parenting and child/adolescent, pastoral counseling, theology; professional counseling (MA); psychology (MS), including developmental psychology (MA, MS), industrial/organizational psychology (MA, MS); school counseling (M Ed). *Program availability:* Part-time, online learning. *Students:* 2,649 full-time (2,085 women), 5,086 part-time (4,015 women); includes 2,275 minority (1,784 Black or African American, non-Hispanic/Latino; 44 American Indian or Alaska Native, non-Hispanic/Latino; 67 Asian, non-Hispanic/Latino; 200 Hispanic/Latino; 11 Native Hawaiian or other Pacific Islander, non-Hispanic/Latino; 169 Two or more races, non-Hispanic/Latino), 145 international. Average age 39. 5,839 applicants, 51% accepted, 1710 enrolled. In 2017, 1,626 master's, 7 doctorates, 61 other advanced degrees awarded. *Application deadline:* Applications are processed on a rolling basis. Application fee: $50. Electronic applications accepted. *Financial support:* Applicants required to submit FAFSA. *Unit head:* Dr. Ronald Hawkins, Founding Dean, School of Behavioral Sciences. *Application contact:* Jay Bridge, Director of Admissions, 800-424-9595, Fax: 800-628-7977, E-mail: gradadmissions@liberty.edu.

Lindenwood University, Graduate Programs, School of Education, St. Charles, MO 63301-1695. Offers behavioral analysis (MA); education (MA), including autism spectrum disorders, character education, early intervention in autism and sensory impairment, gifted, technology; educational administration (MA, Ed D, Ed S); English to speakers of other languages (MA); instructional leadership (Ed D, Ed S); library media (MA); professional counseling (MA); school administration (MA, Ed S); school counseling (MA); teaching (MA). *Program availability:* Part-time, evening/weekend, 100% online, blended/hybrid learning. *Faculty:* 47 full-time (31 women), 213 part-time/adjunct (135 women). *Students:* 434 full-time (319 women), 1,292 part-time (989 women); includes 387 minority (313 Black or African American, non-Hispanic/Latino; 9 American Indian or Alaska Native, non-Hispanic/Latino; 13 Asian, non-Hispanic/Latino; 37 Hispanic/Latino; 1 Native Hawaiian or other Pacific Islander, non-Hispanic/Latino; 14 Two or more races, non-Hispanic/Latino), 20 international. Average age 36. 828 applicants, 61% accepted, 378 enrolled. In 2017, 431 master's, 63 doctorates, 94 other advanced degrees awarded. *Degree requirements:* For master's, thesis (for some programs), minimum GPA of 3.0; for doctorate, thesis/dissertation, minimum GPA of 3.0; for Ed S, comprehensive exam, project, minimum GPA of 3.0. *Entrance requirements:* For master's, interview, minimum undergraduate cumulative GPA of 3.0, writing sample, letter of recommendation; for doctorate, GRE, minimum graduate GPA of 3.4, resume, interview, writing sample, 4 letters of recommendation; for Ed S, master's degree in education, relevant work experience. Additional exam requirements/recommendations for international students: Required—TOEFL (minimum score 550 paper-based; 80 iBT); Recommended—IELTS (minimum score 6.5). *Application deadline:* For fall admission, 8/27 priority date for domestic and international students; for spring admission, 1/14 priority date for domestic and international students; for summer admission, 6/4 priority date for domestic and international students. Applications are processed on a rolling basis. Application fee: $30 ($100 for international students). Electronic applications accepted. *Expenses: Tuition:* Full-time $16,300; part-time $460 per credit. *Required fees:* $660; $330 per credit. Tuition and fees vary according to degree level and program. *Financial support:* In 2017–18, 1,615 students received support. Career-related internships or fieldwork, Federal Work-Study, institutionally sponsored loans, scholarships/grants, tuition waivers (partial), and unspecified assistantships available. Financial award application deadline: 6/30; financial award applicants required to submit FAFSA. *Unit head:* Dr. Anthony Scheffler, Dean, School of Education, 636-949-4618, Fax: 636-949-4197, E-mail: ascheffler@lindenwood.edu. *Application contact:* Kara Schilli, Director, Evening and Graduate Admissions, 636-949-4349, Fax: 636-949-4109, E-mail: adultadmissions@lindenwood.edu.
Website: http://www.lindenwood.edu/academics/academic-schools/school-of-education/

Lindsey Wilson College, School of Professional Counseling, Columbia, KY 42728. Offers counseling and human development (M Ed); counselor education and supervision (PhD). *Accreditation:* ACA (one or more programs are accredited). *Program availability:* Part-time, evening/weekend, online learning.

Lipscomb University, Department of Psychology, Counseling, and Family Science, Nashville, TN 37204-3951. Offers clinical mental health counseling (MS); counseling psychology (Certificate); marriage and family therapy (MMFT); psychology (MS). *Program availability:* Part-time, evening/weekend. *Faculty:* 10 full-time (3 women), 10 part-time/adjunct (4 women). *Students:* 120 full-time (92 women), 30 part-time (27 women); includes 38 minority (22 Black or African American, non-Hispanic/Latino; 1 American Indian or Alaska Native, non-Hispanic/Latino; 1 Asian, non-Hispanic/Latino; 11 Hispanic/Latino; 3 Two or more races, non-Hispanic/Latino), 2 international. Average age 28. 144 applicants, 44% accepted, 42 enrolled. In 2017, 68 master's, 1 other advanced degree awarded. *Degree requirements:* For master's, thesis (for some programs), practicum, internship, capstone. *Entrance requirements:* For master's, GRE, resume, 3 reference letters, transcripts, goals statement. Additional exam requirements/recommendations for international students: Required—TOEFL (minimum score 570 paper-based; 80 iBT). *Application deadline:* For fall admission, 7/1 for domestic students; for spring admission, 11/1 for domestic students. Applications are processed on a rolling basis. Application fee: $50 ($75 for international students). Electronic applications accepted. *Expenses:* Contact institution. *Financial support:* Scholarships/grants and unspecified assistantships available. Financial award applicants required to submit FAFSA. *Faculty research:* Cognitive psychology, neuroscience, health psychology, grief issues. *Unit head:* Dr. Shanna Ray, Director/Professor of Psychology, 615-966-5833, E-mail: shanna.ray@lipscomb.edu. *Application contact:* Kathi Johnson, Recruiting and Marketing Coordinator, 615-966-5237, E-mail: kathi.johnson@lipscomb.edu.
Website: http://www.lipscomb.edu/psychology/graduate-programs

Lock Haven University of Pennsylvania, The Stephen Poorman College of Business, Information Systems, and Human Services, Lock Haven, PA 17745-2390. Offers clinical mental health counseling (MS); sport science (MS). *Program availability:* Online learning. *Degree requirements:* For master's, thesis. *Entrance requirements:* For master's, minimum undergraduate GPA of 3.0. Additional exam requirements/recommendations for international students: Required—TOEFL. Electronic applications accepted.

London Metropolitan University, Graduate Programs, London, United Kingdom. Offers applied psychology (M Sc); architecture (MA); biomedical science (M Sc); blood science (M Sc); cancer pharmacology (M Sc); computer networking and cyber security (M Sc); computing and information systems (M Sc); conference interpreting (MA); counter-terrorism studies (M Sc); creative, digital and professional writing (MA); crime, violence and prevention (M Sc); criminology (M Sc); curating contemporary art (MA); data analytics (M Sc); digital media (MA); early childhood studies (MA); education (MA, Ed D); financial services law, regulation and compliance (LL M); food science (M Sc); forensic psychology (M Sc); health and social care management and policy (M Sc); human nutrition (M Sc); human resource management (MA); human rights and international conflict (MA); information technology (M Sc); intelligence and security studies (M Sc); international oil, gas and energy law (LL M); international relations (MA); interpreting (MA); learning and teaching in higher education (MA); legal practice (LL M); media and entertainment law (LL M); organizational and consumer psychology (M Sc); psychological therapy (M Sc); psychology of mental health (M Sc); public health (M Sc); public policy and management (MPA); security studies (M Sc); social work (M Sc); spatial planning and urban design (MA); sports therapy (M Sc); supporting older children and young people with dyslexia (MA); teaching languages (MA), including Arabic, English; translation (MA); woman and child abuse (MA).

Long Island University–Brentwood Campus, Graduate Programs, Brentwood, NY 11717. Offers childhood education (MS), including grades 1-6; childhood education/literacy B-6 (MS); childhood education/special education (grades 1-6) (MS); clinical mental health counseling (MS, Advanced Certificate); criminal justice (MS); early childhood education (MS); educational leadership (MS Ed); family nurse practitioner (MS, Advanced Certificate); health administration (MPA); library and information science (MS); literacy (B-6) (MS Ed); school counselor (MS, Advanced Certificate); social work (MSW); special education (MS Ed); students with disabilities generalist (grades 7-12)

(Advanced Certificate). *Program availability:* Part-time. *Faculty:* 14 full-time (9 women), 22 part-time/adjunct (11 women). *Students:* 111 full-time (89 women), 47 part-time (34 women); includes 35 minority (8 Black or African American, non-Hispanic/Latino; 1 American Indian or Alaska Native, non-Hispanic/Latino; 3 Asian, non-Hispanic/Latino; 22 Hispanic/Latino; 1 Two or more races, non-Hispanic/Latino), 1 international. Average age 30. 110 applicants, 82% accepted, 63 enrolled. In 2017, 58 master's, 5 other advanced degrees awarded. *Entrance requirements:* For master's and Advanced Certificate, GRE. Additional exam requirements/recommendations for international students: Required—TOEFL or IELTS. *Application deadline:* Applications are processed on a rolling basis. Application fee: $50. Electronic applications accepted. *Expenses: Tuition:* Full-time $21,168; part-time $1201 per credit. *Required fees:* $1840; $920 per term. Tuition and fees vary according to course load. *Financial support:* In 2017–18, 121 students received support. Scholarships/grants available. Support available to part-time students. Financial award application deadline: 2/15; financial award applicants required to submit FAFSA. *Unit head:* Dr. Abby Van Vlerah, Dean and Chief Operating Officer, 631-299-3831, E-mail: abagail.vanvlerah@liu.edu. *Application contact:* Scott Aug, Associate Director of Enrollment Management, 631-287-8506, E-mail: scott.aug@liu.edu.
Website: http://liu.edu/brentwood

Long Island University–Hudson, Graduate School, Purchase, NY 10577. Offers autism (Advanced Certificate); bilingual education (Advanced Certificate); childhood education (MS Ed); crisis management (Advanced Certificate); early childhood education (MS Ed); educational leadership (MS Ed); health administration (MPA); literacy (MS Ed); marriage and family therapy (MS); mental health counseling (MS, Advanced Certificate), including credentialed alcoholism and substance abuse counselor (MS); middle childhood and adolescence education (MS Ed); pharmaceutics (MS), including cosmetic science, industrial pharmacy; public administration (MPA); school counseling (MS Ed, Advanced Certificate); school psychology (MS Ed); special education (MS Ed); TESOL (MS Ed); TESOL (all grades) (Advanced Certificate). *Program availability:* Part-time, evening/weekend. *Faculty:* 8 full-time (6 women), 41 part-time/adjunct (24 women). *Students:* 69 full-time (54 women), 249 part-time (200 women); includes 102 minority (29 Black or African American, non-Hispanic/Latino; 1 American Indian or Alaska Native, non-Hispanic/Latino; 9 Asian, non-Hispanic/Latino; 62 Hispanic/Latino; 1 Native Hawaiian or other Pacific Islander, non-Hispanic/Latino). Average age 33. 153 applicants, 96% accepted, 103 enrolled. In 2017, 138 master's, 36 other advanced degrees awarded. *Entrance requirements:* Additional exam requirements/recommendations for international students: Required—TOEFL. *Application deadline:* Applications are processed on a rolling basis. Application fee: $50. Electronic applications accepted. *Expenses:* Contact institution. *Financial support:* In 2017–18, 32 students received support. Scholarships/grants available. Support available to part-time students. Financial award application deadline: 2/15; financial award applicants required to submit FAFSA. *Unit head:* Dr. Sylvia Blake, Dean and Chief Operating Officer, 914-831-2700, E-mail: westchester@liu.edu. *Application contact:* Dr. Sylvia Blake, Dean and Chief Operating Officer, 914-831-2700, E-mail: westchester@liu.edu.

Long Island University–LIU Brooklyn, School of Education, Brooklyn, NY 11201-8423. Offers adolescence urban education (MS Ed); applied behavior analysis (Advanced Certificate); bilingual education (Advanced Certificate); bilingual education in urban setting (MS Ed); bilingual school counselor (MS Ed, Advanced Certificate); childhood urban education (MS Ed); childhood/early childhood education (MS Ed); childhood/early childhood urban education (MS Ed); early childhood urban education (MS Ed, Advanced Certificate); educational leadership (Advanced Certificate); marriage and family therapy (MS, Advanced Certificate); mental health counseling (MS, Advanced Certificate); school building district leader (Advanced Certificate); school counselor (MS Ed, Advanced Certificate); school psychologist (MS Ed); teaching students with disabilities (MS Ed); teaching urban children with disabilities (MS Ed); TESOL (MS Ed, Advanced Certificate). *Accreditation:* TEAC. *Program availability:* Part-time, evening/weekend, 100% online. *Faculty:* 14 full-time (12 women), 42 part-time/adjunct (32 women). *Students:* 140 full-time (130 women), 563 part-time (414 women); includes 417 minority (183 Black or African American, non-Hispanic/Latino; 1 American Indian or Alaska Native, non-Hispanic/Latino; 32 Asian, non-Hispanic/Latino; 187 Hispanic/Latino; 14 Two or more races, non-Hispanic/Latino), 10 international. Average age 31. 449 applicants, 82% accepted, 264 enrolled. In 2017, 408 master's, 31 other advanced degrees awarded. *Entrance requirements:* For master's, GRE. Additional exam requirements/recommendations for international students: Required—TOEFL (minimum score 527 paper-based, 75 iBT), IELTS, or PTE. *Application deadline:* Applications are processed on a rolling basis. Application fee: $50. Electronic applications accepted. *Expenses: Tuition:* Full-time $21,618; part-time $1201 per credit. *Required fees:* $1840; $920 per term. Tuition and fees vary according to course load. *Financial support:* In 2017–18, 58 students received support. Career-related internships or fieldwork, Federal Work-Study, scholarships/grants, and unspecified assistantships available. Support available to part-time students. Financial award application deadline: 2/15; financial award applicants required to submit FAFSA. *Faculty research:* Diversity issues in education and mental health care, inclusion - disability studies, sustainability, teacher professional development. *Unit head:* Dean, 718-488-1055, E-mail: bkln-admissions@liu.edu. *Application contact:* Bayu Sutrisno, Graduate Admissions Counselor, 718-488-1011, Fax: 718-780-6110, E-mail: bkln-admissions@liu.edu.
Website: http://www.liu.edu/Brooklyn/Academics/School-of-Education

Long Island University–LIU Post, College of Education, Information and Technology, Brookville, NY 11548-1300. Offers adolescence education (MS); adolescence education 7-12 (MS); archives and records management (AC); art education (MS); childhood education (MS); childhood education/literacy B-6 (MS); childhood education/special education (MS); clinical mental health counseling (MS, AC); early childhood education (MS); early childhood education/childhood education (MS); educational leadership (AC); educational technology (MS); information studies (PhD); interdisciplinary educational studies (Ed D); middle childhood education (MS); music education (MS); public library administration (AC); school counselor (MS); special education (MS Ed); speech-language pathology (MA); students with disabilities, 7-12 generalist (AC); TESOL (MA). *Accreditation:* TEAC. *Program availability:* Part-time, 100% online, blended/hybrid learning. *Faculty:* 40 full-time (26 women), 73 part-time/adjunct (38 women). *Students:* 472 full-time (400 women), 696 part-time (543 women); includes 254 minority (93 Black or African American, non-Hispanic/Latino; 46 Asian, non-Hispanic/Latino; 105 Hispanic/Latino; 10 Two or more races, non-Hispanic/Latino), 33 international. Average age 33. 917 applicants, 82% accepted, 357 enrolled. In 2017, 408 master's, 31 other advanced degrees awarded. Terminal master's awarded for partial completion of doctoral program. *Degree requirements:* For master's, variable foreign language requirement, comprehensive exam (for some programs), thesis optional; for doctorate, comprehensive exam, thesis/dissertation. *Entrance requirements:* For master's and AC, GRE (for some programs). Additional exam requirements/recommendations for international students: Required—TOEFL (minimum score 550 paper-based, 75 iBT), IELTS, or PTE. *Application deadline:* Applications are processed on a rolling basis. Application fee: $50. Electronic applications accepted. *Expenses: Tuition:* Full-time $21,618; part-time $1201 per credit. *Required fees:* $1840; $920 per term. Tuition and fees vary according to course load. *Financial support:* In 2017–18, 376 students received support. Career-related internships or fieldwork, Federal Work-Study, institutionally sponsored loans, scholarships/grants, tuition waivers (partial), and unspecified assistantships available. Support available to part-time students. Financial award application deadline: 2/15; financial award applicants required to submit FAFSA. *Faculty research:* Sleep; use of technology to develop executive function by students with disabilities; early childhood literacy development through play; social justice through education; using a structured protocol to discuss Bad News. *Unit head:* Dr. Albert Inserra, Dean, 516-299-2210, E-mail: albert.inserra@liu.edu. *Application contact:* Rita Langdon, Graduate Admissions, 516-299-2900, Fax: 516-299-2137, E-mail: post-enroll@liu.edu.
Website: http://liu.edu/CWPost/Academics/College-of-Education-Information-and-Technology

Louisiana Tech University, Graduate School, College of Education, Ruston, LA 71272. Offers counseling and guidance (MA), including clinical mental health counseling, human services, orientation and mobility; counseling psychology (PhD); curriculum and instruction (M Ed); cyber education (Graduate Certificate); dynamics of domestic and family violence (Graduate Certificate); early childhood education - PreK-3 (MAT); educational leadership (M Ed, Ed D); elementary education and special education mild/moderate grades 1-5 (MAT); higher education administration (Graduate Certificate); industrial/organizational psychology (MA, PhD); kinesiology (MS); middle school education (MAT), including mathematics; orientation and mobility (Graduate Certificate); rehabilitation teaching for the blind (Graduate Certificate); secondary education (MAT), including agriculture, biology, business, chemistry, English; special education: visually impaired (MAT); teacher leader education (Graduate Certificate); visual impairments - blind education (Graduate Certificate). *Accreditation:* NCATE. *Program availability:* Part-time. *Faculty:* 28 full-time (16 women), 23 part-time/adjunct (22 women). *Students:* 269 full-time (192 women), 194 part-time (150 women); includes 127 minority (94 Black or African American, non-Hispanic/Latino; 2 American Indian or Alaska Native, non-Hispanic/Latino; 6 Asian, non-Hispanic/Latino; 16 Hispanic/Latino; 1 Native Hawaiian or other Pacific Islander, non-Hispanic/Latino; 8 Two or more races, non-Hispanic/Latino), 8 international. Average age 34. 226 applicants, 74% accepted, 60 enrolled. In 2017, 5 master's, 2 doctorates, 1 other advanced degree awarded. *Degree requirements:* For master's, thesis; for doctorate, thesis/dissertation. *Entrance requirements:* For master's and doctorate, GRE General Test. Additional exam requirements/recommendations for international students: Required—TOEFL (minimum score 550 paper-based; 80 iBT), IELTS (minimum score 6.5). *Application deadline:* For fall admission, 9/1 priority date for domestic students, 6/1 for international students; for winter admission, 11/1 priority date for domestic students, 9/1 for international students; for spring admission, 2/1 priority date for domestic students, 12/1 for international students; for summer admission, 5/1 priority date for domestic students, 3/1 for international students. Application fee: $40. Electronic applications accepted. *Expenses:* Tuition, state resident: full-time $5146. Tuition, nonresident: full-time $10,147. *International tuition:* $10,267 full-time. *Required fees:* $2273. *Financial support:* In 2017–18, 40 students received support, including 23 research assistantships (averaging $10,346 per year), 15 teaching assistantships (averaging $6,887 per year); fellowships and career-related internships or fieldwork also available. Financial award application deadline: 2/1. *Faculty research:* Blindness and the best methods for increasing independence for individuals who are blind or visually impaired; educating and investigating factors contributing to improvements in human performance across the lifespan and a reduction in injury rates during training. *Total annual research expenditures:* $2.1 million. *Unit head:* Dr. Don Schillinger, Dean, 318-257-3712, E-mail: dschill@latech.edu. *Application contact:* Dr. Dawn Basinger, Associate Dean of Academic Affairs, 318-257-2977, Fax: 318-257-2379, E-mail: dbasing@latech.edu.
Website: http://education.latech.edu/

Loyola Marymount University, School of Education, Program in Counseling, Los Angeles, CA 90045-2659. Offers MA. *Unit head:* Dr. Sheri Atwater, Director, Counseling Program, E-mail: sheri.atwater@lmu.edu. *Application contact:* Chake H. Kouyoumjian, Associate Dean of Graduate Studies, 310-338-2721, Fax: 310-338-6086, E-mail: graduateinfo@lmu.edu.
Website: http://soe.lmu.edu/academics/counseling

Loyola University Chicago, School of Education, Program in Community Counseling, Chicago, IL 60660. Offers clinical mental health counseling (Ed S); community counseling (M Ed, MA). MA offered through the Graduate School. *Program availability:* Part-time. *Faculty:* 5 full-time (2 women), 5 part-time/adjunct (4 women). *Students:* 26 full-time (22 women), 1 (woman) part-time; includes 10 minority (3 Black or African American, non-Hispanic/Latino; 2 Asian, non-Hispanic/Latino; 5 Hispanic/Latino), 2 international. Average age 26. 56 applicants, 77% accepted, 13 enrolled. In 2017, 15 master's awarded. *Degree requirements:* For master's and Ed S, comprehensive exam. *Entrance requirements:* For master's, GRE General Test, minimum GPA of 3.0, letters of recommendation, resume. Additional exam requirements/recommendations for international students: Required—TOEFL (minimum score 550 paper-based; 79 iBT). *Application deadline:* For fall admission, 1/1 for domestic and international students. Application fee: $50. Electronic applications accepted. Application fee is waived when completed online. *Expenses:* $949 per semester hour, $2,847 per course, $8,541-$11,388 full-time semester tuition; $432 per semester fees, $225 additional fees (first semester only). *Financial support:* Career-related internships or fieldwork, institutionally sponsored loans, scholarships/grants, and unspecified assistantships available. Support available to part-time students. Financial award application deadline: 2/1; financial award applicants required to submit FAFSA. *Faculty research:* Career development, prevention, group counseling, family therapy, multicultural counseling. *Unit head:* Dr. Eunju Yoon, Director, 312-915-6461, E-mail: eyoon@luc.edu. *Application contact:* Mirtza Campbell, Information Contact, 312-915-8907, E-mail: mcampbell11@luc.edu.

Loyola University Chicago, School of Education, Program in Counseling Psychology, Chicago, IL 60660. Offers PhD. PhD offered through the Graduate School. *Accreditation:* APA. *Faculty:* 5 full-time (2 women), 5 part-time/adjunct (4 women). *Students:* 18 full-time (14 women); includes 10 minority (5 Black or African American, non-Hispanic/Latino; 3 Asian, non-Hispanic/Latino; 1 Hispanic/Latino; 1 Two or more races, non-Hispanic/Latino), 3 international. Average age 29. 29 applicants, 10% accepted, 3 enrolled. In 2017, 4 doctorates awarded. *Degree requirements:* For doctorate, comprehensive exam, thesis/dissertation. *Entrance requirements:* For doctorate, GRE General Test, GRE Subject Test, interview; minimum graduate GPA of 3.5, undergraduate 3.0; letters of recommendation. Additional exam requirements/recommendations for international students: Required—TOEFL (minimum score 550 paper-based; 79 iBT). *Application deadline:* For fall admission, 12/1 for domestic and international students. Application fee: $50. Electronic applications accepted. Application fee is waived when completed online. *Expenses:* $949 per semester hour, $2,847 per course, $8,541-$11,388 full-time semester tuition; $432 per semester fees, $225 additional fees (first semester only). *Financial support:* In 2017–18, 7 research assistantships with full tuition reimbursements (averaging $14,000 per year), 18 teaching assistantships with full tuition reimbursements (averaging $4,000 per year) were awarded; career-related internships or fieldwork, institutionally sponsored loans, scholarships/grants, traineeships, health care benefits, and unspecified assistantships also available. Financial award application deadline: 2/1; financial award applicants required to submit FAFSA. *Faculty research:* Career choice and development,

multicultural counseling, psychological measurement, prevention and intervention, family therapy. *Unit head:* Dr. Eunju Yoon, Director, 312-915-6461, E-mail: eyoon@luc.edu. *Application contact:* Mirtza Campbell, Information Contact, 312-915-8907, E-mail: mcampbell11@luc.edu.

Loyola University Maryland, Graduate Programs, Loyola College of Arts and Sciences, Department of Psychology, Baltimore, MD 21210-2699. Offers clinical psychology (MS, Psy D, CAS); counseling psychology (MS, CAS). *Accreditation:* APA. *Program availability:* Part-time, evening/weekend. *Faculty:* 64 full-time (37 women), 31 part-time/adjunct (20 women). *Students:* 137 full-time (111 women), 58 part-time (46 women); includes 50 minority (18 Black or African American, non-Hispanic/Latino; 1 American Indian or Alaska Native, non-Hispanic/Latino; 13 Asian, non-Hispanic/Latino; 10 Hispanic/Latino; 8 Two or more races, non-Hispanic/Latino), 6 international. Average age 27. In 2017, 52 master's, 13 doctorates awarded. *Degree requirements:* For doctorate, thesis/dissertation. *Entrance requirements:* For master's, GRE, essay, 3 letters of recommendation, transcript. Additional exam requirements/recommendations for international students: Required—TOEFL (minimum score 550 paper-based), IELTS (minimum score 7). *Application deadline:* For fall admission, 12/1 for domestic students, 3/1 for international students. Application fee: $60. Electronic applications accepted. *Expenses:* Contact institution. *Financial support:* Scholarships/grants and unspecified assistantships available. Financial award application deadline: 4/15; financial award applicants required to submit FAFSA. *Unit head:* Carolyn M. Barry, Chair, 410-617-5325, E-mail: cbarry@loyola.edu. *Application contact:* Office of Graduate Admission, 410-617-5020, E-mail: graduate@loyola.edu.

Lynn University, College of Arts and Sciences, Boca Raton, FL 33431-5598. Offers criminal justice (MS); mental health counseling (MS); psychology (MS), including general psychology, industrial/organizational psychology. *Program availability:* Part-time, evening/weekend, 100% online, blended/hybrid learning. *Faculty:* 59 full-time (26 women), 22 part-time/adjunct (16 women). *Students:* 60 full-time (47 women), 38 part-time (24 women); includes 32 minority (15 Black or African American, non-Hispanic/Latino; 2 Asian, non-Hispanic/Latino; 15 Hispanic/Latino), 6 international. Average age 30. 73 applicants, 82% accepted, 47 enrolled. In 2017, 64 master's awarded. *Degree requirements:* For master's, comprehensive exam (for some programs), thesis (for some programs). *Entrance requirements:* For master's, bachelor's degree from accrediated institution, minimum undergraduate GPA of 3.0, official undergraduate transcripts, two letters of recommendation from academic or professional sources, writing sample demonstrating capacity to perform at graduate level. Additional exam requirements/recommendations for international students: Required—TOEFL (minimum score 550 paper-based; 80 iBT), IELTS (minimum score 6.5). *Application deadline:* For fall admission, 8/18 for domestic students, 8/4 for international students; for spring admission, 12/15 for domestic students, 12/1 for international students; for summer admission, 4/17 for domestic students, 4/3 for international students. Applications are processed on a rolling basis. Application fee: $45. Electronic applications accepted. *Expenses:* $740 per credit. *Financial support:* Career-related internships or fieldwork, Federal Work-Study, scholarships/grants, tuition waivers (full and partial), and unspecified assistantships available. Support available to part-time students. Financial award application deadline: 3/1; financial award applicants required to submit FAFSA. *Faculty research:* Personality and social media, learning strategies, personal health behaviors and compliance, using drums in substance abuse groups, interpersonal behaviors with individuals with autism, case conceptualization, teaching case conceptualization across the curriculum. *Unit head:* Dr. Katrina Carter-Tellison, Dean, 561-237-7412, E-mail: kcartertellison@lynn.edu. *Application contact:* Steven Pruitt, Director of Graduate Admission, 561-237-7834, Fax: 561-237-7100, E-mail: admissionpm@lynn.edu.
Website: https://www.lynn.edu/academics/colleges-schools/arts-and-sciences

Manhattan College, Graduate Programs, School of Education and Health, Program in Mental Health Counseling, Riverdale, NY 10471. Offers MS, Advanced Certificate. *Expenses: Tuition:* Part-time $1034 per credit. *Required fees:* $280 per term. One-time fee: $590 part-time. Tuition and fees vary according to program.

Marian University, Master of Science in Counseling Program, Indianapolis, IN 46222-1997. Offers clinical mental health counseling (MS); school counseling (MS). *Program availability:* Part-time. *Faculty:* 2 full-time (1 woman). *Students:* 8 full-time (7 women); includes 2 minority (both Two or more races, non-Hispanic/Latino). Average age 26. 18 applicants, 44% accepted, 8 enrolled. *Degree requirements:* For master's, 60 credit hours plus 1000 hours of supervised practicum (for clinical mental health counseling track); 48 credit hours plus 700 hours of supervised practicum (for school counseling track). *Entrance requirements:* For master's, GRE (preferred scores: combined 295, verbal 150, quantitative 145, writing 4), bachelor's degree (in related field preferred); minimum undergraduate and major GPA of 3.0; completion of undergraduate psychology courses in development, abnormal psychology, statistics or research methods; official transcripts from all postsecondary institutions attended; personal statement; 3 letters of recommendation; resume; interview. Additional exam requirements/recommendations for international students: Required—TOEFL (minimum score 550 paper-based; 79 iBT). *Application deadline:* For fall admission, 4/13 for domestic students; for spring admission, 11/1 for international students. Applications are processed on a rolling basis. Application fee: $40. Electronic applications accepted. Application fee is waived when completed online. *Expenses:* $505 per credit hour. *Financial support:* Application deadline: 4/15; applicants required to submit FAFSA. *Unit head:* Dr. Sarah Jenkins, 317-955-6399, E-mail: sjenkins@marian.edu. *Application contact:* Bryan Moody, Executive Director of Graduate Admission, 317-955-6284, E-mail: bmoody@marian.edu.
Website: http://www.marian.edu/academics/office-of-graduate-studies/master-of-science-in-counseling

Marist College, Graduate Programs, School of Social and Behavioral Sciences, Poughkeepsie, NY 12601-1387. Offers education (M Ed, MA); mental health counseling (MA); school psychology (MA, Adv C). *Program availability:* Part-time, evening/weekend. *Degree requirements:* For master's, thesis optional. *Entrance requirements:* For master's, GRE General Test, letters of recommendation, minimum undergraduate GPA of 3.0, interview. Additional exam requirements/recommendations for international students: Required—TOEFL (minimum score 550 paper-based; 80 iBT); Recommended—IELTS (minimum score 6.5). Electronic applications accepted. *Faculty research:* AIDS prevention, educational intervention, humanistic counseling research, aging and development, neuroimaging.

Marquette University, Graduate School, College of Education, Department of Counselor Education and Counseling Psychology, Milwaukee, WI 53201-1881. Offers clinical mental health counseling (MS); community counseling (MA); counseling psychology (PhD); school counseling (MA). *Accreditation:* ACA. *Program availability:* Part-time. Terminal master's awarded for partial completion of doctoral program. *Degree requirements:* For master's, comprehensive exam, thesis (for some programs); for doctorate, thesis/dissertation, qualifying exam. *Entrance requirements:* For master's, GRE General Test or MAT, official transcripts from all current and previous colleges/universities except Marquette, three letters of recommendation, statement of purpose; for doctorate, GRE General Test, MAT, sample of written work, official transcripts from all current and previous colleges/universities except Marquette, three letters of recommendation, statement of purpose, resume/curriculum vitae. Additional exam requirements/recommendations for international students: Required—TOEFL (minimum score 530 paper-based). *Faculty research:* Ethical and legal issues in education, anxiety disorders, multicultural counseling, child psychopathology, group counseling and dynamics.

Marymount University, School of Education and Human Services, Program in Counseling, Arlington, VA 22207-4299. Offers clinical mental health counseling (MA); pastoral counseling (MA); school counseling (MA); MA/MA. *Accreditation:* ACA (one or more programs are accredited). *Program availability:* Part-time, evening/weekend. *Faculty:* 9 full-time (7 women), 5 part-time/adjunct (all women). *Students:* 108 full-time (97 women), 38 part-time (32 women); includes 61 minority (28 Black or African American, non-Hispanic/Latino; 1 American Indian or Alaska Native, non-Hispanic/Latino; 5 Asian, non-Hispanic/Latino; 20 Hispanic/Latino; 7 Two or more races, non-Hispanic/Latino). Average age 29. 74 applicants, 92% accepted, 59 enrolled. In 2017, 40 master's awarded. *Degree requirements:* For master's, thesis or alternative, capstone/internship. *Entrance requirements:* For master's, GRE, 2 letters of recommendation, interview, resume, personal statement. Additional exam requirements/recommendations for international students: Required—TOEFL (minimum score 600 paper-based; 96 iBT), IELTS (minimum score 6.5). *Application deadline:* For fall admission, 1/15 priority date for domestic and international students. Applications are processed on a rolling basis. Application fee: $40. Electronic applications accepted. *Expenses: Tuition:* Full-time $17,550; part-time $975 per credit hour. *Required fees:* $198; $11 per credit hour. One-time fee: $250. Tuition and fees vary according to program. *Financial support:* In 2017–18, 19 students received support, including 4 research assistantships with full and partial tuition reimbursements available (averaging $8,325 per year), 8 teaching assistantships with full and partial tuition reimbursements available (averaging $8,016 per year); career-related internships or fieldwork, Federal Work-Study, scholarships/grants, and unspecified assistantships also available. Support available to part-time students. Financial award application deadline: 3/1; financial award applicants required to submit FAFSA. *Unit head:* Dr. Lisa Jackson-Cherry, Chair, Counseling, 703-284-1633, Fax: 703-284-5708, E-mail: lisa.jackson-cherry@marymount.edu. *Application contact:* Francesca Reed, Director, Graduate Admissions, 703-284-5901, Fax: 703-527-3815, E-mail: grad.admissions@marymount.edu.
Website: http://www.marymount.edu/Academics/School-of-Education-Human-Services/Graduate-Programs/Counseling-(M-A-)

Marywood University, Academic Affairs, Reap College of Education and Human Development, Department of Psychology and Counseling, Program in Mental Health Counseling, Scranton, PA 18509-1598. Offers MA. *Accreditation:* ACA. Electronic applications accepted.

McGill University, Faculty of Graduate and Postdoctoral Studies, Faculty of Education, Department of Educational and Counseling Psychology, Montréal, QC H3A 2T5, Canada. Offers counseling psychology (MA, PhD); educational psychology (M Ed, MA, PhD); school/applied child psychology and applied developmental psychology (M Ed, MA, PhD, Diploma), including school psychology. *Accreditation:* APA.

McKendree University, Graduate Programs, Master of Arts Program in Clinical Mental Health Counseling, Lebanon, IL 62254-1299. Offers MA. *Program availability:* Part-time, evening/weekend. *Degree requirements:* For master's, comprehensive exam, internship. *Entrance requirements:* For master's, official transcripts from each college or university attended, minimum undergraduate GPA of 3.0, three letters of recommendation, personal statement, completion of six undergraduate credit hours in a behavior science, curriculum vitae or resume. Electronic applications accepted.

McNeese State University, Doré School of Graduate Studies, Burton College of Education, Department of Psychology, Lake Charles, LA 70609. Offers applied behavior analysis (MA, Graduate Certificate); counseling psychology (MA); general/experimental psychology (MA). *Program availability:* Evening/weekend. *Entrance requirements:* For master's, GRE. *Application deadline:* For fall admission, 5/15 priority date for domestic and international students; for spring admission, 10/15 priority date for domestic and international students. Applications are processed on a rolling basis. Application fee: $20 ($30 for international students). *Financial support:* Application deadline: 5/1. *Unit head:* Dr. Dena L. Matzenbacher, Head, 337-475-5434, Fax: 337-562-4115, E-mail: dena@mcneese.edu. *Application contact:* Dr. Dustin M. Hebert, Director of Dore' School of Graduate Studies, 337-475-5396, Fax: 337-475-5397, E-mail: admissions@mcneese.edu.

Medaille College, Programs in Psychology, Buffalo, NY 14214-2695. Offers clinical psychology (Psy D); marriage and family therapy (MA); mental health counseling (MA); psychology (MA). *Accreditation:* ACA. *Program availability:* Part-time, evening/weekend. *Degree requirements:* For master's, comprehensive exam (for some programs), thesis (for some programs). *Entrance requirements:* For master's, GRE General Test (psychology), minimum GPA of 2.75 (psychology). Additional exam requirements/recommendations for international students: Required—TOEFL (minimum score 550 paper-based). Electronic applications accepted. *Faculty research:* Schizophrenia, Parkinson's Disease, eyewitness testimony, methodology.

Mercy College, School of Social and Behavioral Sciences, Program in Counseling, Dobbs Ferry, NY 10522-1189. Offers counseling (MS); family counseling (Certificate). *Program availability:* Part-time, evening/weekend, 100% online, blended/hybrid learning. *Students:* 144 full-time (117 women), 185 part-time (155 women); includes 251 minority (105 Black or African American, non-Hispanic/Latino; 5 Asian, non-Hispanic/Latino; 135 Hispanic/Latino; 1 Native Hawaiian or other Pacific Islander, non-Hispanic/Latino; 5 Two or more races, non-Hispanic/Latino), 4 international. Average age 34. 127 applicants, 60% accepted, 51 enrolled. In 2017, 92 master's awarded. *Degree requirements:* For master's, comprehensive exam (for some programs). *Entrance requirements:* For master's, essay, two professional letters of recommendation, resume, undergraduate transcript with minimum GPA of 3.0. Additional exam requirements/recommendations for international students: Required—TOEFL (minimum score 600 paper-based; 100 iBT), IELTS (minimum score 8). *Application deadline:* For fall admission, 8/1 for international students. Applications are processed on a rolling basis. Application fee: $40. Electronic applications accepted. *Expenses: Tuition:* Full-time $15,426; part-time $857 per credit hour. *Required fees:* $630; $158 per term. Tuition and fees vary according to course load, degree level and program. *Financial support:* Career-related internships or fieldwork, Federal Work-Study, scholarships/grants, and unspecified assistantships available. Support available to part-time students. Financial award applicants required to submit FAFSA. *Unit head:* Dr. Karol Dean, Dean, School of Social and Behavioral Sciences, 914-674-7517, E-mail: kdean@mercy.edu. *Application contact:* Allison Gurdineer, Senior Director of Admissions, 914-637-2946, Fax: 914-674-7382, E-mail: admissions@mercy.edu.
Website: https://www.mercy.edu/degrees-programs/ms-counseling

Mercy College, School of Social and Behavioral Sciences, Program in Mental Health Counseling, Dobbs Ferry, NY 10522-1189. Offers MS. *Program availability:* Part-time, evening/weekend. *Students:* 75 full-time (60 women), 97 part-time (80 women); includes 133 minority (69 Black or African American, non-Hispanic/Latino; 3 Asian, non-Hispanic/Latino; 58 Hispanic/Latino; 1 Native Hawaiian or other Pacific Islander, non-Hispanic/

Latino; 2 Two or more races, non-Hispanic/Latino), 4 international. Average age 34. 115 applicants, 48% accepted, 37 enrolled. In 2017, 38 master's awarded. *Degree requirements:* For master's, comprehensive exam. *Entrance requirements:* For master's, essay, resume, interview, two letters of recommendation, undergraduate transcript. Additional exam requirements/recommendations for international students: Required—TOEFL (minimum score 600 paper-based; 100 iBT), IELTS (minimum score 8). *Application deadline:* For fall admission, 8/1 for international students. Applications are processed on a rolling basis. Application fee: $40. Electronic applications accepted. *Expenses: Tuition:* Full-time $15,426; part-time $857 per credit hour. *Required fees:* $630; $158 per term. Tuition and fees vary according to course load, degree level and program. *Financial support:* Career-related internships or fieldwork, Federal Work-Study, scholarships/grants, and unspecified assistantships available. Support available to part-time students. Financial award applicants required to submit FAFSA. *Unit head:* Dr. Karol Dean, Dean, School of Social and Behavioral Sciences, 914-674-7809. *Application contact:* Allison Gurdineer, Senior Director of Admissions, 877-637-2946, Fax: 914-674-7382, E-mail: admissions@mercy.edu.
Website: https://www.mercy.edu/degrees-programs/ms-mental-health-counseling

Messiah College, Program in Counseling, Mechanicsburg, PA 17055. Offers clinical mental health counseling (MAC); counseling (CAGS); marriage, couple, and family counseling (MAC); school counseling (MAC). *Accreditation:* ACA. *Program availability:* Part-time, online learning. *Entrance requirements:* For master's, minimum undergraduate cumulative GPA of 3.0, 2 recommendations, resume or curriculum vitae, interview; for CAGS, bachelor's degree, minimum undergraduate cumulative GPA of 3.0, essay, two recommendations, resume or curriculum vitae, interview. Electronic applications accepted.

Mid-America Christian University, Program in Counseling, Oklahoma City, OK 73170-4504. Offers marital and family therapy (MS); pastoral/spiritual direction (MS); professional counselor (MS). *Entrance requirements:* For master's, MAT, bachelor's degree from a regionally accredited college or university, minimum overall cumulative GPA of 2.75 of bachelor course work. Additional exam requirements/recommendations for international students: Required—TOEFL (minimum score 550 paper-based).

Middle Tennessee State University, College of Graduate Studies, College of Education, Department of Educational Leadership, Program in Professional Counseling, Murfreesboro, TN 37132. Offers mental health counseling (M Ed); school counseling (M Ed). *Accreditation:* ACA; NCATE. *Program availability:* Part-time, evening/weekend, online learning. *Degree requirements:* For master's, comprehensive exam, thesis. *Entrance requirements:* For master's, GRE or MAT. Additional exam requirements/recommendations for international students: Required—TOEFL (minimum score 525 paper-based; 71 iBT) or IELTS (minimum score 6). Electronic applications accepted.

Midwestern State University, Billie Doris McAda Graduate School, Prothro-Yeager College of Humanities and Social Sciences, Department of Psychology, Wichita Falls, TX 76308. Offers clinical/counseling psychology (MA). *Program availability:* Part-time, evening/weekend. *Degree requirements:* For master's, one foreign language, comprehensive exam, thesis optional. *Entrance requirements:* For master's, GRE General Test, 3 recommendation forms. Additional exam requirements/recommendations for international students: Required—TOEFL (minimum score 550 paper-based). Electronic applications accepted. *Faculty research:* Child assessment and treatment outcomes, Christianity as it relates to psychology, treatment of behavioral/emotional problems in childhood, people struggling with HIV/AIDS, educational psychology.

Minnesota State University Mankato, College of Graduate Studies and Research, College of Education, Department of Counseling and Student Personnel, Mankato, MN 56001. Offers college student affairs (MS); counselor education and supervision (Ed D); mental health counseling (MS); professional school counseling (K-12) (MS). *Accreditation:* ACA (one or more programs are accredited); NCATE. *Degree requirements:* For master's, comprehensive exam, thesis or alternative. *Entrance requirements:* For master's, GRE General Test or MAT (if GPA less than 3.0 for last 2 years), minimum GPA of 3.0 during previous 2 years, 3 letters of reference. Additional exam requirements/recommendations for international students: Required—TOEFL. Electronic applications accepted.

Mississippi College, Graduate School, School of Education, Department of Psychology and Counseling, Clinton, MS 39058. Offers counseling (Ed S); marriage and family counseling (MS); mental health counseling (MS); school counseling (M Ed). *Program availability:* Part-time. *Degree requirements:* For master's and Ed S, comprehensive exam, thesis optional. *Entrance requirements:* For master's, GRE or NTE. Additional exam requirements/recommendations for international students: Recommended—TOEFL, IELTS. Electronic applications accepted.

Missouri State University, Graduate College, College of Education, Department of Counseling, Leadership, and Special Education, Program in Counseling, Springfield, MO 65897. Offers mental health counseling (MS). *Accreditation:* ACA. *Program availability:* Part-time, evening/weekend. *Faculty:* 9 full-time (6 women), 3 part-time/adjunct (2 women). *Students:* 62 full-time (46 women), 41 part-time (31 women); includes 17 minority (6 Black or African American, non-Hispanic/Latino; 7 Hispanic/Latino; 4 Two or more races, non-Hispanic/Latino), 3 international. Average age 24. 35 applicants, 31% accepted, 11 enrolled. In 2017, 53 master's awarded. *Degree requirements:* For master's, comprehensive exam, thesis or alternative. *Entrance requirements:* For master's, GRE or MAT, minimum GPA of 2.75. Additional exam requirements/recommendations for international students: Required—TOEFL (minimum score 550 paper-based; 79 iBT), IELTS (minimum score 6). *Application deadline:* For fall admission, 2/1 priority date for domestic students, 1/1 priority date for international students; for spring admission, 10/1 priority date for domestic students, 9/1 priority date for international students. Application fee: $35 ($50 for international students). Electronic applications accepted. *Expenses:* Tuition, state resident: full-time $2915; part-time $2021 per credit hour. Tuition, nonresident: full-time $5354; part-time $3647 per credit hour. *International tuition:* $11,992 full-time. *Required fees:* $173; $173 per credit hour. Tuition and fees vary according to class time, course level, course load, degree level, campus/location and program. *Financial support:* Federal Work-Study, institutionally sponsored loans, scholarships/grants, and unspecified assistantships available. Financial award application deadline: 3/31; financial award applicants required to submit FAFSA. *Unit head:* Dr. James Satterfield, Department Head, 417-836-5392, Fax: 417-836-4918, E-mail: clse@missouristate.edu. *Application contact:* Stephanie Praschan, Director, Graduate Enrollment Management, 417-836-5300, Fax: 417-836-6200, E-mail: stephaniepraschan@missouristate.edu.
Website: http://education.missouristate.edu/clse/

Monmouth University, Graduate Studies, Department of Professional Counseling, West Long Branch, NJ 07764-1898. Offers addiction studies (MA); clinical mental health counseling (MS); professional counseling (PMC). *Accreditation:* ACA. *Program availability:* Part-time, evening/weekend. *Faculty:* 11 full-time (5 women), 5 part-time/adjunct (4 women). *Students:* 106 full-time (97 women), 68 part-time (55 women); includes 42 minority (14 Black or African American, non-Hispanic/Latino; 5 Asian, non-Hispanic/Latino; 18 Hispanic/Latino; 5 Two or more races, non-Hispanic/Latino), 3 international. Average age 30. In 2017, 67 master's, 16 other advanced degrees

awarded. *Degree requirements:* For master's, comprehensive exam (for some programs), thesis optional, fieldwork. *Entrance requirements:* For master's, GRE, minimum GPA of 3.0 overall, 12 credits in psychology or closely-related field, two Monmouth University psychological counseling recommendation forms, narrative essay; for PMC, degree or current enrollment in CACREP-accredited master's program in counseling with minimum cumulative GPA of 3.0. Additional exam requirements/recommendations for international students: Required—TOEFL (minimum score 550 paper-based; 79 iBT), IELTS (minimum score 6), Michigan English Language Assessment Battery (minimum score 77) or Certificate of Advanced English (minimum score 160). *Application deadline:* For fall admission, 7/15 priority date for domestic students, 6/1 for international students; for spring admission, 12/1 priority date for domestic students, 11/1 for international students; for summer admission, 5/1 for domestic students. Applications are processed on a rolling basis. Application fee: $50. Electronic applications accepted. *Expenses: Tuition:* Full-time $21,366; part-time $7122 per credit. *Required fees:* $700; $175 per term. *Financial support:* In 2017–18, 82 students received support. Institutionally sponsored loans, scholarships/grants, and unspecified assistantships available. Support available to part-time students. Financial award applicants required to submit FAFSA. *Faculty research:* Violent crime, single parenting, the African-American male, counseling older women, successful behavior for under-achieving youth. *Unit head:* Dr. David Burkholder, Program Director, 732-923-4621, Fax: 732-923-4661, E-mail: dburkhol@monmouth.edu. *Application contact:* Andrea Thompson, Graduate Admission Counselor, 732-571-3452, Fax: 732-263-5123, E-mail: gradadm@monmouth.edu.
Website: https://www.monmouth.edu/school-of-humanities-social-sciences/professional-counseling.aspx

Montana State University Billings, College of Allied Health Professions, Program in Clinical Rehabilitation and Mental Health Counseling, Billings, MT 59101. Offers MS. *Accreditation:* ACA; CORE. *Program availability:* Part-time. *Degree requirements:* For master's, thesis or professional paper and/or field experience. *Entrance requirements:* For master's, GRE General Test or MAT, minimum GPA of 3.0, letters of recommendation, letter of intent. Additional exam requirements/recommendations for international students: Required—TOEFL (minimum score 79 iBT), IELTS (minimum score 6.5). *Application deadline:* For fall admission, 7/15 for international students; for spring admission, 12/1 for international students. Applications are processed on a rolling basis. Application fee: $40. Electronic applications accepted. *Expenses:* Tuition, state resident: full-time $11,740; part-time $7880 per year. Tuition, nonresident: full-time $32,200; part-time $24,140 per year. *Financial support:* Research assistantships with partial tuition reimbursements, teaching assistantships with partial tuition reimbursements, career-related internships or fieldwork, Federal Work-Study, institutionally sponsored loans, scholarships/grants, tuition waivers (partial), and unspecified assistantships available. Support available to part-time students. Financial award application deadline: 5/1; financial award applicants required to submit FAFSA. *Unit head:* Dr. Tom Dell, Chair, 406-896-5837, E-mail: tdell@msubillings.edu. *Application contact:* Dr. Tom Dell, Chair, 406-896-5837, E-mail: tdell@msubillings.edu.
Website: http://msubillings.edu/grad/program-rehab-mental_health_counseling.htm

Moody Theological Seminary–Michigan, Graduate Programs, Plymouth, MI 48170. Offers Bible (Graduate Certificate); Christian education (MA); counseling psychology (MA); divinity (M Div); theological studies (MA). *Accreditation:* ATS. *Program availability:* Part-time, evening/weekend. *Degree requirements:* For master's, one foreign language, thesis. *Faculty research:* Judaism, cults, world religions.

Morehead State University, Graduate Programs, College of Science and Technology, Department of Psychology, Morehead, KY 40351. Offers clinical/counseling psychology (MS); general/experimental psychology (MS). *Program availability:* Part-time, evening/weekend. *Degree requirements:* For master's, comprehensive exam, thesis optional. *Entrance requirements:* For master's, GRE General Test, 18 undergraduate hours in psychology, minimum GPA of 3.0, 3 letters of recommendation. Additional exam requirements/recommendations for international students: Required—TOEFL (minimum score 500 paper-based). Electronic applications accepted. *Faculty research:* Mood induction effects, serotonin receptor activity, stress, perceptual processes.

Mount Mary University, Graduate Programs, Program in Counseling, Milwaukee, WI 53222-4597. Offers clinical mental health counseling (MS, Certificate); clinical rehabilitation counseling (MS, Certificate); school counseling (MS, Certificate); vocational rehabilitation counseling (MS, Certificate). *Accreditation:* ACA. *Program availability:* Part-time, evening/weekend. *Degree requirements:* For master's, comprehensive exam, thesis or alternative. *Entrance requirements:* For master's, minimum GPA of 3.0. Additional exam requirements/recommendations for international students: Required—TOEFL (minimum score 550 paper-based; 80 iBT); Recommended—IELTS (minimum score 6.5). Electronic applications accepted. *Expenses:* Contact institution. *Faculty research:* Cognitive behavioral interventions for depression, eating disorders and compliance, trauma-informed care.

Mount Saint Mary's University, Graduate Division, Los Angeles, CA 90049. Offers business administration (MBA); counseling psychology (MS); creative writing (MFA); education (MS, Certificate); film and television (MFA); health policy and management (MS); humanities (MA); nursing (MSN, Certificate); physical therapy (DPT); religious studies (MA). *Program availability:* Part-time, evening/weekend. *Faculty:* 50 full-time (35 women), 116 part-time/adjunct (81 women). *Students:* 670 full-time (518 women), 147 part-time (116 women); includes 414 minority (73 Black or African American, non-Hispanic/Latino; 4 American Indian or Alaska Native, non-Hispanic/Latino; 60 Asian, non-Hispanic/Latino; 259 Hispanic/Latino; 7 Native Hawaiian or other Pacific Islander, non-Hispanic/Latino; 11 Two or more races, non-Hispanic/Latino), 4 international. Average age 32. 1,398 applicants, 21% accepted, 242 enrolled. In 2017, 170 master's, 28 doctorates, 35 other advanced degrees awarded. *Entrance requirements:* Additional exam requirements/recommendations for international students: Required—TOEFL. *Application deadline:* For fall admission, 6/30 priority date for domestic and international students; for spring admission, 10/30 priority date for domestic and international students; for summer admission, 3/30 priority date for domestic and international students. Applications are processed on a rolling basis. Application fee: $50. Electronic applications accepted. *Expenses: Tuition:* Part-time $905 per unit. One-time fee: $155 part-time. Tuition and fees vary according to degree level and program. *Financial support:* Career-related internships or fieldwork, Federal Work-Study, institutionally sponsored loans, and tuition waivers (full and partial) available. Support available to part-time students. Financial award application deadline: 3/15; financial award applicants required to submit FAFSA. *Unit head:* Albert Ramos, Director of Graduate Admissions, 213-477-2800, E-mail: gradprograms@msmu.edu. *Application contact:* Shawn Peters, Graduate Admission Counselor, 213-477-2676, E-mail: gradprograms@msmu.edu.
Website: http://www.msmu.edu/graduate-programs/

Naropa University, Graduate Programs, Program in Clinical Mental Health Counseling, Boulder, CO 80302-6697. Offers contemplative psychotherapy and Buddhist psychology (MA); mindfulness-based transpersonal counseling (MA); somatic counseling: body psychotherapy (MA); somatic counseling: dance/movement therapy (MA); transpersonal art therapy (MA); transpersonal wilderness therapy (MA). *Faculty:* 16 full-time (10 women), 38 part-time/adjunct (28 women). *Students:* 298 full-time (234 women), 112

part-time (80 women); includes 85 minority (10 Black or African American, non-Hispanic/Latino; 2 American Indian or Alaska Native, non-Hispanic/Latino; 9 Asian, non-Hispanic/Latino; 44 Hispanic/Latino; 1 Native Hawaiian or other Pacific Islander, non-Hispanic/Latino; 19 Two or more races, non-Hispanic/Latino), 18 international. Average age 32. 316 applicants, 77% accepted, 169 enrolled. In 2017, 124 master's awarded. *Degree requirements:* For master's, internships, counseling practicum, paper. *Entrance requirements:* For master's, interview, 2 letters of recommendation, professional resume, statement of interest essay, supplementary essay; minimum 100 hours of paid or volunteer work in a helping profession (for some concentrations); wilderness experience (for some concentrations). Additional exam requirements/recommendations for international students: Required—TOEFL (minimum score 550 paper-based; 80 iBT). *Application deadline:* For fall admission, 1/15 priority date for domestic and international students. Applications are processed on a rolling basis. Application fee: $60. Electronic applications accepted. *Expenses:* $995 per credit. *Financial support:* In 2017–18, 206 students received support, including 8 research assistantships with partial tuition reimbursements available (averaging $2,025 per year); teaching assistantships with partial tuition reimbursements available, career-related internships or fieldwork, Federal Work-Study, scholarships/grants, tuition waivers (partial), and unspecified assistantships also available. Support available to part-time students. Financial award application deadline: 3/1; financial award applicants required to submit FAFSA. *Unit head:* Dr. Kathleen Gregory, Dean, Graduate School of Counseling and Psychology, 303-245-4706, E-mail: kgregory@naropa.edu. *Application contact:* Office of Admissions, 303-546-3572, Fax: 303-546-3583, E-mail: admissions@naropa.edu.

National University, Academic Affairs, College of Letters and Sciences, La Jolla, CA 92037-1011. Offers biology (MS); counseling psychology (MA), including licensed professional clinical counseling, marriage and family therapy; creative writing (MFA); english (MA); film studies (MA); forensic and crime scene investigations (Certificate); forensic sciences (MFS); human behavior (MA); mathematics for educators (MS); performance psychology (MA); strategic communications (MA). *Program availability:* Part-time, evening/weekend, 100% online, blended/hybrid learning. *Degree requirements:* For master's, thesis (for some programs). *Entrance requirements:* For master's, interview, minimum GPA of 2.5. Additional exam requirements/recommendations for international students: Required—TOEFL (minimum score 550 paper-based; 79 iBT), IELTS (minimum score 6). *Application deadline:* Applications are processed on a rolling basis. Application fee: $60 ($65 for international students). Electronic applications accepted. *Expenses: Tuition:* Part-time $430 per quarter hour. *Financial support:* Career-related internships or fieldwork, institutionally sponsored loans, scholarships/grants, and tuition waivers (partial) available. Support available to part-time students. Financial award application deadline: 6/30; financial award applicants required to submit FAFSA. *Unit head:* Dr. Carol Richardson, Dean, 858-642-8450, E-mail: cols@nu.edu. *Application contact:* Brandon Jouganatos, Interim Vice President for Enrollment Services, 800-628-8648, E-mail: advisor@nu.edu.
Website: http://www.nu.edu/OurPrograms/CollegeOfLettersAndSciences.html

New England College, Program in Community Mental Health Counseling, Henniker, NH 03242-3293. Offers human services (MS); mental health counseling (MS). *Program availability:* Part-time, evening/weekend. *Degree requirements:* For master's, internship.

New Mexico Highlands University, Graduate Studies, College of Arts and Sciences, Department of Social and Behavioral Sciences, Las Vegas, NM 87701. Offers psychology (MS), including clinical psychology/counseling, general psychology; public affairs (MA), including applied sociology; Southwest studies (MA), including anthropology. *Program availability:* Part-time. *Degree requirements:* For master's, comprehensive exam, thesis or alternative. *Entrance requirements:* For master's, minimum undergraduate GPA of 3.0. Additional exam requirements/recommendations for international students: Required—TOEFL (minimum score 540 paper-based). *Faculty research:* Southwest Native American resettlement development, community-level interventions, neurochemistry of personality, comparative criminal justice, social theory and activism.

New Mexico State University, College of Education, Department of Counseling and Educational Psychology, Las Cruces, NM 88003. Offers counseling psychology (PhD); educational diagnostics (MA), including counseling and guidance, educational diagnostics; school psychology (Ed S). *Accreditation:* ACA; APA (one or more programs are accredited); NCATE. *Program availability:* Part-time, evening/weekend. *Faculty:* 11 full-time (9 women), 3 part-time/adjunct (all women). *Students:* 80 full-time (57 women), 23 part-time (17 women); includes 68 minority (3 Black or African American, non-Hispanic/Latino; 3 American Indian or Alaska Native, non-Hispanic/Latino; 5 Asian, non-Hispanic/Latino; 56 Hispanic/Latino; 1 Two or more races, non-Hispanic/Latino), 1 international. Average age 31. 103 applicants, 59% accepted, 34 enrolled. In 2017, 18 master's, 5 doctorates, 6 other advanced degrees awarded. *Degree requirements:* For master's, comprehensive exam, thesis optional, internship; for doctorate, comprehensive exam, thesis/dissertation, internship; for Ed S, comprehensive exam, thesis or alternative, internship. *Entrance requirements:* For master's, doctorate, and Ed S, GRE General Test, minimum GPA of 3.0. Additional exam requirements/recommendations for international students: Required—TOEFL (minimum score 550 paper-based; 79 iBT), IELTS (minimum score 6.5). *Application deadline:* For fall admission, 12/15 for domestic and international students; for spring admission, 2/1 priority date for domestic students, 2/1 for international students. Application fee: $40 ($50 for international students). Electronic applications accepted. *Expenses:* Tuition, state resident: full-time $4390. Tuition, nonresident: full-time $15,309. *Required fees:* $853. *Financial support:* In 2017–18, 72 students received support, including 4 fellowships (averaging $4,390 per year), 2 research assistantships (averaging $15,197 per year), 25 teaching assistantships (averaging $14,416 per year); career-related internships or fieldwork, Federal Work-Study, scholarships/grants, traineeships, health care benefits, and unspecified assistantships also available. Support available to part-time students. Financial award application deadline: 3/1. *Faculty research:* Multicultural counseling and training, school and counseling psychology, social justice, integrated primary care behavioral health training, mental health disparities. *Total annual research expenditures:* $110,485. *Unit head:* Dr. Barbara Gormley, Department Head, 575-646-2121, Fax: 575-646-8035, E-mail: bgormley@nmsu.edu. *Application contact:* Norma Arrieta, Student Program Coordinator, 575-646-2121, Fax: 575-646-8035, E-mail: cep@nmsu.edu.
Website: http://cep.education.nmsu.edu

New York University, Steinhardt School of Culture, Education, and Human Development, Department of Applied Psychology, Programs in Counseling, New York, NY 10012. Offers counseling and guidance (MA, Advanced Certificate), including bilingual school counseling K-12 (MA), school counseling K-12 (MA); counseling for mental health and wellness (MA); counseling psychology (PhD); LGBT health, education, and social services (Advanced Certificate); Advanced Certificate/MPH; MA/Advanced Certificate. *Accreditation:* APA (one or more programs are accredited). *Program availability:* Part-time. *Students:* Average age 29. 663 applicants, 33% accepted, 74 enrolled. In 2017, 87 master's, 7 doctorates awarded. *Entrance requirements:* For doctorate, GRE General Test, interview. Additional exam requirements/recommendations for international students: Required—TOEFL (minimum score 100 iBT). *Application deadline:* For fall admission, 12/1 priority date for domestic and international students. Applications are processed on a rolling basis. Application fee: $75. Electronic applications accepted. *Expenses: Tuition:* Full-time $41,352; part-time $19,968 per year. *Required fees:* $2496; $1628 per unit. $814 per term. Tuition and fees vary according to course load and program. *Financial support:* Fellowships with full and partial tuition reimbursements, research assistantships, teaching assistantships with partial tuition reimbursements, career-related internships or fieldwork, Federal Work-Study, institutionally sponsored loans, scholarships/grants, tuition waivers (partial), and unspecified assistantships available. Support available to part-time students. Financial award application deadline: 2/1; financial award applicants required to submit FAFSA. *Faculty research:* Sexual and gender identities, group dynamics, psychopathy and personality, multicultural assessment, working people's lives. *Unit head:* Dr. Randolph Mowry, Co-Director, 212-998-5222, Fax: 212-995-4358, E-mail: randolph.mowry@nyu.edu. *Application contact:* 212-998-5030, Fax: 212-995-4328, E-mail: steinhardt.gradadmissions@nyu.edu.
Website: http://steinhardt.nyu.edu/appsych/counseling

Niagara University, Graduate Division of Education, Niagara University, NY 14109. Offers applied behavior analysis (Certificate); educational leadership (MS Ed, PhD, Certificate), including leadership and policy (PhD), school building leader (MS Ed), school district business leader (Certificate), school district leader (MS Ed, Certificate); literacy instruction (MS Ed); mental health counseling (MS, Certificate); school counseling (MS Ed, Certificate); school psychology (MS); teacher education (MS, MS Ed, Certificate), including early childhood and childhood education (MS Ed, Certificate), early childhood special education (MS), middle and adolescence education (Certificate), special education (MS Ed), special education (grades 1-6) (Certificate), special education (grades 7-12) (Certificate), teaching English to speakers of other languages (TESOL) (Certificate). *Accreditation:* NCATE (one or more programs are accredited). *Program availability:* Part-time, evening/weekend. *Faculty:* 24 full-time, 49 part-time/adjunct. *Students:* 260 full-time (203 women), 311 part-time (239 women); includes 67 minority (35 Black or African American, non-Hispanic/Latino; 3 American Indian or Alaska Native, non-Hispanic/Latino; 3 Asian, non-Hispanic/Latino; 18 Hispanic/Latino; 8 Two or more races, non-Hispanic/Latino), 102 international. Average age 31. In 2017, 202 master's, 10 doctorates, 59 other advanced degrees awarded. *Entrance requirements:* For master's, GRE General Test or MAT. Additional exam requirements/recommendations for international students: Required—TOEFL (minimum score 550 paper-based; 79 iBT), IELTS (minimum score 6). *Application deadline:* For fall admission, 8/1 for domestic students. Applications are processed on a rolling basis. Application fee: $30. *Expenses:* Contact institution. *Financial support:* Research assistantships with tuition reimbursements, teaching assistantships with tuition reimbursements, career-related internships or fieldwork, Federal Work-Study, scholarships/grants, and unspecified assistantships available. Financial award application deadline: 4/15; financial award applicants required to submit FAFSA. *Faculty research:* Instructional supervision, appraisal and evaluation, career opportunities. *Unit head:* Dr. Chandra Foote, Dean, College of Education, 716-286-8549, Fax: 716-286-8561, E-mail: cjf@niagara.edu. *Application contact:* Evan Pierce, Associate Director for Graduate Recruitment, 716-286-8769, Fax: 716-286-8170, E-mail: epierce@niagara.edu.
Website: http://www.niagara.edu/advance/

North Dakota State University, College of Graduate and Interdisciplinary Studies, College of Human Development and Education, School of Education, Program in Counselor Education, Fargo, ND 58102. Offers clinical mental health counseling (M Ed, MS); counselor education and supervision (PhD); school counseling (M Ed, MS). *Accreditation:* ACA; NCATE. *Program availability:* Part-time, online learning. *Degree requirements:* For master's, comprehensive exam, thesis or alternative; for doctorate, comprehensive exam, thesis/dissertation. *Entrance requirements:* For master's, GRE, MAT, interview. Additional exam requirements/recommendations for international students: Required—TOEFL. *Faculty research:* Supervision, program assessment, multicultural issues.

Northeastern University, Bouvé College of Health Sciences, Boston, MA 02115-5096. Offers applied behavior analysis (MS); audiology (Au D); counseling psychology (MS, PhD, CAGS); exercise science (MS); nursing (MS, PhD, CAGS), including administration (MS), adult-gerontology acute care nurse practitioner (MS, CAGS), adult-gerontology primary care nurse practitioner (MS, CAGS), anesthesia (MS), family nurse practitioner (MS, CAGS), neonatal nurse practitioner (MS, CAGS), pediatric nurse practitioner (MS, CAGS), psychiatric mental health nurse practitioner (MS, CAGS); nursing practice (DNP); pharmaceutical sciences (MS, PhD), including interdisciplinary concentration, pharmaceutics and drug delivery systems; pharmacology (MS); pharmacy (Pharm D); school psychology (PhD); speech-language pathology (MS); urban health (MPH); MS/MBA. *Accreditation:* ACPE (one or more programs are accredited). *Program availability:* Part-time, evening/weekend, online learning. *Faculty:* 192 full-time. *Students:* 1,685. In 2017, 352 master's, 312 doctorates, 25 other advanced degrees awarded. *Degree requirements:* For doctorate, thesis/dissertation (for some programs); for CAGS, comprehensive exam. Application fee: $75. Electronic applications accepted. *Expenses:* Contact institution. *Financial support:* Fellowships, research assistantships, teaching assistantships, career-related internships or fieldwork, scholarships/grants, health care benefits, tuition waivers, and unspecified assistantships available. Support available to part-time students. Financial award applicants required to submit FAFSA. *Unit head:* Susan L. Parish, Dean, Bouve College of Health Sciences, 617-373-3321, Fax: 617-373-3030, E-mail: s.parish@northeastern.edu. *Application contact:* 617-373-2708, Fax: 617-373-4701, E-mail: bouvegrad@northeastern.edu.
Website: https://www.northeastern.edu/bouve/

Northern Arizona University, College of Education, Department of Educational Psychology, Flagstaff, AZ 86011. Offers clinical mental health counseling (MA); combined counseling/school psychology (PhD), including counseling psychology; counseling (M Ed), including school counseling, student affairs; human relations (M Ed); psychology of human development and learning (Graduate Certificate); school psychology (Ed S). *Program availability:* Part-time, 100% online, blended/hybrid learning. *Faculty:* 22 full-time (12 women), 6 part-time/adjunct (4 women). *Students:* 184 full-time (139 women), 175 part-time (131 women); includes 118 minority (14 Black or African American, non-Hispanic/Latino; 10 American Indian or Alaska Native, non-Hispanic/Latino; 5 Asian, non-Hispanic/Latino; 79 Hispanic/Latino; 1 Native Hawaiian or other Pacific Islander, non-Hispanic/Latino; 9 Two or more races, non-Hispanic/Latino), 9 international. Average age 33. 244 applicants, 44% accepted, 108 enrolled. In 2017, 147 master's, 4 doctorates awarded. Terminal master's awarded for partial completion of doctoral program. *Degree requirements:* For master's, variable foreign language requirement, comprehensive exam (for some programs), thesis (for some programs); for doctorate, variable foreign language requirement, comprehensive exam (for some programs), thesis/dissertation (for some programs); for other advanced degree, comprehensive exam (for some programs). *Entrance requirements:* Additional exam requirements/recommendations for international students: Required—TOEFL (minimum score 80 iBT), IELTS (minimum score 6.5). *Application deadline:* For fall admission, 12/1 for domestic and international students; for spring admission, 9/15 for domestic and international students. Applications are processed on a rolling basis. Application fee: $65. Electronic applications accepted. *Expenses:* Tuition, state resident: full-time $9240; part-time $458 per credit hour. Tuition, nonresident: full-time $21,588; part-time

$1199 per credit hour. *Required fees:* $1021; $14 per credit hour. $646 per semester. Tuition and fees vary according to course load, campus/location and program. *Financial support:* In 2017–18, 62 students received support, including 1 fellowship with full and partial tuition reimbursement available (averaging $13,927 per year), 2 research assistantships with full and partial tuition reimbursements available (averaging $13,927 per year), 15 teaching assistantships with full and partial tuition reimbursements available (averaging $13,927 per year); institutionally sponsored loans, health care benefits, tuition waivers (full and partial), and unspecified assistantships also available. Financial award application deadline: 2/1; financial award applicants required to submit FAFSA. *Unit head:* Dr. Robert Horn, Chair, 928-523-0545, Fax: 928-523-9284, E-mail: robert.horn@nau.edu. *Application contact:* Hope DeMello, Administrative Assistant, 928-523-7103, Fax: 928-523-9284, E-mail: eps@nau.edu. Website: https://nau.edu/coe/ed-psych/

Northern Kentucky University, Office of Graduate Programs, College of Education and Human Services, Clinical Mental Health Counseling Program, Highland Heights, KY 41099. Offers MS. *Accreditation:* ACA. *Program availability:* Part-time, evening/ weekend. *Degree requirements:* For master's, comprehensive exam. *Entrance requirements:* For master's, GRE or MAT. Additional exam requirements/ recommendations for international students: Required—TOEFL (minimum score 550 paper-based; 79 iBT); Recommended—IELTS (minimum score 6.5). Electronic applications accepted. *Faculty research:* Preferences for college counseling, accreditation, partner violence prevention, data-based school counseling, creativity in counseling.

Northern State University, MS Ed Program in Counseling, Aberdeen, SD 57401-7198. Offers clinical mental health counseling (MS Ed); school counseling (MS Ed). *Accreditation:* ACA; NCATE. *Program availability:* Part-time, online learning. *Degree requirements:* For master's, comprehensive exam, thesis optional. *Entrance requirements:* For master's, minimum GPA of 2.75. Additional exam requirements/ recommendations for international students: Required—TOEFL (minimum score 550 paper-based; 78 iBT), IELTS (minimum score 6). Electronic applications accepted.

Northwest Christian University, School of Education and Counseling, Eugene, OR 97401-3745. Offers clinical mental health counseling (MA); elementary teaching (MAT); English for speakers of other languages (MAT); physical education (MAT); school counseling (MA); secondary teaching (MAT); special education (MAT). *Program availability:* Part-time, evening/weekend, online learning. *Faculty:* 9 full-time (4 women), 14 part-time/adjunct (10 women). *Students:* 77 full-time (60 women), 44 part-time (30 women); includes 19 minority (4 Black or African American, non-Hispanic/Latino; 1 American Indian or Alaska Native, non-Hispanic/Latino; 3 Asian, non-Hispanic/Latino; 2 Hispanic/Latino; 1 Native Hawaiian or other Pacific Islander, non-Hispanic/Latino; 8 Two or more races, non-Hispanic/Latino). Average age 34. In 2017, 58 master's awarded. *Degree requirements:* For master's, thesis (for some programs). *Entrance requirements:* For master's, GRE or MAT, minimum undergraduate GPA of 3.0, interview, 2-3 page statement of purpose, two letters of recommendation, resume, background check. Additional exam requirements/recommendations for international students: Required— TOEFL (minimum score 550 paper-based; 80 iBT). *Application deadline:* Applications are processed on a rolling basis. Electronic applications accepted. *Expenses:* $640 to $660 per credit tuition, $90 per semester technology fee. *Financial support:* Applicants required to submit FAFSA. *Unit head:* Elizabeth Wosley-George, Director, 541-349-7465, Fax: 541-684-7310, E-mail: ewosleygeorge@nwcu.edu. *Application contact:* Billy Dorsch, Admission Counselor for Graduate Studies, 541-684-7279, Fax: 541-349-5281, E-mail: wdorsch@nwcu.edu.

Northwestern Oklahoma State University, School of Professional Studies, Program in Counseling Psychology, Alva, OK 73717-2799. Offers MCP. *Program availability:* Part-time. *Degree requirements:* For master's, comprehensive exam. *Entrance requirements:* For master's, GRE General Test or MAT, minimum GPA of 2.75.

Northwest University, College of Social and Behavioral Sciences, Kirkland, WA 98033. Offers counseling psychology (MA, Psy D); international community development (MA). *Program availability:* Evening/weekend. *Entrance requirements:* For master's, 3 character references. Additional exam requirements/recommendations for international students: Required—TOEFL (minimum score 580 paper-based). *Expenses:* Contact institution.

Nova Southeastern University, College of Psychology, Fort Lauderdale, FL 33314-7796. Offers clinical mental health counseling (MS); clinical psychology (PhD, Psy D); counseling (MS); experimental psychology (MS); forensic psychology (MS); general psychology (MS); school counseling (MS); school psychology (Psy D, Psy S); substance abuse counseling (MS); substance abuse counseling and education (MS). *Accreditation:* APA (one or more programs are accredited). *Program availability:* 100% online, blended/hybrid learning. *Faculty:* 51 full-time (21 women), 120 part-time/adjunct (70 women). *Students:* 751 full-time (618 women), 821 part-time (709 women); includes 787 minority (268 Black or African American, non-Hispanic/Latino; 2 American Indian or Alaska Native, non-Hispanic/Latino; 38 Asian, non-Hispanic/Latino; 431 Hispanic/Latino; 2 Native Hawaiian or other Pacific Islander, non-Hispanic/Latino; 46 Two or more races, non-Hispanic/Latino), 45 international. Average age 31. 1,117 applicants, 38% accepted, 294 enrolled. In 2017, 459 master's, 100 doctorates, 10 other advanced degrees awarded. Terminal master's awarded for partial completion of doctoral program. *Degree requirements:* For master's, comprehensive exam, 3 practica; for doctorate, thesis/dissertation, clinical internship, competency exam; for Psy S, comprehensive exam, internship. *Entrance requirements:* For master's and Psy S, GRE General Test, letters of recommendation, research/personal statement, interview; for doctorate, GRE General Test, GRE Subject Test (recommended), minimum undergraduate GPA of 3.0, letters of recommendation, research/personal statement, interview, curriculum vitae/resume. Additional exam requirements/recommendations for international students: Required—TOEFL (minimum score 550 paper-based). *Application deadline:* Applications are processed on a rolling basis. Application fee: $50. Electronic applications accepted. *Expenses:* Contact institution. *Financial support:* In 2017–18, 197 students received support, including 15 research assistantships (averaging $5,600 per year), 68 teaching assistantships (averaging $2,000 per year); career-related internships or fieldwork, Federal Work-Study, institutionally sponsored loans, scholarships/grants, and unspecified assistantships also available. Support available to part-time students. Financial award application deadline: 4/15; financial award applicants required to submit FAFSA. *Faculty research:* Clinical health psychology, multicultural/diversity psychology, clinical neuropsychology, clinical child psychology, family violence. *Unit head:* Dr. Karen Grosby, Dean, 954-262-5712, Fax: 954-262-3859, E-mail: grosby@nova.edu. *Application contact:* Carlos Perez, Senior Manager of Outreach, 954-262-5702, Fax: 954-262-3893, E-mail: gradschool@nova.edu. Website: http://psychology.nova.edu/

Nyack College, Alliance Graduate School of Counseling, Nyack, NY 10960. Offers marriage and family therapy (MA); mental health counseling (MA). *Program availability:* Part-time, evening/weekend, 100% online. *Students:* 66 full-time (50 women), 162 part-time (136 women); includes 183 minority (78 Black or African American, non-Hispanic/ Latino; 45 Asian, non-Hispanic/Latino; 53 Hispanic/Latino; 7 Two or more races, non-Hispanic/Latino), 10 international. Average age 37. In 2017, 48 master's awarded.

Degree requirements: For master's, comprehensive exam, counselor-in-training therapy, internship, CPCE exam. *Entrance requirements:* For master's, Millon Clinical Multiaxial Inventory-3, Minnesota Multiphasic Personality Inventory-2, transcripts, statement of Christian life and experience, statement of support systems. Additional exam requirements/recommendations for international students: Required—TOEFL (minimum score 550 paper-based; 80 iBT). *Application deadline:* For fall admission, 8/1 for domestic students, 2/15 for international students; for spring admission, 12/15 for domestic students, 7/15 for international students. Applications are processed on a rolling basis. Application fee: $30. Electronic applications accepted. *Expenses:* $800 per credit. *Financial support:* Career-related internships or fieldwork and scholarships/ grants available. Financial award applicants required to submit FAFSA. *Unit head:* Dr. Antoinette Gines-Rivera, Director, 646-378-6160. *Application contact:* Chastity Crespo, Admissions Associate, 646-378-6199, E-mail: admissions.grad@nyack.edu. Website: http://www.nyack.edu/agsc

Oakland University, Graduate Study and Lifelong Learning, School of Education and Human Services, Department of Counseling, Rochester, MI 48309-4401. Offers MA, PhD, Certificate. *Accreditation:* ACA (one or more programs are accredited). *Program availability:* Part-time, evening/weekend. *Degree requirements:* For doctorate, thesis/ dissertation. *Entrance requirements:* Additional exam requirements/recommendations for international students: Required—TOEFL (minimum score 550 paper-based). Electronic applications accepted. *Expenses:* Tuition, state resident: full-time $16,950; part-time $706.25 per credit. Tuition, nonresident: full-time $24,648; part-time $1027 per credit.

Old Dominion University, Darden College of Education, Counseling Program, Norfolk, VA 23529. Offers clinical mental health counseling (MS Ed); college counseling (MS Ed); counseling (Ed S); counselor education (PhD); school counseling (MS Ed). *Accreditation:* ACA. *Program availability:* Part-time, evening/weekend. *Faculty:* 14 full-time (7 women), 9 part-time/adjunct (7 women). *Students:* 134 full-time (113 women), 52 part-time (44 women); includes 72 minority (42 Black or African American, non-Hispanic/ Latino; 1 American Indian or Alaska Native, non-Hispanic/Latino; 4 Asian, non-Hispanic/ Latino; 17 Hispanic/Latino; 8 Two or more races, non-Hispanic/Latino), 6 international. Average age 31. 195 applicants, 57% accepted, 79 enrolled. In 2017, 43 master's, 9 doctorates, 2 other advanced degrees awarded. *Degree requirements:* For master's and Ed S, comprehensive exam; for doctorate, comprehensive exam, thesis/dissertation. *Entrance requirements:* For master's and Ed S, GRE General Test, resume, essay, transcripts, recommendations; for doctorate, GRE General Test, resume, interview, essay, transcripts, recommendations. Additional exam requirements/recommendations for international students: Required—TOEFL. *Application deadline:* For fall admission, 3/ 1 for domestic and international students; for winter admission, 1/10 for domestic students; for spring admission, 10/1 for domestic and international students; for summer admission, 3/1 for domestic students, 2/1 for international students. Application fee: $50. Electronic applications accepted. *Expenses:* $496 per credit hour, plus $9.00 services fee per semester. *Financial support:* In 2017–18, 20 students received support, including 2 fellowships with full tuition reimbursements available (averaging $15,000 per year), 13 research assistantships (averaging $9,000 per year), 20 teaching assistantships with full tuition reimbursements available (averaging $20,000 per year); career-related internships or fieldwork, Federal Work-Study, institutionally sponsored loans, scholarships/grants, tuition waivers (partial), and unspecified assistantships also available. Support available to part-time students. Financial award application deadline: 10/1; financial award applicants required to submit FAFSA. *Faculty research:* Group counseling, counselor education, career counseling, spirituality and counseling, school counseling, LGBT counseling, legal and ethical issues. *Total annual research expenditures:* $75,000. *Unit head:* Dr. Jeff Moe, Director, 757-683-6235, Fax: 757-683-5756, E-mail: jmoe@odu.edu. Website: http://www.odu.edu/chs

Ottawa University, Graduate Studies-Arizona, Program in Professional Counseling, Ottawa, KS 66067-3399. Offers Christian counseling (MA); expressive arts therapy (MA); marriage and family therapy (MA); treatment of trauma, abuse and deprivation (MA). Programs offered in Mesa, Phoenix, Tempe and West Valley, AZ. *Program availability:* Part-time, evening/weekend, online learning. *Degree requirements:* For master's, comprehensive exam, thesis or alternative, field experience, practicum. *Entrance requirements:* For master's, minimum undergraduate GPA of 3.0; course work in theories of personality, abnormal psychology, and human growth and development. Additional exam requirements/recommendations for international students: Required— TOEFL (minimum score 550 paper-based).

Our Lady of the Lake University, College of Professional Studies, Program in Counseling Psychology, San Antonio, TX 78207-4689. Offers Psy D. *Faculty:* 9 full-time (7 women), 10 part-time/adjunct (6 women). *Students:* 34 full-time (30 women), 1 part-time (0 women); includes 23 minority (4 Black or African American, non-Hispanic/Latino; 19 Hispanic/Latino). Average age 32. 27 applicants, 30% accepted, 6 enrolled. In 2017, 6 doctorates awarded. *Degree requirements:* For doctorate, comprehensive exam, thesis/dissertation, internship, 3-years of residency in San Antonio. *Entrance requirements:* For doctorate, GRE General Test, GRE Subject Test (psychology), master's degree in psychology or closely-related discipline of at least 45 hours from regionally-accredited institution; minimum cumulative GPA of 3.5 in the master's program; criminal background check; 3 letters of recommendation; pertinent professional experience; personal statement. Additional exam requirements/ recommendations for international students: Required—TOEFL. *Application deadline:* For fall admission, 1/15 for domestic and international students. Application fee: $40 ($50 for international students). Electronic applications accepted. Application fee is waived when completed online. *Expenses:* Contact institution. *Financial support:* In 2017–18, 8 students received support. Federal Work-Study, scholarships/grants, unspecified assistantships, and tuition discounts available. Support available to part-time students. Financial award application deadline: 5/1; financial award applicants required to submit FAFSA. *Faculty research:* Providing competent services to diverse client populations. *Unit head:* Psychology Department, 210-431-3914. *Application contact:* Office of Graduate Admissions, 210-431-3995, Fax: 210-431-3945, E-mail: gradadm@lake.ollusa.edu. Website: http://www.ollusa.edu/s/1190/hybrid/default-hybrid-ollu.aspx?sid-1190&gid-1&pgid-7957

Pace University, Dyson College of Arts and Sciences, Department of Psychology, Program in Mental Health Counseling, New York, NY 10038. Offers grief and loss (MS); mental health counseling (MS, PhD); substance abuse (MS). Program offered at Pleasantville, NY location only. *Program availability:* Part-time, evening/weekend. *Students:* 72 full-time (57 women), 57 part-time (50 women); includes 42 minority (9 Black or African American, non-Hispanic/Latino; 1 American Indian or Alaska Native, non-Hispanic/Latino; 8 Asian, non-Hispanic/Latino; 24 Hispanic/Latino), 2 international. Average age 30. In 2017, 49 master's awarded. Terminal master's awarded for partial completion of doctoral program. *Degree requirements:* For master's, comprehensive exam, qualifying exams, internship; for doctorate, comprehensive exam, thesis/ dissertation, internships. *Entrance requirements:* For master's, GRE, resume, personal statement, two letters of reference, official transcripts, interview; for doctorate, three letters of recommendation (two of which are academic in nature); personal statement;

official transcripts; internship(s); interview; master's degree in mental health counseling or program with curriculum equivalent to that of Pace's graduate program in mental health counseling. Additional exam requirements/recommendations for international students: Required—TOEFL (minimum score 88 iBT), IELTS (minimum score 7) or PTE (minimum score 60). *Application deadline:* For fall admission, 8/1 priority date for domestic students, 6/1 for international students; for spring admission, 12/1 priority date for domestic students, 10/1 for international students. Applications are processed on a rolling basis. Application fee: $70. Electronic applications accepted. *Financial support:* Research assistantships, teaching assistantships, career-related internships or fieldwork, Federal Work-Study, and tuition waivers (partial) available. Financial award application deadline: 2/15; financial award applicants required to submit FAFSA. *Unit head:* Dr. Ross Robak, Psychology Department Chair/Director, Graduate Program in Counseling, 914-773-3786, E-mail: rrobak@pace.edu. *Application contact:* Susan Ford-Goldschein, Director of Graduate Admissions, 914-422-4283, Fax: 212-346-1585, E-mail: graduateadmission@pace.edu.
Website: http://www.pace.edu/academics/graduate-students/degrees/mental-health-counseling-ms

Pacifica Graduate Institute, Graduate Programs, Carpinteria, CA 93013. Offers clinical psychology (PhD); counseling psychology (MA); depth psychology (MA, PhD); mythological studies (MA, PhD). Terminal master's awarded for partial completion of doctoral program. *Degree requirements:* For master's, thesis (for some programs), practicum; for doctorate, comprehensive exam, thesis/dissertation, internship. *Entrance requirements:* For master's, resume, 3 letters of recommendation, writing sample, interview; for doctorate, resumé, 4 letters of recommendation, writing sample, interview. Additional exam requirements/recommendations for international students: Required—TOEFL. *Faculty research:* Imaginal and archetypal theory; post-Colonial psychoanalytic and Jungian theory; myth literature as it applies to the theory and practice of psychology.

Palm Beach Atlantic University, School of Education and Behavioral Studies, West Palm Beach, FL 33416-4708. Offers counseling psychology (MS), including addictions/mental health, general counseling, marriage and family therapy, mental health counseling, school guidance counseling. *Program availability:* Part-time, evening/weekend. *Entrance requirements:* For master's, GRE or MAT, minimum GPA of 3.0; essay. Additional exam requirements/recommendations for international students: Required—TOEFL (minimum score 550 paper-based; 79 iBT). Electronic applications accepted. *Faculty research:* Group dynamics, phenomenology, spirituality, multicultural psychology.

Palo Alto University, MA in Counseling Program, Palo Alto, CA 94304. Offers clinical mental health (MA); marriage, family and child (MA). *Program availability:* Part-time, 100% online, blended/hybrid learning. *Faculty:* 6 full-time (4 women), 5 part-time/adjunct (4 women). *Students:* 158 full-time (130 women), 131 part-time (113 women); includes 138 minority (9 Black or African American, non-Hispanic/Latino; 35 Asian, non-Hispanic/Latino; 43 Hispanic/Latino; 51 Two or more races, non-Hispanic/Latino). Average age 34. 167 applicants, 74% accepted, 80 enrolled. In 2017, 110 master's awarded. *Degree requirements:* For master's, capstone project. *Entrance requirements:* For master's, undergraduate degree in psychology with minimum GPA of 3.3. Additional exam requirements/recommendations for international students: Required—TOEFL. *Application deadline:* For fall admission, 6/30 priority date for domestic and international students; for spring admission, 3/21 for domestic and international students. Applications are processed on a rolling basis. Application fee: $50. Electronic applications accepted. *Expenses:* Contact institution. *Financial support:* In 2017–18, 12 students received support. Federal Work-Study available. Financial award applicants required to submit FAFSA. *Unit head:* Dr. William Snow, Director of Counseling, 831-246-2440, E-mail: wsnow@paloaltou.edu. *Application contact:* Yukti Singh, Director of Admissions, 650-417-2055, E-mail: ysingh@paloaltou.edu.
Website: http://www.paloaltou.edu/graduate-programs/masters-programs/ma-counseling

Philadelphia College of Osteopathic Medicine, Graduate and Professional Programs, Department of Psychology, Philadelphia, PA 19131-1694. Offers applied behavior analysis (Certificate); clinical health psychology (Post-Doctoral Certificate); clinical neuropsychology (Post-Doctoral Certificate); clinical psychology (Psy D); educational psychology (PhD); mental health counseling (MS); organizational development and leadership (MS); psychology (Certificate); public health management and administration (MS); school psychology (MS, Psy D, Ed S). *Accreditation:* APA. *Faculty:* 19 full-time (11 women), 122 part-time/adjunct (58 women). *Students:* 487 (335 women); includes 138 minority (89 Black or African American, non-Hispanic/Latino; 4 American Indian or Alaska Native, non-Hispanic/Latino; 11 Asian, non-Hispanic/Latino; 12 Hispanic/Latino; 22 Two or more races, non-Hispanic/Latino). 298 applicants, 44% accepted, 100 enrolled. In 2017, 50 master's, 43 doctorates, 10 other advanced degrees awarded. Terminal master's awarded for partial completion of doctoral program. *Degree requirements:* For master's, comprehensive exam (for some programs), thesis (for some programs); for doctorate, comprehensive exam, thesis/dissertation. *Entrance requirements:* For master's, GRE or MAT, minimum GPA of 3.0; bachelor's degree from regionally-accredited college or university; for doctorate, PRAXIS II (for Psy D in school psychology), minimum undergraduate GPA of 3.0; for other advanced degree, GRE (for Ed S). Additional exam requirements/recommendations for international students: Required—TOEFL (minimum score 79 iBT). *Application deadline:* Applications are processed on a rolling basis. Application fee: $50. Electronic applications accepted. *Financial support:* In 2017–18, 28 teaching assistantships were awarded; Federal Work-Study, institutionally sponsored loans, and scholarships/grants also available. Financial award application deadline: 3/15; financial award applicants required to submit FAFSA. *Faculty research:* Adult and childhood anxiety and ADHD; coping with chronic illness; primary care psychology/integrated health care; applied behavior analysis; psychological, educational, and neuropsychological assessment. *Total annual research expenditures:* $533,489. *Unit head:* Dr. Robert DiTomasso, Chairman, 215-871-6442, Fax: 215-871-6458, E-mail: robertd@pcom.edu. *Application contact:* Johnathan Cox, Associate Director of Admissions, 215-871-6700, Fax: 215-871-6719, E-mail: johnathancox@pcom.edu.

See Display on page 982 and Close-Up on page 1203.

Phoenix Seminary, Graduate Programs, Phoenix, AZ 85018. Offers Biblical and theological studies (Graduate Diploma); Biblical communication (M Div); Biblical leadership (MA); Christian counseling (Graduate Diploma); counseling and family (M Div); leadership development (M Div); ministry (D Min); professional counseling (MA). *Accreditation:* ATS (one or more programs are accredited). *Program availability:* Part-time, evening/weekend. *Degree requirements:* For master's, 2 foreign languages, comprehensive exam; for doctorate, 2 foreign languages, thesis/dissertation. *Entrance requirements:* For master's, undergraduate degree with minimum GPA of 2.5; for doctorate, M Div (94 hours) with minimum GPA of 3.0. Additional exam requirements/recommendations for international students: Required—TOEFL (minimum score 587 paper-based; 92 iBT), TWE (minimum score 4.5).

Prescott College, Graduate Programs, Program in Counseling and Psychology, Prescott, AZ 86301. Offers adventure-based psychotherapy (MA); counseling psychology (MA); ecopsychology (MA); ecotherapy (MA); equine-assisted mental health (MA); expressive arts therapy (MA); somatic psychology (MA); student-directed independent study (MA). *Program availability:* Part-time, online learning. Terminal master's awarded for partial completion of doctoral program. *Degree requirements:* For master's, thesis, fieldwork or internship, practicum. *Entrance requirements:* For master's, 2 letters of recommendation, resume. Additional exam requirements/recommendations for international students: Required—TOEFL (minimum score 500 paper-based). Electronic applications accepted.

Providence University College & Theological Seminary, Theological Seminary, Otterburne, MB R0A 1G0, Canada. Offers children's ministry (Certificate); Christian studies (MA, Certificate); counseling (MA); cross-cultural discipleship (Certificate); divinity (M Div); educational studies (MA), including counseling psychology, educational ministries, student development, teaching English to speakers of other languages, training teachers of English to speakers of other languages; global studies (MA); lay counseling (Diploma); ministry (D Min); teaching English to speakers of other languages (Certificate); theological studies (MA); training teacher of English to speakers of other languages (Certificate); youth ministry (Certificate). *Accreditation:* ATS. *Program availability:* Part-time. *Degree requirements:* For master's, variable foreign language requirement, thesis (for some programs); for doctorate, thesis/dissertation. *Entrance requirements:* Additional exam requirements/recommendations for international students: Recommended—TOEFL (minimum score 550 paper-based). *Faculty research:* Studies in Isaiah, theology of sin.

Purdue University Northwest, Graduate Studies Office, School of Education, Program in Counseling, Hammond, IN 46323-2094. Offers human services (MS Ed); mental health counseling (MS Ed); school counseling (MS Ed). *Accreditation:* ACA. *Entrance requirements:* Additional exam requirements/recommendations for international students: Required—TOEFL.

Queens College of the City University of New York, Division of Education, Department of Educational and Community Programs, Queens, NY 11367-1597. Offers bilingual pupil personnel (AC); counselor education (MS Ed); mental health counseling (MS); school building leader (AC); school district leader (AC); school psychologist (MS Ed); special education-childhood education (AC); special education-early childhood (MS Ed); teacher of special education 1-6 (MS Ed); teacher of special education birth-2 (MS Ed); teaching students with disabilities, grades 7-12 (MS Ed, AC). *Program availability:* Part-time. *Faculty:* 20 full-time (14 women), 63 part-time/adjunct (37 women). *Students:* 105 full-time (94 women), 423 part-time (350 women); includes 241 minority (40 Black or African American, non-Hispanic/Latino; 2 American Indian or Alaska Native, non-Hispanic/Latino; 50 Asian, non-Hispanic/Latino; 142 Hispanic/Latino; 1 Native Hawaiian or other Pacific Islander, non-Hispanic/Latino; 6 Two or more races, non-Hispanic/Latino), 5 international. Average age 28. 515 applicants, 57% accepted, 230 enrolled. In 2017, 163 master's, 74 other advanced degrees awarded. *Degree requirements:* For master's, research project; for AC, internship. *Entrance requirements:* For master's, minimum GPA of 3.0. Additional exam requirements/recommendations for international students: Required—TOEFL, IELTS. *Application deadline:* For fall admission, 3/1 for domestic students. Applications are processed on a rolling basis. Application fee: $125. Electronic applications accepted. *Financial support:* Career-related internships or fieldwork available. Financial award application deadline: 4/1; financial award applicants required to submit FAFSA. *Unit head:* Dr. Emilia Lopez, Chair, 718-997-5250, E-mail: emilia.lopez@qc.cuny.edu. *Application contact:* Elizabeth D'Amico-Ramirez, Assistant Director of Graduate Admissions, 718-997-5203, E-mail: elizabeth.damicoramirez@qc.cuny.edu.

Radford University, College of Graduate Studies and Research, Program in Counseling Psychology, Radford, VA 24142. Offers Psy D. *Faculty:* 21 full-time (14 women). *Students:* 12 full-time (6 women), 5 part-time (4 women); includes 4 minority (2 Black or African American, non-Hispanic/Latino; 2 Two or more races, non-Hispanic/Latino). Average age 27. 19 applicants, 42% accepted, 3 enrolled. In 2017, 1 doctorate awarded. *Degree requirements:* For doctorate, comprehensive exam, thesis/dissertation. *Entrance requirements:* For doctorate, GRE General Test, master's degree; minimum graduate GPA of 3.5; letter of interest describing professional and/or research experience; curriculum vitae/resume; essay on cultural background and experiences; 3 letters of recommendation; official transcripts. Additional exam requirements/recommendations for international students: Required—TOEFL (minimum score 550 paper-based; 79 iBT), IELTS (minimum score 6.5). *Application deadline:* For fall admission, 12/1 priority date for domestic students, 12/1 for international students. Applications are processed on a rolling basis. Application fee: $50. Electronic applications accepted. *Expenses:* Tuition, state resident: full-time $8336; part-time $347 per credit hour. Tuition, nonresident: full-time $16,862; part-time $702 per credit hour. *Required fees:* $3220; $135 per credit hour. Tuition and fees vary according to course load and program. *Financial support:* In 2017–18, 12 students received support, including 8 research assistantships (averaging $6,900 per year), 4 teaching assistantships (averaging $13,800 per year); career-related internships or fieldwork, scholarships/grants, and unspecified assistantships also available. Support available to part-time students. Financial award application deadline: 3/1; financial award applicants required to submit FAFSA. *Faculty research:* Human sexuality and conflict in close relationships, rural mental health and psychology practice, self-compassion and body image, effectiveness of multicultural training, treatments for post-traumatic stress disorder. *Unit head:* Dr. Valerie Leake, Program Director, 540-831-5361, Fax: 540-831-6113, E-mail: vleake@radford.edu.
Website: http://www.radford.edu/content/chbs/home/psychology/programs/counseling.html

Regent University, Graduate School, School of Psychology and Counseling, Virginia Beach, VA 23464-9800. Offers clinical mental health counseling (MA); clinical psychology (Psy D); counseling and psychological studies - clinical (PhD); counseling and psychological studies - research (PhD); counseling studies (CAGS); counselor education and supervision (PhD); general psychology (MS); human services (MA), including addictions counseling, Biblical counseling, Christian counseling, conflict and mediation ministry, criminal justice and ministry, grief counseling, human services counseling, human services for student affairs, life coaching, marriage and family ministry, trauma and crisis counseling; marriage, couple, and family counseling (MA); pastoral counseling (MA); school counseling (MA); M Div/MA; M Ed/MA; MBA/MA. *Accreditation:* ACA; APA (one or more programs are accredited). *Program availability:* Part-time, evening/weekend, 100% online, blended/hybrid learning. *Faculty:* 28 full-time (16 women), 51 part-time/adjunct (30 women). *Students:* 294 full-time (236 women), 404 part-time (317 women); includes 286 minority (218 Black or African American, non-Hispanic/Latino; 4 American Indian or Alaska Native, non-Hispanic/Latino; 17 Asian, non-Hispanic/Latino; 30 Hispanic/Latino; 17 Two or more races, non-Hispanic/Latino), 13 international. Average age 37. 2,109 applicants, 18% accepted, 233 enrolled. In 2017, 158 master's, 28 doctorates awarded. *Degree requirements:* For master's, thesis or alternative, internship, practicum, written competency exam; for doctorate, thesis/dissertation or alternative. *Entrance requirements:* For master's, GRE General Test (including writing exam) or MAT, minimum undergraduate GPA of 3.0, resume, transcripts, writing sample, personal goals statement; for doctorate, GRE General Test (including writing exam), minimum undergraduate GPA of 3.0, graduate 3.5; writing sample; 3 recommendations; resume; college transcripts; personal goals statement.

Additional exam requirements/recommendations for international students: Required—TOEFL (minimum score 577 paper-based). *Application deadline:* For fall admission, 4/1 priority date for domestic students; for spring admission, 11/1 priority date for domestic students. Applications are processed on a rolling basis. Application fee: $50. Electronic applications accepted. *Expenses:* Contact institution. *Financial support:* In 2017–18, 557 students received support, including 5 fellowships (averaging $10,000 per year), 11 research assistantships (averaging $3,200 per year); career-related internships or fieldwork, scholarships/grants, and unspecified assistantships also available. Support available to part-time students. *Faculty research:* Marriage enrichment, clinical psychology, troubled youth, faith and learning, trauma. *Unit head:* Dr. William Hathaway, Dean, 757-352-4294, Fax: 757-352-4282, E-mail: willhat@regent.edu. *Application contact:* Heidi Cece, Assistant Vice President of Enrollment Management, 800-373-5504, Fax: 757-352-4381, E-mail: admissions@regent.edu.
Website: https://www.regent.edu/school-of-psychology-and-counseling/

Regis College, Nursing and Health Sciences School, Weston, MA 02493. Offers applied behavior analysis (MS); counseling psychology (MA); health administration (MS); nurse practitioner (Certificate); nursing (MS, DNP); nursing education (Certificate); occupational therapy (MS). *Accreditation:* ACEN. *Program availability:* Part-time, evening/weekend, 100% online, blended/hybrid learning. *Degree requirements:* For doctorate, thesis/dissertation. *Entrance requirements:* For master's, GRE General Test or MAT, minimum GPA of 3.0, official transcripts, recommendations, personal statement, resume/curriculum vitae, interview; for doctorate, MAT or GRE if GPA from master's lower than 3.5. Additional exam requirements/recommendations for international students: Required—TOEFL (minimum score 560 paper-based; 79 iBT); Recommended—IELTS (minimum score 6.5). *Application deadline:* Applications are processed on a rolling basis. Application fee: $75. Electronic applications accepted. *Financial support:* Federal Work-Study, scholarships/grants, traineeships, and unspecified assistantships available. Support available to part-time students. Financial award applicants required to submit FAFSA. *Faculty research:* Global public health, health policy, education, aging, job satisfaction, psychiatric nursing, critical thinking. *Application contact:* Hillary Lyons, Graduate Admission Counselor, 781-768-7746, E-mail: hillary.lyons@regiscollege.edu.

Rhode Island College, School of Graduate Studies, Feinstein School of Education and Human Development, Department of Counseling, Educational Leadership, and School Psychology, Providence, RI 02908-1991. Offers advanced counseling (CGS); agency counseling (MA); clinical mental health counseling (MS); co-occurring disorders (MA, CGS); educational leadership (M Ed); mental health counseling (CAGS); school counseling (MA); school psychology (CAGS); teacher leadership (CGS). *Accreditation:* ACA; NCATE. *Program availability:* Part-time, evening/weekend. *Faculty:* 10. *Students:* 31 full-time (25 women), 75 part-time (65 women); includes 16 minority (4 Black or African American, non-Hispanic/Latino; 11 Hispanic/Latino; 1 Two or more races, non-Hispanic/Latino). Average age 32. In 2017, 40 master's, 15 other advanced degrees awarded. *Degree requirements:* For master's and other advanced degree, comprehensive exam (for some programs), thesis (for some programs). *Entrance requirements:* For master's, GRE General Test or MAT, undergraduate transcripts; minimum undergraduate GPA of 3.0; for other advanced degree, GRE or MAT (for most programs), undergraduate transcripts; minimum undergraduate GPA of 3.0; 3 letters of recommendation; current resume. Additional exam requirements/recommendations for international students: Recommended—TOEFL (minimum score 550 paper-based; 79 iBT). *Application deadline:* For fall admission, 3/1 for domestic students; for spring admission, 11/1 for domestic students. Applications are processed on a rolling basis. Application fee: $50. Electronic applications accepted. *Expenses:* Tuition, state resident: full-time $9768; part-time $407 per credit. Tuition, nonresident: full-time $19,008; part-time $792 per credit. *Required fees:* $696; $29 per credit. One-time fee: $200 full-time; $100 part-time. Tuition and fees vary according to course load. *Financial support:* In 2017–18, 4 teaching assistantships with full tuition reimbursements (averaging $2,063 per year) were awarded; career-related internships or fieldwork, Federal Work-Study, scholarships/grants, health care benefits, and unspecified assistantships also available. Support available to part-time students. Financial award application deadline: 5/15; financial award applicants required to submit FAFSA. *Unit head:* Dr. John Eagle, Chair, 401-456-8023. *Application contact:* Graduate Studies, 401-456-8700.
Website: http://www.ric.edu/counselingEducationalLeadershipSchoolPsychology/index.php

Rivier University, School of Graduate Studies, Department of Education, Nashua, NH 03060. Offers curriculum and instruction (M Ed); early childhood education (M Ed); educational administration (M Ed); educational studies (M Ed); elementary education (M Ed); elementary education and general special education (M Ed); emotional and behavioral disorders (M Ed); general social education (M Ed); leadership and learning (Ed D, CAGS); learning disabilities (M Ed); learning disabilities and reading (M Ed); mental health counseling (MA); reading (M Ed); school counseling (M Ed). *Program availability:* Part-time, evening/weekend. *Degree requirements:* For master's, comprehensive exam (for some programs), internships. *Entrance requirements:* For master's, GRE General Test or MAT.

Robert Morris University, School of Education and Social Sciences, Moon Township, PA 15108-1189. Offers business education (MS); counseling psychology (MS); education (Postbaccalaureate Certificate); higher education (MS); instructional leadership (MS), including education; instructional management and leadership (PhD); literacy (MS); special education (MS). *Accreditation:* TEAC. *Program availability:* Part-time, evening/weekend, online learning. *Faculty:* 18 full-time (10 women), 5 part-time/adjunct (2 women). *Students:* 151 part-time (90 women); includes 23 minority (12 Black or African American, non-Hispanic/Latino; 2 Asian, non-Hispanic/Latino; 2 Hispanic/Latino; 7 Two or more races, non-Hispanic/Latino), 4 international. Average age 34. 51 applicants, 39% accepted, 10 enrolled. In 2017, 31 master's, 16 doctorates awarded. *Degree requirements:* For doctorate, thesis/dissertation. *Entrance requirements:* Additional exam requirements/recommendations for international students: Required—TOEFL (minimum score 550 paper-based; 79 iBT). *Application deadline:* For fall admission, 7/1 priority date for domestic and international students; for spring admission, 11/1 priority date for domestic and international students. Applications are processed on a rolling basis. Application fee: $35. Electronic applications accepted. *Expenses:* $890 per credit tuition, $80 per credit university fee. *Unit head:* Dr. George Semich, Acting Dean, 412-397-6032, Fax: 412-397-6044, E-mail: semich@rmu.edu. *Application contact:* E-mail: graduateadmissions@rmu.edu.
Website: http://www.rmu.edu/web/cms/schools/sess/

Rosemont College, Schools of Graduate and Professional Studies, Counseling Psychology Program, Rosemont, PA 19010-1699. Offers human services (MA); school counseling (MA). *Program availability:* Part-time, evening/weekend. *Degree requirements:* For master's, thesis or alternative, practicum. *Entrance requirements:* For master's, minimum undergraduate GPA of 3.0, 3 letters of recommendation. Additional exam requirements/recommendations for international students: Required—TOEFL. Electronic applications accepted. Application fee is waived when completed online. *Expenses:* Contact institution. *Faculty research:* Addictions counseling.

Rutgers University–New Brunswick, Graduate School of Education, Department of Educational Psychology, Programs in School Counseling and Counseling Psychology, Piscataway, NJ 08854-8097. Offers Ed M. *Accreditation:* ACA. *Program availability:* Part-time, evening/weekend. *Entrance requirements:* For master's, GRE General Test, 3 letters of recommendation. Additional exam requirements/recommendations for international students: Required—TOEFL (minimum score 550 paper-based; 83 iBT). Electronic applications accepted. *Faculty research:* Children and family in cross-cultural context, attachment theory, multicultural counseling, therapy relationship.

Sage Graduate School, School of Health Sciences, Department of Psychology, Program in Counseling and Community Psychology, Troy, NY 12180-4115. Offers MA. *Program availability:* Part-time, evening/weekend. *Faculty:* 6 full-time (all women), 2 part-time/adjunct (both women). *Students:* 30 full-time (27 women), 32 part-time (27 women); includes 12 minority (4 Black or African American, non-Hispanic/Latino; 1 Asian, non-Hispanic/Latino; 4 Hispanic/Latino; 3 Two or more races, non-Hispanic/Latino). Average age 29. 65 applicants, 57% accepted, 20 enrolled. In 2017, 25 master's awarded. *Degree requirements:* For master's, externship, internship, thesis or research seminar. *Entrance requirements:* For master's, official transcripts of all previous undergraduate study; 2 letters of reference (academic or professional); undergraduate courses in statistics, history and systems of psychology; 3 other courses in behavioral science; personal prospectus statement; current resume. Additional exam requirements/recommendations for international students: Required—TOEFL (minimum score 550 paper-based). *Application deadline:* Applications are processed on a rolling basis. Application fee: $30. Electronic applications accepted. Tuition and fees vary according to degree level and program. *Financial support:* Fellowships, research assistantships, scholarships/grants, and unspecified assistantships available. Financial award applicants required to submit FAFSA. *Unit head:* Dr. Theresa Hand, Dean, School of Health Sciences, 518-244-2264, Fax: 518-244-4571, E-mail: handt@sage.edu. *Application contact:* Dr. Gayle Morse, Graduate Program Director, 518-292-1819, E-mail: morseg@sage.edu.
Website: http://www.sage.edu/academics/psychology/programs/counseling/

St. Bonaventure University, School of Graduate Studies, School of Education, Program in Counselor Education, St. Bonaventure, NY 14778-2284. Offers community mental health counseling (MS Ed); rehabilitation counseling (MS Ed); school counseling (MS Ed); school counselor (Adv C). *Accreditation:* ACA. *Program availability:* Part-time, evening/weekend, 100% online. *Faculty:* 4 full-time (2 women), 5 part-time/adjunct (3 women). *Students:* 35 full-time (27 women), 30 part-time (23 women); includes 8 minority (3 Black or African American, non-Hispanic/Latino; 4 Hispanic/Latino; 1 Two or more races, non-Hispanic/Latino), 1 international. Average age 28. 55 applicants, 82% accepted, 29 enrolled. In 2017, 27 master's, 2 Adv Cs awarded. *Degree requirements:* For master's, comprehensive exam, thesis optional, internship, portfolio; for Adv C, internship. *Entrance requirements:* For master's, statement of intent/writing sample; transcripts from all colleges previously attended; two references; interview; minimum undergraduate GPA of 3.0; for Adv C, interview, writing sample, minimum undergraduate GPA of 3.0, two letters of recommendation, master's degree, transcripts from all colleges previously attended. Additional exam requirements/recommendations for international students: Required—TOEFL (minimum score 550 paper-based; 79 iBT). *Application deadline:* For fall admission, 3/15 priority date for domestic students, 2/1 priority date for international students; for spring admission, 11/15 priority date for domestic students, 7/1 priority date for international students. Applications are processed on a rolling basis. Application fee: $0. Electronic applications accepted. *Expenses:* $733 per credit hour, $100 graduation fee. *Financial support:* Career-related internships or fieldwork, Federal Work-Study, scholarships/grants, health care benefits, and unspecified assistantships available. Support available to part-time students. Financial award application deadline: 4/15; financial award applicants required to submit FAFSA. *Faculty research:* Balance between technology and personal contact in counselor education, special education and cyberbullying, school response to child abuse. *Unit head:* Dr. Chris Siuta, Director, 716-375-2114, Fax: 716-375-2360, E-mail: csiuta@sbu.edu. *Application contact:* Bruce Campbell, Director of Graduate Admissions, 716-375-2429, Fax: 716-375-4015, E-mail: gradsch@sbu.edu.
Website: http://www.sbu.edu/academics/msed-in-school-counseling

St. Edward's University, School of Education, Master of Arts in Counseling Program, Austin, TX 78704. Offers MA. *Program availability:* Part-time, evening/weekend. *Students:* 76 full-time (63 women), 131 part-time (112 women); includes 75 minority (13 Black or African American, non-Hispanic/Latino; 5 Asian, non-Hispanic/Latino; 51 Hispanic/Latino; 6 Two or more races, non-Hispanic/Latino), 2 international. Average age 35. 112 applicants, 56% accepted, 43 enrolled. In 2017, 72 master's awarded. *Entrance requirements:* Additional exam requirements/recommendations for international students: Required—TOEFL, IELTS. *Application deadline:* For fall admission, 6/1 priority date for domestic and international students; for spring admission, 10/1 priority date for domestic and international students. Applications are processed on a rolling basis. Application fee: $50. Electronic applications accepted. *Expenses: Tuition:* Full-time $26,406; part-time $1467 per hour. *Required fees:* $75 per trimester. Full-time tuition and fees vary according to course load and program. *Unit head:* Dr. Bill McHenry, Department Chair/Associate Professor of Counseling, 512-448-8733, E-mail: wmchenry@stedwards.edu. *Application contact:* Staci Hanrahan, Graduate Admission Counselor, 512-326-7333, E-mail: shanraha@stedwards.edu.

St. John Fisher College, Wegmans School of Nursing, Program in Mental Health Counseling, Rochester, NY 14618-3597. Offers MS. *Accreditation:* ACA. *Program availability:* Part-time. *Faculty:* 6 full-time (4 women), 1 part-time/adjunct (0 women). *Students:* 59 full-time (43 women), 19 part-time (18 women); includes 14 minority (6 Black or African American, non-Hispanic/Latino; 6 Hispanic/Latino; 2 Two or more races, non-Hispanic/Latino). Average age 27. 78 applicants, 65% accepted, 36 enrolled. In 2017, 32 master's awarded. *Degree requirements:* For master's, practicum experience, internship. *Entrance requirements:* For master's, GRE (if GPA below 3.0), 2 letters of recommendation, personal statement, current resume, interview. Additional exam requirements/recommendations for international students: Required—TOEFL (minimum score 575 paper-based; 80 iBT). *Application deadline:* Applications are processed on a rolling basis. Application fee: $30. Electronic applications accepted. *Expenses:* Contact institution. *Financial support:* Scholarships/grants available. Financial award applicants required to submit FAFSA. *Faculty research:* Social class issues, clinical supervision, counselor education, play therapy. *Unit head:* Dr. Rachel Jordan, Director, 585-899-3858, E-mail: rjordan@sjfc.edu. *Application contact:* Michelle Gosier, Director of Transfer and Graduate Admissions, 585-385-8064, E-mail: mgosier@sjfc.edu.
Website: https://www.sjfc.edu/graduate-programs/ms-in-mental-health-counseling/

St. John's University, The School of Education, Department of Counselor Education, Program in Clinical Mental Health Counseling, Queens, NY 11439. Offers MS Ed, Adv C. Master's program admits in fall only; Advanced Certificate in spring only. *Students:* 45 full-time (34 women), 27 part-time (19 women); includes 40 minority (16 Black or African American, non-Hispanic/Latino; 3 Asian, non-Hispanic/Latino; 20 Hispanic/Latino; 1 Two or more races, non-Hispanic/Latino), 2 international. Average age 27. 67 applicants, 72% accepted, 22 enrolled. In 2017, 27 master's, 1 Adv C awarded. *Entrance requirements:* For master's, 2 letters of recommendation, interview; for Adv C, official master's transcripts, statement of purpose. *Application deadline:* For

fall admission, 8/17 for domestic and international students; for summer admission, 5/15 for domestic and international students. Application fee: $70. Electronic applications accepted. *Expenses: Tuition:* Full-time $44,280; part-time $1230 per credit. *Required fees:* $340; $340 per credit. Tuition and fees vary according to course load, degree level and program. *Financial support:* Fellowships, research assistantships, scholarships/grants, and unspecified assistantships available. Support available to part-time students. Financial award application deadline: 2/1; financial award applicants required to submit FAFSA. *Faculty research:* Psychological issues of veterans as they return to civilian life, career issues of same populations, role of spirituality in recovery from substance abuse, issues around resilience, issues surrounding happiness, effective practice and supervision in on-line format, diversity issues in the presentation of pathology and special requirements for effective treatment. *Unit head:* Dr. Robert K. Eschenauer, Chair, 718-990-2120, E-mail: eschenar@stjohns.edu. *Application contact:* Dr. Robert K. Eschenauer, Chair, 718-990-2120, E-mail: eschenar@stjohns.edu.
Website: https://www.stjohns.edu/academics/schools-and-colleges/school-education/programs-and-majors/clinical-mental-health-counseling-master-science-education

Saint Martin's University, Office of Graduate Studies, Program in Counseling Psychology, Lacey, WA 98503. Offers MAC. *Program availability:* Part-time. *Faculty:* 3 full-time (2 women), 2 part-time/adjunct (both women). *Students:* 5 full-time (4 women), 84 part-time (73 women); includes 30 minority (7 Black or African American, non-Hispanic/Latino; 2 American Indian or Alaska Native, non-Hispanic/Latino; 3 Asian, non-Hispanic/Latino; 13 Hispanic/Latino; 5 Two or more races, non-Hispanic/Latino). Average age 36. 24 applicants, 100% accepted, 18 enrolled. In 2017, 32 master's awarded. *Degree requirements:* For master's, clinical experience, interview. *Entrance requirements:* For master's, clinical experience. Additional exam requirements/recommendations for international students: Required—TOEFL (minimum score 550 paper-based; 79 iBT); Recommended—IELTS (minimum score 6.5). *Application deadline:* For fall admission, 4/1 priority date for domestic and international students; for spring admission, 11/1 priority date for domestic and international students. Applications are processed on a rolling basis. Application fee: $50. Electronic applications accepted. *Expenses: Tuition:* Full-time $21,420; part-time $1190 per credit. *Financial support:* Career-related internships or fieldwork, Federal Work-Study, and institutionally sponsored loans available. Support available to part-time students. Financial award application deadline: 3/1; financial award applicants required to submit FAFSA. *Faculty research:* Alcohol studies, clinical effectiveness, social justice, parent adolescent interaction. *Unit head:* Dr. Godfrey J. Ellis, Director, 360-438-4560, E-mail: gellis@stmartin.edu. *Application contact:* Casey Caronna, Administrative Assistant, 360-412-6128, E-mail: ccaronna@stmartin.edu.
Website: https://www.stmartin.edu

St. Mary's University, Graduate Studies, Program in Clinical Mental Health Counseling, San Antonio, TX 78228. Offers MA. *Program availability:* Part-time, evening/weekend. *Students:* 39 full-time (31 women), 16 part-time (12 women); includes 31 minority (7 Black or African American, non-Hispanic/Latino; 23 Hispanic/Latino; 1 Two or more races, non-Hispanic/Latino), 2 international. Average age 32. 81 applicants, 25% accepted, 15 enrolled. In 2017, 15 master's awarded. *Degree requirements:* For master's, comprehensive exam, 700-hour clinical experience (practicum/internship). *Entrance requirements:* For master's, GRE General Test or MAT, bachelor's degree from accredited college or university; recommendations from past employers and/or from faculty members of previous undergraduate studies; personal statement indicating interest in becoming professional counselor or doing work that requires counseling skills. Additional exam requirements/recommendations for international students: Required—TOEFL (minimum score 550 paper-based; 80 iBT), IELTS (minimum score 6). *Application deadline:* For fall admission, 7/1 for domestic students; for spring admission, 11/15 for domestic students; for summer admission, 4/1 for domestic students. Applications are processed on a rolling basis. Application fee: $0. Electronic applications accepted. *Expenses: Tuition:* Full-time $16,200; part-time $900 per credit hour. *Required fees:* $810; $405 per semester. *Financial support:* Application deadline: 3/31; applicants required to submit FAFSA. *Faculty research:* Relational-cultural theory, aging, human personality, interculturalism. *Unit head:* Dr. Melanie Harper, Program Director, 210-438-6400, E-mail: mharper@stmarytx.edu. *Application contact:* Kim Thornton, Director of Graduate Admission, 210-436-3101, E-mail: kthornton@stmarytx.edu.
Website: https://www.stmarytx.edu/academics/programs/master-clinical-mental-health-counseling/

Saint Mary's University of Minnesota, Schools of Graduate and Professional Programs, Graduate School of Health and Human Services, Counseling and Psychological Services Program, Winona, MN 55987-1399. Offers addiction studies (Certificate); counseling and psychological services (MA). *Unit head:* Dr. Mary Louise Wise, Associate Program Director, 612-728-5104, Fax: 612-728-5121, E-mail: mlwise@smumn.edu. *Application contact:* James Callinan, Director of Admissions for Graduate and Professional Programs, 612-728-5158, Fax: 612-728-5121, E-mail: jcallina@smumn.edu.
Website: http://www.smumn.edu/graduate-home/areas-of-study/graduate-school-of-health-human-services/ma-in-counseling-psychological-services

Saint Mary's University of Minnesota, Schools of Graduate and Professional Programs, Graduate School of Health and Human Services, Counseling Psychology Program, Winona, MN 55987-1399. Offers Psy D. *Unit head:* Dr. Ashley Sovereign, Director, 612-238-4557, E-mail: asoverei@smumn.edu. *Application contact:* James Callinan, Director of Admissions for Graduate and Professional Programs, 612-728-5158, Fax: 612-728-5121, E-mail: jcallina@smumn.edu.
Website: http://www.smumn.edu/graduate-home/areas-of-study/graduate-school-of-health-human-services/doctor-of-psychology-in-counseling-psychology

Saint Paul University, Faculty of Human Sciences, Program in Counseling and Spirituality, Ottawa, ON K1S 1C4, Canada. Offers individual or marital/couple counseling (MA); spiritual care (MA). *Program availability:* Part-time. *Degree requirements:* For master's, research project or thesis. *Entrance requirements:* For master's, honors BA in human sciences, minimum B average, 12 theology credits.

St. Thomas University, Biscayne College, Department of Social Sciences and Counseling, Program in Mental Health Counseling, Miami Gardens, FL 33054-6459. Offers MS. *Program availability:* Part-time, evening/weekend. *Degree requirements:* For master's, comprehensive exam. *Entrance requirements:* For master's, interview, minimum GPA of 3.0 or GRE. Additional exam requirements/recommendations for international students: Required—TOEFL (minimum score 550 paper-based; 79 iBT). Electronic applications accepted.

Salem State University, School of Graduate Studies, Program in Counseling and Psychological Services, Salem, MA 01970-5353. Offers MS, Graduate Certificate. *Program availability:* Part-time, evening/weekend. *Entrance requirements:* For master's, GRE or MAT. Additional exam requirements/recommendations for international students: Required—TOEFL (minimum score 550 paper-based; 80 iBT) or IELTS (minimum score 5.5).

Salem State University, School of Graduate Studies, Program of Advanced Professional Studies in Counseling, Salem, MA 01970-5353. Offers Graduate

Certificate. *Program availability:* Part-time, evening/weekend. *Entrance requirements:* Additional exam requirements/recommendations for international students: Required—TOEFL (minimum score 550 paper-based; 80 iBT) or IELTS (minimum score 5.5).

Salve Regina University, Program in Rehabilitation Counseling, Newport, RI 02840-4192. Offers clinical rehabilitation and mental health counseling (MA); mental health (CAGS), including rehabilitation counseling; rehabilitation (CAGS), including substance abuse counseling; rehabilitation counseling (MA); substance abuse and treatment (CAGS). *Accreditation:* CORE. *Program availability:* Part-time, evening/weekend. *Entrance requirements:* For master's, GMAT, GRE General Test or MAT. Additional exam requirements/recommendations for international students: Required—TOEFL (minimum score 600 paper-based; 100 iBT) or IELTS. Electronic applications accepted.

Santa Clara University, School of Education and Counseling Psychology, Santa Clara, CA 95053. Offers alternative and correctional education (Certificate); Catholic school teaching (MAT); counseling (MA); counseling psychology (MA); educational leadership (MA); interdisciplinary education (MA); teaching multiple subjects (MAT); teaching single subjects (MAT). *Program availability:* Part-time. *Faculty:* 31 full-time (21 women), 37 part-time/adjunct (25 women). *Students:* 253 full-time (195 women), 350 part-time (283 women); includes 296 minority (10 Black or African American, non-Hispanic/Latino; 1 American Indian or Alaska Native, non-Hispanic/Latino; 80 Asian, non-Hispanic/Latino; 179 Hispanic/Latino; 26 Two or more races, non-Hispanic/Latino), 41 international. Average age 31. 211 applicants, 75% accepted, 142 enrolled. In 2017, 266 master's awarded. *Entrance requirements:* For master's, official transcripts, 2-3 letters of recommendation, statement of purpose, resume or curriculum vitae. Additional exam requirements/recommendations for international students: Required—TOEFL (minimum score 90 iBT) or IELTS (6.5). *Application deadline:* For fall admission, 4/16 for international students; for summer admission, 3/12 for domestic students. Applications are processed on a rolling basis. Application fee: $50. Electronic applications accepted. *Expenses:* $607 per unit. *Financial support:* In 2017–18, 355 students received support. Fellowships, research assistantships, teaching assistantships, Federal Work-Study, scholarships/grants, and health care benefits available. Support available to part-time students. Financial award applicants required to submit FAFSA. *Unit head:* Dr. Sabrina Zirkel, Dean, 408-551-3074, Fax: 408-554-4367, E-mail: szirkel@scu.edu. *Application contact:* Victoria Rodriguez, Graduate Admissions Advisor, 408-554-4723, E-mail: v1rodriguez@scu.edu.
Website: http://www.scu.edu/ecp/

Saybrook University, LIOS MA Residential Programs, Kirkland, WA 98033. Offers leadership and organization development (MA); psychology counseling (MA). *Degree requirements:* For master's, thesis (for some programs), oral exams. *Entrance requirements:* For master's, bachelor's degree from an accredited university or college. Additional exam requirements/recommendations for international students: Recommended—TOEFL, IELTS, TWE.

The Seattle School of Theology and Psychology, Graduate Programs, Seattle, WA 98121. Offers Christian studies (MA); counseling psychology (MA); divinity (M Div). *Program availability:* Part-time. *Entrance requirements:* For master's, MAT.

Seton Hall University, College of Education and Human Services, Department of Professional Psychology and Family Therapy, Program in Counseling Psychology, South Orange, NJ 07079-2697. Offers counseling psychology (PhD); school counseling (MA). *Accreditation:* APA. *Degree requirements:* For doctorate, comprehensive exam, thesis/dissertation, internship. *Entrance requirements:* For master's and doctorate, GRE, interview. *Faculty research:* Vocational indecision, coping skills, cognitive behavioral interventions, vocational development.

Siena Heights University, Graduate College, Adrian, MI 49221-1796. Offers clinical mental health counseling (MA); educational leadership (Specialist); leadership (MA), including health care leadership, organizational leadership; teacher education (MA), including early childhood education, early childhood education: Montessori, education leadership: principal, elementary education: reading K-12, leadership: higher education, secondary education: reading K-12, special education: cognitive impairment, special education: learning disabilities. *Program availability:* Part-time, evening/weekend. *Degree requirements:* For master's, thesis, presentation. *Entrance requirements:* For master's, minimum GPA of 3.0, current resume, essay, all post-secondary transcripts, 3 letters of reference, conviction disclosure form; copy of teaching certificate (for some education programs); for Specialist, master's degree, minimum GPA of 3.0, current resume, essay, all post-secondary transcripts, 3 letters of reference, conviction disclosure form; copy of teaching certificate (for some education programs). Electronic applications accepted.

Simpson University, School of Graduate Studies, Redding, CA 96003-8606. Offers counseling psychology (MA); organizational leadership (MA). *Program availability:* Evening/weekend, 100% online, blended/hybrid learning. *Degree requirements:* For master's, thesis optional, portfolio capstone, integrative essay. *Entrance requirements:* For master's, three letters of recommendation, personal statement, resume, transcripts, personal interview, bachelor's degree in psychology or related field with minimum GPA of 3.0 in final 60 credits (for counseling psychology); two references (for organizational leadership). Additional exam requirements/recommendations for international students: Required—TOEFL (minimum score 550 paper-based; 79 iBT). Electronic applications accepted. *Expenses:* Contact institution. *Faculty research:* Development of executive functioning in young children, cognitive neuropsychology, historical issues in the neurosciences, neurotheology.

Slippery Rock University of Pennsylvania, Graduate Studies (Recruitment), College of Education, Department of Counseling and Development, Slippery Rock, PA 16057-1383. Offers clinical mental health (MA); school counseling (M Ed); student affairs in higher education (MA); student affairs in higher education with college counseling (MA). *Accreditation:* ACA (one or more programs are accredited); NCATE. *Program availability:* Part-time, evening/weekend. *Degree requirements:* For master's, comprehensive exam, thesis (for some programs). *Entrance requirements:* For master's, GRE General Test or MAT, official transcripts, personal statement, three letters of recommendation, interview. Additional exam requirements/recommendations for international students: Required—TOEFL (minimum score 550 paper-based; 80 iBT). Electronic applications accepted. *Expenses:* Contact institution.

Sofia University, Residential Programs, Palo Alto, CA 94303. Offers clinical psychology (Psy D); computer science (MS); counseling psychology (MA); transpersonal psychology (MA, PhD). *Program availability:* Part-time, evening/weekend. Terminal master's awarded for partial completion of doctoral program. *Degree requirements:* For doctorate, thesis/dissertation. *Entrance requirements:* For master's, bachelor's degree; for doctorate, bachelor's degree; master's degree (for some programs). Electronic applications accepted.

Sonoma State University, School of Social Sciences, Department of Counseling, Rohnert Park, CA 94928. Offers clinical mental health counseling (MA); school counseling (MA). *Accreditation:* ACA. *Program availability:* Part-time. *Entrance requirements:* For master's, minimum GPA of 3.0. Additional exam requirements/recommendations for international students: Required—TOEFL (minimum score 500 paper-based). *Application deadline:* For fall admission, 11/30 for domestic students. Application fee: $55. *Financial support:* Fellowships and career-related internships or

fieldwork available. Financial award application deadline: 3/2; financial award applicants required to submit FAFSA. *Unit head:* Dr. Adam Zagelbaum, Chair, 707-664-2544, E-mail: adam.zagelbaum@sonoma.edu.
Website: http://www.sonoma.edu/counseling

Southeastern Oklahoma State University, School of Behavioral Sciences, Durant, OK 74701-0609. Offers clinical mental health counseling (MS). *Accreditation:* ACA. *Program availability:* Part-time, evening/weekend. *Degree requirements:* For master's, comprehensive exam, thesis optional. *Entrance requirements:* For master's, GRE General Test, minimum GPA of 3.0 in last 60 hours or 2.75 overall. Additional exam requirements/recommendations for international students: Required—TOEFL (minimum score 550 paper-based; 79 iBT). Electronic applications accepted.

Southeastern University, College of Behavioral and Social Sciences, Lakeland, FL 33801-6099. Offers human services (MA); international community development (MA); marriage and family counseling (MS); professional counseling (MS); school counseling (MS); social work (MSW). *Program availability:* Evening/weekend. *Faculty:* 9 full-time (6 women), 7 part-time/adjunct (4 women). *Students:* 72 full-time (60 women), 9 part-time (all women); includes 28 minority (12 Black or African American, non-Hispanic/Latino; 2 Asian, non-Hispanic/Latino; 13 Hispanic/Latino; 1 Native Hawaiian or other Pacific Islander, non-Hispanic/Latino), 1 international. Average age 29. Application fee: $50. Electronic applications accepted. *Unit head:* Erica H. Sirrine, Dean, 863-667-5341, E-mail: ehsirrine@seu.edu.
Website: http://www.seu.edu/behavior/

Southeast Missouri State University, School of Graduate Studies, Department of Educational Leadership and Counseling, Counseling Program, Cape Girardeau, MO 63701-4799. Offers career counseling (MA); mental health counseling (MA); school counseling (MA). *Accreditation:* ACA; NCATE. *Program availability:* Part-time, evening/weekend. *Faculty:* 5 full-time (4 women), 2 part-time/adjunct (both women). *Students:* 30 full-time (23 women), 30 part-time (26 women); includes 6 minority (4 Black or African American, non-Hispanic/Latino; 2 American Indian or Alaska Native, non-Hispanic/Latino), 1 international. Average age 33. 45 applicants, 78% accepted, 26 enrolled. In 2017, 49 master's, 4 other advanced degrees awarded. *Degree requirements:* For master's and Ed S, comprehensive exam, thesis or alternative. *Entrance requirements:* For master's, personal essay, interview, minimum GPA of 3.5; for Ed S, minimum graduate GPA of 3.7. Additional exam requirements/recommendations for international students: Required—TOEFL (minimum score 550 paper-based; 79 iBT), IELTS (minimum score 6), PTE (minimum score 53). *Application deadline:* For fall admission, 3/1 for domestic and international students; for spring admission, 11/21 for domestic students, 10/1 for international students; for summer admission, 3/1 for domestic students. Applications are processed on a rolling basis. Application fee: $30 ($40 for international students). Electronic applications accepted. *Expenses:* $270.35 per credit hour in-state tuition, $33.40 per credit hour fees. *Financial support:* In 2017–18, 6 students received support. Career-related internships or fieldwork, Federal Work-Study, scholarships/grants, traineeships, tuition waivers (full), and unspecified assistantships available. Financial award application deadline: 6/30; financial award applicants required to submit FAFSA. *Faculty research:* School counseling, mental health, career and family counseling, social justice and spirituality in counseling. *Unit head:* Dr. C. P. Gause, Department Chair, 573-651-2137, Fax: 573-986-6512, E-mail: cpgause@semo.edu. *Application contact:* Dr. Jan Ward, Program Coordinator/Associate Professor, 573-651-2137, Fax: 573-986-6512, E-mail: jward@semo.edu.
Website: http://www.semo.edu/eduleadcounsel/

Southern Adventist University, School of Education and Psychology, Collegedale, TN 37315-0370. Offers clinical mental health counseling (MS); instructional leadership (MS Ed); literacy education (MS Ed); outdoor education (MS Ed); professional school counseling (MS). *Accreditation:* NCATE. *Program availability:* Part-time, evening/weekend. *Degree requirements:* For master's, comprehensive exam (for some programs), thesis optional, position paper (MS), portfolio (MS Ed in outdoor education). *Entrance requirements:* For master's, interview (MS); 9 semester hours of upper-division course work in psychology or related field, including 1 course in psychology research or statistics; 9 semester hours of education (MS Ed). Additional exam requirements/recommendations for international students: Required—TOEFL (minimum score 600 paper-based; 100 iBT). *Application deadline:* For fall admission, 7/1 priority date for domestic students, 6/1 priority date for international students; for winter admission, 11/1 priority date for domestic students, 10/1 priority date for international students; for spring admission, 4/1 priority date for domestic students, 3/1 priority date for international students. Applications are processed on a rolling basis. Application fee: $40. Electronic applications accepted. *Expenses: Tuition:* Full-time $11,430; part-time $635 per credit hour. Tuition and fees vary according to degree level and program. *Financial support:* Research assistantships with full tuition reimbursements, teaching assistantships with full tuition reimbursements, career-related internships or fieldwork, scholarships/grants, tuition waivers (partial), and unspecified assistantships available. Support available to part-time students. Financial award application deadline: 4/1; financial award applicants required to submit FAFSA. *Unit head:* Bonnie Eder, Interim Dean, 423-236-2759, Fax: 423-236-1765, E-mail: beder@southern.edu. *Application contact:* Mikhaile Spence, Graduate Enrollment Counselor, 423-236-2496, Fax: 423-236-1765, E-mail: maspence@southern.edu.
Website: https://www.southern.edu/academics/edpsych.html

Southern California Seminary, Graduate and Professional Programs, El Cajon, CA 92019. Offers Biblical studies (MABS); counseling psychology (MACP); marriage and family therapy (MAMFT); psychology (Psy D); religious studies (MRS); theology (M Div). *Program availability:* Part-time, evening/weekend, online learning. *Degree requirements:* For master's, thesis (for some programs); for doctorate, thesis/dissertation. *Entrance requirements:* For doctorate, master's degree in psychology. Additional exam requirements/recommendations for international students: Required—TOEFL (minimum score 550 paper-based). Electronic applications accepted.

Southern Illinois University Carbondale, Graduate School, College of Liberal Arts, Department of Psychology, Carbondale, IL 62901-4701. Offers clinical psychology (PhD); counseling psychology (PhD); experimental psychology (MA, MS). *Accreditation:* APA (one or more programs are accredited). *Degree requirements:* For master's, thesis; for doctorate, thesis/dissertation. *Entrance requirements:* For master's, GRE General Test, GRE Subject Test, minimum GPA of 2.7; for doctorate, GRE General Test, GRE Subject Test, minimum GPA of 3.25. Additional exam requirements/recommendations for international students: Required—TOEFL. *Faculty research:* Developmental neuropsychology; smoking, affect, and cognition; personality measurement; vocational psychology; program evaluation.

Southern Nazarene University, College of Professional and Graduate Studies, Department of Psychology and Counseling, Bethany, OK 73008. Offers counseling psychology (MA, MSCP); marital and family therapy (MA). *Degree requirements:* For master's, thesis optional. *Entrance requirements:* For master's, English proficiency exam, minimum GPA of 3.0 in last 60 hours/major, 2.7 overall.

Southern Oregon University, Graduate Studies, Department of Psychology, Ashland, OR 97520. Offers MHC. *Accreditation:* ACA. *Program availability:* Part-time, online learning. *Degree requirements:* For master's, thesis, portfolio, oral defense. *Entrance requirements:* For master's, GRE General Test, minimum cumulative GPA of 3.0 in the last 90 quarter credits (60 semester credits) of undergraduate coursework. Additional exam requirements/recommendations for international students: Required—TOEFL (minimum score 540 paper-based; 76 iBT), IELTS (minimum score 6), ELPT (minimum score 964) or ELS (minimum score 112). Electronic applications accepted.

South University, Graduate Programs, College of Arts and Sciences, Program in Clinical Mental Health Counseling, Savannah, GA 31406. Offers MA. *Accreditation:* ACA.

South University, Program in Clinical Mental Health Counseling, Montgomery, AL 36116-1120. Offers MA.

South University, Program in Clinical Mental Health Counseling, Columbia, SC 29203. Offers MA.

South University, Program in Clinical Mental Health Counseling, Royal Palm Beach, FL 33411. Offers MA.

South University, Program in Clinical Mental Health Counseling, Glen Allen, VA 23060. Offers MA. *Accreditation:* ACA.

South University, Program in Clinical Mental Health Counseling, Virginia Beach, VA 23452. Offers MA. *Accreditation:* ACA.

South University, Program in Clinical Mental Health Counseling, Round Rock, TX 78681. Offers MA.

Southwestern Assemblies of God University, Thomas F. Harrison School of Graduate Studies, Program in Counseling Psychology, Waxahachie, TX 75165-5735. Offers counseling psychology (clinical) (MCP); human services counseling (MS). *Program availability:* Part-time. *Degree requirements:* For master's, comprehensive written and oral exams. *Entrance requirements:* For master's, GRE General Test, minimum GPA of 2.5. Electronic applications accepted.

Southwestern College, Program in Art Therapy/Counseling, Santa Fe, NM 87502-4788. Offers MA. *Program availability:* Part-time, evening/weekend. *Degree requirements:* For master's, internship. *Entrance requirements:* For master's, resume, slide portfolio, interview, 3 letters of reference. Additional exam requirements/recommendations for international students: Required—TOEFL.

Southwestern College, Program in Counseling, Santa Fe, NM 87502-4788. Offers MA. *Program availability:* Part-time, evening/weekend. *Degree requirements:* For master's, internship. *Entrance requirements:* For master's, resume, 3 letters of reference, interview. Additional exam requirements/recommendations for international students: Required—TOEFL.

Southwestern College, Program in Grief, Loss and Trauma Counseling, Santa Fe, NM 87502-4788. Offers MA, Certificate. *Program availability:* Part-time, evening/weekend, online learning. *Entrance requirements:* For master's, interview, references, resume; for Certificate, 3 letters of reference, interview.

Spring Arbor University, School of Human Services, Spring Arbor, MI 49283-9799. Offers counseling (MAC); family studies (MAFS); nursing (MSN). *Program availability:* Part-time, evening/weekend, online learning. *Entrance requirements:* For master's, bachelor's degree from regionally-accredited college or university, minimum GPA of 3.0 for at least the last two years of the bachelor's degree, at least two recommendations from professional/academic individuals. Additional exam requirements/recommendations for international students: Required—TOEFL (minimum score 600 paper-based). Electronic applications accepted.

Springfield College, Graduate Programs, Programs in Psychology, Springfield, MA 01109-3797. Offers athletic counseling (MS, CAGS); clinical mental health counseling (M Ed, CAGS); counseling psychology (Psy D); general counseling (M Ed); industrial/organizational psychology (M Ed, CAGS); school counseling (M Ed, CAGS); student personnel administration in higher education (M Ed, CAGS). *Accreditation:* APA. *Program availability:* Part-time. *Students:* 192 applicants, 65% accepted, 64 enrolled. In 2017, 56 master's, 5 doctorates awarded. *Degree requirements:* For master's, research project, portfolio; for doctorate, dissertation project, 1500 hours of counseling psychology practicum, full-year internship. *Entrance requirements:* For doctorate, GRE. Additional exam requirements/recommendations for international students: Required—TOEFL (minimum score 550 paper-based); Recommended—IELTS (minimum score 7). *Application deadline:* For fall admission, 1/15 priority date for domestic students, 1/15 for international students; for winter admission, 11/1 for domestic and international students; for spring admission, 11/1 for domestic and international students. Applications are processed on a rolling basis. Application fee: $50. Electronic applications accepted. *Financial support:* Fellowships with partial tuition reimbursements, teaching assistantships with partial tuition reimbursements, career-related internships or fieldwork, Federal Work-Study, institutionally sponsored loans, scholarships/grants, and unspecified assistantships available. Financial award application deadline: 3/1; financial award applicants required to submit FAFSA. *Unit head:* Dr. Allison Cumming-McCann, Chair, 413-748-3025, Fax: 413-748-3854, E-mail: acumming@springfield.edu. *Application contact:* Anne Griffin, Director of Graduate Admissions, 413-748-3225, E-mail: agriffin2@springfield.edu.
Website: http://springfield.edu/programs

State University of New York at New Paltz, Graduate and Extended Learning School, School of Liberal Arts and Sciences, Department of Psychology, New Paltz, NY 12561. Offers clinical mental health counseling (MS); mental health counseling (AC); psychological science (MS); school counseling (MS); trauma and disaster mental health (AC). *Program availability:* Part-time, evening/weekend. *Faculty:* 12 full-time (9 women), 1 (woman) part-time/adjunct. *Students:* 61 full-time (44 women), 19 part-time (15 women); includes 18 minority (2 Black or African American, non-Hispanic/Latino; 1 Asian, non-Hispanic/Latino; 12 Hispanic/Latino; 1 Native Hawaiian or other Pacific Islander, non-Hispanic/Latino; 2 Two or more races, non-Hispanic/Latino). 109 applicants, 57% accepted, 40 enrolled. In 2017, 16 master's awarded. *Degree requirements:* For master's, comprehensive exam, thesis. *Entrance requirements:* For master's, GRE General Test, minimum GPA of 3.0. Additional exam requirements/recommendations for international students: Required—TOEFL (minimum score 550 paper-based; 80 iBT), IELTS (minimum score 6.5). *Application deadline:* For fall admission, 2/1 priority date for domestic and international students; for spring admission, 11/15 priority date for domestic and international students. Application fee: $50. Electronic applications accepted. *Financial support:* In 2017–18, 6 teaching assistantships with partial tuition reimbursements (averaging $5,000 per year) were awarded. Financial award application deadline: 8/1. *Faculty research:* Disaster mental health, women's objectification, mate selection, cultural psychology, achievement motivation. *Unit head:* Dr. Glenn Geher, Chair, 845-257-3091, E-mail: geherg@newpaltz.edu. *Application contact:* Dr. Tabitha Holmes, Program Coordinator, 845-257-3955, E-mail: holmest@newpaltz.edu.
Website: http://www.newpaltz.edu/psychology/

State University of New York at Oswego, Graduate Studies, School of Education, Department of Counseling and Psychological Services, Oswego, NY 13126. Offers mental health counseling (MS); MS/CAS. *Degree requirements:* For master's, comprehensive exam, thesis optional. *Entrance requirements:* For master's, GRE

General Test, interview, minimum GPA of 3.0. Additional exam requirements/recommendations for international students: Required—TOEFL (minimum score 560 paper-based). *Faculty research:* Lowenfeld mosaics as predictor validation of preschool screening.

State University of New York at Plattsburgh, School of Education, Health, and Human Services, Department of Counselor Education, Plattsburgh, NY 12901-2681. Offers clinical mental health counseling (MS, Advanced Certificate); school counselor (MS Ed, CAS); student affairs counseling (MS). *Accreditation:* ACA (one or more programs are accredited); TEAC. *Program availability:* Part-time. *Entrance requirements:* For master's, GRE General Test or MAT, minimum GPA of 2.8. Additional exam requirements/recommendations for international students: Required—TOEFL. *Faculty research:* Campus violence, program accreditation, substance abuse, vocational assessment, group counseling, divorce.

State University of New York College at Old Westbury, Program in Mental Health Counseling, Old Westbury, NY 11568-0210. Offers MS. *Faculty:* 3 full-time (0 women), 2 part-time/adjunct (both women). *Students:* 34 full-time (29 women); includes 11 minority (4 Black or African American, non-Hispanic/Latino; 2 Asian, non-Hispanic/Latino; 5 Hispanic/Latino). Average age 29. 39 applicants, 64% accepted, 21 enrolled. In 2017, 14 master's awarded. *Entrance requirements:* For master's, essay, letters of recommendation. Application fee: $50. *Financial support:* Applicants required to submit FAFSA. *Unit head:* Dr. Fred Millan, Director, 516-876-3315, E-mail: millanf@oldwestbury.edu. *Application contact:* Philip D'Angelo, Graduate Admissions Office, 516-876-3073, E-mail: enroll@oldwestbury.edu.

Stetson University, College of Arts and Sciences, Division of Education, Department of Counselor Education, DeLand, FL 32723. Offers marriage, couple and family counseling (MS); mental health counseling (MS); school counseling (MS). *Accreditation:* ACA. *Program availability:* Evening/weekend. *Faculty:* 6 full-time (5 women), 5 part-time/adjunct (2 women). *Students:* 100 full-time (82 women), 9 part-time (all women); includes 37 minority (9 Black or African American, non-Hispanic/Latino; 4 American Indian or Alaska Native, non-Hispanic/Latino; 15 Hispanic/Latino; 9 Two or more races, non-Hispanic/Latino), 5 international. Average age 30. 42 applicants, 79% accepted, 22 enrolled. In 2017, 24 master's awarded. *Entrance requirements:* For master's, GRE or MAT, transcripts, three letters of recommendation, group interview. Additional exam requirements/recommendations for international students: Required—TOEFL (minimum score 90 iBT), IELTS (minimum score 7). *Application deadline:* For fall admission, 8/1 priority date for domestic students; for spring admission, 1/1 priority date for domestic students; for summer admission, 5/1 priority date for domestic students. Applications are processed on a rolling basis. Application fee: $50. Electronic applications accepted. *Expenses:* $911 per credit hour. *Financial support:* In 2017–18, 29 students received support. Federal Work-Study, scholarships/grants, unspecified assistantships, and tuition waivers (for staff and dependents) available. Support available to part-time students. Financial award applicants required to submit FAFSA. *Faculty research:* Play therapy, trauma, spirituality and wellness in counseling, gatekeeping and supervision in counselor education, reproductive health in counseling, LBGTQ+ issues in counseling. *Unit head:* Dr. Leila Roach, Chair, 386-822-8992. *Application contact:* Jamie Vanderlip, Director of Admissions for Graduate, Transfer and Adult Programs, 386-822-7100, Fax: 386-822-7112, E-mail: jlvander@stetson.edu.

Suffolk University, College of Arts and Sciences, Department of Psychology, Boston, MA 02108-2770. Offers clinical psychology (PhD); college admission counseling (Certificate); mental health counseling (MS); school counseling (MS). *Accreditation:* APA. *Faculty:* 14 full-time (7 women), 3 part-time/adjunct (all women). *Students:* 52 full-time (47 women), 35 part-time (28 women); includes 17 minority (4 Black or African American, non-Hispanic/Latino; 1 Asian, non-Hispanic/Latino; 11 Hispanic/Latino; 1 Two or more races, non-Hispanic/Latino), 7 international. Average age 27. 266 applicants, 23% accepted, 19 enrolled. In 2017, 23 master's, 7 doctorates, 11 other advanced degrees awarded. Terminal master's awarded for partial completion of doctoral program. *Degree requirements:* For master's, practicum, internship; for doctorate, thesis/dissertation, practicum. *Entrance requirements:* For doctorate, GRE General Test or MAT, 2 letters of recommendation, resume. Additional exam requirements/recommendations for international students: Required—TOEFL (minimum score 550 paper-based; 80 iBT). *Application deadline:* For fall admission, 12/1 for domestic and international students. Applications are processed on a rolling basis. Application fee: $50. Electronic applications accepted. *Expenses:* $36,936 per year full-time, $1,539 per credit part-time (for PhD); $15,675 per year full-time, $1,045 per credit part-time (for MS). *Financial support:* In 2017–18, 57 students received support, including 21 fellowships (averaging $17,193 per year); career-related internships or fieldwork, Federal Work-Study, institutionally sponsored loans, scholarships/grants, and unspecified assistantships also available. Support available to part-time students. Financial award application deadline: 4/1; financial award applicants required to submit FAFSA. *Faculty research:* Assessing exposure in the context of a family-based cognitive behavioral treatment for pediatric OCD, a mindfulness approach to designing and testing the efficacy of a new sexual revictimization prevention program for college women, olfaction and decision-making in substance-dependent individuals, the role of experiential avoidance in Generalized Anxiety Disorder, ego development as a predictor of dogmatism and intolerance in the political right and left. *Unit head:* Dr. Amy Marks, Chairperson, 617-573-8017, E-mail: akmarks@suffolk.edu. *Application contact:* Mara Marzocchi, Associate Director of Graduate Admissions, 617-573-8302, Fax: 617-305-1733, E-mail: grad.admission@suffolk.edu.
Website: http://www.suffolk.edu/college/graduate/69299.php

Tarleton State University, College of Graduate Studies, College of Education, Department of Psychological Sciences, Stephenville, TX 76402. Offers applied psychology (MS). *Program availability:* Part-time, evening/weekend. *Faculty:* 4 full-time (2 women). *Students:* 5 full-time (3 women), 8 part-time (all women); includes 4 minority (2 Black or African American, non-Hispanic/Latino; 2 Hispanic/Latino), 1 international. Average age 28. 11 applicants, 82% accepted, 7 enrolled. *Degree requirements:* For master's, comprehensive exam, thesis optional. *Entrance requirements:* For master's, GRE General Test, minimum GPA of 3.0. Additional exam requirements/recommendations for international students: Required—TOEFL (minimum score 550 paper-based; 80 iBT), IELTS (minimum score 6). *Application deadline:* For fall admission, 8/15 priority date for domestic students; for spring admission, 1/7 for domestic students. Applications are processed on a rolling basis. Application fee: $45 ($145 for international students). Electronic applications accepted. *Expenses:* Contact institution. *Financial support:* Research assistantships, teaching assistantships, career-related internships or fieldwork, Federal Work-Study, institutionally sponsored loans, and tuition waivers (partial) available. Support available to part-time students. Financial award application deadline: 5/1; financial award applicants required to submit FAFSA. *Unit head:* Dr. Kimberly Rynearson, Department Head, 254-968-9916, E-mail: rynearson@tarleton.edu. *Application contact:* Information Contact, 254-968-9104, Fax: 254-968-9670, E-mail: gradoffice@tarleton.edu.

Teachers College, Columbia University, Department of Counseling and Clinical Psychology, New York, NY 10027-6696. Offers clinical psychology (PhD); counseling psychology (Ed M, Ed D, PhD); mental health counseling (ME); psychological counseling (ME, ND); psychology in education (MA, ND); school counselor (ME). *Accreditation:* APA (one or more programs are accredited). *Program availability:* Part-time. *Students:* 430 full-time (364 women), 237 part-time (201 women); includes 243 minority (65 Black or African American, non-Hispanic/Latino; 73 Asian, non-Hispanic/Latino; 83 Hispanic/Latino; 22 Two or more races, non-Hispanic/Latino), 142 international. Average age 28. 1,568 applicants, 38% accepted, 292 enrolled. *Unit head:* Prof. George Bonanno, Head, E-mail: gab38@tc.columbia.edu. *Application contact:* David Estrella, Director of Admission, 212-678-3305, E-mail: estrella@tc.columbia.edu.

Temple University, College of Education, Department of Psychological Studies in Education, Philadelphia, PA 19122-6096. Offers applied behavior analysis (MS Ed); counseling psychology (Ed M), including agency counseling, school counseling; educational psychology (Ed M); school psychology (PhD, Ed S). *Accreditation:* APA (one or more programs are accredited). *Program availability:* Part-time, evening/weekend. *Faculty:* 25 full-time (12 women), 23 part-time/adjunct (11 women). *Students:* 255 full-time (191 women), 188 part-time (137 women); includes 136 minority (90 Black or African American, non-Hispanic/Latino; 1 American Indian or Alaska Native, non-Hispanic/Latino; 18 Asian, non-Hispanic/Latino; 14 Hispanic/Latino; 13 Two or more races, non-Hispanic/Latino), 28 international. 376 applicants, 51% accepted, 109 enrolled. In 2017, 129 master's, 27 doctorates, 21 other advanced degrees awarded. Terminal master's awarded for partial completion of doctoral program. *Degree requirements:* For master's, thesis or alternative; for doctorate, thesis/dissertation. *Entrance requirements:* Additional exam requirements/recommendations for international students: Required—TOEFL (minimum score 550 paper-based; 79 iBT). *Application deadline:* For fall admission, 12/15 for international students; for spring admission, 8/1 for international students. Application fee: $60. *Expenses:* Tuition, state resident: full-time $16,164; part-time $898 per credit hour. Tuition, nonresident: full-time $22,158; part-time $1231 per credit hour. *Required fees:* $890; $445 per semester. Full-time tuition and fees vary according to course load, degree level, campus/location and program. *Financial support:* Fellowships, research assistantships with full tuition reimbursements, and teaching assistantships with full tuition reimbursements available. Financial award application deadline: 1/15; financial award applicants required to submit FAFSA. *Unit head:* Dr. Catherine Fiorello, Chair, 215-204-6254, E-mail: catherine.fiorello@temple.edu.
Website: http://education.temple.edu/pse

Tennessee State University, The School of Graduate Studies and Research, College of Education, Department of Psychology, Nashville, TN 37209-1561. Offers counseling psychology (MS). *Entrance requirements:* For master's, GRE General Test or MAT. Electronic applications accepted.

Texas A&M International University, Office of Graduate Studies and Research, College of Arts and Sciences, Department of Psychology and Communication, Laredo, TX 78041. Offers counseling psychology (MACP); psychology (MS). *Degree requirements:* For master's, thesis (for some programs). *Entrance requirements:* For master's, GRE General Test. Additional exam requirements/recommendations for international students: Required—TOEFL (minimum score 550 paper-based; 79 iBT).

Texas A&M University, College of Education and Human Development, Department of Educational Psychology, College Station, TX 77843. Offers bilingual education (M Ed, MS); counseling psychology (PhD); educational psychology (M Ed, MS, PhD); educational technology (M Ed); school psychology (PhD); special education (M Ed, MS). *Accreditation:* APA (one or more programs are accredited). *Program availability:* Part-time, evening/weekend, blended/hybrid learning. *Faculty:* 45. *Students:* 165 full-time (131 women), 248 part-time (210 women); includes 144 minority (24 Black or African American, non-Hispanic/Latino; 3 American Indian or Alaska Native, non-Hispanic/Latino; 21 Asian, non-Hispanic/Latino; 84 Hispanic/Latino; 2 Native Hawaiian or other Pacific Islander, non-Hispanic/Latino; 10 Two or more races, non-Hispanic/Latino), 45 international. Average age 33. 171 applicants, 44% accepted, 47 enrolled. In 2017, 141 master's, 28 doctorates awarded. *Degree requirements:* For master's, thesis optional; for doctorate, thesis/dissertation. *Entrance requirements:* For master's and doctorate, GRE General Test. Additional exam requirements/recommendations for international students: Required—TOEFL (minimum score 550 paper-based; 80 iBT), IELTS (minimum score 6), PTE (minimum score 53). *Application deadline:* For fall admission, 12/1 for domestic students; for spring admission, 10/15 for domestic students. Application fee: $50 ($90 for international students). Electronic applications accepted. *Expenses:* Contact institution. *Financial support:* In 2017–18, 210 students received support, including 4 fellowships with tuition reimbursements available (averaging $24,775 per year), 102 research assistantships with tuition reimbursements available (averaging $10,698 per year), 19 teaching assistantships with tuition reimbursements available (averaging $7,177 per year); career-related internships or fieldwork, institutionally sponsored loans, scholarships/grants, traineeships, health care benefits, tuition waivers (full and partial), and unspecified assistantships also available. Support available to part-time students. Financial award application deadline: 3/15; financial award applicants required to submit FAFSA. *Unit head:* Dr. Victor Willson, Department Head, 979-845-1394, E-mail: v-willson@tamu.edu. *Application contact:* Kristie Stramaski, Senior Academic Advisor, 979-845-1833, E-mail: epsyadvisor@tamu.edu.
Website: http://epsy.tamu.edu

Texas A&M University–Texarkana, Graduate Studies and Research, College of Health and Behavioral Sciences, Texarkana, TX 75503. Offers counseling psychology (MS). *Program availability:* Part-time, evening/weekend. *Degree requirements:* For master's, comprehensive exam (for some programs), thesis or alternative. *Entrance requirements:* For master's, minimum GPA of 3.0 in last 60 hours of bachelor's degree. Additional exam requirements/recommendations for international students: Required—TOEFL. Electronic applications accepted.

Texas Tech University, Graduate School, College of Arts and Sciences, Department of Psychological Sciences, Lubbock, TX 79409-2051. Offers clinical psychology (PhD); counseling psychology (MA, PhD); general experimental psychology (MA, PhD); psychology (MA). *Accreditation:* APA (one or more programs are accredited). *Faculty:* 31 full-time (14 women), 2 part-time/adjunct (both women). *Students:* 126 full-time (75 women), 10 part-time (5 women); includes 33 minority (4 Black or African American, non-Hispanic/Latino; 1 American Indian or Alaska Native, non-Hispanic/Latino; 10 Asian, non-Hispanic/Latino; 17 Hispanic/Latino; 1 Two or more races, non-Hispanic/Latino), 11 international. Average age 27. 278 applicants, 15% accepted, 28 enrolled. In 2017, 17 master's, 7 doctorates awarded. *Degree requirements:* For doctorate, comprehensive exam, thesis/dissertation, 100 credit hours of organized courses, research credits, and practica. *Entrance requirements:* For master's, GRE General Test, GRE Subject Test, essays, letters of recommendation; for doctorate, GRE General Test, essays, letters of recommendation. Additional exam requirements/recommendations for international students: Required—TOEFL (minimum score 550 paper-based; 79 iBT). *Application deadline:* For fall admission, 6/1 priority date for domestic students, 1/15 priority date for international students; for spring admission, 9/1 priority date for domestic students, 6/15 priority date for international students. Applications are processed on a rolling basis. Application fee: $60. Electronic applications accepted. *Expenses:* Contact institution. *Financial support:* In 2017–18, 132 students received support, including 127 fellowships (averaging $2,830 per year), 58 research assistantships (averaging $8,094 per year), 105 teaching assistantships (averaging $11,486 per year); Federal Work-Study, institutionally sponsored loans, health care benefits, and unspecified

assistantships also available. Financial award application deadline: 4/15; financial award applicants required to submit FAFSA. *Faculty research:* Health psychology, addictive behaviors, depression and suicide risk, sexuality/sexual risk behaviors/HIV, neuroscience/neuroimaging, forensic and correctional psychology. *Total annual research expenditures:* $647,634. *Unit head:* Dr. Robert Morgan, Professor and Chair, 806-834-7117, Fax: 806-742-0818, E-mail: robert.morgan@ttu.edu. *Application contact:* Kay Hill, Admissions Coordinator, 806-834-1350, Fax: 806-742-0818, E-mail: kay.hill@ttu.edu.
Website: http://www.depts.ttu.edu/psy/

Texas Woman's University, Graduate School, College of Arts and Sciences, Department of Psychology and Philosophy, Denton, TX 76204. Offers counseling psychology (MA, PhD); psychological science (MS); school psychology (PhD, SSP). *Accreditation:* APA (one or more programs are accredited). *Faculty:* 15 full-time (10 women), 3 part-time/adjunct (2 women). *Students:* 77 full-time (70 women), 41 part-time (37 women); includes 52 minority (13 Black or African American, non-Hispanic/Latino; 11 Asian, non-Hispanic/Latino; 23 Hispanic/Latino; 5 Two or more races, non-Hispanic/Latino). Average age 28. 120 applicants, 21% accepted, 24 enrolled. In 2017, 4 master's, 13 doctorates, 4 other advanced degrees awarded. Terminal master's awarded for partial completion of doctoral program. *Degree requirements:* For master's, comprehensive exam (for some programs), thesis (for some programs), practica (for MA); for doctorate, comprehensive exam, thesis/dissertation, internship, residency; for SSP, comprehensive exam, internship, capstone evaluation. *Entrance requirements:* For master's, GRE (preferred minimum score 153 [500 old version] Verbal, 144 [500 old version] Quantitative, 4.0 Analytical Writing), BA/BS or 18 hours in psychology; minimum GPA of 3.0, 3.5 in psychology classes; 3 letters of reference; curriculum vitae; essay; for doctorate, GRE (preferred minimum score 153 [500 old version] Verbal, 144 [500 old version] Quantitative, 4 Analytical), 3 letters of reference, minimum GPA of 3.0 overall and 3.5 in psychology classes, MA in psychology or related discipline with thesis, curriculum vitae, essays; for SSP, GRE (preferred minimum score 153 [500 old version] Verbal, 144 [500 old version] Quantitative, 4 Analytical), BA/BS or 18 hours in psychology; minimum GPA of 3.0, 3.5 in psychology classes; 3 letters of reference; curriculum vitae; personal essay. Additional exam requirements/recommendations for international students: Required—TOEFL (minimum score 550 paper-based; 79 iBT); Recommended—IELTS (minimum score 6.5), TSE (minimum score 53). *Application deadline:* For fall admission, 2/1 for domestic and international students; for summer admission, 2/1 for domestic and international students. Applications are processed on a rolling basis. Application fee: $50 ($75 for international students). Electronic applications accepted. *Expenses:* $7,520 per year full-time in-state; $16,820 per year full-time out-of-state. *Financial support:* In 2017–18, 74 students received support, including 11 teaching assistantships (averaging $13,010 per year); research assistantships, career-related internships or fieldwork, Federal Work-Study, institutionally sponsored loans, scholarships/grants, traineeships, health care benefits, and unspecified assistantships also available. Support available to part-time students. Financial award application deadline: 3/1; financial award applicants required to submit FAFSA. *Faculty research:* Victimization, body image, moral and political philosophy, neuropsychology and assessment in children, neurobiology of memory and learning. *Total annual research expenditures:* $51,748. *Unit head:* Dr. Shannon Scott, Chair, 940-898-2303, Fax: 940-898-2301, E-mail: psychology@twu.edu. *Application contact:* Korie Hawkins, Associate Director of Admissions, Graduate Recruitment, 940-898-3188, Fax: 940-898-3081, E-mail: admissions@twu.edu.
Website: http://www.twu.edu/psychology-philosophy/

Touro College, School of Health Sciences, Bay Shore, NY 11706. Offers industrial-organizational psychology (MS); mental health counseling (MS); occupational therapy (MS); physical therapy (DPT); physician assistant (MS); speech-language pathology (MS). *Faculty:* 81 full-time (55 women), 77 part-time/adjunct (46 women). *Students:* 628 full-time (470 women), 113 part-time (73 women); includes 143 minority (31 Black or African American, non-Hispanic/Latino; 1 American Indian or Alaska Native, non-Hispanic/Latino; 61 Asian, non-Hispanic/Latino; 42 Hispanic/Latino; 1 Native Hawaiian or other Pacific Islander, non-Hispanic/Latino; 7 Two or more races, non-Hispanic/Latino), 63 international. Average age 28. *Expenses:* Contact institution. *Financial support:* Fellowships available. *Unit head:* Dr. Louis Primavera, Dean, School of Health Sciences, 516-673-3200, E-mail: louis.primavera@touro.edu. *Application contact:* Brian J. Diele, Director of Student Administrative Services, 631-665-1600 Ext. 6311, E-mail: brian.diele@touro.edu.

Towson University, College of Liberal Arts, Program in Psychology, Towson, MD 21252-0001. Offers clinical psychology (MA); counseling psychology (MA); experimental psychology (MA); school psychology (MA). *Program availability:* Part-time, evening/weekend. *Students:* 98 full-time (75 women), 21 part-time (13 women); includes 32 minority (15 Black or African American, non-Hispanic/Latino; 4 Asian, non-Hispanic/Latino; 8 Hispanic/Latino; 5 Two or more races, non-Hispanic/Latino). *Degree requirements:* For master's, thesis (for some programs). *Entrance requirements:* For master's, GRE, minimum GPA of 3.0, letters of recommendation. *Application deadline:* For fall admission, 1/17 for domestic students, 5/15 for international students; for spring admission, 10/15 for domestic students, 12/1 for international students. Applications are processed on a rolling basis. Application fee: $45. Electronic applications accepted. *Expenses:* Tuition, state resident: full-time $7960; part-time $398 per unit. Tuition, nonresident: full-time $16,480; part-time $824 per unit. *Required fees:* $2600; $130 per year. $390 per term. *Financial support:* Application deadline: 4/1. *Unit head:* Dr. Geoffrey Munro, Department Chair, 410-704-2634, E-mail: psycdept@towson.edu. *Application contact:* Coverley Beidleman, Assistant Director of Graduate Admissions, 410-704-5630, Fax: 410-704-3030, E-mail: cbeidleman@towson.edu.
Website: https://www.towson.edu/cla/departments/psychology/grad/

Trinity Christian College, Program in Counseling Psychology, Palos Heights, IL 60463-0929. Offers MA. *Program availability:* Evening/weekend, online learning.

Trinity International University, Trinity Evangelical Divinity School, Deerfield, IL 60015-1284. Offers academic ministry (M Div); Biblical and Near Eastern archaeology and languages (MA); chaplaincy and ministry care (MA); Christian studies (Certificate); church and parachurch ministry (M Div); church history (MA, Th M); counseling (Th M); educational ministries (MA); educational ministry (Th M); educational studies (PhD); intercultural studies (MA, PhD); leadership and management (D Min); mental health counseling (MA); military chaplaincy (D Min); ministry (MA); missions (Th M); missions and evangelism (D Min); New Testament (MA, Th M); Old Testament (Th M); Old Testament and Semitic languages (MA); pastoral ministry and care (D Min); pastoral theology (Th M); preaching and teaching (D Min); spiritual formation and education (D Min); systematic theology (MA, Th M); theological studies (MA, PhD); urban ministry (MA). *Program availability:* Part-time, online learning. *Degree requirements:* For master's, comprehensive exam, thesis, fieldwork; for doctorate, comprehensive exam (for some programs), thesis/dissertation; for Certificate, comprehensive exam, integrative papers. *Entrance requirements:* For master's, GRE, MAT, minimum cumulative undergraduate GPA of 3.0; for doctorate, GRE, minimum cumulative graduate GPA of 3.2; for Certificate, GRE, MAT, minimum undergraduate GPA of 2.5. Additional exam requirements/recommendations for international students: Required—

TOEFL (minimum score 580 paper-based), TWE (minimum score 4). Electronic applications accepted.

Trinity International University, Trinity Graduate School, Deerfield, IL 60015-1284. Offers athletic training (MA); bioethics (MA); counseling psychology (MA); diverse learning (M Ed); leadership (MA); teaching (MA). *Program availability:* Part-time, evening/weekend, online learning. *Degree requirements:* For master's, comprehensive exam. *Entrance requirements:* For master's, GRE General Test or MAT, minimum undergraduate GPA of 3.0. Additional exam requirements/recommendations for international students: Required—TOEFL (minimum score 580 paper-based), TWE (minimum score 4). Electronic applications accepted.

Trinity International University Florida, Graduate School, Davie, FL 33324. Offers MA.

Trinity Washington University, School of Education, Washington, DC 20017-1094. Offers clinical mental health counseling (MA); early childhood education (MAT); educating for change (M Ed); educational administration (MSA); elementary education (MAT); reading (M Ed); school counseling (MA); secondary education (MAT), including English, social studies; special education (MAT). *Accreditation:* NCATE. *Program availability:* Part-time, evening/weekend. *Degree requirements:* For master's, thesis (for some programs), capstone project(s). *Entrance requirements:* For master's, PRAXIS I, minimum GPA of 2.8. Additional exam requirements/recommendations for international students: Required—TOEFL (minimum score 550 paper-based). *Faculty research:* Technology, literacy, special education, organizations, inclusion models.

Trinity Western University, School of Graduate Studies, Program in Counseling Psychology, Langley, BC V2Y 1Y1, Canada. Offers MA. *Accreditation:* ACA. *Program availability:* Part-time. *Degree requirements:* For master's, comprehensive exam, thesis. *Entrance requirements:* For master's, GRE (if out of school for 5 years prior to applying), BA in honors psychology, minimum GPA of 3.0 for 3rd and 4th year of BA. Additional exam requirements/recommendations for international students: Required—TOEFL (minimum score 600 paper-based). *Faculty research:* Meaning, group counseling, trauma, counseling supervision.

Truett McConnell University, The Leonhard Schiemer School of Psychology and Biblical Counseling, Cleveland, GA 30528. Offers professional counseling (MA). *Program availability:* Part-time. *Faculty:* 2 full-time (1 woman). *Students:* 2 full-time (1 woman), 9 part-time (6 women). *Entrance requirements:* For master's, bachelor's degree from accredited institution, minimum GPA of 2.5, interview with faculty, personal statement. *Application deadline:* For fall admission, 8/1 for domestic students; for spring admission, 12/1 for domestic students; for summer admission, 5/1 for domestic students. Applications are processed on a rolling basis. Electronic applications accepted. *Expenses:* Tuition: Part-time $325 per credit hour. *Required fees:* $910 per year. $455 per semester. *Financial support:* Applicants required to submit FAFSA. *Unit head:* Dr. Holly Haynes, Dean, 706-865-2134 Ext. 1604, E-mail: hhaynes@truett.edu. *Application contact:* Jim Dunnington, Coordinator of Online and Graduate Admissions, 706-865-2134 Ext. 2131, E-mail: jdunnington@truett.edu.
Website: https://truett.edu/degrees/master-arts-professional-counseling/

Union College, Graduate Programs, Department of Psychology, Barbourville, KY 40906-1499. Offers clinical psychology (MA); counseling psychology (MA); school psychology (MA).

United States International University–Africa, School of Arts and Sciences, Nairobi, Kenya. Offers counseling psychology (MA), including chemical dependency, health psychology; international relations (MA), including development studies, diplomacy and foreign policy, peace and conflict studies. *Program availability:* Part-time, evening/weekend. *Degree requirements:* For master's, thesis, practicum. *Entrance requirements:* For master's, GRE General Test, 2 letters of recommendation, resume. Additional exam requirements/recommendations for international students: Required—TOEFL. *Faculty research:* Trauma in children, African intellectualism, psychological assessment tools.

Universidad del Turabo, Graduate Programs, School of Social Sciences and Humanities, Programs in Psychology, Program in Counseling Psychology, Gurabo, PR 00778-3030. Offers M Psych, Psy D, Certificate. *Entrance requirements:* For master's, GRE, GMAT or EXADEP, interview, essay, official transcript, recommendation letters. Electronic applications accepted.

Universidad Metropolitana, School of Social Sciences, Humanities and Communications, Program in Counseling Psychology, San Juan, PR 00928-1150. Offers MA.

University at Albany, State University of New York, School of Education, Department of Educational and Counseling Psychology, Albany, NY 12222-0001. Offers counseling psychology (PhD, CAS); mental health counseling (MS). *Program availability:* Part-time, evening/weekend, 100% online. *Faculty:* 22 full-time (12 women), 26 part-time/adjunct (18 women). *Students:* 198 full-time (163 women), 82 part-time (62 women); includes 54 minority (15 Black or African American, non-Hispanic/Latino; 1 American Indian or Alaska Native, non-Hispanic/Latino; 14 Asian, non-Hispanic/Latino; 15 Hispanic/Latino; 9 Two or more races, non-Hispanic/Latino), 23 international. 254 applicants, 57% accepted, 98 enrolled. In 2017, 60 master's, 5 doctorates, 2 other advanced degrees awarded. *Entrance requirements:* For master's, GRE General Test. Additional exam requirements/recommendations for international students: Required—TOEFL (minimum score 550 paper-based). *Application deadline:* For fall admission, 2/15 for domestic and international students. Application fee: $75. Electronic applications accepted. *Expenses:* Tuition, state resident: full-time $10,870; part-time $453 per credit hour. Tuition, nonresident: full-time $22,210; part-time $925 per credit hour. *Required fees:* $84.68 per credit hour. $508.06 per semester. Part-time tuition and fees vary according to course load and program. *Financial support:* Career-related internships or fieldwork available. *Unit head:* Kevin Quinn, Chair, 518-442-5049, E-mail: kquinn@albany.edu.
Website: http://www.albany.edu/counseling_psych/

University at Buffalo, the State University of New York, Graduate School, Graduate School of Education, Department of Counseling, School, and Educational Psychology, Buffalo, NY 14260. Offers applied statistical analysis (Advanced Certificate); counseling/school psychology (PhD); counselor education (PhD); education studies (Ed M); educational psychology (MA, PhD); mental health counseling (MS, Certificate); mindful counseling for wellness and engagement (Advanced Certificate); rehabilitation counseling (MS, Advanced Certificate); school counseling (Ed M, Certificate). *Accreditation:* CORE (one or more programs are accredited). *Program availability:* Part-time, 100% online. *Faculty:* 21 full-time (11 women), 53 part-time/adjunct (41 women). *Students:* 173 full-time (140 women), 138 part-time (116 women); includes 32 minority (25 Black or African American, non-Hispanic/Latino; 2 American Indian or Alaska Native, non-Hispanic/Latino; 2 Asian, non-Hispanic/Latino; 3 Hispanic/Latino), 16 international. Average age 32. 328 applicants, 59% accepted, 143 enrolled. In 2017, 74 master's, 12 doctorates, 39 other advanced degrees awarded. *Degree requirements:* For master's, comprehensive exam (for some programs), thesis (for some programs); for doctorate, comprehensive exam, thesis/dissertation. *Entrance requirements:* For master's, GRE General Test, interview, letters of reference; for doctorate, GRE General Test, interview, letters of reference, writing sample. Additional exam requirements/recommendations for

international students: Required—TOEFL (minimum score 79 iBT). *Application deadline:* For fall admission, 2/1 priority date for domestic and international students. Application fee: $50. Electronic applications accepted. *Financial support:* In 2017–18, 22 fellowships (averaging $7,823 per year), 41 research assistantships with tuition reimbursements (averaging $10,876 per year) were awarded; teaching assistantships, career-related internships or fieldwork, Federal Work-Study, institutionally sponsored loans, scholarships/grants, tuition waivers (full and partial), and unspecified assistantships also available. Financial award application deadline: 2/1; financial award applicants required to submit FAFSA. *Faculty research:* Multicultural counseling, class size effects, good work in counseling, eating disorders, outcome assessment, change agents and therapeutic factors in group counseling. *Total annual research expenditures:* $1.3 million. *Unit head:* Dr. Jeremy Finn, Chair, 716-645-1126, Fax: 716-645-6616, E-mail: finn@buffalo.edu. *Application contact:* Baylee Richards, Recruitment and Student Services Coordinator, 716-645-2110, Fax: 716-645-7937, E-mail: gse-info@buffalo.edu.
Website: http://gse.buffalo.edu/csep

The University of Akron, Graduate School, Buchtel College of Arts and Sciences, Department of Psychology, Program in Counseling Psychology, Akron, OH 44325. Offers MA, PhD. *Accreditation:* APA (one or more programs are accredited). *Students:* 31 full-time (22 women), 17 part-time (13 women); includes 16 minority (12 Black or African American, non-Hispanic/Latino; 3 Hispanic/Latino; 1 Two or more races, non-Hispanic/Latino), 3 international. Average age 29. 53 applicants, 15% accepted, 6 enrolled. In 2017, 9 doctorates awarded. *Degree requirements:* For doctorate, one foreign language, comprehensive exam, thesis/dissertation. *Entrance requirements:* For doctorate, GRE, bachelor's degree in psychology or 30 credits of psychology coursework; current curriculum vitae; declaration of intent outlining goals and interests; three letters of recommendation. Additional exam requirements/recommendations for international students: Required—TOEFL (minimum score 79 iBT), IELTS (minimum score 6.5). *Application deadline:* For fall admission, 12/1 for domestic and international students. Application fee: $45 ($70 for international students). Electronic applications accepted. *Faculty research:* Counseling process and outcome, suicide, diversity issues and counseling psychology (e.g., gender, race, ethnicity, sexual orientation) vocational psychology, assessment. *Unit head:* Dr. Paul Levy, Department Chair, 330-972-8639, E-mail: pelevy@uakron.edu.
Website: http://www.uakron.edu/psychology/academics/cpp/

The University of Akron, Graduate School, College of Health Professions, School of Counseling, Program in Clinical Mental Health Counseling, Akron, OH 44325. Offers MA. *Accreditation:* ACA; NCATE. *Students:* 41 full-time (33 women), 44 part-time (37 women); includes 17 minority (8 Black or African American, non-Hispanic/Latino; 2 Asian, non-Hispanic/Latino; 4 Hispanic/Latino; 3 Two or more races, non-Hispanic/Latino). Average age 29. 44 applicants, 45% accepted, 9 enrolled. In 2017, 20 master's awarded. *Degree requirements:* For master's, comprehensive exam. *Entrance requirements:* For master's, minimum GPA of 2.75, letters of recommendation, interview. Additional exam requirements/recommendations for international students: Required—TOEFL (minimum score 79 iBT), IELTS (minimum score 6.5). *Application deadline:* Applications are processed on a rolling basis. Application fee: $45 ($70 for international students). Electronic applications accepted. *Application contact:* Dr. Robert Schwartz, Program Coordinator, 330-972-8155, E-mail: rcs@uakron.edu.
Website: http://www.uakron.edu/soc/masters/cmhc/index.dot

University of Alberta, Faculty of Graduate Studies and Research, Department of Educational Psychology, Edmonton, AB T6G 2E1, Canada. Offers counseling psychology (M Ed, PhD); educational psychology (M Ed, PhD); instructional technology (M Ed); school counseling (M Ed); school psychology (M Ed, PhD); special education (M Ed, PhD); special education-deafness studies (M Ed); teaching English as a second language (M Ed). *Program availability:* Part-time. *Degree requirements:* For master's, thesis optional; for doctorate, comprehensive exam, thesis/dissertation. *Entrance requirements:* For master's and doctorate, minimum GPA of 3.0. Additional exam requirements/recommendations for international students: Required—TOEFL. *Faculty research:* Human learning, development and assessment.

The University of Arizona, College of Education, Department of Disability and Psychoeducational Studies, Program in Counseling and Mental Health, Tucson, AZ 85721. Offers rehabilitation counseling (MA); school counseling (MA). *Accreditation:* ACA. *Entrance requirements:* Additional exam requirements/recommendations for international students: Required—TOEFL (minimum score 550 paper-based; 80 iBT). *Faculty research:* Further knowledge and understanding of abilities, disabilities, adaptations, interventions, and support systems; preparing professionals to educate and facilitate the development of individuals with disabilities and special abilities; providing leadership at the local, state, national, and international levels.

University of Baltimore, Graduate School, Yale Gordon College of Arts and Sciences, Program in Applied Psychology, Baltimore, MD 21201-5779. Offers counseling psychology (MS). *Program availability:* Part-time, evening/weekend. *Degree requirements:* For master's, thesis optional. *Entrance requirements:* For master's, GRE, minimum GPA of 3.0. Additional exam requirements/recommendations for international students: Required—TOEFL (minimum score 550 paper-based). Electronic applications accepted. *Expenses:* Contact institution. *Faculty research:* Participatory decision-making, counter-productive workplace behavior, organizational consulting, substance abuse treatment, cognitive functioning in head injured.

University of Bridgeport, School of Arts and Sciences, Department of Counseling, Bridgeport, CT 06604. Offers clinical mental health counseling (MS); college student personnel (MS); community counseling (MS); human resource development (MS); human service (MS). *Program availability:* Part-time, evening/weekend. *Degree requirements:* For master's, thesis, project. *Entrance requirements:* Additional exam requirements/recommendations for international students: Recommended—TOEFL (minimum score 550 paper-based; 80 iBT), IELTS (minimum score 6.5). Electronic applications accepted. *Expenses:* Contact institution.

The University of British Columbia, Faculty of Education, Department of Educational and Counseling Psychology, and Special Education, Vancouver, BC V6T 1Z4, Canada. Offers counseling psychology (M Ed, MA, PhD); guidance studies (Diploma); human development, learning and culture (M Ed, MA, PhD); measurement, evaluation, and research methodology (M Ed, MA, PhD); school psychology (M Ed, MA, PhD); special education (M Ed, MA, PhD, Diploma). *Program availability:* Part-time. *Degree requirements:* For master's, thesis (for some programs); for doctorate, comprehensive exam, thesis/dissertation. *Entrance requirements:* For master's, GRE General Test (for MA in counseling psychology); for doctorate, GRE General Test. Additional exam requirements/recommendations for international students: Required—TOEFL. Electronic applications accepted. *Expenses:* Contact institution. *Faculty research:* Women, family, social problems, career transition, stress and coping problems.

University of Calgary, Faculty of Graduate Studies, Werklund School of Education, Division of Applied Psychology, Calgary, AB T2N 1N4, Canada. Offers counseling psychology (M Sc, MC, PhD); school and applied child psychology (M Ed, M Sc, PhD). *Program availability:* Part-time. *Degree requirements:* For master's, thesis (for some programs), final oral exam; for doctorate, thesis/dissertation, candidacy exam, final oral exam. *Entrance requirements:* For master's, minimum GPA of 3.0, 3 letters of reference; for doctorate, minimum GPA of 3.5, 3 letters of reference. *Faculty research:* Counselor education, family life studies, learning and cognition.

University of California, Berkeley, UC Berkeley Extension, Certificate Programs in Behavioral and Health Sciences, Berkeley, CA 94720-1500. Offers alcohol and drug abuse studies (Certificate). *Accreditation:* APA.

University of California, Santa Barbara, Graduate Division, Gevirtz Graduate School of Education, Santa Barbara, CA 93106-9490. Offers counseling, clinical and school psychology (MA, PhD, Credential), including clinical psychology (PhD), counseling psychology (MA, PhD), pupil personnel services (Credential), school psychology (PhD); education (MA, PhD); teacher education (M Ed, Credential), including multiple subject teaching (Credential), single subject teaching (Credential), special education (Credential), teaching (M Ed); MA/PhD. *Accreditation:* APA (one or more programs are accredited). Terminal master's awarded for partial completion of doctoral program. *Degree requirements:* For master's, comprehensive exam (for some programs), thesis (for some programs); for doctorate, comprehensive exam (for some programs), thesis/dissertation. *Entrance requirements:* For master's and doctorate, GRE; for Credential, GRE or MAT, CSET, CBEST. Additional exam requirements/recommendations for international students: Required—TOEFL (minimum score 550 paper-based; 80 iBT), IELTS (minimum score 7). Electronic applications accepted. *Faculty research:* Needs of diverse students, school accountability and leadership, school violence, language learning and literacy, science/math education.

University of Central Arkansas, Graduate School, College of Health and Behavioral Sciences, Department of Counseling and Psychology, Program in Counseling Psychology, Conway, AR 72035-0001. Offers MS. *Degree requirements:* For master's, comprehensive exam, thesis optional. *Entrance requirements:* For master's, GRE General Test, minimum GPA of 2.7. Additional exam requirements/recommendations for international students: Required—TOEFL (minimum score 550 paper-based). Electronic applications accepted.

University of Central Missouri, The Graduate School, Warrensburg, MO 64093. Offers accountancy (MA); accounting (MBA); applied mathematics (MS); aviation safety (MA); biology (MS); business administration (MBA); career and technical education leadership (MS); college student personnel administration (MS); communication (MA); computer science (MS); counseling (MS); criminal justice (MS); educational leadership (Ed D); educational technology (MS); elementary and early childhood education (MSE); English (MA); environmental studies (MA); finance (MBA); history (MA); human services/educational technology (Ed S); human services/learning resources (Ed S); human services/professional counseling (Ed S); industrial hygiene (MS); industrial management (MS); information systems (MBA); information technology (MS); kinesiology (MS); library science and information services (MS); literacy education (MSE); marketing (MBA); mathematics (MS); music (MA); occupational safety management (MS); psychology (MS); rural family nursing (MS); school administration (MSE); social gerontology (MS); sociology (MA); special education (MSE); speech language pathology (MS); superintendency (Ed S); teaching (MAT); teaching English as a second language (MA); technology (MS); technology management (PhD); theatre (MA). *Program availability:* Part-time, 100% online, blended/hybrid learning. *Faculty:* 337 full-time (145 women), 41 part-time/adjunct (28 women). *Students:* 785 full-time (398 women), 1,633 part-time (1,063 women); includes 231 minority (102 Black or African American, non-Hispanic/Latino; 4 American Indian or Alaska Native, non-Hispanic/Latino; 16 Asian, non-Hispanic/Latino; 52 Hispanic/Latino; 57 Two or more races, non-Hispanic/Latino), 692 international. Average age 30. In 2017, 2,605 master's, 122 other advanced degrees awarded. *Degree requirements:* For master's and Ed S, comprehensive exam (for some programs), thesis (for some programs). *Entrance requirements:* Additional exam requirements/recommendations for international students: Required—TOEFL (minimum score 550 paper-based; 79 iBT). *Application deadline:* For fall admission, 6/1 priority date for domestic and international students; for spring admission, 10/1 priority date for domestic and international students; for summer admission, 4/1 priority date for domestic and international students. Applications are processed on a rolling basis. Application fee: $30 ($75 for international students). Electronic applications accepted. *Expenses:* Tuition, state resident: full-time $8771; part-time $292.35 per credit hour. Tuition, nonresident: full-time $17,541; part-time $584.70 per credit hour. *Required fees:* $372; $24.78 per credit hour. *Financial support:* In 2017–18, 99 students received support. Research assistantships, teaching assistantships, career-related internships or fieldwork, Federal Work-Study, scholarships/grants, and administrative and laboratory assistantships available. Support available to part-time students. Financial award application deadline: 3/1; financial award applicants required to submit FAFSA. *Unit head:* Shellie Hewitt, Director of Graduate and International Student Services, 660-543-4621, Fax: 660-543-4778, E-mail: hewitt@ucmo.edu. *Application contact:* 660-543-4621, E-mail: admit_intl@ucmo.edu.
Website: http://www.ucmo.edu/graduate/

University of Central Oklahoma, The Jackson College of Graduate Studies, College of Education and Professional Studies, Department of Psychology, Edmond, OK 73034-5209. Offers psychology (MA), including counseling psychology, experimental psychology, forensic psychology, general psychology, school psychology. *Faculty:* 13 full-time (7 women), 1 part-time/adjunct (0 women). *Students:* 74 full-time (59 women), 35 part-time (29 women); includes 30 minority (4 Black or African American, non-Hispanic/Latino; 4 American Indian or Alaska Native, non-Hispanic/Latino; 3 Asian, non-Hispanic/Latino; 12 Hispanic/Latino; 7 Two or more races, non-Hispanic/Latino), 5 international. Average age 27. 109 applicants, 71% accepted, 51 enrolled. In 2017, 33 master's awarded. *Degree requirements:* For master's, thesis (for some programs). *Entrance requirements:* For master's, GRE. Additional exam requirements/recommendations for international students: Required—TOEFL (minimum score 550 paper-based; 79 iBT), IELTS (minimum score 6.5). *Application deadline:* For fall admission, 1/15 for domestic and international students; for spring admission, 11/15 for international students. Application fee: $60. Electronic applications accepted. *Expenses:* Tuition, state resident: full-time $5375; part-time $268.75 per credit hour. Tuition, nonresident: full-time $13,295; part-time $664.75 per credit hour. *Required fees:* $626; $31.30 per credit hour. One-time fee: $50. Tuition and fees vary according to program. *Financial support:* In 2017–18, 18 students received support, including 6 research assistantships with partial tuition reimbursements available (averaging $3,943 per year); teaching assistantships, career-related internships or fieldwork, scholarships/grants, tuition waivers (partial), and unspecified assistantships also available. Financial award application deadline: 3/31; financial award applicants required to submit FAFSA. *Unit head:* Dr. Thomas Hancock, Chair, 405-974-5707, Fax: 405-974-3865. *Application contact:* Carlie Wellington, Assistant Director, CEPS Graduate Enrollment, 405-974-5105, Fax: 405-974-3851, E-mail: gradcoll@uco.edu.
Website: http://sites.uco.edu/ceps/dept/Professional-Studies-Programs/psy/index.asp

University of Colorado Denver, School of Education and Human Development, Program in Counseling Psychology and Counselor Education, Denver, CO 80217. Offers counseling (MA), including clinical mental health counseling, couple and family counseling, multicultural counseling, school counseling; school counseling (MA). *Accreditation:* ACA; NCATE. *Program availability:* Part-time, evening/weekend. *Degree requirements:* For master's, comprehensive exam (for some programs), thesis or

alternative, 63-66 hours. *Entrance requirements:* For master's, GRE or MAT (unless applicant already holds a graduate degree), letters of recommendation, interview, resume, transcripts from all colleges/universities attended. Additional exam requirements/recommendations for international students: Required—TOEFL (minimum score 525 paper-based; 71 iBT); Recommended—IELTS (minimum score 6.3). Electronic applications accepted. *Expenses:* Contact institution. *Faculty research:* Spiritual issues in counseling, multicultural and diversity issues in counseling, adolescent suicide, career development.

University of Connecticut, Graduate School, Neag School of Education, Department of Educational Psychology, Program in Counseling Psychology, Storrs, CT 06269. Offers counseling psychology (PhD); school counseling (MA). *Accreditation:* ACA. Terminal master's awarded for partial completion of doctoral program. *Degree requirements:* For master's, comprehensive exam, thesis or alternative; for doctorate, thesis/dissertation. *Entrance requirements:* For doctorate, GRE General Test. Additional exam requirements/recommendations for international students: Required—TOEFL (minimum score 550 paper-based). Electronic applications accepted.

University of Dayton, Department of Counselor Education and Human Services, Dayton, OH 45469. Offers clinical mental health counseling (MS Ed); college student personnel (MS Ed); higher education administration (MS Ed); human services (MS Ed); school counseling (MS Ed); school psychology (MS Ed, Ed S). *Accreditation:* ACA; NCATE. *Program availability:* Part-time. *Faculty:* 11 full-time (6 women), 34 part-time/ adjunct (24 women). *Students:* 194 full-time (153 women), 83 part-time (68 women); includes 58 minority (37 Black or African American, non-Hispanic/Latino; 2 Asian, non-Hispanic/Latino; 9 Hispanic/Latino; 10 Two or more races, non-Hispanic/Latino), 3 international. Average age 30. 426 applicants, 28% accepted. In 2017, 107 master's, 6 Ed Ss awarded. *Degree requirements:* For master's, thesis (for some programs); for Ed S, thesis (for some programs), professional portfolio. *Entrance requirements:* For master's, MAT or GRE (if GPA less than 2.75), essays (for some programs). Additional exam requirements/recommendations for international students: Required—TOEFL (minimum score 550 paper-based; 80 iBT). *Application deadline:* For fall admission, 1/10 priority date for domestic and international students; for spring admission, 9/10 priority date for domestic and international students; for summer admission, 11/10 priority date for domestic and international students. Application fee: $0 ($50 for international students). Electronic applications accepted. *Expenses:* Contact institution. *Financial support:* In 2017–18, 5 research assistantships with partial tuition reimbursements (averaging $9,950 per year) were awarded; career-related internships or fieldwork, institutionally sponsored loans, and unspecified assistantships also available. Financial award application deadline: 3/1; financial award applicants required to submit FAFSA. *Faculty research:* Student school bonding, traumatic brain injuries, wellness and counseling, creativity in education. *Unit head:* Dr. Alan Demmitt, Chair, 937-229-3644, Fax: 937-229-1055, E-mail: ademmitt1@udayton.edu. *Application contact:* Kathleen Brown, Administrative Assistant, 937-229-3644, Fax: 937-229-1055, E-mail: kbrown1@udayton.edu.
Website: https://www.udayton.edu/education/departments_and_programs/edc/

University of Denver, Morgridge College of Education, Denver, CO 80208. Offers child, family and school psychology (MA, PhD, Ed S); counseling psychology (MA, PhD); curriculum and instruction (MA, Ed D, PhD); curriculum instruction and teaching (Certificate); early childhood special education (MA, Certificate); educational leadership and policy studies (MA, Ed D, PhD, Certificate); higher education (Ed D, PhD); library and information science (MLIS); research methods and statistics (MA, PhD). *Accreditation:* ALA; APA (one or more programs are accredited). *Program availability:* Part-time, evening/weekend, online learning. *Faculty:* 39 full-time (29 women), 60 part-time/adjunct (42 women). *Students:* 502 full-time (406 women), 361 part-time (267 women); includes 233 minority (54 Black or African American, non-Hispanic/Latino; 6 American Indian or Alaska Native, non-Hispanic/Latino; 25 Asian, non-Hispanic/Latino; 113 Hispanic/Latino; 35 Two or more races, non-Hispanic/Latino), 52 international. Average age 31. 1,167 applicants, 64% accepted, 415 enrolled. In 2017, 285 master's, 51 doctorates, 157 other advanced degrees awarded. Terminal master's awarded for partial completion of doctoral program. *Degree requirements:* For master's, comprehensive exam; for doctorate, 2 foreign languages, comprehensive exam, thesis/ dissertation. *Entrance requirements:* For master's and doctorate, GRE General Test or GMAT. Additional exam requirements/recommendations for international students: Required—TOEFL (minimum score 550 paper-based; 80 iBT). *Application deadline:* Applications are processed on a rolling basis. Application fee: $65. Electronic applications accepted. *Expenses:* $31,935 per year full-time. *Financial support:* In 2017–18, 765 students received support, including 26 research assistantships with tuition reimbursements available (averaging $10,957 per year), 38 teaching assistantships with tuition reimbursements available (averaging $3,391 per year); career-related internships or fieldwork, Federal Work-Study, institutionally sponsored loans, scholarships/grants, and unspecified assistantships also available. Support available to part-time students. Financial award application deadline: 2/15; financial award applicants required to submit FAFSA. *Faculty research:* Early childhood education, educational leadership, access and opportunity to postsecondary education, marriage and family therapy, data management and archival research. *Unit head:* Dr. Karen Riley, Dean, 303-871-3665, Fax: 303-871-4456, E-mail: karen.riley@du.edu. *Application contact:* Jodi Dye, Director of Admissions, 303-871-2510, Fax: 303-871-4456, E-mail: jodi.dye@du.edu.
Website: http://morgridge.du.edu

University of Florida, Graduate School, College of Liberal Arts and Sciences, Department of Psychology, Gainesville, FL 32611. Offers counseling psychology (PhD); psychology (MA, MS, PhD), including psychology (PhD), women's and gender studies (PhD); JD/PhD. *Degree requirements:* For master's, comprehensive exam, thesis or alternative; for doctorate, comprehensive exam, thesis/dissertation. *Entrance requirements:* For master's and doctorate, GRE General Test, minimum GPA of 3.0. Additional exam requirements/recommendations for international students: Required—TOEFL (minimum score 550 paper-based; 80 iBT), IELTS (minimum score 6). Electronic applications accepted. *Faculty research:* Behavior analysis, behavioral and cognitive neuroscience, counseling, developmental psychology, social psychology.

University of Hawaii at Hilo, Program in Counseling Psychology, Hilo, HI 96720-4091. Offers MA. *Entrance requirements:* Additional exam requirements/recommendations for international students: Required—TOEFL, IELTS.

University of Houston, College of Education, Department of Educational Psychology, Houston, TX 77204. Offers administration and supervision - higher education (M Ed); counseling (M Ed); counseling psychology (PhD); educational psychology (M Ed); school psychology (PhD); school psychology and individual differences (PhD); special education (M Ed). *Accreditation:* NCATE. *Program availability:* Part-time, evening/ weekend, online learning. *Degree requirements:* For master's, comprehensive exam or thesis; for doctorate, comprehensive exam, thesis/dissertation. *Entrance requirements:* For master's, GRE, transcripts, 3 letters of recommendation, curriculum vita, goal statement; for doctorate, GRE, transcripts, 3 letters of recommendation, curriculum vita, goal statement, writing sample, interview. Additional exam requirements/ recommendations for international students: Required—TOEFL (minimum score 550 paper-based; 79 iBT), IELTS (minimum score 6.5). Electronic applications accepted.

Faculty research: Evidence-based assessment and intervention, multicultural issues in psychology, social and cultural context of learning, systemic barriers to college, motivational aspects of self-regulated learning.

University of Houston–Victoria, School of Arts and Sciences, Program in Psychology, Victoria, TX 77901-4450. Offers counseling psychology (MA); forensic psychology (MA); school psychology (MA). *Program availability:* Part-time, evening/weekend, online learning. *Degree requirements:* For master's, project or thesis. *Entrance requirements:* For master's, GRE General Test. Additional exam requirements/recommendations for international students: Required—TOEFL (minimum score 550 paper-based). Electronic applications accepted.

University of Indianapolis, Graduate Programs, School of Psychological Sciences, Indianapolis, IN 46227-3697. Offers clinical psychology (Psy D); clinical psychology/ mental health counseling (MA). *Accreditation:* APA. *Degree requirements:* For master's, practicum; for doctorate, comprehensive exam, thesis/dissertation, 1200 hours of clinical practicum, 2000-hour internship. *Entrance requirements:* For master's, GRE, 3 letters of recommendation; for doctorate, GRE, minimum GPA of 3.0, 18 hours of course work in psychology, 3 letters of recommendation. Additional exam requirements/ recommendations for international students: Required—TOEFL (minimum score 550 paper-based).

The University of Iowa, Graduate College, College of Education, Department of Psychological and Quantitative Foundations, Iowa City, IA 52242-1316. Offers counseling psychology (PhD); educational measurement and statistics (MA, PhD); educational psychology (MA, PhD); school psychology (PhD, Ed S). *Accreditation:* APA. *Degree requirements:* For master's, thesis optional, exam; for doctorate, comprehensive exam, thesis/dissertation; for Ed S, exam. *Entrance requirements:* For master's, doctorate, and Ed S, GRE General Test, minimum GPA of 3.0. Additional exam requirements/recommendations for international students: Required—TOEFL (minimum score 550 paper-based; 81 iBT). Electronic applications accepted.

The University of Iowa, Graduate College, College of Education, Department of Rehabilitation and Counselor Education, Iowa City, IA 52242-1316. Offers counselor education and supervision (PhD); couple and family therapy (PhD); rehabilitation and mental health counseling (MA); rehabilitation counselor education (PhD); school counseling (MA). *Accreditation:* ACA (one or more programs are accredited); CORE (one or more programs are accredited). *Degree requirements:* For master's, thesis optional, exam; for doctorate, comprehensive exam, thesis/dissertation. *Entrance requirements:* For master's and doctorate, GRE General Test, minimum GPA of 3.0. Additional exam requirements/recommendations for international students: Required—TOEFL (minimum score 550 paper-based; 81 iBT). Electronic applications accepted.

The University of Kansas, Graduate Studies, School of Education, Department of Educational Psychology, Program in Counseling Psychology, Lawrence, KS 66045. Offers MS, PhD. *Accreditation:* APA (one or more programs are accredited). *Program availability:* Part-time. *Students:* 58 full-time (41 women), 3 part-time (all women); includes 10 minority (4 Black or African American, non-Hispanic/Latino; 3 Hispanic/ Latino; 3 Two or more races, non-Hispanic/Latino), 4 international. Average age 28. 88 applicants, 31% accepted, 16 enrolled. In 2017, 11 master's, 8 doctorates awarded. *Entrance requirements:* For master's and doctorate, GRE General Test, minimum GPA of 3.0, resume, statement of purpose, official transcript, three letters of recommendation. *Application deadline:* For fall admission, 12/1 priority date for domestic and international students. Application fee: $65 ($85 for international students). Electronic applications accepted. *Financial support:* Fellowships, research assistantships, teaching assistantships, career-related internships or fieldwork, scholarships/grants, and unspecified assistantships available. Financial award application deadline: 12/1. *Faculty research:* Career development, assessment and intervention, multi-cultural counseling, counselor training, positive psychology. *Unit head:* Dr. Changming Duan, Director of Counseling Psychology, 785-864-2426, E-mail: duanc@ku.edu. *Application contact:* Penny Fritts, Graduate Admissions Contact, 785-864-9645, E-mail: fritts@ku.edu.
Website: http://pre.soe.ku.edu/academics/cpsy/masters

University of Kentucky, Graduate School, College of Education, Program in Educational and Counseling Psychology, Lexington, KY 40506-0032. Offers counseling psychology (MS, PhD, Ed S); educational psychology (MS, PhD); school psychology (PhD, Ed S). *Accreditation:* APA (one or more programs are accredited); NCATE. *Degree requirements:* For doctorate, comprehensive exam, thesis/dissertation; for Ed S, comprehensive exam. *Entrance requirements:* For doctorate, GRE General Test, minimum graduate GPA of 3.0; for Ed S, GRE General Test. Additional exam requirements/recommendations for international students: Required—TOEFL (minimum score 550 paper-based). Electronic applications accepted.

University of Lethbridge, School of Graduate Studies, Lethbridge, AB T1K 3M4, Canada. Offers addictions counseling (M Sc); agricultural biotechnology (M Sc); agricultural studies (M Sc, MA); anthropology (MA); archaeology (M Sc, MA); art (MA, MFA); biochemistry (M Sc); biological sciences (M Sc); biomolecular science (PhD); biosystems and biodiversity (PhD); Canadian studies (MA); chemistry (M Sc); computer science (M Sc); computer science and geographical information science (M Sc); counseling (MC); counseling psychology (M Ed); dramatic arts (MA); earth, space, and physical science (PhD); economics (MA); education (MA, PhD); educational leadership (M Ed); English (MA); environmental science (M Sc); evolution and behavior (PhD); exercise science (M Sc); French (MA); French/German (MA); French/Spanish (MA); general education (M Ed); geography (M Sc, MA); German (MA); health sciences (M Sc); individualized multidisciplinary (M Sc, MA); kinesiology (M Sc, MA); management (M Sc), including accounting, finance, human resource management and labor relations, information systems, international management, marketing, policy and strategy; mathematics (M Sc); music (M Mus, MA); Native American studies (MA); neuroscience (M Sc, PhD); new media (MA, MFA); nursing (M Sc, MN); philosophy (MA); physics (M Sc); political science (MA); psychology (M Sc, MA); religious studies (MA); sociology (MA); theatre and dramatic arts (MFA); theoretical and computational science (PhD); urban and regional studies (MA); women and gender studies (MA). *Program availability:* Part-time, evening/weekend. *Degree requirements:* For master's, thesis (for some programs); for doctorate, comprehensive exam, thesis/dissertation. *Entrance requirements:* For master's, GMAT (for M Sc in management), bachelor's degree in related field, minimum GPA of 3.0 during previous 20 graded semester courses, 2 years' teaching or related experience (M Ed); for doctorate, master's degree, minimum graduate GPA of 3.5. Additional exam requirements/recommendations for international students: Required—TOEFL (minimum score 580 paper-based; 93 iBT). Electronic applications accepted. *Faculty research:* Movement and brain plasticity, gibberellin physiology, photosynthesis, carbon cycling, molecular properties of main-group ring components.

University of Louisiana at Monroe, Graduate School, College of Health and Pharmaceutical Sciences, Programs in Counseling Studies, Monroe, LA 71209-0001. Offers clinical mental health counseling (MS); school counseling (MS). *Accreditation:* ACA; NCATE. *Program availability:* Part-time, evening/weekend, online learning. *Faculty:* 3 full-time (all women). *Students:* 34 full-time (28 women), 8 part-time (7 women); includes 14 minority (12 Black or African American, non-Hispanic/Latino; 1 Asian, non-Hispanic/Latino; 1 Hispanic/Latino). Average age 32. 18 applicants, 94%

accepted, 13 enrolled. In 2017, 19 master's awarded. *Degree requirements:* For master's, comprehensive exam, thesis. *Entrance requirements:* For master's, GRE General Test, minimum GPA of 2.8 in last 60 hours. Additional exam requirements/recommendations for international students: Required—TOEFL (minimum score 500 paper-based; 61 iBT). *Application deadline:* For fall admission, 8/24 priority date for domestic students, 7/1 for international students; for winter admission, 12/14 priority date for domestic students; for spring admission, 1/19 for domestic students, 11/1 for international students. Applications are processed on a rolling basis. Application fee: $20 ($30 for international students). Electronic applications accepted. *Expenses:* Tuition, state resident: full-time $6489; part-time $479 per hour. Tuition, nonresident: full-time $12,100; part-time $479 per hour. *Required fees:* $8860; $802 per hour. $3273 per semester. *Financial support:* In 2017–18, 9 students received support. Career-related internships or fieldwork, Federal Work-Study, and unspecified assistantships available. Financial award application deadline: 4/1; financial award applicants required to submit FAFSA. *Unit head:* Dr. David Hale, Director, 318-342-1349, E-mail: dhale@ulm.edu.
Website: http://www.ulm.edu/counseling/

University of Louisville, Graduate School, College of Education and Human Development, Department of Counseling and Human Development, Louisville, KY 40292-0001. Offers counseling and personnel services (M Ed, PhD), including art therapy (M Ed), clinical mental health counseling (M Ed), college student personnel, counseling psychology, counselor education and supervision (PhD), educational psychology, measurement, and evaluation (PhD), school counseling (M Ed). *Accreditation:* APA; NCATE. *Program availability:* Part-time, evening/weekend. *Students:* 144 full-time (107 women), 63 part-time (44 women); includes 49 minority (32 Black or African American, non-Hispanic/Latino; 1 American Indian or Alaska Native, non-Hispanic/Latino; 3 Asian, non-Hispanic/Latino; 7 Hispanic/Latino; 6 Two or more races, non-Hispanic/Latino), 3 international. Average age 28. 178 applicants, 49% accepted, 51 enrolled. In 2017, 35 master's, 3 doctorates awarded. *Degree requirements:* For doctorate, comprehensive exam, thesis/dissertation. *Entrance requirements:* For master's and doctorate, GRE General Test. Application fee: $65. *Expenses:* Tuition, state resident: full-time $12,246; part-time $681 per credit hour. Tuition, nonresident: full-time $25,486; part-time $1417 per credit hour. *Required fees:* $196. Tuition and fees vary according to course load, program and reciprocity agreements. *Financial support:* Fellowships, research assistantships, teaching assistantships, career-related internships or fieldwork, Federal Work-Study, scholarships/grants, health care benefits, and unspecified assistantships available. Financial award application deadline: 6/1; financial award applicants required to submit FAFSA. *Faculty research:* Mental health services and under-served populations; health disparities and outcomes; well-being identity development; measurement and evaluation. *Total annual research expenditures:* $295,684. *Unit head:* Dr. Mark M. Leach, Interim Chair/Professor, 502-852-0588, Fax: 502-852-0629, E-mail: m.leach@louisville.edu. *Application contact:* Betty Hampton, Director of Graduate Student Services, 502-852-5597, Fax: 502-852-1465, E-mail: edadvise@louisville.edu.
Website: http://www.louisville.edu/education/departments/ecpy

University of Lynchburg, Graduate Studies, M Ed Program in Clinical Mental Health Counseling, Lynchburg, VA 24501-3199. Offers M Ed. *Accreditation:* ACA. *Program availability:* Part-time, evening/weekend. *Faculty:* 17 full-time (10 women). *Students:* 31 full-time (27 women), 15 part-time (12 women); includes 6 minority (3 Black or African American, non-Hispanic/Latino; 1 Asian, non-Hispanic/Latino; 1 Hispanic/Latino; 1 Two or more races, non-Hispanic/Latino), 2 international. Average age 27. 24 applicants, 100% accepted, 10 enrolled. In 2017, 7 master's awarded. *Degree requirements:* For master's, counseling internship. *Entrance requirements:* For master's, GRE, minimum GPA of 3.0 (preferred), official transcripts (bachelor's, others as relevant), three letters of recommendation, career goals statement, personal interview. Additional exam requirements/recommendations for international students: Required—TOEFL (minimum score 550 paper-based; 80 iBT), IELTS (minimum score 6). *Application deadline:* For fall admission, 7/31 for domestic students, 6/1 for international students; for spring admission, 11/30 for domestic students, 10/15 for international students. Applications are processed on a rolling basis. Application fee: $30. Electronic applications accepted. Application fee is waived when completed online. *Expenses:* $510 per credit hour tuition, $100 fees. *Financial support:* Federal Work-Study, scholarships/grants, health care benefits, and unspecified assistantships available. Support available to part-time students. Financial award application deadline: 7/31; financial award applicants required to submit FAFSA. *Unit head:* Dr. Karena Heyward, Assistant Professor and Program Director, 434-544-8067, E-mail: heyward.k@lynchburg.edu. *Application contact:* Ellen Thompson, Graduate Admissions Counselor, 434-544-8841, E-mail: thompson_e@lynchburg.edu.
Website: http://www.lynchburg.edu/graduate/master-of-education-in-counselor-education/clinical-mental-health-counseling/

The University of Manchester, School of Education, Manchester, United Kingdom. Offers counseling (D Couns); counseling psychology (D Couns); education (M Phil, Ed D, PhD); educational and child psychology (Ed D); educational psychology (Ed D).

University of Mary Hardin-Baylor, Graduate Studies in Counseling, Belton, TX 76513. Offers clinical and mental health counseling (MA); marriage, family and child counseling (MA); non-clinical professional studies (MA). *Accreditation:* ACA. *Program availability:* Part-time, evening/weekend. *Faculty:* 7 full-time (4 women), 1 part-time/adjunct (0 women). *Students:* 74 full-time (58 women), 13 part-time (8 women); includes 44 minority (23 Black or African American, non-Hispanic/Latino; 18 Hispanic/Latino; 3 Two or more races, non-Hispanic/Latino). Average age 32. 54 applicants, 65% accepted, 29 enrolled. In 2017, 27 master's awarded. *Degree requirements:* For master's, comprehensive exam. *Entrance requirements:* For master's, GRE General Test with minimum cumulative score of 300 on verbal and quantitative portions and 3.0 on analytical section (if overall undergraduate GPA is below a 3.0), minimum cumulative undergraduate GPA of 2.75 or 3.0 on last 60 hours of course work; three letters of recommendation; interview with departmental graduate admissions committee. Additional exam requirements/recommendations for international students: Required—TOEFL (minimum score 60 iBT), IELTS (minimum score 4.5). *Application deadline:* For fall admission, 6/1 for domestic students, 4/30 priority date for international students; for spring admission, 11/1 for domestic students, 9/30 priority date for international students. Applications are processed on a rolling basis. Application fee: $35 ($135 for international students). Electronic applications accepted. *Expenses:* *Tuition:* Full-time $15,570; part-time $10,380 per credit hour. *Required fees:* $1350; $75 per credit hour. $50 per term. Tuition and fees vary according to course load and degree level. *Financial support:* In 2017–18, 55 students received support. Federal Work-Study, unspecified assistantships, and scholarships for some active duty military personnel available. Support available to part-time students. Financial award applicants required to submit FAFSA. *Faculty research:* Teaching mindfulness skills as part of an interdisciplinary training protocol for doctor of physical therapy students; using symbolic art cards and oracle cards in supervision as a method for teaching appropriate self-disclosure, clinical reflection and counselor development reflection; understanding integral breath therapy. *Unit head:* Dr. Dan Williamson, Director, Graduate Counseling, 254-295-5018, E-mail: dwilliamson@umhb.edu. *Application contact:* Sharon Aguilera, Assistant Director, Graduate Admissions, 254-295-4835, E-mail: saguilera@umhb.edu.
Website: https://go.umhb.edu/graduate/counseling/home

University of Maryland, College Park, Academic Affairs, College of Education, Department of Counseling, Higher Education and Special Education, College Park, MD 20742. Offers college student personnel (M Ed, MA); college student personnel administration (PhD); community counseling (CAGS); community/career counseling (M Ed, MA); counseling and personnel services (M Ed, MA, PhD), including art therapy (M Ed), college student personnel (M Ed), counseling and personnel services (PhD), counseling psychology (M Ed), mental health counseling (M Ed), school counseling (M Ed); counseling psychology (PhD); counselor education (PhD); rehabilitation counseling (M Ed, MA, AGSC); school counseling (M Ed, MA); school psychology (M Ed, MA, PhD). *Accreditation:* APA (one or more programs are accredited); NCATE. *Program availability:* Part-time, evening/weekend, online learning. *Degree requirements:* For master's, thesis (for some programs); for doctorate, thesis/dissertation. *Entrance requirements:* For master's, GRE General Test or MAT, minimum GPA of 3.0, 3 letters of recommendation; for doctorate, GRE General Test or MAT, minimum GPA of 3.5, 3 letters of recommendation. Additional exam requirements/recommendations for international students: Required—TOEFL. Electronic applications accepted. *Faculty research:* Educational psychology, counseling, health.

University of Massachusetts Boston, College of Education and Human Development, Program in Counseling and School Psychology, Boston, MA 02125-3393. Offers PhD. *Accreditation:* ACA; CORE. *Program availability:* Part-time, evening/weekend. *Faculty:* 19 full-time (11 women), 8 part-time/adjunct (4 women). *Students:* 39 full-time (34 women), 1 (woman) part-time; includes 8 minority (3 Black or African American, non-Hispanic/Latino; 3 Hispanic/Latino; 2 Two or more races, non-Hispanic/Latino), 3 international. Average age 29. 91 applicants, 20% accepted, 9 enrolled. *Application deadline:* For fall admission, 12/1 for domestic students. *Expenses:* Tuition, state resident: full-time $17,375. Tuition, nonresident: full-time $33,915. *Required fees:* $355. *Financial support:* Research assistantships, teaching assistantships, career-related internships or fieldwork, Federal Work-Study, and unspecified assistantships available. Support available to part-time students. Financial award application deadline: 3/1; financial award applicants required to submit FAFSA. *Faculty research:* Persuasion and power in the counseling process, self-efficacy for counselors and clients, career and biracial issues in family therapy. *Unit head:* Dr. Melissa Pearrow, 617-287-5000. *Application contact:* Graduate Admissions Coordinator, 617-287-6400, Fax: 617-287-6236, E-mail: bos.gadm@dpc.umassp.edu.

University of Massachusetts Boston, College of Education and Human Development, Program in Mental Health Counseling, Boston, MA 02125-3393. Offers MS. *Students:* 64 full-time (52 women), 37 part-time (29 women); includes 20 minority (5 Black or African American, non-Hispanic/Latino; 4 Asian, non-Hispanic/Latino; 9 Hispanic/Latino; 2 Two or more races, non-Hispanic/Latino), 5 international. Average age 34. 141 applicants, 50% accepted, 40 enrolled. In 2017, 41 master's awarded. *Expenses:* Tuition, state resident: full-time $17,375. Tuition, nonresident: full-time $33,915. *Required fees:* $355. *Financial support:* Research assistantships available. *Unit head:* Dr. Boaz Levy, Director, 617-287-7409. *Application contact:* Graduate Admissions Coordinator, 617-287-6400, Fax: 617-287-6236, E-mail: bos.gadm@dpc.umassp.edu.

University of Memphis, Graduate School, College of Education, Department of Counseling, Educational Psychology and Research, Memphis, TN 38152. Offers counseling (MS, Ed D), including clinical mental health counseling (MS), clinical rehabilitation counseling (MS), rehabilitation counseling (MS), school counseling (MS); counseling psychology (PhD); educational psychology and research (MS, PhD), including educational psychology, educational research. *Accreditation:* ACA (one or more programs are accredited); APA (one or more programs are accredited); CORE (one or more programs are accredited); NCATE. *Program availability:* Blended/hybrid learning. *Faculty:* 26 full-time (17 women), 8 part-time/adjunct (5 women). *Students:* 132 full-time (111 women), 87 part-time (66 women); includes 71 minority (51 Black or African American, non-Hispanic/Latino; 4 Asian, non-Hispanic/Latino; 10 Hispanic/Latino; 6 Two or more races, non-Hispanic/Latino), 5 international. Average age 31. 146 applicants, 49% accepted, 49 enrolled. In 2017, 39 master's, 13 doctorates awarded. *Degree requirements:* For master's, comprehensive exam, thesis or alternative, internship; for doctorate, comprehensive exam, thesis/dissertation, practicum, internship, residency, scholarly work. *Entrance requirements:* For master's, GRE General Test or MAT, minimum GPA of 2.5, letters of reference, interview; for doctorate, GRE General Test, master's degree or equivalent, letters of reference, interview, curriculum vitae, personal statement. Additional exam requirements/recommendations for international students: Required—TOEFL (minimum score 550 paper-based; 79 iBT). *Application deadline:* For fall admission, 10/1 priority date for domestic students; for spring admission, 4/1 priority date for domestic students. Applications are processed on a rolling basis. Application fee: $35 ($60 for international students). Electronic applications accepted. *Expenses:* Contact institution. *Financial support:* In 2017–18, 130 students received support, including 15 research assistantships with full tuition reimbursements available (averaging $13,426 per year), 12 teaching assistantships with full tuition reimbursements available (averaging $11,976 per year); fellowships with full tuition reimbursements available, career-related internships or fieldwork, Federal Work-Study, scholarships/grants, and unspecified assistantships also available. Financial award application deadline: 2/1; financial award applicants required to submit FAFSA. *Faculty research:* Anger management, aging and disability, supervision, multicultural counseling. *Unit head:* Dr. Steve West, Chair, 901-678-2841, Fax: 901-678-5114, E-mail: slwest@memphis.edu. *Application contact:* Dr. Suzanne Lease, Interim Assistant Dean of Education and Graduate Programs, 901-678-4476, Fax: 901-678-4778, E-mail: slease@memphis.edu.
Website: http://www.memphis.edu/cepr/

University of Miami, Graduate School, School of Education and Human Development, Department of Educational and Psychological Studies, Program in Counseling Psychology, Coral Gables, FL 33124. Offers PhD. *Accreditation:* APA. *Degree requirements:* For doctorate, thesis/dissertation, qualifying exam. *Entrance requirements:* For doctorate, GRE General Test. Additional exam requirements/recommendations for international students: Required—TOEFL (minimum score 550 paper-based; 80 iBT); Recommended—IELTS (minimum score 6.5). Electronic applications accepted. *Faculty research:* Cocaine recidivism, family systems, behavior and health, nontraditional families, stress and coping.

University of Minnesota, Twin Cities Campus, Graduate School, College of Liberal Arts, Department of Psychology, Program in Counseling Psychology, Minneapolis, MN 55455-0213. Offers PhD. *Accreditation:* APA. *Degree requirements:* For doctorate, comprehensive exam, thesis/dissertation, internship. *Entrance requirements:* For doctorate, GRE General Test, GRE Subject Test (recommended), 12 credits of upper-level psychology courses, including a course in statistics or psychological measurement. Additional exam requirements/recommendations for international students: Required—TOEFL (minimum score 550 paper-based; 79 iBT).

University of Missouri, Office of Research and Graduate Studies, College of Education, Department of Educational, School, and Counseling Psychology, Columbia, MO 65211. Offers counseling psychology (M Ed, MA, PhD, Ed S); educational psychology (M Ed, MA, PhD, Ed S); learning and instruction (M Ed); school psychology

(M Ed, MA, PhD, Ed S). *Accreditation:* APA (one or more programs are accredited). *Program availability:* Part-time. *Degree requirements:* For doctorate, thesis/dissertation. *Entrance requirements:* For master's, doctorate, and Ed S, GRE General Test, minimum GPA of 3.0. Additional exam requirements/recommendations for international students: Required—TOEFL (minimum score 580 paper-based; 92 iBT). Electronic applications accepted.

University of Missouri–Kansas City, School of Education, Kansas City, MO 64110-2499. Offers administration (Ed D); counseling and guidance (MA, Ed S), including mental health counseling (Ed S), school counseling (Ed S); counseling psychology (PhD); curriculum and instruction (MA, Ed S), including language and literacy (Ed S); education (PhD), including higher education administration, PK-12 education administration; educational administration (MA, Ed S), including advanced principal (Ed S), beginning principal (Ed S), district-level administration (Ed S); reading education (MA); special education (MA). PhD in education offered through the School of Graduate Studies. *Accreditation:* NCATE. *Program availability:* Part-time, evening/weekend. *Degree requirements:* For doctorate, thesis/dissertation, internship, practicum. *Entrance requirements:* For master's, GRE, minimum GPA of 2.75, 2 letters of reference, written statement of purpose; for doctorate, GRE, minimum GPA of 3.0; for Ed S, minimum GPA of 3.0. Additional exam requirements/recommendations for international students: Required—TOEFL (minimum score 550 paper-based; 80 iBT). *Faculty research:* Urban education, inquiry-based field study, theories of counseling and psychotherapy, school literacy, educational technology.

University of Montana, Graduate School, Phyllis J. Washington College of Education and Human Sciences, Department of Counselor Education, Missoula, MT 59812. Offers clinical mental health counseling (MA); counseling and supervision (Ed D); counselor education (Ed S); intercultural youth and family development (MA); school counseling (MA). *Accreditation:* ACA. *Degree requirements:* For doctorate, thesis/dissertation. *Entrance requirements:* For master's, doctorate, and Ed S, GRE General Test. Additional exam requirements/recommendations for international students: Required—TOEFL.

University of Nebraska at Kearney, College of Education, Department of Counseling and School Psychology, Kearney, NE 68849-0001. Offers clinical mental health counseling (MS Ed); school counseling (MS Ed), including elementary, secondary; school psychology (Ed S); student affairs (MS Ed). *Accreditation:* ACA; NCATE. *Program availability:* Part-time, evening/weekend, 100% online. *Degree requirements:* For master's, comprehensive exam, thesis optional; for Ed S, thesis. *Entrance requirements:* For master's and Ed S, personal statement, recommendations, resume, interview. Additional exam requirements/recommendations for international students: Recommended—TOEFL (minimum score 550 paper-based; 79 iBT), IELTS (minimum score 6.5). Electronic applications accepted. *Faculty research:* Multicultural counseling and diversity issues, team decision-making, adult development, women's issues, brief therapy.

University of Nebraska–Lincoln, Graduate College, College of Education and Human Sciences, Department of Educational Psychology, Lincoln, NE 68588. Offers cognition, learning and development (MA); counseling psychology (MA); educational psychology (MA, Ed S); psychological studies in education (PhD), including cognition, learning and development, counseling psychology, quantitative, qualitative, and psychometric methods, school psychology; quantitative, qualitative, and psychometric methods (MA); school psychology (MA, Ed S). *Accreditation:* APA (one or more programs are accredited); NCATE. *Degree requirements:* For master's, thesis optional. *Entrance requirements:* For master's, GRE General Test. Additional exam requirements/recommendations for international students: Required—TOEFL (minimum score 500 paper-based). Electronic applications accepted. *Faculty research:* Measurement and assessment, metacognition, academic skills, child development, multicultural education and counseling.

University of Nevada, Las Vegas, Graduate College, College of Education, Department of Educational and Clinical Studies, Las Vegas, NV 89154-3066. Offers addiction studies (Advanced Certificate); counselor education (M Ed, MS), including clinical mental health (MS), school counseling (M Ed); early childhood education (M Ed); early childhood special education (Certificate), including infancy, preschool; English language learning (M Ed); mental health counseling (Advanced Certificate); special education (M Ed, PhD); PhD/JD. *Program availability:* Part-time. *Faculty:* 18 full-time (9 women), 28 part-time/adjunct (22 women). *Students:* 281 full-time (230 women), 193 part-time (148 women); includes 211 minority (54 Black or African American, non-Hispanic/Latino; 2 American Indian or Alaska Native, non-Hispanic/Latino; 28 Asian, non-Hispanic/Latino; 95 Hispanic/Latino; 4 Native Hawaiian or other Pacific Islander, non-Hispanic/Latino; 28 Two or more races, non-Hispanic/Latino), 13 international. Average age 34. 262 applicants, 76% accepted, 161 enrolled. In 2017, 204 master's, 8 doctorates, 1 other advanced degree awarded. *Degree requirements:* For master's, comprehensive exam (for some programs); for doctorate, comprehensive exam, thesis/dissertation; for other advanced degree, final project. *Entrance requirements:* For master's, bachelor's degree; letter of recommendation; statement of purpose; for doctorate, GRE General Test, statement of purpose; writing sample; 3 letters of recommendation. Additional exam requirements/recommendations for international students: Required—TOEFL (minimum score 550 paper-based; 80 iBT), IELTS (minimum score 7). Application fee: $60 ($95 for international students). Electronic applications accepted. *Expenses:* $275 per credit, $850 per course, $7,969 per year resident, $22,157 per year non-resident, $7,094 non-resident fee (7 credits or more), $1,307 annual health insurance fee. *Financial support:* In 2017–18, 35 students received support, including 10 research assistantships with full tuition reimbursements available (averaging $13,775 per year), 25 teaching assistantships with full tuition reimbursements available (averaging $17,140 per year); institutionally sponsored loans, scholarships/grants, health care benefits, and unspecified assistantships also available. Financial award application deadline: 3/15; financial award applicants required to submit FAFSA. *Faculty research:* Multicultural issues in counseling, academic interventions for students with disabilities, establishment of pro-social skills in young children with severe disabilities, inclusive strategies for students with disabilities, language and literacy for English language learners. *Total annual research expenditures:* $1.1 million. *Unit head:* Dr. Monica Brown, Interim Department Chair/Professor, 702-895-3167, Fax: 702-895-3205, E-mail: monica.brown@unlv.edu. *Application contact:* Dr. Joseph Morgan, Graduate Coordinator, 702-895-3329, Fax: 702-895-3205, E-mail: joseph.morgan@unlv.edu.
Website: http://education.unlv.edu/ecs/

The University of North Carolina at Greensboro, Graduate School, School of Education, Department of Counseling and Educational Development, Greensboro, NC 27412-5001. Offers advanced school counseling (PMC); counseling and counselor education (PhD); counseling and educational development (MS); couple and family counseling (PMC); school counseling (PMC); MS/Ed S. *Accreditation:* ACA (one or more programs are accredited); NCATE. *Degree requirements:* For master's, comprehensive exam, practicum, internship; for doctorate, comprehensive exam, thesis/dissertation. *Entrance requirements:* For master's, doctorate, and PMC, GRE General Test. Additional exam requirements/recommendations for international students: Required—TOEFL. Electronic applications accepted. *Faculty research:* Gerontology, invitational theory, career development, marriage and family therapy, drug and alcohol abuse prevention.

The University of North Carolina at Pembroke, The Graduate School, School of Education, Programs in Counseling, Pembroke, NC 28372-1510. Offers clinical mental health counseling (MA Ed); professional school counseling (MA Ed). *Accreditation:* NCATE. *Program availability:* Part-time, evening/weekend. *Degree requirements:* For master's, comprehensive exam, thesis optional. *Entrance requirements:* For master's, GRE General Test or MAT, minimum GPA of 3.0 in major, 2.5 overall. Additional exam requirements/recommendations for international students: Required—TOEFL. *Application deadline:* For fall admission, 7/15 priority date for domestic and international students; for spring admission, 12/1 priority date for domestic and international students. Applications are processed on a rolling basis. Application fee: $45 ($60 for international students). *Financial support:* Application deadline: 4/15; applicants required to submit FAFSA. *Unit head:* Dr. Jeffrey M. Warren, Department Chair, 910-775-4414, Fax: 910-521-6165, E-mail: jeffrey.warren@uncp.edu.

University of North Dakota, Graduate School, College of Education and Human Development, Department of Counseling Psychology and Community Services, Grand Forks, ND 58202. Offers counseling (MA); counseling psychology (PhD). *Degree requirements:* For master's, comprehensive exam, thesis or alternative; for doctorate, comprehensive exam, thesis/dissertation, final examination. *Entrance requirements:* For master's, GRE General Test or MAT, minimum GPA of 3.0; for doctorate, GRE General Test, minimum GPA of 3.0. Additional exam requirements/recommendations for international students: Required—TOEFL (minimum score 550 paper-based; 79 iBT), IELTS (minimum score 6.5). Electronic applications accepted. *Faculty research:* Group dynamics, addictive behavior, item response theory, geopsychology, women's health.

University of Northern Colorado, Graduate School, College of Education and Behavioral Sciences, Department of Applied Psychology and Counselor Education, Program in Counseling Psychology, Greeley, CO 80639. Offers PhD. *Accreditation:* ACA; APA; NCATE. *Program availability:* Part-time, evening/weekend. *Degree requirements:* For doctorate, comprehensive exam, thesis/dissertation. *Entrance requirements:* For doctorate, GRE General Test, 3 letters of reference.

University of Northern Iowa, Graduate College, College of Social and Behavioral Sciences, School of Applied Human Sciences, MA Program in Counseling, Cedar Falls, IA 50614. Offers mental health counseling (MA); school counseling (MA). *Accreditation:* ACA. *Program availability:* Part-time, evening/weekend. *Degree requirements:* For master's, comprehensive exam, thesis or alternative. *Entrance requirements:* For master's, minimum GPA of 3.0. Additional exam requirements/recommendations for international students: Required—TOEFL (minimum score 500 paper-based; 61 iBT). Electronic applications accepted.

University of North Florida, College of Arts and Sciences, Department of Psychology, Jacksonville, FL 32224. Offers counseling psychology (MAC); general psychology (MA). *Program availability:* Part-time, evening/weekend. *Degree requirements:* For master's, comprehensive exam, thesis optional, practicum. *Entrance requirements:* For master's, GRE General Test, 2 letters of recommendation, minimum GPA of 3.0 in last 60 hours of course work. Additional exam requirements/recommendations for international students: Required—TOEFL (minimum score 500 paper-based; 61 iBT). Electronic applications accepted. *Faculty research:* Sensory perception, social cognition, sexual behavior, evolutionary psychology, psychology and law.

University of North Georgia, Department of Counseling, Dahlonega, GA 30597. Offers counseling (MS). *Program availability:* Part-time. *Faculty:* 4 full-time (3 women). *Students:* 29 full-time (24 women), 26 part-time (20 women); includes 13 minority (7 Black or African American, non-Hispanic/Latino; 1 Asian, non-Hispanic/Latino; 3 Hispanic/Latino; 2 Two or more races, non-Hispanic/Latino). Average age 29. 58 applicants, 55% accepted, 20 enrolled. In 2017, 13 master's awarded. *Degree requirements:* For master's, internship, counseling practicum. *Entrance requirements:* For master's, GRE (minimum score of 290 verbal and quantitative combined), official transcripts, group interview, personal statement, 3 UNG recommendation forms, resume, immunization. Additional exam requirements/recommendations for international students: Required—TOEFL (minimum score 550 paper-based; 79 iBT), IELTS (minimum score 6.5). *Application deadline:* For fall admission, 3/1 for domestic students. Application fee: $40. Electronic applications accepted. *Expenses:* Contact institution. *Financial support:* Fellowships, research assistantships, teaching assistantships, and career-related internships or fieldwork available. Financial award application deadline: 3/17; financial award applicants required to submit FAFSA. *Unit head:* Dr. P. Clay Rowell, Department Head, 706-867-2791, E-mail: clay.rowell@ung.edu. *Application contact:* Melinda Maxwell, Director of Graduate Admissions, 706-864-1543, E-mail: melinda.maxwell@ung.edu.
Website: http://ung.edu/clinical-mental-health-counseling/

University of North Texas, Robert B. Toulouse School of Graduate Studies, Denton, TX 76203-5459. Offers accounting (MS); applied anthropology (MA, MS); applied behavior analysis (Certificate); applied geography (MA); applied technology and performance improvement (M Ed, MS); art education (MA); art history (MA); art museum education (Certificate); arts leadership (Certificate); audiology (Au D); behavior analysis (MS); behavioral science (PhD); biochemistry and molecular biology (MS); biology (MA, MS); biomedical engineering (MS); business analysis (MS); chemistry (MS); clinical health psychology (PhD); communication studies (MA, MS); computer engineering (MS); computer science (MS); counseling (M Ed, MS), including clinical mental health counseling (MS), college and university counseling, elementary school counseling, secondary school counseling; creative writing (MA); criminal justice (MS); curriculum and instruction (M Ed); decision sciences (MBA); design (MA, MFA), including fashion design (MFA), innovation studies, interior design (MFA); early childhood studies (MS); economics (MS); educational leadership (M Ed, Ed D); educational psychology (MS, PhD), including family studies (MS), gifted and talented (MS), human development (MS), learning and cognition (MS), research, measurement and evaluation (MS); electrical engineering (MS); emergency management (MPA); engineering technology (MS); English (MA); English as a second language (MA); environmental science (MS); finance (MBA, MS); financial management (MPA); French (MA); health services management (MBA); higher education (M Ed, Ed D); history (MA, MS); hospitality management (MS); human resources management (MPA); information science (MS); information systems (PhD); information technologies (MBA); interdisciplinary studies (MA, MS); international studies (MA); international sustainable tourism (MS); jazz studies (MM); journalism (MA, MJ, Graduate Certificate), including interactive and virtual digital communication (Graduate Certificate), narrative journalism (Graduate Certificate), public relations (Graduate Certificate); kinesiology (MS); linguistics (MA); local government management (MPA); logistics (PhD); logistics and supply chain management (MBA); long-term care, senior housing, and aging services (MA); management (PhD); marketing (MBA); mathematics (MA, MS); mechanical and energy engineering (MS, PhD); music (MA), including ethnomusicology, music theory, musicology, performance; music composition (PhD); music education (MM Ed, PhD); nonprofit management (MPA); operations and supply chain management (MBA); performance (MM, DMA); philosophy (MA); political science (MA); professional and technical communication (MA); radio, television and film (MA, MFA); rehabilitation counseling (Certificate); sociology (MA); Spanish (MA); special education (M Ed); speech-language pathology (MA); strategic

management (MBA); studio art (MFA); teaching (M Ed); MBA/MS. *Program availability:* Part-time, evening/weekend, online learning. Terminal master's awarded for partial completion of doctoral program. *Degree requirements:* For master's, variable foreign language requirement, comprehensive exam (for some programs), thesis (for some programs); for doctorate, variable foreign language requirement, comprehensive exam (for some programs), thesis/dissertation; for other advanced degree, variable foreign language requirement, comprehensive exam (for some programs). *Entrance requirements:* For master's and doctorate, GRE, GMAT. Additional exam requirements/recommendations for international students: Required—TOEFL (minimum score 550 paper-based; 79 iBT). Electronic applications accepted.

University of Notre Dame, Graduate School, College of Arts and Letters, Division of Social Science, Department of Psychology, Notre Dame, IN 46556. Offers cognitive psychology (PhD); counseling psychology (PhD); developmental psychology (PhD); quantitative psychology (PhD). *Accreditation:* APA. *Degree requirements:* For doctorate, comprehensive exam, thesis/dissertation, candidacy exam. *Entrance requirements:* For doctorate, GRE General Test, GRE Subject Test (strongly recommended). Additional exam requirements/recommendations for international students: Required—TOEFL (minimum score 600 paper-based; 80 iBT). Electronic applications accepted. *Faculty research:* Cognitive and socio-emotional development, statistical methods and quantitative models applicable to psychology, interpersonal relations, life span development and developmental delay, childhood depression, structural equation and dynamical systems.

University of Oklahoma, Jeannine Rainbolt College of Education, Department of Educational Psychology, Program in Professional Counseling, Norman, OK 73019. Offers professional counseling (M Ed), including drug and alcohol counseling, Oklahoma licensed professional counseling, school counseling. *Students:* 32 full-time (23 women), 2 part-time (1 woman); includes 13 minority (2 Black or African American, non-Hispanic/Latino; 1 American Indian or Alaska Native, non-Hispanic/Latino; 6 Hispanic/Latino; 4 Two or more races, non-Hispanic/Latino). Average age 31. 43 applicants, 51% accepted, 17 enrolled. In 2017, 16 master's awarded. *Degree requirements:* For master's, comprehensive exam. *Entrance requirements:* For master's, GRE. Additional exam requirements/recommendations for international students: Required—TOEFL (minimum score 79 iBT) or IELTS (minimum score 6.5). *Application deadline:* For fall admission, 1/10 for domestic and international students. Application fee: $50 ($100 for international students). Electronic applications accepted. *Expenses:* Tuition, state resident: full-time $5119; part-time $213.30 per credit hour. Tuition, nonresident: full-time $19,778; part-time $824.10 per credit hour. *Required fees:* $3458; $133.55 per credit hour. $126.50 per semester. *Financial support:* In 2017–18, 12 students received support. Research assistantships with full and partial tuition reimbursements available, teaching assistantships with full and partial tuition reimbursements available, and scholarships/grants available. Financial award application deadline: 6/1; financial award applicants required to submit FAFSA. *Faculty research:* Group therapy interventions; family/child counseling; American Indian psychological issues; diversity issues in counseling; drug and alcohol (addictions) counseling/therapy. *Unit head:* Dr. Nancy E. Marchand-Martella, Chair, Department of Educational Psychology, 405-325-0624, Fax: 405-325-6655, E-mail: nmarchand-martella@ou.edu. *Application contact:* Anna Steele, Graduate Programs Specialist, 405-325-4525, Fax: 405-325-7390, E-mail: jrcoe_gps@ou.edu.
Website: http://www.ou.edu/education/edpy.html

University of Oregon, Graduate School, College of Education, Eugene, OR 97403. Offers communication disorders and sciences (MA, MS, PhD); counseling psychology (PhD); couples and family therapy (MS); critical and sociocultural studies in education (PhD); curriculum and teacher education (MA, MS); educational leadership (MS, D Ed, PhD); prevention science (M Ed, MS, PhD); school psychology (MS, PhD); special education (M Ed, MA, MS, PhD). *Program availability:* Part-time. Terminal master's awarded for partial completion of doctoral program. *Degree requirements:* For master's, exam, paper, or project; for doctorate, comprehensive exam, thesis/dissertation. *Entrance requirements:* Additional exam requirements/recommendations for international students: Required—TOEFL. *Faculty research:* Basic and applied research in teaching, learning and habilitation in all settings, schooling effectiveness.

University of Pennsylvania, Graduate School of Education, Division of Human Development and Quantitative Methods, Program in Counseling and Mental Health Services, Philadelphia, PA 19104. Offers M Phil, MS Ed. *Students:* Average age 25. 202 applicants, 64% accepted, 71 enrolled. In 2017, 69 master's awarded.
Website: http://www.gse.upenn.edu/aphd/cmhs/msed

University of Phoenix–Las Vegas Campus, College of Human Services, Las Vegas, NV 89135. Offers marriage, family, and child therapy (MSC); mental health counseling (MSC); school counseling (MSC). *Program availability:* Online learning. *Entrance requirements:* For master's, minimum undergraduate GPA of 2.5, 3 years of work experience. Additional exam requirements/recommendations for international students: Required—TOEFL (minimum score 550 paper-based; 79 iBT). Electronic applications accepted.

University of Phoenix–Phoenix Campus, College of Social Sciences, Tempe, AZ 85282-2371. Offers counseling (MS), including clinical mental health counseling, community counseling, counseling, marriage, family and child therapy; psychology (MS). *Program availability:* Evening/weekend, online learning. *Entrance requirements:* Additional exam requirements/recommendations for international students: Required—TOEFL, TOEIC (Test of English as an International Communication), Berlitz Online English Proficiency Exam, PTE, or IELTS. Electronic applications accepted. *Expenses:* Contact institution.

University of Providence, Graduate Studies, Program in Counseling, Great Falls, MT 59405. Offers MSC. *Program availability:* Part-time, evening/weekend. *Degree requirements:* For master's, thesis optional, internship. *Entrance requirements:* For master's, GRE General Test, 3 letters of recommendation. Additional exam requirements/recommendations for international students: Required—TOEFL (minimum score 500 paper-based). Electronic applications accepted. *Faculty research:* Self concept and adolescent offenders, juvenile delinquency, community mental health counseling.

University of Puget Sound, School of Education, Program in Counseling, Tacoma, WA 98416. Offers mental health counseling (M Ed); school counseling (M Ed). *Program availability:* Part-time. *Degree requirements:* For master's, capstone course. *Entrance requirements:* For master's, GRE General Test, interview. Additional exam requirements/recommendations for international students: Required—TOEFL (minimum score 550 paper-based; 90 iBT). Electronic applications accepted. *Expenses:* Contact institution. *Faculty research:* Suicide prevention.

University of Rhode Island, Graduate School, College of Health Sciences, Department of Human Development and Family Studies, Kingston, RI 02881. Offers college student personnel (MS); human development and family studies (MS); marriage and family therapy (MS). *Accreditation:* AAMFT/COAMFTE. *Program availability:* Part-time. *Faculty:* 16 full-time (11 women). *Students:* 47 full-time (35 women), 12 part-time (10 women); includes 13 minority (4 Black or African American, non-Hispanic/Latino; 1 American Indian or Alaska Native, non-Hispanic/Latino; 4 Asian, non-Hispanic/Latino; 3 Hispanic/Latino; 1 Two or more races, non-Hispanic/Latino), 2 international. 91 applicants, 43% accepted, 29 enrolled. In 2017, 24 master's awarded. *Entrance requirements:* Additional exam requirements/recommendations for international students: Required—TOEFL. *Application deadline:* For fall admission, 1/15 for domestic and international students. Application fee: $65. Electronic applications accepted. *Expenses:* Tuition, state resident: full-time $12,706; part-time $786 per credit. Tuition, nonresident: full-time $25,216; part-time $1401 per credit. *Required fees:* $1598; $45 per credit. One-time fee: $30 part-time. *Financial support:* In 2017–18, 1 research assistantship (averaging $4,431 per year), 4 teaching assistantships (averaging $10,128 per year) were awarded. Financial award application deadline: 1/15; financial award applicants required to submit FAFSA. *Unit head:* Dr. Karen McCurdy, Chair, 401-874-5960, Fax: 401-874-4020, E-mail: kmccurdy@uri.edu.
Website: http://www.uri.edu/hss/hdf/

University of Saint Francis, Graduate School, Department of Behavioral and Social Sciences, Fort Wayne, IN 46808-3994. Offers clinical mental health counseling (MS, Post Master's Certificate); psychology (MS); school counseling (MS Ed). *Program availability:* Part-time, evening/weekend. *Faculty:* 4 full-time (0 women). *Students:* 23 full-time (18 women), 7 part-time (6 women); includes 8 minority (7 Black or African American, non-Hispanic/Latino; 1 Asian, non-Hispanic/Latino), 1 international. Average age 30. 18 applicants, 83% accepted, 12 enrolled. In 2017, 23 master's awarded. *Entrance requirements:* For master's, GRE with minimum score of 150 if undergraduate GPA is below 3.0 (for MS Ed in school counseling), minimum undergraduate GPA of 3.0; undergraduate coursework in psychology; statement of professional goals (for MS); 2 professional recommendations; interview (for mental health counseling and school counseling). Additional exam requirements/recommendations for international students: Required—TOEFL (minimum score 550 paper-based) or IELTS (minimum score 6.5). *Application deadline:* For fall admission, 7/1 for international students; for spring admission, 11/1 for international students; for summer admission, 3/1 for international students. Applications are processed on a rolling basis. Application fee: $0. Electronic applications accepted. *Expenses:* $905 per credit. *Financial support:* In 2017–18, 3 students received support. Federal Work-Study, scholarships/grants, and unspecified assistantships available. Financial award application deadline: 4/15; financial award applicants required to submit FAFSA. *Unit head:* Dr. John Brinkman, Chair of Department of Behavioral and Social Sciences, 260-399-7700 Ext. 8425, E-mail: jbrinkman@sf.edu. *Application contact:* Kyle Richardson, Associate Director of Enrollment Services for Adult Learning, 260-399-7700 Ext. 6310, Fax: 260-399-8152, E-mail: krichardson@sf.edu.
Website: https://bhvscience.sf.edu/

University of Saint Joseph, Department of Counseling and Applied Behavioral Studies, West Hartford, CT 06117-2700. Offers clinical mental health counseling (MA); school counseling (MA). *Accreditation:* ACA. *Program availability:* Part-time, evening/weekend. *Degree requirements:* For master's, comprehensive exam, thesis optional. *Entrance requirements:* For master's, 2 letters of recommendation. *Application deadline:* Applications are processed on a rolling basis. Application fee: $50. Electronic applications accepted. Application fee is waived when completed online. *Financial support:* Career-related internships or fieldwork and unspecified assistantships available. Support available to part-time students. Financial award applicants required to submit FAFSA.
Website: https://www.usj.edu/academics/schools/sihs/counseling-and-applied-behavioral-studies/

University of Saint Mary, Graduate Programs, Program in Counseling Psychology, Leavenworth, KS 66048-5082. Offers MA. *Program availability:* Part-time, evening/weekend. *Entrance requirements:* For master's, bachelor's degree in psychology from accredited college, official transcripts, minimum GPA of 2.75, three professional recommendations, essay. Electronic applications accepted.

University of St. Thomas, College of Education, Leadership and Counseling, Graduate School of Professional Psychology, St. Paul, MN 55105-1096. Offers counseling psychology (MA, Psy D). *Accreditation:* APA. *Program availability:* Part-time, evening/weekend. *Degree requirements:* For master's, comprehensive exam, practicum; for doctorate, comprehensive exam, thesis/dissertation, qualifying exam, practicum, internship. *Entrance requirements:* For master's, GRE, minimum GPA of 2.75, letters of recommendation, personal statement; for doctorate, GRE, minimum GPA of 3.2, letters of recommendation, personal statement. Additional exam requirements/recommendations for international students: Required—TOEFL (minimum score 550 paper-based; 80 iBT). *Application deadline:* For fall admission, 2/5 priority date for domestic students; for winter admission, 1/5 priority date for domestic students; for spring admission, 10/15 priority date for domestic students, 3/1 for international students. Electronic applications accepted. *Expenses:* Contact institution. *Financial support:* Fellowships with partial tuition reimbursements, research assistantships, teaching assistantships, institutionally sponsored loans, and scholarships/grants available. Support available to part-time students. Financial award application deadline: 8/1; financial award applicants required to submit FAFSA. *Faculty research:* Elderly, neuropsychology, anxiety, family, therapist expertise, business of practice, religion and psychology, early attachment, relationship of science and practice in psychotherapy. *Unit head:* Dr. Christopher S. Vye, Chair, 651-962-4666, E-mail: csvye@stthomas.edu. *Application contact:* Melissa Anderson, Program Manager, 651-962-4669, Fax: 651-962-4651, E-mail: msanderson@stthomas.edu.
Website: https://www.stthomas.edu/counselingpsychology/

University of San Diego, School of Leadership and Education Sciences, Department of Counseling and Marital and Family Therapy, San Diego, CA 92110-2492. Offers clinical mental health counseling (MA); marital and family therapy (MA); school counseling (MA). *Accreditation:* ACA. *Program availability:* Part-time, evening/weekend. *Faculty:* 13 full-time (6 women), 26 part-time/adjunct (18 women). *Students:* 172 full-time (155 women), 50 part-time (42 women); includes 106 minority (13 Black or African American, non-Hispanic/Latino; 1 American Indian or Alaska Native, non-Hispanic/Latino; 20 Asian, non-Hispanic/Latino; 62 Hispanic/Latino; 10 Two or more races, non-Hispanic/Latino), 5 international. Average age 27. 406 applicants, 45% accepted, 92 enrolled. In 2017, 69 master's awarded. *Degree requirements:* For master's, comprehensive exam, international experience. *Entrance requirements:* For master's, GRE or GMAT (minimum overall score in 50th percentile), group interview with faculty. Additional exam requirements/recommendations for international students: Required—TOEFL (minimum score 580 paper-based; 83 iBT), TWE. *Application deadline:* For fall admission, 1/13 priority date for domestic and international students. Applications are processed on a rolling basis. Application fee: $45. Electronic applications accepted. *Financial support:* In 2017–18, 160 students received support. Career-related internships or fieldwork, Federal Work-Study, institutionally sponsored loans, unspecified assistantships, and stipends available. Support available to part-time students. Financial award application deadline: 4/1; financial award applicants required to submit FAFSA. *Faculty research:* Action research, collaboration between family therapists and medical professionals, family therapy training and supervision, multicultural counseling, school counseling. *Unit head:* Dr. Ann Garland, Director, 619-260-7879, E-mail: agarland@sandiego.edu. *Application contact:* Monica Mahon, Director of Admissions and Enrollment, 619-260-

4524, Fax: 619-260-4158, E-mail: grads@sandiego.edu.
Website: http://www.sandiego.edu/soles/counseling-and-marital-and-family-therapy//

University of San Francisco, School of Education, Department of Counseling Psychology, San Francisco, CA 94117-1080. Offers counseling (MA), including educational counseling, life transitions counseling, marital and family therapy. *Program availability:* Part-time. *Entrance requirements:* Additional exam requirements/recommendations for international students: Required—TOEFL, IELTS, PTE. Electronic applications accepted.

The University of Scranton, Panuska College of Professional Studies, Department of Counseling and Human Services, Program in Clinical Mental Health Counseling, Scranton, PA 18510. Offers MS. *Accreditation:* ACA. *Program availability:* Part-time, evening/weekend. *Degree requirements:* For master's, comprehensive exam (for some programs), thesis (for some programs), capstone experience. *Entrance requirements:* For master's, minimum GPA of 3.0, three letters of reference. Additional exam requirements/recommendations for international students: Required—TOEFL (minimum score 500 paper-based; 80 iBT), IELTS (minimum score 6.5). Electronic applications accepted. *Faculty research:* Play therapy, expressive arts, identity development, counseling supervision.

University of South Africa, College of Human Sciences, Pretoria, South Africa. Offers adult education (M Ed); African languages (MA, PhD); African politics (MA, PhD); Afrikaans (MA, PhD); ancient history (MA, PhD); ancient Near Eastern studies (MA, PhD); anthropology (MA, PhD); applied linguistics (MA); Arabic (MA, PhD); archaeology (MA); art history (MA); Biblical archaeology (MA); Biblical studies (M Th, D Th, PhD); Christian spirituality (M Th, D Th); church history (M Th, D Th); classical studies (MA, PhD); clinical psychology (MA); communication (MA, PhD); comparative education (M Ed, Ed D); consulting psychology (D Admin, D Com, PhD); curriculum studies (M Ed, Ed D); development studies (M Admin, MA, D Admin, PhD); didactics (M Ed, Ed D); education (M Tech); education management (M Ed, Ed D); educational psychology (M Ed); English (MA); environmental education (M Ed); French (MA, PhD); German (MA, PhD); Greek (MA); guidance and counseling (M Ed); health studies (MA, PhD), including health sciences education (MA), health services management (MA), medical and surgical nursing science (critical care general) (MA), midwifery and neonatal nursing science (MA), trauma and emergency care (MA); history (MA, PhD); history of education (Ed D); inclusive education (M Ed, Ed D); information and communications technology policy and regulation (MA); information science (MA, MIS, PhD); international politics (MA, PhD); Islamic studies (MA, PhD); Italian (MA, PhD); Judaica (MA, PhD); linguistics (MA, PhD); mathematical education (M Ed); mathematics education (MA); missiology (M Th, D Th); modern Hebrew (MA, PhD); musicology (MA, MMus, D Mus, PhD); natural science education (M Ed); New Testament (M Th, D Th); Old Testament (D Th); pastoral therapy (M Th, D Th); philosophy (MA); philosophy of education (M Ed, Ed D); politics (MA, PhD); Portuguese (MA, PhD); practical theology (M Th, D Th); psychology (MA, MS, PhD); psychology of education (M Ed, Ed D); public health (MA); religious studies (MA, D Th, PhD); Romance languages (MA); Russian (MA, PhD); Semitic languages (MA, PhD); social behavior studies in HIV/AIDS (MA); social science (mental health) (MA); social science in development studies (MA); social science in psychology (MA); social science in social work (MA); social science in sociology (MA); social work (MSW, DSW, PhD); socio-education (M Ed, Ed D); sociolinguistics (MA); sociology (MA, PhD); Spanish (MA, PhD); systematic theology (M Th, D Th); TESOL (teaching English to speakers of other languages) (MA); theological ethics (M Th, D Th); theory of literature (MA, PhD); urban ministries (D Th); urban ministry (M Th).

University of South Alabama, College of Education and Professional Studies, Department of Counseling and Instructional Sciences, Mobile, AL 36688. Offers clinical mental health counseling (MS); educational media (M Ed); educational media and technology (MS); instructional design and development (MS, PhD); instructional leadership (Ed S); school counseling (M Ed). *Accreditation:* NCATE. *Program availability:* Part-time. *Faculty:* 12 full-time (7 women), 10 part-time/adjunct (9 women). *Students:* 110 full-time (85 women), 39 part-time (32 women); includes 43 minority (33 Black or African American, non-Hispanic/Latino; 4 Asian, non-Hispanic/Latino; 5 Hispanic/Latino; 1 Two or more races, non-Hispanic/Latino), 5 international. Average age 34. 68 applicants, 53% accepted, 31 enrolled. In 2017, 32 master's, 9 doctorates, 10 other advanced degrees awarded. *Degree requirements:* For master's, comprehensive exam; for doctorate, comprehensive exam, thesis/dissertation. *Entrance requirements:* For master's, GRE General Test or MAT, minimum GPA of 3.0, three letters of recommendation; for doctorate, GRE, three letters of recommendation, master's degree in field or completion of prerequisites, resume. Additional exam requirements/recommendations for international students: Required—TOEFL (minimum score 525 paper-based; 71 iBT). *Application deadline:* For fall admission, 6/15 for domestic and international students; for spring admission, 12/1 for domestic students, 11/1 for international students; for summer admission, 4/1 for domestic and international students. Applications are processed on a rolling basis. Application fee: $35. Electronic applications accepted. *Expenses:* Tuition, state resident: full-time $10,104; part-time $421 per semester hour. Tuition, nonresident: full-time $20,208; part-time $842 per semester hour. *Financial support:* Fellowships, research assistantships, teaching assistantships, career-related internships or fieldwork, Federal Work-Study, institutionally sponsored loans, scholarships/grants, and unspecified assistantships available. Support available to part-time students. Financial award application deadline: 3/31; financial award applicants required to submit FAFSA. *Faculty research:* Agency counseling, rehabilitation counseling, school psychometry, juvenile delinquency, mixed methods research. *Unit head:* Dr. Tres Stefurak, Department Chair, 251-380-2734, Fax: 251-380-2713, E-mail: jstefurak@southalabama.edu. *Application contact:* Dr. James Van Haneghan, Graduate Coordinator, 251-380-2760, Fax: 251-380-2713, E-mail: jvanhane@southalabama.edu.
Website: http://www.southalabama.edu/colleges/ceps/cins/

University of South Alabama, Graduate School, Program in Clinical and Counseling Psychology, Mobile, AL 36688. Offers PhD. *Accreditation:* ACA. *Faculty:* 7 full-time (2 women). *Students:* 24 full-time (13 women), 6 part-time (5 women); includes 4 minority (2 Black or African American, non-Hispanic/Latino; 1 Hispanic/Latino; 1 Two or more races, non-Hispanic/Latino). Average age 28. 101 applicants, 7% accepted, 7 enrolled. In 2017, 10 doctorates awarded. *Degree requirements:* For doctorate, thesis/dissertation, capstone internship. *Entrance requirements:* For doctorate, GRE, three letters of recommendation, statement of purpose, curriculum vitae. Additional exam requirements/recommendations for international students: Required—TOEFL (minimum score 525 paper-based; 71 iBT). *Application deadline:* For fall admission, 12/15 for domestic students. Application fee: $50. Electronic applications accepted. *Expenses:* Tuition, state resident: full-time $10,104; part-time $421 per semester hour. Tuition, nonresident: full-time $20,208; part-time $842 per semester hour. *Financial support:* Fellowships, research assistantships, teaching assistantships, career-related internships or fieldwork, institutionally sponsored loans, scholarships/grants, and unspecified assistantships available. Support available to part-time students. Financial award application deadline: 3/31; financial award applicants required to submit FAFSA. *Faculty research:* Suicidal behaviors, healthy youth and families, integrated healthcare and undeserved communities following disasters. *Unit head:* Dr. Elise Labbe-coldsmih, Chair, 251-460-6622, E-mail: elabbe@southalabama.edu. *Application contact:* Dr. Joe Currier, Director of Clinical Training, 251-460-6622, E-mail: jcurrier@southalabama.edu.
Website: http://www.southalabama.edu/ccp/

University of South Dakota, Graduate School, School of Education, Division of Counseling and Psychology in Education, Vermillion, SD 57069. Offers counseling (MA, PhD, Ed S); human development and educational psychology (MA, PhD, Ed S); mental health counseling (Certificate); school psychology (PhD, Ed S). *Accreditation:* ACA (one or more programs are accredited); NCATE. *Program availability:* Part-time. *Degree requirements:* For master's and other advanced degree, comprehensive exam, thesis or alternative; for doctorate, comprehensive exam, thesis/dissertation. *Entrance requirements:* For master's and doctorate, GRE General Test, minimum GPA of 3.0. Additional exam requirements/recommendations for international students: Required—TOEFL (minimum score 550 paper-based; 79 iBT). *Application deadline:* Applications are processed on a rolling basis. Application fee: $35. Electronic applications accepted. *Financial support:* Research assistantships with partial tuition reimbursements, teaching assistantships with partial tuition reimbursements, career-related internships or fieldwork, Federal Work-Study, and unspecified assistantships available. Financial award applicants required to submit FAFSA. *Application contact:* Graduate School, 605-658-6140, Fax: 605-677-6118.
Website: http://www.usd.edu/cpe

University of Southern Maine, College of Management and Human Service, School of Education and Human Development, Program in Counselor Education, Portland, ME 04103. Offers clinical mental health counseling (MS); counseling (CAS); culturally responsive practices in education and human development (CGS); mental health rehabilitation technician/community (CGS); rehabilitation counseling (MS); school counseling (MS); substance abuse counseling (CGS). *Accreditation:* ACA (one or more programs are accredited); CORE; TEAC. *Program availability:* Part-time, evening/weekend. *Degree requirements:* For master's, comprehensive exam, thesis or alternative; for other advanced degree, thesis or alternative. *Entrance requirements:* For master's, GRE General Test or MAT, interview; for other advanced degree, master's degree. Additional exam requirements/recommendations for international students: Required—TOEFL (minimum score 550 paper-based; 79 iBT). Electronic applications accepted. *Faculty research:* Counselor licensure, group dynamics, counseling theories, healthy adaptation, counselor educator well-being.

University of South Florida, College of Behavioral and Community Sciences, Department of Child and Family Studies, Tampa, FL 33620-9951. Offers applied behavior analysis (MA, MS, PhD); behavioral and community sciences (PhD); child and adolescent behavioral health (MS), including developmental disabilities, leadership in child and adolescent health, translational research and evaluation, youth and behavioral health; rehabilitation and mental health counseling (MA), including addictions and substance abuse counseling, marriage and family therapy. *Accreditation:* ACA. *Faculty:* 18 full-time (12 women), 2 part-time/adjunct (1 woman). *Students:* 188 full-time (166 women), 115 part-time (92 women); includes 121 minority (40 Black or African American, non-Hispanic/Latino; 8 Asian, non-Hispanic/Latino; 61 Hispanic/Latino; 12 Two or more races, non-Hispanic/Latino), 6 international. Average age 28. 287 applicants, 53% accepted, 89 enrolled. In 2017, 45 master's, 1 doctorate awarded. *Degree requirements:* For master's, comprehensive exam, thesis (for some programs); for doctorate, comprehensive exam, thesis/dissertation, Behavior Analyst Board Certification Exam. *Entrance requirements:* For master's, GRE General Test, minimum GPA of 3.0 in last 60 hours of coursework; letters of recommendation; one-page narrative describing experience, interest, and career goals in applied behavior analysis; resume or curriculum vitae (varies by program); for doctorate, GRE General Test, master's degree in behavioral analysis or closely-related field; minimum GPA of 3.5 in graduate course work; three letters of recommendation; campus visit with faculty interview; personal statement; curriculum vitae; evidence of research experiences and expertise. Additional exam requirements/recommendations for international students: Required—TOEFL (minimum score 550 paper-based; 79 iBT) or IELTS (minimum score 6.5). *Application deadline:* For fall admission, 12/5 for domestic and international students. Application fee: $30. *Financial support:* In 2017–18, 30 students received support. Unspecified assistantships available. *Faculty research:* Applied behavior analysis, autism, behavior management, behavioral intervention, children, developmental disabilities, experimental analysis of behavior, functional assessment, positive behavior support. *Total annual research expenditures:* $17.6 million. *Application contact:* Dr. Raymond G. Miltenberger, Professor/Director of Master's Program, 813-974-5079, Fax: 813-974-6115, E-mail: miltenbe@usf.edu.
Website: http://cfs.cbcs.usf.edu/

University of South Florida, Innovative Education, Tampa, FL 33620-9951. Offers adult, career and higher education (Graduate Certificate), including college teaching, leadership in developing human resources, leadership in higher education; Africana studies (Graduate Certificate), including diasporas and health disparities, genocide and human rights; aging studies (Graduate Certificate), including gerontology; art research (Graduate Certificate), including museum studies; business foundations (Graduate Certificate); chemical and biomedical engineering (Graduate Certificate), including materials science and engineering, water, health and sustainability; child and family studies (Graduate Certificate), including positive behavior support; civil and industrial engineering (Graduate Certificate), including transportation systems analysis; community and family health (Graduate Certificate), including maternal and child health, social marketing and public health, violence and injury: prevention and intervention, women's health; criminology (Graduate Certificate), including criminal justice administration; data science for public administration (Graduate Certificate); digital humanities (Graduate Certificate); educational measurement and research (Graduate Certificate), including evaluation; English (Graduate Certificate), including comparative literary studies, creative writing, professional and technical communication; entrepreneurship (Graduate Certificate); environmental health (Graduate Certificate), including safety management; epidemiology and biostatistics (Graduate Certificate), including applied biostatistics, biostatistics, concepts and tools of epidemiology, epidemiology, epidemiology of infectious diseases; geography, environment and planning (Graduate Certificate), including community development, environmental policy and management, geographical information systems; geology (Graduate Certificate), including hydrogeology; global health (Graduate Certificate), including disaster management, global health and Latin American and Caribbean studies, global health practice, humanitarian assistance, infection control; government and international affairs (Graduate Certificate), including Cuban studies, globalization studies; health policy and management (Graduate Certificate), including health management and leadership, public health policy and programs; hearing specialist: early intervention (Graduate Certificate); industrial and management systems engineering (Graduate Certificate), including systems engineering, technology management; information studies (Graduate Certificate), including school library media specialist; information systems/decision sciences (Graduate Certificate), including analytics and business intelligence; instructional technology (Graduate Certificate), including distance education, Florida digital/virtual educator, instructional design, multimedia design, Web design; internal medicine, bioethics and medical humanities (Graduate Certificate), including biomedical ethics; Latin American and Caribbean studies (Graduate Certificate); leadership for coastal resiliency planning (Graduate Certificate); mass communications (Graduate Certificate), including multimedia journalism; mathematics and statistics (Graduate

Certificate), including mathematics; medicine (Graduate Certificate), including aging and neuroscience, bioinformatics, biotechnology, brain fitness and memory management, clinical investigation, hand and upper limb rehabilitation, health informatics, health sciences, integrative weight management, intellectual property, medicine and gender, metabolic and nutritional medicine, metabolic cardiology, pharmacy sciences; national and competitive intelligence (Graduate Certificate); nursing (Graduate Certificate), including simulation based academic fellowship in advanced pain management; psychological and social foundations (Graduate Certificate), including career counseling, college teaching, diversity in education, mental health counseling, school counseling; public affairs (Graduate Certificate), including nonprofit management, public management, research administration; public health (Graduate Certificate), including assessing chemical toxicity and public health risks, health equity, pharmacoepidemiology, public health generalist, toxicology, translational research in adolescent behavioral health; public health practices (Graduate Certificate), including planning for healthy communities; rehabilitation and mental health counseling (Graduate Certificate), including integrative mental health care, marriage and family therapy, rehabilitation technology; secondary education (Graduate Certificate), including ESOL, foreign language education: culture and content, foreign language education: professional; social work (Graduate Certificate), including geriatric social work/clinical gerontology; special education (Graduate Certificate), including autism spectrum disorder, disabilities education: severe/profound; world languages (Graduate Certificate), including teaching English as a second language (TESL) or foreign language. *Unit head:* Dr. Cynthia DeLuca, Associate Vice President and Assistant Vice Provost, 813-974-3077, Fax: 813-974-7061, E-mail: deluca@usf.edu. *Application contact:* Owen Hooper, Director, Summer and Alternative Calendar Programs, 813-974-6917, E-mail: hooper@usf.edu.
Website: http://www.usf.edu/innovative-education/

The University of Tennessee, Graduate School, College of Education, Health and Human Sciences, Department of Educational Psychology and Counseling, Knoxville, TN 37996. Offers adult education (MS); applied educational psychology (MS); collaborative learning (Ed D); college student personnel (MS); mental health counseling (MS); rehabilitation counseling (MS); school counseling (MS). *Accreditation:* ACA (one or more programs are accredited); CORE (one or more programs are accredited); NCATE. *Program availability:* Part-time, evening/weekend. *Degree requirements:* For master's, thesis optional. *Entrance requirements:* For master's, GRE General Test, minimum GPA of 2.7. Additional exam requirements/recommendations for international students: Required—TOEFL. Electronic applications accepted.

The University of Texas at Austin, Graduate School, College of Education, Department of Educational Psychology, Austin, TX 78712-1111. Offers academic educational psychology (M Ed, MA); counseling psychology (PhD); counselor education (M Ed); human development, culture and learning sciences (PhD); program evaluation (MA); quantitative methods (M Ed, MA, PhD); school psychology (MA, PhD). *Accreditation:* APA (one or more programs are accredited). *Degree requirements:* For master's, thesis optional; for doctorate, thesis/dissertation. *Entrance requirements:* For master's and doctorate, GRE General Test, 3 letters of recommendation. Additional exam requirements/recommendations for international students: Required—TOEFL.

The University of Texas at Tyler, College of Education and Psychology, Department of Psychology and Counseling, Tyler, TX 75799-0001. Offers clinical psychology (MS), including neuropsychology, school psychology; counseling psychology (MA), including general, marriage and family; interdisciplinary studies (MSIS); school counseling (MA). *Program availability:* Part-time, evening/weekend. *Degree requirements:* For master's, comprehensive exam, thesis optional. *Entrance requirements:* For master's, GRE General Test, minimum GPA of 3.0. Additional exam requirements/recommendations for international students: Required—TOEFL. Electronic applications accepted. *Faculty research:* Neuropsychology, child abuse, psychometric properties of psychological instruments, maternal behavior, clinical practice issues, victimization of women, post-traumatic stress disorder.

University of the Cumberlands, Program in Professional Counseling, Williamsburg, KY 40769-1372. Offers MA. Program also offered in San Francisco. *Accreditation:* ACA. *Program availability:* Part-time, evening/weekend, online learning. Electronic applications accepted.

University of the District of Columbia, College of Arts and Sciences, Program in Counseling, Washington, DC 20008-1175. Offers MS. *Accreditation:* ACA.

University of the Southwest, Graduate Programs, Hobbs, NM 88240-9129. Offers business administration (MBA); curriculum and instruction (MSE); curriculum and instruction: bilingual (MSE); curriculum and instruction: TESOL (MSE); early childhood education (MSE); educational administration (MSE); mental health counseling (MSE); school counseling (MSE); special education (MSE); sports management (MBA). *Program availability:* Part-time, evening/weekend, online learning. *Degree requirements:* For master's, comprehensive exam, thesis (for some programs). *Entrance requirements:* Additional exam requirements/recommendations for international students: Recommended—TOEFL. Electronic applications accepted.

University of Utah, Graduate School, College of Education, Department of Educational Psychology, Salt Lake City, UT 84112. Offers clinical mental health counseling (M Ed); counseling psychology (PhD); elementary education (M Ed); instructional design and educational technology (M Ed); instructional design and technology (MS); learning and cognition (MS, PhD); reading and literacy (M Ed, PhD); school counseling (M Ed); school psychology (M Ed, PhD, Ed S); statistics (M Stat). *Accreditation:* APA (one or more programs are accredited). *Faculty:* 19 full-time (9 women), 12 part-time/adjunct (8 women). *Students:* 122 full-time (95 women), 97 part-time (68 women); includes 26 minority (4 Asian, non-Hispanic/Latino; 16 Hispanic/Latino; 6 Two or more races, non-Hispanic/Latino), 7 international. Average age 31. 296 applicants, 27% accepted, 73 enrolled. In 2017, 65 master's, 15 doctorates awarded. Terminal master's awarded for partial completion of doctoral program. *Entrance requirements:* For master's and doctorate, GRE General Test, minimum GPA of 3.0. Additional exam requirements/recommendations for international students: Required—TOEFL (minimum score 80 iBT). *Application deadline:* For fall admission, 12/15 for domestic and international students; for winter admission, 11/1 for domestic and international students; for spring admission, 3/15 for domestic and international students. Application fee: $55 ($65 for international students). Electronic applications accepted. *Expenses:* Contact institution. *Financial support:* In 2017–18, 84 students received support, including 12 fellowships with full and partial tuition reimbursements available (averaging $17,000 per year), 16 research assistantships with full and partial tuition reimbursements available (averaging $15,500 per year), 39 teaching assistantships with full and partial tuition reimbursements available (averaging $15,500 per year); career-related internships or fieldwork, scholarships/grants, traineeships, health care benefits, and unspecified assistantships also available. Financial award application deadline: 4/1; financial award applicants required to submit FAFSA. *Faculty research:* Autism, computer technology and instruction, cognitive behavior, aging, group counseling. *Total annual research expenditures:* $620,935. *Unit head:* Dr. Anne E. Cook, Chair, 801-581-7148, Fax: 801-581-5566, E-mail: anne.cook@utah.edu. *Application contact:* JoLynn N. Yates, Academic Coordinator, 801-581-7148, Fax: 801-581-5566, E-mail: jo.yates@utah.edu.
Website: http://www.ed.utah.edu/edps/

University of Vermont, Graduate College, College of Education and Social Services, Counseling Program, Burlington, VT 05405. Offers counseling (MS), including clinical mental health, school counseling. *Accreditation:* ACA; NCATE. *Students:* 68 (54 women); includes 4 minority (1 American Indian or Alaska Native, non-Hispanic/Latino; 1 Hispanic/Latino; 2 Two or more races, non-Hispanic/Latino). 99 applicants, 64% accepted, 35 enrolled. In 2017, 11 master's awarded. *Entrance requirements:* For master's, resume. Additional exam requirements/recommendations for international students: Required—TOEFL (minimum score 550 paper-based, 90 iBT) or IELTS (6.5). *Application deadline:* For fall admission, 2/1 for domestic and international students. Application fee: $65. Electronic applications accepted. *Expenses:* Tuition, state resident: full-time $11,628; part-time $646 per credit. Tuition, nonresident: full-time $29,340; part-time $1630 per credit. *Required fees:* $1994; $10 per credit. Tuition and fees vary according to course load and program. *Financial support:* In 2017–18, 1 student received support, including 1 teaching assistantship with partial tuition reimbursement available (averaging $8,000 per year); fellowships and research assistantships also available. Financial award application deadline: 2/1. *Faculty research:* Women and tenure, counseling children and adolescents. *Unit head:* Dr. Aaron Kindsvatter, Program Coordinator, 802-656-3888, E-mail: cslgprog@uvm.edu.
Website: https://www.uvm.edu/cess/dlds/counseling

University of Victoria, Faculty of Graduate Studies, Faculty of Education, Department of Educational Psychology and Leadership Studies, Victoria, BC V8W 2Y2, Canada. Offers aboriginal communities counseling (M Ed); counseling (M Ed, MA); educational psychology (M Ed, MA, PhD), including counseling psychology (M Ed, MA), leadership studies (PhD), learning and development (MA, PhD), measurement and evaluation, special education (M Ed, MA); leadership studies (M Ed, MA). *Program availability:* Part-time. *Degree requirements:* For master's, thesis (for some programs), comprehensive exam (M Ed); for doctorate, comprehensive exam, thesis/dissertation, candidacy exam. *Entrance requirements:* For master's, 2 years of work experience in a relevant field; for doctorate, GRE, 2 years of work experience in a relevant field, minimum B average. Additional exam requirements/recommendations for international students: Required—TOEFL (minimum score 575 paper-based), IELTS (minimum score 7). *Faculty research:* Learning and development (child, adolescent and adult), special education and exceptional children.

The University of Western Ontario, Faculty of Graduate Studies, Social Sciences Division, Faculty of Education, Program in Counseling Psychology, London, ON N6A 5B8, Canada. Offers M Ed. *Program availability:* Part-time. *Entrance requirements:* For master's, minimum B average, 3 years' experience in helping profession. *Faculty research:* Women's issues in counseling, causes for sexual harassment in the workplace, counselor memory and confidence in clinical judgements.

University of West Florida, Usha Kundu, MD College of Health, Department of Psychology, Pensacola, FL 32514-5750. Offers applied experimental (MA); counseling (MA); industrial-organizational (MA). *Program availability:* Part-time. *Degree requirements:* For master's, thesis (for some programs). *Entrance requirements:* For master's, GRE, official transcripts; minimum GPA of 3.0; writing sample; three letters of reference; field experience or skill sets; oral interview (for counseling specialization). Additional exam requirements/recommendations for international students: Required—TOEFL (minimum score 550 paper-based). *Faculty research:* Prose recall, brain imaging, peak performance, biofeedback and pain control, comparable worth.

University of Wisconsin–Madison, Graduate School, School of Education, Department of Counseling Psychology, Program in Counseling Psychology, Madison, WI 53706-1380. Offers PhD. *Accreditation:* APA. *Degree requirements:* For doctorate, thesis/dissertation.

University of Wisconsin–Milwaukee, Graduate School, School of Education, Department of Educational Psychology, Milwaukee, WI 53201-0413. Offers children's mental health for school professionals (Graduate Certificate); counseling psychology (PhD); educational statistics and measurement (MS, PhD); learning and development (MS, PhD); multicultural knowledge of mental health practices (Graduate Certificate); school counseling (MS); school counseling (Graduate Certificate); school psychology (MS, PhD, Ed S). *Accreditation:* APA. *Program availability:* Part-time. *Students:* 170 full-time (132 women), 52 part-time (39 women); includes 51 minority (14 Black or African American, non-Hispanic/Latino; 1 American Indian or Alaska Native, non-Hispanic/Latino; 7 Asian, non-Hispanic/Latino; 7 Hispanic/Latino; 1 Native Hawaiian or other Pacific Islander, non-Hispanic/Latino; 21 Two or more races, non-Hispanic/Latino), 4 international. Average age 31. 304 applicants, 39% accepted, 83 enrolled. In 2017, 59 master's, 11 doctorates, 10 other advanced degrees awarded. *Degree requirements:* For master's, comprehensive exam, thesis; for doctorate, thesis/dissertation. *Entrance requirements:* For master's, minimum GPA of 3.0; for doctorate, GRE General Test, minimum GPA of 3.0. Additional exam requirements/recommendations for international students: Required—TOEFL (minimum score 550 paper-based; 79 iBT), IELTS (minimum score 6.5). *Application deadline:* For fall admission, 1/1 priority date for domestic students; for spring admission, 9/1 for domestic students. Application fee: $56 ($96 for international students). Electronic applications accepted. *Financial support:* Fellowships, research assistantships, teaching assistantships, career-related internships or fieldwork, health care benefits, unspecified assistantships, and project assistantships available. Support available to part-time students. Financial award application deadline: 4/15; financial award applicants required to submit FAFSA. *Application contact:* General Information Contact, 414-229-4721, E-mail: soeinfo@uwm.edu.
Website: http://uwm.edu/education/academics/educational-psychology-department/

University of Wisconsin–Stout, Graduate School, College of Education, Health and Human Sciences, School of Education, Program in School Counseling, Menomonie, WI 54751. Offers MS. *Accreditation:* ACA. *Program availability:* Part-time. *Degree requirements:* For master's, thesis. *Entrance requirements:* For master's, minimum GPA of 2.75. Additional exam requirements/recommendations for international students: Required—TOEFL (minimum score 500 paper-based; 61 iBT). Electronic applications accepted. *Faculty research:* Adventure-based learning, body image, domestic violence, resilience, school climate.

Utah State University, School of Graduate Studies, Emma Eccles Jones College of Education and Human Services, Department of Psychology, Logan, UT 84322. Offers clinical/counseling/school psychology (PhD); research and evaluation methodology (PhD); school counseling (MS); school psychology (MS). *Accreditation:* APA (one or more programs are accredited). *Program availability:* Part-time, evening/weekend, online learning. Terminal master's awarded for partial completion of doctoral program. *Degree requirements:* For master's, thesis (for some programs); for doctorate, thesis/dissertation. *Entrance requirements:* For master's, GRE General Test (school psychology), MAT (school counseling), minimum GPA of 3.5; for doctorate, GRE General Test, minimum GPA of 3.5. Additional exam requirements/recommendations for international students: Required—TOEFL. *Faculty research:* Hearing loss detection in infancy, ADHD, eating disorders, domestic violence, neuropsychology, bilingual/Spanish speaking students/parents.

Virginia Commonwealth University, Graduate School, College of Humanities and Sciences, Department of Psychology, Program in Counseling Psychology, Richmond,

VA 23284-9005. Offers PhD. *Accreditation:* ACA; APA. *Degree requirements:* For doctorate, thesis/dissertation. *Entrance requirements:* For doctorate, GRE General Test, GRE Subject Test. Additional exam requirements/recommendations for international students: Required—TOEFL (minimum score 600 paper-based; 100 iBT); Recommended—IELTS (minimum score 6.5). Electronic applications accepted.

Virginia Commonwealth University, Graduate School, School of Allied Health Professions, Program in Patient Counseling, Richmond, VA 23284-9005. Offers MS. *Accreditation:* ACA. *Entrance requirements:* For master's, GRE General Test. Additional exam requirements/recommendations for international students: Required—TOEFL (minimum score 600 paper-based; 100 iBT). Electronic applications accepted.

Viterbo University, Master of Science in Mental Health Counseling Program, La Crosse, WI 54601-4797. Offers addiction counseling (MS); child and adolescent counseling (MS); complementary health and wellness counseling (MS). *Accreditation:* ACA. *Program availability:* Part-time, evening/weekend. *Degree requirements:* For master's, comprehensive exam, thesis, 54 credits of core program courses; 6 elective credits; minimum GPA of 3.0; action research project; practicum/internship experience. *Entrance requirements:* For master's, MAT, BS in a human service or social science discipline; prerequisite coursework in general psychology, behavior disorders/abnormal psychology, and research methods/statistics; minimum undergraduate cumulative GPA of 3.0; background check; personal statement; undergraduate transcripts; interview. Additional exam requirements/recommendations for international students: Required—TOEFL (minimum score 525 paper-based). Electronic applications accepted. Application fee is waived when completed online. *Expenses:* Contact institution. *Faculty research:* Supervision, recovery substance abuse, culture, counseling theory, health and wellness.

Walden University, Graduate Programs, School of Counseling, Minneapolis, MN 55401. Offers addiction counseling (MS), including addictions and public health, child and adolescent counseling, family studies and interventions, forensic counseling, general program, military families and culture, trauma and crisis counseling; clinical mental health counseling (MS), including addiction counseling, forensic counseling, military families and culture, trauma and crisis counseling; counselor education and supervision (PhD), including consultation, counseling and social change, forensic mental health counseling, leadership and program evaluation, trauma and crisis; marriage, couple, and family counseling (MS), including addiction counseling, career counseling, forensic counseling, military families and culture, trauma and crisis counseling; school counseling (MS), including addiction counseling, career counseling, crisis and trauma, military families and culture. *Accreditation:* ACA. *Program availability:* Part-time, evening/weekend, online only, 100% online. *Degree requirements:* For master's, residency, field experience, professional development plan, licensure plan; for doctorate, thesis/dissertation, residency, practicum, internship. *Entrance requirements:* For master's, bachelor's degree or higher; minimum GPA of 2.5; official transcripts; goal statement (for some programs); access to computer and Internet; for doctorate, master's degree or higher; three years of related professional or academic experience (preferred); minimum GPA of 3.0; goal statement and current resume (for select programs); official transcripts; access to computer and Internet. Additional exam requirements/recommendations for international students: Required—TOEFL (minimum score 550 paper-based, 79 iBT), IELTS (minimum score 6.5), Michigan English Language Assessment Battery (minimum score 82), or PTE (minimum score 53). Electronic applications accepted.

Walden University, Graduate Programs, School of Psychology, Minneapolis, MN 55401. Offers clinical psychology (MS), including counseling, general program; forensic psychology (MS), including forensic psychology in the community, general program, mental health applications, program planning and evaluation in forensic settings, psychology and legal systems; industrial organizational (MS, PhD), including consulting psychology, forensic (MS), forensic psychology (PhD), general practice, leadership development and coaching (MS), organizational diversity and social change, research evaluation (PhD); online teaching in psychology (Post-Master's Certificate); organizational psychology and development (Postbaccalaureate Certificate); psychology (MS, PhD), including applied psychology (MS), clinical psychology (PhD), crisis management and response (MS), educational psychology, forensic psychology (PhD), general psychology (MS), general psychology research (PhD), general psychology teaching (PhD), health psychology, leadership development and coaching (MS), psychology of culture (MS), psychology, public administration, and social change (MS), social psychology, terrorism and security (MS); psychology respecialization (Post-Doctoral Certificate). *Program availability:* Part-time, evening/weekend, online only, 100% online. Terminal master's awarded for partial completion of doctoral program. *Degree requirements:* For master's, thesis optional; for doctorate, thesis/dissertation, residency. *Entrance requirements:* For master's, bachelor's degree or higher; minimum GPA of 2.5; official transcripts; goal statement (for some programs); access to computer and Internet; for doctorate, master's degree or higher; three years of related professional or academic experience (preferred); minimum GPA of 3.0; goal statement and current resume (for select programs); official transcripts; access to computer and Internet; for other advanced degree, relevant work experience; access to computer and Internet. Additional exam requirements/recommendations for international students: Required—TOEFL (minimum score 550 paper-based, 79 iBT), IELTS (minimum score 6.5), Michigan English Language Assessment Battery (minimum score 82), or PTE (minimum score 53). Electronic applications accepted.

Walden University, Graduate Programs, School of Social Work and Human Services, Minneapolis, MN 55401. Offers addictions and social work (DSW); advanced clinical practice (MSW); clinical expertise (DSW); criminal justice (DSW); disaster, crisis, and intervention (DSW); family studies and interventions (DSW); human and social services (PhD), including advanced research, community and social services, community intervention and leadership, conflict management, criminal justice, disaster crisis and intervention, family studies and intervention, gerontology, global social services, higher education, human services and nonprofit administration, mental health facilitation; medical social work (DSW); military social work (MSW); policy practice (DSW); social work (PhD), including addictions and social work, clinical expertise, criminal justice, disaster, crisis and intervention, family studies and interventions, medical social work, policy practice, social work administration; social work administration (DSW); social work in healthcare (MSW); social work with children and families (MSW). *Accreditation:* CSWE. *Program availability:* Part-time, evening/weekend, online only, 100% online. *Degree requirements:* For master's, residency (for some programs); for doctorate, thesis/dissertation, residency. *Entrance requirements:* For master's, bachelor's degree or higher; minimum GPA of 2.5; official transcripts; goal statement (for some programs); access to computer and Internet; for doctorate, master's degree or higher; three years of related professional or academic experience (preferred); minimum GPA of 3.0; goal statement and current resume (for select programs); official transcripts; access to computer and Internet. Additional exam requirements/recommendations for international students: Required—TOEFL (minimum score 550 paper-based, 79 iBT), IELTS (minimum score 6.5), Michigan English Language Assessment Battery (minimum score 82), or PTE (minimum score 53). Electronic applications accepted.

Walsh University, Graduate Programs, Program in Counseling and Human Development, North Canton, OH 44720-3396. Offers clinical mental health counseling (MA); school counseling (MA); student affairs in higher education (MA). *Accreditation:* ACA. *Program availability:* Part-time, evening/weekend. *Degree requirements:* For master's, comprehensive exam, internship, practicum. *Entrance requirements:* For master's, GRE (minimum score of 145 verbal and 146 quantitative) or MAT (minimum score of 397), interview, minimum GPA of 3.0, writing sample, reference forms, notarized affidavit of good moral conduct. Additional exam requirements/recommendations for international students: Required—TOEFL (minimum score 500 paper-based; 61 iBT). Electronic applications accepted. Application fee is waived when completed online. *Expenses:* Contact institution. *Faculty research:* Supervision of clinical mental health, clinical mental health practice/issues, clinical mental health skills development, advocacy, teaching and professional development, career development, refugee development in US, supervision in student affairs, offender treatment, domestic violence issues, alcohol and drug treatment issues, Professional identity and advocacy in school counseling, Efficacy in counseling clinic.

Washington Adventist University, Program in Counseling Psychology, Takoma Park, MD 20912. Offers MA. *Program availability:* Part-time. *Students:* 12 full-time (9 women), 20 part-time (14 women); includes 22 minority (15 Black or African American, non-Hispanic/Latino; 3 Asian, non-Hispanic/Latino; 2 Hispanic/Latino; 2 Two or more races, non-Hispanic/Latino), 4 international. Average age 35. In 2017, 16 master's awarded. *Entrance requirements:* Additional exam requirements/recommendations for international students: Required—TOEFL (minimum score 550 paper-based), IELTS (minimum score 5). *Application deadline:* Applications are processed on a rolling basis. *Expenses:* Tuition: Part-time $625 per credit. *Financial support:* Applicants required to submit FAFSA. *Unit head:* Dr. Patrick Wiliams, Associate Provost, 301-891-4116, E-mail: pawillia@wau.edu. *Application contact:* Jessica Ritchie, Program Coordinator, 301-891-4086, Fax: 301-891-4023, E-mail: jritchie@wau.edu.

Washington Adventist University, Program in Professional Counseling Psychology, Takoma Park, MD 20912. Offers MA. *Program availability:* Part-time. *Students:* 12 full-time (9 women), 20 part-time (14 women); includes 18 minority (13 Black or African American, non-Hispanic/Latino; 2 Asian, non-Hispanic/Latino; 2 Hispanic/Latino; 1 Two or more races, non-Hispanic/Latino), 4 international. Average age 35. In 2017, 8 master's awarded. *Entrance requirements:* Additional exam requirements/recommendations for international students: Required—TOEFL (minimum score 550 paper-based), IELTS (minimum score 5). *Application deadline:* Applications are processed on a rolling basis. *Expenses:* Tuition: Part-time $625 per credit. *Financial support:* Applicants required to submit FAFSA. *Unit head:* Dr. Patrick Williams, Associate Provost, 301-891-4116, E-mail: pawillia@wau.edu. *Application contact:* Jessica Ritchie, Program Coordinator, 301-891-4086, Fax: 301-891-4023, E-mail: jritchie@wau.edu.
Website: http://www.wau.edu/index.php?option-com_content&view-article&id-409temid-966

Washington State University, College of Education, Department of Educational Leadership, Sports Studies, and Educational/Counseling Psychology, Pullman, WA 99164-2136. Offers counseling psychology (PhD); educational leadership (Ed M, MA, Ed D, PhD); educational psychology (MA, PhD); sport management (MA). Programs also offered at the Spokane, Tri-Cities, Vancouver and Global (online) campuses. *Program availability:* Part-time, online learning. *Degree requirements:* For master's, comprehensive exam (for some programs), thesis (for some programs), oral or written exam; for doctorate, comprehensive exam, thesis/dissertation, oral and written exam, internship. *Entrance requirements:* For master's and doctorate, GRE General Test, minimum GPA of 3.0, 3 letters of recommendation, transcripts showing all college or university course work, statement of professional objectives, current curriculum vitae/resume. Additional exam requirements/recommendations for international students: Required—TOEFL (minimum score 550 paper-based; 80 iBT). Electronic applications accepted. *Faculty research:* Multicultural counseling and career development, educational and psychological measurement issues, business decision-making process and power relationships, leadership practices and processes as suffused with and constituted by emotion work.

Wayland Baptist University, Graduate Programs, Programs in Behavioral and Social Sciences, Plainview, TX 79072-6998. Offers counseling (MA); criminal justice (MACJ); government administration (MPA); history (MA); homeland security (MPA); humanities (MAH); justice administration (MPA). *Program availability:* Part-time, evening/weekend, 100% online, blended/hybrid learning. *Faculty:* 19 full-time (5 women), 18 part-time/adjunct (8 women). *Students:* 16 full-time (10 women), 322 part-time (183 women); includes 207 minority (82 Black or African American, non-Hispanic/Latino; 8 American Indian or Alaska Native, non-Hispanic/Latino; 8 Asian, non-Hispanic/Latino; 84 Hispanic/Latino; 5 Native Hawaiian or other Pacific Islander, non-Hispanic/Latino; 20 Two or more races, non-Hispanic/Latino), 1 international. Average age 40. 56 applicants, 93% accepted, 39 enrolled. In 2017, 141 master's awarded. *Degree requirements:* For master's, comprehensive exam. *Entrance requirements:* For master's, GRE, MAT. Additional exam requirements/recommendations for international students: Required—TOEFL (minimum score 500 paper-based; 61 iBT). *Application deadline:* Applications are processed on a rolling basis. Application fee: $50. Electronic applications accepted. *Expenses:* Tuition: Full-time $11,250; part-time $625 per credit hour. *Required fees:* $1200. *Financial support:* Federal Work-Study, institutionally sponsored loans, and scholarships/grants available. Support available to part-time students. Financial award application deadline: 5/1; financial award applicants required to submit FAFSA. *Unit head:* Dr. Peter Bowen, Dean, 806-291-1179, Fax: 806-291-1972, E-mail: pbowen@wbu.edu. *Application contact:* Amanda Stanton, Graduate Studies, 806-291-3423, Fax: 806-291-1950, E-mail: stanton@wbu.edu.

Waynesburg University, Graduate and Professional Studies, Canonsburg, PA 15370. Offers business (MBA), including energy management, finance, health systems, human resources, leadership, market development; counseling (MA), including addictions counseling, clinical mental health; counselor education and supervision (PhD); criminal investigation (MA); education (M Ed), including autism, curriculum and instruction, educational leadership, online teaching; nursing (MSN), including administration, education, informatics; nursing practice (DNP); special education (M Ed); technology (M Ed); MSN/MBA. *Accreditation:* AACN. *Program availability:* Part-time, evening/weekend. *Degree requirements:* For doctorate, thesis/dissertation. *Entrance requirements:* Additional exam requirements/recommendations for international students: Required—TOEFL. Electronic applications accepted.

Wayne State University, College of Education, Division of Theoretical and Behavioral Foundations, Detroit, MI 48202. Offers applied behavior analysis (Certificate); counseling (M Ed, MA, Ed D, Ed S); counseling psychology (MA, PhD); education evaluation and research (M Ed, Ed D); educational psychology (M Ed, PhD), including learning and instruction sciences (PhD); rehabilitation counseling and community inclusion (MA); school and community psychology (MA, Certificate). *Accreditation:* ACA (one or more programs are accredited); CORE (one or more programs are accredited). *Program availability:* Evening/weekend. *Students:* Average age 32. 294 applicants, 34% accepted, 72 enrolled. In 2017, 87 master's, 12 doctorates, 14 other advanced degrees awarded. *Entrance requirements:* For master's, GRE, interview, personal statement, portfolio (art therapy); for doctorate, GRE, department-written exam, interview, curriculum vitae, references, master's degree in closely-related field with minimum GPA

of 3.5, demonstration of counseling skills (for Ed D in counseling); for other advanced degree, master's degree in counseling and counseling license (for Ed S); good standing in school and community psychology MA program (for Certificate). Additional exam requirements/recommendations for international students: Required—TOEFL (minimum score 550 paper-based; 79 iBT), Michigan English Language Assessment Battery (minimum score 85); Recommended—IELTS (minimum score 6.5), TWE (minimum score 5.5). *Application deadline:* For fall admission, 6/1 priority date for domestic students, 5/1 priority date for international students; for winter admission, 10/1 priority date for domestic students, 9/1 priority date for international students; for spring admission, 2/1 priority date for domestic students, 1/1 priority date for international students. Applications are processed on a rolling basis. Application fee: $50. Electronic applications accepted. *Expenses:* Contact institution. *Financial support:* In 2017–18, 92 students received support, including 2 research assistantships with tuition reimbursements available (averaging $17,994 per year); fellowships, teaching assistantships, Federal Work-Study, scholarships/grants, health care benefits, and unspecified assistantships also available. Support available to part-time students. Financial award applicants required to submit FAFSA. *Faculty research:* Adolescents at risk, supervision of counseling. *Unit head:* Dr. Cheryl Somers, Assistant Dean, 313-577-1670, E-mail: c.somers@wayne.edu. *Application contact:* Janice Green, Assistant Dean, 313-577-1605, E-mail: jwgreen@wayne.edu.
Website: http://coe.wayne.edu/tbf/index.php

Webster University, College of Arts and Sciences, Department of Professional Counseling, St. Louis, MO 63119-3194. Offers counseling (MA). *Accreditation:* ACA. *Program availability:* Part-time. *Entrance requirements:* Additional exam requirements/recommendations for international students: Required—TOEFL.

Webster University, College of Arts and Sciences, Department of Psychology, St. Louis, MO 63119-3194. Offers counseling psychology (MS); gerontology (MS). *Program availability:* Part-time. *Entrance requirements:* Additional exam requirements/recommendations for international students: Required—TOEFL.

Western Kentucky University, Graduate Studies, College of Education and Behavioral Sciences, Department of Counseling and Student Affairs, Bowling Green, KY 42101. Offers counseling (MA Ed), including marriage and family therapy, mental health counseling; school counseling (P-12) (MA Ed); student affairs in higher education (MA Ed). *Accreditation:* ACA; NCATE. *Program availability:* Part-time, evening/weekend. *Degree requirements:* For master's, comprehensive exam, thesis optional. *Entrance requirements:* For master's, GRE General Test. Additional exam requirements/recommendations for international students: Required—TOEFL (minimum score 555 paper-based; 79 iBT). *Faculty research:* Counselor education, research for residential workers.

Western Michigan University, Graduate College, College of Education and Human Development, Department of Counselor Education and Counseling Psychology, Kalamazoo, MI 49008. Offers counseling psychology (MA, PhD); counselor education (MA, PhD), including counselor education (MA). *Accreditation:* ACA (one or more programs are accredited); APA (one or more programs are accredited); CORE; NCATE. *Degree requirements:* For doctorate, thesis/dissertation.

Western Washington University, Graduate School, College of Humanities and Social Sciences, Department of Psychology, Program in Mental Health Counseling, Bellingham, WA 98225-5996. Offers MS. *Accreditation:* ACA. *Degree requirements:* For master's, thesis optional. *Entrance requirements:* For master's, GRE General Test, minimum GPA of 3.0 in last 60 semester hours or last 90 quarter hours. Additional exam requirements/recommendations for international students: Required—TOEFL (minimum score 567 paper-based). Electronic applications accepted.

Westfield State University, College of Graduate and Continuing Education, Department of Psychology, Program in Counseling, Westfield, MA 01086. Offers forensic mental health counseling (MA); mental health counseling (MA); school adjustment counseling (MA); school guidance counseling (MA). *Program availability:* Part-time, evening/weekend. *Faculty:* 5 full-time (3 women), 4 part-time/adjunct (1 woman). *Students:* 36 full-time (27 women), 14 part-time (10 women); includes 9 minority (1 Black or African American, non-Hispanic/Latino; 1 Asian, non-Hispanic/Latino; 4 Hispanic/Latino; 3 Two or more races, non-Hispanic/Latino). Average age 28. 29 applicants, 79% accepted, 16 enrolled. In 2017, 10 master's awarded. *Degree requirements:* For master's, comprehensive exam, practicum. *Entrance requirements:* For master's, GRE General Test, MAT, minimum undergraduate GPA of 3.0. Additional exam requirements/recommendations for international students: Recommended—TOEFL (minimum score 550 paper-based; 79 iBT). *Application deadline:* For fall admission, 2/1 for domestic students. Applications are processed on a rolling basis. Application fee: $50. *Expenses:* Tuition, state resident: part-time $332 per credit. Tuition, nonresident: part-time $332 per credit. *Required fees:* $75 per semester. Tuition and fees vary according to program. *Financial support:* Unspecified assistantships available. Financial award application deadline: 4/1; financial award applicants required to submit FAFSA. *Unit head:* Dr. Robert Hayes, Professor, 413-572-5700, Fax: 413-572-5227, E-mail: rhayes@westfield.ma.edu. *Application contact:* Shelly Henrichon, Coordinator of College of Graduate and Continuing Education Admissions, 413-572-8022, Fax: 413-572-5227, E-mail: mhenrichon@westfield.ma.edu.

Westminster College, Master of Science in Mental Health Counseling Program, Salt Lake City, UT 84105-3697. Offers MSMHC. *Faculty:* 3 full-time (all women), 3 part-time/adjunct (2 women). *Students:* 19 full-time (15 women), 11 part-time (8 women); includes 4 minority (1 Asian, non-Hispanic/Latino; 2 Hispanic/Latino; 1 Two or more races, non-Hispanic/Latino). Average age 32. 27 applicants, 63% accepted, 11 enrolled. In 2017, 9 master's awarded. *Degree requirements:* For master's, comprehensive exam, internship. *Entrance requirements:* For master's, GRE (waived if undergraduate GPA is 3.4 or higher), baccalaureate degree from regionally-accredited college or university or a recognized international college or university; official copies of transcripts sent by the registrar of each college or university attended; three letters of recommendation; proof of clear state and federal background checks. Additional exam requirements/recommendations for international students: Required—TOEFL (minimum score 84 iBT), IELTS (minimum score 7). *Application deadline:* For fall admission, 2/1 priority date for domestic and international students. Applications are processed on a rolling basis. Application fee: $50. Electronic applications accepted. *Expenses:* $757 per credit hour, plus $13 student fee per credit hour, fall and spring only. *Financial support:* Career-related internships or fieldwork, scholarships/grants, unspecified assistantships, and tuition remission available. Financial award applicants required to submit FAFSA. *Faculty research:* Mental health issues, trauma, eating disorder, anxiety, depression, interpersonal relationships. *Unit head:* Colleen Sandor, Director, 801-832-2422, E-mail: csandor@westminstercollege.edu. *Application contact:* Collin Bess, Enrollment Coordinator/Admissions Recruiter, 801-832-2207, Fax: 801-832-3101, E-mail: cbess@westminstercollege.edu.
Website: https://www.westminstercollege.edu/graduate/programs

West Virginia University, College of Education and Human Services, Morgantown, WV 26506. Offers audiology (Au D); autism spectrum disorder (MA); clinical rehabilitation and mental health counseling (MS); communication science and disorders (PhD); counseling (MA); counseling psychology (PhD); curriculum and instruction (Ed D); early childhood education (MA); early intervention (MA); education (PhD); educational leadership (MA, Ed D); educational leadership/public school administration (MA); educational psychology (MA, Ed D); elementary education (MA); gifted education (MA); higher education administration (MA, Ed D); higher education curriculum and teaching (MA); institutional design and technology (MA); instructional design and technology (Ed D); literacy education (MA); secondary education (MA); secondary education/English (MA); special education (Ed D); speech pathology (MS). *Accreditation:* NCATE. *Program availability:* Part-time, evening/weekend, online learning. *Students:* 423 full-time (347 women), 367 part-time (316 women); includes 57 minority (14 Black or African American, non-Hispanic/Latino; 7 Asian, non-Hispanic/Latino; 20 Hispanic/Latino; 16 Two or more races, non-Hispanic/Latino), 13 international. *Degree requirements:* For master's, content exams; for doctorate, comprehensive exam, thesis/dissertation. *Entrance requirements:* Additional exam requirements/recommendations for international students: Required—TOEFL (minimum score 500 paper-based; 61 iBT). *Application deadline:* For fall admission, 8/1 for domestic students; for spring admission, 1/1 for domestic students; for summer admission, 5/1 for domestic students. Application fee: $60. Electronic applications accepted. *Expenses:* Tuition, state resident: full-time $9450. Tuition, nonresident: full-time $24,390. *Financial support:* Fellowships, research assistantships, teaching assistantships, career-related internships or fieldwork, Federal Work-Study, institutionally sponsored loans, health care benefits, tuition waivers (full and partial), and administrative assistantships available. Financial award applicants required to submit FAFSA. *Faculty research:* Internet training and integration for teachers, rural education, teacher preparation, organization of schools, evaluation of personnel. *Unit head:* Dr. Gypsy Denzine, Dean, 304-293-5703, Fax: 304-293-7565, E-mail: gypsy.denzine@mail.wvu.edu. *Application contact:* Dr. M. Cecil Smith, Associate Dean for Research and Graduate Education, 304-293-2174, Fax: 304-293-3802, E-mail: mcecil.smith@mail.wvu.edu.
Website: http://cehs.wvu.edu/

Wheaton College, Graduate School, Department of Psychology, Wheaton, IL 60187-5593. Offers clinical mental health counseling (MA); clinical psychology (Psy D); marriage and family therapy (MA). *Accreditation:* APA (one or more programs are accredited). *Faculty:* 15 full-time (7 women), 12 part-time/adjunct (9 women). *Students:* 132 full-time (99 women), 26 part-time (13 women); includes 40 minority (12 Black or African American, non-Hispanic/Latino; 2 American Indian or Alaska Native, non-Hispanic/Latino; 12 Asian, non-Hispanic/Latino; 7 Hispanic/Latino; 7 Two or more races, non-Hispanic/Latino), 28 international. Average age 28. 139 applicants, 74% accepted, 69 enrolled. In 2017, 62 master's, 20 doctorates awarded. Terminal master's awarded for partial completion of doctoral program. *Degree requirements:* For master's, thesis or alternative; for doctorate, thesis/dissertation, internship. *Entrance requirements:* For master's, GRE General Test, 18 hours of course work in psychology; for doctorate, GRE General Test. Additional exam requirements/recommendations for international students: Required—TOEFL (minimum score 550 paper-based; 80 iBT), IELTS (minimum score 6.5). *Application deadline:* For fall admission, 3/1 priority date for domestic students, 1/1 for international students. Applications are processed on a rolling basis. Application fee: $30. *Expenses: Tuition:* Full-time $19,800; part-time $825 per credit hour. Tuition and fees vary according to degree level and program. *Financial support:* In 2017–18, 3 research assistantships (averaging $4,800 per year) were awarded; career-related internships or fieldwork, Federal Work-Study, scholarships/grants, and unspecified assistantships also available. Financial award application deadline: 3/1; financial award applicants required to submit FAFSA. *Unit head:* Dr. Terri Watson, Associate Dean of Psychology, 630-752-5104, E-mail: psychology@wheaton.edu. *Application contact:* Director of Graduate Admissions, 630-752-5195, Fax: 630-752-7047, E-mail: graduate.admissions@wheaton.edu.
Website: https://www.wheaton.edu/academics/programs/psychology/graduate-programs/

William Carey University, Department of Psychology and Graduate Counseling, Hattiesburg, MS 39401. Offers counseling psychology (MS). *Program availability:* Part-time. *Entrance requirements:* For master's, GRE, PRAXIS, MAT, minimum GPA of 2.5. Additional exam requirements/recommendations for international students: Required—TOEFL (minimum score 550 paper-based). *Expenses:* Contact institution. *Faculty research:* Addiction prevention, psychometric measurement, crisis counseling, gerontology.

William James College, Graduate Programs, Newton, MA 02459. Offers applied psychology in higher education student personnel administration (MA); clinical psychology (Psy D); counseling psychology (MA); counseling psychology and community mental health (MA); counseling psychology and global mental health (MA); executive coaching (Graduate Certificate); forensic and counseling psychology (MA); leadership psychology (Psy D); organizational psychology (MA); primary care psychology (MA); respecialization in clinical psychology (Certificate); school psychology (Psy D); MA/CAGS. *Accreditation:* APA. *Degree requirements:* For master's, comprehensive exam (for some programs); for doctorate, thesis/dissertation (for some programs). Electronic applications accepted.

William Paterson University of New Jersey, College of Humanities and Social Sciences, Wayne, NJ 07470-8420. Offers applied sociology (MA); assessment and evaluation research (Certificate); bilingual education (Certificate); clinical and counseling psychology (MA); clinical psychology (Psy D); creative and professional writing (MFA); English (MA); history (MA); public policy and international affairs (MA); teaching English as a second language (Certificate). *Program availability:* Part-time. *Faculty:* 36 full-time (21 women), 10 part-time/adjunct (5 women). *Students:* 62 full-time (44 women), 102 part-time (71 women); includes 76 minority (12 Black or African American, non-Hispanic/Latino; 8 Asian, non-Hispanic/Latino; 50 Hispanic/Latino; 6 Two or more races, non-Hispanic/Latino), 6 international. Average age 33. 156 applicants, 51% accepted, 52 enrolled. In 2017, 39 master's awarded. *Degree requirements:* For master's, thesis (for some programs), internship (for some programs). *Entrance requirements:* For master's, GRE/MAT, minimum GPA of 3.0; 2 letters of recommendation; writing sample/personal statement. Additional exam requirements/recommendations for international students: Required—TOEFL (minimum score 550 paper-based; 79 iBT), IELTS (minimum score 6). *Application deadline:* For fall admission, 6/1 for domestic students, 3/1 for international students; for spring admission, 11/1 for domestic students, 10/1 for international students. Applications are processed on a rolling basis. Application fee: $50. Electronic applications accepted. *Expenses:* Tuition, state resident: full-time $13,920; part-time $6264 per year. Tuition, nonresident: full-time $21,700; part-time $9765 per year. *Required fees:* $80; $36 per year. Tuition and fees vary according to course load, degree level and program. *Financial support:* In 2017–18, 3,480 students received support. Career-related internships or fieldwork, Federal Work-Study, scholarships/grants, and unspecified assistantships available. Support available to part-time students. Financial award application deadline: 3/15; financial award applicants required to submit FAFSA. *Faculty research:* Relationship violence, work-family balance, social development of Japan, theories justifying war, reactions to trauma. *Total annual research expenditures:* $32,300. *Unit head:* Dr. Kara Rabbitt, Dean, 973-720-2180, Fax: 973-720-2955, E-mail: rabbittk@wpunj.edu. *Application contact:* Tinu Adeniran, Associate Director, Graduate Admissions, 973-720-2764, Fax: 973-720-2035, E-mail: adenirant@wpunj.edu.
Website: http://www.wpunj.edu/cohss

Wilmington University, College of Social and Behavioral Sciences, New Castle, DE 19720-6491. Offers administration of human services (MS); administration of justice (MS); clinical mental health counseling (MS); homeland security (MS). *Accreditation:* ACA. *Program availability:* Part-time, evening/weekend. *Faculty:* 11 full-time (6 women), 74 part-time/adjunct (34 women). *Students:* 174 full-time (132 women), 428 part-time (334 women); includes 269 minority (229 Black or African American, non-Hispanic/Latino; 5 American Indian or Alaska Native, non-Hispanic/Latino; 7 Asian, non-Hispanic/Latino; 17 Hispanic/Latino; 11 Two or more races, non-Hispanic/Latino), 11 international. Average age 35. 541 applicants, 81% accepted, 292 enrolled. In 2017, 271 master's awarded. *Entrance requirements:* Additional exam requirements/recommendations for international students: Required—TOEFL (minimum score 500 paper-based). *Application deadline:* Applications are processed on a rolling basis. Application fee: $35. Electronic applications accepted. *Expenses: Tuition:* Part-time $466 per credit. *Required fees:* $25 per semester. Tuition and fees vary according to degree level and campus/location. *Financial support:* Applicants required to submit FAFSA. *Unit head:* Dr. Edward L. Guthrie, Dean, 302-356-6870. *Application contact:* Laura Morris, Director of Admissions, 877-967-5464, E-mail: inquire@wilmcoll.edu.
Website: http://www.wilmu.edu/behavioralscience/

Winebrenner Theological Seminary, Graduate Programs, Findlay, OH 45840. Offers clinical counseling (MA); family ministry (MA); practical theology (MA); theological and ministerial studies (M Div, D Min); theological studies (MA). *Accreditation:* ATS (one or more programs are accredited). *Program availability:* Part-time, 100% online, blended/hybrid learning. *Degree requirements:* For master's, variable foreign language requirement, thesis (for some programs); for doctorate, thesis/dissertation. *Entrance requirements:* For doctorate, 3 years of post-M Div full-time ministry. Additional exam requirements/recommendations for international students: Required—TOEFL (minimum score 550 paper-based; 80 iBT). Electronic applications accepted. *Faculty research:* Inductive biblical language grammar; review of Tobias Hagerland's "Jesus and the Scriptures"; Teleios profile of student wholeness; Puritanism; theological aesthetics.

The Wright Institute, Master of Arts in Counseling Psychology Program, Berkeley, CA 94704-1796. Offers MA. *Program availability:* Part-time, evening/weekend. *Degree requirements:* For master's, comprehensive exam. *Entrance requirements:* Additional exam requirements/recommendations for international students: Required—TOEFL. Electronic applications accepted.

Xavier University, College of Social Sciences, Health and Education, School of Education, Department of Counseling, Cincinnati, OH 45207. Offers clinical mental health counseling (MA); school counseling (MA). *Program availability:* Part-time, evening/weekend. *Degree requirements:* For master's, internship. *Entrance requirements:* For master's, GRE or MAT, minimum GPA of 3.0; 2 letters of recommendation; resume; official transcript; statement of purpose. Additional exam requirements/recommendations for international students: Required—TOEFL (minimum score 550 paper-based; 79 iBT). Electronic applications accepted. Application fee is waived when completed online. *Expenses:* Contact institution. *Faculty research:* Supervision, ethics, consultation, self-injury, bullying.

Yeshiva University, Ferkauf Graduate School of Psychology, Program in Mental Health Counseling Psychology, New York, NY 10033-3201. Offers MA. *Program availability:* Part-time. *Entrance requirements:* For master's, GRE General Test. *Faculty research:* Substance abuse treatment, group therapy.

Youngstown State University, Graduate School, Beeghly College of Education, Department of Counseling, Youngstown, OH 44555-0001. Offers community counseling (MS Ed); school counseling (MS Ed). *Accreditation:* ACA; NCATE. *Program availability:* Part-time, evening/weekend. *Degree requirements:* For master's, comprehensive exam. *Entrance requirements:* For master's, MAT, interview, minimum GPA of 2.7. Additional exam requirements/recommendations for international students: Required—TOEFL. *Faculty research:* Suicide, euthanasia, ethical issues, marriage and family.

Developmental Psychology

Andrews University, School of Graduate Studies, School of Education, Department of Graduate Psychology and Counseling, Program in Educational and Developmental Psychology, Berrien Springs, MI 49104. Offers educational and developmental psychology (MA); educational psychology (Ed D, PhD). *Students:* 15 full-time (10 women), 4 part-time (3 women); includes 5 minority (3 Black or African American, non-Hispanic/Latino; 2 Hispanic/Latino), 9 international. Average age 39. 18 applicants, 50% accepted, 6 enrolled. In 2017, 8 master's, 4 doctorates awarded. *Degree requirements:* For master's, thesis optional. *Entrance requirements:* For master's, GRE. Additional exam requirements/recommendations for international students: Required—TOEFL (minimum score 550 paper-based). *Application deadline:* Applications are processed on a rolling basis. Application fee: $40. *Unit head:* Dr. Jimmy Kijai, Coordinator, 269-471-6240. *Application contact:* Justina Clayburn, Supervisor of Graduate Admission, 800-253-2874, Fax: 269-471-6321, E-mail: graduate@andrews.edu.

Arizona State University at the Tempe campus, College of Liberal Arts and Sciences, Department of Psychology, Tempe, AZ 85287-1104. Offers applied behavior analysis (MS); behavioral neuroscience (PhD); clinical psychology (PhD); cognitive science (PhD); developmental psychology (PhD); quantitative psychology (PhD); social psychology (PhD). *Accreditation:* APA. *Degree requirements:* For doctorate, comprehensive exam, thesis/dissertation, interactive Program of Study (iPOS) submitted before completing 50 percent of required credit hours. *Entrance requirements:* For doctorate, GRE General Test, GRE Subject Test, minimum GPA of 3.0 or equivalent in last 2 years of work leading to bachelor's degree. Additional exam requirements/recommendations for international students: Required—TOEFL, IELTS, or PTE. Electronic applications accepted.

Azusa Pacific University, School of Behavioral and Applied Sciences, Department of Psychology, Azusa, CA 91702-7000. Offers child life (MS); research psychology and data analytics (MS).

Bay Path University, Program in Developmental Psychology, Longmeadow, MA 01106-2292. Offers developmental psychology (MS). *Program availability:* Part-time, 100% online. *Students:* 6 full-time (all women), 12 part-time (all women); includes 9 minority (3 Black or African American, non-Hispanic/Latino; 5 Hispanic/Latino; 1 Two or more races, non-Hispanic/Latino). Average age 35. In 2017, 7 master's awarded. *Degree requirements:* For master's, nine core courses (27 credits) and three elective courses (9 credits); 160 hours of community-based field work. *Entrance requirements:* For master's, bachelor's degree in psychology or related field; minimum cumulative GPA of 3.0; working knowledge of statistics, research methods, abnormal psychology, personality, and developmental psychology (strongly recommended). *Application deadline:* Applications are processed on a rolling basis. Application fee: $45. Electronic applications accepted. Application fee is waived when completed online. *Expenses:* $815 per credit. *Financial support:* Unspecified assistantships available. Financial award applicants required to submit FAFSA. *Unit head:* Dr. Mark Benander, Program Director, 413-565-1332, E-mail: mbenander@baypath.edu. *Application contact:* Diane Ranaldi, Dean of Graduate Admissions, 413-565-1332, Fax: 413-565-1250, E-mail: dranaldi@baypath.edu.
Website: http://www.baypath.edu/academics/graduate-programs/developmental-psychology-ms/

Boston College, Lynch School of Education, Program in Applied Developmental and Educational Psychology, Chestnut Hill, MA 02467-3800. Offers MA, PhD. *Program availability:* Part-time, evening/weekend. *Students:* 34 full-time (32 women), 9 part-time (8 women); includes 9 minority (2 Black or African American, non-Hispanic/Latino; 2 Asian, non-Hispanic/Latino; 4 Hispanic/Latino; 1 Two or more races, non-Hispanic/Latino), 10 international. Average age 27. 97 applicants, 61% accepted, 20 enrolled. In 2017, 13 master's, 3 doctorates awarded. Terminal master's awarded for partial completion of doctoral program. *Degree requirements:* For master's, comprehensive exam; for doctorate, comprehensive exam, thesis/dissertation. *Entrance requirements:* For master's and doctorate, GRE General Test. Additional exam requirements/recommendations for international students: Required—TOEFL (minimum score 100 iBT). *Application deadline:* For fall admission, 12/1 priority date for domestic and international students; for spring admission, 11/1 for domestic and international students. Application fee: $65. Electronic applications accepted. *Financial support:* Fellowships with tuition reimbursements, research assistantships with tuition reimbursements, teaching assistantships with tuition reimbursements, career-related internships or fieldwork, Federal Work-Study, scholarships/grants, traineeships, health care benefits, tuition waivers (full and partial), and unspecified assistantships available. Support available to part-time students. Financial award applicants required to submit FAFSA. *Faculty research:* Cognitive learning and culture, effects of social policy reform on children and families, psychosocial trauma, human rights and international justice, positive youth development, children and adolescents living in poverty. *Unit head:* Dr. Rebekah Levine Coley, Chairperson, 617-552-6018, Fax: 617-552-4710. *Application contact:* Kimberly Rose, Graduate Admission Assistant, 617-552-4214, Fax: 617-552-0398, E-mail: roseki@bc.edu.

Boston Graduate School of Psychoanalysis, CAGS and Certificate Programs, Brookline, MA 02446-4602. Offers child and adolescent intervention (CAGS); psychoanalysis (Certificate); psychoanalytic psychotherapy (CAGS). *Program availability:* Part-time. *Degree requirements:* For other advanced degree, thesis. *Entrance requirements:* For degree, interview, BA, writing sample, 3 letters of reference, transcripts. Additional exam requirements/recommendations for international students: Required—TOEFL (minimum score 550 paper-based; 79 iBT). *Faculty research:* Treatment approaches for intractable patients, unconscious symbolic processes, female adolescent development, evaluation of school mental health interventions, development of symbolic processes in early childhood.

Bowling Green State University, Graduate College, College of Arts and Sciences, Department of Psychology, Bowling Green, OH 43403. Offers clinical psychology (MA, PhD); developmental psychology (MA, PhD); experimental psychology (MA, PhD); industrial/organizational psychology (MA, PhD); quantitative psychology (MA, PhD). *Accreditation:* APA (one or more programs are accredited). *Degree requirements:* For doctorate, thesis/dissertation. *Entrance requirements:* For doctorate, GRE General Test, GRE Subject Test. Additional exam requirements/recommendations for international students: Required—TOEFL. Electronic applications accepted. *Faculty research:* Personnel psychology, developmental-mathematical models, behavioral medication, brain process, child/adolescent social cognition.

Brandeis University, Graduate School of Arts and Sciences, Department of Psychology, Waltham, MA 02454-9110. Offers brain, body and behavior (PhD); cognitive neuroscience (PhD); general psychology (MA); social/developmental psychology (PhD). *Program availability:* Part-time. *Faculty:* 14 full-time (7 women), 4 part-time/adjunct (3 women). *Students:* 34 full-time (26 women), 4 part-time (2 women); includes 8 minority (5 Asian, non-Hispanic/Latino; 3 Hispanic/Latino), 10 international. Average age 27. 124 applicants, 31% accepted, 15 enrolled. In 2017, 13 master's, 7 doctorates awarded. Terminal master's awarded for partial completion of doctoral program. *Degree requirements:* For master's, thesis or alternative; for doctorate, thesis/dissertation, research reports. *Entrance requirements:* For master's and doctorate, GRE General Test; GRE Subject Test (recommended), letters of recommendation, statement of purpose, transcripts, resume. Additional exam requirements/recommendations for international students: Required—PTE (minimum score 68), TOEFL (minimum score 600 paper-based, 100 iBT) or IELTS (7). *Application deadline:* For fall admission, 12/1 priority date for domestic students. Applications are processed on a rolling basis. Application fee: $75. Electronic applications accepted. *Expenses: Tuition:* Full-time $48,720. *Required fees:* $88. Tuition and fees vary according to course load, degree level, program and student level. *Financial support:* In 2017–18, 40 students received support, including 20 fellowships with full tuition reimbursements available (averaging $24,480 per year), 26 teaching assistantships with partial tuition reimbursements available (averaging $3,200 per year); Federal Work-Study, scholarships/grants, health care benefits, and tuition waivers (partial) also available. Support available to part-time students. Financial award application deadline: 4/15; financial award applicants required to submit FAFSA. *Faculty research:* Brain, body, and behavior across the lifespan; face perception and nonverbal communication; learning and memory; motor control and spatial orientation; neurophysiology of learning and decision making; personality and cognition in adulthood and old age; social, cultural and affective neuroscience; social relations and health physiology; speech comprehension and memory; taste physiology and psychophysics; visual perception. *Unit head:* Dr. Angela Gutchess, Department Chair, 781-736-3303, E-mail: gutchess@brandeis.edu. *Application contact:* Dr. Sarah Lupis, Department Administrator, 781-736-3303, E-mail: slupis@brandeis.edu.
Website: http://www.brandeis.edu/gsas/programs/psychology.html

Capella University, Harold Abel School of Social and Behavioral Science, Master's Programs in Counseling, Minneapolis, MN 55402. Offers child and adolescent development (MS); general addiction counseling (MS); general marriage and family counseling/therapy (MS); general mental health counseling (MS); general school counseling (MS).

Developmental Psychology

Carnegie Mellon University, Dietrich College of Humanities and Social Sciences, Department of Psychology, Area of Developmental Psychology, Pittsburgh, PA 15213-3891. Offers PhD. *Degree requirements:* For doctorate, comprehensive exam, thesis/dissertation. *Entrance requirements:* For doctorate, GRE General Test. Additional exam requirements/recommendations for international students: Required—TOEFL. *Faculty research:* Cognitive development, language acquisition.

Chatham University, Program in Counseling Psychology, Pittsburgh, PA 15232-2826. Offers child, adolescent and family (MSCP); counseling psychology (Psy D); health and holistic (MSCP); organization and supervision (MSCP); sport and exercise (MSCP). *Accreditation:* APA. *Program availability:* Part-time, evening/weekend. *Faculty:* 11 full-time (10 women). *Students:* 61 full-time (46 women), 25 part-time (22 women); includes 12 minority (9 Black or African American, non-Hispanic/Latino; 2 Hispanic/Latino; 1 Two or more races, non-Hispanic/Latino), 3 international. Average age 30. 124 applicants, 62% accepted, 45 enrolled. In 2017, 38 master's awarded. *Degree requirements:* For master's, thesis optional, supervised internship; for doctorate, thesis/dissertation, internship. *Entrance requirements:* For master's, minimum GPA of 3.0; 2 letters of recommendation; resume; prerequisite coursework in statistics, biology, and psychology; for doctorate, GRE. Additional exam requirements/recommendations for international students: Required—TOEFL (minimum score 600 paper-based; 100 iBT), IELTS (minimum score 7), TWE. *Application deadline:* For fall admission, 4/1 priority date for domestic and international students; for spring admission, 11/1 for domestic students, 10/1 for international students. Applications are processed on a rolling basis. Application fee: $45. Electronic applications accepted. Application fee is waived when completed online. *Expenses: Tuition:* Full-time $16,740; part-time $930 per credit. *Required fees:* $486; $27 per credit. $243 per semester. *Financial support:* Career-related internships or fieldwork available. Financial award applicants required to submit FAFSA. *Faculty research:* Trauma and recovery, hypnosis, psychospiritual dimensions of healing, psychotherapy of schizophrenia. *Unit head:* Dr. Mary Beth Mannarino, Director, 412-365-1196, Fax: 412-365-1505, E-mail: mmannarino@chatham.edu. *Application contact:* Katie Noel, Assistant Director of Graduate Admission, 412-365-2758, Fax: 412-365-1609, E-mail: gradadmissions@chatham.edu. Website: http://www.chatham.edu/mscp

Claremont Graduate University, Graduate Programs, School of Social Science, Policy and Evaluation, Department of Psychology, Claremont, CA 91711-6160. Offers advanced study in evaluation (Certificate); cognitive psychology (MA, PhD); developmental psychology (MA, PhD); evaluation and applied research methods (MA, PhD); health behavior research and evaluation (MA, PhD); human resource development and evaluation (MA); industrial/organizational psychology (MA, PhD); organizational behavior (MA, PhD); organizational psychology (MA, PhD); social psychology (MA, PhD); MBA/PhD. *Program availability:* Part-time. Terminal master's awarded for partial completion of doctoral program. *Entrance requirements:* For master's and doctorate, GRE General Test. Additional exam requirements/recommendations for international students: Required—TOEFL (minimum score 75 iBT). Electronic applications accepted. *Faculty research:* Social intervention, diversity in organizations, eyewitness memory, aging and cognition, drug policy.

Clark University, Graduate School, Hiatt School of Psychology, Program in Developmental Psychology, Worcester, MA 01610-1477. Offers PhD. *Students:* 6 full-time (5 women), 4 international. Average age 28. *Entrance requirements:* For doctorate, GRE General Test. Additional exam requirements/recommendations for international students: Required—TOEFL. *Application deadline:* For fall admission, 12/15 priority date for domestic students, 12/15 for international students. Applications are processed on a rolling basis. Application fee: $75. *Financial support:* Fellowships, research assistantships, teaching assistantships, and tuition waivers (full) available. *Faculty research:* Development of psychological processes in sociocultural context, conceptualizing and reasoning, symbolization, parental structure in families of adolescents, transition to kindergarten. *Unit head:* Dr. Michael Bamberg, Chair, 508-793-7135, E-mail: mbamberg@clarku.edu. *Application contact:* Kelly Boulay, Departmental Administrator, 508-793-7274, Fax: 508-793-7265, E-mail: psychology@clarku.edu.
Website: http://www.clarku.edu/departments/psychology/grad/developmental/index.cfm

Clayton State University, School of Graduate Studies, College of Arts and Sciences, Program in Psychology, Morrow, GA 30260-0285. Offers applied developmental psychology (MS); clinical/counseling psychology (MS). *Entrance requirements:* For master's, GRE, 2 official transcripts; 3 letters of recommendation; statement of purpose; on-campus interview; background check. Additional exam requirements/recommendations for international students: Required—TOEFL (minimum score 550 paper-based). Electronic applications accepted.

Cornell University, Graduate School, Graduate Fields of Human Ecology, Field of Human Development, Ithaca, NY 14853. Offers developmental psychology (MA, PhD), including cognitive development, developmental psychopathology, ecology of human development, social and personality development; human development and family studies (MA, PhD), including ecology of human development, family studies and the life course. *Degree requirements:* For doctorate, comprehensive exam, thesis/dissertation, pre-doctoral research project, teaching experience. *Entrance requirements:* For doctorate, GRE General Test, 2 letters of recommendation. Additional exam requirements/recommendations for international students: Required—TOEFL (minimum score 550 paper-based; 77 iBT). Electronic applications accepted. *Faculty research:* Cognitive development, developmental psychopathology, ecology of human development, family studies and the life course, social and personality development.

Delaware Valley University, Program in Counseling Psychology, Doylestown, PA 18901-2697. Offers child and adolescent therapy (MA); social justice community counseling (MA).

Duke University, Graduate School, Department of Psychology and Neuroscience, Durham, NC 27708. Offers biological psychology (PhD); clinical psychology (PhD); cognitive psychology (PhD); developmental psychology (PhD); experimental psychology (PhD); health psychology (PhD); human social development (PhD); JD/MA. *Accreditation:* APA (one or more programs are accredited). *Degree requirements:* For doctorate, thesis/dissertation. *Entrance requirements:* For doctorate, GRE General Test. Additional exam requirements/recommendations for international students: Required—TOEFL (minimum score 577 paper-based; 90 iBT) or IELTS (minimum score 7). Electronic applications accepted.

Emory University, Laney Graduate School, Department of Psychology, Atlanta, GA 30322-1100. Offers clinical psychology (PhD); cognition and development (PhD); neuroscience and animal behavior (PhD). *Accreditation:* APA. *Degree requirements:* For doctorate, comprehensive exam, thesis/dissertation. *Entrance requirements:* For doctorate, GRE General Test, minimum GPA of 3.25. Additional exam requirements/recommendations for international students: Required—TOEFL. Electronic applications accepted. *Faculty research:* Neuroscience and animal behavior; adult and child psychopathology, cognition development assessment.

Erikson Institute, Academic Programs, Chicago, IL 60654. Offers administration (Certificate); bilingual/ESL (Certificate); child development (MS); early childhood education (MS); infant mental health (Certificate); infant studies (Certificate); MS/MSW.

MS/MSW offered jointly with Loyola University Chicago. *Program availability:* Part-time, evening/weekend. *Degree requirements:* For master's, comprehensive exam, internship; for Certificate, internship. *Entrance requirements:* For master's and Certificate, minimum GPA of 2.75. Additional exam requirements/recommendations for international students: Required—TOEFL. *Faculty research:* Assessment strategies from early childhood through elementary years; language, literacy, and the arts in children's development; inclusive special education; parent-child relationships; cognitive development.

Fielding Graduate University, Graduate Programs, School of Leadership Studies, Programs in Infant and Early Childhood Development, Santa Barbara, CA 93105-3814. Offers infant and early childhood development (MA, PhD, Graduate Certificate), including early childhood development: education, mental health, and disruptive behaviors (MA), infant mental health and neurodevelopment (MA), reflective practice and supervision (Graduate Certificate). *Program availability:* Part-time, evening/weekend, 100% online, blended/hybrid learning. *Faculty:* 1 (woman) full-time, 28 part-time/adjunct (22 women). *Students:* 84 full-time (79 women), 1 (woman) part-time; includes 33 minority (12 Black or African American, non-Hispanic/Latino; 2 American Indian or Alaska Native, non-Hispanic/Latino; 3 Asian, non-Hispanic/Latino; 10 Hispanic/Latino; 6 Two or more races, non-Hispanic/Latino), 1 international. Average age 45. 17 applicants, 94% accepted, 14 enrolled. In 2017, 9 doctorates awarded. Terminal master's awarded for partial completion of doctoral program. *Degree requirements:* For master's, thesis or alternative, capstone; for doctorate, comprehensive exam, thesis/dissertation. *Entrance requirements:* For master's and Graduate Certificate, bachelor's degree from regionally-accredited U.S. institution or equivalent; for doctorate, bachelor's or master's degree from regionally-accredited U.S. institution or equivalent, curriculum vitae, statement of purpose, critical thinking writing sample, 2 letters of recommendation, official transcript. *Application deadline:* For fall admission, 7/16 for domestic and international students; for spring admission, 11/1 for domestic and international students; for summer admission, 3/1 for domestic and international students. Application fee: $75. Electronic applications accepted. *Expenses:* Contact institution. *Financial support:* Research assistantships, teaching assistantships, and scholarships/grants available. Support available to part-time students. Financial award applicants required to submit FAFSA. *Unit head:* Dr. Barbara Mink, Program Director, E-mail: bmink@fielding.edu. *Application contact:* Enrollment Coordinator, 800-340-1099 Ext. 4098, Fax: 805-687-9793, E-mail: hodadmission@fielding.edu.
Website: http://www.fielding.edu/our-programs/school-of-leadership-studies/phd-infant-early-childhood-development/

Florida International University, College of Arts, Sciences, and Education, Department of Psychology, Miami, FL 33199. Offers behavioral analysis (MS); clinical science (PhD); cognitive neuroscience (PhD); counseling psychology (MS); developmental science (MS, PhD); legal psychology (MS, PhD); organizational psychology (MS, PhD). Program has fall admissions only. *Accreditation:* APA. *Program availability:* Part-time, evening/weekend. *Faculty:* 45 full-time (28 women), 48 part-time/adjunct (31 women). *Students:* 162 full-time (122 women), 13 part-time (5 women); includes 94 minority (11 Black or African American, non-Hispanic/Latino; 5 Asian, non-Hispanic/Latino; 75 Hispanic/Latino; 3 Two or more races, non-Hispanic/Latino), 12 international. Average age 27. 290 applicants, 21% accepted, 50 enrolled. In 2017, 43 master's, 13 doctorates awarded. Terminal master's awarded for partial completion of doctoral program. *Degree requirements:* For master's, thesis; for doctorate, comprehensive exam, thesis/dissertation. *Entrance requirements:* For master's, GRE General Test, minimum GPA of 3.0, resume, 3 letters of recommendation; for doctorate, GRE General Test, 3 letters of recommendation, resume, letter of intent, two writing samples, minimum GPA of 3.0. Additional exam requirements/recommendations for international students: Required—TOEFL (minimum score 550 paper-based; 80 iBT). *Application deadline:* For fall admission, 12/15 for domestic and international students. Application fee: $30. Electronic applications accepted. *Expenses:* Tuition, state resident: full-time $8912; part-time $446 per credit hour. Tuition, nonresident: full-time $21,393; part-time $992 per credit hour. *Required fees:* $390; $195 per semester. *Financial support:* Institutionally sponsored loans and scholarships/grants available. Financial award application deadline: 3/1. *Faculty research:* Legal psychology, organizational and industrial psychology, child behavior psychology. *Unit head:* Dr. Jeremy Pettit, Interim Chair, 305-348-1671, Fax: 305-348-3646, E-mail: jeremy.pettit@fiu.edu. *Application contact:* Nanett Rojas, Assistant Director, Graduate Admissions, 305-348-7464, Fax: 305-348-7441, E-mail: gradadm@fiu.edu.

Florida State University, The Graduate School, College of Arts and Sciences, Department of Psychology, Program in Developmental Psychology, Tallahassee, FL 32306. Offers PhD. *Faculty:* 5 full-time (2 women). *Students:* 8 full-time (all women); includes 3 minority (1 Black or African American, non-Hispanic/Latino; 2 Hispanic/Latino). Average age 27. 14 applicants, 29% accepted, 2 enrolled. In 2017, 2 doctorates awarded. Terminal master's awarded for partial completion of doctoral program. *Degree requirements:* For doctorate, comprehensive exam, thesis/dissertation. *Entrance requirements:* For doctorate, GRE General Test, minimum GPA of 3.2, research experience, letters of recommendation. Additional exam requirements/recommendations for international students: Required—TOEFL (minimum score 80 iBT). *Application deadline:* For fall admission, 12/1 for domestic and international students. Application fee: $30. Electronic applications accepted. *Financial support:* In 2017–18, 6 students received support, including 2 fellowships with full tuition reimbursements available (averaging $23,844 per year), 4 research assistantships with full tuition reimbursements available (averaging $23,815 per year), 2 teaching assistantships with full tuition reimbursements available (averaging $19,000 per year); health care benefits also available. Financial award application deadline: 12/1; financial award applicants required to submit FAFSA. *Faculty research:* Learning disabilities, phonological processing, psychology of reading, emergent literacy, aging. *Total annual research expenditures:* $1.6 million. *Unit head:* Dr. Sara Hart, Director, 850-645-9693, Fax: 850-644-7739, E-mail: shart@fcrr.org. *Application contact:* Lynda L. Gibson, Graduate Program Associate, 850-644-2499, Fax: 850-644-7739, E-mail: grad-info@psy.fsu.edu.
Website: http://www.psy.fsu.edu

Fordham University, Graduate School of Arts and Sciences, Department of Psychology, Program in Applied Developmental Psychology, New York, NY 10458. Offers PhD. *Accreditation:* APA. *Students:* 15 full-time (13 women), 3 part-time (all women); includes 4 minority (2 Black or African American, non-Hispanic/Latino; 1 Asian, non-Hispanic/Latino; 1 Hispanic/Latino), 4 international. Average age 31. 36 applicants, 33% accepted, 4 enrolled. In 2017, 5 doctorates awarded. *Degree requirements:* For doctorate, comprehensive exam, thesis/dissertation. *Entrance requirements:* For doctorate, GRE General Test, GRE Subject Test. Additional exam requirements/recommendations for international students: Required—TOEFL (minimum score 600 paper-based). *Application deadline:* For fall admission, 12/14 for domestic students. Application fee: $70. Electronic applications accepted. *Financial support:* In 2017–18, 15 students received support, including 4 fellowships with tuition reimbursements available (averaging $26,065 per year), 2 research assistantships with tuition reimbursements available (averaging $17,529 per year), 2 teaching assistantships with tuition reimbursements available (averaging $10,600 per year); career-related internships or fieldwork, institutionally sponsored loans, tuition waivers (full and partial),

and unspecified assistantships also available. Financial award application deadline: 12/14. *Faculty research:* Development of citizenship, impact of participation in community service, impact of poverty on children, development of moral reasoning and behavior. *Unit head:* Dr. Tiffany Yip, Program Director, 718-817-3797, Fax: 718-817-3785, E-mail: tyip@fordham.edu. *Application contact:* Bernadette Valentino-Morrison, Director of Graduate Admissions, 718-817-4419, Fax: 718-817-3566, E-mail: valentinomor@fordham.edu.

George Mason University, College of Humanities and Social Sciences, Department of Psychology, Fairfax, VA 22030. Offers applied developmental psychology (MA, PhD); clinical psychology (PhD); cognitive and behavioral neuroscience (MA, PhD); cognitive neuroscience (Certificate); human factors/applied cognition (MA, PhD, Certificate), including transportation human factors (Certificate), usability (Certificate); industrial/organizational psychology (MA, PhD). *Accreditation:* APA. *Faculty:* 41 full-time (20 women), 5 part-time/adjunct (all women). *Students:* 152 full-time (101 women), 56 part-time (39 women); includes 47 minority (15 Black or African American, non-Hispanic/Latino; 13 Asian, non-Hispanic/Latino; 13 Hispanic/Latino; 1 Native Hawaiian or other Pacific Islander, non-Hispanic/Latino; 5 Two or more races, non-Hispanic/Latino), 12 international. Average age 27. 719 applicants, 19% accepted, 61 enrolled. In 2017, 55 master's, 18 doctorates, 8 other advanced degrees awarded. *Degree requirements:* For master's, comprehensive exam, thesis or practicum research; for doctorate, comprehensive exam, thesis/dissertation, 2nd-year project. *Entrance requirements:* For master's, GRE, 2 official transcripts; goals statement; 15 undergraduate credits in concentration for which the applicant is applying; for doctorate, GRE, 3 letters of recommendation; resume; goals statement; minimum GPA of 3.0 overall for last 60 undergraduate credits, 3.25 in psychology courses; 15 undergraduate credits in concentration for which the applicant is applying; 2 official transcripts; for Certificate, GRE, 2 official transcripts; expanded goals statement; 3 letters of recommendation. Additional exam requirements/recommendations for international students: Required—TOEFL (minimum score 575 paper-based; 88 iBT), IELTS (minimum score 6.5), PTE (minimum score 59). Application fee: $75 ($80 for international students). Electronic applications accepted. *Expenses:* Tuition, state resident: full-time $11,228; part-time $459.50 per credit. Tuition, nonresident: full-time $30,932; part-time $1280.50 per credit. *Required fees:* $3252; $135.50 per credit. Part-time tuition and fees vary according to course load and program. *Financial support:* In 2017–18, 110 students received support, including 6 fellowships (averaging $4,829 per year), 52 research assistantships with tuition reimbursements available (averaging $10,933 per year), 70 teaching assistantships with tuition reimbursements available (averaging $7,703 per year); career-related internships or fieldwork, Federal Work-Study, scholarships/grants, tuition waivers (partial), unspecified assistantships, and health care benefits (for full-time research or teaching assistantship recipients) also available. Support available to part-time students. Financial award application deadline: 3/1; financial award applicants required to submit FAFSA. *Faculty research:* Applied developmental psychology, biopsychology, clinical psychology, human factors/applied cognition psychology, industrial/organizational psychology, school psychology. *Total annual research expenditures:* $2.6 million. *Unit head:* Reeshad Dalal, Department Chair, 703-993-9487, Fax: 703-993-1359, E-mail: rdalal@gmu.edu. *Application contact:* Michael Hock, Graduate Program Coordinator, 703-993-1548, Fax: 703-993-1359, E-mail: mhock2@gmu.edu.
Website: http://psychology.gmu.edu

Georgia State University, College of Arts and Sciences, Department of Psychology, Atlanta, GA 30302-3083. Offers clinical psychology (PhD); cognitive sciences (PhD); community psychology (PhD); developmental psychology (PhD); neuropsychology and behavioral neuroscience (PhD). *Accreditation:* APA. *Faculty:* 40 full-time (26 women). *Students:* 102 full-time (80 women), 4 part-time (all women); includes 26 minority (7 Black or African American, non-Hispanic/Latino; 10 Asian, non-Hispanic/Latino; 4 Hispanic/Latino; 5 Two or more races, non-Hispanic/Latino), 8 international. Average age 27. 450 applicants, 7% accepted, 16 enrolled. In 2017, 21 doctorates awarded. *Entrance requirements:* For doctorate, GRE. Additional exam requirements/recommendations for international students: Required—TOEFL (minimum score 550 paper-based; 80 iBT). *Application deadline:* For fall admission, 12/1 for domestic and international students. Application fee: $50. Electronic applications accepted. *Expenses:* Tuition, state resident: full-time $7020. Tuition, nonresident: full-time $22,518. *Required fees:* $2128. Tuition and fees vary according to degree level and program. *Financial support:* In 2017–18, fellowships with full tuition reimbursements (averaging $19,282 per year), research assistantships with full tuition reimbursements (averaging $5,173 per year), teaching assistantships with full tuition reimbursements (averaging $6,389 per year) were awarded; scholarships/grants, traineeships, health care benefits, and unspecified assistantships also available. Financial award applicants required to submit FAFSA. *Faculty research:* Clinical psychology, developmental psychology, community psychology, neuropsychology and behavioral neuroscience, cognitive sciences. *Unit head:* Dr. Lisa Armistead, Chair, 404-413-6205, Fax: 404-413-6207, E-mail: lparmistead@gsu.edu. *Application contact:* Dr. Lindsey Cohen, Director of Graduate Studies, 404-413-6263, Fax: 404-413-6207, E-mail: llcohen@gsu.edu.

The Graduate Center, City University of New York, Graduate Studies, Program in Psychology, New York, NY 10016-4039. Offers basic applied neurocognition (PhD); biopsychology (PhD); clinical psychology (PhD); developmental psychology (PhD); environmental psychology (PhD); experimental psychology (PhD); industrial psychology (PhD); learning processes (PhD); neuropsychology (PhD); psychology (PhD); social personality (PhD). *Faculty:* 119 full-time (40 women). *Students:* 428 full-time (308 women); includes 118 minority (31 Black or African American, non-Hispanic/Latino; 31 Asian, non-Hispanic/Latino; 47 Hispanic/Latino; 1 Native Hawaiian or other Pacific Islander, non-Hispanic/Latino; 8 Two or more races, non-Hispanic/Latino), 53 international. Average age 33. 795 applicants, 12% accepted, 56 enrolled. In 2017, 46 doctorates awarded. *Degree requirements:* For doctorate, one foreign language, thesis/dissertation. *Entrance requirements:* For doctorate, GRE General Test. Additional exam requirements/recommendations for international students: Required—TOEFL. *Application deadline:* For fall admission, 12/1 priority date for domestic students. Application fee: $125. Electronic applications accepted. *Financial support:* In 2017–18, 371 students received support, including 340 fellowships, 34 research assistantships, 33 teaching assistantships; career-related internships or fieldwork, Federal Work-Study, institutionally sponsored loans, and tuition waivers (full and partial) also available. Financial award application deadline: 2/1; financial award applicants required to submit FAFSA. *Unit head:* Richard Bodnar, Executive Officer, 212-817-8706, Fax: 212-817-1533, E-mail: rbodnar@gc.cuny.edu. *Application contact:* Les Gribben, Director of Admissions, 212-817-7470, Fax: 212-817-1624, E-mail: lgribben@gc.cuny.edu.

Harvard University, Graduate School of Arts and Sciences, Department of Psychology, Cambridge, MA 02138. Offers psychology (PhD), including behavior and decision analysis, cognition, developmental psychology, experimental psychology, personality, psychobiology, psychopathology; social psychology (PhD). *Accreditation:* APA. *Degree requirements:* For doctorate, thesis/dissertation, general exams. *Entrance requirements:* For doctorate, GRE General Test. Additional exam requirements/recommendations for international students: Required—TOEFL.

Howard University, Graduate School, Department of Psychology, Washington, DC 20059-0002. Offers clinical psychology (PhD); developmental psychology (PhD); experimental psychology (PhD); neuropsychology (PhD); personality psychology (PhD); psychology (MS); social psychology (PhD). *Accreditation:* APA (one or more programs are accredited). *Program availability:* Part-time. *Degree requirements:* For master's, thesis; for doctorate, comprehensive exam, thesis/dissertation, qualifying exam. *Entrance requirements:* For master's, GRE General Test, minimum GPA of 2.5, bachelor's degree in psychology or related field; for doctorate, GRE General Test, minimum GPA of 3.0. *Faculty research:* Personality and psychophysiology, educational and social development of African-American children, child and adult psychopathology.

Humboldt State University, Academic Programs, College of Professional Studies, Department of Psychology, Arcata, CA 95521-8299. Offers psychology (MA), including biological psychology, counseling, developmental psychopathology, school psychology, social and environmental psychology. *Degree requirements:* For master's, thesis. *Entrance requirements:* For master's, appropriate bachelor's degree, minimum GPA of 2.5. Additional exam requirements/recommendations for international students: Required—TOEFL (minimum score 500 paper-based). *Faculty research:* School psychology, counseling, eating disorders, mood induction, depression.

Illinois State University, Graduate School, College of Arts and Sciences, Department of Psychology, Normal, IL 61790. Offers psychology (MA, MS), including clinical-counseling psychology, cognitive and behavioral sciences, developmental psychology, industrial/organizational-social psychology; school psychology (PhD, SSP). *Accreditation:* APA. *Degree requirements:* For master's, thesis or alternative; for doctorate, variable foreign language requirement, thesis/dissertation, 2 terms of residency, internship, practicum. *Entrance requirements:* For master's, GRE General Test, GRE Subject Test, minimum GPA of 3.0 in last 60 hours of course work; for doctorate, GRE General Test. *Faculty research:* Comprehensive evaluation system for the central region professional development grant, Illinois school psychology internship consortium, for children's sake.

Indiana University Bloomington, University Graduate School, College of Arts and Sciences, Department of Psychological and Brain Sciences, Bloomington, IN 47405. Offers clinical science (PhD); cognitive neuroscience (PhD); cognitive psychology (PhD); developmental psychology (PhD); methods of behavior (PhD); molecular systems neuroscience (PhD); social psychology (PhD). *Accreditation:* APA. *Degree requirements:* For doctorate, comprehensive exam, 90 credit hours, 2 advanced statistics/methods courses, 2 written research projects, the teaching of psychology course, teaching 1 semester of undergraduate methods course, qualifying examination, minor or a second major, first-year research seminar course, dissertation defense, written dissertation. *Entrance requirements:* For doctorate, GRE. Additional exam requirements/recommendations for international students: Required—TOEFL (minimum score 550 paper-based; 79 iBT). Electronic applications accepted. *Faculty research:* Clinical science, cognitive neuroscience, cognitive psychology, developmental psychology, mechanisms of behavior, molecular and systems neuroscience, social psychology.

La Salle University, School of Arts and Sciences, Program in Clinical Psychology, Philadelphia, PA 19141-1199. Offers child clinical psychology (Psy D); clinical health psychology (Psy D); clinical psychology (MA); general practice psychology (Psy D). *Accreditation:* AAMFT/COAMFTE. *Program availability:* Part-time, evening/weekend. *Faculty:* 9 full-time (7 women), 7 part-time/adjunct (4 women). *Students:* 82 full-time (69 women), 27 part-time (20 women); includes 12 minority (2 Black or African American, non-Hispanic/Latino; 4 Asian, non-Hispanic/Latino; 4 Hispanic/Latino; 2 Two or more races, non-Hispanic/Latino), 2 international. Average age 27. 400 applicants, 16% accepted, 23 enrolled. In 2017, 19 master's, 24 doctorates awarded. Terminal master's awarded for partial completion of doctoral program. *Degree requirements:* For doctorate, comprehensive exam, thesis/dissertation. *Entrance requirements:* For doctorate, GRE (minimum scores of 148 on both the Verbal Reasoning and Quantitative Reasoning sections strongly recommended); GRE Subject Test in psychology (for those entering with bachelor's degree), baccalaureate degree from accredited institution with major in psychology or related discipline; minimum undergraduate GPA of 3.0, 3.2 graduate; three letters of recommendation; statement of interest and intent; curriculum vitae or resume; personal interview. Additional exam requirements/recommendations for international students: Required—TOEFL. *Application deadline:* For fall admission, 1/15 for domestic students, 1/1 for international students. Application fee: $35. Electronic applications accepted. Application fee is waived when completed online. *Expenses:* Contact institution. *Financial support:* In 2017–18, 31 students received support. Scholarships/grants and unspecified assistantships available. Financial award application deadline: 8/31; financial award applicants required to submit FAFSA. *Unit head:* Dr. Randy Fingerhut, Director, 215-951-1284, Fax: 215-951-5140, E-mail: psyd@lasalle.edu. *Application contact:* Elizabeth Heenan, Director, Graduate and Adult Enrollment, 215-951-1100, Fax: 215-951-1462, E-mail: heenan@lasalle.edu.
Website: http://www.lasalle.edu/doctor-of-psychology/

Liberty University, School of Behavioral Sciences, Lynchburg, VA 24515. Offers applied psychology (MA), including developmental psychology (MA, MS), industrial/organizational psychology (MA, MS); clinical mental health counseling (MA); community care and counseling (Ed D), including marriage and family counseling, pastoral care and counseling, traumatology; counselor education and supervision (PhD); human services counseling (MA), including addictions and recovery, business, child and family law, Christian ministries, criminal justice, crisis response and trauma, executive leadership, health and wellness, life coaching, marriage and family, military resilience; marriage and family counseling (MA); marriage and family therapy (MA); military resilience (Certificate); pastoral counseling (MA), including addictions and recovery, community chaplaincy, crisis response and trauma, discipleship and church ministry, leadership, life coaching, marriage and family, marriage and family studies, military resilience, parenting and child/adolescent, pastoral counseling, theology; professional counseling (MA); psychology (MS), including developmental psychology (MA, MS), industrial/organizational psychology (MA, MS); school counseling (M Ed.) *Program availability:* Part-time, online learning. *Students:* 2,649 full-time (2,085 women), 5,086 part-time (4,015 women); includes 2,275 minority (1,784 Black or African American, non-Hispanic/Latino; 44 American Indian or Alaska Native, non-Hispanic/Latino; 67 Asian, non-Hispanic/Latino; 200 Hispanic/Latino; 11 Native Hawaiian or other Pacific Islander, non-Hispanic/Latino; 169 Two or more races, non-Hispanic/Latino), 145 international. Average age 39. 5,839 applicants, 51% accepted, 1710 enrolled. In 2017, 1,626 master's, 7 doctorates, 61 other advanced degrees awarded. *Application deadline:* Applications are processed on a rolling basis. Application fee: $50. Electronic applications accepted. *Financial support:* Applicants required to submit FAFSA. *Unit head:* Dr. Ronald Hawkins, Founding Dean, School of Behavioral Sciences. *Application contact:* Jay Bridge, Director of Admissions, 800-424-9595, Fax: 800-628-7977, E-mail: gradadmissions@liberty.edu.

Louisiana State University and Agricultural & Mechanical College, Graduate School, College of Humanities and Social Sciences, Department of Psychology, Baton Rouge, LA 70803. Offers biological psychology (MA, PhD); clinical psychology (MA, PhD); cognitive psychology (MA, PhD); developmental psychology (MA, PhD); school psychology (MA, PhD). *Accreditation:* APA (one or more programs are accredited).

Faculty: 29 full-time (11 women). *Students:* 78 full-time (57 women), 18 part-time (14 women); includes 25 minority (8 Black or African American, non-Hispanic/Latino; 5 Asian, non-Hispanic/Latino; 5 Hispanic/Latino; 1 Native Hawaiian or other Pacific Islander, non-Hispanic/Latino; 6 Two or more races, non-Hispanic/Latino), 4 international. Average age 27. 239 applicants, 8% accepted, 18 enrolled. In 2017, 15 master's, 12 doctorates awarded. *Financial support:* In 2017–18, 7 fellowships (averaging $41,483 per year), 9 research assistantships (averaging $19,441 per year), 58 teaching assistantships (averaging $19,688 per year) were awarded. *Total annual research expenditures:* $326,871.

Loyola University Chicago, Graduate School, Programs in Non-Clinical Psychology, Chicago, IL 60660. Offers developmental psychology (PhD). *Faculty:* 7 full-time (2 women), 1 (woman) part-time/adjunct. *Students:* 44 full-time (38 women), 5 part-time (all women); includes 16 minority (6 Black or African American, non-Hispanic/Latino; 2 Asian, non-Hispanic/Latino; 5 Hispanic/Latino; 3 Two or more races, non-Hispanic/Latino), 3 international. Average age 28. 108 applicants, 11% accepted, 6 enrolled. In 2017, 5 master's, 5 doctorates awarded. Terminal master's awarded for partial completion of doctoral program. *Entrance requirements:* For master's and doctorate, GRE General Test, sample of written work. Additional exam requirements/recommendations for international students: Required—TOEFL. *Application deadline:* For fall admission, 1/15 for domestic and international students. Application fee: $50. Electronic applications accepted. Application fee is waived when completed online. *Expenses:* $1,033 per credit hour tuition, $432 pere semester mandatory fees. *Financial support:* In 2017–18, 1 fellowship with tuition reimbursement (averaging $16,000 per year), 5 research assistantships with tuition reimbursements (averaging $16,000 per year), 1 teaching assistantship with tuition reimbursement (averaging $16,000 per year) were awarded; career-related internships or fieldwork, Federal Work-Study, and scholarships/grants also available. Financial award application deadline: 12/15; financial award applicants required to submit FAFSA. *Faculty research:* Program evaluation, attitudes and prejudice, psychological well-being, self esteem and relationships, groups and organizations. *Total annual research expenditures:* $150,000. *Unit head:* Dr. Christine Li-Grine, Graduate Department Head, 773-508-8225, Fax: 773-508-8713, E-mail: cligrining@luc.edu. *Application contact:* Jill Schur, Director, Graduate Enrollment Management, 312-915-8902, E-mail: gradinfo@luc.edu.

McGill University, Faculty of Graduate and Postdoctoral Studies, Faculty of Education, Department of Educational and Counseling Psychology, Montréal, QC H3A 2T5, Canada. Offers counseling psychology (MA, PhD); educational psychology (M Ed, MA, PhD); school/applied child psychology and applied developmental psychology (M Ed, MA, PhD, Diploma), including school psychology. *Accreditation:* APA.

New York University, Steinhardt School of Culture, Education, and Human Development, Department of Applied Psychology, Programs in Educational and Developmental Psychology, New York, NY 10012. Offers developmental psychology (PhD); human development and social intervention (MA); psychology and social intervention (PhD). *Accreditation:* APA (one or more programs are accredited). *Program availability:* Part-time. *Students:* Average age 27. 137 applicants, 26% accepted, 13 enrolled. In 2017, 16 master's, 4 doctorates awarded. *Entrance requirements:* For doctorate, GRE General Test, interview. Additional exam requirements/recommendations for international students: Required—TOEFL. *Application deadline:* For fall admission, 12/1 priority date for domestic and international students. Applications are processed on a rolling basis. Application fee: $75. Electronic applications accepted. *Expenses: Tuition:* Full-time $41,352; part-time $19,968 per year. *Required fees:* $2496; $1628 per unit. $814 per term. Tuition and fees vary according to course load and program. *Financial support:* Teaching assistantships with partial tuition reimbursements, career-related internships or fieldwork, Federal Work-Study, institutionally sponsored loans, and tuition waivers (partial) available. Support available to part-time students. Financial award application deadline: 2/1; financial award applicants required to submit FAFSA. *Faculty research:* Schools and communities, self-regulation and academic achievement, intervention and social change, trauma and resilience, cognition. *Unit head:* Prof. Clancy Blair, Director, 212-998-5853, Fax: 212-995-4358, E-mail: clancy.blair@nyu.edu. *Application contact:* 212-998-5030, Fax: 212-995-4328, E-mail: steinhardt.gradadmissions@nyu.edu.
Website: http://steinhardt.nyu.edu/appsych

North Carolina State University, Graduate School, College of Humanities and Social Sciences, Department of Psychology, Raleigh, NC 27695. Offers developmental psychology (PhD); ergonomics and experimental psychology (PhD); industrial/organizational psychology (PhD); psychology in the public interest (PhD); school psychology (PhD). *Accreditation:* APA. *Degree requirements:* For doctorate, comprehensive exam, thesis/dissertation. *Entrance requirements:* For doctorate, GRE General Test, GRE Subject Test (industrial/organizational psychology), MAT (recommended), minimum GPA of 3.0 in major. Electronic applications accepted. *Faculty research:* Cognitive and social development (human factors, families, the workplace, community issues and health, aging).

North Dakota State University, College of Graduate and Interdisciplinary Studies, College of Human Development and Education, Department of Human Development and Family Science, Program in Developmental Science, Fargo, ND 58102. Offers PhD. Electronic applications accepted.

The Ohio State University, Graduate School, College of Arts and Sciences, Division of Social and Behavioral Sciences, Department of Psychology, Columbus, OH 43210. Offers behavioral neuroscience (PhD); clinical psychology (PhD); cognitive psychology (PhD); developmental psychology (PhD); intellectual and developmental disabilities psychology (PhD); quantitative psychology (PhD); social psychology (PhD). *Accreditation:* APA. *Faculty:* 52. *Students:* 144 full-time (86 women); includes 18 minority (8 Asian, non-Hispanic/Latino; 10 Hispanic/Latino), 28 international. Average age 26. In 2017, 21 doctorates awarded. *Entrance requirements:* For doctorate, GRE General Test. Additional exam requirements/recommendations for international students: Required—TOEFL (minimum score 600 paper-based; 100 iBT); Recommended—IELTS (minimum score 8). *Application deadline:* For fall admission, 12/1 for domestic and international students. Applications are processed on a rolling basis. Application fee: $60 ($70 for international students). Electronic applications accepted. *Financial support:* Fellowships, research assistantships, and teaching assistantships available. *Unit head:* Dr. John Bruno, Chair, 614-292-3038, E-mail: bruno.1@osu.edu. *Application contact:* Graduate and Professional Admissions, 614-292-9444, Fax: 614-292-3895, E-mail: gpadmissions@osu.edu.
Website: http://psychology.osu.edu/

Pace University, Dyson College of Arts and Sciences, Department of Psychology, Program in School-Clinical Child Psychology, New York, NY 10038. Offers school psychology (MS Ed); school-clinical child psychology (Psy D). *Accreditation:* APA (one or more programs are accredited). *Students:* 68 full-time (60 women), 30 part-time (23 women); includes 23 minority (3 Black or African American, non-Hispanic/Latino; 9 Asian, non-Hispanic/Latino; 7 Hispanic/Latino; 1 Native Hawaiian or other Pacific Islander, non-Hispanic/Latino; 3 Two or more races, non-Hispanic/Latino), 5 international. Average age 27. In 2017, 15 master's, 22 doctorates awarded. Terminal master's awarded for partial completion of doctoral program. *Degree requirements:* For master's, qualifying exams, internship; for doctorate, comprehensive exam, thesis/dissertation, qualifying exams, externship, internship. *Entrance requirements:* For master's, GRE General Test, GRE Subject Test in psychology (recommended), interview, 3 letters of recommendation, resume, personal statement; for doctorate, GRE General Test, GRE Subject Test in psychology (recommended), interview, transcripts, 3 letters of recommendation. Additional exam requirements/recommendations for international students: Required—TOEFL (minimum score 88 iBT), IELTS (minimum score 7) or PTE (minimum score 60). *Application deadline:* For fall admission, 1/15 priority date for domestic students. Application fee: $70. Electronic applications accepted. *Financial support:* Scholarships/grants and unspecified assistantships available. Financial award application deadline: 1/15; financial award applicants required to submit FAFSA. *Unit head:* Dr. Barbara Mowder, Director of Graduate Psychology Programs, 212-346-1556, E-mail: bmowder@pace.edu. *Application contact:* Susan Ford-Goldschein, Director of Graduate Admissions, 212-346-1531, Fax: 212-346-1585, E-mail: graduateadmission@pace.edu.
Website: http://www.pace.edu/dyson/academic-departments-and-programs/psychology—nyc/graduate-programs

Pontificia Universidad Catolica Madre y Maestra, Graduate School, Faculty of Social and Administrative Sciences, Santiago, Dominican Republic. Offers business administration (MBA), including business development, finance, international business, management skills (M Mgmt, MBA), marketing, operations, strategic cost management, strategy, tourist destination planning and management; law (LL M), including civil law, corporate business law, criminal law, international relations, real estate law; management (M Mgmt), including higher financial management, insurance program administration, management skills (M Mgmt, MBA); psychology (MA), including clinical child and adolescent psychology, forensic psychology; strategic human resources (EMBA).

Queen's University at Kingston, School of Graduate Studies, Faculty of Arts and Sciences, Department of Psychology, Kingston, ON K7L 3N6, Canada. Offers brain behavior and cognitive science (MA, PhD); clinical psychology (MA, PhD); developmental psychology (MA, PhD); social personality psychology (MA, PhD). *Degree requirements:* For master's, thesis; for doctorate, comprehensive exam, thesis/dissertation. *Entrance requirements:* For master's and doctorate, GRE General Test. Additional exam requirements/recommendations for international students: Required—TOEFL. *Faculty research:* Human development, social, personality, behavioral neuroscience, forensic.

Regis University, Rueckert-Hartman College for Health Professions, Denver, CO 80221-1099. Offers advanced practice nurse (DNP); counseling (MA); counseling children and adolescents (Post-Graduate Certificate); counseling military families (Post-Graduate Certificate); depth psychotherapy (Post-Graduate Certificate); fellowship in orthopedic manual physical therapy (Certificate); health care business management (Certificate); health care quality and patient safety (Certificate); health industry leadership (MBA); health services administration (MS); marriage and family therapy (MA, Post-Graduate Certificate); neonatal nurse practitioner (MSN); nursing education (MSN); nursing leadership (MSN); occupational therapy (OTD); pharmacy (Pharm D); physical therapy (DPT). *Program availability:* Part-time, evening/weekend, 100% online, blended/hybrid learning. *Degree requirements:* For master's, thesis (for some programs), internship. *Entrance requirements:* For master's, official transcript reflecting baccalaureate degree awarded from regionally-accredited college or university. Additional exam requirements/recommendations for international students: Required—TOEFL (minimum score 550 paper-based; 82 iBT). Electronic applications accepted. *Expenses:* Contact institution. *Faculty research:* Normal and pathological balance and gait research, normal/pathological upper limb motor control/biomechanics, exercise energy/metabolism research, optical treatment protocols for therapeutic modalities.

San Francisco State University, Division of Graduate Studies, College of Science and Engineering, Department of Psychology, San Francisco, CA 94132-1722. Offers clinical psychology (MS); developmental psychology (MA); industrial/organizational psychology (MS); mind, brain, and behavior (MA); school psychology (MS, Credential); social psychology (MA). *Financial support:* Teaching assistantships available. Financial award application deadline: 3/1. *Unit head:* Dr. Dawn Terrell, Chair, 415-338-7555, Fax: 415-338-2398, E-mail: schen9@sfsu.edu. *Application contact:* Dr. Diane Harris, Graduate Program Coordinator, 415-338-7064, Fax: 415-338-2398, E-mail: dharris@sfsu.edu.
Website: http://psychology.sfsu.edu/graduate/application.html

Teachers College, Columbia University, Department of Human Development, New York, NY 10027-6696. Offers applied statistics (MS); cognitive studies in education (MA, Ed D, PhD); developmental psychology (MA, Ed D, PhD); educational psychology-human cognition and learning (Ed M, MA, Ed D, PhD); learning analytics (MS); measurement and evaluation (ME, Ed D, PhD); measurement, evaluation, and statistics (MA, MS, Ed D, PhD). *Program availability:* Part-time. *Students:* 155 full-time (105 women), 135 part-time (106 women); includes 93 minority (26 Black or African American, non-Hispanic/Latino; 44 Asian, non-Hispanic/Latino; 21 Hispanic/Latino; 2 Two or more races, non-Hispanic/Latino), 118 international. Average age 29. 459 applicants, 53% accepted, 100 enrolled. *Unit head:* Jim Corter, Chair, E-mail: jec34@tc.columbia.edu. *Application contact:* David Estrella, Director of Admission, 212-678-3305, E-mail: estrella@tc.columbia.edu.
Website: http://www.tc.columbia.edu/human-development/

Texas Christian University, College of Science and Engineering, Department of Psychology, Fort Worth, TX 76129. Offers developmental trauma (MS); experimental psychology (PhD), including cognition/developmental, learning, neuroscience, social. *Faculty:* 13 full-time (6 women), 2 part-time/adjunct (both women). *Students:* 32 full-time (25 women); includes 5 minority (1 Asian, non-Hispanic/Latino; 2 Hispanic/Latino; 2 Two or more races, non-Hispanic/Latino), 2 international. Average age 26. 50 applicants, 34% accepted, 16 enrolled. In 2017, 8 master's, 2 doctorates awarded. Terminal master's awarded for partial completion of doctoral program. *Degree requirements:* For master's, thesis; for doctorate, thesis/dissertation. *Entrance requirements:* For doctorate, GRE General Test. Additional exam requirements/recommendations for international students: Required—TOEFL. *Application deadline:* For fall admission, 2/1 for domestic and international students. Application fee: $60 ($0 for international students). Electronic applications accepted. *Expenses:* Contact institution. *Financial support:* In 2017–18, 23 students received support, including 23 teaching assistantships with full tuition reimbursements available (averaging $19,750 per year); scholarships/grants also available. Financial award application deadline: 2/1; financial award applicants required to submit FAFSA. *Faculty research:* Neuroscience, human and animal learning, cognition, development, experimental social psychology. *Unit head:* Dr. Mauricio R. Papini, Chair, 817-257-7410, Fax: 817-257-7681, E-mail: m.papini@tcu.edu. *Application contact:* Cindy Hayes, Administrative Assistant, 817-257-7410, Fax: 817-257-7681, E-mail: c.hayes@tcu.edu.
Website: https://psychology.tcu.edu/current-graduate-students/

Université de Montréal, Faculty of Arts and Sciences, School of Psychoeducation, Montréal, QC H3C 3J7, Canada. Offers M Sc, PhD. *Program availability:* Part-time. *Degree requirements:* For master's, one foreign language, thesis. Electronic applications accepted. *Faculty research:* Child maladjustment, family, prevention, treatment, antisocial behavior.

The University of Alabama at Birmingham, College of Arts and Sciences, Program in Psychology, Birmingham, AL 35294. Offers behavioral neuroscience (PhD); lifespan developmental psychology (PhD); medical/clinical psychology (PhD); psychology (MA). *Accreditation:* APA (one or more programs are accredited). *Entrance requirements:* For master's and doctorate, GRE General Test, letters of recommendation. Electronic applications accepted. *Faculty research:* Biological basis of behavior structure, function of the nervous system.

The University of British Columbia, Faculty of Arts and Faculty of Graduate Studies, Department of Psychology, Vancouver, BC V6T 1Z4, Canada. Offers behavioral neuroscience (MA, PhD); clinical psychology (MA, PhD); cognitive science (MA, PhD); developmental psychology (MA, PhD); health psychology (MA, PhD); quantitative methods (MA, PhD); social/personality psychology (MA, PhD). *Accreditation:* APA (one or more programs are accredited). Terminal master's awarded for partial completion of doctoral program. *Degree requirements:* For master's, thesis; for doctorate, comprehensive exam, thesis/dissertation. *Entrance requirements:* For master's and doctorate, GRE General Test. Additional exam requirements/recommendations for international students: Required—TOEFL. Electronic applications accepted. *Expenses:* Contact institution. *Faculty research:* Clinical, developmental, social/personality, cognition, behavioral neuroscience.

University of Connecticut, Graduate School, College of Liberal Arts and Sciences, Department of Psychology, Storrs, CT 06269. Offers behavioral neuroscience (PhD); biopsychology (PhD); clinical psychology (MA, PhD); cognition and instruction (PhD); developmental psychology (MA, PhD); ecological psychology (PhD); experimental psychology (PhD); general psychology (MA, PhD); industrial/organizational psychology (PhD); language and cognition (PhD); neuroscience (PhD); social psychology (MA, PhD). *Accreditation:* APA. Terminal master's awarded for partial completion of doctoral program. *Degree requirements:* For master's, comprehensive exam; for doctorate, thesis/dissertation. *Entrance requirements:* For master's and doctorate, GRE General Test, GRE Subject Test. Additional exam requirements/recommendations for international students: Required—TOEFL (minimum score 550 paper-based). Electronic applications accepted.

University of Denver, Division of Arts, Humanities and Social Sciences, Department of Psychology, Denver, CO 80208. Offers affective/cognitive/social psychology (PhD); clinical child psychology (PhD); developmental psychology (PhD). *Accreditation:* APA. *Students:* Average age 28. 294 applicants, 4% accepted, 8 enrolled. In 2017, 8 doctorates awarded. Terminal master's awarded for partial completion of doctoral program. *Degree requirements:* For doctorate, variable foreign language requirement, comprehensive exam (for some programs), thesis/dissertation. *Entrance requirements:* For doctorate, GRE General Test, master's degree, transcripts, biographical statement, three letters of recommendation. Additional exam requirements/recommendations for international students: Required—TOEFL (minimum score 550 paper-based; 80 iBT). *Application deadline:* For fall admission, 12/1 priority date for domestic and international students. Application fee: $65. Electronic applications accepted. *Expenses:* Contact institution. *Financial support:* In 2017–18, 24 students received support, including 5 research assistantships with tuition reimbursements available (averaging $16,000 per year), 12 teaching assistantships with tuition reimbursements available (averaging $17,778 per year); Federal Work-Study, institutionally sponsored loans, scholarships/grants, and unspecified assistantships also available. Support available to part-time students. Financial award application deadline: 2/15; financial award applicants required to submit FAFSA. *Faculty research:* Stress and trauma, developmental science, affect science, clinical science, child psychopathology. *Unit head:* Dr. Anne DePrince, Professor and Chair, 303-871-2939, Fax: 303-871-4747, E-mail: adeprinc@du.edu. *Application contact:* Paula Houghtaling, Graduate Program Administrator, 303-871-3803, Fax: 303-871-4747, E-mail: phoughta@du.edu.
Website: http://www.du.edu/ahss/psychology

University of Houston, College of Liberal Arts and Social Sciences, Department of Psychology, Houston, TX 77204. Offers clinical psychology (PhD); developmental psychology (PhD); industrial/organizational psychology (PhD); psychology (MA); social psychology (PhD). *Accreditation:* APA (one or more programs are accredited). *Degree requirements:* For master's, comprehensive exam, thesis; for doctorate, comprehensive exam, thesis/dissertation. *Entrance requirements:* For master's, GRE General Test, career statement, 3 letters of recommendation; for doctorate, GRE General Test, 3 letters of recommendation. Additional exam requirements/recommendations for international students: Required—TOEFL (minimum score 550 paper-based; 79 iBT). Electronic applications accepted. *Faculty research:* Health psychology, depression, child/family process, organizational effectiveness, close relationships.

University of Illinois at Chicago, College of Education, Department of Educational Psychology, Chicago, IL 60607-7128. Offers early childhood education (M Ed); educational psychology (PhD); measurement, evaluation, statistics, and assessment (M Ed); youth development (M Ed). *Program availability:* Part-time, online learning. *Faculty research:* Children's construction of morality, development of resilience in the face of enduring economical difficulties, cognition and cognitive development, test fairness.

The University of Kansas, Graduate Studies, College of Liberal Arts and Sciences, Department of Psychology, Lawrence, KS 66045. Offers clinical psychology (MA, PhD); cognitive and brain sciences (MA, PhD); developmental psychology (MA, PhD); quantitative psychology (PhD); social psychology (MA, PhD). *Accreditation:* APA (one or more programs are accredited). *Program availability:* Part-time. *Students:* 92 full-time (63 women), 3 part-time (all women); includes 19 minority (7 Black or African American, non-Hispanic/Latino; 4 Asian, non-Hispanic/Latino; 4 Hispanic/Latino; 4 Two or more races, non-Hispanic/Latino), 10 international. Average age 28. 361 applicants, 7% accepted, 16 enrolled. In 2017, 9 master's, 17 doctorates awarded. Terminal master's awarded for partial completion of doctoral program. *Entrance requirements:* For doctorate, GRE General Test, three letters of recommendation, resume/curriculum vitae, statement of purpose/personal statement, writing sample. Additional exam requirements/recommendations for international students: Required—TOEFL. *Application deadline:* For fall admission, 12/1 for domestic and international students. Application fee: $65 ($85 for international students). Electronic applications accepted. *Financial support:* Fellowships, research assistantships, teaching assistantships, career-related internships or fieldwork, Federal Work-Study, scholarships/grants, health care benefits, and unspecified assistantships available. Financial award application deadline: 12/1; financial award applicants required to submit FAFSA. *Faculty research:* Origins, correlates and treatment of depression; health and emotion; concentration on topics related to prejudice, stereotyping, and intergroup relations; memory, cognitive development, language, perception, attention, aging; psychometric methods, item response theory, structural equation modeling. *Unit head:* Ruth Anne Atchley, Chair, 785-864-4131. *Application contact:* Graduate Officer, 785-864-4195, E-mail: psycgrad@ku.edu.
Website: http://www.psych.ku.edu/

The University of Kansas, Graduate Studies, College of Liberal Arts and Sciences, Program in Child Language, Lawrence, KS 66045. Offers MA, PhD. *Students:* 5 full-time (all women); includes 1 minority (Asian, non-Hispanic/Latino). Average age 29. 2 applicants, 50% accepted. In 2017, 2 master's awarded. *Entrance requirements:* For master's and doctorate, GRE, official transcripts, three letters of recommendation, personal statement, curriculum vitae. Additional exam requirements/recommendations for international students: Required—TOEFL. *Application deadline:* For fall admission, 1/15 for domestic and international students. Application fee: $65 ($85 for international students). Electronic applications accepted. *Financial support:* Fellowships, research assistantships, teaching assistantships, career-related internships or fieldwork, traineeships, and unspecified assistantships available. Financial award application deadline: 1/15. *Faculty research:* Language impairments in children, specific language impairment, genetics of language acquisition, brain processing of language, language of aging. *Unit head:* Mabel L. Rice, Director, 785-864-4570, E-mail: mabel@ku.edu. *Application contact:* Linda Mann, Graduate Admissions Contact, 785-864-4804, E-mail: childlang@ku.edu.
Website: http://cldp.ku.edu/

University of Louisville, Graduate School, College of Arts and Sciences, Department of Psychological and Brain Sciences, Louisville, KY 40292-0001. Offers clinical psychology (PhD); experimental psychology (PhD), including cognition and development, vision and hearing. *Accreditation:* APA. *Students:* 55 full-time (44 women), 1 (woman) part-time; includes 7 minority (1 Black or African American, non-Hispanic/Latino; 2 Asian, non-Hispanic/Latino; 2 Hispanic/Latino; 2 Two or more races, non-Hispanic/Latino), 4 international. Average age 29. 9 applicants, 78% accepted. In 2017, 1 doctorate awarded. *Degree requirements:* For doctorate, comprehensive exam, thesis/dissertation, internship (for clinical psychology). *Entrance requirements:* For doctorate, GRE General Test, GRE Subject Test. Additional exam requirements/recommendations for international students: Required—TOEFL. *Application deadline:* For fall and winter admission, 12/1 for domestic and international students. Application fee: $65. *Expenses:* Tuition, state resident: full-time $12,246; part-time $681 per credit hour. Tuition, nonresident: full-time $25,486; part-time $1417 per credit hour. *Required fees:* $196. Tuition and fees vary according to course load, program and reciprocity agreements. *Financial support:* In 2017–18, 8 fellowships with full tuition reimbursements (averaging $22,000 per year), 3 research assistantships with full tuition reimbursements (averaging $22,000 per year), 30 teaching assistantships with full tuition reimbursements (averaging $22,000 per year) were awarded; health care benefits and unspecified assistantships also available. Financial award application deadline: 12/1. *Faculty research:* Cognitive development, hearing/visual science, cognitive neuroscience/imaging, health psychology/mindfulness/stress and trauma, child/adult psychopathology, geropsychology. *Total annual research expenditures:* $923,340. *Unit head:* Dr. Suzanne Meeks, Chair, 502-852-6068, Fax: 502-852-8904, E-mail: smeeks@louisville.edu. *Application contact:* Maggie Leahy, Administrative Assistant, 502-852-4364, Fax: 502-852-8904, E-mail: maggie.leahy@louisville.edu.
Website: http://louisville.edu/psychology

The University of Manchester, School of Education, Manchester, United Kingdom. Offers counseling (D Couns); counseling psychology (D Couns); education (M Phil, Ed D, PhD); educational and child psychology (Ed D); educational psychology (Ed D).

University of Maryland, Baltimore County, The Graduate School, College of Arts, Humanities and Social Sciences, Department of Psychology, Program in Applied Developmental Psychology, Baltimore, MD 21250. Offers PhD. *Faculty:* 8 full-time (6 women), 11 part-time/adjunct (4 women). *Students:* 22 full-time (all women); includes 8 minority (2 Black or African American, non-Hispanic/Latino; 6 Asian, non-Hispanic/Latino), 4 international. Average age 25. 24 applicants, 21% accepted, 3 enrolled. In 2017, 1 doctorate awarded. *Degree requirements:* For doctorate, comprehensive exam, thesis/dissertation. *Entrance requirements:* For doctorate, GRE General Test, minimum GPA of 3.0. Additional exam requirements/recommendations for international students: Required—TOEFL. *Application deadline:* For fall admission, 12/1 for domestic and international students. Application fee: $50. Electronic applications accepted. *Expenses:* Contact institution. *Financial support:* In 2017–18, 17 students received support, including 4 fellowships with partial tuition reimbursements available (averaging $17,250 per year), 5 research assistantships with full tuition reimbursements available (averaging $20,400 per year), 8 teaching assistantships with full tuition reimbursements available (averaging $17,250 per year); career-related internships or fieldwork, Federal Work-Study, health care benefits, and unspecified assistantships also available. Financial award application deadline: 3/1; financial award applicants required to submit FAFSA. *Faculty research:* Early intervention and development, schooling and development, cultural aspects of development, development in high risk children, social-emotional development. *Unit head:* Dr. Susan Sonnenschein, Director, 410-455-2361, Fax: 410-455-1055, E-mail: sonnenschein@umbc.edu. *Application contact:* Beverly McDougall, Program Management Specialist, 410-455-2567, Fax: 410-455-1055, E-mail: psycdept@umbc.edu.
Website: http://psychology.umbc.edu/

University of Maryland, College Park, Academic Affairs, College of Behavioral and Social Sciences, Department of Psychology, College Park, MD 20742. Offers clinical psychology (PhD); developmental psychology (PhD); experimental psychology (PhD); industrial psychology (MA, MS, PhD); social psychology (PhD). *Accreditation:* APA (one or more programs are accredited). *Degree requirements:* For master's, thesis; for doctorate, variable foreign language requirement, comprehensive exam, thesis/dissertation. *Entrance requirements:* For master's and doctorate, GRE General Test, GRE Subject Test, minimum GPA of 3.5, research and/or work experience, 3 letters of recommendation. Electronic applications accepted. *Faculty research:* Social stereotyping and prejudice, anxiety disorders, auditory neuroethology, counseling and social psychology.

University of Massachusetts Amherst, Graduate School, College of Natural Sciences, Department of Psychological and Brain Sciences, Amherst, MA 01003. Offers clinical psychology (MS, PhD); cognitive psychology (MS, PhD); developmental science (MS, PhD); psychology of peace and violence (MS, PhD); social psychology (MS, PhD). *Accreditation:* APA (one or more programs are accredited). Terminal master's awarded for partial completion of doctoral program. *Degree requirements:* For master's, thesis; for doctorate, comprehensive exam, thesis/dissertation. *Entrance requirements:* For master's and doctorate, GRE General Test, 3 letters of recommendation. Additional exam requirements/recommendations for international students: Required—TOEFL (minimum score 550 paper-based; 80 iBT), IELTS (minimum score 6.5). Electronic applications accepted.

University of Miami, Graduate School, College of Arts and Sciences, Department of Psychology, Coral Gables, FL 33124. Offers adult clinical (PhD); behavioral neuroscience (PhD); child clinical (PhD); developmental psychology (PhD); health clinical (PhD); psychology (MS). *Accreditation:* APA (one or more programs are accredited). *Degree requirements:* For doctorate, comprehensive exam, thesis/dissertation. *Entrance requirements:* For doctorate, GRE General Test, minimum GPA of 3.5. Additional exam requirements/recommendations for international students: Required—TOEFL. Electronic applications accepted. *Faculty research:* Behavioral factors in cardiovascular disease and cancer adult psychopathology, developmental disabilities, social and emotional development, mechanisms of coping.

University of Michigan, Rackham Graduate School, College of Literature, Science, and the Arts, Department of Psychology, Ann Arbor, MI 48109. Offers biopsychology (PhD); clinical science (PhD); cognition and cognitive neuroscience (PhD);

developmental psychology (PhD); personality and social contexts (PhD); social psychology (PhD). *Accreditation:* APA. *Faculty:* 66 full-time (31 women), 28 part-time/adjunct (17 women). *Students:* 148 full-time (113 women); includes 61 minority (13 Black or African American, non-Hispanic/Latino; 1 American Indian or Alaska Native, non-Hispanic/Latino; 12 Asian, non-Hispanic/Latino; 28 Hispanic/Latino; 7 Two or more races, non-Hispanic/Latino), 24 international. Average age 27. 691 applicants, 7% accepted, 35 enrolled. In 2017, 34 doctorates awarded. Terminal master's awarded for partial completion of doctoral program. *Degree requirements:* For doctorate, comprehensive exam, thesis/dissertation, oral defense of dissertation, preliminary exam. *Entrance requirements:* For doctorate, GRE General Test. Additional exam requirements/recommendations for international students: Required—TOEFL. *Application deadline:* For fall admission, 12/1 for domestic and international students. Application fee: $75 ($90 for international students). Electronic applications accepted. *Expenses:* $11,184 in-state, $22,578 out-of-state. *Financial support:* In 2017–18, 90 students received support, including 61 fellowships with full tuition reimbursements available (averaging $26,400 per year), 10 research assistantships with full tuition reimbursements available (averaging $26,400 per year), 89 teaching assistantships with full tuition reimbursements available (averaging $26,400 per year); career-related internships or fieldwork, traineeships, and health care benefits also available. Financial award application deadline: 4/15. *Unit head:* Prof. Patricia Reuter-Lorenz, Department Chair, 734-764-7429. *Application contact:* Sheri M. Circele, Psychology Student Academic Affairs, 734-764-2580, Fax: 734-764-3520, E-mail: psych.saa@umich.edu.
Website: http://www.lsa.umich.edu/psych/

University of Montana, Graduate School, College of Humanities and Sciences, Department of Psychology, Missoula, MT 59812. Offers clinical psychology (PhD); experimental psychology (PhD), including animal behavior psychology, developmental psychology; school psychology (MA, PhD, Ed S). *Accreditation:* APA (one or more programs are accredited). Terminal master's awarded for partial completion of doctoral program. *Degree requirements:* For master's, thesis; for doctorate, thesis/dissertation. *Entrance requirements:* For master's, doctorate, and Ed S, GRE General Test. Additional exam requirements/recommendations for international students: Required—TOEFL.

University of Nebraska–Lincoln, Graduate College, College of Arts and Sciences, Department of Psychology, Lincoln, NE 68588. Offers biopsychology (PhD); clinical psychology (PhD); cognitive psychology (PhD); developmental psychology (PhD); psychology (MA); social/personality psychology (PhD); JD/MA; JD/PhD. *Accreditation:* APA (one or more programs are accredited). *Degree requirements:* For master's, thesis optional; for doctorate, comprehensive exam, thesis/dissertation. *Entrance requirements:* For master's and doctorate, GRE General Test. Additional exam requirements/recommendations for international students: Required—TOEFL (minimum score 550 paper-based). Electronic applications accepted. *Faculty research:* Law and psychology, rural mental health, chronic mental illness, neuropsychology, child clinical psychology.

University of Nebraska–Lincoln, Graduate College, College of Education and Human Sciences, Department of Educational Psychology, Lincoln, NE 68588. Offers cognition, learning and development (MA); counseling psychology (MA); educational psychology (MA, Ed S); psychological studies in education (PhD), including cognition, learning and development, counseling psychology, quantitative, qualitative, and psychometric methods, school psychology; quantitative, qualitative, and psychometric methods (MA); school psychology (MA, Ed S). *Accreditation:* APA (one or more programs are accredited); NCATE. *Degree requirements:* For master's, thesis optional. *Entrance requirements:* For master's, GRE General Test. Additional exam requirements/recommendations for international students: Required—TOEFL (minimum score 500 paper-based). Electronic applications accepted. *Faculty research:* Measurement and assessment, metacognition, academic skills, child development, multicultural education and counseling.

University of New Mexico, Graduate Studies, College of Arts and Sciences, Program in Psychology, Albuquerque, NM 87131-2039. Offers behavioral neuroscience (PhD); clinical psychology (PhD); cognitive neuroimaging (PhD); developmental psychology (PhD); evolution (PhD); health psychology (PhD); quantitative methodology (PhD). *Accreditation:* APA. *Students:* Average age 30. 227 applicants, 11% accepted, 16 enrolled. In 2017, 10 doctorates awarded. *Degree requirements:* For doctorate, comprehensive exam, thesis/dissertation. *Entrance requirements:* For doctorate, GRE General Test, GRE Subject Test (psychology), minimum GPA of 3.0. Additional exam requirements/recommendations for international students: Required—TOEFL (minimum score 550 paper-based; 79 iBT), IELTS (minimum score 6.5). *Application deadline:* For fall admission, 12/15 priority date for domestic and international students. Applications are processed on a rolling basis. Application fee: $50. Electronic applications accepted. *Financial support:* Fellowships, research assistantships, teaching assistantships, career-related internships or fieldwork, Federal Work-Study, institutionally sponsored loans, scholarships/grants, health care benefits, tuition waivers (partial), and unspecified assistantships available. Financial award application deadline: 3/1; financial award applicants required to submit FAFSA. *Faculty research:* Addiction, cognition, brain and behavior, developmental, evolutionary, functioning neuroimaging, health psychology, learning and memory, neuroscience. *Total annual research expenditures:* $727,970. *Unit head:* Dr. Jane Ellen Smith, Department Chair, 505-277-4121, Fax: 505-277-1394. *Application contact:* Rikk Murphy, Graduate Program Coordinator, 505-277-5009, Fax: 505-277-1394, E-mail: advising@unm.edu.
Website: http://psych.unm.edu

The University of North Carolina at Chapel Hill, Graduate School, College of Arts and Sciences, Department of Psychology, Chapel Hill, NC 27599-3270. Offers behavioral neuroscience psychology (PhD); clinical psychology (PhD); cognitive psychology (PhD); developmental psychology (PhD); quantitative psychology (PhD); social psychology (PhD). *Accreditation:* APA. *Degree requirements:* For doctorate, comprehensive exam, thesis/dissertation. *Entrance requirements:* For doctorate, GRE General Test, minimum GPA of 3.0. Additional exam requirements/recommendations for international students: Required—TOEFL (minimum score 550 paper-based; 79 iBT), IELTS (minimum score 7). Electronic applications accepted. *Faculty research:* Expressed emotion, cognitive development, social cognitive neuroscience, human memory personality.

The University of North Carolina at Greensboro, Graduate School, College of Arts and Sciences, Department of Psychology, Greensboro, NC 27412-5001. Offers clinical psychology (MA, PhD); cognitive psychology (MA, PhD); developmental psychology (MA, PhD); social psychology (MA, PhD). *Accreditation:* APA (one or more programs are accredited). Terminal master's awarded for partial completion of doctoral program. *Degree requirements:* For master's, comprehensive exam, thesis; for doctorate, one foreign language, thesis/dissertation, preliminary exam. *Entrance requirements:* For master's and doctorate, GRE General Test. Additional exam requirements/recommendations for international students: Required—TOEFL. Electronic applications accepted. *Faculty research:* Sensory and perceptual determinants; evoked potential: disorders, deafness, and development.

University of Notre Dame, Graduate School, College of Arts and Letters, Division of Social Science, Department of Psychology, Notre Dame, IN 46556. Offers cognitive psychology (PhD); counseling psychology (PhD); developmental psychology (PhD); quantitative psychology (PhD). *Accreditation:* APA. *Degree requirements:* For doctorate, comprehensive exam, thesis/dissertation, candidacy exam. *Entrance requirements:* For doctorate, GRE General Test, GRE Subject Test (strongly recommended). Additional exam requirements/recommendations for international students: Required—TOEFL (minimum score 600 paper-based; 80 iBT). Electronic applications accepted. *Faculty research:* Cognitive and socio-emotional development, statistical methods and quantitative models applicable to psychology, interpersonal relations, life span development and developmental delay, childhood depression, structural equation and dynamical systems.

University of Oregon, Graduate School, College of Arts and Sciences, Department of Psychology, Eugene, OR 97403. Offers clinical psychology (PhD); cognitive psychology (MA, MS, PhD); developmental psychology (MA, MS, PhD); physiological psychology (MA, MS, PhD); psychology (MA, MS, PhD); social/personality psychology (MA, MS, PhD). *Accreditation:* APA (one or more programs are accredited). Terminal master's awarded for partial completion of doctoral program. *Degree requirements:* For doctorate, thesis/dissertation. *Entrance requirements:* For master's, GRE General Test, minimum GPA of 3.0; for doctorate, GRE General Test. Additional exam requirements/recommendations for international students: Required—TOEFL.

University of Pittsburgh, Kenneth P. Dietrich School of Arts and Sciences, Department of Psychology, Pittsburgh, PA 15260. Offers biological and health psychology (PhD); clinical psychology (PhD); cognitive psychology (PhD); developmental psychology (PhD); social psychology (PhD). *Accreditation:* APA. *Faculty:* 58 full-time (26 women). *Students:* 90 full-time (72 women); includes 25 minority (5 Black or African American, non-Hispanic/Latino; 11 Asian, non-Hispanic/Latino; 9 Hispanic/Latino), 9 international. Average age 26. 485 applicants, 6% accepted, 14 enrolled. In 2017, 6 doctorates awarded. Terminal master's awarded for partial completion of doctoral program. *Degree requirements:* For doctorate, comprehensive exam, thesis/dissertation. *Entrance requirements:* For doctorate, GRE General Test, minimum GPA of 3.0. Additional exam requirements/recommendations for international students: Required—TOEFL (minimum score 90 iBT) or IELTS (minimum score 7). *Application deadline:* For fall admission, 12/1 for domestic and international students. Application fee: $50. Electronic applications accepted. *Financial support:* In 2017–18, 76 students received support, including 20 fellowships with full tuition reimbursements available (averaging $22,000 per year), 28 research assistantships with full tuition reimbursements available (averaging $18,060 per year), 29 teaching assistantships with full tuition reimbursements available (averaging $19,180 per year); scholarships/grants, traineeships, and health care benefits also available. Financial award application deadline: 12/1. *Faculty research:* Developmental psychopathology; autism spectrum disorder; cardiovascular medicine; STEM research. *Total annual research expenditures:* $20 million. *Unit head:* Dr. Julie Fiez, Chair, 412-624-4500, E-mail: fiez@pitt.edu. *Application contact:* Stacy McLinden, Graduate Administrator, 412-624-4502, E-mail: psygrad@pitt.edu.
Website: http://www.psychology.pitt.edu/

University of Pittsburgh, School of Education, Department of Psychology in Education, Program in Applied Developmental Psychology, Pittsburgh, PA 15260. Offers M Ed, MS, PhD. *Program availability:* Part-time, evening/weekend. *Degree requirements:* For master's, thesis. *Entrance requirements:* For doctorate, GRE. Additional exam requirements/recommendations for international students: Required—TOEFL. Electronic applications accepted.

University of Rochester, School of Arts and Sciences, Department of Clinical and Social Sciences in Psychology, Rochester, NY 14627. Offers clinical psychology (PhD); developmental psychology (PhD); social-personality psychology (PhD). *Accreditation:* APA. *Faculty:* 14 full-time (7 women). *Students:* 46 full-time (39 women), 1 (woman) part-time; includes 9 minority (1 Black or African American, non-Hispanic/Latino; 4 Asian, non-Hispanic/Latino; 3 Hispanic/Latino; 1 Two or more races, non-Hispanic/Latino), 4 international. Average age 28. 246 applicants, 4% accepted, 8 enrolled. In 2017, 6 doctorates awarded. Terminal master's awarded for partial completion of doctoral program. *Degree requirements:* For doctorate, thesis/dissertation. *Entrance requirements:* For doctorate, GRE General Test; GRE Subject Test (required for clinical psychology, recommended for others), personal statement, official transcripts, three letters of recommendation, curriculum vitae, resume. Additional exam requirements/recommendations for international students: Required—TOEFL. *Application deadline:* For fall admission, 12/1 for domestic and international students. Application fee: $60. Electronic applications accepted. *Expenses:* $1,596 per credit hour. *Financial support:* In 2017–18, 37 students received support, including 2 fellowships, 37 research assistantships (averaging $22,000 per year); teaching assistantships, career-related internships or fieldwork, scholarships/grants, and tuition waivers (full) also available. Financial award application deadline: 4/15. *Faculty research:* Multisensory processing in social-communication difficulties, child emotion regulation, interpersonal relationships, social stress, understanding romantic relationships. *Total annual research expenditures:* $4.3 million. *Unit head:* Loisa Bennetto, Chair, 585-275-8712, E-mail: loisa.bennetto@rochester.edu. *Application contact:* April Engram, Academic Coordinator, 585-275-8704, E-mail: april.engram@rochester.edu.
Website: http://www.sas.rochester.edu/psy/graduate/index.html

University of Southern California, Graduate School, Dana and David Dornsife College of Letters, Arts and Sciences, Department of Psychology, Los Angeles, CA 90089. Offers brain and cognitive science (PhD); clinical science (PhD); developmental psychology (PhD); human behavior (MHB); quantitative methods (PhD); social psychology (PhD). *Accreditation:* APA. *Degree requirements:* For doctorate, comprehensive exam, thesis/dissertation, one-year internship (for clinical science students). *Entrance requirements:* For doctorate, GRE. Additional exam requirements/recommendations for international students: Recommended—TOEFL (minimum score 600 paper-based; 100 iBT). Electronic applications accepted. *Faculty research:* Affective neuroscience; children and families; vision, culture and ethnicity; intergroup relations; aggression and violence; language and reading development; substance abuse.

The University of Texas at Austin, Graduate School, College of Liberal Arts, Department of Psychology, Austin, TX 78712-1111. Offers behavioral neuroscience (PhD); clinical psychology (PhD); cognitive systems (PhD); developmental psychology (PhD); individual differences and evolutionary psychology (PhD); perceptual systems (PhD); social psychology (PhD). *Accreditation:* APA. *Degree requirements:* For doctorate, thesis/dissertation. *Entrance requirements:* For doctorate, GRE General Test. Electronic applications accepted. *Faculty research:* Behavioral neuroscience, sensory neuroscience, evolutionary psychology, cognitive processes in psychopathology, cognitive processes and their development.

University of Utah, Graduate School, College of Social and Behavioral Science, Department of Psychology, Salt Lake City, UT 84112. Offers clinical psychology (PhD); psychology (PhD), including cognitive neuroscience, developmental psychology, social psychology. *Accreditation:* APA. *Faculty:* 32 full-time (15 women), 11 part-time/adjunct (7 women). *Students:* 53 full-time (36 women), 10 part-time (7 women); includes 10 minority (2 Black or African American, non-Hispanic/Latino; 1 Asian, non-Hispanic/Latino; 4 Hispanic/Latino; 3 Two or more races, non-Hispanic/Latino), 5 international. Average age 26. 295 applicants, 8% accepted, 13 enrolled. In 2017, 11 doctorates awarded. *Entrance requirements:* For doctorate, GRE General Test. Additional exam requirements/recommendations for international students: Required—TOEFL (minimum

score 500 paper-based). Application fee: $55 ($65 for international students). Electronic applications accepted. *Expenses:* All admitted students are guaranteed funding and full tuition benefit for four years. *Financial support:* In 2017–18, 51 students received support, including 2 fellowships with full tuition reimbursements available (averaging $17,000 per year), 16 research assistantships with full tuition reimbursements available (averaging $16,800 per year), 30 teaching assistantships with full tuition reimbursements available (averaging $16,800 per year); career-related internships or fieldwork, health care benefits, and unspecified assistantships also available. Financial award application deadline: 4/15; financial award applicants required to submit FAFSA. *Faculty research:* Cognitive neuroscience, health, social cognition, psychopathology, cognitive and social development. *Total annual research expenditures:* $1.9 million. *Unit head:* Dr. Lisa G. Aspinwall, Chair, 801-581-8925, Fax: 801-581-5841, E-mail: lisa.aspinwall@utah.edu. *Application contact:* Nancy Seegmiller, Program Manager, 801-581-8925, Fax: 801-581-5841, E-mail: nancy.seegmiller@psych.utah.edu. Website: http://www.psych.utah.edu/

University of Vermont, Graduate College, College of Arts and Sciences, Program in General/Experimental Psychology, Burlington, VT 05405-0134. Offers psychology (PhD), including biobehavioral psychology, developmental psychology, human behavioral pharmacology, social psychology. *Accreditation:* APA. *Students:* 15 (11 women). 22 applicants, 9% accepted, 2 enrolled. In 2017, 2 doctorates awarded. *Degree requirements:* For doctorate, thesis/dissertation. *Entrance requirements:* For doctorate, GRE General Test. Additional exam requirements/recommendations for international students: Required—TOEFL (minimum score 550 paper-based, 100 iBT) or IELTS (7). *Application deadline:* For fall admission, 12/1 for domestic and international students. Application fee: $65. Electronic applications accepted. *Expenses:* Tuition, state resident: full-time $11,628; part-time $646 per credit. Tuition, nonresident: full-time $29,340; part-time $1630 per credit. *Required fees:* $1994; $10 per credit. Tuition and fees vary according to course load and program. *Financial support:* In 2017–18, 15 students received support, including 15 teaching assistantships with full tuition reimbursements available (averaging $20,000 per year); fellowships and research assistantships also available. Financial award application deadline: 12/1. *Unit head:* Dr. Dianna Murray-Close, Coordinator, 802-656-2670, E-mail: dianna.murray-close@uvm.edu.
Website: https://www.uvm.edu/cas/psychology/general/experimental-psychology-phd-program

University of Victoria, Faculty of Graduate Studies, Faculty of Social Sciences, Department of Psychology, Victoria, BC V8W 2Y2, Canada. Offers clinical psychology (PhD); clinical psychology (neuropsychology) (M Sc); cognition and brain science (M Sc, PhD); experimental neuropsychology (M Sc, PhD); individualized study (M Sc, PhD); life span development psychology (PhD); life span developmental psychology (M Sc); social psychology (M Sc, PhD). *Degree requirements:* For master's, thesis; for doctorate, thesis/dissertation, candidacy exam. *Entrance requirements:* For master's and doctorate, GRE General Test. Additional exam requirements/recommendations for international students: Required—TOEFL (minimum score 600 paper-based). Electronic applications accepted. *Faculty research:* Life span development psychology and aging, behavioral neuroscience, cognitive psychology, behavioral psychology, environmental psychology.

University of Washington, Graduate School, College of Arts and Sciences, Department of Psychology, Seattle, WA 98195. Offers animal behavior (PhD); applied child and adolescent psychology: prevention and treatment (MA); behavioral neuroscience (PhD); clinical psychology (PhD); cognition and perception (PhD); developmental psychology (PhD); quantitative psychology (PhD); social psychology and personality (PhD). *Accreditation:* APA (one or more programs are accredited). *Degree requirements:* For doctorate, thesis/dissertation. *Entrance requirements:* For doctorate, GRE General Test, minimum GPA of 3.0. Electronic applications accepted. *Faculty research:* Addictive behaviors, artificial intelligence, child psychopathology, mechanisms and development of vision, physiology of ingestive behaviors.

University of Wisconsin–Madison, Graduate School, College of Letters and Science, Department of Psychology, Program in Developmental Psychology, Madison, WI 53706-1380. Offers PhD. *Degree requirements:* For doctorate, comprehensive exam, thesis/dissertation. *Entrance requirements:* For doctorate, GRE General Test, minimum undergraduate GPA of 3.0. Additional exam requirements/recommendations for international students: Required—TOEFL. Electronic applications accepted.

University of Wisconsin–Milwaukee, Graduate School, School of Education, Department of Educational Psychology, Milwaukee, WI 53201-0413. Offers children's mental health for school professionals (Graduate Certificate); counseling psychology (PhD); educational statistics and measurement (MS, PhD); learning and development (MS, PhD); multicultural knowledge of mental health practices (Graduate Certificate); school counseling (MS); school counseling (Graduate Certificate); school psychology (MS, PhD, Ed S). *Accreditation:* APA. *Program availability:* Part-time. *Students:* 170 full-time (132 women), 52 part-time (39 women); includes 51 minority (14 Black or African American, non-Hispanic/Latino; 1 American Indian or Alaska Native, non-Hispanic/Latino; 7 Asian, non-Hispanic/Latino; 7 Hispanic/Latino; 1 Native Hawaiian or other Pacific Islander, non-Hispanic/Latino; 21 Two or more races, non-Hispanic/Latino), 4 international. Average age 31. 304 applicants, 39% accepted, 83 enrolled. In 2017, 59 master's, 11 doctorates, 10 other advanced degrees awarded. *Degree requirements:* For master's, comprehensive exam, thesis; for doctorate, thesis/dissertation. *Entrance requirements:* For master's, minimum GPA of 3.0; for doctorate, GRE General Test, minimum GPA of 3.0. Additional exam requirements/recommendations for international students: Required—TOEFL (minimum score 550 paper-based; 79 iBT), IELTS (minimum score 6.5). *Application deadline:* For fall admission, 1/1 priority date for domestic students; for spring admission, 9/1 for domestic students. Application fee: $56 ($96 for international students). Electronic applications accepted. *Financial support:* Fellowships, research assistantships, teaching assistantships, career-related internships or fieldwork, health care benefits, unspecified assistantships, and project assistantships available. Support available to part-time students. Financial award application deadline: 4/15; financial award applicants required to submit FAFSA. *Application contact:* General Information Contact, 414-229-4721, E-mail: soeinfo@uwm.edu.
Website: http://uwm.edu/education/academics/educational-psychology-department/

Viterbo University, Master of Science in Mental Health Counseling Program, La Crosse, WI 54601-4797. Offers addiction counseling (MS); child and adolescent counseling (MS); complementary health and wellness counseling (MS). *Accreditation:* ACA. *Program availability:* Part-time, evening/weekend. *Degree requirements:* For master's, comprehensive exam, thesis, 54 credits of core program courses; 6 elective credits; minimum GPA of 3.0; action research project; practicum/internship experience. *Entrance requirements:* For master's, MAT, BS in a human service or social science discipline; prerequisite coursework in general psychology, behavior disorders/abnormal psychology, and research methods/statistics; minimum undergraduate cumulative GPA of 3.0; background check; personal statement; undergraduate transcripts; interview. Additional exam requirements/recommendations for international students: Required—TOEFL (minimum score 525 paper-based). Electronic applications accepted. Application fee is waived when completed online. *Expenses:* Contact institution. *Faculty research:* Supervision, recovery substance abuse, culture, counseling theory, health and wellness.

Washington University in St. Louis, The Graduate School, Department of Psychological and Brain Sciences, St. Louis, MO 63130-4899. Offers aging and development (PhD). Terminal master's awarded for partial completion of doctoral program. *Degree requirements:* For doctorate, thesis/dissertation. *Entrance requirements:* For doctorate, GRE General Test. Additional exam requirements/recommendations for international students: Required—TOEFL. Electronic applications accepted. *Faculty research:* Behavior/brain/cognition; clinical; aging/development; social/personality.

Wilfrid Laurier University, Faculty of Graduate and Postdoctoral Studies, Faculty of Science, Department of Psychology, Waterloo, ON N2L 3C5, Canada. Offers behavioral neuroscience (M Sc, PhD); cognitive neuroscience (M Sc, PhD); community psychology (MA, PhD); social and developmental psychology (MA, PhD). *Program availability:* Part-time. *Degree requirements:* For master's, thesis; for doctorate, thesis/dissertation. *Entrance requirements:* For master's, GRE General Test, honors BA or the equivalent in psychology, minimum B average in undergraduate course work; for doctorate, GRE General Test, master's degree, minimum A- average. Additional exam requirements/recommendations for international students: Required—TOEFL (minimum score 89 iBT). Electronic applications accepted. *Faculty research:* Brain and cognition, community psychology, social and developmental psychology.

Yale University, Graduate School of Arts and Sciences, Department of Psychology, New Haven, CT 06520. Offers behavioral neuroscience (PhD); clinical psychology (PhD); cognitive psychology (PhD); developmental psychology (PhD); social/personality psychology (PhD). *Accreditation:* APA. *Degree requirements:* For doctorate, thesis/dissertation. *Entrance requirements:* For doctorate, GRE General Test.

Experimental Psychology

Azusa Pacific University, School of Behavioral and Applied Sciences, Department of Psychology, Azusa, CA 91702-7000. Offers child life (MS); research psychology and data analytics (MS).

Bowling Green State University, Graduate College, College of Arts and Sciences, Department of Psychology, Bowling Green, OH 43403. Offers clinical psychology (MA, PhD); developmental psychology (MA, PhD); experimental psychology (MA, PhD); industrial/organizational psychology (MA, PhD); quantitative psychology (MA, PhD). *Accreditation:* APA (one or more programs are accredited). *Degree requirements:* For doctorate, thesis/dissertation. *Entrance requirements:* For doctorate, GRE General Test, GRE Subject Test. Additional exam requirements/recommendations for international students: Required—TOEFL. Electronic applications accepted. *Faculty research:* Personnel psychology, developmental-mathematical models, behavioral medication, brain process, child/adolescent social cognition.

Brooklyn College of the City University of New York, School of Natural and Behavioral Sciences, Department of Psychology, Brooklyn, NY 11210-2889. Offers experimental psychology (MA); industrial and organizational psychology (MA), including human relations, organizational behavior; mental health counseling (MA); psychology (PhD). *Program availability:* Part-time. *Degree requirements:* For master's, comprehensive exam, thesis (for some programs). *Entrance requirements:* For master's, minimum GPA of 3.0, 2 letters of recommendation, essay; for doctorate, GRE. Additional exam requirements/recommendations for international students: Required—TOEFL (minimum score 520 paper-based; 69 iBT). Electronic applications accepted.

California State University, Fresno, Division of Research and Graduate Studies, College of Science and Mathematics, Department of Psychology, Fresno, CA 93740-8027. Offers applied behavior analysis (MA); general/experimental psychology (MA); school psychology (Ed S). *Degree requirements:* For master's, thesis. *Entrance requirements:* For master's, GRE General Test, GRE Subject Test, minimum GPA of 3.0. Additional exam requirements/recommendations for international students: Required—TOEFL. Electronic applications accepted. *Faculty research:* Oncology prediction, parenting stress, wellness, aging and memory, retrieval inhibition, anger, minority mental health.

California State University, Northridge, Graduate Studies, College of Social and Behavioral Sciences, Department of Psychology, Northridge, CA 91330. Offers clinical psychology (MA); general experimental psychology (MA). *Students:* 46 full-time (36 women), 7 part-time (4 women); includes 25 minority (2 Black or African American, non-Hispanic/Latino; 4 Asian, non-Hispanic/Latino; 18 Hispanic/Latino; 1 Two or more races, non-Hispanic/Latino), 1 international. Average age 25. 263 applicants, 27% accepted, 23 enrolled. In 2017, 55 master's awarded. *Degree requirements:* For master's, thesis. *Entrance requirements:* For master's, GRE General Test, GRE Subject Test, minimum GPA of 3.0, letters of recommendation. Additional exam requirements/recommendations for international students: Required—TOEFL. *Application deadline:* For fall admission, 11/30 for domestic students. Application fee: $55. *Financial support:* Application deadline: 3/1. *Unit head:* Jill Razani, Chair, 818-677-3506.
Website: http://www.csun.edu/csbs/departments/psychology/index.html

Case Western Reserve University, School of Graduate Studies, Psychological Sciences Department, Program in Experimental Psychology, Cleveland, OH 44106. Offers PhD. *Faculty:* 10 full-time (5 women). *Students:* 7 full-time (4 women), 1 international. Average age 27. 165 applicants, 4% accepted, 3 enrolled. *Degree requirements:* For doctorate, thesis/dissertation, internship. *Entrance requirements:* For doctorate, GRE General Test, GRE Subject Test, personal statement, three letters of recommendation, curriculum vitae. Additional exam requirements/recommendations for international students: Required—TOEFL (minimum score 577 paper-based; 90 iBT); Recommended—IELTS (minimum score 7). *Application deadline:* For fall admission, 1/15 priority date for domestic students. Application fee: $50. Electronic applications

accepted. *Expenses: Tuition:* Full-time $43,854; part-time $1827 per credit hour. *Required fees:* $50; $50 per credit hour. Tuition and fees vary according to course load and program. *Financial support:* Research assistantships and teaching assistantships available. Financial award application deadline: 1/15; financial award applicants required to submit FAFSA. *Faculty research:* Development and evaluation of cognitive behavioral treatments for anxiety and mood disorders, evaluating treatments for post-traumatic stress disorder (PTSD), depression and bipolar disorder in youth, family relations and emotional expressions. *Unit head:* Dr. Heath Demaree, Professor and Chair, 216-368-6468, E-mail: psychsciences@case.edu. *Application contact:* Dr. Elizabeth J. Short, Director of Experimental Training, 216-368-2815, E-mail: psychsciences@case.edu.
Website: http://psychsciences.case.edu/graduate/

The Catholic University of America, School of Arts and Sciences, Department of Psychology, Washington, DC 20064. Offers applied experimental psychology (PhD); clinical psychology (PhD); general psychology (MA); human development psychology (PhD); human factors (MA); MA/JD. MA/JD offered jointly with Columbus School of Law. *Accreditation:* APA (one or more programs are accredited). *Program availability:* Part-time. *Faculty:* 11 full-time (6 women), 9 part-time/adjunct (3 women). *Students:* 38 full-time (27 women), 33 part-time (25 women); includes 22 minority (4 Black or African American, non-Hispanic/Latino; 4 Asian, non-Hispanic/Latino; 5 Hispanic/Latino; 9 Two or more races, non-Hispanic/Latino), 6 international. Average age 29. 183 applicants, 26% accepted, 21 enrolled. In 2017, 18 master's, 9 doctorates awarded. *Degree requirements:* For master's, comprehensive exam, thesis (for some programs); for doctorate, comprehensive exam, thesis/dissertation. *Entrance requirements:* For master's, GRE General Test, statement of purpose, official copies of academic transcripts, three letters of recommendation; for doctorate, GRE General Test, GRE Subject Test, statement of purpose, official copies of academic transcripts, three letters of recommendation. Additional exam requirements/recommendations for international students: Required—TOEFL (minimum score 550 paper-based; 80 iBT). *Application deadline:* For fall admission, 7/15 priority date for domestic students, 7/1 for international students; for spring admission, 11/15 priority date for domestic students, 11/1 for international students. Applications are processed on a rolling basis. Application fee: $55. Electronic applications accepted. *Expenses:* Contact institution. *Financial support:* Fellowships, research assistantships, teaching assistantships, Federal Work-Study, scholarships/grants, tuition waivers (full and partial), and unspecified assistantships available. Financial award application deadline: 2/1; financial award applicants required to submit FAFSA. *Faculty research:* Clinical psychology, applied cognitive science, psychopathology, cognitive neuroscience, psychotherapy. *Total annual research expenditures:* $243,144. *Unit head:* Dr. Marc M. Sebrechts, Chair, 202-319-5750, Fax: 202-319-6263, E-mail: sebrechts@cua.edu. *Application contact:* Dr. Steven Brown, Director of Graduate Admissions, 202-319-5057, Fax: 202-319-6533, E-mail: cua-admissions@cua.edu.
Website: http://psychology.cua.edu/

Central Michigan University, College of Graduate Studies, College of Humanities and Social and Behavioral Sciences, Department of Psychology, Program in Experimental Psychology, Mount Pleasant, MI 48859. Offers applied experimental psychology (PhD); experimental psychology (MS). *Program availability:* Part-time. *Degree requirements:* For master's, thesis or alternative; for doctorate, thesis/dissertation. Electronic applications accepted. *Faculty research:* Behavioral neuroscience, human development, perception and cognition, social/personal problem solving, psychophysiology.

Central Washington University, School of Graduate Studies and Research, College of the Sciences, Department of Psychology, Program in Experimental Psychology, Ellensburg, WA 98926. Offers MS. *Entrance requirements:* For master's, GRE General Test, minimum GPA of 3.0. Additional exam requirements/recommendations for international students: Required—TOEFL (minimum score 550 paper-based; 79 iBT). *Application deadline:* For fall admission, 2/1 priority date for domestic students. Applications are processed on a rolling basis. Application fee: $50. Electronic applications accepted. *Financial support:* Application deadline: 3/1. *Unit head:* Dr. Elizabeth Haviland, Program Director, 509-963-2371, E-mail: haviland@cwu.edu. *Application contact:* Justine Eason, Admissions Program Coordinator, 509-963-3103, Fax: 509-963-1799, E-mail: masters@cwu.edu.

Cornell University, Graduate School, Graduate Fields of Arts and Sciences, Field of Psychology, Ithaca, NY 14853. Offers biopsychology (PhD); human experimental psychology (PhD); personality and social psychology (PhD). *Degree requirements:* For doctorate, comprehensive exam, thesis/dissertation, 2 semesters of teaching experience. *Entrance requirements:* For doctorate, GRE General Test, 3 letters of recommendation. Additional exam requirements/recommendations for international students: Required—TOEFL (minimum score 550 paper-based; 77 iBT). Electronic applications accepted. *Faculty research:* Sensory and perceptual systems, social cognition, cognitive development, quantitative and computational modeling, behavioral neuroscience.

Duke University, Graduate School, Department of Psychology and Neuroscience, Durham, NC 27708. Offers biological psychology (PhD); clinical psychology (PhD); cognitive psychology (PhD); developmental psychology (PhD); experimental psychology (PhD); health psychology (PhD); human social development (PhD); JD/MA. *Accreditation:* APA (one or more programs are accredited). *Degree requirements:* For doctorate, thesis/dissertation. *Entrance requirements:* For doctorate, GRE General Test. Additional exam requirements/recommendations for international students: Required—TOEFL (minimum score 577 paper-based; 90 iBT) or IELTS (minimum score 7). Electronic applications accepted.

Eastern Washington University, Graduate Studies, College of Social Sciences, Department of Psychology, Program in Experimental Psychology, Cheney, WA 99004-2431. Offers MS. *Students:* 8 full-time (7 women), 1 part-time (0 women). Average age 29. 9 applicants, 22% accepted, 2 enrolled. In 2017, 2 master's awarded. *Degree requirements:* For master's, comprehensive exam (for some programs), thesis or research report; practicum. *Entrance requirements:* For master's, GRE, minimum GPA of 3.0 in last 90 quarter or 60 semester graded credits; official transcripts; curriculum vitae; three letters of recommendation. Additional exam requirements/recommendations for international students: Required—TOEFL (minimum score 580 paper-based; 92 iBT), IELTS (minimum score 7), PTE (minimum score 63). *Application deadline:* For fall admission, 3/1 for domestic students. Application fee: $75. Electronic applications accepted. *Expenses:* Tuition, state resident: full-time $11,191; part-time $373.06 per credit. Tuition, nonresident: full-time $25,995; part-time $866.52 per credit. *Financial support:* Application deadline: 2/15; applicants required to submit FAFSA. *Unit head:* Dennis Anderson, Director, 509-359-2087, E-mail: danderson2@ewu.edu. *Application contact:* Kathy White, Advisor/Recruiter for Graduate Studies, 509-359-2491, Fax: 509-359-6044, E-mail: gradprograms@ewu.edu.

East Tennessee State University, School of Graduate Studies, College of Arts and Sciences, Department of Psychology, Johnson City, TN 37614. Offers clinical psychology (PhD); experimental psychology (PhD). *Accreditation:* APA. Terminal master's awarded for partial completion of doctoral program. *Degree requirements:* For doctorate, thesis/dissertation, externship. *Entrance requirements:* For doctorate, GRE General Test, minimum GPA of 3.0, three letters of recommendation, interview, minimum of 18 semester hours in undergraduate psychology. Additional exam requirements/recommendations for international students: Required—TOEFL (minimum score 550 paper-based; 79 iBT). *Application deadline:* For fall admission, 12/1 for domestic and international students. Application fee: $55 ($65 for international students). Electronic applications accepted. *Financial support:* Research assistantships with full tuition reimbursements, teaching assistantships with full tuition reimbursements, career-related internships or fieldwork, institutionally sponsored loans, scholarships/grants, and unspecified assistantships available. Financial award application deadline: 7/1; financial award applicants required to submit FAFSA. *Faculty research:* Women's issues, prenatal stress, childhood obesity, suicide prevention, behavioral pediatrics, self-control, substance dependence, violence. *Unit head:* Dr. Wallace E. Dixon, Jr., Chair, 423-439-6656, Fax: 423-439-5695, E-mail: dixonw@etsu.edu. *Application contact:* Dr. Wallace E. Dixon, Jr., Chair, 423-439-6656, Fax: 423-439-5695, E-mail: dixonw@etsu.edu.
Website: http://www.etsu.edu/cas/psychology/

Fairleigh Dickinson University, Metropolitan Campus, University College: Arts, Sciences, and Professional Studies, School of Psychology, Program in General-Theoretical Psychology, Teaneck, NJ 07666-1914. Offers MA, Certificate.

The Graduate Center, City University of New York, Graduate Studies, Program in Psychology, New York, NY 10016-4039. Offers basic applied neurocognition (PhD); biopsychology (PhD); clinical psychology (PhD); developmental psychology (PhD); environmental psychology (PhD); experimental psychology (PhD); industrial psychology (PhD); learning processes (PhD); neuropsychology (PhD); psychology (PhD); social personality (PhD). *Faculty:* 119 full-time (40 women). *Students:* 428 full-time (308 women); includes 118 minority (31 Black or African American, non-Hispanic/Latino; 31 Asian, non-Hispanic/Latino; 47 Hispanic/Latino; 1 Native Hawaiian or other Pacific Islander, non-Hispanic/Latino; 8 Two or more races, non-Hispanic/Latino), 53 international. Average age 33. 795 applicants, 12% accepted, 56 enrolled. In 2017, 46 doctorates awarded. *Degree requirements:* For doctorate, one foreign language, thesis/dissertation. *Entrance requirements:* For doctorate, GRE General Test. Additional exam requirements/recommendations for international students: Required—TOEFL. *Application deadline:* For fall admission, 12/1 priority date for domestic students. Application fee: $125. Electronic applications accepted. *Financial support:* In 2017–18, 371 students received support, including 340 fellowships, 34 research assistantships, 33 teaching assistantships; career-related internships or fieldwork, Federal Work-Study, institutionally sponsored loans, and tuition waivers (full and partial) also available. Financial award application deadline: 2/1; financial award applicants required to submit FAFSA. *Unit head:* Richard Bodnar, Executive Officer, 212-817-8706, Fax: 212-817-1533, E-mail: rbodnar@gc.cuny.edu. *Application contact:* Les Gribben, Director of Admissions, 212-817-7470, Fax: 212-817-1624, E-mail: lgribben@gc.cuny.edu.

Harvard University, Graduate School of Arts and Sciences, Department of Psychology, Cambridge, MA 02138. Offers psychology (PhD), including behavior and decision analysis, cognition, developmental psychology, experimental psychology, personality, psychobiology, psychopathology; social psychology (PhD). *Accreditation:* APA. *Degree requirements:* For doctorate, thesis/dissertation, general exams. *Entrance requirements:* For doctorate, GRE General Test. Additional exam requirements/recommendations for international students: Required—TOEFL.

Howard University, Graduate School, Department of Psychology, Washington, DC 20059-0002. Offers clinical psychology (PhD); developmental psychology (PhD); experimental psychology (PhD); neuropsychology (PhD); personality psychology (PhD); psychology (MS); social psychology (PhD). *Accreditation:* APA (one or more programs are accredited). *Program availability:* Part-time. *Degree requirements:* For master's, thesis; for doctorate, comprehensive exam, thesis/dissertation, qualifying exam. *Entrance requirements:* For master's, GRE General Test, minimum GPA of 2.5, bachelor's degree in psychology or related field; for doctorate, GRE General Test, minimum GPA of 3.0. *Faculty research:* Personality and psychophysiology, educational and social development of African-American children, child and adult psychopathology.

Idaho State University, Office of Graduate Studies, College of Arts and Letters, Department of Psychology, Program in Experimental Psychology, Pocatello, ID 83209. Offers PhD. *Entrance requirements:* For doctorate, GRE, BA/BS in psychology or the equivalent, minimum undergraduate GPA of 3.0 for the last two years.

Iona College, School of Arts and Science, Department of Psychology, New Rochelle, NY 10801-1890. Offers general-experimental psychology (MA); human resources (Certificate); industrial-organizational psychology (MA); mental health counseling (MA); organizational behavior (Certificate); psychology (MA); school psychology (MA). *Program availability:* Part-time. *Faculty:* 9 full-time (5 women), 7 part-time/adjunct (5 women). *Students:* 75 full-time (55 women), 37 part-time (24 women); includes 46 minority (9 Black or African American, non-Hispanic/Latino; 2 Asian, non-Hispanic/Latino; 34 Hispanic/Latino; 1 Two or more races, non-Hispanic/Latino), 1 international. Average age 25. 88 applicants, 88% accepted, 40 enrolled. In 2017, 23 master's awarded. *Degree requirements:* For master's, thesis (for some programs), literature review (for some programs). *Entrance requirements:* For master's, BA in psychology including 3 credits each in psychology statistics and experimental research methods, or 9 credits in psychology including 3 credits each in psychology statistics, psychology research methods and upper-level coursework. Additional exam requirements/recommendations for international students: Required—TOEFL (minimum score 550 paper-based), IELTS (minimum score 6.5). *Application deadline:* For fall admission, 8/15 for domestic students, 5/1 for international students; for spring admission, 1/15 for domestic students, 9/1 for international students. Applications are processed on a rolling basis. Electronic applications accepted. Tuition and fees vary according to program. *Financial support:* In 2017–18, 27 students received support. Research assistantships with partial tuition reimbursements available, tuition waivers (partial), and unspecified assistantships available. Support available to part-time students. Financial award application deadline: 4/15; financial award applicants required to submit FAFSA. *Faculty research:* Non-suicidal self-injury, trauma response, performance appraisal and evaluation, diversity infusion, assessment and treatment of sexual offenders. *Unit head:* Patricia Oswald, PhD, Chair, 914-633-2374, E-mail: poswald@iona.edu. *Application contact:* Katelyn Brunck, Assistant Director, Graduate Admissions, 914-633-2451, Fax: 914-633-2277, E-mail: kbrunck@iona.edu.
Website: http://www.iona.edu/Academics/School-of-Arts-Science/Departments/Psychology/Graduate-Programs.aspx

James Madison University, The Graduate School, College of Health and Behavioral Studies, Program in Psychological Sciences, Harrisonburg, VA 22801. Offers applied research (MA); behavior analysis (MA); experimental psychology (MA); quantitative psychology (MA). *Program availability:* Part-time, evening/weekend. *Students:* 18 full-time (10 women), 2 part-time (1 woman); includes 3 minority (1 American Indian or Alaska Native, non-Hispanic/Latino; 1 Asian, non-Hispanic/Latino; 1 Two or more races, non-Hispanic/Latino), 1 international. Average age 30. In 2017, 9 master's awarded. Application fee: $55. Electronic applications accepted. *Expenses:* Tuition, state resident: full-time $10,512; part-time $438 per credit hour. Tuition, nonresident: full-time $28,358; part-time $1162 per credit hour. *Required fees:* $1128. *Financial support:* In 2017–18, 18 students received support, including 1 teaching assistantship with full tuition reimbursement available (averaging $9,284 per year); career-related internships or fieldwork, Federal Work-Study, and 16 assistantships (averaging $7911) also

available. Financial award application deadline: 3/1; financial award applicants required to submit FAFSA. *Unit head:* Dr. Jeff S. Dyche, Graduate Program Director, 540-568-4965, E-mail: dychejs@jmu.edu. *Application contact:* Lynette D. Michael, Director of Graduate Admissions, 540-568-6131 Ext. 6395, Fax: 540-568-7860, E-mail: michaeld@jmu.edu.
Website: http://www.psyc.jmu.edu/psycsciences/

Kent State University, College of Arts and Sciences, Department of Psychological Sciences, Kent, OH 44242-0001. Offers clinical psychology (MA, PhD), including gerontology (MA), psychological sciences (MA); experimental psychology (MA, PhD), including gerontology (MA), psychological sciences (MA). *Accreditation:* APA (one or more programs are accredited). *Program availability:* Part-time. *Faculty:* 29 full-time (15 women), 5 part-time/adjunct (2 women). *Students:* 84 full-time (66 women); includes 15 minority (8 Black or African American, non-Hispanic/Latino; 4 Asian, non-Hispanic/Latino; 2 Hispanic/Latino; 1 Two or more races, non-Hispanic/Latino), 3 international. Average age 26. 217 applicants, 10% accepted, 14 enrolled. In 2017, 10 master's, 16 doctorates awarded. Terminal master's awarded for partial completion of doctoral program. *Degree requirements:* For master's, thesis; for doctorate, comprehensive exam, thesis/dissertation. *Entrance requirements:* For master's and doctorate, GRE General Test, statement of goals and motivations, transcripts, 3 letters of recommendation, minimum junior-senior GPA of 3.0, at least one course in statistics and a broad background in psychology. Additional exam requirements/recommendations for international students: Required—TOEFL (minimum score 550 paper-based, 79 iBT), Michigan English Language Assessment Battery (minimum score 77), IELTS (minimum score 6.5) or PTE (minimum score 58). *Application deadline:* For fall admission, 12/1 for domestic and international students. Applications are processed on a rolling basis. Application fee: $45 ($70 for international students). Electronic applications accepted. *Expenses:* Tuition, state resident: full-time $11,310; part-time $515 per credit hour. Tuition, nonresident: full-time $20,396; part-time $928 per credit hour. *International tuition:* $18,544 full-time. *Financial support:* Federal Work-Study, health care benefits, and unspecified assistantships available. Financial award application deadline: 12/1. *Unit head:* Dr. Maria S. Zaragoza, Professor and Chair, 330-672-2166, E-mail: mzaragoz@kent.edu. *Application contact:* Dr. John A. Updegraff, Professor and Graduate Coordinator, 330-672-2166, E-mail: jupdegr1@kent.edu.
Website: https://www.kent.edu/psychology

Lakehead University, Graduate Studies, Department of Psychology, Thunder Bay, ON P7B 5E1, Canada. Offers clinical psychology (PhD); experimental psychology (MA). *Program availability:* Part-time, evening/weekend. *Degree requirements:* For master's, thesis optional; for doctorate, thesis/dissertation, 2 comprehensive exams, internship. *Entrance requirements:* For master's, GRE, honors degree in psychology, advanced course work in statistics, minimum B average; for doctorate, GRE, minimum B average. Additional exam requirements/recommendations for international students: Required—TOEFL. *Faculty research:* Chaos theory, health psychology, counseling psychology, gerontology, women's studies.

Laurentian University, School of Graduate Studies and Research, Programme in Psychology, Sudbury, ON P3E 2C6, Canada. Offers applied psychology (MA); experimental psychology (MA).

McGill University, Faculty of Graduate and Postdoctoral Studies, Faculty of Science, Department of Psychology, Montréal, QC H3A 2T5, Canada. Offers clinical psychology (PhD); experimental psychology (M Sc, MA, PhD).

McNeese State University, Doré School of Graduate Studies, Burton College of Education, Department of Psychology, Lake Charles, LA 70609. Offers applied behavior analysis (MA, Graduate Certificate); counseling psychology (MA); general/experimental psychology (MA). *Program availability:* Evening/weekend. *Entrance requirements:* For master's, GRE. *Application deadline:* For fall admission, 5/15 priority date for domestic and international students; for spring admission, 10/15 priority date for domestic and international students. Applications are processed on a rolling basis. Application fee: $20 ($30 for international students). *Financial support:* Application deadline: 5/1. *Unit head:* Dr. Dena L. Matzenbacher, Head, 337-475-5434, Fax: 337-562-4115, E-mail: dena@mcneese.edu. *Application contact:* Dr. Dustin M. Hebert, Director of Dore' School of Graduate Studies, 337-475-5396, Fax: 337-475-5397, E-mail: admissions@mcneese.edu.

Memorial University of Newfoundland, School of Graduate Studies, Department of Psychology, St. John's, NL A1C 5S7, Canada. Offers applied psychological sciences (MAPS); clinical psychology (Psy D); experimental psychology (M Sc, PhD). *Program availability:* Part-time. *Degree requirements:* For master's, workterms (MASP), thesis (M Sc); for doctorate, comprehensive exam, thesis/dissertation, oral thesis defense. *Entrance requirements:* For master's, GRE, honors bachelor's degree of high second class standing or equivalent; for doctorate, GRE, master's or honors degree. Electronic applications accepted. *Faculty research:* Behavioral neuroscience, cognition, theory and research on abnormal behavior.

Middle Tennessee State University, College of Graduate Studies, College of Behavioral and Health Sciences, Department of Psychology, Murfreesboro, TN 37132. Offers clinical psychology (MA); experimental psychology (MA); industrial/organizational psychology (MA); psychology (MA, Ed S); quantitative psychology (MA); school psychology (MA). *Program availability:* Part-time, evening/weekend, online learning. *Degree requirements:* For master's, comprehensive exam, thesis. *Entrance requirements:* For master's, GRE. Additional exam requirements/recommendations for international students: Required—TOEFL (minimum score 525 paper-based; 71 iBT) or IELTS (minimum score 6). Electronic applications accepted. *Faculty research:* Health psychology, industrial/organizational psychology, experimental psychology.

Missouri State University, Graduate College, College of Health and Human Services, Department of Psychology, Springfield, MO 65897. Offers applied behavior analysis (MS); clinical psychology (MS); experimental psychology (MS); forensic child psychology (Certificate); industrial/organizational psychology (MS). *Faculty:* 25 full-time (11 women), 4 part-time/adjunct (0 women). *Students:* 54 full-time (41 women), 12 part-time (9 women); includes 9 minority (2 Black or African American, non-Hispanic/Latino; 2 Hispanic/Latino; 5 Two or more races, non-Hispanic/Latino), 5 international. Average age 23. 127 applicants, 17% accepted, 21 enrolled. In 2017, 41 master's awarded. *Degree requirements:* For master's, comprehensive exam, thesis. *Entrance requirements:* For master's, GRE General Test, GRE Subject Test, minimum GPA of 3.25 in major, 3.0 overall; 20 hours of course work in psychology. Additional exam requirements/recommendations for international students: Required—TOEFL (minimum score 550 paper-based; 79 iBT), IELTS (minimum score 6). *Application deadline:* For fall admission, 2/15 priority date for domestic and international students. Application fee: $35 ($50 for international students). Electronic applications accepted. *Expenses:* Tuition, state resident: full-time $2915; part-time $2021 per credit hour. Tuition, nonresident: full-time $5354; part-time $3647 per credit hour. *International tuition:* $11,992 full-time. *Required fees:* $173; $173 per credit hour. Tuition and fees vary according to class time, course level, course load, degree level, campus/location and program. *Financial support:* In 2017–18, 9 research assistantships with full tuition reimbursements (averaging $8,772 per year), 8 teaching assistantships with full tuition reimbursements (averaging $8,772 per year) were awarded; career-related internships or fieldwork, Federal Work-Study, institutionally sponsored loans, scholarships/grants, and unspecified assistantships also available. Financial award application deadline: 3/31; financial award applicants required to submit FAFSA. *Faculty research:* Work-family conflict, child forensic psychology, sports psychology, body image assessment, visual learning. *Unit head:* Dr. Paul Deal, Department Head, 417-836-5797, Fax: 417-836-8330, E-mail: psychology@missouristate.edu. *Application contact:* Stephanie Praschan, Director, Graduate Enrollment Management, 417-836-5330, Fax: 417-836-6200, E-mail: stephaniepraschan@missouristate.edu.
Website: http://psychology.missouristate.edu/

Morehead State University, Graduate Programs, College of Science and Technology, Department of Psychology, Morehead, KY 40351. Offers clinical/counseling psychology (MS); general/experimental psychology (MS). *Program availability:* Part-time, evening/weekend. *Degree requirements:* For master's, comprehensive exam, thesis optional. *Entrance requirements:* For master's, GRE General Test, 18 undergraduate hours in psychology, minimum GPA of 3.0, 3 letters of recommendation. Additional exam requirements/recommendations for international students: Required—TOEFL (minimum score 500 paper-based). Electronic applications accepted. *Faculty research:* Mood induction effects, serotonin receptor activity, stress, perceptual processes.

Murray State University, College of Humanities and Fine Arts, Department of Psychology, Murray, KY 42071. Offers clinical psychology (MA, MS); general experimental psychology (MA, MS); research design and analysis (Certificate). *Program availability:* Part-time. *Faculty:* 9 full-time (5 women). *Students:* 21 full-time (16 women), 1 part-time (0 women); includes 2 minority (1 Hispanic/Latino; 1 Two or more races, non-Hispanic/Latino), 1 international. Average age 25. 44 applicants, 68% accepted, 11 enrolled. In 2017, 9 master's awarded. *Entrance requirements:* For master's and Certificate, GRE or GMAT, minimum university GPA of 2.75. Additional exam requirements/recommendations for international students: Required—TOEFL (minimum score 527 paper-based; 71 iBT). *Application deadline:* Applications are processed on a rolling basis. Application fee: $40 ($50 for international students). Electronic applications accepted. *Expenses:* Tuition, state resident: full-time $9504. Tuition, nonresident: full-time $26,811. *International tuition:* $14,400 full-time. Tuition and fees vary according to course load, degree level and reciprocity agreements. *Financial support:* In 2017–18, 5 research assistantships were awarded; Federal Work-Study and unspecified assistantships also available. Financial award applicants required to submit FAFSA. *Unit head:* Dr. Paula Waddill, Chair, Department of Psychology, 270-809-2851, Fax: 270-809-2991, E-mail: pwaddill@murraystate.edu. *Application contact:* Kaitlyn Burzynski, Interim Assistant Director for Graduate Admission and Records, 270-809-5732, Fax: 270-809-3780, E-mail: msu.graduateadmissions@murraystate.edu.
Website: https://www.murraystate.edu/academics/CollegesDepartments/CollegeOfHumanitiesAndFineArts/Psychology/

North Carolina State University, Graduate School, College of Humanities and Social Sciences, Department of Psychology, Raleigh, NC 27695. Offers developmental psychology (PhD); ergonomics and experimental psychology (PhD); industrial/organizational psychology (PhD); psychology in the public interest (PhD); school psychology (PhD). *Accreditation:* APA. *Degree requirements:* For doctorate, comprehensive exam, thesis/dissertation. *Entrance requirements:* For doctorate, GRE General Test, GRE Subject Test (industrial/organizational psychology), MAT (recommended), minimum GPA of 3.0 in major. Electronic applications accepted. *Faculty research:* Cognitive and social development (human factors, families, the workplace, community issues and health, aging).

Nova Southeastern University, College of Psychology, Fort Lauderdale, FL 33314-7796. Offers clinical mental health counseling (MS); clinical psychology (PhD, Psy D); counseling (MS); experimental psychology (MS); forensic psychology (MS); general psychology (MS); school counseling (MS); school psychology (Psy D, Psy S); substance abuse counseling (MS); substance abuse counseling and education (MS). *Accreditation:* APA (one or more programs are accredited). *Program availability:* 100% online, blended/hybrid learning. *Faculty:* 51 full-time (21 women), 120 part-time/adjunct (70 women). *Students:* 751 full-time (618 women), 821 part-time (709 women); includes 787 minority (268 Black or African American, non-Hispanic/Latino; 2 American Indian or Alaska Native, non-Hispanic/Latino; 38 Asian, non-Hispanic/Latino; 431 Hispanic/Latino; 2 Native Hawaiian or other Pacific Islander, non-Hispanic/Latino; 46 Two or more races, non-Hispanic/Latino), 45 international. Average age 31. 1,117 applicants, 38% accepted, 294 enrolled. In 2017, 459 master's, 100 doctorates, 10 other advanced degrees awarded. Terminal master's awarded for partial completion of doctoral program. *Degree requirements:* For master's, comprehensive exam, 3 practica; for doctorate, thesis/dissertation, clinical internship, competency exam; for Psy S, comprehensive exam, internship. *Entrance requirements:* For master's and Psy S, GRE General Test, letters of recommendation, research/personal statement, interview; for doctorate, GRE General Test, GRE Subject Test (recommended), minimum undergraduate GPA of 3.0, letters of recommendation, research/personal statement, interview, curriculum vitae/resume. Additional exam requirements/recommendations for international students: Required—TOEFL (minimum score 550 paper-based). *Application deadline:* Applications are processed on a rolling basis. Application fee: $50. Electronic applications accepted. *Expenses:* Contact institution. *Financial support:* In 2017–18, 197 students received support, including 15 research assistantships (averaging $5,600 per year), 68 teaching assistantships (averaging $2,000 per year); career-related internships or fieldwork, Federal Work-Study, institutionally sponsored loans, scholarships/grants, and unspecified assistantships also available. Support available to part-time students. Financial award application deadline: 4/15; financial award applicants required to submit FAFSA. *Faculty research:* Clinical health psychology, multicultural/diversity psychology, clinical neuropsychology, clinical child psychology, family violence. *Unit head:* Dr. Karen Grosby, Dean, 954-262-5712, Fax: 954-262-3859, E-mail: grosby@nova.edu. *Application contact:* Carlos Perez, Senior Manager of Outreach, 954-262-5702, Fax: 954-262-3893, E-mail: gradschool@nova.edu.
Website: http://psychology.nova.edu/

Ohio University, Graduate College, College of Arts and Sciences, Department of Psychology, Program in Experimental Psychology, Athens, OH 45701-2979. Offers PhD. *Degree requirements:* For doctorate, one foreign language, comprehensive exam, thesis/dissertation. *Entrance requirements:* For doctorate, GRE General Test, GRE Subject Test, minimum graduate GPA of 3.4. Additional exam requirements/recommendations for international students: Required—TOEFL. *Faculty research:* Cognitive psychology, quantitative psychology, social psychology, judgment and decision-making, health psychology.

Radford University, College of Graduate Studies and Research, Program in Psychology, Radford, VA 24142. Offers clinical-counseling psychology (MA, MS); experimental psychology (MA); industrial-organizational psychology (MA, MS). *Program availability:* Part-time. *Faculty:* 21 full-time (14 women). *Students:* 39 full-time (30 women); includes 5 minority (2 Black or African American, non-Hispanic/Latino; 1 Asian, non-Hispanic/Latino; 2 Hispanic/Latino). Average age 23. 87 applicants, 51% accepted, 22 enrolled. In 2017, 28 master's awarded. *Degree requirements:* For master's, comprehensive exam, thesis (for some programs). *Entrance requirements:* For master's, GRE, minimum GPA of 3.0, 3 letters of reference, essay, resume, official transcripts.

Additional exam requirements/recommendations for international students: Required—TOEFL (minimum score 550 paper-based; 79 iBT), IELTS (minimum score 6.5). *Application deadline:* For fall admission, 2/15 priority date for domestic students, 12/1 for international students; for spring admission, 7/1 for international students. Applications are processed on a rolling basis. Application fee: $50. Electronic applications accepted. *Expenses:* Tuition, state resident: full-time $8336; part-time $347 per credit hour. Tuition, nonresident: full-time $16,862; part-time $702 per credit hour. *Required fees:* $3220; $135 per credit hour. Tuition and fees vary according to course load and program. *Financial support:* In 2017–18, 19 students received support, including 2 research assistantships (averaging $7,500 per year), 14 teaching assistantships (averaging $10,500 per year); career-related internships or fieldwork, scholarships/grants, and unspecified assistantships also available. Support available to part-time students. Financial award application deadline: 3/1; financial award applicants required to submit FAFSA. *Faculty research:* Social cognition and interpersonal relationships, relationship between one's self-concept and social interactions, creativity and innovation, organizational politics and ethical decision-making, victimization in childhood. *Unit head:* Dr. Jeffery Aspelmeier, Chair, 540-831-5361, Fax: 540-831-6113, E-mail: jaspelme@radford.edu.
Website: http://www.radford.edu/content/chbs/home/psychology.html

Rivier University, School of Graduate Studies, Department of Psychology, Nashua, NH 03060. Offers clinical psychology (MS); experimental psychology (MS).

Rochester Institute of Technology, Graduate Enrollment Services, College of Liberal Arts, Psychology Department, MS Program in Experimental Psychology, Rochester, NY 14623. Offers MS. *Program availability:* Part-time. *Students:* 7 full-time (5 women), 4 part-time (2 women); includes 2 minority (1 Black or African American, non-Hispanic/Latino; 1 Two or more races, non-Hispanic/Latino). Average age 24. 16 applicants, 31% accepted, 4 enrolled. In 2017, 3 master's awarded. *Degree requirements:* For master's, thesis. *Entrance requirements:* For master's, GRE, minimum GPA of 3.0 (recommended). Additional exam requirements/recommendations for international students: Required—TOEFL (minimum score 550 paper-based; 79 iBT), IELTS (minimum score 6.5), PTE (minimum score 58). *Application deadline:* For fall admission, 2/15 priority date for domestic and international students; for spring admission, 12/15 priority date for domestic and international students. Applications are processed on a rolling basis. Application fee: $65. Electronic applications accepted. *Expenses:* $1,815 per credit hour. *Financial support:* In 2017–18, 7 students received support. Research assistantships with partial tuition reimbursements available, teaching assistantships with partial tuition reimbursements available, career-related internships or fieldwork, scholarships/grants, and unspecified assistantships available. Support available to part-time students. Financial award applicants required to submit FAFSA. *Faculty research:* Human factors in complex systems, human performance measurement and modeling, mental workload, decision-making, human error and reliability, perception, cognitive neuroscience, brain and behavior relationships, human development. *Unit head:* Tina M. Sutton, PhD, Graduate Program Director, 585-475-6773, E-mail: tmsgsh@rit.edu. *Application contact:* Diane Ellison, Senior Associate Vice President, Graduate Enrollment Services, 585-475-2229, Fax: 585-475-7164, E-mail: gradinfo@rit.edu.
Website: http://www.rit.edu/cla/psychology/graduate/ms-experimental-psych/overview

Saint Louis University, Graduate Programs, College of Arts and Sciences and Graduate Programs, Department of Psychology, St. Louis, MO 63103. Offers clinical psychology (MS-R, PhD); experimental psychology (MS-R, PhD); industrial-organizational psychology (PhD); psychology (PhD). *Accreditation:* APA (one or more programs are accredited). *Program availability:* Part-time. *Degree requirements:* For master's, comprehensive exam, thesis; for doctorate, thesis/dissertation, clinical internship (for clinical psychology PhD). *Entrance requirements:* For master's, GRE General Test, interview, letters of recommendation, resume; for doctorate, GRE General Test, interview, letters of recommendation, resumé, transcripts, goal statement. Additional exam requirements/recommendations for international students: Required—TOEFL (minimum score 550 paper-based). Electronic applications accepted. *Faculty research:* Violence and trauma; neural basis of learning and memory function; eating disorders; body image and health behavior; prejudice, stereotyping, and victimization; memory, cognitive aging and language processing.

San Jose State University, Graduate Studies and Research, College of Social Sciences, San Jose, CA 95192-0107. Offers applied anthropology (MA); communication studies (MA); economics (MA), including applied economics, economics; environmental studies (MS); geography (MA); history (MA), including history, history education; Mexican American studies (MA); psychology (MA, MS), including clinical psychology (MS), industrial/organizational psychology (MS), research and experimental psychology (MA); public administration (MPA); social sciences (MS); sociology (MA). *Faculty:* 59 full-time (29 women), 18 part-time/adjunct (5 women). *Students:* 181 full-time (126 women), 221 part-time (127 women); includes 228 minority (15 Black or African American, non-Hispanic/Latino; 48 Asian, non-Hispanic/Latino; 112 Hispanic/Latino; 3 Native Hawaiian or other Pacific Islander, non-Hispanic/Latino; 50 Two or more races, non-Hispanic/Latino), 38 international. Average age 30. 532 applicants, 44% accepted, 156 enrolled. In 2017, 139 master's awarded. *Degree requirements:* For master's, one foreign language, comprehensive exam, thesis (for some programs), project, field work, professional work experience. *Entrance requirements:* Additional exam requirements/recommendations for international students: Required—TOEFL (minimum score 550 paper-based; 80 iBT), IELTS (minimum score 6.5), PTE (minimum score 53). *Application deadline:* For fall admission, 2/1 for domestic and international students. Applications are processed on a rolling basis. Application fee: $55. Electronic applications accepted. *Expenses:* Tuition, state resident: full-time $7176. Tuition, nonresident: full-time $16,680. Tuition and fees vary according to course load and program. *Financial support:* Fellowships, research assistantships, career-related internships or fieldwork, Federal Work-Study, scholarships/grants, tuition waivers (full and partial), and unspecified assistantships available. Support available to part-time students. Financial award application deadline: 4/28; financial award applicants required to submit FAFSA. *Unit head:* Dr. Walt Jacobs, Dean, 408-924-5300, Fax: 408-924-5303, E-mail: walter.jacobs@sjsu.edu.
Website: http://www.sjsu.edu/socialsciences/

Seton Hall University, College of Arts and Sciences, Department of Psychology, South Orange, NJ 07079-2697. Offers experimental psychology (MS). *Program availability:* Part-time, evening/weekend. *Degree requirements:* For master's, thesis optional. *Entrance requirements:* For master's, GRE, minimum of 18 credits in psychology with minimum GPA of 3.0. Additional exam requirements/recommendations for international students: Required—TOEFL. Electronic applications accepted. *Faculty research:* Behavioral neuroscience, cognitive psychology, social psychology, perception/motor skills, memory, depression, anxiety.

Southern Illinois University Carbondale, Graduate School, College of Liberal Arts, Department of Psychology, Carbondale, IL 62901-4701. Offers clinical psychology (PhD); counseling psychology (PhD); experimental psychology (MA, MS). *Accreditation:* APA (one or more programs are accredited). *Degree requirements:* For master's, thesis; for doctorate, thesis/dissertation. *Entrance requirements:* For master's, GRE General Test, GRE Subject Test, minimum GPA of 2.7; for doctorate, GRE General Test, GRE Subject Test, minimum GPA of 3.25. Additional exam requirements/recommendations for international students: Required—TOEFL. *Faculty research:* Developmental neuropsychology; smoking, affect, and cognition; personality measurement; vocational psychology; program evaluation.

Southern Methodist University, Bobby B. Lyle School of Engineering, Department of Environmental and Civil Engineering, Dallas, TX 75275-0340. Offers air pollution control and atmospheric sciences (PhD); civil engineering (MS); environmental engineering (MS); environmental science (MS); structural engineering (PhD); sustainability and development (MA); water and wastewater engineering (PhD). *Program availability:* Part-time, evening/weekend, online learning. Terminal master's awarded for partial completion of doctoral program. *Degree requirements:* For master's, thesis optional; for doctorate, thesis/dissertation, oral and written qualifying exams. *Entrance requirements:* For master's, GRE General Test, minimum GPA of 3.0 in last 2 years; bachelor's degree in engineering, mathematics, or sciences; for doctorate, GRE, BS and MS in related field, minimum GPA of 3.3. Additional exam requirements/recommendations for international students: Required—TOEFL. Electronic applications accepted. *Faculty research:* Human and environmental health effects of endocrine disrupters, development of air pollution control systems for diesel engines, structural analysis and design, modeling and design of waste treatment systems.

Texas A&M University–Central Texas, Graduate Studies and Research, Killeen, TX 76549. Offers accounting (MS); business administration (MBA); clinical mental health counseling (MS); criminal justice (MCJ); curriculum and instruction (M Ed); educational administration (M Ed); educational psychology - experimental psychology (MS); history (MA); human resource management (MS); information systems (MS); liberal studies (MS); management and leadership (MS); marriage and family therapy (MS); mathematics (MS); political science (MA); school counseling (M Ed); school psychology (Ed S).

Texas Christian University, College of Science and Engineering, Department of Psychology, Fort Worth, TX 76129. Offers developmental trauma (MS); experimental psychology (PhD), including cognition/developmental, learning, neuroscience, social. *Faculty:* 13 full-time (6 women), 2 part-time/adjunct (both women). *Students:* 32 full-time (25 women); includes 5 minority (1 Asian, non-Hispanic/Latino; 2 Hispanic/Latino; 2 Two or more races, non-Hispanic/Latino), 2 international. Average age 26. 50 applicants, 34% accepted, 16 enrolled. In 2017, 8 master's, 2 doctorates awarded. Terminal master's awarded for partial completion of doctoral program. *Degree requirements:* For master's, thesis; for doctorate, thesis/dissertation. *Entrance requirements:* For doctorate, GRE General Test. Additional exam requirements/recommendations for international students: Required—TOEFL. *Application deadline:* For fall admission, 2/1 for domestic and international students. Application fee: $60 ($0 for international students). Electronic applications accepted. *Expenses:* Contact institution. *Financial support:* In 2017–18, 23 students received support, including 23 teaching assistantships with full tuition reimbursements available (averaging $19,750 per year); scholarships/grants also available. Financial award application deadline: 2/1; financial award applicants required to submit FAFSA. *Faculty research:* Neuroscience, human and animal learning, cognition, development, experimental social psychology. *Unit head:* Dr. Mauricio R. Papini, Chair, 817-257-7410, Fax: 817-257-7681, E-mail: m.papini@tcu.edu. *Application contact:* Cindy Hayes, Administrative Assistant, 817-257-7410, Fax: 817-257-7681, E-mail: c.hayes@tcu.edu.
Website: https://psychology.tcu.edu/current-graduate-students/

Texas Tech University, Graduate School, College of Arts and Sciences, Department of Psychological Sciences, Lubbock, TX 79409-2051. Offers clinical psychology (PhD); counseling psychology (MA, PhD); general experimental psychology (MA, PhD); psychology (MA). *Accreditation:* APA (one or more programs are accredited). *Faculty:* 31 full-time (14 women), 2 part-time/adjunct (both women). *Students:* 126 full-time (75 women), 10 part-time (5 women); includes 33 minority (4 Black or African American, non-Hispanic/Latino; 1 American Indian or Alaska Native, non-Hispanic/Latino; 10 Asian, non-Hispanic/Latino; 17 Hispanic/Latino; 1 Two or more races, non-Hispanic/Latino), 11 international. Average age 27. 278 applicants, 15% accepted, 28 enrolled. In 2017, 17 master's, 7 doctorates awarded. *Degree requirements:* For doctorate, comprehensive exam, thesis/dissertation, 100 credit hours of organized courses, research credits, and practica. *Entrance requirements:* For master's, GRE General Test, GRE Subject Test, essays, letters of recommendation; for doctorate, GRE General Test, essays, letters of recommendation. Additional exam requirements/recommendations for international students: Required—TOEFL (minimum score 550 paper-based; 79 iBT). *Application deadline:* For fall admission, 6/1 priority date for domestic students, 1/15 priority date for international students; for spring admission, 9/1 priority date for domestic students, 6/15 priority date for international students. Applications are processed on a rolling basis. Application fee: $60. Electronic applications accepted. *Expenses:* Contact institution. *Financial support:* In 2017–18, 132 students received support, including 127 fellowships (averaging $2,830 per year), 58 research assistantships (averaging $8,094 per year), 105 teaching assistantships (averaging $11,486 per year); Federal Work-Study, institutionally sponsored loans, health care benefits, and unspecified assistantships also available. Financial award application deadline: 4/15; financial award applicants required to submit FAFSA. *Faculty research:* Health psychology, addictive behaviors, depression and suicide risk, sexuality/sexual risk behaviors/HIV, neuroscience/neuroimaging, forensic and correctional psychology. *Total annual research expenditures:* $647,634. *Unit head:* Dr. Robert Morgan, Professor and Chair, 806-834-7117, Fax: 806-742-0818, E-mail: robert.morgan@ttu.edu. *Application contact:* Kay Hill, Admissions Coordinator, 806-834-1350, Fax: 806-742-0818, E-mail: kay.hill@ttu.edu.
Website: http://www.depts.ttu.edu/psy/

Towson University, College of Liberal Arts, Program in Psychology, Towson, MD 21252-0001. Offers clinical psychology (MA); counseling psychology (MA); experimental psychology (MA); school psychology (MA). *Program availability:* Part-time, evening/weekend. *Students:* 98 full-time (75 women), 21 part-time (13 women); includes 32 minority (15 Black or African American, non-Hispanic/Latino; 4 Asian, non-Hispanic/Latino; 8 Hispanic/Latino; 5 Two or more races, non-Hispanic/Latino). *Degree requirements:* For master's, thesis (for some programs). *Entrance requirements:* For master's, GRE, minimum GPA of 3.0, letters of recommendation. *Application deadline:* For fall admission, 1/17 for domestic students, 5/15 for international students; for spring admission, 10/15 for domestic students, 12/1 for international students. Applications are processed on a rolling basis. Application fee: $45. Electronic applications accepted. *Expenses:* Tuition, state resident: full-time $7960; part-time $398 per unit. Tuition, nonresident: full-time $16,480; part-time $824 per unit. *Required fees:* $2600; $130 per year. $390 per term. *Financial support:* Application deadline: 4/1. *Unit head:* Dr. Geoffrey Munro, Department Chair, 410-704-2634, E-mail: psycdept@towson.edu. *Application contact:* Coverley Beidleman, Assistant Director of Graduate Admissions, 410-704-5630, Fax: 410-704-3030, E-mail: cbeidleman@towson.edu.
Website: https://www.towson.edu/cla/departments/psychology/grad/

The University of Alabama, Graduate School, College of Arts and Sciences, Department of Psychology, Tuscaloosa, AL 35487. Offers clinical psychology (PhD); experimental psychology (PhD). *Faculty:* 29 full-time (17 women), 4 part-time/adjunct (3 women). *Students:* 84 full-time (65 women), 13 part-time (9 women); includes 14 minority (5 Black or African American, non-Hispanic/Latino; 3 Asian, non-Hispanic/

Latino; 4 Hispanic/Latino; 2 Two or more races, non-Hispanic/Latino), 8 international. Average age 27. 309 applicants, 8% accepted, 15 enrolled. In 2017, 13 doctorates awarded. *Degree requirements:* For doctorate, thesis/dissertation, internship (for clinical psychology). *Entrance requirements:* For doctorate, GRE. Additional exam requirements/recommendations for international students: Required—TOEFL (minimum score 550 paper-based). *Application deadline:* For fall admission, 11/16 for domestic and international students. Application fee: $50 ($60 for international students). Electronic applications accepted. *Financial support:* In 2017–18, 65 students received support, including fellowships with full tuition reimbursements available (averaging $17,000 per year), research assistantships with tuition reimbursements available (averaging $12,744 per year), teaching assistantships with tuition reimbursements available (averaging $13,824 per year); career-related internships or fieldwork, institutionally sponsored loans, scholarships/grants, health care benefits, and unspecified assistantships also available. Financial award application deadline: 11/16. *Faculty research:* Cognitive development/disability, child clinical, psychology and law, health/aging, social psychology. *Total annual research expenditures:* $1.2 million. *Unit head:* Dr. Frances A. Conners, Chair, 205-348-1913, Fax: 205-348-8648, E-mail: fconners@ua.edu. *Application contact:* Mary Beth Hubbard, Information Contact, 205-348-1919, Fax: 205-348-8648, E-mail: mary.b.hubbard@ua.edu.
Website: http://www.psychology.ua.edu

University of Central Oklahoma, The Jackson College of Graduate Studies, College of Education and Professional Studies, Department of Psychology, Edmond, OK 73034-5209. Offers psychology (MA), including counseling psychology, experimental psychology, forensic psychology, general psychology, school psychology. *Faculty:* 13 full-time (7 women), 1 part-time/adjunct (0 women). *Students:* 74 full-time (59 women), 35 part-time (29 women); includes 30 minority (4 Black or African American, non-Hispanic/Latino; 4 American Indian or Alaska Native, non-Hispanic/Latino; 3 Asian, non-Hispanic/Latino; 12 Hispanic/Latino; 7 Two or more races, non-Hispanic/Latino), 5 international. Average age 27. 109 applicants, 71% accepted, 51 enrolled. In 2017, 33 master's awarded. *Degree requirements:* For master's, thesis (for some programs). *Entrance requirements:* For master's, GRE. Additional exam requirements/recommendations for international students: Required—TOEFL (minimum score 550 paper-based; 79 iBT), IELTS (minimum score 6.5). *Application deadline:* For fall admission, 1/15 for domestic and international students; for spring admission, 11/15 for international students. Application fee: $60. Electronic applications accepted. *Expenses:* Tuition, state resident: full-time $5375; part-time $268.75 per credit hour. Tuition, nonresident: full-time $13,295; part-time $664.75 per credit hour. *Required fees:* $626; $31.30 per credit hour. One-time fee: $50. Tuition and fees vary according to program. *Financial support:* In 2017–18, 18 students received support, including 6 research assistantships with partial tuition reimbursements available (averaging $3,943 per year); teaching assistantships, career-related internships or fieldwork, scholarships/grants, tuition waivers (partial), and unspecified assistantships also available. Financial award application deadline: 3/31; financial award applicants required to submit FAFSA. *Unit head:* Dr. Thomas Hancock, Chair, 405-974-5707, Fax: 405-974-3865. *Application contact:* Carlie Wellington, Assistant Director, CEPS Graduate Enrollment, 405-974-5105, Fax: 405-974-3851, E-mail: gradcoll@uco.edu.
Website: http://sites.uco.edu/ceps/dept/Professional-Studies-Programs/psy/index.asp

University of Cincinnati, Graduate School, McMicken College of Arts and Sciences, Department of Psychology, Cincinnati, OH 45221. Offers clinical psychology (PhD); experimental psychology (PhD). *Accreditation:* APA. *Degree requirements:* For doctorate, comprehensive exam, thesis/dissertation. *Entrance requirements:* For doctorate, GRE General Test. Additional exam requirements/recommendations for international students: Required—TOEFL. *Expenses: Tuition, area resident:* Full-time $14,468. Tuition, state resident: full-time $14,968; part-time $754 per credit hour. Tuition, nonresident: full-time $24,210; part-time $1311 per credit hour. *International tuition:* $26,460 full-time. *Required fees:* $3958; $84 per credit hour. One-time fee: $85 full-time. Tuition and fees vary according to course load, degree level and program. *Faculty research:* Neuropsychology, human factors, health.

University of Connecticut, Graduate School, College of Liberal Arts and Sciences, Department of Psychology, Storrs, CT 06269. Offers behavioral neuroscience (PhD); biopsychology (PhD); clinical psychology (MA, PhD); cognition and instruction (PhD); developmental psychology (MA, PhD); ecological psychology (PhD); experimental psychology (PhD); general psychology (MA, PhD); industrial/organizational psychology (PhD); language and cognition (PhD); neuroscience (PhD); social psychology (MA, PhD). *Accreditation:* APA. Terminal master's awarded for partial completion of doctoral program. *Degree requirements:* For master's, comprehensive exam; for doctorate, thesis/dissertation. *Entrance requirements:* For master's and doctorate, GRE General Test, GRE Subject Test. Additional exam requirements/recommendations for international students: Required—TOEFL (minimum score 550 paper-based). Electronic applications accepted.

University of Hartford, College of Arts and Sciences, Department of Psychology, Program in General Experimental Psychology, West Hartford, CT 06117-1599. Offers MA. *Program availability:* Part-time. *Degree requirements:* For master's, comprehensive exam, thesis or alternative. *Entrance requirements:* For master's, GRE General Test, GRE Subject Test, minimum GPA of 3.0, 3 letters of recommendation. Additional exam requirements/recommendations for international students: Required—TOEFL (minimum score 550 paper-based). Electronic applications accepted. *Faculty research:* Decision making, social judgment and stereotyping, stress and health.

University of Idaho, College of Graduate Studies, College of Letters, Arts and Social Sciences, Department of Psychology and Communication Studies, Moscow, ID 83844. Offers experimental psychology (PhD); psychology and communication studies (MS). *Faculty:* 8. *Students:* 18 full-time (5 women), 11 part-time (5 women). Average age 30. In 2017, 11 master's awarded. *Entrance requirements:* For master's, GRE, minimum GPA of 3.0. Additional exam requirements/recommendations for international students: Required—TOEFL (minimum score 79 iBT). *Application deadline:* For fall admission, 8/1 for domestic students; for spring admission, 12/15 for domestic students. Applications are processed on a rolling basis. Application fee: $60. Electronic applications accepted. *Expenses:* Tuition, state resident: full-time $6722; part-time $430 per credit hour. Tuition, nonresident: full-time $23,046; part-time $1337 per credit hour. *Required fees:* $2142; $63 per credit hour. *Financial support:* Fellowships, research assistantships, and teaching assistantships available. Financial award applicants required to submit FAFSA. *Faculty research:* Instructional communication, visual and spatial cognition. *Unit head:* Dr. Todd Thorsteinson, Chair, 208-885-6324, E-mail: psyc-comm@uidaho.edu. *Application contact:* Sean Scoggin, Graduate Recruitment Coordinator, 208-885-4723, Fax: 208-885-4406, E-mail: graduateadmissions@uidaho.edu.
Website: https://www.uidaho.edu/class/psychcomm

University of Louisville, Graduate School, College of Arts and Sciences, Department of Psychological and Brain Sciences, Louisville, KY 40292-0001. Offers clinical psychology (PhD); experimental psychology (PhD), including cognition and development, vision and hearing. *Accreditation:* APA. *Students:* 55 full-time (44 women), 1 (woman) part-time; includes 7 minority (1 Black or African American, non-Hispanic/Latino; 2 Asian, non-Hispanic/Latino; 2 Hispanic/Latino; 2 Two or more races, non-Hispanic/Latino), 4 international. Average age 29. 9 applicants, 78% accepted. In 2017, 1 doctorate awarded. *Degree requirements:* For doctorate, comprehensive exam, thesis/dissertation, internship (for clinical psychology). *Entrance requirements:* For doctorate, GRE General Test, GRE Subject Test. Additional exam requirements/recommendations for international students: Required—TOEFL. *Application deadline:* For fall and winter admission, 12/1 for domestic and international students. Application fee: $65. *Expenses:* Tuition, state resident: full-time $12,246; part-time $681 per credit hour. Tuition, nonresident: full-time $25,486; part-time $1417 per credit hour. *Required fees:* $196. Tuition and fees vary according to course load, program and reciprocity agreements. *Financial support:* In 2017–18, 8 fellowships with full tuition reimbursements (averaging $22,000 per year), 3 research assistantships with full tuition reimbursements (averaging $22,000 per year), 30 teaching assistantships with full tuition reimbursements (averaging $22,000 per year) were awarded; health care benefits and unspecified assistantships also available. Financial award application deadline: 12/1. *Faculty research:* Cognitive development, hearing/visual science, cognitive neuroscience/imaging, health psychology/mindfulness/stress and trauma, child/adult psychopathology, geropsychology. *Total annual research expenditures:* $923,340. *Unit head:* Dr. Suzanne Meeks, Chair, 502-852-6068, Fax: 502-852-8904, E-mail: smeeks@louisville.edu. *Application contact:* Maggie Leahy, Administrative Assistant, 502-852-4364, Fax: 502-852-8904, E-mail: maggie.leahy@louisville.edu.
Website: http://louisville.edu/psychology

University of Maryland, College Park, Academic Affairs, College of Behavioral and Social Sciences, Department of Psychology, College Park, MD 20742. Offers clinical psychology (PhD); developmental psychology (PhD); experimental psychology (PhD); industrial psychology (MA, MS, PhD); social psychology (PhD). *Accreditation:* APA (one or more programs are accredited). *Degree requirements:* For master's, thesis; for doctorate, variable foreign language requirement, comprehensive exam, thesis/dissertation. *Entrance requirements:* For master's and doctorate, GRE General Test, GRE Subject Test, minimum GPA of 3.5, research and/or work experience, 3 letters of recommendation. Electronic applications accepted. *Faculty research:* Social stereotyping and prejudice, anxiety disorders, auditory neuroethology, counseling and social psychology.

University of Massachusetts Dartmouth, Graduate School, College of Arts and Sciences, Department of Psychology, North Dartmouth, MA 02747-2300. Offers autism studies (Graduate Certificate); psychology - applied behavioral analysis (MA, Post-Master's Certificate); psychology - clinical (MA); psychology - research (MA). *Program availability:* Part-time. *Faculty:* 20 full-time (12 women), 8 part-time/adjunct (2 women). *Students:* 40 full-time (31 women), 57 part-time (52 women); includes 19 minority (4 Black or African American, non-Hispanic/Latino; 3 Asian, non-Hispanic/Latino; 7 Hispanic/Latino; 5 Two or more races, non-Hispanic/Latino), 1 international. Average age 29. 96 applicants, 54% accepted, 39 enrolled. In 2017, 21 master's awarded. *Degree requirements:* For master's, comprehensive exam (for some programs), thesis or comprehensive exam (for psychology - clinical); thesis (for psychology - research). *Entrance requirements:* For master's and other advanced degree, statement of purpose (minimum of 300 words), resume, 3 letters of recommendation, official transcripts. Additional exam requirements/recommendations for international students: Required—TOEFL (minimum score 533 paper-based; 72 iBT), IELTS (minimum score 6). *Application deadline:* For fall admission, 3/1 priority date for domestic students, 2/1 priority date for international students. Application fee: $60. Electronic applications accepted. *Expenses:* Tuition, state resident: full-time $15,449; part-time $643.71 per credit. Tuition, nonresident: full-time $27,880; part-time $1161.67 per credit. *Required fees:* $405; $25.88 per credit. Tuition and fees vary according to course load and reciprocity agreements. *Financial support:* In 2017–18, 1 research assistantship (averaging $12,000 per year), 2 teaching assistantships (averaging $14,000 per year) were awarded; tuition waivers (full and partial) and unspecified assistantships also available. Support available to part-time students. Financial award application deadline: 3/1; financial award applicants required to submit FAFSA. *Faculty research:* Health inequities, language and cognitive development, interethnic dating and marriage, executive function and implicit learning in deaf children, behavioral medicine. *Total annual research expenditures:* $344,000. *Unit head:* Mahzad Hojjat, Graduate Program Director, Research Psychology, 508-999-8951, E-mail: mhojjat@umassd.edu. *Application contact:* Steven Briggs, Director of Marketing and Recruitment for Graduate Studies, 508-999-8604, Fax: 508-999-8183, E-mail: graduate@umassd.edu.
Website: http://www.umassd.edu/cas/psychology

University of Memphis, Graduate School, College of Arts and Sciences, Department of Psychology, Memphis, TN 38152-3230. Offers clinical psychology (PhD); experimental psychology (PhD); general psychology (MS); school psychology (MA, PhD, Ed S). *Accreditation:* APA. *Faculty:* 26 full-time (11 women), 3 part-time/adjunct (0 women). *Students:* 94 full-time (69 women), 17 part-time (12 women); includes 25 minority (10 Black or African American, non-Hispanic/Latino; 6 Asian, non-Hispanic/Latino; 6 Hispanic/Latino; 3 Two or more races, non-Hispanic/Latino), 6 international. Average age 27. 291 applicants, 16% accepted, 32 enrolled. In 2017, 23 master's, 13 doctorates, 8 other advanced degrees awarded. *Degree requirements:* For master's, comprehensive exam (for some programs), thesis (for some programs), 37 credit hours (for MA); 33 credit hours with thesis or 36 with exam (for MS); for doctorate, comprehensive exam, thesis/dissertation, 80 semester hours, major area paper; 1-year placement and 1-year internship (for clinical psychology); internship (for school psychology); for Ed S, 30 credit hours. *Entrance requirements:* For master's, GRE, 3 letters of recommendation, 18 undergraduate hours in psychology; for doctorate, GRE, minimum GPA of 2.75, 18 hours of undergraduate psychology courses, transcripts, personal statement, 3 letters of recommendation, interview; for Ed S, GRE, minimum GPA of 2.75, 18 hours of undergraduate psychology courses, 3 letters of recommendation. Additional exam requirements/recommendations for international students: Required—TOEFL (minimum score 550 paper-based; 79 iBT). *Application deadline:* For fall admission, 12/5 for domestic students. Applications are processed on a rolling basis. Application fee: $35 ($60 for international students). Electronic applications accepted. *Expenses:* Contact institution. *Financial support:* In 2017–18, 66 students received support, including 60 research assistantships with full tuition reimbursements available (averaging $11,846 per year), 25 teaching assistantships with full tuition reimbursements available (averaging $6,794 per year); fellowships with full tuition reimbursements available, Federal Work-Study, scholarships/grants, tuition waivers (partial), and unspecified assistantships also available. Financial award application deadline: 2/1; financial award applicants required to submit FAFSA. *Faculty research:* Clinical health; school, child and family psychology; psychotherapy; cognitive and behavioral neuroscience; industrial-organizational psychology. *Unit head:* Dr. Frank Andrasik, Chair, 901-678-2145, Fax: 901-678-2579, E-mail: rcohen@memphis.edu. *Application contact:* Dr. Robert Cohen, Coordinator of Graduate Studies, 901-678-4679, Fax: 901-678-2579, E-mail: rcohen@memphis.edu.
Website: http://www.memphis.edu/psychology

University of Mississippi, Graduate School, College of Liberal Arts, University, MS 38677. Offers anthropology (MA); biology (MS, PhD); chemistry (MS, DA, PhD); creative writing (MFA); documentary expression (MFA); economics (MA, PhD); English (MA, PhD); experimental psychology (PhD); history (MA, PhD); mathematics (MS, PhD); modern languages (MA); music (MM); philosophy (MA); physics (MA, MS, PhD); political science (MA, PhD); Southern studies (MA); studio art (MFA). *Program availability:* Part-

time. *Faculty:* 465 full-time (207 women), 82 part-time/adjunct (46 women). *Students:* 466 full-time (229 women), 72 part-time (34 women); includes 87 minority (38 Black or African American, non-Hispanic/Latino; 18 Asian, non-Hispanic/Latino; 24 Hispanic/Latino; 7 Two or more races, non-Hispanic/Latino), 121 international. Average age 29. *Degree requirements:* For doctorate, thesis/dissertation. *Entrance requirements:* For master's, GRE General Test, minimum GPA of 3.0; for doctorate, GRE General Test. Additional exam requirements/recommendations for international students: Required—TOEFL. *Application deadline:* For fall admission, 2/1 priority date for domestic students; for spring admission, 10/1 for domestic students. Applications are processed on a rolling basis. Application fee: $50. Electronic applications accepted. *Financial support:* Fellowships, research assistantships, teaching assistantships, career-related internships or fieldwork, Federal Work-Study, institutionally sponsored loans, scholarships/grants, and unspecified assistantships available. Financial award application deadline: 3/1; financial award applicants required to submit FAFSA. *Unit head:* Dr. Lee Michael Cohen, Dean, 662-915-7177, Fax: 662-915-5792, E-mail: libarts@olemiss.edu. *Application contact:* Dr. Christy M. Wyandt, Associate Dean of Graduate School, 662-915-7474, Fax: 662-915-7577, E-mail: cwyandt@olemiss.edu.

University of Montana, Graduate School, College of Humanities and Sciences, Department of Psychology, Missoula, MT 59812. Offers clinical psychology (PhD); experimental psychology (PhD), including animal behavior psychology, developmental psychology; school psychology (MA, PhD, Ed S). *Accreditation:* APA (one or more programs are accredited). Terminal master's awarded for partial completion of doctoral program. *Degree requirements:* For master's, thesis; for doctorate, thesis/dissertation. *Entrance requirements:* For master's, doctorate, and Ed S, GRE General Test. Additional exam requirements/recommendations for international students: Required—TOEFL.

University of New Brunswick Saint John, Department of Psychology, Saint John, NB E2L 4L5, Canada. Offers clinical psychology (PhD); experimental psychology (MA, PhD). *Program availability:* Part-time. *Degree requirements:* For master's, thesis. *Entrance requirements:* For master's, GRE General and Subject Tests, honors thesis; minimum GPA of 3.7. Additional exam requirements/recommendations for international students: Required—TOEFL (minimum score 550 paper-based), TWE. Electronic applications accepted. *Faculty research:* Forensic psychology, peer relationships and social skills, polygraph techniques, addictions, attachment and social adjustment, neuroscience, optical illusions, graphical perception, associative learning in animals, bio-psychology.

University of Regina, Faculty of Graduate Studies and Research, Faculty of Arts, Department of Psychology, Regina, SK S4S 0A2, Canada. Offers clinical psychology (MA, PhD); experimental and applied psychology (MA, PhD). *Faculty:* 19 full-time (9 women), 5 part-time/adjunct (2 women). *Students:* 18 full-time (13 women), 2 part-time (0 women). 52 applicants, 19% accepted. In 2017, 4 master's, 4 doctorates awarded. *Degree requirements:* For master's, thesis; for doctorate, comprehensive exam, thesis/dissertation. *Entrance requirements:* For master's, GRE General Test; for doctorate, GRE General Test and GRE Subject Test (optional for those with a master's degree from a Canadian university). Additional exam requirements/recommendations for international students: Required—TOEFL (minimum score 580 paper-based; 80 iBT), IELTS (minimum score 6.5), PTE (minimum score 59). *Application deadline:* For fall admission, 1/15 for domestic and international students. Application fee: $100. Electronic applications accepted. *Expenses:* $10,681. *Financial support:* In 2017–18, 7 fellowships (averaging $6,714 per year), 17 teaching assistantships (averaging $2,562 per year) were awarded; research assistantships, career-related internships or fieldwork, and scholarships/grants also available. Financial award application deadline: 6/15. *Faculty research:* Clinical, experimental, cognitive, and applied psychology; post-traumatic stress disorder, anxiety, and panic disorder; traumatic brain injury; chronic pain; perception and memory. *Unit head:* Dr. Richard MacLennan, Department Head, 306-585-4458, Fax: 306-585-5429, E-mail: richard.maclennan@uregina.ca.
Website: http://www.uregina.ca/arts/psychology

University of South Carolina, The Graduate School, College of Arts and Sciences, Department of Psychology, Program in Experimental Psychology, Columbia, SC 29208. Offers MA, PhD. Terminal master's awarded for partial completion of doctoral program. *Degree requirements:* For master's, comprehensive exam, thesis; for doctorate, comprehensive exam, thesis/dissertation. *Entrance requirements:* For master's and doctorate, GRE General Test. Additional exam requirements/recommendations for international students: Required—TOEFL. Electronic applications accepted. *Faculty research:* Cognition, development, neuroscience.

The University of Tennessee, Graduate School, College of Arts and Sciences, Department of Psychology, Knoxville, TN 37996. Offers clinical psychology (PhD); experimental psychology (MA, PhD); psychology (MA). *Accreditation:* APA (one or more programs are accredited). Terminal master's awarded for partial completion of doctoral program. *Degree requirements:* For master's, thesis; for doctorate, thesis/dissertation. *Entrance requirements:* For master's and doctorate, GRE General Test, GRE Subject Test, minimum GPA of 2.7. Additional exam requirements/recommendations for international students: Required—TOEFL. Electronic applications accepted.

The University of Tennessee at Chattanooga, Program in Psychology, Chattanooga, TN 37403. Offers industrial/organizational psychology (MS); research psychology (MS). *Program availability:* Part-time. *Students:* 46 full-time (28 women), 4 part-time (3 women); includes 5 minority (2 Black or African American, non-Hispanic/Latino; 1 Asian, non-Hispanic/Latino; 2 Hispanic/Latino). Average age 25. 85 applicants, 38% accepted, 25 enrolled. In 2017, 20 master's awarded. *Degree requirements:* For master's, comprehensive exam (for some programs), thesis (for some programs), comprehensive exam or thesis. *Entrance requirements:* For master's, GRE General Test, minimum GPA of 2.5 on all undergraduate coursework or 3.0 in senior year. Additional exam requirements/recommendations for international students: Required—TOEFL (minimum score 550 paper-based; 79 iBT), IELTS (minimum score 6). *Application deadline:* For fall admission, 6/15 priority date for domestic students, 7/1 for international students; for spring admission, 11/1 priority date for domestic students, 11/1 for international students. Applications are processed on a rolling basis. Application fee: $35 ($40 for international students). Electronic applications accepted. *Expenses:* Contact institution. *Financial support:* Research assistantships, teaching assistantships, career-related internships or fieldwork, scholarships/grants, and unspecified assistantships available. Support available to part-time students. Financial award application deadline: 7/1; financial award applicants required to submit FAFSA. *Faculty research:* Decision processes, philosophical psychology, memory, social cognition, employee selection. *Total annual research expenditures:* $44,854. *Unit head:* Dr. Brian O'Leary, Department Head, 423-425-4283, Fax: 423-425-4284, E-mail: brian-o'leary@utc.edu. *Application contact:* Dr. Joanne Romagni, Dean of the Graduate School, 423-425-4478, Fax: 423-425-5223, E-mail: joanne-romagni@utc.edu.
Website: http://www.utc.edu/psychology/

The University of Texas at Arlington, Graduate School, College of Science, Department of Psychology, Arlington, TX 76019. Offers experimental health psychology (PhD); experimental psychology (MS, PhD); health/neuroscience psychology (MS, PhD); industrial and organizational psychology (MS). *Program availability:* Part-time. Terminal master's awarded for partial completion of doctoral program. *Degree requirements:* For master's, comprehensive exam or thesis; for doctorate, thesis/dissertation (for some programs). *Entrance requirements:* For master's and doctorate, GRE General Test, minimum GPA of 3.0 in last 60 hours of course work. Additional exam requirements/recommendations for international students: Required—TOEFL (minimum score 550 paper-based).

The University of Texas at El Paso, Graduate School, College of Liberal Arts, Department of Psychology, El Paso, TX 79968-0001. Offers clinical psychology (MA); experimental psychology (MA); psychology (PhD). *Program availability:* Part-time, evening/weekend. *Degree requirements:* For master's, thesis; for doctorate, thesis/dissertation. *Entrance requirements:* For master's, GRE, letters of recommendation; for doctorate, GRE, statement of purpose, letters of recommendation. Additional exam requirements/recommendations for international students: Required—TOEFL; Recommended—IELTS. Electronic applications accepted.

The University of Texas of the Permian Basin, Office of Graduate Studies, College of Arts and Sciences, Department of Psychology, Odessa, TX 79762-0001. Offers applied research psychology (MA); clinical psychology (MA). *Program availability:* Part-time, evening/weekend. *Degree requirements:* For master's, comprehensive exam, thesis, practicum. *Entrance requirements:* For master's, GRE General Test, 3 letters of recommendation. Additional exam requirements/recommendations for international students: Required—TOEFL (minimum score 550 paper-based).

The University of Texas Rio Grande Valley, College of Liberal Arts, Department of Psychological Science, Edinburg, TX 78539. Offers psychology (MA), including clinical psychology, experimental psychology. *Program availability:* Part-time, evening/weekend. *Faculty:* 12 full-time (1 woman), 3 part-time/adjunct (1 woman). *Students:* 32 full-time (25 women), 20 part-time (15 women); includes 50 minority (all Hispanic/Latino), 2 international. Average age 27. 29 applicants, 69% accepted, 15 enrolled. In 2017, 15 master's awarded. *Degree requirements:* For master's, comprehensive exam, thesis optional, internship. *Entrance requirements:* For master's, GRE, letters of recommendation. Additional exam requirements/recommendations for international students: Required—TOEFL or IELTS. *Application deadline:* For fall admission, 7/1 priority date for domestic and international students; for spring admission, 11/1 priority date for domestic and international students. Application fee: $50 ($100 for international students). *Expenses:* Tuition, state resident: full-time $5550; part-time $417 per credit hour. Tuition, nonresident: full-time $13,020; part-time $832 per credit hour. *Required fees:* $1169. *Faculty research:* Biofeedback, acculturation, health, stress/trauma, neuropsychological assessment, false memories, children's theory of mind. *Unit head:* Pamela Anderson-Mejias, Interim Chair, E-mail: pamela.andersonmejias@utrgv.edu.

The University of Toledo, College of Graduate Studies, College of Languages, Literature and Social Sciences, Department of Psychology, Toledo, OH 43606-3390. Offers clinical psychology (MA, PhD); experimental psychology (MA, PhD). *Accreditation:* APA. *Degree requirements:* For master's, comprehensive exam, thesis; for doctorate, comprehensive exam, thesis/dissertation. *Entrance requirements:* For master's and doctorate, GRE General Test, GRE Subject Test, minimum cumulative point-hour ratio of 2.7 for all previous academic work, three letters of recommendation, statement of purpose, transcripts from all prior institutions attended. Additional exam requirements/recommendations for international students: Required—TOEFL (minimum score 550 paper-based; 80 iBT). Electronic applications accepted. *Faculty research:* Neural taste response.

University of Vermont, Graduate College, College of Arts and Sciences, Program in General/Experimental Psychology, Burlington, VT 05405-0134. Offers psychology (PhD), including biobehavioral psychology, developmental psychology, human behavioral pharmacology, social psychology. *Accreditation:* APA. *Students:* 15 (11 women). 22 applicants, 9% accepted, 2 enrolled. In 2017, 2 doctorates awarded. *Degree requirements:* For doctorate, thesis/dissertation. *Entrance requirements:* For doctorate, GRE General Test. Additional exam requirements/recommendations for international students: Required—TOEFL (minimum score 550 paper-based, 100 iBT) or IELTS (7). *Application deadline:* For fall admission, 12/1 for domestic and international students. Application fee: $65. Electronic applications accepted. *Expenses:* Tuition, state resident: full-time $11,628; part-time $646 per credit. Tuition, nonresident: full-time $29,340; part-time $1630 per credit. *Required fees:* $1994; $10 per credit. Tuition and fees vary according to course load and program. *Financial support:* In 2017–18, 15 students received support, including 15 teaching assistantships with full tuition reimbursements available (averaging $20,000 per year); fellowships and research assistantships also available. Financial award application deadline: 12/1. *Unit head:* Dr. Dianna Murray-Close, Coordinator, 802-656-2670, E-mail: dianna.murray-close@uvm.edu.
Website: https://www.uvm.edu/cas/psychology/general/experimental-psychology-phd-program

University of Victoria, Faculty of Graduate Studies, Faculty of Social Sciences, Department of Psychology, Victoria, BC V8W 2Y2, Canada. Offers clinical psychology (PhD); clinical psychology (neuropsychology) (M Sc); cognition and brain science (M Sc, PhD); experimental neuropsychology (M Sc, PhD); individualized study (M Sc, PhD); life span development psychology (PhD); life span developmental psychology (M Sc); social psychology (M Sc, PhD). *Degree requirements:* For master's, thesis; for doctorate, thesis/dissertation, candidacy exam. *Entrance requirements:* For master's and doctorate, GRE General Test. Additional exam requirements/recommendations for international students: Required—TOEFL (minimum score 600 paper-based). Electronic applications accepted. *Faculty research:* Life span development psychology and aging, behavioral neuroscience, cognitive psychology, behavioral psychology, environmental psychology.

The University of West Alabama, School of Graduate Studies, College of Liberal Arts, Livingston, AL 35470. Offers experimental psychology (MS). *Program availability:* Part-time, evening/weekend, 100% online. *Faculty:* 3 full-time (1 woman), 7 part-time/adjunct (4 women). *Students:* 17 (13 women); includes 5 minority (all Black or African American, non-Hispanic/Latino). Average age 29. 5 applicants, 80% accepted, 3 enrolled. *Degree requirements:* For master's, thesis. *Entrance requirements:* For master's, GRE (minimum score of 280 combined verbal and quantitative, 3 on writing portion), minimum GPA of 2.85, official transcripts, statement of purpose, three academic references. Additional exam requirements/recommendations for international students: Required—TOEFL (minimum score 500 paper-based; 61 iBT). *Application deadline:* Applications are processed on a rolling basis. Application fee: $40. Electronic applications accepted. *Expenses:* Tuition, state resident: part-time $371 per credit hour. Tuition, nonresident: part-time $742 per credit hour. *Required fees:* $130 per semester. *Financial support:* In 2017–18, 3 teaching assistantships (averaging $7,344 per year) were awarded; Federal Work-Study, scholarships/grants, and unspecified assistantships also available. Support available to part-time students. Financial award application deadline: 3/1; financial award applicants required to submit FAFSA. *Unit head:* Dr. Mark Davis, Dean, 205-652-3570, Fax: 205-652-3717, E-mail: mdavis@uwa.edu.
Website: http://www.uwa.edu/academics/collegeofliberalarts

University of West Florida, Usha Kundu, MD College of Health, Department of Psychology, Pensacola, FL 32514-5750. Offers applied experimental (MA); counseling (MA); industrial-organizational (MA). *Program availability:* Part-time. *Degree*

requirements: For master's, thesis (for some programs). *Entrance requirements:* For master's, GRE, official transcripts; minimum GPA of 3.0; writing sample; three letters of reference; field experience or skill sets; oral interview (for counseling specialization). Additional exam requirements/recommendations for international students: Required—TOEFL (minimum score 550 paper-based). *Faculty research:* Prose recall, brain imaging, peak performance, biofeedback and pain control, comparable worth.

University of Wisconsin–Oshkosh, Graduate Studies, College of Letters and Science, Department of Psychology, Oshkosh, WI 54901. Offers experimental psychology (MS); industrial/organizational psychology (MS). *Degree requirements:* For master's, thesis. *Entrance requirements:* For master's, GRE, 10 semester hours of undergraduate course work in psychology. Additional exam requirements/recommendations for international students: Required—TOEFL (minimum score 550 paper-based; 79 iBT). Electronic applications accepted. *Faculty research:* Performance evaluation, training, biological bases of behavior, tactile perception, aging.

Washington State University, College of Arts and Sciences, Department of Psychology, Pullman, WA 99164. Offers clinical psychology (PhD); experimental psychology (PhD). Program applications must be made through the Pullman campus. *Accreditation:* APA (one or more programs are accredited). *Degree requirements:* For doctorate, comprehensive exam, thesis/dissertation, oral exam, written exam. *Entrance requirements:* For doctorate, GRE General Test, three letters of reference; summary data form; at least 18 credits of study in psychology; at least one course in statistics and research methodology; official transcripts; minimum cumulative undergraduate GPA of 3.0 or master's degree in psychology. Additional exam requirements/recommendations for international students: Required—TOEFL, IELTS. Electronic applications accepted. *Faculty research:* Adult psychopathology and therapy, child psychopathology, neuropsychology, health psychology.

Western Illinois University, School of Graduate Studies, College of Arts and Sciences, Department of Psychology, Macomb, IL 61455-1390. Offers clinical/community mental health (MS); general experimental psychology (MS); school psychology (SSP). *Program availability:* Part-time. *Students:* 39 full-time (28 women), 15 part-time (8 women); includes 6 minority (1 Black or African American, non-Hispanic/Latino; 2 Asian, non-Hispanic/Latino; 1 Hispanic/Latino; 2 Two or more races, non-Hispanic/Latino), 2 international. Average age 26. 77 applicants, 77% accepted, 30 enrolled. In 2017, 8 master's, 6 other advanced degrees awarded. *Degree requirements:* For master's, comprehensive exam (for some programs), thesis or alternative. *Entrance requirements:* For master's and SSP, GRE General Test. Additional exam requirements/recommendations for international students: Required—TOEFL (minimum score 550 paper-based; 80 iBT). Application fee: $30. Electronic applications accepted. *Financial support:* In 2017–18, 6 research assistantships with full tuition reimbursements (averaging $7,544 per year) were awarded; unspecified assistantships also available. Financial award applicants required to submit FAFSA. *Unit head:* Dr. Karen Sears, Chairperson, 309-298-1593. *Application contact:* Dr. Nancy Parsons, Associate Provost and Director of Graduate Studies, 309-298-1806, Fax: 309-298-2345, E-mail: grad-office@wiu.edu.
Website: http://wiu.edu/psychology

Western Kentucky University, Graduate Studies, College of Education and Behavioral Sciences, Department of Psychology, Bowling Green, KY 42101. Offers clinical psychology (MA); experimental psychology (MA); general psychology (MA); industrial/organizational psychology (MA); school psychology (Ed S). *Degree requirements:* For master's, comprehensive exam, thesis (for some programs); for Ed S, thesis, oral exam. *Entrance requirements:* For master's, GRE General Test; for Ed S, GRE General Test, minimum GPA of 3.5. Additional exam requirements/recommendations for international students: Required—TOEFL (minimum score 555 paper-based; 79 iBT). *Faculty research:* Neural regeneration, enhancing mobility in the elderly, improvement in visual processing in older adults, lifespan development.

Western Washington University, Graduate School, College of Humanities and Social Sciences, Department of Psychology, Program in Experimental Psychology, Bellingham, WA 98225-5996. Offers MS. *Degree requirements:* For master's, thesis. *Entrance requirements:* For master's, GRE General Test, minimum GPA of 3.0 in last 60 semester hours or last 90 quarter hours. Additional exam requirements/recommendations for international students: Required—TOEFL (minimum score 567 paper-based). Electronic applications accepted.

Forensic Psychology

Adler University, Graduate Programs, MA in Counseling Program: Specialization in Forensic Psychology, Chicago, IL 60602. Offers MAC. *Program availability:* Evening/weekend, online learning. *Entrance requirements:* For master's, baccalaureate degree, minimum GPA of 3.0 (recommended), interview, official transcripts.

Alliant International University–Fresno, California School of Forensic Studies, PhD Program in Clinical Forensic Psychology, Fresno, CA 93727. Offers PhD. *Degree requirements:* For doctorate, comprehensive exam, thesis/dissertation, research internship. *Entrance requirements:* For doctorate, minimum GPA of 3.0, letters of recommendation, essay, interview. Additional exam requirements/recommendations for international students: Required—TOEFL (minimum score 550 paper-based), TWE (minimum score 5). *Faculty research:* Effects of stress in law enforcement officers, treatment for mentally ill offenders, psychotic disorders and violence, behavioral threat assessment/risk analysis, juvenile delinquency.

Alliant International University–Fresno, California School of Forensic Studies, PsyD Program in Clinical Forensic Psychology, Fresno, CA 93727. Offers victimology (Psy D). *Degree requirements:* For doctorate, comprehensive exam, thesis/dissertation, internship. *Entrance requirements:* For doctorate, minimum GPA of 3.0, recommendations, essay, interview. Additional exam requirements/recommendations for international students: Required—TOEFL (minimum score 550 paper-based), TWE (minimum score 5). Electronic applications accepted. *Faculty research:* Correctional psychology, psychopathology, police psychology, substance abuse and ADHD, investigative psychology.

Alliant International University–Irvine, California School of Forensic Studies, Irvine, CA 92606. Offers Psy D. *Degree requirements:* For doctorate, comprehensive exam, thesis/dissertation, internship. *Entrance requirements:* For doctorate, minimum GPA of 3.0, recommendations, essay. Additional exam requirements/recommendations for international students: Required—TOEFL (minimum score 80 iBT), TWE (minimum score 5). Electronic applications accepted. *Faculty research:* Detecting deception, psychological safety of undercover police officers, domestic violence, risk assessment, competency evaluations.

Alliant International University–Los Angeles, California School of Forensic Studies, Alhambra, CA 91803. Offers forensic psychology (Psy D). *Degree requirements:* For doctorate, comprehensive exam, thesis/dissertation. *Entrance requirements:* For doctorate, interview; master's degree in psychology, forensic psychology, criminology, criminal justice, social work or law; minimum GPA of 3.0 in psychology and overall. Additional exam requirements/recommendations for international students: Required—TOEFL (minimum score 600 paper-based), TWE (minimum score 5). *Faculty research:* Court testimony, juvenile offenders, violence risk assessment, Miranda rights, police psychology.

Alliant International University–Sacramento, California School of Forensic Studies, Program in Clinical Forensic Psychology, Sacramento, CA 95833. Offers Psy D. *Degree requirements:* For doctorate, comprehensive exam, thesis/dissertation. *Entrance requirements:* For doctorate, minimum GPA of 3.0, recommendations, essay. Additional exam requirements/recommendations for international students: Required—TOEFL (minimum score 550 paper-based; 80 iBT), TWE (minimum score 5). Electronic applications accepted. *Faculty research:* Correctional mental health treatment, psychopathy, child maltreatment, interventions for delinquent youth, malingering.

Alliant International University–San Diego, California School of Forensic Studies, Psy D Program in Clinical Forensic Psychology, San Diego, CA 92131. Offers Psy D. *Degree requirements:* For doctorate, comprehensive exam, internship. *Entrance requirements:* Additional exam requirements/recommendations for international students: Required—TOEFL (minimum score 550 paper-based; 80 iBT), TWE (minimum score 5).

Alliant International University–San Francisco, California School of Forensic Studies, San Francisco, CA 94133. Offers applied criminology (MS), including victimology; clinical forensic psychology (PhD, Psy D). *Degree requirements:* For doctorate, comprehensive exam, thesis/dissertation, internship. *Entrance requirements:* For master's, minimum GPA of 3.0, recommendations, essay; for doctorate, minimum GPA of 3.0, recommendations, essay, interview. Additional exam requirements/recommendations for international students: Required—TOEFL (minimum score 550 paper-based; 80 iBT), TWE (minimum score 5). *Faculty research:* Post-traumatic stress disorder, correctional mental health.

American International College, School of Business, Arts and Sciences, Springfield, MA 01109-3189. Offers accounting and taxation (MS); business administration (MBA); clinical psychology (MA); educational psychology (Ed D); forensic psychology (MS); general psychology (MA, CAGS); management (CAGS); resort and casino management (MBA, CAGS). *Program availability:* Part-time, evening/weekend. *Faculty:* 4 full-time (2 women), 25 part-time/adjunct (13 women). *Students:* 178 full-time (120 women), 24 part-time (20 women); includes 94 minority (42 Black or African American, non-Hispanic/Latino; 1 American Indian or Alaska Native, non-Hispanic/Latino; 4 Asian, non-Hispanic/Latino; 39 Hispanic/Latino; 8 Two or more races, non-Hispanic/Latino), 13 international. Average age 28. 155 applicants, 83% accepted, 71 enrolled. In 2017, 87 master's, 3 doctorates awarded. *Degree requirements:* For master's, practicum; for doctorate, comprehensive exam, thesis/dissertation, practicum. *Entrance requirements:* For master's, BS or BA, minimum undergraduate GPA of 2.75, 2 letters of recommendation, official transcripts, personal goal statement or essay; for doctorate, 3 letters of recommendation; BS or BA; minimum undergraduate GPA of 3.0 (3.25 recommended); official transcripts; personal goal statement or essay. Additional exam requirements/recommendations for international students: Required—TOEFL (minimum score 550 paper-based; 80 iBT). *Application deadline:* For fall admission, 8/15 for domestic and international students; for spring admission, 12/15 for domestic and international students. Applications are processed on a rolling basis. Application fee: $50. *Expenses:* Contact institution. *Financial support:* In 2017–18, 6 students received support, including 6 research assistantships with full tuition reimbursements available (averaging $1,500 per year). Financial award application deadline: 4/1; financial award applicants required to submit FAFSA. *Faculty research:* Substance abuse, forensic psychology, special education. *Unit head:* Dr. Susanne Swanker, Dean, 413-205-3216, Fax: 413-205-3943, E-mail: susanne.swanker@aic.edu. *Application contact:* Kerry Barnes, Dean of Graduate Admissions, 413-205-3703, Fax: 413-205-3051, E-mail: kerry.barnes@aic.edu.
Website: http://www.aic.edu/school-of-business-arts-and-sciences/

Argosy University, Atlanta, Georgia School of Professional Psychology, Atlanta, GA 30328. Offers clinical psychology (MA, Psy D, Postdoctoral Respecialization Certificate), including child and family psychology (Psy D), general adult clinical (Psy D), health psychology (Psy D), neuropsychology/geropsychology (Psy D); community counseling (MA), including marriage and family therapy; counselor education and supervision (Ed D); forensic psychology (MA); industrial organizational psychology (MA); marriage and family therapy (Certificate); sport-exercise psychology (MA). *Accreditation:* APA.

Argosy University, Chicago, Illinois School of Professional Psychology, Doctoral Program in Clinical Psychology, Chicago, IL 60601. Offers child and adolescent psychology (Psy D); client-centered and experiential psychotherapies (Psy D); diversity and multicultural psychology (Psy D); family psychology (Psy D); forensic psychology (Psy D); health psychology (Psy D); neuropsychology (Psy D); organizational consulting (Psy D); psychoanalytic psychology (Psy D); psychology and spirituality (Psy D). *Accreditation:* APA.

Argosy University, Hawai`i, Hawai'i School of Professional Psychology, Program in Forensic Psychology, Honolulu, HI 96813. Offers MA.

Argosy University, Los Angeles, College of Psychology and Behavioral Sciences, Los Angeles, CA 90045. Offers clinical psychology/marriage and family therapy (MA); counseling psychology (Ed D); counseling psychology/marriage and family therapy (MA); forensic psychology (MA).

Argosy University, Northern Virginia, American School of Professional Psychology, Arlington, VA 22209. Offers clinical psychology (MA, Psy D), including child and family psychology (Psy D), diversity and multicultural psychology (Psy D), forensic psychology (Psy D), health and neuropsychology (Psy D); community counseling (MA); counseling psychology (Ed D), including counselor education and supervision; counselor education and supervision (Ed D); forensic psychology (MA).

Argosy University, Orange County, American School of Professional Psychology, Program in Forensic Psychology, Orange, CA 92868. Offers MA.

Forensic Psychology

Argosy University, Phoenix, Arizona School of Professional Psychology, Program in Forensic Psychology, Phoenix, AZ 85021. Offers MA.

Argosy University, Twin Cities, Minnesota School of Professional Psychology, Eagan, MN 55121. Offers clinical psychology (MA, Psy D), including child and family psychology (Psy D), forensic psychology (Psy D), health and neuropsychology (Psy D), trauma (Psy D); forensic counseling (Post-Graduate Certificate); forensic psychology (MA); industrial organizational psychology (MA); marriage and family therapy (MA, DMFT), including forensic counseling (MA). *Accreditation:* AAMFT; AAMFT/COAMFTE; APA.

California Baptist University, Program in Counseling Psychology, Riverside, CA 92504-3206. Offers counseling psychology (MS); forensic psychology (MS); professional clinical counseling (MS). *Program availability:* Part-time, evening/weekend. *Faculty:* 15 full-time (8 women), 17 part-time/adjunct (12 women). *Students:* 249 full-time (211 women), 91 part-time (76 women); includes 234 minority (58 Black or African American, non-Hispanic/Latino; 2 American Indian or Alaska Native, non-Hispanic/Latino; 11 Asian, non-Hispanic/Latino; 149 Hispanic/Latino; 1 Native Hawaiian or other Pacific Islander, non-Hispanic/Latino; 13 Two or more races, non-Hispanic/Latino), 2 international. Average age 31. 136 applicants, 69% accepted, 77 enrolled. In 2017, 114 master's awarded. *Degree requirements:* For master's, comprehensive exam, 24 (individual) or 50 hours (group) of psychotherapy, practicum. *Entrance requirements:* For master's, minimum undergraduate GPA of 2.75; official transcripts; three recommendations; 500-word essay; interview; 3 prerequisite courses completed with minimum C grade. Additional exam requirements/recommendations for international students: Required—TOEFL (minimum score 80 iBT). *Application deadline:* For fall admission, 8/1 priority date for domestic students, 7/1 for international students; for spring admission, 12/1 priority date for domestic students, 11/1 for international students. Applications are processed on a rolling basis. Application fee: $45. Electronic applications accepted. *Expenses:* Contact institution. *Financial support:* In 2017–18, 79 students received support. Federal Work-Study and scholarships/grants available. Financial award applicants required to submit CSS PROFILE or FAFSA. *Faculty research:* Identify formation, faith integration, psychological assessment, child abuse and child welfare, clinical psychology and crisis intervention techniques. *Unit head:* Dr. Jacqueline Gustafson, Dean, School of Behavioral Sciences, 951-343-4487, E-mail: jcraig@calbaptist.edu. *Application contact:* Deanna Meyer, Graduate Admission Counselor, 951-343-4463, E-mail: dmeyer@calbaptist.edu.
Website: http://www.calbaptist.edu/mft/

California Baptist University, Program in Forensic Psychology, Riverside, CA 92504-3206. Offers MA. *Program availability:* Part-time, evening/weekend. *Faculty:* 4 full-time (3 women), 1 (woman) part-time/adjunct. *Students:* 60 full-time (53 women), 11 part-time (all women); includes 41 minority (8 Black or African American, non-Hispanic/Latino; 27 Hispanic/Latino; 3 Native Hawaiian or other Pacific Islander, non-Hispanic/Latino; 3 Two or more races, non-Hispanic/Latino). Average age 25. 33 applicants, 73% accepted, 21 enrolled. In 2017, 28 master's awarded. *Degree requirements:* For master's, comprehensive exam, thesis or alternative, 9-month practicum. *Entrance requirements:* For master's, minimum undergraduate GPA of 2.75; three recommendations; 500-word essay; interview; four prerequisite courses completed with minimum C grade. Additional exam requirements/recommendations for international students: Required—TOEFL (minimum score 80 iBT). *Application deadline:* For fall admission, 8/1 priority date for domestic students, 7/1 for international students; for spring admission, 12/1 priority date for domestic students, 11/1 for international students. Applications are processed on a rolling basis. Application fee: $45. Electronic applications accepted. *Expenses:* Contact institution. *Financial support:* In 2017–18, 12 students received support. Federal Work-Study and scholarships/grants available. Financial award applicants required to submit CSS PROFILE or FAFSA. *Faculty research:* Criminal profiling, police psychology, post-traumatic stress disorder in law enforcement, religiosity as a protective factor in the incarcerated, media influence on perception of police. *Unit head:* Dr. Jacqueline Gustafson, Dean, School of Behavioral Sciences, 951-343-4487, E-mail: jcraig@calbaptist.edu. *Application contact:* Rudy Villarruel, Graduate Admission Counselor, 951-552-8132, E-mail: rvillarruel@calbaptist.edu.
Website: http://www.calbaptist.edu/for_psych/

Cambridge College, School of Psychology and Counseling, Boston, MA 02129. Offers addiction counseling (M Ed); alcohol and drug counseling (Certificate); counseling psychology (M Ed, CAGS); counseling psychology: forensic counseling (M Ed); marriage and family therapy (M Ed); mental health and addiction counseling (M Ed); mental health counseling (M Ed); mental health counseling for school guidance counselors (Post Master's Certificate); psychological studies (M Ed); school adjustment and mental health counseling (M Ed); school adjustment, mental health and addiction counseling (M Ed); school guidance counselor (M Ed); trauma studies (Certificate). *Program availability:* Part-time, evening/weekend. *Degree requirements:* For master's and other advanced degree, thesis, practicum/internship. *Entrance requirements:* For master's, resume, 2 professional references; for other advanced degree, official transcripts, documents for transfer credit evaluation, resume, written personal statement/essay, 2 professional references, health insurance, immunizations form. Additional exam requirements/recommendations for international students: Required—TOEFL (minimum score 550 paper-based; 79 iBT), Michigan English Language Assessment Battery (minimum score 85); Recommended—IELTS (minimum score 6). Electronic applications accepted. *Expenses:* Contact institution. *Faculty research:* Trauma, drug and alcohol counseling, cross-cultural issues, school counseling, trauma in schools.

Castleton University, Division of Graduate Studies, Department of Psychology, Castleton, VT 05735. Offers forensic psychology (MA). *Degree requirements:* For master's, thesis. *Entrance requirements:* For master's, GRE General Test, minimum undergraduate GPA of 3.5, previous course work in research methodology and statistics. Additional exam requirements/recommendations for international students: Required—TOEFL. *Faculty research:* Psychology and law, juvenile delinquency, criminal psychology, correctional psychology, police psychology.

The Chicago School of Professional Psychology, Program in Clinical Forensic Psychology, Chicago, IL 60610. Offers Psy D. *Degree requirements:* For doctorate, thesis/dissertation. *Entrance requirements:* For doctorate, GRE. Additional exam requirements/recommendations for international students: Required—TOEFL, IELTS.

The Chicago School of Professional Psychology, Program in Forensic Psychology, Chicago, IL 60610. Offers MA. *Degree requirements:* For master's, thesis optional. *Entrance requirements:* For master's, GRE (highly recommended); 1 course each in research methods, statistics, and psychology. Additional exam requirements/recommendations for international students: Required—TOEFL (minimum score 550 paper-based; 79 iBT).

The Chicago School of Professional Psychology at Downtown Los Angeles, Program in Clinical Forensic Psychology, Los Angeles, CA 90017. Offers Psy D.

The Chicago School of Professional Psychology at Irvine, Program in Clinical Forensic Psychology, Irvine, CA 92612. Offers Psy D.

The Chicago School of Professional Psychology: Online, Program in Forensic Psychology, Chicago, IL 60654. Offers MA, Certificate.

Drexel University, College of Arts and Sciences, Department of Psychology, Clinical Psychology Program, Philadelphia, PA 19104-2875. Offers clinical psychology (PhD); forensic psychology (PhD); health psychology (PhD); neuropsychology (PhD). *Accreditation:* APA. Terminal master's awarded for partial completion of doctoral program. *Degree requirements:* For doctorate, thesis/dissertation, qualifying exam. *Entrance requirements:* For doctorate, GRE General Test, GRE Subject Test, minimum GPA of 3.0. Electronic applications accepted. *Expenses:* Contact institution. *Faculty research:* Cognitive behavioral therapy, stress and coping, eating disorders, substance abuse, developmental disabilities.

Fairleigh Dickinson University, Metropolitan Campus, University College: Arts, Sciences, and Professional Studies, School of Psychology, Program in Forensic Psychology, Teaneck, NJ 07666-1914. Offers MA.

The George Washington University, Graduate School of Education and Human Development, Department of Counseling and Human Development, Program in Forensic Rehabilitation Counseling, Washington, DC 20052. Offers Graduate Certificate. *Students:* 30 full-time (17 women), 19 part-time (17 women); includes 17 minority (5 Black or African American, non-Hispanic/Latino; 1 American Indian or Alaska Native, non-Hispanic/Latino; 2 Asian, non-Hispanic/Latino; 7 Hispanic/Latino; 2 Two or more races, non-Hispanic/Latino), 8 international. Average age 35. *Expenses: Tuition:* Full-time $28,800; part-time $1655 per credit hour. *Required fees:* $45; $2.75 per credit hour. *Unit head:* Dr. Kenneth C. Hergenrather, Chair, 202-994-1334, E-mail: hergenkc@gwu.edu. *Application contact:* Sarah Lang, Director of Graduate Admissions, 202-994-1447, Fax: 202-994-7207, E-mail: slang@gwu.edu.
Website: http://gsehd.gwu.edu/

Holy Names University, Graduate Division, Department of Counseling Psychology, Oakland, CA 94619-1699. Offers counseling and forensic counseling (MA); counseling psychology (MA); forensic psychology (MA). *Program availability:* Part-time, evening/weekend. *Degree requirements:* For master's, comprehensive paper, seminars. *Entrance requirements:* For master's, minimum undergraduate GPA of 2.6 overall, 3.0 in major. Additional exam requirements/recommendations for international students: Required—TOEFL (minimum score 550 paper-based; 79 iBT). Electronic applications accepted. Application fee is waived when completed online. *Expenses:* Contact institution. *Faculty research:* Cognitive psychology, anger management, grief and grief counseling, post-modernism and psychotherapy, spirituality and psychology.

Immaculata University, College of Graduate Studies, Department of Psychology, Immaculata, PA 19345. Offers clinical mental health counseling (MA); clinical psychology (Psy D); forensic psychology (Graduate Certificate); integrative psychotherapy (Graduate Certificate); neuropsychology (Graduate Certificate); psychodynamic psychotherapy (Graduate Certificate); psychological testing (Graduate Certificate); school counseling (MA, Graduate Certificate); school psychology (MA). *Accreditation:* APA. *Program availability:* Part-time, evening/weekend. Terminal master's awarded for partial completion of doctoral program. *Degree requirements:* For master's, comprehensive exam, thesis optional; for doctorate, comprehensive exam, thesis/dissertation. *Entrance requirements:* For master's, GRE General Test or MAT, minimum GPA of 3.0; for doctorate, GRE General Test or MAT, minimum GPA of 3.5. Additional exam requirements/recommendations for international students: Required—TOEFL, IELTS. Electronic applications accepted. *Faculty research:* Supervision ethics, psychology of teaching, gender.

John Jay College of Criminal Justice of the City University of New York, Graduate Studies, Program in Forensic Psychology, New York, NY 10019. Offers MA, PhD, MA/JD. MA/JD offered with New York Law School. *Accreditation:* APA. *Program availability:* Part-time, evening/weekend. *Degree requirements:* For master's, thesis or alternative, externship. *Entrance requirements:* For master's, GRE General Test, minimum B average in major. Additional exam requirements/recommendations for international students: Required—TOEFL (minimum score 500 paper-based).

John Jay College of Criminal Justice of the City University of New York, Graduate Studies, Programs in Criminal Justice, New York, NY 10019. Offers criminal justice (MA, PhD); criminology and deviance (PhD); forensic psychology (PhD); forensic science (PhD); international crime and justice (MA); law and philosophy (PhD); organizational behavior (PhD); public policy (PhD). *Program availability:* Part-time, evening/weekend. Terminal master's awarded for partial completion of doctoral program. *Degree requirements:* For master's, thesis or alternative; for doctorate, one foreign language, thesis/dissertation. *Entrance requirements:* For master's, GRE General Test, minimum B average; for doctorate, GRE General Test. Additional exam requirements/recommendations for international students: Required—TOEFL (minimum score 500 paper-based).

Kean University, College of Liberal Arts, Program in Forensic Psychology, Union, NJ 07083. Offers MA. *Faculty:* 18 full-time (14 women). *Students:* 33 full-time (29 women), 8 part-time (7 women); includes 17 minority (9 Black or African American, non-Hispanic/Latino; 1 American Indian or Alaska Native, non-Hispanic/Latino; 7 Hispanic/Latino), 1 international. Average age 26. 42 applicants, 79% accepted, 25 enrolled. In 2017, 1 master's awarded. *Degree requirements:* For master's, project. *Entrance requirements:* For master's, baccalaureate degree from accredited college or university in psychology or related field; minimum cumulative GPA of 3.0; official transcripts; two letters of recommendation; professional resume/curriculum vitae; personal statement. Additional exam requirements/recommendations for international students: Required—TOEFL (minimum score 550 paper-based, 79 iBT) or IELTS (6.5). *Application deadline:* For fall admission, 6/30 for domestic and international students; for spring admission, 12/1 for domestic and international students. Application fee: $75. Electronic applications accepted. *Expenses:* Tuition, state resident: full-time $13,419; part-time $653 per credit. Tuition, nonresident: full-time $18,188; part-time $801 per credit. *Required fees:* $3382; $154 per credit. Tuition and fees vary according to course level, course load, degree level and program. *Financial support:* Scholarships/grants and unspecified assistantships available. Financial award applicants required to submit FAFSA. *Unit head:* Dr. Richard Conti, Director, 908-737-5883, E-mail: rconti@kean.edu. *Application contact:* Amy Clark, Program Assistant, 908-737-7100, E-mail: grad-adm@kean.edu.
Website: http://grad.kean.edu/masters-programs/forensic-psychology

Liberty University, Helms School of Government, Lynchburg, VA 24515. Offers criminal justice (MS), including forensic psychology, homeland security, public administration (MA, MS); international relations (MS); political science (MS); public administration (MPA), including business and government, healthcare, law and public policy, public and non-profit management; public policy (MA), including campaigns and elections, international affairs, Middle East affairs, public administration (MA, MS). *Program availability:* Part-time, online learning. *Students:* 287 full-time (148 women), 639 part-time (248 women); includes 231 minority (173 Black or African American, non-Hispanic/Latino; 4 American Indian or Alaska Native, non-Hispanic/Latino; 8 Asian, non-Hispanic/Latino; 20 Hispanic/Latino; 1 Native Hawaiian or other Pacific Islander, non-Hispanic/Latino; 25 Two or more races, non-Hispanic/Latino), 7 international. Average age 35. 876 applicants, 64% accepted, 277 enrolled. In 2017, 211 master's awarded. *Entrance requirements:* For master's, minimum undergraduate GPA of 3.0. Additional exam requirements/recommendations for international students: Required—TOEFL (minimum score 600 paper-based; 100 iBT). *Application deadline:* Applications are

processed on a rolling basis. Application fee: $50. Electronic applications accepted. *Unit head:* Shawn D. Akers, Dean, 434-592-4986. *Application contact:* Jay Bridge, Director of Admissions, 800-424-9595, Fax: 800-628-7977, E-mail: gradadmissions@liberty.edu.

London Metropolitan University, Graduate Programs, London, United Kingdom. Offers applied psychology (M Sc); architecture (MA); biomedical science (M Sc); blood science (M Sc); cancer pharmacology (M Sc); computer networking and cyber security (M Sc); computing and information systems (M Sc); conference interpreting (MA); counter-terrorism studies (M Sc); creative, digital and professional writing (MA); crime, violence and prevention (M Sc); criminology (M Sc); curating contemporary art (MA); data analytics (M Sc); digital media (MA); early childhood studies (MA); education (MA, Ed D); financial services law, regulation and compliance (LL M); food science (M Sc); forensic psychology (M Sc); health and social care management and policy (M Sc); human nutrition (M Sc); human resource management (MA); human rights and international conflict (MA); information technology (M Sc); intelligence and security studies (M Sc); international oil, gas and energy law (LL M); international relations (MA); interpreting (MA); learning and teaching in higher education (MA); legal practice (LL M); media and entertainment law (LL M); organizational and consumer psychology (M Sc); psychological therapy (M Sc); psychology of mental health (M Sc); public health (M Sc); public policy and management (MPA); security studies (M Sc); social work (M Sc); spatial planning and urban design (MA); sports therapy (M Sc); supporting older children and young people with dyslexia (MA); teaching languages (MA), including Arabic, English; translation (MA); woman and child abuse (MA).

Marymount University, School of Education and Human Services, Program in Forensic and Legal Psychology, Arlington, VA 22207-4299. Offers forensic and legal psychology (MA); intelligence studies (MA); MA/MA. *Program availability:* Part-time, evening/weekend. *Faculty:* 5 full-time (4 women), 10 part-time/adjunct (7 women). *Students:* 114 full-time (106 women), 45 part-time (40 women); includes 28 minority (5 Black or African American, non-Hispanic/Latino; 1 American Indian or Alaska Native, non-Hispanic/Latino; 3 Asian, non-Hispanic/Latino; 13 Hispanic/Latino; 6 Two or more races, non-Hispanic/Latino), 2 international. Average age 25. 162 applicants, 80% accepted, 83 enrolled. In 2017, 76 master's awarded. *Degree requirements:* For master's, thesis or alternative, capstone/internship. *Entrance requirements:* For master's, GRE, 2 letters of recommendation, resume, personal statement. Additional exam requirements/recommendations for international students: Required—TOEFL (minimum score 600 paper-based; 96 iBT), IELTS (minimum score 6.5). *Application deadline:* For fall admission, 2/15 for domestic and international students. Application fee: $40. Electronic applications accepted. *Expenses: Tuition:* Full-time $17,550; part-time $975 per credit hour. *Required fees:* $198; $11 per credit hour. One-time fee: $250. Tuition and fees vary according to program. *Financial support:* In 2017–18, 12 students received support, including 7 research assistantships with full and partial tuition reimbursements available (averaging $10,629 per year), 5 teaching assistantships with full and partial tuition reimbursements available (averaging $10,446 per year); career-related internships or fieldwork, Federal Work-Study, scholarships/grants, and unspecified assistantships also available. Support available to part-time students. Financial award application deadline: 3/1; financial award applicants required to submit FAFSA. *Unit head:* Dr. Mary Lindahl, Chair, Forensic and Legal Psychology, 703-526-6821, Fax: 703-284-5708, E-mail: mary.lindahl@marymount.edu. *Application contact:* Francesca Reed, Director, Graduate Admissions, 703-284-5901, Fax: 703-527-3815, E-mail: grad.admissions@marymount.edu.
Website: http://www.marymount.edu/Academics/School-of-Education-Human-Services/Graduate-Programs/Forensic-Legal-Psychology-(M-A-)

Montclair State University, The Graduate School, College of Humanities and Social Sciences, Family/Civil Forensic Psychology Certificate Program, Montclair, NJ 07043-1624. Offers Certificate.

Montclair State University, The Graduate School, College of Humanities and Social Sciences, Forensic Psychology Certificate Program, Montclair, NJ 07043-1624. Offers Certificate. *Program availability:* Part-time, evening/weekend. *Entrance requirements:* For degree, 2 letters of recommendation, essay. Additional exam requirements/recommendations for international students: Required—TOEFL (minimum score 83 iBT), IELTS (minimum score 6.5). Electronic applications accepted. *Faculty research:* Forensic interviewing, child abuse.

Nova Southeastern University, College of Psychology, Fort Lauderdale, FL 33314-7796. Offers clinical mental health counseling (MS); clinical psychology (PhD, Psy D); counseling (MS); experimental psychology (MS); forensic psychology (MS); general psychology (MS); school counseling (MS); school psychology (Psy D, Psy S); substance abuse counseling (MS); substance abuse counseling and education (MS). *Accreditation:* APA (one or more programs are accredited). *Program availability:* 100% online, blended/hybrid learning. *Faculty:* 51 full-time (21 women), 120 part-time/adjunct (70 women). *Students:* 751 full-time (618 women), 821 part-time (709 women); includes 787 minority (268 Black or African American, non-Hispanic/Latino; 2 American Indian or Alaska Native, non-Hispanic/Latino; 38 Asian, non-Hispanic/Latino; 431 Hispanic/Latino; 2 Native Hawaiian or other Pacific Islander, non-Hispanic/Latino; 46 Two or more races, non-Hispanic/Latino), 45 international. Average age 31. 1,117 applicants, 38% accepted, 294 enrolled. In 2017, 459 master's, 100 doctorates, 10 other advanced degrees awarded. Terminal master's awarded for partial completion of doctoral program. *Degree requirements:* For master's, comprehensive exam, 3 practica; for doctorate, thesis/dissertation, clinical internship, competency exam; for Psy S, comprehensive exam, internship. *Entrance requirements:* For master's and Psy S, GRE General Test, letters of recommendation, research/personal statement, interview; for doctorate, GRE General Test, GRE Subject Test (recommended), minimum undergraduate GPA of 3.0, letters of recommendation, research/personal statement, interview, curriculum vitae/resume. Additional exam requirements/recommendations for international students: Required—TOEFL (minimum score 550 paper-based). *Application deadline:* Applications are processed on a rolling basis. Application fee: $50. Electronic applications accepted. *Expenses:* Contact institution. *Financial support:* In 2017–18, 197 students received support, including 15 research assistantships (averaging $5,600 per year), 68 teaching assistantships (averaging $2,000 per year); career-related internships or fieldwork, Federal Work-Study, institutionally sponsored loans, scholarships/grants, and unspecified assistantships also available. Support available to part-time students. Financial award application deadline: 4/15; financial award applicants required to submit FAFSA. *Faculty research:* Clinical health psychology, multicultural/diversity psychology, clinical neuropsychology, clinical child psychology, family violence. *Unit head:* Dr. Karen Grosby, Dean, 954-262-5712, Fax: 954-262-3859, E-mail: grosby@nova.edu. *Application contact:* Carlos Perez, Senior Manager of Outreach, 954-262-5702, Fax: 954-262-3893, E-mail: gradschool@nova.edu.
Website: http://psychology.nova.edu/

Pontificia Universidad Catolica Madre y Maestra, Graduate School, Faculty of Social and Administrative Sciences, Santiago, Dominican Republic. Offers business administration (MBA), including business development, finance, international business, management skills (M Mgmt, MBA), marketing, operations, strategic cost management, strategy, tourist destination planning and management; law (LL M), including civil law, corporate business law, criminal law, international relations, real estate law; management (M Mgmt), including higher financial management, insurance program administration, management skills (M Mgmt, MBA); psychology (MA), including clinical child and adolescent psychology, forensic psychology; strategic human resources (EMBA).

Post University, Program in Counseling and Human Services, Waterbury, CT 06723-2540. Offers counseling and human services (MS); counseling and human services/alcohol and drug counseling (MS); counseling and human services/clinical mental health counseling (MS); counseling and human services/forensic mental health counseling (MS); counseling and human services/non-profit management (MS). *Program availability:* Part-time, evening/weekend, online learning. *Entrance requirements:* For master's, resume. *Expenses: Tuition:* Part-time $730 per credit hour. Part-time tuition and fees vary according to degree level and program. *Application contact:* Veronica Montalvo, Vice President, Online Education Enrollment Management and Admissions, 203-596-6164, E-mail: vmontalvo@post.edu.
Website: https://post.edu/academics/online-master-of-science-in-counseling-and-human-services

Prairie View A&M University, College of Juvenile Justice and Psychology, Prairie View, TX 77446. Offers clinical adolescent psychology (PhD); juvenile forensic psychology (MSJFP); juvenile justice (MSJJ, PhD). *Program availability:* Part-time, evening/weekend, online only, 100% online. *Faculty:* 7 full-time (5 women), 3 part-time/adjunct (1 woman). *Students:* 23 full-time (18 women), 30 part-time (25 women); includes 50 minority (41 Black or African American, non-Hispanic/Latino; 8 Hispanic/Latino; 1 Two or more races, non-Hispanic/Latino), 2 international. Average age 31. 39 applicants, 82% accepted, 24 enrolled. In 2017, 19 master's, 3 doctorates awarded. *Degree requirements:* For master's, comprehensive exam; for doctorate, thesis/dissertation. *Entrance requirements:* For master's, GRE, minimum GPA of 2.75; for doctorate, GRE, previous course work in clinical adolescent psychology, minimum GPA of 3.5. Additional exam requirements/recommendations for international students: Required—TOEFL (minimum score 550 paper-based; 79 iBT). *Application deadline:* For fall admission, 5/1 priority date for domestic and international students; for spring admission, 10/1 priority date for domestic students, 9/1 priority date for international students; for summer admission, 3/1 priority date for domestic students, 2/1 priority date for international students. Applications are processed on a rolling basis. Application fee: $50. Electronic applications accepted. *Expenses:* Tuition, state resident: part-time $242 per credit. Tuition, nonresident: part-time $695 per credit. *Required fees:* $149 per credit. *Financial support:* Research assistantships, teaching assistantships, scholarships/grants, and unspecified assistantships available. Financial award application deadline: 4/1; financial award applicants required to submit FAFSA. *Faculty research:* Juvenile justice, community policing, adolescent substance use, reducing mental illness stigma and promoting positive psychological well-being in diverse communities, promoting prosocial behavior among at-risk youth. *Unit head:* Dr. Tamara L. Brown, Dean, 936-261-5206, Fax: 936-261-5253, E-mail: tlbrown@pvamu.edu. *Application contact:* Pauline Walker, Executive Secretary, Graduate Program, 936-261-3521, Fax: 936-261-3529, E-mail: gradadmissions@pvamu.edu.

Roger Williams University, Feinstein School of Social and Natural Sciences, Forensic and Legal Psychology, Bristol, RI 02809. Offers forensic psychology (MA). *Expenses:* Contact institution.

Sage Graduate School, School of Health Sciences, Program in Forensic Mental Health, Troy, NY 12180-4115. Offers MS, Certificate. *Program availability:* Part-time, evening/weekend. *Faculty:* 4 part-time/adjunct (all women). *Students:* 19 full-time (17 women), 25 part-time (22 women); includes 15 minority (7 Black or African American, non-Hispanic/Latino; 5 Hispanic/Latino; 3 Two or more races, non-Hispanic/Latino). Average age 28. 31 applicants, 39% accepted, 8 enrolled. In 2017, 11 master's awarded. *Entrance requirements:* Additional exam requirements/recommendations for international students: Required—TOEFL (minimum score 550 paper-based). *Application deadline:* Applications are processed on a rolling basis. Application fee: $30. Electronic applications accepted. Tuition and fees vary according to degree level and program. *Financial support:* Fellowships, research assistantships, scholarships/grants, and unspecified assistantships available. Financial award applicants required to submit FAFSA. *Unit head:* Dr. Maureen McLeod, Coordinator, Forensic Mental Health, 518-244-2211, E-mail: mcleom@sage.edu. *Application contact:* Wendy D. Diefendorf, Director of Graduate and Adult Admission, 518-244-2443, Fax: 518-244-6880, E-mail: diefew@sage.edu.

Tiffin University, Program in Criminal Justice, Tiffin, OH 44883-2161. Offers criminal justice (MS), including crime analysis, criminal behavior, forensic psychology, homeland security administration, justice administration. *Program availability:* Part-time, evening/weekend, 100% online, blended/hybrid learning. *Degree requirements:* For master's, thesis optional. *Entrance requirements:* For master's, minimum undergraduate GPA of 2.5, work experience. Additional exam requirements/recommendations for international students: Required—TOEFL (minimum score 550 paper-based; 79 iBT). Electronic applications accepted. *Expenses:* Contact institution. *Faculty research:* Terrorism, intelligence, homeland security, guns and crime.

Universidad de Iberoamerica, Graduate School, San Jose, Costa Rica. Offers clinical neuropsychology (PhD); clinical psychology (M Psych); educational psychology (M Psych); forensic psychology (M Psych); hospital management (MHA); intensive care nursing (MN); medicine (MD).

Universidad del Turabo, Graduate Programs, School of Social Sciences and Humanities, Programs in Psychology, Gurabo, PR 00778-3030. Offers counseling psychology (M Psych, Psy D, Certificate); forensic psychology (Certificate); psychology (M Psych). *Entrance requirements:* For master's, GRE, GMAT or EXADEP, interview, essay, official transcript, recommendation letters; for doctorate, GRE, GMAT or EXADEP, interview, essay, official transcript, recommendation letters, curriculum vitae. Electronic applications accepted.

University of Central Oklahoma, The Jackson College of Graduate Studies, College of Education and Professional Studies, Department of Psychology, Edmond, OK 73034-5209. Offers psychology (MA), including counseling psychology, experimental psychology, forensic psychology, general psychology, school psychology. *Faculty:* 13 full-time (7 women), 1 part-time/adjunct (0 women). *Students:* 74 full-time (59 women), 35 part-time (29 women); includes 30 minority (4 Black or African American, non-Hispanic/Latino; 4 American Indian or Alaska Native, non-Hispanic/Latino; 3 Asian, non-Hispanic/Latino; 12 Hispanic/Latino; 7 Two or more races, non-Hispanic/Latino), 5 international. Average age 27. 109 applicants, 71% accepted, 51 enrolled. In 2017, 33 master's awarded. *Degree requirements:* For master's, thesis (for some programs). *Entrance requirements:* For master's, GRE. Additional exam requirements/recommendations for international students: Required—TOEFL (minimum score 550 paper-based; 79 iBT), IELTS (minimum score 6.5). *Application deadline:* For fall admission, 1/15 for domestic and international students; for spring admission, 11/15 for international students. Application fee: $60. Electronic applications accepted. *Expenses:* Tuition, state resident: full-time $5375; part-time $268.75 per credit hour. Tuition, nonresident: full-time $13,295; part-time $664.75 per credit hour. *Required fees:* $626; $31.30 per credit hour. One-time fee: $50. Tuition and fees vary according to program. *Financial support:* In 2017–18, 18 students received support, including 6 research

Forensic Psychology

assistantships with partial tuition reimbursements available (averaging $3,943 per year); teaching assistantships, career-related internships or fieldwork, scholarships/grants, tuition waivers (partial), and unspecified assistantships also available. Financial award application deadline: 3/31; financial award applicants required to submit FAFSA. *Unit head:* Dr. Thomas Hancock, Chair, 405-974-5707, Fax: 405-974-3865. *Application contact:* Carlie Wellington, Assistant Director, CEPS Graduate Enrollment, 405-974-5105, Fax: 405-974-3851, E-mail: gradcoll@uco.edu.
Website: http://sites.uco.edu/ceps/dept/Professional-Studies-Programs/psy/index.asp

University of Denver, Graduate School of Professional Psychology, Denver, CO 80208. Offers clinical psychology (Psy D); forensic psychology (MA); international disaster psychology (MA); sport and performance psychology (MA); sport coaching (MA); strength and conditioning and fitness coaching (Certificate). *Accreditation:* APA. *Faculty:* 23 full-time (13 women), 25 part-time/adjunct (14 women). *Students:* 233 full-time (180 women), 79 part-time (46 women); includes 81 minority (22 Black or African American, non-Hispanic/Latino; 9 Asian, non-Hispanic/Latino; 31 Hispanic/Latino; 1 Native Hawaiian or other Pacific Islander, non-Hispanic/Latino; 18 Two or more races, non-Hispanic/Latino), 7 international. Average age 26. 866 applicants, 30% accepted, 135 enrolled. In 2017, 106 master's, 23 doctorates awarded. *Degree requirements:* For master's, comprehensive exam (for some programs); for doctorate, comprehensive exam (for some programs), paper, clinical internship. *Entrance requirements:* For master's and doctorate, GRE General Test, transcripts, resume, two letters of recommendation, essay. Additional exam requirements/recommendations for international students: Required—TOEFL (minimum score 550 paper-based; 80 iBT). *Application deadline:* For fall admission, 1/5 for domestic and international students. Application fee: $65. Electronic applications accepted. *Expenses:* $47,823 per year full-time. *Financial support:* In 2017–18, 235 students received support, including 2 teaching assistantships with tuition reimbursements available (averaging $1,976 per year); career-related internships or fieldwork, Federal Work-Study, institutionally sponsored loans, scholarships/grants, unspecified assistantships, and clinical assistantships also available. Support available to part-time students. Financial award application deadline: 2/15; financial award applicants required to submit FAFSA. *Unit head:* Dr. Shelly Smith-Acuna, Dean, 303-871-3880, Fax: 303-871-4220, E-mail: shelly.smith-acuna@du.edu. *Application contact:* Admissions Counselor, 303-871-3736, Fax: 303-871-4220, E-mail: gsppinfo@du.edu.
Website: http://www.du.edu/gspp

University of Houston–Victoria, School of Arts and Sciences, Program in Psychology, Victoria, TX 77901-4450. Offers counseling psychology (MA); forensic psychology (MA); school psychology (MA). *Program availability:* Part-time, evening/weekend, online learning. *Degree requirements:* For master's, project or thesis. *Entrance requirements:* For master's, GRE General Test. Additional exam requirements/recommendations for international students: Required—TOEFL (minimum score 550 paper-based). Electronic applications accepted.

University of Louisiana at Monroe, Graduate School, College of Business and Social Sciences, Department of Psychology, Monroe, LA 71209-0001. Offers forensic psychology (MS); general psychology (MS); psychometrics (MS). *Program availability:* Part-time, evening/weekend, online learning. *Faculty:* 6 full-time (2 women). *Students:* 35 full-time (30 women), 19 part-time (14 women); includes 19 minority (12 Black or African American, non-Hispanic/Latino; 1 Asian, non-Hispanic/Latino; 3 Hispanic/Latino; 3 Two or more races, non-Hispanic/Latino), 7 international. Average age 26. 53 applicants, 58% accepted, 18 enrolled. In 2017, 18 master's awarded. *Degree requirements:* For master's, comprehensive exam, thesis optional. *Entrance requirements:* For master's, GRE General Test, minimum GPA of 2.75. Additional exam requirements/recommendations for international students: Required—TOEFL (minimum score 500 paper-based; 61 iBT). *Application deadline:* For fall admission, 7/1 for domestic and international students; for winter admission, 12/14 for domestic students; for spring admission, 12/1 for domestic and international students. Applications are processed on a rolling basis. Application fee: $20 ($30 for international students). Electronic applications accepted. *Expenses:* Tuition, state resident: full-time $6489; part-time $479 per hour. Tuition, nonresident: full-time $12,100; part-time $479 per hour. *Required fees:* $8860; $802 per hour. $3273 per semester. *Financial support:* In 2017–18, 19 students received support. Research assistantships, career-related internships or fieldwork, Federal Work-Study, and unspecified assistantships available. Financial award application deadline: 4/1; financial award applicants required to submit FAFSA. *Unit head:* Dr. Ashworth Burton, Director, 318-342-1439, E-mail: ashworth@ulm.edu. *Application contact:* Dr. Jack Palmer, Graduate Coordinator, 318-342-1345, E-mail: palmer@ulm.edu.
Website: http://www.ulm.edu/psychology

★ **University of New Haven,** Graduate School, College of Arts and Sciences, Program in Community Psychology, West Haven, CT 06516. Offers applications of psychology (Graduate Certificate); community clinical services (MA); community psychology (MA); forensic psychology (MA); program development (MA). *Program availability:* Part-time, evening/weekend. *Students:* 32 full-time (30 women), 5 part-time (all women); includes 12 minority (7 Black or African American, non-Hispanic/Latino; 1 American Indian or Alaska Native, non-Hispanic/Latino; 3 Hispanic/Latino; 1 Two or more races, non-Hispanic/Latino). Average age 25. 31 applicants, 84% accepted, 12 enrolled. In 2017, 26 master's awarded. *Degree requirements:* For master's, thesis or alternative, fieldwork. *Entrance requirements:* Additional exam requirements/recommendations for international students: Required—TOEFL (minimum score 80 iBT), IELTS, PTE. *Application deadline:* Applications are processed on a rolling basis. Application fee: $50. Electronic applications accepted. Application fee is waived when completed online. *Expenses:* Tuition: Full-time $16,020; part-time $890 per credit hour. *Required fees:* $220; $90 per term. *Financial support:* Research assistantships with partial tuition reimbursements, teaching assistantships with partial tuition reimbursements, Federal Work-Study, scholarships/grants, and unspecified assistantships available. Support available to part-time students. Financial award application deadline: 5/1; financial award applicants required to submit FAFSA. *Unit head:* Dr. Michael Morris, Coordinator, 203-932-7289, E-mail: mmorris@newhaven.edu.
Website: http://www.newhaven.edu/4725/

See Display below and Close-Up on page 1205.

University of North Dakota, Graduate School, College of Arts and Sciences, Department of Psychology, Grand Forks, ND 58202. Offers clinical psychology (PhD); forensic psychology (MA, MS). *Accreditation:* APA (one or more programs are accredited). *Degree requirements:* For master's, thesis, final exam; for doctorate, comprehensive exam, thesis/dissertation, internship, final exam. *Entrance requirements:* For master's, GRE General Test, GRE Subject Test, minimum GPA of 3.0; for doctorate, GRE General Test, GRE Subject Test, minimum GPA of 3.5. Additional exam requirements/recommendations for international students: Required—TOEFL (minimum score 550 paper-based; 79 iBT), IELTS (minimum score 6.5). Electronic applications accepted. *Faculty research:* Developmental psychology, clinical social psychology, educational psychology, personality disorders.

Walden University, Graduate Programs, School of Counseling, Minneapolis, MN 55401. Offers addiction counseling (MS), including addictions and public health, child and adolescent counseling, family studies and interventions, forensic counseling, general program, military families and culture, trauma and crisis counseling; clinical mental health counseling (MS), including addiction counseling, forensic counseling, military families and culture, trauma and crisis counseling; counselor education and

supervision (PhD), including consultation, counseling and social change, forensic mental health counseling, leadership and program evaluation, trauma and crisis; marriage, couple, and family counseling (MS), including addiction counseling, career counseling, forensic counseling, military families and culture, trauma and crisis counseling; school counseling (MS), including addiction counseling, career counseling, crisis and trauma, military families and culture. *Accreditation:* ACA. *Program availability:* Part-time, evening/weekend, online only, 100% online. *Degree requirements:* For master's, residency, field experience, professional development plan, licensure plan; for doctorate, thesis/dissertation, residency, practicum, internship. *Entrance requirements:* For master's, bachelor's degree or higher; minimum GPA of 2.5; official transcripts; goal statement (for some programs); access to computer and Internet; for doctorate, master's degree or higher; three years of related professional or academic experience (preferred); minimum GPA of 3.0; goal statement and current resume (for select programs); official transcripts; access to computer and Internet. Additional exam requirements/recommendations for international students: Required—TOEFL (minimum score 550 paper-based, 79 iBT), IELTS (minimum score 6.5), Michigan English Language Assessment Battery (minimum score 82), or PTE (minimum score 53). Electronic applications accepted.

Walden University, Graduate Programs, School of Psychology, Minneapolis, MN 55401. Offers clinical psychology (MS), including counseling, general program; forensic psychology (MS), including forensic psychology in the community, general program, mental health applications, program planning and evaluation in forensic settings, psychology and legal systems; industrial organizational (MS, PhD), including consulting psychology, forensic (MS), forensic psychology (PhD), general practice, leadership development and coaching (MS), organizational diversity and social change, research evaluation (PhD); online teaching in psychology (Post-Master's Certificate); organizational psychology and development (Postbaccalaureate Certificate); psychology (MS, PhD), including applied psychology (MS), clinical psychology (PhD), crisis management and response (MS), educational psychology, forensic psychology (PhD), general psychology (MS), general psychology research (PhD), general psychology teaching (PhD), health psychology, leadership development and coaching (MS), psychology of culture (MS), psychology, public administration, and social change (MS), social psychology, terrorism and security (MS); psychology respecialization (Post-Doctoral Certificate). *Program availability:* Part-time, evening/weekend, online only, 100% online. Terminal master's awarded for partial completion of doctoral program. *Degree requirements:* For master's, thesis optional; for doctorate, thesis/dissertation, residency. *Entrance requirements:* For master's, bachelor's degree or higher; minimum GPA of 2.5; official transcripts; goal statement (for some programs); access to computer and Internet; for doctorate, master's degree or higher; three years of related professional or academic experience (preferred); minimum GPA of 3.0; goal statement and current

resume (for select programs); official transcripts; access to computer and Internet; for other advanced degree, relevant work experience; access to computer and Internet. Additional exam requirements/recommendations for international students: Required—TOEFL (minimum score 550 paper-based, 79 iBT), IELTS (minimum score 6.5), Michigan English Language Assessment Battery (minimum score 82), or PTE (minimum score 53). Electronic applications accepted.

Westfield State University, College of Graduate and Continuing Education, Department of Psychology, Program in Counseling, Westfield, MA 01086. Offers forensic mental health counseling (MA); mental health counseling (MA); school adjustment counseling (MA); school guidance counseling (MA). *Program availability:* Part-time, evening/weekend. *Faculty:* 5 full-time (3 women), 4 part-time/adjunct (1 woman). *Students:* 36 full-time (27 women), 14 part-time (10 women); includes 9 minority (1 Black or African American, non-Hispanic/Latino; 1 Asian, non-Hispanic/Latino; 4 Hispanic/Latino; 3 Two or more races, non-Hispanic/Latino). Average age 28. 29 applicants, 79% accepted, 16 enrolled. In 2017, 10 master's awarded. *Degree requirements:* For master's, comprehensive exam, practicum. *Entrance requirements:* For master's, GRE General Test, MAT, minimum undergraduate GPA of 3.0. Additional exam requirements/recommendations for international students: Recommended—TOEFL (minimum score 550 paper-based; 79 iBT). *Application deadline:* For fall admission, 2/1 for domestic students. Applications are processed on a rolling basis. Application fee: $50. *Expenses:* Tuition, state resident: part-time $332 per credit. Tuition, nonresident: part-time $332 per credit. *Required fees:* $75 per semester. Tuition and fees vary according to program. *Financial support:* Unspecified assistantships available. Financial award application deadline: 4/1; financial award applicants required to submit FAFSA. *Unit head:* Dr. Robert Hayes, Professor, 413-572-5700, Fax: 413-572-5227, E-mail: rhayes@westfield.ma.edu. *Application contact:* Shelly Henrichon, Coordinator of College of Graduate and Continuing Education Admissions, 413-572-8022, Fax: 413-572-5227, E-mail: mhenrichon@westfield.ma.edu.

William James College, Graduate Programs, Newton, MA 02459. Offers applied psychology in higher education student personnel administration (MA); clinical psychology (Psy D); counseling psychology (MA); counseling psychology and community mental health (MA); counseling psychology and global mental health (MA); executive coaching (Graduate Certificate); forensic and counseling psychology (MA); leadership psychology (Psy D); organizational psychology (MA); primary care psychology (MA); respecialization in clinical psychology (Certificate); school psychology (Psy D); MA/CAGS. *Accreditation:* APA. *Degree requirements:* For master's, comprehensive exam (for some programs); for doctorate, thesis/dissertation (for some programs). Electronic applications accepted.

Genetic Counseling

Arcadia University, College of Health Sciences, Department of Genetic Counseling, Glenside, PA 19038-3295. Offers MSGC. *Degree requirements:* For master's, thesis. *Entrance requirements:* For master's, GRE. Additional exam requirements/recommendations for international students: Required—TOEFL or IELTS. *Expenses:* Contact institution.

Augustana University, Augustana-Sanford Genetic Counseling Program, Sioux Falls, SD 57197. Offers MS. Program offered in collaboration with Sanford Health. *Faculty:* 1 full-time (0 women), 9 part-time/adjunct (8 women). *Students:* 16 full-time (14 women); includes 1 minority (Asian, non-Hispanic/Latino). Average age 25. 114 applicants, 7% accepted, 8 enrolled. *Degree requirements:* For master's, thesis, clinical rotation with satisfactory evaluations; ACGC logbook with minimum 50 core-qualifying cases. *Entrance requirements:* For master's, GRE or GMAT. Additional exam requirements/recommendations for international students: Required—TOEFL. *Application deadline:* For fall admission, 2/5 for domestic students. Application fee: $60. Electronic applications accepted. *Expenses:* Contact institution. *Financial support:* Application deadline: 7/1; applicants required to submit FAFSA. *Faculty research:* Obesity, genome sequencing in individuals with Autism Spectrum Disorder, newborn screening, cancer risk assessment, professional development for practicing genetic counselors. *Unit head:* Dr. Quinn Stein, Associate Professor and Chair of the Department of Genetic Counseling, E-mail: quinn.stein@augie.edu. *Application contact:* Julia Paluch, Administrative Assistant, Graduate Education, 605-274-4043, Fax: 605-274-4450, E-mail: julia.paluch@augie.edu.

Baylor College of Medicine, School of Allied Health Sciences, Genetic Counseling Program, Houston, TX 77030-3498. Offers MS.

Bay Path University, Program in Genetic Counseling, Longmeadow, MA 01106-2292. Offers MS. *Program availability:* Evening/weekend, blended/hybrid learning. *Students:* 11 full-time (10 women), 1 (woman) part-time. Average age 31. *Degree requirements:* For master's, 50 credits, 4 clinical rotations (840 hours). *Entrance requirements:* For master's, GRE, successful completion of the following courses (undergraduate or graduate level): biology, molecular and/or cellular biology, chemistry, biochemistry, organic chemistry, genetics, psychology (general), developmental biology, embryology, and statistics. *Application deadline:* For fall admission, 2/1 for domestic students. Applications are processed on a rolling basis. Application fee: $45. Electronic applications accepted. Application fee is waived when completed online. *Expenses:* $1,045 per credit. *Financial support:* Scholarships/grants available. Financial award applicants required to submit FAFSA. *Unit head:* Dr. Liz Fleming, Associate Provost/Dean, 413-565-1332, E-mail: lfleming@baypath.edu. *Application contact:* Diane Ranaldi, Dean of Graduate Admissions, 413-565-1332, Fax: 413-565-1250, E-mail: dranaldi@baypath.edu.
Website: http://www.baypath.edu/academics/graduate-programs/genetic-counseling-ms/

Boston University, School of Medicine, Division of Graduate Medical Sciences, Program in Genetic Counseling, Boston, MA 02215. Offers MS. *Application deadline:* For fall admission, 2/1 for domestic students. *Financial support:* In 2017–18, 15 students received support. Institutionally sponsored loans and unspecified assistantships available. Financial award application deadline: 1/1; financial award applicants required to submit FAFSA. *Unit head:* Kathleen Berentsen Swenson, Program Director, 617-638-5980, E-mail: kbb2010@bu.edu. *Application contact:* GMS Admissions Office, 617-638-5255, E-mail: askgms@bu.edu.
Website: http://www.bumc.bu.edu/gms/m-s-genetic-counseling-program/

Brandeis University, Graduate School of Arts and Sciences, Program in Genetic Counseling, Waltham, MA 02454-9110. Offers MS. *Faculty:* 8 part-time/adjunct (all women). *Students:* 20 full-time (all women); includes 3 minority (2 Asian, non-Hispanic/Latino; 1 Hispanic/Latino), 4 international. Average age 28. 183 applicants, 13% accepted, 10 enrolled. In 2017, 9 master's awarded. *Degree requirements:* For master's, thesis, proseminar, journal club, research project, internship/fieldwork. *Entrance requirements:* For master's, GRE General Test, resume, letters of recommendation, statement of purpose, transcripts, list of prerequisite courses, national matching service registration number. Additional exam requirements/recommendations for international students: Required—PTE (minimum score 68), TOEFL (minimum score 600 paper-based, 100 iBT) or IELTS (7). *Application deadline:* For fall admission, 1/1 for domestic students. Application fee: $75. Electronic applications accepted. *Expenses:* $36,540 tuition, $88 fees. *Financial support:* In 2017–18, 20 students received support. Federal Work-Study, scholarships/grants, and tuition waivers (partial) available. Financial award application deadline: 4/15; financial award applicants required to submit FAFSA. *Faculty research:* Genetics, genetic counseling, DNA sequencing, medical genetics. *Unit head:* Dr. Gretchen Schneider, Co-Director, 781-736-3108, E-mail: gretchen@brandeis.edu. *Application contact:* Missy Goldberg, Department Administrator, 781-736-3179, E-mail: goldberg@brandeis.edu.
Website: http://www.brandeis.edu/gsas/programs/genetic_counseling.html

California State University, Stanislaus, College of Natural Sciences, MS Program in Genetic Counseling, Turlock, CA 95382. Offers MS. *Degree requirements:* For master's, thesis. *Entrance requirements:* For master's, GRE, minimum GPA of 3.0, 3 letters of reference, personal statement. Additional exam requirements/recommendations for international students: Required—TOEFL (minimum score 550 paper-based). Electronic applications accepted. *Expenses:* Contact institution.

Case Western Reserve University, School of Medicine and School of Graduate Studies, Graduate Programs in Medicine, Department of Genetics and Genome Sciences, Cleveland, OH 44106. Offers genetic counseling (MS); genetics and genome sciences (PhD); MD/PhD. Terminal master's awarded for partial completion of doctoral program. *Degree requirements:* For master's, thesis; for doctorate, comprehensive exam, thesis/dissertation. *Entrance requirements:* For master's, GRE General Test; for doctorate, GRE General Test, GRE Subject Test. Additional exam requirements/recommendations for international students: Required—TOEFL. *Expenses: Tuition:* Full-time $43,854; part-time $1827 per credit hour. *Required fees:* $50; $50 per credit hour. Tuition and fees vary according to course load and program. *Faculty research:* Eukaryotic genetics, regulation of gene expression, chromosome structure and function.

Emory University, School of Medicine, Programs in Allied Health Professions, Genetic Counseling Training Program, Atlanta, GA 30322. Offers MM Sc. *Degree requirements:* For master's, thesis, capstone project. *Entrance requirements:* For master's, GRE General Test, minimum GPA of 3.0; prerequisites: genetics, statistics, psychology, and biochemistry. Additional exam requirements/recommendations for international students: Required—TOEFL. *Faculty research:* Cancer genetics, lysosomal storage disease, carrier screening, public health genomics, genetic counseling, psychology, molecular genetics.

Icahn School of Medicine at Mount Sinai, Graduate School of Biomedical Sciences, New York, NY 10029-6504. Offers biomedical sciences (MS, PhD); clinical research education (MS, PhD); community medicine (MPH); genetic counseling (MS); neurosciences (PhD); MD/PhD. Terminal master's awarded for partial completion of doctoral program. *Degree requirements:* For master's, thesis; for doctorate, comprehensive exam, thesis/dissertation. *Entrance requirements:* For master's, GRE General Test; for doctorate, GRE General Test, GRE Subject Test, 3 years of college pre-med course work. Additional exam requirements/recommendations for international students: Required—TOEFL. Electronic applications accepted. *Faculty research:* Cancer, genetics and genomics, immunology, neuroscience, developmental and stem cell biology, translational research.

Genetic Counseling

Johns Hopkins University, Bloomberg School of Public Health, Department of Health, Behavior and Society, Baltimore, MD 21218. Offers genetic counseling (Sc M); health education and health communication (MSPH); social and behavioral sciences (PhD); social factors in health (MHS). *Students:* 86 full-time (76 women), 5 part-time (4 women); includes 33 minority (8 Black or African American, non-Hispanic/Latino; 13 Asian, non-Hispanic/Latino; 7 Hispanic/Latino; 5 Two or more races, non-Hispanic/Latino), 13 international. Average age 28. 312 applicants, 29% accepted, 28 enrolled. In 2017, 27 master's, 10 doctorates awarded. *Degree requirements:* For master's, comprehensive exam (for some programs), thesis (for some programs); for doctorate, comprehensive exam, thesis/dissertation. *Entrance requirements:* For master's, GRE, curriculum vitae, 3 letters of recommendation; for doctorate, GRE, transcripts, curriculum vitae, 3 recommendation letters. Additional exam requirements/recommendations for international students: Required—TOEFL (minimum score 100 iBT), IELTS (minimum score 7). *Application deadline:* Applications are processed on a rolling basis. Application fee: $135. Electronic applications accepted. *Financial support:* Fellowships with tuition reimbursements, research assistantships, teaching assistantships, career-related internships or fieldwork, Federal Work-Study, scholarships/grants, traineeships, health care benefits, unspecified assistantships, and stipends available. *Faculty research:* Social determinants of health and structural and community-level inventions to improve health, communication and health education, behavioral and social aspects of genetic counseling. *Unit head:* Margaret Ensminger, Interim Chair, 410-502-4076, Fax: 410-502-4080. *Application contact:* Shenay Johnson, Academic Program Administrator, 410-502-4415, E-mail: shejohns@jhu.edu.
Website: http://jhsph.edu/dept/hbs

Long Island University–LIU Post, College of Liberal Arts and Sciences, Brookville, NY 11548-1300. Offers applied mathematics (MS); behavior analysis (MA); biology (MS); criminal justice (MS); earth science (MS); English (MA); environmental sustainability (MS); genetic counseling (MS); history (MA); interdisciplinary studies (MA, MS); political science (MA); psychology (MA). *Program availability:* Part-time, evening/weekend, blended/hybrid learning. *Faculty:* 41 full-time (21 women), 24 part-time/adjunct (13 women). *Students:* 173 full-time (124 women), 62 part-time (35 women); includes 54 minority (11 Black or African American, non-Hispanic/Latino; 13 Asian, non-Hispanic/Latino; 23 Hispanic/Latino; 7 Two or more races, non-Hispanic/Latino), 12 international. Average age 28. 368 applicants, 54% accepted, 74 enrolled. In 2017, 89 master's, 15 other advanced degrees awarded. Terminal master's awarded for partial completion of doctoral program. *Degree requirements:* For master's, comprehensive exam (for some programs), thesis (for some programs). *Entrance requirements:* Additional exam requirements/recommendations for international students: Required—TOEFL, IELTS, or PTE. *Application deadline:* Applications are processed on a rolling basis. Application fee: $50. Electronic applications accepted. *Expenses: Tuition:* Full-time $21,618; part-time $1201 per credit. *Required fees:* $1840; $920 per term. Tuition and fees vary according to course load. *Financial support:* In 2017–18, 165 students received support. Fellowships, research assistantships, teaching assistantships, career-related internships or fieldwork, Federal Work-Study, scholarships/grants, tuition waivers (partial), and unspecified assistantships available. Support available to part-time students. Financial award application deadline: 2/15; financial award applicants required to submit FAFSA. *Faculty research:* Biology, environmental sustainability, mathematics, psychology, genetic counseling. *Unit head:* Dr. Nathaniel Bowditch, Dean, 516-299-2234, Fax: 516-299-4140, E-mail: nathaniel.bowditch@liu.edu. *Application contact:* Rita Langdon, Graduate Admissions, 516-299-2900, Fax: 516-299-2137, E-mail: post-enroll@liu.edu.
Website: http://liu.edu/CWPost/Academics/Schools/CLAS

McGill University, Faculty of Graduate and Postdoctoral Studies, Faculty of Medicine, Department of Human Genetics, Montréal, QC H3A 2T5, Canada. Offers genetic counseling (M Sc); human genetics (M Sc, PhD).

Northwestern University, The Graduate School, Program in Genetic Counseling, Evanston, IL 60208. Offers MS. *Degree requirements:* For master's, thesis. *Entrance requirements:* For master's, GRE General Test, interview. Additional exam requirements/recommendations for international students: Required—TOEFL. *Faculty research:* Preimplantation genetic diagnosis, gene expression in preimplantation embryos, fetal cells in maternal blood: first trimester prenatal screening for Down's Syndrome, genetic counseling efficacy and counseling issues in prenatal diagnosis.

Sarah Lawrence College, Graduate Studies, Joan H. Marks Graduate Program in Human Genetics, Bronxville, NY 10708-5999. Offers MS. *Program availability:* Part-time. *Degree requirements:* For master's, thesis, fieldwork. *Entrance requirements:* For master's, previous course work in biology, chemistry, developmental biology, genetics, probability and statistics. Additional exam requirements/recommendations for international students: Required—TOEFL (minimum score 600 paper-based). Electronic applications accepted. *Expenses:* Contact institution.

Thomas Jefferson University, Jefferson College of Biomedical Sciences, MS Program in Human Genetics and Genetic Counseling, Philadelphia, PA 19107. Offers MS. *Faculty:* 1 (woman) full-time, 6 part-time/adjunct (all women). *Students:* 6 full-time (all women); includes 1 minority (Hispanic/Latino). 36 applicants, 17% accepted, 6 enrolled. *Entrance requirements:* For master's, BA, personal statement, official transcripts, recommendation letters. Additional exam requirements/recommendations for international students: Required—TOEFL, IELTS (minimum score 7). *Application deadline:* For fall admission, 3/15 for domestic students. Applications are processed on a rolling basis. Application fee: $50. Electronic applications accepted. *Financial support:* Federal Work-Study and institutionally sponsored loans available. Support available to part-time students. Financial award application deadline: 5/1; financial award applicants required to submit FAFSA. *Unit head:* Dr. Rachael Brandt, Program Director, E-mail: rachael.brandt@jefferson.edu. *Application contact:* Marc E. Stearns, Senior Associate Director of Admissions, 215-503-0155, Fax: 215-503-3433, E-mail: jgsbs-info@jefferson.edu.

Université de Montréal, Faculty of Medicine, Program in Genetic Counseling, Montréal, QC H3C 3J7, Canada. Offers DESS.

The University of Alabama at Birmingham, School of Health Professions, Program in Genetic Counseling, Birmingham, AL 35294. Offers MS. *Entrance requirements:* For master's, GRE, minimum undergraduate GPA of 3.0, letters of recommendation, paid or volunteer experience, personal statement. Additional exam requirements/recommendations for international students: Required—TOEFL, TWE. Electronic applications accepted.

University of Arkansas for Medical Sciences, College of Health Professions, Little Rock, AR 72205-7199. Offers audiology (Au D); communication sciences and disorders (MS, PhD); genetic counseling (MS); nuclear medicine advanced associate (MIS); physician assistant studies (MPAS); radiologist assistant (MIS). PhD offered through consortium with University of Arkansas at Little Rock and University of Central Arkansas. *Program availability:* Part-time, online learning. *Degree requirements:* For master's, thesis (for some programs); for doctorate, comprehensive exam (for some programs), thesis/dissertation (for some programs). *Entrance requirements:* For master's, GRE. Additional exam requirements/recommendations for international students: Required—TOEFL (minimum score 550 paper-based; 79 iBT). Electronic

applications accepted. *Expenses:* Contact institution. *Faculty research:* Auditory-based intervention, soy diet, nutrition and cancer.

The University of British Columbia, Faculty of Medicine, Department of Medical Genetics, M Sc Program in Genetic Counselling, Vancouver, BC V6H 3N1, Canada. Offers M Sc. Electronic applications accepted. *Expenses:* Contact institution.

University of California, Irvine, School of Medicine, Program in Genetic Counseling, Irvine, CA 92697. Offers MS. *Students:* 15 full-time (14 women); includes 3 minority (all Hispanic/Latino), 1 international. Average age 27. 155 applicants, 12% accepted, 8 enrolled. In 2017, 7 master's awarded. *Entrance requirements:* For master's, GRE General Test, minimum GPA of 3.0. Additional exam requirements/recommendations for international students: Required—TOEFL (minimum score 550 paper-based). *Application deadline:* For fall admission, 1/15 priority date for domestic students, 1/15 for international students. Applications are processed on a rolling basis. Application fee: $105 ($125 for international students). Electronic applications accepted. *Financial support:* In 2017–18, 3 students received support. Research assistantships with full tuition reimbursements available, teaching assistantships, career-related internships or fieldwork, institutionally sponsored loans, traineeships, health care benefits, and unspecified assistantships available. Financial award application deadline: 3/1; financial award applicants required to submit FAFSA. *Faculty research:* Gene mapping and linkage analysis, delineation of new malformation and chromosomal syndromes, ethical and counseling issues in genetics. *Unit head:* Pamela Flodman, Director, 714-456-8470, E-mail: pflodman@uci.edu.
Website: http://www.pediatrics.uci.edu/masters-genetic-counseling.asp

University of Cincinnati, Graduate School, College of Allied Health Sciences, Program in Genetic Counseling, Cincinnati, OH 45221. Offers medical genetics (MS). *Program availability:* Part-time. *Degree requirements:* For master's, thesis. *Entrance requirements:* For master's, GRE General Test. Additional exam requirements/recommendations for international students: Required—TOEFL. Electronic applications accepted. *Expenses: Tuition, area resident:* Full-time $14,468. Tuition, state resident: full-time $14,968; part-time $754 per credit hour. Tuition, nonresident: full-time $24,210; part-time $1311 per credit hour. *International tuition:* $26,460 full-time. *Required fees:* $3958; $84 per credit hour. One-time fee: $85 full-time. Tuition and fees vary according to course load, degree level and program. *Faculty research:* Lysosomal disease, Tourette's syndrome, epidemiology of Down syndrome, genetic counseling, genetic disease treatment.

University of Colorado Denver, School of Medicine, Graduate Program in Genetic Counseling, Aurora, CO 80045. Offers biophysics and genetics (MS, PhD). *Degree requirements:* For master's, 44 core semester hours, project or thesis; for doctorate, comprehensive exam, thesis/dissertation, 30 hours each of didactic course work and research credits. *Entrance requirements:* For master's, GRE, minimum undergraduate GPA of 3.0; 4 letters of recommendation; prerequisite coursework in biology, general chemistry, general biochemistry, general genetics, general psychology; experience in counseling and laboratory settings and strong understanding of genetic counseling field (highly recommended); for doctorate, GRE, three letters of recommendation, laboratory research experience and solid undergraduate foundation in mathematics and biological sciences. Additional exam requirements/recommendations for international students: Required—TOEFL (minimum score 570 paper-based; 89 iBT). Electronic applications accepted. *Expenses:* Contact institution. *Faculty research:* Psychosocial aspects of genetic counseling, clinical cytogenetics and molecular genetics, human inborn errors of metabolism, congenital malformations and disorders of the newborn, cancer genetics and genetic counseling.

University of Manitoba, Max Rady College of Medicine and Faculty of Graduate Studies, Graduate Programs in Medicine, Department of Biochemistry and Medical Genetics, Winnipeg, MB R3T 2N2, Canada. Offers biochemistry and medical genetics (M Sc, PhD); genetic counseling (M Sc). Terminal master's awarded for partial completion of doctoral program. *Degree requirements:* For master's, thesis; for doctorate, thesis/dissertation. *Faculty research:* Cancer, gene expression, membrane lipids, metabolic control, genetic diseases.

University of Maryland, Baltimore, School of Medicine, Genetic Counseling Training Program, Baltimore, MD 21201. Offers MGC. *Students:* 16 full-time (15 women); includes 5 minority (1 Asian, non-Hispanic/Latino; 4 Hispanic/Latino). Average age 24. 148 applicants, 5% accepted, 8 enrolled. In 2017, 8 master's awarded. *Expenses:* Contact institution. *Unit head:* Shannan DeLany Dixon, Director, 410-706-4713, Fax: 410-706-1644, E-mail: sdelany@som.umaryland.edu.

University of Michigan, Rackham Graduate School, Program in Biomedical Sciences (PIBS), Department of Human Genetics, Ann Arbor, MI 48109. Offers genetic counseling (MS); human genetics (MS, PhD). *Faculty:* 39 full-time (16 women). *Students:* 44 full-time (34 women); includes 5 minority (2 Asian, non-Hispanic/Latino; 1 Hispanic/Latino; 2 Two or more races, non-Hispanic/Latino), 5 international. Average age 29. 257 applicants, 15% accepted, 16 enrolled. In 2017, 12 master's, 3 doctorates awarded. Terminal master's awarded for partial completion of doctoral program. *Degree requirements:* For master's, thesis optional, research project (for MS in genetic counseling); for doctorate, thesis/dissertation, oral preliminary exam, oral defense of dissertation. *Entrance requirements:* For master's, GRE General Test, bachelor's degree; 3 letters of recommendation; advocacy experience (for the MS in genetic counseling); for doctorate, bachelor's degree; 3 letters of recommendation. Additional exam requirements/recommendations for international students: Required—TOEFL (minimum score 84 iBT). Application fee: $75 ($90 for international students). Electronic applications accepted. *Expenses:* $22,742 resident full-time; $45,576 non-resident full-time. *Financial support:* In 2017–18, 42 students received support, including 33 fellowships with tuition reimbursements available, 7 research assistantships with full tuition reimbursements available (averaging $30,600 per year), 7 teaching assistantships with full tuition reimbursements available (averaging $30,600 per year); Federal Work-Study, scholarships/grants, traineeships, and health care benefits also available. Financial award application deadline: 4/30; financial award applicants required to submit CSS PROFILE or FAFSA. *Faculty research:* Molecular and developmental genetics, genetics of Mendelian and complex human disease, genome biology, statistical and population genetics, epigenetics. *Total annual research expenditures:* $5.6 million. *Unit head:* Jeffery R. Holden, Chief Department Administrator, 734-764-6361, Fax: 734-763-3784, E-mail: jholden@umich.edu. *Application contact:* Molly G. Martin, Student Services Coordinator, 734-764-5490, Fax: 734-763-3784, E-mail: mollymu@umich.edu.
Website: http://www.hg.med.umich.edu/

University of Minnesota, Twin Cities Campus, Graduate School, Program in Molecular, Cellular, Developmental Biology and Genetics, Minneapolis, MN 55455-0213. Offers genetic counseling (MS); molecular, cellular, developmental biology and genetics (PhD). Terminal master's awarded for partial completion of doctoral program. *Degree requirements:* For master's, thesis optional; for doctorate, thesis/dissertation. *Entrance requirements:* For master's and doctorate, GRE General Test. Additional exam requirements/recommendations for international students: Required—TOEFL (minimum score 625 paper-based; 80 iBT). Electronic applications accepted. *Faculty research:*

Membrane receptors and membrane transport, cell interactions, cytoskeleton and cell mobility, regulation of gene expression, plant cell and molecular biology.

The University of North Carolina at Greensboro, Graduate School, School of Health and Human Sciences, Program in Genetic Counseling, Greensboro, NC 27412-5001. Offers MS. Electronic applications accepted.

University of Oklahoma Health Sciences Center, College of Medicine and Graduate College, Department of Genetic Counseling, Oklahoma City, OK 73190. Offers MS. *Entrance requirements:* For master's, GRE General Test, 3 letters of recommendation.

University of Pittsburgh, Graduate School of Public Health, Department of Human Genetics, Pittsburgh, PA 15261. Offers genetic counseling (MS); human genetics (MS, PhD); public health genetics (MPH, Certificate); MD/PhD; MS/MPH. *Program availability:* Part-time. *Faculty:* 19. *Students:* 59 full-time (48 women), 13 part-time (all women); includes 8 minority (2 Black or African American, non-Hispanic/Latino; 1 Asian, non-Hispanic/Latino; 2 Hispanic/Latino; 1 Native Hawaiian or other Pacific Islander, non-Hispanic/Latino; 2 Two or more races, non-Hispanic/Latino), 16 international. Average age 27. 226 applicants, 35% accepted, 27 enrolled. *Degree requirements:* For master's, thesis, final paper; comprehensive exam and thesis defense (for MS); for doctorate, comprehensive exam, thesis/dissertation, qualifying examination. *Entrance requirements:* For master's and doctorate, GRE General Test (above the 70th percentile for the verbal and quantitative tests), previous course work in biochemistry and behavioral or social sciences (recommended); bachelor's degree in a discipline related to the biological or behavioral sciences from accredited college or university with minimum GPA of 3.0, introductory courses in genetics and calculus. Additional exam requirements/recommendations for international students: Required—TOEFL (minimum score 550 paper-based, 80 iBT) or IELTS (minimum score 6.5); GRE. *Application deadline:* For fall admission, 4/15 priority date for domestic students, 3/15 priority date for international students; for spring admission, 10/15 priority date for domestic students, 8/1 priority date for international students. Applications are processed on a rolling basis. Application fee: $135. Electronic applications accepted. *Expenses:* $13,068 full-time in-state tuition per term, $21,696 out-of-state. *Financial support:* Fellowships, research assistantships, teaching assistantships, career-related internships or fieldwork, institutionally sponsored loans, scholarships/grants, traineeships, health care benefits, tuition waivers, and unspecified assistantships available. Support available to part-time students. Financial award applicants required to submit CSS PROFILE or FAFSA. *Faculty research:* Search for Alzheimer's disease gene, genetics, factors of oral health, cellular Samoan variant, connections of brain imaging and dementia. *Total annual research expenditures:* $3.9 million. *Unit head:* Dr. Eleanor Feingold, Acting Chair, 412-648-3353, Fax: 412-624-3020. *Application contact:* Jennifer Heinemann, Department Administrator, 412-624-1560, Fax: 412-624-3020, E-mail: jdh150@pitt.edu. Website: http://www.publichealth.pitt.edu/hugen

University of South Carolina, School of Medicine and The Graduate School, Graduate Programs in Medicine, Program in Genetic Counseling, Columbia, SC 29203. Offers MS. *Degree requirements:* For master's, comprehensive exam, internship, practicum. *Entrance requirements:* For master's, GRE General Test. Electronic applications accepted. *Expenses:* Contact institution. *Faculty research:* Genetic counseling, international, transition, prenatal diagnosis.

The University of Texas Health Science Center at Houston, MD Anderson UTHealth Graduate School, Houston, TX 77225-0036. Offers biochemistry and cell biology (PhD); biomedical sciences (MS); cancer biology (PhD); genetic counseling (MS); genetics and epigenetics (PhD); immunology (PhD); medical physics (MS, PhD); microbiology and infectious diseases (PhD); neuroscience (PhD); quantitative sciences (PhD); therapeutics and pharmacology (PhD); MD/PhD. Terminal master's awarded for partial completion of doctoral program. *Degree requirements:* For master's, thesis; for doctorate, thesis/dissertation. *Entrance requirements:* For master's and doctorate, GRE General Test. Additional exam requirements/recommendations for international

students: Required—TOEFL. Electronic applications accepted. *Faculty research:* Biomedical sciences.

University of Toronto, Faculty of Medicine, Department of Molecular Genetics, Toronto, ON M5S 1A1, Canada. Offers genetic counseling (M Sc); molecular genetics (M Sc, PhD). *Degree requirements:* For master's, thesis; for doctorate, thesis/dissertation. *Entrance requirements:* For master's, B Sc or equivalent; for doctorate, M Sc or equivalent, minimum B+ average. Additional exam requirements/recommendations for international students: Required—TOEFL, IELTS (minimum score 7), Michigan English Language Assessment Battery (minimum score 85), or COPE (minimum score 4). Electronic applications accepted. *Faculty research:* Structural biology, developmental genetics, molecular medicine, genetic counseling.

University of Wisconsin–Madison, Graduate School, College of Agricultural and Life Sciences and Graduate Programs in Medicine, Department of Genetics, Madison, WI 53706-1380. Offers genetic counseling (MS); genetics (PhD). *Degree requirements:* For doctorate, thesis/dissertation.

University of Wisconsin–Madison, School of Medicine and Public Health, Master of Genetic Counselor Studies Program, Madison, WI 53706. Offers MGCS. *Unit head:* Catherine Ann Reiser, Associate Professor, 608-262-9722, E-mail: reiser@pediatrics.wisc.edu. *Application contact:* April Meiller, Graduate Coordinator, 608-262-9674, E-mail: ameiller@wisc.edu. Website: http://www.med.wisc.edu/education/graduate-programs/genetic-counseling/main/26910

Wayne State University, School of Medicine, Office of Biomedical Graduate Programs, Detroit, MI 48202. Offers anatomy and cell biology (MS, PhD); basic medical sciences (MS); biochemistry and molecular biology (MS, PhD); cancer biology (MS, PhD); clinical and translational science (Graduate Certificate); family medicine and public health sciences (MPH, Graduate Certificate), including public health practice; genetic counseling (MS); immunology and microbiology (MS, PhD); medical physics (MS, PhD, Graduate Certificate); medical research (MS); molecular medicine and genomics (MS, PhD), including molecular genetics and genomics; pathology (PhD); pharmacology (MS, PhD); physiology (MS, PhD), including physiology, reproductive sciences (PhD); psychiatry and behavioral neurosciences (PhD), including translational neuroscience; MD/MPH; MD/PhD; MPH/MA; MSW/MPH. *Program availability:* Part-time, evening/weekend. *Students:* 268 full-time (152 women), 117 part-time (59 women); includes 108 minority (19 Black or African American, non-Hispanic/Latino; 1 American Indian or Alaska Native, non-Hispanic/Latino; 62 Asian, non-Hispanic/Latino; 9 Hispanic/Latino; 17 Two or more races, non-Hispanic/Latino), 48 international. Average age 26. 1,133 applicants, 21% accepted, 151 enrolled. In 2017, 70 master's, 25 doctorates, 10 other advanced degrees awarded. Terminal master's awarded for partial completion of doctoral program. *Degree requirements:* For master's, thesis (for some programs); for doctorate, thesis/dissertation. *Entrance requirements:* For master's, doctorate, and Graduate Certificate, GRE. Additional exam requirements/recommendations for international students: Required—TOEFL (minimum score 550 paper-based; 100 iBT), Michigan English Language Assessment Battery (minimum score 85); Recommended—IELTS (minimum score 6.5), TWE (minimum score 5.5). *Application deadline:* For fall admission, 2/1 for domestic and international students. Applications are processed on a rolling basis. Application fee: $50. Electronic applications accepted. *Expenses:* Contact institution. *Financial support:* In 2017–18, 177 students received support, including 64 fellowships with full tuition reimbursements available (averaging $24,388 per year), 79 research assistantships with full tuition reimbursements available (averaging $26,894 per year); scholarships/grants, traineeships, and health care benefits also available. *Faculty research:* Cancer biology, neurosciences, vision sciences, molecular biology, pathology, physiology, pharmacology, public health, medical physics. *Unit head:* Dr. Daniel A. Walz, Associate Dean for Biomedical Graduate Programs, 313-577-1455, Fax: 313-577-8796, E-mail: gradprogs@med.wayne.edu. Website: https://www.med.wayne.edu/biomedical-graduate-programs/

Health Psychology

Adler University, Graduate Programs, MA in Counseling Program: Specialization in Sport and Health Psychology, Chicago, IL 60602. Offers MAC. *Degree requirements:* For master's, thesis optional, practicum, internship, externship. *Entrance requirements:* For master's, baccalaureate degree, minimum GPA of 3.0 (recommended), interview, official transcripts, two letters of recommendation.

Alliant International University–Los Angeles, California School of Professional Psychology, Psy D Program in Clinical Psychology, Alhambra, CA 91803. Offers clinical health psychology (Psy D); family/child and couple clinical psychology (Psy D); multi-interest option (Psy D); multicultural community-clinical psychology (Psy D). *Accreditation:* APA. *Degree requirements:* For doctorate, comprehensive exam, thesis/dissertation. *Entrance requirements:* For doctorate, interview, minimum GPA of 3.0 in both psychology and overall. Additional exam requirements/recommendations for international students: Required—TOEFL (minimum score 600 paper-based), TWE. Electronic applications accepted. *Faculty research:* Child and family psychology, multicultural and community psychology, acculturation, lesbian and gay issues, women's health.

Appalachian State University, Cratis D. Williams Graduate School, Department of Psychology, Boone, NC 28608. Offers clinical health psychology (MA). *Program availability:* Part-time. *Degree requirements:* For master's, comprehensive exam, thesis optional, exit exam. *Entrance requirements:* For master's, GRE General Test, 3 letters of recommendation. Additional exam requirements/recommendations for international students: Required—TOEFL (minimum score 550 paper-based; 79 iBT) or IELTS (minimum score 6.5). Electronic applications accepted. *Faculty research:* Eating disorders, school-based consultations, organizational behavior management, brain mechanisms of sound localization, parenting styles.

Argosy University, Atlanta, Georgia School of Professional Psychology, Atlanta, GA 30328. Offers clinical psychology (MA, Psy D, Postdoctoral Respecialization Certificate), including child and family psychology (Psy D), general adult clinical (Psy D), health psychology (Psy D), neuropsychology/geropsychology (Psy D); community counseling (MA), including marriage and family therapy; counselor education and supervision (Ed D); forensic psychology (MA); industrial organizational psychology (MA); marriage and family therapy (Certificate); sport-exercise psychology (MA). *Accreditation:* APA.

Argosy University, Chicago, Illinois School of Professional Psychology, Doctoral Program in Clinical Psychology, Chicago, IL 60601. Offers child and adolescent psychology (Psy D); client-centered and experiential psychotherapies (Psy D); diversity and multicultural psychology (Psy D); family psychology (Psy D); forensic psychology

(Psy D); health psychology (Psy D); neuropsychology (Psy D); organizational consulting (Psy D); psychoanalytic psychology (Psy D); psychology and spirituality (Psy D). *Accreditation:* APA.

Argosy University, Northern Virginia, American School of Professional Psychology, Arlington, VA 22209. Offers clinical psychology (MA, Psy D), including child and family psychology (Psy D), diversity and multicultural psychology (Psy D), forensic psychology (Psy D), health and neuropsychology (Psy D); community counseling (MA); counseling psychology (Ed D), including counselor education and supervision; counselor education and supervision (Ed D); forensic psychology (MA).

Argosy University, Twin Cities, Minnesota School of Professional Psychology, Eagan, MN 55121. Offers clinical psychology (MA, Psy D), including child and family psychology (Psy D), forensic psychology (Psy D), health and neuropsychology (Psy D), trauma (Psy D); forensic counseling (Post-Graduate Certificate); forensic psychology (MA); industrial organizational psychology (MA); marriage and family therapy (MA, DMFT), including forensic counseling (MA). *Accreditation:* AAMFT; AAMFT/COAMFTE; APA.

Bastyr University, School of Natural Health Arts and Sciences, Kenmore, WA 98028-4966. Offers counseling psychology (MA); maternal-child health systems (MA); midwifery (MS); nutrition (Certificate); nutrition and clinical health psychology (MS); nutrition and wellness (MS). *Accreditation:* AND. *Program availability:* Part-time. *Degree requirements:* For master's, thesis optional. *Entrance requirements:* For master's, 1-2 years' basic sciences course work (depending on program). Additional exam requirements/recommendations for international students: Required—TOEFL (minimum score 550 paper-based; 79 iBT). *Application deadline:* For fall admission, 3/15 priority date for domestic and international students. Applications are processed on a rolling basis. Application fee: $75. *Expenses: Tuition:* Part-time $714 per credit hour. *Required fees:* $75. *Financial support:* Career-related internships or fieldwork, Federal Work-Study, and scholarships/grants available. Support available to part-time students. Financial award application deadline: 4/15; financial award applicants required to submit FAFSA. *Faculty research:* Whole-food nutrition for type 2 diabetes; meditation in end-of-life care; stress management; Qi Gong, Tai Chi and yoga for older adults; Echinacea and immunology. *Unit head:* Dr. Lynelle Golden, Dean, 425-602-3110, Fax: 425-823-6222, E-mail: lgolden@bastyr.edu. *Application contact:* Admissions Office, 425-602-3330, Fax: 425-602-3090, E-mail: admissions@bastyr.edu. Website: http://www.bastyr.edu/academics/schools-departments/school-natural-health-arts-sciences

Health Psychology

California Institute of Integral Studies, School of Professional Psychology and Health, San Francisco, CA 94103. Offers clinical psychology (Psy D); community mental health (MA); drama therapy (MA); expressive arts therapy (MA); integral counseling psychology (MA); integrative health studies (MA); psychological studies (MA); somatic psychology (MA). *Program availability:* Part-time, evening/weekend, 100% online, blended/hybrid learning. *Students:* 507 full-time (401 women), 96 part-time (77 women); includes 167 minority (29 Black or African American, non-Hispanic/Latino; 3 American Indian or Alaska Native, non-Hispanic/Latino; 32 Asian, non-Hispanic/Latino; 62 Hispanic/Latino; 2 Native Hawaiian or other Pacific Islander, non-Hispanic/Latino; 39 Two or more races, non-Hispanic/Latino; 60 international. Average age 34. 302 applicants, 89% accepted, 171 enrolled. In 2017, 194 master's, 18 doctorates awarded. *Degree requirements:* For doctorate, comprehensive exam, thesis/dissertation. *Entrance requirements:* For master's, minimum GPA of 3.0, letters of recommendation, writing sample; for doctorate, GRE, MA in psychology or social work with appropriate practical experience for advanced standing, or BA with a minimum GPA of 3.1; letters of recommendation; writing sample. Additional exam requirements/recommendations for international students: Required—TOEFL. *Application deadline:* For fall admission, 2/1 priority date for domestic and international students; for spring admission, 10/15 priority date for domestic and international students. Applications are processed on a rolling basis. Application fee: $65. Electronic applications accepted. *Expenses:* $21,400 (for MA); $32,734 (for PsyD). *Financial support:* Research assistantships with tuition reimbursements, teaching assistantships with tuition reimbursements, career-related internships or fieldwork, Federal Work-Study, and scholarships/grants available. Support available to part-time students. Financial award application deadline: 4/15; financial award applicants required to submit FAFSA. *Faculty research:* Transpersonal psychology, somatic psychology, expressive arts therapy, drama therapy, community mental health, ecopsychology, integrative health, human sexuality. *Unit head:* Nicolle Zapien, Academic Dean, 415-575-5577, E-mail: nzapien@ciis.edu. *Application contact:* Ellen Durst, Director of Admissions, 415-575-6100, Fax: 415-575-1268, E-mail: admissions@ciis.edu.

California State University, Dominguez Hills, College of Natural and Behavioral Sciences, Department of Psychology, Carson, CA 90747-0001. Offers clinical psychology (MA); health psychology (MA). *Program availability:* Part-time, evening/weekend. Terminal master's awarded for partial completion of doctoral program. *Degree requirements:* For master's, comprehensive exam, thesis optional. *Entrance requirements:* For master's, GRE General Test or MAT, interview, minimum GPA of 3.0, prerequisite psychology courses. Additional exam requirements/recommendations for international students: Required—TOEFL (minimum score 550 paper-based). Electronic applications accepted. *Faculty research:* Culture and health, neuropsychology and HIV, psychohistory of the Holocaust, community and adolescents, malingering.

Central Michigan University, College of Graduate Studies, College of Humanities and Social and Behavioral Sciences, Department of Psychology, Program in Industrial and Organizational Psychology, Mount Pleasant, MI 48859. Offers industrial and organizational psychology (MA, PhD); occupational health psychology (PhD). *Degree requirements:* For master's, thesis; for doctorate, comprehensive exam, thesis/dissertation. *Entrance requirements:* For master's and doctorate, GRE. Electronic applications accepted. *Faculty research:* Job stress, retirement, leadership, and careers; personality in the workplace, personnel selection, and structural equation modeling in industrial/organizational psychology; personnel psychology, evolutionary psychology, and influences on HRM utilization; occupational health psychology and job stress; work attitudes, psychological ownership in work, and performance appraisal.

Chatham University, Program in Counseling Psychology, Pittsburgh, PA 15232-2826. Offers child, adolescent and family (MSCP); counseling psychology (Psy D); health and holistic (MSCP); organization and supervision (MSCP); sport and exercise (MSCP). *Accreditation:* APA. *Program availability:* Part-time, evening/weekend. *Faculty:* 11 full-time (10 women). *Students:* 61 full-time (46 women), 25 part-time (22 women); includes 12 minority (9 Black or African American, non-Hispanic/Latino; 2 Hispanic/Latino; 1 Two or more races, non-Hispanic/Latino), 3 international. Average age 30. 124 applicants, 62% accepted, 45 enrolled. In 2017, 38 master's awarded. *Degree requirements:* For master's, thesis optional, supervised internship; for doctorate, thesis/dissertation, internship. *Entrance requirements:* For master's, minimum GPA of 3.0; 2 letters of recommendation; resume; prerequisite coursework in statistics, biology, and psychology; for doctorate, GRE. Additional exam requirements/recommendations for international students: Required—TOEFL (minimum score 600 paper-based; 100 iBT), IELTS (minimum score 7), TWE. *Application deadline:* For fall admission, 4/1 priority date for domestic and international students; for spring admission, 11/1 for domestic students, 10/1 for international students. Applications are processed on a rolling basis. Application fee: $45. Electronic applications accepted. Application fee is waived when completed online. *Expenses: Tuition:* Full-time $16,740; part-time $930 per credit. *Required fees:* $486; $27 per credit. $243 per semester. *Financial support:* Career-related internships or fieldwork available. Financial award applicants required to submit FAFSA. *Faculty research:* Trauma and recovery, hypnosis, psychospiritual dimensions of healing, psychotherapy of schizophrenia. *Unit head:* Dr. Mary Beth Mannarino, Director, 412-365-1196, Fax: 412-365-1505, E-mail: mmannarino@chatham.edu. *Application contact:* Katie Noel, Assistant Director of Graduate Admission, 412-365-2758, Fax: 412-365-1609, E-mail: gradadmissions@chatham.edu. Website: http://www.chatham.edu/mscp

Claremont Graduate University, Graduate Programs, School of Social Science, Policy and Evaluation, Department of Psychology, Claremont, CA 91711-6160. Offers advanced study in evaluation (Certificate); cognitive psychology (MA, PhD); developmental psychology (MA, PhD); evaluation and applied research methods (MA, PhD); health behavior research and evaluation (MA, PhD); human resource development and evaluation (MA); industrial/organizational psychology (MA, PhD); organizational behavior (MA, PhD); organizational psychology (MA, PhD); social psychology (MA, PhD); MBA/PhD. *Program availability:* Part-time. Terminal master's awarded for partial completion of doctoral program. *Entrance requirements:* For master's and doctorate, GRE General Test. Additional exam requirements/recommendations for international students: Required—TOEFL (minimum score 75 iBT). Electronic applications accepted. *Faculty research:* Social intervention, diversity in organizations, eyewitness memory, aging and cognition, drug policy.

Drexel University, College of Arts and Sciences, Department of Psychology, Clinical Psychology Program, Philadelphia, PA 19104-2875. Offers clinical psychology (PhD); forensic psychology (PhD); health psychology (PhD); neuropsychology (PhD). *Accreditation:* APA. Terminal master's awarded for partial completion of doctoral program. *Degree requirements:* For doctorate, thesis/dissertation, qualifying exam. *Entrance requirements:* For doctorate, GRE General Test, GRE Subject Test, minimum GPA of 3.0. Electronic applications accepted. *Expenses:* Contact institution. *Faculty research:* Cognitive behavioral therapy, stress and coping, eating disorders, substance abuse, developmental disabilities.

Drexel University, College of Arts and Sciences, Department of Psychology, Program in Law-Psychology, Philadelphia, PA 19104-2875. Offers JD/PhD. Electronic applications accepted. *Expenses:* Contact institution. *Faculty research:* Mental health law issues, professional ethics, social science applications to law.

Duke University, Graduate School, Department of Psychology and Neuroscience, Durham, NC 27708. Offers biological psychology (PhD); clinical psychology (PhD); cognitive psychology (PhD); developmental psychology (PhD); experimental psychology (PhD); health psychology (PhD); human social development (PhD); JD/MA. *Accreditation:* APA (one or more programs are accredited). *Degree requirements:* For doctorate, thesis/dissertation. *Entrance requirements:* For doctorate, GRE General Test. Additional exam requirements/recommendations for international students: Required—TOEFL (minimum score 577 paper-based; 90 iBT) or IELTS (minimum score 7). Electronic applications accepted.

East Carolina University, Graduate School, Thomas Harriot College of Arts and Sciences, Department of Psychology, Greenville, NC 27858-4353. Offers health psychology (PhD), including clinical health psychology, occupational health psychology, pediatric school psychology; industrial and organizational psychology (MA); quantitative methods for the social and behavioral sciences (Certificate); MA/CAS. *Program availability:* Part-time, evening/weekend. *Students:* 77 full-time (52 women), 17 part-time (15 women); includes 12 minority (8 Black or African American, non-Hispanic/Latino; 3 Hispanic/Latino; 1 Two or more races, non-Hispanic/Latino). Average age 26. 221 applicants, 31% accepted, 22 enrolled. In 2017, 31 master's, 7 doctorates, 21 other advanced degrees awarded. *Degree requirements:* For doctorate, comprehensive exam, thesis/dissertation or alternative. *Entrance requirements:* For master's and doctorate, GRE General Test. Additional exam requirements/recommendations for international students: Recommended—TOEFL (minimum score 78 iBT), IELTS (minimum score 6.5). *Application deadline:* For fall admission, 12/1 priority date for domestic and international students. Applications are processed on a rolling basis. Application fee: $75. Electronic applications accepted. *Expenses:* Tuition, state resident: full-time $4749; part-time $297 per credit hour. Tuition, nonresident: full-time $17,898; part-time $1119 per credit hour. *Required fees:* $2691; $224 per credit hour. Part-time tuition and fees vary according to course load and program. *Financial support:* Research assistantships with partial tuition reimbursements, teaching assistantships with partial tuition reimbursements, Federal Work-Study, and traineeships available. Support available to part-time students. Financial award application deadline: 6/1. *Unit head:* Dr. Susan L. McCammon, Chair, 252-328-6357, E-mail: mccammons@ecu.edu. *Application contact:* Dean of Graduate School, 252-328-6012, Fax: 252-328-6071, E-mail: gradschool@ecu.edu. Website: http://www.ecu.edu/psyc

Georgian Court University, School of Arts and Sciences, Lakewood, NJ 08701-2697. Offers applied behavior analysis (MA); autism spectrum disorders (Certificate); clinical mental health counseling (MA); criminal justice and human rights (MS); holistic health studies (MA, Certificate); homeland security (Certificate); instructional technology (CPC); mercy spirituality (Certificate); parish business management (Certificate); professional counselor (Certificate); school psychology (MA, Certificate); theology (MA, Certificate). *Program availability:* Part-time, evening/weekend. *Faculty:* 18 full-time (11 women), 8 part-time/adjunct (4 women). *Students:* 100 full-time (86 women), 92 part-time (67 women); includes 34 minority (9 Black or African American, non-Hispanic/Latino; 1 Asian, non-Hispanic/Latino; 20 Hispanic/Latino; 4 Two or more races, non-Hispanic/Latino), 2 international. Average age 34. 187 applicants, 56% accepted, 78 enrolled. In 2017, 58 master's, 20 other advanced degrees awarded. *Degree requirements:* For master's, comprehensive exam (for some programs), thesis (for some programs). *Entrance requirements:* For master's, GRE, GMAT, or NTE/PRAXIS, 3 letters of recommendation. Additional exam requirements/recommendations for international students: Required—TOEFL (minimum score 550 paper-based). *Application deadline:* For fall admission, 8/15 for domestic students, 5/1 for international students; for spring admission, 1/15 for domestic students, 10/1 for international students. Applications are processed on a rolling basis. Application fee: $40. Electronic applications accepted. *Expenses: Tuition:* Part-time $839 per credit. *Required fees:* $248 per semester. Tuition and fees vary according to campus/location and program. *Financial support:* Scholarships/grants, health care benefits, and unspecified assistantships available. Financial award application deadline: 4/15; financial award applicants required to submit FAFSA. *Unit head:* Dr. Mary Chinery, Dean, 732-987-2493, Fax: 732-987-2007, E-mail: mchinery@georgian.edu. *Application contact:* Patrick Givens, Director of Graduate and Professional Studies Admissions, 732-987-2736, Fax: 732-987-2000, E-mail: gps@georgian.edu. Website: https://georgian.edu/academics/school-of-arts-sciences/

John F. Kennedy University, Graduate School of Holistic Studies, Department of Counseling Psychology, Program in Counseling Psychology, Pleasant Hill, CA 94523-4817. Offers holistic studies (MA); somatic psychology (MA); transpersonal psychology (MA). *Program availability:* Part-time, evening/weekend. *Degree requirements:* For master's, thesis or alternative. *Entrance requirements:* For master's, interview. Additional exam requirements/recommendations for international students: Required—TOEFL.

La Salle University, School of Arts and Sciences, Program in Clinical Psychology, Philadelphia, PA 19141-1199. Offers child clinical psychology (Psy D); clinical health psychology (Psy D); clinical psychology (MA); general practice psychology (Psy D). *Accreditation:* AAMFT/COAMFTE. *Program availability:* Part-time, evening/weekend. *Faculty:* 9 full-time (7 women), 7 part-time/adjunct (4 women). *Students:* 82 full-time (69 women), 27 part-time (20 women); includes 12 minority (2 Black or African American, non-Hispanic/Latino; 4 Asian, non-Hispanic/Latino; 4 Hispanic/Latino; 2 Two or more races, non-Hispanic/Latino), 2 international. Average age 27. 400 applicants, 16% accepted, 23 enrolled. In 2017, 19 master's, 24 doctorates awarded. Terminal master's awarded for partial completion of doctoral program. *Degree requirements:* For doctorate, comprehensive exam, thesis/dissertation. *Entrance requirements:* For doctorate, GRE (minimum scores of 148 on both the Verbal Reasoning and Quantitative Reasoning sections strongly recommended); GRE Subject Test in psychology (for those entering with bachelor's degree), baccalaureate degree from accredited institution with major in psychology or related discipline; minimum undergraduate GPA of 3.0, 3.2 graduate; three letters of recommendation; statement of interest and intent; curriculum vitae or resume; personal interview. Additional exam requirements/recommendations for international students: Required—TOEFL. *Application deadline:* For fall admission, 1/15 for domestic students, 1/1 for international students. Application fee: $35. Electronic applications accepted. Application fee is waived when completed online. *Expenses:* Contact institution. *Financial support:* In 2017–18, 31 students received support. Scholarships/grants and unspecified assistantships available. Financial award application deadline: 8/31; financial award applicants required to submit FAFSA. *Unit head:* Dr. Randy Fingerhut, Director, 215-951-1284, Fax: 215-951-5140, E-mail: psyd@lasalle.edu. *Application contact:* Elizabeth Heenan, Director, Graduate and Adult Enrollment, 215-951-1100, Fax: 215-951-1462, E-mail: heenan@lasalle.edu. Website: http://www.lasalle.edu/doctor-of-psychology/

Lesley University, Graduate School of Arts and Social Sciences, Cambridge, MA 02138-2790. Offers clinical mental health counseling (MA), including holistic counseling, school and community counseling, trauma studies; counseling psychology (MA, CAGS), including professional counseling (MA), school counseling (MA); creative writing (MFA); expressive therapies (MA, PhD, CAGS), including art (MA), clinical mental health counseling (MA), dance (MA), expressive therapies (MA), music (MA); independent

studies (CAGS); independent study (MA); intercultural relations (MA, CAGS); interdisciplinary studies (MA), including individualized studies, integrative holistic health, mindfulness studies, peace and conflict transformation, trauma sensitive assessment, intervention, and consultation, women's studies; urban environmental leadership (MA). *Program availability:* Part-time, online learning. *Degree requirements:* For master's, internship, practicum, thesis (for expressive therapies); for doctorate, thesis/dissertation, arts apprenticeship, field placement; for CAGS, thesis, internship (for counseling psychology, expressive therapies). *Entrance requirements:* For master's, MAT (counseling psychology), interview, writing samples, art portfolio; for doctorate, GRE or MAT, interview, master's degree; for CAGS, interview, master's degree. Additional exam requirements/recommendations for international students: Required—TOEFL (minimum score 550 paper-based; 80 iBT). Electronic applications accepted. *Faculty research:* Psychotherapy and culture; psychotherapy and psychological trauma; women's issues in art, teaching and psychotherapy; community-based art, psycho-spiritual inquiry.

North Dakota State University, College of Graduate and Interdisciplinary Studies, College of Science and Mathematics, Department of Psychology, Fargo, ND 58102. Offers clinical psychology (MS); health and social psychology (PhD); psychological clinical science (PhD); psychology (MS); visual and cognitive neuroscience (PhD). *Degree requirements:* For master's, thesis; for doctorate, thesis/dissertation. *Entrance requirements:* For master's and doctorate, GRE General Test, GRE Subject Test. Additional exam requirements/recommendations for international students: Required—TOEFL (minimum score 525 paper-based; 71 iBT). Electronic applications accepted. *Faculty research:* Cognition science, neuropsychology, group behavior, applied behavior analysis, behavior therapy.

Northern Kentucky University, Office of Graduate Programs, College of Arts and Sciences, Program in Industrial-Organizational Psychology, Highland Heights, KY 41099. Offers industrial psychology (Certificate); industrial-organizational psychology (MS); occupational health psychology (Certificate); organizational psychology (Certificate). *Program availability:* Part-time, evening/weekend. *Degree requirements:* For master's, thesis optional, capstone. *Entrance requirements:* For master's, GRE General Test (minimum scores of 141 verbal, 144 quantitative, and 3.5 writing), bachelor's degree with minimum GPA of 3.0, nine semester hours of psychology coursework, at least one undergraduate course in statistics with minimum B grade, official transcripts, current resume or vita, statement of personal interest, three letters of recommendation; for Certificate, official transcripts, bachelor's degree, minimum undergraduate GPA of 3.0, no grade lower than B on all graduate coursework previously taken that may apply. Additional exam requirements/recommendations for international students: Required—TOEFL (minimum score 79 iBT); Recommended—IELTS (minimum score 6.5). Electronic applications accepted. *Faculty research:* Workplace bullying and abuse, assessment and situational judgment tasks, human factors and work design, racial and social stereotyping in employment, social conflict.

Oklahoma State University, College of Education, Health and Aviation, School of Applied Health and Educational Psychology, Stillwater, OK 74078. Offers applied behavioral studies (Ed D); applied health and educational psychology (MS, PhD, Ed S). *Accreditation:* APA (one or more programs are accredited). *Program availability:* Part-time. *Faculty:* 31 full-time (20 women), 9 part-time/adjunct (7 women). *Students:* 169 full-time (119 women), 158 part-time (102 women); includes 98 minority (29 Black or African American, non-Hispanic/Latino; 15 American Indian or Alaska Native, non-Hispanic/Latino; 5 Asian, non-Hispanic/Latino; 24 Hispanic/Latino; 25 Two or more races, non-Hispanic/Latino), 22 international. Average age 30. 140 applicants, 56% accepted, 69 enrolled. In 2017, 71 master's, 24 doctorates awarded. *Entrance requirements:* For master's and doctorate, GRE or GMAT. Additional exam requirements/recommendations for international students: Required—TOEFL (minimum score 550 paper-based; 79 iBT). *Application deadline:* For fall admission, 3/1 priority date for international students; for spring admission, 8/1 priority date for international students. Applications are processed on a rolling basis. Application fee: $40 ($75 for international students). Electronic applications accepted. *Expenses:* Tuition, state resident: full-time $4019; part-time $2679.60 per year. Tuition, nonresident: full-time $15,286; part-time $10,190.40 per year. *Required fees:* $2129; $1419 per unit. Tuition and fees vary according to program. *Financial support:* Research assistantships, teaching assistantships, career-related internships or fieldwork, Federal Work-Study, scholarships/grants, health care benefits, tuition waivers (partial), and unspecified assistantships available. Support available to part-time students. Financial award application deadline: 3/1; financial award applicants required to submit FAFSA. *Unit head:* Dr. Aric Warren, Head, 405-744-6040, Fax: 405-744-6779, E-mail: aric.warren@okstate.edu.
Website: http://education.okstate.edu/

Oregon State University, College of Liberal Arts, Program in Psychology, Corvallis, OR 97331. Offers applied cognition (MS, PhD); engineering psychology (MS, PhD); health psychology (MS, PhD). *Application deadline:* For fall admission, 12/15 for domestic and international students. Application fee: $75 ($85 for international students). *Unit head:* Jason McCarley, Graduate Education Chair, E-mail: jason.mccarley@oregonstate.edu. *Application contact:* Aurora Sherman, Associate Professor and Graduate Education Chair, 541-737-1361, E-mail: aurora.sherman@oregonstate.edu.
Website: http://liberalarts.oregonstate.edu/school-psychological-science/psychology/graduate-psychology

Penn State Harrisburg, Graduate School, School of Behavioral Sciences and Education, Middletown, PA 17057. Offers adult education in the health and medical professions (Certificate); applied behavior analysis (MA); applied clinical psychology (MA); applied psychological research (MA); community psychology and social change (MA); English as a second language (ESL) program specialist and leadership (Certificate); health education (M Ed); lifelong learning and adult education (M Ed, D Ed); literacy education (M Ed); literacy leadership (Certificate); psychology: applications in clinical psychology (Certificate); psychology: health psychology (Certificate); teaching and curriculum (M Ed); training and development (M Ed, Certificate). *Program availability:* Part-time, evening/weekend. *Unit head:* Dr. Mukund S. Kulkarni, Chancellor, 717-948-6105, Fax: 717-948-6452. *Application contact:* Robert W. Coffman, Jr., Director of Enrollment Management, Recruitment and Admissions, 717-948-6250, Fax: 717-948-6325, E-mail: hbgadmit@psu.edu.
Website: https://harrisburg.psu.edu/behavioral-sciences-and-education/

Prescott College, Graduate Programs, Program in Counseling and Psychology, Prescott, AZ 86301. Offers adventure-based psychotherapy (MA); counseling psychology (MA); ecopsychology (MA); ecotherapy (MA); equine-assisted mental health (MA); expressive arts therapy (MA); somatic psychology (MA); student-directed independent study (MA). *Program availability:* Part-time, online learning. Terminal master's awarded for partial completion of doctoral program. *Degree requirements:* For master's, thesis, fieldwork or internship, practicum. *Entrance requirements:* For master's, 2 letters of recommendation, resume. Additional exam requirements/recommendations for international students: Required—TOEFL (minimum score 500 paper-based). Electronic applications accepted.

Rhode Island College, School of Graduate Studies, Faculty of Arts and Sciences, Department of Psychology, Providence, RI 02908-1991. Offers health psychology (CGS); psychology (MA). *Program availability:* Part-time, evening/weekend. *Faculty:* 2. *Students:* 3 full-time (all women), 10 part-time (9 women); includes 2 minority (1 Black or African American, non-Hispanic/Latino; 1 American Indian or Alaska Native, non-Hispanic/Latino). Average age 28. In 2017, 2 master's awarded. *Degree requirements:* For master's, comprehensive exam. *Entrance requirements:* For master's, GRE, 3 letters of recommendation. Additional exam requirements/recommendations for international students: Recommended—TOEFL (minimum score 550 paper-based; 79 iBT). *Application deadline:* For fall admission, 3/1 for domestic students; for spring admission, 11/1 for domestic students. Applications are processed on a rolling basis. Application fee: $50. Electronic applications accepted. *Expenses:* Tuition, state resident: full-time $9768; part-time $407 per credit. Tuition, nonresident: full-time $19,008; part-time $792 per credit. *Required fees:* $696; $29 per credit. One-time fee: $200 full-time; $100 part-time. Tuition and fees vary according to course load. *Financial support:* In 2017–18, 3 teaching assistantships with full tuition reimbursements (averaging $3,500 per year) were awarded; Federal Work-Study, scholarships/grants, health care benefits, and unspecified assistantships also available. Support available to part-time students. Financial award application deadline: 5/15; financial award applicants required to submit FAFSA. *Unit head:* Dr. Randi Kim, Chair, 401-456-8015. *Application contact:* Graduate Studies, 401-456-8700.
Website: http://www.ric.edu/psychology/index.php

Rutgers University–New Brunswick, Graduate School-New Brunswick, Program in Psychology, Piscataway, NJ 08854-8097. Offers behavioral neuroscience (PhD); clinical psychology (PhD); cognitive psychology (PhD); interdisciplinary health psychology (PhD); social psychology (PhD). *Accreditation:* APA. *Degree requirements:* For doctorate, comprehensive exam, thesis/dissertation. *Entrance requirements:* For doctorate, GRE General Test, 3 letters of recommendation. Additional exam requirements/recommendations for international students: Required—TOEFL (minimum score 577 paper-based). Electronic applications accepted. *Faculty research:* Learning and memory, behavioral ecology, hormones and behavior, psychopharmacology, anxiety disorders.

San Diego State University, Graduate and Research Affairs, College of Health and Human Services, Graduate School of Public Health, San Diego, CA 92182. Offers environmental health (MPH); epidemiology (MPH, PhD), including biostatistics (MPH); global emergency preparedness and response (MS); global health (PhD); health behavior (PhD); health promotion (MPH); health services administration (MPH); toxicology (MS); MPH/MA; MSW/MPH. *Accreditation:* CAHME (one or more programs are accredited). *Program availability:* Part-time. *Degree requirements:* For master's, comprehensive exam (for some programs), thesis (for some programs); for doctorate, thesis/dissertation. *Entrance requirements:* For master's, GMAT (MPH in health services administration), GRE General Test; for doctorate, GRE General Test. Additional exam requirements/recommendations for international students: Required—TOEFL. *Faculty research:* Evaluation of tobacco, AIDS prevalence and prevention, mammography, infant death project, Alzheimer's in elderly Chinese.

Saybrook University, School of Psychology and Interdisciplinary Inquiry, San Francisco, CA 94612. Offers human science (MA, PhD), including consciousness and spirituality, humanistic and transpersonal psychology, integrative health studies, organizational systems, social transformation; organizational systems (MA, PhD), including consciousness and spirituality, humanistic and transpersonal psychology, integrative health studies, leadership of sustainable systems (MA), organizational systems, social transformation; psychology (MA, PhD), including consciousness and spirituality, creativity studies (MA), humanistic and transpersonal psychology, integrative health studies, Jungian studies, marriage and family therapy (MA), organizational systems, social transformation. *Program availability:* Online learning. Terminal master's awarded for partial completion of doctoral program. *Degree requirements:* For master's, thesis or alternative; for doctorate, thesis/dissertation. *Entrance requirements:* Additional exam requirements/recommendations for international students: Required—TOEFL (minimum score 580 paper-based; 93 iBT). Electronic applications accepted. *Faculty research:* Humanistic theory, health studies, organizational systems, consciousness and spirituality, social transformation.

Southwestern College, Program in Integral Somatic Psychology, Santa Fe, NM 87502-4788. Offers Certificate.

Stony Brook University, State University of New York, Graduate School, College of Arts and Sciences, Department of Psychology, Program in Social and Health Psychology, Stony Brook, NY 11794. Offers PhD. *Students:* 17 full-time (16 women); includes 5 minority (1 Black or African American, non-Hispanic/Latino; 3 Asian, non-Hispanic/Latino; 1 Two or more races, non-Hispanic/Latino), 1 international. Average age 28. 64 applicants, 8% accepted, 2 enrolled. In 2017, 5 doctorates awarded. *Degree requirements:* For doctorate, thesis/dissertation. *Entrance requirements:* For doctorate, GRE General Test, GRE Subject Test. Additional exam requirements/recommendations for international students: Required—TOEFL (minimum score 90 iBT). *Application deadline:* For fall admission, 1/15 for domestic students; for spring admission, 10/1 for domestic students. Application fee: $100. Electronic applications accepted. *Expenses:* Contact institution. *Financial support:* In 2017–18, 1 fellowship, 2 research assistantships, 9 teaching assistantships were awarded. *Unit head:* Dr. Sheri Levy, Chair, 631-632-4355, E-mail: sheri.levy@stonybrook.edu. *Application contact:* Marilynn Wollmuth, Coordinator, 631-632-7855, Fax: 631-632-7876, E-mail: marilyn.wollmuth@stonybrook.edu.
Website: http://www.stonybrook.edu/commcms/psychology/social_health/overview.html

United States International University–Africa, School of Arts and Sciences, Nairobi, Kenya. Offers counseling psychology (MA), including chemical dependency, health psychology; international relations (MA), including development studies, diplomacy and foreign policy, peace and conflict studies. *Program availability:* Part-time, evening/weekend. *Degree requirements:* For master's, thesis, practicum. *Entrance requirements:* For master's, GRE General Test, 2 letters of recommendation, resume. Additional exam requirements/recommendations for international students: Required—TOEFL. *Faculty research:* Trauma in children, African intellectualism, psychological assessment tools.

The University of Alabama at Birmingham, School of Public Health, Program in Public Health, Birmingham, AL 35294. Offers applied epidemiology and pharmacoepidemiology (MSPH); biostatistics (MPH); clinical and translational science (MSPH); environmental health (MPH); environmental health and toxicology (MSPH); epidemiology (MPH); general theory and practice (MPH); health behavior (MPH); health care organization (MPH); health policy quantitative policy analysis (MPH); industrial hygiene (MPH, MSPH); maternal and child health policy (Dr PH); maternal and child health policy and leadership (MPH); occupational health and safety (MPH); outcomes research (MSPH, Dr PH); public health (PhD); public health management (Dr PH); public health preparedness management (MPH). *Program availability:* Part-time, online learning. *Degree requirements:* For doctorate, comprehensive exam, thesis/dissertation. *Entrance requirements:* For master's and doctorate, GRE. Additional exam requirements/recommendations for international students: Recommended—TOEFL (minimum score 550 paper-based; 79 iBT), IELTS (minimum score 6.5). Electronic applications accepted.

Health Psychology

The University of British Columbia, Faculty of Arts and Faculty of Graduate Studies, Department of Psychology, Vancouver, BC V6T 1Z4, Canada. Offers behavioral neuroscience (MA, PhD); clinical psychology (MA, PhD); cognitive science (MA, PhD); developmental psychology (MA, PhD); health psychology (MA, PhD); quantitative methods (MA, PhD); social/personality psychology (MA, PhD). *Accreditation:* APA (one or more programs are accredited). Terminal master's awarded for partial completion of doctoral program. *Degree requirements:* For master's, thesis; for doctorate, comprehensive exam, thesis/dissertation. *Entrance requirements:* For master's and doctorate, GRE General Test. Additional exam requirements/recommendations for international students: Required—TOEFL. Electronic applications accepted. *Expenses:* Contact institution. *Faculty research:* Clinical, developmental, social/personality, cognition, behavioral neuroscience.

University of Colorado Denver, College of Liberal Arts and Sciences, Department of Psychology, Denver, CO 80217. Offers clinical health (PhD); psychology (MA). *Program availability:* Part-time, evening/weekend. *Degree requirements:* For master's, 31-33 semester hours, thesis or internship, minimum GPA of 3.0; for doctorate, comprehensive exam, thesis/dissertation, 69 credits of coursework, minimum of 12 clinical practicum hours, 30 dissertation hours, three credits of pre-doctoral internship. *Entrance requirements:* For master's, GRE General Test; GRE Subject Test (recommended), undergraduate courses in psychological statistics, abnormal psychology and introductory psychology; minimum GPA of 3.0; three letters of recommendation; personal statement; resume; for doctorate, GRE General Test; GRE Subject Test (recommended), minimum GPA of 3.5; undergraduate courses in introductory psychology, psychological statistics, research methods and abnormal psychology; letters of recommendation; personal statement; resume. Additional exam requirements/recommendations for international students: Required—TOEFL (minimum score 537 paper-based; 75 iBT); Recommended—IELTS (minimum score 6.5). Electronic applications accepted. *Faculty research:* Organizational behavior, body image perception, professional ethics, infant perception and cognition, charismatic leadership.

University of Florida, Graduate School, College of Public Health and Health Professions, Department of Clinical and Health Psychology, Gainesville, FL 32611. Offers clinical and translational science (PhD); psychology (MS). *Accreditation:* APA (one or more programs are accredited). *Degree requirements:* For doctorate, comprehensive exam, thesis/dissertation, pre-doctoral internship. *Entrance requirements:* For master's and doctorate, GRE General Test, minimum GPA of 3.0. Additional exam requirements/recommendations for international students: Required—TOEFL (minimum score 550 paper-based; 80 iBT), IELTS (minimum score 6). Electronic applications accepted. *Faculty research:* Clinical child and pediatric psychology, medical psychology, neuropsychology, health promotion and aging.

University of Michigan–Dearborn, College of Arts, Sciences, and Letters, Master of Science in Psychology Program, Dearborn, MI 48128. Offers clinical health psychology (MS); health psychology (MS). *Program availability:* Part-time. *Faculty:* 17 full-time (10 women). *Students:* 21 full-time (15 women), 8 part-time (6 women); includes 5 minority (2 Black or African American, non-Hispanic/Latino; 1 Asian, non-Hispanic/Latino; 2 Hispanic/Latino), 2 international. Average age 27. 44 applicants, 55% accepted, 13 enrolled. In 2017, 18 master's awarded. *Degree requirements:* For master's, thesis optional. *Entrance requirements:* For master's, GRE, 3 letters of recommendation. Additional exam requirements/recommendations for international students: Required—TOEFL (minimum score 560 paper-based; 84 iBT), IELTS (minimum score 6.5). *Application deadline:* For fall admission, 3/15 for domestic and international students. Application fee: $60. Electronic applications accepted. *Expenses:* $683 per credit hour in-state; $1,176 per credit hour out-state. *Financial support:* In 2017–18, 15 students received support. Career-related internships or fieldwork, scholarships/grants, and non-resident tuition scholarships available. Financial award application deadline: 3/1; financial award applicants required to submit FAFSA. *Faculty research:* Stress and health, adjustment to and coping with chronic illness, interpersonal relationships, personality and multicultural assessment, physiology and behavioral health. *Unit head:* Dr. Michelle Leonard, Program Director, 313-593-5608, E-mail: mtleon@umich.edu. *Application contact:* Office of Graduate Studies, 313-583-6321, E-mail: umd-graduatestudies@umich.edu. Website: http://umdearborn.edu/casl/psychology/

University of New Mexico, Graduate Studies, College of Arts and Sciences, Program in Psychology, Albuquerque, NM 87131-2039. Offers behavioral neuroscience (PhD); clinical psychology (PhD); cognitive neuroimaging (PhD); developmental psychology (PhD); evolution (PhD); health psychology (PhD); quantitative methodology (PhD). *Accreditation:* APA. *Students:* Average age 30. 227 applicants, 11% accepted, 16 enrolled. In 2017, 10 doctorates awarded. *Degree requirements:* For doctorate, comprehensive exam, thesis/dissertation. *Entrance requirements:* For doctorate, GRE General Test, GRE Subject Test (psychology), minimum GPA of 3.0. Additional exam requirements/recommendations for international students: Required—TOEFL (minimum score 550 paper-based; 79 iBT), IELTS (minimum score 6.5). *Application deadline:* For fall admission, 12/15 priority date for domestic and international students. Applications are processed on a rolling basis. Application fee: $50. Electronic applications accepted. *Financial support:* Fellowships, research assistantships, teaching assistantships, career-related internships or fieldwork, Federal Work-Study, institutionally sponsored loans, scholarships/grants, health care benefits, tuition waivers (partial), and unspecified assistantships available. Financial award application deadline: 3/1; financial award applicants required to submit FAFSA. *Faculty research:* Addiction, cognition, brain and behavior, developmental, evolutionary, functioning neuroimaging, health psychology, learning and memory, neuroscience. *Total annual research expenditures:* $727,970. *Unit head:* Dr. Jane Ellen Smith, Department Chair, 505-277-4121, Fax: 505-277-1394. *Application contact:* Rikk Murphy, Graduate Program Coordinator, 505-277-5009, Fax: 505-277-1394, E-mail: advising@unm.edu. Website: http://psych.unm.edu

The University of North Carolina at Chapel Hill, Graduate School, Gillings School of Global Public Health, Department of Health Behavior, Chapel Hill, NC 27599. Offers MPH, PhD, MPH/MCRP, MSPH/PhD. *Accreditation:* CEPH (one or more programs are accredited). *Faculty:* 24 full-time (19 women), 35 part-time/adjunct (24 women). *Students:* 134 full-time (117 women), 4 part-time (3 women); includes 51 minority (14 Black or African American, non-Hispanic/Latino; 15 Asian, non-Hispanic/Latino; 12 Hispanic/Latino; 10 Two or more races, non-Hispanic/Latino), 8 international. Average age 27. 350 applicants, 44% accepted, 55 enrolled. In 2017, 36 master's, 8 doctorates awarded. *Degree requirements:* For master's, comprehensive exam, thesis or alternative, major paper, capstone, practicum; for doctorate, comprehensive exam, thesis/dissertation, practicum. *Entrance requirements:* For master's, GRE General Test or MCAT, three letters of recommendation (academic and/or professional); for doctorate, GRE General Test, master's degree, three letters of recommendation (academic and/or professional). Additional exam requirements/recommendations for international students: Required—TOEFL (minimum score 90 iBT), IELTS (minimum score 7). *Application deadline:* For fall admission, 12/1 for domestic and international students. Applications are processed on a rolling basis. Application fee: $85. Electronic applications accepted. *Financial support:* Fellowships with tuition reimbursements, research assistantships with tuition reimbursements, teaching assistantships with tuition reimbursements, career-related internships or fieldwork, Federal Work-Study, institutionally sponsored loans, scholarships/grants, traineeships, health care benefits, and unspecified assistantships available. Financial award application deadline: 12/10; financial award applicants required to submit FAFSA. *Faculty research:* Cancer prevention and control, aging health promotion and disease prevention, adolescent health, nutrition intervention. *Unit head:* Dr. Kurt M. Ribisl, Chair, 919-843-8042, E-mail: kurt_ribisl@unc.edu. *Application contact:* Da'esha McPhaul, Student Services Manager, 919-966-5771, E-mail: hbstudentservices@unc.edu. Website: https://sph.unc.edu/hb/health-behavior-home/

The University of North Carolina at Charlotte, College of Liberal Arts and Sciences, Department of Psychology, Charlotte, NC 28223-0001. Offers cognitive science (Graduate Certificate); health psychology (PhD); industrial/organizational psychology (MA); psychology (MA). *Accreditation:* APA. *Program availability:* Part-time. *Faculty:* 29 full-time (19 women), 2 part-time/adjunct (both women). *Students:* 42 full-time (38 women), 32 part-time (21 women); includes 22 minority (11 Black or African American, non-Hispanic/Latino; 8 Hispanic/Latino; 3 Two or more races, non-Hispanic/Latino), 1 international. Average age 28. 196 applicants, 12% accepted, 16 enrolled. In 2017, 13 master's, 9 doctorates, 1 other advanced degree awarded. *Degree requirements:* For master's, thesis (for some programs); for doctorate, comprehensive exam, thesis/dissertation, internship (clinical health students only). *Entrance requirements:* For master's, GRE, GMAT, MAT; for doctorate, GRE, at least 18 hours of coursework in psychology including introductory psychology and research methods, undergraduate course in statistics, transcripts of all academic work attempted since high school including evidence of the completion of a bachelor's degree, at least three references, personal statement, resume or curriculum vitae; for Graduate Certificate, enrolled and in good standing in a graduate degree program at UNC Charlotte, or have minimum GPA of 3.0 for undergraduate courses. Additional exam requirements/recommendations for international students: Required—TOEFL (minimum score 523 paper-based, 70 iBT) or IELTS (6.5). *Application deadline:* For fall admission, 11/15 for domestic and international students. Applications are processed on a rolling basis. Application fee: $75. Electronic applications accepted. *Expenses:* Contact institution. *Financial support:* In 2017–18, 32 students received support, including 1 fellowship (averaging $47,476 per year), 13 research assistantships (averaging $14,282 per year), 18 teaching assistantships (averaging $14,405 per year); career-related internships or fieldwork, Federal Work-Study, institutionally sponsored loans, scholarships/grants, and unspecified assistantships also available. Support available to part-time students. Financial award application deadline: 3/1; financial award applicants required to submit FAFSA. *Total annual research expenditures:* $440,921. *Unit head:* Dr. Eric Heggestad, Interim Chair, 704-687-1315. *Application contact:* Kathy B. Giddings, Director of Graduate Admissions, 704-687-5503, Fax: 704-687-1668, E-mail: gradadm@uncc.edu. Website: http://psych.uncc.edu

University of Pittsburgh, Kenneth P. Dietrich School of Arts and Sciences, Department of Psychology, Pittsburgh, PA 15260. Offers biological and health psychology (PhD); clinical psychology (PhD); cognitive psychology (PhD); developmental psychology (PhD); social psychology (PhD). *Accreditation:* APA. *Faculty:* 58 full-time (26 women). *Students:* 90 full-time (72 women); includes 25 minority (5 Black or African American, non-Hispanic/Latino; 11 Asian, non-Hispanic/Latino; 9 Hispanic/Latino), 9 international. Average age 26. 485 applicants, 6% accepted, 14 enrolled. In 2017, 6 doctorates awarded. Terminal master's awarded for partial completion of doctoral program. *Degree requirements:* For doctorate, comprehensive exam, thesis/dissertation. *Entrance requirements:* For doctorate, GRE General Test, minimum GPA of 3.0. Additional exam requirements/recommendations for international students: Required—TOEFL (minimum score 90 iBT) or IELTS (minimum score 7). *Application deadline:* For fall admission, 12/1 for domestic and international students. Application fee: $50. Electronic applications accepted. *Financial support:* In 2017–18, 76 students received support, including 20 fellowships with full tuition reimbursements available (averaging $22,000 per year), 28 research assistantships with full tuition reimbursements available (averaging $18,060 per year), 29 teaching assistantships with full tuition reimbursements available (averaging $19,180 per year); scholarships/grants, traineeships, and health care benefits also available. Financial award application deadline: 12/1. *Faculty research:* Developmental psychopathology; autism spectrum disorder; cardiovascular medicine; STEM research. *Total annual research expenditures:* $20 million. *Unit head:* Dr. Julie Fiez, Chair, 412-624-4500, E-mail: fiez@pitt.edu. *Application contact:* Stacy McLinden, Graduate Administrator, 412-624-4502, E-mail: psygrad@pitt.edu. Website: http://www.psychology.pitt.edu/

The University of Texas at Arlington, Graduate School, College of Science, Department of Psychology, Arlington, TX 76019. Offers experimental health psychology (PhD); experimental psychology (MS, PhD); health/neuroscience psychology (MS, PhD); industrial and organizational psychology (MS). *Program availability:* Part-time. Terminal master's awarded for partial completion of doctoral program. *Degree requirements:* For master's, comprehensive exam or thesis; for doctorate, thesis/dissertation (for some programs). *Entrance requirements:* For master's and doctorate, GRE General Test, minimum GPA of 3.0 in last 60 hours of course work. Additional exam requirements/recommendations for international students: Required—TOEFL (minimum score 550 paper-based).

University of the Sciences, Program in Health Psychology, Philadelphia, PA 19104-4495. Offers MS. *Entrance requirements:* For master's, bachelor's degree in related field, minimum GPA of 3.0 in major. Additional exam requirements/recommendations for international students: Required—TOEFL, TWE. *Expenses:* Contact institution. *Faculty research:* Stress and immune system, women's health and breast cancer, memory, health care policy.

Virginia Commonwealth University, Graduate School, College of Humanities and Sciences, Department of Psychology, Richmond, VA 23284-9005. Offers clinical psychology (PhD), including behavioral medicine, clinical child psychology; counseling psychology (PhD); health psychology (PhD). *Accreditation:* APA. *Degree requirements:* For doctorate, thesis/dissertation. *Entrance requirements:* For doctorate, GRE General Test. Additional exam requirements/recommendations for international students: Required—TOEFL (minimum score 600 paper-based; 100 iBT); Recommended—IELTS (minimum score 6.5). Electronic applications accepted. *Faculty research:* Biopsychology, clinical psychology, counseling psychology, developmental psychology, health psychology, social psychology.

Virginia State University, College of Graduate Studies, College of Natural and Health Sciences, Department of Psychology, Petersburg, VA 23806-0001. Offers behavioral and community health sciences (PhD); clinical health psychology (PhD); clinical psychology (MS); general psychology (MS). *Degree requirements:* For master's, one foreign language, thesis. *Entrance requirements:* For master's, GRE General Test.

Viterbo University, Master of Science in Mental Health Counseling Program, La Crosse, WI 54601-4797. Offers addiction counseling (MS); child and adolescent counseling (MS); complementary health and wellness counseling (MS). *Accreditation:* ACA. *Program availability:* Part-time, evening/weekend. *Degree requirements:* For master's, comprehensive exam, thesis, 54 credits of core program courses; 6 elective credits; minimum GPA of 3.0; action research project; practicum/internship experience. *Entrance requirements:* For master's, MAT, BS in a human service or social science

discipline; prerequisite coursework in general psychology, behavior disorders/abnormal psychology, and research methods/statistics; minimum undergraduate cumulative GPA of 3.0; background check; personal statement; undergraduate transcripts; interview. Additional exam requirements/recommendations for international students: Required—TOEFL (minimum score 525 paper-based). Electronic applications accepted. Application fee is waived when completed online. *Expenses:* Contact institution. *Faculty research:* Supervision, recovery substance abuse, culture, counseling theory, health and wellness.

Walden University, Graduate Programs, School of Psychology, Minneapolis, MN 55401. Offers clinical psychology (MS), including counseling, general program; forensic psychology (MS), including forensic psychology in the community, general program, mental health applications, program planning and evaluation in forensic settings, psychology and legal systems; industrial organizational (MS, PhD), including consulting psychology, forensic (MS), forensic psychology (PhD), general practice, leadership development and coaching (MS), organizational diversity and social change, research evaluation (PhD); online teaching in psychology (Post-Master's Certificate); organizational psychology and development (Postbaccalaureate Certificate); psychology (MS, PhD), including applied psychology (MS), clinical psychology (PhD), crisis management and response (MS), educational psychology, forensic psychology (PhD), general psychology (MS), general psychology research (PhD), general psychology teaching (PhD), health psychology, leadership development and coaching

(MS), psychology of culture (MS), psychology, public administration, and social change (MS), social psychology, terrorism and security (MS); psychology respecialization (Post-Doctoral Certificate). *Program availability:* Part-time, evening/weekend, online only, 100% online. Terminal master's awarded for partial completion of doctoral program. *Degree requirements:* For master's, thesis optional; for doctorate, thesis/dissertation, residency. *Entrance requirements:* For master's, bachelor's degree or higher; minimum GPA of 2.5; official transcripts; goal statement (for some programs); access to computer and Internet; for doctorate, master's degree or higher; three years of related professional or academic experience (preferred); minimum GPA of 3.0; goal statement and current resume (for select programs); official transcripts; access to computer and Internet; for other advanced degree, relevant work experience; access to computer and Internet. Additional exam requirements/recommendations for international students: Required—TOEFL (minimum score 550 paper-based, 79 iBT), IELTS (minimum score 6.5), Michigan English Language Assessment Battery (minimum score 82), or PTE (minimum score 53). Electronic applications accepted.

Yeshiva University, Ferkauf Graduate School of Psychology, Program in Clinical Health Psychology, New York, NY 10033-3201. Offers PhD. *Accreditation:* APA. *Program availability:* Part-time. *Degree requirements:* For doctorate, comprehensive exam, thesis/dissertation. *Entrance requirements:* For doctorate, GRE General Test. *Faculty research:* Dieting, substance abuse, adolescent depression and suicide, cancer research, MS research.

Human Development

Alabama Agricultural and Mechanical University, School of Graduate Studies, College of Agricultural, Life and Natural Sciences, Department of Family and Consumer Sciences, Huntsville, AL 35811. Offers apparel, merchandising and design (MS); family and consumer sciences (MS); human development and family studies (MS); nutrition and hospitality management (MS). *Program availability:* Part-time, evening/weekend. *Degree requirements:* For master's, comprehensive exam, thesis optional. *Entrance requirements:* For master's, GRE General Test. Additional exam requirements/ recommendations for international students: Required—TOEFL (minimum score 500 paper-based; 61 iBT). Electronic applications accepted. *Faculty research:* Food biotechnology, nutrition, food microbiology, food engineering, food chemistry.

Argosy University, Chicago, Illinois School of Professional Psychology, Doctoral Program in Clinical Psychology, Chicago, IL 60601. Offers child and adolescent psychology (Psy D); client-centered and experiential psychotherapies (Psy D); diversity and multicultural psychology (Psy D); family psychology (Psy D); forensic psychology (Psy D); health psychology (Psy D); neuropsychology (Psy D); organizational consulting (Psy D); psychoanalytic psychology (Psy D); psychology and spirituality (Psy D). *Accreditation:* APA.

Arizona State University at the Tempe campus, College of Liberal Arts and Sciences, School of Social and Family Dynamics, Tempe, AZ 85287-3701. Offers family and human development (MS, PhD); infant-family practice (MAS); marriage and family therapy (MAS); sociology (MA, PhD). Terminal master's awarded for partial completion of doctoral program. *Degree requirements:* For master's, thesis or alternative, interactive Program of Study (iPOS) submitted before completing 50 percent of required credit hours; for doctorate, thesis/dissertation, interactive Program of Study (iPOS) submitted before completing 50 percent of required credit hours. *Entrance requirements:* For master's and doctorate, GRE, minimum GPA of 3.0 or equivalent in last 2 years of work leading to bachelor's degree. Additional exam requirements/recommendations for international students: Required—TOEFL, IELTS, or PTE. Electronic applications accepted. *Expenses:* Contact institution.

Auburn University, Graduate School, College of Human Sciences, Department of Human Development and Family Studies, Auburn University, AL 36849. Offers MS, PhD. *Accreditation:* AAMFT/COAMFTE (one or more programs are accredited). *Program availability:* Part-time. *Faculty:* 24 full-time (16 women). *Students:* 21 full-time (all women), 16 part-time (12 women); includes 12 minority (6 Black or African American, non-Hispanic/Latino; 1 Asian, non-Hispanic/Latino; 3 Hispanic/Latino; 1 Native Hawaiian or other Pacific Islander, non-Hispanic/Latino; 1 Two or more races, non-Hispanic/Latino). Average age 27. 50 applicants, 22% accepted, 11 enrolled. In 2017, 8 master's, 4 doctorates awarded. *Degree requirements:* For master's, thesis, oral exam; for doctorate, thesis/dissertation. *Entrance requirements:* For master's, GRE General Test; for doctorate, GRE General Test, master's degree. *Application deadline:* Applications are processed on a rolling basis. Application fee: $50 ($60 for international students). *Expenses:* Tuition, state resident: full-time $10,974; part-time $519 per credit hour. Tuition, nonresident: full-time $29,658; part-time $1557 per credit hour. *Required fees:* $816 per semester. Tuition and fees vary according to degree level and program. *Financial support:* Research assistantships, teaching assistantships, and Federal Work-Study available. Support available to part-time students. Financial award application deadline: 3/15; financial award applicants required to submit FAFSA. *Faculty research:* Family influences on personality and social development, parent-child relations, infancy, day care, parent education. *Unit head:* Dr. Joe F. Pittman, Jr., Head, 334-844-3242, E-mail: mbradbar@humsci.auburn.edu. *Application contact:* Dr. George Flowers, Dean of the Graduate School, 334-844-2125.
Website: http://www.humsci.auburn.edu/hdfs/

Ball State University, Graduate School, Teachers College, Department of Educational Psychology, Muncie, IN 47306. Offers educational psychology (MA, MS), including educational psychology (MA, MS, PhD); educational psychology (PhD), including educational psychology (MA, MS, PhD); gifted and talented education (Certificate); human development and learning (Certificate); instructional design and assessment (Certificate); neuropsychology (Certificate); quantitative psychology (MS); response to intervention (Certificate); school psychology (MA, PhD), including school psychology (MA, PhD, Ed S); school psychology (Ed S), including school psychology (MA, PhD, Ed S). *Program availability:* 100% online. *Faculty:* 24 full-time (15 women), 3 part-time/adjunct (all women). *Students:* 68 full-time (49 women), 122 part-time (106 women); includes 33 minority (16 Black or African American, non-Hispanic/Latino; 4 Asian, non-Hispanic/Latino; 7 Hispanic/Latino; 6 Two or more races, non-Hispanic/Latino), 3 international. Average age 32. 146 applicants, 42% accepted, 47 enrolled. In 2017, 49 master's, 8 doctorates, 20 other advanced degrees awarded. *Degree requirements:* For doctorate, thesis/dissertation; for other advanced degree, thesis. *Entrance requirements:* For master's, GRE General Test, minimum baccalaureate GPA of 2.75 or 3.0 in latter half of baccalaureate, professional goals and self-assessment; for doctorate, GRE General Test, minimum graduate GPA of 3.2; for other advanced degree, GRE General Test. Additional exam requirements/recommendations for international students: Required—TOEFL (minimum score 550 paper-based; 79 iBT), IELTS

(minimum score 6.5). *Application deadline:* Applications are processed on a rolling basis. Application fee: $60. Electronic applications accepted. *Financial support:* In 2017–18, 40 students received support, including 29 research assistantships with partial tuition reimbursements available (averaging $12,276 per year), 3 teaching assistantships with partial tuition reimbursements available (averaging $11,167 per year); unspecified assistantships also available. Financial award application deadline: 3/1; financial award applicants required to submit FAFSA. *Unit head:* Dr. Jerell Cassady, Chairperson, 765-285-8503, E-mail: jccassady@bsu.edu. *Application contact:* Dr. Jerrell Cassady, Chairperson, 765-285-8503, Fax: 765-285-5455, E-mail: jccassady@bsu.edu. Website: http://www.bsu.edu/edpsych

Bradley University, The Graduate School, College of Education and Health Sciences, Department of Leadership in Education, Nonprofits and Counseling, Peoria, IL 61625-0002. Offers counseling (MA), including clinical mental health counseling, professional school counseling; leadership in educational administration (MA); nonprofit leadership (MA). *Accreditation:* ACA; NCATE. *Program availability:* Part-time, evening/weekend. *Degree requirements:* For master's, comprehensive exam, thesis optional. *Entrance requirements:* For master's, GRE General Test or MAT, interview, 3 letters of recommendation. Additional exam requirements/recommendations for international students: Required—TOEFL (minimum score 550 paper-based; 79 iBT), IELTS (minimum score 6.5). Electronic applications accepted.

Brigham Young University, Graduate Studies, College of Family, Home, and Social Sciences, Program in Marriage, Family and Human Development, Provo, UT 84602. Offers MS, PhD. *Accreditation:* AAMFT/COAMFTE. *Faculty:* 21 full-time (4 women). *Students:* 22 full-time (16 women), 3 international. Average age 26. 26 applicants, 42% accepted, 11 enrolled. In 2017, 10 master's, 1 doctorate awarded. *Degree requirements:* For master's, thesis; for doctorate, comprehensive exam, thesis/dissertation. *Entrance requirements:* For master's and doctorate, GRE General Test, minimum GPA of 3.0 in last 60 semester hours, letters of recommendation. Additional exam requirements/recommendations for international students: Required—TOEFL (minimum score 580 paper-based; 85 iBT), IELTS (minimum score 7). *Application deadline:* For fall admission, 1/10 for domestic and international students. Application fee: $50. Electronic applications accepted. *Expenses:* Contact institution. *Financial support:* In 2017–18, 22 students received support, including 22 research assistantships with full and partial tuition reimbursements available (averaging $8,736 per year), 3 teaching assistantships with tuition reimbursements available (averaging $2,800 per year); scholarships/grants and unspecified assistantships also available. Financial award application deadline: 3/25. *Faculty research:* Family studies and family process, marriage, adolescence and emerging adulthood, adult development and aging, child development. *Unit head:* Dr. Dean M. Busby, Director, School of Life, 801-422-2069, Fax: 801-422-0230, E-mail: dean_busby@byu.edu. *Application contact:* Graduate Secretary, 801-422-2060, E-mail: mfhdgrad@byu.edu.
Website: http://mfhd.byu.edu

Brock University, Faculty of Graduate Studies, Faculty of Social Sciences, Program in Psychology, St. Catharines, ON L2S 3A1, Canada. Offers behavioral neuroscience (MA, PhD); life span development (MA, PhD); social personality (MA, PhD). *Program availability:* Part-time. *Degree requirements:* For master's, thesis; for doctorate, thesis/dissertation. *Entrance requirements:* For master's, GRE, honors degree; for doctorate, GRE, master's degree. Additional exam requirements/recommendations for international students: Required—TOEFL (minimum score 550 paper-based; 80 iBT), IELTS (minimum score 6.5), TWE (minimum score 4). Electronic applications accepted. *Faculty research:* Social personality, behavioral neuroscience, life-span development.

California State University, Fresno, Division of Research and Graduate Studies, Kremen School of Education and Human Development, Fresno, CA 93740-8027. Offers MA, MS, Ed D. *Accreditation:* NCATE. *Program availability:* Part-time, evening/weekend. *Degree requirements:* For master's, thesis or alternative; for doctorate, thesis/dissertation. *Entrance requirements:* For master's, GRE General Test, MAT; for doctorate, GRE or MAT, minimum GPA of 3.2, master's degree. Additional exam requirements/recommendations for international students: Required—TOEFL. Electronic applications accepted. *Faculty research:* Adult community education, parenting, gifted and talented curriculum and instruction, peer mediation and conflict resolution.

Central Michigan University, College of Graduate Studies, College of Education and Human Services, Department of Human Environmental Studies, Mount Pleasant, MI 48859. Offers apparel product development and merchandising technology (MS); gerontology (Graduate Certificate); human development and family studies (MA); nutrition and dietetics (MS). *Program availability:* Part-time, evening/weekend. *Degree requirements:* For master's, thesis or alternative. Electronic applications accepted. *Faculty research:* Human growth and development, family studies and human sexuality, human nutrition and dietetics, apparel and textile retailing, computer-aided design for apparel.

Human Development

Claremont Graduate University, Graduate Programs, School of Educational Studies, Claremont, CA 91711-6160. Offers Africana education (Certificate); education and policy (MA, PhD); higher education/student affairs (MA, PhD); human development (MA, PhD); public school administration (MA, PhD); quantitative evaluation (MA, PhD); special education (MA, PhD); teacher education (MA); teaching and learning (MA, PhD); urban leadership (PhD); MBA/PhD. PhD program offered jointly with San Diego State University. *Program availability:* Part-time. Terminal master's awarded for partial completion of doctoral program. *Entrance requirements:* For master's and doctorate, GRE General Test. Additional exam requirements/recommendations for international students: Required—TOEFL (minimum score 75 iBT). Electronic applications accepted. *Faculty research:* Education administration, K-12 and higher education, multicultural education, education policy, diversity in higher education, faculty issues.

Colorado State University, College of Health and Human Sciences, Department of Human Development and Family Studies, Fort Collins, CO 80523-1570. Offers applied developmental science (PhD); family and developmental studies (MS); marriage and family therapy (MS). *Accreditation:* AAMFT/COAMFTE. *Faculty:* 18 full-time (15 women), 3 part-time/adjunct (1 woman). *Students:* 31 full-time (28 women), 3 part-time (all women); includes 6 minority (2 Asian, non-Hispanic/Latino; 4 Hispanic/Latino), 1 international. Average age 27. 95 applicants, 26% accepted, 14 enrolled. In 2017, 13 master's, 3 doctorates awarded. Terminal master's awarded for partial completion of doctoral program. *Degree requirements:* For master's, thesis; for doctorate, comprehensive exam, thesis/dissertation. *Entrance requirements:* For master's and doctorate, GRE General Test, 3 letters of recommendation; minimum GPA of 3.0; bachelor's degree; curriculum vitae/resume. Additional exam requirements/recommendations for international students: Required—TOEFL (minimum score 550 paper-based; 80 iBT), IELTS (minimum score 6.5), PTE (minimum score 58). *Application deadline:* For fall admission, 1/2 priority date for domestic and international students. Application fee: $60 ($70 for international students). Electronic applications accepted. *Expenses:* Tuition, state resident: full-time $9917. Tuition, nonresident: full-time $24,312. *Required fees:* $2284. Tuition and fees vary according to course load and program. *Financial support:* In 2017–18, 2 fellowships with full and partial tuition reimbursements (averaging $7,128 per year), 10 research assistantships with full and partial tuition reimbursements (averaging $12,830 per year), 17 teaching assistantships with full and partial tuition reimbursements (averaging $9,224 per year) were awarded; Federal Work-Study, scholarships/grants, health care benefits, and unspecified assistantships also available. *Faculty research:* Risk, resilience, and developmental psychopathology; treatment, intervention, and prevention science; emotion, regulation, and relational processes; adult development and aging; cultural context and diversity. *Total annual research expenditures:* $1.7 million. *Unit head:* Dr. Lise Youngblade, Department Head, 970-491-3581, Fax: 970-491-7975, E-mail: lise.youngblade@colostate.edu. *Application contact:* Mary Daughtrey, Administrative Assistant III, 970-491-2872, Fax: 970-491-7975, E-mail: mary.daughtrey@colostate.edu.
Website: http://www.hdfs.chhs.colostate.edu/

Cornell University, Graduate School, Graduate Fields of Human Ecology, Field of Human Development, Ithaca, NY 14853. Offers developmental psychology (MA, PhD), including cognitive development, developmental psychopathology, ecology of human development, social and personality development; human development and family studies (MA, PhD), including ecology of human development, family studies and the life course. *Degree requirements:* For doctorate, comprehensive exam, thesis/dissertation, pre-doctoral research project, teaching experience. *Entrance requirements:* For doctorate, GRE General Test, 2 letters of recommendation. Additional exam requirements/recommendations for international students: Required—TOEFL (minimum score 550 paper-based; 77 iBT). Electronic applications accepted. *Faculty research:* Cognitive development, developmental psychopathology, ecology of human development, family studies and the life course, social and personality development.

Duke University, Graduate School, Department of Psychology and Neuroscience, Durham, NC 27708. Offers biological psychology (PhD); clinical psychology (PhD); cognitive psychology (PhD); developmental psychology (PhD); experimental psychology (PhD); health psychology (PhD); human social development (PhD); JD/MA. *Accreditation:* APA (one or more programs are accredited). *Degree requirements:* For doctorate, thesis/dissertation. *Entrance requirements:* For doctorate, GRE General Test. Additional exam requirements/recommendations for international students: Required—TOEFL (minimum score 577 paper-based; 90 iBT) or IELTS (minimum score 7). Electronic applications accepted.

Eastern Illinois University, Graduate School, College of Health and Human Services, Program in Human Services Program Development, Charleston, IL 61920. Offers MHS. *Program availability:* Part-time, evening/weekend, online learning. *Degree requirements:* For master's, comprehensive exam (for some programs), thesis (for some programs). *Entrance requirements:* For master's, GMAT or GRE. Additional exam requirements/recommendations for international students: Required—TOEFL (minimum score 500 paper-based; 61 iBT), IELTS (minimum score 6). *Application deadline:* For fall admission, 5/15 for domestic and international students; for spring admission, 10/15 for domestic and international students. Applications are processed on a rolling basis. Application fee: $30. Electronic applications accepted. *Financial support:* Research assistantships with full tuition reimbursements, teaching assistantships with full tuition reimbursements, career-related internships or fieldwork, Federal Work-Study, and unspecified assistantships available. Support available to part-time students. Financial award application deadline: 3/1; financial award applicants required to submit FAFSA. *Unit head:* Linda Simpson, Coordinator, 217-581-2315, Fax: 217-581-6090, E-mail: ldsimpson@eiu.edu. *Application contact:* Linda Simpson, Coordinator, 217-581-2315, Fax: 217-581-6090, E-mail: ldsimpson@eiu.edu.
Website: https://www.eiu.edu/mhs/

Erikson Institute, Academic Programs, Chicago, IL 60654. Offers administration (Certificate); bilingual/ESL (Certificate); child development (MS); early childhood education (MS); infant mental health (Certificate); infant studies (Certificate); MS/MSW. MS/MSW offered jointly with Loyola University Chicago. *Program availability:* Part-time, evening/weekend. *Degree requirements:* For master's, comprehensive exam, internship; for Certificate, internship. *Entrance requirements:* For master's and Certificate, minimum GPA of 2.75. Additional exam requirements/recommendations for international students: Required—TOEFL. *Faculty research:* Assessment strategies from early childhood through elementary years; language, literacy, and the arts in children's development; inclusive special education; parent-child relationships; cognitive development.

Fielding Graduate University, Graduate Programs, School of Leadership Studies, Programs in Human and Organizational Development, Santa Barbara, CA 93105-3814. Offers human development (PhD); organizational consulting (Graduate Certificate); organizational development and change (PhD); organizational development and leadership (MA, Graduate Certificate). *Program availability:* Part-time, evening/weekend, 100% online, blended/hybrid learning. *Faculty:* 12 full-time (7 women), 36 part-time/adjunct (20 women). *Students:* 189 full-time (132 women), 29 part-time (20 women); includes 68 minority (30 Black or African American, non-Hispanic/Latino; 10 Asian, non-Hispanic/Latino; 15 Hispanic/Latino; 2 Native Hawaiian or other Pacific Islander, non-Hispanic/Latino; 11 Two or more races, non-Hispanic/Latino), 3 international. Average age 50. 54 applicants, 93% accepted, 30 enrolled. In 2017, 16 master's, 57 doctorates, 3 other advanced degrees awarded. *Degree requirements:* For doctorate, comprehensive exam, thesis/dissertation. *Entrance requirements:* For master's and Graduate Certificate, bachelor's or master's degree, resume, statement of purpose, official transcript; for doctorate, bachelor's or master's degree, resume, statement of purpose, reflexive essay, official transcript. *Application deadline:* For fall admission, 7/16 for domestic and international students; for spring admission, 11/1 for domestic and international students; for summer admission, 3/1 for domestic and international students. Application fee: $75. Electronic applications accepted. *Expenses:* Contact institution. *Financial support:* In 2017–18, 36 students received support, including 1 research assistantship; teaching assistantships and scholarships/grants also available. Support available to part-time students. Financial award applicants required to submit FAFSA. *Unit head:* Dr. Dorothy Agger-Gupta, Program Director, E-mail: dotagger@fielding.edu. *Application contact:* Enrollment Coordinator, 800-340-1099 Ext. 4098, Fax: 805-687-9793, E-mail: admissions@fielding.edu.
Website: http://www.fielding.edu/our-programs/school-of-leadership-studies/

Florida State University, The Graduate School, College of Human Sciences, Department of Family and Child Sciences, Tallahassee, FL 32306-1491. Offers family and child sciences (MS); human development and family sciences (PhD); marriage and family therapy (PhD). *Accreditation:* AAMFT/COAMFTE. *Program availability:* Part-time. *Faculty:* 14 full-time (8 women). *Students:* 28 full-time (21 women); includes 9 minority (6 Black or African American, non-Hispanic/Latino; 1 Asian, non-Hispanic/Latino; 1 Hispanic/Latino; 1 Two or more races, non-Hispanic/Latino), 2 international. 21 applicants, 33% accepted, 5 enrolled. In 2017, 6 master's, 7 doctorates awarded. Terminal master's awarded for partial completion of doctoral program. *Degree requirements:* For master's, thesis optional; for doctorate, thesis/dissertation, preliminary examination; clinical examination (for marriage and family therapy). *Entrance requirements:* For master's and doctorate, GRE General Test, writing assessment, minimum GPA of 3.0. Additional exam requirements/recommendations for international students: Required—TOEFL (minimum score 550 paper-based; 80 iBT). *Application deadline:* For fall admission, 12/1 for domestic and international students. Applications are processed on a rolling basis. Application fee: $30. Electronic applications accepted. *Expenses:* $480 per credit hour in-state; $1,111 per credit hour out-of-state. *Financial support:* In 2017–18, 33 students received support, including 12 research assistantships with full tuition reimbursements available (averaging $6,062 per year), 32 teaching assistantships with full tuition reimbursements available (averaging $16,142 per year); fellowships with partial tuition reimbursements available, career-related internships or fieldwork, Federal Work-Study, institutionally sponsored loans, scholarships/grants, health care benefits, and unspecified assistantships also available. Financial award application deadline: 1/5; financial award applicants required to submit FAFSA. *Faculty research:* Family therapy, parent-child relations, distressed families and foster care, marital processes, relational interventions, family structural complexity. *Total annual research expenditures:* $1.3 million. *Unit head:* Dr. Joseph Grzywacz, Department Chair, 850-644-3217, Fax: 850-644-3439, E-mail: jgrzywacz@fsu.edu. *Application contact:* Mary-Sue McLemore, Academic Support Assistant, 850-644-1117, E-mail: mmclemore@fsu.edu.
Website: https://humansciences.fsu.edu/family-child-sciences/students/graduate-programs/

Georgetown University, Graduate School of Arts and Sciences, Department of Psychology, Washington, DC 20057. Offers human development and public policy (PhD); lifespan cognitive neuroscience (PhD); PhD/MPP. PhD/MPP offered jointly with McCourt School of Public Policy. *Faculty:* 13 full-time (9 women). *Students:* 17 full-time (11 women), 3 international. 105 applicants, 5 enrolled. *Degree requirements:* For doctorate, thesis/dissertation, area paper. *Entrance requirements:* For doctorate, GRE General Test, GRE Subject Test. Additional exam requirements/recommendations for international students: Required—TOEFL. *Application deadline:* For fall admission, 12/1 for domestic and international students. Application fee: $50 ($55 for international students). Electronic applications accepted. *Financial support:* In 2017–18, 16 students received support, including 16 teaching assistantships with full tuition reimbursements available (averaging $28,000 per year); research assistantships also available. Financial award application deadline: 2/1; financial award applicants required to submit FAFSA. *Unit head:* Dr. Chandan Vaidya, Chair, 202-687-4274, Fax: 202-687-6050, E-mail: cjv2@georgetown.edu. *Application contact:* Graduate School Admissions Office, 202-687-5568, E-mail: gradmail@georgetown.edu.
Website: https://psychology.georgetown.edu

Georgetown University, Graduate School of Arts and Sciences, Walsh School of Foreign Service, Program in Global Human Development, Washington, DC 20057. Offers MA.

The George Washington University, Graduate School of Education and Human Development, Department of Educational Leadership, Individualized Master's Program, Washington, DC 20052. Offers MA Ed. *Students:* 15 part-time (12 women); includes 6 minority (4 Black or African American, non-Hispanic/Latino; 2 Hispanic/Latino). Average age 41. 5 applicants, 80% accepted, 2 enrolled. In 2017, 14 master's awarded. *Entrance requirements:* For master's, GRE General Test or MAT, minimum GPA of 2.75. *Application deadline:* For fall admission, 3/1 priority date for domestic students; for spring admission, 10/1 for domestic students. Applications are processed on a rolling basis. Application fee: $75. *Expenses: Tuition:* Full-time $28,800; part-time $1655 per credit hour. *Required fees:* $45; $2.75 per credit hour. *Financial support:* Application deadline: 1/15; applicants required to submit FAFSA. *Unit head:* Michael Feuer, Dean, 202-994-6161, Fax: 202-994-7207, E-mail: mjfeuer@gwu.edu. *Application contact:* Sarah Lang, Director of Graduate Admissions, 202-994-1447, Fax: 202-994-7207, E-mail: slang@gwu.edu.

Georgia State University, College of Education and Human Development, Atlanta, GA 30302-3083. Offers M Ed, MAT, MS, Ed D, PhD, Ed S. *Accreditation:* NCATE. *Program availability:* Part-time, evening/weekend, online learning. *Faculty:* 103 full-time (64 women). *Students:* 874 full-time (662 women), 472 part-time (324 women); includes 656 minority (460 Black or African American, non-Hispanic/Latino; 1 American Indian or Alaska Native, non-Hispanic/Latino; 52 Asian, non-Hispanic/Latino; 92 Hispanic/Latino; 1 Native Hawaiian or other Pacific Islander, non-Hispanic/Latino; 50 Two or more races, non-Hispanic/Latino), 36 international. Average age 31. 1,084 applicants, 43% accepted, 333 enrolled. In 2017, 333 master's, 64 doctorates, 36 other advanced degrees awarded. Terminal master's awarded for partial completion of doctoral program. *Degree requirements:* For master's, comprehensive exam (for some programs), thesis (for some programs), minimum GPA of 3.0; for doctorate, comprehensive exam, thesis/dissertation, minimum GPA of 3.5; for Ed S, thesis or alternative, minimum GPA of 3.0. *Entrance requirements:* For master's, GRE, MAT (for some programs), minimum GPA of 2.5 on all undergraduate work attempted in which letter grades were awarded; for doctorate, GRE, MAT (for some programs), minimum GPA of 3.3 on all graduate coursework for which letter grades were awarded (for PhD); for Ed S, GRE, MAT (for some programs), graduate degree from regionally-accredited college or university unless specified otherwise by the program with minimum GPA of 3.25 on all graduate coursework for which letter grades were awarded. Application fee:

$50. Electronic applications accepted. *Expenses:* Tuition, state resident: full-time $7020. Tuition, nonresident: full-time $22,518. *Required fees:* $2128. Tuition and fees vary according to degree level and program. *Financial support:* In 2017–18, fellowships with full tuition reimbursements (averaging $25,000 per year), research assistantships with tuition reimbursements (averaging $4,867 per year), teaching assistantships with tuition reimbursements (averaging $4,683 per year) were awarded; career-related internships or fieldwork, Federal Work-Study, scholarships/grants, tuition waivers (partial), and unspecified assistantships also available. Support available to part-time students. Financial award applicants required to submit FAFSA. *Faculty research:* Literacy: early, middle-secondary, adult and deaf/hard of hearing; teacher professional development, evaluation and urban education; STEM teacher education; health, physical activity and exercise science; school safety and counseling. *Unit head:* Dr. Paul A. Alberto, Interim Dean, 404-413-8100, Fax: 404-413-8103, E-mail: palberto@gsu.edu. *Application contact:* Nancy Keita, Director, Office of Academic Assistance and Graduate Admissions, 404-413-8001, E-mail: nkeita@gsu.edu.
Website: http://education.gsu.edu/main/

Harvard University, Harvard Graduate School of Education, Master's Programs in Education, Cambridge, MA 02138. Offers arts in education (Ed M); education policy and management (Ed M); higher education (Ed M); human development and psychology (Ed M); international education policy (Ed M); language and literacy (Ed M); learning and teaching (Ed M); mind, brain, and education (Ed M); prevention science and practice (Ed M); school leadership (Ed M); special studies (Ed M); teacher education (Ed M); technology, innovation, and education (Ed M). *Program availability:* Part-time. *Entrance requirements:* For master's, GRE General Test, statement of purpose, 3 letters of recommendation, resume, official transcripts. Additional exam requirements/recommendations for international students: Required—TOEFL (minimum score 613 paper-based; 104 iBT), TWE (minimum score 5). Electronic applications accepted. *Faculty research:* Learning and development, educational leadership and organizations, education policy analysis.

Hofstra University, School of Education, Programs in Teacher Education, Hempstead, NY 11549. Offers bilingual education (MA); bilingual extension (Advanced Certificate), including education/speech language pathology, intensive teacher institute; business education (MS Ed); curriculum studies (MS Ed); early childhood and childhood education (MS Ed); early childhood education (MA, MS Ed); educational technology (Advanced Certificate); elementary education (MA, MS Ed), including science, technology, engineering, and mathematics (STEM) (MA); English education (MS Ed); family and consumer science (MS Ed); fine arts and music education (Advanced Certificate); fine arts education (MS Ed); foreign language and TESOL (MS Ed); foreign language education (MA, MS Ed), including Arabic (MS Ed), biology, chemistry, Chinese (MS Ed), earth science, French, German, Italian (MS Ed), Mandarin (MS Ed), physics, Russian, Spanish; foundations of education (Advanced Certificate), including grades 5-6, grades 7-9; languages other than English and teaching English as a second language (MA); learning and teaching (Ed D), including applied linguistics, art education, arts and humanities, early childhood education, English education, human development, math education, math, science, and technology, multicultural education, physical education, science education, social studies education, special education; mathematics education (MA, MS Ed); music education (MA, MS Ed); science education (MA), including biology (MA, MS Ed), chemistry (MA, MS Ed), earth science (MA, MS Ed), physics (MA, MS Ed); secondary education (Advanced Certificate); social studies education (MA, MS Ed); teaching languages other than English and TESOL (MS Ed); technology for learning (MA); TESOL (MS Ed, Advanced Certificate); TESOL with specialization in STEM (MA); work based learning extension (Advanced Certificate). *Program availability:* Part-time, evening/weekend, blended/hybrid learning. *Students:* 119 full-time (83 women), 124 part-time (90 women); includes 54 minority (15 Black or African American, non-Hispanic/Latino; 9 Asian, non-Hispanic/Latino; 29 Hispanic/Latino; 1 Native Hawaiian or other Pacific Islander, non-Hispanic/Latino), 12 international. Average age 29. 205 applicants, 88% accepted, 93 enrolled. In 2017, 103 master's, 4 doctorates, 32 other advanced degrees awarded. *Degree requirements:* For master's, comprehensive exam, thesis (for some programs), exit project, student teaching, fieldwork, electronic portfolio, curriculum project, minimum GPA of 3.0; for doctorate, thesis/dissertation; for Advanced Certificate, 3 foreign languages, comprehensive exam (for some programs), thesis project. *Entrance requirements:* For master's, GRE, 2 letters of recommendation, portfolio, teacher certification (MA), interview, essay; for doctorate, GMAT, GRE, LSAT, or MAT; for Advanced Certificate, 2 letters of recommendation, essay, interview and/or portfolio, teaching certificate. Additional exam requirements/recommendations for international students: Required—TOEFL (minimum score 550 paper-based; 80 iBT). *Application deadline:* Applications are processed on a rolling basis. Application fee: $75. Electronic applications accepted. *Expenses: Tuition:* Full-time $1292. *Required fees:* $970. Tuition and fees vary according to program. *Financial support:* In 2017–18, 112 students received support, including 56 fellowships with full and partial tuition reimbursements available (averaging $4,998 per year), 2 research assistantships with full and partial tuition reimbursements available (averaging $8,753 per year); career-related internships or fieldwork, Federal Work-Study, institutionally sponsored loans, scholarships/grants, traineeships, tuition waivers (full and partial), and unspecified assistantships also available. Support available to part-time students. Financial award applicants required to submit FAFSA. *Faculty research:* Educational interventions that foster critical-thinking skills; teachers' attitudes about professional development; threats to teacher quality. *Unit head:* Dr. Eustace Thompson, Chairperson, 516-463-5749, Fax: 516-463-6275, E-mail: eustace.g.thompson@hofstra.edu. *Application contact:* Sunil Samuel, Assistant Vice President of Admissions, 516-463-4723, Fax: 516-463-4664, E-mail: graduateadmission@hofstra.edu.
Website: http://www.hofstra.edu/education

Hood College, Graduate School, Programs in Human Behavior, Frederick, MD 21701-8575. Offers interdisciplinary studies in human behavior (MA), including psychology; thanatology (Certificate). *Program availability:* Part-time, evening/weekend. *Faculty:* 1 (woman) full-time, 2 part-time/adjunct (0 women). *Students:* 9 full-time (6 women), 22 part-time (16 women); includes 4 minority (2 Black or African American, non-Hispanic/Latino; 2 Two or more races, non-Hispanic/Latino), 2 international. Average age 37. 7 applicants, 100% accepted, 2 enrolled. In 2017, 9 master's, 11 other advanced degrees awarded. *Degree requirements:* For master's, comprehensive exam, thesis optional, capstone/research project. *Entrance requirements:* For master's, minimum GPA of 2.75, essay; for Certificate, minimum GPA of 2.75, essay, resume. Additional exam requirements/recommendations for international students: Required—TOEFL (minimum score 575 paper-based; 89 iBT), IELTS (minimum score 6.5). *Application deadline:* For fall admission, 8/15 priority date for domestic students, 8/5 for international students; for spring admission, 12/1 priority date for domestic students, 12/1 for international students; for summer admission, 5/1 priority date for domestic students, 4/15 for international students. Applications are processed on a rolling basis. Application fee: $35. Electronic applications accepted. *Expenses:* $465 per credit hour plus $110 comprehensive fee per semester. *Financial support:* Research assistantships with full tuition reimbursements, tuition waivers (partial), and unspecified assistantships available. Financial award applicants required to submit FAFSA. *Faculty research:* Mind-body medicine and multicultural healing, the New Orleans jazz funeral, death practices in African-American culture, bereavement theories and gender differences, Piaget's

theory of cognitive development as a formal mathematical model. *Unit head:* Dr. April M. Boulton, Dean of the Graduate School, 301-696-3600, E-mail: gofurther@hood.edu. *Application contact:* Jan Marcus, Assistant Director of Graduate Admissions, 301-696-3600, E-mail: gofurther@hood.edu.
Website: http://www.hood.edu/graduate

Iowa State University of Science and Technology, Department of Human Development and Family Studies, Ames, IA 50011. Offers human development and family studies (MFCS, MS, PhD). *Degree requirements:* For master's, thesis; for doctorate, thesis/dissertation. *Entrance requirements:* For master's and doctorate, GRE General Test. Additional exam requirements/recommendations for international students: Required—TOEFL (minimum score 550 paper-based; 79 iBT), IELTS (minimum score 6.5). Electronic applications accepted. *Faculty research:* Child development, early childhood education, family resource management and housing, life span studies.

Kansas State University, Graduate School, College of Human Ecology, Doctorate in Human Ecology Program, Manhattan, KS 66506-1407. Offers apparel and textiles (PhD); applied family sciences (PhD); couple and family therapy (PhD); hospitality administration (PhD); kinesiology (PhD); life-span human development (PhD). *Program availability:* Part-time. *Degree requirements:* For doctorate, thesis/dissertation. *Entrance requirements:* Additional exam requirements/recommendations for international students: Required—TOEFL. Electronic applications accepted.

Kansas State University, Graduate School, College of Human Ecology, School of Family Studies and Human Services, Manhattan, KS 66506-1403. Offers applied family sciences (MS); communication sciences and disorders (MS); conflict resolution (Graduate Certificate); couple and family therapy (MS); early childhood education (MS); family and community service (MS); life-span human development (MS); personal financial planning (MS, PhD, Graduate Certificate); youth development (MS, Graduate Certificate). *Accreditation:* AAMFT/COAMFTE; ASHA. *Program availability:* Part-time, online learning. *Degree requirements:* For master's, comprehensive exam (for some programs), thesis optional. *Entrance requirements:* For master's, GRE, minimum GPA of 3.0 in last 2 years (60 semester hours) of undergraduate study; for doctorate, GRE. Additional exam requirements/recommendations for international students: Required—TOEFL (minimum score 600 paper-based). Electronic applications accepted. *Faculty research:* Health and security of military families, training in and evaluation of professional human services (marriage and couple therapy, family life education, treatment of speech and swallowing disorders, financial therapy), disorders of communication and swallowing, family and relationship development and health, financial decision-making.

Kent State University, College of Education, Health and Human Services, School of Lifespan Development and Educational Sciences, Program in Counseling and Human Development Services, Kent, OH 44242-0001. Offers PhD. *Accreditation:* ACA; NCATE. *Degree requirements:* For doctorate, comprehensive exam, thesis/dissertation. *Entrance requirements:* For doctorate, GRE General Test, preliminary written exam, 2 letters of reference, resume, interview. Additional exam requirements/recommendations for international students: Required—TOEFL (minimum score 550 paper-based; 80 iBT). Electronic applications accepted. *Expenses:* Tuition, state resident: full-time $11,310; part-time $515 per credit hour. Tuition, nonresident: full-time $20,396; part-time $928 per credit hour. *International tuition:* $18,544 full-time. *Faculty research:* Family/child therapy, clinical supervision, group work, experiential training methods.

Kent State University, College of Education, Health and Human Services, School of Lifespan Development and Educational Sciences, Program in Human Development and Family Studies, Kent, OH 44242-0001. Offers MA. *Degree requirements:* For master's, thesis optional. *Entrance requirements:* For master's, minimum undergraduate GPA of 3.0, 3 letters of reference, goals statement. Additional exam requirements/recommendations for international students: Required—TOEFL (minimum score 550 paper-based; 80 iBT). *Expenses:* Tuition, state resident: full-time $11,310; part-time $515 per credit hour. Tuition, nonresident: full-time $20,396; part-time $928 per credit hour. *International tuition:* $18,544 full-time.

Laurentian University, School of Graduate Studies and Research, Programme in Human Development, Sudbury, ON P3E 2C6, Canada. Offers M Sc, MA. Interdisciplinary program consisting of the Departments of Psychology, Sociology, and Human Movement. *Program availability:* Part-time. *Degree requirements:* For master's, thesis or alternative. *Entrance requirements:* For master's, honors degree with second class or better. *Faculty research:* Aging and well-being, physical, social and cognitive development of children, social cognition and social relationships including peers and family, education and schooling.

Lindsey Wilson College, School of Professional Counseling, Columbia, KY 42728. Offers counseling and human development (M Ed); counselor education and supervision (PhD). *Accreditation:* ACA (one or more programs are accredited). *Program availability:* Part-time, evening/weekend, online learning.

Marywood University, Academic Affairs, Center for Interdisciplinary Studies, Scranton, PA 18509-1598. Offers human development (PhD), including educational administration, health promotion, higher education administration, instructional leadership, social work. *Program availability:* Part-time. Electronic applications accepted. *Expenses:* Contact institution.

Mississippi State University, College of Agriculture and Life Sciences, School of Human Sciences, Mississippi State, MS 39762. Offers agriculture and extension education (MS), including communication, leadership; agriculture science (PhD), including agriculture and extension education; fashion design and merchandising (MS), including design and product development, merchandising; human development and family studies (MS, PhD). *Accreditation:* NCATE (one or more programs are accredited). *Program availability:* Part-time. *Faculty:* 20 full-time (11 women). *Students:* 31 full-time (23 women), 54 part-time (38 women); includes 19 minority (15 Black or African American, non-Hispanic/Latino; 1 Hispanic/Latino; 3 Two or more races, non-Hispanic/Latino), 5 international. Average age 36. 26 applicants, 65% accepted, 15 enrolled. In 2017, 19 master's, 2 doctorates awarded. *Degree requirements:* For master's, thesis optional, comprehensive oral or written exam. *Entrance requirements:* For master's, GRE, minimum GPA of 2.75 in last 4 semesters of course work; for doctorate, minimum GPA of 3.0 on prior graduate work. Additional exam requirements/recommendations for international students: Required—TOEFL (minimum score 477 paper-based; 53 iBT); Recommended—IELTS (minimum score 4.5). *Application deadline:* For fall admission, 7/1 for domestic students, 5/1 for international students; for spring admission, 11/1 for domestic students, 9/1 for international students. Applications are processed on a rolling basis. Application fee: $60 ($80 for international students). Electronic applications accepted. *Expenses:* Tuition, state resident: full-time $8318; part-time $462.12 per credit hour. Tuition, nonresident: full-time $22,358; part-time $1242.12 per credit hour. *Required fees:* $110; $12.24 per credit hour. $6.12 per semester. *Financial support:* In 2017–18, 13 research assistantships (averaging $13,718 per year) were awarded; Federal Work-Study, institutionally sponsored loans, and unspecified assistantships also available. Financial award application deadline: 4/1; financial award applicants required to submit FAFSA. *Faculty research:* Animal welfare, agroscience, information technology, learning styles, problem solving. *Unit head:* Dr. Michael Newman, Professor

and Director, 662-325-2950, E-mail: mnewman@humansci.msstate.edu. *Application contact:* Marina Hunt, Admissions and Enrollment Assistant, 662-325-5188, E-mail: mhunt@grad.msstate.edu.
Website: http://www.humansci.msstate.edu

Montana State University, The Graduate School, College of Education, Health, and Human Development, Department of Health and Human Development, Bozeman, MT 59717. Offers family and consumer sciences (MS). *Accreditation:* ACA. *Program availability:* Part-time, online learning. *Degree requirements:* For master's, comprehensive exam. *Entrance requirements:* For master's, GRE (minimum scores: verbal 480; quantitative 480). Additional exam requirements/recommendations for international students: Required—TOEFL (minimum score 550 paper-based). Electronic applications accepted. *Faculty research:* Community food systems, ethic of care for teachers and coaches, influence of public policy on families and communities, cost effectiveness of early childhood education, exercise metabolism, winter sport performance enhancement, assessment of physical activity.

Murray State University, College of Education and Human Services, Department of Community Leadership and Human Services, Murray, KY 42071. Offers nonprofit leadership studies (MS, Certificate). *Program availability:* Part-time, evening/weekend, 100% online, blended/hybrid learning. *Faculty:* 6 full-time (2 women), 1 part-time/adjunct (0 women). *Students:* 4 full-time (all women), 14 part-time (12 women); includes 3 minority (2 Black or African American, non-Hispanic/Latino; 1 American Indian or Alaska Native, non-Hispanic/Latino), 1 international. Average age 41. 7 applicants, 57% accepted, 2 enrolled. In 2017, 3 master's awarded. *Entrance requirements:* For master's, GRE or GMAT, minimum university GPA of 2.75. Additional exam requirements/recommendations for international students: Required—TOEFL (minimum score 527 paper-based; 71 iBT). *Application deadline:* Applications are processed on a rolling basis. Application fee: $40 ($50 for international students). Electronic applications accepted. *Expenses:* Tuition, state resident: full-time $9504. Tuition, nonresident: full-time $26,811. *International tuition:* $14,400 full-time. Tuition and fees vary according to course load, degree level and reciprocity agreements. *Financial support:* Federal Work-Study and unspecified assistantships available. Financial award applicants required to submit FAFSA. *Faculty research:* Service learning, engaged citizenship, volunteer development, youth programming, philanthropy. *Unit head:* Dr. Paul Lucko, Chair, Community Leadership and Human Services, 270-809-2785, E-mail: plucko@murraystate.edu. *Application contact:* Kaitlyn Burzynski, Interim Assistant Director for Graduate Admission and Records, 270-809-5732, Fax: 270-809-3780, E-mail: msu.graduateadmissions@murraystate.edu.
Website: https://www.murraystate.edu/academics/CollegesDepartments/CollegeOfEducationandHumanServices/coehsacademicunits/CLHS/index.aspx

Murray State University, College of Education and Human Services, Department of Educational Studies, Leadership and Counseling, Murray, KY 42071. Offers college advising (Certificate); education administration (MA Ed); human development and leadership (MS, Certificate); library media (MA Ed); middle school teacher leader (MA Ed); P-20 and community leadership (Ed D); postsecondary education administration (MA Ed); school counseling (MA Ed); school guidance and counseling (Ed S); secondary teacher leader (MA Ed). *Program availability:* Part-time, evening/weekend, 100% online, blended/hybrid learning. *Faculty:* 38 full-time (16 women), 3 part-time/adjunct (1 woman). *Students:* 45 full-time (22 women), 190 part-time (140 women); includes 33 minority (25 Black or African American, non-Hispanic/Latino; 4 Asian, non-Hispanic/Latino; 3 Hispanic/Latino; 1 Two or more races, non-Hispanic/Latino), 6 international. Average age 35. 87 applicants, 77% accepted, 51 enrolled. In 2017, 21 master's, 16 doctorates, 12 other advanced degrees awarded. *Entrance requirements:* For master's and other advanced degree, GRE or GMAT, minimum university GPA of 2.75. Additional exam requirements/recommendations for international students: Required—TOEFL (minimum score 527 paper-based; 71 iBT). *Application deadline:* Applications are processed on a rolling basis. Application fee: $40 ($50 for international students). Electronic applications accepted. *Expenses:* Tuition, state resident: full-time $9504. Tuition, nonresident: full-time $26,811. *International tuition:* $14,400 full-time. Tuition and fees vary according to course load, degree level and reciprocity agreements. *Financial support:* Federal Work-Study and unspecified assistantships available. Financial award applicants required to submit FAFSA. *Unit head:* Dr. Susana Bloomdahl, Chair, Department of Educational Studies, Leadership, and Counseling, 270-809-6471, Fax: 270-809-3799, E-mail: sbloomdahl@murraystate.edu. *Application contact:* Kaitlyn Burzynski, Interim Assistant Director for Graduate Admission and Records, 270-809-5732, Fax: 270-809-3780, E-mail: msu.graduateadmissions@murraystate.edu.
Website: http://www.murraystate.edu/academics/CollegesDepartments/CollegeOfEducationandHumanServices/coehsacademicunits/EducationalStudiesLeadershipandCounseli

National Louis University, National College of Education, Chicago, IL 60603. Offers administration and supervision (M Ed, Ed D, CAS, Ed S); curriculum and instruction (M Ed, MS Ed, CAS); early childhood administration (M Ed, CAS); early childhood education (M Ed, MAT, MS Ed, CAS); education (Ed D); educational psychology/human learning and development (M Ed, MS Ed, CAS, Ed S); elementary education (MAT); interdisciplinary curriculum and instruction (M Ed); mathematics education (M Ed, MS Ed, CAS); middle grades education (MAT); reading and language (M Ed, MS Ed, CAS); school psychology (M Ed, Ed S); science education (M Ed, MS Ed, CAS); secondary education (MAT); special education (M Ed, MAT, CAS); technology in education (M Ed, CAS). *Accreditation:* NCATE. *Program availability:* Part-time, evening/weekend. *Degree requirements:* For doctorate, comprehensive exam, thesis/dissertation. *Entrance requirements:* For master's, MAT or GRE, minimum GPA of 3.0; for doctorate, GRE General Test, minimum GPA of 3.25, interview, resume, writing sample, 4 recommendations. Additional exam requirements/recommendations for international students: Required—TOEFL (minimum score 550 paper-based; 79 iBT).

New York University, Steinhardt School of Culture, Education, and Human Development, New York, NY 10003. Offers MA, MFA, MM, MPH, MS, DPS, DPT, Ed D, PhD, Advanced Certificate, Post Master's Certificate, Postbaccalaureate Certificate, Advanced Certificate/MPH, MA/Advanced Certificate, MA/MA, MA/MS, MLIS/MA. *Accreditation:* TEAC. *Program availability:* Part-time. *Students:* Average age 31. 6,757 applicants, 42% accepted, 1245 enrolled. In 2017, 1,316 master's, 109 doctorates, 36 other advanced degrees awarded. *Entrance requirements:* For doctorate, GRE General Test, interview. Additional exam requirements/recommendations for international students: Required—TOEFL (minimum score 100 iBT). *Application deadline:* Applications are processed on a rolling basis. Application fee: $75. Electronic applications accepted. *Expenses:* Contact institution. *Financial support:* Fellowships, research assistantships, teaching assistantships, career-related internships or fieldwork, Federal Work-Study, institutionally sponsored loans, scholarships/grants, traineeships, tuition waivers (partial), and unspecified assistantships available. Support available to part-time students. Financial award application deadline: 2/1; financial award applicants required to submit FAFSA. *Faculty research:* Equity, urban adolescents, arts in education, globalization, multivariate analysis, psychometrics. *Total annual research expenditures:* $30.4 million. *Unit head:* Dr. Dominic Brewer, Dean, 212-998-5000. *Application contact:* John Myers, Director of Enrollment Management, 212-998-5030, Fax: 212-995-4328, E-mail: steinhardt.gradadmissions@nyu.edu.
Website: http://steinhardt.nyu.edu/

New York University, Steinhardt School of Culture, Education, and Human Development, Department of Applied Psychology, Programs in Educational and Developmental Psychology, New York, NY 10012. Offers developmental psychology (PhD); human development and social intervention (MA); psychology and social intervention (PhD). *Accreditation:* APA (one or more programs are accredited). *Program availability:* Part-time. *Students:* Average age 27. 137 applicants, 26% accepted, 13 enrolled. In 2017, 16 master's, 4 doctorates awarded. *Entrance requirements:* For doctorate, GRE General Test, interview. Additional exam requirements/recommendations for international students: Required—TOEFL. *Application deadline:* For fall admission, 12/1 priority date for domestic and international students. Applications are processed on a rolling basis. Application fee: $75. Electronic applications accepted. *Expenses: Tuition:* Full-time $41,352; part-time $19,968 per year. *Required fees:* $2496; $1628 per unit. $814 per term. Tuition and fees vary according to course load and program. *Financial support:* Teaching assistantships with partial tuition reimbursements, career-related internships or fieldwork, Federal Work-Study, institutionally sponsored loans, and tuition waivers (partial) available. Support available to part-time students. Financial award application deadline: 2/1; financial award applicants required to submit FAFSA. *Faculty research:* Schools and communities, self-regulation and academic achievement, intervention and social change, trauma and resilience, cognition. *Unit head:* Prof. Clancy Blair, Director, 212-998-5853, Fax: 212-995-4358, E-mail: clancy.blair@nyu.edu. *Application contact:* 212-998-5030, Fax: 212-995-4328, E-mail: steinhardt.gradadmissions@nyu.edu.
Website: http://steinhardt.nyu.edu/appsych

Northern Arizona University, College of Social and Behavioral Sciences, Institute for Human Development, Flagstaff, AZ 86011. Offers assistive technology (Graduate Certificate). *Program availability:* Part-time. *Students:* 4 part-time (3 women); includes 2 minority (both Hispanic/Latino). Average age 36. 3 applicants, 100% accepted, 3 enrolled. In 2017, 8 Graduate Certificates awarded. *Degree requirements:* For Graduate Certificate, comprehensive exam (for some programs). *Entrance requirements:* For degree, undergraduate degree from regionally-accredited institution with minimum GPA of 3.0, or the equivalent. Additional exam requirements/recommendations for international students: Required—TOEFL (minimum score 80 iBT), IELTS (minimum score 6.5). *Application deadline:* For fall admission, 3/1 for domestic and international students; for spring admission, 10/1 for domestic and international students. Applications are processed on a rolling basis. Application fee: $65. Electronic applications accepted. *Expenses:* Tuition, state resident: full-time $9240; part-time $458 per credit hour. Tuition, nonresident: full-time $21,588; part-time $1199 per credit hour. *Required fees:* $1021; $14 per credit hour. $646 per semester. Tuition and fees vary according to course load, campus/location and program. *Financial support:* Institutionally sponsored loans available. Financial award application deadline: 2/1; financial award applicants required to submit FAFSA. *Unit head:* Richard Carroll, Executive Director, 928-523-7033, Fax: 928-523-9127, E-mail: richard.carroll@nau.edu. *Application contact:* Karen Applequist, Graduate Coordinator, 928-523-9276, E-mail: karen.applequist@nau.edu.
Website: http://nau.edu/sbs/ihd/

Northwestern University, The Graduate School, School of Education and Social Policy, Program in Human Development and Social Policy, Evanston, IL 60208. Offers PhD. Admissions and degrees offered through The Graduate School. *Degree requirements:* For doctorate, comprehensive exam, thesis/dissertation. *Entrance requirements:* For doctorate, GRE General Test. Additional exam requirements/recommendations for international students: Required—TOEFL (minimum score 600 paper-based; 100 iBT). Electronic applications accepted. *Faculty research:* Individual development and the personal narrative; the life course and culture; development, intervention and culture; the life course and policy; analysis of policy effects on lives.

The Ohio State University, Graduate School, College of Education and Human Ecology, Department of Human Sciences, Columbus, OH 43210. Offers consumer sciences (MS, PhD); human development and family science (PhD); human nutrition (MS, PhD); kinesiology (MA, Ed D, PhD). *Program availability:* Part-time. *Faculty:* 55. *Students:* 127 full-time (71 women), 14 part-time (12 women). Average age 27. In 2017, 31 master's, 14 doctorates awarded. *Degree requirements:* For master's, thesis optional; for doctorate, thesis/dissertation. *Entrance requirements:* For master's and doctorate, GRE. Additional exam requirements/recommendations for international students: Required—TOEFL (minimum score 550 paper-based; 79 iBT), Michigan English Language Assessment Battery (minimum score 82); Recommended—IELTS (minimum score 7). *Application deadline:* For fall admission, 12/1 priority date for domestic and international students. Applications are processed on a rolling basis. Application fee: $60 ($70 for international students). Electronic applications accepted. *Financial support:* Fellowships with tuition reimbursements, research assistantships with tuition reimbursements, teaching assistantships with tuition reimbursements, Federal Work-Study, and institutionally sponsored loans available. Support available to part-time students. *Unit head:* Dr. Brian Focht, Associate Chair and Professor, E-mail: focht.10@osu.edu. *Application contact:* Graduate and Professional Admissions, 614-292-9444, Fax: 614-292-3895, E-mail: gpadmissions@osu.edu.
Website: http://ehe.osu.edu/human-sciences/

Oregon State University, College of Public Health and Human Sciences, Program in Human Development and Family Studies, Corvallis, OR 97331. Offers MS, PhD. *Entrance requirements:* For master's, GRE; for doctorate, GRE, master's degree (including thesis). Additional exam requirements/recommendations for international students: Required—TOEFL (minimum score 80 iBT), IELTS (minimum score 6.5). *Application deadline:* For fall admission, 4/15 for domestic and international students. *Financial support:* Application deadline: 1/2. *Unit head:* Megan Ferris, Advisor, 541-737-0781, E-mail: megan.ferris@oregonstate.edu. *Application contact:* Megan Ferris, Doctoral Programs Manager, 541-737-0781, E-mail: megan.ferris@oregonstate.edu.
Website: http://health.oregonstate.edu/degrees/graduate/hdfs

Pacific Oaks College, Graduate School, Program in Human Development, Pasadena, CA 91103. Offers MA. *Program availability:* Part-time, evening/weekend, online learning. *Degree requirements:* For master's, thesis. *Entrance requirements:* Additional exam requirements/recommendations for international students: Required—TOEFL (minimum score 550 paper-based). *Faculty research:* Bicultural development, teaching adults, art education, literacy development, adolescent development.

Penn State University Park, Graduate School, College of Health and Human Development, Department of Human Development and Family Studies, University Park, PA 16802. Offers MS, PhD. *Unit head:* Dr. Ann C. Crouter, Dean, 814-865-1420, Fax: 814-865-3282. *Application contact:* Lori Hawn, Director, Graduate Student Services, 814-865-1795, Fax: 814-863-4627, E-mail: l-gswww@lists.psu.edu.
Website: http://hhd.psu.edu/hdfs/

Purdue University, Graduate School, College of Health and Human Sciences, Department of Child Development and Family Studies, West Lafayette, IN 47907. Offers developmental studies (MS, PhD); family studies (MS, PhD); marriage and family therapy (MS, PhD). *Program availability:* Part-time. *Faculty:* 19 full-time (11 women), 1

(woman) part-time/adjunct. *Students:* 22 full-time (21 women), 1 (woman) part-time; includes 3 minority (1 Black or African American, non-Hispanic/Latino; 1 Hispanic/Latino; 1 Two or more races, non-Hispanic/Latino), 5 international. Average age 26. 41 applicants, 29% accepted, 8 enrolled. In 2017, 4 master's, 3 doctorates awarded. Terminal master's awarded for partial completion of doctoral program. *Degree requirements:* For master's, thesis; for doctorate, thesis/dissertation. *Entrance requirements:* For master's and doctorate, GRE General Test (minimum score 1000 combined verbal and quantitative), minimum undergraduate GPA of 3.0 or equivalent. Additional exam requirements/recommendations for international students: Required—TOEFL (minimum score 600 paper-based; 90 iBT), TWE (minimum score 4). *Application deadline:* For fall admission, 1/4 for domestic and international students. Applications are processed on a rolling basis. Application fee: $60 ($75 for international students). Electronic applications accepted. *Financial support:* Fellowships with full tuition reimbursements, research assistantships with full tuition reimbursements, teaching assistantships with full tuition reimbursements, and career-related internships or fieldwork available. Support available to part-time students. Financial award application deadline: 1/15; financial award applicants required to submit FAFSA. *Faculty research:* Inclusion of children with special needs, families as learning environments, relationships in child care, work-family relations, AIDS prevention. *Unit head:* Dr. Doran C. French, Head, 765-494-9511, E-mail: dcfrench@purdue.edu. *Application contact:* Tina Putz, Graduate Contact, 765-496-3816, E-mail: tputz@purdue.edu.
Website: http://www.purdue.edu/hhs/hdfs/

St. Lawrence University, Department of Education, Program in Counseling and Human Development, Canton, NY 13617. Offers mental health counseling (MS); school counseling (M Ed, CAS). *Program availability:* Part-time, evening/weekend. *Entrance requirements:* For master's, GRE General Test. *Faculty research:* Defense mechanisms and mediation.

Saint Mary's University of Minnesota, Schools of Graduate and Professional Programs, Graduate School of Business and Technology, Human Development Program, Winona, MN 55987-1399. Offers MA. *Unit head:* Dr. Jim Ollhoff, Director, 651-295-2454, Fax: 612-728-5121, E-mail: jollhoff@smumn.edu. *Application contact:* James Callinan, Director of Admissions for Graduate and Professional Programs, 612-728-5158, Fax: 612-728-5121, E-mail: jcallina@smumn.edu.
Website: http://www.smumn.edu/graduate-home/areas-of-study/graduate-school-of-business-technology/ma-in-human-development

Syracuse University, David B. Falk College of Sport and Human Dynamics, Programs in Human Development and Family Science, Syracuse, NY 13244. Offers MA, MS, PhD. *Accreditation:* AAMFT/COAMFTE (one or more programs are accredited). *Program availability:* Part-time. *Degree requirements:* For master's, comprehensive exam (for some programs), thesis; for doctorate, comprehensive exam, thesis/dissertation. *Entrance requirements:* For master's and doctorate, GRE General Test, personal statement, official transcripts, three letters of recommendation, resume. Additional exam requirements/recommendations for international students: Required—TOEFL (minimum score 100 iBT). *Application deadline:* For fall admission, 2/15 priority date for domestic and international students; for spring admission, 11/15 priority date for domestic and international students. Application fee: $75. Electronic applications accepted. *Financial support:* Fellowships with full tuition reimbursements, research assistantships with tuition reimbursements, teaching assistantships with tuition reimbursements, career-related internships or fieldwork, and tuition waivers available. Financial award application deadline: 1/1. *Faculty research:* Family and child theories, research methods, family dynamics, child development. *Unit head:* Dr. Rachel R. Razza, Associate Professor/Graduate Program Director, 315-443-7377, Fax: 315-443-9402, E-mail: rrazza@syr.edu. *Application contact:* Felicia Otero, Director of Admissions, 315-443-5555, E-mail: falk@syr.edu.
Website: http://falk.syr.edu/ChildFamilyStudies/Default.aspx

Texas A&M University–Corpus Christi, College of Graduate Studies, College of Education and Human Development, Corpus Christi, TX 78412. Offers counseling (MS), including counseling; counselor education (PhD); curriculum and instruction (MS, PhD); early childhood education (MS); educational administration (MS); educational leadership (Ed D); elementary education (MS); instructional design and educational technology (MS); kinesiology (MS); reading (MS); secondary education (MS); special education (MS). *Program availability:* Part-time, evening/weekend, blended/hybrid learning. *Faculty:* 50 full-time (29 women), 29 part-time/adjunct (18 women). *Students:* 160 full-time (127 women), 366 part-time (293 women); includes 279 minority (40 Black or African American, non-Hispanic/Latino; 3 Asian, non-Hispanic/Latino; 228 Hispanic/Latino; 8 Two or more races, non-Hispanic/Latino), 18 international. Average age 35. 296 applicants, 65% accepted, 155 enrolled. In 2017, 103 master's, 27 doctorates awarded. *Degree requirements:* For master's, comprehensive exam, capstone; for doctorate, thesis/dissertation. *Entrance requirements:* For master's, GRE General Test, essay (300 words); for doctorate, GRE, essay, resume, 3-4 reference forms. *Application deadline:* For fall admission, 7/15 priority date for domestic students, 5/1 priority date for international students; for spring admission, 11/15 priority date for domestic students, 9/1 priority date for international students. Applications are processed on a rolling basis. Application fee: $50 ($70 for international students). Electronic applications accepted. *Expenses:* Tuition, state resident: full-time $3568; part-time $198.24 per credit hour. Tuition, nonresident: full-time $11,038; part-time $613.24 per credit hour. *Required fees:* $2129; $1422.58 per semester. Tuition and fees vary according to program. *Financial support:* Research assistantships, teaching assistantships, career-related internships or fieldwork, Federal Work-Study, institutionally sponsored loans, scholarships/grants, health care benefits, and unspecified assistantships available. Support available to part-time students. Financial award application deadline: 3/15; financial award applicants required to submit FAFSA. *Unit head:* Dr. David Scott, Dean, 361-825-2660, E-mail: david.scott@tamucc.edu. *Application contact:* Graduate Admissions Coordinator, 361-825-2177, Fax: 361-825-2755, E-mail: gradweb@tamucc.edu.
Website: http://education.tamucc.edu/

Texas Tech University, Graduate School, College of Human Sciences, Department of Human Development and Family Studies, Lubbock, TX 79409-1230. Offers human development and family studies (MS, PhD), including gerontology (MS). *Accreditation:* AAMFT/COAMFTE (one or more programs are accredited). *Faculty:* 25 full-time (21 women), 7 part-time/adjunct (all women). *Students:* 23 full-time (20 women), 41 part-time (26 women); includes 15 minority (5 Black or African American, non-Hispanic/Latino; 9 Hispanic/Latino; 1 Two or more races, non-Hispanic/Latino), 9 international. Average age 33. 34 applicants, 29% accepted, 6 enrolled. In 2017, 5 master's, 8 doctorates awarded. *Degree requirements:* For master's, thesis; for doctorate, comprehensive exam, thesis/dissertation. *Entrance requirements:* For master's and doctorate, GRE General Test. Additional exam requirements/recommendations for international students: Required—TOEFL (minimum score 550 paper-based; 79 iBT). *Application deadline:* For fall admission, 6/1 priority date for domestic students, 1/15 priority date for international students; for spring admission, 9/1 priority date for domestic students, 6/15 priority date for international students. Applications are processed on a rolling basis. Application fee: $60. Electronic applications accepted. *Expenses:* Contact institution. *Financial support:* In 2017–18, 31 students received support, including 30 fellowships (averaging $5,499 per year), 15 research assistantships (averaging $11,129 per year), 19 teaching assistantships (averaging $10,544 per year); scholarships/grants and unspecified assistantships also available. Financial award application deadline: 12/1; financial award applicants required to submit FAFSA. *Faculty research:* Parenting (including family relationships and parent-child interactions), marital and premarital relationships, adolescence (risk and resilience), life span, child development (including factors that influence developmental outcomes: poverty, risk, genetic and environmental factors). *Total annual research expenditures:* $79,092. *Unit head:* Dr. Ann M. Mastergeorge, Chairperson/Professor, 806-834-7162, Fax: 806-742-3042, E-mail: ann.mastergeorge@ttu.edu. *Application contact:* Dr. Malinda Colwell, Graduate Program Director, 806-834-4179, Fax: 806-742-0285, E-mail: malinda.colwell@ttu.edu.
Website: http://www.depts.ttu.edu/hdfs

Tufts University, Graduate School of Arts and Sciences, Eliot-Pearson Department of Child Study and Human Development, Medford, MA 02155. Offers child study and human development (MA, PhD). *Program availability:* Part-time. *Students:* 78 full-time (66 women), 1 (woman) part-time; includes 19 minority (4 Black or African American, non-Hispanic/Latino; 8 Asian, non-Hispanic/Latino; 5 Hispanic/Latino; 2 Two or more races, non-Hispanic/Latino), 17 international. Average age 27. 129 applicants, 59% accepted, 37 enrolled. In 2017, 26 master's, 7 doctorates awarded. *Degree requirements:* For master's, thesis (for some programs); for doctorate, comprehensive exam, thesis/dissertation. *Entrance requirements:* For master's and doctorate, GRE General Test. Additional exam requirements/recommendations for international students: Required—TOEFL (minimum score 550 paper-based; 80 iBT), IELTS (minimum score 6.5). *Application deadline:* For fall admission, 12/1 priority date for domestic and international students. Applications are processed on a rolling basis. Application fee: $85. Electronic applications accepted. *Expenses:* Contact institution. *Financial support:* Fellowships, research assistantships, teaching assistantships, Federal Work-Study, scholarships/grants, tuition waivers (full and partial), and unspecified assistantships available. Support available to part-time students. Financial award application deadline: 1/15. *Unit head:* Dr. David Henry Feldman, Graduate Program Director, 617-627-3355. *Application contact:* Office of Graduate Admissions, 617-627-3395, E-mail: gradadmissions@tufts.edu.
Website: http://ase.tufts.edu/epcd

The University of Alabama, Graduate School, College of Human Environmental Sciences, Department of Human Development and Family Studies, Tuscaloosa, AL 35487. Offers human development and family studies (MSHES); marriage and family therapy (MSHES); parent and family life education (MSHES). *Faculty:* 11 full-time (8 women), 2 part-time/adjunct (both women). *Students:* 25 full-time (19 women), 1 (woman) part-time; includes 6 minority (4 Black or African American, non-Hispanic/Latino; 1 Hispanic/Latino; 1 Two or more races, non-Hispanic/Latino). Average age 26. 24 applicants, 75% accepted, 14 enrolled. In 2017, 14 master's awarded. Terminal master's awarded for partial completion of doctoral program. *Degree requirements:* For master's, comprehensive exam (for some programs), thesis (for some programs). *Entrance requirements:* For master's, GRE General Test or MAT, minimum GPA of 3.0. Additional exam requirements/recommendations for international students: Required—TOEFL (minimum score 79 iBT), IELTS (minimum score 6.5). *Application deadline:* For fall admission, 12/15 priority date for domestic and international students. Applications are processed on a rolling basis. Application fee: $50 ($60 for international students). Electronic applications accepted. *Financial support:* In 2017–18, 15 students received support, including research assistantships with full tuition reimbursements available (averaging $13,140 per year), teaching assistantships (averaging $13,140 per year); fellowships, career-related internships or fieldwork, Federal Work-Study, scholarships/grants, health care benefits, and unspecified assistantships also available. Financial award application deadline: 3/15. *Faculty research:* Parent/child relationships, preschool curricula and quality measures for child care programs, family strengths and adolescent behaviors, depression in mothers and infants, word association and word learning in young children, bullying behaviors in children, attachment parenting, medical play therapy, socialization of young children, impact of daily experiences on relationship quality, re-entry of service members into civilian roles. *Unit head:* Dr. Carroll M. Tingle, Chair, 205-348-6158, Fax: 205-348-8153, E-mail: ctingle@ches.ua.edu. *Application contact:* Dr. Maria Hernandez-Reif, Professor, 205-348-5894, Fax: 205-348-8153, E-mail: mhernandez-reif@ches.ua.edu.
Website: http://www.hdfs.ches.ua.edu/

The University of Arizona, College of Education, Department of Disability and Psychoeducational Studies, Tucson, AZ 85721. Offers counseling and mental health (MA), including rehabilitation counseling, school counseling; family studies and human development (M Ed); rehabilitation counseling (PhD); school counseling (MA); school psychology (PhD, Ed S); special education (MA, PhD), including cross-categorical special education (MA), deaf and hard of hearing (MA), learning disabilities (MA), severe and multiple disabilities (MA), special education (PhD), visual impairment (MA). *Accreditation:* CORE. *Program availability:* Part-time. Terminal master's awarded for partial completion of doctoral program. *Degree requirements:* For master's, comprehensive exam, thesis optional; for doctorate, comprehensive exam, thesis/dissertation. *Entrance requirements:* For master's, statement of purpose; for doctorate, GRE General Test (minimum score 1100) or MAT, 3 letters of recommendation. Additional exam requirements/recommendations for international students: Required—TOEFL (minimum score 550 paper-based; 79 iBT).

The University of British Columbia, Faculty of Education, Department of Educational and Counseling Psychology, and Special Education, Vancouver, BC V6T 1Z4, Canada. Offers counseling psychology (M Ed, MA, PhD); guidance studies (Diploma); human development, learning and culture (M Ed, MA, PhD); measurement, evaluation, and research methodology (M Ed, MA, PhD); school psychology (M Ed, MA, PhD); special education (M Ed, MA, PhD, Diploma). *Program availability:* Part-time. *Degree requirements:* For master's, thesis (for some programs); for doctorate, comprehensive exam, thesis/dissertation. *Entrance requirements:* For master's, GRE General Test (for MA in counseling psychology); for doctorate, GRE General Test. Additional exam requirements/recommendations for international students: Required—TOEFL. Electronic applications accepted. *Expenses:* Contact institution. *Faculty research:* Women, family, social problems, career transition, stress and coping problems.

University of California, Berkeley, Graduate Division, School of Education, Programs in Education, Berkeley, CA 94720-1500. Offers development in mathematics and science (MA); education in mathematics, science, and technology (MA, PhD); human development and education (MA, PhD); leadership education (MA); special education (PhD); teacher education (MA); MA/Credential; PhD/Credential; PhD/MA. Terminal master's awarded for partial completion of doctoral program. *Degree requirements:* For master's, exam or thesis; for doctorate, thesis/dissertation, oral qualifying exam. *Entrance requirements:* For master's and doctorate, GRE General Test, minimum GPA of 3.0 during last 2 years of undergraduate course work. Electronic applications accepted. *Faculty research:* Human development, social and moral educational psychology, developmental teacher preparation.

University of California, Davis, Graduate Studies, Graduate Group in Human Development, Davis, CA 95616. Offers PhD. *Degree requirements:* For doctorate, thesis/dissertation. *Entrance requirements:* For doctorate, GRE General Test, GRE Subject Test, minimum GPA of 3.0. Additional exam requirements/recommendations for

international students: Required—TOEFL (minimum score 550 paper-based). Electronic applications accepted. *Faculty research:* Life span socioemotional and cognitive development, individual differences, relationship between biological and behavioral development, cross-cultural and cross-generational development.

University of Central Oklahoma, The Jackson College of Graduate Studies, College of Education and Professional Studies, Department of Human Environmental Sciences, Edmond, OK 73034-5209. Offers family and child studies (MS), including family life education, infant/child specialist, marriage and family therapy; nutrition-food science (MS). *Program availability:* Part-time. *Faculty:* 5 full-time (4 women), 8 part-time/adjunct (6 women). *Students:* 46 full-time (38 women), 65 part-time (62 women); includes 48 minority (27 Black or African American, non-Hispanic/Latino; 3 American Indian or Alaska Native, non-Hispanic/Latino; 3 Asian, non-Hispanic/Latino; 7 Hispanic/Latino; 8 Two or more races, non-Hispanic/Latino), 13 international. Average age 29. 68 applicants, 93% accepted, 31 enrolled. In 2017, 37 master's awarded. *Degree requirements:* For master's, comprehensive exam (for some programs), thesis (for some programs). *Entrance requirements:* For master's, GRE, essay, physical, CPR and First Aid training. Additional exam requirements/recommendations for international students: Required—TOEFL (minimum score 550 paper-based; 79 iBT), IELTS (minimum score 6.5). *Application deadline:* For fall admission, 1/15 for domestic students, 7/15 for international students; for spring admission, 11/15 for international students. Applications are processed on a rolling basis. Application fee: $60. Electronic applications accepted. *Expenses:* Tuition, state resident: full-time $5375; part-time $268.75 per credit hour. Tuition, nonresident: full-time $13,295; part-time $664.75 per credit hour. *Required fees:* $626; $31.30 per credit hour. One-time fee: $50. Tuition and fees vary according to program. *Financial support:* In 2017–18, 11 students received support, including 8 research assistantships with partial tuition reimbursements available (averaging $4,436 per year); teaching assistantships, career-related internships or fieldwork, scholarships/grants, tuition waivers (partial), and unspecified assistantships also available. Financial award application deadline: 3/31; financial award applicants required to submit FAFSA. *Unit head:* Dr. Kaye Sears, Chair, 405-974-5551, Fax: 405-974-3850. *Application contact:* Carlie Wellington, Assistant Director, CEPS Graduate Enrollment, 405-974-5105, Fax: 405-974-3851, E-mail: gradcoll@uco.edu. Website: http://sites.uco.edu/ceps/dept/Professional-Studies-Programs/hes/index.asp

University of Chicago, Division of the Social Sciences, Department of Comparative Human Development, Chicago, IL 60637. Offers PhD. *Faculty:* 16. *Students:* 52 full-time (44 women); includes 14 minority (8 Black or African American, non-Hispanic/Latino; 3 Asian, non-Hispanic/Latino; 2 Hispanic/Latino; 1 Two or more races, non-Hispanic/Latino), 8 international. Average age 30. 50 applicants, 14% accepted, 4 enrolled. In 2017, 6 doctorates awarded. *Degree requirements:* For doctorate, one foreign language, thesis/dissertation, trial research project. *Entrance requirements:* For doctorate, GRE General Test, 3 letters of recommendation, statement of purpose, transcripts, resume or curriculum vitae, writing sample (dependent on department). Additional exam requirements/recommendations for international students: Required—TOEFL (minimum score 104 iBT), IELTS (minimum score 7). *Application deadline:* For fall admission, 12/15 priority date for domestic and international students. Application fee: $90. Electronic applications accepted. *Financial support:* In 2017–18, 5 students received support, including 5 fellowships with full tuition reimbursements available (averaging $27,000 per year); research assistantships, teaching assistantships, career-related internships or fieldwork, Federal Work-Study, institutionally sponsored loans, scholarships/grants, and health care benefits also available. Financial award application deadline: 12/15. *Unit head:* Margaret Beale Spencer, Chair, E-mail: olivergarland@uchicago.edu. *Application contact:* Office of the Dean of Students, 773-702-8415, E-mail: ssd-admissions@uchicago.edu. Website: http://humdev.uchicago.edu

University of Colorado Denver, School of Education and Human Development, Programs in Educational and School Psychology, Denver, CO 80217. Offers educational psychology (MA), including educational assessment, educational psychology, human development, human learning, research and evaluation; school psychology (Psy D, Ed S). MA program also offered in partnership with Boulder Journey School, Friends School and Stanley British Primary School. *Program availability:* Part-time, evening/weekend. *Degree requirements:* For master's, comprehensive exam, 9 hours of core courses, embedded within a minimum of 36 to 38 hours of relevant coursework, including an educational psychology practicum, independent study project or thesis (recommended); for Ed S, comprehensive exam, minimum of 75 semester hours (61 hours of coursework, 6 of 500-hour practicum in field, and 8 of 1200-hour internship); PRAXIS II. *Entrance requirements:* For master's, GRE if undergraduate GPA below 2.75, resume, three letters of recommendation, transcripts; for Ed S, GRE, resume, letters of recommendation, transcripts. Additional exam requirements/recommendations for international students: Required—TOEFL (minimum score 537 paper-based; 75 iBT); Recommended—IELTS (minimum score 6.5). Electronic applications accepted. *Expenses:* Contact institution. *Faculty research:* Crisis response and intervention, school violence prevention, immigrant experience, educational environments for English language learners, culturally competent assessment and intervention, child and youth suicide.

University of Connecticut, Graduate School, College of Liberal Arts and Sciences, Department of Human Development and Family Studies, Storrs, CT 06269. Offers MA, PhD. *Accreditation:* AAMFT/COAMFTE (one or more programs are accredited). Terminal master's awarded for partial completion of doctoral program. *Degree requirements:* For master's, comprehensive exam; for doctorate, thesis/dissertation. *Entrance requirements:* For doctorate, GRE General Test. Additional exam requirements/recommendations for international students: Required—TOEFL (minimum score 550 paper-based). Electronic applications accepted.

University of Dayton, Department of Counselor Education and Human Services, Dayton, OH 45469. Offers clinical mental health counseling (MS Ed); college student personnel (MS Ed); higher education administration (MS Ed); human services (MS Ed); school counseling (MS Ed); school psychology (MS Ed, Ed S). *Accreditation:* ACA; NCATE. *Program availability:* Part-time. *Faculty:* 11 full-time (6 women), 34 part-time/adjunct (24 women). *Students:* 194 full-time (153 women), 83 part-time (68 women); includes 58 minority (37 Black or African American, non-Hispanic/Latino; 2 Asian, non-Hispanic/Latino; 9 Hispanic/Latino; 10 Two or more races, non-Hispanic/Latino), 3 international. Average age 30. 426 applicants, 28% accepted. In 2017, 107 master's, 6 Ed Ss awarded. *Degree requirements:* For master's, thesis (for some programs); for Ed S, thesis (for some programs), professional portfolio. *Entrance requirements:* For master's, MAT or GRE (if GPA less than 2.75), essays (for some programs). Additional exam requirements/recommendations for international students: Required—TOEFL (minimum score 550 paper-based; 80 iBT). *Application deadline:* For fall admission, 1/10 priority date for domestic and international students; for spring admission, 9/10 priority date for domestic and international students; for summer admission, 11/10 priority date for domestic and international students. Application fee: $0 ($50 for international students). Electronic applications accepted. *Expenses:* Contact institution. *Financial support:* In 2017–18, 5 research assistantships with partial tuition reimbursements (averaging $9,950 per year) were awarded; career-related internships or fieldwork,

institutionally sponsored loans, and unspecified assistantships also available. Financial award application deadline: 3/1; financial award applicants required to submit FAFSA. *Faculty research:* Student school bonding, traumatic brain injuries, wellness and counseling, creativity in education. *Unit head:* Dr. Alan Demmitt, Chair, 937-229-3644, Fax: 937-229-1055, E-mail: ademmitt1@udayton.edu. *Application contact:* Kathleen Brown, Administrative Assistant, 937-229-3644, Fax: 937-229-1055, E-mail: kbrown1@udayton.edu. Website: https://www.udayton.edu/education/departments_and_programs/edc/

University of Delaware, College of Education and Human Development, Department of Human Development and Family Studies, Newark, DE 19716. Offers MS, PhD. *Program availability:* Part-time. Terminal master's awarded for partial completion of doctoral program. *Degree requirements:* For master's, thesis or alternative; for doctorate, comprehensive exam, thesis/dissertation. *Entrance requirements:* For master's and doctorate, GRE General Test, 3 letters of recommendation. Additional exam requirements/recommendations for international students: Required—TOEFL. Electronic applications accepted. *Faculty research:* Early childhood inclusive education, relationships, family risk and resilience, disability issues, program development and evaluation.

University of Guelph, Graduate Studies, College of Social and Applied Human Sciences, Department of Family Relations and Applied Nutrition, Guelph, ON N1G 2W1, Canada. Offers applied nutrition (MAN); family relations and human development (M Sc, PhD), including applied human nutrition, couple and family therapy (M Sc), family relations and human development. *Accreditation:* AAMFT/COAMFTE (one or more programs are accredited). *Program availability:* Part-time. *Degree requirements:* For master's, thesis (for some programs); for doctorate, comprehensive exam, thesis/dissertation. *Entrance requirements:* For master's, minimum B+ average; for doctorate, master's degree in family relations and human development or related field with a minimum B+ average or master's degree in applied human nutrition. Additional exam requirements/recommendations for international students: Required—TOEFL (minimum score 600 paper-based). Electronic applications accepted. *Faculty research:* Child and adolescent development, social gerontology, family roles and relations, couple and family therapy, applied human nutrition.

University of Illinois at Chicago, College of Applied Health Sciences, Department of Disability and Human Development, Chicago, IL 60607-7128. Offers MS, PhD. *Accreditation:* AOTA. *Program availability:* Part-time. *Degree requirements:* For master's, thesis optional; for doctorate, thesis/dissertation. *Entrance requirements:* For master's and doctorate, GRE General Test. Additional exam requirements/recommendations for international students: Required—TOEFL. Electronic applications accepted. *Faculty research:* Emerging trends in disability, demography and financial structure of disability services, aging and disability, empowerment of people with disabilities, health promotion in disabilities.

University of Illinois at Springfield, Graduate Programs, College of Education and Human Services, Program in Human Development Counseling, Springfield, IL 62703-5407. Offers MA. *Accreditation:* ACA. *Program availability:* Part-time, evening/weekend. *Faculty:* 6 full-time (4 women), 2 part-time/adjunct (both women). *Students:* 58 full-time (50 women), 41 part-time (34 women); includes 15 minority (8 Black or African American, non-Hispanic/Latino; 3 Hispanic/Latino; 4 Two or more races, non-Hispanic/Latino), 2 international. Average age 30. 50 applicants, 48% accepted, 22 enrolled. In 2017, 19 master's awarded. *Degree requirements:* For master's, comprehensive exam. *Entrance requirements:* For master's, minimum undergraduate GPA of 3.0 in last 60 hours of coursework or cumulative; essay; personal references; group interview. Additional exam requirements/recommendations for international students: Required—TOEFL (minimum score 500 paper-based; 61 iBT). *Application deadline:* Applications are processed on a rolling basis. Application fee: $60 ($75 for international students). Electronic applications accepted. *Expenses:* Tuition, state resident: full-time $7896; part-time $329 per credit hour. Tuition, nonresident: full-time $16,200; part-time $675 per credit hour. Tuition and fees vary according to program. *Financial support:* In 2017–18, research assistantships with full tuition reimbursements (averaging $10,249 per year), teaching assistantships with full tuition reimbursements (averaging $10,303 per year) were awarded; fellowships, career-related internships or fieldwork, Federal Work-Study, scholarships/grants, health care benefits, and unspecified assistantships also available. Support available to part-time students. Financial award application deadline: 11/15; financial award applicants required to submit FAFSA. *Unit head:* Dr. William Abler, Program Administrator, 217-206-7567, Fax: 217-206-6775, E-mail: abler.bill@uis.edu. Website: http://www.uis.edu/hdc

University of Illinois at Urbana–Champaign, Graduate College, College of Agricultural, Consumer and Environmental Sciences, Department of Human and Community Development, Champaign, IL 61820. Offers MS, PhD.

University of Maine, Graduate School, College of Education and Human Development, School of Educational Leadership, Higher Education, and Human Development, Orono, ME 04469. Offers educational leadership (M Ed, CAS); higher education (CAS); human development (MS). *Program availability:* Part-time. *Faculty:* 11 full-time (7 women), 10 part-time/adjunct (5 women). *Students:* 42 full-time (31 women), 67 part-time (49 women); includes 8 minority (1 Black or African American, non-Hispanic/Latino; 2 American Indian or Alaska Native, non-Hispanic/Latino; 3 Hispanic/Latino; 2 Two or more races, non-Hispanic/Latino). Average age 36. 73 applicants, 82% accepted, 25 enrolled. In 2017, 30 master's, 4 doctorates, 16 other advanced degrees awarded. *Degree requirements:* For master's, thesis (for some programs); for doctorate, comprehensive exam, thesis/dissertation. *Entrance requirements:* For master's, GRE General Test, MAT; for doctorate, GRE. Additional exam requirements/recommendations for international students: Required—TOEFL (minimum score 550 paper-based; 80 iBT), IELTS (minimum score 6.5). *Application deadline:* For fall admission, 2/1 priority date for domestic students. Applications are processed on a rolling basis. Application fee: $65. Electronic applications accepted. *Expenses:* Tuition, state resident: full-time $7722; part-time $429 per credit hour. Tuition, nonresident: full-time $25,146; part-time $1397 per credit hour. *Required fees:* $1162; $581 per credit hour. *Financial support:* In 2017–18, 30 students received support, including 5 teaching assistantships with full tuition reimbursements available (averaging $14,600 per year); career-related internships or fieldwork, Federal Work-Study, institutionally sponsored loans, tuition waivers (full and partial), and unspecified assistantships also available. Financial award application deadline: 3/1. *Faculty research:* Student hazing and hazing prevention, sexuality education, cross cultural perspectives on family, early childhood development, fatherhood/parenting, campus climate, social justice, rural higher education, gender in higher education, discourse, rural sociology, school-community relationships, instructional supervision, rural educational leadership. *Total annual research expenditures:* $130,000. *Unit head:* Dr. Jim Artesani, Associate Dean of Accreditation and Graduate Affairs, 207-581-4061, Fax: 207-581-3120. *Application contact:* Scott G. Delcourt, Senior Associate Dean of the Graduate School, 207-581-3291, Fax: 207-581-3232, E-mail: graduate@maine.edu. Website: http://www.umaine.edu/edhd/

University of Maryland, College Park, Academic Affairs, College of Education, Department of Human Development and Quantitative Methodology, College Park, MD 20742. Offers MA, Ed D, PhD. *Entrance requirements:* Additional exam requirements/recommendations for international students: Required—TOEFL.

University of Missouri, Office of Research and Graduate Studies, College of Human Environmental Sciences, Department of Human Development and Family Studies, Columbia, MO 65211. Offers MA, MS, PhD. *Entrance requirements:* For master's, GRE General Test, minimum GPA of 3.0. Additional exam requirements/recommendations for international students: Required—TOEFL (minimum score 550 paper-based; 80 iBT). Electronic applications accepted.

University of Nebraska–Lincoln, Graduate College, College of Education and Human Sciences, Department of Child, Youth and Family Studies, Lincoln, NE 68588. Offers child development/early childhood education (MS, PhD); child, youth and family studies (MS); family and consumer sciences education (MS, PhD); family financial planning (MS); family science (MS, PhD); gerontology (PhD); human sciences (PhD), including child, youth and family studies, gerontology, medical family therapy; marriage and family therapy (MS); medical family therapy (PhD); youth development (MS). *Accreditation:* AAMFT/COAMFTE (one or more programs are accredited). *Program availability:* Online learning. *Degree requirements:* For master's, thesis optional. *Entrance requirements:* For master's, GRE. Additional exam requirements/recommendations for international students: Required—TOEFL (minimum score 550 paper-based). Electronic applications accepted. *Faculty research:* Marriage and family therapy, child development/early childhood education, family financial management.

University of Nebraska–Lincoln, Graduate College, College of Education and Human Sciences, Department of Special Education and Communication Disorders, Lincoln, NE 68588. Offers audiology research (PhD); clinical audiology (Au D); educational studies (PhD); human sciences (PhD), including communication disorders; special education (M Ed, MA, Ed S), including special education (M Ed, MA), special education and communication disorders (Ed S); speech-language pathology and audiology (MS, Au D), including audiology and hearing science (Au D), speech-language pathology (Au D), speech-language pathology and audiology (MS). *Accreditation:* ASHA (one or more programs are accredited); NCATE. *Degree requirements:* For master's, thesis optional. *Entrance requirements:* For master's, GRE General Test. Additional exam requirements/recommendations for international students: Required—TOEFL. Electronic applications accepted. *Faculty research:* Curriculum-based assessment, paraprofessional and parent training, behavior management for special needs individuals, augmentative communication, speech/language disorders.

University of Nebraska–Lincoln, Graduate College, College of Education and Human Sciences, Department of Textiles, Clothing and Design, Lincoln, NE 68588. Offers human sciences (PhD), including textiles, clothing and design (MS, PhD); merchandising (MS); textile history/quilt studies (MA); textile science (MS); textile-apparel (MA); textiles, clothing and design (MA, MS), including textiles, clothing and design (MS, PhD). *Program availability:* Part-time, online learning. *Degree requirements:* For master's, thesis optional. *Entrance requirements:* For master's, GRE General Test. Additional exam requirements/recommendations for international students: Required—TOEFL (minimum score 550 paper-based). Electronic applications accepted. *Faculty research:* Merchandising, textile science, fiber arts, textile history, quilt studies.

University of Nevada, Reno, Graduate School, College of Education, Department of Human Development and Family Studies, Reno, NV 89557. Offers MS. *Degree requirements:* For master's, thesis optional. *Entrance requirements:* For master's, GRE General Test, minimum GPA of 2.75. Additional exam requirements/recommendations for international students: Required—TOEFL (minimum score 500 paper-based; 61 iBT), IELTS (minimum score 6). Electronic applications accepted. *Faculty research:* Early childhood/adolescent development, family studies.

University of New Mexico, Graduate Studies, College of Education, Program in Family Studies, Albuquerque, NM 87131-2039. Offers family life education (MA); family relations (MA); family studies (PhD); human development in families (MA). *Program availability:* Part-time, evening/weekend. *Faculty:* 5 full-time (2 women). *Students:* 10 full-time (9 women), 14 part-time (12 women); includes 12 minority (3 American Indian or Alaska Native, non-Hispanic/Latino; 9 Hispanic/Latino), 3 international. Average age 38. 4 applicants, 50% accepted, 2 enrolled. In 2017, 2 master's, 1 doctorate awarded. *Degree requirements:* For master's, comprehensive exam, thesis (for some programs); for doctorate, comprehensive exam, thesis/dissertation. *Entrance requirements:* For master's, written paper, 3 letters of recommendation, personal statement; for doctorate, GRE General Test, written paper, 3 letters of recommendation, personal statement, interview. Additional exam requirements/recommendations for international students: Required—TOEFL (minimum score 550 paper-based). *Application deadline:* For fall admission, 3/15 priority date for domestic and international students; for spring admission, 10/15 priority date for domestic and international students. Applications are processed on a rolling basis. Application fee: $50. Electronic applications accepted. *Financial support:* Fellowships, teaching assistantships, and unspecified assistantships available. Financial award application deadline: 3/1; financial award applicants required to submit FAFSA. *Faculty research:* Home, community and school relations; multicultural issues; parent-child interactions; grandparents as primary caretakers for grandchildren; fathering; early childhood evaluation; early childhood development; globalization and indigenous cultures. *Unit head:* Dr. Ziarat Hossain, Program Coordinator, 505-277-4162, Fax: 505-277-8361, E-mail: zhossain@unm.edu. *Application contact:* Cynthia Salas, Department Administrator, 505-277-4535, Fax: 505-277-8361, E-mail: divbse@unm.edu.
Website: https://coe.unm.edu/departments-programs/ifce/family-studies/

The University of North Carolina at Greensboro, Graduate School, School of Health and Human Sciences, Department of Human Development and Family Studies, Greensboro, NC 27412-5001. Offers M Ed, MS, PhD. *Degree requirements:* For master's, one foreign language; for doctorate, one foreign language, thesis/dissertation. *Entrance requirements:* For master's and doctorate, GRE General Test. Additional exam requirements/recommendations for international students: Required—TOEFL. Electronic applications accepted. *Expenses:* Contact institution. *Faculty research:* Adolescent mothers, multi-handicapped, older adults.

University of North Texas, Robert B. Toulouse School of Graduate Studies, Denton, TX 76203-5459. Offers accounting (MS); applied anthropology (MA, MS); applied behavior analysis (Certificate); applied geography (MA); applied technology and performance improvement (M Ed, MS); art education (MA); art history (MA); art museum education (Certificate); arts leadership (Certificate); audiology (Au D); behavior analysis (MS); behavioral science (PhD); biochemistry and molecular biology (MS); biology (MA, MS); biomedical engineering (MS); business analysis (MS); chemistry (MS); clinical health psychology (PhD); communication studies (MA, MS); computer engineering (MS); computer science (MS); counseling (M Ed, MS), including clinical mental health counseling (MS), college and university counseling, elementary school counseling, secondary school counseling; creative writing (MA); criminal justice (MS); curriculum and instruction (M Ed); decision sciences (MBA); design (MA, MFA), including fashion design (MFA), innovation studies, interior design (MFA); early childhood studies (MS); economics (MS); educational leadership (M Ed, Ed D); educational psychology (MS, PhD), including family studies (MS), gifted and talented (MS), human development (MS), learning and cognition (MS), research, measurement and evaluation (MS); electrical engineering (MS); emergency management (MPA); engineering technology (MS); English (MA); English as a second language (MA); environmental science (MS); finance (MBA, MS); financial management (MPA); French (MA); health services management (MBA); higher education (M Ed, Ed D); history (MA, MS); hospitality management (MS); human resources management (MPA); information science (MS); information systems (PhD); information technologies (MBA); interdisciplinary studies (MA, MS); international studies (MA); international sustainable tourism (MS); jazz studies (MM); journalism (MA, MJ, Graduate Certificate), including interactive and virtual digital communication (Graduate Certificate), narrative journalism (Graduate Certificate), public relations (Graduate Certificate); kinesiology (MS); linguistics (MA); local government management (MPA); logistics (PhD); logistics and supply chain management (MBA); long-term care, senior housing, and aging services (MA); management (PhD); marketing (MBA); mathematics (MA, MS); mechanical and energy engineering (MS, PhD); music (MA), including ethnomusicology, music theory, musicology, performance; music composition (PhD); music education (MM Ed, PhD); nonprofit management (MPA); operations and supply chain management (MBA); performance (MM, DMA); philosophy (MA); political science (MA); professional and technical communication (MA); radio, television and film (MA, MFA); rehabilitation counseling (Certificate); sociology (MA); Spanish (MA); special education (M Ed); speech-language pathology (MA); strategic management (MBA); studio art (MFA); teaching (M Ed); MBA/MS. *Program availability:* Part-time, evening/weekend, online learning. Terminal master's awarded for partial completion of doctoral program. *Degree requirements:* For master's, variable foreign language requirement, comprehensive exam (for some programs), thesis (for some programs); for doctorate, variable foreign language requirement, comprehensive exam (for some programs), thesis/dissertation; for other advanced degree, variable foreign language requirement, comprehensive exam (for some programs). *Entrance requirements:* For master's and doctorate, GRE, GMAT. Additional exam requirements/recommendations for international students: Required—TOEFL (minimum score 550 paper-based; 79 iBT). Electronic applications accepted.

University of Pennsylvania, Graduate School of Education, Division of Human Development and Quantitative Methods, Program in Interdisciplinary Studies in Human Development, Philadelphia, PA 19104. Offers MS Ed, PhD. *Program availability:* Part-time. *Students:* Average age 28. 135 applicants, 50% accepted, 28 enrolled. In 2017, 15 master's awarded. Terminal master's awarded for partial completion of doctoral program.
Website: http://www.gse.upenn.edu/aphd/ishd/msed

University of Rhode Island, Graduate School, College of Health Sciences, Department of Human Development and Family Studies, Kingston, RI 02881. Offers college student personnel (MS); human development and family studies (MS); marriage and family therapy (MS). *Accreditation:* AAMFT/COAMFTE. *Program availability:* Part-time. *Faculty:* 16 full-time (11 women). *Students:* 47 full-time (35 women), 12 part-time (10 women); includes 13 minority (4 Black or African American, non-Hispanic/Latino; 1 American Indian or Alaska Native, non-Hispanic/Latino; 4 Asian, non-Hispanic/Latino; 3 Hispanic/Latino; 1 Two or more races, non-Hispanic/Latino), 2 international. 91 applicants, 43% accepted, 29 enrolled. In 2017, 24 master's awarded. *Entrance requirements:* Additional exam requirements/recommendations for international students: Required—TOEFL. *Application deadline:* For fall admission, 1/15 for domestic and international students. Application fee: $65. Electronic applications accepted. *Expenses:* Tuition, state resident: full-time $12,706; part-time $786 per credit. Tuition, nonresident: full-time $25,216; part-time $1401 per credit. *Required fees:* $1598; $45 per credit. One-time fee: $30 part-time. *Financial support:* In 2017–18, 1 research assistantship (averaging $4,431 per year), 4 teaching assistantships (averaging $10,128 per year) were awarded. Financial award application deadline: 1/15; financial award applicants required to submit FAFSA. *Unit head:* Dr. Karen McCurdy, Chair, 401-874-5960, Fax: 401-874-4020, E-mail: kmccurdy@uri.edu.
Website: http://www.uri.edu/hss/hdf/

University of Rochester, Margaret Warner Graduate School of Education and Human Development, Doctoral Programs in Education, Rochester, NY 14627. Offers counseling (Ed D); educational administration (Ed D); educational policy and theory (PhD); higher education (PhD); human development in educational context (PhD); teaching, curriculum, and change (PhD).

University of Rochester, Margaret Warner Graduate School of Education and Human Development, Master's Program in Human Development, Rochester, NY 14627. Offers MS.

University of St. Thomas, College of Education, Leadership and Counseling, Department of Organization Learning and Development, St. Paul, MN 55105-1096. Offers organization development and change (Ed D). *Program availability:* Part-time, evening/weekend. *Degree requirements:* For doctorate, comprehensive exam, thesis/dissertation. *Entrance requirements:* For doctorate, minimum GPA of 3.5, interview, 5-7 years of organization development or leadership experience. Additional exam requirements/recommendations for international students: Required—TOEFL (minimum score 550 paper-based). *Application deadline:* For fall admission, 7/15 priority date for domestic and international students; for spring admission, 12/9 priority date for domestic and international students; for summer admission, 4/3 priority date for domestic students, 4/3 for international students. Applications are processed on a rolling basis. Electronic applications accepted. *Expenses:* Contact institution. *Financial support:* Fellowships, research assistantships, institutionally sponsored loans, and scholarships/grants available. Support available to part-time students. Financial award application deadline: 8/1; financial award applicants required to submit FAFSA. *Faculty research:* Workplace conflict, physician leaders, virtual teams, technology use in schools/workplace, developing masterful practitioners. *Application contact:* Liz G. Knight, Program Manager, 651-962-4459, Fax: 651-962-4169, E-mail: egknight@stthomas.edu.

University of South Africa, College of Human Sciences, Pretoria, South Africa. Offers adult education (M Ed); African languages (MA, PhD); African politics (MA, PhD); Afrikaans (MA, PhD); ancient history (MA, PhD); ancient Near Eastern studies (MA, PhD); anthropology (MA, PhD); applied linguistics (MA); Arabic (MA, PhD); archaeology (MA); art history (MA); Biblical archaeology (MA); Biblical studies (M Th, D Th, PhD); Christian spirituality (M Th, D Th); church history (M Th, D Th); classical studies (MA, PhD); clinical psychology (MA); communication (MA, PhD); comparative education (M Ed, Ed D); consulting psychology (D Admin, D Com, PhD); curriculum studies (M Ed, Ed D); development studies (M Admin, MA, D Admin, PhD); didactics (M Ed, Ed D); education (M Tech); education management (M Ed, Ed D); educational psychology (M Ed); English (MA); environmental education (M Ed); French (MA, PhD); German (MA, PhD); Greek (MA); guidance and counseling (M Ed); health studies (MA, PhD), including health sciences education (MA), health services management (MA), medical and surgical nursing science (critical care general) (MA), midwifery and neonatal nursing science (MA), trauma and emergency care (MA); history (MA, PhD); history of education (Ed D); inclusive education (M Ed, Ed D); information and communications technology policy and regulation (MA); information science (MA, MIS, PhD); international politics (MA, PhD); Islamic studies (MA, PhD); Italian (MA, PhD); Judaica (MA, PhD); linguistics (MA, PhD); mathematical education (M Ed); mathematics education (MA); missiology (M Th, D Th); modern Hebrew (MA, PhD); musicology (MA, MMus, D Mus, PhD); natural

science education (M Ed); New Testament (M Th, D Th); Old Testament (D Th); pastoral therapy (M Th, D Th); philosophy (MA); philosophy of education (M Ed, Ed D); politics (MA, PhD); Portuguese (MA, PhD); practical theology (M Th, D Th); psychology (MA, MS, PhD); psychology of education (M Ed, Ed D); public health (MA); religious studies (MA, D Th, PhD); Romance languages (MA); Russian (MA, PhD); Semitic languages (MA, PhD); social behavior studies in HIV/AIDS (MA); social science (mental health) (MA); social science in development studies (MA); social science in psychology (MA); social science in social work (MA); social science in sociology (MA); social work (MSW, DSW, PhD); socio-education (M Ed, Ed D); sociolinguistics (MA); sociology (MA, PhD); Spanish (MA, PhD); systematic theology (M Th, D Th); TESOL (teaching English to speakers of other languages) (MA); theological ethics (M Th, D Th); theory of literature (MA, PhD); urban ministries (D Th); urban ministry (M Th).

University of South Dakota, Graduate School, School of Education, Division of Counseling and Psychology in Education, Vermillion, SD 57069. Offers counseling (MA, PhD, Ed S); human development and educational psychology (MA, PhD, Ed S); mental health counseling (Certificate); school psychology (PhD, Ed S). *Accreditation:* ACA (one or more programs are accredited); NCATE. *Program availability:* Part-time. *Degree requirements:* For master's and other advanced degree, comprehensive exam, thesis or alternative; for doctorate, comprehensive exam, thesis/dissertation. *Entrance requirements:* For master's and doctorate, GRE General Test, minimum GPA of 3.0. Additional exam requirements/recommendations for international students: Required—TOEFL (minimum score 550 paper-based; 79 iBT). *Application deadline:* Applications are processed on a rolling basis. Application fee: $35. Electronic applications accepted. *Financial support:* Research assistantships with partial tuition reimbursements, teaching assistantships with partial tuition reimbursements, career-related internships or fieldwork, Federal Work-Study, and unspecified assistantships available. Financial award applicants required to submit FAFSA. *Application contact:* Graduate School, 605-658-6140, Fax: 605-677-6118.
Website: http://www.usd.edu/cpe

The University of Texas at Austin, Graduate School, College of Education, Department of Educational Psychology, Austin, TX 78712-1111. Offers academic educational psychology (M Ed, MA); counseling psychology (PhD); counselor education (M Ed); human development, culture and learning sciences (PhD); program evaluation (MA); quantitative methods (M Ed, MA, PhD); school psychology (MA, PhD). *Accreditation:* APA (one or more programs are accredited). *Degree requirements:* For master's, thesis optional; for doctorate, thesis/dissertation. *Entrance requirements:* For master's and doctorate, GRE General Test, 3 letters of recommendation. Additional exam requirements/recommendations for international students: Required—TOEFL.

The University of Texas at Austin, Graduate School, College of Fine Arts, Sarah and Ernest Butler School of Music, Austin, TX 78712-1111. Offers band and wind conducting (M Music, DMA); brass/woodwind/percussion (MM, DMA); chamber music (MM); choral conducting (MM, DMA); collaborative piano (MM, DMA); composition (MM, DMA), including composition, jazz, jazz (DMA); ethnomusicology (MM, PhD); literature and pedagogy (MM); music and human learning (MM, PhD); music and human learning (DMA), including jazz (MM, DMA), piano pedagogy; musicology (MM, PhD); opera performance (MM, DMA); orchestral conducting (MM, DMA); organ (MM), including sacred music; organ performance (MM, DMA); performance (MM), including jazz (MM, DMA); performance (DMA), including jazz (MM, DMA); piano (DMA), including jazz (MM, DMA); piano literature and pedagogy (MM); piano performance (MM, DMA); string performance (MM, DMA); theory (MM, PhD); vocal performance (MM, DMA); voice (DMA), including opera; voice performance pedagogy (DMA); woodwind, brass, percussion performance (MM). *Accreditation:* NASM. *Program availability:* Part-time. *Degree requirements:* For master's, one foreign language, comprehensive exam, thesis (for some programs), recital (performance or composition majors); for doctorate, one foreign language, comprehensive exam, thesis/dissertation (for some programs), recital (for performance or composition majors). *Entrance requirements:* For master's and doctorate, GRE General Test (except for performance or composition majors), audition (performance majors). Electronic applications accepted.

University of Utah, Graduate School, College of Social and Behavioral Science, Department of Family and Consumer Studies, Salt Lake City, UT 84112-0080. Offers human development and social policy (MS). *Program availability:* Part-time. *Faculty:* 15 full-time (7 women), 7 part-time/adjunct (4 women). *Students:* 9 full-time (8 women), 1 (woman) part-time. Average age 26. 12 applicants, 67% accepted, 7 enrolled. In 2017, 7 master's awarded. *Degree requirements:* For master's, comprehensive exam (for some programs), thesis (for some programs), thesis or project. *Entrance requirements:* For master's, GRE General Test, minimum undergraduate GPA of 3.0, courses in research methods and statistics. Additional exam requirements/recommendations for international students: Required—TOEFL (minimum score 550 paper-based). *Application deadline:* For fall admission, 2/15 priority date for domestic and international students. Applications are processed on a rolling basis. Application fee: $55 ($65 for international students). Electronic applications accepted. *Financial support:* In 2017–18, 6 students received support, including 2 research assistantships with full tuition reimbursements available (averaging $15,000 per year), 4 teaching assistantships with full tuition reimbursements available (averaging $15,000 per year); scholarships/grants also available. Financial award application deadline: 2/15. *Faculty research:* Social, physical, educational and economic contexts of individuals, families and communities; autism spectrum disorder; play/flow; division of labor. *Unit head:* Prof. Lori Kowaleski-Jones, PhD, Chair, 801-585-0074, Fax: 801-581-5156, E-mail: lk2700@fcs.utah.edu. *Application contact:* Prof. Jessie Fan, PhD, Graduate Director, 801-581-4170, E-mail: jessie.fan@fcs.utah.edu.
Website: http://fcs.utah.edu/

University of Victoria, Faculty of Graduate Studies, Faculty of Education, Department of Educational Psychology and Leadership Studies, Victoria, BC V8W 2Y2, Canada. Offers aboriginal communities counseling (M Ed); counseling (M Ed, MA); educational psychology (M Ed, MA, PhD), including counseling psychology (M Ed, MA), leadership studies (PhD), learning and development (MA, PhD), measurement and evaluation, special education (M Ed, MA); leadership studies (M Ed, MA). *Program availability:* Part-time. *Degree requirements:* For master's, thesis (for some programs), comprehensive exam (M Ed); for doctorate, comprehensive exam, thesis/dissertation, candidacy exam. *Entrance requirements:* For master's, 2 years of work experience in a relevant field; for doctorate, GRE, 2 years of work experience in a relevant field, minimum B average. Additional exam requirements/recommendations for international students: Required—TOEFL (minimum score 575 paper-based), IELTS (minimum score 7). *Faculty research:* Learning and development (child, adolescent and adult), special education and exceptional children.

University of Victoria, Faculty of Graduate Studies, Faculty of Human and Social Development, Studies in Policy and Practice Program, Victoria, BC V8W 2Y2, Canada. Offers MA. *Program availability:* Part-time. *Degree requirements:* For master's, thesis. *Entrance requirements:* For master's, resume. Additional exam requirements/recommendations for international students: Required—TOEFL (minimum score 575 paper-based), IELTS (minimum score 7). Electronic applications accepted. *Faculty research:* Women's issues, public policy formation and implementation, health promotion and education, children, youth and families.

University of Washington, Graduate School, College of Education, Program in Educational Psychology, Seattle, WA 98195. Offers educational psychology (PhD); human development and cognition (M Ed); learning sciences (M Ed, PhD); measurement, statistics and research design (M Ed); school psychology (M Ed). *Accreditation:* APA. *Degree requirements:* For master's, thesis optional; for doctorate, thesis/dissertation. *Entrance requirements:* For master's and doctorate, GRE General Test, minimum GPA of 3.0. Additional exam requirements/recommendations for international students: Required—TOEFL.

University of Wisconsin–Madison, Graduate School, School of Human Ecology, Program in Human Development and Family Studies, Madison, WI 53706-1380. Offers MS, PhD. *Program availability:* Part-time. Terminal master's awarded for partial completion of doctoral program. *Degree requirements:* For master's, thesis; for doctorate, comprehensive exam, thesis/dissertation. *Entrance requirements:* For master's, GRE General Test, 3 letters of recommendation; for doctorate, GRE General Test, MS or MA, 3 letters of recommendation. Additional exam requirements/recommendations for international students: Required—TOEFL (minimum score 580 paper-based; 92 iBT). Electronic applications accepted. *Faculty research:* Human development, adolescence, adulthood, prevention, intervention.

University of Wisconsin–Stevens Point, College of Professional Studies, School of Health Promotion and Human Development, Stevens Point, WI 54481-3897. Offers human and community resources (MS); nutritional sciences (MS). *Program availability:* Part-time. *Degree requirements:* For master's, thesis or alternative. *Entrance requirements:* For master's, minimum GPA of 2.75.

Utah State University, School of Graduate Studies, Emma Eccles Jones College of Education and Human Services, Department of Family, Consumer, and Human Development, Logan, UT 84322. Offers family and human development (MFHD); family, consumer, and human development (MS, PhD), including adolescence/youth (MS), adult development/aging (MS), consumer science (MS), infancy/childhood (MS), marriage and family relations (MS), marriage and family therapy (MS). *Accreditation:* AAMFT/COAMFTE (one or more programs are accredited). *Program availability:* Part-time, evening/weekend, online learning. *Degree requirements:* For master's, thesis; for doctorate, comprehensive exam, thesis/dissertation, competencies. *Entrance requirements:* For master's, GRE General Test or MAT, minimum GPA of 3.0, 3 letters of recommendation; for doctorate, GRE, minimum GPA of 3.0, 3 letters of recommendation. Additional exam requirements/recommendations for international students: Required—TOEFL. Electronic applications accepted. *Faculty research:* Marriage and family relations, adolescent problem behavior, family financial management, early literacy, mental health in the elderly, parent child attachment.

Vanderbilt University, Peabody College, Department of Human and Organizational Development, Nashville, TN 37240-1001. Offers community development and action (M Ed); human development counseling (M Ed). *Accreditation:* ACA; NCATE. *Program availability:* Blended/hybrid learning, on-campus immersion once every semester. *Faculty:* 31 full-time (20 women), 19 part-time/adjunct (9 women). *Students:* 104 full-time (87 women), 21 part-time (20 women); includes 18 minority (8 Black or African American, non-Hispanic/Latino; 2 Asian, non-Hispanic/Latino; 4 Hispanic/Latino; 4 Two or more races, non-Hispanic/Latino), 2 international. Average age 26. 186 applicants, 64% accepted, 55 enrolled. In 2017, 52 master's awarded. *Degree requirements:* For master's, comprehensive exam, thesis optional. *Entrance requirements:* For master's, GRE General Test. Additional exam requirements/recommendations for international students: Required—TOEFL (minimum score 550 paper-based; 80 iBT). *Application deadline:* For fall admission, 12/31 priority date for domestic and international students; for spring admission, 11/1 priority date for domestic and international students. Applications are processed on a rolling basis. Application fee: $0. Electronic applications accepted. *Financial support:* Fellowships with partial tuition reimbursements, research assistantships with partial tuition reimbursements, teaching assistantships with partial tuition reimbursements, Federal Work-Study, institutionally sponsored loans, scholarships/grants, tuition waivers (partial), and unspecified assistantships available. Support available to part-time students. Financial award application deadline: 1/15; financial award applicants required to submit FAFSA. *Faculty research:* Community psychology and community development; counseling and mental health services, prevention and positive youth development; organizational and community change; youth physical and behavioral health in schools and communities. *Unit head:* Dr. Paul Speer, Chair, 615-322-6881, Fax: 615-322-1141, E-mail: paul.w.speer@vanderbilt.edu. *Application contact:* Sherrie Lane, Educational Coordinator, 615-322-8484, Fax: 615-322-1141, E-mail: sherrie.a.lane@vanderbilt.edu.

Washington State University, College of Agricultural, Human, and Natural Resource Sciences, Department of Human Development, Pullman, WA 99164-4852. Offers prevention science (PhD). Program also offered at the Spokane campus. *Program availability:* Part-time. *Degree requirements:* For doctorate, comprehensive exam, thesis/dissertation. *Entrance requirements:* For doctorate, GRE General Test, bachelor's or master's degree in prevention science related field (e.g., communication, educational psychology, human development, nursing, psychology, sociology); written statement specifying qualifications, educational goals, and career objectives; official copies of all college transcripts; three letters of reference. Additional exam requirements/recommendations for international students: Required—TOEFL, IELTS. Electronic applications accepted. *Faculty research:* Prevention science, program implementation and dissemination, drug and alcohol prevention, health communication, equine assisted interventions, obesity prevention, health promotion in emerging adulthood, family processes, disenfranchised youth, rural poverty, adolescent sexuality, cultural competency, community collaborations, parent-child relationships, healthy aging.

Industrial and Organizational Psychology

Adler University, Graduate Programs, MA in Industrial and Organizational Psychology Program, Chicago, IL 60602. Offers MA. *Program availability:* Online learning.

Adler University, Graduate Programs, MA in Organizational Psychology Program, Chicago, IL 60602. Offers MA. Program offered at Vancouver campus. *Program availability:* Part-time.

Adler University, Graduate Programs, PhD in Industrial and Organizational Psychology Program, Chicago, IL 60602. Offers PhD. *Program availability:* Online learning. *Degree requirements:* For doctorate, thesis/dissertation.

Alliant International University–Fresno, California School of Professional Psychology, Organizational Psychology Programs, Fresno, CA 93727. Offers organizational behavior (MA); organizational development (Psy D); MA/PhD; Psy D/MA. *Program availability:* Part-time, evening/weekend. *Degree requirements:* For doctorate, thesis/dissertation. *Entrance requirements:* For doctorate, interview, minimum GPA of 3.0. Additional exam requirements/recommendations for international students: Required—TOEFL (minimum score 550 paper-based; 80 iBT), TWE (minimum score 5). Electronic applications accepted. *Faculty research:* Team development, international organizational development, mergers and acquisitions, strategic change, information technology implementations.

Alliant International University–Los Angeles, California School of Professional Psychology, Organizational Psychology Division, Alhambra, CA 91803. Offers MA, PhD. *Accreditation:* APA. *Program availability:* Part-time. Terminal master's awarded for partial completion of doctoral program. *Degree requirements:* For doctorate, comprehensive exam, thesis/dissertation. *Entrance requirements:* For master's and doctorate, interview, minimum GPA of 3.0 in both psychology and overall. Additional exam requirements/recommendations for international students: Required—TOEFL (minimum score 600 paper-based), TWE (minimum score 5). Electronic applications accepted. *Faculty research:* Organizational transitions, productivity, workforce demographics, management technology, comparative and international research.

Alliant International University–San Diego, California School of Professional Psychology, Organizational Psychology Division, San Diego, CA 92131. Offers clinical/industrial organizational psychology (PhD); consulting psychology (PhD); industrial/organizational psychology (MA, MS, PhD); leadership (PhD). *Program availability:* Part-time, evening/weekend. Terminal master's awarded for partial completion of doctoral program. *Degree requirements:* For doctorate, comprehensive exam, thesis/dissertation, internship/practicum. *Entrance requirements:* For master's and doctorate, minimum GPA of 3.0, recommendations, essay, interview. Additional exam requirements/recommendations for international students: Required—TOEFL (minimum score 550 paper-based; 80 iBT), TWE (minimum score 5). Electronic applications accepted. *Faculty research:* Cultural diversity in the workplace, work motivation, personnel and performance management, organizational diagnosis.

Alliant International University–San Francisco, California School of Professional Psychology, Organizational Psychology Division, San Francisco, CA 94133. Offers MA, PhD. *Accreditation:* APA. *Program availability:* Part-time, evening/weekend. Terminal master's awarded for partial completion of doctoral program. *Degree requirements:* For doctorate, comprehensive exam, thesis/dissertation, field placement. *Entrance requirements:* For master's and doctorate, minimum GPA of 3.0, interview. Additional exam requirements/recommendations for international students: Required—TOEFL (minimum score 550 paper-based; 80 iBT), TWE (minimum score 5). Electronic applications accepted. *Faculty research:* Leadership, ethics and management, career development, organizational behavior, strategic change.

American InterContinental University Online, Program in Business Administration, Schaumburg, IL 60173. Offers accounting and finance (MBA); finance (MBA); healthcare management (MBA); human resource management (MBA); international business (MBA); management (MBA); marketing (MBA); operations management (MBA); organizational psychology and development (MBA); project management (MBA). *Accreditation:* ACBSP. *Program availability:* Evening/weekend, online learning. *Entrance requirements:* Additional exam requirements/recommendations for international students: Required—TOEFL (minimum score 550 paper-based). Electronic applications accepted.

Angelo State University, College of Graduate Studies and Research, Archer College of Health and Human Services, Department of Psychology and Sociology, San Angelo, TX 76909. Offers industrial-organizational psychology (MS). *Program availability:* Part-time, evening/weekend. *Students:* 83 full-time (55 women), 41 part-time (28 women); includes 39 minority (8 Black or African American, non-Hispanic/Latino; 1 Asian, non-Hispanic/Latino; 28 Hispanic/Latino; 2 Two or more races, non-Hispanic/Latino), 6 international. Average age 32. *Degree requirements:* For master's, comprehensive exam, thesis optional. *Entrance requirements:* For master's, GRE General Test (for industrial and organizational psychology only), essay, letters of recommendation (for industrial and organizational psychology only). Additional exam requirements/recommendations for international students: Required—TOEFL or IELTS. *Application deadline:* For fall admission, 7/15 priority date for domestic students, 6/10 for international students; for spring admission, 12/1 priority date for domestic students, 11/1 for international students. Applications are processed on a rolling basis. Application fee: $40 ($50 for international students). Electronic applications accepted. *Expenses:* Tuition, state resident: full-time $3856. Tuition, nonresident: full-time $11,324. *Required fees:* $2650. *Financial support:* Teaching assistantships, career-related internships or fieldwork, Federal Work-Study, scholarships/grants, and unspecified assistantships available. Support available to part-time students. Financial award application deadline: 3/1; financial award applicants required to submit FAFSA. *Unit head:* Dr. James N. Forbes, Chair, 325-486-6120, Fax: 325-942-2290, E-mail: james.forbes@angelo.edu. Website: http://www.angelo.edu/dept/psychology_sociology/

Anna Maria College, Graduate Division, Program in Industrial/Organizational Psychology, Paxton, MA 01612. Offers MS.

Argosy University, Atlanta, Georgia School of Professional Psychology, Atlanta, GA 30328. Offers clinical psychology (MA, Psy D, Postdoctoral Respecialization Certificate), including child and family psychology (Psy D); general adult clinical (Psy D); health psychology (Psy D), neuropsychology/geropsychology (Psy D); community counseling (MA), including marriage and family therapy; counselor education and supervision (Ed D); forensic psychology (MA); industrial organizational psychology (MA); marriage and family therapy (Certificate); sport-exercise psychology (MA). *Accreditation:* APA.

Argosy University, Chicago, Illinois School of Professional Psychology, Chicago, IL 60601. Offers clinical psychology (MA, Psy D), including child and adolescent psychology (Psy D), client-centered and experiential psychotherapies (Psy D), diversity and multicultural psychology (Psy D), family psychology (Psy D), forensic psychology (Psy D), health psychology (Psy D), neuropsychology (Psy D), organizational consulting (Psy D), psychoanalytic psychology (Psy D), psychology and spirituality (Psy D); community counseling (MA); counseling psychology (Ed D), including counselor education and supervision; counselor education and supervision (Ed D); industrial organizational psychology (MA). *Accreditation:* APA (one or more programs are accredited). *Program availability:* Online learning.

Argosy University, Phoenix, Arizona School of Professional Psychology, Program in Industrial Organizational Psychology, Phoenix, AZ 85021. Offers MA.

Argosy University, Tampa, Florida School of Professional Psychology, Tampa, FL 33607. Offers clinical psychology (MA, Psy D), including clinical psychology; counselor education and supervision (Ed D); industrial organizational psychology (MA); marriage and family therapy (MA); mental health counseling (MA).

Argosy University, Twin Cities, Minnesota School of Professional Psychology, Eagan, MN 55121. Offers clinical psychology (MA, Psy D), including child and family psychology (Psy D), forensic psychology (Psy D), health and neuropsychology (Psy D), trauma (Psy D); forensic counseling (Post-Graduate Certificate); forensic psychology (MA); industrial organizational psychology (MA); marriage and family therapy (MA, DMFT), including forensic counseling (MA). *Accreditation:* AAMFT; AAMFT/COAMFTE; APA.

Austin Peay State University, College of Graduate Studies, College of Behavioral and Health Sciences, Department of Psychological Science and Counseling, Clarksville, TN 37044. Offers industrial-organizational psychology (MS); mental health counseling (MS), including clinical mental health, school counseling; school counseling (MS). *Program availability:* Part-time, online learning. *Faculty:* 11 full-time (6 women), 1 (woman) part-time/adjunct. *Students:* 60 full-time (46 women), 12 part-time (10 women); includes 16 minority (11 Black or African American, non-Hispanic/Latino; 4 Hispanic/Latino; 1 Two or more races, non-Hispanic/Latino). Average age 29. 59 applicants, 69% accepted, 31 enrolled. In 2017, 30 master's awarded. *Degree requirements:* For master's, comprehensive exam, thesis (for some programs). *Entrance requirements:* For master's, GRE General Test, minimum undergraduate GPA of 2.5, 3 letters of recommendation, bachelor's degree. Additional exam requirements/recommendations for international students: Required—TOEFL (minimum score 500 paper-based). *Application deadline:* For fall admission, 8/8 priority date for domestic students. Applications are processed on a rolling basis. Application fee: $45 ($55 for international students). Electronic applications accepted. *Expenses:* Tuition, state resident: full-time $7686; part-time $427 per credit hour. Tuition, nonresident: full-time $20,268; part-time $1126 per credit hour. *Required fees:* $1529; $76.45 per credit hour. *Financial support:* Research assistantships with full tuition reimbursements, career-related internships or fieldwork, Federal Work-Study, institutionally sponsored loans, scholarships/grants, and unspecified assistantships available. Support available to part-time students. Financial award application deadline: 4/1; financial award applicants required to submit FAFSA. *Unit head:* Dr. Nicole Knickmeyer, Chair, 931-221-7232, Fax: 931-221-6267, E-mail: knickmeyer@apsu.edu. *Application contact:* Brad Averitt, Coordinator of Graduate Admissions, 800-859-4723, Fax: 931-221-7641, E-mail: gradadmissions@apsu.edu. Website: http://www.apsu.edu/psychology/index.php

Azusa Pacific University, School of Behavioral and Applied Sciences, Department of Leadership and Organizational Psychology, Program in Organizational Psychology, Azusa, CA 91702-7000. Offers MS. *Expenses:* Contact institution.

Baruch College of the City University of New York, Weissman School of Arts and Sciences, Program in Industrial/Organizational Psychology, New York, NY 10010-5585. Offers MS. *Program availability:* Part-time, evening/weekend. Terminal master's awarded for partial completion of doctoral program. *Degree requirements:* For master's, thesis or alternative. *Entrance requirements:* For master's, GRE, 2 letters of recommendation, personal essay, resume. Additional exam requirements/recommendations for international students: Required—TOEFL. Electronic applications accepted. *Faculty research:* Examining possible explanations for race-based differences on intelligence and cognitive ability tests; developing alternative formats and types of intelligence tests as well as examining the role of previous experience, test taking skills, and test characteristics on performance on these types of tests; identified employee surveys; personnel staffing and equal employment opportunity issues; leadership development; organizational culture.

Baruch College of the City University of New York, Zicklin School of Business, Program in Industrial and Organizational Psychology, New York, NY 10010-5585. Offers MBA, MS, PhD. PhD offered jointly with Graduate School and University Center of the City University of New York. *Program availability:* Part-time, evening/weekend. *Degree requirements:* For master's, thesis or alternative; for doctorate, comprehensive exam, thesis/dissertation. *Entrance requirements:* For master's, GMAT or GRE General Test, 2 letters of recommendation, resumé, 2 years of work experience; for doctorate, GMAT or GRE General Test. Additional exam requirements/recommendations for international students: Required—TOEFL (minimum score 590 paper-based), TWE. *Faculty research:* Job attitudes, power and leadership in organizations, measurement issues in organizational behavior, work motivation, fair employment practices.

Bayamón Central University, Graduate Programs, Program in Organizational Psychology, Bayamón, PR 00960-1725. Offers MA. *Program availability:* Part-time, evening/weekend. *Degree requirements:* For master's, comprehensive exam. *Entrance requirements:* For master's, EXADEP, bachelor's degree in psychology or related field.

Bowling Green State University, Graduate College, College of Arts and Sciences, Department of Psychology, Bowling Green, OH 43403. Offers clinical psychology (MA, PhD); developmental psychology (MA, PhD); experimental psychology (MA, PhD); industrial/organizational psychology (MA, PhD); quantitative psychology (MA, PhD). *Accreditation:* APA (one or more programs are accredited). *Degree requirements:* For doctorate, thesis/dissertation. *Entrance requirements:* For doctorate, GRE General Test, GRE Subject Test. Additional exam requirements/recommendations for international students: Required—TOEFL. Electronic applications accepted. *Faculty research:* Personnel psychology, developmental-mathematical models, behavioral medication, brain process, child/adolescent social cognition.

Brooklyn College of the City University of New York, School of Natural and Behavioral Sciences, Department of Psychology, Brooklyn, NY 11210-2889. Offers experimental psychology (MA); industrial and organizational psychology (MA), including human relations, organizational behavior; mental health counseling (MA); psychology (PhD). *Program availability:* Part-time. *Degree requirements:* For master's, comprehensive exam, thesis (for some programs). *Entrance requirements:* For master's, minimum GPA of 3.0, 2 letters of recommendation, essay; for doctorate, GRE. Additional exam requirements/recommendations for international students: Required—TOEFL (minimum score 520 paper-based; 69 iBT). Electronic applications accepted.

California State University, Long Beach, Graduate Studies, College of Liberal Arts, Department of Psychology, Long Beach, CA 90840. Offers human factors (MS);

industrial/organizational psychology (MS); psychology (MA). *Program availability:* Part-time, evening/weekend. *Degree requirements:* For master's, comprehensive exam, thesis. *Entrance requirements:* For master's, GRE General Test, GRE Subject Test. Electronic applications accepted. *Faculty research:* Physiological psychology, social and personality psychology, community-clinical psychology, industrial-organizational psychology, developmental psychology.

California State University, Sacramento, College of Social Sciences and Interdisciplinary Studies, Department of Psychology, Sacramento, CA 95819. Offers applied behavior analysis (MA); industrial/organizational psychology (MA). *Program availability:* Part-time. *Students:* 19 full-time (11 women), 29 part-time (21 women); includes 17 minority (4 Asian, non-Hispanic/Latino; 11 Hispanic/Latino; 2 Native Hawaiian or other Pacific Islander, non-Hispanic/Latino), 1 international. Average age 27. 77 applicants, 32% accepted, 17 enrolled. In 2017, 9 master's awarded. *Degree requirements:* For master's, thesis, project; writing proficiency exam. *Entrance requirements:* For master's, GRE, minimum GPA of 3.0 during previous 2 years. Additional exam requirements/recommendations for international students: Required—TOEFL (minimum score 550 paper-based; 80 iBT); Recommended—IELTS, TSE. *Application deadline:* For fall admission, 3/1 for domestic and international students. Applications are processed on a rolling basis. Application fee: $55. Electronic applications accepted. *Expenses:* Contact institution. *Financial support:* Teaching assistantships, career-related internships or fieldwork, Federal Work-Study, and scholarships/grants available. Support available to part-time students. Financial award application deadline: 3/1; financial award applicants required to submit FAFSA. *Unit head:* Dr. Rebecca Cameron, Interim Department Chair, 916-278-6254, E-mail: cameron@csus.edu. *Application contact:* Jose Martinez, Graduate Admissions Supervisor, 916-278-7871, E-mail: martinj@skymail.csus.edu.
Website: http://www.csus.edu/psyc

California State University, San Bernardino, Graduate Studies, College of Social and Behavioral Sciences, Department of Psychology, San Bernardino, CA 92407. Offers child development (MA); clinical/counseling psychology (MS); industrial/organizational psychology (MS); psychological science (MA). *Faculty:* 13 full-time (4 women), 2 part-time/adjunct (both women). *Students:* 61 full-time (41 women), 17 part-time (14 women); includes 47 minority (2 Black or African American, non-Hispanic/Latino; 3 Asian, non-Hispanic/Latino; 33 Hispanic/Latino; 9 Two or more races, non-Hispanic/Latino), 3 international. Average age 28. 190 applicants, 19% accepted, 33 enrolled. In 2017, 28 master's awarded. *Degree requirements:* For master's, comprehensive exam, thesis (for some programs). *Entrance requirements:* Additional exam requirements/recommendations for international students: Required—TOEFL. Application fee: $55. *Financial support:* Fellowships, research assistantships, and teaching assistantships available. *Faculty research:* Perceptual development, human memory, psychopharmacology, psychology of women, language acquisition. *Unit head:* Dr. Robert Ricco, Chair, 909-537-5485, Fax: 909-537-7003, E-mail: rricco@csusb.edu. *Application contact:* Dr. Dorota Huizinga, Dean of Graduate Studies, 909-537-3064, E-mail: dorota.huizinga@csusb.edu.
Website: https://csbs.csusb.edu/psychology

Capella University, Harold Abel School of Social and Behavioral Science, Doctoral Programs in Psychology, Minneapolis, MN 55402. Offers addiction psychology (PhD); clinical psychology (Psy D); educational psychology (PhD); general advanced studies in human behavior (PhD); general psychology (PhD); industrial/organizational psychology (PhD); school psychology (Psy D).

Capella University, Harold Abel School of Social and Behavioral Science, Master's Programs in Psychology, Minneapolis, MN 55402. Offers applied behavior analysis (MS); clinical psychology (MS); counseling psychology (MS); educational psychology (MS); evaluation, research, and measurement (MS); general advanced studies in human behavior (MS); general psychology (MS); industrial/organizational psychology (MS); leadership coaching psychology (MS); school psychology (MS); sport psychology (MS).

Carlos Albizu University, Graduate Programs, San Juan, PR 00901. Offers clinical psychology (MS, PhD, Psy D); general psychology (PhD); industrial/organizational psychology (MS, PhD); speech and language pathology (MS). *Accreditation:* APA (one or more programs are accredited). *Program availability:* Part-time, evening/weekend. Terminal master's awarded for partial completion of doctoral program. *Degree requirements:* For master's, one foreign language, comprehensive exam, thesis; for doctorate, one foreign language, comprehensive exam, thesis/dissertation, written qualifying exams. *Entrance requirements:* For master's, GRE General Test or EXADEP, interview; minimum GPA of 2.8 (industrial/organizational psychology); for doctorate, GRE General Test or EXADEP, interview; minimum GPA of 3.0 (PhD in industrial/organizational psychology and clinical psychology), 3.25 (Psy D). *Faculty research:* Psychotherapeutic techniques for Hispanics, psychology of the aged, school dropouts, stress, violence.

Carlos Albizu University, Miami Campus, Graduate Programs, Miami, FL 33172-2209. Offers clinical psychology (PhD, Psy D); entrepreneurship (MBA); exceptional student education (MS); human services (PhD); industrial/organizational psychology (MS); marriage and family therapy (MS); mental health counseling (MS); nonprofit management (MBA); organizational management (MBA); psychology (MS); speech and language pathology (MS); teaching English for speakers of other languages (MS). *Accreditation:* APA. *Program availability:* Part-time, evening/weekend, 100% online, blended/hybrid learning. *Faculty:* 32 full-time (24 women), 27 part-time/adjunct (15 women). *Students:* 411 full-time (345 women), 248 part-time (215 women); includes 562 minority (53 Black or African American, non-Hispanic/Latino; 4 Asian, non-Hispanic/Latino; 498 Hispanic/Latino; 7 Two or more races, non-Hispanic/Latino), 23 international. Average age 34. 391 applicants, 42% accepted, 154 enrolled. In 2017, 96 master's, 54 doctorates awarded. Terminal master's awarded for partial completion of doctoral program. *Degree requirements:* For master's, comprehensive exam (for some programs), integrative project (for MBA); research project (for exceptional student education, teaching English as a second language); for doctorate, comprehensive examinations, internship, project/dissertation. *Entrance requirements:* For master's, GRE/EXADEP, bachelor's degree from accredited institution, minimum GPA of 3.0, 3 letters of recommendation, interview, resume, statement of purpose, official transcripts; for doctorate, GRE (for Psy D), 3 letters of recommendation, resume, interview, statement of purpose, official transcripts; bachelor's degree and minimum GPA of 3.25 (for Psy D); master's degree and minimum GPA of 3.0 (for PhD). Additional exam requirements/recommendations for international students: Required—Michigan Test of English Language Proficiency. *Application deadline:* For fall admission, 4/1 priority date for domestic students, 5/1 priority date for international students; for spring admission, 11/1 priority date for domestic students, 9/1 priority date for international students. Applications are processed on a rolling basis. Application fee: $50. Electronic applications accepted. Application fee is waived when completed online. *Expenses:* Contact institution. *Financial support:* In 2017–18, 145 students received support. Federal Work-Study, scholarships/grants, unspecified assistantships, and tuition discounts available. Financial award application deadline: 6/1; financial award applicants required to submit FAFSA. *Faculty research:* Psychotherapy, forensic psychology, neuropsychology, special education, speech-language pathology, criminal justice. *Unit head:* Dr. Etiony Aldarondo, Provost, 305-593-1223 Ext. 3138, Fax: 305-592-7930, E-mail: ealdarondo@albizu.edu. *Application contact:* Sonia Feliciano, Institutional Director of Student Recruitment, 305-593-1223 Ext. 3108, Fax: 305-477-8983, E-mail: sfeliciano@albizu.edu.

Central Michigan University, College of Graduate Studies, College of Humanities and Social and Behavioral Sciences, Department of Psychology, Program in Industrial and Organizational Psychology, Mount Pleasant, MI 48859. Offers industrial and organizational psychology (MA, PhD); occupational health psychology (PhD). *Degree requirements:* For master's, thesis; for doctorate, comprehensive exam, thesis/dissertation. *Entrance requirements:* For master's and doctorate, GRE. Electronic applications accepted. *Faculty research:* Job stress, retirement, leadership, and careers; personality in the workplace, personnel selection, and structural equation modeling in industrial/organizational psychology; personnel psychology, evolutionary psychology, and influences on HRM utilization; occupational health psychology and job stress; work attitudes, psychological ownership in work, and performance appraisal.

Chatham University, Program in Counseling Psychology, Pittsburgh, PA 15232-2826. Offers child, adolescent and family (MSCP); counseling psychology (Psy D); health and holistic (MSCP); organization and supervision (MSCP); sport and exercise (MSCP). *Accreditation:* APA. *Program availability:* Part-time, evening/weekend. *Faculty:* 11 full-time (10 women). *Students:* 61 full-time (46 women), 25 part-time (22 women); includes 12 minority (9 Black or African American, non-Hispanic/Latino; 2 Hispanic/Latino; 1 Two or more races, non-Hispanic/Latino), 3 international. Average age 30. 124 applicants, 62% accepted, 45 enrolled. In 2017, 38 master's awarded. *Degree requirements:* For master's, thesis optional, supervised internship; for doctorate, thesis/dissertation, internship. *Entrance requirements:* For master's, minimum GPA of 3.0; 2 letters of recommendation; resume; prerequisite coursework in statistics, biology, and psychology; for doctorate, GRE. Additional exam requirements/recommendations for international students: Required—TOEFL (minimum score 600 paper-based; 100 iBT), IELTS (minimum score 7), TWE. *Application deadline:* For fall admission, 4/1 priority date for domestic and international students; for spring admission, 11/1 for domestic students, 10/1 for international students. Applications are processed on a rolling basis. Application fee: $45. Electronic applications accepted. Application fee is waived when completed online. *Expenses: Tuition:* Full-time $16,740; part-time $930 per credit. *Required fees:* $486; $27 per credit. $243 per semester. *Financial support:* Career-related internships or fieldwork available. Financial award applicants required to submit FAFSA. *Faculty research:* Trauma and recovery, hypnosis, psychospiritual dimensions of healing, psychotherapy of schizophrenia. *Unit head:* Dr. Mary Beth Mannarino, Director, 412-365-1196, Fax: 412-365-1505, E-mail: mmannarino@chatham.edu. *Application contact:* Katie Noel, Assistant Director of Graduate Admission, 412-365-2758, Fax: 412-365-1609, E-mail: gradadmissions@chatham.edu.
Website: http://www.chatham.edu/mscp

The Chicago School of Professional Psychology, Program in Business Psychology, Chicago, IL 60610. Offers business psychology (PhD); industrial and organizational business psychology (Psy D); industrial and organizational psychology (MA); organizational leadership (MA, PhD). *Degree requirements:* For doctorate, thesis/dissertation optional. *Entrance requirements:* For doctorate, GRE. Additional exam requirements/recommendations for international students: Required—TOEFL.

The Chicago School of Professional Psychology, Program in Industrial and Organizational Psychology, Chicago, IL 60610. Offers business psychology (Psy D); industrial and organizational psychology (MA). *Program availability:* Part-time, evening/weekend. *Degree requirements:* For master's, internship; for doctorate, thesis/dissertation, internship. *Entrance requirements:* For master's, 1 course each in psychology, statistics, and research methods. Additional exam requirements/recommendations for international students: Required—TOEFL (minimum score 550 paper-based; 79 iBT).

The Chicago School of Professional Psychology at Downtown Los Angeles, Program in Industrial and Organizational Psychology, Los Angeles, CA 90017. Offers MA.

The Chicago School of Professional Psychology: Online, PhD Program in Organizational Leadership, Chicago, IL 60654. Offers PhD.

The Chicago School of Professional Psychology: Online, Program in Applied Industrial and Organizational Psychology, Chicago, IL 60654. Offers MA, Certificate.

Claremont Graduate University, Graduate Programs, School of Social Science, Policy and Evaluation, Department of Psychology, Claremont, CA 91711-6160. Offers advanced study in evaluation (Certificate); cognitive psychology (MA, PhD); developmental psychology (MA, PhD); evaluation and applied research methods (MA, PhD); health behavior research and evaluation (MA, PhD); human resource development and evaluation (MA); industrial/organizational psychology (MA, PhD); organizational behavior (MA, PhD); organizational psychology (MA, PhD); social psychology (MA, PhD); MBA/PhD. *Program availability:* Part-time. Terminal master's awarded for partial completion of doctoral program. *Entrance requirements:* For master's and doctorate, GRE General Test. Additional exam requirements/recommendations for international students: Required—TOEFL (minimum score 75 iBT). Electronic applications accepted. *Faculty research:* Social intervention, diversity in organizations, eyewitness memory, aging and cognition, drug policy.

Clemson University, Graduate School, College of Behavioral, Social and Health Sciences, Department of Psychology, Clemson, SC 29634. Offers applied psychology (MS); human factors psychology (PhD); industrial-organizational psychology (PhD). *Faculty:* 30 full-time (13 women), 1 (woman) part-time/adjunct. *Students:* 39 full-time (23 women), 4 part-time (3 women); includes 4 minority (1 Black or African American, non-Hispanic/Latino; 3 Hispanic/Latino). Average age 27. 214 applicants, 8% accepted, 10 enrolled. In 2017, 7 master's, 6 doctorates awarded. *Degree requirements:* For master's, thesis; for doctorate, comprehensive exam, thesis/dissertation. *Entrance requirements:* For master's and doctorate, GRE General Test, unofficial transcripts, letters of recommendation, statement of intent. Additional exam requirements/recommendations for international students: Required—TOEFL (minimum score 80 iBT), IELTS (minimum score 7), PTE (minimum score 54). *Application deadline:* For fall admission, 1/15 priority date for domestic and international students. Application fee: $80 ($90 for international students). Electronic applications accepted. *Expenses:* $6,564 per semester full-time resident, $12,538 per semester full-time non-resident, $743 per credit hour part-time resident, $1,486 per credit hour part-time non-resident, $1,203 per credit hour online, other fees may apply per session. *Financial support:* In 2017–18, 18 students received support, including 4 fellowships with partial tuition reimbursements available (averaging $8,750 per year), 2 research assistantships with partial tuition reimbursements available (averaging $12,000 per year), 11 teaching assistantships with partial tuition reimbursements available (averaging $13,386 per year); career-related internships or fieldwork and unspecified assistantships also available. Financial award application deadline: 1/15. *Faculty research:* Occupational health and organizational psychology; transportation safety; human factors in health care; ergonomics and human-computer interaction; aging, retirement, and return to work. *Total annual research expenditures:* $436,382. *Unit head:* Dr. Patrick Raymark, Chair, 864-656-4715, E-mail: praymar@clemson.edu. *Application contact:* Dr. Robert Sinclair, Graduate Program

Coordinator, 864-656-3931, E-mail: rsincla@clemson.edu.
Website: http://www.clemson.edu/cbshs/departments/psychology/index.html

East Carolina University, Graduate School, Thomas Harriot College of Arts and Sciences, Department of Psychology, Greenville, NC 27858-4353. Offers health psychology (PhD), including clinical health psychology, occupational health psychology, pediatric school psychology; industrial and organizational psychology (MA); quantitative methods for the social and behavioral sciences (Certificate); MA/CAS. *Program availability:* Part-time, evening/weekend. *Students:* 77 full-time (52 women), 17 part-time (15 women); includes 12 minority (8 Black or African American, non-Hispanic/Latino; 3 Hispanic/Latino; 1 Two or more races, non-Hispanic/Latino). Average age 26. 221 applicants, 31% accepted, 22 enrolled. In 2017, 31 master's, 7 doctorates, 21 other advanced degrees awarded. *Degree requirements:* For doctorate, comprehensive exam, thesis/dissertation or alternative. *Entrance requirements:* For master's and doctorate, GRE General Test. Additional exam requirements/recommendations for international students: Recommended—TOEFL (minimum score 78 iBT), IELTS (minimum score 6.5). *Application deadline:* For fall admission, 12/1 priority date for domestic and international students. Applications are processed on a rolling basis. Application fee: $75. Electronic applications accepted. *Expenses:* Tuition, state resident: full-time $4749; part-time $297 per credit hour. Tuition, nonresident: full-time $17,898; part-time $1119 per credit hour. *Required fees:* $2691; $224 per credit hour. Part-time tuition and fees vary according to course load and program. *Financial support:* Research assistantships with partial tuition reimbursements, teaching assistantships with partial tuition reimbursements, Federal Work-Study, and traineeships available. Support available to part-time students. Financial award application deadline: 6/1. *Unit head:* Dr. Susan L. McCammon, Chair, 252-328-6357, E-mail: mccammons@ecu.edu. *Application contact:* Dean of Graduate School, 252-328-6012, Fax: 252-328-6071, E-mail: gradschool@ecu.edu.
Website: http://www.ecu.edu/psyc/

Eastern Kentucky University, The Graduate School, College of Arts and Sciences, Department of Psychology, Richmond, KY 40475-3102. Offers clinical psychology (MS); industrial/organizational psychology (MS); school psychology (Psy S). *Program availability:* Part-time. *Entrance requirements:* For master's and Psy S, GRE General Test, minimum GPA of 2.5. *Faculty research:* Autism, social psychology, parenting, assessment of depression/anxiety, reading.

Elmhurst College, Graduate Programs, Program in Industrial/Organizational Psychology, Elmhurst, IL 60126-3296. Offers MA. *Program availability:* Part-time, evening/weekend. *Faculty:* 2 full-time (1 woman), 5 part-time/adjunct (1 woman). *Students:* 6 full-time (2 women), 55 part-time (37 women); includes 15 minority (4 Black or African American, non-Hispanic/Latino; 5 Asian, non-Hispanic/Latino; 4 Hispanic/Latino; 2 Two or more races, non-Hispanic/Latino). Average age 25. 68 applicants, 47% accepted, 31 enrolled. In 2017, 28 master's awarded. *Degree requirements:* For master's, thesis optional. *Entrance requirements:* For master's, GRE General Test, 3 recommendations, resume, statement of purpose. Additional exam requirements/recommendations for international students: Required—TOEFL (minimum score 550 paper-based; 79 iBT). *Application deadline:* Applications are processed on a rolling basis. Application fee: $0. Electronic applications accepted. *Expenses:* Contact institution. *Financial support:* In 2017–18, 47 students received support. Scholarships/grants and unspecified assistantships available. Support available to part-time students. Financial award application deadline: 3/1; financial award applicants required to submit FAFSA. *Unit head:* Carrie Hewitt, Director, 630-617-3735, E-mail: hewittc@elmhurst.edu. *Application contact:* Timothy J. Panfil, Director of Enrollment Management, 630-617-3300 Ext. 3256, Fax: 630-617-6471, E-mail: panfilt@elmhurst.edu.
Website: http://www.elmhurst.edu/iop

Emporia State University, Program in Psychology, Emporia, KS 66801-5415. Offers general psychology (MS); industrial/organizational psychology (MS). *Program availability:* Part-time. *Faculty:* 8 full-time (4 women). *Students:* 9 full-time (5 women), 4 part-time (2 women); includes 1 minority (Black or African American, non-Hispanic/Latino), 2 international. 20 applicants, 75% accepted, 5 enrolled. In 2017, 3 master's awarded. *Degree requirements:* For master's, comprehensive exam or thesis, internship. *Entrance requirements:* For master's, GRE General Test or MAT, essay exam, appropriate bachelor's degree, letters of recommendation. Additional exam requirements/recommendations for international students: Required—TOEFL (minimum score 520 paper-based; 68 iBT). *Application deadline:* For fall admission, 6/1 priority date for domestic students; for spring admission, 10/1 for domestic students. Applications are processed on a rolling basis. Application fee: $30 ($75 for international students). Electronic applications accepted. *Expenses:* Tuition, state resident: full-time $6084; part-time $253.50 per credit hour. Tuition, nonresident: full-time $18,924; part-time $788.50 per credit hour. *Required fees:* $1943; $80.95 per credit hour. Tuition and fees vary according to campus/location. *Financial support:* In 2017–18, 11 teaching assistantships with full tuition reimbursements (averaging $7,344 per year) were awarded; career-related internships or fieldwork, Federal Work-Study, institutionally sponsored loans, health care benefits, and unspecified assistantships also available. Financial award application deadline: 3/15; financial award applicants required to submit FAFSA. *Faculty research:* Driving under the influence (DUI) personality, lifestyles and imposter phenomenon. *Unit head:* Dr. Jim Persinger, Chair, 620-341-5317, E-mail: jpersing@emporia.edu. *Application contact:* Mary Sewell, Admissions Coordinator, 800-950-GRAD, Fax: 620-341-5909, E-mail: msewell@emporia.edu.

Fairleigh Dickinson University, Florham Campus, Maxwell Becton College of Arts and Sciences, Department of Psychology, Program in Industrial/Organizational Psychology, Madison, NJ 07940-1099. Offers MA, MA/MBA. *Entrance requirements:* For master's, GRE General Test.

Florida Institute of Technology, College of Psychology and Liberal Arts, Program in Industrial/Organizational Psychology, Melbourne, FL 32901-6975. Offers MS, PhD. *Program availability:* Part-time. *Students:* Average age 30. 187 applicants, 21% accepted, 17 enrolled. In 2017, 8 master's, 4 doctorates awarded. *Degree requirements:* For master's, comprehensive exam (for some programs), thesis (for some programs), minimum of 45 credit hours; for doctorate, thesis/dissertation, minimum of 90 credit hours beyond bachelor's degree. *Entrance requirements:* For master's, GRE General Test, minimum GPA of 3.0, 3 letters of recommendation, resume, statement of objectives, bachelor's degree in psychology; for doctorate, GRE General Test, minimum GPA of 3.2, 3 letters of recommendation, statement of objectives, resume. Additional exam requirements/recommendations for international students: Required—TOEFL (minimum score 550 paper-based; 79 iBT). *Application deadline:* For fall admission, 3/15 for domestic students. Applications are processed on a rolling basis. Electronic applications accepted. *Expenses: Tuition:* Part-time $1241 per credit hour. Part-time tuition and fees vary according to campus/location. *Financial support:* Fellowships, research assistantships, teaching assistantships, career-related internships or fieldwork, and tuition waivers (partial) available. Financial award application deadline: 3/1; financial award applicants required to submit FAFSA. *Faculty research:* Faking, personality measures, team performance, behavioral change, strategies for programming, analysis of verbal behavior. *Unit head:* Dr. Lisa Steelman, Chair of Industrial and Organizational Psychology Programs, 321-674-7316, E-mail: lsteelma@fit.edu. *Application contact:* Cheryl A. Brown, Associate Director of Graduate Admissions, 321-674-7581, Fax: 321-674-9468, E-mail: cbrown@fit.edu.
Website: http://cpla.fit.edu/programs.php

Florida International University, College of Arts, Sciences, and Education, Department of Psychology, Miami, FL 33199. Offers behavioral analysis (MS); clinical science (PhD); cognitive neuroscience (PhD); counseling psychology (MS); developmental science (MS, PhD); legal psychology (MS, PhD); organizational psychology (MS, PhD). Program has fall admissions only. *Accreditation:* APA. *Program availability:* Part-time, evening/weekend. *Faculty:* 45 full-time (28 women), 48 part-time/adjunct (31 women). *Students:* 162 full-time (122 women), 13 part-time (5 women); includes 94 minority (11 Black or African American, non-Hispanic/Latino; 5 Asian, non-Hispanic/Latino; 75 Hispanic/Latino; 3 Two or more races, non-Hispanic/Latino), 12 international. Average age 27. 290 applicants, 21% accepted, 50 enrolled. In 2017, 43 master's, 13 doctorates awarded. Terminal master's awarded for partial completion of doctoral program. *Degree requirements:* For master's, thesis; for doctorate, comprehensive exam, thesis/dissertation. *Entrance requirements:* For master's, GRE General Test, minimum GPA of 3.0, resume, 3 letters of recommendation; for doctorate, GRE General Test, 3 letters of recommendation, resume, letter of intent, two writing samples, minimum GPA of 3.0. Additional exam requirements/recommendations for international students: Required—TOEFL (minimum score 550 paper-based; 80 iBT). *Application deadline:* For fall admission, 12/15 for domestic and international students. Application fee: $30. Electronic applications accepted. *Expenses:* Tuition, state resident: full-time $8912; part-time $446 per credit hour. Tuition, nonresident: full-time $21,393; part-time $992 per credit hour. *Required fees:* $390; $195 per semester. *Financial support:* Institutionally sponsored loans and scholarships/grants available. Financial award application deadline: 3/1. *Faculty research:* Legal psychology, organizational and industrial psychology, child behavior psychology. *Unit head:* Dr. Jeremy Pettit, Interim Chair, 305-348-1671, Fax: 305-348-3646, E-mail: jeremy.pettit@fiu.edu. *Application contact:* Nanett Rojas, Assistant Director, Graduate Admissions, 305-348-7464, Fax: 305-348-7441, E-mail: gradadm@fiu.edu.

George Mason University, College of Humanities and Social Sciences, Department of Psychology, Fairfax, VA 22030. Offers applied developmental psychology (MA, PhD); clinical psychology (PhD); cognitive and behavioral neuroscience (MA, PhD); cognitive neuroscience (Certificate); human factors/applied cognition (MA, PhD, Certificate), including transportation human factors (Certificate), usability (Certificate); industrial/organizational psychology (MA, PhD). *Accreditation:* APA. *Faculty:* 41 full-time (20 women), 5 part-time/adjunct (all women). *Students:* 152 full-time (101 women), 56 part-time (39 women); includes 47 minority (15 Black or African American, non-Hispanic/Latino; 13 Asian, non-Hispanic/Latino; 13 Hispanic/Latino; 1 Native Hawaiian or other Pacific Islander, non-Hispanic/Latino; 5 Two or more races, non-Hispanic/Latino), 12 international. Average age 27. 719 applicants, 19% accepted, 61 enrolled. In 2017, 55 master's, 18 doctorates, 8 other advanced degrees awarded. *Degree requirements:* For master's, comprehensive exam, thesis or practicum research; for doctorate, comprehensive exam, thesis/dissertation, 2nd-year project. *Entrance requirements:* For master's, GRE, 2 official transcripts; goals statement; 15 undergraduate credits in concentration for which the applicant is applying; for doctorate, GRE, 3 letters of recommendation; resume; goals statement; minimum GPA of 3.0 overall for last 60 undergraduate credits, 3.25 in psychology courses; 15 undergraduate credits in concentration for which the applicant is applying; 2 official transcripts; for Certificate, GRE, 2 official transcripts; expanded goals statement; 3 letters of recommendation. Additional exam requirements/recommendations for international students: Required—TOEFL (minimum score 575 paper-based; 88 iBT), IELTS (minimum score 6.5), PTE (minimum score 59). Application fee: $75 ($80 for international students). Electronic applications accepted. *Expenses:* Tuition, state resident: full-time $11,228; part-time $459.50 per credit. Tuition, nonresident: full-time $30,932; part-time $1280.50 per credit. *Required fees:* $3252; $135.50 per credit. Part-time tuition and fees vary according to course load and program. *Financial support:* In 2017–18, 110 students received support, including 6 fellowships (averaging $4,829 per year), 52 research assistantships with tuition reimbursements available (averaging $10,933 per year), 70 teaching assistantships with tuition reimbursements available (averaging $7,703 per year); career-related internships or fieldwork, Federal Work-Study, scholarships/grants, tuition waivers (partial), unspecified assistantships, and health care benefits (for full-time research or teaching assistantship recipients) also available. Support available to part-time students. Financial award application deadline: 3/1; financial award applicants required to submit FAFSA. *Faculty research:* Applied developmental psychology, biopsychology, clinical psychology, human factors/applied cognition psychology, industrial/organizational psychology, school psychology. *Total annual research expenditures:* $2.6 million. *Unit head:* Reeshad Dalal, Department Chair, 703-993-9487, Fax: 703-993-1359, E-mail: rdalal@gmu.edu. *Application contact:* Michael Hock, Graduate Program Coordinator, 703-993-1548, Fax: 703-993-1359, E-mail: mhock2@gmu.edu.
Website: http://psychology.gmu.edu

The Graduate Center, City University of New York, Graduate Studies, Program in Psychology, New York, NY 10016-4039. Offers basic applied neurocognition (PhD); biopsychology (PhD); clinical psychology (PhD); developmental psychology (PhD); environmental psychology (PhD); experimental psychology (PhD); industrial psychology (PhD); learning processes (PhD); neuropsychology (PhD); psychology (PhD); social personality (PhD). *Faculty:* 119 full-time (40 women). *Students:* 428 full-time (308 women); includes 118 minority (31 Black or African American, non-Hispanic/Latino; 31 Asian, non-Hispanic/Latino; 47 Hispanic/Latino; 1 Native Hawaiian or other Pacific Islander, non-Hispanic/Latino; 8 Two or more races, non-Hispanic/Latino), 53 international. Average age 33. 795 applicants, 12% accepted, 56 enrolled. In 2017, 46 doctorates awarded. *Degree requirements:* For doctorate, one foreign language, thesis/dissertation. *Entrance requirements:* For doctorate, GRE General Test. Additional exam requirements/recommendations for international students: Required—TOEFL. *Application deadline:* For fall admission, 12/1 priority date for domestic students. Application fee: $125. Electronic applications accepted. *Financial support:* In 2017–18, 371 students received support, including 340 fellowships, 34 research assistantships, 33 teaching assistantships; career-related internships or fieldwork, Federal Work-Study, institutionally sponsored loans, and tuition waivers (full and partial) also available. Financial award application deadline: 2/1; financial award applicants required to submit FAFSA. *Unit head:* Richard Bodnar, Executive Officer, 212-817-8706, Fax: 212-817-1533, E-mail: rbodnar@gc.cuny.edu. *Application contact:* Les Gribben, Director of Admissions, 212-817-7470, Fax: 212-817-1624, E-mail: lgribben@gc.cuny.edu.

Grand Canyon University, College of Doctoral Studies, Phoenix, AZ 85017-1097. Offers data analytics (DBA); general psychology (PhD), including cognition and instruction, industrial and organizational psychology, integrating technology, learning, and psychology, performance psychology; management (DBA); marketing (DBA); organizational leadership (Ed D), including behavioral health, Christian ministry, health care administration, organizational development. *Degree requirements:* For doctorate, comprehensive exam, thesis/dissertation. *Entrance requirements:* For doctorate, minimum GPA of 3.4 on earned advanced degree from regionally-accredited institution; transcripts; goals statement.

Industrial and Organizational Psychology

Hofstra University, College of Liberal Arts and Sciences, Programs in Psychology, Hempstead, NY 11549. Offers applied organizational psychology (PhD); clinical psychology (PhD); industrial/organizational psychology (MA); school-community psychology (Psy D). *Accreditation:* APA. *Program availability:* Part-time, evening/weekend. *Students:* 199 full-time (130 women), 24 part-time (20 women); includes 44 minority (5 Black or African American, non-Hispanic/Latino; 12 Asian, non-Hispanic/Latino; 25 Hispanic/Latino; 1 Native Hawaiian or other Pacific Islander, non-Hispanic/Latino; 1 Two or more races, non-Hispanic/Latino), 19 international. Average age 27. 314 applicants, 45% accepted, 60 enrolled. In 2017, 47 master's, 25 doctorates awarded. *Degree requirements:* For master's, comprehensive exam, thesis optional, internship, minimum GPA of 3.0; for doctorate, comprehensive exam, thesis/dissertation, 1st year qualifying examination, 2nd year research project, successful practicum/externship placements, written presentation and successful oral defense of dissertation, completion of full-time internship. *Entrance requirements:* For master's, GRE General Test, minimum GPA of 3.0, essay, interview; for doctorate, GRE General Test, GRE Subject Test (psychology), 3 letters of recommendation, interview, essay, curriculum vitae. Additional exam requirements/recommendations for international students: Required—TOEFL (minimum score 550 paper-based; 80 iBT). *Application deadline:* For fall admission, 12/31 for domestic and international students. Application fee: $75. Electronic applications accepted. *Expenses: Tuition:* Full-time $1292. *Required fees:* $970. Tuition and fees vary according to program. *Financial support:* In 2017–18, 131 students received support, including 126 fellowships with full and partial tuition reimbursements available (averaging $7,840 per year), 4 research assistantships with full and partial tuition reimbursements available (averaging $5,974 per year); career-related internships or fieldwork, Federal Work-Study, institutionally sponsored loans, scholarships/grants, traineeships, tuition waivers (full and partial), and unspecified assistantships also available. Support available to part-time students. Financial award applicants required to submit FAFSA. *Faculty research:* Coping with job stress; schizophrenia; positive clinical psychology; treatments (including virtual reality based) for phobias, trauma, and PTSD; scientific reasoning in children and adults. *Unit head:* Dr. Craig Johnson, Chairperson, 516-463-5636, E-mail: craig.a.johnson@hofstra.edu. *Application contact:* Sunil Samuel, Assistant Vice President of Admissions, 516-463-4723, Fax: 516-463-4664, E-mail: graduateadmission@hofstra.edu.
Website: http://www.hofstra.edu/hclas

Illinois Institute of Technology, Graduate College, Lewis College of Human Sciences, Department of Psychology, Chicago, IL 60616. Offers clinical psychology (PhD); industrial and organizational psychology (PhD); personnel and human resource development (MS); rehabilitation and mental health counseling (MS); rehabilitation counseling education (PhD). *Accreditation:* APA (one or more programs are accredited); CORE. *Program availability:* Part-time, evening/weekend. Terminal master's awarded for partial completion of doctoral program. *Degree requirements:* For master's, thesis (for some programs); for doctorate, comprehensive exam, thesis/dissertation, minimum of 107 credit hours, 1-year full-time internship. *Entrance requirements:* For master's, GRE General Test (minimum score 298 Quantitative and Verbal, 3.0 Analytical Writing), minimum GPA of 3.0; 3 letters of recommendation; bachelor's degree from accredited institution (for personnel and human resource development); for doctorate, GRE General Test (minimum score 298 Quantitative and Verbal, 3.0 Analytical Writing), bachelor's or master's degree from accredited institution, recommendations. Additional exam requirements/recommendations for international students: Required—TOEFL (minimum score 550 paper-based; 80 iBT). Electronic applications accepted. *Faculty research:* Clinical psychology, rehabilitation and mental health counseling, industrial organizational psychology.

Illinois State University, Graduate School, College of Arts and Sciences, Department of Psychology, Normal, IL 61790. Offers psychology (MA, MS), including clinical-counseling psychology, cognitive and behavioral sciences, developmental psychology, industrial/organizational-social psychology; school psychology (PhD, SSP). *Accreditation:* APA. *Degree requirements:* For master's, thesis or alternative; for doctorate, variable foreign language requirement, thesis/dissertation, 2 terms of residency, internship, practicum. *Entrance requirements:* For master's, GRE General Test, GRE Subject Test, minimum GPA of 3.0 in last 60 hours of course work; for doctorate, GRE General Test. *Faculty research:* Comprehensive evaluation system for the central region professional development grant, Illinois school psychology internship consortium, for children's sake.

Indiana University–Purdue University Indianapolis, School of Science, Department of Psychology, Indianapolis, IN 46202-3275. Offers addiction neuroscience (PhD); applied social and organizational psychology (PhD); clinical psychology (PhD); industrial/organizational psychology (MS). *Accreditation:* APA (one or more programs are accredited). Terminal master's awarded for partial completion of doctoral program. *Degree requirements:* For master's, thesis; for doctorate, thesis/dissertation. *Entrance requirements:* For master's, GRE General Test, minimum undergraduate GPA of 3.0; for doctorate, GRE General Test, GRE Subject Test (clinical psychology), minimum undergraduate GPA of 3.2. Additional exam requirements/recommendations for international students: Required—TOEFL (minimum score 567 paper-based; 86 iBT), IELTS (minimum score 6.5). Electronic applications accepted. *Faculty research:* Severe mental illness, health psychology, neurological research, alcoholism and psychopathology, functional activities within organizations.

Inter American University of Puerto Rico, Metropolitan Campus, Graduate Programs, Program in Psychology, San Juan, PR 00919-1293. Offers counseling psychology (MA, PhD); industrial/organizational psychology (MA, PhD); labor relations (MA); school psychology (MA, PhD). *Degree requirements:* For master's, comprehensive exam. *Entrance requirements:* For master's, GRE or EXADEP, interview. Electronic applications accepted.

Iona College, School of Arts and Science, Department of Psychology, New Rochelle, NY 10801-1890. Offers general-experimental psychology (MA); human resources (Certificate); industrial-organizational psychology (MA); mental health counseling (MA); organizational behavior (Certificate); psychology (MA); school psychology (MA). *Program availability:* Part-time. *Faculty:* 9 full-time (5 women), 7 part-time/adjunct (5 women). *Students:* 75 full-time (55 women), 37 part-time (24 women); includes 46 minority (9 Black or African American, non-Hispanic/Latino; 2 Asian, non-Hispanic/Latino; 34 Hispanic/Latino; 1 Two or more races, non-Hispanic/Latino), 1 international. Average age 25. 88 applicants, 88% accepted, 40 enrolled. In 2017, 23 master's awarded. *Degree requirements:* For master's, thesis (for some programs), literature review (for some programs). *Entrance requirements:* For master's, BA in psychology including 3 credits each in psychology statistics and experimental research methods, or 9 credits in psychology including 3 credits each in psychology statistics, psychology research methods and upper-level coursework. Additional exam requirements/recommendations for international students: Required—TOEFL (minimum score 550 paper-based), IELTS (minimum score 6.5). *Application deadline:* For fall admission, 8/15 for domestic students, 5/1 for international students; for spring admission, 1/15 for domestic students, 9/1 for international students. Applications are processed on a rolling basis. Electronic applications accepted. Tuition and fees vary according to program. *Financial support:* In 2017–18, 27 students received support. Research assistantships with partial tuition reimbursements available, tuition waivers (partial), and unspecified assistantships available. Support available to part-time students. Financial award application deadline: 4/15; financial award applicants required to submit FAFSA. *Faculty research:* Non-suicidal self-injury, trauma response, performance appraisal and evaluation, diversity infusion, assessment and treatment of sexual offenders. *Unit head:* Patricia Oswald, PhD, Chair, 914-633-2374, E-mail: poswald@iona.edu. *Application contact:* Katelyn Brunck, Assistant Director, Graduate Admissions, 914-633-2451, Fax: 914-633-2277, E-mail: kbrunck@iona.edu.
Website: http://www.iona.edu/Academics/School-of-Arts-Science/Departments/Psychology/Graduate-Programs.aspx

John F. Kennedy University, Graduate School of Professional Psychology, Program in Organizational Psychology, Pleasant Hill, CA 94523-4817. Offers MA, Certificate. *Program availability:* Part-time, evening/weekend. *Degree requirements:* For master's, thesis or alternative. *Entrance requirements:* For master's, interview. Additional exam requirements/recommendations for international students: Required—TOEFL.

Kean University, College of Liberal Arts, Program in Psychology, Union, NJ 07083. Offers human behavior and organizational psychology (MA); psychological services (MA). *Program availability:* Part-time. *Faculty:* 18 full-time (14 women). *Students:* 65 full-time (46 women), 49 part-time (34 women); includes 74 minority (26 Black or African American, non-Hispanic/Latino; 13 Asian, non-Hispanic/Latino; 31 Hispanic/Latino; 1 Native Hawaiian or other Pacific Islander, non-Hispanic/Latino; 3 Two or more races, non-Hispanic/Latino), 2 international. Average age 28. 82 applicants, 89% accepted, 48 enrolled. In 2017, 25 master's awarded. *Degree requirements:* For master's, comprehensive exam, research component, two semesters of advanced seminar. *Entrance requirements:* For master's, GRE General Test, minimum GPA of 3.0; official transcripts from all institutions attended; two letters of recommendation; professional resume/curriculum vitae; 12 credits in behavioral sciences on the undergraduate level. Additional exam requirements/recommendations for international students: Required—TOEFL (minimum score 550 paper-based; 79 iBT), IELTS (minimum score 6.5). *Application deadline:* For fall admission, 6/30 for domestic and international students; for spring admission, 12/1 for domestic and international students. Applications are processed on a rolling basis. Application fee: $75. Electronic applications accepted. *Expenses:* Tuition, state resident: full-time $13,419; part-time $653 per credit. Tuition, nonresident: full-time $18,188; part-time $801 per credit. *Required fees:* $3382; $154 per credit. Tuition and fees vary according to course level, course load, degree level and program. *Financial support:* Scholarships/grants and unspecified assistantships available. Financial award applicants required to submit FAFSA. *Unit head:* Dr. Zandra Gratz, Program Coordinator, 908-737-5881, E-mail: zgratz@kean.edu. *Application contact:* Amy Clark, Program Assistant, 908-737-7100, E-mail: gradadmissions@kean.edu.
Website: http://grad.kean.edu/masters-programs/psychological-services

Keiser University, MS in Organizational Psychology Program, Fort Lauderdale, FL 33309. Offers MS.
Website: http://www.keiseruniversity.edu/graduateschool/organizational-psychology.php

Keiser University, PhD in Industrial and Organizational Psychology Program, Fort Lauderdale, FL 33309. Offers PhD. *Unit head:* Craig D. Marker, Chair.
Website: http://www.keiseruniversity.edu/graduateschool/industrial-organizational-psychology.php

Lamar University, College of Graduate Studies, College of Arts and Sciences, Department of Psychology, Beaumont, TX 77701. Offers clinical psychology (MS); industrial/organizational psychology (MS). *Program availability:* Part-time. *Faculty:* 9 full-time (5 women), 4 part-time/adjunct (1 woman). *Students:* 9 full-time (7 women), 6 part-time (4 women); includes 7 minority (2 Black or African American, non-Hispanic/Latino; 4 Hispanic/Latino; 1 Two or more races, non-Hispanic/Latino), 1 international. Average age 28. 24 applicants, 75% accepted, 7 enrolled. In 2017, 5 master's awarded. *Degree requirements:* For master's, thesis, practicum. *Entrance requirements:* For master's, GRE General Test, minimum GPA of 2.75 in last 60 hours of undergraduate course work. Additional exam requirements/recommendations for international students: Required—TOEFL (minimum score 550 paper-based; 79 iBT), IELTS (minimum score 6.5). *Application deadline:* For fall admission, 8/10 for domestic students, 7/1 for international students; for spring admission, 1/5 for domestic students, 12/1 for international students. Application fee: $25 ($50 for international students). *Expenses:* Contact institution. *Financial support:* In 2017–18, 12 students received support, including 3 teaching assistantships (averaging $4,500 per year); fellowships, research assistantships, career-related internships or fieldwork, Federal Work-Study, scholarships/grants, and tuition waivers (partial) also available. Support available to part-time students. Financial award application deadline: 4/1. *Faculty research:* Group think, health psychology, school psychology, behavioral neuroscience. *Unit head:* Dr. Edythe E. Kirk, Chair, 409-880-8285, Fax: 409-880-1710. *Application contact:* Deidre Mayer, Interim Director, Admissions and Academic Services, 409-880-8888, Fax: 409-880-7419, E-mail: gradmissions@lamar.edu.
Website: http://artssciences.lamar.edu/psychology

La Salle University, School of Arts and Sciences, Program in Counseling and Family Therapy, Philadelphia, PA 19141-1199. Offers industrial/organizational psychology (MA); marriage and family therapy (MA); professional clinical counseling (MA). *Accreditation:* ACA; APA. *Program availability:* Part-time, evening/weekend. *Faculty:* 7 full-time (2 women), 18 part-time/adjunct (10 women). *Students:* 47 full-time (38 women), 159 part-time (123 women); includes 63 minority (29 Black or African American, non-Hispanic/Latino; 4 Asian, non-Hispanic/Latino; 26 Hispanic/Latino; 4 Two or more races, non-Hispanic/Latino), 5 international. Average age 30. 125 applicants, 78% accepted, 42 enrolled. In 2017, 73 master's awarded. *Degree requirements:* For master's, comprehensive exam. *Entrance requirements:* For master's, GRE or MAT (waived for applicants that already possess a master's degree in any field or for applicants that have a cumulative GPA of 3.5 or higher), minimum of 15 hours in psychology, counseling, or marriage and family studies; minimum GPA of 3.0; three letters of recommendation; personal statement; work experience (paid or volunteer). Additional exam requirements/recommendations for international students: Required—TOEFL. *Application deadline:* For fall admission, 8/15 priority date for domestic students, 7/15 for international students; for spring admission, 12/15 priority date for domestic students, 11/15 for international students; for summer admission, 4/15 priority date for domestic students, 3/15 for international students. Applications are processed on a rolling basis. Application fee: $35. Electronic applications accepted. Application fee is waived when completed online. *Expenses:* Contact institution. *Financial support:* In 2017–18, 34 students received support. Scholarships/grants and unspecified assistantships available. Support available to part-time students. Financial award application deadline: 8/31; financial award applicants required to submit FAFSA. *Faculty research:* Cognitive therapy, attribution theory, work habits, single parent families, treatment of addictions. *Unit head:* Dr. Donna A. Tonrey, Director, 215-951-1767, Fax: 215-951-1843, E-mail: psyma@lasalle.edu. *Application contact:* Elizabeth Heenan, Director, Graduate and Adult Enrollment, 215-951-1100, Fax: 215-951-1462, E-mail: heenan@lasalle.edu.
Website: http://www.lasalle.edu/counseling-family-therapy/

Liberty University, School of Behavioral Sciences, Lynchburg, VA 24515. Offers applied psychology (MA), including developmental psychology (MA, MS), industrial/organizational psychology (MA, MS); clinical mental health counseling (MA); community care and counseling (Ed D), including marriage and family counseling, pastoral care and counseling, traumatology; counselor education and supervision (PhD); human services counseling (MA), including addictions and recovery, business, child and family law, Christian ministries, criminal justice, crisis response and trauma, executive leadership, health and wellness, life coaching, marriage and family, military resilience; marriage and family counseling (MA); marriage and family therapy (MA); military resilience (Certificate); pastoral counseling (MA), including addictions and recovery, community chaplaincy, crisis response and trauma, discipleship and church ministry, leadership, life coaching, marriage and family, marriage and family studies, military resilience, parenting and child/adolescent, pastoral counseling, theology; professional counseling (MA); psychology (MS), including developmental psychology (MA, MS), industrial/organizational psychology (MA, MS); school counseling (M Ed). *Program availability:* Part-time, online learning. *Students:* 2,649 full-time (2,085 women), 5,086 part-time (4,015 women); includes 2,275 minority (1,784 Black or African American, non-Hispanic/Latino; 44 American Indian or Alaska Native, non-Hispanic/Latino; 67 Asian, non-Hispanic/Latino; 200 Hispanic/Latino; 11 Native Hawaiian or other Pacific Islander, non-Hispanic/Latino; 169 Two or more races, non-Hispanic/Latino), 145 international. Average age 39. 5,839 applicants, 51% accepted, 1710 enrolled. In 2017, 1,626 master's, 7 doctorates, 61 other advanced degrees awarded. *Application deadline:* Applications are processed on a rolling basis. Application fee: $50. Electronic applications accepted. *Financial support:* Applicants required to submit FAFSA. *Unit head:* Dr. Ronald Hawkins, Founding Dean, School of Behavioral Sciences. *Application contact:* Jay Bridge, Director of Admissions, 800-424-9595, Fax: 800-628-7977, E-mail: gradadmissions@liberty.edu.

London Metropolitan University, Graduate Programs, London, United Kingdom. Offers applied psychology (M Sc); architecture (MA); biomedical science (M Sc); blood science (M Sc); cancer pharmacology (M Sc); computer networking and cyber security (M Sc); computing and information systems (M Sc); conference interpreting (MA); counter-terrorism studies (M Sc); creative, digital and professional writing (MA); crime, violence and prevention (M Sc); criminology (M Sc); curating contemporary art (MA); data analytics (M Sc); digital media (MA); early childhood studies (MA); education (MA, Ed D); financial services law, regulation and compliance (LL M); food science (M Sc); forensic psychology (M Sc); health and social care management and policy (M Sc); human nutrition (M Sc); human resource management (MA); human rights and international conflict (MA); information technology (M Sc); intelligence and security studies (M Sc); international oil, gas and energy law (LL M); international relations (MA); interpreting (MA); learning and teaching in higher education (MA); legal practice (LL M); media and entertainment law (LL M); organizational and consumer psychology (M Sc); psychological therapy (M Sc); psychology of mental health (M Sc); public health (M Sc); public policy and management (MPA); security studies (M Sc); social work (M Sc); spatial planning and urban design (MA); sports therapy (M Sc); supporting older children and young people with dyslexia (MA); teaching languages (MA), including Arabic, English; translation (MA); woman and child abuse (MA).

Louisiana Tech University, Graduate School, College of Education, Ruston, LA 71272. Offers counseling and guidance (MA), including clinical mental health counseling, human services, orientation and mobility; counseling psychology (PhD); curriculum and instruction (M Ed); cyber education (Graduate Certificate); dynamics of domestic and family violence (Graduate Certificate); early childhood education - PreK-3 (MAT); educational leadership (M Ed, Ed D); elementary education and special education mild/moderate grades 1-5 (MAT); higher education administration (Graduate Certificate); industrial/organizational psychology (MA, PhD); kinesiology (MS); middle school education (MAT), including mathematics; orientation and mobility (Graduate Certificate); rehabilitation teaching for the blind (Graduate Certificate); secondary education (MAT), including agriculture, biology, business, chemistry, English; special education: visually impaired (MAT); teacher leader education (Graduate Certificate); visual impairments - blind education (Graduate Certificate). *Accreditation:* NCATE. *Program availability:* Part-time. *Faculty:* 28 full-time (16 women), 23 part-time/adjunct (22 women). *Students:* 269 full-time (192 women), 194 part-time (150 women); includes 127 minority (94 Black or African American, non-Hispanic/Latino; 2 American Indian or Alaska Native, non-Hispanic/Latino; 6 Asian, non-Hispanic/Latino; 16 Hispanic/Latino; 1 Native Hawaiian or other Pacific Islander, non-Hispanic/Latino; 8 Two or more races, non-Hispanic/Latino), 8 international. Average age 34. 226 applicants, 74% accepted, 60 enrolled. In 2017, 5 master's, 2 doctorates, 1 other advanced degree awarded. *Degree requirements:* For master's, thesis; for doctorate, thesis/dissertation. *Entrance requirements:* For master's and doctorate, GRE General Test. Additional exam requirements/recommendations for international students: Required—TOEFL (minimum score 550 paper-based; 80 iBT), IELTS (minimum score 6.5). *Application deadline:* For fall admission, 9/1 priority date for domestic students, 6/1 for international students; for winter admission, 11/1 priority date for domestic students, 9/1 for international students; for spring admission, 2/1 priority date for domestic students, 12/1 for international students; for summer admission, 5/1 priority date for domestic students, 3/1 for international students. Application fee: $40. Electronic applications accepted. *Expenses:* Tuition, state resident: full-time $5146. Tuition, nonresident: full-time $10,147. *International tuition:* $10,267 full-time. *Required fees:* $2273. *Financial support:* In 2017–18, 40 students received support, including 23 research assistantships (averaging $10,346 per year), 15 teaching assistantships (averaging $6,887 per year); fellowships and career-related internships or fieldwork also available. Financial award application deadline: 2/1. *Faculty research:* Blindness and the best methods for increasing independence for individuals who are blind or visually impaired; educating and investigating factors contributing to improvements in human performance across the lifespan and a reduction in injury rates during training. *Total annual research expenditures:* $2.1 million. *Unit head:* Dr. Don Schillinger, Dean, 318-257-3712, E-mail: dschill@latech.edu. *Application contact:* Dr. Dawn Basinger, Associate Dean of Academic Affairs, 318-257-2977, Fax: 318-257-2379, E-mail: dbasing@latech.edu.
Website: http://education.latech.edu/

Lynn University, College of Arts and Sciences, Boca Raton, FL 33431-5598. Offers criminal justice (MS); mental health counseling (MS); psychology (MS), including general psychology, industrial/organizational psychology. *Program availability:* Part-time, evening/weekend, 100% online, blended/hybrid learning. *Faculty:* 59 full-time (26 women), 22 part-time/adjunct (16 women). *Students:* 60 full-time (47 women), 38 part-time (24 women); includes 32 minority (15 Black or African American, non-Hispanic/Latino; 2 Asian, non-Hispanic/Latino; 15 Hispanic/Latino), 6 international. Average age 30. 73 applicants, 82% accepted, 47 enrolled. In 2017, 64 master's awarded. *Degree requirements:* For master's, comprehensive exam (for some programs), thesis (for some programs). *Entrance requirements:* For master's, bachelor's degree from accredited institution, minimum undergraduate GPA of 3.0, official undergraduate transcripts, two letters of recommendation from academic or professional sources, writing sample demonstrating capacity to perform at graduate level. Additional exam requirements/recommendations for international students: Required—TOEFL (minimum score 550 paper-based; 80 iBT), IELTS (minimum score 6.5). *Application deadline:* For fall admission, 8/18 for domestic students, 8/4 for international students; for spring admission, 12/15 for domestic students, 12/1 for international students; for summer admission, 4/17 for domestic students, 4/3 for international students. Applications are processed on a rolling basis. Application fee: $45. Electronic applications accepted. *Expenses:* $740 per credit. *Financial support:* Career-related internships or fieldwork, Federal Work-Study, scholarships/grants, tuition waivers (full and partial), and unspecified assistantships available. Support available to part-time students. Financial award application deadline: 3/1; financial award applicants required to submit FAFSA. *Faculty research:* Personality and social media, learning strategies, personal health behaviors and compliance, using drums in substance abuse groups, interpersonal behaviors with individuals with autism, case conceptualization, teaching case conceptualization across the curriculum. *Unit head:* Dr. Katrina Carter-Tellison, Dean, 561-237-7412, E-mail: kcartertellison@lynn.edu. *Application contact:* Steven Pruitt, Director of Graduate Admission, 561-237-7834, Fax: 561-237-7100, E-mail: admissionpm@lynn.edu.
Website: https://www.lynn.edu/academics/colleges-schools/arts-and-sciences

Meredith College, School of Education, Health and Human Sciences, Master of Arts in Psychology Program, Raleigh, NC 27607-5298. Offers industrial/organizational psychology (MA). *Degree requirements:* For master's, internship. *Entrance requirements:* For master's, GRE, official transcripts, two recommendation forms, resume or curriculum vitae, essay. *Application deadline:* Applications are processed on a rolling basis. Application fee: $60. Tuition and fees vary according to course load and program. *Unit head:* Lori Kelley, Program Manager/Admissions Counselor, 919-760-8723, E-mail: lrkelley@meredith.edu.
Website: https://www.meredith.edu/master-of-psychology

Middle Tennessee State University, College of Graduate Studies, College of Behavioral and Health Sciences, Department of Psychology, Murfreesboro, TN 37132. Offers clinical psychology (MA); experimental psychology (MA); industrial/organizational psychology (MA); psychology (MA, Ed S); quantitative psychology (MA); school psychology (MA). *Program availability:* Part-time, evening/weekend, online learning. *Degree requirements:* For master's, comprehensive exam, thesis. *Entrance requirements:* For master's, GRE. Additional exam requirements/recommendations for international students: Required—TOEFL (minimum score 525 paper-based; 71 iBT) or IELTS (minimum score 6). Electronic applications accepted. *Faculty research:* Health psychology, industrial/organizational psychology, experimental psychology.

Minnesota State University Mankato, College of Graduate Studies and Research, College of Social and Behavioral Sciences, Department of Psychology, Mankato, MN 56001. Offers clinical psychology (MA); industrial/organizational psychology (MA); school psychology (Psy D). *Program availability:* Part-time. *Degree requirements:* For master's, one foreign language, comprehensive exam, thesis (for some programs). *Entrance requirements:* For master's, GRE General Test, GRE Subject Test (clinical psychology), minimum GPA of 3.0 during previous 2 years, 3 letters of reference. Additional exam requirements/recommendations for international students: Required—TOEFL. Electronic applications accepted.

Missouri State University, Graduate College, College of Health and Human Services, Department of Psychology, Springfield, MO 65897. Offers applied behavior analysis (MS); clinical psychology (MS); experimental psychology (MS); forensic child psychology (Certificate); industrial/organizational psychology (MS). *Faculty:* 25 full-time (11 women), 4 part-time/adjunct (0 women). *Students:* 54 full-time (41 women), 12 part-time (9 women); includes 9 minority (2 Black or African American, non-Hispanic/Latino; 2 Hispanic/Latino; 5 Two or more races, non-Hispanic/Latino), 5 international. Average age 23. 127 applicants, 17% accepted, 21 enrolled. In 2017, 41 master's awarded. *Degree requirements:* For master's, comprehensive exam, thesis. *Entrance requirements:* For master's, GRE General Test, GRE Subject Test, minimum GPA of 3.25 in major, 3.0 overall; 20 hours of course work in psychology. Additional exam requirements/recommendations for international students: Required—TOEFL (minimum score 550 paper-based; 79 iBT), IELTS (minimum score 6). *Application deadline:* For fall admission, 2/15 priority date for domestic and international students. Application fee: $35 ($50 for international students). Electronic applications accepted. *Expenses:* Tuition, state resident: full-time $2915; part-time $2021 per credit hour. Tuition, nonresident: full-time $5354; part-time $3647 per credit hour. *International tuition:* $11,992 full-time. *Required fees:* $173; $173 per credit hour. Tuition and fees vary according to class time, course level, course load, degree level, campus/location and program. *Financial support:* In 2017–18, 9 research assistantships with full tuition reimbursements (averaging $8,772 per year), 8 teaching assistantships with full tuition reimbursements (averaging $8,772 per year) were awarded; career-related internships or fieldwork, Federal Work-Study, institutionally sponsored loans, scholarships/grants, and unspecified assistantships also available. Financial award application deadline: 3/31; financial award applicants required to submit FAFSA. *Faculty research:* Work-family conflict, child forensic psychology, sports psychology, body image assessment, visual learning. *Unit head:* Dr. Paul Deal, Department Head, 417-836-5797, Fax: 417-836-8330, E-mail: psychology@missouristate.edu. *Application contact:* Stephanie Praschan, Director, Graduate Enrollment Management, 417-836-5330, Fax: 417-836-6200, E-mail: stephaniepraschan@missouristate.edu.
Website: http://psychology.missouristate.edu/

Missouri University of Science and Technology, Department of Psychological Science, Rolla, MO 65409. Offers industrial-organizational psychology (MS). *Expenses:* Tuition, state resident: full-time $7391; part-time $3696 per year. Tuition, nonresident: full-time $21,712; part-time $10,857 per year. *Required fees:* $728; $564 per unit. Tuition and fees vary according to course load.

Montclair State University, The Graduate School, College of Humanities and Social Sciences, Program in Industrial and Organizational Psychology, Montclair, NJ 07043-1624. Offers MA. *Program availability:* Part-time, evening/weekend. *Degree requirements:* For master's, thesis. *Entrance requirements:* For master's, GRE General Test, 2 letters of recommendation, essay. Additional exam requirements/recommendations for international students: Required—TOEFL (minimum score 83 iBT), IELTS (minimum score 6.5). Electronic applications accepted. *Faculty research:* Study of behavior in the work place; job satisfaction, organizational commitment and how to select individuals for given positions in an organization.

New York University, Graduate School of Arts and Science, Department of Psychology, New York, NY 10012-1019. Offers cognition and perception (PhD); general psychology (MA); industrial/organizational psychology (MA); psychotherapy and psychoanalysis (Advanced Certificate); social psychology (PhD). *Program availability:* Part-time. *Students:* Average age 31. 874 applicants, 46% accepted, 153 enrolled. In 2017, 102 master's, 9 doctorates, 10 other advanced degrees awarded. Terminal master's awarded for partial completion of doctoral program. *Degree requirements:* For master's, comprehensive exam, thesis or alternative; for doctorate, thesis/dissertation. *Entrance requirements:* For master's and doctorate, GRE General Test. Additional exam requirements/recommendations for international students: Required—TOEFL. *Application deadline:* For fall admission, 12/12 for domestic and international students. Application fee: $100. *Expenses: Tuition:* Full-time $41,352; part-time $19,968 per year. *Required fees:* $2496; $1628 per unit. $814 per term. Tuition and fees vary according to course load and program. *Financial support:* Fellowships, research assistantships, teaching assistantships, career-related internships or fieldwork, Federal Work-Study,

institutionally sponsored loans, scholarships/grants, traineeships, health care benefits, and unspecified assistantships available. Financial award application deadline: 12/12; financial award applicants required to submit FAFSA. *Faculty research:* Vision, memory, social cognition, social and cognitive development, relationships. *Unit head:* Gabriele Oettingen, Director of Graduate Studies, PhD Program, 212-998-7900, Fax: 212-995-4018, E-mail: psychq@psych.nyu.edu. *Application contact:* Adrienne Gans, Director of Graduate Studies, MA Program, 212-998-7900, Fax: 212-995-4018, E-mail: psychq@psych.nyu.edu.
Website: http://www.psych.nyu.edu/

North Carolina State University, Graduate School, College of Humanities and Social Sciences, Department of Psychology, Raleigh, NC 27695. Offers developmental psychology (PhD); ergonomics and experimental psychology (PhD); industrial/organizational psychology (PhD); psychology in the public interest (PhD); school psychology (PhD). *Accreditation:* APA. *Degree requirements:* For doctorate, comprehensive exam, thesis/dissertation. *Entrance requirements:* For doctorate, GRE General Test, GRE Subject Test (industrial/organizational psychology), MAT (recommended), minimum GPA of 3.0 in major. Electronic applications accepted. *Faculty research:* Cognitive and social development (human factors, families, the workplace, community issues and health, aging).

Northern Kentucky University, Office of Graduate Programs, College of Arts and Sciences, Program in Industrial-Organizational Psychology, Highland Heights, KY 41099. Offers industrial psychology (Certificate); industrial-organizational psychology (MS); occupational health psychology (Certificate); organizational psychology (Certificate). *Program availability:* Part-time, evening/weekend. *Degree requirements:* For master's, thesis optional, capstone. *Entrance requirements:* For master's, GRE General Test (minimum scores of 141 verbal, 144 quantitative, and 3.5 writing), bachelor's degree with minimum GPA of 3.0, nine semester hours of psychology coursework, at least one undergraduate course in statistics with minimum B grade, official transcripts, current resume or vita, statement of personal interest, three letters of recommendation; for Certificate, official transcripts, bachelor's degree, minimum undergraduate GPA of 3.0, no grade lower than B on all graduate coursework previously taken that may apply. Additional exam requirements/recommendations for international students: Required—TOEFL (minimum score 79 iBT); Recommended—IELTS (minimum score 6.5). Electronic applications accepted. *Faculty research:* Workplace bullying and abuse, assessment and situational judgment tasks, human factors and work design, racial and social stereotyping in employment, social conflict.

Ohio University, Graduate College, College of Arts and Sciences, Department of Psychology, Program in Organizational Psychology, Athens, OH 45701-2979. Offers PhD. *Degree requirements:* For doctorate, one foreign language, comprehensive exam, thesis/dissertation. *Entrance requirements:* For doctorate, GRE General Test, GRE Subject Test. Additional exam requirements/recommendations for international students: Required—TOEFL. *Faculty research:* Performance appraisal, job satisfaction, organizational entry, sexual harassment.

Old Dominion University, College of Sciences, Doctoral Program in Psychology, Norfolk, VA 23529. Offers applied psychological sciences (PhD); human factors psychology (PhD); industrial/organizational psychology (PhD). *Faculty:* 21 full-time (8 women). *Students:* 14 full-time (9 women), 14 part-time (8 women); includes 4 minority (1 Black or African American, non-Hispanic/Latino; 3 Hispanic/Latino). Average age 29. 99 applicants, 11% accepted, 6 enrolled. In 2017, 9 doctorates awarded. *Degree requirements:* For doctorate, comprehensive exam, thesis/dissertation, candidacy exam. *Entrance requirements:* For doctorate, GRE General Test, GRE Subject Test, 3 recommendation letters. Additional exam requirements/recommendations for international students: Required—TOEFL. *Application deadline:* For fall and winter admission, 1/5 for domestic and international students. Application fee: $50. Electronic applications accepted. *Expenses:* Contact institution. *Financial support:* In 2017–18, 26 students received support, including 4 research assistantships with full tuition reimbursements available (averaging $15,000 per year), 22 teaching assistantships with full tuition reimbursements available (averaging $15,000 per year); scholarships/grants also available. Financial award application deadline: 1/15. *Faculty research:* Human factors, industrial psychology, organizational psychology, applied psychological sciences (health, developmental, community, quantitative). *Total annual research expenditures:* $1.2 million. *Unit head:* Dr. Debra A. Major, Graduate Program Director, 757-683-4235, Fax: 757-683-5087, E-mail: dmajor@odu.edu. *Application contact:* William Heffelfinger, Director of Graduate Admissions, 757-683-5554, Fax: 757-683-3255, E-mail: gradadmit@odu.edu.
Website: http://www.odu.edu/psychology/

Philadelphia College of Osteopathic Medicine, Graduate and Professional Programs, Department of Psychology, Philadelphia, PA 19131-1694. Offers applied behavior analysis (Certificate); clinical health psychology (Post-Doctoral Certificate); clinical neuropsychology (Post-Doctoral Certificate); clinical psychology (Psy D); educational psychology (PhD); mental health counseling (MS); organizational development and leadership (MS); psychology (Certificate); public health management and administration (MS); school psychology (MS, Psy D, Ed S). *Accreditation:* APA. *Faculty:* 19 full-time (11 women), 122 part-time/adjunct (58 women). *Students:* 487 (335 women); includes 138 minority (89 Black or African American, non-Hispanic/Latino; 4 American Indian or Alaska Native, non-Hispanic/Latino; 11 Asian, non-Hispanic/Latino; 12 Hispanic/Latino; 22 Two or more races, non-Hispanic/Latino). 298 applicants, 44% accepted, 100 enrolled. In 2017, 50 master's, 43 doctorates, 10 other advanced degrees awarded. Terminal master's awarded for partial completion of doctoral program. *Degree requirements:* For master's, comprehensive exam (for some programs), thesis (for some programs); for doctorate, comprehensive exam, thesis/dissertation. *Entrance requirements:* For master's, GRE or MAT, minimum GPA of 3.0; bachelor's degree from regionally-accredited college or university; for doctorate, PRAXIS II (for Psy D in school psychology), minimum undergraduate GPA of 3.0; for other advanced degree, GRE (for Ed S). Additional exam requirements/recommendations for international students: Required—TOEFL (minimum score 79 iBT). *Application deadline:* Applications are processed on a rolling basis. Application fee: $50. Electronic applications accepted. *Financial support:* In 2017–18, 28 teaching assistantships were awarded; Federal Work-Study, institutionally sponsored loans, and scholarships/grants also available. Financial award application deadline: 3/15; financial award applicants required to submit FAFSA. *Faculty research:* Adult and childhood anxiety and ADHD; coping with chronic illness; primary care psychology/integrated health care; applied behavior analysis; psychological, educational, and neuropsychological assessment. *Total annual research expenditures:* $533,489. *Unit head:* Dr. Robert DiTomasso, Chairman, 215-871-6442, Fax: 215-871-6458, E-mail: robertd@pcom.edu. *Application contact:* Johnathan Cox, Associate Director of Admissions, 215-871-6700, Fax: 215-871-6719, E-mail: johnathancox@pcom.edu.

See Display on page 982 and Close-Up on page 1203.

Pontifical Catholic University of Puerto Rico, College of Graduate Studies in Behavioral Science and Community Affairs, Program in Industrial Psychology (Doctorate), Ponce, PR 00717-0777. Offers PhD. *Program availability:* Part-time, evening/weekend. *Entrance requirements:* For doctorate, EXADEP, minimum GPA of 2.75.

Purdue University, Graduate School, College of Health and Human Sciences, Department of Psychological Sciences, West Lafayette, IN 47907. Offers behavioral neuroscience (PhD); clinical psychology (PhD); cognitive psychology (PhD); industrial/organizational psychology (PhD); mathematical and computational cognitive science (PhD). *Accreditation:* APA. *Faculty:* 46 full-time (18 women), 1 part-time/adjunct (0 women). *Students:* 64 full-time (41 women), 4 part-time (3 women); includes 13 minority (1 Black or African American, non-Hispanic/Latino; 4 Asian, non-Hispanic/Latino; 6 Hispanic/Latino; 2 Two or more races, non-Hispanic/Latino), 12 international. Average age 27. 288 applicants, 8% accepted, 16 enrolled. In 2017, 9 doctorates awarded. Terminal master's awarded for partial completion of doctoral program. *Degree requirements:* For doctorate, thesis/dissertation. *Entrance requirements:* For doctorate, GRE General Test, minimum undergraduate GPA of 3.0 or equivalent. Additional exam requirements/recommendations for international students: Required—TOEFL (minimum score 550 paper-based; 77 iBT); Recommended—TWE. *Application deadline:* For fall admission, 12/3 for domestic and international students. Applications are processed on a rolling basis. Application fee: $60 ($75 for international students). Electronic applications accepted. *Financial support:* Fellowships with partial tuition reimbursements, research assistantships with partial tuition reimbursements, teaching assistantships with partial tuition reimbursements, and career-related internships or fieldwork available. Support available to part-time students. Financial award applicants required to submit FAFSA. *Faculty research:* Career development of women in science, development of friendships during childhood and adolescence, social competence, human information processing. *Unit head:* Dr. David Rollock, Head, 765-494-6061, E-mail: rollock@purdue.edu. *Application contact:* Nancy A. O'Brien, Graduate Contact, 765-494-6067, E-mail: nobrien@psych.pardue.edu.
Website: http://www.psych.purdue.edu/

Radford University, College of Graduate Studies and Research, Program in Psychology, Radford, VA 24142. Offers clinical-counseling psychology (MA, MS); experimental psychology (MA); industrial-organizational psychology (MA, MS). *Program availability:* Part-time. *Faculty:* 21 full-time (14 women). *Students:* 39 full-time (30 women); includes 5 minority (2 Black or African American, non-Hispanic/Latino; 1 Asian, non-Hispanic/Latino; 2 Hispanic/Latino). Average age 23. 87 applicants, 51% accepted, 22 enrolled. In 2017, 28 master's awarded. *Degree requirements:* For master's, comprehensive exam, thesis (for some programs). *Entrance requirements:* For master's, GRE, minimum GPA of 3.0, 3 letters of reference, essay, resume, official transcripts. Additional exam requirements/recommendations for international students: Required—TOEFL (minimum score 550 paper-based; 79 iBT), IELTS (minimum score 6.5). *Application deadline:* For fall admission, 2/15 priority date for domestic students, 12/1 for international students; for spring admission, 7/1 for international students. Applications are processed on a rolling basis. Application fee: $50. Electronic applications accepted. *Expenses:* Tuition, state resident: full-time $8336; part-time $347 per credit hour. Tuition, nonresident: full-time $16,862; part-time $702 per credit hour. *Required fees:* $3220; $135 per credit hour. Tuition and fees vary according to course load and program. *Financial support:* In 2017–18, 19 students received support, including 2 research assistantships (averaging $7,500 per year), 14 teaching assistantships (averaging $10,500 per year); career-related internships or fieldwork, scholarships/grants, and unspecified assistantships also available. Support available to part-time students. Financial award application deadline: 3/1; financial award applicants required to submit FAFSA. *Faculty research:* Social cognition and interpersonal relationships, relationship between one's self-concept and social interactions, creativity and innovation, organizational politics and ethical decision-making, victimization in childhood. *Unit head:* Dr. Jeffery Aspelmeier, Chair, 540-831-5361, Fax: 540-831-6113, E-mail: jaspelme@radford.edu.
Website: http://www.radford.edu/content/chbs/home/psychology.html

Rice University, Graduate Programs, School of Social Sciences, Department of Psychology, Houston, TX 77251-1892. Offers cognitive sciences (MA, PhD); industrial-organizational/social psychology (MA, PhD); psychology (MA, PhD). Terminal master's awarded for partial completion of doctoral program. *Degree requirements:* For master's, thesis; for doctorate, thesis/dissertation. *Entrance requirements:* For doctorate, GRE General Test, minimum GPA of 3.0. Additional exam requirements/recommendations for international students: Required—TOEFL. Electronic applications accepted. *Faculty research:* Cognitive, cognitive neuropsychology, human factors, human-computer interaction, industrial-organizational psychology.

Roosevelt University, Graduate Division, College of Arts and Sciences, Department of Psychology, Program in Industrial/Organizational Psychology, Chicago, IL 60605. Offers MA, PhD. *Students:* 67 full-time (41 women), 41 part-time (27 women); includes 38 minority (6 Black or African American, non-Hispanic/Latino; 14 Asian, non-Hispanic/Latino; 12 Hispanic/Latino; 6 Two or more races, non-Hispanic/Latino), 3 international. Average age 27. 90 applicants, 88% accepted, 30 enrolled. In 2017, 26 master's, 1 doctorate awarded. Application fee: $40. Electronic applications accepted. *Financial support:* Scholarships/grants and unspecified assistantships available. *Application contact:* Sivling Lam, Graduate Admission Counselor, 312-281-3252, E-mail: slam02@roosevelt.edu.

Sacred Heart University, Graduate Programs, College of Arts and Sciences, Department of Psychology, Fairfield, CT 06825. Offers applied psychology (MS), including community psychology, general applied psychology, industrial-organizational psychology. *Program availability:* Part-time, evening/weekend, online learning. *Faculty:* 9 full-time (7 women). *Students:* 17 full-time (15 women), 76 part-time (58 women); includes 18 minority (6 Black or African American, non-Hispanic/Latino; 1 Asian, non-Hispanic/Latino; 8 Hispanic/Latino; 3 Two or more races, non-Hispanic/Latino), 2 international. Average age 31. 50 applicants, 54% accepted, 16 enrolled. In 2017, 42 master's awarded. *Degree requirements:* For master's, comprehensive exam, thesis optional. *Entrance requirements:* For master's, minimum overall GPA of 3.0, bachelor's degree from accredited college or university. Additional exam requirements/recommendations for international students: Required—TOEFL (minimum score 570 paper-based, 80 iBT), TWE, or IELTS (6.5). *Application deadline:* Applications are processed on a rolling basis. Application fee: $75. Electronic applications accepted. *Expenses:* Contact institution. *Financial support:* Unspecified assistantships available. Financial award applicants required to submit FAFSA. *Unit head:* Rachel Bowman, Interim Chair/Associate Professor, 203-396-8243, E-mail: bowmanr@sacredheart.edu. *Application contact:* Pam Pillo, Executive Director of Graduate Admissions, 203-365-7916, Fax: 203-365-4732, E-mail: gradstudies@sacredheart.edu.
Website: http://www.sacredheart.edu/academics/collegeofartssciences/academicdepartments/psychology/mastersinappliedpsychology/

St. Cloud State University, School of Graduate Studies, College of Liberal Arts, Program in Industrial-Organizational Psychology, St. Cloud, MN 56301-4498. Offers MS. *Degree requirements:* For master's, thesis or portfolio. *Entrance requirements:* For master's, GRE General Test, minimum GPA of 2.75. Additional exam requirements/recommendations for international students: Required—TOEFL (minimum score 550 paper-based) or IELTS (minimum score 6.5). Electronic applications accepted.

Saint Louis University, Graduate Programs, College of Arts and Sciences and Graduate Programs, Department of Psychology, St. Louis, MO 63103. Offers clinical psychology (MS-R, PhD); experimental psychology (MS-R, PhD); industrial-organizational psychology (PhD); psychology (PhD). *Accreditation:* APA (one or more programs are accredited). *Program availability:* Part-time. *Degree requirements:* For master's, comprehensive exam, thesis; for doctorate, thesis/dissertation, clinical internship (for clinical psychology PhD). *Entrance requirements:* For master's, GRE General Test, interview, letters of recommendation, resume; for doctorate, GRE General Test, interview, letters of recommendation, resumé, transcripts, goal statement. Additional exam requirements/recommendations for international students: Required—TOEFL (minimum score 550 paper-based). Electronic applications accepted. *Faculty research:* Violence and trauma; neural basis of learning and memory function; eating disorders; body image and health behavior; prejudice, stereotyping, and victimization; memory, cognitive aging and language processing.

Saint Mary's University, Faculty of Science, Department of Psychology, Halifax, NS B3H 3C3, Canada. Offers applied psychology (M Sc, PhD), including industrial/organizational psychology (M Sc). *Program availability:* Part-time. *Degree requirements:* For master's, thesis, 500-hour internship; for doctorate, comprehensive exam, thesis/dissertation, research project. *Entrance requirements:* For master's and doctorate, GRE General Test. *Faculty research:* Assessment, health psychology, social psychology, cognition.

St. Mary's University, Graduate Studies, Program in Industrial/Organizational Psychology, San Antonio, TX 78228. Offers MA, MS. *Program availability:* Part-time, evening/weekend. *Students:* 22 full-time (15 women), 5 part-time (3 women); includes 16 minority (1 Black or African American, non-Hispanic/Latino; 3 Asian, non-Hispanic/Latino; 12 Hispanic/Latino). Average age 27. 60 applicants, 28% accepted, 12 enrolled. In 2017, 8 master's awarded. *Degree requirements:* For master's, comprehensive exam, thesis optional. *Entrance requirements:* For master's, GRE (minimum combined score on verbal and quantitative sections of 294; no less than 146 on the verbal section or 140 on the quantitative section), bachelor's degree from accredited institution; satisfactory completion of the following prerequisite courses or their equivalent (12 credit hours): general psychology, introductory statistics, research methods or experimental psychology, or upper-level psychology course. Additional exam requirements/ recommendations for international students: Required—TOEFL (minimum score 550 paper-based; 80 iBT), IELTS (minimum score 6). *Application deadline:* For fall admission, 3/1 priority date for domestic students. Application fee: $0. Electronic applications accepted. *Expenses: Tuition:* Full-time $16,200; part-time $900 per credit hour. *Required fees:* $810; $405 per semester. *Financial support:* Fellowships, research assistantships, career-related internships or fieldwork, Federal Work-Study, institutionally sponsored loans, scholarships/grants, health care benefits, and unspecified assistantships available. Financial award application deadline: 3/31; financial award applicants required to submit FAFSA. *Faculty research:* Social undermining in the workplace, majority and minority influence, multivariate statistics, development, social influence. *Unit head:* Dr. Gregory Pool, Graduate Program Director, 210-431-2020, E-mail: gpool@stmarytx.edu. *Application contact:* Kim Thornton, Director of Graduate Admission, 210-436-3101, E-mail: kthornton@stmarytx.edu.
Website: https://www.stmarytx.edu/academics/programs/master-industrial-organizational-psychology/

San Diego State University, Graduate and Research Affairs, College of Sciences, Department of Psychology, San Diego, CA 92182. Offers clinical psychology (MS, PhD); industrial and organizational psychology (MS); program evaluation (MS); psychology (MA). PhD offered jointly with University of California, San Diego. *Accreditation:* APA (one or more programs are accredited). Terminal master's awarded for partial completion of doctoral program. *Degree requirements:* For master's, thesis, oral exam; for doctorate, thesis/dissertation. *Entrance requirements:* For master's, GRE General Test, GRE Subject Test, 3 letters of recommendation; for doctorate, GRE General Test, GRE Subject Test, minimum GPA of 3.0, 3 letters of recommendation. Additional exam requirements/recommendations for international students: Required—TOEFL. Electronic applications accepted.

San Francisco State University, Division of Graduate Studies, College of Science and Engineering, Department of Psychology, San Francisco, CA 94132-1722. Offers clinical psychology (MS); developmental psychology (MA); industrial/organizational psychology (MS); mind, brain, and behavior (MA); school psychology (MS, Credential); social psychology (MA). *Financial support:* Teaching assistantships available. Financial award application deadline: 3/1. *Unit head:* Dr. Dawn Terrell, Chair, 415-338-7555, Fax: 415-338-2398, E-mail: schen9@sfsu.edu. *Application contact:* Dr. Diane Harris, Graduate Program Coordinator, 415-338-7064, Fax: 415-338-2398, E-mail: dharris@sfsu.edu.
Website: http://psychology.sfsu.edu/graduate/application.html

San Jose State University, Graduate Studies and Research, College of Social Sciences, San Jose, CA 95192-0107. Offers applied anthropology (MA); communication studies (MA); economics (MA), including applied economics, economics; environmental studies (MS); geography (MA); history (MA), including history, history education; Mexican American studies (MA); psychology (MA, MS), including clinical psychology (MS), industrial/organizational psychology (MS), research and experimental psychology (MA); public administration (MPA); social sciences (MS); sociology (MA). *Faculty:* 59 full-time (29 women), 18 part-time/adjunct (5 women). *Students:* 181 full-time (126 women), 221 part-time (127 women); includes 228 minority (15 Black or African American, non-Hispanic/Latino; 48 Asian, non-Hispanic/Latino; 112 Hispanic/Latino; 3 Native Hawaiian or other Pacific Islander, non-Hispanic/Latino; 50 Two or more races, non-Hispanic/Latino), 38 international. Average age 30. 532 applicants, 44% accepted, 156 enrolled. In 2017, 139 master's awarded. *Degree requirements:* For master's, one foreign language, comprehensive exam, thesis (for some programs), project, field work, professional work experience. *Entrance requirements:* Additional exam requirements/ recommendations for international students: Required—TOEFL (minimum score 550 paper-based; 80 iBT), IELTS (minimum score 6.5), PTE (minimum score 53). *Application deadline:* For fall admission, 2/1 for domestic and international students. Applications are processed on a rolling basis. Application fee: $55. Electronic applications accepted. *Expenses:* Tuition, state resident: full-time $7176. Tuition, nonresident: full-time $16,680. Tuition and fees vary according to course load and program. *Financial support:* Fellowships, research assistantships, career-related internships or fieldwork, Federal Work-Study, scholarships/grants, tuition waivers (full and partial), and unspecified assistantships available. Support available to part-time students. Financial award application deadline: 4/28; financial award applicants required to submit FAFSA. *Unit head:* Dr. Walt Jacobs, Dean, 408-924-5300, Fax: 408-924-5303, E-mail: walter.jacobs@sjsu.edu.
Website: http://www.sjsu.edu/socialsciences/

Seattle Pacific University, Industrial-Organizational Psychology Program, Seattle, WA 98119-1997. Offers MA, PhD. *Students:* 51 full-time (41 women), 33 part-time (23 women); includes 9 minority (2 Black or African American, non-Hispanic/Latino; 1 American Indian or Alaska Native, non-Hispanic/Latino; 5 Asian, non-Hispanic/Latino; 1 Two or more races, non-Hispanic/Latino), 2 international. Average age 28. 67 applicants, 72% accepted, 31 enrolled. In 2017, 33 master's, 8 doctorates awarded. *Degree requirements:* For master's, research project; for doctorate, thesis/dissertation, field placement. *Entrance requirements:* For master's, GRE (administered within five

years of application to program, with minimum combined score of 950/295 new scoring on verbal and quantitative sections preferred), personal statement; recommendations; language competency; statement of financial support; for doctorate, GRE (administered within five years of application to program, with minimum combined score of 1100/300 new scoring on verbal and quantitative sections preferred), personal statement; recommendations; language competency; statement of financial support. Additional exam requirements/recommendations for international students: Required—TOEFL (minimum score 550 paper-based). *Application deadline:* For fall admission, 12/15 for domestic and international students. Application fee: $50. Electronic applications accepted. *Financial support:* Applicants required to submit FAFSA. *Unit head:* Dr. Robert B. McKenna, Chair, 206-281-2629, E-mail: rmckenna@spu.edu. *Application contact:* The Graduate Center, 206-281-2091.
Website: http://spu.edu/academics/school-of-psychology-family-community/graduate-programs/industrial-organizational-psychology

South Dakota State University, Graduate School, College of Arts and Science, Department of Psychology, Brookings, SD 57007. Offers industrial/organizational psychology (MS). *Degree requirements:* For master's, thesis, internship.

Southeastern Louisiana University, College of Arts, Humanities and Social Sciences, Department of Psychology, Hammond, LA 70402. Offers industrial/organizational psychology (MA). *Program availability:* Part-time. *Faculty:* 7 full-time (5 women). *Students:* 23 full-time (14 women), 15 part-time (11 women); includes 8 minority (1 Black or African American, non-Hispanic/Latino; 1 Asian, non-Hispanic/Latino; 3 Hispanic/ Latino; 3 Two or more races, non-Hispanic/Latino). Average age 26. 38 applicants, 61% accepted, 12 enrolled. In 2017, 10 master's awarded. *Degree requirements:* For master's, comprehensive exam, thesis, 38 hours of psychology course work including core courses in statistics, social psychology, cognition, and physiological psychology. *Entrance requirements:* For master's, GRE (minimum combined score of 294 on Verbal and Quantitative sections). Additional exam requirements/recommendations for international students: Required—TOEFL (minimum score 500 paper-based; 61 iBT). *Application deadline:* For fall admission, 7/15 priority date for domestic students, 6/1 priority date for international students; for spring admission, 12/1 priority date for domestic students, 10/1 priority date for international students. Applications are processed on a rolling basis. Application fee: $20 ($30 for international students). Electronic applications accepted. *Expenses:* Tuition, state resident: full-time $6684. Tuition, nonresident: full-time $19,162. *Required fees:* $2088. *Financial support:* In 2017–18, 17 students received support, including 15 research assistantships (averaging $8,624 per year); career-related internships or fieldwork, Federal Work-Study, institutionally sponsored loans, scholarships/grants, and traineeships also available. Support available to part-time students. Financial award application deadline: 5/1; financial award applicants required to submit FAFSA. *Faculty research:* Eating disorders, evolutionary psychology, violence exposure effects on children, parental behavior, neurobiology of mental disorders and addiction. *Unit head:* Dr. Susan Coats, Department Head, 985-549-2154, Fax: 985-549-6892, E-mail: scoats@southeastern.edu. *Application contact:* Amanda Harper, Graduate Admissions Analyst, 985-549-5620, Fax: 985-549-5632, E-mail: admissions@southeastern.edu.
Website: http://www.southeastern.edu/acad_research/depts/psyc/index.html

Southern Illinois University Edwardsville, Graduate School, School of Education, Health, and Human Behavior, Department of Psychology, Program in Industrial-Organizational Psychology, Edwardsville, IL 62026. Offers MA. *Program availability:* Part-time. *Degree requirements:* For master's, thesis. *Entrance requirements:* For master's, GRE. Additional exam requirements/recommendations for international students: Required—TOEFL (minimum score 550 paper-based, 79 iBT), IELTS (minimum score 6.5), Michigan Test of English Language Proficiency or PTE. Electronic applications accepted.

Springfield College, Graduate Programs, Programs in Psychology, Springfield, MA 01109-3797. Offers athletic counseling (MS, CAGS); clinical mental health counseling (M Ed, CAGS); counseling psychology (Psy D); general counseling (M Ed); industrial/ organizational psychology (M Ed, CAGS); school counseling (M Ed, CAGS); student personnel administration in higher education (M Ed, CAGS). *Accreditation:* APA. *Program availability:* Part-time. *Students:* 192 applicants, 65% accepted, 64 enrolled. In 2017, 56 master's, 5 doctorates awarded. *Degree requirements:* For master's, research project, portfolio; for doctorate, dissertation project, 1500 hours of counseling psychology practicum, full-year internship. *Entrance requirements:* For doctorate, GRE. Additional exam requirements/recommendations for international students: Required— TOEFL (minimum score 550 paper-based); Recommended—IELTS (minimum score 7). *Application deadline:* For fall admission, 1/15 priority date for domestic students, 1/15 for international students; for winter admission, 11/1 for domestic and international students; for spring admission, 11/1 for domestic and international students. Applications are processed on a rolling basis. Application fee: $50. Electronic applications accepted. *Financial support:* Fellowships with partial tuition reimbursements, teaching assistantships with partial tuition reimbursements, career-related internships or fieldwork, Federal Work-Study, institutionally sponsored loans, scholarships/grants, and unspecified assistantships available. Financial award application deadline: 3/1; financial award applicants required to submit FAFSA. *Unit head:* Dr. Allison Cumming-McCann, Chair, 413-748-3025, Fax: 413-748-3854, E-mail: acumming@springfield.edu. *Application contact:* Anne Griffin, Director of Graduate Admissions, 413-748-3225, E-mail: agriffin2@springfield.edu.
Website: http://springfield.edu/programs

Teachers College, Columbia University, Department of Organization and Leadership, New York, NY 10027-6696. Offers adult education guided intensive study (Ed D); adult learning and leadership (Ed M, MA, Ed D); educational leadership (Ed D); higher and postsecondary education (MA, Ed D); leadership, policy and politics (Ed D); nurse executive (MA, Ed D), including administration studies (MA); professorial studies (MA); private school leadership (Ed M, MA); public school building leadership (Ed M, MA); social and organizational psychology (MA); urban education leaders (Ed D); MA/MBA. *Program availability:* Part-time, evening/weekend. *Students:* 342 full-time (244 women), 378 part-time (256 women); includes 288 minority (106 Black or African American, non-Hispanic/Latino; 69 Asian, non-Hispanic/Latino; 92 Hispanic/Latino; 21 Two or more races, non-Hispanic/Latino), 86 international. Average age 33. 1,063 applicants, 59% accepted, 405 enrolled. *Degree requirements:* For doctorate, thesis/dissertation. *Unit head:* Prof. Bill Baldwin, Chair, E-mail: wjb12@tc.columbia.edu. *Application contact:* David Estrella, Director of Admission, 212-678-3305, E-mail: estrella@tc.columbia.edu.

Texas A&M University, College of Liberal Arts, Department of Psychology, College Station, TX 77843. Offers clinical psychology (PhD); industrial/organizational psychology (PhD); psychology (MS, PhD), including clinical psychology (PhD). *Accreditation:* APA (one or more programs are accredited). *Faculty:* 50. *Students:* 84 full-time (42 women), 15 part-time (9 women); includes 41 minority (8 Black or African American, non-Hispanic/ Latino; 7 Asian, non-Hispanic/Latino; 23 Hispanic/Latino; 3 Two or more races, non-Hispanic/Latino), 12 international. Average age 28. 292 applicants, 12% accepted, 22 enrolled. In 2017, 10 master's, 18 doctorates awarded. *Degree requirements:* For doctorate, comprehensive exam (for some programs), thesis/dissertation. *Entrance requirements:* For doctorate, GRE General Test. Additional exam requirements/ recommendations for international students: Required—TOEFL (minimum score 550

paper-based; 80 iBT), IELTS (minimum score 6), PTE (minimum score 53). *Application deadline:* For fall admission, 12/1 for domestic and international students. Application fee: $50 ($90 for international students). Electronic applications accepted. *Expenses:* Contact institution. *Financial support:* In 2017–18, 83 students received support, including 19 fellowships with tuition reimbursements available (averaging $37,600 per year), 30 research assistantships with tuition reimbursements available (averaging $11,994 per year), 58 teaching assistantships with tuition reimbursements available (averaging $11,425 per year); career-related internships or fieldwork, institutionally sponsored loans, scholarships/grants, traineeships, health care benefits, tuition waivers (full and partial), and unspecified assistantships also available. Support available to part-time students. Financial award application deadline: 3/15; financial award applicants required to submit FAFSA. *Unit head:* Dr. Heather Lench, Department Head, 979-845-0377, E-mail: hlench@tamu.edu. *Application contact:* Dr. Charles D. Samuelson, Director of Graduate Studies, 979-845-0880, Fax: 979-845-4727, E-mail: c-samuelson@tamu.edu.
Website: http://psychology.tamu.edu/

Thomas Edison State University, Heavin School of Arts and Sciences, Program in Liberal Studies, Trenton, NJ 08608. Offers digital humanities (MALS, Graduate Certificate); geropsychology (MALS, Graduate Certificate); industrial-organizational psychology (MALS, Graduate Certificate); learner-designed area of study (MALS); professional communications (MALS, Graduate Certificate). *Program availability:* Part-time, online learning. *Degree requirements:* For master's, final project. *Entrance requirements:* For master's, bachelor's degree from a regionally-accredited college or university; minimum 2 letters of recommendation; 3-5 years of related working experience; current resume. Additional exam requirements/recommendations for international students: Required—TOEFL (minimum score 550 paper-based; 79 iBT). Electronic applications accepted.

Touro College, School of Health Sciences, Bay Shore, NY 11706. Offers industrial-organizational psychology (MS); mental health counseling (MS); occupational therapy (MS); physical therapy (DPT); physician assistant (MS); speech-language pathology (MS). *Faculty:* 81 full-time (55 women), 77 part-time/adjunct (46 women). *Students:* 628 full-time (470 women), 113 part-time (73 women); includes 143 minority (31 Black or African American, non-Hispanic/Latino; 1 American Indian or Alaska Native, non-Hispanic/Latino; 61 Asian, non-Hispanic/Latino; 42 Hispanic/Latino; 1 Native Hawaiian or other Pacific Islander, non-Hispanic/Latino; 7 Two or more races, non-Hispanic/Latino), 63 international. Average age 28. *Expenses:* Contact institution. *Financial support:* Fellowships available. *Unit head:* Dr. Louis Primavera, Dean, School of Health Sciences, 516-673-3200, E-mail: louis.primavera@touro.edu. *Application contact:* Brian J. Diele, Director of Student Administrative Services, 631-665-1600 Ext. 6311, E-mail: brian.diele@touro.edu.

University at Albany, State University of New York, College of Arts and Sciences, Department of Psychology, Albany, NY 12222-0001. Offers behavioral neuroscience (PhD); clinical psychology (PhD); cognitive psychology (PhD); industrial/organizational psychology (MA, PhD); social-personality psychology (PhD). *Accreditation:* APA (one or more programs are accredited). *Faculty:* 31 full-time (13 women). *Students:* 63 full-time (42 women), 49 part-time (33 women); includes 25 minority (4 Black or African American, non-Hispanic/Latino; 8 Asian, non-Hispanic/Latino; 4 Hispanic/Latino; 9 Two or more races, non-Hispanic/Latino), 11 international. 295 applicants, 14% accepted, 28 enrolled. In 2017, 13 master's, 5 doctorates awarded. *Degree requirements:* For doctorate, thesis/dissertation. *Entrance requirements:* For doctorate, GRE General Test, GRE Subject Test. Additional exam requirements/recommendations for international students: Required—TOEFL (minimum score 550 paper-based). *Application deadline:* For fall admission, 1/15 for domestic and international students. Application fee: $75. Electronic applications accepted. *Expenses:* Tuition, state resident: full-time $10,870; part-time $453 per credit hour. Tuition, nonresident: full-time $22,210; part-time $925 per credit hour. *Required fees:* $84.68 per credit hour. $508.06 per semester. Part-time tuition and fees vary according to course load and program. *Financial support:* Fellowships, research assistantships, teaching assistantships, and career-related internships or fieldwork available. Financial award application deadline: 2/1. *Unit head:* Christine K. Wagner, Chair, 518-442-4820, Fax: 518-442-4867, E-mail: cwagner@albany.edu. *Application contact:* Michael DeRensis, Director, Graduate Admissions, 518-442-3980, Fax: 518-442-3922, E-mail: graduate@albany.edu.
Website: http://www.albany.edu/psychology/

The University of Akron, Graduate School, Buchtel College of Arts and Sciences, Department of Psychology, Program in Industrial/Organizational Psychology, Akron, OH 44325. Offers MA, PhD. *Students:* 22 full-time (14 women), 14 part-time (8 women); includes 8 minority (1 Black or African American, non-Hispanic/Latino; 5 Asian, non-Hispanic/Latino; 2 Hispanic/Latino), 4 international. Average age 26. 60 applicants, 17% accepted, 4 enrolled. In 2017, 3 master's, 3 doctorates awarded. Terminal master's awarded for partial completion of doctoral program. *Degree requirements:* For master's, thesis or specialty exam; for doctorate, one foreign language, comprehensive exam, thesis/dissertation. *Entrance requirements:* For master's, GRE General Test, minimum GPA of 2.75, three letters of recommendation, personal statement, curriculum vitae; for doctorate, GRE General Test, minimum graduate GPA of 3.25, three letters of recommendation, personal statement, curriculum vitae. Additional exam requirements/recommendations for international students: Required—TOEFL (minimum score 79 iBT), IELTS (minimum score 6.5). *Application deadline:* For fall admission, 1/15 for domestic and international students. Application fee: $45 ($70 for international students). Electronic applications accepted. *Faculty research:* Personnel selection, performance management, leadership, self-regulation, affect. *Unit head:* Dr. Paul Levy, Department Chair, 330-972-8369, E-mail: pelevy@uakron.edu.
Website: http://www.uakron.edu/psychology/academics/industrial-organizational-psychology/

The University of Alabama in Huntsville, School of Graduate Studies, College of Arts, Humanities, and Social Sciences, Department of Psychology, Huntsville, AL 35899. Offers industrial/organizational psychology (MA); psychology (MA). *Program availability:* Part-time, evening/weekend. *Degree requirements:* For master's, comprehensive exam, thesis or alternative, oral and written exams. *Entrance requirements:* For master's, GRE General Test, 15 hours of course work in psychology, minimum GPA of 3.25, sample of written work. Additional exam requirements/recommendations for international students: Required—TOEFL (minimum score 500 paper-based; 80 iBT), IELTS (minimum score 6.5). Electronic applications accepted. *Faculty research:* Virtual teams and teamwork, eyewitness identification, aging and memory, psychology of natural disasters and emergency preparedness, pain and pain management research.

University of Central Florida, College of Sciences, Department of Psychology, Program in Industrial/Organizational Psychology, Orlando, FL 32816. Offers MS, PhD. *Students:* 47 full-time (31 women), 3 part-time (1 woman); includes 14 minority (5 Black or African American, non-Hispanic/Latino; 4 Asian, non-Hispanic/Latino; 5 Hispanic/Latino), 4 international. Average age 25. 129 applicants, 32% accepted, 14 enrolled. In 2017, 16 master's awarded. *Degree requirements:* For master's, comprehensive exam, thesis, practicum; for doctorate, thesis/dissertation, candidacy examination. *Entrance requirements:* For master's, GRE General Test, bachelor's degree with major in psychology or allied area, or baccalaureate degree with completion of undergraduate courses in statistics and research methods, and preference of four additional upper-division psychology courses (12 credit hours); resume; goal statement; letters of recommendation; for doctorate, GRE General Test, bachelor's or master's degree in psychology or another allied area, resume, personal statement, letters of recommendation. Additional exam requirements/recommendations for international students: Required—TOEFL. *Application deadline:* For fall admission, 12/15 for domestic students. Application fee: $30. Electronic applications accepted. *Expenses:* Tuition, state resident: part-time $288.16 per credit hour. Tuition, nonresident: part-time $1073.31 per credit hour. Tuition and fees vary according to program. *Financial support:* In 2017–18, 29 students received support, including 8 fellowships (averaging $12,742 per year), 10 research assistantships with partial tuition reimbursements available (averaging $7,241 per year), 18 teaching assistantships with partial tuition reimbursements available (averaging $14,341 per year); career-related internships or fieldwork, Federal Work-Study, institutionally sponsored loans, health care benefits, tuition waivers (partial), and unspecified assistantships also available. Financial award application deadline: 3/1; financial award applicants required to submit FAFSA. *Unit head:* Dr. Barbara Fritzsche, Program Director, 407-823-0674, E-mail: barbara.fritzsche@ucf.edu. *Application contact:* Associate Director, Graduate Admissions, 407-823-2766, Fax: 407-823-6442, E-mail: gradadmissions@ucf.edu.
Website: http://psychology.cos.ucf.edu/graduate/

University of Connecticut, Graduate School, College of Liberal Arts and Sciences, Department of Psychology, Storrs, CT 06269. Offers behavioral neuroscience (PhD); biopsychology (PhD); clinical psychology (MA, PhD); cognition and instruction (PhD); developmental psychology (MA, PhD); ecological psychology (PhD); experimental psychology (PhD); general psychology (MA, PhD); industrial/organizational psychology (PhD); language and cognition (PhD); neuroscience (PhD); social psychology (MA, PhD). *Accreditation:* APA. Terminal master's awarded for partial completion of doctoral program. *Degree requirements:* For master's, comprehensive exam; for doctorate, thesis/dissertation. *Entrance requirements:* For master's and doctorate, GRE General Test, GRE Subject Test. Additional exam requirements/recommendations for international students: Required—TOEFL (minimum score 550 paper-based). Electronic applications accepted.

University of Detroit Mercy, College of Liberal Arts and Education, Detroit, MI 48221. Offers addiction counseling (MA); addiction studies (Certificate); clinical mental health counseling (MA); clinical psychology (MA, PhD); computer and information systems (MS); criminal justice (MA); curriculum and instruction (MA); economics (MA); educational administration (MA); financial economics (MA); industrial/organizational psychology (MA); information assurance (MS); intelligence analysis (MA); liberal studies (MALS); religious studies (MA); school counseling (MA, Certificate); school psychology (Spec); security administration (MS); special education: emotionally impaired/behaviorally disordered (MA); special education: learning disabilities (MA). *Program availability:* Part-time, evening/weekend. *Degree requirements:* For doctorate, departmental qualifying exam. *Faculty research:* Psychology of aging, history of technology, Renaissance humanism, U.S. and Japanese economic relations.

University of Guelph, Graduate Studies, College of Social and Applied Human Sciences, Department of Psychology, Guelph, ON N1G 2W1, Canada. Offers applied social psychology (MA, PhD); clinical psychology: applied development emphasis (PhD); clinical psychology: applied developmental emphasis (MA); industrial/organizational psychology (MA, PhD); neuroscience and applied cognitive science (MA, PhD). *Degree requirements:* For master's, thesis; for doctorate, comprehensive exam, thesis/dissertation. *Entrance requirements:* For master's, GRE General Test, GRE Subject Test, minimum B+ average during previous 2 years of course work; for doctorate, GRE General Test, GRE Subject Test, minimum A- average. Additional exam requirements/recommendations for international students: Required—TOEFL (minimum score 89 iBT). Electronic applications accepted. *Faculty research:* Organizational psychology, reading comprehension and mathematical ability, drug addiction and relapse, gender issues and culture, memory, clinical psychology.

University of Houston, College of Liberal Arts and Social Sciences, Department of Psychology, Houston, TX 77204. Offers clinical psychology (PhD); developmental psychology (PhD); industrial/organizational psychology (PhD); psychology (MA); social psychology (PhD). *Accreditation:* APA (one or more programs are accredited). *Degree requirements:* For master's, comprehensive exam, thesis; for doctorate, comprehensive exam, thesis/dissertation. *Entrance requirements:* For master's, GRE General Test, career statement, 3 letters of recommendation; for doctorate, GRE General Test, 3 letters of recommendation. Additional exam requirements/recommendations for international students: Required—TOEFL (minimum score 550 paper-based; 79 iBT). Electronic applications accepted. *Faculty research:* Health psychology, depression, child/family process, organizational effectiveness, close relationships.

The University of Manchester, Alliance Manchester Business School, M15 6PB, United Kingdom. Offers accounting and finance (M Sc); business (M Ent); business analysis and strategic management (M Sc); business analytics: operational research and risk analysis (M Sc); business psychology (M Sc); corporate communications and reputation management (M Sc); finance (M Sc); finance and business economics (M Sc); human resource management and industrial relations (M Sc); innovation management and entrepreneurship (M Sc); international business and management (M Sc); international human resource management and comparative industrial relations (M Sc); management (M Sc); marketing (M Sc); operations, project and supply chain management (M Sc); organizational psychology (M Sc); quantitative finance (M Sc). *Entrance requirements:* For master's, UK 2:1 honours degree or overseas equivalent. Additional exam requirements/recommendations for international students: Required—TOEFL (minimum score 100 iBT), IELTS (minimum score 7), PTE. Electronic applications accepted. *Faculty research:* Accounting and finance, management sciences and marketing, people management and organization, innovation management and policy, decision sciences.

University of Maryland, Baltimore County, The Graduate School, College of Arts, Humanities and Social Sciences, Department of Psychology, Program in Industrial/Organizational Psychology, Rockville, MD 20850. Offers MPS. *Program availability:* Part-time, evening/weekend. *Faculty:* 2 full-time (1 woman), 13 part-time/adjunct (4 women). *Students:* 14 full-time (11 women), 92 part-time (66 women); includes 49 minority (22 Black or African American, non-Hispanic/Latino; 8 Asian, non-Hispanic/Latino; 12 Hispanic/Latino; 7 Two or more races, non-Hispanic/Latino), 4 international. Average age 28. 135 applicants, 70% accepted, 54 enrolled. In 2017, 33 master's awarded. *Entrance requirements:* Additional exam requirements/recommendations for international students: Required—TOEFL (minimum score 99 iBT), IELTS (minimum score 7). *Application deadline:* For fall admission, 4/1 for domestic students, 1/1 for international students. Applications are processed on a rolling basis. Application fee: $50. Electronic applications accepted. *Expenses:* Contact institution. *Financial support:* In 2017–18, 1 teaching assistantship with full tuition reimbursement (averaging $14,000 per year) was awarded; unspecified assistantships also available. *Faculty research:* Organizations, human factors, group dynamics, change management. *Unit head:* Dr. Elliot Lasson, Program Director, 301-738-6171, E-mail: elasson@umbc.edu. *Application contact:* Rickeysha Jones, Program Coordinator, 301-738-6285, E-mail: rcjones@umbc.edu.
Website: http://www.umbc.edu/shadygrove/io/

University of Maryland, College Park, Academic Affairs, College of Behavioral and Social Sciences, Department of Psychology, College Park, MD 20742. Offers clinical psychology (PhD); developmental psychology (PhD); experimental psychology (PhD); industrial psychology (MA, MS, PhD); social psychology (PhD). *Accreditation:* APA (one or more programs are accredited). *Degree requirements:* For master's, thesis; for doctorate, variable foreign language requirement, comprehensive exam, thesis/dissertation. *Entrance requirements:* For master's and doctorate, GRE General Test, GRE Subject Test, minimum GPA of 3.5, research and/or work experience, 3 letters of recommendation. Electronic applications accepted. *Faculty research:* Social stereotyping and prejudice, anxiety disorders, auditory neuroethology, counseling and social psychology.

University of Minnesota, Twin Cities Campus, Graduate School, College of Liberal Arts, Department of Psychology, Program in Industrial/Organizational Psychology, Minneapolis, MN 55455-0213. Offers PhD. *Degree requirements:* For doctorate, comprehensive exam, thesis/dissertation. *Entrance requirements:* For doctorate, GRE General Test, GRE Subject Test (recommended), 12 credits of upper-level psychology courses, including a course in statistics or psychological measurement. Additional exam requirements/recommendations for international students: Required—TOEFL (minimum score 550 paper-based; 79 iBT).

University of Nebraska at Omaha, Graduate Studies, College of Arts and Sciences, Department of Psychology, Omaha, NE 68182. Offers applied behavior analysis (Certificate); human resources and training (Certificate); industrial/organizational psychology (MS); psychology (MA, PhD); school psychology (MS, Ed S). *Program availability:* Part-time. *Degree requirements:* For master's, comprehensive exam, thesis (for some programs); for doctorate, comprehensive exam, thesis/dissertation. *Entrance requirements:* For master's and doctorate, GRE, minimum GPA of 3.0, official transcripts, 3 letters of recommendation, statement of purpose, writing sample, resume. Additional exam requirements/recommendations for international students: Required—TOEFL, IELTS, PTE. Electronic applications accepted.

★ **University of New Haven,** Graduate School, College of Arts and Sciences, Program in Industrial and Organizational Psychology, West Haven, CT 06516. Offers conflict management (MA); industrial organizational psychology (MA); industrial-human resources psychology (MA); organizational development and consultation (MA); psychology of conflict management (Graduate Certificate). *Program availability:* Part-time, evening/weekend. *Students:* 80 full-time (53 women), 10 part-time (6 women); includes 17 minority (8 Black or African American, non-Hispanic/Latino; 4 Asian, non-Hispanic/Latino; 5 Hispanic/Latino), 3 international. Average age 26. 116 applicants, 89% accepted, 47 enrolled. In 2017, 45 master's awarded. *Degree requirements:* For master's, thesis or alternative, internship or practicum. *Entrance requirements:* Additional exam requirements/recommendations for international students: Required—TOEFL (minimum score 80 iBT), IELTS, PTE. *Application deadline:* Applications are processed on a rolling basis. Application fee: $50. Electronic applications accepted. Application fee is waived when completed online. *Expenses:* Contact institution. *Financial support:* Research assistantships with partial tuition reimbursements, teaching assistantships with partial tuition reimbursements, career-related internships or fieldwork, Federal Work-Study, scholarships/grants, and unspecified assistantships available. Support available to part-time students. Financial award applicants required to submit FAFSA. *Unit head:* Dr. Eric Marcus, Coordinator, 203-932-1242, E-mail: emarcus@newhaven.edu. *Application contact:* Michelle Mason, Director of Graduate Enrollment, 203-932-7067.
Website: http://www.newhaven.edu/4730/

See Display below and Close-Up on page 1207.

The University of North Carolina at Charlotte, College of Liberal Arts and Sciences, Department of Psychology, Charlotte, NC 28223-0001. Offers cognitive science (Graduate Certificate); health psychology (PhD); industrial/organizational psychology (MA); psychology (MA). *Accreditation:* APA. *Program availability:* Part-time. *Faculty:* 29 full-time (19 women), 2 part-time/adjunct (both women). *Students:* 42 full-time (38 women), 32 part-time (21 women); includes 22 minority (11 Black or African American, non-Hispanic/Latino; 8 Hispanic/Latino; 3 Two or more races, non-Hispanic/Latino), 1 international. Average age 28. 196 applicants, 12% accepted, 16 enrolled. In 2017, 13 master's, 9 doctorates, 1 other advanced degree awarded. *Degree requirements:* For master's, thesis (for some programs); for doctorate, comprehensive exam, thesis/dissertation, internship (clinical health students only). *Entrance requirements:* For master's, GRE, GMAT, MAT; for doctorate, GRE, at least 18 hours of coursework in psychology including introductory psychology and research methods, undergraduate course in statistics, transcripts of all academic work attempted since high school including evidence of the completion of a bachelor's degree, at least three references, personal statement, resume or curriculum vitae; for Graduate Certificate, enrolled and in good standing in a graduate degree program at UNC Charlotte, or have minimum GPA of 3.0 for undergraduate courses. Additional exam requirements/recommendations for international students: Required—TOEFL (minimum score 523 paper-based, 70 iBT) or IELTS (6.5). *Application deadline:* For fall admission, 11/15 for domestic and international students. Applications are processed on a rolling basis. Application fee: $75. Electronic applications accepted. *Expenses:* Contact institution. *Financial support:* In 2017–18, 32 students received support, including 1 fellowship (averaging $47,476 per year), 13 research assistantships (averaging $14,282 per year), 18 teaching assistantships (averaging $14,405 per year); career-related internships or fieldwork, Federal Work-Study, institutionally sponsored loans, scholarships/grants, and unspecified assistantships also available. Support available to part-time students. Financial award application deadline: 3/1; financial award applicants required to submit FAFSA. *Total annual research expenditures:* $440,921. *Unit head:* Dr. Eric Heggestad, Interim Chair, 704-687-1315. *Application contact:* Kathy B. Giddings, Director of Graduate Admissions, 704-687-5503, Fax: 704-687-1668, E-mail: gradadm@uncc.edu. Website: http://psych.uncc.edu

University of Oklahoma, College of Arts and Sciences, Department of Psychology, Program in Psychology, Norman, OK 73019. Offers psychology (MS, PhD), including general (MS), industrial-organizational psychology, standard (PhD). *Students:* 72 full-time (38 women), 15 part-time (10 women); includes 19 minority (2 American Indian or Alaska Native, non-Hispanic/Latino; 5 Asian, non-Hispanic/Latino; 8 Hispanic/Latino; 4 Two or more races, non-Hispanic/Latino), 6 international. Average age 27. 94 applicants, 11% accepted, 10 enrolled. In 2017, 7 master's, 7 doctorates awarded. Terminal master's awarded for partial completion of doctoral program. *Degree requirements:* For master's, comprehensive exam, thesis; for doctorate, comprehensive exam, thesis/dissertation. *Entrance requirements:* For master's and doctorate, GRE. Additional exam requirements/recommendations for international students: Required—TOEFL (minimum score 79 iBT) or IELTS (minimum score 6.5). *Application deadline:* For fall admission, 1/1 for domestic and international students. Application fee: $50 ($100 for international students). Electronic applications accepted. *Expenses:* Tuition, state resident: full-time $5119; part-time $213.30 per credit hour. Tuition, nonresident: full-time $19,778; part-time $824.10 per credit hour. *Required fees:* $3458; $133.55 per credit hour. $126.50 per semester. *Financial support:* In 2017–18, 57 students received support. Fellowships with full tuition reimbursements available, research assistantships with full tuition reimbursements available, and teaching assistantships with full tuition reimbursements available available. Financial award application deadline: 6/1; financial award applicants required to submit FAFSA. *Faculty research:* Behavioral statistics; social and cognitive development; ethics in organizations; creativity in the workplace;

training, complex skill acquisition and adaptable performance. *Unit head:* Dr. Eric Day, Chair, 405-325-4511, Fax: 405-325-4737, E-mail: eday@ou.edu. *Application contact:* Dr. Shane Connelly, Professor/Chair, 405-325-4580, Fax: 405-325-4737, E-mail: sconnelly@ou.edu.
Website: http://www.ou.edu/psychology

University of Phoenix–Online Campus, College of Social Science, Phoenix, AZ 85034-7209. Offers mediation (Certificate); psychology (MS), including behavioral health, industrial-organizational, psychology. *Program availability:* Evening/weekend, online learning. *Entrance requirements:* Additional exam requirements/recommendations for international students: Required—TOEFL, TOEIC (Test of English as an International Communication), Berlitz Online English Proficiency Exam, PTE, or IELTS. Electronic applications accepted. *Expenses:* Contact institution.

University of Phoenix–Online Campus, School of Advanced Studies, Phoenix, AZ 85034-7209. Offers business administration (DBA); education (Ed S); educational leadership (Ed D), including curriculum and instruction, education technology, educational leadership; health administration (DHA); higher education administration (PhD); industrial/organizational psychology (PhD); nursing (PhD); organizational leadership (DM), including information systems and technology, organizational leadership. *Program availability:* Evening/weekend, online learning. *Degree requirements:* For doctorate, thesis/dissertation. *Entrance requirements:* Additional exam requirements/recommendations for international students: Required—TOEFL, TOEIC (Test of English as an International Communication), Berlitz Online English Proficiency Exam, PTE, or IELTS. Electronic applications accepted. *Expenses:* Contact institution.

University of Puerto Rico–Río Piedras, College of Social Sciences, Department of Psychology, San Juan, PR 00931-3300. Offers clinical psychology (MA); industrial organizational psychology (MA); investigative academic psychology (MA); psychology (PhD); social-community psychology (MA). *Program availability:* Part-time. *Degree requirements:* For master's, comprehensive exam, thesis; for doctorate, comprehensive exam, thesis/dissertation, internship. *Entrance requirements:* For master's, GRE or PAEG, interview, minimum GPA of 3.0; for doctorate, GRE or PAEG, interview, master's degree, minimum GPA of 3.0. *Faculty research:* Intervention on depressed Latino youth, biosychosocial training.

University of South Africa, College of Economic and Management Sciences, Pretoria, South Africa. Offers accounting (D Admin, D Com); accounting science (DA); auditing (D Admin, D Com); business administration (M Tech); business economics (D Admin); business leadership (DBL); business management (D Admin, D Com); economic management analysis (M Tech); economics (D Admin, D Com, PhD); human resource development (M Tech); industrial psychology (D Admin, D Com, PhD); logistics (D Com); marketing (M Tech); public administration (D Admin, D Com, DPA, PhD); public management (M Tech); quantitative management (D Admin, D Com); real estate (M Tech); statistics (D Admin, PhD); tourism management (D Admin, D Com); transport economics (D Admin, D Com).

University of South Africa, College of Human Sciences, Pretoria, South Africa. Offers adult education (M Ed); African languages (MA, PhD); African politics (MA, PhD); Afrikaans (MA, PhD); ancient history (MA, PhD); ancient Near Eastern studies (MA, PhD); anthropology (MA, PhD); applied linguistics (MA); Arabic (MA, PhD); archaeology (MA); art history (MA); Biblical archaeology (MA); Biblical studies (M Th, D Th, PhD); Christian spirituality (M Th, D Th); church history (M Th, D Th); classical studies (MA, PhD); clinical psychology (MA); communication (MA, PhD); comparative education (M Ed, Ed D); consulting psychology (D Admin, D Com, PhD); curriculum studies (M Ed, Ed D); development studies (M Admin, MA, D Admin, PhD); didactics (M Ed, Ed D); education (M Tech); education management (M Ed, Ed D); educational psychology (M Ed); English (MA); environmental education (M Ed); French (MA, PhD); German (MA, PhD); Greek (MA); guidance and counseling (M Ed); health studies (MA, PhD), including health sciences education (MA), health services management (MA), medical and surgical nursing science (critical care general) (MA), midwifery and neonatal nursing science (MA), trauma and emergency care (MA); history (MA, PhD); history of education (Ed D); inclusive education (M Ed, Ed D); information and communications technology policy and regulation (MA); information science (MA, MIS, PhD); international politics (MA, PhD); Islamic studies (MA, PhD); Italian (MA, PhD); Judaica (MA, PhD); linguistics (MA, PhD); mathematical education (M Ed); mathematics education (MA); missiology (M Th, D Th); modern Hebrew (MA, PhD); musicology (MA, MMus, D Mus, PhD); natural science education (M Ed); New Testament (M Th, D Th); Old Testament (D Th); pastoral therapy (M Th, D Th); philosophy (MA); philosophy of education (M Ed, Ed D); politics (MA, PhD); Portuguese (MA, PhD); practical theology (M Th, D Th); psychology (MA, MS, PhD); psychology of education (M Ed, Ed D); public health (MA); religious studies (MA, D Th, PhD); Romance languages (MA); Russian (MA, PhD); Semitic languages (MA, PhD); social behavior studies in HIV/AIDS (MA); social science (mental health) (MA); social science in development studies (MA); social science in psychology (MA); social science in social work (MA); social science in sociology (MA); social work (MSW, DSW, PhD); socio-education (M Ed, Ed D); sociolinguistics (MA); sociology (MA, PhD); Spanish (MA, PhD); systematic theology (M Th, D Th); TESOL (teaching English to speakers of other languages) (MA); theological ethics (M Th, D Th); theory of literature (MA, PhD); urban ministries (D Th); urban ministry (M Th).

University of South Florida, College of Arts and Sciences, Department of Psychology, Tampa, FL 33620-9951. Offers psychology (PhD), including clinical psychology, cognition, neuroscience and social psychology, industrial-organizational psychology. *Accreditation:* APA. *Faculty:* 30 full-time (11 women). *Students:* 79 full-time (53 women), 11 part-time (8 women); includes 12 minority (1 Black or African American, non-Hispanic/Latino; 5 Asian, non-Hispanic/Latino; 4 Hispanic/Latino; 2 Two or more races, non-Hispanic/Latino), 7 international. Average age 28. 393 applicants, 3% accepted, 11 enrolled. In 2017, 17 doctorates awarded. *Degree requirements:* For doctorate, comprehensive exam, thesis/dissertation, internship. *Entrance requirements:* For doctorate, GRE General Test, minimum upper-division GPA of 3.4, three letters of recommendation, personal goals statement. Additional exam requirements/recommendations for international students: Required—TOEFL (minimum score 550 paper-based; 79 iBT) or IELTS (minimum score 6.5). *Application deadline:* For fall admission, 12/1 priority date for domestic and international students. Application fee: $30. Electronic applications accepted. *Expenses:* Contact institution. *Financial support:* In 2017–18, 43 students received support, including 18 research assistantships with tuition reimbursements available (averaging $14,727 per year), 57 teaching assistantships with tuition reimbursements available (averaging $14,543 per year); tuition waivers (partial) and unspecified assistantships also available. Financial award applicants required to submit FAFSA. *Faculty research:* Clinical, cognitive, neuroscience, social, and industrial/organizational. *Total annual research expenditures:* $2 million. *Unit head:* Dr. Toru Shimizu, Chairperson, 813-974-0352, Fax: 813-974-4617, E-mail: shimizu@usf.edu. *Application contact:* Dr. Sandra Schneider, Professor and Graduate Program Director, 813-974-0928, E-mail: sandra@usf.edu.
Website: http://psychology.usf.edu/

The University of Tennessee, Graduate School, College of Business Administration, Program in Industrial and Organizational Psychology, Knoxville, TN 37996. Offers PhD. *Degree requirements:* For doctorate, thesis/dissertation. *Entrance requirements:* For doctorate, GRE General Test, minimum GPA of 2.7. Additional exam requirements/recommendations for international students: Required—TOEFL. Electronic applications accepted.

The University of Tennessee at Chattanooga, Program in Psychology, Chattanooga, TN 37403. Offers industrial/organizational psychology (MS); research psychology (MS). *Program availability:* Part-time. *Students:* 46 full-time (28 women), 4 part-time (3 women); includes 5 minority (2 Black or African American, non-Hispanic/Latino; 1 Asian, non-Hispanic/Latino; 2 Hispanic/Latino). Average age 25. 85 applicants, 38% accepted, 25 enrolled. In 2017, 20 master's awarded. *Degree requirements:* For master's, comprehensive exam (for some programs), thesis (for some programs), comprehensive exam or thesis. *Entrance requirements:* For master's, GRE General Test, minimum GPA of 2.5 on all undergraduate coursework or 3.0 in senior year. Additional exam requirements/recommendations for international students: Required—TOEFL (minimum score 550 paper-based; 79 iBT), IELTS (minimum score 6). *Application deadline:* For fall admission, 6/15 priority date for domestic students, 7/1 for international students; for spring admission, 11/1 priority date for domestic students, 11/1 for international students. Applications are processed on a rolling basis. Application fee: $35 ($40 for international students). Electronic applications accepted. *Expenses:* Contact institution. *Financial support:* Research assistantships, teaching assistantships, career-related internships or fieldwork, scholarships/grants, and unspecified assistantships available. Support available to part-time students. Financial award application deadline: 7/1; financial award applicants required to submit FAFSA. *Faculty research:* Decision processes, philosophical psychology, memory, social cognition, employee selection. *Total annual research expenditures:* $44,854. *Unit head:* Dr. Brian O'Leary, Department Head, 423-425-4283, Fax: 423-425-4284, E-mail: brian-o'leary@utc.edu. *Application contact:* Dr. Joanne Romagni, Dean of the Graduate School, 423-425-4478, Fax: 423-425-5223, E-mail: joanne-romagni@utc.edu.
Website: http://www.utc.edu/psychology/

The University of Texas at Arlington, Graduate School, College of Science, Department of Psychology, Arlington, TX 76019. Offers experimental health psychology (PhD); experimental psychology (MS, PhD); health/neuroscience psychology (MS, PhD); industrial and organizational psychology (MS). *Program availability:* Part-time. Terminal master's awarded for partial completion of doctoral program. *Degree requirements:* For master's, comprehensive exam or thesis; for doctorate, thesis/dissertation (for some programs). *Entrance requirements:* For master's and doctorate, GRE General Test, minimum GPA of 3.0 in last 60 hours of course work. Additional exam requirements/recommendations for international students: Required—TOEFL (minimum score 550 paper-based).

University of the Incarnate Word, School of Professional Studies, San Antonio, TX 78209-6397. Offers communication arts (MAA), including applied administration, communication arts, healthcare administration, industrial and organizational psychology, organizational development; organizational development and leadership (MS); professional studies (DBA). *Program availability:* Part-time, evening/weekend, 100% online, blended/hybrid learning. *Faculty:* 9 full-time (3 women), 25 part-time/adjunct (10 women). *Students:* 528 full-time (263 women), 348 part-time (141 women); includes 543 minority (122 Black or African American, non-Hispanic/Latino; 3 American Indian or Alaska Native, non-Hispanic/Latino; 26 Asian, non-Hispanic/Latino; 365 Hispanic/Latino; 6 Native Hawaiian or other Pacific Islander, non-Hispanic/Latino; 21 Two or more races, non-Hispanic/Latino). In 2017, 377 master's, 10 doctorates awarded. *Degree requirements:* For master's, comprehensive exam (for some programs), thesis or alternative. *Entrance requirements:* For master's, GMAT, GRE, official transcripts from all other colleges attended. Additional exam requirements/recommendations for international students: Required—TOEFL (minimum score 560 paper-based; 83 iBT). *Application deadline:* Applications are processed on a rolling basis. Electronic applications accepted. *Expenses:* $915 per credit hour (for master's programs); $940 per credit hour (for doctoral program). *Financial support:* Scholarships/grants and unspecified assistantships available. Financial award applicants required to submit FAFSA. *Unit head:* Dr. Cyndi Porter, Vice President, 877-603-1130, E-mail: porter@uiwtx.edu. *Application contact:* Julie Weber, Director of Marketing and Recruitment, 210-318-1876, Fax: 210-829-2756, E-mail: eapadmission@uiwtx.edu.
Website: http://sps.uiw.edu/

The University of Tulsa, Graduate School, Kendall College of Arts and Sciences, Department of Psychology, Program in Industrial/Organizational Psychology, Tulsa, OK 74104-3189. Offers MA, PhD, JD/MA. *Program availability:* Part-time. *Faculty:* 5 full-time (2 women). *Students:* 18 full-time (10 women), 1 (woman) part-time; includes 6 minority (2 Asian, non-Hispanic/Latino; 2 Hispanic/Latino; 2 Two or more races, non-Hispanic/Latino), 1 international. Average age 26. 90 applicants, 16% accepted, 5 enrolled. In 2017, 7 master's, 1 doctorate awarded. Terminal master's awarded for partial completion of doctoral program. *Degree requirements:* For master's, comprehensive exam, thesis (for some programs), 100-hour internship; for doctorate, comprehensive exam, thesis/dissertation, 100-hour internship. *Entrance requirements:* For master's and doctorate, GRE General Test. Additional exam requirements/recommendations for international students: Required—TOEFL (minimum score 577 paper-based; 91 iBT), IELTS (minimum score 6.5). *Application deadline:* For fall admission, 12/15 for domestic and international students. Application fee: $55. Electronic applications accepted. *Expenses: Tuition:* Full-time $22,230. *Required fees:* $2000. Tuition and fees vary according to course load and program. *Financial support:* In 2017–18, 25 students received support, including 5 fellowships with full tuition reimbursements available (averaging $12,500 per year), 4 research assistantships with full tuition reimbursements available (averaging $8,500 per year), 15 teaching assistantships with full tuition reimbursements available (averaging $10,500 per year); career-related internships or fieldwork, Federal Work-Study, scholarships/grants, health care benefits, tuition waivers (full and partial), and unspecified assistantships also available. Support available to part-time students. Financial award application deadline: 2/1; financial award applicants required to submit FAFSA. *Faculty research:* Personnel testing and selection, training, performance appraisal, organizational development, job attitudes and motivation, leadership. *Unit head:* Dr. Robert Tett, Director, 918-631-2737, Fax: 918-631-2833, E-mail: robert-tett@utulsa.edu. *Application contact:* Information Contact, 800-882-4723, E-mail: grad@utulsa.edu.

University of West Florida, Usha Kundu, MD College of Health, Department of Psychology, Pensacola, FL 32514-5750. Offers applied experimental (MA); counseling (MA); industrial-organizational (MA). *Program availability:* Part-time. *Degree requirements:* For master's, thesis (for some programs). *Entrance requirements:* For master's, GRE, official transcripts; minimum GPA of 3.0; writing sample; three letters of reference; field experience or skill sets; oral interview (for counseling specialization). Additional exam requirements/recommendations for international students: Required—TOEFL (minimum score 550 paper-based). *Faculty research:* Prose recall, brain imaging, peak performance, biofeedback and pain control, comparable worth.

University of Wisconsin–Oshkosh, Graduate Studies, College of Letters and Science, Department of Psychology, Oshkosh, WI 54901. Offers experimental psychology (MS); industrial/organizational psychology (MS). *Degree requirements:* For master's, thesis. *Entrance requirements:* For master's, GRE, 10 semester hours of undergraduate course work in psychology. Additional exam requirements/recommendations for international

students: Required—TOEFL (minimum score 550 paper-based; 79 iBT). Electronic applications accepted. *Faculty research:* Performance evaluation, training, biological bases of behavior, tactile perception, aging.

Valdosta State University, Department of Psychology, Counseling, and Family Therapy, Valdosta, GA 31698. Offers industrial/organizational psychology (MS); marriage and family therapy (MS); school counseling (M Ed, Ed S). *Accreditation:* AAMFT/COAMFTE. *Program availability:* Part-time, evening/weekend, 100% online, blended/hybrid learning. *Degree requirements:* For master's, thesis or alternative, comprehensive written and/or oral exams; for Ed S, thesis. *Entrance requirements:* For master's, GRE General Test or MAT, GACE; for Ed S, GRE General Test or MAT. Additional exam requirements/recommendations for international students: Required— TOEFL (minimum score 523 paper-based); Recommended—IELTS. *Application deadline:* For fall admission, 7/1 for domestic and international students; for spring admission, 11/15 for domestic and international students. Applications are processed on a rolling basis. Application fee: $45. Electronic applications accepted. *Expenses:* Contact institution. *Financial support:* Research assistantships with full tuition reimbursements, institutionally sponsored loans, and unspecified assistantships available. Support available to part-time students. Financial award application deadline: 7/1; financial award applicants required to submit FAFSA. *Unit head:* Dr. Kate Warner, Head, 229-293-6264, Fax: 229-259-5576, E-mail: kwarner@valdosta.edu. *Application contact:* Jessica Powers, Admission Specialist, 229-333-5694, Fax: 229-245-3853, E-mail: jldevane@valdosta.edu.
Website: https://www.valdosta.edu/colleges/education/pcft/

Walden University, Graduate Programs, School of Psychology, Minneapolis, MN 55401. Offers clinical psychology (MS), including counseling, general program; forensic psychology (MS), including forensic psychology in the community, general program, mental health applications, program planning and evaluation in forensic settings, psychology and legal systems; industrial organizational (MS, PhD), including consulting psychology, forensic (MS), forensic psychology (PhD), general practice, leadership development and coaching (MS), organizational diversity and social change, research evaluation (PhD); online teaching in psychology (Post-Master's Certificate); organizational psychology and development (Postbaccalaureate Certificate); psychology (MS, PhD), including applied psychology (MS), clinical psychology (PhD), crisis management and response (MS), educational psychology, forensic psychology (PhD), general psychology (MS), general psychology research (PhD), general psychology teaching (PhD), health psychology, leadership development and coaching (MS), psychology of culture (MS), psychology, public administration, and social change (MS), social psychology, terrorism and security (MS); psychology respecialization (Post-Doctoral Certificate). *Program availability:* Part-time, evening/weekend, online only, 100% online. Terminal master's awarded for partial completion of doctoral program. *Degree requirements:* For master's, thesis optional; for doctorate, thesis/dissertation, residency. *Entrance requirements:* For master's, bachelor's degree or higher; minimum GPA of 2.5; official transcripts; goal statement (for some programs); access to computer and Internet; for doctorate, master's degree or higher; three years of related professional or academic experience (preferred); minimum GPA of 3.0; goal statement and current resume (for select programs); official transcripts; access to computer and Internet; for other advanced degree, relevant work experience; access to computer and Internet. Additional exam requirements/recommendations for international students: Required— TOEFL (minimum score 550 paper-based, 79 iBT), IELTS (minimum score 6.5), Michigan English Language Assessment Battery (minimum score 82), or PTE (minimum score 53). Electronic applications accepted.

Wayne State University, College of Liberal Arts and Sciences, Department of Psychology, Detroit, MI 48202. Offers behavioral and cognitive neuroscience (PhD); clinical psychology (PhD); developmental science (PhD); industrial/organizational psychology (MA, PhD); social personality (PhD). Doctoral program admits for fall only. *Accreditation:* APA (one or more programs are accredited). *Faculty:* 38. *Students:* 94 full-time (63 women), 43 part-time (29 women); includes 23 minority (6 Black or African American, non-Hispanic/Latino; 3 Asian, non-Hispanic/Latino; 10 Hispanic/Latino; 4 Two or more races, non-Hispanic/Latino), 12 international. Average age 27. 478 applicants, 11% accepted, 39 enrolled. In 2017, 29 master's, 27 doctorates awarded. Terminal master's awarded for partial completion of doctoral program. *Degree requirements:* For master's, thesis (for some programs); for doctorate, thesis/dissertation, training assignments. *Entrance requirements:* For master's, GRE General Test, minimum undergraduate upper-division cumulative GPA of 3.0, courses in psychology and statistics; for doctorate, GRE General Test, bachelor's, master's, or other advanced degree; at least twelve credits in psychology with minimum GPA of 3.0; courses in laboratory psychology and statistical methods in psychology; at least three letters of recommendation; statement of purpose. Additional exam requirements/ recommendations for international students: Required—TOEFL (minimum score 550 paper-based; 79 iBT), TWE (minimum score 5.5), Michigan English Language Assessment Battery (minimum score 85); Recommended—IELTS (minimum score 6.5). Application fee: $50. Electronic applications accepted. *Expenses:* Tuition, state resident: full-time $10,224; part-time $638.98 per credit hour. Tuition, nonresident: full-time $22,145; part-time $1384.04 per credit hour. Tuition and fees vary according to course load and program. *Financial support:* In 2017–18, 90 students received support, including 13 fellowships with tuition reimbursements available (averaging $11,212 per year), 8 research assistantships with tuition reimbursements available (averaging $18,534 per year), 50 teaching assistantships with tuition reimbursements available (averaging $18,534 per year); scholarships/grants, health care benefits, and unspecified assistantships also available. Financial award applicants required to submit FAFSA. *Faculty research:* Behavioral neuroscience, cognitive/neuroscience of development and aging research, children, adolescents, and family research, cognition research, emotion research, health psychology research, homelessness and poverty research, memory research, neuropsychology research, personality/cognition, relationships research,

substance use and abuse research, workplace adaptation, well-being and evaluation research. *Unit head:* Boris Baltes, PhD, Chair/Professor, 313-577-2803, E-mail: b.baltes@wayne.edu. *Application contact:* Alia Allen, Academic Services Officer, 313-577-2823, E-mail: aallen@wayne.edu.
Website: http://clas.wayne.edu/psychology/

West Chester University of Pennsylvania, College of the Sciences and Mathematics, Department of Psychology, West Chester, PA 19383. Offers clinical psychology (Psy D); industrial/organizational psychology (Certificate); psychology (MA), including general psychology, industrial/organizational psychology. *Program availability:* Part-time, evening/weekend, 100% online. *Students:* 56 full-time (37 women), 28 part-time (20 women); includes 18 minority (9 Black or African American, non-Hispanic/Latino; 2 Asian, non-Hispanic/Latino; 4 Hispanic/Latino; 3 Two or more races, non-Hispanic/Latino). Average age 26. 125 applicants, 62% accepted, 42 enrolled. In 2017, 47 master's awarded. Terminal master's awarded for partial completion of doctoral program. *Degree requirements:* For master's, comprehensive exam (for some programs), thesis optional; for doctorate, comprehensive exam, thesis/dissertation, year-long pre-doctoral internship. *Entrance requirements:* For master's, GRE General Test, minimum GPA of 3.0 overall, psychology 3.25; three letters of reference; for doctorate, GRE General Test, minimum undergraduate GPA of 3.0 or graduate 3.3; three letters of reference; curriculum vitae; completion of courses (at the undergraduate level) in abnormal/clinical psychology, personality, research methods, and statistics; professional goals statement. Additional exam requirements/recommendations for international students: Required—TOEFL or IELTS. *Application deadline:* For fall admission, 5/15 for international students; for spring admission, 10/15 for international students. Applications are processed on a rolling basis. Application fee: $50. Electronic applications accepted. *Expenses:* Tuition, state resident: full-time $9000; part-time $500 per credit. Tuition, nonresident: full-time $13,500; part-time $750 per credit. *Required fees:* $2959; $149.79 per credit. *Financial support:* Scholarships/grants and unspecified assistantships available. Financial award application deadline: 2/15; financial award applicants required to submit FAFSA. *Faculty research:* Child and adolescent mental health, trauma, stress, coping and resilience, preventative interventions workplace stress, organizational leadership, eating disorders, several other areas including diversity, cognition, and animal behavior. *Unit head:* Dr. Sandra Kerr, Chairperson, 610-436-2945, E-mail: skerr@wcupa.edu. *Application contact:* Dr. Angela Clarke, Director of Clinical Training, Clinical Psychology PsyD Program, 610-436-3136, E-mail: aclarke@wcupa.edu.
Website: http://www.wcupa.edu/sciences-mathematics/psychology/

Western Kentucky University, Graduate Studies, College of Education and Behavioral Sciences, Department of Psychology, Bowling Green, KY 42101. Offers clinical psychology (MA); experimental psychology (MA); general psychology (MA); industrial/ organizational psychology (MA); school psychology (Ed S). *Degree requirements:* For master's, comprehensive exam, thesis (for some programs); for Ed S, thesis, oral exam. *Entrance requirements:* For master's, GRE General Test; for Ed S, GRE General Test, minimum GPA of 3.5. Additional exam requirements/recommendations for international students: Required—TOEFL (minimum score 555 paper-based; 79 iBT). *Faculty research:* Neural regeneration, enhancing mobility in the elderly, improvement in visual processing in older adults, lifespan development.

Western Michigan University, Graduate College, College of Arts and Sciences, Department of Psychology, Kalamazoo, MI 49008. Offers behavior analysis (MA, PhD); clinical psychology (PhD); industrial/organizational behavior management (MA). *Accreditation:* APA (one or more programs are accredited). *Degree requirements:* For master's, variable foreign language requirement, thesis; for doctorate, 2 foreign languages, comprehensive exam, thesis/dissertation.

William James College, Graduate Programs, Newton, MA 02459. Offers applied psychology in higher education student personnel administration (MA); clinical psychology (Psy D); counseling psychology (MA); counseling psychology and community mental health (MA); counseling psychology and global mental health (MA); executive coaching (Graduate Certificate); forensic and counseling psychology (MA); leadership psychology (Psy D); organizational psychology (MA); primary care psychology (MA); respecialization in clinical psychology (Certificate); school psychology (Psy D); MA/CAGS. *Accreditation:* APA. *Degree requirements:* For master's, comprehensive exam (for some programs); for doctorate, thesis/dissertation (for some programs). Electronic applications accepted.

Wright State University, Graduate School, College of Science and Mathematics, Department of Psychology, Program in Human Factors and Industrial/Organizational Psychology, Dayton, OH 45435. Offers MS, PhD. *Degree requirements:* For master's, thesis; for doctorate, thesis/dissertation.

Xavier University, College of Social Sciences, Health and Education, Department of Psychology, Cincinnati, OH 45207. Offers clinical psychology (Psy D); industrial-organizational psychology (MA). *Accreditation:* APA (one or more programs are accredited). *Degree requirements:* For master's, one foreign language, comprehensive exam, thesis, internship; for doctorate, one foreign language, comprehensive exam, thesis/dissertation, internship. *Entrance requirements:* For master's, GRE, official transcript; 3 letters of recommendation; for doctorate, GRE General Test; GRE Subject Test in psychology (if no undergraduate degree in psychology), bachelor's or master's degree; 18 semester hours of psychology coursework; minimum GPA of 3.0; work and research experience; official transcript; 3 letters of recommendation; statement of purpose. Additional exam requirements/recommendations for international students: Required—TOEFL (minimum score 550 paper-based; 79 iBT), IELTS (minimum score 6.5). Electronic applications accepted. *Expenses:* Contact institution. *Faculty research:* Older adults, clinical child and adolescent issues, personnel selection and employee behavior, at-risk youth, sexual abuse.

Marriage and Family Therapy

Abilene Christian University, College of Graduate and Professional Studies, Marriage and Family Therapy Online Program, Addison, TX 75001. Offers child and adolescent therapy (MMFT); medical family therapy (MMFT); therapy with military families (MMFT); treatment of trauma (MMFT). *Program availability:* Part-time, online only. *Faculty:* 3 full-time (1 woman), 10 part-time/adjunct (6 women). *Students:* 143 full-time (121 women), 36 part-time (32 women); includes 55 minority (43 Black or African American, non-Hispanic/Latino; 2 American Indian or Alaska Native, non-Hispanic/Latino; 5 Asian, non-Hispanic/Latino; 5 Hispanic/Latino). 162 applicants, 50% accepted, 61 enrolled. *Entrance requirements:* For master's, statement of purpose, three letters of

recommendation. Additional exam requirements/recommendations for international students: Required—TOEFL (minimum score 80 iBT), IELTS (minimum score 6). *Application deadline:* For fall admission, 8/15 for domestic students; for winter admission, 10/1 for domestic students; for spring admission, 12/15 for domestic students; for summer admission, 4/15 for domestic students. Applications are processed on a rolling basis. Application fee: $50. *Expenses:* $800 per hour. *Financial support:* Application deadline: 4/1; applicants required to submit FAFSA. *Unit head:* Dr. Sara Salkil, Program Director, 325-829-2131, Fax: 325-674-6717, E-mail: seb04b@acu.edu. *Application contact:* Graduate Advisor, 855-219-7300, E-mail: gradonline@acu.edu.

Marriage and Family Therapy

Abilene Christian University, Graduate Programs, College of Biblical Studies, Program in Marriage and Family Therapy, Abilene, TX 79699. Offers MMFT. *Accreditation:* AAMFT/COAMFTE. *Faculty:* 4 full-time (2 women), 7 part-time/adjunct (3 women). *Students:* 32 full-time (22 women), 1 (woman) part-time; includes 11 minority (8 Black or African American, non-Hispanic/Latino; 3 Hispanic/Latino), 1 international. 41 applicants, 66% accepted, 14 enrolled. In 2017, 16 master's awarded. *Degree requirements:* For master's, comprehensive exam, internship. *Entrance requirements:* For master's, GRE General Test, interview, writing sample. Additional exam requirements/recommendations for international students: Required—TOEFL (minimum score 80 iBT), IELTS (minimum score 6), PTE. *Application deadline:* For fall admission, 2/15 for domestic students. Applications are processed on a rolling basis. Application fee: $50. Electronic applications accepted. *Expenses:* $1,081 per hour. *Financial support:* In 2017–18, 10 students received support. Research assistantships, career-related internships or fieldwork, and scholarships/grants available. Support available to part-time students. Financial award application deadline: 4/1; financial award applicants required to submit FAFSA. *Faculty research:* Overeating variables, family systems, intervention strategies. *Unit head:* Dr. Dale Bertram, Program Director, 325-674-3780, Fax: 325-674-3779, E-mail: deb12a@acu.edu. *Application contact:* Graduate Admissions, 325-674-6911, Fax: 325-674-6717, E-mail: gradinfo@acu.edu. Website: http://www.acu.edu/graduate/academics/marriage-and-family-therapy.html

Adler Graduate School, Program in Adlerian Counseling and Psychotherapy, Richfield, MN 55423. Offers Adlerian studies (MA); art therapy (MA); clinical mental health counseling (MA); co-occurring substance use and mental health disorders (MA); marriage and family therapy (MA); school counseling (MA). *Program availability:* Part-time, evening/weekend. *Faculty:* 71 part-time/adjunct (55 women). *Students:* 317 part-time (259 women); includes 51 minority (40 Black or African American, non-Hispanic/Latino; 6 American Indian or Alaska Native, non-Hispanic/Latino; 5 Hispanic/Latino). *Degree requirements:* For master's, thesis or alternative, 500-700 hour internship (depending on license choice). *Entrance requirements:* For master's, interview, official transcripts, minimum cumulative GPA of 3.0. *Application deadline:* Applications are processed on a rolling basis. Application fee: $50. Electronic applications accepted. *Expenses:* $575 per credit tuition. *Financial support:* Career-related internships or fieldwork and tuition waivers available. Support available to part-time students. Financial award applicants required to submit FAFSA. *Unit head:* Dr. Jeffrey Allen, President, 612-767-7048, Fax: 612-861-7559, E-mail: jeffrey.allen@alfredadler.edu. *Application contact:* Christina Hilpipre-Frischman, Director of Admissions, 612-767-7055, Fax: 612-861-7559, E-mail: christina@alfredadler.edu. Website: http://alfredadler.edu/programs/masters-level-programs

Adler University, Graduate Programs, Certificate Programs, Chicago, IL 60602. Offers couple and family therapy (Certificate); substance abuse counseling (Certificate). *Entrance requirements:* For degree, baccalaureate degree, minimum GPA of 3.0.

Adler University, Graduate Programs, MA in Couple and Family Therapy Program, Chicago, IL 60602. Offers MA. *Degree requirements:* For master's, practicum, comprehensive qualifying exam.

Adler University, Graduate Programs, PhD in Couple and Family Therapy Program, Chicago, IL 60602. Offers PhD.

Alliant International University–Irvine, California School of Professional Psychology, Program in Couple and Family Therapy, Irvine, CA 92606. Offers MA, Psy D. *Accreditation:* AAMFT/COAMFTE. *Program availability:* Part-time. *Degree requirements:* For doctorate, thesis/dissertation. *Entrance requirements:* For master's, minimum GPA of 3.0, letters of recommendation, interview; for doctorate, letters of recommendation, minimum GPA of 3.0, interview. Additional exam requirements/recommendations for international students: Required—TOEFL (minimum score 550 paper-based; 80 iBT), TWE (minimum score 5). Electronic applications accepted. *Faculty research:* Chemical dependency, gender issues in couples relationships, multicultural competence in therapy, contextual family therapy, relationship quality and stability.

Alliant International University–Los Angeles, California School of Professional Psychology, Program in Couple and Family Therapy, Alhambra, CA 91803. Offers chemical dependency (MA); gerontology (MA); Latin American family therapy (MA). *Accreditation:* AAMFT/COAMFTE. *Program availability:* Part-time, evening/weekend. Terminal master's awarded for partial completion of doctoral program. *Degree requirements:* For master's, comprehensive exam, 50 hours of professional development activities. *Entrance requirements:* Additional exam requirements/recommendations for international students: Required—TOEFL (minimum score 550 paper-based). Electronic applications accepted. *Faculty research:* Foster care, therapy with minority couples, parenting, marriage, trauma.

Alliant International University–Los Angeles, California School of Professional Psychology, Psy D Program in Clinical Psychology, Alhambra, CA 91803. Offers clinical health psychology (Psy D); family/child and couple clinical psychology (Psy D); multi-interest option (Psy D); multicultural community-clinical psychology (Psy D). *Accreditation:* APA. *Degree requirements:* For doctorate, comprehensive exam, thesis/dissertation. *Entrance requirements:* For doctorate, interview, minimum GPA of 3.0 in both psychology and overall. Additional exam requirements/recommendations for international students: Required—TOEFL (minimum score 600 paper-based), TWE. Electronic applications accepted. *Faculty research:* Child and family psychology, multicultural and community psychology, acculturation, lesbian and gay issues, women's health.

Alliant International University–Sacramento, California School of Professional Psychology, Program in Couple and Family Therapy, Sacramento, CA 95833. Offers MA, Psy D. *Accreditation:* AAMFT/COAMFTE. *Degree requirements:* For master's, practicum; for doctorate, thesis/dissertation, practicum. *Entrance requirements:* For master's and doctorate, minimum GPA of 3.0, letters of recommendation, interview. Additional exam requirements/recommendations for international students: Required—TOEFL (minimum score 600 paper-based), TWE (minimum score 5). Electronic applications accepted. *Faculty research:* Adolescent risky behaviors including substance abuse, family therapy process, cultural issues, therapy with the LGBT community, commonalities of healthy and distressed couples.

Alliant International University–San Diego, California School of Professional Psychology, Program in Couple and Family Therapy, San Diego, CA 92131. Offers marital and family therapy (MA, Psy D). *Accreditation:* AAMFT/COAMFTE. *Program availability:* Part-time. *Degree requirements:* For doctorate, thesis/dissertation. *Entrance requirements:* For master's and doctorate, minimum GPA of 3.0, letters of recommendation, interview. Additional exam requirements/recommendations for international students: Required—TOEFL (minimum score 550 paper-based; 80 iBT), TWE (minimum score 5). Electronic applications accepted. *Faculty research:* Chemical dependency, women's issues, emotionally-focused therapy, couple relationships, work/family/parenting.

Amberton University, Graduate School, Programs in Counseling, Garland, TX 75041-5595. Offers marriage and family therapy (MA); professional counseling (MA); school counseling (MA). *Entrance requirements:* For master's, minimum GPA of 3.0.

Application deadline: Applications are processed on a rolling basis. Application fee: $0. *Expenses: Tuition:* Part-time $795 per course. *Unit head:* Dr. Don Hebbard, Academic Dean, 972-635-8641 Ext. 157, Fax: 972-279-9773, E-mail: dhebbard@amberton.edu. *Application contact:* Adviser, 972-279-6511 Ext. 180, Fax: 972-279-9773, E-mail: advisor@amberton.edu.

Amridge University, Graduate and Professional Programs, Montgomery, AL 36117. Offers Biblical studies (MA, PhD); Christian ministry (MS); family therapy (D Min); human services (MS); leadership and management (MS); marriage and family therapy (M Div, MA, PhD); ministerial leadership (M Div, MS); New Testament studies (MA); Old Testament studies (MA); professional counseling (M Div, MA, PhD); theology (M Div, D Min). *Program availability:* Part-time, evening/weekend, online learning. *Faculty:* 23 full-time (3 women), 9 part-time/adjunct (5 women). *Students:* 105 full-time (55 women), 250 part-time (152 women); includes 217 minority (167 Black or African American, non-Hispanic/Latino; 4 Asian, non-Hispanic/Latino; 42 Hispanic/Latino; 4 Native Hawaiian or other Pacific Islander, non-Hispanic/Latino). Average age 42. 160 applicants, 100% accepted, 110 enrolled. *Degree requirements:* For master's, one foreign language, comprehensive exam (for some programs), thesis (for some programs); for doctorate, one foreign language, comprehensive exam (for some programs), thesis/dissertation (for some programs). *Entrance requirements:* For master's, official transcript showing an earned 4-year BA or BS from regionally- or nationally-accredited institution; for doctorate, official transcript showing earned graduate degree from regionally- or nationally-accredited institution; writing sample (e.g. career monograph, published journal article, term paper from master's degree or doctoral dissertation); interview. Additional exam requirements/recommendations for international students: Required—TOEFL (minimum score 79 iBT). *Application deadline:* Applications are processed on a rolling basis. Application fee: $50. Electronic applications accepted. *Financial support:* In 2017–18, 33 students received support. Federal Work-Study and scholarships/grants available. Support available to part-time students. Financial award applicants required to submit FAFSA. *Faculty research:* Technology and mental healthcare, resilience in black families, theology and congregational ministry. *Unit head:* Laina Costanza, Vice President, Student Affairs, 888-790-8080 Ext. 1, Fax: 334-387-3878, E-mail: cc@amridgeuniversity.edu. *Application contact:* Brooks Housley, Student Affairs Coordinator, 888-790-8080 Ext. 1, Fax: 334-387-3878, E-mail: admissions@amridgeuniversity.edu.

Antioch University New England, Graduate School, Department of Applied Psychology, Program in Marriage and Family Therapy, Keene, NH 03431-3552. Offers MA, PhD, Certificate. *Accreditation:* AAMFT/COAMFTE. *Degree requirements:* For master's, internship, practicum. *Entrance requirements:* For master's, previous course work and work experience in psychology; resume; 3 letters of recommendation. Additional exam requirements/recommendations for international students: Required—TOEFL (minimum score 550 paper-based). Electronic applications accepted. *Expenses:* Contact institution. *Faculty research:* Use of reflective team model in case teaching and in organizational consulting, executive mentoring and coaching.

Antioch University Seattle, Program in Counseling, Therapy and Wellness, Seattle, WA 98121. Offers clinical mental health counseling (MA); counselor education and supervision (PhD); couple and family therapy (MA). *Students:* 258 full-time (220 women), 100 part-time (84 women); includes 81 minority (9 Black or African American, non-Hispanic/Latino; 3 American Indian or Alaska Native, non-Hispanic/Latino; 19 Asian, non-Hispanic/Latino; 30 Hispanic/Latino; 20 Two or more races, non-Hispanic/Latino), 1 international. Average age 35. *Unit head:* Peter Rojcewicz, Vice President of Academic Affairs, 206-268-4108, E-mail: projcewicz@antioch.edu. *Application contact:* Eileen Knight, Recruitment and Admissions Director, 206-268-4200, E-mail: psmith-mentz@antiochsea.edu.

Appalachian State University, Cratis D. Williams Graduate School, Department of Human Development and Psychological Counseling, Boone, NC 28608. Offers clinical mental health counseling (MA); college student development (MA); marriage and family therapy (MA); school counseling (MA). *Accreditation:* AAMFT/COAMFTE; ACA; NCATE. *Program availability:* Part-time. *Degree requirements:* For master's, comprehensive exam (for some programs), thesis optional, internships. *Entrance requirements:* For master's, GRE General Test, 3 letters of recommendation. Additional exam requirements/recommendations for international students: Required—TOEFL (minimum score 570 paper-based; 79 iBT), IELTS (minimum score 6.5). Electronic applications accepted. *Faculty research:* Multicultural counseling, addictions counseling, play therapy, expressive arts, child and adolescent therapy, sexual abuse counseling.

Arcadia University, College of Arts and Sciences, Department of Psychology, Glenside, PA 19038-3295. Offers applied behavior analysis (MAC); autism (MAC); child/family therapy (MAC); community public health (MAC); counseling/international peace and conflict resolution dual degree (MAC); mental health counseling (MAC); trauma (MAC). *Program availability:* Part-time. *Degree requirements:* For master's, practicum. *Entrance requirements:* For master's, GRE General Test or MAT. *Expenses:* Contact institution.

Argosy University, Atlanta, Georgia School of Professional Psychology, Atlanta, GA 30328. Offers clinical psychology (MA, Psy D, Postdoctoral Respecialization Certificate), including child and family psychology (Psy D), general adult clinical (Psy D), health psychology (Psy D), neuropsychology/geropsychology (Psy D); community counseling (MA), including marriage and family therapy; counselor education and supervision (Ed D); forensic psychology (MA); industrial organizational psychology (MA); marriage and family therapy (Certificate); sport-exercise psychology (MA). *Accreditation:* APA.

Argosy University, Chicago, Illinois School of Professional Psychology, Doctoral Program in Clinical Psychology, Chicago, IL 60601. Offers child and adolescent psychology (Psy D); client-centered and experiential psychotherapies (Psy D); diversity and multicultural psychology (Psy D); family psychology (Psy D); forensic psychology (Psy D); health psychology (Psy D); neuropsychology (Psy D); organizational consulting (Psy D); psychoanalytic psychology (Psy D); psychology and spirituality (Psy D). *Accreditation:* APA.

Argosy University, Hawai`i, Hawai'i School of Professional Psychology, Program in Marriage and Family Therapy, Honolulu, HI 96813. Offers MA.

Argosy University, Los Angeles, College of Psychology and Behavioral Sciences, Los Angeles, CA 90045. Offers clinical psychology/marriage and family therapy (MA); counseling psychology (Ed D); counseling psychology/marriage and family therapy (MA); forensic psychology (MA).

Argosy University, Northern Virginia, American School of Professional Psychology, Arlington, VA 22209. Offers clinical psychology (MA, Psy D), including child and family psychology (Psy D), diversity and multicultural psychology (Psy D), forensic psychology (Psy D), health and neuropsychology (Psy D); community counseling (MA); counseling psychology (Ed D), including counselor education and supervision; counselor education and supervision (Ed D); forensic psychology (MA).

Argosy University, Orange County, American School of Professional Psychology, Program in Clinical Psychology, Orange, CA 92868. Offers child and adolescent psychology (Psy D); forensic psychology (Psy D); marriage and family therapy (MA).

Argosy University, Orange County, American School of Professional Psychology, Program in Counseling Psychology, Orange, CA 92868. Offers counseling psychology (Ed D); marriage and family therapy (MA).

Argosy University, Tampa, Florida School of Professional Psychology, Program in Clinical Psychology, Tampa, FL 33607. Offers clinical psychology (MA, Psy D), including child and adolescent psychology (Psy D), geropsychology (Psy D), marriage/couples and family therapy (Psy D), neuropsychology (Psy D). *Accreditation:* APA.

Argosy University, Twin Cities, Minnesota School of Professional Psychology, Eagan, MN 55121. Offers clinical psychology (MA, Psy D), including child and family psychology (Psy D), forensic psychology (Psy D), health and neuropsychology (Psy D), trauma (Psy D); forensic counseling (Post-Graduate Certificate); forensic psychology (MA); industrial organizational psychology (MA); marriage and family therapy (MA, DMFT), including forensic counseling (MA). *Accreditation:* AAMFT; AAMFT/COAMFTE; APA.

Arizona State University at the Tempe campus, College of Liberal Arts and Sciences, School of Social and Family Dynamics, Tempe, AZ 85287-3701. Offers family and human development (MS, PhD); infant-family practice (MAS); marriage and family therapy (MAS); sociology (MA, PhD). Terminal master's awarded for partial completion of doctoral program. *Degree requirements:* For master's, thesis or alternative, interactive Program of Study (iPOS) submitted before completing 50 percent of required credit hours; for doctorate, thesis/dissertation, interactive Program of Study (iPOS) submitted before completing 50 percent of required credit hours. *Entrance requirements:* For master's and doctorate, GRE, minimum GPA of 3.0 or equivalent in last 2 years of work leading to bachelor's degree. Additional exam requirements/recommendations for international students: Required—TOEFL, IELTS, or PTE. Electronic applications accepted. *Expenses:* Contact institution.

Azusa Pacific University, School of Behavioral and Applied Sciences, Department of Clinical Psychology, Azusa, CA 91702-7000. Offers family psychology (Psy D). *Accreditation:* APA. *Program availability:* Part-time, evening/weekend. *Degree requirements:* For doctorate, comprehensive exam. *Entrance requirements:* Additional exam requirements/recommendations for international students: Required—TOEFL (minimum score 600 paper-based). *Expenses:* Contact institution.

Barry University, School of Education, Program in Marital, Couple and Family Counseling/Therapy, Miami Shores, FL 33161-6695. Offers MS, Ed S. *Program availability:* Part-time, evening/weekend. *Degree requirements:* For master's, comprehensive exam, scholarly paper; for Ed S, comprehensive exam. *Entrance requirements:* For master's, GRE General Test or MAT, minimum GPA of 3.0; for Ed S, GRE General Test, minimum GPA of 3.0. Electronic applications accepted.

Bayamón Central University, Graduate Programs, Program in Education, Bayamón, PR 00960-1725. Offers administration and supervision (MA Ed); commercial education (MA Ed); elementary education (K–3) (MA Ed); family counseling (Graduate Certificate); guidance and counseling (MA Ed); pre-elementary teacher (MA Ed); rehabilitation counseling (MA Ed); special education (MA Ed), including attention deficit disorder, education of the autistic, learning disabilities. *Program availability:* Part-time, evening/weekend. *Degree requirements:* For master's, comprehensive exam. *Entrance requirements:* For master's, EXADEP, bachelor's degree in education or related field.

Bethel Seminary, Graduate and Professional Programs, St. Paul, MN 55112-6998. Offers Anglican studies (Certificate); children's and family ministry (MA); Christian studies (Certificate); Christian thought (MA); church planting (Certificate); Greek and Hebrew language (M Div); Greek language (M Div); Hebrew language (M Div); marriage and family therapy (MA, Certificate); mental health counseling (MA); ministry (MA, D Min); ministry practice (Certificate); theological studies (MA, Certificate); transformational leadership (MA); young life youth ministry (Certificate). *Accreditation:* ACIPE. *Program availability:* Part-time, evening/weekend, 100% online, blended/hybrid learning. *Faculty:* 16 full-time (4 women), 31 part-time/adjunct (15 women). *Students:* 380 full-time (170 women), 167 part-time (55 women); includes 161 minority (65 Black or African American, non-Hispanic/Latino; 52 Asian, non-Hispanic/Latino; 31 Hispanic/Latino; 1 Native Hawaiian or other Pacific Islander, non-Hispanic/Latino; 12 Two or more races, non-Hispanic/Latino), 5 international. Average age 38. 356 applicants, 62% accepted, 156 enrolled. In 2017, 120 master's, 15 doctorates, 4 other advanced degrees awarded. *Degree requirements:* For master's, variable foreign language requirement, thesis (for some programs); for doctorate, thesis/dissertation. *Entrance requirements:* For master's, letters of reference, transcripts, personal statement; for doctorate, M Div, letters of reference, organizational support; for Certificate, letters of reference, family essay, personal statement, and family of origin paper (for marriage and family therapy). Additional exam requirements/recommendations for international students: Required—TOEFL (minimum score 550 paper-based; 87 iBT). *Application deadline:* For fall admission, 8/1 priority date for domestic students, 8/1 for international students; for winter admission, 12/1 priority date for domestic students; for spring admission, 1/1 priority date for domestic students. Applications are processed on a rolling basis. Application fee: $0. Electronic applications accepted. *Expenses:* Contact institution. *Financial support:* Teaching assistantships, career-related internships or fieldwork, Federal Work-Study, and scholarships/grants available. Financial award applicants required to submit FAFSA. *Faculty research:* Nature of theology, ethics, Biblical commentaries, nature of God, science and theology. *Unit head:* Dr. Randy Bergen, Associate Provost, 651-635-8000, E-mail: r-bergen@bethel.edu. *Application contact:* Director of Admissions, 651-638-8000, Fax: 651-638-6002, E-mail: seminary-admissions@bethel.edu.
Website: https://www.bethel.edu/seminary

Brandman University, School of Arts and Sciences, Irvine, CA 92618. Offers psychology (MA), including counseling, marriage and family therapy, professional clinical counseling; social work (MSW). *Expenses:* Tuition: Part-time $640 per credit hour. Tuition and fees vary according to degree level and program. *Unit head:* Dr. Jeremy Korr, Dean, 949-341-9831. *Application contact:* Dr. Jeremy Korr, Dean, 949-341-9831.
Website: https://www.brandman.edu/academic-programs/arts-and-sciences

Briercrest Seminary, Graduate Programs, Program in Christian Ministries, Caronport, SK S0H 0S0, Canada. Offers leadership (MA); marriage and family counseling (MA); missions (MA); pastoral counseling (MA); worship (MA); youth and family ministry (MA). *Program availability:* Part-time. *Degree requirements:* For master's, comprehensive exam, thesis optional. *Entrance requirements:* Additional exam requirements/recommendations for international students: Required—TOEFL (minimum score 550 paper-based).

Brigham Young University, Graduate Studies, College of Family, Home, and Social Sciences, Marriage and Family Therapy Program, Provo, UT 84602. Offers MS, PhD. *Accreditation:* AAMFT/COAMFTE. *Faculty:* 8 full-time (2 women), 3 part-time/adjunct (2 women). *Students:* 32 full-time (23 women); includes 6 minority (1 Black or African American, non-Hispanic/Latino; 2 Asian, non-Hispanic/Latino; 2 Hispanic/Latino; 1 Native Hawaiian or other Pacific Islander, non-Hispanic/Latino). Average age 29. 94 applicants, 16% accepted, 15 enrolled. In 2017, 8 master's, 3 doctorates awarded. *Degree requirements:* For master's, thesis or alternative, 500 clinical hours; for doctorate, comprehensive exam, thesis/dissertation, 500 clinical hours, portfolio. *Entrance requirements:* For master's and doctorate, GRE General Test, minimum GPA of 3.0 in last 60 hours of course work. Additional exam requirements/recommendations for international students: Required—TOEFL (minimum score 85 iBT). *Application*

deadline: For fall admission, 12/1 for domestic and international students. Application fee: $50. Electronic applications accepted. *Expenses:* Contact institution. *Financial support:* In 2017–18, 29 students received support, including 29 research assistantships with tuition reimbursements available (averaging $8,736 per year); teaching assistantships, career-related internships or fieldwork, scholarships/grants, and tuition waivers (full and partial) also available. *Faculty research:* Therapy processes and outcomes, family relationships across the life cycle, adjustment to medical illnesses, health family processes. *Unit head:* Jonathan Sandberg, Program Director, 801-422-6512, Fax: 801-422-0163, E-mail: jonathan_sandberg@byu.edu. *Application contact:* Dr. Lauren A. Barnes, Director of Clinical Training, 801-422-3889, Fax: 801-422-0163, E-mail: lauren_barnes@byu.edu.
Website: http://mft.byu.edu

California Lutheran University, Graduate Studies, Department of Psychology, Thousand Oaks, CA 91360-2787. Offers clinical psychology (MS, Psy D); marital and family therapy (MS). *Accreditation:* APA. *Program availability:* Part-time. *Faculty:* 10 full-time (6 women), 19 part-time/adjunct (15 women). *Students:* 155 full-time (122 women), 35 part-time (10 women); includes 72 minority (4 Black or African American, non-Hispanic/Latino; 3 American Indian or Alaska Native, non-Hispanic/Latino; 4 Asian, non-Hispanic/Latino; 57 Hispanic/Latino; 4 Two or more races, non-Hispanic/Latino), 6 international. Average age 30. 261 applicants, 46% accepted, 66 enrolled. In 2017, 37 master's, 7 doctorates awarded. *Degree requirements:* For master's, thesis or comprehensive exams; for doctorate, thesis/dissertation, internship. *Entrance requirements:* For master's, GRE General Test, interview, minimum GPA of 3.0; for doctorate, GRE General Test. *Application deadline:* For fall admission, 12/1 priority date for domestic and international students. Applications are processed on a rolling basis. Application fee: $50. Electronic applications accepted. *Expenses: Tuition:* Full-time $15,000. Full-time tuition and fees vary according to degree level and program. *Unit head:* Dr. Richard Holigrock, Dean, 805-493-3723. *Application contact:* 805-493-3325, Fax: 805-493-3861, E-mail: clugrad@callutheran.edu.

California State University, Chico, Office of Graduate Studies, College of Behavioral and Social Sciences, Department of Psychology, Program in Marriage and Family Therapy, Chico, CA 95929-0722. Offers MS. *Degree requirements:* For master's, oral exam and thesis or analytical review and written exam. *Entrance requirements:* For master's, GRE General Test or MAT, 3 letters of recommendation, statement of purpose. Additional exam requirements/recommendations for international students: Required—TOEFL (minimum score 550 paper-based; 80 iBT), IELTS (minimum score 6.5), PTE. Electronic applications accepted.

California State University, Dominguez Hills, College of Health, Human Services and Nursing, Program in Marital and Family Therapy, Carson, CA 90747-0001. Offers MS. *Program availability:* Part-time, evening/weekend. *Degree requirements:* For master's, comprehensive exam. *Entrance requirements:* For master's, minimum GPA of 3.0. Additional exam requirements/recommendations for international students: Required—TOEFL (minimum score 550 paper-based). Electronic applications accepted. *Faculty research:* Sociology of the family, clinical psychology theory, employee assistance programs, race and sport, secondary trauma.

California State University, East Bay, Office of Graduate Studies, College of Education and Allied Studies, Department of Educational Psychology, Hayward, CA 94542-3000. Offers counseling (MS), including marriage and family therapy; special education (MS), including mild-moderate disabilities, moderate-severe disabilities. *Program availability:* Part-time. *Faculty:* 8 full-time (5 women), 21 part-time/adjunct (16 women). *Students:* 129 full-time (112 women), 13 part-time (11 women); includes 70 minority (5 Black or African American, non-Hispanic/Latino; 22 Asian, non-Hispanic/Latino; 32 Hispanic/Latino; 11 Two or more races, non-Hispanic/Latino), 1 international. Average age 31. 206 applicants, 35% accepted, 62 enrolled. In 2017, 50 master's awarded. *Degree requirements:* For master's, comprehensive exam, project or thesis. *Entrance requirements:* For master's, GRE or MAT, interview; minimum GPA of 3.0 during previous 2 years of course work; 3 letters of recommendation; valid teaching credential; negative TB test. Additional exam requirements/recommendations for international students: Required—TOEFL (minimum score 550 paper-based). *Application deadline:* For fall admission, 6/1 for domestic and international students. Application fee: $55. Electronic applications accepted. *Financial support:* Fellowships, career-related internships or fieldwork, Federal Work-Study, institutionally sponsored loans, and scholarships/grants available. Support available to part-time students. Financial award application deadline: 3/2; financial award applicants required to submit FAFSA. *Faculty research:* Mental health, learning disabilities, therapy. *Unit head:* Dr. Jack Davis, Chair, 510-885-3052, E-mail: jack.davis@csueastbay.edu. *Application contact:* Prof. Greg Jennings, Graduate Advisor, 510-885-2296, Fax: 510-885-4642, E-mail: greg.jennings@csueastbay.edu.
Website: http://www20.csueastbay.edu/ceas/departments/epsy/

California State University, Fresno, Division of Research and Graduate Studies, Kremen School of Education and Human Development, Department of Counselor Education and Rehabilitation, Program in Marriage, Family and Child Counseling, Fresno, CA 93740-8027. Offers MS. *Accreditation:* ACA. *Program availability:* Part-time, evening/weekend. *Degree requirements:* For master's, thesis or alternative. *Entrance requirements:* For master's, GRE General Test, MAT, minimum GPA of 3.0. Additional exam requirements/recommendations for international students: Required—TOEFL. Electronic applications accepted. *Faculty research:* Child abuse prevention, early childhood education.

California State University, Long Beach, Graduate Studies, College of Education, Department of Advanced Studies in Education and Counseling, Long Beach, CA 90840. Offers counseling (MS), including marriage and family therapy, school counseling, student development in higher education; education (MA, Ed D); educational administration (MA, Ed D); educational psychology (MA); special education (MS). *Program availability:* Part-time, evening/weekend. *Entrance requirements:* For master's, GRE General Test, minimum GPA of 2.75. Electronic applications accepted.

California State University, Northridge, Graduate Studies, Michael D. Eisner College of Education, Department of Educational Psychology and Counseling, Northridge, CA 91330. Offers counseling (MS), including career counseling, college counseling and student services, marriage and family therapy, school counseling, school psychology; educational psychology (MA Ed), including development, learning, and instruction, early childhood education. *Accreditation:* ACA (one or more programs are accredited); NCATE. *Program availability:* Part-time, evening/weekend. *Students:* 288 full-time (244 women), 84 part-time (76 women); includes 190 minority (13 Black or African American, non-Hispanic/Latino; 24 Asian, non-Hispanic/Latino; 139 Hispanic/Latino; 14 Two or more races, non-Hispanic/Latino), 11 international. Average age 29. 427 applicants, 34% accepted, 136 enrolled. In 2017, 103 master's awarded. *Entrance requirements:* For master's, GRE General Test or minimum GPA of 3.0. Additional exam requirements/recommendations for international students: Required—TOEFL. *Application deadline:* For fall admission, 11/30 for domestic students. Application fee: $55. *Financial support:* Scholarships/grants available. Support available to part-time students. Financial award application deadline: 3/1. *Unit head:* Dr. Alberto Restori, Chair, 818-677-2599. *Application contact:* 818-677-3755.
Website: http://www.csun.edu/eisner-education/educational-psychology-counseling

Marriage and Family Therapy

Cambridge College, School of Psychology and Counseling, Boston, MA 02129. Offers addiction counseling (M Ed); alcohol and drug counseling (Certificate); counseling psychology (M Ed, CAGS); counseling psychology: forensic counseling (M Ed); marriage and family therapy (M Ed); mental health and addiction counseling (M Ed); mental health counseling (M Ed); mental health counseling for school guidance counselors (Post Master's Certificate); psychological studies (M Ed); school adjustment and mental health counseling (M Ed); school adjustment, mental health and addiction counseling (M Ed); school guidance counselor (M Ed); trauma studies (Certificate). *Program availability:* Part-time, evening/weekend. *Degree requirements:* For master's and other advanced degree, thesis, practicum/internship. *Entrance requirements:* For master's, resume, 2 professional references; for other advanced degree, official transcripts, documents for transfer credit evaluation, resume, written personal statement/essay, 2 professional references, health insurance, immunizations form. Additional exam requirements/recommendations for international students: Required— TOEFL (minimum score 550 paper-based; 79 iBT), Michigan English Language Assessment Battery (minimum score 85); Recommended—IELTS (minimum score 6). Electronic applications accepted. *Expenses:* Contact institution. *Faculty research:* Trauma, drug and alcohol counseling, cross-cultural issues, school counseling, trauma in schools.

Campbellsville University, School of Theology, Campbellsville, KY 42718-2799. Offers marriage and family therapy (MMFT); theology (M Th). *Program availability:* Part-time, evening/weekend, 100% online, blended/hybrid learning. *Faculty:* 14 full-time (3 women), 2 part-time/adjunct (0 women). *Students:* 7 full-time (6 women), 83 part-time (44 women); includes 32 minority (30 Black or African American, non-Hispanic/Latino; 2 Hispanic/Latino). Average age 43. 58 applicants, 64% accepted, 29 enrolled. In 2017, 32 master's awarded. *Degree requirements:* For master's, comprehensive exam, thesis optional. *Entrance requirements:* For master's, GRE General Test, minimum GPA of 3.0 in major, 2.75 overall; 18 hours of undergraduate coursework in Christian studies; college transcripts; letters of recommendation. Additional exam requirements/ recommendations for international students: Recommended—TOEFL (minimum score 550 paper-based; 79 iBT), IELTS (minimum score 6). *Application deadline:* Applications are processed on a rolling basis. Application fee: $25. Electronic applications accepted. Application fee is waived when completed online. *Expenses:* $299 per credit hour (Th M), $399 per credit hour (MMFT). *Financial support:* In 2017–18, 22 students received support. Unspecified assistantships and employee tuition waivers available. Financial award application deadline: 6/1; financial award applicants required to submit FAFSA. *Faculty research:* Clergy needing graduate theology education, trinity and Christian faith, Old Testament David narratives, leadership principles on Christian university integration of Christian principles in counseling process, church history; Women in Church History. *Unit head:* Dr. John E. Hurtgen, Dean, 270-789-5077, Fax: 270-789-5050, E-mail: jehurtgen@campbellsville.edu. *Application contact:* Monica Bamwine, Assistant Director of Graduate Admissions, 270-789-5221, Fax: 270-789-5071, E-mail: mkbamwine@campbellsville.edu.
Website: http://www.campbellsville.edu/

Capella University, Harold Abel School of Social and Behavioral Science, Master's Programs in Counseling, Minneapolis, MN 55402. Offers child and adolescent development (MS); general addiction counseling (MS); general marriage and family counseling/therapy (MS); general mental health counseling (MS); general school counseling (MS).

Carlos Albizu University, Miami Campus, Graduate Programs, Miami, FL 33172-2209. Offers clinical psychology (PhD, Psy D); entrepreneurship (MBA); exceptional student education (MS); human services (PhD); industrial/organizational psychology (MS); marriage and family therapy (MS); mental health counseling (MS); nonprofit management (MBA); organizational management (MBA); psychology (MS); speech and language pathology (MS); teaching English for speakers of other languages (MS). *Accreditation:* APA. *Program availability:* Part-time, evening/weekend, 100% online, blended/hybrid learning. *Faculty:* 32 full-time (24 women), 27 part-time/adjunct (15 women). *Students:* 411 full-time (345 women), 248 part-time (215 women); includes 562 minority (53 Black or African American, non-Hispanic/Latino; 4 Asian, non-Hispanic/ Latino; 498 Hispanic/Latino; 7 Two or more races, non-Hispanic/Latino), 23 international. Average age 34. 391 applicants, 42% accepted, 154 enrolled. In 2017, 96 master's, 54 doctorates awarded. Terminal master's awarded for partial completion of doctoral program. *Degree requirements:* For master's, comprehensive exam (for some programs), integrative project (for MBA); research project (for exceptional student education, teaching English as a second language); for doctorate, comprehensive examinations, internship, project/dissertation. *Entrance requirements:* For master's, GRE/EXADEP, bachelor's degree from accredited institution, minimum GPA of 3.0, 3 letters of recommendation, interview, resume, statement of purpose, official transcripts; for doctorate, GRE (for Psy D), 3 letters of recommendation, resume, interview, statement of purpose, official transcripts; bachelor's degree and minimum GPA of 3.25 (for Psy D); master's degree and minimum GPA of 3.0 (for PhD). Additional exam requirements/recommendations for international students: Required—Michigan Test of English Language Proficiency. *Application deadline:* For fall admission, 4/1 priority date for domestic students, 5/1 priority date for international students; for spring admission, 11/1 priority date for domestic students, 9/1 priority date for international students. Applications are processed on a rolling basis. Application fee: $50. Electronic applications accepted. Application fee is waived when completed online. *Expenses:* Contact institution. *Financial support:* In 2017–18, 145 students received support. Federal Work-Study, scholarships/grants, unspecified assistantships, and tuition discounts available. Financial award application deadline: 6/1; financial award applicants required to submit FAFSA. *Faculty research:* Psychotherapy, forensic psychology, neuropsychology, special education, speech-language pathology, criminal justice. *Unit head:* Dr. Etiony Aldarondo, Provost, 305-593-1223 Ext. 3138, Fax: 305-592-7930, E-mail: ealdarondo@albizu.edu. *Application contact:* Sonia Feliciano, Institutional Director of Student Recruitment, 305-593-1223 Ext. 3108, Fax: 305-477-8983, E-mail: sfeliciano@albizu.edu.

Central Connecticut State University, School of Graduate Studies, School of Education and Professional Studies, Department of Counselor Education and Family Therapy, New Britain, CT 06050-4010. Offers marriage and family therapy (MS); professional counseling (MS, AC, Certificate); school counseling (MS); student development in higher education (MS). *Accreditation:* AAMFT/COAMFTE; ACA. *Program availability:* Part-time, evening/weekend. *Faculty:* 9 full-time (6 women), 27 part-time/adjunct (23 women). *Students:* 184 full-time (141 women), 189 part-time (144 women); includes 131 minority (51 Black or African American, non-Hispanic/Latino; 3 Asian, non-Hispanic/Latino; 66 Hispanic/Latino; 11 Two or more races, non-Hispanic/ Latino), 1 international. Average age 34. 217 applicants, 64% accepted, 105 enrolled. In 2017, 94 master's, 7 other advanced degrees awarded. *Degree requirements:* For master's, comprehensive exam, thesis or alternative; for other advanced degree, qualifying exam. *Entrance requirements:* For master's, minimum undergraduate GPA of 2.7, essay, interview, letters of recommendation. Additional exam requirements/ recommendations for international students: Required—TOEFL (minimum score 550 paper-based; 79 iBT); Recommended—IELTS (minimum score 6.5). *Application deadline:* For fall admission, 3/1 for domestic and international students; for summer

admission, 3/1 for domestic and international students. Applications are processed on a rolling basis. Application fee: $50. Electronic applications accepted. *Expenses: Tuition, area resident:* Full-time $6757. Tuition, state resident: full-time $9750; part-time $374 per credit. Tuition, nonresident: full-time $18,102; part-time $374 per credit. *Required fees:* $4635; $255 per credit. *Financial support:* In 2017–18, 77 students received support. Career-related internships or fieldwork, Federal Work-Study, scholarships/ grants, and unspecified assistantships available. Support available to part-time students. Financial award application deadline: 3/1; financial award applicants required to submit FAFSA. *Faculty research:* Elementary and secondary school counseling, marriage and family therapy, rehabilitation counseling, counseling in higher educational settings. *Unit head:* Dr. Cherie King, Chair, 860-832-2154, E-mail: kingche@ccsu.edu. *Application contact:* Patricia Gardner, Associate Director of Graduate Studies, 860-832-2350, Fax: 860-832-2362.
Website: http://www.ccsu.edu/ceft/

Chaminade University of Honolulu, Office of Professional and Continuing Education, Program in Counseling Psychology, Honolulu, HI 96816-1578. Offers marriage and family counseling (MSCP); mental health counseling (MSCP); school counseling (MSCP). *Program availability:* Part-time, evening/weekend, blended/hybrid learning. *Faculty:* 6 full-time (3 women), 16 part-time/adjunct (7 women). *Students:* 158 full-time (118 women), 34 part-time (26 women); includes 131 minority (13 Black or African American, non-Hispanic/Latino; 2 American Indian or Alaska Native, non-Hispanic/ Latino; 61 Asian, non-Hispanic/Latino; 14 Hispanic/Latino; 39 Native Hawaiian or other Pacific Islander, non-Hispanic/Latino; 2 Two or more races, non-Hispanic/Latino), 3 international. Average age 31. 53 applicants, 96% accepted, 37 enrolled. In 2017, 78 master's awarded. *Degree requirements:* For master's, comprehensive exam, internship/practicum. *Entrance requirements:* For master's, minimum undergraduate GPA of 3.0, 3 letters of recommendation, resume. Additional exam requirements/ recommendations for international students: Required—TOEFL (minimum score 550 paper-based; 79 iBT). *Application deadline:* Applications are processed on a rolling basis. Application fee: $40. Electronic applications accepted. *Expenses:* $860 per credit hour plus $93 fee per online course. *Financial support:* Applicants required to submit FAFSA. *Unit head:* Dr. Robert G. Santee, Dean, 808-735-4751, Fax: 808-739-4670, E-mail: mscp@chaminade.edu. *Application contact:* 808-735-4755, E-mail: gradserv@chaminade.edu.
Website: https://pace.chaminade.edu/graduate-programs/mscp-program/

Chapman University, Crean College of Health and Behavioral Sciences, Marriage and Family Therapy Program, Orange, CA 92866. Offers MA. *Accreditation:* AAMFT/ COAMFTE. *Program availability:* Part-time, evening/weekend. *Faculty:* 2 full-time (1 woman), 3 part-time/adjunct (2 women). *Students:* 34 full-time (31 women), 31 part-time (25 women); includes 26 minority (1 Black or African American, non-Hispanic/Latino; 5 Asian, non-Hispanic/Latino; 18 Hispanic/Latino; 2 Two or more races, non-Hispanic/ Latino), 3 international. Average age 27. 99 applicants, 37% accepted, 18 enrolled. In 2017, 25 master's awarded. *Degree requirements:* For master's, comprehensive exam, thesis optional. *Entrance requirements:* For master's, GRE (if undergraduate GPA less than 3.3). *Application deadline:* For fall admission, 2/1 priority date for domestic students. Applications are processed on a rolling basis. Application fee: $60. Electronic applications accepted. *Expenses:* Contact institution. *Financial support:* Fellowships, Federal Work-Study, and scholarships/grants available. Financial award applicants required to submit FAFSA. *Unit head:* Dr. Naveen Jonathan, Director, 714-997-6932, E-mail: jonathan@chapman.edu. *Application contact:* Melissa Liberman, Graduate Admission Counselor, 714-628-2847, E-mail: liberman@chapman.edu.

Chatham University, Program in Counseling Psychology, Pittsburgh, PA 15232-2826. Offers child, adolescent and family (MSCP); counseling psychology (Psy D); health and holistic (MSCP); organization and supervision (MSCP); sport and exercise (MSCP). *Accreditation:* APA. *Program availability:* Part-time, evening/weekend. *Faculty:* 11 full-time (10 women). *Students:* 61 full-time (46 women), 25 part-time (22 women); includes 12 minority (9 Black or African American, non-Hispanic/Latino; 2 Hispanic/Latino; 1 Two or more races, non-Hispanic/Latino), 3 international. Average age 30. 124 applicants, 62% accepted, 45 enrolled. In 2017, 38 master's awarded. *Degree requirements:* For master's, thesis optional, supervised internship; for doctorate, thesis/dissertation, internship. *Entrance requirements:* For master's, minimum GPA of 3.0; 2 letters of recommendation; resume; prerequisite coursework in statistics, biology, and psychology; for doctorate, GRE. Additional exam requirements/recommendations for international students: Required—TOEFL (minimum score 600 paper-based; 100 iBT), IELTS (minimum score 7), TWE. *Application deadline:* For fall admission, 4/1 priority date for domestic and international students; for spring admission, 11/1 for domestic students, 10/1 for international students. Applications are processed on a rolling basis. Application fee: $45. Electronic applications accepted. Application fee is waived when completed online. *Expenses: Tuition:* Full-time $16,740; part-time $930 per credit. *Required fees:* $486; $27 per credit. $243 per semester. *Financial support:* Career-related internships or fieldwork available. Financial award applicants required to submit FAFSA. *Faculty research:* Trauma and recovery, hypnosis, psychospiritual dimensions of healing, psychotherapy of schizophrenia. *Unit head:* Dr. Mary Beth Mannarino, Director, 412-365-1196, Fax: 412-365-1505, E-mail: mmannarino@chatham.edu. *Application contact:* Katie Noel, Assistant Director of Graduate Admission, 412-365-2758, Fax: 412-365-1609, E-mail: gradadmissions@chatham.edu.
Website: http://www.chatham.edu/mscp

Chestnut Hill College, School of Graduate Studies, Division of Psychology, Program in Clinical and Counseling Psychology, Philadelphia, PA 19118-2693. Offers clinical and counseling psychology (MS, CAS), including child and adolescent therapy, child and adolescent therapy with autism spectrum disorders, co-occurring disorders, couple and family therapy, diverse and underserved communities, generalist (MS), trauma studies. *Program availability:* Part-time, evening/weekend. *Degree requirements:* For master's, thesis optional, practica. *Entrance requirements:* For master's, GRE General Test, writing sample, letters of recommendation. Additional exam requirements/ recommendations for international students: Required—TOEFL (minimum score 500 paper-based), IELTS (minimum score 6.0), or TWE (minimum score 22). Electronic applications accepted. *Expenses:* Contact institution. *Faculty research:* Play therapy, eating disorders, addictions, group psychology and group therapy, health psychology.

Chestnut Hill College, School of Graduate Studies, Division of Psychology, Program in Clinical Psychology, Philadelphia, PA 19118-2693. Offers clinical psychology (Psy D), including clinical psychology, couple and family therapy, psychological assessment. *Accreditation:* APA. *Program availability:* Part-time, evening/weekend. *Degree requirements:* For doctorate, comprehensive exam, thesis/dissertation, internship, practica, clinical competency exam. *Entrance requirements:* For doctorate, GRE General Test, letters of recommendation, writing sample, master's degree in clinical/ counseling psychology or closely-related field. Additional exam requirements/ recommendations for international students: Required—TOEFL (minimum score 500 paper-based), IELTS (minimum score 6.0), or TWE (minimum score 22). Electronic applications accepted. *Expenses:* Contact institution. *Faculty research:* Psychological testing and assessment, LGBT issues, autism and developmental disorders, stepfamilies, gender issues.

The Chicago School of Professional Psychology at Downtown Los Angeles, Program in Clinical Psychology, Los Angeles, CA 90017. Offers applied behavior analysis (MA); clinical psychology (Psy D); marital and family therapy (MA).

The Chicago School of Professional Psychology at Irvine, Program in Marital and Family Therapy, Irvine, CA 92612. Offers clinical psychology (MA), including marital and family therapy; management practice (Psy D); psychodynamic psychotherapy (Psy D).

Christian Theological Seminary, Graduate and Professional Programs, Indianapolis, IN 46208-3301. Offers educational and arts ministries (MA); marriage and family therapy (MA); pastoral care and counseling (D Min); psychotherapy and faith (MA); theological studies (MTS); theology (M Div). *Accreditation:* AAMFT/COAMFTE (one or more programs are accredited); ACIPE; ATS. *Program availability:* Part-time. Terminal master's awarded for partial completion of doctoral program. *Degree requirements:* For master's, comprehensive exam (for some programs), thesis (for some programs), missionary and cross-cultural experience (for M Div); for doctorate, comprehensive exam, thesis/dissertation. *Entrance requirements:* For doctorate, M Div. Additional exam requirements/recommendations for international students: Recommended—TOEFL. Electronic applications accepted. *Faculty research:* Faith formation, peer learning post graduation.

The College of New Jersey, Office of Graduate and Advancing Education, School of Education, Department of Counselor Education, Program in Marriage and Family Therapy, Ewing, NJ 08628. Offers Ed S. *Program availability:* Part-time. *Entrance requirements:* For degree, previous master's degree or higher. Additional exam requirements/recommendations for international students: Required—TOEFL.

The College of New Rochelle, Graduate School, Division of Human Services, Program in Marriage and Family Therapy, New Rochelle, NY 10805-2308. Offers MMFT. *Degree requirements:* For master's, practica. *Entrance requirements:* For master's, minimum GPA of 3.0 in baccalaureate or other graduate-level work (overall and major field); undergraduate major in psychology, social work, or related field; personal statement; two letters of recommendation; official transcripts from all colleges/universities attended; proof of immunizations. *Expenses:* Tuition: Full-time $17,406. *Required fees:* $1120.

The College of William and Mary, School of Education, Program in Counselor Education, Williamsburg, VA 23187-8795. Offers addictions counseling (M Ed); community counseling (M Ed); counselor education (PhD); family counseling (M Ed); school counseling (M Ed). *Accreditation:* ACA; NCATE. *Program availability:* Part-time, evening/weekend, 100% online with required residency. *Faculty:* 12 full-time (4 women), 6 part-time/adjunct (5 women). *Students:* 64 full-time (50 women), 3 part-time (2 women); includes 14 minority (1 Black or African American, non-Hispanic/Latino; 2 Asian, non-Hispanic/Latino; 6 Hispanic/Latino; 5 Two or more races, non-Hispanic/Latino), 2 international. Average age 28. 163 applicants, 43% accepted, 32 enrolled. In 2017, 33 master's, 8 doctorates awarded. *Degree requirements:* For doctorate, comprehensive exam, thesis/dissertation. *Entrance requirements:* For master's, GRE, minimum GPA of 3.0; for doctorate, GRE, minimum GPA of 3.5. Additional exam requirements/recommendations for international students: Required—TOEFL (minimum score 100 iBT), IELTS (minimum score 7). *Application deadline:* For fall admission, 1/15 for domestic and international students. Application fee: $50. Electronic applications accepted. *Expenses:* $9,630 resident full-time, $535 resident part-time per credit hour; $25,920 nonresident full-time, $1,265 nonresident part-time per credit hour; $5,944 full-time fees. *Financial support:* In 2017–18, 34 students received support, including 26 research assistantships (averaging $18,723 per year); scholarships/grants also available. Financial award application deadline: 1/15; financial award applicants required to submit FAFSA. *Faculty research:* Sexuality, multicultural education, addiction counseling, transpersonal psychology, measurement and evaluation in counseling. *Unit head:* Dr. Charles F. Gressard, Department Chair, 757-221-2352, E-mail: cfgres@wm.edu. *Application contact:* Dorothy Smith Osborne, Assistant Dean for Academic Programs and Student Services, 757-221-2317, E-mail: dsosbo@wm.edu. Website: http://education.wm.edu

Colorado State University, College of Health and Human Sciences, Department of Human Development and Family Studies, Fort Collins, CO 80523-1570. Offers applied developmental science (PhD); family and developmental studies (MS); marriage and family therapy (MS). *Accreditation:* AAMFT/COAMFTE. *Faculty:* 18 full-time (15 women), 3 part-time/adjunct (1 woman). *Students:* 31 full-time (28 women), 3 part-time (all women); includes 6 minority (2 Asian, non-Hispanic/Latino; 4 Hispanic/Latino), 1 international. Average age 27. 95 applicants, 26% accepted, 14 enrolled. In 2017, 13 master's, 3 doctorates awarded. Terminal master's awarded for partial completion of doctoral program. *Degree requirements:* For master's, thesis; for doctorate, comprehensive exam, thesis/dissertation. *Entrance requirements:* For master's and doctorate, GRE General Test, 3 letters of recommendation; minimum GPA of 3.0; bachelor's degree; curriculum vitae/resume. Additional exam requirements/recommendations for international students: Required—TOEFL (minimum score 550 paper-based; 80 iBT), IELTS (minimum score 6.5), PTE (minimum score 58). *Application deadline:* For fall admission, 1/2 priority date for domestic and international students. Application fee: $60 ($70 for international students). Electronic applications accepted. *Expenses:* Tuition, state resident: full-time $9917. Tuition, nonresident: full-time $24,312. *Required fees:* $2284. Tuition and fees vary according to course load and program. *Financial support:* In 2017–18, 2 fellowships with full and partial tuition reimbursements (averaging $7,128 per year), 10 research assistantships with full and partial tuition reimbursements (averaging $12,830 per year), 17 teaching assistantships with full and partial tuition reimbursements (averaging $9,224 per year) were awarded; Federal Work-Study, scholarships/grants, health care benefits, and unspecified assistantships also available. *Faculty research:* Risk, resilience, and developmental psychopathology; treatment, intervention, and prevention science; emotion, regulation, and relational processes; adult development and aging; cultural context and diversity. *Total annual research expenditures:* $1.7 million. *Unit head:* Dr. Lise Youngblade, Department Head, 970-491-3581, Fax: 970-491-7975, E-mail: lise.youngblade@colostate.edu. *Application contact:* Mary Daughtrey, Administrative Assistant III, 970-491-2872, Fax: 970-491-7975, E-mail: mary.daughtrey@colostate.edu. Website: http://www.hdfs.chhs.colostate.edu/

Converse College, Program in Marriage and Family Therapy, Spartanburg, SC 29302. Offers MMFT. *Accreditation:* AAMFT/COAMFTE. *Unit head:* Lienne Medford, Dean of Graduate Studies and Distance Education, 864-596-9082, E-mail: lienne.medford@converse.edu. *Application contact:* 864-596-9404, E-mail: graduate@converse.edu.

Denver Seminary, Graduate and Professional Programs, Littleton, CO 80120. Offers apologetics (Certificate); biblical studies (MA); Christian formation and soul care (MA, Certificate); Christian studies (MA, Certificate); church and parachurch leadership (D Min); counseling licensure (MA); counseling ministry (MA); intercultural ministry (Certificate); leadership (MA, Certificate); marriage and family counseling (D Min); pastoral ministry (D Min); philosophy of religion (MA); spiritual guidance (Certificate); theology (M Div, Certificate); worship (Certificate); youth and family ministry (MA). *Accreditation:* ACA; ACIPE; ATS (one or more programs are accredited). *Program availability:* Part-time, evening/weekend, online learning. *Degree requirements:* For

master's, 2 foreign languages, thesis (for some programs); for doctorate, 2 foreign languages, thesis/dissertation. *Entrance requirements:* For doctorate, M Div, 3 years of ministry experience. Additional exam requirements/recommendations for international students: Required—TOEFL (minimum score 575 paper-based; 90 iBT). Electronic applications accepted.

Dominican University of California, School of Health and Natural Sciences, Counseling Psychology Department, San Rafael, CA 94901-2298. Offers general (MS); marriage and family therapy (MS). *Program availability:* Part-time, evening/weekend. *Faculty:* 4 full-time (2 women), 7 part-time/adjunct (5 women). *Students:* 48 full-time (40 women), 28 part-time (25 women); includes 21 minority (2 Black or African American, non-Hispanic/Latino; 1 Asian, non-Hispanic/Latino; 14 Hispanic/Latino; 1 Native Hawaiian or other Pacific Islander, non-Hispanic/Latino; 3 Two or more races, non-Hispanic/Latino), 1 international. Average age 38. 28 applicants, 100% accepted, 17 enrolled. In 2017, 12 master's awarded. *Degree requirements:* For master's, comprehensive exam (for some programs), thesis (for some programs). *Entrance requirements:* For master's, minimum GPA of 3.0 for last 60 units, autobiography, response to scenario. Additional exam requirements/recommendations for international students: Required—TOEFL (minimum score 550 paper-based; 80 iBT), IELTS (minimum score 6.5). *Application deadline:* For fall admission, 4/1 priority date for domestic and international students; for spring admission, 11/15 priority date for domestic and international students. Applications are processed on a rolling basis. Application fee: $0. Electronic applications accepted. *Expenses:* $1,100 per unit. *Financial support:* In 2017–18, 15 students received support. Career-related internships or fieldwork, scholarships/grants, and health care benefits available. Support available to part-time students. Financial award application deadline: 3/2; financial award applicants required to submit FAFSA. *Unit head:* Dr. Robin R. Gayle, Chair, 415-485-3263. *Application contact:* Michael Lavigna, Assistant Director, Graduate Admissions, 415-485-3253, Fax: 415-485-3214, E-mail: gradmissions@dominican.edu. Website: https://www.dominican.edu/academics/hns2/counpsych

Drexel University, College of Nursing and Health Professions, Department of Couple and Family Therapy, Philadelphia, PA 19104-2875. Offers MFT, PhD. *Accreditation:* AAMFT/COAMFTE (one or more programs are accredited). *Program availability:* Part-time. Terminal master's awarded for partial completion of doctoral program. *Degree requirements:* For master's, comprehensive exam, thesis; for doctorate, thesis/dissertation, qualifying exam. *Entrance requirements:* For master's, GRE General Test or MAT, minimum GPA of 2.75; for doctorate, GRE General Test, minimum GPA of 3.0. Electronic applications accepted. *Faculty research:* Family assessment, gender issues, chronic illness, early intervention.

Duquesne University, School of Education, Department of Counseling, Psychology, and Special Education, Program in Counselor Education, Pittsburgh, PA 15282-0001. Offers clinical mental health counseling (MS Ed, Post-Master's Certificate); counselor education and supervision (Ed D); counselor licensure (Post-Master's Certificate); marriage and family counseling (MS Ed); school counseling (MS Ed). *Accreditation:* ACA (one or more programs are accredited). *Program availability:* Part-time, evening/weekend. *Faculty:* 8 full-time (3 women). *Students:* 194 full-time (140 women), 10 part-time (6 women); includes 41 minority (21 Black or African American, non-Hispanic/Latino; 1 American Indian or Alaska Native, non-Hispanic/Latino; 5 Asian, non-Hispanic/Latino; 6 Hispanic/Latino; 8 Two or more races, non-Hispanic/Latino), 8 international. Average age 28. 149 applicants, 78% accepted, 66 enrolled. In 2017, 53 master's, 6 doctorates awarded. *Degree requirements:* For master's, thesis optional; for doctorate, thesis/dissertation. *Entrance requirements:* For master's, letters of recommendation, essay, interview, bachelor's degree; for doctorate, GRE, letters of recommendation, essay, interview, master's degree; for Post-Master's Certificate, GRE, letters of recommendation, essay, interview, bachelor's/master's degree. Additional exam requirements/recommendations for international students: Required—TOEFL (minimum score 550 paper-based), IELTS (minimum score 6.5). *Application deadline:* For fall admission, 4/2 for domestic students; for spring admission, 9/1 for domestic students. Applications are processed on a rolling basis. Application fee: $0. Electronic applications accepted. *Expenses:* $1,259 per credit. *Financial support:* Research assistantships, teaching assistantships, and Federal Work-Study available. Support available to part-time students. *Faculty research:* Trauma counseling, counseling supervision, purpose and meaning, Internet addictions, bullying and relational aggression. *Unit head:* Dr. Jered Kolbert, Professor/Director, 412-396-4471, Fax: 412-396-1340, E-mail: kolbertj@duq.edu. *Application contact:* Kelly McGinley, Graduate Admissions Assistant, 412-396-1559, Fax: 412-396-5585, E-mail: mcginleyk@duq.edu.

East Carolina University, Graduate School, College of Health and Human Performance, Department of Human Development and Family Science, Greenville, NC 27858-4353. Offers birth through kindergarten education (MA Ed); human development and family science (MS); marriage and family therapy (MS); medical family therapy (PhD). *Accreditation:* AAMFT/COAMFTE. *Program availability:* Part-time. *Students:* 73 full-time (69 women), 24 part-time (21 women); includes 20 minority (14 Black or African American, non-Hispanic/Latino; 3 American Indian or Alaska Native, non-Hispanic/Latino; 2 Hispanic/Latino; 1 Native Hawaiian or other Pacific Islander, non-Hispanic/Latino), 2 international. Average age 28. 98 applicants, 50% accepted, 35 enrolled. In 2017, 26 master's, 3 doctorates awarded. *Degree requirements:* For master's, comprehensive exam, thesis optional. *Entrance requirements:* Additional exam requirements/recommendations for international students: Recommended—TOEFL (minimum score 78 iBT), IELTS (minimum score 6.5). *Application deadline:* For fall admission, 1/15 for domestic students; for spring admission, 10/15 for domestic students. Applications are processed on a rolling basis. Application fee: $75. *Expenses:* Tuition, state resident: full-time $4749; part-time $297 per credit hour. Tuition, nonresident: full-time $17,898; part-time $1119 per credit hour. *Required fees:* $2691; $224 per credit hour. Part-time tuition and fees vary according to course load and program. *Financial support:* Research assistantships, teaching assistantships, career-related internships or fieldwork, Federal Work-Study, institutionally sponsored loans, and scholarships/grants available. Support available to part-time students. Financial award application deadline: 6/1. *Faculty research:* Child care quality, mental health delivery systems for children, family violence. *Unit head:* Dr. Sharon Ballard, Interim Chair, 252-328-1356, E-mail: ballards@ecu.edu. Website: https://hhp.ecu.edu/hdfs/

Eastern Nazarene College, Adult and Graduate Studies, Program in Marriage and Family Therapy, Quincy, MA 02170. Offers MS. *Program availability:* Part-time, evening/weekend. *Entrance requirements:* For master's, 3 letters of recommendation, resume. Additional exam requirements/recommendations for international students: Required—TOEFL (minimum score 550 paper-based).

Eastern University, Department of Marriage and Family Therapy, St. Davids, PA 19087-3696. Offers marriage and family therapy (PhD); marriage and family therapy studies (DA). *Program availability:* Evening/weekend, online learning. *Students:* 63 full-time (45 women); includes 42 minority (33 Black or African American, non-Hispanic/Latino; 2 Asian, non-Hispanic/Latino; 5 Hispanic/Latino; 2 Two or more races, non-Hispanic/Latino), 1 international. Average age 43. In 2017, 7 doctorates awarded. *Application deadline:* Applications are processed on a rolling basis. Application fee: $75. Electronic applications accepted. Application fee is waived when completed online.

Expenses: Contact institution. *Unit head:* Michael Dziedziak, Executive Director of Enrollment, 800-452-0996, E-mail: gpsadmissions@eastern.edu.
Website: https://www.eastern.edu/academics/programs/department-marriage-and-family-therapy

East Tennessee State University, School of Graduate Studies, College of Education, Department of Counseling and Human Services, Johnson City, TN 37614. Offers clinical mental health counseling (MA); college counseling/student affairs higher education (MA); couples and family therapy (MA); human services (MS); school counseling (MA). *Accreditation:* ACA; NCATE. *Program availability:* Part-time. *Degree requirements:* For master's, comprehensive exam, thesis optional, internship, student teaching, culminating experience. *Entrance requirements:* For master's, GRE General Test, minimum GPA of 3.0, three letters of recommendation, interview, 2-3 page essay detailing experiences that have shaped pursuit of degree, resume. Additional exam requirements/recommendations for international students: Required—TOEFL (minimum score 550 paper-based; 79 iBT). *Application deadline:* For fall admission, 1/31 priority date for domestic and international students. Application fee: $55 ($65 for international students). Electronic applications accepted. *Financial support:* Research assistantships with full tuition reimbursements, teaching assistantships with full tuition reimbursements, career-related internships or fieldwork, institutionally sponsored loans, scholarships/grants, traineeships, and unspecified assistantships available. Financial award application deadline: 7/1; financial award applicants required to submit FAFSA. *Faculty research:* Intervention and assistance with at-risk and under-served youth and high conflict families; service and social justice; women and girls' issues in counseling; counseling competence with LGBTQ individuals; counselor education and supervision. *Unit head:* Dr. Janna Scarborough, Chair, 423-439-4191, Fax: 423-439-7790, E-mail: scarboro@etsu.edu. *Application contact:* Dr. Janna Scarborough, Chair, 423-439-4191, Fax: 423-439-7790, E-mail: scarboro@etsu.edu.
Website: http://www.etsu.edu/coe/chs/

Evangelical Seminary, Graduate and Professional Programs, Myerstown, PA 17067-1212. Offers Biblical studies (MAR); congregational ministry (M Div); global and contextual studies (M Div, MAR); historical and theological studies (MAR); interdisciplinary studies (MAR); marriage and family counseling (M Div); marriage and family therapy (MA); New Testament (MAR); Old Testament (MAR); spiritual formation (MAR); teaching ministry (M Div); youth ministry (M Div). *Accreditation:* ATS (one or more programs are accredited). *Program availability:* Part-time, online learning. *Degree requirements:* For master's, 2 foreign languages. *Entrance requirements:* For master's, minimum GPA of 2.5. Additional exam requirements/recommendations for international students: Required—TOEFL (minimum score 550 paper-based). *Faculty research:* Literary form and structure within the Hebrew and Greek scriptures, Wesley studies, esoteric biblical languages, the Mosaic law and the Christian, ethics.

Fairfield University, Graduate School of Education and Allied Professions, Fairfield, CT 06824. Offers applied behavior analysis (ATC); applied psychology (MA); clinical mental health counseling (MA, CAS); educational technology (MA); elementary education (MA, CAS); family studies (MA); integration of spirituality and religion in counseling (ATC); marriage and family therapy (MA); reading and language development (Sixth Year Certificate); school counseling (MA, CAS); school psychology (MA, CAS); school-based marriage and family therapy (ATC); secondary education (MA); special education (MA, CAS); substance abuse counseling (ATC); teaching (Certificate); teaching and foundations (MA, CAS); TESOL, world languages, and bilingual education (MA, CAS). *Accreditation:* NCATE. *Program availability:* Part-time, evening/weekend. *Faculty:* 23 full-time (17 women), 39 part-time/adjunct (28 women). *Students:* 199 full-time (168 women), 251 part-time (206 women); includes 85 minority (21 Black or African American, non-Hispanic/Latino; 9 Asian, non-Hispanic/Latino; 49 Hispanic/Latino; 6 Two or more races, non-Hispanic/Latino), 4 international. Average age 32. 370 applicants, 56% accepted, 125 enrolled. In 2017, 136 master's, 28 other advanced degrees awarded. *Degree requirements:* For master's, comprehensive exam. *Entrance requirements:* For master's, minimum GPA of 3.0, 2 recommendations, resume. Additional exam requirements/recommendations for international students: Required—TOEFL (minimum score 550 paper-based; 84 iBT) or IELTS (minimum score 7.5). *Application deadline:* For fall admission, 2/15 for international students; for spring admission, 10/1 for international students. Application fee: $60. Electronic applications accepted. *Expenses:* $750 per credit hour. *Financial support:* In 2017–18, 34 students received support. Career-related internships or fieldwork and unspecified assistantships available. Support available to part-time students. Financial award applicants required to submit FAFSA. *Faculty research:* Reading and literacy, writing, social justice and inequality in education, addictions and mental health issues, therapeutic relationships and clinical supervision. *Unit head:* Dr. Robert D. Hannafin, Dean, 203-254-4250, Fax: 203-254-4241, E-mail: rhannafin@fairfield.edu. *Application contact:* Marianne Gumpper, Director of Graduate Admission, 203-254-4184, Fax: 203-254-4073, E-mail: gradadmis@fairfield.edu.
Website: http://www.fairfield.edu/gseap

Fielding Graduate University, Graduate Programs, School of Leadership Studies, Program in Couples/Marriage and Family Therapy, Santa Barbara, CA 93105-3814. Offers MA. *Entrance requirements:* For master's, bachelor's degree, minimum GPA of 3.0, resume, statement of purpose, 2 letters of recommendation, official transcripts, interview. *Application deadline:* For fall admission, 7/26 for domestic students. Tuition and fees vary according to course load, degree level and program. *Unit head:* Dr. Karen Westbrooks, Director. *Application contact:* Enrollment Coordinator, 800-340-1099 Ext. 4098, Fax: 805-687-9793, E-mail: hodadmission@fielding.edu.
Website: http://www.fielding.edu/our-programs/school-of-leadership-studies/ma-couples-marriage-and-family-therapy/

Florida State University, The Graduate School, College of Human Sciences, Department of Family and Child Sciences, Tallahassee, FL 32306-1491. Offers family and child sciences (MS); human development and family sciences (PhD); marriage and family therapy (PhD). *Accreditation:* AAMFT/COAMFTE. *Program availability:* Part-time. *Faculty:* 14 full-time (8 women). *Students:* 28 full-time (21 women); includes 9 minority (6 Black or African American, non-Hispanic/Latino; 1 Asian, non-Hispanic/Latino; 1 Hispanic/Latino; 1 Two or more races, non-Hispanic/Latino), 2 international. 21 applicants, 33% accepted, 5 enrolled. In 2017, 6 master's, 7 doctorates awarded. Terminal master's awarded for partial completion of doctoral program. *Degree requirements:* For master's, thesis optional; for doctorate, thesis/dissertation, preliminary examination; clinical examination (for marriage and family therapy). *Entrance requirements:* For master's and doctorate, GRE General Test, writing assessment, minimum GPA of 3.0. Additional exam requirements/recommendations for international students: Required—TOEFL (minimum score 550 paper-based; 80 iBT). *Application deadline:* For fall admission, 12/1 for domestic and international students. Applications are processed on a rolling basis. Application fee: $30. Electronic applications accepted. *Expenses:* $480 per credit hour in-state; $1,111 per credit hour out-of-state. *Financial support:* In 2017–18, 33 students received support, including 12 research assistantships with full tuition reimbursements available (averaging $6,062 per year), 32 teaching assistantships with full tuition reimbursements available (averaging $16,142 per year); fellowships with partial tuition reimbursements available, career-related internships or fieldwork, Federal Work-Study, institutionally sponsored loans, scholarships/grants, health care benefits, and unspecified assistantships also available. Financial award application deadline: 1/5; financial award applicants required to submit FAFSA. *Faculty research:* Family therapy, parent-child relations, distressed families and foster care, marital processes, relational interventions, family structural complexity. *Total annual research expenditures:* $1.3 million. *Unit head:* Dr. Joseph Grzywacz, Department Chair, 850-644-3217, Fax: 850-644-3439, E-mail: jgrzywacz@fsu.edu. *Application contact:* Mary-Sue McLemore, Academic Support Assistant, 850-644-1117, E-mail: mmclemore@fsu.edu.
Website: https://humansciences.fsu.edu/family-child-sciences/students/graduate-programs/

Fresno Pacific University, Biblical Seminary, Program in Marriage and Family Therapy, Fresno, CA 93702-4709. Offers MA. *Degree requirements:* For master's, thesis or alternative. *Entrance requirements:* For master's, minimum GPA of 3.0. Additional exam requirements/recommendations for international students: Required—TOEFL (minimum score 550 paper-based). *Expenses:* Contact institution.

Friends University, Graduate School, Wichita, KS 67213. Offers family therapy (MSFT); global business administration (MBA), including accounting, business law, change management, health care leadership, management information systems, supply chain management and logistics; health care leadership (MHCL); management information systems (MMIS); professional business administration (MBA), including accounting, business law, change management, health care leadership, management information systems, supply chain management and logistics. *Program availability:* Part-time, evening/weekend, online learning. *Degree requirements:* For master's, research project. *Entrance requirements:* For master's, bachelor's degree from accredited institution, official transcripts, interview with program director, letter(s) of recommendation. Additional exam requirements/recommendations for international students: Required—TOEFL (minimum score 560 paper-based). Electronic applications accepted.

Fuller Theological Seminary, Graduate Programs, Pasadena, CA 91182. Offers Christian leadership (MACL); clinical psychology (PhD, Psy D); family studies (MA); global leadership (MA); global ministries (D Min); global ministries (Korean language) (D Min); intercultural studies (MA, Th M, PhD); intercultural studies (Korean language) (MA); marital and family therapy (MS); marriage and family enrichment (Certificate); ministry (M Div, D Min); missiology (D Miss); missiology (Korean language) (Th M); theology (MA, Th M, PhD), including evangelism (MA), family life education (MA), pastoral ministry (MA), recovery ministry (MA), worship music ministry (MA), worship, theology, and the arts (MA), youth, family, and culture (MA); theology and ministry (MA).

Geneva College, Master of Arts in Counseling Program, Beaver Falls, PA 15010-3599. Offers clinical mental health counseling (MA); marriage and family counseling (MA); school counseling (MA). *Accreditation:* ACA. *Program availability:* Part-time, evening/weekend. *Faculty:* 6 full-time (3 women), 3 part-time/adjunct (1 woman). *Students:* 34 full-time (26 women), 20 part-time (16 women); includes 12 minority (11 Black or African American, non-Hispanic/Latino; 1 Hispanic/Latino), 1 international. Average age 33. In 2017, 34 master's awarded. *Degree requirements:* For master's, comprehensive exam, 60 credits including practicum and internship. *Entrance requirements:* For master's, minimum GPA of 3.0 (preferred), 3 letters of recommendation, essay on career goals, resume of educational and professional experiences. Additional exam requirements/recommendations for international students: Required—TOEFL. *Application deadline:* For fall admission, 9/1 for domestic students; for spring admission, 1/10 for domestic students. Applications are processed on a rolling basis. Electronic applications accepted. *Expenses:* $670 per credit. *Financial support:* Research assistantships, teaching assistantships, career-related internships or fieldwork, and unspecified assistantships available. Financial award application deadline: 8/1; financial award applicants required to submit FAFSA. *Faculty research:* Blended family counseling; premarital and newlywed couples; religion in clinical supervision; conceptual mapping in research, supervision, and clinical work. *Unit head:* Dr. Shannan Shiderly, Program Director, 724-847-6649, Fax: 724-847-6101, E-mail: slshider@geneva.edu. *Application contact:* Marina Frazier, Graduate Program Manager, 724-847-6697, E-mail: counseling@geneva.edu.
Website: http://www.geneva.edu/page/grad_counseling

George Fox University, College of Education, Graduate Department of Counseling, Newberg, OR 97132-2697. Offers clinical mental health counseling (MA); marriage, couple and family counseling (MA, Certificate); school counseling (MA, Certificate); school psychology (Ed S). *Program availability:* Part-time. *Degree requirements:* For master's, clinical project. *Entrance requirements:* For master's, MAT or GRE, bachelor's degree from regionally-accredited college or university, minimum cumulative GPA of 3.0, 1 professional and 1 academic reference, resume, on-campus interview, official transcripts. Additional exam requirements/recommendations for international students: Required—TOEFL (minimum score 577 paper-based; 90 iBT), IELTS (minimum score 7). Electronic applications accepted. *Expenses:* Contact institution.

Gonzaga University, School of Education, Spokane, WA 99258. Offers clinical mental health counseling (MA); educational leadership (M Ed, Ed D); elementary education (MIT); marriage and family counseling (MA); school counseling (MA); secondary education (MIT); special education (M Ed, MIT); sport and athletic administration (MA). *Accreditation:* NCATE. *Program availability:* Part-time, evening/weekend, 100% online, blended/hybrid learning. *Faculty:* 16 full-time (11 women), 31 part-time/adjunct (19 women). *Students:* 108 full-time (90 women), 225 part-time (140 women); includes 34 minority (4 Black or African American, non-Hispanic/Latino; 2 American Indian or Alaska Native, non-Hispanic/Latino; 5 Asian, non-Hispanic/Latino; 18 Hispanic/Latino; 5 Two or more races, non-Hispanic/Latino), 114 international. Average age 31. 367 applicants, 74% accepted, 160 enrolled. In 2017, 175 master's awarded. *Degree requirements:* For master's, comprehensive exam. *Entrance requirements:* For master's, GRE, MAT, and/or Washington Educator Skills Test-Basic (WEST-B), Washington Educator Skills Test-Endorsements (WEST-E), official transcripts from all colleges or universities attended, interview, two letters of recommendation, resume, essay, minimum GPA of 3.0. Additional exam requirements/recommendations for international students: Required—TOEFL (minimum score 580 paper-based, 88 iBT) or IELTS (minimum score 6.5). *Application deadline:* Applications are processed on a rolling basis. Application fee: $50. Electronic applications accepted. *Expenses:* $990 per credit. *Financial support:* In 2017–18, 51 students received support. Scholarships/grants and unspecified assistantships available. Support available to part-time students. Financial award applicants required to submit FAFSA. *Unit head:* Dr. Vincent Alfonso, Dean, 509-313-3594, Fax: 509-313-5821, E-mail: alfonso@gonzaga.edu. *Application contact:* Meg Martens, Graduate Admissions Program Specialist, 509-313-4314, E-mail: martens@gonzaga.edu.
Website: https://www.gonzaga.edu/school-of-education

Hampton University, School of Liberal Arts and Education, Program in Psychology, Hampton, VA 23668. Offers marriage and family studies (MS); psychology (MS). *Program availability:* Part-time. *Students:* 1 (woman) full-time, 6 part-time (5 women); all minorities (all Black or African American, non-Hispanic/Latino). Average age 24. 13 applicants, 8% accepted. *Degree requirements:* For master's, thesis. *Entrance requirements:* For master's, GRE. Additional exam requirements/recommendations for international students: Required—TOEFL (minimum score 525 paper-based) or IELTS

(6.5). *Application deadline:* For fall admission, 6/1 priority date for domestic students, 4/1 priority date for international students; for spring admission, 11/1 priority date for domestic students, 9/1 priority date for international students; for summer admission, 4/1 priority date for domestic and international students. Application fee: $35. Electronic applications accepted. *Expenses:* Contact institution. *Financial support:* Unspecified assistantships available. Financial award application deadline: 6/30; financial award applicants required to submit FAFSA. *Faculty research:* Marriage and family studies, violence prevention, racial identity and race relations, learning styles, psychosocial factors influencing health. *Unit head:* Dr. Tamara Williams, Interim Chairperson, 757-727-5301.

Hardin-Simmons University, Graduate School, Cynthia Ann Parker College of Liberal Arts, Department of Psychology, Abilene, TX 79698-0001. Offers clinical counseling and marriage and family therapy (MA). *Program availability:* Part-time. *Faculty:* 9 full-time (7 women). *Students:* 25 full-time (19 women), 2 part-time (both women); includes 3 minority (1 Black or African American, non-Hispanic/Latino; 1 Hispanic/Latino; 1 Two or more races, non-Hispanic/Latino), 1 international. Average age 31. 20 applicants, 85% accepted, 15 enrolled. In 2017, 11 master's awarded. *Degree requirements:* For master's, comprehensive exam, clinical experience, project. *Entrance requirements:* For master's, 21 semester hours of course work in psychology (18 in upper-division classes); minimum undergraduate GPA of 3.0 in major, 2.7 overall; writing sample; letters of recommendation. Additional exam requirements/recommendations for international students: Required—TOEFL (minimum score 550 paper-based; 79 iBT). *Application deadline:* For fall admission, 8/15 priority date for domestic students, 4/1 for international students; for spring admission, 1/5 priority date for domestic students, 9/1 for international students. Applications are processed on a rolling basis. Application fee: $50 ($150 for international students). Electronic applications accepted. *Expenses: Tuition:* Full-time $13,500; part-time $750 per semester hour. *Required fees:* $220 per term. One-time fee: $50. Tuition and fees vary according to course load, campus/location and program. *Financial support:* In 2017–18, 21 students received support, including 17 fellowships (averaging $1,047 per year); career-related internships or fieldwork and scholarships/grants also available. Support available to part-time students. Financial award application deadline: 6/30; financial award applicants required to submit FAFSA. *Faculty research:* Spirituality in marriage, intimacy and sexuality in marriage, sex education in the church, role of faith in marital satisfaction, family stress management. *Unit head:* Dr. Sherry Rosenblad, Program Director, 325-671-2271, Fax: 325-670-1458, E-mail: sherry.rosenblad@hsutx.edu. *Application contact:* Dr. Nancy Kucinski, Dean of Graduate Studies, 325-670-1298, Fax: 325-670-1564, E-mail: gradoff@hsutx.edu.
Website: http://www.hsutx.edu/academics/cap/psychology/

Hofstra University, School of Health Professions and Human Services, Programs in Counseling, Hempstead, NY 11549. Offers counseling (MS Ed, PD); creative arts therapy (MA); interdisciplinary transition specialist (Advanced Certificate); marriage and family therapy (MA); mental health counseling (MA, Advanced Certificate), including alcohol and substance abuse (Advanced Certificate); rehabilitation administration (PD); rehabilitation counseling (MS Ed, Advanced Certificate); rehabilitation counseling in mental health (MS Ed, Advanced Certificate). *Accreditation:* ACA. *Program availability:* Part-time, evening/weekend. *Students:* 103 full-time (87 women), 67 part-time (60 women); includes 50 minority (21 Black or African American, non-Hispanic/Latino; 11 Asian, non-Hispanic/Latino; 15 Hispanic/Latino; 1 Native Hawaiian or other Pacific Islander, non-Hispanic/Latino; 2 Two or more races, non-Hispanic/Latino), 6 international. Average age 30. 131 applicants, 79% accepted, 52 enrolled. In 2017, 66 master's, 4 other advanced degrees awarded. *Degree requirements:* For master's, comprehensive exam (for some programs), thesis (for some programs), internship, practicum, student teaching, seminars, minimum GPA of 3.0. *Entrance requirements:* For master's, GRE, interview, letters of recommendation, portfolio, essay, professional experience, certification; for other advanced degree, GRE, interview, letters of recommendation, essay, professional experience, resume, master's degree. Additional exam requirements/recommendations for international students: Required—TOEFL (minimum score 550 paper-based; 80 iBT). *Application deadline:* Applications are processed on a rolling basis. Application fee: $75. Electronic applications accepted. *Expenses: Tuition:* Full-time $1292. *Required fees:* $970. Tuition and fees vary according to program. *Financial support:* In 2017–18, 78 students received support, including 47 fellowships with full and partial tuition reimbursements available (averaging $3,138 per year), 5 research assistantships with full and partial tuition reimbursements available (averaging $5,702 per year); career-related internships or fieldwork, Federal Work-Study, institutionally sponsored loans, scholarships/grants, traineeships, tuition waivers (full and partial), and unspecified assistantships also available. Support available to part-time students. Financial award applicants required to submit FAFSA. *Faculty research:* Couple and family therapy infidelity; creative arts impact on Parkinson's disease; LGBTQ inclusion; substance abuse/heroin addiction's racial identity, multicultural issues, white privilege, Latinos, school counseling and the intensity of the high school curriculum. *Unit head:* Dr. Jamie Mitus, Chairperson, 516-463-5759, E-mail: jamie.s.mitus@hofstra.edu. *Application contact:* Sunil Samuel, Assistant Vice President of Admissions, 516-463-4723, Fax: 516-463-4664, E-mail: graduateadmission@hofstra.edu.
Website: http://www.hofstra.edu/academics/colleges/healthscienceshumanservices/

Hope International University, School of Graduate and Professional Studies, Program in Marriage and Family Therapy, Fullerton, CA 92831-3138. Offers MA, MFT. *Accreditation:* AAMFT/COAMFTE. *Degree requirements:* For master's, comprehensive exam, thesis (for some programs), final exam, practicum. *Entrance requirements:* For master's, minimum GPA of 3.0, interview, bachelor's degree, 2 references. Additional exam requirements/recommendations for international students: Required—TOEFL (minimum score 550 paper-based; 86 iBT); Recommended—IELTS (minimum score 6.5). Electronic applications accepted. *Expenses:* Contact institution.

Houston Baptist University, College of Education and Behavioral Sciences, Program in Counseling, Houston, TX 77074-3298. Offers Christian counseling (MACC); counseling (MAC); marriage and family therapy (MA); pastoral counseling (MA), including addiction and recovery, crisis response, human sexuality, marriage and family therapy, military and veteran care and counseling, professional life coaching. *Program availability:* Part-time, evening/weekend, 100% online. *Students:* 42 full-time (35 women), 103 part-time (91 women); includes 80 minority (31 Black or African American, non-Hispanic/Latino; 10 Asian, non-Hispanic/Latino; 36 Hispanic/Latino; 3 Two or more races, non-Hispanic/Latino), 4 international. Average age 29. 178 applicants, 16% accepted, 16 enrolled. In 2017, 22 master's awarded. *Degree requirements:* For master's, comprehensive exam, practicum. *Entrance requirements:* For master's, GRE (waived if GPA is 3.0 or higher), two academic or professional recommendations, bachelor's degree conferred transcript, resume, interview. Additional exam requirements/recommendations for international students: Required—TOEFL (minimum score 80 iBT), IELTS (minimum score 6.5). *Application deadline:* For fall admission, 8/1 for domestic students, 6/1 for international students; for spring admission, 1/1 for domestic students, 11/1 for international students; for summer admission, 5/1 for domestic students, 3/1 for international students. Applications are processed on a rolling basis. Application fee: $0 ($100 for international students). Electronic applications accepted. Application fee is waived when completed online. *Expenses:* $33,000 tuition;

$4,500 fees (general, technology and parking). *Financial support:* In 2017–18, 9 students received support. Career-related internships or fieldwork, Federal Work-Study, and scholarships/grants available. Support available to part-time students. Financial award application deadline: 4/1; financial award applicants required to submit FAFSA. *Faculty research:* Multicultural psychology, counseling: technology integration. *Unit head:* Dr. Maria Soto-Leggett, Program Coordinator, 281-649-3310, E-mail: msotoleggett@hbu.edu. *Application contact:* Victoria Humphreys, Administrative Assistant to the Dean, 281-649-3131, E-mail: vhumphreys@hbu.edu.
Website: http://www.hbu.edu/mac

Idaho State University, Office of Graduate Studies, School of Health Professions, Department of Counseling, Pocatello, ID 83209-8120. Offers counseling (M Coun, Ed S), including marriage and family counseling (M Coun), mental health counseling (M Coun), school counseling (M Coun), student affairs and college counseling (M Coun); counselor education and counseling (PhD). *Accreditation:* ACA (one or more programs are accredited). *Program availability:* Part-time. *Degree requirements:* For master's, comprehensive exam, thesis, 4 semesters resident graduate study, practicum/internship; for doctorate, comprehensive exam, thesis/dissertation, 3 semesters internship, 4 consecutive semesters doctoral-level study on campus; for Ed S, comprehensive exam, thesis, case studies, oral exam. *Entrance requirements:* For master's, GRE General Test, MAT, minimum GPA of 3.0, bachelors degree, interview, 3 letters of recommendation; for doctorate, GRE General Test, MAT, minimum graduate GPA of 3.0, resume, interview, counseling license, master's degree; for Ed S, GRE General Test, minimum graduate GPA of 3.0, master's degree in counseling, 3 letters of recommendation, 2 years work experience. Additional exam requirements/recommendations for international students: Required—TOEFL (minimum score 600 paper-based; 80 iBT). Electronic applications accepted. *Faculty research:* Group counseling, multicultural counseling, family counseling, child therapy, supervision.

Indiana University–Purdue University Fort Wayne, College of Education and Public Policy, Department of Professional Studies, Fort Wayne, IN 46805-1499. Offers couple and family counseling (MS Ed); educational leadership (MS Ed); school counseling (MS Ed); special education (MS Ed, Certificate). *Program availability:* Part-time. *Degree requirements:* For master's, comprehensive exam, practicum, internship, portfolio. *Entrance requirements:* For master's, minimum GPA of 2.5, three professional letters of recommendation. Additional exam requirements/recommendations for international students: Required—TOEFL (minimum score 550 paper-based; 79 iBT). *Faculty research:* Learning opportunities with deafness and the hearing impaired, adolescent emotion, student evaluation of teaching.

Indiana University South Bend, School of Education, South Bend, IN 46615. Offers addiction counseling (MS Ed); alcohol and drug counseling (Graduate Certificate); clinical mental health counseling (MS Ed); educational leadership (MS Ed); elementary education (MS Ed); marriage, couple, and family counseling (MS Ed); school counseling (MS Ed); secondary education (MS Ed); special education (MAT, MS Ed), including intense intervention (MS Ed), mild intervention (MS Ed). *Accreditation:* NCATE. *Program availability:* Part-time, evening/weekend. *Degree requirements:* For master's, thesis or alternative, exit project. *Entrance requirements:* For master's, letters of recommendation, GRE or minimum GPA of 3.0. Additional exam requirements/recommendations for international students: Required—TOEFL. Electronic applications accepted. *Expenses:* Contact institution. *Faculty research:* Professional dispositions, early childhood literacy, online learning, program assessments, problem-based learning.

Indiana Wesleyan University, Graduate School, College of Arts and Sciences, Marion, IN 46953. Offers addictions counseling (MS); clinical mental health counseling (MS); community counseling (MS); marriage and family therapy (MS); school counseling (MS); student development counseling and administration (MS). *Accreditation:* ACA. *Program availability:* Part-time. *Degree requirements:* For master's, thesis or alternative. *Entrance requirements:* For master's, GRE General Test. Additional exam requirements/recommendations for international students: Required—TOEFL. Electronic applications accepted. *Expenses:* Contact institution. *Faculty research:* Community counseling, multicultural counseling, addictions.

Instituto Tecnologico de Santo Domingo, Graduate School, Area of Humanities and Social Sciences, Santo Domingo, Dominican Republic. Offers accounting (Certificate); adult education (Certificate); applied linguistics (MA); economics (MA); education (M Ed); educational psychology (MA, Certificate); gender and development (MA, Certificate); humanistic studies (MA); international marketing management (Certificate); international relations in the Caribbean basin (Certificate); intervention systems in family therapy (MA); linguistic and literary communication (Certificate); pedagogical support (MA); social science education (M Ed); sustainable human development (MA); terminal illness and death psychology (Certificate); youth and adult education (M Ed).

Iona College, School of Arts and Science, Marriage and Family Therapy Program, New Rochelle, NY 10801-1890. Offers MS. *Accreditation:* AAMFT/COAMFTE. *Program availability:* Part-time. *Faculty:* 3 full-time (1 woman), 2 part-time/adjunct (1 woman). *Students:* 34 full-time (33 women), 3 part-time (all women); includes 20 minority (9 Black or African American, non-Hispanic/Latino; 3 Asian, non-Hispanic/Latino; 8 Hispanic/Latino), 2 international. Average age 31. 22 applicants, 100% accepted, 15 enrolled. In 2017, 11 master's awarded. *Degree requirements:* For master's, thesis, project. *Entrance requirements:* For master's, interview, minimum GPA of 3.0. *Application deadline:* For fall admission, 8/1 priority date for domestic students, 7/1 for international students. Applications are processed on a rolling basis. Application fee: $50. Electronic applications accepted. *Expenses:* Contact institution. *Financial support:* In 2017–18, 8 students received support. Career-related internships or fieldwork, tuition waivers (partial), and unspecified assistantships available. Support available to part-time students. Financial award application deadline: 4/15; financial award applicants required to submit FAFSA. *Unit head:* Robert Burns, PhD, Program Director, 914-633-2418, E-mail: rburns@iona.edu. *Application contact:* Katelyn Brunck, Assistant Director of Graduate Admissions, 914-633-2451, Fax: 914-633-2277, E-mail: kbrunck@iona.edu.
Website: http://www.iona.edu/Academics/School-of-Arts-Science/Departments/Marriage-and-Family-Therapy/Graduate-Programs.aspx

Jacksonville University, Brooks Rehabilitation College of Healthcare Sciences, School of Applied Health Sciences, Program in Clinical Mental Health Counseling, Jacksonville, FL 32211. Offers clinical mental health counseling (MS), including marriage and family therapy. *Program availability:* Part-time, blended/hybrid learning. *Faculty:* 3 full-time (2 women), 3 part-time/adjunct (0 women). *Students:* 53 full-time (41 women); includes 24 minority (20 Black or African American, non-Hispanic/Latino; 4 Hispanic/Latino). Average age 35. 39 applicants, 72% accepted, 24 enrolled. *Degree requirements:* For master's, 1,000-hour community-based clinical field experience. *Entrance requirements:* For master's, baccalaureate degree from accredited college or university with minimum GPA of 3.0; background check; 1-2 page essay stating intent; resume (education, work experience); 3 letters of recommendation; interview. Additional exam requirements/recommendations for international students: Required—TOEFL (minimum score 650 paper-based; 114 iBT), IELTS (minimum score 8). *Application deadline:* For fall admission, 2/1 for domestic and international students. Applications are processed on a rolling basis. Application fee: $50. Electronic applications accepted. *Expenses:* $680 per credit hour. *Financial support:* Federal Work-Study, institutionally sponsored loans, scholarships/grants, and health care benefits available. Support available to part-time

students. Financial award application deadline: 3/15; financial award applicants required to submit FAFSA. *Unit head:* Dr. Whitney George, Department Chair, Clinical Mental Health Counseling, 904-256-7620, E-mail: wgeorge@ju.edu. *Application contact:* Pamela Adrian, Assistant Director, Graduate Admissions, 904-256-7245, E-mail: padrian@ju.edu.
Website: https://www.ju.edu/mentalhealth/

John Brown University, Graduate Counseling Programs, Siloam Springs, AR 72761-2121. Offers clinical mental health counseling (MS); marriage and family therapy (MS); play therapy (Graduate Certificate); school counseling (MS). *Accreditation:* NCATE. *Program availability:* Part-time, evening/weekend. *Degree requirements:* For master's, practica or internships. *Entrance requirements:* For master's, GRE (minimum score of 300), recommendation forms from three people, 200-word essay describing professional plans and reason for seeking acceptance. Additional exam requirements/recommendations for international students: Required—TOEFL (minimum score 550 paper-based; 79 iBT). Electronic applications accepted. *Expenses:* Contact institution.

Kansas State University, Graduate School, College of Human Ecology, Doctorate in Human Ecology Program, Manhattan, KS 66506-1407. Offers apparel and textiles (PhD); applied family sciences (PhD); couple and family therapy (PhD); hospitality administration (PhD); kinesiology (PhD); life-span human development (PhD). *Program availability:* Part-time. *Degree requirements:* For doctorate, thesis/dissertation. *Entrance requirements:* Additional exam requirements/recommendations for international students: Required—TOEFL. Electronic applications accepted.

Kansas State University, Graduate School, College of Human Ecology, School of Family Studies and Human Services, Manhattan, KS 66506-1403. Offers applied family sciences (MS); communication sciences and disorders (MS); conflict resolution (Graduate Certificate); couple and family therapy (MS); early childhood education (MS); family and community service (MS); life-span human development (MS); personal financial planning (MS, PhD, Graduate Certificate); youth development (MS, Graduate Certificate). *Accreditation:* AAMFT/COAMFTE; ASHA. *Program availability:* Part-time, online learning. *Degree requirements:* For master's, comprehensive exam (for some programs), thesis optional. *Entrance requirements:* For master's, GRE, minimum GPA of 3.0 in last 2 years (60 semester hours) of undergraduate study; for doctorate, GRE. Additional exam requirements/recommendations for international students: Required—TOEFL (minimum score 600 paper-based). Electronic applications accepted. *Faculty research:* Health and security of military families, training in and evaluation of professional human services (marriage and couple therapy, family life education, treatment of speech and swallowing disorders, financial therapy), disorders of communication and swallowing, family and relationship development and health, financial decision-making.

Kean University, College of Liberal Arts, Program in Marriage and Family Therapy, Union, NJ 07083. Offers MA. *Program availability:* Part-time. *Faculty:* 18 full-time (14 women). *Students:* 30 full-time (28 women), 10 part-time (9 women); includes 26 minority (16 Black or African American, non-Hispanic/Latino; 1 Asian, non-Hispanic/Latino; 9 Hispanic/Latino), 1 international. Average age 31. 23 applicants, 91% accepted, 16 enrolled. In 2017, 8 master's awarded. *Entrance requirements:* Additional exam requirements/recommendations for international students: Required—TOEFL (minimum score 550 paper-based; 79 iBT), IELTS (minimum score 6.5). *Application deadline:* For fall admission, 6/30 for domestic and international students; for spring admission, 12/1 for domestic and international students. Applications are processed on a rolling basis. Application fee: $75. Electronic applications accepted. *Expenses:* Tuition, state resident: full-time $13,419; part-time $653 per credit. Tuition, nonresident: full-time $18,188; part-time $801 per credit. *Required fees:* $3382; $154 per credit. Tuition and fees vary according to course level, course load, degree level and program. *Financial support:* Scholarships/grants and unspecified assistantships available. Financial award applicants required to submit FAFSA. *Unit head:* Dr. Zandra Gratz, Program Coordinator, 908-737-5881, E-mail: zgratz@kean.edu. *Application contact:* Amy Clark, Program Assistant, 908-737-7100, E-mail: gradadmissions@kean.edu.
Website: http://grad.kean.edu/professional-diploma-programs/marriage-family-therapy

Kutztown University of Pennsylvania, College of Education, Program in Counseling Psychology, Kutztown, PA 19530-0730. Offers clinical mental health counseling (MA); marriage, couple and family counseling (MA). *Program availability:* Part-time, evening/weekend. *Faculty:* 4 full-time (3 women), 1 part-time/adjunct (0 women). *Students:* 75 full-time (68 women), 54 part-time (45 women); includes 31 minority (14 Black or African American, non-Hispanic/Latino; 1 Asian, non-Hispanic/Latino; 14 Hispanic/Latino; 2 Two or more races, non-Hispanic/Latino), 1 international. Average age 29. 73 applicants, 67% accepted, 27 enrolled. In 2017, 36 master's awarded. *Degree requirements:* For master's, comprehensive exam, thesis optional. *Entrance requirements:* For master's, GRE General Test, 3 letters of recommendation, minimum undergraduate GPA of 3.0, psychobiographical statement, resume. Additional exam requirements/recommendations for international students: Required—TOEFL (minimum score 550 paper-based, 79 iBT), IELTS (minimum score 6.5), or PTE (minimum score 53). *Application deadline:* For fall admission, 3/1 for domestic and international students; for spring admission, 10/1 for domestic and international students. Application fee: $35. Electronic applications accepted. *Expenses:* Tuition, state resident: part-time $500 per credit. Tuition, nonresident: part-time $750 per credit. *Required fees:* $115 per credit. One-time fee: $50 part-time. Tuition and fees vary according to degree level. *Financial support:* Career-related internships or fieldwork, Federal Work-Study, and unspecified assistantships available. Financial award application deadline: 3/1; financial award applicants required to submit FAFSA. *Faculty research:* Family addictions. *Unit head:* Dr. Helen S Hamlet, Department Chair, 610-683-4204, Fax: 610-683-1585, E-mail: hamlet@kutztown.edu.
Website: https://www.kutztown.edu/academics/graduate-programs/counseling.htm

Lancaster Bible College, Graduate School, Lancaster, PA 17601-5036. Offers adult ministries (MA); Bible (MA); children and family ministry (MA); church planting (MA); consulting resource teacher (M Ed); elementary school counseling (M Ed); leadership (PhD); leadership studies (MA); marriage and family counseling (MA); mental health counseling (MA); pastoral studies (MA); secondary school counseling (M Ed); sports ministry (MA); student ministry (MA); town and country ministry (MA). *Program availability:* Part-time, evening/weekend. *Degree requirements:* For master's, comprehensive exam (for some programs), thesis (for some programs). *Entrance requirements:* For master's, bachelor's degree with a minimum of 30 credits of course work in Bible, minimum undergraduate GPA of 3.0, interview. Additional exam requirements/recommendations for international students: Required—TOEFL.

La Salle University, School of Arts and Sciences, Program in Counseling and Family Therapy, Philadelphia, PA 19141-1199. Offers industrial/organizational psychology (MA); marriage and family therapy (MA); professional clinical counseling (MA). *Accreditation:* ACA; APA. *Program availability:* Part-time, evening/weekend. *Faculty:* 7 full-time (2 women), 18 part-time/adjunct (10 women). *Students:* 47 full-time (38 women), 159 part-time (123 women); includes 63 minority (29 Black or African American, non-Hispanic/Latino; 4 Asian, non-Hispanic/Latino; 26 Hispanic/Latino; 4 Two or more races, non-Hispanic/Latino), 5 international. Average age 30. 125 applicants, 78% accepted, 42 enrolled. In 2017, 73 master's awarded. *Degree requirements:* For master's, comprehensive exam. *Entrance requirements:* For master's, GRE or MAT (waived for applicants that already possess a master's degree in any field or for applicants that have a cumulative GPA of 3.5 or higher), minimum of 15 hours in psychology, counseling, or marriage and family studies; minimum GPA of 3.0; three letters of recommendation; personal statement; work experience (paid or volunteer). Additional exam requirements/recommendations for international students: Required—TOEFL. *Application deadline:* For fall admission, 8/15 priority date for domestic students, 7/15 for international students; for spring admission, 12/15 priority date for domestic students, 11/15 for international students; for summer admission, 4/15 priority date for domestic students, 3/15 for international students. Applications are processed on a rolling basis. Application fee: $35. Electronic applications accepted. Application fee is waived when completed online. *Expenses:* Contact institution. *Financial support:* In 2017–18, 34 students received support. Scholarships/grants and unspecified assistantships available. Support available to part-time students. Financial award application deadline: 8/31; financial award applicants required to submit FAFSA. *Faculty research:* Cognitive therapy, attribution theory, work habits, single parent families, treatment of addictions. *Unit head:* Dr. Donna A. Tonrey, Director, 215-951-1767, Fax: 215-951-1843, E-mail: psyma@lasalle.edu. *Application contact:* Elizabeth Heenan, Director, Graduate and Adult Enrollment, 215-951-1100, Fax: 215-951-1462, E-mail: heenan@lasalle.edu.
Website: http://www.lasalle.edu/counseling-family-therapy/

Lee University, Graduate Studies in Counseling, Cleveland, TN 37320-3450. Offers holistic child development (MS); marriage and family studies (MS); marriage and family therapy (MS); school counseling (MS). *Program availability:* Part-time, 100% online. *Faculty:* 7 full-time (3 women), 3 part-time/adjunct (0 women). *Students:* 95 full-time (71 women), 24 part-time (18 women); includes 27 minority (5 Black or African American, non-Hispanic/Latino; 19 Hispanic/Latino; 3 Two or more races, non-Hispanic/Latino), 7 international. Average age 30. 47 applicants, 87% accepted, 33 enrolled. In 2017, 32 master's awarded. *Degree requirements:* For master's, variable foreign language requirement, comprehensive exam (for some programs), thesis (for some programs), internship. *Entrance requirements:* For master's, GRE General Test or MAT (waived if undergraduate GPA is greater than 3.0 or if applicant already has a graduate degree), minimum undergraduate GPA of 3.0, 3 letters of recommendation, interview, official transcripts, essay. Additional exam requirements/recommendations for international students: Required—TOEFL (minimum score 61 iBT). *Application deadline:* For fall admission, 4/1 priority date for domestic and international students; for spring admission, 11/1 priority date for domestic and international students. Applications are processed on a rolling basis. Application fee: $25. Electronic applications accepted. *Expenses: Tuition:* Full-time $12,780; part-time $710 per credit hour. *Required fees:* $60; $60 per term. Tuition and fees vary according to program. *Financial support:* In 2017–18, 36 students received support. Career-related internships or fieldwork, Federal Work-Study, institutionally sponsored loans, scholarships/grants, and unspecified assistantships available. Financial award application deadline: 3/1; financial award applicants required to submit FAFSA. *Unit head:* Dr. Trevor Milliron, Director, 423-614-8126, Fax: 423-614-8124, E-mail: tmilliron@leeuniversity.edu.
Website: http://www.leeuniversity.edu/academics/graduate/counseling/

LeTourneau University, Graduate Programs, Longview, TX 75607-7001. Offers business (MBA); counseling (MA), including licensed professional counselor, marriage and family therapy, school counseling; curriculum and instruction (M Ed); educational administration (M Ed); engineering (ME, MS); engineering management (MEM); health care administration (MS); marriage and family therapy (MA); psychology (MA); strategic leadership (MSL); teacher leadership (M Ed); teaching and learning (M Ed). *Program availability:* Part-time, 100% online, blended/hybrid learning. *Students:* 55 full-time (35 women), 337 part-time (266 women); includes 218 minority (140 Black or African American, non-Hispanic/Latino; 2 American Indian or Alaska Native, non-Hispanic/Latino; 5 Asian, non-Hispanic/Latino; 32 Hispanic/Latino; 39 Two or more races, non-Hispanic/Latino), 3 international. Average age 37. *Entrance requirements:* Additional exam requirements/recommendations for international students: Required—TOEFL. *Application deadline:* For fall admission, 8/22 for domestic students, 8/29 for international students; for winter admission, 10/10 for domestic students; for spring admission, 1/2 for domestic students, 1/10 for international students; for summer admission, 5/1 for domestic and international students. Applications are processed on a rolling basis. Electronic applications accepted. *Expenses:* Contact institution. *Financial support:* Research assistantships, institutionally sponsored loans, and unspecified assistantships available. Financial award applicants required to submit FAFSA.
Website: http://www.letu.edu

Lewis & Clark College, Graduate School of Education and Counseling, Department of Counseling Psychology, Program in Marriage, Couple, and Family Therapy, Portland, OR 97219-7899. Offers MA, MS. *Accreditation:* AAMFT/COAMFTE. *Program availability:* Part-time, evening/weekend. *Degree requirements:* For master's, thesis (MS). *Entrance requirements:* For master's, GRE General Test, minimum undergraduate GPA of 2.75. Additional exam requirements/recommendations for international students: Required—TOEFL (minimum score 575 paper-based). Electronic applications accepted.

Liberty University, School of Behavioral Sciences, Lynchburg, VA 24515. Offers applied psychology (MA), including developmental psychology (MA, MS), industrial/organizational psychology (MA, MS); clinical mental health counseling (MA); community care and counseling (Ed D), including marriage and family counseling, pastoral care and counseling, traumatology; counselor education and supervision (PhD); human services counseling (MA), including addictions and recovery, business, child and family law, Christian ministries, criminal justice, crisis response and trauma, executive leadership, health and wellness, life coaching, marriage and family, military resilience; marriage and family counseling (MA); marriage and family therapy (MA); military resilience (Certificate); pastoral counseling (MA), including addictions and recovery, community chaplaincy, crisis response and trauma, discipleship and church ministry, leadership, life coaching, marriage and family, marriage and family studies, military resilience, parenting and child/adolescent, pastoral counseling, theology; professional counseling (MA); psychology (MS), including developmental psychology (MA, MS), industrial/organizational psychology (MA, MS); school counseling (M Ed). *Program availability:* Part-time, online learning. *Students:* 2,649 full-time (2,085 women), 5,086 part-time (4,015 women); includes 2,275 minority (1,784 Black or African American, non-Hispanic/Latino; 44 American Indian or Alaska Native, non-Hispanic/Latino; 67 Asian, non-Hispanic/Latino; 200 Hispanic/Latino; 11 Native Hawaiian or other Pacific Islander, non-Hispanic/Latino; 169 Two or more races, non-Hispanic/Latino), 145 international. Average age 39. 5,839 applicants, 51% accepted, 1710 enrolled. In 2017, 1,626 master's, 7 doctorates, 61 other advanced degrees awarded. *Application deadline:* Applications are processed on a rolling basis. Application fee: $50. Electronic applications accepted. *Financial support:* Applicants required to submit FAFSA. *Unit head:* Dr. Ronald Hawkins, Founding Dean, School of Behavioral Sciences. *Application contact:* Jay Bridge, Director of Admissions, 800-424-9595, Fax: 800-628-7977, E-mail: gradadmissions@liberty.edu.

Liberty University, School of Divinity, Lynchburg, VA 24515. Offers Biblical exposition (MA); Biblical languages (M Div); Biblical studies (M Div, MA, MAR, Th M, D Min); chaplaincy (M Div, D Min); Christian apologetics (M Div, MA, MAR, Th M); Christian

leadership and church ministries (M Div); Christian ministries (M Div); Christian ministry (MA); Christian thought (M Div); church history (M Div, MAR, Th M); community chaplaincy (M Div, MAR); discipleship (D Min); discipleship and church ministry (M Div, MAR, MCM); evangelism and church planting (MAR, MCM, D Min); expository preaching (D Min); global ministry (MA); global studies (M Div, MAR, MCM, MGS, Th M); healthcare chaplaincy (M Div); homiletics (M Div, MAR, Th M); leadership (M Div, MAR); marketplace chaplaincy (M Div, MCM); ministry leadership (Ed D); pastoral counseling (M Div, MA, MAR, D Min), including addictions and recovery (MA), crisis response and trauma (MA), discipleship and church ministries (MA), leadership (MA), life coaching (MA), marketplace chaplaincy (MA), marriage and family (MA), military resilience (MA), pastoral counseling (MA); pastoral leadership (D Min); pastoral ministries (M Div, M Serv Soc, MCM); religious education (MRE); sports chaplaincy (MA); theology (M Div, MAR, MTS, Th M); theology and apologetics (D Min, PhD); worship (M Div, MAR, MCM, D Min); youth and family ministries (M Div). *Program availability:* Part-time, online learning. *Students:* 2,140 full-time (615 women), 3,020 part-time (906 women); includes 1,312 minority (1,016 Black or African American, non-Hispanic/Latino; 9 American Indian or Alaska Native, non-Hispanic/Latino; 100 Asian, non-Hispanic/Latino; 90 Hispanic/Latino; 7 Native Hawaiian or other Pacific Islander, non-Hispanic/Latino; 90 Two or more races, non-Hispanic/Latino), 158 international. Average age 42. 4,673 applicants, 33% accepted, 977 enrolled. In 2017, 904 master's, 54 doctorates awarded. *Degree requirements:* For master's, 2 foreign languages, thesis (for some programs); for doctorate, 2 foreign languages, thesis/dissertation. *Entrance requirements:* For master's, minimum undergraduate GPA of 2.0; for doctorate, GRE General Test or MAT, minimum graduate GPA of 3.0. Additional exam requirements/recommendations for international students: Required—TOEFL (minimum score 600 paper-based; 100 iBT). *Application deadline:* For fall admission, 6/1 for domestic students; for spring admission, 11/1 for domestic students. Applications are processed on a rolling basis. Application fee: $50. Electronic applications accepted. *Expenses:* Contact institution. *Financial support:* Teaching assistantships with tuition reimbursements, career-related internships or fieldwork, and Federal Work-Study available. Financial award applicants required to submit FAFSA. *Unit head:* Dr. Ed Hindson, Dean, 434-592-4140, Fax: 434-522-0415, E-mail: ehindson@liberty.edu. *Application contact:* Jay Bridge, Director of Graduate Admissions, 800-424-9595, Fax: 800-628-7977, E-mail: gradadmissions@liberty.edu.
Website: https://www.liberty.edu/divinity/.

Lipscomb University, Department of Psychology, Counseling, and Family Science, Nashville, TN 37204-3951. Offers clinical mental health counseling (MS); counseling psychology (Certificate); marriage and family therapy (MMFT); psychology (MS). *Program availability:* Part-time, evening/weekend. *Faculty:* 10 full-time (3 women), 10 part-time/adjunct (4 women). *Students:* 120 full-time (92 women), 30 part-time (27 women); includes 38 minority (22 Black or African American, non-Hispanic/Latino; 1 American Indian or Alaska Native, non-Hispanic/Latino; 1 Asian, non-Hispanic/Latino; 11 Hispanic/Latino; 3 Two or more races, non-Hispanic/Latino), 2 international. Average age 28. 144 applicants, 44% accepted, 42 enrolled. In 2017, 68 master's, 1 other advanced degree awarded. *Degree requirements:* For master's, thesis (for some programs), practicum, internship, capstone. *Entrance requirements:* For master's, GRE, resume, 3 reference letters, transcripts, goals statement. Additional exam requirements/recommendations for international students: Required—TOEFL (minimum score 570 paper-based; 80 iBT). *Application deadline:* For fall admission, 7/1 for domestic students; for spring admission, 11/1 for domestic students. Applications are processed on a rolling basis. Application fee: $50 ($75 for international students). Electronic applications accepted. *Expenses:* Contact institution. *Financial support:* Scholarships/grants and unspecified assistantships available. Financial award applicants required to submit FAFSA. *Faculty research:* Cognitive psychology, neuroscience, health psychology, grief issues. *Unit head:* Dr. Shanna Ray, Director/Professor of Psychology, 615-966-5833, E-mail: shanna.ray@lipscomb.edu. *Application contact:* Kathi Johnson, Recruiting and Marketing Coordinator, 615-966-5237, E-mail: kathi.johnson@lipscomb.edu.
Website: http://www.lipscomb.edu/psychology/graduate-programs

Loma Linda University, School of Behavioral Health, Department of Counseling and Family Sciences, Loma Linda, CA 92350. Offers child life specialist (MS); clinical mediation (Certificate); counseling (MS); drug and alcohol counseling (Certificate); family life education (Certificate); marital and family therapy (DMFT); school counseling (Certificate). *Degree requirements:* For master's, comprehensive exam, thesis optional; for doctorate, comprehensive exam, thesis/dissertation (for some programs). *Entrance requirements:* For master's, minimum GPA of 3.0; for doctorate, GRE. Additional exam requirements/recommendations for international students: Required—TOEFL (minimum score 550 paper-based). Electronic applications accepted.

Long Island University–Hudson, Graduate School, Purchase, NY 10577. Offers autism (Advanced Certificate); bilingual education (Advanced Certificate); childhood education (MS Ed); crisis management (Advanced Certificate); early childhood education (MS Ed); educational leadership (MS Ed); health administration (MPA); literacy (MS Ed); marriage and family therapy (MS); mental health counseling (MS, Advanced Certificate), including credentialed alcoholism and substance abuse counselor (MS); middle childhood and adolescence education (MS Ed); pharmaceutics (MS), including cosmetic science, industrial pharmacy; public administration (MPA); school counseling (MS Ed, Advanced Certificate); school psychology (MS Ed); special education (MS Ed); TESOL (MS Ed); TESOL (all grades) (Advanced Certificate). *Program availability:* Part-time, evening/weekend. *Faculty:* 8 full-time (6 women), 41 part-time/adjunct (24 women). *Students:* 69 full-time (54 women), 249 part-time (200 women); includes 102 minority (29 Black or African American, non-Hispanic/Latino; 1 American Indian or Alaska Native, non-Hispanic/Latino; 9 Asian, non-Hispanic/Latino; 62 Hispanic/Latino; 1 Native Hawaiian or other Pacific Islander, non-Hispanic/Latino). Average age 33. 153 applicants, 96% accepted, 103 enrolled. In 2017, 138 master's, 36 other advanced degrees awarded. *Entrance requirements:* Additional exam requirements/recommendations for international students: Required—TOEFL. *Application deadline:* Applications are processed on a rolling basis. Application fee: $50. Electronic applications accepted. *Expenses:* Contact institution. *Financial support:* In 2017–18, 32 students received support. Scholarships/grants available. Support available to part-time students. Financial award application deadline: 2/15; financial award applicants required to submit FAFSA. *Unit head:* Dr. Sylvia Blake, Dean and Chief Operating Officer, 914-831-2700, E-mail: westchester@liu.edu. *Application contact:* Dr. Sylvia Blake, Dean and Chief Operating Officer, 914-831-2700, E-mail: westchester@liu.edu.

Long Island University–LIU Brooklyn, School of Education, Brooklyn, NY 11201-8423. Offers adolescence urban education (MS Ed); applied behavior analysis (Advanced Certificate); bilingual education (Advanced Certificate); bilingual education in urban setting (MS Ed); bilingual school counselor (MS Ed, Advanced Certificate); childhood urban education (MS Ed); childhood/early childhood education (MS Ed); childhood/early childhood urban education (MS Ed); early childhood urban education (MS Ed, Advanced Certificate); educational leadership (Advanced Certificate); marriage and family therapy (MS, Advanced Certificate); mental health counseling (MS, Advanced Certificate); school building district leader (Advanced Certificate); school counselor (MS Ed, Advanced Certificate); school psychologist (MS Ed); teaching

students with disabilities (MS Ed); teaching urban children with disabilities (MS Ed); TESOL (MS Ed, Advanced Certificate). *Accreditation:* TEAC. *Program availability:* Part-time, evening/weekend, 100% online. *Faculty:* 14 full-time (12 women), 42 part-time/adjunct (32 women). *Students:* 140 full-time (130 women), 563 part-time (414 women); includes 417 minority (183 Black or African American, non-Hispanic/Latino; 1 American Indian or Alaska Native, non-Hispanic/Latino; 32 Asian, non-Hispanic/Latino; 187 Hispanic/Latino; 14 Two or more races, non-Hispanic/Latino), 10 international. Average age 31. 449 applicants, 82% accepted, 264 enrolled. In 2017, 408 master's, 31 other advanced degrees awarded. *Entrance requirements:* For master's, GRE. Additional exam requirements/recommendations for international students: Required—TOEFL (minimum score 527 paper-based, 75 iBT), IELTS, or PTE. *Application deadline:* Applications are processed on a rolling basis. Application fee: $50. Electronic applications accepted. *Expenses: Tuition:* Full-time $21,618; part-time $1201 per credit. *Required fees:* $1840; $920 per term. Tuition and fees vary according to course load. *Financial support:* In 2017–18, 58 students received support. Career-related internships or fieldwork, Federal Work-Study, scholarships/grants, and unspecified assistantships available. Support available to part-time students. Financial award application deadline: 2/15; financial award applicants required to submit FAFSA. *Faculty research:* Diversity issues in education and mental health care, inclusion - disability studies, sustainability, teacher professional development. *Unit head:* Dean, 718-488-1055, E-mail: bkln-admissions@liu.edu. *Application contact:* Bayu Sutrisno, Graduate Admissions Counselor, 718-488-1011, Fax: 718-780-6110, E-mail: bkln-admissions@liu.edu.
Website: http://www.liu.edu/Brooklyn/Academics/School-of-Education

Loyola Marymount University, College of Communication and Fine Arts, Program in Marital and Family Therapy, Los Angeles, CA 90045-2659. Offers MA. *Unit head:* Dr. Debra B. Linesch, Director, Marital and Family Therapy, 310-338-7674, Fax: 310-338-4518, E-mail: dlinesch@lmu.edu. *Application contact:* Chake H. Kouyoumjian, Associate Dean of Graduate Studies, 310-338-2721, Fax: 310-338-6086, E-mail: graduateinfo@lmu.edu.
Website: http://cfa.lmu.edu/programs/mft

Loyola University New Orleans, College of Nursing and Health, Department of Counseling, New Orleans, LA 70118-6195. Offers counseling (MS), including marriage and family. *Program availability:* Part-time, evening/weekend. *Faculty:* 5 full-time (2 women). *Students:* 25 full-time (23 women), 42 part-time (40 women); includes 11 minority (6 Black or African American, non-Hispanic/Latino; 5 Hispanic/Latino), 2 international. Average age 29. 50 applicants, 84% accepted, 24 enrolled. In 2017, 17 master's awarded. *Degree requirements:* For master's, comprehensive exam, minimum GPA of 3.0 in counseling coursework. *Entrance requirements:* For master's, GRE, resume, transcripts, letters of recommendation, statement of objectives, degree from regionally-accredited institution, interview, writing sample. Additional exam requirements/recommendations for international students: Required—TOEFL (minimum score 550 paper-based; 79 iBT). *Application deadline:* For fall admission, 12/1 priority date for domestic and international students. Applications are processed on a rolling basis. Application fee: $0. Electronic applications accepted. *Expenses:* $818 per hour tuition; $738 per semester full-time fees, $376.50 part-time. *Financial support:* Research assistantships, career-related internships or fieldwork, and tuition waivers (partial) available. Support available to part-time students. Financial award application deadline: 5/1; financial award applicants required to submit FAFSA. *Faculty research:* Counseling theory, spirituality issues, group counseling, multicultural applications. *Unit head:* Dr. Thomas Foster, Chair, 504-864-7867, Fax: 504-864-7844, E-mail: counselingdept@loyno.edu. *Application contact:* Dianna Whitfield, Department Assistant, 504-864-7848, Fax: 504-864-7844, E-mail: counselingdept@loyno.edu.
Website: http://css.loyno.edu/counseling

Manhattan College, Graduate Programs, School of Education and Health, Program in Marriage and Family Therapy, Riverdale, NY 10471. Offers MS. *Expenses: Tuition:* Part-time $1034 per credit. *Required fees:* $280 per term. One-time fee: $590 part-time. Tuition and fees vary according to program.

Maryville University of Saint Louis, Myrtle E. and Earl E. Walker College of Health Professions, Program in Rehabilitation Counseling, St. Louis, MO 63141-7299. Offers marriage and family therapy (MARC); music therapy (MARC); substance abuse (MARC). *Accreditation:* CORE. *Program availability:* Part-time. *Faculty:* 3 full-time (1 woman), 1 (woman) part-time/adjunct. *Students:* 17 full-time (all women), 15 part-time (10 women); includes 7 minority (6 Black or African American, non-Hispanic/Latino; 1 Hispanic/Latino). Average age 32. In 2017, 18 master's awarded. *Degree requirements:* For master's, internship, seminar. *Entrance requirements:* For master's, minimum cumulative GPA of 3.0, 2 letters of recommendation, interview, essay, transcripts, resume. Additional exam requirements/recommendations for international students: Required—TOEFL (minimum score 563 paper-based). *Application deadline:* For fall admission, 1/15 for domestic students; for spring admission, 10/1 for domestic students. Applications are processed on a rolling basis. Electronic applications accepted. *Expenses:* $663 per credit hour; $350 per semester fees. *Financial support:* Career-related internships or fieldwork, Federal Work-Study, and campus employment available. Financial award application deadline: 4/1; financial award applicants required to submit FAFSA. *Unit head:* Dr. Michael Kiener, Director, 314-529-9443, Fax: 314-529-9495, E-mail: mkiener@maryville.edu. *Application contact:* Jeannie DeLuca, Director, Admissions and Advising, 314-529-9355, Fax: 314-529-9927, E-mail: jdeluca@maryville.edu.
Website: http://www.maryville.edu/hp/rehabilitation-counseling/

Medaille College, Programs in Psychology, Buffalo, NY 14214-2695. Offers clinical psychology (Psy D); marriage and family therapy (MA); mental health counseling (MA); psychology (MA). *Accreditation:* ACA. *Program availability:* Part-time, evening/weekend. *Degree requirements:* For master's, comprehensive exam (for some programs), thesis (for some programs). *Entrance requirements:* For master's, GRE General Test (psychology), minimum GPA of 2.75 (psychology). Additional exam requirements/recommendations for international students: Required—TOEFL (minimum score 550 paper-based). Electronic applications accepted. *Faculty research:* Schizophrenia, Parkinson's Disease, eyewitness testimony, methodology.

Mercy College, School of Social and Behavioral Sciences, Program in Counseling, Dobbs Ferry, NY 10522-1189. Offers counseling (MS); family counseling (Certificate). *Program availability:* Part-time, evening/weekend, 100% online, blended/hybrid learning. *Students:* 144 full-time (117 women), 185 part-time (155 women); includes 251 minority (105 Black or African American, non-Hispanic/Latino; 5 Asian, non-Hispanic/Latino; 135 Hispanic/Latino; 1 Native Hawaiian or other Pacific Islander, non-Hispanic/Latino; 5 Two or more races, non-Hispanic/Latino), 4 international. Average age 34. 127 applicants, 60% accepted, 51 enrolled. In 2017, 92 master's awarded. *Degree requirements:* For master's, comprehensive exam (for some programs). *Entrance requirements:* For master's, essay, two professional letters of recommendation, resume, undergraduate transcript with minimum GPA of 3.0. Additional exam requirements/recommendations for international students: Required—TOEFL (minimum score 600 paper-based; 100 iBT), IELTS (minimum score 8). *Application deadline:* For fall admission, 8/1 for international students. Applications are processed on a rolling basis. Application fee: $40. Electronic applications accepted. *Expenses: Tuition:* Full-time $15,426; part-time $857 per credit hour. *Required fees:* $630; $158 per term. Tuition and fees vary

according to course load, degree level and program. *Financial support:* Career-related internships or fieldwork, Federal Work-Study, scholarships/grants, and unspecified assistantships available. Support available to part-time students. Financial award applicants required to submit FAFSA. *Unit head:* Dr. Karol Dean, Dean, School of Social and Behavioral Sciences, 914-674-7517, E-mail: kdean@mercy.edu. *Application contact:* Allison Gurdineer, Senior Director of Admissions, 914-637-2946, Fax: 914-674-7382, E-mail: admissions@mercy.edu.
Website: https://www.mercy.edu/degrees-programs/ms-counseling

Mercy College, School of Social and Behavioral Sciences, Program in Marriage and Family Therapy, Dobbs Ferry, NY 10522-1189. Offers MS. *Program availability:* Part-time, evening/weekend. *Students:* 18 full-time (15 women), 13 part-time (11 women); includes 23 minority (8 Black or African American, non-Hispanic/Latino; 3 Asian, non-Hispanic/Latino; 12 Hispanic/Latino), 2 international. Average age 34. 29 applicants, 55% accepted, 12 enrolled. In 2017, 11 master's awarded. *Degree requirements:* For master's, thesis (for some programs), practicum, research project. *Entrance requirements:* For master's, essay, resume, interview, two letters of recommendation, undergraduate transcript. Additional exam requirements/recommendations for international students: Required—TOEFL (minimum score 600 paper-based; 100 iBT), IELTS (minimum score 8). *Application deadline:* For fall admission, 8/1 for international students. Applications are processed on a rolling basis. Application fee: $40. Electronic applications accepted. *Expenses: Tuition:* Full-time $15,426; part-time $857 per credit hour. *Required fees:* $630; $158 per term. Tuition and fees vary according to course load, degree level and program. *Financial support:* Career-related internships or fieldwork, Federal Work-Study, scholarships/grants, and unspecified assistantships available. Support available to part-time students. Financial award applicants required to submit FAFSA. *Unit head:* Dr. Karol Dean, Dean, School of Social and Behavioral Sciences, 914-674-7517, E-mail: kdean@mercy.edu. *Application contact:* Allison Gurdineer, Senior Director of Admissions, 877-637-2946, Fax: 914-674-7382, E-mail: admissions@mercy.edu.
Website: https://www.mercy.edu/degrees-programs/ms-marriage-and-family-therapy

Messiah College, Program in Counseling, Mechanicsburg, PA 17055. Offers clinical mental health counseling (MAC); counseling (CAGS); marriage, couple, and family counseling (MAC); school counseling (MAC). *Accreditation:* ACA. *Program availability:* Part-time, online learning. *Entrance requirements:* For master's, minimum undergraduate cumulative GPA of 3.0, 2 recommendations, resume or curriculum vitae, interview; for CAGS, bachelor's degree, minimum undergraduate cumulative GPA of 3.0, essay, two recommendations, resume or curriculum vitae, interview. Electronic applications accepted.

Michigan State University, The Graduate School, College of Social Science, Department of Family and Child Ecology, East Lansing, MI 48824. Offers child development (MA); community services (MS); family and child ecology (PhD); family studies (MA); marriage and family therapy (MA); youth development (MA). *Accreditation:* AAMFT/COAMFTE (one or more programs are accredited). *Entrance requirements:* For master's, GRE General Test, minimum GPA of 3.0 in last 2 years of undergraduate course work, 3 letters of recommendation; for doctorate, GRE General Test, minimum GPA of 3.0, 3 letters of recommendation, background in behavioral sciences. Additional exam requirements/recommendations for international students: Required—TOEFL. Electronic applications accepted.

Mid-America Christian University, Program in Counseling, Oklahoma City, OK 73170-4504. Offers marital and family therapy (MS); pastoral/spiritual direction (MS); professional counselor (MS). *Entrance requirements:* For master's, MAT, bachelor's degree from a regionally accredited college or university, minimum overall cumulative GPA of 2.75 of bachelor course work. Additional exam requirements/recommendations for international students: Required—TOEFL (minimum score 550 paper-based).

MidAmerica Nazarene University, School of Behavioral Sciences and Counseling, Olathe, KS 66062-1899. Offers counseling (MA), including clinical mental health, marriage, couple and family, school counseling, spiritual formation in counseling. *Accreditation:* ACA. *Program availability:* Evening/weekend. *Degree requirements:* For master's, comprehensive exam. *Entrance requirements:* For master's, on-site writing assessment, official transcript, three recommendations, personal interview. Additional exam requirements/recommendations for international students: Required—TOEFL (minimum score 81 iBT). Electronic applications accepted. *Expenses:* Contact institution. *Faculty research:* Technology and intimacy, play therapy, interpersonal neurobiology, sexual addiction.

Mississippi College, Graduate School, School of Education, Department of Psychology and Counseling, Clinton, MS 39058. Offers counseling (Ed S); marriage and family counseling (MS); mental health counseling (MS); school counseling (M Ed). *Program availability:* Part-time. *Degree requirements:* For master's and Ed S, comprehensive exam, thesis optional. *Entrance requirements:* For master's, GRE or NTE. Additional exam requirements/recommendations for international students: Recommended—TOEFL, IELTS. Electronic applications accepted.

Mount Mercy University, Program in Marriage and Family Therapy, Cedar Rapids, IA 52402-4797. Offers MA. *Accreditation:* AAMFT/COAMFTE. *Program availability:* Evening/weekend.

National University, Academic Affairs, College of Letters and Sciences, La Jolla, CA 92037-1011. Offers biology (MS); counseling psychology (MA), including licensed professional clinical counseling, marriage and family therapy; creative writing (MFA); english (MA); film studies (MA); forensic and crime scene investigations (Certificate); forensic sciences (MFS); human behavior (MA); mathematics for educators (MS); performance psychology (MA); strategic communications (MA). *Program availability:* Part-time, evening/weekend, 100% online, blended/hybrid learning. *Degree requirements:* For master's, thesis (for some programs). *Entrance requirements:* For master's, interview, minimum GPA of 2.5. Additional exam requirements/recommendations for international students: Required—TOEFL (minimum score 550 paper-based; 79 iBT), IELTS (minimum score 6). *Application deadline:* Applications are processed on a rolling basis. Application fee: $60 ($65 for international students). Electronic applications accepted. *Expenses: Tuition:* Part-time $430 per quarter hour. *Financial support:* Career-related internships or fieldwork, institutionally sponsored loans, scholarships/grants, and tuition waivers (partial) available. Support available to part-time students. Financial award application deadline: 6/30; financial award applicants required to submit FAFSA. *Unit head:* Dr. Carol Richardson, Dean, 858-642-8450, E-mail: cols@nu.edu. *Application contact:* Brandon Jouganatos, Interim Vice President for Enrollment Services, 800-628-8648, E-mail: advisor@nu.edu.
Website: http://www.nu.edu/OurPrograms/CollegeOfLettersAndSciences.html

Northcentral University, Graduate Studies, San Diego, CA 92106. Offers business (MBA, DBA, PhD, Postbaccalaureate Certificate); education (M Ed, Ed D, PhD, Ed S, Post-Master's Certificate, Postbaccalaureate Certificate); marriage and family therapy (MA, DMFT, PhD, Post-Master's Certificate, Postbaccalaureate Certificate); psychology (MA, PhD, Post-Master's Certificate, Postbaccalaureate Certificate); technology (MS, PhD), including computer science, cybersecurity (MS), data science, technology and innovation management (PhD). *Program availability:* Part-time, evening/weekend, online only, 100% online. *Faculty:* 98 full-time (63 women), 385 part-time/adjunct (203 women). *Students:* 5,036 full-time (3,291 women), 5,747 part-time (3,977 women); includes 3,777 minority (2,550 Black or African American, non-Hispanic/Latino; 76 American Indian or Alaska Native, non-Hispanic/Latino; 192 Asian, non-Hispanic/Latino; 603 Hispanic/Latino; 39 Native Hawaiian or other Pacific Islander, non-Hispanic/Latino; 317 Two or more races, non-Hispanic/Latino). Average age 45. In 2017, 929 master's, 782 doctorates, 278 other advanced degrees awarded. *Degree requirements:* For doctorate, comprehensive exam, thesis/dissertation. *Entrance requirements:* For master's, bachelor's degree from regionally- or nationally-accredited institution, current resume or curriculum vitae, statement of intent, interview, and background check (for marriage and family therapy); for doctorate, post-baccalaureate master's degree and/or doctoral degree from nationally- or regionally-accredited academic institution; for other advanced degree, bachelor's-level or higher degree from accredited institution or university (for Post-Baccalaureate Certificate); master's and/or doctoral degree from regionally- or nationally-accredited academic institution (for Post-Master's Certificate). Additional exam requirements/recommendations for international students: Required—TOEFL (minimum score 550 paper-based; 79 iBT), IELTS (minimum score 6.5), PTE (minimum score 53). *Application deadline:* Applications are processed on a rolling basis. Application fee: $0. Electronic applications accepted. Tuition and fees vary according to program. *Financial support:* Scholarships/grants available. *Faculty research:* Business management, curriculum and instruction, educational leadership, health psychology, organizational behavior. *Unit head:* Dr. David Harpool, Acting Provost, 888-327-2877 Ext. 8181, E-mail: provost@ncu.edu. *Application contact:* Ken Boutelle, Vice President, Enrollment Services, 888-628-4979, E-mail: enrollmentservices@ncu.edu.

North Dakota State University, College of Graduate and Interdisciplinary Studies, College of Human Development and Education, Department of Human Development and Family Science, Program in Couple and Family Therapy, Fargo, ND 58102. Offers PhD. *Degree requirements:* For doctorate, thesis/dissertation, 180 hours of supervisory experience; one year of research, teaching, or clinical internship experience; scholarly portfolio; oral examination.

Northeastern Illinois University, College of Graduate Studies and Research, Daniel L. Goodwin College of Education, Program in Family Counseling, Chicago, IL 60625. Offers MA. *Expenses:* Tuition, state resident: full-time $7274; part-time $404.11 per credit hour. Tuition, nonresident: full-time $14,548; part-time $808.23 per credit hour. *Required fees:* $1284. *Unit head:* Dr. Charles Pistorio, Department Chair, 773-442-5551, E-mail: c-pistorio@neiu.edu. *Application contact:* Martha Narvaez, Graduate Admission Representative, 773-442-6006, E-mail: m-narvaez@neiu.edu.

Northern Kentucky University, Office of Graduate Programs, College of Informatics, Program in Communication, Highland Heights, KY 41099. Offers communication (MA); communication teaching (Certificate); documentary studies (Certificate); public relations (Certificate); relationships (Certificate). *Program availability:* Part-time, evening/weekend. Terminal master's awarded for partial completion of doctoral program. *Degree requirements:* For master's, comprehensive exams, thesis or applied capstone project. *Entrance requirements:* For master's, GRE, minimum GPA of 3.0, 3 letters of recommendation, letter of intent. Additional exam requirements/recommendations for international students: Required—TOEFL (minimum score 79 iBT); Recommended—IELTS (minimum score 6.5). Electronic applications accepted. *Faculty research:* Mediating effect of health communication, organizational communication, quantitative and qualitative research methods, family and interpersonal communication.

Northwestern University, The Graduate School, Program in Marital and Family Therapy, Evanston, IL 60208. Offers MS. *Entrance requirements:* For master's, GRE General Test. *Faculty research:* Marital and family therapy training, gender, psychotherapy outcome, adolescents and pre-school children at risk, families.

Northwest Nazarene University, Program in Counselor Education, Nampa, ID 83686-5897. Offers clinical counseling (MS); marriage and family counseling (MS); school counseling (MS). *Program availability:* Part-time. *Students:* Average age 35. 47 applicants, 66% accepted, 25 enrolled. In 2017, 33 master's awarded. *Entrance requirements:* For master's, minimum GPA of 3.0, BA. Additional exam requirements/recommendations for international students: Required—TOEFL. *Application deadline:* For fall admission, 2/15 for domestic and international students; for spring admission, 9/15 for domestic and international students. Application fee: $50. Electronic applications accepted. *Unit head:* Dr. Michael Pitts, Chair, 208-467-8040, Fax: 208-467-8339. *Application contact:* Lynette Kingsmore, Graduate Admissions Counselor, 208-467-8107, E-mail: lkingsmore@nnu.edu.

Notre Dame de Namur University, Division of Academic Affairs, School of Education and Psychology, Program in Clinical Psychology: Marital and Family Therapy, Belmont, CA 94002-1908. Offers MS. *Program availability:* Part-time. *Students:* 45 full-time (43 women), 46 part-time (43 women). Average age 31. *Degree requirements:* For master's, thesis. *Entrance requirements:* Additional exam requirements/recommendations for international students: Required—TOEFL (minimum score 550 paper-based; 79 iBT). *Application deadline:* For fall admission, 8/1 for domestic students; for spring admission, 12/1 for domestic students. Applications are processed on a rolling basis. Application fee: $60. Electronic applications accepted. *Expenses: Tuition:* Full-time $16,128; part-time $8064 per credit hour. *Required fees:* $80; $80 per credit hour. $40 per semester. *Financial support:* Career-related internships or fieldwork available. Support available to part-time students. Financial award applicants required to submit FAFSA. *Unit head:* Helen Marlo, Chair, Graduate Psychology Department, 650-508-3723, E-mail: hmarlo@ndnu.edu.

Nova Southeastern University, College of Arts, Humanities, and Social Sciences, Fort Lauderdale, FL 33314-7796. Offers advanced conflict resolution practice (Graduate Certificate); child protection (MHS); college student affairs (MS); conflict analysis and resolution (MS, PhD); criminal justice (MS, PhD); cross-disciplinary studies (MA); developmental disabilities (MS); family studies (Graduate Certificate); family systems health care (Graduate Certificate); family therapy (MS, PhD); marriage and family therapy (DMFT); peace studies (Graduate Certificate); qualitative research (Graduate Certificate); solution focused coaching (Graduate Certificate). *Accreditation:* AAMFT/COAMFTE (one or more programs are accredited). *Program availability:* Part-time, evening/weekend, 100% online, blended/hybrid learning. *Faculty:* 29 full-time (18 women), 27 part-time/adjunct (21 women). *Students:* 303 full-time (238 women), 903 part-time (677 women); includes 689 minority (385 Black or African American, non-Hispanic/Latino; 4 American Indian or Alaska Native, non-Hispanic/Latino; 31 Asian, non-Hispanic/Latino; 234 Hispanic/Latino; 1 Native Hawaiian or other Pacific Islander, non-Hispanic/Latino; 34 Two or more races, non-Hispanic/Latino), 60 international. Average age 37. 624 applicants, 61% accepted, 285 enrolled. In 2017, 277 master's, 62 doctorates, 25 other advanced degrees awarded. *Degree requirements:* For master's, thesis optional, comprehensive exams, portfolios (for some programs), table-top exams (for some programs); for doctorate, comprehensive exam, thesis/dissertation, qualifying exams, portfolios (for some programs). *Entrance requirements:* For master's, interview, minimum GPA of 3.0, writing sample; for doctorate, interview, minimum GPA of 3.5, master's degree in related field, writing sample; for Graduate Certificate, minimum GPA of 3.0. Additional exam requirements/recommendations for international students: Required—TOEFL. *Application deadline:* For fall admission, 5/17 priority date for domestic and international students; for winter admission, 12/1 priority date for domestic and international students; for spring admission, 4/1 priority date for domestic and

international students. Applications are processed on a rolling basis. Application fee: $50. Electronic applications accepted. *Expenses:* Contact institution. *Financial support:* In 2017–18, 170 students received support. Career-related internships or fieldwork, Federal Work-Study, scholarships/grants, and unspecified assistantships available. Financial award application deadline: 4/1; financial award applicants required to submit CSS PROFILE. *Faculty research:* Conflict resolution, family therapy, peace research, international conflict, multi-disciplinary studies, college student affairs, national security affairs, health care conflict resolution, family systems health care, advanced family systems, qualitative research, solution-focused coaching. *Unit head:* Dr. Honggang Yang, Dean, 954-262-3016, Fax: 954-262-3968, E-mail: yangh@nova.edu. *Application contact:* Marcia Arango, Student Recruitment Coordinator, 954-262-3006, Fax: 954-262-3968, E-mail: marango@nsu.nova.edu.
Website: http://cahss.nova.edu/

Nyack College, Alliance Graduate School of Counseling, Nyack, NY 10960. Offers marriage and family therapy (MA); mental health counseling (MA). *Program availability:* Part-time, evening/weekend, 100% online. *Students:* 66 full-time (50 women), 162 part-time (136 women); includes 183 minority (78 Black or African American, non-Hispanic/Latino; 45 Asian, non-Hispanic/Latino; 53 Hispanic/Latino; 7 Two or more races, non-Hispanic/Latino), 10 international. Average age 37. In 2017, 48 master's awarded. *Degree requirements:* For master's, comprehensive exam, counselor-in-training therapy, internship, CPCE exam. *Entrance requirements:* For master's, Millon Clinical Multiaxial Inventory-3, Minnesota Multiphasic Personality Inventory-2, transcripts, statement of Christian life and experience, statement of support systems. Additional exam requirements/recommendations for international students: Required—TOEFL (minimum score 550 paper-based; 80 iBT). *Application deadline:* For fall admission, 8/1 for domestic students, 2/15 for international students; for spring admission, 12/15 for domestic students, 7/15 for international students. Applications are processed on a rolling basis. Application fee: $30. Electronic applications accepted. *Expenses:* $800 per credit. *Financial support:* Career-related internships or fieldwork and scholarships/grants available. Financial award applicants required to submit FAFSA. *Unit head:* Dr. Antoinette Gines-Rivera, Director, 646-378-6160. *Application contact:* Chastity Crespo, Admissions Associate, 646-378-6199, E-mail: admissions.grad@nyack.edu.
Website: http://www.nyack.edu/agsc

Oklahoma Baptist University, Program in Marriage and Family Therapy, Shawnee, OK 74804. Offers MS. *Program availability:* Part-time, evening/weekend. *Degree requirements:* For master's, thesis optional, practicum. *Entrance requirements:* For master's, GRE General Test. Additional exam requirements/recommendations for international students: Required—TOEFL. Electronic applications accepted. *Faculty research:* Marriage and family therapy supervision, intimate partner violence in migrant populations, medical family therapy, violence and aggression, protective factors and adolescent delinquency.

Oral Roberts University, School of Theology and Missions, Tulsa, OK 74171. Offers biblical literature (MA), including advanced languages, Judaic-Christian studies; church ministries and leadership (D Min); clinical pastoral education (M Div); missions (MA); pastoral care and chaplaincy (M Div, D Min); practical theology (MA), including teaching ministries, urban ministries; professional counseling (MA), including addiction studies, marriage and family therapy; theological/historical studies (MA). *Accreditation:* ATS. *Program availability:* Part-time, online learning. *Faculty:* 17 full-time (2 women). *Students:* 371 full-time (156 women), 110 part-time (65 women); includes 177 minority (127 Black or African American, non-Hispanic/Latino; 5 American Indian or Alaska Native, non-Hispanic/Latino; 20 Asian, non-Hispanic/Latino; 25 Hispanic/Latino), 82 international. Average age 36. 159 applicants, 95% accepted, 124 enrolled. In 2017, 52 master's, 10 doctorates awarded. *Degree requirements:* For master's, thesis (for some programs), practicum/internship; for doctorate, thesis/dissertation, applied research project. *Entrance requirements:* For master's, GRE General Test or MAT (waived for those with undergraduate degree from regionally accredited institution and 3.0 or higher GPA), minimum GPA of 2.5 (professional) or 3.0 (academic); for doctorate, M Div, minimum GPA of 3.0, 3 years of full-time ministry experience. Additional exam requirements/recommendations for international students: Recommended—TOEFL (minimum score 550 paper-based; 79 iBT), IELTS (minimum score 7). *Application deadline:* Applications are processed on a rolling basis. Application fee: $35. Electronic applications accepted. Application fee is waived when completed online. *Financial support:* Fellowships and scholarships/grants available. Financial award application deadline: 6/1. *Unit head:* Dr. Bill Buker, Chair, 918-495-6493, E-mail: bbuker@oru.edu. *Application contact:* Michael Thomas, Enrollment Counselor, 918-495-6618, E-mail: mthomas@oru.edu.
Website: http://www.gradtheology.oru.edu/

Ottawa University, Graduate Studies-Arizona, Program in Professional Counseling, Ottawa, KS 66067-3399. Offers Christian counseling (MA); expressive arts therapy (MA); marriage and family therapy (MA); treatment of trauma, abuse and deprivation (MA). Programs offered in Mesa, Phoenix, Tempe and West Valley, AZ. *Program availability:* Part-time, evening/weekend, online learning. *Degree requirements:* For master's, comprehensive exam, thesis or alternative, field experience, practicum. *Entrance requirements:* For master's, minimum undergraduate GPA of 3.0; course work in theories of personality, abnormal psychology, and human growth and development. Additional exam requirements/recommendations for international students: Required—TOEFL (minimum score 550 paper-based).

Our Lady of the Lake University, College of Professional Studies, Program in Psychology, San Antonio, TX 78207-4689. Offers marriage and family therapy (MS); school psychology (MS). *Accreditation:* APA. *Program availability:* Part-time. *Faculty:* 2 full-time (both women), 2 part-time/adjunct (1 woman). *Students:* 101 full-time (87 women), 14 part-time (13 women); includes 78 minority (12 Black or African American, non-Hispanic/Latino; 66 Hispanic/Latino). Average age 30. 81 applicants, 78% accepted, 37 enrolled. In 2017, 40 master's awarded. *Degree requirements:* For master's, comprehensive exam, practicum. *Entrance requirements:* For master's, GRE General Test or MAT, bachelor's degree with at least 12 undergraduate semester hours in psychology including one course in statistics and minimum cumulative GPA of 3.0; criminal background check; personal statement addressing background in psychology, expectations of the MS program, and professional goals; statement of purpose; 2 letters of recommendation. Additional exam requirements/recommendations for international students: Required—TOEFL. *Application deadline:* For fall admission, 3/1 priority date for domestic and international students. Application fee: $40 ($50 for international students). Electronic applications accepted. Application fee is waived when completed online. *Expenses: Tuition:* Full-time $10,668; part-time $5334 per year. *Required fees:* $816; $816 per year. $408 per semester. *Financial support:* In 2017–18, 2 students received support. Federal Work-Study, scholarships/grants, unspecified assistantships, and tuition discounts available. Support available to part-time students. Financial award application deadline: 5/1; financial award applicants required to submit FAFSA. *Faculty research:* Providing competent services to diverse client populations. *Unit head:* Dr. Deborah Healy, Psychology Department, 210-431-7118, E-mail: dahealy@ollusa.edu. *Application contact:* Office of Graduate Admissions, 210-431-3995, Fax: 210-431-3945, E-mail: gradadm@lake.ollusa.edu.
Website: http://www.ollusa.edu/s/1190/hybrid/default-hybrid-ollu.aspx?sid-1190&gid-1&pgid-7908

Pacific Lutheran University, Division of Social Sciences, Program in Marriage and Family Therapy, Tacoma, WA 98447. Offers MA. *Accreditation:* AAMFT/COAMFTE. *Program availability:* Part-time. *Degree requirements:* For master's, thesis optional, clinical competency. *Entrance requirements:* Additional exam requirements/recommendations for international students: Required—TOEFL (minimum score 550 paper-based; 88 iBT). Electronic applications accepted.

Pacific Oaks College, Graduate School, Program in Marriage and Family Therapy, Pasadena, CA 91103. Offers marriage, family and child counseling (MA). *Program availability:* Part-time, evening/weekend. *Degree requirements:* For master's, thesis. *Entrance requirements:* For master's, interview. Additional exam requirements/recommendations for international students: Required—TOEFL (minimum score 550 paper-based). *Faculty research:* Family systems, cross-cultural development, therapeutic intervention and Latino families, battered women.

Palm Beach Atlantic University, School of Education and Behavioral Studies, West Palm Beach, FL 33416-4708. Offers counseling psychology (MS), including addictions/mental health, general counseling, marriage and family therapy, mental health counseling, school guidance counseling. *Program availability:* Part-time, evening/weekend. *Entrance requirements:* For master's, GRE or MAT, minimum GPA of 3.0; essay. Additional exam requirements/recommendations for international students: Required—TOEFL (minimum score 550 paper-based; 79 iBT). Electronic applications accepted. *Faculty research:* Group dynamics, phenomenology, spirituality, multicultural psychology.

Palo Alto University, MA in Counseling Program, Palo Alto, CA 94304. Offers clinical mental health (MA); marriage, family and child (MA). *Program availability:* Part-time, 100% online, blended/hybrid learning. *Faculty:* 6 full-time (4 women), 5 part-time/adjunct (4 women). *Students:* 158 full-time (130 women), 131 part-time (113 women); includes 138 minority (9 Black or African American, non-Hispanic/Latino; 35 Asian, non-Hispanic/Latino; 43 Hispanic/Latino; 51 Two or more races, non-Hispanic/Latino). Average age 34. 167 applicants, 74% accepted, 80 enrolled. In 2017, 110 master's awarded. *Degree requirements:* For master's, capstone project. *Entrance requirements:* For master's, undergraduate degree in psychology with minimum GPA of 3.3. Additional exam requirements/recommendations for international students: Required—TOEFL. *Application deadline:* For fall admission, 6/30 priority date for domestic and international students; for spring admission, 3/21 for domestic and international students. Applications are processed on a rolling basis. Application fee: $50. Electronic applications accepted. *Expenses:* Contact institution. *Financial support:* In 2017–18, 12 students received support. Federal Work-Study available. Financial award applicants required to submit FAFSA. *Unit head:* Dr. William Snow, Director of Counseling, 831-246-2440, E-mail: wsnow@paloaltou.edu. *Application contact:* Yukti Singh, Director of Admissions, 650-417-2055, E-mail: ysingh@paloaltou.edu.
Website: http://www.paloaltou.edu/graduate-programs/masters-programs/ma-counseling

Pepperdine University, Graduate School of Education and Psychology, Division of Psychology, Los Angeles, CA 90263. Offers behavioral psychology (MS); clinical psychology (Psy D); clinical psychology (MA), including marriage and family therapy; clinical psychology with Latinos (MA); psychology (MA). *Program availability:* Part-time, evening/weekend. *Students:* 499 full-time (417 women), 416 part-time (343 women); includes 401 minority (90 Black or African American, non-Hispanic/Latino; 4 American Indian or Alaska Native, non-Hispanic/Latino; 68 Asian, non-Hispanic/Latino; 205 Hispanic/Latino; 5 Native Hawaiian or other Pacific Islander, non-Hispanic/Latino; 29 Two or more races, non-Hispanic/Latino), 68 international. Average age 31. 574 applicants, 75% accepted, 254 enrolled. In 2017, 253 master's, 34 doctorates awarded. *Entrance requirements:* For master's and doctorate, GRE General Test. Additional exam requirements/recommendations for international students: Required—TOEFL. *Application deadline:* For fall admission, 2/1 for domestic students. Applications are processed on a rolling basis. Application fee: $55. Electronic applications accepted. *Expenses:* Contact institution. *Financial support:* Research assistantships, teaching assistantships, career-related internships or fieldwork, and scholarships/grants available. Support available to part-time students. Financial award application deadline: 7/1; financial award applicants required to submit FAFSA. *Unit head:* Dr. Robert A. deMayo, Associate Dean, Psychology Division, 310-568-5747, E-mail: robert.demayo@pepperdine.edu. *Application contact:* Chris Costa, Director of Enrollment, 310-568-2850, E-mail: chris.costa@pepperdine.edu.
Website: http://gsep.pepperdine.edu/masters-psychology/

Phillips Graduate University, Master's Program in Psychology, Chatsworth, CA 91311. Offers art therapy (MA); marriage and family therapy (MA); school counseling (MA); school psychology (MA). *Program availability:* Evening/weekend. *Degree requirements:* For master's, comprehensive exam, thesis. *Entrance requirements:* For master's, minimum GPA of 2.5. *Application deadline:* For fall admission, 4/16 priority date for domestic students; for spring admission, 11/15 for domestic students. Applications are processed on a rolling basis. Application fee: $80. Electronic applications accepted. *Expenses: Tuition:* Part-time $897 per unit. *Required fees:* $375 per semester. Part-time tuition and fees vary according to degree level and program. *Financial support:* Federal Work-Study and tuition waivers (full and partial) available. Financial award application deadline: 8/15; financial award applicants required to submit FAFSA. *Faculty research:* Integration of interpersonal psychological theory, systems approach, firsthand experiential learning. *Application contact:* Christine Montagna, Admissions Advisor, 818-600-4945, Fax: 818-386-5699, E-mail: cmontagna@pgu.edu.

Pillar College, Program in Counseling, Newark, NJ 07102. Offers MA.

Point Loma Nazarene University, College of Extended Learning, Program in Clinical Counseling, San Diego, CA 92108. Offers marriage and family therapy (MA); professional clinical counselor (MA). *Faculty:* 2 full-time (0 women), 12 part-time/adjunct (6 women). *Students:* 43 full-time (33 women), 4 part-time (all women); includes 23 minority (3 Black or African American, non-Hispanic/Latino; 3 Asian, non-Hispanic/Latino; 16 Hispanic/Latino; 1 Two or more races, non-Hispanic/Latino), 1 international. Average age 28. 33 applicants, 100% accepted, 25 enrolled. *Degree requirements:* For master's, comprehensive exam. *Expenses:* Contact institution. *Financial support:* Scholarships/grants available. Financial award applicants required to submit FAFSA. *Unit head:* Dr. Daniel Lee Jenkins, Program Director, 619-849-2282, E-mail: danieljenkins@pointloma.edu. *Application contact:* Joanie Joy, Senior Director of Enrollment Management, 619-329-6785, E-mail: gradinfo@pointloma.edu.
Website: https://www.pointloma.edu/graduate-studies/programs/clinical-counseling-ma

Pontifical John Paul II Institute for Studies on Marriage and Family, Graduate Programs, Washington, DC 20064. Offers biotechnology and ethics (MTS); marriage and family (MTS, STD, STL); theology (PhD).

Purdue University, Graduate School, College of Health and Human Sciences, Department of Child Development and Family Studies, West Lafayette, IN 47907. Offers developmental studies (MS, PhD); family studies (MS, PhD); marriage and family therapy (MS, PhD). *Program availability:* Part-time. *Faculty:* 19 full-time (11 women), 1 (woman) part-time/adjunct. *Students:* 22 full-time (21 women), 1 (woman) part-time;

includes 3 minority (1 Black or African American, non-Hispanic/Latino; 1 Hispanic/Latino; 1 Two or more races, non-Hispanic/Latino), 5 international. Average age 26. 41 applicants, 29% accepted, 8 enrolled. In 2017, 4 master's, 3 doctorates awarded. Terminal master's awarded for partial completion of doctoral program. *Degree requirements:* For master's, thesis; for doctorate, thesis/dissertation. *Entrance requirements:* For master's and doctorate, GRE General Test (minimum score 1000 combined verbal and quantitative), minimum undergraduate GPA of 3.0 or equivalent. Additional exam requirements/recommendations for international students: Required—TOEFL (minimum score 600 paper-based; 90 iBT), TWE (minimum score 4). *Application deadline:* For fall admission, 1/4 for domestic and international students. Applications are processed on a rolling basis. Application fee: $60 ($75 for international students). Electronic applications accepted. *Financial support:* Fellowships with full tuition reimbursements, research assistantships with full tuition reimbursements, teaching assistantships with full tuition reimbursements, and career-related internships or fieldwork available. Support available to part-time students. Financial award application deadline: 1/15; financial award applicants required to submit FAFSA. *Faculty research:* Inclusion of children with special needs, families as learning environments, relationships in child care, work-family relations, AIDS prevention. *Unit head:* Dr. Doran C. French, Head, 765-494-9511, E-mail: dcfrench@purdue.edu. *Application contact:* Tina Putz, Graduate Contact, 765-496-3816, E-mail: tputz@purdue.edu.
Website: http://www.purdue.edu/hhs/hdfs/

Purdue University Northwest, Graduate Studies Office, School of Liberal Arts and Social Sciences, Department of Behavioral Sciences, Hammond, IN 46323-2094. Offers child development and family studies (MS); marriage and family therapy (MS). *Accreditation:* AAMFT/COAMFTE. *Program availability:* Part-time. *Degree requirements:* For master's, thesis. *Entrance requirements:* For master's, GRE, interview. Additional exam requirements/recommendations for international students: Required—TOEFL. *Faculty research:* Substance abuse, sexual abuse, couple therapy, professional issues, adolescent therapy.

Reformed Theological Seminary–Jackson Campus, Graduate and Professional Programs, Jackson, MS 39209-3004. Offers Bible, theology, and missions (Certificate); Biblical exegesis (M Div); biblical studies (MA); Christian education (MA); counseling (M Div); marriage and family therapy (MA); ministry (D Min); missions (M Div, MA, D Min); theological studies (MA). *Accreditation:* AAMFT/COAMFTE (one or more programs are accredited); ATS (one or more programs are accredited). *Degree requirements:* For master's, thesis (for some programs), fieldwork; for doctorate, 2 foreign languages, thesis/dissertation. *Entrance requirements:* For master's, minimum GPA of 2.6; for doctorate, minimum GPA of 3.0. Additional exam requirements/recommendations for international students: Required—TOEFL.

Regent University, Graduate School, School of Psychology and Counseling, Virginia Beach, VA 23464-9800. Offers clinical mental health counseling (MA); clinical psychology (Psy D); counseling and psychological studies - clinical (PhD); counseling and psychological studies - research (PhD); counseling studies (CAGS); counselor education and supervision (PhD); general psychology (MS); human services (MA), including addictions counseling, Biblical counseling, Christian counseling, conflict and mediation ministry, criminal justice and ministry, grief counseling, human services counseling, human services for student affairs, life coaching, marriage and family ministry, trauma and crisis counseling; marriage, couple, and family counseling (MA); pastoral counseling (MA); school counseling (MA); M Div/MA; M Ed/MA; MBA/MA. *Accreditation:* ACA; APA (one or more programs are accredited). *Program availability:* Part-time, evening/weekend, 100% online, blended/hybrid learning. *Faculty:* 28 full-time (16 women), 51 part-time/adjunct (30 women). *Students:* 294 full-time (236 women), 404 part-time (317 women); includes 286 minority (218 Black or African American, non-Hispanic/Latino; 4 American Indian or Alaska Native, non-Hispanic/Latino; 17 Asian, non-Hispanic/Latino; 30 Hispanic/Latino; 17 Two or more races, non-Hispanic/Latino), 13 international. Average age 37. 2,109 applicants, 18% accepted, 233 enrolled. In 2017, 158 master's, 28 doctorates awarded. *Degree requirements:* For master's, thesis or alternative, internship, practicum, written competency exam; for doctorate, thesis/dissertation or alternative. *Entrance requirements:* For master's, GRE General Test (including writing exam) or MAT, minimum undergraduate GPA of 3.0, resume, transcripts, writing sample, personal goals statement; for doctorate, GRE General Test (including writing exam), minimum undergraduate GPA of 3.0, graduate 3.5; writing sample; 3 recommendations; resume; college transcripts; personal goals statement. Additional exam requirements/recommendations for international students: Required—TOEFL (minimum score 577 paper-based). *Application deadline:* For fall admission, 4/1 priority date for domestic students; for spring admission, 11/1 priority date for domestic students. Applications are processed on a rolling basis. Application fee: $50. Electronic applications accepted. *Expenses:* Contact institution. *Financial support:* In 2017–18, 557 students received support, including 5 fellowships (averaging $10,000 per year), 11 research assistantships (averaging $3,200 per year); career-related internships or fieldwork, scholarships/grants, and unspecified assistantships also available. Support available to part-time students. *Faculty research:* Marriage enrichment, clinical psychology, troubled youth, faith and learning, trauma. *Unit head:* Dr. William Hathaway, Dean, 757-352-4294, Fax: 757-352-4282, E-mail: willhat@regent.edu. *Application contact:* Heidi Cece, Assistant Vice President of Enrollment Management, 800-373-5504, Fax: 757-352-4381, E-mail: admissions@regent.edu.
Website: https://www.regent.edu/school-of-psychology-and-counseling/

Regis University, Rueckert-Hartman College for Health Professions, Denver, CO 80221-1099. Offers advanced practice nurse (DNP); counseling (MA); counseling children and adolescents (Post-Graduate Certificate); counseling military families (Post-Graduate Certificate); depth psychotherapy (Post-Graduate Certificate); fellowship in orthopedic manual physical therapy (Certificate); health care business management (Certificate); health care quality and patient safety (Certificate); health industry leadership (MBA); health services administration (MS); marriage and family therapy (MA, Post-Graduate Certificate); neonatal nurse practitioner (MSN); nursing education (MSN); nursing leadership (MSN); occupational therapy (OTD); pharmacy (Pharm D); physical therapy (DPT). *Program availability:* Part-time, evening/weekend, 100% online, blended/hybrid learning. *Degree requirements:* For master's, thesis (for some programs), internship. *Entrance requirements:* For master's, official transcript reflecting baccalaureate degree awarded from regionally-accredited college or university. Additional exam requirements/recommendations for international students: Required—TOEFL (minimum score 550 paper-based; 82 iBT). Electronic applications accepted. *Expenses:* Contact institution. *Faculty research:* Normal and pathological balance and gait research, normal/pathological upper limb motor control/biomechanics, exercise energy/metabolism research, optical treatment protocols for therapeutic modalities.

Richmont Graduate University, School of Counseling, Atlanta, GA 30339. Offers clinical mental health counseling (MA); marriage and family therapy (MA). *Accreditation:* ACA. *Program availability:* Part-time, evening/weekend. *Degree requirements:* For master's, comprehensive exam, thesis optional. *Entrance requirements:* For master's, GRE or MAT. Electronic applications accepted.

St. Cloud State University, School of Graduate Studies, School of Health and Human Services, Department of Counseling and Community Psychology, Program in Marriage and Family Therapy, St. Cloud, MN 56301-4498. Offers MS. *Accreditation:* AAMFT/COAMFTE. *Entrance requirements:* Additional exam requirements/recommendations for international students: Required—Michigan English Language Assessment Battery; Recommended—TOEFL (minimum score 550 paper-based), IELTS (minimum score 6.5). Electronic applications accepted.

Saint Mary's College of California, Kalmanovitz School of Education, Program in Counseling, Moraga, CA 94575. Offers career counseling (MA); college student services (Credential); general counseling (MA); marriage and family therapy (MA); pupil personnel services (Credential), including school counseling, school psychology; school counseling (MA); school psychology (MA). *Program availability:* Part-time, evening/weekend. *Degree requirements:* For master's, thesis or alternative. *Entrance requirements:* For master's, interview, minimum GPA of 3.0. *Faculty research:* Counselor training effectiveness, multicultural development, empathy, the interface of spirituality and psychotherapy, gender issues.

Saint Mary's University of Minnesota, Schools of Graduate and Professional Programs, Graduate School of Health and Human Services, Marriage and Family Therapy Program, Winona, MN 55987-1399. Offers MA. *Unit head:* Dr. Samantha Zaid, Program Director, 612-728-5140, Fax: 612-728-5121, E-mail: szaid@smumn.edu. *Application contact:* James Callinan, Director of Admissions for Graduate and Professional Programs, 612-728-5158, Fax: 612-728-5121, E-mail: jcallina@smumn.edu.
Website: http://www.smumn.edu/graduate-home/areas-of-study/graduate-school-of-health-human-services/ma-in-marriage-family-therapy

Saint Paul University, Faculty of Human Sciences, Program in Counseling and Spirituality, Ottawa, ON K1S 1C4, Canada. Offers individual or marital/couple counseling (MA); spiritual care (MA). *Program availability:* Part-time. *Degree requirements:* For master's, research project or thesis. *Entrance requirements:* For master's, honors BA in human sciences, minimum B average, 12 theology credits.

St. Thomas University, Biscayne College, Department of Social Sciences and Counseling, Program in Marriage and Family Therapy, Miami Gardens, FL 33054-6459. Offers MS, Post-Master's Certificate. *Program availability:* Part-time, evening/weekend. *Degree requirements:* For master's, comprehensive exam. *Entrance requirements:* For master's, interview, minimum GPA of 3.0 or GRE. Additional exam requirements/recommendations for international students: Required—TOEFL. Electronic applications accepted.

San Francisco State University, Division of Graduate Studies, College of Health and Social Sciences, Department of Counseling, San Francisco, CA 94132-1722. Offers clinical mental health counseling (MS); marriage, family and child counseling (MS). *Accreditation:* ACA. *Program availability:* Part-time. *Application deadline:* Applications are processed on a rolling basis. *Unit head:* Dr. Graciela Orozco, Chair, 415-338-2005, Fax: 415-338-0594, E-mail: counsel@sfsu.edu. *Application contact:* Dr. Alison Cerezo, College Counseling Coordinator, 415-338-1064, Fax: 415-338-0594, E-mail: acerezo@sfsu.edu.
Website: http://counseling.sfsu.edu

Saybrook University, School of Psychology and Interdisciplinary Inquiry, San Francisco, CA 94612. Offers human science (MA, PhD), including consciousness and spirituality, humanistic and transpersonal psychology, integrative health studies, organizational systems, social transformation; organizational systems (MA, PhD), including consciousness and spirituality, humanistic and transpersonal psychology, integrative health studies, leadership of sustainable systems (MA), organizational systems, social transformation; psychology (MA, PhD), including consciousness and spirituality, creativity studies (MA), humanistic and transpersonal psychology, integrative health studies, Jungian studies, marriage and family therapy (MA), organizational systems, social transformation. *Program availability:* Online learning. Terminal master's awarded for partial completion of doctoral program. *Degree requirements:* For master's, thesis or alternative; for doctorate, thesis/dissertation. *Entrance requirements:* Additional exam requirements/recommendations for international students: Required—TOEFL (minimum score 580 paper-based; 93 iBT). Electronic applications accepted. *Faculty research:* Humanistic theory, health studies, organizational systems, consciousness and spirituality, social transformation.

Seattle Pacific University, MS in Marriage and Family Therapy Program, Seattle, WA 98119-1997. Offers marriage and family therapy (MS); medical family therapy (Certificate). *Accreditation:* AAMFT/COAMFTE. *Program availability:* Part-time. *Students:* 52 full-time (38 women), 8 part-time (all women); includes 6 minority (1 Black or African American, non-Hispanic/Latino; 1 Asian, non-Hispanic/Latino; 3 Hispanic/Latino; 1 Two or more races, non-Hispanic/Latino). Average age 28. 81 applicants, 62% accepted, 36 enrolled. In 2017, 37 master's awarded. *Degree requirements:* For master's, thesis optional, internship, clinical portfolio. *Entrance requirements:* For master's, GRE General Test or MAT, interview. Additional exam requirements/recommendations for international students: Required—TOEFL (minimum score 550 paper-based). *Application deadline:* For fall admission, 1/23 for domestic students, 2/1 for international students. Applications are processed on a rolling basis. Application fee: $50. Electronic applications accepted. *Expenses:* Contact institution. *Financial support:* Fellowships and Federal Work-Study available. Financial award applicants required to submit FAFSA. *Faculty research:* Roles of therapists, models of collaboration, medical and mental health theories of marriage and family therapy. *Unit head:* Dr. Scott Edwards, Chair, 206-281-2681, E-mail: sedwards@spu.edu.
Website: http://spu.edu/academics/school-of-psychology-family-community/graduate-programs/marriage-and-family-therapy

Seattle University, School of Theology and Ministry, Program in Couples and Family Therapy, Seattle, WA 98122-1090. Offers MA. *Program availability:* Part-time, evening/weekend. *Faculty:* 15 full-time (7 women), 18 part-time/adjunct (11 women). *Students:* 16 full-time (14 women), 16 part-time (14 women); includes 9 minority (2 Black or African American, non-Hispanic/Latino; 4 American Indian or Alaska Native, non-Hispanic/Latino; 2 Hispanic/Latino; 1 Two or more races, non-Hispanic/Latino). Average age 35. 25 applicants, 48% accepted, 8 enrolled. In 2017, 7 master's awarded. *Entrance requirements:* For master's, minimum GPA of 2.75 (3.0 for international students); two years of experience in some form of education, ministry, or service as a profession or volunteer; recommendations; interview with admissions committee. *Application deadline:* For fall admission, 7/1 for domestic students. *Expenses:* Contact institution. *Financial support:* In 2017–18, 22 students received support. Scholarships/grants available. *Unit head:* Rev. Clinton McNair, Director, 206-296-6968. *Application contact:* Catherine Kehoe Fallon, Admissions Coordinator, 206-296-5333, Fax: 206-296-5329, E-mail: fallon@seattleu.edu.
Website: https://www.seattleu.edu/stm/degrees/macft/

Seton Hall University, College of Education and Human Services, Department of Professional Psychology and Family Therapy, Program in Psychological Studies, South Orange, NJ 07079-2697. Offers individualized (MA); marriage and family therapy (MA); sport and exercise psychology (MA). *Program availability:* Part-time, evening/weekend. *Degree requirements:* For master's, comprehensive exam. *Entrance requirements:* For master's, GRE or MAT. *Faculty research:* Cognitive style, self-esteem anxiety in preadolescence, object relation, bonding.

Seton Hill University, MA Program in Marriage and Family Therapy, Greensburg, PA 15601. Offers MA. *Accreditation:* AAMFT/COAMFTE. *Entrance requirements:* For master's, 3 letters of recommendation, interview, resume, letter of intent, transcripts. Additional exam requirements/recommendations for international students: Required—TOEFL (minimum score 650 paper-based; 114 iBT), IELTS (minimum score 7). *Application deadline:* For fall admission, 8/15 for domestic students; for spring admission, 12/15 for domestic students. Applications are processed on a rolling basis. Electronic applications accepted. *Expenses: Tuition:* Part-time $734 per credit. Tuition and fees vary according to class time, course level, course load and program. *Financial support:* Federal Work-Study, scholarships/grants, and unspecified assistantships available. Financial award application deadline: 8/15; financial award applicants required to submit FAFSA.
Website: http://www.setonhill.edu/academics/graduate_programs/marriage_and_family_therapy

Sioux Falls Seminary, Graduate and Professional Programs, Master of Divinity Program, Sioux Falls, SD 57105-1599. Offers marriage and family therapy (M Div); pastoral care and counseling (M Div). Program also offered in Omaha, NE. *Accreditation:* ACIPE. *Program availability:* Part-time, online learning.

Southeastern University, College of Behavioral and Social Sciences, Lakeland, FL 33801-6099. Offers human services (MA); international community development (MA); marriage and family counseling (MS); professional counseling (MS); school counseling (MS); social work (MSW). *Program availability:* Evening/weekend. *Faculty:* 9 full-time (6 women), 7 part-time/adjunct (4 women). *Students:* 72 full-time (60 women), 9 part-time (all women); includes 28 minority (12 Black or African American, non-Hispanic/Latino; 2 Asian, non-Hispanic/Latino; 13 Hispanic/Latino; 1 Native Hawaiian or other Pacific Islander, non-Hispanic/Latino), 1 international. Average age 29. Application fee: $50. Electronic applications accepted. *Unit head:* Erica H. Sirrine, Dean, 863-667-5341, E-mail: ehsirrine@seu.edu.
Website: http://www.seu.edu/behavior/

Southern California Seminary, Graduate and Professional Programs, El Cajon, CA 92019. Offers Biblical studies (MABS); counseling psychology (MACP); marriage and family therapy (MAMFT); psychology (Psy D); religious studies (MRS); theology (M Div). *Program availability:* Part-time, evening/weekend, online learning. *Degree requirements:* For master's, thesis (for some programs); for doctorate, thesis/dissertation. *Entrance requirements:* For doctorate, master's degree in psychology. Additional exam requirements/recommendations for international students: Required—TOEFL (minimum score 550 paper-based). Electronic applications accepted.

Southern Nazarene University, College of Professional and Graduate Studies, Department of Psychology and Counseling, Bethany, OK 73008. Offers counseling psychology (MA, MSCP); marital and family therapy (MA). *Degree requirements:* For master's, thesis optional. *Entrance requirements:* For master's, English proficiency exam, minimum GPA of 3.0 in last 60 hours/major, 2.7 overall.

Stetson University, College of Arts and Sciences, Division of Education, Department of Counselor Education, DeLand, FL 32723. Offers marriage, couple and family counseling (MS); mental health counseling (MS); school counseling (MS). *Accreditation:* ACA. *Program availability:* Evening/weekend. *Faculty:* 6 full-time (5 women), 5 part-time/adjunct (2 women). *Students:* 100 full-time (82 women), 9 part-time (all women); includes 37 minority (9 Black or African American, non-Hispanic/Latino; 4 American Indian or Alaska Native, non-Hispanic/Latino; 15 Hispanic/Latino; 9 Two or more races, non-Hispanic/Latino), 5 international. Average age 30. 42 applicants, 79% accepted, 22 enrolled. In 2017, 24 master's awarded. *Entrance requirements:* For master's, GRE or MAT, transcripts, three letters of recommendation, group interview. Additional exam requirements/recommendations for international students: Required—TOEFL (minimum score 90 iBT), IELTS (minimum score 7). *Application deadline:* For fall admission, 8/1 priority date for domestic students; for spring admission, 1/1 priority date for domestic students; for summer admission, 5/1 priority date for domestic students. Applications are processed on a rolling basis. Application fee: $50. Electronic applications accepted. *Expenses:* $911 per credit hour. *Financial support:* In 2017–18, 29 students received support. Federal Work-Study, scholarships/grants, unspecified assistantships, and tuition waivers (for staff and dependents) available. Support available to part-time students. Financial award applicants required to submit FAFSA. *Faculty research:* Play therapy, trauma, spirituality and wellness in counseling, gatekeeping and supervision in counselor education, reproductive health in counseling, LBGTQ+ issues in counseling. *Unit head:* Dr. Leila Roach, Chair, 386-822-8992. *Application contact:* Jamie Vanderlip, Director of Admissions for Graduate, Transfer and Adult Programs, 386-822-7100, Fax: 386-822-7112, E-mail: jlvander@stetson.edu.

Syracuse University, David B. Falk College of Sport and Human Dynamics, Dual Master's Program in Social Work and Marriage and Family Therapy (MSW/MA), Syracuse, NY 13244. Offers MSW/MA. *Accreditation:* AAMFT/COAMFTE. *Entrance requirements:* Additional exam requirements/recommendations for international students: Required—TOEFL or IELTS. *Application deadline:* For fall admission, 2/15 priority date for domestic and international students; for summer admission, 1/15 priority date for domestic students, 1/15 for international students. Application fee: $75. Electronic applications accepted. *Financial support:* Fellowships, research assistantships, teaching assistantships, career-related internships or fieldwork, and scholarships/grants available. Financial award application deadline: 1/1. *Faculty research:* Human diversity in social context, foundations of social work practice, policy and services in child welfare, child and family policy, social welfare policy and services. *Unit head:* Prof. Keith Alford, Director, School of Social Work, 315-443-5562, Fax: 315-443-2562, E-mail: kalford@syr.edu. *Application contact:* Felicia Otero, Director of College Admissions, 315-443-5555, Fax: 315-443-2562, E-mail: falk@syr.edu.
Website: https://falk.syr.edu/marriage-family-therapy/academic-programs/#mswmft

Syracuse University, David B. Falk College of Sport and Human Dynamics, Programs in Marriage and Family Therapy, Syracuse, NY 13202. Offers MA, PhD. *Accreditation:* AAMFT/COAMFTE. *Program availability:* Part-time. *Degree requirements:* For master's, thesis or alternative, internship; for doctorate, comprehensive exam, thesis/dissertation. *Entrance requirements:* For master's and doctorate, GRE, personal statement, three letters of recommendation, official transcripts, resume. Additional exam requirements/recommendations for international students: Required—TOEFL (minimum score 100 iBT). *Application deadline:* For fall admission, 2/15 priority date for domestic and international students; for spring admission, 11/1 priority date for domestic students, 11/15 priority date for international students. Application fee: $75. Electronic applications accepted. *Financial support:* Fellowships with full tuition reimbursements, research assistantships with tuition reimbursements, teaching assistantships with tuition reimbursements, career-related internships or fieldwork, and tuition waivers available. Financial award application deadline: 1/1; financial award applicants required to submit FAFSA. *Faculty research:* Marriage and family therapy theory and techniques. *Unit head:* Dr. Thom deLara, Chair, 315-443-9830, E-mail: tdelara@syr.edu. *Application contact:* Felicia Otero, Director of Graduate Admissions, 315-443-5555, E-mail: falk@syr.edu.
Website: https://falk.syr.edu/marriage-family-therapy/

Texas A&M University–Central Texas, Graduate Studies and Research, Killeen, TX 76549. Offers accounting (MS); business administration (MBA); clinical mental health counseling (MS); criminal justice (MCJ); curriculum and instruction (M Ed); educational administration (M Ed); educational psychology - experimental psychology (MS); history (MA); human resource management (MS); information systems (MS); liberal studies (MS); management and leadership (MS); marriage and family therapy (MS); mathematics (MS); political science (MA); school counseling (M Ed); school psychology (Ed S).

Texas A&M University–San Antonio, Department of Counseling, Health and Kinesiology, San Antonio, TX 78224. Offers clinical mental health counseling (MA); counseling and guidance (MA); kinesiology (MS); marriage and family counseling (MA). *Program availability:* Part-time, evening/weekend, online learning. *Faculty:* 12 full-time (5 women), 6 part-time/adjunct (4 women). *Students:* 48 full-time (35 women), 146 part-time (118 women); includes 135 minority (24 Black or African American, non-Hispanic/Latino; 3 Asian, non-Hispanic/Latino; 103 Hispanic/Latino; 5 Two or more races, non-Hispanic/Latino), 2 international. Average age 34. 201 applicants, 56% accepted, 62 enrolled. In 2017, 68 master's awarded. *Degree requirements:* For master's, comprehensive exam, thesis or alternative. *Entrance requirements:* For master's, MAT or GRE (composite quantitative and verbal). Additional exam requirements/recommendations for international students: Required—TOEFL (minimum score 550 paper-based; 79 iBT), IELTS (minimum score 6). *Application deadline:* For fall admission, 3/15 priority date for domestic and international students; for spring admission, 11/1 priority date for domestic and international students; for summer admission, 4/1 priority date for domestic and international students. Applications are processed on a rolling basis. Application fee: $35 ($50 for international students). Electronic applications accepted. *Expenses:* Tuition, state resident: full-time $3475; part-time $1930 per semester. Tuition, nonresident: full-time $10,945; part-time $6080 per semester. *Required fees:* $2148; $1412 per year. $706 per semester. Tuition and fees vary according to course load. *Financial support:* In 2017–18, 10 students received support. Federal Work-Study, scholarships/grants, and tuition waivers available. Financial award application deadline: 3/15; financial award applicants required to submit FAFSA. *Unit head:* Dr. Suzanne Mudge, Department Chair. *Application contact:* Caitie Garza, Graduate Admissions Coordinator, 210-784-1300, E-mail: beajaguar@tamusa.edu.
Website: http://www.tamusa.edu/collegeofeducationandhumandevelopment/counselinghealthkinesiology/index.html

Texas State University, The Graduate College, College of Education, Program in Professional Counseling, San Marcos, TX 78666. Offers clinical mental health counseling (MA); marriage and family counseling (MA); school counseling (MA). *Accreditation:* ACA. *Program availability:* Part-time. *Faculty:* 12 full-time (11 women), 12 part-time/adjunct (9 women). *Students:* 87 full-time (71 women), 99 part-time (80 women); includes 49 minority (6 Black or African American, non-Hispanic/Latino; 6 Asian, non-Hispanic/Latino; 30 Hispanic/Latino; 7 Two or more races, non-Hispanic/Latino). Average age 31. 144 applicants, 46% accepted, 23 enrolled. In 2017, 57 master's awarded. *Degree requirements:* For master's, comprehensive exam, thesis optional, internship. *Entrance requirements:* For master's, GRE General Test (minimum preferred score of 291 [150 verbal, 141 quantitative]), baccalaureate degree from regionally-accredited institution with minimum GPA of 3.0 in last 60 hours of undergraduate work; resume; statement of purpose addressing professional goals, reasoning for specified emphasis (i.e., community, school, marital), strengths and weaknesses, and perspective on diversity; 3 references. Additional exam requirements/recommendations for international students: Required—TOEFL (minimum iBT scores: 22 listening, 22 reading, 24 speaking, 21 writing). *Application deadline:* For fall admission, 2/15 for domestic and international students; for spring admission, 10/1 for domestic and international students; for summer admission, 2/15 for domestic and international students. Applications are processed on a rolling basis. Application fee: $40 ($90 for international students). Electronic applications accepted. *Expenses:* Tuition, state resident: full-time $7868; part-time $3934 per semester. Tuition, nonresident: full-time $17,828; part-time $8914 per semester. *Required fees:* $2092; $1435 per semester. Tuition and fees vary according to course load. *Financial support:* In 2017–18, 97 students received support, including 11 research assistantships (averaging $7,298 per year); teaching assistantships, Federal Work-Study, institutionally sponsored loans, and scholarships/grants also available. Support available to part-time students. Financial award application deadline: 3/1; financial award applicants required to submit FAFSA. *Unit head:* Dr. Kevin Fall, Graduate Advisor, 512-245-2081, Fax: 512-245-8872, E-mail: kf22@txstate.edu. *Application contact:* Dr. Andrea Golato, Dean of Graduate School, 512-245-2581, Fax: 512-245-8365, E-mail: gradcollege@txstate.edu.
Website: http://www.gradcollege.txstate.edu/programs/counseling.html

Texas Tech University, Graduate School, College of Human Sciences, Department of Community, Family, and Addiction Sciences, Lubbock, TX 79409-1250. Offers marriage and family therapy (MS, PhD). *Accreditation:* AAMFT/COAMFTE. *Faculty:* 15 full-time (5 women), 2 part-time/adjunct (1 woman). *Students:* 50 full-time (36 women), 13 part-time (6 women); includes 16 minority (4 Black or African American, non-Hispanic/Latino; 9 Hispanic/Latino; 3 Two or more races, non-Hispanic/Latino), 4 international. Average age 28. 50 applicants, 46% accepted, 19 enrolled. In 2017, 13 master's, 8 doctorates awarded. *Degree requirements:* For master's, comprehensive exam, thesis optional; for doctorate, thesis/dissertation. *Entrance requirements:* For master's and doctorate, GRE. Additional exam requirements/recommendations for international students: Required—TOEFL (minimum score 550 paper-based; 79 iBT). *Application deadline:* For fall admission, 6/1 priority date for domestic students, 1/15 priority date for international students; for spring admission, 9/1 priority date for domestic students, 6/15 priority date for international students. Applications are processed on a rolling basis. Application fee: $60. Electronic applications accepted. *Expenses:* Contact institution. *Financial support:* In 2017–18, 52 students received support, including 49 fellowships (averaging $4,977 per year), 10 research assistantships (averaging $10,956 per year), 19 teaching assistantships (averaging $14,655 per year); career-related internships or fieldwork, Federal Work-Study, scholarships/grants, health care benefits, and unspecified assistantships also available. Financial award application deadline: 2/1; financial award applicants required to submit FAFSA. *Faculty research:* Medical family therapy, systemic intervention for intimate partner violence, gene-environment influences on substance use behaviors and the effect of language on substance users, the influence of technology on individuals, couples, families, systemic understanding of contemporary sexual issues within couple relationships. *Total annual research expenditures:* $858,877. *Unit head:* Dr. Sterling T. Shumway, Department Chair, 806-742-3060, Fax: 806-742-0053, E-mail: sterling.shumway@ttu.edu. *Application contact:* Lori Minner, Coordinator, 806-742-3060, Fax: 806-742-0053, E-mail: lori.minner@ttu.edu.
Website: http://www.depts.ttu.edu/hs/cfas

Texas Woman's University, Graduate School, College of Professional Education, Department of Family Sciences, Denton, TX 76204. Offers child development (MS); child life (MS); counseling and development (MS); early childhood development and education (PhD); early childhood education (M Ed); family studies (MS, PhD); family therapy (MS, PhD). *Accreditation:* ACA (one or more programs are accredited). *Program availability:* Part-time, evening/weekend. *Faculty:* 24 full-time (19 women), 17 part-time/adjunct (15 women). *Students:* 153 full-time (146 women), 237 part-time (220 women);

includes 169 minority (81 Black or African American, non-Hispanic/Latino; 9 Asian, non-Hispanic/Latino; 68 Hispanic/Latino; 11 Two or more races, non-Hispanic/Latino), 10 international. Average age 32. 235 applicants, 55% accepted, 87 enrolled. In 2017, 77 master's, 15 doctorates awarded. Terminal master's awarded for partial completion of doctoral program. *Degree requirements:* For master's, comprehensive exam (for some programs), thesis, professional paper, or coursework; practicums (for some programs); for doctorate, comprehensive exam, thesis/dissertation. *Entrance requirements:* For master's, GRE with preferred minimum score 147 Verbal, 144 Quantitative, 4.0 Analytical (for MS in child development and M Ed), minimum GPA of 3.0 (3.25 for family therapy), 3 letters of recommendations (1 for child life), letter of intent, curriculum vitae/resume, interview, writing sample; for doctorate, GRE (preferred minimum score 147 Verbal, 144 Quantitative, 4.0 Analytical), minimum GPA of 3.5 (3.35 for family studies) on all prior graduate work, curriculum vitae/resume, letter of intent. Additional exam requirements/recommendations for international students: Required—TOEFL (minimum score 550 paper-based; 79 iBT); Recommended—IELTS (minimum score 6.5), TSE (minimum score 53). *Application deadline:* For fall admission, 3/1 priority date for domestic and international students; for spring admission, 11/1 priority date for domestic students, 7/1 priority date for international students. Applications are processed on a rolling basis. Application fee: $50 ($75 for international students). Electronic applications accepted. *Expenses:* $7,520 per year full-time in-state; $16,820 per year full-time out-of-state. *Financial support:* In 2017–18, 104 students received support, including 12 teaching assistantships (averaging $22,972 per year); career-related internships or fieldwork, Federal Work-Study, institutionally sponsored loans, scholarships/grants, traineeships, health care benefits, and unspecified assistantships also available. Support available to part-time students. Financial award application deadline: 3/1; financial award applicants required to submit FAFSA. *Faculty research:* Parenting/parent education, play therapy, healthy relationships, child development, technology integration. *Unit head:* Dr. Jerry Whitworth, Interim Chair, 940-898-2685, Fax: 940-898-2676, E-mail: famsci@twu.edu. *Application contact:* Korie Hawkins, Associate Director of Admissions, Graduate Recruitment, 940-898-3188, Fax: 940-898-3081, E-mail: admissions@twu.edu.
Website: http://www.twu.edu/family-sciences/

Thomas Jefferson University, Jefferson College of Health Professions, Department of Couple and Family Therapy, Philadelphia, PA 19107. Offers MFT. *Accreditation:* AAMFT/COAMFTE. *Entrance requirements:* Additional exam requirements/recommendations for international students: Required—TOEFL (minimum score 87 iBT). Electronic applications accepted. *Faculty research:* Developing multicultural therapy competence: exploring the impact of a clinical practicum with marginalized clients in non-traditional settings.

Trevecca Nazarene University, Graduate Counseling Program, Nashville, TN 37210-2877. Offers clinical counseling: teaching and supervision (PhD); clinical mental health counseling (MA); marriage and family counseling/therapy (MMFC/T). *Accreditation:* ACA. *Program availability:* Part-time, evening/weekend. *Faculty:* 7 full-time (3 women), 11 part-time/adjunct (8 women). *Students:* 157 full-time (129 women), 73 part-time (50 women); includes 49 minority (38 Black or African American, non-Hispanic/Latino; 5 Hispanic/Latino; 6 Two or more races, non-Hispanic/Latino). Average age 35. In 2017, 47 master's, 3 doctorates awarded. *Degree requirements:* For master's, comprehensive exam; for doctorate, comprehensive exam, thesis/dissertation. *Entrance requirements:* For master's, MAT (minimum score of 380) or GRE (minimum score of 290 combined verbal and quantitative), minimum GPA of 2.7, official transcript from regionally accredited institution, 2 reference assessment forms; for doctorate, GRE (minimum scores: 300 combined verbal and quantitative, 3.5 analytical writing), minimum GPA of 3.25, official transcript of master's degree from regionally accredited institution, 3 recommendation forms, 400-word letter of intent, professional vita, interview. Additional exam requirements/recommendations for international students: Required—TOEFL (minimum score 600 paper-based; 100 iBT). *Application deadline:* Applications are processed on a rolling basis. Application fee: $0. Electronic applications accepted. *Expenses:* $636 per credit hour (MA and MMFC/T); $799 per credit hour (PhD). *Financial support:* Applicants required to submit FAFSA. *Unit head:* Dr. Susan Lahey, Director, 615-248-1384, Fax: 615-248-1662, E-mail: admissions_gradcouns@trevecca.edu. *Application contact:* 615-248-1384, Fax: 615-248-1662, E-mail: admissions_gradcouns@trevecca.edu.
Website: http://trevecca.edu/gradcounseling

Universidad de las Americas, A.C., Program in Psychology, Mexico City, Mexico. Offers family therapy (MA).

The University of Akron, Graduate School, College of Health Professions, School of Counseling, Program in Marriage and Family Counseling/Therapy, Akron, OH 44325. Offers MA, MS. *Accreditation:* AAMFT/COAMFTE; ACA. *Students:* 47 full-time (39 women), 38 part-time (31 women); includes 26 minority (12 Black or African American, non-Hispanic/Latino; 1 American Indian or Alaska Native, non-Hispanic/Latino; 1 Asian, non-Hispanic/Latino; 4 Hispanic/Latino; 8 Two or more races, non-Hispanic/Latino), 1 international. Average age 30. 33 applicants, 73% accepted, 15 enrolled. In 2017, 36 master's awarded. *Degree requirements:* For master's, comprehensive exam. *Entrance requirements:* For master's, minimum GPA of 2.75, three letters of recommendation. Additional exam requirements/recommendations for international students: Required—TOEFL (minimum score 79 iBT), IELTS (minimum score 6.5). *Application deadline:* For fall admission, 3/15 for domestic and international students; for spring admission, 10/1 for domestic and international students. Application fee: $45 ($70 for international students). Electronic applications accepted. *Application contact:* Dr. Heather Katafiasz, Program Director, 330-972-6637, E-mail: hkatafiasz@uakron.edu.
Website: https://www.uakron.edu/soc/masters/mft-masters/index.dot

The University of Alabama, Graduate School, College of Human Environmental Sciences, Department of Human Development and Family Studies, Tuscaloosa, AL 35487. Offers human development and family studies (MSHES); marriage and family therapy (MSHES); parent and family life education (MSHES). *Faculty:* 11 full-time (8 women), 2 part-time/adjunct (both women). *Students:* 25 full-time (19 women), 1 (woman) part-time; includes 6 minority (4 Black or African American, non-Hispanic/Latino; 1 Hispanic/Latino; 1 Two or more races, non-Hispanic/Latino). Average age 26. 24 applicants, 75% accepted, 14 enrolled. In 2017, 14 master's awarded. Terminal master's awarded for partial completion of doctoral program. *Degree requirements:* For master's, comprehensive exam (for some programs), thesis (for some programs). *Entrance requirements:* For master's, GRE General Test or MAT, minimum GPA of 3.0. Additional exam requirements/recommendations for international students: Required—TOEFL (minimum score 79 iBT), IELTS (minimum score 6.5). *Application deadline:* For fall admission, 12/15 priority date for domestic and international students. Applications are processed on a rolling basis. Application fee: $50 ($60 for international students). Electronic applications accepted. *Financial support:* In 2017–18, 15 students received support, including research assistantships with full tuition reimbursements available (averaging $13,140 per year), teaching assistantships (averaging $13,140 per year); fellowships, career-related internships or fieldwork, Federal Work-Study, scholarships/grants, health care benefits, and unspecified assistantships also available. Financial award application deadline: 3/15. *Faculty research:* Parent/child relationships, preschool curricula and quality measures for child care programs, family strengths and adolescent behaviors, depression in mothers and infants, word association and word learning in young children, bullying behaviors in children, attachment parenting, medical play therapy, socialization of young children, impact of daily experiences on relationship quality, re-entry of service members into civilian roles. *Unit head:* Dr. Carroll M. Tingle, Chair, 205-348-6158, Fax: 205-348-8153, E-mail: ctingle@ches.ua.edu. *Application contact:* Dr. Maria Hernandez-Reif, Professor, 205-348-5894, Fax: 205-348-8153, E-mail: mhernandez-reif@ches.ua.edu.
Website: http://www.hdfs.ches.ua.edu/

University of Central Florida, College of Community Innovation and Education, Department of Counselor Education and School Psychology, Program in Marriage, Couple, and Family Therapy, Orlando, FL 32816. Offers MA, Certificate. *Students:* 47 full-time (37 women), 7 part-time (all women); includes 21 minority (11 Black or African American, non-Hispanic/Latino; 1 Asian, non-Hispanic/Latino; 9 Hispanic/Latino), 2 international. Average age 28. 55 applicants, 60% accepted, 25 enrolled. In 2017, 23 master's, 15 other advanced degrees awarded. *Degree requirements:* For master's, thesis or alternative. *Entrance requirements:* For master's, GRE, letters of recommendation, resume, goal statement. Additional exam requirements/recommendations for international students: Required—TOEFL. *Application deadline:* For fall admission, 2/15 for domestic students. Application fee: $30. Electronic applications accepted. *Expenses:* Tuition, state resident: part-time $288.16 per credit hour. Tuition, nonresident: part-time $1073.31 per credit hour. Tuition and fees vary according to program. *Financial support:* In 2017–18, 9 students received support, including 2 fellowships with partial tuition reimbursements available (averaging $5,800 per year), 8 research assistantships with partial tuition reimbursements available (averaging $9,517 per year); tuition waivers also available. Financial award application deadline: 3/1; financial award applicants required to submit FAFSA. *Unit head:* Dr. Sejal Barden, Program Coordinator, 407-823-6106, E-mail: sejal.barden@ucf.edu. *Application contact:* Associate Director, Graduate Admissions, 407-823-2766, Fax: 407-823-6442, E-mail: gradadmissions@ucf.edu.
Website: http://education.ucf.edu/counselored/progDetail.cfm?pid=ma#1

University of Central Oklahoma, The Jackson College of Graduate Studies, College of Education and Professional Studies, Department of Human Environmental Sciences, Edmond, OK 73034-5209. Offers family and child studies (MS), including family life education, infant/child specialist, marriage and family therapy; nutrition-food science (MS). *Program availability:* Part-time. *Faculty:* 5 full-time (4 women), 8 part-time/adjunct (6 women). *Students:* 46 full-time (38 women), 65 part-time (62 women); includes 48 minority (27 Black or African American, non-Hispanic/Latino; 3 American Indian or Alaska Native, non-Hispanic/Latino; 3 Asian, non-Hispanic/Latino; 7 Hispanic/Latino; 8 Two or more races, non-Hispanic/Latino), 13 international. Average age 29. 68 applicants, 93% accepted, 31 enrolled. In 2017, 37 master's awarded. *Degree requirements:* For master's, comprehensive exam (for some programs), thesis (for some programs). *Entrance requirements:* For master's, GRE, essay, physical, CPR and First Aid training. Additional exam requirements/recommendations for international students: Required—TOEFL (minimum score 550 paper-based; 79 iBT), IELTS (minimum score 6.5). *Application deadline:* For fall admission, 1/15 for domestic students, 7/15 for international students; for spring admission, 11/15 for international students. Applications are processed on a rolling basis. Application fee: $60. Electronic applications accepted. *Expenses:* Tuition, state resident: full-time $5375; part-time $268.75 per credit hour. Tuition, nonresident: full-time $13,295; part-time $664.75 per credit hour. *Required fees:* $626; $31.30 per credit hour. One-time fee: $50. Tuition and fees vary according to program. *Financial support:* In 2017–18, 11 students received support, including 8 research assistantships with partial tuition reimbursements available (averaging $4,436 per year); teaching assistantships, career-related internships or fieldwork, scholarships/grants, tuition waivers (partial), and unspecified assistantships also available. Financial award application deadline: 3/31; financial award applicants required to submit FAFSA. *Unit head:* Dr. Kaye Sears, Chair, 405-974-5551, Fax: 405-974-3850. *Application contact:* Carlie Wellington, Assistant Director, CEPS Graduate Enrollment, 405-974-5105, Fax: 405-974-3851, E-mail: gradcoll@uco.edu.
Website: http://sites.uco.edu/ceps/dept/Professional-Studies-Programs/hes/index.asp

University of Colorado Denver, School of Education and Human Development, Program in Counseling Psychology and Counselor Education, Denver, CO 80217. Offers counseling (MA), including clinical mental health counseling, couple and family counseling, multicultural counseling, school counseling; school counseling (MA). *Accreditation:* ACA; NCATE. *Program availability:* Part-time, evening/weekend. *Degree requirements:* For master's, comprehensive exam (for some programs), thesis or alternative, 63-66 hours. *Entrance requirements:* For master's, GRE or MAT (unless applicant already holds a graduate degree), letters of recommendation, interview, resume, transcripts from all colleges/universities attended. Additional exam requirements/recommendations for international students: Required—TOEFL (minimum score 525 paper-based; 71 iBT); Recommended—IELTS (minimum score 6.3). Electronic applications accepted. *Expenses:* Contact institution. *Faculty research:* Spiritual issues in counseling, multicultural and diversity issues in counseling, adolescent suicide, career development.

University of Denver, Graduate School of Social Work, Denver, CO 80208. Offers animal-assisted social work (Certificate); couples and family therapy (Certificate); social work (MSW, PhD); social work with Latinos/as (Certificate). *Accreditation:* CSWE (one or more programs are accredited). *Program availability:* Part-time, evening/weekend. *Faculty:* 40 full-time (27 women), 103 part-time/adjunct (88 women). *Students:* 511 full-time (457 women), 11 part-time (10 women); includes 117 minority (19 Black or African American, non-Hispanic/Latino; 7 American Indian or Alaska Native, non-Hispanic/Latino; 14 Asian, non-Hispanic/Latino; 58 Hispanic/Latino; 19 Two or more races, non-Hispanic/Latino), 1 international. Average age 28. 919 applicants, 79% accepted, 302 enrolled. In 2017, 278 master's, 7 doctorates, 55 other advanced degrees awarded. *Degree requirements:* For doctorate, comprehensive exam, thesis/dissertation. *Entrance requirements:* For master's, 20 undergraduate semester hours in the arts and humanities, social/behavioral sciences, and biological sciences; for doctorate, master's degree in social work or in one of the social sciences with substantial professional experience in the social work field; two years of post-master's practice experience (preferred). Additional exam requirements/recommendations for international students: Required—TOEFL (minimum score 587 paper-based; 95 iBT). *Application deadline:* For fall admission, 1/15 priority date for domestic and international students. Applications are processed on a rolling basis. Application fee: $65. Electronic applications accepted. *Expenses:* $47,823 per year on-campus full-time. *Financial support:* In 2017–18, 492 students received support, including 1 teaching assistantship with tuition reimbursement available (averaging $16,000 per year); Federal Work-Study, scholarships/grants, and unspecified assistantships also available. Support available to part-time students. Financial award application deadline: 2/15; financial award applicants required to submit FAFSA. *Faculty research:* Aging, youth, community, mental health, families. *Unit head:* Dr. Amanda Moore McBride, Dean, 303-871-2203, Fax: 303-871-2845. *Application contact:* Roberto Garcia, Director of Enrollment Management, 303-871-2602, E-mail: gssw-admission@du.edu.
Website: http://www.du.edu/socialwork

University of Florida, Graduate School, College of Education, School of Human Development and Organizational Studies in Education, Gainesville, FL 32611. Offers counseling and counselor education (Ed D, PhD), including counseling and counselor education, marriage and family counseling, mental health counseling, school counseling and guidance; educational leadership (M Ed, MAE, Ed D, PhD, Ed S), including educational leadership (Ed D, PhD), educational policy (Ed D, PhD); higher education administration (Ed D, PhD), including education policy (Ed D), educational policy, higher education administration; marriage and family counseling (M Ed, MAE, Ed D, PhD, Ed S); mental health counseling (M Ed, MAE, Ed D, PhD, Ed S); research and evaluation methodology (M Ed, MAE, Ed D, PhD); school counseling and guidance (M Ed, MAE, Ed D, PhD, Ed S); student personnel in higher education (M Ed, MAE). *Accreditation:* ACA (one or more programs are accredited); NCATE. *Program availability:* Part-time, online learning. Terminal master's awarded for partial completion of doctoral program. *Degree requirements:* For master's, thesis optional; for doctorate, comprehensive exam, thesis/dissertation. *Entrance requirements:* For master's and doctorate, GRE General Test, minimum GPA of 3.0 (undergraduate), 3.5 (graduate); for Ed S, GRE General Test. Additional exam requirements/recommendations for international students: Required—TOEFL (minimum score 550 paper-based; 80 iBT), IELTS (minimum score 6). Electronic applications accepted.

University of Guelph, Graduate Studies, College of Social and Applied Human Sciences, Department of Family Relations and Applied Nutrition, Guelph, ON N1G 2W1, Canada. Offers applied nutrition (MAN); family relations and human development (M Sc, PhD), including applied human nutrition, couple and family therapy (M Sc), family relations and human development. *Accreditation:* AAMFT/COAMFTE (one or more programs are accredited). *Program availability:* Part-time. *Degree requirements:* For master's, thesis (for some programs); for doctorate, comprehensive exam, thesis/dissertation. *Entrance requirements:* For master's, minimum B+ average; for doctorate, master's degree in family relations and human development or related field with a minimum B+ average or master's degree in applied human nutrition. Additional exam requirements/recommendations for international students: Required—TOEFL (minimum score 600 paper-based). Electronic applications accepted. *Faculty research:* Child and adolescent development, social gerontology, family roles and relations, couple and family therapy, applied human nutrition.

University of Holy Cross, Graduate Programs, New Orleans, LA 70131-7399. Offers biomedical sciences (MS); Catholic theology (MA); counseling (MA, PhD), including community counseling (MA), marriage and family counseling (MA), school counseling (MA); educational leadership (M Ed); executive leadership (Ed D); management (MS), including healthcare management, operations management; teaching and learning (M Ed). *Accreditation:* ACA; NCATE. *Program availability:* Part-time, evening/weekend, online learning. *Faculty:* 7 full-time (4 women), 8 part-time/adjunct (3 women). *Students:* 67 full-time (55 women), 69 part-time (55 women); includes 51 minority (46 Black or African American, non-Hispanic/Latino; 2 American Indian or Alaska Native, non-Hispanic/Latino; 1 Asian, non-Hispanic/Latino; 2 Hispanic/Latino). Average age 30. 20 applicants, 50% accepted. In 2017, 28 degrees awarded. *Degree requirements:* For master's, thesis. *Entrance requirements:* For master's, GRE General Test, minimum GPA of 2.7. *Application deadline:* For fall admission, 9/1 for domestic students. Application fee: $15. *Expenses: Tuition:* Full-time $10,890; part-time $605 per credit hour. *Required fees:* $1624; $812 per semester. One-time fee: $50. *Financial support:* Federal Work-Study and tuition waivers (partial) available. Support available to part-time students. Financial award application deadline: 6/1. *Unit head:* Dr. Myles Seghers, Dean of Humanities, Education, and Counseling, 504-394-7744 Ext. 214, Fax: 504-391-2421, E-mail: mseghers@olhcc.edu. *Application contact:* Anne-Katherine Lene, Director of Student Enrollment, 504-394-7744 Ext. 110, Fax: 504-391-2421, E-mail: aklene@olhcc.edu.

University of Houston–Clear Lake, School of Human Sciences and Humanities, Programs in Human Sciences, Houston, TX 77058-1002. Offers behavioral sciences (MA), including criminology, cross cultural studies, general psychology, sociology; clinical psychology (MA); criminology (MA); cross cultural studies (MA); family therapy (MA); fitness and human performance (MA); school psychology (MA). *Accreditation:* AAMFT/COAMFTE. *Program availability:* Part-time, evening/weekend, online learning. *Degree requirements:* For master's, thesis or alternative. *Entrance requirements:* For master's, GRE General Test. Additional exam requirements/recommendations for international students: Required—TOEFL (minimum score 550 paper-based). Electronic applications accepted. *Faculty research:* Smoking cessation, adolescent sexuality, white collar crime, serial murder, human factors/human computer interaction.

The University of Iowa, Graduate College, College of Education, Department of Rehabilitation and Counselor Education, Iowa City, IA 52242-1316. Offers counselor education and supervision (PhD); couple and family therapy (PhD); rehabilitation and mental health counseling (MA); rehabilitation counselor education (PhD); school counseling (MA). *Accreditation:* ACA (one or more programs are accredited); CORE (one or more programs are accredited). *Degree requirements:* For master's, thesis optional, exam; for doctorate, comprehensive exam, thesis/dissertation. *Entrance requirements:* For master's and doctorate, GRE General Test, minimum GPA of 3.0. Additional exam requirements/recommendations for international students: Required—TOEFL (minimum score 550 paper-based; 81 iBT). Electronic applications accepted.

University of La Verne, College of Arts and Sciences, Department of Psychology, Program in Marriage and Family Therapy, La Verne, CA 91750-4443. Offers MFT. *Program availability:* Part-time. *Faculty:* 3 full-time (2 women), 12 part-time/adjunct (9 women). *Students:* 27 full-time (26 women), 20 part-time (18 women); includes 34 minority (3 Black or African American, non-Hispanic/Latino; 31 Hispanic/Latino). Average age 27. *Degree requirements:* For master's, thesis, competency exam, fieldwork, culminating project. *Entrance requirements:* For master's, minimum undergraduate GPA of 3.0, 5- to 7-page statement of purpose and autobiography, 3 letters of recommendation, interview, curriculum vitae. Additional exam requirements/recommendations for international students: Required—TOEFL (minimum score 600 paper-based; 100 iBT), IELTS (minimum score 6.5). *Application deadline:* For fall admission, 3/15 for domestic and international students. Application fee: $50. *Expenses:* Contact institution. *Financial support:* Career-related internships or fieldwork, institutionally sponsored loans, scholarships/grants, and unspecified assistantships available. Financial award application deadline: 3/2; financial award applicants required to submit FAFSA. *Unit head:* Dr. Amy Demyan, Department Chair, 909-448-4181, E-mail: ademyan@laverne.edu. *Application contact:* Christy Ranells, Associate Director of Graduate Admissions, 909-448-4644, Fax: 909-392-2744, E-mail: cranells@laverne.edu.
Website: http://sites.laverne.edu/psychology/mft_program/

University of Louisiana at Monroe, Graduate School, College of Health and Pharmaceutical Sciences, Program in Marriage and Family Therapy, Monroe, LA 71209-0001. Offers MA, PhD. *Accreditation:* AAMFT/COAMFTE (one or more programs are accredited); ACA. *Program availability:* Part-time, evening/weekend. *Faculty:* 6 full-time (2 women), 2 part-time/adjunct (1 woman). *Students:* 46 full-time (33 women), 32 part-time (19 women); includes 32 minority (26 Black or African American, non-Hispanic/Latino; 1 American Indian or Alaska Native, non-Hispanic/Latino; 2 Asian, non-Hispanic/Latino; 1 Native Hawaiian or other Pacific Islander, non-Hispanic/Latino; 2 Two or more races, non-Hispanic/Latino), 2 international. Average age 34. 53 applicants, 42% accepted, 19 enrolled. In 2017, 13 master's, 8 doctorates awarded. *Degree requirements:* For master's, thesis optional; for doctorate, comprehensive exam, thesis/dissertation, clinical experience. *Entrance requirements:* For master's, GRE General Test, minimum GPA of 2.8; for doctorate, GRE General Test, minimum GPA of 3.5. Additional exam requirements/recommendations for international students: Required—TOEFL (minimum score 500 paper-based; 61 iBT). *Application deadline:* For fall admission, 8/24 priority date for domestic students, 7/1 for international students; for winter admission, 12/14 priority date for domestic students; for spring admission, 1/19 for domestic students, 11/1 for international students. Applications are processed on a rolling basis. Application fee: $20 ($30 for international students). Electronic applications accepted. *Expenses:* Tuition, state resident: full-time $6489; part-time $479 per hour. Tuition, nonresident: full-time $12,100; part-time $479 per hour. *Required fees:* $8860; $802 per hour. $3273 per semester. *Financial support:* In 2017–18, 21 students received support. Career-related internships or fieldwork, Federal Work-Study, and unspecified assistantships available. Financial award application deadline: 4/1; financial award applicants required to submit FAFSA. *Faculty research:* Family systems, substance abuse. *Unit head:* Dr. David Hale, Director, 318-342-1246, E-mail: dhale@ulm.edu.
Website: http://www.ulm.edu/mft/

University of Louisville, Graduate School, Kent School of Social Work, Louisville, KY 40292-0001. Offers marriage and family therapy (PMC), including mental health; social work (MSSW, PhD), including alcohol and drug counseling (MSSW), gerontology (MSSW), marriage and family (PhD), school social work (MSSW). *Accreditation:* AAMFT/COAMFTE; CSWE (one or more programs are accredited). *Program availability:* Part-time, evening/weekend, 100% online, blended/hybrid learning. *Faculty:* 31 full-time (22 women), 44 part-time/adjunct (35 women). *Students:* 402 full-time (357 women), 103 part-time (88 women); includes 119 minority (68 Black or African American, non-Hispanic/Latino; 1 American Indian or Alaska Native, non-Hispanic/Latino; 8 Asian, non-Hispanic/Latino; 16 Hispanic/Latino; 26 Two or more races, non-Hispanic/Latino), 5 international. Average age 31. 396 applicants, 78% accepted, 228 enrolled. In 2017, 179 master's awarded. *Degree requirements:* For doctorate, comprehensive exam, thesis/dissertation. *Entrance requirements:* For master's, GRE or minimum GPA of 2.75; for doctorate, GRE General Test, interview, writing sample. Additional exam requirements/recommendations for international students: Required—TOEFL (minimum score 550 paper-based; 79 iBT), IELTS (minimum score 6.5). *Application deadline:* For fall admission, 5/30 for domestic and international students; for spring admission, 9/30 for domestic and international students; for summer admission, 2/28 for domestic and international students. Applications are processed on a rolling basis. Application fee: $65. Electronic applications accepted. *Expenses:* Contact institution. *Financial support:* In 2017–18, 11 research assistantships with full tuition reimbursements (averaging $21,500 per year), 1 teaching assistantship with full tuition reimbursement (averaging $19,000 per year) were awarded; scholarships/grants, health care benefits, and unspecified assistantships also available. Financial award application deadline: 5/15; financial award applicants required to submit FAFSA. *Faculty research:* Equipping young children with skills, assisting abused or neglected children, helping juveniles with sexual behavioral problems, illuminating the contributions that men and women make to their families, managing chronic conditions, enhancing trauma-informed services, addressing social and health issues of older adults, palliative and end-of-life care. *Total annual research expenditures:* $6.1 million. *Unit head:* Dr. David Jenkins, Dean, 502-852-3944, Fax: 502-852-0422, E-mail: dajenk03@exchange.louisville.edu. *Application contact:* Misty Kupka, Program Manager for Admissions and Recruitment, 502-852-0414, Fax: 502-852-0422, E-mail: misty.kupka@louisville.edu.
Website: http://www.louisville.edu/kent

University of Mary Hardin-Baylor, Graduate Studies in Counseling, Belton, TX 76513. Offers clinical and mental health counseling (MA); marriage, family and child counseling (MA); non-clinical professional studies (MA). *Accreditation:* ACA. *Program availability:* Part-time, evening/weekend. *Faculty:* 7 full-time (4 women), 1 part-time/adjunct (0 women). *Students:* 74 full-time (58 women), 13 part-time (8 women); includes 44 minority (23 Black or African American, non-Hispanic/Latino; 18 Hispanic/Latino; 3 Two or more races, non-Hispanic/Latino). Average age 32. 54 applicants, 65% accepted, 29 enrolled. In 2017, 27 master's awarded. *Degree requirements:* For master's, comprehensive exam. *Entrance requirements:* For master's, GRE General Test with minimum cumulative score of 300 on verbal and quantitative portions and 3.0 on analytical section (if overall undergraduate GPA is below a 3.0), minimum cumulative undergraduate GPA of 2.75 or 3.0 on last 60 hours of course work; three letters of recommendation; interview with departmental graduate admissions committee. Additional exam requirements/recommendations for international students: Required—TOEFL (minimum score 60 iBT), IELTS (minimum score 4.5). *Application deadline:* For fall admission, 6/1 for domestic students, 4/30 priority date for international students; for spring admission, 11/1 for domestic students, 9/30 priority date for international students. Applications are processed on a rolling basis. Application fee: $35 ($135 for international students). Electronic applications accepted. *Expenses: Tuition:* Full-time $15,570; part-time $10,380 per credit hour. *Required fees:* $1350; $75 per credit hour. $50 per term. Tuition and fees vary according to course load and degree level. *Financial support:* In 2017–18, 55 students received support. Federal Work-Study, unspecified assistantships, and scholarships for some active duty military personnel available. Support available to part-time students. Financial award applicants required to submit FAFSA. *Faculty research:* Teaching mindfulness skills as part of an interdisciplinary training protocol for doctor of physical therapy students; using symbolic art cards and oracle cards in supervision as a method for teaching appropriate self-disclosure, clinical reflection and counselor development reflection; understanding integral breath therapy. *Unit head:* Dr. Dan Williamson, Director, Graduate Counseling, 254-295-5018, E-mail: dwilliamson@umhb.edu. *Application contact:* Sharon Aguilera, Assistant Director, Graduate Admissions, 254-295-4835, E-mail: saguilera@umhb.edu.
Website: https://go.umhb.edu/graduate/counseling/home

University of Maryland, College Park, Academic Affairs, School of Public Health, Department of Family Science, College Park, MD 20742. Offers family studies (PhD); marriage and family therapy (MS); maternal and child health (PhD). *Accreditation:* AAMFT/COAMFTE. *Program availability:* Part-time, evening/weekend. *Degree requirements:* For master's, thesis or alternative; for doctorate, comprehensive exam, thesis/dissertation, oral defense. *Entrance requirements:* For master's, GRE General Test, minimum GPA of 3.0, 3 letters of recommendation; for doctorate, GRE General Test, minimum GPA of 3.0, 3 letters of recommendation, research sample. Electronic applications accepted. *Faculty research:* Family life quality, interracial couples, child support, homeless families, family and child well-being.

University of Massachusetts Boston, College of Education and Human Development, Program in Family Therapy, Boston, MA 02125-3393. Offers MS. *Students:* 2 part-time (both women); includes 1 minority (Black or African American, non-Hispanic/Latino). Average age 36. 4 applicants, 75% accepted. In 2017, 19 master's awarded. *Expenses:* Tuition, state resident: full-time $17,375. Tuition, nonresident: full-time $33,915. *Required fees:* $355. *Financial support:* Research assistantships available. *Unit head:* Dr. Gonzalo Bacigalupe, Director, 617-287-7631, E-mail: gonzalo.bacigalupe@umb.edu. *Application contact:* Graduate Admissions Coordinator, 617-287-6400, Fax: 617-287-6236, E-mail: bos.gadm@dpc.umassp.edu.

Marriage and Family Therapy

University of Miami, Graduate School, School of Education and Human Development, Department of Educational and Psychological Studies, Program in Counseling, Coral Gables, FL 33124. Offers counseling and research (MS Ed); Latino mental health (Certificate); marriage and family therapy (MS Ed); mental health counseling (MS Ed). *Program availability:* Part-time, evening/weekend. *Degree requirements:* For master's, comprehensive exam, personal growth experience. *Entrance requirements:* For master's, GRE General Test. Additional exam requirements/recommendations for international students: Required—TOEFL (minimum score 550 paper-based; 80 iBT); Recommended—IELTS (minimum score 6.5). Electronic applications accepted. *Faculty research:* Cocaine recidivism, HIV, non-traditional families, health psychology, diversity.

University of Minnesota, Twin Cities Campus, Graduate School, College of Education and Human Development, Department of Family Social Science, Minneapolis, MN 55455-0213. Offers family education (M Ed); marriage and family therapy (MA, PhD); prevention science (MA). *Accreditation:* AAMFT/COAMFTE (one or more programs are accredited). *Faculty:* 19 full-time (13 women). *Students:* 60 full-time (53 women), 35 part-time (32 women); includes 17 minority (7 Black or African American, non-Hispanic/Latino; 5 Asian, non-Hispanic/Latino; 3 Hispanic/Latino; 2 Two or more races, non-Hispanic/Latino), 7 international. Average age 35. 57 applicants, 61% accepted, 33 enrolled. In 2017, 18 master's, 6 doctorates awarded. *Degree requirements:* For master's, thesis; for doctorate, thesis/dissertation. *Entrance requirements:* For master's and doctorate, GRE General Test, minimum undergraduate GPA of 3.0 (preferred). Additional exam requirements/recommendations for international students: Required—TOEFL. *Application deadline:* For fall admission, 12/15 for domestic students. Application fee: $75 ($95 for international students). *Financial support:* In 2017–18, 3 fellowships, 33 research assistantships (averaging $11,720 per year), 13 teaching assistantships (averaging $8,528 per year) were awarded; career-related internships or fieldwork, Federal Work-Study, institutionally sponsored loans, and tuition waivers (partial) also available. Financial award application deadline: 6/30; financial award applicants required to submit FAFSA. *Faculty research:* Ethnicity, culture and diverse families in social context; family stress, loss, and trauma; family finances; parenting; family transitions, and child adjustment in a family context. *Total annual research expenditures:* $2.5 million. *Unit head:* Dr. Lynne Borden, Head, 612-625-1900, Fax: 612-625-4227, E-mail: lmborden@umn.edu. *Application contact:* Dr. Jodi Dworkin, Director of Graduate Studies, 612-624-3732, Fax: 612-625-4227, E-mail: jdworkin@umn.edu.
Website: http://www.cehd.umn.edu/fsos/

University of Mobile, Graduate Studies, Program in Marriage and Family Counseling, Mobile, AL 36613. Offers MA. *Program availability:* Part-time, evening/weekend. *Degree requirements:* For master's, comprehensive exam, thesis optional. *Entrance requirements:* For master's, GRE, official transcripts, essay, 2 letters of recommendation, interview. Additional exam requirements/recommendations for international students: Required—TOEFL (minimum score 550 paper-based; 80 iBT). *Application deadline:* For fall admission, 8/3 priority date for domestic and international students; for spring admission, 12/23 priority date for domestic and international students. Applications are processed on a rolling basis. Application fee: $40 ($50 for international students). Electronic applications accepted. *Expenses:* $535 per credit hour. *Financial support:* Application deadline: 8/1; applicants required to submit FAFSA. *Unit head:* Dr. Buddy Landry, Chair, 251-442-2293, Fax: 251-442-2523, E-mail: rlandry@umobile.edu. *Application contact:* Brian Boyle, Director of Recruitment, 251-442-2727, Fax: 251-442-2523.
Website: https://umobile.edu/academics/college-of-health-professions/school-of-allied-health/master-arts-marriage-family-counseling/

University of Nebraska–Lincoln, Graduate College, College of Education and Human Sciences, Department of Child, Youth and Family Studies, Lincoln, NE 68588. Offers child development/early childhood education (MS, PhD); child, youth and family studies (MS); family and consumer sciences education (MS, PhD); family financial planning (MS); family science (MS, PhD); gerontology (PhD); human sciences (PhD), including child, youth and family studies, gerontology, medical family therapy; marriage and family therapy (MS); medical family therapy (PhD); youth development (MS). *Accreditation:* AAMFT/COAMFTE (one or more programs are accredited). *Program availability:* Online learning. *Degree requirements:* For master's, thesis optional. *Entrance requirements:* For master's, GRE. Additional exam requirements/recommendations for international students: Required—TOEFL (minimum score 550 paper-based). Electronic applications accepted. *Faculty research:* Marriage and family therapy, child development/early childhood education, family financial management.

University of Nevada, Las Vegas, Graduate College, Greenspun College of Urban Affairs, Couple and Family Therapy Program, Las Vegas, NV 89154-3045. Offers MS. *Accreditation:* AAMFT/COAMFTE; ACA. *Faculty:* 2 full-time (both women), 8 part-time/adjunct (6 women). *Students:* 63 full-time (53 women), 20 part-time (16 women); includes 24 minority (3 Black or African American, non-Hispanic/Latino; 3 Asian, non-Hispanic/Latino; 15 Hispanic/Latino; 3 Two or more races, non-Hispanic/Latino), 3 international. Average age 30. 82 applicants, 39% accepted, 28 enrolled. In 2017, 21 master's awarded. *Degree requirements:* For master's, thesis optional. *Entrance requirements:* For master's, GRE General Test, bachelor's degree; 3 letters of recommendation; 2 writing samples. Additional exam requirements/recommendations for international students: Required—TOEFL (minimum score 550 paper-based; 80 iBT), IELTS (minimum score 7). *Application deadline:* For fall admission, 1/15 for domestic students. Application fee: $60 ($95 for international students). Electronic applications accepted. *Expenses:* $275 per credit, $850 per course, $7,969 per year resident, $22,157 per year non-resident, $7,094 non-resident fee (7 credits or more), $1,307 annual health insurance fee. *Financial support:* In 2017–18, 18 students received support, including 7 research assistantships with partial tuition reimbursements available (averaging $12,221 per year), 11 teaching assistantships with partial tuition reimbursements available (averaging $11,727 per year); institutionally sponsored loans, scholarships/grants, health care benefits, and unspecified assistantships also available. Financial award application deadline: 3/15; financial award applicants required to submit FAFSA. *Faculty research:* Forgiveness, couple change processes, sex therapy, infidelity, technology in couples and families. *Unit head:* Dr. Katherine Hertlein, Director, 702-895-3210, Fax: 702-895-1869, E-mail: katherine.hertlein@unlv.edu.
Website: http://mft.unlv.edu/grad.html

University of New Hampshire, Graduate School, College of Health and Human Services, Department of Human Development and Family Studies, Durham, NH 03824. Offers adolescent development (Postbaccalaureate Certificate); human development and family studies (MS); human development and family studies: marriage and family therapy (MS). *Accreditation:* AAMFT/COAMFTE. *Program availability:* Part-time. *Students:* 11 full-time (10 women), 7 part-time (6 women); includes 3 minority (1 Asian, non-Hispanic/Latino; 2 Hispanic/Latino), 1 international. Average age 29. 33 applicants, 39% accepted, 8 enrolled. In 2017, 8 master's awarded. *Entrance requirements:* Additional exam requirements/recommendations for international students: Required—TOEFL (minimum score 550 paper-based; 80 iBT). *Application deadline:* For fall admission, 1/15 priority date for domestic students, 4/1 for international students. Application fee: $65. Electronic applications accepted. *Financial support:* In 2017–18, 10 students received support, including 4 teaching assistantships; fellowships, research

assistantships, career-related internships or fieldwork, Federal Work-Study, scholarships/grants, and tuition waivers (full and partial) also available. Support available to part-time students. Financial award application deadline: 2/15. *Unit head:* Kerry Kazura, Chair, 603-862-2135. *Application contact:* Corinna Tucker, Administrative Assistant, 603-862-2153, E-mail: cjtucker@unh.edu.
Website: http://www.chhs.unh.edu/hdfs

The University of North Carolina at Greensboro, Graduate School, School of Education, Department of Counseling and Educational Development, Greensboro, NC 27412-5001. Offers advanced school counseling (PMC); counseling and counselor education (PhD); counseling and educational development (MS); couple and family counseling (PMC); school counseling (PMC); MS/Ed S. *Accreditation:* ACA (one or more programs are accredited); NCATE. *Degree requirements:* For master's, comprehensive exam, practicum, internship; for doctorate, comprehensive exam, thesis/dissertation. *Entrance requirements:* For master's, doctorate, and PMC, GRE General Test. Additional exam requirements/recommendations for international students: Required—TOEFL. Electronic applications accepted. *Faculty research:* Gerontology, invitational theory, career development, marriage and family therapy, drug and alcohol abuse prevention.

University of Oregon, Graduate School, College of Education, Eugene, OR 97403. Offers communication disorders and sciences (MA, MS, PhD); counseling psychology (PhD); couples and family therapy (MS); critical and sociocultural studies in education (PhD); curriculum and teacher education (MA, MS); educational leadership (MS, D Ed, PhD); prevention science (M Ed, MS, PhD); school psychology (MS, PhD); special education (M Ed, MA, MS, PhD). *Program availability:* Part-time. Terminal master's awarded for partial completion of doctoral program. *Degree requirements:* For master's, exam, paper, or project; for doctorate, comprehensive exam, thesis/dissertation. *Entrance requirements:* Additional exam requirements/recommendations for international students: Required—TOEFL. *Faculty research:* Basic and applied research in teaching, learning and habilitation in all settings, schooling effectiveness.

University of Phoenix–Bay Area Campus, College of Social Sciences, San Jose, CA 95134-1805. Offers marriage, family, and child therapy (MSC). *Program availability:* Evening/weekend. *Degree requirements:* For master's, thesis or alternative. *Entrance requirements:* For master's, Comprehensive Cognitive Assessment, minimum undergraduate GPA of 2.5, 3 years of work experience.

University of Phoenix–Central Valley Campus, College of Human Services, Fresno, CA 93720-1552. Offers marriage, family and child therapy (MSC).

University of Phoenix–Las Vegas Campus, College of Human Services, Las Vegas, NV 89135. Offers marriage, family, and child therapy (MSC); mental health counseling (MSC); school counseling (MSC). *Program availability:* Online learning. *Entrance requirements:* For master's, minimum undergraduate GPA of 2.5, 3 years of work experience. Additional exam requirements/recommendations for international students: Required—TOEFL (minimum score 550 paper-based; 79 iBT). Electronic applications accepted.

University of Phoenix–Phoenix Campus, College of Social Sciences, Tempe, AZ 85282-2371. Offers counseling (MS), including clinical mental health counseling, community counseling, counseling, marriage, family and child therapy; psychology (MS). *Program availability:* Evening/weekend, online learning. *Entrance requirements:* Additional exam requirements/recommendations for international students: Required—TOEFL, TOEIC (Test of English as an International Communication), Berlitz Online English Proficiency Exam, PTE, or IELTS. Electronic applications accepted. *Expenses:* Contact institution.

University of Rhode Island, Graduate School, College of Health Sciences, Department of Human Development and Family Studies, Kingston, RI 02881. Offers college student personnel (MS); human development and family studies (MS); marriage and family therapy (MS). *Accreditation:* AAMFT/COAMFTE. *Program availability:* Part-time. *Faculty:* 16 full-time (11 women). *Students:* 47 full-time (35 women), 12 part-time (10 women); includes 13 minority (4 Black or African American, non-Hispanic/Latino; 1 American Indian or Alaska Native, non-Hispanic/Latino; 4 Asian, non-Hispanic/Latino; 3 Hispanic/Latino; 1 Two or more races, non-Hispanic/Latino), 2 international. 91 applicants, 43% accepted, 29 enrolled. In 2017, 24 master's awarded. *Entrance requirements:* Additional exam requirements/recommendations for international students: Required—TOEFL. *Application deadline:* For fall admission, 1/15 for domestic and international students. Application fee: $65. Electronic applications accepted. *Expenses:* Tuition, state resident: full-time $12,706; part-time $786 per credit. Tuition, nonresident: full-time $25,216; part-time $1401 per credit. *Required fees:* $1598; $45 per credit. One-time fee: $30 part-time. *Financial support:* In 2017–18, 1 research assistantship (averaging $4,431 per year), 4 teaching assistantships (averaging $10,128 per year) were awarded. Financial award application deadline: 1/15; financial award applicants required to submit FAFSA. *Unit head:* Dr. Karen McCurdy, Chair, 401-874-5960, Fax: 401-874-4020, E-mail: kmccurdy@uri.edu.
Website: http://www.uri.edu/hss/hdf

University of Rochester, School of Medicine and Dentistry, Graduate Programs in Medicine and Dentistry, Department of Psychiatry, Rochester, NY 14627. Offers marriage and family therapy (MS). *Accreditation:* AAMFT/COAMFTE. *Program availability:* Part-time. *Degree requirements:* For master's, projects. *Entrance requirements:* For master's, GRE General Test.

University of Saint Joseph, Program in Marriage and Family Therapy, West Hartford, CT 06117-2700. Offers MA. *Accreditation:* AAMFT/COAMFTE. *Program availability:* Part-time, evening/weekend. *Degree requirements:* For master's, comprehensive exam, thesis or alternative, practicum, internship. *Entrance requirements:* For master's, 2 letters of recommendation. *Application deadline:* Applications are processed on a rolling basis. Application fee: $50. Electronic applications accepted. Application fee is waived when completed online. *Financial support:* Career-related internships or fieldwork and unspecified assistantships available. Support available to part-time students. Financial award applicants required to submit FAFSA. *Unit head:* Dr. Rachel Diamond, Director, E-mail: rdiamond@usj.edu.

University of San Diego, School of Leadership and Education Sciences, Department of Counseling and Marital and Family Therapy, San Diego, CA 92110-2492. Offers clinical mental health counseling (MA); marital and family therapy (MA); school counseling (MA). *Accreditation:* ACA. *Program availability:* Part-time, evening/weekend. *Faculty:* 13 full-time (6 women), 26 part-time/adjunct (18 women). *Students:* 172 full-time (155 women), 50 part-time (42 women); includes 106 minority (13 Black or African American, non-Hispanic/Latino; 1 American Indian or Alaska Native, non-Hispanic/Latino; 20 Asian, non-Hispanic/Latino; 62 Hispanic/Latino; 10 Two or more races, non-Hispanic/Latino), 5 international. Average age 27. 406 applicants, 45% accepted, 92 enrolled. In 2017, 69 master's awarded. *Degree requirements:* For master's, comprehensive exam, international experience. *Entrance requirements:* For master's, GRE or GMAT (minimum overall score in 50th percentile), group interview with faculty. Additional exam requirements/recommendations for international students: Required—TOEFL (minimum score 580 paper-based; 83 iBT), TWE. *Application deadline:* For fall admission, 1/13 priority date for domestic and international students. Applications are processed on a rolling basis. Application fee: $45. Electronic applications accepted. *Financial support:*

In 2017–18, 160 students received support. Career-related internships or fieldwork, Federal Work-Study, institutionally sponsored loans, unspecified assistantships, and stipends available. Support available to part-time students. Financial award application deadline: 4/1; financial award applicants required to submit FAFSA. *Faculty research:* Action research, collaboration between family therapists and medical professionals, family therapy training and supervision, multicultural counseling, school counseling. *Unit head:* Dr. Ann Garland, Director, 619-260-7879, E-mail: agarland@sandiego.edu. *Application contact:* Monica Mahon, Director of Admissions and Enrollment, 619-260-4524, Fax: 619-260-4158, E-mail: grads@sandiego.edu.
Website: http://www.sandiego.edu/soles/counseling-and-marital-and-family-therapy//

University of San Francisco, School of Education, Department of Counseling Psychology, San Francisco, CA 94117-1080. Offers counseling (MA), including educational counseling, life transitions counseling, marital and family therapy. *Program availability:* Part-time. *Entrance requirements:* Additional exam requirements/recommendations for international students: Required—TOEFL, IELTS, PTE. Electronic applications accepted.

University of Southern California, Graduate School, Rossier School of Education, Master's Programs in Education, Los Angeles, CA 90089-4038. Offers educational counseling (ME); marriage, family and child counseling (MMFT); postsecondary administration and student affairs [PASA] (ME); school counseling (ME); teaching (online) (MAT); teaching and teaching credential (MAT); teaching English to speakers of other languages (MAT). *Program availability:* Part-time, evening/weekend, online learning. *Degree requirements:* For master's, thesis optional. *Entrance requirements:* For master's, GRE (for all programs except MAT). Additional exam requirements/recommendations for international students: Required—TOEFL (minimum score 100 iBT). Electronic applications accepted. *Faculty research:* College access and equity, preparing teachers for culturally diverse populations, sociocultural basis of learning as mediated by instruction with focus on reading and literacy in English learners, social and political aspects of teaching and learning English, school counselor development and training.

University of South Florida, College of Behavioral and Community Sciences, Department of Child and Family Studies, Tampa, FL 33620-9951. Offers applied behavior analysis (MA, MS, PhD); behavioral and community sciences (PhD); child and adolescent behavioral health (MS), including developmental disabilities, leadership in child and adolescent health, translational research and evaluation, youth and behavioral health; rehabilitation and mental health counseling (MA), including addictions and substance abuse counseling, marriage and family therapy. *Accreditation:* ACA. *Faculty:* 18 full-time (12 women), 2 part-time/adjunct (1 woman). *Students:* 188 full-time (166 women), 115 part-time (92 women); includes 121 minority (40 Black or African American, non-Hispanic/Latino; 8 Asian, non-Hispanic/Latino; 61 Hispanic/Latino; 12 Two or more races, non-Hispanic/Latino), 6 international. Average age 28. 287 applicants, 53% accepted, 89 enrolled. In 2017, 45 master's, 1 doctorate awarded. *Degree requirements:* For master's, comprehensive exam, thesis (for some programs); for doctorate, comprehensive exam, thesis/dissertation, Behavior Analyst Board Certification Exam. *Entrance requirements:* For master's, GRE General Test, minimum GPA of 3.0 in last 60 hours of coursework; letters of recommendation; one-page narrative describing experience, interest, and career goals in applied behavior analysis; resume or curriculum vitae (varies by program); for doctorate, GRE General Test, master's degree in behavioral analysis or closely-related field; minimum GPA of 3.5 in graduate course work; three letters of recommendation; campus visit with faculty interview; personal statement; curriculum vitae; evidence of research experiences and expertise. Additional exam requirements/recommendations for international students: Required—TOEFL (minimum score 550 paper-based; 79 iBT) or IELTS (minimum score 6.5). *Application deadline:* For fall admission, 12/5 for domestic and international students. Application fee: $30. *Financial support:* In 2017–18, 30 students received support. Unspecified assistantships available. *Faculty research:* Applied behavior analysis, autism, behavior management, behavioral intervention, children, developmental disabilities, experimental analysis of behavior, functional assessment, positive behavior support. *Total annual research expenditures:* $17.6 million. *Application contact:* Dr. Raymond G. Miltenberger, Professor/Director of Master's Program, 813-974-5079, Fax: 813-974-6115, E-mail: miltenbe@usf.edu.
Website: http://cfs.cbcs.usf.edu/

University of South Florida, Innovative Education, Tampa, FL 33620-9951. Offers adult, career and higher education (Graduate Certificate), including college teaching, leadership in developing human resources, leadership in higher education; Africana studies (Graduate Certificate), including diasporas and health disparities, genocide and human rights; aging studies (Graduate Certificate), including gerontology; art research (Graduate Certificate), including museum studies; business foundations (Graduate Certificate); chemical and biomedical engineering (Graduate Certificate), including materials science and engineering, water, health and sustainability; child and family studies (Graduate Certificate), including positive behavior support; civil and industrial engineering (Graduate Certificate), including transportation systems analysis; community and family health (Graduate Certificate), including maternal and child health, social marketing and public health, violence and injury: prevention and intervention, women's health; criminology (Graduate Certificate), including criminal justice administration; data science for public administration (Graduate Certificate); digital humanities (Graduate Certificate); educational measurement and research (Graduate Certificate), including evaluation; English (Graduate Certificate), including comparative literary studies, creative writing, professional and technical communication; entrepreneurship (Graduate Certificate); environmental health (Graduate Certificate), including safety management; epidemiology and biostatistics (Graduate Certificate), including applied biostatistics, biostatistics, concepts and tools of epidemiology, epidemiology, epidemiology of infectious diseases; geography, environment and planning (Graduate Certificate), including community development, environmental policy and management, geographical information systems; geology (Graduate Certificate), including hydrogeology; global health (Graduate Certificate), including disaster management, global health and Latin American and Caribbean studies, global health practice, humanitarian assistance, infection control; government and international affairs (Graduate Certificate), including Cuban studies, globalization studies; health policy and management (Graduate Certificate), including health management and leadership, public health policy and programs; hearing specialist: early intervention (Graduate Certificate); industrial and management systems engineering (Graduate Certificate), including systems engineering, technology management; information studies (Graduate Certificate), including school library media specialist; information systems/decision sciences (Graduate Certificate), including analytics and business intelligence; instructional technology (Graduate Certificate), including distance education, Florida digital/virtual educator, instructional design, multimedia design, Web design; internal medicine, bioethics and medical humanities (Graduate Certificate), including biomedical ethics; Latin American and Caribbean studies (Graduate Certificate); leadership for coastal resiliency planning (Graduate Certificate); mass communications (Graduate Certificate), including multimedia journalism; mathematics and statistics (Graduate Certificate), including mathematics; medicine (Graduate Certificate), including aging and neuroscience, bioinformatics, biotechnology, brain fitness and memory management, clinical investigation, hand and upper limb rehabilitation, health informatics, health sciences, integrative weight management, intellectual property, medicine and gender, metabolic and nutritional medicine, metabolic cardiology, pharmacy sciences; national and competitive intelligence (Graduate Certificate); nursing (Graduate Certificate), including simulation based academic fellowship in advanced pain management; psychological and social foundations (Graduate Certificate), including career counseling, college teaching, diversity in education, mental health counseling, school counseling; public affairs (Graduate Certificate), including nonprofit management, public management, research administration; public health (Graduate Certificate), including assessing chemical toxicity and public health risks, health equity, pharmacoepidemiology, public health generalist, toxicology, translational research in adolescent behavioral health; public health practices (Graduate Certificate), including planning for healthy communities; rehabilitation and mental health counseling (Graduate Certificate), including integrative mental health care, marriage and family therapy, rehabilitation technology; secondary education (Graduate Certificate), including ESOL, foreign language education: culture and content, foreign language education: professional; social work (Graduate Certificate), including geriatric social work/clinical gerontology; special education (Graduate Certificate), including autism spectrum disorder, disabilities education: severe/profound; world languages (Graduate Certificate), including teaching English as a second language (TESL) or foreign language. *Unit head:* Dr. Cynthia DeLuca, Associate Vice President and Assistant Vice Provost, 813-974-3077, Fax: 813-974-7061, E-mail: deluca@usf.edu. *Application contact:* Owen Hooper, Director, Summer and Alternative Calendar Programs, 813-974-6917, E-mail: hooper@usf.edu.
Website: http://www.usf.edu/innovative-education/

The University of Texas at Tyler, College of Education and Psychology, Department of Psychology and Counseling, Tyler, TX 75799-0001. Offers clinical psychology (MS), including neuropsychology, school psychology; counseling psychology (MA), including general, marriage and family; interdisciplinary studies (MSIS); school counseling (MA). *Program availability:* Part-time, evening/weekend. *Degree requirements:* For master's, comprehensive exam, thesis optional. *Entrance requirements:* For master's, GRE General Test, minimum GPA of 3.0. Additional exam requirements/recommendations for international students: Required—TOEFL. Electronic applications accepted. *Faculty research:* Neuropsychology, child abuse, psychometric properties of psychological instruments, maternal behavior, clinical practice issues, victimization of women, post-traumatic stress disorder.

The University of West Alabama, School of Graduate Studies, College of Education, Program in Family Counseling, Livingston, AL 35470. Offers MS. *Program availability:* Part-time, evening/weekend, 100% online. *Faculty:* 8 full-time (6 women), 17 part-time/adjunct (12 women). *Students:* 42 (38 women); includes 36 minority (32 Black or African American, non-Hispanic/Latino; 1 American Indian or Alaska Native, non-Hispanic/Latino; 3 Hispanic/Latino). Average age 35. 20 applicants, 100% accepted, 13 enrolled. *Degree requirements:* For master's, comprehensive exam. *Entrance requirements:* For master's, GRE, minimum GPA of 2.75. Additional exam requirements/recommendations for international students: Required—TOEFL (minimum score 500 paper-based; 61 iBT). *Application deadline:* Applications are processed on a rolling basis. Application fee: $40. Electronic applications accepted. *Expenses:* Tuition, state resident: part-time $371 per credit hour. Tuition, nonresident: part-time $742 per credit hour. *Required fees:* $130 per semester. *Financial support:* Teaching assistantships, Federal Work-Study, scholarships/grants, and unspecified assistantships available. Support available to part-time students. Financial award application deadline: 3/1; financial award applicants required to submit FAFSA. *Unit head:* Dr. Reenay Rogers, Chair of Instructional Leadership and Support, 205-652-5423, E-mail: rrogers@uwa.edu. *Application contact:* Dr. B. J. Kimbrough, Dean of Graduate Studies, 205-652-3647, Fax: 205-652-3670, E-mail: bkimbrough@uwa.edu.

The University of Winnipeg, Faculty of Theology, Winnipeg, MB R3B 2E9, Canada. Offers marriage and family therapy (MMFT, Certificate); sacred theology (STM); theology (M Div). *Accreditation:* AAMFT/COAMFTE. *Program availability:* Part-time.

University of Wisconsin–Stout, Graduate School, College of Education, Health and Human Sciences, Program in Marriage and Family Therapy, Menomonie, WI 54751. Offers MS. *Accreditation:* AAMFT/COAMFTE. *Program availability:* Part-time. *Degree requirements:* For master's, thesis or alternative. *Entrance requirements:* For master's, minimum GPA of 2.75. Additional exam requirements/recommendations for international students: Required—TOEFL (minimum score 500 paper-based; 61 iBT). Electronic applications accepted. *Faculty research:* Abuse, addiction, resilience, diversity, narrative therapy.

Utah State University, School of Graduate Studies, Emma Eccles Jones College of Education and Human Services, Department of Family, Consumer, and Human Development, Logan, UT 84322. Offers family and human development (MFHD); family, consumer, and human development (MS, PhD), including adolescence/youth (MS), adult development/aging (MS), consumer science (MS), infancy/childhood (MS), marriage and family relations (MS), marriage and family therapy (MS). *Accreditation:* AAMFT/COAMFTE (one or more programs are accredited). *Program availability:* Part-time, evening/weekend, online learning. *Degree requirements:* For master's, thesis; for doctorate, comprehensive exam, thesis/dissertation, competencies. *Entrance requirements:* For master's, GRE General Test or MAT, minimum GPA of 3.0, 3 letters of recommendation; for doctorate, GRE, minimum GPA of 3.0, 3 letters of recommendation. Additional exam requirements/recommendations for international students: Required—TOEFL. Electronic applications accepted. *Faculty research:* Marriage and family relations, adolescent problem behavior, family financial management, early literacy, mental health in the elderly, parent child attachment.

Valdosta State University, Department of Psychology, Counseling, and Family Therapy, Valdosta, GA 31698. Offers industrial/organizational psychology (MS); marriage and family therapy (MS); school counseling (M Ed, Ed S). *Accreditation:* AAMFT/COAMFTE. *Program availability:* Part-time, evening/weekend, 100% online, blended/hybrid learning. *Degree requirements:* For master's, thesis or alternative, comprehensive written and/or oral exams; for Ed S, thesis. *Entrance requirements:* For master's, GRE General Test or MAT, GACE; for Ed S, GRE General Test or MAT. Additional exam requirements/recommendations for international students: Required—TOEFL (minimum score 523 paper-based); Recommended—IELTS. *Application deadline:* For fall admission, 7/1 for domestic and international students; for spring admission, 11/15 for domestic and international students. Applications are processed on a rolling basis. Application fee: $45. Electronic applications accepted. *Expenses:* Contact institution. *Financial support:* Research assistantships with full tuition reimbursements, institutionally sponsored loans, and unspecified assistantships available. Support available to part-time students. Financial award application deadline: 7/1; financial award applicants required to submit FAFSA. *Unit head:* Dr. Kate Warner, Head, 229-293-6264, Fax: 229-259-5576, E-mail: kwarner@valdosta.edu. *Application contact:* Jessica Powers, Admission Specialist, 229-333-5694, Fax: 229-245-3853, E-mail: jldevane@valdosta.edu.
Website: https://www.valdosta.edu/colleges/education/pcft/

Walden University, Graduate Programs, School of Counseling, Minneapolis, MN 55401. Offers addiction counseling (MS), including addictions and public health, child and adolescent counseling, family studies and interventions, forensic counseling,

general program, military families and culture, trauma and crisis counseling; clinical mental health counseling (MS), including addiction counseling, forensic counseling, military families and culture, trauma and crisis counseling; counselor education and supervision (PhD), including consultation, counseling and social change, forensic mental health counseling, leadership and program evaluation, trauma and crisis; marriage, couple, and family counseling (MS), including addiction counseling, career counseling, forensic counseling, military families and culture, trauma and crisis counseling; school counseling (MS), including addiction counseling, career counseling, crisis and trauma, military families and culture. *Accreditation:* ACA. *Program availability:* Part-time, evening/weekend, online only, 100% online. *Degree requirements:* For master's, residency, field experience, professional development plan, licensure plan; for doctorate, thesis/dissertation, residency, practicum, internship. *Entrance requirements:* For master's, bachelor's degree or higher; minimum GPA of 2.5; official transcripts; goal statement (for some programs); access to computer and Internet; for doctorate, master's degree or higher; three years of related professional or academic experience (preferred); minimum GPA of 3.0; goal statement and current resume (for select programs); official transcripts; access to computer and Internet. Additional exam requirements/recommendations for international students: Required—TOEFL (minimum score 550 paper-based, 79 iBT), IELTS (minimum score 6.5), Michigan English Language Assessment Battery (minimum score 82), or PTE (minimum score 53). Electronic applications accepted.

Western Kentucky University, Graduate Studies, College of Education and Behavioral Sciences, Department of Counseling and Student Affairs, Bowling Green, KY 42101. Offers counseling (MA Ed), including marriage and family therapy, mental health counseling; school counseling (P-12) (MA Ed); student affairs in higher education (MA Ed). *Accreditation:* ACA; NCATE. *Program availability:* Part-time, evening/weekend. *Degree requirements:* For master's, comprehensive exam, thesis optional. *Entrance requirements:* For master's, GRE General Test. Additional exam requirements/recommendations for international students: Required—TOEFL (minimum score 555 paper-based; 79 iBT). *Faculty research:* Counselor education, research for residential workers.

Western Seminary–Sacramento Campus, Program in Marital and Family Therapy, Rocklin, CA 95765. Offers MA. *Entrance requirements:* For master's, essays, undergraduate transcripts, 4 recommendations. Additional exam requirements/recommendations for international students: Required—TOEFL.

Western Seminary–San Jose Campus, Graduate Programs, Milpitas, CA 95035. Offers Bible and theology (Graduate Diploma); Bible, camp and conference ministry (CGS); Biblical and theological studies (MA), including exegetical track, theological track; coaching (CGS); expositional ministry (M Div); marital and family therapy (MA); ministry (Graduate Diploma); ministry and leadership (MA), including camp and conference ministry, coaching, pastoral care to women, youth ministry; pastoral care to women (CGS, Graduate Diploma); pastoral ministry (M Div); theology (CGS); youth and family (CGS). *Program availability:* Part-time, evening/weekend, online learning. *Entrance requirements:* For master's, minimum GPA of 3.0. Electronic applications accepted.

Wheaton College, Graduate School, Department of Psychology, Wheaton, IL 60187-5593. Offers clinical mental health counseling (MA); clinical psychology (Psy D); marriage and family therapy (MA). *Accreditation:* APA (one or more programs are accredited). *Faculty:* 15 full-time (7 women), 12 part-time/adjunct (9 women). *Students:* 132 full-time (99 women), 26 part-time (13 women); includes 40 minority (12 Black or African American, non-Hispanic/Latino; 2 American Indian or Alaska Native, non-Hispanic/Latino; 12 Asian, non-Hispanic/Latino; 7 Hispanic/Latino; 7 Two or more races, non-Hispanic/Latino), 28 international. Average age 28. 139 applicants, 74% accepted, 69 enrolled. In 2017, 62 master's, 20 doctorates awarded. Terminal master's awarded for partial completion of doctoral program. *Degree requirements:* For master's, thesis or alternative; for doctorate, thesis/dissertation, internship. *Entrance requirements:* For master's, GRE General Test, 18 hours of course work in psychology; for doctorate, GRE General Test. Additional exam requirements/recommendations for international students: Required—TOEFL (minimum score 550 paper-based; 80 iBT), IELTS (minimum score 6.5). *Application deadline:* For fall admission, 3/1 priority date for domestic students, 1/1 for international students. Applications are processed on a rolling basis. Application fee: $30. *Expenses: Tuition:* Full-time $19,800; part-time $825 per credit hour. Tuition and fees vary according to degree level and program. *Financial support:* In 2017–18, 3 research assistantships (averaging $4,800 per year) were awarded; career-related internships or fieldwork, Federal Work-Study, scholarships/grants, and unspecified assistantships also available. Financial award application deadline: 3/1; financial award applicants required to submit FAFSA. *Unit head:* Dr. Terri Watson, Associate Dean of Psychology, 630-752-5104, E-mail: psychology@wheaton.edu. *Application contact:* Director of Graduate Admissions, 630-752-5195, Fax: 630-752-7047, E-mail: graduate.admissions@wheaton.edu. Website: https://www.wheaton.edu/academics/programs/psychology/graduate-programs/

Psychoanalysis and Psychotherapy

Adler Graduate School, Program in Adlerian Counseling and Psychotherapy, Richfield, MN 55423. Offers Adlerian studies (MA); art therapy (MA); clinical mental health counseling (MA); co-occurring substance use and mental health disorders (MA); marriage and family therapy (MA); school counseling (MA). *Program availability:* Part-time, evening/weekend. *Faculty:* 71 part-time/adjunct (55 women). *Students:* 317 part-time (259 women); includes 51 minority (40 Black or African American, non-Hispanic/Latino; 6 American Indian or Alaska Native, non-Hispanic/Latino; 5 Hispanic/Latino). *Degree requirements:* For master's, thesis or alternative, 500-700 hour internship (depending on license choice). *Entrance requirements:* For master's, interview, official transcripts, minimum cumulative GPA of 3.0. *Application deadline:* Applications are processed on a rolling basis. Application fee: $50. Electronic applications accepted. *Expenses:* $575 per credit tuition. *Financial support:* Career-related internships or fieldwork and tuition waivers available. Support available to part-time students. Financial award applicants required to submit FAFSA. *Unit head:* Dr. Jeffrey Allen, President, 612-767-7048, Fax: 612-861-7559, E-mail: jeffrey.allen@alfredadler.edu. *Application contact:* Christina Hilpipre-Frischman, Director of Admissions, 612-767-7055, Fax: 612-861-7559, E-mail: christina@alfredadler.edu.
Website: http://alfredadler.edu/programs/masters-level-programs

Argosy University, Chicago, Illinois School of Professional Psychology, Doctoral Program in Clinical Psychology, Chicago, IL 60601. Offers child and adolescent psychology (Psy D); client-centered and experiential psychotherapies (Psy D); diversity and multicultural psychology (Psy D); family psychology (Psy D); forensic psychology (Psy D); health psychology (Psy D); neuropsychology (Psy D); organizational consulting (Psy D); psychoanalytic psychology (Psy D); psychology and spirituality (Psy D). *Accreditation:* APA.

Atlantic University, Program in Integrated Imagery: Regression Hypnosis, Virginia Beach, VA 23451-2061. Offers Graduate Certificate. *Program availability:* Blended/hybrid learning. *Entrance requirements:* For degree, bachelor's degree, minimum undergraduate GPA of 3.0, official transcripts, 1000-word essay. *Application deadline:* For fall admission, 9/3 for domestic students; for winter admission, 3/12 for domestic students; for spring admission, 12/4 for domestic students; for summer admission, 6/11 for domestic students. Applications are processed on a rolling basis. Application fee: $50. Electronic applications accepted. *Expenses:* $360 per credit. *Application contact:* Rachel Alvidrez, Educational Services Manager, 757-631-8101, Fax: 757-631-8096, E-mail: info@atlanticuniv.edu.
Website: https://www.atlanticuniv.edu/academics/programs/integrated-imagery-regression-hypnosis-grad-certificate/

Boston Graduate School of Psychoanalysis, BGSP-New Jersey, Brookline, MA 02446-4602. Offers psychoanalysis (MA); psychoanalytic counseling (MA). Programs offered in conjunction with Academic of Clinical and Applied Psychoanalysis in Livingston, NJ.

Boston Graduate School of Psychoanalysis, CAGS and Certificate Programs, Brookline, MA 02446-4602. Offers child and adolescent intervention (CAGS); psychoanalysis (Certificate); psychoanalytic psychotherapy (CAGS). *Program availability:* Part-time. *Degree requirements:* For other advanced degree, thesis. *Entrance requirements:* For degree, interview, BA, writing sample, 3 letters of reference, transcripts. Additional exam requirements/recommendations for international students: Required—TOEFL (minimum score 550 paper-based; 79 iBT). *Faculty research:* Treatment approaches for intractable patients, unconscious symbolic processes, female adolescent development, evaluation of school mental health interventions, development of symbolic processes in early childhood.

Boston Graduate School of Psychoanalysis, Doctoral Programs, Brookline, MA 02446-4602. Offers psychoanalysis (Psya D); psychoanalysis, society and culture (Psya D). *Program availability:* Part-time. *Degree requirements:* For doctorate, thesis/dissertation. *Entrance requirements:* For doctorate, interview, BA, personal statement, writing sample, 3 letters of recommendation. Additional exam requirements/recommendations for international students: Required—TOEFL (minimum score 550 paper-based; 79 iBT). *Faculty research:* Unconscious symbolic processes, female adolescent development, psychodynamics of social processes, dreams and other symbolic processes, cultural expressions of psychopathology.

Boston Graduate School of Psychoanalysis, Master's Programs, Brookline, MA 02446-4602. Offers mental health counseling (MA); psychoanalysis (MA); psychoanalysis, society and culture (MA). *Program availability:* Part-time. Terminal master's awarded for partial completion of doctoral program. *Degree requirements:* For master's, thesis. *Entrance requirements:* For master's, interview, BA, personal statement, writing sample, 3 letters of recommendation. Additional exam requirements/recommendations for international students: Required—TOEFL (minimum score 550 paper-based; 79 iBT). *Faculty research:* Qualitative and narrative research methodologies, ethical conflicts and dual loyalties in health professionals, psychodynamics of social processes, treatment approaches for intractable patients, psychoanalytic research methodologies.

Boston Graduate School of Psychoanalysis, New York Graduate School of Psychoanalysis, New York, NY 10011. Offers MA. *Program availability:* Part-time. *Degree requirements:* For master's, thesis. *Entrance requirements:* For master's, interview, BA, writing sample, letters of recommendation. Additional exam requirements/recommendations for international students: Required—TOEFL.

Immaculata University, College of Graduate Studies, Department of Psychology, Immaculata, PA 19345. Offers clinical mental health counseling (MA); clinical psychology (Psy D); forensic psychology (Graduate Certificate); integrative psychotherapy (Graduate Certificate); neuropsychology (Graduate Certificate); psychodynamic psychotherapy (Graduate Certificate); psychological testing (Graduate Certificate); school counseling (MA, Graduate Certificate); school psychology (MA). *Accreditation:* APA. *Program availability:* Part-time, evening/weekend. Terminal master's awarded for partial completion of doctoral program. *Degree requirements:* For master's, comprehensive exam, thesis optional; for doctorate, comprehensive exam, thesis/dissertation. *Entrance requirements:* For master's, GRE General Test or MAT, minimum GPA of 3.0; for doctorate, GRE General Test or MAT, minimum GPA of 3.5. Additional exam requirements/recommendations for international students: Required—TOEFL, IELTS. Electronic applications accepted. *Faculty research:* Supervision ethics, psychology of teaching, gender.

Naropa University, Graduate Programs, Program in Clinical Mental Health Counseling, Concentration in Contemplative Psychotherapy and Buddhist Psychology, Boulder, CO 80302-6697. Offers MA. *Faculty:* 2 full-time (0 women), 7 part-time/adjunct (4 women). *Students:* 62 full-time (31 women), 23 part-time (14 women); includes 20 minority (2 Black or African American, non-Hispanic/Latino; 1 American Indian or Alaska Native, non-Hispanic/Latino; 1 Asian, non-Hispanic/Latino; 11 Hispanic/Latino; 1 Native Hawaiian or other Pacific Islander, non-Hispanic/Latino; 4 Two or more races, non-Hispanic/Latino), 6 international. Average age 34. 68 applicants, 84% accepted, 34 enrolled. In 2017, 35 master's awarded. *Degree requirements:* For master's, thesis, internship. *Entrance requirements:* For master's, interview; curriculum vitae/resume with pertinent academic, employment and volunteer activities; 2 letters of recommendation; statement of interest essay; transcripts; paid or volunteer experience in a clinical setting (recommended). Additional exam requirements/recommendations for international students: Required—TOEFL (minimum score 550 paper-based; 80 iBT). *Application deadline:* For fall admission, 1/15 priority date for domestic and international students. Applications are processed on a rolling basis. Application fee: $60. Electronic applications accepted. *Expenses:* $995 per credit. *Financial support:* In 2017–18, 39 students received support, including 3 research assistantships with partial tuition reimbursements available (averaging $2,500 per year), teaching assistantships with partial tuition reimbursements available (averaging $3,000 per year); career-related internships or fieldwork, Federal Work-Study, scholarships/grants, tuition waivers (partial), and unspecified assistantships also available. Support available to part-time

students. Financial award application deadline: 3/1; financial award applicants required to submit FAFSA. *Unit head:* Dr. Kathleen Gregory, Dean, Graduate School of Counseling and Psychology, 303-245-4706, E-mail: kgregory@naropa.edu. *Application contact:* Office of Admissions, 303-546-3572, Fax: 303-546-3583.
Website: http://www.naropa.edu/academics/masters/clinical-mental-health-counseling/contemplative-psychotherapy-buddhist-psychology/index.php

Naropa University, Graduate Programs, Program in Clinical Mental Health Counseling, Concentration in Somatic Counseling: Body Psychotherapy, Boulder, CO 80302-6697. Offers MA. *Faculty:* 3 full-time (2 women), 9 part-time/adjunct (all women). *Students:* 19 full-time (16 women), 7 part-time (5 women); includes 4 minority (1 Asian, non-Hispanic/Latino; 3 Hispanic/Latino), 1 international. Average age 32. 19 applicants, 84% accepted, 10 enrolled. In 2017, 17 master's awarded. *Degree requirements:* For master's, thesis, internship, clinical practicum. *Entrance requirements:* For master's, BA (preferably in field related to the helping professions); minimum of 100 hours of paid or volunteer experience in mental health field or community facility/service organization; interview; state of interest essay; supplemental essays; 2 letters of recommendation; transcripts. Additional exam requirements/recommendations for international students: Required—TOEFL (minimum score 550 paper-based; 80 iBT). *Application deadline:* For fall admission, 1/15 priority date for domestic and international students. Applications are processed on a rolling basis. Application fee: $60. Electronic applications accepted. *Expenses:* $995 per credit. *Financial support:* In 2017–18, 8 students received support, including 1 research assistantship with partial tuition reimbursement available (averaging $1,500 per year), teaching assistantships with partial tuition reimbursements available (averaging $3,000 per year); career-related internships or fieldwork, Federal Work-Study, scholarships/grants, tuition waivers (partial), and unspecified assistantships also available. Support available to part-time students. Financial award application deadline: 3/1; financial award applicants required to submit FAFSA. *Unit head:* Dr. Kathleen Gregory, Dean, Graduate School of Counseling and Psychology, 303-245-4706, E-Mail: kgregory@naropa.edu. *Application contact:* Office of Admissions, 303-546-3572, Fax: 303-546-3583, E-mail: admissions@naropa.edu.
Website: http://www.naropa.edu/academics/masters/clinical-mental-health-counseling/somatic-counseling/body-psychotherapy/index.php

The New School, The New School for Social Research, Department of Philosophy, New York, NY 10003. Offers philosophy (MA); psychoanalysis (PhD). *Program availability:* Part-time. *Faculty:* 10 full-time (4 women), 6 part-time/adjunct (0 women). *Students:* 129 full-time (39 women), 18 part-time (4 women); includes 21 minority (2 Black or African American, non-Hispanic/Latino; 1 Asian, non-Hispanic/Latino; 11 Hispanic/Latino; 7 Two or more races, non-Hispanic/Latino), 37 international. Average age 33. 154 applicants, 65% accepted, 20 enrolled. In 2017, 20 master's, 13 doctorates awarded. Terminal master's awarded for partial completion of doctoral program. *Degree requirements:* For master's, one foreign language, comprehensive exam, thesis; for doctorate, one foreign language, comprehensive exam, thesis/dissertation. *Entrance requirements:* For master's, GRE, letters of recommendation, writing sample, essays, transcript; for doctorate, letters of recommendation, writing sample, essays, transcript. Additional exam requirements/recommendations for international students: Required—TOEFL (minimum score 100 iBT), IELTS (minimum score 7), PTE (minimum score 68). *Application deadline:* For fall admission, 1/5 priority date for domestic and international students; for spring admission, 10/15 priority date for domestic and international students. Applications are processed on a rolling basis. Application fee: $50. Electronic applications accepted. *Expenses:* $2,180 per credit. *Financial support:* In 2017–18, 90 students received support, including 13 fellowships (averaging $23,707 per year), 2 research assistantships (averaging $17,240 per year), 22 teaching assistantships with full and partial tuition reimbursements available (averaging $9,841 per year); Federal Work-Study and scholarships/grants also available. Support available to part-time students. Financial award application deadline: 2/1; financial award applicants required to submit FAFSA. *Unit head:* Dr. William Milberg, Dean, The New School for Social Research, 212-229-5777, E-mail: milbergw@newschool.edu. *Application contact:* Dana Messinger, Director of Graduate Admission, 212-229-5150 Ext. 2300, E-mail: socialresearchadmit@newschool.edu.
Website: http://www.newschool.edu/nssr/philosophy/

New York University, Graduate School of Arts and Science, Department of Psychology, New York, NY 10012-1019. Offers cognition and perception (PhD); general psychology (MA); industrial/organizational psychology (MA); psychotherapy and psychoanalysis (Advanced Certificate); social psychology (PhD). *Program availability:* Part-time. *Students:* Average age 31. 874 applicants, 46% accepted, 153 enrolled. In 2017, 102 master's, 9 doctorates, 10 other advanced degrees awarded. Terminal master's awarded for partial completion of doctoral program. *Degree requirements:* For master's, comprehensive exam, thesis or alternative; for doctorate, thesis/dissertation. *Entrance requirements:* For master's and doctorate, GRE General Test. Additional exam requirements/recommendations for international students: Required—TOEFL. *Application deadline:* For fall admission, 12/12 for domestic and international students. Application fee: $100. *Expenses:* Tuition: Full-time $41,352; part-time $19,968 per year. *Required fees:* $2496; $1628 per unit. $814 per term. Tuition and fees vary according to course load and program. *Financial support:* Fellowships, research assistantships, teaching assistantships, career-related internships or fieldwork, Federal Work-Study, institutionally sponsored loans, scholarships/grants, traineeships, health care benefits, and unspecified assistantships available. Financial award application deadline: 12/12; financial award applicants required to submit FAFSA. *Faculty research:* Vision, memory, social cognition, social and cognitive development, relationships. *Unit head:* Gabriele Oettingen, Director of Graduate Studies, PhD Program, 212-998-7900, Fax: 212-995-4018, E-mail: psychq@psych.nyu.edu. *Application contact:* Adrienne Gans, Director of Graduate Studies, MA Program, 212-998-7900, Fax: 212-995-4018, E-mail: psychq@psych.nyu.edu.
Website: http://www.psych.nyu.edu/

Prescott College, Graduate Programs, Program in Counseling and Psychology, Prescott, AZ 86301. Offers adventure-based psychotherapy (MA); counseling psychology (MA); ecopsychology (MA); ecotherapy (MA); equine-assisted mental health (MA); expressive arts therapy (MA); somatic psychology (MA); student-directed independent study (MA). *Program availability:* Part-time, online learning. Terminal master's awarded for partial completion of doctoral program. *Degree requirements:* For master's, thesis, fieldwork or internship, practicum. *Entrance requirements:* For master's, 2 letters of recommendation, resume. Additional exam requirements/recommendations for international students: Required—TOEFL (minimum score 500 paper-based). Electronic applications accepted.

University of Manitoba, Max Rady College of Medicine and Faculty of Graduate Studies, Graduate Programs in Medicine, Department of Psychiatry, Winnipeg, MB R3T 2N2, Canada. Offers M Sc. *Degree requirements:* For master's, thesis (for some programs). *Faculty research:* Child and adolescent psychiatry, mood disorders, anxiety disorders, psycho-oncology, psychiatric education.

Rehabilitation Counseling

Adler University, Graduate Programs, MA in Counseling Program: Specialization in Rehabilitation Counseling, Chicago, IL 60602. Offers MAC. *Program availability:* Part-time. *Degree requirements:* For master's, thesis optional, practicum, internship.

Alabama Agricultural and Mechanical University, School of Graduate Studies, College of Education, Humanities, and Behavioral Sciences, Department of Social Work, Psychology and Counseling, Huntsville, AL 35811. Offers psychology and counseling (MS, Ed S), including clinical psychology (MS), counseling psychology (MS), guidance and counseling, rehabilitation counseling (MS), school counseling (MS), school psychology (MS), school psychometry (MS); social work (MSW). *Accreditation:* CORE; NCATE. *Program availability:* Part-time, evening/weekend. *Degree requirements:* For master's, comprehensive exam. *Entrance requirements:* For master's, GRE General Test. Additional exam requirements/recommendations for international students: Required—TOEFL (minimum score 500 paper-based; 61 iBT). *Faculty research:* Increasing numbers of minorities in special education and speech-language pathology.

Alabama State University, College of Health Sciences, Department of Rehabilitation Studies, Montgomery, AL 36101-0271. Offers rehabilitation counseling (MRC). *Accreditation:* CORE. *Faculty:* 5 full-time (3 women). *Students:* 19 full-time (11 women), 1 (woman) part-time; includes 18 minority (all Black or African American, non-Hispanic/Latino), 1 international. Average age 22. 17 applicants, 65% accepted, 11 enrolled. In 2017, 13 master's awarded. *Degree requirements:* For master's, comprehensive exam. *Entrance requirements:* Additional exam requirements/recommendations for international students: Required—TOEFL (minimum score 500 paper-based). *Application deadline:* For fall admission, 4/15 priority date for domestic students, 4/15 for international students; for spring admission, 11/15 for domestic and international students; for summer admission, 3/15 for domestic and international students. Application fee: $25. Electronic applications accepted. *Expenses:* Tuition, state resident: part-time $412 per credit hour. Tuition, nonresident: part-time $824 per credit hour. *Required fees:* $685 per semester. *Financial support:* Research assistantships available. Financial award application deadline: 6/30; financial award applicants required to submit FAFSA. *Unit head:* Dr. Naoko Y. Yasui, Interim Chair/Program Coordinator, 334-229-8776, E-mail: nyasui@alasu.edu. *Application contact:* Dr. William Person, Dean of Graduate Studies, 334-229-4274, Fax: 334-229-4928, E-mail: wperson@alasu.edu.
Website: http://www.alasu.edu/academics/colleges—departments/health-sciences/rehabilitation-studies/master-of-rehabilitation-counseling/index.aspx

Arkansas State University, Graduate School, College of Education and Behavioral Science, Department of Psychology and Counseling, State University, AR 72467. Offers clinical mental health counseling (Graduate Certificate); college student personnel services (MS); dyslexia therapy (Graduate Certificate); psychological science (MS); psychology and counseling (Ed S); rehabilitation counseling (MRC); school counseling (MSE); student affairs (Graduate Certificate). *Accreditation:* ACA (one or more programs are accredited); CORE (one or more programs are accredited); NCATE. *Program availability:* Part-time. *Degree requirements:* For master's and other advanced degree, comprehensive exam, thesis or alternative. *Entrance requirements:* For master's, GRE General Test or MAT (for MSE), appropriate bachelor's degree, interview, letters of reference, official transcripts, immunization records, written statement, 2-3 page autobiography; for other advanced degree, GRE General Test, interview, master's degree, letters of reference, official transcript, personal statement, immunization records. Additional exam requirements/recommendations for international students: Required—TOEFL (minimum score 550 paper-based; 79 iBT), IELTS (minimum score 6), PTE (minimum score 56). Electronic applications accepted.

Assumption College, Rehabilitation Counseling Program, Worcester, MA 01609-1296. Offers MA, CAGS. *Accreditation:* CORE. *Program availability:* Part-time, evening/weekend, blended/hybrid learning. *Faculty:* 2 full-time (0 women), 15 part-time/adjunct (10 women). *Students:* 26 full-time (18 women), 35 part-time (30 women); includes 15 minority (10 Black or African American, non-Hispanic/Latino; 1 American Indian or Alaska Native, non-Hispanic/Latino; 3 Hispanic/Latino; 1 Two or more races, non-Hispanic/Latino). Average age 35. 19 applicants, 89% accepted, 14 enrolled. In 2017, 33 master's awarded. *Degree requirements:* For master's, comprehensive exam, internship, practicum. *Entrance requirements:* For master's, bachelor's degree with at least 15 semester hours of undergraduate course work in the behavioral and social sciences and minimum GPA of 2.75; three letters of recommendation; official transcripts; personal statement; current resume; interview; for CAGS, master's degree in human service, counseling, education, social work or related field; three letters of recommendation; official transcripts; personal statement; current resume; interview. Additional exam requirements/recommendations for international students: Required—TOEFL (minimum score 540 paper-based; 76 iBT), IELTS (minimum score 6). *Application deadline:* For fall admission, 7/1 for domestic and international students; for spring admission, 12/1 for domestic and international students; for summer admission, 4/15 for domestic and international students. Application fee: $30. Electronic applications accepted. *Expenses:* Tuition: Full-time $11,952; part-time $664 per credit. *Required fees:* $70 per term. *Financial support:* In 2017–18, 12 students received support. Scholarships/grants, tuition waivers (full and partial), unspecified assistantships, and institutional discounts available. Financial award application deadline: 4/15; financial award applicants required to submit FAFSA. *Faculty research:* Job placement for severe disabilities, vocational counseling, conflict resolution, health issues in mental illness. *Unit head:* Dr. Nicholas Cioe, Director, 508-767-7370, Fax: 508-798-2872, E-mail: nj.cioe@assumption.edu. *Application contact:* Karen Stoyanoff, Director of Recruitment for Graduate Enrollment, 508-767-7442, Fax: 508-799-4915, E-mail: graduate@assumption.edu.
Website: http://graduate.assumption.edu/rehabilitation-counseling/masterofarts

Ball State University, Graduate School, College of Health, Department of Counseling Psychology, Social Psychology, and Counseling, Program in Counseling Psychology, Muncie, IN 47306. Offers counseling (MA), including clinical mental health counseling, mental health counseling, rehabilitation counseling, school counseling; counseling

psychology (PhD). *Accreditation:* ACA; APA. *Program availability:* Part-time. *Students:* 88 full-time (57 women), 29 part-time (24 women); includes 18 minority (3 Black or African American, non-Hispanic/Latino; 1 Asian, non-Hispanic/Latino; 7 Hispanic/Latino; 7 Two or more races, non-Hispanic/Latino), 4 international. Average age 26. 133 applicants, 29% accepted, 39 enrolled. In 2017, 29 master's, 9 doctorates awarded. *Degree requirements:* For doctorate, thesis/dissertation. *Entrance requirements:* For master's, GRE General Test (minimum scores 144 quantitative, 153 verbal), minimum baccalaureate GPA of 2.75 or 3.0 in latter half of baccalaureate, minimum GPA of 3.0 in psychology coursework, three letters of recommendation; for doctorate, GRE General Test, interview, minimum graduate GPA of 3.2, resume. Additional exam requirements/recommendations for international students: Required—TOEFL (minimum score 550 paper-based; 79 iBT), IELTS (minimum score 6.5). *Application deadline:* For fall admission, 3/1 priority date for domestic students, 1/1 for international students. Applications are processed on a rolling basis. Application fee: $60. Electronic applications accepted. *Financial support:* Research assistantships with partial tuition reimbursements, teaching assistantships with partial tuition reimbursements, and unspecified assistantships available. Financial award application deadline: 3/1; financial award applicants required to submit FAFSA. *Unit head:* Dr. Sharon Bowman, Chairperson, 765-285-8040, Fax: 765-285-2067, E-mail: sbowman@bsu.edu.
Website: http://www.bsu.edu/teachers/counseling/cpsy/

Barry University, School of Education, Program in Rehabilitation Counseling, Miami Shores, FL 33161-6695. Offers MS, Ed S. *Program availability:* Part-time, evening/weekend. *Degree requirements:* For master's, comprehensive exam, scholarly paper; for Ed S, comprehensive exam. *Entrance requirements:* For master's, GRE General Test or MAT, minimum GPA of 3.0; for Ed S, GRE General Test, minimum GPA of 3.0. Electronic applications accepted.

Bayamón Central University, Graduate Programs, Program in Education, Bayamón, PR 00960-1725. Offers administration and supervision (MA Ed); commercial education (MA Ed); elementary education (K–3) (MA Ed); family counseling (Graduate Certificate); guidance and counseling (MA Ed); pre-elementary teacher (MA Ed); rehabilitation counseling (MA Ed); special education (MA Ed), including attention deficit disorder, education of the autistic, learning disabilities. *Program availability:* Part-time, evening/weekend. *Degree requirements:* For master's, comprehensive exam. *Entrance requirements:* For master's, EXADEP, bachelor's degree in education or related field.

California State University, Fresno, Division of Research and Graduate Studies, Kremen School of Education and Human Development, Department of Counselor Education and Rehabilitation, Program in Clinical Rehabilitation and Mental Health Counseling, Fresno, CA 93740-8027. Offers MS. *Accreditation:* ACA; CORE. *Program availability:* Part-time, evening/weekend. *Degree requirements:* For master's, internship; project, thesis, or comprehensive exam. *Entrance requirements:* For master's, GRE General Test, MAT, minimum GPA of 3.0, official transcripts. Additional exam requirements/recommendations for international students: Required—TOEFL. Electronic applications accepted. *Faculty research:* Aging, career development, job retention, rehabilitation administration.

California State University, Los Angeles, Graduate Studies, Charter College of Education, Division of Special Education and Counseling, Los Angeles, CA 90032-8530. Offers counseling (MS), including applied behavior analysis, community college counseling, rehabilitation counseling, school counseling, school psychology; special education (MA, PhD). *Accreditation:* ACA. *Program availability:* Part-time, evening/weekend. *Entrance requirements:* For master's, minimum GPA of 2.75 in last 90 units of course work, teaching certificate. Additional exam requirements/recommendations for international students: Required—TOEFL (minimum score 500 paper-based). Electronic applications accepted.

California State University, San Bernardino, Graduate Studies, College of Education, Program in Counseling and Guidance, San Bernardino, CA 92407. Offers counseling and guidance (MS); rehabilitation counseling (MA). *Accreditation:* NCATE. *Program availability:* Part-time, evening/weekend. *Students:* 120 full-time (99 women), 6 part-time (3 women); includes 93 minority (6 Black or African American, non-Hispanic/Latino; 4 Asian, non-Hispanic/Latino; 81 Hispanic/Latino; 2 Two or more races, non-Hispanic/Latino), 3 international. Average age 29. 99 applicants, 65% accepted, 49 enrolled. In 2017, 54 master's awarded. *Degree requirements:* For master's, comprehensive exam, thesis or alternative. *Entrance requirements:* Additional exam requirements/recommendations for international students: Required—TOEFL. *Application deadline:* For fall admission, 7/16 for domestic students. Application fee: $55. *Unit head:* Dr. Judith Sylva, Chair, 909-537-5606, E-mail: jsylva@csusb.edu. *Application contact:* Dr. Dorota Huizinga, Dean of Graduate Studies, 909-537-3064, E-mail: dorota.huizinga@csusb.edu.

California State University, San Bernardino, Graduate Studies, College of Education, Program in Rehabilitation Counseling, San Bernardino, CA 92407. Offers MA. *Accreditation:* CORE; NCATE. *Program availability:* Part-time, evening/weekend. *Students:* 5 full-time (3 women), 49 part-time (41 women); includes 36 minority (10 Black or African American, non-Hispanic/Latino; 3 Asian, non-Hispanic/Latino; 21 Hispanic/Latino; 2 Two or more races, non-Hispanic/Latino). Average age 36. 38 applicants, 82% accepted, 16 enrolled. In 2017, 12 master's awarded. *Degree requirements:* For master's, thesis or alternative. *Entrance requirements:* Additional exam requirements/recommendations for international students: Required—TOEFL. *Application deadline:* For fall admission, 7/16 for domestic students. Application fee: $55. *Financial support:* Career-related internships or fieldwork and Federal Work-Study available. Support available to part-time students. *Unit head:* Dr. Judith Sylva, Chair, 909-537-5606, E-mail: jsylva@csusb.edu. *Application contact:* Dr. Dorota Huizinga, Dean of Graduate Studies, 909-537-3064, E-mail: dorota.huizinga@csusb.edu.

Central Connecticut State University, School of Graduate Studies, School of Education and Professional Studies, Department of Counselor Education and Family Therapy, New Britain, CT 06050-4010. Offers marriage and family therapy (MS); professional counseling (MS, AC, Certificate); school counseling (MS); student development in higher education (MS). *Accreditation:* AAMFT/COAMFTE; ACA. *Program availability:* Part-time, evening/weekend. *Faculty:* 9 full-time (6 women), 27 part-time/adjunct (23 women). *Students:* 184 full-time (141 women), 189 part-time (144 women); includes 131 minority (51 Black or African American, non-Hispanic/Latino; 3 Asian, non-Hispanic/Latino; 66 Hispanic/Latino; 11 Two or more races, non-Hispanic/Latino), 1 international. Average age 34. 217 applicants, 64% accepted, 105 enrolled. In 2017, 94 master's, 7 other advanced degrees awarded. *Degree requirements:* For master's, comprehensive exam, thesis or alternative; for other advanced degree, qualifying exam. *Entrance requirements:* For master's, minimum undergraduate GPA of 2.7, essay, interview, letters of recommendation. Additional exam requirements/recommendations for international students: Required—TOEFL (minimum score 550 paper-based; 79 iBT); Recommended—IELTS (minimum score 6.5). *Application deadline:* For fall admission, 3/1 for domestic and international students; for summer admission, 3/1 for domestic and international students. Applications are processed on a rolling basis. Application fee: $50. Electronic applications accepted. *Expenses: Tuition, area resident:* Full-time $6757. Tuition, state resident: full-time $9750; part-time $374 per credit. Tuition, nonresident: full-time $18,102; part-time $374 per credit. *Required fees:* $4635; $255 per credit. *Financial support:* In 2017–18, 77 students received support. Career-related internships or fieldwork, Federal Work-Study, scholarships/grants, and unspecified assistantships available. Support available to part-time students. Financial award application deadline: 3/1; financial award applicants required to submit FAFSA. *Faculty research:* Elementary and secondary school counseling, marriage and family therapy, rehabilitation counseling, counseling in higher educational settings. *Unit head:* Dr. Cherie King, Chair, 860-832-2154, E-mail: kingche@ccsu.edu. *Application contact:* Patricia Gardner, Associate Director of Graduate Studies, 860-832-2350, Fax: 860-832-2362.
Website: http://www.ccsu.edu/ceft/

Coppin State University, Division of Graduate Studies, Division of Arts and Sciences, Department of Applied Psychology and Rehabilitation Counseling, Program in Rehabilitation Counseling, Baltimore, MD 21216-3698. Offers M Ed. *Accreditation:* CORE. *Program availability:* Part-time. *Degree requirements:* For master's, comprehensive exam (for some programs), thesis optional, internship, clinical requirements. *Entrance requirements:* For master's, GRE General Test, interview, minimum GPA of 3.0.

East Carolina University, Graduate School, College of Allied Health Sciences, Department of Addictions and Rehabilitation Studies, Greenville, NC 27858-4353. Offers clinical counseling (MS); military and trauma counseling (Certificate); rehabilitation and career counseling (MS); rehabilitation counseling (Certificate); rehabilitation counseling and administration (PhD); substance abuse counseling (Certificate); vocational evaluation (Certificate). *Accreditation:* CORE. *Program availability:* Part-time, evening/weekend. *Students:* 82 full-time (64 women), 55 part-time (43 women); includes 39 minority (28 Black or African American, non-Hispanic/Latino; 1 American Indian or Alaska Native, non-Hispanic/Latino; 2 Asian, non-Hispanic/Latino; 5 Hispanic/Latino; 3 Two or more races, non-Hispanic/Latino). Average age 33. 51 applicants, 73% accepted, 31 enrolled. In 2017, 19 master's, 5 doctorates, 34 other advanced degrees awarded. *Degree requirements:* For master's, comprehensive exam, thesis or alternative, internship; for doctorate, thesis/dissertation, internship. *Entrance requirements:* For master's and doctorate, GRE General Test or MAT. Additional exam requirements/recommendations for international students: Recommended—TOEFL (minimum score 78 iBT), IELTS (minimum score 6.5). *Application deadline:* For fall admission, 3/1 priority date for domestic students; for spring admission, 10/1 priority date for domestic students. Applications are processed on a rolling basis. Application fee: $75. Electronic applications accepted. *Expenses:* Tuition, state resident: full-time $4749; part-time $297 per credit hour. Tuition, nonresident: full-time $17,898; part-time $1119 per credit hour. *Required fees:* $2691; $224 per credit hour. Part-time tuition and fees vary according to course load and program. *Financial support:* Research assistantships with partial tuition reimbursements, teaching assistantships with partial tuition reimbursements, Federal Work-Study, scholarships/grants, and unspecified assistantships available. Support available to part-time students. Financial award application deadline: 3/1; financial award applicants required to submit FAFSA. *Unit head:* Dr. Paul Toriello, Chair, 252-744-6292, E-mail: toriellop@ecu.edu.
Website: http://www.ecu.edu/rehb/

East Central University, School of Graduate Studies, Department of Professional Programs in Human Services, Ada, OK 74820. Offers clinical rehabilitation and clinical mental health counseling (MSHR); criminal justice (MSHR); human resources (MSHR). *Accreditation:* CORE. *Program availability:* Part-time, evening/weekend. *Degree requirements:* For master's, thesis optional. *Entrance requirements:* For master's, GRE General Test, MAT, minimum GPA of 2.5. *Application deadline:* Applications are processed on a rolling basis. Application fee: $0 ($50 for international students). Electronic applications accepted. *Unit head:* Regina Robertson, Chair, 580-559-5647, E-mail: rrobrtsn@ecok.edu. *Application contact:* Regina Robertson, Chair, 580-559-5647, E-mail: rrobrtsn@ecok.edu.
Website: http://www.ecok.edu/academics/colleges-and-schools/college-liberal-arts-and-social-sciences/department-human-resources

Edinboro University of Pennsylvania, Department of Counseling, School Psychology and Special Education, Edinboro, PA 16444. Offers counseling (MA), including art therapy, clinical mental health counseling, college counseling, rehabilitation counseling, school counseling; educational psychology (M Ed); school psychology (Ed S); special education (M Ed), including autism, behavior management. *Accreditation:* ACA. *Program availability:* Part-time, evening/weekend. *Degree requirements:* For master's, thesis or alternative, competency exam; for Ed S, thesis or alternative. *Entrance requirements:* For master's and Ed S, GRE or MAT, minimum QPA of 2.5. Electronic applications accepted.

Emporia State University, Program in Rehabilitation Counseling, Emporia, KS 66801-5415. Offers MS. *Accreditation:* CORE. *Program availability:* Part-time. *Faculty:* 13 full-time (9 women). *Students:* 13 full-time (10 women), 2 part-time (1 woman); includes 1 minority (Hispanic/Latino). 6 applicants, 67% accepted, 2 enrolled. In 2017, 17 master's awarded. *Degree requirements:* For master's, comprehensive exam or thesis, practicum. *Entrance requirements:* For master's, GRE or MAT, essay exam, appropriate bachelor's degree, interview, letters of recommendation. *Application deadline:* For fall admission, 8/15 priority date for domestic students. Applications are processed on a rolling basis. Application fee: $30 ($75 for international students). Electronic applications accepted. *Expenses:* Tuition, state resident: full-time $6084; part-time $253.50 per credit hour. Tuition, nonresident: full-time $18,924; part-time $788.50 per credit hour. *Required fees:* $1943; $80.95 per credit hour. Tuition and fees vary according to campus/location. *Financial support:* Career-related internships or fieldwork, Federal Work-Study, institutionally sponsored loans, health care benefits, and unspecified assistantships available. Financial award application deadline: 3/15; financial award applicants required to submit FAFSA. *Unit head:* Dr. Katrina Miller, Chair/Graduate Co-Coordinator, 620-341-5791, E-mail: kmille12@emporia.edu. *Application contact:* Mary Sewell, Admissions Coordinator, 800-950-GRAD, Fax: 620-341-5909, E-mail: msewell@emporia.edu.

Florida International University, College of Arts, Sciences, and Education, Department of Leadership and Professional Studies, Miami, FL 33199. Offers adult education and human resource development (MS, Ed D); counseling (MS), including rehabilitation counseling, school counseling; counselor education (MS), including clinical mental health counseling; educational administration and supervision (Ed D); educational leadership (MS, Certificate, Ed S); higher education (Ed D); higher education administration (MS); international and comparative education (MS); recreation and sport management (MS), including recreation and sport management, recreational therapy; school psychology (Ed S); urban education (MS), including instruction in urban settings, learning technologies, multicultural/bilingual, multicultural/TESOL, urban education. *Program availability:* Part-time, evening/weekend. *Faculty:* 60 full-time (41 women), 112 part-time/adjunct (77 women). *Students:* 221 full-time (162 women), 301 part-time (239 women); includes 418 minority (127 Black or African American, non-Hispanic/Latino; 9 Asian, non-Hispanic/Latino; 271 Hispanic/Latino; 11 Two or more races, non-Hispanic/Latino), 10 international. Average age 31. 330 applicants, 55% accepted, 100 enrolled. In 2017, 181 master's, 6 doctorates awarded. *Degree requirements:* For doctorate, thesis/dissertation. *Entrance requirements:* For master's, minimum GPA of 3.0; for doctorate and other advanced degree, GRE General Test. Additional exam requirements/recommendations for international students: Required—

TOEFL (minimum score 550 paper-based; 80 iBT), IELTS (minimum score 6.3). *Application deadline:* For fall admission, 6/1 priority date for domestic students, 4/1 for international students; for winter admission, 10/1 priority date for domestic students, 9/1 for international students; for spring admission, 3/1 priority date for domestic students, 2/1 for international students. Applications are processed on a rolling basis. Application fee: $30. Electronic applications accepted. *Expenses:* Tuition, state resident: full-time $8912; part-time $446 per credit hour. Tuition, nonresident: full-time $21,393; part-time $992 per credit hour. *Required fees:* $390; $195 per semester. *Financial support:* Fellowships, research assistantships with tuition reimbursements, teaching assistantships with tuition reimbursements, Federal Work-Study, and tuition waivers (full and partial) available. Support available to part-time students. Financial award applicants required to submit FAFSA. *Unit head:* Dr. Benjamin Baez, Chair, 305-348-3214, Fax: 305-348-1515, E-mail: benjamin.baez@fiu.edu. *Application contact:* Nanett Rojas, Assistant Director, Graduate Admissions, 305-348-7464, Fax: 305-348-7441, E-mail: gradadm@fiu.edu.
Website: http://education.fiu.edu

Fort Valley State University, College of Graduate Studies and Extended Education, Department of Counseling Psychology, Program in Rehabilitation Counseling, Fort Valley, GA 31030. Offers MS. *Accreditation:* CORE. *Program availability:* Part-time. *Degree requirements:* For master's, comprehensive exam (for some programs), thesis optional. *Entrance requirements:* For master's, GRE General Test or MAT. Additional exam requirements/recommendations for international students: Recommended—TOEFL.

The George Washington University, Graduate School of Education and Human Development, Department of Counseling and Human Development, Program in Rehabilitation Counseling, Washington, DC 20052. Offers autism spectrum disorder (MA Ed/HD); substance abuse and psychiatric disabilities (MA Ed/HD); traumatic brain injury (MA Ed/HD). *Accreditation:* CORE. *Program availability:* Online learning. *Students:* 30 full-time (17 women), 19 part-time (17 women); includes 17 minority (5 Black or African American, non-Hispanic/Latino; 1 American Indian or Alaska Native, non-Hispanic/Latino; 2 Asian, non-Hispanic/Latino; 7 Hispanic/Latino; 2 Two or more races, non-Hispanic/Latino), 8 international. Average age 35. 39 applicants, 74% accepted, 14 enrolled. In 2017, 22 master's awarded. *Entrance requirements:* For master's, GRE or MAT, two letters of recommendation, 1- to 2-page statement of purpose, official transcripts from all institutions attended, resume. Additional exam requirements/recommendations for international students: Required—TOEFL or IELTS. Electronic applications accepted. *Expenses: Tuition:* Full-time $28,800; part-time $1655 per credit hour. *Required fees:* $45; $2.75 per credit hour. *Unit head:* Dr. Kenneth C. Hergenrather, Director, 202-994-1334, E-mail: hergenkc@gwu.edu. *Application contact:* Sarah Lang, Director of Graduate Admissions, 202-994-1447, Fax: 202-994-7207, E-mail: slang@gwu.edu.
Website: http://gsehd.gwu.edu/rehabilitation-counseling-masters

Georgia State University, College of Education and Human Development, Department of Counseling and Psychological Services, Program in Rehabilitation Counseling, Atlanta, GA 30302-3083. Offers MS. *Accreditation:* CORE. *Program availability:* Online learning. *Entrance requirements:* For master's, GRE, goal statement, resume, 3 letters of recommendation, transcripts. Additional exam requirements/recommendations for international students: Required—TOEFL. Application fee: $50. Electronic applications accepted. *Expenses:* Tuition, state resident: full-time $7020. Tuition, nonresident: full-time $22,518. *Required fees:* $2128. Tuition and fees vary according to degree level and program. *Financial support:* Research assistantships, teaching assistantships, career-related internships or fieldwork, institutionally sponsored loans, scholarships/grants, health care benefits, tuition waivers, and unspecified assistantships available. Financial award application deadline: 4/1. *Faculty research:* Career counseling; sexual and gender minority issues; trauma, stress and coping; disability services; disability employment. *Unit head:* Dr. Brian Dew, Department Chair, 404-413-8168, Fax: 404-413-8013, E-mail: bdew@gsu.edu. *Application contact:* CPS Admissions Office, 404-413-8200.
Website: http://cps.education.gsu.edu/programs/clinical-rehabilitation-counseling/

Hofstra University, School of Health Professions and Human Services, Programs in Counseling, Hempstead, NY 11549. Offers counseling (MS Ed, PD); creative arts therapy (MA); interdisciplinary transition specialist (Advanced Certificate); marriage and family therapy (MA); mental health counseling (MA, Advanced Certificate), including alcohol and substance abuse (Advanced Certificate); rehabilitation administration (PD); rehabilitation counseling (MS Ed, Advanced Certificate); rehabilitation counseling in mental health (MS Ed, Advanced Certificate). *Accreditation:* ACA. *Program availability:* Part-time, evening/weekend. *Students:* 103 full-time (87 women), 67 part-time (60 women); includes 50 minority (21 Black or African American, non-Hispanic/Latino; 11 Asian, non-Hispanic/Latino; 15 Hispanic/Latino; 1 Native Hawaiian or other Pacific Islander, non-Hispanic/Latino; 2 Two or more races, non-Hispanic/Latino), 6 international. Average age 30. 131 applicants, 79% accepted, 52 enrolled. In 2017, 66 master's, 4 other advanced degrees awarded. *Degree requirements:* For master's, comprehensive exam (for some programs), thesis (for some programs), internship, practicum, student teaching, seminars, minimum GPA of 3.0. *Entrance requirements:* For master's, GRE, interview, letters of recommendation, portfolio, essay, professional experience, certification; for other advanced degree, GRE, interview, letters of recommendation, essay, professional experience, resume, master's degree. Additional exam requirements/recommendations for international students: Required—TOEFL (minimum score 550 paper-based; 80 iBT). *Application deadline:* Applications are processed on a rolling basis. Application fee: $75. Electronic applications accepted. *Expenses: Tuition:* Full-time $1292. *Required fees:* $970. Tuition and fees vary according to program. *Financial support:* In 2017–18, 78 students received support, including 47 fellowships with full and partial tuition reimbursements available (averaging $3,138 per year), 5 research assistantships with full and partial tuition reimbursements available (averaging $5,702 per year); career-related internships or fieldwork, Federal Work-Study, institutionally sponsored loans, scholarships/grants, traineeships, tuition waivers (full and partial), and unspecified assistantships also available. Support available to part-time students. Financial award applicants required to submit FAFSA. *Faculty research:* Couple and family therapy infidelity; creative arts impact on Parkinson's disease; LGBTQ inclusion; substance abuse/heroin addiction's racial identity, multicultural issues, white privilege, Latinos, school counseling and the intensity of the high school curriculum. *Unit head:* Dr. Jamie Mitus, Chairperson, 516-463-5759, E-mail: jamie.s.mitus@hofstra.edu. *Application contact:* Sunil Samuel, Assistant Vice President of Admissions, 516-463-4723, Fax: 516-463-4664, E-mail: graduateadmission@hofstra.edu.
Website: http://www.hofstra.edu/academics/colleges/healthscienceshumanservices/

Hunter College of the City University of New York, Graduate School, School of Education, Department of Educational Foundations and Counseling, Program in Rehabilitation Counseling, New York, NY 10065-5085. Offers MS Ed. *Accreditation:* CORE. *Degree requirements:* For master's, thesis, seminar. *Entrance requirements:* For master's, interview, minimum GPA of 2.7, recommendations. Additional exam requirements/recommendations for international students: Required—TOEFL, TWE.

Illinois Institute of Technology, Graduate College, Lewis College of Human Sciences, Department of Psychology, Chicago, IL 60616. Offers clinical psychology (PhD); industrial and organizational psychology (PhD); personnel and human resource development (MS); rehabilitation and mental health counseling (MS); rehabilitation counseling education (PhD). *Accreditation:* APA (one or more programs are accredited); CORE. *Program availability:* Part-time, evening/weekend. Terminal master's awarded for partial completion of doctoral program. *Degree requirements:* For master's, thesis (for some programs); for doctorate, comprehensive exam, thesis/dissertation, minimum of 107 credit hours, 1-year full-time internship. *Entrance requirements:* For master's, GRE General Test (minimum score 298 Quantitative and Verbal, 3.0 Analytical Writing, minimum GPA of 3.0; 3 letters of recommendation; bachelor's degree from accredited institution (for personnel and human resource development); for doctorate, GRE General Test (minimum score 298 Quantitative and Verbal, 3.0 Analytical Writing), bachelor's or master's degree from accredited institution, recommendations. Additional exam requirements/recommendations for international students: Required—TOEFL (minimum score 550 paper-based; 80 iBT). Electronic applications accepted. *Faculty research:* Clinical psychology, rehabilitation and mental health counseling, industrial organizational psychology.

Kent State University, College of Education, Health and Human Services, School of Lifespan Development and Educational Sciences, Program in Rehabilitation Counseling, Kent, OH 44242-0001. Offers M Ed. *Accreditation:* CORE. *Entrance requirements:* For master's, 2 letters of reference, goals statement, minimum undergraduate GPA of 2.75, interview. Additional exam requirements/recommendations for international students: Required—TOEFL (minimum score 550 paper-based; 80 iBT). Electronic applications accepted. *Expenses:* Tuition, state resident: full-time $11,310; part-time $515 per credit hour. Tuition, nonresident: full-time $20,396; part-time $928 per credit hour. *International tuition:* $18,544 full-time.

Langston University, School of Education and Behavioral Sciences, Langston, OK 73050. Offers bilingual/multicultural (M Ed); elementary education (M Ed); English as a second language (M Ed); rehabilitation counseling (M Sc); urban education (M Ed). *Accreditation:* CORE; NCATE (one or more programs are accredited). *Program availability:* Part-time. *Degree requirements:* For master's, comprehensive exam, thesis optional. *Entrance requirements:* For master's, GRE, writing skills test, minimum GPA of 2.5, 3 letters of recommendation. Additional exam requirements/recommendations for international students: Required—TOEFL, TWE. *Faculty research:* Bilingual/multicultural education, financing post-secondary education.

Louisiana State University Health Sciences Center, School of Allied Health Professions, Department of Clinical Rehabilitation and Counseling, New Orleans, LA 70112-2262. Offers MHS. *Accreditation:* CORE. *Faculty:* 4 full-time (3 women). *Students:* 20 full-time (18 women); includes 7 minority (5 Black or African American, non-Hispanic/Latino; 1 Hispanic/Latino; 1 Two or more races, non-Hispanic/Latino). Average age 25. 12 applicants, 83% accepted, 10 enrolled. In 2017, 9 master's awarded. *Degree requirements:* For master's, clinical internship. *Entrance requirements:* For master's, GRE General Test, minimum GPA of 2.5, 2 letters of recommendation. Additional exam requirements/recommendations for international students: Required—TOEFL (minimum score 550 paper-based; 79 iBT). *Application deadline:* For fall admission, 4/15 priority date for domestic students. Applications are processed on a rolling basis. Application fee: $50. *Expenses:* Contact institution. *Financial support:* Traineeships available. Financial award application deadline: 4/15; financial award applicants required to submit FAFSA. *Faculty research:* Job placement, clinical judgment, counseling process, consumer satisfaction, vocational assessment. *Total annual research expenditures:* $10,000. *Unit head:* Dr. Erin M. Dugan, Interim Head, 504-556-3403, Fax: 504-556-7540, E-mail: emart3@lsuhsc.edu. *Application contact:* Yudialys Delgado Cazanas, Student Affairs Director, 504-568-4253, Fax: 504-568-3185, E-mail: ydelga@lsuhsc.edu.
Website: http://alliedhealth.lsuhsc.edu/crc/default.aspx

Maryville University of Saint Louis, Myrtle E. and Earl E. Walker College of Health Professions, Program in Rehabilitation Counseling, St. Louis, MO 63141-7299. Offers marriage and family therapy (MARC); music therapy (MARC); substance abuse (MARC). *Accreditation:* CORE. *Program availability:* Part-time. *Faculty:* 3 full-time (1 woman), 1 (woman) part-time/adjunct. *Students:* 17 full-time (all women), 15 part-time (10 women); includes 7 minority (6 Black or African American, non-Hispanic/Latino; 1 Hispanic/Latino). Average age 32. In 2017, 18 master's awarded. *Degree requirements:* For master's, internship, seminar. *Entrance requirements:* For master's, minimum cumulative GPA of 3.0, 2 letters of recommendation, interview, essay, transcripts, resume. Additional exam requirements/recommendations for international students: Required—TOEFL (minimum score 563 paper-based). *Application deadline:* For fall admission, 1/15 for domestic students; for spring admission, 10/1 for domestic students. Applications are processed on a rolling basis. Electronic applications accepted. *Expenses:* $663 per credit hour; $350 per semester fees. *Financial support:* Career-related internships or fieldwork, Federal Work-Study, and campus employment available. Financial award application deadline: 4/1; financial award applicants required to submit FAFSA. *Unit head:* Dr. Michael Kiener, Director, 314-529-9443, Fax: 314-529-9495, E-mail: mkiener@maryville.edu. *Application contact:* Jeannie DeLuca, Director, Admissions and Advising, 314-529-9355, Fax: 314-529-9927, E-mail: jdeluca@maryville.edu.
Website: http://www.maryville.edu/hp/rehabilitation-counseling/

Mercer University, Graduate Studies, Cecil B. Day Campus, Penfield College, Atlanta, GA 30341. Offers certified rehabilitation counseling (MS); clinical mental health (MS); counselor education and supervision (PhD); criminal justice and public safety leadership (MS); health informatics (MS); human services (MS), including child and adolescent services, gerontology services; organizational leadership (MS), including leadership for the health care professional, leadership for the nonprofit organization, organizational development and change; school counseling (MS). *Program availability:* Part-time, evening/weekend, 100% online, blended/hybrid learning. *Faculty:* 17 full-time (10 women), 27 part-time/adjunct (24 women). *Students:* 199 full-time (165 women), 266 part-time (218 women); includes 268 minority (226 Black or African American, non-Hispanic/Latino; 1 American Indian or Alaska Native, non-Hispanic/Latino; 19 Asian, non-Hispanic/Latino; 19 Hispanic/Latino; 3 Two or more races, non-Hispanic/Latino). Average age 32. 300 applicants, 45% accepted, 114 enrolled. In 2017, 101 master's, 5 doctorates awarded. *Degree requirements:* For master's, comprehensive exam (for some programs), thesis (for some programs); for doctorate, thesis/dissertation. *Entrance requirements:* For master's, GRE or MAT, Georgia Professional Standards Commission (GPSC) Certification at the SC-5 level; for doctorate, GRE or MAT. Additional exam requirements/recommendations for international students: Recommended—TOEFL (minimum score 550 paper-based; 80 iBT), IELTS (minimum score 6.5). *Application deadline:* For fall admission, 7/1 priority date for domestic and international students; for spring admission, 11/1 priority date for domestic and international students; for summer admission, 4/1 priority date for domestic and international students. Application fee: $35. Electronic applications accepted. Application fee is waived when completed online. *Expenses:* $637 per credit. *Financial support:* In 2017–18, 32 students received support. Federal Work-Study, scholarships/grants, and unspecified assistantships available. Financial award applicants required to submit FAFSA. *Faculty research:*

Marriage and families issues, leadership and ethics, cyber-bullying, trauma, narrative counseling and theory. *Total annual research expenditures:* $85,000. *Unit head:* Dr. Priscilla R. Danheiser, Dean, 678-547-6028, Fax: 678-547-6008, E-mail: danheiser_p@mercer.edu. *Application contact:* Dr. Melissa McCants Cruz, Director of Graduate Admissions, 678-547-6024, E-mail: penfield.admissions@mercer.edu.
Website: http://penfield.mercer.edu/programs/graduate-professional/

Michigan State University, The Graduate School, College of Education, Department of Counseling, Educational Psychology and Special Education, East Lansing, MI 48824. Offers counseling (MA); educational psychology and educational technology (PhD); educational technology (MA); measurement and quantitative methods (PhD); rehabilitation counseling (MA); rehabilitation counselor education (PhD); school psychology (MA, PhD, Ed S); special education (MA, PhD). *Accreditation:* APA (one or more programs are accredited); CORE (one or more programs are accredited). *Program availability:* Part-time. *Entrance requirements:* Additional exam requirements/recommendations for international students: Required—TOEFL. Electronic applications accepted.

Minnesota State University Mankato, College of Graduate Studies and Research, College of Allied Health and Nursing, Program in Rehabilitation Counseling, Mankato, MN 56001. Offers MS. *Accreditation:* CORE. *Degree requirements:* For master's, comprehensive exam. *Entrance requirements:* For master's, GRE General Test, minimum GPA of 3.0 during previous 2 years, references.

Mississippi State University, College of Education, Department of Counseling, Educational Psychology, and Foundations, Mississippi State, MS 39762. Offers clinical mental health (MS); college counseling (MS); counseling/mental health (PhD); counseling/school psychology (PhD); counselor education (Ed S); educational psychology/general educational psychology (PhD); educational psychology/school psychology (PhD); general educational psychology (MS); psychometry (MS); rehabilitation counseling (MS); school counseling (MS); school psychology (Ed S); student affairs (MS). *Accreditation:* ACA (one or more programs are accredited); APA; CORE (one or more programs are accredited); NCATE. *Program availability:* Part-time, blended/hybrid learning. *Faculty:* 21 full-time (14 women), 3 part-time/adjunct (2 women). *Students:* 106 full-time (85 women), 51 part-time (43 women); includes 55 minority (44 Black or African American, non-Hispanic/Latino; 1 American Indian or Alaska Native, non-Hispanic/Latino; 1 Asian, non-Hispanic/Latino; 5 Hispanic/Latino; 4 Two or more races, non-Hispanic/Latino), 5 international. Average age 29. 136 applicants, 55% accepted, 54 enrolled. In 2017, 50 master's, 7 doctorates, 10 other advanced degrees awarded. Terminal master's awarded for partial completion of doctoral program. *Degree requirements:* For master's, comprehensive exam, thesis optional; for doctorate, thesis/dissertation, comprehensive oral and written exam. *Entrance requirements:* For master's, GRE (taken within the last five years), BS with minimum GPA of 2.75 on last 60 hours; for doctorate, GRE, MS from CACREP- or CORE-accredited program in counseling; for Ed S, GRE, MS in counseling or related field, minimum GPA of 3.3 on all graduate work. Additional exam requirements/recommendations for international students: Required—TOEFL (minimum score 550 paper-based; 79 iBT); Recommended—IELTS (minimum score 6.5). *Application deadline:* For fall admission, 2/1 priority date for domestic and international students. Applications are processed on a rolling basis. Application fee: $60 ($80 for international students). Electronic applications accepted. *Expenses:* Tuition, state resident: full-time $8318; part-time $462.12 per credit hour. Tuition, nonresident: full-time $22,358; part-time $1242.12 per credit hour. *Required fees:* $110; $12.24 per credit hour. $6.12 per semester. *Financial support:* In 2017–18, 4 research assistantships (averaging $9,000 per year), 10 teaching assistantships with full tuition reimbursements (averaging $8,401 per year) were awarded; career-related internships or fieldwork, Federal Work-Study, institutionally sponsored loans, and unspecified assistantships also available. Financial award application deadline: 2/1; financial award applicants required to submit FAFSA. *Faculty research:* HIV/AIDS in college population, substance abuse in youth and college students, ADHD and conduct disorders in youth, assessment and identification of early childhood disabilities, assessment and vocational transition of the disabled. *Unit head:* Dr. David Morse, Professor and Head, 662-325-3426, Fax: 662-325-3263, E-mail: dmorse@colled.msstate.edu. *Application contact:* Marina Hunt, Admissions and Enrollment Assistant, 662-325-3363, E-mail: mhunt@grad.msstate.edu.
Website: http://www.cep.msstate.edu/

Montana State University Billings, College of Allied Health Professions, Program in Clinical Rehabilitation and Mental Health Counseling, Billings, MT 59101. Offers MS. *Accreditation:* ACA; CORE. *Program availability:* Part-time. *Degree requirements:* For master's, thesis or professional paper and/or field experience. *Entrance requirements:* For master's, GRE General Test or MAT, minimum GPA of 3.0, letters of recommendation, letter of intent. Additional exam requirements/recommendations for international students: Required—TOEFL (minimum score 79 iBT), IELTS (minimum score 6.5). *Application deadline:* For fall admission, 7/15 for international students; for spring admission, 12/1 for international students. Applications are processed on a rolling basis. Application fee: $40. Electronic applications accepted. *Expenses:* Tuition, state resident: full-time $11,740; part-time $7880 per year. Tuition, nonresident: full-time $32,200; part-time $24,140 per year. *Financial support:* Research assistantships with partial tuition reimbursements, teaching assistantships with partial tuition reimbursements, career-related internships or fieldwork, Federal Work-Study, institutionally sponsored loans, scholarships/grants, tuition waivers (partial), and unspecified assistantships available. Support available to part-time students. Financial award application deadline: 5/1; financial award applicants required to submit FAFSA. *Unit head:* Dr. Tom Dell, Chair, 406-896-5837, E-mail: tdell@msubillings.edu. *Application contact:* Dr. Tom Dell, Chair, 406-896-5837, E-mail: tdell@msubillings.edu.
Website: http://msubillings.edu/grad/program-rehab-mental_health_counseling.htm

Mount Mary University, Graduate Programs, Program in Counseling, Milwaukee, WI 53222-4597. Offers clinical mental health counseling (MS, Certificate); clinical rehabilitation counseling (MS, Certificate); school counseling (MS, Certificate); vocational rehabilitation counseling (MS, Certificate). *Accreditation:* ACA. *Program availability:* Part-time, evening/weekend. *Degree requirements:* For master's, comprehensive exam, thesis or alternative. *Entrance requirements:* For master's, minimum GPA of 3.0. Additional exam requirements/recommendations for international students: Required—TOEFL (minimum score 550 paper-based; 80 iBT); Recommended—IELTS (minimum score 6.5). Electronic applications accepted. *Expenses:* Contact institution. *Faculty research:* Cognitive behavioral interventions for depression, eating disorders and compliance, trauma-informed care.

Northeastern Illinois University, College of Graduate Studies and Research, Daniel L. Goodwin College of Education, Program in Rehabilitation Counseling, Chicago, IL 60625. Offers MA. *Accreditation:* CORE. *Expenses:* Tuition, state resident: full-time $7274; part-time $404.11 per credit hour. Tuition, nonresident: full-time $14,548; part-time $808.23 per credit hour. *Required fees:* $1284. *Unit head:* Dr. Charles Pistorio, Department Chair, 773-442-5551, E-mail: c-pistorio@neiu.edu. *Application contact:* Martha Narvaez, Graduate Admission Representative, 773-442-6006, E-mail: m-narvaez@neiu.edu.

Ohio University, Graduate College, Gladys W. and David H. Patton College of Education and Human Services, Department of Counseling and Higher Education, Athens, OH 45701-2979. Offers college student personnel (M Ed); community/agency counseling (M Ed); counselor education (PhD); higher education (PhD); rehabilitation counseling (M Ed); school counseling (M Ed). *Accreditation:* ACA; CORE. *Program availability:* Part-time, evening/weekend. *Degree requirements:* For master's, comprehensive exam (for some programs), thesis or alternative; for doctorate, comprehensive exam, thesis/dissertation. *Entrance requirements:* For master's, GRE General Test or MAT (if GPA less than 2.9), 3 letters of reference; for doctorate, GRE General Test, work experience, minimum GPA of 3.4. Additional exam requirements/recommendations for international students: Required—TOEFL (minimum score 550 paper-based; 80 iBT) or IELTS (minimum score 6.5). Electronic applications accepted. *Faculty research:* Youth violence, gender studies, student affairs, chemical dependency, disabilities issues.

Pontifical Catholic University of Puerto Rico, College of Graduate Studies in Behavioral Science and Community Affairs, Program in Rehabilitation Counseling, Ponce, PR 00717-0777. Offers MA. *Accreditation:* CORE. *Program availability:* Part-time. *Degree requirements:* For master's, thesis. *Entrance requirements:* For master's, EXADEP, GRE General Test, 3 letters of recommendation, interview, minimum GPA of 2.75.

Rutgers University–Newark, School of Health Related Professions, Department of Psychiatric Rehabilitation and Counseling Professions, Program in Psychiatric Rehabilitation, Newark, NJ 07102. Offers MS, PhD. *Accreditation:* CORE. *Program availability:* Part-time, evening/weekend, online learning. *Degree requirements:* For doctorate, comprehensive exam, thesis/dissertation. *Entrance requirements:* For master's, all transcripts, interview, statement of interest, bachelor's degree, 2 reference letters; for doctorate, GRE General Test, all transcripts, bachelor's degree, personal statement, 3 reference letters. Additional exam requirements/recommendations for international students: Required—TOEFL (minimum score 500 paper-based; 79 iBT). Electronic applications accepted.

Rutgers University–Newark, School of Health Related Professions, Department of Psychiatric Rehabilitation and Counseling Professions, Program in Rehabilitation Counseling, Newark, NJ 07102. Offers community counseling (MS). Programs offered at Scotch Plains and Stratford campuses. *Accreditation:* CORE. *Program availability:* Part-time, evening/weekend. *Degree requirements:* For master's, internship, practicum. *Entrance requirements:* For master's, bachelor's degree with transcript, interview, personal goals statement, 2 reference letters. Additional exam requirements/recommendations for international students: Required—TOEFL (minimum score 500 paper-based; 79 iBT). Electronic applications accepted.

St. Bonaventure University, School of Graduate Studies, School of Education, Program in Counselor Education, St. Bonaventure, NY 14778-2284. Offers community mental health counseling (MS Ed); rehabilitation counseling (MS Ed); school counseling (MS Ed); school counselor (Adv C). *Accreditation:* ACA. *Program availability:* Part-time, evening/weekend, 100% online. *Faculty:* 4 full-time (2 women), 5 part-time/adjunct (3 women). *Students:* 35 full-time (27 women), 30 part-time (23 women); includes 8 minority (3 Black or African American, non-Hispanic/Latino; 4 Hispanic/Latino; 1 Two or more races, non-Hispanic/Latino), 1 international. Average age 28. 55 applicants, 82% accepted, 29 enrolled. In 2017, 27 master's, 2 Adv Cs awarded. *Degree requirements:* For master's, comprehensive exam, thesis optional, internship, portfolio; for Adv C, internship. *Entrance requirements:* For master's, statement of intent/writing sample; transcripts from all colleges previously attended; two references; interview; minimum undergraduate GPA of 3.0; for Adv C, interview, writing sample, minimum undergraduate GPA of 3.0, two letters of recommendation, master's degree, transcripts from all colleges previously attended. Additional exam requirements/recommendations for international students: Required—TOEFL (minimum score 550 paper-based; 79 iBT). *Application deadline:* For fall admission, 3/15 priority date for domestic students, 2/1 priority date for international students; for spring admission, 11/15 priority date for domestic students, 7/1 priority date for international students. Applications are processed on a rolling basis. Application fee: $0. Electronic applications accepted. *Expenses:* $733 per credit hour, $100 graduation fee. *Financial support:* Career-related internships or fieldwork, Federal Work-Study, scholarships/grants, health care benefits, and unspecified assistantships available. Support available to part-time students. Financial award application deadline: 4/15; financial award applicants required to submit FAFSA. *Faculty research:* Balance between technology and personal contact in counselor education, special education and cyberbullying, school response to child abuse. *Unit head:* Dr. Chris Siuta, Director, 716-375-2114, Fax: 716-375-2360, E-mail: csiuta@sbu.edu. *Application contact:* Bruce Campbell, Director of Graduate Admissions, 716-375-2429, Fax: 716-375-4015, E-mail: gradsch@sbu.edu.
Website: http://www.sbu.edu/academics/msed-in-school-counseling

St. Cloud State University, School of Graduate Studies, School of Education, Department of Educational Leadership and Higher Education, Program in Rehabilitation Counseling, St. Cloud, MN 56301-4498. Offers MS. *Accreditation:* CORE. *Degree requirements:* For master's, comprehensive exam (for some programs), thesis or alternative. *Entrance requirements:* For master's, GRE General Test, minimum GPA of 2.75. Additional exam requirements/recommendations for international students: Required—Michigan English Language Assessment Battery; Recommended—TOEFL (minimum score 550 paper-based), IELTS (minimum score 6.5). Electronic applications accepted.

Salve Regina University, Program in Rehabilitation Counseling, Newport, RI 02840-4192. Offers clinical rehabilitation and mental health counseling (MA); mental health (CAGS), including rehabilitation counseling; rehabilitation (CAGS), including substance abuse counseling; rehabilitation counseling (MA); substance abuse and treatment (CAGS). *Accreditation:* CORE. *Program availability:* Part-time, evening/weekend. *Entrance requirements:* For master's, GMAT, GRE General Test or MAT. Additional exam requirements/recommendations for international students: Required—TOEFL (minimum score 600 paper-based; 100 iBT) or IELTS. Electronic applications accepted.

San Diego State University, Graduate and Research Affairs, College of Education, Department of Administration, Rehabilitation and Post-Secondary Education, San Diego, CA 92182. Offers educational leadership in post-secondary education (MA); rehabilitation counseling (MS), including deafness. *Program availability:* Evening/weekend, online learning. *Degree requirements:* For master's, comprehensive exam (for some programs), thesis (for some programs). *Entrance requirements:* For master's, GRE General Test, letters of reference. Additional exam requirements/recommendations for international students: Required—TOEFL. Electronic applications accepted. *Faculty research:* Rehabilitation in cultural diversity, distance learning technology.

South Carolina State University, College of Graduate and Professional Studies, Department of Human Services, Orangeburg, SC 29117-0001. Offers counselor education (M Ed); rehabilitation counseling (MA). *Accreditation:* CORE. *Program availability:* Part-time, evening/weekend. *Faculty:* 8 full-time (6 women), 3 part-time/adjunct (all women). *Students:* 87 full-time (74 women), 25 part-time (17 women); includes 106 minority (all Black or African American, non-Hispanic/Latino). Average age 32. 60 applicants, 93% accepted, 51 enrolled. In 2017, 38 master's awarded. *Degree requirements:* For master's, comprehensive exam (for some programs), departmental

qualifying exam, internship. *Entrance requirements:* For master's, GRE, MAT, minimum GPA of 2.7. *Application deadline:* For fall admission, 6/15 priority date for domestic students, 6/15 for international students; for spring admission, 11/1 for domestic and international students. Application fee: $25. Electronic applications accepted. *Expenses:* Tuition, state resident: full-time $9388; part-time $607 per credit hour. Tuition, nonresident: full-time $19,968; part-time $1194 per credit hour. *Required fees:* $766; $766 per credit hour. *Financial support:* Fellowships, career-related internships or fieldwork, scholarships/grants, and unspecified assistantships available. Financial award application deadline: 6/1. *Unit head:* Dr. Michelle Maultsby-Priester, Interim Chair, Department of Human Services, 803-536-7075, Fax: 803-533-3636, E-mail: mmaultsb@scsu.edu. *Application contact:* Curtis Foskey, Coordinator of Graduate Admissions, 803-536-8419, Fax: 803-536-8812, E-mail: cfoskey@scsu.edu.

Southern University and Agricultural and Mechanical College, Graduate School, College of Sciences, Department of Psychology, Program in Rehabilitation Counseling, Baton Rouge, LA 70813. Offers MS. *Accreditation:* CORE. *Degree requirements:* For master's, comprehensive exam, thesis optional. *Entrance requirements:* For master's, GMAT or GRE General Test. Additional exam requirements/recommendations for international students: Required—TOEFL. *Faculty research:* Cultural diversity, professional preparation and participation of minorities, needs and satisfaction of students with disabilities, prediction model for rehabilitation outcome, diabetes.

Springfield College, Graduate Programs, Programs in Rehabilitation Counseling, Springfield, MA 01109-3797. Offers rehabilitation counseling (M Ed, MS). *Accreditation:* CORE (one or more programs are accredited). *Program availability:* Part-time. *Students:* 9 applicants, 89% accepted, 4 enrolled. In 2017, 9 master's awarded. *Degree requirements:* For master's, comprehensive exam. *Entrance requirements:* Additional exam requirements/recommendations for international students: Required—TOEFL (minimum score 550 paper-based); Recommended—IELTS (minimum score 7). *Application deadline:* For fall admission, 1/15 for domestic and international students; for winter admission, 11/1 for international students; for spring admission, 11/1 for domestic and international students. Applications are processed on a rolling basis. Application fee: $50. Electronic applications accepted. *Financial support:* Fellowships with partial tuition reimbursements, teaching assistantships with partial tuition reimbursements, career-related internships or fieldwork, Federal Work-Study, institutionally sponsored loans, scholarships/grants, and unspecified assistantships available. Financial award application deadline: 3/1; financial award applicants required to submit FAFSA. *Unit head:* Dr. Kathleen Glynn, Graduate Coordinator, 413-748-3318, E-mail: kglynn@springfield.edu. *Application contact:* Anne Griffin, Director of Graduate Admissions, 413-748-3225, Fax: 413-748-3694, E-mail: agriffin2@springfield.edu. Website: http://springfield.edu/gradrehab

Texas Tech University Health Sciences Center, School of Health Professions, Program in Clinical Rehabilitation Counseling, Lubbock, TX 79430. Offers MRC. *Accreditation:* CORE. *Program availability:* Part-time, online only. *Faculty:* 5 full-time (2 women). *Students:* 23 full-time (17 women), 45 part-time (30 women); includes 32 minority (9 Black or African American, non-Hispanic/Latino; 1 Asian, non-Hispanic/Latino; 19 Hispanic/Latino; 1 Native Hawaiian or other Pacific Islander, non-Hispanic/Latino; 2 Two or more races, non-Hispanic/Latino). Average age 38. 38 applicants, 79% accepted, 24 enrolled. In 2017, 25 master's awarded. *Entrance requirements:* Additional exam requirements/recommendations for international students: Required—TOEFL (minimum score 550 paper-based; 79 iBT), IELTS. *Application deadline:* For fall admission, 6/1 for domestic students; for spring admission, 11/1 for domestic students. Applications are processed on a rolling basis. Application fee: $75. Electronic applications accepted. *Financial support:* Career-related internships or fieldwork and institutionally sponsored loans available. Financial award application deadline: 9/1; financial award applicants required to submit FAFSA. *Unit head:* Dr. Sara Johnston, Program Director, 806-743-2590, Fax: 806-743-3244, E-mail: sara.johnston@ttuhsc.edu. *Application contact:* Lindsay Johnson, Associate Dean for Admissions and Student Affairs, 806-743-3220, Fax: 806-743-2994, E-mail: lindsay.johnson@ttuhsc.edu. Website: http://www.ttuhsc.edu/health-professions/master-of-science-clinical-rehabilitation-counseling/

Thomas University, Department of Human Services, Thomasville, GA 31792-7499. Offers community counseling (MSCC); rehabilitation counseling (MRC). *Accreditation:* CORE. *Program availability:* Part-time. *Entrance requirements:* For master's, resume, 3 academic/professional references. Additional exam requirements/recommendations for international students: Required—TOEFL (minimum score 600 paper-based). Electronic applications accepted.

University at Buffalo, the State University of New York, Graduate School, Graduate School of Education, Department of Counseling, School, and Educational Psychology, Buffalo, NY 14260. Offers applied statistical analysis (Advanced Certificate); counseling/school psychology (PhD); counselor education (PhD); education studies (Ed M); educational psychology (MA, PhD); mental health counseling (MS, Certificate); mindful counseling for wellness and engagement (Advanced Certificate); rehabilitation counseling (MS, Advanced Certificate); school counseling (Ed M, Certificate). *Accreditation:* CORE (one or more programs are accredited). *Program availability:* Part-time, 100% online. *Faculty:* 21 full-time (11 women), 53 part-time/adjunct (41 women). *Students:* 173 full-time (140 women), 138 part-time (116 women); includes 32 minority (25 Black or African American, non-Hispanic/Latino; 2 American Indian or Alaska Native, non-Hispanic/Latino; 2 Asian, non-Hispanic/Latino; 3 Hispanic/Latino), 16 international. Average age 32. 328 applicants, 59% accepted, 143 enrolled. In 2017, 74 master's, 12 doctorates, 39 other advanced degrees awarded. *Degree requirements:* For master's, comprehensive exam (for some programs), thesis (for some programs); for doctorate, comprehensive exam, thesis/dissertation. *Entrance requirements:* For master's, GRE General Test, interview, letters of reference; for doctorate, GRE General Test, interview, letters of reference, writing sample. Additional exam requirements/recommendations for international students: Required—TOEFL (minimum score 79 iBT). *Application deadline:* For fall admission, 2/1 priority date for domestic and international students. Application fee: $50. Electronic applications accepted. *Financial support:* In 2017–18, 22 fellowships (averaging $7,823 per year), 41 research assistantships with tuition reimbursements (averaging $10,876 per year) were awarded; teaching assistantships, career-related internships or fieldwork, Federal Work-Study, institutionally sponsored loans, scholarships/grants, tuition waivers (full and partial), and unspecified assistantships also available. Financial award application deadline: 2/1; financial award applicants required to submit FAFSA. *Faculty research:* Multicultural counseling, class size effects, good work in counseling, eating disorders, outcome assessment, change agents and therapeutic factors in group counseling. *Total annual research expenditures:* $1.3 million. *Unit head:* Dr. Jeremy Finn, Chair, 716-645-1126, Fax: 716-645-6616, E-mail: finn@buffalo.edu. *Application contact:* Baylee Richards, Recruitment and Student Services Coordinator, 716-645-2110, Fax: 716-645-7937, E-mail: gse-info@buffalo.edu. Website: http://gse.buffalo.edu/csep

The University of Arizona, College of Education, Department of Disability and Psychoeducational Studies, Program in Counseling and Mental Health, Tucson, AZ 85721. Offers rehabilitation counseling (MA); school counseling (MA). *Accreditation:* ACA. *Entrance requirements:* Additional exam requirements/recommendations for international students: Required—TOEFL (minimum score 550 paper-based; 80 iBT). *Faculty research:* Further knowledge and understanding of abilities, disabilities, adaptations, interventions, and support systems; preparing professionals to educate and facilitate the development of individuals with disabilities and special abilities; providing leadership at the local, state, national, and international levels.

The University of Arizona, College of Education, Department of Disability and Psychoeducational Studies, Program in Rehabilitation Counseling, Tucson, AZ 85721. Offers PhD. *Accreditation:* CORE. *Entrance requirements:* For doctorate, GMAT, 3 letters of recommendation. Additional exam requirements/recommendations for international students: Required—TOEFL (minimum score 550 paper-based; 79 iBT). Electronic applications accepted.

University of Arkansas, Graduate School, College of Education and Health Professions, Department of Rehabilitation, Human Resources and Communication Disorders, Program in Rehabilitation, Fayetteville, AR 72701. Offers MS, PhD. *Accreditation:* CORE (one or more programs are accredited). *Program availability:* Part-time. In 2017, 12 master's, 3 doctorates awarded. *Degree requirements:* For doctorate, thesis/dissertation. *Entrance requirements:* For doctorate, GRE General Test. *Application deadline:* For fall admission, 8/1 for domestic students, 4/1 for international students; for spring admission, 12/1 for domestic students, 10/1 for international students; for summer admission, 4/15 for domestic students, 3/1 for international students. Applications are processed on a rolling basis. Application fee: $60. Electronic applications accepted. *Expenses:* Tuition, state resident: full-time $3782. Tuition, nonresident: full-time $10,238. *Financial support:* In 2017–18, 6 research assistantships were awarded; fellowships with tuition reimbursements, teaching assistantships, career-related internships or fieldwork, and Federal Work-Study also available. Support available to part-time students. Financial award application deadline: 4/1; financial award applicants required to submit FAFSA. *Unit head:* Dr. Kate Mamiseishvili, Department Chairperson, 479-575-4758, Fax: 479-575-3319, E-mail: kmamisei@uark.edu. *Application contact:* Dr. Brent Williams, Graduate Coordinator, 479-575-4758, E-mail: btwilli@uark.edu. Website: http://rhrc.uark.edu

University of Arkansas at Little Rock, Graduate School, College of Education and Health Professions, Department of Counseling, Adult and Rehabilitation Education, Little Rock, AR 72204-1099. Offers adult education (M Ed); counselor education (M Ed); rehabilitation counseling (MA, Graduate Certificate); rehabilitation for the blind: orientation and mobility (MA). *Accreditation:* CORE; NCATE. *Program availability:* Part-time. *Entrance requirements:* For master's, interview, minimum GPA of 2.75. *Faculty research:* Low vision, orientation and mobility instruction.

University of Idaho, College of Graduate Studies, College of Education, Health and Human Sciences, Department of Leadership and Counseling, Boise, ID 83844-2282. Offers adult/organizational learning and leadership (Ed S); educational leadership (Ed S); rehabilitation counseling and human services (M Ed); school counseling (M Ed, MS). *Faculty:* 14 full-time, 6 part-time/adjunct. *Students:* 29 full-time (20 women), 147 part-time (78 women). Average age 38. In 2017, 62 master's, 32 other advanced degrees awarded. *Entrance requirements:* For master's, minimum GPA of 3.0, writing sample. Additional exam requirements/recommendations for international students: Required—TOEFL (minimum score 79 iBT). *Application deadline:* Applications are processed on a rolling basis. Application fee: $60. Electronic applications accepted. *Expenses:* Tuition, state resident: full-time $6722; part-time $430 per credit hour. Tuition, nonresident: full-time $23,046; part-time $1337 per credit hour. *Required fees:* $2142; $63 per credit hour. *Financial support:* Applicants required to submit FAFSA. *Unit head:* Dr. Kathy Canfield-Davis, Chair, 208-364-4047, E-mail: lead@uidaho.edu. *Application contact:* Sean Scoggin, Graduate Recruitment Coordinator, 208-885-4723, Fax: 208-885-4406, E-mail: graduateadmissions@uidaho.edu. Website: https://www.uidaho.edu/ed/lc

The University of Iowa, Graduate College, College of Education, Department of Rehabilitation and Counselor Education, Iowa City, IA 52242-1316. Offers counselor education and supervision (PhD); couple and family therapy (PhD); rehabilitation and mental health counseling (MA); rehabilitation counselor education (PhD); school counseling (MA). *Accreditation:* ACA (one or more programs are accredited); CORE (one or more programs are accredited). *Degree requirements:* For master's, thesis optional, exam; for doctorate, comprehensive exam, thesis/dissertation. *Entrance requirements:* For master's and doctorate, GRE General Test, minimum GPA of 3.0. Additional exam requirements/recommendations for international students: Required—TOEFL (minimum score 550 paper-based; 81 iBT). Electronic applications accepted.

University of Kentucky, Graduate School, College of Education, Program in Special Education, Lexington, KY 40506-0032. Offers early childhood (MS Ed); rehabilitation counseling (MRC, PhD); special education (MS Ed, PhD). *Accreditation:* CORE; NCATE. Terminal master's awarded for partial completion of doctoral program. *Degree requirements:* For master's, comprehensive exam, thesis optional; for doctorate, comprehensive exam, thesis/dissertation. *Entrance requirements:* For master's, GRE General Test, minimum undergraduate GPA of 2.75; for doctorate, GRE General Test, minimum graduate GPA of 3.0. Additional exam requirements/recommendations for international students: Required—TOEFL (minimum score 550 paper-based). Electronic applications accepted. *Faculty research:* Applied behavior analysis applications in special education, single subject research design in classroom settings, transition research across life span, rural special education personnel.

University of Louisiana at Lafayette, College of Liberal Arts, Department of Psychology, Program in Rehabilitation Counseling, Lafayette, LA 70504. Offers MS. *Entrance requirements:* For master's, GRE General Test, minimum GPA of 3.0. Additional exam requirements/recommendations for international students: Required—TOEFL (minimum score 550 paper-based). Electronic applications accepted. *Faculty research:* Vocational assessment, psychology.

University of Maryland, College Park, Academic Affairs, College of Education, Department of Counseling, Higher Education and Special Education, College Park, MD 20742. Offers college student personnel (M Ed, MA); college student personnel administration (PhD); community counseling (CAGS); community/career counseling (M Ed, MA); counseling and personnel services (M Ed, MA, PhD), including art therapy (M Ed), college student personnel (M Ed), counseling and personnel services (PhD), counseling psychology (M Ed), mental health counseling (M Ed), school counseling (M Ed); counseling psychology (PhD); counselor education (PhD); rehabilitation counseling (M Ed, MA, AGSC); school counseling (M Ed, MA); school psychology (M Ed, MA, PhD). *Accreditation:* APA (one or more programs are accredited); NCATE. *Program availability:* Part-time, evening/weekend, online learning. *Degree requirements:* For master's, thesis (for some programs); for doctorate, thesis/dissertation. *Entrance requirements:* For master's, GRE General Test or MAT, minimum GPA of 3.0, 3 letters of recommendation; for doctorate, GRE General Test or MAT, minimum GPA of 3.5, 3 letters of recommendation. Additional exam requirements/recommendations for international students: Required—TOEFL. Electronic applications accepted. *Faculty research:* Educational psychology, counseling, health.

Rehabilitation Counseling

University of Maryland Eastern Shore, Graduate Programs, Department of Rehabilitation Services, Princess Anne, MD 21853. Offers rehabilitation counseling (MS). *Accreditation:* CORE. *Program availability:* Part-time, evening/weekend. *Degree requirements:* For master's, internship. *Entrance requirements:* For master's, interview. Additional exam requirements/recommendations for international students: Required—TOEFL (minimum score 80 iBT). Electronic applications accepted. *Faculty research:* Long-term rehabilitation training.

University of Massachusetts Boston, Graduate School of Global Inclusion and Social Development, Program in Rehabilitation Counseling, Boston, MA 02125-3393. Offers MS. *Accreditation:* CORE. *Students:* 18 full-time (15 women), 16 part-time (12 women); includes 11 minority (2 Black or African American, non-Hispanic/Latino; 3 Asian, non-Hispanic/Latino; 4 Hispanic/Latino; 2 Two or more races, non-Hispanic/Latino). Average age 38. 24 applicants, 75% accepted, 13 enrolled. In 2017, 8 master's awarded. *Expenses:* Tuition, state resident: full-time $17,375. Tuition, nonresident: full-time $33,915. *Required fees:* $355. *Application contact:* Graduate Admissions Coordinator, 617-287-6400, Fax: 617-287-6236, E-mail: bos.gadm@dpc.umassp.edu.

University of Memphis, Graduate School, College of Education, Department of Counseling, Educational Psychology and Research, Memphis, TN 38152. Offers counseling (MS, Ed D), including clinical mental health counseling (MS), clinical rehabilitation counseling (MS), rehabilitation counseling (MS), school counseling (MS); counseling psychology (PhD); educational psychology and research (MS, PhD), including educational psychology, educational research. *Accreditation:* ACA (one or more programs are accredited); APA (one or more programs are accredited); CORE (one or more programs are accredited); NCATE. *Program availability:* Blended/hybrid learning. *Faculty:* 26 full-time (17 women), 8 part-time/adjunct (5 women). *Students:* 132 full-time (111 women), 87 part-time (66 women); includes 71 minority (51 Black or African American, non-Hispanic/Latino; 4 Asian, non-Hispanic/Latino; 10 Hispanic/Latino; 6 Two or more races, non-Hispanic/Latino), 5 international. Average age 31. 146 applicants, 49% accepted, 49 enrolled. In 2017, 39 master's, 13 doctorates awarded. *Degree requirements:* For master's, comprehensive exam, thesis or alternative, internship; for doctorate, comprehensive exam, thesis/dissertation, practicum, internship, residency, scholarly work. *Entrance requirements:* For master's, GRE General Test or MAT, minimum GPA of 2.5, letters of reference, interview; for doctorate, GRE General Test, master's degree or equivalent, letters of reference, interview, curriculum vitae, personal statement. Additional exam requirements/recommendations for international students: Required—TOEFL (minimum score 550 paper-based; 79 iBT). *Application deadline:* For fall admission, 10/1 priority date for domestic students; for spring admission, 4/1 priority date for domestic students. Applications are processed on a rolling basis. Application fee: $35 ($60 for international students). Electronic applications accepted. *Expenses:* Contact institution. *Financial support:* In 2017–18, 130 students received support, including 15 research assistantships with full tuition reimbursements available (averaging $13,426 per year), 12 teaching assistantships with full tuition reimbursements available (averaging $11,976 per year); fellowships with full tuition reimbursements available, career-related internships or fieldwork, Federal Work-Study, scholarships/grants, and unspecified assistantships also available. Financial award application deadline: 2/1; financial award applicants required to submit FAFSA. *Faculty research:* Anger management, aging and disability, supervision, multicultural counseling. *Unit head:* Dr. Steve West, Chair, 901-678-2841, Fax: 901-678-5114, E-mail: slwest@memphis.edu. *Application contact:* Dr. Suzanne Lease, Interim Assistant Dean of Education and Graduate Programs, 901-678-4476, Fax: 901-678-4778, E-mail: slease@memphis.edu.
Website: http://www.memphis.edu/cepr/

The University of North Carolina at Chapel Hill, School of Medicine and Graduate School, Graduate Programs in Medicine, Department of Allied Health Sciences, Division of Clinical Rehabilitation and Mental Health Counseling, Chapel Hill, NC 27599. Offers MS. *Accreditation:* CORE. *Degree requirements:* For master's, comprehensive exam, thesis or alternative, internship. *Entrance requirements:* For master's, GRE. Additional exam requirements/recommendations for international students: Required—TOEFL (minimum score 550 paper-based). *Faculty research:* Motor development, motor control; treatment of sports/orthopedic patient problems; movement in older adults; postural control across the lifespan; research in clinical practice; fetal, preterm, and infant movement; functional assessment across the lifespan.

University of Northern Colorado, Graduate School, College of Natural and Health Sciences, School of Human Sciences, Program in Rehabilitation Counseling and Sciences, Greeley, CO 80639. Offers rehabilitation counseling (MA); rehabilitation sciences (PhD). *Accreditation:* CORE (one or more programs are accredited). *Program availability:* Part-time. *Degree requirements:* For master's, comprehensive exam, thesis or alternative; for doctorate, comprehensive exam, thesis/dissertation. *Entrance requirements:* For master's, GRE General Test or MAT, 2 letters of recommendation; for doctorate, GRE General Test, 2 letters of recommendation. Electronic applications accepted.

University of North Texas, Robert B. Toulouse School of Graduate Studies, Denton, TX 76203-5459. Offers accounting (MS); applied anthropology (MA, MS); applied behavior analysis (Certificate); applied geography (MA); applied technology and performance improvement (M Ed, MS); art education (MA); art history (MA); art museum education (Certificate); arts leadership (Certificate); audiology (Au D); behavior analysis (MS); behavioral science (PhD); biochemistry and molecular biology (MS); biology (MA, MS); biomedical engineering (MS); business analysis (MS); chemistry (MS); clinical health psychology (PhD); communication studies (MA, MS); computer engineering (MS); computer science (MS); counseling (M Ed, MS), including clinical mental health counseling (MS), college and university counseling, elementary school counseling, secondary school counseling; creative writing (MA); criminal justice (MS); curriculum and instruction (M Ed); decision sciences (MBA); design (MA, MFA), including fashion design (MFA), innovation studies, interior design (MFA); early childhood studies (MS); economics (MS); educational leadership (M Ed, Ed D); educational psychology (MS, PhD), including family studies (MS), gifted and talented (MS), human development (MS), learning and cognition (MS), research, measurement and evaluation (MS); electrical engineering (MS); emergency management (MPA); engineering technology (MS); English (MA); English as a second language (MA); environmental science (MS); finance (MBA, MS); financial management (MPA); French (MA); health services management (MBA); higher education (M Ed, Ed D); history (MA, MS); hospitality management (MS); human resources management (MPA); information science (MS); information systems (PhD); information technologies (MBA); interdisciplinary studies (MA, MS); international studies (MA); international sustainable tourism (MS); jazz studies (MM); journalism (MA, MJ, Graduate Certificate), including interactive and virtual digital communication (Graduate Certificate), narrative journalism (Graduate Certificate), public relations (Graduate Certificate); kinesiology (MS); linguistics (MA); local government management (MPA); logistics (PhD); logistics and supply chain management (MBA); long-term care, senior housing, and aging services (MA); management (PhD); marketing (MBA); mathematics (MA, MS); mechanical and energy engineering (MS, PhD); music (MA), including ethnomusicology, music theory, musicology, performance; music composition (PhD); music education (MM Ed, PhD); nonprofit management (MPA);

operations and supply chain management (MBA); performance (MM, DMA); philosophy (MA); political science (MA); professional and technical communication (MA); radio, television and film (MA, MFA); rehabilitation counseling (Certificate); sociology (MA); Spanish (MA); special education (M Ed); speech-language pathology (MA); strategic management (MBA); studio art (MFA); teaching (M Ed); MBA/MS. *Program availability:* Part-time, evening/weekend, online learning. Terminal master's awarded for partial completion of doctoral program. *Degree requirements:* For master's, variable foreign language requirement, comprehensive exam (for some programs), thesis (for some programs); for doctorate, variable foreign language requirement, comprehensive exam (for some programs), thesis/dissertation; for other advanced degree, variable foreign language requirement, comprehensive exam (for some programs). *Entrance requirements:* For master's and doctorate, GRE, GMAT. Additional exam requirements/recommendations for international students: Required—TOEFL (minimum score 550 paper-based; 79 iBT). Electronic applications accepted.

University of Pittsburgh, School of Health and Rehabilitation Sciences, Department of Rehabilitation Science and Technology, Pittsburgh, PA 15260. Offers clinical rehabilitation and mental health counseling (MS); physician assistant studies (MS); prosthetics and orthotics (DPT); rehabilitation technology (MS). *Program availability:* Online learning. *Faculty:* 27 full-time (14 women), 7 part-time/adjunct (3 women). *Students:* 177 full-time (118 women), 9 part-time (8 women); includes 26 minority (6 Black or African American, non-Hispanic/Latino; 5 Asian, non-Hispanic/Latino; 9 Hispanic/Latino; 6 Two or more races, non-Hispanic/Latino), 12 international. Average age 25. 611 applicants, 25% accepted, 101 enrolled. In 2017, 72 master's awarded. *Degree requirements:* For master's, comprehensive exam (for some programs). *Entrance requirements:* For master's, GRE General Test, hands-on patient care experience, CPR certification. Additional exam requirements/recommendations for international students: Required—TOEFL (minimum score 550 paper-based; 80 iBT), IELTS (minimum score 6.5). *Application deadline:* For fall admission, 12/31 for domestic and international students; for spring admission, 11/1 for domestic students, 9/1 for international students. Application fee: $177. Electronic applications accepted. *Financial support:* In 2017–18, 14 research assistantships (averaging $23,650 per year) were awarded; career-related internships or fieldwork, Federal Work-Study, scholarships/grants, traineeships, and unspecified assistantships also available. *Faculty research:* Assistive and rehabilitation technology development; prevention and management of chronic conditions; universal design and accessibility; environmental optimization; rehabilitation outcomes measurement. *Total annual research expenditures:* $9.2 million. *Unit head:* Dr. Rory Cooper, Associate Dean for Inclusion/Chair/Professor, 412-822-3700, E-mail: rcooper@pitt.edu. *Application contact:* Jessica Maguire, Director of Admissions, 412-383-6557, Fax: 412-383-6535, E-mail: maguire@pitt.edu. Website: http://www.shrs.pitt.edu/rst

University of Puerto Rico–Río Piedras, College of Social Sciences, Graduate School of Rehabilitation Counseling, San Juan, PR 00931-3300. Offers MRC. *Accreditation:* CORE. *Program availability:* Part-time. *Degree requirements:* For master's, comprehensive exam, thesis, internship. *Entrance requirements:* For master's, GRE or PAEG, interview, minimum GPA of 3.0, letter of recommendation.

The University of Scranton, Panuska College of Professional Studies, Department of Counseling and Human Services, Program in Rehabilitation Counseling, Scranton, PA 18510. Offers MS. *Accreditation:* CORE. *Program availability:* Part-time, evening/weekend. *Degree requirements:* For master's, comprehensive exam (for some programs), thesis (for some programs), capstone experience. *Entrance requirements:* For master's, minimum GPA of 3.0, three letters of reference. Additional exam requirements/recommendations for international students: Required—TOEFL (minimum score 500 paper-based; 80 iBT), IELTS (minimum score 6.5). Electronic applications accepted.

University of South Carolina, School of Medicine and The Graduate School, Graduate Programs in Medicine, Program in Rehabilitation Counseling, Columbia, SC 29208. Offers psychiatric rehabilitation (Certificate); rehabilitation counseling (MRC). *Accreditation:* CORE. *Program availability:* Part-time, evening/weekend. *Degree requirements:* For master's, comprehensive exam, internship, practicum. *Entrance requirements:* For master's and Certificate, GRE General Test or GMAT. Electronic applications accepted. *Expenses:* Contact institution. *Faculty research:* Quality of life, alcohol dependency, technology for disabled, psychiatric rehabilitation, women with disabilities.

University of Southern Maine, College of Management and Human Service, School of Education and Human Development, Program in Counselor Education, Portland, ME 04103. Offers clinical mental health counseling (MS); counseling (CAS); culturally responsive practices in education and human development (CGS); mental health rehabilitation technician/community (CGS); rehabilitation counseling (MS); school counseling (MS); substance abuse counseling (CGS). *Accreditation:* ACA (one or more programs are accredited); CORE; TEAC. *Program availability:* Part-time, evening/weekend. *Degree requirements:* For master's, comprehensive exam, thesis or alternative; for other advanced degree, thesis or alternative. *Entrance requirements:* For master's, GRE General Test or MAT, interview; for other advanced degree, master's degree. Additional exam requirements/recommendations for international students: Required—TOEFL (minimum score 550 paper-based; 79 iBT). Electronic applications accepted. *Faculty research:* Counselor licensure, group dynamics, counseling theories, healthy adaptation, counselor educator well-being.

University of South Florida, College of Behavioral and Community Sciences, Department of Child and Family Studies, Tampa, FL 33620-9951. Offers applied behavior analysis (MA, MS, PhD); behavioral and community sciences (PhD); child and adolescent behavioral health (MS), including developmental disabilities, leadership in child and adolescent health, translational research and evaluation, youth and behavioral health; rehabilitation and mental health counseling (MA), including addictions and substance abuse counseling, marriage and family therapy. *Accreditation:* ACA. *Faculty:* 18 full-time (12 women), 2 part-time/adjunct (1 woman). *Students:* 188 full-time (166 women), 115 part-time (92 women); includes 121 minority (40 Black or African American, non-Hispanic/Latino; 8 Asian, non-Hispanic/Latino; 61 Hispanic/Latino; 12 Two or more races, non-Hispanic/Latino), 6 international. Average age 28. 287 applicants, 53% accepted, 89 enrolled. In 2017, 45 master's, 1 doctorate awarded. *Degree requirements:* For master's, comprehensive exam, thesis (for some programs); for doctorate, comprehensive exam, thesis/dissertation, Behavior Analyst Board Certification Exam. *Entrance requirements:* For master's, GRE General Test, minimum GPA of 3.0 in last 60 hours of coursework; letters of recommendation; one-page narrative describing experience, interest, and career goals in applied behavior analysis; resume or curriculum vitae (varies by program); for doctorate, GRE General Test, master's degree in behavioral analysis or closely-related field; minimum GPA of 3.5 in graduate course work; three letters of recommendation; campus visit with faculty interview; personal statement; curriculum vitae; evidence of research experiences and expertise. Additional exam requirements/recommendations for international students: Required—TOEFL (minimum score 550 paper-based; 79 iBT) or IELTS (minimum score 6.5). *Application deadline:* For fall admission, 12/5 for domestic and international students. Application fee: $30. *Financial support:* In 2017–18, 30 students received

support. Unspecified assistantships available. *Faculty research:* Applied behavior analysis, autism, behavior management, behavioral intervention, children, developmental disabilities, experimental analysis of behavior, functional assessment, positive behavior support. *Total annual research expenditures:* $17.6 million. *Application contact:* Dr. Raymond G. Miltenberger, Professor/Director of Master's Program, 813-974-5079, Fax: 813-974-6115, E-mail: miltenbe@usf.edu.
Website: http://cfs.cbcs.usf.edu/

University of South Florida, Innovative Education, Tampa, FL 33620-9951. Offers adult, career and higher education (Graduate Certificate), including college teaching, leadership in developing human resources, leadership in higher education; Africana studies (Graduate Certificate), including diasporas and health disparities, genocide and human rights; aging studies (Graduate Certificate), including gerontology; art research (Graduate Certificate), including museum studies; business foundations (Graduate Certificate); chemical and biomedical engineering (Graduate Certificate), including materials science and engineering, water, health and sustainability; child and family studies (Graduate Certificate), including positive behavior support; civil and industrial engineering (Graduate Certificate), including transportation systems analysis; community and family health (Graduate Certificate), including maternal and child health, social marketing and public health, violence and injury: prevention and intervention, women's health; criminology (Graduate Certificate), including criminal justice administration; data science for public administration (Graduate Certificate); digital humanities (Graduate Certificate); educational measurement and research (Graduate Certificate), including evaluation; English (Graduate Certificate), including comparative literary studies, creative writing, professional and technical communication; entrepreneurship (Graduate Certificate); environmental health (Graduate Certificate), including safety management; epidemiology and biostatistics (Graduate Certificate), including applied biostatistics, biostatistics, concepts and tools of epidemiology, epidemiology, epidemiology of infectious diseases; geography, environment and planning (Graduate Certificate), including community development, environmental policy and management, geographical information systems; geology (Graduate Certificate), including hydrogeology; global health (Graduate Certificate), including disaster management, global health and Latin American and Caribbean studies, global health practice, humanitarian assistance, infection control; government and international affairs (Graduate Certificate), including Cuban studies, globalization studies; health policy and management (Graduate Certificate), including health management and leadership, public health policy and programs; hearing specialist: early intervention (Graduate Certificate); industrial and management systems engineering (Graduate Certificate), including systems engineering, technology management; information studies (Graduate Certificate), including school library media specialist; information systems/decision sciences (Graduate Certificate), including analytics and business intelligence; instructional technology (Graduate Certificate), including distance education, Florida digital/virtual educator, instructional design, multimedia design, Web design; internal medicine, bioethics and medical humanities (Graduate Certificate), including biomedical ethics; Latin American and Caribbean studies (Graduate Certificate); leadership for coastal resiliency planning (Graduate Certificate); mass communications (Graduate Certificate), including multimedia journalism; mathematics and statistics (Graduate Certificate), including mathematics; medicine (Graduate Certificate), including aging and neuroscience, bioinformatics, biotechnology, brain fitness and memory management, clinical investigation, hand and upper limb rehabilitation, health informatics, health sciences, integrative weight management, intellectual property, medicine and gender, metabolic and nutritional medicine, metabolic cardiology, pharmacy sciences; national and competitive intelligence (Graduate Certificate); nursing (Graduate Certificate), including simulation based academic fellowship in advanced pain management; psychological and social foundations (Graduate Certificate), including career counseling, college teaching, diversity in education, mental health counseling, school counseling; public affairs (Graduate Certificate), including nonprofit management, public management, research administration; public health (Graduate Certificate), including assessing chemical toxicity and public health risks, health equity, pharmacoepidemiology, public health generalist, toxicology, translational research in adolescent behavioral health; public health practices (Graduate Certificate), including planning for healthy communities; rehabilitation and mental health counseling (Graduate Certificate), including integrative mental health care, marriage and family therapy, rehabilitation technology; secondary education (Graduate Certificate), including ESOL, foreign language education: culture and content, foreign language education: professional; social work (Graduate Certificate), including geriatric social work/clinical gerontology; special education (Graduate Certificate), including autism spectrum disorder, disabilities education: severe/profound; world languages (Graduate Certificate), including teaching English as a second language (TESL) or foreign language. *Unit head:* Dr. Cynthia DeLuca, Associate Vice President and Assistant Vice Provost, 813-974-3077, Fax: 813-974-7061, E-mail: deluca@usf.edu. *Application contact:* Owen Hooper, Director, Summer and Alternative Calendar Programs, 813-974-6917, E-mail: hooper@usf.edu.
Website: http://www.usf.edu/innovative-education/

The University of Tennessee, Graduate School, College of Education, Health and Human Sciences, Department of Educational Psychology and Counseling, Knoxville, TN 37996. Offers adult education (MS); applied educational psychology (MS); collaborative learning (Ed D); college student personnel (MS); mental health counseling (MS); rehabilitation counseling (MS); school counseling (MS). *Accreditation:* ACA (one or more programs are accredited); CORE (one or more programs are accredited); NCATE. *Program availability:* Part-time, evening/weekend. *Degree requirements:* For master's, thesis optional. *Entrance requirements:* For master's, GRE General Test, minimum GPA of 2.7. Additional exam requirements/recommendations for international students: Required—TOEFL. Electronic applications accepted.

The University of Texas at Austin, Graduate School, College of Education, Department of Special Education, Austin, TX 78712-1111. Offers autism and developmental disabilities (Ed D, PhD); autism and developmental disability (M Ed, MA); early childhood special education (M Ed, MA, Ed D, PhD); learning disabilities (Ed D, PhD); learning disabilities/behavior disorders (M Ed, MA); multicultural special education (M Ed, MA, Ed D, PhD); rehabilitation counselor (M Ed); rehabilitation counselor education (Ed D, PhD); special education administration (Ed D, PhD). *Accreditation:* CORE. *Program availability:* Part-time, evening/weekend, online learning. *Degree requirements:* For master's, thesis or alternative; for doctorate, thesis/dissertation. *Entrance requirements:* For master's and doctorate, GRE General Test. *Faculty research:* Anchored instruction, reading disabilities, multicultural/bilingual.

The University of Texas at El Paso, Graduate School, College of Health Sciences, Rehabilitation Counseling Program, El Paso, TX 79968-0001. Offers MRC. *Accreditation:* CORE. *Program availability:* Part-time, evening/weekend. *Degree requirements:* For master's, comprehensive exam, thesis optional. *Entrance requirements:* For master's, GRE, minimum GPA of 3.0, statement of professional goals, letters of recommendation. Additional exam requirements/recommendations for international students: Required—TOEFL; Recommended—IELTS. Electronic applications accepted. *Faculty research:* Psychosocial adjustment to disability, attribution regarding disability, self-regulation, professional issues in rehabilitation counseling, rehabilitation education.

The University of Texas Rio Grande Valley, College of Health Affairs, School of Rehabilitation Services and Counseling, Edinburg, TX 78539. Offers MS, PhD. *Accreditation:* CORE. *Program availability:* Part-time, evening/weekend. *Faculty:* 16 full-time (8 women), 1 (woman) part-time/adjunct. *Students:* 109 full-time (91 women), 89 part-time (75 women); includes 186 minority (4 Black or African American, non-Hispanic/Latino; 4 Asian, non-Hispanic/Latino; 178 Hispanic/Latino). Average age 26. 88 applicants, 67% accepted, 54 enrolled. In 2017, 77 master's, 1 doctorate awarded. *Degree requirements:* For master's, comprehensive exam; for doctorate, comprehensive exam, thesis/dissertation. *Entrance requirements:* For master's, minimum GPA of 3.0; for doctorate, GRE, master's degree in related counseling field, minimum GPA of 3.25. *Application deadline:* For fall admission, 2/15 for domestic and international students; for spring admission, 10/15 for domestic and international students; for summer admission, 2/15 for domestic and international students. Application fee: $50. Electronic applications accepted. *Expenses:* $25,824 (for MS); $28,406 (for PhD). *Financial support:* In 2017–18, 60 students received support, including 12 research assistantships (averaging $25,500 per year), 10 teaching assistantships (averaging $12,600 per year); career-related internships or fieldwork, Federal Work-Study, institutionally sponsored loans, scholarships/grants, traineeships, and unspecified assistantships also available. *Faculty research:* Attitudes and disability, substance abuse, multicultural counseling, Hispanics and disability, Social Security beneficiary characteristics. *Total annual research expenditures:* $25,000. *Unit head:* Dr. Bruce J. Reed, Director/Professor, 956-665-7036, Fax: 956-665-5237, E-mail: bruce.reed@utrgv.edu. *Application contact:* Dr. Elizabeth Chavez-Palacios, Clinical Assistant Professor/Graduate Coordinator, 956-665-3734, Fax: 956-665-5237, E-mail: elizabeth.palacios@utrgv.edu.
Website: http://www.utrgv.edu/rehab-counseling/index.htm

The University of Texas Southwestern Medical Center, Southwestern School of Health Professions, Rehabilitation Counseling Psychology Program, Dallas, TX 75390. Offers MRC. *Accreditation:* CORE. *Degree requirements:* For master's, thesis. *Entrance requirements:* For master's, GRE General Test, minimum GPA of 3.0. Electronic applications accepted. *Faculty research:* Psychophysiology of stress and emotion, psychosocial rehabilitation, assessment of learning disabilities.

University of the District of Columbia, College of Arts and Sciences, Program in Rehabilitation Counseling, Washington, DC 20008-1175. Offers MA.

University of Wisconsin–Madison, Graduate School, School of Education, Department of Rehabilitation Psychology and Special Education, Program in Rehabilitation Psychology, Madison, WI 53706-1380. Offers MA, MS, PhD. *Accreditation:* CORE (one or more programs are accredited). *Degree requirements:* For doctorate, thesis/dissertation.

University of Wisconsin–Stout, Graduate School, College of Education, Health and Human Sciences, Program in Vocational Rehabilitation, Menomonie, WI 54751. Offers MS. *Accreditation:* CORE. *Program availability:* Part-time, online learning. *Degree requirements:* For master's, comprehensive exam or thesis. *Entrance requirements:* For master's, minimum GPA of 2.75. Additional exam requirements/recommendations for international students: Required—TOEFL (minimum score 500 paper-based; 61 iBT). Electronic applications accepted. *Faculty research:* Aging/gerontology, athletics, neuropsychology, recreation, transition to work.

Utah State University, School of Graduate Studies, Emma Eccles Jones College of Education and Human Services, Department of Special Education and Rehabilitation, Program in Rehabilitation Counseling, Logan, UT 84322. Offers MRC. *Accreditation:* CORE. *Program availability:* Part-time, online learning. *Degree requirements:* For master's, internship. *Entrance requirements:* For master's, GRE General Test, minimum GPA of 3.0. Additional exam requirements/recommendations for international students: Required—TOEFL (minimum score 550 paper-based). Electronic applications accepted. *Expenses:* Contact institution. *Faculty research:* Distance education, Hispanic rehabilitation, transition from school to work.

Virginia Commonwealth University, Graduate School, School of Allied Health Professions, Department of Rehabilitation Counseling, Richmond, VA 23284-9005. Offers MS. *Accreditation:* CORE. *Entrance requirements:* For master's, GRE General Test or MAT. Additional exam requirements/recommendations for international students: Required—TOEFL (minimum score 600 paper-based; 100 iBT). Electronic applications accepted. *Faculty research:* Substance abuse/addictions, lifelong disabilities, consumer empowerment, counseling models, adjustment to disability.

Wayne State University, College of Education, Division of Theoretical and Behavioral Foundations, Detroit, MI 48202. Offers applied behavior analysis (Certificate); counseling (M Ed, MA, Ed D, Ed S); counseling psychology (MA, PhD); education evaluation and research (M Ed, Ed D); educational psychology (M Ed, PhD), including learning and instruction sciences (PhD); rehabilitation counseling and community inclusion (MA); school and community psychology (MA, Certificate). *Accreditation:* ACA (one or more programs are accredited); CORE (one or more programs are accredited). *Program availability:* Evening/weekend. *Students:* Average age 32. 294 applicants, 34% accepted, 72 enrolled. In 2017, 87 master's, 12 doctorates, 14 other advanced degrees awarded. *Entrance requirements:* For master's, GRE, interview, personal statement, portfolio (art therapy); for doctorate, GRE, department-written exam, interview, curriculum vitae, references, master's degree in closely-related field with minimum GPA of 3.5, demonstration of counseling skills (for Ed D in counseling); for other advanced degree, master's degree in counseling and counseling license (for Ed S); good standing in school and community psychology MA program (for Certificate). Additional exam requirements/recommendations for international students: Required—TOEFL (minimum score 550 paper-based; 79 iBT), Michigan English Language Assessment Battery (minimum score 85); Recommended—IELTS (minimum score 6.5), TWE (minimum score 5.5). *Application deadline:* For fall admission, 6/1 priority date for domestic students, 5/1 priority date for international students; for winter admission, 10/1 priority date for domestic students, 9/1 priority date for international students; for spring admission, 2/1 priority date for domestic students, 1/1 priority date for international students. Applications are processed on a rolling basis. Application fee: $50. Electronic applications accepted. *Expenses:* Contact institution. *Financial support:* In 2017–18, 92 students received support, including 2 research assistantships with tuition reimbursements available (averaging $17,994 per year); fellowships, teaching assistantships, Federal Work-Study, scholarships/grants, health care benefits, and unspecified assistantships also available. Support available to part-time students. Financial award applicants required to submit FAFSA. *Faculty research:* Adolescents at risk, supervision of counseling. *Unit head:* Dr. Cheryl Somers, Assistant Dean, 313-577-1670, E-mail: c.somers@wayne.edu. *Application contact:* Janice Green, Assistant Dean, 313-577-1605, E-mail: jwgreen@wayne.edu.
Website: http://coe.wayne.edu/tbf/index.php

Western Michigan University, Graduate College, College of Health and Human Services, Department of Blindness and Low Vision Studies, Kalamazoo, MI 49008. Offers orientation and mobility (MA); orientation and mobility of children (MA); vision rehabilitation therapy (MA). *Accreditation:* CORE.

Western Oregon University, Graduate Programs, College of Education, Division of Special Education, Program in Rehabilitation Counseling, Monmouth, OR 97361. Offers MS. *Accreditation:* CORE. *Degree requirements:* For master's, thesis optional, oral exam, portfolio. *Entrance requirements:* For master's, interview, minimum GPA of 3.0. Additional exam requirements/recommendations for international students: Required—TOEFL (minimum score 550 paper-based; 79 iBT), IELTS (minimum score 6.5). *Faculty research:* Deafness, rehabilitation counseling.

Western Washington University, Graduate School, Woodring College of Education, Program in Rehabilitation Counseling, Bellingham, WA 98225-5996. Offers MA. *Accreditation:* CORE. *Program availability:* Part-time, evening/weekend, online learning. *Degree requirements:* For master's, research project. *Entrance requirements:* For master's, GRE General Test or MAT, minimum GPA of 3.0 in last 60 semester hours or last 90 quarter hours of course work. Additional exam requirements/recommendations for international students: Required—TOEFL (minimum score 567 paper-based). Electronic applications accepted. *Faculty research:* Employment issues for individuals with significant disabilities, research and statistics techniques, rehabilitation counselor education.

West Virginia University, College of Education and Human Services, Morgantown, WV 26506. Offers audiology (Au D); autism spectrum disorder (MA); clinical rehabilitation and mental health counseling (MS); communication science and disorders (PhD); counseling (MA); counseling psychology (PhD); curriculum and instruction (Ed D); early childhood education (MA); early intervention (MA); education (PhD); educational leadership (MA, Ed D); educational leadership/public school administration (MA); educational psychology (MA, Ed D); elementary education (MA); gifted education (MA); higher education administration (MA, Ed D); higher education curriculum and teaching (MA); institutional design and technology (MA); instructional design and technology (Ed D); literacy education (MA); secondary education (MA); secondary education/English (MA); special education (Ed D); speech pathology (MS). *Accreditation:* NCATE. *Program availability:* Part-time, evening/weekend, online learning. *Students:* 423 full-time (347 women), 367 part-time (316 women); includes 57 minority (14 Black or African American, non-Hispanic/Latino; 7 Asian, non-Hispanic/Latino; 20 Hispanic/Latino; 16 Two or more races, non-Hispanic/Latino), 13 international. *Degree requirements:* For master's, content exams; for doctorate, comprehensive exam, thesis/dissertation.

Entrance requirements: Additional exam requirements/recommendations for international students: Required—TOEFL (minimum score 500 paper-based; 61 iBT). *Application deadline:* For fall admission, 8/1 for domestic students; for spring admission, 1/1 for domestic students; for summer admission, 5/1 for domestic students. Application fee: $60. Electronic applications accepted. *Expenses:* Tuition, state resident: full-time $9450. Tuition, nonresident: full-time $24,390. *Financial support:* Fellowships, research assistantships, teaching assistantships, career-related internships or fieldwork, Federal Work-Study, institutionally sponsored loans, health care benefits, tuition waivers (full and partial), and administrative assistantships available. Financial award applicants required to submit FAFSA. *Faculty research:* Internet training and integration for teachers, rural education, teacher preparation, organization of schools, evaluation of personnel. *Unit head:* Dr. Gypsy Denzine, Dean, 304-293-5703, Fax: 304-293-7565, E-mail: gypsy.denzine@mail.wvu.edu. *Application contact:* Dr. M. Cecil Smith, Associate Dean for Research and Graduate Education, 304-293-2174, Fax: 304-293-3802, E-mail: mcecil.smith@mail.wvu.edu.
Website: http://cehs.wvu.edu/

Wilberforce University, Program in Rehabilitation Counseling, Wilberforce, OH 45384. Offers MS. *Entrance requirements:* For master's, bachelor's degree, 3 letters of recommendation, interview. Additional exam requirements/recommendations for international students: Required—TOEFL.

Winston-Salem State University, Program in Rehabilitation Counseling, Winston-Salem, NC 27110-0003. Offers MRC. *Program availability:* Part-time, online learning. *Degree requirements:* For master's, thesis optional. *Entrance requirements:* For master's, GRE, 3 letters of recommendation. Electronic applications accepted. *Faculty research:* Drug addiction, recovery, HIV/AIDS interventions.

Wright State University, Graduate School, College of Education and Human Services, Department of Human Services, Program in Rehabilitation Counseling, Dayton, OH 45435. Offers chemical dependency (MRC). *Accreditation:* CORE. *Degree requirements:* For master's, comprehensive exam. *Entrance requirements:* For master's, GRE General Test, MAT, interview. Additional exam requirements/recommendations for international students: Required—TOEFL.

School Psychology

Abilene Christian University, Graduate Programs, College of Arts and Sciences, Department of Psychology, Specialist in School Psychology Program, Abilene, TX 79699. Offers Specialist. *Students:* 10 full-time (8 women), 7 part-time (5 women); includes 3 minority (2 Black or African American, non-Hispanic/Latino; 1 Hispanic/Latino), 1 international. 21 applicants, 67% accepted, 6 enrolled. *Entrance requirements:* Additional exam requirements/recommendations for international students: Required—TOEFL (minimum score 80 iBT), IELTS (minimum score 6), PTE. *Application deadline:* For fall admission, 3/30 priority date for domestic students; for spring admission, 11/1 for domestic students. Applications are processed on a rolling basis. Application fee: $50. Electronic applications accepted. *Expenses:* $1,148 per hour. *Financial support:* In 2017–18, 9 students received support. Federal Work-Study and scholarships/grants available. Support available to part-time students. Financial award application deadline: 4/1; financial award applicants required to submit FAFSA. *Unit head:* Dr. Cherisse Flanagan, Graduate Director, 325-674-4826, Fax: 325-674-6968, E-mail: cherisse.flanagan@acu.edu. *Application contact:* Graduate Admissions, 325-674-6911, Fax: 325-674-6717, E-mail: gradinfo@acu.edu.
Website: http://www.acu.edu/graduate/academics/school-psychology.html

Adelphi University, Gordon F. Derner School of Psychology, Program in School Psychology, Garden City, NY 11530-0701. Offers MA. *Program availability:* Part-time. *Students:* 41 full-time (37 women), 18 part-time (17 women); includes 16 minority (5 Black or African American, non-Hispanic/Latino; 3 Asian, non-Hispanic/Latino; 7 Hispanic/Latino; 1 Two or more races, non-Hispanic/Latino), 1 international. Average age 25. 104 applicants, 42% accepted, 26 enrolled. In 2017, 15 master's awarded. *Degree requirements:* For master's, comprehensive exam. *Entrance requirements:* For master's, minimum GPA of 3.0; 15 credits of course work in psychology including general psychology, developmental child or adolescent psychology, abnormal personality in school psychology, tests and measurements, statistics; 3 letters of recommendation. Additional exam requirements/recommendations for international students: Required—TOEFL (minimum score 550 paper-based; 80 iBT), IELTS (minimum score 6.5). *Application deadline:* For fall admission, 5/1 for domestic students, 4/1 for international students. Application fee: $50. Electronic applications accepted. *Expenses:* Contact institution. *Financial support:* Research assistantships with full and partial tuition reimbursements, teaching assistantships, career-related internships or fieldwork, institutionally sponsored loans, scholarships/grants, traineeships, and unspecified assistantships available. Support available to part-time students. *Unit head:* Dr. Ionas Sapountzis, Director, 516-877-4743, E-mail: isapountzis@adelphi.edu. *Application contact:* E-mail: graduateadmissions@adelphi.edu.
Website: http://derner.adelphi.edu/psychology/graduate/ma-in-school-psychology/

Adler University, Graduate Programs, MA in Counseling Psychology Program: School and Youth Concentration, Chicago, IL 60602. Offers MACP. Program offered at Vancouver campus. *Entrance requirements:* For master's, baccalaureate degree, minimum GPA of 3.0, official transcripts, three letters of recommendation.

Adler University, Graduate Programs, Master of Counseling Psychology Program: School and Youth Concentration, Chicago, IL 60602. Offers MCP. Program offered at Vancouver campus. *Program availability:* Evening/weekend. *Entrance requirements:* For master's, baccalaureate degree, minimum GPA of 3.0, official transcripts, three letters of recommendation.

Alabama Agricultural and Mechanical University, School of Graduate Studies, College of Education, Humanities, and Behavioral Sciences, Department of Social Work, Psychology and Counseling, Huntsville, AL 35811. Offers psychology and counseling (MS, Ed S), including clinical psychology (MS), counseling psychology (MS), guidance and counseling, rehabilitation counseling (MS), school counseling (MS), school psychology (MS), school psychometry (MS); social work (MSW). *Accreditation:* CORE; NCATE. *Program availability:* Part-time, evening/weekend. *Degree requirements:* For master's, comprehensive exam. *Entrance requirements:* For master's, GRE General Test. Additional exam requirements/recommendations for international students: Required—TOEFL (minimum score 500 paper-based; 61 iBT). *Faculty research:* Increasing numbers of minorities in special education and speech-language pathology.

Alfred University, Graduate School, Counseling and School Psychology Program, Alfred, NY 14802-1205. Offers mental health counseling (MS Ed); school counseling (MS Ed, CAS); school psychology (MA, Psy D, CAS). *Accreditation:* APA. *Degree requirements:* For master's, internship; for doctorate, thesis/dissertation, internship. *Entrance requirements:* For master's and doctorate, GRE General Test. Additional exam requirements/recommendations for international students: Required—TOEFL (minimum score 590 paper-based; 90 iBT), IELTS (minimum score 6.5). Electronic applications accepted. *Faculty research:* Family processes, alternative assessment approaches, behavior disorders in children, parent involvement, school psychology training issues.

Alliant International University–Irvine, Shirley M. Hufstedler School of Education, Educational Psychology Programs, Irvine, CA 92606. Offers educational psychology (Psy D); pupil personnel services (Credential); school psychology (MA). *Program availability:* Part-time. *Degree requirements:* For doctorate, thesis/dissertation. *Entrance requirements:* For master's, minimum GPA of 2.5, letters of recommendation; for doctorate, interview, minimum GPA of 3.0, letters of recommendation. Additional exam requirements/recommendations for international students: Required—TOEFL (minimum score 550 paper-based; 80 iBT), TWE (minimum score 5). *Faculty research:* School-based mental health.

Alliant International University–Los Angeles, Shirley M. Hufstedler School of Education, Educational Psychology Programs, Alhambra, CA 91803. Offers educational psychology (Psy D); pupil personnel services (Credential); school psychology (MA). *Program availability:* Part-time. *Degree requirements:* For doctorate, comprehensive exam, thesis/dissertation. *Entrance requirements:* For master's, minimum GPA of 2.5, letters of recommendation; for doctorate, interview, minimum GPA of 3.0, letters of recommendation. Additional exam requirements/recommendations for international students: Required—TOEFL (minimum score 550 paper-based), TWE (minimum score 5). Electronic applications accepted. *Faculty research:* Early identification and intervention with high-risk preschoolers, pediatric neuropsychology, interpersonal violence, ADHD, learning theories.

Alliant International University–San Diego, Shirley M. Hufstedler School of Education, Educational Psychology Programs, San Diego, CA 92131. Offers educational psychology (Psy D); pupil personnel services (Credential); school neuropsychology (Certificate); school psychology (MA); school-based mental health (Certificate). *Program availability:* Part-time. *Degree requirements:* For doctorate, comprehensive exam, thesis/dissertation, internship. *Entrance requirements:* For master's, minimum GPA of 2.5, letters of recommendation; for doctorate, minimum GPA of 3.0, letters of recommendation. Additional exam requirements/recommendations for international students: Required—TOEFL (minimum score 550 paper-based; 80 iBT), TWE (minimum score 5). Electronic applications accepted. *Faculty research:* School-based mental health, pupil personnel services, childhood mood, school-based assessment.

Alliant International University–San Francisco, Shirley M. Hufstedler School of Education, Educational Psychology Programs, San Francisco, CA 94133. Offers educational psychology (Psy D); pupil personnel services (Credential); school psychology (MA). *Program availability:* Part-time. Terminal master's awarded for partial completion of doctoral program. *Degree requirements:* For doctorate, thesis/dissertation. *Entrance requirements:* For master's, minimum GPA of 3.0, letters of recommendation; for doctorate, interview, minimum GPA of 3.0, letters of recommendation. Additional exam requirements/recommendations for international students: Required—TOEFL (minimum score 550 paper-based), TWE (minimum score 5). Electronic applications accepted. *Faculty research:* Social skills, ADHD, cognitive functioning and learning, innovative teaching methods.

American University of Beirut, Graduate Programs, Faculty of Arts and Sciences, 1107 2020, Lebanon. Offers anthropology (MA); Arab and Middle Eastern history (PhD); Arabic language and literature (MA, PhD); archaeology (MA); art history and curating (MA); biology (MS); cell and molecular biology (PhD); chemistry (MS); clinical psychology (MA); computational sciences (MS); computer science (MS); economics (MA); education (MA), including administration and policy studies, elementary education, mathematics education, psychology school guidance, psychology test and

measurements, science education, teaching English as a foreign language; English language (MA); English literature (MA); environmental policy planning (MS); financial economics (MAFE); general psychology (MA); geology (MS); history (MA); Islamic studies (MA); mathematics (MS); media studies (MA); Middle East studies (MA); philosophy (MA); physics (MS); political studies (MA); public administration (MA); public policy and international affairs (MA); sociology (MA); theoretical physics (PhD). *Program availability:* Part-time. *Faculty:* 108 full-time (36 women), 5 part-time/adjunct (4 women). *Students:* 251 full-time (180 women), 233 part-time (172 women). Average age 26. 425 applicants, 65% accepted, 121 enrolled. In 2017, 47 master's, 2 doctorates awarded. *Degree requirements:* For master's, one foreign language, comprehensive exam, thesis (for some programs), project; for doctorate, one foreign language, comprehensive exam, thesis/dissertation. *Entrance requirements:* For master's, GRE General Test (for some programs); for doctorate, GRE General Test (GRE Subject Test for theoretical physics). Additional exam requirements/recommendations for international students: Required— TOEFL (minimum score 583 paper-based; 97 iBT), IELTS (minimum score 7). *Application deadline:* For fall admission, 2/8 for domestic students; for spring admission, 11/3 for domestic students. Application fee: $50. Electronic applications accepted. *Expenses:* Contact institution. *Financial support:* In 2017–18, 29 fellowships, 40 research assistantships were awarded; teaching assistantships, scholarships/grants, tuition waivers (full and partial), and unspecified assistantships also available. Financial award application deadline: 4/4. *Unit head:* Dr. Nadia Maria El Cheikh, Dean, Faculty of Arts and Sciences, 961-1-374374 Ext. 3800, Fax: 961-1-744461, E-mail: nmcheikh@aub.edu.lb. *Application contact:* Rima Rassi, Graduate Studies Officer, 961-1-350000 Ext. 3833, Fax: 961-1-744461, E-mail: rr46@aub.edu.lb.
Website: http://www.aub.edu.lb/fas/pages/default.aspx

Andrews University, School of Graduate Studies, School of Education, Department of Graduate Psychology and Counseling, Program in School Counseling, Berrien Springs, MI 49104. Offers MA. *Students:* 3 full-time (2 women), 1 (woman) part-time; includes 2 minority (1 Black or African American, non-Hispanic/Latino; 1 Hispanic/Latino); 1 international. Average age 28. 4 applicants, 75% accepted, 2 enrolled. In 2017, 1 master's awarded. *Degree requirements:* For master's, thesis optional. *Entrance requirements:* For master's, GRE. Additional exam requirements/recommendations for international students: Required—TOEFL (minimum score 550 paper-based). Application fee: $40. *Unit head:* Dr. Rudolph N. Bailey, Coordinator, 269-471-3466. *Application contact:* Justina Clayburn, Supervisor of Graduate Admission, 800-253-2874, Fax: 269-471-6321, E-mail: graduate@andrews.edu.

Andrews University, School of Graduate Studies, School of Education, Department of Graduate Psychology and Counseling, Program in School Psychology, Berrien Springs, MI 49104. Offers Ed S. *Program availability:* Part-time. *Students:* 9 full-time (all women); includes 2 minority (both Black or African American, non-Hispanic/Latino), 3 international. Average age 33. 5 applicants, 40% accepted, 2 enrolled. In 2017, 8 Ed Ss awarded. *Entrance requirements:* Additional exam requirements/recommendations for international students: Required—TOEFL (minimum score 550 paper-based). *Application deadline:* Applications are processed on a rolling basis. Application fee: $40. *Unit head:* Dr. Elizabeth Lundy, Coordinator, 269-471-6251. *Application contact:* Justina Clayburn, Supervisor of Graduate Admission, 800-253-2874, Fax: 269-471-6321, E-mail: graduate@andrews.edu.

Appalachian State University, Cratis D. Williams Graduate School, Department of Human Development and Psychological Counseling, Boone, NC 28608. Offers clinical mental health counseling (MA); college student development (MA); marriage and family therapy (MA); school counseling (MA). *Accreditation:* AAMFT/COAMFTE; ACA; NCATE. *Program availability:* Part-time. *Degree requirements:* For master's, comprehensive exam (for some programs), thesis optional, internships. *Entrance requirements:* For master's, GRE General Test, 3 letters of recommendation. Additional exam requirements/recommendations for international students: Required—TOEFL (minimum score 570 paper-based; 79 iBT), IELTS (minimum score 6.5). Electronic applications accepted. *Faculty research:* Multicultural counseling, addictions counseling, play therapy, expressive arts, child and adolescent therapy, sexual abuse counseling.

Argosy University, Hawai`i, College of Education, Program in School Psychology, Honolulu, HI 96813. Offers MA.

Argosy University, Phoenix, College of Education, Program in School Psychology, Phoenix, AZ 85021. Offers MA, Psy D.

Arkansas State University, Graduate School, College of Education and Behavioral Science, Department of Psychology and Counseling, State University, AR 72467. Offers clinical mental health counseling (Graduate Certificate); college student personnel services (MS); dyslexia therapy (Graduate Certificate); psychological science (MS); psychology and counseling (Ed S); rehabilitation counseling (MRC); school counseling (MSE); student affairs (Graduate Certificate). *Accreditation:* ACA (one or more programs are accredited); CORE (one or more programs are accredited); NCATE. *Program availability:* Part-time. *Degree requirements:* For master's and other advanced degree, comprehensive exam, thesis or alternative. *Entrance requirements:* For master's, GRE General Test or MAT (for MSE), appropriate bachelor's degree, interview, letters of reference, official transcripts, immunization records, written statement, 2-3 page autobiography; for other advanced degree, GRE General Test, interview, master's degree, letters of reference, official transcript, personal statement, immunization records. Additional exam requirements/recommendations for international students: Required—TOEFL (minimum score 550 paper-based; 79 iBT), IELTS (minimum score 6), PTE (minimum score 56). Electronic applications accepted.

Assumption College, School Counseling Program, Worcester, MA 01609-1296. Offers school counseling (MA, CAGS). *Program availability:* Part-time, evening/weekend. *Faculty:* 3 full-time (2 women), 5 part-time/adjunct (2 women). *Students:* 29 full-time (24 women), 32 part-time (26 women); includes 8 minority (3 Black or African American, non-Hispanic/Latino; 4 Hispanic/Latino; 1 Two or more races, non-Hispanic/Latino). Average age 28. 29 applicants, 83% accepted, 15 enrolled. In 2017, 20 master's, 10 other advanced degrees awarded. *Degree requirements:* For master's, comprehensive exam, internship, practicum; for CAGS, comprehensive exam, practicum. *Entrance requirements:* For master's, bachelor's degree with minimum GPA of 3.0, three letters of recommendation, official transcripts, personal statement, current resume, interview; for CAGS, master's degree in counseling or closely-related field, three letters of recommendation, official transcripts, personal statement, current resume, interview. Additional exam requirements/recommendations for international students: Required— TOEFL (minimum score 540 paper-based; 76 iBT), IELTS (minimum score 6). *Application deadline:* Applications are processed on a rolling basis. Application fee: $30. Electronic applications accepted. *Expenses: Tuition:* Full-time $11,952; part-time $664 per credit. *Required fees:* $70 per term. *Financial support:* In 2017–18, 11 students received support. Tuition waivers (full and partial), unspecified assistantships, and institutional discounts available. Financial award applicants required to submit FAFSA. *Faculty research:* Low dose stress reduction interventions for elementary school teachers. *Unit head:* Dr. Susan Scully-Hill, Director, 508-767-7319, Fax: 508-798-2872, E-mail: sscully@assumption.edu. *Application contact:* Karen Stoyanoff, Director of Recruitment for Graduate Enrollment, 508-767-7442, Fax: 508-799-4915, E-mail: graduate@assumption.edu.
Website: http://graduate.assumption.edu/school-counseling/masterofarts

Auburn University at Montgomery, College of Education, Department of Counselor, Leadership, and Special Education, Montgomery, AL 36124-4023. Offers counselor education (M Ed, Ed S), including clinical mental health counseling, school counseling; early childhood special education (M Ed); instructional leadership (M Ed, Ed S); special education/collaborative teacher (M Ed, Ed S). *Accreditation:* ACA; NCATE. *Program availability:* Part-time, evening/weekend. *Faculty:* 7 full-time (4 women), 2 part-time/adjunct (both women). *Students:* 27 full-time (23 women), 57 part-time (51 women); includes 40 minority (38 Black or African American, non-Hispanic/Latino; 2 Hispanic/Latino). Average age 34. 76 applicants, 72% accepted, 26 enrolled. In 2017, 37 master's awarded. *Degree requirements:* For master's and Ed S, comprehensive exam. *Entrance requirements:* For master's, GRE General Test or MAT, certification, BS in teaching; for Ed S, GRE General Test or MAT, certification. Additional exam requirements/recommendations for international students: Recommended—TOEFL (minimum score 500 paper-based; 61 iBT), IELTS (minimum score 5.5), TSE (minimum score 44). *Application deadline:* For fall admission, 7/15 for international students; for spring admission, 11/15 for international students; for summer admission, 4/15 for international students. Applications are processed on a rolling basis. Electronic applications accepted. *Expenses:* Tuition, state resident: full-time $6930; part-time $385 per credit hour. Tuition, nonresident: full-time $15,588; part-time $866 per credit hour. *Required fees:* $640. *Financial support:* Career-related internships or fieldwork and scholarships/grants available. Support available to part-time students. Financial award application deadline: 3/1; financial award applicants required to submit FAFSA. *Unit head:* Dr. Samuel Flynt, Head, 334-244-3835, Fax: 334-244-3101, E-mail: sflynt@aum.edu. *Application contact:* Dr. Rhonda Morton, Associate Dean/Graduate Coordinator, 334-244-3287, Fax: 334-244-3978, E-mail: rmorton@aum.edu.
Website: http://education.aum.edu/academic-departments/counselor-leadership-and-special-education

Augusta University, College of Education, Department of Counselor Education, Leadership, and Research, Augusta, GA 30912. Offers counselor education (M Ed, Ed S), including clinical mental health counseling (M Ed), school counselor (M Ed). *Accreditation:* ACA; NCATE. *Program availability:* Part-time, evening/weekend. *Degree requirements:* For master's, comprehensive exam; for Ed S, comprehensive exam, thesis. *Entrance requirements:* For master's, GRE, MAT, minimum GPA of 2.5; for Ed S, GRE, MAT. *Faculty research:* Restructuring schools, financing education, student transition.

Azusa Pacific University, School of Behavioral and Applied Sciences, Department of Higher Education, Azusa, CA 91702-7000. Offers college counseling and student development (MS); higher education (PhD); higher education leadership (Ed D).

Azusa Pacific University, School of Education, Department of School Counseling and School Psychology, Program in Educational Psychology, Azusa, CA 91702-7000. Offers MA Ed. *Accreditation:* APA.

Ball State University, Graduate School, Teachers College, Department of Educational Psychology, Program in School Psychology, Muncie, IN 47306. Offers MA, PhD, Ed S. *Accreditation:* APA (one or more programs are accredited); NCATE. *Program availability:* Part-time. *Students:* 36 full-time (29 women), 8 part-time (all women); includes 5 minority (4 Black or African American, non-Hispanic/Latino; 1 Hispanic/Latino), 1 international. Average age 26. 44 applicants, 27% accepted, 12 enrolled. In 2017, 9 master's awarded. *Degree requirements:* For doctorate, thesis/dissertation; for Ed S, thesis. *Entrance requirements:* For doctorate, GRE General Test, interview, minimum graduate GPA of 3.2; for Ed S, GRE General Test. Additional exam requirements/recommendations for international students: Required—TOEFL (minimum score 550 paper-based; 79 iBT), IELTS (minimum score 6.5). *Application deadline:* Applications are processed on a rolling basis. Application fee: $60. Electronic applications accepted. *Financial support:* Research assistantships with partial tuition reimbursements, teaching assistantships with partial tuition reimbursements, and unspecified assistantships available. Financial award application deadline: 3/1; financial award applicants required to submit FAFSA. *Unit head:* Dr. Jerell Cassady, Chairperson, 765-285-8500, Fax: 785-285-5455, E-mail: spaulson@bsu.edu.
Website: http://www.bsu.edu/edpsych

Barry University, College of Arts and Sciences, Department of Psychology, Miami Shores, FL 33161-6695. Offers clinical psychology (MS); school psychology (MS, SSP). *Program availability:* Part-time, evening/weekend. *Degree requirements:* For master's, thesis, practicum. *Entrance requirements:* For master's, GRE General Test, minimum GPA of 3.0, course work in psychology. Electronic applications accepted. *Faculty research:* Closed head injury, memory and aging, infant/mother interaction, evolutionary aspects of behavior, gender roles.

Baylor University, Graduate School, School of Education, Department of Educational Psychology, Waco, TX 76798. Offers applied behavior analysis (MS Ed); educational psychology (MA, MS Ed, PhD); exceptionalities (PhD); gifted and talented studies (MS Ed); learning and development (PhD); quantitative methods (MA); school psychology (Ed S). *Accreditation:* NCATE. *Faculty:* 11 full-time (6 women). *Students:* 45 full-time (41 women), 11 part-time (10 women); includes 16 minority (1 Black or African American, non-Hispanic/Latino; 3 Asian, non-Hispanic/Latino; 10 Hispanic/Latino; 2 Two or more races, non-Hispanic/Latino), 4 international. Average age 29. 90 applicants, 33% accepted, 30 enrolled. In 2017, 24 master's, 1 doctorate, 7 other advanced degrees awarded. Terminal master's awarded for partial completion of doctoral program. *Degree requirements:* For master's, thesis optional; for doctorate, comprehensive exam, thesis/dissertation; for Ed S, comprehensive exam, thesis or alternative. *Entrance requirements:* For master's, GRE, minimum GPA of 3.0; for doctorate, GRE General Test, master's degree; for Ed S, GRE General Test. Additional exam requirements/recommendations for international students: Required—TOEFL (minimum score 550 paper-based; 80 iBT), IELTS (minimum score 6.5). *Application deadline:* For fall admission, 2/1 priority date for domestic and international students. Application fee: $80. Electronic applications accepted. *Financial support:* In 2017–18, 42 students received support, including 20 fellowships with full and partial tuition reimbursements available, 22 research assistantships with full and partial tuition reimbursements available; career-related internships or fieldwork, Federal Work-Study, institutionally sponsored loans, scholarships/grants, health care benefits, tuition waivers (full and partial), unspecified assistantships, and stipends also available. Financial award application deadline: 2/1; financial award applicants required to submit FAFSA. *Faculty research:* Individual differences, quantitative methods, gifted and talented, special education, school psychology, autism, applied behavior analysis, learning, human development. *Total annual research expenditures:* $300,000. *Unit head:* Dr. Susan K. Johnsen, Professor and Interim Chair, 254-710-6116, E-mail: susan_johnsen@baylor.edu. *Application contact:* Heather Tindle, Office Manager, 254-710-3112, E-mail: heather_tindle@baylor.edu.
Website: http://www.baylor.edu/soe/EDP/

Brigham Young University, Graduate Studies, David O. McKay School of Education, Department of Counseling Psychology and Special Education, Provo, UT 84602. Offers counseling psychology (PhD); school psychology (Ed S); special education (MS). *Program availability:* Part-time. *Faculty:* 14 full-time (4 women), 9 part-time/adjunct (4 women). *Students:* 70 full-time (47 women), 20 part-time (18 women); includes 11 minority (1 Black or African American, non-Hispanic/Latino; 2 American Indian or Alaska

Native, non-Hispanic/Latino; 1 Asian, non-Hispanic/Latino; 4 Hispanic/Latino; 3 Native Hawaiian or other Pacific Islander, non-Hispanic/Latino), 4 international. Average age 29. 76 applicants, 38% accepted, 28 enrolled. In 2017, 1 master's, 6 doctorates, 10 other advanced degrees awarded. *Degree requirements:* For master's and Ed S, comprehensive exam, thesis; for doctorate, comprehensive exam, thesis/dissertation. *Entrance requirements:* For master's, GRE General Test, minimum cumulative GPA of 3.0 in undergraduate coursework; for doctorate and Ed S, GRE General Test, minimum cumulative GPA of 3.0 in undergraduate coursework. Additional exam requirements/ recommendations for international students: Required—TOEFL (minimum score 580 paper-based; 85 iBT), IELTS (minimum score 7). *Application deadline:* For fall admission, 1/15 for domestic and international students. Application fee: $50. Electronic applications accepted. *Expenses: Tuition:* Full-time $6880; part-time $405 per credit hour. Tuition and fees vary according to course load, program and student's religious affiliation. *Financial support:* In 2017–18, 64 students received support, including 64 research assistantships (averaging $9,270 per year); institutionally sponsored loans and tuition waivers (partial) also available. Financial award application deadline: 3/31. *Faculty research:* Autism, religious and spiritual values in counseling, school-based crisis intervention, behavior interventions in MTSS framework, counseling and psychotherapy process and outcomes. *Unit head:* Dr. Lane Fischer, Department Chair, 801-422-3857, E-mail: lane_fischer@byu.edu. *Application contact:* Diane E. Hancock, Executive Secretary, 801-422-3859, E-mail: diane_hancock@byu.edu.
Website: http://education.byu.edu/cpse/

Brooklyn College of the City University of New York, School of Education, Program in School Psychologist, Brooklyn, NY 11210-2889. Offers play therapy (AC); school psychologist (MS Ed). *Program availability:* Part-time, evening/weekend. *Degree requirements:* For master's, internship. *Entrance requirements:* For master's, interview, previous course work in education and psychology, teaching certificate, resume, 2 letters of recommendation. Additional exam requirements/recommendations for international students: Required—TOEFL (minimum score 500 paper-based; 61 iBT). Electronic applications accepted.

Caldwell University, School of Psychology and Counseling, Caldwell, NJ 07006-6195. Offers art therapy (MA); counseling (MA), including art therapy, mental health, school counseling; director of school counseling (Post-Master's Certificate); professional counselor (Post-Master's Certificate); school counselor (Post-Master's Certificate). *Accreditation:* ACA. *Program availability:* Part-time. *Faculty:* 16 full-time (13 women), 13 part-time/adjunct (7 women). *Students:* 88 full-time (79 women), 84 part-time (82 women); includes 33 minority (12 Black or African American, non-Hispanic/Latino; 6 Asian, non-Hispanic/Latino; 15 Hispanic/Latino). Average age 30. 104 applicants, 100% accepted, 44 enrolled. In 2017, 31 master's awarded. *Degree requirements:* For master's, comprehensive exam, practicum, internship; for Post-Master's Certificate, comprehensive exam. *Entrance requirements:* For master's, minimum GPA of 3.2; two letters of recommendation; interview; writing sample. Additional exam requirements/ recommendations for international students: Required—TOEFL (minimum score 580 paper-based, 92 iBT) or IELTS (7.5). *Application deadline:* For fall admission, 6/1 for domestic students, 7/1 for international students; for spring admission, 12/1 for domestic and international students; for summer admission, 4/1 for domestic and international students. Applications are processed on a rolling basis. Application fee: $50. Electronic applications accepted. *Expenses:* $975 per credit. *Financial support:* 2 general assistantships available. Financial award applicants required to submit FAFSA. *Faculty research:* Mental health counseling, school counseling, art therapy. *Unit head:* Dr. Thomson Ling, Associate Dean, 973-618-3596, E-mail: tling@caldwell.edu. *Application contact:* Tom Disch, Senior Graduate Admissions Counselor, 973-618-3544, E-mail: graduate@caldwell.edu.

California Baptist University, Program in School Psychology, Riverside, CA 92504-3206. Offers MS. *Program availability:* Part-time, evening/weekend. *Faculty:* 2 full-time (both women), 6 part-time/adjunct (3 women). *Students:* 39 full-time (34 women), 30 part-time (29 women); includes 35 minority (5 Black or African American, non-Hispanic/ Latino; 6 Asian, non-Hispanic/Latino; 23 Hispanic/Latino; 1 Two or more races, non-Hispanic/Latino). Average age 29. 62 applicants, 66% accepted, 39 enrolled. In 2017, 14 master's awarded. *Degree requirements:* For master's, 450 hours of introductory fieldwork, 1200 hours of field experience/internship, PRAXIS. *Entrance requirements:* For master's, CBEST, minimum GPA of 3.0, completion of prerequisites with minimum C grade, three letters of recommendation, 500-word essay. Additional exam requirements/ recommendations for international students: Required—TOEFL (minimum score 80 iBT). *Application deadline:* For fall admission, 7/1 priority date for domestic and international students; for spring admission, 12/1 priority date for domestic students, 11/ 1 priority date for international students. Applications are processed on a rolling basis. Application fee: $45. Electronic applications accepted. *Expenses:* Contact institution. *Financial support:* In 2017–18, 16 students received support. Federal Work-Study and scholarships/grants available. Financial award applicants required to submit CSS PROFILE or FAFSA. *Faculty research:* Cultural competence, learning handicapped, cognitive development, school neuropsychology, behavioral assessment. *Unit head:* Dr. John Shoup, Dean, School of Education, 951-343-4205, E-mail: jshoup@calbaptist.edu. *Application contact:* David Little, Graduate Admissions Counselor, 951-552-8093, E-mail: dlittle@calbaptist.edu.
Website: https://calbaptist.edu/programs/master-of-science-school-psychology/

California State University, Chico, Office of Graduate Studies, College of Behavioral and Social Sciences, Department of Psychology, Program in Applied/School Psychology, Chico, CA 95929-0722. Offers MA. *Degree requirements:* For master's, thesis or comprehensive exam. *Entrance requirements:* For master's, GRE General Test or MAT, 3 letters of recommendation, statement of purpose. Additional exam requirements/recommendations for international students: Required—TOEFL (minimum score 550 paper-based; 80 iBT), IELTS (minimum score 6.5), PTE. Electronic applications accepted.

California State University, Dominguez Hills, College of Education, Division of Graduate Education, Program in Counseling, Carson, CA 90747-0001. Offers college counseling (MS); school counseling (MS). *Program availability:* Part-time, evening/ weekend. *Degree requirements:* For master's, comprehensive exam. *Entrance requirements:* For master's, minimum GPA of 3.0. Additional exam requirements/ recommendations for international students: Required—TOEFL. *Faculty research:* Social development.

California State University, Fresno, Division of Research and Graduate Studies, College of Science and Mathematics, Department of Psychology, Fresno, CA 93740-8027. Offers applied behavior analysis (MA); general/experimental psychology (MA); school psychology (Ed S). *Degree requirements:* For master's, thesis. *Entrance requirements:* For master's, GRE General Test, GRE Subject Test, minimum GPA of 3.0. Additional exam requirements/recommendations for international students: Required—TOEFL. Electronic applications accepted. *Faculty research:* Oncology prediction, parenting stress, wellness, aging and memory, retrieval inhibition, anger, minority mental health.

California State University, Los Angeles, Graduate Studies, Charter College of Education, Division of Special Education and Counseling, Los Angeles, CA 90032-8530. Offers counseling (MS), including applied behavior analysis, community college counseling, rehabilitation counseling, school counseling, school psychology; special education (MA, PhD). *Accreditation:* ACA. *Program availability:* Part-time, evening/ weekend. *Entrance requirements:* For master's, minimum GPA of 2.75 in last 90 units of course work, teaching certificate. Additional exam requirements/recommendations for international students: Required—TOEFL (minimum score 500 paper-based). Electronic applications accepted.

California State University, Northridge, Graduate Studies, Michael D. Eisner College of Education, Department of Educational Psychology and Counseling, Northridge, CA 91330. Offers counseling (MS), including career counseling, college counseling and student services, marriage and family therapy, school counseling, school psychology; educational psychology (MA Ed), including development, learning, and instruction, early childhood education. *Accreditation:* ACA (one or more programs are accredited); NCATE. *Program availability:* Part-time, evening/weekend. *Students:* 288 full-time (244 women), 84 part-time (76 women); includes 190 minority (13 Black or African American, non-Hispanic/Latino; 24 Asian, non-Hispanic/Latino; 139 Hispanic/Latino; 14 Two or more races, non-Hispanic/Latino), 11 international. Average age 29. 427 applicants, 34% accepted, 136 enrolled. In 2017, 103 master's awarded. *Entrance requirements:* For master's, GRE General Test or minimum GPA of 3.0. Additional exam requirements/ recommendations for international students: Required—TOEFL. *Application deadline:* For fall admission, 11/30 for domestic students. Application fee: $55. *Financial support:* Scholarships/grants available. Support available to part-time students. Financial award application deadline: 3/1. *Unit head:* Dr. Alberto Restori, Chair, 818-677-2599. *Application contact:* 818-677-3755.
Website: http://www.csun.edu/eisner-education/educational-psychology-counseling

California State University, Sacramento, College of Education, Graduate and Professional Studies in Education, Sacramento, CA 95819. Offers behavioral science and gender equity (MA); child development (MA); counseling (MS); curriculum and instruction (MA); education (Ed D), including K-12 and community college; education leadership and policy studies (MA), including higher education, PreK-12; education specialist (Ed S), including school psychology; educational technology (MA); language and literacy (MA); multicultural education (MA); school psychology (MA); special education (MA); workforce development advocacy (MA). *Program availability:* Part-time, evening/weekend, blended/hybrid learning. *Students:* 381 full-time (294 women), 135 part-time (101 women); includes 296 minority (44 Black or African American, non-Hispanic/Latino; 1 American Indian or Alaska Native, non-Hispanic/Latino; 94 Asian, non-Hispanic/Latino; 153 Hispanic/Latino; 4 Native Hawaiian or other Pacific Islander, non-Hispanic/Latino), 3 international. Average age 32. 553 applicants, 53% accepted, 292 enrolled. In 2017, 147 master's, 13 doctorates, 10 other advanced degrees awarded. *Degree requirements:* For master's, thesis or project; writing proficiency exam; for doctorate, thesis/dissertation. *Entrance requirements:* For master's and doctorate, GRE. Additional exam requirements/recommendations for international students: Required—TOEFL (minimum score 550 paper-based; 80 iBT); Recommended—IELTS (minimum score 7), TSE. *Application deadline:* For fall admission, 2/15 for domestic students, 1/15 for international students. Applications are processed on a rolling basis. Application fee: $55. Electronic applications accepted. *Expenses:* Contact institution. *Financial support:* Career-related internships or fieldwork, Federal Work-Study, and scholarships/grants available. Support available to part-time students. Financial award application deadline: 3/1; financial award applicants required to submit FAFSA. *Unit head:* Dr. Elizabeth Liles, Chair, 916-278-5942, E-mail: coe@csus.edu. *Application contact:* Jose Martinez, Graduate Admissions Supervisor, 916-278-7871, E-mail: martinj@skymail.csus.edu.
Website: http://www.csus.edu/coe/academics/graduate/index.html

California University of Pennsylvania, School of Graduate Studies and Research, College of Liberal Arts, Program in School Psychology, California, PA 15419-1394. Offers MS. *Accreditation:* NCATE. *Program availability:* Part-time, evening/weekend. *Degree requirements:* For master's, comprehensive exam, thesis optional, internship. *Entrance requirements:* For master's, MAT or GRE, minimum GPA of 3.0, work experience in psychology, letters of reference. Additional exam requirements/ recommendations for international students: Required—TOEFL (minimum score 550 paper-based; 80 iBT). *Application deadline:* For summer admission, 2/25 for domestic and international students. Applications are processed on a rolling basis. Application fee: $25. Electronic applications accepted. *Financial support:* Applicants required to submit FAFSA. *Unit head:* Dr. Angela Bloomquist, Chair, 724-938-4488, Fax: 724-938-4406, E-mail: bloomquist@calu.edu. *Application contact:* Suzanne C. Powers, Director of Graduate Admissions and Recruitment, 724-938-4029, Fax: 724-938-5712, E-mail: powers_s@cup.edu.
Website: http://www.calu.edu/academics/graduate-programs/school-psychology/

Cambridge College, School of Education, Boston, MA 02129. Offers autism specialist (M Ed); autism/behavior analyst (M Ed); behavior analyst (Post-Master's Certificate); behavioral management (M Ed); early childhood teacher (M Ed); education specialist in curriculum and instruction (CAGS); educational leadership (Ed D); elementary teacher (M Ed); English as a second language (M Ed, Certificate); general science (M Ed); health education (Post-Master's Certificate); health/family and consumer sciences (M Ed); history (M Ed); individualized (M Ed); information technology literacy (M Ed); instructional technology (M Ed); interdisciplinary studies (M Ed); library teacher (M Ed); literacy education (M Ed); mathematics (M Ed); mathematics specialist (Certificate); middle school mathematics and science (M Ed); school administration (M Ed, CAGS); school guidance counselor (M Ed); school nurse education (M Ed); school social worker/ school adjustment counselor (M Ed); special education administrator (CAGS); special education/moderate disabilities (M Ed); teaching skills and methodologies (M Ed). *Program availability:* Part-time, evening/weekend, online learning. *Degree requirements:* For master's, thesis, internship/practicum (licensure program only); for doctorate, thesis/ dissertation; for other advanced degree, thesis. *Entrance requirements:* For master's, interview, resume, documentation of licensure, 2 professional references; for doctorate, official transcripts, interview, resume, documentation of licensure (if any), written personal statement/essay, portfolio of scholarly and professional work, qualifying assessment, 2 professional references, health insurance, immunizations form; for other advanced degree, official transcripts, interview, resume, documentation of licensure (if any), written personal statement/essay, 2 professional references, health insurance, immunizations form. Additional exam requirements/recommendations for international students: Required—TOEFL (minimum score 550 paper-based; 79 iBT), Michigan English Language Assessment Battery (minimum score 85); Recommended—IELTS (minimum score 6). Electronic applications accepted. *Expenses:* Contact institution. *Faculty research:* Adult education, accelerated learning, mathematics education, brain compatible learning, special education and law.

Cambridge College, School of Psychology and Counseling, Boston, MA 02129. Offers addiction counseling (M Ed); alcohol and drug counseling (Certificate); counseling psychology (M Ed, CAGS); counseling psychology: forensic counseling (M Ed); marriage and family therapy (M Ed); mental health and addiction counseling (M Ed); mental health counseling (M Ed); mental health counseling for school guidance counselors (Post Master's Certificate); psychological studies (M Ed); school adjustment and mental health counseling (M Ed); school adjustment, mental health and addiction counseling (M Ed); school guidance counselor (M Ed); trauma studies (Certificate).

Program availability: Part-time, evening/weekend. *Degree requirements:* For master's and other advanced degree, thesis, practicum/internship. *Entrance requirements:* For master's, resume, 2 professional references; for other advanced degree, official transcripts, documents for transfer credit evaluation, resume, written personal statement/essay, 2 professional references, health insurance, immunizations form. Additional exam requirements/recommendations for international students: Required—TOEFL (minimum score 550 paper-based; 79 iBT), Michigan English Language Assessment Battery (minimum score 85); Recommended—IELTS (minimum score 6). Electronic applications accepted. *Expenses:* Contact institution. *Faculty research:* Trauma, drug and alcohol counseling, cross-cultural issues, school counseling, trauma in schools.

Campbellsville University, School of Education, Campbellsville, KY 42718-2799. Offers education (MA); school counseling (MA); school improvement (MA); special education (MASE); special education-teacher leader (MA); teacher leader (MA); teaching (MAT), including middle grades biology, middle grades chemistry, middle grades English. *Accreditation:* NCATE. *Program availability:* Part-time, evening/weekend, 100% online, blended/hybrid learning. *Faculty:* 15 full-time (10 women), 14 part-time/adjunct (9 women). *Students:* 26 full-time (20 women), 155 part-time (122 women); includes 14 minority (13 Black or African American, non-Hispanic/Latino; 1 Hispanic/Latino). Average age 35. 199 applicants, 34% accepted, 57 enrolled. In 2017, 96 master's awarded. *Degree requirements:* For master's, comprehensive exam (for some programs), thesis, research paper. *Entrance requirements:* For master's, GRE or PRAXIS, minimum undergraduate GPA of 2.75, teaching certificate, professional growth plan, letters of recommendation, interview. Additional exam requirements/recommendations for international students: Recommended—TOEFL (minimum score 550 paper-based; 79 iBT), IELTS (minimum score 6). *Application deadline:* Applications are processed on a rolling basis. Application fee: $25. Electronic applications accepted. Application fee is waived when completed online. *Expenses:* $399 per credit hour. *Financial support:* Unspecified assistantships and employee tuition waivers available. Financial award applicants required to submit FAFSA. *Faculty research:* Professional development, curriculum development, school governance, assessment, special education. *Unit head:* Dr. Beverly Ennis, Dean, 270-789-5344, Fax: 270-789-5206, E-mail: bcennis@campbellsville.edu. *Application contact:* Monica Bamwine, Assistant Director of Graduate Admissions, 270-789-5221, Fax: 270-789-5071, E-mail: mkbamwine@campbellsville.edu.

Canisius College, Graduate Division, School of Education and Human Services, Programs in Counseling and Human Services, Buffalo, NY 14208-1098. Offers community mental health counseling (MS); counseling and human services (MS); school agency counseling (MS). *Accreditation:* ACA. *Program availability:* Part-time, evening/weekend. *Faculty:* 5 full-time (2 women), 11 part-time/adjunct (8 women). *Students:* 80 full-time (68 women), 40 part-time (31 women); includes 21 minority (13 Black or African American, non-Hispanic/Latino; 6 Hispanic/Latino; 2 Two or more races, non-Hispanic/Latino), 5 international. Average age 29. 89 applicants, 85% accepted, 31 enrolled. In 2017, 39 master's awarded. *Degree requirements:* For master's, thesis, research project. *Entrance requirements:* For master's, GRE (if cumulative GPA less than 2.7), transcripts, two letters of recommendation, interview, BA. Additional exam requirements/recommendations for international students: Required—TOEFL (minimum score 550 paper-based, 79 iBT), IELTS (minimum score 6.5), or CAEL (minimum score 70). *Application deadline:* Applications are processed on a rolling basis. Application fee: $0. Electronic applications accepted. *Expenses: Tuition:* Full-time $22,860; part-time $820 per credit. *Required fees:* $720; $25 per credit. $65 per semester. One-time fee: $425. *Financial support:* Career-related internships or fieldwork, Federal Work-Study, scholarships/grants, tuition waivers (partial), and unspecified assistantships available. Support available to part-time students. Financial award application deadline: 4/30; financial award applicants required to submit FAFSA. *Faculty research:* Impact of trauma on adults, long term psych-social impact on police officers. *Unit head:* Dr. Christine Moll, Chair, 716-888-3287, E-mail: moll@canisius.edu.
Website: http://www.canisius.edu/masters-counseling/

Capella University, Harold Abel School of Social and Behavioral Science, Doctoral Programs in Psychology, Minneapolis, MN 55402. Offers addiction psychology (PhD); clinical psychology (Psy D); educational psychology (PhD); general advanced studies in human behavior (PhD); general psychology (PhD); industrial/organizational psychology (PhD); school psychology (Psy D).

Capella University, Harold Abel School of Social and Behavioral Science, Master's Programs in Psychology, Minneapolis, MN 55402. Offers applied behavior analysis (MS); clinical psychology (MS); counseling psychology (MS); educational psychology (MS); evaluation, research, and measurement (MS); general advanced studies in human behavior (MS); general psychology (MS); industrial/organizational psychology (MS); leadership coaching psychology (MS); school psychology (MS); sport psychology (MS).

Central Connecticut State University, School of Graduate Studies, School of Education and Professional Studies, Department of Counselor Education and Family Therapy, New Britain, CT 06050-4010. Offers marriage and family therapy (MS); professional counseling (MS, AC, Certificate); school counseling (MS); student development in higher education (MS). *Accreditation:* AAMFT/COAMFTE; ACA. *Program availability:* Part-time, evening/weekend. *Faculty:* 9 full-time (6 women), 27 part-time/adjunct (23 women). *Students:* 184 full-time (141 women), 189 part-time (144 women); includes 131 minority (51 Black or African American, non-Hispanic/Latino; 3 Asian, non-Hispanic/Latino; 66 Hispanic/Latino; 11 Two or more races, non-Hispanic/Latino), 1 international. Average age 34. 217 applicants, 64% accepted, 105 enrolled. In 2017, 94 master's, 7 other advanced degrees awarded. *Degree requirements:* For master's, comprehensive exam, thesis or alternative; for other advanced degree, qualifying exam. *Entrance requirements:* For master's, minimum undergraduate GPA of 2.7, essay, interview, letters of recommendation. Additional exam requirements/recommendations for international students: Required—TOEFL (minimum score 550 paper-based; 79 iBT); Recommended—IELTS (minimum score 6.5). *Application deadline:* For fall admission, 3/1 for domestic and international students; for summer admission, 3/1 for domestic and international students. Applications are processed on a rolling basis. Application fee: $50. Electronic applications accepted. *Expenses: Tuition, area resident:* Full-time $6757. Tuition, state resident: full-time $9750; part-time $374 per credit. Tuition, nonresident: full-time $18,102; part-time $374 per credit. *Required fees:* $4635; $255 per credit. *Financial support:* In 2017–18, 77 students received support. Career-related internships or fieldwork, Federal Work-Study, scholarships/grants, and unspecified assistantships available. Support available to part-time students. Financial award application deadline: 3/1; financial award applicants required to submit FAFSA. *Faculty research:* Elementary and secondary school counseling, marriage and family therapy, rehabilitation counseling, counseling in higher educational settings. *Unit head:* Dr. Cherie King, Chair, 860-832-2154, E-mail: kingche@ccsu.edu. *Application contact:* Patricia Gardner, Associate Director of Graduate Studies, 860-832-2350, Fax: 860-832-2362.
Website: http://www.ccsu.edu/ceft/

Central Michigan University, College of Graduate Studies, College of Humanities and Social and Behavioral Sciences, Department of Psychology, Program in School Psychology, Mount Pleasant, MI 48859. Offers PhD, S Psy S. *Accreditation:* APA. *Degree requirements:* For doctorate, thesis/dissertation; for S Psy S, thesis. *Entrance requirements:* For doctorate, GRE. Electronic applications accepted. *Faculty research:* Psychology and education foundations, psychology and education assessment, intervention strategies.

Central Washington University, School of Graduate Studies and Research, College of the Sciences, Department of Psychology, Program in School Psychology, Ellensburg, WA 98926. Offers Ed S. *Entrance requirements:* Additional exam requirements/recommendations for international students: Required—TOEFL (minimum score 550 paper-based; 79 iBT). *Application deadline:* For fall admission, 2/1 priority date for domestic students. Applications are processed on a rolling basis. Application fee: $50. Electronic applications accepted. *Financial support:* Application deadline: 3/1; applicants required to submit FAFSA. *Unit head:* Dr. Heath Marrs, Director, 509-963-2349, E-mail: heath.marrs@cwu.edu. *Application contact:* Justine Eason, Admissions Program Coordinator, 509-963-3103, Fax: 509-963-1799, E-mail: masters@cwu.edu.

Chaminade University of Honolulu, Office of Professional and Continuing Education, Program in Counseling Psychology, Honolulu, HI 96816-1578. Offers marriage and family counseling (MSCP); mental health counseling (MSCP); school counseling (MSCP). *Program availability:* Part-time, evening/weekend, blended/hybrid learning. *Faculty:* 6 full-time (3 women), 16 part-time/adjunct (7 women). *Students:* 158 full-time (118 women), 34 part-time (26 women); includes 131 minority (13 Black or African American, non-Hispanic/Latino; 2 American Indian or Alaska Native, non-Hispanic/Latino; 61 Asian, non-Hispanic/Latino; 14 Hispanic/Latino; 39 Native Hawaiian or other Pacific Islander, non-Hispanic/Latino; 2 Two or more races, non-Hispanic/Latino), 3 international. Average age 31. 53 applicants, 96% accepted, 37 enrolled. In 2017, 78 master's awarded. *Degree requirements:* For master's, comprehensive exam, internship/practicum. *Entrance requirements:* For master's, minimum undergraduate GPA of 3.0, 3 letters of recommendation, resume. Additional exam requirements/recommendations for international students: Required—TOEFL (minimum score 550 paper-based; 79 iBT). *Application deadline:* Applications are processed on a rolling basis. Application fee: $40. Electronic applications accepted. *Expenses:* $860 per credit hour plus $93 fee per online course. *Financial support:* Applicants required to submit FAFSA. *Unit head:* Dr. Robert G. Santee, Dean, 808-735-4751, Fax: 808-739-4670, E-mail: mscp@chaminade.edu. *Application contact:* 808-735-4755, E-mail: gradserv@chaminade.edu.
Website: https://pace.chaminade.edu/graduate-programs/mscp-program/

Chapman University, Donna Ford Attallah College of Educational Studies, Orange, CA 92866. Offers counseling (MA), including school counseling (MA, Credential); curriculum and instruction (MA), including elementary education, secondary education; education (PhD), including cultural and curricular studies, disability studies, leadership studies, school psychology (PhD, Credential); educational psychology (MA); leadership development (MA); multiple subjects (Credential), including Spanish/English bilingual; pupil personnel services (Credential), including school counseling (MA, Credential), school psychology (PhD, Credential); school psychology (Ed S); single subject (Credential); special education (MA, Credential), including mild/moderate (Credential), moderate/severe (Credential); teaching (MA), including elementary education, secondary education, secondary music education. *Accreditation:* TEAC. *Program availability:* Part-time, evening/weekend. *Faculty:* 32 full-time (18 women), 37 part-time/adjunct (26 women). *Students:* 170 full-time (140 women), 180 part-time (129 women); includes 164 minority (6 Black or African American, non-Hispanic/Latino; 38 Asian, non-Hispanic/Latino; 101 Hispanic/Latino; 1 Native Hawaiian or other Pacific Islander, non-Hispanic/Latino; 18 Two or more races, non-Hispanic/Latino), 10 international. Average age 28. 143 applicants, 63% accepted, 64 enrolled. In 2017, 126 master's, 18 doctorates awarded. *Application deadline:* Applications are processed on a rolling basis. Application fee: $60. Electronic applications accepted. *Expenses:* Contact institution. *Financial support:* Fellowships and scholarships/grants available. Financial award application deadline: 3/2; financial award applicants required to submit FAFSA. *Unit head:* Dr. Margaret Grogan, Dean, 714-516-5968, E-mail: grogan@chapman.edu. *Application contact:* Shannon McCance, Graduate Admission Counselor, 714-516-5236, E-mail: smccance@chapman.edu.
Website: http://www.chapman.edu/CES/

The Chicago School of Professional Psychology, Program in School Psychology, Chicago, IL 60610. Offers Ed D, Psy D, Ed S. *Program availability:* Part-time. *Entrance requirements:* For degree, GRE (recommended), minimum GPA of 3.2 (recommended); completion of one course in statistics or research methods and one course in psychology. Additional exam requirements/recommendations for international students: Required—TOEFL (minimum score 550 paper-based; 79 iBT).

The Chicago School of Professional Psychology at Washington DC, Program in School Psychology, Washington, DC 20005. Offers Ed S. *Program availability:* Part-time.

The Citadel, The Military College of South Carolina, Citadel Graduate College, School of Humanities and Social Sciences, Department of Psychology, Charleston, SC 29409. Offers psychology (MA), including clinical counseling; school psychology (Ed S). *Program availability:* Part-time, evening/weekend. *Degree requirements:* For master's, comprehensive exam, practicum; internship (written and oral presentation of a case study as part of internship); for Ed S, comprehensive exam, thesis (for some programs), practicum, internship. *Entrance requirements:* For master's, GRE (minimum combined score of 297, 150 on verbal reasoning and 141 on quantitative reasoning) or MAT (minimum score of 410), minimum undergraduate GPA of 3.0; 12 credit hours in psychology or minimum score on GRE Subject Test in psychology of 600; 2 letters of recommendation; for Ed S, GRE (minimum combined score of 297, 150 on verbal reasoning and 147 on quantitative reasoning) or MAT (minimum score of 410), minimum undergraduate or graduate GPA of 3.0; 2 letters of recommendation. Additional exam requirements/recommendations for international students: Required—TOEFL (minimum score 550 paper-based; 79 iBT). Electronic applications accepted. *Expenses:* Tuition, state resident: part-time $587 per credit hour. Tuition, nonresident: part-time $988 per credit hour. *Required fees:* $90 per term.

The Citadel, The Military College of South Carolina, Citadel Graduate College, Zucker Family School of Education, Charleston, SC 29409. Offers elementary/secondary school administration and supervision (M Ed); elementary/secondary school counseling (M Ed); interdisciplinary STEM education (M Ed); literacy education (M Ed, Graduate Certificate); middle grades (MAT), including English, mathematics, science, social studies; physical education (grades K-12) (MAT); school superintendency (Ed S); secondary education (MAT), including biology, English, mathematics, social studies; student affairs (Graduate Certificate); student affairs and college counseling (M Ed). *Accreditation:* NCATE. *Program availability:* Part-time, evening/weekend, 100% online, blended/hybrid learning. *Degree requirements:* For master's, comprehensive exam (for some programs). *Entrance requirements:* For master's, GRE (minimum combined verbal and quantitative score of 290) or MAT (minimum score 396). Additional exam requirements/recommendations for international students: Required—TOEFL (minimum score 550 paper-based; 79 iBT). Electronic applications accepted. *Expenses:* Tuition, state resident: part-time $587 per credit hour. Tuition, nonresident: part-time $988 per credit hour. *Required fees:* $90 per term.

School Psychology

The College of New Rochelle, Graduate School, Division of Human Services, Program in School Psychology, New Rochelle, NY 10805-2308. Offers MS. *Degree requirements:* For master's, comprehensive exam, clinical fieldwork journal. *Entrance requirements:* For master's, interview, minimum GPA of 3.0, course work in psychology, sample of written work. *Expenses: Tuition:* Full-time $17,406. *Required fees:* $1120.

College of Saint Elizabeth, Department of Psychology, Morristown, NJ 07960-6989. Offers counseling psychology (MA, Psy D), including mental health counseling (MA), school counseling (MA). *Program availability:* Part-time. *Faculty:* 4 full-time (3 women), 7 part-time/adjunct (all women). *Students:* 37 full-time (32 women), 40 part-time (37 women); includes 30 minority (12 Black or African American, non-Hispanic/Latino; 1 Asian, non-Hispanic/Latino; 16 Hispanic/Latino; 1 Two or more races, non-Hispanic/Latino). Average age 31. 37 applicants, 81% accepted, 24 enrolled. In 2017, 17 master's, 3 doctorates awarded. *Degree requirements:* For master's, thesis or alternative; for doctorate, thesis/dissertation. *Entrance requirements:* For master's, minimum GPA of 3.0, BA in psychology (preferred), 12 credits of course work in psychology; for doctorate, GRE, 3 letters of recommendation from professionals who can comment on the applicant's qualifications for doctoral study; master's degree in counseling psychology, forensic psychology and counseling, or its equivalent. Additional exam requirements/recommendations for international students: Required—TOEFL (minimum score 550 paper-based; 79 iBT), IELTS (minimum score 6.5). *Application deadline:* For fall admission, 5/1 for international students. Applications are processed on a rolling basis. Application fee: $35. Electronic applications accepted. Application fee is waived when completed online. *Expenses:* Contact institution. *Financial support:* Career-related internships or fieldwork, scholarships/grants, tuition waivers (partial), and unspecified assistantships available. Support available to part-time students. Financial award applicants required to submit FAFSA. *Unit head:* Dr. Michelle M. Barrett, Director, Graduate and Doctoral Programs in Psychology, 973-290-4027, Fax: 973-290-4676, E-mail: mbarrett01@cse.edu. *Application contact:* Lori J. Fragoso, Director of Graduate and Continuing Studies Admissions, 973-290-4413, Fax: 973-290-4710, E-mail: apply@cse.edu.
Website: https://www.cse.edu/academics/prof-studies/psychology/

College of St. Joseph, Graduate Programs, Division of Psychology and Human Services, Program in School Guidance Counseling, Rutland, VT 05701-3899. Offers MS. *Program availability:* Part-time, evening/weekend. *Degree requirements:* For master's, comprehensive exam, thesis optional. *Entrance requirements:* For master's, PRAXIS I, official college transcripts; 2 letters of reference. Additional exam requirements/recommendations for international students: Required—TOEFL (minimum score 550 paper-based). Electronic applications accepted.

The College of Saint Rose, Graduate Studies, Thelma P. Lally School of Education, Educational and School Psychology Programs, Albany, NY 12203-1419. Offers educational psychology (MS Ed, Certificate); school psychology (MS Ed). *Students:* 35 full-time (31 women), 5 part-time (2 women); includes 3 minority (1 Black or African American, non-Hispanic/Latino; 1 Hispanic/Latino; 1 Two or more races, non-Hispanic/Latino), 1 international. Average age 25. 40 applicants, 75% accepted, 18 enrolled. In 2017, 20 master's awarded. *Entrance requirements:* For master's, minimum undergraduate GPA of 3.0. Additional exam requirements/recommendations for international students: Required—TOEFL (minimum score 550 paper-based; 80 iBT), IELTS (minimum score 6), PTE (minimum score 56). *Application deadline:* For fall admission, 2/15 priority date for domestic and international students. Applications are processed on a rolling basis. Application fee: $40. Electronic applications accepted. *Expenses: Tuition:* Full-time $7191; part-time $799 per credit hour. *Required fees:* $924; $462 per credit hour. Tuition and fees vary according to course load. *Financial support:* Career-related internships or fieldwork, scholarships/grants, tuition waivers (partial), and unspecified assistantships available. Support available to part-time students. Financial award application deadline: 4/15. *Unit head:* Dr. Andrew Shanock, Chair, 518-337-5694, E-mail: shanocka@strose.edu. *Application contact:* Cris Murray, Assistant Vice President for Graduate Recruitment and Enrollment, 518-485-3390, Fax: 518-458-5479, E-mail: grad@strose.edu.
Website: https://www.strose.edu/school-psychology/

The College of William and Mary, School of Education, Program in School Psychology, Williamsburg, VA 23187-8795. Offers M Ed, Ed S. *Accreditation:* NCATE. *Faculty:* 2 full-time (1 woman), 7 part-time/adjunct (6 women). *Students:* 17 full-time (15 women), 1 (woman) part-time; includes 1 minority (Hispanic/Latino), 1 international. Average age 26. 45 applicants, 47% accepted, 10 enrolled. In 2017, 9 Ed Ss awarded. *Degree requirements:* For Ed S, internship. *Entrance requirements:* For master's and Ed S, GRE, minimum GPA of 3.5. Additional exam requirements/recommendations for international students: Required—TOEFL (minimum score 100 iBT), IELTS (minimum score 7). *Application deadline:* For fall admission, 1/15 for domestic and international students. Application fee: $50. Electronic applications accepted. *Expenses:* $9,630 resident full-time, $535 resident part-time per credit hour; $25,920 nonresident full-time, $1,265 nonresident part-time per credit hour; $5,944 full-time fees. *Financial support:* In 2017–18, 15 students received support, including 15 research assistantships (averaging $10,616 per year); unspecified assistantships also available. Financial award application deadline: 1/15; financial award applicants required to submit FAFSA. *Faculty research:* Assessment, diagnostic decision making, quantitative methods, multi-tiered interventions, behavioral interventions. *Unit head:* Dr. Ryan McGill, Assistant Professor, 757-221-6072, E-mail: rmcgill@wm.edu. *Application contact:* Dorothy Smith Osborne, Assistant Dean for Academic Programs and Student Services, 757-221-2317, E-mail: dsosbo@wm.edu.
Website: http://education.wm.edu

Creighton University, Graduate School, College of Arts and Sciences, Department of Education, Program in School Counseling and Preventive Mental Health, Omaha, NE 68178-0001. Offers elementary school guidance (MS); secondary school guidance (MS). *Program availability:* Part-time, online only, 100% online, blended/hybrid learning. *Faculty:* 3 full-time (1 woman). *Students:* 27 full-time (23 women), 42 part-time (34 women); includes 4 minority (1 Black or African American, non-Hispanic/Latino; 2 American Indian or Alaska Native, non-Hispanic/Latino; 1 Native Hawaiian or other Pacific Islander, non-Hispanic/Latino), 1 international. Average age 31. In 2017, 18 master's awarded. *Degree requirements:* For master's, comprehensive exam. *Entrance requirements:* For master's, resume, 3 letters of recommendation, personal statement, background check. Additional exam requirements/recommendations for international students: Required—TOEFL (minimum score 90 iBT). *Application deadline:* For fall admission, 7/1 for domestic students, 3/1 for international students; for winter admission, 10/1 for domestic students, 7/1 for international students; for spring admission, 3/1 for domestic students, 9/1 for international students; for summer admission, 3/1 for domestic and international students. Application fee: $50. Electronic applications accepted. Part-time tuition and fees vary according to course load, degree level, campus/location and program. *Financial support:* Scholarships/grants available. Support available to part-time students. Financial award applicants required to submit FAFSA. *Unit head:* Dr. Timothy Dickel, Professor of Education, 402-280-2230, E-mail: ctdickel@creighton.edu. *Application contact:* Lindsay Johnson, Director of Graduate and Adult Recruitment, 402-280-2703, Fax: 402-280-2423, E-mail: gradschool@creighton.edu.

DePaul University, College of Education, Chicago, IL 60614. Offers bilingual-bicultural education (M Ed, MA); counseling (M Ed, MA), including clinical mental health counseling, college student development, school counseling; curriculum studies (M Ed, MA, Ed D); early childhood education (M Ed, MA, Ed D); educational leadership (M Ed, MA, Ed D), including Catholic leadership (M Ed, MA), general (M Ed, MA), higher education (M Ed, MA), physical education (M Ed, MA), principal preparation (M Ed), teacher preparation (M Ed); elementary education (M Ed, MA); middle grades education (M Ed); middle school mathematics education (MS); reading specialist (M Ed, MA); secondary education (M Ed, MA); social and cultural foundations in education (M Ed, MA); special education (M Ed); sport, fitness and recreation leadership (MS); value-creating education for global citizenship (M Ed); world languages education (M Ed, MA). *Program availability:* Part-time, evening/weekend, online learning. *Degree requirements:* For doctorate, thesis/dissertation. *Application deadline:* Applications are processed on a rolling basis. Application fee: $40. Electronic applications accepted. *Financial support:* Application deadline: 12/31; applicants required to submit FAFSA. *Unit head:* Dr. Paul Zionts, Dean, 773-325-7581, Fax: 773-325-7713, E-mail: pzionts@depaul.edu. *Application contact:* Dr. Paul Zionts, Dean, 773-325-7581, Fax: 773-325-7713, E-mail: pzionts@depaul.edu.
Website: http://education.depaul.edu

Doane University, Program in Education, Crete, NE 68333-2430. Offers curriculum and instruction (M Ed); curriculum leadership (Ed S); education (Ed D); educational leadership (M Ed); school counseling (M Ed). *Accreditation:* NCATE. *Program availability:* Part-time, evening/weekend. *Faculty:* 10 full-time (7 women), 66 part-time/adjunct (50 women). *Students:* 228 full-time (172 women), 541 part-time (433 women); includes 51 minority (21 Black or African American, non-Hispanic/Latino; 4 American Indian or Alaska Native, non-Hispanic/Latino; 4 Asian, non-Hispanic/Latino; 12 Hispanic/Latino; 1 Native Hawaiian or other Pacific Islander, non-Hispanic/Latino; 9 Two or more races, non-Hispanic/Latino). Average age 33. In 2017, 284 master's, 1 other advanced degree awarded. *Degree requirements:* For master's, thesis; for doctorate, thesis/dissertation. *Entrance requirements:* For master's, minimum GPA of 2.5. Additional exam requirements/recommendations for international students: Required—TOEFL. *Application deadline:* Applications are processed on a rolling basis. Electronic applications accepted. *Expenses:* Contact institution. *Financial support:* Applicants required to submit FAFSA. *Unit head:* Dr. Lyn C. Forester, Dean, 402-826-8604, Fax: 402-826-8278. *Application contact:* Leah Schaber, Assistant Dean, 402-464-1223, Fax: 402-466-4228, E-mail: leah.schaber@doane.edu.
Website: http://www.doane.edu/masters-degrees

Duquesne University, School of Education, Department of Counseling, Psychology, and Special Education, Program in School Psychology, Pittsburgh, PA 15282-0001. Offers child psychology (MS Ed). *Program availability:* Part-time, evening/weekend. *Faculty:* 8 full-time (5 women). *Students:* 76 full-time (63 women), 2 part-time (0 women); includes 4 minority (2 Black or African American, non-Hispanic/Latino; 1 Hispanic/Latino; 1 Two or more races, non-Hispanic/Latino), 1 international. Average age 27. 75 applicants, 71% accepted, 26 enrolled. In 2017, 16 master's, 16 doctorates awarded. *Entrance requirements:* For master's, bachelor's degree; for doctorate, GRE, letters of reference, letter of intent, interview, master's degree. Additional exam requirements/recommendations for international students: Required—TOEFL (minimum score 550 paper-based), IELTS (minimum score 6.5). *Application deadline:* For fall admission, 4/2 for domestic students; for spring admission, 9/1 for domestic students. Applications are processed on a rolling basis. Application fee: $0. Electronic applications accepted. *Expenses:* $1,259 per credit. *Financial support:* Research assistantships and Federal Work-Study available. Support available to part-time students. *Faculty research:* Interventions for social, emotional, and behavior problems; academic interventions; prevention; neuropsychological assessment; consultation. *Unit head:* Dr. Kara McGoey, Professor/Program Director, 412-396-4105, Fax: 412-396-1340, E-mail: mcgoeyk@duq.edu. *Application contact:* Kelly McGinley, Graduate Admissions Assistant, 412-396-1559, Fax: 412-396-5585, E-mail: mcginleyk@duq.edu.

Eastern Illinois University, Graduate School, College of Liberal Arts and Sciences, Department of Psychology, Charleston, IL 61920. Offers clinical psychology (MA); school psychology (SSP). *Program availability:* Part-time, evening/weekend. *Degree requirements:* For master's, comprehensive exam, thesis; for SSP, thesis. *Entrance requirements:* For master's and SSP, GMAT or GRE. Additional exam requirements/recommendations for international students: Required—TOEFL (minimum score 500 paper-based; 61 iBT), IELTS (minimum score 6). *Application deadline:* For fall admission, 5/15 for domestic and international students; for spring admission, 10/15 for domestic and international students. Applications are processed on a rolling basis. Application fee: $30. Electronic applications accepted. *Financial support:* Research assistantships with full tuition reimbursements, teaching assistantships with full tuition reimbursements, career-related internships or fieldwork, Federal Work-Study, and unspecified assistantships available. Support available to part-time students. Financial award application deadline: 3/1; financial award applicants required to submit FAFSA. *Unit head:* John H. Mace, Chair, 217-581-2127, Fax: 217-581-6764, E-mail: jhmace@eiu.edu. *Application contact:* John H. Mace, Chair, 217-581-2127, Fax: 217-581-6764, E-mail: jhmace@eiu.edu.
Website: http://www.eiu.edu/psych/index.php

Eastern Kentucky University, The Graduate School, College of Arts and Sciences, Department of Psychology, Richmond, KY 40475-3102. Offers clinical psychology (MS); industrial/organizational psychology (MS); school psychology (Psy S). *Program availability:* Part-time. *Entrance requirements:* For master's and Psy S, GRE General Test, minimum GPA of 2.5. *Faculty research:* Autism, social psychology, parenting, assessment of depression/anxiety, reading.

Eastern University, Graduate Education Programs, St. Davids, PA 19087-3696. Offers ESL program specialist (K-12) (Certificate); general supervisor (PreK-12) (Certificate); health and physical education (K-12) (Certificate); middle level (4-8) (Certificate); multicultural education (M Ed); music (K-12) (Certificate); Pre K-4 (Certificate); Pre K-4 with special education (Certificate); reading (M Ed); reading specialist (K-12) (Certificate); reading supervisor (K-12) (Certificate); school counseling (MA, CAGS); school principalship (preK-12) (Certificate); school psychology (MS, CAGS); secondary biology education (7-12) (Certificate); secondary chemistry education (7-12) (Certificate); secondary communication education (7-12) (Certificate); secondary English education (7-12) (Certificate); secondary math education (7-12) (Certificate); secondary social studies education (7-12) (Certificate); special education (M Ed); special education (7-12) (Certificate); special education (Pre K-8) (Certificate); special education supervisor (K-12) (Certificate); TESOL (M Ed); world language (Certificate), including Spanish. *Program availability:* Part-time, evening/weekend, online learning. *Students:* 46 full-time (40 women), 115 part-time (93 women); includes 65 minority (42 Black or African American, non-Hispanic/Latino; 3 Asian, non-Hispanic/Latino; 14 Hispanic/Latino; 6 Two or more races, non-Hispanic/Latino), 1 international. Average age 32. In 2017, 72 master's awarded. *Entrance requirements:* Additional exam requirements/recommendations for international students: Required—TOEFL. *Application deadline:* Applications are processed on a rolling basis. Application fee: $35. Electronic applications accepted. Application fee is waived when completed online. *Expenses:* Contact institution. *Unit head:* Michael Dziedziak, Executive Director of

Enrollment, 800-452-0996, E-mail: gpsadmissions@eastern.edu.
Website: https://www.eastern.edu/academics/programs/education-department-graduate-programs/graduate-programs

Eastern Washington University, Graduate Studies, College of Social Sciences, Department of Psychology, Program in School Psychology Respecialization, Cheney, WA 99004-2431. Offers Ed S. *Students:* 36 full-time (28 women), 33 part-time (27 women); includes 6 minority (1 Black or African American, non-Hispanic/Latino; 1 American Indian or Alaska Native, non-Hispanic/Latino; 4 Hispanic/Latino), 1 international. Average age 27. 32 applicants, 44% accepted, 10 enrolled. *Entrance requirements:* Additional exam requirements/recommendations for international students: Required—TOEFL (minimum score 580 paper-based; 92 iBT), IELTS (minimum score 7), PTE (minimum score 63). *Application deadline:* Applications are processed on a rolling basis. Application fee: $75. Electronic applications accepted. *Expenses:* Tuition, state resident: full-time $11,191; part-time $373.06 per credit. Tuition, nonresident: full-time $25,995; part-time $866.52 per credit. *Financial support:* In 2017–18, teaching assistantships with partial tuition reimbursements (averaging $10,000 per year) were awarded; career-related internships or fieldwork, Federal Work-Study, institutionally sponsored loans, scholarships/grants, tuition waivers (partial), and unspecified assistantships also available. Support available to part-time students. Financial award application deadline: 2/1; financial award applicants required to submit FAFSA. *Unit head:* Dr. Jamie Chaffin, 509-359-4736, E-mail: edsonline@ewu.edu. *Application contact:* Kathy White, Advisor/Recruiter for Graduate Studies, 509-359-6297, Fax: 509-359-6044, E-mail: gradprograms@ewu.edu.

East Tennessee State University, School of Graduate Studies, College of Education, Department of Counseling and Human Services, Johnson City, TN 37614. Offers clinical mental health counseling (MA); college counseling/student affairs higher education (MA); couples and family therapy (MA); human services (MS); school counseling (MA). *Accreditation:* ACA; NCATE. *Program availability:* Part-time. *Degree requirements:* For master's, comprehensive exam, thesis optional, internship, student teaching, culminating experience. *Entrance requirements:* For master's, GRE General Test, minimum GPA of 3.0, three letters of recommendation, interview, 2-3 page essay detailing experiences that have shaped pursuit of degree, resume. Additional exam requirements/recommendations for international students: Required—TOEFL (minimum score 550 paper-based; 79 iBT). *Application deadline:* For fall admission, 1/31 priority date for domestic and international students. Application fee: $55 ($65 for international students). Electronic applications accepted. *Financial support:* Research assistantships with full tuition reimbursements, teaching assistantships with full tuition reimbursements, career-related internships or fieldwork, institutionally sponsored loans, scholarships/grants, traineeships, and unspecified assistantships available. Financial award application deadline: 7/1; financial award applicants required to submit FAFSA. *Faculty research:* Intervention and assistance with at-risk and under-served youth and high conflict families; service and social justice; women and girls' issues in counseling; counseling competence with LGBTQ individuals; counselor education and supervision. *Unit head:* Dr. Janna Scarborough, Chair, 423-439-4191, Fax: 423-439-7790, E-mail: scarboro@etsu.edu. *Application contact:* Dr. Janna Scarborough, Chair, 423-439-4191, Fax: 423-439-7790, E-mail: scarboro@etsu.edu.
Website: http://www.etsu.edu/coe/chs/

Edinboro University of Pennsylvania, Department of Counseling, School Psychology and Special Education, Edinboro, PA 16444. Offers counseling (MA), including art therapy, clinical mental health counseling, college counseling, rehabilitation counseling, school counseling; educational psychology (M Ed); school psychology (Ed S); special education (M Ed), including autism, behavior management. *Accreditation:* ACA. *Program availability:* Part-time, evening/weekend. *Degree requirements:* For master's, thesis or alternative, competency exam; for Ed S, thesis or alternative. *Entrance requirements:* For master's and Ed S, GRE or MAT, minimum QPA of 2.5. Electronic applications accepted.

Emporia State University, Program in School Psychology, Emporia, KS 66801-5415. Offers MS, Ed S. *Accreditation:* NCATE. *Program availability:* Part-time. *Faculty:* 8 full-time (4 women). *Students:* 26 full-time (23 women), 7 part-time (all women); includes 2 minority (1 Hispanic/Latino; 1 Two or more races, non-Hispanic/Latino). 38 applicants, 74% accepted, 14 enrolled. In 2017, 16 master's awarded. *Degree requirements:* For master's, comprehensive exam or thesis, internship; for Ed S, comprehensive exam, thesis or alternative, internship. *Entrance requirements:* For master's, GRE General Test or MAT, essay exam, appropriate bachelor's degree, teacher certification, letters of recommendation; for Ed S, GRE, essay exam, letters of recommendation, teacher certification. Additional exam requirements/recommendations for international students: Required—TOEFL (minimum score 520 paper-based; 68 iBT). *Application deadline:* For fall admission, 8/15 priority date for domestic students. Applications are processed on a rolling basis. Application fee: $30 ($75 for international students). Electronic applications accepted. *Expenses:* Tuition, state resident: full-time $6084; part-time $253.50 per credit hour. Tuition, nonresident: full-time $18,924; part-time $788.50 per credit hour. *Required fees:* $1943; $80.95 per credit hour. Tuition and fees vary according to campus/location. *Financial support:* Career-related internships or fieldwork, Federal Work-Study, institutionally sponsored loans, health care benefits, and unspecified assistantships available. Financial award application deadline: 3/15; financial award applicants required to submit FAFSA. *Unit head:* Dr. Jim Persinger, Chair, 620-341-5317, E-mail: jpersing@emporia.edu. *Application contact:* Mary Sewell, Admissions Coordinator, 800-950-GRAD, Fax: 620-341-5909, E-mail: msewell@emporia.edu.

Evangel University, School Counseling Program, Springfield, MO 65802. Offers MS. *Program availability:* Part-time, evening/weekend. *Faculty:* 17 full-time (12 women), 4 part-time/adjunct (3 women). *Students:* 24 full-time (19 women), 21 part-time (19 women); includes 3 minority (2 Black or African American, non-Hispanic/Latino; 1 Hispanic/Latino). Average age 31. 16 applicants, 100% accepted, 11 enrolled. In 2017, 14 master's awarded. *Degree requirements:* For master's, comprehensive exam. *Entrance requirements:* For master's, MAT (preferred) or GRE. Additional exam requirements/recommendations for international students: Required—TOEFL (minimum score 550 paper-based). *Application deadline:* For fall admission, 7/15 priority date for domestic students, 7/1 for international students; for spring admission, 11/15 priority date for domestic students, 12/1 for international students. Applications are processed on a rolling basis. Application fee: $25. Electronic applications accepted. *Expenses:* *Tuition:* Full-time $7200; part-time $4800 per credit hour. *Required fees:* $210; $155 per semester. *Financial support:* In 2017–18, 6 students received support. Scholarships/grants and unspecified assistantships available. Financial award application deadline: 4/1; financial award applicants required to submit FAFSA. *Unit head:* Dr. Christine Arnzen, Program Coordinator, 417-865-2815 Ext. 8678, Fax: 417-575-5484, E-mail: arnzenc@evangel.edu. *Application contact:* Michael Mann, Enrollment Coordinator, Graduate Studies, 417-865-2815 Ext. 8276, Fax: 417-575-5484, E-mail: mannm@evangel.edu.
Website: http://www.evangel.edu/academics/graduate-studies/graduate-programs

Fairfield University, Graduate School of Education and Allied Professions, Fairfield, CT 06824. Offers applied behavior analysis (ATC); applied psychology (MA); clinical mental health counseling (MA, CAS); educational technology (MA); elementary education (MA, CAS); family studies (MA); integration of spirituality and religion in counseling (ATC); marriage and family therapy (MA); reading and language development (Sixth Year Certificate); school counseling (MA, CAS); school psychology (MA, CAS); school-based marriage and family therapy (ATC); secondary education (MA); special education (MA, CAS); substance abuse counseling (ATC); teaching (Certificate); teaching and foundations (MA, CAS); TESOL, world languages, and bilingual education (MA, CAS). *Accreditation:* NCATE. *Program availability:* Part-time, evening/weekend. *Faculty:* 23 full-time (17 women), 39 part-time/adjunct (28 women). *Students:* 199 full-time (168 women), 251 part-time (206 women); includes 85 minority (21 Black or African American, non-Hispanic/Latino; 9 Asian, non-Hispanic/Latino; 49 Hispanic/Latino; 6 Two or more races, non-Hispanic/Latino), 4 international. Average age 32. 370 applicants, 56% accepted, 125 enrolled. In 2017, 136 master's, 28 other advanced degrees awarded. *Degree requirements:* For master's, comprehensive exam. *Entrance requirements:* For master's, minimum GPA of 3.0, 2 recommendations, resume. Additional exam requirements/recommendations for international students: Required—TOEFL (minimum score 550 paper-based; 84 iBT) or IELTS (minimum score 7.5). *Application deadline:* For fall admission, 2/15 for international students; for spring admission, 10/1 for international students. Application fee: $60. Electronic applications accepted. *Expenses:* $750 per credit hour. *Financial support:* In 2017–18, 34 students received support. Career-related internships or fieldwork and unspecified assistantships available. Support available to part-time students. Financial award applicants required to submit FAFSA. *Faculty research:* Reading and literacy, writing, social justice and inequality in education, addictions and mental health issues, therapeutic relationships and clinical supervision. *Unit head:* Dr. Robert D. Hannafin, Dean, 203-254-4250, Fax: 203-254-4241, E-mail: rhannafin@fairfield.edu. *Application contact:* Marianne Gumpper, Director of Graduate Admission, 203-254-4184, Fax: 203-254-4073, E-mail: gradadmis@fairfield.edu.
Website: http://www.fairfield.edu/gseap

Fairleigh Dickinson University, Metropolitan Campus, University College: Arts, Sciences, and Professional Studies, School of Psychology, Program in School Psychology, Teaneck, NJ 07666-1914. Offers MA, Psy D.

Florida Gulf Coast University, Elaine Nicpon Marieb College of Health and Human Services, Program in School Counseling, Fort Myers, FL 33965-6565. Offers clinical mental health counseling (MA); school counseling (MA). *Accreditation:* ACA. *Program availability:* Part-time, evening/weekend. *Faculty:* 71 full-time (49 women), 49 part-time/adjunct (32 women). *Students:* 12 full-time (9 women), 27 part-time (21 women); includes 6 minority (3 Black or African American, non-Hispanic/Latino; 3 Hispanic/Latino). Average age 30. 27 applicants, 89% accepted, 21 enrolled. In 2017, 12 master's awarded. *Degree requirements:* For master's, thesis or alternative. *Entrance requirements:* For master's, GRE General Test, MAT, minimum GPA of 3.0. Additional exam requirements/recommendations for international students: Required—TOEFL (minimum score 550 paper-based). *Application deadline:* For fall admission, 2/15 priority date for domestic students; for summer admission, 2/15 priority date for domestic students. Applications are processed on a rolling basis. Application fee: $30. Electronic applications accepted. *Expenses:* Tuition, state resident: part-time $290 per credit hour. Tuition, nonresident: part-time $1173 per credit hour. *Required fees:* $127 per credit hour. Tuition and fees vary according to course load. *Financial support:* In 2017–18, 9 students received support. Application deadline: 6/30; applicants required to submit FAFSA. *Faculty research:* Sexuality, confidentiality, school counselor roles, distance learning, exceptional students. *Unit head:* Dr. Madelyn Isaacs, Department Chair, 239-590-7785, Fax: 239-590-7801, E-mail: misaacs@fgcu.edu. *Application contact:* Ana Hill, Graduate Studies Admissions, 239-590-7408, Fax: 239-590-7843, E-mail: graduate@fgcu.edu.

Florida International University, College of Arts, Sciences, and Education, Department of Leadership and Professional Studies, Miami, FL 33199. Offers adult education and human resource development (MS, Ed D); counseling (MS), including rehabilitation counseling, school counseling; counselor education (MS), including clinical mental health counseling; educational administration and supervision (Ed D); educational leadership (MS, Certificate, Ed S); higher education (Ed D); higher education administration (MS); international and comparative education (MS); recreation and sport management (MS), including recreation and sport management, recreational therapy; school psychology (Ed S); urban education (MS), including instruction in urban settings, learning technologies, multicultural/bilingual, multicultural/TESOL, urban education. *Program availability:* Part-time, evening/weekend. *Faculty:* 60 full-time (41 women), 112 part-time/adjunct (77 women). *Students:* 221 full-time (162 women), 301 part-time (239 women); includes 418 minority (127 Black or African American, non-Hispanic/Latino; 9 Asian, non-Hispanic/Latino; 271 Hispanic/Latino; 11 Two or more races, non-Hispanic/Latino), 10 international. Average age 31. 330 applicants, 55% accepted, 100 enrolled. In 2017, 181 master's, 6 doctorates awarded. *Degree requirements:* For doctorate, thesis/dissertation. *Entrance requirements:* For master's, minimum GPA of 3.0; for doctorate and other advanced degree, GRE General Test. Additional exam requirements/recommendations for international students: Required—TOEFL (minimum score 550 paper-based; 80 iBT), IELTS (minimum score 6.3). *Application deadline:* For fall admission, 6/1 priority date for domestic students, 4/1 for international students; for winter admission, 10/1 priority date for domestic students, 9/1 for international students; for spring admission, 3/1 priority date for domestic students, 2/1 for international students. Applications are processed on a rolling basis. Application fee: $30. Electronic applications accepted. *Expenses:* Tuition, state resident: full-time $8912; part-time $446 per credit hour. Tuition, nonresident: full-time $21,393; part-time $992 per credit hour. *Required fees:* $390; $195 per semester. *Financial support:* Fellowships, research assistantships with tuition reimbursements, teaching assistantships with tuition reimbursements, Federal Work-Study, and tuition waivers (full and partial) available. Support available to part-time students. Financial award applicants required to submit FAFSA. *Unit head:* Dr. Benjamin Baez, Chair, 305-348-3214, Fax: 305-348-1515, E-mail: benjamin.baez@fiu.edu. *Application contact:* Nanett Rojas, Assistant Director, Graduate Admissions, 305-348-7464, Fax: 305-348-7441, E-mail: gradadm@fiu.edu.
Website: http://education.fiu.edu

Florida State University, The Graduate School, College of Education, Department of Educational Psychology and Learning Systems, Tallahassee, FL 32306. Offers counseling and human systems (PhD), including counseling psychology and school psychology; educational psychology (MS, PhD), including learning and cognition, sport psychology; human performance and technology (Certificate); instructional systems and learning technologies (MS, PhD); measurement and statistics (MS, PhD, Certificate); online instructional development (Certificate); MS/Ed S. *Program availability:* Part-time, evening/weekend, 100% online, blended/hybrid learning, asynchronous, minimal on-campus study. *Faculty:* 28 full-time (17 women), 12 part-time/adjunct (7 women). *Students:* 339 full-time (238 women), 136 part-time (93 women); includes 126 minority (47 Black or African American, non-Hispanic/Latino; 4 American Indian or Alaska Native, non-Hispanic/Latino; 7 Asian, non-Hispanic/Latino; 48 Hispanic/Latino; 20 Two or more races, non-Hispanic/Latino), 110 international. Average age 31. 419 applicants, 39% accepted, 82 enrolled. In 2017, 84 master's, 27 doctorates, 38 other advanced degrees awarded. Terminal master's awarded for partial completion of doctoral program. *Degree requirements:* For master's and Certificate, comprehensive exam, thesis optional; for doctorate, comprehensive exam, thesis/dissertation, diagnostic exam, preliminary exam,

prospectus defense. *Entrance requirements:* For master's, doctorate, and Certificate, GRE General Test, minimum GPA of 3.0. Additional exam requirements/ recommendations for international students: Required—TOEFL (minimum score 550 paper-based, 80 iBT), IELTS (minimum score 6.5) or Michigan English Language Assessment Battery (minimum score 77). Application fee: $30. Electronic applications accepted. *Financial support:* Fellowships, research assistantships, teaching assistantships, scholarships/grants, tuition waivers (full and partial), and unspecified assistantships available. Financial award application deadline: 1/15; financial award applicants required to submit FAFSA. *Faculty research:* Learning and cognition, counseling and school psychology, instructional systems, measurement and evaluation. *Unit head:* Dr. Betsy Becker, Chair, 850-644-4592, Fax: 850-644-8776, E-mail: bbecker@fsu.edu. *Application contact:* Deborah Kelly, Academic Program Specialist, 850-644-8046, Fax: 850-644-8781, E-mail: dhamkelly@fsu.edu.

Fordham University, Graduate School of Education, Division of Psychological and Educational Services, New York, NY 10023. Offers counseling and personnel services (MSE); counseling psychology (PhD); school psychology (PhD). *Accreditation:* APA (one or more programs are accredited); NCATE. *Program availability:* Part-time, evening/weekend. Terminal master's awarded for partial completion of doctoral program. *Degree requirements:* For master's, comprehensive exam (for some programs); for doctorate, comprehensive exam (for some programs), thesis/dissertation. *Entrance requirements:* For doctorate, GRE General Test. Additional exam requirements/recommendations for international students: Required—TOEFL (minimum score 577 paper-based; 90 iBT), IELTS (minimum score 7). Electronic applications accepted.

Fort Hays State University, Graduate School, College of Arts and Sciences, Department of Psychology, Program in School Psychology, Hays, KS 67601-4099. Offers Ed S. *Accreditation:* NCATE. *Degree requirements:* For Ed S, comprehensive exam, thesis. *Entrance requirements:* Additional exam requirements/recommendations for international students: Required—TOEFL (minimum score 550 paper-based). Electronic applications accepted.

Francis Marion University, Graduate Programs, Department of Psychology, Florence, SC 29502-0547. Offers applied psychology (MS), including clinical/counseling psychology, school psychology; school psychology (SSP). *Program availability:* Part-time, evening/weekend. *Degree requirements:* For master's, internship. *Entrance requirements:* For master's, GRE General Test, official transcripts, two letters of recommendation. Additional exam requirements/recommendations for international students: Required—TOEFL (minimum score 550 paper-based; 79 iBT). *Faculty research:* Parenting and family relationships, child development, applied behavioral analysis, post-traumatic stress disorder, clinical psychology in adults.

Fresno Pacific University, Graduate Programs, School of Education, Division of Pupil Personnel Services, Program in School Psychology, Fresno, CA 93702-4709. Offers MA. *Program availability:* Part-time, evening/weekend. *Degree requirements:* For master's, thesis or alternative. *Entrance requirements:* Additional exam requirements/ recommendations for international students: Required—TOEFL (minimum score 550 paper-based). *Expenses:* Contact institution.

Gallaudet University, The Graduate School, Washington, DC 20002-3625. Offers American Sign Language/English bilingual early childhood deaf education: birth to 5 (Certificate); audiology (Au D); clinical psychology (PhD); deaf and hard of hearing infants, toddlers, and their families (Certificate); deaf education (MA, Ed S); deaf history (Certificate); deaf studies (Certificate); educating deaf students with disabilities (Certificate); education: teacher preparation (MA), including deaf education, early childhood education and deaf education, elementary education and deaf education, secondary education and deaf education; educational neuroscience (PhD); hearing, speech and language sciences (MS, PhD); international development (MA); interpretation (MA, PhD), including combined interpreting practice and research (MA), interpreting research (MA); linguistics (MA, PhD); mental health counseling (MA); peer mentoring (Certificate); public administration (MPA); school counseling (MA); school psychology (Psy S); sign language teaching (MA); social work (MSW); speech-language pathology (MS). *Program availability:* Part-time. Terminal master's awarded for partial completion of doctoral program. *Degree requirements:* For master's, comprehensive exam (for some programs), thesis optional; for doctorate, comprehensive exam, thesis/ dissertation. *Entrance requirements:* For master's and doctorate, GRE General Test or MAT, letters of recommendation, interviews, goals statement, American Sign Language proficiency interview, written English competency. Additional exam requirements/ recommendations for international students: Required—TOEFL. Electronic applications accepted. *Faculty research:* Signing math dictionaries, telecommunications access, cancer genetics, linguistics, visual language and visual learning, integrated quantum materials, deaf legal discourse, advance recruitment and retention in geosciences.

Gardner-Webb University, Graduate School, School of Psychology, Boiling Springs, NC 28017. Offers mental health counseling (MA); school counseling (MA). *Program availability:* Part-time, evening/weekend. *Faculty:* 5 full-time (4 women), 4 part-time/ adjunct (2 women). *Students:* 1 full-time (0 women), 88 part-time (76 women); includes 19 minority (13 Black or African American, non-Hispanic/Latino; 1 American Indian or Alaska Native, non-Hispanic/Latino; 3 Hispanic/Latino; 2 Two or more races, non-Hispanic/Latino). Average age 31. *Degree requirements:* For master's, comprehensive exam. *Entrance requirements:* For master's, GRE General Test, MAT, minimum GPA of 2.7. *Application deadline:* For fall admission, 7/1 priority date for domestic students. Applications are processed on a rolling basis. Electronic applications accepted. *Expenses:* Contact institution. *Financial support:* Unspecified assistantships available. *Unit head:* Dr. David Carscaddon, Chair, 704-406-4437, Fax: 704-406-4329, E-mail: dcarscaddon@gardner-webb.edu. *Application contact:* Office of Graduate Admissions, 877-498-4723, Fax: 704-406-3895, E-mail: gradinfo@gardner-webb.edu.

George Fox University, College of Education, Graduate Department of Counseling, Newberg, OR 97132-2697. Offers clinical mental health counseling (MA); marriage, couple and family counseling (MA, Certificate); school counseling (MA, Certificate); school psychology (Ed S). *Program availability:* Part-time. *Degree requirements:* For master's, clinical project. *Entrance requirements:* For master's, MAT or GRE, bachelor's degree from regionally-accredited college or university, minimum cumulative GPA of 3.0, 1 professional and 1 academic reference, resume, on-campus interview, official transcripts. Additional exam requirements/recommendations for international students: Required—TOEFL (minimum score 577 paper-based; 90 iBT), IELTS (minimum score 7). Electronic applications accepted. *Expenses:* Contact institution.

Georgian Court University, School of Arts and Sciences, Lakewood, NJ 08701-2697. Offers applied behavior analysis (MA); autism spectrum disorders (Certificate); clinical mental health counseling (MA); criminal justice and human rights (MS); holistic health studies (MA, Certificate); homeland security (Certificate); instructional technology (CPC); mercy spirituality (Certificate); parish business management (Certificate); professional counselor (Certificate); school psychology (MA, Certificate); theology (MA, Certificate). *Program availability:* Part-time, evening/weekend. *Faculty:* 18 full-time (11 women), 8 part-time/adjunct (4 women). *Students:* 100 full-time (86 women), 92 part-time (67 women); includes 34 minority (9 Black or African American, non-Hispanic/ Latino; 1 Asian, non-Hispanic/Latino; 20 Hispanic/Latino; 4 Two or more races, non-Hispanic/Latino), 2 international. Average age 34. 187 applicants, 56% accepted, 78 enrolled. In 2017, 58 master's, 20 other advanced degrees awarded. *Degree requirements:* For master's, comprehensive exam (for some programs), thesis (for some programs). *Entrance requirements:* For master's, GRE, GMAT, or NTE/PRAXIS, 3 letters of recommendation. Additional exam requirements/recommendations for international students: Required—TOEFL (minimum score 550 paper-based). *Application deadline:* For fall admission, 8/15 for domestic students, 5/1 for international students; for spring admission, 1/15 for domestic students, 10/1 for international students. Applications are processed on a rolling basis. Application fee: $40. Electronic applications accepted. *Expenses: Tuition:* Part-time $839 per credit. *Required fees:* $248 per semester. Tuition and fees vary according to campus/location and program. *Financial support:* Scholarships/grants, health care benefits, and unspecified assistantships available. Financial award application deadline: 4/15; financial award applicants required to submit FAFSA. *Unit head:* Dr. Mary Chinery, Dean, 732-987-2493, Fax: 732-987-2007, E-mail: mchinery@georgian.edu. *Application contact:* Patrick Givens, Director of Graduate and Professional Studies Admissions, 732-987-2736, Fax: 732-987-2000, E-mail: gps@georgian.edu.
Website: https://georgian.edu/academics/school-of-arts-sciences/

Georgia Southern University, Jack N. Averitt College of Graduate Studies, College of Education, Department of Leadership, Technology, and Human Development, Program in Counselor Education, Statesboro, GA 30460. Offers mental health counseling (M Ed); school counseling (M Ed). *Accreditation:* ACA; NCATE. *Program availability:* Part-time, evening/weekend. *Students:* 39 full-time (30 women), 9 part-time (6 women); includes 21 minority (20 Black or African American, non-Hispanic/Latino; 1 Asian, non-Hispanic/ Latino). Average age 28. 34 applicants, 53% accepted, 11 enrolled. In 2017, 22 master's awarded. *Degree requirements:* For master's, comprehensive exam, transition point assessments. *Entrance requirements:* For master's, minimum GPA of 2.5, letters of recommendation, interview. Additional exam requirements/recommendations for international students: Required—TOEFL (minimum score 550 paper-based; 80 iBT), IELTS (minimum score 6). *Application deadline:* For fall admission, 3/2 for domestic students, 3/15 for international students; for spring admission, 3/2 for domestic students, 10/1 for international students. Application fee: $50. Electronic applications accepted. *Expenses:* Tuition, state resident: full-time $4986; part-time $3324 per year. Tuition, nonresident: full-time $21,982; part-time $15,352 per year. *Required fees:* $2092; $1802 per credit hour. $901 per semester. Tuition and fees vary according to course load, campus/location and program. *Financial support:* In 2017–18, 25 students received support, including 3 research assistantships with full tuition reimbursements available (averaging $7,750 per year); career-related internships or fieldwork, scholarships/ grants, and unspecified assistantships also available. Financial award application deadline: 4/15; financial award applicants required to submit FAFSA. *Faculty research:* School counseling, test development, gender equity, career counseling, mental health counseling, best practices for preparing counselors. *Unit head:* Dr. Brandon Hunt, Program Director, 912-478-0502, Fax: 912-478-7104, E-mail: bhunt@georgiasouthern.edu. *Application contact:* Dr. Lydia Cross, Graduate Academic Services Center, 912-478-8664, E-mail: lcross@georgiasouthern.edu.
Website: http://coe.georgiasouthern.edu/coun/

Georgia Southern University, Jack N. Averitt College of Graduate Studies, College of Education, Department of Leadership, Technology, and Human Development, Program in School Psychology, Statesboro, GA 30460. Offers M Ed, Ed S. *Accreditation:* NCATE. *Program availability:* Part-time, evening/weekend. *Students:* 41 full-time (40 women), 24 part-time (21 women); includes 22 minority (20 Black or African American, non-Hispanic/Latino; 2 Hispanic/Latino). Average age 28. 21 applicants, 95% accepted, 13 enrolled. In 2017, 24 master's, 11 Ed Ss awarded. *Degree requirements:* For Ed S, comprehensive exam, field-based research project. *Entrance requirements:* For degree, minimum graduate GPA of 3.25, letters of reference, interview. Additional exam requirements/recommendations for international students: Required—TOEFL (minimum score 550 paper-based; 80 iBT), IELTS (minimum score 6). *Application deadline:* For fall admission, 4/10 for domestic students, 3/1 priority date for international students; for spring admission, 11/10 for domestic students, 10/1 for international students. Application fee: $50. Electronic applications accepted. *Expenses:* Tuition, state resident: full-time $4986; part-time $3324 per year. Tuition, nonresident: full-time $21,982; part-time $15,352 per year. *Required fees:* $2092; $1802 per credit hour. $901 per semester. Tuition and fees vary according to course load, campus/location and program. *Financial support:* In 2017–18, 30 students received support, including 3 fellowships with full tuition reimbursements available (averaging $7,750 per year); research assistantships with partial tuition reimbursements available, teaching assistantships with partial tuition reimbursements available, career-related internships or fieldwork, Federal Work-Study, scholarships/grants, tuition waivers (full), and unspecified assistantships also available. Support available to part-time students. Financial award application deadline: 4/15; financial award applicants required to submit FAFSA. *Faculty research:* K-12 online learning as it applies to school psychology, supervision, training in school psychology, cyber bullying. *Unit head:* Dr. Dawn Tysinger, Director, 912-478-5792, Fax: 912-478-7104, E-mail: dtysinger@georgiasouthern.edu. *Application contact:* Dr. Lydia Cross, Coordinator for Graduate Student Recruitment, 912-478-8664, E-mail: lcross@georgiasouthern.edu.
Website: http://coe.georgiasouthern.edu/espy/

Georgia State University, College of Education and Human Development, Department of Counseling and Psychological Services, Program in School Psychology, Atlanta, GA 30302-3083. Offers M Ed, PhD, Ed S. *Accreditation:* APA (one or more programs are accredited); NCATE. Terminal master's awarded for partial completion of doctoral program. *Entrance requirements:* For master's and doctorate, GRE, writing sample, resume, 3 letters of recommendation, goal statement, transcripts. Additional exam requirements/recommendations for international students: Required—TOEFL. Application fee: $50. Electronic applications accepted. *Expenses:* Tuition, state resident: full-time $7020. Tuition, nonresident: full-time $22,518. *Required fees:* $2128. Tuition and fees vary according to degree level and program. *Financial support:* Fellowships, research assistantships, teaching assistantships, career-related internships or fieldwork, institutionally sponsored loans, scholarships/grants, health care benefits, and unspecified assistantships available. Financial award application deadline: 4/1. *Faculty research:* School safety, school climate, and classroom management; alternative schools; children with disabilities; prevention of bullying, cyberbullying, and the commercial sexual exploitation of children; school psychology professional diversity. *Unit head:* Dr. Brian Dew, Chairperson, 404-413-8168, Fax: 404-413-8013, E-mail: bdew@gsu.edu. *Application contact:* Nancy Keita, Director, Office of Academic Assistance and Graduate Admissions, 404-413-8001, E-mail: nkeita@gsu.edu.
Website: http://education.gsu.edu/CPS/4514.html

Grand Valley State University, College of Education, Program in School Counseling, Allendale, MI 49401-9403. Offers M Ed. *Program availability:* Part-time. *Students:* 18 full-time (15 women), 21 part-time (19 women); includes 4 minority (1 Asian, non-Hispanic/Latino; 2 Hispanic/Latino; 1 Two or more races, non-Hispanic/Latino), 2 international. Average age 29. 29 applicants, 86% accepted, 16 enrolled. In 2017, 14 master's awarded. *Degree requirements:* For master's, project or thesis. *Entrance requirements:* For master's, GRE General Test or minimum GPA of 3.0; last 60 credits from regionally-accredited college/university; 3 letters of recommendation. Additional

exam requirements/recommendations for international students: Required—TOEFL (minimum iBT score of 80), IELTS (6.5), or Michigan English Language Assessment Battery (77). *Application deadline:* Applications are processed on a rolling basis. Application fee: $30. Electronic applications accepted. *Expenses:* $652 per credit hour. *Financial support:* In 2017–18, 7 students received support, including 4 fellowships, 2 research assistantships with full and partial tuition reimbursements available (averaging $8,000 per year); career-related internships or fieldwork and unspecified assistantships also available. *Faculty research:* Multicultural issues in counselor education, use of technology in counseling programs. *Unit head:* Dr. Shawn Bultsma, Program Director, 616-331-6648, E-mail: bultsmas@gvsu.edu. *Application contact:* Dr. Judy Williams, Graduate Program Director, 616-331-6492, Fax: 616-331-6422, E-mail: willjud@gvsu.edu.

Grand Valley State University, College of Liberal Arts and Sciences, Program in School Psychology, Allendale, MI 49401-9403. Offers MS, Psy S. *Program availability:* Part-time. *Faculty:* 6 full-time (all women). *Students:* 25 full-time (21 women), 17 part-time (all women); includes 4 minority (2 Black or African American, non-Hispanic/Latino; 2 Two or more races, non-Hispanic/Latino). Average age 28. 33 applicants, 48% accepted, 14 enrolled. In 2017, 10 master's, 10 other advanced degrees awarded. *Degree requirements:* For master's, project, internship. *Entrance requirements:* For master's, GRE, bachelor's degree in psychology, special education, or related field with minimum GPA of 3.0; completion of prerequisite courses in child development, statistics, and research methods; professional vitae or resume; 3 letters of recommendation; personal statement. Additional exam requirements/recommendations for international students: Required—TOEFL (minimum iBT score of 80), IELTS (6.5), or Michigan English Language Assessment Battery (77). *Application deadline:* For fall admission, 12/15 for domestic and international students. Applications are processed on a rolling basis. Application fee: $30. Electronic applications accepted. *Expenses:* $652 per credit hour. *Financial support:* In 2017–18, 11 students received support, including 2 fellowships, 1 research assistantship with full and partial tuition reimbursement available (averaging $8,000 per year); unspecified assistantships also available. *Unit head:* Dr. Robert Hendersen, Director, 616-331-2195, Fax: 616-331-2480, E-mail: hendersr@gvsu.edu. *Application contact:* Dr. Amy Campbell, Graduate Program Director, 616-331-2409, Fax: 616-331-2480, E-mail: campbeam@gvsu.edu. Website: http://www.gvsu.edu/grad/schoolpsy/

Heidelberg University, Master of Arts in Counseling Program, Tiffin, OH 44883-2462. Offers clinical mental health counseling (MA); school counseling (MA). *Accreditation:* ACA. *Program availability:* Part-time, evening/weekend. *Students:* 19 full-time (15 women), 25 part-time (19 women). In 2017, 10 master's awarded. *Degree requirements:* For master's, counseling practicum, internship. *Entrance requirements:* For master's, bachelor's degree with minimum GPA of 2.9; 12 hours of coursework in behavioral sciences; 3 letters of recommendation; 2-3 page goal statement. Additional exam requirements/recommendations for international students: Required—TOEFL (minimum score 550 paper-based, 79 iBT) or IELTS (minimum score 6.5). *Application deadline:* Applications are processed on a rolling basis. Application fee: $0. Electronic applications accepted. *Expenses:* $525 per hour. *Financial support:* Scholarships/grants and unspecified assistantships available. Financial award applicants required to submit FAFSA. *Unit head:* Dr. Marjorie Shavers, Director of Graduate Studies in Counseling, 419-448-2308, E-mail: mshavers@heidelberg.edu. *Application contact:* Katie Zeyen, Graduate Admissions Coordinator, 419-448-2602, Fax: 419-448-2565, E-mail: kzeyen@heidelberg.edu. Website: https://www.heidelberg.edu/academics/programs/master-of-counseling

Hofstra University, College of Liberal Arts and Sciences, Programs in Psychology, Hempstead, NY 11549. Offers applied organizational psychology (PhD); clinical psychology (PhD); industrial/organizational psychology (MA); school-community psychology (Psy D). *Accreditation:* APA. *Program availability:* Part-time, evening/weekend. *Students:* 199 full-time (130 women), 24 part-time (20 women); includes 44 minority (5 Black or African American, non-Hispanic/Latino; 12 Asian, non-Hispanic/Latino; 25 Hispanic/Latino; 1 Native Hawaiian or other Pacific Islander, non-Hispanic/Latino; 1 Two or more races, non-Hispanic/Latino), 19 international. Average age 27. 314 applicants, 45% accepted, 60 enrolled. In 2017, 47 master's, 25 doctorates awarded. *Degree requirements:* For master's, comprehensive exam, thesis optional, internship, minimum GPA of 3.0; for doctorate, comprehensive exam, thesis/dissertation, 1st year qualifying examination, 2nd year research project, successful practicum/externship placements, written presentation and successful oral defense of dissertation, completion of full-time internship. *Entrance requirements:* For master's, GRE General Test, minimum GPA of 3.0, essay, interview; for doctorate, GRE General Test, GRE Subject Test (psychology), 3 letters of recommendation, interview, essay, curriculum vitae. Additional exam requirements/recommendations for international students: Required—TOEFL (minimum score 550 paper-based; 80 iBT). *Application deadline:* For fall admission, 12/31 for domestic and international students. Application fee: $75. Electronic applications accepted. *Expenses: Tuition:* Full-time $1292. *Required fees:* $970. Tuition and fees vary according to program. *Financial support:* In 2017–18, 131 students received support, including 126 fellowships with full and partial tuition reimbursements available (averaging $7,840 per year), 4 research assistantships with full and partial tuition reimbursements available (averaging $5,974 per year); career-related internships or fieldwork, Federal Work-Study, institutionally sponsored loans, scholarships/grants, traineeships, tuition waivers (full and partial), and unspecified assistantships also available. Support available to part-time students. Financial award applicants required to submit FAFSA. *Faculty research:* Coping with job stress; schizophrenia; positive clinical psychology; treatments (including virtual reality based) for phobias, trauma, and PTSD; scientific reasoning in children and adults. *Unit head:* Dr. Craig Johnson, Chairperson, 516-463-5636, E-mail: craig.a.johnson@hofstra.edu. *Application contact:* Sunil Samuel, Assistant Vice President of Admissions, 516-463-4723, Fax: 516-463-4664, E-mail: graduateadmission@hofstra.edu. Website: http://www.hofstra.edu/hclas

Hood College, Graduate School, Program in Counseling, Frederick, MD 21701-8575. Offers clinical mental health counseling (MS); school counseling (MS). *Program availability:* Part-time, evening/weekend. *Faculty:* 2 full-time (1 woman), 2 part-time/adjunct (both women). *Students:* 36 full-time (32 women), 26 part-time (24 women); includes 12 minority (4 Black or African American, non-Hispanic/Latino; 1 American Indian or Alaska Native, non-Hispanic/Latino; 4 Hispanic/Latino; 3 Two or more races, non-Hispanic/Latino), 1 international. Average age 31. 27 applicants, 85% accepted, 18 enrolled. In 2017, 3 master's awarded. *Degree requirements:* For master's, practicum, internship. *Entrance requirements:* For master's, minimum GPA of 3.0, personal statement, resume, two letters of recommendation. Additional exam requirements/recommendations for international students: Required—TOEFL (minimum score 575 paper-based; 89 iBT), IELTS (minimum score 6.5). *Application deadline:* For fall admission, 6/15 for domestic and international students; for winter admission, 11/15 for domestic and international students. Application fee: $35. Electronic applications accepted. *Expenses:* $660 per credit plus $110 comprehensive fee per semester. *Financial support:* Research assistantships with full tuition reimbursements, tuition waivers (partial), and unspecified assistantships available. Financial award applicants required to submit FAFSA. *Unit head:* Dr. April M. Boulton, Dean of the Graduate

School, 301-696-3600, E-mail: gofurther@hood.edu. *Application contact:* Jan Marcus, Assistant Director of Graduate Admissions, 301-696-3600, E-mail: gofurther@hood.edu.

Houston Baptist University, College of Education and Behavioral Sciences, Program in Psychology, Houston, TX 77074-3298. Offers school psychology (MAP). *Program availability:* Part-time, evening/weekend. *Students:* 47 full-time (42 women), 53 part-time (46 women); includes 70 minority (36 Black or African American, non-Hispanic/Latino; 10 Asian, non-Hispanic/Latino; 23 Hispanic/Latino; 1 Two or more races, non-Hispanic/Latino), 4 international. Average age 32. 129 applicants, 25% accepted, 16 enrolled. In 2017, 23 master's awarded. *Degree requirements:* For master's, comprehensive exam, thesis. *Entrance requirements:* For master's, GRE (waived with a cumulative GPA of 3.0 or higher), minimum GPA of 2.5, two recommendations, resume, bachelor's degree conferred transcript. Additional exam requirements/recommendations for international students: Required—TOEFL (minimum score 80 iBT), IELTS (minimum score 6.5). *Application deadline:* For fall admission, 8/1 for domestic students, 6/1 for international students; for spring admission, 1/1 for domestic students, 11/1 for international students; for summer admission, 5/1 for domestic students, 3/1 for international students. Applications are processed on a rolling basis. Application fee: $0 ($100 for international students). Electronic applications accepted. Application fee is waived when completed online. *Expenses:* $20,350 tuition; $4,500 fees (general, technology and parking). *Financial support:* In 2017–18, 11 students received support. Federal Work-Study and scholarships/grants available. Support available to part-time students. Financial award application deadline: 4/1; financial award applicants required to submit FAFSA. *Faculty research:* Drug and alcohol abuse in relation to delinquency, mental health and school factors, chronic stress, coping strategies. *Unit head:* Dr. Renata Nero, Chair, 281-649-3171, Fax: 281-649-3361, E-mail: rnero@hbu.edu. *Application contact:* Victoria Humphreys, Administrative Assistant to the Dean, 281-649-3131, E-mail: vhumphreys@hbu.edu. Website: http://www.hbu.edu/MAP

Howard University, School of Education, Department of Human Development and Psychoeducational Studies, Program in School Psychology, Washington, DC 20059-0002. Offers M Ed, PhD. *Accreditation:* NCATE. *Students:* Average age 31. 61 applicants, 69% accepted, 36 enrolled. In 2017, 5 master's awarded. *Degree requirements:* For doctorate, one foreign language, comprehensive exam, thesis/dissertation, expository writing exam, internship. *Entrance requirements:* For doctorate, GRE General Test, minimum GPA of 3.4. Additional exam requirements/recommendations for international students: Required—TOEFL (minimum score 550 paper-based; 79 iBT). *Application deadline:* For fall admission, 2/15 priority date for domestic students; for spring admission, 11/1 for domestic students. Applications are processed on a rolling basis. Application fee: $45. Electronic applications accepted. *Financial support:* In 2017–18, 5 students received support, including 5 fellowships with full and partial tuition reimbursements available (averaging $15,000 per year); career-related internships or fieldwork, Federal Work-Study, institutionally sponsored loans, scholarships/grants, tuition waivers (full and partial), and unspecified assistantships also available. Financial award application deadline: 3/15; financial award applicants required to submit FAFSA. *Faculty research:* Psychopathology, maltreatment abuse and neglect, children exposed to political unrest, family conflict and community violence. *Unit head:* Dr. Gregory Reed, Associate Professor/Coordinator, 202-806-5334, Fax: 202-806-7018, E-mail: g_reed@howard.edu. *Application contact:* Georgina Jarrett, Administration Assistant, Department of Human Development and Psychoeducational Studies, 202-806-7351, Fax: 202-806-5205, E-mail: georgina.jarrett@howard.edu.

Humboldt State University, Academic Programs, College of Professional Studies, Department of Psychology, Arcata, CA 95521-8299. Offers psychology (MA), including biological psychology, counseling, developmental psychopathology, school psychology, social and environmental psychology. *Degree requirements:* For master's, thesis. *Entrance requirements:* For master's, appropriate bachelor's degree, minimum GPA of 2.5. Additional exam requirements/recommendations for international students: Required—TOEFL (minimum score 500 paper-based). *Faculty research:* School psychology, counseling, eating disorders, mood induction, depression.

Husson University, Graduate Programs in Counseling and Human Relations, Bangor, ME 04401-2999. Offers clinical mental health counseling (MS); human relations (MS); school counseling (MS). *Accreditation:* ACA. *Program availability:* Part-time, evening/weekend. *Faculty:* 3 full-time (2 women), 5 part-time/adjunct (all women). *Students:* 21 full-time (18 women), 44 part-time (39 women); includes 2 minority (1 Black or African American, non-Hispanic/Latino; 1 Hispanic/Latino), 1 international. Average age 31. 49 applicants, 41% accepted, 13 enrolled. In 2017, 17 master's awarded. *Degree requirements:* For master's, comprehensive exam (for some programs), thesis optional. *Entrance requirements:* For master's, BS with minimum GPA of 3.0, letters of recommendation, interview. Additional exam requirements/recommendations for international students: Required—TOEFL (minimum score 550 paper-based; 80 iBT), IELTS (minimum score 6.5). *Application deadline:* For fall admission, 2/1 for domestic students. Application fee: $50. Electronic applications accepted. *Expenses:* $577 per credit; fees depend on number of credits. *Financial support:* In 2017–18, 2 students received support. Federal Work-Study, scholarships/grants, and unspecified assistantships available. Financial award application deadline: 4/15; financial award applicants required to submit FAFSA. *Faculty research:* Challenges and rewards of counseling practice in rural, small town and neighborhood settings. *Unit head:* Dr. Deborah Drew, Director, Graduate Counseling Programs, 207-992-4912, Fax: 207-992-4952, E-mail: drewd@husson.edu. *Application contact:* Kristen Card, Director of Graduate Admissions, 207-404-5660, Fax: 207-941-7935, E-mail: cardk@husson.edu. Website: http://www.husson.edu/college-of-health-and-education/school-of-education/graduate-programs/

Idaho State University, Office of Graduate Studies, College of Education, Department of School Psychology and Educational Leadership, Pocatello, ID 83209-8059. Offers educational administration (M Ed, 6th Year Certificate, Ed S); educational leadership (Ed D), including higher education administration, K-12 school administration; school psychology (M Ed, Ed S). *Program availability:* Part-time. *Degree requirements:* For master's, comprehensive exam, thesis optional, internship, oral exam or deferred thesis; for doctorate, comprehensive exam, thesis/dissertation, written exam; for other advanced degree, comprehensive exam, thesis (for some programs), written and oral exam. *Entrance requirements:* For master's, MAT, bachelor's degree, minimum GPA of 3.0, 1 year of training experience; for doctorate, GRE General Test or MAT, minimum GPA of 3.0 (undergraduate), 3.5 (graduate); departmental interview; for other advanced degree, GRE General Test, minimum GPA of 3.0, master's degree. Additional exam requirements/recommendations for international students: Required—TOEFL (minimum score 550 paper-based; 80 iBT). Electronic applications accepted. *Faculty research:* Educational leadership, gender issues in education and sport, staff development.

Idaho State University, Office of Graduate Studies, School of Health Professions, Department of Counseling, Pocatello, ID 83209-8120. Offers counseling (M Coun, Ed S), including marriage and family counseling (M Coun), mental health counseling (M Coun), school counseling (M Coun), student affairs and college counseling (M Coun); counselor education and counseling (PhD). *Accreditation:* ACA (one or more programs are accredited). *Program availability:* Part-time. *Degree requirements:* For master's, comprehensive exam, thesis, 4 semesters resident graduate study, practicum/

internship; for doctorate, comprehensive exam, thesis/dissertation, 3 semesters internship, 4 consecutive semesters doctoral-level study on campus; for Ed S, comprehensive exam, thesis, case studies, oral exam. *Entrance requirements:* For master's, GRE General Test, MAT, minimum GPA of 3.0, bachelors degree, interview, 3 letters of recommendation; for doctorate, GRE General Test, MAT, minimum graduate GPA of 3.0, resume, interview, counseling license, master's degree; for Ed S, GRE General Test, minimum graduate GPA of 3.0, master's degree in counseling, 3 letters of recommendation, 2 years work experience. Additional exam requirements/recommendations for international students: Required—TOEFL (minimum score 600 paper-based; 80 iBT). Electronic applications accepted. *Faculty research:* Group counseling, multicultural counseling, family counseling, child therapy, supervision.

Illinois State University, Graduate School, College of Arts and Sciences, Department of Psychology, Program in School Psychology, Normal, IL 61790. Offers PhD, SSP. *Accreditation:* APA (one or more programs are accredited); NCATE (one or more programs are accredited). *Degree requirements:* For doctorate, variable foreign language requirement, thesis/dissertation, 2 terms of residency, internship, practicum. *Entrance requirements:* For doctorate, GRE General Test.

Immaculata University, College of Graduate Studies, Department of Psychology, Immaculata, PA 19345. Offers clinical mental health counseling (MA); clinical psychology (Psy D); forensic psychology (Graduate Certificate); integrative psychotherapy (Graduate Certificate); neuropsychology (Graduate Certificate); psychodynamic psychotherapy (Graduate Certificate); psychological testing (Graduate Certificate); school counseling (MA, Graduate Certificate); school psychology (MA). *Accreditation:* APA. *Program availability:* Part-time, evening/weekend. Terminal master's awarded for partial completion of doctoral program. *Degree requirements:* For master's, comprehensive exam, thesis optional; for doctorate, comprehensive exam, thesis/dissertation. *Entrance requirements:* For master's, GRE General Test or MAT, minimum GPA of 3.0; for doctorate, GRE General Test or MAT, minimum GPA of 3.5. Additional exam requirements/recommendations for international students: Required—TOEFL, IELTS. Electronic applications accepted. *Faculty research:* Supervision ethics, psychology of teaching, gender.

Indiana State University, College of Graduate and Professional Studies, Bayh College of Education, Department of Communication Disorders and Counseling, School, and Educational Psychology, Terre Haute, IN 47809. Offers clinical mental health counseling (MS); communication disorders (MS); school counseling (M Ed); school psychology (PhD, Ed S); MA/MS. *Accreditation:* ACA; ASHA; NCATE. *Program availability:* Part-time, evening/weekend. *Degree requirements:* For master's, thesis optional; for doctorate, thesis/dissertation, research tools proficiency tests. *Entrance requirements:* For master's, GRE General Test or MAT, minimum undergraduate GPA of 2.75; for doctorate, GRE General Test, master's degree, minimum undergraduate GPA of 3.5. Electronic applications accepted. *Faculty research:* Vocational development supervision.

Indiana University Bloomington, School of Education, Department of Counseling and Educational Psychology, Bloomington, IN 47405-1006. Offers counseling (MS, PhD, Ed S); counselor education (MS, Ed S); educational psychology (MS, PhD); inquiry methodology (PhD); learning and developmental sciences (MS, PhD); school psychology (PhD, Ed S). *Accreditation:* ACA (one or more programs are accredited); APA (one or more programs are accredited); NCATE. Terminal master's awarded for partial completion of doctoral program. *Degree requirements:* For master's, thesis optional; for doctorate, thesis/dissertation; for Ed S, comprehensive exam or project. *Entrance requirements:* For master's, doctorate, and Ed S, GRE General Test. Additional exam requirements/recommendations for international students: Required—TOEFL. Electronic applications accepted. *Faculty research:* Counseling psychology, inquiry methodology, school psychology, learning sciences, human development, educational psychology.

Indiana University of Pennsylvania, School of Graduate Studies and Research, College of Education and Communications, Department of Educational and School Psychology, Program in School Psychology, Indiana, PA 15705. Offers D Ed, Certificate. *Accreditation:* NCATE. *Program availability:* Part-time, evening/weekend. *Faculty:* 7 full-time (3 women). *Students:* 18 full-time (14 women), 44 part-time (32 women); includes 5 minority (3 Black or African American, non-Hispanic/Latino; 1 Hispanic/Latino; 1 Two or more races, non-Hispanic/Latino). Average age 28. 26 applicants, 54% accepted, 7 enrolled. In 2017, 5 doctorates, 11 Certificates awarded. *Degree requirements:* For doctorate, comprehensive exam, thesis/dissertation. *Entrance requirements:* For doctorate, GRE General Test, PRAXIS II School Psychology Exam, 2 letters of recommendation. Additional exam requirements/recommendations for international students: Required—TOEFL (minimum score 540 paper-based). *Application deadline:* For fall admission, 2/1 priority date for domestic students. Applications are processed on a rolling basis. Application fee: $50. Electronic applications accepted. *Expenses:* Tuition, state resident: full-time $12,000; part-time $500 per credit. Tuition, nonresident: full-time $18,000; part-time $750 per credit. *Required fees:* $4073; $165.55 per credit. $64 per term. *Financial support:* In 2017–18, 7 fellowships with full tuition reimbursements (averaging $607 per year), 3 teaching assistantships with partial tuition reimbursements (averaging $11,652 per year) were awarded; research assistantships with tuition reimbursements, career-related internships or fieldwork, Federal Work-Study, scholarships/grants, and unspecified assistantships also available. Support available to part-time students. Financial award application deadline: 4/15; financial award applicants required to submit FAFSA. *Unit head:* Dr. Courtney McLaughlin, Graduate Coordinator, 724-357-2299, E-mail: cmc@iup.edu.
Website: http://www.iup.edu/schoolpsychology/grad/school-psychology-ded/default.aspx

Indiana University South Bend, School of Education, South Bend, IN 46615. Offers addiction counseling (MS Ed); alcohol and drug counseling (Graduate Certificate); clinical mental health counseling (MS Ed); educational leadership (MS Ed); elementary education (MS Ed); marriage, couple, and family counseling (MS Ed); school counseling (MS Ed); secondary education (MS Ed); special education (MAT, MS Ed), including intense intervention (MS Ed), mild intervention (MS Ed). *Accreditation:* NCATE. *Program availability:* Part-time, evening/weekend. *Degree requirements:* For master's, thesis or alternative, exit project. *Entrance requirements:* For master's, letters of recommendation, GRE or minimum GPA of 3.0. Additional exam requirements/recommendations for international students: Required—TOEFL. Electronic applications accepted. *Expenses:* Contact institution. *Faculty research:* Professional dispositions, early childhood literacy, online learning, program assessments, problem-based learning.

Inter American University of Puerto Rico, Metropolitan Campus, Graduate Programs, Program in Psychology, San Juan, PR 00919-1293. Offers counseling psychology (MA, PhD); industrial/organizational psychology (MA, PhD); labor relations (MA); school psychology (MA, PhD). *Degree requirements:* For master's, comprehensive exam. *Entrance requirements:* For master's, GRE or EXADEP, interview. Electronic applications accepted.

Inter American University of Puerto Rico, San Germán Campus, Graduate Studies Center, Program in Psychology, San Germán, PR 00683-5008. Offers counseling psychology (MA, PhD); school psychology (MA, PhD). *Program availability:* Part-time, evening/weekend. *Degree requirements:* For master's, comprehensive exam, thesis; for doctorate, comprehensive exam, thesis/dissertation. *Entrance requirements:* For master's, GRE General Test or EXADEP, minimum GPA of 3.0; for doctorate, GRE, EXADEP or MAT, minimum GPA of 3.0.

Iona College, School of Arts and Science, Department of Psychology, New Rochelle, NY 10801-1890. Offers general-experimental psychology (MA); human resources (Certificate); industrial-organizational psychology (MA); mental health counseling (MA); organizational behavior (Certificate); psychology (MA); school psychology (MA). *Program availability:* Part-time. *Faculty:* 9 full-time (5 women), 7 part-time/adjunct (5 women). *Students:* 75 full-time (55 women), 37 part-time (24 women); includes 46 minority (9 Black or African American, non-Hispanic/Latino; 2 Asian, non-Hispanic/Latino; 34 Hispanic/Latino; 1 Two or more races, non-Hispanic/Latino), 1 international. Average age 25. 88 applicants, 88% accepted, 40 enrolled. In 2017, 23 master's awarded. *Degree requirements:* For master's, thesis (for some programs), literature review (for some programs). *Entrance requirements:* For master's, BA in psychology including 3 credits each in psychology statistics and experimental research methods, or 9 credits in psychology including 3 credits each in psychology statistics, psychology research methods and upper-level coursework. Additional exam requirements/recommendations for international students: Required—TOEFL (minimum score 550 paper-based), IELTS (minimum score 6.5). *Application deadline:* For fall admission, 8/15 for domestic students, 5/1 for international students; for spring admission, 1/15 for domestic students, 9/1 for international students. Applications are processed on a rolling basis. Electronic applications accepted. Tuition and fees vary according to program. *Financial support:* In 2017–18, 27 students received support. Research assistantships with partial tuition reimbursements available, tuition waivers (partial), and unspecified assistantships available. Support available to part-time students. Financial award application deadline: 4/15; financial award applicants required to submit FAFSA. *Faculty research:* Non-suicidal self-injury, trauma response, performance appraisal and evaluation, diversity infusion, assessment and treatment of sexual offenders. *Unit head:* Patricia Oswald, PhD, Chair, 914-633-2374, E-mail: poswald@iona.edu. *Application contact:* Katelyn Brunck, Assistant Director, Graduate Admissions, 914-633-2451, Fax: 914-633-2277, E-mail: kbrunck@iona.edu.
Website: http://www.iona.edu/Academics/School-of-Arts-Science/Departments/Psychology/Graduate-Programs.aspx

Jackson State University, Graduate School, College of Education and Human Development, Department of Counseling, Rehabilitation and Psychometric Services, Jackson, MS 39217. Offers clinical mental health (MS); rehabilitation counseling (MS); school counseling (MS Ed). *Accreditation:* ACA; CORE (one or more programs are accredited); NCATE. *Program availability:* Part-time, evening/weekend, 100% online, blended/hybrid learning. *Degree requirements:* For master's, comprehensive exam, thesis. *Entrance requirements:* For master's, GRE General Test. Additional exam requirements/recommendations for international students: Required—TOEFL (minimum score 520 paper-based; 67 iBT). Electronic applications accepted. *Expenses:* Contact institution.

James Madison University, The Graduate School, College of Health and Behavioral Studies, Program in Combined-Integrated Clinical and School Psychology, Harrisonburg, VA 22801. Offers Psy D. *Program availability:* Part-time, evening/weekend. *Students:* 22 full-time (18 women), 3 part-time (1 woman); includes 4 minority (2 Black or African American, non-Hispanic/Latino; 2 Hispanic/Latino), 1 international. Average age 30. In 2017, 5 doctorates awarded. Application fee: $55. Electronic applications accepted. *Expenses:* Tuition, state resident: full-time $10,512; part-time $438 per credit hour. Tuition, nonresident: full-time $28,358; part-time $1162 per credit hour. *Required fees:* $1128. *Financial support:* In 2017–18, 17 students received support. Fellowships, teaching assistantships, Federal Work-Study, unspecified assistantships, and 17 doctoral assistantships (stipend varies) available. Financial award application deadline: 3/1; financial award applicants required to submit FAFSA. *Unit head:* Dr. Gregg R. Henriques, Graduate Program Director, 540-568-7857, E-mail: henrigg@jmu.edu. *Application contact:* Lynette D. Michael, Director of Graduate Admissions, 540-568-6131 Ext. 6395, Fax: 540-568-7860, E-mail: michaeld@jmu.edu.
Website: http://www.psyc.jmu.edu/cipsyd/

James Madison University, The Graduate School, College of Health and Behavioral Studies, Program in School Psychology, Harrisonburg, VA 22801. Offers MA, Ed S. *Accreditation:* APA (one or more programs are accredited); NCATE (one or more programs are accredited). *Program availability:* Part-time, evening/weekend. *Students:* 20 full-time (16 women), 7 part-time (all women); includes 4 minority (3 Black or African American, non-Hispanic/Latino; 1 Two or more races, non-Hispanic/Latino), 1 international. Average age 30. In 2017, 8 master's, 9 other advanced degrees awarded. Application fee: $55. Electronic applications accepted. *Expenses:* Tuition, state resident: full-time $10,512; part-time $438 per credit hour. Tuition, nonresident: full-time $28,358; part-time $1162 per credit hour. *Required fees:* $1128. *Financial support:* In 2017–18, 17 students received support, including 1 teaching assistantship with full tuition reimbursement available (averaging $9,284 per year); fellowships, career-related internships or fieldwork, Federal Work-Study, and 16 assistantships (averaging $7911) also available. Financial award application deadline: 3/1; financial award applicants required to submit FAFSA. *Unit head:* Dr. Tammy D. Gilligan, Graduate Program Director, 540-568-6564, E-mail: gilligtd@jmu.edu. *Application contact:* Lynette D. Michael, Director of Graduate Admissions, 540-568-6131 Ext. 6395, Fax: 540-568-7860, E-mail: michaeld@jmu.edu.
Website: http://psyc.jmu.edu/school/

Kean University, Nathan Weiss Graduate College, Doctorate Program in Combined School and Clinical Psychology, Union, NJ 07083. Offers Psy D. *Program availability:* Part-time. *Faculty:* 7 full-time (4 women). *Students:* 42 full-time (33 women), 9 part-time (7 women); includes 18 minority (2 Black or African American, non-Hispanic/Latino; 5 Asian, non-Hispanic/Latino; 10 Hispanic/Latino; 1 Two or more races, non-Hispanic/Latino). Average age 27. 66 applicants, 50% accepted, 12 enrolled. In 2017, 9 doctorates awarded. *Degree requirements:* For doctorate, comprehensive exam, thesis/dissertation, externship. *Entrance requirements:* For doctorate, GRE General Test, GRE Subject Test in psychology (taken within last 5 years), minimum undergraduate GPA of 3.3, graduate 3.5; 3 letters of recommendation; personal interview; prerequisite coursework in theories of personality, abnormal psychology, tests and measurements, statistics, and experimental psychology; personal statement. Additional exam requirements/recommendations for international students: Required—TOEFL (minimum score 550 paper-based; 79 iBT), IELTS (minimum score 6.5). *Application deadline:* For fall admission, 1/1 for domestic and international students. Applications are processed on a rolling basis. Application fee: $75. Electronic applications accepted. *Expenses:* Contact institution. *Financial support:* Scholarships/grants and unspecified assistantships available. Financial award applicants required to submit FAFSA. *Unit head:* Dr. Jennifer Block-Lerner, Program Coordinator, 908-737-5864, E-mail: jlerner@kean.edu. *Application contact:* Pedro Lopes, Admissions Counselor, 908-737-7100, E-mail: gradadmissions@kean.edu.
Website: http://grad.kean.edu/doctoral-programs/combined-school-and-clinical-psychology

Kean University, Nathan Weiss Graduate College, Program in School Psychology, Union, NJ 07083. Offers Diploma. *Accreditation:* APA. *Program availability:* Part-time. *Faculty:* 7 full-time (4 women). *Students:* 24 full-time (22 women), 11 part-time (10 women); includes 9 minority (2 Asian, non-Hispanic/Latino; 7 Hispanic/Latino). Average age 24. 32 applicants, 69% accepted, 14 enrolled. In 2017, 11 Diplomas awarded. *Degree requirements:* For Diploma, comprehensive exam, practicum, externship. *Entrance requirements:* For degree, GRE General Test, minimum GPA of 3.0, interview, 3 letters of recommendation, prerequisites in psychology, official transcripts from all institutions attended, resume. Additional exam requirements/recommendations for international students: Required—TOEFL (minimum score 550 paper-based; 79 iBT), IELTS. *Application deadline:* For fall admission, 2/5 for domestic and international students. Application fee: $75. Electronic applications accepted. *Expenses:* Tuition, state resident: full-time $13,419; part-time $653 per credit. Tuition, nonresident: full-time $18,188; part-time $801 per credit. *Required fees:* $3382; $154 per credit. Tuition and fees vary according to course level, course load, degree level and program. *Financial support:* Scholarships/grants and unspecified assistantships available. Financial award applicants required to submit FAFSA. *Unit head:* Dr. Adrienne Garro, Program Coordinator, 908-737-5863, E-mail: agarro@kean.edu. *Application contact:* Pedro Lopes, Admissions Counselor, 908-737-7100, E-mail: gradadmissions@kean.edu. Website: http://grad.kean.edu/professional-diploma-programs/school-psychology

Keene State College, School of Professional and Graduate Studies, Keene, NH 03435. Offers curriculum and instruction (M Ed); education leadership (PMC); educational leadership (M Ed); school counselor (M Ed, PMC); special education (M Ed). *Accreditation:* NCATE. *Program availability:* Part-time, evening/weekend. *Faculty:* 6 full-time (3 women), 7 part-time/adjunct (2 women). *Students:* 20 full-time (14 women), 42 part-time (20 women); includes 2 minority (1 Black or African American, non-Hispanic/Latino; 1 Asian, non-Hispanic/Latino), 1 international. Average age 31. 33 applicants, 58% accepted, 17 enrolled. In 2017, 39 master's awarded. *Degree requirements:* For master's, thesis (for some programs). *Entrance requirements:* For master's, PRAXIS I, 3 references; official transcripts; minimum GPA of 2.5; interview; essay; teacher/educator certificate; work/internship experience. Additional exam requirements/recommendations for international students: Required—TOEFL (minimum score 550 paper-based; 61 iBT). *Application deadline:* For fall admission, 4/1 for domestic and international students; for spring admission, 11/1 for domestic and international students; for summer admission, 3/1 for domestic and international students. Applications are processed on a rolling basis. Application fee: $50. Electronic applications accepted. *Expenses:* Tuition, state resident: full-time $9360; part-time $520 per credit. Tuition, nonresident: full-time $10,260; part-time $570 per credit. *Required fees:* $1908; $106 per credit. Tuition and fees vary according to course load. *Financial support:* In 2017–18, 19 students received support. Career-related internships or fieldwork, Federal Work-Study, institutionally sponsored loans, scholarships/grants, and unspecified assistantships available. Support available to part-time students. Financial award application deadline: 3/1; financial award applicants required to submit FAFSA. *Unit head:* Dr. Karrie Kalich, Dean of Professional and Graduate Studies, 603-358-2885, E-mail: kkalich@keene.edu. *Application contact:* Carl Ditkoff, Graduate Program Assistant, 603-358-2497, E-mail: kscgraduatestudies@keene.edu. Website: http://www.keene.edu/academics/graduate/

Kent State University, College of Education, Health and Human Services, School of Lifespan Development and Educational Sciences, Program in School Psychology, Kent, OH 44242-0001. Offers M Ed, PhD, Ed S. *Accreditation:* APA; NCATE. *Degree requirements:* For doctorate, comprehensive exam, thesis/dissertation. *Entrance requirements:* For master's, doctorate, and Ed S, GRE General Test, 2 letters of reference, goals statement, moral character form, sample of written work, resume, interview. Additional exam requirements/recommendations for international students: Required—TOEFL (minimum score 550 paper-based; 80 iBT). Electronic applications accepted. *Expenses:* Tuition, state resident: full-time $11,310; part-time $515 per credit hour. Tuition, nonresident: full-time $20,396; part-time $928 per credit hour. *International tuition:* $18,544 full-time. *Faculty research:* Special education policy and practice, treatment fidelity, school-based consultation.

La Sierra University, School of Education, Department of School Psychology and Counseling, Riverside, CA 92505. Offers counseling (MA); educational psychology (Ed S); school psychology (Ed S). *Program availability:* Part-time, evening/weekend. *Degree requirements:* For master's, thesis optional; for Ed S, practicum (educational psychology). *Entrance requirements:* For master's, California Basic Educational Skills Test, NTE, minimum GPA of 3.0; for Ed S, minimum GPA of 3.3. *Faculty research:* Equivalent score scales, self perception.

Lehigh University, College of Education, Program in School Psychology, Bethlehem, PA 18015. Offers PhD, Ed S. *Accreditation:* APA (one or more programs are accredited). *Faculty:* 6 full-time (5 women), 1 part-time/adjunct (0 women). *Students:* 35 full-time (34 women), 5 part-time (4 women); includes 4 minority (2 Black or African American, non-Hispanic/Latino; 1 Asian, non-Hispanic/Latino; 1 Hispanic/Latino), 1 international. Average age 25. 52 applicants, 38% accepted, 12 enrolled. In 2017, 4 doctorates awarded. *Degree requirements:* For doctorate, comprehensive exam, thesis/dissertation, internship, research qualifying exam; for Ed S, comprehensive exam, internship. *Entrance requirements:* For doctorate and Ed S, GRE General Test, minimum GPA of 3.0, 2 letters of recommendation (at least one academic), transcripts, vitae. Additional exam requirements/recommendations for international students: Required—TOEFL (minimum score 93 iBT). *Application deadline:* For fall admission, 12/1 for domestic and international students. Application fee: $65. Electronic applications accepted. *Expenses:* $565 per credit. *Financial support:* In 2017–18, 34 students received support, including 30 research assistantships (averaging $11,513 per year); fellowships and unspecified assistantships also available. Financial award application deadline: 1/31. *Faculty research:* Applied behavior analysis, developmental disabilities, at-risk students, learning and behavior problems, pediatric psychology, ADHD, school readiness. *Total annual research expenditures:* $13,309. *Unit head:* Dr. Robin Hojnoski, Program Director/Associate Professor, 610-758-3268, Fax: 610-758-6223, E-mail: roh206@lehigh.edu. *Application contact:* Kristi Ball, Coordinator, 610-758-3250, Fax: 610-758-6223, E-mail: kmb618@lehigh.edu. Website: https://ed.lehigh.edu/academics/programs/school-psychology

Lesley University, Graduate School of Arts and Social Sciences, Cambridge, MA 02138-2790. Offers clinical mental health counseling (MA), including holistic counseling, school and community counseling, trauma studies; counseling psychology (MA, CAGS), including professional counseling (MA), school counseling (MA); creative writing (MFA); expressive therapies (MA, PhD, CAGS), including art (MA), clinical mental health counseling (MA), dance (MA), expressive therapies (MA), music (MA); independent studies (CAGS); independent study (MA); intercultural relations (MA, CAGS); interdisciplinary studies (MA), including individualized studies, integrative holistic health, mindfulness studies, peace and conflict transformation, trauma sensitive assessment, intervention, and consultation, women's studies; urban environmental leadership (MA). *Program availability:* Part-time, online learning. *Degree requirements:* For master's, internship, practicum, thesis (for expressive therapies); for doctorate, thesis/dissertation, arts apprenticeship, field placement; for CAGS, thesis, internship (for counseling psychology, expressive therapies). *Entrance requirements:* For master's, MAT

(counseling psychology), interview, writing samples, art portfolio; for doctorate, GRE or MAT, interview, master's degree; for CAGS, interview, master's degree. Additional exam requirements/recommendations for international students: Required—TOEFL (minimum score 550 paper-based; 80 iBT). Electronic applications accepted. *Faculty research:* Psychotherapy and culture; psychotherapy and psychological trauma; women's issues in art, teaching and psychotherapy; community-based art, psycho-spiritual inquiry.

LeTourneau University, Graduate Programs, Longview, TX 75607-7001. Offers business (MBA); counseling (MA), including licensed professional counselor, marriage and family therapy, school counseling; curriculum and instruction (M Ed); educational administration (M Ed); engineering (ME, MS); engineering management (MEM); health care administration (MS); marriage and family therapy (MA); psychology (MA); strategic leadership (MSL); teacher leadership (M Ed); teaching and learning (M Ed). *Program availability:* Part-time, 100% online, blended/hybrid learning. *Students:* 55 full-time (35 women), 337 part-time (266 women); includes 218 minority (140 Black or African American, non-Hispanic/Latino; 2 American Indian or Alaska Native, non-Hispanic/Latino; 5 Asian, non-Hispanic/Latino; 32 Hispanic/Latino; 39 Two or more races, non-Hispanic/Latino), 3 international. Average age 37. *Entrance requirements:* Additional exam requirements/recommendations for international students: Required—TOEFL. *Application deadline:* For fall admission, 8/22 for domestic students, 8/29 for international students; for winter admission, 10/10 for domestic students; for spring admission, 1/2 for domestic students, 1/10 for international students; for summer admission, 5/1 for domestic and international students. Applications are processed on a rolling basis. Electronic applications accepted. *Expenses:* Contact institution. *Financial support:* Research assistantships, institutionally sponsored loans, and unspecified assistantships available. Financial award applicants required to submit FAFSA. Website: http://www.letu.edu

Lewis & Clark College, Graduate School of Education and Counseling, Department of Counseling Psychology, Program in School Psychology, Portland, OR 97219-7899. Offers Ed S. *Program availability:* Part-time, evening/weekend. *Entrance requirements:* Additional exam requirements/recommendations for international students: Required—TOEFL (minimum score 575 paper-based). Electronic applications accepted.

Lewis & Clark College, Graduate School of Education and Counseling, Department of Educational Leadership, Program in School Counseling, Portland, OR 97219-7899. Offers M Ed. *Program availability:* Part-time, evening/weekend. *Entrance requirements:* For master's, minimum undergraduate GPA of 2.75. Additional exam requirements/recommendations for international students: Required—TOEFL (minimum score 575 paper-based). Electronic applications accepted.

Liberty University, School of Behavioral Sciences, Lynchburg, VA 24515. Offers applied psychology (MA), including developmental psychology (MA, MS), industrial/organizational psychology (MA, MS); clinical mental health counseling (MA); community care and counseling (Ed D), including marriage and family counseling, pastoral care and counseling, traumatology; counselor education and supervision (PhD); human services counseling (MA), including addictions and recovery, business, child and family law, Christian ministries, criminal justice, crisis response and trauma, executive leadership, health and wellness, life coaching, marriage and family, military resilience; marriage and family counseling (MA); marriage and family therapy (MA); military resilience (Certificate); pastoral counseling (MA), including addictions and recovery, community chaplaincy, crisis response and trauma, discipleship and church ministry, leadership, life coaching, marriage and family, marriage and family studies, military resilience, parenting and child/adolescent, pastoral counseling, theology; professional counseling (MA); psychology (MS), including developmental psychology (MA, MS), industrial/organizational psychology (MA, MS); school counseling (M Ed). *Program availability:* Part-time, online learning. *Students:* 2,649 full-time (2,085 women), 5,086 part-time (4,015 women); includes 2,275 minority (1,784 Black or African American, non-Hispanic/Latino; 44 American Indian or Alaska Native, non-Hispanic/Latino; 67 Asian, non-Hispanic/Latino; 200 Hispanic/Latino; 11 Native Hawaiian or other Pacific Islander, non-Hispanic/Latino; 169 Two or more races, non-Hispanic/Latino), 145 international. Average age 39. 5,839 applicants, 51% accepted, 1710 enrolled. In 2017, 1,626 master's, 7 doctorates, 61 other advanced degrees awarded. *Application deadline:* Applications are processed on a rolling basis. Application fee: $50. Electronic applications accepted. *Financial support:* Applicants required to submit FAFSA. *Unit head:* Dr. Ronald Hawkins, Founding Dean, School of Behavioral Sciences. *Application contact:* Jay Bridge, Director of Admissions, 800-424-9595, Fax: 800-628-7977, E-mail: gradadmissions@liberty.edu.

Lindenwood University, Graduate Programs, School of Education, St. Charles, MO 63301-1695. Offers behavioral analysis (MA); education (MA), including autism spectrum disorders, character education, early intervention in autism and sensory impairment, gifted, technology; educational administration (MA, Ed D, Ed S); English to speakers of other languages (MA); instructional leadership (Ed D, Ed S); library media (MA); professional counseling (MA); school administration (MA, Ed S); school counseling (MA); teaching (MA). *Program availability:* Part-time, evening/weekend, 100% online, blended/hybrid learning. *Faculty:* 47 full-time (31 women), 213 part-time/adjunct (135 women). *Students:* 434 full-time (319 women), 1,292 part-time (989 women); includes 387 minority (313 Black or African American, non-Hispanic/Latino; 9 American Indian or Alaska Native, non-Hispanic/Latino; 13 Asian, non-Hispanic/Latino; 37 Hispanic/Latino; 1 Native Hawaiian or other Pacific Islander, non-Hispanic/Latino; 14 Two or more races, non-Hispanic/Latino), 20 international. Average age 36. 828 applicants, 61% accepted, 378 enrolled. In 2017, 431 master's, 63 doctorates, 94 other advanced degrees awarded. *Degree requirements:* For master's, thesis (for some programs), minimum GPA of 3.0; for doctorate, thesis/dissertation, minimum GPA of 3.0; for Ed S, comprehensive exam, project, minimum GPA of 3.0. *Entrance requirements:* For master's, interview, minimum undergraduate cumulative GPA of 3.0, writing sample, letter of recommendation; for doctorate, GRE, minimum graduate GPA of 3.4, resume, interview, writing sample, 4 letters of recommendation; for Ed S, master's degree in education, relevant work experience. Additional exam requirements/recommendations for international students: Required—TOEFL (minimum score 550 paper-based; 80 iBT); Recommended—IELTS (minimum score 6.5). *Application deadline:* For fall admission, 8/27 priority date for domestic and international students; for spring admission, 1/14 priority date for domestic and international students; for summer admission, 6/4 priority date for domestic and international students. Applications are processed on a rolling basis. Application fee: $30 ($100 for international students). Electronic applications accepted. *Expenses:* Tuition: Full-time $16,300; part-time $460 per credit. *Required fees:* $660; $330 per credit. Tuition and fees vary according to degree level and program. *Financial support:* In 2017–18, 1,615 students received support. Career-related internships or fieldwork, Federal Work-Study, institutionally sponsored loans, scholarships/grants, tuition waivers (partial), and unspecified assistantships available. Financial award application deadline: 6/30; financial award applicants required to submit FAFSA. *Unit head:* Dr. Anthony Scheffler, Dean, School of Education, 636-949-4618, Fax: 636-949-4197, E-mail: ascheffler@lindenwood.edu. *Application contact:* Kara Schilli, Director, Evening and Graduate Admissions, 636-949-4349, Fax: 636-949-4109, E-mail: adultadmissions@lindenwood.edu. Website: http://www.lindenwood.edu/academics/academic-schools/school-of-education/

School Psychology

Lipscomb University, College of Education, Nashville, TN 37204-3951. Offers applied behavior analysis (MS, Certificate); coaching for learning (M Ed, Certificate, Ed S); educational leadership (M Ed, Ed S); English language learning (M Ed, Ed S); instructional coaching (M Ed, Certificate, Ed S); instructional practice (M Ed); learning organizations and strategic change (Ed D); literacy coaching (Certificate, Ed S); reading specialty (M Ed, Ed S); school counseling (M Ed, Ed S); special education (M Ed); teaching, learning, and leading (M Ed); technology integration (M Ed, Ed S); technology integration specialist (Certificate). *Accreditation:* NCATE. *Program availability:* Part-time, evening/weekend, 100% online. *Faculty:* 21 full-time (14 women), 42 part-time/adjunct (29 women). *Students:* 565 full-time (452 women), 59 part-time (45 women); includes 154 minority (102 Black or African American, non-Hispanic/Latino; 2 American Indian or Alaska Native, non-Hispanic/Latino; 8 Asian, non-Hispanic/Latino; 26 Hispanic/Latino; 16 Two or more races, non-Hispanic/Latino). Average age 32. 395 applicants, 54% accepted, 196 enrolled. In 2017, 162 master's, 30 doctorates, 54 other advanced degrees awarded. *Degree requirements:* For master's, comprehensive exam, portfolio, research project and presentation; for doctorate, practical capstone project in experiential setting. *Entrance requirements:* For master's, MAT (minimum score 31) or GRE General Test (minimum score 294), 2 reference letters, goals statement, writing sample, interview; for doctorate, MAT or GRE General Test, 3 reference letters, artifact of demonstrated academic excellence, written personal statements, interview. Additional exam requirements/recommendations for international students: Required—TOEFL (minimum score 570 paper-based; 80 iBT). *Application deadline:* For fall admission, 8/29 priority date for domestic students; for spring admission, 1/15 priority date for domestic students. Applications are processed on a rolling basis. Application fee: $50 ($75 for international students). Electronic applications accepted. *Expenses:* Contact institution. *Financial support:* Scholarships/grants, unspecified assistantships, and partnerships with local school districts available. Financial award applicants required to submit FAFSA. *Faculty research:* Facilitative learning styles, leadership, student assessment, interactive multimedia inclusion, learning organizations and strategic change. *Unit head:* Dr. Deborah Boyd, Director of Graduate Studies, 615-966-6263, E-mail: deborah.boyd@lipscomb.edu. *Application contact:* Amanda Logsdon, Director of Enrollment and Outreach, 615-966-7199, E-mail: amanda.logsdon@lipscomb.edu.
Website: http://www.lipscomb.edu/education/graduate-programs

Long Island University–Hudson, Graduate School, Purchase, NY 10577. Offers autism (Advanced Certificate); bilingual education (Advanced Certificate); childhood education (MS Ed); crisis management (Advanced Certificate); early childhood education (MS Ed); educational leadership (MS Ed); health administration (MPA); literacy (MS Ed); marriage and family therapy (MS); mental health counseling (MS, Advanced Certificate), including credentialed alcoholism and substance abuse counselor (MS); middle childhood and adolescence education (MS Ed); pharmaceutics (MS), including cosmetic science, industrial pharmacy; public administration (MPA); school counseling (MS Ed, Advanced Certificate); school psychology (MS Ed); special education (MS Ed); TESOL (MS Ed); TESOL (all grades) (Advanced Certificate). *Program availability:* Part-time, evening/weekend. *Faculty:* 8 full-time (6 women), 41 part-time/adjunct (24 women). *Students:* 69 full-time (54 women), 249 part-time (200 women); includes 102 minority (29 Black or African American, non-Hispanic/Latino; 1 American Indian or Alaska Native, non-Hispanic/Latino; 9 Asian, non-Hispanic/Latino; 62 Hispanic/Latino; 1 Native Hawaiian or other Pacific Islander, non-Hispanic/Latino). Average age 33. 153 applicants, 96% accepted, 103 enrolled. In 2017, 138 master's, 36 other advanced degrees awarded. *Entrance requirements:* Additional exam requirements/recommendations for international students: Required—TOEFL. *Application deadline:* Applications are processed on a rolling basis. Application fee: $50. Electronic applications accepted. *Expenses:* Contact institution. *Financial support:* In 2017–18, 32 students received support. Scholarships/grants available. Support available to part-time students. Financial award application deadline: 2/15; financial award applicants required to submit FAFSA. *Unit head:* Dr. Sylvia Blake, Dean and Chief Operating Officer, 914-831-2700, E-mail: westchester@liu.edu. *Application contact:* Dr. Sylvia Blake, Dean and Chief Operating Officer, 914-831-2700, E-mail: westchester@liu.edu.

Long Island University–LIU Post, College of Education, Information and Technology, Brookville, NY 11548-1300. Offers adolescence education (MS); adolescence education 7-12 (MS); archives and records management (AC); art education (MS); childhood education (MS); childhood education/literacy B-6 (MS); childhood education/special education (MS); clinical mental health counseling (MS, AC); early childhood education (MS); early childhood education/childhood education (MS); educational leadership (AC); educational technology (MS); information studies (PhD); interdisciplinary educational studies (Ed D); middle childhood education (MS); music education (MS); public library administration (AC); school counselor (MS); special education (MS Ed); speech-language pathology (MA); students with disabilities, 7-12 generalist (AC); TESOL (MA). *Accreditation:* TEAC. *Program availability:* Part-time, 100% online, blended/hybrid learning. *Faculty:* 40 full-time (26 women), 73 part-time/adjunct (38 women). *Students:* 472 full-time (400 women), 696 part-time (543 women); includes 254 minority (93 Black or African American, non-Hispanic/Latino; 46 Asian, non-Hispanic/Latino; 105 Hispanic/Latino; 10 Two or more races, non-Hispanic/Latino), 33 international. Average age 33. 917 applicants, 82% accepted, 357 enrolled. In 2017, 408 master's, 31 other advanced degrees awarded. Terminal master's awarded for partial completion of doctoral program. *Degree requirements:* For master's, variable foreign language requirement, comprehensive exam (for some programs), thesis optional; for doctorate, comprehensive exam, thesis/dissertation. *Entrance requirements:* For master's and AC, GRE (for some programs). Additional exam requirements/recommendations for international students: Required—TOEFL (minimum score 550 paper-based, 75 iBT), IELTS, or PTE. *Application deadline:* Applications are processed on a rolling basis. Application fee: $50. Electronic applications accepted. *Expenses: Tuition:* Full-time $21,618; part-time $1201 per credit. *Required fees:* $1840; $920 per term. Tuition and fees vary according to course load. *Financial support:* In 2017–18, 376 students received support. Career-related internships or fieldwork, Federal Work-Study, institutionally sponsored loans, scholarships/grants, tuition waivers (partial), and unspecified assistantships available. Support available to part-time students. Financial award application deadline: 2/15; financial award applicants required to submit FAFSA. *Faculty research:* Sleep; use of technology to develop executive function by students with disabilities; early childhood literacy development through play; social justice through education; using a structured protocol to discuss Bad News. *Unit head:* Dr. Albert Inserra, Dean, 516-299-2210, E-mail: albert.inserra@liu.edu. *Application contact:* Rita Langdon, Graduate Admissions, 516-299-2900, Fax: 516-299-2137, E-mail: post-enroll@liu.edu.
Website: http://liu.edu/CWPost/Academics/College-of-Education-Information-and-Technology

Louisiana State University and Agricultural & Mechanical College, Graduate School, College of Humanities and Social Sciences, Department of Psychology, Baton Rouge, LA 70803. Offers biological psychology (MA, PhD); clinical psychology (MA, PhD); cognitive psychology (MA, PhD); developmental psychology (MA, PhD); school psychology (MA, PhD). *Accreditation:* APA (one or more programs are accredited). *Faculty:* 29 full-time (11 women). *Students:* 78 full-time (57 women), 18 part-time (14 women); includes 25 minority (8 Black or African American, non-Hispanic/Latino; 5 Asian, non-Hispanic/Latino; 5 Hispanic/Latino; 1 Native Hawaiian or other Pacific Islander, non-Hispanic/Latino; 6 Two or more races, non-Hispanic/Latino), 4 international. Average age 27. 239 applicants, 8% accepted, 18 enrolled. In 2017, 15 master's, 12 doctorates awarded. *Financial support:* In 2017–18, 7 fellowships (averaging $41,483 per year), 9 research assistantships (averaging $19,441 per year), 58 teaching assistantships (averaging $19,688 per year) were awarded. *Total annual research expenditures:* $326,871.

Louisiana State University in Shreveport, College of Business, Education, and Human Development, Program in School Psychology, Shreveport, LA 71115-2399. Offers SSP. *Students:* 15 full-time (14 women), 9 part-time (4 women); includes 6 minority (2 Black or African American, non-Hispanic/Latino; 4 Two or more races, non-Hispanic/Latino). Average age 28. 23 applicants, 100% accepted, 11 enrolled. In 2017, 5 SSPs awarded. *Entrance requirements:* For degree, GRE General Test, minimum GPA of 2.75, references, letter of intent, interview. Additional exam requirements/recommendations for international students: Required—TOEFL (minimum score 550 paper-based; 61 iBT). *Application deadline:* For fall admission, 6/30 for domestic and international students; for spring admission, 11/30 for domestic and international students; for summer admission, 4/30 for domestic and international students. Applications are processed on a rolling basis. Application fee: $20 ($30 for international students). Electronic applications accepted. *Expenses:* Tuition, state resident: full-time $3098; part-time $344 per credit hour. Tuition, nonresident: full-time $9923; part-time $1103 per credit hour. *Required fees:* $384 per semester. Tuition and fees vary according to program. *Financial support:* Unspecified assistantships available. Financial award applicants required to submit FAFSA. *Unit head:* Dr. Kevin Jones, Program Director, 318-797-5050, Fax: 318-798-4171, E-mail: ssp@lsus.edu. *Application contact:* Mary Catherine Harvison, Director of Admissions, 318-797-2400, Fax: 318-797-5286, E-mail: mary.harvison@lsus.edu.

Loyola Marymount University, School of Education, Program in School Psychology, Los Angeles, CA 90045-2659. Offers MA. *Unit head:* Dr. Brian P. Leung, Director, School Psychology, 310-338-7313, E-mail: bleung@lmu.edu. *Application contact:* Chake H. Kouyoumjian, Associate Dean of Graduate Studies, 310-338-2721, Fax: 310-338-6086, E-mail: graduateinfo@lmu.edu.
Website: http://soe.lmu.edu/academics/schoolpsychology

Loyola University Chicago, School of Education, Program in School Psychology, Chicago, IL 60660. Offers Ed D, PhD, Ed S. PhD offered through the Graduate School. *Program availability:* Blended/hybrid learning. *Faculty:* 6 full-time (5 women), 8 part-time/adjunct (4 women). *Students:* 78 full-time (70 women), 17 part-time (13 women); includes 34 minority (14 Black or African American, non-Hispanic/Latino; 5 Asian, non-Hispanic/Latino; 13 Hispanic/Latino; 2 Two or more races, non-Hispanic/Latino), 2 international. Average age 30. 150 applicants, 50% accepted, 32 enrolled. In 2017, 6 doctorates awarded. Terminal master's awarded for partial completion of doctoral program. *Degree requirements:* For doctorate, comprehensive exam, thesis/dissertation; for Ed S, comprehensive exam. *Entrance requirements:* For doctorate, GRE, interview, letters of recommendation, minimum GPA of 3.0. Additional exam requirements/recommendations for international students: Required—TOEFL (minimum score 550 paper-based; 79 iBT). *Application deadline:* For fall admission, 12/1 for domestic and international students. Application fee: $50. Electronic applications accepted. Application fee is waived when completed online. *Expenses:* $949 per semester hour, $2,847 per course, $8,541-$11,388 full-time semester tuition; $432 per semester fees, $225 additional fees (first semester only). *Financial support:* In 2017–18, 31 fellowships with partial tuition reimbursements, 11 research assistantships with full tuition reimbursements (averaging $14,000 per year), 20 teaching assistantships (averaging $4,000 per year) were awarded; career-related internships or fieldwork, institutionally sponsored loans, scholarships/grants, health care benefits, and unspecified assistantships also available. Support available to part-time students. Financial award application deadline: 2/1. *Faculty research:* Learning theory and teaching, school reform, instructional intervention, violence prevention, mental health programming in schools and communities. *Unit head:* Dr. Markeda Newell, Program Chair, 312-915-6918, E-mail: mnewell2@luc.edu. *Application contact:* Mirtza Campbell, Information Contact, 312-915-8907, E-mail: mcampbell11@luc.edu.

Marist College, Graduate Programs, School of Social and Behavioral Sciences, Poughkeepsie, NY 12601-1387. Offers education (M Ed, MA); mental health counseling (MA); school psychology (MA, Adv C). *Program availability:* Part-time, evening/weekend. *Degree requirements:* For master's, thesis optional. *Entrance requirements:* For master's, GRE General Test, letters of recommendation, minimum undergraduate GPA of 3.0, interview. Additional exam requirements/recommendations for international students: Required—TOEFL (minimum score 550 paper-based; 80 iBT); Recommended—IELTS (minimum score 6.5). Electronic applications accepted. *Faculty research:* AIDS prevention, educational intervention, humanistic counseling research, aging and development, neuroimaging.

Marshall University, Academic Affairs Division, College of Education and Professional Development, Program in School Psychology, Huntington, WV 25755. Offers Ed S. *Accreditation:* NCATE. *Program availability:* Part-time, evening/weekend. *Students:* 13 full-time (all women), 17 part-time (all women); includes 3 minority (2 Black or African American, non-Hispanic/Latino; 1 Two or more races, non-Hispanic/Latino). Average age 31. In 2017, 16 Ed Ss awarded. *Entrance requirements:* For degree, master's degree in psychology. Application fee: $40. *Financial support:* Career-related internships or fieldwork and tuition waivers (full) available. Support available to part-time students. Financial award applicants required to submit FAFSA. *Unit head:* Dr. Sandra Stroebel, Program Director, 304-746-2032, E-mail: stroebel@marshall.edu. *Application contact:* Information Contact, 304-746-1900, Fax: 304-746-1902, E-mail: services@marshall.edu.

McGill University, Faculty of Graduate and Postdoctoral Studies, Faculty of Education, Department of Educational and Counseling Psychology, Montréal, QC H3A 2T5, Canada. Offers counseling psychology (MA, PhD); educational psychology (M Ed, MA, PhD); school/applied child psychology and applied developmental psychology (M Ed, MA, PhD, Diploma), including school psychology. *Accreditation:* APA.

McNeese State University, Doré School of Graduate Studies, Burton College of Education, Department of Education Professions, Lake Charles, LA 70609. Offers curriculum and instruction (M Ed), including academically gifted education, elementary education, reading, secondary education, special education; early childhood education grades PK-3 (Postbaccalaureate Certificate); educational leadership (M Ed, Ed S), including educational leadership, educational technology (Ed S); educational technology leadership (M Ed); elementary education (MAT); elementary education grades 1-5 (Postbaccalaureate Certificate); instructional technology (MS); middle school education grades 4-8 (Postbaccalaureate Certificate), including middle school education grades 4-8; multiple levels grades K-12 (Postbaccalaureate Certificate), including multiple levels grades K-12; school counseling (M Ed); school librarian (Postbaccalaureate Certificate); secondary education (MAT); secondary education grades 6-12 (Postbaccalaureate Certificate); special education (M Ed), including advanced professional, autism, educational diagnostician; special education - mild/moderate grades 1-12 (MAT); special education, mild/moderate for elementary education grades 1-5 (Postbaccalaureate Certificate). *Program availability:* Evening/weekend. *Entrance requirements:* For

master's, GRE. *Application deadline:* For fall admission, 5/15 priority date for domestic and international students; for spring admission, 10/15 priority date for domestic and international students. Applications are processed on a rolling basis. Application fee: $20 ($30 for international students). *Financial support:* Application deadline: 5/1. *Unit head:* Dr. Deborah King, Department Head, 337-475-5437, Fax: 337-475-5402, E-mail: deborah@mcneese.edu. *Application contact:* Dr. Dustin M. Hebert, Director of Dore' School of Graduate Studies, 337-475-5396, Fax: 337-475-5397, E-mail: admissions@mcneese.edu.

Mercer University, Graduate Studies, Cecil B. Day Campus, Penfield College, Atlanta, GA 30341. Offers certified rehabilitation counseling (MS); clinical mental health (MS); counselor education and supervision (PhD); criminal justice and public safety leadership (MS); health informatics (MS); human services (MS), including child and adolescent services, gerontology services; organizational leadership (MS), including leadership for the health care professional, leadership for the nonprofit organization, organizational development and change; school counseling (MS). *Program availability:* Part-time, evening/weekend, 100% online, blended/hybrid learning. *Faculty:* 17 full-time (10 women), 27 part-time/adjunct (24 women). *Students:* 199 full-time (165 women), 266 part-time (218 women); includes 268 minority (226 Black or African American, non-Hispanic/Latino; 1 American Indian or Alaska Native, non-Hispanic/Latino; 19 Asian, non-Hispanic/Latino; 19 Hispanic/Latino; 3 Two or more races, non-Hispanic/Latino). Average age 32. 300 applicants, 45% accepted, 114 enrolled. In 2017, 101 master's, 5 doctorates awarded. *Degree requirements:* For master's, comprehensive exam (for some programs), thesis (for some programs); for doctorate, thesis/dissertation. *Entrance requirements:* For master's, GRE or MAT, Georgia Professional Standards Commission (GPSC) Certification at the SC-5 level; for doctorate, GRE or MAT. Additional exam requirements/recommendations for international students: Recommended—TOEFL (minimum score 550 paper-based; 80 iBT), IELTS (minimum score 6.5). *Application deadline:* For fall admission, 7/1 priority date for domestic and international students; for spring admission, 11/1 priority date for domestic and international students; for summer admission, 4/1 priority date for domestic and international students. Application fee: $35. Electronic applications accepted. Application fee is waived when completed online. *Expenses:* $637 per credit. *Financial support:* In 2017–18, 32 students received support. Federal Work-Study, scholarships/grants, and unspecified assistantships available. Financial award applicants required to submit FAFSA. *Faculty research:* Marriage and families issues, leadership and ethics, cyber-bullying, trauma, narrative counseling and theory. *Total annual research expenditures:* $85,000. *Unit head:* Dr. Priscilla R. Danheiser, Dean, 678-547-6028, Fax: 678-547-6008, E-mail: danheiser_p@mercer.edu. *Application contact:* Dr. Melissa McCants Cruz, Director of Graduate Admissions, 678-547-6024, E-mail: penfield.admissions@mercer.edu. Website: http://penfield.mercer.edu/programs/graduate-professional/

Mercy College, School of Social and Behavioral Sciences, Program in School Psychology, Dobbs Ferry, NY 10522-1189. Offers MS. *Program availability:* Part-time, evening/weekend. *Students:* 175 full-time (147 women), 196 part-time (164 women); includes 271 minority (109 Black or African American, non-Hispanic/Latino; 5 Asian, non-Hispanic/Latino; 151 Hispanic/Latino; 1 Native Hawaiian or other Pacific Islander, non-Hispanic/Latino; 5 Two or more races, non-Hispanic/Latino), 4 international. Average age 34. 271 applicants, 49% accepted, 72 enrolled. In 2017, 103 master's awarded. *Degree requirements:* For master's, thesis (for some programs), practicum, fieldwork, internship, integrative project. *Entrance requirements:* For master's, interview, 3 letters of recommendation, undergraduate transcript. Additional exam requirements/recommendations for international students: Required—TOEFL (minimum score 600 paper-based; 100 iBT), IELTS (minimum score 8). *Application deadline:* For fall admission, 8/1 for international students. Applications are processed on a rolling basis. Application fee: $40. Electronic applications accepted. *Expenses:* Tuition: Full-time $15,426; part-time $857 per credit hour. *Required fees:* $630; $158 per term. Tuition and fees vary according to course load, degree level and program. *Financial support:* Career-related internships or fieldwork, Federal Work-Study, scholarships/grants, and unspecified assistantships available. Support available to part-time students. Financial award applicants required to submit FAFSA. *Unit head:* Dr. Karol Dean, Dean, School of Social and Behavioral Sciences, 914-674-7517, E-mail: kdean@mercy.edu. *Application contact:* Allison Gurdineer, Senior Director of Admissions, 877-637-2946, Fax: 914-674-7382, E-mail: admissions@mercy.edu. Website: https://www.mercy.edu/degrees-programs/ms-school-psychology

Merrimack College, School of Education and Social Policy, North Andover, MA 01845-5800. Offers community engagement (M Ed), including community organizations, higher education, PreK-12 education; criminology and criminal justice (MS); curriculum and instruction (M Ed); early childhood education (M Ed); educational leadership (CAGS), including instructional leadership; elementary education (M Ed); English as a second language (PreK-6) (M Ed); high school education (M Ed); higher education (M Ed), including leadership and organizational development, student affairs; middle school education (M Ed); moderate disabilities (PreK-8) (M Ed); school counseling (M Ed). *Program availability:* Part-time, evening/weekend, 100% online courses with immersion events and in-classroom practicum close to home. *Faculty:* 15 full-time, 36 part-time/adjunct. *Students:* 212 full-time (175 women), 121 part-time (101 women); includes 42 minority (6 Black or African American, non-Hispanic/Latino; 6 Asian, non-Hispanic/Latino; 27 Hispanic/Latino; 3 Two or more races, non-Hispanic/Latino), 3 international. Average age 27. 420 applicants, 84% accepted, 250 enrolled. In 2017, 177 master's awarded. *Degree requirements:* For master's, practicum, portfolio, and state test (for licensure track); capstone (for higher education, curriculum and instruction, and community engagement tracks); for CAGS, capstone. *Entrance requirements:* For master's, Massachusetts Teacher Education Licensure (MTEL), official transcripts from other colleges, resume, personal statement, 2 letters of recommendation. Additional exam requirements/recommendations for international students: Required—TOEFL (minimum score 84 iBT), IELTS (minimum score 6.5), PTE (minimum score 56). *Application deadline:* For fall admission, 8/24 for domestic students, 7/30 for international students; for spring admission, 1/10 for domestic students, 12/10 for international students; for summer admission, 5/10 for domestic students, 4/10 for international students. Applications are processed on a rolling basis. Application fee: $0. Electronic applications accepted. *Expenses:* Contact institution. *Financial support:* Fellowships with full tuition reimbursements, career-related internships or fieldwork, scholarships/grants, and health care benefits available. Support available to part-time students. Financial award application deadline: 5/1; financial award applicants required to submit FAFSA. *Application contact:* Alyssa Orlando, Graduate Admissions Counselor, 978-837-3563, E-mail: orlandoaf@merrimack.edu. Website: http://www.merrimack.edu/academics/graduate/education/

Michigan State University, The Graduate School, College of Education, Department of Counseling, Educational Psychology and Special Education, East Lansing, MI 48824. Offers counseling (MA); educational psychology and educational technology (PhD); educational technology (MA); measurement and quantitative methods (PhD); rehabilitation counseling (MA); rehabilitation counselor education (PhD); school psychology (MA, PhD, Ed S); special education (MA, PhD). *Accreditation:* APA (one or more programs are accredited); CORE (one or more programs are accredited). *Program availability:* Part-time. *Entrance requirements:* Additional exam requirements/

recommendations for international students: Required—TOEFL. Electronic applications accepted.

MidAmerica Nazarene University, School of Behavioral Sciences and Counseling, Olathe, KS 66062-1899. Offers counseling (MA), including clinical mental health, marriage, couple and family, school counseling, spiritual formation in counseling. *Accreditation:* ACA. *Program availability:* Evening/weekend. *Degree requirements:* For master's, comprehensive exam. *Entrance requirements:* For master's, on-site writing assessment, official transcript, three recommendations, personal interview. Additional exam requirements/recommendations for international students: Required—TOEFL (minimum score 81 iBT). Electronic applications accepted. *Expenses:* Contact institution. *Faculty research:* Technology and intimacy, play therapy, interpersonal neurobiology, sexual addiction.

Middle Tennessee State University, College of Graduate Studies, College of Behavioral and Health Sciences, Department of Psychology, Murfreesboro, TN 37132. Offers clinical psychology (MA); experimental psychology (MA); industrial/organizational psychology (MA); psychology (MA, Ed S); quantitative psychology (MA); school psychology (MA). *Program availability:* Part-time, evening/weekend, online learning. *Degree requirements:* For master's, comprehensive exam, thesis. *Entrance requirements:* For master's, GRE. Additional exam requirements/recommendations for international students: Required—TOEFL (minimum score 525 paper-based; 71 iBT) or IELTS (minimum score 6). Electronic applications accepted. *Faculty research:* Health psychology, industrial/organizational psychology, experimental psychology.

Millersville University of Pennsylvania, College of Graduate Studies and Adult Learning, College of Education and Human Services, Department of Psychology, Program in School Counseling, Millersville, PA 17551-0302. Offers M Ed. *Accreditation:* NCATE. *Program availability:* Part-time, evening/weekend. *Faculty:* 12 full-time (8 women), 1 part-time/adjunct (0 women). *Students:* 12 full-time (10 women), 23 part-time (20 women); includes 4 minority (1 Black or African American, non-Hispanic/Latino; 3 Hispanic/Latino). Average age 31. 21 applicants, 95% accepted, 11 enrolled. In 2017, 12 master's awarded. *Degree requirements:* For master's, thesis optional, practicum, portfolio, internship, competency project. *Entrance requirements:* For master's, GRE or MAT (if cumulative GPA is lower than 3.0), at least 1 academic reference; interview; 6 undergraduate credits in psychology. Additional exam requirements/recommendations for international students: Required—TOEFL (minimum score 80 iBT), IELTS (minimum score 6.5), PTE (minimum score 60). *Application deadline:* For fall admission, 1/15 for domestic students; for winter admission, 6/1 for domestic students; for spring admission, 10/1 for domestic students. Application fee: $40. Electronic applications accepted. *Expenses:* $500 per credit resident tuition and fees; $750 per credit non-resident tuition and fees; $114.75 per credit general fee (maximum of 12 credits); technology fee $27 per credit (resident), $39 per credit (non-resident). *Financial support:* In 2017–18, 4 students received support. Unspecified assistantships available. Financial award application deadline: 3/15; financial award applicants required to submit FAFSA. *Faculty research:* Solution-focused counseling, the psychological and social impact of urban gardening with children, comprehensive developmental school counseling programs, sustainability education and research, national model implementation. *Unit head:* Dr. Jason B. Baker, Coordinator, 717-871-7267, Fax: 717-871-7946, E-mail: jason.baker@millersville.edu. *Application contact:* Dr. Victor S. DeSantis, Dean of College of Graduate Studies and Adult Learning/Associate Provost for Civic and Community Engagement, 717-871-7619, Fax: 717-871-7954, E-mail: victor.desantis@millersville.edu. Website: http://www.millersville.edu/psychology/Graduate%20Programs%20Webpages/School%20Counseling/index.php

Millersville University of Pennsylvania, College of Graduate Studies and Adult Learning, College of Education and Human Services, Department of Psychology, Program in School Psychology, Millersville, PA 17551-0302. Offers MS. *Program availability:* Part-time, evening/weekend. *Faculty:* 12 full-time (8 women), 1 part-time/adjunct (0 women). *Students:* 29 full-time (25 women), 11 part-time (10 women); includes 9 minority (4 Black or African American, non-Hispanic/Latino; 3 Hispanic/Latino; 2 Two or more races, non-Hispanic/Latino). Average age 27. 34 applicants, 94% accepted, 20 enrolled. In 2017, 7 master's awarded. *Degree requirements:* For master's, comprehensive exam, thesis optional, portfolio, practicum, internship. *Entrance requirements:* For master's, GRE or MAT (if cumulative GPA is lower than 3.0), at least 1 academic reference; interview; 18 undergraduate credits in psychology. Additional exam requirements/recommendations for international students: Required—TOEFL (minimum score 80 iBT), IELTS (minimum score 6.5), PTE (minimum score 60). *Application deadline:* For fall admission, 1/15 for domestic students; for winter admission, 6/1 for domestic students; for spring admission, 10/1 for domestic students. Application fee: $40. Electronic applications accepted. *Expenses:* $500 per credit resident tuition and fees; $750 per credit non-resident tuition and fees; $114.75 per credit general fee (maximum of 12 credits); technology fee $27 per credit (resident), $39 per credit (non-resident). *Financial support:* In 2017–18, 18 students received support. Unspecified assistantships available. Financial award application deadline: 3/15; financial award applicants required to submit FAFSA. *Faculty research:* Modification of ELL reading and writing instruction based on CALP, parent participation in ELL education, assessment tools for diverse children. *Unit head:* Dr. Helena Tuleya-Payne, Coordinator, 717-871-4420, Fax: 717-871-7946, E-mail: helena.tuleya-payne@millersville.edu. *Application contact:* Dr. Victor S. DeSantis, Dean of College of Graduate Studies and Adult Learning/Associate Provost for Civic and Community Engagement, 717-871-7619, Fax: 717-871-7954, E-mail: victor.desantis@millersville.edu. Website: http://www.millersville.edu/psychology/Graduate%20Programs%20Webpages/School%20Psychology%20Home%20Webpage.php

Minnesota State University Mankato, College of Graduate Studies and Research, College of Social and Behavioral Sciences, Department of Psychology, Mankato, MN 56001. Offers clinical psychology (MA); industrial/organizational psychology (MA); school psychology (Psy D). *Program availability:* Part-time. *Degree requirements:* For master's, one foreign language, comprehensive exam, thesis (for some programs). *Entrance requirements:* For master's, GRE General Test, GRE Subject Test (clinical psychology), minimum GPA of 3.0 during previous 2 years, 3 letters of reference. Additional exam requirements/recommendations for international students: Required—TOEFL. Electronic applications accepted.

Minnesota State University Moorhead, Graduate Studies, College of Science, Health and the Environment, Moorhead, MN 56563. Offers healthcare administration (MHA); nursing (MS); school psychology (MS, Psy S). *Program availability:* Part-time. *Faculty:* 24. *Students:* 34 full-time (25 women), 104 part-time (84 women). Average age 32. 42 applicants, 74% accepted. In 2017, 34 master's, 11 other advanced degrees awarded. *Degree requirements:* For master's, comprehensive exam (for some programs), thesis, final oral defense. *Entrance requirements:* For master's, GRE (for school psychology program), minimum GPA of 3.0, essay, letters of reference. Additional exam requirements/recommendations for international students: Required—TOEFL (minimum score 550 paper-based). *Application deadline:* Applications are processed on a rolling basis. Application fee: $20. Electronic applications accepted. *Expenses:* Tuition, state resident: full-time $9000; part-time $374 per credit. Tuition, nonresident: full-time

$18,000; part-time $748 per credit. *Required fees:* $1055; $43.96 per credit. Tuition and fees vary according to degree level, program and reciprocity agreements. *Financial support:* Federal Work-Study and unspecified assistantships available. Financial award application deadline: 10/1; financial award applicants required to submit FAFSA. *Unit head:* Dr. Jeffrey Bodwin, Dean, 218-477-5892, E-mail: jeffrey.bodwin@mnstate.edu. *Application contact:* Karla Wenger, Graduate Studies Office Manager, 218-477-2344, Fax: 218-477-2482, E-mail: wengerk@mnstate.edu. Website: http://www.mnstate.edu/cshe/

Minot State University, Graduate School, Program in School Psychology, Minot, ND 58707-0002. Offers Ed Sp. *Degree requirements:* For Ed Sp, comprehensive exam, thesis optional. *Entrance requirements:* For degree, GRE General Test, minimum GPA of 3.0. Additional exam requirements/recommendations for international students: Required—TOEFL (minimum score 79 iBT), IELTS (minimum score 6).

Mississippi State University, College of Education, Department of Counseling, Educational Psychology, and Foundations, Mississippi State, MS 39762. Offers clinical mental health (MS); college counseling (MS); counseling/mental health (PhD); counseling/school psychology (PhD); counselor education (Ed S); educational psychology/general educational psychology (PhD); educational psychology/school psychology (PhD); general educational psychology (MS); psychometry (MS); rehabilitation counseling (MS); school counseling (MS); school psychology (Ed S); student affairs (MS). *Accreditation:* ACA (one or more programs are accredited); APA; CORE (one or more programs are accredited); NCATE. *Program availability:* Part-time, blended/hybrid learning. *Faculty:* 21 full-time (14 women), 3 part-time/adjunct (2 women). *Students:* 106 full-time (85 women), 51 part-time (43 women); includes 55 minority (44 Black or African American, non-Hispanic/Latino; 1 American Indian or Alaska Native, non-Hispanic/Latino; 1 Asian, non-Hispanic/Latino; 5 Hispanic/Latino; 4 Two or more races, non-Hispanic/Latino), 5 international. Average age 29. 136 applicants, 55% accepted, 54 enrolled. In 2017, 50 master's, 7 doctorates, 10 other advanced degrees awarded. Terminal master's awarded for partial completion of doctoral program. *Degree requirements:* For master's, comprehensive exam, thesis optional; for doctorate, thesis/dissertation, comprehensive oral and written exam. *Entrance requirements:* For master's, GRE (taken within the last five years), BS with minimum GPA of 2.75 on last 60 hours; for doctorate, GRE, MS from CACREP- or CORE-accredited program in counseling; for Ed S, GRE, MS in counseling or related field, minimum GPA of 3.3 on all graduate work. Additional exam requirements/recommendations for international students: Required—TOEFL (minimum score 550 paper-based; 79 iBT); Recommended—IELTS (minimum score 6.5). *Application deadline:* For fall admission, 2/1 priority date for domestic and international students. Applications are processed on a rolling basis. Application fee: $60 ($80 for international students). Electronic applications accepted. *Expenses:* Tuition, state resident: full-time $8318; part-time $462.12 per credit hour. Tuition, nonresident: full-time $22,358; part-time $1242.12 per credit hour. *Required fees:* $110; $12.24 per credit hour. $6.12 per semester. *Financial support:* In 2017–18, 4 research assistantships (averaging $9,000 per year), 10 teaching assistantships with full tuition reimbursements (averaging $8,401 per year) were awarded; career-related internships or fieldwork, Federal Work-Study, institutionally sponsored loans, and unspecified assistantships also available. Financial award application deadline: 2/1; financial award applicants required to submit FAFSA. *Faculty research:* HIV/AIDS in college population, substance abuse in youth and college students, ADHD and conduct disorders in youth, assessment and identification of early childhood disabilities, assessment and vocational transition of the disabled. *Unit head:* Dr. David Morse, Professor and Head, 662-325-3426, Fax: 662-325-3263, E-mail: dmorse@colled.msstate.edu. *Application contact:* Marina Hunt, Admissions and Enrollment Assistant, 662-325-3363, E-mail: mhunt@grad.msstate.edu. Website: http://www.cep.msstate.edu/

Monmouth University, Graduate Studies, School of Education, West Long Branch, NJ 07764-1898. Offers applied behavior analysis (Certificate); autism (Certificate); director of school counseling services (Post-Master's Certificate); early childhood (M Ed); educational leadership (Ed D); elementary education (MAT), including elementary level, secondary level; English as a second language (M Ed); learning disabilities teacher-consultant (Post-Master's Certificate); literacy (MS Ed); school counseling (MS Ed); special education (MS Ed), including autism, learning disabilities teacher-consultant, teacher of students with disabilities, teaching in inclusive settings; speech-language pathology (MS Ed); student affairs and college counseling (MS Ed); supervisor (Post-Master's Certificate); teaching English to speakers of other languages (Certificate). *Accreditation:* NCATE. *Program availability:* Part-time, evening/weekend, 100% online, blended/hybrid learning. *Faculty:* 23 full-time (19 women), 33 part-time/adjunct (25 women). *Students:* 175 full-time (163 women), 168 part-time (142 women); includes 54 minority (10 Black or African American, non-Hispanic/Latino; 4 Asian, non-Hispanic/Latino; 32 Hispanic/Latino; 8 Two or more races, non-Hispanic/Latino). Average age 27. In 2017, 160 master's, 3 other advanced degrees awarded. *Entrance requirements:* For master's, GRE taken within last 5 years (for MS Ed in speech-language pathology); SAT (minimum combined score of 1660 in 3 sections), ACT (23), GRE (minimum score of 4.0 on analytical writing section and minimum combined score of 310 on quantitative and verbal sections), or passing scores on 3 parts of Core Academic Skills Educators, minimum GPA of 3.0 in major; 2 letters of recommendation (for some programs); resume, personal statement or essay (depending on program). Additional exam requirements/recommendations for international students: Required—TOEFL (minimum score 550 paper-based; 79 iBT), IELTS (minimum score 6), Michigan English Language Assessment Battery (minimum score 77) or Certificate of Advanced English (minimum score 160). *Application deadline:* For fall admission, 7/15 priority date for domestic students, 7/1 for international students; for spring admission, 12/1 priority date for domestic students, 11/1 for international students; for summer admission, 5/1 for domestic students. Applications are processed on a rolling basis. Application fee: $50. Electronic applications accepted. *Expenses: Tuition:* Full-time $21,366; part-time $7122 per credit. *Required fees:* $700; $175 per term. *Financial support:* In 2017–18, 125 students received support. Institutionally sponsored loans, scholarships/grants, and unspecified assistantships available. Support available to part-time students. Financial award applicants required to submit FAFSA. *Faculty research:* Multicultural literacy, science and mathematics teaching strategies, teacher as reflective practitioner, children with disabilities. *Unit head:* Dr. John E. Henning, Dean, 732-263-5513, Fax: 732-263-5277. *Application contact:* Laurie Kuhn, Associate Director of Graduate Admission, 732-571-3452, Fax: 732-263-5123, E-mail: gradadm@monmouth.edu. Website: http://www.monmouth.edu/academics/schools/education/default.asp

Montana State University, The Graduate School, College of Education, Health, and Human Development, Department of Education, Bozeman, MT 59717. Offers adult and higher education (Ed D); curriculum and instruction (M Ed, Ed D), including professional educator (M Ed), technology education (M Ed); education (M Ed), including adult and higher education, educational leadership, school counseling; educational leadership (Ed D, Ed S). *Accreditation:* TEAC. *Program availability:* Part-time, online learning. *Degree requirements:* For master's, comprehensive exam; for doctorate, comprehensive exam, thesis/dissertation. *Entrance requirements:* For master's, GRE, 3 letters of reference, essays, BA transcripts; for doctorate, GRE, MAT, 3 letters of reference, essay, BA and M Ed transcripts; for Ed S, PRAXIS. Additional exam requirements/recommendations for international students: Required—TOEFL (minimum

score 550 paper-based). Electronic applications accepted. *Faculty research:* Critical literacy; standards-based education; school improvement, organizational change, leadership in rural education, leadership in Indian education; student Learning; multicultural/culturally responsive education for social justice Native American indigenous education, community-centered education teacher preparation.

Mount Saint Vincent University, Graduate Programs, Faculty of Education, Program in School Psychology, Halifax, NS B3M 2J6, Canada. Offers MASP. *Degree requirements:* For master's, thesis, 500 hour practicum. *Entrance requirements:* For master's, bachelor's degree in psychology or equivalent, related work experience. Electronic applications accepted. *Faculty research:* Relationship between cognitive and emotional development, expression of emotions, cognitive-behavioral constituents of racism.

Murray State University, College of Education and Human Services, Department of Educational Studies, Leadership and Counseling, Murray, KY 42071. Offers college advising (Certificate); education administration (MA Ed); human development and leadership (MS, Certificate); library media (MA Ed); middle school teacher leader (MA Ed); P-20 and community leadership (Ed D); postsecondary education administration (MA Ed); school counseling (MA Ed); school guidance and counseling (Ed S); secondary teacher leader (MA Ed). *Program availability:* Part-time, evening/weekend, 100% online, blended/hybrid learning. *Faculty:* 38 full-time (16 women), 3 part-time/adjunct (1 woman). *Students:* 45 full-time (22 women), 190 part-time (140 women); includes 33 minority (25 Black or African American, non-Hispanic/Latino; 4 Asian, non-Hispanic/Latino; 3 Hispanic/Latino; 1 Two or more races, non-Hispanic/Latino), 6 international. Average age 35. 87 applicants, 77% accepted, 51 enrolled. In 2017, 21 master's, 16 doctorates, 12 other advanced degrees awarded. *Entrance requirements:* For master's and other advanced degree, GRE or GMAT, minimum university GPA of 2.75. Additional exam requirements/recommendations for international students: Required—TOEFL (minimum score 527 paper-based; 71 iBT). *Application deadline:* Applications are processed on a rolling basis. Application fee: $40 ($50 for international students). Electronic applications accepted. *Expenses:* Tuition, state resident: full-time $9504. Tuition, nonresident: full-time $26,811. *International tuition:* $14,400 full-time. Tuition and fees vary according to course load, degree level and reciprocity agreements. *Financial support:* Federal Work-Study and unspecified assistantships available. Financial award applicants required to submit FAFSA. *Unit head:* Dr. Susana Bloomdahl, Chair, Department of Educational Studies, Leadership, and Counseling, 270-809-6471, Fax: 270-809-3799, E-mail: sbloomdahl@murraystate.edu. *Application contact:* Kaitlyn Burzynski, Interim Assistant Director for Graduate Admission and Records, 270-809-5732, Fax: 270-809-3780, E-mail: msu.graduateadmissions@murraystate.edu. Website: http://www.murraystate.edu/academics/CollegesDepartments/CollegeOfEducationandHumanServices/coehsacademicunits/EducationalStudiesLeadershipandCounseli

National Louis University, National College of Education, Chicago, IL 60603. Offers administration and supervision (M Ed, Ed D, CAS, Ed S); curriculum and instruction (M Ed, MS Ed, CAS); early childhood administration (M Ed, CAS); early childhood education (M Ed, MAT, MS Ed, CAS); education (Ed D); educational psychology/human learning and development (M Ed, MS Ed, CAS, Ed S); elementary education (MAT); interdisciplinary curriculum and instruction (M Ed); mathematics education (M Ed, MS Ed, CAS); middle grades education (MAT); reading and language (M Ed, MS Ed, CAS); school psychology (M Ed, Ed S); science education (M Ed, MS Ed, CAS); secondary education (MAT); special education (M Ed, MAT, CAS); technology in education (M Ed, CAS). *Accreditation:* NCATE. *Program availability:* Part-time, evening/weekend. *Degree requirements:* For doctorate, comprehensive exam, thesis/dissertation. *Entrance requirements:* For master's, MAT or GRE, minimum GPA of 3.0; for doctorate, GRE General Test, minimum GPA of 3.25, interview, resume, writing sample, 4 recommendations. Additional exam requirements/recommendations for international students: Required—TOEFL (minimum score 550 paper-based; 79 iBT).

National University, Academic Affairs, Sanford College of Education, La Jolla, CA 92037-1011. Offers advanced teaching practices (MS); applied behavior analysis (MS); applied school leadership (MS); e-teaching and learning (Certificate); education (MA); educational administration (MS); educational and instructional technology (MS); educational counseling (MS); higher education administration (MS); inspired teaching and learning (M Ed); school psychology (MS); special education (MA, MS). *Program availability:* Part-time, evening/weekend, 100% online, blended/hybrid learning. *Degree requirements:* For master's, thesis (for some programs). *Entrance requirements:* For master's, interview, minimum GPA of 2.5. Additional exam requirements/recommendations for international students: Required—TOEFL (minimum score 550 paper-based; 79 iBT), IELTS (minimum score 6). *Application deadline:* Applications are processed on a rolling basis. Application fee: $60 ($65 for international students). Electronic applications accepted. *Expenses: Tuition:* Part-time $430 per quarter hour. *Financial support:* Career-related internships or fieldwork, institutionally sponsored loans, scholarships/grants, and tuition waivers (partial) available. Support available to part-time students. Financial award application deadline: 6/30. *Faculty research:* Teacher education, special education, educational effectiveness, teaching abroad, school counseling. *Unit head:* Dr. Judy Mantle, Dean, 858-642-8320, E-mail: soe@nu.edu. *Application contact:* Brandon Jouganatos, Vice President for Enrollment Services, 800-628-8648, E-mail: advisor@nu.edu. Website: http://www.nu.edu/OurPrograms/SchoolOfEducation.html

New Mexico State University, College of Education, Department of Counseling and Educational Psychology, Las Cruces, NM 88003. Offers counseling psychology (PhD); educational diagnostics (MA), including counseling and guidance, educational diagnostics; school psychology (Ed S). *Accreditation:* ACA; APA (one or more programs are accredited); NCATE. *Program availability:* Part-time, evening/weekend. *Faculty:* 11 full-time (9 women), 3 part-time/adjunct (all women). *Students:* 80 full-time (57 women), 23 part-time (17 women); includes 68 minority (3 Black or African American, non-Hispanic/Latino; 3 American Indian or Alaska Native, non-Hispanic/Latino; 5 Asian, non-Hispanic/Latino; 56 Hispanic/Latino; 1 Two or more races, non-Hispanic/Latino), 1 international. Average age 31. 103 applicants, 59% accepted, 34 enrolled. In 2017, 18 master's, 5 doctorates, 6 other advanced degrees awarded. *Degree requirements:* For master's, comprehensive exam, thesis optional, internship; for doctorate, comprehensive exam, thesis/dissertation, internship; for Ed S, comprehensive exam, thesis or alternative, internship. *Entrance requirements:* For master's, doctorate, and Ed S, GRE General Test, minimum GPA of 3.0. Additional exam requirements/recommendations for international students: Required—TOEFL (minimum score 550 paper-based; 79 iBT), IELTS (minimum score 6.5). *Application deadline:* For fall admission, 12/15 for domestic and international students; for spring admission, 2/1 priority date for domestic students, 2/1 for international students. Application fee: $40 ($50 for international students). Electronic applications accepted. *Expenses:* Tuition, state resident: full-time $4390. Tuition, nonresident: full-time $15,309. *Required fees:* $853. *Financial support:* In 2017–18, 72 students received support, including 4 fellowships (averaging $4,390 per year), 2 research assistantships (averaging $15,197 per year), 25 teaching assistantships (averaging $14,416 per year); career-related internships or fieldwork, Federal Work-Study, scholarships/grants, traineeships, health

care benefits, and unspecified assistantships also available. Support available to part-time students. Financial award application deadline: 3/1. *Faculty research:* Multicultural counseling and training, school and counseling psychology, social justice, integrated primary care behavioral health training, mental health disparities. *Total annual research expenditures:* \$110,485. *Unit head:* Dr. Barbara Gormley, Department Head, 575-646-2121, Fax: 575-646-8035, E-mail: bgormley@nmsu.edu. *Application contact:* Norma Arrieta, Student Program Coordinator, 575-646-2121, Fax: 575-646-8035, E-mail: cep@nmsu.edu.
Website: http://cep.education.nmsu.edu

Niagara University, Graduate Division of Education, Concentration in School Psychology, Niagara University, NY 14109. Offers MS. *Program availability:* Part-time. *Students:* 19 full-time (16 women), 11 part-time (8 women); includes 5 minority (2 Black or African American, non-Hispanic/Latino; 3 Hispanic/Latino), 2 international. Average age 26. In 2017, 14 master's awarded. *Entrance requirements:* For master's, GRE. Additional exam requirements/recommendations for international students: Required—TOEFL (minimum score 550 paper-based; 79 iBT), IELTS (minimum score 6). *Application deadline:* For fall admission, 8/1 for domestic students. Application fee: \$30. *Expenses:* Contact institution. *Financial support:* Research assistantships with tuition reimbursements, teaching assistantships with tuition reimbursements, career-related internships or fieldwork, Federal Work-Study, scholarships/grants, and unspecified assistantships available. Financial award application deadline: 4/15; financial award applicants required to submit FAFSA. *Unit head:* Dr. Lisa Kilanowski, Associate Professor of School Psychology, 716-286-8797, E-mail: lak@niagara.edu. *Application contact:* Evan Pierce, Associate Director, Graduate Studies, 716-286-8769, Fax: 716-286-8170, E-mail: epierce@niagara.edu.
Website: http://www.niagara.edu/school-psychology

Nicholls State University, Graduate Studies, College of Education, Department of Psychology, Counseling and Family Studies, Thibodaux, LA 70310. Offers clinical mental health counseling (MA); school counseling (M Ed); school psychology (SSP). *Accreditation:* NCATE. *Program availability:* Part-time, evening/weekend. *Degree requirements:* For master's, comprehensive exam; for SSP, comprehensive exam, internship. *Entrance requirements:* For master's, GRE General Test. Electronic applications accepted.

North Carolina State University, Graduate School, College of Humanities and Social Sciences, Department of Psychology, Raleigh, NC 27695. Offers developmental psychology (PhD); ergonomics and experimental psychology (PhD); industrial/organizational psychology (PhD); psychology in the public interest (PhD); school psychology (PhD). *Accreditation:* APA. *Degree requirements:* For doctorate, comprehensive exam, thesis/dissertation. *Entrance requirements:* For doctorate, GRE General Test, GRE Subject Test (industrial/organizational psychology), MAT (recommended), minimum GPA of 3.0 in major. Electronic applications accepted. *Faculty research:* Cognitive and social development (human factors, families, the workplace, community issues and health, aging).

North Dakota State University, College of Graduate and Interdisciplinary Studies, College of Human Development and Education, School of Education, Program in Counselor Education, Fargo, ND 58102. Offers clinical mental health counseling (M Ed, MS); counselor education and supervision (PhD); school counseling (M Ed, MS). *Accreditation:* ACA; NCATE. *Program availability:* Part-time, online learning. *Degree requirements:* For master's, comprehensive exam, thesis or alternative; for doctorate, comprehensive exam, thesis/dissertation. *Entrance requirements:* For master's, GRE, MAT, interview. Additional exam requirements/recommendations for international students: Required—TOEFL. *Faculty research:* Supervision, program assessment, multicultural issues.

Northeastern University, Bouvé College of Health Sciences, Boston, MA 02115-5096. Offers applied behavior analysis (MS); audiology (Au D); counseling psychology (MS, PhD, CAGS); exercise science (MS); nursing (MS, PhD, CAGS), including administration (MS), adult-gerontology acute care nurse practitioner (MS, CAGS), adult-gerontology primary care nurse practitioner (MS, CAGS), anesthesia (MS), family nurse practitioner (MS, CAGS), neonatal nurse practitioner (MS, CAGS), pediatric nurse practitioner (MS, CAGS), psychiatric mental health nurse practitioner (MS, CAGS); nursing practice (DNP); pharmaceutical sciences (MS, PhD), including interdisciplinary concentration, pharmaceutics and drug delivery systems; pharmacology (MS); pharmacy (Pharm D); school psychology (PhD); speech-language pathology (MS); urban health (MPH); MS/MBA. *Accreditation:* ACPE (one or more programs are accredited). *Program availability:* Part-time, evening/weekend, online learning. *Faculty:* 192 full-time. *Students:* 1,685. In 2017, 352 master's, 312 doctorates, 25 other advanced degrees awarded. *Degree requirements:* For doctorate, thesis/dissertation (for some programs); for CAGS, comprehensive exam. Application fee: \$75. Electronic applications accepted. *Expenses:* Contact institution. *Financial support:* Fellowships, research assistantships, teaching assistantships, career-related internships or fieldwork, scholarships/grants, health care benefits, tuition waivers, and unspecified assistantships available. Support available to part-time students. Financial award applicants required to submit FAFSA. *Unit head:* Susan L. Parish, Dean, Bouve College of Health Sciences, 617-373-3321, Fax: 617-373-3030, E-mail: s.parish@northeastern.edu. *Application contact:* 617-373-2708, Fax: 617-373-4701, E-mail: bouvegrad@northeastern.edu.
Website: https://www.northeastern.edu/bouve/

Northern Arizona University, College of Education, Department of Educational Psychology, Flagstaff, AZ 86011. Offers clinical mental health counseling (MA); combined counseling/school psychology (PhD), including counseling psychology; counseling (M Ed), including school counseling, student affairs; human relations (M Ed); psychology of human development and learning (Graduate Certificate); school psychology (Ed S). *Program availability:* Part-time, 100% online, blended/hybrid learning. *Faculty:* 22 full-time (12 women), 6 part-time/adjunct (4 women). *Students:* 184 full-time (139 women), 175 part-time (131 women); includes 118 minority (14 Black or African American, non-Hispanic/Latino; 10 American Indian or Alaska Native, non-Hispanic/Latino; 5 Asian, non-Hispanic/Latino; 79 Hispanic/Latino; 1 Native Hawaiian or other Pacific Islander, non-Hispanic/Latino; 9 Two or more races, non-Hispanic/Latino), 9 international. Average age 33. 244 applicants, 44% accepted, 108 enrolled. In 2017, 147 master's, 4 doctorates awarded. Terminal master's awarded for partial completion of doctoral program. *Degree requirements:* For master's, variable foreign language requirement, comprehensive exam (for some programs), thesis (for some programs); for doctorate, variable foreign language requirement, comprehensive exam (for some programs), thesis/dissertation (for some programs); for other advanced degree, comprehensive exam (for some programs). *Entrance requirements:* Additional exam requirements/recommendations for international students: Required—TOEFL (minimum score 80 iBT), IELTS (minimum score 6.5). *Application deadline:* For fall admission, 12/1 for domestic and international students; for spring admission, 9/15 for domestic and international students. Applications are processed on a rolling basis. Application fee: \$65. Electronic applications accepted. *Expenses:* Tuition, state resident: full-time \$9240; part-time \$458 per credit hour. Tuition, nonresident: full-time \$21,588; part-time \$1199 per credit hour. *Required fees:* \$1021; \$14 per credit hour. \$646 per semester. Tuition and fees vary according to course load, campus/location and program. *Financial support:* In 2017–18, 62 students received support, including 1 fellowship with full and

partial tuition reimbursement available (averaging \$13,927 per year), 2 research assistantships with full and partial tuition reimbursements available (averaging \$13,927 per year), 15 teaching assistantships with full and partial tuition reimbursements available (averaging \$13,927 per year); institutionally sponsored loans, health care benefits, tuition waivers (full and partial), and unspecified assistantships also available. Financial award application deadline: 2/1; financial award applicants required to submit FAFSA. *Unit head:* Dr. Robert Horn, Chair, 928-523-0545, Fax: 928-523-9284, E-mail: robert.horn@nau.edu. *Application contact:* Hope DeMello, Administrative Assistant, 928-523-7103, Fax: 928-523-9284, E-mail: eps@nau.edu.
Website: https://nau.edu/coe/ed-psych/

Northern Vermont University–Johnson, Program in Counseling, Johnson, VT 05656. Offers addictions counseling (MA); clinical mental health counseling (MA); general counseling (MA); school counseling (MA). *Program availability:* Part-time. *Faculty:* 2 full-time (1 woman), 11 part-time/adjunct (6 women). *Students:* 2 full-time (1 woman), 15 part-time (9 women). In 2017, 50 master's awarded. *Degree requirements:* For master's, comprehensive exam. *Entrance requirements:* For master's, interview. Additional exam requirements/recommendations for international students: Required—TOEFL. *Application deadline:* For fall admission, 7/1 for domestic students, 2/1 for international students; for spring admission, 11/1 for domestic students, 7/1 for international students; for summer admission, 4/1 for domestic students. Applications are processed on a rolling basis. Electronic applications accepted. *Expenses:* Tuition, state resident: part-time \$572 per credit hour. Tuition, nonresident: part-time \$832 per credit hour. *Financial support:* Career-related internships or fieldwork and unspecified assistantships available. Support available to part-time students. Financial award application deadline: 3/1; financial award applicants required to submit FAFSA. *Unit head:* Dr. Kimberly Donovan, Coordinator, 802-635-1453, Fax: 802-635-1465, E-mail: kimberly.donovan@northernvermont.edu. *Application contact:* Catherine H. Higley, Administrative Assistant, 800-635-2356 Ext. 1244, Fax: 802-635-1248, E-mail: catherine.higley@jsc.edu.

Northwest Nazarene University, Program in Counselor Education, Nampa, ID 83686-5897. Offers clinical counseling (MS); marriage and family counseling (MS); school counseling (MS). *Program availability:* Part-time. *Students:* Average age 35. 47 applicants, 66% accepted, 25 enrolled. In 2017, 33 master's awarded. *Entrance requirements:* For master's, minimum GPA of 3.0, BA. Additional exam requirements/recommendations for international students: Required—TOEFL. *Application deadline:* For fall admission, 2/15 for domestic and international students; for spring admission, 9/15 for domestic and international students. Application fee: \$50. Electronic applications accepted. *Unit head:* Dr. Michael Pitts, Chair, 208-467-8040, Fax: 208-467-8339. *Application contact:* Lynette Kingsmore, Graduate Admissions Counselor, 208-467-8107, E-mail: lkingsmore@nnu.edu.

Nova Southeastern University, College of Psychology, Fort Lauderdale, FL 33314-7796. Offers clinical mental health counseling (MS); clinical psychology (PhD, Psy D); counseling (MS); experimental psychology (MS); forensic psychology (MS); general psychology (MS); school counseling (MS); school psychology (Psy D, Psy S); substance abuse counseling (MS); substance abuse counseling and education (MS). *Accreditation:* APA (one or more programs are accredited). *Program availability:* 100% online, blended/hybrid learning. *Faculty:* 51 full-time (21 women), 120 part-time/adjunct (70 women). *Students:* 751 full-time (618 women), 821 part-time (709 women); includes 787 minority (268 Black or African American, non-Hispanic/Latino; 2 American Indian or Alaska Native, non-Hispanic/Latino; 38 Asian, non-Hispanic/Latino; 431 Hispanic/Latino; 2 Native Hawaiian or other Pacific Islander, non-Hispanic/Latino; 46 Two or more races, non-Hispanic/Latino), 45 international. Average age 31. 1,117 applicants, 38% accepted, 294 enrolled. In 2017, 459 master's, 100 doctorates, 10 other advanced degrees awarded. Terminal master's awarded for partial completion of doctoral program. *Degree requirements:* For master's, comprehensive exam, 3 practica; for doctorate, thesis/dissertation, clinical internship, competency exam; for Psy S, comprehensive exam, internship. *Entrance requirements:* For master's and Psy S, GRE General Test, letters of recommendation, research/personal statement, interview; for doctorate, GRE General Test, GRE Subject Test (recommended), minimum undergraduate GPA of 3.0, letters of recommendation, research/personal statement, interview, curriculum vitae/resume. Additional exam requirements/recommendations for international students: Required—TOEFL (minimum score 550 paper-based). *Application deadline:* Applications are processed on a rolling basis. Application fee: \$50. Electronic applications accepted. *Expenses:* Contact institution. *Financial support:* In 2017–18, 197 students received support, including 15 research assistantships (averaging \$5,600 per year), 68 teaching assistantships (averaging \$2,000 per year); career-related internships or fieldwork, Federal Work-Study, institutionally sponsored loans, scholarships/grants, and unspecified assistantships also available. Support available to part-time students. Financial award application deadline: 4/15; financial award applicants required to submit FAFSA. *Faculty research:* Clinical health psychology, multicultural/diversity psychology, clinical neuropsychology, clinical child psychology, family violence. *Unit head:* Dr. Karen Grosby, Dean, 954-262-5712, Fax: 954-262-3859, E-mail: grosby@nova.edu. *Application contact:* Carlos Perez, Senior Manager of Outreach, 954-262-5702, Fax: 954-262-3893, E-mail: gradschool@nova.edu.
Website: http://psychology.nova.edu/

Old Dominion University, Darden College of Education, Counseling Program, Norfolk, VA 23529. Offers clinical mental health counseling (MS Ed); college counseling (MS Ed); counseling (Ed S); counselor education (PhD); school counseling (MS Ed). *Accreditation:* ACA. *Program availability:* Part-time, evening/weekend. *Faculty:* 14 full-time (7 women), 9 part-time/adjunct (7 women). *Students:* 134 full-time (113 women), 52 part-time (44 women); includes 72 minority (42 Black or African American, non-Hispanic/Latino; 1 American Indian or Alaska Native, non-Hispanic/Latino; 4 Asian, non-Hispanic/Latino; 17 Hispanic/Latino; 8 Two or more races, non-Hispanic/Latino), 6 international. Average age 31. 195 applicants, 57% accepted, 79 enrolled. In 2017, 43 master's, 9 doctorates, 2 other advanced degrees awarded. *Degree requirements:* For master's and Ed S, comprehensive exam; for doctorate, comprehensive exam, thesis/dissertation. *Entrance requirements:* For master's and Ed S, GRE General Test, resume, essay, transcripts, recommendations; for doctorate, GRE General Test, resume, interview, essay, transcripts, recommendations. Additional exam requirements/recommendations for international students: Required—TOEFL. *Application deadline:* For fall admission, 3/1 for domestic and international students; for winter admission, 1/10 for domestic students; for spring admission, 10/1 for domestic and international students; for summer admission, 3/1 for domestic students, 2/1 for international students. Application fee: \$50. Electronic applications accepted. *Expenses:* \$496 per credit hour, plus \$9.00 services fee per semester. *Financial support:* In 2017–18, 20 students received support, including 2 fellowships with full tuition reimbursements available (averaging \$15,000 per year), 13 research assistantships (averaging \$9,000 per year), 20 teaching assistantships with full tuition reimbursements available (averaging \$20,000 per year); career-related internships or fieldwork, Federal Work-Study, institutionally sponsored loans, scholarships/grants, tuition waivers (partial), and unspecified assistantships also available. Support available to part-time students. Financial award application deadline: 10/1; financial award applicants required to submit FAFSA. *Faculty research:* Group counseling, counselor education, career counseling, spirituality and counseling, school

counseling, LGBT counseling, legal and ethical issues. *Total annual research expenditures:* $75,000. *Unit head:* Dr. Jeff Moe, Director, 757-683-6235, Fax: 757-683-5756, E-mail: jmoe@odu.edu.
Website: http://www.odu.edu/chs

Oregon State University, College of Education, Program in Counseling, Corvallis, OR 97331. Offers clinical mental health counseling (M Coun); counseling (PhD); school counseling (M Coun). *Accreditation:* ACA (one or more programs are accredited); NCATE. *Program availability:* Part-time, blended/hybrid learning. *Degree requirements:* For master's, thesis or alternative; for doctorate, one foreign language, thesis/dissertation. *Entrance requirements:* For master's, minimum GPA of 3.0 in last 90 hours; for doctorate, GRE or MAT, master's degree, minimum GPA of 3.0 in last 90 hours of course work, 2 years of teaching experience. Additional exam requirements/recommendations for international students: Required—TOEFL (minimum score 575 paper-based). *Application deadline:* For fall admission, 1/31 for domestic students. Application fee: $75 ($85 for international students). *Financial support:* Application deadline: 3/1. *Faculty research:* Counseling and guidance improvement in social services agencies, elementary and secondary schools. *Unit head:* Lisa Schulz, Counseling Lead, 541-737-5959, E-mail: lisa.schulz@oregonstate.edu. *Application contact:* Mary Aguilera, Advisor, 541-737-2232, E-mail: mary.aguilera@oregonstate.edu.
Website: http://education.oregonstate.edu/counseling

Oregon State University–Cascades, Program in Counseling, Bend, OR 97701. Offers community counseling (MS); school counseling (MS).

Ottawa University, Graduate Studies-Arizona, Program in Education, Ottawa, KS 66067-3399. Offers community college counseling (MA); curriculum and instruction (MA); early childhood (MA); education intervention (MA); education leadership (MA); education technology (MA); Montessori early childhood education (MA); Montessori elementary education (MA); professional development (MA); school guidance counseling (MA); special education - cross categorical (MA). Programs offered in Mesa, Phoenix, Tempe and West Valley, AZ. *Accreditation:* NCATE. *Program availability:* Part-time. *Degree requirements:* For master's, thesis or alternative. *Entrance requirements:* For master's, minimum undergraduate GPA of 3.0, copy of current state certification or teaching license. Additional exam requirements/recommendations for international students: Required—TOEFL (minimum score 550 paper-based). Electronic applications accepted. *Expenses:* Contact institution.

Our Lady of the Lake University, College of Professional Studies, Program in Psychology, San Antonio, TX 78207-4689. Offers marriage and family therapy (MS); school psychology (MS). *Accreditation:* APA. *Program availability:* Part-time. *Faculty:* 2 full-time (both women), 2 part-time/adjunct (1 woman). *Students:* 101 full-time (87 women), 14 part-time (13 women); includes 78 minority (12 Black or African American, non-Hispanic/Latino; 66 Hispanic/Latino). Average age 30. 81 applicants, 78% accepted, 37 enrolled. In 2017, 40 master's awarded. *Degree requirements:* For master's, comprehensive exam, practicum. *Entrance requirements:* For master's, GRE General Test or MAT, bachelor's degree with at least 12 undergraduate semester hours in psychology including one course in statistics and minimum cumulative GPA of 3.0; criminal background check; personal statement addressing background in psychology, expectations of the MS program, and professional goals; statement of purpose; 2 letters of recommendation. Additional exam requirements/recommendations for international students: Required—TOEFL. *Application deadline:* For fall admission, 3/1 priority date for domestic and international students. Application fee: $40 ($50 for international students). Electronic applications accepted. Application fee is waived when completed online. *Expenses: Tuition:* Full-time $10,668; part-time $5334 per year. *Required fees:* $816; $816 per year. $408 per semester. *Financial support:* In 2017–18, 2 students received support. Federal Work-Study, scholarships/grants, unspecified assistantships, and tuition discounts available. Support available to part-time students. Financial award application deadline: 5/1; financial award applicants required to submit FAFSA. *Faculty research:* Providing competent services to diverse client populations. *Unit head:* Dr. Deborah Healy, Psychology Department, 210-431-7118, E-mail: dahealy@ollusa.edu. *Application contact:* Office of Graduate Admissions, 210-431-3995, Fax: 210-431-3945, E-mail: gradadm@lake.ollusa.edu.
Website: http://www.ollusa.edu/s/1190/hybrid/default-hybrid-ollu.aspx?sid-1190&gid-1&pgid-7908

Pace University, Dyson College of Arts and Sciences, Department of Psychology, Program in School-Clinical Child Psychology, New York, NY 10038. Offers school psychology (MS Ed); school-clinical child psychology (Psy D). *Accreditation:* APA (one or more programs are accredited). *Students:* 68 full-time (60 women), 30 part-time (23 women); includes 23 minority (3 Black or African American, non-Hispanic/Latino; 9 Asian, non-Hispanic/Latino; 7 Hispanic/Latino; 1 Native Hawaiian or other Pacific Islander, non-Hispanic/Latino; 3 Two or more races, non-Hispanic/Latino), 5 international. Average age 27. In 2017, 15 master's, 22 doctorates awarded. Terminal master's awarded for partial completion of doctoral program. *Degree requirements:* For master's, qualifying exams, internship; for doctorate, comprehensive exam, thesis/dissertation, qualifying exams, externship, internship. *Entrance requirements:* For master's, GRE General Test, GRE Subject Test in psychology (recommended), interview, 3 letters of recommendation, resume, personal statement; for doctorate, GRE General Test, GRE Subject Test in psychology (recommended), interview, transcripts, 3 letters of recommendation. Additional exam requirements/recommendations for international students: Required—TOEFL (minimum score 88 iBT), IELTS (minimum score 7) or PTE (minimum score 60). *Application deadline:* For fall admission, 1/15 priority date for domestic students. Application fee: $70. Electronic applications accepted. *Financial support:* Scholarships/grants and unspecified assistantships available. Financial award application deadline: 1/15; financial award applicants required to submit FAFSA. *Unit head:* Dr. Barbara Mowder, Director of Graduate Psychology Programs, 212-346-1556, E-mail: bmowder@pace.edu. *Application contact:* Susan Ford-Goldschein, Director of Graduate Admissions, 212-346-1531, Fax: 212-346-1585, E-mail: graduateadmission@pace.edu.
Website: http://www.pace.edu/dyson/academic-departments-and-programs/psychology—nyc/graduate-programs

Penn State University Park, Graduate School, College of Education, Department of Educational Psychology, Counseling, and Special Education, University Park, PA 16802. Offers counselor education (M Ed, D Ed, PhD, Certificate); educational psychology (MS, PhD, Certificate); school psychology (M Ed, MS, PhD, Certificate); special education (M Ed, MS, PhD). *Unit head:* Dr. David H. Monk, Dean, 814-865-2523, Fax: 814-865-0555. *Application contact:* Lori Hawn, Director, Graduate Student Services, 814-865-1795, Fax: 814-863-4627, E-mail: l-gswww@lists.psu.edu.
Website: http://ed.psu.edu/epcse

Philadelphia College of Osteopathic Medicine, Graduate and Professional Programs, Department of Psychology, Philadelphia, PA 19131-1694. Offers applied behavior analysis (Certificate); clinical health psychology (Post-Doctoral Certificate); clinical neuropsychology (Post-Doctoral Certificate); clinical psychology (Psy D); educational psychology (PhD); mental health counseling (MS); organizational development and leadership (MS); psychology (Certificate); public health management and administration (MS); school psychology (MS, Psy D, Ed S). *Accreditation:* APA. *Faculty:* 19 full-time (11 women), 122 part-time/adjunct (58 women). *Students:* 487 (335 women); includes 138 minority (89 Black or African American, non-Hispanic/Latino; 4 American Indian or Alaska Native, non-Hispanic/Latino; 11 Asian, non-Hispanic/Latino; 12 Hispanic/Latino; 22 Two or more races, non-Hispanic/Latino). 298 applicants, 44% accepted, 100 enrolled. In 2017, 50 master's, 43 doctorates, 10 other advanced degrees awarded. Terminal master's awarded for partial completion of doctoral program. *Degree requirements:* For master's, comprehensive exam (for some programs), thesis (for some programs); for doctorate, comprehensive exam, thesis/dissertation. *Entrance requirements:* For master's, GRE or MAT, minimum GPA of 3.0; bachelor's degree from regionally-accredited college or university; for doctorate, PRAXIS II (for Psy D in school psychology), minimum undergraduate GPA of 3.0; for other advanced degree, GRE (for Ed S). Additional exam requirements/recommendations for international students: Required—TOEFL (minimum score 79 iBT). *Application deadline:* Applications are processed on a rolling basis. Application fee: $50. Electronic applications accepted. *Financial support:* In 2017–18, 28 teaching assistantships were awarded; Federal Work-Study, institutionally sponsored loans, and scholarships/grants also available. Financial award application deadline: 3/15; financial award applicants required to submit FAFSA. *Faculty research:* Adult and childhood anxiety and ADHD; coping with chronic illness; primary care psychology/integrated health care; applied behavior analysis; psychological, educational, and neuropsychological assessment. *Total annual research expenditures:* $533,489. *Unit head:* Dr. Robert DiTomasso, Chairman, 215-871-6442, Fax: 215-871-6458, E-mail: robertd@pcom.edu. *Application contact:* Johnathan Cox, Associate Director of Admissions, 215-871-6700, Fax: 215-871-6719, E-mail: johnathancox@pcom.edu.

See Display on page 982 and Close-Up on page 1203.

Phillips Graduate University, Master's Program in Psychology, Chatsworth, CA 91311. Offers art therapy (MA); marriage and family therapy (MA); school counseling (MA); school psychology (MA). *Program availability:* Evening/weekend. *Degree requirements:* For master's, comprehensive exam, thesis. *Entrance requirements:* For master's, minimum GPA of 2.5. *Application deadline:* For fall admission, 4/16 priority date for domestic students; for spring admission, 11/15 for domestic students. Applications are processed on a rolling basis. Application fee: $80. Electronic applications accepted. *Expenses: Tuition:* Part-time $897 per unit. *Required fees:* $375 per semester. Part-time tuition and fees vary according to degree level and program. *Financial support:* Federal Work-Study and tuition waivers (full and partial) available. Financial award application deadline: 8/15; financial award applicants required to submit FAFSA. *Faculty research:* Integration of interpersonal psychological theory, systems approach, firsthand experiential learning. *Application contact:* Christine Montagna, Admissions Advisor, 818-600-4945, Fax: 818-386-5699, E-mail: cmontagna@pgu.edu.

Pittsburg State University, Graduate School, College of Education, Department of Psychology and Counseling, Program in School Psychology, Pittsburg, KS 66762. Offers Ed S. *Accreditation:* NCATE. *Program availability:* Part-time. *Students:* 6. In 2017, 2 Ed Ss awarded. *Degree requirements:* For Ed S, thesis or alternative. *Entrance requirements:* For degree, GRE General Test, minimum GPA of 3.0. Additional exam requirements/recommendations for international students: Required—TOEFL (minimum score 550 paper-based; 79 iBT), IELTS (minimum score 6.5), PTE (minimum score 53). *Application deadline:* Applications are processed on a rolling basis. Application fee: $35 ($60 for international students). Electronic applications accepted. *Expenses:* Contact institution. *Financial support:* Teaching assistantships, career-related internships or fieldwork, and Federal Work-Study available. Financial award application deadline: 2/1; financial award applicants required to submit FAFSA. *Unit head:* Dr. David Hurford, Chairperson, 620-235-4521. *Application contact:* Lisa Allen, Assistant Director of Graduate and Continuing Studies, 620-235-4218, Fax: 620-235-4219, E-mail: lallen@pittstate.edu.

Plymouth State University, College of Graduate Studies, Graduate Studies in Education, Certificate of Advanced Graduate Studies Programs, Plymouth, NH 03264-1595. Offers clinical mental health counseling (CAGS); educational leadership (CAGS); higher education (CAGS); school psychology (CAGS). *Program availability:* Part-time, evening/weekend.

Plymouth State University, College of Graduate Studies, Graduate Studies in Education, Programs in Counseling, Plymouth, NH 03264-1595. Offers human relations (M Ed); school counseling (M Ed); school psychology (M Ed). *Accreditation:* ACA; NCATE. *Program availability:* Part-time, evening/weekend. *Degree requirements:* For master's, PRAXIS I. *Entrance requirements:* For master's, MAT, minimum GPA of 3.0.

Purdue University Northwest, Graduate Studies Office, School of Education, Program in Counseling, Hammond, IN 46323-2094. Offers human services (MS Ed); mental health counseling (MS Ed); school counseling (MS Ed). *Accreditation:* ACA. *Entrance requirements:* Additional exam requirements/recommendations for international students: Required—TOEFL.

Queens College of the City University of New York, Division of Education, Department of Educational and Community Programs, Queens, NY 11367-1597. Offers bilingual pupil personnel (AC); counselor education (MS Ed); mental health counseling (MS); school building leader (AC); school district leader (AC); school psychologist (MS Ed); special education-childhood education (AC); special education-early childhood (MS Ed); teacher of special education 1-6 (MS Ed); teacher of special education birth-2 (MS Ed); teaching students with disabilities, grades 7-12 (MS Ed, AC). *Program availability:* Part-time. *Faculty:* 20 full-time (14 women), 63 part-time/adjunct (37 women). *Students:* 105 full-time (94 women), 423 part-time (350 women); includes 241 minority (40 Black or African American, non-Hispanic/Latino; 2 American Indian or Alaska Native, non-Hispanic/Latino; 50 Asian, non-Hispanic/Latino; 142 Hispanic/Latino; 1 Native Hawaiian or other Pacific Islander, non-Hispanic/Latino; 6 Two or more races, non-Hispanic/Latino), 5 international. Average age 28. 515 applicants, 57% accepted, 230 enrolled. In 2017, 163 master's, 74 other advanced degrees awarded. *Degree requirements:* For master's, research project; for AC, internship. *Entrance requirements:* For master's, minimum GPA of 3.0. Additional exam requirements/recommendations for international students: Required—TOEFL, IELTS. *Application deadline:* For fall admission, 3/1 for domestic students. Applications are processed on a rolling basis. Application fee: $125. Electronic applications accepted. *Financial support:* Career-related internships or fieldwork available. Financial award application deadline: 4/1; financial award applicants required to submit FAFSA. *Unit head:* Dr. Emilia Lopez, Chair, 718-997-5250, E-mail: emilia.lopez@qc.cuny.edu. *Application contact:* Elizabeth D'Amico-Ramirez, Assistant Director of Graduate Admissions, 718-997-5203, E-mail: elizabeth.damicoramirez@qc.cuny.edu.

Quincy University, Master of Science in Education Counseling Program, Quincy, IL 62301-2699. Offers clinical mental health counseling (MS Ed); college student personnel (MS Ed); school counseling (MS Ed). *Program availability:* Part-time, evening/weekend. *Degree requirements:* For master's, comprehensive exam, practicum, internship. *Entrance requirements:* For master's, MAT or GRE. Additional exam requirements/recommendations for international students: Required—TOEFL (minimum score 550 paper-based; 79 iBT). *Application deadline:* Applications are processed on a rolling basis. Application fee: $25. Electronic applications accepted. *Expenses: Tuition:* Part-time $450 per credit hour. *Financial support:* Applicants required to submit FAFSA.

Unit head: Dr. Kenneth Oliver, Director, 217-228-5432 Ext. 3113, E-mail: oliveke@quincy.edu. *Application contact:* Office of Admissions, 217-228-5210, Fax: 217-228-5479, E-mail: admissions@quincy.edu.
Website: http://www.quincy.edu/academics/graduate-programs/counseling/

Radford University, College of Graduate Studies and Research, Program in School Psychology, Radford, VA 24142. Offers Ed S. *Accreditation:* NCATE. *Faculty:* 21 full-time (14 women). *Students:* 12 full-time (11 women), 9 part-time (8 women); includes 2 minority (1 Black or African American, non-Hispanic/Latino; 1 Hispanic/Latino), 1 international. Average age 25. 25 applicants, 76% accepted, 5 enrolled. In 2017, 7 Ed Ss awarded. *Degree requirements:* For Ed S, comprehensive exam. *Entrance requirements:* For degree, GRE, minimum GPA of 3.0, 2 letters of reference, essay, resume, official transcripts. Additional exam requirements/recommendations for international students: Required—TOEFL (minimum score 550 paper-based; 79 iBT), IELTS (minimum score 6.5). *Application deadline:* For fall admission, 2/15 priority date for domestic students, 12/1 for international students; for spring admission, 7/1 for international students. Applications are processed on a rolling basis. Application fee: $50. Electronic applications accepted. *Expenses:* Tuition, state resident: full-time $8336; part-time $347 per credit hour. Tuition, nonresident: full-time $16,862; part-time $702 per credit hour. *Required fees:* $3220; $135 per credit hour. Tuition and fees vary according to course load and program. *Financial support:* In 2017–18, 2 students received support, including 2 teaching assistantships (averaging $7,500 per year); career-related internships or fieldwork, scholarships/grants, and unspecified assistantships also available. Support available to part-time students. Financial award application deadline: 3/1; financial award applicants required to submit FAFSA. *Faculty research:* Civility in the classroom, intellectual assessment and identification of learning difficulties, behaviorally-based academic interventions in students experiencing learning difficulties, pediatric neuropsychology. *Unit head:* Dr. Eric Mesmer, Coordinator, 540-831-5361, Fax: 540-831-6113, E-mail: emesmer@radford.edu.
Website: http://www.radford.edu/content/chbs/home/psychology/programs/school.html

Rhode Island College, School of Graduate Studies, Feinstein School of Education and Human Development, Department of Counseling, Educational Leadership, and School Psychology, Providence, RI 02908-1991. Offers advanced counseling (CGS); agency counseling (MA); clinical mental health counseling (MS); co-occurring disorders (MA, CGS); educational leadership (M Ed); mental health counseling (CAGS); school counseling (MA); school psychology (CAGS); teacher leadership (CGS). *Accreditation:* ACA; NCATE. *Program availability:* Part-time, evening/weekend. *Faculty:* 10. *Students:* 31 full-time (25 women), 75 part-time (65 women); includes 16 minority (4 Black or African American, non-Hispanic/Latino; 11 Hispanic/Latino; 1 Two or more races, non-Hispanic/Latino). Average age 32. In 2017, 40 master's, 15 other advanced degrees awarded. *Degree requirements:* For master's and other advanced degree, comprehensive exam (for some programs), thesis (for some programs). *Entrance requirements:* For master's, GRE General Test or MAT, undergraduate transcripts; minimum undergraduate GPA of 3.0; for other advanced degree, GRE or MAT (for most programs), undergraduate transcripts; minimum undergraduate GPA of 3.0; 3 letters of recommendation; current resume. Additional exam requirements/recommendations for international students: Recommended—TOEFL (minimum score 550 paper-based; 79 iBT). *Application deadline:* For fall admission, 3/1 for domestic students; for spring admission, 11/1 for domestic students. Applications are processed on a rolling basis. Application fee: $50. Electronic applications accepted. *Expenses:* Tuition, state resident: full-time $9768; part-time $407 per credit. Tuition, nonresident: full-time $19,008; part-time $792 per credit. *Required fees:* $696; $29 per credit. One-time fee: $200 full-time; $100 part-time. Tuition and fees vary according to course load. *Financial support:* In 2017–18, 4 teaching assistantships with full tuition reimbursements (averaging $2,063 per year) were awarded; career-related internships or fieldwork, Federal Work-Study, scholarships/grants, health care benefits, and unspecified assistantships also available. Support available to part-time students. Financial award application deadline: 5/15; financial award applicants required to submit FAFSA. *Unit head:* Dr. John Eagle, Chair, 401-456-8023. *Application contact:* Graduate Studies, 401-456-8700.
Website: http://www.ric.edu/counselingEducationalLeadershipSchoolPsychology/index.php

Rider University, College of Education and Human Services, Program in School Psychology, Lawrenceville, NJ 08648-3001. Offers Certificate, Ed S. *Entrance requirements:* For degree, GRE or MAT, resume, 2 professional references, interview, 1 year of counseling experience. Additional exam requirements/recommendations for international students: Required—TOEFL (minimum score 550 paper-based). *Faculty research:* Prenatal factors on child development, child abuse developmental assessments.

Roberts Wesleyan College, Graduate Psychology Programs, Rochester, NY 14624-1997. Offers clinical/school psychology (Psy D); school counseling (MS); school psychology (MS). *Program availability:* Part-time, evening/weekend. *Degree requirements:* For master's, comprehensive exam, PRAXIS II (for school psychology). *Entrance requirements:* For master's, GRE. Electronic applications accepted. Application fee is waived when completed online. *Faculty research:* Counselor supervision, forgiveness, community health psychology, applied research in group process.

Rochester Institute of Technology, Graduate Enrollment Services, College of Liberal Arts, Psychology Department, Advanced Certificate Program in School Psychology, Rochester, NY 14623. Offers Advanced Certificate. *Program availability:* Part-time. *Students:* 1 (woman) full-time. Average age 23. 6 applicants. In 2017, 8 Advanced Certificates awarded. *Entrance requirements:* For degree, minimum GPA of 3.0 (recommended). Additional exam requirements/recommendations for international students: Required—TOEFL (minimum score 600 paper-based; 100 iBT), IELTS (minimum score 7), PTE (minimum score 68). *Application deadline:* For fall admission, 2/15 priority date for domestic and international students; for spring admission, 12/15 priority date for domestic students, 11/15 priority date for international students. Applications are processed on a rolling basis. Application fee: $65. Electronic applications accepted. *Expenses:* $1,815 per credit hour. *Financial support:* Scholarships/grants available. Support available to part-time students. Financial award applicants required to submit FAFSA. *Unit head:* Dr. Suzanne Bamonto, Graduate Program Director, 585-475-2765, E-mail: sbggsp@rit.edu. *Application contact:* Diane Ellison, Senior Associate Vice President, Graduate Enrollment Services, 585-475-2229, Fax: 585-475-7164, E-mail: gradinfo@rit.edu.
Website: http://www.rit.edu/cla/psychology/advanced-certificates/school-psychology

Rochester Institute of Technology, Graduate Enrollment Services, College of Liberal Arts, Psychology Department, MS Program in School Psychology, Rochester, NY 14623. Offers MS. *Program availability:* Part-time. *Students:* 21 full-time (18 women); includes 1 minority (Black or African American, non-Hispanic/Latino). Average age 25. 29 applicants, 69% accepted, 9 enrolled. In 2017, 7 master's awarded. *Degree requirements:* For master's, internship, portfolio. *Entrance requirements:* For master's, GRE, minimum GPA of 3.0 (recommended). Additional exam requirements/recommendations for international students: Required—TOEFL (minimum score 600 paper-based; 100 iBT), IELTS (minimum score 7), PTE (minimum score 68). *Application*

deadline: For fall admission, 2/15 priority date for domestic and international students; for spring admission, 12/15 priority date for domestic and international students. Applications are processed on a rolling basis. Application fee: $65. Electronic applications accepted. *Expenses:* $1,815 per credit hour. *Financial support:* In 2017–18, 14 students received support. Teaching assistantships with partial tuition reimbursements available, career-related internships or fieldwork, scholarships/grants, and unspecified assistantships available. Support available to part-time students. Financial award applicants required to submit FAFSA. *Faculty research:* Personality assessment, autism spectrum disorders, developmental disabilities, psychometrics, curriculum-based measurement, multi-tier system of supports, psychophysiological and neuropsychological assessment, impulsivity, aggression, attention. *Unit head:* Dr. Suzanne Bamonto, Graduate Program Director, 585-475-2765, E-mail: sbggsp@rit.edu. *Application contact:* Diane Ellison, Senior Associate Vice President, Graduate Enrollment Services, 585-475-2229, Fax: 585-475-7164, E-mail: gradinfo@rit.edu.
Website: http://www.rit.edu/cla/psychology/graduate/ms-school-psych/overview

Roosevelt University, Graduate Division, College of Education, Program in Clinical Mental Health Counseling and School Counseling, Chicago, IL 60605. Offers clinical mental health counseling (MA); school counseling (MA). *Accreditation:* ACA. *Students:* 64 full-time (52 women), 33 part-time (25 women); includes 45 minority (25 Black or African American, non-Hispanic/Latino; 1 Asian, non-Hispanic/Latino; 15 Hispanic/Latino; 4 Two or more races, non-Hispanic/Latino), 2 international. Average age 28. 65 applicants, 98% accepted, 36 enrolled. In 2017, 35 master's awarded. Application fee: $40. *Financial support:* Scholarships/grants and unspecified assistantships available. *Application contact:* Laura Lag, Associate Dean for Graduate Admission, 312-853-4753, E-mail: llag@roosevelt.edu.

Rowan University, Graduate School, College of Education, Department of Educational Services and Leadership, Ed S in School Psychology Program, Glassboro, NJ 08028-1701. Offers Ed S. *Degree requirements:* For Ed S, practicum, internship. *Entrance requirements:* For degree, master's degree, official transcripts, current professional resume, statement of professional objectives, two letters of recommendation, interview. Electronic applications accepted. *Expenses:* Tuition, state resident: full-time $15,020; part-time $751 per semester hour. Tuition, nonresident: full-time $15,020; part-time $751 per semester hour. *Required fees:* $3158; $157.90 per semester hour. Tuition and fees vary according to course load, campus/location and program.

Rowan University, Graduate School, College of Education, Department of Educational Services and Leadership, MA in School Psychology Program, Glassboro, NJ 08028-1701. Offers MA. *Accreditation:* NCATE. *Program availability:* Part-time, evening/weekend. *Degree requirements:* For master's, comprehensive exam, thesis. *Entrance requirements:* For master's, GRE General Test, GRE Subject Test, interview, minimum GPA of 3.0. Additional exam requirements/recommendations for international students: Required—TOEFL. *Expenses:* Tuition, state resident: full-time $15,020; part-time $751 per semester hour. Tuition, nonresident: full-time $15,020; part-time $751 per semester hour. *Required fees:* $3158; $157.90 per semester hour. Tuition and fees vary according to course load, campus/location and program.

Rutgers University–New Brunswick, Graduate School of Applied and Professional Psychology, Program in School Psychology, Piscataway, NJ 08854-8097. Offers Psy M, Psy D. *Accreditation:* APA (one or more programs are accredited). *Degree requirements:* For doctorate, comprehensive exam, thesis/dissertation, 1 year internship. *Entrance requirements:* For doctorate, GRE General Test, GRE Subject Test, bachelor's degree in psychology or equivalent. Additional exam requirements/recommendations for international students: Required—TOEFL. Electronic applications accepted. *Expenses:* Contact institution. *Faculty research:* Consultation, program evaluation, applied educational psychology, exceptional children, crisis intervention.

St. John's University, St. John's College of Liberal Arts and Sciences, Department of Psychology, Program in School Psychology, Queens, NY 11439. Offers MS, Psy D. *Students:* 100 full-time (90 women), 25 part-time (21 women); includes 37 minority (6 Black or African American, non-Hispanic/Latino; 8 Asian, non-Hispanic/Latino; 22 Hispanic/Latino; 1 Two or more races, non-Hispanic/Latino), 9 international. Average age 26. 130 applicants, 47% accepted, 31 enrolled. In 2017, 23 master's, 15 doctorates awarded. Terminal master's awarded for partial completion of doctoral program. *Degree requirements:* For master's, comprehensive exam, internship; for doctorate, comprehensive exam, thesis/dissertation, 105 credits, 2 practica, 2 externships, internship. *Entrance requirements:* For master's and doctorate, GRE General Test, letters of recommendation, transcripts, resume, personal statement, 24 credits of psychology prerequisites, lab paper, term paper. Additional exam requirements/recommendations for international students: Required—TOEFL (minimum score 80 iBT), IELTS (minimum score 6.5). *Application deadline:* For fall admission, 3/15 priority date for domestic students. Application fee: $70. Electronic applications accepted. *Expenses:* $23,724 per year. *Financial support:* Fellowships, research assistantships, teaching assistantships, scholarships/grants, tuition waivers, and unspecified assistantships available. Support available to part-time students. Financial award application deadline: 2/1; financial award applicants required to submit FAFSA. *Faculty research:* Identification of learning disabilities; nondiscriminatory assessment; anger; behavioral assessment and intervention for children with autism spectrum disorders and other developmental disabilities. *Unit head:* Dr. Marlene Sotelo-Dynega, Director, 718-990-1545, Fax: 718-990-6705, E-mail: sotelodmj@stjohns.edu. *Application contact:* Robert Medrano, Director of Graduate Admission, 718-990-1601, Fax: 718-990-5686, E-mail: gradhelp@stjohns.edu.
Website: https://www.stjohns.edu/academics/schools-and-colleges/st-johns-college-liberal-arts-and-sciences/psychology/school-psychology-psyd

Saint Mary's College of California, Kalmanovitz School of Education, Program in Counseling, Moraga, CA 94575. Offers career counseling (MA); college student services (Credential); general counseling (MA); marriage and family therapy (MA); pupil personnel services (Credential), including school counseling, school psychology; school counseling (MA); school psychology (MA). *Program availability:* Part-time, evening/weekend. *Degree requirements:* For master's, thesis or alternative. *Entrance requirements:* For master's, interview, minimum GPA of 3.0. *Faculty research:* Counselor training effectiveness, multicultural development, empathy, the interface of spirituality and psychotherapy, gender issues.

Sam Houston State University, College of Humanities and Social Sciences, Department of Psychology and Philosophy, Huntsville, TX 77341. Offers psychology (MA, PhD, SSP), including clinical psychology (MA, PhD), psychology (MA), school psychology (SSP). *Accreditation:* APA. *Program availability:* Part-time. Terminal master's awarded for partial completion of doctoral program. *Degree requirements:* For master's, comprehensive exam, thesis optional; for doctorate, comprehensive exam, thesis/dissertation. *Entrance requirements:* For master's, GRE General Test, personal statement, letters of recommendation; for doctorate, GRE General Test, GRE Subject Test (advanced psychology), personal essay, letters of recommendation, resume. Additional exam requirements/recommendations for international students: Required—TOEFL (minimum score 550 paper-based; 79 iBT), IELTS (minimum score 6.5). Electronic applications accepted.

School Psychology

San Diego State University, Graduate and Research Affairs, College of Education, Department of Counseling and School Psychology, San Diego, CA 92182. Offers MS. *Accreditation:* NCATE. *Program availability:* Evening/weekend. *Degree requirements:* For master's, comprehensive exam (for some programs), thesis (for some programs). *Entrance requirements:* For master's, GRE General Test, interview, letters of reference. Additional exam requirements/recommendations for international students: Required—TOEFL. Electronic applications accepted. *Faculty research:* Multicultural and cross-cultural counseling and training, AIDS counseling.

San Francisco State University, Division of Graduate Studies, College of Science and Engineering, Department of Psychology, San Francisco, CA 94132-1722. Offers clinical psychology (MS); developmental psychology (MA); industrial/organizational psychology (MS); mind, brain, and behavior (MA); school psychology (MS, Credential); social psychology (MA). *Financial support:* Teaching assistantships available. Financial award application deadline: 3/1. *Unit head:* Dr. Dawn Terrell, Chair, 415-338-7555, Fax: 415-338-2398, E-mail: schen9@sfsu.edu. *Application contact:* Dr. Diane Harris, Graduate Program Coordinator, 415-338-7064, Fax: 415-338-2398, E-mail: dharris@sfsu.edu. Website: http://psychology.sfsu.edu/graduate/application.html

Seattle University, College of Education, Program in Counseling and School Psychology, Seattle, WA 98122-1090. Offers MA, Certificate, Ed S. *Accreditation:* ACA; NCATE. *Program availability:* Part-time, evening/weekend. *Faculty:* 13 full-time (7 women), 3 part-time/adjunct (2 women). *Students:* 122 full-time (107 women), 90 part-time (74 women); includes 71 minority (8 Black or African American, non-Hispanic/Latino; 3 American Indian or Alaska Native, non-Hispanic/Latino; 21 Asian, non-Hispanic/Latino; 28 Hispanic/Latino; 11 Two or more races, non-Hispanic/Latino), 3 international. Average age 29. 212 applicants, 55% accepted, 54 enrolled. In 2017, 40 master's, 27 other advanced degrees awarded. *Degree requirements:* For master's, comprehensive exam. *Entrance requirements:* For master's, interview; GRE, MAT, or minimum GPA of 3.0; related work experience. Additional exam requirements/recommendations for international students: Required—TOEFL. *Application deadline:* For fall admission, 7/1 for domestic students; for winter admission, 10/20 for domestic students; for spring admission, 1/20 for domestic students. Application fee: $55. *Expenses:* Tuition: Full-time $12,960. *Required fees:* $570. Tuition and fees vary according to program. *Financial support:* In 2017–18, 39 students received support. *Unit head:* Hutch Haney, Director, 206-296-5750, E-mail: schpsy@seattleu.edu. *Application contact:* Janet Shandley, Associate Dean of Graduate Admissions, 206-296-5900, Fax: 206-298-5656, E-mail: grad_admissions@seattleu.edu. Website: https://www.seattleu.edu/education/psychology/

Seton Hall University, College of Education and Human Services, Department of Professional Psychology and Family Therapy, Program in School Psychology, South Orange, NJ 07079-2697. Offers MA. *Degree requirements:* For master's, comprehensive exam, thesis, internship. *Entrance requirements:* For master's, GRE or MAT, interview. *Faculty research:* Family systems, ethical behavior, childhood depression.

Slippery Rock University of Pennsylvania, Graduate Studies (Recruitment), College of Education, Department of Counseling and Development, Slippery Rock, PA 16057-1383. Offers clinical mental health (MA); school counseling (M Ed); student affairs in higher education (MA); student affairs in higher education with college counseling (MA). *Accreditation:* ACA (one or more programs are accredited); NCATE. *Program availability:* Part-time, evening/weekend. *Degree requirements:* For master's, comprehensive exam, thesis (for some programs). *Entrance requirements:* For master's, GRE General Test or MAT, official transcripts, personal statement, three letters of recommendation, interview. Additional exam requirements/recommendations for international students: Required—TOEFL (minimum score 550 paper-based; 80 iBT). Electronic applications accepted. *Expenses:* Contact institution.

Sonoma State University, School of Social Sciences, Department of Counseling, Rohnert Park, CA 94928. Offers clinical mental health counseling (MA); school counseling (MA). *Accreditation:* ACA. *Program availability:* Part-time. *Entrance requirements:* For master's, minimum GPA of 3.0. Additional exam requirements/recommendations for international students: Required—TOEFL (minimum score 500 paper-based). *Application deadline:* For fall admission, 11/30 for domestic students. Application fee: $55. *Financial support:* Fellowships and career-related internships or fieldwork available. Financial award application deadline: 3/2; financial award applicants required to submit FAFSA. *Unit head:* Dr. Adam Zagelbaum, Chair, 707-664-2544, E-mail: adam.zagelbaum@sonoma.edu. Website: http://www.sonoma.edu/counseling

Southern Connecticut State University, School of Graduate Studies, School of Education, Department of Counseling and School Psychology, New Haven, CT 06515-1355. Offers community counseling (MS); counseling (Diploma); school counseling (MS); school psychology (MS, Diploma). *Accreditation:* ACA (one or more programs are accredited); NCATE. *Program availability:* Part-time, evening/weekend. *Degree requirements:* For master's, comprehensive exam. *Entrance requirements:* For master's, interview, previous course work in behavioral sciences, minimum QPA of 2.7. Electronic applications accepted.

Southern Illinois University Edwardsville, Graduate School, School of Education, Health, and Human Behavior, Department of Psychology, Program in School Psychology, Edwardsville, IL 62026. Offers SD. *Accreditation:* NCATE. *Program availability:* Part-time, evening/weekend. *Degree requirements:* For SD, thesis. *Entrance requirements:* For degree, GRE. Additional exam requirements/recommendations for international students: Required—TOEFL (minimum score 550 paper-based; 79 iBT), IELTS (minimum score 6.5). Electronic applications accepted.

Southwestern Oklahoma State University, College of Professional and Graduate Studies, School of Behavioral Sciences and Education, Specialization in School Psychology, Weatherford, OK 73096-3098. Offers MS.

State University of New York at Plattsburgh, School of Arts and Sciences, Department of Psychology, Plattsburgh, NY 12901-2681. Offers school psychology (MA, CAS). *Program availability:* Part-time. *Entrance requirements:* For master's, GRE General Test, minimum GPA of 3.0. Additional exam requirements/recommendations for international students: Required—TOEFL. *Faculty research:* Alzheimer's disease, adolescent behavior, intellectual assessment, learning disabilities, reading skill acquisition.

Stephen F. Austin State University, Graduate School, College of Education, Department of Human Services, Nacogdoches, TX 75962. Offers counseling (MA); school psychology (MA); special education (M Ed); speech-language pathology (MS). *Accreditation:* ACA (one or more programs are accredited); ASHA (one or more programs are accredited); CORE; NCATE. *Degree requirements:* For master's, comprehensive exam, thesis (for some programs). *Entrance requirements:* For master's, GRE General Test, minimum GPA of 2.8. Additional exam requirements/recommendations for international students: Required—TOEFL.

Syracuse University, College of Arts and Sciences, Department of Psychology, Syracuse, NY 13244. Offers clinical psychology (PhD); cognition, brain, and behavior (PhD); school psychology (PhD); social psychology (PhD). *Accreditation:* APA. In 2017, 1 doctorate awarded. Terminal master's awarded for partial completion of doctoral program. *Degree requirements:* For doctorate, comprehensive exam, thesis/dissertation. *Entrance requirements:* For doctorate, GRE General Test, GRE Subject Test, resume, personal statement, three letters of recommendation. Additional exam requirements/recommendations for international students: Required—TOEFL (minimum score 100 iBT). *Application deadline:* For fall admission, 12/1 priority date for domestic and international students. Application fee: $75. Electronic applications accepted. *Financial support:* Fellowships with full tuition reimbursements, research assistantships with tuition reimbursements, teaching assistantships with tuition reimbursements, and scholarships/grants available. Financial award application deadline: 1/1. *Faculty research:* Clinical psychology; cognition, brain, and behavior; school psychology; social psychology. *Unit head:* Dr. Amy Criss, Professor and Department Chair, Psychology, 315-443-1210, E-mail: acriss@syr.edu. *Application contact:* Alecia Zema, Curriculum Coordinator, 315-443-2760, E-mail: azema@syr.edu. Website: http://psychology.syr.edu/graduate/overview.html

Syracuse University, School of Education, Programs in School Counseling, Syracuse, NY 13244. Offers MS, CAS. *Accreditation:* APA. *Program availability:* Part-time. *Students:* Average age 24. *Entrance requirements:* For master's, GRE or MAT, baccalaureate degree from regionally-accredited college/university, three letters of recommendation, transcripts, personal statement, interview; for CAS, master's degree in counseling; minimum of 60 credits beyond the baccalaureate, of which 30 credits must be taken at Syracuse University. Additional exam requirements/recommendations for international students: Required—TOEFL (minimum score 100 iBT). *Application deadline:* For fall admission, 6/1 priority date for domestic and international students; for spring admission, 10/15 priority date for domestic and international students; for summer admission, 1/15 priority date for domestic and international students. Applications are processed on a rolling basis. Application fee: $75. Electronic applications accepted. *Financial support:* Fellowships with full tuition reimbursements, research assistantships, teaching assistantships, career-related internships or fieldwork, and scholarships/grants available. Financial award application deadline: 1/15; financial award applicants required to submit FAFSA. *Faculty research:* Group work in counseling, social and cultural dimensions of counseling, life-span human development, counseling in the schools, assessment in counseling. *Unit head:* Dr. Jing Lei, Professor/Chair of the Department of Counseling and Human Service, 315-443-2266, E-mail: dxseward@syr.edu. *Application contact:* Speranza Migliore, Graduate Admissions Recruiter, 315-443-2505, E-mail: gradrcrt@syr.edu. Website: http://soe.syr.edu/academic/counseling_and_human_services/

Teachers College, Columbia University, Department of Counseling and Clinical Psychology, New York, NY 10027-6696. Offers clinical psychology (PhD); counseling psychology (Ed M, Ed D, PhD); mental health counseling (ME); psychological counseling (ME, ND); psychology in education (MA, ND); school counselor (ME). *Accreditation:* APA (one or more programs are accredited). *Program availability:* Part-time. *Students:* 430 full-time (364 women), 237 part-time (201 women); includes 243 minority (65 Black or African American, non-Hispanic/Latino; 73 Asian, non-Hispanic/Latino; 83 Hispanic/Latino; 22 Two or more races, non-Hispanic/Latino), 142 international. Average age 28. 1,568 applicants, 38% accepted, 292 enrolled. *Unit head:* Prof. George Bonanno, Head, E-mail: gab38@tc.columbia.edu. *Application contact:* David Estrella, Director of Admission, 212-678-3305, E-mail: estrella@tc.columbia.edu.

Teachers College, Columbia University, Department of Health and Behavior Studies, New York, NY 10027-6696. Offers applied behavior analysis (MA, PhD); applied educational psychology: school psychology (Ed M, PhD); behavioral nutrition (PhD), including nutrition (Ed D, PhD); community health education (MS); community nutrition education (Ed M), including community nutrition education; education of deaf and hard of hearing (MA, PhD); health education (MA, Ed D); hearing impairment (Ed D); intellectual disability/autism (MA, Ed D, PhD); nursing education (Ed D, Advanced Certificate); nutrition and education (MS); nutrition and exercise physiology (MS); nutrition and public health (MS); nutrition education (Ed D), including nutrition (Ed D, PhD); physical disabilities (Ed D); reading specialist (MA); severe or multiple disabilities (MA); special education (Ed M, MA, Ed D); teaching of sign language (MA). *Program availability:* Part-time, evening/weekend. *Students:* 245 full-time (226 women), 242 part-time (219 women); includes 167 minority (52 Black or African American, non-Hispanic/Latino; 2 American Indian or Alaska Native, non-Hispanic/Latino; 55 Asian, non-Hispanic/Latino; 48 Hispanic/Latino; 1 Native Hawaiian or other Pacific Islander, non-Hispanic/Latino; 9 Two or more races, non-Hispanic/Latino), 60 international. Average age 30. 480 applicants, 59% accepted, 157 enrolled. Terminal master's awarded for partial completion of doctoral program. *Unit head:* Prof. Dolores Perin, Chair, E-mail: dp111@tc.columbia.edu. *Application contact:* David Estrella, Director of Admission, 212-678-3305, E-mail: estrella@tc.columbia.edu. Website: http://www.tc.columbia.edu/health-and-behavior-studies/

Temple University, College of Education, Department of Psychological Studies in Education, Philadelphia, PA 19122-6096. Offers applied behavior analysis (MS Ed); counseling psychology (Ed M), including agency counseling, school counseling; educational psychology (Ed M); school psychology (PhD, Ed S). *Accreditation:* APA (one or more programs are accredited). *Program availability:* Part-time, evening/weekend. *Faculty:* 25 full-time (12 women), 23 part-time/adjunct (11 women). *Students:* 255 full-time (191 women), 188 part-time (137 women); includes 136 minority (90 Black or African American, non-Hispanic/Latino; 1 American Indian or Alaska Native, non-Hispanic/Latino; 18 Asian, non-Hispanic/Latino; 14 Hispanic/Latino; 13 Two or more races, non-Hispanic/Latino), 28 international. 376 applicants, 51% accepted, 109 enrolled. In 2017, 129 master's, 27 doctorates, 21 other advanced degrees awarded. Terminal master's awarded for partial completion of doctoral program. *Degree requirements:* For master's, thesis or alternative; for doctorate, thesis/dissertation. *Entrance requirements:* Additional exam requirements/recommendations for international students: Required—TOEFL (minimum score 550 paper-based; 79 iBT). *Application deadline:* For fall admission, 12/15 for international students; for spring admission, 8/1 for international students. Application fee: $60. *Expenses:* Tuition, state resident: full-time $16,164; part-time $898 per credit hour. Tuition, nonresident: full-time $22,158; part-time $1231 per credit hour. *Required fees:* $890; $445 per semester. Full-time tuition and fees vary according to course load, degree level, campus/location and program. *Financial support:* Fellowships, research assistantships with full tuition reimbursements, and teaching assistantships with full tuition reimbursements available. Financial award application deadline: 1/15; financial award applicants required to submit FAFSA. *Unit head:* Dr. Catherine Fiorello, Chair, 215-204-6254, E-mail: catherine.fiorello@temple.edu. Website: http://education.temple.edu/pse

Texas A&M University, College of Education and Human Development, Department of Educational Psychology, College Station, TX 77843. Offers bilingual education (M Ed, MS); counseling psychology (PhD); educational psychology (M Ed, MS, PhD); educational technology (M Ed); school psychology (PhD); special education (M Ed, MS). *Accreditation:* APA (one or more programs are accredited). *Program availability:* Part-time, evening/weekend, blended/hybrid learning. *Faculty:* 45. *Students:* 165 full-time (131 women), 248 part-time (210 women); includes 144 minority (24 Black or African American, non-Hispanic/Latino; 3 American Indian or Alaska Native, non-Hispanic/

Latino; 21 Asian, non-Hispanic/Latino; 84 Hispanic/Latino; 2 Native Hawaiian or other Pacific Islander, non-Hispanic/Latino; 10 Two or more races, non-Hispanic/Latino), 45 international. Average age 33. 171 applicants, 44% accepted, 47 enrolled. In 2017, 141 master's, 28 doctorates awarded. *Degree requirements:* For master's, thesis optional; for doctorate, thesis/dissertation. *Entrance requirements:* For master's and doctorate, GRE General Test. Additional exam requirements/recommendations for international students: Required—TOEFL (minimum score 550 paper-based; 80 iBT), IELTS (minimum score 6), PTE (minimum score 53). *Application deadline:* For fall admission, 12/1 for domestic students; for spring admission, 10/15 for domestic students. Application fee: $50 ($90 for international students). Electronic applications accepted. *Expenses:* Contact institution. *Financial support:* In 2017–18, 210 students received support, including 4 fellowships with tuition reimbursements available (averaging $24,775 per year), 102 research assistantships with tuition reimbursements available (averaging $10,698 per year), 19 teaching assistantships with tuition reimbursements available (averaging $7,177 per year); career-related internships or fieldwork, institutionally sponsored loans, scholarships/grants, traineeships, health care benefits, tuition waivers (full and partial), and unspecified assistantships also available. Support available to part-time students. Financial award application deadline: 3/15; financial award applicants required to submit FAFSA. *Unit head:* Dr. Victor Willson, Department Head, 979-845-1394, E-mail: v-willson@tamu.edu. *Application contact:* Kristie Stramaski, Senior Academic Advisor, 979-845-1833, E-mail: epsyadvisor@tamu.edu.
Website: http://epsy.tamu.edu

Texas A&M University–Central Texas, Graduate Studies and Research, Killeen, TX 76549. Offers accounting (MS); business administration (MBA); clinical mental health counseling (MS); criminal justice (MCJ); curriculum and instruction (M Ed); educational administration (M Ed); educational psychology - experimental psychology (MS); history (MA); human resource management (MS); information systems (MS); liberal studies (MS); management and leadership (MS); marriage and family therapy (MS); mathematics (MS); political science (MA); school counseling (M Ed); school psychology (Ed S).

Texas State University, The Graduate College, College of Education, Program in School Psychology, San Marcos, TX 78666. Offers SSP. *Program availability:* Part-time. *Faculty:* 7 full-time (4 women), 8 part-time/adjunct (2 women). *Students:* 43 full-time (40 women), 28 part-time (23 women); includes 42 minority (3 Black or African American, non-Hispanic/Latino; 1 Asian, non-Hispanic/Latino; 37 Hispanic/Latino; 1 Two or more races, non-Hispanic/Latino). Average age 27. 61 applicants, 61% accepted, 16 enrolled. *Entrance requirements:* Additional exam requirements/recommendations for international students: Required—TOEFL (minimum score 550 paper-based; 78 iBT), IELTS (minimum score 6.5). *Application deadline:* For fall admission, 2/15 for domestic and international students. Applications are processed on a rolling basis. Application fee: $40 ($90 for international students). Electronic applications accepted. *Expenses:* Tuition, state resident: full-time $7868; part-time $3934 per semester. Tuition, nonresident: full-time $17,828; part-time $8914 per semester. *Required fees:* $2092; $1435 per semester. Tuition and fees vary according to course load. *Financial support:* In 2017–18, 61 students received support, including 3 research assistantships (averaging $6,076 per year), 2 teaching assistantships (averaging $6,076 per year); career-related internships or fieldwork, Federal Work-Study, institutionally sponsored loans, scholarships/grants, and unspecified assistantships also available. Support available to part-time students. Financial award application deadline: 3/1; financial award applicants required to submit FAFSA. *Faculty research:* Using psychology and education in reaching bilinguals. *Total annual research expenditures:* $271,440. *Unit head:* Dr. Jon Lasser, Graduate Advisor, 512-245-3413, Fax: 512-245-8872, E-mail: jl30@txstate.edu. *Application contact:* Dr. Andrea Golato, Dean of Graduate School, 512-245-2581, Fax: 512-245-8365, E-mail: gradcollege@txstate.edu.
Website: http://www.gradcollege.txstate.edu/programs/ssp.html

Texas Woman's University, Graduate School, College of Arts and Sciences, Department of Psychology and Philosophy, Denton, TX 76204. Offers counseling psychology (MA, PhD); psychological science (MS); school psychology (PhD, SSP). *Accreditation:* APA (one or more programs are accredited). *Faculty:* 15 full-time (10 women), 3 part-time/adjunct (2 women). *Students:* 77 full-time (70 women), 41 part-time (37 women); includes 52 minority (13 Black or African American, non-Hispanic/Latino; 11 Asian, non-Hispanic/Latino; 23 Hispanic/Latino; 5 Two or more races, non-Hispanic/Latino). Average age 28. 120 applicants, 21% accepted, 24 enrolled. In 2017, 4 master's, 13 doctorates, 4 other advanced degrees awarded. Terminal master's awarded for partial completion of doctoral program. *Degree requirements:* For master's, comprehensive exam (for some programs), thesis (for some programs), practica (for MA); for doctorate, comprehensive exam, thesis/dissertation, internship, residency; for SSP, comprehensive exam, internship, capstone evaluation. *Entrance requirements:* For master's, GRE (preferred minimum score 153 [500 old version] Verbal, 144 [500 old version] Quantitative, 4.0 Analytical Writing), BA/BS or 18 hours in psychology; minimum GPA of 3.0, 3.5 in psychology classes; 3 letters of reference; curriculum vitae; essay; for doctorate, GRE (preferred minimum score 153 [500 old version] Verbal, 144 [500 old version] Quantitative, 4 Analytical), 3 letters of reference, minimum GPA of 3.0 overall and 3.5 in psychology classes, MA in psychology or related discipline with thesis, curriculum vitae, essays; for SSP, GRE (preferred minimum score 153 [500 old version] Verbal, 144 [500 old version] Quantitative, 4 Analytical), BA/BS or 18 hours in psychology; minimum GPA of 3.0, 3.5 in psychology classes; 3 letters of reference; curriculum vitae; personal essay. Additional exam requirements/recommendations for international students: Required—TOEFL (minimum score 550 paper-based; 79 iBT); Recommended—IELTS (minimum score 6.5), TSE (minimum score 53). *Application deadline:* For fall admission, 2/1 for domestic and international students; for summer admission, 2/1 for domestic and international students. Applications are processed on a rolling basis. Application fee: $50 ($75 for international students). Electronic applications accepted. *Expenses:* $7,520 per year full-time in-state; $16,820 per year full-time out-of-state. *Financial support:* In 2017–18, 74 students received support, including 11 teaching assistantships (averaging $13,010 per year); research assistantships, career-related internships or fieldwork, Federal Work-Study, institutionally sponsored loans, scholarships/grants, traineeships, health care benefits, and unspecified assistantships also available. Support available to part-time students. Financial award application deadline: 3/1; financial award applicants required to submit FAFSA. *Faculty research:* Victimization, body image, moral and political philosophy, neuropsychology and assessment in children, neurobiology of memory and learning. *Total annual research expenditures:* $51,748. *Unit head:* Dr. Shannon Scott, Chair, 940-898-2303, Fax: 940-898-2301, E-mail: psychology@twu.edu. *Application contact:* Korie Hawkins, Associate Director of Admissions, Graduate Recruitment, 940-898-3188, Fax: 940-898-3081, E-mail: admissions@twu.edu.
Website: http://www.twu.edu/psychology-philosophy/

Towson University, College of Liberal Arts, Program in Psychology, Towson, MD 21252-0001. Offers clinical psychology (MA); counseling psychology (MA); experimental psychology (MA); school psychology (MA). *Program availability:* Part-time, evening/weekend. *Students:* 98 full-time (75 women), 21 part-time (13 women); includes 32 minority (15 Black or African American, non-Hispanic/Latino; 4 Asian, non-Hispanic/Latino; 8 Hispanic/Latino; 5 Two or more races, non-Hispanic/Latino). *Degree requirements:* For master's, thesis (for some programs). *Entrance requirements:* For master's, GRE, minimum GPA of 3.0, letters of recommendation. *Application deadline:* For fall admission, 1/17 for domestic students, 5/15 for international students; for spring admission, 10/15 for domestic students, 12/1 for international students. Applications are processed on a rolling basis. Application fee: $45. Electronic applications accepted. *Expenses:* Tuition, state resident: full-time $7960; part-time $398 per unit. Tuition, nonresident: full-time $16,480; part-time $824 per unit. *Required fees:* $2600; $130 per year. $390 per term. *Financial support:* Application deadline: 4/1. *Unit head:* Dr. Geoffrey Munro, Department Chair, 410-704-2634, E-mail: psycdept@towson.edu. *Application contact:* Coverley Beidleman, Assistant Director of Graduate Admissions, 410-704-5630, Fax: 410-704-3030, E-mail: cbeidleman@towson.edu.
Website: https://www.towson.edu/cla/departments/psychology/grad/

Trinity University, Department of Education, Master of Arts in School Psychology Program, San Antonio, TX 78212-7200. Offers MA. *Accreditation:* NCATE. *Entrance requirements:* For master's, GRE or master's degree, minimum GPA of 3.0, academic and professional references, interview with program director. *Application deadline:* For fall admission, 2/1 for domestic and international students. Application fee: $50. Electronic applications accepted. *Financial support:* Institutionally sponsored loans, scholarships/grants, and unspecified assistantships available. Support available to part-time students. Financial award application deadline: 5/1; financial award applicants required to submit FAFSA. *Unit head:* Dr. Laurie Klose, Director, 210-999-7595, E-mail: lklose@trinity.edu. *Application contact:* Sonia Mireles, Academic Office Manager, 210-999-8835, E-mail: smireles@trinity.edu.
Website: https://new.trinity.edu/academics/departments/education/master-arts-school-psychology

Tufts University, Graduate School of Arts and Sciences, Department of Education, Program in School Psychology, Medford, MA 02155. Offers MA, Ed S. *Students:* 45 full-time (40 women); includes 8 minority (2 Black or African American, non-Hispanic/Latino; 4 Asian, non-Hispanic/Latino; 1 Hispanic/Latino; 1 Two or more races, non-Hispanic/Latino). Average age 25. 77 applicants, 36% accepted, 16 enrolled. In 2017, 13 master's, 14 other advanced degrees awarded. *Degree requirements:* For master's, internship. *Entrance requirements:* For master's, GRE General Test. Additional exam requirements/recommendations for international students: Required—TOEFL (minimum score 550 paper-based; 80 iBT), IELTS (minimum score 6.5). *Application deadline:* For fall admission, 1/2 for domestic and international students. Applications are processed on a rolling basis. Application fee: $85. Electronic applications accepted. *Expenses:* Contact institution. *Financial support:* Federal Work-Study, scholarships/grants, and tuition waivers (full and partial) available. Financial award application deadline: 1/2. *Unit head:* Dr. Steve Luz-Alterman, Graduate Program Director, 617-627-2390. *Application contact:* Office of Graduate Admissions, 617-627-3395, E-mail: gradadmissions@tufts.edu.
Website: http://ase.tufts.edu/education/programs/schoolPsych/

Union College, Graduate Programs, Department of Psychology, Barbourville, KY 40906-1499. Offers clinical psychology (MA); counseling psychology (MA); school psychology (MA).

The University of Akron, Graduate School, College of Health Professions, School of Counseling, Program in Classroom Guidance for Teachers, Akron, OH 44325. Offers MA, MS. *Accreditation:* NCATE. *Degree requirements:* For master's, comprehensive exam. *Entrance requirements:* For master's, minimum GPA of 2.75, interview, letters of recommendation. Additional exam requirements/recommendations for international students: Required—TOEFL (minimum score 550 paper-based; 79 iBT). Electronic applications accepted.

University of Alberta, Faculty of Graduate Studies and Research, Department of Educational Psychology, Edmonton, AB T6G 2E1, Canada. Offers counseling psychology (M Ed, PhD); educational psychology (M Ed, PhD); instructional technology (M Ed); school counseling (M Ed); school psychology (M Ed, PhD); special education (M Ed, PhD); special education-deafness studies (M Ed); teaching English as a second language (M Ed). *Program availability:* Part-time. *Degree requirements:* For master's, thesis optional; for doctorate, comprehensive exam, thesis/dissertation. *Entrance requirements:* For master's and doctorate, minimum GPA of 3.0. Additional exam requirements/recommendations for international students: Required—TOEFL. *Faculty research:* Human learning, development and assessment.

The University of Arizona, College of Education, Department of Disability and Psychoeducational Studies, Program in School Psychology, Tucson, AZ 85721. Offers PhD, Ed S. *Program availability:* Part-time. *Entrance requirements:* For doctorate, GRE General Test; for Ed S, minimum GPA of 3.5, 3 letters of recommendation, curriculum vitae, writing sample. Additional exam requirements/recommendations for international students: Required—TOEFL (minimum score 550 paper-based; 79 iBT). Electronic applications accepted.

The University of British Columbia, Faculty of Education, Department of Educational and Counseling Psychology, and Special Education, Vancouver, BC V6T 1Z4, Canada. Offers counseling psychology (M Ed, MA, PhD); guidance studies (Diploma); human development, learning and culture (M Ed, MA, PhD); measurement, evaluation, and research methodology (M Ed, MA, PhD); school psychology (M Ed, MA, PhD); special education (M Ed, MA, PhD, Diploma). *Program availability:* Part-time. *Degree requirements:* For master's, thesis (for some programs); for doctorate, comprehensive exam, thesis/dissertation. *Entrance requirements:* For master's, GRE General Test (for MA in counseling psychology); for doctorate, GRE General Test. Additional exam requirements/recommendations for international students: Required—TOEFL. Electronic applications accepted. *Expenses:* Contact institution. *Faculty research:* Women, family, social problems, career transition, stress and coping problems.

University of Calgary, Faculty of Graduate Studies, Werklund School of Education, Division of Applied Psychology, Calgary, AB T2N 1N4, Canada. Offers counseling psychology (M Sc, MC, PhD); school and applied child psychology (M Ed, M Sc, PhD). *Program availability:* Part-time. *Degree requirements:* For master's, thesis (for some programs), final oral exam; for doctorate, thesis/dissertation, candidacy exam, final oral exam. *Entrance requirements:* For master's, minimum GPA of 3.0, 3 letters of reference; for doctorate, minimum GPA of 3.5, 3 letters of reference. *Faculty research:* Counselor education, family life studies, learning and cognition.

University of California, Riverside, Graduate Division, Graduate School of Education, Riverside, CA 92521. Offers applied behavior analysis (M Ed); diversity and equity (M Ed); education policy analysis and leadership (PhD); education specialist (Credential); education, society, and culture (MA, PhD); educational psychology (MA, PhD); general education (M Ed); higher education administration and policy (M Ed, PhD); multiple subject (Credential); research, evaluation, measurement and statistics (MA); school psychology (PhD); single subject (Credential); special education (M Ed, PhD); special education and autism (MA); TESOL (M Ed). *Faculty:* 29 full-time (16 women), 2 part-time/adjunct (1 woman). *Students:* 241 full-time (188 women). 396 applicants, 42% accepted, 166 enrolled. In 2017, 130 master's, 15 doctorates, 14 other advanced degrees awarded. Terminal master's awarded for partial completion of doctoral program. *Degree requirements:* For master's, comprehensive exams or thesis (MA), case study or analytical report (M Ed); for doctorate, comprehensive exam, thesis/dissertation, written and oral qualifying exams, college teaching practicum. *Entrance*

requirements: For master's, GRE General Test (for MA); CBEST and CSET (for M Ed in general education only), UCR Extension TESOL certificate (for M Ed with TESOL emphasis only); for doctorate, GRE General Test, writing sample; for Credential, CBEST, CSET. Additional exam requirements/recommendations for international students: Required—TOEFL (minimum score 550 paper-based; 80 iBT), IELTS (minimum score 7). *Application deadline:* For fall admission, 9/1 for domestic students, 6/1 for international students; for winter admission, 11/15 for domestic students, 9/1 for international students; for spring admission, 3/1 for domestic students, 12/1 for international students. Applications are processed on a rolling basis. Application fee: $80 ($100 for international students). Electronic applications accepted. *Expenses:* Tuition, state resident: full-time $5746. Tuition, nonresident: full-time $10,780. Tuition and fees vary according to campus/location and program. *Financial support:* In 2017–18, 105 students received support, including 16 fellowships with full tuition reimbursements available (averaging $31,000 per year), 25 research assistantships with full tuition reimbursements available (averaging $31,000 per year), 10 teaching assistantships with full tuition reimbursements available (averaging $31,000 per year); career-related internships or fieldwork, Federal Work-Study, institutionally sponsored loans, scholarships/grants, and unspecified assistantships also available. Financial award application deadline: 12/15. *Faculty research:* Responsiveness to intervention, faculty core, response to intervention of English language learners, advanced modeling techniques, study on social capital, trust, and motivation. *Total annual research expenditures:* $1.7 million. *Unit head:* Thomas Smith, Dean, 951-827-4633, E-mail: thomas.smith@ucr.edu. *Application contact:* Heather Killeen, Graduate Program Coordinator, 951-827-6362, E-mail: heather.killeen@ucr.edu.
Website: http://www.education.ucr.edu/

University of California, Santa Barbara, Graduate Division, Gevirtz Graduate School of Education, Santa Barbara, CA 93106-9490. Offers counseling, clinical and school psychology (MA, PhD, Credential), including clinical psychology (PhD), counseling psychology (MA, PhD), pupil personnel services (Credential), school psychology (PhD); education (MA, PhD); teacher education (M Ed, Credential), including multiple subject teaching (Credential), single subject teaching (Credential), special education (Credential), teaching (M Ed); MA/PhD. *Accreditation:* APA (one or more programs are accredited). Terminal master's awarded for partial completion of doctoral program. *Degree requirements:* For master's, comprehensive exam (for some programs), thesis (for some programs); for doctorate, comprehensive exam (for some programs), thesis/dissertation. *Entrance requirements:* For master's and doctorate, GRE; for Credential, GRE or MAT, CSET, CBEST. Additional exam requirements/recommendations for international students: Required—TOEFL (minimum score 550 paper-based; 80 iBT), IELTS (minimum score 7). Electronic applications accepted. *Faculty research:* Needs of diverse students, school accountability and leadership, school violence, language learning and literacy, science/math education.

University of Central Arkansas, Graduate School, College of Health and Behavioral Sciences, Department of Counseling and Psychology, Program in School Psychology, Conway, AR 72035-0001. Offers MS, PhD, PMC. *Accreditation:* APA; NCATE. Terminal master's awarded for partial completion of doctoral program. *Degree requirements:* For master's, comprehensive exam, thesis optional; for doctorate, comprehensive exam, thesis/dissertation. *Entrance requirements:* For master's, GRE General Test, minimum GPA of 2.7; for doctorate, GRE General Test. Additional exam requirements/recommendations for international students: Required—TOEFL (minimum score 550 paper-based). Electronic applications accepted.

University of Central Florida, College of Community Innovation and Education, Department of Counselor Education and School Psychology, Program in School Psychology, Orlando, FL 32816. Offers Ed S. *Program availability:* Part-time, evening/weekend. *Students:* 40 full-time (35 women), 1 (woman) part-time; includes 10 minority (4 Black or African American, non-Hispanic/Latino; 1 Asian, non-Hispanic/Latino; 5 Hispanic/Latino). Average age 27. 59 applicants, 25% accepted, 11 enrolled. In 2017, 15 Ed Ss awarded. *Degree requirements:* For Ed S, thesis or alternative, practicum, internship. *Entrance requirements:* For degree, GRE General Test, minimum GPA of 3.0, resume, letters of recommendation, goal statement, interview. Additional exam requirements/recommendations for international students: Required—TOEFL. *Application deadline:* For fall admission, 3/1 for domestic students. Application fee: $30. Electronic applications accepted. *Expenses:* Tuition, state resident: part-time $288.16 per credit hour. Tuition, nonresident: part-time $1073.31 per credit hour. Tuition and fees vary according to program. *Financial support:* In 2017–18, 5 students received support, including 2 research assistantships with partial tuition reimbursements available (averaging $9,141 per year), 3 teaching assistantships with partial tuition reimbursements available (averaging $9,088 per year); fellowships, career-related internships or fieldwork, Federal Work-Study, institutionally sponsored loans, health care benefits, and tuition waivers (partial) also available. Financial award application deadline: 3/1; financial award applicants required to submit FAFSA. *Unit head:* Dr. Oliver Edwards, Program Coordinator, 407-823-2401, E-mail: oliver.edwards@ucf.edu. *Application contact:* Associate Director, Graduate Admissions, 407-823-2766, Fax: 407-823-6442, E-mail: gradadmissions@ucf.edu.
Website: http://education.ucf.edu/schpsy/

University of Central Oklahoma, The Jackson College of Graduate Studies, College of Education and Professional Studies, Department of Psychology, Edmond, OK 73034-5209. Offers psychology (MA), including counseling psychology, experimental psychology, forensic psychology, general psychology, school psychology. *Faculty:* 13 full-time (7 women), 1 part-time/adjunct (0 women). *Students:* 74 full-time (59 women), 35 part-time (29 women); includes 30 minority (4 Black or African American, non-Hispanic/Latino; 4 American Indian or Alaska Native, non-Hispanic/Latino; 3 Asian, non-Hispanic/Latino; 12 Hispanic/Latino; 7 Two or more races, non-Hispanic/Latino), 5 international. Average age 27. 109 applicants, 71% accepted, 51 enrolled. In 2017, 33 master's awarded. *Degree requirements:* For master's, thesis (for some programs). *Entrance requirements:* For master's, GRE. Additional exam requirements/recommendations for international students: Required—TOEFL (minimum score 550 paper-based; 79 iBT), IELTS (minimum score 6.5). *Application deadline:* For fall admission, 1/15 for domestic and international students; for spring admission, 11/15 for international students. Application fee: $60. Electronic applications accepted. *Expenses:* Tuition, state resident: full-time $5375; part-time $268.75 per credit hour. Tuition, nonresident: full-time $13,295; part-time $664.75 per credit hour. *Required fees:* $626; $31.30 per credit hour. One-time fee: $50. Tuition and fees vary according to program. *Financial support:* In 2017–18, 18 students received support, including 6 research assistantships with partial tuition reimbursements available (averaging $3,943 per year); teaching assistantships, career-related internships or fieldwork, scholarships/grants, tuition waivers (partial), and unspecified assistantships also available. Financial award application deadline: 3/31; financial award applicants required to submit FAFSA. *Unit head:* Dr. Thomas Hancock, Chair, 405-974-5707, Fax: 405-974-3865. *Application contact:* Carlie Wellington, Assistant Director, CEPS Graduate Enrollment, 405-974-5105, Fax: 405-974-3851, E-mail: gradcoll@uco.edu.
Website: http://sites.uco.edu/ceps/dept/Professional-Studies-Programs/psy/index.asp

University of Cincinnati, Graduate School, College of Education, Criminal Justice, and Human Services, School of Human Services, School Psychology Program, Cincinnati, OH 45221. Offers PhD, Ed S. *Accreditation:* NCATE. *Program availability:* Online only, 100% online. Terminal master's awarded for partial completion of doctoral program. *Degree requirements:* For doctorate, comprehensive exam, thesis/dissertation. *Entrance requirements:* For doctorate, GRE General Test, GRE Subject Test. Additional exam requirements/recommendations for international students: Required—TOEFL (minimum score 520 paper-based; 68 iBT). Electronic applications accepted. *Expenses:* *Tuition, area resident:* Full-time $14,468. Tuition, state resident: full-time $14,968; part-time $754 per credit hour. Tuition, nonresident: full-time $24,210; part-time $1311 per credit hour. *International tuition:* $26,460 full-time. *Required fees:* $3958; $84 per credit hour. One-time fee: $85 full-time. Tuition and fees vary according to course load, degree level and program. *Faculty research:* School psychology services delivery, direct assessment and intervention.

University of Colorado Denver, School of Education and Human Development, Program in Counseling Psychology and Counselor Education, Denver, CO 80217. Offers counseling (MA), including clinical mental health counseling, couple and family counseling, multicultural counseling, school counseling; school counseling (MA). *Accreditation:* ACA; NCATE. *Program availability:* Part-time, evening/weekend. *Degree requirements:* For master's, comprehensive exam (for some programs), thesis or alternative, 63-66 hours. *Entrance requirements:* For master's, GRE or MAT (unless applicant already holds a graduate degree), letters of recommendation, interview, resume, transcripts from all colleges/universities attended. Additional exam requirements/recommendations for international students: Required—TOEFL (minimum score 525 paper-based; 71 iBT); Recommended—IELTS (minimum score 6.3). Electronic applications accepted. *Expenses:* Contact institution. *Faculty research:* Spiritual issues in counseling, multicultural and diversity issues in counseling, adolescent suicide, career development.

University of Colorado Denver, School of Education and Human Development, Programs in Educational and School Psychology, Denver, CO 80217. Offers educational psychology (MA), including educational assessment, educational psychology, human development, human learning, research and evaluation; school psychology (Psy D, Ed S). MA program also offered in partnership with Boulder Journey School, Friends School and Stanley British Primary School. *Program availability:* Part-time, evening/weekend. *Degree requirements:* For master's, comprehensive exam, 9 hours of core courses, embedded within a minimum of 36 to 38 hours of relevant coursework, including an educational psychology practicum, independent study project or thesis (recommended); for Ed S, comprehensive exam, minimum of 75 semester hours (61 hours of coursework, 6 of 500-hour practicum in field, and 8 of 1200-hour internship); PRAXIS II. *Entrance requirements:* For master's, GRE if undergraduate GPA below 2.75, resume, three letters of recommendation, transcripts; for Ed S, GRE, resume, letters of recommendation, transcripts. Additional exam requirements/recommendations for international students: Required—TOEFL (minimum score 537 paper-based; 75 iBT); Recommended—IELTS (minimum score 6.5). Electronic applications accepted. *Expenses:* Contact institution. *Faculty research:* Crisis response and intervention, school violence prevention, immigrant experience, educational environments for English language learners, culturally competent assessment and intervention, child and youth suicide.

University of Dayton, Department of Counselor Education and Human Services, Dayton, OH 45469. Offers clinical mental health counseling (MS Ed); college student personnel (MS Ed); higher education administration (MS Ed); human services (MS Ed); school counseling (MS Ed); school psychology (MS Ed, Ed S). *Accreditation:* ACA; NCATE. *Program availability:* Part-time. *Faculty:* 11 full-time (6 women), 34 part-time/adjunct (24 women). *Students:* 194 full-time (153 women), 83 part-time (68 women); includes 58 minority (37 Black or African American, non-Hispanic/Latino; 2 Asian, non-Hispanic/Latino; 9 Hispanic/Latino; 10 Two or more races, non-Hispanic/Latino), 3 international. Average age 30. 426 applicants, 28% accepted. In 2017, 107 master's, 6 Ed Ss awarded. *Degree requirements:* For master's, thesis (for some programs); for Ed S, thesis (for some programs), professional portfolio. *Entrance requirements:* For master's, MAT or GRE (if GPA less than 2.75), essays (for some programs). Additional exam requirements/recommendations for international students: Required—TOEFL (minimum score 550 paper-based; 80 iBT). *Application deadline:* For fall admission, 1/10 priority date for domestic and international students; for spring admission, 9/10 priority date for domestic and international students; for summer admission, 11/10 priority date for domestic and international students. Application fee: $0 ($50 for international students). Electronic applications accepted. *Expenses:* Contact institution. *Financial support:* In 2017–18, 5 research assistantships with partial tuition reimbursements (averaging $9,950 per year) were awarded; career-related internships or fieldwork, institutionally sponsored loans, and unspecified assistantships also available. Financial award application deadline: 3/1; financial award applicants required to submit FAFSA. *Faculty research:* Student school bonding, traumatic brain injuries, wellness and counseling, creativity in education. *Unit head:* Dr. Alan Demmitt, Chair, 937-229-3644, Fax: 937-229-1055, E-mail: ademmitt1@udayton.edu. *Application contact:* Kathleen Brown, Administrative Assistant, 937-229-3644, Fax: 937-229-1055, E-mail: kbrown1@udayton.edu.
Website: https://www.udayton.edu/education/departments_and_programs/edc/

University of Delaware, College of Education and Human Development, School of Education, Newark, DE 19716. Offers education (PhD); educational leadership (Ed D); higher education (M Ed); instruction (MI); reading (M Ed); school leadership (M Ed); school psychology (MA, Ed S); teaching English as a second language (TESL) (MA). *Accreditation:* NCATE. *Program availability:* Part-time, evening/weekend. Terminal master's awarded for partial completion of doctoral program. *Degree requirements:* For master's, comprehensive exam (for some programs), thesis (for some programs); for doctorate, comprehensive exam (for some programs), thesis/dissertation. *Entrance requirements:* For master's and doctorate, GRE, 3 letters of recommendation. Additional exam requirements/recommendations for international students: Required—TOEFL (minimum score 600 paper-based). Electronic applications accepted. *Faculty research:* Teacher education; curriculum theory and development; community based education models, educational leadership.

University of Denver, Morgridge College of Education, Denver, CO 80208. Offers child, family and school psychology (MA, PhD, Ed S); counseling psychology (MA, PhD); curriculum and instruction (MA, Ed D, PhD); curriculum instruction and teaching (Certificate); early childhood special education (MA, Certificate); educational leadership and policy studies (MA, Ed D, PhD, Certificate); higher education (Ed D, PhD); library and information science (MLIS); research methods and statistics (MA, PhD). *Accreditation:* ALA; APA (one or more programs are accredited). *Program availability:* Part-time, evening/weekend, online learning. *Faculty:* 39 full-time (29 women), 60 part-time/adjunct (42 women). *Students:* 502 full-time (406 women), 361 part-time (267 women); includes 233 minority (54 Black or African American, non-Hispanic/Latino; 6 American Indian or Alaska Native, non-Hispanic/Latino; 25 Asian, non-Hispanic/Latino; 113 Hispanic/Latino; 35 Two or more races, non-Hispanic/Latino), 52 international. Average age 31. 1,167 applicants, 64% accepted, 415 enrolled. In 2017, 285 master's, 51 doctorates, 157 other advanced degrees awarded. Terminal master's awarded for partial completion of doctoral program. *Degree requirements:* For master's, comprehensive exam; for doctorate, 2 foreign languages, comprehensive exam, thesis/

dissertation. *Entrance requirements:* For master's and doctorate, GRE General Test or GMAT. Additional exam requirements/recommendations for international students: Required—TOEFL (minimum score 550 paper-based; 80 iBT). *Application deadline:* Applications are processed on a rolling basis. Application fee: $65. Electronic applications accepted. *Expenses:* $31,935 per year full-time. *Financial support:* In 2017–18, 765 students received support, including 26 research assistantships with tuition reimbursements available (averaging $10,957 per year), 38 teaching assistantships with tuition reimbursements available (averaging $3,391 per year); career-related internships or fieldwork, Federal Work-Study, institutionally sponsored loans, scholarships/grants, and unspecified assistantships also available. Support available to part-time students. Financial award application deadline: 2/15; financial award applicants required to submit FAFSA. *Faculty research:* Early childhood education, educational leadership, access and opportunity to postsecondary education, marriage and family therapy, data management and archival research. *Unit head:* Dr. Karen Riley, Dean, 303-871-3665, Fax: 303-871-4456, E-mail: karen.riley@du.edu. *Application contact:* Jodi Dye, Director of Admissions, 303-871-2510, Fax: 303-871-4456, E-mail: jodi.dye@du.edu.
Website: http://morgridge.du.edu

University of Detroit Mercy, College of Liberal Arts and Education, Detroit, MI 48221. Offers addiction counseling (MA); addiction studies (Certificate); clinical mental health counseling (MA); clinical psychology (MA, PhD); computer and information systems (MS); criminal justice (MA); curriculum and instruction (MA); economics (MA); educational administration (MA); financial economics (MA); industrial/organizational psychology (MA); information assurance (MS); intelligence analysis (MA); liberal studies (MALS); religious studies (MA); school counseling (MA, Certificate); school psychology (Spec); security administration (MS); special education: emotionally impaired/behaviorally disordered (MA); special education: learning disabilities (MA). *Program availability:* Part-time, evening/weekend. *Degree requirements:* For doctorate, departmental qualifying exam. *Faculty research:* Psychology of aging, history of technology, Renaissance humanism, U.S. and Japanese economic relations.

University of Florida, Graduate School, College of Education, School of Special Education, School Psychology and Early Childhood Studies, Gainesville, FL 32611. Offers early childhood education (M Ed, MAE); school psychology (M Ed, MAE, Ed D, PhD, Ed S); special education (M Ed, MAE, Ed D, PhD, Ed S). *Accreditation:* NCATE. *Program availability:* Part-time, evening/weekend, online learning. *Degree requirements:* For master's, comprehensive exam (for some programs), thesis (MAE); for doctorate, comprehensive exam, thesis/dissertation. *Entrance requirements:* For master's and doctorate, GRE General Test, minimum GPA of 3.0; for Ed S, GRE General Test. Additional exam requirements/recommendations for international students: Required—TOEFL (minimum score 550 paper-based; 80 iBT), IELTS (minimum score 6). Electronic applications accepted. *Faculty research:* Teacher quality/teacher education, early childhood, autism, academic and behavioral assessment and interventions.

University of Hartford, College of Arts and Sciences, Department of Psychology, Program in School Psychology, West Hartford, CT 06117-1599. Offers MS. *Accreditation:* NCATE. *Program availability:* Part-time. *Degree requirements:* For master's, comprehensive exam. *Entrance requirements:* For master's, GRE General Test, GRE Subject Test, minimum GPA of 3.0, 3 letters of recommendation. Additional exam requirements/recommendations for international students: Required—TOEFL (minimum score 550 paper-based). Electronic applications accepted. *Faculty research:* Family therapy, child developments, clinical supervision.

University of Houston–Clear Lake, School of Human Sciences and Humanities, Programs in Human Sciences, Houston, TX 77058-1002. Offers behavioral sciences (MA), including criminology, cross cultural studies, general psychology, sociology; clinical psychology (MA); criminology (MA); cross cultural studies (MA); family therapy (MA); fitness and human performance (MA); school psychology (MA). *Accreditation:* AAMFT/COAMFTE. *Program availability:* Part-time, evening/weekend, online learning. *Degree requirements:* For master's, thesis or alternative. *Entrance requirements:* For master's, GRE General Test. Additional exam requirements/recommendations for international students: Required—TOEFL (minimum score 550 paper-based). Electronic applications accepted. *Faculty research:* Smoking cessation, adolescent sexuality, white collar crime, serial murder, human factors/human computer interaction.

University of Houston–Victoria, School of Arts and Sciences, Program in Psychology, Victoria, TX 77901-4450. Offers counseling psychology (MA); forensic psychology (MA); school psychology (MA). *Program availability:* Part-time, evening/weekend, online learning. *Degree requirements:* For master's, project or thesis. *Entrance requirements:* For master's, GRE General Test. Additional exam requirements/recommendations for international students: Required—TOEFL (minimum score 550 paper-based). Electronic applications accepted.

The University of Iowa, Graduate College, College of Education, Department of Psychological and Quantitative Foundations, Iowa City, IA 52242-1316. Offers counseling psychology (PhD); educational measurement and statistics (MA, PhD); educational psychology (MA, PhD); school psychology (PhD, Ed S). *Accreditation:* APA. *Degree requirements:* For master's, thesis optional, exam; for doctorate, comprehensive exam, thesis/dissertation; for Ed S, exam. *Entrance requirements:* For master's, doctorate, and Ed S, GRE General Test, minimum GPA of 3.0. Additional exam requirements/recommendations for international students: Required—TOEFL (minimum score 550 paper-based; 81 iBT). Electronic applications accepted.

The University of Kansas, Graduate Studies, School of Education, Department of Educational Psychology, Program in School Psychology, Lawrence, KS 66045. Offers PhD, Ed S. *Accreditation:* APA (one or more programs are accredited); NCATE. *Students:* 26 full-time (24 women), 1 (woman) part-time; includes 2 minority (both Hispanic/Latino), 2 international. Average age 25. 35 applicants, 51% accepted, 8 enrolled. In 2017, 6 doctorates awarded. *Entrance requirements:* For doctorate and Ed S, GRE General Test, minimum GPA of 3.0, resume, statement of purpose, official transcript, three letters of recommendation. *Application deadline:* For fall admission, 12/15 for domestic and international students. Application fee: $65 ($85 for international students). Electronic applications accepted. *Financial support:* Fellowships, research assistantships, teaching assistantships, scholarships/grants, and unspecified assistantships available. Financial award application deadline: 12/15. *Faculty research:* Classroom management, anxiety in children and youth, child behavior and learning problems, behavioral and personality assessment, home/school/community partnerships. *Unit head:* Dr. Steven Lee, Chair, 785-864-3931, Fax: 785-864-3820, E-mail: swlee@ku.edu. *Application contact:* Penny Fritts, Admissions Coordinator, 785-864-9645, E-mail: fritts@ku.edu.
Website: http://epsy.ku.edu/

University of Kentucky, Graduate School, College of Education, Program in Educational and Counseling Psychology, Lexington, KY 40506-0032. Offers counseling psychology (MS, PhD, Ed S); educational psychology (MS, PhD); school psychology (PhD, Ed S). *Accreditation:* APA (one or more programs are accredited); NCATE. *Degree requirements:* For doctorate, comprehensive exam, thesis/dissertation; for Ed S, comprehensive exam. *Entrance requirements:* For doctorate, GRE General Test, minimum graduate GPA of 3.0; for Ed S, GRE General Test. Additional exam

requirements/recommendations for international students: Required—TOEFL (minimum score 550 paper-based). Electronic applications accepted.

University of La Verne, LaFetra College of Education, Program in Educational Counseling, La Verne, CA 91750-4443. Offers educational counseling (MS); pupil personnel services (Credential); school psychology (MS). *Program availability:* Part-time. *Students:* 64 full-time (57 women), 123 part-time (101 women); includes 131 minority (8 Black or African American, non-Hispanic/Latino; 5 Asian, non-Hispanic/Latino; 116 Hispanic/Latino; 2 Two or more races, non-Hispanic/Latino), 1 international. Average age 31. *Entrance requirements:* For master's, California Basic Educational Skills Test, minimum undergraduate GPA of 2.75, graduate 3.0; interview; 1 year's experience working with children; 3 letters of reference. Additional exam requirements/recommendations for international students: Required—TOEFL (minimum score 550 paper-based). *Application deadline:* Applications are processed on a rolling basis. Application fee: $50. *Expenses:* Contact institution. *Financial support:* Scholarships/grants and traineeships available. Financial award application deadline: 3/2; financial award applicants required to submit FAFSA. *Unit head:* Everett Lovelace, Assistant Professor, Education Counseling, 909-448-1495, E-mail: elovelace@laverne.edu. *Application contact:* Kristen Ahn, Assistant Director of Graduate Admissions, 909-448-4480, E-mail: sahn@laverne.edu.
Website: https://education.laverne.edu/counseling/

University of Louisville, Graduate School, College of Education and Human Development, Department of Counseling and Human Development, Louisville, KY 40292-0001. Offers counseling and personnel services (M Ed, PhD), including art therapy (M Ed), clinical mental health counseling (M Ed), college student personnel, counseling psychology, counselor education and supervision (PhD), educational psychology, measurement, and evaluation (PhD), school counseling (M Ed). *Accreditation:* APA; NCATE. *Program availability:* Part-time, evening/weekend. *Students:* 144 full-time (107 women), 63 part-time (44 women); includes 49 minority (32 Black or African American, non-Hispanic/Latino; 1 American Indian or Alaska Native, non-Hispanic/Latino; 3 Asian, non-Hispanic/Latino; 7 Hispanic/Latino; 6 Two or more races, non-Hispanic/Latino), 3 international. Average age 28. 178 applicants, 49% accepted, 51 enrolled. In 2017, 35 master's, 3 doctorates awarded. *Degree requirements:* For doctorate, comprehensive exam, thesis/dissertation. *Entrance requirements:* For master's and doctorate, GRE General Test. Application fee: $65. *Expenses:* Tuition, state resident: full-time $12,246; part-time $681 per credit hour. Tuition, nonresident: full-time $25,486; part-time $1417 per credit hour. *Required fees:* $196. Tuition and fees vary according to course load, program and reciprocity agreements. *Financial support:* Fellowships, research assistantships, teaching assistantships, career-related internships or fieldwork, Federal Work-Study, scholarships/grants, health care benefits, and unspecified assistantships available. Financial award application deadline: 6/1; financial award applicants required to submit FAFSA. *Faculty research:* Mental health services and under-served populations; health disparities and outcomes; well-being identity development; measurement and evaluation. *Total annual research expenditures:* $295,684. *Unit head:* Dr. Mark M. Leach, Interim Chair/Professor, 502-852-0588, Fax: 502-852-0629, E-mail: m.leach@louisville.edu. *Application contact:* Betty Hampton, Director of Graduate Student Services, 502-852-5597, Fax: 502-852-1465, E-mail: edadvise@louisville.edu.
Website: http://www.louisville.edu/education/departments/ecpy

University of Lynchburg, Graduate Studies, M Ed Program in School Counseling, Lynchburg, VA 24501-3199. Offers M Ed. *Accreditation:* ACA. *Program availability:* Part-time, evening/weekend. *Faculty:* 17 full-time (10 women). *Students:* 8 full-time (all women), 4 part-time (3 women); includes 5 minority (3 Black or African American, non-Hispanic/Latino; 1 Hispanic/Latino; 1 Two or more races, non-Hispanic/Latino). Average age 32. 12 applicants, 100% accepted, 3 enrolled. In 2017, 9 master's awarded. *Degree requirements:* For master's, counseling internship. *Entrance requirements:* For master's, GRE, minimum GPA of 3.0 (preferred), official transcripts (bachelor's, others as relevant), three letters of recommendation, career goals statement, personal interview. Additional exam requirements/recommendations for international students: Required—TOEFL (minimum score 550 paper-based; 80 iBT), IELTS (minimum score 6). *Application deadline:* For fall admission, 7/31 for domestic students, 6/1 for international students; for spring admission, 11/30 for domestic students, 10/15 for international students. Applications are processed on a rolling basis. Application fee: $30. Electronic applications accepted. Application fee is waived when completed online. *Expenses:* $510 per credit tuition, $100 fees. *Financial support:* Federal Work-Study, scholarships/grants, health care benefits, and unspecified assistantships available. Support available to part-time students. Financial award application deadline: 7/31; financial award applicants required to submit FAFSA. *Unit head:* Dr. Jeanne Booth, Program Advisor of M Ed in School Counseling, 434-544-8551, E-mail: booth@lynchburg.edu. *Application contact:* Ellen Thompson, Graduate Admissions Counselor, 434-544-8841, E-mail: thompson_e@lynchburg.edu.
Website: http://www.lynchburg.edu/graduate/master-of-education-in-counselor-education/school-counseling/

University of Manitoba, Faculty of Graduate Studies, Faculty of Arts, Department of Psychology, Winnipeg, MB R3T 2N2, Canada. Offers clinical psychology (PhD); psychology (MA, PhD); school psychology (MA). *Degree requirements:* For master's, thesis; for doctorate, one foreign language, thesis/dissertation. *Entrance requirements:* For master's and doctorate, GRE General Test.

University of Maryland, College Park, Academic Affairs, College of Education, Department of Counseling, Higher Education and Special Education, College Park, MD 20742. Offers college student personnel (M Ed, MA); college student personnel administration (PhD); community counseling (CAGS); community/career counseling (M Ed, MA); counseling and personnel services (M Ed, MA, PhD), including art therapy (M Ed), college student personnel (M Ed), counseling and personnel services (PhD), counseling psychology (M Ed), mental health counseling (M Ed), school counseling (M Ed); counseling psychology (PhD); counselor education (PhD); rehabilitation counseling (M Ed, MA, AGSC); school counseling (M Ed, MA); school psychology (M Ed, MA, PhD). *Accreditation:* APA (one or more programs are accredited); NCATE. *Program availability:* Part-time, evening/weekend, online learning. *Degree requirements:* For master's, thesis (for some programs); for doctorate, thesis/dissertation. *Entrance requirements:* For master's, GRE General Test or MAT, minimum GPA of 3.0, 3 letters of recommendation; for doctorate, GRE General Test or MAT, minimum GPA of 3.5, 3 letters of recommendation. Additional exam requirements/recommendations for international students: Required—TOEFL. Electronic applications accepted. *Faculty research:* Educational psychology, counseling, health.

University of Massachusetts Amherst, Graduate School, College of Education, Program in Education, Amherst, MA 01003. Offers bilingual, English as a second language, and multicultural education (M Ed, Ed S); child study and early education (M Ed); children, families and schools (Ed D, Ed S); early childhood and elementary teacher education (M Ed); educational leadership (M Ed); educational policy and leadership (Ed D); higher education (M Ed); international education (M Ed); language, literacy and culture (Ed D); learning, media and technology (M Ed, Ed S); mathematics, science, and learning technologies (Ed D); reading and writing (M Ed); research, educational measurement and psychometrics (Ed D); school counselor education

(M Ed, Ed S); school psychology (Ed S); science education (Ed S); secondary teacher education (M Ed); social justice education (M Ed, Ed D, Ed S); special education (M Ed, Ed D, Ed S); teacher education and school improvement (Ed D, Ed S). *Accreditation:* NCATE. *Program availability:* Part-time, online learning. Terminal master's awarded for partial completion of doctoral program. *Degree requirements:* For doctorate, comprehensive exam, thesis/dissertation. *Entrance requirements:* Additional exam requirements/recommendations for international students: Required—TOEFL (minimum score 550 paper-based; 80 iBT), IELTS (minimum score 6.5). Electronic applications accepted.

University of Massachusetts Amherst, Graduate School, College of Education, Program in School Psychology, Amherst, MA 01003. Offers M Ed, PhD, Ed S. *Accreditation:* APA; NCATE. *Program availability:* Part-time. Terminal master's awarded for partial completion of doctoral program. *Degree requirements:* For doctorate, comprehensive exam, thesis/dissertation. *Entrance requirements:* For doctorate, 3 letters of recommendation. Additional exam requirements/recommendations for international students: Required—TOEFL (minimum score 550 paper-based; 80 iBT), IELTS (minimum score 6.5). Electronic applications accepted.

University of Massachusetts Boston, College of Education and Human Development, Program in Counseling and School Psychology, Boston, MA 02125-3393. Offers PhD. *Accreditation:* ACA; CORE. *Program availability:* Part-time, evening/weekend. *Faculty:* 19 full-time (11 women), 8 part-time/adjunct (4 women). *Students:* 39 full-time (34 women), 1 (woman) part-time; includes 8 minority (3 Black or African American, non-Hispanic/Latino; 3 Hispanic/Latino; 2 Two or more races, non-Hispanic/Latino), 3 international. Average age 29. 91 applicants, 20% accepted, 9 enrolled. *Application deadline:* For fall admission, 12/1 for domestic students. *Expenses:* Tuition, state resident: full-time $17,375. Tuition, nonresident: full-time $33,915. *Required fees:* $355. *Financial support:* Research assistantships, teaching assistantships, career-related internships or fieldwork, Federal Work-Study, and unspecified assistantships available. Support available to part-time students. Financial award application deadline: 3/1; financial award applicants required to submit FAFSA. *Faculty research:* Persuasion and power in the counseling process, self-efficacy for counselors and clients, career and biracial issues in family therapy. *Unit head:* Dr. Melissa Pearrow, 617-287-5000. *Application contact:* Graduate Admissions Coordinator, 617-287-6400, Fax: 617-287-6236, E-mail: bos.gadm@dpc.umassp.edu.

University of Massachusetts Boston, College of Education and Human Development, Program in School Psychology, Boston, MA 02125-3393. Offers M Ed. *Program availability:* Part-time, evening/weekend. *Students:* 17 full-time (16 women), 5 part-time (all women); includes 4 minority (1 Black or African American, non-Hispanic/Latino; 1 Asian, non-Hispanic/Latino; 2 Hispanic/Latino), 2 international. Average age 26. 86 applicants, 41% accepted, 17 enrolled. In 2017, 6 master's awarded. *Entrance requirements:* For master's, GRE General Test or MAT, minimum GPA of 3.0. *Application deadline:* For fall admission, 3/1 for domestic students; for spring admission, 11/1 for domestic students. *Expenses:* Tuition, state resident: full-time $17,375. Tuition, nonresident: full-time $33,915. *Required fees:* $355. *Financial support:* Research assistantships, teaching assistantships, career-related internships or fieldwork, Federal Work-Study, and unspecified assistantships available. Support available to part-time students. Financial award application deadline: 3/1; financial award applicants required to submit FAFSA. *Faculty research:* School psychology services, assessment of children, cultural and gender differences on psychological adjustment to disabilities. *Unit head:* Dr. Amy Cook, 617-287-5000. *Application contact:* Graduate Admissions Coordinator, 617-287-6400, Fax: 617-287-6236, E-mail: bos.gadm@dpc.umassp.edu.

University of Memphis, Graduate School, College of Arts and Sciences, Department of Psychology, Memphis, TN 38152-3230. Offers clinical psychology (PhD); experimental psychology (PhD); general psychology (MS); school psychology (MA, PhD, Ed S). *Accreditation:* APA. *Faculty:* 26 full-time (11 women), 3 part-time/adjunct (0 women). *Students:* 94 full-time (69 women), 17 part-time (12 women); includes 25 minority (10 Black or African American, non-Hispanic/Latino; 6 Asian, non-Hispanic/Latino; 6 Hispanic/Latino; 3 Two or more races, non-Hispanic/Latino), 6 international. Average age 27. 291 applicants, 16% accepted, 32 enrolled. In 2017, 23 master's, 13 doctorates, 8 other advanced degrees awarded. *Degree requirements:* For master's, comprehensive exam (for some programs), thesis (for some programs), 37 credit hours (for MA); 33 credit hours with thesis or 36 with exam (for MS); for doctorate, comprehensive exam, thesis/dissertation, 80 semester hours, major area paper; 1-year placement and 1-year internship (for clinical psychology); internship (for school psychology); for Ed S, 30 credit hours. *Entrance requirements:* For master's, GRE, 3 letters of recommendation, 18 undergraduate hours in psychology; for doctorate, GRE, minimum GPA of 2.75, 18 hours of undergraduate psychology courses, transcripts, personal statement, 3 letters of recommendation, interview; for Ed S, GRE, minimum GPA of 2.75, 18 hours of undergraduate psychology courses, 3 letters of recommendation. Additional exam requirements/recommendations for international students: Required—TOEFL (minimum score 550 paper-based; 79 iBT). *Application deadline:* For fall admission, 12/5 for domestic students. Applications are processed on a rolling basis. Application fee: $35 ($60 for international students). Electronic applications accepted. *Expenses:* Contact institution. *Financial support:* In 2017–18, 66 students received support, including 60 research assistantships with full tuition reimbursements available (averaging $11,846 per year), 25 teaching assistantships with full tuition reimbursements available (averaging $6,794 per year); fellowships with full tuition reimbursements available, Federal Work-Study, scholarships/grants, tuition waivers (partial), and unspecified assistantships also available. Financial award application deadline: 2/1; financial award applicants required to submit FAFSA. *Faculty research:* Clinical health; school, child and family psychology; psychotherapy; cognitive and behavioral neuroscience; industrial-organizational psychology. *Unit head:* Dr. Frank Andrasik, Chair, 901-678-2145, Fax: 901-678-2579, E-mail: rcohen@memphis.edu. *Application contact:* Dr. Robert Cohen, Coordinator of Graduate Studies, 901-678-4679, Fax: 901-678-2579, E-mail: rcohen@memphis.edu.
Website: http://www.memphis.edu/psychology

University of Minnesota, Twin Cities Campus, Graduate School, College of Education and Human Development, Department of Educational Psychology, Program in School Psychology, Minneapolis, MN 55455-0213. Offers MA, PhD, Ed S. *Accreditation:* APA. *Students:* 35 full-time (30 women), 21 part-time (19 women); includes 6 minority (2 Black or African American, non-Hispanic/Latino; 1 Asian, non-Hispanic/Latino; 1 Hispanic/Latino; 2 Two or more races, non-Hispanic/Latino), 4 international. Average age 27. 20 applicants, 15% accepted, 2 enrolled. In 2017, 16 master's, 5 doctorates, 9 other advanced degrees awarded. Application fee: $75 ($95 for international students). *Unit head:* Dr. Geoffrey Maruyama, Chair, 612-625-5861, Fax: 612-624-8241, E-mail: geoff@umn.edu. *Application contact:* Dr. Ernest Davenport, Director of Graduate Studies, 612-624-1040, E-mail: lqr6576@umn.edu.
Website: http://www.cehd.umn.edu/EdPsych/programs/SchoolPsych/

University of Minnesota, Twin Cities Campus, Graduate School, College of Liberal Arts, Department of Psychology, Minneapolis, MN 55455-0213. Offers biological psychopathology (PhD); clinical psychology (PhD); cognitive and biological psychology (PhD); counseling psychology (PhD); industrial/organizational psychology (PhD); personality, individual differences, and behavior genetics (PhD); quantitative/psychometric methods (PhD); school psychology (PhD); social psychology (PhD). *Accreditation:* APA. *Degree requirements:* For doctorate, comprehensive exam, thesis/dissertation. *Entrance requirements:* For doctorate, GRE General Test, GRE Subject Test (recommended), 12 credits of upper-level psychology courses, including a course in statistics or psychological measurement. Additional exam requirements/recommendations for international students: Required—TOEFL (minimum score 79 iBT).

University of Missouri, Office of Research and Graduate Studies, College of Education, Department of Educational, School, and Counseling Psychology, Columbia, MO 65211. Offers counseling psychology (M Ed, MA, PhD, Ed S); educational psychology (M Ed, MA, PhD, Ed S); learning and instruction (M Ed); school psychology (M Ed, MA, PhD, Ed S). *Accreditation:* APA (one or more programs are accredited). *Program availability:* Part-time. *Degree requirements:* For doctorate, thesis/dissertation. *Entrance requirements:* For master's, doctorate, and Ed S, GRE General Test, minimum GPA of 3.0. Additional exam requirements/recommendations for international students: Required—TOEFL (minimum score 580 paper-based; 92 iBT). Electronic applications accepted.

University of Missouri–St. Louis, College of Education, Department of Education Sciences and Professional Programs, St. Louis, MO 63121. Offers adult and higher education (M Ed); educational psychology (M Ed), including character and citizenship education, research and program evaluation; program evaluation (Certificate); school psychology (Ed S). *Students:* 19 full-time (17 women), 13 part-time (12 women); includes 4 minority (2 Black or African American, non-Hispanic/Latino; 2 Hispanic/Latino). 16 applicants, 56% accepted, 9 enrolled. *Degree requirements:* For other advanced degree, comprehensive exam, thesis or alternative, internship. *Entrance requirements:* For degree, GRE General Test, 2-4 letters of recommendation, personal interview. Additional exam requirements/recommendations for international students: Required—IELTS (minimum score 6.5); Recommended—TOEFL (minimum score 550 paper-based; 79 iBT). *Application deadline:* For fall admission, 2/15 priority date for domestic students, 2/15 for international students. Application fee: $50 ($40 for international students). Electronic applications accepted. *Expenses:* Tuition, state resident: part-time $476.50 per credit hour. Tuition, nonresident: part-time $1169.70 per credit hour. *Financial support:* Application deadline: 4/1; applicants required to submit FAFSA. *Faculty research:* Child/adolescent psychology, quantitative and qualitative methodology, evaluation processes, measurement and assessment. *Unit head:* Dr. Donald Gouwens, Chairperson, 314-516-4773, Fax: 314-516-5784, E-mail: gouwensd@umsl.edu. *Application contact:* 314-516-5458, Fax: 314-516-6996, E-mail: gradadm@umsl.edu.
Website: https://coe.umsl.edu/dept/espp.html

University of Montana, Graduate School, College of Humanities and Sciences, Department of Psychology, Program in School Psychology, Missoula, MT 59812. Offers MA, PhD, Ed S. *Degree requirements:* For master's, oral exam, professional paper; for Ed S, thesis. *Entrance requirements:* For master's, GRE General Test, GRE Subject Test, minimum GPA of 3.25 during previous 2 years; for Ed S, GRE General Test. Additional exam requirements/recommendations for international students: Required—TOEFL. *Faculty research:* Child development and creativity, psychological measurement.

University of Nebraska at Kearney, College of Education, Department of Counseling and School Psychology, Kearney, NE 68849-0001. Offers clinical mental health counseling (MS Ed); school counseling (MS Ed), including elementary, secondary; school psychology (Ed S); student affairs (MS Ed). *Accreditation:* ACA; NCATE. *Program availability:* Part-time, evening/weekend, 100% online. *Degree requirements:* For master's, comprehensive exam, thesis optional; for Ed S, thesis. *Entrance requirements:* For master's and Ed S, personal statement, recommendations, resume, interview. Additional exam requirements/recommendations for international students: Recommended—TOEFL (minimum score 550 paper-based; 79 iBT), IELTS (minimum score 6.5). Electronic applications accepted. *Faculty research:* Multicultural counseling and diversity issues, team decision-making, adult development, women's issues, brief therapy.

University of Nebraska at Omaha, Graduate Studies, College of Arts and Sciences, Department of Psychology, Omaha, NE 68182. Offers applied behavior analysis (Certificate); human resources and training (Certificate); industrial/organizational psychology (MS); psychology (MA, PhD); school psychology (MS, Ed S). *Program availability:* Part-time. *Degree requirements:* For master's, comprehensive exam, thesis (for some programs); for doctorate, comprehensive exam, thesis/dissertation. *Entrance requirements:* For master's and doctorate, GRE, minimum GPA of 3.0, official transcripts, 3 letters of recommendation, statement of purpose, writing sample, resume. Additional exam requirements/recommendations for international students: Required—TOEFL, IELTS, PTE. Electronic applications accepted.

University of Nebraska–Lincoln, Graduate College, College of Education and Human Sciences, Department of Educational Psychology, Lincoln, NE 68588. Offers cognition, learning and development (MA); counseling psychology (MA); educational psychology (MA, Ed S); psychological studies in education (PhD), including cognition, learning and development, counseling psychology, quantitative, qualitative, and psychometric methods, school psychology; quantitative, qualitative, and psychometric methods (MA); school psychology (MA, Ed S). *Accreditation:* APA (one or more programs are accredited); NCATE. *Degree requirements:* For master's, thesis optional. *Entrance requirements:* For master's, GRE General Test. Additional exam requirements/recommendations for international students: Required—TOEFL (minimum score 500 paper-based). Electronic applications accepted. *Faculty research:* Measurement and assessment, metacognition, academic skills, child development, multicultural education and counseling.

The University of North Carolina at Chapel Hill, Graduate School, School of Education, Program in School Psychology, Chapel Hill, NC 27599. Offers M Ed, MA, PhD. *Accreditation:* APA (one or more programs are accredited); NCATE. *Degree requirements:* For master's, comprehensive exam, thesis (for some programs); for doctorate, comprehensive exam, thesis/dissertation. *Entrance requirements:* For master's and doctorate, GRE General Test, minimum GPA of 3.0 during last 2 years of undergraduate course work. Additional exam requirements/recommendations for international students: Required—TOEFL (minimum score 550 paper-based). Electronic applications accepted.

The University of North Carolina at Greensboro, Graduate School, School of Education, Department of Counseling and Educational Development, Greensboro, NC 27412-5001. Offers advanced school counseling (PMC); counseling and counselor education (PhD); counseling and educational development (MS); couple and family counseling (PMC); school counseling (PMC); MS/Ed S. *Accreditation:* ACA (one or more programs are accredited); NCATE. *Degree requirements:* For master's, comprehensive exam, practicum, internship; for doctorate, comprehensive exam, thesis/dissertation. *Entrance requirements:* For master's, doctorate, and PMC, GRE General Test. Additional exam requirements/recommendations for international students: Required—TOEFL. Electronic applications accepted. *Faculty research:* Gerontology, invitational

theory, career development, marriage and family therapy, drug and alcohol abuse prevention.

University of Northern Colorado, Graduate School, College of Education and Behavioral Sciences, Department of School Psychology, Greeley, CO 80639. Offers Ed S. *Accreditation:* APA; NCATE. *Program availability:* Part-time, evening/weekend. *Degree requirements:* For Ed S, comprehensive exam. Electronic applications accepted.

University of Northern Iowa, Graduate College, College of Education, Department of Educational Psychology and Foundations, Ed S Program in School Psychology, Cedar Falls, IA 50614. Offers Ed S.

University of Northern Iowa, Graduate College, College of Social and Behavioral Sciences, School of Applied Human Sciences, Cedar Falls, IA 50614. Offers counseling (MA), including mental health counseling, school counseling; mental health counseling (MA); school counseling (MA). *Program availability:* Part-time. *Degree requirements:* For master's, comprehensive exam, thesis (for some programs). *Entrance requirements:* Additional exam requirements/recommendations for international students: Required—TOEFL (minimum score 550 paper-based; 79 iBT). Electronic applications accepted.

University of Oklahoma, Jeannine Rainbolt College of Education, Department of Educational Psychology, Program in Professional Counseling, Norman, OK 73019. Offers professional counseling (M Ed), including drug and alcohol counseling, Oklahoma licensed professional counseling, school counseling. *Students:* 32 full-time (23 women), 2 part-time (1 woman); includes 13 minority (2 Black or African American, non-Hispanic/Latino; 1 American Indian or Alaska Native, non-Hispanic/Latino; 6 Hispanic/Latino; 4 Two or more races, non-Hispanic/Latino). Average age 31. 43 applicants, 51% accepted, 17 enrolled. In 2017, 16 master's awarded. *Degree requirements:* For master's, comprehensive exam. *Entrance requirements:* For master's, GRE. Additional exam requirements/recommendations for international students: Required—TOEFL (minimum score 79 iBT) or IELTS (minimum score 6.5). *Application deadline:* For fall admission, 1/10 for domestic and international students. Application fee: $50 ($100 for international students). Electronic applications accepted. *Expenses:* Tuition, state resident: full-time $5119; part-time $213.30 per credit hour. Tuition, nonresident: full-time $19,778; part-time $824.10 per credit hour. *Required fees:* $3458; $133.55 per credit hour. $126.50 per semester. *Financial support:* In 2017–18, 12 students received support. Research assistantships with full and partial tuition reimbursements available, teaching assistantships with full and partial tuition reimbursements available, and scholarships/grants available. Financial award application deadline: 6/1; financial award applicants required to submit FAFSA. *Faculty research:* Group therapy interventions; family/child counseling; American Indian psychological issues; diversity issues in counseling; drug and alcohol (addictions) counseling/therapy. *Unit head:* Dr. Nancy E. Marchand-Martella, Chair, Department of Educational Psychology, 405-325-0624, Fax: 405-325-6655, E-mail: nmarchand-martella@ou.edu. *Application contact:* Anna Steele, Graduate Programs Specialist, 405-325-4525, Fax: 405-325-7390, E-mail: jrcoe_gps@ou.edu.
Website: http://www.ou.edu/education/edpy.html

University of Oregon, Graduate School, College of Education, Eugene, OR 97403. Offers communication disorders and sciences (MA, MS, PhD); counseling psychology (PhD); couples and family therapy (MS); critical and sociocultural studies in education (PhD); curriculum and teacher education (MA, MS); educational leadership (MS, D Ed, PhD); prevention science (M Ed, MS, PhD); school psychology (MS, PhD); special education (M Ed, MA, MS, PhD). *Program availability:* Part-time. Terminal master's awarded for partial completion of doctoral program. *Degree requirements:* For master's, exam, paper, or project; for doctorate, comprehensive exam, thesis/dissertation. *Entrance requirements:* Additional exam requirements/recommendations for international students: Required—TOEFL. *Faculty research:* Basic and applied research in teaching, learning and habilitation in all settings, schooling effectiveness.

University of Phoenix–Las Vegas Campus, College of Education, Las Vegas, NV 89135. Offers administration and supervision (MA Ed); curriculum and instruction (MA Ed); school counseling (MSC); teacher education-elementary licensure (MA Ed). *Program availability:* Evening/weekend. *Degree requirements:* For master's, thesis (for some programs). *Entrance requirements:* For master's, minimum undergraduate GPA of 2.5, 3 years of work experience. Additional exam requirements/recommendations for international students: Required—TOEFL (minimum score 550 paper-based; 79 iBT). Electronic applications accepted.

University of Rhode Island, Graduate School, College of Health Sciences, Department of Psychology, Kingston, RI 02881. Offers behavioral science (PhD); clinical psychology (PhD); school psychology (MS, PhD). *Accreditation:* APA (one or more programs are accredited). *Program availability:* Part-time. *Faculty:* 17 full-time (11 women), 1 part-time/adjunct (0 women). *Students:* 63 full-time (49 women), 11 part-time (9 women); includes 12 minority (6 Black or African American, non-Hispanic/Latino; 1 American Indian or Alaska Native, non-Hispanic/Latino; 3 Asian, non-Hispanic/Latino; 2 Hispanic/Latino), 5 international. 253 applicants, 4% accepted, 7 enrolled. In 2017, 8 master's, 21 doctorates awarded. *Entrance requirements:* Additional exam requirements/recommendations for international students: Required—TOEFL. *Application deadline:* For fall admission, 12/1 for domestic and international students. Application fee: $65. Electronic applications accepted. *Expenses:* Tuition, state resident: full-time $12,706; part-time $786 per credit. Tuition, nonresident: full-time $25,216; part-time $1401 per credit. *Required fees:* $1598; $45 per credit. One-time fee: $30 part-time. *Financial support:* In 2017–18, 10 research assistantships with tuition reimbursements (averaging $17,979 per year), 24 teaching assistantships with tuition reimbursements (averaging $13,572 per year) were awarded. Financial award application deadline: 12/1; financial award applicants required to submit FAFSA. *Faculty research:* Health psychology, multicultural psychology, research methodology, child/family/developmental neuropsychology. *Unit head:* Dr. Mark Robbins, Chair, 401-874-5082, E-mail: markrobb@uri.edu.
Website: http://www.uri.edu/artsci/psy/

University of San Diego, School of Leadership and Education Sciences, Department of Counseling and Marital and Family Therapy, San Diego, CA 92110-2492. Offers clinical mental health counseling (MA); marital and family therapy (MA); school counseling (MA). *Accreditation:* ACA. *Program availability:* Part-time, evening/weekend. *Faculty:* 13 full-time (6 women), 26 part-time/adjunct (18 women). *Students:* 172 full-time (155 women), 50 part-time (42 women); includes 106 minority (13 Black or African American, non-Hispanic/Latino; 1 American Indian or Alaska Native, non-Hispanic/Latino; 20 Asian, non-Hispanic/Latino; 62 Hispanic/Latino; 10 Two or more races, non-Hispanic/Latino), 5 international. Average age 27. 406 applicants, 45% accepted, 92 enrolled. In 2017, 69 master's awarded. *Degree requirements:* For master's, comprehensive exam, international experience. *Entrance requirements:* For master's, GRE or GMAT (minimum overall score in 50th percentile), group interview with faculty. Additional exam requirements/recommendations for international students: Required—TOEFL (minimum score 580 paper-based; 83 iBT), TWE. *Application deadline:* For fall admission, 1/13 priority date for domestic and international students. Applications are processed on a rolling basis. Application fee: $45. Electronic applications accepted. *Financial support:* In 2017–18, 160 students received support. Career-related internships or fieldwork, Federal Work-Study, institutionally sponsored loans, unspecified assistantships, and stipends available. Support available to part-time students. Financial award application deadline: 4/1; financial award applicants required to submit FAFSA. *Faculty research:* Action research, collaboration between family therapists and medical professionals, family therapy training and supervision, multicultural counseling, school counseling. *Unit head:* Dr. Ann Garland, Director, 619-260-7879, E-mail: agarland@sandiego.edu. *Application contact:* Monica Mahon, Director of Admissions and Enrollment, 619-260-4524, Fax: 619-260-4158, E-mail: grads@sandiego.edu.
Website: http://www.sandiego.edu/soles/counseling-and-marital-and-family-therapy//

University of South Carolina, The Graduate School, College of Arts and Sciences, Department of Psychology, Program in School Psychology, Columbia, SC 29208. Offers PhD. *Accreditation:* APA; NCATE. *Degree requirements:* For doctorate, thesis/dissertation. *Entrance requirements:* For doctorate, GRE General Test, minimum GPA of 3.0. Additional exam requirements/recommendations for international students: Required—TOEFL. Electronic applications accepted. *Faculty research:* Preschool services, families and diversity life satisfaction, ADHD intervention, attachment.

University of South Dakota, Graduate School, School of Education, Division of Counseling and Psychology in Education, Vermillion, SD 57069. Offers counseling (MA, PhD, Ed S); human development and educational psychology (MA, PhD, Ed S); mental health counseling (Certificate); school psychology (PhD, Ed S). *Accreditation:* ACA (one or more programs are accredited); NCATE. *Program availability:* Part-time. *Degree requirements:* For master's and other advanced degree, comprehensive exam, thesis or alternative; for doctorate, comprehensive exam, thesis/dissertation. *Entrance requirements:* For master's and doctorate, GRE General Test, minimum GPA of 3.0. Additional exam requirements/recommendations for international students: Required—TOEFL (minimum score 550 paper-based; 79 iBT). *Application deadline:* Applications are processed on a rolling basis. Application fee: $35. Electronic applications accepted. *Financial support:* Research assistantships with partial tuition reimbursements, teaching assistantships with partial tuition reimbursements, career-related internships or fieldwork, Federal Work-Study, and unspecified assistantships available. Financial award applicants required to submit FAFSA. *Application contact:* Graduate School, 605-658-6140, Fax: 605-677-6118.
Website: http://www.usd.edu/cpe

University of Southern Maine, College of Management and Human Service, School of Education and Human Development, Program in School Psychology, Portland, ME 04103. Offers MS, Psy D. *Program availability:* Part-time, evening/weekend. *Degree requirements:* For doctorate, comprehensive exam, thesis/dissertation, dissertation defense. *Entrance requirements:* For doctorate, GRE General Test, interview. Additional exam requirements/recommendations for international students: Required—TOEFL (minimum score 550 paper-based; 79 iBT). Electronic applications accepted. *Faculty research:* Academic interventions, applied behavior analysis, assessment methods, response to intervention, school psychology practices, positive behavioral interventions and supports, multi-tier systems of support.

University of South Florida, College of Education, Department of Educational and Psychological Studies, Tampa, FL 33620-9951. Offers college student affairs (M Ed); counselor education (MA, PhD, Ed S); interdisciplinary education (PhD, Ed S); school psychology (PhD, Ed S). *Faculty:* 28 full-time (13 women). *Students:* 115 full-time (77 women), 107 part-time (80 women); includes 59 minority (29 Black or African American, non-Hispanic/Latino; 6 Asian, non-Hispanic/Latino; 18 Hispanic/Latino; 1 Native Hawaiian or other Pacific Islander, non-Hispanic/Latino; 5 Two or more races, non-Hispanic/Latino), 23 international. Average age 33. 163 applicants, 72% accepted, 84 enrolled. In 2017, 46 master's, 5 doctorates, 1 other advanced degree awarded. Application fee: $30. *Faculty research:* College student affairs, counselor education, educational psychology, school psychology, social foundations. *Total annual research expenditures:* $9 million. *Unit head:* Dr. Barabara Shircliff, Chair, 813-974-4001, E-mail: shirclif@usf.edu.

The University of Tennessee, Graduate School, College of Education, Health and Human Sciences, Program in Education, Knoxville, TN 37996. Offers art education (MS); counseling education (PhD); cultural studies in education (PhD); curriculum (MS, Ed S); curriculum, educational research and evaluation (Ed D, PhD); early childhood education (PhD); early childhood special education (MS); education of deaf and hard of hearing (MS); educational administration and policy studies (Ed D, PhD); educational administration and supervision (Ed S); educational psychology (Ed D, PhD); elementary education (MS, Ed S); elementary teaching (MS); English education (MS, Ed S); exercise science (PhD); foreign language/ESL education (MS, Ed S); instructional technology (MS, Ed D, PhD, Ed S); literacy, language and ESL education (PhD); literacy, language education, and ESL education (Ed D); mathematics education (MS, Ed S); modified and comprehensive special education (MS); reading education (MS, Ed S); school counseling (Ed S); school psychology (PhD, Ed S); science education (MS, Ed S); secondary teaching (MS); social foundations (MS); social science education (MS, Ed S); socio-cultural foundations of sports and education (PhD); special education (Ed S); teacher education (Ed D, PhD). *Accreditation:* NCATE. *Program availability:* Part-time, evening/weekend. *Degree requirements:* For master's and Ed S, thesis optional; for doctorate, variable foreign language requirement, thesis/dissertation. *Entrance requirements:* For master's, minimum GPA of 2.7; for doctorate and Ed S, GRE General Test, minimum GPA of 2.7. Additional exam requirements/recommendations for international students: Required—TOEFL. Electronic applications accepted.

The University of Tennessee at Chattanooga, Program in Counseling, Chattanooga, TN 37403. Offers mental health (M Ed); school counseling (M Ed, Post Master's Certificate). *Students:* 44 full-time (36 women), 11 part-time (10 women); includes 13 minority (8 Black or African American, non-Hispanic/Latino; 1 Hispanic/Latino; 4 Two or more races, non-Hispanic/Latino). Average age 26. 49 applicants, 67% accepted, 24 enrolled. In 2017, 13 master's awarded. *Degree requirements:* For master's, comprehensive exam, internship. *Entrance requirements:* For master's, MAT or GRE, 2 letters of reference, interview; for Post Master's Certificate, graduate degree in counseling, 2 letters of reference. Additional exam requirements/recommendations for international students: Required—TOEFL (minimum score 550 paper-based; 79 iBT), IELTS (minimum score 6). *Application deadline:* For fall admission, 6/15 priority date for domestic students, 7/1 for international students; for spring admission, 11/1 priority date for domestic students, 11/1 for international students. Applications are processed on a rolling basis. Application fee: $35 ($40 for international students). Electronic applications accepted. *Expenses:* Tuition, state resident: full-time $8244; part-time $458 per credit hour. Tuition, nonresident: full-time $24,362; part-time $1353 per credit hour. *Required fees:* $1776; $487 per semester. Tuition and fees vary according to course load. *Financial support:* Research assistantships, career-related internships or fieldwork, scholarships/grants, and unspecified assistantships available. Support available to part-time students. Financial award application deadline: 7/1; financial award applicants required to submit FAFSA. *Faculty research:* Play therapy; clinical supervision; technology in marital infidelity; female inmates and recidivism; grief, loss and trauma in children. *Unit head:* Dr. Elizabeth O'Brien, Director, 423-425-4544, E-mail: elizabeth-o'brien@utc.edu. *Application contact:* Dr. Joanne Romagni, Dean of the Graduate School, 423-425-4478, Fax: 423-425-4052, E-mail: joanne-romagni@utc.edu.
Website: https://www.utc.edu/counselor-education-program/

School Psychology

The University of Tennessee at Chattanooga, School of Education, Chattanooga, TN 37403. Offers counseling (M Ed), including community counseling, school counseling; education (M Ed, Post-Master's Certificate), including elementary education (M Ed), school leadership (Post-Master's Certificate); elementary education (M Ed); learning and leadership (Ed D), including educational leadership; school leadership (Post-Master's Certificate); school leadership: principal licensure (Ed S); secondary education (M Ed); special education (M Ed). *Accreditation:* ACA; NCATE. *Program availability:* Part-time. *Students:* 43 full-time (30 women), 58 part-time (47 women); includes 18 minority (9 Black or African American, non-Hispanic/Latino; 1 Asian, non-Hispanic/Latino; 1 Hispanic/Latino; 7 Two or more races, non-Hispanic/Latino). Average age 31. 118 applicants, 75% accepted, 33 enrolled. In 2017, 59 master's, 7 other advanced degrees awarded. *Degree requirements:* For master's, comprehensive exam, thesis optional, culminating experience; for other advanced degree, internship. *Entrance requirements:* For master's, GRE General Test, PPST 1, teaching certificate; for other advanced degree, two letters of recommendation, graduate degree in education, teaching certificate with three years of experience. Additional exam requirements/recommendations for international students: Required—TOEFL (minimum score 550 paper-based; 79 iBT), IELTS (minimum score 6). *Application deadline:* For fall admission, 6/15 for domestic students, 7/1 for international students; for spring admission, 11/1 for domestic and international students. Applications are processed on a rolling basis. Application fee: $35 ($40 for international students). Electronic applications accepted. *Expenses:* Contact institution. *Financial support:* Research assistantships, teaching assistantships, career-related internships or fieldwork, institutionally sponsored loans, scholarships/grants, and unspecified assistantships available. Support available to part-time students. Financial award application deadline: 7/1; financial award applicants required to submit FAFSA. *Faculty research:* School counseling, community counseling, elementary and secondary education, school leadership and administration. *Total annual research expenditures:* $576,495. *Unit head:* Dr. Renee Murley, Director, 423-425-4684, Fax: 423-425-5380, E-mail: renee-murley@utc.edu. *Application contact:* Dr. Joanne Romagni, Dean of the Graduate School, 423-425-4478, Fax: 423-425-5223, E-mail: joanne-romagni@utc.edu. Website: https://www.utc.edu/school-education/

The University of Texas at Austin, Graduate School, College of Education, Department of Educational Psychology, Austin, TX 78712-1111. Offers academic educational psychology (M Ed, MA); counseling psychology (PhD); counselor education (M Ed); human development, culture and learning sciences (PhD); program evaluation (MA); quantitative methods (M Ed, MA, PhD); school psychology (MA, PhD). *Accreditation:* APA (one or more programs are accredited). *Degree requirements:* For master's, thesis optional; for doctorate, thesis/dissertation. *Entrance requirements:* For master's and doctorate, GRE General Test, 3 letters of recommendation. Additional exam requirements/recommendations for international students: Required—TOEFL.

The University of Texas at San Antonio, College of Education and Human Development, Department of Educational Psychology, San Antonio, TX 78207. Offers applied behavior analysis (Certificate); educational psychology (MA), including applied educational psychology, behavior assessment and intervention, general educational psychology, program evaluation; language acquisition and bilingual psychoeducational assessment (Certificate); school psychology (MA). *Program availability:* Part-time. *Faculty:* 9 full-time (5 women), 1 (woman) part-time/adjunct. *Students:* 34 full-time (27 women), 40 part-time (35 women); includes 52 minority (5 Black or African American, non-Hispanic/Latino; 1 Asian, non-Hispanic/Latino; 43 Hispanic/Latino; 3 Two or more races, non-Hispanic/Latino). Average age 28. 46 applicants, 72% accepted, 23 enrolled. In 2017, 16 master's, 23 other advanced degrees awarded. *Degree requirements:* For master's, comprehensive exam, thesis (for some programs). *Entrance requirements:* For master's, GRE, bachelor's degree with 18 credit hours in field of study or in another appropriate field of study, two letters of recommendation, statement of purpose; for Certificate, 18 hours in psychology, sociology, education, or anything related (for applied behavioral analysis); minimum GPA of 2.7 in last 30 hours (for language acquisition and bilingual psychoeducational assessment). Additional exam requirements/recommendations for international students: Required—TOEFL (minimum score 550 paper-based; 79 iBT), IELTS (minimum score 6.5). *Application deadline:* For fall admission, 6/15 for domestic students, 3/1 for international students; for spring admission, 10/15 for domestic students, 9/15 for international students; for summer admission, 3/1 for international students. Applications are processed on a rolling basis. Application fee: $50 ($90 for international students). Electronic applications accepted. *Expenses:* Tuition, state resident: full-time $5495. Tuition, nonresident: full-time $21,938. *Required fees:* $1915. Tuition and fees vary according to program. *Financial support:* Research assistantships available. Financial award applicants required to submit FAFSA. *Faculty research:* Teacher consultation and culturally responsive school psychology practices, youth mentoring, cross-age peer mentoring, adolescent connectedness, pair counseling. *Total annual research expenditures:* $168,976. *Unit head:* Dr. Jeremy Sullivan, Department Chair, 210-458-2650, Fax: 210-458-2019, E-mail: jeremy.sullivan@utsa.edu. Website: http://education.utsa.edu/educational_psychology

The University of Texas at Tyler, College of Education and Psychology, Department of Psychology and Counseling, Tyler, TX 75799-0001. Offers clinical psychology (MS), including neuropsychology, school psychology; counseling psychology (MA), including general, marriage and family; interdisciplinary studies (MSIS); school counseling (MA). *Program availability:* Part-time, evening/weekend. *Degree requirements:* For master's, comprehensive exam, thesis optional. *Entrance requirements:* For master's, GRE General Test, minimum GPA of 3.0. Additional exam requirements/recommendations for international students: Required—TOEFL. Electronic applications accepted. *Faculty research:* Neuropsychology, child abuse, psychometric properties of psychological instruments, maternal behavior, clinical practice issues, victimization of women, post-traumatic stress disorder.

The University of Texas Rio Grande Valley, College of Education and P-16 Integration, Department of Human Development and School Services, Edinburg, TX 78539. Offers early childhood education (M Ed); early childhood special education (M Ed); school psychology (MA); special education (M Ed). *Program availability:* Part-time, evening/weekend. *Faculty:* 14. *Students:* 131. In 2017, 164 master's awarded. *Degree requirements:* For master's, comprehensive exam (for some programs). *Entrance requirements:* For master's, minimum GPA of 3.0. Additional exam requirements/recommendations for international students: Required—TOEFL (minimum score 550 paper-based; 79 iBT), IELTS (minimum score 6.5). *Application deadline:* For fall admission, 4/15 for domestic students; for spring admission, 11/1 for domestic students; for summer admission, 3/1 for domestic students. Applications are processed on a rolling basis. Application fee: $50 ($75 for international students). Electronic applications accepted. *Expenses:* Tuition, state resident: full-time $5550; part-time $417 per credit hour. Tuition, nonresident: full-time $13,020; part-time $832 per credit hour. *Required fees:* $1169. *Financial support:* Research assistantships, career-related internships or fieldwork, institutionally sponsored loans, and scholarships/grants available. Financial award application deadline: 4/15; financial award applicants required to submit FAFSA. *Faculty research:* Special education, assessment practice, behavior interventions, mental retardation, early childhood. *Unit head:* Dr. John Lowdermilk, Chair, 956-665-3466, E-mail: john.lowdermilk@utrgv.edu. *Application contact:* Stephanie Ozuna, Graduate Student Recruiter, 956-665-3661, E-mail: stephanie.ozuna@utrgv.edu.

University of the Pacific, Gladys L. Benerd School of Education, Stockton, CA 95211-0197. Offers curriculum and instruction (MA, Ed D); education (M Ed); educational administration and leadership (MA, Ed D); educational and school psychology (MA, Ed D); school psychology (Ed S); special education (MA); teacher education (MA). *Accreditation:* NCATE. *Faculty:* 19 full-time (12 women), 48 part-time/adjunct (39 women). *Students:* 141 full-time (115 women), 305 part-time (236 women); includes 219 minority (41 Black or African American, non-Hispanic/Latino; 44 Asian, non-Hispanic/Latino; 105 Hispanic/Latino; 2 Native Hawaiian or other Pacific Islander, non-Hispanic/Latino; 27 Two or more races, non-Hispanic/Latino), 7 international. Average age 33. 144 applicants, 83% accepted, 94 enrolled. In 2017, 231 master's, 8 doctorates awarded. *Degree requirements:* For doctorate, thesis/dissertation. *Entrance requirements:* For master's, GRE General Test; for doctorate, GRE General Test, GRE Subject Test. Additional exam requirements/recommendations for international students: Required—TOEFL. *Application deadline:* For fall admission, 3/1 priority date for domestic students; for spring admission, 10/15 for domestic students. Applications are processed on a rolling basis. Application fee: $75. *Financial support:* Teaching assistantships and institutionally sponsored loans available. Support available to part-time students. Financial award application deadline: 3/1; financial award applicants required to submit FAFSA. *Unit head:* Dr. Vanessa Sheared, Dean, 209-946-2683, E-mail: lwebster@pacific.edu. *Application contact:* Office of Graduate Admissions, 209-946-2344.

University of the Virgin Islands, School of Education, St. Thomas, VI 00802. Offers creative leadership for innovation and change (PhD); educational leadership (MA); school counseling (MA); school psychology (Ed S). *Program availability:* Part-time, evening/weekend. *Degree requirements:* For master's, comprehensive exam, thesis or alternative; for doctorate, comprehensive exam, thesis/dissertation, qualifying examination; for Ed S, comprehensive exam. *Entrance requirements:* For master's, GRE, minimum GPA of 2.5, BA degree from accredited institution. Additional exam requirements/recommendations for international students: Required—TOEFL (minimum score 550 paper-based). Electronic applications accepted. *Expenses:* Contact institution.

The University of Toledo, College of Graduate Studies, College of Health and Human Services, School of Intervention and Wellness, Toledo, OH 43606-3390. Offers counselor education (MA, PhD); school psychology (Ed S); speech-language pathology (MA). *Accreditation:* ACA (one or more programs are accredited); NCATE. *Degree requirements:* For master's, seminar paper. *Entrance requirements:* For master's, GRE General Test, interview, minimum GPA of 3.0. Electronic applications accepted. *Faculty research:* Training and supervision, ethics and standards, therapist development, multicultural issues, substance abuse screening.

The University of Toledo, College of Graduate Studies, College of Social Justice and Human Service, Department of School Psychology, Higher Education and Counselor Education, Toledo, OH 43606-3390. Offers counselor education (MA, PhD); higher education (ME, PhD, Certificate); school psychology (MA, Ed S). *Program availability:* Part-time. *Degree requirements:* For master's, comprehensive exam, thesis or alternative; for doctorate, comprehensive exam, thesis/dissertation; for other advanced degree, thesis optional. *Entrance requirements:* For master's, doctorate, and other advanced degree, minimum cumulative GPA of 2.7 for all previous academic work, letters of recommendation. Additional exam requirements/recommendations for international students: Required—TOEFL (minimum score 550 paper-based; 80 iBT). Electronic applications accepted.

University of Utah, Graduate School, College of Education, Department of Educational Psychology, Salt Lake City, UT 84112. Offers clinical mental health counseling (M Ed); counseling psychology (PhD); elementary education (M Ed); instructional design and educational technology (M Ed); instructional design and technology (MS); learning and cognition (MS, PhD); reading and literacy (M Ed, PhD); school counseling (M Ed); school psychology (M Ed, PhD, Ed S); statistics (M Stat). *Accreditation:* APA (one or more programs are accredited). *Faculty:* 19 full-time (9 women), 12 part-time/adjunct (8 women). *Students:* 122 full-time (95 women), 97 part-time (68 women); includes 26 minority (4 Asian, non-Hispanic/Latino; 16 Hispanic/Latino; 6 Two or more races, non-Hispanic/Latino), 7 international. Average age 31. 296 applicants, 27% accepted, 73 enrolled. In 2017, 65 master's, 15 doctorates awarded. Terminal master's awarded for partial completion of doctoral program. *Entrance requirements:* For master's and doctorate, GRE General Test, minimum GPA of 3.0. Additional exam requirements/recommendations for international students: Required—TOEFL (minimum score 80 iBT). *Application deadline:* For fall admission, 12/15 for domestic and international students; for winter admission, 11/1 for domestic and international students; for spring admission, 3/15 for domestic and international students. Application fee: $55 ($65 for international students). Electronic applications accepted. *Expenses:* Contact institution. *Financial support:* In 2017–18, 84 students received support, including 12 fellowships with full and partial tuition reimbursements available (averaging $17,000 per year), 16 research assistantships with full and partial tuition reimbursements available (averaging $15,500 per year), 39 teaching assistantships with full and partial tuition reimbursements available (averaging $15,500 per year); career-related internships or fieldwork, scholarships/grants, traineeships, health care benefits, and unspecified assistantships also available. Financial award application deadline: 4/1; financial award applicants required to submit FAFSA. *Faculty research:* Autism, computer technology and instruction, cognitive behavior, aging, group counseling. *Total annual research expenditures:* $620,935. *Unit head:* Dr. Anne E. Cook, Chair, 801-581-7148, Fax: 801-581-5566, E-mail: anne.cook@utah.edu. *Application contact:* JoLynn N. Yates, Academic Coordinator, 801-581-7148, Fax: 801-581-5566, E-mail: jo.yates@utah.edu. Website: http://www.ed.utah.edu/edps/

University of Vermont, Graduate College, College of Education and Social Services, Counseling Program, Burlington, VT 05405. Offers counseling (MS), including clinical mental health, school counseling. *Accreditation:* ACA; NCATE. *Students:* 68 (54 women); includes 4 minority (1 American Indian or Alaska Native, non-Hispanic/Latino; 1 Hispanic/Latino; 2 Two or more races, non-Hispanic/Latino). 99 applicants, 64% accepted, 35 enrolled. In 2017, 11 master's awarded. *Entrance requirements:* For master's, resume. Additional exam requirements/recommendations for international students: Required—TOEFL (minimum score 550 paper-based, 90 iBT) or IELTS (6.5). *Application deadline:* For fall admission, 2/1 for domestic and international students. Application fee: $65. Electronic applications accepted. *Expenses:* Tuition, state resident: full-time $11,628; part-time $646 per credit. Tuition, nonresident: full-time $29,340; part-time $1630 per credit. *Required fees:* $1994; $10 per credit. Tuition and fees vary according to course load and program. *Financial support:* In 2017–18, 1 student received support, including 1 teaching assistantship with partial tuition reimbursement available (averaging $8,000 per year); fellowships and research assistantships also available. Financial award application deadline: 2/1. *Faculty research:* Women and tenure, counseling children and adolescents. *Unit head:* Dr. Aaron Kindsvatter, Program Coordinator, 802-656-3888, E-mail: cslgprog@uvm.edu. Website: https://www.uvm.edu/cess/dlds/counseling

University of Virginia, Curry School of Education, Department of Human Services, Program in Clinical and School Psychology, Charlottesville, VA 22903. Offers PhD. *Students:* 23 full-time (22 women); includes 4 minority (2 Black or African American, non-Hispanic/Latino; 1 Hispanic/Latino; 1 Two or more races, non-Hispanic/Latino). Average age 26. 179 applicants, 4% accepted, 7 enrolled. In 2017, 5 doctorates awarded. *Unit head:* Peter Sheras, Chair, 434-924-0795, E-mail: pls@virginia.edu. *Application contact:* E-mail: curry-admissions@virginia.edu. Website: http://curry.virginia.edu/academics/areas-of-study/clinical-school-psychology

University of Virginia, Curry School of Education, Program in Education, Charlottesville, VA 22903. Offers administration and supervision (PhD); applied developmental science (PhD); counselor education (PhD); curriculum and instruction (PhD); early childhood special education (MT); education evaluation (PhD); educational psychology (PhD); educational research (PhD); elementary education (MT); English education (MT, PhD); foreign language education (MT); higher education (PhD); instructional technology (PhD); kinesiology (MT, PhD); math education (PhD); reading education (PhD); research, statistics and evaluation (PhD); school psychology (PhD); science education (PhD); social studies education (MT, PhD); special education (PhD); world languages education (MT). *Students:* 431 full-time (353 women), 15 part-time (14 women); includes 100 minority (32 Black or African American, non-Hispanic/Latino; 33 Asian, non-Hispanic/Latino; 16 Hispanic/Latino; 19 Two or more races, non-Hispanic/Latino), 14 international. Average age 25. 264 applicants, 49% accepted, 83 enrolled. In 2017, 142 master's, 33 doctorates awarded. *Degree requirements:* For master's, comprehensive exam (for some programs), field project; for doctorate, comprehensive exam, thesis/dissertation. *Entrance requirements:* For doctorate, GRE General Test. Additional exam requirements/recommendations for international students: Required—TOEFL (minimum score 600 paper-based; 90 iBT), IELTS (minimum score 7). *Application deadline:* Applications are processed on a rolling basis. Application fee: $60. Electronic applications accepted. *Financial support:* Fellowships, research assistantships, and teaching assistantships available. Financial award application deadline: 1/5; financial award applicants required to submit FAFSA. *Unit head:* Robert C. Pianta, Dean, 434-924-3334, E-mail: pianta@virginia.edu. *Application contact:* E-mail: curry-admissions@virginia.edu. Website: http://curry.virginia.edu/teacher-education

University of Washington, Graduate School, College of Education, Program in Educational Psychology, Seattle, WA 98195. Offers educational psychology (PhD); human development and cognition (M Ed); learning sciences (M Ed, PhD); measurement, statistics and research design (M Ed); school psychology (M Ed). *Accreditation:* APA. *Degree requirements:* For master's, thesis optional; for doctorate, thesis/dissertation. *Entrance requirements:* For master's and doctorate, GRE General Test, minimum GPA of 3.0. Additional exam requirements/recommendations for international students: Required—TOEFL.

University of Wisconsin–Eau Claire, College of Arts and Sciences, Department of Psychology, Eau Claire, WI 54702-4004. Offers school psychology (MSE, Ed S). *Program availability:* Part-time. *Degree requirements:* For master's, comprehensive exam, thesis, National Certified School Psychologist Professional Exam, written exam, externship. *Entrance requirements:* For master's, GRE, minimum undergraduate GPA of 3.0; courses in exceptional children and youth, statistics, psychopathology, and theories of counseling. Additional exam requirements/recommendations for international students: Required—TOEFL (minimum score 79 iBT).

University of Wisconsin–La Crosse, College of Liberal Studies, Department of Psychology, La Crosse, WI 54601-3742. Offers school psychology (MS Ed, Ed S). *Students:* 24 full-time (22 women), 12 part-time (10 women). Average age 24. 45 applicants, 42% accepted, 12 enrolled. In 2017, 11 master's, 11 Ed Ss awarded. *Degree requirements:* For master's, thesis, seminar, or comprehensive exams. *Entrance requirements:* For master's and Ed S, GRE. Additional exam requirements/recommendations for international students: Required—TOEFL (minimum score 550 paper-based; 79 iBT). *Application deadline:* For fall admission, 1/31 for domestic and international students. Electronic applications accepted. *Financial support:* Research assistantships, Federal Work-Study, scholarships/grants, and health care benefits available. Support available to part-time students. *Unit head:* Dr. Robert Dixon, Director of the School Psychology Program, 608-785-6893, E-mail: rdixon@uwlax.edu. *Application contact:* Brandon Schaller, Senior Graduate Student Status Examiner, 608-785-8941, E-mail: admissions@uwlax.edu. Website: https://www.uwlax.edu/Psychology/Graduate-program/

University of Wisconsin–Milwaukee, Graduate School, School of Education, Department of Educational Psychology, Milwaukee, WI 53201-0413. Offers children's mental health for school professionals (Graduate Certificate); counseling psychology (PhD); educational statistics and measurement (MS, PhD); learning and development (MS, PhD); multicultural knowledge of mental health practices (Graduate Certificate); school counseling (MS); school counseling (Graduate Certificate); school psychology (MS, PhD, Ed S). *Accreditation:* APA. *Program availability:* Part-time. *Students:* 170 full-time (132 women), 52 part-time (39 women); includes 51 minority (14 Black or African American, non-Hispanic/Latino; 1 American Indian or Alaska Native, non-Hispanic/Latino; 7 Asian, non-Hispanic/Latino; 7 Hispanic/Latino; 1 Native Hawaiian or other Pacific Islander, non-Hispanic/Latino; 21 Two or more races, non-Hispanic/Latino), 4 international. Average age 31. 304 applicants, 39% accepted, 83 enrolled. In 2017, 59 master's, 11 doctorates, 10 other advanced degrees awarded. *Degree requirements:* For master's, comprehensive exam, thesis; for doctorate, thesis/dissertation. *Entrance requirements:* For master's, minimum GPA of 3.0; for doctorate, GRE General Test, minimum GPA of 3.0. Additional exam requirements/recommendations for international students: Required—TOEFL (minimum score 550 paper-based; 79 iBT), IELTS (minimum score 6.5). *Application deadline:* For fall admission, 1/1 priority date for domestic students; for spring admission, 9/1 for domestic students. Application fee: $56 ($96 for international students). Electronic applications accepted. *Financial support:* Fellowships, research assistantships, teaching assistantships, career-related internships or fieldwork, health care benefits, unspecified assistantships, and project assistantships available. Support available to part-time students. Financial award application deadline: 4/15; financial award applicants required to submit FAFSA. *Application contact:* General Information Contact, 414-229-4721, E-mail: soeinfo@uwm.edu. Website: http://uwm.edu/education/academics/educational-psychology-department/

University of Wisconsin–River Falls, Outreach and Graduate Studies, College of Education and Professional Studies, Department of Counseling and School Psychology, River Falls, WI 54022. Offers counseling (MSE); school psychology (MSE, Ed S). *Accreditation:* ACA. *Program availability:* Part-time. *Entrance requirements:* For master's, minimum GPA of 2.75, resume, 3 letters of reference, vita. Additional exam requirements/recommendations for international students: Required—TOEFL (minimum score 500 paper-based; 65 iBT), IELTS (minimum score 5.5). Electronic applications accepted.

University of Wisconsin–Stout, Graduate School, College of Education, Health and Human Sciences, School of Education, Program in School Psychology, Menomonie, WI 54751. Offers MS Ed, Ed S. *Program availability:* Part-time. *Degree requirements:* For master's and Ed S, thesis. *Entrance requirements:* For master's, minimum GPA of 3.0; for Ed S, minimum GPA of 3.25. Additional exam requirements/recommendations for

international students: Required—TOEFL (minimum score 500 paper-based; 61 iBT). Electronic applications accepted. *Faculty research:* Intelligence assessment, eating disorders, intervention models, resilience, school violence.

University of Wisconsin–Superior, Graduate Division, Department of Counseling and Psychological Professions, Superior, WI 54880-4500. Offers community counseling (MSE); human relations (MSE); school counseling (MSE). *Program availability:* Part-time, evening/weekend. *Degree requirements:* For master's, position paper, practicum. *Entrance requirements:* For master's, GRE and/or MAT, minimum GPA of 2.75. Electronic applications accepted. *Faculty research:* Women and power, intrafamily dynamics.

University of Wisconsin–Whitewater, School of Graduate Studies, College of Letters and Sciences, Department of Psychology, Program in School Psychology, Whitewater, WI 53190-1790. Offers MSE, Ed S. *Program availability:* Evening/weekend, online learning. *Degree requirements:* For Ed S, project. *Entrance requirements:* For degree, master's degree in school psychology from an accredited school. Additional exam requirements/recommendations for international students: Required—TOEFL (minimum score 550 paper-based; 80 iBT), IELTS (minimum score 6). Electronic applications accepted.

Utah State University, School of Graduate Studies, Emma Eccles Jones College of Education and Human Services, Department of Psychology, Logan, UT 84322. Offers clinical/counseling/school psychology (PhD); research and evaluation methodology (PhD); school counseling (MS); school psychology (MS). *Accreditation:* APA (one or more programs are accredited). *Program availability:* Part-time, evening/weekend, online learning. Terminal master's awarded for partial completion of doctoral program. *Degree requirements:* For master's, thesis (for some programs); for doctorate, thesis/dissertation. *Entrance requirements:* For master's, GRE General Test (school psychology), MAT (school counseling), minimum GPA of 3.5; for doctorate, GRE General Test, minimum GPA of 3.5. Additional exam requirements/recommendations for international students: Required—TOEFL. *Faculty research:* Hearing loss detection in infancy, ADHD, eating disorders, domestic violence, neuropsychology, bilingual/Spanish speaking students/parents.

Valparaiso University, Graduate School and Continuing Education, Programs in Education, Valparaiso, IN 46383. Offers initial licensure (M Ed), including Chinese teaching, elementary education, secondary education; instructional leadership (M Ed); school psychology (Ed S); secondary education (M Ed); M Ed/Ed S. *Accreditation:* NCATE. *Program availability:* Part-time, evening/weekend, online learning. *Entrance requirements:* For master's, GRE General Test, minimum GPA of 3.0. Additional exam requirements/recommendations for international students: Required—TOEFL (minimum score 550 paper-based; 80 iBT), IELTS (minimum score 6). Electronic applications accepted. *Expenses:* Tuition: Full-time $11,340; part-time $630 per credit hour. *Required fees:* $520; $250 per year. $125 per semester. Tuition and fees vary according to program and reciprocity agreements.

Wayne State University, College of Education, Division of Theoretical and Behavioral Foundations, Detroit, MI 48202. Offers applied behavior analysis (Certificate); counseling (M Ed, MA, Ed D, Ed S); counseling psychology (MA, PhD); education evaluation and research (M Ed, Ed D); educational psychology (M Ed, PhD), including learning and instruction sciences (PhD); rehabilitation counseling and community inclusion (MA); school and community psychology (MA, Certificate). *Accreditation:* ACA (one or more programs are accredited); CORE (one or more programs are accredited). *Program availability:* Evening/weekend. *Students:* Average age 32. 294 applicants, 34% accepted, 72 enrolled. In 2017, 87 master's, 12 doctorates, 14 other advanced degrees awarded. *Entrance requirements:* For master's, GRE, interview, personal statement, portfolio (art therapy); for doctorate, GRE, department-written exam, interview, curriculum vitae, references, master's degree in closely-related field with minimum GPA of 3.5, demonstration of counseling skills (for Ed D in counseling); for other advanced degree, master's degree in counseling and counseling license (for Ed S); good standing in school and community psychology MA program (for Certificate). Additional exam requirements/recommendations for international students: Required—TOEFL (minimum score 550 paper-based; 79 iBT), Michigan English Language Assessment Battery (minimum score 85); Recommended—IELTS (minimum score 6.5), TWE (minimum score 5.5). *Application deadline:* For fall admission, 6/1 priority date for domestic students, 5/1 priority date for international students; for winter admission, 10/1 priority date for domestic students, 9/1 priority date for international students; for spring admission, 2/1 priority date for domestic students, 1/1 priority date for international students. Applications are processed on a rolling basis. Application fee: $50. Electronic applications accepted. *Expenses:* Contact institution. *Financial support:* In 2017–18, 92 students received support, including 2 research assistantships with tuition reimbursements available (averaging $17,994 per year); fellowships, teaching assistantships, Federal Work-Study, scholarships/grants, health care benefits, and unspecified assistantships also available. Support available to part-time students. Financial award applicants required to submit FAFSA. *Faculty research:* Adolescents at risk, supervision of counseling. *Unit head:* Dr. Cheryl Somers, Assistant Dean, 313-577-1670, E-mail: c.somers@wayne.edu. *Application contact:* Janice Green, Assistant Dean, 313-577-1605, E-mail: jwgreen@wayne.edu. Website: http://coe.wayne.edu/tbf/index.php

Western Illinois University, School of Graduate Studies, College of Arts and Sciences, Department of Psychology, Macomb, IL 61455-1390. Offers clinical/community mental health (MS); general experimental psychology (MS); school psychology (SSP). *Program availability:* Part-time. *Students:* 39 full-time (28 women), 15 part-time (8 women); includes 6 minority (1 Black or African American, non-Hispanic/Latino; 2 Asian, non-Hispanic/Latino; 1 Hispanic/Latino; 2 Two or more races, non-Hispanic/Latino), 2 international. Average age 26. 77 applicants, 77% accepted, 30 enrolled. In 2017, 8 master's, 6 other advanced degrees awarded. *Degree requirements:* For master's, comprehensive exam (for some programs), thesis or alternative. *Entrance requirements:* For master's and SSP, GRE General Test. Additional exam requirements/recommendations for international students: Required—TOEFL (minimum score 550 paper-based; 80 iBT). Application fee: $30. Electronic applications accepted. *Financial support:* In 2017–18, 6 research assistantships with full tuition reimbursements (averaging $7,544 per year) were awarded; unspecified assistantships also available. Financial award applicants required to submit FAFSA. *Unit head:* Dr. Karen Sears, Chairperson, 309-298-1593. *Application contact:* Dr. Nancy Parsons, Associate Provost and Director of Graduate Studies, 309-298-1806, Fax: 309-298-2345, E-mail: grad-office@wiu.edu. Website: http://wiu.edu/psychology

Western Kentucky University, Graduate Studies, College of Education and Behavioral Sciences, Department of Psychology, Bowling Green, KY 42101. Offers clinical psychology (MA); experimental psychology (MA); general psychology (MA); industrial/organizational psychology (MA); school psychology (Ed S). *Degree requirements:* For master's, comprehensive exam, thesis (for some programs); for Ed S, thesis, oral exam. *Entrance requirements:* For master's, GRE General Test; for Ed S, GRE General Test, minimum GPA of 3.5. Additional exam requirements/recommendations for international students: Required—TOEFL (minimum score 555 paper-based; 79 iBT). *Faculty research:* Neural regeneration, enhancing mobility in the elderly, improvement in visual processing in older adults, lifespan development.

Wichita State University, Graduate School, College of Education, Department of Counseling, Educational Leadership, Educational and School Psychology, Wichita, KS 67260. Offers counseling (M Ed); educational leadership (M Ed, Ed D); educational psychology (M Ed); school psychology (Ed S). *Accreditation:* NCATE. *Program availability:* Part-time, evening/weekend. Application fee: $50 ($65 for international students). *Unit head:* Dr. Jody Fiorini, Department Head, 316-978-3325, Fax: 316-978-3102, E-mail: jody.fiorini@wichita.edu. *Application contact:* Jordan Oleson, Admissions Coordinator, 316-978-3095, Fax: 316-978-3253, E-mail: jordan.oleson@wichita.edu. Website: http://www.wichita.edu/cles

William James College, Graduate Programs, Newton, MA 02459. Offers applied psychology in higher education student personnel administration (MA); clinical psychology (Psy D); counseling psychology (MA); counseling psychology and community mental health (MA); counseling psychology and global mental health (MA); executive coaching (Graduate Certificate); forensic and counseling psychology (MA); leadership psychology (Psy D); organizational psychology (MA); primary care psychology (MA); respecialization in clinical psychology (Certificate); school psychology (Psy D); MA/CAGS. *Accreditation:* APA. *Degree requirements:* For master's, comprehensive exam (for some programs); for doctorate, thesis/dissertation (for some programs). Electronic applications accepted.

Worcester State University, Graduate School, Department of Education, Program in School Psychology, Worcester, MA 01602-2597. Offers M Ed, Ed S. *Students:* 30 full-time (28 women), 7 part-time (all women); includes 4 minority (1 Black or African American, non-Hispanic/Latino; 2 Hispanic/Latino; 1 Two or more races, non-Hispanic/Latino). Average age 27. 41 applicants, 49% accepted, 17 enrolled. In 2017, 10 master's, 10 Ed Ss awarded. *Degree requirements:* For master's, comprehensive exam, thesis optional, practicum; internship. *Entrance requirements:* For degree, MTEL Communication and Literacy Skills test (strongly recommended), undergraduate major or concentration in psychology. Additional exam requirements/recommendations for international students: Required—TOEFL (minimum score 550 paper-based; 79 iBT). *Application deadline:* For fall admission, 3/1 priority date for domestic and international students. Applications are processed on a rolling basis. Application fee: $50. Electronic applications accepted. *Expenses:* Tuition, state resident: full-time $3042; part-time $169 per credit hour. Tuition, nonresident: full-time $3042; part-time $169 per credit hour. *Required fees:* $2754; $153 per credit hour. *Financial support:* Career-related internships or fieldwork, scholarships/grants, and unspecified assistantships available. Financial award application deadline: 3/1; financial award applicants required to submit FAFSA. *Unit head:* Dr. Diane Tighe Cooke, Coordinator, 508-929-8673. *Application contact:* Sara Grady, Associate Dean for Graduate Studies and Professional Development, 508-929-8130, Fax: 508-929-8100, E-mail: sara.grady@worcester.edu.

Yeshiva University, Ferkauf Graduate School of Psychology, Program in School/Clinical-Child Psychology, New York, NY 10033-3201. Offers Psy D. *Accreditation:* APA. *Program availability:* Part-time. *Degree requirements:* For doctorate, comprehensive exam, thesis/dissertation. *Entrance requirements:* For doctorate, GRE General Test. *Faculty research:* Testing, early childhood intervention, child and adolescent psychotherapy, clinical child psychology.

Youngstown State University, Graduate School, Beeghly College of Education, Department of Counseling, Youngstown, OH 44555-0001. Offers community counseling (MS Ed); school counseling (MS Ed). *Accreditation:* ACA; NCATE. *Program availability:* Part-time, evening/weekend. *Degree requirements:* For master's, comprehensive exam. *Entrance requirements:* For master's, MAT, interview, minimum GPA of 2.7. Additional exam requirements/recommendations for international students: Required—TOEFL. *Faculty research:* Suicide, euthanasia, ethical issues, marriage and family.

Social Psychology

Adler University, Graduate Programs, Master of Public Policy and Administration Program: Social Change Leadership, Chicago, IL 60602. Offers MPPA. Program offered at Vancouver campus. *Program availability:* Evening/weekend.

Alliant International University–Los Angeles, California School of Professional Psychology, Psy D Program in Clinical Psychology, Alhambra, CA 91803. Offers clinical health psychology (Psy D); family/child and couple clinical psychology (Psy D); multi-interest option (Psy D); multicultural community-clinical psychology (Psy D). *Accreditation:* APA. *Degree requirements:* For doctorate, comprehensive exam, thesis/dissertation. *Entrance requirements:* For doctorate, interview, minimum GPA of 3.0 in both psychology and overall. Additional exam requirements/recommendations for international students: Required—TOEFL (minimum score 600 paper-based), TWE. Electronic applications accepted. *Faculty research:* Child and family psychology, multicultural and community psychology, acculturation, lesbian and gay issues, women's health.

Alvernia University, School of Graduate Studies, Department of Psychology and Counseling, Reading, PA 19607-1799. Offers community counseling (MA). *Entrance requirements:* For master's, GRE or MAT.

Alverno College, School of Arts and Sciences, Milwaukee, WI 53234-3922. Offers community-based research and consultation (MSCP); professional counselor (MSCP). *Program availability:* Part-time, evening/weekend. *Faculty:* 6 full-time (all women), 6 part-time/adjunct (all women). *Students:* 78 full-time (76 women), 12 part-time (all women); includes 37 minority (24 Black or African American, non-Hispanic/Latino; 1 Asian, non-Hispanic/Latino; 11 Hispanic/Latino; 1 Two or more races, non-Hispanic/Latino), 2 international. Average age 34. 34 applicants, 100% accepted, 23 enrolled. In 2017, 20 master's awarded. *Entrance requirements:* Additional exam requirements/recommendations for international students: Required—TOEFL. *Application deadline:* For fall admission, 7/15 priority date for domestic and international students; for spring admission, 12/15 priority date for domestic and international students. Applications are processed on a rolling basis. Application fee: $0. Electronic applications accepted. *Expenses:* Contact institution. *Financial support:* Federal Work-Study and scholarships/grants available. Support available to part-time students. Financial award applicants required to submit FAFSA. *Unit head:* Dr. Kimberly Skerven, Director, Master of Science in Community Psychology, 414-382-6461, Fax: 414-382-6354, E-mail: kimberly.skerven@alverno.edu. *Application contact:* Katie Kipp, Graduate Admissions Counselor, 414-382-6045, Fax: 414-382-6354, E-mail: katie.kipp@alverno.edu.

Andrews University, School of Graduate Studies, School of Education, Department of Graduate Psychology and Counseling, Program in Community Counseling, Berrien Springs, MI 49104. Offers clinical mental health counseling (MA); community counseling (MA). *Students:* 23 full-time (13 women), 3 part-time (all women); includes 7 minority (3 Black or African American, non-Hispanic/Latino; 4 Hispanic/Latino), 9 international. Average age 30. 25 applicants, 76% accepted, 7 enrolled. In 2017, 12 master's awarded. *Degree requirements:* For master's, thesis optional. *Entrance requirements:* For master's, GRE. Additional exam requirements/recommendations for international students: Required—TOEFL (minimum score 550 paper-based). Application fee: $40. *Unit head:* Dr. Nancy Carbonell, Coordinator, 269-471-3472. *Application contact:* Justina Clayburn, Supervisor of Graduate Admission, 800-253-2874, Fax: 269-471-6321, E-mail: graduate@andrews.edu.

Argosy University, Atlanta, Georgia School of Professional Psychology, Atlanta, GA 30328. Offers clinical psychology (MA, Psy D, Postdoctoral Respecialization Certificate), including child and family psychology (Psy D), general adult clinical (Psy D), health psychology (Psy D), neuropsychology/geropsychology (Psy D); community counseling (MA), including marriage and family therapy; counselor education and supervision (Ed D); forensic psychology (MA); industrial organizational psychology (MA); marriage and family therapy (Certificate); sport-exercise psychology (MA). *Accreditation:* APA.

Argosy University, Chicago, Illinois School of Professional Psychology, Chicago, IL 60601. Offers clinical psychology (MA, Psy D), including child and adolescent psychology (Psy D), client-centered and experiential psychotherapies (Psy D), diversity and multicultural psychology (Psy D), family psychology (Psy D), forensic psychology (Psy D), health psychology (Psy D), neuropsychology (Psy D), organizational consulting (Psy D), psychoanalytic psychology (Psy D), psychology and spirituality (Psy D); community counseling (MA); counseling psychology (Ed D), including counselor education and supervision; counselor education and supervision (Ed D); industrial organizational psychology (MA). *Accreditation:* APA (one or more programs are accredited). *Program availability:* Online learning.

Argosy University, Northern Virginia, American School of Professional Psychology, Arlington, VA 22209. Offers clinical psychology (MA, Psy D), including child and family psychology (Psy D), diversity and multicultural psychology (Psy D), forensic psychology (Psy D), health and neuropsychology (Psy D); community counseling (MA); counseling psychology (Ed D), including counselor education and supervision; counselor education and supervision (Ed D); forensic psychology (MA).

Arizona State University at the Tempe campus, College of Liberal Arts and Sciences, Department of Psychology, Tempe, AZ 85287-1104. Offers applied behavior analysis (MS); behavioral neuroscience (PhD); clinical psychology (PhD); cognitive science (PhD); developmental psychology (PhD); quantitative psychology (PhD); social psychology (PhD). *Accreditation:* APA. *Degree requirements:* For doctorate, comprehensive exam, thesis/dissertation, interactive Program of Study (iPOS) submitted before completing 50 percent of required credit hours. *Entrance requirements:* For doctorate, GRE General Test, GRE Subject Test, minimum GPA of 3.0 or equivalent in last 2 years of work leading to bachelor's degree. Additional exam requirements/recommendations for international students: Required—TOEFL, IELTS, or PTE. Electronic applications accepted.

Ball State University, Graduate School, College of Health, Department of Counseling Psychology, Social Psychology, and Counseling, Program in Social Psychology, Muncie, IN 47306. Offers social psychology (MA); social psychology and clinical mental health counseling (MA). *Students:* 4 full-time (2 women), 4 part-time (all women); includes 2 minority (1 Black or African American, non-Hispanic/Latino; 1 Asian, non-Hispanic/Latino). Average age 27. 20 applicants, 15% accepted, 2 enrolled. In 2017, 4 master's awarded. *Entrance requirements:* For master's, GRE General Test (minimum scores 144 quantitative, 153 verbal), minimum baccalaureate GPA of 2.75 or 3.0 in latter half of baccalaureate, minimum GPA of 3.0 in psychology coursework, three letters of recommendation. Additional exam requirements/recommendations for international students: Required—TOEFL (minimum score 550 paper-based; 79 iBT), IELTS (minimum score 6.5). *Application deadline:* For fall admission, 3/1 priority date for domestic students, 1/1 priority date for international students. Applications are processed on a rolling basis. Application fee: $60. Electronic applications accepted. *Financial support:* Teaching assistantships with partial tuition reimbursements and unspecified assistantships available. Financial award application deadline: 3/1; financial award applicants required to submit FAFSA. *Unit head:* Dr. Sharon Bowman, Head, 765-285-8040, Fax: 765-285-2067, E-mail: sbowman@bsu.edu.

Becker College, Program in Mental Health Counseling, Worcester, MA 01609. Offers community mental health (MA); school consultation (MA). *Entrance requirements:* For master's, GRE, interview, official transcript, three letters of recommendation, essay. Electronic applications accepted.

Bowling Green State University, Graduate College, College of Arts and Sciences, Department of Sociology, Bowling Green, OH 43403. Offers demography and population studies (MA); social psychology (MA); sociology (PhD). *Program availability:* Part-time. *Degree requirements:* For master's, thesis or alternative; for doctorate, comprehensive exam, thesis/dissertation. *Entrance requirements:* For master's and doctorate, GRE General Test. Additional exam requirements/recommendations for international students: Required—TOEFL. Electronic applications accepted. *Faculty research:* Applied demography, criminology and deviance, family studies, population studies, social psychology.

Brandeis University, Graduate School of Arts and Sciences, Department of Psychology, Waltham, MA 02454-9110. Offers brain, body and behavior (PhD); cognitive neuroscience (PhD); general psychology (MA); social/developmental psychology (PhD). *Program availability:* Part-time. *Faculty:* 14 full-time (7 women), 4 part-time/adjunct (3 women). *Students:* 34 full-time (26 women), 4 part-time (2 women); includes 8 minority (5 Asian, non-Hispanic/Latino; 3 Hispanic/Latino), 10 international. Average age 27. 124 applicants, 31% accepted, 15 enrolled. In 2017, 13 master's, 7 doctorates awarded. Terminal master's awarded for partial completion of doctoral program. *Degree requirements:* For master's, thesis or alternative; for doctorate, thesis/dissertation, research reports. *Entrance requirements:* For master's and doctorate, GRE General Test; GRE Subject Test (recommended), letters of recommendation, statement of purpose, transcripts, resume. Additional exam requirements/recommendations for international students: Required—PTE (minimum score 68), TOEFL (minimum score 600 paper-based, 100 iBT) or IELTS (7). *Application deadline:* For fall admission, 12/1 priority date for domestic students. Applications are processed on a rolling basis. Application fee: $75. Electronic applications accepted. *Expenses: Tuition:* Full-time $48,720. *Required fees:* $88. Tuition and fees vary according to course load, degree level, program and student level. *Financial support:* In 2017–18, 40 students received support, including 20 fellowships with full tuition reimbursements available (averaging $24,480 per year), 26 teaching assistantships with partial tuition reimbursements

available (averaging $3,200 per year); Federal Work-Study, scholarships/grants, health care benefits, and tuition waivers (partial) also available. Support available to part-time students. Financial award application deadline: 4/15; financial award applicants required to submit FAFSA. *Faculty research:* Brain, body, and behavior across the lifespan; face perception and nonverbal communication; learning and memory; motor control and spatial orientation; neurophysiology of learning and decision making; personality and cognition in adulthood and old age; social, cultural and affective neuroscience; social relations and health physiology; speech comprehension and memory; taste physiology and psychophysics; visual perception. *Unit head:* Dr. Angela Gutchess, Department Chair, 781-736-3303, E-mail: gutchess@brandeis.edu. *Application contact:* Dr. Sarah Lupis, Department Administrator, 781-736-3303, E-mail: slupis@brandeis.edu. Website: http://www.brandeis.edu/gsas/programs/psychology.html

Brock University, Faculty of Graduate Studies, Faculty of Social Sciences, Program in Psychology, St. Catharines, ON L2S 3A1, Canada. Offers behavioral neuroscience (MA, PhD); life span development (MA, PhD); social personality (MA, PhD). *Program availability:* Part-time. *Degree requirements:* For master's, thesis; for doctorate, thesis/dissertation. *Entrance requirements:* For master's, GRE, honors degree; for doctorate, GRE, master's degree. Additional exam requirements/recommendations for international students: Required—TOEFL (minimum score 550 paper-based; 80 iBT), IELTS (minimum score 6.5), TWE (minimum score 4). Electronic applications accepted. *Faculty research:* Social personality, behavioral neuroscience, life-span development.

Brooklyn College of the City University of New York, School of Natural and Behavioral Sciences, Department of Psychology, Brooklyn, NY 11210-2889. Offers experimental psychology (MA); industrial and organizational psychology (MA), including human relations, organizational behavior; mental health counseling (MA); psychology (PhD). *Program availability:* Part-time. *Degree requirements:* For master's, comprehensive exam, thesis (for some programs). *Entrance requirements:* For master's, minimum GPA of 3.0, 2 letters of recommendation, essay; for doctorate, GRE. Additional exam requirements/recommendations for international students: Required—TOEFL (minimum score 520 paper-based; 69 iBT). Electronic applications accepted.

California Institute of Integral Studies, School of Professional Psychology and Health, San Francisco, CA 94103. Offers clinical psychology (Psy D); community mental health (MA); drama therapy (MA); expressive arts therapy (MA); integral counseling psychology (MA); integrative health studies (MA); psychological studies (MA); somatic psychology (MA). *Program availability:* Part-time, evening/weekend, 100% online, blended/hybrid learning. *Students:* 507 full-time (401 women), 96 part-time (77 women); includes 167 minority (29 Black or African American, non-Hispanic/Latino; 3 American Indian or Alaska Native, non-Hispanic/Latino; 32 Asian, non-Hispanic/Latino; 62 Hispanic/Latino; 2 Native Hawaiian or other Pacific Islander, non-Hispanic/Latino; 39 Two or more races, non-Hispanic/Latino), 60 international. Average age 34. 302 applicants, 89% accepted, 171 enrolled. In 2017, 194 master's, 18 doctorates awarded. *Degree requirements:* For doctorate, comprehensive exam, thesis/dissertation. *Entrance requirements:* For master's, minimum GPA of 3.0, letters of recommendation, writing sample; for doctorate, GRE, MA in psychology or social work with appropriate practical experience for advanced standing, or BA with a minimum GPA of 3.1; letters of recommendation; writing sample. Additional exam requirements/recommendations for international students: Required—TOEFL. *Application deadline:* For fall admission, 2/1 priority date for domestic and international students; for spring admission, 10/15 priority date for domestic and international students. Applications are processed on a rolling basis. Application fee: $65. Electronic applications accepted. *Expenses:* $21,400 (for MA); $32,734 (for PsyD). *Financial support:* Research assistantships with tuition reimbursements, teaching assistantships with tuition reimbursements, career-related internships or fieldwork, Federal Work-Study, and scholarships/grants available. Support available to part-time students. Financial award application deadline: 4/15; financial award applicants required to submit FAFSA. *Faculty research:* Transpersonal psychology, somatic psychology, expressive arts therapy, drama therapy, community mental health, ecopsychology, integrative health, human sexuality. *Unit head:* Nicolle Zapien, Academic Dean, 415-575-5577, E-mail: nzapien@ciis.edu. *Application contact:* Ellen Durst, Director of Admissions, 415-575-6100, Fax: 415-575-1268, E-mail: admissions@ciis.edu.

California State University, East Bay, Office of Graduate Studies, College of Letters, Arts, and Social Sciences, Department of Social Work, Hayward, CA 94542-3000. Offers children, youth, and family services (MSW); community mental health services (MSW). *Accreditation:* CSWE. *Faculty:* 8 full-time (7 women), 10 part-time/adjunct (9 women). *Students:* 137 full-time (108 women), 1 (woman) part-time; includes 118 minority (34 Black or African American, non-Hispanic/Latino; 19 Asian, non-Hispanic/Latino; 58 Hispanic/Latino; 1 Native Hawaiian or other Pacific Islander, non-Hispanic/Latino; 6 Two or more races, non-Hispanic/Latino), 5 international. Average age 32. 334 applicants, 26% accepted, 71 enrolled. In 2017, 90 master's awarded. *Degree requirements:* For master's, comprehensive exam. *Entrance requirements:* For master's, minimum GPA of 2.8; courses in statistics and either human biology, physiology, or anatomy; liberal arts or social science baccalaureate degree; 3 letters of recommendation; personal statement; criminal background check; student professional liability insurance. Additional exam requirements/recommendations for international students: Required—TOEFL (minimum score 550 paper-based). *Application deadline:* For fall admission, 12/1 for domestic and international students. Applications are processed on a rolling basis. Application fee: $55. Electronic applications accepted. *Financial support:* Fellowships, career-related internships or fieldwork, Federal Work-Study, institutionally sponsored loans, and scholarships/grants available. Support available to part-time students. Financial award application deadline: 3/2; financial award applicants required to submit FAFSA. *Unit head:* Dr. Holly Vugia, Interim Chair, 510-885-2121, E-mail: holly.vugia@csueastbay.edu. *Application contact:* Philip Cole-Regis, Administrative Support Coordinator, 510-885-3286, E-mail: philip.coleregis@csueastbay.edu. Website: http://www20.csueastbay.edu/class/departments/socialwork/

California State University, Fullerton, Graduate Studies, College of Health and Human Development, Department of Social Work, Fullerton, CA 92831-3599. Offers aging (MSW); child welfare (MSW); community mental health (MSW). *Accreditation:* CSWE. *Program availability:* Part-time. *Faculty:* 15 full-time (10 women), 8 part-time/adjunct (7 women). *Students:* 167 full-time (145 women), 3 part-time (2 women); includes 118 minority (5 Black or African American, non-Hispanic/Latino; 1 American Indian or Alaska Native, non-Hispanic/Latino; 25 Asian, non-Hispanic/Latino; 81 Hispanic/Latino; 6 Two or more races, non-Hispanic/Latino), 3 international. Average age 27. 571 applicants, 23% accepted, 84 enrolled. *Entrance requirements:* For master's, minimum GPA of 3.0 for last 60 semester or 90 quarter units. Application fee: $55. *Financial support:* Career-related internships or fieldwork, Federal Work-Study, institutionally sponsored loans, and scholarships/grants available. Support available to part-time students. Financial award application deadline: 3/1; financial award applicants required to submit FAFSA. *Unit head:* Dr. David Chenot, Chair, 657-278-8452, E-mail: dchenot@fullerton.edu. *Application contact:* Admissions/Applications, 657-278-2371. Website: http://hhd.fullerton.edu/msw

Canisius College, Graduate Division, School of Education and Human Services, Programs in Counseling and Human Services, Buffalo, NY 14208-1098. Offers

community mental health counseling (MS); counseling and human services (MS); school agency counseling (MS). *Accreditation:* ACA. *Program availability:* Part-time, evening/weekend. *Faculty:* 5 full-time (2 women), 11 part-time/adjunct (8 women). *Students:* 80 full-time (68 women), 40 part-time (31 women); includes 21 minority (13 Black or African American, non-Hispanic/Latino; 6 Hispanic/Latino; 2 Two or more races, non-Hispanic/Latino), 5 international. Average age 29. 89 applicants, 85% accepted, 31 enrolled. In 2017, 39 master's awarded. *Degree requirements:* For master's, thesis, research project. *Entrance requirements:* For master's, GRE (if cumulative GPA less than 2.7), transcripts, two letters of recommendation, interview, BA. Additional exam requirements/recommendations for international students: Required—TOEFL (minimum score 550 paper-based, 79 iBT), IELTS (minimum score 6.5), or CAEL (minimum score 70). *Application deadline:* Applications are processed on a rolling basis. Application fee: $0. Electronic applications accepted. *Expenses: Tuition:* Full-time $22,860; part-time $820 per credit. *Required fees:* $720; $25 per credit. $65 per semester. One-time fee: $425. *Financial support:* Career-related internships or fieldwork, Federal Work-Study, scholarships/grants, tuition waivers (partial), and unspecified assistantships available. Support available to part-time students. Financial award application deadline: 4/30; financial award applicants required to submit FAFSA. *Faculty research:* Impact of trauma on adults, long term psych-social impact on police officers. *Unit head:* Dr. Christine Moll, Chair, 716-888-3287, E-mail: moll@canisius.edu. Website: http://www.canisius.edu/masters-counseling/

Carnegie Mellon University, Dietrich College of Humanities and Social Sciences, Department of Psychology, Program in Social/Personality/Health Psychology, Pittsburgh, PA 15213-3891. Offers PhD. *Degree requirements:* For doctorate, comprehensive exam, thesis/dissertation. *Entrance requirements:* For doctorate, GRE General Test. Additional exam requirements/recommendations for international students: Required—TOEFL.

Claremont Graduate University, Graduate Programs, School of Social Science, Policy and Evaluation, Department of Psychology, Claremont, CA 91711-6160. Offers advanced study in evaluation (Certificate); cognitive psychology (MA, PhD); developmental psychology (MA, PhD); evaluation and applied research methods (MA, PhD); health behavior research and evaluation (MA, PhD); human resource development and evaluation (MA); industrial/organizational psychology (MA, PhD); organizational behavior (MA, PhD); organizational psychology (MA, PhD); social psychology (MA, PhD); MBA/PhD. *Program availability:* Part-time. Terminal master's awarded for partial completion of doctoral program. *Entrance requirements:* For master's and doctorate, GRE General Test. Additional exam requirements/recommendations for international students: Required—TOEFL (minimum score 75 iBT). Electronic applications accepted. *Faculty research:* Social intervention, diversity in organizations, eyewitness memory, aging and cognition, drug policy.

Clark University, Graduate School, Hiatt School of Psychology, Program in Social Psychology, Worcester, MA 01610-1477. Offers PhD. *Students:* 7 full-time (all women); includes 3 minority (1 Black or African American, non-Hispanic/Latino; 1 Asian, non-Hispanic/Latino; 1 Hispanic/Latino), 3 international. Average age 28. *Entrance requirements:* For doctorate, GRE General Test. Additional exam requirements/recommendations for international students: Required—TOEFL. *Application deadline:* For fall admission, 12/15 priority date for domestic and international students. Applications are processed on a rolling basis. Application fee: $75. *Financial support:* Fellowships, research assistantships, teaching assistantships, and tuition waivers (full) available. *Faculty research:* Conceptualizing and reasoning, symbolization, psychotherapy, metaphor, emotions and personalities. *Unit head:* Dr. Johanna Ray Vollhardt, 508-793-7274, E-mail: jvollhardt@clarku.edu. *Application contact:* Kelly Boulay, Graduate School Secretary, 508-793-7274, Fax: 508-793-7265, E-mail: psychology@clarku.edu. Website: http://www.clarku.edu/departments/psychology/grad/social/index.cfm

College of St. Joseph, Graduate Programs, Division of Psychology and Human Services, Program in Community Counseling, Rutland, VT 05701-3899. Offers MS. *Program availability:* Part-time, evening/weekend. *Degree requirements:* For master's, comprehensive exam, thesis optional. *Entrance requirements:* For master's, official college transcripts; 2 letters of reference. Additional exam requirements/recommendations for international students: Required—TOEFL (minimum score 550 paper-based). Electronic applications accepted.

Cornell University, Graduate School, Graduate Fields of Arts and Sciences, Field of Psychology, Ithaca, NY 14853. Offers biopsychology (PhD); human experimental psychology (PhD); personality and social psychology (PhD). *Degree requirements:* For doctorate, comprehensive exam, thesis/dissertation, 2 semesters of teaching experience. *Entrance requirements:* For doctorate, GRE General Test, 3 letters of recommendation. Additional exam requirements/recommendations for international students: Required—TOEFL (minimum score 550 paper-based; 77 iBT). Electronic applications accepted. *Faculty research:* Sensory and perceptual systems, social cognition, cognitive development, quantitative and computational modeling, behavioral neuroscience.

Cornell University, Graduate School, Graduate Fields of Arts and Sciences, Field of Sociology, Ithaca, NY 14853. Offers economy and society (MA, PhD); gender and life course (MA, PhD); methodology (MA, PhD); organizations (MA, PhD); policy analysis (MA, PhD); political sociology/social movements (MA, PhD); racial and ethnic relations (MA, PhD); social networks (MA, PhD); social psychology (MA, PhD); social stratification (MA, PhD). Terminal master's awarded for partial completion of doctoral program. *Degree requirements:* For master's, thesis; for doctorate, thesis/dissertation, 1 year of teaching experience. *Entrance requirements:* For master's and doctorate, GRE General Test, 2 letters of recommendation, writing sample. Additional exam requirements/recommendations for international students: Required—TOEFL (minimum score 550 paper-based; 77 iBT). Electronic applications accepted. *Faculty research:* Comparative societal analysis, work and family, simulations, social class and mobility, racial segregation and inequality.

Delaware Valley University, Program in Counseling Psychology, Doylestown, PA 18901-2697. Offers child and adolescent therapy (MA); social justice community counseling (MA).

Florida Agricultural and Mechanical University, Division of Graduate Studies, Research, and Continuing Education, College of Social Sciences, Arts and Humanities, Department of Psychology, Program in Community Psychology, Tallahassee, FL 32307-3200. Offers MS. *Degree requirements:* For master's, thesis, internship. *Entrance requirements:* For master's, GRE General Test, minimum GPA of 3.0, letters of recommendation (3). Additional exam requirements/recommendations for international students: Required—TOEFL. *Faculty research:* African-American personality and mental health, racism in the socialization of black children.

Florida State University, The Graduate School, College of Arts and Sciences, Department of Psychology, Program in Social Psychology, Tallahassee, FL 32306. Offers PhD. *Faculty:* 6 full-time (2 women). *Students:* 16 full-time (12 women); includes 4 minority (3 Hispanic/Latino; 1 Two or more races, non-Hispanic/Latino). Average age 28. 62 applicants, 3% accepted, 2 enrolled. In 2017, 3 doctorates awarded. Terminal master's awarded for partial completion of doctoral program. *Degree requirements:* For

Social Psychology

doctorate, comprehensive exam, thesis/dissertation. *Entrance requirements:* For doctorate, GRE General Test, minimum GPA of 3.0, research experience, letters of recommendation. Additional exam requirements/recommendations for international students: Required—TOEFL (minimum score 80 iBT). *Application deadline:* For fall admission, 12/15 for domestic and international students. Application fee: $30. Electronic applications accepted. *Financial support:* In 2017–18, 16 students received support, including 2 fellowships with full tuition reimbursements available (averaging $22,815 per year), 1 research assistantship with full tuition reimbursement available (averaging $23,815 per year), 13 teaching assistantships with full tuition reimbursements available (averaging $19,000 per year); health care benefits also available. Financial award application deadline: 12/15; financial award applicants required to submit FAFSA. *Faculty research:* Self and identity, prejudice and intergroup relations, evolutionary psychology, emotion, health. *Total annual research expenditures:* $288,152. *Unit head:* Dr. Ashby Plant, Director of Social Psychology, 850-644-5533, Fax: 850-644-7739, E-mail: plant@psy.fsu.edu. *Application contact:* Lynda L. Gibson, Graduate Program Associate, 850-644-2499, Fax: 850-644-7739, E-mail: grad-info@psy.fsu.edu.
Website: http://www.psy.fsu.edu/

Future Generations University, Program in Applied Community Change, Franklin, WV 26807. Offers conservation (MA). *Program availability:* Blended/hybrid learning. *Faculty:* 9 full-time (3 women), 12 part-time/adjunct (4 women). *Students:* 16 full-time (7 women); includes 13 minority (6 Black or African American, non-Hispanic/Latino; 4 Asian, non-Hispanic/Latino; 3 Hispanic/Latino). In 2017, 11 master's awarded. *Degree requirements:* For master's, portfolio. *Entrance requirements:* For master's, bachelor's degree, community involvement. Additional exam requirements/recommendations for international students: Recommended—TOEFL. *Application deadline:* Applications are processed on a rolling basis. Application fee: $0. Electronic applications accepted. *Financial support:* Scholarships/grants and tuition waivers (partial) available. Financial award applicants required to submit FAFSA. *Faculty research:* Sustainable communities, community engagement, peacebuilding, seed-scale community development. *Unit head:* Christie Hand, Chief Academic Officer, 304-358-2000. *Application contact:* Jodie Wimer, Registrar, 304-358-2000, E-mail: jwimer@future.edu.
Website: http://www.future.edu

The George Washington University, Columbian College of Arts and Sciences, Department of Psychology, Washington, DC 20052. Offers applied social psychology (PhD); clinical psychology (PhD); cognitive neuroscience (PhD). *Accreditation:* APA. *Program availability:* Part-time, evening/weekend. *Faculty:* 26 full-time (15 women), 10 part-time/adjunct (7 women). *Students:* 41 full-time (27 women), 25 part-time (17 women); includes 24 minority (10 Black or African American, non-Hispanic/Latino; 8 Asian, non-Hispanic/Latino; 4 Hispanic/Latino; 2 Two or more races, non-Hispanic/Latino), 6 international. Average age 28. 452 applicants, 35% accepted, 87 enrolled. In 2017, 10 doctorates awarded. *Degree requirements:* For doctorate, thesis/dissertation or alternative, general exam. *Entrance requirements:* For doctorate, GRE General Test, minimum GPA of 3.0. Additional exam requirements/recommendations for international students: Required—TOEFL (minimum score 550 paper-based; 80 iBT). *Application deadline:* For fall admission, 1/15 for domestic and international students. Application fee: $75. *Expenses: Tuition:* Full-time $28,800; part-time $1655 per credit hour. *Required fees:* $45; $2.75 per credit hour. *Financial support:* In 2017–18, 62 students received support. Fellowships with tuition reimbursements available, teaching assistantships with tuition reimbursements available, career-related internships or fieldwork, Federal Work-Study, and tuition waivers available. *Unit head:* Dr. Carol Sigelman, Chair, 202-994-8422, E-mail: carol@gwu.edu. *Application contact:* Information Contact, 202-994-6320, Fax: 202-994-1602, E-mail: psych@gwu.edu.
Website: http://psychology.columbian.gwu.edu/

Georgia State University, College of Arts and Sciences, Department of Psychology, Atlanta, GA 30302-3083. Offers clinical psychology (PhD); cognitive sciences (PhD); community psychology (PhD); developmental psychology (PhD); neuropsychology and behavioral neuroscience (PhD). *Accreditation:* APA. *Faculty:* 40 full-time (26 women). *Students:* 102 full-time (80 women), 4 part-time (all women); includes 26 minority (7 Black or African American, non-Hispanic/Latino; 10 Asian, non-Hispanic/Latino; 4 Hispanic/Latino; 5 Two or more races, non-Hispanic/Latino), 8 international. Average age 27. 450 applicants, 7% accepted, 16 enrolled. In 2017, 21 doctorates awarded. *Entrance requirements:* For doctorate, GRE. Additional exam requirements/recommendations for international students: Required—TOEFL (minimum score 550 paper-based; 80 iBT). *Application deadline:* For fall admission, 12/1 for domestic and international students. Application fee: $50. Electronic applications accepted. *Expenses:* Tuition, state resident: full-time $7020. Tuition, nonresident: full-time $22,518. *Required fees:* $2128. Tuition and fees vary according to degree level and program. *Financial support:* In 2017–18, fellowships with full tuition reimbursements (averaging $19,282 per year), research assistantships with full tuition reimbursements (averaging $5,173 per year), teaching assistantships with full tuition reimbursements (averaging $6,389 per year) were awarded; scholarships/grants, traineeships, health care benefits, and unspecified assistantships also available. Financial award applicants required to submit FAFSA. *Faculty research:* Clinical psychology, developmental psychology, community psychology, neuropsychology and behavioral neuroscience, cognitive sciences. *Unit head:* Dr. Lisa Armistead, Chair, 404-413-6205, Fax: 404-413-6207, E-mail: lparmistead@gsu.edu. *Application contact:* Dr. Lindsey Cohen, Director of Graduate Studies, 404-413-6263, Fax: 404-413-6207, E-mail: llcohen@gsu.edu.

The Graduate Center, City University of New York, Graduate Studies, Program in Psychology, New York, NY 10016-4039. Offers basic applied neurocognition (PhD); biopsychology (PhD); clinical psychology (PhD); developmental psychology (PhD); environmental psychology (PhD); experimental psychology (PhD); industrial psychology (PhD); learning processes (PhD); neuropsychology (PhD); psychology (PhD); social personality (PhD). *Faculty:* 119 full-time (40 women). *Students:* 428 full-time (308 women); includes 118 minority (31 Black or African American, non-Hispanic/Latino; 31 Asian, non-Hispanic/Latino; 47 Hispanic/Latino; 1 Native Hawaiian or other Pacific Islander, non-Hispanic/Latino; 8 Two or more races, non-Hispanic/Latino), 53 international. Average age 33. 795 applicants, 12% accepted, 56 enrolled. In 2017, 46 doctorates awarded. *Degree requirements:* For doctorate, one foreign language, thesis/dissertation. *Entrance requirements:* For doctorate, GRE General Test. Additional exam requirements/recommendations for international students: Required—TOEFL. *Application deadline:* For fall admission, 12/1 priority date for domestic students. Application fee: $125. Electronic applications accepted. *Financial support:* In 2017–18, 371 students received support, including 340 fellowships, 34 research assistantships, 33 teaching assistantships; career-related internships or fieldwork, Federal Work-Study, institutionally sponsored loans, and tuition waivers (full and partial) also available. Financial award application deadline: 2/1; financial award applicants required to submit FAFSA. *Unit head:* Richard Bodnar, Executive Officer, 212-817-8706, Fax: 212-817-1533, E-mail: rbodnar@gc.cuny.edu. *Application contact:* Les Gribben, Director of Admissions, 212-817-7470, Fax: 212-817-1624, E-mail: lgribben@gc.cuny.edu.

Harvard University, Graduate School of Arts and Sciences, Department of Psychology, Cambridge, MA 02138. Offers psychology (PhD), including behavior and decision analysis, cognition, developmental psychology, experimental psychology, personality,

psychobiology, psychopathology; social psychology (PhD). *Accreditation:* APA. *Degree requirements:* For doctorate, thesis/dissertation, general exams. *Entrance requirements:* For doctorate, GRE General Test. Additional exam requirements/recommendations for international students: Required—TOEFL.

Hofstra University, College of Liberal Arts and Sciences, Programs in Psychology, Hempstead, NY 11549. Offers applied organizational psychology (PhD); clinical psychology (PhD); industrial/organizational psychology (MA); school-community psychology (Psy D). *Accreditation:* APA. *Program availability:* Part-time, evening/weekend. *Students:* 199 full-time (130 women), 24 part-time (20 women); includes 44 minority (5 Black or African American, non-Hispanic/Latino; 12 Asian, non-Hispanic/Latino; 25 Hispanic/Latino; 1 Native Hawaiian or other Pacific Islander, non-Hispanic/Latino; 1 Two or more races, non-Hispanic/Latino), 19 international. Average age 27. 314 applicants, 45% accepted, 60 enrolled. In 2017, 47 master's, 25 doctorates awarded. *Degree requirements:* For master's, comprehensive exam, thesis optional, internship, minimum GPA of 3.0; for doctorate, comprehensive exam, thesis/dissertation, 1st year qualifying examination, 2nd year research project, successful practicum/externship placements, written presentation and successful oral defense of dissertation, completion of full-time internship. *Entrance requirements:* For master's, GRE General Test, minimum GPA of 3.0, essay, interview; for doctorate, GRE General Test, GRE Subject Test (psychology), 3 letters of recommendation, interview, essay, curriculum vitae. Additional exam requirements/recommendations for international students: Required—TOEFL (minimum score 550 paper-based; 80 iBT). *Application deadline:* For fall admission, 12/31 for domestic and international students. Application fee: $75. Electronic applications accepted. *Expenses: Tuition:* Full-time $1292. *Required fees:* $970. Tuition and fees vary according to program. *Financial support:* In 2017–18, 131 students received support, including 126 fellowships with full and partial tuition reimbursements available (averaging $7,840 per year), 4 research assistantships with full and partial tuition reimbursements available (averaging $5,974 per year); career-related internships or fieldwork, Federal Work-Study, institutionally sponsored loans, scholarships/grants, traineeships, tuition waivers (full and partial), and unspecified assistantships also available. Support available to part-time students. Financial award applicants required to submit FAFSA. *Faculty research:* Coping with job stress; schizophrenia; positive clinical psychology; treatments (including virtual reality based) for phobias, trauma, and PTSD; scientific reasoning in children and adults. *Unit head:* Dr. Craig Johnson, Chairperson, 516-463-5636, E-mail: craig.a.johnson@hofstra.edu. *Application contact:* Sunil Samuel, Assistant Vice President of Admissions, 516-463-4723, Fax: 516-463-4664, E-mail: graduateadmission@hofstra.edu.
Website: http://www.hofstra.edu/hclas

Howard University, Graduate School, Department of Psychology, Washington, DC 20059-0002. Offers clinical psychology (PhD); developmental psychology (PhD); experimental psychology (PhD); neuropsychology (PhD); personality psychology (PhD); psychology (MS); social psychology (PhD). *Accreditation:* APA (one or more programs are accredited). *Program availability:* Part-time. *Degree requirements:* For master's, thesis; for doctorate, comprehensive exam, thesis/dissertation, qualifying exam. *Entrance requirements:* For master's, GRE General Test, minimum GPA of 2.5, bachelor's degree in psychology or related field; for doctorate, GRE General Test, minimum GPA of 3.0. *Faculty research:* Personality and psychophysiology, educational and social development of African-American children, child and adult psychopathology.

Humboldt State University, Academic Programs, College of Professional Studies, Department of Psychology, Arcata, CA 95521-8299. Offers psychology (MA), including biological psychology, counseling, developmental psychopathology, school psychology, social and environmental psychology. *Degree requirements:* For master's, thesis. *Entrance requirements:* For master's, appropriate bachelor's degree, minimum GPA of 2.5. Additional exam requirements/recommendations for international students: Required—TOEFL (minimum score 500 paper-based). *Faculty research:* School psychology, counseling, eating disorders, mood induction, depression.

Husson University, Graduate Programs in Counseling and Human Relations, Bangor, ME 04401-2999. Offers clinical mental health counseling (MS); human relations (MS); school counseling (MS). *Accreditation:* ACA. *Program availability:* Part-time, evening/weekend. *Faculty:* 3 full-time (2 women), 5 part-time/adjunct (all women). *Students:* 21 full-time (18 women), 44 part-time (39 women); includes 2 minority (1 Black or African American, non-Hispanic/Latino; 1 Hispanic/Latino), 1 international. Average age 31. 49 applicants, 41% accepted, 13 enrolled. In 2017, 17 master's awarded. *Degree requirements:* For master's, comprehensive exam (for some programs), thesis optional. *Entrance requirements:* For master's, BS with minimum GPA of 3.0, letters of recommendation, interview. Additional exam requirements/recommendations for international students: Required—TOEFL (minimum score 550 paper-based; 80 iBT), IELTS (minimum score 6.5). *Application deadline:* For fall admission, 2/1 for domestic students. Application fee: $50. Electronic applications accepted. *Expenses:* $577 per credit; fees depend on number of credits. *Financial support:* In 2017–18, 2 students received support. Federal Work-Study, scholarships/grants, and unspecified assistantships available. Financial award application deadline: 4/15; financial award applicants required to submit FAFSA. *Faculty research:* Challenges and rewards of counseling practice in rural, small town and neighborhood settings. *Unit head:* Dr. Deborah Drew, Director, Graduate Counseling Programs, 207-992-4912, Fax: 207-992-4952, E-mail: drewd@husson.edu. *Application contact:* Kristen Card, Director of Graduate Admissions, 207-404-5660, Fax: 207-941-7935, E-mail: cardk@husson.edu.
Website: http://www.husson.edu/college-of-health-and-education/school-of-education/graduate-programs/

Indiana University Bloomington, University Graduate School, College of Arts and Sciences, Department of Psychological and Brain Sciences, Bloomington, IN 47405. Offers clinical science (PhD); cognitive neuroscience (PhD); cognitive psychology (PhD); developmental psychology (PhD); methods of behavior (PhD); molecular systems neuroscience (PhD); social psychology (PhD). *Accreditation:* APA. *Degree requirements:* For doctorate, comprehensive exam, 90 credit hours, 2 advanced statistics/methods courses, 2 written research projects, the teaching of psychology course, teaching 1 semester of undergraduate methods course, qualifying examination, minor or a second major, first-year research seminar course, dissertation defense, written dissertation. *Entrance requirements:* For doctorate, GRE. Additional exam requirements/recommendations for international students: Required—TOEFL (minimum score 550 paper-based; 79 iBT). Electronic applications accepted. *Faculty research:* Clinical science, cognitive neuroscience, cognitive psychology, developmental psychology, mechanisms of behavior, molecular and systems neuroscience, social psychology.

Indiana University of Pennsylvania, School of Graduate Studies and Research, College of Education and Communications, Department of Counseling, Program in Community Counseling, Indiana, PA 15705. Offers MA. *Program availability:* Part-time. *Faculty:* 11 full-time (10 women), 5 part-time/adjunct (4 women). *Entrance requirements:* For master's, goal statement, 2 letters of recommendation. Additional exam requirements/recommendations for international students: Required—TOEFL (minimum score 540 paper-based). *Application deadline:* For fall admission, 3/17 priority date for domestic students. Application fee: $50. Electronic applications accepted. *Expenses:* Tuition, state resident: full-time $12,000; part-time $500 per credit. Tuition, nonresident:

full-time $18,000; part-time $750 per credit. *Required fees:* $4073; $165.55 per credit. $64 per term. *Financial support:* Research assistantships with full tuition reimbursements available. Financial award application deadline: 4/15; financial award applicants required to submit FAFSA. *Unit head:* Dr. Claire Dandeaneau, Chairperson/Graduate Coordinator, 724-357-2306, E-mail: candean@iup.edu.
Website: http://www.iup.edu/grad/communitycounseling/default.aspx

Indiana University–Purdue University Indianapolis, School of Science, Department of Psychology, Indianapolis, IN 46202-3275. Offers addiction neuroscience (PhD); applied social and organizational psychology (PhD); clinical psychology (PhD); industrial/organizational psychology (MS). *Accreditation:* APA (one or more programs are accredited). Terminal master's awarded for partial completion of doctoral program. *Degree requirements:* For master's, thesis; for doctorate, thesis/dissertation. *Entrance requirements:* For master's, GRE General Test, minimum undergraduate GPA of 3.0; for doctorate, GRE General Test, GRE Subject Test (clinical psychology), minimum undergraduate GPA of 3.2. Additional exam requirements/recommendations for international students: Required—TOEFL (minimum score 567 paper-based; 86 iBT), IELTS (minimum score 6.5). Electronic applications accepted. *Faculty research:* Severe mental illness, health psychology, neurological research, alcoholism and psychopathology, functional activities within organizations.

Indiana Wesleyan University, Graduate School, College of Arts and Sciences, Marion, IN 46953. Offers addictions counseling (MS); clinical mental health counseling (MS); community counseling (MS); marriage and family therapy (MS); school counseling (MS); student development counseling and administration (MS). *Accreditation:* ACA. *Program availability:* Part-time. *Degree requirements:* For master's, thesis or alternative. *Entrance requirements:* For master's, GRE General Test. Additional exam requirements/recommendations for international students: Required—TOEFL. Electronic applications accepted. *Expenses:* Contact institution. *Faculty research:* Community counseling, multicultural counseling, addictions.

Iowa State University of Science and Technology, Department of Psychology, Ames, IA 50011. Offers cognitive psychology (PhD); counseling psychology (PhD); psychology (MS, PhD); social psychology (PhD). *Accreditation:* APA (one or more programs are accredited). *Entrance requirements:* For doctorate, GRE General Test, GRE Subject Test (psychology), 3 letters of recommendation. Additional exam requirements/recommendations for international students: Required—TOEFL (minimum score 560 paper-based; 79 iBT), IELTS (minimum score 6.5). Electronic applications accepted. *Faculty research:* Counseling psychology, cognitive psychology, social psychology, health psychology, psychology and public policy.

Lesley University, Graduate School of Arts and Social Sciences, Cambridge, MA 02138-2790. Offers clinical mental health counseling (MA), including holistic counseling, school and community counseling, trauma studies; counseling psychology (MA, CAGS), including professional counseling (MA), school counseling (MA); creative writing (MFA); expressive therapies (MA, PhD, CAGS), including art (MA), clinical mental health counseling (MA), dance (MA), expressive therapies (MA), music (MA); independent studies (CAGS); independent study (MA); intercultural relations (MA, CAGS); interdisciplinary studies (MA), including individualized studies, integrative holistic health, mindfulness studies, peace and conflict transformation, trauma sensitive assessment, intervention, and consultation, women's studies; urban environmental leadership (MA). *Program availability:* Part-time, online learning. *Degree requirements:* For master's, internship, practicum, thesis (for expressive therapies); for doctorate, thesis/dissertation, arts apprenticeship, field placement; for CAGS, thesis, internship (for counseling psychology, expressive therapies). *Entrance requirements:* For master's, MAT (counseling psychology), interview, writing samples, art portfolio; for doctorate, GRE or MAT, interview, master's degree; for CAGS, interview, master's degree. Additional exam requirements/recommendations for international students: Required—TOEFL (minimum score 550 paper-based; 80 iBT). Electronic applications accepted. *Faculty research:* Psychotherapy and culture; psychotherapy and psychological trauma; women's issues in art, teaching and psychotherapy; community-based art, psycho-spiritual inquiry.

Loyola University Chicago, School of Education, Program in Community Counseling, Chicago, IL 60660. Offers clinical mental health counseling (Ed S); community counseling (M Ed, MA). MA offered through the Graduate School. *Program availability:* Part-time. *Faculty:* 5 full-time (2 women), 5 part-time/adjunct (4 women). *Students:* 26 full-time (22 women), 1 (woman) part-time; includes 10 minority (3 Black or African American, non-Hispanic/Latino; 2 Asian, non-Hispanic/Latino; 5 Hispanic/Latino), 2 international. Average age 26. 56 applicants, 77% accepted, 13 enrolled. In 2017, 15 master's awarded. *Degree requirements:* For master's and Ed S, comprehensive exam. *Entrance requirements:* For master's, GRE General Test, minimum GPA of 3.0, letters of recommendation, resume. Additional exam requirements/recommendations for international students: Required—TOEFL (minimum score 550 paper-based; 79 iBT). *Application deadline:* For fall admission, 1/1 for domestic and international students. Application fee: $50. Electronic applications accepted. Application fee is waived when completed online. *Expenses:* $949 per semester hour, $2,847 per course, $8,541–$11,388 full-time semester tuition; $432 per semester fees, $225 additional fees (first semester only). *Financial support:* Career-related internships or fieldwork, institutionally sponsored loans, scholarships/grants, and unspecified assistantships available. Support available to part-time students. Financial award application deadline: 2/1; financial award applicants required to submit FAFSA. *Faculty research:* Career development, prevention, group counseling, family therapy, multicultural counseling. *Unit head:* Dr. Eunju Yoon, Director, 312-915-6461, E-mail: eyoon@luc.edu. *Application contact:* Mirtza Campbell, Information Contact, 312-915-8907, E-mail: mcampbell11@luc.edu.

Marquette University, Graduate School, College of Education, Department of Counselor Education and Counseling Psychology, Milwaukee, WI 53201-1881. Offers clinical mental health counseling (MS); community counseling (MA); counseling psychology (PhD); school counseling (MA). *Accreditation:* ACA. *Program availability:* Part-time. Terminal master's awarded for partial completion of doctoral program. *Degree requirements:* For master's, comprehensive exam, thesis (for some programs); for doctorate, thesis/dissertation, qualifying exam. *Entrance requirements:* For master's, GRE General Test or MAT, official transcripts from all current and previous colleges/universities except Marquette, three letters of recommendation, statement of purpose; for doctorate, GRE General Test, MAT, sample of written work, official transcripts from all current and previous colleges/universities except Marquette, three letters of recommendation, statement of purpose, resume/curriculum vitae. Additional exam requirements/recommendations for international students: Required—TOEFL (minimum score 530 paper-based). *Faculty research:* Ethical and legal issues in education, anxiety disorders, multicultural counseling, child psychopathology, group counseling and dynamics.

Martin University, Division of Psychology, Indianapolis, IN 46218-3867. Offers community psychology (MS). *Program availability:* Part-time, evening/weekend. *Degree requirements:* For master's, thesis. *Entrance requirements:* For master's, GRE General Test, GRE Subject Test.

Marymount California University, Program in Community Psychology, Rancho Palos Verdes, CA 90275-6299. Offers MS.

Missouri Valley College, Graduate Studies, Marshall, MO 65340-3197. Offers community counseling (MA).

Mount Aloysius College, Program in Community Counseling, Cresson, PA 16630-1999. Offers MS. *Program availability:* Evening/weekend. *Entrance requirements:* Additional exam requirements/recommendations for international students: Required—IELTS (minimum score 5.5); Recommended—TOEFL. *Application deadline:* For fall admission, 8/1 for domestic students; for spring admission, 12/1 for domestic students. Applications are processed on a rolling basis. Application fee: $30. Electronic applications accepted. Application fee is waived when completed online. *Expenses:* Tuition: Full-time $14,000; part-time $790 per credit hour. *Financial support:* Unspecified assistantships available. Financial award applicants required to submit FAFSA. *Application contact:* Matthew P. Bodenschatz, Director of Graduate and Continuing Education Admissions, 814-886-6556, Fax: 814-886-6441, E-mail: mbodenschatz@mtaloy.edu.

The New School, The New School for Social Research, Department of Psychology, New York, NY 10011. Offers clinical psychology (PhD); cognitive, social, and developmental psychology (PhD); psychology (MA). *Accreditation:* APA (one or more programs are accredited). *Program availability:* Part-time. *Faculty:* 14 full-time (8 women), 4 part-time/adjunct (0 women). *Students:* 154 full-time (121 women), 77 part-time (58 women); includes 42 minority (8 Black or African American, non-Hispanic/Latino; 12 Asian, non-Hispanic/Latino; 17 Hispanic/Latino; 5 Two or more races, non-Hispanic/Latino), 39 international. Average age 29. 250 applicants, 83% accepted, 71 enrolled. In 2017, 45 master's, 18 doctorates awarded. Terminal master's awarded for partial completion of doctoral program. *Degree requirements:* For master's, comprehensive exam, thesis (for some programs); for doctorate, comprehensive exam, thesis/dissertation. *Entrance requirements:* For master's, GRE, letters of recommendation, writing sample, essays, transcripts; for doctorate, letters of recommendation, writing sample, essays, transcripts. Additional exam requirements/recommendations for international students: Required—TOEFL (minimum score 100 iBT), IELTS (minimum score 7), PTE (minimum score 68). *Application deadline:* For fall admission, 1/5 priority date for domestic and international students; for spring admission, 10/15 priority date for domestic and international students. Applications are processed on a rolling basis. Application fee: $50. Electronic applications accepted. *Expenses:* $2,180 per credit. *Financial support:* In 2017–18, 191 students received support, including 21 fellowships with full and partial tuition reimbursements available (averaging $19,453 per year), 45 teaching assistantships with full and partial tuition reimbursements available (averaging $9,505 per year); career-related internships or fieldwork, Federal Work-Study, scholarships/grants, and tuition waivers (full and partial) also available. Support available to part-time students. Financial award application deadline: 2/1; financial award applicants required to submit FAFSA. *Unit head:* Dr. William Milberg, Dean, The New School for Social Research, 212-229-5777, E-mail: milbergw@newschool.edu. *Application contact:* Dana Messinger, Director of Graduate Admission, 212-229-5150 Ext. 2300, E-mail: socialresearchadmit@newschool.edu.

New York University, Graduate School of Arts and Science, Department of Psychology, New York, NY 10012-1019. Offers cognition and perception (PhD); general psychology (MA); industrial/organizational psychology (MA); psychotherapy and psychoanalysis (Advanced Certificate); social psychology (PhD). *Program availability:* Part-time. *Students:* Average age 31. 874 applicants, 46% accepted, 153 enrolled. In 2017, 102 master's, 9 doctorates, 10 other advanced degrees awarded. Terminal master's awarded for partial completion of doctoral program. *Degree requirements:* For master's, comprehensive exam, thesis or alternative; for doctorate, thesis/dissertation. *Entrance requirements:* For master's and doctorate, GRE General Test. Additional exam requirements/recommendations for international students: Required—TOEFL. *Application deadline:* For fall admission, 12/12 for domestic and international students. Application fee: $100. *Expenses: Tuition:* Full-time $41,352; part-time $19,968 per year. *Required fees:* $2496; $1628 per unit. $814 per term. Tuition and fees vary according to course load and program. *Financial support:* Fellowships, research assistantships, teaching assistantships, career-related internships or fieldwork, Federal Work-Study, institutionally sponsored loans, scholarships/grants, traineeships, health care benefits, and unspecified assistantships available. Financial award application deadline: 12/12; financial award applicants required to submit FAFSA. *Faculty research:* Vision, memory, social cognition, social and cognitive development, relationships. *Unit head:* Gabriele Oettingen, Director of Graduate Studies, PhD Program, 212-998-7900, Fax: 212-995-4018, E-mail: psychq@psych.nyu.edu. *Application contact:* Adrienne Gans, Director of Graduate Studies, MA Program, 212-998-7900, Fax: 212-995-4018, E-mail: psychq@psych.nyu.edu.
Website: http://www.psych.nyu.edu/

Norfolk State University, School of Graduate Studies, School of Liberal Arts, Department of Psychology, Program in Community/Clinical Psychology, Norfolk, VA 23504. Offers MA. *Degree requirements:* For master's, comprehensive exam, thesis or alternative. *Entrance requirements:* For master's, minimum GPA of 2.7.

North Carolina State University, Graduate School, College of Education, Department of Curriculum and Instruction, Program in Agency Counseling, Raleigh, NC 27695. Offers M Ed, MS. *Accreditation:* APA. *Degree requirements:* For master's, thesis optional. *Entrance requirements:* For master's, GRE General Test or MAT, minimum GPA of 3.0 in major. Electronic applications accepted. *Faculty research:* Cross-cultural issues, non-cognitive variables, achievement gaps, identity development, counseling supervision.

North Dakota State University, College of Graduate and Interdisciplinary Studies, College of Science and Mathematics, Department of Psychology, Fargo, ND 58102. Offers clinical psychology (MS); health and social psychology (PhD); psychological clinical science (PhD); psychology (MS); visual and cognitive neuroscience (PhD). *Degree requirements:* For master's, thesis; for doctorate, thesis/dissertation. *Entrance requirements:* For master's and doctorate, GRE General Test, GRE Subject Test. Additional exam requirements/recommendations for international students: Required—TOEFL (minimum score 525 paper-based; 71 iBT). Electronic applications accepted. *Faculty research:* Cognition science, neuropsychology, group behavior, applied behavior analysis, behavior therapy.

Northwestern University, The Graduate School, Judd A. and Marjorie Weinberg College of Arts and Sciences, Department of Psychology, Evanston, IL 60208. Offers brain, behavior and cognition (PhD); clinical psychology (PhD); cognitive psychology (PhD); personality psychology (PhD); social psychology (PhD); JD/PhD. Admissions and degrees offered through The Graduate School. *Accreditation:* APA (one or more programs are accredited). *Program availability:* Part-time. *Degree requirements:* For doctorate, thesis/dissertation. *Entrance requirements:* For doctorate, GRE General Test, GRE Subject Test. Additional exam requirements/recommendations for international students: Required—TOEFL. Electronic applications accepted. *Faculty research:* Memory and higher order cognition, anxiety and depression, effectiveness of psychotherapy, social cognition, molecular basis of memory.

The Ohio State University, Graduate School, College of Arts and Sciences, Division of Social and Behavioral Sciences, Department of Psychology, Columbus, OH 43210. Offers behavioral neuroscience (PhD); clinical psychology (PhD); cognitive psychology

(PhD); developmental psychology (PhD); intellectual and developmental disabilities psychology (PhD); quantitative psychology (PhD); social psychology (PhD). *Accreditation:* APA. *Faculty:* 52. *Students:* 144 full-time (86 women); includes 18 minority (8 Asian, non-Hispanic/Latino; 10 Hispanic/Latino), 28 international. Average age 26. In 2017, 21 doctorates awarded. *Entrance requirements:* For doctorate, GRE General Test. Additional exam requirements/recommendations for international students: Required—TOEFL (minimum score 600 paper-based; 100 iBT); Recommended—IELTS (minimum score 8). *Application deadline:* For fall admission, 12/1 for domestic and international students. Applications are processed on a rolling basis. Application fee: $60 ($70 for international students). Electronic applications accepted. *Financial support:* Fellowships, research assistantships, and teaching assistantships available. *Unit head:* Dr. John Bruno, Chair, 614-292-3038, E-mail: bruno.1@osu.edu. *Application contact:* Graduate and Professional Admissions, 614-292-9444, Fax: 614-292-3895, E-mail: gpadmissions@osu.edu.
Website: http://psychology.osu.edu/

Oregon State University–Cascades, Program in Counseling, Bend, OR 97701. Offers community counseling (MS); school counseling (MS).

Penn State Harrisburg, Graduate School, School of Behavioral Sciences and Education, Middletown, PA 17057. Offers adult education in the health and medical professions (Certificate); applied behavior analysis (MA); applied clinical psychology (MA); applied psychological research (MA); community psychology and social change (MA); English as a second language (ESL) program specialist and leadership (Certificate); health education (M Ed); lifelong learning and adult education (M Ed, D Ed); literacy education (M Ed); literacy leadership (Certificate); psychology: applications in clinical psychology (Certificate); psychology: health psychology (Certificate); teaching and curriculum (M Ed); training and development (M Ed, Certificate). *Program availability:* Part-time, evening/weekend. *Unit head:* Dr. Mukund S. Kulkarni, Chancellor, 717-948-6105, Fax: 717-948-6452. *Application contact:* Robert W. Coffman, Jr., Director of Enrollment Management, Recruitment and Admissions, 717-948-6250, Fax: 717-948-6325, E-mail: hbgadmit@psu.edu.
Website: https://harrisburg.psu.edu/behavioral-sciences-and-education/

Queen's University at Kingston, School of Graduate Studies, Faculty of Arts and Sciences, Department of Psychology, Kingston, ON K7L 3N6, Canada. Offers brain behavior and cognitive science (MA, PhD); clinical psychology (MA, PhD); developmental psychology (MA, PhD); social personality psychology (MA, PhD). *Degree requirements:* For master's, thesis; for doctorate, comprehensive exam, thesis/dissertation. *Entrance requirements:* For master's and doctorate, GRE General Test. Additional exam requirements/recommendations for international students: Required—TOEFL. *Faculty research:* Human development, social, personality, behavioral neuroscience, forensic.

Rutgers University–Newark, Graduate School, Program in Psychology, Newark, NJ 07102. Offers cognitive neuroscience (PhD); cognitive science (PhD); perception (PhD); psychobiology (PhD); social cognition (PhD). *Degree requirements:* For doctorate, comprehensive exam, thesis/dissertation. *Entrance requirements:* For doctorate, GRE General Test, GRE Subject Test, minimum undergraduate B average. Electronic applications accepted. *Faculty research:* Visual perception (luminance, motion), neuroendocrine mechanisms in behavior (reproduction, pain), attachment theory, connectionist modeling of cognition.

Rutgers University–New Brunswick, Graduate School-New Brunswick, Program in Psychology, Piscataway, NJ 08854-8097. Offers behavioral neuroscience (PhD); clinical psychology (PhD); cognitive psychology (PhD); interdisciplinary health psychology (PhD); social psychology (PhD). *Accreditation:* APA. *Degree requirements:* For doctorate, comprehensive exam, thesis/dissertation. *Entrance requirements:* For doctorate, GRE General Test, 3 letters of recommendation. Additional exam requirements/recommendations for international students: Required—TOEFL (minimum score 577 paper-based). Electronic applications accepted. *Faculty research:* Learning and memory, behavioral ecology, hormones and behavior, psychopharmacology, anxiety disorders.

Sacred Heart University, Graduate Programs, College of Arts and Sciences, Department of Psychology, Fairfield, CT 06825. Offers applied psychology (MS), including community psychology, general applied psychology, industrial-organizational psychology. *Program availability:* Part-time, evening/weekend, online learning. *Faculty:* 9 full-time (7 women). *Students:* 17 full-time (15 women), 76 part-time (58 women); includes 18 minority (6 Black or African American, non-Hispanic/Latino; 1 Asian, non-Hispanic/Latino; 8 Hispanic/Latino; 3 Two or more races, non-Hispanic/Latino), 2 international. Average age 31. 50 applicants, 54% accepted, 16 enrolled. In 2017, 42 master's awarded. *Degree requirements:* For master's, comprehensive exam, thesis optional. *Entrance requirements:* For master's, minimum overall GPA of 3.0, bachelor's degree from accredited college or university. Additional exam requirements/recommendations for international students: Required—TOEFL (minimum score 570 paper-based, 80 iBT), TWE, or IELTS (6.5). *Application deadline:* Applications are processed on a rolling basis. Application fee: $75. Electronic applications accepted. *Expenses:* Contact institution. *Financial support:* Unspecified assistantships available. Financial award applicants required to submit FAFSA. *Unit head:* Rachel Bowman, Interim Chair/Associate Professor, 203-396-8243, E-mail: bowmanr@sacredheart.edu. *Application contact:* Pam Pillo, Executive Director of Graduate Admissions, 203-365-7916, Fax: 203-365-4732, E-mail: gradstudies@sacredheart.edu.
Website: http://www.sacredheart.edu/academics/collegeofartssciences/academicdepartments/psychology/mastersinappliedpsychology/

Sage Graduate School, School of Health Sciences, Department of Psychology, Program in Community Psychology, Troy, NY 12180-4115. Offers MA. *Program availability:* Part-time, evening/weekend. *Faculty:* 6 full-time (all women), 2 part-time/adjunct (both women). *Students:* 1 full-time (0 women), 2 part-time (1 woman); includes 2 minority (1 Asian, non-Hispanic/Latino; 1 Two or more races, non-Hispanic/Latino). Average age 23. 7 applicants, 43% accepted, 1 enrolled. In 2017, 1 master's awarded. *Degree requirements:* For master's, thesis or alternative. *Entrance requirements:* For master's, official transcripts of all previous undergraduate study; 2 letters of reference (academic or professional); undergraduate courses in statistics, history and systems of psychology; 3 other courses in behavioral science; personal prospectus statement; current resume. Additional exam requirements/recommendations for international students: Required—TOEFL (minimum score 550 paper-based). *Application deadline:* Applications are processed on a rolling basis. Application fee: $30. Electronic applications accepted. Tuition and fees vary according to degree level and program. *Financial support:* Fellowships, research assistantships, scholarships/grants, and unspecified assistantships available. Financial award application deadline: 3/1; financial award applicants required to submit FAFSA. *Unit head:* Dr. Theresa Hand, Dean, School of Health Sciences, 518-244-2264, Fax: 518-244-4571, E-mail: handt@sage.edu. *Application contact:* Dr. Gayle Morse, Graduate Program Director, 518-292-1819, E-mail: morseg@sage.edu.

Sage Graduate School, School of Health Sciences, Department of Psychology, Program in Counseling and Community Psychology, Troy, NY 12180-4115. Offers MA. *Program availability:* Part-time, evening/weekend. *Faculty:* 6 full-time (all women), 2 part-time/adjunct (both women). *Students:* 30 full-time (27 women), 32 part-time (27 women); includes 12 minority (4 Black or African American, non-Hispanic/Latino; 1 Asian, non-Hispanic/Latino; 4 Hispanic/Latino; 3 Two or more races, non-Hispanic/Latino). Average age 29. 65 applicants, 57% accepted, 20 enrolled. In 2017, 25 master's awarded. *Degree requirements:* For master's, externship, internship, thesis or research seminar. *Entrance requirements:* For master's, official transcripts of all previous undergraduate study; 2 letters of reference (academic or professional); undergraduate courses in statistics, history and systems of psychology; 3 other courses in behavioral science; personal prospectus statement; current resume. Additional exam requirements/recommendations for international students: Required—TOEFL (minimum score 550 paper-based). *Application deadline:* Applications are processed on a rolling basis. Application fee: $30. Electronic applications accepted. Tuition and fees vary according to degree level and program. *Financial support:* Fellowships, research assistantships, scholarships/grants, and unspecified assistantships available. Financial award applicants required to submit FAFSA. *Unit head:* Dr. Theresa Hand, Dean, School of Health Sciences, 518-244-2264, Fax: 518-244-4571, E-mail: handt@sage.edu. *Application contact:* Dr. Gayle Morse, Graduate Program Director, 518-292-1819, E-mail: morseg@sage.edu.
Website: http://www.sage.edu/academics/psychology/programs/counseling/

St. Bonaventure University, School of Graduate Studies, School of Education, Program in Counselor Education, St. Bonaventure, NY 14778-2284. Offers community mental health counseling (MS Ed); rehabilitation counseling (MS Ed); school counseling (MS Ed); school counselor (Adv C). *Accreditation:* ACA. *Program availability:* Part-time, evening/weekend, 100% online. *Faculty:* 4 full-time (2 women), 5 part-time/adjunct (3 women). *Students:* 35 full-time (27 women), 30 part-time (23 women); includes 8 minority (3 Black or African American, non-Hispanic/Latino; 4 Hispanic/Latino; 1 Two or more races, non-Hispanic/Latino), 1 international. Average age 28. 55 applicants, 82% accepted, 29 enrolled. In 2017, 27 master's, 2 Adv Cs awarded. *Degree requirements:* For master's, comprehensive exam, thesis optional, internship, portfolio; for Adv C, internship. *Entrance requirements:* For master's, statement of intent/writing sample; transcripts from all colleges previously attended; two references; interview; minimum undergraduate GPA of 3.0; for Adv C, interview, writing sample, minimum undergraduate GPA of 3.0, two letters of recommendation, master's degree, transcripts from all colleges previously attended. Additional exam requirements/recommendations for international students: Required—TOEFL (minimum score 550 paper-based; 79 iBT). *Application deadline:* For fall admission, 3/15 priority date for domestic students, 2/1 priority date for international students; for spring admission, 11/15 priority date for domestic students, 7/1 priority date for international students. Applications are processed on a rolling basis. Application fee: $0. Electronic applications accepted. *Expenses:* $733 per credit hour, $100 graduation fee. *Financial support:* Career-related internships or fieldwork, Federal Work-Study, scholarships/grants, health care benefits, and unspecified assistantships available. Support available to part-time students. Financial award application deadline: 4/15; financial award applicants required to submit FAFSA. *Faculty research:* Balance between technology and personal contact in counselor education, special education and cyberbullying, school response to child abuse. *Unit head:* Dr. Chris Siuta, Director, 716-375-2114, Fax: 716-375-2360, E-mail: csiuta@sbu.edu. *Application contact:* Bruce Campbell, Director of Graduate Admissions, 716-375-2429, Fax: 716-375-4015, E-mail: gradsch@sbu.edu.
Website: http://www.sbu.edu/academics/msed-in-school-counseling

St. Cloud State University, School of Graduate Studies, School of Health and Human Services, Department of Counseling and Community Psychology, Program in Community Counseling, St. Cloud, MN 56301-4498. Offers MS. *Degree requirements:* For master's, comprehensive exam (for some programs), thesis or alternative. *Entrance requirements:* For master's, GRE General Test, minimum GPA of 2.75. Additional exam requirements/recommendations for international students: Required—Michigan English Language Assessment Battery; Recommended—TOEFL (minimum score 550 paper-based), IELTS (minimum score 6.5). Electronic applications accepted.

Saint Martin's University, Office of Graduate Studies, Program in Counseling Psychology, Lacey, WA 98503. Offers MAC. *Program availability:* Part-time. *Faculty:* 3 full-time (2 women), 2 part-time/adjunct (both women). *Students:* 5 full-time (4 women), 84 part-time (73 women); includes 30 minority (7 Black or African American, non-Hispanic/Latino; 2 American Indian or Alaska Native, non-Hispanic/Latino; 3 Asian, non-Hispanic/Latino; 13 Hispanic/Latino; 5 Two or more races, non-Hispanic/Latino). Average age 36. 24 applicants, 100% accepted, 18 enrolled. In 2017, 32 master's awarded. *Degree requirements:* For master's, clinical experience, interview. *Entrance requirements:* For master's, clinical experience. Additional exam requirements/recommendations for international students: Required—TOEFL (minimum score 550 paper-based; 79 iBT); Recommended—IELTS (minimum score 6.5). *Application deadline:* For fall admission, 4/1 priority date for domestic and international students; for spring admission, 11/1 priority date for domestic and international students. Applications are processed on a rolling basis. Application fee: $50. Electronic applications accepted. *Expenses:* Tuition: Full-time $21,420; part-time $1190 per credit. *Financial support:* Career-related internships or fieldwork, Federal Work-Study, and institutionally sponsored loans available. Support available to part-time students. Financial award application deadline: 3/1; financial award applicants required to submit FAFSA. *Faculty research:* Alcohol studies, clinical effectiveness, social justice, parent adolescent interaction. *Unit head:* Dr. Godfrey J. Ellis, Director, 360-438-4560, E-mail: gellis@stmartin.edu. *Application contact:* Casey Caronna, Administrative Assistant, 360-412-6128, E-mail: ccaronna@stmartin.edu.
Website: https://www.stmartin.edu

San Francisco State University, Division of Graduate Studies, College of Science and Engineering, Department of Psychology, San Francisco, CA 94132-1722. Offers clinical psychology (MS); developmental psychology (MA); industrial/organizational psychology (MS); mind, brain, and behavior (MA); school psychology (MS, Credential); social psychology (MA). *Financial support:* Teaching assistantships available. Financial award application deadline: 3/1. *Unit head:* Dr. Dawn Terrell, Chair, 415-338-7555, Fax: 415-338-2398, E-mail: schen9@sfsu.edu. *Application contact:* Dr. Diane Harris, Graduate Program Coordinator, 415-338-7064, Fax: 415-338-2398, E-mail: dharris@sfsu.edu.
Website: http://psychology.sfsu.edu/graduate/application.html

Southwestern College, Program in Transformational Ecopsychology, Santa Fe, NM 87502-4788. Offers Certificate. *Entrance requirements:* For degree, 3 letters of reference, interview.

Stony Brook University, State University of New York, Graduate School, College of Arts and Sciences, Department of Psychology, Program in Social and Health Psychology, Stony Brook, NY 11794. Offers PhD. *Students:* 17 full-time (16 women); includes 5 minority (1 Black or African American, non-Hispanic/Latino; 3 Asian, non-Hispanic/Latino; 1 Two or more races, non-Hispanic/Latino), 1 international. Average age 28. 64 applicants, 8% accepted, 2 enrolled. In 2017, 5 doctorates awarded. *Degree requirements:* For doctorate, thesis/dissertation. *Entrance requirements:* For doctorate, GRE General Test, GRE Subject Test. Additional exam requirements/recommendations for international students: Required—TOEFL (minimum score 90 iBT). *Application deadline:* For fall admission, 1/15 for domestic students; for spring admission, 10/1 for domestic students. Application fee: $100. Electronic applications accepted. *Expenses:*

Contact institution. *Financial support:* In 2017–18, 1 fellowship, 2 research assistantships, 9 teaching assistantships were awarded. *Unit head:* Dr. Sheri Levy, Chair, 631-632-4355, E-mail: sheri.levy@stonybrook.edu. *Application contact:* Marilynn Wollmuth, Coordinator, 631-632-7855, Fax: 631-632-7876, E-mail: marilyn.wollmuth@stonybrook.edu.
Website: http://www.stonybrook.edu/commcms/psychology/social_health/overview.html

Syracuse University, College of Arts and Sciences, Department of Psychology, Syracuse, NY 13244. Offers clinical psychology (PhD); cognition, brain, and behavior (PhD); school psychology (PhD); social psychology (PhD). *Accreditation:* APA. In 2017, 1 doctorate awarded. Terminal master's awarded for partial completion of doctoral program. *Degree requirements:* For doctorate, comprehensive exam, thesis/dissertation. *Entrance requirements:* For doctorate, GRE General Test, GRE Subject Test, resume, personal statement, three letters of recommendation. Additional exam requirements/recommendations for international students: Required—TOEFL (minimum score 100 iBT). *Application deadline:* For fall admission, 12/1 priority date for domestic and international students. Application fee: $75. Electronic applications accepted. *Financial support:* Fellowships with full tuition reimbursements, research assistantships with tuition reimbursements, teaching assistantships with tuition reimbursements, and scholarships/grants available. Financial award application deadline: 1/1. *Faculty research:* Clinical psychology; cognition, brain, and behavior; school psychology; social psychology. *Unit head:* Dr. Amy Criss, Professor and Department Chair, Psychology, 315-443-1210, E-mail: acriss@syr.edu. *Application contact:* Alecia Zema, Curriculum Coordinator, 315-443-2760, E-mail: azema@syr.edu.
Website: http://psychology.syr.edu/graduate/overview.html

Teachers College, Columbia University, Department of Organization and Leadership, New York, NY 10027-6696. Offers adult education guided intensive study (Ed D); adult learning and leadership (Ed M, MA, Ed D); educational leadership (Ed D); higher and postsecondary education (MA, Ed D); leadership, policy and politics (Ed D); nurse executive (MA, Ed D), including administration studies (MA), professorial studies (MA); private school leadership (Ed M, MA); public school building leadership (Ed M, MA); social and organizational psychology (MA); urban education leaders (Ed D); MA/MBA. *Program availability:* Part-time, evening/weekend. *Students:* 342 full-time (244 women), 378 part-time (256 women); includes 288 minority (106 Black or African American, non-Hispanic/Latino; 69 Asian, non-Hispanic/Latino; 92 Hispanic/Latino; 21 Two or more races, non-Hispanic/Latino), 86 international. Average age 33. 1,063 applicants, 59% accepted, 405 enrolled. *Degree requirements:* For doctorate, thesis/dissertation. *Unit head:* Prof. Bill Baldwin, Chair, E-mail: wjb12@tc.columbia.edu. *Application contact:* David Estrella, Director of Admission, 212-678-3305, E-mail: estrella@tc.columbia.edu.

Temple University, College of Education, Department of Psychological Studies in Education, Philadelphia, PA 19122-6096. Offers applied behavior analysis (MS Ed); counseling psychology (Ed M), including agency counseling, school counseling; educational psychology (Ed M); school psychology (PhD, Ed S). *Accreditation:* APA (one or more programs are accredited). *Program availability:* Part-time, evening/weekend. *Faculty:* 25 full-time (12 women), 23 part-time/adjunct (11 women). *Students:* 255 full-time (191 women), 188 part-time (137 women); includes 136 minority (90 Black or African American, non-Hispanic/Latino; 1 American Indian or Alaska Native, non-Hispanic/Latino; 18 Asian, non-Hispanic/Latino; 14 Hispanic/Latino; 13 Two or more races, non-Hispanic/Latino), 28 international. 376 applicants, 51% accepted, 109 enrolled. In 2017, 129 master's, 27 doctorates, 21 other advanced degrees awarded. Terminal master's awarded for partial completion of doctoral program. *Degree requirements:* For master's, thesis or alternative; for doctorate, thesis/dissertation. *Entrance requirements:* Additional exam requirements/recommendations for international students: Required—TOEFL (minimum score 550 paper-based; 79 iBT). *Application deadline:* For fall admission, 12/15 for international students; for spring admission, 8/1 for international students. Application fee: $60. *Expenses:* Tuition, state resident: full-time $16,164; part-time $898 per credit hour. Tuition, nonresident: full-time $22,158; part-time $1231 per credit hour. *Required fees:* $890; $445 per semester. Full-time tuition and fees vary according to course load, degree level, campus/location and program. *Financial support:* Fellowships, research assistantships with full tuition reimbursements, and teaching assistantships with full tuition reimbursements available. Financial award application deadline: 1/15; financial award applicants required to submit FAFSA. *Unit head:* Dr. Catherine Fiorello, Chair, 215-204-6254, E-mail: catherine.fiorello@temple.edu.
Website: http://education.temple.edu/pse

Texas Christian University, College of Science and Engineering, Department of Psychology, Fort Worth, TX 76129. Offers developmental trauma (MS); experimental psychology (PhD), including cognition/developmental, learning, neuroscience, social. *Faculty:* 13 full-time (6 women), 2 part-time/adjunct (both women). *Students:* 32 full-time (25 women); includes 5 minority (1 Asian, non-Hispanic/Latino; 2 Hispanic/Latino; 2 Two or more races, non-Hispanic/Latino), 2 international. Average age 26. 50 applicants, 34% accepted, 16 enrolled. In 2017, 8 master's, 2 doctorates awarded. Terminal master's awarded for partial completion of doctoral program. *Degree requirements:* For master's, thesis; for doctorate, thesis/dissertation. *Entrance requirements:* For doctorate, GRE General Test. Additional exam requirements/recommendations for international students: Required—TOEFL. *Application deadline:* For fall admission, 2/1 for domestic and international students. Application fee: $60 ($0 for international students). Electronic applications accepted. *Expenses:* Contact institution. *Financial support:* In 2017–18, 23 students received support, including 23 teaching assistantships with full tuition reimbursements available (averaging $19,750 per year); scholarships/grants also available. Financial award application deadline: 2/1; financial award applicants required to submit FAFSA. *Faculty research:* Neuroscience, human and animal learning, cognition, development, experimental social psychology. *Unit head:* Dr. Mauricio R. Papini, Chair, 817-257-7410, Fax: 817-257-7681, E-mail: m.papini@tcu.edu. *Application contact:* Cindy Hayes, Administrative Assistant, 817-257-7410, Fax: 817-257-7681, E-mail: c.hayes@tcu.edu.
Website: https://psychology.tcu.edu/current-graduate-students/

Thomas Jefferson University, College of Science, Health and the Liberal Arts, Program in Community and Trauma Counseling, Philadelphia, PA 19107. Offers MS.

Thomas University, Department of Human Services, Thomasville, GA 31792-7499. Offers community counseling (MSCC); rehabilitation counseling (MRC). *Accreditation:* CORE. *Program availability:* Part-time. *Entrance requirements:* For master's, resume, 3 academic/professional references. Additional exam requirements/recommendations for international students: Required—TOEFL (minimum score 600 paper-based). Electronic applications accepted.

Université du Québec à Rimouski, Graduate Programs, Program in Psychosocial Studies, Rimouski, QC G5L 3A1, Canada. Offers MA.

Université Laval, Faculty of Social Sciences, School of Psychology, Programs in Psychology, Québec, QC G1K 7P4, Canada. Offers clinical psychology (PhD); community psychology (PhD); psychology (PhD, Psy D). *Degree requirements:* For doctorate, comprehensive exam, thesis/dissertation. *Entrance requirements:* For doctorate, comprehension of written English, knowledge of French, interview. Electronic applications accepted.

University at Albany, State University of New York, College of Arts and Sciences, Department of Psychology, Albany, NY 12222-0001. Offers behavioral neuroscience (PhD); clinical psychology (PhD); cognitive psychology (PhD); industrial/organizational psychology (MA, PhD); social-personality psychology (PhD). *Accreditation:* APA (one or more programs are accredited). *Faculty:* 31 full-time (13 women). *Students:* 63 full-time (42 women), 49 part-time (33 women); includes 25 minority (4 Black or African American, non-Hispanic/Latino; 8 Asian, non-Hispanic/Latino; 4 Hispanic/Latino; 9 Two or more races, non-Hispanic/Latino), 11 international. 295 applicants, 14% accepted, 28 enrolled. In 2017, 13 master's, 5 doctorates awarded. *Degree requirements:* For doctorate, thesis/dissertation. *Entrance requirements:* For doctorate, GRE General Test, GRE Subject Test. Additional exam requirements/recommendations for international students: Required—TOEFL (minimum score 550 paper-based). *Application deadline:* For fall admission, 1/15 for domestic and international students. Application fee: $75. Electronic applications accepted. *Expenses:* Tuition, state resident: full-time $10,870; part-time $453 per credit hour. Tuition, nonresident: full-time $22,210; part-time $925 per credit hour. *Required fees:* $84.68 per credit hour. $508.06 per semester. Part-time tuition and fees vary according to course load and program. *Financial support:* Fellowships, research assistantships, teaching assistantships, and career-related internships or fieldwork available. Financial award application deadline: 2/1. *Unit head:* Christine K. Wagner, Chair, 518-442-4820, Fax: 518-442-4867, E-mail: cwagner@albany.edu. *Application contact:* Michael DeRensis, Director, Graduate Admissions, 518-442-3980, Fax: 518-442-3922, E-mail: graduate@albany.edu.
Website: http://www.albany.edu/psychology/

University of Alaska Anchorage, College of Arts and Sciences, Department of Psychology, Anchorage, AK 99508. Offers clinical psychology (MS); clinical-community psychology with rural-indigenous emphasis (PhD). *Accreditation:* APA. *Program availability:* Part-time. *Degree requirements:* For master's, thesis. *Entrance requirements:* For master's, GRE General Test, GRE Subject Test, interview, references; for doctorate, interview, bachelor's or master's degree in psychology. Additional exam requirements/recommendations for international students: Required—TOEFL (minimum score 550 paper-based). *Faculty research:* Substance abuse, childhood autism, biofeedback, psychological assessment, mental health in Native Alaskans.

University of Alaska Fairbanks, College of Liberal Arts, Department of Psychology, Fairbanks, AK 99775-6480. Offers clinical-community psychology (PhD). Program offered jointly with University of Alaska Anchorage. *Degree requirements:* For doctorate, comprehensive exam, thesis/dissertation, oral defense of dissertation. *Entrance requirements:* For doctorate, bachelor's degree from accredited institution with minimum cumulative undergraduate and major GPA of 3.0; criminal background check; interview; course work in abnormal psychology, statistics, and research methods. Additional exam requirements/recommendations for international students: Required—TOEFL (minimum score 550 paper-based; 80 iBT), IELTS (minimum score 6.5). Electronic applications accepted. *Faculty research:* Clinical and community psychology; rural, indigenous, and cultural psychology.

University of Alaska Fairbanks, School of Education, Program in Counseling, Fairbanks, AK 99775-7480. Offers community counseling (M Ed). *Program availability:* 100% online, blended/hybrid learning. *Degree requirements:* For master's, comprehensive exam, oral defense of project or thesis. *Entrance requirements:* For master's, bachelor's degree from accredited institution with minimum cumulative undergraduate and major GPA of 3.0; for Graduate Certificate, master's degree from accredited institution with minimum GPA of 3.0. Additional exam requirements/recommendations for international students: Required—TOEFL (minimum score 550 paper-based; 79 iBT), IELTS (minimum score 6.5). Electronic applications accepted.

University of Bridgeport, School of Arts and Sciences, Department of Counseling, Bridgeport, CT 06604. Offers clinical mental health counseling (MS); college student personnel (MS); community counseling (MS); human resource development (MS); human service (MS). *Program availability:* Part-time, evening/weekend. *Degree requirements:* For master's, thesis, project. *Entrance requirements:* Additional exam requirements/recommendations for international students: Recommended—TOEFL (minimum score 550 paper-based; 80 iBT), IELTS (minimum score 6.5). Electronic applications accepted. *Expenses:* Contact institution.

The University of British Columbia, Faculty of Arts and Faculty of Graduate Studies, Department of Psychology, Vancouver, BC V6T 1Z4, Canada. Offers behavioral neuroscience (MA, PhD); clinical psychology (MA, PhD); cognitive science (MA, PhD); developmental psychology (MA, PhD); health psychology (MA, PhD); quantitative methods (MA, PhD); social/personality psychology (MA, PhD). *Accreditation:* APA (one or more programs are accredited). Terminal master's awarded for partial completion of doctoral program. *Degree requirements:* For master's, thesis; for doctorate, comprehensive exam, thesis/dissertation. *Entrance requirements:* For master's and doctorate, GRE General Test. Additional exam requirements/recommendations for international students: Required—TOEFL. Electronic applications accepted. *Expenses:* Contact institution. *Faculty research:* Clinical, developmental, social/personality, cognition, behavioral neuroscience.

University of Central Arkansas, Graduate School, College of Health and Behavioral Sciences, Department of Counseling and Psychology, Program in Community Counseling, Conway, AR 72035-0001. Offers MS. *Degree requirements:* For master's, comprehensive exam, thesis optional. *Entrance requirements:* For master's, GRE General Test, minimum GPA of 2.7. Additional exam requirements/recommendations for international students: Required—TOEFL (minimum score 550 paper-based). Electronic applications accepted.

University of Connecticut, Graduate School, College of Liberal Arts and Sciences, Department of Psychology, Storrs, CT 06269. Offers behavioral neuroscience (PhD); biopsychology (PhD); clinical psychology (MA, PhD); cognition and instruction (PhD); developmental psychology (MA, PhD); ecological psychology (PhD); experimental psychology (PhD); general psychology (MA, PhD); industrial/organizational psychology (PhD); language and cognition (PhD); neuroscience (PhD); social psychology (MA, PhD). *Accreditation:* APA. Terminal master's awarded for partial completion of doctoral program. *Degree requirements:* For master's, comprehensive exam; for doctorate, thesis/dissertation. *Entrance requirements:* For master's and doctorate, GRE General Test, GRE Subject Test. Additional exam requirements/recommendations for international students: Required—TOEFL (minimum score 550 paper-based). Electronic applications accepted.

University of Delaware, College of Arts and Sciences, Department of Psychology, Newark, DE 19716. Offers behavioral neuroscience (PhD); clinical psychology (PhD); cognitive psychology (PhD); social psychology (PhD). *Accreditation:* APA. *Degree requirements:* For doctorate, thesis/dissertation. *Entrance requirements:* For doctorate, GRE General Test. Additional exam requirements/recommendations for international students: Required—TOEFL (minimum score 600 paper-based). Electronic applications accepted. *Faculty research:* Emotion development, neural and cognitive aspects of memory, neural control of feeding, intergroup relations, social cognition and communication.

Social Psychology

University of Denver, Division of Arts, Humanities and Social Sciences, Department of Psychology, Denver, CO 80208. Offers affective/cognitive/social psychology (PhD); clinical child psychology (PhD); developmental psychology (PhD). *Accreditation:* APA. *Students:* Average age 28. 294 applicants, 4% accepted, 8 enrolled. In 2017, 8 doctorates awarded. Terminal master's awarded for partial completion of doctoral program. *Degree requirements:* For doctorate, variable foreign language requirement, comprehensive exam (for some programs), thesis/dissertation. *Entrance requirements:* For doctorate, GRE General Test, master's degree, transcripts, biographical statement, three letters of recommendation. Additional exam requirements/recommendations for international students: Required—TOEFL (minimum score 550 paper-based; 80 iBT). *Application deadline:* For fall admission, 12/1 priority date for domestic and international students. Application fee: $65. Electronic applications accepted. *Expenses:* Contact institution. *Financial support:* In 2017–18, 24 students received support, including 5 research assistantships with tuition reimbursements available (averaging $16,000 per year), 12 teaching assistantships with tuition reimbursements available (averaging $17,778 per year); Federal Work-Study, institutionally sponsored loans, scholarships/grants, and unspecified assistantships also available. Support available to part-time students. Financial award application deadline: 2/15; financial award applicants required to submit FAFSA. *Faculty research:* Stress and trauma, developmental science, affect science, clinical science, child psychopathology. *Unit head:* Dr. Anne DePrince, Professor and Chair, 303-871-2939, Fax: 303-871-4747, E-mail: adeprinc@du.edu. *Application contact:* Paula Houghtaling, Graduate Program Administrator, 303-871-3803, Fax: 303-871-4747, E-mail: phoughta@du.edu.
Website: http://www.du.edu/ahss/psychology

University of Guelph, Graduate Studies, College of Social and Applied Human Sciences, Department of Psychology, Guelph, ON N1G 2W1, Canada. Offers applied social psychology (MA, PhD); clinical psychology: applied development emphasis (PhD); clinical psychology: applied developmental emphasis (MA); industrial/organizational psychology (MA, PhD); neuroscience and applied cognitive science (MA, PhD). *Degree requirements:* For master's, thesis; for doctorate, comprehensive exam, thesis/dissertation. *Entrance requirements:* For master's, GRE General Test, GRE Subject Test, minimum B+ average during previous 2 years of course work; for doctorate, GRE General Test, GRE Subject Test, minimum A- average. Additional exam requirements/recommendations for international students: Required—TOEFL (minimum score 89 iBT). Electronic applications accepted. *Faculty research:* Organizational psychology, reading comprehension and mathematical ability, drug addiction and relapse, gender issues and culture, memory, clinical psychology.

University of Hawaii at Manoa, Office of Graduate Education, College of Social Sciences, Department of Psychology, Honolulu, HI 96822. Offers clinical psychology (PhD); community and cultural psychology (PhD); community and culture (MA); psychology (MA, PhD, Graduate Certificate). *Accreditation:* APA (one or more programs are accredited). *Program availability:* Part-time. Terminal master's awarded for partial completion of doctoral program. *Degree requirements:* For master's, comprehensive exam, thesis; for doctorate, comprehensive exam, thesis/dissertation. *Entrance requirements:* For master's and doctorate, GRE General Test, GRE Subject Test. Additional exam requirements/recommendations for international students: Required—TOEFL (minimum score 600 paper-based; 100 iBT), IELTS (minimum score 7). *Faculty research:* Cross-cultural psychology, health psychology, marine mammals, child/adult psychopathology.

University of Houston, College of Liberal Arts and Social Sciences, Department of Psychology, Houston, TX 77204. Offers clinical psychology (PhD); developmental psychology (PhD); industrial/organizational psychology (PhD); psychology (MA); social psychology (PhD). *Accreditation:* APA (one or more programs are accredited). *Degree requirements:* For master's, comprehensive exam, thesis; for doctorate, comprehensive exam, thesis/dissertation. *Entrance requirements:* For master's, GRE General Test, career statement, 3 letters of recommendation; for doctorate, GRE General Test, 3 letters of recommendation. Additional exam requirements/recommendations for international students: Required—TOEFL (minimum score 550 paper-based; 79 iBT). Electronic applications accepted. *Faculty research:* Health psychology, depression, child/family process, organizational effectiveness, close relationships.

The University of Kansas, Graduate Studies, College of Liberal Arts and Sciences, Department of Psychology, Lawrence, KS 66045. Offers clinical psychology (MA, PhD); cognitive and brain sciences (MA, PhD); developmental psychology (MA, PhD); quantitative psychology (PhD); social psychology (MA, PhD). *Accreditation:* APA (one or more programs are accredited). *Program availability:* Part-time. *Students:* 92 full-time (63 women), 3 part-time (all women); includes 19 minority (7 Black or African American, non-Hispanic/Latino; 4 Asian, non-Hispanic/Latino; 4 Hispanic/Latino; 4 Two or more races, non-Hispanic/Latino), 10 international. Average age 28. 361 applicants, 7% accepted, 16 enrolled. In 2017, 9 master's, 17 doctorates awarded. Terminal master's awarded for partial completion of doctoral program. *Entrance requirements:* For doctorate, GRE General Test, three letters of recommendation, resume/curriculum vitae, statement of purpose/personal statement, writing sample. Additional exam requirements/recommendations for international students: Required—TOEFL. *Application deadline:* For fall admission, 12/1 for domestic and international students. Application fee: $65 ($85 for international students). Electronic applications accepted. *Financial support:* Fellowships, research assistantships, teaching assistantships, career-related internships or fieldwork, Federal Work-Study, scholarships/grants, health care benefits, and unspecified assistantships available. Financial award application deadline: 12/1; financial award applicants required to submit FAFSA. *Faculty research:* Origins, correlates and treatment of depression; health and emotion; concentration on topics related to prejudice, stereotyping, and intergroup relations; memory, cognitive development, language, perception, attention, aging; psychometric methods, item response theory, structural equation modeling. *Unit head:* Ruth Anne Atchley, Chair, 785-864-4131. *Application contact:* Graduate Officer, 785-864-4195, E-mail: psycgrad@ku.edu.
Website: http://www.psych.ku.edu/

University of Maryland, Baltimore County, The Graduate School, College of Arts, Humanities and Social Sciences, Department of Psychology, Program in Human Services Psychology, Baltimore, MD 21250. Offers applied behavioral analysis (MA); human services psychology (PhD), including behavioral medicine, clinical psychology, community psychology. *Faculty:* 17 full-time (9 women), 11 part-time/adjunct (4 women). *Students:* 82 full-time (65 women), 1 (woman) part-time; includes 26 minority (10 Black or African American, non-Hispanic/Latino; 6 Asian, non-Hispanic/Latino; 9 Hispanic/Latino; 1 Two or more races, non-Hispanic/Latino). Average age 25. 136 applicants, 21% accepted, 18 enrolled. In 2017, 25 master's, 7 doctorates awarded. *Degree requirements:* For master's, thesis; for doctorate, comprehensive exam, thesis/dissertation. *Entrance requirements:* For master's, GRE General Test, minimum GPA of 3.0; for doctorate, GRE General Test, GRE Subject Test, minimum GPA of 3.0. Additional exam requirements/recommendations for international students: Required—TOEFL. *Application deadline:* For fall admission, 12/1 for domestic and international students. Application fee: $50. Electronic applications accepted. *Expenses:* Contact institution. *Financial support:* In 2017–18, 43 students received support, including 3 fellowships with full tuition reimbursements available (averaging $26,000 per year), 27 research assistantships with full tuition reimbursements available (averaging $20,400 per year), 8 teaching assistantships with full tuition reimbursements available (averaging $17,250 per year); career-related internships or fieldwork, Federal Work-Study, scholarships/grants, health care benefits, tuition waivers, and unspecified assistantships also available. Financial award application deadline: 3/1; financial award applicants required to submit FAFSA. *Faculty research:* Addictive behaviors, cardiovascular and cerebrovascular disease, family violence, pediatric psychology, community prevention. *Unit head:* Dr. Lynnda Dahlquist, Director, 410-455-2567, Fax: 410-455-1055, E-mail: dahlquis@umbc.edu. *Application contact:* Beverly McDougall, Program Management Specialist, 410-455-2567, Fax: 410-455-1055, E-mail: psycdept@umbc.edu.
Website: http://psychology.umbc.edu/

University of Maryland, College Park, Academic Affairs, College of Behavioral and Social Sciences, Department of Psychology, College Park, MD 20742. Offers clinical psychology (PhD); developmental psychology (PhD); experimental psychology (PhD); industrial psychology (MA, MS, PhD); social psychology (PhD). *Accreditation:* APA (one or more programs are accredited). *Degree requirements:* For master's, thesis; for doctorate, variable foreign language requirement, comprehensive exam, thesis/dissertation. *Entrance requirements:* For master's and doctorate, GRE General Test, GRE Subject Test, minimum GPA of 3.5, research and/or work experience, 3 letters of recommendation. Electronic applications accepted. *Faculty research:* Social stereotyping and prejudice, anxiety disorders, auditory neuroethology, counseling and social psychology.

University of Massachusetts Amherst, Graduate School, College of Natural Sciences, Department of Psychological and Brain Sciences, Amherst, MA 01003. Offers clinical psychology (MS, PhD); cognitive psychology (MS, PhD); developmental science (MS, PhD); psychology of peace and violence (MS, PhD); social psychology (MS, PhD). *Accreditation:* APA (one or more programs are accredited). Terminal master's awarded for partial completion of doctoral program. *Degree requirements:* For master's, thesis; for doctorate, comprehensive exam, thesis/dissertation. *Entrance requirements:* For master's and doctorate, GRE General Test, 3 letters of recommendation. Additional exam requirements/recommendations for international students: Required—TOEFL (minimum score 550 paper-based; 80 iBT), IELTS (minimum score 6.5). Electronic applications accepted.

University of Massachusetts Lowell, College of Fine Arts, Humanities and Social Sciences, Department of Psychology, Lowell, MA 01854. Offers community social psychology (MA). *Program availability:* Part-time. *Degree requirements:* For master's, thesis optional. *Entrance requirements:* For master's, GRE General Test or MAT. Electronic applications accepted. *Faculty research:* Domestic violence, youth sports, teen pregnancy, substance abuse, family and work roles.

University of Michigan, Rackham Graduate School, College of Literature, Science, and the Arts, Department of Psychology, Ann Arbor, MI 48109. Offers biopsychology (PhD); clinical science (PhD); cognition and cognitive neuroscience (PhD); developmental psychology (PhD); personality and social contexts (PhD); social psychology (PhD). *Accreditation:* APA. *Faculty:* 66 full-time (31 women), 28 part-time/adjunct (17 women). *Students:* 148 full-time (113 women); includes 61 minority (13 Black or African American, non-Hispanic/Latino; 1 American Indian or Alaska Native, non-Hispanic/Latino; 12 Asian, non-Hispanic/Latino; 28 Hispanic/Latino; 7 Two or more races, non-Hispanic/Latino), 24 international. Average age 27. 691 applicants, 7% accepted, 35 enrolled. In 2017, 34 doctorates awarded. Terminal master's awarded for partial completion of doctoral program. *Degree requirements:* For doctorate, comprehensive exam, thesis/dissertation, oral defense of dissertation, preliminary exam. *Entrance requirements:* For doctorate, GRE General Test. Additional exam requirements/recommendations for international students: Required—TOEFL. *Application deadline:* For fall admission, 12/1 for domestic and international students. Application fee: $75 ($90 for international students). Electronic applications accepted. *Expenses:* $11,184 in-state, $22,578 out-of-state. *Financial support:* In 2017–18, 90 students received support, including 61 fellowships with full tuition reimbursements available (averaging $26,400 per year), 10 research assistantships with full tuition reimbursements available (averaging $26,400 per year), 89 teaching assistantships with full tuition reimbursements available (averaging $26,400 per year); career-related internships or fieldwork, traineeships, and health care benefits also available. Financial award application deadline: 4/15. *Unit head:* Prof. Patricia Reuter-Lorenz, Department Chair, 734-764-7429. *Application contact:* Sheri M. Circele, Psychology Student Academic Affairs, 734-764-2580, Fax: 734-764-3520, E-mail: psych.saa@umich.edu.
Website: http://www.lsa.umich.edu/psych/

University of Minnesota, Twin Cities Campus, Graduate School, College of Liberal Arts, Department of Psychology, Program in Social Psychology, Minneapolis, MN 55455-0213. Offers PhD. *Degree requirements:* For doctorate, comprehensive exam, thesis/dissertation. *Entrance requirements:* For doctorate, GRE General Test, GRE Subject Test (recommended), 12 credits of upper-level psychology courses, including a course in statistics or psychological measurement. Additional exam requirements/recommendations for international students: Required—TOEFL (minimum score 550 paper-based; 79 iBT).

University of Missouri–Kansas City, College of Arts and Sciences, Department of Psychology, Kansas City, MO 64110-2499. Offers community psychology (PhD). PhD (interdisciplinary) offered through the School of Graduate Studies. *Accreditation:* APA. Terminal master's awarded for partial completion of doctoral program. *Degree requirements:* For master's, thesis; for doctorate, comprehensive exam, thesis/dissertation, residency. *Entrance requirements:* For master's, GRE, minimum GPA of 3.5, letter of recommendation; for doctorate, GRE, minimum GPA of 3.25. Additional exam requirements/recommendations for international students: Required—TOEFL (minimum score 550 paper-based; 80 iBT). Electronic applications accepted. *Faculty research:* HIV/AIDS research group, psycho-oncology, sensory and cognitive neuroscience, cognitive psychophysiology, obesity and related metabolic disorders.

University of Nebraska–Lincoln, Graduate College, College of Arts and Sciences, Department of Psychology, Lincoln, NE 68588. Offers biopsychology (PhD); clinical psychology (PhD); cognitive psychology (PhD); developmental psychology (PhD); psychology (MA); social/personality psychology (PhD); JD/MA; JD/PhD. *Accreditation:* APA (one or more programs are accredited). *Degree requirements:* For master's, thesis optional; for doctorate, comprehensive exam, thesis/dissertation. *Entrance requirements:* For master's and doctorate, GRE General Test. Additional exam requirements/recommendations for international students: Required—TOEFL (minimum score 550 paper-based). Electronic applications accepted. *Faculty research:* Law and psychology, rural mental health, chronic mental illness, neuropsychology, child clinical psychology.

University of Nevada, Reno, Graduate School, Interdisciplinary Program in Social Psychology, Reno, NV 89557. Offers PhD. *Degree requirements:* For doctorate, one foreign language, thesis/dissertation. *Entrance requirements:* For doctorate, GRE General Test, GRE Subject Test (psychology or sociology), minimum GPA of 3.0. Additional exam requirements/recommendations for international students: Required—TOEFL (minimum score 500 paper-based; 61 iBT), IELTS (minimum score 6). Electronic applications accepted. *Faculty research:* Social psychological theory, social psychology of law.

★ **University of New Haven,** Graduate School, College of Arts and Sciences, Program in Community Psychology, West Haven, CT 06516. Offers applications of psychology (Graduate Certificate); community clinical services (MA); community psychology (MA); forensic psychology (MA); program development (MA). *Program availability:* Part-time, evening/weekend. *Students:* 32 full-time (30 women), 5 part-time (all women); includes 12 minority (7 Black or African American, non-Hispanic/Latino; 1 American Indian or Alaska Native, non-Hispanic/Latino; 3 Hispanic/Latino; 1 Two or more races, non-Hispanic/Latino). Average age 25. 31 applicants, 84% accepted, 12 enrolled. In 2017, 26 master's awarded. *Degree requirements:* For master's, thesis or alternative, fieldwork. *Entrance requirements:* Additional exam requirements/recommendations for international students: Required—TOEFL (minimum score 80 iBT), IELTS, PTE. *Application deadline:* Applications are processed on a rolling basis. Application fee: $50. Electronic applications accepted. Application fee is waived when completed online. *Expenses: Tuition:* Full-time $16,020; part-time $890 per credit hour. *Required fees:* $220; $90 per term. *Financial support:* Research assistantships with partial tuition reimbursements, teaching assistantships with partial tuition reimbursements, Federal Work-Study, scholarships/grants, and unspecified assistantships available. Support available to part-time students. Financial award application deadline: 5/1; financial award applicants required to submit FAFSA. *Unit head:* Dr. Michael Morris, Coordinator, 203-932-7289, E-mail: mmorris@newhaven.edu.
Website: http://www.newhaven.edu/4725/

See Display on page 1116 and Close-Up on page 1205.

The University of North Carolina at Chapel Hill, Graduate School, College of Arts and Sciences, Department of Psychology, Chapel Hill, NC 27599-3270. Offers behavioral neuroscience psychology (PhD); clinical psychology (PhD); cognitive psychology (PhD); developmental psychology (PhD); quantitative psychology (PhD); social psychology (PhD). *Accreditation:* APA. *Degree requirements:* For doctorate, comprehensive exam, thesis/dissertation. *Entrance requirements:* For doctorate, GRE General Test, minimum GPA of 3.0. Additional exam requirements/recommendations for international students: Required—TOEFL (minimum score 550 paper-based; 79 iBT), IELTS (minimum score 7). Electronic applications accepted. *Faculty research:* Expressed emotion, cognitive development, social cognitive neuroscience, human memory personality.

The University of North Carolina at Greensboro, Graduate School, College of Arts and Sciences, Department of Psychology, Greensboro, NC 27412-5001. Offers clinical psychology (MA, PhD); cognitive psychology (MA, PhD); developmental psychology (MA, PhD); social psychology (MA, PhD). *Accreditation:* APA (one or more programs are accredited). Terminal master's awarded for partial completion of doctoral program. *Degree requirements:* For master's, comprehensive exam, thesis; for doctorate, one foreign language, thesis/dissertation, preliminary exam. *Entrance requirements:* For master's and doctorate, GRE General Test. Additional exam requirements/recommendations for international students: Required—TOEFL. Electronic applications accepted. *Faculty research:* Sensory and perceptual determinants; evoked potential: disorders, deafness, and development.

University of Oregon, Graduate School, College of Arts and Sciences, Department of Psychology, Eugene, OR 97403. Offers clinical psychology (PhD); cognitive psychology (MA, MS, PhD); developmental psychology (MA, MS, PhD); physiological psychology (MA, MS, PhD); psychology (MA, MS, PhD); social/personality psychology (MA, MS, PhD). *Accreditation:* APA (one or more programs are accredited). Terminal master's awarded for partial completion of doctoral program. *Degree requirements:* For doctorate, thesis/dissertation. *Entrance requirements:* For master's, GRE General Test, minimum GPA of 3.0; for doctorate, GRE General Test. Additional exam requirements/recommendations for international students: Required—TOEFL.

University of Phoenix–Phoenix Campus, College of Social Sciences, Tempe, AZ 85282-2371. Offers counseling (MS), including clinical mental health counseling, community counseling, counseling, marriage, family and child therapy; psychology (MS). *Program availability:* Evening/weekend, online learning. *Entrance requirements:* Additional exam requirements/recommendations for international students: Required—TOEFL, TOEIC (Test of English as an International Communication), Berlitz Online English Proficiency Exam, PTE, or IELTS. Electronic applications accepted. *Expenses:* Contact institution.

University of Pittsburgh, Kenneth P. Dietrich School of Arts and Sciences, Department of Psychology, Pittsburgh, PA 15260. Offers biological and health psychology (PhD); clinical psychology (PhD); cognitive psychology (PhD); developmental psychology (PhD); social psychology (PhD). *Accreditation:* APA. *Faculty:* 58 full-time (26 women). *Students:* 90 full-time (72 women); includes 25 minority (5 Black or African American, non-Hispanic/Latino; 11 Asian, non-Hispanic/Latino; 9 Hispanic/Latino), 9 international. Average age 26. 485 applicants, 6% accepted, 14 enrolled. In 2017, 6 doctorates awarded. Terminal master's awarded for partial completion of doctoral program. *Degree requirements:* For doctorate, comprehensive exam, thesis/dissertation. *Entrance requirements:* For doctorate, GRE General Test, minimum GPA of 3.0. Additional exam requirements/recommendations for international students: Required—TOEFL (minimum score 90 iBT) or IELTS (minimum score 7). *Application deadline:* For fall admission, 12/1 for domestic and international students. Application fee: $50. Electronic applications accepted. *Financial support:* In 2017–18, 76 students received support, including 20 fellowships with full tuition reimbursements available (averaging $22,000 per year), 28 research assistantships with full tuition reimbursements available (averaging $18,060 per year), 29 teaching assistantships with full tuition reimbursements available (averaging $19,180 per year); scholarships/grants, traineeships, and health care benefits also available. Financial award application deadline: 12/1. *Faculty research:* Developmental psychopathology; autism spectrum disorder; cardiovascular medicine; STEM research. *Total annual research expenditures:* $20 million. *Unit head:* Dr. Julie Fiez, Chair, 412-624-4500, E-mail: fiez@pitt.edu. *Application contact:* Stacy McLinden, Graduate Administrator, 412-624-4502, E-mail: psygrad@pitt.edu.
Website: http://www.psychology.pitt.edu/

University of Puerto Rico–Río Piedras, College of Social Sciences, Department of Psychology, San Juan, PR 00931-3300. Offers clinical psychology (MA); industrial organizational psychology (MA); investigative academic psychology (MA); psychology (PhD); social-community psychology (MA). *Program availability:* Part-time. *Degree requirements:* For master's, comprehensive exam, thesis; for doctorate, comprehensive exam, thesis/dissertation, internship. *Entrance requirements:* For master's, GRE or PAEG, interview, minimum GPA of 3.0; for doctorate, GRE or PAEG, interview, master's degree, minimum GPA of 3.0. *Faculty research:* Intervention on depressed Latino youth, biosychosocial training.

University of Rochester, Margaret Warner Graduate School of Education and Human Development, Master's Program in Counseling, Rochester, NY 14627. Offers school and community counseling (MS); school counseling (MS).

University of Rochester, School of Arts and Sciences, Department of Clinical and Social Sciences in Psychology, Rochester, NY 14627. Offers clinical psychology (PhD); developmental psychology (PhD); social-personality psychology (PhD). *Accreditation:* APA. *Faculty:* 14 full-time (7 women). *Students:* 46 full-time (39 women), 1 (woman) part-time; includes 9 minority (1 Black or African American, non-Hispanic/Latino; 4 Asian, non-Hispanic/Latino; 3 Hispanic/Latino; 1 Two or more races, non-Hispanic/Latino), 4 international. Average age 28. 246 applicants, 4% accepted, 8 enrolled. In 2017, 6 doctorates awarded. Terminal master's awarded for partial completion of doctoral program. *Degree requirements:* For doctorate, thesis/dissertation. *Entrance requirements:* For doctorate, GRE General Test; GRE Subject Test (required for clinical psychology, recommended for others), personal statement, official transcripts, three letters of recommendation, curriculum vitae, resume. Additional exam requirements/recommendations for international students: Required—TOEFL. *Application deadline:* For fall admission, 12/1 for domestic and international students. Application fee: $60. Electronic applications accepted. *Expenses:* $1,596 per credit hour. *Financial support:* In 2017–18, 37 students received support, including 2 fellowships, 37 research assistantships (averaging $22,000 per year); teaching assistantships, career-related internships or fieldwork, scholarships/grants, and tuition waivers (full) also available. Financial award application deadline: 4/15. *Faculty research:* Multisensory processing in social-communication difficulties, child emotion regulation, interpersonal relationships, social stress, understanding romantic relationships. *Total annual research expenditures:* $4.3 million. *Unit head:* Loisa Bennetto, Chair, 585-275-8712, E-mail: loisa.bennetto@rochester.edu. *Application contact:* April Engram, Academic Coordinator, 585-275-8704, E-mail: april.engram@rochester.edu.
Website: http://www.sas.rochester.edu/psy/graduate/index.html

University of South Carolina, The Graduate School, College of Arts and Sciences, Department of Psychology, Program in Clinical/Community Psychology, Columbia, SC 29208. Offers clinical/community psychology (PhD); general psychology (MA). *Accreditation:* APA. *Degree requirements:* For master's, comprehensive exam, thesis; for doctorate, comprehensive exam, thesis/dissertation. *Entrance requirements:* For doctorate, GRE General Test, minimum GPA of 3.2. Additional exam requirements/recommendations for international students: Required—TOEFL. Electronic applications accepted. *Faculty research:* Developmental psychopathology, health disparities, community-level interventions for psychological well being.

University of Southern California, Graduate School, Dana and David Dornsife College of Letters, Arts and Sciences, Department of Psychology, Los Angeles, CA 90089. Offers brain and cognitive science (PhD); clinical science (PhD); developmental psychology (PhD); human behavior (MHB); quantitative methods (PhD); social psychology (PhD). *Accreditation:* APA. *Degree requirements:* For doctorate, comprehensive exam, thesis/dissertation, one-year internship (for clinical science students). *Entrance requirements:* For doctorate, GRE. Additional exam requirements/recommendations for international students: Recommended—TOEFL (minimum score 600 paper-based; 100 iBT). Electronic applications accepted. *Faculty research:* Affective neuroscience; children and families; vision, culture and ethnicity; intergroup relations; aggression and violence; language and reading development; substance abuse.

The University of Tennessee at Chattanooga, School of Education, Chattanooga, TN 37403. Offers counseling (M Ed), including community counseling, school counseling; education (M Ed, Post-Master's Certificate), including elementary education (M Ed), school leadership (Post-Master's Certificate); elementary education (M Ed); learning and leadership (Ed D), including educational leadership; school leadership (Post-Master's Certificate); school leadership: principal licensure (Ed S); secondary education (M Ed); special education (M Ed). *Accreditation:* ACA; NCATE. *Program availability:* Part-time. *Students:* 43 full-time (30 women), 58 part-time (47 women); includes 18 minority (9 Black or African American, non-Hispanic/Latino; 1 Asian, non-Hispanic/Latino; 1 Hispanic/Latino; 7 Two or more races, non-Hispanic/Latino). Average age 31. 118 applicants, 75% accepted, 33 enrolled. In 2017, 59 master's, 7 other advanced degrees awarded. *Degree requirements:* For master's, comprehensive exam, thesis optional, culminating experience; for other advanced degree, internship. *Entrance requirements:* For master's, GRE General Test, PPST 1, teaching certificate; for other advanced degree, two letters of recommendation, graduate degree in education, teaching certificate with three years of experience. Additional exam requirements/recommendations for international students: Required—TOEFL (minimum score 550 paper-based; 79 iBT), IELTS (minimum score 6). *Application deadline:* For fall admission, 6/15 for domestic students, 7/1 for international students; for spring admission, 11/1 for domestic and international students. Applications are processed on a rolling basis. Application fee: $35 ($40 for international students). Electronic applications accepted. *Expenses:* Contact institution. *Financial support:* Research assistantships, teaching assistantships, career-related internships or fieldwork, institutionally sponsored loans, scholarships/grants, and unspecified assistantships available. Support available to part-time students. Financial award application deadline: 7/1; financial award applicants required to submit FAFSA. *Faculty research:* School counseling, community counseling, elementary and secondary education, school leadership and administration. *Total annual research expenditures:* $576,495. *Unit head:* Dr. Renee Murley, Director, 423-425-4684, Fax: 423-425-5380, E-mail: renee-murley@utc.edu. *Application contact:* Dr. Joanne Romagni, Dean of the Graduate School, 423-425-4478, Fax: 423-425-5223, E-mail: joanne-romagni@utc.edu.
Website: https://www.utc.edu/school-education/

The University of Tennessee at Martin, Graduate Programs, College of Education, Health and Behavioral Sciences, Program in Counseling, Martin, TN 38238. Offers addictions counseling (MS Ed); community counseling (MS Ed); school counseling (MS Ed); student affairs and college counseling (MS Ed). *Accreditation:* NCATE. *Program availability:* Part-time, online only, 100% online. *Students:* 17 full-time (15 women), 54 part-time (51 women); includes 7 minority (6 Black or African American, non-Hispanic/Latino; 1 Two or more races, non-Hispanic/Latino). Average age 34. 35 applicants, 54% accepted, 12 enrolled. In 2017, 14 master's awarded. *Degree requirements:* For master's, comprehensive exam. *Entrance requirements:* For master's, GRE General Test, minimum GPA of 2.5, resume, letters of reference. Additional exam requirements/recommendations for international students: Required—TOEFL (minimum score 525 paper-based; 71 iBT). *Application deadline:* For fall admission, 7/27 priority date for domestic and international students; for spring admission, 12/17 priority date for domestic and international students; for summer admission, 5/10 priority date for domestic and international students. Applications are processed on a rolling basis. Application fee: $30 ($130 for international students). Electronic applications accepted. *Expenses:* Tuition, state resident: full-time $8658; part-time $481 per credit hour. Tuition, nonresident: full-time $14,418; part-time $801 per credit hour. *International tuition:* $22,602 full-time. *Required fees:* $1404; $79 per credit hour. Part-time tuition and fees vary according to course load. *Financial support:* In 2017–18, 14 students received support, including 1 research assistantship with full tuition reimbursement available (averaging $7,540 per year), 2 teaching assistantships with full tuition reimbursements available (averaging $6,283 per year); scholarships/grants and tuition waivers (full and partial) also available. Financial award application deadline: 2/1; financial award applicants required to submit FAFSA. *Unit head:* Cynthia West, Dean, 731-881-7125, Fax: 731-881-7975, E-mail: cwest@utm.edu. *Application contact:* Jolene L. Cunningham, Student Services Specialist, 731-881-7012, Fax: 731-881-7499, E-mail: jcunningham@utm.edu.

University of Utah, Graduate School, College of Social and Behavioral Science, Department of Psychology, Salt Lake City, UT 84112. Offers clinical psychology (PhD); psychology (PhD), including cognitive neuroscience, developmental psychology, social psychology. *Accreditation:* APA. *Faculty:* 32 full-time (15 women), 11 part-time/adjunct

(7 women). *Students:* 53 full-time (36 women), 10 part-time (7 women); includes 10 minority (2 Black or African American, non-Hispanic/Latino; 1 Asian, non-Hispanic/Latino; 4 Hispanic/Latino; 3 Two or more races, non-Hispanic/Latino), 5 international. Average age 26. 295 applicants, 8% accepted, 13 enrolled. In 2017, 11 doctorates awarded. *Entrance requirements:* For doctorate, GRE General Test. Additional exam requirements/recommendations for international students: Required—TOEFL (minimum score 500 paper-based). Application fee: $55 ($65 for international students). Electronic applications accepted. *Expenses:* All admitted students are guaranteed funding and full tuition benefit for four years. *Financial support:* In 2017–18, 51 students received support, including 2 fellowships with full tuition reimbursements available (averaging $17,000 per year), 16 research assistantships with full tuition reimbursements available (averaging $16,800 per year), 30 teaching assistantships with full tuition reimbursements available (averaging $16,800 per year); career-related internships or fieldwork, health care benefits, and unspecified assistantships also available. Financial award application deadline: 4/15; financial award applicants required to submit FAFSA. *Faculty research:* Cognitive neuroscience, health, social cognition, psychopathology, cognitive and social development. *Total annual research expenditures:* $1.9 million. *Unit head:* Dr. Lisa G. Aspinwall, Chair, 801-581-8925, Fax: 801-581-5841, E-mail: lisa.aspinwall@utah.edu. *Application contact:* Nancy Seegmiller, Program Manager, 801-581-8925, Fax: 801-581-5841, E-mail: nancy.seegmiller@psych.utah.edu.
Website: http://www.psych.utah.edu/

University of Vermont, Graduate College, College of Arts and Sciences, Program in General/Experimental Psychology, Burlington, VT 05405-0134. Offers psychology (PhD), including biobehavioral psychology, developmental psychology, human behavioral pharmacology, social psychology. *Accreditation:* APA. *Students:* 15 (11 women). 22 applicants, 9% accepted, 2 enrolled. In 2017, 2 doctorates awarded. *Degree requirements:* For doctorate, thesis/dissertation. *Entrance requirements:* For doctorate, GRE General Test. Additional exam requirements/recommendations for international students: Required—TOEFL (minimum score 550 paper-based, 100 iBT) or IELTS (7). *Application deadline:* For fall admission, 12/1 for domestic and international students. Application fee: $65. Electronic applications accepted. *Expenses:* Tuition, state resident: full-time $11,628; part-time $646 per credit. Tuition, nonresident: full-time $29,340; part-time $1630 per credit. *Required fees:* $1994; $10 per credit. Tuition and fees vary according to course load and program. *Financial support:* In 2017–18, 15 students received support, including 15 teaching assistantships with full tuition reimbursements available (averaging $20,000 per year); fellowships and research assistantships also available. Financial award application deadline: 12/1. *Unit head:* Dr. Dianna Murray-Close, Coordinator, 802-656-2670, E-mail: dianna.murray-close@uvm.edu.
Website: https://www.uvm.edu/cas/psychology/general/experimental-psychology-phd-program

University of Victoria, Faculty of Graduate Studies, Faculty of Education, Department of Educational Psychology and Leadership Studies, Victoria, BC V8W 2Y2, Canada. Offers aboriginal communities counseling (M Ed); counseling (M Ed, MA); educational psychology (M Ed, MA, PhD), including counseling psychology (M Ed, MA), leadership studies (PhD), learning and development (MA, PhD), measurement and evaluation, special education (M Ed, MA); leadership studies (M Ed, MA). *Program availability:* Part-time. *Degree requirements:* For master's, thesis (for some programs), comprehensive exam (M Ed); for doctorate, comprehensive exam, thesis/dissertation, candidacy exam. *Entrance requirements:* For master's, 2 years of work experience in a relevant field; for doctorate, GRE, 2 years of work experience in a relevant field, minimum B average. Additional exam requirements/recommendations for international students: Required—TOEFL (minimum score 575 paper-based), IELTS (minimum score 7). *Faculty research:* Learning and development (child, adolescent and adult), special education and exceptional children.

University of Victoria, Faculty of Graduate Studies, Faculty of Social Sciences, Department of Psychology, Victoria, BC V8W 2Y2, Canada. Offers clinical psychology (PhD); clinical psychology (neuropsychology) (M Sc); cognition and brain science (M Sc, PhD); experimental neuropsychology (M Sc, PhD); individualized study (M Sc, PhD); life span development psychology (PhD); life span developmental psychology (M Sc); social psychology (M Sc, PhD). *Degree requirements:* For master's, thesis; for doctorate, thesis/dissertation, candidacy exam. *Entrance requirements:* For master's and doctorate, GRE General Test. Additional exam requirements/recommendations for international students: Required—TOEFL (minimum score 600 paper-based). Electronic applications accepted. *Faculty research:* Life span development psychology and aging, behavioral neuroscience, cognitive psychology, behavioral psychology, environmental psychology.

University of Washington, Graduate School, College of Arts and Sciences, Department of Psychology, Seattle, WA 98195. Offers animal behavior (PhD); applied child and adolescent psychology: prevention and treatment (MA); behavioral neuroscience (PhD); clinical psychology (PhD); cognition and perception (PhD); developmental psychology (PhD); quantitative psychology (PhD); social psychology and personality (PhD). *Accreditation:* APA (one or more programs are accredited). *Degree requirements:* For doctorate, thesis/dissertation. *Entrance requirements:* For doctorate, GRE General Test, minimum GPA of 3.0. Electronic applications accepted. *Faculty research:* Addictive behaviors, artificial intelligence, child psychopathology, mechanisms and development of vision, physiology of ingestive behaviors.

University of Windsor, Faculty of Graduate Studies, Faculty of Arts and Social Sciences, Department of Psychology, Windsor, ON N9B 3P4, Canada. Offers adult clinical (MA, PhD); applied social psychology (MA, PhD); child clinical (MA, PhD); clinical neuropsychology (MA, PhD). *Degree requirements:* For master's, thesis; for doctorate, comprehensive exam, thesis/dissertation. *Entrance requirements:* For master's, GRE General Test, GRE Subject Test in psychology, minimum B average; for doctorate, GRE General Test, GRE Subject Test in psychology, master's degree. Additional exam requirements/recommendations for international students: Required—TOEFL (minimum score 600 paper-based). Electronic applications accepted. *Faculty research:* Gambling, suicidology, emotional competence, psychotherapy and trauma.

University of Wisconsin–Madison, Graduate School, College of Letters and Science, Department of Psychology, Program in Social and Personality Psychology, Madison, WI 53706-1380. Offers PhD. *Degree requirements:* For doctorate, comprehensive exam, thesis/dissertation. *Entrance requirements:* For doctorate, GRE General Test, minimum undergraduate GPA of 3.0. Additional exam requirements/recommendations for international students: Required—TOEFL. Electronic applications accepted.

University of Wisconsin–Superior, Graduate Division, Department of Counseling and Psychological Professions, Superior, WI 54880-4500. Offers community counseling (MSE); human relations (MSE); school counseling (MSE). *Program availability:* Part-time, evening/weekend. *Degree requirements:* For master's, position paper, practicum. *Entrance requirements:* For master's, GRE and/or MAT, minimum GPA of 2.75. Electronic applications accepted. *Faculty research:* Women and power, intrafamily dynamics.

Walden University, Graduate Programs, School of Psychology, Minneapolis, MN 55401. Offers clinical psychology (MS), including counseling, general program; forensic psychology (MS), including forensic psychology in the community, general program, mental health applications, program planning and evaluation in forensic settings, psychology and legal systems; industrial organizational (MS, PhD), including consulting psychology, forensic (MS), forensic psychology (PhD), general practice, leadership development and coaching (MS), organizational diversity and social change, research evaluation (PhD); online teaching in psychology (Post-Master's Certificate); organizational psychology and development (Postbaccalaureate Certificate); psychology (MS, PhD), including applied psychology (MS), clinical psychology (PhD), crisis management and response (MS), educational psychology, forensic psychology (PhD), general psychology (MS), general psychology research (PhD), general psychology teaching (PhD), health psychology, leadership development and coaching (MS), psychology of culture (MS), psychology, public administration, and social change (MS), social psychology, terrorism and security (MS); psychology respecialization (Post-Doctoral Certificate). *Program availability:* Part-time, evening/weekend, online only, 100% online. Terminal master's awarded for partial completion of doctoral program. *Degree requirements:* For master's, thesis optional; for doctorate, thesis/dissertation, residency. *Entrance requirements:* For master's, bachelor's degree or higher; minimum GPA of 2.5; official transcripts; goal statement (for some programs); access to computer and Internet; for doctorate, master's degree or higher; three years of related professional or academic experience (preferred); minimum GPA of 3.0; goal statement and current resume (for select programs); official transcripts; access to computer and Internet; for other advanced degree, relevant work experience; access to computer and Internet. Additional exam requirements/recommendations for international students: Required—TOEFL (minimum score 550 paper-based, 79 iBT), IELTS (minimum score 6.5), Michigan English Language Assessment Battery (minimum score 82), or PTE (minimum score 53). Electronic applications accepted.

Wayne State University, College of Education, Division of Theoretical and Behavioral Foundations, Detroit, MI 48202. Offers applied behavior analysis (Certificate); counseling (M Ed, MA, Ed D, Ed S); counseling psychology (MA, PhD); education evaluation and research (M Ed, Ed D); educational psychology (M Ed, PhD), including learning and instruction sciences (PhD); rehabilitation counseling and community inclusion (MA); school and community psychology (MA, Certificate). *Accreditation:* ACA (one or more programs are accredited); CORE (one or more programs are accredited). *Program availability:* Evening/weekend. *Students:* Average age 32. 294 applicants, 34% accepted, 72 enrolled. In 2017, 87 master's, 12 doctorates, 14 other advanced degrees awarded. *Entrance requirements:* For master's, GRE, interview, personal statement, portfolio (art therapy); for doctorate, GRE, department-written exam, interview, curriculum vitae, references, master's degree in closely-related field with minimum GPA of 3.5, demonstration of counseling skills (for Ed D in counseling); for other advanced degree, master's degree in counseling and counseling license (for Ed S); good standing in school and community psychology MA program (for Certificate). Additional exam requirements/recommendations for international students: Required—TOEFL (minimum score 550 paper-based; 79 iBT), Michigan English Language Assessment Battery (minimum score 85); Recommended—IELTS (minimum score 6.5), TWE (minimum score 5.5). *Application deadline:* For fall admission, 6/1 priority date for domestic students, 5/1 priority date for international students; for winter admission, 10/1 priority date for domestic students, 9/1 priority date for international students; for spring admission, 2/1 priority date for domestic students, 1/1 priority date for international students. Applications are processed on a rolling basis. Application fee: $50. Electronic applications accepted. *Expenses:* Contact institution. *Financial support:* In 2017–18, 92 students received support, including 2 research assistantships with tuition reimbursements available (averaging $17,994 per year); fellowships, teaching assistantships, Federal Work-Study, scholarships/grants, health care benefits, and unspecified assistantships also available. Support available to part-time students. Financial award applicants required to submit FAFSA. *Faculty research:* Adolescents at risk, supervision of counseling. *Unit head:* Dr. Cheryl Somers, Assistant Dean, 313-577-1670, E-mail: c.somers@wayne.edu. *Application contact:* Janice Green, Assistant Dean, 313-577-1605, E-mail: jwgreen@wayne.edu.
Website: http://coe.wayne.edu/tbf/index.php

Western Illinois University, School of Graduate Studies, College of Arts and Sciences, Department of Psychology, Macomb, IL 61455-1390. Offers clinical/community mental health (MS); general experimental psychology (MS); school psychology (SSP). *Program availability:* Part-time. *Students:* 39 full-time (28 women), 15 part-time (8 women); includes 6 minority (1 Black or African American, non-Hispanic/Latino; 2 Asian, non-Hispanic/Latino; 1 Hispanic/Latino; 2 Two or more races, non-Hispanic/Latino), 2 international. Average age 26. 77 applicants, 77% accepted, 30 enrolled. In 2017, 8 master's, 6 other advanced degrees awarded. *Degree requirements:* For master's, comprehensive exam (for some programs), thesis or alternative. *Entrance requirements:* For master's and SSP, GRE General Test. Additional exam requirements/recommendations for international students: Required—TOEFL (minimum score 550 paper-based; 80 iBT). Application fee: $30. Electronic applications accepted. *Financial support:* In 2017–18, 6 research assistantships with full tuition reimbursements (averaging $7,544 per year) were awarded; unspecified assistantships also available. Financial award applicants required to submit FAFSA. *Unit head:* Dr. Karen Sears, Chairperson, 309-298-1593. *Application contact:* Dr. Nancy Parsons, Associate Provost and Director of Graduate Studies, 309-298-1806, Fax: 309-298-2345, E-mail: grad-office@wiu.edu.
Website: http://wiu.edu/psychology

Wichita State University, Graduate School, Fairmount College of Liberal Arts and Sciences, Department of Psychology, Wichita, KS 67260. Offers clinical (PhD); community (PhD); human factors (PhD). *Accreditation:* APA. *Program availability:* Part-time. *Application deadline:* For fall admission, 12/1 for domestic and international students. Application fee: $50 ($65 for international students). *Unit head:* Dr. Rhonda K. Lewis, Chair, 316-978-3170, Fax: 316-978-3006, E-mail: rhonda.lewis@wichita.edu. *Application contact:* Jordan Oleson, Admissions Coordinator, 316-978-3095, Fax: 316-978-3253, E-mail: jordan.oleson@wichita.edu.
Website: http://www.wichita.edu/psychology

Wilfrid Laurier University, Faculty of Graduate and Postdoctoral Studies, Faculty of Science, Department of Psychology, Waterloo, ON N2L 3C5, Canada. Offers behavioral neuroscience (M Sc, PhD); cognitive neuroscience (M Sc, PhD); community psychology (MA, PhD); social and developmental psychology (MA, PhD). *Program availability:* Part-time. *Degree requirements:* For master's, thesis; for doctorate, thesis/dissertation. *Entrance requirements:* For master's, GRE General Test, honors BA or the equivalent in psychology, minimum B average in undergraduate course work; for doctorate, GRE General Test, master's degree, minimum A- average. Additional exam requirements/recommendations for international students: Required—TOEFL (minimum score 89 iBT). Electronic applications accepted. *Faculty research:* Brain and cognition, community psychology, social and developmental psychology.

Yale University, Graduate School of Arts and Sciences, Department of Psychology, New Haven, CT 06520. Offers behavioral neuroscience (PhD); clinical psychology (PhD); cognitive psychology (PhD); developmental psychology (PhD); social/personality psychology (PhD). *Accreditation:* APA. *Degree requirements:* For doctorate, thesis/dissertation. *Entrance requirements:* For doctorate, GRE General Test.

Sport Psychology

Adams State University, Office of Graduate Studies, Department of Human Performance and Physical Education, Alamosa, CO 81101. Offers human performance and physical education (MA, MS), including applied sport psychology, coaching (MA), exercise science (MA), sport management (MA). *Program availability:* Part-time. *Entrance requirements:* For master's, GRE General Test or MAT, minimum undergraduate GPA of 2.75. *Application deadline:* For fall admission, 5/15 priority date for domestic students; for spring admission, 10/15 for domestic students. Applications are processed on a rolling basis. Application fee: $30. *Expenses:* Tuition, state resident: full-time $4800; part-time $2400 per credit. Tuition, nonresident: full-time $7100; part-time $3550 per credit. *Required fees:* $213; $106 per credit. One-time fee: $100. Tuition and fees vary according to campus/location and program. *Financial support:* In 2017–18, fellowships with partial tuition reimbursements (averaging $4,000 per year), teaching assistantships with partial tuition reimbursements (averaging $4,000 per year) were awarded; career-related internships or fieldwork, Federal Work-Study, institutionally sponsored loans, and unspecified assistantships also available. Support available to part-time students. Financial award application deadline: 4/15; financial award applicants required to submit FAFSA. *Unit head:* Dr. Marty Jones, Interim Chair, 719-587-7271, E-mail: hppe@adams.edu. *Application contact:* Caryn Chavez, Administrative Assistant III, 719-587-7208, Fax: 719-587-8230, E-mail: hppe@adams.edu. Website: http://hppe.adams.edu

Adler University, Graduate Programs, MA in Counseling Program: Specialization in Sport and Health Psychology, Chicago, IL 60602. Offers MAC. *Degree requirements:* For master's, thesis optional, practicum, internship, externship. *Entrance requirements:* For master's, baccalaureate degree, minimum GPA of 3.0 (recommended), interview, official transcripts, two letters of recommendation.

Argosy University, Atlanta, Georgia School of Professional Psychology, Atlanta, GA 30328. Offers clinical psychology (MA, Psy D, Postdoctoral Respecialization Certificate), including child and family psychology (Psy D), general adult clinical (Psy D), health psychology (Psy D), neuropsychology/geropsychology (Psy D); community counseling (MA), including marriage and family therapy; counselor education and supervision (Ed D); forensic psychology (MA); industrial organizational psychology (MA); marriage and family therapy (Certificate); sport-exercise psychology (MA). *Accreditation:* APA.

Argosy University, Orange County, American School of Professional Psychology, Program in Sport-Exercise Psychology, Orange, CA 92868. Offers MA.

Argosy University, Phoenix, Arizona School of Professional Psychology, Program in Clinical Psychology, Phoenix, AZ 85021. Offers clinical psychology (MA); neuropsychology (Psy D); sports-exercise psychology (Psy D).

Argosy University, Phoenix, Arizona School of Professional Psychology, Program in Sport–Exercise Psychology, Phoenix, AZ 85021. Offers MA.

A.T. Still University, College of Graduate Health Studies, Kirksville, MO 63501. Offers dental public health (MPH); exercise and sport psychology (Certificate); fundamentals of education (Certificate); geriatric exercise science (Certificate); global health (Certificate); health administration (MHA, DHA); health professions (Ed D); health sciences (DH Sc); kinesiology (MS); leadership and organizational behavior (Certificate); public health (MPH); sports conditioning (Certificate). *Program availability:* Part-time, evening/weekend, online only, 100% online, blended/hybrid learning. *Faculty:* 28 full-time (18 women), 83 part-time/adjunct (43 women). *Students:* 537 full-time (334 women), 516 part-time (316 women); includes 397 minority (171 Black or African American, non-Hispanic/Latino; 14 American Indian or Alaska Native, non-Hispanic/Latino; 84 Asian, non-Hispanic/Latino; 106 Hispanic/Latino; 1 Native Hawaiian or other Pacific Islander, non-Hispanic/Latino; 21 Two or more races, non-Hispanic/Latino), 43 international. Average age 36. 392 applicants, 84% accepted, 270 enrolled. In 2017, 138 master's, 102 doctorates, 116 other advanced degrees awarded. *Degree requirements:* For master's, thesis, integrated terminal project, practicum; for doctorate, thesis/dissertation. *Entrance requirements:* For master's, minimum GPA of 2.5, bachelor's degree or equivalent, essay, resume, English proficiency; for doctorate, minimum GPA of 2.5, master's or terminal degree, essay, past experience in relevant field, resume, English proficiency. Additional exam requirements/recommendations for international students: Required—TOEFL (minimum score 550 paper-based; 80 iBT). *Application deadline:* For fall admission, 6/26 for domestic students, 5/20 for international students; for winter admission, 9/11 for domestic students, 9/12 for international students; for spring admission, 12/11 for domestic students, 12/12 for international students; for summer admission, 3/5 for domestic students, 3/6 for international students. Applications are processed on a rolling basis. Application fee: $70. Electronic applications accepted. *Financial support:* In 2017–18, 18 students received support. Scholarships/grants available. Financial award applicants required to submit FAFSA. *Faculty research:* Public health: influence of availability of comprehensive wellness resources online, student wellness, oral health care needs assessment of community, oral health knowledge and behaviors of Medicaid-eligible pregnant women and mothers of young children in relations to early childhood caries and tooth decay, alcohol use and alcohol related problems among college students. *Unit head:* Dr. Donald Altman, Dean, 480-219-6008, Fax: 660-626-2826, E-mail: daltman@atsu.edu. *Application contact:* Amie Waldemer, Associate Director, Online Admissions, 480-219-6146, E-mail: awaldemer@atsu.edu.
Website: http://www.atsu.edu/college-of-graduate-health-studies

Ball State University, Graduate School, College of Health, School of Kinesiology, Program in Physical Education and Sport, Muncie, IN 47306. Offers physical education and sport (MA, MS), including athletic coaching education, sport administration, sport and exercise psychology. *Program availability:* Part-time, 100% online. *Students:* 19 full-time (5 women), 69 part-time (25 women); includes 6 minority (2 Black or African American, non-Hispanic/Latino; 4 Hispanic/Latino), 1 international. Average age 26. 83 applicants, 35% accepted, 27 enrolled. In 2017, 32 master's awarded. *Entrance requirements:* For master's, GRE General Test, minimum baccalaureate GPA of 2.75 or 3.0 in latter half of baccalaureate, curriculum vitae, three letters of recommendation; campus visit to meet faculty and see facilities (strongly encouraged). Additional exam requirements/recommendations for international students: Required—TOEFL (minimum score 550 paper-based; 79 iBT), IELTS (minimum score 6.5). *Application deadline:* For fall admission, 1/15 for domestic students. Applications are processed on a rolling basis. Application fee: $60. Electronic applications accepted. *Financial support:* Research assistantships with partial tuition reimbursements and unspecified assistantships available. Financial award application deadline: 3/1; financial award applicants required to submit FAFSA. *Unit head:* Dr. Tom Weidner, Chairperson, 765-285-5039, Fax: 765-285-8254, E-mail: tweidner@bsu.edu.

Barry University, School of Human Performance and Leisure Sciences, Programs in Movement Science, Specialization in Sport and Exercise Psychology, Miami Shores, FL 33161-6695. Offers MS. *Entrance requirements:* For master's, GRE.

California State University, Fresno, Division of Research and Graduate Studies, College of Health and Human Services, Department of Kinesiology, Fresno, CA 93740-8027. Offers exercise science (MA); general kinesiology (MA); sport administration (MA); sport psychology (MA). *Program availability:* Part-time, evening/weekend. *Degree requirements:* For master's, thesis or alternative. *Entrance requirements:* For master's, GRE General Test, minimum GPA of 2.7. Additional exam requirements/recommendations for international students: Required—TOEFL. Electronic applications accepted. *Faculty research:* Refugee education, homeless, geriatrics, fitness.

California State University, Long Beach, Graduate Studies, College of Health and Human Services, Department of Kinesiology, Long Beach, CA 90840. Offers adapted physical education (MA); coaching and student athlete development (MA); exercise physiology and nutrition (MS); exercise science (MS); individualized studies (MA); kinesiology (MA); pedagogical studies (MA); sport and exercise psychology (MS); sport management (MA); sports medicine and injury studies (MS). *Program availability:* Part-time. *Degree requirements:* For master's, oral and written comprehensive exams or thesis. *Entrance requirements:* For master's, GRE General Test, minimum GPA of 2.75 during previous 2 years of course work. Electronic applications accepted. *Faculty research:* Pulmonary functioning, feedback and practice structure, strength training, history and politics of sports, special population research issues.

California University of Pennsylvania, School of Graduate Studies and Research, College of Education and Human Services, Department of Exercise Science and Sport Studies, California, PA 15419-1394. Offers applied sport science (MS); exercise science (MS), including group fitness leadership, nutrition, performance enhancement and injury prevention, rehabilitation science; group fitness leadership (MS); nutrition (MS); wellness coaching (MS). *Program availability:* Part-time, evening/weekend, online learning. *Degree requirements:* For master's, comprehensive exam, thesis optional. *Entrance requirements:* For master's, minimum GPA of 3.0. Additional exam requirements/recommendations for international students: Required—TOEFL (minimum score 550 paper-based; 80 iBT). *Application deadline:* For winter admission, 12/1 priority date for domestic and international students. Applications are processed on a rolling basis. Application fee: $25. Electronic applications accepted. *Expenses:* Contact institution. *Financial support:* Applicants required to submit FAFSA. *Faculty research:* Reducing obesity in children, sport performance, creating unique biomechanical assessment techniques, web-based training for fitness professionals, webcams. *Unit head:* Dr. William B. Biddington, Interim Dean, 724-938-4356, E-mail: biddington_w@calu.edu. *Application contact:* Suzanne C. Powers, Director of Graduate Admissions and Recruitment, 724-938-4029, Fax: 724-938-5712, E-mail: powers_s@cup.edu.

Capella University, Harold Abel School of Social and Behavioral Science, Master's Programs in Psychology, Minneapolis, MN 55402. Offers applied behavior analysis (MS); clinical psychology (MS); counseling psychology (MS); educational psychology (MS); evaluation, research, and measurement (MS); general advanced studies in human behavior (MS); general psychology (MS); industrial/organizational psychology (MS); leadership coaching psychology (MS); school psychology (MS); sport psychology (MS).

Chatham University, Program in Counseling Psychology, Pittsburgh, PA 15232-2826. Offers child, adolescent and family (MSCP); counseling psychology (Psy D); health and holistic (MSCP); organization and supervision (MSCP); sport and exercise (MSCP). *Accreditation:* APA. *Program availability:* Part-time, evening/weekend. *Faculty:* 11 full-time (10 women). *Students:* 61 full-time (46 women), 25 part-time (22 women); includes 12 minority (9 Black or African American, non-Hispanic/Latino; 2 Hispanic/Latino; 1 Two or more races, non-Hispanic/Latino), 3 international. Average age 30. 124 applicants, 62% accepted, 45 enrolled. In 2017, 38 master's awarded. *Degree requirements:* For master's, thesis optional, supervised internship; for doctorate, thesis/dissertation, internship. *Entrance requirements:* For master's, minimum GPA of 3.0; 2 letters of recommendation; resume; prerequisite coursework in statistics, biology, and psychology; for doctorate, GRE. Additional exam requirements/recommendations for international students: Required—TOEFL (minimum score 600 paper-based; 100 iBT), IELTS (minimum score 7), TWE. *Application deadline:* For fall admission, 4/1 priority date for domestic and international students; for spring admission, 11/1 for domestic students, 10/1 for international students. Applications are processed on a rolling basis. Application fee: $45. Electronic applications accepted. Application fee is waived when completed online. *Expenses:* Tuition: Full-time $16,740; part-time $930 per credit. *Required fees:* $486; $27 per credit. $243 per semester. *Financial support:* Career-related internships or fieldwork available. Financial award applicants required to submit FAFSA. *Faculty research:* Trauma and recovery, hypnosis, psychospiritual dimensions of healing, psychotherapy of schizophrenia. *Unit head:* Dr. Mary Beth Mannarino, Director, 412-365-1196, Fax: 412-365-1505, E-mail: mmannarino@chatham.edu. *Application contact:* Katie Noel, Assistant Director of Graduate Admission, 412-365-2758, Fax: 412-365-1609, E-mail: gradadmissions@chatham.edu.
Website: http://www.chatham.edu/mscp

Florida State University, The Graduate School, College of Education, Department of Educational Psychology and Learning Systems, Tallahassee, FL 32306. Offers counseling and human systems (PhD), including counseling psychology and school psychology; educational psychology (MS, PhD), including learning and cognition, sport psychology; human performance and technology (Certificate); instructional systems and learning technologies (MS, PhD); measurement and statistics (MS, PhD, Certificate); online instructional development (Certificate); MS/Ed S. *Program availability:* Part-time, evening/weekend, 100% online, blended/hybrid learning, asynchronous, minimal on-campus study. *Faculty:* 28 full-time (17 women), 12 part-time/adjunct (7 women). *Students:* 339 full-time (238 women), 136 part-time (93 women); includes 126 minority (47 Black or African American, non-Hispanic/Latino; 4 American Indian or Alaska Native, non-Hispanic/Latino; 7 Asian, non-Hispanic/Latino; 48 Hispanic/Latino; 20 Two or more races, non-Hispanic/Latino), 110 international. Average age 31. 419 applicants, 39% accepted, 82 enrolled. In 2017, 84 master's, 27 doctorates, 38 other advanced degrees awarded. Terminal master's awarded for partial completion of doctoral program. *Degree requirements:* For master's and Certificate, comprehensive exam, thesis optional; for doctorate, comprehensive exam, thesis/dissertation, diagnostic exam, preliminary exam, prospectus defense. *Entrance requirements:* For master's, doctorate, and Certificate, GRE General Test, minimum GPA of 3.0. Additional exam requirements/recommendations for international students: Required—TOEFL (minimum score 550 paper-based, 80 iBT), IELTS (minimum score 6.5) or Michigan English Language Assessment Battery (minimum score 77). Application fee: $30. Electronic applications accepted. *Financial support:* Fellowships, research assistantships, teaching assistantships, scholarships/grants, tuition waivers (full and partial), and unspecified assistantships available. Financial award application deadline: 1/15; financial award applicants required to submit FAFSA. *Faculty research:* Learning and cognition,

counseling and school psychology, instructional systems, measurement and evaluation. *Unit head:* Dr. Betsy Becker, Chair, 850-644-4592, Fax: 850-644-8776, E-mail: bbecker@fsu.edu. *Application contact:* Deborah Kelly, Academic Program Specialist, 850-644-8046, Fax: 850-644-8781, E-mail: dhamkelly@fsu.edu.

John F. Kennedy University, Graduate School of Professional Psychology, Program in Sport Psychology, Pleasant Hill, CA 94523-4817. Offers MA. *Program availability:* Part-time, evening/weekend. *Degree requirements:* For master's, thesis or alternative. *Entrance requirements:* For master's, interview. Additional exam requirements/recommendations for international students: Required—TOEFL.

Lock Haven University of Pennsylvania, The Stephen Poorman College of Business, Information Systems, and Human Services, Lock Haven, PA 17745-2390. Offers clinical mental health counseling (MS); sport science (MS). *Program availability:* Online learning. *Degree requirements:* For master's, thesis. *Entrance requirements:* For master's, minimum undergraduate GPA of 3.0. Additional exam requirements/recommendations for international students: Required—TOEFL. Electronic applications accepted.

Purdue University, Graduate School, College of Health and Human Sciences, Department of Health and Kinesiology, West Lafayette, IN 47907. Offers athletic training education administration (MS, PhD); biomechanics (MS, PhD); exercise physiology (MS, PhD); health education (MS, PhD); history/philosophy of sport (MS, PhD); motor control and development (MS, PhD); physical education pedagogy (PhD); physical education teacher education (MS); recreation and sport management (MS, PhD); sport and exercise psychology (MS, PhD). *Program availability:* Part-time. *Faculty:* 19 full-time (7 women). *Students:* 30 full-time (13 women), 10 part-time (5 women); includes 2 minority (1 Asian, non-Hispanic/Latino; 1 Two or more races, non-Hispanic/Latino), 6 international. Average age 26. 77 applicants, 29% accepted, 18 enrolled. In 2017, 18 master's, 9 doctorates awarded. *Degree requirements:* For master's, thesis optional; for doctorate, comprehensive exam, thesis/dissertation, qualifying examination, preliminary examination. *Entrance requirements:* For master's, GRE General Test (minimum score 1000 combined verbal and quantitative), minimum undergraduate GPA of 3.0 or equivalent; for doctorate, GRE General Test (minimum score 1100 combined verbal and quantitative), minimum undergraduate GPA of 3.0 or equivalent; master's degree with minimum GPA of 3.25 (recommended). Additional exam requirements/recommendations for international students: Required—TOEFL (minimum score 77 iBT); Recommended—TWE. *Application deadline:* For fall admission, 4/30 for domestic and international students; for spring admission, 10/15 for domestic and international students. Applications are processed on a rolling basis. Application fee: $60 ($75 for international students). Electronic applications accepted. *Financial support:* Fellowships with partial tuition reimbursements, research assistantships with partial tuition reimbursements, teaching assistantships with partial tuition reimbursements, and Federal Work-Study available. Support available to part-time students. Financial award applicants required to submit FAFSA. *Faculty research:* Wellness, motivation, teaching effectiveness, learning and development. *Unit head:* Dr. Timothy P. Gavin, Head of the Graduate Program, 765-494-3178, Fax: 765-494-1239, E-mail: gavin1@purdue.edu. *Application contact:* David B. Klenosky, Graduate Contact, 765-494-0865, E-mail: klenosky@purdue.edu.
Website: http://www.purdue.edu/hhs/hk/

Queen's University at Kingston, School of Graduate Studies, School of Kinesiology and Health Studies, Kingston, ON K7L 3N6, Canada. Offers applied exercise science (PhD); biomechanics/ergonomics (M Sc); exercise physiology (M Sc); social psychology of sport and exercise rehabilitation (MA); sociology of sport (MA). *Program availability:* Part-time. *Degree requirements:* For master's, thesis (for some programs); for doctorate, comprehensive exam, thesis/dissertation. *Entrance requirements:* For master's and doctorate, minimum B+ average. Additional exam requirements/recommendations for international students: Required—TOEFL. Electronic applications accepted. *Faculty research:* Expert performance ergonomics, obesity research, pregnancy and exercise, gender and sport participation.

Seton Hall University, College of Education and Human Services, Department of Professional Psychology and Family Therapy, Program in Psychological Studies, South Orange, NJ 07079-2697. Offers individualized (MA); marriage and family therapy (MA); sport and exercise psychology (MA). *Program availability:* Part-time, evening/weekend. *Degree requirements:* For master's, comprehensive exam. *Entrance requirements:* For master's, GRE or MAT. *Faculty research:* Cognitive style, self-esteem anxiety in preadolescence, object relation, bonding.

Southern Illinois University Edwardsville, Graduate School, School of Education, Health, and Human Behavior, Department of Kinesiology and Health Education, Program in Exercise and Sport Psychology, Edwardsville, IL 62026. Offers MS. *Program availability:* Part-time, evening/weekend. *Degree requirements:* For master's, comprehensive exam (for some programs), thesis (for some programs). *Entrance requirements:* Additional exam requirements/recommendations for international students: Required—TOEFL (minimum score 550 paper-based, 79 iBT), IELTS (minimum score 6.5), Michigan Test of English Language Proficiency or PTE. Electronic applications accepted.

Springfield College, Graduate Programs, Programs in Exercise Science and Sport Studies, Springfield, MA 01109-3797. Offers athletic training (MS); clinical exercise physiology (MS); exercise physiology (MS); sport and exercise psychology (MS); strength and conditioning (MS). *Program availability:* Part-time. *Students:* 121 applicants, 60% accepted, 36 enrolled. In 2017, 19 master's awarded. Terminal master's awarded for partial completion of doctoral program. *Degree requirements:* For master's, comprehensive exam, research project or thesis. *Entrance requirements:* For master's, GRE General Test. Additional exam requirements/recommendations for international students: Required—TOEFL (minimum score 550 paper-based); Recommended—IELTS (minimum score 7). *Application deadline:* For fall admission, 1/15 for domestic and international students; for winter admission, 11/1 for domestic and international students; for spring admission, 11/1 for domestic and international students. Application fee: $50. Electronic applications accepted. *Financial support:* Fellowships with partial tuition reimbursements, teaching assistantships with partial tuition reimbursements, career-related internships or fieldwork, Federal Work-Study, institutionally sponsored loans, scholarships/grants, and unspecified assistantships available. Financial award application deadline: 3/1; financial award applicants required to submit FAFSA. *Unit head:* Dr. Sue Guyer, Chair, 413-748-3404, E-mail: mguyer@springfield.edu. *Application contact:* Anne Griffin, Director of Graduate Admissions, 413-748-3225, Fax: 413-748-3694, E-mail: agriffin2@springfield.edu.
Website: http://springfield.edu/gradesss

Springfield College, Graduate Programs, Programs in Psychology, Springfield, MA 01109-3797. Offers athletic counseling (MS, CAGS); clinical mental health counseling (M Ed, CAGS); counseling psychology (Psy D); general counseling (M Ed); industrial/organizational psychology (M Ed, CAGS); school counseling (M Ed, CAGS); student personnel administration in higher education (M Ed, CAGS). *Accreditation:* APA. *Program availability:* Part-time. *Students:* 192 applicants, 65% accepted, 64 enrolled. In 2017, 56 master's, 5 doctorates awarded. *Degree requirements:* For master's, research project, portfolio; for doctorate, dissertation project, 1500 hours of counseling psychology practicum, full-year internship. *Entrance requirements:* For doctorate, GRE. Additional exam requirements/recommendations for international students: Required—TOEFL (minimum score 550 paper-based); Recommended—IELTS (minimum score 7). *Application deadline:* For fall admission, 1/15 priority date for domestic students, 1/15 for international students; for winter admission, 11/1 for domestic and international students; for spring admission, 11/1 for domestic and international students. Applications are processed on a rolling basis. Application fee: $50. Electronic applications accepted. *Financial support:* Fellowships with partial tuition reimbursements, teaching assistantships with partial tuition reimbursements, career-related internships or fieldwork, Federal Work-Study, institutionally sponsored loans, scholarships/grants, and unspecified assistantships available. Financial award application deadline: 3/1; financial award applicants required to submit FAFSA. *Unit head:* Dr. Allison Cumming-McCann, Chair, 413-748-3025, Fax: 413-748-3854, E-mail: acumming@springfield.edu. *Application contact:* Anne Griffin, Director of Graduate Admissions, 413-748-3225, E-mail: agriffin2@springfield.edu.
Website: http://springfield.edu/programs

University of Denver, Graduate School of Professional Psychology, Denver, CO 80208. Offers clinical psychology (Psy D); forensic psychology (MA); international disaster psychology (MA); sport and performance psychology (MA); sport coaching (MA); strength and conditioning and fitness coaching (Certificate). *Accreditation:* APA. *Faculty:* 23 full-time (13 women), 25 part-time/adjunct (14 women). *Students:* 233 full-time (180 women), 79 part-time (46 women); includes 81 minority (22 Black or African American, non-Hispanic/Latino; 9 Asian, non-Hispanic/Latino; 31 Hispanic/Latino; 1 Native Hawaiian or other Pacific Islander, non-Hispanic/Latino; 18 Two or more races, non-Hispanic/Latino), 7 international. Average age 26. 866 applicants, 30% accepted, 135 enrolled. In 2017, 106 master's, 23 doctorates awarded. *Degree requirements:* For master's, comprehensive exam (for some programs); for doctorate, comprehensive exam (for some programs), paper, clinical internship. *Entrance requirements:* For master's and doctorate, GRE General Test, transcripts, resume, two letters of recommendation, essay. Additional exam requirements/recommendations for international students: Required—TOEFL (minimum score 550 paper-based; 80 iBT). *Application deadline:* For fall admission, 1/5 for domestic and international students. Application fee: $65. Electronic applications accepted. *Expenses:* $47,823 per year full-time. *Financial support:* In 2017–18, 235 students received support, including 2 teaching assistantships with tuition reimbursements available (averaging $1,976 per year); career-related internships or fieldwork, Federal Work-Study, institutionally sponsored loans, scholarships/grants, unspecified assistantships, and clinical assistantships also available. Support available to part-time students. Financial award application deadline: 2/15; financial award applicants required to submit FAFSA. *Unit head:* Dr. Shelly Smith-Acuna, Dean, 303-871-3880, Fax: 303-871-4220, E-mail: shelly.smith-acuna@du.edu. *Application contact:* Admissions Counselor, 303-871-3736, Fax: 303-871-4220, E-mail: gsppinfo@du.edu.
Website: http://www.du.edu/gspp

University of Rhode Island, Graduate School, College of Health Sciences, Department of Kinesiology, Kingston, RI 02881. Offers cultural studies of sport and physical culture (MS); exercise science (MS); psychosocial/behavioral aspects of physical activity (MS). *Accreditation:* NCATE. *Program availability:* Part-time. *Faculty:* 14 full-time (9 women). *Students:* 10 full-time (4 women), 3 part-time (1 woman), 1 international. 8 applicants, 100% accepted, 6 enrolled. In 2017, 7 master's awarded. *Entrance requirements:* Additional exam requirements/recommendations for international students: Required—TOEFL. *Application deadline:* For fall admission, 7/15 for domestic students, 2/1 for international students; for spring admission, 11/15 for domestic students, 7/15 for international students. Application fee: $65. Electronic applications accepted. *Expenses:* Tuition, state resident: full-time $12,706; part-time $786 per credit. Tuition, nonresident: full-time $25,216; part-time $1401 per credit. *Required fees:* $1598; $45 per credit. One-time fee: $30 part-time. *Financial support:* In 2017–18, 5 teaching assistantships with tuition reimbursements (averaging $11,078 per year) were awarded. Financial award application deadline: 2/1; financial award applicants required to submit FAFSA. *Unit head:* Dr. Disa Hatfield, Interim Chair, 401-874-5183, E-mail: doch@uri.edu. *Application contact:* Dr. Matthew Delmonico, Graduate Program Director, 401-874-5440, E-mail: delmonico@uri.edu.
Website: http://web.uri.edu/kinesiology/

The University of Texas at Austin, Graduate School, College of Education, Department of Kinesiology and Health Education, Austin, TX 78712-1111. Offers behavioral health (PhD); exercise and sport psychology (M Ed, MA); exercise science (M Ed, MS, PhD); health education (M Ed, MS, Ed D, PhD). *Program availability:* Part-time. Terminal master's awarded for partial completion of doctoral program. *Degree requirements:* For master's, thesis (for some programs); for doctorate, thesis/dissertation. *Entrance requirements:* For master's and doctorate, GRE General Test. Additional exam requirements/recommendations for international students: Required—TOEFL. Electronic applications accepted. *Faculty research:* Health promotion, human performance and exercise biochemistry, motor behavior and biomechanics, sport management, aging and pediatric development.

West Virginia University, College of Physical Activity and Sport Sciences, Morgantown, WV 26506. Offers athletic training (MS); coaching and sport education (MS); coaching and teaching studies (Ed D, PhD), including curriculum and instruction (PhD); physical education/teacher education (MS); sport and exercise psychology (MS); sport coaching (MS); sport management (MS). *Students:* 104 full-time (37 women), 75 part-time (28 women); includes 30 minority (12 Black or African American, non-Hispanic/Latino; 2 Asian, non-Hispanic/Latino; 9 Hispanic/Latino; 7 Two or more races, non-Hispanic/Latino), 12 international. *Degree requirements:* For doctorate, comprehensive exam, thesis/dissertation, oral exam. *Entrance requirements:* For master's, GRE or MAT, minimum GPA of 3.0; for doctorate, GRE General Test or MAT, minimum GPA of 3.5. Additional exam requirements/recommendations for international students: Required—TOEFL (minimum score 550 paper-based). *Application deadline:* For fall admission, 12/15 for domestic students, 10/1 for international students. Application fee: $60. Electronic applications accepted. *Expenses:* Tuition, state resident: full-time $9450. Tuition, nonresident: full-time $24,390. *Financial support:* Research assistantships, teaching assistantships, career-related internships or fieldwork, Federal Work-Study, institutionally sponsored loans, health care benefits, tuition waivers (full and partial), and administrative assistantships available. Support available to part-time students. Financial award application deadline: 2/1; financial award applicants required to submit FAFSA. *Faculty research:* Sport psych sociology, teacher education, exercise psychology, counseling. *Unit head:* Sean Bulger, Online Program Coordinator, 304-293-0845, Fax: 304-293-4641, E-mail: sean.bulger@mail.wvu.edu.
Website: http://www.cpass.wvu.edu

Thanatology

Brooklyn College of the City University of New York, School of Natural and Behavioral Sciences, Department of Health and Nutrition Sciences, Program in Community Health, Brooklyn, NY 11210-2889. Offers community health education (MA); thanatology (MA). *Accreditation:* CEPH. *Degree requirements:* For master's, thesis or alternative. *Entrance requirements:* For master's, 2 letters of recommendation, essay. Additional exam requirements/recommendations for international students: Required—TOEFL. Electronic applications accepted. *Faculty research:* Diet restriction, religious practices in bereavement, diabetes, stress management, palliative care.

The College of New Rochelle, Graduate School, Division of Human Services, Program in Mental Health Counseling, New Rochelle, NY 10805-2308. Offers mental health counseling (MS); thanatology (Certificate). *Degree requirements:* For Certificate, internship. *Expenses: Tuition:* Full-time $17,406. *Required fees:* $1120.

Hood College, Graduate School, Programs in Human Behavior, Frederick, MD 21701-8575. Offers interdisciplinary studies in human behavior (MA), including psychology; thanatology (Certificate). *Program availability:* Part-time, evening/weekend. *Faculty:* 1 (woman) full-time, 2 part-time/adjunct (0 women). *Students:* 9 full-time (6 women), 22 part-time (16 women); includes 4 minority (2 Black or African American, non-Hispanic/Latino; 2 Two or more races, non-Hispanic/Latino), 2 international. Average age 37. 7 applicants, 100% accepted, 2 enrolled. In 2017, 9 master's, 11 other advanced degrees awarded. *Degree requirements:* For master's, comprehensive exam, thesis optional, capstone/research project. *Entrance requirements:* For master's, minimum GPA of 2.75, essay; for Certificate, minimum GPA of 2.75, essay, resume. Additional exam requirements/recommendations for international students: Required—TOEFL (minimum score 575 paper-based; 89 iBT), IELTS (minimum score 6.5). *Application deadline:* For fall admission, 8/15 priority date for domestic students, 8/5 for international students; for spring admission, 12/1 priority date for domestic students, 12/1 for international students; for summer admission, 5/1 priority date for domestic students, 4/15 for international students. Applications are processed on a rolling basis. Application fee: $35. Electronic applications accepted. *Expenses:* $465 per credit hour plus $110 comprehensive fee per semester. *Financial support:* Research assistantships with full tuition reimbursements, tuition waivers (partial), and unspecified assistantships available. Financial award applicants required to submit FAFSA. *Faculty research:* Mind-body medicine and multicultural healing, the New Orleans jazz funeral, death practices in African-American culture, bereavement theories and gender differences, Piaget's theory of cognitive development as a formal mathematical model. *Unit head:* Dr. April M.

Boulton, Dean of the Graduate School, 301-696-3600, E-mail: gofurther@hood.edu. *Application contact:* Jan Marcus, Assistant Director of Graduate Admissions, 301-696-3600, E-mail: gofurther@hood.edu.
Website: http://www.hood.edu/graduate

Marian University, School of Nursing and Health Professions, Fond du Lac, WI 54935-4699. Offers adult nurse practitioner (MSN); nurse educator (MSN); thanatology (MS). *Accreditation:* AACN. *Program availability:* Part-time, evening/weekend. *Degree requirements:* For master's, thesis, 675 clinical practicum hours. *Entrance requirements:* For master's, 3 letters of professional recommendation; undergraduate work in nursing research, statistics, health assessment. Additional exam requirements/recommendations for international students: Required—TOEFL (minimum score 525 paper-based; 70 iBT). Electronic applications accepted. *Expenses:* Contact institution.

Southwestern College, Program in Grief, Loss and Trauma Counseling, Santa Fe, NM 87502-4788. Offers MA, Certificate. *Program availability:* Part-time, evening/weekend, online learning. *Entrance requirements:* For master's, interview, references, resume; for Certificate, 3 letters of reference, interview.

University of Maryland, Baltimore, Graduate School, Program in Thanatology, Baltimore, MD 21201. Offers Certificate. *Students:* 9 part-time (7 women); includes 1 minority (Hispanic/Latino). Average age 45. 19 applicants, 47% accepted, 6 enrolled. In 2017, 15 Certificates awarded. *Entrance requirements:* For degree, minimum GPA of 3.0, curriculum vitae, essay. Additional exam requirements/recommendations for international students: Required—TOEFL (minimum score 80 iBT); Recommended—IELTS (minimum score 7). *Application deadline:* For fall admission, 7/15 for domestic students; for spring admission, 12/15 for domestic students. Applications are processed on a rolling basis. Application fee: $75. Electronic applications accepted. *Expenses:* Contact institution. *Financial support:* Application deadline: 3/1; applicants required to submit FAFSA. *Unit head:* Dr. Michelle Pearce, Graduate Program Director, 410-706-6164, E-mail: mpearce@som.umaryland.edu. *Application contact:* Jade Grant, Academic Program Specialist, 410-706-7131, Fax: 410-706-3473, E-mail: jgrant@umaryland.edu.

Washington & Jefferson College, Graduate and Continuing Studies, Washington, PA 15301. Offers applied health care economics and outcomes management (MS); professional accounting (MAC); professional writing (Graduate Certificate); thanatology (Graduate Certificate).

Transpersonal and Humanistic Psychology

Atlantic University, Program in Transpersonal Psychology, Virginia Beach, VA 23451-2061. Offers applied spirituality (MA); consciousness (MA); creativity (MA); general studies (MA); leadership and conflict transformation (MA). *Program availability:* Part-time, evening/weekend, online learning. *Degree requirements:* For master's, culminating project. *Entrance requirements:* For master's, official transcripts, 1000-word essay, interview. Additional exam requirements/recommendations for international students: Required—TOEFL (minimum score 550 paper-based). *Application deadline:* For fall admission, 9/3 for domestic students; for winter admission, 6/11 for domestic students; for spring admission, 12/4 for domestic students; for summer admission, 3/12 for domestic students. Applications are processed on a rolling basis. Application fee: $50. Electronic applications accepted. *Expenses:* $360 per credit. *Application contact:* Rachel Alvidrez, Associate Vice President of Enrollment Management Services, 757-631-8101, Fax: 757-631-8096, E-mail: info@atlanticuniv.edu.
Website: https://www.atlanticuniv.edu/academics/programs/transpersonal-psychology-m-a/

California Institute of Integral Studies, School of Consciousness and Transformation, San Francisco, CA 94103. Offers anthropology and social change (MA, PhD); Asian philosophies and cultures (MA); creative inquiry/interdisciplinary arts (MFA); East-West psychology (MA, PhD); integral and transpersonal psychology (PhD); philosophy and religion (PhD), including ecology, spirituality, and religion, philosophy, cosmology, and consciousness, women's spirituality; philosophy, cosmology, and consciousness (Certificate); transformative leadership (MA); transformative studies (PhD); women, gender, spirituality and social justice (MA); writing and consciousness (MFA). *Program availability:* Part-time, evening/weekend, 100% online, blended/hybrid learning. *Students:* 392 full-time (265 women), 141 part-time (98 women); includes 145 minority (40 Black or African American, non-Hispanic/Latino; 1 American Indian or Alaska Native, non-Hispanic/Latino; 19 Asian, non-Hispanic/Latino; 54 Hispanic/Latino; 31 Two or more races, non-Hispanic/Latino), 61 international. Average age 43. 212 applicants, 96% accepted, 153 enrolled. In 2017, 49 master's, 36 doctorates awarded. Terminal master's awarded for partial completion of doctoral program. *Degree requirements:* For master's, thesis optional; for doctorate, comprehensive exam, thesis/dissertation, 1 foreign language (for Asian philosophies and cultures). *Entrance requirements:* For master's, minimum GPA of 3.0, letters of recommendation, writing sample; for doctorate, master's degree, minimum GPA of 3.0, letters of recommendation, writing sample. Additional exam requirements/recommendations for international students: Required—TOEFL. *Application deadline:* For fall admission, 2/1 priority date for domestic and international students; for spring admission, 10/15 priority date for domestic and international students. Applications are processed on a rolling basis. Application fee: $65. Electronic applications accepted. *Expenses:* $21,400 tuition and fees (for MA); $28,390 (for MFA); $24,658 (for PhD). *Financial support:* Fellowships, research assistantships, teaching assistantships, career-related internships or fieldwork, Federal Work-Study, and scholarships/grants available. Support available to part-time students. Financial award application deadline: 4/15; financial award applicants required to submit FAFSA. *Faculty research:* Ecology and sustainability, philosophy and religion, East-West psychology, integrative health, social and cultural anthropology, transformative leadership. *Unit head:* Kathy Littles, Academic Dean, 415-575-6100, E-mail: klittles@ciis.edu. *Application contact:* Ellen Durst, Director of Admissions, 415-575-6100, Fax: 415-575-1268, E-mail: admissions@ciis.edu.
Website: http://www.ciis.edu/

John F. Kennedy University, Graduate School of Holistic Studies, Department of Counseling Psychology, Program in Counseling Psychology, Pleasant Hill, CA 94523-4817. Offers holistic studies (MA); somatic psychology (MA); transpersonal psychology

(MA). *Program availability:* Part-time, evening/weekend. *Degree requirements:* For master's, thesis or alternative. *Entrance requirements:* For master's, interview. Additional exam requirements/recommendations for international students: Required—TOEFL.

John F. Kennedy University, Graduate School of Holistic Studies, Department of Integral Studies, Program in Consciousness and Transformative Studies, Pleasant Hill, CA 94523-4817. Offers MA. *Program availability:* Part-time, evening/weekend. *Degree requirements:* For master's, thesis or alternative. *Entrance requirements:* For master's, interview. Additional exam requirements/recommendations for international students: Required—TOEFL.

Michigan School of Professional Psychology, MA and Psy D Programs in Clinical Psychology, Farmington Hills, MI 48334. Offers MA, Psy D. *Accreditation:* APA. *Program availability:* Part-time, evening/weekend. *Faculty:* 11 full-time (7 women), 21 part-time/adjunct (17 women). *Students:* 109 full-time (85 women), 64 part-time (51 women); includes 46 minority (30 Black or African American, non-Hispanic/Latino; 3 Asian, non-Hispanic/Latino; 2 Hispanic/Latino; 11 Two or more races, non-Hispanic/Latino), 1 international. Average age 31. 194 applicants, 47% accepted, 80 enrolled. In 2017, 37 master's, 16 doctorates awarded. *Degree requirements:* For master's, practicum; for doctorate, comprehensive exam, thesis/dissertation, internship, practicum. *Entrance requirements:* For master's, undergraduate degree from accredited institution with minimum GPA of 2.5; major in psychology, social work, or counseling; for doctorate, GRE General Test, undergraduate degree from accredited institution with minimum GPA of 2.5; graduate degree in psychology, social work, or counseling from accredited institution with minimum GPA of 3.25; graduate-level practicum. Additional exam requirements/recommendations for international students: Required—TOEFL (minimum score 550 paper-based; 79 iBT). *Application deadline:* For fall admission, 8/15 for domestic students. Applications are processed on a rolling basis. Application fee: $75. Electronic applications accepted. *Expenses:* $35,871 per academic year full-time tuition and fees (doctoral); $32,518 per academic year full-time tuition and fees (for master's). *Financial support:* In 2017–18, 12 students received support, including 1 research assistantship (averaging $8,566 per year), 5 teaching assistantships (averaging $14,436 per year); institutionally sponsored loans, scholarships/grants, and unspecified assistantships also available. Financial award application deadline: 8/30; financial award applicants required to submit FAFSA. *Faculty research:* Health psychology, trauma, multicultural, humanistic, applied behavior analysis. *Unit head:* Dr. Frances Brown, Program Director, 248-476-1122, Fax: 248-476-1125. *Application contact:* Carrie Hauser, Coordinator of Admissions and Student Engagement, 248-476-1122 Ext. 117, Fax: 248-476-1125, E-mail: chauser@mispp.edu.
Website: http://www.mispp.edu

Saybrook University, School of Psychology and Interdisciplinary Inquiry, San Francisco, CA 94612. Offers human science (MA, PhD), including consciousness and spirituality, humanistic and transpersonal psychology, integrative health studies, organizational systems, social transformation; organizational systems (MA, PhD), including consciousness and spirituality, humanistic and transpersonal psychology, integrative health studies, leadership of sustainable systems (MA), organizational systems, social transformation; psychology (MA, PhD), including consciousness and spirituality, creativity studies (MA), humanistic and transpersonal psychology, integrative health studies, Jungian studies, marriage and family therapy (MA), organizational systems, social transformation. *Program availability:* Online learning. Terminal master's awarded for partial completion of doctoral program. *Degree requirements:* For master's, thesis or alternative; for doctorate, thesis/dissertation. *Entrance requirements:*

Transpersonal and Humanistic Psychology

Additional exam requirements/recommendations for international students: Required—TOEFL (minimum score 580 paper-based; 93 iBT). Electronic applications accepted. *Faculty research:* Humanistic theory, health studies, organizational systems, consciousness and spirituality, social transformation.

Seattle University, College of Arts and Sciences, Department of Psychology, Seattle, WA 98122-1090. Offers existential and phenomenological therapeutic psychology (MA Psych). *Faculty:* 7 full-time (4 women), 5 part-time/adjunct (3 women). *Students:* 31 full-time (22 women), 1 (woman) part-time; includes 3 minority (all Hispanic/Latino), 1 international. Average age 32. 57 applicants, 47% accepted, 20 enrolled. In 2017, 19 master's awarded. *Degree requirements:* For master's, thesis optional. *Entrance requirements:* For master's, interview, minimum GPA of 3.0, previous undergraduate course work in psychology, experience (paid or volunteer) in counseling or human services. *Application deadline:* For fall admission, 1/15 for domestic and international students. Application fee: $55. Electronic applications accepted. *Expenses: Tuition:* Full-time $12,960. *Required fees:* $570. Tuition and fees vary according to program. *Financial support:* In 2017–18, 23 students received support. Career-related internships or fieldwork and Federal Work-Study available. Support available to part-time students. Financial award applicants required to submit FAFSA. *Faculty research:* Interpersonal relations, psychotherapy, qualitative research, trauma, philosophy and psychology. *Unit head:* Dr. Kevin Krycka, Director of Graduate Programs, 206-296-5398, Fax: 206-296-2141, E-mail: krycka@seattleu.edu. *Application contact:* Janet Shandley, Associate Dean of Graduate Admissions, 206-296-5900, Fax: 206-298-5656, E-mail: grad_admissions@seattleu.edu.
Website: http://www.seattleu.edu/artsci/departments/psychology/

Sofia University, Hybrid: Face-to-Face/Online Programs, Palo Alto, CA 94303. Offers transpersonal psychology (MA, PhD), including transpersonal psychology (PhD). *Program availability:* Online learning. *Entrance requirements:* For master's, bachelor's degree; for doctorate, bachelor's degree; master's degree. Electronic applications accepted.

Sofia University, Residential Programs, Palo Alto, CA 94303. Offers clinical psychology (Psy D); computer science (MS); counseling psychology (MA); transpersonal psychology (MA, PhD). *Program availability:* Part-time, evening/weekend. Terminal master's awarded for partial completion of doctoral program. *Degree requirements:* For doctorate, thesis/dissertation. *Entrance requirements:* For master's, bachelor's degree; for doctorate, bachelor's degree; master's degree (for some programs). Electronic applications accepted.

PHILADELPHIA COLLEGE OF OSTEOPATHIC MEDICINE

Graduate Programs in Clinical Psychology, Counseling and Clinical Health Psychology, and School Psychology

 For more information, visit http://petersons.to/philiadephiacollegepsychology

Programs of Study

The Philadelphia College of Osteopathic Medicine (PCOM) Department of Psychology offers numerous graduate programs taught by a nationally renowned, highly credentialed faculty. All faculty members in PCOM's psychology department are teaching faculty members who work closely with students to help them achieve their professional goals. Students often have the opportunity to coauthor scholarly papers, books, and professional presentations with faculty members. The Department of Psychology at PCOM offers a cognitive-behavioral theoretical orientation and teaches students to apply empirically-supported approaches in delivering clinical services. PCOM has one of the only psychology departments in the country that provides a standardized patient program for student training. The standardized patient program presents authentic clinical learning and skills situations in which "patients" simulate mental health conditions. Students conduct sessions with the patients, which are videotaped and reviewed by the faculty members to help train and assess students' skills. Students in the psychology programs may also have the opportunity for clinical experience at any of the College's urban health-care centers. In addition, the department trains leadership and change practitioners in multiple sectors including the areas of public health, not-for-profit and profit sectors. The programs have an emphasis on advocacy, diversity and inclusiveness, and serving the underserved.

The **Ph.D. in educational psychology** is approximately 35 to 40-credits. It is designed to be completed in three years, including coursework and dissertation. Graduates of this program may choose to pursue careers teaching in a higher education setting, or assume leadership roles within educational systems. The 89-credit **Psy.D. in clinical psychology program** is designed to be completed in five years, including course work, practicum, internship, and dissertation. Graduates of this program are prepared to assume responsibilities in a broad range of clinical settings. **Post-doctoral certificates in clinical health psychology and clinical neuropsychology** will each provide one year (16 and 19 credits respectively) of post-doctoral specialty training to doctoral-level psychologists. The 108-credit **Psy.D. in school psychology program** is designed to train, develop, and prepare school psychologists with a focus on applied behavior analysis, empirically supported cognitive behavioral techniques, and advanced interventions in neuropsychology. Adopting the practitioner-scholar model of training and a competency-based model of education, the program prepares graduates to provide empirically-based and ethnically-sound direct and indirect school psychological services that promote learning and well-being of all children with sensitivity to culture and diversity. The fourteen-month, 33-credit **M.S. in school psychology program** has an applied behavior analysis emphasis and prepares professionals in community and school settings to provide mental health services to children, youth, and families. This program, taken in sequence with the Ed.S. degree program, leads to certification in school psychology and also provides the required coursework to continue to accrue supervised experience towards behavior analysis certification (BCBA). The three-year, 45-credit **Ed.S. program** provides students with the knowledge and skills to assume the role of a school psychologist in diverse settings. The two-year 60-credit **M.S. in mental health counseling program** trains graduates to offer assessment, therapy, consultation, program evaluation, social justice advocacy, and follow-up services. Students in this program may complete concentrations in addictions and offender counseling or professional counseling. This curriculum fulfills the course requirements for becoming a Licensed Professional Counselor (LPC) in many states, including Pennsylvania and New Jersey. The two-year, 48-credit **M.S. in counseling and clinical health psychology** program also trains graduates to offer assessment, therapy, consultation, program evaluation, social justice advocacy, and follow-up services. This program prepares master's-level graduates to pursue further doctoral training and/or credentialing as a licensed professional counselor to work in the mental

health field. A **Certificate of Advanced Graduate Study (CAGS)** is offered for students who have already earned a master's degree and wish to complete an additional 12–18 credits at the master's level. The 36-credit **M.S. in organizational development and leadership (ODL) program** uses a unique combination of organizational theory and individual self-discovery to provide an essential leadership perspective in creating organizational change. The 36-credit **M.S. in aging and long-term care administration (ALTCA) program** is designed to address the need for leaders in critically important long-term care services, from home- and community-based care to assisted living and skilled nursing facilities. A key component of the ALTCA program is the Nursing Home Administration 120-hour program, which satisfies the educational requirement for licensure in Pennsylvania. The 36-credit **M.S. in public health management and administration program** prepares leaders in public health, advocacy and public policy who can successfully manage change in the fast-moving arena of public health organizations. The 36-credit **M.S. in nonprofit leadership and population health management** engages students in learning that focuses on leadership, administration, and the challenges and opportunities within the field of population health practice.

All on-site classes for the M.S., Ed.S., CAGS, Psy.D., and Ph.D. programs are held in the late afternoon/evening or on weekends on the Philadelphia campus, supplemented by online content. The CAGS in Applied Behavior Analysis is offered entirely online. The M.S. in public health management and administration program is offered on weekends at Public Health Management Corporations' office facilities located in the heart of Center City, Philadelphia. The M.S. in non profit leadership and population health management program is offered on Fridays and Saturdays at Woods Services in Langhorne, PA.

Research Facilities

The academic facilities at PCOM include state-of-the-art amphitheaters, classroom facilities, and standardized patient labs; a wireless campus and computer laboratories with extensive software, including PsycLIT and SPSS; a comfortable, sophisticated library with online access to electronic textbooks, journals, databases, and Internet guides; and access to the digital library and statistical programs through the Internet.

Financial Aid

The Financial Aid Office at PCOM offers financial assistance to students through the Federal Direct Loan program, institutional grants, and various alternative private loan programs.

Cost of Study

In 2018–19, the direct tuition costs of attending PCOM (including tuition, fees, books, and supplies) for the first year were approximately $27,896 for mental health counseling M.S. students, based on enrollment of 30 credits; $30,745 for school psychology M.S. students, based on enrollment of 33 credits; $7,838 for ODL M.S. students, based on enrollment of 9 credits; $21,861 for Ed.S. students, based on enrollment of 21 credits; $38,933 for Psy.D. in clinical psychology students, based on enrollment of 31 credits; and $31,858 for Psy.D. in school psychology students, based on enrollment of 32 credits.

Living and Housing Costs

Students live off-campus within the Philadelphia metropolitan and suburban areas, as there is no on-campus housing. Room and board costs vary by individual preferences.

Student Group

The programs seek a diverse group of students who are committed to excellence. The Psy.D. in clinical psychology program recruits in-practice professionals who have earned master's degrees in psychology, social work, counseling, psychiatric nursing, or a related field and are working in human services. This population brings to their studies a high level of maturity, established skills, diverse backgrounds, and a strong motivation to succeed. The Psy.D. in school psychology seeks to attract students with a BA/BS degree in psychology, behavioral sciences, education/special education, and social work. Students entering the Ed.S. program typically have completed master's degrees in psychology or education and have been working with school-aged children in some capacity. The Ph.D. in educational psychology recruits school psychologists, educators, social workers, and other master's level professionals. Candidates for the M.S. programs typically are working professionals and have bachelor's degrees in varying fields, having completed specific prerequisite courses, who want to be leaders in psychoeducational and mental health services to children, youth, and families.

The Faculty

The Department of Psychology has extraordinarily committed, experienced, and dedicated faculty members who are student-centered and have themselves been trained and mentored by some of the most foremost authorities in cognitive-behavioral therapy.

Faculty members are career teachers, devoted to mentoring students and fostering their professional and personal growth.

A full listing of PCOM Psychology Department faculty can be found at https://www.pcom.edu/academics/academic-departments/psychology/faculty-and-staff.html.

Location

Philadelphia College of Osteopathic Medicine is one of the largest of thirty-one osteopathic colleges in the United States, with campuses in both Philadelphia, suburban Atlanta, and South Georgia. Psychology programs are offered only on the Philadelphia campus, which is located in a suburban setting on City Avenue, minutes away from Fairmount Park, Philadelphia's historic district, art museums, theaters, restaurants, and professional sports complexes. PCOM's facilities include two large lecture halls, small classrooms, labs for teaching and research, a state-of-the-art library, and scenic landscaping, all in a suburban setting.

The College and the Programs

PCOM, chartered in 1899, enrolls approximately 2,800 students in its various programs across both campuses. The clinical and teaching facility in Philadelphia makes an ideal home for psychology graduate programs. The graduate psychology programs at PCOM are approved by the Department of Education of the Commonwealth of Pennsylvania and the college is accredited by the Middle States Commission on Higher Education. The Psy.D. in clinical psychology program is accredited by the American Psychological Association and fulfills the requirements of the National Register for Healthcare Providers in Psychology. Clinical Psy.D. graduates qualify to take the Examination for Professional Practice of Psychology Licensure in Pennsylvania and New Jersey. The curriculum provides Psy.D. in school psychology students with the knowledge and skills to assume the role of a school psychologist and practice in a variety of settings. The school psychology M.S. (when taken in conjunction with the Ed.S. program) and Ed.S. programs have been approved by the National Association of School Psychologists. The M.S. in School Psychology course sequence is approved by the Behavior Analyst Certification Board (BACB). The M.S. in school psychology and CAGS in applied behavioral analysis course sequences are approved by the Behavior Analyst Certification Board (BACB). The M.S. program in mental health counseling has been designed to fulfill the Licensed Professional Counselor curriculum requirements in Pennsylvania and New Jersey.

Applying

M.S. applicants to the mental health counseling and the counseling and clinical health psychology programs need to have a baccalaureate degree from a regionally accredited institution, with basic psychology course work (introduction to psychology, abnormal psychology or psychopathology, and statistics). Psy.D. in clinical psychology applicants must have completed a master's degree in psychology or a related field at a regionally accredited institution and also completed developmental psychology, theories of personality, abnormal psychology or psychopathology, and statistics. Those applying to the certificate of advanced graduate studies program must have completed a master's degree in psychology or related field. Candidates for the post-doctoral certificate programs must have completed a doctoral degree in clinical psychology at a regionally accredited institution. Applicants to the M.S. in school psychology program need to have a baccalaureate degree in psychology, education, or a related field from a regionally accredited institution and must have completed 6 credits each of English and math plus 15 credits in psychology or a related field. Applicants to the Psy.D. program in School Psychology program need to have a baccalaureate degree in psychology from a regionally accredited institution and must have completed statistics, introductory biology, developmental psychology, and an additional 15 credits in psychology. Applicants must also submit test scores from the GRE Psychology Subtest #81. Applicants to the M.S. program in school psychology or mental health counseling must have taken the GRE or MAT exam. Applicants to the ODL, ALTCA, and non-profit leadership programs must have completed a bachelor's degree from a regionally accredited institution. Applicants to the Ed.S. program must have a master's degree in school psychology or a related field and must submit test scores from the GRE Psychology Subtest #81. Ph.D. applicants must have a master's degree in psychology, counseling, education or a related field a nd must have completed statistics, abnormal psychology or psychopathology, and developmental or lifespan psychology.

All applicants to Psychology Department programs must submit official college transcripts from all schools attended and as many as three letters of recommendation using either PsyCAS or the college's online application. See pcom.edu for details. Most programs require a specified writing sample and autobiographical statement. All programs utilize a rolling admissions policy. Finalists for all programs interview with the Admissions Committee and are then notified in writing of the committee's decision.

Correspondence and Information

Office of Admissions
Philadelphia College of Osteopathic Medicine
4170 City Avenue
Philadelphia, Pennsylvania 19131-1694
Phone: 215-871-6700 or 800-999-6998 (toll-free)
Fax: 215-871-6719
E-mail: Admissions@pcom.edu
Website: http://admissions.pcom.edu
Twitter: @PCOMAdmissions

PCOM provides a collaborative learning environment for students.

UNIVERSITY OF NEW HAVEN
Community Psychology

University of
New Haven

Programs of Study

The College of Arts and Sciences at the University of New Haven offers a Master of Arts (M.A.) degree program in Community Psychology. The program, developed over four decades, offers three areas of concentration: program development, forensic psychology, and community-clinical services. These programs are designed to help mental health and human services professionals develop the knowledge and experience they need to build and run service programs, work with criminal offenders and law enforcement agencies, and help communities and individuals cope with mental health challenges.

The M.A. in Community Psychology requires students to complete 45 credits, including 24 core-curriculum credits, 12 concentration credits, and 9 elective credits. Core coursework includes: Survey of Community Psychology, Psychometrics and Statistics, Research Methods, Program Evaluation, Consultation Seminar, Consultation Fieldwork, Individual or Systems Intervention Seminar, and Individual or Systems Intervention Fieldwork.

Together, the core courses give students in the program a thorough grounding in the history and current state of community psychology theories and best practices, tools for researching and evaluating methodologies, and practical experience with consultation and intervention. Upon graduation, students will have 45 of the 60 credits needed for professional licensure as counselors. The program can generally be completed in two years or less.

Concentration in Community-Clinical Services: This concentration is recommended for students who work or plan to work in clinical, mental health, and related human-service settings. Students must complete four of the following six classes for this concentration:

- Life Span Developmental Psychology, which covers normal and abnormal development as well as the influences of factors like family, community, and education as well as age, gender, race, social class, and more.
- The Interview, which uses role-playing and other learning methods to help students improve their skills at gathering client information, diagnosing issues, and finding solutions with clients.
- Introduction to Psychotherapy and Counseling, which delves into theory, research, and best practices.
- Group Counseling, which covers the broad goals, ethics, and practices of group therapy as well as the finer points of managing group dynamics and taking diverse experiences into account.
- Family Therapy, which focuses on the skills and communication patterns that are specific to effective family therapy.
- Abnormal Psychology, which covers a range of abnormal development pathways, mental health issues, and personality disorders.

The goal is for students who complete this concentration to refine their skill at working with individuals.

Concentration in Program Development: This concentration prepares students for careers that emphasize the administration of both traditional and non-traditional programs and services and addresses planning, development, and evaluation of innovative approaches to treatment and prevention in the public and private human service sectors as well as in business and industry. The following four courses are required for this concentration:

- Organizational Behavior, which covers theories of group behavior related to its structure and processes, predicting behavior within group frameworks, fostering positive behavior, and managing conflict.
- The Interview, which helps students develop their information gathering and interpersonal relationship gathering skills.

- Public Policy Formation and Implementation, which explores the ways in which program administrators can connect with other change agents to pursue policy change.
- History and Development of Health Care Institutions, which gives students background and perspective on the current system of care.

Students also complete practical work in a community care setting or service organization.

Concentration in Forensic Psychology: This concentration includes both psychology and criminal justice department coursework and prepares students for careers in the management and care of offenders in forensic settings. The four required courses for the concentration are:

- Mental Health Law, which covers criminal and civil statues, professional responsibility and ethics, and other elements of the intersection between mental health and the legal system.
- Abnormal Psychology in Forensic Populations, which builds on previous abnormal psychology coursework to focus on behaviors that are predatory, violent, and psychopathic.
- Forensic Assessment, which covers evaluation and treatment approaches for offenders, along with risk and potential violence assessment tools.
- Forensic Treatment Models, which covers methods such as medication, therapy, life skills development, and high-risk population management.

This concentration is designed to meet the career development needs of working law enforcement, legal system, and community service professionals, as well as students who intend to work with inmate populations.

Fieldwork and Career Support

Graduate students in the community psychology program work with local organizations and community groups to practice their assessment, intervention, counseling, and related skills. They also have access to the University's top-rated Career Development Center, which offers internship location help, interview practice, and other services. Program graduates have gone on to pursue work in public defense, risk-mitigation services, shelter and supportive housing programs, and mentorship programs.

Financial Aid

The University is committed to assisting graduate students by offering a comprehensive financial aid program. The financial aid that is offered generally consists of student loans and, when applicable, grants and student employment.

A number of merit-based assistantships are available for full-time graduate students to defray the cost of tuition and provide an earned wage. These include the Provost's Assistantship, which offsets 75 percent of tuition expenses and provides 15 to 20 hours per week of research or teaching experience, and the Dean's Scholarship, which covers up to half of the recipients' tuition.

Cost of Study

Full-time graduate tuition for the 2018–19 academic year is $16,470; half-time tuition is $10,980. Books are estimated at $400–$600 and fees are $220 for full-time students, $180 for half-time students.

Living and Housing

There are two graduate student housing options sponsored by the University. The Atwood Apartments are located just across the street from the northeast end of campus and the Savin Court apartments

are located approximately 1.5 miles from campus. Other off-campus housing is also available.

The University's Office of Graduate Student Services offers many resources to assist participants in the program.

Location

The University's main campus is located on 82 acres in West Haven, Connecticut, a suburban hillside community minutes from the bustling city of New Haven and miles of Connecticut shoreline and beaches. The campus is 90 minutes from New York City and 2 1/2 hours from Boston and is also accessible by train from those cities.

Situated on 82 acres atop a hill overlooking the New Haven skyline with views of Long Island Sound, this residential campus is conveniently located a mile north of Interstate 95. The campus has experienced significant growth in the last decade with more than $220 million in construction projects completed or underway.

The University

The University of New Haven is a small private, secular school established in 1920 in West Haven, Connecticut. Today, the university has four campuses in Connecticut as well as one in Italy. It has been named one of *U.S. News & World Report*'s "Best Regional Universities–North" and one of The Princeton Review's "Best 382 Colleges" and "Best Northeastern Colleges." The Princeton Review has also named the University of New Haven to its top-20 U.S. colleges for "Best Career Services." The institution has also been recognized by multiple organizations for its service to military veteran students.

The Graduate School offers over 60 graduate degree and certificate programs to help prepare students for success in their careers and lives. The various courses of study deliver skills and experiences that will help students make the most of real-world opportunities and maximize your career potential. Graduate programs follow a semester schedule. Courses are generally in the evenings, offering flexibility for those continuing to work while pursuing their studies.

Faculty

The University of New Haven is a recognized leader in experiential education, promoting a philosophy and methodology of education in which educators purposefully engage with learners in direct experience and focused reflection in order to increase knowledge, develop skills, and clarify values.

Notable community psychology faculty at University of New Haven include program coordinator Dr. Melissa Whitson, an expert in childhood trauma who examines the risks, protective factors, and effectiveness of mental health services for low-income children and families; Dr. Amy Nicole Baker, an expert on workplace romance and dual-earner couples whose research interests also include reading motivation, teacher mentoring, and reducing criminal recidivism for probationers with mental illness; and Dr. Stuart Sidle, a national expert on leadership development, gender bias in the workplace, job stress, and workplace humor.

Applying

The Office of Graduate Admissions strives to provide a personalized admission process. Interested students are welcome to visit campus, meet with a graduate admissions counselor, go on a campus tour, meet a faculty advisor in the program, and meet with a financial aid officer.

Applicants to the Forensic Science programs must submit the following:

- Online application
- $50 nonrefundable fee
- Official university transcripts and proof of bachelor's degree completion. An explanation of the grading system that conferred the degree must be provided with the transcripts.
- Two letters of recommendation from professors or employers
- A statement of purpose is required. A resume is highly recommended.

Applications are considered on a rolling basis, but there are recommended deadlines: June 1 (domestic) and May 1 (international) for fall admission and November 15 for spring admission.

Conditional acceptance is offered in most majors to those who are academically admissible but who have not met the University's required English test scores. Students who do not submit proof of English proficiency will be recommended to enroll in the Academic Preparatory Program (APP).

Contact

University of New Haven
Office of Graduate Admissions
Maxy Hall Room 129
300 Boston Post Road
West Haven, Connecticut 06516
Phone: 800-342-5864
Fax: 203-932-7364
E-mail: SOToole@newhaven.edu
Website: https://www.newhaven.edu/arts-sciences/graduate-programs/community-psychology/

UNIVERSITY OF NEW HAVEN
Master of Arts in Industrial/Organizational Psychology

University of
New Haven

Programs of Study

The Master of Arts (M.A.) in Industrial/Organizational Psychology program at the University of New Haven is one of the best-regarded programs in the region, placing a strong emphasis on preparing students for careers in human resource management, organizational development, and management consulting.

The program enables its graduates to apply psychological principles in the workplace to benefit both employees and employers. Students learn to work with individuals and groups on organizational change and development, leadership and management development, conflict management, team dynamics, and strategic human resource management.

The program offers a flexible curriculum and schedule that accommodates graduate assistantships, internships, or full-time jobs; as well as completing the program in two or three years. Students may opt to participate in internships or complete thesis research. They may also conduct a practicum within their own workplaces.

The program provides 45 credits of coursework and can be completed in two years of full-time study or three years of part-time study.

There are three optional program concentrations: industrial-human resources psychology, organization development and consultation, or psychology of conflict management. A graduate certificate in psychology of conflict management is also available.

The M.A. in Industrial/Organizational Psychology program provides students with a strong foundational knowledge with courses that include:

- Industrial Motivation and Morale
- Worker Well-Being
- The Psychology of Communication and Influence in Organizations
- Organization Change and Development
- Psychology of Negotiation and Mediation

Fieldwork and Career Support

For more than 20 years, the MAIOP internship program has provided students with meaningful experiential learning opportunities to apply knowledge and theory learned in the classroom. Interns typically work in human resources or organizational development and may be compensated. New Haven students have offered their talents to companies like Pratt & Whitney, Translux, MetroNorth, Yale University, Dale Carnegie Training, and others. These experiences may lead to employment opportunities following graduation from the program. Program graduates have applied their skills in many fields, and some have gone on to leadership development programs in well-known corporations.

Students in the master's degree program in Industrial/Organizational Psychology have the opportunity to network and gain experience through local and national professional organizations, including the Society for Industrial and Organizational Psychology, the Southern Connecticut Chapter of the Association for Talent Development, and the Human Resource Association of Central Connecticut.

All University of New Haven students have access to the many resources available through the University's Career Development Center, which has been named one of the best in the nation by The Princeton Review.

Financial Aid

The University is committed to assisting graduate students by offering a comprehensive financial aid program. The financial aid that is offered generally consists of student loans and, when applicable, grants and student employment.

A number of merit-based assistantships are available for full-time graduate students to defray the cost of tuition and provide an earned wage. These include the Provost's Assistantship, which offsets 75 percent of tuition expenses and provides 15 to 20 hours per week of research or teaching experience, and the Dean's Scholarship, which covers up to half of the recipients' tuition.

Cost of Study

Full-time graduate tuition for the 2018–19 academic year is $16,470; half-time tuition is $10,980. Books are estimated at $400–$600 and fees are $220 for full-time students, $180 for half-time students.

Living and Housing

There are two graduate student housing options sponsored by the University. The Atwood Apartments are located just across the street from the northeast end of campus and the Savin Court apartments are located approximately 1.5 miles from campus. Other off-campus housing is also available.

The University's Office of Graduate Student Services offers many resources to assist participants in the program.

Location

The University's main campus is located on 82 acres in West Haven, Connecticut, a suburban hillside community minutes from the bustling city of New Haven and miles of Connecticut shoreline and beaches. The campus is 90 minutes from New York City and 2 1/2 hours from Boston and is also accessible by train from those cities.

Situated on 82 acres atop a hill overlooking the New Haven skyline with views of Long Island Sound, this residential campus is conveniently located a mile north of Interstate 95. The campus has experienced significant growth in the last decade with more than $220 million in construction projects completed or underway.

The University

The University of New Haven is a small private, secular school established in 1920 in West Haven, Connecticut. Today, the university has four campuses in Connecticut as well as one in Italy. It has been named one of *U.S. News & World Report*'s "Best Regional Universities–North" and one of The Princeton Review's "Best 382 Colleges" and "Best Northeastern Colleges." The Princeton Review has also named the University of New Haven to its top-20 U.S. colleges for "Best Career Services." The institution has also been recognized by multiple organizations for its service to military veteran students.

The University of New Haven offers over 60 graduate degree and certificate programs to help prepare students for success in their careers and lives. The various courses of study deliver skills and experiences that will help students make the most of real-world opportunities and maximize your career potential. Graduate programs follow a semester schedule. Courses are generally in the evenings, offering flexibility for those continuing to work while pursuing their studies.

University of New Haven

Faculty

The University of New Haven is a recognized leader in experiential education, promoting a philosophy and methodology of education in which educators purposefully engage with learners in direct experience and focused reflection in order to increase knowledge, develop skills, and clarify values.

Program Coordinator, Dr. Eric Marcus has been working as a consulting social psychologist for almost three decades, specializing in building the capacity of individuals, groups, and organizations for a wide variety of public- and private-sector client systems. Dr. Marcus also conducts workshops on group dynamics, conflict resolution, feedback, team development, and variations of these focused on particular client needs. He has published a variety of articles related to change and conflict.

Dr. Maurice Cayer has extensive industry and corporate experience improving organizational and human resource effectiveness. This includes developing, delivering, and evaluating a wide range of human resources, management, leadership and organizational development interventions, and learning experiences. Over the course of his long career, he has worked with organizations such as the American Management Association, Bayer Healthcare/Pharmaceutical, GE Capital, and JCPenney. He continues to consult to private- and public-sector organizations and researches and speaks on human resource strategies, leadership and executive development, organizational development and change, and strategic thinking.

Applying

The Office of Graduate Admissions strives to provide a personalized admission process. Interested students are welcome to visit campus, meet with a graduate admissions counselor, go on a campus tour, meet a faculty advisor in the program, and meet with a financial aid officer.

Applicants to the Forensic Science programs must submit the following:

- Online application
- $50 nonrefundable fee
- Official university transcripts and proof of bachelor's degree completion. An explanation of the grading system that conferred the degree must be provided with the transcripts.
- Two letters of recommendation from professors or employers
- A statement of purpose is required. A resume is highly recommended.

Applications are considered on a rolling basis, but there are recommended deadlines: June 1 (domestic) and May 1 (international) for fall admission and November 15 for spring admission.

Conditional acceptance is offered in most majors to those who are academically admissible but who have not met the University's required English test scores. Students who do not submit proof of English proficiency will be recommended to enroll in the Academic Preparatory Program (APP).

Contact

University of New Haven

Office of Graduate Admissions

Maxcy Hall, 129

300 Boston Post Road

West Haven, Connecticut 06516

Phone: 800-342-5864

      203-932-7364

Fax:

E-mail: SOToole@newhaven.edu

Website: https://www.newhaven.edu/arts-sciences/graduate-programs/industrial-organizational-psychology/

Section 25
Public, Regional, and Industrial Affairs

This section contains a directory of institutions offering graduate work in public, regional, and industrial affairs, followed by in-depth entries submitted by institutions that chose to prepare detailed program descriptions. Additional information about programs listed in the directory but not augmented by an in-depth entry may be obtained by writing directly to the dean of a graduate school or chair of a department at the address given in the directory.

For programs offering related work, see also in this book *Architecture, Area and Cultural Studies, Criminology and Forensics, Economics, Humanities, Political Science and International Affairs,* and *Sociology, Anthropology, and Archaeology.* In the other guides in this series:

Graduate Programs in the Biological/Biomedical Sciences & Health-Related Medical Professions
See *Public Health*

Graduate Programs in the Physical Sciences, Mathematics, Agricultural Sciences, the Environment & Natural Resources
See *Environmental Sciences and Management*

Graduate Programs in Engineering & Applied Sciences
See *Management of Engineering and Technology*

Graduate Programs in Business, Education, Information Studies, Law & Social Work
See *Business Administration and Management* and *Law*

CONTENTS

Disability Studies

Brandeis University, The Heller School for Social Policy and Management, Program in Social Policy, Waltham, MA 02454-9110. Offers assets and inequalities (PhD); children, youth and families (PhD); global health and development (PhD); health and behavioral health (PhD). *Degree requirements:* For doctorate, comprehensive exam, thesis/dissertation, qualifying paper, 2-year residency. *Entrance requirements:* For doctorate, GRE General Test, 3 letters of recommendation, statement of purpose, writing sample, at least 3-5 years of professional experience. Additional exam requirements/recommendations for international students: Required—TOEFL (minimum score 600 paper-based; 100 iBT). Electronic applications accepted. *Expenses: Tuition:* Full-time $48,720. *Required fees:* $88. Tuition and fees vary according to course load, degree level, program and student level. *Faculty research:* Health; mental health; substance abuse; children, youth, and families; aging; international and community development; disabilities; work and inequality; hunger and poverty.

Brock University, Faculty of Graduate Studies, Faculty of Social Sciences, Program in Applied Disability Studies, St. Catharines, ON L2S 3A1, Canada. Offers MA, MADS, Diploma. *Program availability:* Part-time. *Degree requirements:* For master's, thesis (for some programs). *Entrance requirements:* For master's, honors degree. Additional exam requirements/recommendations for international students: Required—TOEFL (minimum score 550 paper-based; 80 iBT), IELTS (minimum score 6.5). Electronic applications accepted.

California Baptist University, Program in Disability Studies, Riverside, CA 92503. Offers disability ministry (MA); disability policy (MA). *Program availability:* Part-time, evening/weekend, 100% online. *Faculty:* 1 full-time (0 women). In 2017, 1 master's awarded. *Degree requirements:* For master's, research thesis or capstone project. *Entrance requirements:* For master's, minimum undergraduate GPA of 2.75; transcripts of bachelor's degree; background in disability studies through coursework, degree, or experience; three recommendations; 500-word essay; interview. Additional exam requirements/recommendations for international students: Required—TOEFL (minimum score 80 iBT). *Application deadline:* For fall admission, 8/1 priority date for domestic students, 7/1 for international students; for spring admission, 12/1 priority date for domestic students, 11/1 for international students. Applications are processed on a rolling basis. Application fee: $45. Electronic applications accepted. *Expenses:* Contact institution. *Financial support:* Federal Work-Study and scholarships/grants available. Financial award applicants required to submit CSS PROFILE or FAFSA. *Faculty research:* Community integration of adults with disability, models of disability, Biblical perspectives on disability, building social competence in adolescents with Asperger's syndrome. *Unit head:* Dr. Jeff McNair, Program Director, MA in Disability Studies, 951-343-4489, E-mail: jmcnair@calbaptist.edu. *Application contact:* Gavin Andrew, Assistant Director, Graduate Admissions, 951-552-8437, E-mail: gandrew@calbaptist.edu. Website: https://www.cbuonline.edu/degrees/master-of-science-in-education-specialization-in-disability-studies

Chapman University, Donna Ford Attallah College of Educational Studies, Orange, CA 92866. Offers counseling (MA), including school counseling (MA, Credential); curriculum and instruction (MA), including elementary education, secondary education; education (PhD), including cultural and curricular studies, disability studies, leadership studies, school psychology (PhD, Credential); educational psychology (MA); leadership development (MA); multiple subjects (Credential), including Spanish/English bilingual; pupil personnel services (Credential), including school counseling (MA, Credential), school psychology (PhD, Credential); school psychology (Ed S); single subject (Credential); special education (MA, Credential), including mild/moderate (Credential), moderate/severe (Credential); teaching (MA), including elementary education, secondary education, secondary music education. *Accreditation:* TEAC. *Program availability:* Part-time, evening/weekend. *Faculty:* 32 full-time (18 women), 37 part-time/adjunct (26 women). *Students:* 170 full-time (140 women), 180 part-time (129 women); includes 164 minority (6 Black or African American, non-Hispanic/Latino; 38 Asian, non-Hispanic/Latino; 101 Hispanic/Latino; 1 Native Hawaiian or other Pacific Islander, non-Hispanic/Latino; 18 Two or more races, non-Hispanic/Latino), 10 international. Average age 28. 143 applicants, 63% accepted, 64 enrolled. In 2017, 126 master's, 18 doctorates awarded. *Application deadline:* Applications are processed on a rolling basis. Application fee: $60. Electronic applications accepted. *Expenses:* Contact institution. *Financial support:* Fellowships and scholarships/grants available. Financial award application deadline: 3/2; financial award applicants required to submit FAFSA. *Unit head:* Dr. Margaret Grogan, Dean, 714-516-5968, E-mail: grogan@chapman.edu. *Application contact:* Shannon McCance, Graduate Admission Counselor, 714-516-5236, E-mail: smccance@chapman.edu. Website: http://www.chapman.edu/CES/

Montclair State University, The Graduate School, College of Education and Human Services, Developmental Models of Autism Intervention Certificate Program, Montclair, NJ 07043-1624. Offers Certificate. *Program availability:* Part-time, evening/weekend. *Entrance requirements:* Additional exam requirements/recommendations for international students: Required—TOEFL (minimum score 83 iBT), IELTS (minimum score 6.5). Electronic applications accepted.

Montclair State University, The Graduate School, College of Education and Human Services, Program in Learning Disabilities, Montclair, NJ 07043-1624. Offers M Ed.

Program availability: Part-time, evening/weekend. *Degree requirements:* For master's, comprehensive exam, thesis or alternative. *Entrance requirements:* For master's, GRE General Test, interview, 2 letters of recommendation. Additional exam requirements/recommendations for international students: Required—TOEFL (minimum score 83 iBT), IELTS (minimum score 6.5). Electronic applications accepted.

Syracuse University, School of Education, CAS Program in Disability Studies, Syracuse, NY 13244. Offers CAS. *Program availability:* Part-time. In 2017, 8 CASs awarded. *Entrance requirements:* For degree, baccalaureate degree from regionally-accredited college/university, two letters of recommendation. Additional exam requirements/recommendations for international students: Required—TOEFL (minimum score 100 iBT). *Application deadline:* For fall admission, 2/1 priority date for domestic and international students; for summer admission, 2/1 priority date for domestic and international students. Applications are processed on a rolling basis. Application fee: $75. Electronic applications accepted. *Financial support:* Fellowships, research assistantships, teaching assistantships, career-related internships or fieldwork, and scholarships/grants available. Financial award application deadline: 1/15. *Unit head:* Dr. Alan Foley, Program Coordinator, 315-443-5087, E-mail: disabilitystudies@syr.edu. *Application contact:* Speranza Migliore, Graduate Admissions Recruiter, 315-443-2505, E-mail: gradrcrt@syr.edu. Website: http://disabilitystudies.syr.edu/academic-programs/cas/

University of Hawaii at Manoa, Office of Graduate Education, College of Education, Program in Disability and Diversity Studies, Honolulu, HI 96822. Offers Graduate Certificate. *Program availability:* Part-time. *Entrance requirements:* Additional exam requirements/recommendations for international students: Required—TOEFL (minimum score 500 paper-based; 61 iBT), IELTS (minimum score 5).

University of Illinois at Chicago, College of Applied Health Sciences, Department of Disability and Human Development, Chicago, IL 60607-7128. Offers MS, PhD. *Accreditation:* AOTA. *Program availability:* Part-time. *Degree requirements:* For master's, thesis optional; for doctorate, thesis/dissertation. *Entrance requirements:* For master's and doctorate, GRE General Test. Additional exam requirements/recommendations for international students: Required—TOEFL. Electronic applications accepted. *Faculty research:* Emerging trends in disability, demography and financial structure of disability services, aging and disability, empowerment of people with disabilities, health promotion in disabilities.

University of Manitoba, Faculty of Graduate Studies, Interdisciplinary Programs, Program in Disability Studies, Winnipeg, MB R3T 2N2, Canada. Offers M Sc, MA.

University of Northern British Columbia, Office of Graduate Studies, Prince George, BC V2N 4Z9, Canada. Offers business administration (Diploma); community health science (M Sc); disability management (MA); education (M Ed); first nations studies (MA); gender studies (MA); history (MA); interdisciplinary studies (MA); international studies (MA); mathematical, computer and physical sciences (M Sc); natural resources and environmental studies (M Sc, MA, MNRES, PhD); political science (MA); psychology (M Sc, PhD); social work (MSW). *Program availability:* Part-time, evening/weekend, online learning. *Degree requirements:* For master's, thesis; for doctorate, thesis/dissertation. *Entrance requirements:* For master's, GRE, minimum B average in undergraduate course work; for doctorate, candidacy exam, minimum A average in graduate course work.

University of Pittsburgh, School of Law, Certificate Program in Disability Legal Studies, Pittsburgh, PA 15260. Offers Certificate. *Faculty:* 47 full-time (22 women), 116 part-time/adjunct (29 women). *Entrance requirements:* For degree, official transcript, two letters of recommendation, essay. Additional exam requirements/recommendations for international students: Required—TOEFL. *Application deadline:* Applications are processed on a rolling basis. Application fee: $0. *Unit head:* Prof. Alan Meisel, Director, 412-648-7120, Fax: 412-648-2649, E-mail: dlcert@pitt.edu. *Application contact:* Beth Ann Pischke, Administrator, 412-648-7120, Fax: 412-648-2649, E-mail: dlcert@pitt.edu. Website: http://www.law.pitt.edu/academics/programs-non-lawyers/

Utah State University, School of Graduate Studies, Emma Eccles Jones College of Education and Human Services, Department of Special Education and Rehabilitation, Logan, UT 84322. Offers disability disciplines (PhD); rehabilitation counseling (MRC); special education (M Ed, MS, Ed S). *Program availability:* Part-time, online learning. *Degree requirements:* For master's, thesis (for some programs), internships (for some programs); for doctorate, comprehensive exam, thesis/dissertation. *Entrance requirements:* For master's and doctorate, GRE General Test, minimum GPA of 3.0. Additional exam requirements/recommendations for international students: Required—TOEFL (minimum score 550 paper-based). Electronic applications accepted. *Faculty research:* Applied behavior analysis, effective instructional practices, early childhood teacher training research, distance education, multicultural rehabilitation.

York University, Faculty of Graduate Studies, Faculty of Health, Program in Critical Disability Studies, Toronto, ON M3J 1P3, Canada. Offers MA, PhD. *Degree requirements:* For master's, thesis or alternative. *Entrance requirements:* Additional exam requirements/recommendations for international students: Required—TOEFL (minimum score 600 paper-based). Electronic applications accepted.

Emergency Management

Adelphi University, College of Professional and Continuing Studies, Graduate Certificate in Emergency Management Program, Garden City, NY 11530-0701. Offers Certificate. *Program availability:* Part-time, evening/weekend. *Students:* 2 full-time (0 women), 13 part-time (7 women); includes 7 minority (5 Black or African American, non-Hispanic/Latino; 2 Hispanic/Latino). Average age 38. 28 applicants, 71% accepted, 6 enrolled. In 2017, 1 Certificate awarded. *Entrance requirements:* Additional exam requirements/recommendations for international students: Required—TOEFL (minimum score 550 paper-based; 80 iBT), IELTS (minimum score 6.5). *Application deadline:* For fall admission, 5/1 for international students; for spring admission, 12/1 for international students. Applications are processed on a rolling basis. Application fee: $50. Electronic applications accepted. *Financial support:* Research assistantships, teaching assistantships, career-related internships or fieldwork, institutionally sponsored loans,

scholarships/grants, traineeships, and unspecified assistantships available. Support available to part-time students. *Faculty research:* Emergency nursing, disaster management, disaster preparedness. *Unit head:* Dr. Shawn O'Riley, Dean, 516-877-3412, E-mail: ucinfo@adelphi.edu. Website: http://academics.adelphi.edu/universitycollege/emergency-management-certificate.php

Adler University, Graduate Programs, MA in Emergency Management Leadership Program, Chicago, IL 60602. Offers MA. *Program availability:* Online learning. *Degree requirements:* For master's, capstone project.

Anna Maria College, Graduate Division, Program in Health Emergency Management, Paxton, MA 01612. Offers MS, Graduate Certificate. *Program availability:* Part-time, evening/weekend. *Degree requirements:* For master's, thesis. *Entrance requirements:*

For master's, minimum GPA of 2.7. Additional exam requirements/recommendations for international students: Required—TOEFL (minimum score 500 paper-based). Electronic applications accepted.

Arizona State University at the Tempe campus, College of Public Programs, School of Public Affairs, Phoenix, AZ 85004-0687. Offers emergency management and homeland security (MA); program evaluation (MS); public administration (MPA, PhD), including nonprofit administration (MPA), urban management (MPA); public policy (MPP); MPA/MSW. *Accreditation:* NASPAA (one or more programs are accredited). *Program availability:* Part-time, evening/weekend. Terminal master's awarded for partial completion of doctoral program. *Degree requirements:* For master's, thesis or alternative, policy analysis or capstone project; interactive Program of Study (iPOS) submitted before completing 50 percent of required credit hours; for doctorate, comprehensive exam, thesis/dissertation, interactive Program of Study (iPOS) submitted before completing 50 percent of required credit hours. *Entrance requirements:* For master's, GRE, minimum GPA of 3.0 or equivalent in last 2 years of work leading to bachelor's degree; for doctorate, GRE, minimum GPA of 3.0 or equivalent in last 2 years of work leading to bachelor's degree, 3 letters of recommendation, resume, statement of goals, samples of research reports. Additional exam requirements/recommendations for international students: Required—TOEFL (minimum score 600 paper-based; 100 iBT), IELTS (minimum score 6.5). Electronic applications accepted. *Expenses:* Contact institution.

Arkansas State University, Graduate School, College of Nursing and Health Professions, Disaster Preparedness Program, State University, AR 72467. Offers disaster preparedness and emergency management (MS); healthcare emergency management (Graduate Certificate). *Program availability:* Part-time. *Degree requirements:* For master's and Graduate Certificate, comprehensive exam, thesis or alternative. *Entrance requirements:* For master's, GRE General Test or MAT, appropriate bachelor's degree, TB skin test, TB mask fit test, CPR certification, liability insurance; for Graduate Certificate, bachelor's degree, TB skin test, TB mask fit test, CPR certification, liability insurance. Additional exam requirements/recommendations for international students: Required—TOEFL (minimum score 550 paper-based; 79 iBT), IELTS (minimum score 6), PTE (minimum score 56). Electronic applications accepted. *Expenses:* Contact institution.

Arkansas Tech University, College of Engineering and Applied Sciences, Russellville, AR 72801. Offers electrical engineering (M Engr); emergency management (MS); information technology (MS); mechanical engineering (M Engr). *Program availability:* Part-time, evening/weekend, 100% online, blended/hybrid learning. *Students:* 45 full-time (8 women), 68 part-time (18 women); includes 22 minority (9 Black or African American, non-Hispanic/Latino; 3 American Indian or Alaska Native, non-Hispanic/Latino; 4 Asian, non-Hispanic/Latino; 3 Hispanic/Latino; 3 Two or more races, non-Hispanic/Latino), 36 international. Average age 32. In 2017, 36 master's awarded. *Degree requirements:* For master's, comprehensive exam (for some programs), thesis (for some programs). *Entrance requirements:* Additional exam requirements/recommendations for international students: Required—TOEFL (minimum score 550 paper-based; 79 iBT), IELTS (minimum score 6.5), PTE (minimum score 58). *Application deadline:* For fall admission, 3/1 priority date for domestic students, 5/1 priority date for international students; for spring admission, 10/1 priority date for domestic and international students. Applications are processed on a rolling basis. Application fee: $40 ($90 for international students). Electronic applications accepted. *Expenses:* Tuition, state resident: full-time $6816; part-time $284 per credit hour. Tuition, nonresident: full-time $13,632; part-time $568 per credit hour. *Required fees:* $420 per semester. Tuition and fees vary according to course load. *Financial support:* In 2017–18, research assistantships with full and partial tuition reimbursements (averaging $4,800 per year), teaching assistantships with full and partial tuition reimbursements (averaging $4,800 per year) were awarded; career-related internships or fieldwork, Federal Work-Study, scholarships/grants, health care benefits, and unspecified assistantships also available. Support available to part-time students. Financial award application deadline: 4/15; financial award applicants required to submit FAFSA. *Unit head:* Dr. Douglas Barlow, Dean, 479-968-0353, E-mail: dbarlow@atu.edu. *Application contact:* Dr. Mary B. Gunter, Dean of Graduate College, 479-968-0398, Fax: 479-964-0542, E-mail: gradcollege@atu.edu.
Website: http://www.atu.edu/appliedsci/

Auburn University at Montgomery, College of Public Policy and Justice, Department of Justice and Public Safety, Montgomery, AL 36124-4023. Offers criminal studies (MSJPS); homeland security (MSJPS); homeland security and emergency management (MS); legal studies (MSJPS); organizational leadership (MSJPS). *Program availability:* Part-time, evening/weekend. *Faculty:* 5 full-time (2 women). *Students:* 9 full-time (3 women), 33 part-time (20 women); includes 23 minority (22 Black or African American, non-Hispanic/Latino; 1 Asian, non-Hispanic/Latino). Average age 30. 24 applicants, 75% accepted, 9 enrolled. In 2017, 23 master's awarded. *Degree requirements:* For master's, comprehensive exam, thesis optional. *Entrance requirements:* For master's, GRE General Test or MAT. Additional exam requirements/recommendations for international students: Recommended—TOEFL (minimum score 500 paper-based; 61 iBT), IELTS (minimum score 5.5), TSE (minimum score 44). *Application deadline:* For fall admission, 7/15 for international students; for spring admission, 11/15 for international students; for summer admission, 4/15 for international students. Applications are processed on a rolling basis. Application fee: $25. Electronic applications accepted. *Expenses:* Tuition, state resident: full-time $6930; part-time $385 per credit hour. Tuition, nonresident: full-time $15,588; part-time $866 per credit hour. *Required fees:* $640. *Financial support:* Career-related internships or fieldwork and scholarships/grants available. Support available to part-time students. Financial award application deadline: 3/1; financial award applicants required to submit FAFSA. *Faculty research:* Law enforcement, corrections, juvenile justice. *Unit head:* Dr. Ralph Ioimo, Head, 334-244-3691, Fax: 334-244-3244, E-mail: rioimo@aum.edu.
Website: http://cppj.aum.edu/departments/justice-and-public-safety

Ball State University, Graduate School, College of Sciences and Humanities, Department of Natural Resources and Environmental Management, Muncie, IN 47306. Offers emergency management and homeland security (Certificate); natural resources and environmental management (MA, MS). *Program availability:* Part-time. *Faculty:* 5 full-time (2 women). *Students:* 4 full-time (2 women), 9 part-time (5 women); includes 1 minority (Two or more races, non-Hispanic/Latino). Average age 28. 12 applicants, 67% accepted, 4 enrolled. In 2017, 4 master's, 3 other advanced degrees awarded. *Degree requirements:* For master's, thesis (for some programs). *Entrance requirements:* For master's, GRE General Test, minimum baccalaureate GPA of 2.75 or 3.0 in latter half of baccalaureate, two letters of reference. Additional exam requirements/recommendations for international students: Required—TOEFL (minimum score 550 paper-based; 79 iBT), IELTS (minimum score 6.5). *Application deadline:* For fall admission, 3/1 priority date for domestic students. Applications are processed on a rolling basis. Application fee: $60. Electronic applications accepted. *Financial support:* In 2017–18, 8 students received support, including 2 research assistantships with partial tuition reimbursements available (averaging $12,250 per year), 6 teaching assistantships with partial tuition reimbursements available (averaging $9,907 per year); unspecified assistantships also available. Financial award application deadline: 3/1; financial award applicants required to submit FAFSA. *Faculty research:* Acid rain, indoor air pollution, land reclamation. *Unit head:* Dr. Amy Gregg, Chairperson, 765-285-5781, Fax: 765-285-2606, E-mail: algregg2@bsu.edu.
Website: http://www.bsu.edu/nrem/

Ball State University, Graduate School, College of Sciences and Humanities, Department of Political Science, Program in Public Administration, Muncie, IN 47306. Offers public administration (MPA, Certificate), including community and economic development (MPA), criminal justice (MPA), emergency management and homeland security (MPA), information and communication technology (MPA). *Program availability:* Part-time. *Students:* 20 full-time (7 women), 14 part-time (8 women); includes 4 minority (2 Black or African American, non-Hispanic/Latino; 2 Hispanic/Latino), 1 international. Average age 29. 28 applicants, 89% accepted, 15 enrolled. In 2017, 10 master's awarded. *Degree requirements:* For master's, comprehensive exam. *Entrance requirements:* For master's, GRE General Test, minimum baccalaureate GPA of 2.8, two letters of recommendation. Additional exam requirements/recommendations for international students: Required—TOEFL (minimum score 550 paper-based; 79 iBT), IELTS (minimum score 6.5). *Application deadline:* Applications are processed on a rolling basis. Application fee: $60. Electronic applications accepted. *Financial support:* Research assistantships with partial tuition reimbursements and unspecified assistantships available. Financial award application deadline: 3/1; financial award applicants required to submit FAFSA. *Faculty research:* Employment training programs, personnel and labor relations, planning. *Unit head:* Dr. Daniel Reagan, Chairperson, 765-285-8789, Fax: 765-285-5345, E-mail: jlosco@bsu.edu. *Application contact:* Dr. Charles Taylor, Associate Professor/Graduate Advisor, 765-285-8794, Fax: 765-285-5345, E-mail: cdtaylor@bsu.edu.
Website: http://www.bsu.edu/poli-sci

Benedictine University, Graduate Programs, Program in Public Health, Lisle, IL 60532. Offers administration of health care institutions (MPH); dietetics (MPH); disaster management (MPH); health education (MPH); health information systems (MPH); MBA/MPH; MPH/MS. *Accreditation:* CEPH. *Program availability:* Part-time, evening/weekend, online learning. *Entrance requirements:* For master's, MAT, GRE, or GMAT. Additional exam requirements/recommendations for international students: Required—TOEFL (minimum score 550 paper-based).

Boston University, School of Medicine, Division of Graduate Medical Sciences, Program in Healthcare Emergency Management, Boston, MA 02215. Offers MS. *Financial support:* Applicants required to submit FAFSA. *Unit head:* Dr. Kevin Thomas, Director, 617-414-2316, Fax: 617-414-2332, E-mail: kipthoma@bu.edu. *Application contact:* GMS Admissions Office, 617-638-5255, E-mail: askgms@bu.edu.
Website: http://www.bumc.bu.edu/bmcm/

California State University, Long Beach, Graduate Studies, College of Health and Human Services, Department of Criminal Justice, Long Beach, CA 90840. Offers criminal justice (MS); emergency services administration (MS). *Program availability:* Part-time. *Degree requirements:* For master's, comprehensive course or thesis. *Entrance requirements:* For master's, minimum GPA of 3.0. Electronic applications accepted.

California State University Maritime Academy, Graduate Studies, Vallejo, CA 94590. Offers transportation and engineering management (MS), including engineering management, humanitarian disaster management, transportation. *Program availability:* Evening/weekend, online only, 100% online. *Faculty:* 16 part-time/adjunct (2 women). *Students:* 41 full-time (7 women); includes 10 minority (2 Black or African American, non-Hispanic/Latino; 5 Asian, non-Hispanic/Latino; 2 Hispanic/Latino; 1 Native Hawaiian or other Pacific Islander, non-Hispanic/Latino), 2 international. Average age 33. 32 applicants, 84% accepted, 22 enrolled. In 2017, 16 master's awarded. *Degree requirements:* For master's, comprehensive exam (for some programs), thesis, minimum GPA of 3.0 in 10 required courses including capstone course and project. *Entrance requirements:* For master's, GMAT/GRE (for applicants with fewer than five years of post-baccalaureate professional experience), equivalent of four-year U.S. bachelor's degree with minimum GPA of 2.5 during last two years (60 semester units or 90 quarter units) of coursework in degree program. Additional exam requirements/recommendations for international students: Required—TOEFL (minimum score 550 paper-based). *Application deadline:* Applications are processed on a rolling basis. Application fee: $55. Electronic applications accepted. *Expenses:* $900 per credit. *Financial support:* Applicants required to submit FAFSA. *Unit head:* Dr. Graham Benton, Associate Vice President, Academic Affairs, 707-654-1147. *Application contact:* Kathy Arnold, Program Coordinator, 707-654-1271, Fax: 707-654-1158, E-mail: karnold@csum.edu.
Website: http://www.csum.edu/web/industry/graduate-studies

Capella University, School of Public Service Leadership, Doctoral Programs in Healthcare, Minneapolis, MN 55402. Offers criminal justice (PhD); emergency management (PhD); epidemiology (Dr PH); general health administration (DHA); general public administration (DPA); health advocacy and leadership (Dr PH); health care administration (PhD); health care leadership (DHA); health policy advocacy (DHA); multidisciplinary human services (PhD); nonprofit management and leadership (PhD); public safety leadership (PhD); social and community services (PhD).

Capella University, School of Public Service Leadership, Master's Programs in Healthcare, Minneapolis, MN 55402. Offers criminal justice (MS); emergency management (MS); general public health (MPH); gerontology (MS); health administration (MHA); health care operations (MHA); health management policy (MPH); health policy (MHA); homeland security (MS); multidisciplinary human services (MS); public administration (MPA); public safety leadership (MS); social and community services (MS); social behavioral sciences (MPH); MS/MPA.

Columbia Southern University, College of Safety and Emergency Services, Orange Beach, AL 36561. Offers criminal justice administration (MS); emergency services management (MS); occupational safety and health (MS), including environmental management. *Program availability:* Part-time, evening/weekend, online learning. *Entrance requirements:* For master's, bachelor's degree from accredited/approved institution. Additional exam requirements/recommendations for international students: Required—TOEFL. Electronic applications accepted.

Drexel University, College of Nursing and Health Professions, Emergency and Public Safety Services Program, Philadelphia, PA 19104-2875. Offers MS. *Program availability:* Part-time, evening/weekend. *Degree requirements:* For master's, comprehensive exam. *Entrance requirements:* For master's, GRE General Test, minimum GPA of 2.75.

Endicott College, Van Loan School of Graduate and Professional Studies, Program in Homeland Security, Beverly, MA 01915-2096. Offers cybersecurity (MS, Postbaccalaureate Certificate); emergency management (MS). *Program availability:* Part-time. *Faculty:* 2 full-time (1 woman), 5 part-time/adjunct (2 women). *Students:* 21 full-time (8 women), 1 part-time (0 women); includes 5 minority (1 Black or African American, non-Hispanic/Latino; 2 Hispanic/Latino; 2 Native Hawaiian or other Pacific Islander, non-Hispanic/Latino). Average age 28. 18 applicants, 100% accepted, 16 enrolled. In 2017, 16 master's awarded. *Degree requirements:* For master's, thesis. *Entrance requirements:* For master's, undergraduate transcript, two recommendations,

personal statement. Additional exam requirements/recommendations for international students: Required—TOEFL. *Application deadline:* Applications are processed on a rolling basis. Application fee: $50. Electronic applications accepted. *Expenses:* Contact institution. *Financial support:* In 2017–18, 2 students received support. Applicants required to submit FAFSA. *Unit head:* Paul Joyce, Director, 978-232-2740, Fax: 978-232-3000, E-mail: pjoyce@endicott.edu. *Application contact:* Ian Menchini, Director, Graduate Enrollment and Advising, 978-232-5292, Fax: 978-232-3000, E-mail: imenchin@endicott.edu.
Website: https://vanloan.endicott.edu/programs-of-study/masters-programs/homeland-security-studies-program

Excelsior College, School of Public Service, Albany, NY 12203-5159. Offers criminal justice (MSCI); homeland security and emergency management (MSCJ); justice administration (MSCI); mediation and arbitration (MPA); public administration (MPA). *Program availability:* Part-time, evening/weekend, online learning. *Faculty:* 6 part-time/adjunct (5 women). *Students:* 173 part-time (49 women); includes 70 minority (32 Black or African American, non-Hispanic/Latino; 1 American Indian or Alaska Native, non-Hispanic/Latino; 3 Asian, non-Hispanic/Latino; 28 Hispanic/Latino; 1 Native Hawaiian or other Pacific Islander, non-Hispanic/Latino; 5 Two or more races, non-Hispanic/Latino). Average age 40. In 2017, 45 master's awarded. *Application deadline:* Applications are processed on a rolling basis. Application fee: $50. Electronic applications accepted. *Expenses: Tuition:* Part-time $645 per credit. *Required fees:* $265 per credit. *Financial support:* Scholarships/grants available. *Unit head:* Dr. Robert Waters, Dean, School of Public Service, 518-464-8500, Fax: 518-464-8777. *Application contact:* Admissions Counselor, 888-647-2388, Fax: 518-464-8777, E-mail: gradadmissions@excelsior.edu.
Website: http://www.excelsior.edu/programs/public-service

Florida Institute of Technology, Extended Studies Division, Melbourne, FL 32901-6975. Offers acquisition and contract management (MS); aerospace engineering (MS); business administration (MBA, DBA); computer information systems (MS); computer science (MS); electrical engineering (MS); engineering management (MS); human resources management (MS); logistics management (MS), including humanitarian and disaster relief logistics; management (MS), including acquisition and contract management, e-business, human resources management, information systems, logistics management, management, transportation management; material acquisition management (MS); mechanical engineering (MS); operations research (MS); project management (MS), including information systems, operations research; public administration (MPA); quality management (MS); software engineering (MS); space systems (MS); space systems management (MS); supply chain management (MS); systems management (MS), including information systems, operations research; technology management (MS). *Program availability:* Part-time, evening/weekend, online learning. *Students:* Average age 36. 962 applicants, 48% accepted, 323 enrolled. In 2017, 403 master's awarded. *Entrance requirements:* For master's, GMAT or resume showing 8 years of supervised experience, minimum GPA of 3.0, 2 letters of recommendation, resume. Additional exam requirements/recommendations for international students: Required—TOEFL (minimum score 550 paper-based; 79 iBT). *Application deadline:* For fall admission, 4/1 for international students; for spring admission, 9/30 for international students. Applications are processed on a rolling basis. Electronic applications accepted. *Expenses:* Contact institution. *Financial support:* Application deadline: 3/1; applicants required to submit FAFSA. *Unit head:* Dr. Theodore R. Richardson, III, Dean, 321-674-8123, Fax: 321-674-7597, E-mail: trichardson@fit.edu. *Application contact:* Carolyn Farrior, Director of Graduate Admissions, Online Learning and Off-Campus Programs, 321-674-7118, Fax: 321-674-8216, E-mail: cfarrior@fit.edu.
Website: http://es.fit.edu

Florida International University, Steven J. Green School of International and Public Affairs, Department of Emergency Management, Miami, FL 33199. Offers disaster management (MA). *Accreditation:* AACSB. *Program availability:* Part-time, evening/weekend. *Students:* 40 full-time (17 women), 1 part-time (0 women); includes 34 minority (9 Black or African American, non-Hispanic/Latino; 24 Hispanic/Latino; 1 Two or more races, non-Hispanic/Latino), 1 international. Average age 35. 99 applicants, 55% accepted, 40 enrolled. In 2017, 39 master's awarded. *Entrance requirements:* For master's, minimum GPA of 3.0 in upper-level coursework; resume. *Application deadline:* For fall admission, 6/1 for domestic and international students; for spring admission, 10/1 for domestic students, 9/1 for international students. Applications are processed on a rolling basis. Application fee: $30. Electronic applications accepted. *Expenses:* Tuition, state resident: full-time $8912; part-time $446 per credit hour. Tuition, nonresident: full-time $21,393; part-time $992 per credit hour. *Required fees:* $390; $195 per semester. *Financial support:* Institutionally sponsored loans and scholarships/grants available. Financial award application deadline: 3/1; financial award applicants required to submit FAFSA. *Faculty research:* Emergency management, crisis intervention, disaster preparedness. *Unit head:* Ruben D. Almaguer, Director, 305-348-4779, E-mail: ruben.almaguer@fiu.edu. *Application contact:* Nanett Rojas, Manager, Admissions Operations, 305-348-7464, Fax: 305-348-7441, E-mail: nanett.rojas@fiu.edu.

Fordham University, Graduate School of Arts and Sciences, Program in International Humanitarian Action, New York, NY 10458. Offers MA. Program offered in collaboration with the Institute for International Humanitarian Affairs (IIHA). *Students:* 1 (woman) full-time, 5 part-time (3 women); includes 1 minority (Black or African American, non-Hispanic/Latino), 1 international. Average age 37. 18 applicants, 22% accepted, 1 enrolled. In 2017, 4 master's awarded. *Entrance requirements:* For master's, official transcripts, 3 letters of recommendation, resume, statement of interest. Application fee: $70. Electronic applications accepted. *Unit head:* Dr. Brendan Cahill, Executive Director, 212-636-6294, Fax: 212-636-7060, E-mail: iiha@fordham.edu. *Application contact:* Bernadette Valentino-Morrison, Director of Graduate Admissions, 718-817-4419, Fax: 718-817-3566, E-mail: valentinomor@fordham.edu.
Website: http://www.fordham.edu/academics/programs_at_fordham_/international_humani/index.asp

Georgetown University, Graduate School of Arts and Sciences, School of Continuing Studies, Washington, DC 20057. Offers American studies (MALS); applied intelligence (MPS); Catholic studies (MALS); classical civilizations (MALS); emergency and disaster management (MPS); ethics and the professions (MALS); global strategic communications (MPS); hospitality management (MPS); human resources management (MPS); humanities (MALS); individualized study (MALS); integrated marketing communications (MPS); international affairs (MALS); Islam and Muslim-Christian relations (MALS); journalism (MPS); liberal studies (DLS); literature and society (MALS); medieval and early modern European studies (MALS); public relations and corporate communications (MPS); real estate (MPS); religious studies (MALS); social and public policy (MALS); sports industry management (MPS); systems engineering management (MPS); technology management (MPS); the theory and practice of American democracy (MALS); urban and regional planning (MPS); visual culture (MALS). MPS in systems engineering management offered jointly with Stevens Institute of Technology. *Entrance requirements:* Additional exam requirements/recommendations for international students: Required—TOEFL.

The George Washington University, School of Medicine and Health Sciences, Health Sciences Programs, Washington, DC 20052. Offers clinical practice management (MSHS); clinical research administration (MSHS); emergency services management (MSHS); end-of-life care (MSHS); immunohematology (MSHS); immunohematology and biotechnology (MSHS); physical therapy (DPT); physician assistant (MSHS). *Program availability:* Online learning. *Faculty:* 31 full-time (23 women), 4 part-time/adjunct (2 women). *Students:* 304 full-time (233 women), 321 part-time (248 women); includes 212 minority (70 Black or African American, non-Hispanic/Latino; 1 American Indian or Alaska Native, non-Hispanic/Latino; 64 Asian, non-Hispanic/Latino; 59 Hispanic/Latino; 3 Native Hawaiian or other Pacific Islander, non-Hispanic/Latino; 15 Two or more races, non-Hispanic/Latino), 18 international. Average age 33. 2,366 applicants, 19% accepted, 246 enrolled. In 2017, 159 master's, 49 doctorates, 2 other advanced degrees awarded. *Entrance requirements:* Additional exam requirements/recommendations for international students: Required—TOEFL (minimum score 550 paper-based). *Application deadline:* Applications are processed on a rolling basis. Application fee: $75. *Expenses:* Contact institution. *Unit head:* Jean E. Johnson, Senior Associate Dean, 202-994-3725, E-mail: jejohns@gwu.edu. *Application contact:* Joke Ogundiran, Director of Admission, 202-994-1668, Fax: 202-994-0870, E-mail: jokeogun@gwu.edu.

Georgia State University, Andrew Young School of Policy Studies, Department of Public Management and Policy, Atlanta, GA 30303. Offers criminal justice (MPA); disaster management (Certificate); disaster policy (MPA); environmental policy (PhD); health policy (PhD); management and finance (MPA); nonprofit management (MPA, Certificate); nonprofit policy (MPA); planning and economic development (MPP, Certificate); policy analysis and evaluation (MPA), including planning and economic development; public and nonprofit management (PhD); public finance and budgeting (PhD), including science and technology policy, urban and regional economic development; public finance policy (MPA), including social policy; public health (MPA). *Accreditation:* NASPAA (one or more programs are accredited). *Program availability:* Part-time. *Faculty:* 17 full-time (9 women). *Students:* 125 full-time (75 women), 78 part-time (51 women); includes 90 minority (67 Black or African American, non-Hispanic/Latino; 5 Asian, non-Hispanic/Latino; 9 Hispanic/Latino; 9 Two or more races, non-Hispanic/Latino), 34 international. Average age 30. 275 applicants, 62% accepted, 88 enrolled. In 2017, 71 master's, 5 doctorates, 12 other advanced degrees awarded. Terminal master's awarded for partial completion of doctoral program. *Degree requirements:* For master's, thesis optional; for doctorate, comprehensive exam, thesis/dissertation. *Entrance requirements:* For master's and doctorate, GRE. Additional exam requirements/recommendations for international students: Required—TOEFL (minimum score 603 paper-based; 100 iBT) or IELTS (minimum score 7). *Application deadline:* For fall admission, 1/15 for domestic and international students. Application fee: $50. Electronic applications accepted. *Expenses:* Tuition, state resident: full-time $7020. Tuition, nonresident: full-time $22,518. *Required fees:* $2128. Tuition and fees vary according to degree level and program. *Financial support:* In 2017–18, fellowships (averaging $8,194 per year), research assistantships (averaging $8,068 per year), teaching assistantships (averaging $3,600 per year) were awarded; institutionally sponsored loans, scholarships/grants, health care benefits, and unspecified assistantships also available. Financial award application deadline: 2/1. *Faculty research:* Public budgeting and finance, public management, nonprofit management, performance measurement and management, urban development. *Unit head:* Dr. Carolyn Bourdeaux, Chair and Professor, 404-413-0013, Fax: 404-413-0104, E-mail: cbourdeaux@gsu.edu.
Website: http://aysps.gsu.edu/pmap/

Grand Canyon University, Colangelo College of Business, Phoenix, AZ 85017-1097. Offers accounting (MBA, MS); business analytics (MS); disaster preparedness and executive fire service leadership (MS); finance (MBA); general management (MBA); health systems management (MBA); information technology management (MS); leadership (MBA, MS); marketing (MBA); organizational leadership and entrepreneurship (MS); project management (MBA); sports business (MBA); strategic human resource management (MBA). *Accreditation:* ACBSP. *Program availability:* Part-time, evening/weekend, online learning. *Entrance requirements:* For master's, equivalent of two years' full-time professional work experience. Additional exam requirements/recommendations for international students: Required—TOEFL (minimum score 575 paper-based; 90 iBT), IELTS (minimum score 7). Electronic applications accepted.

Indiana University–Purdue University Indianapolis, School of Public and Environmental Affairs, Indianapolis, IN 46202. Offers criminal justice and public safety (MS); homeland security and emergency management (Graduate Certificate); library management (Graduate Certificate); nonprofit management (Graduate Certificate); public affairs (MPA); public management (Graduate Certificate); social entrepreneurship: nonprofit and public benefit organizations (Graduate Certificate); JD/MPA; MLS/NMC; MLS/PMC; MPA/MA. *Accreditation:* CAHME (one or more programs are accredited); NASPAA. *Program availability:* Part-time, evening/weekend, online learning. *Entrance requirements:* For master's, GRE General Test, GMAT or LSAT, minimum GPA of 3.0 (preferred). Additional exam requirements/recommendations for international students: Required—TOEFL (minimum score 93 iBT), IELTS (minimum score 6.5). Electronic applications accepted. *Faculty research:* Nonprofit and public management, public policy, urban policy, sustainability policy, disaster preparedness and recovery, vehicular safety, homicide, offender rehabilitation and re-entry.

Jacksonville State University, College of Graduate Studies and Continuing Education, College of Arts and Sciences, Program in Emergency Management, Jacksonville, AL 36265-1602. Offers MS, D Sc. *Program availability:* Part-time, evening/weekend. *Degree requirements:* For master's, comprehensive exam, thesis (for some programs); for doctorate, comprehensive exam, thesis/dissertation. *Entrance requirements:* Additional exam requirements/recommendations for international students: Required—TOEFL (minimum score 500 paper-based; 61 iBT). Electronic applications accepted.

Lander University, Graduate Studies, Greenwood, SC 29649-2099. Offers clinical nurse leader (MSN); emergency management (MS); Montessori education (M Ed); teaching and learning (M Ed). *Accreditation:* NCATE. *Program availability:* Part-time, online learning. *Degree requirements:* For master's, comprehensive exam, thesis or alternative. *Entrance requirements:* For master's, GRE General Test. Additional exam requirements/recommendations for international students: Required—TOEFL (minimum score 550 paper-based). Electronic applications accepted.

Lasell College, Graduate and Professional Studies in Criminal Justice, Newton, MA 02466-2709. Offers emergency and crisis management (MS, Certificate); homeland security and global justice (MS, Certificate); violence prevention and advocacy (MS, Certificate). *Program availability:* Part-time, evening/weekend, online only, 100% online. *Faculty:* 2 full-time (1 woman), 2 part-time/adjunct (0 women). *Students:* 20 full-time (9 women), 31 part-time (16 women); includes 11 minority (3 Black or African American, non-Hispanic/Latino; 1 Asian, non-Hispanic/Latino; 5 Hispanic/Latino; 2 Two or more races, non-Hispanic/Latino). Average age 31. 33 applicants, 73% accepted, 23 enrolled. In 2017, 2 master's awarded. *Degree requirements:* For master's, minimum GPA of 3.0; internship or research paper. *Entrance requirements:* For master's, one-page personal statement, 2 letters of recommendation, resume, bachelor's degree transcript; for Certificate, bachelor's transcript, 2 letters of recommendation, 1-page statement, resume. Additional exam requirements/recommendations for international students: Required—TOEFL (minimum score 550 paper-based, 79 iBT) or IELTS (minimum score

6). *Application deadline:* For fall admission, 8/31 priority date for domestic students, 6/30 priority date for international students; for spring admission, 12/31 priority date for domestic students, 10/31 priority date for international students. Applications are processed on a rolling basis. Electronic applications accepted. *Expenses:* $600 per credit. *Financial support:* Federal Work-Study, scholarships/grants, and tuition discounts available. Support available to part-time students. Financial award application deadline: 8/31; financial award applicants required to submit FAFSA. *Faculty research:* Children aging out of foster care and the criminal justice system; police departments' attitudes toward the mentally ill and jail diversion programs for those offenders. *Unit head:* Eric Turner, Vice President of Graduate and Professional Studies, 617-243-2071, Fax: 617-243-2450, E-mail: gradinfo@lasell.edu. *Application contact:* Adrienne Franciosi, Director of Graduate Enrollment, 617-243-2214, Fax: 617-243-2450, E-mail: gradinfo@lasell.edu.
Website: http://www.lasell.edu/academics/graduate-and-professional-studies/programs-of-study/master-of-science-in-criminal-justice-.html

Liberty University, School of Behavioral Sciences, Lynchburg, VA 24515. Offers applied psychology (MA), including developmental psychology (MA, MS), industrial/organizational psychology (MA, MS); clinical mental health counseling (MA); community care and counseling (Ed D), including marriage and family counseling, pastoral care and counseling, traumatology; counselor education and supervision (PhD); human services counseling (MA), including addictions and recovery, business, child and family law, Christian ministries, criminal justice, crisis response and trauma, executive leadership, health and wellness, life coaching, marriage and family, military resilience; marriage and family counseling (MA); marriage and family therapy (MA); military resilience (Certificate); pastoral counseling (MA), including addictions and recovery, community chaplaincy, crisis response and trauma, discipleship and church ministry, leadership, life coaching, marriage and family, marriage and family studies, military resilience, parenting and child/adolescent, pastoral counseling, theology; professional counseling (MA); psychology (MS), including developmental psychology (MA, MS), industrial/organizational psychology (MA, MS); school counseling (M Ed). *Program availability:* Part-time, online learning. *Students:* 2,649 full-time (2,085 women), 5,086 part-time (4,015 women); includes 2,275 minority (1,784 Black or African American, non-Hispanic/Latino; 44 American Indian or Alaska Native, non-Hispanic/Latino; 67 Asian, non-Hispanic/Latino; 200 Hispanic/Latino; 11 Native Hawaiian or other Pacific Islander, non-Hispanic/Latino; 169 Two or more races, non-Hispanic/Latino), 145 international. Average age 39. 5,839 applicants, 51% accepted, 1710 enrolled. In 2017, 1,626 master's, 7 doctorates, 61 other advanced degrees awarded. *Application deadline:* Applications are processed on a rolling basis. Application fee: $50. Electronic applications accepted. *Financial support:* Applicants required to submit FAFSA. *Unit head:* Dr. Ronald Hawkins, Founding Dean, School of Behavioral Sciences. *Application contact:* Jay Bridge, Director of Admissions, 800-424-9595, Fax: 800-628-7977, E-mail: gradadmissions@liberty.edu.

London Metropolitan University, Graduate Programs, London, United Kingdom. Offers applied psychology (M Sc); architecture (MA); biomedical science (M Sc); blood science (M Sc); cancer pharmacology (M Sc); computer networking and cyber security (M Sc); computing and information systems (M Sc); conference interpreting (MA); counter-terrorism studies (M Sc); creative, digital and professional writing (MA); crime, violence and prevention (M Sc); criminology (M Sc); curating contemporary art (MA); data analytics (M Sc); digital media (MA); early childhood studies (MA); education (MA, Ed D); financial services law, regulation and compliance (LL M); food science (M Sc); forensic psychology (M Sc); health and social care management and policy (M Sc); human nutrition (M Sc); human resource management (MA); human rights and international conflict (MA); information technology (M Sc); intelligence and security studies (M Sc); international oil, gas and energy law (LL M); international relations (MA); interpreting (MA); learning and teaching in higher education (MA); legal practice (LL M); media and entertainment law (LL M); organizational and consumer psychology (M Sc); psychological therapy (M Sc); psychology of mental health (M Sc); public health (M Sc); public policy and management (MPA); security studies (M Sc); social work (M Sc); spatial planning and urban design (MA); sports therapy (M Sc); supporting older children and young people with dyslexia (MA); teaching languages (MA), including Arabic, English; translation (MA); woman and child abuse (MA).

Massachusetts Maritime Academy, Program in Emergency Management, Buzzards Bay, MA 02532-1803. Offers MS. *Program availability:* Part-time-only, evening/weekend. Electronic applications accepted.

Metropolitan College of New York, Program in Public Administration, New York, NY 10013. Offers emergency and disaster management (MPA); public affairs and administration (MPA). *Program availability:* Evening/weekend. *Students:* 102 full-time (70 women), 10 part-time (9 women); includes 99 minority (71 Black or African American, non-Hispanic/Latino; 1 Asian, non-Hispanic/Latino; 25 Hispanic/Latino; 2 Two or more races, non-Hispanic/Latino), 3 international. Average age 39. 122 applicants, 45% accepted, 52 enrolled. In 2017, 129 master's awarded. *Degree requirements:* For master's, thesis. *Entrance requirements:* For master's, appropriate work experience, interview, minimum GPA of 2.7, internship or job in administrative setting. Additional exam requirements/recommendations for international students: Required—TOEFL (minimum score 600 paper-based). *Application deadline:* For fall admission, 7/30 priority date for domestic students, 7/1 for international students; for winter admission, 11/30 priority date for domestic students, 11/1 for international students; for spring admission, 3/30 priority date for domestic students, 3/1 for international students. Applications are processed on a rolling basis. Application fee: $45. Electronic applications accepted. *Expenses:* $842 per credit, $395 fee per semester. *Financial support:* Fellowships with tuition reimbursements, career-related internships or fieldwork, scholarships/grants, and tuition waivers (partial) available. Financial award application deadline: 8/15; financial award applicants required to submit FAFSA. *Faculty research:* Transnational politics and culture, women and social policy, confidentiality in the human services, concepts of marginality, ethics in social policy. *Unit head:* Prof. Humphrey Crookendale, Dean, Graduate School for Public Affairs Administration, 212-343-1234 Ext. 2209, E-mail: hcrookendale@mcny.edu. *Application contact:* Steebo Varghese, Assistant Director of Admissions, 212-343-1234 Ext. 2708, Fax: 212-343-8474, E-mail: svarghese@mcny.edu.
Website: https://www.mcny.edu/academics/school-public-affairs-administration/

Millersville University of Pennsylvania, College of Graduate Studies and Adult Learning, College of Science and Technology, Center for Disaster Research and Education, Millersville, PA 17551-0302. Offers emergency management (MS). *Program availability:* Part-time, evening/weekend, online only, 100% online. *Faculty:* 18 full-time (9 women), 13 part-time/adjunct (7 women). *Students:* 7 full-time (5 women), 39 part-time (16 women); includes 1 minority (Hispanic/Latino). Average age 34. 14 applicants, 93% accepted, 8 enrolled. In 2017, 19 master's awarded. *Degree requirements:* For master's, field practicum. *Entrance requirements:* For master's, GRE or MAT (if undergraduate cumulative GPA is lower than 2.8), three professional letters of recommendation; goal statement; resume. Additional exam requirements/recommendations for international students: Required—TOEFL (minimum score 80 iBT), IELTS (minimum score 6.5), PTE (minimum score 60). *Application deadline:* Applications are processed on a rolling basis. Application fee: $40. Electronic applications accepted. *Expenses:* $500 per credit resident tuition, $581.75 per credit non-resident tuition; $59.25 academic support fee. *Financial support:* In 2017–18, 4 students received support. Unspecified assistantships available. Financial award application deadline: 3/15; financial award applicants required to submit FAFSA. *Faculty research:* Emergency management, continuity of operations, regional planning and preparedness, disaster law and policy, community preparedness and mitigation efforts. *Total annual research expenditures:* $2,500. *Unit head:* Dr. Sepideh Yalda, Director, 717-871-7433, Fax: 717-871-2429, E-mail: sepi.yalda@millersville.edu. *Application contact:* Dr. Victor S. DeSantis, Dean of College of Graduate Studies and Adult Learning/Associate Provost for Civic and Community Engagement, 717-871-7619, Fax: 717-871-7954, E-mail: victor.desantis@millersville.edu.
Website: http://www.millersville.edu/cdre/

National University, Academic Affairs, School of Professional Studies, La Jolla, CA 92037-1011. Offers criminal justice (MCJ); digital cinema production (MFA); digital journalism (MA); homeland security and emergency management (MS); juvenile justice (MS); professional screenwriting (MFA); public administration (MPA), including human resource management, organizational leadership. *Program availability:* Part-time, evening/weekend, 100% online, blended/hybrid learning. *Degree requirements:* For master's, thesis (for some programs). *Entrance requirements:* For master's, interview, minimum GPA of 2.5. Additional exam requirements/recommendations for international students: Required—TOEFL (minimum score 550 paper-based; 79 iBT), IELTS (minimum score 6). *Application deadline:* Applications are processed on a rolling basis. Application fee: $60 ($65 for international students). Electronic applications accepted. *Expenses: Tuition:* Part-time $430 per quarter hour. *Financial support:* Career-related internships or fieldwork, institutionally sponsored loans, scholarships/grants, and tuition waivers (partial) available. Support available to part-time students. Financial award application deadline: 6/30; financial award applicants required to submit FAFSA. *Unit head:* Dr. Daniel Donaldson, Dean, 858-642-8480, E-mail: sops@nu.edu. *Application contact:* Brandon Jouganatos, Vice President for Enrollment Services, 800-628-8648, E-mail: advisor@nu.edu.
Website: http://www.nu.edu/OurPrograms/School-of-Professional-Studies.html

New Jersey Institute of Technology, Ying Wu College of Computing, Newark, NJ 07102. Offers big data management and mining (Certificate); business and information systems (Certificate); computer science (MS, PhD), including bioinformatics (MS), computer science, computing and business (MS), cyber security and privacy (MS), software engineering (MS); data mining (Certificate); information security (Certificate); information systems (MS, PhD), including business and information systems (MS), emergency management and business continuity (MS), information systems; information technology administration and security (MS); IT administration (Certificate); network security and information assurance (Certificate); software engineering analysis/design (Certificate); Web systems development (Certificate). *Program availability:* Part-time, evening/weekend. *Faculty:* 64 full-time (10 women), 38 part-time/adjunct (4 women). *Students:* 818 full-time (241 women), 225 part-time (53 women); includes 162 minority (35 Black or African American, non-Hispanic/Latino; 77 Asian, non-Hispanic/Latino; 41 Hispanic/Latino; 9 Two or more races, non-Hispanic/Latino), 772 international. Average age 27. 2,666 applicants, 51% accepted, 377 enrolled. In 2017, 398 master's, 10 doctorates, 9 other advanced degrees awarded. Terminal master's awarded for partial completion of doctoral program. *Degree requirements:* For master's, thesis optional; for doctorate, thesis/dissertation. *Entrance requirements:* For master's, GRE General Test; for doctorate, GRE General Test, minimum graduate GPA of 3.5. Additional exam requirements/recommendations for international students: Required—TOEFL (minimum score 550 paper-based; 79 iBT). *Application deadline:* For fall admission, 6/1 priority date for domestic students, 5/1 priority date for international students; for spring admission, 11/15 priority date for domestic and international students. Applications are processed on a rolling basis. Application fee: $75. Electronic applications accepted. *Expenses:* Contact institution. *Financial support:* In 2017–18, 57 students received support, including 2 fellowships (averaging $23,254 per year), 47 research assistantships (averaging $24,412 per year), 44 teaching assistantships (averaging $23,528 per year); career-related internships or fieldwork, Federal Work-Study, institutionally sponsored loans, and unspecified assistantships also available. Financial award application deadline: 1/15. *Faculty research:* Computer systems, communications and networking, artificial intelligence, database engineering, systems analysis, analytics and optimization in crowdsourcing. *Total annual research expenditures:* $3 million. *Unit head:* Dr. Craig Gotsman, Dean, 973-542-5488, Fax: 973-596-5777, E-mail: marek.rusinkiewicz@njit.edu. *Application contact:* Stephen Eck, Director of Admissions, 973-596-3300, Fax: 973-596-3461, E-mail: admissions@njit.edu.
Website: http://computing.njit.edu/

New York Medical College, School of Health Sciences and Practice, Valhalla, NY 10595. Offers behavioral sciences and health promotion (MPH); biostatistics (MS); children with special health care (Graduate Certificate); emergency preparedness (Graduate Certificate); environmental health science (MPH); epidemiology (MPH, MS); global health (Graduate Certificate); health education (Graduate Certificate); health policy and management (MPH, Dr PH); industrial hygiene (Graduate Certificate); pediatric dysphagia (Post-Graduate Certificate); physical therapy (DPT); public health (Graduate Certificate); speech-language pathology (MS). *Accreditation:* CEPH. *Program availability:* Part-time, evening/weekend, 100% online, blended/hybrid learning. *Faculty:* 48 full-time (33 women), 235 part-time/adjunct (141 women). *Students:* 221 full-time (153 women), 270 part-time (194 women); includes 202 minority (83 Black or African American, non-Hispanic/Latino; 2 American Indian or Alaska Native, non-Hispanic/Latino; 64 Asian, non-Hispanic/Latino; 47 Hispanic/Latino; 1 Native Hawaiian or other Pacific Islander, non-Hispanic/Latino; 5 Two or more races, non-Hispanic/Latino), 19 international. Average age 29. 1,118 applicants, 38% accepted, 169 enrolled. In 2017, 110 master's, 41 doctorates awarded. *Degree requirements:* For master's, comprehensive exam (for some programs), thesis (for some programs); for doctorate, thesis/dissertation. *Entrance requirements:* For master's, GRE (for MS in speech-language pathology); for doctorate, GRE. Additional exam requirements/recommendations for international students: Required—TOEFL, IELTS. *Application deadline:* For fall admission, 8/1 for domestic students, 4/15 for international students; for spring admission, 12/1 for domestic students; for summer admission, 5/1 for domestic students, 4/15 for international students. Application fee: $125. Electronic applications accepted. *Expenses:* $1,125 per credit, $245 fees. *Financial support:* In 2017–18, 10,000 students received support. Scholarships/grants and unspecified assistantships available. Financial award application deadline: 4/30; financial award applicants required to submit FAFSA. *Unit head:* Ben Watson, PhD, Vice Dean, 914-594-4531, E-mail: ben_watson@nymc.edu. *Application contact:* Irene Bundziak, Assistant to Director of Admissions, 914-594-4905, E-mail: irene_bundziak@nymc.edu.
Website: http://www.nymc.edu/school-of-health-sciences-and-practice-shsp/

Norwich University, College of Graduate and Continuing Studies, Master of Public Administration Program, Northfield, VT 05663. Offers criminal justice and public safety (MPA); fiscal management (MPA); international development and influence (MPA); municipal governance (MPA); nonprofit management (MPA); policy analysis and analytics (MPA); public administration leadership and crisis management (MPA); public works and sustainability (MPA). *Program availability:* Evening/weekend, online only,

mostly all online with a week-long residency requirement. *Degree requirements:* For master's, capstone. *Entrance requirements:* For master's, minimum undergraduate GPA of 2.75. Additional exam requirements/recommendations for international students: Required—TOEFL (minimum score 550 paper-based; 80 iBT), IELTS (minimum score 6.5). Electronic applications accepted. *Expenses:* Contact institution.

Nova Southeastern University, Dr. Kiran C. Patel College of Osteopathic Medicine, Fort Lauderdale, FL 33328. Offers biomedical informatics (MS, Graduate Certificate), including biomedical informatics (MS), clinical informatics (Graduate Certificate); public health informatics (Graduate Certificate); disaster and emergency management (MS); medical education (MS); nutrition (MS, Graduate Certificate), including functional nutrition and herbal therapy (Graduate Certificate); osteopathic medicine (DO); public health (MPH, Graduate Certificate), including health education (Graduate Certificate); social medicine (Graduate Certificate); DO/DMD. *Accreditation:* AOsA. *Faculty:* 98 full-time (58 women), 1,484 part-time/adjunct (401 women). *Students:* 1,032 full-time (479 women), 197 part-time (129 women); includes 656 minority (97 Black or African American, non-Hispanic/Latino; 308 Asian, non-Hispanic/Latino; 215 Hispanic/Latino; 1 Native Hawaiian or other Pacific Islander, non-Hispanic/Latino; 35 Two or more races, non-Hispanic/Latino; 67 international. Average age 26. 5,226 applicants, 9% accepted, 248 enrolled. In 2017, 110 master's, 239 doctorates, 7 other advanced degrees awarded. *Degree requirements:* For master's, comprehensive exam (for MPH); field/special projects; for doctorate, comprehensive exam, COMLEX Board Exams; for Graduate Certificate, thesis or alternative. *Entrance requirements:* For master's, GRE; for doctorate, MCAT, coursework in biology, chemistry, organic chemistry, physics (all with labs), biochemistry, and English. *Application deadline:* For fall admission, 1/15 for domestic students. Applications are processed on a rolling basis. Application fee: $50. Electronic applications accepted. *Expenses:* Contact institution. *Financial support:* In 2017–18, 83 students received support, including 24 fellowships with tuition reimbursements available; Federal Work-Study and scholarships/grants also available. Financial award application deadline: 6/1; financial award applicants required to submit FAFSA. *Faculty research:* Teaching strategies, simulated patient use, HIV/AIDS education, minority health issues, immune disorders. *Unit head:* Elaine M. Wallace, Dean, 954-262-1457, Fax: 954-262-2250, E-mail: ewallace@nova.edu. *Application contact:* HPD Admissions, 877-640-0218, E-mail: hpdinfo@nova.edu.
Website: https://www.osteopathic.nova.edu/

Oklahoma State University, College of Arts and Sciences, Department of Political Science, Stillwater, OK 74078. Offers fire and emergency management administration (MS, PhD); political science (MA). *Faculty:* 21 full-time (7 women), 2 part-time/adjunct (0 women). *Students:* 29 full-time (7 women), 45 part-time (6 women); includes 13 minority (2 Black or African American, non-Hispanic/Latino; 2 Asian, non-Hispanic/Latino; 9 Hispanic/Latino), 13 international. Average age 36. 33 applicants, 52% accepted, 15 enrolled. In 2017, 11 master's, 5 doctorates awarded. *Entrance requirements:* For master's and doctorate, GRE. Additional exam requirements/recommendations for international students: Required—TOEFL (minimum score 550 paper-based; 79 iBT). *Application deadline:* For fall admission, 3/1 priority date for international students; for spring admission, 8/1 priority date for international students. Applications are processed on a rolling basis. Application fee: $40 ($75 for international students). Electronic applications accepted. *Expenses:* Tuition, state resident: full-time $4019; part-time $2679.60 per year. Tuition, nonresident: full-time $15,286; part-time $10,190.40 per year. *Required fees:* $2129; $1419 per unit. Tuition and fees vary according to program. *Financial support:* Research assistantships, teaching assistantships, career-related internships or fieldwork, Federal Work-Study, scholarships/grants, health care benefits, tuition waivers (partial), and unspecified assistantships available. Support available to part-time students. Financial award application deadline: 3/1; financial award applicants required to submit FAFSA. *Faculty research:* Fire and emergency management, environmental dispute resolution, voting and elections, women and politics, urban politics. *Unit head:* Dr. Jeanette Mendez, Department Head, 405-744-5607, E-mail: jeanette.mendez@okstate.edu.
Website: http://polsci.okstate.edu

Pace University, Dyson College of Arts and Sciences, MA Program in Management for Public Safety and Homeland Security Professionals, New York, NY 10038. Offers MA. *Program availability:* Evening/weekend, blended/hybrid learning. *Students:* 3 full-time (2 women), 11 part-time (5 women); includes 6 minority (2 Black or African American, non-Hispanic/Latino; 1 Asian, non-Hispanic/Latino; 3 Hispanic/Latino). Average age 27. In 2017, 7 master's awarded. *Degree requirements:* For master's, project. *Entrance requirements:* For master's, 2 letters of recommendation, resume, personal statement, official transcripts. Additional exam requirements/recommendations for international students: Required—TOEFL. *Application deadline:* For fall admission, 8/1 for domestic students. Applications are processed on a rolling basis. Application fee: $70. Electronic applications accepted. *Financial support:* Research assistantships, scholarships/grants, and unspecified assistantships available. Financial award application deadline: 2/15; financial award applicants required to submit FAFSA. *Unit head:* Dr. Joseph Ryan, Chair, Criminal Justice and Security Department, 914-773-3814, E-mail: jryan@pace.edu. *Application contact:* Susan Ford-Goldschein, Director of Admissions, 914-422-4283, Fax: 212-346-1585, E-mail: graduateadmission@pace.edu.
Website: http://www.pace.edu/dyson/programs/ma-public-safety-homeland-security

Park University, School of Graduate and Professional Studies, Kansas City, MO 54105. Offers adult education (M Ed); business and government leadership (Graduate Certificate); business, government, and global society (MPA); communication and leadership (MA); creative and life writing (Graduate Certificate); disaster and emergency management (MPA, Graduate Certificate); educational leadership (M Ed); finance (MBA, Graduate Certificate); general business (MBA); global business (Graduate Certificate); healthcare administration (MHA); healthcare services management and leadership (Graduate Certificate); international business (MBA); language and literacy (M Ed), including English for speakers of other languages, special reading teacher/literacy coach; leadership of international healthcare organizations (Graduate Certificate); management information systems (MBA, Graduate Certificate); music performance (ADP, Graduate Certificate), including cello (MM, ADP), piano (MM, ADP), viola (MM, ADP), violin (MM, ADP); nonprofit and community services management (MPA); nonprofit leadership (Graduate Certificate); performance (MM), including cello (MM, ADP), piano (MM, ADP), viola (MM, ADP), violin (MM, ADP); public management (MPA); social work (MSW); teacher leadership (M Ed), including curriculum and assessment, instructional leader. *Program availability:* Part-time, evening/weekend, online learning. *Degree requirements:* For master's, comprehensive exam (for some programs), thesis (for some programs), internship (for some programs); exam (for some programs). *Entrance requirements:* For master's, GRE or GMAT (for some programs), teacher certification (for some M Ed programs), letters of recommendation, essay, resume (for some programs). Additional exam requirements/recommendations for international students: Required—TOEFL (minimum score 550 paper-based; 79 iBT), IELTS (minimum score 6). Electronic applications accepted.

Post University, Program in Public Administration, Waterbury, CT 06723-2540. Offers emergency management and homeland security (MPA). *Program availability:* Online learning. *Degree requirements:* For master's, capstone project. *Entrance requirements:* For master's, resume. *Expenses: Tuition:* Part-time $730 per credit hour. Part-time

tuition and fees vary according to degree level and program. *Application contact:* Veronica Montalvo, Vice President, Online Education Enrollment Management and Admissions, 203-596-6164, E-mail: vmontalvo@post.edu.
Website: https://post.edu/academics/online-master-of-public-administration

Regent University, Graduate School, Robertson School of Government, Virginia Beach, VA 23464. Offers government (MA), including American government, healthcare policy and ethics (MA, MPA), international relations, law and public policy, national security studies, political communication, political theory, religion and politics; national security studies (MA), including cybersecurity, homeland security, international security, Middle East politics; public administration (MPA), including emergency management and homeland security, federal government, general public administration, healthcare policy and ethics (MA, MPA), law, nonprofit administration and faith-based organizations, public leadership and management, servant leadership. *Program availability:* Part-time, evening/weekend, 100% online, blended/hybrid learning. *Faculty:* 8 full-time (1 woman), 20 part-time/adjunct (3 women). *Students:* 39 full-time (23 women), 137 part-time (78 women); includes 83 minority (49 Black or African American, non-Hispanic/Latino; 1 American Indian or Alaska Native, non-Hispanic/Latino; 7 Asian, non-Hispanic/Latino; 15 Hispanic/Latino; 11 Two or more races, non-Hispanic/Latino). Average age 35. 345 applicants, 31% accepted, 57 enrolled. In 2017, 38 master's awarded. *Degree requirements:* For master's, thesis optional, internship. *Entrance requirements:* For master's, GRE General Test or LSAT, personal essay, writing sample, resume, college transcripts. Additional exam requirements/recommendations for international students: Required—TOEFL (minimum score 577 paper-based). *Application deadline:* For fall admission, 5/1 priority date for domestic students; for spring admission, 11/1 priority date for domestic students. Applications are processed on a rolling basis. Application fee: $50. Electronic applications accepted. *Expenses:* $650 per credit; $300 technology fee per semester. *Financial support:* In 2017–18, 116 students received support. Career-related internships or fieldwork, scholarships/grants, and unspecified assistantships available. Support available to part-time students. *Faculty research:* International relations and politics, public administration, leadership and ethics, Biblical law, Constitutional law and Supreme Court. *Unit head:* Dr. Eric Patterson, Dean, 757-352-4616, Fax: 757-352-4735, E-mail: epatterson@regent.edu. *Application contact:* Heidi Cece, Assistant Vice President of Enrollment Management, 800-373-5504, Fax: 757-352-4381, E-mail: admissions@regent.edu.
Website: https://www.regent.edu/robertson-school-of-government/

Royal Roads University, Graduate Studies, Peace and Conflict Studies Program, Victoria, BC V9B 5Y2, Canada. Offers conflict analysis (G Dip); conflict analysis and management (MA); disaster and emergency management (MA, G Dip); human security and peacebuilding (MA, G Dip); justice studies (G Dip); peace and conflict studies (MAIS). *Program availability:* Blended/hybrid learning. *Degree requirements:* For master's, thesis. *Entrance requirements:* For master's, 5-7 years of related work experience. Additional exam requirements/recommendations for international students: Required—TOEFL (minimum score 570 paper-based) or IELTS (7) recommended. *Application deadline:* Applications are processed on a rolling basis. Application fee: $120 ($240 for international students). Electronic applications accepted. *Financial support:* Federal Work-Study, institutionally sponsored loans, and scholarships/grants available. Support available to part-time students. *Faculty research:* Conflict analysis, ethno-political conflict reconciliation, international relations, displaced persons, resiliency. *Unit head:* Dr. Brigitte Harris, Dean, 250-391-2511, E-mail: admissions@royalroads.ca. *Application contact:* E-mail: admissions@royalroads.ca.
Website: http://www.royalroads.ca/

Rutgers University–New Brunswick, School of Public Health, Piscataway, NJ 08854. Offers biostatistics (MPH, MS, Dr PH, PhD); clinical epidemiology (Certificate); environmental and occupational health (MPH, Dr PH, PhD, Certificate); epidemiology (MPH, Dr PH, PhD); general public health (Certificate); health education and behavioral science (MPH, Dr PH, PhD); health systems and policy (MPH, PhD); public health (MPH, Dr PH, PhD); public health preparedness (Certificate); DO/MPH; JD/MPH; MBA/MPH; MD/MPH; MPH/MBA; MPH/MSPA; MS/MPH; Psy D/MPH. *Accreditation:* CEPH. *Program availability:* Part-time, evening/weekend. *Degree requirements:* For master's, thesis, internship; for doctorate, comprehensive exam, thesis/dissertation. *Entrance requirements:* For master's, GRE General Test; for doctorate, GRE General Test, MPH (Dr PH); MA, MPH, or MS (PhD). Additional exam requirements/recommendations for international students: Required—TOEFL. Electronic applications accepted.

Saint Leo University, Graduate Studies in Public Safety Administration, Saint Leo, FL 33574-6665. Offers criminal justice (MS), including behavioral studies, corrections, criminal investigation, criminal justice, emergency and disaster management, forensic science, legal studies; emergency and disaster management (MS), including emergency and disaster management, fire science. *Program availability:* Part-time, evening/weekend, 100% online, blended/hybrid learning. *Faculty:* 8 full-time (3 women), 32 part-time/adjunct (7 women). *Students:* 7 full-time (6 women), 617 part-time (385 women); includes 313 minority (235 Black or African American, non-Hispanic/Latino; 5 American Indian or Alaska Native, non-Hispanic/Latino; 3 Asian, non-Hispanic/Latino; 54 Hispanic/Latino; 1 Native Hawaiian or other Pacific Islander, non-Hispanic/Latino; 15 Two or more races, non-Hispanic/Latino). Average age 36. 336 applicants, 63% accepted, 197 enrolled. In 2017, 267 master's awarded. *Degree requirements:* For master's, comprehensive project. *Entrance requirements:* For master's, official transcripts, bachelor's degree from regionally-accredited university with minimum GPA of 3.0. Additional exam requirements/recommendations for international students: Required—TOEFL (minimum score 550 paper-based; 78 iBT). *Application deadline:* For fall admission, 7/1 priority date for domestic and international students; for spring admission, 11/1 priority date for domestic and international students. Applications are processed on a rolling basis. Application fee: $80. Electronic applications accepted. *Expenses:* $555 per credit hour. *Financial support:* In 2017–18, 21 students received support. Scholarships/grants, health care benefits, unspecified assistantships, and tuition remission for Saint Leo employees and their dependents available. Financial award application deadline: 3/1; financial award applicants required to submit FAFSA. *Faculty research:* Emergency management, fire science, community policing. *Unit head:* Dr. Robert Diemer, Director of Graduate Studies in Safety Administration, 352-588-8974, Fax: 352-588-8289, E-mail: graduatepublicsafety@saintleo.edu. *Application contact:* Mark Russum, Assistant Vice President, Enrollment, 800-707-8846, Fax: 352-588-7873, E-mail: grad.admissions@saintleo.edu.
Website: https://www.saintleo.edu/criminal-justice-master-degree

Saint Louis University, Graduate Programs, College for Public Health and Social Justice, Program in Criminology and Criminal Justice, St. Louis, MO 63103. Offers administration of justice (MA); emergency management (MA); treatment and rehabilitation (MA). *Program availability:* Part-time. *Degree requirements:* For master's, comprehensive exam. *Entrance requirements:* For master's, GRE General Test, two letters of recommendation, resume, transcripts. Additional exam requirements/recommendations for international students: Required—TOEFL (minimum score 525 paper-based).

San Diego State University, Graduate and Research Affairs, College of Health and Human Services, Graduate School of Public Health, San Diego, CA 92182. Offers environmental health (MPH); epidemiology (MPH, PhD), including biostatistics (MPH);

global emergency preparedness and response (MS); global health (PhD); health behavior (PhD); health promotion (MPH); health services administration (MPH); toxicology (MS); MPH/MA; MSW/MPH. *Accreditation:* CAHME (one or more programs are accredited). *Program availability:* Part-time. *Degree requirements:* For master's, comprehensive exam (for some programs), thesis (for some programs); for doctorate, thesis/dissertation. *Entrance requirements:* For master's, GMAT (MPH in health services administration), GRE General Test; for doctorate, GRE General Test. Additional exam requirements/recommendations for international students: Required—TOEFL. *Faculty research:* Evaluation of tobacco, AIDS prevalence and prevention, mammography, infant death project, Alzheimer's in elderly Chinese.

Sul Ross State University, College of Professional Studies, Department of Criminal Justice, Alpine, TX 79832. Offers criminal justice (MS); homeland security (MS); MS/MA. *Entrance requirements:* For master's, GRE General Test, minimum GPA of 2.5 in last 60 hours of undergraduate work.

Syracuse University, David B. Falk College of Sport and Human Dynamics, CAS Program in Trauma-Informed Practice, Syracuse, NY 13202. Offers CAS. *Program availability:* Part-time. *Entrance requirements:* For degree, three letters of recommendation, transcripts, personal statement, resume. Additional exam requirements/recommendations for international students: Required—TOEFL or IELTS. *Application deadline:* For fall admission, 2/15 priority date for domestic and international students; for summer admission, 11/15 priority date for domestic and international students. Application fee: $75. Electronic applications accepted. *Financial support:* Application deadline: 1/1. *Faculty research:* Trauma-informed practice, understanding of the vulnerabilities or triggers of trauma survivors, theoretical foundations of trauma, evidenced based approaches and techniques, trauma response and intervention. *Unit head:* Dr. Thom deLara, Department Chair/Professor of Practice, 315-443-9830, E-mail: tdelara@syr.edu. *Application contact:* Felicia Otero, Director of College Admissions, 315-443-5555, E-mail: falk@syr.edu.
Website: http://falk.syr.edu/MarriageFamilyTherapy/CAS.aspx

Thomas Jefferson University, College of Science, Health and the Liberal Arts, Program in Disaster Medicine and Management, Philadelphia, PA 19107. Offers MS. *Program availability:* Online learning.

Trident University International, College of Health Sciences, Program in Health Sciences, Cypress, CA 90630. Offers clinical research administration (MS, Certificate); emergency and disaster management (MS, Certificate); environmental health science (Certificate); health care administration (PhD); health care management (MS), including health informatics; health education (MS, Certificate); health informatics (Certificate); health sciences (PhD); international health (MS); international health: educator or researcher option (PhD); international health: practitioner option (PhD); law and expert witness studies (MS, Certificate); public health (MS); quality assurance (Certificate). *Program availability:* Part-time, evening/weekend, online learning. *Degree requirements:* For doctorate, comprehensive exam, thesis/dissertation, defense of dissertation. *Entrance requirements:* For master's, minimum GPA of 2.5 (students with GPA 3.0 or greater may transfer up to 30% of graduate level credits); for doctorate, minimum GPA of 3.4, curriculum vitae, course work in research methods or statistics. Additional exam requirements/recommendations for international students: Required—TOEFL. Electronic applications accepted.

Trine University, Program in Criminal Justice, Angola, IN 46703-1764. Offers emergency management (MS). *Program availability:* Part-time, evening/weekend, online only, 100% online, blended/hybrid learning. *Faculty:* 8. *Students:* 42 (31 women). In 2017, 23 master's awarded. *Entrance requirements:* Additional exam requirements/recommendations for international students: Required—TOEFL. *Application deadline:* Applications are processed on a rolling basis. Electronic applications accepted. *Expenses:* $550 per credit hour tuition. *Financial support:* Application deadline: 3/1; applicants required to submit FAFSA. *Unit head:* Ryan Dombkowski, Dean, College of Graduate and Professional Studies/Associate Professor, 260-203-2695, E-mail: dombkowskir@trine.edu. *Application contact:* Jacqueline Delagrange, Director, Master of Science in Criminal Justice, 260-203-2693, E-mail: delagrangej@trine.edu.
Website: https://www.trine.edu/adult-studies/academics/graduate/ms-criminal-justice.aspx

Tulane University, School of Social Work, New Orleans, LA 70118-5669. Offers city, culture and community (PhD); disaster resilience leadership (MS); social work (MSW, DSW). *Accreditation:* CSWE (one or more programs are accredited). *Program availability:* Part-time. *Degree requirements:* For master's, thesis. *Entrance requirements:* Additional exam requirements/recommendations for international students: Required—TOEFL. Electronic applications accepted. *Expenses: Tuition:* Full-time $50,920; part-time $2829 per credit hour. *Required fees:* $2040; $44.50 per credit hour. $580 per term. Tuition and fees vary according to course load, degree level and program.

Université de Montréal, Faculty of Medicine, Programs in Environment and Prevention, Montréal, QC H3C 3J7, Canada. Offers environment, health and disaster management (DESS). Electronic applications accepted. *Faculty research:* Health, environment, pollutants, protection, waste.

University at Albany, State University of New York, College of Emergency Preparedness, Homeland Security and Cybersecurity, Albany, NY 12222-0001. Offers cybersecurity (Certificate); emergency preparedness (Certificate); homeland security (Certificate); information science (MS, PhD). *Faculty:* 10 full-time (4 women), 14 part-time/adjunct (5 women). *Students:* 59 full-time (40 women), 77 part-time (49 women); includes 23 minority (4 Black or African American, non-Hispanic/Latino; 6 Asian, non-Hispanic/Latino; 10 Hispanic/Latino; 3 Two or more races, non-Hispanic/Latino), 14 international. 90 applicants, 67% accepted, 36 enrolled. In 2017, 30 master's, 1 doctorate, 24 other advanced degrees awarded. *Entrance requirements:* Additional exam requirements/recommendations for international students: Required—TOEFL. *Expenses:* Tuition, state resident: full-time $10,870; part-time $453 per credit hour. Tuition, nonresident: full-time $22,210; part-time $925 per credit hour. *Required fees:* $84.68 per credit hour. $508.06 per semester. Part-time tuition and fees vary according to course load and program. *Faculty research:* Electrical and computer engineering, environmental and sustainability engineering, computer science. *Unit head:* Dr. Robert Griffin, Dean, 518-442-5258. *Application contact:* Michael DeRensis, Director, Graduate Admissions, 518-442-3980, Fax: 518-442-3922, E-mail: graduate@albany.edu.
Website: http://www.albany.edu/cehc

University of Alaska Fairbanks, School of Management, Program in Security and Disaster Management, Fairbanks, AK 99775-6080. Offers MSDM. *Program availability:* Part-time, evening/weekend, 100% online, blended/hybrid learning. *Entrance requirements:* For master's, Watson-Glaser Critical Thinking Appraisal. Additional exam requirements/recommendations for international students: Required—TOEFL (minimum score 79 iBT), IELTS (minimum score 6.5). Electronic applications accepted. *Expenses:* Contact institution.

University of Central Florida, College of Community Innovation and Education, School of Public Administration, Orlando, FL 32816. Offers emergency management and homeland security (Certificate); fundraising (Certificate); nonprofit management (MNM, Certificate); public administration (MPA); research administration (MRA); urban and regional planning (MS). *Accreditation:* NASPAA. *Program availability:* Part-time,

evening/weekend. *Students:* 110 full-time (76 women), 290 part-time (215 women); includes 193 minority (96 Black or African American, non-Hispanic/Latino; 2 American Indian or Alaska Native, non-Hispanic/Latino; 13 Asian, non-Hispanic/Latino; 74 Hispanic/Latino; 8 Two or more races, non-Hispanic/Latino), 6 international. Average age 32. 255 applicants, 78% accepted, 152 enrolled. In 2017, 95 master's, 34 other advanced degrees awarded. *Degree requirements:* For master's, comprehensive exam, thesis or alternative, research report. *Entrance requirements:* For master's, letters of recommendation, goal statement, resume. Additional exam requirements/recommendations for international students: Required—TOEFL. *Application deadline:* For fall admission, 6/15 for domestic students; for spring admission, 11/1 for domestic students. Application fee: $30. Electronic applications accepted. *Expenses:* Tuition, state resident: part-time $288.16 per credit hour. Tuition, nonresident: part-time $1073.31 per credit hour. Tuition and fees vary according to program. *Financial support:* In 2017–18, 11 students received support, including 2 fellowships with partial tuition reimbursements available (averaging $5,300 per year), 6 research assistantships with partial tuition reimbursements available (averaging $9,637 per year), 3 teaching assistantships with partial tuition reimbursements available (averaging $9,390 per year); career-related internships or fieldwork, Federal Work-Study, institutionally sponsored loans, health care benefits, tuition waivers (partial), and unspecified assistantships also available. Financial award application deadline: 3/1; financial award applicants required to submit FAFSA. *Unit head:* Dr. Naim Kapucu, Director, 407-823-6096, Fax: 407-823-5651, E-mail: kapucu@ucf.edu. *Application contact:* Associate Director, Graduate Admissions, 407-823-2766, Fax: 407-823-6442, E-mail: gradadmissions@ucf.edu.
Website: https://www.cohpa.ucf.edu/publicadmin/

University of Chicago, Graham School of Continuing Liberal and Professional Studies, Program in Threat and Response Management, Chicago, IL 60637. Offers M Sc. *Program availability:* Part-time-only, evening/weekend. *Faculty:* 13. *Students:* 38 part-time (14 women); includes 13 minority (5 Black or African American, non-Hispanic/Latino; 3 Asian, non-Hispanic/Latino; 5 Hispanic/Latino), 1 international. Average age 37. 18 applicants, 67% accepted, 11 enrolled. In 2017, 6 master's awarded. *Entrance requirements:* For master's, 3 letters of recommendation, statement of purpose, transcripts, resume or curriculum vitae, U.S. citizen or permanent resident. Additional exam requirements/recommendations for international students: Required—TOEFL (minimum score 104 iBT), IELTS (minimum score 7). *Application deadline:* For fall admission, 6/15 for domestic students. Application fee: $75. Electronic applications accepted. *Financial support:* Yellow Ribbon Program available. *Unit head:* E-mail: msctrm@uchicago.edu. *Application contact:* 773-834-2765, E-mail: msctrm@uchicago.edu.
Website: https://grahamschool.uchicago.edu/credit/master-science-threat-response-management/index

University of Colorado Denver, School of Public Affairs, Program in Criminology and Criminal Justice, Denver, CO 80217. Offers criminal justice (MCJ), including criminal justice, domestic violence, emergency management and homeland security. *Program availability:* Part-time, evening/weekend. *Degree requirements:* For master's, thesis or alternative, 36-39 semester credit hours. *Entrance requirements:* For master's, GRE, GMAT, LSAT, recommendations, official transcripts, current resume, essay. Additional exam requirements/recommendations for international students: Required—TOEFL (minimum score 537 paper-based; 75 iBT); Recommended—IELTS (minimum score 6.5). Electronic applications accepted. *Expenses:* Contact institution. *Faculty research:* White collar crime, women and the criminal justice system, applied family violence issues, intimate partner violence and domestic violence interventions, juvenile delinquency.

University of Colorado Denver, School of Public Affairs, Program in Public Affairs and Administration, Denver, CO 80127. Offers public administration (MPA), including domestic violence, emergency management and homeland security, environmental policy, management and law, homeland security and defense, local government, nonprofit management, public administration; public affairs (PhD). *Accreditation:* NASPAA. *Program availability:* Part-time, evening/weekend, online learning. *Degree requirements:* For master's, thesis or alternative, 36-39 credit hours; for doctorate, comprehensive exam, thesis/dissertation, minimum of 66 semester hours, including at least 30 hours of dissertation. *Entrance requirements:* For master's, GRE, GMAT or LSAT, resume, essay, transcripts, recommendations; for doctorate, GRE, resume, essay, transcripts, recommendations. Additional exam requirements/recommendations for international students: Required—TOEFL (minimum score 550 paper-based; 80 iBT); Recommended—IELTS (minimum score 6.5). Electronic applications accepted. *Expenses:* Contact institution. *Faculty research:* Housing, education and the social and economic issues of vulnerable populations; nonprofit governance and management; education finance, effectiveness and reform; P-20 education initiatives; municipal government accountability.

University of Delaware, College of Arts and Sciences, School of Public Policy and Administration, Program in Disaster Science and Management, Newark, DE 19716. Offers MS, PhD.

University of Denver, University College, Denver, CO 80208. Offers arts and culture (MA, Certificate); communication management (MS, Certificate), including translation studies (Certificate); world history and culture (Certificate); environmental policy and management (MS); geographic information systems (MS); global affairs (MA, Certificate), including human capital in organizations (Certificate), philanthropic leadership (Certificate), project management (Certificate), strategic innovation and change (Certificate); healthcare leadership (MS); information communications and technology (MS); leadership and organizations (MS); professional creative writing (MA, Certificate), including emergency planning and response (Certificate), organizational security (Certificate); security management (MS, Certificate); strategic human resources (Certificate). *Program availability:* Part-time, evening/weekend, online learning. *Faculty:* 118 part-time/adjunct (62 women). *Students:* 56 full-time (32 women), 1,287 part-time (707 women); includes 330 minority (99 Black or African American, non-Hispanic/Latino; 7 American Indian or Alaska Native, non-Hispanic/Latino; 43 Asian, non-Hispanic/Latino; 141 Hispanic/Latino; 3 Native Hawaiian or other Pacific Islander, non-Hispanic/Latino; 37 Two or more races, non-Hispanic/Latino), 84 international. Average age 34. 783 applicants, 86% accepted, 420 enrolled. In 2017, 461 master's, 173 other advanced degrees awarded. *Degree requirements:* For master's, capstone project. *Entrance requirements:* For master's, transcripts, two letters of recommendation, personal statement, resume. Additional exam requirements/recommendations for international students: Required—TOEFL (minimum score 550 paper-based; 80 iBT). *Application deadline:* For fall admission, 6/21 priority date for domestic students, 5/1 priority date for international students; for winter admission, 9/14 priority date for domestic students, 9/19 priority date for international students; for spring admission, 1/11 priority date for domestic students, 12/12 priority date for international students; for summer admission, 3/29 priority date for domestic students, 3/6 priority date for international students. Applications are processed on a rolling basis. Application fee: $75. Electronic applications accepted. *Expenses:* $7,968 per year half-time. *Financial support:* In 2017–18, 29 students received support. Teaching assistantships available. Financial award applicants required to submit FAFSA. *Unit head:* Dr. Michael McGuire, Dean, 303-871-3518, Fax: 303-871-3303, E-mail: mmcguire@du.edu. *Application contact:* Information Contact, 303-871-2291, E-mail: ucoladm@du.edu.
Website: http://universitycollege.du.edu/

Emergency Management

University of Florida, Graduate School, College of Design, Construction and Planning, M.E. Rinker, Sr. School of Construction Management, Gainesville, FL 32611. Offers construction management (MSCM); fire and emergency services (MFES); historic preservation (MSCM); international construction (MICM), including historic preservation; sustainable construction (MSCM); sustainable design (MSCM). *Program availability:* Part-time, online learning. *Degree requirements:* For master's, thesis. *Entrance requirements:* For master's, GRE General Test, minimum GPA of 3.0. Additional exam requirements/recommendations for international students: Required—TOEFL (minimum score 550 paper-based; 80 iBT), IELTS (minimum score 6). Electronic applications accepted. *Faculty research:* Safety, affordable housing, construction management, environmental issues, sustainable construction.

University of Hawaii at Manoa, Office of Graduate Education, College of Social Sciences, Department of Urban and Regional Planning, Program in Disaster Preparedness and Emergency Management, Honolulu, HI 96822. Offers Graduate Certificate. *Program availability:* Part-time. *Entrance requirements:* Additional exam requirements/recommendations for international students: Required—TOEFL (minimum score 500 paper-based; 61 iBT), IELTS (minimum score 5).

University of Illinois at Springfield, Graduate Programs, College of Public Affairs and Administration, Program in Public Health, Springfield, IL 62703-5407. Offers community health education (Graduate Certificate); emergency preparedness and homeland security (Graduate Certificate); environmental health (MPH, Graduate Certificate); environmental risk assessment (Graduate Certificate); epidemiology (Graduate Certificate); public health (MPH). *Program availability:* Part-time, evening/weekend, 100% online. *Faculty:* 7 full-time (4 women). *Students:* 38 full-time (23 women), 46 part-time (34 women); includes 27 minority (16 Black or African American, non-Hispanic/Latino; 4 Asian, non-Hispanic/Latino; 5 Hispanic/Latino; 2 Two or more races, non-Hispanic/Latino), 22 international. Average age 32. 47 applicants, 51% accepted, 18 enrolled. In 2017, 28 master's, 17 other advanced degrees awarded. *Degree requirements:* For master's, comprehensive exam, internship. *Entrance requirements:* For master's, GRE, minimum undergraduate GPA of 3.0, 3 letters of recommendation, statement of personal goals. Additional exam requirements/recommendations for international students: Required—TOEFL (minimum score 500 paper-based; 61 iBT). *Application deadline:* Applications are processed on a rolling basis. Application fee: $60 ($75 for international students). Electronic applications accepted. *Expenses:* Tuition, state resident: full-time $7896; part-time $329 per credit hour. Tuition, nonresident: full-time $16,200; part-time $675 per credit hour. Tuition and fees vary according to program. *Financial support:* In 2017–18, research assistantships with full tuition reimbursements (averaging $10,249 per year), teaching assistantships with full tuition reimbursements (averaging $10,303 per year) were awarded; fellowships, career-related internships or fieldwork, Federal Work-Study, scholarships/grants, health care benefits, and unspecified assistantships also available. Support available to part-time students. Financial award application deadline: 11/15; financial award applicants required to submit FAFSA. *Unit head:* Dr. Josiah Alamu, Program Administrator, 217-206-7874, Fax: 217-206-7279, E-mail: jalam3@uis.edu.
Website: http://www.uis.edu/publichealth/

University of Maryland, Baltimore County, The Graduate School, College of Arts, Humanities and Social Sciences, Department of Emergency Health Services, Baltimore, MD 21250. Offers emergency health services (MS), including administration, planning, and policy, preventive medicine and epidemiology; emergency management (Postbaccalaureate Certificate); public policy (PhD), including emergency health, emergency management. Some of the required/elective courses within the Preventative Medicine and Epidemiology track are offered in collaboration with the University of Maryland, Baltimore (UMB) and other University System Schools. *Program availability:* Part-time, evening/weekend, 100% online, blended/hybrid learning. *Faculty:* 4 full-time (2 women), 8 part-time/adjunct (3 women). *Students:* 18 full-time (11 women), 4 part-time (3 women); includes 9 minority (6 Black or African American, non-Hispanic/Latino; 1 Asian, non-Hispanic/Latino; 1 Hispanic/Latino; 1 Two or more races, non-Hispanic/Latino). Average age 28. 22 applicants, 91% accepted, 18 enrolled. In 2017, 12 master's awarded. Terminal master's awarded for partial completion of doctoral program. *Degree requirements:* For master's, comprehensive exam (for some programs), capstone project or thesis. *Entrance requirements:* For master's, GRE General Test if GPA is below 3.2, minimum GPA of 3.2. Additional exam requirements/recommendations for international students: Required—TOEFL (minimum score 80 iBT), IELTS, or PTE. *Application deadline:* For fall admission, 6/15 for domestic students, 3/1 for international students; for spring admission, 12/1 for domestic students, 10/1 for international students. Applications are processed on a rolling basis. Application fee: $50. Electronic applications accepted. *Expenses:* $753 per credit hour. *Financial support:* In 2017–18, 6 students received support, including 7 research assistantships with full tuition reimbursements available (averaging $16,875 per year); career-related internships or fieldwork, Federal Work-Study, scholarships/grants, health care benefits, and unspecified assistantships also available. Financial award application deadline: 5/30; financial award applicants required to submit FAFSA. *Faculty research:* EMS management, disaster health services, emergency management, epidemiology, risk profiles, infectious disease control, stress management for care providers, climate change and public health. *Total annual research expenditures:* $715,419. *Unit head:* Dr. J. Lee Jenkins, Department Chair, 410-455-3216, Fax: 410-455-3045, E-mail: jleejenkins@umbc.edu. *Application contact:* Dr. Rick Bissell, Program Director, 410-455-3776, Fax: 410-455-3045, E-mail: bissell@umbc.edu.
Website: http://ehs.umbc.edu/

University of Nebraska Medical Center, Program in Emergency Preparedness, Omaha, NE 68198. Offers MS. *Program availability:* Part-time, 100% online, blended/hybrid learning. *Degree requirements:* For master's, thesis. *Entrance requirements:* For master's, GRE. Additional exam requirements/recommendations for international students: Required—TOEFL (minimum score 550 paper-based; 80 iBT). Electronic applications accepted. *Expenses:* Tuition, state resident: full-time $8451; part-time $4225 per semester. Tuition, nonresident: full-time $24,219; part-time $11,295 per semester. *Required fees:* $589; $117 per term.

University of Nevada, Las Vegas, Graduate College, Greenspun College of Urban Affairs, School of Public Policy and Leadership, Las Vegas, NV 89154-4030. Offers crisis and emergency management (MS); emergency crisis management cybersecurity (Certificate); environmental science (MS, PhD); non-profit management (Certificate); public administration (MPA); public affairs (PhD); public management (Certificate); urban leadership (MA). *Program availability:* Part-time. *Faculty:* 13 full-time (5 women), 10 part-time/adjunct (3 women). *Students:* 76 full-time (40 women), 107 part-time (66 women); includes 79 minority (19 Black or African American, non-Hispanic/Latino; 1 American Indian or Alaska Native, non-Hispanic/Latino; 6 Asian, non-Hispanic/Latino; 40 Hispanic/Latino; 3 Native Hawaiian or other Pacific Islander, non-Hispanic/Latino; 10 Two or more races, non-Hispanic/Latino), 1 international. Average age 37. 86 applicants, 80% accepted, 47 enrolled. In 2017, 61 master's, 6 doctorates, 14 other advanced degrees awarded. *Degree requirements:* For master's, comprehensive exam (for some programs), thesis (for some programs), oral exam; for doctorate, comprehensive exam, thesis/dissertation; for Certificate, portfolio. *Entrance requirements:* For master's, GRE General Test or GMAT, bachelor's degree with minimum GPA 2.75; statement of purpose; 3 letters of recommendation; for doctorate, GRE General Test, master's degree with minimum GPA of 3.5; 3 letters of recommendation; statement of purpose; writing sample; personal interview; for Certificate, bachelor's degree; 2 letters of recommendation; writing sample. Additional exam requirements/recommendations for international students: Required—TOEFL (minimum score 550 paper-based; 80 iBT), IELTS (minimum score 7). *Application deadline:* For fall admission, 6/1 for domestic and international students; for spring admission, 11/1 for domestic and international students; for summer admission, 3/1 for domestic students. Application fee: $60 ($95 for international students). Electronic applications accepted. *Expenses:* $275 per credit, $850 per course, $7,969 per year resident, $22,157 per year non-resident, $7,094 non-resident fee (7 credits or more), $1,307 annual health insurance fee. *Financial support:* In 2017–18, 23 students received support, including 7 research assistantships with partial tuition reimbursements available (averaging $15,995 per year), 16 teaching assistantships with partial tuition reimbursements available (averaging $15,547 per year); institutionally sponsored loans, scholarships/grants, health care benefits, and unspecified assistantships also available. Financial award application deadline: 3/15; financial award applicants required to submit FAFSA. *Total annual research expenditures:* $63,202. *Unit head:* Dr. Christopher Stream, Director, 702-895-5120, Fax: 702-895-4436, E-mail: chris.stream@unlv.edu. *Application contact:* Dr. Jayce Farmer, Graduate Coordinator, 702-895-4828, E-mail: jayce.farmer@unlv.edu.
Website: https://www.unlv.edu/publicpolicy

University of New Haven, Graduate School, Henry C. Lee College of Criminal Justice and Forensic Sciences, Program in Emergency Management, West Haven, CT 06516. Offers MS, Graduate Certificate. *Program availability:* Part-time, 100% online. *Students:* 22 full-time (7 women), 60 part-time (10 women); includes 8 minority (2 Black or African American, non-Hispanic/Latino; 2 Asian, non-Hispanic/Latino; 3 Hispanic/Latino; 1 Two or more races, non-Hispanic/Latino), 8 international. Average age 35. 60 applicants, 98% accepted, 28 enrolled. In 2017, 31 master's, 3 other advanced degrees awarded. Application fee: $50. *Expenses: Tuition:* Full-time $16,020; part-time $890 per credit hour. *Required fees:* $220; $90 per term. *Unit head:* Wayne Sandford, Coordinator, 203-479-4891, E-mail: wsandford@newhaven.edu. *Application contact:* Michelle Mason, Director of Graduate Enrollment, 203-932-7067, E-mail: mmason@newhaven.edu.
Website: http://www.newhaven.edu/lee-college/programs/graduate/emergency-management/

See Display on page 784 and Close-Up on page 799.

The University of North Carolina at Charlotte, College of Liberal Arts and Sciences, Department of Political Science and Public Administration, Charlotte, NC 28223-0001. Offers emergency management (Graduate Certificate); non-profit management (Graduate Certificate); public administration (MPA), including arts administration, emergency management, non-profit management, public budgeting and finance, urban management and policy; public budgeting and finance (Graduate Certificate); urban management and policy (Graduate Certificate). *Accreditation:* NASPAA. *Program availability:* Part-time, evening/weekend. *Faculty:* 19 full-time (9 women), 4 part-time/adjunct (1 woman). *Students:* 20 full-time (11 women), 61 part-time (41 women); includes 21 minority (12 Black or African American, non-Hispanic/Latino; 2 American Indian or Alaska Native, non-Hispanic/Latino; 1 Asian, non-Hispanic/Latino; 4 Hispanic/Latino; 2 Two or more races, non-Hispanic/Latino), 1 international. Average age 28. 48 applicants, 67% accepted, 22 enrolled. In 2017, 25 master's, 15 other advanced degrees awarded. *Degree requirements:* For master's, research project or thesis. *Entrance requirements:* For master's, GRE General Test, bachelor's degree, or its equivalent, from accredited college or university; minimum undergraduate GPA of 3.0; 3 letters of recommendation; statement of purpose; for Graduate Certificate, statement of purpose (1-2 pages in length) explaining applicant's career goals, how the Graduate Certificate fits into achieving those goals, and any relevant work experience; official transcripts; letters of recommendation. Additional exam requirements/recommendations for international students: Required—TOEFL (minimum score 523 paper-based, 70 iBT) or IELTS (6.5). *Application deadline:* For fall admission, 8/1 for domestic and international students; for spring admission, 12/1 for domestic and international students. Applications are processed on a rolling basis. Application fee: $75. Electronic applications accepted. *Expenses:* Tuition, state resident: full-time $4337. Tuition, nonresident: full-time $17,771. *Required fees:* $3211. Tuition and fees vary according to course load and program. *Financial support:* In 2017–18, 14 students received support, including 13 research assistantships (averaging $9,015 per year), 1 teaching assistantship (averaging $19,500 per year); career-related internships or fieldwork, Federal Work-Study, institutionally sponsored loans, scholarships/grants, and unspecified assistantships also available. Support available to part-time students. Financial award application deadline: 3/1; financial award applicants required to submit FAFSA. *Total annual research expenditures:* $419,411. *Unit head:* Dr. Greg Weeks, Chair, 704-687-7574, E-mail: gbweeks@uncc.edu. *Application contact:* Kathy B. Giddings, Director of Graduate Admissions, 704-687-5503, Fax: 704-687-1668, E-mail: gradadm@uncc.edu.
Website: http://politicalscience.uncc.edu/

The University of North Carolina at Pembroke, The Graduate School, Department of Political Science and Public Administration, Pembroke, NC 28372-1510. Offers criminal justice (MPA); emergency management (MPA); health administration (MPA); public management (MPA). *Program availability:* Part-time, evening/weekend, online learning. *Degree requirements:* For master's, comprehensive exam, thesis optional. *Entrance requirements:* For master's, GRE General Test or MAT, minimum GPA of 3.0 in major, 2.5 overall; interview. Additional exam requirements/recommendations for international students: Required—TOEFL. *Application deadline:* Applications are processed on a rolling basis. Application fee: $45 ($60 for international students). *Financial support:* Application deadline: 4/15; applicants required to submit FAFSA. *Unit head:* Dr. Emily Neff-Sharum, Interim Director, 910-775-4409, E-mail: emily.neffsharum@uncp.edu.

University of North Texas, Robert B. Toulouse School of Graduate Studies, Denton, TX 76203-5459. Offers accounting (MS); applied anthropology (MA, MS); applied behavior analysis (Certificate); applied geography (MA); applied technology and performance improvement (M Ed, MS); art education (MA); art history (MA); art museum education (Certificate); arts leadership (Certificate); audiology (Au D); behavior analysis (MS); behavioral science (PhD); biochemistry and molecular biology (MS); biology (MA, MS); biomedical engineering (MS); business analysis (MS); chemistry (MS); clinical health psychology (PhD); communication studies (MA, MS); computer engineering (MS); computer science (MS); counseling (M Ed, MS), including clinical mental health counseling (MS), college and university counseling, elementary school counseling, secondary school counseling; creative writing (MA); criminal justice (MS); curriculum and instruction (M Ed); decision sciences (MBA); design (MA, MFA), including fashion design (MFA), innovation studies, interior design (MFA); early childhood studies (MS); economics (MS); educational leadership (M Ed, Ed D); educational psychology (MS, PhD), including family studies (MS), gifted and talented (MS), human development (MS), learning and cognition (MS), research, measurement and evaluation (MS); electrical engineering (MS); emergency management (MPA); engineering technology (MS); English (MA); English as a second language (MA); environmental science (MS); finance (MBA, MS); financial management (MPA); French (MA); health services management

(MBA); higher education (M Ed, Ed D); history (MA, MS); hospitality management (MS); human resources management (MPA); information science (MS); information systems (PhD); information technologies (MBA); interdisciplinary studies (MA, MS); international studies (MA); international sustainable tourism (MS); jazz studies (MM); journalism (MA, MJ, Graduate Certificate), including interactive and virtual digital communication (Graduate Certificate), narrative journalism (Graduate Certificate), public relations (Graduate Certificate); kinesiology (MS); linguistics (MA); local government management (MPA); logistics (PhD); logistics and supply chain management (MBA); long-term care, senior housing, and aging services (MA); management (PhD); marketing (MBA); mathematics (MA, MS); mechanical and energy engineering (MS, PhD); music (MA), including ethnomusicology, music theory, musicology, performance; music composition (PhD); music education (MM Ed, PhD); nonprofit management (MPA); operations and supply chain management (MBA); performance (MM, DMA); philosophy (MA); political science (MA); professional and technical communication (MA); radio, television and film (MA, MFA); rehabilitation counseling (Certificate); sociology (MA); Spanish (MA); special education (M Ed); speech-language pathology (MA); strategic management (MBA); studio art (MFA); teaching (M Ed); MBA/MS. *Program availability:* Part-time, evening/weekend, online learning. Terminal master's awarded for partial completion of doctoral program. *Degree requirements:* For master's, variable foreign language requirement, comprehensive exam (for some programs), thesis (for some programs); for doctorate, variable foreign language requirement, comprehensive exam (for some programs), thesis/dissertation; for other advanced degree, variable foreign language requirement, comprehensive exam (for some programs). *Entrance requirements:* For master's and doctorate, GRE, GMAT. Additional exam requirements/recommendations for international students: Required—TOEFL (minimum score 550 paper-based; 79 iBT). Electronic applications accepted.

University of South Florida, Innovative Education, Tampa, FL 33620-9951. Offers adult, career and higher education (Graduate Certificate), including college teaching, leadership in developing human resources, leadership in higher education; Africana studies (Graduate Certificate), including diasporas and health disparities, genocide and human rights; aging studies (Graduate Certificate), including gerontology; art research (Graduate Certificate), including museum studies; business foundations (Graduate Certificate); chemical and biomedical engineering (Graduate Certificate), including materials science and engineering, water, health and sustainability; child and family studies (Graduate Certificate), including positive behavior support; civil and industrial engineering (Graduate Certificate), including transportation systems analysis; community and family health (Graduate Certificate), including maternal and child health, social marketing and public health, violence and injury: prevention and intervention, women's health; criminology (Graduate Certificate), including criminal justice administration; data science for public administration (Graduate Certificate); digital humanities (Graduate Certificate); educational measurement and research (Graduate Certificate), including evaluation; English (Graduate Certificate), including comparative literary studies, creative writing, professional and technical communication; entrepreneurship (Graduate Certificate); environmental health (Graduate Certificate), including safety management; epidemiology and biostatistics (Graduate Certificate), including applied biostatistics, biostatistics, concepts and tools of epidemiology, epidemiology, epidemiology of infectious diseases; geography, environment and planning (Graduate Certificate), including community development, environmental policy and management, geographical information systems; geology (Graduate Certificate), including hydrogeology; global health (Graduate Certificate), including disaster management, global health and Latin American and Caribbean studies, global health practice, humanitarian assistance, infection control; government and international affairs (Graduate Certificate), including Cuban studies, globalization studies; health policy and management (Graduate Certificate), including health management and leadership, public health policy and programs; hearing specialist: early intervention (Graduate Certificate); industrial and management systems engineering (Graduate Certificate), including systems engineering, technology management; information studies (Graduate Certificate), including school library media specialist; information systems/decision sciences (Graduate Certificate), including analytics and business intelligence; instructional technology (Graduate Certificate), including distance education, Florida digital/virtual educator, instructional design, multimedia design, Web design; internal medicine, bioethics and medical humanities (Graduate Certificate), including biomedical ethics; Latin American and Caribbean studies (Graduate Certificate); leadership for coastal resiliency planning (Graduate Certificate); mass communications (Graduate Certificate), including multimedia journalism; mathematics and statistics (Graduate Certificate), including mathematics; medicine (Graduate Certificate), including aging and neuroscience, bioinformatics, biotechnology, brain fitness and memory management, clinical investigation, hand and upper limb rehabilitation, health informatics, health sciences, integrative weight management, intellectual property, medicine and gender, metabolic and nutritional medicine, metabolic cardiology, pharmacy sciences; national and competitive intelligence (Graduate Certificate); nursing (Graduate Certificate), including simulation based academic fellowship in advanced pain management; psychological and social foundations (Graduate Certificate), including career counseling, college teaching, diversity in education, mental health counseling, school counseling; public affairs (Graduate Certificate), including nonprofit management, public management, research administration; public health (Graduate Certificate), including assessing chemical toxicity and public health risks, health equity, pharmacoepidemiology, public health generalist, toxicology, translational research in adolescent behavioral health; public health practices (Graduate Certificate), including planning for healthy communities; rehabilitation and mental health counseling (Graduate Certificate), including integrative mental health care, marriage and family therapy, rehabilitation technology; secondary education (Graduate Certificate), including ESOL, foreign language education: culture and content, foreign language education: professional; social work (Graduate Certificate), including geriatric social work/clinical gerontology; special education (Graduate Certificate), including autism spectrum disorder, disabilities education: severe/profound; world languages (Graduate Certificate), including teaching English as a second language (TESL) or foreign language. *Unit head:* Dr. Cynthia DeLuca, Associate Vice President and Assistant Vice Provost, 813-974-3077, Fax: 813-974-7061, E-mail: deluca@usf.edu. *Application contact:* Owen Hooper, Director, Summer and Alternative Calendar Programs, 813-974-6917, E-mail: hooper@usf.edu.
Website: http://www.usf.edu/innovative-education/

The University of Texas Rio Grande Valley, College of Liberal Arts, Department of Sociology and Anthropology, Edinburg, TX 78539. Offers disaster studies (MA); sociology (MS). *Program availability:* Part-time, evening/weekend. *Faculty:* 14 full-time (4 women). *Students:* 16 full-time (12 women), 8 part-time (6 women); includes 21 minority (all Hispanic/Latino). Average age 30. 6 applicants, 83% accepted, 4 enrolled. In 2017, 4 master's awarded. *Entrance requirements:* For master's, GRE General Test, minimum undergraduate GPA of 3.0, bachelor's degree, official transcripts, personal statement, two letters of recommendation. Additional exam requirements/recommendations for international students: Required—TOEFL or IELTS. *Application deadline:* Applications are processed on a rolling basis. Application fee: $50 ($100 for international students). *Expenses:* Tuition, state resident: full-time $5550; part-time $417 per credit hour. Tuition, nonresident: full-time $13,020; part-time $832 per credit hour. *Required fees:* $1169. *Faculty research:* Sociology of education, sociology of health, sociology of religion, migration, race and ethnicity, gender, border studies, disaster studies. *Unit head:* Ramon Guerra, Chair, E-mail: ramon.guerra@utrgv.edu.

The University of Toledo, College of Graduate Studies, College of Medicine and Life Sciences, Department of Public Health and Preventative Medicine, Toledo, OH 43606-3390. Offers biostatistics and epidemiology (Certificate); contemporary gerontological practice (Certificate); environmental and occupational health and safety (MPH); epidemiology (Certificate); global public health (Certificate); health promotion and education (MPH); industrial hygiene (MSOH); medical and health science teaching and learning (Certificate); occupational health (Certificate); public health administration (MPH); public health and emergency response (Certificate); public health epidemiology (MPH); public health nutrition (MPH); MD/MPH. *Program availability:* Part-time, evening/weekend. *Degree requirements:* For master's, thesis or alternative. *Entrance requirements:* For master's, GRE, minimum undergraduate GPA of 3.0, three letters of recommendation, statement of purpose, transcripts from all prior institutions attended, resume; for Certificate, minimum undergraduate GPA of 3.0, three letters of recommendation, statement of purpose, transcripts from all prior institutions attended, resume. Additional exam requirements/recommendations for international students: Required—TOEFL (minimum score 550 paper-based; 80 iBT), IELTS (minimum score 6.5). Electronic applications accepted.

Upper Iowa University, Online Master's Programs, Fayette, IA 52142-1857. Offers accounting (MBA); corporate financial management (MBA); emergency management and homeland security (MPA); general management (MBA); general studies (MPA); government administration (MPA); health and human services (MPA); human resources management (MBA); nonprofit organizational management (MPA); organizational development (MBA); public management (MPA); sport administration (MSA). MBA also available at Madison, WI campus. *Program availability:* Part-time, online learning. *Degree requirements:* For master's, research project. *Entrance requirements:* For master's, GMAT, GRE, or minimum GPA of 2.7 during last 60 hours. Additional exam requirements/recommendations for international students: Required—TOEFL (minimum score 570 paper-based). Electronic applications accepted. *Faculty research:* Total quality management, teams, organization culture and climate, management.

Virginia Commonwealth University, Graduate School, L. Douglas Wilder School of Government and Public Affairs, Program in Homeland Security and Emergency Preparedness, Richmond, VA 23284-9005. Offers MA, Graduate Certificate. *Program availability:* Part-time, online learning. *Entrance requirements:* For master's, GRE, GMAT, MAT or LSAT, minimum GPA of 2.7; for Graduate Certificate, minimum GPA of 2.7. Additional exam requirements/recommendations for international students: Required—TOEFL (minimum score 600 paper-based; 100 iBT); Recommended—IELTS (minimum score 6.5). Electronic applications accepted.

Walden University, Graduate Programs, School of Counseling, Minneapolis, MN 55401. Offers addiction counseling (MS), including addictions and public health, child and adolescent counseling, family studies and interventions, forensic counseling, general program, military families and culture, trauma and crisis counseling; clinical mental health counseling (MS), including addiction counseling, forensic counseling, military families and culture, trauma and crisis counseling; counselor education and supervision (PhD), including consultation, counseling and social change, forensic mental health counseling, leadership and program evaluation, trauma and crisis; marriage, couple, and family counseling (MS), including addiction counseling, career counseling, forensic counseling, military families and culture, trauma and crisis counseling; school counseling (MS), including addiction counseling, career counseling, crisis and trauma, military families and culture. *Accreditation:* ACA. *Program availability:* Part-time, evening/weekend, online only, 100% online. *Degree requirements:* For master's, residency, field experience, professional development plan, licensure plan; for doctorate, thesis/dissertation, residency, practicum, internship. *Entrance requirements:* For master's, bachelor's degree or higher; minimum GPA of 2.5; official transcripts; goal statement (for some programs); access to computer and Internet; for doctorate, master's degree or higher; three years of related professional or academic experience (preferred); minimum GPA of 3.0; goal statement and current resume (for select programs); official transcripts; access to computer and Internet. Additional exam requirements/recommendations for international students: Required—TOEFL (minimum score 550 paper-based, 79 iBT), IELTS (minimum score 6.5), Michigan English Language Assessment Battery (minimum score 82), or PTE (minimum score 53). Electronic applications accepted.

Walden University, Graduate Programs, School of Health Sciences, Minneapolis, MN 55401. Offers clinical research administration (MS, Graduate Certificate); health education and promotion (MS, PhD), including behavioral health (PhD), disease surveillance (PhD), emergency preparedness (MS), general (MHA, MS), global health (PhD), health policy (PhD), health policy and advocacy (MS), population health (PhD); health informatics (MS); health services (PhD), including community health, healthcare administration, leadership, public health policy, self-designed; healthcare administration (MHA, DHA), including general (MHA, MS); leadership and organizational development (MHA); public health (MPH, Dr PH, PhD, Graduate Certificate), including community health education (PhD), epidemiology (PhD); systems policy (MHA). *Program availability:* Part-time, evening/weekend, online only, 100% online. *Degree requirements:* For doctorate, thesis/dissertation, residency. *Entrance requirements:* For master's, bachelor's degree or higher; minimum GPA of 2.5; official transcripts; goal statement (for some programs); access to computer and Internet; for doctorate, master's degree or higher; three years of related professional or academic experience (preferred); minimum GPA of 3.0; goal statement and current resume (for select programs); official transcripts; access to computer and Internet; for Graduate Certificate, relevant work experience; access to computer and Internet. Additional exam requirements/recommendations for international students: Required—TOEFL (minimum score 550 paper-based, 79 iBT), IELTS (minimum score 6.5), Michigan English Language Assessment Battery (minimum score 82), or PTE (minimum score 53). Electronic applications accepted.

Walden University, Graduate Programs, School of Public Policy and Administration, Minneapolis, MN 55401. Offers criminal justice (MPA, MPP, MS, Graduate Certificate), including emergency management (MS, PhD), general program (MS), global leadership (MS, PhD), homeland security and policy coordination (MS, PhD), law and public policy (MS, PhD), policy analysis (MS, PhD), public management and leadership (MS, PhD), self-designed (MS), terrorism, mediation, and peace (MS, PhD); criminal justice and executive management (MS), including global leadership (MS, PhD); criminal justice leadership and executive management (MS), including emergency management (MS, PhD), general program, homeland security and policy coordination (MS, PhD), law and public policy (MS, PhD), policy analysis (MS, PhD), public management and leadership (MS, PhD), self-designed, terrorism, mediation, and peace (MS, PhD); emergency management (MPA, MPP, MS), including criminal justice (MS, PhD), general program (MS), homeland security (MS), public management and leadership (MS, PhD), terrorism and emergency management (MS); general program (MPA, MPP); global leadership (MPA, MPP); government management (Graduate Certificate); health policy (MPA, MPP); homeland security (Graduate Certificate); homeland security and policy coordination (MPA, MPP); international nongovernmental organizations (MPA, MPP);

law and public policy (MPA, MPP); local government management for sustainable communities (MPA, MPP); nonprofit management (Graduate Certificate); nonprofit management and leadership (MPA, MPP, MS), including global leadership (MS, PhD), international nongovernmental organization (MS), local government for sustainable communities (MS), self designed (MS); online teaching in higher education (Post-Master's Certificate); policy analysis (MPA); public management and leadership (MPA, MPP, Graduate Certificate); public policy (Graduate Certificate); public policy and administration (PhD), including criminal justice (MS, PhD), emergency management (MS, PhD), global leadership (MS, PhD), health policy, homeland security and policy coordination (MS, PhD), international nongovernmental organizations, law and public policy (MS, PhD), local government management for sustainable communities, nonprofit management and leadership, policy analysis (MS, PhD), public management and leadership (MS, PhD), terrorism, mediation, and peace (MS, PhD); strategic planning and public policy (Graduate Certificate); terrorism, mediation, and peace (MPA, MPP). *Program availability:* Part-time, evening/weekend, online only, 100% online. *Degree requirements:* For doctorate, thesis/dissertation, residency. *Entrance requirements:* For master's, bachelor's degree or higher; minimum GPA of 2.5; official transcripts; goal statement (for some programs); access to computer and Internet; for doctorate, master's degree or higher; three years of related professional or academic experience (preferred); minimum GPA of 3.0; goal statement and current resume (for select programs); official transcripts; access to computer and Internet; for other advanced degree, relevant work experience; access to computer and Internet. Additional exam requirements/recommendations for international students: Required—TOEFL (minimum score 550 paper-based, 79 iBT), IELTS (minimum score 6.5), Michigan English Language Assessment Battery (minimum score 82), or PTE (minimum score 53). Electronic applications accepted.

Waldorf University, Program in Organizational Leadership, Forest City, IA 50436. Offers criminal justice leadership (MA); emergency management leadership (MA); fire/rescue executive leadership (MA); human resource development (MA); public administration (MA); sport management (MA); teacher leader (MA).

Wheaton College, Graduate School, Humanitarian Disaster Institute, Wheaton, IL 60187-5593. Offers humanitarian and disaster leadership (MA). *Faculty:* 1 full-time (0 women). *Degree requirements:* For master's, thesis or alternative. *Entrance requirements:* Additional exam requirements/recommendations for international students: Required—TOEFL (minimum score 550 paper-based; 80 iBT), IELTS (minimum score 6.5). Electronic applications accepted. *Expenses: Tuition:* Full-time $19,800; part-time $825 per credit hour. Tuition and fees vary according to degree level and program. *Unit head:* Dr. Jamie Aten, Executive Director, 630-752-7659, E-mail: jamie.aten@wheaton.edu. *Application contact:* Director of Graduate Admissions, 630-752-5195, Fax: 630-752-7047, E-mail: graduate.admissions@wheaton.edu.
Website: https://www.wheaton.edu/graduate-school/degrees/ma-in-humanitarian-and-disaster-leadership/

York University, Faculty of Graduate Studies, Faculty of Liberal Arts and Professional Studies, Program in Disaster and Emergency Management, Toronto, ON M3J 1P3, Canada. Offers MA.

Homeland Security

Angelo State University, College of Graduate Studies and Research, College of Arts and Humanities, Department of Security Studies and Criminal Justice, San Angelo, TX 76909. Offers criminal justice (MS); homeland security (MS); intelligence, security studies, and analysis (MSS); security studies (MSS). *Program availability:* Part-time, evening/weekend, online learning. *Students:* 56 full-time (28 women), 146 part-time (44 women); includes 81 minority (27 Black or African American, non-Hispanic/Latino; 2 American Indian or Alaska Native, non-Hispanic/Latino; 10 Asian, non-Hispanic/Latino; 35 Hispanic/Latino; 7 Two or more races, non-Hispanic/Latino). Average age 32. *Degree requirements:* For master's, comprehensive exam. *Entrance requirements:* For master's, essay, letters of recommendation. Additional exam requirements/recommendations for international students: Required—TOEFL or IELTS. *Application deadline:* For fall admission, 7/15 priority date for domestic students, 6/10 for international students; for spring admission, 12/1 priority date for domestic students, 11/1 for international students. Applications are processed on a rolling basis. Application fee: $40 ($50 for international students). Electronic applications accepted. *Expenses:* Tuition, state resident: full-time $3856. Tuition, nonresident: full-time $11,324. *Required fees:* $2650. *Financial support:* Federal Work-Study and scholarships/grants available. Support available to part-time students. Financial award application deadline: 3/1; financial award applicants required to submit FAFSA. *Unit head:* Dr. William A. Taylor, Chair, 325-486-6689, Fax: 325-942-2544, E-mail: william.taylor@angelo.edu.
Website: http://www.angelo.edu/dept/security_studies_criminal_justice/

Arizona State University at the Tempe campus, College of Public Programs, School of Public Affairs, Phoenix, AZ 85004-0687. Offers emergency management and homeland security (MA); program evaluation (MS); public administration (MPA, PhD), including nonprofit administration (MPA), urban management (MPA); public policy (MPP); MPA/MSW. *Accreditation:* NASPAA (one or more programs are accredited). *Program availability:* Part-time, evening/weekend. Terminal master's awarded for partial completion of doctoral program. *Degree requirements:* For master's, thesis or alternative, policy analysis or capstone project; interactive Program of Study (iPOS) submitted before completing 50 percent of required credit hours; for doctorate, comprehensive exam, thesis/dissertation, interactive Program of Study (iPOS) submitted before completing 50 percent of required credit hours. *Entrance requirements:* For master's, GRE, minimum GPA of 3.0 or equivalent in last 2 years of work leading to bachelor's degree; for doctorate, GRE, minimum GPA of 3.0 or equivalent in last 2 years of work leading to bachelor's degree, 3 letters of recommendation, resume, statement of goals, samples of research reports. Additional exam requirements/recommendations for international students: Required—TOEFL (minimum score 600 paper-based; 100 iBT), IELTS (minimum score 6.5). Electronic applications accepted. *Expenses:* Contact institution.

Auburn University at Montgomery, College of Public Policy and Justice, Department of Justice and Public Safety, Montgomery, AL 36124-4023. Offers criminal studies (MSJPS); homeland security (MSJPS); homeland security and emergency management (MS); legal studies (MSJPS); organizational leadership (MSJPS). *Program availability:* Part-time, evening/weekend. *Faculty:* 5 full-time (2 women). *Students:* 9 full-time (3 women), 33 part-time (20 women); includes 23 minority (22 Black or African American, non-Hispanic/Latino; 1 Asian, non-Hispanic/Latino). Average age 30. 24 applicants, 75% accepted, 9 enrolled. In 2017, 23 master's awarded. *Degree requirements:* For master's, comprehensive exam, thesis optional. *Entrance requirements:* For master's, GRE General Test or MAT. Additional exam requirements/recommendations for international students: Recommended—TOEFL (minimum score 500 paper-based; 61 iBT), IELTS (minimum score 5.5), TSE (minimum score 44). *Application deadline:* For fall admission, 7/15 for international students; for spring admission, 11/15 for international students; for summer admission, 4/15 for international students. Applications are processed on a rolling basis. Application fee: $25. Electronic applications accepted. *Expenses:* Tuition, state resident: full-time $6930; part-time $385 per credit hour. Tuition, nonresident: full-time $15,588; part-time $866 per credit hour. *Required fees:* $640. *Financial support:* Career-related internships or fieldwork and scholarships/grants available. Support available to part-time students. Financial award application deadline: 3/1; financial award applicants required to submit FAFSA. *Faculty research:* Law enforcement, corrections, juvenile justice. *Unit head:* Dr. Ralph Ioimo, Head, 334-244-3691, Fax: 334-244-3244, E-mail: rioimo@aum.edu.
Website: http://cppj.aum.edu/departments/justice-and-public-safety

Aurora University, College of Arts and Sciences, Aurora, IL 60506-4892. Offers homeland security (MS); mathematics (MS); mathematics and science education for elementary teachers (MA); mathematics educaton (MA); science education (MA). *Program availability:* Part-time, evening/weekend, 100% online. *Faculty:* 3 full-time (2 women), 6 part-time/adjunct (3 women). *Students:* 47 full-time (28 women), 45 part-time (10 women); includes 12 minority (5 Black or African American, non-Hispanic/Latino; 4 Asian, non-Hispanic/Latino; 3 Hispanic/Latino). Average age 36. 68 applicants, 96% accepted, 15 enrolled. *Degree requirements:* For master's, research seminars. *Entrance requirements:* For master's, bachelor's degree in mathematics or in some other field with extensive course work in mathematics (for MS in mathematics). Additional exam requirements/recommendations for international students: Required—TOEFL (minimum score 550 paper-based; 79 iBT). *Application deadline:* For fall admission, 6/1 for international students; for spring admission, 10/1 for international students. Applications are processed on a rolling basis. Application fee: $0. Electronic applications accepted. *Expenses:* Contact institution. *Financial support:* Federal Work-Study, scholarships/grants, and unspecified assistantships available. Support available to part-time students. Financial award application deadline: 4/1; financial award applicants required to submit FAFSA. *Unit head:* Dr. Frank Buscher, Vice President for Academic Affairs, 630-844-5252, E-mail: fbuscher@aurora.edu. *Application contact:* Judson Curry, Dean of Adult and Graduate Studies, 630-947-8946, E-mail: jcurry@aurora.edu.

Ball State University, Graduate School, College of Sciences and Humanities, Department of Natural Resources and Environmental Management, Muncie, IN 47306. Offers emergency management and homeland security (Certificate); natural resources and environmental management (MA, MS). *Program availability:* Part-time. *Faculty:* 5 full-time (2 women). *Students:* 4 full-time (2 women), 9 part-time (5 women); includes 1 minority (Two or more races, non-Hispanic/Latino). Average age 28. 12 applicants, 67% accepted, 4 enrolled. In 2017, 4 master's, 3 other advanced degrees awarded. *Degree requirements:* For master's, thesis (for some programs). *Entrance requirements:* For master's, GRE General Test, minimum baccalaureate GPA of 2.75 or 3.0 in latter half of baccalaureate, two letters of reference. Additional exam requirements/recommendations for international students: Required—TOEFL (minimum score 550 paper-based; 79 iBT), IELTS (minimum score 6.5). *Application deadline:* For fall admission, 3/1 priority date for domestic students. Applications are processed on a rolling basis. Application fee: $60. Electronic applications accepted. *Financial support:* In 2017–18, 8 students received support, including 2 research assistantships with partial tuition reimbursements available (averaging $12,250 per year), 6 teaching assistantships with partial tuition reimbursements available (averaging $9,907 per year); unspecified assistantships also available. Financial award application deadline: 3/1; financial award applicants required to submit FAFSA. *Faculty research:* Acid rain, indoor air pollution, land reclamation. *Unit head:* Dr. Amy Gregg, Chairperson, 765-285-5781, Fax: 765-285-2606, E-mail: algregg2@bsu.edu.
Website: http://www.bsu.edu/nrem/

Ball State University, Graduate School, College of Sciences and Humanities, Department of Political Science, Program in Public Administration, Muncie, IN 47306. Offers public administration (MPA, Certificate), including community and economic development (MPA), criminal justice (MPA), emergency management and homeland security (MPA), information and communication technology (MPA). *Program availability:* Part-time. *Students:* 20 full-time (7 women), 14 part-time (8 women); includes 4 minority (2 Black or African American, non-Hispanic/Latino; 2 Hispanic/Latino), 1 international. Average age 29. 28 applicants, 89% accepted, 15 enrolled. In 2017, 10 master's awarded. *Degree requirements:* For master's, comprehensive exam. *Entrance requirements:* For master's, GRE General Test, minimum baccalaureate GPA of 2.8, two letters of recommendation. Additional exam requirements/recommendations for international students: Required—TOEFL (minimum score 550 paper-based; 79 iBT), IELTS (minimum score 6.5). *Application deadline:* Applications are processed on a rolling basis. Application fee: $60. Electronic applications accepted. *Financial support:* Research assistantships with partial tuition reimbursements and unspecified assistantships available. Financial award application deadline: 3/1; financial award applicants required to submit FAFSA. *Faculty research:* Employment training programs, personnel and labor relations, planning. *Unit head:* Dr. Daniel Reagan, Chairperson, 765-285-8789, Fax: 765-285-5345, E-mail: jlosco@bsu.edu. *Application contact:* Dr. Charles Taylor, Associate Professor/Graduate Advisor, 765-285-8794, Fax: 765-285-5345, E-mail: cdtaylor@bsu.edu.
Website: http://www.bsu.edu/poli-sci

Capella University, School of Public Service Leadership, Master's Programs in Healthcare, Minneapolis, MN 55402. Offers criminal justice (MS); emergency management (MS); general public health (MPH); gerontology (MS); health administration (MHA); health care operations (MHA); health management policy (MPH); health policy (MHA); homeland security (MS); multidisciplinary human services (MS); public administration (MPA); public safety leadership (MS); social and community services (MS); social behavioral sciences (MPH); MS/MPA.

The Citadel, The Military College of South Carolina, Citadel Graduate College, School of Humanities and Social Sciences, Department of Criminal Justice, Charleston, SC 29409. Offers homeland security (Graduate Certificate); intelligence analysis (Graduate Certificate); intelligence and security studies (MA). *Program availability:* Part-time, evening/weekend, 100% online, blended/hybrid learning. *Entrance requirements:* For master's, GRE or MAT, writing sample that demonstrates strong critical thinking and communication skills. Additional exam requirements/recommendations for international students: Required—TOEFL (minimum score 550 paper-based; 79 iBT). Electronic

applications accepted. *Expenses:* Tuition, state resident: part-time $587 per credit hour. Tuition, nonresident: part-time $988 per credit hour. *Required fees:* $90 per term.

Columbus State University, Graduate Studies, College of Letters and Sciences, Program in Public Safety Administration, Columbus, GA 31907-5645. Offers MPSA. *Program availability:* Part-time. *Faculty:* 1 (woman) full-time, 9 part-time/adjunct (0 women). *Students:* 32 full-time (7 women), 172 part-time (33 women); includes 55 minority (48 Black or African American, non-Hispanic/Latino; 1 American Indian or Alaska Native, non-Hispanic/Latino; 1 Asian, non-Hispanic/Latino; 4 Hispanic/Latino; 1 Two or more races, non-Hispanic/Latino). Average age 44. 45 applicants, 91% accepted, 36 enrolled. In 2017, 83 master's awarded. *Entrance requirements:* For master's, baccalaureate degree, employment in a public safety profession. Additional exam requirements/recommendations for international students: Required—TOEFL (minimum score 550 paper-based; 79 iBT). *Application deadline:* For fall admission, 6/30 for domestic students, 4/1 for international students; for spring admission, 11/1 for domestic and international students; for summer admission, 3/1 for domestic students, 2/1 for international students. Applications are processed on a rolling basis. Application fee: $50. Electronic applications accepted. *Expenses:* Tuition, state resident: full-time $3708; part-time $2472 per year. Tuition, nonresident: full-time $14,418; part-time $9612 per year. *International tuition:* $19,218 full-time. *Required fees:* $1605. Tuition and fees vary according to program. *Financial support:* Application deadline: 5/1; applicants required to submit FAFSA. *Unit head:* Dr. Dennis Rome, Dean, 706-568-2056, E-mail: rome_dennis@columbusstate.edu. *Application contact:* Catrina Smith-Edmond, Assistant Director for Graduate and Global Admission, 706-507-8824, Fax: 706-568-5091, E-mail: smithedmond_catrina@columbusstate.edu.
Website: http://cols.columbusstate.edu

Drexel University, Goodwin College of Professional Studies, School of Technology and Professional Studies, Philadelphia, PA 19104-2875. Offers construction management (MS); creativity and innovation (MS); engineering technology (MS); food science (MS); hospitality management (MS); professional studies: creativity studies (MS); professional studies: e-learning leadership (MS); professional studies: homeland security management (MS); project management (MS); property management (MS); sport management (MS). *Program availability:* Part-time, evening/weekend. *Entrance requirements:* Additional exam requirements/recommendations for international students: Required—TOEFL, IELTS. Electronic applications accepted. Application fee is waived when completed online.

Endicott College, Van Loan School of Graduate and Professional Studies, Program in Homeland Security, Beverly, MA 01915-2096. Offers cybersecurity (MS, Postbaccalaureate Certificate); emergency management (MS). *Program availability:* Part-time. *Faculty:* 2 full-time (1 woman), 5 part-time/adjunct (2 women). *Students:* 21 full-time (8 women), 1 part-time (0 women); includes 5 minority (1 Black or African American, non-Hispanic/Latino; 2 Hispanic/Latino; 2 Native Hawaiian or other Pacific Islander, non-Hispanic/Latino). Average age 28. 18 applicants, 100% accepted, 16 enrolled. In 2017, 16 master's awarded. *Degree requirements:* For master's, thesis. *Entrance requirements:* For master's, undergraduate transcript, two recommendations, personal statement. Additional exam requirements/recommendations for international students: Required—TOEFL. *Application deadline:* Applications are processed on a rolling basis. Application fee: $50. Electronic applications accepted. *Expenses:* Contact institution. *Financial support:* In 2017–18, 2 students received support. Applicants required to submit FAFSA. *Unit head:* Paul Joyce, Director, 978-232-2740, Fax: 978-232-3000, E-mail: pjoyce@endicott.edu. *Application contact:* Ian Menchini, Director, Graduate Enrollment and Advising, 978-232-5292, Fax: 978-232-3000, E-mail: imenchin@endicott.edu.
Website: https://vanloan.endicott.edu/programs-of-study/masters-programs/homeland-security-studies-program

Excelsior College, School of Public Service, Albany, NY 12203-5159. Offers criminal justice (MSCI); homeland security and emergency management (MSCJ); justice administration (MSCI); mediation and arbitration (MPA); public administration (MPA). *Program availability:* Part-time, evening/weekend, online learning. *Faculty:* 6 part-time/adjunct (5 women). *Students:* 173 part-time (49 women); includes 70 minority (32 Black or African American, non-Hispanic/Latino; 1 American Indian or Alaska Native, non-Hispanic/Latino; 3 Asian, non-Hispanic/Latino; 28 Hispanic/Latino; 1 Native Hawaiian or other Pacific Islander, non-Hispanic/Latino; 5 Two or more races, non-Hispanic/Latino). Average age 40. In 2017, 45 master's awarded. *Application deadline:* Applications are processed on a rolling basis. Application fee: $50. Electronic applications accepted. *Expenses:* Tuition: Part-time $645 per credit. *Required fees:* $265 per credit. *Financial support:* Scholarships/grants available. *Unit head:* Dr. Robert Waters, Dean, School of Public Service, 518-464-8500, Fax: 518-464-8777. *Application contact:* Admissions Counselor, 888-647-2388, Fax: 518-464-8777, E-mail: gradadmissions@excelsior.edu.
Website: http://www.excelsior.edu/programs/public-service

Fairleigh Dickinson University, Metropolitan Campus, Anthony J. Petrocelli College of Continuing Studies, School of Administrative Science, Program in Homeland Security, Teaneck, NJ 07666-1914. Offers MSHS.

Georgian Court University, School of Arts and Sciences, Lakewood, NJ 08701-2697. Offers applied behavior analysis (MA); autism spectrum disorders (Certificate); clinical mental health counseling (MA); criminal justice and human rights (MS); holistic health studies (MA, Certificate); homeland security (Certificate); instructional technology (CPC); mercy spirituality (Certificate); parish business management (Certificate); professional counselor (Certificate); school psychology (MA, Certificate); theology (MA, Certificate). *Program availability:* Part-time, evening/weekend. *Faculty:* 18 full-time (11 women), 8 part-time/adjunct (4 women). *Students:* 100 full-time (86 women), 92 part-time (67 women); includes 34 minority (9 Black or African American, non-Hispanic/Latino; 1 Asian, non-Hispanic/Latino; 20 Hispanic/Latino; 4 Two or more races, non-Hispanic/Latino), 2 international. Average age 34. 187 applicants, 56% accepted, 78 enrolled. In 2017, 58 master's, 20 other advanced degrees awarded. *Degree requirements:* For master's, comprehensive exam (for some programs), thesis (for some programs). *Entrance requirements:* For master's, GRE, GMAT, or NTE/PRAXIS, 3 letters of recommendation. Additional exam requirements/recommendations for international students: Required—TOEFL (minimum score 550 paper-based). *Application deadline:* For fall admission, 8/15 for domestic students, 5/1 for international students; for spring admission, 1/15 for domestic students, 10/1 for international students. Applications are processed on a rolling basis. Application fee: $40. Electronic applications accepted. *Expenses:* Tuition: Part-time $839 per credit. *Required fees:* $248 per semester. Tuition and fees vary according to campus/location and program. *Financial support:* Scholarships/grants, health care benefits, and unspecified assistantships available. Financial award application deadline: 4/15; financial award applicants required to submit FAFSA. *Unit head:* Dr. Mary Chinery, Dean, 732-987-2493, Fax: 732-987-2007, E-mail: mchinery@georgian.edu. *Application contact:* Patrick Givens, Director of Graduate and Professional Studies Admissions, 732-987-2736, Fax: 732-987-2000, E-mail: gps@georgian.edu.
Website: https://georgian.edu/academics/school-of-arts-sciences/

Henley-Putnam School of Strategic Security, Master of Science Program in Intelligence Management, Rapid City, SD 57701. Offers MS. *Program availability:* Part-time, online learning. *Degree requirements:* For master's, thesis. *Entrance*

requirements: For master's, bachelor's degree from an institution accredited by an agency recognized by the U.S. Department of Education and/or the Council for Higher Education Accreditation; background check. Additional exam requirements/recommendations for international students: Required—TOEFL (minimum score 650 paper-based; 79 iBT); Recommended—IELTS (minimum score 7). *Expenses:* Contact institution.

Henley-Putnam School of Strategic Security, Master of Science Program in Strategic Security and Protection Management, Rapid City, SD 57701. Offers extremist organizations (MS). *Program availability:* Part-time, online learning. *Degree requirements:* For master's, comprehensive exam, thesis. *Entrance requirements:* For master's, bachelor's degree from institution accredited by an agency recognized by the U.S. Department of Education and/or the Council for Higher Education Accreditation, background check. Additional exam requirements/recommendations for international students: Required—TOEFL (minimum score 650 paper-based; 79 iBT); Recommended—IELTS. *Expenses:* Contact institution.

Henley-Putnam School of Strategic Security, Master of Science Program in Terrorism and Counterterrorism Studies, Rapid City, SD 57701. Offers intelligence operations (MS); protective intelligence (MS). *Program availability:* Part-time, online learning. *Degree requirements:* For master's, thesis. *Entrance requirements:* For master's, bachelor's degree from institution accredited by an agency recognized by the U.S. Department of Education and/or the Council for Higher Education Accreditation, background check. Additional exam requirements/recommendations for international students: Required—TOEFL (minimum score 650 paper-based; 79 iBT); Recommended—IELTS (minimum score 7). *Expenses:* Contact institution.

Indiana University–Purdue University Indianapolis, School of Public and Environmental Affairs, Indianapolis, IN 46202. Offers criminal justice and public safety (MS); homeland security and emergency management (Graduate Certificate); library management (Graduate Certificate); nonprofit management (Graduate Certificate); public affairs (MPA); public management (Graduate Certificate); social entrepreneurship: nonprofit and public benefit organizations (Graduate Certificate); JD/MPA; MLS/NMC; MLS/PMC; MPA/MA. *Accreditation:* CAHME (one or more programs are accredited); NASPAA. *Program availability:* Part-time, evening/weekend, online learning. *Entrance requirements:* For master's, GRE General Test, GMAT or LSAT, minimum GPA of 3.0 (preferred). Additional exam requirements/recommendations for international students: Required—TOEFL (minimum score 93 iBT), IELTS (minimum score 6.5). Electronic applications accepted. *Faculty research:* Nonprofit and public management, public policy, urban policy, sustainability policy, disaster preparedness and recovery, vehicular safety, homicide, offender rehabilitation and re-entry.

Johns Hopkins University, Zanvyl Krieger School of Arts and Sciences, Advanced Academic Programs, Program in Government, Washington, DC 20036. Offers global security studies (MA); government (MA); national securities study (Certificate); nonprofit management (Certificate); public management (MA); research administration (MS); MA/MBA. *Program availability:* Part-time, evening/weekend, online learning. *Degree requirements:* For master's, thesis. *Entrance requirements:* For master's, minimum GPA of 3.0. Additional exam requirements/recommendations for international students: Required—TOEFL (minimum score 100 iBT). Electronic applications accepted.

Keiser University, MA in Homeland Security Program, Fort Lauderdale, FL 33309. Offers MA.
Website: https://www.keiseruniversity.edu/master-arts-criminal-justice-homeland-security-macjhs/

Lasell College, Graduate and Professional Studies in Criminal Justice, Newton, MA 02466-2709. Offers emergency and crisis management (MS, Certificate); homeland security and global justice (MS, Certificate); violence prevention and advocacy (MS, Certificate). *Program availability:* Part-time, evening/weekend, online only, 100% online. *Faculty:* 2 full-time (1 woman), 2 part-time/adjunct (0 women). *Students:* 20 full-time (9 women), 31 part-time (16 women); includes 11 minority (3 Black or African American, non-Hispanic/Latino; 1 Asian, non-Hispanic/Latino; 5 Hispanic/Latino; 2 Two or more races, non-Hispanic/Latino). Average age 31. 33 applicants, 73% accepted, 23 enrolled. In 2017, 2 master's awarded. *Degree requirements:* For master's, minimum GPA of 3.0; internship or research paper. *Entrance requirements:* For master's, one-page personal statement, 2 letters of recommendation, resume, bachelor's degree transcript; for Certificate, bachelor's transcript, 2 letters of recommendation, 1-page statement, resume. Additional exam requirements/recommendations for international students: Required—TOEFL (minimum score 550 paper-based, 79 iBT) or IELTS (minimum score 6). *Application deadline:* For fall admission, 8/31 priority date for domestic students, 6/30 priority date for international students; for spring admission, 12/31 priority date for domestic students, 10/31 priority date for international students. Applications are processed on a rolling basis. Electronic applications accepted. *Expenses:* $600 per credit. *Financial support:* Federal Work-Study, scholarships/grants, and tuition discounts available. Support available to part-time students. Financial award application deadline: 8/31; financial award applicants required to submit FAFSA. *Faculty research:* Children aging out of foster care and the criminal justice system; police departments' attitudes toward the mentally ill and jail diversion programs for those offenders. *Unit head:* Eric Turner, Vice President of Graduate and Professional Studies, 617-243-2071, Fax: 617-243-2450, E-mail: gradinfo@lasell.edu. *Application contact:* Adrienne Franciosi, Director of Graduate Enrollment, 617-243-2214, Fax: 617-243-2450, E-mail: gradinfo@lasell.edu.
Website: http://www.lasell.edu/academics/graduate-and-professional-studies/programs-of-study/master-of-science-in-criminal-justice-.html

Liberty University, Helms School of Government, Lynchburg, VA 24515. Offers criminal justice (MS), including forensic psychology, homeland security, public administration (MA, MS); international relations (MS); political science (MS); public administration (MPA), including business and government, healthcare, law and public policy, public and non-profit management; public policy (MA), including campaigns and elections, international affairs, Middle East affairs, public administration (MA, MS). *Program availability:* Part-time, online learning. *Students:* 287 full-time (148 women), 639 part-time (248 women); includes 231 minority (173 Black or African American, non-Hispanic/Latino; 4 American Indian or Alaska Native, non-Hispanic/Latino; 8 Asian, non-Hispanic/Latino; 20 Hispanic/Latino; 1 Native Hawaiian or other Pacific Islander, non-Hispanic/Latino; 25 Two or more races, non-Hispanic/Latino), 7 international. Average age 35. 876 applicants, 64% accepted, 277 enrolled. In 2017, 211 master's awarded. *Entrance requirements:* For master's, minimum undergraduate GPA of 3.0. Additional exam requirements/recommendations for international students: Required—TOEFL (minimum score 600 paper-based; 100 iBT). *Application deadline:* Applications are processed on a rolling basis. Application fee: $50. Electronic applications accepted. *Unit head:* Shawn D. Akers, Dean, 434-592-4986. *Application contact:* Jay Bridge, Director of Admissions, 800-424-9595, Fax: 800-628-7977, E-mail: gradadmissions@liberty.edu.

London Metropolitan University, Graduate Programs, London, United Kingdom. Offers applied psychology (M Sc); architecture (MA); biomedical science (M Sc); blood science (M Sc); cancer pharmacology (M Sc); computer networking and cyber security (M Sc); computing and information systems (M Sc); conference interpreting (MA); counter-terrorism studies (M Sc); creative, digital and professional writing (MA); crime,

violence and prevention (M Sc); criminology (M Sc); curating contemporary art (MA); data analytics (M Sc); digital media (MA); early childhood studies (MA); education (MA, Ed D); financial services law, regulation and compliance (LL M); food science (M Sc); forensic psychology (M Sc); health and social care management and policy (M Sc); human nutrition (M Sc); human resource management (MA); human rights and international conflict (MA); information technology (M Sc); intelligence and security studies (M Sc); international oil, gas and energy law (LL M); international relations (MA); interpreting (MA); learning and teaching in higher education (MA); legal practice (LL M); media and entertainment law (LL M); organizational and consumer psychology (M Sc); psychological therapy (M Sc); psychology of mental health (M Sc); public health (M Sc); public policy and management (MPA); security studies (M Sc); social work (M Sc); spatial planning and urban design (MA); sports therapy (M Sc); supporting older children and young people with dyslexia (MA); teaching languages (MA), including Arabic, English; translation (MA); woman and child abuse (MA).

Long Island University–Riverhead, Graduate Programs, Riverhead, NY 11901. Offers applied behavior analysis (Advanced Certificate); childhood education (MS), including grades 1-6; cybersecurity policy (Advanced Certificate); homeland security management (MS, Advanced Certificate); literacy education (MS); literacy education B-6 (MS); teaching students with disabilities (MS), including grades 1-6; TESOL (Advanced Certificate). *Accreditation:* TEAC. *Program availability:* Part-time. *Faculty:* 4 full-time (1 woman), 11 part-time/adjunct (5 women). *Students:* 17 full-time (14 women), 58 part-time (36 women); includes 14 minority (4 Black or African American, non-Hispanic/Latino; 1 American Indian or Alaska Native, non-Hispanic/Latino; 1 Asian, non-Hispanic/Latino; 6 Hispanic/Latino; 2 Two or more races, non-Hispanic/Latino). Average age 32. 68 applicants, 79% accepted, 26 enrolled. In 2017, 30 master's, 7 other advanced degrees awarded. *Entrance requirements:* Additional exam requirements/recommendations for international students: Required—TOEFL or IELTS. *Application deadline:* Applications are processed on a rolling basis. Application fee: $50. Electronic applications accepted. *Expenses:* Contact institution. *Financial support:* In 2017–18, 53 students received support. Scholarships/grants available. Support available to part-time students. Financial award application deadline: 2/15; financial award applicants required to submit FAFSA. *Unit head:* Dr. Abagail VanVlerah, Dean and Chief Operating Officer, 631-299-3831, E-mail: abagail.vanvlerah@liu.edu. *Application contact:* Jean Conroy, Associate Dean, 631-287-8301, E-mail: jean.conroy@liu.edu.

Missouri State University, Graduate College, College of Humanities and Public Affairs, Department of Criminology and Criminal Justice, Springfield, MO 65897. Offers community corrections (Certificate); criminology and criminal justice (MS); homeland security and defense (Certificate). *Program availability:* Part-time, 100% online, blended/hybrid learning. *Faculty:* 7 full-time (2 women). *Students:* 19 full-time (12 women), 18 part-time (7 women); includes 2 minority (both Black or African American, non-Hispanic/Latino). Average age 26. 23 applicants, 83% accepted, 11 enrolled. In 2017, 25 master's awarded. *Degree requirements:* For master's, comprehensive exam, thesis or alternative. *Entrance requirements:* For master's, bachelor's degree in criminology, criminal justice, or sociology; minimum undergraduate GPA of 3.0. Additional exam requirements/recommendations for international students: Required—TOEFL (minimum score 550 paper-based; 79 iBT), IELTS (minimum score 6). *Application deadline:* For fall admission, 7/20 priority date for domestic students, 5/1 for international students; for spring admission, 12/20 priority date for domestic students, 9/1 for international students; for summer admission, 5/20 priority date for domestic students. Applications are processed on a rolling basis. Application fee: $35 ($50 for international students). Electronic applications accepted. *Expenses:* Tuition, state resident: full-time $2915; part-time $2021 per credit hour. Tuition, nonresident: full-time $5354; part-time $3647 per credit hour. *International tuition:* $11,992 full-time. *Required fees:* $173; $173 per credit hour. Tuition and fees vary according to class time, course level, course load, degree level, campus/location and program. *Financial support:* Federal Work-Study, institutionally sponsored loans, and unspecified assistantships available. Financial award application deadline: 3/31; financial award applicants required to submit FAFSA. *Faculty research:* Homeland security initiatives, juvenile policy and programs, law enforcement and drug abuse. *Unit head:* Dr. Brett Garland, Department Head, 417-836-6954, E-mail: brettgarland@missouristate.edu. *Application contact:* Stephanie Praschan, Director, Graduate Enrollment Management, 417-836-5388, Fax: 417-836-6200, E-mail: stephaniepraschan@missouristate.edu.
Website: http://criminology.missouristate.edu/

Missouri State University, Graduate College, Interdisciplinary Program in Professional Studies, Springfield, MO 65897. Offers administrative studies (Certificate); applied communication (MS); criminal justice (MS); environmental management (MS); homeland security (MS); individualized (MS); professional studies (MS); screenwriting and producing (MS); sports management (MS). *Program availability:* Part-time, evening/weekend, 100% online, blended/hybrid learning. *Students:* 51 full-time (33 women), 95 part-time (41 women); includes 21 minority (8 Black or African American, non-Hispanic/Latino; 1 Asian, non-Hispanic/Latino; 7 Hispanic/Latino; 5 Two or more races, non-Hispanic/Latino), 37 international. Average age 24. 71 applicants, 69% accepted, 35 enrolled. In 2017, 50 master's awarded. *Degree requirements:* For master's, comprehensive exam, thesis or alternative. *Entrance requirements:* For master's, GRE, GMAT (if GPA less than 3.0). Additional exam requirements/recommendations for international students: Required—TOEFL (minimum score 550 paper-based; 79 iBT), IELTS (minimum score 6). *Application deadline:* For fall admission, 7/15 priority date for domestic students; for spring admission, 12/1 priority date for domestic students; for summer admission, 5/1 for domestic students. Applications are processed on a rolling basis. Application fee: $35 ($50 for international students). Electronic applications accepted. *Expenses:* Tuition, state resident: full-time $2915; part-time $2021 per credit hour. Tuition, nonresident: full-time $5354; part-time $3647 per credit hour. *International tuition:* $11,992 full-time. *Required fees:* $173; $173 per credit hour. Tuition and fees vary according to class time, course level, course load, degree level, campus/location and program. *Financial support:* Career-related internships or fieldwork, Federal Work-Study, institutionally sponsored loans, scholarships/grants, and unspecified assistantships available. Support available to part-time students. Financial award application deadline: 3/31; financial award applicants required to submit FAFSA. *Unit head:* Dr. Gerald Masterson, Program Director, 417-836-5251, Fax: 417-836-6888, E-mail: mps@missouristate.edu. *Application contact:* Stephanie Praschan, Director, Graduate Enrollment Management, 417-836-5330, Fax: 417-836-6200, E-mail: stephaniepraschan@missouristate.edu.
Website: http://mps.missouristate.edu

Monmouth University, Graduate Studies, Department of Criminal Justice, West Long Branch, NJ 07764-1898. Offers criminal justice (MA), including homeland security; criminal justice administration (Certificate). *Program availability:* Part-time, evening/weekend, 100% online. *Faculty:* 5 full-time (1 woman), 2 part-time/adjunct (0 women). *Students:* 12 full-time (8 women), 15 part-time (8 women); includes 9 minority (4 Black or African American, non-Hispanic/Latino; 4 Hispanic/Latino; 1 Two or more races, non-Hispanic/Latino). Average age 29. In 2017, 11 master's, 1 other advanced degree awarded. *Degree requirements:* For master's, comprehensive exam (for some programs), thesis (for some programs). *Entrance requirements:* For master's and Certificate, baccalaureate degree with minimum GPA of 3.0 in major, 2.5 overall; two letters of recommendation; personal essay. Additional exam requirements/

recommendations for international students: Required—TOEFL (minimum score 550 paper-based; 79 iBT), IELTS (minimum score 6), Michigan English Language Assessment Battery (minimum score 77) or Certificate of Advanced English (minimum score 160). *Application deadline:* For fall admission, 7/15 priority date for domestic students, 6/1 for international students; for spring admission, 12/1 priority date for domestic students, 11/1 for international students; for summer admission, 5/1 for domestic students. Applications are processed on a rolling basis. Application fee: $50. Electronic applications accepted. *Expenses: Tuition:* Full-time $21,366; part-time $7122 per credit. *Required fees:* $700; $175 per term. *Financial support:* In 2017–18, 7 students received support. Institutionally sponsored loans, scholarships/grants, and unspecified assistantships available. Support available to part-time students. Financial award applicants required to submit FAFSA. *Faculty research:* Violent crimes, criminal pathology, terrorism, computer crime, comparative criminal justice systems, homeland security. *Unit head:* Dr. Brian Lockwood, Program Director, 732-571-7567, Fax: 732-263-5148, E-mail: lockwood@monmouth.edu. *Application contact:* Andrea Thompson, Graduate Admission Counselor, 732-571-3452, Fax: 732-263-5123, E-mail: gradadm@monmouth.edu.
Website: http://www.monmouth.edu/academics/criminal_justice/default.asp

National Defense University, College of International Security Affairs, Washington, DC 20319-5066. Offers strategic security studies (MA), including counterterrorism, homeland defense, international security studies. *Program availability:* Part-time, evening/weekend. *Degree requirements:* For master's, thesis. *Entrance requirements:* Additional exam requirements/recommendations for international students: Required—TOEFL.

The National Graduate School of Quality Management, Graduate Programs, Falmouth, MA 02541. Offers homeland security (MS); quality systems management (MS, DBA).

National University, Academic Affairs, School of Professional Studies, La Jolla, CA 92037-1011. Offers criminal justice (MCJ); digital cinema production (MFA); digital journalism (MA); homeland security and emergency management (MS); juvenile justice (MS); professional screenwriting (MFA); public administration (MPA), including human resource management, organizational leadership. *Program availability:* Part-time, evening/weekend, 100% online, blended/hybrid learning. *Degree requirements:* For master's, thesis (for some programs). *Entrance requirements:* For master's, interview, minimum GPA of 2.5. Additional exam requirements/recommendations for international students: Required—TOEFL (minimum score 550 paper-based; 79 iBT), IELTS (minimum score 6). *Application deadline:* Applications are processed on a rolling basis. Application fee: $60 ($65 for international students). Electronic applications accepted. *Expenses: Tuition:* Part-time $430 per quarter hour. *Financial support:* Career-related internships or fieldwork, institutionally sponsored loans, scholarships/grants, and tuition waivers (partial) available. Support available to part-time students. Financial award application deadline: 6/30; financial award applicants required to submit FAFSA. *Unit head:* Dr. Daniel Donaldson, Dean, 858-642-8480, E-mail: sops@nu.edu. *Application contact:* Brandon Jouganatos, Vice President for Enrollment Services, 800-628-8648, E-mail: advisor@nu.edu.
Website: http://www.nu.edu/OurPrograms/School-of-Professional-Studies.html

Naval Postgraduate School, Departments and Academic Groups, Department of National Security Affairs, Monterey, CA 93943. Offers national security affairs (MA); security studies (MA), including civil-military relations, combating terrorism: policy and strategy, defense decision-making and planning, Europe and Eurasia, Far East, Southeast Asia, the Pacific, homeland security and defense, Middle East, South Asia, Sub-Saharan Africa, stabilization and reconstruction, western hemisphere. Program only open to commissioned officers of the United States and friendly nations and selected United States federal civilian employees. *Program availability:* Part-time. *Degree requirements:* For master's, thesis (for some programs). *Faculty research:* Privatizing welfare in the Middle East; social construction of Russia's resurgence; institutions, ethnicity and political mobilization in South Africa; Hezbollah; China's strategic interests in Cambodia.

Nichols College, Graduate and Professional Studies, Dudley, MA 01571-5000. Offers business administration (MBA); counterterrorism (MS); organizational leadership (MSOL). *Program availability:* Part-time, evening/weekend, online learning. *Degree requirements:* For master's, project (for MOL). *Entrance requirements:* For master's, 2 letters of recommendation, current resume, official transcripts, 800-word personal statement. Additional exam requirements/recommendations for international students: Required—TOEFL (minimum score 500 paper-based). Electronic applications accepted.

Northeastern University, College of Professional Studies, Boston, MA 02115-5096. Offers applied nutrition (MS); college athletics administration (MSL); commerce and economic development (MS); corporate and organizational communication (MS); criminal justice (MS); digital media (MPS); elearning and instructional design (M Ed); elementary education (MAT); geographic information technology (MPS); global studies and international relations (MS); higher education administration (M Ed); homeland security (MA); human services (MS); informatics (MPS); leadership (MS); learning analytics (M Ed); learning and instruction (M Ed); nonprofit management (MS); professional sports administration (MSL); project management (MS); regulatory affairs for drugs, biologics, and medical devices (MS); respiratory care leadership (MS); special education (M Ed); technical communication (MS). *Program availability:* Part-time, evening/weekend, 100% online, blended/hybrid learning. *Faculty:* 82 full-time (51 women), 853 part-time/adjunct (366 women). *Students:* 5,278 part-time (3,230 women). In 2017, 1,586 master's awarded. *Application deadline:* Applications are processed on a rolling basis. Application fee: $0. Electronic applications accepted. *Expenses:* Contact institution. *Financial support:* Applicants required to submit FAFSA. *Unit head:* Dr. Mary Loeffelholz, Dean of the College of Professional Studies. *Application contact:* E-mail: cpsadmissions@northeastern.edu.
Website: https://cps.northeastern.edu/

Northeastern University, College of Social Sciences and Humanities, Boston, MA 02115. Offers criminology and criminal justice (MSCJ); criminology and justice policy (PhD); economics (MA, PhD); English (MA, PhD); international affairs (MA); law and public policy (PhD); political science (MA, PhD); public administration (MPA); public policy (MPP); security and resilience studies (MS); sociology (MA, PhD); urban and regional policy (MS); urban informatics (MS); world history (MA, PhD). *Program availability:* Online learning. *Faculty:* 242. *Students:* 491. In 2017, 143 master's, 38 doctorates awarded. *Degree requirements:* For doctorate, variable foreign language requirement, comprehensive exam, thesis/dissertation. *Entrance requirements:* For master's and doctorate, GRE. Additional exam requirements/recommendations for international students: Required—TOEFL, IELTS. Application fee: $75. Electronic applications accepted. *Expenses:* Contact institution. *Financial support:* Teaching assistantships, career-related internships or fieldwork, scholarships/grants, health care benefits, tuition waivers (full and partial), and unspecified assistantships available. Support available to part-time students. Financial award applicants required to submit FAFSA. *Unit head:* Dr. Uta Poiger, Dean, 617-373-5173, E-mail: college_of_social_sciences_and_humanities@neu.edu. *Application contact:* 617-373-5990, E-mail: gradcssh@northeastern.edu.
Website: http://www.northeastern.edu/cssh/

Northwestern State University of Louisiana, Graduate Studies and Research, Department of Criminal Justice, History and Social Sciences, Program in Homeland Security, Natchitoches, LA 71497. Offers MS. *Degree requirements:* For master's, comprehensive exam, thesis or alternative. *Entrance requirements:* For master's, GRE General Test. Additional exam requirements/recommendations for international students: Required—TOEFL. Electronic applications accepted.

Notre Dame College, Graduate Programs, South Euclid, OH 44121-4293. Offers mild/moderate needs (M Ed); reading (M Ed); security policy studies (MA, Graduate Certificate); technology (M Ed). *Program availability:* Part-time, evening/weekend. *Degree requirements:* For master's, thesis. *Entrance requirements:* For master's, GRE General Test, MAT, minimum undergraduate GPA of 2.75, valid teaching certificate, bachelor's degree in an education-related field from accredited college or university, official transcripts of most recent college work. *Faculty research:* Cognitive psychology, teaching critical thinking in the classroom.

Pace University, Dyson College of Arts and Sciences, MA Program in Management for Public Safety and Homeland Security Professionals, New York, NY 10038. Offers MA. *Program availability:* Evening/weekend, blended/hybrid learning. *Students:* 3 full-time (2 women), 11 part-time (5 women); includes 6 minority (2 Black or African American, non-Hispanic/Latino; 1 Asian, non-Hispanic/Latino; 3 Hispanic/Latino). Average age 27. In 2017, 7 master's awarded. *Degree requirements:* For master's, project. *Entrance requirements:* For master's, 2 letters of recommendation, resume, personal statement, official transcripts. Additional exam requirements/recommendations for international students: Required—TOEFL. *Application deadline:* For fall admission, 8/1 for domestic students. Applications are processed on a rolling basis. Application fee: $70. Electronic applications accepted. *Financial support:* Research assistantships, scholarships/grants, and unspecified assistantships available. Financial award application deadline: 2/15; financial award applicants required to submit FAFSA. *Unit head:* Dr. Joseph Ryan, Chair, Criminal Justice and Security Department, 914-773-3814, E-mail: jryan@pace.edu. *Application contact:* Susan Ford-Goldschein, Director of Admissions, 914-422-4283, Fax: 212-346-1585, E-mail: graduateadmission@pace.edu.
Website: http://www.pace.edu/dyson/programs/ma-public-safety-homeland-security

Penn State Harrisburg, Graduate School, School of Public Affairs, Middletown, PA 17057. Offers criminal justice (MA); health administration (MHA); health administration: long term care (Certificate); homeland security (MPS, Certificate); public administration (MPA, PhD); public administration: non-profit administration (Certificate); public budgeting and financial management (Certificate); public sector human resource management (Certificate). *Accreditation:* NASPAA. *Unit head:* Dr. Mukund S. Kulkarni, Chancellor, 717-948-6105, Fax: 717-948-6452. *Application contact:* Robert W. Coffman, Jr., Director of Enrollment Management, Recruitment and Admissions, 717-948-6250, Fax: 717-948-6325, E-mail: hbgadmit@psu.edu.
Website: https://harrisburg.psu.edu/public-affairs

Post University, Program in Public Administration, Waterbury, CT 06723-2540. Offers emergency management and homeland security (MPA). *Program availability:* Online learning. *Degree requirements:* For master's, capstone project. *Entrance requirements:* For master's, resume. *Expenses: Tuition:* Part-time $730 per credit hour. Part-time tuition and fees vary according to degree level and program. *Application contact:* Veronica Montalvo, Vice President, Online Education Enrollment Management and Admissions, 203-596-6164, E-mail: vmontalvo@post.edu.
Website: https://post.edu/academics/online-master-of-public-administration

Regent University, Graduate School, Robertson School of Government, Virginia Beach, VA 23464. Offers government (MA), including American government, healthcare policy and ethics (MA, MPA), international relations, law and public policy, national security studies, political communication, political theory, religion and politics; national security studies (MA), including cybersecurity, homeland security, international security, Middle East politics; public administration (MPA), including emergency management and homeland security, federal government, general public administration, healthcare policy and ethics (MA, MPA), law, nonprofit administration and faith-based organizations, public leadership and management, servant leadership. *Program availability:* Part-time, evening/weekend, 100% online, blended/hybrid learning. *Faculty:* 8 full-time (1 woman), 20 part-time/adjunct (3 women). *Students:* 39 full-time (23 women), 137 part-time (78 women); includes 83 minority (49 Black or African American, non-Hispanic/Latino; 1 American Indian or Alaska Native, non-Hispanic/Latino; 7 Asian, non-Hispanic/Latino; 15 Hispanic/Latino; 11 Two or more races, non-Hispanic/Latino). Average age 35. 345 applicants, 31% accepted, 57 enrolled. In 2017, 38 master's awarded. *Degree requirements:* For master's, thesis optional, internship. *Entrance requirements:* For master's, GRE General Test or LSAT, personal essay, writing sample, resume, college transcripts. Additional exam requirements/recommendations for international students: Required—TOEFL (minimum score 577 paper-based). *Application deadline:* For fall admission, 5/1 priority date for domestic students; for spring admission, 11/1 priority date for domestic students. Applications are processed on a rolling basis. Application fee: $50. Electronic applications accepted. *Expenses:* $650 per credit; $300 technology fee per semester. *Financial support:* In 2017–18, 116 students received support. Career-related internships or fieldwork, scholarships/grants, and unspecified assistantships available. Support available to part-time students. *Faculty research:* International relations and politics, public administration, leadership and ethics, Biblical law, Constitutional law and Supreme Court. *Unit head:* Dr. Eric Patterson, Dean, 757-352-4616, Fax: 757-352-4735, E-mail: epatterson@regent.edu. *Application contact:* Heidi Cece, Assistant Vice President of Enrollment Management, 800-373-5504, Fax: 757-352-4381, E-mail: admissions@regent.edu.
Website: https://www.regent.edu/robertson-school-of-government/

Rider University, College of Liberal Arts and Sciences, Program in Homeland Security, Lawrenceville, NJ 08648-3001. Offers domestic security (MA); global security (MA). *Program availability:* Evening/weekend, online learning. *Entrance requirements:* For master's, bachelor's degree with minimum cumulative GPA of 2.7.

St. John's University, College of Professional Studies, Department of Criminal Justice, Legal Studies, and Homeland Security, Queens, NY 11439. Offers homeland security and criminal justice leadership (MPS). *Faculty:* 22 full-time (5 women), 33 part-time/adjunct (25 women). *Students:* 70 full-time (25 women), 20 part-time (10 women); includes 42 minority (12 Black or African American, non-Hispanic/Latino; 4 Asian, non-Hispanic/Latino; 18 Hispanic/Latino; 8 Two or more races, non-Hispanic/Latino). Average age 29. 52 applicants, 90% accepted, 42 enrolled. In 2017, 35 master's awarded. *Entrance requirements:* For master's, letters of recommendation, transcripts, resume, personal statement, proficiency in a foreign language. Additional exam requirements/recommendations for international students: Required—TOEFL (minimum score 90 iBT), IELTS (minimum score 6.5). *Application deadline:* For fall admission, 5/1 for domestic students; for spring admission, 11/1 for domestic students. Applications are processed on a rolling basis. Application fee: $70. Electronic applications accepted. *Expenses: Tuition:* Full-time $44,280; part-time $1230 per credit. *Required fees:* $340; $340 per credit. Tuition and fees vary according to course load, degree level and program. *Financial support:* Research assistantships, teaching assistantships, scholarships/grants, and unspecified assistantships available. Financial award application deadline: 2/1; financial award applicants required to submit FAFSA. *Unit head:* Dr. Antoinette Collarini-Schlossberg, Acting Chair, 718-990-7531, E-mail: schlossa@stjohns.edu. *Application contact:* Robert Medrano, Director of Graduate Admission, 718-990-1601, Fax: 718-990-5686, E-mail: gradhelp@stjohns.edu.
Website: https://www.stjohns.edu/academics/schools-and-colleges/college-professional-studies/criminal-justice-legal-studies-and-homeland-security

St. Mary's University, Graduate Studies, Program in International Relations, San Antonio, TX 78228. Offers conflict transformation (Certificate); international conflict resolution (MA); international development (MA); international relations (MA); security policy (MA); JD/MA. *Program availability:* Part-time, evening/weekend, 100% online. *Students:* 22 full-time (12 women), 48 part-time (16 women); includes 38 minority (5 Black or African American, non-Hispanic/Latino; 1 American Indian or Alaska Native, non-Hispanic/Latino; 1 Asian, non-Hispanic/Latino; 30 Hispanic/Latino; 1 Two or more races, non-Hispanic/Latino), 5 international. Average age 31. 89 applicants, 39% accepted, 19 enrolled. In 2017, 36 master's awarded. *Degree requirements:* For master's, one foreign language, comprehensive exam (for some programs), thesis (for some programs), thesis or comprehensive exam. *Entrance requirements:* For master's, minimum undergraduate cumulative GPA of 3.0. Additional exam requirements/recommendations for international students: Required—TOEFL (minimum score 550 paper-based; 80 iBT), IELTS (minimum score 6). *Application deadline:* For fall admission, 7/1 for domestic students; for spring admission, 11/15 for domestic students; for summer admission, 4/1 for domestic students. Applications are processed on a rolling basis. Application fee: $0. Electronic applications accepted. *Expenses: Tuition:* Full-time $16,200; part-time $900 per credit hour. *Required fees:* $810; $405 per semester. *Financial support:* Research assistantships, Federal Work-Study, tuition waivers (full), unspecified assistantships, and grants for active-duty and retired military, DOD employees, and their spouses available. Financial award application deadline: 3/31; financial award applicants required to submit FAFSA. *Faculty research:* Anthropology and ethics, states in crisis and socioeconomic development, politics and society of South Asia, political psychology, international relations theory. *Unit head:* Dr. Larry Hufford, Graduate International Relations, 210-431-6790, E-mail: lhufford@stmarytx.edu. *Application contact:* Kim Thornton, Director of Graduate Admission, 210-436-3101, E-mail: kthornton@stmarytx.edu.
Website: https://www.stmarytx.edu/academics/programs/master-international-relations/

Salve Regina University, Program in Administration of Justice and Homeland Security, Newport, RI 02840-4192. Offers administration of justice and homeland security (MS); cybersecurity and intelligence (CGS); digital forensics (CGS); leadership in justice (CGS). *Program availability:* Part-time, evening/weekend, online learning. *Entrance requirements:* For master's, GMAT, GRE General Test, or MAT. Additional exam requirements/recommendations for international students: Required—TOEFL (minimum score 600 paper-based; 100 iBT). Electronic applications accepted.

Sam Houston State University, College of Criminal Justice, Department of Security Studies, Huntsville, TX 77341. Offers homeland security studies (MS). *Program availability:* Part-time, online learning. *Degree requirements:* For master's, thesis optional. *Entrance requirements:* For master's, undergraduate degree, official transcripts, three letters of recommendation, current resume, personal essay. Additional exam requirements/recommendations for international students: Required—TOEFL (minimum score 550 paper-based; 79 iBT); Recommended—IELTS (minimum score 6.5). Electronic applications accepted.

Southern Illinois University Carbondale, Graduate School, College of Applied Science, Program in Fire Service and Homeland Security, Carbondale, IL 62901-4701. Offers MS. *Program availability:* Part-time, evening/weekend, online learning. *Entrance requirements:* Additional exam requirements/recommendations for international students: Required—TOEFL. Electronic applications accepted.

Texas A&M University, Bush School of Government and Public Service, College Station, TX 77845. Offers homeland security (Certificate); international affairs (MIA, Certificate); national security affairs (Certificate); non-profit management (Certificate); public service and administration (MPSA). *Accreditation:* NASPAA. *Faculty:* 66. *Students:* 332 full-time (182 women), 54 part-time (16 women); includes 94 minority (19 Black or African American, non-Hispanic/Latino; 10 Asian, non-Hispanic/Latino; 56 Hispanic/Latino; 9 Two or more races, non-Hispanic/Latino), 41 international. Average age 28. 297 applicants, 94% accepted, 164 enrolled. In 2017, 154 master's awarded. *Degree requirements:* For master's, summer internship. *Entrance requirements:* For master's, GRE (preferred) or GMAT. Additional exam requirements/recommendations for international students: Required—TOEFL (minimum score 550 paper-based; 80 iBT), IELTS (minimum score 6), PTE (minimum score 53). *Application deadline:* For fall admission, 1/15 for domestic and international students. Application fee: $50 ($90 for international students). Electronic applications accepted. *Expenses:* Contact institution. *Financial support:* In 2017–18, 417 students received support, including 29 fellowships with tuition reimbursements available (averaging $20,966 per year), 71 research assistantships with tuition reimbursements available (averaging $9,778 per year); teaching assistantships, career-related internships or fieldwork, institutionally sponsored loans, scholarships/grants, traineeships, health care benefits, tuition waivers (full and partial), and unspecified assistantships also available. Support available to part-time students. Financial award application deadline: 3/15; financial award applicants required to submit FAFSA. *Faculty research:* Public policy, Presidential studies, public leadership, economic policy, social policy. *Unit head:* Dr. Mark Welsh, Dean, 979-862-8007, E-mail: mwelsh@tamu.edu. *Application contact:* Kathryn Meyer, Director of Recruitment and Admissions, 979-458-4767, Fax: 979-845-4155, E-mail: bushschooladmissions@tamu.edu.
Website: http://bush.tamu.edu/

Texas A&M University–Commerce, College of Humanities, Social Sciences and Arts, Commerce, TX 75429. Offers applied criminology (MS); applied linguistics (MA, MS); art (MA, MFA); computational linguistics (Graduate Certificate); creative writing (Graduate Certificate); criminal justice management (Graduate Certificate); criminal justice studies (Graduate Certificate); English (MA, MS, PhD); film studies (Graduate Certificate); history (MA, MS); history of Christianity (Graduate Certificate); Holocaust studies (Graduate Certificate); homeland security (Graduate Certificate); music education (MM); music performance (MM); political science (MA, MS); public history (Graduate Certificate); sociology (MS); Spanish (MA); studies in children's and adolescent literature and culture (Graduate Certificate); teaching English to speakers of other languages (Graduate Certificate); theater (MA, MS); world history (Graduate Certificate). *Program availability:* Part-time. *Faculty:* 56 full-time (26 women), 10 part-time/adjunct (5 women). *Students:* 133 full-time (85 women), 439 part-time (311 women); includes 204 minority (79 Black or African American, non-Hispanic/Latino; 4 American Indian or Alaska Native, non-Hispanic/Latino; 9 Asian, non-Hispanic/Latino; 98 Hispanic/Latino; 14 Two or more races, non-Hispanic/Latino), 26 international. Average age 36. 261 applicants, 50% accepted, 113 enrolled. In 2017, 105 master's, 5 doctorates awarded. *Degree requirements:* For master's, one foreign language, comprehensive exam, thesis (for some programs); for doctorate, one foreign language, comprehensive exam, thesis/dissertation, departmental qualifying exam. *Entrance requirements:* For master's and doctorate, GRE General Test. Additional exam requirements/recommendations for international students: Required—TOEFL (minimum score 550 paper-based; 79 iBT), IELTS (minimum score 6). *Application deadline:* Applications are processed on a rolling basis. Application fee: $50. Electronic applications accepted. *Expenses:* Contact

institution. *Financial support:* In 2017–18, 43 students received support, including 9 research assistantships with partial tuition reimbursements available (averaging $9,000 per year), 68 teaching assistantships with partial tuition reimbursements available (averaging $9,000 per year); Federal Work-Study, institutionally sponsored loans, scholarships/grants, health care benefits, and unspecified assistantships also available. Financial award application deadline: 5/1; financial award applicants required to submit FAFSA. *Unit head:* Dr. William F. Kuracina, Interim Dean, 903-886-5166, Fax: 903-886-5774, E-mail: william.kuracina@tamuc.edu. *Application contact:* Vicky Turner, Doctoral Degree and Special Programs Coordinator, 903-886-5167, E-mail: vicky.turner@tamuc.edu.
Website: http://www.tamuc.edu/academics/graduateSchool/programs/humanitiesSocialScienceArts/default.aspx

Thomas Edison State University, John S. Watson School of Public Service and Continuing Studies, Trenton, NJ 08608. Offers community and economic development (MSM); environmental policy/environmental justice (MSM); homeland security (MSHS, MSM); information and technology for public service (MSM); nonprofit management (MSM); public and municipal finance (MSM); public health (MSM); public service administration and leadership (MSM); public service leadership (MPSL). *Program availability:* Part-time, online learning. *Entrance requirements:* Additional exam requirements/recommendations for international students: Required—TOEFL (minimum score 550 paper-based; 79 iBT). Electronic applications accepted.

Tiffin University, Program in Criminal Justice, Tiffin, OH 44883-2161. Offers criminal justice (MS), including crime analysis, criminal behavior, forensic psychology, homeland security administration, justice administration. *Program availability:* Part-time, evening/weekend, 100% online, blended/hybrid learning. *Degree requirements:* For master's, thesis optional. *Entrance requirements:* For master's, minimum undergraduate GPA of 2.5, work experience. Additional exam requirements/recommendations for international students: Required—TOEFL (minimum score 550 paper-based; 79 iBT). Electronic applications accepted. *Expenses:* Contact institution. *Faculty research:* Terrorism, intelligence, homeland security, guns and crime.

Towson University, College of Liberal Arts, Program in Integrated Homeland Security Management, Towson, MD 21252-0001. Offers integrated homeland security management (MS); security assessment and management (Postbaccalaureate Certificate). *Program availability:* Part-time, evening/weekend. *Students:* 2 full-time (1 woman), 24 part-time (11 women); includes 10 minority (9 Black or African American, non-Hispanic/Latino; 1 Asian, non-Hispanic/Latino). *Entrance requirements:* For master's and Postbaccalaureate Certificate, BA in related field, 3 years of related work experience, resume, 2 letters of reference, minimum GPA of 3.0. *Application deadline:* For fall admission, 1/17 for domestic students, 5/15 for international students; for spring admission, 10/15 for domestic students, 12/1 for international students. Applications are processed on a rolling basis. Application fee: $45. Electronic applications accepted. *Expenses:* Tuition, state resident: full-time $7960; part-time $398 per unit. Tuition, nonresident: full-time $16,480; part-time $824 per unit. *Required fees:* $2600; $130 per year. $390 per term. *Financial support:* Application deadline: 4/1. *Unit head:* Dr. Joseph Clark, Graduate Program Director, 410-704-4490, E-mail: jrclark@towson.edu. *Application contact:* Coverley Beidleman, Assistant Director of Graduate Admissions, 410-704-5630, Fax: 410-704-3030, E-mail: cbeidleman@towson.edu.
Website: http://www.towson.edu/cla/departments/interdisciplinary/grad/homelandsecurity/index.html

Tulane University, School of Professional Advancement, New Orleans, LA 70118-5669. Offers health and wellness management (MPS); homeland security studies (MPS); information technology management (MPS); liberal arts (MLA). *Program availability:* Part-time. *Degree requirements:* For master's, thesis. *Entrance requirements:* For master's, GRE General Test, minimum B average in undergraduate course work. Additional exam requirements/recommendations for international students: Required—TOEFL. *Expenses:* Tuition: Full-time $50,920; part-time $2829 per credit hour. *Required fees:* $2040; $44.50 per credit hour. $580 per term. Tuition and fees vary according to course load, degree level and program.

University at Albany, State University of New York, College of Emergency Preparedness, Homeland Security and Cybersecurity, Albany, NY 12222-0001. Offers cybersecurity (Certificate); emergency preparedness (Certificate); homeland security (Certificate); information science (MS, PhD). *Faculty:* 10 full-time (4 women), 14 part-time/adjunct (5 women). *Students:* 59 full-time (40 women), 77 part-time (49 women); includes 23 minority (4 Black or African American, non-Hispanic/Latino; 6 Asian, non-Hispanic/Latino; 10 Hispanic/Latino; 3 Two or more races, non-Hispanic/Latino), 14 international. 90 applicants, 67% accepted, 36 enrolled. In 2017, 30 master's, 1 doctorate, 24 other advanced degrees awarded. *Entrance requirements:* Additional exam requirements/recommendations for international students: Required—TOEFL. *Expenses:* Tuition, state resident: full-time $10,870; part-time $453 per credit hour. Tuition, nonresident: full-time $22,210; part-time $925 per credit hour. *Required fees:* $84.68 per credit hour. $508.06 per semester. Part-time tuition and fees vary according to course load and program. *Faculty research:* Electrical and computer engineering, environmental and sustainability engineering, computer science. *Unit head:* Dr. Robert Griffin, Dean, 518-442-5258. *Application contact:* Michael DeRensis, Director, Graduate Admissions, 518-442-3980, Fax: 518-442-3922, E-mail: graduate@albany.edu.
Website: http://www.albany.edu/cehc

University at Albany, State University of New York, Nelson A. Rockefeller College of Public Affairs and Policy, Department of Public Administration and Policy, Albany, NY 12222-0001. Offers financial management and public economics (MPA); financial market regulation (MPA); health policy (MPA); healthcare management (MPA); homeland security (MPA); human resources management (MPA); information strategy and management (MPA); local government management (MPA); nonprofit management (MPA); nonprofit management and leadership (Certificate); organizational behavior and theory (MPA, PhD); planning and policy analysis (CAS); policy analysis (MPA); politics and administration (PhD); public finance (PhD); public management (PhD); public policy (PhD); public sector management (Certificate); women and public policy (Certificate); JD/MPA. JD/MPA offered jointly with Albany Law School. *Accreditation:* NASPAA (one or more programs are accredited). *Faculty:* 21 full-time (7 women), 14 part-time/adjunct (7 women). *Students:* 115 full-time (59 women), 93 part-time (56 women); includes 41 minority (11 Black or African American, non-Hispanic/Latino; 9 Asian, non-Hispanic/Latino; 18 Hispanic/Latino; 3 Two or more races, non-Hispanic/Latino), 32 international. 236 applicants, 69% accepted, 86 enrolled. In 2017, 57 master's, 1 doctorate, 14 other advanced degrees awarded. *Degree requirements:* For doctorate, one foreign language, thesis/dissertation. *Entrance requirements:* For doctorate, GRE General Test. Additional exam requirements/recommendations for international students: Required—TOEFL (minimum score 550 paper-based). *Application deadline:* For fall admission, 2/1 priority date for domestic students, 5/1 for international students; for spring admission, 12/1 for domestic students. Applications are processed on a rolling basis. Application fee: $75. Electronic applications accepted. *Expenses:* Tuition, state resident: full-time $10,870; part-time $453 per credit hour. Tuition, nonresident: full-time $22,210; part-time $925 per credit hour. *Required fees:* $84.68 per credit hour. $508.06 per semester. Part-time tuition and fees vary according to course load and program. *Financial support:* Application deadline: 2/1. *Unit head:* Victor Asal, Chair, 518-591-8729, E-mail:

vasal@albany.edu.
Website: http://www.albany.edu/rockefeller/pad.shtml

University of Alaska Fairbanks, School of Management, Program in Security and Disaster Management, Fairbanks, AK 99775-6080. Offers MSDM. *Program availability:* Part-time, evening/weekend, 100% online, blended/hybrid learning. *Entrance requirements:* For master's, Watson-Glaser Critical Thinking Appraisal. Additional exam requirements/recommendations for international students: Required—TOEFL (minimum score 79 iBT), IELTS (minimum score 6.5). Electronic applications accepted. *Expenses:* Contact institution.

University of Central Florida, College of Community Innovation and Education, School of Public Administration, Orlando, FL 32816. Offers emergency management and homeland security (Certificate); fundraising (Certificate); nonprofit management (MNM, Certificate); public administration (MPA); research administration (MRA); urban and regional planning (MS). *Accreditation:* NASPAA. *Program availability:* Part-time, evening/weekend. *Students:* 110 full-time (76 women), 290 part-time (215 women); includes 193 minority (96 Black or African American, non-Hispanic/Latino; 2 American Indian or Alaska Native, non-Hispanic/Latino; 13 Asian, non-Hispanic/Latino; 74 Hispanic/Latino; 8 Two or more races, non-Hispanic/Latino), 6 international. Average age 32. 255 applicants, 78% accepted, 152 enrolled. In 2017, 95 master's, 34 other advanced degrees awarded. *Degree requirements:* For master's, comprehensive exam, thesis or alternative, research report. *Entrance requirements:* For master's, letters of recommendation, goal statement, resume. Additional exam requirements/recommendations for international students: Required—TOEFL. *Application deadline:* For fall admission, 6/15 for domestic students; for spring admission, 11/1 for domestic students. Application fee: $30. Electronic applications accepted. *Expenses:* Tuition, state resident: part-time $288.16 per credit hour. Tuition, nonresident: part-time $1073.31 per credit hour. Tuition and fees vary according to program. *Financial support:* In 2017–18, 11 students received support, including 2 fellowships with partial tuition reimbursements available (averaging $5,300 per year), 6 research assistantships with partial tuition reimbursements available (averaging $9,637 per year), 3 teaching assistantships with partial tuition reimbursements available (averaging $9,390 per year); career-related internships or fieldwork, Federal Work-Study, institutionally sponsored loans, health care benefits, tuition waivers (partial), and unspecified assistantships also available. Financial award application deadline: 3/1; financial award applicants required to submit FAFSA. *Unit head:* Dr. Naim Kapucu, Director, 407-823-6096, Fax: 407-823-5651, E-mail: kapucu@ucf.edu. *Application contact:* Associate Director, Graduate Admissions, 407-823-2766, Fax: 407-823-6442, E-mail: gradadmissions@ucf.edu.
Website: https://www.cohpa.ucf.edu/publicadmin/

University of Colorado Denver, School of Public Affairs, Program in Public Affairs and Administration, Denver, CO 80127. Offers public administration (MPA), including domestic violence, emergency management and homeland security, environmental policy, management and law, homeland security and defense, local government, nonprofit management, public administration; public affairs (PhD). *Accreditation:* NASPAA. *Program availability:* Part-time, evening/weekend, online learning. *Degree requirements:* For master's, thesis or alternative, 36-39 credit hours; for doctorate, comprehensive exam, thesis/dissertation, minimum of 66 semester hours, including at least 30 hours of dissertation. *Entrance requirements:* For master's, GRE, GMAT or LSAT, resume, essay, transcripts, recommendations; for doctorate, GRE, resume, essay, transcripts, recommendations. Additional exam requirements/recommendations for international students: Required—TOEFL (minimum score 550 paper-based; 80 iBT); Recommended—IELTS (minimum score 6.5). Electronic applications accepted. *Expenses:* Contact institution. *Faculty research:* Housing, education and the social and economic issues of vulnerable populations; nonprofit governance and management; education finance, effectiveness and reform; P-20 education initiatives; municipal government accountability.

University of Denver, Josef Korbel School of International Studies, Denver, CO 80208. Offers conflict resolution (MA); global business and corporate social responsibility (Certificate); global finance, trade and economic integration (MA); global health affairs (Certificate); homeland security (Certificate); humanitarian assistance (Certificate); international administration (MA); international development (MA); international human rights (MA); international security (MA); international studies (MA, PhD); public policy studies (MPP); religion and international affairs (Certificate). *Program availability:* Part-time. *Faculty:* 46 full-time (16 women), 28 part-time/adjunct (8 women). *Students:* 245 full-time (132 women), 40 part-time (21 women); includes 58 minority (8 Black or African American, non-Hispanic/Latino; 2 American Indian or Alaska Native, non-Hispanic/Latino; 11 Asian, non-Hispanic/Latino; 27 Hispanic/Latino; 10 Two or more races, non-Hispanic/Latino), 22 international. Average age 27. 627 applicants, 74% accepted, 106 enrolled. In 2017, 218 master's, 6 doctorates, 25 other advanced degrees awarded. *Degree requirements:* For master's, one foreign language, thesis (for some programs); for doctorate, one foreign language, comprehensive exam, thesis/dissertation, two extended research papers. *Entrance requirements:* For master's, GRE General Test, bachelor's degree, transcripts, two letters of recommendation, statement of purpose, resume or curriculum vitae; for doctorate, GRE General Test, master's degree, transcripts, three letters of recommendation, statement of purpose, resume or curriculum vitae, writing sample; for Certificate, bachelor's degree, transcripts, two letters of recommendation, statement of purpose, resume or curriculum vitae. Additional exam requirements/recommendations for international students: Required—TOEFL (minimum score 587 paper-based; 95 iBT). *Application deadline:* For fall admission, 1/15 priority date for domestic and international students; for winter admission, 11/1 for domestic and international students. Applications are processed on a rolling basis. Application fee: $65. Electronic applications accepted. *Expenses:* $47,823 per year full-time. *Financial support:* In 2017–18, 225 students received support, including 1 teaching assistantship with tuition reimbursement available (averaging $2,236 per year); research assistantships with tuition reimbursements available, career-related internships or fieldwork, Federal Work-Study, institutionally sponsored loans, scholarships/grants, and unspecified assistantships also available. Support available to part-time students. Financial award application deadline: 2/15; financial award applicants required to submit FAFSA. *Faculty research:* Human rights and international security, international politics and economics, economic-social and political development, international technology analysis and management. *Unit head:* Dr. Pardis Mahdavi, Dean, 303-871-6338, E-mail: pardis.mahdavi@du.edu. *Application contact:* Admissions Contact, E-mail: korbeladm@du.edu.
Website: http://www.du.edu/korbel

University of Illinois at Springfield, Graduate Programs, College of Public Affairs and Administration, Program in Public Health, Springfield, IL 62703-5407. Offers community health education (Graduate Certificate); emergency preparedness and homeland security (Graduate Certificate); environmental health (MPH, Graduate Certificate); environmental risk assessment (Graduate Certificate); epidemiology (Graduate Certificate); public health (MPH). *Program availability:* Part-time, evening/weekend, 100% online. *Faculty:* 7 full-time (4 women). *Students:* 38 full-time (23 women), 46 part-time (34 women); includes 27 minority (16 Black or African American, non-Hispanic/Latino; 4 Asian, non-Hispanic/Latino; 5 Hispanic/Latino; 2 Two or more races, non-Hispanic/Latino), 22 international. Average age 32. 47 applicants, 51% accepted, 18

enrolled. In 2017, 28 master's, 17 other advanced degrees awarded. *Degree requirements:* For master's, comprehensive exam, internship. *Entrance requirements:* For master's, GRE, minimum undergraduate GPA of 3.0, 3 letters of recommendation, statement of personal goals. Additional exam requirements/recommendations for international students: Required—TOEFL (minimum score 500 paper-based; 61 iBT). *Application deadline:* Applications are processed on a rolling basis. Application fee: $60 ($75 for international students). Electronic applications accepted. *Expenses:* Tuition, state resident: full-time $7896; part-time $329 per credit hour. Tuition, nonresident: full-time $16,200; part-time $675 per credit hour. Tuition and fees vary according to program. *Financial support:* In 2017–18, research assistantships with full tuition reimbursements (averaging $10,249 per year), teaching assistantships with full tuition reimbursements (averaging $10,303 per year) were awarded; fellowships, career-related internships or fieldwork, Federal Work-Study, scholarships/grants, health care benefits, and unspecified assistantships also available. Support available to part-time students. Financial award application deadline: 11/15; financial award applicants required to submit FAFSA. *Unit head:* Dr. Josiah Alamu, Program Administrator, 217-206-7874, Fax: 217-206-7279, E-mail: jalam3@uis.edu.
Website: http://www.uis.edu/publichealth/

University of Management and Technology, Program in Criminal Justice, Arlington, VA 22209-1609. Offers homeland security (MS). *Program availability:* Part-time, evening/weekend, online learning. *Entrance requirements:* Additional exam requirements/recommendations for international students: Required—TOEFL (minimum score 530 paper-based; 71 iBT).

University of Management and Technology, Program in Homeland Security, Arlington, VA 22209-1609. Offers MS. *Degree requirements:* For master's, capstone course.

University of Oklahoma Health Sciences Center, Graduate College, College of Public Health, Program in Preparedness and Terrorism, Oklahoma City, OK 73190. Offers MPH.

University of Phoenix–Online Campus, College of Justice and Security, Phoenix, AZ 85034-7209. Offers administration of justice and security (MS), including administration of justice and security, global and homeland security, law enforcement organizations; public administration (MPA). *Program availability:* Evening/weekend, online learning. *Entrance requirements:* Additional exam requirements/recommendations for international students: Required—TOEFL, TOEIC (Test of English as an International Communication), Berlitz Online English Proficiency Exam, PTE, or IELTS. Electronic applications accepted. *Expenses:* Contact institution.

University of Phoenix–Phoenix Campus, College of Criminal Justice and Security, Tempe, AZ 85282-2371. Offers administration of justice and security (MS); global and homeland security (MS); law enforcement organizations (MS); public administration (MPA). *Program availability:* Evening/weekend, online learning. *Entrance requirements:* Additional exam requirements/recommendations for international students: Required—TOEFL, TOEIC (Test of English as an International Communication), Berlitz Online English Proficiency Exam, PTE, or IELTS. Electronic applications accepted. *Expenses:* Contact institution.

University of Southern California, Graduate School, Sol Price School of Public Policy, Public Policy Programs, Los Angeles, CA 90089. Offers homeland security and public policy (Graduate Certificate); public policy (MPP, Graduate Certificate); M Pl/MPP; MPP/JD. *Program availability:* Part-time. Terminal master's awarded for partial completion of doctoral program. *Degree requirements:* For master's, practicum. *Entrance requirements:* For master's, GRE. Additional exam requirements/recommendations for international students: Required—TOEFL (minimum score 600 paper-based; 100 iBT). Electronic applications accepted. *Faculty research:* Urban political economy, community and economic development, environmental policy, transportation policy, housing policy.

University of the District of Columbia, College of Arts and Sciences, Program in Homeland Security, Washington, DC 20008-1175. Offers MS. *Degree requirements:* For master's, thesis or public policy paper.

Upper Iowa University, Online Master's Programs, Fayette, IA 52142-1857. Offers accounting (MBA); corporate financial management (MBA); emergency management and homeland security (MPA); general management (MBA); general studies (MPA); government administration (MPA); health and human services (MPA); human resources management (MBA); nonprofit organizational management (MPA); organizational development (MBA); public management (MPA); sport administration (MSA). MBA also available at Madison, WI campus. *Program availability:* Part-time, online learning. *Degree requirements:* For master's, research project. *Entrance requirements:* For master's, GMAT, GRE, or minimum GPA of 2.7 during last 60 hours. Additional exam requirements/recommendations for international students: Required—TOEFL (minimum score 570 paper-based). Electronic applications accepted. *Faculty research:* Total quality management, teams, organization culture and climate, management.

Virginia Commonwealth University, Graduate School, L. Douglas Wilder School of Government and Public Affairs, Program in Homeland Security and Emergency Preparedness, Richmond, VA 23284-9005. Offers MA, Graduate Certificate. *Program availability:* Part-time, online learning. *Entrance requirements:* For master's, GRE, GMAT, MAT or LSAT, minimum GPA of 2.7; for Graduate Certificate, minimum GPA of 2.7. Additional exam requirements/recommendations for international students: Required—TOEFL (minimum score 600 paper-based; 100 iBT); Recommended—IELTS (minimum score 6.5). Electronic applications accepted.

Walden University, Graduate Programs, School of Psychology, Minneapolis, MN 55401. Offers clinical psychology (MS), including counseling, general program; forensic psychology (MS), including forensic psychology in the community, general program, mental health applications, program planning and evaluation in forensic settings, psychology and legal systems; industrial organizational (MS, PhD), including consulting psychology, forensic (MS), forensic psychology (PhD), general practice, leadership development and coaching (MS), organizational diversity and social change, research evaluation (PhD); online teaching in psychology (Post-Master's Certificate); organizational psychology and development (Postbaccalaureate Certificate); psychology (MS, PhD), including applied psychology (MS), clinical psychology (PhD), crisis management and response (MS), educational psychology, forensic psychology (PhD), general psychology (MS), general psychology research (PhD), general psychology teaching (PhD), health psychology, leadership development and coaching (MS), psychology of culture (MS), psychology, public administration, and social change (MS), social psychology, terrorism and security (MS); psychology respecialization (Post-Doctoral Certificate). *Program availability:* Part-time, evening/weekend, online only, 100% online. Terminal master's awarded for partial completion of doctoral program. *Degree requirements:* For master's, thesis optional; for doctorate, thesis/dissertation, residency. *Entrance requirements:* For master's, bachelor's degree or higher; minimum GPA of 2.5; official transcripts; goal statement (for some programs); access to computer and Internet; for doctorate, master's degree or higher; three years of related professional or academic experience (preferred); minimum GPA of 3.0; goal statement and current resume (for select programs); official transcripts; access to computer and Internet; for other advanced degree, relevant work experience; access to computer and Internet. Additional exam requirements/recommendations for international students: Required—TOEFL (minimum score 550 paper-based, 79 iBT), IELTS (minimum score 6.5), Michigan English Language Assessment Battery (minimum score 82), or PTE (minimum score 53). Electronic applications accepted.

Walden University, Graduate Programs, School of Public Policy and Administration, Minneapolis, MN 55401. Offers criminal justice (MPA, MPP, MS, Graduate Certificate), including emergency management (MS, PhD), general program (MS), global leadership (MS, PhD), homeland security and policy coordination (MS, PhD), law and public policy (MS, PhD), policy analysis (MS, PhD), public management and leadership (MS, PhD), self-designed (MS), terrorism, mediation, and peace (MS, PhD); criminal justice and executive management (MS), including global leadership (MS, PhD); criminal justice leadership and executive management (MS), including emergency management (MS, PhD), general program, homeland security and policy coordination (MS, PhD), law and public policy (MS, PhD), policy analysis (MS, PhD), public management and leadership (MS, PhD), self-designed, terrorism, mediation, and peace (MS, PhD); emergency management (MPA, MPP, MS), including criminal justice (MS, PhD), general program (MS), homeland security (MS), public management and leadership (MS, PhD), terrorism and emergency management (MS); general program (MPA, MPP); global leadership (MPA, MPP); government management (Graduate Certificate); health policy (MPA, MPP); homeland security (Graduate Certificate); homeland security and policy coordination (MPA, MPP); international nongovernmental organizations (MPA, MPP); law and public policy (MPA, MPP); local government management for sustainable communities (MPA, MPP); nonprofit management (Graduate Certificate); nonprofit management and leadership (MPA, MPP, MS), including global leadership (MS, PhD), international nongovernmental organization (MS), local government for sustainable communities (MS), self designed (MS); online teaching in higher education (Post-Master's Certificate); policy analysis (MPA); public management and leadership (MPA, MPP, Graduate Certificate); public policy (Graduate Certificate); public policy and administration (PhD), including criminal justice (MS, PhD), emergency management (MS, PhD), global leadership (MS, PhD), health policy, homeland security and policy coordination (MS, PhD), international nongovernmental organizations, law and public policy (MS, PhD), local government management for sustainable communities, nonprofit management and leadership, policy analysis (MS, PhD), public management and leadership (MS, PhD), terrorism, mediation, and peace (MS, PhD); strategic planning and public policy (Graduate Certificate); terrorism, mediation, and peace (MPA, MPP). *Program availability:* Part-time, evening/weekend, online only, 100% online. *Degree requirements:* For doctorate, thesis/dissertation, residency. *Entrance requirements:* For master's, bachelor's degree or higher; minimum GPA of 2.5; official transcripts; goal statement (for some programs); access to computer and Internet; for doctorate, master's degree or higher; three years of related professional or academic experience (preferred); minimum GPA of 3.0; goal statement and current resume (for select programs); official transcripts; access to computer and Internet; for other advanced degree, relevant work experience; access to computer and Internet. Additional exam requirements/recommendations for international students: Required—TOEFL (minimum score 550 paper-based, 79 iBT), IELTS (minimum score 6.5), Michigan English Language Assessment Battery (minimum score 82), or PTE (minimum score 53). Electronic applications accepted.

Wayland Baptist University, Graduate Programs, Programs in Behavioral and Social Sciences, Plainview, TX 79072-6998. Offers counseling (MA); criminal justice (MACJ); government administration (MPA); history (MA); homeland security (MPA); humanities (MAH); justice administration (MPA). *Program availability:* Part-time, evening/weekend, 100% online, blended/hybrid learning. *Faculty:* 19 full-time (5 women), 18 part-time/adjunct (8 women). *Students:* 16 full-time (10 women), 322 part-time (183 women); includes 207 minority (82 Black or African American, non-Hispanic/Latino; 8 American Indian or Alaska Native, non-Hispanic/Latino; 8 Asian, non-Hispanic/Latino; 84 Hispanic/Latino; 5 Native Hawaiian or other Pacific Islander, non-Hispanic/Latino; 20 Two or more races, non-Hispanic/Latino), 1 international. Average age 40. 56 applicants, 93% accepted, 39 enrolled. In 2017, 141 master's awarded. *Degree requirements:* For master's, comprehensive exam. *Entrance requirements:* For master's, GRE, MAT. Additional exam requirements/recommendations for international students: Required—TOEFL (minimum score 500 paper-based; 61 iBT). *Application deadline:* Applications are processed on a rolling basis. Application fee: $50. Electronic applications accepted. *Expenses: Tuition:* Full-time $11,250; part-time $625 per credit hour. *Required fees:* $1200. *Financial support:* Federal Work-Study, institutionally sponsored loans, and scholarships/grants available. Support available to part-time students. Financial award application deadline: 5/1; financial award applicants required to submit FAFSA. *Unit head:* Dr. Peter Bowen, Dean, 806-291-1179, Fax: 806-291-1972, E-mail: pbowen@wbu.edu. *Application contact:* Amanda Stanton, Graduate Studies, 806-291-3423, Fax: 806-291-1950, E-mail: stanton@wbu.edu.

Western Kentucky University, Graduate Studies, Ogden College of Science and Engineering, Department of Physics and Astronomy, Bowling Green, KY 42101. Offers homeland security sciences (MS); physics (MA Ed).

Western Michigan University Thomas M. Cooley Law School, Graduate Programs, Lansing, MI 48901-3038. Offers administrative law (public law) (JD); business transactions (JD); Canadian law practice (JD); corporate law and finance (LL M); environmental law (public law) (JD); general practice (JD), including solo and small firm; general studies (LL M); homeland and national security law (LL M); insurance law (LL M); intellectual property (JD); intellectual property law (LL M); international law (JD); litigation (JD); taxation (LL M); U.S. legal studies for foreign attorneys (LL M); JD/LL M; JD/MBA; JD/MHA; JD/MPA; JD/MSW. *Program availability:* Part-time, evening/weekend, 100% online, blended/hybrid learning. *Degree requirements:* For master's, thesis (for some programs); for doctorate, minimum of 3 credits of clinical experience. *Entrance requirements:* For master's, JD or LL B; for doctorate, LSAT. Additional exam requirements/recommendations for international students: Required—TOEFL (for U.S. legal studies for foreign attorneys LL M program); Recommended—TOEFL. Electronic applications accepted. *Expenses:* Contact institution. *Faculty research:* Wrongful convictions, civil rights, environmental law, litigation techniques, data mining, intellectual property, practical and skills-based legal education.

Wilmington University, College of Business, New Castle, DE 19720-6491. Offers accounting (MBA, MS); business administration (MBA, DBA); environmental stewardship (MBA); finance (MBA); health care administration (MBA, MSM); homeland security (MBA, MSM); human resource management (MSM); management information systems (MBA, MSN); marketing (MSM); marketing management (MBA); military leadership (MSM); organizational leadership (MBA, MSM); public administration (MSM). *Program availability:* Part-time, evening/weekend. *Faculty:* 16 full-time (8 women), 106 part-time/adjunct (49 women). *Students:* 525 full-time (294 women), 1,212 part-time (780 women); includes 557 minority (412 Black or African American, non-Hispanic/Latino; 14 American Indian or Alaska Native, non-Hispanic/Latino; 55 Asian, non-Hispanic/Latino; 25 Hispanic/Latino; 3 Native Hawaiian or other Pacific Islander, non-Hispanic/Latino; 48 Two or more races, non-Hispanic/Latino), 157 international. Average age 35. 1,484 applicants, 70% accepted, 685 enrolled. In 2017, 543 master's, 16 doctorates awarded. *Entrance requirements:* Additional exam requirements/recommendations for international students: Required—TOEFL (minimum score 500 paper-based). *Application deadline:* Applications are processed on a rolling basis.

Application fee: $35. Electronic applications accepted. *Expenses: Tuition:* Part-time $466 per credit. *Required fees:* $25 per semester. Tuition and fees vary according to degree level and campus/location. *Financial support:* Applicants required to submit FAFSA. *Unit head:* Dr. Kathy S. Kennedy Ratajack, Dean, 302-356-2481. *Application contact:* Laura Morris, Director of Admissions, 877-967-5456, E-mail: infocenter@wilmu.edu.
Website: http://www.wilmu.edu/business/

Wilmington University, College of Social and Behavioral Sciences, New Castle, DE 19720-6491. Offers administration of human services (MS); administration of justice (MS); clinical mental health counseling (MS); homeland security (MS). *Accreditation:* ACA. *Program availability:* Part-time, evening/weekend. *Faculty:* 11 full-time (6 women), 74 part-time/adjunct (34 women). *Students:* 174 full-time (132 women), 428 part-time (334 women); includes 269 minority (229 Black or African American, non-Hispanic/Latino; 5 American Indian or Alaska Native, non-Hispanic/Latino; 7 Asian, non-Hispanic/Latino; 17 Hispanic/Latino; 11 Two or more races, non-Hispanic/Latino), 11 international. Average age 35. 541 applicants, 81% accepted, 292 enrolled. In 2017, 271 master's awarded. *Entrance requirements:* Additional exam requirements/recommendations for international students: Required—TOEFL (minimum score 500 paper-based). *Application deadline:* Applications are processed on a rolling basis. Application fee: $35. Electronic applications accepted. *Expenses: Tuition:* Part-time $466 per credit. *Required fees:* $25 per semester. Tuition and fees vary according to degree level and campus/location. *Financial support:* Applicants required to submit FAFSA. *Unit head:* Dr. Edward L. Guthrie, Dean, 302-356-6870. *Application contact:* Laura Morris, Director of Admissions, 877-967-5464, E-mail: inquire@wilmcoll.edu.
Website: http://www.wilmu.edu/behavioralscience/

Industrial and Labor Relations

Baruch College of the City University of New York, Zicklin School of Business, Zicklin Executive Programs, Baruch Executive Master of Science in Industrial and Labor Relations Program, New York, NY 10010-5585. Offers MS. *Program availability:* Part-time, evening/weekend. *Entrance requirements:* For master's, professional experience in HR or labor relations. Additional exam requirements/recommendations for international students: Required—TOEFL. *Expenses:* Contact institution.

Carnegie Mellon University, Dietrich College of Humanities and Social Sciences, Department of History, Pittsburgh, PA 15213-3891. Offers African and African-American diaspora (PhD); culture and power (PhD); labor, politics and social movements (PhD); technology, environment, science and health (PhD); women, gender and the family (PhD). *Program availability:* Part-time. *Degree requirements:* For doctorate, oral and written comprehensive exams, dissertation defense. *Entrance requirements:* For doctorate, GRE General Test. Additional exam requirements/recommendations for international students: Required—TOEFL. Electronic applications accepted. *Faculty research:* Anthropology and history, African-American history, technology/environment, cultural history analysis.

Cleveland State University, College of Graduate Studies, Monte Ahuja College of Business, Department of Management, Cleveland, OH 44115. Offers health care administration (MBA); labor relations and human resources (MLRHR). *Program availability:* Part-time, evening/weekend. *Faculty:* 6 full-time (3 women), 8 part-time/adjunct (1 woman). *Students:* 101 full-time (45 women), 41 part-time (22 women); includes 19 minority (9 Black or African American, non-Hispanic/Latino; 6 Asian, non-Hispanic/Latino; 3 Hispanic/Latino; 1 Two or more races, non-Hispanic/Latino), 81 international. Average age 27. In 2017, 12 master's awarded. *Entrance requirements:* For master's, GMAT or GRE, minimum GPA of 3.0. Additional exam requirements/recommendations for international students: Required—TOEFL (minimum score 550 paper-based; 78 iBT). *Application deadline:* For fall admission, 7/15 for domestic students; for spring admission, 12/15 for domestic students. Applications are processed on a rolling basis. Application fee: $40. Electronic applications accepted. *Financial support:* In 2017–18, 3 students received support. Career-related internships or fieldwork, scholarships/grants, and unspecified assistantships available. Financial award application deadline: 5/1; financial award applicants required to submit FAFSA. *Faculty research:* Employee selection, individual differences, leadership, emotions, interviews. *Unit head:* Dr. Kenneth J. Dunegan, Chairperson, 216-687-4747, Fax: 216-687-4708, E-mail: t.degroot@csuohio.edu. *Application contact:* Lisa Marie Sample, Administrative Assistant, 216-687-4726, Fax: 216-687-6888, E-mail: l.m.sample@csuohio.edu.
Website: https://www.csuohio.edu/business/management/management

Cornell University, Graduate School, Graduate Fields of Industrial and Labor Relations, Ithaca, NY 14853. Offers collective bargaining, labor law and labor history (MILR, MPS, MS, PhD); economic and social statistics (MILR); human resource studies (MILR, MPS, MS, PhD); industrial and labor relations problems (MILR, MPS, MS, PhD); international and comparative labor (MILR, MPS, MS, PhD); labor economics (MILR, MPS, MS, PhD); organizational behavior (MILR, MPS, MS, PhD). *Degree requirements:* For master's, thesis (MS); for doctorate, comprehensive exam, thesis/dissertation, teaching experience. *Entrance requirements:* For master's and doctorate, GMAT or GRE General Test, 2 academic recommendations. Additional exam requirements/recommendations for international students: Required—TOEFL (minimum score 550 paper-based; 77 iBT). Electronic applications accepted. *Expenses:* Contact institution.

Georgetown University, Graduate School of Arts and Sciences, Department of Economics, Washington, DC 20057. Offers econometrics (PhD); economic development (PhD); economic theory (PhD); industrial organization (PhD); international macro and finance (PhD); international trade (PhD); labor economics (PhD); macroeconomics (PhD); public economics and political economy (PhD); MA/PhD; MS/MA. *Degree requirements:* For doctorate, comprehensive exam, thesis/dissertation. *Entrance requirements:* For doctorate, GRE General Test. Additional exam requirements/recommendations for international students: Required—TOEFL. *Faculty research:* International economics, economic development.

Georgia State University, Andrew Young School of Policy Studies, Department of Economics, Atlanta, GA 30302. Offers economics (MA); environmental economics (PhD); experimental economics (PhD); labor economics (PhD); policy (MA); public finance (PhD); urban and regional economics (PhD). MA offered through the College of Arts and Sciences. *Program availability:* Part-time. *Faculty:* 26 full-time (4 women). *Students:* 110 full-time (39 women), 14 part-time (5 women); includes 26 minority (14 Black or African American, non-Hispanic/Latino; 4 Asian, non-Hispanic/Latino; 4 Hispanic/Latino; 4 Two or more races, non-Hispanic/Latino), 61 international. Average age 28. 204 applicants, 50% accepted, 37 enrolled. In 2017, 26 master's, 13 doctorates awarded. Terminal master's awarded for partial completion of doctoral program. *Degree requirements:* For master's, thesis optional; for doctorate, comprehensive exam, thesis/dissertation. *Entrance requirements:* For master's and doctorate, GRE. Additional exam requirements/recommendations for international students: Required—TOEFL (minimum score 603 paper-based; 100 iBT) or IELTS (minimum score 7). *Application deadline:* For fall admission, 1/15 for domestic and international students. Application fee: $50. Electronic applications accepted. *Expenses:* Tuition, state resident: full-time $7020. Tuition, nonresident: full-time $22,518. *Required fees:* $2128. Tuition and fees vary according to degree level and program. *Financial support:* In 2017–18, fellowships with full tuition reimbursements (averaging $11,333 per year), research assistantships with full tuition reimbursements (averaging $9,788 per year), teaching assistantships with full tuition reimbursements (averaging $3,000 per year) were awarded; career-related internships or fieldwork also available. Financial award application deadline: 2/15; financial award applicants required to submit FAFSA. *Faculty research:* Public, experimental, urban/environmental, labor, and health economics. *Unit head:* Dr. Rusty Tchernis, Director of the Doctoral Program, 404-413-0154, Fax: 404-413-0145, E-mail: rtchernis@gsu.edu.
Website: http://economics.gsu.edu/

Indiana University of Pennsylvania, School of Graduate Studies and Research, College of Health and Human Services, Department of Employment and Labor Relations, Program in Employment and Labor Relations, Indiana, PA 15705. Offers MA. *Program availability:* Part-time, evening/weekend, online learning. *Faculty:* 4 full-time (1 woman), 1 part-time/adjunct (0 women). *Students:* 25 full-time (11 women), 21 part-time (17 women); includes 1 minority (Two or more races, non-Hispanic/Latino), 2 international. Average age 29. 48 applicants, 81% accepted, 21 enrolled. In 2017, 47 master's awarded. *Entrance requirements:* Additional exam requirements/recommendations for international students: Required—TOEFL (minimum score 550 paper-based). *Application deadline:* Applications are processed on a rolling basis. Application fee: $50. Electronic applications accepted. *Expenses:* Tuition, state resident: full-time $12,000; part-time $500 per credit. Tuition, nonresident: full-time $18,000; part-time $750 per credit. *Required fees:* $4073; $165.55 per credit. $64 per term. *Financial support:* In 2017–18, 15 research assistantships with tuition reimbursements (averaging $3,247 per year) were awarded; fellowships with full tuition reimbursements, career-related internships or fieldwork, Federal Work-Study, scholarships/grants, and unspecified assistantships also available. Financial award application deadline: 4/15; financial award applicants required to submit FAFSA. *Unit head:* Dr. David M. Piper, Coordinator, 724-357-4471, E-mail: david.piper@iup.edu.
Website: http://www.iup.edu/elr/programs/ma/

Inter American University of Puerto Rico, Metropolitan Campus, Graduate Programs, Program in Labor Relations, San Juan, PR 00919-1293. Offers MA. *Degree requirements:* For master's, comprehensive exam. *Entrance requirements:* For master's, GRE or EXADEP, interview. Electronic applications accepted.

Inter American University of Puerto Rico, Metropolitan Campus, Graduate Programs, Program in Psychology, San Juan, PR 00919-1293. Offers counseling psychology (MA, PhD); industrial/organizational psychology (MA, PhD); labor relations (MA); school psychology (MA, PhD). *Degree requirements:* For master's, comprehensive exam. *Entrance requirements:* For master's, GRE or EXADEP, interview. Electronic applications accepted.

McMaster University, School of Graduate Studies, Faculty of Social Sciences, Program in Labour Studies, Hamilton, ON L8S 4M2, Canada. Offers work and society (MA).

Memorial University of Newfoundland, School of Graduate Studies, Interdisciplinary Program in Employment Relations, St. John's, NL A1C 5S7, Canada. Offers MER. *Program availability:* Part-time. *Degree requirements:* For master's, major supervised paper. *Entrance requirements:* For master's, undergraduate degree in related field, minimum B average. Electronic applications accepted.

Michigan State University, The Graduate School, College of Social Science, School of Labor and Industrial Relations, East Lansing, MI 48824. Offers human resources and labor relations (MLRHR); industrial relations and human resources (PhD). *Entrance requirements:* Additional exam requirements/recommendations for international students: Required—TOEFL.

New York Institute of Technology, School of Management, Department of Human Resource Management Studies, Old Westbury, NY 11568-8000. Offers human resource management (Advanced Certificate); human resource management and labor relations (MS). *Program availability:* Part-time. *Faculty:* 5 full-time (1 woman), 4 part-time/adjunct (1 woman). *Students:* 16 full-time (15 women), 29 part-time (25 women); includes 23 minority (7 Black or African American, non-Hispanic/Latino; 6 Asian, non-Hispanic/Latino; 10 Hispanic/Latino), 10 international. Average age 30. 57 applicants, 61% accepted, 10 enrolled. In 2017, 18 master's, 1 other advanced degree awarded. *Degree requirements:* For master's, seminar and comprehensive exam, or thesis. *Entrance requirements:* For master's, bachelor's degree; minimum undergraduate GPA of 3.0; interview; for Advanced Certificate, bachelor's degree; minimum undergraduate GPA of 3.0. Additional exam requirements/recommendations for international students: Required—TOEFL (minimum score 79 iBT), IELTS (minimum score 6). *Application deadline:* Applications are processed on a rolling basis. Application fee: $50. Electronic applications accepted. *Expenses:* $1,285 per credit plus fees. *Financial support:* Career-related internships or fieldwork, Federal Work-Study, scholarships/grants, tuition waivers (full and partial), and unspecified assistantships available. Support available to part-time students. Financial award application deadline: 2/15; financial award applicants required to submit FAFSA. *Faculty research:* Conflict resolution; adapting human resource practices to the needs of a global workforce; effect of leadership styles and human resource practices on employee productivity; human resource management practices as a source of competitive advantage; influence of personality on work-life balance and work-home domain boundaries. *Unit head:* Dr. Maya Kroumova, Chairperson, 212-261-1667, Fax: 516-686-7425, E-mail: mkroumov@nyit.edu. *Application contact:* Alice Dolitsky, Director, Graduate Admissions, 516-686-7520, Fax: 516-686-1116, E-mail: nyitgrad@nyit.edu.
Website: http://www.nyit.edu/degrees/human_resources_management_labor_relations_ms

The Ohio State University, Graduate School, Max M. Fisher College of Business, Program in Human Resource Management, Columbus, OH 43210. Offers human resource management (MHRM, PhD); labor and human resources (PhD). *Program availability:* Part-time. *Faculty:* 25. *Students:* 85 full-time (64 women), 23 part-time (15

women). Average age 26. In 2017, 54 master's, 3 doctorates awarded. *Degree requirements:* For doctorate, thesis/dissertation. *Entrance requirements:* For master's and doctorate, GRE General Test or GMAT. Additional exam requirements/recommendations for international students: Required—Michigan English Language Assessment Battery (minimum score 86); Recommended—TOEFL (minimum score 600 paper-based; 100 iBT), IELTS (minimum score 7). *Application deadline:* For fall admission, 11/15 priority date for domestic and international students. Applications are processed on a rolling basis. Application fee: $60 ($70 for international students). Electronic applications accepted. *Financial support:* Fellowships with tuition reimbursements, research assistantships with tuition reimbursements, and teaching assistantships with tuition reimbursements available. *Unit head:* Dr. Bennett J. Tepper, Chair, 614-688-2129, E-mail: tepper.15@osu.edu. *Application contact:* Graduate and Professional Admissions, 614-292-9444, Fax: 614-292-3895, E-mail: gpadmissions@osu.edu.
Website: http://fisher.osu.edu/departments/management-and-hr/

Penn State University Park, Graduate School, College of the Liberal Arts, School of Labor and Employment Relations, University Park, PA 16802. Offers human resources and employment relations (MS); labor and global workers' rights (MPS). *Unit head:* Dr. Susan Welch, Dean, 814-865-7691, Fax: 814-863-2085. *Application contact:* Lori Hawn, Director, Graduate Student Services, 814-865-1795, Fax: 814-863-4627, E-mail: l-gswww@lists.psu.edu.
Website: http://lser.la.psu.edu/

Queen's University at Kingston, School of Graduate Studies, School of Industrial Relations, Kingston, ON K7L 3N6, Canada. Offers MIR. *Program availability:* Part-time. *Degree requirements:* For master's, research essay, skill seminars and modules. *Entrance requirements:* For master's, course work in micro-economics, macro-economics, and quantitative statistics. Additional exam requirements/recommendations for international students: Required—TOEFL (minimum score 600 paper-based). *Faculty research:* Collective bargaining and labor law, personnel and human relations, labor market analysis and policy, change management, teams.

Rutgers University–New Brunswick, School of Management and Labor Relations, Program in Industrial Relations and Human Resources, Piscataway, NJ 08854-8097. Offers PhD. *Program availability:* Part-time. *Degree requirements:* For doctorate, comprehensive exam, thesis/dissertation. *Entrance requirements:* For doctorate, GRE or GMAT, 3 letters of recommendation. Additional exam requirements/recommendations for international students: Required—TOEFL (minimum score 575 paper-based; 91 iBT). Electronic applications accepted. *Faculty research:* Strategic human resources, labor relations, organizational change, worker representation.

Rutgers University–New Brunswick, School of Management and Labor Relations, Program in Labor and Employment Relations, Piscataway, NJ 08854-8097. Offers MLER. *Program availability:* Part-time, online learning. *Degree requirements:* For master's, thesis optional. *Entrance requirements:* For master's, GRE General Test. Additional exam requirements/recommendations for international students: Required—TOEFL. Electronic applications accepted. *Expenses:* Contact institution. *Faculty research:* Labor history, women and work, labor education, comparative labor movements, labor involvement and corporate decision making.

State University of New York Empire State College, School for Graduate Studies, Program in Labor and Policy Studies, Saratoga Springs, NY 12866-4391. Offers MA. *Program availability:* Part-time, evening/weekend, online learning. *Degree requirements:* For master's, thesis, exam, final project. *Entrance requirements:* Additional exam requirements/recommendations for international students: Required—TOEFL (minimum score 600 paper-based). Electronic applications accepted. *Faculty research:* Work and technology, collective bargaining, labor law, human resources management, trade union governance.

Temple University, Beasley School of Law, Master's and Certificate Programs, Philadelphia, PA 19122-6096. Offers Asian law (LL M); business law (Certificate); employee benefits (Certificate); estate planning (Certificate); trial advocacy (LL M); trial advocacy and litigation (Certificate). *Expenses:* Tuition, state resident: full-time $16,164; part-time $898 per credit hour. Tuition, nonresident: full-time $22,158; part-time $1231 per credit hour. *Required fees:* $890; $445 per semester. Full-time tuition and fees vary according to course load, degree level, campus/location and program.

Université de Montréal, Faculty of Arts and Sciences, School of Industrial Relations, Montréal, QC H3C 3J7, Canada. Offers M Sc, PhD, DESS. *Program availability:* Part-time. *Degree requirements:* For master's, thesis; for doctorate, thesis/dissertation, general exam. *Entrance requirements:* For master's, BS in industrial relations. Electronic applications accepted. *Faculty research:* Labor law, health and safety at work, stress, job satisfaction, labor economics.

Université du Québec à Trois-Rivières, Graduate Programs, Program in Labor Relations, Trois-Rivières, QC G9A 5H7, Canada. Offers DESS.

Université du Québec en Outaouais, Graduate Programs, Department of Industrial Relations, Gatineau, QC J8X 3X7, Canada. Offers M Sc, MA, PhD, Diploma. *Program availability:* Part-time. *Degree requirements:* For master's, thesis (for some programs), internship (for some programs); for doctorate, thesis/dissertation. *Entrance requirements:* For master's, appropriate bachelor's degree, proficiency in French; for doctorate, appropriate master's degree, proficiency in French.

Université Laval, Faculty of Social Sciences, Department of Industrial Relations, Programs in Industrial Relations, Québec, QC G1K 7P4, Canada. Offers MA, PhD. Terminal master's awarded for partial completion of doctoral program. *Degree requirements:* For master's, thesis (for some programs); for doctorate, comprehensive exam, thesis/dissertation. *Entrance requirements:* For master's and doctorate, knowledge of French, comprehension of written English. Electronic applications accepted.

University of Alberta, Faculty of Graduate Studies and Research, Doctoral Program in Business, Edmonton, AB T6G 2E1, Canada. Offers accounting (PhD); finance (PhD); human resources/industrial relations (PhD); management science (PhD); marketing (PhD); organizational analysis (PhD); MBA/PhD. *Accreditation:* AACSB. *Program availability:* Part-time. *Degree requirements:* For doctorate, comprehensive exam, thesis/dissertation. *Entrance requirements:* For doctorate, GMAT. Additional exam requirements/recommendations for international students: Required—TOEFL (minimum score 550 paper-based). Electronic applications accepted. *Faculty research:* Accounting, capital markets and corporate finance, organizational change and human resource management, marketing, strategic management.

University of California, Berkeley, Graduate Division, Haas School of Business, PhD in Business Administration Program, Berkeley, CA 94720-1500. Offers accounting (PhD); business and public policy (PhD); finance (PhD); management of organizations (PhD); marketing (PhD); real estate (PhD). *Accreditation:* AACSB. *Students:* 72 full-time (20 women); includes 30 minority (26 Asian, non-Hispanic/Latino; 4 Hispanic/Latino). Average age 27. *Degree requirements:* For doctorate, comprehensive exam, thesis/dissertation, written preliminary exams, oral qualifying exam. *Entrance requirements:* For doctorate, GMAT or GRE, minimum GPA of 3.0 in undergraduate and graduate coursework. Additional exam requirements/recommendations for international students: Required—TOEFL (minimum score 570 paper-based; 70 iBT), IELTS (minimum score 7). *Application deadline:* For fall admission, 12/1 for domestic and international students. Application fee: $105 ($125 for international students). Electronic applications accepted. *Expenses:* Contact institution. *Financial support:* Fellowships with tuition reimbursements, research assistantships with tuition reimbursements, teaching assistantships with tuition reimbursements, scholarships/grants, health care benefits, tuition waivers (full), unspecified assistantships, and transit passes, travel grants available. Financial award application deadline: 12/1. *Faculty research:* Accounting, business and public policy, entrepreneurship, finance, management of organizations, marketing, operations and information technology management, real estate. *Unit head:* Dr. Nicolae Garleanu, Director, 510-643-6349, Fax: 510-643-4255. *Application contact:* Melissa Hacker, Director, Student Affairs, 510-642-3944, Fax: 510-643-4255, E-mail: melhacker@haas.berkeley.edu.
Website: http://www.haas.berkeley.edu/Phd/

University of Cincinnati, Graduate School, McMicken College of Arts and Sciences, Center for Organizational Leadership, Program in Labor and Employment Relations, Cincinnati, OH 45221. Offers MALER. *Program availability:* Part-time, evening/weekend. *Degree requirements:* For master's, thesis or alternative, final experience project. *Entrance requirements:* For master's, minimum undergraduate GPA of 3.0. Additional exam requirements/recommendations for international students: Required—TOEFL (minimum score 560 paper-based). Electronic applications accepted. *Expenses: Tuition, area resident:* Full-time $14,468. Tuition, state resident: full-time $14,968; part-time $754 per credit hour. Tuition, nonresident: full-time $24,210; part-time $1311 per credit hour. *International tuition:* $26,460 full-time. *Required fees:* $3958; $84 per credit hour. One-time fee: $85 full-time. Tuition and fees vary according to course load, degree level and program. *Faculty research:* Human resource management, diversity, leadership.

University of Illinois at Urbana–Champaign, Graduate College, School of Labor and Employment Relations, Champaign, IL 61820. Offers human resources and industrial relations (MHRIR, PhD); MHRIR/JD; MHRIR/MBA. Terminal master's awarded for partial completion of doctoral program.

The University of Manchester, Alliance Manchester Business School, M15 6PB, United Kingdom. Offers accounting and finance (M Sc); business (M Ent); business analysis and strategic management (M Sc); business analytics: operational research and risk analysis (M Sc); business psychology (M Sc); corporate communications and reputation management (M Sc); finance (M Sc); finance and business economics (M Sc); human resource management and industrial relations (M Sc); innovation management and entrepreneurship (M Sc); international business and management (M Sc); international human resource management and comparative industrial relations (M Sc); management (M Sc); marketing (M Sc); operations, project and supply chain management (M Sc); organizational psychology (M Sc); quantitative finance (M Sc). *Entrance requirements:* For master's, UK 2:1 honours degree or overseas equivalent. Additional exam requirements/recommendations for international students: Required—TOEFL (minimum score 100 iBT), IELTS (minimum score 7), PTE. Electronic applications accepted. *Faculty research:* Accounting and finance, management sciences and marketing, people management and organization, innovation management and policy, decision sciences.

University of Massachusetts Amherst, Graduate School, College of Social and Behavioral Sciences, The Labor Center, Amherst, MA 01003. Offers labor studies (MS); union leadership and administration (MS). *Program availability:* Part-time, online learning. *Degree requirements:* For master's, thesis or alternative. *Entrance requirements:* Additional exam requirements/recommendations for international students: Required—TOEFL (minimum score 550 paper-based; 80 iBT), IELTS (minimum score 6.5). Electronic applications accepted.

University of Minnesota, Twin Cities Campus, Carlson School of Management, Master of Arts Program in Human Resources and Industrial Relations, Minneapolis, MN 55455. Offers MA. *Accreditation:* AACSB. *Program availability:* Part-time, evening/weekend. *Faculty:* 16 full-time (9 women), 14 part-time/adjunct (7 women). *Students:* 122 full-time (85 women), 38 part-time (32 women); includes 20 minority (8 Black or African American, non-Hispanic/Latino; 1 American Indian or Alaska Native, non-Hispanic/Latino; 7 Asian, non-Hispanic/Latino; 4 Hispanic/Latino), 60 international. Average age 25. 204 applicants, 61% accepted, 69 enrolled. In 2017, 70 master's awarded. *Degree requirements:* For master's, thesis or alternative, 48 course credits. *Entrance requirements:* For master's, GMAT or GRE General Test, undergraduate degree from accredited institution, course in microeconomics. Additional exam requirements/recommendations for international students: Required—TOEFL (minimum score 550 paper-based; 79 iBT), IELTS (minimum score 6.5). *Application deadline:* For fall admission, 2/1 for domestic and international students. Applications are processed on a rolling basis. Application fee: $75 ($95 for international students). Electronic applications accepted. *Expenses:* $22,336 resident or reciprocity full-time per year; $33,556 nonresident full-time per year; $1,003 resident part-time per credit; $1,706 nonresident part-time per credit. *Financial support:* In 2017–18, 61 students received support, including 61 fellowships (averaging $7,500 per year), 1 research assistantship with partial tuition reimbursement available (averaging $16,225 per year), 5 teaching assistantships with partial tuition reimbursements available (averaging $9,000 per year); scholarships/grants, health care benefits, tuition waivers (partial), and unspecified assistantships also available. Financial award application deadline: 2/1; financial award applicants required to submit FAFSA. *Faculty research:* Staffing, training, and development; compensation and benefits; organization theory; collective bargaining. *Total annual research expenditures:* $27,000. *Unit head:* Stacy Doepner-Hove, Director, 612-625-8732, Fax: 612-624-8360, E-mail: doepn002@umn.edu. *Application contact:* Amy Danzeisen, Assistant Director for Admissions and Recruiting, 612-624-5704, Fax: 612-624-8360, E-mail: hrirgrad@umn.edu.
Website: https://carlsonschool.umn.edu/degrees/master-arts-human-resources-industrial-relations

University of Rhode Island, Graduate School, College of Business, Schmidt Labor Research Center, Kingston, RI 02881. Offers labor relations and human resources (MS, Graduate Certificate); MS/JD. *Program availability:* Part-time, evening/weekend. *Faculty:* 1 (woman) full-time, 2 part-time/adjunct (1 woman). *Students:* 6 full-time (3 women), 19 part-time (15 women); includes 8 minority (4 Black or African American, non-Hispanic/Latino; 1 American Indian or Alaska Native, non-Hispanic/Latino; 3 Hispanic/Latino), 1 international. 24 applicants, 96% accepted, 10 enrolled. In 2017, 3 master's, 20 other advanced degrees awarded. *Entrance requirements:* Additional exam requirements/recommendations for international students: Required—TOEFL. *Application deadline:* For fall admission, 7/15 for domestic students, 2/1 for international students; for spring admission, 11/15 for domestic students, 7/15 for international students; for summer admission, 4/15 for domestic students. Application fee: $65. Electronic applications accepted. *Expenses:* Tuition, state resident: full-time $12,706; part-time $786 per credit. Tuition, nonresident: full-time $25,216; part-time $1401 per credit. *Required fees:* $1598; $45 per credit. One-time fee: $30 part-time. *Financial support:* In 2017–18, 2 teaching assistantships with tuition reimbursements (averaging $17,724 per year) were awarded; institutionally sponsored loans also available. Financial award application deadline: 2/1; financial award applicants required to submit FAFSA. *Unit head:* Dr. Aimee Phelps, Acting Director, 401-874-4693, E-mail: aimee@uri.edu.
Website: http://www.uri.edu/research/lrc/

Industrial and Labor Relations

University of Toronto, School of Graduate Studies, Faculty of Arts and Science, Centre for Industrial Relations and Human Resources, Toronto, ON M5S 1A1, Canada. Offers MIRHR, PhD. *Program availability:* Part-time. *Degree requirements:* For doctorate, thesis/dissertation. *Entrance requirements:* For master's, GRE or GMAT (for applicants who completed degree outside of Canada), minimum B+ in final 2 years of bachelor's degree completion, 2 letters of reference, resume; for doctorate, GRE or GMAT, MIR or equivalent, minimum B+ average, 3 letters of reference, resume. Additional exam requirements/recommendations for international students: Required—TOEFL (minimum score 600 paper-based; 100 iBT), IELTS, TWE (minimum score 5), Michigan English Language Assessment Battery, or COPE. Electronic applications accepted. *Expenses:* Contact institution.

University of Wisconsin–Milwaukee, Graduate School, College of Letters and Science, Interdepartmental Program in Human Resources and Labor Relations, Milwaukee, WI 53201-0413. Offers human resources and labor relations (MHRLR); international human resources and labor relations (Graduate Certificate); mediation and negotiation (Graduate Certificate). *Program availability:* Part-time. *Students:* 14 full-time (10 women), 18 part-time (13 women); includes 8 minority (6 Black or African American, non-Hispanic/Latino; 1 Asian, non-Hispanic/Latino; 1 Two or more races, non-Hispanic/Latino), 1 international. Average age 31. 17 applicants, 65% accepted, 10 enrolled. In 2017, 13 master's awarded. *Entrance requirements:* For master's, GMAT or GRE General Test. Additional exam requirements/recommendations for international students: Required—TOEFL (minimum score 80 iBT), IELTS (minimum score 6.5). Application fee: $56 ($96 for international students). Electronic applications accepted. *Financial support:* Career-related internships or fieldwork available. Support available to part-time students. Financial award application deadline: 4/15; financial award applicants required to submit FAFSA. *Unit head:* Susan M. Donohue-Davies, Assistant Director, 414-299-4009, Fax: 414-229-5915, E-mail: suedono@uwm.edu. Website: http://uwm.edu/human-resources-labor-relations/

Wayne State University, College of Liberal Arts and Sciences, Department of Economics, Detroit, MI 48202. Offers applied macroeconomics (MA, PhD); health economics (MA, PhD); industrial organization (MA, PhD); international economics (MA, PhD); labor and human resources (MA, PhD); JD/MA. *Faculty:* 11. *Students:* 34 full-time (8 women), 9 part-time (3 women); includes 5 minority (4 Black or African American, non-Hispanic/Latino; 1 Asian, non-Hispanic/Latino), 17 international. Average age 30. 90 applicants, 30% accepted, 13 enrolled. In 2017, 10 master's, 6 doctorates awarded. *Degree requirements:* For master's, comprehensive exam; for doctorate, comprehensive exam, thesis/dissertation, oral examination on research, completion of course work in quantitative methods, final lecture. *Entrance requirements:* For master's, minimum upper-division GPA of 3.0; prior coursework in intermediate microeconomic and macroeconomic theory, statistics, and elementary calculus; for doctorate, GRE, minimum upper-division GPA of 3.0, prior coursework in intermediate microeconomic and macroeconomic theory, statistics, two courses in calculus, three letters of recommendation from officials or teaching staff at institution(s) most recently attended, statement of purpose. Additional exam requirements/recommendations for international students: Required—TOEFL (minimum score 550 paper-based; 79 iBT), TWE (minimum score 5.5), Michigan English Language Assessment Battery (minimum score 85); Recommended—IELTS (minimum score 6.5). *Application deadline:* For fall admission, 5/1 for domestic and international students; for winter admission, 10/1 priority date for domestic students, 9/1 priority date for international students; for spring admission, 1/1 priority date for domestic and international students. Applications are processed on a rolling basis. Application fee: $50. Electronic applications accepted. *Expenses:* Tuition, state resident: full-time $10,224; part-time $638.98 per credit hour. Tuition, nonresident: full-time $22,145; part-time $1384.04 per credit hour. Tuition and fees vary according to course load and program. *Financial support:* In 2017–18, 25 students received support, including 2 fellowships with tuition reimbursements available (averaging $16,000 per year), 17 teaching assistantships with tuition reimbursements available (averaging $18,534 per year); research assistantships with tuition reimbursements available, scholarships/grants, health care benefits, and unspecified assistantships also available. Support available to part-time students. Financial award applicants required to submit FAFSA. *Faculty research:* Health economics, international economics, macro-economics, urban and labor economics, econometrics. *Unit head:* Dr. Kevin Cotter, Interim Chair, 313-577-3345, E-mail: kevin.cotter@wayne.edu. *Application contact:* Dr. Li Way Lee, Professor and Director of Graduate Studies, 313-577-3345, E-mail: aa1313@wayne.edu. Website: http://clas.wayne.edu/economics/

Wayne State University, College of Liberal Arts and Sciences, Program in Employment and Labor Relations, Detroit, MI 48202. Offers MA. *Program availability:* Part-time, evening/weekend. *Students:* 8 full-time (7 women), 17 part-time (12 women); includes 14 minority (11 Black or African American, non-Hispanic/Latino; 3 Hispanic/Latino), 2 international. Average age 35. 8 applicants, 63% accepted, 1 enrolled. In 2017, 9 master's awarded. *Entrance requirements:* For master's, GRE or GMAT, personal statement, three letters of recommendation written by former college or university

professors and/or current employers, baccalaureate degree from accredited institution, writing sample. Additional exam requirements/recommendations for international students: Required—TOEFL (minimum score 550 paper-based; 79 iBT), IELTS (minimum score 6.5), Michigan English Language Assessment Battery (minimum score 85). *Application deadline:* For fall admission, 6/1 priority date for domestic students, 5/1 priority date for international students; for winter admission, 10/1 priority date for domestic students, 9/1 priority date for international students; for spring admission, 2/1 priority date for domestic students, 1/1 priority date for international students. Application fee: $50. Electronic applications accepted. *Expenses:* Tuition, state resident: full-time $10,224; part-time $638.98 per credit hour. Tuition, nonresident: full-time $22,145; part-time $1384.04 per credit hour. Tuition and fees vary according to course load and program. *Financial support:* In 2017–18, 15 students received support. Scholarships/grants available. Financial award applicants required to submit FAFSA. *Unit head:* Dr. Marick Masters, Director, 313-577-5358, E-mail: marickm@wayne.edu. *Application contact:* Linda Johnson, Academic Services Officer, 313-577-0175, E-mail: ab1232@wayne.edu. Website: http://clas.wayne.edu/labor/maelr

Wayne State University, Law School, Detroit, MI 48202. Offers corporate and finance law (LL M); labor and employment law (LL M); law (JD); taxation (LL M); United States law (LL M); JD/MA; JD/MADR; JD/MBA; JD/MS. *Accreditation:* ABA. *Program availability:* Part-time, evening/weekend. *Faculty:* 43 full-time (18 women), 17 part-time/adjunct (9 women). *Students:* 409 full-time (184 women), 46 part-time (22 women); includes 61 minority (33 Black or African American, non-Hispanic/Latino; 1 American Indian or Alaska Native, non-Hispanic/Latino; 14 Asian, non-Hispanic/Latino; 3 Hispanic/Latino; 10 Two or more races, non-Hispanic/Latino), 11 international. Average age 26. 811 applicants, 54% accepted, 146 enrolled. In 2017, 4 master's, 113 doctorates awarded. *Degree requirements:* For master's, thesis (for some programs). *Entrance requirements:* For master's, JD or LL B from ABA-accredited institution and member institution of the AALS; for doctorate, LSAT, LDAS report, bachelor's degree from accredited institution, personal statement, transcripts from all U.S. undergraduate schools attended and an analysis and summary of the transcripts; letter of recommendation (up to two are accepted). Additional exam requirements/recommendations for international students: Required—TOEFL, Michigan English Language Assessment Battery (minimum score 85); Recommended—IELTS. *Application deadline:* For fall admission, 7/1 for domestic students, 5/1 priority date for international students. Applications are processed on a rolling basis. Application fee: $0. Electronic applications accepted. *Expenses:* Contact institution. *Financial support:* In 2017–18, 386 students received support. Fellowships, Federal Work-Study, and scholarships/grants available. Support available to part-time students. Financial award application deadline: 6/30; financial award applicants required to submit FAFSA. *Unit head:* Richard A. Bierschbach, Dean and Professor of Law, 313-577-3933, E-mail: rbierschbach@wayne.edu. *Application contact:* Kathy Fox, Assistant Dean of Admissions, 313-577-3937, Fax: 313-993-8129, E-mail: lawinquire@wayne.edu. Website: http://law.wayne.edu/

West Virginia University, College of Business and Economics, Morgantown, WV 26506. Offers accountancy (M Acc); accounting (PhD); business administration (MBA); business cyber security management (MS); business data analytics (MS); economics (MA, PhD); finance (MS, PhD); forensic and fraud examination (MS); industrial relations (MS); management (PhD); marketing (PhD). *Program availability:* Part-time, online learning. *Students:* 343 full-time (141 women), 43 part-time (12 women); includes 59 minority (22 Black or African American, non-Hispanic/Latino; 11 Asian, non-Hispanic/Latino; 12 Hispanic/Latino; 14 Two or more races, non-Hispanic/Latino), 54 international. Terminal master's awarded for partial completion of doctoral program. *Degree requirements:* For master's, thesis optional; for doctorate, comprehensive exam, thesis/dissertation. *Entrance requirements:* For doctorate, GRE General Test, minimum GPA of 3.0. Additional exam requirements/recommendations for international students: Required—TOEFL (minimum score 550 paper-based; 92 iBT). *Application deadline:* For fall admission, 10/15 priority date for domestic and international students; for spring admission, 3/1 priority date for domestic and international students. Applications are processed on a rolling basis. Application fee: $60. Electronic applications accepted. *Expenses:* Contact institution. *Financial support:* Fellowships, research assistantships, teaching assistantships, career-related internships or fieldwork, Federal Work-Study, institutionally sponsored loans, scholarships/grants, health care benefits, tuition waivers (full and partial), unspecified assistantships, and administrative assistantships available. Financial award application deadline: 2/1; financial award applicants required to submit FAFSA. *Faculty research:* Regional labor market studies, economic development, market research, economic forecasting, energy analysis. *Unit head:* Dr. Javier Reyes, Dean, 304-293-7800, Fax: 304-293-4056, E-mail: javier.reyes@mail.wvu.edu. *Application contact:* Dr. Mark Gavin, Associate Dean for Graduate Programs, 304-293-7952, Fax: 304-293-7188, E-mail: mark.gavin@mail.wvu.edu. Website: http://www.be.wvu.edu

Philanthropic Studies

Indiana University–Purdue University Indianapolis, Lilly Family School of Philanthropy, Indianapolis, IN 46202. Offers MA, XMA, PhD. *Degree requirements:* For master's, thesis optional; for doctorate, thesis/dissertation. *Entrance requirements:* For master's, GRE General Test (minimum score 500 quantitative, 500 verbal, 4.5 analytical writing), minimum undergraduate GPA of 3.0; for doctorate, GRE General Test (minimum score 500 quantitative, 500 verbal, 4.5 analytical writing), minimum GPA of 3.0, master's degree.

Saint Mary's University of Minnesota, Schools of Graduate and Professional Programs, Graduate School of Business and Technology, Philanthropy and Development Program, Winona, MN 55987-1399. Offers MA. *Unit head:* Cheryl Pray, Executive Director, 612-728-5137, E-mail: cpray@smumn.edu. *Application contact:* Jami Spitzer, Information Contact, 507-457-7500, E-mail: jspitzer@smumn.edu. Website: http://www.smumn.edu/graduate-home/areas-of-study/graduate-school-of-business-technology/ma-in-philanthropy-development

Public Administration

Adams State University, Office of Graduate Studies, Department of History, Government and Philosophy, Alamosa, CO 81101. Offers humanities (MA), including cultural resource management, public administration, U.S. history. Application fee: $30. *Expenses:* Tuition, state resident: full-time $4800; part-time $2400 per credit. Tuition, nonresident: full-time $7100; part-time $3550 per credit. *Required fees:* $213; $106 per

credit. One-time fee: $100. Tuition and fees vary according to campus/location and program. *Unit head:* Dr. Edward Crowther, Chair, 719-587-7771, Fax: 719-587-7176, E-mail: ascgrad@adams.edu. *Application contact:* Eileen Tilton, Administrative Assistant III, 719-587-7771, Fax: 719-587-7176, E-mail: ascgrad@adams.edu. Website: http://www2.adams.edu/academics/hgp/

Adler University, Graduate Programs, Master of Public Administration Program, Chicago, IL 60602. Offers criminal justice (MPA); sustainable communities (MPA). *Program availability:* Part-time, evening/weekend.

Albany State University, College of Arts and Humanities, Albany, GA 31705-2717. Offers criminal justice (MS); English education (M Ed); public administration (MPA), including community and economic development, criminal justice administration, health administration and policy, human resources management, public management, public policy, water resources management and policy; social work (MSW). *Accreditation:* NASPAA. *Program availability:* Part-time. *Degree requirements:* For master's, comprehensive exam, professional portfolio (for MPA), internship, capstone report. *Entrance requirements:* For master's, GRE, MAT, minimum GPA of 3.0, official transcript, pre-medical record/certificate of immunization, letters of reference. Electronic applications accepted. *Faculty research:* HIV prevention for minority students.

Albany State University, College of Business, Albany, GA 31705-2717. Offers accounting (MBA); general business administration (MBA); healthcare (MBA); public administration (MBA); supply chain and logistics (MBA). *Accreditation:* ACBSP. *Program availability:* Part-time, evening/weekend. *Degree requirements:* For master's, comprehensive exam, internship, 3 hours of physical education. *Entrance requirements:* For master's, GMAT (minimum score of 450)/GRE (minimum score of 800) for those without earned master's degree or higher, minimum undergraduate GPA of 2.5, 2 letters of reference, official transcript, pre-entrance medical record and certificate of immunization. Electronic applications accepted. *Faculty research:* Diversity issues, ancestry, understanding finance through use of technology.

Alfred University, Graduate School, Public Administration Program, Alfred, NY 14802-1205. Offers MPA. *Program availability:* Part-time, evening/weekend.

American University, School of Public Affairs, Department of Public Administration and Policy, Washington, DC 20016-8070. Offers organization development (MSOD, Certificate), including leadership for organizational change (Certificate), organization development (MSOD); public administration (MPA, PhD, Certificate), including nonprofit management (Certificate), public financial management (Certificate), public management (Certificate); public administration and policy (MPAP), including public administration policy; public policy (MPP), including public policy; public policy (Certificate), including public policy analysis; LL M/MPA; MPA/JD; MPP/JD; MPP/LL M. *Program availability:* Part-time, evening/weekend, online learning. *Faculty:* 31 full-time (12 women), 36 part-time/adjunct (13 women). *Students:* 211 full-time (129 women), 305 part-time (202 women); includes 132 minority (84 Black or African American, non-Hispanic/Latino; 4 American Indian or Alaska Native, non-Hispanic/Latino; 24 Asian, non-Hispanic/Latino; 10 Hispanic/Latino; 10 Two or more races, non-Hispanic/Latino), 34 international. Average age 31. 658 applicants, 86% accepted, 230 enrolled. In 2017, 178 master's, 6 doctorates, 7 other advanced degrees awarded. *Degree requirements:* For master's, comprehensive exam; for doctorate, comprehensive exam, thesis/dissertation. *Entrance requirements:* For master's, GRE, statement of purpose, 2 recommendations, resume, transcript; for doctorate, GRE, 3 recommendations, statement of purpose, resume, writing sample, transcript; for Certificate, bachelor's degree. Additional exam requirements/recommendations for international students: Required—TOEFL (minimum score 600 paper-based; 100 iBT). *Application deadline:* For fall admission, 2/15 priority date for domestic students, 5/1 for international students; for spring admission, 11/1 for domestic students, 9/15 for international students. Application fee: $55. *Expenses:* Contact institution. *Financial support:* Research assistantships, teaching assistantships, institutionally sponsored loans, scholarships/grants, and unspecified assistantships available. Financial award application deadline: 2/1; financial award applicants required to submit FAFSA. *Unit head:* Dr. Dave Marcotte, Department Chair, 202-885-3108, E-mail: marcotte@american.edu. *Application contact:* Jennifer Forney, Assistant Dean, Graduate Enrollment, E-mail: forney@american.edu.
Website: http://www.american.edu/spa/dpap/

The American University in Cairo, School of Global Affairs and Public Policy, Cairo, Egypt. Offers gender and women's studies (MA); global affairs (MGA); international and comparative law (LL M); international human rights law (MA); journalism and mass communication (MA); Middle East studies (MA); migration and refugee studies (MA, Diploma); public administration (MPA); public policy (MPP); television and digital journalism (MA). *Program availability:* Part-time, evening/weekend. *Faculty:* 26 full-time (11 women), 4 part-time/adjunct (3 women). *Students:* 65 full-time (50 women), 201 part-time (136 women), 39 international. Average age 29. 357 applicants, 51% accepted, 72 enrolled. In 2017, 94 master's awarded. *Degree requirements:* For master's, comprehensive exam (for some programs), thesis (for some programs). *Entrance requirements:* Additional exam requirements/recommendations for international students: Required—TOEFL (minimum score 450 paper-based; 45 iBT), IELTS (minimum score 5). *Application deadline:* For fall admission, 2/1 for domestic and international students; for spring admission, 10/15 for domestic and international students. Applications are processed on a rolling basis. Application fee: $85. Electronic applications accepted. *Expenses:* Contact institution. *Financial support:* Fellowships with partial tuition reimbursements, scholarships/grants, and unspecified assistantships available. Financial award application deadline: 3/10. *Faculty research:* Law, media and journalism; public policy and public administration; gender studies; Middle East Studies; global affairs; refugees studies. *Unit head:* Dr. Nabil Fahmy, Dean, 20-2-2615-2671, E-mail: nfahmy@aucegypt.edu. *Application contact:* Maha Hegazi, Director for Graduate Admissions, 20-2-2615-1462, E-mail: mahahegazi@aucegypt.edu.
Website: http://www.aucegypt.edu/GAPP/Pages/default.aspx

American University of Beirut, Graduate Programs, Faculty of Arts and Sciences, 1107 2020, Lebanon. Offers anthropology (MA); Arab and Middle Eastern history (PhD); Arabic language and literature (MA, PhD); archaeology (MA); art history and curating (MA); biology (MS); cell and molecular biology (PhD); chemistry (MS); clinical psychology (MA); computational sciences (MS); computer science (MS); economics (MA); education (MA), including administration and policy studies, elementary education, mathematics education, psychology school guidance, psychology test and measurements, science education, teaching English as a foreign language; English language (MA); English literature (MA); environmental policy planning (MS); financial economics (MAFE); general psychology (MA); geology (MS); history (MA); Islamic studies (MA); mathematics (MS); media studies (MA); Middle East studies (MA); philosophy (MA); physics (MS); political studies (MA); public administration (MA); public policy and international affairs (MA); sociology (MA); theoretical physics (PhD). *Program availability:* Part-time. *Faculty:* 108 full-time (36 women), 5 part-time/adjunct (4 women). *Students:* 251 full-time (180 women), 233 part-time (172 women). Average age 26. 425 applicants, 65% accepted, 121 enrolled. In 2017, 47 master's, 2 doctorates awarded. *Degree requirements:* For master's, one foreign language, comprehensive exam, thesis (for some programs), project; for doctorate, one foreign language, comprehensive exam, thesis/dissertation. *Entrance requirements:* For master's, GRE General Test (for some programs); for doctorate, GRE General Test (GRE Subject Test for theoretical physics). Additional exam requirements/recommendations for international students: Required—TOEFL (minimum score 583 paper-based; 97 iBT), IELTS (minimum score 7). *Application deadline:* For fall admission, 2/8 for domestic students; for spring admission, 11/3 for domestic students. Application fee: $50. Electronic applications accepted. *Expenses:* Contact institution. *Financial support:* In 2017–18, 29 fellowships, 40 research assistantships were awarded; teaching assistantships, scholarships/grants, tuition waivers (full and partial), and unspecified assistantships also available. Financial award application deadline: 4/4. *Unit head:* Dr. Nadia Maria El Cheikh, Dean, Faculty of Arts and Sciences, 961-1-374374 Ext. 3800, Fax: 961-1-744461, E-mail: nmcheikh@aub.edu.lb. *Application contact:* Rima Rassi, Graduate Studies Officer, 961-1-350000 Ext. 3833, Fax: 961-1-744461, E-mail: rr46@aub.edu.lb.
Website: http://www.aub.edu.lb/fas/pages/default.aspx

Anabaptist Mennonite Biblical Seminary, Graduate and Professional Programs, Elkhart, IN 46517-1999. Offers chaplaincy (M Div); Christian faith formation (M Div); Christian formation (MA); Christian spiritual formation (Certificate); divinity (M Div); pastoral ministry (M Div); pastoral theology for financial professionals (Certificate); peace studies (M Div), including environmental sustainability leadership (M Div, MA); theological studies (M Div, Certificate), including peace studies (M Div), theology and ethics (M Div); theology and peace studies (MA), including conflict transformation, environmental sustainability leadership (M Div, MA), international development administration; United Methodist leadership (M Div). Conflict transformation and environmental sustainability leadership concentrations offered in cooperation with Goshen College; international development administration offered in cooperation with Andrews University. *Accreditation:* ACIPE; ATS. *Program availability:* Part-time, 100% online, blended/hybrid learning. *Degree requirements:* For master's, variable foreign language requirement, comprehensive exam (for some programs), thesis optional, senior interview. *Entrance requirements:* For master's, undergraduate degree transcripts, 3 letters of reference, essay. Additional exam requirements/recommendations for international students: Required—TOEFL (minimum score 90 iBT); Recommended—IELTS (minimum score 7). Electronic applications accepted. *Faculty research:* Biblical studies, peace studies, theology, ethics, creation care or environmental ethics, church history, church leadership, mission, ministry, preaching, pastoral leadership, social justice, peacemaking, Jesus Christ, Christianity, Anabaptism, Mennonite, Scripture, Bible, Old Testament, New Testament, spirituality, clinical pastoral education, teaching, faith formation, pastoral care, Koine Greek, Hebrew, Aramaic, Syriac, Ugaritic.

Anna Maria College, Graduate Division, Program in Public Administration, Paxton, MA 01612. Offers MPA.

Appalachian State University, Cratis D. Williams Graduate School, Department of Government and Justice Studies, Boone, NC 28608. Offers political science (MA), including American government; public administration (MPA), including public management. *Accreditation:* NASPAA. *Program availability:* Part-time, online learning. *Degree requirements:* For master's, variable foreign language requirement, comprehensive exam, thesis optional. *Entrance requirements:* For master's, GRE General Test, 3 letters of recommendation. Additional exam requirements/recommendations for international students: Required—TOEFL (minimum score 570 paper-based; 79 iBT), IELTS (minimum score 6.5). Electronic applications accepted. *Faculty research:* Campaign finance, emerging democracies, bureaucratic politics, judicial behavior, administration of justice.

Argosy University, Chicago, College of Business, Chicago, IL 60601. Offers accounting (DBA); customized professional concentration (MBA, DBA); finance (MBA); fraud examination (MBA); global business sustainability (DBA); healthcare administration (MBA); information systems (DBA); information systems management (MBA); international business (MBA, DBA); management (MBA, MSM, DBA); marketing (MBA, DBA); organizational leadership (Ed D); public administration (MBA); sustainable management (MBA). *Accreditation:* ACBSP. *Program availability:* Online learning.

Argosy University, Los Angeles, College of Business, Los Angeles, CA 90045. Offers accounting (DBA); corporate compliance (MBA); customized professional concentration (MBA, DBA); finance (MBA); fraud examination (MBA); global business sustainability (DBA); healthcare administration (MBA); information systems (DBA); information systems management (MBA); international business (MBA, DBA); management (MBA, MSM, DBA); marketing (MBA, DBA); organizational leadership (Ed D); public administration (MBA); sustainable management (MBA).

Argosy University, Northern Virginia, College of Business, Arlington, VA 22209. Offers accounting (DBA); customized professional concentration (MBA, DBA); finance (MBA); fraud examination (MBA); global business sustainability (DBA); healthcare administration (MBA); information systems (DBA); information systems management (MBA); international business (MBA, DBA, Certificate); management (MBA, MSM, DBA); marketing (MBA, DBA, Certificate); organizational leadership (Ed D); public administration (MBA); sustainable management (MBA).

Argosy University, Orange County, College of Business, Orange, CA 92868. Offers accounting (DBA, Adv C); corporate compliance (MBA); customized professional concentration (MBA, DBA); finance (MBA, Certificate); fraud examination (MBA); global business sustainability (DBA); healthcare administration (MBA, Certificate); information systems (DBA, Adv C, Certificate); information systems management (MBA); international business (MBA, DBA, Adv C, Certificate); management (MBA, MSM, DBA, Adv C); marketing (MBA, DBA, Adv C, Certificate); organizational leadership (Ed D); public administration (MBA, Certificate); sustainable management (MBA).

Argosy University, Phoenix, College of Business, Phoenix, AZ 85021. Offers accounting (DBA); corporate compliance (MBA); customized professional concentration (MBA, DBA); finance (MBA); fraud examination (MBA); global business sustainability (DBA); healthcare administration (MBA); information systems (DBA); information systems management (MBA); international business (MBA, DBA); management (MBA, DBA); marketing (MBA, DBA); public administration (MBA); sustainable management (MBA).

Argosy University, Seattle, College of Business, Seattle, WA 98121. Offers accounting (DBA); corporate compliance (MBA); customized professional concentration (MBA, DBA); finance (MBA); fraud examination (MBA); global business sustainability (DBA); healthcare administration (MBA); information systems (DBA); information systems management (MBA); international business (MBA, DBA); management (MBA, MSM, DBA); marketing (MBA, DBA); organizational leadership (Ed D); public administration (MBA); sustainable management (MBA).

Argosy University, Tampa, College of Business, Tampa, FL 33607. Offers accounting (DBA); corporate compliance (MBA); customized professional concentration (MBA, DBA); finance (MBA); fraud examination (MBA); global business sustainability (DBA); healthcare administration (MBA); information systems (DBA); information systems management (MBA); international business (MBA, DBA); management (MBA, MSM, DBA); marketing (MBA, DBA); organizational leadership (Ed D); public administration (MBA); sustainable management (MBA).

Argosy University, Twin Cities, College of Business, Eagan, MN 55121. Offers accounting (DBA); customized professional concentration (MBA, DBA); finance (MBA); fraud examination (MBA); global business sustainability (DBA); healthcare administration (MBA); information systems (DBA); information systems management (MBA); international business (MBA, DBA); management (MBA, MSM, DBA); marketing (MBA, DBA); organizational leadership (Ed D); public administration (MBA); sustainable management (MBA).

Public Administration

Arizona State University at the Tempe campus, College of Public Programs, School of Public Affairs, Phoenix, AZ 85004-0687. Offers emergency management and homeland security (MA); program evaluation (MS); public administration (MPA, PhD), including nonprofit administration (MPA), urban management (MPA); public policy (MPP); MPA/MSW. *Accreditation:* NASPAA (one or more programs are accredited). *Program availability:* Part-time, evening/weekend. Terminal master's awarded for partial completion of doctoral program. *Degree requirements:* For master's, thesis or alternative, policy analysis or capstone project; interactive Program of Study (iPOS) submitted before completing 50 percent of required credit hours; for doctorate, comprehensive exam, thesis/dissertation, interactive Program of Study (iPOS) submitted before completing 50 percent of required credit hours. *Entrance requirements:* For master's, GRE, minimum GPA of 3.0 or equivalent in last 2 years of work leading to bachelor's degree; for doctorate, GRE, minimum GPA of 3.0 or equivalent in last 2 years of work leading to bachelor's degree, 3 letters of recommendation, resume, statement of goals, samples of research reports. Additional exam requirements/recommendations for international students: Required—TOEFL (minimum score 600 paper-based; 100 iBT), IELTS (minimum score 6.5). Electronic applications accepted. *Expenses:* Contact institution.

Arkansas State University, Graduate School, College of Humanities and Social Sciences, Department of Political Science, State University, AR 72467. Offers political science (MA); political science education (SCCT); public administration (MPA). *Accreditation:* NASPAA (one or more programs are accredited). *Program availability:* Part-time. *Degree requirements:* For master's, comprehensive exam, thesis or alternative; for SCCT, comprehensive exam. *Entrance requirements:* For master's, GRE General Test or MAT, GMAT, appropriate bachelor's degree, letters of recommendation, official transcripts, immunization records, statement of purpose; for SCCT, GRE General Test or MAT, GMAT, interview, master's degree, official transcript, letters of recommendation, immunization records. Additional exam requirements/recommendations for international students: Required—TOEFL (minimum score 550 paper-based; 79 iBT), IELTS (minimum score 6), PTE (minimum score 56). Electronic applications accepted.

Auburn University, Graduate School, College of Liberal Arts, Department of Political Science, Program in Public Administration, Auburn University, AL 36849. Offers MPA, PhD, Graduate Certificate, MPA/MCP. PhD offered jointly with Auburn University Montgomery. *Accreditation:* NASPAA (one or more programs are accredited). *Program availability:* Part-time. *Faculty:* 28 full-time (16 women), 4 part-time/adjunct (3 women). *Students:* 70 full-time (41 women), 38 part-time (15 women); includes 15 minority (13 Black or African American, non-Hispanic/Latino; 1 American Indian or Alaska Native, non-Hispanic/Latino; 1 Hispanic/Latino), 43 international. Average age 32. 45 applicants, 82% accepted, 17 enrolled. In 2017, 12 master's, 3 doctorates awarded. *Degree requirements:* For master's, internship or research project; for doctorate, thesis/dissertation. *Entrance requirements:* For master's, GRE General Test, sample of written work; for doctorate, GRE General Test. *Application deadline:* Applications are processed on a rolling basis. Application fee: $50 ($60 for international students). Electronic applications accepted. *Expenses:* Tuition, state resident: full-time $10,974; part-time $519 per credit hour. Tuition, nonresident: full-time $29,658; part-time $1557 per credit hour. *Required fees:* $816 per semester. Tuition and fees vary according to degree level and program. *Financial support:* Fellowships, research assistantships, teaching assistantships, career-related internships or fieldwork, and Federal Work-Study available. Support available to part-time students. Financial award application deadline: 3/15; financial award applicants required to submit FAFSA. *Faculty research:* Privatization studies, policy evolution, water resources, election administration. *Unit head:* Dr. Kathleen Hale, Head, 334-844-6155. *Application contact:* Dr. George Flowers, Dean of the Graduate School, 334-844-2125.
Website: http://www.cla.auburn.edu/polisci/

Auburn University at Montgomery, College of Public Policy and Justice, Department of Political Science and Public Administration, Montgomery, AL 36124-4023. Offers political science (MPS); public administration (MPA); public administration and public policy (PhD). PhD offered jointly with Auburn University. *Accreditation:* NASPAA (one or more programs are accredited). *Program availability:* Part-time, evening/weekend. *Faculty:* 4 full-time (1 woman). *Students:* 11 full-time (5 women), 22 part-time (15 women); includes 18 minority (all Black or African American, non-Hispanic/Latino), 4 international. Average age 31. 23 applicants, 78% accepted, 9 enrolled. In 2017, 5 master's awarded. *Degree requirements:* For master's, comprehensive exam; for doctorate, thesis/dissertation. *Entrance requirements:* For master's, GRE General Test or MAT; for doctorate, GRE General Test. Additional exam requirements/recommendations for international students: Recommended—TOEFL (minimum score 500 paper-based; 61 iBT), IELTS (minimum score 5.5), TSE (minimum score 44). *Application deadline:* For fall admission, 7/15 for international students; for spring admission, 11/15 for international students; for summer admission, 4/15 for international students. Applications are processed on a rolling basis. Application fee: $25. Electronic applications accepted. *Expenses:* Tuition, state resident: full-time $6930; part-time $385 per credit hour. Tuition, nonresident: full-time $15,588; part-time $866 per credit hour. *Required fees:* $640. *Financial support:* Research assistantships, teaching assistantships, career-related internships or fieldwork, and scholarships/grants available. Support available to part-time students. Financial award application deadline: 3/1; financial award applicants required to submit FAFSA. *Unit head:* Dr. Andrew Cortell, Head, 334-244-3622, E-mail: acortell@aum.edu.
Website: http://cppj.aum.edu/departments/political-science

Ball State University, Graduate School, College of Sciences and Humanities, Department of Political Science, Program in Public Administration, Muncie, IN 47306. Offers public administration (MPA, Certificate), including community and economic development (MPA), criminal justice (MPA), emergency management and homeland security (MPA), information and communication technology (MPA). *Program availability:* Part-time. *Students:* 20 full-time (7 women), 14 part-time (8 women); includes 4 minority (2 Black or African American, non-Hispanic/Latino; 2 Hispanic/Latino), 1 international. Average age 29. 28 applicants, 89% accepted, 15 enrolled. In 2017, 10 master's awarded. *Degree requirements:* For master's, comprehensive exam. *Entrance requirements:* For master's, GRE General Test, minimum baccalaureate GPA of 2.8, two letters of recommendation. Additional exam requirements/recommendations for international students: Required—TOEFL (minimum score 550 paper-based; 79 iBT), IELTS (minimum score 6.5). *Application deadline:* Applications are processed on a rolling basis. Application fee: $60. Electronic applications accepted. *Financial support:* Research assistantships with partial tuition reimbursements and unspecified assistantships available. Financial award application deadline: 3/1; financial award applicants required to submit FAFSA. *Faculty research:* Employment training programs, personnel and labor relations, planning. *Unit head:* Dr. Daniel Reagan, Chairperson, 765-285-8789, Fax: 765-285-5345, E-mail: jlosco@bsu.edu. *Application contact:* Dr. Charles Taylor, Associate Professor/Graduate Advisor, 765-285-8794, Fax: 765-285-5345, E-mail: cdtaylor@bsu.edu.
Website: http://www.bsu.edu/poli-sci

Barry University, School of Adult and Continuing Education, Program in Public Administration, Miami Shores, FL 33161-6695. Offers MPA. *Program availability:* Part-time, evening/weekend. *Entrance requirements:* For master's, GMAT, GRE or MAT, recommendations. Electronic applications accepted.

Baruch College of the City University of New York, Austin W. Marxe School of Public and International Affairs, Program in Public Administration, New York, NY 10010-5585. Offers general public administration (MPA); health care policy (MPA); nonprofit administration (MPA); policy analysis and evaluation (MPA); public management (MPA); urban development and sustainability (MPA); MS/MPA. *Accreditation:* NASPAA. *Program availability:* Part-time, evening/weekend. *Degree requirements:* For master's, thesis, capstone. *Entrance requirements:* For master's, GRE General Test. Additional exam requirements/recommendations for international students: Required—TOEFL. Electronic applications accepted. *Expenses:* Contact institution. *Faculty research:* Urbanization, population and poverty in the developing world, housing and community development, labor unions and housing, government-nongovernment relations, immigration policy, social network analysis, cross-sectoral governance, comparative healthcare systems, program evaluation, social welfare policy, health outcomes, educational policy and leadership, transnationalism, infant health, welfare reform, racial/ethnic disparities in health, urban politics, homelessness, race and ethnic relations.
See Display on page 910 and Close-Up on page 955.

Baylor University, Graduate School, College of Arts and Sciences, Department of Political Science, Waco, TX 76798. Offers international studies (MA); political science (MA, PhD); public policy and administration (MPPA); JD/MPPA. *Faculty:* 19 full-time (3 women), 1 part-time/adjunct (0 women). *Students:* 28 full-time (14 women); includes 1 minority (Hispanic/Latino). Average age 26. 27 applicants, 22% accepted, 4 enrolled. In 2017, 4 master's, 5 doctorates awarded. Terminal master's awarded for partial completion of doctoral program. *Degree requirements:* For master's, variable foreign language requirement, comprehensive exam (for some programs), thesis (for some programs); for doctorate, variable foreign language requirement, comprehensive exam, thesis/dissertation. *Entrance requirements:* For master's and doctorate, GRE General Test. Additional exam requirements/recommendations for international students: Required—TOEFL. *Application deadline:* For fall admission, 12/20 for domestic and international students. Application fee: $50. Electronic applications accepted. *Financial support:* In 2017–18, 26 students received support, including 26 research assistantships with full tuition reimbursements available (averaging $16,000 per year); career-related internships or fieldwork, Federal Work-Study, and institutionally sponsored loans also available. Financial award application deadline: 12/20; financial award applicants required to submit FAFSA. *Unit head:* Dr. Timothy Burns, Graduate Program Director, 254-710-6237, Fax: 254-710-3122, E-mail: timothy_burns@baylor.edu. *Application contact:* Jenice Langston, Office Manager, 254-710-3161, Fax: 254-710-3122, E-mail: jenice_langston@baylor.edu.
Website: http://www.baylor.edu/political_science/

Belhaven University, School of Business, Jackson, MS 39202-1789. Offers business administration (MBA); health administration (MBA, MHA); human resources (MBA, MSL); leadership (MBA); public administration (MPA); sports administration (MBA, MSA). *Program availability:* Part-time, evening/weekend, 100% online. *Faculty:* 11 full-time (4 women), 93 part-time/adjunct (39 women). *Students:* 20 full-time (12 women), 1,441 part-time (1,061 women); includes 1,168 minority (1,100 Black or African American, non-Hispanic/Latino; 22 American Indian or Alaska Native, non-Hispanic/Latino; 2 Asian, non-Hispanic/Latino; 23 Hispanic/Latino; 1 Native Hawaiian or other Pacific Islander, non-Hispanic/Latino; 20 Two or more races, non-Hispanic/Latino), 21 international. Average age 35. 501 applicants, 74% accepted, 261 enrolled. In 2017, 326 master's awarded. *Degree requirements:* For master's, comprehensive exam (for some programs), thesis or alternative. *Entrance requirements:* For master's, minimum GPA of 2.8 (for MBA and MHA), 2.5 (for MSL, MPA and MSA). *Application deadline:* Applications are processed on a rolling basis. Application fee: $25. Electronic applications accepted. *Expenses:* Contact institution. *Financial support:* Applicants required to submit FAFSA. *Unit head:* Dr. Ralph Mason, Dean, 601-968-8949, Fax: 601-968-8951, E-mail: cmason@belhaven.edu. *Application contact:* Dr. Audrey Kelleher, Vice President of Adult and Graduate Marketing and Development, 407-804-1424, Fax: 407-620-5210, E-mail: akelleher@belhaven.edu.
Website: http://www.belhaven.edu/campuses/index.htm

Bellevue University, Graduate School, College of Professional Studies, Bellevue, NE 68005-3098. Offers instructional design and development (MS); justice administration and criminal management (MS); leadership (MA); organizational performance (MS); public administration (MPA); security management (MS).

Binghamton University, State University of New York, Graduate School, College of Community and Public Affairs, Department of Public Administration, Binghamton, NY 13902-6000. Offers MPA. *Accreditation:* NASPAA. *Program availability:* Part-time. *Faculty:* 8 full-time (4 women). *Students:* 76 full-time (43 women), 45 part-time (30 women); includes 29 minority (11 Black or African American, non-Hispanic/Latino; 6 Asian, non-Hispanic/Latino; 10 Hispanic/Latino; 2 Two or more races, non-Hispanic/Latino), 15 international. Average age 28. 160 applicants, 78% accepted, 46 enrolled. In 2017, 55 master's awarded. *Degree requirements:* For master's, thesis. *Entrance requirements:* Additional exam requirements/recommendations for international students: Required—TOEFL (minimum score 80 iBT). *Application deadline:* Applications are processed on a rolling basis. Application fee: $75. Electronic applications accepted. *Financial support:* In 2017–18, 38 students received support. Fellowships, research assistantships, career-related internships or fieldwork, Federal Work-Study, institutionally sponsored loans, scholarships/grants, health care benefits, tuition waivers (full and partial), and unspecified assistantships available. Financial award application deadline: 1/15; financial award applicants required to submit FAFSA. *Unit head:* Brianna King, Director of Admissions and Student Services, 607-777-2719, E-mail: bking@binghamton.edu. *Application contact:* Ben Balkaya, Assistant Dean and Director, 607-777-2151, Fax: 607-777-2501, E-mail: balkaya@binghamton.edu.

Boise State University, School of Public Service, Department of Public Policy and Administration, Boise, ID 83725-0399. Offers public policy and administration (MPA, PhD, Graduate Certificate), including environmental, natural resource and energy policy and administration (MPA), general public administration (MPA), state and local government policy and administration (MPA). *Accreditation:* NASPAA. *Program availability:* Part-time. *Faculty:* 16. *Students:* 38 full-time (19 women), 85 part-time (56 women); includes 15 minority (1 American Indian or Alaska Native, non-Hispanic/Latino; 1 Asian, non-Hispanic/Latino; 12 Hispanic/Latino; 1 Two or more races, non-Hispanic/Latino), 1 international. Average age 37. 81 applicants, 43% accepted, 29 enrolled. In 2017, 22 master's awarded. Terminal master's awarded for partial completion of doctoral program. *Degree requirements:* For master's, comprehensive exam, thesis optional, directed research project, internship; for doctorate, thesis/dissertation. *Entrance requirements:* For master's, GRE General Test, minimum GPA of 3.0. Additional exam requirements/recommendations for international students: Required—TOEFL (minimum score 550 paper-based; 80 iBT), IELTS (minimum score 6). *Application deadline:* For fall admission, 2/1 for domestic and international students; for spring admission, 10/1 for domestic and international students. Application fee: $65 ($95 for international students). Electronic applications accepted. *Expenses:* Tuition, state resident: full-time $6471; part-time $390 per credit. Tuition, nonresident: full-time

$21,787; part-time $685 per credit. *Required fees:* $2283; $100 per term. Part-time tuition and fees vary according to course load and program. *Financial support:* Research assistantships, scholarships/grants, and unspecified assistantships available. Financial award application deadline: 2/1; financial award applicants required to submit FAFSA. *Unit head:* Dr. Gregory Hill, Department Chair, 208-426-2917, E-mail: greghill@boisestate.edu. *Application contact:* Dr. Luke Fowler, MPA Director, 208-426-5527, E-mail: lukefowler@boisestate.edu.
Website: http://sps.boisestate.edu/publicpolicy/

Bowie State University, Graduate Programs, Program in Public Administration, Bowie, MD 20715-9465. Offers MPA. *Accreditation:* NASPAA. *Program availability:* Part-time, evening/weekend. *Degree requirements:* For master's, comprehensive exam. *Entrance requirements:* For master's, minimum undergraduate GPA of 2.5. Electronic applications accepted.

Bowling Green State University, Graduate College, College of Arts and Sciences, Department of Political Science, Bowling Green, OH 43403. Offers public administration (MPA). *Degree requirements:* For master's, comprehensive exam or thesis. *Entrance requirements:* For master's, GRE General Test. Additional exam requirements/recommendations for international students: Required—TOEFL. Electronic applications accepted. *Faculty research:* Public law, international relations, American government, economic development.

Brandman University, School of Business and Professional Studies, Irvine, CA 92618. Offers accounting (MBA); business administration (MBA); business intelligence and data analytics (MBA); e-business strategic management (MBA); entrepreneurship (MBA); finance (MBA); health administration (MBA); human resources (MBA, MS); international business (MBA); marketing (MBA); organizational leadership (MA, MBA, MPA); public administration (MPA). *Expenses: Tuition:* Part-time $640 per credit hour. Tuition and fees vary according to degree level and program. *Unit head:* Dr. Glenn Worthington, Dean, 253-861-1024, E-mail: gworthin@brandman.edu. *Application contact:* Dr. Glenn Worthington, Dean, 253-861-1024, E-mail: gworthin@brandman.edu.
Website: https://www.brandman.edu/academic-programs/business-and-professional-studies

Bridgewater State University, College of Graduate Studies, College of Humanities and Social Sciences, Department of Political Science, Program in Public Administration, Bridgewater, MA 02325. Offers MPA. *Accreditation:* NASPAA. *Entrance requirements:* For master's, GRE General Test.

Brigham Young University, Graduate Studies, BYU Marriott School of Business, Executive Master of Public Administration Program, Provo, UT 84602. Offers MPA. *Program availability:* Part-time-only, evening/weekend. *Faculty:* 134 full-time (15 women), 65 part-time/adjunct (16 women). *Students:* 124 part-time (59 women); includes 13 minority (1 Black or African American, non-Hispanic/Latino; 4 Asian, non-Hispanic/Latino; 3 Hispanic/Latino; 5 Native Hawaiian or other Pacific Islander, non-Hispanic/Latino), 3 international. Average age 40. 51 applicants, 100% accepted, 45 enrolled. In 2017, 46 master's awarded. *Entrance requirements:* For master's, GRE or GMAT, 4 years of work experience, 3 letters of recommendation, statement of intent, resume. Additional exam requirements/recommendations for international students: Required—TOEFL (minimum score 580 paper-based; 79 iBT). *Application deadline:* For fall admission, 5/1 for domestic and international students. Application fee: $50. Electronic applications accepted. *Expenses:* Contact institution. *Financial support:* Scholarships/grants available. Financial award applicants required to submit FAFSA. *Faculty research:* Taxes, budgeting, nonprofit, ethics, decision modeling, work balance, organizational behavior. *Unit head:* Dr. Jeffery Thompson, Director, 801-422-4221, Fax: 801-422-0311, E-mail: mpa@byu.edu. *Application contact:* Catherine Cooper, Associate Director, 801-422-4221, Fax: 801-422-0311, E-mail: mpa@byu.edu.
Website: http://empa.byu.edu

Brigham Young University, Graduate Studies, BYU Marriott School of Business, Master of Public Administration Program, Provo, UT 84602. Offers healthcare (MPA); local government (MPA); nonprofit management (MPA); state and federal government (MPA); JD/MPA. *Accreditation:* NASPAA. *Faculty:* 134 full-time (15 women), 65 part-time/adjunct (16 women). *Students:* 105 full-time (50 women); includes 10 minority (3 Black or African American, non-Hispanic/Latino; 3 Asian, non-Hispanic/Latino; 3 Hispanic/Latino; 1 Native Hawaiian or other Pacific Islander, non-Hispanic/Latino), 14 international. Average age 27. 95 applicants, 73% accepted, 50 enrolled. In 2017, 41 master's awarded. *Entrance requirements:* For master's, GMAT or GRE, commitment to BYU Honor Code. Additional exam requirements/recommendations for international students: Required—TOEFL (minimum score 580 paper-based; 85 iBT). *Application deadline:* For fall admission, 1/15 for domestic and international students. Application fee: $50. Electronic applications accepted. *Expenses:* Contact institution. *Financial support:* Research assistantships, teaching assistantships, career-related internships or fieldwork, institutionally sponsored loans, and scholarships/grants available. Financial award application deadline: 4/15; financial award applicants required to submit FAFSA. *Faculty research:* Taxes, budgeting, nonprofit, ethics, decision modeling, work balance, organizational behavior. *Unit head:* Dr. Lori Wadsworth, Director, 801-422-5956, E-mail: mpa@byu.edu. *Application contact:* Catherine Cooper, Associate Director, 801-422-9173, E-mail: mpa@byu.edu.
Website: https://marriottschool.byu.edu/mpa/

California Baptist University, Program in Public Administration, Riverside, CA 92503. Offers public administration (MPA). *Program availability:* Part-time, evening/weekend. *Faculty:* 4 full-time (all women), 2 part-time/adjunct (0 women). *Students:* 39 full-time (24 women), 71 part-time (32 women); includes 71 minority (13 Black or African American, non-Hispanic/Latino; 1 American Indian or Alaska Native, non-Hispanic/Latino; 8 Asian, non-Hispanic/Latino; 42 Hispanic/Latino; 2 Native Hawaiian or other Pacific Islander, non-Hispanic/Latino; 5 Two or more races, non-Hispanic/Latino), 1 international. Average age 37. 35 applicants, 60% accepted, 19 enrolled. In 2017, 60 master's awarded. *Degree requirements:* For master's, comprehensive exam or thesis. *Entrance requirements:* For master's, minimum GPA of 2.75; bachelor's degree in applicable field or any field with five years of managerial experience; three recommendations; resume; 500-word essay. Additional exam requirements/recommendations for international students: Required—TOEFL (minimum score 80 iBT). *Application deadline:* For fall admission, 8/1 priority date for domestic students, 7/1 for international students; for spring admission, 12/1 priority date for domestic students, 11/1 for international students. Applications are processed on a rolling basis. Application fee: $45. Electronic applications accepted. *Expenses:* Contact institution. *Financial support:* In 2017–18, 37 students received support. Federal Work-Study and scholarships/grants available. Financial award applicants required to submit CSS PROFILE or FAFSA. *Faculty research:* Policy networks, water policy, democratic theory, international relations, political theory and philosophy. *Unit head:* Dr. David Poole, Vice President, Online and Professional Studies, 951-343-3902, E-mail: dpoole@calbaptist.edu. *Application contact:* Dr. Elaine Ahumada, Director, MPA Program, 951-343-3929, Fax: 951-343-4661, E-mail: eahumada@calbaptist.edu.
Website: http://www.cbuonline.edu/programs/program/master-of-public-administration

California State Polytechnic University, Pomona, Program in Public Administration, Pomona, CA 91768-2557. Offers MPA. *Accreditation:* NASPAA. *Program availability:* Part-time, evening/weekend. *Students:* 6 full-time (2 women), 36 part-time (23 women); includes 28 minority (3 Black or African American, non-Hispanic/Latino; 6 Asian, non-Hispanic/Latino; 18 Hispanic/Latino; 1 Two or more races, non-Hispanic/Latino), 3 international. Average age 33. 29 applicants, 52% accepted, 11 enrolled. In 2017, 11 master's awarded. *Entrance requirements:* Additional exam requirements/recommendations for international students: Required—TOEFL (minimum score 550 paper-based). *Application deadline:* Applications are processed on a rolling basis. Application fee: $55. Electronic applications accepted. *Expenses:* Contact institution. *Financial support:* Application deadline: 3/2; applicants required to submit FAFSA. *Unit head:* Dr. Sandra M. Emerson, Professor/MPA Coordinator, 909-869-3879, Fax: 909-869-6995, E-mail: smemerson@cpp.edu. *Application contact:* Deborah L. Brandon, Executive Director of Admissions and Enrollment Planning, 909-869-3427, Fax: 909-869-5315, E-mail: dlbrandon@cpp.edu.
Website: http://www.cpp.edu/~class/mpa/index.shtml

California State University, Bakersfield, Division of Graduate Studies, School of Business and Public Administration, Program in Public Administration, Bakersfield, CA 93311. Offers MPA. *Accreditation:* NASPAA. *Faculty:* 4 full-time (0 women), 2 part-time/adjunct (1 woman). *Students:* 29 full-time (19 women), 31 part-time (19 women); includes 40 minority (9 Black or African American, non-Hispanic/Latino; 4 Asian, non-Hispanic/Latino; 27 Hispanic/Latino), 2 international. Average age 30. 50 applicants, 78% accepted, 31 enrolled. In 2017, 30 master's awarded. *Degree requirements:* For master's, thesis or alternative. *Entrance requirements:* For master's, minimum GPA of 3.0, official transcripts, personal statement. Additional exam requirements/recommendations for international students: Required—TOEFL (minimum score 550 paper-based; 79 iBT), IELTS (minimum score 7). *Application deadline:* Applications are processed on a rolling basis. Application fee: $55. Electronic applications accepted. *Expenses:* Tuition, state resident: full-time $7176; part-time $4164 per year. *Financial support:* In 2017–18, fellowships (averaging $1,850 per year) were awarded; Federal Work-Study, scholarships/grants, and tuition waivers (full and partial) also available. Financial award application deadline: 3/2; financial award applicants required to submit FAFSA. *Unit head:* Dr. Thomas Martinez, Coordinator, 661-654-3064, E-mail: tmartinez@csub.edu. *Application contact:* Debbie Blowers, Assistant Director of Admissions and Evaluations, 661-654-3381, E-mail: dblowers@csub.edu.
Website: https://bpa.csub.edu/departments/Department-of-Public-Policy-and-Administration.html

California State University, Chico, Office of Graduate Studies, College of Behavioral and Social Sciences, Department of Political Science and Criminal Justice, Program in Public Administration, Chico, CA 95929-0722. Offers health administration (MPA); local government management (MPA). *Accreditation:* NASPAA. *Program availability:* Part-time. *Degree requirements:* For master's, thesis or culminating practicum. *Entrance requirements:* For master's, 2 letters of recommendation. Additional exam requirements/recommendations for international students: Required—TOEFL (minimum score 550 paper-based; 80 iBT), IELTS (minimum score 6.5), PTE. Electronic applications accepted.

California State University, Dominguez Hills, College of Business Administration and Public Policy, Program in Public Administration, Carson, CA 90747-0001. Offers MPA. *Accreditation:* NASPAA. *Program availability:* Part-time, evening/weekend, online learning. *Degree requirements:* For master's, thesis or alternative, capstone project. *Entrance requirements:* For master's, GRE, minimum GPA of 2.75. Additional exam requirements/recommendations for international students: Required—TOEFL (minimum score 550 paper-based; 79 iBT). *Faculty research:* Applied public management.

California State University, East Bay, Office of Graduate Studies, College of Letters, Arts, and Social Sciences, Department of Public Affairs and Administration, Program in Public Administration, Hayward, CA 94542-3000. Offers health care administration (MPA); public management and policy analysis (MPA). *Program availability:* Part-time, evening/weekend. *Students:* 3 full-time (2 women), 125 part-time (79 women); includes 92 minority (30 Black or African American, non-Hispanic/Latino; 2 American Indian or Alaska Native, non-Hispanic/Latino; 19 Asian, non-Hispanic/Latino; 30 Hispanic/Latino; 3 Native Hawaiian or other Pacific Islander, non-Hispanic/Latino; 8 Two or more races, non-Hispanic/Latino), 9 international. Average age 33. 88 applicants, 74% accepted, 38 enrolled. In 2017, 87 master's awarded. *Degree requirements:* For master's, comprehensive exam (for some programs), comprehensive exam or thesis. *Entrance requirements:* For master's, minimum GPA of 2.5; statement of purpose; 2 letters of recommendation; professional resume/curriculum vitae. Additional exam requirements/recommendations for international students: Required—TOEFL (minimum score 550 paper-based; 79 iBT). *Application deadline:* For fall admission, 6/1 for domestic and international students. Application fee: $55. Electronic applications accepted. *Financial support:* Fellowships, teaching assistantships, career-related internships or fieldwork, Federal Work-Study, institutionally sponsored loans, and scholarships/grants available. Support available to part-time students. Financial award application deadline: 3/2; financial award applicants required to submit FAFSA. *Unit head:* Dr. Toni Fogarty, Chair, 510-885-2268, E-mail: toni.fogarty@csueastbay.edu. *Application contact:* Prof. Michael Moon, Public Administration Graduate Advisor, 510-885-2545, Fax: 510-885-3726, E-mail: michael.moon@csueastbay.edu.

California State University, Fresno, Division of Research and Graduate Studies, College of Social Sciences, Department of Political Science, Program in Public Administration, Fresno, CA 93740-8027. Offers MPA. *Accreditation:* NASPAA. *Program availability:* Part-time, evening/weekend. *Degree requirements:* For master's, thesis or alternative. *Entrance requirements:* For master's, GRE General Test or GMAT, minimum GPA of 3.0. Additional exam requirements/recommendations for international students: Required—TOEFL. Electronic applications accepted.

California State University, Fullerton, Graduate Studies, College of Humanities and Social Sciences, Division of Politics, Administration, and Justice, Fullerton, CA 92831-3599. Offers political science (MA); public administration (MPA). *Accreditation:* NASPAA (one or more programs are accredited). *Program availability:* Part-time. *Faculty:* 12 full-time (6 women). *Students:* 20 full-time (8 women), 102 part-time (53 women); includes 84 minority (8 Black or African American, non-Hispanic/Latino; 11 Asian, non-Hispanic/Latino; 61 Hispanic/Latino; 4 Two or more races, non-Hispanic/Latino), 4 international. Average age 29. 99 applicants, 60% accepted, 30 enrolled. *Degree requirements:* For master's, comprehensive exam, project or thesis. *Entrance requirements:* For master's, minimum GPA of 2.5 in last 60 units of course work, 12 units of course work in social sciences. Application fee: $55. *Financial support:* Career-related internships or fieldwork, Federal Work-Study, institutionally sponsored loans, and scholarships/grants available. Support available to part-time students. Financial award application deadline: 3/1; financial award applicants required to submit FAFSA. *Faculty research:* Emergency management plans. *Unit head:* Dr. Stephen Stambough, Chair, 657-278-2933. *Application contact:* Admissions/Applications, 657-278-2371.

California State University, Long Beach, Graduate Studies, College of Health and Human Services, Graduate Center for Public Policy and Administration, Long Beach, CA 90840. Offers MPA, Graduate Certificate. *Accreditation:* NASPAA (one or more programs are accredited). *Program availability:* Part-time, evening/weekend. *Degree requirements:* For master's, comprehensive exam. *Entrance requirements:* For master's, minimum GPA of 2.75. Electronic applications accepted. *Faculty research:* Transportation access, air quality controls, coastal issues, intergovernmental relations.

California State University, Los Angeles, Graduate Studies, College of Natural and Social Sciences, Department of Political Science, Los Angeles, CA 90032-8530. Offers political science (MA); public administration (MS). *Program availability:* Part-time, evening/weekend. *Degree requirements:* For master's, comprehensive exam or thesis. *Entrance requirements:* Additional exam requirements/recommendations for international students: Required—TOEFL (minimum score 500 paper-based). Electronic applications accepted. *Faculty research:* Government; public policy and law; international, political, and economic relations; comparative politics.

California State University, Northridge, Graduate Studies, Tseng College, Northridge, CA 91330. Offers business administration (Graduate Certificate); health administration (MPA); health education (MPH); knowledge management (MKM); music industry administration (MA); nonprofit-sector management (Graduate Certificate); public administration (MPA); public sector management and leadership (MPA); social work (MSW); taxation (MS); tourism, hospitality and recreation management (MS). *Students:* 4 part-time (all women); includes 1 minority (Black or African American, non-Hispanic/Latino). Average age 37. In 2017, 2 master's awarded. *Entrance requirements:* For master's, GRE (if cumulative undergraduate GPA less than 3.0). *Unit head:* Joyce Feucht-Haviar, Dean, 866-873-6439.

California State University, Sacramento, College of Social Sciences and Interdisciplinary Studies, Program in Public Policy and Administration, Sacramento, CA 95819. Offers MPPA. *Program availability:* Part-time. *Students:* 19 full-time (8 women), 37 part-time (28 women); includes 20 minority (1 Black or African American, non-Hispanic/Latino; 6 Asian, non-Hispanic/Latino; 11 Hispanic/Latino; 2 Native Hawaiian or other Pacific Islander, non-Hispanic/Latino). Average age 31. 52 applicants, 67% accepted, 26 enrolled. In 2017, 11 master's awarded. *Degree requirements:* For master's, thesis or writing proficiency exam. *Entrance requirements:* For master's, GRE, minimum GPA of 3.0 for all undergraduate coursework and in last 60 units. Additional exam requirements/recommendations for international students: Required—TOEFL (minimum score 560 paper-based; 83 iBT); Recommended—IELTS, TSE. *Application deadline:* For fall admission, 3/1 priority date for domestic and international students. Applications are processed on a rolling basis. Application fee: $55. Electronic applications accepted. *Expenses:* Contact institution. *Financial support:* Teaching assistantships, career-related internships or fieldwork, Federal Work-Study, and scholarships/grants available. Support available to part-time students. Financial award application deadline: 3/1; financial award applicants required to submit FAFSA. *Faculty research:* Education policy, urban policy, collaborative governance, judicial administration, and California state/local governance. *Unit head:* Dr. Ted Lascher, Chair, 916-278-6557, E-mail: tedl@csus.edu. *Application contact:* Jose Martinez, Graduate Admissions Supervisor, 916-278-7871, E-mail: martinj@skymail.csus.edu.
Website: http://www.csus.edu/ppa

California State University, San Bernardino, Graduate Studies, College of Business and Public Administration, Program in Public Administration, San Bernardino, CA 92407. Offers MPA. *Accreditation:* NASPAA. *Program availability:* Part-time, evening/weekend. *Faculty:* 7 full-time (1 woman), 3 part-time/adjunct (2 women). *Students:* 19 full-time (11 women), 164 part-time (103 women); includes 122 minority (24 Black or African American, non-Hispanic/Latino; 12 Asian, non-Hispanic/Latino; 81 Hispanic/Latino; 1 Native Hawaiian or other Pacific Islander, non-Hispanic/Latino; 4 Two or more races, non-Hispanic/Latino), 22 international. Average age 33. 88 applicants, 65% accepted, 39 enrolled. In 2017, 89 master's awarded. *Degree requirements:* For master's, comprehensive exam. *Entrance requirements:* Additional exam requirements/recommendations for international students: Required—TOEFL. *Application deadline:* For fall admission, 7/16 for domestic students; for winter admission, 10/23 for domestic students; for spring admission, 1/22 for domestic students. Application fee: $55. *Financial support:* Institutionally sponsored loans available. Financial award application deadline: 3/1. *Unit head:* Dr. Jonathan Anderson, Chair, 909-537-5759, E-mail: jfanders@csusb.edu. *Application contact:* Dr. Dorota Huizinga, Dean of Graduate Studies, 909-537-3064, E-mail: dorota.huizinga@csusb.edu.

California State University, Stanislaus, College of the Arts, Humanities and Social Sciences, Master of Public Administration Program, Turlock, CA 95382. Offers MPA. *Accreditation:* NASPAA. *Program availability:* Part-time, evening/weekend. *Degree requirements:* For master's, comprehensive exam, thesis or alternative. *Entrance requirements:* For master's, minimum GPA of 2.7, 3 letters of reference, personal statement. Additional exam requirements/recommendations for international students: Required—TOEFL (minimum score 550 paper-based), ELPT (minimum score 954). Electronic applications accepted. *Faculty research:* Blogging in the Middle East, incumbency and electoral competitiveness, legislative acceptance of gubernatorial budget proposals.

Capella University, School of Public Service Leadership, Doctoral Programs in Healthcare, Minneapolis, MN 55402. Offers criminal justice (PhD); emergency management (PhD); epidemiology (Dr PH); general health administration (DHA); general public administration (DPA); health advocacy and leadership (Dr PH); health care administration (PhD); health care leadership (DHA); health policy advocacy (DHA); multidisciplinary human services (PhD); nonprofit management and leadership (PhD); public safety leadership (PhD); social and community services (PhD).

Capella University, School of Public Service Leadership, Master's Programs in Healthcare, Minneapolis, MN 55402. Offers criminal justice (MS); emergency management (MS); general public health (MPH); gerontology (MS); health administration (MHA); health care operations (MHA); health management policy (MPH); health policy (MHA); homeland security (MS); multidisciplinary human services (MS); public administration (MPA); public safety leadership (MS); social and community services (MS); social behavioral sciences (MPH); MS/MPA.

Carleton University, Faculty of Graduate Studies, Faculty of Public Affairs and Management, School of Public Policy and Administration, Ottawa, ON K1S 5B6, Canada. Offers public administration (MA, DPA); public policy (PhD). *Program availability:* Part-time. *Degree requirements:* For master's, thesis optional; for doctorate, one foreign language, comprehensive exam, thesis/dissertation. *Entrance requirements:* For master's, GRE, honors degree; for doctorate, master's degree. Additional exam requirements/recommendations for international students: Required—TOEFL. *Faculty research:* Canadian public administration and policy, development administration, public policy analysis, public management.

Carnegie Mellon University, Heinz College, School of Public Policy and Management, Master of Public Management Program, Pittsburgh, PA 15213-3891. Offers MPM. *Accreditation:* NASPAA. *Program availability:* Part-time, evening/weekend. *Degree requirements:* For master's, internship. *Entrance requirements:* For master's, undergraduate degree; five years of full-time, relevant work experience.

Central European University, School of Public Policy, 1051, Hungary. Offers public administration (MPA); public policy (MA, PhD). *Faculty:* 22 full-time (7 women), 7 part-time/adjunct (5 women). *Students:* 123 full-time (76 women). Average age 28. 696 applicants, 32% accepted, 62 enrolled. In 2017, 74 master's, 4 doctorates awarded. *Degree requirements:* For master's, one foreign language, thesis; for doctorate, one foreign language, comprehensive exam, thesis/dissertation. *Entrance requirements:* For master's and doctorate, interview. Additional exam requirements/recommendations for international students: Required—TOEFL (minimum score 570 paper-based); Recommended—IELTS (minimum score 6.5). *Application deadline:* For fall admission, 2/4 for domestic and international students. Application fee: $30. Electronic applications accepted. *Expenses: Tuition:* Full-time 12,000 euros. *Required fees:* 230 euros. One-time fee: 30 euros full-time. Tuition and fees vary according to course level, course load, degree level and program. *Financial support:* Fellowships, career-related internships or fieldwork, scholarships/grants, health care benefits, and tuition waivers (full and partial) available. *Faculty research:* Multi-disciplinary study of public policy, innovative teaching and research, as well as meaningful engagement with policy practice, public health, law, humanitarian assistance, anti-corruption, conflict and post-conflict recovery, natural resource management. *Unit head:* Dr. Martin Kahanec, Head, 36 1 327-3110, E-mail: spp@ceu.edu. *Application contact:* Zsuzsanna Jaszberenyi, Admissions Officer, 361-324-3009, Fax: 367-327-3211, E-mail: admissions@ceu.edu.
Website: http://spp.ceu.edu

Central Michigan University, Central Michigan University Global Campus, Program in Administration, Mount Pleasant, MI 48859. Offers acquisitions administration (MSA, Certificate); engineering management administration (MSA, Certificate); general administration (MSA, Certificate); health services administration (MSA, Certificate); human resources administration (MSA, Certificate); information resource management (MSA); information resource management administration (Certificate); international administration (MSA, Certificate); leadership (MSA, Certificate); philanthropy and fundraising administration (MSA, Certificate); public administration (MSA, Certificate); recreation and park administration (MSA); research administration (MSA, Certificate). *Program availability:* Part-time, evening/weekend, online learning. *Entrance requirements:* For master's, minimum GPA of 2.7 in major. Electronic applications accepted.

Central Michigan University, Central Michigan University Global Campus, Program in Public Administration, Mount Pleasant, MI 48859. Offers general public administration (MPA); public management (MPA); state and local government (MPA). *Accreditation:* NASPAA. *Program availability:* Part-time, evening/weekend. *Entrance requirements:* For master's, minimum GPA of 2.8. Additional exam requirements/recommendations for international students: Required—TOEFL. Electronic applications accepted.

Central Michigan University, College of Graduate Studies, College of Humanities and Social and Behavioral Sciences, Department of Political Science and Public Administration, Program in Public Administration, Mount Pleasant, MI 48859. Offers professional development in public administration (Graduate Certificate); public administration (MPA); public management (MPA); state and local government (MPA). *Accreditation:* NASPAA. *Program availability:* Part-time. *Degree requirements:* For master's, thesis or alternative. Electronic applications accepted.

Central Michigan University, College of Graduate Studies, Interdisciplinary Administration Programs, Mount Pleasant, MI 48859. Offers acquisitions administration (MSA, Graduate Certificate); general administration (MSA, Graduate Certificate); health services administration (MSA, Graduate Certificate); human resource administration (Graduate Certificate); human resources administration (MSA); information resource management (MSA, Graduate Certificate); international administration (MSA, Graduate Certificate); leadership (MSA, Graduate Certificate); public administration (MSA, Graduate Certificate); research administration (Graduate Certificate); sport administration (MSA). *Accreditation:* AACSB. *Program availability:* Part-time, evening/weekend, online learning. *Degree requirements:* For master's, thesis or alternative. *Entrance requirements:* For master's, bachelor's degree with minimum GPA of 2.7. Electronic applications accepted. *Faculty research:* Interdisciplinary studies in acquisitions administration, health services administration, sport administration, recreation and park administration, and international administration.

Cheyney University of Pennsylvania, Graduate Programs, Program in Public Administration, Cheyney, PA 19319. Offers MPA.

City College of the City University of New York, Graduate School, Colin Powell School for Civic and Global Leadership, New York, NY 10031-9198. Offers economics and business (MA), including economics; international relations (MA); psychology (MA, PhD), including clinical psychology (PhD), general psychology (MA), mental health counseling (MA); public service management (MPA); sociology (MA). *Program availability:* Part-time. *Entrance requirements:* For master's, GRE. Additional exam requirements/recommendations for international students: Required—TOEFL (minimum score 500 paper-based; 61 iBT). Electronic applications accepted.

Clark Atlanta University, School of Arts and Sciences, Department of Public Administration, Atlanta, GA 30314. Offers MPA. *Accreditation:* NASPAA. *Program availability:* Part-time. *Faculty:* 5 full-time (3 women). *Students:* 29 full-time (17 women), 14 part-time (7 women); includes 27 minority (all Black or African American, non-Hispanic/Latino), 12 international. Average age 28. 21 applicants, 81% accepted, 9 enrolled. In 2017, 17 master's awarded. *Degree requirements:* For master's, one foreign language, thesis or alternative. *Entrance requirements:* For master's, GRE General Test, minimum GPA of 2.5. Additional exam requirements/recommendations for international students: Required—TOEFL (minimum score 500 paper-based; 61 iBT). *Application deadline:* For fall admission, 4/1 for domestic and international students; for spring admission, 11/1 for domestic and international students. Applications are processed on a rolling basis. Application fee: $40 ($55 for international students). *Financial support:* Scholarships/grants and unspecified assistantships available. Financial award application deadline: 4/30; financial award applicants required to submit FAFSA. *Faculty research:* Nutrition education, Africa. *Unit head:* Dr. Henry Elonge, Chairperson, 404-880-6653, E-mail: helonge@cau.edu.

Clark University, Graduate School, School of Professional Studies, Program in Public Administration, Worcester, MA 01610-1477. Offers MPA, Certificate. *Program availability:* Part-time, evening/weekend. *Students:* 35 full-time (21 women), 20 part-time (11 women); includes 10 minority (3 Black or African American, non-Hispanic/Latino; 7 Hispanic/Latino), 11 international. Average age 31. 107 applicants, 60% accepted, 41 enrolled. In 2017, 21 master's awarded. *Degree requirements:* For master's, thesis optional. *Entrance requirements:* For master's, 2 references, resume or curriculum vitae, personal statement. Additional exam requirements/recommendations for international students: Required—TOEFL (minimum score 575 paper-based; 90 iBT), IELTS (minimum score 6.5). *Application deadline:* Applications are processed on a rolling basis. Application fee: $75. Electronic applications accepted. *Expenses:* $2,750 tuition per 14-week course; $40 activity fee (full-time students only); $40 miscellaneous one-time fee; $300 student services fee. *Financial support:* Career-related internships or fieldwork available. Support available to part-time students. *Unit head:* Mary Piecewicz, Assistant Dean, 508-793-7212, E-mail: mpiecewicz@clarku.edu.
Website: http://www.clarku.edu/programs/masters-public-administration

Clemson University, Graduate School, College of Behavioral, Social and Health Sciences, Department of Parks, Recreation, and Tourism Management, Clemson, SC 29634. Offers international parks and tourism (Certificate); parks, recreation and tourism management (MS, PhD), including recreational therapy (PhD); public administration (MPA, Certificate); recreational therapy (MS); youth development leadership (MS, Certificate). *Program availability:* Part-time, evening/weekend, 100% online. *Faculty:* 31 full-time (10 women), 3 part-time/adjunct (0 women). *Students:* 90 full-time (62 women),

193 part-time (114 women); includes 57 minority (44 Black or African American, non-Hispanic/Latino; 1 American Indian or Alaska Native, non-Hispanic/Latino; 1 Asian, non-Hispanic/Latino; 8 Hispanic/Latino; 3 Two or more races, non-Hispanic/Latino), 14 international. Average age 32. 245 applicants, 80% accepted, 129 enrolled. In 2017, 37 master's, 5 doctorates, 38 other advanced degrees awarded. *Degree requirements:* For master's, comprehensive exam (for some programs), thesis (for some programs); for doctorate, comprehensive exam, thesis/dissertation; for Certificate, portfolio. *Entrance requirements:* For master's and doctorate, GRE General Test, unofficial transcripts, letter of intent, letters of reference; for Certificate, letter of recommendation, unofficial transcripts, personal statement, resume. Additional exam requirements/recommendations for international students: Required—TOEFL (minimum score 610 paper-based; 80 iBT), IELTS (minimum score 6.5), PTE (minimum score 54). *Application deadline:* For fall admission, 1/15 priority date for domestic and international students; for spring admission, 11/15 priority date for domestic and international students. Applications are processed on a rolling basis. Application fee: $80 ($90 for international students). Electronic applications accepted. *Expenses:* $5,767 per semester full-time resident, $10,918 per semester full-time non-resident, $656 per credit hour part-time resident, $1,310 per credit hour part-time non-resident, $915 per credit hour online; $5,174 per semester full-time resident, $9,714 per semester full-time non-resident, $511 per credit hour part-time resident, $1,017 per credit hour part-time non-resident, $741 per credit hour online (for online non-thesis ms and doctoral programs); $613 per credit hour (for online youth development leadership); other fees may apply per session. *Financial support:* In 2017–18, 68 students received support, including 4 fellowships with partial tuition reimbursements available (averaging $5,250 per year), 7 research assistantships with partial tuition reimbursements available (averaging $11,653 per year), 52 teaching assistantships with partial tuition reimbursements available (averaging $8,517 per year); career-related internships or fieldwork and unspecified assistantships also available. Financial award application deadline: 1/15. *Faculty research:* Human behavior, land use, recreational therapy, sustainability, tourism. *Total annual research expenditures:* $400,772. *Unit head:* Dr. Fran McGuire, Interim Chair, 864-656-3036, E-mail: lefty@clemson.edu. *Application contact:* Dr. Jeff Hallo, Graduate Coordinator, 864-656-3237, E-mail: jhallo@clemson.edu.
Website: http://www.clemson.edu/hehd/departments/prtm/

Cleveland State University, College of Graduate Studies, Maxine Goodman Levin College of Urban Affairs, Program in Public Administration, Cleveland, OH 44115. Offers economic development (MPA); non-profit management (MPA); public management (MPA); JD/MPA. *Accreditation:* NASPAA. *Program availability:* Part-time, evening/weekend. *Faculty:* 16 full-time (8 women), 13 part-time/adjunct (5 women). *Students:* 23 full-time (15 women), 45 part-time (24 women); includes 19 minority (14 Black or African American, non-Hispanic/Latino; 1 Asian, non-Hispanic/Latino; 1 Hispanic/Latino; 3 Two or more races, non-Hispanic/Latino), 3 international. Average age 32. 79 applicants, 77% accepted, 12 enrolled. In 2017, 35 master's awarded. *Degree requirements:* For master's, thesis or alternative, exit project. *Entrance requirements:* For master's, GRE General Test (minimum scores in 40th percentile verbal and quantitative, 4.0 writing), minimum GPA of 3.0. Additional exam requirements/recommendations for international students: Required—TOEFL (minimum score 550 paper-based; 78 iBT), IELTS (6.0), or International Test of English Proficiency (iTEP). *Application deadline:* For fall admission, 7/1 priority date for domestic students, 5/15 for international students; for spring admission, 11/15 for domestic students, 11/1 for international students; for summer admission, 4/1 for domestic students, 3/15 for international students. Applications are processed on a rolling basis. Application fee: $40. Electronic applications accepted. *Expenses:* Contact institution. *Financial support:* In 2017–18, 16 students received support, including 5 research assistantships with full tuition reimbursements available (averaging $7,200 per year), 1 teaching assistantship with partial tuition reimbursement available (averaging $2,400 per year); scholarships/grants, tuition waivers (full and partial), and unspecified assistantships also available. Support available to part-time students. Financial award application deadline: 3/1; financial award applicants required to submit FAFSA. *Faculty research:* City management, nonprofit management, health care administration, public management, economic development. *Unit head:* Dr. Nicholas Zingale, Director, 216-802-3389, Fax: 216-687-9342, E-mail: n.zingale@csuohio.edu. *Application contact:* David Arrighi, Graduate Academic Advisor, 216-523-7522, Fax: 216-687-5398, E-mail: d.arrighi@csuohio.edu.
Website: http://urban.csuohio.edu/academics/graduate/mpa/

Cleveland State University, College of Graduate Studies, Maxine Goodman Levin College of Urban Affairs, Program in Urban Studies and Public Affairs, Cleveland, OH 44115. Offers communication (PhD); public administration (PhD); urban policy and development (PhD). *Program availability:* Part-time, evening/weekend. *Faculty:* 16 full-time (8 women), 13 part-time/adjunct (5 women). *Students:* 3 full-time (2 women), 24 part-time (14 women); includes 6 minority (4 Black or African American, non-Hispanic/Latino; 1 Hispanic/Latino; 1 Two or more races, non-Hispanic/Latino), 4 international. Average age 41. 32 applicants, 34% accepted, 2 enrolled. In 2017, 4 doctorates awarded. *Degree requirements:* For doctorate, comprehensive exam, thesis/dissertation. *Entrance requirements:* For doctorate, GRE General Test (minimum score: verbal and quantitative 50th percentile, analytical writing 4.0), minimum GPA of 3.5. Additional exam requirements/recommendations for international students: Required—TOEFL (minimum score 550 paper-based; 78 iBT), IELTS (6.0), or International Test of English Proficiency (iTEP). *Application deadline:* For fall admission, 1/31 for domestic and international students. Application fee: $40. Electronic applications accepted. *Expenses:* Contact institution. *Financial support:* In 2017–18, 15 students received support, including 1 research assistantship with full tuition reimbursement available (averaging $11,800 per year), 2 teaching assistantships with full tuition reimbursements available (averaging $11,800 per year); scholarships/grants, tuition waivers (full and partial), and unspecified assistantships also available. Support available to part-time students. Financial award application deadline: 3/1; financial award applicants required to submit FAFSA. *Faculty research:* Urban and public policy, public affairs. *Unit head:* Dr. Bill Bowen, Professor/PhD Program Director, 216-687-9226, E-mail: w.bowen@csuohio.edu. *Application contact:* David Arrighi, Graduate Academic Advisor, 216-523-7522, Fax: 216-687-5398, E-mail: d.arrighi@csuohio.edu.
Website: http://urban.csuohio.edu/academics/graduate/phd/

The College at Brockport, State University of New York, School of Business and Management, Department of Public Administration, Brockport, NY 14420-2997. Offers arts administration (AGC); nonprofit management (AGC); public administration (MPA), including health care management, nonprofit management, poverty studies, public management, public safety. *Accreditation:* NASPAA. *Program availability:* Part-time, evening/weekend. *Faculty:* 5 full-time (3 women), 5 part-time/adjunct (1 woman). *Students:* 54 full-time (38 women), 95 part-time (57 women); includes 38 minority (19 Black or African American, non-Hispanic/Latino; 3 Asian, non-Hispanic/Latino; 11 Hispanic/Latino; 5 Two or more races, non-Hispanic/Latino), 4 international. 53 applicants, 91% accepted, 31 enrolled. In 2017, 59 master's, 6 other advanced degrees awarded. *Degree requirements:* For master's, thesis or alternative. *Entrance requirements:* For master's, GRE or minimum GPA of 3.0, letters of recommendation, statement of objectives, current resume. Additional exam requirements/recommendations for international students: Required—TOEFL (minimum score 550 paper-based; 79 iBT), IELTS (minimum score 6.5). *Application deadline:* For fall admission, 8/15 priority date for domestic and international students; for spring admission, 1/15 priority date for domestic and international students; for summer admission, 4/15 priority date for domestic and international students. Application fee: $50. Electronic applications accepted. *Expenses:* Tuition, state resident: full-time $10,870; part-time $453 per credit hour. Tuition, nonresident: full-time $22,210. *Required fees:* $988; $246 per semester. *Financial support:* In 2017–18, 1 fellowship with full tuition reimbursement (averaging $7,500 per year), 1 teaching assistantship with full tuition reimbursement (averaging $6,000 per year) were awarded; Federal Work-Study, scholarships/grants, and unspecified assistantships also available. Support available to part-time students. Financial award application deadline: 3/15; financial award applicants required to submit FAFSA. *Faculty research:* E-government, performance management, nonprofits and policy implementation, Medicaid and disabilities. *Unit head:* Dr. Celia Watt, Graduate Director, 585-395-5538, Fax: 585-395-2172, E-mail: cwatt@brockport.edu. *Application contact:* Danielle A. Welch, Graduate Admissions Counselor, 585-395-2525, Fax: 585-395-2515.
Website: https://www.brockport.edu/academics/public_administration/graduate/masters.html

College of Charleston, Graduate School, School of Humanities and Social Sciences, Program in Public Administration, Charleston, SC 29424-0001. Offers MPA. Program offered jointly with University of South Carolina. *Accreditation:* NASPAA. *Program availability:* Part-time, evening/weekend. *Degree requirements:* For master's, thesis optional, internship, capstone seminar. *Entrance requirements:* For master's, GRE General Test, previous course work in statistics, 3 letters of recommendation, minimum GPA of 3.0. Additional exam requirements/recommendations for international students: Required—TOEFL (minimum score 81 iBT). Electronic applications accepted. *Faculty research:* Local government, environmental policy, budgeting, ethics.

The College of New Rochelle, Graduate School, Division of Human Services, Program in Public Administration, New Rochelle, NY 10805-2308. Offers long term care administration (MPA); public administration (MPA). *Degree requirements:* For master's, comprehensive exam, internship. *Entrance requirements:* For master's, minimum GPA of 3.0, personal statement, two letters of recommendation, official transcripts of all colleges/universities attended, proof of immunizations. *Expenses: Tuition:* Full-time $17,406. *Required fees:* $1120.

College of Saint Elizabeth, Program in Justice Administration and Public Service, Morristown, NJ 07960-6989. Offers counter terrorism (Certificate); cyber security investigation (Certificate); justice administration and public service (MA); leadership in community policing (Certificate). *Program availability:* Part-time, 100% online, blended/hybrid learning. *Faculty:* 3 full-time (1 woman), 1 (woman) part-time/adjunct. *Students:* 4 full-time (2 women), 21 part-time (12 women); includes 12 minority (8 Black or African American, non-Hispanic/Latino; 1 Asian, non-Hispanic/Latino; 2 Hispanic/Latino; 1 Two or more races, non-Hispanic/Latino). Average age 31. 15 applicants, 100% accepted, 10 enrolled. In 2017, 13 master's awarded. *Degree requirements:* For master's, thesis. *Entrance requirements:* Additional exam requirements/recommendations for international students: Required—TOEFL (minimum score 550 paper-based; 79 iBT), IELTS (minimum score 6.5). *Application deadline:* For fall admission, 5/1 for international students. Applications are processed on a rolling basis. Application fee: $35. Electronic applications accepted. Application fee is waived when completed online. *Expenses:* Contact institution. *Financial support:* Career-related internships or fieldwork, scholarships/grants, and unspecified assistantships available. Support available to part-time students. Financial award applicants required to submit FAFSA. *Unit head:* Dr. James Ford, Associate Professor, 973-290-4324, E-mail: jford@cse.edu. *Application contact:* Lori J. Fragoso, Director of Graduate and Continuing Studies Admissions, 973-290-4413, Fax: 973-290-4710, E-mail: apply@cse.edu.
Website: http://www.cse.edu/academics/prof-studies/criminal-justice/

Columbia University, School of International and Public Affairs, Program in Public Policy and Administration, New York, NY 10027. Offers MPA, JD/MPA, MPA/MS, MPH/MPA. *Accreditation:* NASPAA. *Entrance requirements:* For master's, GRE General Test. Additional exam requirements/recommendations for international students: Required—TOEFL (minimum score 600 paper-based; 100 iBT), IELTS (minimum score 7), PTE (minimum score 68). Electronic applications accepted. *Expenses: Tuition:* Full-time $44,864; part-time $1704 per credit. *Required fees:* $2370 per semester. One-time fee: $105.

Columbus State University, Graduate Studies, College of Letters and Sciences, Department of Political Science and Public Administration, Columbus, GA 31907-5645. Offers public administration (MPA), including criminal justice, environmental policy, government administration, health services administration, political campaigning, urban policy. *Program availability:* Part-time, evening/weekend, 100% online, blended/hybrid learning. *Faculty:* 15 full-time (6 women), 14 part-time/adjunct (0 women). *Students:* 34 full-time (21 women), 44 part-time (24 women); includes 40 minority (32 Black or African American, non-Hispanic/Latino; 2 Asian, non-Hispanic/Latino; 3 Hispanic/Latino; 1 Native Hawaiian or other Pacific Islander, non-Hispanic/Latino; 2 Two or more races, non-Hispanic/Latino), 3 international. Average age 33. 68 applicants, 43% accepted, 21 enrolled. In 2017, 38 master's awarded. *Degree requirements:* For master's, comprehensive exam. *Entrance requirements:* For master's, GRE General Test, minimum GPA of 2.75, three letters of recommendation. Additional exam requirements/recommendations for international students: Required—TOEFL (minimum score 550 paper-based; 79 iBT). *Application deadline:* For fall admission, 6/30 for domestic students, 5/1 for international students; for spring admission, 11/1 for domestic and international students; for summer admission, 3/1 for domestic and international students. Applications are processed on a rolling basis. Application fee: $50. Electronic applications accepted. *Expenses:* Tuition, state resident: full-time $3708; part-time $2472 per year. Tuition, nonresident: full-time $14,418; part-time $9612 per year. *International tuition:* $19,218 full-time. *Required fees:* $1605. Tuition and fees vary according to program. *Financial support:* In 2017–18, 4 students received support, including 6 research assistantships with partial tuition reimbursements available (averaging $3,000 per year); career-related internships or fieldwork, Federal Work-Study, institutionally sponsored loans, scholarships/grants, tuition waivers (partial), and unspecified assistantships also available. Support available to part-time students. Financial award application deadline: 5/1; financial award applicants required to submit FAFSA. *Unit head:* Dr. Frederick Gordon, Director, 706-565-7875, E-mail: gordon_frederick@colstate.edu. *Application contact:* Catrina Smith-Edmond, Assistant Director for Graduate and Global Admission, 706-507-8824, Fax: 706-568-5091, E-mail: smithedmond_catrina@columbusstate.edu.
Website: http://politicalscience.columbusstate.edu/

Concordia University, School of Graduate Studies, Faculty of Arts and Science, Department of Political Science, Montréal, QC H3G 1M8, Canada. Offers political science (PhD); public policy and public administration (MA), including geography. *Degree requirements:* For master's, one foreign language, comprehensive exam, thesis optional, internship. *Entrance requirements:* For master's, honors degree or equivalent. Additional exam requirements/recommendations for international students: Required—TOEFL. *Faculty research:* International public policy and administration, Quebec public administration, public policy and social/political theory, geography and public policy, public administration and decision making.

Public Administration

Concordia University Wisconsin, Graduate Programs, School of Business Administration, MBA Program, Mequon, WI 53097-2402. Offers finance (MBA); health care administration (MBA); human resource management (MBA); international business (MBA); international business-bilingual English/Chinese (MBA); management (MBA); management information systems (MBA); managerial communications (MBA); marketing (MBA); public administration (MBA); risk management (MBA). *Program availability:* Online learning. *Degree requirements:* For master's, comprehensive exam, thesis or alternative. *Entrance requirements:* Additional exam requirements/recommendations for international students: Required—TOEFL. *Expenses:* Contact institution.

Copenhagen Business School, Graduate Programs, Copenhagen, Denmark. Offers business administration (Exec MBA, MBA, PhD); business administration and information systems (M Sc); business, language and culture (M Sc); economics and business administration (M Sc); health management (MHM); international business and politics (M Sc); public administration (MPA); shipping and logistics (Exec MBA); technology, market and organization (MBA).

Cumberland University, Program in Public Service Administration, Lebanon, TN 37087. Offers MS. *Program availability:* Part-time, evening/weekend. *Degree requirements:* For master's, comprehensive exam. *Entrance requirements:* For master's, MAT, 3 letters of recommendation. Additional exam requirements/recommendations for international students: Required—TOEFL (minimum score 500 paper-based).

Dalhousie University, Faculty of Management, School of Public Administration, Halifax, NS B3H 3J5, Canada. Offers management (MPA); public administration (MPA, GDPA); LL B/MPA; MLIS/MPA. *Program availability:* Part-time. *Entrance requirements:* For master's, GMAT. Additional exam requirements/recommendations for international students: Required—TOEFL, IELTS, CANTEST, CAEL, or Michigan English Language Assessment Battery. Electronic applications accepted. *Expenses:* Contact institution. *Faculty research:* Municipal management, policy and program management, environmental policy, economic and social policy, business and government.

DePaul University, College of Liberal Arts and Social Sciences, Chicago, IL 60614. Offers Arabic (MA); Chinese (MA); critical ethnic studies (MA); English (MA); French (MA); German (MA); history (MA); interdisciplinary studies (MA, MS); international public service (MS); international studies (MA); Italian (MA); Japanese (MA); liberal studies (MA); nonprofit management (MNM); public administration (MPA); public health (MPH); public policy (MPP); public service management (MS); refugee and forced migration studies (MS); social work (MSW); sociology (MA); Spanish (MA); sustainable urban development (MA); women's and gender studies (MA); writing and publishing (MA); writing, rhetoric and discourse (MA); MA/PhD. *Program availability:* Part-time, evening/weekend, online learning. Terminal master's awarded for partial completion of doctoral program. *Degree requirements:* For master's, variable foreign language requirement, comprehensive exam (for some programs), thesis (for some programs). *Application deadline:* Applications are processed on a rolling basis. Application fee: $40. Electronic applications accepted. *Financial support:* Applicants required to submit FAFSA. *Unit head:* Dr. Guillermo Vasquez de Velasco, Dean, 773-325-7305. *Application contact:* Ann Spittle, Director of Graduate Admission, 773-325-8369, Fax: 312-476-3244, E-mail: graddepaul@depaul.edu.
Website: http://las.depaul.edu/

DeVry University–Folsom Campus, Graduate Programs, Folsom, CA 95630. Offers accounting (M Acc); accounting and financial management (MAFM); business administration (MBA); curriculum leadership (M Ed); educational leadership (M Ed); educational technology (M Ed); higher education leadership (M Ed); human resource management (MHRM); information systems management (MISM); network and communications management (MNCM); project management (MPM); public administration (MPA).

Drake University, College of Business and Public Administration, Des Moines, IA 50311-4516. Offers accounting (M Acc); business administration (MBA); public administration (MPA); JD/MBA; JD/MPA; Pharm D/MBA; Pharm D/MPA. *Program availability:* Part-time, evening/weekend. *Degree requirements:* For master's, comprehensive exam (for some programs), thesis (for some programs), internships. *Entrance requirements:* For master's, GMAT, letters of recommendation, resume. Additional exam requirements/recommendations for international students: Required—TOEFL (minimum score 550 paper-based). *Application deadline:* For fall admission, 8/15 priority date for domestic students; for winter admission, 12/20 priority date for domestic students; for spring admission, 12/1 priority date for domestic students. Applications are processed on a rolling basis. Application fee: $25. Electronic applications accepted. *Expenses:* Contact institution. *Financial support:* Fellowships with tuition reimbursements, teaching assistantships, career-related internships or fieldwork, and institutionally sponsored loans available. Support available to part-time students. Financial award application deadline: 3/1; financial award applicants required to submit FAFSA. *Faculty research:* Venture capital, online commerce, professional ethics, process improvement, project management. *Unit head:* Dr. Daniel J. Connolly, Dean, 515-271-2872, Fax: 515-271-4518, E-mail: daniel.connolly@drake.edu. *Application contact:* Danette Kenne, Assistant Dean, 515-271-2188, Fax: 515-271-4518, E-mail: cbpa.gradprograms@drake.edu.
Website: http://www.drake.edu/cbpa/

East Carolina University, Graduate School, Thomas Harriot College of Arts and Sciences, Department of Political Science, Greenville, NC 27858-4353. Offers public administration (MPA); security studies (MS, Certificate). *Accreditation:* NASPAA. *Program availability:* Part-time, evening/weekend, online learning. *Students:* 29 full-time (13 women), 76 part-time (30 women); includes 27 minority (16 Black or African American, non-Hispanic/Latino; 1 American Indian or Alaska Native, non-Hispanic/Latino; 1 Asian, non-Hispanic/Latino; 9 Hispanic/Latino), 1 international. Average age 34. 28 applicants, 100% accepted, 18 enrolled. In 2017, 21 master's, 10 other advanced degrees awarded. *Degree requirements:* For master's, internship, professional paper. *Entrance requirements:* For master's, GRE General Test. Additional exam requirements/recommendations for international students: Recommended—TOEFL (minimum score 78 iBT), IELTS (minimum score 6.5). *Application deadline:* For fall admission, 6/1 priority date for domestic students; for spring admission, 10/15 for domestic students. Applications are processed on a rolling basis. Application fee: $75. Electronic applications accepted. *Expenses:* Tuition, state resident: full-time $4749; part-time $297 per credit hour. Tuition, nonresident: full-time $17,898; part-time $1119 per credit hour. *Required fees:* $2691; $224 per credit hour. Part-time tuition and fees vary according to course load and program. *Financial support:* Research assistantships with partial tuition reimbursements, teaching assistantships with partial tuition reimbursements, and Federal Work-Study available. Support available to part-time students. Financial award application deadline: 3/1. *Unit head:* Dr. Alethia Cook, Chair, 252-328-5869, E-mail: cooka@ecu.edu. *Application contact:* Dean of Graduate School, 252-328-6012, Fax: 252-328-6071, E-mail: gradschool@ecu.edu.
Website: http://www.ecu.edu/polsci/

Eastern Kentucky University, The Graduate School, College of Arts and Sciences, Department of Government, Program in General Public Administration, Richmond, KY 40475-3102. Offers community development (MPA); community health administration (MPA); general public administration (MPA). *Accreditation:* NASPAA. *Program availability:* Part-time, evening/weekend. *Entrance requirements:* For master's, GRE General Test, minimum GPA of 2.5.

Eastern Michigan University, Graduate School, College of Arts and Sciences, Department of Political Science, Programs in Public Administration, Ypsilanti, MI 48197. Offers general public management (Graduate Certificate); local government management (Graduate Certificate); management of public healthcare services (Graduate Certificate); nonprofit management (Graduate Certificate); public administration (MPA); public budget management (Graduate Certificate); public land planning and development management (Graduate Certificate); public personnel management (Graduate Certificate); public policy analysis (Graduate Certificate). *Accreditation:* NASPAA. *Students:* 11 full-time (6 women), 41 part-time (19 women); includes 18 minority (13 Black or African American, non-Hispanic/Latino; 1 Hispanic/Latino; 4 Two or more races, non-Hispanic/Latino). Average age 34. 42 applicants, 79% accepted, 14 enrolled. In 2017, 23 master's, 4 other advanced degrees awarded. Application fee: $45. *Application contact:* Dr. Jeffrey L. Bernstein, Program Advisor, 734-487-6970, Fax: 734-487-3340, E-mail: jeffrey.bernstein@emich.edu.
Website: http://www.emich.edu/polisci/

Eastern University, Program in Organizational Leadership, St. Davids, PA 19087-3696. Offers leadership studies (CAGS); organizational leadership (PhD), including business management, educational administration, public and nonprofit administration. *Students:* 98 full-time (60 women); includes 31 minority (26 Black or African American, non-Hispanic/Latino; 2 Asian, non-Hispanic/Latino; 2 Hispanic/Latino; 1 Two or more races, non-Hispanic/Latino), 4 international. Average age 47. In 2017, 8 doctorates, 10 other advanced degrees awarded. *Application deadline:* Applications are processed on a rolling basis. Application fee: $75. Electronic applications accepted. *Expenses:* Contact institution. *Unit head:* Michael Dziedziak, Executive Director of Enrollment, 800-452-0996, E-mail: gpsadmissions@eastern.edu.
Website: https://www.eastern.edu/academics/programs/phd-organizational-leadership/phd-organizational-leadership-0

Eastern Washington University, Graduate Studies, College of Business and Public Administration, Program in Public Administration, Cheney, WA 99004-2431. Offers MPA, MPA/MURP. *Accreditation:* NASPAA. *Program availability:* Part-time, evening/weekend. *Faculty:* 9. *Students:* 36 full-time (25 women), 16 part-time (11 women); includes 6 minority (5 American Indian or Alaska Native, non-Hispanic/Latino; 1 Asian, non-Hispanic/Latino), 1 international. Average age 36. 55 applicants, 64% accepted, 28 enrolled. In 2017, 38 master's awarded. *Degree requirements:* For master's, comprehensive exam, thesis optional. *Entrance requirements:* For master's, minimum GPA of 3.0. Additional exam requirements/recommendations for international students: Required—TOEFL (minimum score 580 paper-based; 92 iBT), IELTS (minimum score 7), PTE (minimum score 63). *Application deadline:* For fall admission, 4/1 priority date for domestic students; for spring admission, 1/15 for domestic students. Applications are processed on a rolling basis. Application fee: $75. Electronic applications accepted. *Expenses:* Tuition, state resident: full-time $11,191; part-time $373.06 per credit. Tuition, nonresident: full-time $25,995; part-time $866.52 per credit. *Financial support:* Teaching assistantships with partial tuition reimbursements, career-related internships or fieldwork, Federal Work-Study, institutionally sponsored loans, scholarships/grants, health care benefits, tuition waivers (partial), and unspecified assistantships available. Support available to part-time students. Financial award application deadline: 2/1; financial award applicants required to submit FAFSA. *Unit head:* Dr. Kerry Brooks, 509-828-1230, E-mail: kbrooks@ewu.edu. *Application contact:* Kathy White, Student Application Contact, 509-359-7870, E-mail: gradprograms@ewu.edu.
Website: http://www.ewu.edu/CBPA/Programs/Public-Administration.xml

East Stroudsburg University of Pennsylvania, Graduate and Extended Studies, College of Arts and Sciences, Department of Political Science and Economics, East Stroudsburg, PA 18301-2999. Offers management and leadership in public administration (MS); political science (MA). *Program availability:* Part-time, evening/weekend. *Faculty:* 5 full-time (1 woman), 1 (woman) part-time/adjunct. *Students:* 9 full-time (5 women), 10 part-time (6 women); includes 7 minority (1 Asian, non-Hispanic/Latino; 5 Hispanic/Latino; 1 Two or more races, non-Hispanic/Latino), 2 international. Average age 30. 17 applicants, 82% accepted, 8 enrolled. In 2017, 7 master's awarded. *Degree requirements:* For master's, variable foreign language requirement, comprehensive exam, thesis or alternative. *Entrance requirements:* Additional exam requirements/recommendations for international students: Recommended—TOEFL (minimum score 560 paper-based; 83 iBT), IELTS. *Application deadline:* For fall admission, 7/31 priority date for domestic students, 6/30 priority date for international students; for spring admission, 11/30 for domestic students, 10/31 for international students. Applications are processed on a rolling basis. Application fee: $50. Electronic applications accepted. *Expenses:* Tuition, state resident: full-time $4500; part-time $3000 per credit. Tuition, nonresident: full-time $6750; part-time $4500 per credit. *Required fees:* $2642; $1756 per credit. $878 per semester. Tuition and fees vary according to course load, campus/location and program. *Financial support:* Research assistantships with tuition reimbursements, Federal Work-Study, and unspecified assistantships available. Support available to part-time students. Financial award application deadline: 3/1; financial award applicants required to submit FAFSA. *Unit head:* Ko Mishima, Graduate Coordinator, 570-422-3248. *Application contact:* Kevin Quintero, Associate Director, Graduate and Extended Studies, 570-422-3890, Fax: 570-422-2711, E-mail: kquintero@esu.edu.
Website: http://www.esu.edu/academics/departments/polisci-econ/index.cfm

East Tennessee State University, School of Graduate Studies, College of Arts and Sciences, Department of Political Science, International Affairs and Public Administration, Johnson City, TN 37614. Offers economic development (Postbaccalaureate Certificate); economic development and planning (MPA); local government management (MPA); nonprofit and public financial management (MPA); urban planning (Postbaccalaureate Certificate). *Program availability:* Part-time. *Degree requirements:* For master's, internship, capstone. *Entrance requirements:* For master's, GRE General Test, three letters of recommendation. Additional exam requirements/recommendations for international students: Required—TOEFL (minimum score 550 paper-based; 79 iBT). *Application deadline:* For fall admission, 6/1 for domestic students, 4/29 for international students; for spring admission, 11/1 for domestic students, 9/29 for international students. Application fee: $55 ($65 for international students). Electronic applications accepted. *Financial support:* Research assistantships with full tuition reimbursements, teaching assistantships with full tuition reimbursements, career-related internships or fieldwork, institutionally sponsored loans, scholarships/grants, and unspecified assistantships available. Financial award application deadline: 7/1; financial award applicants required to submit FAFSA. *Faculty research:* Labor issues, presidency, public law in American politics, East Asian politics, European politics, Middle Eastern politics, development in comparative politics, international political economy, international relations, world politics in international affairs. *Unit head:* Dr. Andrew Battista, Chair, 423-439-6628, Fax: 423-439-4348, E-mail: battista@etsu.edu. *Application contact:* Dr. Andrew Battista, Chair, 423-439-6628, Fax:

423-439-4348, E-mail: battista@etsu.edu.
Website: http://www.etsu.edu/cas/polisci/

The Evergreen State College, Graduate Programs, Program in Public Administration, Olympia, WA 98505. Offers MPA. *Program availability:* Part-time, evening/weekend. *Faculty:* 6 full-time (3 women), 9 part-time/adjunct (5 women). *Students:* 74 full-time (54 women), 68 part-time (46 women); includes 59 minority (9 Black or African American, non-Hispanic/Latino; 18 American Indian or Alaska Native, non-Hispanic/Latino; 2 Asian, non-Hispanic/Latino; 15 Hispanic/Latino; 2 Native Hawaiian or other Pacific Islander, non-Hispanic/Latino; 13 Two or more races, non-Hispanic/Latino), 1 international. Average age 35. 119 applicants, 53% accepted, 50 enrolled. In 2017, 49 master's awarded. *Degree requirements:* For master's, 6-credit capstone course or 8-credit thesis. *Entrance requirements:* For master's, minimum GPA of 3.0 in last 90 quarter hours toward BA/BS; 4 quarter credits in statistics within past 3 years; evidence of writing, analytical, and general communication skills at appropriate level for graduate study. *Application deadline:* For fall admission, 2/1 priority date for domestic and international students. Application fee: $50. Electronic applications accepted. *Expenses:* Contact institution. *Financial support:* In 2017–18, 81 students received support, including 26 fellowships with partial tuition reimbursements available (averaging $988 per year); career-related internships or fieldwork, Federal Work-Study, scholarships/grants, and tuition waivers (partial) also available. Support available to part-time students. Financial award application deadline: 2/1; financial award applicants required to submit FAFSA. *Faculty research:* Public administration, public policy, women's studies, political science. *Unit head:* Dr. Doreen Swetkis, MPA Program Director, 360-867-5320, E-mail: swetkisd@evergreen.edu. *Application contact:* Anna Rhoads, Associate MPA Program Director, 360-867-6554, E-mail: rhoadsa@evergreen.edu. Website: http://www.evergreen.edu/mpa/

Excelsior College, School of Public Service, Albany, NY 12203-5159. Offers criminal justice (MSCI); homeland security and emergency management (MSCJ); justice administration (MSCI); mediation and arbitration (MPA); public administration (MPA). *Program availability:* Part-time, evening/weekend, online learning. *Faculty:* 6 part-time/adjunct (5 women). *Students:* 173 part-time (49 women); includes 70 minority (32 Black or African American, non-Hispanic/Latino; 1 American Indian or Alaska Native, non-Hispanic/Latino; 3 Asian, non-Hispanic/Latino; 28 Hispanic/Latino; 1 Native Hawaiian or other Pacific Islander, non-Hispanic/Latino; 5 Two or more races, non-Hispanic/Latino). Average age 40. In 2017, 45 master's awarded. *Application deadline:* Applications are processed on a rolling basis. Application fee: $50. Electronic applications accepted. *Expenses: Tuition:* Part-time $645 per credit. *Required fees:* $265 per credit. *Financial support:* Scholarships/grants available. *Unit head:* Dr. Robert Waters, Dean, School of Public Service, 518-464-8500, Fax: 518-464-8777. *Application contact:* Admissions Counselor, 888-647-2388, Fax: 518-464-8777, E-mail: gradadmissions@excelsior.edu. Website: http://www.excelsior.edu/programs/public-service

Fairfield University, College of Arts and Sciences, Fairfield, CT 06824. Offers American studies (MA); communication (MA); creative writing (MFA); mathematics (MS); public administration (MPA). *Program availability:* Part-time, evening/weekend, online learning. *Faculty:* 16 full-time (8 women), 12 part-time/adjunct (8 women). *Students:* 67 full-time (46 women), 64 part-time (35 women); includes 27 minority (8 Black or African American, non-Hispanic/Latino; 1 Asian, non-Hispanic/Latino; 14 Hispanic/Latino; 4 Two or more races, non-Hispanic/Latino), 10 international. Average age 32. 80 applicants, 81% accepted, 43 enrolled. In 2017, 38 master's awarded. *Degree requirements:* For master's, capstone research course. *Entrance requirements:* For master's, minimum GPA of 3.0, 2 letters of recommendation, resume, personal statement. Additional exam requirements/recommendations for international students: Required—TOEFL (minimum score 550 paper-based; 80 iBT) or IELTS (minimum score 6.5). *Application deadline:* For fall admission, 5/15 for international students; for spring admission, 10/15 for international students. Applications are processed on a rolling basis. Application fee: $60. Electronic applications accepted. *Expenses:* $725 per credit hour (for American studies, communication and math programs); $575 per credit hour (for MFA); $775 per credit hour (for MPA). *Financial support:* In 2017–18, 11 students received support. Scholarships/grants and unspecified assistantships available. Financial award applicants required to submit FAFSA. *Faculty research:* Nutrition and physiology, media industries, community-based teaching and learning, non commutative algebra and partial differential equations, cancer research in biology and physics. *Unit head:* Dr. Richard Greenwald, Dean, 203-254-4000 Ext. 2221, Fax: 203-254-4119, E-mail: rgreenwald@fairfield.edu. *Application contact:* Marianne Gumpper, Director of Graduate Admission, 203-254-4184, Fax: 203-254-4073, E-mail: gradadmis@fairfield.edu. Website: http://www.fairfield.edu/cas

Fairleigh Dickinson University, Florham Campus, Anthony J. Petrocelli College of Continuing Studies, Public Administration Institute, Program in Public Administration, Madison, NJ 07940-1099. Offers MPA.

Fairleigh Dickinson University, Metropolitan Campus, Anthony J. Petrocelli College of Continuing Studies, Public Administration Institute, Program in Public Administration, Teaneck, NJ 07666-1914. Offers MPA, Certificate.

Florida Agricultural and Mechanical University, Division of Graduate Studies, Research, and Continuing Education, College of Social Sciences, Arts and Humanities, Department of History and Political Science, Program in Applied Social Science, Tallahassee, FL 32307-3200. Offers criminal justice (MASS); history (MASS); political science (MASS); public administration (MASS). *Program availability:* Part-time. *Degree requirements:* For master's, thesis optional. *Entrance requirements:* For master's, GRE General Test, minimum GPA of 3.0. *Faculty research:* Southern history, black history, election trends, Presidential history.

Florida Atlantic University, College for Design and Social Inquiry, School of Public Administration, Boca Raton, FL 33431-0991. Offers MPA, PhD. *Accreditation:* NASPAA (one or more programs are accredited). *Program availability:* Part-time, evening/weekend. *Faculty:* 12 full-time (4 women), 1 part-time/adjunct (0 women). *Students:* 28 full-time (14 women), 77 part-time (44 women); includes 48 minority (24 Black or African American, non-Hispanic/Latino; 3 Asian, non-Hispanic/Latino; 19 Hispanic/Latino; 2 Two or more races, non-Hispanic/Latino), 5 international. Average age 34. 80 applicants, 31% accepted, 16 enrolled. In 2017, 56 master's, 6 doctorates awarded. *Degree requirements:* For master's, thesis optional; for doctorate, comprehensive exam, thesis/dissertation. *Entrance requirements:* For master's, GRE General Test, minimum GPA of 3.0; for doctorate, GRE General Test, faculty reference, scholarly writing samples, letters of recommendation. Additional exam requirements/recommendations for international students: Required—TOEFL (minimum score 500 paper-based; 61 iBT), IELTS (minimum score 6). *Application deadline:* For fall admission, 5/1 priority date for domestic students, 2/15 for international students; for spring admission, 11/1 for domestic students, 7/15 for international students. Applications are processed on a rolling basis. Application fee: $30. *Expenses:* Tuition, state resident: full-time $7400; part-time $369.82 per credit. Tuition, nonresident: full-time $20,496; part-time $1042.81 per credit. *Financial support:* Fellowships with full tuition reimbursements, research assistantships with partial tuition reimbursements, teaching assistantships with partial tuition reimbursements, career-related internships or fieldwork, Federal Work-Study, institutionally sponsored loans, and tuition waivers (partial) available. Support available to part-time students. Financial award application deadline: 4/1. *Faculty research:* Public

finance and budgeting, public management, evaluation, criminal justice, postmodern public administration. *Unit head:* Leslie Leip, Program Coordinator, 954-924-8818, E-mail: lleip@fau.edu.
Website: http://www.fau.edu/spa/

Florida Gulf Coast University, College of Arts and Sciences, Program in Public Administration, Fort Myers, FL 33965-6565. Offers environmental policy (MPA); management (MPA). *Accreditation:* NASPAA. *Program availability:* Part-time. *Faculty:* 245 full-time (104 women), 155 part-time/adjunct (71 women). *Students:* 16 full-time (8 women), 51 part-time (33 women); includes 20 minority (9 Black or African American, non-Hispanic/Latino; 11 Hispanic/Latino). Average age 34. 25 applicants, 76% accepted, 14 enrolled. In 2017, 17 master's awarded. *Degree requirements:* For master's, thesis. *Entrance requirements:* For master's, GRE General Test, MAT, minimum GPA of 3.0. Additional exam requirements/recommendations for international students: Required—TOEFL (minimum score 550 paper-based). *Application deadline:* For fall admission, 2/15 priority date for domestic students, 5/1 for international students; for spring admission, 12/1 for domestic students, 9/15 for international students. Applications are processed on a rolling basis. Application fee: $30. Electronic applications accepted. *Expenses:* Tuition, state resident: part-time $290 per credit hour. Tuition, nonresident: part-time $1173 per credit hour. *Required fees:* $127 per credit hour. Tuition and fees vary according to course load. *Financial support:* In 2017–18, 5 students received support. Research assistantships, career-related internships or fieldwork, and tuition waivers (full and partial) available. Support available to part-time students. Financial award application deadline: 6/30; financial award applicants required to submit FAFSA. *Faculty research:* Personnel, public policy, public finance, housing policy. *Unit head:* Dr. Roger Green, Chair, 239-590-7838, E-mail: rgreen@fgcu.edu. *Application contact:* Dr. Margaret Banyan, Assistant Professor/Director of MPA Program, 239-590-7850, Fax: 239-590-7846, E-mail: mbanyan@fgcu.edu.

Florida Institute of Technology, Extended Studies Division, Melbourne, FL 32901-6975. Offers acquisition and contract management (MS); aerospace engineering (MS); business administration (MBA, DBA); computer information systems (MS); computer science (MS); electrical engineering (MS); engineering management (MS); human resources management (MS); logistics management (MS), including humanitarian and disaster relief logistics; management (MS), including acquisition and contract management, e-business, human resources management, information systems, logistics management, management, transportation management; material acquisition management (MS); mechanical engineering (MS); operations research (MS); project management (MS), including information systems, operations research; public administration (MPA); quality management (MS); software engineering (MS); space systems (MS); space systems management (MS); supply chain management (MS); systems management (MS), including information systems, operations research; technology management (MS). *Program availability:* Part-time, evening/weekend, online learning. *Students:* Average age 36. 962 applicants, 48% accepted, 323 enrolled. In 2017, 403 master's awarded. *Entrance requirements:* For master's, GMAT or resume showing 8 years of supervised experience, minimum GPA of 3.0, 2 letters of recommendation, resume. Additional exam requirements/recommendations for international students: Required—TOEFL (minimum score 550 paper-based; 79 iBT). *Application deadline:* For fall admission, 4/1 for international students; for spring admission, 9/30 for international students. Applications are processed on a rolling basis. Electronic applications accepted. *Expenses:* Contact institution. *Financial support:* Application deadline: 3/1; applicants required to submit FAFSA. *Unit head:* Dr. Theodore R. Richardson, III, Dean, 321-674-8123, Fax: 321-674-7597, E-mail: trichardson@fit.edu. *Application contact:* Carolyn Farrior, Director of Graduate Admissions, Online Learning and Off-Campus Programs, 321-674-7118, Fax: 321-674-8216, E-mail: cfarrior@fit.edu.
Website: http://es.fit.edu

Florida International University, Steven J. Green School of International and Public Affairs, Department of Public Administration, Miami, FL 33199. Offers public administration (MPA); public affairs (PhD); JD/MPA; MS/MPA. *Accreditation:* NASPAA (one or more programs are accredited). *Program availability:* Part-time, evening/weekend. *Faculty:* 13 full-time (5 women), 12 part-time/adjunct (8 women). *Students:* 111 full-time (73 women), 147 part-time (97 women); includes 201 minority (60 Black or African American, non-Hispanic/Latino; 2 American Indian or Alaska Native, non-Hispanic/Latino; 4 Asian, non-Hispanic/Latino; 131 Hispanic/Latino; 4 Two or more races, non-Hispanic/Latino), 17 international. Average age 33. 173 applicants, 62% accepted, 82 enrolled. In 2017, 90 master's, 4 doctorates awarded. *Degree requirements:* For doctorate, comprehensive exam, thesis/dissertation. *Entrance requirements:* For master's, minimum undergraduate GPA of 3.0 in upper-level coursework, letter of recommendation, letter of intent; for doctorate, GRE, minimum undergraduate GPA of 3.0 in upper-level coursework, 3 letters of recommendation, samples of scholarly written work, interview (when student lives within 50 miles of campus). Additional exam requirements/recommendations for international students: Required—TOEFL (minimum score 550 paper-based; 80 iBT). *Application deadline:* For fall admission, 6/1 for domestic students, 4/1 for international students; for spring admission, 10/1 for domestic students, 9/1 for international students. Applications are processed on a rolling basis. Application fee: $30. Electronic applications accepted. *Expenses:* Tuition, state resident: full-time $8912; part-time $446 per credit hour. Tuition, nonresident: full-time $21,393; part-time $992 per credit hour. *Required fees:* $390; $195 per semester. *Financial support:* Institutionally sponsored loans and scholarships/grants available. Financial award application deadline: 3/1; financial award applicants required to submit FAFSA. *Unit head:* Dr. Howard Frank, Chair, 305-348-0410, E-mail: howard.frank@fiu.edu. *Application contact:* Nanett Rojas, Manager, Admissions Operations, 305-348-7464, E-mail: gradadm@fiu.edu.
Website: http://cas.fiu.edu/

Florida National University, Program in Business Administration, Hialeah, FL 33012. Offers accounting (MBA); finance (MBA); general management (MBA); health services administration (MBA); marketing (MBA); public management and leadership (MBA). *Program availability:* Part-time, blended/hybrid learning. *Degree requirements:* For master's, capstone. *Entrance requirements:* For master's, writing assessment, bachelor's degree from accredited institution; official undergraduate transcripts; minimum undergraduate GPA of 2.5, GMAT (minimum score of 400), or GRE (minimum score of 900); two letters of recommendation; resume. Additional exam requirements/recommendations for international students: Required—TOEFL (minimum score 500 paper-based; 62 iBT), IELTS (minimum score 5.5). *Application deadline:* Applications are processed on a rolling basis. Electronic applications accepted. *Expenses:* Contact institution. *Financial support:* Federal Work-Study, institutionally sponsored loans, scholarships/grants, and tuition waivers available. Financial award applicants required to submit FAFSA. *Unit head:* Dr. Ernesto Gonzalez, Business and Economics Department Head, 305-821-3333 Ext. 1070, Fax: 305-362-0595, E-mail: egonzalez@fnu.edu. Website: https://www.fnu.edu/prospective-students/our-programs/select-a-program/master-of-business-administration/business-administration-mba-masters/

Florida State University, The Graduate School, College of Social Sciences and Public Policy, Reubin O'D. Askew School of Public Administration and Policy, Tallahassee, FL 32306-2250. Offers public administration (MPA, PhD); public administration and policy

(Certificate); JD/MPA; MPA/MSC; MPA/MSP; MPA/MSW. *Accreditation:* NASPAA (one or more programs are accredited). *Program availability:* Part-time, evening/weekend. *Faculty:* 10 full-time (2 women), 10 part-time/adjunct (3 women). *Students:* 78 full-time (39 women), 68 part-time (41 women); includes 74 minority (12 Black or African American, non-Hispanic/Latino; 41 Asian, non-Hispanic/Latino; 6 Hispanic/Latino; 15 Two or more races, non-Hispanic/Latino). Average age 25. 115 applicants, 67% accepted, 37 enrolled. In 2017, 82 master's, 9 doctorates awarded. *Degree requirements:* For master's, action report; for doctorate, comprehensive exam, thesis/dissertation. *Entrance requirements:* For master's, GRE General Test, GMAT, MAT, LSAT, minimum undergraduate upper-division GPA of 3.0; for doctorate, GRE General Test (minimum score of 1100 or equivalent on current grading scale); GMAT; MAT; LSAT, minimum undergraduate GPA of 3.0, graduate 3.5. Additional exam requirements/recommendations for international students: Required—TOEFL (minimum score 550 paper-based; 80 iBT), IELTS (minimum score 6.5), PTE (minimum score 55), Michigan English Language Assessment Battery (minimum score 77). *Application deadline:* For fall admission, 7/1 for domestic students, 5/1 for international students; for spring admission, 11/1 for domestic students, 9/1 for international students; for summer admission, 3/1 for domestic students, 1/1 for international students. Applications are processed on a rolling basis. Application fee: $30. Electronic applications accepted. *Financial support:* In 2017–18, 22 students received support, including 8 fellowships with full tuition reimbursements available (averaging $18,000 per year), 4 research assistantships with full tuition reimbursements available (averaging $15,000 per year), 8 teaching assistantships with full tuition reimbursements available (averaging $15,000 per year); career-related internships or fieldwork, Federal Work-Study, institutionally sponsored loans, scholarships/grants, tuition waivers (full and partial), and unspecified assistantships also available. Support available to part-time students. Financial award application deadline: 2/1; financial award applicants required to submit FAFSA. *Faculty research:* Public financial management, policy analysis and evaluation methods, leadership and strategic management, state and local government administration, public and nonprofit management, international and nongovernmental organizations. *Unit head:* Dr. Keon-Hyung Lee, Director, 850-645-8210, Fax: 850-644-7617, E-mail: klee2@fsu.edu. *Application contact:* Velda Williams, Academic Program Specialist, 850-644-3060, Fax: 850-644-7617, E-mail: vwilliams3@fsu.edu.
Website: http://askew.fsu.edu/

Framingham State University, Graduate Studies, Program in Public Administration, Framingham, MA 01701-9101. Offers MPA. *Program availability:* Part-time, evening/weekend. *Unit head:* Dr. David Stender, Program Coordinator, E-mail: dstender@framingham.edu. *Application contact:* 508-626-4550, Fax: 508-626-4030, E-mail: dgce@frc.mass.edu.

Gallaudet University, The Graduate School, Washington, DC 20002-3625. Offers American Sign Language/English bilingual early childhood deaf education: birth to 5 (Certificate); audiology (Au D); clinical psychology (PhD); deaf and hard of hearing infants, toddlers, and their families (Certificate); deaf education (MA, Ed S); deaf history (Certificate); deaf studies (Certificate); educating deaf students with disabilities (Certificate); education: teacher preparation (MA), including deaf education, early childhood education and deaf education, elementary education and deaf education, secondary education and deaf education; educational neuroscience (PhD); hearing, speech and language sciences (MS, PhD); international development (MA); interpretation (MA, PhD), including combined interpreting practice and research (MA), interpreting research (MA); linguistics (MA, PhD); mental health counseling (MA); peer mentoring (Certificate); public administration (MPA); school counseling (MA); school psychology (Psy S); sign language teaching (MA); social work (MSW); speech-language pathology (MS). *Program availability:* Part-time. Terminal master's awarded for partial completion of doctoral program. *Degree requirements:* For master's, comprehensive exam (for some programs), thesis optional; for doctorate, comprehensive exam, thesis/dissertation. *Entrance requirements:* For master's and doctorate, GRE General Test or MAT, letters of recommendation, interviews, goals statement, American Sign Language proficiency interview, written English competency. Additional exam requirements/recommendations for international students: Required—TOEFL. Electronic applications accepted. *Faculty research:* Signing math dictionaries, telecommunications access, cancer genetics, linguistics, visual language and visual learning, integrated quantum materials, deaf legal discourse, advance recruitment and retention in geosciences.

Gannon University, School of Graduate Studies, College of Engineering and Business, Dahlkemper School of Business, Program in Public Administration, Erie, PA 16541-0001. Offers MPA. *Program availability:* Part-time, evening/weekend, 100% online, blended/hybrid learning. *Degree requirements:* For master's, thesis or alternative, research project. *Entrance requirements:* For master's, GRE, bachelor's degree in any discipline from accredited college or university, transcripts, 3 letters of recommendation. Additional exam requirements/recommendations for international students: Required—TOEFL (minimum score 79 iBT). Electronic applications accepted. Application fee is waived when completed online.

George Mason University, Schar School of Policy and Government, Program in Public Administration, Arlington, VA 22201. Offers public administration (MPA). *Accreditation:* NASPAA. *Faculty:* 17 full-time (6 women), 13 part-time/adjunct (5 women). *Students:* 68 full-time (37 women), 183 part-time (103 women); includes 96 minority (42 Black or African American, non-Hispanic/Latino; 21 Asian, non-Hispanic/Latino; 25 Hispanic/Latino; 8 Two or more races, non-Hispanic/Latino), 9 international. Average age 32. 157 applicants, 91% accepted, 63 enrolled. In 2017, 113 master's awarded. *Degree requirements:* For master's, thesis or alternative, professional experience. *Entrance requirements:* Additional exam requirements/recommendations for international students: Required—TOEFL (minimum score 575 paper-based; 88 iBT), IELTS (minimum score 6.5), PTE (minimum score 59). *Application deadline:* For fall admission, 2/1 priority date for domestic and international students; for spring admission, 11/1 priority date for domestic and international students. Application fee: $75 ($80 for international students). Electronic applications accepted. *Expenses:* $795 per credit in-state tuition, $1,516 out-of-state. *Financial support:* In 2017–18, 6 students received support, including 5 research assistantships with tuition reimbursements available (averaging $14,000 per year), 1 teaching assistantship; career-related internships or fieldwork, Federal Work-Study, scholarships/grants, unspecified assistantships, and health care benefits (for full-time research or teaching assistantship recipients) also available. Support available to part-time students. Financial award application deadline: 3/1; financial award applicants required to submit FAFSA. *Unit head:* Paul Posner, Director, 703-993-8138, Fax: 703-993-1399, E-mail: pposner@gmu.edu. *Application contact:* Stephanie Ellis, Graduate Admissions Coordinator, 703-993-4478, E-mail: sellis11@gmu.edu.
Website: http://spgia.gmu.edu/programs/graduate-degrees/mpa-in-public-administration/

The George Washington University, Columbian College of Arts and Sciences, Trachtenberg School of Public Policy and Public Administration, Washington, DC 20052. Offers environmental resource policy (MA); public administration (MPA); public policy (MPP); public policy and administration (PhD); JD/MPP; MPA/JD; PhD/MPP. *Program availability:* Part-time, evening/weekend, online learning. *Faculty:* 13 full-time (7 women), 20 part-time/adjunct (8 women). *Students:* 102 full-time (63 women), 127 part-time (76 women); includes 66 minority (25 Black or African American, non-Hispanic/Latino; 10 Asian, non-Hispanic/Latino; 24 Hispanic/Latino; 2 Native Hawaiian or other Pacific Islander, non-Hispanic/Latino; 5 Two or more races, non-Hispanic/Latino), 28 international. Average age 30. 630 applicants, 59% accepted, 91 enrolled. In 2017, 122 master's, 13 doctorates awarded. *Degree requirements:* For master's, capstone project; for doctorate, comprehensive exam, thesis/dissertation. *Entrance requirements:* For master's and doctorate, minimum GPA of 3.0. Additional exam requirements/recommendations for international students: Required—TOEFL (minimum score 600 paper-based; 100 iBT). *Application deadline:* For fall admission, 1/5 priority date for domestic and international students; for spring admission, 10/1 priority date for domestic students, 10/1 for international students. Application fee: $75. Electronic applications accepted. *Expenses:* Contact institution. *Financial support:* In 2017–18, 57 students received support. Fellowships, research assistantships, teaching assistantships, Federal Work-Study, scholarships/grants, health care benefits, and unspecified assistantships available. Financial award application deadline: 1/5; financial award applicants required to submit FAFSA. *Faculty research:* Education policy, budget and finance, health policy, regulatory policy, program evaluation. *Unit head:* Dr. Kathyrn E. Newcomer, Director, 202-994-3959, Fax: 202-994-6792, E-mail: newcomer@gwu.edu. *Application contact:* Denee' Bottoms, Assistant Director of Graduate Studies, 202-994-6662, Fax: 202-994-6792, E-mail: dbottoms@gwu.edu.
Website: http://www.tspppa.gwu.edu/

Georgia College & State University, Graduate School, College of Arts and Sciences, Department of Government and Sociology, Program in Public Administration, Milledgeville, GA 31061. Offers MPA. *Accreditation:* NASPAA. *Program availability:* Part-time, evening/weekend. *Students:* 18 full-time (11 women), 63 part-time (48 women); includes 25 minority (22 Black or African American, non-Hispanic/Latino; 1 Hispanic/Latino; 2 Two or more races, non-Hispanic/Latino). Average age 32. 38 applicants, 92% accepted, 25 enrolled. In 2017, 7 master's awarded. *Degree requirements:* For master's, capstone project or thesis, minimum GPA of 3.0. *Entrance requirements:* For master's, transcript of all undergraduate and graduate work, current resume, minimum undergraduate GPA of 3.0. *Application deadline:* For fall admission, 8/1 priority date for domestic students, 4/1 priority date for international students; for spring admission, 11/1 priority date for domestic students, 9/1 priority date for international students; for summer admission, 4/1 priority date for domestic students. Applications are processed on a rolling basis. Application fee: $40. Electronic applications accepted. *Expenses:* $338 per semester hour full-time, $3,042 per term; $343 per semester fees. *Financial support:* In 2017–18, 2 students received support. Unspecified assistantships available. Financial award application deadline: 3/1; financial award applicants required to submit FAFSA. *Unit head:* Dr. Min Kim, Graduate Coordinator for MPA Program, 478-445-7393, E-mail: min.kim@gcsu.edu. *Application contact:* Kate Marshall, Graduate Admissions Coordinator, 478-445-1184, E-mail: kate.marshall@gcsu.edu.
Website: http://www.gcsu.edu/artsandsciences/gov/public-administration-mpa

Georgia Southern University, Jack N. Averitt College of Graduate Studies, College of Liberal Arts and Social Sciences, Institute for Public and Nonprofit Studies, Program in Public Administration, Statesboro, GA 30460. Offers MPA. *Program availability:* Part-time, evening/weekend. *Faculty:* 2 full-time (1 woman). *Students:* 30 full-time (19 women), 22 part-time (17 women); includes 21 minority (17 Black or African American, non-Hispanic/Latino; 2 Asian, non-Hispanic/Latino; 1 Hispanic/Latino; 1 Two or more races, non-Hispanic/Latino), 2 international. Average age 27. 35 applicants, 94% accepted, 20 enrolled. In 2017, 14 master's awarded. *Degree requirements:* For master's, comprehensive exam, internship, terminal exam. *Entrance requirements:* For master's, GRE General Test, minimum GPA of 2.5, resume, undergraduate major appropriate to field, letters of reference. Additional exam requirements/recommendations for international students: Required—TOEFL (minimum score 550 paper-based; 80 iBT), IELTS (minimum score 6). *Application deadline:* For fall admission, 3/1 priority date for domestic and international students; for spring admission, 10/1 priority date for domestic students, 10/1 for international students. Applications are processed on a rolling basis. Application fee: $50. Electronic applications accepted. *Expenses:* Tuition, state resident: full-time $4986; part-time $3324 per year. Tuition, nonresident: full-time $21,982; part-time $15,352 per year. *Required fees:* $2092; $1802 per credit hour. $901 per semester. Tuition and fees vary according to course load, campus/location and program. *Financial support:* In 2017–18, 20 students received support, including 3 fellowships with full tuition reimbursements available (averaging $7,750 per year); career-related internships or fieldwork, Federal Work-Study, scholarships/grants, tuition waivers (full), and unspecified assistantships also available. Support available to part-time students. Financial award application deadline: 4/15; financial award applicants required to submit FAFSA. *Faculty research:* Comparative public administration, equal employment policies, gangs, environmental policy, AIDS policy. *Unit head:* Dr. Trenton Davis, Director, 912-478-5430, Fax: 912-478-8029, E-mail: tjdavis@georgiasouthern.edu.
Website: http://centers.georgiasouthern.edu/ipns/mpa/

Georgia State University, Andrew Young School of Policy Studies, Department of Public Management and Policy, Atlanta, GA 30303. Offers criminal justice (MPA); disaster management (Certificate); disaster policy (MPA); environmental policy (PhD); health policy (PhD); management and finance (MPA); nonprofit management (MPA, Certificate); nonprofit policy (MPA); planning and economic development (MPP, Certificate); policy analysis and evaluation (MPA), including planning and economic development; public and nonprofit management (PhD); public finance and budgeting (PhD), including science and technology policy, urban and regional economic development; public finance policy (MPA), including social policy; public health (MPA). *Accreditation:* NASPAA (one or more programs are accredited). *Program availability:* Part-time. *Faculty:* 17 full-time (9 women). *Students:* 125 full-time (75 women), 78 part-time (51 women); includes 90 minority (67 Black or African American, non-Hispanic/Latino; 5 Asian, non-Hispanic/Latino; 9 Hispanic/Latino; 9 Two or more races, non-Hispanic/Latino), 34 international. Average age 30. 275 applicants, 62% accepted, 88 enrolled. In 2017, 71 master's, 5 doctorates, 12 other advanced degrees awarded. Terminal master's awarded for partial completion of doctoral program. *Degree requirements:* For master's, thesis optional; for doctorate, comprehensive exam, thesis/dissertation. *Entrance requirements:* For master's and doctorate, GRE. Additional exam requirements/recommendations for international students: Required—TOEFL (minimum score 603 paper-based; 100 iBT) or IELTS (minimum score 7). *Application deadline:* For fall admission, 1/15 for domestic and international students. Application fee: $50. Electronic applications accepted. *Expenses:* Tuition, state resident: full-time $7020. Tuition, nonresident: full-time $22,518. *Required fees:* $2128. Tuition and fees vary according to degree level and program. *Financial support:* In 2017–18, fellowships (averaging $8,194 per year), research assistantships (averaging $8,068 per year), teaching assistantships (averaging $3,600 per year) were awarded; institutionally sponsored loans, scholarships/grants, health care benefits, and unspecified assistantships also available. Financial award application deadline: 2/1. *Faculty research:* Public budgeting and finance, public management, nonprofit management, performance measurement and management, urban development. *Unit head:* Dr. Carolyn Bourdeaux, Chair and Professor, 404-413-0013, Fax: 404-413-0104, E-mail:

cbourdeaux@gsu.edu.
Website: http://aysps.gsu.edu/pmap/

Golden Gate University, Ageno School of Business, San Francisco, CA 94105-2968. Offers accounting (MBA); adaptive leadership (MBA); advanced financial planning (MS); business administration (EMBA, MBA, DBA); business analytics (MBA, MS); entrepreneurship (MBA); finance (MBA, MS, Certificate); financial life planning (Certificate); financial planning (MS, Certificate); global supply chain management (MBA, Certificate); human resource management (MBA, MS, Certificate); information technology management (MBA, MS, Certificate); international business (MBA); marketing (MBA, MS, Certificate); project management (MBA, MS, Certificate); psychology (MA, Certificate); public administration (EMPA, MBA); public administration leadership (Certificate); JD/MBA. *Program availability:* Part-time, evening/weekend. *Faculty:* 17 full-time (7 women), 280 part-time/adjunct (95 women). *Students:* 309 full-time (147 women), 527 part-time (266 women); includes 286 minority (56 Black or African American, non-Hispanic/Latino; 1 American Indian or Alaska Native, non-Hispanic/Latino; 131 Asian, non-Hispanic/Latino; 83 Hispanic/Latino; 4 Native Hawaiian or other Pacific Islander, non-Hispanic/Latino; 11 Two or more races, non-Hispanic/Latino), 209 international. Average age 35. 549 applicants, 66% accepted, 185 enrolled. *Degree requirements:* For doctorate, thesis/dissertation, qualifying examination. *Entrance requirements:* For master's, GMAT (for MBA), minimum GPA of 2.5 (MS). Additional exam requirements/recommendations for international students: Required—TOEFL (minimum score 550 paper-based; 79 iBT). *Application deadline:* For fall admission, 5/15 for domestic and international students; for winter admission, 1/15 for domestic and international students; for spring admission, 9/15 for domestic and international students. Applications are processed on a rolling basis. Application fee: $65 ($105 for international students). Electronic applications accepted. *Expenses:* $3,150 per 3-unit course. *Financial support:* Career-related internships or fieldwork, Federal Work-Study, institutionally sponsored loans, and scholarships/grants available. Support available to part-time students. Financial award applicants required to submit FAFSA. *Unit head:* Marianne Koch, Associate Dean, 415-442-6542, Fax: 415-442-6579, E-mail: mkoch@ggu.edu. *Application contact:* Angela Melero, Enrollment Services, 415-442-7800, Fax: 415-442-7807, E-mail: info@ggu.edu.
Website: http://www.ggu.edu/programs/business-and-management

Governors State University, College of Arts and Sciences, Program in Public Administration, University Park, IL 60484. Offers MPA. *Accreditation:* NASPAA. *Program availability:* Part-time. *Faculty:* 60 full-time (34 women), 115 part-time/adjunct (58 women). *Students:* 4 full-time (2 women), 65 part-time (45 women); includes 46 minority (43 Black or African American, non-Hispanic/Latino; 3 Hispanic/Latino), 2 international. Average age 38. 24 applicants, 54% accepted, 11 enrolled. In 2017, 15 master's awarded. *Application deadline:* For fall admission, 4/1 for domestic students. Applications are processed on a rolling basis. Application fee: $50. Electronic applications accepted. *Expenses:* Tuition, state resident: full-time $8472; part-time $353 per credit hour. Tuition, nonresident: full-time $16,944; part-time $706 per credit hour. *Required fees:* $1824; $76 per credit hour. $38 per term. Tuition and fees vary according to course load, degree level and program. *Financial support:* Application deadline: 5/1; applicants required to submit FAFSA. *Unit head:* Lori Montalbano, Chair, Division of Arts and Letters, 708-534-5000 Ext. 2802, E-mail: lmontalbano@govst.edu.

Grambling State University, School of Graduate Studies and Research, College of Arts and Sciences, Department of Political Science and Public Administration, Grambling, LA 71270. Offers health services administration (MPA); human resource management (MPA); public management (MPA); state and local government (MPA). *Accreditation:* NASPAA. *Program availability:* Part-time. *Degree requirements:* For master's, comprehensive exam (for some programs), thesis optional. *Entrance requirements:* For master's, GRE, minimum GPA of 2.75 on last degree. Additional exam requirements/recommendations for international students: Required—TOEFL (minimum score 500 paper-based; 62 iBT). Electronic applications accepted.

Grand Valley State University, College of Community and Public Service, School of Public, Nonprofit and Health Administration, Allendale, MI 49401-9403. Offers MHA, MPA, MPNL. *Accreditation:* NASPAA. *Program availability:* Part-time, evening/weekend. *Faculty:* 13 full-time (6 women), 6 part-time/adjunct (3 women). *Students:* 33 full-time (18 women), 88 part-time (65 women); includes 22 minority (10 Black or African American, non-Hispanic/Latino; 1 American Indian or Alaska Native, non-Hispanic/Latino; 2 Asian, non-Hispanic/Latino; 6 Hispanic/Latino; 3 Two or more races, non-Hispanic/Latino), 6 international. Average age 30. 67 applicants, 79% accepted, 22 enrolled. In 2017, 44 master's awarded. *Degree requirements:* For master's, capstone course. *Entrance requirements:* For master's, three references from informed sources; essay on career and educational objectives (250 to 750 words); resume. Additional exam requirements/recommendations for international students: Required—TOEFL (minimum iBT score of 80), IELTS (6.5), or Michigan English Language Assessment Battery (77). *Application deadline:* For fall admission, 5/1 priority date for domestic students; for winter admission, 11/1 priority date for domestic students. Applications are processed on a rolling basis. Application fee: $30. Electronic applications accepted. *Expenses:* $627 per credit hour. *Financial support:* In 2017–18, 17 students received support, including 9 fellowships, 9 research assistantships with full and partial tuition reimbursements available (averaging $4,000 per year); career-related internships or fieldwork, Federal Work-Study, scholarships/grants, and unspecified assistantships also available. Financial award application deadline: 5/1. *Faculty research:* Comparative urban systems, ethics and public management, local economic development, public and nonprofit boards and governance. *Unit head:* Dr. Richard Jelier, Director, 616-331-6575, Fax: 616-331-7120, E-mail: jelierr@gvsu.edu. *Application contact:* Davia Downey, Graduate Program Director/Recruiting Contact, 616-331-6681, Fax: 616-331-7120, E-mail: downeyd@gvsu.edu.
Website: http://www.gvsu.edu/spnha/

Hamline University, School of Business, St. Paul, MN 55104-1284. Offers business administration (MBA); nonprofit management (MNM); public administration (MPA, DPA); MBA/MNM; MBA/MPA; MPA/MNM. *Program availability:* Part-time, evening/weekend, blended/hybrid learning. *Faculty:* 16 full-time (6 women), 15 part-time/adjunct (4 women). *Students:* 18 full-time (8 women), 309 part-time (165 women); includes 89 minority (43 Black or African American, non-Hispanic/Latino; 3 American Indian or Alaska Native, non-Hispanic/Latino; 22 Asian, non-Hispanic/Latino; 12 Hispanic/Latino; 9 Two or more races, non-Hispanic/Latino), 15 international. Average age 34. 174 applicants, 61% accepted, 68 enrolled. In 2017, 152 master's, 4 doctorates awarded. *Degree requirements:* For master's, thesis (for some programs); for doctorate, comprehensive exam, thesis/dissertation. *Entrance requirements:* For master's and doctorate, personal statement, official transcripts, resume or curriculum vitae, letters of recommendation, writing sample. Additional exam requirements/recommendations for international students: Required—TOEFL (minimum score 550 paper-based; 80 iBT), IELTS (minimum score 6.5). *Application deadline:* For fall admission, 6/1 for domestic and international students; for spring admission, 11/1 for domestic students, 10/1 for international students; for summer admission, 3/1 for domestic students, 2/1 for international students. Applications are processed on a rolling basis. Application fee: $0 ($100 for international students). Electronic applications accepted. *Expenses:* $530 per credit (for MPA), $495 per credit (for MNM), $775 per credit plus fees (for DPA).

Financial support: Career-related internships or fieldwork, Federal Work-Study, scholarships/grants, and unspecified assistantships available. Support available to part-time students. Financial award application deadline: 4/20; financial award applicants required to submit FAFSA. *Faculty research:* Experiential learning, organizational process/politics, gender differences, social equity, pyramid schemes. *Unit head:* Dr. Anne McCarthy, Dean, 651-523-2284, Fax: 651-523-3098, E-mail: hsb@hamline.edu. *Application contact:* Shawn Skoog, Director of Graduate Recruitment and Admission, 651-523-2900, Fax: 651-523-3058, E-mail: gradprog@hamline.edu.
Website: http://www.hamline.edu/business

Harvard University, John F. Kennedy School of Government, Master in Public Administration in International Development Program, Cambridge, MA 02138. Offers MPAID. *Students:* 130 full-time (59 women); includes 15 minority (5 Black or African American, non-Hispanic/Latino; 5 Asian, non-Hispanic/Latino; 3 Hispanic/Latino; 2 Two or more races, non-Hispanic/Latino), 103 international. Average age 29. 251 applicants, 39% accepted, 61 enrolled. In 2017, 64 master's awarded. *Entrance requirements:* For master's, one course each in microeconomics and macroeconomics; two college-level calculus courses (one must contain multivariable calculus); bachelor's degree; 2-3 years of professional experience in development (strongly encouraged). Additional exam requirements/recommendations for international students: Required—TOEFL (minimum score 600 paper-based; 100 iBT). *Application deadline:* For fall admission, 12/1 for domestic students. Application fee: $100. Electronic applications accepted. *Financial support:* In 2017–18, 75 fellowships (averaging $45,739 per year) were awarded; career-related internships or fieldwork, Federal Work-Study, scholarships/grants, health care benefits, and unspecified assistantships also available. Financial award application deadline: 2/24; financial award applicants required to submit FAFSA. *Unit head:* Carol Finney, Director, 617-495-7799, E-mail: carol_finney@harvard.edu. *Application contact:* 617-495-2133, E-mail: mpaid_program@hks.harvard.edu.
Website: http://www.hks.harvard.edu/degrees/masters/mpa-id

Harvard University, John F. Kennedy School of Government, Mid-Career Program in Public Administration, Cambridge, MA 02138. Offers MPA. *Students:* 213 full-time (85 women), 10 part-time (5 women); includes 34 minority (11 Black or African American, non-Hispanic/Latino; 1 American Indian or Alaska Native, non-Hispanic/Latino; 11 Asian, non-Hispanic/Latino; 9 Hispanic/Latino; 2 Two or more races, non-Hispanic/Latino), 122 international. Average age 39. 693 applicants, 42% accepted, 183 enrolled. In 2017, 206 master's awarded. *Entrance requirements:* For master's, GMAT or GRE General Test, minimum 7 years of professional experience. Additional exam requirements/recommendations for international students: Required—TOEFL (minimum score 600 paper-based; 100 iBT), TWE. *Application deadline:* For fall admission, 12/1 for domestic students. Application fee: $100. Electronic applications accepted. *Expenses:* Contact institution. *Financial support:* In 2017–18, 104 fellowships (averaging $63,013 per year) were awarded; Federal Work-Study, scholarships/grants, health care benefits, and unspecified assistantships also available. Financial award application deadline: 2/24; financial award applicants required to submit FAFSA. *Unit head:* Emma Heffern, Director, 617-496-4313, E-mail: emma_heffern@hks.harvard.edu. *Application contact:* 617-495-1155, E-mail: admissions@hks.harvard.edu.
Website: http://www.hks.harvard.edu/

Harvard University, John F. Kennedy School of Government, Program in Public Administration, Cambridge, MA 02138. Offers MPA. *Students:* 183 full-time (86 women); includes 34 minority (4 Black or African American, non-Hispanic/Latino; 1 American Indian or Alaska Native, non-Hispanic/Latino; 18 Asian, non-Hispanic/Latino; 6 Hispanic/Latino; 5 Two or more races, non-Hispanic/Latino), 91 international. Average age 30. 174 applicants, 56% accepted, 65 enrolled. In 2017, 74 master's awarded. *Entrance requirements:* For master's, GMAT or GRE General Test, minimum of 3 years of work experience. Additional exam requirements/recommendations for international students: Required—TOEFL (minimum score 600 paper-based; 100 iBT), TWE. *Application deadline:* For fall admission, 12/1 for domestic students. Application fee: $100. Electronic applications accepted. *Financial support:* In 2017–18, 72 fellowships (averaging $37,476 per year) were awarded; career-related internships or fieldwork, Federal Work-Study, scholarships/grants, health care benefits, and unspecified assistantships also available. Financial award application deadline: 2/24; financial award applicants required to submit FAFSA. *Unit head:* Emma Heffern, Director, 617-496-4312, E-mail: emma_heffern@hks.harvard.edu. *Application contact:* 617-495-1155.
Website: http://www.hks.harvard.edu/

Hawai`i Pacific University, College of Professional Studies, Program in Public Administration, Honolulu, HI 96813. Offers MPA. *Program availability:* Part-time, evening/weekend, 100% online, blended/hybrid learning. *Faculty:* 3 full-time (1 woman), 2 part-time/adjunct (both women). *Students:* 3 full-time (0 women), 2 part-time (1 woman); includes 3 minority (1 Asian, non-Hispanic/Latino; 1 Native Hawaiian or other Pacific Islander, non-Hispanic/Latino; 1 Two or more races, non-Hispanic/Latino). Average age 28. 5 applicants, 100% accepted, 5 enrolled. *Entrance requirements:* For master's, official transcript reflecting conferred bachelor's degree, resume, statement of purpose/essay. Additional exam requirements/recommendations for international students: Recommended—TOEFL (minimum score 550 paper-based; 80 iBT), IELTS (minimum score 6), TWE (minimum score 5). *Application deadline:* For fall admission, 1/15 priority date for domestic students; for spring admission, 10/15 priority date for domestic students. Applications are processed on a rolling basis. Application fee: $50. Electronic applications accepted. *Expenses:* Tuition: Full-time $18,000; part-time $1000 per credit. *Required fees:* $200; $26 per credit. Tuition and fees vary according to course load and program. *Financial support:* Career-related internships or fieldwork, Federal Work-Study, scholarships/grants, tuition waivers (partial), and unspecified assistantships available. Financial award application deadline: 3/1; financial award applicants required to submit FAFSA. *Unit head:* Sheryl Sunia, Department Chair, 808-544-0215, E-mail: ssunia@hpu.edu. *Application contact:* Danny Lam, Assistant Director of Graduate Admissions, 808-544-1135, E-mail: graduate@hpu.edu.
Website: https://www.hpu.edu/cps/public-service/mpa.html

Hilbert College, Program in Public Administration, Hamburg, NY 14075-1597. Offers health administration (MPA); public administration (MPA). *Program availability:* Evening/weekend. *Faculty:* 1 full-time (0 women), 12 part-time/adjunct (6 women). *Students:* 27 full-time (22 women), 1 part-time (0 women); includes 8 minority (3 Black or African American, non-Hispanic/Latino; 1 American Indian or Alaska Native, non-Hispanic/Latino; 1 Hispanic/Latino; 3 Two or more races, non-Hispanic/Latino), 1 international. Average age 30. In 2017, 14 master's awarded. *Degree requirements:* For master's, final capstone project. *Entrance requirements:* For master's, essay, official transcripts from all prior colleges, two letters of recommendation, current resume, relevant work experience, baccalaureate degree from accredited college or university with minimum cumulative GPA of 3.0, personal interview. Additional exam requirements/recommendations for international students: Recommended—TOEFL. *Application deadline:* Applications are processed on a rolling basis. Application fee: $25. Electronic applications accepted. Application fee is waived when completed online. *Expenses:* $800 per credit hour; $20 technology fee per course; $20 one-time orientation fee; $50 one-time graduation fee. *Financial support:* Scholarships/grants and tuition waivers (partial) available. Financial award application deadline: 7/1; financial award applicants required to submit FAFSA. *Unit head:* Kathryn Eskew, Director of Adult and Graduate

Studies, 716-649-7900 Ext. 305, Fax: 716-649-0702, E-mail: keskew@hilbert.edu. *Application contact:* Kim Chiarmonte, Director for Adult and Graduate Recruitment, 716-926-8948, Fax: 716-649-0702, E-mail: kchiarmonte@hilbert.edu. Website: http://www.hilbert.edu/grad/mpa

Hood College, Graduate School, Department of Economics and Business Administration, Frederick, MD 21701-8575. Offers accounting (MBA, Certificate); finance (MBA); financial management (Certificate); human resource management (MBA); information systems (MBA); marketing (MBA); organizational management (Certificate); public management (MBA). *Accreditation:* ACBSP. *Program availability:* Part-time, evening/weekend. *Faculty:* 4 full-time (2 women), 7 part-time/adjunct (1 woman). *Students:* 21 full-time (12 women), 91 part-time (47 women); includes 19 minority (8 Black or African American, non-Hispanic/Latino; 3 Asian, non-Hispanic/Latino; 8 Hispanic/Latino), 15 international. Average age 31. 34 applicants, 97% accepted, 23 enrolled. In 2017, 42 master's awarded. *Degree requirements:* For master's, capstone/final research project. *Entrance requirements:* For master's, minimum GPA of 3.0 (or resume and two letters of recommendation), copy of official transcripts, essay. Additional exam requirements/recommendations for international students: Required—TOEFL (minimum score 575 paper-based; 89 iBT), IELTS (minimum score 6.5). *Application deadline:* For fall admission, 8/15 for domestic students, 8/5 for international students; for spring admission, 12/1 for domestic and international students; for summer admission, 5/1 for domestic students, 4/15 for international students. Applications are processed on a rolling basis. Application fee: $35. Electronic applications accepted. *Expenses:* $550 per credit hour plus $110 per semester comprehensive fee. *Financial support:* Tuition waivers (partial) and unspecified assistantships available. Financial award applicants required to submit FAFSA. *Faculty research:* Corporate strategy and sustainable competitive advantages, business ethics, entrepreneurship, investments management, economic development. *Unit head:* Dr. April M. Boulton, Dean of the Graduate School, 301-696-3600, Fax: 301-696-3597, E-mail: gofurther@hood.edu. *Application contact:* Jan Marcus, Assistant Director of Graduate Admissions, 301-696-3603, E-mail: gofurther@hood.edu.

Howard University, Graduate School, Department of Political Science, Program in Public Administration, Washington, DC 20059-0002. Offers MAPA. *Program availability:* Part-time. *Degree requirements:* For master's, comprehensive exam. *Entrance requirements:* For master's, GRE General Test, minimum GPA of 3.0.

Idaho State University, Office of Graduate Studies, College of Arts and Letters, Department of Political Science, Program in Public Administration, Pocatello, ID 83209-8073. Offers MPA. *Program availability:* Part-time. *Degree requirements:* For master's, comprehensive exam, thesis optional, public service internship. *Entrance requirements:* For master's, GRE General Test, course work in humanities and social sciences, 3 letters of recommendation. Additional exam requirements/recommendations for international students: Required—TOEFL (minimum score 550 paper-based; 80 iBT). Electronic applications accepted. *Faculty research:* Constitutional law, policy theory, public administration, international affairs.

IGlobal University, Graduate Programs, Vienna, VA 22182. Offers accounting (MBA); data management and analytics (MSIT); entrepreneurship (MBA); finance (MBA); global business management (MBA); health care management (MBA); hospitality and tourism management (MBA); human resources management (MBA); information technology (MBA); information technology systems and management (MSIT); leadership and management (MBA); project management (MBA); public service and administration (MBA); software design and management (MSIT).

Illinois Institute of Technology, Stuart School of Business, Program in Public Administration, Chicago, IL 60661. Offers MPA, JD/MPA, MBA/MPA. *Program availability:* Part-time, evening/weekend. *Entrance requirements:* For master's, minimum cumulative undergraduate GPA of 3.0. Additional exam requirements/recommendations for international students: Required—TOEFL (minimum score 575 paper-based; 90 iBT); Recommended—IELTS (minimum score 7). Electronic applications accepted. *Faculty research:* Comparative public administration and policy, migration and ethnic politics, social dimension and impact of science and technology, urban politics, urban ethnography.

Indiana State University, College of Graduate and Professional Studies, College of Arts and Sciences, Department of Political Science, Terre Haute, IN 47809. Offers public administration (MPA). *Degree requirements:* For master's, thesis (for some programs), capstone project. *Entrance requirements:* For master's, GRE or minimum undergraduate GPA of 2.75, 18 semester hours of course work in political science. Additional exam requirements/recommendations for international students: Required—TOEFL (minimum score 550 paper-based). Electronic applications accepted.

Indiana University Bloomington, School of Public and Environmental Affairs, Public Affairs Programs, Bloomington, IN 47405. Offers economic development (MPA); energy (MPA); environmental policy (PhD); environmental policy and natural resource management (MPA); information systems (MPA); international development (MPA); local government management (MPA); nonprofit management (MPA, Certificate); policy analysis (MPA); public budgeting and financial management (Certificate); public finance (PhD); public financial administration (MPA); public management (MPA, PhD, Certificate); public policy analysis (PhD); social entrepreneurship (Certificate); specialized public affairs (MPA); sustainability and sustainable development (MPA); JD/MPA; MPA/MA; MPA/MIS; MPA/MLS; MSES/MPA. *Accreditation:* NASPAA (one or more programs are accredited). *Program availability:* Part-time. *Degree requirements:* For master's, capstone, internship; for doctorate, comprehensive exam, thesis/dissertation. *Entrance requirements:* For master's, GRE General Test or GMAT, official transcripts, 3 letters of recommendation, resume, personal statement; for doctorate, GRE General Test, official transcripts, 3 letters of recommendation, statement of purpose. Additional exam requirements/recommendations for international students: Required—TOEFL (minimum score 600 paper-based; 96 iBT); Recommended—IELTS (minimum score 7). Electronic applications accepted. *Faculty research:* International development, environmental policy and resource management, policy analysis, public finance, public management, urban management, nonprofit management, energy policy, social policy, public finance.

Indiana University Kokomo, Department of Public Administration and Health Management, Kokomo, IN 46904. Offers health management (MPM, Graduate Certificate); public management (Graduate Certificate); public management and policy (MPM). *Program availability:* Part-time, evening/weekend. *Entrance requirements:* For master's, GRE/GMAT for GPAs lower than 3.0, letters of recommendation. Additional exam requirements/recommendations for international students: Required—TOEFL (minimum score 550 paper-based; 73 iBT). Electronic applications accepted. *Expenses:* Contact institution.

Indiana University Northwest, School of Public and Environmental Affairs, Gary, IN 46408. Offers criminal justice (MPA); environmental affairs (Graduate Certificate); health services (MPA); nonprofit management (Certificate); public management (MPA, Graduate Certificate). *Accreditation:* NASPAA (one or more programs are accredited). *Program availability:* Part-time. *Entrance requirements:* For master's, GRE General Test (minimum combined verbal and quantitative score of 280), GMAT, or LSAT, letters of recommendation. Electronic applications accepted. *Faculty research:* Employment in

income security policies, evidence in criminal justice, equal employment law, social welfare policy and welfare reform, public finance in developing countries.

Indiana University–Purdue University Indianapolis, School of Public and Environmental Affairs, Indianapolis, IN 46202. Offers criminal justice and public safety (MS); homeland security and emergency management (Graduate Certificate); library management (Graduate Certificate); nonprofit management (Graduate Certificate); public affairs (MPA); public management (Graduate Certificate); social entrepreneurship: nonprofit and public benefit organizations (Graduate Certificate); JD/MPA; MLS/NMC; MLS/PMC; MPA/MA. *Accreditation:* CAHME (one or more programs are accredited); NASPAA. *Program availability:* Part-time, evening/weekend, online learning. *Entrance requirements:* For master's, GRE General Test, GMAT or LSAT, minimum GPA of 3.0 (preferred). Additional exam requirements/recommendations for international students: Required—TOEFL (minimum score 93 iBT), IELTS (minimum score 6.5). Electronic applications accepted. *Faculty research:* Nonprofit and public management, public policy, urban policy, sustainability policy, disaster preparedness and recovery, vehicular safety, homicide, offender rehabilitation and re-entry.

Indiana University South Bend, College of Liberal Arts and Sciences, South Bend, IN 46615. Offers advanced computer programming (Graduate Certificate); applied informatics (Graduate Certificate); applied mathematics and computer science (MS); behavior modification (Graduate Certificate); computer applications (Graduate Certificate); computer programming (Graduate Certificate); correctional management and supervision (Graduate Certificate); English (MA); health systems management (Graduate Certificate); international studies (Graduate Certificate); liberal studies (MLS); nonprofit management (Graduate Certificate); paralegal studies (Graduate Certificate); professional writing (Graduate Certificate); public affairs (MPA); public management (Graduate Certificate); social and cultural diversity (Graduate Certificate); strategic sustainability leadership (Graduate Certificate); technology for administration (Graduate Certificate). *Program availability:* Part-time, evening/weekend. *Degree requirements:* For master's, variable foreign language requirement, thesis (for some programs). *Entrance requirements:* For master's, minimum GPA of 3.0. Additional exam requirements/recommendations for international students: Required—TOEFL (minimum score 550 paper-based; 80 iBT). *Expenses:* Contact institution. *Faculty research:* Artificial intelligence, bioinformatics, English language and literature, creative writing, computer networks.

Institute of Public Administration, Programs in Public Administration, Dublin, Ireland. Offers healthcare management (MA); local government management (MA); public management (MA, Diploma).

Instituto Tecnológico y de Estudios Superiores de Monterrey, Campus Ciudad Juárez, Program in Applied Public Management, Ciudad Juárez, Mexico. Offers MPM.

International University in Geneva, Leadership Programs, Geneva, Switzerland. Offers international relations and diplomacy (MIRD); media and communication (MA); public administration (DPA). *Degree requirements:* For master's, comprehensive exam. *Entrance requirements:* Additional exam requirements/recommendations for international students: Required—TOEFL. Electronic applications accepted.

Iowa State University of Science and Technology, Department of Political Science, Ames, IA 50011. Offers political science (MA); public administration (MPA); JD/MA. JD/MA offered jointly with Drake University. *Degree requirements:* For master's, thesis (for some programs). *Entrance requirements:* For master's, GRE General Test, GMAT or LSAT. Additional exam requirements/recommendations for international students: Required—TOEFL (minimum score 570 paper-based; 80 iBT), IELTS (minimum score 6.5). Electronic applications accepted.

Jackson State University, Graduate School, College of Public Service, Department of Public Policy and Administration, Jackson, MS 39217. Offers public administration (PhD); public policy and administration (MPPA). *Accreditation:* NASPAA (one or more programs are accredited). *Program availability:* Evening/weekend. *Degree requirements:* For master's, comprehensive exam, thesis optional; for doctorate, comprehensive exam, thesis/dissertation. *Entrance requirements:* For master's, GRE General Test; for doctorate, GRE, GMAT, MAT. Additional exam requirements/recommendations for international students: Required—TOEFL (minimum score 520 paper-based; 67 iBT).

James Madison University, The Graduate School, College of Arts and Letters, Program in Public Administration, Harrisonburg, VA 22801. Offers individualized (MPA); public management (MPA), including international stabilization and recovery, management in international non-governmental organizations, nonprofit management, public management. Public and nonprofit management program offered in Roanoke. *Accreditation:* NASPAA. *Program availability:* Part-time. *Students:* 23 full-time (11 women), 16 part-time (7 women); includes 7 minority (4 Black or African American, non-Hispanic/Latino; 1 Hispanic/Latino; 2 Two or more races, non-Hispanic/Latino). Average age 30. In 2017, 19 master's awarded. Application fee: $55. Electronic applications accepted. *Expenses:* Tuition, state resident: full-time $10,512; part-time $438 per credit hour. Tuition, nonresident: full-time $28,358; part-time $1162 per credit hour. Required fees: $1128. *Financial support:* In 2017–18, 14 students received support, including 14 fellowships; Federal Work-Study and assistantships (averaging $7911) also available. Financial award application deadline: 3/1; financial award applicants required to submit FAFSA. *Unit head:* Dr. Charles Blake, Department Head, 540-568-6149, E-mail: blakech@jmu.edu. *Application contact:* Lynette D. Michael, Director of Graduate Admissions, 540-568-6131, Fax: 540-568-7860, E-mail: michaeld@jmu.edu. Website: http://www.jmu.edu/mpa

John Jay College of Criminal Justice of the City University of New York, Graduate Studies, Program in Public Administration, New York, NY 10019. Offers MPA. *Accreditation:* NASPAA. *Program availability:* Part-time, evening/weekend. *Degree requirements:* For master's, thesis or alternative. *Entrance requirements:* For master's, minimum B average. Additional exam requirements/recommendations for international students: Required—TOEFL (minimum score 500 paper-based).

Johns Hopkins University, Zanvyl Krieger School of Arts and Sciences, Advanced Academic Programs, Program in Government, Washington, DC 20036. Offers global security studies (MA); government (MA); national securities study (Certificate); nonprofit management (Certificate); public management (MA); research administration (MS); MA/MBA. *Program availability:* Part-time, evening/weekend, online learning. *Degree requirements:* For master's, thesis. *Entrance requirements:* For master's, minimum GPA of 3.0. Additional exam requirements/recommendations for international students: Required—TOEFL (minimum score 100 iBT). Electronic applications accepted.

Kansas State University, Graduate School, College of Arts and Sciences, Department of Political Science, Manhattan, KS 66506. Offers political science (MA); public administration (MPA). *Accreditation:* NASPAA. *Program availability:* Part-time. *Degree requirements:* For master's, comprehensive exam, thesis or alternative. *Entrance requirements:* For master's, GRE (recommended), minimum GPA of 3.0. Additional exam requirements/recommendations for international students: Required—TOEFL (minimum score 550 paper-based; 79 iBT); Recommended—IELTS (minimum score 6.5), TSE (minimum score 58). Electronic applications accepted. *Faculty research:*

Armed conflict, civil military relations, comparative public administration and policy, electoral competition, legislative studies.

Kean University, College of Business and Public Management, Program in Public Administration, Union, NJ 07083. Offers health services administration (MPA); non-profit management (MPA); public administration (MPA). *Accreditation:* NASPAA. *Program availability:* Part-time. *Faculty:* 14 full-time (4 women). *Students:* 55 full-time (40 women), 47 part-time (35 women); includes 86 minority (51 Black or African American, non-Hispanic/Latino; 10 Asian, non-Hispanic/Latino; 22 Hispanic/Latino; 3 Two or more races, non-Hispanic/Latino), 3 international. Average age 31. 62 applicants, 94% accepted, 33 enrolled. In 2017, 57 master's awarded. *Degree requirements:* For master's, thesis, internship, research seminar. *Entrance requirements:* For master's, minimum cumulative GPA of 3.0, official transcripts from all institutions attended, two letters of recommendation, personal statement, writing sample, professional resume/curriculum vitae. Additional exam requirements/recommendations for international students: Required—TOEFL (minimum score 550 paper-based; 79 iBT), IELTS (minimum score 6.5). *Application deadline:* For fall admission, 6/30 for domestic and international students; for spring admission, 12/1 for domestic and international students. Applications are processed on a rolling basis. Application fee: $75. Electronic applications accepted. *Expenses:* Tuition, state resident: full-time $13,419; part-time $653 per credit. Tuition, nonresident: full-time $18,188; part-time $801 per credit. *Required fees:* $3382; $154 per credit. Tuition and fees vary according to course level, course load, degree level and program. *Financial support:* Scholarships/grants and unspecified assistantships available. Financial award applicants required to submit FAFSA. *Unit head:* Dr. Patricia Moore, Program Coordinator, 908-737-4314, E-mail: pmoore@kean.edu. *Application contact:* Pedro Lopes, Admissions Counselor, 908-737-7100, E-mail: gradadmissions@kean.edu.
Website: http://grad.kean.edu/masters-programs/public-administration

Kennesaw State University, College of Humanities and Social Sciences, Program in Public Administration, Kennesaw, GA 30144. Offers MPA. *Accreditation:* NASPAA. *Program availability:* Part-time, evening/weekend. *Degree requirements:* For master's, thesis optional. *Entrance requirements:* For master's, GRE General Test, minimum GPA of 2.75. Additional exam requirements/recommendations for international students: Required—TOEFL (minimum score 550 paper-based; 80 iBT), IELTS (minimum score 6.5). Electronic applications accepted.

Kent State University, College of Arts and Sciences, Department of Political Science, Kent, OH 44242-0001. Offers political science (MA, PhD), including American politics and policy, conflict analysis and management, transnational and comparative politics and policy; public administration (MPA). *Accreditation:* NASPAA. *Program availability:* Part-time, online learning. *Faculty:* 16 full-time (4 women), 3 part-time/adjunct (2 women). *Students:* 28 full-time (11 women), 58 part-time (36 women); includes 13 minority (8 Black or African American, non-Hispanic/Latino; 1 American Indian or Alaska Native, non-Hispanic/Latino; 3 Asian, non-Hispanic/Latino; 1 Hispanic/Latino), 9 international. Average age 35. 46 applicants, 83% accepted, 24 enrolled. In 2017, 34 master's, 4 doctorates awarded. *Degree requirements:* For master's, thesis optional; for doctorate, comprehensive exam, thesis/dissertation. *Entrance requirements:* For master's, GRE, goal statement, transcripts, writing sample, 3 letters of recommendation, minimum GPA of 3.0, resume; for doctorate, GRE, goal statement, transcripts, writing sample, 3 letters of recommendation, minimum GPA of 3.0. Additional exam requirements/recommendations for international students: Required—TOEFL (minimum score 550 paper-based, 79 iBT), Michigan English Language Assessment Battery (minimum score 77), IELTS (minimum score 6.5) or PTE (minimum score 58). *Application deadline:* For fall admission, 1/31 for domestic and international students. Applications are processed on a rolling basis. Application fee: $45 ($70 for international students). Electronic applications accepted. *Expenses:* Tuition, state resident: full-time $11,310; part-time $515 per credit hour. Tuition, nonresident: full-time $20,396; part-time $928 per credit hour. *International tuition:* $18,544 full-time. *Financial support:* Research assistantships with full tuition reimbursements, teaching assistantships with full tuition reimbursements, and unspecified assistantships available. Financial award application deadline: 1/31. *Unit head:* Dr. Andrew Barnes, Associate Professor and Chair, 330-672-2060, E-mail: abarnes3@kent.edu. *Application contact:* Julie Mazzei, Associate Professor and Graduate Coordinator, 330-672-8934, E-mail: jmazzei@kent.edu.
Website: http://www.kent.edu/polisci

Kentucky State University, College of Professional Studies, Frankfort, KY 40601. Offers nursing (DNP); public administration (MPA), including human resource management; special education (MA). *Program availability:* Part-time, evening/weekend, 100% online, blended/hybrid learning. *Faculty:* 9 full-time (7 women), 3 part-time/adjunct (all women). *Students:* 29 full-time (18 women), 29 part-time (24 women); includes 42 minority (40 Black or African American, non-Hispanic/Latino; 1 Asian, non-Hispanic/Latino; 1 Two or more races, non-Hispanic/Latino). Average age 35. 17 applicants, 53% accepted, 7 enrolled. In 2017, 11 master's, 4 doctorates awarded. *Degree requirements:* For master's, comprehensive exam, thesis optional; for doctorate, comprehensive exam, thesis/dissertation optional, 180 clinical hours. *Entrance requirements:* For master's, GMAT, GRE, transcript, essay, letters of recommendation; for doctorate, RN license; resume; graduate research and statistics courses (strongly recommended). Additional exam requirements/recommendations for international students: Required—TOEFL (minimum score 525 paper-based, 41 iBT) or IELTS (minimum score 4). *Application deadline:* For fall admission, 7/1 for domestic students, 4/1 for international students; for spring admission, 11/15 for domestic students, 8/15 for international students; for summer admission, 5/1 for domestic students, 2/1 for international students. Applications are processed on a rolling basis. Application fee: $30 ($100 for international students). Electronic applications accepted. *Expenses:* Contact institution. *Financial support:* In 2017–18, 54 students received support, including 1 research assistantship (averaging $1,350 per year); scholarships/grants, tuition waivers (partial), and unspecified assistantships also available. Financial award application deadline: 4/15; financial award applicants required to submit FAFSA. *Faculty research:* Risk assessment and failure modeling for the public sector implication of property rights on economic development, the social stability of communities, civil peace of nations. *Total annual research expenditures:* $414,831. *Unit head:* Dr. Kristen Broady, Assistant Vice President and Dean of Graduate Programs, 502-597-6386, E-mail: kristen.broady@kysu.edu. *Application contact:* Dr. James Obielodan, Director of Graduate Studies, 502-597-4723, E-mail: james.obielodan@kysu.edu.
Website: http://kysu.edu/academics/college-of-professional-studies/

Kutztown University of Pennsylvania, College of Liberal Arts and Sciences, Program in Public Administration, Kutztown, PA 19530-0730. Offers MPA. *Program availability:* Part-time, evening/weekend. *Faculty:* 4 full-time (2 women). *Students:* 12 full-time (8 women), 12 part-time (7 women); includes 7 minority (5 Black or African American, non-Hispanic/Latino; 1 Hispanic/Latino; 1 Two or more races, non-Hispanic/Latino). Average age 32. 21 applicants, 90% accepted, 9 enrolled. In 2017, 15 master's awarded. *Degree requirements:* For master's, comprehensive exam, thesis optional. *Entrance requirements:* For master's, GRE, GMAT, MAT, or LSAT, 3 letters of recommendation. Additional exam requirements/recommendations for international students: Required—TOEFL (minimum score 550 paper-based, 79 iBT), IELTS (minimum score 6.5), or PTE (minimum score 53). *Application deadline:* For fall admission, 8/1 for domestic and international students; for spring admission, 12/1 for domestic and international students. Application fee: $35. Electronic applications accepted. *Expenses:* Tuition, state resident: part-time $500 per credit. Tuition, nonresident: part-time $750 per credit. *Required fees:* $115 per credit. One-time fee: $50 part-time. Tuition and fees vary according to degree level. *Financial support:* Career-related internships or fieldwork, Federal Work-Study, and unspecified assistantships available. Financial award application deadline: 3/1; financial award applicants required to submit FAFSA. *Faculty research:* Structure of code enforcement offices in smaller developing communities. *Unit head:* Dr. Steve Lem, Department Chair, 610-683-4471, Fax: 610-683-4603, E-mail: lem@kutztown.edu. *Application contact:* Stacy Kushner, Academic Department Secretary, 610-683-4449, E-mail: kushner@kutztown.edu.
Website: https://www.kutztown.edu/academics/graduate-programs/public-administration.htm

Lamar University, College of Graduate Studies, College of Arts and Sciences, Department of Political Science, Beaumont, TX 77701. Offers public administration (MPA). *Program availability:* Part-time. *Faculty:* 8 full-time (3 women), 1 part-time/adjunct (0 women). *Students:* 10 part-time (6 women); includes 3 minority (all Black or African American, non-Hispanic/Latino), 1 international. Average age 28. 7 applicants, 100% accepted, 7 enrolled. In 2017, 3 master's awarded. *Entrance requirements:* For master's, GRE General Test. Additional exam requirements/recommendations for international students: Required—TOEFL (minimum score 550 paper-based; 79 iBT), IELTS (minimum score 6.5). *Application deadline:* For fall admission, 8/10 for domestic students, 7/1 for international students; for spring admission, 1/5 for domestic students, 12/1 for international students. Applications are processed on a rolling basis. Application fee: $25 ($50 for international students). Electronic applications accepted. *Expenses:* Contact institution. *Financial support:* Fellowships, research assistantships, teaching assistantships, career-related internships or fieldwork, Federal Work-Study, and institutionally sponsored loans available. Financial award application deadline: 4/1; financial award applicants required to submit FAFSA. *Faculty research:* Political activities of administrators, administrative response to Hurricane Rita, budgeting, environmental politics, urban planning. *Unit head:* Dr. Terri Davis, Chair, 409-880-8285, Fax: 409-880-8710. *Application contact:* Deidre Mayer, Interim Director, Admissions and Academic Services, 409-880-8888, Fax: 409-880-7419, E-mail: gradmissions@lamar.edu.
Website: http://artssciences.lamar.edu/political-science

Liberty University, Helms School of Government, Lynchburg, VA 24515. Offers criminal justice (MS), including forensic psychology, homeland security, public administration (MA, MS); international relations (MS); political science (MS); public administration (MPA), including business and government, healthcare, law and public policy, public and non-profit management; public policy (MA), including campaigns and elections, international affairs, Middle East affairs, public administration (MA, MS). *Program availability:* Part-time, online learning. *Students:* 287 full-time (148 women), 639 part-time (248 women); includes 231 minority (173 Black or African American, non-Hispanic/Latino; 4 American Indian or Alaska Native, non-Hispanic/Latino; 8 Asian, non-Hispanic/Latino; 20 Hispanic/Latino; 1 Native Hawaiian or other Pacific Islander, non-Hispanic/Latino; 25 Two or more races, non-Hispanic/Latino), 7 international. Average age 35. 876 applicants, 64% accepted, 277 enrolled. In 2017, 211 master's awarded. *Entrance requirements:* For master's, minimum undergraduate GPA of 3.0. Additional exam requirements/recommendations for international students: Required—TOEFL (minimum score 600 paper-based; 100 iBT). *Application deadline:* Applications are processed on a rolling basis. Application fee: $50. Electronic applications accepted. *Unit head:* Shawn D. Akers, Dean, 434-592-4986. *Application contact:* Jay Bridge, Director of Admissions, 800-424-9595, Fax: 800-628-7977, E-mail: gradadmissions@liberty.edu.

Liberty University, School of Business, Lynchburg, VA 24515. Offers accounting (MBA, MS), including audit and financial reporting (MS), business (MS), financial services (MS), forensic accounting (MS), leadership (MS), taxation (MS); criminal justice (MBA); cyber security (MS); executive leadership (MA); information systems (MS), including information assurance, technology management; international business (MBA, DBA); leadership (DBA); marketing (MBA, MS, DBA), including digital marketing and advertising (MS), project management (MS), public relations (MS), sports marketing and media (MS); project management (MBA, DBA); public administration (MBA); public relations (MBA). *Program availability:* Part-time, online learning. *Students:* 1,887 full-time (1,003 women), 4,223 part-time (1,950 women); includes 1,570 minority (1,133 Black or African American, non-Hispanic/Latino; 30 American Indian or Alaska Native, non-Hispanic/Latino; 118 Asian, non-Hispanic/Latino; 149 Hispanic/Latino; 13 Native Hawaiian or other Pacific Islander, non-Hispanic/Latino; 127 Two or more races, non-Hispanic/Latino), 109 international. Average age 35. 5,680 applicants, 51% accepted, 1510 enrolled. In 2017, 1,290 master's, 17 doctorates awarded. *Entrance requirements:* For master's, minimum undergraduate GPA of 3.0, 15 hours of upper-level business courses. Additional exam requirements/recommendations for international students: Required—TOEFL (minimum score 600 paper-based; 100 iBT). *Application deadline:* Applications are processed on a rolling basis. Application fee: $50. Electronic applications accepted. *Expenses:* Contact institution. *Financial support:* Applicants required to submit FAFSA. *Unit head:* Dr. Scott Hicks, Dean, 434-592-4808, Fax: 434-582-2366, E-mail: smhicks@liberty.edu. *Application contact:* Jay Bridge, Director of Graduate Admissions, 800-424-9595, Fax: 800-628-7977, E-mail: gradadmissions@liberty.edu.
Website: http://www.liberty.edu/academics/business/index.cfm?PID-149

Lincoln University, Graduate Studies, Jefferson City, MO 65101. Offers business administration (MBA), including accounting, management, management information systems, public administration/policy; elementary teaching (M Ed); environmental science (MS); guidance and counseling (M Ed), including community/agency counseling, elementary school, secondary school; higher education (MA); history (MA); integrated agricultural systems (MS); middle school (M Ed); natural sciences (MS); secondary teaching (M Ed); sociology (MA); sociology/criminal justice (MA). *Program availability:* Part-time, evening/weekend, 100% online, blended/hybrid learning. *Students:* 40 full-time (23 women), 64 part-time (32 women); includes 33 minority (30 Black or African American, non-Hispanic/Latino; 2 Hispanic/Latino; 1 Two or more races, non-Hispanic/Latino), 12 international. Average age 33. 48 applicants, 81% accepted, 22 enrolled. In 2017, 46 master's awarded. *Degree requirements:* For master's, comprehensive exam, thesis optional. *Entrance requirements:* For master's, GRE, MAT, or GMAT, minimum GPA of 2.75 overall, 3.0 in courses related to specialization; 3 letters of recommendation; minimum C average in English composition; personal statement of purpose. Additional exam requirements/recommendations for international students: Required—TOEFL (minimum score 500 paper-based; 61 iBT), IELTS (minimum score 5.5), Michigan English Language Assessment Battery (minimum score 80). *Application deadline:* For fall admission, 7/1 priority date for domestic students, 5/1 priority date for international students; for spring admission, 11/1 priority date for domestic students, 10/1 priority date for international students; for summer admission, 6/1 priority date for domestic students. Applications are processed on a rolling basis. Application fee: $30. Electronic applications accepted. *Expenses:* Tuition, state resident: part-time $291 per credit hour. Tuition, nonresident: part-time $541.50 per credit hour. *Financial support:* In 2017–18, 2 fellowships with tuition reimbursements, 3

research assistantships with tuition reimbursements were awarded; Federal Work-Study, scholarships/grants, and unspecified assistantships also available. Support available to part-time students. Financial award application deadline: 3/1; financial award applicants required to submit FAFSA. *Unit head:* Dr. Debra F. Greene, Interim Provost, 573-681-5247, Fax: 573-681-5106, E-mail: gradschool@lincolnu.edu. *Application contact:* Irasema Steck, Administrative Assistant, 573-681-5247, Fax: 573-681-5106, E-mail: gradschool@lincolnu.edu.
Website: http://www.lincolnu.edu/web/graduate-studies/graduate-studies

Lindenwood University, Graduate Programs, Plaster School of Business and Entrepreneurship, St. Charles, MO 63301-1695. Offers accountancy (M Acc); accounting (MBA); business administration (MBA); entrepreneurial studies (MBA); finance (MBA, MS); human resource management (MBA); international business (MBA); leadership (MA); management (MBA); marketing (MBA, MS); nonprofit administration (MA); public administration (MBA); sport management (MA); supply chain management (MBA). *Accreditation:* ACBSP. *Program availability:* Part-time, evening/weekend, 100% online. *Faculty:* 15 full-time (8 women), 26 part-time/adjunct (9 women). *Students:* 201 full-time (116 women), 253 part-time (153 women); includes 102 minority (80 Black or African American, non-Hispanic/Latino; 2 American Indian or Alaska Native, non-Hispanic/Latino; 6 Asian, non-Hispanic/Latino; 7 Hispanic/Latino; 7 Two or more races, non-Hispanic/Latino), 61 international. Average age 32. 370 applicants, 42% accepted, 134 enrolled. In 2017, 178 master's awarded. *Degree requirements:* For master's, comprehensive exam (for some programs), thesis (for some programs), minimum GPA of 3.0. *Entrance requirements:* For master's, interview, minimum undergraduate cumulative GPA of 3.0, letter of recommendation. Additional exam requirements/recommendations for international students: Required—TOEFL (minimum score 550 paper-based; 80 iBT); Recommended—IELTS (minimum score 6.5). *Application deadline:* For fall admission, 8/27 priority date for domestic and international students; for winter admission, 1/14 priority date for domestic and international students; for spring admission, 3/18 for domestic students, 3/18 priority date for international students; for summer admission, 6/3 priority date for domestic and international students. Applications are processed on a rolling basis. Application fee: $30 ($100 for international students). Electronic applications accepted. *Expenses:* Contact institution. *Financial support:* In 2017–18, 439 students received support. Career-related internships or fieldwork, Federal Work-Study, institutionally sponsored loans, scholarships/grants, tuition waivers (partial), and unspecified assistantships available. Financial award application deadline: 6/30; financial award applicants required to submit FAFSA. *Unit head:* Roger Ellis, Dean, School of Business and Entrepreneurship, 636-949-4839, E-mail: rellis@lindenwood.edu. *Application contact:* Kara Schilli, Director, Evening and Graduate Admissions, 636-949-4349, Fax: 636-949-4109, E-mail: adultadmissions@lindenwood.edu.
Website: http://www.lindenwood.edu/academics/academic-schools/robert-w-plaster-school-of-business-entrepreneurship/

Lipscomb University, School of Public Policy, Nashville, TN 37204-3951. Offers leadership and public service (MA). *Faculty:* 2 full-time (1 woman). *Students:* 12 full-time (9 women); includes 6 minority (all Black or African American, non-Hispanic/Latino). Average age 27. 33 applicants, 48% accepted, 12 enrolled. In 2017, 15 master's awarded. *Entrance requirements:* For master's, GRE or GMAT, references, resume, goals statement. Additional exam requirements/recommendations for international students: Required—TOEFL (minimum score 550 paper-based). *Application deadline:* Applications are processed on a rolling basis. Application fee: $50 ($75 for international students). Electronic applications accepted. *Expenses:* $1,290. *Faculty research:* African American family strengths and their relationship to health and mental health prevention and intervention, application of hope theories, systems theories and positive psychology principles in systems and organizations at multiples levels. *Unit head:* Dr. Kristine LaLonde, Academic Director, 615-966-6692, E-mail: kristine.lalonde@lipscomb.edu. *Application contact:* Amy Goode, New Student Enrollment Manager, 615-966-6691, E-mail: amy.goode@lipscomb.edu.

London Metropolitan University, Graduate Programs, London, United Kingdom. Offers applied psychology (M Sc); architecture (MA); biomedical science (M Sc); blood science (M Sc); cancer pharmacology (M Sc); computer networking and cyber security (M Sc); computing and information systems (M Sc); conference interpreting (MA); counter-terrorism studies (M Sc); creative, digital and professional writing (MA); crime, violence and prevention (M Sc); criminology (M Sc); curating contemporary art (MA); data analytics (M Sc); digital media (MA); early childhood studies (MA); education (MA, Ed D); financial services law, regulation and compliance (LL M); food science (M Sc); forensic psychology (M Sc); health and social care management and policy (M Sc); human nutrition (M Sc); human resource management (MA); human rights and international conflict (MA); information technology (M Sc); intelligence and security studies (M Sc); international oil, gas and energy law (LL M); international relations (MA); interpreting (MA); learning and teaching in higher education (MA); legal practice (LL M); media and entertainment law (LL M); organizational and consumer psychology (M Sc); psychological therapy (M Sc); psychology of mental health (M Sc); public health (M Sc); public policy and management (MPA); security studies (M Sc); social work (M Sc); spatial planning and urban design (MA); sports therapy (M Sc); supporting older children and young people with dyslexia (MA); teaching languages (MA), including Arabic, English; translation (MA); woman and child abuse (MA).

Long Island University–Hudson, Graduate School, Purchase, NY 10577. Offers autism (Advanced Certificate); bilingual education (Advanced Certificate); childhood education (MS Ed); crisis management (Advanced Certificate); early childhood education (MS Ed); educational leadership (MS Ed); health administration (MPA); literacy (MS Ed); marriage and family therapy (MS); mental health counseling (MS, Advanced Certificate), including credentialed alcoholism and substance abuse counselor (MS); middle childhood and adolescence education (MS Ed); pharmaceutics (MS), including cosmetic science, industrial pharmacy; public administration (MPA); school counseling (MS Ed, Advanced Certificate); school psychology (MS Ed); special education (MS Ed); TESOL (MS Ed); TESOL (all grades) (Advanced Certificate). *Program availability:* Part-time, evening/weekend. *Faculty:* 8 full-time (6 women), 41 part-time/adjunct (24 women). *Students:* 69 full-time (54 women), 249 part-time (200 women); includes 102 minority (29 Black or African American, non-Hispanic/Latino; 1 American Indian or Alaska Native, non-Hispanic/Latino; 9 Asian, non-Hispanic/Latino; 62 Hispanic/Latino; 1 Native Hawaiian or other Pacific Islander, non-Hispanic/Latino). Average age 33. 153 applicants, 96% accepted, 103 enrolled. In 2017, 138 master's, 36 other advanced degrees awarded. *Entrance requirements:* Additional exam requirements/recommendations for international students: Required—TOEFL. *Application deadline:* Applications are processed on a rolling basis. Application fee: $50. Electronic applications accepted. *Expenses:* Contact institution. *Financial support:* In 2017–18, 32 students received support. Scholarships/grants available. Support available to part-time students. Financial award application deadline: 2/15; financial award applicants required to submit FAFSA. *Unit head:* Dr. Sylvia Blake, Dean and Chief Operating Officer, 914-831-2700, E-mail: westchester@liu.edu. *Application contact:* Dr. Sylvia Blake, Dean and Chief Operating Officer, 914-831-2700, E-mail: westchester@liu.edu.

Long Island University–LIU Brooklyn, School of Business, Public Administration and Information Sciences, Brooklyn, NY 11201-8423. Offers accounting (MBA); accounting (MS); business administration (MBA); computer science (MS); gerontology (Advanced Certificate); health administration (MPA); human resources management (MS); not-for-profit management (Advanced Certificate); public administration (MPA); taxation (MS). *Program availability:* Part-time, evening/weekend. *Faculty:* 18 full-time (7 women), 28 part-time/adjunct (8 women). *Students:* 226 full-time (140 women), 232 part-time (150 women); includes 272 minority (192 Black or African American, non-Hispanic/Latino; 2 American Indian or Alaska Native, non-Hispanic/Latino; 35 Asian, non-Hispanic/Latino; 40 Hispanic/Latino; 3 Two or more races, non-Hispanic/Latino), 88 international. Average age 32. 495 applicants, 64% accepted, 149 enrolled. In 2017, 189 master's, 13 other advanced degrees awarded. *Entrance requirements:* Additional exam requirements/recommendations for international students: Required—TOEFL (minimum score 550 paper-based; 75 iBT). *Application deadline:* Applications are processed on a rolling basis. Application fee: $50. Electronic applications accepted. *Expenses: Tuition:* Full-time $21,618; part-time $1201 per credit. *Required fees:* $1840; $920 per term. Tuition and fees vary according to course load. *Financial support:* In 2017–18, 78 students received support. Career-related internships or fieldwork, Federal Work-Study, scholarships/grants, and unspecified assistantships available. Support available to part-time students. Financial award application deadline: 2/15; financial award applicants required to submit FAFSA. *Faculty research:* Tax policy; public sector budgeting and gender inequities; technology and innovation; game theory; knowledge management. *Unit head:* Dr. Edward Rogoff, Dean, 718-488-1159, E-mail: edward.rogoff@liu.edu. *Application contact:* Luis Santiago, Dean of Enrollment, 718-488-1011, Fax: 718-780-6110, E-mail: bkln-admissions@liu.edu.
Website: http://liu.edu/Brooklyn/Academics/School-of-Business-Public-Administration-and-Information-Sciences

Long Island University–LIU Post, School of Health Professions and Nursing, Brookville, NY 11548-1300. Offers biomedical science (MS); cardiovascular perfusion (MS); clinical lab sciences (MS); clinical laboratory management (MS); dietetic internship (Advanced Certificate); family nurse practitioner (MS, Advanced Certificate); forensic social work (Advanced Certificate); gerontology (Advanced Certificate); health administration (MPA); non-profit management (Advanced Certificate); nursing education (MS); nutrition (MS); public administration (MPA); social work (MSW). *Program availability:* Part-time, blended/hybrid learning. *Faculty:* 23 full-time (17 women), 33 part-time/adjunct (19 women). *Students:* 228 full-time (174 women), 227 part-time (185 women); includes 172 minority (76 Black or African American, non-Hispanic/Latino; 1 American Indian or Alaska Native, non-Hispanic/Latino; 44 Asian, non-Hispanic/Latino; 48 Hispanic/Latino; 3 Two or more races, non-Hispanic/Latino), 60 international. Average age 31. 392 applicants, 67% accepted, 138 enrolled. In 2017, 180 master's, 26 other advanced degrees awarded. *Degree requirements:* For master's, comprehensive exam (for some programs), thesis (for some programs). *Entrance requirements:* Additional exam requirements/recommendations for international students: Required—TOEFL (minimum score 85 iBT) or IELTS (7.5). *Application deadline:* Applications are processed on a rolling basis. Application fee: $50. Electronic applications accepted. *Expenses: Tuition:* Full-time $21,618; part-time $1201 per credit. *Required fees:* $1840; $920 per term. Tuition and fees vary according to course load. *Financial support:* In 2017–18, 102 students received support. Research assistantships, teaching assistantships, career-related internships or fieldwork, Federal Work-Study, scholarships/grants, and unspecified assistantships available. Support available to part-time students. Financial award application deadline: 2/15; financial award applicants required to submit FAFSA. *Faculty research:* Antibiotic resistance, evidence-based practice, family care, interprofessional learning, simulation learning. *Unit head:* Dr. Stacy Gropack, Dean, 516-299-2485, Fax: 516-299-2527, E-mail: post-shpn@liu.edu. *Application contact:* Kathy Riley, Associate Director of Graduate Admissions, 516-299-2900, Fax: 516-299-2137, E-mail: post-enroll@liu.edu.
Website: http://liu.edu/post/health

Louisiana State University and Agricultural & Mechanical College, Graduate School, E. J. Ourso College of Business, Public Administration Institute, Baton Rouge, LA 70803. Offers MPA, JD/MPA. *Accreditation:* NASPAA. *Faculty:* 7 full-time (3 women). *Students:* 31 full-time (20 women), 38 part-time (26 women); includes 32 minority (28 Black or African American, non-Hispanic/Latino; 2 Hispanic/Latino; 1 Native Hawaiian or other Pacific Islander, non-Hispanic/Latino; 1 Two or more races, non-Hispanic/Latino). Average age 29. 34 applicants, 100% accepted, 26 enrolled. In 2017, 29 master's awarded. *Financial support:* In 2017–18, 9 research assistantships (averaging $16,419 per year), 1 teaching assistantship (averaging $10,320 per year) were awarded. *Total annual research expenditures:* $29,327.

Louisiana State University and Agricultural & Mechanical College, Graduate School, Manship School of Mass Communication, Baton Rouge, LA 70803. Offers MMC, PhD, JD/MMC. *Accreditation:* ACEJMC. *Faculty:* 24 full-time (10 women). *Students:* 50 full-time (34 women), 9 part-time (5 women); includes 17 minority (16 Black or African American, non-Hispanic/Latino; 1 Two or more races, non-Hispanic/Latino), 9 international. Average age 27. 51 applicants, 65% accepted, 22 enrolled. In 2017, 16 master's, 6 doctorates awarded. *Financial support:* In 2017–18, 29 research assistantships (averaging $21,011 per year), 13 teaching assistantships (averaging $25,523 per year) were awarded. *Total annual research expenditures:* $93,684.

Marist College, Graduate Programs, School of Management, Program in Public Administration, Poughkeepsie, NY 12601-1387. Offers MPA. *Accreditation:* NASPAA. *Program availability:* Part-time, evening/weekend, online learning. *Entrance requirements:* For master's, GRE General Test, resume. Additional exam requirements/recommendations for international students: Required—TOEFL (minimum score 550 paper-based; 80 iBT); Recommended—IELTS (minimum score 6.5). Electronic applications accepted. *Faculty research:* Public policy analysis, health administration.

Marshall University, Academic Affairs Division, College of Liberal Arts, Department of Political Science, Huntington, WV 25755. Offers MA, MPA. *Students:* 19 full-time (12 women), 5 part-time (1 woman); includes 4 minority (1 Black or African American, non-Hispanic/Latino; 1 American Indian or Alaska Native, non-Hispanic/Latino; 2 Hispanic/Latino). Average age 27. In 2017, 8 master's awarded. *Degree requirements:* For master's, thesis optional. *Entrance requirements:* For master's, GRE General Test. Application fee: $40. *Unit head:* Dr. George Davis, Chair, 304-696-2766, Fax: 304-696-3245, E-mail: davg@marshall.edu. *Application contact:* Graduate Admissions, 304-746-1900, Fax: 304-746-1902, E-mail: services@marshall.edu.
Website: http://www.marshall.edu/polsci/

Marywood University, Academic Affairs, College of Health and Human Services, School of Social Work, Program in Public Administration, Scranton, PA 18509-1598. Offers MPA. *Program availability:* Part-time. Electronic applications accepted.

McMaster University, School of Graduate Studies, Faculty of Social Sciences, Department of Political Science, Hamilton, ON L8S 4M2, Canada. Offers international relations (PhD); political science (MA); public and the global economy (MA); public policy (PhD); public policy and administration (MA). MA program in public policy and administration offered jointly with University of Guelph. *Program availability:* Part-time. *Degree requirements:* For master's, thesis or alternative. *Entrance requirements:* For master's, minimum B+ average. Additional exam requirements/recommendations for

international students: Required—TOEFL (minimum score 580 paper-based). *Faculty research:* Organizational theory, internationalization of public policy, water resource policies, political interest intermediation, comparative politics.

Metropolitan College of New York, Program in Public Administration, New York, NY 10013. Offers emergency and disaster management (MPA); public affairs and administration (MPA). *Program availability:* Evening/weekend. *Students:* 102 full-time (70 women), 10 part-time (9 women); includes 99 minority (71 Black or African American, non-Hispanic/Latino; 1 Asian, non-Hispanic/Latino; 25 Hispanic/Latino; 2 Two or more races, non-Hispanic/Latino; 3 international. Average age 39. 122 applicants, 45% accepted, 52 enrolled. In 2017, 129 master's awarded. *Degree requirements:* For master's, thesis. *Entrance requirements:* For master's, appropriate work experience, interview, minimum GPA of 2.7, internship or job in administrative setting. Additional exam requirements/recommendations for international students: Required—TOEFL (minimum score 600 paper-based). *Application deadline:* For fall admission, 7/30 priority date for domestic students, 7/1 for international students; for winter admission, 11/30 priority date for domestic students, 11/1 for international students; for spring admission, 3/30 priority date for domestic students, 3/1 for international students. Applications are processed on a rolling basis. Application fee: $45. Electronic applications accepted. *Expenses:* $842 per credit, $395 fee per semester. *Financial support:* Fellowships with tuition reimbursements, career-related internships or fieldwork, scholarships/grants, and tuition waivers (partial) available. Financial award application deadline: 8/15; financial award applicants required to submit FAFSA. *Faculty research:* Transnational politics and culture, women and social policy, confidentiality in the human services, concepts of marginality, ethics in social policy. *Unit head:* Prof. Humphrey Crookendale, Dean, Graduate School for Public Affairs Administration, 212-343-1234 Ext. 2209, E-mail: hcrookendale@mcny.edu. *Application contact:* Steebo Varghese, Assistant Director of Admissions, 212-343-1234 Ext. 2708, Fax: 212-343-8474, E-mail: svarghese@mcny.edu.
Website: https://www.mcny.edu/academics/school-public-affairs-administration/

Mid-America Christian University, Program in Public Administration, Oklahoma City, OK 73170-4504. Offers MA. *Entrance requirements:* For master's, bachelor's degree from a regionally accredited college or university, minimum overall cumulative GPA of 2.75 of bachelor course work. Additional exam requirements/recommendations for international students: Required—TOEFL (minimum score 550 paper-based).

Middlebury Institute of International Studies at Monterey, Graduate School of International Policy and Management, Program in Public Administration, Monterey, CA 93940-2691. Offers MPA. *Degree requirements:* For master's, one foreign language. *Entrance requirements:* For master's, minimum GPA of 3.0, proficiency in a foreign language. Additional exam requirements/recommendations for international students: Required—TOEFL (minimum score 550 paper-based; 80 iBT). Electronic applications accepted.

Minnesota State University Mankato, College of Graduate Studies and Research, College of Social and Behavioral Sciences, Department of Government, Program in Public Administration, Mankato, MN 56001. Offers MPA. *Accreditation:* NASPAA. *Degree requirements:* For master's, one foreign language, comprehensive exam, thesis or alternative. *Entrance requirements:* For master's, minimum GPA of 3.0 during previous 2 years. Additional exam requirements/recommendations for international students: Required—TOEFL. Electronic applications accepted.

Mississippi State University, College of Arts and Sciences, Department of Political Science and Public Administration, Mississippi State, MS 39762. Offers political science (MA); public policy and administration (MPPA, PhD). *Accreditation:* NASPAA (one or more programs are accredited). *Program availability:* Evening/weekend, blended/hybrid learning. *Faculty:* 15 full-time (6 women). *Students:* 30 full-time (14 women), 31 part-time (18 women); includes 24 minority (21 Black or African American, non-Hispanic/Latino; 1 American Indian or Alaska Native, non-Hispanic/Latino; 2 Hispanic/Latino), 3 international. Average age 32. 54 applicants, 87% accepted, 33 enrolled. In 2017, 13 master's, 7 doctorates awarded. *Degree requirements:* For master's, thesis optional, comprehensive oral or written exam; for doctorate, thesis/dissertation, comprehensive oral and written exam. *Entrance requirements:* For master's, GRE, minimum GPA of 3.0 on the last two years of undergraduate courses or graduate work; for doctorate, GRE General Test, minimum graduate GPA of 3.35. Additional exam requirements/recommendations for international students: Required—TOEFL (minimum score 600 paper-based; 100 iBT); Recommended—IELTS (minimum score 7.5). *Application deadline:* For fall admission, 8/1 priority date for domestic students, 5/1 for international students; for spring admission, 12/1 priority date for domestic students, 9/1 for international students. Applications are processed on a rolling basis. Application fee: $60 ($80 for international students). Electronic applications accepted. *Expenses:* Tuition, state resident: full-time $8318; part-time $462.12 per credit hour. Tuition, nonresident: full-time $22,358; part-time $1242.12 per credit hour. *Required fees:* $110; $12.24 per credit hour. $6.12 per semester. *Financial support:* In 2017–18, 8 teaching assistantships with full tuition reimbursements (averaging $10,469 per year) were awarded; Federal Work-Study, institutionally sponsored loans, scholarships/grants, and unspecified assistantships also available. Financial award application deadline: 4/1; financial award applicants required to submit FAFSA. *Faculty research:* American politics, international relations, state and local government, comparative government, public administration. *Total annual research expenditures:* $811,000. *Unit head:* Dr. P. Edward French, Professor and Head, 662-325-2711, Fax: 662-325-2716, E-mail: efrench@pspa.msstate.edu. *Application contact:* Nathan Drake, Admissions and Enrollment Assistant, 662-325-3804, E-mail: ndrake@grad.msstate.edu.
Website: http://www.pspa.msstate.edu/

Missouri State University, Graduate College, College of Humanities and Public Affairs, Department of Political Science, Program in Public Administration, Springfield, MO 65897. Offers MPA. *Accreditation:* NASPAA. *Program availability:* Part-time. *Faculty:* 6 full-time (2 women). *Students:* 7 full-time (4 women), 9 part-time (5 women), 3 international. Average age 28. 10 applicants, 70% accepted, 6 enrolled. In 2017, 10 master's awarded. *Degree requirements:* For master's, comprehensive exam, thesis or alternative, internship. *Entrance requirements:* For master's, GRE, minimum GPA of 3.0. Additional exam requirements/recommendations for international students: Required—TOEFL (minimum score 550 paper-based; 79 iBT), IELTS (minimum score 6). *Application deadline:* For fall admission, 7/20 priority date for domestic students, 5/1 for international students; for spring admission, 12/20 priority date for domestic students, 9/1 for international students; for summer admission, 5/20 priority date for domestic students. Applications are processed on a rolling basis. Application fee: $35 ($50 for international students). Electronic applications accepted. *Expenses:* Tuition, state resident: full-time $2915; part-time $2021 per credit hour. Tuition, nonresident: full-time $5354; part-time $3647 per credit hour. *International tuition:* $11,992 full-time. *Required fees:* $173; $173 per credit hour. Tuition and fees vary according to class time, course level, course load, degree level, campus/location and program. *Financial support:* Career-related internships or fieldwork, Federal Work-Study, institutionally sponsored loans, scholarships/grants, and unspecified assistantships available. Support available to part-time students. Financial award application deadline: 3/31; financial award applicants required to submit FAFSA. *Faculty research:* Public management, environmental policy, health care policy, law and religion. *Unit head:* Dr. George Connor,

Department Head, 417-836-5630, Fax: 417-836-6655, E-mail: georgeconnor@missouristate.edu. *Application contact:* Stephanie Praschan, Director, Graduate Enrollment Management, 417-836-5330, Fax: 417-836-6200, E-mail: stephaniepraschan@missouristate.edu.
Website: http://polsci.missouristate.edu/mpa/

Missouri State University, Graduate College, Interdisciplinary Program in Professional Studies, Springfield, MO 65897. Offers administrative studies (Certificate); applied communication (MS); criminal justice (MS); environmental management (MS); homeland security (MS); individualized (MS); professional studies (MS); screenwriting and producing (MS); sports management (MS). *Program availability:* Part-time, evening/weekend, 100% online, blended/hybrid learning. *Students:* 51 full-time (33 women), 95 part-time (41 women); includes 21 minority (8 Black or African American, non-Hispanic/Latino; 1 Asian, non-Hispanic/Latino; 7 Hispanic/Latino; 5 Two or more races, non-Hispanic/Latino), 37 international. Average age 24. 71 applicants, 69% accepted, 35 enrolled. In 2017, 50 master's awarded. *Degree requirements:* For master's, comprehensive exam, thesis or alternative. *Entrance requirements:* For master's, GRE, GMAT (if GPA less than 3.0). Additional exam requirements/recommendations for international students: Required—TOEFL (minimum score 550 paper-based; 79 iBT), IELTS (minimum score 6). *Application deadline:* For fall admission, 7/15 priority date for domestic students; for spring admission, 12/1 priority date for domestic students; for summer admission, 5/1 for domestic students. Applications are processed on a rolling basis. Application fee: $35 ($50 for international students). Electronic applications accepted. *Expenses:* Tuition, state resident: full-time $2915; part-time $2021 per credit hour. Tuition, nonresident: full-time $5354; part-time $3647 per credit hour. *International tuition:* $11,992 full-time. *Required fees:* $173; $173 per credit hour. Tuition and fees vary according to class time, course level, course load, degree level, campus/location and program. *Financial support:* Career-related internships or fieldwork, Federal Work-Study, institutionally sponsored loans, scholarships/grants, and unspecified assistantships available. Support available to part-time students. Financial award application deadline: 3/31; financial award applicants required to submit FAFSA. *Unit head:* Dr. Gerald Masterson, Program Director, 417-836-5251, Fax: 417-836-6888, E-mail: mps@missouristate.edu. *Application contact:* Stephanie Praschan, Director, Graduate Enrollment Management, 417-836-5330, Fax: 417-836-6200, E-mail: stephaniepraschan@missouristate.edu.
Website: http://mps.missouristate.edu

Montana State University, The Graduate School, College of Letters and Science, Department of Political Science, Bozeman, MT 59717. Offers public administration (MPA). Program offered jointly with The University of Montana. *Program availability:* Part-time. *Degree requirements:* For master's, comprehensive exam, thesis (for some programs). *Entrance requirements:* For master's, GRE General Test. Additional exam requirements/recommendations for international students: Required—TOEFL (minimum score 550 paper-based). Electronic applications accepted. *Faculty research:* National resource policy, political economy of agriculture, qualitative methods, organizational theory.

Morehead State University, Graduate Programs, Institute for Regional Analysis and Public Policy, Morehead, KY 40351. Offers public administration (MPA). *Entrance requirements:* For master's, GRE. Additional exam requirements/recommendations for international students: Required—TOEFL (minimum score 500 paper-based). Electronic applications accepted.

National University, Academic Affairs, School of Professional Studies, La Jolla, CA 92037-1011. Offers criminal justice (MCJ); digital cinema production (MFA); digital journalism (MA); homeland security and emergency management (MS); juvenile justice (MS); professional screenwriting (MFA); public administration (MPA), including human resource management, organizational leadership. *Program availability:* Part-time, evening/weekend, 100% online, blended/hybrid learning. *Degree requirements:* For master's, thesis (for some programs). *Entrance requirements:* For master's, interview, minimum GPA of 2.5. Additional exam requirements/recommendations for international students: Required—TOEFL (minimum score 550 paper-based; 79 iBT), IELTS (minimum score 6). *Application deadline:* Applications are processed on a rolling basis. Application fee: $60 ($65 for international students). Electronic applications accepted. *Expenses:* Tuition: Part-time $430 per quarter hour. *Financial support:* Career-related internships or fieldwork, institutionally sponsored loans, scholarships/grants, and tuition waivers (partial) available. Support available to part-time students. Financial award application deadline: 6/30; financial award applicants required to submit FAFSA. *Unit head:* Dr. Daniel Donaldson, Dean, 858-642-8480, E-mail: sops@nu.edu. *Application contact:* Brandon Jouganatos, Vice President for Enrollment Services, 800-628-8648, E-mail: advisor@nu.edu.
Website: http://www.nu.edu/OurPrograms/School-of-Professional-Studies.html

New Charter University, College of Public Policy and Administration, Program in Public Administration, Salt Lake City, UT 84101. Offers MPA. *Program availability:* Part-time, evening/weekend, online learning. *Entrance requirements:* For master's, course work in calculus, statistics. Additional exam requirements/recommendations for international students: Required—TOEFL (minimum score 550 paper-based). Electronic applications accepted.

New Mexico State University, College of Arts and Sciences, Department of Government, Las Cruces, NM 88003. Offers government (MA); public administration (MPA). *Accreditation:* NASPAA (one or more programs are accredited). *Program availability:* Part-time. *Faculty:* 8 full-time (3 women), 1 (woman) part-time/adjunct. *Students:* 22 full-time (9 women), 13 part-time (7 women); includes 22 minority (3 Black or African American, non-Hispanic/Latino; 18 Hispanic/Latino; 1 Two or more races, non-Hispanic/Latino), 1 international. Average age 31. 25 applicants, 76% accepted, 14 enrolled. In 2017, 6 master's awarded. *Degree requirements:* For master's, comprehensive exam (for some programs), thesis optional. *Entrance requirements:* For master's, GRE (if GPA less than 3.0), writing sample, 3 letters of recommendation, resume. Additional exam requirements/recommendations for international students: Required—TOEFL (minimum score 550 paper-based; 79 iBT), IELTS (minimum score 6.5). *Application deadline:* For fall admission, 10/1 for domestic and international students; for spring admission, 3/1 for domestic and international students; for summer admission, 3/1 for domestic and international students. Application fee: $40 ($50 for international students). Electronic applications accepted. *Expenses:* Tuition, state resident: full-time $4390. Tuition, nonresident: full-time $15,309. *Required fees:* $853. *Financial support:* In 2017–18, 19 students received support, including 11 teaching assistantships (averaging $12,723 per year); career-related internships or fieldwork, Federal Work-Study, scholarships/grants, health care benefits, and unspecified assistantships also available. Support available to part-time students. Financial award application deadline: 3/1. *Faculty research:* U.S.-Mexico border studies, public administration and policy, international relations, Latin America, American politics and theory, Native American policy. *Total annual research expenditures:* $6,901. *Unit head:* Dr. Neil Harvey, Department Head, 575-646-4935, Fax: 575-646-2052, E-mail: nharvey@nmsu.edu. *Application contact:* Dr. Neil Harvey, Director of Master of Arts in Government Program, 575-646-4935, Fax: 575-646-2052, E-mail: nharvey@nmsu.edu.
Website: http://deptofgov.nmsu.edu

New York University, Wagner Graduate School of Public Service, Executive Master of Public Administration Program, New York, NY 10012. Offers global public policy and management (EMPA); MSW/EMPA. EMPA in global public policy and management offered jointly with University College London. *Accreditation:* AACSB. *Program availability:* Part-time. *Students:* Average age 38. 94 applicants, 74% accepted, 46 enrolled. In 2017, 45 master's awarded. *Entrance requirements:* Additional exam requirements/recommendations for international students: Required—TOEFL (minimum score 100 iBT), IELTS (minimum score 7.5), TWE. *Application deadline:* For fall admission, 5/1 for domestic and international students. Application fee: $85. Electronic applications accepted. *Expenses:* Contact institution. *Financial support:* In 2017–18, 5 students received support, including 10 fellowships with partial tuition reimbursements available (averaging $22,046 per year); scholarships/grants and health care benefits also available. Support available to part-time students. Financial award application deadline: 5/1; financial award applicants required to submit FAFSA. *Unit head:* David Elcott, Director, 212-992-9894, Fax: 212-995-4164, E-mail: david.elcott@nyu.edu. *Application contact:* Jay Esposito, Associate Director of Admissions, 212-998-7414, Fax: 212-995-4611, E-mail: wagner.admissions@nyu.edu.
Website: http://wagner.nyu.edu/executivempa/

New York University, Wagner Graduate School of Public Service, Program in Public Administration, New York, NY 10012. Offers public administration (PhD); public and nonprofit management and policy (MPA, Advanced Certificate), including financial management and public finance (MPA), international policy and management (MPA), management for public and nonprofit organizations, public policy analysis, social impact, innovation, and investment (MPA); JD/MPA; MBA/MPA; MPA/MA. *Accreditation:* NASPAA (one or more programs are accredited). *Program availability:* Part-time. *Students:* Average age 27. 951 applicants, 63% accepted, 238 enrolled. In 2017, 233 master's, 6 doctorates, 1 other advanced degree awarded. *Degree requirements:* For master's, thesis or alternative, capstone end event; for doctorate, one foreign language, comprehensive exam, thesis/dissertation, preliminary qualifying examination. *Entrance requirements:* Additional exam requirements/recommendations for international students: Required—TOEFL (minimum score 100 iBT), IELTS (minimum score 7.5), TWE. *Application deadline:* For fall admission, 1/5 for domestic and international students; for spring admission, 10/1 for domestic and international students. Application fee: $85. Electronic applications accepted. *Expenses:* Contact institution. *Financial support:* In 2017–18, 152 students received support, including 137 fellowships with full and partial tuition reimbursements available (averaging $16,683 per year), 2 research assistantships with full tuition reimbursements available (averaging $56,524 per year); career-related internships or fieldwork, Federal Work-Study, scholarships/grants, health care benefits, and unspecified assistantships also available. Support available to part-time students. Financial award application deadline: 1/5; financial award applicants required to submit FAFSA. *Unit head:* Prof. Katherine O'Regan, Associate Professor of Public Policy, 212-998-7498, E-mail: katherine.oregan@nyu.edu. *Application contact:* Sandra Oliveira, Admissions Officer, 212-998-7414, Fax: 212-995-4611, E-mail: wagner.admissions@nyu.edu.
Website: http://wagner.nyu.edu/

North Carolina Central University, College of Behavioral and Social Sciences, Department of Public Administration, Durham, NC 27707-3129. Offers MPA. *Program availability:* Part-time, evening/weekend. *Degree requirements:* For master's, one foreign language, comprehensive exam, thesis or alternative. *Entrance requirements:* For master's, GRE, minimum GPA of 3.0 in major, 2.5 overall. Additional exam requirements/recommendations for international students: Required—TOEFL. *Application deadline:* For fall admission, 8/1 for domestic students. Application fee: $30. *Expenses:* Tuition, state resident: full-time $2770; part-time $692.50 per credit hour. Tuition, nonresident: full-time $9247; part-time $2311.75 per credit hour. *Financial support:* Application deadline: 5/1; applicants required to submit FAFSA. *Unit head:* Christopher M. Kimaru, Director, 919-530-7264, E-mail: ckimaru@nccu.edu. *Application contact:* Christopher M. Kimaru, Director, 919-530-7264, E-mail: ckimaru@nccu.edu.

North Carolina State University, Graduate School, College of Humanities and Social Sciences, School of Public and International Affairs, Program in Public Administration, Raleigh, NC 27695. Offers MPA, PhD. *Accreditation:* NASPAA. *Degree requirements:* For master's, thesis optional; for doctorate, thesis/dissertation. *Entrance requirements:* For master's, GRE General Test, minimum GPA of 3.0 during previous 2 years; for doctorate, GRE General Test. Electronic applications accepted. *Faculty research:* Public budgeting, human resources, public information technology, nonprofit management, environmental policy.

Northeastern University, College of Social Sciences and Humanities, Boston, MA 02115. Offers criminology and criminal justice (MSCJ); criminology and justice policy (PhD); economics (MA, PhD); English (MA, PhD); international affairs (MA); law and public policy (PhD); political science (MA, PhD); public administration (MPA); public policy (MPP); security and resilience studies (MS); sociology (MA, PhD); urban and regional policy (MS); urban informatics (MS); world history (MA, PhD). *Program availability:* Online learning. *Faculty:* 242. *Students:* 491. In 2017, 143 master's, 38 doctorates awarded. *Degree requirements:* For doctorate, variable foreign language requirement, comprehensive exam, thesis/dissertation. *Entrance requirements:* For master's and doctorate, GRE. Additional exam requirements/recommendations for international students: Required—TOEFL, IELTS. Application fee: $75. Electronic applications accepted. *Expenses:* Contact institution. *Financial support:* Teaching assistantships, career-related internships or fieldwork, scholarships/grants, health care benefits, tuition waivers (full and partial), and unspecified assistantships available. Support available to part-time students. Financial award applicants required to submit FAFSA. *Unit head:* Dr. Uta Poiger, Dean, 617-373-5173, E-mail: college_of_social_sciences_and_humanities@neu.edu. *Application contact:* 617-373-5990, E-mail: gradcssh@northeastern.edu.
Website: http://www.northeastern.edu/cssh/

Northern Arizona University, College of Social and Behavioral Sciences, Department of Politics and International Affairs, Flagstaff, AZ 86011. Offers political science (MA, PhD, Graduate Certificate); public administration (MPA); public management (Graduate Certificate). *Program availability:* Part-time, 100% online, blended/hybrid learning. *Faculty:* 20 full-time (6 women), 1 (woman) part-time/adjunct. *Students:* 26 full-time (15 women), 18 part-time (10 women); includes 15 minority (1 Black or African American, non-Hispanic/Latino; 6 American Indian or Alaska Native, non-Hispanic/Latino; 2 Asian, non-Hispanic/Latino; 4 Hispanic/Latino; 2 Two or more races, non-Hispanic/Latino), 8 international. Average age 33. 36 applicants, 69% accepted, 23 enrolled. In 2017, 10 master's, 5 doctorates, 1 other advanced degree awarded. *Degree requirements:* For master's, variable foreign language requirement, comprehensive exam (for some programs), thesis (for some programs); for doctorate, variable foreign language requirement, comprehensive exam (for some programs), thesis/dissertation (for some programs); for Graduate Certificate, comprehensive exam (for some programs). *Entrance requirements:* For master's and doctorate, GRE General Test. Additional exam requirements/recommendations for international students: Required—TOEFL (minimum score 93 iBT), IELTS (minimum score 6.5). *Application deadline:* For fall admission, 2/1 for domestic and international students; for spring admission, 10/1 for domestic and international students. Applications are processed on a rolling basis. Application fee: $65. Electronic applications accepted. *Expenses:* Tuition, state resident: full-time $9240; part-time $458 per credit hour. Tuition, nonresident: full-time $21,588; part-time $1199 per credit hour. *Required fees:* $1021; $14 per credit hour. $646 per semester. Tuition and fees vary according to course load, campus/location and program. *Financial support:* In 2017–18, 12 students received support, including 12 teaching assistantships with full and partial tuition reimbursements available (averaging $13,500 per year); institutionally sponsored loans, health care benefits, tuition waivers (full and partial), and unspecified assistantships also available. Financial award application deadline: 2/1; financial award applicants required to submit FAFSA. *Unit head:* Dr. Lori Poloni-Staudinger, Chair, 928-523-6546, Fax: 928-523-6777, E-mail: lori.poloni-staudinger@nau.edu. *Application contact:* Pamela Ruth Bowen, Administrative Associate, 928-523-6544, Fax: 928-523-6777, E-mail: political.science@nau.edu.
Website: http://www.nau.edu/SBS/Politics

Northern Illinois University, Graduate School, College of Liberal Arts and Sciences, Department of Public Administration, De Kalb, IL 60115-2854. Offers MPA. *Accreditation:* NASPAA. *Program availability:* Part-time, evening/weekend. *Faculty:* 5 full-time (1 woman), 3 part-time/adjunct (1 woman). *Students:* 39 full-time (14 women), 40 part-time (18 women); includes 18 minority (4 Black or African American, non-Hispanic/Latino; 1 Asian, non-Hispanic/Latino; 12 Hispanic/Latino; 1 Two or more races, non-Hispanic/Latino), 3 international. Average age 31. 55 applicants, 62% accepted, 19 enrolled. In 2017, 44 master's awarded. *Degree requirements:* For master's, comprehensive exam, internship, research paper. *Entrance requirements:* For master's, GRE General Test, minimum GPA of 2.75, 9 hours in social science. Additional exam requirements/recommendations for international students: Required—TOEFL (minimum score 550 paper-based). *Application deadline:* For fall admission, 3/1 priority date for domestic students, 5/1 for international students; for spring admission, 10/1 priority date for domestic students, 10/1 for international students. Applications are processed on a rolling basis. Application fee: $40. Electronic applications accepted. *Financial support:* In 2017–18, 22 research assistantships with full tuition reimbursements, 2 teaching assistantships were awarded; fellowships with full tuition reimbursements, career-related internships or fieldwork, Federal Work-Study, scholarships/grants, tuition waivers (full), and unspecified assistantships also available. Support available to part-time students. Financial award applicants required to submit FAFSA. *Faculty research:* Urban service and management, manpower public policy, performance appraisal, bureaucratic politics. *Unit head:* Dr. Kurt Thurmaier, Chair, 815-753-0311, Fax: 815-753-2539, E-mail: kthur@niu.edu. *Application contact:* Graduate School Office, 815-753-0395, E-mail: gradsch@niu.edu.
Website: http://www.niu.edu/pub_ad/

Northern Kentucky University, Office of Graduate Programs, College of Arts and Sciences, Program in Public Administration, Highland Heights, KY 41099. Offers non-profit management (Certificate); public administration (MPA). *Accreditation:* NASPAA. *Program availability:* Part-time. *Degree requirements:* For master's, 39 semester hours, including completion of the capstone course. *Entrance requirements:* For master's, GRE, minimum GPA of 2.5, letters of references, portfolios; for Certificate, minimum GPA of 2.0. Additional exam requirements/recommendations for international students: Required—TOEFL (minimum score 79 iBT); Recommended—IELTS (minimum score 6.5). Electronic applications accepted. *Faculty research:* Nonprofit management, human resource management, urban planning, service-learning, homeland security.

Northwestern University, School of Professional Studies, Program in Public Policy and Administration, Evanston, IL 60208. Offers global policy (MA); health services policy (MA); public administration (MA); public policy (MA). *Program availability:* Part-time, evening/weekend, online learning.
Website: https://sps.northwestern.edu/masters/public-policy/index.php

Norwich University, College of Graduate and Continuing Studies, Master of Public Administration Program, Northfield, VT 05663. Offers criminal justice and public safety (MPA); fiscal management (MPA); international development and influence (MPA); municipal governance (MPA); nonprofit management (MPA); policy analysis and analytics (MPA); public administration leadership and crisis management (MPA); public works and sustainability (MPA). *Program availability:* Evening/weekend, online only, mostly all online with a week-long residency requirement. *Degree requirements:* For master's, capstone. *Entrance requirements:* For master's, minimum undergraduate GPA of 2.75. Additional exam requirements/recommendations for international students: Required—TOEFL (minimum score 550 paper-based; 80 iBT), IELTS (minimum score 6.5). Electronic applications accepted. *Expenses:* Contact institution.

Notre Dame de Namur University, Division of Academic Affairs, School of Business and Management, Program in Public Administration, Belmont, CA 94002-1908. Offers human resource management (MPA); public affairs administration (MPA). *Program availability:* Part-time, evening/weekend, online learning. *Students:* 2 full-time (1 woman), 32 part-time (29 women). Average age 35. *Entrance requirements:* For master's, interview, minimum GPA of 2.5. Additional exam requirements/recommendations for international students: Required—TOEFL (minimum score 550 paper-based; 79 iBT). *Application deadline:* For fall admission, 8/1 priority date for domestic students; for spring admission, 12/1 priority date for domestic students. Applications are processed on a rolling basis. Application fee: $60. Electronic applications accepted. *Expenses: Tuition:* Full-time $16,128; part-time $8064 per credit hour. *Required fees:* $80; $80 per credit hour. $40 per semester. *Financial support:* Available to part-time students. Applicants required to submit FAFSA. *Unit head:* Jordan Holtzman, Program Director, Graduate Business Programs, 510-375-1348, E-mail: jholtzman@ndnu.edu.
Website: http://www.ndnu.edu/academics/schools-programs/school-business/graduate/mpa.aspx

Nova Southeastern University, H. Wayne Huizenga College of Business and Entrepreneurship, Fort Lauderdale, FL 33314-7796. Offers accounting (M Acc); business (MBA); business intelligence/analytics (MBA); complex health systems (MBA); enterprise informatics (MBA); entrepreneurship (MBA); finance (MBA); human resource management (MBA); international business (MBA); management (MBA); marketing (MBA); process improvement (MBA); public administration (MPA); real estate development (MS); sport revenue generation (MBA); supply chain management (MBA). *Accreditation:* NASPAA. *Program availability:* Part-time, evening/weekend, 100% online, blended/hybrid learning. *Faculty:* 85 full-time (37 women), 59 part-time/adjunct (19 women). *Students:* 1,999 full-time (1,225 women), 335 part-time (210 women); includes 1,516 minority (597 Black or African American, non-Hispanic/Latino; 4 American Indian or Alaska Native, non-Hispanic/Latino; 92 Asian, non-Hispanic/Latino; 789 Hispanic/Latino; 3 Native Hawaiian or other Pacific Islander, non-Hispanic/Latino; 31 Two or more races, non-Hispanic/Latino), 291 international. Average age 34. 1,269 applicants, 59% accepted, 551 enrolled. In 2017, 1,055 master's awarded. *Entrance requirements:* For master's, GMAT or GRE (depending on undergraduate GPA), official transcripts from all schools attended while in pursuit of bachelor's degree; minimum GPA of 2.5 from regionally-accredited institution. Additional exam requirements/recommendations for international students: Required—TOEFL (minimum score 550 paper-based; 79 iBT), IELTS (minimum score 6), PTE (minimum score 54). *Application deadline:* For fall admission, 8/5 priority date for domestic students, 7/29 priority date for international students; for winter admission, 12/16 priority date for domestic students, 12/9 priority

date for international students; for summer admission, 4/21 priority date for domestic and international students. Applications are processed on a rolling basis. Application fee: $50. Electronic applications accepted. *Expenses:* $37,785 (online), $35,640 (in-classroom). *Financial support:* In 2017–18, 325 students received support. Federal Work-Study and scholarships/grants available. Support available to part-time students. Financial award application deadline: 4/15; financial award applicants required to submit FAFSA. *Faculty research:* Entrepreneurship and venture capital, ethics and social responsibility, global commerce and cultures, business process management. *Unit head:* Dr. J. Preston Jones, Dean, 954-262-5127, E-mail: prestonj@nova.edu. *Application contact:* Zeida Rodriguez, Associate Director of Enrollment Services, 954-262-5163, Fax: 954-262-3822, E-mail: zeida@nova.edu.
Website: http://www.huizenga.nova.edu

Oakland University, Graduate Study and Lifelong Learning, College of Arts and Sciences, Department of Political Science, Rochester, MI 48309-4401. Offers local government management (Graduate Certificate); non-profit and organizational management (PMC); public administration (MPA). *Accreditation:* NASPAA. *Program availability:* Part-time, evening/weekend. *Entrance requirements:* For master's, minimum GPA of 3.0. Additional exam requirements/recommendations for international students: Required—TOEFL (minimum score 550 paper-based). Electronic applications accepted. *Expenses:* Tuition, state resident: full-time $16,950; part-time $706.25 per credit. Tuition, nonresident: full-time $24,648; part-time $1027 per credit.

The Ohio State University, Graduate School, John Glenn College of Public Affairs, Columbus, OH 43210. Offers public administration (MA, MPA); public policy and management (PhD). *Accreditation:* NASPAA (one or more programs are accredited). *Program availability:* Part-time. *Faculty:* 21. *Students:* 136 full-time (71 women), 37 part-time (25 women). Average age 30. In 2017, 77 master's, 4 doctorates awarded. *Degree requirements:* For doctorate, thesis/dissertation. *Entrance requirements:* For master's, GRE General Test (for MPA), minimum GPA of 3.0 (for MA); for doctorate, GRE General Test. Additional exam requirements/recommendations for international students: Required—TOEFL (minimum score 600 paper-based; 100 iBT); Recommended—IELTS (minimum score 7.5). *Application deadline:* For fall admission, 12/1 priority date for domestic students, 11/30 priority date for international students; for spring admission, 11/15 for domestic and international students; for summer admission, 4/1 for domestic and international students. Applications are processed on a rolling basis. Application fee: $60 ($70 for international students). Electronic applications accepted. *Financial support:* Fellowships, research assistantships, teaching assistantships, Federal Work-Study, institutionally sponsored loans, and unspecified assistantships available. Support available to part-time students. *Unit head:* Dr. Trevor Brown, Dean, 614-292-4533, Fax: 614-292-4868, E-mail: brown.2296@osu.edu. *Application contact:* Graduate and Professional Admissions, 614-292-6031, Fax: 614-292-3656, E-mail: gpadmissions@osu.edu.
Website: http://glenn.osu.edu/

Ohio University, Graduate College, Voinovich School of Leadership and Public Affairs, Athens, OH 45701-2979. Offers environmental studies (MS, Certificate); public administration (MPA). Electronic applications accepted.

Old Dominion University, Strome College of Business, Master of Public Administration Program, Norfolk, VA 23529. Offers multi-sector public service (MPA); public administration (MPA). *Accreditation:* NASPAA. *Program availability:* Part-time, evening/weekend, 100% online, blended/hybrid learning. *Faculty:* 9 full-time (3 women), 4 part-time/adjunct (1 woman). *Students:* 32 full-time (17 women), 100 part-time (54 women); includes 53 minority (39 Black or African American, non-Hispanic/Latino; 1 Asian, non-Hispanic/Latino; 3 Hispanic/Latino; 10 Two or more races, non-Hispanic/Latino). Average age 35. 66 applicants, 58% accepted, 35 enrolled. In 2017, 60 master's awarded. *Degree requirements:* For master's, capstone seminar. *Entrance requirements:* For master's, GRE (waived for work experience or undergraduate GPA greater than or equal to 3.5). Additional exam requirements/recommendations for international students: Required—TOEFL (minimum score 550 paper-based; 79 iBT), IELTS (minimum score 6.5). *Application deadline:* For fall admission, 7/15 for domestic and international students; for spring admission, 11/15 for domestic and international students. Applications are processed on a rolling basis. Application fee: $50. Electronic applications accepted. *Expenses:* Contact institution. *Financial support:* In 2017–18, 5 students received support, including 5 research assistantships (averaging $10,000 per year); unspecified assistantships also available. Financial award application deadline: 4/15; financial award applicants required to submit FAFSA. *Faculty research:* Environment and resilience, policy analysis, non-profit management, transportation policy, public budgeting. *Unit head:* Dr. David W. Chapman, Graduate Program Director, 757-683-7053, E-mail: mpa@odu.edu. *Application contact:* Megan S. Jones, Graduate Program Manager, 757-683-3961, E-mail: mmjones@odu.edu.
Website: http://www.odu.edu/mpa

Pace University, Dyson College of Arts and Sciences, Department of Public Administration, New York, NY 10038. Offers government management (MPA); health care administration (MPA); not-for-profit management (MPA); JD/MPA. *Program availability:* Part-time, evening/weekend. *Faculty:* 6 full-time (4 women), 4 part-time/adjunct (1 woman). *Students:* 34 full-time (18 women), 66 part-time (45 women); includes 59 minority (38 Black or African American, non-Hispanic/Latino; 9 Asian, non-Hispanic/Latino; 11 Hispanic/Latino; 1 Two or more races, non-Hispanic/Latino), 8 international. Average age 31. In 2017, 53 master's awarded. *Degree requirements:* For master's, comprehensive exam, thesis (for some programs), capstone project. *Entrance requirements:* For master's, 2 letters of recommendation, resume, personal statement, official transcripts, essay. Additional exam requirements/recommendations for international students: Required—TOEFL (minimum score 88 iBT), IELTS (minimum score 7) or PTE (minimum score 60). *Application deadline:* For fall admission, 8/1 priority date for domestic students, 6/1 for international students; for spring admission, 12/1 priority date for domestic students, 10/1 for international students. Applications are processed on a rolling basis. Application fee: $70. Electronic applications accepted. *Financial support:* Research assistantships, career-related internships or fieldwork, Federal Work-Study, and tuition waivers (partial) available. Support available to part-time students. Financial award application deadline: 2/15; financial award applicants required to submit FAFSA. *Unit head:* Dr. Hillary Knepper, Chairperson, 914-773-3140, E-mail: hknepper@pace.edu. *Application contact:* Susan Ford-Goldschein, Director of Admissions, 914-422-4283, Fax: 212-346-1585, E-mail: graduateadmission@pace.edu.
Website: http://www.pace.edu/dyson/academic-departments-and-programs/public-admin

Park University, School of Graduate and Professional Studies, Kansas City, MO 54105. Offers adult education (M Ed); business and government leadership (Graduate Certificate); business, government, and global society (MPA); communication and leadership (MA); creative and life writing (Graduate Certificate); disaster and emergency management (MPA, Graduate Certificate); educational leadership (M Ed); finance (MBA, Graduate Certificate); general business (MBA); global business (Graduate Certificate); healthcare administration (MHA); healthcare services management and leadership (Graduate Certificate); international business (MBA); language and literacy (M Ed), including English for speakers of other languages, special reading teacher/literacy coach; leadership of international healthcare organizations (Graduate Certificate); management information systems (MBA, Graduate Certificate); music performance (ADP, Graduate Certificate), including cello (MM, ADP), piano (MM, ADP), viola (MM, ADP), violin (MM, ADP); nonprofit and community services management (MPA); nonprofit leadership (Graduate Certificate); performance (MM), including cello (MM, ADP), piano (MM, ADP), viola (MM, ADP), violin (MM, ADP); public management (MPA); social work (MSW); teacher leadership (M Ed), including curriculum and assessment, instructional leader. *Program availability:* Part-time, evening/weekend, online learning. *Degree requirements:* For master's, comprehensive exam (for some programs), thesis (for some programs), internship (for some programs); exam (for some programs). *Entrance requirements:* For master's, GRE or GMAT (for some programs), teacher certification (for some M Ed programs), letters of recommendation, essay, resume (for some programs). Additional exam requirements/recommendations for international students: Required—TOEFL (minimum score 550 paper-based; 79 iBT), IELTS (minimum score 6). Electronic applications accepted.

Penn State Harrisburg, Graduate School, School of Public Affairs, Middletown, PA 17057. Offers criminal justice (MA); health administration (MHA); health administration: long term care (Certificate); homeland security (MPS, Certificate); public administration (MPA, PhD); public administration: non-profit administration (Certificate); public budgeting and financial management (Certificate); public sector human resource management (Certificate). *Accreditation:* NASPAA. *Unit head:* Dr. Mukund S. Kulkarni, Chancellor, 717-948-6105, Fax: 717-948-6452. *Application contact:* Robert W. Coffman, Jr., Director of Enrollment Management, Recruitment and Admissions, 717-948-6250, Fax: 717-948-6325, E-mail: hbgadmit@psu.edu.
Website: https://harrisburg.psu.edu/public-affairs

Pontifical Catholic University of Puerto Rico, College of Graduate Studies in Behavioral Science and Community Affairs, Program in Public Administration, Ponce, PR 00717-0777. Offers MSS. *Program availability:* Part-time, evening/weekend. *Degree requirements:* For master's, thesis. *Entrance requirements:* For master's, EXADEP, 3 letters of recommendation, interview, minimum GPA of 2.75.

Portland State University, Graduate Studies, College of Urban and Public Affairs, Hatfield School of Government, Division of Public Administration, Portland, OR 97207-0751. Offers collaborative governance (Certificate); energy policy and management (Certificate); global management and leadership (MPA); health administration (MPA); human resource management (MPA); local government (MPA); natural resource policy and administration (MPA); nonprofit and public management (Certificate); nonprofit management (MPA); public administration (EMPA); public affairs and policy (PhD); sustainable food systems (Certificate). *Accreditation:* NASPAA (one or more programs are accredited). *Program availability:* Part-time, evening/weekend. *Faculty:* 15 full-time (6 women), 6 part-time/adjunct (4 women). *Students:* 84 full-time (54 women), 109 part-time (75 women); includes 40 minority (8 Black or African American, non-Hispanic/Latino; 5 American Indian or Alaska Native, non-Hispanic/Latino; 8 Asian, non-Hispanic/Latino; 12 Hispanic/Latino; 1 Native Hawaiian or other Pacific Islander, non-Hispanic/Latino; 6 Two or more races, non-Hispanic/Latino), 14 international. Average age 35. 118 applicants, 84% accepted, 56 enrolled. In 2017, 60 master's, 1 doctorate awarded. *Degree requirements:* For master's, integrative field experience (MPA), practicum (MPH); for doctorate, comprehensive exam, thesis/dissertation. *Entrance requirements:* For master's, GRE (minimum scores: verbal 150, quantitative 149, and analytic writing 4.5), minimum GPA of 3.0, 3 recommendation letters, resume, 500-word statement of intent; for doctorate, GRE, 3 recommendation letters, resume, 500-word personal essay. Additional exam requirements/recommendations for international students: Required—TOEFL (minimum score 550 paper-based; 80 iBT), IELTS (minimum score 7). *Application deadline:* For fall admission, 4/1 for domestic students, 3/1 for international students; for winter admission, 9/1 for domestic students, 8/1 for international students; for spring admission, 11/1 for domestic and international students. Application fee: $65. *Expenses:* Tuition, state resident: full-time $14,436; part-time $401 per credit. Tuition, nonresident: full-time $21,780; part-time $605 per credit. *Required fees:* $1380; $22 per credit. $119 per quarter. One-time fee: $325. Tuition and fees vary according to program. *Financial support:* In 2017–18, 39 students received support, including 5 research assistantships with full and partial tuition reimbursements available (averaging $8,341 per year), 4 teaching assistantships (averaging $5,292 per year); career-related internships or fieldwork, Federal Work-Study, scholarships/grants, and unspecified assistantships also available. Support available to part-time students. Financial award application deadline: 3/1; financial award applicants required to submit FAFSA. *Faculty research:* Public budgeting, program evaluation, nonprofit management, natural resources policy and administration. *Total annual research expenditures:* $679,077. *Unit head:* Dr. Masami Nishishiba, Chair, 503-725-5151, E-mail: nishism@pdx.edu. *Application contact:* Megan Heljeson, Office Coordinator, 503-725-3921, Fax: 503-725-8250, E-mail: publicad@pdx.edu.
Website: https://www.pdx.edu/hatfieldschool/public-administration

Post University, Program in Public Administration, Waterbury, CT 06723-2540. Offers emergency management and homeland security (MPA). *Program availability:* Online learning. *Degree requirements:* For master's, capstone project. *Entrance requirements:* For master's, resume. *Expenses: Tuition:* Part-time $730 per credit hour. Part-time tuition and fees vary according to degree level and program. *Application contact:* Veronica Montalvo, Vice President, Online Education Enrollment Management and Admissions, 203-596-6164, E-mail: vmontalvo@post.edu.
Website: https://post.edu/academics/online-master-of-public-administration

Regent University, Graduate School, Robertson School of Government, Virginia Beach, VA 23464. Offers government (MA), including American government, healthcare policy and ethics (MA, MPA), international relations, law and public policy, national security studies, political communication, political theory, religion and politics; national security studies (MA), including cybersecurity, homeland security, international security, Middle East politics; public administration (MPA), including emergency management and homeland security, federal government, general public administration, healthcare policy and ethics (MA, MPA), law, nonprofit administration and faith-based organizations, public leadership and management, servant leadership. *Program availability:* Part-time, evening/weekend, 100% online, blended/hybrid learning. *Faculty:* 8 full-time (1 woman), 20 part-time/adjunct (3 women). *Students:* 39 full-time (23 women), 137 part-time (78 women); includes 83 minority (49 Black or African American, non-Hispanic/Latino; 1 American Indian or Alaska Native, non-Hispanic/Latino; 7 Asian, non-Hispanic/Latino; 15 Hispanic/Latino; 11 Two or more races, non-Hispanic/Latino). Average age 35. 345 applicants, 31% accepted, 57 enrolled. In 2017, 38 master's awarded. *Degree requirements:* For master's, thesis optional, internship. *Entrance requirements:* For master's, GRE General Test or LSAT, personal essay, writing sample, resume, college transcripts. Additional exam requirements/recommendations for international students: Required—TOEFL (minimum score 577 paper-based). *Application deadline:* For fall admission, 5/1 priority date for domestic students; for spring admission, 11/1 priority date for domestic students. Applications are processed on a rolling basis. Application fee: $50. Electronic applications accepted. *Expenses:* $650 per credit; $300 technology fee per semester. *Financial support:* In 2017–18, 116 students received support. Career-related internships or fieldwork, scholarships/grants, and unspecified assistantships available. Support available to part-time students. *Faculty research:* International relations and politics, public administration, leadership

and ethics, Biblical law, Constitutional law and Supreme Court. *Unit head:* Dr. Eric Patterson, Dean, 757-352-4616, Fax: 757-352-4735, E-mail: epatterson@regent.edu. *Application contact:* Heidi Cece, Assistant Vice President of Enrollment Management, 800-373-5504, Fax: 757-352-4381, E-mail: admissions@regent.edu. Website: https://www.regent.edu/robertson-school-of-government/

Reinhardt University, Program in Public Administration, Waleska, GA 30183-2981. Offers MPA.

Rhode Island College, School of Graduate Studies, Faculty of Arts and Sciences, Department of Political Science, Providence, RI 02908-1991. Offers public administration (MPA). *Program availability:* Part-time, evening/weekend. *Faculty:* 4 full-time (1 woman). *Entrance requirements:* For master's, GRE, GMAT, or MAT. Additional exam requirements/recommendations for international students: Recommended—TOEFL (minimum score 550 paper-based; 79 iBT). *Application deadline:* For fall admission, 3/1 for domestic students; for spring admission, 11/1 for domestic students. Applications are processed on a rolling basis. Application fee: $50. *Expenses:* Tuition, state resident: full-time $9768; part-time $407 per credit. Tuition, nonresident: full-time $19,008; part-time $792 per credit. *Required fees:* $696; $29 per credit. One-time fee: $200 full-time; $100 part-time. Tuition and fees vary according to course load. *Financial support:* Career-related internships or fieldwork, Federal Work-Study, scholarships/grants, health care benefits, and unspecified assistantships available. Support available to part-time students. Financial award application deadline: 5/15; financial award applicants required to submit FAFSA. *Unit head:* Dr. Thomas Schmeling, Chair, 401-456-8056. *Application contact:* Graduate Studies, 401-456-8700. Website: http://www.ric.edu/politicalscience/index.php

Roger Williams University, School of Justice Studies, Bristol, RI 02809. Offers criminal justice (MS); cybersecurity (MS); leadership (MS), including health care administration (MPA, MS); public management (MPA, MS); public administration (MPA), including health care administration (MPA, MS), public management (MPA, MS); MS/JD. *Program availability:* Part-time, evening/weekend, 100% online, blended/hybrid learning. *Faculty:* 10 full-time (5 women), 7 part-time/adjunct (1 woman). *Students:* 16 full-time (11 women), 114 part-time (57 women); includes 33 minority (14 Black or African American, non-Hispanic/Latino; 1 American Indian or Alaska Native, non-Hispanic/Latino; 1 Asian, non-Hispanic/Latino; 17 Hispanic/Latino), 1 international. Average age 35. 58 applicants, 83% accepted, 33 enrolled. In 2017, 27 master's awarded. *Degree requirements:* For master's, thesis optional. *Entrance requirements:* For master's, 2 letters of recommendation, college transcript, and resume (for MS in leadership and MPA programs); criminal background check (for MS in cybersecurity). Additional exam requirements/recommendations for international students: Required—TOEFL (minimum score 85 iBT), IELTS (minimum score 6.5). *Application deadline:* For fall admission, 8/1 for domestic students; for spring admission, 1/1 for domestic students. Applications are processed on a rolling basis. Application fee: $50. Electronic applications accepted. Application fee is waived when completed online. *Expenses:* Contact institution. *Financial support:* In 2017–18, 1 student received support, including 1 research assistantship (averaging $6,942 per year). Financial award application deadline: 4/1; financial award applicants required to submit FAFSA. *Faculty research:* Opioid addiction and treatment, community policing. *Unit head:* Dr. Eric Bronson, Dean, 401-254-3336, E-mail: ebronson@rwu.edu. *Application contact:* Marcus Hanscom, Director of Graduate Admissions, 401-254-3345, Fax: 401-254-3557, E-mail: gradadmit@rwu.edu. Website: http://www.rwu.edu/academics/departments/criminaljustice.htm#graduate

Rutgers University–Camden, Graduate School of Arts and Sciences, Department of Public Policy and Administration, Camden, NJ 08102. Offers education policy and leadership (MPA); international public service and development (MPA); public management (MPA); JD/MPA; MPA/MA. *Accreditation:* NASPAA. *Program availability:* Part-time, evening/weekend. *Degree requirements:* For master's, directed study, research workshop, 42 credits. *Entrance requirements:* For master's, GRE General Test, GMAT or LSAT, 3 letters of recommendation; resume. Additional exam requirements/recommendations for international students: Required—TOEFL (minimum score 550 paper-based), IELTS. Electronic applications accepted. *Faculty research:* Nonprofit management, county and municipal administration, health and human services, government communication, administrative law, educational finance.

Rutgers University–Newark, Graduate School, Program in Public Administration, Newark, NJ 07102. Offers health care administration (MPA); human resources administration (MPA); public administration (PhD); public management (MPA); public policy analysis (MPA); urban systems and issues (MPA). *Accreditation:* NASPAA (one or more programs are accredited). *Program availability:* Part-time, evening/weekend. *Degree requirements:* For master's, comprehensive exam, thesis or alternative; for doctorate, thesis/dissertation. *Entrance requirements:* For master's, GRE, minimum undergraduate B average; for doctorate, GRE, MPA, minimum B average. Electronic applications accepted. *Faculty research:* Government finance, municipal and state government, public productivity.

Sacred Heart University, Graduate Programs, College of Arts and Sciences, Department of Government, Politics and Global Studies, Fairfield, CT 06825. Offers public administration (MPA). *Program availability:* Part-time, online learning. *Entrance requirements:* For master's, BA or BS, minimum GPA of 3.0. *Expenses:* Tuition: Full-time $28,114; part-time $739 per credit. *Unit head:* Dr. Gary L. Rose, Chair, 203-371-7745, Fax: 203-365-7587, E-mail: roseg@sacredheart.edu. *Application contact:* Dr. Lesley DeNardis, Program Director, 203-371-7834, E-mail: denardisl@sacredheart.edu. Website: http://www.sacredheart.edu/academics/collegeofartssciences/academicdepartments/governmentpoliticsglobalstudies/

Saginaw Valley State University, College of Arts and Behavioral Sciences, Program in Public Administration, University Center, MI 48710. Offers MA. *Program availability:* Part-time, evening/weekend. *Students:* 16 full-time (11 women), 33 part-time (21 women); includes 10 minority (6 Black or African American, non-Hispanic/Latino; 2 Hispanic/Latino; 2 Two or more races, non-Hispanic/Latino), 2 international. Average age 31. 19 applicants, 89% accepted, 14 enrolled. In 2017, 11 master's awarded. *Degree requirements:* For master's, thesis optional. *Entrance requirements:* For master's, minimum GPA of 2.75. Additional exam requirements/recommendations for international students: Required—TOEFL (minimum score 580 paper-based; 92 iBT). *Application deadline:* For fall admission, 7/15 for international students; for winter admission, 11/15 for international students; for spring admission, 4/15 for international students. Applications are processed on a rolling basis. Application fee: $30 ($90 for international students). Electronic applications accepted. *Expenses:* Tuition, state resident: full-time $10,156; part-time $564.20 per credit hour. Tuition, nonresident: full-time $19,336; part-time $1074.20 per credit hour. *Required fees:* $263; $14.60 per credit hour. Tuition and fees vary according to degree level and program. *Financial support:* Federal Work-Study and scholarships/grants available. Support available to part-time students. Financial award application deadline: 4/1; financial award applicants required to submit FAFSA. *Unit head:* Dr. Joseph Jaksa, Program Coordinator, 989-964-2178, E-mail: jjjaksa@svsu.edu. *Application contact:* Jenna Briggs, Director, Graduate and International Admissions, 989-964-6096, Fax: 989-964-2788, E-mail: gradadm@svsu.edu.

St. John's University, St. John's College of Liberal Arts and Sciences, Department of Government and Politics, Program in Government and Politics, Queens, NY 11439. Offers government and politics (MA); international law and diplomacy (Adv C); public administration (Adv C); JD/MA. *Program availability:* Part-time, evening/weekend. *Students:* 39 full-time (19 women), 18 part-time (15 women); includes 36 minority (17 Black or African American, non-Hispanic/Latino; 1 American Indian or Alaska Native, non-Hispanic/Latino; 1 Asian, non-Hispanic/Latino; 13 Hispanic/Latino; 4 Two or more races, non-Hispanic/Latino), 1 international. Average age 27. 85 applicants, 78% accepted, 28 enrolled. In 2017, 25 master's awarded. *Degree requirements:* For master's, comprehensive exam, thesis optional. *Entrance requirements:* For master's, letters of recommendation, transcripts, resume, personal statement. Additional exam requirements/recommendations for international students: Required—TOEFL (minimum score 80 iBT), IELTS (minimum score 6.5). *Application deadline:* For fall admission, 5/1 for domestic students; for spring admission, 11/1 for domestic students. Applications are processed on a rolling basis. Application fee: $70. Electronic applications accepted. *Expenses: Tuition:* Full-time $44,280; part-time $1230 per credit. *Required fees:* $340; $340 per credit. Tuition and fees vary according to course load, degree level and program. *Financial support:* Fellowships, research assistantships, teaching assistantships, scholarships/grants, tuition waivers, and unspecified assistantships available. Support available to part-time students. Financial award application deadline: 2/1; financial award applicants required to submit FAFSA. *Faculty research:* Presidential leadership, morality and politics, U.S. foreign policy, U.S. national security policy, NY state and local government and politics, state building and social policy, public opinion, campaigns and elections, education politics, North African politics, energy and European Union politics. *Unit head:* Dr. Fred Pompeo Cocozzelli, Chair, 718-990-5267, E-mail: cocozzef@stjohns.edu. *Application contact:* Robert Medrano, Director of Graduate Admissions, 718-990-1601, Fax: 718-990-5686, E-mail: gradhelp@stjohns.edu. Website: https://www.stjohns.edu/academics/schools-and-colleges/st-johns-college-liberal-arts-and-sciences/programs-and-majors/government-and-politics-master-a

St. Mary's University, Graduate Studies, Program in Public Administration, San Antonio, TX 78228. Offers public administration (MPA); public communication, public policy and public leadership (Certificate); JD/MPA. *Program availability:* Part-time, evening/weekend, online learning. *Students:* 21 full-time (14 women), 17 part-time (8 women); includes 24 minority (2 Black or African American, non-Hispanic/Latino; 22 Hispanic/Latino), 10 international. Average age 29. 46 applicants, 61% accepted, 16 enrolled. In 2017, 11 master's awarded. *Degree requirements:* For master's, comprehensive exam, 6-hour internship or applied public service. *Entrance requirements:* For master's, GRE General Test, letters of recommendation, writing sample, essay. Additional exam requirements/recommendations for international students: Required—TOEFL (minimum score 550 paper-based; 80 iBT), IELTS (minimum score 6). *Application deadline:* For fall admission, 7/1 for domestic students; for spring admission, 11/15 for domestic students; for summer admission, 4/1 for domestic students. Applications are processed on a rolling basis. Application fee: $0. Electronic applications accepted. *Expenses: Tuition:* Full-time $16,200; part-time $900 per credit hour. *Required fees:* $810; $405 per semester. *Financial support:* Career-related internships or fieldwork, Federal Work-Study, and institutionally sponsored loans available. Financial award application deadline: 3/31; financial award applicants required to submit FAFSA. *Faculty research:* Municipal service delivery, election systems, urban management and planning. *Unit head:* Dr. Arturo Veha, Director, Graduate Public Administration, 210-431-8028, E-mail: avega2@stmarytx.edu. *Application contact:* Kim Thornton, Director of Graduate Admission, 210-436-3101, E-mail: kthornton@stmarytx.edu. Website: https://www.stmarytx.edu/academics/programs/master-public-administration/

Saint Mary's University of Minnesota, Schools of Graduate and Professional Programs, Graduate School of Business and Technology, Public Administration Program, Winona, MN 55987-1399. Offers MA. *Unit head:* George Diaz, Director, 612-238-4510, E-mail: gdiaz@smumn.edu. *Application contact:* James Callinan, Director of Admissions for Graduate and Professional Programs, 612-728-5158, Fax: 612-728-5121, E-mail: jcallina@smumn.edu. Website: https://onlineprograms.smumn.edu/mpa/masters-in-public-administration?_ga=2.254655304.1736907137.1523547391-1359115499.1515170921

Saint Peter's University, Program in Public Administration, Jersey City, NJ 07306-5997. Offers MPA. *Degree requirements:* For master's, capstone project.

St. Thomas University, School of Business, Department of Management, Miami Gardens, FL 33054-6459. Offers accounting (MBA); general management (MSM, Certificate); health management (MBA, MSM, Certificate); human resource management (MBA, MSM, Certificate); international business (MBA, MIB, MSM, Certificate); justice administration (MSM, Certificate); management accounting (MSM, Certificate); public management (MSM, Certificate); sports administration (MS). *Program availability:* Part-time, evening/weekend. *Degree requirements:* For master's, comprehensive exam. *Entrance requirements:* For master's, interview, minimum GPA of 3.0 or GMAT. Additional exam requirements/recommendations for international students: Required—TOEFL (minimum score 550 paper-based; 79 iBT). Electronic applications accepted.

Sam Houston State University, College of Humanities and Social Sciences, Department of Political Science, Huntsville, TX 77341. Offers political science (MA); public administration (MPA). *Program availability:* Part-time, online learning. *Degree requirements:* For master's, comprehensive exam, thesis optional, internship. *Entrance requirements:* For master's, GRE General Test, GMAT, writing sample of scholarly work, letters of recommendation, statement of purpose, resume. Additional exam requirements/recommendations for international students: Required—TOEFL (minimum score 550 paper-based; 79 iBT), IELTS (minimum score 6.5). Electronic applications accepted.

San Diego State University, Graduate and Research Affairs, College of Professional Studies and Fine Arts, School of Public Affairs, Program in Public Administration, San Diego, CA 92182. Offers MPA. *Accreditation:* NASPAA. *Program availability:* Part-time. *Entrance requirements:* For master's, GRE General Test, 2 letters of reference. Additional exam requirements/recommendations for international students: Required—TOEFL. Electronic applications accepted.

San Francisco State University, Division of Graduate Studies, College of Health and Social Sciences, Public Administration Program, San Francisco, CA 94132-1722. Offers criminal justice administration (MPA); environmental administration and policy (MPA); gerontology (MPA); nonprofit administration (MPA); public management (MPA); public policy (MPA); urban administration (MPA). *Accreditation:* NASPAA. *Unit head:* Dr. Jennifer Shea, Graduate Coordinator, 415-817-4462, Fax: 415-817-4464, E-mail: jshea@sfsu.edu. Website: http://mpa.sfsu.edu/

San Jose State University, Graduate Studies and Research, College of Social Sciences, San Jose, CA 95192-0107. Offers applied anthropology (MA); communication studies (MA); economics (MA), including applied economics, economics; environmental studies (MS); geography (MA); history (MA), including history, history education;

Mexican American studies (MA); psychology (MA, MS), including clinical psychology (MS), industrial/organizational psychology (MS), research and experimental psychology (MA); public administration (MPA); social sciences (MS); sociology (MA). *Faculty:* 59 full-time (29 women), 18 part-time/adjunct (5 women). *Students:* 181 full-time (126 women), 221 part-time (127 women); includes 228 minority (15 Black or African American, non-Hispanic/Latino; 48 Asian, non-Hispanic/Latino; 112 Hispanic/Latino; 3 Native Hawaiian or other Pacific Islander, non-Hispanic/Latino; 50 Two or more races, non-Hispanic/Latino), 38 international. Average age 30. 532 applicants, 44% accepted, 156 enrolled. In 2017, 139 master's awarded. *Degree requirements:* For master's, one foreign language, comprehensive exam, thesis (for some programs), project, field work, professional work experience. *Entrance requirements:* Additional exam requirements/recommendations for international students: Required—TOEFL (minimum score 550 paper-based; 80 iBT), IELTS (minimum score 6.5), PTE (minimum score 53). *Application deadline:* For fall admission, 2/1 for domestic and international students. Applications are processed on a rolling basis. Application fee: $55. Electronic applications accepted. *Expenses:* Tuition, state resident: full-time $7176. Tuition, nonresident: full-time $16,680. Tuition and fees vary according to course load and program. *Financial support:* Fellowships, research assistantships, career-related internships or fieldwork, Federal Work-Study, scholarships/grants, tuition waivers (full and partial), and unspecified assistantships available. Support available to part-time students. Financial award application deadline: 4/28; financial award applicants required to submit FAFSA. *Unit head:* Dr. Walt Jacobs, Dean, 408-924-5300, Fax: 408-924-5303, E-mail: walter.jacobs@sjsu.edu.
Website: http://www.sjsu.edu/socialsciences/

Savannah State University, Master of Public Administration Program, Savannah, GA 31404. Offers city management (MPA); human resources (MPA). *Accreditation:* NASPAA. *Program availability:* Part-time. *Degree requirements:* For master's, comprehensive exam, thesis, public service internship, capstone seminar. *Entrance requirements:* For master's, GRE General Test, GMAT, or MAT, minimum cumulative GPA of 2.5, 3 letters of recommendation, essay, official transcripts, resume, essay of 500-1000 words detailing reasons for pursuing degree. Additional exam requirements/recommendations for international students: Required—TOEFL. Electronic applications accepted. *Expenses:* Contact institution. *Faculty research:* Community development, human resources, leadership, conflict resolution, city management, non-profit management.

Seattle University, College of Arts and Sciences, Institute of Public Service, Seattle, WA 98122-1090. Offers MNPL, MPA. *Accreditation:* NASPAA. *Program availability:* Part-time, evening/weekend. *Faculty:* 11 full-time (5 women), 6 part-time/adjunct (2 women). *Students:* 15 full-time (8 women), 122 part-time (79 women); includes 52 minority (11 Black or African American, non-Hispanic/Latino; 2 American Indian or Alaska Native, non-Hispanic/Latino; 10 Asian, non-Hispanic/Latino; 20 Hispanic/Latino; 9 Two or more races, non-Hispanic/Latino), 8 international. Average age 31. 61 applicants, 75% accepted, 33 enrolled. In 2017, 42 master's awarded. *Degree requirements:* For master's, thesis. *Entrance requirements:* For master's, minimum GPA of 3.0, letters of recommendation, current resume reflecting two years of relevant professional experience in nonprofit organization (preferred). Additional exam requirements/recommendations for international students: Required—TOEFL, IELTS. *Application deadline:* For fall admission, 7/20 priority date for domestic students, 7/20 for international students; for winter admission, 10/20 priority date for domestic students, 10/20 for international students; for spring admission, 2/20 priority date for domestic students, 2/20 for international students. Applications are processed on a rolling basis. Application fee: $55. Electronic applications accepted. *Expenses: Tuition:* Full-time $12,960. *Required fees:* $570. Tuition and fees vary according to program. *Financial support:* In 2017–18, 15 students received support. Career-related internships or fieldwork, Federal Work-Study, and unspecified assistantships available. Support available to part-time students. Financial award applicants required to submit FAFSA. *Faculty research:* Leadership development, decision-making, and advocacy; government and nonprofit management, processes, and program analysis; organizational theory and structure; policy formation and analysis, financial analysis and planning. *Unit head:* Dr. John Collins, Interim Director, Institute of Public Service, 206-296-5442, Fax: 206-296-5997, E-mail: collinsj@seattleu.edu. *Application contact:* Janet Shandley, Associate Dean of Graduate Admissions, 206-296-5900, Fax: 206-298-5656, E-mail: grad_admissions@seattleu.edu.
Website: http://www.seattleu.edu/artsci/departments/ips/

Seton Hall University, College of Arts and Sciences, Department of Political Science and Public Affairs, South Orange, NJ 07079-2697. Offers nonprofit organization management (Graduate Certificate); public administration (MPA), including health policy and management, nonprofit organization management, public service: leadership, governance, and policy. *Accreditation:* CAHME; NASPAA. *Program availability:* Part-time, evening/weekend. *Degree requirements:* For master's, thesis or alternative, internship or practicum. *Entrance requirements:* Additional exam requirements/recommendations for international students: Required—TOEFL. Electronic applications accepted.

Shippensburg University of Pennsylvania, School of Graduate Studies, College of Arts and Sciences, Department of Political Science, Shippensburg, PA 17257-2299. Offers public administration (MPA). *Program availability:* Part-time, evening/weekend. *Faculty:* 5 full-time (2 women). *Students:* 12 full-time (7 women), 17 part-time (8 women); includes 2 minority (both Black or African American, non-Hispanic/Latino), 3 international. Average age 31. 29 applicants, 76% accepted, 12 enrolled. In 2017, 13 master's awarded. *Degree requirements:* For master's, thesis or internship. *Entrance requirements:* For master's, current resume, official transcript showing minimum cumulative GPA of 2.75 or sufficient work experience, personal goals statement. Additional exam requirements/recommendations for international students: Required—TOEFL (minimum score 550 paper-based, 68 iBT) or IELTS (minimum score 6). *Application deadline:* For fall admission, 4/30 for international students; for spring admission, 9/30 for international students. Applications are processed on a rolling basis. Application fee: $45. Electronic applications accepted. *Expenses:* Tuition, state resident: part-time $500 per credit. Tuition, nonresident: part-time $750 per credit. *Required fees:* $145 per credit. *Financial support:* In 2017–18, 3 students received support. Career-related internships or fieldwork, scholarships/grants, unspecified assistantships, and resident hall director and student payroll positions available. Support available to part-time students. Financial award application deadline: 3/1; financial award applicants required to submit FAFSA. *Unit head:* Dr. C. Niel Brasher, Department Chair and Program Coordinator, 717-477-1718, Fax: 717-477-4030, E-mail: cnbras@ship.edu. *Application contact:* Maya T. Mapp, Director of Admissions, 717-477-1231, Fax: 717-477-4016, E-mail: mtmapp@ship.edu.
Website: http://www.ship.edu/political_science/

Sonoma State University, School of Social Sciences, Department of Political Science, Rohnert Park, CA 94928. Offers public administration (MPA). *Program availability:* Part-time, evening/weekend. *Entrance requirements:* For master's, GRE General Test, minimum GPA of 3.0. Additional exam requirements/recommendations for international students: Required—TOEFL (minimum score 500 paper-based). *Application deadline:* For fall admission, 11/30 for domestic students; for spring admission, 8/31 for domestic

students. Application fee: $55. *Financial support:* Research assistantships, teaching assistantships, career-related internships or fieldwork, and Federal Work-Study available. Support available to part-time students. Financial award application deadline: 3/2; financial award applicants required to submit FAFSA. *Unit head:* David McCuan, Department Chair, 707-664-2179, E-mail: mccuan@sonoma.edu. *Application contact:* Emily Ray, Graduate Program Coordinator, 707-664-2731, Fax: 707-664-3920, E-mail: emily.ray@sonoma.edu.
Website: http://www.sonoma.edu/polisci/

Southeast Missouri State University, School of Graduate Studies, Department of Political Science, Philosophy and Religion, Cape Girardeau, MO 63701-4799. Offers MPA. *Program availability:* Part-time, evening/weekend, 100% online, blended/hybrid learning. *Faculty:* 5 full-time (1 woman). *Students:* 8 full-time (6 women), 17 part-time (9 women); includes 3 minority (all Black or African American, non-Hispanic/Latino), 3 international. Average age 32. 17 applicants, 76% accepted, 6 enrolled. In 2017, 7 master's awarded. *Degree requirements:* For master's, thesis or alternative, internship paper. *Entrance requirements:* For master's, statement of interest, minimum GPA of 2.7. Additional exam requirements/recommendations for international students: Required—TOEFL (minimum score 550 paper-based; 79 iBT), IELTS (minimum score 6), PTE (minimum score 53). *Application deadline:* For fall admission, 8/1 for domestic students, 6/1 for international students; for spring admission, 11/21 for domestic students, 10/1 for international students; for summer admission, 5/15 for domestic students. Applications are processed on a rolling basis. Application fee: $30 ($40 for international students). Electronic applications accepted. *Expenses:* $270.35 per credit hour in-state tuition, $33.40 per credit hour fees. *Financial support:* In 2017–18, 2 students received support. Career-related internships or fieldwork, Federal Work-Study, scholarships/grants, traineeships, tuition waivers (full), and unspecified assistantships available. Financial award application deadline: 6/30; financial award applicants required to submit FAFSA. *Faculty research:* Rural public administration, public policy analysis, budgeting, emergency management. *Unit head:* Dr. Hamner Hill, Chairperson, Department of Political Science, Philosophy, and Religion, 573-651-2816, Fax: 573-651-2695, E-mail: hhill@semo.edu. *Application contact:* Dr. Rick Althaus, Graduate Coordinator, Department of Political Science, Philosophy, and Religion, 573-651-2700, Fax: 573-651-2695, E-mail: ralthaus@semo.edu.
Website: http://www.semo.edu/polisci

Southern Arkansas University–Magnolia, School of Graduate Studies, Magnolia, AR 71753. Offers agriculture (MS); business administration (MBA), including agribusiness, social entrepreneurship, supply chain management; clinical and mental health counseling (MS); computer and information sciences (MS), including cyber security and privacy, data science, information technology; gifted and talented (M Ed), including curriculum and instruction, educational administration and supervision, gifted and talented P-8/7-12, instructional specialist P-4; higher, adult and lifelong education (M Ed); kinesiology (M Ed), including coaching; library media and information specialist (M Ed); public administration (MPA); school counseling K-12 (M Ed); student affairs and college counseling (M Ed); teaching (MAT). *Accreditation:* NCATE. *Program availability:* Part-time, 100% online, blended/hybrid learning. *Faculty:* 36 full-time (20 women), 31 part-time/adjunct (12 women). *Students:* 242 full-time (89 women), 889 part-time (459 women); includes 167 minority (143 Black or African American, non-Hispanic/Latino; 7 American Indian or Alaska Native, non-Hispanic/Latino; 7 Asian, non-Hispanic/Latino; 3 Hispanic/Latino; 7 Two or more races, non-Hispanic/Latino), 562 international. Average age 28. 400 applicants, 100% accepted, 239 enrolled. In 2017, 875 master's awarded. *Degree requirements:* For master's, comprehensive exam (for some programs), thesis optional. *Entrance requirements:* For master's, GRE, MAT or GMAT, minimum GPA of 2.5. Additional exam requirements/recommendations for international students: Required—TOEFL (minimum score 550 paper-based), IELTS (minimum score 6). *Application deadline:* For fall admission, 7/20 for domestic students, 7/10 for international students; for spring admission, 12/1 for domestic students, 11/15 for international students; for summer admission, 4/1 for domestic students, 5/1 for international students. Applications are processed on a rolling basis. Application fee: $25 ($50 for international students). Electronic applications accepted. *Expenses:* Tuition, state resident: full-time $6038. Tuition, nonresident: full-time $8558. *Required fees:* $804. One-time fee: $110 full-time. Tuition and fees vary according to course load. *Financial support:* Career-related internships or fieldwork, Federal Work-Study, scholarships/grants, tuition waivers (full), and unspecified assistantships available. Financial award applicants required to submit FAFSA. *Faculty research:* Alternative certification for teachers, supervision of instruction, instructional leadership, counseling. *Unit head:* Dr. Kim Bloss, Dean, School of Graduate Studies, 870-235-4150, Fax: 870-235-5227, E-mail: kkbloss@saumag.edu. *Application contact:* Shrijana Malakar, Admissions Specialist, 870-235-4150, Fax: 870-235-5227, E-mail: smalakar@saumag.edu.
Website: http://www.saumag.edu/graduate

Southern Illinois University Carbondale, Graduate School, College of Liberal Arts, Department of Political Science, Public Administration Program, Carbondale, IL 62901-4701. Offers MPA, JD/MPA. *Accreditation:* NASPAA. *Program availability:* Part-time. *Degree requirements:* For master's, thesis or alternative. *Entrance requirements:* For master's, minimum GPA of 3.0. Additional exam requirements/recommendations for international students: Required—TOEFL (minimum score 600 paper-based; 100 iBT). *Faculty research:* Natural resources and environmental management, intergovernmental relations, state mandates, rural administration, economic development policy, nonprofit management.

Southern Illinois University Edwardsville, Graduate School, College of Arts and Sciences, Department of Public Administration and Policy Analysis, Edwardsville, IL 62026. Offers public administration (MPA). *Accreditation:* NASPAA. *Program availability:* Part-time, evening/weekend. *Degree requirements:* For master's, comprehensive exam. *Entrance requirements:* Additional exam requirements/recommendations for international students: Required—TOEFL (minimum score 550 paper-based; 79 iBT), IELTS (minimum score 6.5). Electronic applications accepted.

Southern New Hampshire University, School of Business, Manchester, NH 03106-1045. Offers accounting (MBA, Graduate Certificate); accounting finance (MS); accounting/auditing (MS); accounting/forensic accounting (MS); accounting/management accounting (MS); accounting/taxation (MS); applied economics (MS); athletic administration (MBA, Graduate Certificate); business administration (IMBA, Certificate), including business information systems (Certificate), human resource management (Certificate); business analytics (MBA); business intelligence (MBA); communication (MA), including new media and marketing, public relations; community economic development (MBA); criminal justice (MBA); data analytics (MS); economics (MBA); engineering management (MBA); entrepreneurship (MBA); finance (MBA, MS, Graduate Certificate); finance/corporate finance (MS); finance/investments (MS); forensic accounting (MBA); forensic accounting and fraud examination (Graduate Certificate); healthcare informatics (MBA); healthcare management (MBA); human resource management (MS); human resources (MBA); information technology (MS); information technology management (MBA); international business (PhD); Internet marketing (MBA); leadership (MBA); leadership of nonprofit organizations (Graduate Certificate); management (MS); marketing (MBA, MS, Graduate Certificate); music

business (MBA); operations and project management (MS); operations and supply chain management (MBA, Graduate Certificate); organizational leadership (MS); project management (MBA, Graduate Certificate); public administration (MBA, Graduate Certificate); quantitative analysis (MBA); Six Sigma (Graduate Certificate); Six Sigma quality (MBA); social media marketing (MBA, Graduate Certificate); sport management (MBA, MS, Graduate Certificate); sustainability and environmental compliance (MBA); MBA/Certificate. *Accreditation:* ACBSP. *Program availability:* Part-time, evening/weekend, online learning. Terminal master's awarded for partial completion of doctoral program. *Degree requirements:* For master's, one foreign language, comprehensive exam (for some programs), thesis or alternative; for doctorate, one foreign language, comprehensive exam, thesis/dissertation. *Entrance requirements:* For master's, minimum GPA of 2.5; for doctorate, GMAT. Additional exam requirements/recommendations for international students: Required—TOEFL (minimum score 500 paper-based). *Application deadline:* Applications are processed on a rolling basis. Application fee: $40. Electronic applications accepted. *Expenses: Tuition:* Part-time $627 per credit hour. Part-time tuition and fees vary according to campus/location and program. *Financial support:* Career-related internships or fieldwork, Federal Work-Study, institutionally sponsored loans, scholarships/grants, tuition waivers (partial), and unspecified assistantships available. Support available to part-time students. Financial award applicants required to submit FAFSA. *Unit head:* Dr. Bill Lightfoot, Dean, 603-644-3102, Fax: 603-644-3144. *Application contact:* Office of Graduate Admission, 888-327-SNHU, Fax: 603-644-3144, E-mail: enroll@snhu.edu.

Southern University and Agricultural and Mechanical College, Graduate School, Nelson Mandela School of Public Policy and Urban Affairs, Department of Public Administration, Baton Rouge, LA 70813. Offers MPA. *Accreditation:* NASPAA. *Program availability:* Part-time, evening/weekend. *Degree requirements:* For master's, thesis. *Entrance requirements:* For master's, GRE General Test. Additional exam requirements/recommendations for international students: Required—TOEFL (minimum score 525 paper-based). *Faculty research:* Fiscal policy, public finance policy and practitioner interests; minority politics, healthcare and political economy.

Southern Utah University, Program in Public Administration, Cedar City, UT 84720-2498. Offers MPA. *Accreditation:* NASPAA. *Program availability:* Part-time, evening/weekend, 100% online. *Faculty:* 4 full-time (0 women), 6 part-time/adjunct (4 women). *Students:* 42 full-time (21 women), 73 part-time (33 women); includes 18 minority (2 Black or African American, non-Hispanic/Latino; 2 American Indian or Alaska Native, non-Hispanic/Latino; 3 Asian, non-Hispanic/Latino; 8 Hispanic/Latino; 3 Native Hawaiian or other Pacific Islander, non-Hispanic/Latino), 3 international. Average age 33. 47 applicants, 70% accepted, 30 enrolled. In 2017, 36 master's awarded. *Entrance requirements:* For master's, GMAT, GRE, MAT, or LSAT. Additional exam requirements/recommendations for international students: Required—TOEFL (minimum score 550 paper-based, 79 iBT) or IELTS (minimum score 6). *Application deadline:* For fall admission, 7/15 for domestic and international students; for spring admission, 11/15 for domestic and international students; for summer admission, 4/15 for domestic and international students. Applications are processed on a rolling basis. Application fee: $60 ($65 for international students). Electronic applications accepted. *Expenses:* Contact institution. *Financial support:* Tuition waivers (full and partial) and unspecified assistantships available. Financial award application deadline: 5/31. *Unit head:* Dr. Angela Pool-Funai, MPA Program Director, 435-865-8153, Fax: 435-586-1925, E-mail: angelapoolfunai@suu.edu.
Website: https://www.suu.edu/hss/polscj/mpa/

South University, Graduate Programs, College of Business, Program in Public Administration, Savannah, GA 31406. Offers MPA.

South University, Program in Public Administration, Montgomery, AL 36116-1120. Offers MPA.

South University, Program in Public Administration, Royal Palm Beach, FL 33411. Offers MPA.

Stephen F. Austin State University, Graduate School, College of Liberal Arts, Department of Political Science and Geography, Nacogdoches, TX 75962. Offers public administration (MPA). *Degree requirements:* For master's, thesis optional. *Entrance requirements:* For master's, GRE General Test. Additional exam requirements/recommendations for international students: Required—TOEFL.

Strayer University, Graduate Studies, Washington, DC 20005-2603. Offers accounting (MS); acquisition (MBA); business administration (MBA); communications technology (MS); educational management (M Ed); finance (MBA); health services administration (MHSA); hospitality and tourism management (MBA); human resource management (MBA); information systems (MS), including computer security management, decision support system management, enterprise resource management, network management, software engineering management, systems development management; management (MBA); management information systems (MS); marketing (MBA); professional accounting (MS), including accounting information systems, controllership, taxation; public administration (MPA); supply chain management (MBA); technology in education (M Ed). Programs also offered at campus locations in Birmingham, AL; Chamblee, GA; Cobb County, GA; Morrow, GA; White Marsh, MD; Charleston, SC; Columbia, SC; Greensboro, NC; Greenville, SC; Lexington, KY; Louisville, KY; Nashville, TN; North Raleigh, NC; Washington, DC. *Accreditation:* ACBSP. *Program availability:* Part-time, evening/weekend, online learning. *Degree requirements:* For master's, thesis. *Entrance requirements:* For master's, GMAT, GRE General Test, bachelor's degree from an accredited college or university, minimum undergraduate GPA of 2.75. Electronic applications accepted.

Suffolk University, Sawyer Business School, Department of Public Administration, Boston, MA 02108-2770. Offers community health (MPA); information systems, performance management, and big data analytics (MPA); nonprofit management (MPA); state and local government (MPA); JD/MPA; MPA/MS; MPA/MSCJ; MPA/MSMHC; MPA/MSPS. *Accreditation:* NASPAA (one or more programs are accredited). *Program availability:* Part-time, evening/weekend. *Faculty:* 6 full-time (3 women), 8 part-time/adjunct (6 women). *Students:* 25 full-time (12 women), 90 part-time (56 women); includes 43 minority (20 Black or African American, non-Hispanic/Latino; 7 Asian, non-Hispanic/Latino; 14 Hispanic/Latino; 2 Two or more races, non-Hispanic/Latino), 2 international. Average age 34. 134 applicants, 38% accepted, 5 enrolled. In 2017, 44 master's awarded. *Entrance requirements:* Additional exam requirements/recommendations for international students: Required—TOEFL (minimum score 550 paper-based; 80 iBT). *Application deadline:* For fall admission, 3/15 priority date for domestic and international students; for spring admission, 10/15 priority date for domestic and international students. Applications are processed on a rolling basis. Application fee: $50. Electronic applications accepted. *Expenses:* $35,130 per year full-time tuition; $1,171 per credit part-time. *Financial support:* In 2017–18, 76 students received support, including 2 fellowships (averaging $4,650 per year); career-related internships or fieldwork, Federal Work-Study, institutionally sponsored loans, and scholarships/grants also available. Support available to part-time students. Financial award application deadline: 4/1; financial award applicants required to submit FAFSA. *Faculty research:* Local government, health care, federal policy, mental health, HIV/AIDS. *Unit head:* Brenda Bond, Director/Department Chair, 617-305-1768, E-mail: bbond@suffolk.edu. *Application contact:* Mara Marzocchi, Associate Director of Graduate Admissions, 617-573-8302, Fax: 617-305-1733, E-mail: grad.admission@suffolk.edu.
Website: http://www.suffolk.edu/mpa

Syracuse University, Maxwell School of Citizenship and Public Affairs, Dual MPA/IR Program in Public Administration and International Relations, Syracuse, NY 13244. Offers MPA/MA. *Students:* Average age 27. *Entrance requirements:* Additional exam requirements/recommendations for international students: Required—TOEFL (minimum score 100 iBT). *Application deadline:* For fall admission, 2/1 priority date for domestic and international students. Application fee: $75. Electronic applications accepted. *Financial support:* Fellowships with full tuition reimbursements, research assistantships, and teaching assistantships available. Financial award application deadline: 1/1; financial award applicants required to submit FAFSA. *Faculty research:* Economics for public decisions, comparative foreign policy, international and development administration, public and nonprofit management, quantitative analysis. *Unit head:* Dr. Robert Bifulco, Associate Dean and Chair, Department of Public Administration and International Affairs, 315-443-3232, E-mail: rbifulco@maxwell.syr.edu. *Application contact:* Christine Omolino, Director, 315-443-4000, E-mail: comolino@syr.edu.
Website: https://www.maxwell.syr.edu/paia.aspx?id=6442451202

Syracuse University, Maxwell School of Citizenship and Public Affairs, EMPA Program of Public Administration Program, Syracuse, NY 13244. Offers EMPA. *Program availability:* Part-time. *Entrance requirements:* For master's, 7 years of mid-level professional experience, resume, personal statement, official transcripts, three letters of recommendation. Additional exam requirements/recommendations for international students: Required—TOEFL (minimum score 100 iBT). *Application deadline:* For fall admission, 2/1 for domestic and international students; for spring admission, 8/15 for domestic and international students. Applications are processed on a rolling basis. Application fee: $75. Electronic applications accepted. *Financial support:* Application deadline: 2/1. *Unit head:* Steven Lux, Director, Executive Education Programs, 315-443-3759, E-mail: sjlux@maxwell.syr.edu. *Application contact:* Margaret Lane, Assistant Director, Executive Education Programs, 315-443-8708, E-mail: melane02@maxwell.syr.edu.
Website: http://www.maxwell.syr.edu/

Syracuse University, Maxwell School of Citizenship and Public Affairs, Programs in Public Administration, Syracuse, NY 13244. Offers MPA, PhD, JD/MPA, MPA/MA. *Accreditation:* NASPAA (one or more programs are accredited). *Program availability:* Part-time. In 2017, 124 master's awarded. *Degree requirements:* For doctorate, comprehensive exam, thesis/dissertation. *Entrance requirements:* For master's and doctorate, GRE General Test, resume, three letters of recommendation, personal statement, official transcripts. Additional exam requirements/recommendations for international students: Required—TOEFL (minimum score 100 iBT). *Application deadline:* For fall admission, 2/1 priority date for domestic and international students. Application fee: $75. Electronic applications accepted. *Financial support:* Fellowships with full tuition reimbursements, research assistantships, teaching assistantships, scholarships/grants, and unspecified assistantships available. Financial award application deadline: 1/1; financial award applicants required to submit FAFSA. *Faculty research:* Public and nonprofit management, government contracting, public-private partnerships, policy implementation, strategic management. *Unit head:* Dr. Robert Bifulco, Associate Dean and Chair, Public Administration and International Affairs, 315-443-3232, E-mail: rbifulco@maxwell.syr.edu. *Application contact:* Christine Omolino, Associate Director, 315-443-3712, Fax: 315-443-5330, E-mail: comolino@syr.edu.
Website: http://www.maxwell.syr.edu/

Tarleton State University, College of Graduate Studies, College of Liberal and Fine Arts, Master of Public Administration Program, Stephenville, TX 76402. Offers MPA. *Program availability:* Part-time, evening/weekend, 100% online, blended/hybrid learning. *Faculty:* 1 (woman) full-time, 8 part-time/adjunct (3 women). *Students:* 20 full-time (8 women), 79 part-time (50 women); includes 35 minority (20 Black or African American, non-Hispanic/Latino; 11 Hispanic/Latino; 4 Two or more races, non-Hispanic/Latino), 1 international. Average age 35. 61 applicants, 89% accepted, 47 enrolled. In 2017, 3 master's awarded. *Degree requirements:* For master's, comprehensive exam, thesis optional. *Entrance requirements:* For master's, GRE General Test, minimum GPA of 3.0. Additional exam requirements/recommendations for international students: Required—TOEFL (minimum score 550 paper-based; 80 iBT), IELTS (minimum score 6). *Application deadline:* For fall admission, 8/15 priority date for domestic students; for spring admission, 1/5 for domestic students. Applications are processed on a rolling basis. Application fee: $45 ($145 for international students). Electronic applications accepted. *Expenses:* Contact institution. *Financial support:* Application deadline: 5/1; applicants required to submit FAFSA. *Unit head:* Dr. Alex del Carmen, Executive Director of School of Criminology, Criminal Justice, and Strategic Studies, 817-717-3669, E-mail: delcarmen@tarleton.edu. *Application contact:* Information Contact, 254-968-9104, Fax: 254-968-9670, E-mail: gradoffice@tarleton.edu.
Website: http://www.tarleton.edu/degrees/masters/mpa/

Tennessee State University, The School of Graduate Studies and Research, College of Public Service, Nashville, TN 37209-1561. Offers human resource management (MPS); public administration (MPA, PhD); social work (MSW); strategic leadership (MPS); training and development (MPS). *Accreditation:* NASPAA (one or more programs are accredited). *Program availability:* Part-time, evening/weekend. *Degree requirements:* For master's, comprehensive exam, thesis optional; for doctorate, comprehensive exam, thesis/dissertation. *Entrance requirements:* For master's, GRE General Test, minimum GPA of 2.5, writing sample; for doctorate, GRE General Test, minimum GPA of 3.25, writing sample. *Faculty research:* Total quality management and process improvement, national health care policy and administration, starting non-profit ventures, public service ethics, state education financing across the U.S. public.

Texas A&M International University, Office of Graduate Studies and Research, College of Arts and Sciences, Department of Public Affairs and Social Research, Laredo, TX 78041. Offers criminal justice (MS); history and political thought (MA); political science (MA); public administration (MPA). *Degree requirements:* For master's, comprehensive exam (for some programs), thesis (for some programs). *Entrance requirements:* For master's, GRE General Test. Additional exam requirements/recommendations for international students: Required—TOEFL (minimum score 550 paper-based; 79 iBT).

Texas A&M University, Bush School of Government and Public Service, College Station, TX 77845. Offers homeland security (Certificate); international affairs (MIA, Certificate); national security affairs (Certificate); non-profit management (Certificate); public service and administration (MPSA). *Accreditation:* NASPAA. *Faculty:* 66. *Students:* 332 full-time (182 women), 54 part-time (16 women); includes 94 minority (19 Black or African American, non-Hispanic/Latino; 10 Asian, non-Hispanic/Latino; 56 Hispanic/Latino; 9 Two or more races, non-Hispanic/Latino), 41 international. Average age 28. 297 applicants, 94% accepted, 164 enrolled. In 2017, 154 master's awarded. *Degree requirements:* For master's, summer internship. *Entrance requirements:* For master's, GRE (preferred) or GMAT. Additional exam requirements/recommendations for international students: Required—TOEFL (minimum score 550 paper-based; 80 iBT), IELTS (minimum score 6), PTE (minimum score 53). *Application deadline:* For fall admission, 1/15 for domestic and international students. Application fee: $50 ($90 for

international students). Electronic applications accepted. *Expenses:* Contact institution. *Financial support:* In 2017–18, 417 students received support, including 29 fellowships with tuition reimbursements available (averaging $20,966 per year), 71 research assistantships with tuition reimbursements available (averaging $9,778 per year); teaching assistantships, career-related internships or fieldwork, institutionally sponsored loans, scholarships/grants, traineeships, health care benefits, tuition waivers (full and partial), and unspecified assistantships also available. Support available to part-time students. Financial award application deadline: 3/15; financial award applicants required to submit FAFSA. *Faculty research:* Public policy, Presidential studies, public leadership, economic policy, social policy. *Unit head:* Dr. Mark Welsh, Dean, 979-862-8007, E-mail: mwelsh@tamu.edu. *Application contact:* Kathryn Meyer, Director of Recruitment and Admissions, 979-458-4767, Fax: 979-845-4155, E-mail: bushschooladmissions@tamu.edu.
Website: http://bush.tamu.edu/

Texas A&M University–Corpus Christi, College of Graduate Studies, College of Liberal Arts, Corpus Christi, TX 78412. Offers communication (MA); English (MA); history (MA); psychology (MA), including clinical psychology, general psychology; public administration (MPA); studio art (MFA). *Program availability:* Part-time, evening/weekend. *Faculty:* 76 full-time (39 women), 9 part-time/adjunct (4 women). *Students:* 83 full-time (56 women), 109 part-time (78 women); includes 112 minority (9 Black or African American, non-Hispanic/Latino; 100 Hispanic/Latino; 3 Two or more races, non-Hispanic/Latino). Average age 32. 119 applicants, 67% accepted, 65 enrolled. In 2017, 65 master's awarded. *Degree requirements:* For master's, comprehensive exam (for some programs). *Entrance requirements:* For master's, portfolio. Additional exam requirements/recommendations for international students: Required—TOEFL (minimum score 550 paper-based; 79 iBT), IELTS (minimum score 6.5). *Application deadline:* For fall admission, 7/15 for domestic students, 5/1 for international students; for spring admission, 11/15 priority date for domestic students, 9/1 priority date for international students. Applications are processed on a rolling basis. Application fee: $50 ($70 for international students). Electronic applications accepted. *Expenses:* Tuition, state resident: full-time $3568; part-time $198.24 per credit hour. Tuition, nonresident: full-time $11,038; part-time $613.24 per credit hour. *Required fees:* $2129; $1422.58 per semester. Tuition and fees vary according to program. *Financial support:* Research assistantships, teaching assistantships, career-related internships or fieldwork, Federal Work-Study, institutionally sponsored loans, scholarships/grants, health care benefits, and unspecified assistantships available. Support available to part-time students. Financial award application deadline: 3/15; financial award applicants required to submit FAFSA. *Unit head:* Dr. Mark Hartlaub, Dean, 361-825-2659, Fax: 361-825-5844, E-mail: mark.hartlaub@tamucc.edu. *Application contact:* Graduate Admissions Coordinator, 361-825-2177, Fax: 361-825-2755, E-mail: gradweb@tamucc.edu.
Website: http://cla.tamucc.edu/

Texas Southern University, Barbara Jordan-Mickey Leland School of Public Affairs, Program in Public Administration, Houston, TX 77004-4584. Offers MPA. *Accreditation:* NASPAA. *Degree requirements:* For master's, comprehensive exam, thesis optional. *Entrance requirements:* For master's, GRE General Test, minimum GPA of 2.5. Additional exam requirements/recommendations for international students: Required—TOEFL. Electronic applications accepted.

Texas State University, The Graduate College, College of Liberal Arts, Program in Public Administration, San Marcos, TX 78666. Offers international relations (MPA); legal and judicial administration (MPA). *Accreditation:* NASPAA. *Program availability:* Part-time, evening/weekend. *Faculty:* 7 full-time (3 women), 1 (woman) part-time/adjunct. *Students:* 31 full-time (14 women), 64 part-time (36 women); includes 45 minority (11 Black or African American, non-Hispanic/Latino; 4 Asian, non-Hispanic/Latino; 29 Hispanic/Latino; 1 Two or more races, non-Hispanic/Latino), 2 international. Average age 30. 89 applicants, 76% accepted, 31 enrolled. In 2017, 37 master's awarded. *Degree requirements:* For master's, comprehensive exam, applied research project. *Entrance requirements:* For master's, baccalaureate degree from regionally-accredited university with minimum GPA of 3.0 on last 60 undergraduate semester hours, statement of purpose, 2 letters of recommendation. Additional exam requirements/recommendations for international students: Required—TOEFL (minimum score 550 paper-based; 78 iBT), IELTS (minimum score 6.5). *Application deadline:* For fall admission, 2/1 priority date for domestic and international students; for spring admission, 10/15 for domestic students, 10/1 for international students; for summer admission, 4/15 for domestic students, 3/15 for international students. Applications are processed on a rolling basis. Application fee: $40 ($90 for international students). Electronic applications accepted. *Expenses:* Tuition, state resident: full-time $7868; part-time $3934 per semester. Tuition, nonresident: full-time $17,828; part-time $8914 per semester. *Required fees:* $2092; $1435 per semester. Tuition and fees vary according to course load. *Financial support:* In 2017–18, 51 students received support, including 10 teaching assistantships (averaging $12,194 per year); research assistantships, career-related internships or fieldwork, Federal Work-Study, institutionally sponsored loans, scholarships/grants, and unspecified assistantships also available. Support available to part-time students. Financial award application deadline: 3/1; financial award applicants required to submit FAFSA. *Unit head:* Dr. Patricia Shields, Graduate Advisor, 512-245-3256, Fax: 512-245-7815, E-mail: ps07@txstate.edu. *Application contact:* Dr. Andrea Golato, Dean of Graduate School, 512-245-2581, Fax: 512-245-8365, E-mail: gradcollege@txstate.edu.
Website: http://mpa.polisci.txstate.edu/

Texas Tech University, Graduate School, College of Arts and Sciences, Department of Political Science, Lubbock, TX 79409. Offers political science (MA, PhD); public administration (MPA); JD/MPA. *Accreditation:* NASPAA (one or more programs are accredited). *Program availability:* 100% online, blended/hybrid learning. *Faculty:* 33 full-time (7 women). *Students:* 50 full-time (22 women), 25 part-time (10 women); includes 15 minority (4 Black or African American, non-Hispanic/Latino; 2 Asian, non-Hispanic/Latino; 8 Hispanic/Latino; 1 Two or more races, non-Hispanic/Latino), 18 international. Average age 32. 58 applicants, 62% accepted, 17 enrolled. In 2017, 20 master's, 2 doctorates awarded. *Degree requirements:* For master's, thesis or alternative; for doctorate, thesis/dissertation. *Entrance requirements:* For master's and doctorate, GRE General Test, 3 letters of reference. Additional exam requirements/recommendations for international students: Required—TOEFL (minimum score 550 paper-based; 79 iBT). *Application deadline:* For fall admission, 6/1 priority date for domestic students, 1/15 priority date for international students; for spring admission, 9/1 priority date for domestic students, 6/15 priority date for international students. Applications are processed on a rolling basis. Application fee: $60. Electronic applications accepted. *Expenses:* Contact institution. *Financial support:* In 2017–18, 48 students received support, including 36 fellowships (averaging $2,419 per year), 42 teaching assistantships (averaging $11,039 per year); research assistantships, scholarships/grants, tuition waivers, and grader positions also available. Financial award application deadline: 4/15; financial award applicants required to submit FAFSA. *Faculty research:* State politics, American institutions and behavior, Asian politics, international and comparative political relations and economics, public administration and organizations. *Total annual research expenditures:* $76,298. *Unit head:* Dr. Timothy Nokken, Department Chairperson, 806-834-2988, Fax: 806-742-0850, E-mail: timothy.nokken@ttu.edu. *Application contact:* Dr. Toby Rider, Graduate Director, 806-834-

8640, Fax: 806-742-0850, E-mail: toby.rider@ttu.edu.
Website: http://www.depts.ttu.edu/politicalscience/

Thomas Edison State University, John S. Watson School of Public Service and Continuing Studies, Trenton, NJ 08608. Offers community and economic development (MSM); environmental policy/environmental justice (MSM); homeland security (MSHS, MSM); information and technology for public service (MSM); nonprofit management (MSM); public and municipal finance (MSM); public health (MSM); public service administration and leadership (MSM); public service leadership (MPSL). *Program availability:* Part-time, online learning. *Entrance requirements:* Additional exam requirements/recommendations for international students: Required—TOEFL (minimum score 550 paper-based; 79 iBT). Electronic applications accepted.

Trident University International, College of Business Administration, Program in Business Administration, Cypress, CA 90630. Offers business administration (PhD); conflict and negotiation management (MBA); criminal justice administration (MBA); entrepreneurship (MBA); finance (MBA); general management (MBA); government accounting (MBA); human resource management (MBA); information security and digital assurance management (MBA); information technology management (MBA); international business (MBA); logistics management (MBA); marketing (MBA); project management (MBA); public management (MBA); quality management (MBA); strategic leadership (MBA). *Program availability:* Part-time, evening/weekend, online learning. *Degree requirements:* For doctorate, comprehensive exam, thesis/dissertation, defense of dissertation. *Entrance requirements:* For master's, minimum GPA of 2.5 (students with GPA 3.0 or greater may transfer up to 30% of graduate level credits); for doctorate, minimum GPA of 3.4, curriculum vitae, course work in research methods or statistics. Additional exam requirements/recommendations for international students: Required—TOEFL. Electronic applications accepted.

Troy University, Graduate School, College of Arts and Sciences, Program in Public Administration, Troy, AL 36082. Offers government contracting (MPA). *Accreditation:* NASPAA. *Program availability:* Part-time, evening/weekend, online learning. *Faculty:* 15 full-time (10 women), 3 part-time/adjunct (1 woman). *Students:* 45 full-time (28 women), 196 part-time (120 women); includes 84 minority (74 Black or African American, non-Hispanic/Latino; 2 Asian, non-Hispanic/Latino; 5 Hispanic/Latino; 3 Two or more races, non-Hispanic/Latino). Average age 33. 163 applicants, 88% accepted, 85 enrolled. In 2017, 71 master's awarded. *Degree requirements:* For master's, capstone course with minimum B grade, minimum GPA of 3.0, admission to candidacy. *Entrance requirements:* For master's, GRE (minimum score of 920 on old exam or 294 on new exam), MAT (minimum score of 400) or GMAT (minimum score of 490), bachelor's degree, minimum undergraduate GPA of 2.5 or 3.0 on last 30 semester hours, letter of recommendation, essay, resume. Additional exam requirements/recommendations for international students: Required—TOEFL (minimum score 523 paper-based; 70 iBT), IELTS (minimum score 6). *Application deadline:* Applications are processed on a rolling basis. Application fee: $50. Electronic applications accepted. *Expenses:* Tuition, state resident: part-time $417 per credit hour. Tuition, nonresident: part-time $834 per credit hour. *Required fees:* $42 per credit hour. $50 per semester. Tuition and fees vary according to campus/location. *Financial support:* Fellowships, career-related internships or fieldwork, and scholarships/grants available. Support available to part-time students. Financial award applicants required to submit FAFSA. *Unit head:* Dr. Terry Anderson, Director, 850-301-2144, E-mail: tanderson@troy.edu. *Application contact:* Jessica A. Kimbro, Director of Graduate Admissions, 334-670-3178, E-mail: jacord@troy.edu.

Tufts University, Graduate School of Arts and Sciences, Graduate Certificate Programs, Program Evaluation Program, Medford, MA 02155. Offers Certificate. *Program availability:* Part-time, evening/weekend. Electronic applications accepted. *Expenses:* Contact institution.

Université de Moncton, Faculty of Arts and Social Sciences, Department of Public Administration, Moncton, NB E1A 3E9, Canada. Offers MPA, LL B/MPA. *Program availability:* Part-time, evening/weekend. *Degree requirements:* For master's, one foreign language. *Entrance requirements:* For master's, minimum GPA of 3.0. *Faculty research:* Public sector reform, privatization, economic modeling, public policy.

Université de Sherbrooke, Faculty of Administration, Program in Public Management, Sherbrooke, QC J1K 2R1, Canada. Offers M Adm. *Degree requirements:* For master's, one foreign language, thesis. *Entrance requirements:* For master's, bachelor's degree in related field, minimum GPA of 3.0 (on 4.3 scale). Electronic applications accepted.

Université du Québec à Montréal, Graduate Programs, Program in Urban Analysis and Management, Montréal, QC H3C 3P8, Canada. Offers MA. Program offered jointly with Université du Québec, École nationale d'administration publique and Université du Québec, Institut National de la Recherche Scientifique. *Program availability:* Part-time. *Entrance requirements:* For master's, appropriate bachelor's degree or equivalent and proficiency in French.

Université du Québec, École nationale d'administration publique, Graduate Programs in Public Administration, Diploma Program in Public Administration, Quebec, QC G1K 9E5, Canada. Offers Diploma.

Université du Québec, École nationale d'administration publique, Graduate Programs in Public Administration, Doctorate Program in Public Administration, Quebec, QC G1K 9E5, Canada. Offers PhD.

University at Albany, State University of New York, Nelson A. Rockefeller College of Public Affairs and Policy, Department of Public Administration and Policy, Albany, NY 12222-0001. Offers financial management and public economics (MPA); financial market regulation (MPA); health policy (MPA); healthcare management (MPA); homeland security (MPA); human resources management (MPA); information strategy and management (MPA); local government management (MPA); nonprofit management (MPA); nonprofit management and leadership (Certificate); organizational behavior and theory (MPA, PhD); planning and policy analysis (CAS); policy analysis (MPA); politics and administration (PhD); public finance (PhD); public management (PhD); public policy (PhD); public sector management (Certificate); women and public policy (Certificate); JD/MPA. JD/MPA offered jointly with Albany Law School. *Accreditation:* NASPAA (one or more programs are accredited). *Faculty:* 21 full-time (7 women), 14 part-time/adjunct (7 women). *Students:* 115 full-time (59 women), 93 part-time (56 women); includes 41 minority (11 Black or African American, non-Hispanic/Latino; 9 Asian, non-Hispanic/Latino; 18 Hispanic/Latino; 3 Two or more races, non-Hispanic/Latino), 32 international. 236 applicants, 69% accepted, 86 enrolled. In 2017, 57 master's, 1 doctorate, 14 other advanced degrees awarded. *Degree requirements:* For doctorate, one foreign language, thesis/dissertation. *Entrance requirements:* For doctorate, GRE General Test. Additional exam requirements/recommendations for international students: Required—TOEFL (minimum score 550 paper-based). *Application deadline:* For fall admission, 2/1 priority date for domestic students, 5/1 for international students; for spring admission, 12/1 for domestic students. Applications are processed on a rolling basis. Application fee: $75. Electronic applications accepted. *Expenses:* Tuition, state resident: full-time $10,870; part-time $453 per credit hour. Tuition, nonresident: full-time $22,210; part-time $925 per credit hour. *Required fees:* $84.68 per credit hour. $508.06 per semester. Part-time tuition and fees vary according to course load and program. *Financial support:* Application deadline: 2/1. *Unit head:* Victor Asal, Chair, 518-591-8729, E-mail: vasal@albany.edu.

Public Administration

The University of Akron, Graduate School, Buchtel College of Arts and Sciences, Department of Public Administration and Urban Studies, Program in Public Administration, Akron, OH 44325. Offers MPA, JD/MPA. *Students:* 28 full-time (13 women), 27 part-time (17 women); includes 15 minority (13 Black or African American, non-Hispanic/Latino; 2 Two or more races, non-Hispanic/Latino), 13 international. Average age 34. 36 applicants, 94% accepted, 20 enrolled. In 2017, 28 master's awarded. *Entrance requirements:* For master's, GRE, GMAT, LSAT, MAT (if undergraduate cumulative GPA less than 3.0), minimum GPA of 3.0, resume, one-page personal essay, three letters of recommendation. Additional exam requirements/recommendations for international students: Required—TOEFL (minimum score 79 iBT). *Application deadline:* For fall admission, 7/1 priority date for domestic and international students; for spring admission, 11/15 priority date for domestic and international students; for summer admission, 4/1 priority date for domestic and international students. Applications are processed on a rolling basis. Application fee: $45 ($70 for international students). Electronic applications accepted. *Unit head:* Dr. Nancy Marion, Department Chair, 330-972-5551, E-mail: nmarion@uakron.edu. *Application contact:* Francois Doamekpor, Graduate Director, 330-972-5408, E-mail: francoi@uakron.edu.
Website: http://www.uakron.edu/paus/academics/

The University of Alabama, Graduate School, College of Arts and Sciences, Department of Political Science, Tuscaloosa, AL 35487. Offers political science (MA, PhD); public administration (MPA). *Program availability:* Part-time. *Faculty:* 15 full-time (3 women). *Students:* 46 full-time (15 women), 19 part-time (7 women); includes 11 minority (7 Black or African American, non-Hispanic/Latino; 1 American Indian or Alaska Native, non-Hispanic/Latino; 2 Asian, non-Hispanic/Latino; 1 Two or more races, non-Hispanic/Latino), 6 international. Average age 30. 38 applicants, 66% accepted, 13 enrolled. In 2017, 16 master's, 3 doctorates awarded. Terminal master's awarded for partial completion of doctoral program. *Degree requirements:* For master's, comprehensive exam, thesis optional; for doctorate, comprehensive exam, thesis/dissertation. *Entrance requirements:* For master's and doctorate, GRE, minimum undergraduate GPA of 3.0. Additional exam requirements/recommendations for international students: Required—TOEFL. *Application deadline:* For fall admission, 6/30 for domestic and international students; for spring admission, 10/15 for domestic and international students. Applications are processed on a rolling basis. Application fee: $50 ($60 for international students). Electronic applications accepted. *Financial support:* In 2017–18, 19 students received support, including fellowships with full tuition reimbursements available (averaging $15,000 per year), teaching assistantships with full tuition reimbursements available (averaging $12,500 per year); career-related internships or fieldwork and Federal Work-Study also available. Financial award application deadline: 2/15. *Faculty research:* American politics, comparative politics, international relations, public policy and administration, political theory. *Total annual research expenditures:* $13,262. *Unit head:* Dr. Joseph Smith, Chair and Professor, 205-348-5981, E-mail: josmith@bama.ua.edu. *Application contact:* Dr. Douglas Gibler, Graduate Advisor, 205-348-5528, Fax: 205-348-5298, E-mail: dmgibler@bama.ua.edu.
Website: http://www.as.ua.edu/psc/

The University of Alabama at Birmingham, College of Arts and Sciences, Master of Public Administration Program, Birmingham, AL 35233. Offers MPA, MPA/JD, MPA/MPH, MPA/MSCJ. *Accreditation:* NASPAA (one or more programs are accredited). *Program availability:* Part-time, evening/weekend, 100% online, blended/hybrid learning. *Degree requirements:* For master's, portfolio or thesis. *Entrance requirements:* For master's, GRE General Test (preferred), references. Additional exam requirements/recommendations for international students: Required—TOEFL (minimum score 500 paper-based; 70 iBT), IELTS (minimum score 6.5). Electronic applications accepted. *Expenses:* Contact institution. *Faculty research:* Information management and technology, nonprofit management, education policy and planning, political philosophy, program evaluation, Geographic Information System, administrative ethics, administrative theory and behavior.

University of Alaska Anchorage, College of Business and Public Policy, Program in Public Administration, Anchorage, AK 99508. Offers MPA. *Program availability:* Part-time. *Degree requirements:* For master's, comprehensive exam, thesis or alternative, capstone project. *Entrance requirements:* For master's, GRE General Test. Additional exam requirements/recommendations for international students: Required—TOEFL (minimum score 550 paper-based). *Faculty research:* Policy analysis, policy and administration issues in the North, hypothetical government policies, public management in health care.

University of Alaska Southeast, Graduate Programs, Program in Public Administration, Juneau, AK 99801. Offers MPA. *Program availability:* Part-time, evening/weekend, online learning. *Degree requirements:* For master's, capstone course or thesis. *Entrance requirements:* For master's, minimum GPA of 3.0, resume or curriculum vitae, three letters of reference. Additional exam requirements/recommendations for international students: Recommended—TOEFL. Electronic applications accepted. *Faculty research:* Democratic governance, public administrative theory, local government.

The University of Arizona, College of Social and Behavioral Sciences, Program in Public Administration, Tucson, AZ 85721. Offers public administration (MPA); public administration and policy (PhD). *Accreditation:* NASPAA. *Degree requirements:* For master's, internship of 400 hours; for doctorate, comprehensive exam, thesis/dissertation. *Entrance requirements:* For doctorate, GMAT or GRE, minimum graduate GPA of 3.5, letter of interest, 3 letters of recommendation, resume. Additional exam requirements/recommendations for international students: Required—TOEFL (minimum score 650 paper-based; 115 iBT). Electronic applications accepted. *Expenses:* Contact institution.

University of Arkansas, Graduate School, J. William Fulbright College of Arts and Sciences, Department of Political Science, Program in Public Administration, Fayetteville, AR 72701. Offers MPA. In 2017, 10 master's awarded. *Degree requirements:* For master's, comprehensive exam, thesis or alternative. *Entrance requirements:* For master's, GRE General Test. *Application deadline:* For fall admission, 8/1 for domestic students, 4/1 for international students; for spring admission, 12/1 for domestic students, 10/1 for international students; for summer admission, 4/15 for domestic students, 3/1 for international students. Applications are processed on a rolling basis. Application fee: $60. Electronic applications accepted. *Expenses:* Tuition, state resident: full-time $3782. Tuition, nonresident: full-time $10,238. *Financial support:* In 2017–18, 2 research assistantships, 1 teaching assistantship were awarded; fellowships with tuition reimbursements, career-related internships or fieldwork, and Federal Work-Study also available. Support available to part-time students. Financial award application deadline: 4/1; financial award applicants required to submit FAFSA. *Unit head:* Dr. Pearl K. Dowe, Department Chair, 479-575-3356, Fax: 479-575-6432, E-mail: pkford@uark.edu. *Application contact:* Dr. Pearl Dowe, Graduate Coordinator, 479-575-3356, Fax: 479-575-6432, E-mail: pkford@uark.edu.
Website: https://fulbright.uark.edu/departments/political-science/

University of Arkansas at Little Rock, Graduate School, College of Social Sciences and Communication, Program in Public Administration, Little Rock, AR 72204-1099. Offers MPA. *Accreditation:* NASPAA. *Program availability:* Part-time, evening/weekend.

Degree requirements: For master's, comprehensive exam. *Entrance requirements:* For master's, GRE General Test or MAT, minimum GPA of 2.7. *Faculty research:* State and local administration, nonprofit management.

University of Baltimore, Graduate School, College of Public Affairs, Doctoral Program in Public Administration, Baltimore, MD 21201-5779. Offers DPA. *Program availability:* Part-time, evening/weekend. *Degree requirements:* For doctorate, thesis/dissertation. *Entrance requirements:* For doctorate, GRE. Additional exam requirements/recommendations for international students: Required—TOEFL.

University of Baltimore, Graduate School, College of Public Affairs, Master's Program in Public Administration, Baltimore, MD 21201-5779. Offers MPA, JD/MPA. *Accreditation:* NASPAA. *Program availability:* Part-time, evening/weekend, online learning. *Entrance requirements:* For master's, interview, minimum GPA of 3.0. Additional exam requirements/recommendations for international students: Required—TOEFL (minimum score 550 paper-based). Electronic applications accepted. *Expenses:* Contact institution. *Faculty research:* Welfare policy, public administration ethics, bureaucratic politics, public sector budgeting, program evaluation.

University of Central Florida, College of Community Innovation and Education, School of Public Administration, Orlando, FL 32816. Offers emergency management and homeland security (Certificate); fundraising (Certificate); nonprofit management (MNM, Certificate); public administration (MPA); research administration (MRA); urban and regional planning (MS). *Accreditation:* NASPAA. *Program availability:* Part-time, evening/weekend. *Students:* 110 full-time (76 women), 290 part-time (215 women); includes 193 minority (96 Black or African American, non-Hispanic/Latino; 2 American Indian or Alaska Native, non-Hispanic/Latino; 13 Asian, non-Hispanic/Latino; 74 Hispanic/Latino; 8 Two or more races, non-Hispanic/Latino), 6 international. Average age 32. 255 applicants, 78% accepted, 152 enrolled. In 2017, 95 master's, 34 other advanced degrees awarded. *Degree requirements:* For master's, comprehensive exam, thesis or alternative, research report. *Entrance requirements:* For master's, letters of recommendation, goal statement, resume. Additional exam requirements/recommendations for international students: Required—TOEFL. *Application deadline:* For fall admission, 6/15 for domestic students; for spring admission, 11/1 for domestic students. Application fee: $30. Electronic applications accepted. *Expenses:* Tuition, state resident: part-time $288.16 per credit hour. Tuition, nonresident: part-time $1073.31 per credit hour. Tuition and fees vary according to program. *Financial support:* In 2017–18, 11 students received support, including 2 fellowships with partial tuition reimbursements available (averaging $5,300 per year), 6 research assistantships with partial tuition reimbursements available (averaging $9,637 per year), 3 teaching assistantships with partial tuition reimbursements available (averaging $9,390 per year); career-related internships or fieldwork, Federal Work-Study, institutionally sponsored loans, health care benefits, tuition waivers (partial), and unspecified assistantships also available. Financial award application deadline: 3/1; financial award applicants required to submit FAFSA. *Unit head:* Dr. Naim Kapucu, Director, 407-823-6096, Fax: 407-823-5651, E-mail: kapucu@ucf.edu. *Application contact:* Associate Director, Graduate Admissions, 407-823-2766, Fax: 407-823-6442, E-mail: gradadmissions@ucf.edu.
Website: https://www.cohpa.ucf.edu/publicadmin/

University of Central Oklahoma, The Jackson College of Graduate Studies, College of Liberal Arts, Department of Political Science, Edmond, OK 73034-5209. Offers political science (MA), including international affairs; public administration (MPA), including public and nonprofit management, urban management. *Program availability:* Part-time. *Faculty:* 11 full-time (4 women), 1 part-time/adjunct (0 women). *Students:* 42 full-time (21 women), 58 part-time (26 women); includes 33 minority (14 Black or African American, non-Hispanic/Latino; 3 American Indian or Alaska Native, non-Hispanic/Latino; 10 Hispanic/Latino; 6 Two or more races, non-Hispanic/Latino), 18 international. Average age 32. 127 applicants, 84% accepted, 29 enrolled. In 2017, 32 master's awarded. *Degree requirements:* For master's, comprehensive exam (for some programs), thesis (for some programs). *Entrance requirements:* For master's, 18 undergraduate hours in political science. Additional exam requirements/recommendations for international students: Required—TOEFL (minimum score 550 paper-based; 79 iBT), IELTS (minimum score 6.5). *Application deadline:* For fall admission, 7/15 for international students; for spring admission, 11/15 for international students. Applications are processed on a rolling basis. Application fee: $60. Electronic applications accepted. *Expenses:* Tuition, state resident: full-time $5375; part-time $268.75 per credit hour. Tuition, nonresident: full-time $13,295; part-time $664.75 per credit hour. *Required fees:* $626; $31.30 per credit hour. One-time fee: $50. Tuition and fees vary according to program. *Financial support:* In 2017–18, 20 students received support, including 3 research assistantships with partial tuition reimbursements available (averaging $3,943 per year), 4 teaching assistantships with partial tuition reimbursements available (averaging $7,394 per year); career-related internships or fieldwork, scholarships/grants, tuition waivers (partial), and unspecified assistantships also available. Financial award application deadline: 3/31; financial award applicants required to submit FAFSA. *Unit head:* Dr. Lou Furmanski, Department Chair, 405-974-5540, Fax: 405-974-3823. *Application contact:* Dr. Jan Hardt, Graduate Advisor, 405-974-5840, Fax: 405-974-3823, E-mail: gradcoll@uco.edu.
Website: http://sites.uco.edu/la/political-science/index.asp

University of Colorado Colorado Springs, School of Public Affairs, Colorado Springs, CO 80918. Offers criminal justice (MCJ); public administration (MPA). *Accreditation:* NASPAA. *Program availability:* Part-time, evening/weekend, 100% online, blended/hybrid learning. *Faculty:* 13 full-time (6 women), 16 part-time/adjunct (3 women). *Students:* 19 full-time (11 women), 164 part-time (101 women); includes 57 minority (6 Black or African American, non-Hispanic/Latino; 1 American Indian or Alaska Native, non-Hispanic/Latino; 5 Asian, non-Hispanic/Latino; 37 Hispanic/Latino; 8 Two or more races, non-Hispanic/Latino). Average age 35. 61 applicants, 95% accepted, 40 enrolled. In 2017, 44 master's awarded. *Degree requirements:* For master's, internship, capstone project, or thesis. *Entrance requirements:* For master's, GRE General Test, GMAT, LSAT, minimum GPA of 3.0. Additional exam requirements/recommendations for international students: Recommended—TOEFL (minimum score 550 paper-based; 80 iBT), IELTS (minimum score 6.5). *Application deadline:* Applications are processed on a rolling basis. Application fee: $60 ($100 for international students). Electronic applications accepted. *Expenses:* $10,350 per year resident tuition, $20,935 nonresident, $11,961 nonresidential online; annual costs vary depending on program, course-load, and residency status. *Financial support:* In 2017–18, 25 students received support. Career-related internships or fieldwork, scholarships/grants, and tuition waivers available. Support available to part-time students. Financial award application deadline: 3/1; financial award applicants required to submit FAFSA. *Faculty research:* Antiquated prison environments; public management; intersections of gender, class, race and crime; national security/U.S. foreign policy; leadership, ethics, organizational theory and behavior. *Total annual research expenditures:* $486,455. *Unit head:* Dr. George Reed, Dean, 719-255-4109, E-mail: george.reed@uccs.edu. *Application contact:* Crista Hill, Outreach Student Services Specialist, 719-255-4993, Fax: 719-255-4183, E-mail: chill12@uccs.edu.
Website: http://www.uccs.edu/spa/

University of Colorado Denver, School of Public Affairs, Program in Public Affairs and Administration, Denver, CO 80127. Offers public administration (MPA), including

domestic violence, emergency management and homeland security, environmental policy, management and law, homeland security and defense, local government, nonprofit management, public administration; public affairs (PhD). *Accreditation:* NASPAA. *Program availability:* Part-time, evening/weekend, online learning. *Degree requirements:* For master's, thesis or alternative, 36-39 credit hours; for doctorate, comprehensive exam, thesis/dissertation, minimum of 66 semester hours, including at least 30 hours of dissertation. *Entrance requirements:* For master's, GRE, GMAT or LSAT, resume, essay, transcripts, recommendations; for doctorate, GRE, resume, essay, transcripts, recommendations. Additional exam requirements/recommendations for international students: Required—TOEFL (minimum score 550 paper-based; 80 iBT); Recommended—IELTS (minimum score 6.5). Electronic applications accepted. *Expenses:* Contact institution. *Faculty research:* Housing, education and the social and economic issues of vulnerable populations; nonprofit governance and management; education finance, effectiveness and reform; P-20 education initiatives; municipal government accountability.

University of Connecticut, Graduate School, College of Liberal Arts and Sciences, Department of Public Policy, Field of Public Administration, Storrs, CT 06269. Offers MPA. *Accreditation:* NASPAA. *Degree requirements:* For master's, comprehensive exam, internship. *Entrance requirements:* For master's, GRE General Test. Additional exam requirements/recommendations for international students: Required—TOEFL (minimum score 550 paper-based). Electronic applications accepted.

University of Dayton, Master of Public Administration Program, Dayton, OH 45469. Offers MPA. *Accreditation:* NASPAA. *Program availability:* Part-time, evening/weekend. *Faculty:* 8 full-time (2 women), 5 part-time/adjunct (3 women). *Students:* 20 full-time (12 women), 8 part-time (6 women); includes 4 minority (2 Black or African American, non-Hispanic/Latino; 2 Two or more races, non-Hispanic/Latino). Average age 29. 54 applicants, 19% accepted. In 2017, 10 master's awarded. *Degree requirements:* For master's, internship or public service project. *Entrance requirements:* For master's, GRE. Additional exam requirements/recommendations for international students: Required—TOEFL (minimum score 550 paper-based; 80 iBT). *Application deadline:* Applications are processed on a rolling basis. Application fee: $0 ($50 for international students). Electronic applications accepted. *Expenses:* Contact institution. *Financial support:* In 2017–18, 3 research assistantships with full tuition reimbursements (averaging $11,868 per year) were awarded; unspecified assistantships also available. Financial award application deadline: 3/1; financial award applicants required to submit FAFSA. *Faculty research:* Urban policy, environmental policy, NGO leadership, ethics in public management, government on TV/film. *Unit head:* Dr. Joshua D. Ambrosius, Director of MPA Program, 937-229-3924, Fax: 937-229-1400, E-mail: jambrosius1@udayton.edu.
Website: https://www.udayton.edu/artssciences/academics/politicalscience/grad/index.php

University of Delaware, College of Arts and Sciences, School of Public Policy and Administration, Program in Public Administration, Newark, DE 19716. Offers MPA. *Accreditation:* NASPAA. *Program availability:* Part-time, evening/weekend. *Degree requirements:* For master's, internship or thesis. *Entrance requirements:* For master's, GRE General Test. Additional exam requirements/recommendations for international students: Required—TOEFL. Electronic applications accepted. *Faculty research:* State and local management, community development and nonprofit leadership, drug and alcohol epidemiology, fiscal and financial policy, transportation impacts and management.
See Display below and Close-Up on page 1307.

University of Evansville, Center for Adult Education, Evansville, IN 47722. Offers public service administration (MS). *Program availability:* Part-time, evening/weekend. *Entrance requirements:* For master's, GRE or MAT, minimum undergraduate GPA of 3.0, resume, minimum of 3 years' work experience, 2 letters of reference. Additional exam requirements/recommendations for international students: Required—TOEFL (minimum score 79 iBT), IELTS (minimum score 6.5). *Expenses:* Contact institution.

The University of Findlay, Office of Graduate Admissions, Findlay, OH 45840. Offers applied security and analytics (MSAS); athletic training (MAT); business (MBA), including certified management accountant, certified public accountant, health care management, hospitality management; education (MA Ed, Ed D), including children's literature (MA Ed), curriculum and teaching (MA Ed), education (MA Ed), educational administration (MA Ed), human resource development (MA Ed), mathematics (MA Ed), reading (MA Ed), science education (MA Ed), superintendent (Ed D), teaching (Ed D), technology (MA Ed); environmental, safety, and health management (MSEM); health informatics (MS); occupational therapy (MOT); pharmacy (Pharm D); physical therapy (DPT); physician assistant (MPA); rhetoric and writing (MA); teaching English to speakers of other languages (TESOL) and applied linguistics (MA). *Program availability:* Part-time, evening/weekend, 100% online, blended/hybrid learning. *Students:* 688 full-time (430 women), 553 part-time (308 women), 170 international. Average age 28. In 2017, 366 master's, 137 doctorates awarded. *Degree requirements:* For master's, comprehensive exam (for some programs), thesis (for some programs), cumulative project, capstone project; for doctorate, thesis/dissertation (for some programs). *Entrance requirements:* For master's, GRE/GMAT, bachelor's degree from accredited institution, minimum undergraduate GPA of 2.5 in last 64 hours of course work; for doctorate, GRE, MAT, minimum cumulative GPA of 3.0. Additional exam requirements/recommendations for international students: Required—TOEFL (minimum score 79 iBT), IELTS (minimum score 7), PTE (minimum score 61). *Application deadline:* Applications are processed on a rolling basis. Electronic applications accepted. *Financial support:* In 2017–18, 10 research assistantships with partial tuition reimbursements (averaging $7,200 per year), 35 teaching assistantships with partial tuition reimbursements (averaging $7,200 per year) were awarded; Federal Work-Study, institutionally sponsored loans, and unspecified assistantships also available. Financial award applicants required to submit FAFSA. *Unit head:* Christopher M. Harris, Director of Admissions, 419-434-4347, E-mail: harrisc1@findlay.edu. *Application contact:* Madeline Fauser Brennan, Graduate Admissions Counselor, 419-434-4636, Fax: 419-434-4898, E-mail: fauserbrennan@findlay.edu.
Website: http://www.findlay.edu/admissions/graduate/Pages/default.aspx

University of Georgia, School of Public and International Affairs, Department of Public Administration and Policy, Athens, GA 30602. Offers public administration (MPA, PhD). *Accreditation:* NASPAA (one or more programs are accredited). *Degree requirements:* For master's, internship; for doctorate, thesis/dissertation. *Entrance requirements:* For master's and doctorate, GRE General Test. Electronic applications accepted.

University of Guam, Office of Graduate Studies, School of Business and Public Administration, Public Administration Program, Mangilao, GU 96923. Offers MPA. *Entrance requirements:* For master's, GRE General Test. Additional exam requirements/recommendations for international students: Required—TOEFL.

University of Guelph, Graduate Studies, College of Social and Applied Human Sciences, Department of Political Science, Guelph, ON N1G 2W1, Canada. Offers comparative politics (MA); international development (MA); political science (MA); public policy and public administration (MA); the Americas (Canada emphasis) (MA). MA in public policy and public administration offered in collaboration with Department of Political Science of McMaster University. *Degree requirements:* For master's, thesis or paper. *Entrance requirements:* For master's, minimum B average during previous 2 years of course work, 4 year Honours Degree in Political Science. Additional exam requirements/recommendations for international students: Required—TOEFL. Electronic applications accepted. *Faculty research:* Political ethics, constitutional power.

Public Administration

University of Hawaii at Manoa, Office of Graduate Education, College of Social Sciences, Department of Public Administration, Honolulu, HI 96822. Offers MPA, Graduate Certificate. *Program availability:* Part-time. *Degree requirements:* For master's, thesis optional, practicum. *Entrance requirements:* Additional exam requirements/recommendations for international students: Required—TOEFL (minimum score 540 paper-based; 76 iBT), IELTS (minimum score 5). *Faculty research:* Public sector finance and the budget process, collaboration between sectors, organizational problem solving and communication processes, system reform in government organizations, public policy analysis.

University of Houston, College of Liberal Arts and Social Sciences, Department of Political Science, Houston, TX 77204. Offers political science (MA, PhD); public administration (MA). *Program availability:* Part-time. Terminal master's awarded for partial completion of doctoral program. *Degree requirements:* For master's, thesis optional; for doctorate, thesis/dissertation. *Entrance requirements:* For master's and doctorate, GRE. Additional exam requirements/recommendations for international students: Required—TOEFL (minimum score 550 paper-based; 79 iBT). *Faculty research:* American politics, political theory, judicial process, public policy, comparative politics.

University of Idaho, College of Graduate Studies, College of Letters, Arts and Social Sciences, Department of Politics and Philosophy, Moscow, ID 83844. Offers political science (MA, PhD); public administration (MPA). *Faculty:* 5 full-time. *Students:* 7 full-time, 10 part-time. Average age 31. In 2017, 7 master's, 1 doctorate awarded. *Entrance requirements:* For master's, GRE, minimum GPA of 3.0. Additional exam requirements/ recommendations for international students: Required—TOEFL (minimum score 96 iBT). *Expenses:* Tuition, state resident: full-time $6722; part-time $430 per credit hour. Tuition, nonresident: full-time $23,046; part-time $1337 per credit hour. *Required fees:* $2142; $63 per credit hour. *Faculty research:* Political socialization, international and domestic conflict processes, constitutional law. *Unit head:* Dr. Brian Ellison, Chair, 208-885-6328, E-mail: politicsphilosophy@uidaho.edu. *Application contact:* Sean Scoggin, Graduate Recruitment Coordinator, 208-885-4723, E-mail: graduateadmissions@uidaho.edu.
Website: https://www.uidaho.edu/class/politics-and-philosophy

University of Illinois at Chicago, College of Urban Planning and Public Affairs, Department of Public Administration, Chicago, IL 60607-7128. Offers MPA, PhD. *Accreditation:* NASPAA (one or more programs are accredited). *Program availability:* Part-time, evening/weekend. Terminal master's awarded for partial completion of doctoral program. *Degree requirements:* For master's, internship/project. *Entrance requirements:* For master's, GRE General Test, minimum GPA of 3.0. Additional exam requirements/recommendations for international students: Required—TOEFL. Electronic applications accepted. *Expenses:* Contact institution. *Faculty research:* E-government, science and technology policy, financial management, urban policy, nonprofit management, public management.

University of Illinois at Springfield, Graduate Programs, College of Public Affairs and Administration, Program in Public Administration, Springfield, IL 62703-5407. Offers management of nonprofit organizations (Graduate Certificate); public administration (MPA, DPA). *Accreditation:* NASPAA. *Program availability:* Part-time, evening/weekend, 100% online, blended/hybrid learning. *Faculty:* 12 full-time (6 women), 7 part-time/ adjunct (4 women). *Students:* 59 full-time (36 women), 167 part-time (83 women); includes 68 minority (45 Black or African American, non-Hispanic/Latino; 10 Asian, non-Hispanic/Latino; 9 Hispanic/Latino; 4 Two or more races, non-Hispanic/Latino), 7 international. Average age 35. 148 applicants, 47% accepted, 59 enrolled. In 2017, 62 master's, 6 other advanced degrees awarded. *Degree requirements:* For master's, capstone seminar; for doctorate, comprehensive exam, thesis/dissertation. *Entrance requirements:* For master's, minimum undergraduate GPA of 2.5; completion of prerequisites that include undergraduate coursework in political science in American national government, microeconomics or a market-based economics survey course, basic statistics, and competence in one computer spreadsheet application package; resume; career goals statement; writing skills; for doctorate, GRE, master's degree with minimum GPA of 3.25; educational and professional goals statement of at least 600 words, including possible research interest; evidence of significant work experience in public affairs field; at least one sample of professional writing; current vitae; 3 letters of recommendation. Additional exam requirements/recommendations for international students: Required—TOEFL (minimum score 550 paper-based). *Application deadline:* Applications are processed on a rolling basis. Application fee: $60 ($75 for international students). Electronic applications accepted. *Expenses:* Contact institution. *Financial support:* In 2017–18, research assistantships with full tuition reimbursements (averaging $10,249 per year), teaching assistantships with full tuition reimbursements (averaging $10,303 per year) were awarded; fellowships, career-related internships or fieldwork, Federal Work-Study, scholarships/grants, health care benefits, and unspecified assistantships also available. Support available to part-time students. Financial award application deadline: 11/15; financial award applicants required to submit FAFSA. *Unit head:* Dr. Robert Blankenberger, Program Administrator, 217-206-8327, E-mail: rblan2@uis.edu.
Website: http://www.uis.edu/publicadministration/

The University of Kansas, Graduate Studies, College of Liberal Arts and Sciences, School of Public Affairs and Administration, Lawrence, KS 66045-3129. Offers city and county management (Graduate Certificate); performance management (Graduate Certificate); public administration (MPA, PhD); urban planning (MUP); JD/MPA; MUP/ MPA. *Accreditation:* NASPAA. *Program availability:* Part-time, evening/weekend. *Students:* 87 full-time (40 women), 73 part-time (45 women); includes 30 minority (9 Black or African American, non-Hispanic/Latino; 5 American Indian or Alaska Native, non-Hispanic/Latino; 3 Asian, non-Hispanic/Latino; 12 Hispanic/Latino; 1 Two or more races, non-Hispanic/Latino), 9 international. Average age 32. 123 applicants, 61% accepted, 49 enrolled. In 2017, 45 master's, 3 doctorates, 6 other advanced degrees awarded. Terminal master's awarded for partial completion of doctoral program. *Entrance requirements:* For master's and doctorate, GRE General Test, official transcript, current resume, personal statement, writing sample, three letters of recommendation. Additional exam requirements/recommendations for international students: Required—TOEFL or IELTS. *Application deadline:* For fall admission, 1/25 priority date for domestic and international students; for spring admission, 5/1 priority date for domestic and international students; for summer admission, 2/1 for domestic and international students. Application fee: $65 ($85 for international students). Electronic applications accepted. *Financial support:* Fellowships, research assistantships, teaching assistantships, career-related internships or fieldwork, institutionally sponsored loans, scholarships/grants, and unspecified assistantships available. Financial award application deadline: 1/25. *Faculty research:* Collaboration, law and society, social equity, performance management, sustainability. *Unit head:* Reggie Robinson, Director, 785-864-3527, E-mail: rlrobinson@ku.edu. *Application contact:* Angie Soden, Graduate Admissions Contact, 785-864-3527, E-mail: padept@ku.edu.
Website: http://kupa.ku.edu/

University of Kentucky, Graduate School, Martin School of Public Policy and Administration, Lexington, KY 40506-0027. Offers public administration (MPA); public

financial management (MPFM, Graduate Certificate); public policy (MPP); public policy and administration (PhD). *Accreditation:* NASPAA (one or more programs are accredited). *Program availability:* Part-time, evening/weekend, 100% online. Terminal master's awarded for partial completion of doctoral program. *Degree requirements:* For master's, thesis; for doctorate, comprehensive exam, thesis/dissertation. *Entrance requirements:* For master's, GMAT or GRE General Test, minimum undergraduate GPA of 2.75; for doctorate, GMAT or GRE General Test, minimum graduate GPA of 3.0. Additional exam requirements/recommendations for international students: Required— TOEFL (minimum score 550 paper-based; 79 iBT); Recommended—IELTS (minimum score 6.5). Electronic applications accepted. *Expenses:* Contact institution. *Faculty research:* Public financial management, education finance and policy, tax policy, environmental policy, public organizations and management.

University of La Verne, College of Business and Public Management, Doctoral Program in Public Administration, La Verne, CA 91750-4443. Offers DPA. *Program availability:* Part-time. *Faculty:* 6 full-time (3 women), 1 (woman) part-time/adjunct. *Students:* 61 part-time (31 women); includes 36 minority (14 Black or African American, non-Hispanic/Latino; 1 American Indian or Alaska Native, non-Hispanic/Latino; 2 Asian, non-Hispanic/Latino; 18 Hispanic/Latino; 1 Native Hawaiian or other Pacific Islander, non-Hispanic/Latino), 6 international. Average age 42. *Degree requirements:* For doctorate, thesis/dissertation. *Entrance requirements:* For doctorate, MAT, GMAT or GRE, minimum undergraduate GPA of 3.25, interview, 3 letters of recommendation, statement of purpose. Additional exam requirements/recommendations for international students: Required—TOEFL (minimum score 550 paper-based). Application fee: $75. *Expenses:* Contact institution. *Financial support:* Institutionally sponsored loans and scholarships/grants available. Financial award application deadline: 3/2; financial award applicants required to submit FAFSA. *Unit head:* Dr. Suzanne Beaumaster, Chairperson, 909-448-4166, E-mail: sbeaumaster@laverne.edu. *Application contact:* Cathy Cook, Associate Director of Graduate Admission, 909-448-4719, Fax: 909-971-2295, E-mail: ccook2@laverne.edu.
Website: http://laverne.edu/business-and-public-administration/doctor-of-public-administration/

University of La Verne, College of Business and Public Management, Master's Program in Public Administration, La Verne, CA 91750-4443. Offers gerontology (MPA); nonprofit (MPA); public health (MPA); urban management and affairs (MPA). *Accreditation:* NASPAA. *Program availability:* Part-time. *Faculty:* 11 full-time (5 women), 1 part-time/adjunct (0 women). *Students:* 33 full-time (18 women), 21 part-time (15 women); includes 40 minority (3 Black or African American, non-Hispanic/Latino; 2 Asian, non-Hispanic/Latino; 35 Hispanic/Latino), 1 international. Average age 33. *Entrance requirements:* For master's, minimum undergraduate GPA of 3.0, statement of purpose, 2 letters of recommendation, resume. Additional exam requirements/ recommendations for international students: Required—TOEFL (minimum score 550 paper-based). *Application deadline:* Applications are processed on a rolling basis. Application fee: $50. *Expenses:* Contact institution. *Financial support:* Institutionally sponsored loans and scholarships/grants available. Financial award application deadline: 3/2; financial award applicants required to submit FAFSA. *Unit head:* Marcia Godwin, Chairperson, 909-448-4103, E-mail: mgodwin@laverne.edu. *Application contact:* Cathy Cook, Associate Director of Graduate Admissions, 909-448-4719, Fax: 909-971-2295, E-mail: ccook2@laverne.edu.
Website: https://business.laverne.edu/mpa/

University of Louisiana at Monroe, Graduate School, College of Business and Social Sciences, Program in Public Administration, Monroe, LA 71209-0001. Offers MPA. *Program availability:* Online learning. *Faculty:* 3 full-time (1 woman). *Students:* 3 full-time (all women), 41 part-time (24 women); includes 17 minority (14 Black or African American, non-Hispanic/Latino; 1 Hispanic/Latino; 2 Two or more races, non-Hispanic/ Latino). Average age 30. 31 applicants, 77% accepted, 15 enrolled. In 2017, 17 master's awarded. *Entrance requirements:* For master's, GRE. *Expenses:* Tuition, state resident: full-time $6489; part-time $479 per hour. Tuition, nonresident: full-time $12,100; part-time $479 per hour. *Required fees:* $8860; $802 per hour. $3273 per semester. *Financial support:* In 2017–18, 18 students received support. *Unit head:* Dr. Leigh Hersey, Director, 318-342-1332, E-mail: hersey@ulm.edu.
Website: http://www.ulm.edu/onlinedegrees/m_pa.html

University of Louisville, Graduate School, College of Arts and Sciences, Department of Urban and Public Affairs, Louisville, KY 40208. Offers public administration (MPA), including human resources management, non-profit management, public policy and administration; urban and public affairs (PhD), including urban planning and development, urban policy and administration; urban planning (MUP), including administration of planning organizations, housing and community development, land use and environmental planning, spatial analysis. *Program availability:* Part-time, evening/ weekend. *Faculty:* 12 full-time (5 women), 4 part-time/adjunct (1 woman). *Students:* 50 full-time (19 women), 20 part-time (17 women); includes 17 minority (6 Black or African American, non-Hispanic/Latino; 1 Asian, non-Hispanic/Latino; 4 Hispanic/Latino; 6 Two or more races, non-Hispanic/Latino), 4 international. Average age 31. 47 applicants, 70% accepted, 22 enrolled. In 2017, 20 master's, 2 doctorates awarded. Terminal master's awarded for partial completion of doctoral program. *Degree requirements:* For master's, internship; for doctorate, comprehensive exam, thesis/dissertation. *Entrance requirements:* For master's, GRE General Test, minimum GPA of 3.0; for doctorate, GRE General Test, master's degree in appropriate field. Additional exam requirements/ recommendations for international students: Required—TOEFL (minimum score 550 paper-based; 79 iBT). *Application deadline:* Applications are processed on a rolling basis. Application fee: $65. *Expenses:* Contact institution. *Financial support:* Fellowships, research assistantships, tuition waivers (full and partial), and unspecified assistantships available. Financial award application deadline: 2/1. *Faculty research:* Urban theory, sustainability, public administration, urban planning, urban management. *Total annual research expenditures:* $240,308. *Unit head:* Dr. David Simpson, Chair, 502-852-8019, Fax: 502-852-4558, E-mail: dave.simpson@louisville.edu. *Application contact:* Latonia Craig, Director of Graduate Recruitment and Diversity Retention, 502-852-5207, Fax: 502-852-4558, E-mail: gradadm@louisville.edu.
Website: http://supa.louisville.edu

University of Management and Technology, Program in Public Administration, Arlington, VA 22209-1609. Offers MPA, Advanced Certificate.

University of Manitoba, Faculty of Graduate Studies, Faculty of Arts, Department of Political Studies, Program in Public Administration, Winnipeg, MB R3T 2N2, Canada. Offers MPA. Program offered jointly with The University of Winnipeg. *Degree requirements:* For master's, thesis or alternative.

University of Maryland, College Park, Academic Affairs, Joint Program in Business and Management/Public Policy, College Park, MD 20742. Offers MBA/MPM. *Accreditation:* AACSB. Electronic applications accepted.

University of Maryland, College Park, Academic Affairs, School of Public Policy, Joint Program in Public Policy/Law, College Park, MD 20742. Offers JD/MPM. Electronic applications accepted.

University of Maryland, College Park, Academic Affairs, School of Public Policy, Public Management Program, College Park, MD 20742. Offers MPM. *Degree*

requirements: For master's, internship. *Entrance requirements:* For master's, GRE General Test, minimum GPA of 3.0. Additional exam requirements/recommendations for international students: Required—TOEFL. Electronic applications accepted. *Faculty research:* International security, economic policy, financial management, social policy.

University of Massachusetts Amherst, Graduate School, College of Social and Behavioral Sciences, Center for Public Policy and Administration, Amherst, MA 01003. Offers MPP, MPPA, MPH/MPPA, MPPA/M Ed, MPPA/MBA, MRP/MPPA. *Program availability:* Part-time. *Degree requirements:* For master's, thesis or alternative. *Entrance requirements:* For master's, GRE General Test. Additional exam requirements/ recommendations for international students: Required—TOEFL (minimum score 550 paper-based; 80 iBT), IELTS (minimum score 6.5). Electronic applications accepted.

University of Massachusetts Amherst, Graduate School, Interdisciplinary Programs, Dual Degree Program in Education and Public Policy and Administration, Amherst, MA 01003. Offers MPPA/M Ed. *Entrance requirements:* Additional exam requirements/ recommendations for international students: Required—TOEFL (minimum score 550 paper-based; 80 iBT), IELTS (minimum score 6.5). Electronic applications accepted.

University of Massachusetts Amherst, Graduate School, Interdisciplinary Programs, Dual Degree Program in Management and Public Policy and Administration, Amherst, MA 01003. Offers MPPA/MBA. *Accreditation:* AACSB. *Program availability:* Part-time. *Entrance requirements:* Additional exam requirements/recommendations for international students: Required—TOEFL (minimum score 600 paper-based; 100 iBT), IELTS (minimum score 7). Electronic applications accepted.

University of Massachusetts Amherst, Graduate School, Interdisciplinary Programs, Dual Degree Program in Public Policy and Administration and Public Health, Amherst, MA 01003. Offers MPH/MPPA. *Entrance requirements:* Additional exam requirements/ recommendations for international students: Required—TOEFL (minimum score 550 paper-based; 80 iBT), IELTS (minimum score 6.5). Electronic applications accepted.

University of Massachusetts Amherst, Graduate School, Interdisciplinary Programs, Dual Degree Program in Regional Planning and Public Policy and Administration, Amherst, MA 01003. Offers MPPA/MRP. *Entrance requirements:* Additional exam requirements/recommendations for international students: Required—TOEFL (minimum score 550 paper-based; 80 iBT), IELTS (minimum score 6.5). Electronic applications accepted.

University of Massachusetts Boston, McCormack Graduate School of Policy and Global Studies, Program in Global Comparative Public Administration, Boston, MA 02125-3393. Offers MPA. *Program availability:* Online learning. *Students:* 23 full-time (16 women), 6 part-time (1 woman); includes 10 minority (6 Black or African American, non-Hispanic/Latino; 2 Asian, non-Hispanic/Latino; 2 Hispanic/Latino), 6 international. Average age 31. 24 applicants, 88% accepted, 17 enrolled. *Application deadline:* For fall admission, 5/1 for domestic students. *Expenses:* Tuition, state resident: full-time $17,375. Tuition, nonresident: full-time $33,915. *Required fees:* $355. *Unit head:* Dr. Aroon Manoharan, Director, 617-287-5935, E-mail: aroon.manoharan@umb.edu. *Application contact:* Graduate Admissions Coordinator, 617-287-6400, Fax: 617-287-6236, E-mail: bos.gadm@dpc.umassp.edu.

University of Massachusetts Boston, McCormack Graduate School of Policy and Global Studies, Program in Public Administration, Boston, MA 02125-3393. Offers MPA. *Program availability:* Part-time, evening/weekend. *Faculty:* 10 full-time (3 women), 4 part-time/adjunct (2 women). *Students:* 9 full-time (8 women), 30 part-time (15 women); includes 8 minority (3 Black or African American, non-Hispanic/Latino; 1 Asian, non-Hispanic/Latino; 4 Hispanic/Latino). Average age 32. 45 applicants, 69% accepted, 20 enrolled. In 2017, 28 master's awarded. *Entrance requirements:* For master's, GRE General Test or MAT, minimum GPA of 2.75. *Application deadline:* For fall admission, 3/1 for domestic students. *Expenses:* Tuition, state resident: full-time $17,375. Tuition, nonresident: full-time $33,915. *Required fees:* $355. *Financial support:* Research assistantships, teaching assistantships, career-related internships or fieldwork, Federal Work-Study, and unspecified assistantships available. Support available to part-time students. Financial award application deadline: 3/1; financial award applicants required to submit FAFSA. *Faculty research:* Leadership and policy implementation, public management, disability; human services and sound policy. *Unit head:* Dr. David Cash, Dean, 617-287-5000. *Application contact:* Graduate Admissions Coordinator, 617-287-6400, Fax: 617-287-6236, E-mail: bos.gadm@dpc.umassp.edu.

University of Massachusetts Dartmouth, Graduate School, College of Arts and Sciences, Department of Public Policy, North Dartmouth, MA 02747-2300. Offers educational policy (Graduate Certificate); environmental policy (Graduate Certificate); public management (Graduate Certificate); public policy (MPP). *Program availability:* Part-time, 100% online, blended/hybrid learning. *Faculty:* 4 full-time (0 women), 1 part-time/adjunct (0 women). *Students:* 6 full-time (2 women), 69 part-time (43 women); includes 18 minority (6 Black or African American, non-Hispanic/Latino; 2 Asian, non-Hispanic/Latino; 7 Hispanic/Latino; 3 Two or more races, non-Hispanic/Latino). Average age 36. 59 applicants, 95% accepted, 41 enrolled. In 2017, 10 master's, 18 other advanced degrees awarded. *Degree requirements:* For master's, e-portfolio. *Entrance requirements:* For master's, GRE or GMAT (waived if applicant has already earned a graduate degree from accredited school or if applicant has successfully completed the educational, environmental or public management certificate program), statement of purpose (minimum of 300 words), resume, 2 letters of recommendation, official transcripts; for Graduate Certificate, statement of purpose (minimum of 300 words), resume, official transcripts. Additional exam requirements/recommendations for international students: Required—TOEFL (minimum score 600 paper-based; 100 iBT). *Application deadline:* Applications are processed on a rolling basis. Application fee: $60. Electronic applications accepted. *Expenses:* Tuition, state resident: full-time $15,449; part-time $643.71 per credit. Tuition, nonresident: full-time $27,880; part-time $1161.67 per credit. *Required fees:* $405; $25.88 per credit. Tuition and fees vary according to course load and reciprocity agreements. *Financial support:* In 2017–18, 2 research assistantships (averaging $12,900 per year) were awarded; teaching assistantships, tuition waivers (full), and unspecified assistantships also available. Support available to part-time students. Financial award application deadline: 3/1; financial award applicants required to submit FAFSA. *Faculty research:* Environmental justice, sustainability, international trade and finance, corporate social responsibility, global governance. *Total annual research expenditures:* $6,000. *Unit head:* Chad McGuire, Graduate Program Director, Public Policy, 508-999-8520, E-mail: cmcguire@umassd.edu. *Application contact:* Steven Briggs, Director of Marketing and Recruitment for Graduate Studies, 508-999-8604, Fax: 508-999-8183, E-mail: graduate@umassd.edu. Website: http://www.umassd.edu/cas/departmentsanddegreeprograms/publicpolicy/

University of Memphis, Graduate School, College of Arts and Sciences, Division of Public and Nonprofit Administration, Memphis, TN 38152. Offers local government management (Graduate Certificate); philanthropy and nonprofit leadership (Graduate Certificate). *Accreditation:* NASPAA. *Program availability:* Part-time, evening/weekend, blended/hybrid learning. *Faculty:* 6 full-time (3 women), 1 part-time/adjunct (0 women). *Students:* 13 full-time (5 women), 28 part-time (19 women); includes 22 minority (21 Black or African American, non-Hispanic/Latino; 1 Two or more races, non-Hispanic/Latino), 1 international. Average age 36. 26 applicants, 96% accepted, 14 enrolled. In 2017, 16 master's, 13 other advanced degrees awarded. *Degree requirements:* For

master's, comprehensive exam, thesis or alternative, internship. *Entrance requirements:* For master's, GRE General Test, GMAT, MAT, or LSAT, minimum GPA of 3.0, resume, two references, statement of interest. Additional exam requirements/recommendations for international students: Required—TOEFL. *Application deadline:* For fall admission, 7/1 for domestic students, 5/1 for international students; for spring admission, 12/1 for domestic students, 9/15 for international students; for summer admission, 5/1 for domestic students, 2/1 for international students. Applications are processed on a rolling basis. Application fee: $35 ($60 for international students). Electronic applications accepted. *Expenses:* Contact institution. *Financial support:* In 2017–18, 37 students received support, including 5 fellowships (averaging $11,200 per year); research assistantships with full tuition reimbursements available, career-related internships or fieldwork, Federal Work-Study, scholarships/grants, health care benefits, and unspecified assistantships also available. Support available to part-time students. Financial award application deadline: 2/1; financial award applicants required to submit FAFSA. *Faculty research:* Nonprofit organization governance, local government management, community collaboration, urban problems, accountability. *Unit head:* Dr. Michael Howell-Moroney, Chair, 901-678-3360, Fax: 901-678-2981, E-mail: mhwllmrn@memphis.edu. *Application contact:* Dr. Sharon Wrobel, MPA Coordinator, 901-678-4720, Fax: 901-678-2981, E-mail: swrobel@memphis.edu. Website: http://www.memphis.edu/padm/

University of Michigan–Dearborn, College of Arts, Sciences, and Letters, Master of Public Administration Program, Dearborn, MI 48128. Offers MPA. *Program availability:* Part-time, evening/weekend. *Faculty:* 6 full-time (3 women), 10 part-time/adjunct (5 women). *Students:* 5 full-time (3 women), 33 part-time (23 women); includes 16 minority (8 Black or African American, non-Hispanic/Latino; 2 Asian, non-Hispanic/Latino; 4 Hispanic/Latino; 2 Two or more races, non-Hispanic/Latino). Average age 38. 9 applicants, 44% accepted, 2 enrolled. In 2017, 20 master's awarded. *Degree requirements:* For master's, assessment seminar. *Entrance requirements:* Additional exam requirements/recommendations for international students: Required—TOEFL (minimum score 560 paper-based; 84 iBT), IELTS (minimum score 6.5). *Application deadline:* For fall admission, 8/1 priority date for domestic students, 5/1 priority date for international students; for winter admission, 12/1 priority date for domestic students, 9/1 priority date for international students; for spring admission, 4/1 priority date for domestic students, 1/1 priority date for international students. Applications are processed on a rolling basis. Application fee: $60. Electronic applications accepted. *Expenses:* $683 per credit hour in-state; $1,176 per credit hour out-state. *Financial support:* In 2017–18, 19 students received support. Career-related internships or fieldwork, scholarships/grants, and non-resident tuition scholarships available. Financial award application deadline: 3/1; financial award applicants required to submit FAFSA. *Faculty research:* Leadership and performance management in public and non-profit organizations, human resource management, open government and information technologies, public policy, community development and organization. *Unit head:* Dr. Natalia Czap, Director, 313-583-6354, E-mail: nczap@umich.edu. *Application contact:* Office of Graduate Studies, 313-583-6321, E-mail: umd-graduatestudies@umich.edu. Website: http://umdearborn.edu/casl/mpad/

University of Michigan–Flint, Graduate Programs, Program in Public Administration, Flint, MI 48502-1950. Offers administration of non-profit agencies (MPA); criminal justice administration (MPA); educational administration (MPA); general public administration (MPA); healthcare administration (MPA). *Program availability:* Part-time. *Faculty:* 1 full-time (0 women), 2 part-time/adjunct (both women). *Students:* 13 full-time (6 women), 88 part-time (59 women); includes 38 minority (29 Black or African American, non-Hispanic/Latino; 3 American Indian or Alaska Native, non-Hispanic/Latino; 2 Asian, non-Hispanic/Latino; 4 Two or more races, non-Hispanic/Latino), 3 international. Average age 37. 63 applicants, 81% accepted, 37 enrolled. In 2017, 55 master's awarded. *Degree requirements:* For master's, thesis or alternative, internship. *Entrance requirements:* For master's, bachelor's degree from regionally-accredited institution, minimum overall undergraduate GPA of 3.0. Additional exam requirements/recommendations for international students: Required—TOEFL (minimum score 84 iBT), IELTS (minimum score 6.5). *Application deadline:* For fall admission, 8/1 for domestic students, 5/1 for international students; for winter admission, 11/15 for domestic students, 9/1 for international students; for spring admission, 3/15 for domestic students, 1/1 for international students; for summer admission, 5/15 for domestic students. Applications are processed on a rolling basis. Application fee: $55. Electronic applications accepted. *Expenses:* Contact institution. *Financial support:* Career-related internships or fieldwork, Federal Work-Study, and scholarships/grants available. Support available to part-time students. Financial award application deadline: 3/1; financial award applicants required to submit FAFSA. *Unit head:* Dr. Kathryn Schellenberg, Director, 810-762-3340, E-mail: kathsch@umflint.edu. *Application contact:* Bradley T. Maki, Director of Graduate Admissions, 810-762-3171, Fax: 810-766-6789, E-mail: bmaki@umflint.edu. Website: http://www.umflint.edu/graduateprograms/public-administration-mpa

University of Missouri, Office of Research and Graduate Studies, Harry S Truman School of Public Affairs, Columbia, MO 65211. Offers grantsmanship (Graduate Certificate); nonprofit management (Graduate Certificate); organizational change (Graduate Certificate); public affairs (MPA, PhD); public management (Graduate Certificate); science and public policy (Graduate Certificate). *Accreditation:* NASPAA. *Entrance requirements:* For master's, GRE General Test, minimum GPA of 3.0. Additional exam requirements/recommendations for international students: Required—TOEFL (minimum score 550 paper-based; 80 iBT), IELTS (minimum score 6.5). Electronic applications accepted.

University of Missouri–Kansas City, Henry W. Bloch School of Management, Kansas City, MO 64110-2499. Offers accounting (MS); finance (MS); public affairs (MPA, PhD); JD/MBA; LL M/MPA. PhD (interdisciplinary) offered through the School of Graduate Studies. *Accreditation:* AACSB; NASPAA. *Program availability:* Part-time, evening/ weekend. Terminal master's awarded for partial completion of doctoral program. *Entrance requirements:* For master's, GMAT, GRE, 2 essays, 2 references, support of employer; for doctorate, GRE, minimum GPA of 3.0. Additional exam requirements/ recommendations for international students: Required—TOEFL (minimum score 550 paper-based; 80 iBT). Electronic applications accepted. *Faculty research:* Entrepreneurship, finance, non-profit, risk management.

University of Missouri–St. Louis, College of Arts and Sciences, Department of Political Science, St. Louis, MO 63121. Offers American politics (MA); comparative politics (MA); international politics (MA); political process and behavior (MA); political science (PhD); public administration and public policy (MA); urban and regional politics (MA). *Program availability:* Part-time, evening/weekend. *Faculty:* 15 full-time (5 women), 9 part-time/adjunct (2 women). *Students:* 32 full-time (11 women), 21 part-time (9 women); includes 11 minority (10 Black or African American, non-Hispanic/Latino; 1 Hispanic/Latino), 4 international. 10 applicants, 80% accepted, 7 enrolled. Terminal master's awarded for partial completion of doctoral program. *Degree requirements:* For master's, thesis optional; for doctorate, thesis/dissertation. *Entrance requirements:* For master's, GRE General Test, 2 letters of recommendation, statement of purpose; for doctorate, GRE General Test, 3 letters of recommendation, statement of purpose. Additional exam requirements/recommendations for international students: Required— TOEFL (minimum score 550 paper-based; 79 iBT), IELTS (minimum score 6.5).

Application deadline: For fall admission, 2/15 priority date for domestic and international students; for winter admission, 10/15 for domestic and international students; for spring admission, 10/15 priority date for domestic and international students. Applications are processed on a rolling basis. Application fee: $50 ($40 for international students). Electronic applications accepted. *Expenses:* Tuition, state resident: part-time $476.50 per credit hour. Tuition, nonresident: part-time $1169.70 per credit hour. *Financial support:* Fellowships, research assistantships with tuition reimbursements, teaching assistantships with tuition reimbursements, and career-related internships or fieldwork available. Support available to part-time students. Financial award application deadline: 3/15; financial award applicants required to submit FAFSA. *Faculty research:* Public policy, urban politics and administration, American government. *Unit head:* Dave Robertson, Chairperson, 314-516-5521, Fax: 314-516-7236. *Application contact:* 314-516-5458, Fax: 314-516-6996, E-mail: gradadm@umsl.edu.
Website: http://www.umsl.edu/~polisci/

University of Missouri–St. Louis, Graduate School, Program in Public Policy Administration, St. Louis, MO 63121. Offers local government management (MPPA, Certificate); nonprofit management and leadership (MPPA, Certificate); policy and program evaluation (MPPA, Certificate). *Accreditation:* NASPAA. *Program availability:* Part-time, evening/weekend. *Faculty:* 2 full-time (1 woman), 4 part-time/adjunct (3 women). *Students:* 9 full-time (5 women), 34 part-time (19 women); includes 10 minority (6 Black or African American, non-Hispanic/Latino; 2 Asian, non-Hispanic/Latino; 1 Hispanic/Latino; 1 Two or more races, non-Hispanic/Latino). 34 applicants, 79% accepted, 14 enrolled. *Degree requirements:* For master's, exit project. *Entrance requirements:* For master's, 3 letters of recommendation, personal statement. Additional exam requirements/recommendations for international students: Recommended—TOEFL (minimum score 550 paper-based), IELTS (minimum score 6.5). *Application deadline:* For fall admission, 7/1 priority date for domestic and international students; for spring admission, 12/1 priority date for domestic and international students. Applications are processed on a rolling basis. Application fee: $50 ($40 for international students). Electronic applications accepted. *Expenses:* Tuition, state resident: part-time $476.50 per credit hour. Tuition, nonresident: part-time $1169.70 per credit hour. *Financial support:* Research assistantships with tuition reimbursements and career-related internships or fieldwork available. Financial award application deadline: 4/1; financial award applicants required to submit FAFSA. *Faculty research:* Urban policy, public finance, evaluation. *Unit head:* Daniel Sise, Interim Director, 314-516-6378, Fax: 314-516-5210, E-mail: sised@umsl.edu. *Application contact:* 314-516-5458, Fax: 314-516-6996, E-mail: gradadm@umsl.edu.
Website: http://www.umsl.edu/gradschool/ppa/

University of Montana, Graduate School, College of Humanities and Sciences, Department of Political Science, Program in Public Administration, Missoula, MT 59812. Offers MPA, JD/MPA. MPA offered jointly with Montana State University. *Degree requirements:* For master's, professional paper. *Entrance requirements:* For master's, GRE General Test.

University of Nebraska at Omaha, Graduate Studies, College of Public Affairs and Community Service, School of Public Administration, Omaha, NE 68182. Offers public administration (MPA, PhD); public management (Certificate); urban studies (MS). *Accreditation:* NASPAA (one or more programs are accredited). *Program availability:* Part-time, evening/weekend, online learning. *Degree requirements:* For master's, comprehensive exam (for some programs), thesis (for some programs); for doctorate, comprehensive exam, thesis/dissertation. *Entrance requirements:* For master's, GRE General Test, minimum GPA of 3.0, 2 letters of recommendation, statement of purpose, resume, official transcripts; for doctorate, GRE General Test, master's degree, minimum GPA of 3.2, 3 letters of recommendation, statement of purpose, resume, official transcripts; for Certificate, 3 years of work experience in the public sector, official transcripts, resume, statement of purpose, minimum undergraduate GPA of 3.0. Additional exam requirements/recommendations for international students: Required—TOEFL (minimum score 550 paper-based; 80 iBT), IELTS (minimum score 5.5), PTE (minimum score 44). Electronic applications accepted.

University of Nevada, Las Vegas, Graduate College, Greenspun College of Urban Affairs, School of Public Policy and Leadership, Las Vegas, NV 89154-4030. Offers crisis and emergency management (MS); emergency crisis management cybersecurity (Certificate); environmental science (MS, PhD); non-profit management (Certificate); public administration (MPA); public affairs (PhD); public management (Certificate); urban leadership (MA). *Program availability:* Part-time. *Faculty:* 13 full-time (5 women), 10 part-time/adjunct (3 women). *Students:* 76 full-time (40 women), 107 part-time (66 women); includes 79 minority (19 Black or African American, non-Hispanic/Latino; 1 American Indian or Alaska Native, non-Hispanic/Latino; 6 Asian, non-Hispanic/Latino; 40 Hispanic/Latino; 3 Native Hawaiian or other Pacific Islander, non-Hispanic/Latino; 10 Two or more races, non-Hispanic/Latino), 1 international. Average age 37. 86 applicants, 80% accepted, 47 enrolled. In 2017, 61 master's, 6 doctorates, 14 other advanced degrees awarded. *Degree requirements:* For master's, comprehensive exam (for some programs), thesis (for some programs), oral exam; for doctorate, comprehensive exam, thesis/dissertation; for Certificate, portfolio. *Entrance requirements:* For master's, GRE General Test or GMAT, bachelor's degree with minimum GPA 2.75; statement of purpose; 3 letters of recommendation; for doctorate, GRE General Test, master's degree with minimum GPA of 3.5; 3 letters of recommendation; statement of purpose; writing sample; personal interview; for Certificate, bachelor's degree; 2 letters of recommendation; writing sample. Additional exam requirements/recommendations for international students: Required—TOEFL (minimum score 550 paper-based; 80 iBT), IELTS (minimum score 7). *Application deadline:* For fall admission, 6/1 for domestic and international students; for spring admission, 11/1 for domestic and international students; for summer admission, 3/1 for domestic students. Application fee: $60 ($95 for international students). Electronic applications accepted. *Expenses:* $275 per credit, $850 per course, $7,969 per year resident, $22,157 per year non-resident, $7,094 non-resident fee (7 credits or more), $1,307 annual health insurance fee. *Financial support:* In 2017–18, 23 students received support, including 7 research assistantships with partial tuition reimbursements available (averaging $15,995 per year), 16 teaching assistantships with partial tuition reimbursements available (averaging $15,547 per year); institutionally sponsored loans, scholarships/grants, health care benefits, and unspecified assistantships also available. Financial award application deadline: 3/15; financial award applicants required to submit FAFSA. *Total annual research expenditures:* $63,202. *Unit head:* Dr. Christopher Stream, Director, 702-895-5120, Fax: 702-895-4436, E-mail: chris.stream@unlv.edu. *Application contact:* Dr. Jayce Farmer, Graduate Coordinator, 702-895-4828, E-mail: jayce.farmer@unlv.edu.
Website: https://www.unlv.edu/publicpolicy

University of Nevada, Reno, Graduate School, College of Liberal Arts, Department of Political Science, Program in Public Administration and Policy, Reno, NV 89557. Offers public administration (MPA). *Degree requirements:* For master's, comprehensive exam, oral exam/thesis or professional paper. *Entrance requirements:* For master's, GRE General Test, GMAT, or LSAT, minimum GPA of 2.75. Additional exam requirements/recommendations for international students: Required—TOEFL (minimum score 500 paper-based; 61 iBT), IELTS (minimum score 6). Electronic applications accepted. *Faculty research:* Administrative processes and problems, public policy issues.

University of New Brunswick Fredericton, School of Graduate Studies, Faculty of Business Administration, Fredericton, NB E3B 5A3, Canada. Offers business administration (MBA); engineering management (MBA); entrepreneurship (MBA); sports and recreation management (MBA); MBA/LL B. *Program availability:* Part-time. *Degree requirements:* For master's, thesis optional. *Entrance requirements:* For master's, GMAT (minimum score 550), minimum GPA of 3.0; 3-5 years of work experience; 3 letters of reference with at least one academic reference. Additional exam requirements/recommendations for international students: Required—TOEFL (minimum score 580 paper-based; 92 iBT) or IELTS (minimum score 7). Electronic applications accepted. *Faculty research:* Entrepreneurship, finance, law, sport and recreation management, engineering management.

University of New Hampshire, Graduate School, Carsey School of Public Policy, Program in Public Administration, Durham, NH 03824. Offers MPA. *Program availability:* Part-time. *Entrance requirements:* For master's, GMAT or GRE General Test. Additional exam requirements/recommendations for international students: Required—TOEFL (minimum score 550 paper-based; 80 iBT). *Application deadline:* For fall admission, 6/1 priority date for domestic students, 4/1 for international students; for spring admission, 12/1 for domestic students. Applications are processed on a rolling basis. Application fee: $65. Electronic applications accepted. *Financial support:* Fellowships, research assistantships, teaching assistantships, career-related internships or fieldwork, Federal Work-Study, scholarships/grants, and tuition waivers (full and partial) available. Support available to part-time students. Financial award application deadline: 2/15. *Unit head:* Marla Brettschneider, Chair, 603-862-1750. *Application contact:* Michael Cole, Administrative Assistant, 603-862-1750, E-mail: m.cole@unh.edu.
Website: http://cola.unh.edu/political-science/program/public-administration-mpa

University of New Hampshire, Graduate School Manchester Campus, Manchester, NH 03101. Offers business administration (MBA); cybersecurity policy and risk management (MS); educational administration and supervision (Ed S); educational studies (M Ed); elementary education (M Ed); information technology (MS); public administration (MPA); public health (MPH, Certificate); secondary education (M Ed, MAT); social work (MSW); substance use disorders (Certificate). *Program availability:* Part-time, evening/weekend. *Students:* 13 full-time (6 women), 17 part-time (0 women); includes 7 minority (1 Black or African American, non-Hispanic/Latino; 4 Asian, non-Hispanic/Latino; 1 Hispanic/Latino; 1 Two or more races, non-Hispanic/Latino), 10 international. Average age 33. 42 applicants, 71% accepted, 8 enrolled. In 2017, 4 master's awarded. *Entrance requirements:* Additional exam requirements/recommendations for international students: Required—TOEFL (minimum score 550 paper-based; 80 iBT). *Application deadline:* For fall admission, 6/1 for domestic students, 4/1 for international students; for spring admission, 12/1 for domestic students. Application fee: $65. Electronic applications accepted. *Financial support:* Fellowships, research assistantships, teaching assistantships, Federal Work-Study, scholarships/grants, health care benefits, and unspecified assistantships available. Support available to part-time students. Financial award application deadline: 2/15; financial award applicants required to submit FAFSA. *Unit head:* Candice Morey, Educational Programs Coordinator, 603-641-4313, E-mail: unhm.gradcenter@unh.edu.
Website: http://www.gradschool.unh.edu/manchester/

University of New Haven, Graduate School, Henry C. Lee College of Criminal Justice and Forensic Sciences, Program in National Security, West Haven, CT 06516. Offers national security (MS, Graduate Certificate); national security administration (Graduate Certificate). *Program availability:* Part-time, evening/weekend. *Students:* 31 full-time (14 women), 35 part-time (19 women); includes 14 minority (3 Black or African American, non-Hispanic/Latino; 8 Hispanic/Latino; 3 Two or more races, non-Hispanic/Latino), 4 international. Average age 32. 38 applicants, 97% accepted, 17 enrolled. In 2017, 38 master's, 3 other advanced degrees awarded. *Entrance requirements:* Additional exam requirements/recommendations for international students: Required—TOEFL (minimum score 70 iBT), IELTS, or PTE (minimum score of 53). *Application deadline:* Applications are processed on a rolling basis. Application fee: $50. Electronic applications accepted. Application fee is waived when completed online. *Expenses: Tuition:* Full-time $16,020; part-time $890 per credit hour. *Required fees:* $220; $90 per term. *Financial support:* Research assistantships with partial tuition reimbursements, teaching assistantships with partial tuition reimbursements, Federal Work-Study, scholarships/grants, and unspecified assistantships available. Support available to part-time students. Financial award applicants required to submit FAFSA. *Unit head:* Dr. Jibey Asthappan, Director, 203-479-4147, E-mail: jasthappan@newhaven.edu. *Application contact:* Michelle Mason, Director of Graduate Enrollment, 203-932-7067, E-mail: mmason@newhaven.edu.
Website: http://www.newhaven.edu/5924/

See Display on page 784 and Close-Up on page 799.

University of New Haven, Graduate School, Henry C. Lee College of Criminal Justice and Forensic Sciences, Program in Public Administration, West Haven, CT 06516. Offers fire and emergency medical services (MPA); municipal management (MPA); nonprofit organization management (MPA); public administration (MPA, Graduate Certificate); public finance (MPA); public safety (MPA). *Program availability:* Part-time, evening/weekend. *Students:* 36 full-time (20 women), 25 part-time (10 women); includes 21 minority (15 Black or African American, non-Hispanic/Latino; 1 American Indian or Alaska Native, non-Hispanic/Latino; 1 Asian, non-Hispanic/Latino; 3 Hispanic/Latino; 1 Two or more races, non-Hispanic/Latino), 3 international. Average age 37. 46 applicants, 91% accepted, 21 enrolled. In 2017, 15 master's, 1 other advanced degree awarded. *Entrance requirements:* Additional exam requirements/recommendations for international students: Required—TOEFL (minimum score 80 iBT), IELTS, PTE. *Application deadline:* Applications are processed on a rolling basis. Application fee: $50. Electronic applications accepted. Application fee is waived when completed online. *Expenses: Tuition:* Full-time $16,020; part-time $890 per credit hour. *Required fees:* $220; $90 per term. *Financial support:* Research assistantships with partial tuition reimbursements, teaching assistantships with partial tuition reimbursements, career-related internships or fieldwork, Federal Work-Study, scholarships/grants, and unspecified assistantships available. Support available to part-time students. Financial award application deadline: 5/1; financial award applicants required to submit FAFSA. *Unit head:* Dr. Cynthia Conrad, Associate Professor, 203-932-7486, E-mail: cconrad@newhaven.edu. *Application contact:* Michelle Mason, Director of Graduate Enrollment, 203-932-7067, E-mail: mmason@newhaven.edu.
Website: http://www.newhaven.edu/lee-college/graduate-programs/public-administration/

See Display on page 784 and Close-Up on page 799.

University of New Mexico, Graduate Studies, School of Public Administration, Program in Public Administration, Albuquerque, NM 87131-2039. Offers MPA. *Accreditation:* NASPAA. *Faculty:* 11 full-time (3 women), 1 part-time/adjunct (0 women). *Students:* 43 full-time (29 women), 101 part-time (71 women); includes 86 minority (4 Black or African American, non-Hispanic/Latino; 23 American Indian or Alaska Native, non-Hispanic/Latino; 3 Asian, non-Hispanic/Latino; 56 Hispanic/Latino), 8 international.

Average age 36. 66 applicants, 76% accepted, 43 enrolled. In 2017, 94 master's awarded. *Entrance requirements:* For master's, baccalaureate degree from accredited college or university with minimum undergraduate GPA of 3.0 for last 60 hours or overall major; letter of intent; three letters of recommendation; resume; official transcripts. *Application deadline:* For fall admission, 4/1 for domestic students, 3/1 for international students; for spring admission, 10/1 for domestic students, 8/1 for international students. Application fee: $50. Electronic applications accepted. *Unit head:* Dr. Uday Desai, Director, 505-277-1092, Fax: 505-277-2529, E-mail: ucdesai@unm.edu. *Application contact:* Gene V. Henley, Associate Director and Graduate Academic Advisor, 505-277-9196, Fax: 505-277-2529, E-mail: spadvise@unm.edu.
Website: http://spa.unm.edu/mpa-graduate-program/

University of New Orleans, Graduate School, College of Liberal Arts, Department of Political Science, Program in Public Administration, New Orleans, LA 70148. Offers MPA. *Accreditation:* NASPAA. *Degree requirements:* For master's, thesis. *Entrance requirements:* For master's, GRE General Test. Additional exam requirements/recommendations for international students: Required—TOEFL (minimum score 550 paper-based; 79 iBT), IELTS (minimum score 6.5). Electronic applications accepted.

The University of North Carolina at Chapel Hill, Graduate School, School of Government, Chapel Hill, NC 27599. Offers MPA, JD/MPA, MPA/MRP, MPA/MSW. *Accreditation:* NASPAA. *Degree requirements:* For master's, comprehensive exam. *Entrance requirements:* For master's, GRE General Test, minimum GPA of 3.0. Additional exam requirements/recommendations for international students: Required—TOEFL. Electronic applications accepted. *Faculty research:* Local government management, nonprofit management.

The University of North Carolina at Charlotte, College of Liberal Arts and Sciences, Department of Political Science and Public Administration, Charlotte, NC 28223-0001. Offers emergency management (Graduate Certificate); non-profit management (Graduate Certificate); public administration (MPA), including arts administration, emergency management, non-profit management, public budgeting and finance, urban management and policy; public budgeting and finance (Graduate Certificate); urban management and policy (Graduate Certificate). *Accreditation:* NASPAA. *Program availability:* Part-time, evening/weekend. *Faculty:* 19 full-time (9 women), 4 part-time/adjunct (1 woman). *Students:* 20 full-time (11 women), 61 part-time (41 women); includes 21 minority (12 Black or African American, non-Hispanic/Latino; 2 American Indian or Alaska Native, non-Hispanic/Latino; 1 Asian, non-Hispanic/Latino; 4 Hispanic/Latino; 2 Two or more races, non-Hispanic/Latino), 1 international. Average age 28. 48 applicants, 67% accepted, 22 enrolled. In 2017, 25 master's, 15 other advanced degrees awarded. *Degree requirements:* For master's, research project or thesis. *Entrance requirements:* For master's, GRE General Test, bachelor's degree, or its equivalent, from accredited college or university; minimum undergraduate GPA of 3.0; 3 letters of recommendation; statement of purpose; for Graduate Certificate, statement of purpose (1-2 pages in length) explaining applicant's career goals, how the Graduate Certificate fits into achieving those goals, and any relevant work experience; official transcripts; letters of recommendation. Additional exam requirements/recommendations for international students: Required—TOEFL (minimum score 523 paper-based, 70 iBT) or IELTS (6.5). *Application deadline:* For fall admission, 8/1 for domestic and international students; for spring admission, 12/1 for domestic and international students. Applications are processed on a rolling basis. Application fee: $75. Electronic applications accepted. *Expenses:* Tuition, state resident: full-time $4337. Tuition, nonresident: full-time $17,771. *Required fees:* $3211. Tuition and fees vary according to course load and program. *Financial support:* In 2017–18, 14 students received support, including 13 research assistantships (averaging $9,015 per year), 1 teaching assistantship (averaging $19,500 per year); career-related internships or fieldwork, Federal Work-Study, institutionally sponsored loans, scholarships/grants, and unspecified assistantships also available. Support available to part-time students. Financial award application deadline: 3/1; financial award applicants required to submit FAFSA. *Total annual research expenditures:* $419,411. *Unit head:* Dr. Greg Weeks, Chair, 704-687-7574, E-mail: gbweeks@uncc.edu. *Application contact:* Kathy B. Giddings, Director of Graduate Admissions, 704-687-5503, Fax: 704-687-1668, E-mail: gradadm@uncc.edu.
Website: http://politicalscience.uncc.edu/

The University of North Carolina at Pembroke, The Graduate School, Department of Political Science and Public Administration, Pembroke, NC 28372-1510. Offers criminal justice (MPA); emergency management (MPA); health administration (MPA); public management (MPA). *Program availability:* Part-time, evening/weekend, online learning. *Degree requirements:* For master's, comprehensive exam, thesis optional. *Entrance requirements:* For master's, GRE General Test or MAT, minimum GPA of 3.0 in major, 2.5 overall; interview. Additional exam requirements/recommendations for international students: Required—TOEFL. *Application deadline:* Applications are processed on a rolling basis. Application fee: $45 ($60 for international students). *Financial support:* Application deadline: 4/15; applicants required to submit FAFSA. *Unit head:* Dr. Emily Neff-Sharum, Interim Director, 910-775-4409, E-mail: emily.neffsharum@uncp.edu.

The University of North Carolina Wilmington, College of Arts and Sciences, Department of Public and International Affairs, Wilmington, NC 28403-3297. Offers coastal and ocean policy (MS); conflict management and resolution (MA); public administration (MPA), including coastal management. *Accreditation:* NASPAA. *Program availability:* Blended/hybrid learning. *Faculty:* 10 full-time (6 women). *Students:* 50 full-time (30 women), 52 part-time (30 women); includes 22 minority (9 Black or African American, non-Hispanic/Latino; 1 American Indian or Alaska Native, non-Hispanic/Latino; 1 Asian, non-Hispanic/Latino; 6 Hispanic/Latino; 5 Two or more races, non-Hispanic/Latino), 1 international. Average age 32. 46 applicants, 74% accepted, 27 enrolled. In 2017, 64 master's awarded. *Degree requirements:* For master's, thesis (for some programs), internship, practicum, capstone project. *Entrance requirements:* For master's, GRE, GMAT, 3 letters of recommendation, statement of interest, resume, essay. Additional exam requirements/recommendations for international students: Required—TOEFL (minimum score 550 paper-based; 79 iBT), IELTS (minimum score 6.5). *Application deadline:* For fall admission, 4/15 for domestic students; for spring admission, 11/15 for domestic students. Applications are processed on a rolling basis. Application fee: $75. Electronic applications accepted. *Expenses:* Tuition, state resident: full-time $4626; part-time $226.76 per credit hour. Tuition, nonresident: full-time $17,834; part-time $874.22 per credit hour. *Required fees:* $2124. Tuition and fees vary according to program. *Financial support:* Teaching assistantships and scholarships/grants available. Financial award application deadline: 1/1; financial award applicants required to submit FAFSA. *Unit head:* Dr. Raymond Burt, Interim Chair, 910-962-3220, Fax: 910-962-3286, E-mail: burtr@uncw.edu. *Application contact:* Dr. Mark Imperial, MPA Program Director, 910-962-7928, Fax: 910-962-3286, E-mail: imperialm@uncw.edu.
Website: http://www.uncw.edu/pia/graduate/index.html

University of North Dakota, Graduate School, College of Business and Public Administration, Program in Public Administration, Grand Forks, ND 58202. Offers MPA, MPA/JD. *Accreditation:* NASPAA. *Program availability:* Part-time, online learning. *Degree requirements:* For master's, comprehensive exam, thesis or alternative, final exam. *Entrance requirements:* For master's, GRE General Test, GMAT or LSAT, minimum GPA of 3.0. Additional exam requirements/recommendations for international students: Required—TOEFL (minimum score 550 paper-based; 79 iBT), IELTS (minimum score 6.5). Electronic applications accepted.

University of North Florida, College of Arts and Sciences, Department of Political Science and Public Administration, Jacksonville, FL 32224. Offers nonprofit management (Graduate Certificate); public administration (MPA). *Accreditation:* NASPAA. *Program availability:* Part-time. *Degree requirements:* For master's, thesis or alternative, internship. *Entrance requirements:* For master's, GRE General Test, minimum GPA of 3.0 in last 60 hours, 2 letters of recommendation, interview. Additional exam requirements/recommendations for international students: Required—TOEFL (minimum score 500 paper-based; 61 iBT). Electronic applications accepted. *Faculty research:* America's usage of the Internet, use of information communication technologies by educators and children.

University of North Georgia, Program in Public Administration, Dahlonega, GA 30597. Offers MPA. *Program availability:* Part-time, evening/weekend, online only, 100% online. *Faculty:* 2 full-time (1 woman), 1 (woman) part-time/adjunct. *Students:* 9 full-time (6 women), 19 part-time (14 women); includes 5 minority (3 Black or African American, non-Hispanic/Latino; 1 Hispanic/Latino; 1 Two or more races, non-Hispanic/Latino), 1 international. Average age 29. 38 applicants, 76% accepted, 24 enrolled. In 2017, 4 master's awarded. *Degree requirements:* For master's, comprehensive exam. *Entrance requirements:* For master's, GRE, official transcripts, 2 recommendation forms, certificate of immunizations, baccalaureate degree with minimum cumulative GPA of 2.75; 600-word personal statement. Additional exam requirements/recommendations for international students: Required—TOEFL (minimum score 550 paper-based; 79 iBT), IELTS (minimum score 6.5). *Application deadline:* For fall admission, 8/10 for domestic students; for spring admission, 12/10 for domestic students; for summer admission, 5/10 for domestic students. Application fee: $40. Electronic applications accepted. *Expenses:* Contact institution. *Financial support:* Teaching assistantships available. Financial award application deadline: 3/17; financial award applicants required to submit FAFSA. *Unit head:* Dr. Dlynn Williams, Department Head, 706-864-1869, E-mail: dlynn.williams@ung.edu. *Application contact:* Melinda Maxwell, Director of Graduate Admissions, 706-864-1543, E-mail: melinda.maxwell@ung.edu.
Website: https://ung.edu/graduate-admissions/programs/master-of-public-administration.php

University of North Texas, Robert B. Toulouse School of Graduate Studies, Denton, TX 76203-5459. Offers accounting (MS); applied anthropology (MA, MS); applied behavior analysis (Certificate); applied geography (MA); applied technology and performance improvement (M Ed, MS); art education (MA); art history (MA); art museum education (Certificate); arts leadership (Certificate); audiology (Au D); behavior analysis (MS); behavioral science (PhD); biochemistry and molecular biology (MS); biology (MA, MS); biomedical engineering (MS); business analysis (MS); chemistry (MS); clinical health psychology (PhD); communication studies (MA, MS); computer engineering (MS); computer science (MS); counseling (M Ed, MS), including clinical mental health counseling (MS), college and university counseling, elementary school counseling, secondary school counseling; creative writing (MA); criminal justice (MS); curriculum and instruction (M Ed); decision sciences (MBA); design (MA, MFA), including fashion design (MFA), innovation studies, interior design (MFA); early childhood studies (MS); economics (MS); educational leadership (M Ed, Ed D); educational psychology (MS, PhD), including family studies (MS), gifted and talented (MS), human development (MS), learning and cognition (MS), research, measurement and evaluation (MS); electrical engineering (MS); emergency management (MPA); engineering technology (MS); English (MA); English as a second language (MA); environmental science (MS); finance (MBA, MS); financial management (MPA); French (MA); health services management (MBA); higher education (M Ed, Ed D); history (MA, MS); hospitality management (MS); human resources management (MPA); information science (MS); information systems (PhD); information technologies (MBA); interdisciplinary studies (MA, MS); international studies (MA); international sustainable tourism (MS); jazz studies (MM); journalism (MA, MJ, Graduate Certificate), including interactive and virtual digital communication (Graduate Certificate), narrative journalism (Graduate Certificate), public relations (Graduate Certificate); kinesiology (MS); linguistics (MA); local government management (MPA); logistics (PhD); logistics and supply chain management (MBA); long-term care, senior housing, and aging services (MA); management (PhD); marketing (MBA); mathematics (MA, MS); mechanical and energy engineering (MS, PhD); music (MA), including ethnomusicology, music theory, musicology, performance; music composition (PhD); music education (MM Ed, PhD); nonprofit management (MPA); operations and supply chain management (MBA); performance (MM, DMA); philosophy (MA); political science (MA); professional and technical communication (MA); radio, television and film (MA, MFA); rehabilitation counseling (Certificate); sociology (MA); Spanish (MA); special education (M Ed); speech-language pathology (MA); strategic management (MBA); studio art (MFA); teaching (M Ed); MBA/MS. *Program availability:* Part-time, evening/weekend, online learning. Terminal master's awarded for partial completion of doctoral program. *Degree requirements:* For master's, variable foreign language requirement, comprehensive exam (for some programs), thesis (for some programs); for doctorate, variable foreign language requirement, comprehensive exam (for some programs), thesis/dissertation; for other advanced degree, variable foreign language requirement, comprehensive exam (for some programs). *Entrance requirements:* For master's and doctorate, GRE, GMAT. Additional exam requirements/recommendations for international students: Required—TOEFL (minimum score 550 paper-based; 79 iBT). Electronic applications accepted.

University of North Texas at Dallas, Graduate School, Dallas, TX 75241. Offers accounting (MBA); counseling (M Ed, MS); criminal justice (MS); curriculum and instruction (M Ed); educational administration (M Ed); human resources and organizational behavior (MBA); public leadership (MS); strategic management (MBA).

University of Oklahoma, College of Arts and Sciences, Department of Political Science, Program in Public Administration, Norman, OK 73019. Offers general (MPA); nonprofit management (MPA); public management (MPA); public policy (MPA). *Program availability:* Part-time, evening/weekend. *Students:* 36 full-time (22 women), 60 part-time (35 women); includes 27 minority (7 Black or African American, non-Hispanic/Latino; 5 American Indian or Alaska Native, non-Hispanic/Latino; 3 Asian, non-Hispanic/Latino; 7 Hispanic/Latino; 1 Native Hawaiian or other Pacific Islander, non-Hispanic/Latino; 4 Two or more races, non-Hispanic/Latino), 2 international. Average age 31. 30 applicants, 77% accepted, 20 enrolled. In 2017, 18 master's awarded. Terminal master's awarded for partial completion of doctoral program. *Degree requirements:* For master's, comprehensive exam, thesis or alternative, 36 hours. *Entrance requirements:* For master's, GRE, purpose statement, resume, two letters of recommendation. Additional exam requirements/recommendations for international students: Required—TOEFL (minimum score 100 iBT) or IELTS (minimum score 7.0). *Application deadline:* Applications are processed on a rolling basis. Application fee: $50 ($100 for international students). Electronic applications accepted. *Expenses:* Tuition, state resident: full-time $5119; part-time $213.30 per credit hour. Tuition, nonresident: full-time $19,778; part-time $824.10 per credit hour. *Required fees:* $3458; $133.55 per credit hour. $126.50 per semester. *Financial support:* In 2017–18, 44 students received support. Research assistantships with full tuition reimbursements available, teaching assistantships with full

tuition reimbursements available, career-related internships or fieldwork, scholarships/grants, health care benefits, unspecified assistantships, and travel and conference attendance funding available. Financial award application deadline: 6/1; financial award applicants required to submit FAFSA. *Faculty research:* Public and nonprofit management, public policy analysis, program evaluation, public finance and budgeting. *Unit head:* Prof. Scott Robinson, Chair, 405-325-2061, Fax: 405-325-0718, E-mail: pscgradprog@ou.edu. *Application contact:* Jeff Alexander, Graduate Programs Coordinator, 405-325-1845, Fax: 405-325-0718, E-mail: pscgradprog@ou.edu. Website: http://www.ou.edu/content/cas/psc/graduate/mpa.html

University of Oregon, Graduate School, College of Design, School of Planning, Public Policy and Management, Program in Public Administration, Eugene, OR 97403. Offers MPA. *Accreditation:* NASPAA. *Program availability:* Part-time, evening/weekend. *Degree requirements:* For master's, thesis. *Entrance requirements:* For master's, minimum GPA of 3.0. Additional exam requirements/recommendations for international students: Required—TOEFL. *Faculty research:* Community economic development, families in poverty, health services.

University of Ottawa, Faculty of Graduate and Postdoctoral Studies, Interdisciplinary Programs, Ottawa, ON K1N 6N5, Canada. Offers e-business (Certificate); e-commerce (Certificate); finance (Certificate); health services and policies research (Diploma); population health (PhD); population health risk assessment and management (Certificate); public management and governance (Certificate); systems science (Certificate).

University of Pennsylvania, School of Arts and Sciences, Fels Institute of Government, Philadelphia, PA 19104. Offers economic development and growth (Certificate); government administration (MGA); nonprofit administration (Certificate); organization dynamics (MS); politics (Certificate); public administration (MPA); public finance (Certificate). *Program availability:* Part-time, evening/weekend. *Students:* 44 full-time (27 women), 78 part-time (41 women); includes 30 minority (9 Black or African American, non-Hispanic/Latino; 8 Asian, non-Hispanic/Latino; 10 Hispanic/Latino; 3 Two or more races, non-Hispanic/Latino), 10 international. Average age 31. 333 applicants, 47% accepted, 88 enrolled. In 2017, 57 master's, 9 other advanced degrees awarded. *Financial support:* Application deadline: 1/1.
Website: http://www.fels.upenn.edu/

University of Phoenix–Bay Area Campus, School of Business, San Jose, CA 95134-1805. Offers accountancy (MS); accounting (MBA); business administration (MBA, DBA); energy management (MBA); global management (MBA); health care management (MBA); human resource management (MBA); human resources management (MM); management (MM); marketing (MBA); organizational leadership (DM); project management (MBA); public administration (MPA); technology management (MBA). *Accreditation:* ACBSP. *Program availability:* Evening/weekend, online learning. *Degree requirements:* For master's, thesis (for some programs). *Entrance requirements:* For master's, minimum undergraduate GPA of 3.0, 3 years of work experience. Additional exam requirements/recommendations for international students: Required—TOEFL (minimum score 550 paper-based; 79 iBT). Electronic applications accepted.

University of Phoenix–Central Valley Campus, School of Business, Fresno, CA 93720-1552. Offers accounting (MBA); business administration (MBA); global management (MBA); human resources management (MBA, MM); management (MM); marketing (MBA); public administration (MBA, MM). *Accreditation:* ACBSP.

University of Phoenix–Dallas Campus, School of Business, Dallas, TX 75251. Offers accounting (MBA); business administration (MBA); global management (MBA); human resources management (MBA, MM); management (MM); marketing (MBA); public administration (MBA, MM). *Accreditation:* ACBSP. *Program availability:* Evening/weekend, online learning. *Degree requirements:* For master's, thesis (for some programs). *Entrance requirements:* For master's, 3 years of work experience, minimum undergraduate GPA of 3.0. Additional exam requirements/recommendations for international students: Required—TOEFL (minimum score 550 paper-based; 79 iBT). Electronic applications accepted.

University of Phoenix–Hawaii Campus, School of Business, Honolulu, HI 96813-3800. Offers accounting (MBA); business administration (MBA); global management (MBA); human resources management (MBA, MM); management (MM); marketing (MBA); public administration (MBA, MM). *Accreditation:* ACBSP. *Program availability:* Evening/weekend. *Degree requirements:* For master's, thesis (for some programs). *Entrance requirements:* For master's, minimum undergraduate GPA of 3.0, 3 years of work experience. Additional exam requirements/recommendations for international students: Required—TOEFL (minimum score 550 paper-based; 79 iBT). Electronic applications accepted.

University of Phoenix–Houston Campus, School of Business, Houston, TX 77079-2004. Offers accounting (MBA); business administration (MBA); global management (MBA); human resources management (MBA, MM); management (MM); marketing (MBA); public administration (MBA, MM). *Accreditation:* ACBSP. *Program availability:* Evening/weekend, online learning. *Degree requirements:* For master's, thesis (for some programs). *Entrance requirements:* For master's, 3 years of work experience, minimum undergraduate GPA of 3.0. Additional exam requirements/recommendations for international students: Required—TOEFL (minimum score 550 paper-based; 79 iBT). Electronic applications accepted.

University of Phoenix–Las Vegas Campus, School of Business, Las Vegas, NV 89135. Offers accounting (MBA); business administration (MBA); global management (MBA); human resources management (MBA, MM); management (MM); marketing (MBA); public administration (MM). *Accreditation:* ACBSP. *Program availability:* Evening/weekend, online learning. *Degree requirements:* For master's, thesis (for some programs). *Entrance requirements:* For master's, minimum undergraduate GPA of 3.0, 3 years of work experience. Additional exam requirements/recommendations for international students: Required—TOEFL (minimum score 550 paper-based; 79 iBT). Electronic applications accepted.

University of Phoenix–Online Campus, College of Justice and Security, Phoenix, AZ 85034-7209. Offers administration of justice and security (MS), including administration of justice and security, global and homeland security, law enforcement organizations; public administration (MPA). *Program availability:* Evening/weekend, online learning. *Entrance requirements:* Additional exam requirements/recommendations for international students: Required—TOEFL, TOEIC (Test of English as an International Communication), Berlitz Online English Proficiency Exam, PTE, or IELTS. Electronic applications accepted. *Expenses:* Contact institution.

University of Phoenix–Online Campus, School of Business, Phoenix, AZ 85034-7209. Offers accountancy (MS); accounting (MBA, Certificate); business administration (MBA); energy management (MBA); global management (MBA); health care management (MBA); human resource management (MBA, Certificate); human resources management (MM); management (MM); marketing (MBA, Certificate); project management (MBA, Certificate); public administration (MBA, MM); technology management (MBA). *Program availability:* Evening/weekend, online learning. *Entrance requirements:* Additional exam requirements/recommendations for international

students: Required—TOEFL, TOEIC (Test of English as an International Communication), Berlitz Online English Proficiency Exam, PTE, or IELTS. Electronic applications accepted. *Expenses:* Contact institution.

University of Phoenix–Phoenix Campus, College of Criminal Justice and Security, Tempe, AZ 85282-2371. Offers administration of justice and security (MS); global and homeland security (MS); law enforcement organizations (MS); public administration (MPA). *Program availability:* Evening/weekend, online learning. *Entrance requirements:* Additional exam requirements/recommendations for international students: Required—TOEFL, TOEIC (Test of English as an International Communication), Berlitz Online English Proficiency Exam, PTE, or IELTS. Electronic applications accepted. *Expenses:* Contact institution.

University of Phoenix–Sacramento Valley Campus, School of Business, Sacramento, CA 95833-4334. Offers accounting (MBA); business administration (MBA); global management (MBA); human resources management (MBA, MM); management (MM); marketing (MBA); public administration (MBA, MM). *Accreditation:* ACBSP. *Program availability:* Evening/weekend. *Degree requirements:* For master's, thesis (for some programs). *Entrance requirements:* For master's, minimum undergraduate GPA of 3.0, 3 years work experience. Additional exam requirements/recommendations for international students: Required—TOEFL (minimum score 550 paper-based; 79 iBT). Electronic applications accepted.

University of Phoenix–San Antonio Campus, School of Business, San Antonio, TX 78230. Offers accounting (MBA); business administration (MBA); e-business (MBA); global management (MBA); human resources management (MBA, MM); management (MM); marketing (MBA); public administration (MBA, MM). *Accreditation:* ACBSP.

University of Phoenix–San Diego Campus, School of Business, San Diego, CA 92123. Offers accounting (MBA); business administration (MBA); global management (MBA); human resources management (MBA, MM); management (MM); marketing (MBA); public administration (MBA). *Accreditation:* ACBSP. *Program availability:* Evening/weekend. *Degree requirements:* For master's, thesis (for some programs). *Entrance requirements:* For master's, 3 years of work experience, minimum undergraduate GPA of 3.0. Additional exam requirements/recommendations for international students: Required—TOEFL (minimum score 550 paper-based; 79 iBT). Electronic applications accepted.

University of Pittsburgh, Graduate School of Public and International Affairs, Master of Public Administration Program, Pittsburgh, PA 15260. Offers energy and environment (MPA); governance and international public management (MPA); policy research and analysis (MPA); public and nonprofit management (MPA); urban affairs and planning (MPA); JD/MPA; MPH/MPA; MSIS/MPA; MSW/MPA. *Accreditation:* NASPAA. *Program availability:* Part-time, evening/weekend. *Faculty:* 30 full-time (11 women), 14 part-time/adjunct (5 women). *Students:* 100 full-time (75 women), 18 part-time (12 women); includes 13 minority (6 Black or African American, non-Hispanic/Latino; 3 Asian, non-Hispanic/Latino; 4 Hispanic/Latino), 54 international. Average age 26. 220 applicants, 87% accepted, 44 enrolled. In 2017, 54 master's awarded. *Degree requirements:* For master's, thesis optional, capstone seminar. *Entrance requirements:* For master's, GRE General Test or GMAT, 2 letters of recommendation, resume, undergraduate transcripts, personal statement. Additional exam requirements/recommendations for international students: Required—TOEFL (minimum score 80 iBT); Recommended—IELTS (minimum score 7). *Application deadline:* For fall admission, 2/1 priority date for domestic students, 1/15 priority date for international students; for spring admission, 11/1 priority date for domestic students, 8/1 priority date for international students. Application fee: $50. Electronic applications accepted. *Expenses:* $23,140 per year in-state, $37,830 out-of-state. *Financial support:* In 2017–18, 23 students received support, including 1 fellowship with full tuition reimbursement available (averaging $37,000 per year), 1 research assistantship with full tuition reimbursement available (averaging $37,000 per year); career-related internships or fieldwork and scholarships/grants also available. Financial award application deadline: 2/1; financial award applicants required to submit FAFSA. *Faculty research:* Urban affairs and planning, governance and international public management, public and nonprofit management, policy research and analysis, energy and environment. *Total annual research expenditures:* $1.6 million. *Unit head:* Dr. John Keeler, Dean, 412-648-7605, Fax: 412-648-7601, E-mail: gspia@pitt.edu. *Application contact:* Dr. Michael Rizzi, Director of Student Services, 412-648-7643, Fax: 412-648-7641, E-mail: rizzim@pitt.edu. Website: http://www.gspia.pitt.edu/

University of Pittsburgh, Graduate School of Public and International Affairs, PhD Program in Public and International Affairs, Pittsburgh, PA 15260. Offers international affairs (PhD); international development (PhD); public administration (PhD); public policy (PhD). *Program availability:* Part-time, online learning. *Faculty:* 30 full-time (11 women), 14 part-time/adjunct (5 women). *Students:* 31 full-time (11 women), 2 part-time (0 women); includes 5 minority (1 Black or African American, non-Hispanic/Latino; 2 Asian, non-Hispanic/Latino; 2 Hispanic/Latino), 12 international. Average age 37. 69 applicants, 13% accepted, 8 enrolled. In 2017, 2 doctorates awarded. *Degree requirements:* For doctorate, thesis/dissertation, mid-term evaluation, preliminary exam, annual review. *Entrance requirements:* For doctorate, GRE or GMAT, 2 letters of recommendation, resume, undergraduate transcripts, personal statement, writing sample. Additional exam requirements/recommendations for international students: Required—TOEFL (minimum score 80 iBT); Recommended—IELTS (minimum score 7). *Application deadline:* For fall admission, 1/15 for domestic and international students. Application fee: $50. Electronic applications accepted. *Expenses:* $23,140 per year in-state, $37,830 out-of-state. *Financial support:* In 2017–18, 19 students received support, including 19 research assistantships with full tuition reimbursements available (averaging $37,000 per year); fellowships, teaching assistantships, and unspecified assistantships also available. Financial award application deadline: 1/15; financial award applicants required to submit FAFSA. *Faculty research:* International development, international affairs, public policy, public administration. *Total annual research expenditures:* $1.6 million. *Unit head:* Dr. John Keeler, Dean, 412-648-7605, Fax: 412-648-7601, E-mail: gspia@pitt.edu. *Application contact:* Dr. Michael Rizzi, Director of Student Services, 412-648-7640, Fax: 412-648-7641, E-mail: rizzim@pitt.edu. Website: http://www.gspia.pitt.edu/

University of Puerto Rico–Río Piedras, College of Social Sciences, School of Public Administration, San Juan, PR 00931-3300. Offers MPA. *Accreditation:* NASPAA. *Program availability:* Part-time. *Degree requirements:* For master's, comprehensive exam, thesis. *Entrance requirements:* For master's, GRE or PAEG, interview, minimum GPA of 3.0, letter of recommendation.

University of Regina, Faculty of Graduate Studies and Research, Johnson-Shoyama Graduate School of Public Policy, Regina, SK S4S 0A2, Canada. Offers economic analysis for public policy (Master's Certificate); health administration (MHA); health systems management (Master's Certificate); public management (MPA, Master's Certificate); public policy (MPA, MPP, PhD); public policy analysis (Master's Certificate). *Program availability:* Part-time. *Faculty:* 9 full-time (4 women), 26 part-time/adjunct (10 women). *Students:* 104 full-time (65 women), 189 part-time (123 women). 285 applicants, 52% accepted. In 2017, 30 master's awarded. *Degree requirements:* For master's, thesis (for some programs); for doctorate, thesis/dissertation. *Entrance*

requirements: For doctorate, master's degree, intended research program in an area of public policy. Additional exam requirements/recommendations for international students: Required—TOEFL (minimum score 580 paper-based; 80 iBT), IELTS (minimum score 6.5), PTE (minimum score 59). *Application deadline:* For fall admission, 5/1 for domestic and international students; for winter admission, 11/1 for domestic and international students; for spring admission, 3/15 for domestic and international students. Application fee: $100. Electronic applications accepted. *Expenses:* CAD$10,626 per year (for master's degrees); CAD$8,783 per year (for PhD). *Financial support:* In 2017–18, fellowships (averaging $6,059 per year), teaching assistantships (averaging $2,562 per year) were awarded; research assistantships, career-related internships or fieldwork, and scholarships/grants also available. Financial award application deadline: 6/15. *Faculty research:* Governance and administration, public finance, public policy analysis, non-governmental organizations and alternative service delivery, micro-economics for policy analysis. *Unit head:* Dr. Kathleen McNutt, Executive Director, Main Campus, 306-585-4759, Fax: 306-585-5461, E-mail: kathy.mcnutt@uregina.ca. *Application contact:* John Bird, Manager, Main Campus, 306-585-5469, Fax: 306-585-5461, E-mail: john.bird@uregina.ca.
Website: http://www.schoolofpublicpolicy.sk.ca/

University of Rhode Island, Graduate School, College of Arts and Sciences, Department of Political Science, Kingston, RI 02881. Offers international relations (MA), including American politics; public policy and administration (MPA). *Program availability:* Part-time. *Faculty:* 13 full-time (6 women). *Students:* 17 full-time (10 women), 36 part-time (19 women); includes 7 minority (2 Black or African American, non-Hispanic/Latino; 2 Asian, non-Hispanic/Latino; 2 Hispanic/Latino; 1 Two or more races, non-Hispanic/Latino). 34 applicants, 94% accepted, 25 enrolled. In 2017, 21 master's awarded. *Entrance requirements:* For master's, GRE, GMAT, or MAT if undergraduate GPA below 3.0, 2 letters of recommendation. Additional exam requirements/recommendations for international students: Required—TOEFL. *Application deadline:* For fall admission, 11/15 for domestic students, 2/1 for international students; for spring admission, 7/15 for domestic students, 7/15 priority date for international students. Application fee: $65. Electronic applications accepted. *Expenses:* Tuition, state resident: full-time $12,706; part-time $786 per credit. Tuition, nonresident: full-time $25,216; part-time $1401 per credit. *Required fees:* $1598; $45 per credit. One-time fee: $30 part-time. *Financial support:* In 2017–18, 4 teaching assistantships with tuition reimbursements (averaging $10,761 per year) were awarded. Financial award application deadline: 2/1; financial award applicants required to submit FAFSA. *Unit head:* Dr. Brian Krueger, Department Chair, 401-874-4058, Fax: 401-874-4072, E-mail: bkrueger@uri.edu. *Application contact:* Dr. Marc Hutchison, Director/Associate Professor, 401-874-4054, Fax: 401-874-4072, E-mail: mlhutch@uri.edu.
Website: http://www.uri.edu/artsci/psc/

University of St. Thomas, School of Arts and Sciences, Houston, TX 77006-4696. Offers public policy administration (MPPA); sacred music (MSM). *Program availability:* Part-time. *Faculty:* 2 full-time (0 women), 5 part-time/adjunct (3 women). *Students:* 4 full-time (3 women), 21 part-time (13 women); includes 18 minority (8 Black or African American, non-Hispanic/Latino; 10 Hispanic/Latino), 1 international. Average age 34. 8 applicants, 100% accepted, 8 enrolled. In 2017, 8 master's awarded. *Entrance requirements:* Additional exam requirements/recommendations for international students: Required—TOEFL (minimum score 79 iBT), IELTS (minimum score 6.5), PTE (minimum score 53). *Application deadline:* For fall admission, 7/15 priority date for domestic and international students; for spring admission, 12/1 priority date for domestic and international students; for summer admission, 5/1 priority date for domestic and international students. Applications are processed on a rolling basis. Application fee: $35. Electronic applications accepted. *Expenses: Tuition:* Full-time $20,934; part-time $1163 per credit hour. *Required fees:* $250; $210 per semester. *Financial support:* In 2017–18, 6 students received support. Federal Work-Study, scholarships/grants, and state work-study, institutional employment available. Support available to part-time students. Financial award application deadline: 4/15; financial award applicants required to submit FAFSA. *Unit head:* Dr. Christopher Evans, Dean, School of Arts and Sciences, 713-525-7863, E-mail: evanscp@stthom.edu. *Application contact:* Elizabeth Kimes, 713-942-3491, E-mail: kimese@stthom.edu.
Website: http://www.stthom.edu/Academics/School_of_Arts_and_Sciences/Index.aqf

University of San Francisco, School of Management, Master of Public Administration Program, San Francisco, CA 94117. Offers health services administration (MPA); public administration (MPA). *Program availability:* Part-time, evening/weekend, online learning. *Entrance requirements:* For master's, resume demonstrating minimum of two years of professional work experience, transcripts from each college or university attended, two letters of recommendation, personal statement. Additional exam requirements/recommendations for international students: Required—TOEFL (minimum score 600 paper-based, 100 iBT), IELTS (minimum score 7) or PTE (minimum score 68). Electronic applications accepted. *Expenses:* Contact institution.

University of South Africa, College of Economic and Management Sciences, Pretoria, South Africa. Offers accounting (D Admin, D Com); accounting science (DA); auditing (D Admin, D Com); business administration (M Tech); business economics (D Admin); business leadership (DBL); business management (D Admin, D Com); economic management analysis (M Tech); economics (D Admin, D Com, PhD); human resource development (M Tech); industrial psychology (D Admin, D Com, PhD); logistics (D Com); marketing (M Tech); public administration (D Admin, D Com, DPA, PhD); public management (M Tech); quantitative management (D Admin, D Com); real estate (M Tech); statistics (D Admin, PhD); tourism management (D Admin, D Com); transport economics (D Admin, D Com).

University of South Alabama, College of Arts and Sciences, Department of Political Science and Criminal Justice, Mobile, AL 36688. Offers public administration (MPA). *Program availability:* Part-time, evening/weekend. *Faculty:* 3 full-time (1 woman). *Students:* 21 full-time (17 women), 5 part-time (2 women); includes 13 minority (10 Black or African American, non-Hispanic/Latino; 1 Asian, non-Hispanic/Latino; 1 Hispanic/Latino; 1 Two or more races, non-Hispanic/Latino). Average age 26. 19 applicants, 63% accepted, 12 enrolled. In 2017, 12 master's awarded. *Degree requirements:* For master's, comprehensive exam, thesis optional. *Entrance requirements:* For master's, GRE, minimum GPA of 3.0. Additional exam requirements/recommendations for international students: Required—TOEFL. *Application deadline:* For fall admission, 7/1 priority date for domestic students, 6/1 priority date for international students; for spring admission, 12/1 priority date for domestic students, 11/1 priority date for international students; for summer admission, 5/1 priority date for domestic students, 4/1 for international students. Applications are processed on a rolling basis. Application fee: $35. Electronic applications accepted. *Expenses:* Tuition, state resident: full-time $10,104; part-time $421 per semester hour. Tuition, nonresident: full-time $20,208; part-time $842 per semester hour. *Financial support:* Fellowships, research assistantships, teaching assistantships, career-related internships or fieldwork, Federal Work-Study, institutionally sponsored loans, scholarships/grants, and unspecified assistantships available. Support available to part-time students. Financial award application deadline: 3/31; financial award applicants required to submit FAFSA. *Faculty research:* Legislatures, public opinion, research and quantitative methods, public administration, public policy. *Unit head:* Dr. Philip Habel, Chair, Political Science/Criminal Justice, 251-460-7161, E-mail: habel@southalabama.edu. *Application contact:* Dr. Samuel Fisher, Director of Graduate Studies, Political Science/Criminal Justice, 251-460-7204, Fax: 251-460-7928, E-mail: sfisher@southalabama.edu.
Website: http://www.southalabama.edu/colleges/artsandsci/pscj/

University of South Carolina, The Graduate School, College of Arts and Sciences, Department of Political Science, Program in Public Administration, Columbia, SC 29208. Offers MPA, JD/MPA, MSW/MPA. MPA offered jointly with Clemson University, The Graduate School of the College of Charleston. *Accreditation:* NASPAA. *Program availability:* Part-time, evening/weekend. *Degree requirements:* For master's, capstone seminar. *Entrance requirements:* For master's, GRE General Test, minimum GPA of 3.0. Additional exam requirements/recommendations for international students: Required—TOEFL. Electronic applications accepted. *Faculty research:* Public policy, organizational theory, personnel administration, budgeting, finance.

University of Southern California, Graduate School, Sol Price School of Public Policy, Master of Public Administration Program, Los Angeles, CA 90089. Offers nonprofit management and policy (Graduate Certificate); political management (Graduate Certificate); public administration (MPA); public management (Graduate Certificate); MPA/JD; MPA/M Pl; MPA/MA; MPA/MAJCS; MPA/MS; MPA/MSW. *Accreditation:* NASPAA (one or more programs are accredited). *Program availability:* Part-time, evening/weekend, online learning. Terminal master's awarded for partial completion of doctoral program. *Degree requirements:* For master's, capstone, internship. *Entrance requirements:* For master's, GRE, GMAT. Additional exam requirements/recommendations for international students: Required—TOEFL (minimum score 600 paper-based; 100 iBT). Electronic applications accepted. *Faculty research:* Collaborative governance and decision-making, nonprofit management, environmental management, institutional analysis, local government, civic engagement.

University of Southern Indiana, Graduate Studies, College of Liberal Arts, Program in Public Administration, Evansville, IN 47712-3590. Offers nonprofit administration (MPA); public sector administration (MPA). *Program availability:* Part-time, evening/weekend. *Faculty:* 5 full-time (2 women). *Students:* 22 full-time (13 women), 8 part-time (6 women); includes 6 minority (5 Black or African American, non-Hispanic/Latino; 1 Hispanic/Latino), 2 international. Average age 32. In 2017, 6 master's awarded. *Entrance requirements:* For master's, resume, 2 letters of reference, personal statement, minimum GPA of 3.0. Additional exam requirements/recommendations for international students: Required—TOEFL (minimum score 550 paper-based; 79 iBT), IELTS (minimum score 6). *Application deadline:* For fall admission, 8/15 priority date for domestic students, 3/1 priority date for international students; for spring admission, 1/5 for domestic students, 11/15 for international students. Applications are processed on a rolling basis. Application fee: $40. Electronic applications accepted. *Expenses:* Tuition, state resident: full-time $9394. Tuition, nonresident: full-time $17,917. *Required fees:* $510. *Financial support:* In 2017–18, 4 students received support. Federal Work-Study, scholarships/grants, tuition waivers (full and partial), and unspecified assistantships available. Financial award application deadline: 3/1; financial award applicants required to submit FAFSA. *Unit head:* Dr. Matthew J. Hanka, Director, 812-461-5204, E-mail: mjhanka@usi.edu. *Application contact:* Dr. Mayola Rowser, Director, Graduate Studies, 812-465-7015, E-mail: mrowser@usi.edu.
Website: http://www.usi.edu/liberal-arts/master-of-public-administration

University of South Florida, Innovative Education, Tampa, FL 33620-9951. Offers adult, career and higher education (Graduate Certificate), including college teaching, leadership in developing human resources, leadership in higher education; Africana studies (Graduate Certificate), including diasporas and health disparities, genocide and human rights; aging studies (Graduate Certificate), including gerontology; art research (Graduate Certificate), including museum studies; business foundations (Graduate Certificate); chemical and biomedical engineering (Graduate Certificate), including materials science and engineering, water, health and sustainability; child and family studies (Graduate Certificate), including positive behavior support; civil and industrial engineering (Graduate Certificate), including transportation systems analysis; community and family health (Graduate Certificate), including maternal and child health, social marketing and public health, violence and injury: prevention and intervention, women's health; criminology (Graduate Certificate), including criminal justice administration; data science for public administration (Graduate Certificate); digital humanities (Graduate Certificate); educational measurement and research (Graduate Certificate), including evaluation; English (Graduate Certificate), including comparative literary studies, creative writing, professional and technical communication; entrepreneurship (Graduate Certificate); environmental health (Graduate Certificate), including safety management; epidemiology and biostatistics (Graduate Certificate), including applied biostatistics, biostatistics, concepts and tools of epidemiology, epidemiology, epidemiology of infectious diseases; geography, environment and planning (Graduate Certificate), including community development, environmental policy and management, geographical information systems; geology (Graduate Certificate), including hydrogeology; global health (Graduate Certificate), including disaster management, global health and Latin American and Caribbean studies, global health practice, humanitarian assistance, infection control; government and international affairs (Graduate Certificate), including Cuban studies, globalization studies; health policy and management (Graduate Certificate), including health management and leadership, public health policy and programs; hearing specialist: early intervention (Graduate Certificate); industrial and management systems engineering (Graduate Certificate), including systems engineering, technology management; information studies (Graduate Certificate), including school library media specialist; information systems/decision sciences (Graduate Certificate), including analytics and business intelligence; instructional technology (Graduate Certificate), including distance education, Florida digital/virtual educator, instructional design, multimedia design, Web design; internal medicine, bioethics and medical humanities (Graduate Certificate), including biomedical ethics; Latin American and Caribbean studies (Graduate Certificate); leadership for coastal resiliency planning (Graduate Certificate); mass communications (Graduate Certificate), including multimedia journalism; mathematics and statistics (Graduate Certificate), including mathematics; medicine (Graduate Certificate), including aging and neuroscience, bioinformatics, biotechnology, brain fitness and memory management, clinical investigation, hand and upper limb rehabilitation, health informatics, health sciences, integrative weight management, intellectual property, medicine and gender, metabolic and nutritional medicine, metabolic cardiology, pharmacy sciences; national and competitive intelligence (Graduate Certificate); nursing (Graduate Certificate), including simulation based academic fellowship in advanced pain management; psychological and social foundations (Graduate Certificate), including career counseling, college teaching, diversity in education, mental health counseling, school counseling; public affairs (Graduate Certificate), including nonprofit management, public management, research administration; public health (Graduate Certificate), including assessing chemical toxicity and public health risks, health equity, pharmacoepidemiology, public health generalist, toxicology, translational research in adolescent behavioral health; public health practices (Graduate Certificate), including planning for healthy communities; rehabilitation and mental health counseling (Graduate Certificate), including integrative mental health care, marriage and family therapy, rehabilitation technology; secondary education (Graduate Certificate), including ESOL, foreign language education: culture and content, foreign language education:

professional; social work (Graduate Certificate), including geriatric social work/clinical gerontology; special education (Graduate Certificate), including autism spectrum disorder, disabilities education: severe/profound; world languages (Graduate Certificate), including teaching English as a second language (TESL) or foreign language. *Unit head:* Dr. Cynthia DeLuca, Associate Vice President and Assistant Vice Provost, 813-974-3077, Fax: 813-974-7061, E-mail: deluca@usf.edu. *Application contact:* Owen Hooper, Director, Summer and Alternative Calendar Programs, 813-974-6917, E-mail: hooper@usf.edu.
Website: http://www.usf.edu/innovative-education/

The University of Tennessee, Graduate School, College of Arts and Sciences, Department of Political Science, Program in Public Administration, Knoxville, TN 37996. Offers MPA, JD/MPA. *Accreditation:* NASPAA. *Program availability:* Part-time. *Degree requirements:* For master's, thesis or alternative. *Entrance requirements:* For master's, GRE General Test, minimum GPA of 2.7. Additional exam requirements/recommendations for international students: Required—TOEFL. Electronic applications accepted.

The University of Tennessee at Chattanooga, Department of Political Science and Public Service, Chattanooga, TN 37403. Offers local government management (MPA); non profit management (MPA); public administration (MPA); public administration and non-profit management (Postbaccalaureate Certificate). *Program availability:* Part-time, evening/weekend. *Students:* 14 full-time (7 women), 12 part-time (9 women); includes 8 minority (5 Black or African American, non-Hispanic/Latino; 2 Asian, non-Hispanic/Latino; 1 Two or more races, non-Hispanic/Latino). Average age 30. 18 applicants, 100% accepted, 11 enrolled. In 2017, 7 master's, 1 other advanced degree awarded. *Degree requirements:* For master's, comprehensive exam, thesis or alternative, internship. *Entrance requirements:* For master's, GRE General Test; for Postbaccalaureate Certificate, bachelor's degree with related experience or master's degree. Additional exam requirements/recommendations for international students: Required—TOEFL (minimum score 550 paper-based; 79 iBT), IELTS (minimum score 6). *Application deadline:* For fall admission, 6/15 priority date for domestic students, 7/1 for international students; for spring admission, 11/1 priority date for domestic students, 11/1 for international students. Applications are processed on a rolling basis. Application fee: $35 ($40 for international students). Electronic applications accepted. *Expenses:* Contact institution. *Financial support:* Research assistantships, career-related internships or fieldwork, scholarships/grants, and unspecified assistantships available. Support available to part-time students. Financial award application deadline: 7/1; financial award applicants required to submit FAFSA. *Faculty research:* Organizational cultures and renewal, management theory, public policy, policy analysis, nonprofit organization. *Unit head:* Dr. Michelle D. Deardorf, Department Head, 423-425-4231, Fax: 423-425-2373, E-mail: michelle-deardorff@utc.edu. *Application contact:* Dr. Joanne Romagni, Dean of the Graduate School, 423-425-4478, Fax: 423-425-5223, E-mail: joanne-romagni@utc.edu.
Website: http://www.utc.edu/political-science-public-service/

The University of Texas at Arlington, Graduate School, College of Architecture, Planning and Public Affairs, Program in Public Administration, Arlington, TX 76019. Offers MPA. *Accreditation:* NASPAA. *Program availability:* Part-time, evening/weekend, online learning. *Degree requirements:* For master's, comprehensive exam, thesis or alternative. *Entrance requirements:* For master's, GRE General Test, three letters of recommendation, essay (approximately 250 words), minimum GPA of 3.0. Additional exam requirements/recommendations for international students: Required—TOEFL (minimum score 550 paper-based). Electronic applications accepted. *Faculty research:* Environment, statistics, public administration, social welfare, economic development, economics, budgeting, planning.

The University of Texas at Austin, Graduate School, Lyndon B. Johnson School of Public Affairs, Austin, TX 78712-1111. Offers global policy studies (MGPS); public affairs (MP Aff); public leadership (EMPL); public policy (PhD); JD/MP Aff; MBA/MP Aff; MP Aff/MA; MP Aff/MSE. *Accreditation:* NASPAA (one or more programs are accredited). *Program availability:* Part-time. *Degree requirements:* For master's, thesis, summer internship; for doctorate, thesis/dissertation. *Entrance requirements:* For master's, GRE General Test (for MP Aff and MGPS), minimum GPA of 3.0 in upper-division classes, seven years of experience in the public sector, and interview (for EMPL); for doctorate, GRE General Test, master's degree in policy-related field. Additional exam requirements/recommendations for international students: Required—TOEFL. Electronic applications accepted. *Faculty research:* Human resource development, health and social policy, philanthropy and community service, ethical leadership, urban and international policy, science and technology policy.

The University of Texas at Dallas, School of Economic, Political and Policy Sciences, Program in Public and Nonprofit Management, Richardson, TX 75080. Offers applied sociology (MS); public affairs (MPA, PhD). *Accreditation:* NASPAA. *Program availability:* Part-time, evening/weekend. *Faculty:* 12 full-time (5 women), 3 part-time/adjunct (1 woman). *Students:* 37 full-time (27 women), 81 part-time (53 women); includes 48 minority (17 Black or African American, non-Hispanic/Latino; 1 American Indian or Alaska Native, non-Hispanic/Latino; 6 Asian, non-Hispanic/Latino; 17 Hispanic/Latino; 7 Two or more races, non-Hispanic/Latino), 19 international. Average age 37. 60 applicants, 62% accepted, 21 enrolled. In 2017, 14 master's, 4 doctorates awarded. *Degree requirements:* For master's, internship; for doctorate, thesis/dissertation. *Entrance requirements:* For master's and doctorate, GRE (minimum combined score of 1000 on verbal and quantitative), minimum GPA of 3.0 in upper-level course work in field. Additional exam requirements/recommendations for international students: Required—TOEFL (minimum score 550 paper-based). *Application deadline:* For fall admission, 7/15 for domestic students, 5/1 priority date for international students; for spring admission, 11/15 for domestic students, 9/1 priority date for international students. Applications are processed on a rolling basis. Application fee: $50 ($100 for international students). Electronic applications accepted. *Expenses:* Tuition, state resident: full-time $12,916; part-time $718 per credit hour. Tuition, nonresident: full-time $25,252; part-time $1403 per credit hour. *Financial support:* In 2017–18, 68 students received support, including 10 teaching assistantships with partial tuition reimbursements available (averaging $13,100 per year); research assistantships with partial tuition reimbursements available, career-related internships or fieldwork, Federal Work-Study, institutionally sponsored loans, and scholarships/grants also available. Support available to part-time students. Financial award application deadline: 4/30; financial award applicants required to submit FAFSA. *Faculty research:* Corporate citizenship and urban problem solving, policy analysis, presidential decision-making, hazardous material safety, emergency management. *Unit head:* Dr. Doug Goodman, Program Head, 972-883-4969, Fax: 972-883-2735, E-mail: doug.goodman@utdallas.edu. *Application contact:* Rita Medford, Graduate Program Administrator, 972-883-4932, Fax: 972-883-2735, E-mail: medford@utdallas.edu.
Website: http://www.utdallas.edu/epps/public-affairs/

The University of Texas at San Antonio, College of Public Policy, Department of Public Administration, San Antonio, TX 78207. Offers MPA. *Accreditation:* NASPAA. *Program availability:* Part-time, evening/weekend. *Faculty:* 9 full-time (5 women), 4 part-time/adjunct (2 women). *Students:* 40 full-time (17 women), 127 part-time (79 women); includes 125 minority (18 Black or African American, non-Hispanic/Latino; 2 Asian, non-Hispanic/Latino; 102 Hispanic/Latino; 1 Native Hawaiian or other Pacific Islander, non-Hispanic/Latino; 2 Two or more races, non-Hispanic/Latino), 3 international. Average age 33. 56 applicants, 91% accepted, 39 enrolled. In 2017, 47 master's awarded. *Degree requirements:* For master's, comprehensive exam, final exit paper. *Entrance requirements:* For master's, bachelor's degree with 18 credit hours in field of study or in another appropriate field of study, two letters of recommendation, statement of purpose. Additional exam requirements/recommendations for international students: Required—TOEFL (minimum score 550 paper-based; 79 iBT), IELTS (minimum score 6.5). *Application deadline:* For fall admission, 6/15 for domestic students, 3/1 for international students; for spring admission, 10/15 for domestic students, 9/15 for international students; for summer admission, 4/15 for domestic students, 2/15 for international students. Application fee: $50 ($90 for international students). Electronic applications accepted. *Expenses:* Tuition, state resident: full-time $5495. Tuition, nonresident: full-time $21,938. *Required fees:* $1915. Tuition and fees vary according to program. *Financial support:* Scholarships/grants and unspecified assistantships available. *Faculty research:* Public administration, public policy, nonprofit management, urban and regional planning, urban and regional management. *Total annual research expenditures:* $6,434. *Unit head:* Dr. Christopher G. Reddick, Department Chair, 210-458-2501, E-mail: chris.reddick@utsa.edu. *Application contact:* Dr. Patricia Jaramillo, Graduate Advisor of Record, 210-458-2716, E-mail: patricia.jaramillo@utsa.edu.
Website: http://copp.utsa.edu/public-administration/

The University of Texas at Tyler, College of Arts and Sciences, Department of Social Sciences, Tyler, TX 75799-0001. Offers criminal justice (MS); public administration (MPA); sociology (MS). *Program availability:* Part-time, evening/weekend. *Degree requirements:* For master's, comprehensive exam, thesis optional. *Entrance requirements:* For master's, GRE General Test, minimum GPA of 3.0. Additional exam requirements/recommendations for international students: Required—TOEFL. *Faculty research:* Urban segregation, minority business, violent crime, gender discrimination.

The University of Texas Rio Grande Valley, College of Liberal Arts, Department of Public Affairs and Security Studies, Edinburg, TX 78539. Offers global security studies and leadership (MPA); public administration (MPA); public policy and management (MPA). *Program availability:* Part-time, evening/weekend. *Faculty:* 8 full-time (5 women). *Students:* 6 full-time (3 women), 127 part-time (57 women); includes 96 minority (5 Black or African American, non-Hispanic/Latino; 2 Asian, non-Hispanic/Latino; 89 Hispanic/Latino), 4 international. Average age 33. 67 applicants, 97% accepted, 40 enrolled. In 2017, 77 master's awarded. *Degree requirements:* For master's, comprehensive exam (for some programs), thesis optional. *Entrance requirements:* For master's, minimum undergraduate GPA of 3.0, official transcripts, personal statement, three recommendations. Additional exam requirements/recommendations for international students: Required—TOEFL or IELTS. *Application deadline:* For fall admission, 7/1 for domestic students, 6/1 for international students; for spring admission, 11/15 for domestic students, 11/1 for international students. Applications are processed on a rolling basis. Application fee: $50 ($100 for international students). Electronic applications accepted. *Expenses:* Tuition, state resident: full-time $5550; part-time $417 per credit hour. Tuition, nonresident: full-time $13,020; part-time $832 per credit hour. *Required fees:* $1169. *Financial support:* Application deadline: 6/1. *Faculty research:* Immigration policy reform, agriculture food policy, social service delivery systems, community development, social welfare policy reform, urban/city management. *Unit head:* Terrence Garett, Chair, E-mail: terence.garrett@utrgv.edu.
Website: http://www.utrgv.edu/pass/

University of the District of Columbia, School of Business and Public Administration, Program in Public Administration, Washington, DC 20008-1175. Offers MPA. *Program availability:* Part-time, evening/weekend. *Degree requirements:* For master's, comprehensive exam, thesis optional. *Entrance requirements:* For master's, GMAT or GRE General Test, writing proficiency exam. Additional exam requirements/recommendations for international students: Required—TOEFL. *Faculty research:* Government management, public personnel management, urban management, management information systems, public financial management.

The University of Toledo, College of Graduate Studies, College of Languages, Literature and Social Sciences, Department of Political Science and Public Administration, Toledo, OH 43606-3390. Offers health care policy and administration (Certificate); management of non-profit organizations (Certificate); municipal administration (Certificate); political science (MA); public administration (MPA); JD/MPA. *Program availability:* Part-time. *Degree requirements:* For master's, comprehensive exam (for some programs), thesis. *Entrance requirements:* For master's, GRE General Test, minimum cumulative point-hour ratio of 2.7 (3.0 for MPA) for all previous academic work, three letters of recommendation, statement of purpose, transcripts from all prior institutions attended; for Certificate, minimum cumulative point-hour ratio of 2.7 for all previous academic work, three letters of recommendation, statement of purpose, transcripts from all prior institutions attended. Additional exam requirements/recommendations for international students: Required—TOEFL (minimum score 550 paper-based; 80 iBT). Electronic applications accepted. *Faculty research:* Economic development, health care, Third World, criminal justice, Eastern Europe.

University of Utah, Graduate School, College of Social and Behavioral Science, Department of Political Science, Program in Political Science, Salt Lake City, UT 84112. Offers American politics (MA, MS, PhD); comparative politics (MA, MS, PhD); international relations (MA, MS, PhD); political theory (MA, MS, PhD); public administration (MA, MS, PhD). *Faculty:* 23 full-time (6 women), 10 part-time/adjunct (2 women). *Students:* 23 full-time (9 women), 28 part-time (8 women); includes 6 minority (2 Asian, non-Hispanic/Latino; 2 Hispanic/Latino; 2 Two or more races, non-Hispanic/Latino), 4 international. Average age 35. 44 applicants, 45% accepted, 11 enrolled. In 2017, 3 master's, 4 doctorates awarded. Terminal master's awarded for partial completion of doctoral program. *Degree requirements:* For master's, variable foreign language requirement, thesis or research paper; for doctorate, comprehensive exam, thesis/dissertation. *Entrance requirements:* For master's and doctorate, GRE General Test, minimum GPA of 3.2. Additional exam requirements/recommendations for international students: Required—TOEFL (minimum score 580 paper-based; 61 iBT), IELTS (minimum score 6). *Application deadline:* For fall admission, 1/15 priority date for domestic and international students. Application fee: $55 ($65 for international students). Electronic applications accepted. *Expenses:* $1,489 for 1 credit hour, $267 for each additional hour (resident); $4,233 for 1 credit hour, $908 for each additional hour (non-resident). *Financial support:* In 2017–18, 10 students received support, including 5 fellowships with full tuition reimbursements available (averaging $15,250 per year), 13 teaching assistantships with full tuition reimbursements available (averaging $15,000 per year); career-related internships or fieldwork, scholarships/grants, health care benefits, and unspecified assistantships also available. Financial award application deadline: 1/15; financial award applicants required to submit FAFSA. *Faculty research:* International politics, comparative politics, political theory, American politics, public administration. *Total annual research expenditures:* $15,000. *Unit head:* Mark Button, Chair, 801-585-7987, Fax: 801-585-6492, E-mail: mark.button@poli-sci.utah.edu. *Application contact:* Sandy Hiskey, Graduate Academic Advisor, 801-581-8608, Fax: 801-585-6492, E-mail: sandy.hiskey@utah.edu.
Website: http://www.poli-sci.utah.edu/

University of Utah, Graduate School, College of Social and Behavioral Science, Department of Political Science, Program in Public Administration, Salt Lake City, UT 84112. Offers Exec MPA, MPA, JD/MPA, MHA/MPA, MPA/Ed D, MPA/MPH, MPA/MSW, MPA/PhD. *Accreditation:* NASPAA (one or more programs are accredited). *Program availability:* Part-time, evening/weekend. *Students:* 42 full-time (30 women), 104 part-time (66 women); includes 24 minority (1 Black or African American, non-Hispanic/Latino; 1 American Indian or Alaska Native, non-Hispanic/Latino; 2 Asian, non-Hispanic/Latino; 16 Hispanic/Latino; 4 Two or more races, non-Hispanic/Latino), 1 international. Average age 33. 76 applicants, 88% accepted, 62 enrolled. In 2017, 53 master's awarded. *Entrance requirements:* For master's, GMAT, GRE General Test, LSAT, MAT, minimum GPA of 3.2. Additional exam requirements/recommendations for international students: Required—TOEFL (minimum score 580 paper-based; 92 iBT), IELTS (minimum score 7). Application fee: $55 ($65 for international students). *Expenses:* Contact institution. *Financial support:* In 2017–18, 4 students received support. Fellowships and unspecified assistantships available. Financial award application deadline: 3/1. *Faculty research:* Non-profit organizations, health policy, environmental policy and natural resources, law and ethics, human resource management, local government, education, conflict resolution, organization theory and behavior, crisis management, policy analysis and program evaluation. *Unit head:* Lina Svedin, MPA Director, 801-581-7031, E-mail: lina.svedin@poli-sci.utah.edu. *Application contact:* Clint Curry, Program Assistant, 801-581-6781, Fax: 801-585-6492, E-mail: clint.curry@utah.edu.
Website: http://www.mpa.utah.edu

University of Vermont, Graduate College, College of Agriculture and Life Sciences, Program in Public Administration, Burlington, VT 05405. Offers MPA. *Accreditation:* NASPAA. *Students:* 23 full-time (14 women). Average age 30. 35 applicants, 89% accepted, 13 enrolled. In 2017, 10 master's awarded. *Entrance requirements:* For master's, GRE General Test. Additional exam requirements/recommendations for international students: Required—TOEFL (minimum score 550 paper-based, 90 iBT) or IELTS (6.5). *Application deadline:* For fall admission, 1/15 priority date for domestic and international students. Applications are processed on a rolling basis. Application fee: $65. Electronic applications accepted. *Expenses:* Contact institution. *Financial support:* In 2017–18, 2 students received support, including 2 research assistantships with full tuition reimbursements available (averaging $21,500 per year); fellowships, teaching assistantships, and health care benefits also available. Financial award application deadline: 1/15. *Unit head:* Dr. Christopher Koliba, Coordinator, 802-656-0009, E-mail: mpa@uvm.edu.
Website: https://www.uvm.edu/cals/cdae/mpa

University of Victoria, Faculty of Graduate Studies, Faculty of Human and Social Development, School of Public Administration, Victoria, BC V8W 2Y2, Canada. Offers dispute resolution (MADR); public administration (MPA, PhD); MPA/LL B. *Program availability:* Part-time, evening/weekend, online learning. *Degree requirements:* For master's, thesis (for some programs), report; for doctorate, thesis/dissertation, candidacy exam. *Entrance requirements:* For master's, GMAT or GRE General Test, professional resume; for doctorate, GMAT or GRE General Test. Additional exam requirements/recommendations for international students: Required—TOEFL (minimum score 610 paper-based). Electronic applications accepted. *Faculty research:* Policy analysis, local government, performance management, energy markets, labor markets.

University of Washington, Graduate School, Evans School of Public Policy and Governance, Seattle, WA 98195. Offers public administration (MPA); public policy and management (PhD); JD/MPA; MPA/MAIS; MPA/MPH; MPA/MS; MPA/MUP. *Accreditation:* NASPAA. *Program availability:* Part-time, evening/weekend. *Degree requirements:* For master's, thesis, internship or cooperative experience. *Entrance requirements:* For master's and doctorate, GRE General Test, minimum GPA of 3.0. Additional exam requirements/recommendations for international students: Required—TOEFL (minimum score 580 paper-based; 92 iBT). Electronic applications accepted. *Faculty research:* Environmental policy, education and social policy, nonprofit management, international affairs, urban and regional development.

University of West Florida, College of Education and Professional Studies, Department of Legal Studies, Public Administration and Sport Management, Pensacola, FL 32514-5750. Offers MSA. *Program availability:* Part-time, evening/weekend. *Degree requirements:* For master's, thesis or alternative. *Entrance requirements:* For master's, GRE General Test, minimum GPA of 3.0. Additional exam requirements/recommendations for international students: Required—TOEFL (minimum score 550 paper-based). *Faculty research:* Law enforcement, growth management.

University of West Georgia, College of Social Sciences, Carrollton, GA 30118. Offers criminology (MA); data analysis and evaluation methods (Postbaccalaureate Certificate); European Union studies (Postbaccalaureate Certificate); integrative health systems (Postbaccalaureate Certificate); nonprofit management and community development (Postbaccalaureate Certificate); psychology (MA, PhD), including consciousness and society (PhD); public administration (MPA); public management (Postbaccalaureate Certificate); sociology (MA). *Program availability:* Part-time, evening/weekend, 100% online, blended/hybrid learning. *Faculty:* 48 full-time (22 women). *Students:* 124 full-time (84 women), 73 part-time (46 women); includes 69 minority (56 Black or African American, non-Hispanic/Latino; 4 Asian, non-Hispanic/Latino; 6 Hispanic/Latino; 3 Two or more races, non-Hispanic/Latino), 10 international. Average age 32. 95 applicants, 89% accepted, 63 enrolled. In 2017, 44 master's, 2 doctorates, 4 other advanced degrees awarded. *Entrance requirements:* Additional exam requirements/recommendations for international students: Required—TOEFL (minimum score 523 paper-based; 69 iBT); Recommended—IELTS (minimum score 6.5). *Application deadline:* For fall admission, 7/15 for domestic students, 6/1 for international students; for spring admission, 11/30 for domestic students, 10/15 for international students; for summer admission, 5/15 for domestic students, 3/30 for international students. Applications are processed on a rolling basis. Application fee: $40. Electronic applications accepted. Tuition and fees vary according to degree level and program. *Financial support:* Fellowships, research assistantships, teaching assistantships, career-related internships or fieldwork, Federal Work-Study, institutionally sponsored loans, scholarships/grants, and unspecified assistantships available. Support available to part-time students. Financial award application deadline: 4/1; financial award applicants required to submit FAFSA. *Unit head:* Dr. N. Jane McCandless, Dean of Social Sciences, 678-839-5170, Fax: 678-839-5171, E-mail: jmccandl@westga.edu. *Application contact:* Dr. Toby Ziglar, Assistant Dean of the Graduate School, 678-839-1394, Fax: 678-839-1395, E-mail: graduate@westga.edu.
Website: https://www.westga.edu/coss

The University of Winnipeg, Graduate Studies, Program in Public Administration, Winnipeg, MB R3B 2E9, Canada. Offers MPA. Program offered jointly with University of Manitoba. *Program availability:* Part-time. *Degree requirements:* For master's, comprehensive exam, thesis optional. *Entrance requirements:* For master's, minimum GPA of 3.0 in last 60 credit hours. *Faculty research:* Policy evaluation, federalism, administrative innovation, administrative ethics, economic development/administration.

University of Wisconsin–Milwaukee, Graduate School, College of Letters and Science, Department of Public and Nonprofit Administration, Milwaukee, WI 53201-0413. Offers public administration (MPA), including general public administration,

municipal management, non-profit management. *Program availability:* Part-time. *Students:* 15 full-time (8 women), 10 part-time (5 women); includes 9 minority (1 Black or African American, non-Hispanic/Latino; 8 Two or more races, non-Hispanic/Latino). Average age 31. 17 applicants, 76% accepted, 9 enrolled. In 2017, 12 master's awarded. *Entrance requirements:* For master's, GRE General Test, minimum GPA of 3.0. Additional exam requirements/recommendations for international students: Required—TOEFL (minimum score 550 paper-based; 79 iBT), IELTS (minimum score 6.5). *Application deadline:* For fall admission, 1/1 priority date for domestic students; for spring admission, 9/1 for domestic students. Application fee: $56 ($96 for international students). Electronic applications accepted. *Financial support:* Fellowships, research assistantships, teaching assistantships, career-related internships or fieldwork, health care benefits, and unspecified assistantships available. Support available to part-time students. Financial award application deadline: 4/15; financial award applicants required to submit FAFSA. *Unit head:* Douglas Ihrke, Department Chair, 414-229-4732, E-mail: dihrke@uwm.edu. *Application contact:* General Information Contact, 414-229-4982, Fax: 414-229-6967, E-mail: gradschool@uwm.edu.
Website: https://uwm.edu/public-nonprofit-administration/

University of Wisconsin–Oshkosh, Graduate Studies, College of Letters and Science, Department of Public Administration, Oshkosh, WI 54901. Offers general agency (MPA); health care (MPA). *Program availability:* Part-time, evening/weekend. *Degree requirements:* For master's, thesis or alternative. *Entrance requirements:* For master's, public service-related experience, resume, sample of written work. Additional exam requirements/recommendations for international students: Required—TOEFL (minimum score 550 paper-based; 79 iBT). Electronic applications accepted. *Faculty research:* Drug policy, local government state revenues and expenditures, health care regulation.

University of Wyoming, College of Arts and Sciences, Department of Political Science, Program in Public Administration, Laramie, WY 82071. Offers MPA. *Program availability:* Part-time, online learning. *Degree requirements:* For master's, comprehensive exam (for some programs), thesis (for some programs). *Entrance requirements:* For master's, GRE General Test, minimum GPA of 3.0. Additional exam requirements/recommendations for international students: Required—TOEFL (minimum score 525 paper-based). Electronic applications accepted. *Faculty research:* Public policy, public ethics, administrative theory, natural resource policy.

Upper Iowa University, Online Master's Programs, Fayette, IA 52142-1857. Offers accounting (MBA); corporate financial management (MBA); emergency management and homeland security (MPA); general management (MBA); general studies (MPA); government administration (MPA); health and human services (MPA); human resources management (MBA); nonprofit organizational management (MPA); organizational development (MBA); public management (MPA); sport administration (MSA). MBA also available at Madison, WI campus. *Program availability:* Part-time, online learning. *Degree requirements:* For master's, research project. *Entrance requirements:* For master's, GMAT, GRE, or minimum GPA of 2.7 during last 60 hours. Additional exam requirements/recommendations for international students: Required—TOEFL (minimum score 570 paper-based). Electronic applications accepted. *Faculty research:* Total quality management, teams, organization culture and climate, management.

Valdosta State University, Department of Political Science, Valdosta, GA 31698. Offers public administration (MPA, DPA). *Accreditation:* NASPAA. *Program availability:* Part-time, evening/weekend, online learning. *Degree requirements:* For master's, comprehensive written and/or oral exams, internship; for doctorate, portfolio/dissertation. *Entrance requirements:* For master's, GMAT, GRE General Test, or MAT, minimum GPA of 2.5; for doctorate, GRE, recommendations. Additional exam requirements/recommendations for international students: Required—TOEFL (minimum score 523 paper-based). *Application deadline:* For fall admission, 7/1 for domestic and international students; for spring admission, 11/15 for domestic and international students. Applications are processed on a rolling basis. Application fee: $45. Electronic applications accepted. *Financial support:* Research assistantships with full tuition reimbursements, institutionally sponsored loans, scholarships/grants, and unspecified assistantships available. Support available to part-time students. Financial award application deadline: 7/1; financial award applicants required to submit FAFSA. *Faculty research:* Powers of state attorneys general; health, transportation, and environmental policy; public administration theory.
Website: https://www.valdosta.edu/polsci/

Villanova University, Graduate School of Liberal Arts and Sciences, Department of Public Administration, Villanova, PA 19085-1699. Offers city management (Certificate); nonprofit management (Certificate); public administration (MPA, Certificate). *Accreditation:* NASPAA. *Program availability:* Part-time, evening/weekend, 100% online. *Faculty:* 19. *Students:* 136 full-time (71 women), 64 part-time (30 women); includes 57 minority (29 Black or African American, non-Hispanic/Latino; 2 American Indian or Alaska Native, non-Hispanic/Latino; 6 Asian, non-Hispanic/Latino; 16 Hispanic/Latino; 4 Two or more races, non-Hispanic/Latino), 4 international. Average age 35. 66 applicants, 100% accepted, 22 enrolled. In 2017, 79 master's, 29 other advanced degrees awarded. *Degree requirements:* For master's, comprehensive exam. *Entrance requirements:* For master's, GRE General Test, minimum GPA of 3.0, statement of goals, 3 letters of recommendation. Additional exam requirements/recommendations for international students: Required—TOEFL. *Application deadline:* For fall admission, 5/1 for international students; for spring admission, 10/15 for international students. Applications are processed on a rolling basis. Application fee: $50. Electronic applications accepted. *Financial support:* Career-related internships or fieldwork, scholarships/grants, and unspecified assistantships available. Financial award application deadline: 3/15; financial award applicants required to submit FAFSA. *Unit head:* Dr. Catherine Wilson, Program Director, 610-519-7851.
Website: http://www1.villanova.edu/villanova/artsci/publicadmin.html

Virginia Commonwealth University, Graduate School, L. Douglas Wilder School of Government and Public Affairs, Program in Public Administration, Richmond, VA 23284-9005. Offers financial management (MPA); human resource management (MPA); state and local government management (MPA). *Accreditation:* NASPAA. *Program availability:* Part-time. *Entrance requirements:* For master's, GRE, GMAT or LSAT. Additional exam requirements/recommendations for international students: Required—TOEFL (minimum score 600 paper-based; 100 iBT); Recommended—IELTS (minimum score 6.5). Electronic applications accepted. *Faculty research:* Environmental policy, executive leadership, human resource management, local government management, nonprofit management, public financial management, public policy analysis and evaluation.

Virginia International University, School of Public and International Affairs, Fairfax, VA 22030. Offers international relations (MS); public administration (MPA).

Virginia Polytechnic Institute and State University, Graduate School, College of Architecture and Urban Studies, Blacksburg, VA 24061. Offers architecture (M Arch, MS); architecture and design research (PhD); building construction science management (MS); creative technologies (MFA); environmental design and planning (PhD); government and international affairs (MPIA); landscape architecture (MLA, PhD); planning, governance, and globalization (PhD); public administration and public affairs (MPA, PhD); urban and regional planning (MURPL). *Accreditation:* ASLA (one or more

programs are accredited). *Faculty:* 139 full-time (58 women), 1 (woman) part-time/adjunct. *Students:* 339 full-time (165 women), 210 part-time (97 women); includes 115 minority (49 Black or African American, non-Hispanic/Latino; 1 American Indian or Alaska Native, non-Hispanic/Latino; 30 Asian, non-Hispanic/Latino; 29 Hispanic/Latino; 6 Two or more races, non-Hispanic/Latino), 136 international. Average age 32. 649 applicants, 49% accepted, 105 enrolled. In 2017, 142 master's, 18 doctorates awarded. *Degree requirements:* For master's, comprehensive exam (for some programs), thesis (for some programs); for doctorate, comprehensive exam (for some programs), thesis/dissertation (for some programs). *Entrance requirements:* For master's and doctorate, GRE/GMAT. Additional exam requirements/recommendations for international students: Required—TOEFL (minimum score 80 iBT). *Application deadline:* For fall admission, 8/1 for domestic students, 4/1 for international students; for spring admission, 1/1 for domestic students, 9/1 for international students. Applications are processed on a rolling basis. Application fee: $75. Electronic applications accepted. *Expenses:* Tuition, state resident: full-time $15,072; part-time $718.50 per credit hour. Tuition, nonresident: full-time $28,810; part-time $1448.25 per credit hour. *Required fees:* $2741; $502 per semester. Tuition and fees vary according to course load, campus/location and program. *Financial support:* In 2017–18, 17 research assistantships with full tuition reimbursements (averaging $18,561 per year), 41 teaching assistantships with full tuition reimbursements (averaging $17,340 per year) were awarded. Financial award application deadline: 3/1; financial award applicants required to submit FAFSA. *Total annual research expenditures:* $3.1 million. *Unit head:* Dr. Richard Blythe, Dean, 540-231-6416, Fax: 540-231-6332, E-mail: richbl1@vt.edu. *Application contact:* Christine Mattsson-Coon, Executive Assistant, 540-231-6416, Fax: 540-231-6332, E-mail: cmattsso@vt.edu.
Website: http://www.caus.vt.edu/

Walden University, Graduate Programs, School of Public Policy and Administration, Minneapolis, MN 55401. Offers criminal justice (MPA, MPP, MS, Graduate Certificate), including emergency management (MS, PhD), general program (MS), global leadership (MS, PhD), homeland security and policy coordination (MS, PhD), law and public policy (MS, PhD), policy analysis (MS, PhD), public management and leadership (MS, PhD), self-designed (MS), terrorism, mediation, and peace (MS, PhD); criminal justice and executive management (MS), including global leadership (MS, PhD); criminal justice leadership and executive management (MS), including emergency management (MS, PhD), general program, homeland security and policy coordination (MS, PhD), law and public policy (MS, PhD), policy analysis (MS, PhD), public management and leadership (MS, PhD), self-designed, terrorism, mediation, and peace (MS, PhD); emergency management (MPA, MPP, MS), including criminal justice (MS, PhD), general program (MS), homeland security (MS), public management and leadership (MS, PhD), terrorism and emergency management (MS); general program (MPA, MPP); global leadership (MPA, MPP); government management (Graduate Certificate); health policy (MPA, MPP); homeland security (Graduate Certificate); homeland security and policy coordination (MPA, MPP); international nongovernmental organizations (MPA, MPP); law and public policy (MPA, MPP); local government management for sustainable communities (MPA, MPP); nonprofit management (Graduate Certificate); nonprofit management and leadership (MPA, MPP, MS), including global leadership (MS, PhD), international nongovernmental organization (MS), local government for sustainable communities (MS), self designed (MS); online teaching in higher education (Post-Master's Certificate); policy analysis (MPA); public management and leadership (MPA, MPP, Graduate Certificate); public policy (Graduate Certificate); public policy and administration (PhD), including criminal justice (MS, PhD), emergency management (MS, PhD), global leadership (MS, PhD), health policy, homeland security and policy coordination (MS, PhD), international nongovernmental organizations, law and public policy (MS, PhD), local government management for sustainable communities, nonprofit management and leadership, policy analysis (MS, PhD), public management and leadership (MS, PhD), terrorism, mediation, and peace (MS, PhD); strategic planning and public policy (Graduate Certificate); terrorism, mediation, and peace (MPA, MPP). *Program availability:* Part-time, evening/weekend, online only, 100% online. *Degree requirements:* For doctorate, thesis/dissertation, residency. *Entrance requirements:* For master's, bachelor's degree or higher; minimum GPA of 2.5; official transcripts; goal statement (for some programs); access to computer and Internet; for doctorate, master's degree or higher; three years of related professional or academic experience (preferred); minimum GPA of 3.0; goal statement and current resume (for select programs); official transcripts; access to computer and Internet; for other advanced degree, relevant work experience; access to computer and Internet. Additional exam requirements/recommendations for international students: Required—TOEFL (minimum score 550 paper-based, 79 iBT), IELTS (minimum score 6.5), Michigan English Language Assessment Battery (minimum score 82), or PTE (minimum score 53). Electronic applications accepted.

Waldorf University, Program in Organizational Leadership, Forest City, IA 50436. Offers criminal justice leadership (MA); emergency management leadership (MA); fire/rescue executive leadership (MA); human resource development (MA); public administration (MA); sport management (MA); teacher leader (MA).

Washington Adventist University, Program in Public Administration, Takoma Park, MD 20912. Offers MPA. *Program availability:* Part-time. *Students:* 4 full-time (all women), 9 part-time (6 women); includes 7 minority (6 Black or African American, non-Hispanic/Latino; 1 Two or more races, non-Hispanic/Latino), 3 international. Average age 39. In 2017, 13 master's awarded. *Entrance requirements:* Additional exam requirements/recommendations for international students: Required—TOEFL (minimum score 550 paper-based), IELTS (minimum score 5). *Application deadline:* Applications are processed on a rolling basis. *Expenses: Tuition:* Part-time $625 per credit. *Financial support:* Applicants required to submit FAFSA. *Unit head:* Dr. Patrick Williams, Associate Provost, 301-891-4116, E-mail: pawillia@wau.edu. *Application contact:* Jessica Ritchie, Program Coordinator, 301-891-4086, Fax: 301-891-4023, E-mail: jritchie@wau.edu.
Website: http://www.wau.edu/index.php?option-com_content&view-article&id-410temid-967

Wayne State University, College of Liberal Arts and Sciences, Department of Political Science, Detroit, MI 48202. Offers political science (MA, PhD); public administration (MPA), including economic development policy and management, health and human services policy and management, human and fiscal resource management, nonprofit policy and management, organizational behavior and management, urban and metropolitan policy and management; JD/MA. *Accreditation:* NASPAA. *Faculty:* 18. *Students:* 48 full-time (20 women), 68 part-time (36 women); includes 37 minority (26 Black or African American, non-Hispanic/Latino; 3 Asian, non-Hispanic/Latino; 2 Hispanic/Latino; 6 Two or more races, non-Hispanic/Latino), 6 international. Average age 32. 105 applicants, 39% accepted, 20 enrolled. In 2017, 17 master's, 3 doctorates awarded. *Degree requirements:* For master's, comprehensive exam (for some programs), thesis (for some programs); for doctorate, thesis/dissertation. *Entrance requirements:* For master's, GRE General Test, substantial undergraduate preparation in the social sciences, minimum upper-division undergraduate GPA of 3.0, two letters of recommendation, personal statement; for doctorate, GRE General Test, 3 letters of recommendation; personal statement; interview. Additional exam requirements/recommendations for international students: Required—TOEFL (minimum score 550

paper-based; 79 iBT), TWE (minimum score 5.5), Michigan English Language Assessment Battery (minimum score 85); Recommended—IELTS (minimum score 6.5). *Application deadline:* For fall admission, 5/15 for domestic students, 5/1 priority date for international students; for winter admission, 10/15 for domestic students, 9/1 priority date for international students. Applications are processed on a rolling basis. Application fee: $50. Electronic applications accepted. *Expenses:* Contact institution. *Financial support:* In 2017–18, 44 students received support, including 6 fellowships with tuition reimbursements available (averaging $11,698 per year), 12 teaching assistantships with tuition reimbursements available (averaging $18,534 per year); research assistantships with tuition reimbursements available, scholarships/grants, health care benefits, and unspecified assistantships also available. Financial award applicants required to submit FAFSA. *Faculty research:* American government and politics, comparative politics, political methodology, political theory, public administration, public law, public policy, world politics/international relations, formal theory/modeling, gender and politics, international law, peace research, political economy, political psychology, politics of developing countries, race, religion, and ethnicity, urban politics. *Unit head:* Dr. Daniel Geller, Professor and Chair, 313-577-6328, E-mail: dgeller@wayne.edu. *Application contact:* Dr. Sharon Lean, Graduate Director, 313-577-2630, E-mail: gradpolisci@wayne.edu.
Website: http://clas.wayne.edu/politicalscience/

Webster University, George Herbert Walker School of Business and Technology, Department of Management, St. Louis, MO 63119-3194. Offers business and organizational security management (MA); digital marketing management (Graduate Certificate); government contracting (Graduate Certificate); health administration (MHA); health care management (MA); health services management (MA); human resources development (MA); human resources management (MA); information technology management (MA, MS); management (D Mgt); management and leadership (MA); marketing (MA); nonprofit leadership (MA); nonprofit revenue development (Graduate Certificate); organizational development (Graduate Certificate); procurement and acquisitions management (MA); public administration (MPA); space systems operations management (MS). *Program availability:* Part-time, evening/weekend, online learning. *Degree requirements:* For master's, thesis (for some programs); for doctorate, thesis/dissertation, written exam. *Entrance requirements:* For doctorate, GMAT, 3 years of work experience, MBA. Additional exam requirements/recommendations for international students: Required—TOEFL.

West Chester University of Pennsylvania, College of Business and Public Management, Department of Public Policy and Administration, West Chester, PA 19383. Offers administration (Certificate); non profit administration (Certificate); nonprofit administration (MPA); public administration (MPA); public policy and administration (MPA, DPA). *Accreditation:* NASPAA. *Program availability:* Part-time, evening/weekend, 100% online. *Students:* 69 full-time (32 women), 149 part-time (77 women); includes 82 minority (67 Black or African American, non-Hispanic/Latino; 1 Asian, non-Hispanic/Latino; 11 Hispanic/Latino; 3 Two or more races, non-Hispanic/Latino), 8 international. Average age 34. 117 applicants, 86% accepted, 67 enrolled. In 2017, 32 master's, 12 other advanced degrees awarded. Terminal master's awarded for partial completion of doctoral program. *Degree requirements:* For master's, capstone project. *Entrance requirements:* For master's, statement of professional goals, resume, two letters of reference, academic transcripts. Additional exam requirements/recommendations for international students: Required—TOEFL or IELTS. *Application deadline:* For fall admission, 5/15 for international students; for spring admission, 10/15 for international students. Applications are processed on a rolling basis. Application fee: $50. Electronic applications accepted. *Expenses:* Tuition, state resident: full-time $9000; part-time $500 per credit. Tuition, nonresident: full-time $13,500; part-time $750 per credit. *Required fees:* $2959; $149.79 per credit. *Financial support:* Scholarships/grants and unspecified assistantships available. Financial award application deadline: 2/15; financial award applicants required to submit FAFSA. *Faculty research:* Public policy, economic development, research methodology, public administration, nonprofit administration. *Unit head:* Dr. Jeremy Phillips, Department Chair/Director of DPA Program, 610-436-2016, E-mail: jphillips@wcupa.edu. *Application contact:* Dr. Alison Turner, MPA Graduate Coordinator, 610-436-2438, E-mail: aturner@wcupa.edu.
Website: http://www.wcupa.edu/business-publicManagement/mpa/

Western Kentucky University, Graduate Studies, Potter College of Arts and Letters, Department of Political Science, Bowling Green, KY 42101. Offers MPA. *Accreditation:* NASPAA. *Program availability:* Part-time, evening/weekend. *Degree requirements:* For master's, comprehensive exam, final exam. *Entrance requirements:* For master's, GRE General Test, minimum GPA of 2.75. Additional exam requirements/recommendations for international students: Required—TOEFL (minimum score 555 paper-based; 79 iBT). *Faculty research:* Role of non-profits, comparative policy analysis, social welfare policy, rural administration, ethics and bureaucracy.

Western Michigan University, Graduate College, College of Arts and Sciences, Department of Political Science, Kalamazoo, MI 49008. Offers international development administration (MIDA), including Peace Corps; political science (MA, PhD). *Degree requirements:* For master's, thesis optional; for doctorate, thesis/dissertation.

Western Michigan University, Graduate College, College of Arts and Sciences, School of Public Affairs and Administration, Kalamazoo, MI 49008. Offers health care administration (MPA, Graduate Certificate); nonprofit leadership and administration (Graduate Certificate); public administration (PhD). *Accreditation:* NASPAA (one or more programs are accredited). *Degree requirements:* For doctorate, thesis/dissertation.

Westfield State University, College of Graduate and Continuing Education, Department of Political Science, Westfield, MA 01086. Offers criminal justice administration (MPA); non-profit management (MPA); public management (MPA). *Program availability:* Part-time, evening/weekend. *Faculty:* 3 full-time (1 woman), 3 part-time/adjunct (2 women). *Students:* 9 full-time (2 women), 40 part-time (17 women); includes 13 minority (2 Black or African American, non-Hispanic/Latino; 2 American Indian or Alaska Native, non-Hispanic/Latino; 8 Hispanic/Latino; 1 Two or more races, non-Hispanic/Latino). Average age 33. 19 applicants, 100% accepted, 14 enrolled. In 2017, 16 master's awarded. *Degree requirements:* For master's, comprehensive exam, thesis (for some programs). *Entrance requirements:* For master's, GRE General Test or MAT, minimum undergraduate GPA of 2.8. Additional exam requirements/recommendations for international students: Recommended—TOEFL (minimum score 550 paper-based; 79 iBT). *Application deadline:* For fall admission, 7/1 for domestic students; for spring admission, 11/1 for domestic students; for summer admission, 4/1 for domestic students. Applications are processed on a rolling basis. Application fee: $50. *Expenses: Tuition,* state resident: part-time $332 per credit. Tuition, nonresident: part-time $332 per credit. *Required fees:* $75 per semester. Tuition and fees vary according to program. *Financial support:* Unspecified assistantships available. Financial award application deadline: 3/1; financial award applicants required to submit FAFSA. *Unit head:* Dr. Hugh Jo, Chair, 413-572-8806, Fax: 413-572-8168, E-mail: hjo@westfield.ma.edu. *Application contact:* Shelly Henrichon, Admissions Coordinator, 413-572-8022, Fax: 413-572-5227, E-mail: mhenrichon@westfield.ma.edu.

West Virginia University, Eberly College of Arts and Sciences, Morgantown, WV 26506. Offers biology (MS, PhD); chemistry (MS, PhD); communication studies (MA, PhD); computational statistics (PhD); creative writing (MFA); English (MA, PhD);

forensic and investigative science (MS); forensic science (PhD); geography (MA); geology (MA, PhD); history (MA, PhD); legal studies (MLS); math (MS); physics (MS, PhD); political science (MA, PhD); professional writing and editing (MA); psychology (MA); public administration (MPA); social work (MSW); sociology (MA, PhD); statistics (MS). *Program availability:* Part-time, evening/weekend, online learning. *Students:* 831 full-time (437 women), 236 part-time (142 women); includes 112 minority (35 Black or African American, non-Hispanic/Latino; 15 Asian, non-Hispanic/Latino; 29 Hispanic/Latino; 33 Two or more races, non-Hispanic/Latino), 235 international. Terminal master's awarded for partial completion of doctoral program. *Degree requirements:* For master's, thesis (for some programs); for doctorate, comprehensive exam, thesis/dissertation. *Entrance requirements:* For master's and doctorate, GRE. Additional exam requirements/recommendations for international students: Required—TOEFL (minimum score 600 paper-based); Recommended—TWE. *Application deadline:* For spring admission, 2/15 priority date for domestic and international students. Applications are processed on a rolling basis. Application fee: $45. Electronic applications accepted. *Expenses:* Tuition, state resident: full-time $9450. Tuition, nonresident: full-time $24,390. *Financial support:* Fellowships with full tuition reimbursements, research assistantships with full tuition reimbursements, teaching assistantships with full tuition reimbursements, career-related internships or fieldwork, Federal Work-Study, institutionally sponsored loans, scholarships/grants, health care benefits, tuition waivers (full and partial), unspecified assistantships, and administrative assistantships available. Financial award application deadline: 2/1; financial award applicants required to submit FAFSA. *Faculty research:* Humanities, social sciences, life science, physical sciences, mathematics. *Unit head:* Dr. Mary Ellen Mazey, Dean, 304-293-4611, Fax: 304-293-6858, E-mail: mary.mazey@mail.wvu.edu. *Application contact:* Dr. Fred L. King, Associate Dean for Graduate Studies, 304-293-4611 Ext. 5205, Fax: 304-293-6858, E-mail: fred.king@mail.wvu.edu.
Website: http://www.as.wvu.edu/

Wichita State University, Graduate School, Fairmount College of Liberal Arts and Sciences, Hugo Wall School of Public Affairs, Wichita, KS 67260. Offers public administration (MPA). *Accreditation:* NASPAA. *Program availability:* Part-time, 100% online, blended/hybrid learning. *Unit head:* Dr. Samuel L. Brown, Director, 316-978-7240, Fax: 316-978-6533, E-mail: sam.brown@wichita.edu. *Application contact:* Jordan Oleson, Admissions Coordinator, 316-978-3095, E-mail: jordan.oleson@wichita.edu.

Widener University, College of Arts and Sciences, Program in Public Administration, Chester, PA 19013-5792. Offers MPA, Psy D/MPA. *Program availability:* Part-time, evening/weekend. *Faculty:* 1 full-time (0 women), 3 part-time/adjunct (0 women). *Students:* 12 part-time (5 women); includes 6 minority (3 Black or African American, non-Hispanic/Latino; 2 Asian, non-Hispanic/Latino; 1 Hispanic/Latino). Average age 33. 21 applicants, 86% accepted. In 2017, 9 master's awarded. *Degree requirements:* For master's, thesis or comprehensive exam. *Entrance requirements:* For master's, minimum undergraduate GPA of 3.0. *Application deadline:* For fall admission, 8/1 priority date for domestic students; for spring admission, 12/1 priority date for domestic students. Applications are processed on a rolling basis. Application fee: $25 ($300 for international students). Electronic applications accepted. *Expenses:* Contact institution. *Financial support:* In 2017–18, 8 students received support. Career-related internships or fieldwork and institutionally sponsored loans available. Support available to part-time students. Financial award application deadline: 5/1. *Faculty research:* Intergovernmental relations, nonprofit organizations, public policy, political economy, bureaucratic politics. *Unit head:* Dr. James E. Vike, Director, 610-499-1120, Fax: 610-499-4603, E-mail: james.vike@widener.edu.
Website: http://www.widener.edu/academics/schools/arts_sciences/public_admin/default.aspx

Wilmington University, College of Business, New Castle, DE 19720-6491. Offers accounting (MBA, MS); business administration (MBA, DBA); environmental stewardship (MBA); finance (MBA); health care administration (MBA, MSM); homeland security (MBA, MSM); human resource management (MSM); management information systems (MBA, MSN); marketing (MSM); marketing management (MBA); military leadership (MSM); organizational leadership (MBA, MSM); public administration (MSM). *Program availability:* Part-time, evening/weekend. *Faculty:* 16 full-time (8 women), 106 part-time/adjunct (49 women). *Students:* 525 full-time (294 women), 1,212 part-time (780 women); includes 557 minority (412 Black or African American, non-Hispanic/Latino; 14 American Indian or Alaska Native, non-Hispanic/Latino; 55 Asian, non-Hispanic/Latino; 25 Hispanic/Latino; 3 Native Hawaiian or other Pacific Islander, non-Hispanic/Latino; 48 Two or more races, non-Hispanic/Latino), 157 international. Average age 35. 1,484 applicants, 70% accepted, 685 enrolled. In 2017, 543 master's, 16 doctorates awarded. *Entrance requirements:* Additional exam requirements/recommendations for international students: Required—TOEFL (minimum score 500 paper-based). *Application deadline:* Applications are processed on a rolling basis. Application fee: $35. Electronic applications accepted. *Expenses: Tuition:* Part-time $466 per credit. *Required fees:* $25 per semester. Tuition and fees vary according to degree level and campus/location. *Financial support:* Applicants required to submit FAFSA. *Unit head:* Dr. Kathy S. Kennedy Ratajack, Dean, 302-356-2481. *Application contact:* Laura Morris, Director of Admissions, 877-967-5456, E-mail: infocenter@wilmu.edu.
Website: http://www.wilmu.edu/business/

Wright State University, Graduate School, College of Liberal Arts, Department of Urban Affairs and Geography, Dayton, OH 45435. Offers public administration (MPA). *Accreditation:* NASPAA. *Degree requirements:* For master's, thesis optional. *Entrance requirements:* For master's, interview, minimum GPA of 2.7. Additional exam requirements/recommendations for international students: Required—TOEFL. *Faculty research:* Strategic planning, economic development, housing and public management.

York University, Faculty of Graduate Studies, Faculty of Liberal Arts and Professional Studies, Program in Public Policy, Administration and Law, Toronto, ON M3J 1P3, Canada. Offers MPPAL.

Public Affairs

Arizona State University at the Tempe campus, College of Public Programs, School of Public Affairs, Phoenix, AZ 85004-0687. Offers emergency management and homeland security (MA); program evaluation (MS); public administration (MPA, PhD), including nonprofit administration (MPA), urban management (MPA); public policy (MPP); MPA/MSW. *Accreditation:* NASPAA (one or more programs are accredited). *Program availability:* Part-time, evening/weekend. Terminal master's awarded for partial completion of doctoral program. *Degree requirements:* For master's, thesis or alternative, policy analysis or capstone project; interactive Program of Study (iPOS) submitted before completing 50 percent of required credit hours; for doctorate, comprehensive exam, thesis/dissertation, interactive Program of Study (iPOS) submitted before completing 50 percent of required credit hours. *Entrance requirements:* For master's, GRE, minimum GPA of 3.0 or equivalent in last 2 years of work leading to bachelor's degree; for doctorate, GRE, minimum GPA of 3.0 or equivalent in last 2 years of work leading to bachelor's degree, 3 letters of recommendation, resume, statement of goals, samples of research reports. Additional exam requirements/recommendations for international students: Required—TOEFL (minimum score 600 paper-based; 100 iBT), IELTS (minimum score 6.5). Electronic applications accepted. *Expenses:* Contact institution.

Binghamton University, State University of New York, Graduate School, College of Community and Public Affairs, Program in Community Research and Action, Binghamton, NY 13902-6000. Offers PhD. *Students:* 13 full-time (6 women), 23 part-time (17 women); includes 8 minority (5 Black or African American, non-Hispanic/Latino; 1 Hispanic/Latino; 2 Two or more races, non-Hispanic/Latino), 7 international. Average age 37. 28 applicants, 32% accepted, 9 enrolled. In 2017, 2 doctorates awarded. *Entrance requirements:* For doctorate, undergraduate and graduate transcripts, minimum undergraduate and graduate GPA of 3.0, personal statement, resume or curriculum vitae, three letters of recommendation, writing sample. Additional exam requirements/recommendations for international students: Required—TOEFL (minimum score 100 iBT), IELTS (minimum score 7). *Financial support:* In 2017–18, 11 students received support. *Unit head:* Dr. Laura Bronstein, Dean, 607-777-5572, Fax: 607-777-2406, E-mail: lbronst@binghamton.edu. *Application contact:* Ben Balkaya, Assistant Dean and Director, 607-777-2151, Fax: 607-777-2501, E-mail: balkaya@binghamton.edu.

Cleveland State University, College of Graduate Studies, Maxine Goodman Levin College of Urban Affairs, Program in Urban Studies and Public Affairs, Cleveland, OH 44115. Offers communication (PhD); public administration (PhD); urban policy and development (PhD). *Program availability:* Part-time, evening/weekend. *Faculty:* 16 full-time (8 women), 13 part-time/adjunct (5 women). *Students:* 3 full-time (2 women), 24 part-time (14 women); includes 6 minority (4 Black or African American, non-Hispanic/Latino; 1 Hispanic/Latino; 1 Two or more races, non-Hispanic/Latino), 4 international. Average age 41. 32 applicants, 34% accepted, 2 enrolled. In 2017, 4 doctorates awarded. *Degree requirements:* For doctorate, comprehensive exam, thesis/dissertation. *Entrance requirements:* For doctorate, GRE General Test (minimum score: verbal and quantitative 50th percentile, analytical writing 4.0), minimum GPA of 3.5. Additional exam requirements/recommendations for international students: Required—TOEFL (minimum score 550 paper-based; 78 iBT), IELTS (6.0), or International Test of English Proficiency (iTEP). *Application deadline:* For fall admission, 1/31 for domestic and international students. Application fee: $40. Electronic applications accepted. *Expenses:* Contact institution. *Financial support:* In 2017–18, 15 students received support, including 1 research assistantship with full tuition reimbursement available (averaging $11,800 per year), 2 teaching assistantships with full tuition reimbursements available (averaging $11,800 per year); scholarships/grants, tuition waivers (full and partial), and unspecified assistantships also available. Support available to part-time students. Financial award application deadline: 3/1; financial award applicants required to submit FAFSA. *Faculty research:* Urban and public policy, public affairs. *Unit head:* Dr. Bill Bowen, Professor/PhD Program Director, 216-687-9226, E-mail: w.bowen@csuohio.edu. *Application contact:* David Arrighi, Graduate Academic Advisor, 216-523-7522, Fax: 216-687-5398, E-mail: d.arrighi@csuohio.edu.
Website: http://urban.csuohio.edu/academics/graduate/phd/

Concordia University, School of Graduate Studies, Faculty of Arts and Science, School of Community and Public Affairs, Montréal, QC H3G 1M8, Canada. Offers community economic development (Diploma).

Cornell University, Graduate School, Graduate Fields of Human Ecology, Field of Public Affairs, Ithaca, NY 14853. Offers MPA. *Degree requirements:* For master's, thesis, research project, paper. *Entrance requirements:* For master's, GRE General Test, 2 letters of recommendation. Additional exam requirements/recommendations for international students: Required—TOEFL (minimum score 550 paper-based; 77 iBT). Electronic applications accepted.

Drake University, School of Journalism and Mass Communication, Des Moines, IA 50311-4516. Offers brand communication (MCL); communication leadership (MCL); public affairs and advocacy (MCL). *Program availability:* Part-time, evening/weekend. *Expenses: Tuition:* Part-time $600 per credit hour. *Required fees:* $120 per credit hour. Tuition and fees vary according to course load and program. *Unit head:* Dr. Kathleen Richardson, Dean, 515-271-2295, Fax: 515-271-4518, E-mail: kathleen.richardson@drake.edu.
Website: http://www.drake.edu/sjmc/

Florida International University, Steven J. Green School of International and Public Affairs, Department of Public Administration, Miami, FL 33199. Offers public administration (MPA); public affairs (PhD); JD/MPA; MS/MPA. *Accreditation:* NASPAA (one or more programs are accredited). *Program availability:* Part-time, evening/weekend. *Faculty:* 13 full-time (5 women), 12 part-time/adjunct (8 women). *Students:* 111 full-time (73 women), 147 part-time (97 women); includes 201 minority (60 Black or African American, non-Hispanic/Latino; 2 American Indian or Alaska Native, non-Hispanic/Latino; 4 Asian, non-Hispanic/Latino; 131 Hispanic/Latino; 4 Two or more races, non-Hispanic/Latino), 17 international. Average age 33. 173 applicants, 62% accepted, 82 enrolled. In 2017, 90 master's, 4 doctorates awarded. *Degree requirements:* For doctorate, comprehensive exam, thesis/dissertation. *Entrance requirements:* For master's, minimum undergraduate GPA of 3.0 in upper-level coursework, letter of recommendation, letter of intent; for doctorate, GRE, minimum undergraduate GPA of 3.0 in upper-level coursework, 3 letters of recommendation, samples of scholarly written work, interview (when student lives within 50 miles of campus). Additional exam requirements/recommendations for international students: Required—TOEFL (minimum score 550 paper-based; 80 iBT). *Application deadline:* For fall admission, 6/1 for domestic students, 4/1 for international students; for spring admission, 10/1 for domestic students, 9/1 for international students. Applications are processed on a rolling basis. Application fee: $30. Electronic applications accepted. *Expenses:* Tuition, state resident: full-time $8912; part-time $446 per credit hour. Tuition, nonresident: full-time $21,393; part-time $992 per credit hour. *Required fees:* $390; $195 per semester. *Financial support:* Institutionally sponsored loans and scholarships/grants available. Financial award application deadline: 3/1; financial award

applicants required to submit FAFSA. *Unit head:* Dr. Howard Frank, Chair, 305-348-0410, E-mail: howard.frank@fiu.edu. *Application contact:* Nanett Rojas, Manager, Admissions Operations, 305-348-7464, E-mail: gradadm@fiu.edu.
Website: http://cas.fiu.edu/

George Mason University, College of Humanities and Social Sciences, Department of Philosophy, Fairfax, VA 22030. Offers ethics and public affairs (MA); philosophy and cultural theory (MA). *Faculty:* 11 full-time (3 women), 8 part-time/adjunct (0 women). *Students:* 10 part-time (3 women); includes 1 minority (Hispanic/Latino). Average age 39. 9 applicants, 67% accepted, 1 enrolled. In 2017, 4 master's awarded. *Degree requirements:* For master's, thesis optional. *Entrance requirements:* For master's, college transcripts, goals statement, 2 letters of recommendation, resume, writing sample; completion of certain undergraduate preparation coursework with grades of B or higher in each course (for philosophy and cultural theory). Additional exam requirements/recommendations for international students: Required—TOEFL (minimum score 575 paper-based, 88 iBT), IELTS (6.5), or PTE (59). *Application deadline:* For fall admission, 3/1 for domestic and international students; for spring admission, 11/1 for domestic and international students. Application fee: $75 ($80 for international students). Electronic applications accepted. *Expenses:* Tuition, state resident: full-time $11,228; part-time $459.50 per credit. Tuition, nonresident: full-time $30,932; part-time $1280.50 per credit. *Required fees:* $3252; $135.50 per credit. Part-time tuition and fees vary according to course load and program. *Financial support:* In 2017–18, 1 student received support, including 1 research assistantship with tuition reimbursement available; career-related internships or fieldwork, Federal Work-Study, scholarships/grants, unspecified assistantships, and health care benefits (for full-time research or teaching assistantship recipients) also available. Financial award application deadline: 3/1; financial award applicants required to submit FAFSA. *Faculty research:* History of philosophy (particularly Asian and modern); Anglo-American and analytic philosophy; continental philosophy; ethics (including bioethics and feminist ethics); philosophy and public policy. *Total annual research expenditures:* $131,560. *Unit head:* Ted Kinnaman, Chair/Associate Professor, 703-993-4328, Fax: 703-993-1297, E-mail: tkinnama@gmu.edu. *Application contact:* Rose Cherubin, Associate Professor and Graduate Coordinator, 703-993-1332, Fax: 703-993-1297, E-mail: rcherubi@gmu.edu.
Website: http://philosophy.gmu.edu/

The George Washington University, Columbian College of Arts and Sciences, School of Media and Public Affairs, Washington, DC 20052. Offers MA, Graduate Certificate. *Faculty:* 24 full-time (10 women), 27 part-time/adjunct (7 women). *Students:* 33 full-time (20 women), 17 part-time (13 women); includes 11 minority (4 Black or African American, non-Hispanic/Latino; 5 Hispanic/Latino; 2 Two or more races, non-Hispanic/Latino), 7 international. Average age 27. 98 applicants, 55% accepted, 20 enrolled. In 2017, 23 master's, 13 other advanced degrees awarded. *Entrance requirements:* For master's, GRE General Test. Additional exam requirements/recommendations for international students: Required—TOEFL (minimum score 550 paper-based; 80 iBT). *Application deadline:* For fall admission, 4/1 priority date for domestic students, 1/15 priority date for international students; for spring admission, 10/1 priority date for domestic students, 9/1 priority date for international students. Applications are processed on a rolling basis. Application fee: $75. Electronic applications accepted. *Expenses: Tuition:* Full-time $28,800; part-time $1655 per credit hour. *Required fees:* $45; $2.75 per credit hour. *Financial support:* In 2017–18, fellowships with tuition reimbursements (averaging $10,000 per year), teaching assistantships with tuition reimbursements (averaging $5,000 per year) were awarded. Financial award application deadline: 1/15. *Unit head:* Frank Sesno, Director, 202-994-9553, E-mail: sesno@gwu.edu. *Application contact:* Information Contact, 202-994-6227, Fax: 202-994-5806, E-mail: smpa@gwu.edu.
Website: http://smpa.gwu.edu/

Indiana University Bloomington, School of Public and Environmental Affairs, Public Affairs Programs, Bloomington, IN 47405. Offers economic development (MPA); energy (MPA); environmental policy (PhD); environmental policy and natural resource management (MPA); information systems (MPA); international development (MPA); local government management (MPA); nonprofit management (MPA, Certificate); policy analysis (MPA); public budgeting and financial management (Certificate); public finance (PhD); public financial administration (MPA); public management (MPA, PhD, Certificate); public policy analysis (PhD); social entrepreneurship (Certificate); specialized public affairs (MPA); sustainability and sustainable development (MPA); JD/MPA; MPA/MA; MPA/MIS; MPA/MLS; MSES/MPA. *Accreditation:* NASPAA (one or more programs are accredited). *Program availability:* Part-time. *Degree requirements:* For master's, capstone, internship; for doctorate, comprehensive exam, thesis/dissertation. *Entrance requirements:* For master's, GRE General Test or GMAT, official transcripts, 3 letters of recommendation, resume, personal statement; for doctorate, GRE General Test, official transcripts, 3 letters of recommendation, statement of purpose. Additional exam requirements/recommendations for international students: Required—TOEFL (minimum score 600 paper-based; 96 iBT); Recommended—IELTS (minimum score 7). Electronic applications accepted. *Faculty research:* International development, environmental policy and resource management, policy analysis, public finance, public management, urban management, nonprofit management, energy policy, social policy, public finance.

Indiana University Northwest, School of Public and Environmental Affairs, Gary, IN 46408. Offers criminal justice (MPA); environmental affairs (Graduate Certificate); health services (MPA); nonprofit management (Certificate); public management (MPA, Graduate Certificate). *Accreditation:* NASPAA (one or more programs are accredited). *Program availability:* Part-time. *Entrance requirements:* For master's, GRE General Test (minimum combined verbal and quantitative score of 280), GMAT, or LSAT, letters of recommendation. Electronic applications accepted. *Faculty research:* Employment in income security policies, evidence in criminal justice, equal employment law, social welfare policy and welfare reform, public finance in developing countries.

Indiana University of Pennsylvania, School of Graduate Studies and Research, College of Humanities and Social Sciences, Department of Political Science, Program in Public Affairs, Indiana, PA 15705. Offers MA. *Program availability:* Part-time. *Faculty:* 6 full-time (4 women), 1 part-time/adjunct (0 women). *Students:* 16 full-time (7 women), 5 part-time (2 women); includes 3 minority (2 Black or African American, non-Hispanic/Latino; 1 Hispanic/Latino), 7 international. Average age 25. 22 applicants, 59% accepted, 8 enrolled. In 2017, 9 master's awarded. *Degree requirements:* For master's, thesis optional. *Entrance requirements:* For master's, 2 letters of recommendation. Additional exam requirements/recommendations for international students: Required—TOEFL (minimum score 550 paper-based). *Application deadline:* Applications are processed on a rolling basis. Application fee: $50. Electronic applications accepted. *Expenses:* Tuition, state resident: full-time $12,000; part-time $500 per credit. Tuition, nonresident: full-time $18,000; part-time $750 per credit. *Required fees:* $4073; $165.55 per credit. $64 per term. *Financial support:* In 2017–18, 10 research assistantships with tuition reimbursements (averaging $2,748 per year) were awarded; fellowships with full tuition reimbursements, career-related internships or fieldwork, Federal Work-Study, scholarships/grants, and unspecified assistantships also available. Support available to part-time students. Financial award application deadline: 4/15; financial award applicants required to submit FAFSA. *Unit head:* Dr. Sarah Wheeler, Graduate Coordinator, 724-357-2290, E-mail: wheeler@iup.edu.
Website: http://www.iup.edu/grad/publicaffairs/default.aspx

Indiana University–Purdue University Indianapolis, School of Public and Environmental Affairs, Indianapolis, IN 46202. Offers criminal justice and public safety (MS); homeland security and emergency management (Graduate Certificate); library management (Graduate Certificate); nonprofit management (Graduate Certificate); public affairs (MPA); public management (Graduate Certificate); social entrepreneurship: nonprofit and public benefit organizations (Graduate Certificate); JD/MPA; MLS/NMC; MLS/PMC; MPA/MA. *Accreditation:* CAHME (one or more programs are accredited); NASPAA. *Program availability:* Part-time, evening/weekend, online learning. *Entrance requirements:* For master's, GRE General Test, GMAT or LSAT, minimum GPA of 3.0 (preferred). Additional exam requirements/recommendations for international students: Required—TOEFL (minimum score 93 iBT), IELTS (minimum score 6.5). Electronic applications accepted. *Faculty research:* Nonprofit and public management, public policy, urban policy, sustainability policy, disaster preparedness and recovery, vehicular safety, homicide, offender rehabilitation and re-entry.

Indiana University South Bend, College of Liberal Arts and Sciences, South Bend, IN 46615. Offers advanced computer programming (Graduate Certificate); applied informatics (Graduate Certificate); applied mathematics and computer science (MS); behavior modification (Graduate Certificate); computer applications (Graduate Certificate); computer programming (Graduate Certificate); correctional management and supervision (Graduate Certificate); English (MA); health systems management (Graduate Certificate); international studies (Graduate Certificate); liberal studies (MLS); nonprofit management (Graduate Certificate); paralegal studies (Graduate Certificate); professional writing (Graduate Certificate); public affairs (MPA); public management (Graduate Certificate); social and cultural diversity (Graduate Certificate); strategic sustainability leadership (Graduate Certificate); technology for administration (Graduate Certificate). *Program availability:* Part-time, evening/weekend. *Degree requirements:* For master's, variable foreign language requirement, thesis (for some programs). *Entrance requirements:* For master's, minimum GPA of 3.0. Additional exam requirements/recommendations for international students: Required—TOEFL (minimum score 550 paper-based; 80 iBT). *Expenses:* Contact institution. *Faculty research:* Artificial intelligence, bioinformatics, English language and literature, creative writing, computer networks.

The Institute of World Politics, Graduate Programs in National Security, Intelligence, and International Affairs, Washington, DC 20036. Offers American foreign policy (Certificate); comparative political culture (Certificate); counterintelligence (Certificate); democracy building (Certificate); intelligence (Certificate); international politics (Certificate); national security affairs (Certificate); public diplomacy and political warfare (Certificate); statecraft and national security affairs (MA); statecraft and world politics (MA); strategic intelligence studies (MA). *Program availability:* Part-time, evening/weekend. *Degree requirements:* For master's, comprehensive exam, thesis optional. *Entrance requirements:* For master's, GRE General Test. Additional exam requirements/recommendations for international students: Required—TOEFL. Electronic applications accepted. *Faculty research:* Intelligence, national security, statecraft.

Jackson State University, Graduate School, College of Public Service, Jackson, MS 39217. Offers MA, MPPA, MSW, PhD. *Degree requirements:* For master's, comprehensive exam. *Entrance requirements:* For master's, GRE General Test. Additional exam requirements/recommendations for international students: Required—TOEFL.

McMaster University, School of Graduate Studies, Faculty of Social Sciences, Department of Political Science, Hamilton, ON L8S 4M2, Canada. Offers international relations (PhD); political science (MA); public and the global economy (MA); public policy (PhD); public policy and administration (MA). MA program in public policy and administration offered jointly with University of Guelph. *Program availability:* Part-time. *Degree requirements:* For master's, thesis or alternative. *Entrance requirements:* For master's, minimum B+ average. Additional exam requirements/recommendations for international students: Required—TOEFL (minimum score 580 paper-based). *Faculty research:* Organizational theory, internationalization of public policy, water resource policies, political interest intermediation, comparative politics.

Merrimack College, School of Liberal Arts, North Andover, MA 01845-5800. Offers clinical mental health counseling (MS); interfaith spirituality (Certificate); public affairs (MPA); spiritual direction (MA, Certificate); spirituality (MA). *Program availability:* Part-time, evening/weekend. *Faculty:* 7 full-time, 4 part-time/adjunct. *Students:* 30 full-time (23 women), 3 part-time (2 women); includes 3 minority (2 Black or African American, non-Hispanic/Latino; 1 Hispanic/Latino), 1 international. Average age 30. 40 applicants, 88% accepted, 20 enrolled. In 2017, 9 master's awarded. *Degree requirements:* For master's, internship/strategic capstone (for MPA); 700-hour fieldwork placement (for MS); practicum (for MA in spiritual direction); for Certificate, practicum (for spiritual direction). *Entrance requirements:* For master's, official college transcripts, resume, personal statement, 2 recommendations (3 for MS in clinical mental health counseling); interview (for MA in spirituality). Additional exam requirements/recommendations for international students: Required—TOEFL (minimum score 84 iBT), IELTS (minimum score 6.5), PTE (minimum score 56). *Application deadline:* For fall admission, 8/24 for domestic students, 7/30 for international students; for spring admission, 1/10 for domestic students, 12/10 for international students; for summer admission, 5/10 for domestic students, 4/10 for international students. Applications are processed on a rolling basis. Electronic applications accepted. *Expenses:* $865 per credit hour tuition; comprehensive fees are $165 for 1-8 credit hours per semester, $320 for 9+ credit hours per semester. *Financial support:* Career-related internships or fieldwork, scholarships/grants, and health care benefits available. Support available to part-time students. Financial award application deadline: 5/1; financial award applicants required to submit FAFSA. *Application contact:* Jennifer Greenwood, Graduate Admissions Counselor, 978-837-3563, E-mail: greenwoodjl@merrimack.edu.

Metropolitan College of New York, Program in Public Administration, New York, NY 10013. Offers emergency and disaster management (MPA); public affairs and administration (MPA). *Program availability:* Evening/weekend. *Students:* 102 full-time (70 women), 10 part-time (9 women); includes 99 minority (71 Black or African American, non-Hispanic/Latino; 1 Asian, non-Hispanic/Latino; 25 Hispanic/Latino; 2 Two or more races, non-Hispanic/Latino), 3 international. Average age 39. 122 applicants, 45% accepted, 52 enrolled. In 2017, 129 master's awarded. *Degree requirements:* For master's, thesis. *Entrance requirements:* For master's, appropriate work experience, interview, minimum GPA of 2.7, internship or job in administrative setting. Additional exam requirements/recommendations for international students: Required—TOEFL (minimum score 600 paper-based). *Application deadline:* For fall admission, 7/30 priority date for domestic students, 7/1 for international students; for winter admission, 11/30 priority date for domestic students, 11/1 for international students; for spring admission, 3/30 priority date for domestic students, 3/1 for international students. Applications are processed on a rolling basis. Application fee: $45. Electronic applications accepted. *Expenses:* $842 per credit, $395 fee per semester. *Financial support:* Fellowships with tuition reimbursements, career-related internships or fieldwork, scholarships/grants, and tuition waivers (partial) available. Financial award application deadline: 8/15; financial award applicants required to submit FAFSA. *Faculty research:* Transnational politics

and culture, women and social policy, confidentiality in the human services, concepts of marginality, ethics in social policy. *Unit head:* Prof. Humphrey Crookendale, Dean, Graduate School for Public Affairs Administration, 212-343-1234 Ext. 2209, E-mail: hcrookendale@mcny.edu. *Application contact:* Steebo Varghese, Assistant Director of Admissions, 212-343-1234 Ext. 2708, Fax: 212-343-8474, E-mail: svarghese@mcny.edu.
Website: https://www.mcny.edu/academics/school-public-affairs-administration/

New Mexico Highlands University, Graduate Studies, College of Arts and Sciences, Department of History, Political Science, and Languages and Culture, Las Vegas, NM 87701. Offers public affairs (MA), including historical and cross-cultural perspectives, history/political science, political and governmental processes. *Degree requirements:* For master's, comprehensive exam, thesis or alternative. *Entrance requirements:* Additional exam requirements/recommendations for international students: Required—TOEFL (minimum score 540 paper-based).

New Mexico Highlands University, Graduate Studies, College of Arts and Sciences, Department of Social and Behavioral Sciences, Las Vegas, NM 87701. Offers psychology (MS), including clinical psychology/counseling, general psychology; public affairs (MA), including applied sociology; Southwest studies (MA), including anthropology. *Program availability:* Part-time. *Degree requirements:* For master's, comprehensive exam, thesis or alternative. *Entrance requirements:* For master's, minimum undergraduate GPA of 3.0. Additional exam requirements/recommendations for international students: Required—TOEFL (minimum score 540 paper-based). *Faculty research:* Southwest Native American resettlement development, community-level interventions, neurochemistry of personality, comparative criminal justice, social theory and activism.

Notre Dame de Namur University, Division of Academic Affairs, School of Business and Management, Program in Public Administration, Belmont, CA 94002-1908. Offers human resource management (MPA); public affairs administration (MPA). *Program availability:* Part-time, evening/weekend, online learning. *Students:* 2 full-time (1 woman), 32 part-time (29 women). Average age 35. *Entrance requirements:* For master's, interview, minimum GPA of 2.5. Additional exam requirements/recommendations for international students: Required—TOEFL (minimum score 550 paper-based; 79 iBT). *Application deadline:* For fall admission, 8/1 priority date for domestic students; for spring admission, 12/1 priority date for domestic students. Applications are processed on a rolling basis. Application fee: $60. Electronic applications accepted. *Expenses: Tuition:* Full-time $16,128; part-time $8064 per credit hour. *Required fees:* $80; $80 per credit hour. $40 per semester. *Financial support:* Available to part-time students. Applicants required to submit FAFSA. *Unit head:* Jordan Holtzman, Program Director, Graduate Business Programs, 510-375-1348, E-mail: jholtzman@ndnu.edu.
Website: http://www.ndnu.edu/academics/schools-programs/school-business/graduate/mpa.aspx

The Ohio State University, Graduate School, John Glenn College of Public Affairs, Columbus, OH 43210. Offers public administration (MA, MPA); public policy and management (PhD). *Accreditation:* NASPAA (one or more programs are accredited). *Program availability:* Part-time. *Faculty:* 21. *Students:* 136 full-time (71 women), 37 part-time (25 women). Average age 30. In 2017, 77 master's, 4 doctorates awarded. *Degree requirements:* For doctorate, thesis/dissertation. *Entrance requirements:* For master's, GRE General Test (for MPA), minimum GPA of 3.0 (for MA); for doctorate, GRE General Test. Additional exam requirements/recommendations for international students: Required—TOEFL (minimum score 600 paper-based; 100 iBT); Recommended—IELTS (minimum score 7.5). *Application deadline:* For fall admission, 12/1 priority date for domestic students, 11/30 priority date for international students; for spring admission, 11/15 for domestic and international students; for summer admission, 4/1 for domestic and international students. Applications are processed on a rolling basis. Application fee: $60 ($70 for international students). Electronic applications accepted. *Financial support:* Fellowships, research assistantships, teaching assistantships, Federal Work-Study, institutionally sponsored loans, and unspecified assistantships available. Support available to part-time students. *Unit head:* Dr. Trevor Brown, Dean, 614-292-4533, Fax: 614-292-4868, E-mail: brown.2296@osu.edu. *Application contact:* Graduate and Professional Admissions, 614-292-6031, Fax: 614-292-3656, E-mail: gpadmissions@osu.edu.
Website: http://glenn.osu.edu/

Park University, School of Graduate and Professional Studies, Kansas City, MO 54105. Offers adult education (M Ed); business and government leadership (Graduate Certificate); business, government, and global society (MPA); communication and leadership (MA); creative and life writing (Graduate Certificate); disaster and emergency management (MPA, Graduate Certificate); educational leadership (M Ed); finance (MBA, Graduate Certificate); general business (MBA); global business (Graduate Certificate); healthcare administration (MHA); healthcare services management and leadership (Graduate Certificate); international business (MBA); language and literacy (M Ed), including English for speakers of other languages, special reading teacher/literacy coach; leadership of international healthcare organizations (Graduate Certificate); management information systems (MBA, Graduate Certificate); music performance (ADP, Graduate Certificate), including cello (MM, ADP), piano (MM, ADP), viola (MM, ADP), violin (MM, ADP); nonprofit and community services management (MPA); nonprofit leadership (Graduate Certificate); performance (MM), including cello (MM, ADP), piano (MM, ADP), viola (MM, ADP), violin (MM, ADP); public management (MPA); social work (MSW); teacher leadership (M Ed), including curriculum and assessment, instructional leader. *Program availability:* Part-time, evening/weekend, online learning. *Degree requirements:* For master's, comprehensive exam (for some programs), thesis (for some programs), internship (for some programs); exam (for some programs). *Entrance requirements:* For master's, GRE or GMAT (for some programs), teacher certification (for some M Ed programs), letters of recommendation, essay, resume (for some programs). Additional exam requirements/recommendations for international students: Required—TOEFL (minimum score 550 paper-based; 79 iBT), IELTS (minimum score 6). Electronic applications accepted.

Penn State Harrisburg, Graduate School, School of Public Affairs, Middletown, PA 17057. Offers criminal justice (MA); health administration (MHA); health administration: long term care (Certificate); homeland security (MPS, Certificate); public administration (MPA, PhD); public administration: non-profit administration (Certificate); public budgeting and financial management (Certificate); public sector human resource management (Certificate). *Accreditation:* NASPAA. *Unit head:* Dr. Mukund S. Kulkarni, Chancellor, 717-948-6105, Fax: 717-948-6452. *Application contact:* Robert W. Coffman, Jr., Director of Enrollment Management, Recruitment and Admissions, 717-948-6250, Fax: 717-948-6325, E-mail: hbgadmit@psu.edu.
Website: https://harrisburg.psu.edu/public-affairs

Portland State University, Graduate Studies, College of Urban and Public Affairs, Hatfield School of Government, Division of Public Administration, Portland, OR 97207-0751. Offers collaborative governance (Certificate); energy policy and management (Certificate); global management and leadership (MPA); health administration (MPA); human resource management (MPA); local government (MPA); natural resource policy and administration (MPA); nonprofit and public management (Certificate); nonprofit management (MPA); public administration (EMPA); public affairs and policy (PhD); sustainable food systems (Certificate). *Accreditation:* NASPAA (one or more programs are accredited). *Program availability:* Part-time, evening/weekend. *Faculty:* 15 full-time (6 women), 6 part-time/adjunct (4 women). *Students:* 84 full-time (54 women), 109 part-time (75 women); includes 40 minority (8 Black or African American, non-Hispanic/Latino; 5 American Indian or Alaska Native, non-Hispanic/Latino; 8 Asian, non-Hispanic/Latino; 12 Hispanic/Latino; 1 Native Hawaiian or other Pacific Islander, non-Hispanic/Latino; 6 Two or more races, non-Hispanic/Latino), 14 international. Average age 35. 118 applicants, 84% accepted, 56 enrolled. In 2017, 60 master's, 1 doctorate awarded. *Degree requirements:* For master's, integrative field experience (MPA), practicum (MPH); for doctorate, comprehensive exam, thesis/dissertation. *Entrance requirements:* For master's, GRE (minimum scores: verbal 150, quantitative 149, and analytic writing 4.5), minimum GPA of 3.0, 3 recommendation letters, resume, 500-word statement of intent; for doctorate, GRE, 3 recommendation letters, resume, 500-word personal essay. Additional exam requirements/recommendations for international students: Required—TOEFL (minimum score 550 paper-based; 80 iBT), IELTS (minimum score 7). *Application deadline:* For fall admission, 4/1 for domestic students, 3/1 for international students; for winter admission, 9/1 for domestic students, 8/1 for international students; for spring admission, 11/1 for domestic and international students. Application fee: $65. *Expenses:* Tuition, state resident: full-time $14,436; part-time $401 per credit. Tuition, nonresident: full-time $21,780; part-time $605 per credit. *Required fees:* $1380; $22 per credit. $119 per quarter. One-time fee: $325. Tuition and fees vary according to program. *Financial support:* In 2017–18, 39 students received support, including 5 research assistantships with full and partial tuition reimbursements available (averaging $8,341 per year), 4 teaching assistantships (averaging $5,292 per year); career-related internships or fieldwork, Federal Work-Study, scholarships/grants, and unspecified assistantships also available. Support available to part-time students. Financial award application deadline: 3/1; financial award applicants required to submit FAFSA. *Faculty research:* Public budgeting, program evaluation, nonprofit management, natural resources policy and administration. *Total annual research expenditures:* $679,077. *Unit head:* Dr. Masami Nishishiba, Chair, 503-725-5151, E-mail: nishism@pdx.edu. *Application contact:* Megan Heljeson, Office Coordinator, 503-725-3921, Fax: 503-725-8250, E-mail: publicad@pdx.edu.
Website: https://www.pdx.edu/hatfieldschool/public-administration

Princeton University, Graduate School, Program in Population Studies, Princeton, NJ 08544-1019. Offers demography (PhD, Certificate); economics and demography (PhD); public affairs and demography (PhD); sociology and demography (PhD). *Degree requirements:* For doctorate, thesis/dissertation. *Entrance requirements:* For doctorate, GRE General Test. Additional exam requirements/recommendations for international students: Required—TOEFL (minimum score 600 paper-based). Electronic applications accepted. *Faculty research:* Models, fertility, infant and child mortality, migration.

Princeton University, Graduate School, Woodrow Wilson School of Public and International Affairs, Princeton, NJ 08544-1019. Offers public affairs (MPA, PhD); public policy (MPP); JD/MPA. JD/MPA offered jointly with Columbia University, New York University, Stanford University. Terminal master's awarded for partial completion of doctoral program. *Degree requirements:* For master's, internship; for doctorate, one foreign language, thesis/dissertation. *Entrance requirements:* For master's, GRE General Test, original policy memo; for doctorate, GRE General Test. Additional exam requirements/recommendations for international students: Required—TOEFL (minimum score 600 paper-based). Electronic applications accepted.

Syracuse University, Maxwell School of Citizenship and Public Affairs, MA/MS Program in Public Diplomacy, Syracuse, NY 13244. Offers MS/MA. *Students:* Average age 26. *Entrance requirements:* Additional exam requirements/recommendations for international students: Required—TOEFL (minimum score 100 iBT). *Application deadline:* For fall admission, 2/1 for domestic students, 2/1 priority date for international students. Application fee: $75. Electronic applications accepted. *Financial support:* Fellowships with full tuition reimbursements, research assistantships, and teaching assistantships available. Financial award application deadline: 1/1. *Faculty research:* Public diplomacy and communications, economic dimensions of global power, comparative foreign policy, development and sustainability, culture in world affairs. *Unit head:* Dr. Dennis Kinsey, Director, Program in International Relations and Public Relations/Professor of Public Relations, S.I. Newhouse School of Public Communications, 315-443-3801, E-mail: dfkinsey@syr.edu. *Application contact:* Martha Coria, Program Contact, 315-443-5749, Fax: 315-443-1834, E-mail: pcgrad@syr.edu.
Website: http://publicdiplomacy.syr.edu/

Syracuse University, S. I. Newhouse School of Public Communications, MS/MA in Public Diplomacy Program, Syracuse, NY 13244. Offers MS/MA. *Students:* Average age 26. *Entrance requirements:* Additional exam requirements/recommendations for international students: Required—TOEFL (minimum score 100 iBT). *Application deadline:* For fall admission, 2/1 priority date for domestic and international students. Application fee: $45. Electronic applications accepted. *Financial support:* Fellowships with full tuition reimbursements, research assistantships with partial tuition reimbursements, and teaching assistantships with partial tuition reimbursements available. Financial award application deadline: 1/15. *Faculty research:* Media law, public diplomacy, public relation theory, international relations. *Unit head:* Dr. Dennis Kinsey, Director, 315-443-3801, E-mail: publicdiplomacy@syr.edu. *Application contact:* Martha Coria, Graduate Records Office, 315-443-4039, Fax: 315-443-1834, E-mail: pcgrad@syr.edu.
Website: http://publicdiplomacy.syr.edu/

Texas A&M University, Bush School of Government and Public Service, College Station, TX 77845. Offers homeland security (Certificate); international affairs (MIA, Certificate); national security affairs (Certificate); non-profit management (Certificate); public service and administration (MPSA). *Accreditation:* NASPAA. *Faculty:* 66. *Students:* 332 full-time (182 women), 54 part-time (16 women); includes 94 minority (19 Black or African American, non-Hispanic/Latino; 10 Asian, non-Hispanic/Latino; 56 Hispanic/Latino; 9 Two or more races, non-Hispanic/Latino), 41 international. Average age 28. 297 applicants, 94% accepted, 164 enrolled. In 2017, 154 master's awarded. *Degree requirements:* For master's, summer internship. *Entrance requirements:* For master's, GRE (preferred) or GMAT. Additional exam requirements/recommendations for international students: Required—TOEFL (minimum score 550 paper-based; 80 iBT), IELTS (minimum score 6), PTE (minimum score 53). *Application deadline:* For fall admission, 1/15 for domestic and international students. Application fee: $50 ($90 for international students). Electronic applications accepted. *Expenses:* Contact institution. *Financial support:* In 2017–18, 417 students received support, including 29 fellowships with tuition reimbursements available (averaging $20,966 per year), 71 research assistantships with tuition reimbursements available (averaging $9,778 per year); teaching assistantships, career-related internships or fieldwork, institutionally sponsored loans, scholarships/grants, traineeships, health care benefits, tuition waivers (full and partial), and unspecified assistantships also available. Support available to part-time students. Financial award application deadline: 3/15; financial award applicants required to submit FAFSA. *Faculty research:* Public policy, Presidential studies, public leadership, economic policy, social policy. *Unit head:* Dr. Mark Welsh, Dean, 979-862-8007, E-mail: mwelsh@tamu.edu. *Application contact:* Kathryn Meyer, Director of Recruitment and Admissions, 979-458-4767, Fax: 979-845-4155, E-mail: bushschooladmissions@tamu.edu.
Website: http://bush.tamu.edu/

Public Affairs

The University of Alabama in Huntsville, School of Graduate Studies, College of Arts, Humanities, and Social Sciences, Program in Public Affairs, Huntsville, AL 35899. Offers MA. *Program availability:* Part-time, evening/weekend. *Degree requirements:* For master's, comprehensive exam, thesis or alternative, oral and written exams. *Entrance requirements:* For master's, GRE General Test, minimum GPA of 3.0. Additional exam requirements/recommendations for international students: Required—TOEFL (minimum score 500 paper-based; 80 iBT), IELTS (minimum score 6.5). Electronic applications accepted. *Faculty research:* Public policy and the law, middle eastern engagements, globalization, American politics, politics in south and central America.

University of Arkansas at Little Rock, Graduate School, Clinton School of Public Service, Little Rock, AR 72204-1099. Offers MPS, Graduate Certificate.

University of Baltimore, Graduate School, College of Public Affairs, Baltimore, MD 21201-5779. Offers MPA, MS, DPA, JD/MPA, JD/MS.

University of California, Berkeley, Graduate Division, Graduate School of Public Policy, Program in Public Affairs, Berkeley, CA 94720-1500. Offers MPA. *Program availability:* Part-time-only.

University of California, Los Angeles, Graduate Division, Luskin School of Public Affairs, Los Angeles, CA 90095. Offers MA, MPP, MSW, PhD, JD/MA, JD/MSW, MA/MA, MBA/MA, MD/PhD. *Accreditation:* CSWE. *Degree requirements:* For doctorate, thesis/dissertation, oral and written qualifying exams. *Entrance requirements:* For master's, minimum GPA of 3.0; for doctorate, minimum undergraduate GPA of 3.0. Additional exam requirements/recommendations for international students: Required—TOEFL. Electronic applications accepted.

University of Central Florida, College of Community Innovation and Education, Program in Public Affairs, Orlando, FL 32816. Offers PhD. *Program availability:* Part-time, evening/weekend. *Students:* 35 full-time (22 women), 54 part-time (40 women); includes 30 minority (16 Black or African American, non-Hispanic/Latino; 1 Asian, non-Hispanic/Latino; 11 Hispanic/Latino; 2 Two or more races, non-Hispanic/Latino), 9 international. Average age 36. 66 applicants, 58% accepted, 26 enrolled. In 2017, 12 doctorates awarded. *Degree requirements:* For doctorate, comprehensive exam, thesis/dissertation, candidacy and qualifying exams. *Entrance requirements:* For doctorate, GRE General Test, letters of recommendation, resume, writing sample. Additional exam requirements/recommendations for international students: Required—TOEFL. *Application deadline:* For fall admission, 3/1 for domestic students. Application fee: $30. Electronic applications accepted. *Expenses:* Tuition, state resident: part-time $288.16 per credit hour. Tuition, nonresident: part-time $1073.31 per credit hour. Tuition and fees vary according to program. *Financial support:* In 2017–18, 20 students received support, including 10 fellowships with partial tuition reimbursements available (averaging $8,284 per year), 10 research assistantships with partial tuition reimbursements available (averaging $11,159 per year), 9 teaching assistantships with partial tuition reimbursements available (averaging $10,258 per year); career-related internships or fieldwork, Federal Work-Study, institutionally sponsored loans, health care benefits, tuition waivers (partial), and unspecified assistantships also available. Financial award application deadline: 3/1; financial award applicants required to submit FAFSA. *Unit head:* Dr. Robyne Stevenson, Program Director, 407-823-3459, Fax: 407-823-0822, E-mail: robyne.stevenson@ucf.edu. *Application contact:* Associate Director, Graduate Admissions, 407-823-2766, Fax: 407-823-6442, E-mail: gradadmissions@ucf.edu.
Website: https://www.cohpa.ucf.edu/publicaffairs/

University of Colorado Colorado Springs, School of Public Affairs, Colorado Springs, CO 80918. Offers criminal justice (MCJ); public administration (MPA). *Accreditation:* NASPAA. *Program availability:* Part-time, evening/weekend, 100% online, blended/hybrid learning. *Faculty:* 13 full-time (6 women), 16 part-time/adjunct (3 women). *Students:* 19 full-time (11 women), 164 part-time (101 women); includes 57 minority (6 Black or African American, non-Hispanic/Latino; 1 American Indian or Alaska Native, non-Hispanic/Latino; 5 Asian, non-Hispanic/Latino; 37 Hispanic/Latino; 8 Two or more races, non-Hispanic/Latino). Average age 35. 61 applicants, 95% accepted, 40 enrolled. In 2017, 44 master's awarded. *Degree requirements:* For master's, internship, capstone project, or thesis. *Entrance requirements:* For master's, GRE General Test, GMAT, LSAT, minimum GPA of 3.0. Additional exam requirements/recommendations for international students: Recommended—TOEFL (minimum score 550 paper-based; 80 iBT), IELTS (minimum score 6.5). *Application deadline:* Applications are processed on a rolling basis. Application fee: $60 ($100 for international students). Electronic applications accepted. *Expenses:* $10,350 per year resident tuition, $20,935 nonresident, $11,961 nonresidential online; annual costs vary depending on program, course-load, and residency status. *Financial support:* In 2017–18, 25 students received support. Career-related internships or fieldwork, scholarships/grants, and tuition waivers available. Support available to part-time students. Financial award application deadline: 3/1; financial award applicants required to submit FAFSA. *Faculty research:* Antiquated prison environments; public management; intersections of gender, class, race and crime; national security/U.S. foreign policy; leadership, ethics, organizational theory and behavior. *Total annual research expenditures:* $486,455. *Unit head:* Dr. George Reed, Dean, 719-255-4109, E-mail: george.reed@uccs.edu. *Application contact:* Crista Hill, Outreach Student Services Specialist, 719-255-4993, Fax: 719-255-4183, E-mail: chill12@uccs.edu.
Website: http://www.uccs.edu/spa/

University of Colorado Denver, School of Public Affairs, Program in Public Affairs and Administration, Denver, CO 80127. Offers public administration (MPA), including domestic violence, emergency management and homeland security, environmental policy, management and law, homeland security and defense, local government, nonprofit management, public administration; public affairs (PhD). *Accreditation:* NASPAA. *Program availability:* Part-time, evening/weekend, online learning. *Degree requirements:* For master's, thesis or alternative, 36-39 credit hours; for doctorate, comprehensive exam, thesis/dissertation, minimum of 66 semester hours, including at least 30 hours of dissertation. *Entrance requirements:* For master's, GRE, GMAT or LSAT, resume, essay, transcripts, recommendations; for doctorate, GRE, resume, essay, transcripts, recommendations. Additional exam requirements/recommendations for international students: Required—TOEFL (minimum score 550 paper-based; 80 iBT); Recommended—IELTS (minimum score 6.5). Electronic applications accepted. *Expenses:* Contact institution. *Faculty research:* Housing, education and the social and economic issues of vulnerable populations; nonprofit governance and management; education finance, effectiveness and reform; P-20 education initiatives; municipal government accountability.

University of Florida, Graduate School, College of Liberal Arts and Sciences, Department of Political Science, Gainesville, FL 32611. Offers educational policy (PhD); international development policy and administration (MA, Certificate); international relations (MA, MAT); political campaigning (MA, Certificate); political science (MA, PhD); public affairs (MA, Certificate); tropical conservation and development (MA, PhD); JD/MA. Terminal master's awarded for partial completion of doctoral program. *Degree requirements:* For master's, variable foreign language requirement, comprehensive exam (for some programs), thesis or alternative, internship (for some programs); for doctorate, variable foreign language requirement, comprehensive exam, thesis/dissertation. *Entrance requirements:* For master's and doctorate, GRE General Test (minimum score: 308 combined verbal/quantitative), minimum GPA of 3.5. Additional exam requirements/recommendations for international students: Required—TOEFL (minimum score 550 paper-based; 80 iBT), IELTS (minimum score 6). Electronic applications accepted. *Faculty research:* American electoral politics and political institutions, comparative democratization and development, theories of international relation, and political theory.

University of Louisville, Graduate School, College of Arts and Sciences, Department of Urban and Public Affairs, Louisville, KY 40208. Offers public administration (MPA), including human resources management, non-profit management, public policy and administration; urban and public affairs (PhD), including urban planning and development, urban policy and administration; urban planning (MUP), including administration of planning organizations, housing and community development, land use and environmental planning, spatial analysis. *Program availability:* Part-time, evening/weekend. *Faculty:* 12 full-time (5 women), 4 part-time/adjunct (1 woman). *Students:* 50 full-time (19 women), 20 part-time (17 women); includes 17 minority (6 Black or African American, non-Hispanic/Latino; 1 Asian, non-Hispanic/Latino; 4 Hispanic/Latino; 6 Two or more races, non-Hispanic/Latino), 4 international. Average age 31. 47 applicants, 70% accepted, 22 enrolled. In 2017, 20 master's, 2 doctorates awarded. Terminal master's awarded for partial completion of doctoral program. *Degree requirements:* For master's, internship; for doctorate, comprehensive exam, thesis/dissertation. *Entrance requirements:* For master's, GRE General Test, minimum GPA of 3.0; for doctorate, GRE General Test, master's degree in appropriate field. Additional exam requirements/recommendations for international students: Required—TOEFL (minimum score 550 paper-based; 79 iBT). *Application deadline:* Applications are processed on a rolling basis. Application fee: $65. *Expenses:* Contact institution. *Financial support:* Fellowships, research assistantships, tuition waivers (full and partial), and unspecified assistantships available. Financial award application deadline: 2/1. *Faculty research:* Urban theory, sustainability, public administration, urban planning, urban management. *Total annual research expenditures:* $240,308. *Unit head:* Dr. David Simpson, Chair, 502-852-8019, Fax: 502-852-4558, E-mail: dave.simpson@louisville.edu. *Application contact:* Latonia Craig, Director of Graduate Recruitment and Diversity Retention, 502-852-5207, Fax: 502-852-4558, E-mail: gradadm@louisville.edu.
Website: http://supa.louisville.edu

University of Minnesota, Twin Cities Campus, Graduate School, Humphrey School of Public Affairs, PhD Program in Public Affairs, Minneapolis, MN 55455. Offers management and governance (PhD); public policy (PhD); science, technology, and environmental policy (PhD); urban planning (PhD). *Program availability:* Part-time. *Degree requirements:* For doctorate, comprehensive exam, thesis/dissertation. *Entrance requirements:* For doctorate, GRE General Test. Additional exam requirements/recommendations for international students: Required—TOEFL (minimum score 650 paper-based; 100 iBT), IELTS (minimum score 7). Electronic applications accepted. *Expenses:* Contact institution. *Faculty research:* Public policy, urban/regional planning, public/nonprofit management and governance, science/technology/environmental policy.

University of Minnesota, Twin Cities Campus, Graduate School, Humphrey School of Public Affairs, Program in Public Affairs, Minneapolis, MN 55455. Offers MPA. *Program availability:* Part-time-only, evening/weekend. *Entrance requirements:* For master's, 10 years of work experience, minimum undergraduate GPA of 3.0. Additional exam requirements/recommendations for international students: Required—TOEFL (minimum score 600 paper-based; 100 iBT), IELTS (minimum score 7). Electronic applications accepted. *Expenses:* Contact institution. *Faculty research:* Public and non-profit leadership and management, social policy, urban and regional planning, economic and community development, foreign policy and international affairs.

University of Missouri, Office of Research and Graduate Studies, Harry S Truman School of Public Affairs, Columbia, MO 65211. Offers grantsmanship (Graduate Certificate); nonprofit management (Graduate Certificate); organizational change (Graduate Certificate); public affairs (MPA, PhD); public management (Graduate Certificate); science and public policy (Graduate Certificate). *Accreditation:* NASPAA. *Entrance requirements:* For master's, GRE General Test, minimum GPA of 3.0. Additional exam requirements/recommendations for international students: Required—TOEFL (minimum score 550 paper-based; 80 iBT), IELTS (minimum score 6.5). Electronic applications accepted.

University of Missouri–Kansas City, Henry W. Bloch School of Management, Kansas City, MO 64110-2499. Offers accounting (MS); finance (MS); public affairs (MPA, PhD); JD/MBA; LL M/MPA. PhD (interdisciplinary) offered through the School of Graduate Studies. *Accreditation:* AACSB; NASPAA. *Program availability:* Part-time, evening/weekend. Terminal master's awarded for partial completion of doctoral program. *Entrance requirements:* For master's, GMAT, GRE, 2 essays, 2 references, support of employer; for doctorate, GRE, minimum GPA of 3.0. Additional exam requirements/recommendations for international students: Required—TOEFL (minimum score 550 paper-based; 80 iBT). Electronic applications accepted. *Faculty research:* Entrepreneurship, finance, non-profit, risk management.

University of Nevada, Las Vegas, Graduate College, Greenspun College of Urban Affairs, School of Public Policy and Leadership, Las Vegas, NV 89154-4030. Offers crisis and emergency management (MS); emergency crisis management cybersecurity (Certificate); environmental science (MS, PhD); non-profit management (Certificate); public administration (MPA); public affairs (PhD); public management (Certificate); urban leadership (MA). *Program availability:* Part-time. *Faculty:* 13 full-time (5 women), 10 part-time/adjunct (3 women). *Students:* 76 full-time (40 women), 107 part-time (66 women); includes 79 minority (19 Black or African American, non-Hispanic/Latino; 1 American Indian or Alaska Native, non-Hispanic/Latino; 6 Asian, non-Hispanic/Latino; 40 Hispanic/Latino; 3 Native Hawaiian or other Pacific Islander, non-Hispanic/Latino; 10 Two or more races, non-Hispanic/Latino), 1 international. Average age 37. 86 applicants, 80% accepted, 47 enrolled. In 2017, 61 master's, 6 doctorates, 14 other advanced degrees awarded. *Degree requirements:* For master's, comprehensive exam (for some programs), thesis (for some programs), oral exam; for doctorate, comprehensive exam, thesis/dissertation; for Certificate, portfolio. *Entrance requirements:* For master's, GRE General Test or GMAT, bachelor's degree with minimum GPA 2.75; statement of purpose; 3 letters of recommendation; for doctorate, GRE General Test, master's degree with minimum GPA of 3.5; 3 letters of recommendation; statement of purpose; writing sample; personal interview; for Certificate, bachelor's degree; 2 letters of recommendation; writing sample. Additional exam requirements/recommendations for international students: Required—TOEFL (minimum score 550 paper-based; 80 iBT), IELTS (minimum score 7). *Application deadline:* For fall admission, 6/1 for domestic and international students; for spring admission, 11/1 for domestic and international students; for summer admission, 3/1 for domestic students. Application fee: $60 ($95 for international students). Electronic applications accepted. *Expenses:* $275 per credit, $850 per course, $7,969 per year resident, $22,157 per year non-resident, $7,094 non-resident fee (7 credits or more), $1,307 annual health insurance fee. *Financial support:* In 2017–18, 23 students received support, including 7 research assistantships with partial tuition reimbursements available (averaging $15,995 per year), 16 teaching assistantships with partial tuition reimbursements available (averaging $15,547 per year); institutionally sponsored loans,

scholarships/grants, health care benefits, and unspecified assistantships also available. Financial award application deadline: 3/15; financial award applicants required to submit FAFSA. *Total annual research expenditures:* $63,202. *Unit head:* Dr. Christopher Stream, Director, 702-895-5120, Fax: 702-895-4436, E-mail: chris.stream@unlv.edu. *Application contact:* Dr. Jayce Farmer, Graduate Coordinator, 702-895-4828, E-mail: jayce.farmer@unlv.edu.
Website: https://www.unlv.edu/publicpolicy

The University of North Carolina at Greensboro, Graduate School, College of Arts and Sciences, Department of Political Science, Greensboro, NC 27412-5001. Offers nonprofit management (Certificate); public affairs (MPA); urban and economic development (Certificate). *Accreditation:* NASPAA. *Degree requirements:* For master's, comprehensive exam. *Entrance requirements:* For master's, GRE General Test. Additional exam requirements/recommendations for international students: Required—TOEFL. Electronic applications accepted. *Faculty research:* U.S. Constitution, Canadian parliament, public management, ethical challenge of public service.

University of San Francisco, College of Arts and Sciences, Public Affairs Program, San Francisco, CA 94117-1080. Offers MPA. *Accreditation:* NASPAA. *Program availability:* Part-time. *Degree requirements:* For master's, internship, capstone project. *Entrance requirements:* Additional exam requirements/recommendations for international students: Required—TOEFL, IELTS, PTE. Electronic applications accepted.

University of Saskatchewan, College of Graduate Studies and Research, School of Public Policy, Saskatoon, SK S7N 5A2, Canada. Offers MIT, MPA, MPP, PhD.

University of South Florida, Innovative Education, Tampa, FL 33620-9951. Offers adult, career and higher education (Graduate Certificate), including college teaching, leadership in developing human resources, leadership in higher education; Africana studies (Graduate Certificate), including diasporas and health disparities, genocide and human rights; aging studies (Graduate Certificate), including gerontology; art research (Graduate Certificate), including museum studies; business foundations (Graduate Certificate); chemical and biomedical engineering (Graduate Certificate), including materials science and engineering, water, health and sustainability; child and family studies (Graduate Certificate), including positive behavior support; civil and industrial engineering (Graduate Certificate), including transportation systems analysis; community and family health (Graduate Certificate), including maternal and child health, social marketing and public health, violence and injury: prevention and intervention, women's health; criminology (Graduate Certificate), including criminal justice administration; data science for public administration (Graduate Certificate); digital humanities (Graduate Certificate); educational measurement and research (Graduate Certificate), including evaluation; English (Graduate Certificate), including comparative literary studies, creative writing, professional and technical communication; entrepreneurship (Graduate Certificate); environmental health (Graduate Certificate), including safety management; epidemiology and biostatistics (Graduate Certificate), including applied biostatistics, biostatistics, concepts and tools of epidemiology, epidemiology, epidemiology of infectious diseases; geography, environment and planning (Graduate Certificate), including community development, environmental policy and management, geographical information systems; geology (Graduate Certificate), including hydrogeology; global health (Graduate Certificate), including disaster management, global health and Latin American and Caribbean studies, global health practice, humanitarian assistance, infection control; government and international affairs (Graduate Certificate), including Cuban studies, globalization studies; health policy and management (Graduate Certificate), including health management and leadership, public health policy and programs; hearing specialist: early intervention (Graduate Certificate); industrial and management systems engineering (Graduate Certificate), including systems engineering, technology management; information studies (Graduate Certificate), including school library media specialist; information systems/decision sciences (Graduate Certificate), including analytics and business intelligence; instructional technology (Graduate Certificate), including distance education, Florida digital/virtual educator, instructional design, multimedia design, Web design; internal medicine, bioethics and medical humanities (Graduate Certificate), including biomedical ethics; Latin American and Caribbean studies (Graduate Certificate); leadership for coastal resiliency planning (Graduate Certificate); mass communications (Graduate Certificate), including multimedia journalism; mathematics and statistics (Graduate Certificate), including mathematics; medicine (Graduate Certificate), including aging and neuroscience, bioinformatics, biotechnology, brain fitness and memory management, clinical investigation, hand and upper limb rehabilitation, health informatics, health sciences, integrative weight management, intellectual property, medicine and gender, metabolic and nutritional medicine, metabolic cardiology, pharmacy sciences; national and competitive intelligence (Graduate Certificate); nursing (Graduate Certificate), including simulation based academic fellowship in advanced pain management; psychological and social foundations (Graduate Certificate), including career counseling, college teaching, diversity in education, mental health counseling, school counseling; public affairs (Graduate Certificate), including nonprofit management, public management, research administration; public health (Graduate Certificate), including assessing chemical toxicity and public health risks, health equity, pharmacoepidemiology, public health generalist, toxicology, translational research in adolescent behavioral health; public health practices (Graduate Certificate), including planning for healthy communities; rehabilitation and mental health counseling (Graduate Certificate), including integrative mental health care, marriage and family therapy, rehabilitation technology; secondary education (Graduate Certificate), including ESOL, foreign language education: culture and content, foreign language education: professional; social work (Graduate Certificate), including geriatric social work/clinical gerontology; special education (Graduate Certificate), including autism spectrum disorder, disabilities education: severe/profound; world languages (Graduate Certificate), including teaching English as a second language (TESL) or foreign language. *Unit head:* Dr. Cynthia DeLuca, Associate Vice President and Assistant Vice Provost, 813-974-3077, Fax: 813-974-7061, E-mail: deluca@usf.edu. *Application contact:* Owen Hooper, Director, Summer and Alternative Calendar Programs, 813-974-6917, E-mail: hooper@usf.edu.
Website: http://www.usf.edu/innovative-education/

The University of Texas at Austin, Graduate School, Lyndon B. Johnson School of Public Affairs, Austin, TX 78712-1111. Offers global policy studies (MGPS); public affairs (MP Aff); public leadership (EMPL); public policy (PhD); JD/MP Aff; MBA/MP Aff; MP Aff/MA; MP Aff/MSE. *Accreditation:* NASPAA (one or more programs are accredited). *Program availability:* Part-time. *Degree requirements:* For master's, thesis, summer internship; for doctorate, thesis/dissertation. *Entrance requirements:* For master's, GRE General Test (for MP Aff and MGPS), minimum GPA of 3.0 in upper-division classes, seven years of experience in the public sector, and interview (for EMPL); for doctorate, GRE General Test, master's degree in policy-related field. Additional exam requirements/recommendations for international students: Required—TOEFL. Electronic applications accepted. *Faculty research:* Human resource development, health and social policy, philanthropy and community service, ethical leadership, urban and international policy, science and technology policy.

The University of Texas Rio Grande Valley, College of Liberal Arts, Department of Public Affairs and Security Studies, Edinburg, TX 78539. Offers global security studies and leadership (MPA); public administration (MPA); public policy and management (MPA). *Program availability:* Part-time, evening/weekend. *Faculty:* 8 full-time (5 women). *Students:* 6 full-time (3 women), 127 part-time (57 women); includes 96 minority (5 Black or African American, non-Hispanic/Latino; 2 Asian, non-Hispanic/Latino; 89 Hispanic/Latino; 4 international. Average age 33. 67 applicants, 97% accepted, 40 enrolled. In 2017, 77 master's awarded. *Degree requirements:* For master's, comprehensive exam (for some programs), thesis optional. *Entrance requirements:* For master's, minimum undergraduate GPA of 3.0, official transcripts, personal statement, three recommendations. Additional exam requirements/recommendations for international students: Required—TOEFL or IELTS. *Application deadline:* For fall admission, 7/1 for domestic students, 6/1 for international students; for spring admission, 11/15 for domestic students, 11/1 for international students. Applications are processed on a rolling basis. Application fee: $50 ($100 for international students). Electronic applications accepted. *Expenses:* Tuition, state resident: full-time $5550; part-time $417 per credit hour. Tuition, nonresident: full-time $13,020; part-time $832 per credit hour. *Required fees:* $1169. *Financial support:* Application deadline: 6/1. *Faculty research:* Immigration policy reform, agriculture food policy, social service delivery systems, community development, social welfare policy reform, urban/city management. *Unit head:* Terrence Garett, Chair, E-mail: terence.garrett@utrgv.edu.
Website: http://www.utrgv.edu/pass/

University of Washington, Graduate School, Evans School of Public Policy and Governance, Seattle, WA 98195. Offers public administration (MPA); public policy and management (PhD); JD/MPA; MPA/MAIS; MPA/MPH; MPA/MS; MPA/MUP. *Accreditation:* NASPAA. *Program availability:* Part-time, evening/weekend. *Degree requirements:* For master's, thesis, internship or cooperative experience. *Entrance requirements:* For master's and doctorate, GRE General Test, minimum GPA of 3.0. Additional exam requirements/recommendations for international students: Required—TOEFL (minimum score 580 paper-based; 92 iBT). Electronic applications accepted. *Faculty research:* Environmental policy, education and social policy, nonprofit management, international affairs, urban and regional development.

University of Waterloo, Graduate Studies, Faculty of Arts, Department of Anthropology, Waterloo, ON N2L 3G1, Canada. Offers anthropology (MA); public issues (MA). *Entrance requirements:* Additional exam requirements/recommendations for international students: Required—TOEFL, IELTS, PTE. Electronic applications accepted. *Faculty research:* Applied socio-cultural anthropology and archaeology.

University of Wisconsin–Madison, Graduate School, College of Letters and Science, Robert M. La Follette School of Public Affairs, Public Policy and Administration Program, Madison, WI 53706-1380. Offers MIPA, MPA. *Program availability:* Part-time. Electronic applications accepted.

Virginia Commonwealth University, Graduate School, L. Douglas Wilder School of Government and Public Affairs, Richmond, VA 23284-9005. Offers MA, MPA, MS, MURP, PhD, Certificate, Graduate Certificate, Postbaccalaureate Certificate.

Virginia Polytechnic Institute and State University, Graduate School, College of Architecture and Urban Studies, Blacksburg, VA 24061. Offers architecture (M Arch, MS); architecture and design research (PhD); building construction science management (MS); creative technologies (MFA); environmental design and planning (PhD); government and international affairs (MPIA); landscape architecture (MLA, PhD); planning, governance, and globalization (PhD); public administration and public affairs (MPA, PhD); urban and regional planning (MURPL). *Accreditation:* ASLA (one or more programs are accredited). *Faculty:* 139 full-time (58 women), 1 (woman) part-time/adjunct. *Students:* 339 full-time (165 women), 210 part-time (97 women); includes 115 minority (49 Black or African American, non-Hispanic/Latino; 1 American Indian or Alaska Native, non-Hispanic/Latino; 30 Asian, non-Hispanic/Latino; 29 Hispanic/Latino; 6 Two or more races, non-Hispanic/Latino), 136 international. Average age 32. 649 applicants, 49% accepted, 105 enrolled. In 2017, 142 master's, 18 doctorates awarded. *Degree requirements:* For master's, comprehensive exam (for some programs), thesis (for some programs); for doctorate, comprehensive exam (for some programs), thesis/dissertation (for some programs). *Entrance requirements:* For master's and doctorate, GRE/GMAT. Additional exam requirements/recommendations for international students: Required—TOEFL (minimum score 80 iBT). *Application deadline:* For fall admission, 8/1 for domestic students, 4/1 for international students; for spring admission, 1/1 for domestic students, 9/1 for international students. Applications are processed on a rolling basis. Application fee: $75. Electronic applications accepted. *Expenses:* Tuition, state resident: full-time $15,072; part-time $718.50 per credit hour. Tuition, nonresident: full-time $28,810; part-time $1448.25 per credit hour. *Required fees:* $2741; $502 per semester. Tuition and fees vary according to course load, campus/location and program. *Financial support:* In 2017–18, 17 research assistantships with full tuition reimbursements (averaging $18,561 per year), 41 teaching assistantships with full tuition reimbursements (averaging $17,340 per year) were awarded. Financial award application deadline: 3/1; financial award applicants required to submit FAFSA. *Total annual research expenditures:* $3.1 million. *Unit head:* Dr. Richard Blythe, Dean, 540-231-6416, Fax: 540-231-6332, E-mail: richbl1@vt.edu. *Application contact:* Christine Mattsson-Coon, Executive Assistant, 540-231-6416, Fax: 540-231-6332, E-mail: cmattsso@vt.edu.
Website: http://www.caus.vt.edu/

Washington State University, College of Arts and Sciences, School of Politics, Philosophy and Public Affairs, Pullman, WA 99164-4880. Offers bioethics (Graduate Certificate); political science (MA, PhD); public affairs (MPA). MPA, MA, and PhD programs also offered at the Vancouver campus; Graduate Certificate offered through Global (online) campus. *Accreditation:* NASPAA. *Program availability:* Online learning. Terminal master's awarded for partial completion of doctoral program. *Degree requirements:* For master's, comprehensive exam (for some programs), thesis, oral exam; for doctorate, comprehensive exam, thesis/dissertation, oral exam, written exam. *Entrance requirements:* For master's, GRE General Test, minimum GPA of 3.0; for doctorate, GRE General Test, minimum GPA of 3.5. Additional exam requirements/recommendations for international students: Required—TOEFL. Electronic applications accepted. *Faculty research:* Political psychology and image theory, grass roots environmental policy, federal juvenile policy.

West Chester University of Pennsylvania, College of Business and Public Management, West Chester, PA 19383. Offers MA, MBA, MPA, MS, MURP, Certificate, DPA. *Program availability:* Part-time, evening/weekend, 100% online, blended/hybrid learning. *Faculty:* 34 full-time (13 women), 11 part-time/adjunct (5 women). *Students:* 146 full-time (70 women), 608 part-time (270 women); includes 180 minority (119 Black or African American, non-Hispanic/Latino; 25 Asian, non-Hispanic/Latino; 29 Hispanic/Latino; 7 Two or more races, non-Hispanic/Latino), 8 international. Average age 32. 460 applicants, 76% accepted, 271 enrolled. In 2017, 137 master's, 44 other advanced degrees awarded. *Degree requirements:* For master's, comprehensive exam (for some programs), thesis (for some programs). *Entrance requirements:* Additional exam requirements/recommendations for international students: Required—TOEFL or IELTS. *Application deadline:* For fall admission, 5/15 for international students; for spring admission, 10/15 for international students. Applications are processed on a rolling

basis. Application fee: $50. Electronic applications accepted. *Expenses:* Tuition, state resident: full-time $9000; part-time $500 per credit. Tuition, nonresident: full-time $13,500; part-time $750 per credit. *Required fees:* $2959; $149.79 per credit. *Financial support:* Scholarships/grants and unspecified assistantships available. Financial award application deadline: 2/15; financial award applicants required to submit FAFSA. *Unit head:* Dr. Anthony Wheeler, Dean, 610-436-2930, Fax: 610-436-3170, E-mail: awheeler@wcupa.edu. *Application contact:* Office of Graduate Studies and Extended Education, 610-436-2943, Fax: 610-436-2763, E-mail: gradstudy@wcupa.edu. Website: http://www.wcupa.edu/business-publicManagement/

Western Carolina University, Graduate School, College of Arts and Sciences, Department of Political Science and Public Affairs, Cullowhee, NC 28723. Offers MPA. *Accreditation:* NASPAA. *Program availability:* Part-time, evening/weekend. *Students:* 37. *Degree requirements:* For master's, comprehensive exam. *Entrance requirements:* For master's, GRE General Test, appropriate undergraduate degree, 3 letters of recommendation, resume, 1-2 page essay. Additional exam requirements/recommendations for international students: Required—TOEFL (minimum score 550 paper-based, 79 iBT) or IELTS (6.5). *Application deadline:* For fall admission, 4/15 priority date for domestic and international students; for spring admission, 11/15 priority date for domestic students, 10/15 priority date for international students. Applications are processed on a rolling basis. Application fee: $65. Electronic applications accepted. *Expenses:* $20,000 per year in-state full-time; $20,308 per year out-of-state full-time.

Financial support: In 2017–18, 6 research assistantships with full and partial tuition reimbursements (averaging $9,000 per year), 4 teaching assistantships with full and partial tuition reimbursements (averaging $9,000 per year) were awarded; career-related internships or fieldwork, institutionally sponsored loans, scholarships/grants, and unspecified assistantships also available. Financial award application deadline: 4/15; financial award applicants required to submit FAFSA. *Faculty research:* Press-government relations, comparative governments, gender in politics, Latin American political systems, foreign policy, trust in government, zoning. *Unit head:* Dr. Chris Cooper, Department Head, E-mail: ccooper@email.wcu.edu. *Application contact:* Bobbi Smith, Graduate Admissions Coordinator, E-mail: bobbismith@email.wcu.edu. Website: https://www.wcu.edu/learn/departments-schools-colleges/cas/social-sciences/poliscipublicaffairs/mpa/

Western Michigan University, Graduate College, College of Arts and Sciences, School of Public Affairs and Administration, Kalamazoo, MI 49008. Offers health care administration (MPA, Graduate Certificate); nonprofit leadership and administration (Graduate Certificate); public administration (PhD). *Accreditation:* NASPAA (one or more programs are accredited). *Degree requirements:* For doctorate, thesis/dissertation.

York University, Faculty of Graduate Studies, Glendon Campus, Program in Public and International Affairs, Toronto, ON M3J 1P3, Canada. Offers MA.

Public Policy

Adler University, Graduate Programs, Master of Public Policy and Administration Program: Immigration Policy and Practice, Chicago, IL 60602. Offers MPPA. Program offered at Vancouver campus.

Adler University, Graduate Programs, Master of Public Policy Program, Chicago, IL 60602. Offers community health (MPP); human rights advocacy (MPP). *Program availability:* Part-time, evening/weekend.

Albany State University, College of Arts and Humanities, Albany, GA 31705-2717. Offers criminal justice (MS); English education (M Ed); public administration (MPA), including community and economic development, criminal justice administration, health administration and policy, human resources management, public management, public policy, water resources management and policy; social work (MSW). *Accreditation:* NASPAA. *Program availability:* Part-time. *Degree requirements:* For master's, comprehensive exam, professional portfolio (for MPA), internship, capstone report. *Entrance requirements:* For master's, GRE, MAT, minimum GPA of 3.0, official transcript, pre-medical record/certificate of immunization, letters of reference. Electronic applications accepted. *Faculty research:* HIV prevention for minority students.

American Public University System, AMU/APU Graduate Programs, Charles Town, WV 25414. Offers accounting (MS); applied business analytics (MS); business administration (MBA); criminal justice (MA); cybersecurity studies (MS); educational leadership (M Ed); environmental policy and management (MS); global security (DGS); health information management (MS); history (MA), including American military history, American Revolution, civil war, war since 1945, World War II; information technology (MS); international relations and conflict resolution (MA), including American politics and government, comparative government and development, general, international relations, public policy; national security studies (MA); nursing (MSN); political science (MA); public policy (MPP); reverse logistics management (MA), including comparative and security issues, conflict resolution, international and transnational security issues, peacekeeping; space studies (MS); sports management (MS); strategic intelligence (DSI); teaching (M Ed), including secondary social studies; transportation and logistics management (MA). *Program availability:* Part-time, evening/weekend, online only, 100% online. *Students:* 455 full-time (227 women), 7,939 part-time (3,353 women); includes 2,793 minority (1,429 Black or African American, non-Hispanic/Latino; 48 American Indian or Alaska Native, non-Hispanic/Latino; 205 Asian, non-Hispanic/Latino; 766 Hispanic/Latino; 62 Native Hawaiian or other Pacific Islander, non-Hispanic/Latino; 283 Two or more races, non-Hispanic/Latino), 101 international. Average age 37. In 2017, 2,977 master's awarded. *Degree requirements:* For master's, comprehensive exam or practicum. *Entrance requirements:* For master's, official transcript showing earned bachelor's degree from institution accredited by recognized accrediting body. Additional exam requirements/recommendations for international students: Required—TOEFL (minimum score 550 paper-based), IELTS (minimum score 6.5). *Application deadline:* Applications are processed on a rolling basis. Application fee: $0. Electronic applications accepted. *Expenses:* Tuition: Full-time $6300; part-time $350 per credit. *Required fees:* $300; $50 per course. *Financial support:* Scholarships/grants available. Financial award applicants required to submit FAFSA. *Unit head:* Dr. Wallace Boston, President, 877-468-6268, Fax: 304-728-2348, E-mail: president@apus.edu. *Application contact:* Yoci Deal, Associate Vice President, Graduate and International Admissions, 877-468-6268, Fax: 304-724-3764, E-mail: info@apus.edu. Website: http://www.apus.edu

American University, School of Public Affairs, Department of Public Administration and Policy, Washington, DC 20016-8070. Offers organization development (MSOD, Certificate), including leadership for organizational change (Certificate), organization development (MSOD); public administration (MPA, PhD, Certificate), including nonprofit management (Certificate), public financial management (Certificate), public management (Certificate); public administration and policy (MPAP), including public administration policy; public policy (MPP), including public policy; public policy (Certificate), including public policy analysis; LL M/MPA; MPA/JD; MPP/JD; MPP/LL M. *Program availability:* Part-time, evening/weekend, online learning. *Faculty:* 31 full-time (12 women), 36 part-time/adjunct (13 women). *Students:* 211 full-time (129 women), 305 part-time (202 women); includes 132 minority (84 Black or African American, non-Hispanic/Latino; 4 American Indian or Alaska Native, non-Hispanic/Latino; 24 Asian, non-Hispanic/Latino; 10 Hispanic/Latino; 10 Two or more races, non-Hispanic/Latino), 34 international. Average age 31. 658 applicants, 86% accepted, 230 enrolled. In 2017, 178 master's, 6 doctorates, 7 other advanced degrees awarded. *Degree requirements:* For master's, comprehensive exam; for doctorate, comprehensive exam, thesis/dissertation. *Entrance requirements:* For master's, GRE, statement of purpose, 2 recommendations, resume, transcript; for doctorate, GRE, 3 recommendations, statement of purpose, resume, writing sample, transcript; for Certificate, bachelor's degree. Additional exam requirements/recommendations for international students: Required—TOEFL (minimum score 600 paper-based; 100 iBT). *Application deadline:* For fall admission, 2/15 priority date for domestic students, 5/1 for international students; for spring admission, 11/1 for domestic students, 9/15 for international students. Application fee: $55. *Expenses:* Contact institution. *Financial support:* Research

assistantships, teaching assistantships, institutionally sponsored loans, scholarships/grants, and unspecified assistantships available. Financial award application deadline: 2/1; financial award applicants required to submit FAFSA. *Unit head:* Dr. Dave Marcotte, Department Chair, 202-885-3108, E-mail: marcotte@american.edu. *Application contact:* Jennifer Forney, Assistant Dean, Graduate Enrollment, E-mail: forney@american.edu. Website: http://www.american.edu/spa/dpap/

The American University in Cairo, School of Global Affairs and Public Policy, Cairo, Egypt. Offers gender and women's studies (MA); global affairs (MGA); international and comparative law (LL M); international human rights law (MA); journalism and mass communication (MA); Middle East studies (MA); migration and refugee studies (MA, Diploma); public administration (MPA); public policy (MPP); television and digital journalism (MA). *Program availability:* Part-time, evening/weekend. *Faculty:* 26 full-time (11 women), 4 part-time/adjunct (3 women). *Students:* 65 full-time (50 women), 201 part-time (136 women), 39 international. Average age 29. 357 applicants, 51% accepted, 72 enrolled. In 2017, 94 master's awarded. *Degree requirements:* For master's, comprehensive exam (for some programs), thesis (for some programs). *Entrance requirements:* Additional exam requirements/recommendations for international students: Required—TOEFL (minimum score 450 paper-based; 45 iBT), IELTS (minimum score 5). *Application deadline:* For fall admission, 2/1 for domestic and international students; for spring admission, 10/15 for domestic and international students. Applications are processed on a rolling basis. Application fee: $85. Electronic applications accepted. *Expenses:* Contact institution. *Financial support:* Fellowships with partial tuition reimbursements, scholarships/grants, and unspecified assistantships available. Financial award application deadline: 3/10. *Faculty research:* Law, media and journalism; public policy and public administration; gender studies; Middle East Studies; global affairs; refugees studies. *Unit head:* Dr. Nabil Fahmy, Dean, 20-2-2615-2671, E-mail: nfahmy@aucegypt.edu. *Application contact:* Maha Hegazi, Director for Graduate Admissions, 20-2-2615-1462, E-mail: mahahegazi@aucegypt.edu. Website: http://www.aucegypt.edu/GAPP/Pages/default.aspx

American University of Beirut, Graduate Programs, Faculty of Arts and Sciences, 1107 2020, Lebanon. Offers anthropology (MA); Arab and Middle Eastern history (PhD); Arabic language and literature (MA, PhD); archaeology (MA); art history and curating (MA); biology (MS); cell and molecular biology (PhD); chemistry (MS); clinical psychology (MA); computational sciences (MS); computer science (MS); economics (MA); education (MA), including administration and policy studies, elementary education, mathematics education, psychology school guidance, psychology test and measurements, science education, teaching English as a foreign language; English language (MA); English literature (MA); environmental policy planning (MS); financial economics (MAFE); general psychology (MA); geology (MS); history (MA); Islamic studies (MA); mathematics (MS); media studies (MA); Middle East studies (MA); philosophy (MA); physics (MS); political studies (MA); public administration (MA); public policy and international affairs (MA); sociology (MA); theoretical physics (PhD). *Program availability:* Part-time. *Faculty:* 108 full-time (36 women), 5 part-time/adjunct (4 women). *Students:* 251 full-time (180 women), 233 part-time (172 women). Average age 26. 425 applicants, 65% accepted, 121 enrolled. In 2017, 47 master's, 2 doctorates awarded. *Degree requirements:* For master's, one foreign language, comprehensive exam, thesis (for some programs), project; for doctorate, one foreign language, comprehensive exam, thesis/dissertation. *Entrance requirements:* For master's, GRE General Test (for some programs); for doctorate, GRE General Test (GRE Subject Test for theoretical physics). Additional exam requirements/recommendations for international students: Required—TOEFL (minimum score 583 paper-based; 97 iBT), IELTS (minimum score 7). *Application deadline:* For fall admission, 2/8 for domestic students; for spring admission, 11/3 for domestic students. Application fee: $50. Electronic applications accepted. *Expenses:* Contact institution. *Financial support:* In 2017–18, 29 fellowships, 40 research assistantships were awarded; teaching assistantships, scholarships/grants, tuition waivers (full and partial), and unspecified assistantships also available. Financial award application deadline: 4/4. *Unit head:* Dr. Nadia Maria El Cheikh, Dean, Faculty of Arts and Sciences, 961-1-374374 Ext. 3800, Fax: 961-1-744461, E-mail: nmcheikh@aub.edu.lb. *Application contact:* Rima Rassi, Graduate Studies Officer, 961-1-350000 Ext. 3833, Fax: 961-1-744461, E-mail: rr46@aub.edu.lb. Website: http://www.aub.edu.lb/fas/pages/default.aspx

The American University of Paris, Graduate Programs, Paris, France. Offers cross-cultural and sustainable business management (MA); cultural translation (MA); global communications (MA); global communications and civil society (MA); international affairs (MA); international affairs, conflict resolution and civil society development (MA); Middle East and Islamic studies (MA); Middle East and Islamic studies and international affairs (MA); public policy and international affairs (MA); public policy and international law (MA). *Degree requirements:* For master's, thesis (for some programs). *Entrance requirements:* For master's, minimum undergraduate GPA of 3.0. Additional exam requirements/recommendations for international students: Recommended—TOEFL, IELTS. Electronic applications accepted.

Arizona State University at the Tempe campus, College of Public Programs, School of Public Affairs, Phoenix, AZ 85004-0687. Offers emergency management and homeland security (MA); program evaluation (MS); public administration (MPA, PhD), including nonprofit administration (MPA), urban management (MPA); public policy (MPP); MPA/MSW. *Accreditation:* NASPAA (one or more programs are accredited). *Program availability:* Part-time, evening/weekend. Terminal master's awarded for partial completion of doctoral program. *Degree requirements:* For master's, thesis or alternative, policy analysis or capstone project; interactive Program of Study (iPOS) submitted before completing 50 percent of required credit hours; for doctorate, comprehensive exam, thesis/dissertation, interactive Program of Study (iPOS) submitted before completing 50 percent of required credit hours. *Entrance requirements:* For master's, GRE, minimum GPA of 3.0 or equivalent in last 2 years of work leading to bachelor's degree; for doctorate, GRE, minimum GPA of 3.0 or equivalent in last 2 years of work leading to bachelor's degree, 3 letters of recommendation, resume, statement of goals, samples of research reports. Additional exam requirements/recommendations for international students: Required—TOEFL (minimum score 600 paper-based; 100 iBT), IELTS (minimum score 6.5). Electronic applications accepted. *Expenses:* Contact institution.

Arizona State University at the Tempe campus, Sandra Day O'Connor College of Law, Phoenix, AZ 85287-7906. Offers biotechnology and genomics (LL M); law (JD); legal studies (MLS); patent practice (MLS); sports law and business (MSLB); tribal policy, law and government (LL M); JD/MBA; JD/MD; JD/MSW; JD/PhD. JD/MD offered jointly with Mayo Medical School. *Accreditation:* ABA. *Program availability:* 100% online. *Faculty:* 69 full-time (30 women), 115 part-time/adjunct (29 women). *Students:* 777 full-time (337 women); includes 207 minority (21 Black or African American, non-Hispanic/Latino; 14 American Indian or Alaska Native, non-Hispanic/Latino; 32 Asian, non-Hispanic/Latino; 104 Hispanic/Latino; 3 Native Hawaiian or other Pacific Islander, non-Hispanic/Latino; 33 Two or more races, non-Hispanic/Latino), 15 international. Average age 28. 2,056 applicants, 41% accepted, 215 enrolled. In 2017, 52 master's, 198 doctorates awarded. *Entrance requirements:* For master's, bachelor's degree and JD (for LL M); for doctorate, LSAT, bachelor's degree. Additional exam requirements/recommendations for international students: Required—TOEFL (minimum score 550 paper-based; 80 iBT). *Application deadline:* For fall admission, 3/1 priority date for domestic and international students. Applications are processed on a rolling basis. Electronic applications accepted. *Expenses:* Contact institution. *Financial support:* In 2017–18, 430 students received support. Institutionally sponsored loans and scholarships/grants available. Financial award application deadline: 3/15; financial award applicants required to submit FAFSA. *Faculty research:* Emerging technologies and the law, Indian law, international law, intellectual property, health law, sports law and business. *Total annual research expenditures:* $2.4 million. *Unit head:* Douglas Sylvester, Dean/Professor, 480-965-6188, Fax: 480-965-6521, E-mail: douglas.sylvester@asu.edu. *Application contact:* Chitra Damania, Director, 480-965-1474, Fax: 480-727-7930, E-mail: law.admissions@asu.edu.
Website: http://www.law.asu.edu/

Arizona State University at the Tempe campus, School of Letters and Sciences, Program in Applied Ethics, Tempe, AZ 85287-4503. Offers biomedical and health ethics (MA); ethics and emerging technologies (MA); public administration, policy and ethics (MA); science, technology and ethics (MA). *Program availability:* Part-time, evening/weekend. *Degree requirements:* For master's, thesis or alternative, applied project, interactive Program of Study (iPOS) submitted before completing 50 percent of required credit hours. *Entrance requirements:* For master's, GRE (for ethics and emerging technologies concentration), minimum GPA of 3.0 or equivalent in last 2 years of work leading to bachelor's degree, 2 letters of recommendation, resume, personal statement of interest and qualifications. Additional exam requirements/recommendations for international students: Required—TOEFL (minimum score 550 paper-based; 80 iBT). Electronic applications accepted.

Auburn University at Montgomery, College of Public Policy and Justice, Department of Political Science and Public Administration, Montgomery, AL 36124-4023. Offers political science (MPS); public administration (MPA); public administration and public policy (PhD). PhD offered jointly with Auburn University. *Accreditation:* NASPAA (one or more programs are accredited). *Program availability:* Part-time, evening/weekend. *Faculty:* 4 full-time (1 woman). *Students:* 11 full-time (5 women), 22 part-time (15 women); includes 18 minority (all Black or African American, non-Hispanic/Latino), 4 international. Average age 31. 23 applicants, 78% accepted, 9 enrolled. In 2017, 5 master's awarded. *Degree requirements:* For master's, comprehensive exam; for doctorate, thesis/dissertation. *Entrance requirements:* For master's, GRE General Test or MAT; for doctorate, GRE General Test. Additional exam requirements/recommendations for international students: Recommended—TOEFL (minimum score 500 paper-based; 61 iBT), IELTS (minimum score 5.5), TSE (minimum score 44). *Application deadline:* For fall admission, 7/15 for international students; for spring admission, 11/15 for international students; for summer admission, 4/15 for international students. Applications are processed on a rolling basis. Application fee: $25. Electronic applications accepted. *Expenses:* Tuition, state resident: full-time $6930; part-time $385 per credit hour. Tuition, nonresident: full-time $15,588; part-time $866 per credit hour. *Required fees:* $640. *Financial support:* Research assistantships, teaching assistantships, career-related internships or fieldwork, and scholarships/grants available. Support available to part-time students. Financial award application deadline: 3/1; financial award applicants required to submit FAFSA. *Unit head:* Dr. Andrew Cortell, Head, 334-244-3622, E-mail: acortell@aum.edu.
Website: http://cppj.aum.edu/departments/political-science

Aurora University, Dunham School of Business and Public Policy, Aurora, IL 60506-4892. Offers accountancy (MS); business (MBA). *Program availability:* Part-time, evening/weekend, 100% online. *Faculty:* 4 full-time (0 women), 22 part-time/adjunct (9 women). *Students:* 193 full-time (106 women), 34 part-time (20 women); includes 83 minority (31 Black or African American, non-Hispanic/Latino; 6 Asian, non-Hispanic/Latino; 36 Hispanic/Latino; 1 Native Hawaiian or other Pacific Islander, non-Hispanic/Latino; 9 Two or more races, non-Hispanic/Latino), 2 international. Average age 33. 135 applicants, 100% accepted, 52 enrolled. In 2017, 122 master's awarded. *Entrance requirements:* For master's, minimum GPA of 3.0, 2 years of work experience, resume. Additional exam requirements/recommendations for international students: Required—TOEFL (minimum score 550 paper-based; 79 iBT). *Application deadline:* For fall admission, 6/1 for international students; for spring admission, 10/1 for international students. Applications are processed on a rolling basis. Application fee: $0. Electronic applications accepted. *Expenses:* Contact institution. *Financial support:* In 2017–18, 58 students received support. Federal Work-Study, scholarships/grants, and unspecified assistantships available. Support available to part-time students. Financial award applicants required to submit FAFSA. *Unit head:* Dr. Toby Arquette, Dean, School of Business and Policy, 630-844-5614, E-mail: tarquett@aurora.edu. *Application contact:* Tom Gergits, Recruiter for Graduate Programs, 630-947-8945, E-mail: tgergits@aurora.edu.

Baruch College of the City University of New York, Austin W. Marxe School of Public and International Affairs, Program in Public Administration, New York, NY 10010-5585. Offers general public administration (MPA); health care policy (MPA); nonprofit administration (MPA); policy analysis and evaluation (MPA); public management (MPA); urban development and sustainability (MPA); MS/MPA. *Accreditation:* NASPAA. *Program availability:* Part-time, evening/weekend. *Degree requirements:* For master's, thesis, capstone. *Entrance requirements:* For master's, GRE General Test. Additional exam requirements/recommendations for international students: Required—TOEFL. Electronic applications accepted. *Expenses:* Contact institution. *Faculty research:* Urbanization, population and poverty in the developing world, housing and community development, labor unions and housing, government-nongovernment relations, immigration policy, social network analysis, cross-sectoral governance, comparative healthcare systems, program evaluation, social welfare policy, health outcomes, educational policy and leadership, transnationalism, infant health, welfare reform, racial/ethnic disparities in health, urban politics, homelessness, race and ethnic relations.
See Display on page 910 and Close-Up on page 955.

Baylor University, Graduate School, College of Arts and Sciences, Department of Political Science, Waco, TX 76798. Offers international studies (MA); political science (MA, PhD); public policy and administration (MPPA); JD/MPPA. *Faculty:* 19 full-time (3 women), 1 part-time/adjunct (0 women). *Students:* 28 full-time (14 women); includes 1 minority (Hispanic/Latino). Average age 26. 27 applicants, 22% accepted, 4 enrolled. In 2017, 4 master's, 5 doctorates awarded. Terminal master's awarded for partial completion of doctoral program. *Degree requirements:* For master's, variable foreign language requirement, comprehensive exam (for some programs), thesis (for some programs); for doctorate, variable foreign language requirement, comprehensive exam, thesis/dissertation. *Entrance requirements:* For master's and doctorate, GRE General Test. Additional exam requirements/recommendations for international students: Required—TOEFL. *Application deadline:* For fall admission, 12/20 for domestic and international students. Application fee: $50. Electronic applications accepted. *Financial support:* In 2017–18, 26 students received support, including 26 research assistantships with full tuition reimbursements available (averaging $16,000 per year); career-related internships or fieldwork, Federal Work-Study, and institutionally sponsored loans also available. Financial award application deadline: 12/20; financial award applicants required to submit FAFSA. *Unit head:* Dr. Timothy Burns, Graduate Program Director, 254-710-6237, Fax: 254-710-3122, E-mail: timothy_burns@baylor.edu. *Application contact:* Jenice Langston, Office Manager, 254-710-3161, Fax: 254-710-3122, E-mail: jenice_langston@baylor.edu.
Website: http://www.baylor.edu/political_science

Boise State University, School of Public Service, Department of Public Policy and Administration, Boise, ID 83725-0399. Offers public policy and administration (MPA, PhD, Graduate Certificate), including environmental, natural resource and energy policy and administration (MPA), general public administration (MPA), state and local government policy and administration (MPA). *Accreditation:* NASPAA. *Program availability:* Part-time. *Faculty:* 16. *Students:* 38 full-time (19 women), 85 part-time (56 women); includes 15 minority (1 American Indian or Alaska Native, non-Hispanic/Latino; 1 Asian, non-Hispanic/Latino; 12 Hispanic/Latino; 1 Two or more races, non-Hispanic/Latino), 1 international. Average age 37. 81 applicants, 43% accepted, 29 enrolled. In 2017, 22 master's awarded. Terminal master's awarded for partial completion of doctoral program. *Degree requirements:* For master's, comprehensive exam, thesis optional, directed research project, internship; for doctorate, thesis/dissertation. *Entrance requirements:* For master's, GRE General Test, minimum GPA of 3.0. Additional exam requirements/recommendations for international students: Required—TOEFL (minimum score 550 paper-based; 80 iBT), IELTS (minimum score 6). *Application deadline:* For fall admission, 2/1 for domestic and international students; for spring admission, 10/1 for domestic and international students. Application fee: $65 ($95 for international students). Electronic applications accepted. *Expenses:* Tuition, state resident: full-time $6471; part-time $390 per credit. Tuition, nonresident: full-time $21,787; part-time $685 per credit. *Required fees:* $2283; $100 per term. Part-time tuition and fees vary according to course load and program. *Financial support:* Research assistantships, scholarships/grants, and unspecified assistantships available. Financial award application deadline: 2/1; financial award applicants required to submit FAFSA. *Unit head:* Dr. Gregory Hill, Department Chair, 208-426-2917, E-mail: greghill@boisestate.edu. *Application contact:* Dr. Luke Fowler, MPA Director, 208-426-5527, E-mail: lukefowler@boisestate.edu.
Website: http://sps.boisestate.edu/publicpolicy/

Brandeis University, Graduate School of Arts and Sciences, Program in Women's, Gender, and Sexuality Studies, Waltham, MA 02454-9110. Offers anthropology/women's, gender, and sexuality studies (MA); English/women's, gender, and sexuality studies (MA); near Eastern and Judaic studies /women's, gender, and sexuality studies (MA); public policy/women's, gender, and sexuality studies (MA); sociology/women's, gender, and sexuality studies (MA); sustainable international development/women's, gender, and sexuality studies (MA); women's, gender, and sexuality studies (MA). Offered jointly with The Heller School of Social Policy and Management. *Students:* 10 full-time (all women); includes 2 minority (1 Hispanic/Latino; 1 Two or more races, non-Hispanic/Latino). Average age 25. 42 applicants, 48% accepted, 8 enrolled. In 2017, 8 master's awarded. *Degree requirements:* For master's, thesis. *Entrance requirements:* For master's, GRE General Test, critical writing sample, resume, statement of purpose, transcripts, letters of recommendation. Additional exam requirements/recommendations for international students: Required—PTE (minimum score 68), TOEFL (minimum score 600 paper-based, 100 iBT) or IELTS (7). *Application deadline:* For fall admission, 1/15 for domestic students. Application fee: $75. Electronic applications accepted. *Expenses:* Tuition: Full-time $48,720. *Required fees:* $88. Tuition and fees vary according to course load, degree level, program and student level. *Financial support:* In 2017–18, 6 students received support, including 7 teaching assistantships with partial tuition reimbursements available (averaging $3,200 per year); fellowships, scholarships/grants, and tuition waivers (partial) also available. Financial award application deadline: 4/15; financial award applicants required to submit FAFSA. *Unit head:* Dr. ChaeRan Freeze, Director of Graduate Study, 781-736-2987, E-mail: cfreeze@brandeis.edu. *Application contact:* Shannon Kearns, Department Administrator, 781-736-3045, E-mail: skearns@brandeis.edu.
Website: http://www.brandeis.edu/gsas/programs/wgs.html

Brandeis University, The Heller School for Social Policy and Management, Program in Public Policy, Waltham, MA 02454-9110. Offers aging (MPP); behavioral health (MPP); children, youth and families (MPP); general social policy (MPP); health (MPP); poverty alleviation and development (MPP); MPP/MA. *Degree requirements:* For master's, thesis. *Entrance requirements:* For master's, GRE, 3 letters of recommendation, statement of purpose, 3 to 5 years of professional experience. Additional exam requirements/recommendations for international students: Required—TOEFL (minimum score 600 paper-based; 100 iBT). Electronic applications accepted. *Expenses:* Tuition: Full-time $48,720. *Required fees:* $88. Tuition and fees vary according to course load, degree level, program and student level. *Faculty research:* Health and behavioral health, children and families, disabilities, aging policy, substance abuse, work, inequality and social change, women/gender, poverty alleviation.

Brock University, Faculty of Graduate Studies, Faculty of Social Sciences, Program in Political Science, St. Catharines, ON L2S 3A1, Canada. Offers Canadian politics (MA); comparative politics (MA); international relations (MA); political theory or philosophy

(MA); public policy (MA). *Program availability:* Part-time. *Degree requirements:* For master's, thesis optional. *Entrance requirements:* For master's, honors degree. Additional exam requirements/recommendations for international students: Required—TOEFL (minimum score 550 paper-based; 80 iBT), IELTS (minimum score 6.5), TWE (minimum score 4). Electronic applications accepted. *Faculty research:* Public administration reform, economic and social justice, politics of societies, Canadian politics, international relations.

Brooklyn College of the City University of New York, School of Humanities and Social Sciences, Department of Political Science, Brooklyn, NY 11210-2889. Offers international affairs (MA); political science (MA); urban policy and administration (MA). *Program availability:* Part-time, evening/weekend. *Degree requirements:* For master's, comprehensive exam (for some programs), thesis or alternative, foreign language exam (for international affairs program). *Entrance requirements:* For master's, 2 letters of recommendation, personal statement. Additional exam requirements/recommendations for international students: Required—TOEFL (minimum score 500 paper-based; 61 iBT). *Faculty research:* Ethics and politics, politics of criminal justice, Western Europe, international law and politics, labor politics.

Brown University, Graduate School, A. Alfred Taubman Center for Public Policy and American Institutions, Providence, RI 02912. Offers MPA, MPP, MD/MPP. *Entrance requirements:* For master's, GRE, 3 letters of recommendation. Additional exam requirements/recommendations for international students: Required—TOEFL.

California Lutheran University, Graduate Studies, School of Management, Thousand Oaks, CA 91360-2787. Offers business (IMBA); entrepreneurship (MBA, Certificate); finance (MBA, Certificate); financial planning (MBA, MS, Certificate); human capital management (MBA, Certificate); information technology (MS); information technology management (MBA, Certificate); international business (MBA, Certificate); marketing (MBA, Certificate); public policy and administration (MPPA); quantitative economics (MS). *Program availability:* Part-time, evening/weekend, 100% online, blended/hybrid learning. *Faculty:* 17 full-time (4 women), 40 part-time/adjunct (9 women). *Students:* 423 full-time (168 women), 153 part-time (72 women); includes 124 minority (11 Black or African American, non-Hispanic/Latino; 1 American Indian or Alaska Native, non-Hispanic/Latino; 21 Asian, non-Hispanic/Latino; 75 Hispanic/Latino; 16 Two or more races, non-Hispanic/Latino), 294 international. Average age 31. 467 applicants, 72% accepted, 108 enrolled. In 2017, 306 master's awarded. *Degree requirements:* For master's, comprehensive exam (for some programs). *Entrance requirements:* For master's, GMAT, interview, minimum GPA of 3.0. *Application deadline:* Applications are processed on a rolling basis. Application fee: $50. Electronic applications accepted. *Expenses:* Contact institution. *Unit head:* Dr. Gerhard Apfelthaler, Dean, 805-493-3360. *Application contact:* 805-493-3325, Fax: 805-493-3861, E-mail: clugrad@callutheran.edu.
Website: http://www.callutheran.edu/management/

California State University, East Bay, Office of Graduate Studies, College of Letters, Arts, and Social Sciences, Department of Public Affairs and Administration, Program in Public Administration, Hayward, CA 94542-3000. Offers health care administration (MPA); public management and policy analysis (MPA). *Program availability:* Part-time, evening/weekend. *Students:* 3 full-time (2 women), 125 part-time (79 women); includes 92 minority (30 Black or African American, non-Hispanic/Latino; 2 American Indian or Alaska Native, non-Hispanic/Latino; 19 Asian, non-Hispanic/Latino; 30 Hispanic/Latino; 3 Native Hawaiian or other Pacific Islander, non-Hispanic/Latino; 8 Two or more races, non-Hispanic/Latino), 9 international. Average age 33. 88 applicants, 74% accepted, 38 enrolled. In 2017, 87 master's awarded. *Degree requirements:* For master's, comprehensive exam (for some programs), comprehensive exam or thesis. *Entrance requirements:* For master's, minimum GPA of 2.5; statement of purpose; 2 letters of recommendation; professional resume/curriculum vitae. Additional exam requirements/recommendations for international students: Required—TOEFL (minimum score 550 paper-based; 79 iBT). *Application deadline:* For fall admission, 6/1 for domestic and international students. Application fee: $55. Electronic applications accepted. *Financial support:* Fellowships, teaching assistantships, career-related internships or fieldwork, Federal Work-Study, institutionally sponsored loans, and scholarships/grants available. Support available to part-time students. Financial award application deadline: 3/2; financial award applicants required to submit FAFSA. *Unit head:* Dr. Toni Fogarty, Chair, 510-885-2268, E-mail: toni.fogarty@csueastbay.edu. *Application contact:* Prof. Michael Moon, Public Administration Graduate Advisor, 510-885-2545, Fax: 510-885-3726, E-mail: michael.moon@csueastbay.edu.

California State University, Long Beach, Graduate Studies, College of Health and Human Services, Graduate Center for Public Policy and Administration, Long Beach, CA 90840. Offers MPA, Graduate Certificate. *Accreditation:* NASPAA (one or more programs are accredited). *Program availability:* Part-time, evening/weekend. *Degree requirements:* For master's, comprehensive exam. *Entrance requirements:* For master's, minimum GPA of 2.75. Electronic applications accepted. *Faculty research:* Transportation access, air quality controls, coastal issues, intergovernmental relations.

California State University, Sacramento, College of Social Sciences and Interdisciplinary Studies, Program in Public Policy and Administration, Sacramento, CA 95819. Offers MPPA. *Program availability:* Part-time. *Students:* 19 full-time (8 women), 37 part-time (28 women); includes 20 minority (1 Black or African American, non-Hispanic/Latino; 6 Asian, non-Hispanic/Latino; 11 Hispanic/Latino; 2 Native Hawaiian or other Pacific Islander, non-Hispanic/Latino). Average age 31. 52 applicants, 67% accepted, 26 enrolled. In 2017, 11 master's awarded. *Degree requirements:* For master's, thesis or writing proficiency exam. *Entrance requirements:* For master's, GRE, minimum GPA of 3.0 for all undergraduate coursework and in last 60 units. Additional exam requirements/recommendations for international students: Required—TOEFL (minimum score 560 paper-based; 83 iBT); Recommended—IELTS, TSE. *Application deadline:* For fall admission, 3/1 priority date for domestic and international students. Applications are processed on a rolling basis. Application fee: $55. Electronic applications accepted. *Expenses:* Contact institution. *Financial support:* Teaching assistantships, career-related internships or fieldwork, Federal Work-Study, and scholarships/grants available. Support available to part-time students. Financial award application deadline: 3/1; financial award applicants required to submit FAFSA. *Faculty research:* Education policy, urban policy, collaborative governance, judicial administration, and California state/local governance. *Unit head:* Dr. Ted Lascher, Chair, 916-278-6557, E-mail: tedl@csus.edu. *Application contact:* Jose Martinez, Graduate Admissions Supervisor, 916-278-7871, E-mail: martinj@skymail.csus.edu.
Website: http://www.csus.edu/ppa

Carleton University, Faculty of Graduate Studies, Faculty of Public Affairs and Management, School of Public Policy and Administration, Ottawa, ON K1S 5B6, Canada. Offers public administration (MA, DPA); public policy (PhD). *Program availability:* Part-time. *Degree requirements:* For master's, thesis optional; for doctorate, one foreign language, comprehensive exam, thesis/dissertation. *Entrance requirements:* For master's, GRE, honors degree; for doctorate, master's degree. Additional exam requirements/recommendations for international students: Required—TOEFL. *Faculty research:* Canadian public administration and policy, development administration, public policy analysis, public management.

Carnegie Mellon University, Dietrich College of Humanities and Social Sciences, Department of Statistics, Pittsburgh, PA 15213-3891. Offers machine learning and statistics (PhD); mathematical finance (PhD); statistics (MS, PhD), including applied statistics (PhD), computational statistics (PhD), theoretical statistics (PhD); statistics and public policy (PhD). Terminal master's awarded for partial completion of doctoral program. *Degree requirements:* For doctorate, comprehensive exam, thesis/dissertation. *Entrance requirements:* For master's and doctorate, GRE General Test. Additional exam requirements/recommendations for international students: Required—TOEFL. *Faculty research:* Stochastic processes, Bayesian statistics, statistical computing, decision theory, psychiatric statistics.

Carnegie Mellon University, Heinz College Australia, Master of Science in Public Policy and Management Program (Adelaide, South Australia), Adelaide SA 5000, Australia. Offers MS. *Entrance requirements:* For master's, GRE or GMAT, college-level course in advanced algebra/pre-calculus; college-level courses in economics and statistics (recommended). Additional exam requirements/recommendations for international students: Required—TOEFL or IELTS.

Carnegie Mellon University, Heinz College, School of Public Policy and Management, Master of Science in Public Policy and Management Program, Pittsburgh, PA 15213-3891. Offers MS. Program also offered with second-year study in Washington, DC. *Accreditation:* NASPAA. *Degree requirements:* For master's, internship. *Entrance requirements:* For master's, GRE or GMAT, college-level course in advanced algebra/pre-calculus; college-level courses in economics and statistics (recommended). Additional exam requirements/recommendations for international students: Required—TOEFL or IELTS. Electronic applications accepted.

Carnegie Mellon University, Heinz College, School of Public Policy and Management, PhD in Public Policy and Management Program, Pittsburgh, PA 15213-3891. Offers PhD. *Entrance requirements:* For doctorate, GRE or GMAT. Additional exam requirements/recommendations for international students: Required—TOEFL or IELTS.

The Catholic University of America, School of Arts and Sciences, Department of Sociology, Washington, DC 20064. Offers crime and justice studies (MA); global and comparative sociology (MA); public policy (MA). *Program availability:* Part-time. *Faculty:* 3 full-time (2 women), 3 part-time/adjunct (0 women). *Students:* 1 (woman) full-time, 1 (woman) part-time; includes 1 minority (Hispanic/Latino). Average age 24. 2 applicants. *Degree requirements:* For master's, comprehensive exam, thesis or alternative, two seminar papers. *Entrance requirements:* For master's, GRE General Test, statement of purpose, official copies of academic transcripts, three letters of recommendation. Additional exam requirements/recommendations for international students: Required—TOEFL (minimum score 550 paper-based; 80 iBT). *Application deadline:* For fall admission, 7/15 priority date for domestic students, 7/1 for international students; for spring admission, 11/15 priority date for domestic students, 11/1 for international students. Applications are processed on a rolling basis. Application fee: $55. Electronic applications accepted. *Expenses:* Contact institution. *Financial support:* Fellowships, research assistantships, teaching assistantships, Federal Work-Study, scholarships/grants, tuition waivers (full and partial), and unspecified assistantships available. Financial award application deadline: 2/1; financial award applicants required to submit FAFSA. *Faculty research:* Social movements, gender structure, political sociology, race and ethnic relations, evaluation methodologies. *Unit head:* Dr. David Walsh, Chair, 202-319-5445, Fax: 202-319-4980, E-mail: pumar@cua.edu. *Application contact:* Dr. Steven Brown, Director of Graduate Admissions, 202-319-5057, Fax: 202-319-6533, E-mail: cua-admissions@cua.edu.
Website: http://sociology.cua.edu/

Central European University, School of Public Policy, 1051, Hungary. Offers public administration (MPA); public policy (MA, PhD). *Faculty:* 22 full-time (7 women), 7 part-time/adjunct (5 women). *Students:* 123 full-time (76 women). Average age 28. 696 applicants, 32% accepted, 62 enrolled. In 2017, 74 master's, 4 doctorates awarded. *Degree requirements:* For master's, one foreign language, thesis; for doctorate, one foreign language, comprehensive exam, thesis/dissertation. *Entrance requirements:* For master's and doctorate, interview. Additional exam requirements/recommendations for international students: Required—TOEFL (minimum score 570 paper-based); Recommended—IELTS (minimum score 6.5). *Application deadline:* For fall admission, 2/4 for domestic and international students. Application fee: $30. Electronic applications accepted. *Expenses: Tuition:* Full-time 12,000 euros. *Required fees:* 230 euros. One-time fee: 30 euros full-time. Tuition and fees vary according to course level, course load, degree level and program. *Financial support:* Fellowships, career-related internships or fieldwork, scholarships/grants, health care benefits, and tuition waivers (full and partial) available. *Faculty research:* Multi-disciplinary study of public policy, innovative teaching and research, as well as meaningful engagement with policy practice, public health, law, humanitarian assistance, anti-corruption, conflict and post-conflict recovery, natural resource management. *Unit head:* Dr. Martin Kahanec, Head, 36 1 327-3110, E-mail: spp@ceu.edu. *Application contact:* Zsuzsanna Jaszberenyi, Admissions Officer, 361-324-3009, Fax: 367-327-3211, E-mail: admissions@ceu.edu.
Website: http://spp.ceu.edu

Claremont Graduate University, Graduate Programs, School of Social Science, Policy and Evaluation, Department of Economics, Claremont, CA 91711-6160. Offers behavioral economics and neuroeconomics (PhD); business and financial economics (MA, PhD); economic development (Certificate); international economic and development policy (PhD); international economics policy and development (MA); international money and finance (PhD); political economy and public economics (PhD); political economy and public policy (MA); MBA/PhD. *Program availability:* Part-time. *Entrance requirements:* For master's and doctorate, GRE General Test or GMAT. Additional exam requirements/recommendations for international students: Required—TOEFL (minimum score 75 iBT). Electronic applications accepted. *Faculty research:* International and financial economics, law and economics, regulation, public choice economics.

Claremont Graduate University, Graduate Programs, School of Social Science, Policy and Evaluation, Department of Politics and Policy, Claremont, CA 91711-6160. Offers American politics (MA, PhD); comparative politics (PhD); international political economy (MA); international studies (MA); political philosophy (PhD); political science (PhD); politics, economics and business (MA); public policy (MA, PhD); world politics (PhD); MBA/PhD. *Program availability:* Part-time. Terminal master's awarded for partial completion of doctoral program. *Entrance requirements:* For master's and doctorate, GRE General Test. Additional exam requirements/recommendations for international students: Required—TOEFL (minimum score 75 iBT). Electronic applications accepted. *Faculty research:* Environmental policy, international debt, global democratization, Third World development, public sector discrimination.

Claremont Graduate University, Graduate Programs, School of Social Science, Policy and Evaluation, Program in Public Policy and Evaluation, Claremont, CA 91711-6160. Offers MA. *Entrance requirements:* For master's, GRE General Test. Additional exam requirements/recommendations for international students: Required—TOEFL (minimum score 75 iBT). Electronic applications accepted.

Clemson University, Graduate School, College of Behavioral, Social and Health Sciences, PhD Program in Policy Studies, Clemson, SC 29634. Offers PhD, Certificate.

Program availability: Part-time, 100% online. *Faculty:* 5 full-time (2 women). *Students:* 21 full-time (3 women), 9 part-time (6 women), 9 international. Average age 40. 1 applicant, 100% accepted. In 2017, 3 doctorates awarded. *Degree requirements:* For doctorate, comprehensive exam, thesis/dissertation. *Entrance requirements:* For doctorate, GRE General Test, letters of recommendation, unofficial transcripts, biographical statement, statement of interest. Additional exam requirements/recommendations for international students: Required—TOEFL (minimum score 80 iBT), IELTS (minimum score 6.5), PTE (minimum score 54). *Application deadline:* For fall admission, 7/15 for domestic students, 5/1 for international students; for spring admission, 12/15 for domestic students, 10/1 for international students. Applications are processed on a rolling basis. Application fee: $80 ($90 for international students). Electronic applications accepted. *Expenses:* $4,318 per semester full-time resident, $8,036 per semester full-time non-resident, $425 per credit hour part-time resident, $837 per credit hour part-time non-resident; $467 per credit hour online; other fees may apply per session. *Financial support:* In 2017–18, 8 students received support, including 1 fellowship with partial tuition reimbursement available (averaging $10,000 per year), 2 research assistantships with partial tuition reimbursements available (averaging $15,000 per year), 4 teaching assistantships with partial tuition reimbursements available (averaging $13,463 per year); career-related internships or fieldwork and unspecified assistantships also available. Financial award application deadline: 4/1. *Faculty research:* Public issues, public policy making, public policy analysis. *Unit head:* Dr. Bruce Ransom, II, Program Chair, 864-656-0214, E-mail: bii@clemson.edu. *Application contact:* Carolyn Benson, Administrative Specialist, 864-656-4463, E-mail: cbenson@clemson.edu.
Website: https://www.clemson.edu/cbshs/departments/political-science/academics/policy-studies/index.html

The College of William and Mary, Faculty of Arts and Sciences, Public Policy Program, Williamsburg, VA 23187-8795. Offers international development and policy (MPP); public policy analysis (MPP); JD/MPP; MBA/MPP; MS/MPP. *Faculty:* 32 full-time (10 women), 5 part-time/adjunct (1 woman). *Students:* 31 full-time (18 women); includes 5 minority (1 Black or African American, non-Hispanic/Latino; 1 American Indian or Alaska Native, non-Hispanic/Latino; 2 Hispanic/Latino; 1 Two or more races, non-Hispanic/Latino), 2 international. Average age 24. 71 applicants, 65% accepted, 21 enrolled. In 2017, 18 master's awarded. *Entrance requirements:* For master's, GRE General Test. Additional exam requirements/recommendations for international students: Required—TOEFL (minimum score 600 paper-based; 100 iBT), IELTS (minimum score 7.5). *Application deadline:* For fall admission, 2/15 priority date for domestic and international students. Application fee: $50. Electronic applications accepted. *Financial support:* In 2017–18, 33 students received support, including 20 research assistantships with partial tuition reimbursements available (averaging $7,000 per year), 15 teaching assistantships with partial tuition reimbursements available (averaging $8,000 per year); career-related internships or fieldwork and unspecified assistantships also available. Financial award application deadline: 1/15; financial award applicants required to submit FAFSA. *Faculty research:* Social policy, international development, health care policy, environmental policy, state and local policy, education policy, regulatory policy. *Total annual research expenditures:* $225,421. *Unit head:* Dr. John Gilmour, Director, 757-221-2368, Fax: 757-221-1175, E-mail: jbgilm@wm.edu. *Application contact:* Sarah Fowkes, Director of Admissions, 757-221-2384, Fax: 757-221-2390, E-mail: sefowk@wm.edu.
Website: http://www.wm.edu/publicpolicy

Columbia University, School of International and Public Affairs, Program in Public Policy and Administration, New York, NY 10027. Offers MPA, JD/MPA, MPA/MS, MPH/MPA. *Accreditation:* NASPAA. *Entrance requirements:* For master's, GRE General Test. Additional exam requirements/recommendations for international students: Required—TOEFL (minimum score 600 paper-based; 100 iBT), IELTS (minimum score 7), PTE (minimum score 68). Electronic applications accepted. *Expenses: Tuition:* Full-time $44,864; part-time $1704 per credit. *Required fees:* $2370 per semester. One-time fee: $105.

Concordia University, School of Graduate Studies, Faculty of Arts and Science, Department of Political Science, Montréal, QC H3G 1M8, Canada. Offers political science (PhD); public policy and public administration (MA), including geography. *Degree requirements:* For master's, one foreign language, comprehensive exam, thesis optional, internship. *Entrance requirements:* For master's, honors degree or equivalent. Additional exam requirements/recommendations for international students: Required—TOEFL. *Faculty research:* International public policy and administration, Quebec public administration, public policy and social/political theory, geography and public policy, public administration and decision making.

Cornell University, Graduate School, Graduate Fields of Arts and Sciences, Field of Government, Ithaca, NY 14853. Offers American politics (PhD); comparative politics (PhD); international relations (PhD); political methodology (PhD); political thought (PhD); public policy (PhD). *Degree requirements:* For doctorate, comprehensive exam, thesis/dissertation. *Entrance requirements:* For doctorate, GRE General Test, sample of written work, 3 letters of recommendation. Additional exam requirements/recommendations for international students: Required—TOEFL (minimum score 550 paper-based; 77 iBT). Electronic applications accepted. *Faculty research:* Political theory, American politics, comparative politics, international relations, methodology.

Cornell University, Graduate School, Graduate Fields of Human Ecology, Field of Policy Analysis and Management, Ithaca, NY 14853. Offers consumer policy (PhD); family and social welfare policy (PhD); health administration (MHA); health management and policy (PhD); public policy (PhD). *Degree requirements:* For master's, thesis; for doctorate, thesis/dissertation. *Entrance requirements:* For master's, GRE General Test or GMAT, 2 letters of recommendation; for doctorate, GRE General Test, 2 letters of recommendation. Additional exam requirements/recommendations for international students: Required—TOEFL (minimum score 550 paper-based; 77 iBT). Electronic applications accepted. *Faculty research:* Health policy, family policy, social welfare policy, program evaluation, consumer policy.

DePaul University, College of Liberal Arts and Social Sciences, Chicago, IL 60614. Offers Arabic (MA); Chinese (MA); critical ethnic studies (MA); English (MA); French (MA); German (MA); history (MA); interdisciplinary studies (MA, MS); international public service (MS); international studies (MA); Italian (MA); Japanese (MA); liberal studies (MA); nonprofit management (MNM); public administration (MPA); public health (MPH); public policy (MPP); public service management (MS); refugee and forced migration studies (MS); social work (MSW); sociology (MA); Spanish (MA); sustainable urban development (MA); women's and gender studies (MA); writing and publishing (MA); writing, rhetoric and discourse (MA); MA/PhD. *Program availability:* Part-time, evening/weekend, online learning. Terminal master's awarded for partial completion of doctoral program. *Degree requirements:* For master's, variable foreign language requirement, comprehensive exam (for some programs), thesis (for some programs). *Application deadline:* Applications are processed on a rolling basis. Application fee: $40. Electronic applications accepted. *Financial support:* Applicants required to submit FAFSA. *Unit head:* Dr. Guillermo Vasquez de Velasco, Dean, 773-325-7305. *Application contact:* Ann Spittle, Director of Graduate Admission, 773-325-8369, Fax: 312-476-3244, E-mail: graddepaul@depaul.edu.
Website: http://las.depaul.edu/

Duke University, Graduate School, PhD Program in Public Policy, Durham, NC 27708. Offers PhD. *Entrance requirements:* For doctorate, GRE General Test. Additional exam requirements/recommendations for international students: Required—TOEFL (minimum score 577 paper-based; 90 iBT) or IELTS. Electronic applications accepted.

Duke University, Sanford School of Public Policy, MPP Program, Durham, NC 27708. Offers MPP, MBA/MPP, MD/MPP, MEM/MPP, MPP/JD, MPP/M Div. MPP/JD offered with North Carolina Central University; MBA/MPP with The University of North Carolina at Chapel Hill; JD/MPP with the University of North Carolina at Chapel Hill. *Faculty:* 70 full-time (24 women), 25 part-time/adjunct (7 women). *Students:* 155 full-time (93 women); includes 66 minority (14 Black or African American, non-Hispanic/Latino; 1 American Indian or Alaska Native, non-Hispanic/Latino; 36 Asian, non-Hispanic/Latino; 14 Hispanic/Latino; 1 Native Hawaiian or other Pacific Islander, non-Hispanic/Latino). Average age 27. 392 applicants, 81 enrolled. In 2017, 66 master's awarded. Terminal master's awarded for partial completion of doctoral program. *Degree requirements:* For master's, thesis, internship. *Entrance requirements:* For master's, GRE. Additional exam requirements/recommendations for international students: Required—TOEFL (minimum score 100 iBT), IELTS. *Application deadline:* For fall admission, 1/5 for domestic and international students. Application fee: $80. Electronic applications accepted. *Expenses:* $49,502 (for MPP); $59,562 (for MBA/MPP); $59,161 (for JD/MPP); $46,230 (for MEM/MPP). *Financial support:* In 2017–18, 161 fellowships with partial tuition reimbursements (averaging $16,735 per year), 10 research assistantships (averaging $4,000 per year), 117 teaching assistantships (averaging $4,000 per year) were awarded; career-related internships or fieldwork, Federal Work-Study, scholarships/grants, and unspecified assistantships also available. Financial award application deadline: 1/5; financial award applicants required to submit FAFSA. *Unit head:* Ken Rogerson, Director of Graduate Studies, 919-613-9206, E-mail: rogerson@duke.edu. *Application contact:* Jessica Pan, Director of Admissions and Scholarships, 919-613-9205, E-mail: mppadmit@duke.edu.
Website: https://www.sanford.duke.edu

Eastern Michigan University, Graduate School, College of Arts and Sciences, Department of Political Science, Programs in Public Administration, Ypsilanti, MI 48197. Offers general public management (Graduate Certificate); local government management (Graduate Certificate); management of public healthcare services (Graduate Certificate); nonprofit management (Graduate Certificate); public administration (MPA); public budget management (Graduate Certificate); public land planning and development management (Graduate Certificate); public personnel management (Graduate Certificate); public policy analysis (Graduate Certificate). *Accreditation:* NASPAA. *Students:* 11 full-time (6 women), 41 part-time (19 women); includes 18 minority (13 Black or African American, non-Hispanic/Latino; 1 Hispanic/Latino; 4 Two or more races, non-Hispanic/Latino). Average age 34. 42 applicants, 79% accepted, 14 enrolled. In 2017, 23 master's, 4 other advanced degrees awarded. Application fee: $45. *Application contact:* Dr. Jeffrey L. Bernstein, Program Advisor, 734-487-6970, Fax: 734-487-3340, E-mail: jeffrey.bernstein@emich.edu.
Website: http://www.emich.edu/polisci/

Excelsior College, School of Business and Technology, Albany, NY 12203-5159. Offers business administration (MBA); cybersecurity - information assurance (MS); cybersecurity - medical data security (MS); cybersecurity - policy administration (MS); cybersecurity management (MBA, Graduate Certificate); general business management (MS); health care management (MBA); human performance technology (MBA); human resource management (MS); human resources management (MBA); leadership (MBA, MS); mediation and arbitration (MBA, MS); social media management (MBA); technology management (MBA). *Program availability:* Part-time, evening/weekend, online learning. *Faculty:* 30 part-time/adjunct (12 women). *Students:* 1,204 part-time (333 women); includes 560 minority (310 Black or African American, non-Hispanic/Latino; 7 American Indian or Alaska Native, non-Hispanic/Latino; 42 Asian, non-Hispanic/Latino; 140 Hispanic/Latino; 10 Native Hawaiian or other Pacific Islander, non-Hispanic/Latino; 51 Two or more races, non-Hispanic/Latino). Average age 40. In 2017, 294 master's awarded. *Application deadline:* Applications are processed on a rolling basis. Application fee: $50. Electronic applications accepted. *Expenses: Tuition:* Part-time $645 per credit. *Required fees:* $265 per credit. *Financial support:* Scholarships/grants available. *Unit head:* Dr. Lifang Shih, Dean, 888-647-2388. *Application contact:* Admissions, 888-647-2388 Ext. 133, Fax: 518-464-8777, E-mail: admissions@excelsior.edu.

Florida State University, The Graduate School, College of Social Sciences and Public Policy, Reubin O'D. Askew School of Public Administration and Policy, Tallahassee, FL 32306-2250. Offers public administration (MPA, PhD); public administration and policy (Certificate); JD/MPA; MPA/MSC; MPA/MSP; MPA/MSW. *Accreditation:* NASPAA (one or more programs are accredited). *Program availability:* Part-time, evening/weekend. *Faculty:* 10 full-time (2 women), 10 part-time/adjunct (3 women). *Students:* 78 full-time (39 women), 68 part-time (41 women); includes 74 minority (12 Black or African American, non-Hispanic/Latino; 41 Asian, non-Hispanic/Latino; 6 Hispanic/Latino; 15 Two or more races, non-Hispanic/Latino). Average age 25. 115 applicants, 67% accepted, 37 enrolled. In 2017, 82 master's, 9 doctorates awarded. *Degree requirements:* For master's, action report; for doctorate, comprehensive exam, thesis/dissertation. *Entrance requirements:* For master's, GRE General Test, GMAT, MAT, LSAT, minimum undergraduate upper-division GPA of 3.0; for doctorate, GRE General Test (minimum score of 1100 or equivalent on current grading scale); GMAT; MAT; LSAT, minimum undergraduate GPA of 3.0, graduate 3.5. Additional exam requirements/recommendations for international students: Required—TOEFL (minimum score 550 paper-based; 80 iBT), IELTS (minimum score 6.5), PTE (minimum score 55), Michigan English Language Assessment Battery (minimum score 77). *Application deadline:* For fall admission, 7/1 for domestic students, 5/1 for international students; for spring admission, 11/1 for domestic students, 9/1 for international students; for summer admission, 3/1 for domestic students, 1/1 for international students. Applications are processed on a rolling basis. Application fee: $30. Electronic applications accepted. *Financial support:* In 2017–18, 22 students received support, including 8 fellowships with full tuition reimbursements available (averaging $18,000 per year), 4 research assistantships with full tuition reimbursements available (averaging $15,000 per year), 8 teaching assistantships with full tuition reimbursements available (averaging $15,000 per year); career-related internships or fieldwork, Federal Work-Study, institutionally sponsored loans, scholarships/grants, tuition waivers (full and partial), and unspecified assistantships also available. Support available to part-time students. Financial award application deadline: 2/1; financial award applicants required to submit FAFSA. *Faculty research:* Public financial management, policy analysis and evaluation methods, leadership and strategic management, state and local government administration, public and nonprofit management, international and nongovernmental organizations. *Unit head:* Dr. Keon-Hyung Lee, Director, 850-645-8210, Fax: 850-644-7617, E-mail: klee2@fsu.edu. *Application contact:* Velda Williams, Academic Program Specialist, 850-644-3060, Fax: 850-644-7617, E-mail: vwilliams3@fsu.edu.
Website: http://askew.fsu.edu/

Public Policy

Frederick S. Pardee RAND Graduate School, Program in Policy Analysis, Santa Monica, CA 90407-2138. Offers PhD. *Students:* 107; includes 20 minority (3 Black or African American, non-Hispanic/Latino; 9 Asian, non-Hispanic/Latino; 8 Hispanic/Latino), 38 international. Average age 31. 136 applicants, 29% accepted, 22 enrolled. In 2017, 19 doctorates awarded. *Degree requirements:* For doctorate, comprehensive exam, thesis/dissertation. *Entrance requirements:* For doctorate, GMAT or GRE General Test, resume or curriculum vitae, three essays, three letters of recommendation. Additional exam requirements/recommendations for international students: Required—TOEFL (minimum score 100 iBT). *Application deadline:* For fall admission, 1/10 for domestic and international students. Application fee: $50. Electronic applications accepted. *Expenses:* Contact institution. *Financial support:* In 2017–18, 107 students received support, including 107 fellowships (averaging $46,000 per year), 30 teaching assistantships (averaging $2,000 per year); scholarships/grants and health care benefits also available. Financial award application deadline: 7/1. *Faculty research:* Education, defense policy, health, labor and population, justice. *Unit head:* Dr. Susan L. Marquis, Dean, 310-393-0411 Ext. 7075, Fax: 310-451-6978. *Application contact:* Mary Parker, Registrar/Admissions Manager, 310-393-0411 Ext. 7690, Fax: 310-451-6978, E-mail: mfparker@prgs.edu.
Website: http://www.prgs.edu

George Mason University, Schar School of Policy and Government, Program in Public Policy, Arlington, VA 22201. Offers MPP, PhD. *Faculty:* 24 full-time (11 women), 7 part-time/adjunct (2 women). *Students:* 104 full-time (54 women), 188 part-time (90 women); includes 102 minority (40 Black or African American, non-Hispanic/Latino; 19 Asian, non-Hispanic/Latino; 28 Hispanic/Latino; 1 Native Hawaiian or other Pacific Islander, non-Hispanic/Latino; 14 Two or more races, non-Hispanic/Latino), 33 international. Average age 32. 197 applicants, 81% accepted, 64 enrolled. In 2017, 88 master's, 12 doctorates awarded. *Degree requirements:* For master's, thesis or alternative, professional experience; for doctorate, comprehensive exam, thesis/dissertation, field studies. *Entrance requirements:* For master's, GRE/GMAT (for students seeking merit-based scholarships), bachelor's degree with minimum GPA of 3.0, current resume, 2 letters of recommendation, expanded goals statement, 2 copies of official transcripts; for doctorate, GMAT or GRE General Test, master's degree with minimum GPA of 3.0; current resume; expanded goals statement; 2 official copies of transcripts; writing sample. Additional exam requirements/recommendations for international students: Required—TOEFL (minimum score 575 paper-based; 88 iBT), IELTS (minimum score 6.5), PTE (minimum score 59). *Application deadline:* For fall admission, 2/1 priority date for domestic and international students; for spring admission, 11/1 priority date for domestic and international students. Application fee: $75 ($80 for international students). Electronic applications accepted. *Expenses:* $795 per credit in-state tuition, $1,516 out-of-state. *Financial support:* In 2017–18, 27 students received support, including 26 research assistantships with tuition reimbursements available (averaging $17,840 per year), 1 teaching assistantship; career-related internships or fieldwork, Federal Work-Study, scholarships/grants, unspecified assistantships, and health care benefits (for full-time research or teaching assistantship recipients) also available. Support available to part-time students. Financial award application deadline: 3/1; financial award applicants required to submit FAFSA. *Faculty research:* Regional development; science and technology policy; international development; health policy; economic policy. *Unit head:* Siona Listokin-Smith, Director, Master of Public Policy, 703-703-9756, Fax: 703-993-8215, E-mail: slistoki@gmu.edu. *Application contact:* Stephanie Ellis, Graduate Admissions Coordinator, 703-993-4478, E-mail: sellis11@gmu.edu.
Website: http://spgia.gmu.edu/programs/graduate-degrees/master-of-public-policy-mpp/

Georgetown University, Graduate School of Arts and Sciences, Department of Government, Washington, DC 20057. Offers American government (MA); conflict resolution (MA); democracy and governance (MA); development, management and policy (MA); government (PhD); MA/PhD. Terminal master's awarded for partial completion of doctoral program. *Degree requirements:* For master's, one foreign language, comprehensive exam; for doctorate, one foreign language, comprehensive exam, thesis/dissertation. *Entrance requirements:* For master's, GRE General Test, minimum B average; for doctorate, GRE General Test, MA. Additional exam requirements/recommendations for international students: Required—TOEFL. *Faculty research:* Western Europe, Latin America, the Middle East, political theory, international relations and law, methodology, American politics and institutions.

Georgetown University, Graduate School of Arts and Sciences, School of Continuing Studies, Washington, DC 20057. Offers American studies (MALS); applied intelligence (MPS); Catholic studies (MALS); classical civilizations (MALS); emergency and disaster management (MPS); ethics and the professions (MALS); global strategic communications (MPS); hospitality management (MPS); human resources management (MPS); humanities (MALS); individualized study (MALS); integrated marketing communications (MPS); international affairs (MALS); Islam and Muslim-Christian relations (MALS); journalism (MPS); liberal studies (DLS); literature and society (MALS); medieval and early modern European studies (MALS); public relations and corporate communications (MPS); real estate (MPS); religious studies (MALS); social and public policy (MALS); sports industry management (MPS); systems engineering management (MPS); technology management (MPS); the theory and practice of American democracy (MALS); urban and regional planning (MPS); visual culture (MALS). MPS in systems engineering management offered jointly with Stevens Institute of Technology. *Entrance requirements:* Additional exam requirements/recommendations for international students: Required—TOEFL.

Georgetown University, McCourt School of Public Policy, Washington, DC 20057. Offers data science for public policy (MDSPP); international development policy (MIDP); policy leadership (EMPL); policy management (MPM); public policy (MPP); MBA/MPP; MPP/JD; MPP/MA; MPP/MSFS; MPP/PhD. *Program availability:* Part-time. *Entrance requirements:* For master's, GRE General Test or GMAT, minimum B average. Additional exam requirements/recommendations for international students: Required—TOEFL (minimum score 100 iBT). *Application deadline:* For fall admission, 1/15 priority date for domestic students. Applications are processed on a rolling basis. Application fee: $90. Electronic applications accepted. *Financial support:* Research assistantships, teaching assistantships, career-related internships or fieldwork, scholarships/grants, and unspecified assistantships available. Financial award application deadline: 2/1; financial award applicants required to submit FAFSA. *Faculty research:* Analytic methods, data analysis, development policy, economic policy, education policy, environmental and energy policy, federalism, health and healthcare policy, international economic policy, leadership, policy analysis, politics and political strategy, poverty and social policy, public and nonprofit management, state and local government, urban policy. *Unit head:* Dr. Michael A. Bailey, Dean, McCourt School of Public Policy, 202-687-6163. *Application contact:* Dr. Adam Thomas, Director of Admissions, 202-687-9186, E-mail: mccourtadmissions@georgetown.edu.
Website: https://mccourt.georgetown.edu/

The George Washington University, Columbian College of Arts and Sciences, Department of Philosophy, Washington, DC 20052. Offers philosophy and social policy (MA). *Faculty:* 10 full-time (4 women), 9 part-time/adjunct (1 woman). *Students:* 3 full-time (2 women), 5 part-time (2 women); includes 2 minority (1 Asian, non-Hispanic/Latino; 1 Hispanic/Latino). Average age 26. 26 applicants, 92% accepted, 4 enrolled. *Degree requirements:* For master's, comprehensive exam, thesis or alternative. *Entrance requirements:* For master's, GRE General Test, interview, minimum GPA of 3.0. Additional exam requirements/recommendations for international students: Required—TOEFL (minimum score 600 paper-based; 100 iBT). *Application deadline:* For fall admission, 4/1 priority date for domestic and international students; for spring admission, 10/1 priority date for domestic students, 9/1 priority date for international students. Applications are processed on a rolling basis. Application fee: $60. Electronic applications accepted. *Expenses: Tuition:* Full-time $28,800; part-time $1655 per credit hour. *Required fees:* $45; $2.75 per credit hour. *Financial support:* Fellowships with tuition reimbursements, Federal Work-Study, and institutionally sponsored loans available. Financial award application deadline: 1/15. *Unit head:* Tad Zawidzki, Chair, 202-994-6444, E-mail: zawidzki@gwu.edu. *Application contact:* Amanda McLaughlin, Executive Aide, 202-994-6265, Fax: 202-994-8683, E-mail: philosop@gwu.edu.
Website: https://philosophy.columbian.gwu.edu/

The George Washington University, Columbian College of Arts and Sciences, Trachtenberg School of Public Policy and Public Administration, Washington, DC 20052. Offers environmental resource policy (MA); public administration (MPA); public policy (MPP); public policy and administration (PhD); JD/MPP; MPA/JD; PhD/MPP. *Program availability:* Part-time, evening/weekend, online learning. *Faculty:* 13 full-time (7 women), 20 part-time/adjunct (8 women). *Students:* 102 full-time (63 women), 127 part-time (76 women); includes 66 minority (25 Black or African American, non-Hispanic/Latino; 10 Asian, non-Hispanic/Latino; 24 Hispanic/Latino; 2 Native Hawaiian or other Pacific Islander, non-Hispanic/Latino; 5 Two or more races, non-Hispanic/Latino), 28 international. Average age 30. 630 applicants, 59% accepted, 91 enrolled. In 2017, 122 master's, 13 doctorates awarded. *Degree requirements:* For master's, capstone project; for doctorate, comprehensive exam, thesis/dissertation. *Entrance requirements:* For master's and doctorate, minimum GPA of 3.0. Additional exam requirements/recommendations for international students: Required—TOEFL (minimum score 600 paper-based; 100 iBT). *Application deadline:* For fall admission, 1/5 priority date for domestic and international students; for spring admission, 10/1 priority date for domestic students, 10/1 for international students. Application fee: $75. Electronic applications accepted. *Expenses:* Contact institution. *Financial support:* In 2017–18, 57 students received support. Fellowships, research assistantships, teaching assistantships, Federal Work-Study, scholarships/grants, health care benefits, and unspecified assistantships available. Financial award application deadline: 1/5; financial award applicants required to submit FAFSA. *Faculty research:* Education policy, budget and finance, health policy, regulatory policy, program evaluation. *Unit head:* Dr. Kathyrn E. Newcomer, Director, 202-994-3959, Fax: 202-994-6792, E-mail: newcomer@gwu.edu. *Application contact:* Denee' Bottoms, Assistant Director of Graduate Studies, 202-994-6662, Fax: 202-994-6792, E-mail: dbottoms@gwu.edu.
Website: http://www.tspppa.gwu.edu/

The George Washington University, School of Business, Department of Strategic Management and Public Policy, Washington, DC 20052. Offers MBA, PhD. *Accreditation:* NASPAA. *Program availability:* Part-time, evening/weekend. *Faculty:* 13 full-time (3 women). *Students:* 170 full-time (74 women); includes 35 minority (7 Black or African American, non-Hispanic/Latino; 13 Asian, non-Hispanic/Latino; 9 Hispanic/Latino; 6 Two or more races, non-Hispanic/Latino), 73 international. Average age 28. 452 applicants, 54% accepted, 82 enrolled. In 2017, 87 master's awarded. *Entrance requirements:* For master's, GMAT; for doctorate, GMAT or GRE. Additional exam requirements/recommendations for international students: Required—TOEFL. *Application deadline:* For fall admission, 4/1 priority date for domestic students; for spring admission, 10/1 for domestic students. Applications are processed on a rolling basis. Application fee: $75. *Expenses: Tuition:* Full-time $28,800; part-time $1655 per credit hour. *Required fees:* $45; $2.75 per credit hour. *Financial support:* In 2017–18, 1 student received support. Fellowships, teaching assistantships, career-related internships or fieldwork, Federal Work-Study, and institutionally sponsored loans available. Financial award application deadline: 4/1. *Unit head:* Dr. Jennifer Griffin, Chair, 202-994-2536, E-mail: jgriffin@gwu.edu. *Application contact:* Christopher Storer, Executive Director, Graduate Admissions, 202-994-1212, E-mail: gwmba@gwu.edu.
Website: http://business.gwu.edu/smpp/

Georgia Institute of Technology, Graduate Studies, Ivan Allen College of Liberal Arts, School of Public Policy, Atlanta, GA 30332-0001. Offers MS, PhD. *Program availability:* Part-time. Terminal master's awarded for partial completion of doctoral program. *Degree requirements:* For master's, professional paper, public policy workshop or thesis; internship; minimum overall GPA of 3.0; for doctorate, comprehensive exam, thesis/dissertation, minimum overall GPA of 3.0, one year of full-time residency. *Entrance requirements:* For master's and doctorate, GRE, three letters of recommendation, transcripts from each college/university attended, essays. Additional exam requirements/recommendations for international students: Required—TOEFL (minimum score 600 paper-based; 100 iBT). Electronic applications accepted. *Faculty research:* National/regional science and technology policy, environmental policy, urban policy and planning, telecommunications policy.

Georgia State University, Andrew Young School of Policy Studies, Department of Public Management and Policy, Atlanta, GA 30303. Offers criminal justice (MPA); disaster management (Certificate); disaster policy (MPA); environmental policy (PhD); health policy (PhD); management and finance (MPA); nonprofit management (MPA, Certificate); nonprofit policy (MPA); planning and economic development (MPP, Certificate); policy analysis and evaluation (MPA), including planning and economic development; public and nonprofit management (PhD); public finance and budgeting (PhD), including science and technology policy, urban and regional economic development; public finance policy (MPA), including social policy; public health (MPA). *Accreditation:* NASPAA (one or more programs are accredited). *Program availability:* Part-time. *Faculty:* 17 full-time (9 women). *Students:* 125 full-time (75 women), 78 part-time (51 women); includes 90 minority (67 Black or African American, non-Hispanic/Latino; 5 Asian, non-Hispanic/Latino; 9 Hispanic/Latino; 9 Two or more races, non-Hispanic/Latino), 34 international. Average age 30. 275 applicants, 62% accepted, 88 enrolled. In 2017, 71 master's, 5 doctorates, 12 other advanced degrees awarded. Terminal master's awarded for partial completion of doctoral program. *Degree requirements:* For master's, thesis optional; for doctorate, comprehensive exam, thesis/dissertation. *Entrance requirements:* For master's and doctorate, GRE. Additional exam requirements/recommendations for international students: Required—TOEFL (minimum score 603 paper-based; 100 iBT) or IELTS (minimum score 7). *Application deadline:* For fall admission, 1/15 for domestic and international students. Application fee: $50. Electronic applications accepted. *Expenses:* Tuition, state resident: full-time $7020. Tuition, nonresident: full-time $22,518. *Required fees:* $2128. Tuition and fees vary according to degree level and program. *Financial support:* In 2017–18, fellowships (averaging $8,194 per year), research assistantships (averaging $8,068 per year), teaching assistantships (averaging $3,600 per year) were awarded; institutionally sponsored loans, scholarships/grants, health care benefits, and unspecified assistantships also available. Financial award application deadline: 2/1. *Faculty research:* Public budgeting and finance, public management, nonprofit management, performance measurement and management, urban development. *Unit head:* Dr. Carolyn Bourdeaux, Chair and Professor, 404-413-0013, Fax: 404-413-0104, E-mail:

cbourdeaux@gsu.edu.
Website: http://aysps.gsu.edu/pmap/

Harvard University, Graduate School of Arts and Sciences and John F. Kennedy School of Government, Committee on Public Policy, Cambridge, MA 02138. Offers PhD. *Degree requirements:* For doctorate, thesis/dissertation, exams. *Entrance requirements:* For doctorate, GRE General Test or GMAT, Harvard MPP degree. Additional exam requirements/recommendations for international students: Required—TOEFL.

Harvard University, Graduate School of Arts and Sciences, Program in Social Policy, Cambridge, MA 02138. Offers PhD.

Harvard University, John F. Kennedy School of Government, Doctoral Programs in Government, Cambridge, MA 02138. Offers political economy and government (PhD); public policy (PhD). *Students:* 20 full-time (11 women); includes 3 minority (all Two or more races, non-Hispanic/Latino), 6 international. Average age 27. 243 applicants, 7% accepted, 12 enrolled. *Degree requirements:* For doctorate, comprehensive exam, thesis/dissertation. *Entrance requirements:* For doctorate, GRE General Test, course work in macroeconomics, multi-variable calculus. Additional exam requirements/recommendations for international students: Required—TOEFL (minimum score 600 paper-based; 100 iBT), TWE. *Application deadline:* For fall admission, 12/1 for domestic students. Application fee: $100. Electronic applications accepted. *Financial support:* Fellowships, research assistantships, teaching assistantships, Federal Work-Study, institutionally sponsored loans, scholarships/grants, health care benefits, and unspecified assistantships available. *Unit head:* Nicole Tateosian, Director, 617-495-1190, E-mail: nicole_tateosian@harvard.edu. *Application contact:* 617-495-1155, Fax: 617-496-1165, E-mail: ksg_admissions@harvard.edu.
Website: http://www.hks.harvard.edu/

Harvard University, John F. Kennedy School of Government, Program in Public Policy, Cambridge, MA 02138. Offers MPP, JD/MPP, MBA/MPP, MD/MPP. *Students:* 423 full-time (197 women); includes 114 minority (20 Black or African American, non-Hispanic/Latino; 57 Asian, non-Hispanic/Latino; 22 Hispanic/Latino; 15 Two or more races, non-Hispanic/Latino), 129 international. Average age 28. 1,601 applicants, 25% accepted, 196 enrolled. In 2017, 196 master's awarded. *Entrance requirements:* For master's, GMAT or GRE General Test. Additional exam requirements/recommendations for international students: Required—TOEFL (minimum score 600 paper-based; 100 iBT), TWE. *Application deadline:* For fall admission, 12/1 for domestic students. Application fee: $100. Electronic applications accepted. *Financial support:* In 2017–18, 199 students received support, including 199 fellowships (averaging $42,260 per year); career-related internships or fieldwork, Federal Work-Study, scholarships/grants, health care benefits, and unspecified assistantships also available. Financial award application deadline: 2/24; financial award applicants required to submit FAFSA. *Unit head:* Eleni Cortis, Director, 617-496-8593, E-mail: eleni_cortis@hks.harvard.edu. *Application contact:* 617-495-1155.
Website: http://www.hks.harvard.edu/

Indiana University Bloomington, School of Public and Environmental Affairs, Public Affairs Programs, Bloomington, IN 47405. Offers economic development (MPA); energy (MPA); environmental policy (PhD); environmental policy and natural resource management (MPA); information systems (MPA); international development (MPA); local government management (MPA); nonprofit management (MPA, Certificate); policy analysis (MPA); public budgeting and financial management (Certificate); public finance (PhD); public financial administration (MPA); public management (MPA, PhD, Certificate); public policy analysis (PhD); social entrepreneurship (Certificate); specialized public affairs (MPA); sustainability and sustainable development (MPA); JD/MPA; MPA/MA; MPA/MIS; MPA/MLS; MSES/MPA. *Accreditation:* NASPAA (one or more programs are accredited). *Program availability:* Part-time. *Degree requirements:* For master's, capstone, internship; for doctorate, comprehensive exam, thesis/dissertation. *Entrance requirements:* For master's, GRE General Test or GMAT, official transcripts, 3 letters of recommendation, resume, personal statement; for doctorate, GRE General Test, official transcripts, 3 letters of recommendation, statement of purpose. Additional exam requirements/recommendations for international students: Required—TOEFL (minimum score 600 paper-based; 96 iBT); Recommended—IELTS (minimum score 7). Electronic applications accepted. *Faculty research:* International development, environmental policy and resource management, policy analysis, public finance, public management, urban management, nonprofit management, energy policy, social policy, public finance.

Indiana University Kokomo, Department of Public Administration and Health Management, Kokomo, IN 46904. Offers health management (MPM, Graduate Certificate); public management (Graduate Certificate); public management and policy (MPM). *Program availability:* Part-time, evening/weekend. *Entrance requirements:* For master's, GRE/GMAT for GPAs lower than 3.0, letters of recommendation. Additional exam requirements/recommendations for international students: Required—TOEFL (minimum score 550 paper-based; 73 iBT). Electronic applications accepted. *Expenses:* Contact institution.

Indiana University–Purdue University Fort Wayne, College of Education and Public Policy, Department of Public Policy, Fort Wayne, IN 46805-1499. Offers public management (MPM, Certificate). *Program availability:* Part-time. *Degree requirements:* For master's, internship. *Entrance requirements:* For master's, GRE General Test or GMAT, minimum GPA of 3.0, 3 letters of reference. Additional exam requirements/recommendations for international students: Required—TOEFL (minimum score 550 paper-based; 79 iBT). *Faculty research:* Opioid safety, homeless and stigma.

The Institute of World Politics, Graduate Programs in National Security, Intelligence, and International Affairs, Washington, DC 20036. Offers American foreign policy (Certificate); comparative political culture (Certificate); counterintelligence (Certificate); democracy building (Certificate); intelligence (Certificate); international politics (Certificate); national security affairs (Certificate); public diplomacy and political warfare (Certificate); statecraft and national security affairs (MA); statecraft and world politics (MA); strategic intelligence studies (MA). *Program availability:* Part-time, evening/weekend. *Degree requirements:* For master's, comprehensive exam, thesis optional. *Entrance requirements:* For master's, GRE General Test. Additional exam requirements/recommendations for international students: Required—TOEFL. Electronic applications accepted. *Faculty research:* Intelligence, national security, statecraft.

Jackson State University, Graduate School, College of Public Service, Department of Public Policy and Administration, Jackson, MS 39217. Offers public administration (PhD); public policy and administration (MPPA). *Accreditation:* NASPAA (one or more programs are accredited). *Program availability:* Evening/weekend. *Degree requirements:* For master's, comprehensive exam, thesis optional; for doctorate, comprehensive exam, thesis/dissertation. *Entrance requirements:* For master's, GRE General Test; for doctorate, GRE, GMAT, MAT. Additional exam requirements/recommendations for international students: Required—TOEFL (minimum score 520 paper-based; 67 iBT).

Jacksonville University, Public Policy Institute, Jacksonville, FL 32211. Offers MPP, MBA/MPP, MPP/JD, MPP/MS. MPP/JD offered in partnership with Florida Coastal School of Law; MPP/MBA with JU's Davis College of Business; MPP/MS with JU's Marine Science Research Institute. *Program availability:* Part-time, evening/weekend. *Faculty:* 3 full-time (1 woman), 3 part-time/adjunct (2 women). *Students:* 10 full-time (4 women), 19 part-time (10 women); includes 7 minority (3 Black or African American, non-Hispanic/Latino; 3 Hispanic/Latino; 1 Two or more races, non-Hispanic/Latino). Average age 34. 39 applicants, 54% accepted, 15 enrolled. In 2017, 4 master's awarded. *Degree requirements:* For master's, thesis, internship, capstone project. *Entrance requirements:* For master's, GRE, GMAT, LSAT, resume, essay, statement of intent, two current references, official transcripts of academic work. Additional exam requirements/recommendations for international students: Recommended—TOEFL (minimum score 540 paper-based; 76 iBT). *Application deadline:* For fall admission, 2/15 priority date for domestic students, 2/15 for international students. Applications are processed on a rolling basis. Application fee: $50. Electronic applications accepted. *Expenses:* $805 per credit hour. *Financial support:* In 2017–18, 11 students received support, including 2 fellowships (averaging $40,000 per year); career-related internships or fieldwork, Federal Work-Study, scholarships/grants, and unspecified assistantships also available. Support available to part-time students. Financial award application deadline: 4/1. *Unit head:* Dr. Richard A. Mullaney, Director of Public Policy Institute, 904-256-7342, E-mail: rmullan1@ju.edu. *Application contact:* Rakia Naze, Assistant Director of Graduate Admissions, 904-256-7004, E-mail: rnaze@ju.edu.
Website: https://www.ju.edu/publicpolicy/master-public-policy/index.php

John Jay College of Criminal Justice of the City University of New York, Graduate Studies, Programs in Criminal Justice, New York, NY 10019. Offers criminal justice (MA, PhD); criminology and deviance (PhD); forensic psychology (PhD); forensic science (PhD); international crime and justice (MA); law and philosophy (PhD); organizational behavior (PhD); public policy (PhD). *Program availability:* Part-time, evening/weekend. Terminal master's awarded for partial completion of doctoral program. *Degree requirements:* For master's, thesis or alternative; for doctorate, one foreign language, thesis/dissertation. *Entrance requirements:* For master's, GRE General Test, minimum B average; for doctorate, GRE General Test. Additional exam requirements/recommendations for international students: Required—TOEFL (minimum score 500 paper-based).

Johns Hopkins University, Bloomberg School of Public Health, Department of Health Policy and Management, Baltimore, MD 21205-1996. Offers bioethics and policy (PhD); health administration (MHA); health and public policy (PhD); health economics (MHS); health economics and policy (PhD); health finance and management (MHS); health policy (MSPH); health policy and management (Dr PH); health services research and policy (PhD); public policy (MPP). *Accreditation:* CAHME (one or more programs are accredited). *Program availability:* Part-time. *Students:* 190 full-time (123 women), 135 part-time (73 women); includes 90 minority (10 Black or African American, non-Hispanic/Latino; 53 Asian, non-Hispanic/Latino; 17 Hispanic/Latino; 1 Native Hawaiian or other Pacific Islander, non-Hispanic/Latino; 9 Two or more races, non-Hispanic/Latino), 107 international. Average age 31. 729 applicants, 31% accepted, 96 enrolled. In 2017, 80 master's, 26 doctorates awarded. *Degree requirements:* For master's, thesis (for some programs), internship (for some programs); for doctorate, comprehensive exam, thesis/dissertation, 1-year full-time residency (for some programs), oral and written exams. *Entrance requirements:* For master's, GRE General Test or GMAT, 3 letters of recommendation, curriculum vitae/resume; for doctorate, GRE General Test or GMAT, 3 letters of recommendation, curriculum vitae, transcripts. Additional exam requirements/recommendations for international students: Required—TOEFL (minimum score 100 iBT), IELTS (minimum score 7). *Application deadline:* Applications are processed on a rolling basis. Application fee: $135. Electronic applications accepted. *Financial support:* Fellowships, research assistantships, teaching assistantships, career-related internships or fieldwork, Federal Work-Study, scholarships/grants, traineeships, and stipends available. Support available to part-time students. *Faculty research:* Quality of care and health outcomes, health care finance and technology, health disparities and vulnerable populations, injury prevention, health policy and health care policy. *Unit head:* Dr. Colleen Barry, Chairman. *Application contact:* Mary Sewell, Coordinator, 410-955-2489, Fax: 410-614-9152, E-mail: msewell@jhsph.edu.

Liberty University, Helms School of Government, Lynchburg, VA 24515. Offers criminal justice (MS), including forensic psychology, homeland security, public administration (MA, MS); international relations (MS); political science (MS); public administration (MPA), including business and government, healthcare, law and public policy, public and non-profit management; public policy (MA), including campaigns and elections, international affairs, Middle East affairs, public administration (MA, MS). *Program availability:* Part-time, online learning. *Students:* 287 full-time (148 women), 639 part-time (248 women); includes 231 minority (173 Black or African American, non-Hispanic/Latino; 4 American Indian or Alaska Native, non-Hispanic/Latino; 8 Asian, non-Hispanic/Latino; 20 Hispanic/Latino; 1 Native Hawaiian or other Pacific Islander, non-Hispanic/Latino; 25 Two or more races, non-Hispanic/Latino), 7 international. Average age 35. 876 applicants, 64% accepted, 277 enrolled. In 2017, 211 master's awarded. *Entrance requirements:* For master's, minimum undergraduate GPA of 3.0. Additional exam requirements/recommendations for international students: Required—TOEFL (minimum score 600 paper-based; 100 iBT). *Application deadline:* Applications are processed on a rolling basis. Application fee: $50. Electronic applications accepted. *Unit head:* Shawn D. Akers, Dean, 434-592-4986. *Application contact:* Jay Bridge, Director of Admissions, 800-424-9595, Fax: 800-628-7977, E-mail: gradadmissions@liberty.edu.

Lincoln University, Graduate Studies, Jefferson City, MO 65101. Offers business administration (MBA), including accounting, management, management information systems, public administration/policy; elementary teaching (M Ed); environmental science (MS); guidance and counseling (M Ed), including community/agency counseling, elementary school, secondary school; higher education (MA); history (MA); integrated agricultural systems (MS); middle school (M Ed); natural sciences (MS); secondary teaching (M Ed); sociology (MA); sociology/criminal justice (MA). *Program availability:* Part-time, evening/weekend, 100% online, blended/hybrid learning. *Students:* 40 full-time (23 women), 64 part-time (32 women); includes 33 minority (30 Black or African American, non-Hispanic/Latino; 2 Hispanic/Latino; 1 Two or more races, non-Hispanic/Latino), 12 international. Average age 33. 48 applicants, 81% accepted, 22 enrolled. In 2017, 46 master's awarded. *Degree requirements:* For master's, comprehensive exam, thesis optional. *Entrance requirements:* For master's, GRE, MAT, or GMAT, minimum GPA of 2.75 overall, 3.0 in courses related to specialization; 3 letters of recommendation; minimum C average in English composition; personal statement of purpose. Additional exam requirements/recommendations for international students: Required—TOEFL (minimum score 500 paper-based; 61 iBT), IELTS (minimum score 5.5), Michigan English Language Assessment Battery (minimum score 80). *Application deadline:* For fall admission, 7/1 priority date for domestic students, 5/1 priority date for international students; for spring admission, 11/1 priority date for domestic students, 10/1 priority date for international students; for summer admission, 6/1 priority date for domestic students. Applications are processed on a rolling basis. Application fee: $30. Electronic applications accepted. *Expenses:* Tuition, state resident: part-time $291 per credit hour. Tuition, nonresident: part-time $541.50 per credit hour. *Financial support:* In 2017–18, 2 fellowships with tuition reimbursements, 3 research assistantships with tuition reimbursements were awarded; Federal Work-Study, scholarships/grants, and unspecified assistantships also available. Support available to part-time students. Financial award application deadline: 3/1; financial award applicants required to submit FAFSA. *Unit head:* Dr. Debra F. Greene, Interim

Provost, 573-681-5247, Fax: 573-681-5106, E-mail: gradschool@lincolnu.edu. *Application contact:* Irasema Steck, Administrative Assistant, 573-681-5247, Fax: 573-681-5106, E-mail: gradschool@lincolnu.edu.
Website: http://www.lincolnu.edu/web/graduate-studies/graduate-studies

Lipscomb University, School of Public Policy, Nashville, TN 37204-3951. Offers leadership and public service (MA). *Faculty:* 2 full-time (1 woman). *Students:* 12 full-time (9 women); includes 6 minority (all Black or African American, non-Hispanic/Latino). Average age 27. 33 applicants, 48% accepted, 12 enrolled. In 2017, 15 master's awarded. *Entrance requirements:* For master's, GRE or GMAT, references, resume, goals statement. Additional exam requirements/recommendations for international students: Required—TOEFL (minimum score 550 paper-based). *Application deadline:* Applications are processed on a rolling basis. Application fee: $50 ($75 for international students). Electronic applications accepted. *Expenses:* $1,290. *Faculty research:* African American family strengths and their relationship to health and mental health prevention and intervention, application of hope theories, systems theories and positive psychology principles in systems and organizations at multiples levels. *Unit head:* Dr. Kristine LaLonde, Academic Director, 615-966-6692, E-mail: kristine.lalonde@lipscomb.edu. *Application contact:* Amy Goode, New Student Enrollment Manager, 615-966-6691, E-mail: amy.goode@lipscomb.edu.

London Metropolitan University, Graduate Programs, London, United Kingdom. Offers applied psychology (M Sc); architecture (MA); biomedical science (M Sc); blood science (M Sc); cancer pharmacology (M Sc); computer networking and cyber security (M Sc); computing and information systems (M Sc); conference interpreting (MA); counter-terrorism studies (M Sc); creative, digital and professional writing (MA); crime, violence and prevention (M Sc); criminology (M Sc); curating contemporary art (MA); data analytics (M Sc); digital media (MA); early childhood studies (MA); education (MA, Ed D); financial services law, regulation and compliance (LL M); food science (M Sc); forensic psychology (M Sc); health and social care management and policy (M Sc); human nutrition (M Sc); human resource management (MA); human rights and international conflict (MA); information technology (M Sc); intelligence and security studies (M Sc); international oil, gas and energy law (LL M); international relations (MA); interpreting (MA); learning and teaching in higher education (MA); legal practice (LL M); media and entertainment law (LL M); organizational and consumer psychology (M Sc); psychological therapy (M Sc); psychology of mental health (M Sc); public health (M Sc); public policy and management (MPA); security studies (M Sc); social work (M Sc); spatial planning and urban design (MA); sports therapy (M Sc); supporting older children and young people with dyslexia (MA); teaching languages (MA), including Arabic, English; translation (MA); woman and child abuse (MA).

Loyola University Chicago, Graduate School, Program in Public Policy, Chicago, IL 60660. Offers MPP. *Program availability:* Part-time, evening/weekend. *Faculty:* 2 full-time (both women), 3 part-time/adjunct (1 woman). *Students:* 13 full-time (8 women), 5 part-time (3 women); includes 9 minority (7 Black or African American, non-Hispanic/Latino; 2 Hispanic/Latino). Average age 27. 39 applicants, 67% accepted, 7 enrolled. In 2017, 11 master's awarded. *Degree requirements:* For master's, internship or capstone experience. *Entrance requirements:* For master's, GRE, three letters of recommendation, transcripts, statement of purpose. Additional exam requirements/recommendations for international students: Required—TOEFL (minimum score 550 paper-based). *Application deadline:* For fall admission, 6/30 for domestic students. Applications are processed on a rolling basis. Application fee: $0. Electronic applications accepted. *Expenses:* $1,033 per credit hour tuition, $432 pere semester mandatory fees. *Financial support:* In 2017–18, 5 students received support, including 5 fellowships (averaging $5,000 per year), 1 research assistantship with partial tuition reimbursement available (averaging $12,000 per year); unspecified assistantships and Fulbright scholarships also available. Financial award application deadline: 2/15; financial award applicants required to submit FAFSA. *Faculty research:* Urban public policy. *Unit head:* Dr. Annette Steinacker, Director, 773-508-3396. *Application contact:* Jill Schur, Director, Graduate Enrollment Management, 312-915-8902, E-mail: gradinfo@luc.edu.

McMaster University, School of Graduate Studies, Faculty of Social Sciences, Department of Political Science, Hamilton, ON L8S 4M2, Canada. Offers international relations (PhD); political science (MA); public and the global economy (MA); public policy (PhD); public policy and administration (MA). MA program in public policy and administration offered jointly with University of Guelph. *Program availability:* Part-time. *Degree requirements:* For master's, thesis or alternative. *Entrance requirements:* For master's, minimum B+ average. Additional exam requirements/recommendations for international students: Required—TOEFL (minimum score 580 paper-based). *Faculty research:* Organizational theory, internationalization of public policy, water resource policies, political interest intermediation, comparative politics.

Mills College, Graduate Studies, Joint MBA/MPP Program, Oakland, CA 94613-1000. Offers MBA/MPP. *Faculty:* 5 full-time (3 women), 14 part-time/adjunct (10 women). *Students:* 16 full-time (13 women), 4 part-time (all women); includes 10 minority (5 Black or African American, non-Hispanic/Latino; 4 Hispanic/Latino; 1 Two or more races, non-Hispanic/Latino). Average age 34. 13 applicants, 69% accepted, 6 enrolled. *Entrance requirements:* Additional exam requirements/recommendations for international students: Required—TOEFL (minimum score 550 paper-based; 80 iBT) or IELTS (minimum score 6). *Application deadline:* For winter admission, 2/1 priority date for domestic students, 12/15 priority date for international students. Application fee: $50. Electronic applications accepted. *Expenses:* Contact institution. *Financial support:* In 2017–18, 19 students received support, including 19 fellowships (averaging $8,957 per year). Financial award application deadline: 2/1; financial award applicants required to submit FAFSA. *Faculty research:* Diversity and inclusion, applied econometrics, non-profit management, business communication and effective public speaking, social media, Internet marketing, organizational and cultural chance, economics of the family, urbanization and land conservation, gender and science, comparative race and ethnic relations. *Unit head:* Dr. Lorien Rice, Professor of Public Policy, 510-430-3113, Fax: 510-430-2159, E-mail: lrice@mills.edu. *Application contact:* Robynne Lofton, Director of Admissions, 510-430-3295, Fax: 510-430-2159, E-mail: grad-admission@mills.edu.
Website: http://www.mills.edu/academics/graduate/ppol/program/joint_MPPMBA.php

Mills College, Graduate Studies, Program in Public Policy, Oakland, CA 94613-1000. Offers MPP. *Faculty:* 1 full-time (0 women), 7 part-time/adjunct (6 women). *Students:* 25 full-time (20 women), 4 part-time (all women); includes 13 minority (4 Black or African American, non-Hispanic/Latino; 1 American Indian or Alaska Native, non-Hispanic/Latino; 6 Hispanic/Latino; 2 Two or more races, non-Hispanic/Latino), 1 international. Average age 32. 39 applicants, 79% accepted, 16 enrolled. In 2017, 14 master's awarded. *Degree requirements:* For master's, thesis. *Entrance requirements:* For master's, GRE, SAT, or ACT, statement of purpose, resume. Additional exam requirements/recommendations for international students: Required—TOEFL (minimum score 550 paper-based; 80 iBT) or IELTS (minimum score 6). *Application deadline:* For fall admission, 1/15 for domestic students, 12/15 for international students. Applications are processed on a rolling basis. Application fee: $50. Electronic applications accepted. *Expenses:* Contact institution. *Financial support:* In 2017–18, 29 students received support, including 29 fellowships with tuition reimbursements available (averaging $7,580 per year); teaching assistantships with tuition reimbursements available and scholarships/grants also available. Financial award application deadline: 2/1; financial award applicants required to submit FAFSA. *Faculty research:* Organizational culture and change, economics of the family, urbanization and land conservation, gender and science, comparative race and ethnic relations. *Unit head:* Dr. Mark Henderson, Associate Professor of Public Policy, 510-430-3169, E-mail: mhenderson@mills.edu. *Application contact:* Robynne Lofton, Director of Admissions, 510-430-3295, Fax: 510-430-2159, E-mail: grad-admission@mills.edu.
Website: http://www.mills.edu/publicpolicy

Mississippi State University, College of Arts and Sciences, Department of Political Science and Public Administration, Mississippi State, MS 39762. Offers political science (MA); public policy and administration (MPPA, PhD). *Accreditation:* NASPAA (one or more programs are accredited). *Program availability:* Evening/weekend, blended/hybrid learning. *Faculty:* 15 full-time (6 women). *Students:* 30 full-time (14 women), 31 part-time (18 women); includes 24 minority (21 Black or African American, non-Hispanic/Latino; 1 American Indian or Alaska Native, non-Hispanic/Latino; 2 Hispanic/Latino), 3 international. Average age 32. 54 applicants, 87% accepted, 33 enrolled. In 2017, 13 master's, 7 doctorates awarded. *Degree requirements:* For master's, thesis optional, comprehensive oral or written exam; for doctorate, thesis/dissertation, comprehensive oral and written exam. *Entrance requirements:* For master's, GRE, minimum GPA of 3.0 on the last two years of undergraduate courses or graduate work; for doctorate, GRE General Test, minimum graduate GPA of 3.35. Additional exam requirements/recommendations for international students: Required—TOEFL (minimum score 600 paper-based; 100 iBT); Recommended—IELTS (minimum score 7.5). *Application deadline:* For fall admission, 8/1 priority date for domestic students, 5/1 for international students; for spring admission, 12/1 priority date for domestic students, 9/1 for international students. Applications are processed on a rolling basis. Application fee: $60 ($80 for international students). Electronic applications accepted. *Expenses:* Tuition, state resident: full-time $8318; part-time $462.12 per credit hour. Tuition, nonresident: full-time $22,358; part-time $1242.12 per credit hour. *Required fees:* $110; $12.24 per credit hour. $6.12 per semester. *Financial support:* In 2017–18, 8 teaching assistantships with full tuition reimbursements (averaging $10,469 per year) were awarded; Federal Work-Study, institutionally sponsored loans, scholarships/grants, and unspecified assistantships also available. Financial award application deadline: 4/1; financial award applicants required to submit FAFSA. *Faculty research:* American politics, international relations, state and local government, comparative government, public administration. *Total annual research expenditures:* $811,000. *Unit head:* Dr. P. Edward French, Professor and Head, 662-325-2711, Fax: 662-325-2716, E-mail: efrench@pspa.msstate.edu. *Application contact:* Nathan Drake, Admissions and Enrollment Assistant, 662-325-3804, E-mail: ndrake@grad.msstate.edu.
Website: http://www.pspa.msstate.edu/

Morehead State University, Graduate Programs, College of Business and Public Affairs, School of Public Affairs, Morehead, KY 40351. Offers public policy (MPA). *Accreditation:* NASPAA. *Program availability:* Part-time, evening/weekend. *Degree requirements:* For master's, comprehensive exam, thesis. *Entrance requirements:* For master's, GRE, thesis (two-page paper to be used as writing sample on personal, education or career goals). Additional exam requirements/recommendations for international students: Required—TOEFL (minimum score 500 paper-based). Electronic applications accepted.

National Louis University, College of Arts and Sciences, Chicago, IL 60603. Offers adult education (Ed D); counseling and human services (MS); language and academic development (M Ed, Certificate); psychology (MA, PhD, Certificate); public policy (MA); written communication (MS, Certificate). *Program availability:* Part-time, evening/weekend, online learning. *Degree requirements:* For master's and Certificate, comprehensive exam (for some programs), thesis (for some programs); for doctorate, thesis/dissertation. *Entrance requirements:* For master's, MAT or GRE, 3 professional or academic references, interview, minimum GPA of 3.0; for doctorate, GRE General Test, MAT, or Watson-Glaser Critical Thinking Appraisal, three professional or academic references, statement of academic and professional goals, 3 years of experience in field, interview, master's degree, resume, writing sample; for Certificate, GRE, MAT, or Watson-Glaser Critical Thinking Appraisal, three professional or academic references, statement of academic and professional goals, interview, minimum GPA of 3.0. Additional exam requirements/recommendations for international students: Required—Department of Language Studies Assessment or TOEFL (minimum score 550 paper-based; 79 iBT). Electronic applications accepted.

New England College, Program in Public Policy, Henniker, NH 03242-3293. Offers MA. *Program availability:* Part-time, evening/weekend, online learning. *Degree requirements:* For master's, thesis. *Entrance requirements:* Additional exam requirements/recommendations for international students: Recommended—TOEFL (minimum score 600 paper-based). Electronic applications accepted.

The New School, Schools of Public Engagement, Program in Public and Urban Policy, New York, NY 10011. Offers public and urban policy (PhD). *Accreditation:* NASPAA. *Program availability:* Part-time, evening/weekend. *Faculty:* 22 full-time (11 women), 4 part-time/adjunct (3 women). *Students:* 39 full-time (25 women), 32 part-time (19 women); includes 31 minority (15 Black or African American, non-Hispanic/Latino; 4 Asian, non-Hispanic/Latino; 10 Hispanic/Latino; 2 Two or more races, non-Hispanic/Latino), 19 international. Average age 37. 74 applicants, 38% accepted, 8 enrolled. In 2017, 1 doctorate awarded. Terminal master's awarded for partial completion of doctoral program. *Degree requirements:* For master's, thesis; for doctorate, comprehensive exam, thesis/dissertation. *Entrance requirements:* For master's, transcripts, recommendation letters, resume, statement of goals and purpose; for doctorate, transcripts, recommendation letters, resume, statement of goals and purpose, example of scholarly work. Additional exam requirements/recommendations for international students: Required—TOEFL (minimum score 92 iBT), IELTS (minimum score 7), PTE (minimum score 68). *Application deadline:* For fall admission, 1/15 priority date for domestic and international students. Applications are processed on a rolling basis. Application fee: $50. Electronic applications accepted. *Expenses:* $1,650 per credit. *Financial support:* In 2017–18, 41 students received support, including 4 teaching assistantships (averaging $4,335 per year); career-related internships or fieldwork, Federal Work-Study, scholarships/grants, and unspecified assistantships also available. Support available to part-time students. Financial award application deadline: 2/1; financial award applicants required to submit FAFSA. *Unit head:* Darrick Hamilton, Director, 212-229-5400 Ext. 1503, E-mail: hamiltod@newschool.edu. *Application contact:* Gabriela Garcia Juarez, Assistant Director, Graduate Admission, 212-229-5600 Ext. 1666, E-mail: garciajg@newschool.edu.
Website: https://www.newschool.edu/public-engagement/ms-public-urban-policy/

New York University, Wagner Graduate School of Public Service, Executive Master of Public Administration Program, New York, NY 10012. Offers global public policy and management (EMPA); MSW/EMPA. EMPA in global public policy and management offered jointly with University College London. *Accreditation:* AACSB. *Program availability:* Part-time. *Students:* Average age 38. 94 applicants, 74% accepted, 46 enrolled. In 2017, 45 master's awarded. *Entrance requirements:* Additional exam requirements/recommendations for international students: Required—TOEFL (minimum score 100 iBT), IELTS (minimum score 7.5), TWE. *Application deadline:* For fall

admission, 5/1 for domestic and international students. Application fee: $85. Electronic applications accepted. *Expenses:* Contact institution. *Financial support:* In 2017–18, 5 students received support, including 10 fellowships with partial tuition reimbursements available (averaging $22,046 per year); scholarships/grants and health care benefits also available. Support available to part-time students. Financial award application deadline: 5/1; financial award applicants required to submit FAFSA. *Unit head:* David Elcott, Director, 212-992-9894, Fax: 212-995-4164, E-mail: david.elcott@nyu.edu. *Application contact:* Jay Esposito, Associate Director of Admissions, 212-998-7414, Fax: 212-995-4611, E-mail: wagner.admissions@nyu.edu.
Website: http://wagner.nyu.edu/executivempa

Northeastern University, College of Engineering, Boston, MA 02115-5096. Offers bioengineering (MS, PhD); chemical engineering (MS, PhD); civil engineering (MS, PhD); computer engineering (PhD); computer systems engineering (MS); electrical and computer engineering (MS); electrical and computer engineering leadership (MS); electrical engineering (PhD); energy systems (MS); engineering and public policy (MS); engineering management (MS, Certificate); environmental engineering (MS); industrial engineering (MS, PhD); information assurance (PhD); information systems (MS); interdisciplinary engineering (PhD); mechanical engineering (PhD); operations research (MS); telecommunication systems management (MS). *Program availability:* Part-time, online learning. *Faculty:* 225 full-time. *Students:* 3,720. In 2017, 851 master's, 74 doctorates awarded. Application fee: $75. Electronic applications accepted. *Expenses:* Contact institution. *Financial support:* Fellowships, research assistantships, teaching assistantships, career-related internships or fieldwork, scholarships/grants, health care benefits, tuition waivers, and unspecified assistantships available. Support available to part-time students. Financial award applicants required to submit FAFSA. *Unit head:* Dr. Nadine Aubry, Dean, College of Engineering, 617-373-5847, E-mail: n.aubry@neu.edu. *Application contact:* Jeffery Hengel, Director of Graduate Admissions, 617-373-2711, E-mail: j.hengel@northeastern.edu.
Website: http://www.coe.neu.edu/

Northeastern University, College of Social Sciences and Humanities, Boston, MA 02115. Offers criminology and criminal justice (MSCJ); criminology and justice policy (PhD); economics (MA, PhD); English (MA, PhD); international affairs (MA); law and public policy (PhD); political science (MA, PhD); public administration (MPA); public policy (MPP); security and resilience studies (MS); sociology (MA, PhD); urban and regional policy (MS); urban informatics (MS); world history (MA, PhD). *Program availability:* Online learning. *Faculty:* 242. *Students:* 491. In 2017, 143 master's, 38 doctorates awarded. *Degree requirements:* For doctorate, variable foreign language requirement, comprehensive exam, thesis/dissertation. *Entrance requirements:* For master's and doctorate, GRE. Additional exam requirements/recommendations for international students: Required—TOEFL, IELTS. Application fee: $75. Electronic applications accepted. *Expenses:* Contact institution. *Financial support:* Teaching assistantships, career-related internships or fieldwork, scholarships/grants, health care benefits, tuition waivers (full and partial), and unspecified assistantships available. Support available to part-time students. Financial award applicants required to submit FAFSA. *Unit head:* Dr. Uta Poiger, Dean, 617-373-5173, E-mail: college_of_social_sciences_and_humanities@neu.edu. *Application contact:* 617-373-5990, E-mail: gradcssh@northeastern.edu.
Website: http://www.northeastern.edu/cssh/

Northwestern University, The Graduate School, School of Education and Social Policy, Program in Human Development and Social Policy, Evanston, IL 60208. Offers PhD. Admissions and degrees offered through The Graduate School. *Degree requirements:* For doctorate, comprehensive exam, thesis/dissertation. *Entrance requirements:* For doctorate, GRE General Test. Additional exam requirements/recommendations for international students: Required—TOEFL (minimum score 600 paper-based; 100 iBT). Electronic applications accepted. *Faculty research:* Individual development and the personal narrative; the life course and culture; development, intervention and culture; the life course and policy; analysis of policy effects on lives.

Northwestern University, School of Professional Studies, Program in Public Policy and Administration, Evanston, IL 60208. Offers global policy (MA); health services policy (MA); public administration (MA); public policy (MA). *Program availability:* Part-time, evening/weekend, online learning.
Website: https://sps.northwestern.edu/masters/public-policy/index.php

Norwich University, College of Graduate and Continuing Studies, Master of Public Administration Program, Northfield, VT 05663. Offers criminal justice and public safety (MPA); fiscal management (MPA); international development and influence (MPA); municipal governance (MPA); nonprofit management (MPA); policy analysis and analytics (MPA); public administration leadership and crisis management (MPA); public works and sustainability (MPA). *Program availability:* Evening/weekend, online only, mostly all online with a week-long residency requirement. *Degree requirements:* For master's, capstone. *Entrance requirements:* For master's, minimum undergraduate GPA of 2.75. Additional exam requirements/recommendations for international students: Required—TOEFL (minimum score 550 paper-based; 80 iBT), IELTS (minimum score 6.5). Electronic applications accepted. *Expenses:* Contact institution.

The Ohio State University, Graduate School, John Glenn College of Public Affairs, Columbus, OH 43210. Offers public administration (MA, MPA); public policy and management (PhD). *Accreditation:* NASPAA (one or more programs are accredited). *Program availability:* Part-time. *Faculty:* 21. *Students:* 136 full-time (71 women), 37 part-time (25 women). Average age 30. In 2017, 77 master's, 4 doctorates awarded. *Degree requirements:* For doctorate, thesis/dissertation. *Entrance requirements:* For master's, GRE General Test (for MPA), minimum GPA of 3.0 (for MA); for doctorate, GRE General Test. Additional exam requirements/recommendations for international students: Required—TOEFL (minimum score 600 paper-based; 100 iBT); Recommended—IELTS (minimum score 7.5). *Application deadline:* For fall admission, 12/1 priority date for domestic students, 11/30 priority date for international students; for spring admission, 11/15 for domestic and international students; for summer admission, 4/1 for domestic and international students. Applications are processed on a rolling basis. Application fee: $60 ($70 for international students). Electronic applications accepted. *Financial support:* Fellowships, research assistantships, teaching assistantships, Federal Work-Study, institutionally sponsored loans, and unspecified assistantships available. Support available to part-time students. *Unit head:* Dr. Trevor Brown, Dean, 614-292-4533, Fax: 614-292-4868, E-mail: brown.2296@osu.edu. *Application contact:* Graduate and Professional Admissions, 614-292-6031, Fax: 614-292-3656, E-mail: gpadmissions@osu.edu.
Website: http://glenn.osu.edu/

Oregon State University, College of Liberal Arts, Program in Public Policy, Corvallis, OR 97331. Offers energy policy (MPP, PhD); environmental policy (MPP, PhD); international policy (MPP, PhD); law, crime and policy (MPP, PhD); rural policy (MPP, PhD); science and technology policy (MPP, PhD); social policy (MPP, PhD). *Accreditation:* NASPAA. *Program availability:* Part-time, 100% online. *Entrance requirements:* For master's and doctorate, GRE. Additional exam requirements/recommendations for international students: Required—TOEFL, IELTS (minimum score 6.5). *Application deadline:* For fall admission, 8/1 for domestic students, 4/1 for international students; for winter admission, 12/1 for domestic students, 7/1 for

international students; for spring admission, 2/1 for domestic students, 10/1 for international students; for summer admission, 5/1 for domestic students, 1/1 for international students. Application fee: $75 ($85 for international students). *Financial support:* Application deadline: 1/15. *Unit head:* Brent Steel, Public Policy Advisor, 541-737-6133, E-mail: bsteel@oregonstate.edu. *Application contact:* Dr. Brent Steel, Professor and Director, Public Policy Graduate Program, 541-737-6133, E-mail: schoolofpublicpolicy@oregonstate.edu.
Website: http://oregonstate.edu/cla/spp/

Pepperdine University, School of Public Policy, Malibu, CA 90263. Offers American politics (MPP); economics (MPP); international relations (MPP); state and local policy (MPP); JD/MPP; MBA/MPP; MDR/MPP. *Students:* Average age 25. 174 applicants, 55% accepted, 29 enrolled. In 2017, 34 master's awarded. *Entrance requirements:* For master's, GRE or GMAT, 2 letters of recommendation, resume, two essays. Additional exam requirements/recommendations for international students: Required—TOEFL. *Application deadline:* For fall admission, 6/15 for domestic students. Applications are processed on a rolling basis. Application fee: $50. Electronic applications accepted. *Expenses:* Contact institution. *Financial support:* Institutionally sponsored loans and scholarships/grants available. Financial award application deadline: 5/1; financial award applicants required to submit FAFSA. *Unit head:* Dr. Pete Peterson, Dean, School of Public Policy, 310-506-7490, Fax: 310-506-7494, E-mail: pete.n.peterson@pepperdine.edu. *Application contact:* Carson Bruno, Assistant Dean for Admission and Program Relations, 310-506-7493, E-mail: carson.bruno@pepperdine.edu.
Website: http://publicpolicy.pepperdine.edu/

Portland State University, Graduate Studies, College of Urban and Public Affairs, Hatfield School of Government, Division of Public Administration, Portland, OR 97207-0751. Offers collaborative governance (Certificate); energy policy and management (Certificate); global management and leadership (MPA); health administration (MPA); human resource management (MPA); local government (MPA); natural resource policy and administration (MPA); nonprofit and public management (Certificate); nonprofit management (MPA); public administration (EMPA); public affairs and policy (PhD); sustainable food systems (Certificate). *Accreditation:* NASPAA (one or more programs are accredited). *Program availability:* Part-time, evening/weekend. *Faculty:* 15 full-time (6 women), 6 part-time/adjunct (4 women). *Students:* 84 full-time (54 women), 109 part-time (75 women); includes 40 minority (8 Black or African American, non-Hispanic/Latino; 5 American Indian or Alaska Native, non-Hispanic/Latino; 8 Asian, non-Hispanic/Latino; 12 Hispanic/Latino; 1 Native Hawaiian or other Pacific Islander, non-Hispanic/Latino; 6 Two or more races, non-Hispanic/Latino), 14 international. Average age 35. 118 applicants, 84% accepted, 56 enrolled. In 2017, 60 master's, 1 doctorate awarded. *Degree requirements:* For master's, integrative field experience (MPA), practicum (MPH); for doctorate, comprehensive exam, thesis/dissertation. *Entrance requirements:* For master's, GRE (minimum scores: verbal 150, quantitative 149, and analytic writing 4.5), minimum GPA of 3.0, 3 recommendation letters, resume, 500-word statement of intent; for doctorate, GRE, 3 recommendation letters, resume, 500-word personal essay. Additional exam requirements/recommendations for international students: Required—TOEFL (minimum score 550 paper-based; 80 iBT), IELTS (minimum score 7). *Application deadline:* For fall admission, 4/1 for domestic students, 3/1 for international students; for winter admission, 9/1 for domestic students, 8/1 for international students; for spring admission, 11/1 for domestic and international students. Application fee: $65. *Expenses:* Tuition, state resident: full-time $14,436; part-time $401 per credit. Tuition, nonresident: full-time $21,780; part-time $605 per credit. *Required fees:* $1380; $22 per credit. $119 per quarter. One-time fee: $325. Tuition and fees vary according to program. *Financial support:* In 2017–18, 39 students received support, including 5 research assistantships with full and partial tuition reimbursements available (averaging $8,341 per year), 4 teaching assistantships (averaging $5,292 per year); career-related internships or fieldwork, Federal Work-Study, scholarships/grants, and unspecified assistantships also available. Support available to part-time students. Financial award application deadline: 3/1; financial award applicants required to submit FAFSA. *Faculty research:* Public budgeting, program evaluation, nonprofit management, natural resources policy and administration. *Total annual research expenditures:* $679,077. *Unit head:* Dr. Masami Nishishiba, Chair, 503-725-5151, E-mail: nishism@pdx.edu. *Application contact:* Megan Heljeson, Office Coordinator, 503-725-3921, Fax: 503-725-8250, E-mail: publicad@pdx.edu.
Website: https://www.pdx.edu/hatfieldschool/public-administration

Princeton University, Graduate School, Woodrow Wilson School of Public and International Affairs, Princeton, NJ 08544-1019. Offers public affairs (MPA, PhD); public policy (MPP); JD/MPA. JD/MPA offered jointly with Columbia University, New York University, Stanford University. Terminal master's awarded for partial completion of doctoral program. *Degree requirements:* For master's, internship; for doctorate, one foreign language, thesis/dissertation. *Entrance requirements:* For master's, GRE General Test, original policy memo; for doctorate, GRE General Test. Additional exam requirements/recommendations for international students: Required—TOEFL (minimum score 600 paper-based). Electronic applications accepted.

Queen's University at Kingston, School of Graduate Studies, School of Policy Studies, Kingston, ON K7L 3N6, Canada. Offers MIR, MPA. *Program availability:* Part-time. *Entrance requirements:* For master's, minimum B+ average. Additional exam requirements/recommendations for international students: Required—TOEFL. *Faculty research:* Public management, social policy, defense management, health policy, the third sector.

Regent University, Graduate School, Robertson School of Government, Virginia Beach, VA 23464. Offers government (MA), including American government, healthcare policy and ethics (MA, MPA), international relations, law and public policy, national security studies, political communication, political theory, religion and politics; national security studies (MA), including cybersecurity, homeland security, international security, Middle East politics; public administration (MPA), including emergency management and homeland security, federal government, general public administration, healthcare policy and ethics (MA, MPA), law, nonprofit administration and faith-based organizations, public leadership and management, servant leadership. *Program availability:* Part-time, evening/weekend, 100% online, blended/hybrid learning. *Faculty:* 8 full-time (1 woman), 20 part-time/adjunct (3 women). *Students:* 39 full-time (23 women), 137 part-time (78 women); includes 83 minority (49 Black or African American, non-Hispanic/Latino; 1 American Indian or Alaska Native, non-Hispanic/Latino; 7 Asian, non-Hispanic/Latino; 15 Hispanic/Latino; 11 Two or more races, non-Hispanic/Latino). Average age 35. 345 applicants, 31% accepted, 57 enrolled. In 2017, 38 master's awarded. *Degree requirements:* For master's, thesis optional, internship. *Entrance requirements:* For master's, GRE General Test or LSAT, personal essay, writing sample, resume, college transcripts. Additional exam requirements/recommendations for international students: Required—TOEFL (minimum score 577 paper-based). *Application deadline:* For fall admission, 5/1 priority date for domestic students; for spring admission, 11/1 priority date for domestic students. Applications are processed on a rolling basis. Application fee: $50. Electronic applications accepted. *Expenses:* $650 per credit; $300 technology fee per semester. *Financial support:* In 2017–18, 116 students received support. Career-related internships or fieldwork, scholarships/grants,

and unspecified assistantships available. Support available to part-time students. *Faculty research:* International relations and politics, public administration, leadership and ethics, Biblical law, Constitutional law and Supreme Court. *Unit head:* Dr. Eric Patterson, Dean, 757-352-4616, Fax: 757-352-4735, E-mail: epatterson@regent.edu. *Application contact:* Heidi Cece, Assistant Vice President of Enrollment Management, 800-373-5504, Fax: 757-352-4381, E-mail: admissions@regent.edu.
Website: https://www.regent.edu/robertson-school-of-government/

Rochester Institute of Technology, Graduate Enrollment Services, College of Liberal Arts, Department of Public Policy, MS Program in Science, Technology and Public Policy, Rochester, NY 14623. Offers MS. *Program availability:* Part-time. *Students:* 8 full-time (5 women), 2 part-time (1 woman). Average age 24. 11 applicants, 64% accepted, 5 enrolled. In 2017, 4 master's awarded. *Degree requirements:* For master's, thesis. *Entrance requirements:* For master's, GRE, minimum GPA of 3.0 (recommended). Additional exam requirements/recommendations for international students: Required—TOEFL (minimum score 570 paper-based; 88 iBT), IELTS (minimum score 6.5), PTE (minimum score 61). *Application deadline:* For fall admission, 2/15 priority date for domestic and international students; for spring admission, 12/15 priority date for domestic and international students. Applications are processed on a rolling basis. Application fee: $65. Electronic applications accepted. *Expenses:* $1,815 per credit hour. *Financial support:* In 2017–18, 14 students received support. Research assistantships with partial tuition reimbursements available, teaching assistantships with partial tuition reimbursements available, career-related internships or fieldwork, scholarships/grants, and unspecified assistantships available. Support available to part-time students. Financial award applicants required to submit FAFSA. *Faculty research:* Environmental management, innovation, and policy; technological innovation, environmental economics and policy; alternative energy and climate change; cybersecurity economics and Internet policy; e-democracy and digital government. *Unit head:* Dr. Franz Foltz, Graduate Program Director, 585-475-5368, E-mail: fafgsh@rit.edu. *Application contact:* Diane Ellison, Senior Associate Vice President, Graduate Enrollment Services, 585-475-2229, Fax: 585-475-7164, E-mail: gradinfo@rit.edu.
Website: http://www.rit.edu/cla/publicpolicy/academics/science-technology-and-public-policy-ms

Rutgers University–Camden, Graduate School of Arts and Sciences, Department of Public Policy and Administration, Camden, NJ 08102. Offers education policy and leadership (MPA); international public service and development (MPA); public management (MPA); JD/MPA; MPA/MA. *Accreditation:* NASPAA. *Program availability:* Part-time, evening/weekend. *Degree requirements:* For master's, directed study, research workshop, 42 credits. *Entrance requirements:* For master's, GRE General Test, GMAT or LSAT, 3 letters of recommendation; resume. Additional exam requirements/recommendations for international students: Required—TOEFL (minimum score 550 paper-based), IELTS. Electronic applications accepted. *Faculty research:* Nonprofit management, county and municipal administration, health and human services, government communication, administrative law, educational finance.

Rutgers University–Newark, Graduate School, Program in Public Administration, Newark, NJ 07102. Offers health care administration (MPA); human resources administration (MPA); public administration (PhD); public management (MPA); public policy analysis (MPA); urban systems and issues (MPA). *Accreditation:* NASPAA (one or more programs are accredited). *Program availability:* Part-time, evening/weekend. *Degree requirements:* For master's, comprehensive exam, thesis or alternative; for doctorate, thesis/dissertation. *Entrance requirements:* For master's, GRE, minimum undergraduate B average; for doctorate, GRE, MPA, minimum B average. Electronic applications accepted. *Faculty research:* Government finance, municipal and state government, public productivity.

Rutgers University–Newark, School of Public Health, Newark, NJ 07107-1709. Offers clinical epidemiology (Certificate); dental public health (MPH); general public health (Certificate); public policy and oral health services administration (Certificate); quantitative methods (MPH); urban health (MPH); DMD/MPH; MD/MPH; MS/MPH. *Program availability:* Part-time, evening/weekend. *Degree requirements:* For master's, thesis, internship. *Entrance requirements:* For master's, GRE General Test. Additional exam requirements/recommendations for international students: Required—TOEFL. Electronic applications accepted.

Rutgers University–New Brunswick, Edward J. Bloustein School of Planning and Public Policy, Doctoral Program in Planning and Public Policy, New Brunswick, NJ 08901. Offers PhD. *Program availability:* Part-time. *Degree requirements:* For doctorate, comprehensive exam, thesis/dissertation. *Entrance requirements:* For doctorate, GRE, master's degree. Additional exam requirements/recommendations for international students: Required—TOEFL (minimum score 575 paper-based; 88 iBT). Electronic applications accepted. *Faculty research:* Housing and community development, land use and transportation, politics and policy analysis, urban and regional economics, international development.

Rutgers University–New Brunswick, Edward J. Bloustein School of Planning and Public Policy, Program in Public Policy, New Brunswick, NJ 08901. Offers MPAP, MPP, JD/MPAP, MBA/MPP, MCRP/MPP. JD/MPAP offered jointly with Rutgers, The State University of New Jersey, Camden. *Accreditation:* NASPAA. *Program availability:* Part-time, evening/weekend. *Entrance requirements:* For master's, GRE General Test. Additional exam requirements/recommendations for international students: Required—TOEFL (minimum score 575 paper-based; 88 iBT). Electronic applications accepted. *Faculty research:* Environment, social and health policy, public opinion, economics, education policy, community development.

San Francisco State University, Division of Graduate Studies, College of Health and Social Sciences, Public Administration Program, San Francisco, CA 94132-1722. Offers criminal justice administration (MPA); environmental administration and policy (MPA); gerontology (MPA); nonprofit administration (MPA); public management (MPA); public policy (MPA); urban administration (MPA). *Accreditation:* NASPAA. *Unit head:* Dr. Jennifer Shea, Graduate Coordinator, 415-817-4462, Fax: 415-817-4464, E-mail: jshea@sfsu.edu.
Website: http://mpa.sfsu.edu/

Seton Hall University, College of Arts and Sciences, Department of Political Science and Public Affairs, South Orange, NJ 07079-2697. Offers nonprofit organization management (Graduate Certificate); public administration (MPA), including health policy and management, nonprofit organization management, public service: leadership, governance, and policy. *Accreditation:* CAHME; NASPAA. *Program availability:* Part-time, evening/weekend. *Degree requirements:* For master's, thesis or alternative, internship or practicum. *Entrance requirements:* Additional exam requirements/recommendations for international students: Required—TOEFL. Electronic applications accepted.

Simmons College, College of Arts and Sciences, Boston, MA 02115. Offers English (MA); gender/cultural studies (MA); history (MA); public health (MPH); public policy (MPP). *Program availability:* Part-time. *Faculty:* 19 full-time (13 women), 2 part-time/adjunct (both women). *Students:* 4 full-time (3 women), 39 part-time (34 women); includes 11 minority (7 Black or African American, non-Hispanic/Latino; 1 Hispanic/Latino; 3 Two or more races, non-Hispanic/Latino). Average age 26. 99 applicants, 57% accepted, 27 enrolled. In 2017, 23 master's awarded. Terminal master's awarded for partial completion of doctoral program. *Degree requirements:* For master's, thesis optional. *Entrance requirements:* For master's, GRE, bachelor's degree from accredited college or university; minimum B average (preferred). Additional exam requirements/recommendations for international students: Required—TOEFL (minimum score 600 paper-based; 100 iBT). *Application deadline:* For fall admission, 8/1 for domestic and international students; for spring admission, 12/15 for domestic and international students; for summer admission, 5/1 for domestic and international students. Applications are processed on a rolling basis. Application fee: $35. Electronic applications accepted. *Expenses:* $1,052 per credit, $55 activity fee per semester. *Financial support:* In 2017–18, 4 fellowships with partial tuition reimbursements, 22 teaching assistantships with partial tuition reimbursements were awarded; scholarships/grants and unspecified assistantships also available. Support available to part-time students. Financial award applicants required to submit FAFSA. *Faculty research:* Film and media studies, postcolonial literature, critical theory, arts and culture. *Unit head:* Dr. Leanne Doherty, Dean, 617-521-2581, E-mail: leanne.doherty@simmons.edu. *Application contact:* Patricia Flaherty, Director, Graduate Studies Admission, 617-521-3902, Fax: 617-521-3058, E-mail: gsa@simmons.edu.
Website: http://www.simmons.edu/gradstudies/

Simon Fraser University, Office of Graduate Studies and Postdoctoral Fellows, Faculty of Arts and Social Sciences, School of Public Policy, Vancouver, BC V6B 5K3, Canada. Offers MPP. *Degree requirements:* For master's, thesis or alternative, internship. *Entrance requirements:* For master's, GRE (for applicants with non-Canadian degrees), minimum GPA of 3.0 (on scale of 4.33) or 3.33 based on last 60 credits of undergraduate courses. Additional exam requirements/recommendations for international students: Recommended—TOEFL (minimum score 580 paper-based; 93 iBT), IELTS (minimum score 7), TWE (minimum score 5). Electronic applications accepted. *Expenses:* Contact institution. *Faculty research:* Health policy, labor market and immigration, gender and discrimination, taxation policy, environmental policy.

Southern University and Agricultural and Mechanical College, Graduate School, Nelson Mandela School of Public Policy and Urban Affairs, Program in Public Policy, Baton Rouge, LA 70813. Offers PhD. *Degree requirements:* For doctorate, comprehensive exam, thesis/dissertation. *Entrance requirements:* For doctorate, GRE General Test. Additional exam requirements/recommendations for international students: Required—TOEFL (minimum score 525 paper-based).

State University of New York Empire State College, School for Graduate Studies, Program in Social Policy, Saratoga Springs, NY 12866-4391. Offers MA. *Program availability:* Part-time, evening/weekend, online learning. *Degree requirements:* For master's, thesis, exam, final project. *Entrance requirements:* Additional exam requirements/recommendations for international students: Required—TOEFL (minimum score 600 paper-based). Electronic applications accepted. *Faculty research:* Study of culture, society and mass communications, urban culture and policy, social decision-making processes.

Stony Brook University, State University of New York, Graduate School, College of Arts and Sciences, Department of Political Science, Program in Public Policy and Urban Development, Stony Brook, NY 11794. Offers MA. *Students:* 22 full-time (11 women), 14 part-time (3 women); includes 10 minority (4 Black or African American, non-Hispanic/Latino; 3 Asian, non-Hispanic/Latino; 3 Hispanic/Latino), 2 international. 42 applicants, 81% accepted, 23 enrolled. In 2017, 34 master's awarded. *Entrance requirements:* For master's, GRE, three letters of recommendation, statement of purpose. Additional exam requirements/recommendations for international students: Required—TOEFL (minimum score 85 iBT). *Application deadline:* For fall admission, 7/1 for domestic students, 5/15 for international students; for spring admission, 12/5 for domestic students, 10/15 for international students. Application fee: $100. Electronic applications accepted. *Expenses:* Contact institution. *Unit head:* Dr. Matthew Lebo, Chair, 631-632-7554, Fax: 631-632-4116, E-mail: matthew.lebo@stonybrook.edu. *Application contact:* Carri Ann Horner, Graduate Program Coordinator, 631-632-7667, Fax: 631-632-4116, E-mail: carri.horner@stonybrook.edu.

Suffolk University, College of Arts and Sciences, Department of Philosophy, Boston, MA 02108-2770. Offers administration of higher education (M Ed, CAGS); disability services (Certificate); ethics and public policy (MS). *Program availability:* Part-time, evening/weekend. *Faculty:* 4 full-time (0 women), 2 part-time/adjunct (0 women). *Students:* 23 full-time (11 women), 37 part-time (27 women); includes 17 minority (6 Black or African American, non-Hispanic/Latino; 2 Asian, non-Hispanic/Latino; 7 Hispanic/Latino; 2 Two or more races, non-Hispanic/Latino), 2 international. Average age 31. 24 applicants, 75% accepted, 3 enrolled. In 2017, 21 master's awarded. *Degree requirements:* For master's, internship or thesis; practicum (for M Ed). *Entrance requirements:* For master's, GRE General Test, MAT, GMAT, statement of professional goals, official transcripts, 2 letters of recommendation, resume. Additional exam requirements/recommendations for international students: Required—TOEFL (minimum score 550 paper-based; 80 iBT). *Application deadline:* For fall admission, 3/15 priority date for domestic and international students; for spring admission, 10/15 priority date for domestic and international students. Applications are processed on a rolling basis. Application fee: $50. Electronic applications accepted. *Expenses:* $29,520 per year full-time tuition; $1,230 per credit part-time. *Financial support:* In 2017–18, 50 students received support, including 13 fellowships (averaging $5,915 per year); career-related internships or fieldwork, Federal Work-Study, institutionally sponsored loans, and unspecified assistantships also available. Support available to part-time students. Financial award application deadline: 4/1; financial award applicants required to submit FAFSA. *Faculty research:* Predicting competent Head Start preschoolers, cultural differences, school counseling technology, sibling attachment in divorce cases, consequences of ethical breaches by human resource professionals. *Unit head:* Dr. Greg Fried, Chair of Philosophy Department, 617-573-8109, E-mail: gfried@suffolk.edu. *Application contact:* Mara Marzocchi, Associate Director of Graduate Admissions, 617-573-8302, Fax: 617-305-1733, E-mail: grad.admission@suffolk.edu.
Website: http://www.suffolk.edu/college/graduate/69296.php

Trinity College, Graduate Programs, Program in Public Policy, Hartford, CT 06106-3100. Offers health care policy (MA); public policy studies (MA). *Program availability:* Part-time, evening/weekend. *Degree requirements:* For master's, thesis optional, departmental qualifying exam. *Entrance requirements:* For master's, minimum GPA of 3.0, two letters of recommendation, statement of purpose.

Tufts University, The Fletcher School of Law and Diplomacy, Medford, MA 02155. Offers economics and public policy (PhD); international affairs (PhD); international business (MIB); international law (LL M); law and diplomacy (MA, MALD); transatlantic affairs (MA); DVM/MA; JD/MALD; MALD/MA; MALD/MBA; MALD/MS; MD/MA. MA in transatlantic affairs offered jointly with The College of Europe; PhD in economics and public policy with Tufts' Graduate School of Arts and Sciences. *Program availability:* Online learning. *Degree requirements:* For master's, one foreign language, thesis; for doctorate, one foreign language, comprehensive exam, thesis/dissertation, dissertation defense. *Entrance requirements:* For master's and doctorate, GMAT or GRE General Test. Additional exam requirements/recommendations for international students: Required—TOEFL (minimum score 600 paper-based; 100 iBT), IELTS (minimum score

7). Electronic applications accepted. *Expenses:* Contact institution. *Faculty research:* Negotiation and conflict resolution, international organizations, international business and economic law, security studies, development economics.

Tufts University, Graduate School of Arts and Sciences, Department of Urban and Environmental Policy and Planning, Medford, MA 02155. Offers community development (MA); environmental policy (MA); health and human welfare (MA); housing policy (MA); international environment/development policy (MA); public policy (MPP); MA/JD; MA/MBA; MA/MPH; MA/MS; MALD/MA. MALD/MA offered in connection with The Fletcher School of Law and Diplomacy; MA/MPH with School of Medicine; MA/MS with School of Nutrition Science and Policy or School of Engineering; MA/MBA with Boston College, Carroll School of Management; MA/JD with Boston College Law School. *Accreditation:* ACSP (one or more programs are accredited). *Program availability:* Part-time. *Students:* 95 full-time (68 women), 17 part-time (14 women); includes 34 minority (14 Black or African American, non-Hispanic/Latino; 10 Asian, non-Hispanic/Latino; 6 Hispanic/Latino; 4 Two or more races, non-Hispanic/Latino), 14 international. Average age 30. 153 applicants, 78% accepted, 51 enrolled. In 2017, 45 master's awarded. *Degree requirements:* For master's, thesis or alternative, internship. *Entrance requirements:* For master's, GRE General Test. Additional exam requirements/recommendations for international students: Required—TOEFL (minimum score 550 paper-based; 80 iBT), IELTS (minimum score 6.5). *Application deadline:* For fall admission, 1/15 for domestic and international students. Applications are processed on a rolling basis. Application fee: $85. Electronic applications accepted. *Expenses:* Contact institution. *Financial support:* Fellowships, research assistantships, teaching assistantships, career-related internships or fieldwork, Federal Work-Study, scholarships/grants, tuition waivers (full and partial), and unspecified assistantships available. Support available to part-time students. Financial award application deadline: 1/15. *Unit head:* Dr. Mary Davis, Graduate Program Director, 617-627-3394. *Application contact:* Office of Graduate Admissions, 617-627-3395, E-mail: gradadmissions@tufts.edu.
Website: http://ase.tufts.edu/uep/

Union Institute & University, Master of Arts Program, Cincinnati, OH 45206-1925. Offers creativity studies (MA); health and wellness (MA); history and culture (MA); leadership, public policy, and social issues (MA); literature and writing (MA). *Program availability:* Part-time, online only, 100% online. *Students:* 9 full-time (7 women), 70 part-time (56 women); includes 33 minority (22 Black or African American, non-Hispanic/Latino; 1 American Indian or Alaska Native, non-Hispanic/Latino; 6 Hispanic/Latino; 4 Two or more races, non-Hispanic/Latino). Average age 40. *Degree requirements:* For master's, thesis. *Entrance requirements:* For master's, transcript, essay, 3 letters of recommendation, resume. Additional exam requirements/recommendations for international students: Recommended—TOEFL. *Application deadline:* For spring admission, 3/13 for domestic students. Applications are processed on a rolling basis. Application fee: $50. Electronic applications accepted. *Expenses:* Contact institution. *Financial support:* Career-related internships or fieldwork and tuition waivers available. Financial award applicants required to submit FAFSA. *Unit head:* Elden Golden, Director, 513-487-1153, E-mail: elden.golden@myunion.edu. *Application contact:* Director of Admissions, 800-861-6400.

Union Institute & University, PhD Program in Interdisciplinary Studies, Cincinnati, OH 45206-1925. Offers educational studies (PhD), including Martin Luther King studies; ethical and creative leadership (PhD); humanities and culture (PhD); public policy and social change (PhD). Program requires participation in brief on-campus residencies twice each year (January and July). *Program availability:* Part-time, online only, blended/hybrid learning. *Degree requirements:* For doctorate, comprehensive exam, thesis/dissertation. *Entrance requirements:* For doctorate, master's degree, three letters of recommendation, statement of purpose. Additional exam requirements/recommendations for international students: Required—TOEFL. *Application deadline:* Applications are processed on a rolling basis. Application fee: $50. Electronic applications accepted. *Expenses:* Contact institution. *Financial support:* Federal Work-Study and scholarships/grants available. Financial award application deadline: 5/1; financial award applicants required to submit FAFSA. *Faculty research:* Social responsibility, ethical leadership, Martin Luther King studies. *Unit head:* Dr. Michael Raffanti, Dean of Graduate College, 800-641-6400 Ext. 1237, E-mail: michael.raffanti@myunion.edu. *Application contact:* Admissions Counselor, 800-486-3116.
Website: https://myunion.edu/academics/doctoral/

Universidad Autonoma de Guadalajara, Graduate Programs, Guadalajara, Mexico. Offers administrative law and justice (LL M); advertising and corporate communications (MA); architecture (M Arch); business (MBA); computational science (MCC); education (Ed M, Ed D); English-Spanish translation (MA); entrepreneurship and management (MBA); integrated management of digital animation (MA); international business (MIB); international corporate law (LL M); internet technologies (MS); manufacturing systems (MMS); occupational health (MS); philosophy (MA, PhD); power electronics (MS); quality systems (MQS); renewable energy (MS); social evaluation of projects (MBA); strategic market research (MBA); tax law (MA); teaching mathematics (MA).

Universidad del Este, Graduate School, Carolina, PR 00984. Offers accounting (MBA); adult education (M Ed); agribusiness (MBA); criminal justice and criminology (MA); curriculum and instruction - early education (M Ed); curriculum and instruction - elementary (M Ed); curriculum and instruction - English (M Ed); curriculum and instruction - Spanish (M Ed); human resources (MBA); information security management (MBA); information technology and Web business development (MBA); management (MBA); public policy (MPA); social work (MA), including clinical social work; special education (M Ed); strategic leadership (MBA).

Université de Montréal, Faculty of Arts and Sciences, Program in Societies, Public Policies and Health, Montréal, QC H3C 3J7, Canada. Offers DESS.

University at Albany, State University of New York, Nelson A. Rockefeller College of Public Affairs and Policy, Department of Public Administration and Policy, Albany, NY 12222-0001. Offers financial management and public economics (MPA); financial market regulation (MPA); health policy (MPA); healthcare management (MPA); homeland security (MPA); human resources management (MPA); information strategy and management (MPA); local government management (MPA); nonprofit management (MPA); nonprofit management and leadership (Certificate); organizational behavior and theory (MPA, PhD); planning and policy analysis (CAS); policy analysis (MPA); politics and administration (PhD); public finance (PhD); public management (PhD); public policy (PhD); public sector management (Certificate); women and public policy (Certificate); JD/MPA. JD/MPA offered jointly with Albany Law School. *Accreditation:* NASPAA (one or more programs are accredited). *Faculty:* 21 full-time (7 women), 14 part-time/adjunct (7 women). *Students:* 115 full-time (59 women), 93 part-time (56 women); includes 41 minority (11 Black or African American, non-Hispanic/Latino; 9 Asian, non-Hispanic/Latino; 18 Hispanic/Latino; 3 Two or more races, non-Hispanic/Latino), 32 international. 236 applicants, 69% accepted, 86 enrolled. In 2017, 57 master's, 1 doctorate, 14 other advanced degrees awarded. *Degree requirements:* For doctorate, one foreign language, thesis/dissertation. *Entrance requirements:* For doctorate, GRE General Test. Additional exam requirements/recommendations for international students: Required—TOEFL (minimum score 550 paper-based). *Application deadline:* For fall admission, 2/1 priority

date for domestic students, 5/1 for international students; for spring admission, 12/1 for domestic students. Applications are processed on a rolling basis. Application fee: $75. Electronic applications accepted. *Expenses:* Tuition, state resident: full-time $10,870; part-time $453 per credit hour. Tuition, nonresident: full-time $22,210; part-time $925 per credit hour. *Required fees:* $84.68 per credit hour. $508.06 per semester. Part-time tuition and fees vary according to course load and program. *Financial support:* Application deadline: 2/1. *Unit head:* Victor Asal, Chair, 518-591-8729, E-mail: vasal@albany.edu.
Website: http://www.albany.edu/rockefeller/pad.shtml

The University of Arizona, College of Social and Behavioral Sciences, Program in Public Administration, Tucson, AZ 85721. Offers public administration (MPA); public administration and policy (PhD). *Accreditation:* NASPAA. *Degree requirements:* For master's, internship of 400 hours; for doctorate, comprehensive exam, thesis/dissertation. *Entrance requirements:* For doctorate, GMAT or GRE, minimum graduate GPA of 3.5, letter of interest, 3 letters of recommendation, resume. Additional exam requirements/recommendations for international students: Required—TOEFL (minimum score 650 paper-based; 115 iBT). Electronic applications accepted. *Expenses:* Contact institution.

University of Arkansas, Graduate School, Interdisciplinary Program in Public Policy, Fayetteville, AR 72701. Offers PhD. In 2017, 8 doctorates awarded. *Degree requirements:* For doctorate, thesis/dissertation. *Application deadline:* For fall admission, 8/1 for domestic students, 4/1 for international students; for spring admission, 10/1 for international students; for summer admission, 4/15 for domestic students, 3/1 for international students. Applications are processed on a rolling basis. Application fee: $60. Electronic applications accepted. *Expenses:* Tuition, state resident: full-time $3782. Tuition, nonresident: full-time $10,238. *Financial support:* In 2017–18, 10 research assistantships, 1 teaching assistantship were awarded; fellowships with tuition reimbursements also available. Financial award application deadline: 4/1; financial award applicants required to submit FAFSA. *Unit head:* Dr. Brinck Kerr, Director, 479-575-3356, Fax: 479-575-5908, E-mail: jbkerr@uark.edu. *Application contact:* Valerie H. Hunt, Associate Director, 479-575-5865, Fax: 479-575-5908, E-mail: vhunt@uark.edu.
Website: https://policy.uark.edu

The University of British Columbia, Institute of Asian Research, Vancouver, BC V6T 1Z2, Canada. Offers Asia Pacific policy studies (MAAPPS); public policy and global affairs (MPPGA). *Degree requirements:* For master's, thesis optional. *Entrance requirements:* Additional exam requirements/recommendations for international students: Required—TOEFL. Electronic applications accepted. *Expenses:* Contact institution. *Faculty research:* Social cohesion, globalization, social safety nets, policy research, research and development alliances, knowledge-based workshops on Asia-Pacific studies.

University of Calgary, Faculty of Graduate Studies, The School of Public Policy, Calgary, AB T2N 1N4, Canada. Offers MPP. *Program availability:* Part-time. *Degree requirements:* For master's, capstone project. *Entrance requirements:* For master's, minimum GPA of 3.3 in last two years of undergraduate program or over last 60 units; baccalaureate degree; personal statement; current resume/curriculum vitae; official transcripts; two reference letters. Additional exam requirements/recommendations for international students: Required—TOEFL (minimum score 600 paper-based; 105 iBT), IELTS (minimum score 7.5).

University of California, Berkeley, Graduate Division, Graduate School of Public Policy, Program in Public Policy, Berkeley, CA 94720-1500. Offers MPP, PhD. Electronic applications accepted.

University of California, Berkeley, Graduate Division, Haas School of Business, PhD in Business Administration Program, Berkeley, CA 94720-1500. Offers accounting (PhD); business and public policy (PhD); finance (PhD); management of organizations (PhD); marketing (PhD); real estate (PhD). *Accreditation:* AACSB. *Students:* 72 full-time (20 women); includes 30 minority (26 Asian, non-Hispanic/Latino; 4 Hispanic/Latino). Average age 27. *Degree requirements:* For doctorate, comprehensive exam, thesis/dissertation, written preliminary exams, oral qualifying exam. *Entrance requirements:* For doctorate, GMAT or GRE, minimum GPA of 3.0 in undergraduate and graduate coursework. Additional exam requirements/recommendations for international students: Required—TOEFL (minimum score 570 paper-based; 70 iBT), IELTS (minimum score 7). *Application deadline:* For fall admission, 12/1 for domestic and international students. Application fee: $105 ($125 for international students). Electronic applications accepted. *Expenses:* Contact institution. *Financial support:* Fellowships with tuition reimbursements, research assistantships with tuition reimbursements, teaching assistantships with tuition reimbursements, scholarships/grants, health care benefits, tuition waivers (full), unspecified assistantships, and transit passes, travel grants available. Financial award application deadline: 12/1. *Faculty research:* Accounting, business and public policy, entrepreneurship, finance, management of organizations, marketing, operations and information technology management, real estate. *Unit head:* Dr. Nicolae Garleanu, Director, 510-643-6349, Fax: 510-643-4255. *Application contact:* Melissa Hacker, Director, Student Affairs, 510-642-3944, Fax: 510-643-4255, E-mail: melhacker@haas.berkeley.edu.
Website: http://www.haas.berkeley.edu/Phd/

University of California, Los Angeles, Graduate Division, Luskin School of Public Affairs, Program in Public Policy, Los Angeles, CA 90095. Offers MPP. *Accreditation:* NASPAA. *Entrance requirements:* For master's, GRE General Test, minimum GPA of 3.0. Additional exam requirements/recommendations for international students: Required—TOEFL. Electronic applications accepted.

University of California, Riverside, Graduate Division, School of Public Policy, Riverside, CA 92521-0102. Offers global health (MS); public policy (MPP, PhD); MD/MPP. MD/MPP offered in partnership with School of Medicine. *Expenses:* Tuition, state resident: full-time $5746. Tuition, nonresident: full-time $10,780. Tuition and fees vary according to campus/location and program.

University of California, San Diego, Graduate Division, School of Global Policy and Strategy, Master of Public Policy Program, La Jolla, CA 92093. Offers American policy in global context (MPP); business, government and regulation (MPP); energy and environmental policy (MPP); health policy (MPP); program design and evaluation (MPP); security policy (MPP). *Entrance requirements:* For master's, GMAT or GRE General Test. Additional exam requirements/recommendations for international students: Required—TOEFL (minimum score 90 iBT), IELTS (minimum score 7). Electronic applications accepted. *Expenses:* Contact institution.

University of Chicago, Harris School of Public Policy, Master of Arts in Public Policy Program, Chicago, IL 60637. Offers public policy studies (AM). *Program availability:* Part-time, evening/weekend. *Students:* 29 full-time (12 women), 1 part-time (0 women); includes 5 minority (2 Black or African American, non-Hispanic/Latino; 2 Asian, non-Hispanic/Latino; 1 Hispanic/Latino), 20 international. Average age 27. 184 applicants, 60% accepted, 30 enrolled. In 2017, 15 master's awarded. *Entrance requirements:* For master's, GRE General Test, graduate degree; transcripts; resume or curriculum vitae; letters of recommendation. Additional exam requirements/recommendations for international students: Required—TOEFL (minimum score 600 paper-based; 104 iBT),

IELTS (minimum score 7). *Application deadline:* For fall admission, 1/23 priority date for domestic students, 1/23 for international students. Applications are processed on a rolling basis. Application fee: $50. Electronic applications accepted. *Financial support:* Fellowships with partial tuition reimbursements, Federal Work-Study, institutionally sponsored loans, and scholarships/grants available. Financial award application deadline: 4/17. *Unit head:* Katherine Baicker, Dean, E-mail: harrisadmissions@uchicago.edu. *Application contact:* Ranjan Daniels, Director of Admissions, 773-702-8401, E-mail: harrisadmissions@uchicago.edu.
Website: http://harris.uchicago.edu/academics/programs-degrees/degrees/ma-public-policy-ma

University of Chicago, Harris School of Public Policy, Master of Public Policy Program, Chicago, IL 60637. Offers MPP. *Students:* 353 full-time (199 women), 6 part-time (4 women); includes 58 minority (11 Black or African American, non-Hispanic/Latino; 2 American Indian or Alaska Native, non-Hispanic/Latino; 26 Asian, non-Hispanic/Latino; 13 Hispanic/Latino; 6 Two or more races, non-Hispanic/Latino), 202 international. Average age 26. 1,091 applicants, 62% accepted, 249 enrolled. In 2017, 133 master's awarded. *Entrance requirements:* For master's, GRE General Test, transcripts, resume, 3 letters of recommendation. Additional exam requirements/recommendations for international students: Required—TOEFL (minimum score 600 paper-based; 104 iBT), IELTS (minimum score 7). *Application deadline:* For fall admission, 1/10 priority date for domestic and international students. Applications are processed on a rolling basis. Application fee: $50. Electronic applications accepted. *Financial support:* Federal Work-Study, institutionally sponsored loans, and scholarships/grants available. Financial award application deadline: 4/17. *Unit head:* Katherine Baicker, Dean, 773-702-8400, E-mail: harrisadmissions@uchicago.edu. *Application contact:* Ranjan Daniels, Director of Admissions, 773-702-8401, E-mail: harrisadmissions@uchicago.edu.
Website: http://harris.uchicago.edu/academics/programs-degrees/degrees/master-public-policy-mpp

University of Chicago, Harris School of Public Policy, PhD Program in Public Policy, Chicago, IL 60637. Offers PhD. *Students:* 29 full-time (16 women); includes 4 minority (1 Black or African American, non-Hispanic/Latino; 2 Asian, non-Hispanic/Latino; 1 Two or more races, non-Hispanic/Latino), 16 international. Average age 29. 304 applicants, 7% accepted, 7 enrolled. In 2017, 10 doctorates awarded. *Degree requirements:* For doctorate, comprehensive exam, thesis/dissertation. *Entrance requirements:* For doctorate, GRE General Test, transcripts, resume, 3 letters of recommendation, writing sample. Additional exam requirements/recommendations for international students: Required—TOEFL (minimum score 600 paper-based; 104 iBT), IELTS (minimum score 7). *Application deadline:* For fall admission, 12/3 for domestic and international students. Application fee: $50. Electronic applications accepted. *Financial support:* In 2017–18, fellowships with full tuition reimbursements (averaging $27,000 per year) were awarded; research assistantships, teaching assistantships, institutionally sponsored loans, scholarships/grants, and health care benefits also available. Financial award application deadline: 12/3. *Faculty research:* Health policy, municipal finance, cultural policy, urban policy, data science. *Unit head:* Scott Ashworth, Director, 773-251-9563, E-mail: sashwort@uchicago.edu. *Application contact:* Jenny Erickson, Director of Recruitment, 773-702-8401, E-mail: harrisadmissions@uchicago.edu.
Website: http://harris.uchicago.edu/academics/programs-degrees/degrees/phd

University of Delaware, Center for Energy and Environmental Policy, Newark, DE 19716. Offers energy and environmental policy (MA, MEEP, PhD); urban affairs and public policy (PhD), including technology, environment, and society. *Degree requirements:* For master's, analytical paper or thesis; for doctorate, comprehensive exam, thesis/dissertation. *Entrance requirements:* For master's, GRE General Test, minimum GPA of 3.0; for doctorate, GRE General Test, minimum GPA of 3.5. Additional exam requirements/recommendations for international students: Required—TOEFL. Electronic applications accepted. *Faculty research:* Sustainable development, renewable energy, climate change, environmental policy, environmental justice, disaster policy.

University of Delaware, College of Arts and Sciences, School of Public Policy and Administration, Program in Urban Affairs and Public Policy, Newark, DE 19716. Offers governance planning and management (PhD); historic preservation (MA); social and urban policy (PhD); technology, environment and society (PhD); urban affairs and public policy (MA). *Program availability:* Part-time. Terminal master's awarded for partial completion of doctoral program. *Degree requirements:* For master's, analytical paper or thesis; for doctorate, thesis/dissertation. *Entrance requirements:* For master's, GRE General Test, minimum GPA of 3.0; for doctorate, GRE General Test, minimum GPA of 3.5. Additional exam requirements/recommendations for international students: Required—TOEFL. Electronic applications accepted. *Faculty research:* Political economy; social policy analysis; technology and society; historic preservation; urban policy.

University of Denver, Josef Korbel School of International Studies, Institute for Public Policy Studies, Denver, CO 80208. Offers MPP. *Students:* Average age 26. 21 applicants, 81% accepted, 4 enrolled. In 2017, 9 master's awarded. *Degree requirements:* For master's, thesis or alternative, policy memorandum capstone. *Entrance requirements:* For master's, GRE General Test, bachelor's degree, transcripts, personal statement, three letters of recommendation, interview. Additional exam requirements/recommendations for international students: Required—TOEFL (minimum score 570 paper-based; 88 iBT). *Application deadline:* For fall admission, 7/1 priority date for domestic and international students; for winter admission, 11/15 priority date for domestic and international students. Applications are processed on a rolling basis. Application fee: $65. Electronic applications accepted. *Expenses:* Contact institution. *Financial support:* In 2017–18, 17 students received support, including 2 teaching assistantships with tuition reimbursements available (averaging $3,750 per year); Federal Work-Study, scholarships/grants, and unspecified assistantships also available. Financial award application deadline: 2/15; financial award applicants required to submit FAFSA. *Faculty research:* Health policy, politics of mobility and migration, aging and later life migration, immigration policy. *Unit head:* Dr. Richard Caldwell, Co-Director, 303-871-2468, Fax: 303-871-3066, E-mail: richard.caldwell@du.edu.
Website: http://www.du.edu/korbel/ipps/index.html

University of Georgia, School of Public and International Affairs, Department of Public Administration and Policy, Athens, GA 30602. Offers public administration (MPA, PhD). *Accreditation:* NASPAA (one or more programs are accredited). *Degree requirements:* For master's, internship; for doctorate, thesis/dissertation. *Entrance requirements:* For master's and doctorate, GRE General Test. Electronic applications accepted.

University of Guelph, Graduate Studies, College of Social and Applied Human Sciences, Department of Political Science, Guelph, ON N1G 2W1, Canada. Offers comparative politics (MA); international development (MA); political science (MA); public policy and public administration (MA); the Americas (Canada emphasis) (MA). MA in public policy and public administration offered in collaboration with Department of Political Science of McMaster University. *Degree requirements:* For master's, thesis or paper. *Entrance requirements:* For master's, minimum B average during previous 2 years of course work, 4 year Honours Degree in Political Science. Additional exam requirements/recommendations for international students: Required—TOEFL. Electronic applications accepted. *Faculty research:* Political ethics, constitutional power.

University of Hawaii at Manoa, Office of Graduate Education, College of Social Sciences, Public Policy Center, Honolulu, HI 96822. Offers Graduate Certificate. *Program availability:* Part-time. *Entrance requirements:* Additional exam requirements/recommendations for international students: Required—TOEFL (minimum score 500 paper-based; 61 iBT), IELTS (minimum score 5).

University of Houston, College of Liberal Arts and Social Sciences, Hobby School of Public Affairs, Houston, TX 77204-5021. Offers public policy (MPP). *Program availability:* Part-time. *Faculty:* 5 full-time (0 women), 4 part-time/adjunct (2 women). *Students:* 30 full-time (18 women), 5 part-time (3 women); includes 17 minority (9 Black or African American, non-Hispanic/Latino; 1 American Indian or Alaska Native, non-Hispanic/Latino; 1 Asian, non-Hispanic/Latino; 4 Hispanic/Latino; 2 Two or more races, non-Hispanic/Latino). Average age 25. 30 applicants, 83% accepted, 21 enrolled. In 2017, 9 master's awarded. *Entrance requirements:* For master's, GRE General Test. Additional exam requirements/recommendations for international students: Required—TOEFL (minimum score 550 paper-based; 79 iBT), IELTS (minimum score 6.5). *Application deadline:* For fall admission, 6/15 for domestic and international students. Applications are processed on a rolling basis. Application fee: $75 ($125 for international students). Electronic applications accepted. *Financial support:* In 2017–18, 35 students received support. Career-related internships or fieldwork, Federal Work-Study, institutionally sponsored loans, scholarships/grants, traineeships, health care benefits, and unspecified assistantships available. Support available to part-time students. Financial award application deadline: 6/15; financial award applicants required to submit FAFSA. *Faculty research:* Policy analysis, political economy, political philosophy, macroeconomic policy, quantitative methods. *Unit head:* Dr. Jim Granato, Executive Director, 713-743-3887, Fax: 713-743-3978, E-mail: jgranato@uh.edu. *Application contact:* Scott Mason, Program Manager II, 713-743-5572, E-mail: smason@uh.edu.
Website: http://www.uh.edu/hobby/

University of Kentucky, Graduate School, Martin School of Public Policy and Administration, Lexington, KY 40506-0027. Offers public administration (MPA); public financial management (MPFM, Graduate Certificate); public policy (MPP); public policy and administration (PhD). *Accreditation:* NASPAA (one or more programs are accredited). *Program availability:* Part-time, evening/weekend, 100% online. Terminal master's awarded for partial completion of doctoral program. *Degree requirements:* For master's, thesis; for doctorate, comprehensive exam, thesis/dissertation. *Entrance requirements:* For master's, GMAT or GRE General Test, minimum undergraduate GPA of 2.75; for doctorate, GMAT or GRE General Test, minimum graduate GPA of 3.0. Additional exam requirements/recommendations for international students: Required—TOEFL (minimum score 550 paper-based; 79 iBT); Recommended—IELTS (minimum score 6.5). Electronic applications accepted. *Expenses:* Contact institution. *Faculty research:* Public financial management, education finance and policy, tax policy, environmental policy, public organizations and management.

University of Louisville, Graduate School, College of Arts and Sciences, Department of Urban and Public Affairs, Louisville, KY 40208. Offers public administration (MPA), including human resources management, non-profit management, public policy and administration; urban and public affairs (PhD), including urban planning and development, urban policy and administration; urban planning (MUP), including administration of planning organizations, housing and community development, land use and environmental planning, spatial analysis. *Program availability:* Part-time, evening/weekend. *Faculty:* 12 full-time (5 women), 4 part-time/adjunct (1 woman). *Students:* 50 full-time (19 women), 20 part-time (17 women); includes 17 minority (6 Black or African American, non-Hispanic/Latino; 1 Asian, non-Hispanic/Latino; 4 Hispanic/Latino; 6 Two or more races, non-Hispanic/Latino), 4 international. Average age 31. 47 applicants, 70% accepted, 22 enrolled. In 2017, 20 master's, 2 doctorates awarded. Terminal master's awarded for partial completion of doctoral program. *Degree requirements:* For master's, internship; for doctorate, comprehensive exam, thesis/dissertation. *Entrance requirements:* For master's, GRE General Test, minimum GPA of 3.0; for doctorate, GRE General Test, master's degree in appropriate field. Additional exam requirements/recommendations for international students: Required—TOEFL (minimum score 550 paper-based; 79 iBT). *Application deadline:* Applications are processed on a rolling basis. Application fee: $65. *Expenses:* Contact institution. *Financial support:* Fellowships, research assistantships, tuition waivers (full and partial), and unspecified assistantships available. Financial award application deadline: 2/1. *Faculty research:* Urban theory, sustainability, public administration, urban planning, urban management. *Total annual research expenditures:* $240,308. *Unit head:* Dr. David Simpson, Chair, 502-852-8019, Fax: 502-852-4558, E-mail: dave.simpson@louisville.edu. *Application contact:* Latonia Craig, Director of Graduate Recruitment and Diversity Retention, 502-852-5207, Fax: 502-852-4558, E-mail: gradadm@louisville.edu.
Website: http://supa.louisville.edu

University of Maryland, Baltimore County, The Graduate School, College of Arts, Humanities and Social Sciences, Department of Emergency Health Services, Baltimore, MD 21250. Offers emergency health services (MS), including administration, planning, and policy, preventive medicine and epidemiology; emergency management (Postbaccalaureate Certificate); public policy (PhD), including emergency health, emergency management. Some of the required/elective courses within the Preventative Medicine and Epidemiology track are offered in collaboration with the University of Maryland, Baltimore (UMB) and other University System Schools. *Program availability:* Part-time, evening/weekend, 100% online, blended/hybrid learning. *Faculty:* 4 full-time (2 women), 8 part-time/adjunct (3 women). *Students:* 18 full-time (11 women), 4 part-time (3 women); includes 9 minority (6 Black or African American, non-Hispanic/Latino; 1 Asian, non-Hispanic/Latino; 1 Hispanic/Latino; 1 Two or more races, non-Hispanic/Latino). Average age 28. 22 applicants, 91% accepted, 18 enrolled. In 2017, 12 master's awarded. Terminal master's awarded for partial completion of doctoral program. *Degree requirements:* For master's, comprehensive exam (for some programs), capstone project or thesis. *Entrance requirements:* For master's, GRE General Test if GPA is below 3.2, minimum GPA of 3.2. Additional exam requirements/recommendations for international students: Required—TOEFL (minimum score 80 iBT), IELTS, or PTE. *Application deadline:* For fall admission, 6/15 for domestic students, 3/1 for international students; for spring admission, 12/1 for domestic students, 10/1 for international students. Applications are processed on a rolling basis. Application fee: $50. Electronic applications accepted. *Expenses:* $753 per credit hour. *Financial support:* In 2017–18, 6 students received support, including 7 research assistantships with full tuition reimbursements available (averaging $16,875 per year); career-related internships or fieldwork, Federal Work-Study, scholarships/grants, health care benefits, and unspecified assistantships also available. Financial award application deadline: 5/30; financial award applicants required to submit FAFSA. *Faculty research:* EMS management, disaster health services, emergency management, epidemiology, risk profiles, infectious disease control, stress management for care providers, climate change and public health. *Total annual research expenditures:* $715,419. *Unit head:* Dr. J. Lee Jenkins, Department Chair, 410-455-3216, Fax: 410-455-3045, E-mail: jleejenkins@umbc.edu. *Application contact:* Dr. Rick Bissell, Program Director, 410-455-3776, Fax: 410-455-3045, E-mail: bissell@umbc.edu.
Website: http://ehs.umbc.edu/

University of Maryland, Baltimore County, The Graduate School, College of Arts, Humanities and Social Sciences, Program in Economic Policy Analysis, Baltimore, MD 21250. Offers MA. *Program availability:* Part-time. *Faculty:* 17 full-time (6 women), 4 part-time/adjunct (2 women). *Students:* 6 full-time (2 women), 8 part-time (4 women); includes 1 minority (Black or African American, non-Hispanic/Latino), 2 international. Average age 26. 17 applicants, 88% accepted, 6 enrolled. In 2017, 4 master's awarded. *Degree requirements:* For master's, comprehensive exam, capstone research project. *Entrance requirements:* For master's, GRE General Test, undergraduate coursework in economic theory, econometrics, and calculus; letters of reference; statement of purpose; transcripts. Additional exam requirements/recommendations for international students: Required—TOEFL (minimum score 80 iBT). *Application deadline:* For fall admission, 7/1 priority date for domestic students, 3/1 priority date for international students; for spring admission, 1/1 priority date for domestic students, 9/15 priority date for international students. Applications are processed on a rolling basis. Application fee: $45. Electronic applications accepted. *Expenses:* Contact institution. *Financial support:* In 2017–18, 6 students received support, including 5 research assistantships with tuition reimbursements available (averaging $12,560 per year), 1 teaching assistantship with partial tuition reimbursement available (averaging $6,500 per year); Federal Work-Study, health care benefits, tuition waivers (full and partial), and unspecified assistantships also available. Support available to part-time students. Financial award application deadline: 4/15; financial award applicants required to submit FAFSA. *Faculty research:* Health and hospital policy evaluation, environmental policy analysis, economics of education, economic growth and development, cost-benefit and risk analysis. *Total annual research expenditures:* $28,539. *Unit head:* Dr. David F. Mitch, Chair, 410-455-2157, Fax: 410-455-1054, E-mail: mitch@umbc.edu. *Application contact:* Dr. Tim H. Gindling, Graduate Program Director, 410-455-3629, Fax: 410-455-1054, E-mail: econ-masters@umbc.edu.
Website: http://www.umbc.edu/economics/grad_intro.html

University of Maryland, Baltimore County, The Graduate School, College of Arts, Humanities and Social Sciences, School of Public Policy, Baltimore, MD 21250. Offers public policy (MPP, PhD), including economics (PhD), educational policy, emergency services (PhD), environmental policy (MPP), evaluation and analytical methods, health policy, policy history (PhD), public management, urban policy. *Program availability:* Part-time, evening/weekend. *Faculty:* 10 full-time (5 women). *Students:* 50 full-time (24 women), 69 part-time (37 women); includes 35 minority (17 Black or African American, non-Hispanic/Latino; 1 American Indian or Alaska Native, non-Hispanic/Latino; 8 Asian, non-Hispanic/Latino; 5 Hispanic/Latino; 1 Native Hawaiian or other Pacific Islander, non-Hispanic/Latino; 3 Two or more races, non-Hispanic/Latino), 6 international. Average age 37. 60 applicants, 68% accepted, 25 enrolled. In 2017, 15 master's, 3 doctorates awarded. Terminal master's awarded for partial completion of doctoral program. *Degree requirements:* For master's, thesis, policy analysis paper, internship for pre-service; for doctorate, comprehensive exam, thesis/dissertation, comprehensive and field qualifying exams. *Entrance requirements:* For master's, GRE General Test, 3 academic letters of reference, resume, official transcripts; for doctorate, GRE General Test, 3 academic letters of reference, resume, research paper, official transcripts. Additional exam requirements/recommendations for international students: Required—TOEFL (minimum score 550 paper-based; 80 iBT), IELTS (minimum score 6.5). *Application deadline:* For fall admission, 1/15 priority date for domestic students, 1/1 priority date for international students; for spring admission, 11/1 priority date for domestic students, 5/1 priority date for international students. Applications are processed on a rolling basis. Application fee: $50. Electronic applications accepted. *Expenses:* $28,061 in-state, $39,356 out-of-state to complete the degree (for MPP); $43,823 in-state, $61,508 out-of-state to complete the degree (for PhD). *Financial support:* In 2017–18, 26 students received support, including 26 research assistantships with full tuition reimbursements available (averaging $20,000 per year); Federal Work-Study, scholarships/grants, health care benefits, and unspecified assistantships also available. Financial award application deadline: 1/1; financial award applicants required to submit FAFSA. *Faculty research:* Education policy, health policy, urban and environmental policy, public management, evaluation and analytical method. *Unit head:* Dr. Susan Sterett, Director, 410-455-2140, Fax: 410-455-1172, E-mail: ssterett@umbc.edu. *Application contact:* Sally F. Helms, Administrator of Academic Affairs, 410-455-3202, Fax: 410-455-1172, E-mail: gradpubpol@umbc.edu.
Website: http://publicpolicy.umbc.edu/

University of Maryland, College Park, Academic Affairs, A. James Clark School of Engineering and School of Public Policy, Program in Engineering and Public Policy, College Park, MD 20742. Offers MS.

University of Maryland, College Park, Academic Affairs, School of Public Policy, Policy Studies Program, College Park, MD 20742. Offers PhD. *Degree requirements:* For doctorate, comprehensive exam, thesis/dissertation, written and oral exams. *Entrance requirements:* For doctorate, GRE General Test, writing sample. Electronic applications accepted.

University of Maryland, College Park, Academic Affairs, School of Public Policy, Programs in Public Policy, College Park, MD 20742. Offers MPP. *Accreditation:* NASPAA. *Entrance requirements:* Additional exam requirements/recommendations for international students: Required—TOEFL. Electronic applications accepted.

University of Massachusetts Amherst, Graduate School, College of Social and Behavioral Sciences, Center for Public Policy and Administration, Amherst, MA 01003. Offers MPP, MPPA, MPH/MPPA, MPPA/M Ed, MPPA/MBA, MRP/MPPA. *Program availability:* Part-time. *Degree requirements:* For master's, thesis or alternative. *Entrance requirements:* For master's, GRE General Test. Additional exam requirements/recommendations for international students: Required—TOEFL (minimum score 550 paper-based; 80 iBT), IELTS (minimum score 6.5). Electronic applications accepted.

University of Massachusetts Amherst, Graduate School, Interdisciplinary Programs, Dual Degree Program in Education and Public Policy and Administration, Amherst, MA 01003. Offers MPPA/M Ed. *Entrance requirements:* Additional exam requirements/recommendations for international students: Required—TOEFL (minimum score 550 paper-based; 80 iBT), IELTS (minimum score 6.5). Electronic applications accepted.

University of Massachusetts Amherst, Graduate School, Interdisciplinary Programs, Dual Degree Program in Management and Public Policy and Administration, Amherst, MA 01003. Offers MPPA/MBA. *Accreditation:* AACSB. *Program availability:* Part-time. *Entrance requirements:* Additional exam requirements/recommendations for international students: Required—TOEFL (minimum score 600 paper-based; 100 iBT), IELTS (minimum score 7). Electronic applications accepted.

University of Massachusetts Amherst, Graduate School, Interdisciplinary Programs, Dual Degree Program in Public Policy and Administration and Public Health, Amherst, MA 01003. Offers MPH/MPPA. *Entrance requirements:* Additional exam requirements/recommendations for international students: Required—TOEFL (minimum score 550 paper-based; 80 iBT), IELTS (minimum score 6.5). Electronic applications accepted.

University of Massachusetts Amherst, Graduate School, Interdisciplinary Programs, Dual Degree Program in Regional Planning and Public Policy and Administration, Amherst, MA 01003. Offers MPPA/MRP. *Entrance requirements:* Additional exam requirements/recommendations for international students: Required—TOEFL (minimum score 550 paper-based; 80 iBT), IELTS (minimum score 6.5). Electronic applications accepted.

University of Massachusetts Boston, McCormack Graduate School of Policy and Global Studies, Program in Public Policy, Boston, MA 02125-3393. Offers MS, PhD. *Program availability:* Evening/weekend. *Faculty:* 9 full-time (3 women), 4 part-time/adjunct (2 women). *Students:* 18 full-time (12 women), 29 part-time (17 women); includes 5 minority (3 Asian, non-Hispanic/Latino; 2 Hispanic/Latino), 15 international. Average age 34. 41 applicants, 44% accepted, 8 enrolled. In 2017, 1 master's, 2 doctorates awarded. *Entrance requirements:* For doctorate, GRE General Test. *Application deadline:* For fall admission, 1/15 for domestic students. *Expenses:* Tuition, state resident: full-time $17,375. Tuition, nonresident: full-time $33,915. *Required fees:* $355. *Financial support:* Research assistantships, teaching assistantships, career-related internships or fieldwork, Federal Work-Study, and unspecified assistantships available. Support available to part-time students. Financial award application deadline: 3/1; financial award applicants required to submit FAFSA. *Faculty research:* Political economy, public managerial control, healthcare policy, planning and public policy theory, economic development. *Unit head:* Dr. David Cash, Dean, 617-287-5000. *Application contact:* Graduate Admissions Coordinator, 617-287-6400, Fax: 617-287-6236, E-mail: bos.gadm@dpc.umassp.edu.

University of Massachusetts Dartmouth, Graduate School, College of Arts and Sciences, Department of Public Policy, North Dartmouth, MA 02747-2300. Offers educational policy (Graduate Certificate); environmental policy (Graduate Certificate); public management (Graduate Certificate); public policy (MPP). *Program availability:* Part-time, 100% online, blended/hybrid learning. *Faculty:* 4 full-time (0 women), 1 part-time/adjunct (0 women). *Students:* 6 full-time (2 women), 69 part-time (43 women); includes 18 minority (6 Black or African American, non-Hispanic/Latino; 2 Asian, non-Hispanic/Latino; 7 Hispanic/Latino; 3 Two or more races, non-Hispanic/Latino). Average age 36. 59 applicants, 95% accepted, 41 enrolled. In 2017, 10 master's, 18 other advanced degrees awarded. *Degree requirements:* For master's, e-portfolio. *Entrance requirements:* For master's, GRE or GMAT (waived if applicant has already earned a graduate degree from accredited school or if applicant has successfully completed the educational, environmental or public management certificate program), statement of purpose (minimum of 300 words), resume, 2 letters of recommendation, official transcripts; for Graduate Certificate, statement of purpose (minimum of 300 words), resume, official transcripts. Additional exam requirements/recommendations for international students: Required—TOEFL (minimum score 600 paper-based; 100 iBT). *Application deadline:* Applications are processed on a rolling basis. Application fee: $60. Electronic applications accepted. *Expenses:* Tuition, state resident: full-time $15,449; part-time $643.71 per credit. Tuition, nonresident: full-time $27,880; part-time $1161.67 per credit. *Required fees:* $405; $25.88 per credit. Tuition and fees vary according to course load and reciprocity agreements. *Financial support:* In 2017–18, 2 research assistantships (averaging $12,900 per year) were awarded; teaching assistantships, tuition waivers (full), and unspecified assistantships also available. Support available to part-time students. Financial award application deadline: 3/1; financial award applicants required to submit FAFSA. *Faculty research:* Environmental justice, sustainability, international trade and finance, corporate social responsibility, global governance. *Total annual research expenditures:* $6,000. *Unit head:* Chad McGuire, Graduate Program Director, Public Policy, 508-999-8520, E-mail: cmcguire@umassd.edu. *Application contact:* Steven Briggs, Director of Marketing and Recruitment for Graduate Studies, 508-999-8604, Fax: 508-999-8183, E-mail: graduate@umassd.edu.
Website: http://www.umassd.edu/cas/departmentsanddegreeprograms/publicpolicy/

University of Memphis, Graduate School, College of Arts and Sciences, Division of Public and Nonprofit Administration, Memphis, TN 38152. Offers local government management (Graduate Certificate); philanthropy and nonprofit leadership (Graduate Certificate). *Accreditation:* NASPAA. *Program availability:* Part-time, evening/weekend, blended/hybrid learning. *Faculty:* 6 full-time (3 women), 1 part-time/adjunct (0 women). *Students:* 13 full-time (5 women), 28 part-time (19 women); includes 22 minority (21 Black or African American, non-Hispanic/Latino; 1 Two or more races, non-Hispanic/Latino), 1 international. Average age 36. 26 applicants, 96% accepted, 14 enrolled. In 2017, 16 master's, 13 other advanced degrees awarded. *Degree requirements:* For master's, comprehensive exam, thesis or alternative, internship. *Entrance requirements:* For master's, GRE General Test, GMAT, MAT, or LSAT, minimum GPA of 3.0, resume, two references, statement of interest. Additional exam requirements/recommendations for international students: Required—TOEFL. *Application deadline:* For fall admission, 7/1 for domestic students, 5/1 for international students; for spring admission, 12/1 for domestic students, 9/15 for international students; for summer admission, 5/1 for domestic students, 2/1 for international students. Applications are processed on a rolling basis. Application fee: $35 ($60 for international students). Electronic applications accepted. *Expenses:* Contact institution. *Financial support:* In 2017–18, 37 students received support, including 5 fellowships (averaging $11,200 per year); research assistantships with full tuition reimbursements available, career-related internships or fieldwork, Federal Work-Study, scholarships/grants, health care benefits, and unspecified assistantships also available. Support available to part-time students. Financial award application deadline: 2/1; financial award applicants required to submit FAFSA. *Faculty research:* Nonprofit organization governance, local government management, community collaboration, urban problems, accountability. *Unit head:* Dr. Michael Howell-Moroney, Chair, 901-678-3360, Fax: 901-678-2981, E-mail: mhwllmrn@memphis.edu. *Application contact:* Dr. Sharon Wrobel, MPA Coordinator, 901-678-4720, Fax: 901-678-2981, E-mail: swrobel@memphis.edu.
Website: http://www.memphis.edu/padm/

University of Michigan, Gerald R. Ford School of Public Policy, Ann Arbor, MI 48109. Offers MPA, MPP, PhD, JD/MPP, MBA/MPP, MD/MPP, MHSA/MPP, MPH/MPP, MPP/AM, MPP/MA, MPP/MIS, MPP/MS, MPP/MUP, MSW/MPP. *Faculty:* 36 full-time (16 women), 34 part-time/adjunct (13 women). *Students:* 272 full-time (141 women); includes 86 minority (26 Black or African American, non-Hispanic/Latino; 26 Asian, non-Hispanic/Latino; 24 Hispanic/Latino; 10 Two or more races, non-Hispanic/Latino), 52 international. Average age 28. 633 applicants, 66% accepted, 106 enrolled. In 2017, 84 master's, 7 doctorates awarded. *Degree requirements:* For doctorate, comprehensive exam, thesis/dissertation. *Entrance requirements:* For master's and doctorate, GRE. Additional exam requirements/recommendations for international students: Required—TOEFL (minimum score 560 paper-based; 84 iBT). *Application deadline:* For fall admission, 1/15 priority date for domestic students, 1/15 for international students. Application fee: $75 ($90 for international students). Electronic applications accepted. *Expenses:* $25,502 per year in-state, $46,234 out-of-state; $11,908 per year (for PhD). *Financial support:* In 2017–18, 213 students received support, including 181 fellowships with tuition reimbursements available, 27 teaching assistantships with tuition reimbursements available; research assistantships, career-related internships or fieldwork, traineeships, health care benefits, and unspecified assistantships also available. Financial award application deadline: 1/15; financial award applicants required to submit FAFSA. *Faculty research:* Quantitative policy analysis; U.S. social policy; international economic policy; environmental policy; health policy. *Total annual research expenditures:* $3 million. *Unit head:* Michael S. Barr, Dean of Public Policy, 734-764-2258, E-mail: ford.school.dean@umich.edu. *Application contact:* Beth Soboleski, Director, Admissions and Recruiting, 734-764-0453, Fax: 734-647-7486, E-mail: fspp-admissions@umich.edu.
Website: http://fordschool.umich.edu/

Public Policy

University of Michigan, Rackham Graduate School, College of Literature, Science, and the Arts, Department of Economics, Ann Arbor, MI 48109. Offers applied economics (AM); economics (AM, PhD); public policy and economics (PhD); social work and economics (PhD); JD/PhD; MPP/AM. Terminal master's awarded for partial completion of doctoral program. *Degree requirements:* For doctorate, comprehensive exam, thesis/dissertation, oral defense of dissertation; preliminary exams in microeconomics, macroeconomics, and 2 fields. *Entrance requirements:* For master's and doctorate, GRE General Test. Additional exam requirements/recommendations for international students: Required—TOEFL (minimum score 600 paper-based; 100 iBT). Electronic applications accepted. *Expenses:* Tuition, state resident: full-time $22,368; part-time $1201 per credit hour. Tuition, nonresident: full-time $45,156; part-time $2467 per credit hour. *Required fees:* $376 per term. Tuition and fees vary according to course load, degree level and program. *Faculty research:* Econometric analysis, finance, industrial organization, international trade, public finance, economic development, economic history, health, labor, natural resources, population studies, macro theory, micro theory.

University of Michigan, Rackham Graduate School, College of Literature, Science, and the Arts, Department of Political Science, Ann Arbor, MI 48109-1045. Offers political science (PhD); political science and public policy (PhD); social work and political science (PhD). *Faculty:* 48 full-time (17 women), 6 part-time/adjunct (4 women). *Students:* 118 full-time (51 women); includes 17 minority (5 Black or African American, non-Hispanic/Latino; 4 Asian, non-Hispanic/Latino; 6 Hispanic/Latino; 2 Two or more races, non-Hispanic/Latino), 29 international. Average age 29. 442 applicants, 8% accepted, 21 enrolled. In 2017, 27 doctorates awarded. Terminal master's awarded for partial completion of doctoral program. *Degree requirements:* For doctorate, comprehensive exam, thesis/dissertation, oral defense of dissertation, preliminary exams. *Entrance requirements:* For doctorate, GRE General Test. Additional exam requirements/recommendations for international students: Required—TOEFL. *Application deadline:* For fall admission, 12/15 for domestic and international students. Application fee: $75 ($90 for international students). Electronic applications accepted. *Expenses:* $22,442 in-state, $44,230 out-of-state/international. *Financial support:* In 2017–18, 100 students received support, including 14 fellowships with full tuition reimbursements available (averaging $23,399 per year), 17 research assistantships with full tuition reimbursements available (averaging $23,399 per year), 46 teaching assistantships with full tuition reimbursements available (averaging $23,399 per year); scholarships/grants, health care benefits, tuition waivers (full), and unspecified assistantships also available. Financial award application deadline: 12/15. *Faculty research:* Political theory; American politics; world politics; comparative politics; research methods; law, courts, and politics. *Unit head:* Nancy Burns, Chair, 734-764-6313, Fax: 734-764-3522. *Application contact:* Kimberly Smith, Graduate Program Coordinator, 734-764-6313, Fax: 734-764-3522, E-mail: psgradinfo@umich.edu.
Website: http://www.lsa.umich.edu/polisci

University of Michigan, Rackham Graduate School, College of Literature, Science, and the Arts, Department of Sociology, Ann Arbor, MI 48109. Offers public policy and sociology (PhD); social work and sociology (PhD); sociology (PhD). *Faculty:* 41 full-time (21 women), 10 part-time/adjunct (4 women). *Students:* 72 full-time (50 women); includes 27 minority (8 Black or African American, non-Hispanic/Latino; 4 Asian, non-Hispanic/Latino; 8 Hispanic/Latino; 7 Two or more races, non-Hispanic/Latino), 10 international. Average age 28. 253 applicants, 12% accepted, 17 enrolled. In 2017, 2 doctorates awarded. *Degree requirements:* For doctorate, comprehensive exam, thesis/dissertation, oral defense of dissertation, preliminary exam, dissertation prospectus. *Entrance requirements:* For doctorate, GRE General Test, letters of recommendation, writing sample, academic statement of purpose, personal statement, transcript. Additional exam requirements/recommendations for international students: Required—TOEFL (minimum score 560 paper-based; 84 iBT), IELTS (minimum score 6.5). *Application deadline:* For fall admission, 12/15 for domestic and international students. Application fee: $75 ($90 for international students). Electronic applications accepted. *Expenses:* Tuition, state resident: full-time $22,368; part-time $1201 per credit hour. Tuition, nonresident: full-time $45,156; part-time $2467 per credit hour. *Required fees:* $376 per term. Tuition and fees vary according to course load, degree level and program. *Financial support:* In 2017–18, 77 students received support, including 17 fellowships with full tuition reimbursements available (averaging $23,940 per year), 28 teaching assistantships with full tuition reimbursements available (averaging $23,782 per year); scholarships/grants, traineeships, health care benefits, and tuition waivers (full) also available. Financial award application deadline: 12/15. *Faculty research:* Power, history and social change; gender and sexuality; race and ethnicity; economic sociology; social demography. *Total annual research expenditures:* $269,377. *Unit head:* Karin A. Martin, Chair, 734-764-5554, Fax: 734-763-6887, E-mail: soc-chair@umich.edu. *Application contact:* Jessica Parks-Piatt, Graduate Program Coordinator, 734-647-4428, Fax: 734-763-6887, E-mail: lsa-soc-gradprogram@umich.edu.
Website: http://www.lsa.umich.edu/soc/

University of Minnesota, Twin Cities Campus, Graduate School, Humphrey School of Public Affairs, PhD Program in Public Affairs, Minneapolis, MN 55455. Offers management and governance (PhD); public policy (PhD); science, technology, and environmental policy (PhD); urban planning (PhD). *Program availability:* Part-time. *Degree requirements:* For doctorate, comprehensive exam, thesis/dissertation. *Entrance requirements:* For doctorate, GRE General Test. Additional exam requirements/recommendations for international students: Required—TOEFL (minimum score 650 paper-based; 100 iBT), IELTS (minimum score 7). Electronic applications accepted. *Expenses:* Contact institution. *Faculty research:* Public policy, urban/regional planning, public/nonprofit management and governance, science/technology/environmental policy.

University of Minnesota, Twin Cities Campus, Graduate School, Humphrey School of Public Affairs, Program in Public Policy, Minneapolis, MN 55455. Offers MPP, JD/MPP, MBA/MPP, MPP/MPH, MSW/MPP. *Accreditation:* NASPAA. *Program availability:* Part-time. *Degree requirements:* For master's, thesis or alternative, internship or equivalent work experience. *Entrance requirements:* For master's, GRE General Test, minimum undergraduate GPA of 3.0. Additional exam requirements/recommendations for international students: Required—TOEFL (minimum score 600 paper-based; 100 iBT), IELTS (minimum score 7). Electronic applications accepted. *Expenses:* Contact institution. *Faculty research:* Social policy, public and non-profit management and leadership, community and economic development, foreign policy and international affairs, women and public policy.

University of Missouri, Office of Research and Graduate Studies, Harry S Truman School of Public Affairs, Columbia, MO 65211. Offers grantsmanship (Graduate Certificate); nonprofit management (Graduate Certificate); organizational change (Graduate Certificate); public affairs (MPA, PhD); public management (Graduate Certificate); science and public policy (Graduate Certificate). *Accreditation:* NASPAA. *Entrance requirements:* For master's, GRE General Test, minimum GPA of 3.0. Additional exam requirements/recommendations for international students: Required—TOEFL (minimum score 550 paper-based; 80 iBT), IELTS (minimum score 6.5). Electronic applications accepted.

University of Missouri–St. Louis, College of Arts and Sciences, Department of Political Science, St. Louis, MO 63121. Offers American politics (MA); comparative politics (MA); international politics (MA); political process and behavior (MA); political science (PhD); public administration and public policy (MA); urban and regional politics (MA). *Program availability:* Part-time, evening/weekend. *Faculty:* 15 full-time (5 women), 9 part-time/adjunct (2 women). *Students:* 32 full-time (11 women), 21 part-time (9 women); includes 11 minority (10 Black or African American, non-Hispanic/Latino; 1 Hispanic/Latino), 4 international. 10 applicants, 80% accepted, 7 enrolled. Terminal master's awarded for partial completion of doctoral program. *Degree requirements:* For master's, thesis optional; for doctorate, thesis/dissertation. *Entrance requirements:* For master's, GRE General Test, 2 letters of recommendation, statement of purpose; for doctorate, GRE General Test, 3 letters of recommendation, statement of purpose. Additional exam requirements/recommendations for international students: Required—TOEFL (minimum score 550 paper-based; 79 iBT), IELTS (minimum score 6.5). *Application deadline:* For fall admission, 2/15 priority date for domestic and international students; for winter admission, 10/15 for domestic and international students; for spring admission, 10/15 priority date for domestic and international students. Applications are processed on a rolling basis. Application fee: $50 ($40 for international students). Electronic applications accepted. *Expenses:* Tuition, state resident: part-time $476.50 per credit hour. Tuition, nonresident: part-time $1169.70 per credit hour. *Financial support:* Fellowships, research assistantships with tuition reimbursements, teaching assistantships with tuition reimbursements, and career-related internships or fieldwork available. Support available to part-time students. Financial award application deadline: 3/15; financial award applicants required to submit FAFSA. *Faculty research:* Public policy, urban politics and administration, American government. *Unit head:* Dave Robertson, Chairperson, 314-516-5521, Fax: 314-516-7236. *Application contact:* 314-516-5458, Fax: 314-516-6996, E-mail: gradadm@umsl.edu.
Website: http://www.umsl.edu/~polisci/

University of Missouri–St. Louis, Graduate School, Program in Public Policy Administration, St. Louis, MO 63121. Offers local government management (MPPA, Certificate); nonprofit management and leadership (MPPA, Certificate); policy and program evaluation (MPPA, Certificate). *Accreditation:* NASPAA. *Program availability:* Part-time, evening/weekend. *Faculty:* 2 full-time (1 woman), 4 part-time/adjunct (3 women). *Students:* 9 full-time (5 women), 34 part-time (19 women); includes 10 minority (6 Black or African American, non-Hispanic/Latino; 2 Asian, non-Hispanic/Latino; 1 Hispanic/Latino; 1 Two or more races, non-Hispanic/Latino). 34 applicants, 79% accepted, 14 enrolled. *Degree requirements:* For master's, exit project. *Entrance requirements:* For master's, 3 letters of recommendation, personal statement. Additional exam requirements/recommendations for international students: Recommended—TOEFL (minimum score 550 paper-based), IELTS (minimum score 6.5). *Application deadline:* For fall admission, 7/1 priority date for domestic and international students; for spring admission, 12/1 priority date for domestic and international students. Applications are processed on a rolling basis. Application fee: $50 ($40 for international students). Electronic applications accepted. *Expenses:* Tuition, state resident: part-time $476.50 per credit hour. Tuition, nonresident: part-time $1169.70 per credit hour. *Financial support:* Research assistantships with tuition reimbursements and career-related internships or fieldwork available. Financial award application deadline: 4/1; financial award applicants required to submit FAFSA. *Faculty research:* Urban policy, public finance, evaluation. *Unit head:* Daniel Sise, Interim Director, 314-516-6378, Fax: 314-516-5210, E-mail: sised@umsl.edu. *Application contact:* 314-516-5458, Fax: 314-516-6996, E-mail: gradadm@umsl.edu.
Website: http://www.umsl.edu/gradschool/ppa/

University of Nebraska–Lincoln, Graduate College, College of Arts and Sciences, Department of Political Science, Lincoln, NE 68588. Offers political science (MA, PhD); public policy analysis (Graduate Certificate). *Degree requirements:* For master's, thesis optional; for doctorate, variable foreign language requirement, comprehensive exam, thesis/dissertation. *Entrance requirements:* For master's and doctorate, GRE General Test, writing sample. Additional exam requirements/recommendations for international students: Required—TOEFL (minimum score 600 paper-based). Electronic applications accepted. *Faculty research:* Public policy; comparative politics; international relations; political theory, behavior, and methodology; American politics.

University of Nevada, Las Vegas, Graduate College, Greenspun College of Urban Affairs, School of Public Policy and Leadership, Las Vegas, NV 89154-4030. Offers crisis and emergency management (MS); emergency crisis management cybersecurity (Certificate); environmental science (MS, PhD); non-profit management (Certificate); public administration (MPA); public affairs (PhD); public management (Certificate); urban leadership (MA). *Program availability:* Part-time. *Faculty:* 13 full-time (5 women), 10 part-time/adjunct (3 women). *Students:* 76 full-time (40 women), 107 part-time (66 women); includes 79 minority (19 Black or African American, non-Hispanic/Latino; 1 American Indian or Alaska Native, non-Hispanic/Latino; 6 Asian, non-Hispanic/Latino; 40 Hispanic/Latino; 3 Native Hawaiian or other Pacific Islander, non-Hispanic/Latino; 10 Two or more races, non-Hispanic/Latino), 1 international. Average age 37. 86 applicants, 80% accepted, 47 enrolled. In 2017, 61 master's, 6 doctorates, 14 other advanced degrees awarded. *Degree requirements:* For master's, comprehensive exam (for some programs), thesis (for some programs), oral exam; for doctorate, comprehensive exam, thesis/dissertation; for Certificate, portfolio. *Entrance requirements:* For master's, GRE General Test or GMAT, bachelor's degree with minimum GPA 2.75; statement of purpose; 3 letters of recommendation; for doctorate, GRE General Test, master's degree with minimum GPA of 3.5; 3 letters of recommendation; statement of purpose; writing sample; personal interview; for Certificate, bachelor's degree; 2 letters of recommendation; writing sample. Additional exam requirements/recommendations for international students: Required—TOEFL (minimum score 550 paper-based; 80 iBT), IELTS (minimum score 7). *Application deadline:* For fall admission, 6/1 for domestic and international students; for spring admission, 11/1 for domestic and international students; for summer admission, 3/1 for domestic students. Application fee: $60 ($95 for international students). Electronic applications accepted. *Expenses:* $275 per credit, $850 per course, $7,969 per year resident, $22,157 per year non-resident, $7,094 non-resident fee (7 credits or more), $1,307 annual health insurance fee. *Financial support:* In 2017–18, 23 students received support, including 7 research assistantships with partial tuition reimbursements available (averaging $15,995 per year), 16 teaching assistantships with partial tuition reimbursements available (averaging $15,547 per year); institutionally sponsored loans, scholarships/grants, health care benefits, and unspecified assistantships also available. Financial award application deadline: 3/15; financial award applicants required to submit FAFSA. *Total annual research expenditures:* $63,202. *Unit head:* Dr. Christopher Stream, Director, 702-895-5120, Fax: 702-895-4436, E-mail: chris.stream@unlv.edu. *Application contact:* Dr. Jayce Farmer, Graduate Coordinator, 702-895-4828, E-mail: jayce.farmer@unlv.edu.
Website: https://www.unlv.edu/publicpolicy

University of New Brunswick Fredericton, School of Graduate Studies, Policy Studies Program, Fredericton, NB E3B 5A3, Canada. Offers citizen engagement/dispute resolution (M Phil); community development (M Phil); international development (M Phil); leadership (M Phil); sustainability/environmental issues (M Phil); worldviews (M Phil). *Program availability:* Part-time. *Degree requirements:* For master's, thesis,

report. *Entrance requirements:* For master's, minimum GPA of 3.5. Additional exam requirements/recommendations for international students: Required—TWE (minimum score 5.5), TOEFL (minimum score 600 paper-based; 100 iBT) or IELTS (minimum score 7). Electronic applications accepted. *Faculty research:* International development, worldviews, citizenship/dispute resolution, sustainability/environmental issues, leadership, community development.

University of New Hampshire, Graduate School, Carsey School of Public Policy, Program in Public Policy, Durham, NH 03824. Offers MPP. *Students:* 19 full-time (10 women), 3 part-time (1 woman); includes 2 minority (both Hispanic/Latino), 4 international. Average age 26. 23 applicants, 70% accepted, 10 enrolled. *Entrance requirements:* For master's, GRE. Additional exam requirements/recommendations for international students: Required—TOEFL (minimum score 80 iBT), IELTS (minimum score 6.5). *Application deadline:* For fall admission, 7/15 for domestic students; for spring admission, 12/15 for domestic students; for summer admission, 4/15 for domestic students. Electronic applications accepted. *Financial support:* Fellowships and scholarships/grants available. Financial award application deadline: 2/15; financial award applicants required to submit FAFSA. *Unit head:* Michael Swack, Chair, 603-862-2821, Fax: 603-862-0275, E-mail: michael.swack@unh.edu. *Application contact:* Sarah Dorner, Administrative Assistant, 603-862-2338, E-mail: sarah.dorner@unh.edu.
Website: https://carsey.unh.edu/mpp

The University of North Carolina at Chapel Hill, Graduate School, College of Arts and Sciences, Department of Public Policy, Chapel Hill, NC 27599. Offers PhD. *Degree requirements:* For doctorate, thesis/dissertation. *Entrance requirements:* For doctorate, GRE General Test. Electronic applications accepted. *Faculty research:* Environmental policy; energy policy; economic development and science and technology policy; social policy; welfare, education and low-income communities.

The University of North Carolina at Charlotte, College of Liberal Arts and Sciences, Department of Political Science and Public Administration, Charlotte, NC 28223-0001. Offers emergency management (Graduate Certificate); non-profit management (Graduate Certificate); public administration (MPA), including arts administration, emergency management, non-profit management, public budgeting and finance, urban management and policy; public budgeting and finance (Graduate Certificate); urban management and policy (Graduate Certificate). *Accreditation:* NASPAA. *Program availability:* Part-time, evening/weekend. *Faculty:* 19 full-time (9 women), 4 part-time/adjunct (1 woman). *Students:* 20 full-time (11 women), 61 part-time (41 women); includes 21 minority (12 Black or African American, non-Hispanic/Latino; 2 American Indian or Alaska Native, non-Hispanic/Latino; 1 Asian, non-Hispanic/Latino; 4 Hispanic/Latino; 2 Two or more races, non-Hispanic/Latino), 1 international. Average age 28. 48 applicants, 67% accepted, 22 enrolled. In 2017, 25 master's, 15 other advanced degrees awarded. *Degree requirements:* For master's, research project or thesis. *Entrance requirements:* For master's, GRE General Test, bachelor's degree, or its equivalent, from accredited college or university; minimum undergraduate GPA of 3.0; 3 letters of recommendation; statement of purpose; for Graduate Certificate, statement of purpose (1-2 pages in length) explaining applicant's career goals, how the Graduate Certificate fits into achieving those goals, and any relevant work experience; official transcripts; letters of recommendation. Additional exam requirements/recommendations for international students: Required—TOEFL (minimum score 523 paper-based, 70 iBT) or IELTS (6.5). *Application deadline:* For fall admission, 8/1 for domestic and international students; for spring admission, 12/1 for domestic and international students. Applications are processed on a rolling basis. Application fee: $75. Electronic applications accepted. *Expenses:* Tuition, state resident: full-time $4337. Tuition, nonresident: full-time $17,771. *Required fees:* $3211. Tuition and fees vary according to course load and program. *Financial support:* In 2017–18, 14 students received support, including 13 research assistantships (averaging $9,015 per year), 1 teaching assistantship (averaging $19,500 per year); career-related internships or fieldwork, Federal Work-Study, institutionally sponsored loans, scholarships/grants, and unspecified assistantships also available. Support available to part-time students. Financial award application deadline: 3/1; financial award applicants required to submit FAFSA. *Total annual research expenditures:* $419,411. *Unit head:* Dr. Greg Weeks, Chair, 704-687-7574, E-mail: gbweeks@uncc.edu. *Application contact:* Kathy B. Giddings, Director of Graduate Admissions, 704-687-5503, Fax: 704-687-1668, E-mail: gradadm@uncc.edu.
Website: http://politicalscience.uncc.edu/

The University of North Carolina at Charlotte, College of Liberal Arts and Sciences, Interdisciplinary Liberal Arts and Sciences Programs, Charlotte, NC 28223-0001. Offers gender, sexuality, and women's studies (Graduate Certificate); gerontology (MA, Graduate Certificate); Latin American studies (MA); liberal studies (MA); organizational science (PhD); public policy (PhD). *Program availability:* Part-time, evening/weekend. *Faculty:* 1 full-time (0 women). *Students:* 66 full-time (48 women), 66 part-time (52 women); includes 41 minority (14 Black or African American, non-Hispanic/Latino; 2 Asian, non-Hispanic/Latino; 24 Hispanic/Latino; 1 Two or more races, non-Hispanic/Latino), 16 international. Average age 27. 129 applicants, 53% accepted, 43 enrolled. In 2017, 22 master's, 10 doctorates, 9 other advanced degrees awarded. *Degree requirements:* For master's, comprehensive exam (for some programs), thesis (for some programs), practicum, project; for doctorate, comprehensive exam, thesis/dissertation; for Graduate Certificate, practicum (for gerontology). *Entrance requirements:* For master's, GRE General Test or MAT, bachelor's degree from accredited college or university; official transcripts of all previous academic work attempted beyond high school with minimum overall GPA of 3.0; statement of purpose; recommendation letters; for doctorate, GRE or GMAT, statement of purpose discussing interest in program and objectives for pursuing degree, current resume or curriculum vitae, unofficial transcripts; for Graduate Certificate, bachelor's degree from accredited university and either enrolled and in good standing in a graduate degree program at UNC Charlotte or have a minimum undergraduate GPA of 3.0. Additional exam requirements/recommendations for international students: Required—TOEFL (minimum score 523 paper-based, 70 iBT) or IELTS (6.5). *Application deadline:* For fall admission, 2/15 for domestic and international students; for spring admission, 10/1 for domestic and international students; for summer admission, 4/1 for domestic and international students. Applications are processed on a rolling basis. Application fee: $75. Electronic applications accepted. *Expenses:* Tuition, state resident: full-time $4337. Tuition, nonresident: full-time $17,771. *Required fees:* $3211. Tuition and fees vary according to course load and program. *Financial support:* In 2017–18, 21 students received support, including 19 research assistantships (averaging $12,011 per year), 1 teaching assistantship (averaging $18,600 per year); career-related internships or fieldwork, institutionally sponsored loans, scholarships/grants, unspecified assistantships, and administrative assistantships also available. Support available to part-time students. Financial award application deadline: 3/1; financial award applicants required to submit FAFSA. *Unit head:* Dr. Nancy A. Gutierrez, Dean, 704-687-0081, E-mail: ngutierr@uncc.edu. *Application contact:* Kathy B. Giddings, Director of Graduate Admissions, 704-687-5503, Fax: 704-687-3279, E-mail: gradadm@uncc.edu.
Website: http://clas.uncc.edu/academics

University of Northern Iowa, Graduate College, College of Social and Behavioral Sciences, MPP Program in Public Policy, Cedar Falls, IA 50614. Offers MPP. *Program availability:* Part-time. *Degree requirements:* For master's, comprehensive exam (for some programs). *Entrance requirements:* For master's, minimum GPA of 3.0. Additional exam requirements/recommendations for international students: Required—TOEFL (minimum score 500 paper-based; 61 iBT). Electronic applications accepted.

University of Oklahoma, College of Arts and Sciences, Department of Political Science, Program in Public Administration, Norman, OK 73019. Offers general (MPA); nonprofit management (MPA); public management (MPA); public policy (MPA). *Program availability:* Part-time, evening/weekend. *Students:* 36 full-time (22 women), 60 part-time (35 women); includes 27 minority (7 Black or African American, non-Hispanic/Latino; 5 American Indian or Alaska Native, non-Hispanic/Latino; 3 Asian, non-Hispanic/Latino; 7 Hispanic/Latino; 1 Native Hawaiian or other Pacific Islander, non-Hispanic/Latino; 4 Two or more races, non-Hispanic/Latino), 2 international. Average age 31. 30 applicants, 77% accepted, 20 enrolled. In 2017, 18 master's awarded. Terminal master's awarded for partial completion of doctoral program. *Degree requirements:* For master's, comprehensive exam, thesis or alternative, 36 hours. *Entrance requirements:* For master's, GRE, purpose statement, resume, two letters of recommendation. Additional exam requirements/recommendations for international students: Required—TOEFL (minimum score 100 iBT) or IELTS (minimum score 7.0). *Application deadline:* Applications are processed on a rolling basis. Application fee: $50 ($100 for international students). Electronic applications accepted. *Expenses:* Tuition, state resident: full-time $5119; part-time $213.30 per credit hour. Tuition, nonresident: full-time $19,778; part-time $824.10 per credit hour. *Required fees:* $3458; $133.55 per credit hour. $126.50 per semester. *Financial support:* In 2017–18, 44 students received support. Research assistantships with full tuition reimbursements available, teaching assistantships with full tuition reimbursements available, career-related internships or fieldwork, scholarships/grants, health care benefits, unspecified assistantships, and travel and conference attendance funding available. Financial award application deadline: 6/1; financial award applicants required to submit FAFSA. *Faculty research:* Public and nonprofit management, public policy analysis, program evaluation, public finance and budgeting. *Unit head:* Prof. Scott Robinson, Chair, 405-325-2061, Fax: 405-325-0718, E-mail: pscgradprog@ou.edu. *Application contact:* Jeff Alexander, Graduate Programs Coordinator, 405-325-1845, Fax: 405-325-0718, E-mail: pscgradprog@ou.edu.
Website: http://www.ou.edu/content/cas/psc/graduate/mpa.html

University of Pennsylvania, Wharton School, Department of Business and Public Policy, Philadelphia, PA 19104. Offers MBA, PhD. *Degree requirements:* For doctorate, thesis/dissertation. *Entrance requirements:* For doctorate, GRE General Test. *Faculty research:* International policy, business and government, regulation, urban development and policy, transportation.

University of Pittsburgh, Graduate School of Public and International Affairs, Master of Public Administration Program, Pittsburgh, PA 15260. Offers energy and environment (MPA); governance and international public management (MPA); policy research and analysis (MPA); public and nonprofit management (MPA); urban affairs and planning (MPA); JD/MPA; MPH/MPA; MSIS/MPA; MSW/MPA. *Accreditation:* NASPAA. *Program availability:* Part-time, evening/weekend. *Faculty:* 30 full-time (11 women), 14 part-time/adjunct (5 women). *Students:* 100 full-time (75 women), 18 part-time (12 women); includes 13 minority (6 Black or African American, non-Hispanic/Latino; 3 Asian, non-Hispanic/Latino; 4 Hispanic/Latino), 54 international. Average age 26. 220 applicants, 87% accepted, 44 enrolled. In 2017, 54 master's awarded. *Degree requirements:* For master's, thesis optional, capstone seminar. *Entrance requirements:* For master's, GRE General Test or GMAT, 2 letters of recommendation, resume, undergraduate transcripts, personal statement. Additional exam requirements/recommendations for international students: Required—TOEFL (minimum score 80 iBT); Recommended—IELTS (minimum score 7). *Application deadline:* For fall admission, 2/1 priority date for domestic students, 1/15 priority date for international students; for spring admission, 11/1 priority date for domestic students, 8/1 priority date for international students. Application fee: $50. Electronic applications accepted. *Expenses:* $23,140 per year in-state, $37,830 out-of-state. *Financial support:* In 2017–18, 23 students received support, including 1 fellowship with full tuition reimbursement available (averaging $37,000 per year), 1 research assistantship with full tuition reimbursement available (averaging $37,000 per year); career-related internships or fieldwork and scholarships/grants also available. Financial award application deadline: 2/1; financial award applicants required to submit FAFSA. *Faculty research:* Urban affairs and planning, governance and international public management, public and nonprofit management, policy research and analysis, energy and environment. *Total annual research expenditures:* $1.6 million. *Unit head:* Dr. John Keeler, Dean, 412-648-7605, Fax: 412-648-7601, E-mail: gspia@pitt.edu. *Application contact:* Dr. Michael Rizzi, Director of Student Services, 412-648-7643, Fax: 412-648-7641, E-mail: rizzim@pitt.edu.
Website: http://www.gspia.pitt.edu/

University of Pittsburgh, Graduate School of Public and International Affairs, Master of Public Policy and Management Program, Pittsburgh, PA 15260. Offers MPPM. *Program availability:* Part-time, evening/weekend, 100% online. *Faculty:* 30 full-time (11 women), 14 part-time/adjunct (5 women). *Students:* 17 full-time (6 women), 104 part-time (63 women); includes 13 minority (6 Black or African American, non-Hispanic/Latino; 2 Asian, non-Hispanic/Latino; 5 Hispanic/Latino), 11 international. Average age 42. 61 applicants, 85% accepted, 47 enrolled. In 2017, 37 master's awarded. *Entrance requirements:* For master's, 2 letters of recommendation, resume, personal statement, 5 years of full-time supervisory or budgetary experience. Additional exam requirements/recommendations for international students: Required—TOEFL (minimum score 80 iBT); Recommended—IELTS (minimum score 7). *Application deadline:* For fall admission, 6/1 priority date for domestic students, 1/15 priority date for international students; for spring admission, 11/1 priority date for domestic students, 8/1 priority date for international students; for summer admission, 3/1 priority date for domestic students, 1/15 priority date for international students. Application fee: $50. *Expenses:* $898 per credit in-state and online, $1,512 out-of-state; $425 per term fees full-time, $270 per term part-time. *Financial support:* In 2017–18, 20 students received support. Career-related internships or fieldwork and scholarships/grants available. Financial award application deadline: 1/1; financial award applicants required to submit FAFSA. *Faculty research:* Public and nonprofit management, policy research and analysis, security and intelligence studies, urban affairs and planning, human security. *Total annual research expenditures:* $1.6 million. *Unit head:* Dr. John Keeler, Dean, 412-648-7605, Fax: 412-648-7601, E-mail: gspia@pitt.edu. *Application contact:* Dr. Michael Rizzi, Director of Student Services, 412-648-7643, Fax: 412-648-7641, E-mail: rizzim@pitt.edu.
Website: http://www.gspia.pitt.edu/

University of Pittsburgh, Graduate School of Public and International Affairs, PhD Program in Public and International Affairs, Pittsburgh, PA 15260. Offers international affairs (PhD); international development (PhD); public administration (PhD); public policy (PhD). *Program availability:* Part-time, online learning. *Faculty:* 30 full-time (11 women), 14 part-time/adjunct (5 women). *Students:* 31 full-time (11 women), 2 part-time (0 women); includes 5 minority (1 Black or African American, non-Hispanic/Latino; 2 Asian, non-Hispanic/Latino; 2 Hispanic/Latino), 12 international. Average age 37. 69 applicants, 13% accepted, 8 enrolled. In 2017, 2 doctorates awarded. *Degree requirements:* For doctorate, thesis/dissertation, mid-term evaluation, preliminary exam, annual review. *Entrance requirements:* For doctorate, GRE or GMAT, 2 letters of

recommendation, resume, undergraduate transcripts, personal statement, writing sample. Additional exam requirements/recommendations for international students: Required—TOEFL (minimum score 80 iBT); Recommended—IELTS (minimum score 7). *Application deadline:* For fall admission, 1/15 for domestic and international students. Application fee: $50. Electronic applications accepted. *Expenses:* $23,140 per year in-state, $37,830 out-of-state. *Financial support:* In 2017–18, 19 students received support, including 19 research assistantships with full tuition reimbursements available (averaging $37,000 per year); fellowships, teaching assistantships, and unspecified assistantships also available. Financial award application deadline: 1/15; financial award applicants required to submit FAFSA. *Faculty research:* International development, international affairs, public policy, public administration. *Total annual research expenditures:* $1.6 million. *Unit head:* Dr. John Keeler, Dean, 412-648-7605, Fax: 412-648-7601, E-mail: gspia@pitt.edu. *Application contact:* Dr. Michael Rizzi, Director of Student Services, 412-648-7640, Fax: 412-648-7641, E-mail: rizzim@pitt.edu.
Website: http://www.gspia.pitt.edu/

University of Puerto Rico–Río Piedras, Graduate School of Planning, San Juan, PR 00931-3300. Offers economic planning systems (MP); environmental planning (MP); social policy and planning (MP); urban and territorial planning (MP). *Accreditation:* ACSP. *Program availability:* Part-time. *Degree requirements:* For master's, comprehensive exam, thesis, planning project defense. *Entrance requirements:* For master's, PAEG, GRE, minimum GPA of 3.0, 2 letters of recommendation. *Faculty research:* Municipalities, historic Atlas, Puerto Rico, economic future.

University of Regina, Faculty of Graduate Studies and Research, Johnson-Shoyama Graduate School of Public Policy, Regina, SK S4S 0A2, Canada. Offers economic analysis for public policy (Master's Certificate); health administration (MHA); health systems management (Master's Certificate); public management (MPA, Master's Certificate); public policy (MPA, MPP, PhD); public policy analysis (Master's Certificate). *Program availability:* Part-time. *Faculty:* 9 full-time (4 women), 26 part-time/adjunct (10 women). *Students:* 104 full-time (65 women), 189 part-time (123 women). 285 applicants, 52% accepted. In 2017, 30 master's awarded. *Degree requirements:* For master's, thesis (for some programs); for doctorate, thesis/dissertation. *Entrance requirements:* For doctorate, master's degree, intended research program in an area of public policy. Additional exam requirements/recommendations for international students: Required—TOEFL (minimum score 580 paper-based; 80 iBT), IELTS (minimum score 6.5), PTE (minimum score 59). *Application deadline:* For fall admission, 5/1 for domestic and international students; for winter admission, 11/1 for domestic and international students; for spring admission, 3/15 for domestic and international students. Application fee: $100. Electronic applications accepted. *Expenses:* CAD$10,626 per year (for master's degrees); CAD$8,783 per year (for PhD). *Financial support:* In 2017–18, fellowships (averaging $6,059 per year), teaching assistantships (averaging $2,562 per year) were awarded; research assistantships, career-related internships or fieldwork, and scholarships/grants also available. Financial award application deadline: 6/15. *Faculty research:* Governance and administration, public finance, public policy analysis, non-governmental organizations and alternative service delivery, micro-economics for policy analysis. *Unit head:* Dr. Kathleen McNutt, Executive Director, Main Campus, 306-585-4759, Fax: 306-585-5461, E-mail: kathy.mcnutt@uregina.ca. *Application contact:* John Bird, Manager, Main Campus, 306-585-5469, Fax: 306-585-5461, E-mail: john.bird@uregina.ca.
Website: http://www.schoolofpublicpolicy.sk.ca/

University of Rhode Island, Graduate School, College of Arts and Sciences, Department of Political Science, Kingston, RI 02881. Offers international relations (MA), including American politics; public policy and administration (MPA). *Program availability:* Part-time. *Faculty:* 13 full-time (6 women). *Students:* 17 full-time (10 women), 36 part-time (19 women); includes 7 minority (2 Black or African American, non-Hispanic/Latino; 2 Asian, non-Hispanic/Latino; 2 Hispanic/Latino; 1 Two or more races, non-Hispanic/Latino). 34 applicants, 94% accepted, 25 enrolled. In 2017, 21 master's awarded. *Entrance requirements:* For master's, GRE, GMAT, or MAT if undergraduate GPA below 3.0, 2 letters of recommendation. Additional exam requirements/recommendations for international students: Required—TOEFL. *Application deadline:* For fall admission, 11/15 for domestic students, 2/1 for international students; for spring admission, 7/15 for domestic students, 7/15 priority date for international students. Application fee: $65. Electronic applications accepted. *Expenses:* Tuition, state resident: full-time $12,706; part-time $786 per credit. Tuition, nonresident: full-time $25,216; part-time $1401 per credit. *Required fees:* $1598; $45 per credit. One-time fee: $30 part-time. *Financial support:* In 2017–18, 4 teaching assistantships with tuition reimbursements (averaging $10,761 per year) were awarded. Financial award application deadline: 2/1; financial award applicants required to submit FAFSA. *Unit head:* Dr. Brian Krueger, Department Chair, 401-874-4058, Fax: 401-874-4072, E-mail: bkrueger@uri.edu. *Application contact:* Dr. Marc Hutchison, Director/Associate Professor, 401-874-4054, Fax: 401-874-4072, E-mail: mlhutch@uri.edu.
Website: http://www.uri.edu/artsci/psc/

University of St. Thomas, School of Arts and Sciences, Houston, TX 77006-4696. Offers public policy administration (MPPA); sacred music (MSM). *Program availability:* Part-time. *Faculty:* 2 full-time (0 women), 5 part-time/adjunct (3 women). *Students:* 4 full-time (3 women), 21 part-time (13 women); includes 18 minority (8 Black or African American, non-Hispanic/Latino; 10 Hispanic/Latino), 1 international. Average age 34. 8 applicants, 100% accepted, 8 enrolled. In 2017, 8 master's awarded. *Entrance requirements:* Additional exam requirements/recommendations for international students: Required—TOEFL (minimum score 79 iBT), IELTS (minimum score 6.5), PTE (minimum score 53). *Application deadline:* For fall admission, 7/15 priority date for domestic and international students; for spring admission, 12/1 priority date for domestic and international students; for summer admission, 5/1 priority date for domestic and international students. Applications are processed on a rolling basis. Application fee: $35. Electronic applications accepted. *Expenses: Tuition:* Full-time $20,934; part-time $1163 per credit hour. *Required fees:* $250; $210 per semester. *Financial support:* In 2017–18, 6 students received support. Federal Work-Study, scholarships/grants, and state work-study, institutional employment available. Support available to part-time students. Financial award application deadline: 4/15; financial award applicants required to submit FAFSA. *Unit head:* Dr. Christopher Evans, Dean, School of Arts and Sciences, 713-525-7863, E-mail: evanscp@stthom.edu. *Application contact:* Elizabeth Kimes, 713-942-3491, E-mail: kimese@stthom.edu.
Website: http://www.stthom.edu/Academics/School_of_Arts_and_Sciences/Index.aqf

University of Saskatchewan, College of Graduate Studies and Research, School of Public Policy, Saskatoon, SK S7N 5A2, Canada. Offers MIT, MPA, MPP, PhD.

University of Southern California, Graduate School, Sol Price School of Public Policy, Doctor of Philosophy in Public Policy and Management Program, Los Angeles, CA 90089. Offers PhD. *Degree requirements:* For doctorate, thesis/dissertation. *Entrance requirements:* For doctorate, GRE. Additional exam requirements/recommendations for international students: Required—TOEFL (minimum score 600 paper-based; 100 iBT). Electronic applications accepted. *Faculty research:* Governance: effective institutions, leadership, management, community and economic development, institutional analysis, civic engagement.

University of Southern California, Graduate School, Sol Price School of Public Policy, Public Policy Programs, Los Angeles, CA 90089. Offers homeland security and public policy (Graduate Certificate); public policy (MPP, Graduate Certificate); M Pl/MPP; MPP/JD. *Program availability:* Part-time. Terminal master's awarded for partial completion of doctoral program. *Degree requirements:* For master's, practicum. *Entrance requirements:* For master's, GRE. Additional exam requirements/recommendations for international students: Required—TOEFL (minimum score 600 paper-based; 100 iBT). Electronic applications accepted. *Faculty research:* Urban political economy, community and economic development, environmental policy, transportation policy, housing policy.

University of Southern Maine, College of Management and Human Service, Muskie School of Public Service, Program in Public Policy and Management, Portland, ME 04103. Offers MPPM, JD/MPPM. *Program availability:* Part-time, evening/weekend, online learning. *Degree requirements:* For master's, thesis, capstone project, field experience. *Entrance requirements:* For master's, GRE General Test or LSAT. Additional exam requirements/recommendations for international students: Required—TOEFL. Electronic applications accepted. *Faculty research:* State and local public finance, education finance, applied social science methodology, nonprofit and higher education organizational management, public service ethics, comparative public policy.

The University of Texas at Arlington, Graduate School, College of Architecture, Planning and Public Affairs, Program in Public Policy, Arlington, TX 76019. Offers MPP. *Accreditation:* NASPAA. *Program availability:* Part-time, evening/weekend. Electronic applications accepted. *Faculty research:* Environment urban policy personnel, research theoretical foundations, urban problems.

The University of Texas at Arlington, Graduate School, College of Architecture, Planning and Public Affairs, Program in Urban Planning and Public Policy, Arlington, TX 76019. Offers PhD. *Accreditation:* ACSP. *Program availability:* Part-time, evening/weekend. *Entrance requirements:* Additional exam requirements/recommendations for international students: Required—TOEFL (minimum score 550 paper-based). Electronic applications accepted. *Faculty research:* Urban structure, GIS environmental resolutions, qualitative methods, planning history/theory.

The University of Texas at Austin, Graduate School, Lyndon B. Johnson School of Public Affairs, Austin, TX 78712-1111. Offers global policy studies (MGPS); public affairs (MP Aff); public leadership (EMPL); public policy (PhD); JD/MP Aff; MBA/MP Aff; MP Aff/MA; MP Aff/MSE. *Accreditation:* NASPAA (one or more programs are accredited). *Program availability:* Part-time. *Degree requirements:* For master's, thesis, summer internship; for doctorate, thesis/dissertation. *Entrance requirements:* For master's, GRE General Test (for MP Aff and MGPS), minimum GPA of 3.0 in upper-division classes, seven years of experience in the public sector, and interview (for EMPL); for doctorate, GRE General Test, master's degree in policy-related field. Additional exam requirements/recommendations for international students: Required—TOEFL. Electronic applications accepted. *Faculty research:* Human resource development, health and social policy, philanthropy and community service, ethical leadership, urban and international policy, science and technology policy.

The University of Texas at Dallas, School of Economic, Political and Policy Sciences, Program in Public Policy and Political Economy, Richardson, TX 75080. Offers international political economy (MS); public policy (MPP); public policy and political economy (PhD); social data analytics and research (MS). *Program availability:* Part-time, evening/weekend. *Faculty:* 12 full-time (1 woman), 1 part-time/adjunct (0 women). *Students:* 46 full-time (22 women), 33 part-time (14 women); includes 27 minority (8 Black or African American, non-Hispanic/Latino; 8 Asian, non-Hispanic/Latino; 10 Hispanic/Latino; 1 Two or more races, non-Hispanic/Latino), 21 international. Average age 33. 69 applicants, 52% accepted, 22 enrolled. In 2017, 21 master's, 3 doctorates awarded. *Degree requirements:* For doctorate, thesis/dissertation. *Entrance requirements:* For master's and doctorate, GRE General Test, minimum GPA of 3.0 in upper-level course work in field. Additional exam requirements/recommendations for international students: Required—TOEFL (minimum score 550 paper-based). *Application deadline:* For fall admission, 7/15 for domestic students, 5/1 priority date for international students; for spring admission, 11/15 for domestic students, 9/1 priority date for international students. Applications are processed on a rolling basis. Application fee: $50 ($100 for international students). Electronic applications accepted. *Expenses:* Tuition, state resident: full-time $12,916; part-time $718 per credit hour. Tuition, nonresident: full-time $25,252; part-time $1403 per credit hour. *Financial support:* In 2017–18, 46 students received support, including 4 research assistantships with partial tuition reimbursements available (averaging $17,697 per year), 14 teaching assistantships with partial tuition reimbursements available (averaging $13,100 per year); career-related internships or fieldwork, Federal Work-Study, institutionally sponsored loans, scholarships/grants, and unspecified assistantships also available. Support available to part-time students. Financial award application deadline: 4/30; financial award applicants required to submit FAFSA. *Faculty research:* Ethnicity, community and local public good provision; community mental health policy; Texas Schools Project; biological and chemical arms control; cross-disciplinary applications of quantitative methodology. *Unit head:* Dr. Jennifer Holmes, Program Head, 972-883-6843, Fax: 972-883-6297, E-mail: jholmes@utdallas.edu. *Application contact:* Marjorie McDonald, Graduate Program Administrator, 972-883-6406, Fax: 972-883-6297, E-mail: pppe@utdallas.edu.
Website: http://www.utdallas.edu/epps/public-policy-and-political-economy/

The University of Texas Rio Grande Valley, College of Liberal Arts, Department of Public Affairs and Security Studies, Edinburg, TX 78539. Offers global security studies and leadership (MPA); public administration (MPA); public policy and management (MPA). *Program availability:* Part-time, evening/weekend. *Faculty:* 8 full-time (5 women). *Students:* 6 full-time (3 women), 127 part-time (57 women); includes 96 minority (5 Black or African American, non-Hispanic/Latino; 2 Asian, non-Hispanic/Latino; 89 Hispanic/Latino), 4 international. Average age 33. 67 applicants, 97% accepted, 40 enrolled. In 2017, 77 master's awarded. *Degree requirements:* For master's, comprehensive exam (for some programs), thesis optional. *Entrance requirements:* For master's, minimum undergraduate GPA of 3.0, official transcripts, personal statement, three recommendations. Additional exam requirements/recommendations for international students: Required—TOEFL or IELTS. *Application deadline:* For fall admission, 7/1 for domestic students, 6/1 for international students; for spring admission, 11/15 for domestic students, 11/1 for international students. Applications are processed on a rolling basis. Application fee: $50 ($100 for international students). Electronic applications accepted. *Expenses:* Tuition, state resident: full-time $5550; part-time $417 per credit hour. Tuition, nonresident: full-time $13,020; part-time $832 per credit hour. *Required fees:* $1169. *Financial support:* Application deadline: 6/1. *Faculty research:* Immigration policy reform, agriculture food policy, social service delivery systems, community development, social welfare policy reform, urban/city management. *Unit head:* Terrence Garett, Chair, E-mail: terence.garrett@utrgv.edu.
Website: http://www.utrgv.edu/pass/

University of the Pacific, McGeorge School of Law, Sacramento, CA 95817. Offers advocacy (JD); international water resources law (JSD); public policy and law (LL M); JD/MBA; JD/MPPA. *Accreditation:* ABA. *Program availability:* Part-time, evening/weekend. *Faculty:* 39 full-time (18 women), 38 part-time/adjunct (14 women). *Students:* 376 full-time (200 women), 219 part-time (126 women); includes 199 minority (22 Black

or African American, non-Hispanic/Latino; 4 American Indian or Alaska Native, non-Hispanic/Latino; 40 Asian, non-Hispanic/Latino; 119 Hispanic/Latino; 2 Native Hawaiian or other Pacific Islander, non-Hispanic/Latino; 12 Two or more races, non-Hispanic/Latino), 181 international. Average age 29. 1,063 applicants, 61% accepted, 201 enrolled. In 2017, 26 master's, 135 doctorates awarded. *Degree requirements:* For master's, thesis (for some programs); for doctorate, thesis/dissertation (for some programs). *Entrance requirements:* For master's, JD; for doctorate, LSAT (for JD), LL M (for JSD). Additional exam requirements/recommendations for international students: Required—TOEFL (minimum score 600 paper-based; 100 iBT). *Application deadline:* For fall admission, 3/15 priority date for domestic students. Applications are processed on a rolling basis. Application fee: $50. Electronic applications accepted. *Expenses:* Contact institution. *Financial support:* Fellowships, research assistantships, teaching assistantships, career-related internships or fieldwork, Federal Work-Study, institutionally sponsored loans, and scholarships/grants available. Support available to part-time students. Financial award applicants required to submit FAFSA. *Faculty research:* International legal studies, public policy and law, advocacy, intellectual property law, taxation, criminal law. *Unit head:* Michael Schwartz, Dean, 916-739-7151, E-mail: jmootz@pacific.edu. *Application contact:* 916-739-7105, Fax: 916-739-7301, E-mail: mcgeorge@pacific.edu.
Website: http://www.mcgeorge.edu/

University of Utah, Graduate School, College of Social and Behavioral Science, Program in Public Policy, Salt Lake City, UT 84112. Offers MPP, MPP/JD, MPP/MPH, MPP/PhD. *Program availability:* Part-time, evening/weekend. *Students:* 16 full-time (13 women), 10 part-time (all women); includes 5 minority (1 Black or African American, non-Hispanic/Latino; 1 Asian, non-Hispanic/Latino; 2 Hispanic/Latino; 1 Two or more races, non-Hispanic/Latino). Average age 30. In 2017, 7 master's awarded. *Degree requirements:* For master's, project. *Entrance requirements:* For master's, GRE, LSAT, GMAT, or MAT. Additional exam requirements/recommendations for international students: Required—TOEFL (minimum score 583 paper-based; 93 iBT). *Application deadline:* For fall admission, 3/1 for domestic and international students. Application fee: $55 ($65 for international students). Electronic applications accepted. *Expenses:* Contact institution. *Financial support:* Fellowships with partial tuition reimbursements and unspecified assistantships available. Financial award application deadline: 2/15. *Unit head:* Lina Svedin, Director, 801-585-7834, E-mail: mppinfo@cppa.utah.edu. *Application contact:* Elizabeth Henke, Program Manager, 801-585-7834, E-mail: elizabeth.henke@cppa.utah.edu.
Website: http://www.mpp.utah.edu

University of Virginia, Frank Batten Sr. School of Leadership and Public Policy, Charlottesville, VA 22903. Offers MPP, JD/MPP, MBA/MPP, MPP/MPH, MPP/MUEP, MPP/PhD. *Faculty:* 21 full-time (8 women), 4 part-time/adjunct (1 woman). *Students:* 111 full-time (63 women), 2 part-time (both women); includes 21 minority (3 Black or African American, non-Hispanic/Latino; 9 Asian, non-Hispanic/Latino; 6 Hispanic/Latino; 3 Two or more races, non-Hispanic/Latino), 8 international. Average age 24. 227 applicants, 67% accepted, 81 enrolled. In 2017, 75 master's awarded. *Entrance requirements:* Additional exam requirements/recommendations for international students: Required—TOEFL, IELTS. *Application deadline:* For fall admission, 2/20 for domestic and international students. Applications are processed on a rolling basis. Electronic applications accepted. *Expenses:* Contact institution. *Unit head:* Allan C. Stam, Dean, 434-924-0812, Fax: 434-243-2318, E-mail: stam@virginia.edu. *Application contact:* Patti Edson, Assistant Director of Admissions, 434-982-2583, Fax: 434-243-2318, E-mail: patti.edson@virginia.edu.
Website: http://batten.virginia.edu/

University of Washington, Graduate School, Evans School of Public Policy and Governance, Seattle, WA 98195. Offers public administration (MPA); public policy and management (PhD); JD/MPA; MPA/MAIS; MPA/MPH; MPA/MS; MPA/MUP. *Accreditation:* NASPAA. *Program availability:* Part-time, evening/weekend. *Degree requirements:* For master's, thesis, internship or cooperative experience. *Entrance requirements:* For master's and doctorate, GRE General Test, minimum GPA of 3.0. Additional exam requirements/recommendations for international students: Required—TOEFL (minimum score 580 paper-based; 92 iBT). Electronic applications accepted. *Faculty research:* Environmental policy, education and social policy, nonprofit management, international affairs, urban and regional development.

University of Washington, Bothell, Master of Arts in Policy Studies Program, Bothell, WA 98011. Offers MA. *Program availability:* Evening/weekend. *Degree requirements:* For master's, thesis. *Entrance requirements:* For master's, GRE, statistics and microeconomics courses. Additional exam requirements/recommendations for international students: Required—TOEFL. Electronic applications accepted. *Faculty research:* Policy studies, cultural studies, cultural and environmental politics, disability studies, public policy.

Vanderbilt University, Program in Community Research and Action, Nashville, TN 37240-1001. Offers PhD. *Students:* 25 full-time (18 women); includes 13 minority (6 Black or African American, non-Hispanic/Latino; 4 Asian, non-Hispanic/Latino; 1 Hispanic/Latino; 2 Two or more races, non-Hispanic/Latino), 4 international. Average age 31. 101 applicants, 11% accepted, 5 enrolled. In 2017, 4 doctorates awarded. *Degree requirements:* For doctorate, thesis/dissertation, internship, fundable grant proposal. *Entrance requirements:* For doctorate, GRE General Test. Additional exam requirements/recommendations for international students: Required—TOEFL (minimum score 570 paper-based; 88 iBT). *Application deadline:* For fall admission, 12/1 for domestic and international students. Application fee: $0. Electronic applications accepted. *Expenses:* Contact institution. *Financial support:* In 2017–18, 16 students received support. Fellowships with tuition reimbursements available, research assistantships with full tuition reimbursements available, teaching assistantships with full tuition reimbursements available, Federal Work-Study, scholarships/grants, health care benefits, tuition waivers, and unspecified assistantships available. Financial award application deadline: 1/15; financial award applicants required to submit FAFSA. *Faculty research:* Applied psychological research, community theory, mental health, public policy, race dynamics. *Unit head:* Dr. Douglas Perkins, Director of Graduate Studies, 615-322-7213, Fax: 615-322-1769, E-mail: douglas.d.perkins@vanderbilt.edu. *Application contact:* Sherrie Lane, Administrative Assistant, 615-322-8484, Fax: 615-322-1141, E-mail: sherrie.a.lane@vanderbilt.edu.
Website: http://peabody.vanderbilt.edu/departments/hod/graduate-programs/phd_in_community_research_and_action/community_research_and_action_program.php

Virginia Commonwealth University, Graduate School, L. Douglas Wilder School of Government and Public Affairs, Center for Public Policy, Richmond, VA 23284-9005. Offers public policy and administration (PhD). *Degree requirements:* For doctorate, thesis/dissertation. *Entrance requirements:* For doctorate, GMAT, GRE General Test, LSAT, or MAT. Additional exam requirements/recommendations for international students: Required—TOEFL (minimum score 600 paper-based; 100 iBT); Recommended—IELTS (minimum score 6.5). Electronic applications accepted.

Virginia Polytechnic Institute and State University, Graduate School, College of Science, Blacksburg, VA 24061. Offers biological sciences (MS, PhD); biomedical technology development and management (MS); chemistry (MS, PhD); data analysis and applied statistics (MA); economics (PhD); geosciences (MS, PhD); mathematics (MS, PhD); physics (MS, PhD); psychology (MS, PhD); statistics (MS, PhD). *Faculty:* 321 full-time (103 women). *Students:* 557 full-time (205 women), 39 part-time (18 women); includes 68 minority (13 Black or African American, non-Hispanic/Latino; 1 American Indian or Alaska Native, non-Hispanic/Latino; 14 Asian, non-Hispanic/Latino; 32 Hispanic/Latino; 8 Two or more races, non-Hispanic/Latino), 238 international. Average age 27. 1,060 applicants, 15% accepted, 121 enrolled. In 2017, 75 master's, 89 doctorates awarded. *Degree requirements:* For master's, comprehensive exam (for some programs), thesis (for some programs); for doctorate, comprehensive exam (for some programs), thesis/dissertation (for some programs). *Entrance requirements:* For master's and doctorate, GRE/GMAT. Additional exam requirements/recommendations for international students: Required—TOEFL (minimum score 80 iBT). *Application deadline:* For fall admission, 8/1 for domestic students, 4/1 for international students; for spring admission, 1/1 for domestic students, 9/1 for international students. Applications are processed on a rolling basis. Application fee: $75. Electronic applications accepted. *Expenses:* Tuition, state resident: full-time $15,072; part-time $718.50 per credit hour. Tuition, nonresident: full-time $28,810; part-time $1448.25 per credit hour. *Required fees:* $2741; $502 per semester. Tuition and fees vary according to course load, campus/location and program. *Financial support:* In 2017–18, 2 fellowships with full tuition reimbursements (averaging $12,267 per year), 140 research assistantships with full tuition reimbursements (averaging $23,004 per year), 351 teaching assistantships with full tuition reimbursements (averaging $20,157 per year) were awarded. Financial award application deadline: 3/1; financial award applicants required to submit FAFSA. *Total annual research expenditures:* $24.3 million. *Unit head:* Dr. Sally C. Morton, Dean, 540-231-5422, Fax: 540-231-3380, E-mail: scmorton@vt.edu. *Application contact:* Allison Craft, Executive Assistant, 540-231-6394, Fax: 540-231-3380, E-mail: crafta@vt.edu.
Website: http://www.science.vt.edu/

Walden University, Graduate Programs, Richard W. Riley College of Education and Leadership, Minneapolis, MN 55401. Offers adult education (Post-Master's Certificate); adult learning (Graduate Certificate); college teaching and learning (Graduate Certificate); community college leadership (Ed D); curriculum, instruction and assessment (Ed D, Ed S, Graduate Certificate); developmental education (Graduate Certificate); early childhood administration, management, and leadership (Graduate Certificate); early childhood education (Ed D, Ed S); early childhood public policy and advocacy (Graduate Certificate); early childhood studies (MS), including administration, management and leadership, early childhood public policy and advocacy, teaching adults in the early childhood field, teaching and diversity in early childhood education; education (MS, PhD), including adolescent literacy and learning (MS), curriculum, instruction, and assessment (grades K-12) (MS), curriculum, instruction, assessment, and evaluation (PhD), early childhood leadership and advocacy (PhD), early childhood special education (PhD), educational leadership (MS), educational leadership and administration (principal preparation) (MS), educational technology and design (PhD), elementary reading and literacy (PreK-6) (MS), elementary reading and mathematics (grades K-6) (MS), global and comparative education (PhD), higher education leadership management and policy (PhD), integrating technology in the classroom (grades K-12) (MS), learning, instruction and innovation (PhD), mathematics (grades 5-8) (MS), mathematics (grades K-6) (MS), mathematics and science (grades K-8) (MS), organizational research, assessment, and evaluation (PhD), reading and literacy with a reading K-12 endorsement (MS), reading literacy assessment and evaluation (PhD), science (grades K-8) (MS), special education (non-licensure) (grades K-12) (MS), teacher leadership (grades K-12) (MS), teaching English language learners (grades K-12) (MS); educational administration and leadership (Ed D); educational leadership and administration (principal preparation) (Ed S); educational technology (Ed D, Ed S, Post Master's Certificate); elementary reading and literacy (Graduate Certificate); engaging culturally diverse learners (Graduate Certificate); enrollment management and institutional marketing (Graduate Certificate); higher education (MS), including adult learning, college teaching and learning, enrollment management and institutional marketing, global higher education, leadership for student success, online and distance learning; higher education and adult learning (Ed D); higher education leadership and management (Ed D); higher education leadership for student success (Graduate Certificate); instructional design and technology (MS, Postbaccalaureate Certificate), including general program (MS), online learning (MS), training and performance improvement (MS); integrating technology in the classroom (Graduate Certificate); mathematics 5-8 (Graduate Certificate); mathematics K-6 (Graduate Certificate); online teaching for adult educators (Graduate Certificate); reading, literacy, and assessment (Ed D, Ed S); science K-8 (Graduate Certificate); special education (Ed D, Ed S, Graduate Certificate); special education (K-age 21) (MAT); teacher leadership (Graduate Certificate); teaching adults English as a second language (Graduate Certificate); teaching adults in the early childhood field (Graduate Certificate); teaching and diversity in early childhood education (Graduate Certificate); teaching English language learners (grades K-12) (Graduate Certificate); teaching K-12 students online (Graduate Certificate). *Accreditation:* NCATE. *Program availability:* Part-time, evening/weekend, online only, 100% online. *Degree requirements:* For doctorate, thesis/dissertation (for some programs), residency; for other advanced degree, residency (for some programs). *Entrance requirements:* For master's, bachelor's degree or higher; minimum GPA of 2.5; official transcripts; goal statement (for some programs); access to computer and Internet; for doctorate, master's degree or higher; three years of related professional or academic experience (preferred); minimum GPA of 3.0; goal statement and current resume (for select programs); official transcripts; access to computer and Internet; for other advanced degree, relevant work experience; access to computer and Internet. Additional exam requirements/recommendations for international students: Required—TOEFL (minimum score 550 paper-based, 79 iBT), IELTS (minimum score 6.5), Michigan English Language Assessment Battery (minimum score 82), or PTE (minimum score 53). Electronic applications accepted.

Walden University, Graduate Programs, School of Public Policy and Administration, Minneapolis, MN 55401. Offers criminal justice (MPA, MPP, MS, Graduate Certificate), including emergency management (MS, PhD), general program (MS), global leadership (MS, PhD), homeland security and policy coordination (MS, PhD), law and public policy (MS, PhD), policy analysis (MS, PhD), public management and leadership (MS, PhD), self-designed (MS), terrorism, mediation, and peace (MS, PhD); criminal justice and executive management (MS), including global leadership (MS, PhD); criminal justice leadership and executive management (MS), including emergency management (MS, PhD), general program, homeland security and policy coordination (MS, PhD), law and public policy (MS, PhD), policy analysis (MS, PhD), public management and leadership (MS, PhD), self-designed, terrorism, mediation, and peace (MS, PhD); emergency management (MPA, MPP, MS), including criminal justice (MS, PhD), general program (MS), homeland security (MS), public management and leadership (MS, PhD), terrorism and emergency management (MS); general program (MPA, MPP); global leadership (MPA, MPP); government management (Graduate Certificate); health policy (MPA, MPP); homeland security (Graduate Certificate); homeland security and policy coordination (MPA, MPP); international nongovernmental organizations (MPA, MPP); law and public policy (MPA, MPP); local government management for sustainable communities (MPA, MPP); nonprofit management (Graduate Certificate); nonprofit

management and leadership (MPA, MPP, MS), including global leadership (MS, PhD); international nongovernmental organization (MS), local government for sustainable communities (MS), self designed (MS); online teaching in higher education (Post-Master's Certificate); policy analysis (MPA); public management and leadership (MPA, MPP, Graduate Certificate); public policy (Graduate Certificate); public policy and administration (PhD), including criminal justice (MS, PhD), emergency management (MS, PhD), global leadership (MS, PhD), health policy, homeland security and policy coordination (MS, PhD), international nongovernmental organizations, law and public policy (MS, PhD), local government management for sustainable communities, nonprofit management and leadership, policy analysis (MS, PhD), public management and leadership (MS, PhD), terrorism, mediation, and peace (MS, PhD); strategic planning and public policy (Graduate Certificate); terrorism, mediation, and peace (MPA, MPP). *Program availability:* Part-time, evening/weekend, online only, 100% online. *Degree requirements:* For doctorate, thesis/dissertation, residency. *Entrance requirements:* For master's, bachelor's degree or higher; minimum GPA of 2.5; official transcripts; goal statement (for some programs); access to computer and Internet; for doctorate, master's degree or higher; three years of related professional or academic experience (preferred); minimum GPA of 3.0; goal statement and current resume (for select programs); official transcripts; access to computer and Internet; for other advanced degree, relevant work experience; access to computer and Internet. Additional exam requirements/recommendations for international students: Required—TOEFL (minimum score 550 paper-based, 79 iBT), IELTS (minimum score 6.5), Michigan English Language Assessment Battery (minimum score 82), or PTE (minimum score 53). Electronic applications accepted.

Walden University, Graduate Programs, School of Social Work and Human Services, Minneapolis, MN 55401. Offers addictions and social work (DSW); advanced clinical practice (MSW); clinical expertise (DSW); criminal justice (DSW); disaster, crisis, and intervention (DSW); family studies and interventions (DSW); human and social services (PhD), including advanced research, community and social services, community intervention and leadership, conflict management, criminal justice, disaster crisis and intervention, family studies and intervention, gerontology, global social services, higher education, human services and nonprofit administration, mental health facilitation; medical social work (DSW); military social work (MSW); policy practice (DSW); social work (PhD), including addictions and social work, clinical expertise, criminal justice, disaster, crisis and intervention, family studies and interventions, medical social work, policy practice, social work administration; social work administration (DSW); social work in healthcare (MSW); social work with children and families (MSW). *Accreditation:* CSWE. *Program availability:* Part-time, evening/weekend, online only, 100% online. *Degree requirements:* For master's, residency (for some programs); for doctorate, thesis/dissertation, residency. *Entrance requirements:* For master's, bachelor's degree or higher; minimum GPA of 2.5; official transcripts; goal statement (for some programs); access to computer and Internet; for doctorate, master's degree or higher; three years of related professional or academic experience (preferred); minimum GPA of 3.0; goal statement and current resume (for select programs); official transcripts; access to computer and Internet. Additional exam requirements/recommendations for international students: Required—TOEFL (minimum score 550 paper-based, 79 iBT), IELTS (minimum score 6.5), Michigan English Language Assessment Battery (minimum score 82), or PTE (minimum score 53). Electronic applications accepted.

Wayne State University, College of Liberal Arts and Sciences, Department of History, Detroit, MI 48202. Offers history (MA, PhD); public history (MA), including African American history and culture, cultural resource management, gender, sexuality, and women's studies, labor and urban history, museum studies, public policy; world history (Graduate Certificate); JD/MA; M Ed/MA; MLIS/MA. Doctoral program admits for fall only. *Program availability:* Evening/weekend. *Faculty:* 17. *Students:* 21 full-time (7 women), 20 part-time (7 women); includes 9 minority (5 Black or African American, non-Hispanic/Latino; 1 Hispanic/Latino; 3 Two or more races, non-Hispanic/Latino). Average age 40. 50 applicants, 16% accepted, 5 enrolled. In 2017, 11 master's, 2 doctorates awarded. *Degree requirements:* For master's, comprehensive exam, thesis (for some programs), final oral exam on thesis or essay and seminar; internship and project (for public history); for doctorate, variable foreign language requirement, comprehensive exam, thesis/dissertation, qualifying exam in 4 fields of history. *Entrance requirements:* For master's, GRE General Test, minimum undergraduate GPA of 3.25 in history, 3.0 overall; at least 18 credits in history and related subjects at the advanced undergraduate level; foreign language; letter of intent; research paper; at least two letters of recommendation from former instructors; for doctorate, GRE General Test, minimum GPA of 3.0, 3.25 in minimum of 18 semester credits in history and related subjects; letter of intent; research paper; at least three letters of recommendation from former professors; for Graduate Certificate, baccalaureate degree from accredited college or university; minimum GPA of 3.0, 3.25 in a minimum of eighteen semester credits in history and related subjects at the advanced undergraduate level. Additional exam requirements/recommendations for international students: Required—TOEFL (minimum score 550 paper-based; 79 iBT), TWE (minimum score 5.5), Michigan English Language Assessment Battery (minimum score 85); Recommended—IELTS (minimum score 6.5). *Application deadline:* For fall admission, 2/1 priority date for domestic and international students; for winter admission, 11/1 for domestic students, 10/1 priority date for international students; for spring admission, 2/1 for domestic students, 1/1 priority date for international students. Application fee: $50. Electronic applications accepted. *Expenses:* Tuition, state resident: full-time $10,224; part-time $638.98 per credit hour. Tuition, nonresident: full-time $22,145; part-time $1384.04 per credit hour. Tuition and fees vary according to course load and program. *Financial support:* In 2017–18, 17 students received support, including 3 fellowships with tuition reimbursements available (averaging $17,198 per year), 1 research assistantship with tuition reimbursement available (averaging $22,241 per year), 6 teaching assistantships with tuition reimbursements available (averaging $18,534 per year); scholarships/grants, health care benefits, and unspecified assistantships also available. Financial award applicants required to submit FAFSA. *Faculty research:* Urban history, labor, political history, history of gender and women. *Unit head:* Dr. Elizabeth V. Faue, Professor/Chair, 313-577-2525, E-mail: evfaue@wayne.edu. *Application contact:* Dr. Eric Ash, Associate Professor and Director of Graduate Studies, 313-577-2525, E-mail: ericash@wayne.edu.
Website: http://clas.wayne.edu/history/

Wayne State University, College of Liberal Arts and Sciences, Department of Political Science, Detroit, MI 48202. Offers political science (MA, PhD); public administration (MPA), including economic development policy and management, health and human services policy and management, human and fiscal resource management, nonprofit policy and management, organizational behavior and management, urban and metropolitan policy and management; JD/MA. *Accreditation:* NASPAA. *Faculty:* 18. *Students:* 48 full-time (20 women), 68 part-time (36 women); includes 37 minority (26 Black or African American, non-Hispanic/Latino; 3 Asian, non-Hispanic/Latino; 2 Hispanic/Latino; 6 Two or more races, non-Hispanic/Latino), 6 international. Average age 32. 105 applicants, 39% accepted, 20 enrolled. In 2017, 17 master's, 3 doctorates awarded. *Degree requirements:* For master's, comprehensive exam (for some programs), thesis (for some programs); for doctorate, thesis/dissertation. *Entrance requirements:* For master's, GRE General Test, substantial undergraduate preparation in the social sciences, minimum upper-division undergraduate GPA of 3.0, two letters of recommendation, personal statement; for doctorate, GRE General Test, 3 letters of recommendation; personal statement; interview. Additional exam requirements/recommendations for international students: Required—TOEFL (minimum score 550 paper-based; 79 iBT), TWE (minimum score 5.5), Michigan English Language Assessment Battery (minimum score 85); Recommended—IELTS (minimum score 6.5). *Application deadline:* For fall admission, 5/15 for domestic students, 5/1 priority date for international students; for winter admission, 10/15 for domestic students, 9/1 priority date for international students. Applications are processed on a rolling basis. Application fee: $50. Electronic applications accepted. *Expenses:* Contact institution. *Financial support:* In 2017–18, 44 students received support, including 6 fellowships with tuition reimbursements available (averaging $11,698 per year), 12 teaching assistantships with tuition reimbursements available (averaging $18,534 per year); research assistantships with tuition reimbursements available, scholarships/grants, health care benefits, and unspecified assistantships also available. Financial award applicants required to submit FAFSA. *Faculty research:* American government and politics, comparative politics, political methodology, political theory, public administration, public law, public policy, world politics/international relations, formal theory/modeling, gender and politics, international law, peace research, political economy, political psychology, politics of developing countries, race, religion, and ethnicity, urban politics. *Unit head:* Dr. Daniel Geller, Professor and Chair, 313-577-6328, E-mail: dgeller@wayne.edu. *Application contact:* Dr. Sharon Lean, Graduate Director, 313-577-2630, E-mail: gradpolisci@wayne.edu.
Website: http://clas.wayne.edu/politicalscience/

Wilfrid Laurier University, Faculty of Graduate and Postdoctoral Studies, School of International Policy and Governance, International Public Policy Program, Waterloo, ON N2L 3C5, Canada. Offers global governance (MIPP); human security (MIPP); international economic relations (MIPP); international environmental policy (MIPP). Offered jointly with University of Waterloo. *Entrance requirements:* For master's, honours BA with minimum B average. Additional exam requirements/recommendations for international students: Required—TOEFL (minimum score 89 iBT). Electronic applications accepted. *Faculty research:* International environmental policy, international economic relations, human security, global governance.

William Paterson University of New Jersey, College of Humanities and Social Sciences, Wayne, NJ 07470-8420. Offers applied sociology (MA); assessment and evaluation research (Certificate); bilingual education (Certificate); clinical and counseling psychology (MA); clinical psychology (Psy D); creative and professional writing (MFA); English (MA); history (MA); public policy and international affairs (MA); teaching English as a second language (Certificate). *Program availability:* Part-time. *Faculty:* 36 full-time (21 women), 10 part-time/adjunct (5 women). *Students:* 62 full-time (44 women), 102 part-time (71 women); includes 76 minority (12 Black or African American, non-Hispanic/Latino; 8 Asian, non-Hispanic/Latino; 50 Hispanic/Latino; 6 Two or more races, non-Hispanic/Latino), 6 international. Average age 33. 156 applicants, 51% accepted, 52 enrolled. In 2017, 39 master's awarded. *Degree requirements:* For master's, thesis (for some programs), internship (for some programs). *Entrance requirements:* For master's, GRE/MAT, minimum GPA of 3.0; 2 letters of recommendation; writing sample/personal statement. Additional exam requirements/recommendations for international students: Required—TOEFL (minimum score 550 paper-based; 79 iBT), IELTS (minimum score 6). *Application deadline:* For fall admission, 6/1 for domestic students, 3/1 for international students; for spring admission, 11/1 for domestic students, 10/1 for international students. Applications are processed on a rolling basis. Application fee: $50. Electronic applications accepted. *Expenses:* Tuition, state resident: full-time $13,920; part-time $6264 per year. Tuition, nonresident: full-time $21,700; part-time $9765 per year. *Required fees:* $80; $36 per year. Tuition and fees vary according to course load, degree level and program. *Financial support:* In 2017–18, 3,480 students received support. Career-related internships or fieldwork, Federal Work-Study, scholarships/grants, and unspecified assistantships available. Support available to part-time students. Financial award application deadline: 3/15; financial award applicants required to submit FAFSA. *Faculty research:* Relationship violence, work-family balance, social development of Japan, theories justifying war, reactions to trauma. *Total annual research expenditures:* $32,300. *Unit head:* Dr. Kara Rabbitt, Dean, 973-720-2180, Fax: 973-720-2955, E-mail: rabbittk@wpunj.edu. *Application contact:* Tinu Adeniran, Associate Director, Graduate Admissions, 973-720-2764, Fax: 973-720-2035, E-mail: adenirant@wpunj.edu.
Website: http://www.wpunj.edu/cohss

York University, Faculty of Graduate Studies, Faculty of Liberal Arts and Professional Studies, Program in Public Policy, Administration and Law, Toronto, ON M3J 1P3, Canada. Offers MPPAL.

Rural Planning and Studies

Brandon University, Department of Rural Development, Brandon, MB R7A 6A9, Canada. Offers MRD, Diploma. *Degree requirements:* For master's, thesis. *Entrance requirements:* For master's, minimum GPA of 3.0, 2 letters of reference. Additional exam requirements/recommendations for international students: Required—TOEFL (minimum score 580 paper-based). Electronic applications accepted. *Faculty research:* Regional development, healthy communities, economic impact analysis, rural tourism, resource management.

Dalhousie University, Faculty of Architecture and Planning, School of Planning, Halifax, NS B3J 2X4, Canada. Offers M Eng, M Plan, MPS. *Degree requirements:* For master's, thesis. *Entrance requirements:* Additional exam requirements/recommendations for international students: Required—TOEFL, IELTS, CANTEST, CAEL, or Michigan English Language Assessment Battery. Electronic applications accepted.

East Carolina University, Graduate School, Thomas Harriot College of Arts and Sciences, Department of Geography, Planning, and Environment, Greenville, NC 27858-4353. Offers development and environmental planning (Certificate); economic development (Certificate); geographic information science and technology (Certificate); geography (MA), including geography, planning, rural development. *Program availability:* Part-time, evening/weekend, online learning. *Students:* 15 full-time (8 women), 6 part-time (2 women); includes 4 minority (3 Black or African American, non-Hispanic/Latino; 1 Hispanic/Latino). Average age 27. 14 applicants, 93% accepted, 8 enrolled. In 2017, 5 master's, 1 other advanced degree awarded. *Degree requirements:* For master's, comprehensive exam, thesis optional. *Entrance requirements:* For master's, GRE General Test. Additional exam requirements/recommendations for international students: Recommended—TOEFL (minimum score 78 iBT), IELTS (minimum score 6.5). *Application deadline:* For fall admission, 4/1 priority date for domestic and international students. Applications are processed on a rolling basis. Application fee: $75. Electronic applications accepted. *Expenses:* Tuition, state resident: full-time $4749; part-time $297 per credit hour. Tuition, nonresident: full-time $17,898; part-time $1119 per credit hour. *Required fees:* $2691; $224 per credit hour. Part-time tuition and fees vary according to course load and program. *Financial support:* Research assistantships with partial tuition reimbursements, teaching assistantships with partial tuition reimbursements, and Federal Work-Study available. Support available to part-time students. Financial award application deadline: 3/1. *Faculty research:* Coastal vulnerability and adaptation, emergency management, public understanding of risk, catastrophic events. *Unit head:* Dr. Thad Wasklewicz, Chair, 252-328-6230, E-mail: wasklewiczt@ecu.edu. *Application contact:* Dean of Graduate School, 252-328-6012, Fax: 252-328-6071, E-mail: gradschool@ecu.edu.
Website: http://www.ecu.edu/geog/

Iowa State University of Science and Technology, Rural, Agricultural, Technological, and Environmental History Program, Ames, IA 50011-1054. Offers PhD. *Entrance requirements:* Additional exam requirements/recommendations for international students: Required—TOEFL (minimum score 600 paper-based; 79 iBT), IELTS (minimum score 7). Electronic applications accepted.

Université Laval, Faculty of Agricultural and Food Sciences, Program in Integrated Rural Development, Québec, QC G1K 7P4, Canada. Offers Diploma. *Entrance requirements:* For degree, good knowledge of French. Electronic applications accepted.

University of Alaska Fairbanks, College of Rural and Community Development, Department of Alaska Native Studies and Rural Development, Fairbanks, AK 99775-6500. Offers rural development (MA). *Program availability:* Part-time, online only, blended/hybrid learning. *Degree requirements:* For master's, comprehensive exam, oral defense of project or thesis. *Entrance requirements:* For master's, bachelor's degree from accredited institution with minimum cumulative undergraduate and major GPA of 3.0. Additional exam requirements/recommendations for international students: Required—TOEFL (minimum score 550 paper-based; 79 iBT). Electronic applications accepted. *Faculty research:* International indigenous leadership development, interrelationships between rural communities and global economy.

University of Guelph, Graduate Studies, Ontario Agricultural College, School of Environmental Design and Rural Development, Interdisciplinary Program in Rural Studies, Guelph, ON N1G 2W1, Canada. Offers PhD. Offered in cooperation with the Department of Food, Agricultural and Resource Economics, and the Department of Geography. *Program availability:* Part-time. *Degree requirements:* For doctorate, thesis/dissertation, qualifying exam. *Entrance requirements:* Additional exam requirements/recommendations for international students: Required—TOEFL (minimum score 600 paper-based), IELTS (minimum score 7). Electronic applications accepted. *Faculty research:* Sustainable rural communities, human resource development, rural planning and development.

University of Guelph, Graduate Studies, Ontario Agricultural College, School of Environmental Design and Rural Development, Program in Capacity Development and Extension, Guelph, ON N1G 2W1, Canada. Offers M Sc. *Program availability:* Part-time. *Degree requirements:* For master's, thesis optional. *Entrance requirements:* For master's, minimum B- average in previous 2 years of course work. Additional exam requirements/recommendations for international students: Required—TOEFL (minimum score 550 paper-based; 89 iBT), IELTS (minimum score 6.5). Electronic applications accepted. *Faculty research:* Adult learning in non-formal settings, communication technology for remote areas, rural quality of life.

University of Guelph, Graduate Studies, Ontario Agricultural College, School of Environmental Design and Rural Development, Program in Rural Planning and Development, Guelph, ON N1G 2W1, Canada. Offers international rural planning and development (M Sc); rural planning and development in Canada (M Sc). M Sc offered in cooperation with Departments of Food, Agricultural and Resource Economics; Geography; Land Resource Science; and others by arrangement. *Program availability:* Part-time. *Degree requirements:* For master's, thesis or alternative. *Entrance requirements:* For master's, minimum B- average during previous 2 years of course work. Additional exam requirements/recommendations for international students: Required—TOEFL (minimum score 550 paper-based), IELTS (minimum score 6.5). Electronic applications accepted. *Faculty research:* Canadian and international rural planning, resource and economic development, tourism.

University of Montana, Graduate School, College of Humanities and Sciences, Department of Geography, Missoula, MT 59812. Offers community and environmental planning (MA); geography (MA, MS). *Entrance requirements:* For master's, GRE General Test. Additional exam requirements/recommendations for international students: Required—TOEFL.

University of Wyoming, College of Arts and Sciences, Department of Geography, Program in Rural Planning and Natural Resources, Laramie, WY 82071. Offers community and regional planning and natural resources (MP). *Degree requirements:* For master's, thesis or alternative. *Entrance requirements:* For master's, GRE General Test, minimum GPA of 3.0. Additional exam requirements/recommendations for international students: Required—TOEFL. *Faculty research:* Rural and small town planning, public land management.

Sustainable Development

American University, School of International Service, Washington, DC 20016-8071. Offers comparative and regional studies (Certificate); cross-cultural communication (Certificate); development management (MS); ethics, peace, and global affairs (MA); European studies (Certificate); global environmental policy (MA, Certificate); global information technology (Certificate); global media (MA); international affairs (MA), including comparative and regional studies, global governance, politics, and security, international economic relations, natural resources and sustainable development, U.S. foreign policy and national security; international arts management (Certificate); international communication (MA, Certificate); international development (MA); international economic policy (Certificate); international economic relations (Certificate); international economics (MA); international peace and conflict resolution (MA, Certificate); international politics (Certificate); international relations (MA, PhD); international service (MIS); peacebuilding (Certificate); social enterprise (MA); the Americas (Certificate); United States foreign policy (Certificate); JD/MA. *Program availability:* Part-time, evening/weekend, 100% online. *Faculty:* 112 full-time (50 women), 46 part-time/adjunct (19 women). *Students:* 495 full-time (333 women), 518 part-time (276 women); includes 360 minority (95 Black or African American, non-Hispanic/Latino; 2 American Indian or Alaska Native, non-Hispanic/Latino; 60 Asian, non-Hispanic/Latino; 164 Hispanic/Latino; 39 Two or more races, non-Hispanic/Latino), 98 international. Average age 30. 1,559 applicants, 81% accepted, 356 enrolled. In 2017, 427 master's, 9 doctorates, 5 other advanced degrees awarded. Terminal master's awarded for partial completion of doctoral program. *Degree requirements:* For master's, one foreign language, comprehensive exam, thesis or alternative; for doctorate, one foreign language, comprehensive exam, thesis/dissertation. *Entrance requirements:* For master's, GRE; GMAT or GRE (for MA in social enterprise), transcripts, resume, 2 letters of recommendation, statement of purpose; for doctorate, GRE, transcripts, resume, 3 letters of recommendation, statement of purpose. Additional exam requirements/recommendations for international students: Required—TOEFL (minimum score 600 paper-based; 100 iBT). *Application deadline:* For fall admission, 1/15 for domestic students, 1/1 for international students; for spring admission, 10/1 for domestic students, 9/15 for international students. Application fee: $55. Electronic applications accepted. *Expenses:* Contact institution. *Financial support:* Research assistantships, teaching assistantships, institutionally sponsored loans, scholarships/grants, and unspecified assistantships available. Financial award application deadline: 1/15; financial award applicants required to submit FAFSA. *Application contact:* 202-885-1646, Fax: 202-885-1109, E-mail: sisgrad@american.edu.
Website: http://www.american.edu/sis/

The American University in Cairo, School of Sciences and Engineering, Cairo, Egypt. Offers biotechnology (MS); chemistry (MS); computer science (MS); computing (M Comp); construction engineering (M Eng, MS); electronics and communications engineering (M Eng); environmental engineering (MS); environmental system design (M Eng); mechanical engineering (M Eng, MS); nanotechnology (MS); physics (MS); robotics, control and smart systems (MS); sciences and engineering (PhD); sustainable development (MS, Graduate Diploma). *Program availability:* Part-time, evening/weekend. *Faculty:* 53 full-time (8 women), 12 part-time/adjunct (0 women). *Students:* 62 full-time (26 women), 210 part-time (104 women), 14 international. Average age 28. 252 applicants, 39% accepted, 51 enrolled. In 2017, 71 master's, 10 doctorates awarded. *Degree requirements:* For master's, comprehensive exam (for some programs), thesis (for some programs); for doctorate, comprehensive exam (for some programs), thesis/ dissertation. *Entrance requirements:* Additional exam requirements/recommendations for international students: Required—TOEFL (minimum score 450 paper-based; 45 iBT), IELTS (minimum score 5). *Application deadline:* For fall admission, 2/1 priority date for domestic and international students; for spring admission, 10/15 priority date for domestic and international students. Applications are processed on a rolling basis. Application fee: $85. Electronic applications accepted. *Financial support:* Fellowships with partial tuition reimbursements, scholarships/grants, and unspecified assistantships available. Financial award application deadline: 3/10. *Faculty research:* Construction, mechanical, and electronics engineering; physics; computer science; biotechnology; nanotechnology; chemistry; robotics. *Unit head:* Dr. Hassan El Fawal, Dean, 20-2-2615-2926, E-mail: hassan.elfawal@aucegypt.edu. *Application contact:* Maha Hegazi, Director for Graduate Admissions, 20-2-2615-1462, E-mail: mahahegazi@aucegypt.edu.
Website: http://www.aucegypt.edu/sse/Pages/default.aspx

Antioch University Los Angeles, Program in Urban Sustainability, Culver City, CA 90230. Offers MA. *Students:* 20 full-time (14 women), 1 part-time (0 women); includes 15 minority (4 Black or African American, non-Hispanic/Latino; 1 Asian, non-Hispanic/Latino; 3 Hispanic/Latino; 7 Two or more races, non-Hispanic/Latino). Average age 43. *Unit head:* Dr. LucyAnn Gelselman, President, 310-578-1080 Ext. 112, Fax: 310-822-4824. *Application contact:* Information Contact, 310-578-1090, Fax: 310-822-4824, E-mail: admissions@antiochla.edu.
Website: http://www.antiochla.edu/academics/ma-urban-sustainability/

Antioch University New England, Graduate School, Department of Education, Experienced Educators Program, Keene, NH 03431-3552. Offers foundations of education (M Ed), including applied behavioral analysis, autism spectrum disorders, educating for sustainability, next-generation learning using technology, problem-based learning using critical skills, teacher leadership; principal certification (PMC). *Degree requirements:* For master's, thesis, practicum. *Entrance requirements:* For master's, previous course work and work experience in education. Additional exam requirements/recommendations for international students: Required—TOEFL (minimum score 550 paper-based). Electronic applications accepted. *Expenses:* Contact institution. *Faculty research:* Classroom action research, school restructuring, problem-based learning, brain-based learning.

Antioch University New England, Graduate School, Department of Environmental Studies, Program in Advocacy for Social Justice and Sustainability, Keene, NH 03431-3552. Offers MS. *Degree requirements:* For master's, practicum, seminar. *Entrance requirements:* For master's, samples of written work, portfolio, letters of recommendation, interview. Additional exam requirements/recommendations for international students: Required—TOEFL (minimum score 550 paper-based). Electronic applications accepted.

Arizona State University at the Tempe campus, School of Sustainability, Tempe, AZ 85287-5502. Offers sustainability (MA, MS, PhD); sustainable technology and management (Graduate Certificate). *Program availability:* Part-time, evening/weekend. Terminal master's awarded for partial completion of doctoral program. *Degree requirements:* For master's, thesis, interactive Program of Study (iPOS) submitted before completing 50 percent of required credit hours; for doctorate, comprehensive exam, thesis/dissertation, interactive Program of Study (iPOS) submitted before completing 50 percent of required credit hours. *Entrance requirements:* For master's, GRE; for doctorate,

GRE, minimum GPA of 3.0 or equivalent in last 2 years of work leading to bachelor's degree. Additional exam requirements/recommendations for international students: Required—TOEFL, IELTS, or PTE. Electronic applications accepted.

Baruch College of the City University of New York, Austin W. Marxe School of Public and International Affairs, Program in Public Administration, New York, NY 10010-5585. Offers general public administration (MPA); health care policy (MPA); nonprofit administration (MPA); policy analysis and evaluation (MPA); public management (MPA); urban development and sustainability (MPA); MS/MPA. *Accreditation:* NASPAA. *Program availability:* Part-time, evening/weekend. *Degree requirements:* For master's, thesis, capstone. *Entrance requirements:* For master's, GRE General Test. Additional exam requirements/recommendations for international students: Required—TOEFL. Electronic applications accepted. *Expenses:* Contact institution. *Faculty research:* Urbanization, population and poverty in the developing world, housing and community development, labor unions and housing, government-nongovernment relations, immigration policy, social network analysis, cross-sectoral governance, comparative healthcare systems, program evaluation, social welfare policy, health outcomes, educational policy and leadership, transnationalism, infant health, welfare reform, racial/ethnic disparities in health, urban politics, homelessness, race and ethnic relations.

See Display on page 910 and Close-Up on page 955.

Binghamton University, State University of New York, Graduate School, Program in Sustainable Communities, Binghamton, NY 13902-6000. Offers MA, MS. *Program availability:* Part-time. *Faculty:* 12 full-time (11 women). *Students:* 11 full-time (8 women); includes 2 minority (1 Black or African American, non-Hispanic/Latino; 1 Asian, non-Hispanic/Latino). Average age 25. 14 applicants, 86% accepted, 6 enrolled. *Entrance requirements:* For master's, undergraduate transcripts, minimum GPA of 3.0, personal statement, resume or curriculum vitae, two letters of recommendation, professional writing sample or essay. Additional exam requirements/recommendations for international students: Required—TOEFL, IELTS, or PTE. *Application deadline:* Applications are processed on a rolling basis. *Financial support:* In 2017–18, 2 students received support. *Unit head:* George Homsy, Program Advisor, 607-777-9184, E-mail: ghomsy@binghamton.edu. *Application contact:* Ben Balkaya, Assistant Dean and Director, 607-777-2151, Fax: 607-777-2501, E-mail: balkaya@binghamton.edu. Website: https://www.binghamton.edu/sustainable-communities/

Boston Architectural College, Graduate Programs, Boston, MA 02115-2795. Offers architecture (M Arch); historic preservation (MDS); interior design (MID); landscape architecture (MLA); sustainable design (MDS). *Accreditation:* CIDA. *Degree requirements:* For master's, thesis. *Entrance requirements:* For master's, portfolio (recommended). Electronic applications accepted.

Brandeis University, The Heller School for Social Policy and Management, Program in Nonprofit Management, Waltham, MA 02454-9110. Offers child, youth, and family management (MBA); health care management (MBA); social impact management (MBA); social policy and management (MBA); sustainable development (MBA); MBA/MA; MBA/MD. MBA/MD program offered in conjunction with Tufts University School of Medicine. *Accreditation:* AACSB. *Program availability:* Part-time. *Degree requirements:* For master's, team consulting project. *Entrance requirements:* For master's, GMAT (preferred) or GRE, 2 letters of recommendation, problem statement analysis, 3-5 years of professional experience. Additional exam requirements/recommendations for international students: Required—TOEFL (minimum score 600 paper-based; 100 iBT). Electronic applications accepted. *Expenses:* Contact institution. *Faculty research:* Health care; children and families; elder and disabled services; social impact management; organizations in the non-profit, for-profit, or public sector.

Brandeis University, The Heller School for Social Policy and Management, Program in Sustainable International Development, Waltham, MA 02454-9110. Offers international development (MA); MA/JD; MA/MA; MBA/MA. MA/JD program offered in conjunction with Northeastern University School of Law. *Degree requirements:* For master's, 2nd year fieldwork or internship; capstone paper and presentation. *Entrance requirements:* For master's, 3 letters of recommendation, curriculum vitae or resume, 3 years of development experience (international experience preferred). Additional exam requirements/recommendations for international students: Required—TOEFL (minimum score 600 paper-based; 100 iBT). Electronic applications accepted. *Expenses: Tuition:* Full-time $48,720. *Required fees:* $88. Tuition and fees vary according to course load, degree level, program and student level. *Faculty research:* Water resource management, human rights, biosphere management, rural development, public policy and governance, gender, conservation, civil society, poverty eradication, project planning and implementation, evaluation, organizational management.

California State University, Stanislaus, College of Natural Sciences, MS Program in Ecology and Sustainability, Turlock, CA 95382. Offers ecological conservation (MS). *Program availability:* Part-time. *Degree requirements:* For master's, thesis. *Entrance requirements:* For master's, GRE, minimum GPA of 3.0, 3 letters of recommendation, personal statement. Additional exam requirements/recommendations for international students: Required—TOEFL (minimum score 550 paper-based). Electronic applications accepted.

Carnegie Mellon University, Carnegie Institute of Technology, Department of Civil and Environmental Engineering, Pittsburgh, PA 15213. Offers advanced infrastructure systems (MS, PhD); advanced infrastructure systems technology development and application (MS); air quality engineering and science (MS); civil and environmental engineering (MS, PhD); civil and environmental engineering/engineering and public policy (PhD); civil engineering (MS, PhD); computational mechanics (MS, PhD); computational modeling and monitoring for resilient structural and material systems (MS); energy infrastructure systems (MS); environmental engineering (MS, PhD); environmental management and science (MS, PhD); IT-based sustainable global infrastructure and construction management (MS); sustainability and green design (MS); water quality engineering and science (MS). *Program availability:* Part-time. *Faculty:* 23 full-time (5 women), 12 part-time/adjunct (3 women). *Students:* 272 full-time (103 women); includes 20 minority (4 Black or African American, non-Hispanic/Latino; 16 Asian, non-Hispanic/Latino), 214 international. Average age 25. 630 applicants, 64% accepted, 114 enrolled. In 2017, 145 master's, 15 doctorates awarded. Terminal master's awarded for partial completion of doctoral program. *Degree requirements:* For master's, thesis optional; for doctorate, comprehensive exam, thesis/dissertation, two-part qualifying exam, public defense of dissertation. *Entrance requirements:* For master's, GRE General Test, BS in engineering, science or mathematics; for doctorate, GRE General Test, BS or MS in engineering, science or mathematics. Additional exam requirements/recommendations for international students: Required—TOEFL (minimum score 84 iBT) or IELTS (6.0). *Application deadline:* For fall admission, 1/5 priority date for domestic and international students; for spring admission, 9/1 priority date for domestic and international students. Applications are processed on a rolling basis. Application fee: $75. Electronic applications accepted. *Expenses:* Contact institution. *Financial support:* In 2017–18, 129 students received support. Fellowships with tuition reimbursements available, research assistantships with tuition reimbursements available, scholarships/grants, tuition waivers (full and partial), unspecified assistantships, and service assistantships available. Financial award application deadline: 1/5. *Faculty research:* Advanced infrastructure systems; environmental engineering, sustainability, and science; mechanics, materials, and computing. *Total annual research expenditures:* $7.4 million. *Unit head:* Dr. David A. Dzombak, Professor and Department Head, 412-268-2941, Fax: 412-268-7813, E-mail: dzombak@cmu.edu. *Application contact:* David A. Vey, Graduate Admissions Manager, 412-268-2292, Fax: 412-268-7813, E-mail: dvey@andrew.cmu.edu. Website: http://www.cmu.edu/cee/

The Catholic University of America, School of Architecture and Planning, Washington, DC 20064. Offers architecture and planning (M Arch, MS Arch St); city and regional planning (M Arch); facilities management (MS Arch); regional development (Certificate); sustainable design (M Arch, Certificate). *Program availability:* Part-time. *Faculty:* 19 full-time (7 women), 9 part-time/adjunct (1 woman). *Students:* 61 full-time (24 women), 13 part-time (7 women); includes 31 minority (12 Black or African American, non-Hispanic/Latino; 1 American Indian or Alaska Native, non-Hispanic/Latino; 3 Asian, non-Hispanic/Latino; 8 Hispanic/Latino; 7 Two or more races, non-Hispanic/Latino), 11 international. Average age 28. 61 applicants, 90% accepted, 28 enrolled. In 2017, 46 master's awarded. *Degree requirements:* For master's, thesis. *Entrance requirements:* For master's, GRE (minimum score: 1000), minimum GPA of 2.8, portfolio, statement of purpose, official copies of academic transcripts, three letters of recommendation. Additional exam requirements/recommendations for international students: Required—TOEFL (minimum score 550 paper-based; 80 iBT). *Application deadline:* For fall admission, 1/15 priority date for domestic students, 7/1 for international students; for spring admission, 10/15 priority date for domestic students, 11/1 for international students. Applications are processed on a rolling basis. Application fee: $55. Electronic applications accepted. *Expenses:* Contact institution. *Financial support:* Fellowships, research assistantships, teaching assistantships, Federal Work-Study, scholarships/grants, tuition waivers (full and partial), and unspecified assistantships available. Financial award application deadline: 2/1; financial award applicants required to submit FAFSA. *Faculty research:* Architectural history, cultural studies/sacred space, design technologies, digital media, real estate development, urban design. *Total annual research expenditures:* $106,977. *Unit head:* Randall Ott, Dean, 202-319-5784, Fax: 202-319-2023, E-mail: ott@cua.edu. *Application contact:* Dr. Steven Brown, Director of Graduate Admissions, 202-319-5057, Fax: 202-319-6533, E-mail: cua-admissions@cua.edu. Website: https://architecture.catholic.edu/

City College of the City University of New York, Graduate School, Program in Sustainability in the Urban Environment, New York, NY 10031-9198. Offers MS. *Degree requirements:* For master's, capstone project.

Clarkson University, Institute for a Sustainable Environment, Potsdam, NY 13699. Offers MS, PhD. *Faculty:* 5 full-time (2 women), 6 part-time/adjunct (2 women). *Students:* 22 full-time (9 women), 12 international. In 2017, 4 master's, 1 doctorate awarded. *Expenses: Tuition:* Full-time $24,210; part-time $1345 per credit hour. Tuition and fees vary according to campus/location and program. *Unit head:* Dr. Susan Powers, Director of the Institute for a Sustainable Environment/Associate Director of Sustainability, 315-268-6542, E-mail: spowers@clarkson.edu. *Application contact:* Dan Capogna, Director of Graduate Admissions, 518-631-9910, E-mail: graduate@clarkson.edu.

Clark University, Graduate School, Department of International Development, Community, and Environment, Worcester, MA 01610-1477. Offers community and global health (MHS); community development and planning (MA); environmental science and policy (MS); geographic information science for development and environment (MS); international development and social change (MA); MA/MBA; MBA/MS. *Faculty:* 19 full-time (10 women), 4 part-time/adjunct (3 women). *Students:* 150 full-time (90 women); includes 23 minority (10 Black or African American, non-Hispanic/Latino; 3 Asian, non-Hispanic/Latino; 5 Hispanic/Latino; 5 Two or more races, non-Hispanic/Latino), 38 international. Average age 27. 364 applicants, 86% accepted, 113 enrolled. In 2017, 85 master's awarded. *Entrance requirements:* For master's, 3 references, resume or curriculum vitae. Additional exam requirements/recommendations for international students: Required—TOEFL (minimum score 575 paper-based; 90 iBT) or IELTS (minimum score 6.5). *Application deadline:* For fall admission, 1/15 for domestic students. Application fee: $75. *Financial support:* Fellowships, research assistantships, teaching assistantships, institutionally sponsored loans, and scholarships/grants available. *Faculty research:* Community action research, gender analysis, environmental risk assessment, land-use planning, geographic information systems, HIV and AIDS, global health and social justice, environmental health, climate change and sustainability. *Unit head:* Dr. Ed Carr, Director, 508-421-3895, Fax: 508-793-8820, E-mail: edcarr@clarku.edu. *Application contact:* Erika Paradis, Student and Academic Services Director, 508-793-7201, Fax: 508-793-8820, E-mail: eparadis@clarku.edu. Website: http://www2.clarku.edu/departments/international-development-community-environment/

Cleveland State University, College of Graduate Studies, Maxine Goodman Levin College of Urban Affairs, Program in Urban Planning and Development, Cleveland, OH 44115. Offers economic development (MUPD); environmental sustainability (MUPD); historic preservation (MUPD); housing and neighborhood development (MUPD); real estate development and finance (MUPD); urban economic development (Certificate); urban geographic information systems (MUPD); JD/MUPDD. *Accreditation:* ACSP. *Program availability:* Part-time, evening/weekend. *Faculty:* 16 full-time (8 women), 13 part-time/adjunct (5 women). *Students:* 20 full-time (7 women), 15 part-time (5 women); includes 1 minority (Black or African American, non-Hispanic/Latino), 2 international. Average age 28. 48 applicants, 56% accepted, 14 enrolled. In 2017, 24 master's awarded. *Degree requirements:* For master's, thesis or alternative, exit project. *Entrance requirements:* For master's, GRE General Test (minimum score: 50th percentile combined verbal and quantitative, 4.0 analytical writing), minimum GPA of 3.0. Additional exam requirements/recommendations for international students: Required—TOEFL (minimum score 550 paper-based; 78 iBT), IELTS (6.0), or International Test of English Proficiency (iTEP). *Application deadline:* For fall admission, 7/1 priority date for domestic students, 5/15 for international students; for spring admission, 11/15 for domestic students, 11/1 for international students; for summer admission, 4/1 for domestic students, 3/15 for international students. Applications are processed on a rolling basis. Application fee: $40. Electronic applications accepted. *Expenses:* Contact institution. *Financial support:* In 2017–18, 10 students received support, including 5 research assistantships with full tuition reimbursements available (averaging $7,200 per year), 3 teaching assistantships with partial tuition reimbursements available (averaging $2,400 per year); scholarships/grants, tuition waivers (full and partial), and unspecified assistantships also available. Support available to part-time students. Financial award application deadline: 3/1; financial award applicants required to submit FAFSA. *Faculty research:* Housing and neighborhood development, urban housing policy, environmental sustainability, economic development, GIS and planning decision support. *Unit head:* Dr. Stephanie Ryberg-Webster, Assistant Professor/Program Director, 216-802-3386, Fax: 216-687-2013, E-mail: s.ryberg@csuohio.edu. *Application contact:* David Arrighi, Graduate Academic Advisor, 216-523-7522, Fax: 216-687-5398, E-mail: d.arrighi@csuohio.edu. Website: http://www.csuohio.edu/urban/mupd/mupd

Colorado State University, Interdisciplinary College, School of Global Environmental Sustainability, Fort Collins, CO 80523. Offers applied global stability: agriculture (Graduate Certificate). *Program availability:* Part-time-only, online only, 100% online. *Students:* 11 part-time (9 women); includes 2 minority (1 Black or African American, non-Hispanic/Latino; 1 Two or more races, non-Hispanic/Latino). Average age 35. *Entrance requirements:* For degree, bachelor's degree; transcripts. Additional exam requirements/recommendations for international students: Required—TOEFL (minimum score 550 paper-based), IELTS. *Application deadline:* For fall admission, 7/15 for domestic and international students; for spring admission, 12/15 for domestic and international students; for summer admission, 4/15 for domestic and international students. Applications are processed on a rolling basis. Application fee: $60 ($70 for international students). Electronic applications accepted. *Expenses:* $624 - $936 per credit hour. *Unit head:* Dr. Diana Wall, Director, School of Global Environmental Sustainability, E-mail: diana.wall@colostate.edu. *Application contact:* Sandra Dailey, Graduate School Academic Progress and Special Admissions Coordinator, 970-491-6817, Fax: 970-491-2194, E-mail: gradschool@colostate.edu.
Website: http://graduateschool.colostate.edu/Programs/applied-global-stability/

Colorado State University, Warner College of Natural Resources, Department of Ecosystem Science and Sustainability, Fort Collins, CO 80523-1476. Offers greenhouse gas management and accounting (MGMA); watershed science (MS). *Faculty:* 10 full-time (3 women), 3 part-time/adjunct (2 women). *Students:* 14 full-time (5 women), 18 part-time (12 women); includes 5 minority (4 Hispanic/Latino; 1 Two or more races, non-Hispanic/Latino), 4 international. Average age 30. 34 applicants, 62% accepted, 12 enrolled. In 2017, 9 master's awarded. *Degree requirements:* For master's, thesis (for some programs). *Entrance requirements:* For master's, GRE (70th percentile or higher), minimum GPA of 3.0; resume; transcript; letters of recommendation; statement of purpose; undergraduate degree in a related field. Additional exam requirements/recommendations for international students: Required—TOEFL (minimum score 550 paper-based; 80 iBT), IELTS (minimum score 6.5). *Application deadline:* For fall admission, 2/1 priority date for domestic and international students. Application fee: $60 ($70 for international students). Electronic applications accepted. *Expenses:* $1,250 per semester (for MGMA). *Financial support:* In 2017–18, 9 research assistantships (averaging $23,945 per year), 8 teaching assistantships (averaging $11,583 per year) were awarded; scholarships/grants and unspecified assistantships also available. *Faculty research:* Animal-habitat relationships; pastoral ecology and simulation; solving applied problems in ecosystem science and sustainable ecosystem management; intersections and boundaries of human activities, physical processes, and ecosystems; theoretical and applied ecology. *Total annual research expenditures:* $2.1 million. *Unit head:* Dr. John Moore, Department Head, 970-491-5589, Fax: 970-491-1965, E-mail: john.moore@colostate.edu. *Application contact:* Nikki Foxley, ESS Department and Academic Success Coordinator, 970-491-5589, Fax: 970-491-1965, E-mail: nikki.foxley@colostate.edu.
Website: http://warnercnr.colostate.edu/departments/ess

Columbia University, Graduate School of Arts and Sciences, New York, NY 10027. Offers African-American studies (MA); American studies (MA); anthropology (MA, PhD); art history and archaeology (MA, PhD); astronomy (PhD); biological sciences (PhD); biotechnology (MA); chemical physics (PhD); chemistry (PhD); classical studies (MA, PhD); classics (MA, PhD); climate and society (MA); conservation biology (MA); earth and environmental sciences (PhD); East Asia: regional studies (MA); East Asian languages and cultures (MA, PhD); ecology, evolution and environmental biology (MA), including conservation biology; ecology, evolution, and environmental biology (PhD), including ecology and evolutionary biology, evolutionary primatology; economics (MA, PhD); English and comparative literature (MA, PhD); French and Romance philology (MA, PhD); Germanic languages (MA, PhD); global French studies (MA); global thought (MA); Hispanic cultural studies (MA); history (PhD); history and literature (MA); human rights studies (MA); Islamic studies (MA); Italian (MA, PhD); Japanese pedagogy (MA); Jewish studies (MA); Latin America and the Caribbean: regional studies (MA); Latin American and Iberian cultures (PhD); mathematics (MA, PhD), including finance (MA); medieval and Renaissance studies (MA); Middle Eastern, South Asian, and African studies (MA, PhD); modern art: critical and curatorial studies (MA); modern European studies (MA); museum anthropology (MA); music (DMA, PhD); oral history (MA); philosophical foundations of physics (MA); philosophy (MA, PhD); physics (PhD); political science (MA, PhD); psychology (PhD); quantitative methods in the social sciences (MA); religion (MA, PhD); Russia, Eurasia and East Europe: regional studies (MA); Russian translation (MA); Slavic cultures (MA); Slavic languages (MA, PhD); sociology (MA, PhD); South Asian studies (MA); statistics (MA, PhD); theatre (PhD). Dual-degree programs require admission to both Graduate School of Arts and Sciences and another Columbia school. *Program availability:* Part-time. Terminal master's awarded for partial completion of doctoral program. *Degree requirements:* For master's, variable foreign language requirement, comprehensive exam (for some programs), thesis (for some programs); for doctorate, variable foreign language requirement, comprehensive exam (for some programs), thesis/dissertation. *Entrance requirements:* For master's and doctorate, GRE General Test, GRE Subject Test (for some programs). Additional exam requirements/recommendations for international students: Required—TOEFL, IELTS. Electronic applications accepted. *Expenses: Tuition:* Full-time $44,864; part-time $1704 per credit. *Required fees:* $2370 per semester. One-time fee: $105.

Columbia University, School of International and Public Affairs, Program in Development Practice, New York, NY 10027. Offers MPA. Offered through The Earth Institute. *Entrance requirements:* For master's, GRE. Additional exam requirements/recommendations for international students: Required—TOEFL (minimum score 100 iBT), IELTS (minimum score 7), PTE (minimum score 68). *Expenses: Tuition:* Full-time $44,864; part-time $1704 per credit. *Required fees:* $2370 per semester. One-time fee: $105.

Cornell University, Graduate School, Graduate Fields of Agriculture and Life Sciences and Graduate Fields of Engineering, Field of Biological and Environmental Engineering, Ithaca, NY 14853. Offers bioenergy and integrated energy systems (M Eng, MPS, MS, PhD); biological engineering (M Eng, MPS, MS, PhD); bioprocess engineering (M Eng, MPS, MS, PhD); ecohydrology (M Eng, MPS, MS, PhD); environmental engineering (M Eng, MPS, MS, PhD); environmental management (MPS); food engineering (M Eng, MPS, MS, PhD); industrial biotechnology (M Eng, MPS, MS, PhD); nanobiotechnology (M Eng, MPS, MS, PhD); sustainable systems (M Eng, MPS, MS, PhD); synthetic biology (MS); syntheticbiology (M Eng, MPS, PhD). Terminal master's awarded for partial completion of doctoral program. *Degree requirements:* For master's, thesis (MS); for doctorate, comprehensive exam, thesis/dissertation. *Entrance requirements:* For master's, letters of recommendation (3 for MS, 2 for M Eng and MPS); for doctorate, GRE General Test, 3 letters of recommendation. Additional exam requirements/recommendations for international students: Required—TOEFL (minimum score 550 paper-based; 77 iBT). Electronic applications accepted. *Faculty research:* Biological and food engineering, environmental, soil and water engineering, international agricultural engineering, structures and controlled environments, machine systems and energy.

Dartmouth College, School of Graduate and Advanced Studies, Program in Ecology, Evolution, Ecosystems, and Society, Hanover, NH 03755. Offers ecology and evolutionary biology (PhD); sustainability, ecosystems, and environment (PhD). *Faculty:* 9 full-time (5 women). *Students:* 22 full-time (14 women); includes 1 minority (Hispanic/Latino), 3 international. Average age 28. 40 applicants, 15% accepted, 3 enrolled. In 2017, 1 doctorate awarded. *Entrance requirements:* For doctorate, GRE General Test, GRE Subject Test in biology (highly recommended). Additional exam requirements/recommendations for international students: Required—TOEFL. *Application deadline:* For fall admission, 12/1 for domestic students. Electronic applications accepted. *Financial support:* Fellowships, research assistantships, teaching assistantships, institutionally sponsored loans, traineeships, and unspecified assistantships available. Financial award applicants required to submit FAFSA. *Unit head:* Dr. Mathew Ayres, Chair, 603-646-2788. *Application contact:* Amy Layne, Administrative Assistant, 603-646-3847.
Website: http://sites.dartmouth.edu/EEES/

DePaul University, College of Liberal Arts and Social Sciences, Chicago, IL 60614. Offers Arabic (MA); Chinese (MA); critical ethnic studies (MA); English (MA); French (MA); German (MA); history (MA); interdisciplinary studies (MA, MS); international public service (MS); international studies (MA); Italian (MA); Japanese (MA); liberal studies (MA); nonprofit management (MNM); public administration (MPA); public health (MPH); public policy (MPP); public service management (MS); refugee and forced migration studies (MS); social work (MSW); sociology (MA); Spanish (MA); sustainable urban development (MA); women's and gender studies (MA); writing and publishing (MA); writing, rhetoric and discourse (MA); MA/PhD. *Program availability:* Part-time, evening/weekend, online learning. Terminal master's awarded for partial completion of doctoral program. *Degree requirements:* For master's, variable foreign language requirement, comprehensive exam (for some programs), thesis (for some programs). *Application deadline:* Applications are processed on a rolling basis. Application fee: $40. Electronic applications accepted. *Financial support:* Applicants required to submit FAFSA. *Unit head:* Dr. Guillermo Vasquez de Velasco, Dean, 773-325-7305. *Application contact:* Ann Spittle, Director of Graduate Admission, 773-325-8369, Fax: 312-476-3244, E-mail: graddepaul@depaul.edu.
Website: http://las.depaul.edu/

Eastern Illinois University, Graduate School, Lumpkin College of Business and Technology, School of Technology, Program in Sustainable Energy, Charleston, IL 61920. Offers MS, MS/MBA, MS/MS. *Program availability:* Part-time, evening/weekend. *Degree requirements:* For master's, comprehensive exam. *Entrance requirements:* For master's, GMAT or GRE. Additional exam requirements/recommendations for international students: Required—TOEFL (minimum score 500 paper-based; 61 iBT), IELTS (minimum score 6). *Application deadline:* For fall admission, 5/15 for domestic and international students; for spring admission, 10/15 for domestic and international students. Applications are processed on a rolling basis. Application fee: $30. Electronic applications accepted. *Financial support:* Research assistantships with full tuition reimbursements, career-related internships or fieldwork, Federal Work-Study, and unspecified assistantships available. Support available to part-time students. Financial award application deadline: 3/1; financial award applicants required to submit FAFSA. *Unit head:* Peter Ping Liu, Assistant Chair, 217-581-7426, Fax: 217-581-6607, E-mail: pliu@eiu.edu. *Application contact:* Peter Ping Liu, Assistant Chair, 217-581-7426, Fax: 217-581-6607, E-mail: pliu@eiu.edu.
Website: http://www.eiu.edu/sustainable/

Eastern Michigan University, Graduate School, College of Technology, School of Visual and Built Environments, Programs in Construction Management, Ypsilanti, MI 48197. Offers construction (Certificate); construction management (MS); project leadership (Certificate); sustainable construction (Certificate). *Program availability:* Part-time, evening/weekend, online learning. *Students:* 17 full-time (2 women), 11 part-time (5 women); includes 1 minority (Black or African American, non-Hispanic/Latino), 16 international. Average age 32. 54 applicants, 44% accepted, 5 enrolled. In 2017, 5 master's awarded. *Entrance requirements:* Additional exam requirements/recommendations for international students: Required—TOEFL. *Application deadline:* Applications are processed on a rolling basis. Application fee: $45. *Financial support:* Fellowships, research assistantships with full tuition reimbursements, teaching assistantships with full tuition reimbursements, career-related internships or fieldwork, Federal Work-Study, institutionally sponsored loans, scholarships/grants, tuition waivers (partial), and unspecified assistantships available. Support available to part-time students. Financial award applicants required to submit FAFSA. *Application contact:* Dr. Armagan Korkmaz, Advisor, 734-487-2492, Fax: 734-487-8755, E-mail: kkorkmaz@emich.edu.

Emory University, Laney Graduate School, Program in Development Practice, Atlanta, GA 30322-1100. Offers MDP. *Entrance requirements:* Additional exam requirements/recommendations for international students: Recommended—TOEFL.

Future Generations University, Program in Applied Community Change, Franklin, WV 26807. Offers conservation (MA). *Program availability:* Blended/hybrid learning. *Faculty:* 9 full-time (3 women), 12 part-time/adjunct (4 women). *Students:* 16 full-time (7 women); includes 13 minority (6 Black or African American, non-Hispanic/Latino; 4 Asian, non-Hispanic/Latino; 3 Hispanic/Latino). In 2017, 11 master's awarded. *Degree requirements:* For master's, portfolio. *Entrance requirements:* For master's, bachelor's degree, community involvement. Additional exam requirements/recommendations for international students: Recommended—TOEFL. *Application deadline:* Applications are processed on a rolling basis. Application fee: $0. Electronic applications accepted. *Financial support:* Scholarships/grants and tuition waivers (partial) available. Financial award applicants required to submit FAFSA. *Faculty research:* Sustainable communities, community engagement, peacebuilding, seed-scale community development. *Unit head:* Christie Hand, Chief Academic Officer, 304-358-2000. *Application contact:* Jodie Wimer, Registrar, 304-358-2000, E-mail: jwimer@future.edu.
Website: http://www.future.edu

Hawai`i Pacific University, College of Liberal Arts, Program in Global Leadership and Sustainable Development, Honolulu, HI 96813. Offers MA. *Program availability:* Part-time, evening/weekend. *Faculty:* 10 full-time (2 women), 2 part-time/adjunct (0 women). *Students:* 22 full-time (14 women), 8 part-time (4 women); includes 11 minority (3 Black or African American, non-Hispanic/Latino; 1 Asian, non-Hispanic/Latino; 4 Hispanic/Latino; 3 Two or more races, non-Hispanic/Latino), 7 international. Average age 30. 27 applicants, 74% accepted, 9 enrolled. In 2017, 6 master's awarded. *Entrance requirements:* Additional exam requirements/recommendations for international students: Recommended—TOEFL (minimum score 550 paper-based; 80 iBT), IELTS (minimum score 6), TWE (minimum score 5). *Application deadline:* For fall admission, 1/15 priority date for domestic students; for spring admission, 10/15 priority date for domestic students. Applications are processed on a rolling basis. Application fee: $50. Electronic applications accepted. *Expenses: Tuition:* Full-time $18,000; part-time $1000 per credit. *Required fees:* $200; $26 per credit. Tuition and fees vary according to course load and program. *Financial support:* In 2017–18, 8 students received support. Career-related internships or fieldwork, Federal Work-Study, scholarships/grants, tuition waivers (partial), and unspecified assistantships available. Financial award application deadline: 3/1; financial award applicants required to submit FAFSA. *Unit head:* Dr. Regina Ostergaard-Klem, Director, 808-236-2492, E-mail: rostergaardklem@hpu.edu. *Application contact:* Danny Lam, Assistant Director of Graduate Admissions, 808-544-1135, E-mail: graduate@hpu.edu.
Website: https://www.hpu.edu/cla/history-intstudies/maglsd/index.html

Sustainable Development

HEC Montreal, School of Business Administration, Graduate Diploma Programs in Administration, Program in Management and Sustainable Development, Montréal, QC H3T 2A7, Canada. Offers Graduate Diploma. All courses are given in French. *Students:* 15 full-time (7 women), 34 part-time (23 women). 36 applicants, 86% accepted, 24 enrolled. In 2017, 12 Graduate Diplomas awarded. *Entrance requirements:* For degree, bachelor's degree. *Application deadline:* For fall admission, 4/15 for domestic and international students; for winter admission, 9/15 for domestic and international students. Applications are processed on a rolling basis. Application fee: $88 ($184 for international students). Electronic applications accepted. *Expenses:* Tuition, state resident: full-time $2869 Canadian dollars; part-time $79.70 Canadian dollars per credit. Tuition, nonresident: full-time $8883 Canadian dollars; part-time $246.76 Canadian dollars per credit. *International tuition:* $19,648 Canadian dollars full-time. *Required fees:* $41.20 Canadian dollars per credit. $67.94 Canadian dollars per term. Tuition and fees vary according to degree level and program. *Financial support:* Research assistantships, teaching assistantships, and scholarships/grants available. Financial award application deadline: 9/2. *Unit head:* Renaud Lachance, Director, 514-340-7165, E-mail: renaud.lachance@hec.ca. *Application contact:* Anny Caron, Administrative Director, 514-340-6151, Fax: 514-340-6411, E-mail: aide@hec.ca.
Website: http://www.hec.ca/programmes/dess/dess-gestion-developpement-durable/index.html

Hofstra University, College of Liberal Arts and Sciences, Program in Sustainability Studies, Hempstead, NY 11549. Offers MA. *Accreditation:* APA; NCATE. *Program availability:* Part-time, evening/weekend. *Students:* 4 full-time (2 women), 10 part-time (6 women); includes 1 minority (Asian, non-Hispanic/Latino), 1 international. Average age 32. 15 applicants, 93% accepted, 6 enrolled. In 2017, 1 master's awarded. *Entrance requirements:* For master's, minimum GPA of 3.0, essay, 3 letters of recommendation. Additional exam requirements/recommendations for international students: Required—TOEFL (minimum score 550 paper-based; 80 iBT). *Application deadline:* Applications are processed on a rolling basis. Application fee: $75. Electronic applications accepted. *Expenses: Tuition:* Full-time $1292. *Required fees:* $970. Tuition and fees vary according to program. *Financial support:* In 2017–18, 10 students received support, including 8 fellowships with full and partial tuition reimbursements available (averaging $3,360 per year), 2 research assistantships with full and partial tuition reimbursements available (averaging $6,065 per year); career-related internships or fieldwork, Federal Work-Study, institutionally sponsored loans, scholarships/grants, tuition waivers (full and partial), and unspecified assistantships also available. Support available to part-time students. Financial award applicants required to submit FAFSA. *Faculty research:* Storm preparedness and storm response, municipality sustainable energy policy, soil and water pollution management, urban and suburban agriculture. *Unit head:* Dr. Bret Bennington, Chairperson, 516-463-5568, E-mail: j.b.bennington@hofstra.edu. *Application contact:* Sunil Samuel, Assistant Vice President of Admissions, 516-463-4723, Fax: 516-463-4664, E-mail: graduateadmission@hofstra.edu.
Website: http://www.hofstra.edu/hclas

Hunter College of the City University of New York, Graduate School, School of Arts and Sciences, Department of Psychology, New York, NY 10065-5085. Offers animal behavior and conservation (MA, Certificate); general psychology (MA). *Program availability:* Part-time, evening/weekend. *Degree requirements:* For master's, comprehensive exam, thesis. *Entrance requirements:* For master's, GRE General Test, minimum 12 credits of course work in psychology, including statistics and experimental psychology; 2 letters of recommendation. Additional exam requirements/recommendations for international students: Required—TOEFL. *Faculty research:* Personality, cognitive and linguistic development, hormonal and neural control of behavior, gender and culture, social cognition of health and attitudes.

Instituto Centroamericano de Administración de Empresas, Graduate Programs, La Garita, Costa Rica. Offers agribusiness management (MIAM); business administration (EMBA); finance (MBA); real estate management (MGREM); sustainable development (MBA); technology (MBA). *Degree requirements:* For master's, comprehensive exam, essay. *Entrance requirements:* For master's, GMAT or GRE General Test, fluency in Spanish, interview, letters of recommendation, minimum 1 year of work experience. Additional exam requirements/recommendations for international students: Recommended—TOEFL. Electronic applications accepted. *Faculty research:* Competitiveness, production.

Instituto Tecnologico de Santo Domingo, Graduate School, Area of Humanities and Social Sciences, Santo Domingo, Dominican Republic. Offers accounting (Certificate); adult education (Certificate); applied linguistics (MA); economics (MA); education (M Ed); educational psychology (MA, Certificate); gender and development (MA, Certificate); humanistic studies (MA); international marketing management (Certificate); international relations in the Caribbean basin (Certificate); intervention systems in family therapy (MA); linguistic and literary communication (Certificate); pedagogical support (MA); social science education (M Ed); sustainable human development (MA); terminal illness and death psychology (Certificate); youth and adult education (M Ed).

Iowa State University of Science and Technology, Program in Sustainable Agriculture, Ames, IA 50011. Offers MS, PhD. *Entrance requirements:* For master's and doctorate, GRE General Test. Additional exam requirements/recommendations for international students: Required—TOEFL (minimum score 570 paper-based; 80 iBT), IELTS (minimum score 6.5). Electronic applications accepted.

Johnson & Wales University, Graduate Studies, MS Program in Global Tourism and Sustainable Economic Development, Providence, RI 02903-3703. Offers MS. *Program availability:* Online learning. *Expenses: Tuition:* Full-time $12,636; part-time $702 per credit hour. *Unit head:* Dr. Eldad Boker, Director, 401-598-4638, E-mail: eldad.boker@jwu.edu. *Application contact:* Graduate School Admissions, 401-598-1015, Fax: 401-598-1286, E-mail: pvdgrad@admissions.jwu.edu.
Website: https://www.jwu.edu/academics/programs-by-campus/providence-programs/global-tourism-and-sustainable-economic-development-ms.html

Judson University, Master of Architecture Program, Elgin, IL 60123-1498. Offers architecture (M Arch); sustainable design (M Arch); traditional architecture and urbanism (M Arch). *Program availability:* Part-time. *Faculty:* 9 full-time (3 women), 3 part-time/adjunct (1 woman). *Students:* 11 full-time (4 women). Average age 23. 24 applicants, 83% accepted, 11 enrolled. In 2017, 6 master's awarded. *Degree requirements:* For master's, thesis optional, 1600-hour practicum/preceptorship completed prior to enrollment. *Entrance requirements:* For master's, GRE, Judson BA in architecture or equivalent; minimum cumulative undergraduate GPA of 2.75, 3.0 in architecture; comprehensive portfolio; letter of intent. Additional exam requirements/recommendations for international students: Required—TOEFL (minimum score 550 paper-based), IELTS (minimum score 6.5). *Application deadline:* For fall admission, 2/15 priority date for domestic and international students; for winter admission, 11/15 for domestic students; for spring admission, 11/15 for domestic and international students. Applications are processed on a rolling basis. Application fee: $100. Electronic applications accepted. *Expenses:* Contact institution. *Financial support:* In 2017–18, 9 students received support. Fellowships, research assistantships, teaching assistantships, scholarships/grants, and 8 assistantships available. Financial award application deadline: 5/1; financial award applicants required to submit FAFSA. *Faculty research:* Sustainable design, urbanism, daylighting, acoustics, digital media and fabrication. *Unit head:* Dr. David M. Ogoli, Chair, 847-628-1018, E-mail: dogoli@judsonu.edu. *Application contact:* Molly Smith, Director of Admissions, 847-628-2521, E-mail: molly.smith@judsonu.edu.
Website: http://www.judsonu.edu/ArchMaster/

Lehigh University, College of Arts and Sciences, Environmental Policy Program, Bethlehem, PA 18015. Offers environmental health (Graduate Certificate); environmental justice (Graduate Certificate); environmental policy and law (Graduate Certificate); environmental policy design (MA); sustainable development (Graduate Certificate); urban environmental policy (Graduate Certificate). *Faculty:* 6 full-time (2 women). *Students:* 6 full-time (3 women), 1 (woman) part-time; includes 1 minority (Black or African American, non-Hispanic/Latino). Average age 28. 6 applicants, 83% accepted, 3 enrolled. In 2017, 3 master's awarded. *Degree requirements:* For master's, thesis or additional course work. *Entrance requirements:* For master's, GRE, minimum GPA of 2.75, 3.0 for last two undergraduate semesters; essay; 2 letters of recommendation. Additional exam requirements/recommendations for international students: Required—TOEFL (minimum score 85 iBT), IELTS (minimum score 6.5). *Application deadline:* For fall admission, 1/1 for domestic and international students; for spring admission, 12/1 for domestic and international students. Applications are processed on a rolling basis. Application fee: $75. Electronic applications accepted. *Expenses:* $1,460 per credit. *Financial support:* In 2017–18, 6 students received support. Teaching assistantships and community fellowship and tuition remission available. Financial award application deadline: 1/1. *Faculty research:* Environmental policy, environmental law, urban policy, urban politics, urban environmental policy, sustainability, sustainable development, international environmental law, international environmental policy, environmental justice, social justice. *Unit head:* Dr. Karen B. Pooley, Director, 610-758-1238, E-mail: kbp312@lehigh.edu. *Application contact:* Gary Burgess, Academic Coordinator, 610-758-4281, Fax: 610-758-6232, E-mail: glb215@lehigh.edu.
Website: http://ei.cas2.lehigh.edu/

Lenoir-Rhyne University, Graduate Programs, School of Natural Sciences, Program in Sustainability Studies, Hickory, NC 28601. Offers MS. *Program availability:* Part-time, evening/weekend, online learning. *Entrance requirements:* For master's, GRE General Test or MAT, official transcripts, essay. Additional exam requirements/recommendations for international students: Required—TOEFL (minimum score 600 paper-based). Electronic applications accepted. *Expenses:* Contact institution.

Lesley University, Graduate School of Arts and Social Sciences, Cambridge, MA 02138-2790. Offers clinical mental health counseling (MA), including holistic counseling, school and community counseling, trauma studies; counseling psychology (MA, CAGS), including professional counseling (MA), school counseling (MA); creative writing (MFA); expressive therapies (MA, PhD, CAGS), including art (MA), clinical mental health counseling (MA), dance (MA), expressive therapies (MA), music (MA); independent studies (CAGS); independent study (MA); intercultural relations (MA, CAGS); interdisciplinary studies (MA), including individualized studies, integrative holistic health, mindfulness studies, peace and conflict transformation, trauma sensitive assessment, intervention, and consultation, women's studies; urban environmental leadership (MA). *Program availability:* Part-time, online learning. *Degree requirements:* For master's, internship, practicum, thesis (for expressive therapies); for doctorate, thesis/dissertation, arts apprenticeship, field placement; for CAGS, thesis, internship (for counseling psychology, expressive therapies). *Entrance requirements:* For master's, MAT (counseling psychology), interview, writing samples, art portfolio; for doctorate, GRE or MAT, interview, master's degree; for CAGS, interview, master's degree. Additional exam requirements/recommendations for international students: Required—TOEFL (minimum score 550 paper-based; 80 iBT). Electronic applications accepted. *Faculty research:* Psychotherapy and culture; psychotherapy and psychological trauma; women's issues in art, teaching and psychotherapy; community-based art, psycho-spiritual inquiry.

Lipscomb University, Institute for Sustainable Practice, Nashville, TN 37204-3951. Offers MS, Certificate. *Program availability:* Part-time, evening/weekend, online learning. *Faculty:* 3 full-time (1 woman), 3 part-time/adjunct (1 woman). *Students:* 21 full-time (11 women), 5 part-time (4 women); includes 2 minority (1 Black or African American, non-Hispanic/Latino; 1 Hispanic/Latino). Average age 31. 24 applicants, 71% accepted, 6 enrolled. In 2017, 8 master's awarded. *Degree requirements:* For master's, capstone project. *Entrance requirements:* For master's, GRE or GMAT, 2 references, interview. Additional exam requirements/recommendations for international students: Required—TOEFL (minimum score 570 paper-based; 80 iBT). *Application deadline:* For fall admission, 7/15 for domestic students; for spring admission, 12/15 for domestic students. Applications are processed on a rolling basis. Application fee: $50 ($75 for international students). Electronic applications accepted. *Expenses:* $1,290. *Financial support:* Unspecified assistantships available. Financial award applicants required to submit FAFSA. *Faculty research:* Water and energy sustainability practices, sociology of conversation and natural resource management, new sustainability practices in forestry. *Unit head:* G. Dodd Galbreath, Executive Director, 615-966-1771, E-mail: dodd.galbreath@lipscomb.edu. *Application contact:* Emily Stutzman Jones, Academic Director, 615-966-5076, E-mail: emily.jones@lipscomb.edu.
Website: http://lipscomb.edu/sustainability

Long Island University–LIU Post, College of Liberal Arts and Sciences, Brookville, NY 11548-1300. Offers applied mathematics (MS); behavior analysis (MA); biology (MS); criminal justice (MS); earth science (MS); English (MA); environmental sustainability (MS); genetic counseling (MS); history (MA); interdisciplinary studies (MA, MS); political science (MA); psychology (MA). *Program availability:* Part-time, evening/weekend, blended/hybrid learning. *Faculty:* 41 full-time (21 women), 24 part-time/adjunct (13 women). *Students:* 173 full-time (124 women), 62 part-time (35 women); includes 54 minority (11 Black or African American, non-Hispanic/Latino; 13 Asian, non-Hispanic/Latino; 23 Hispanic/Latino; 7 Two or more races, non-Hispanic/Latino), 12 international. Average age 28. 368 applicants, 54% accepted, 74 enrolled. In 2017, 89 master's, 15 other advanced degrees awarded. Terminal master's awarded for partial completion of doctoral program. *Degree requirements:* For master's, comprehensive exam (for some programs), thesis (for some programs). *Entrance requirements:* Additional exam requirements/recommendations for international students: Required—TOEFL, IELTS, or PTE. *Application deadline:* Applications are processed on a rolling basis. Application fee: $50. Electronic applications accepted. *Expenses: Tuition:* Full-time $21,618; part-time $1201 per credit. *Required fees:* $1840; $920 per term. Tuition and fees vary according to course load. *Financial support:* In 2017–18, 165 students received support. Fellowships, research assistantships, teaching assistantships, career-related internships or fieldwork, Federal Work-Study, scholarships/grants, tuition waivers (partial), and unspecified assistantships available. Support available to part-time students. Financial award application deadline: 2/15; financial award applicants required to submit FAFSA. *Faculty research:* Biology, environmental sustainability, mathematics, psychology, genetic counseling. *Unit head:* Dr. Nathaniel Bowditch, Dean, 516-299-2234, Fax: 516-299-4140, E-mail: nathaniel.bowditch@liu.edu. *Application contact:* Rita Langdon, Graduate Admissions, 516-299-2900, Fax: 516-299-2137, E-mail: post-enroll@liu.edu.
Website: http://liu.edu/CWPost/Academics/Schools/CLAS

Manhattanville College, School of Education, Program in Middle Childhood/Adolescence Education (Grades 5-12), Purchase, NY 10577-2132. Offers biology (MAT, Advanced Certificate); biology and special education (MPS); chemistry (MAT, Advanced Certificate); chemistry and special education (MPS); earth science (Advanced Certificate); education for sustainability (Advanced Certificate); English (MAT, Advanced Certificate); English and special education (MPS); literacy and special education (MPS); literacy specialist (MPS); math and special education (MPS); mathematics (MAT, Advanced Certificate); physics (MAT, Advanced Certificate); social studies (MAT); social studies and special education (MPS); special education generalist (MPS). *Program availability:* Part-time, evening/weekend. *Faculty:* 2 full-time (both women), 5 part-time/adjunct (1 woman). *Students:* 8 full-time (7 women), 28 part-time (16 women); includes 4 minority (1 Asian, non-Hispanic/Latino; 2 Hispanic/Latino; 1 Two or more races, non-Hispanic/Latino). Average age 31. 7 applicants, 86% accepted, 4 enrolled. In 2017, 13 master's, 1 other advanced degree awarded. *Degree requirements:* For master's, comprehensive exam (for some programs), thesis (for some programs), student teaching, research seminars, portfolios, internships, writing assessment; for Advanced Certificate, comprehensive exam (for some programs). *Entrance requirements:* For master's, GRE or MAT (for programs leading to certification), minimum GPA of 3.0, 2 letters of recommendation, interview, essay (2-3 page personal statement that describes reasons for choosing teaching or educational leadership as profession and philosophy of education), proof of immunization (for those born after 1957). Additional exam requirements/recommendations for international students: Required—TOEFL (minimum score 600 paper-based; 110 iBT); Recommended—IELTS (minimum score 8). *Application deadline:* Applications are processed on a rolling basis. Application fee: $75. Electronic applications accepted. *Expenses:* $915 per credit. *Financial support:* Teaching assistantships, career-related internships or fieldwork, Federal Work-Study, institutionally sponsored loans, scholarships/grants, and unspecified assistantships available. Financial award application deadline: 3/15; financial award applicants required to submit FAFSA. *Faculty research:* Education for sustainability. *Unit head:* Dr. Shelly Wepner, Dean, 914-323-3153, Fax: 914-323-5493, E-mail: shelly.wepner@mville.edu. *Application contact:* Alissa Wilson, Director, Graduate Admissions, 914-323-3150, Fax: 914-694-1732, E-mail: edschool@mville.edu.
Website: http://www.mville.edu/programs#/search/19

Minneapolis College of Art and Design, Certificate Programs, Minneapolis, MN 55404-4347. Offers graphic design (Certificate); media (Certificate); sustainable design (Certificate). *Program availability:* Part-time, 100% online, blended/hybrid learning. *Faculty:* 42 full-time (29 women). *Students:* 29 full-time (21 women), 5 part-time (all women); includes 6 minority (2 Black or African American, non-Hispanic/Latino; 1 Asian, non-Hispanic/Latino; 3 Hispanic/Latino), 1 international. In 2017, 15 Certificates awarded. *Degree requirements:* For Certificate, final project. *Entrance requirements:* For degree, resume, portfolio, letter of recommendation. Additional exam requirements/recommendations for international students: Required—TOEFL (minimum score 550 paper-based; 79 iBT). *Application deadline:* For fall admission, 1/15 for domestic and international students; for spring admission, 10/15 for domestic and international students. Application fee: $50. Electronic applications accepted. *Expenses: Tuition:* Full-time $38,670. *Required fees:* $450. One-time fee: $300 full-time. *Financial support:* Career-related internships or fieldwork and scholarships/grants available. Financial award application deadline: 3/15; financial award applicants required to submit FAFSA. *Faculty research:* Visual arts. *Unit head:* Lara Roy, Senior Director of Continuing Education, 612-874-3778, E-mail: continuing_education@mcad.edu.
Website: http://www.mcad.edu/showPage.php?pageID-1216

Minneapolis College of Art and Design, Program in Sustainable Design, Minneapolis, MN 55404-4347. Offers MA. *Expenses: Tuition:* Full-time $38,670. *Required fees:* $450. One-time fee: $300 full-time.

Mississippi State University, College of Forest Resources, Department of Sustainable Bioproducts, Mississippi State, MS 39762. Offers forest resources (PhD), including sustainable bioproducts; sustainable bioproducts (MS). *Faculty:* 11 full-time (1 woman), 1 part-time/adjunct (0 women). *Students:* 26 full-time (15 women), 3 part-time (2 women); includes 1 minority (Asian, non-Hispanic/Latino), 22 international. Average age 28. 12 applicants, 50% accepted, 6 enrolled. In 2017, 4 master's, 8 doctorates awarded. *Degree requirements:* For master's, thesis optional; for doctorate, comprehensive exam, thesis/dissertation. *Entrance requirements:* For master's, GRE (if undergraduate GPA of last two years less than 3.0); for doctorate, GRE if undergraduate GPA of last two years is below 3.0. Additional exam requirements/recommendations for international students: Required—TOEFL (minimum score 550 paper-based; 79 iBT); Recommended—IELTS (minimum score 6.5). *Application deadline:* For fall admission, 7/1 for domestic students, 5/1 for international students; for spring admission, 11/1 for domestic students, 9/1 for international students. Applications are processed on a rolling basis. Application fee: $60 ($80 for international students). Electronic applications accepted. *Expenses:* Tuition, state resident: full-time $8318; part-time $462.12 per credit hour. Tuition, nonresident: full-time $22,358; part-time $1242.12 per credit hour. *Required fees:* $110; $12.24 per credit hour. $6.12 per semester. *Financial support:* In 2017–18, 100 students received support, including 23 research assistantships with full tuition reimbursements available (averaging $17,249 per year); Federal Work-Study, institutionally sponsored loans, and unspecified assistantships also available. Financial award application deadline: 4/1; financial award applicants required to submit FAFSA. *Faculty research:* Wood property enhancement and durability, environmental science and chemistry, wood-based composites, primary wood production, furniture manufacturing and management. *Unit head:* Dr. Rubin Shmulsky, Professor and Head, 662-325-2116, Fax: 662-325-8126, E-mail: rshmulsky@cfr.msstate.edu. *Application contact:* Nathan Drake, Admissions and Enrollment Assistant, 662-325-3804, E-mail: ndrake@grad.msstate.edu.
Website: http://www.cfr.msstate.edu/forestp//index.asp

Montclair State University, The Graduate School, College of Science and Mathematics, Program in Sustainability Science, Montclair, NJ 07043-1624. Offers MS.

New Jersey Institute of Technology, College of Science and Liberal Arts, Newark, NJ 07102. Offers applied mathematics (MS); applied physics (MS, PhD); applied statistics (MS, Certificate); biology (MS, PhD); biostatistics (MS); chemistry (MS, PhD); environmental and sustainability policy (MS); environmental science (MS, PhD); history (MA, MAT); materials science and engineering (MS, PhD); mathematical and computational finance (MS); mathematical sciences (PhD); pharmaceutical chemistry (MS); professional and technical communications (MS); technical communication essentials (Certificate). *Program availability:* Part-time, evening/weekend. *Students:* Average age 28. 504 applicants, 64% accepted, 65 enrolled. In 2017, 81 master's, 18 doctorates, 1 other advanced degree awarded. Terminal master's awarded for partial completion of doctoral program. *Entrance requirements:* For master's, GRE General Test; for doctorate, GRE General Test, minimum graduate GPA of 3.5. Additional exam requirements/recommendations for international students: Required—TOEFL (minimum score 550 paper-based; 79 iBT). *Application deadline:* For fall admission, 6/1 priority date for domestic students, 5/1 priority date for international students; for spring admission, 11/15 priority date for domestic and international students. Applications are processed on a rolling basis. Application fee: $75. Electronic applications accepted. *Expenses:* Contact institution. *Financial support:* In 2017–18, 106 students received

support, including 8 fellowships (averaging $3,436 per year), 51 research assistantships (averaging $23,452 per year), 91 teaching assistantships (averaging $25,553 per year); scholarships/grants, traineeships, and unspecified assistantships also available. Financial award application deadline: 1/15. *Faculty research:* Biophotonics and bioimaging, morphogenetic patterning, embryogenesis, biological fluid dynamics, applied research in the mathematical sciences. *Unit head:* Dr. Kevin Belfield, Dean, 973-596-3676, Fax: 973-565-0586, E-mail: kevin.d.belfield@njit.edu. *Application contact:* Stephen Eck, Director of Admissions, 973-596-3300, Fax: 973-596-3461, E-mail: admissions@njit.edu.
Website: http://csla.njit.edu/

New York School of Interior Design, Program in Sustainable Interior Environments, New York, NY 10021-5110. Offers MPS. *Entrance requirements:* For master's, degree in interior design, architecture, or closely-related field; portfolio. Additional exam requirements/recommendations for international students: Required—TOEFL (minimum score 550 paper-based; 79 iBT). Electronic applications accepted.

New York University, Graduate School of Arts and Science, Program in Historical and Sustainable Architecture, New York, NY 10012-1019. Offers MA. *Students:* Average age 25. 17 applicants, 100% accepted, 12 enrolled. In 2017, 14 master's awarded. *Entrance requirements:* For master's, GRE, writing sample. *Application deadline:* For fall admission, 3/1 for domestic and international students. Application fee: $100. *Expenses: Tuition:* Full-time $41,352; part-time $19,968 per year. *Required fees:* $2496; $1628 per unit. $814 per term. Tuition and fees vary according to course load and program. *Financial support:* Application deadline: 3/1. *Unit head:* Mosette Broderick, Director of Graduate Studies, 212-998-8180, Fax: 212-995-4152, E-mail: histsust@nyu.edu. *Application contact:* Jon Ritter, Assistant Director, 212-998-8180, Fax: 212-995-4152, E-mail: histsust@nyu.edu.
Website: http://arthistory.as.nyu.edu/

New York University, School of Professional Studies, Schack Institute of Real Estate, Program in Real Estate Development, New York, NY 10012-1019. Offers real estate development (MS), including global real estate, sustainable development, the business of development. *Program availability:* Part-time, evening/weekend. *Students:* 78 full-time (26 women), 140 part-time (35 women); includes 34 minority (8 Black or African American, non-Hispanic/Latino; 1 American Indian or Alaska Native, non-Hispanic/Latino; 7 Asian, non-Hispanic/Latino; 14 Hispanic/Latino; 1 Native Hawaiian or other Pacific Islander, non-Hispanic/Latino; 3 Two or more races, non-Hispanic/Latino), 51 international. Average age 28. 176 applicants, 67% accepted, 68 enrolled. In 2017, 126 master's awarded. *Degree requirements:* For master's, thesis, capstone project. *Entrance requirements:* For master's, GRE or GMAT (only upon request), bachelor's degree, resume with relevant professional work, internship or volunteer experience, two letters of recommendation, statement of purpose. Additional exam requirements/recommendations for international students: Required—TOEFL (minimum score 600 paper-based; 100 iBT), IELTS (minimum score 7). *Application deadline:* For fall admission, 2/1 priority date for domestic and international students; for spring admission, 10/15 priority date for domestic students, 8/15 priority date for international students; for summer admission, 5/1 priority date for domestic students, 1/15 priority date for international students. Applications are processed on a rolling basis. Application fee: $150. Electronic applications accepted. *Expenses:* $20,244 per term. *Financial support:* Fellowships, career-related internships or fieldwork, Federal Work-Study, scholarships/grants, and health care benefits available. Support available to part-time students. Financial award application deadline: 6/30; financial award applicants required to submit FAFSA. *Unit head:* Sam Chandan, Associate Dean/Chair/Clinical Professor, 212-992-3335. *Application contact:* Office of Admissions, 212-998-7100, E-mail: sps.gradadmissions@nyu.edu.
Website: http://www.sps.nyu.edu/academics/departments/schack/academic-offerings/graduate/ms-in-real-estate-development.html

Northern Arizona University, College of Social and Behavioral Sciences, Sustainable Communities Program, Flagstaff, AZ 86011. Offers MA. *Program availability:* Part-time. *Faculty:* 4 full-time (3 women), 3 part-time/adjunct (2 women). *Students:* 27 full-time (19 women), 10 part-time (7 women); includes 11 minority (4 American Indian or Alaska Native, non-Hispanic/Latino; 7 Hispanic/Latino), 2 international. Average age 32. 18 applicants, 72% accepted, 12 enrolled. In 2017, 8 master's awarded. *Degree requirements:* For master's, variable foreign language requirement, comprehensive exam (for some programs), thesis, fieldwork experience/internship, oral defense. *Entrance requirements:* Additional exam requirements/recommendations for international students: Required—TOEFL (minimum score 80 iBT), IELTS (minimum score 6.5). *Application deadline:* For fall admission, 3/1 for domestic and international students; for spring admission, 10/1 for domestic and international students. Applications are processed on a rolling basis. Application fee: $65. Electronic applications accepted. *Expenses:* Tuition, state resident: full-time $9240; part-time $458 per credit hour. Tuition, nonresident: full-time $21,588; part-time $1199 per credit hour. *Required fees:* $1021; $14 per credit hour. $646 per semester. Tuition and fees vary according to course load, campus/location and program. *Financial support:* In 2017–18, 6 students received support, including 4 research assistantships with partial tuition reimbursements available (averaging $9,000 per year), 1 teaching assistantship with partial tuition reimbursement available (averaging $9,000 per year); institutionally sponsored loans, health care benefits, tuition waivers (full and partial), and unspecified assistantships also available. Financial award application deadline: 2/1; financial award applicants required to submit FAFSA. *Unit head:* Luis Fernandez, Director, 928-523-2382, Fax: 928-523-2020, E-mail: luis.fernandez@nau.edu. *Application contact:* Ginger Christenson, Program Coordinator, 928-523-0499, Fax: 928-523-2020, E-mail: sustainable.communities@nau.edu.
Website: http://nau.edu/sbs/sus/

Penn State University Park, Graduate School, Intercollege Graduate Programs, Intercollege Program in Renewable Energy and Sustainability Systems, University Park, PA 16802. Offers MPS. *Unit head:* Dr. Regina Vasilatos-Younken, Dean, 814-865-2516, Fax: 814-863-4627. *Application contact:* Lori Hawn, Director, Graduate Student Services, 814-865-1795, Fax: 814-863-4627, E-mail: l-gswww@lists.psu.edu.
Website: https://www.ress.psu.edu/

Pratt Institute, School of Architecture, Program in Sustainable Environmental Systems, Brooklyn, NY 11205-3899. Offers MS. *Program availability:* Part-time. *Students:* 19 full-time (17 women), 9 part-time (7 women); includes 7 minority (1 Black or African American, non-Hispanic/Latino; 3 Asian, non-Hispanic/Latino; 3 Hispanic/Latino), 14 international. Average age 29. 34 applicants, 76% accepted, 10 enrolled. In 2017, 10 master's awarded. *Degree requirements:* For master's, thesis. *Entrance requirements:* For master's, portfolio or writing sample, letters of recommendation. Additional exam requirements/recommendations for international students: Required—TOEFL (minimum score 550 paper-based; 79 iBT). *Application deadline:* For fall admission, 1/5 for domestic and international students; for spring admission, 10/1 for domestic and international students. Application fee: $50 ($90 for international students). Electronic applications accepted. *Expenses: Tuition:* Full-time $30,834. *Required fees:* $1974. *Financial support:* Career-related internships or fieldwork, Federal Work-Study, institutionally sponsored loans, scholarships/grants, health care benefits, and unspecified assistantships available. Support available to part-time students. Financial

award application deadline: 2/1; financial award applicants required to submit FAFSA. *Unit head:* Eve Baron, Chairperson, 718-687-5641, Fax: 718-636-3709, E-mail: ebaron@pratt.edu. *Application contact:* Natalie Capannelli, Director of Graduate Admissions, 718-636-3551, Fax: 718-399-4242, E-mail: ncapanne@pratt.edu.
Website: https://www.pratt.edu/academics/architecture/sustainable-environmental-systems/

See Display on page 105 and Close-Up on page 125.

Rochester Institute of Technology, Graduate Enrollment Services, Golisano Institute for Sustainability, Architecture and Sustainability Department, MS Program in Sustainable Systems, Rochester, NY 14623. Offers MS. *Program availability:* Part-time. *Students:* 14 full-time (8 women), 4 part-time (0 women), 9 international. Average age 28. 43 applicants, 79% accepted, 12 enrolled. In 2017, 10 master's awarded. *Entrance requirements:* For master's, GRE, minimum GPA of 3.0 (recommended). Additional exam requirements/recommendations for international students: Required—TOEFL (minimum score 600 paper-based; 100 iBT), IELTS (minimum score 6.5), PTE (minimum score 68). *Application deadline:* For fall admission, 2/15 priority date for domestic and international students; for spring admission, 12/15 priority date for domestic and international students. Applications are processed on a rolling basis. Application fee: $65. Electronic applications accepted. *Expenses:* $1,815 per credit hour. *Financial support:* In 2017–18, 18 students received support. Research assistantships with partial tuition reimbursements available, teaching assistantships with partial tuition reimbursements available, career-related internships or fieldwork, scholarships/grants, and unspecified assistantships available. Financial award applicants required to submit FAFSA. *Faculty research:* Renewable energy and energy policy; food systems; material extraction and recycling; green transportation and logistics; eco-design and circular economy. *Unit head:* Dr. Gabrielle Gaustad, Graduate Director, 585-475-6089, E-mail: info@sustainability.rit.edu. *Application contact:* Diane Ellison, Senior Associate Vice President, Graduate Enrollment Services, 585-475-2229, Fax: 585-475-7164, E-mail: gradinfo@rit.edu.
Website: http://www.rit.edu/gis/academics/ms-sustainability/

Rochester Institute of Technology, Graduate Enrollment Services, Golisano Institute for Sustainability, Architecture and Sustainability Department, PhD Program in Sustainability, Rochester, NY 14623. Offers PhD. *Students:* 16 full-time (11 women), 3 part-time (1 woman); includes 1 minority (Two or more races, non-Hispanic/Latino), 13 international. Average age 32. 53 applicants, 11% accepted, 4 enrolled. In 2017, 1 doctorate awarded. *Entrance requirements:* For doctorate, GRE, minimum GPA of 3.0 (recommended). Additional exam requirements/recommendations for international students: Required—TOEFL (minimum score 600 paper-based; 100 iBT), IELTS (minimum score 6.5), PTE (minimum score 68). *Application deadline:* For fall admission, 1/15 priority date for domestic and international students. Applications are processed on a rolling basis. Application fee: $65. Electronic applications accepted. *Expenses:* $1,815 per credit hour. *Financial support:* In 2017–18, 21 students received support. Research assistantships with full tuition reimbursements available, teaching assistantships with full tuition reimbursements available, career-related internships or fieldwork, scholarships/grants, health care benefits, and unspecified assistantships available. Financial award applicants required to submit FAFSA. *Faculty research:* Renewable energy and energy policy; food systems; material extraction and recycling; green transportation and logistics; eco-design and circular economy. *Unit head:* Prof. Thomas Trabold, Head, Sustainability Department/Associate Professor, 585-475-4696, E-mail: info@sustainability.rit.edu. *Application contact:* Diane Ellison, Senior Associate Vice President, Graduate Enrollment Services, 585-475-2229, Fax: 585-475-7164, E-mail: gradinfo@rit.edu.
Website: https://www.rit.edu/gis/academics/sustainability-phd/overview

Rochester Institute of Technology, Graduate Enrollment Services, Kate Gleason College of Engineering, Industrial and Systems Engineering Department, ME Program in Sustainable Engineering, Rochester, NY 14623-5603. Offers ME. *Program availability:* Part-time. *Students:* 12 full-time (6 women), 2 part-time (1 woman); includes 3 minority (1 Asian, non-Hispanic/Latino; 1 Hispanic/Latino; 1 Two or more races, non-Hispanic/Latino), 5 international. Average age 24. 29 applicants, 66% accepted, 6 enrolled. In 2017, 7 master's awarded. *Degree requirements:* For master's, capstone project. *Entrance requirements:* For master's, minimum GPA of 3.0 (recommended). Additional exam requirements/recommendations for international students: Required—TOEFL (minimum score 550 paper-based; 79 iBT), IELTS (minimum score 6.5), PTE (minimum score 58). *Application deadline:* For fall admission, 2/15 priority date for domestic and international students; for spring admission, 12/15 priority date for domestic and international students. Applications are processed on a rolling basis. Application fee: $65. Electronic applications accepted. *Expenses:* $1,815 per credit hour. *Financial support:* In 2017–18, 11 students received support. Research assistantships with partial tuition reimbursements available, teaching assistantships with partial tuition reimbursements available, career-related internships or fieldwork, scholarships/grants, and unspecified assistantships available. Support available to part-time students. Financial award applicants required to submit FAFSA. *Faculty research:* Renewable and alternative energies; grid optimization and Smart Grid applications; life cycle assessment; product/process design methodologies; sanitation, water supply, soil fertility; off grid energy applications; human centered design. *Unit head:* Dr. Brian Thorn, Associate Professor, 585-475-6166, E-mail: bkteie@rit.edu. *Application contact:* Diane Ellison, Senior Associate Vice President, Graduate Enrollment Services, 585-475-2229, Fax: 585-475-7164, E-mail: gradinfo@rit.edu.
Website: http://www.rit.edu/kgcoe/ise/program/master-engineering-degrees/master-engineering-sustainable-engineering

Rochester Institute of Technology, Graduate Enrollment Services, Kate Gleason College of Engineering, Industrial and Systems Engineering Department, MS Program in Sustainable Engineering, Rochester, NY 14623-5603. Offers MS. *Program availability:* Part-time. *Students:* 6 full-time (3 women), 1 part-time (0 women), 6 international. Average age 24. 30 applicants, 57% accepted, 5 enrolled. In 2017, 1 master's awarded. *Degree requirements:* For master's, thesis. *Entrance requirements:* For master's, GRE, minimum GPA of 3.0 (recommended). Additional exam requirements/recommendations for international students: Required—TOEFL (minimum score 550 paper-based; 79 iBT), IELTS (minimum score 6.5), PTE (minimum score 58). *Application deadline:* For fall admission, 2/15 priority date for domestic and international students; for spring admission, 12/15 priority date for domestic and international students. Applications are processed on a rolling basis. Application fee: $65. Electronic applications accepted. *Expenses:* $1,815 per credit hour. *Financial support:* In 2017–18, 8 students received support. Research assistantships with partial tuition reimbursements available, teaching assistantships with partial tuition reimbursements available, career-related internships or fieldwork, scholarships/grants, and unspecified assistantships available. Support available to part-time students. Financial award applicants required to submit FAFSA. *Faculty research:* Renewable and alternative energies; grid optimization and Smart Grid applications; life cycle assessment; product/process design methodologies; sanitation, water supply, soil fertility; off grid energy applications; human centered design. *Unit head:* Dr. Brian Thorn, Associate Professor, 585-475-6166, E-mail: bkteie@rit.edu. *Application contact:* Diane Ellison, Senior Associate Vice President, Graduate Enrollment Services, 585-475-2229, Fax: 585-475-7164, E-mail: gradinfo@rit.edu.
Website: http://www.rit.edu/kgcoe/ise/program/master-science-degrees/master-science-sustainable-engineering

St. Edward's University, School of Behavioral and Social Sciences, Austin, TX 78704. Offers environmental management and sustainability (PSM). *Students:* 20 full-time (14 women); includes 8 minority (1 Asian, non-Hispanic/Latino; 6 Hispanic/Latino; 1 Native Hawaiian or other Pacific Islander, non-Hispanic/Latino). Average age 28. 71 applicants, 35% accepted, 7 enrolled. In 2017, 33 master's awarded. *Entrance requirements:* Additional exam requirements/recommendations for international students: Required—TOEFL, IELTS. *Application deadline:* For fall admission, 6/1 priority date for domestic and international students; for spring admission, 10/1 priority date for domestic and international students. Applications are processed on a rolling basis. Application fee: $50. Electronic applications accepted. *Expenses: Tuition:* Full-time $26,406; part-time $1467 per hour. *Required fees:* $75 per trimester. Full-time tuition and fees vary according to course load and program. *Unit head:* Dr. Peter Beck, Program Director/Associate Professor, 512-428-1249, Fax: 512-233-1664, E-mail: peterab@stedwards.edu. *Application contact:* Dave Bralower, Director of Graduate Admission, 512-233-1424, Fax: 512-464-8877, E-mail: davidcb@stedwards.edu.
Website: http://www.stedwards.edu

Savannah College of Art and Design, Program in Design for Sustainability, Savannah, GA 31402-3146. Offers built environment (MFA); management (MFA); packaging and print media (MFA); products (MFA). *Program availability:* Part-time. *Students:* 19 full-time (15 women); includes 2 minority (both Hispanic/Latino), 11 international. Average age 26. 30 applicants, 53% accepted, 8 enrolled. In 2017, 4 master's awarded. *Degree requirements:* For master's, final project (for MA); thesis (for MFA). *Entrance requirements:* For master's, GRE (recommended), portfolio (submitted in digital format), audition or writing submission, resume, statement of purpose, two letters of recommendation. Additional exam requirements/recommendations for international students: Recommended—TOEFL (minimum score 550 paper-based; 85 iBT), IELTS (minimum score 6.5). *Application deadline:* For fall admission, 4/1 for domestic and international students. Applications are processed on a rolling basis. Application fee: $40. Electronic applications accepted. *Expenses: Tuition:* Full-time $36,765; part-time $817 per credit hour. One-time fee: $500. *Financial support:* Career-related internships or fieldwork, Federal Work-Study, and scholarships/grants available. Financial award application deadline: 4/1; financial award applicants required to submit FAFSA. *Unit head:* Victor Ermoli, Dean, School of Design. *Application contact:* Jenny Jaquillard, Executive Director of Admissions, Recruitment and Events, 912-525-5100, Fax: 912-525-5985, E-mail: admission@scad.edu.
Website: http://www.scad.edu/academics/programs/design-sustainability

Saybrook University, School of Psychology and Interdisciplinary Inquiry, San Francisco, CA 94612. Offers human science (MA, PhD), including consciousness and spirituality, humanistic and transpersonal psychology, integrative health studies, organizational systems, social transformation; organizational systems (MA, PhD), including consciousness and spirituality, humanistic and transpersonal psychology, integrative health studies, leadership of sustainable systems (MA), organizational systems, social transformation; psychology (MA, PhD), including consciousness and spirituality, creativity studies (MA), humanistic and transpersonal psychology, integrative health studies, Jungian studies, marriage and family therapy (MA), organizational systems, social transformation. *Program availability:* Online learning. Terminal master's awarded for partial completion of doctoral program. *Degree requirements:* For master's, thesis or alternative; for doctorate, thesis/dissertation. *Entrance requirements:* Additional exam requirements/recommendations for international students: Required—TOEFL (minimum score 580 paper-based; 93 iBT). Electronic applications accepted. *Faculty research:* Humanistic theory, health studies, organizational systems, consciousness and spirituality, social transformation.

SIT Graduate Institute, Graduate Programs, Master's Programs in Intercultural Service, Leadership, and Management, Master's Program in Sustainable Development, Washington, DC 20005. Offers MA.

Southern Illinois University Edwardsville, Graduate School, Program in Integrative Studies, Edwardsville, IL 62026. Offers cultural heritage and resources management (MA, MS); diversity training (MA, MS); organizational design thinking (MS); sustainability (MS). *Program availability:* Part-time, evening/weekend. *Degree requirements:* For master's, variable foreign language requirement, comprehensive exam (for some programs), thesis (for some programs). *Entrance requirements:* Additional exam requirements/recommendations for international students: Required—TOEFL (minimum score 550 paper-based; 79 iBT), IELTS (minimum score 6.5). Electronic applications accepted.

Southern Methodist University, Bobby B. Lyle School of Engineering, Department of Environmental and Civil Engineering, Dallas, TX 75275-0340. Offers air pollution control and atmospheric sciences (PhD); civil engineering (MS); environmental engineering (MS); environmental science (MS); structural engineering (PhD); sustainability and development (MA); water and wastewater engineering (PhD). *Program availability:* Part-time, evening/weekend, online learning. Terminal master's awarded for partial completion of doctoral program. *Degree requirements:* For master's, thesis optional; for doctorate, thesis/dissertation, oral and written qualifying exams. *Entrance requirements:* For master's, GRE General Test, minimum GPA of 3.0 in last 2 years; bachelor's degree in engineering, mathematics, or sciences; for doctorate, GRE, BS and MS in related field, minimum GPA of 3.3. Additional exam requirements/recommendations for international students: Required—TOEFL. Electronic applications accepted. *Faculty research:* Human and environmental health effects of endocrine disrupters, development of air pollution control systems for diesel engines, structural analysis and design, modeling and design of waste treatment systems.

Stanford University, School of Engineering, Department of Civil and Environmental Engineering, Stanford, CA 94305-2004. Offers atmosphere and energy (MS, PhD); construction (MS), including construction engineering and management, design-construction integration, sustainable design and construction; environmental engineering and science (MS, PhD, Eng); environmental fluid mechanics and hydrology (PhD); geomechanics (MS); structural engineering (MS). Terminal master's awarded for partial completion of doctoral program. *Degree requirements:* For doctorate, thesis/dissertation, qualifying exam; for Eng, thesis. *Entrance requirements:* For master's, doctorate, and Eng, GRE General Test. Additional exam requirements/recommendations for international students: Required—TOEFL. Electronic applications accepted. *Expenses: Tuition:* Full-time $48,987; part-time $10,620 per quarter. One-time fee: $400. Tuition and fees vary according to program.

State University of New York College of Environmental Science and Forestry, Department of Paper and Bioprocess Engineering, Syracuse, NY 13210-2779. Offers biomaterials engineering (MS, PhD); bioprocess engineering (MPS, MS, PhD); bioprocessing (Advanced Certificate); paper science and engineering (MPS, MS, PhD); sustainable engineering management (MPS). *Program availability:* Part-time. *Faculty:* 13 full-time (2 women), 1 part-time/adjunct (0 women). *Students:* 25 full-time (12 women), 2 part-time (1 woman), 17 international. Average age 28. 23 applicants, 87% accepted, 13 enrolled. In 2017, 7 master's, 3 doctorates awarded. Terminal master's

awarded for partial completion of doctoral program. *Degree requirements:* For master's, thesis; for doctorate, comprehensive exam, thesis/dissertation; for Advanced Certificate, 15 credit hours. *Entrance requirements:* For master's and doctorate, GRE General Test, minimum GPA of 3.0; for Advanced Certificate, BS, calculus plus science major. Additional exam requirements/recommendations for international students: Required—TOEFL (minimum score 550 paper-based; 80 iBT), IELTS (minimum score 6). *Application deadline:* For fall admission, 2/1 priority date for domestic and international students; for spring admission, 11/1 priority date for domestic and international students. Applications are processed on a rolling basis. Application fee: $60. Electronic applications accepted. *Expenses:* Tuition, state resident: full-time $10,870; part-time $453 per credit. Tuition, nonresident: full-time $22,210; part-time $925 per credit. *Required fees:* $1435; $70.85 per credit. One-time fee: $25 full-time. Part-time tuition and fees vary according to course load. *Financial support:* In 2017–18, 12 students received support. Unspecified assistantships available. Financial award application deadline: 6/30; financial award applicants required to submit FAFSA. *Faculty research:* Sustainable products and processes, biorefinery, pulping and papermaking, nanocellulose, bioconversions, process control and modeling. *Total annual research expenditures:* $1.2 million. *Unit head:* Dr. Bandaru Ramarao, Interim Chair, 315-470-6502, Fax: 315-470-6945, E-mail: bvramara@esf.edu. *Application contact:* Scott Shannon, Associate Provost and Dean, Instruction and Graduate Studies, 315-470-6599, Fax: 315-470-6978, E-mail: esfgrad@esf.edu.
Website: http://www.esf.edu/pbe/

Temple University, Tyler School of Art, Department of Planning and Community Development, Ambler, PA 19335. Offers city and regional planning (MS); sustainable community planning (Graduate Certificate); transportation planning (Graduate Certificate). *Accreditation:* ACSP. *Program availability:* Part-time, evening/weekend. *Faculty:* 3 full-time (1 woman), 8 part-time/adjunct (5 women). *Students:* 1 (woman) part-time. 23 applicants, 70% accepted, 1 enrolled. In 2017, 2 master's awarded. *Entrance requirements:* For master's, GRE or GMAT, 2 letters of recommendation, minimum undergraduate GPA of 3.0, statement of goals. Additional exam requirements/recommendations for international students: Required—TOEFL (minimum score 550 paper-based; 79 iBT). *Application deadline:* For fall admission, 3/1 for domestic students, 12/15 for international students; for spring admission, 11/1 for domestic students, 8/1 for international students. Applications are processed on a rolling basis. Application fee: $60. *Expenses:* Tuition, state resident: full-time $16,164; part-time $898 per credit hour. Tuition, nonresident: full-time $22,158; part-time $1231 per credit hour. *Required fees:* $890; $445 per semester. Full-time tuition and fees vary according to course load, degree level, campus/location and program. *Financial support:* Fellowships with full tuition reimbursements, research assistantships with full tuition reimbursements, Federal Work-Study, scholarships/grants, health care benefits, and unspecified assistantships available. Financial award application deadline: 1/15; financial award applicants required to submit FAFSA. *Faculty research:* Regional environmental planning, collaboration, management community development through sustainable food systems, storm water management and floodplain mapping, land use policy innovations, community planning for aging. *Unit head:* Lynn Mandarano, Chair, 267-468-8300, Fax: 267-468-8315, E-mail: lynn.mandarano@temple.edu.
Website: http://tyler.temple.edu/programs/planning-community-development

Texas A&M University–Kingsville, College of Graduate Studies, Frank H. Dotterweich College of Engineering, Program in Sustainable Energy Systems Engineering, Kingsville, TX 78363. Offers PhD. *Degree requirements:* For doctorate, variable foreign language requirement, comprehensive exam, thesis/dissertation (for some programs). *Entrance requirements:* For doctorate, GRE, MAT, GMAT, bachelor's or master's degree in engineering or science, curriculum vitae, official transcripts, statement of purpose, three letters of recommendation. Additional exam requirements/recommendations for international students: Required—TOEFL (minimum score 550 paper-based; 79 iBT). Electronic applications accepted.

Texas State University, The Graduate College, College of Liberal Arts, Interdisciplinary Studies Program in Sustainability, San Marcos, TX 78666. Offers MA, MS. *Program availability:* Part-time. *Faculty:* 14 full-time (8 women). *Students:* 17 full-time (13 women), 14 part-time (9 women); includes 6 minority (1 Asian, non-Hispanic/Latino; 3 Hispanic/Latino; 2 Two or more races, non-Hispanic/Latino), 1 international. Average age 30. 25 applicants, 68% accepted, 10 enrolled. In 2017, 4 master's awarded. *Degree requirements:* For master's, comprehensive exam, thesis optional. *Entrance requirements:* For master's, bachelor's degree from accredited institution, minimum GPA of 3.0 on last 60 hours of undergraduate work, statement of personal goals, letter of intent to mentor from faculty member who will serve as research advisor and chair the master's committee. Additional exam requirements/recommendations for international students: Required—TOEFL (minimum score 550 paper-based; 78 iBT), IELTS (minimum score 6). *Application deadline:* For fall admission, 1/15 priority date for domestic students, 1/1 priority date for international students; for spring admission, 10/15 for domestic students, 10/1 for international students; for summer admission, 5/15 for domestic students, 3/15 for international students. Applications are processed on a rolling basis. Application fee: $40 ($90 for international students). Electronic applications accepted. *Expenses:* Tuition, state resident: full-time $7868; part-time $3934 per semester. Tuition, nonresident: full-time $17,828; part-time $8914 per semester. *Required fees:* $2092; $1435 per semester. Tuition and fees vary according to course load. *Financial support:* In 2017–18, 19 students received support, including 1 research assistantship (averaging $11,855 per year), 11 teaching assistantships (averaging $12,549 per year); Federal Work-Study, scholarships/grants, and unspecified assistantships also available. Support available to part-time students. Financial award application deadline: 3/1; financial award applicants required to submit FAFSA. *Faculty research:* Composting, surveying college students attitudes toward exotic species, aerial vehicle monitoring of spectral response to plant productivity, irrigation water use exploring the effects of volume controls, the effect of nature hikes on knowledge and attitudes. *Total annual research expenditures:* $20,842. *Unit head:* Dr. Patti Giuffre, Graduate Advisor, 512-245-8983, E-mail: pg07@txstate.edu. *Application contact:* Dr. Andrea Golato, Dean of Graduate School, 512-245-2581, Fax: 512-245-8365, E-mail: gradcollege@txstate.edu.
Website: http://www.gradcollege.txstate.edu/programs/sustainability.html

Texas Tech University, Graduate School, Interdisciplinary Programs, Lubbock, TX 79409. Offers arid land studies (MS); biotechnology (MS); heritage and museum sciences (MA); interdisciplinary studies (MA, MS); wind science and engineering (PhD); JD/MS. *Program availability:* Part-time, blended/hybrid learning. *Faculty:* 11 full-time (5 women). *Students:* 106 full-time (56 women), 85 part-time (52 women); includes 65 minority (23 Black or African American, non-Hispanic/Latino; 2 American Indian or Alaska Native, non-Hispanic/Latino; 3 Asian, non-Hispanic/Latino; 32 Hispanic/Latino; 5 Two or more races, non-Hispanic/Latino), 30 international. Average age 30. 116 applicants, 67% accepted, 55 enrolled. In 2017, 52 master's, 1 doctorate awarded. Terminal master's awarded for partial completion of doctoral program. *Degree requirements:* For master's, comprehensive exam (for some programs), thesis (for some programs); for doctorate, comprehensive exam, thesis/dissertation (for some programs). *Entrance requirements:* Additional exam requirements/recommendations for international students: Required—TOEFL (minimum score 550 paper-based; 79 iBT), IELTS (minimum score 6.5), PTE (minimum score 60), Cambridge advanced (B), Cambridge Proficiency (C), ELS English for Academic Purposes (Level 112). *Application deadline:* For fall admission, 6/1 priority date for domestic students, 1/15 priority date for international students; for spring admission, 9/1 priority date for domestic students, 6/15 priority date for international students. Applications are processed on a rolling basis. Application fee: $60. Electronic applications accepted. *Expenses:* Tuition, state resident: full-time $7632; part-time $318 per credit hour. Tuition, nonresident: full-time $17,424; part-time $726 per credit hour. *Required fees:* $2428; $50.50 per credit hour. $608 per semester. Tuition and fees vary according to program. *Financial support:* In 2017–18, 124 students received support, including 106 fellowships (averaging $4,660 per year), 25 research assistantships (averaging $16,239 per year), 16 teaching assistantships (averaging $10,391 per year); scholarships/grants and unspecified assistantships also available. Financial award application deadline: 4/15; financial award applicants required to submit FAFSA. *Total annual research expenditures:* $2.2 million. *Unit head:* Dr. Mark Sheridan, Vice Provost for Graduate and Postdoctoral Affairs/Dean of the Graduate School, 806-742-2787, Fax: 806-742-1746, E-mail: mark.sheridan@ttu.edu. *Application contact:* Claudia Simon, Senior Academic Advisor, 806-834-8290, Fax: 806-742-4038, E-mail: claudia.simon@ttu.edu.
Website: http://www.depts.ttu.edu/gradschool/

Thomas Jefferson University, College of Architecture and the Built Environment, Program in Sustainable Design, Philadelphia, PA 19107. Offers MS. *Program availability:* Part-time, online learning.

Unity College, Program in Professional Science, Unity, ME 04988. Offers sustainability science (MS); sustainable natural resource management (MS). *Program availability:* Online learning.

University at Buffalo, the State University of New York, Graduate School, School of Engineering and Applied Sciences, Department of Civil, Structural, and Environmental Engineering, Buffalo, NY 14260. Offers civil engineering (MS, PhD); engineering science (MS), including data sciences, green energy, Internet of Things, nanoelectronics; environmental and water resources engineering (MS). *Program availability:* Part-time, online learning. Terminal master's awarded for partial completion of doctoral program. *Degree requirements:* For master's, project, thesis, or comprehensive exam; for doctorate, thesis/dissertation. *Entrance requirements:* For master's and doctorate, GRE General Test, letters of reference. Additional exam requirements/recommendations for international students: Required—TOEFL (minimum score 550 paper-based; 79 iBT). Electronic applications accepted. *Faculty research:* Structural and earthquake engineering; geomechanics, geotechnical and geoenvironmental engineering; computational engineering mechanics; bridge engineering; environmental and water resources engineering; transportation systems engineering.

The University of Alabama at Birmingham, School of Engineering, Program in Engineering Management, Birmingham, AL 35294. Offers advanced safety engineering and management (M Eng); construction engineering management (M Eng); design and commercialization (M Eng); information engineering management (M Eng); structural engineering (M Eng); sustainable smart cities (M Eng). *Program availability:* Part-time, evening/weekend, 100% online, blended/hybrid learning. *Faculty:* 4 full-time (1 woman), 11 part-time/adjunct (2 women). *Students:* 27 full-time (12 women), 280 part-time (49 women); includes 98 minority (61 Black or African American, non-Hispanic/Latino; 14 Asian, non-Hispanic/Latino; 14 Hispanic/Latino; 3 Native Hawaiian or other Pacific Islander, non-Hispanic/Latino; 6 Two or more races, non-Hispanic/Latino), 17 international. Average age 37. 146 applicants, 79% accepted, 97 enrolled. In 2017, 103 master's awarded. *Entrance requirements:* Additional exam requirements/recommendations for international students: Required—TOEFL (minimum score 90 iBT); Recommended—IELTS (minimum score 6.5). *Application deadline:* For fall admission, 8/1 for domestic and international students; for spring admission, 12/1 for domestic and international students; for summer admission, 5/1 for domestic and international students. Applications are processed on a rolling basis. Application fee: $50 ($60 for international students). Electronic applications accepted. *Expenses:* Contact institution. *Faculty research:* Orthopedic biomechanics, translational rehabilitation and assistive devices, innovation and entrepreneurship, anthropogenic activities and the natural environment, prestressed and spun concrete. *Unit head:* Dr. Dale Callahan, Head, 205-934-8480, E-mail: dcallahan@uab.edu. *Application contact:* Holly Hebard, Director of Graduate School Operations, 205-934-8227, Fax: 205-934-8413, E-mail: gradschool@uab.edu.

University of Alaska Fairbanks, School of Natural Resources and Extension, Fairbanks, AK 99775-7140. Offers natural resources and sustainability (PhD); natural resources management (MS). *Program availability:* Part-time. *Degree requirements:* For master's, comprehensive exam, thesis (for some programs), oral defense of project or thesis; for doctorate, comprehensive exam, thesis/dissertation, defense of the dissertation. *Entrance requirements:* For master's, GRE General Test, bachelor's degree from accredited institution with minimum cumulative undergraduate and major GPA of 3.0; for doctorate, minimum cumulative GPA of 3.0. Additional exam requirements/recommendations for international students: Required—TOEFL (minimum score 550 paper-based; 89 iBT), IELTS (minimum score 6.5). Electronic applications accepted. *Faculty research:* Conservation biology, soil/water conservation, land use policy and planning in the arctic and subarctic, forest ecosystem management, subarctic agricultural production.

The University of British Columbia, Faculty of Applied Science, Clean Energy Research Center, Vancouver, BC V6T 1Z1, Canada. Offers MEL. *Entrance requirements:* For master's, undergraduate degree in engineering or BS in environmental science; undergraduate thermodynamics course; three or more years of relevant work experience.

University of Calgary, Faculty of Graduate Studies, Faculty of Environmental Design, Calgary, AB T2N 1N4, Canada. Offers architecture (M Arch); environmental design (M Env Des, PhD); landscape architecture (MLA); planning (M Plan). *Degree requirements:* For master's, thesis; for doctorate, thesis/dissertation. *Entrance requirements:* For master's, minimum GPA of 3.0; for doctorate, minimum GPA of 3.5. Additional exam requirements/recommendations for international students: Required—TOEFL (minimum score 550 paper-based). *Faculty research:* Sustainable development in architecture, planning and product design, energy and environment, impact assessment, ecotourism.

University of California, Berkeley, Graduate Division, College of Natural Resources, Master of Development Practice Program, Berkeley, CA 94720-1500. Offers MDP.

University of California, Berkeley, UC Berkeley Extension, Certificate Programs in Sustainability Studies, Berkeley, CA 94720-1500. Offers leadership in sustainability and environmental management (Professional Certificate); solar energy and green building (Professional Certificate); sustainable design (Professional Certificate).

University of California, Santa Barbara, Graduate Division, College of Letters and Sciences, Division of Social Sciences, Department of Global Studies, Santa Barbara, CA 93106-7065. Offers global culture, ideology, and religion (MA, PhD); global government, human rights, and civil society (MA, PhD); political economy, sustainable development, and the environment (MA, PhD). *Degree requirements:* For master's, one foreign language, thesis, 2 years of a second language; for doctorate, one foreign

language, thesis/dissertation, reading proficiency in at least one language other than English. *Entrance requirements:* For master's, GRE, 2 years of a second language with minimum B grade in the final term, statement of purpose, resume or curriculum vitae, 3 letters of recommendation, transcripts (from all post-secondary institutions attended), writing sample (15-20 pages); for doctorate, GRE, statement of purpose, personal achievements/contributions statement, resume or curriculum vitae, 3 letters of recommendation, transcripts from all post-secondary institutions attended, writing sample (15-20 pages). Additional exam requirements/recommendations for international students: Required—TOEFL (minimum score 600 paper-based; 94 iBT), IELTS (minimum score 7). Electronic applications accepted.

University of Colorado Denver, College of Architecture and Planning, Program in Design and Planning, Denver, CO 80217. Offers history of architecture, landscape and urbanism (PhD); sustainable and healthy environments (PhD). *Program availability:* Part-time. *Degree requirements:* For doctorate, comprehensive exam, thesis/dissertation. *Entrance requirements:* For doctorate, GRE (minimum score of 158 for both verbal and quantitative; writing 4.0), minimum undergraduate GPA of 3.0, graduate 3.5; writing sample; three letters of recommendation; statement of personal and professional goals. Additional exam requirements/recommendations for international students: Required—TOEFL (minimum score 80 iBT); Recommended—IELTS (minimum score 6.8). Electronic applications accepted. *Expenses:* Contact institution. *Faculty research:* Land use and environmental planning and design; design and planning processes and practices; history, theory, and criticism of the built environment.

University of Colorado Denver, College of Engineering and Applied Science, Department of Civil Engineering, Denver, CO 80217. Offers civil engineering (EASPh D); civil engineering systems (PhD); environmental and sustainability engineering (MS, PhD); geographic information systems (MS); geotechnical engineering (MS, PhD); hydrology and hydraulics (MS, PhD); structural engineering (MS, PhD); transportation engineering (MS, PhD). *Program availability:* Part-time, evening/weekend. *Degree requirements:* For master's, comprehensive exam, 30 credit hours, project or thesis; for doctorate, comprehensive exam, thesis/dissertation, 60 credit hours (30 of which are dissertation research). *Entrance requirements:* For master's, GRE, statement of purpose, transcripts, three references; for doctorate, GRE, statement of purpose, transcripts, references, letter of support from faculty stating willingness to serve as dissertation advisor and outlining plan for financial support. Additional exam requirements/recommendations for international students: Required—TOEFL (minimum score 537 paper-based; 75 iBT); Recommended—IELTS (minimum score 6.5). Electronic applications accepted. *Expenses:* Contact institution. *Faculty research:* Earthquake source physics, environmental biotechnology, hydrologic and hydraulic engineering, sustainability assessments, transportation energy use and greenhouse gas emissions.

University of Colorado Denver, College of Liberal Arts and Sciences, Department of Anthropology, Denver, CO 80217. Offers archaeological studies (MA); biological anthropology (MA); medical anthropology (MA); sustainable development and political ecology (MA). *Program availability:* Part-time, evening/weekend. *Degree requirements:* For master's, comprehensive exam, thesis or alternative, 30-36 credit hours. *Entrance requirements:* For master's, GRE General Test, minimum GPA of 3.0 for all undergraduate studies, transcripts from all undergraduate/graduate institutions attended, prior training in anthropology, three letters of recommendation, statement of purpose. Additional exam requirements/recommendations for international students: Required—TOEFL (minimum score 537 paper-based; 75 iBT); Recommended—IELTS (minimum score 6.5). Electronic applications accepted. *Faculty research:* Applied medical anthropology, primate social behavior, environmental anthropology, Southwestern and Mexican archaeology, human ecology.

University of Florida, Graduate School, College of Liberal Arts and Sciences, Center for Latin American Studies, Gainesville, FL 32611. Offers Latin American studies (MA, Certificate); sustainable development practice (MDP); tropical conservation and development (MA); JD/MA. *Program availability:* Part-time. *Degree requirements:* For master's, thesis. *Entrance requirements:* For master's, GRE General Test, minimum GPA of 3.0. Additional exam requirements/recommendations for international students: Required—TOEFL (minimum score 550 paper-based; 80 iBT), IELTS (minimum score 6). Electronic applications accepted. *Faculty research:* Tropical conservation and development; ethnicity in the Americas, Brazil, and Cuba; North American Free Trade Agreement (NAFTA).

University of Georgia, Eugene P. Odum School of Ecology, Athens, GA 30602. Offers conservation ecology and sustainable development (MS); ecology (PhD). *Degree requirements:* For master's, thesis; for doctorate, one foreign language, thesis/dissertation. *Entrance requirements:* For master's and doctorate, GRE General Test. Electronic applications accepted.

University of Hawaii at Manoa, Office of Graduate Education, College of Social Sciences, Department of Urban and Regional Planning, Honolulu, HI 96822. Offers community planning (MURP); disaster management and humanitarian assistance (Graduate Certificate); environmental planning and sustainability (MURP); international development planning (MURP); land use, transportation and infrastructure planning (MURP); planning studies (Graduate Certificate); urban and regional planning (PhD, Graduate Certificate). *Accreditation:* ACSP. *Program availability:* Part-time. *Entrance requirements:* For master's, GRE General Test, minimum GPA of 3.0; for doctorate, GRE General Test. Additional exam requirements/recommendations for international students: Required—TOEFL (minimum score 500 paper-based; 61 iBT), IELTS (minimum score 5).

University of Houston, Gerald D. Hines College of Architecture and Design, Houston, TX 77204-4000. Offers architectural studies (MA); architecture (M Arch, MS), including media and fabrication (MS), sustainable design (MS), sustainable urban systems (MS), urban design (MS); industrial design (MS). *Faculty:* 15 full-time (4 women), 13 part-time/adjunct (3 women). *Students:* 92 full-time (40 women), 6 part-time (2 women); includes 23 minority (1 Black or African American, non-Hispanic/Latino; 1 American Indian or Alaska Native, non-Hispanic/Latino; 9 Asian, non-Hispanic/Latino; 9 Hispanic/Latino; 3 Two or more races, non-Hispanic/Latino), 20 international. Average age 28. 192 applicants, 45% accepted, 47 enrolled. In 2017, 21 master's awarded. *Degree requirements:* For master's, thesis (for some programs). *Entrance requirements:* For master's, GRE General Test, digital portfolio. Additional exam requirements/recommendations for international students: Required—TOEFL (minimum score 550 paper-based; 79 iBT), IELTS (minimum score 6.5). *Application deadline:* For fall admission, 2/1 priority date for domestic students, 2/1 for international students. Applications are processed on a rolling basis. Application fee: $50. Electronic applications accepted. *Expenses:* Contact institution. *Financial support:* In 2017–18, 15 students received support, including 2 research assistantships with partial tuition reimbursements available (averaging $7,720 per year), 11 teaching assistantships with partial tuition reimbursements available (averaging $5,264 per year); career-related internships or fieldwork, Federal Work-Study, institutionally sponsored loans, scholarships/grants, health care benefits, and unspecified assistantships also available. Support available to part-time students. Financial award application deadline: 2/1. *Faculty research:* Community-based design; twentieth-century architecture, urbanism, and design; extreme environments; design build; green building components; digital technology; preservation; industrial design; interior architecture. *Total annual research expenditures:* $150,000. *Unit head:* Patricia Belton Oliver, Dean, 713-743-2400, Fax: 713-743-2358, E-mail: poliver@central.uh.edu. *Application contact:* Trang Phan, Assistant Dean, 713-743-2400, Fax: 713-743-2358, E-mail: tphan@uh.edu.
Website: http://www.uh.edu/architecture/

The University of Iowa, Graduate College, College of Engineering, Department of Civil and Environmental Engineering, Iowa City, IA 52242-1316. Offers environmental engineering and science (MS, PhD); hydraulics and water resources (MS, PhD); structures, mechanics and materials (MS, PhD); sustainable water development (MS, PhD); transportation engineering (MS, PhD). *Program availability:* Part-time. *Faculty:* 22 full-time (2 women), 5 part-time/adjunct (0 women). *Students:* 61 full-time (23 women), 12 part-time (4 women); includes 6 minority (1 Black or African American, non-Hispanic/Latino; 2 Hispanic/Latino; 3 Two or more races, non-Hispanic/Latino), 24 international. Average age 26. 185 applicants, 28% accepted, 22 enrolled. In 2017, 16 master's, 8 doctorates awarded. Terminal master's awarded for partial completion of doctoral program. *Degree requirements:* For master's, thesis optional, exam; for doctorate, comprehensive exam, thesis/dissertation, exam. *Entrance requirements:* For master's, GRE (minimum combined score of 301 on verbal and quantitative), minimum undergraduate GPA of 3.0; for doctorate, GRE (minimum combined score of 301 on verbal and quantitative), minimum graduate GPA of 3.0. Additional exam requirements/recommendations for international students: Required—TOEFL (minimum score 550 paper-based; 81 iBT), IELTS (minimum score 7). *Application deadline:* For fall admission, 1/15 priority date for domestic and international students; for spring admission, 12/1 for domestic students, 10/1 for international students; for summer admission, 4/15 for domestic students, 3/1 for international students. Applications are processed on a rolling basis. Application fee: $60 ($100 for international students). Electronic applications accepted. *Financial support:* In 2017–18, 57 students received support, including 13 fellowships with partial tuition reimbursements available (averaging $26,000 per year), 34 research assistantships with partial tuition reimbursements available (averaging $23,489 per year), 8 teaching assistantships with partial tuition reimbursements available (averaging $19,225 per year); career-related internships or fieldwork, Federal Work-Study, scholarships/grants, traineeships, and unspecified assistantships also available. Support available to part-time students. Financial award application deadline: 1/15; financial award applicants required to submit FAFSA. *Faculty research:* Water resources; environmental engineering and science; hydraulics and hydrology; structures, mechanics, and materials; transportation engineering. *Total annual research expenditures:* $10.9 million. *Unit head:* Dr. Michelle Scherer, Department Executive Officer, 319-335-5654, Fax: 319-335-5660, E-mail: michelle-scherer@uiowa.edu. *Application contact:* Kim Lebeck, Academic Program Specialist, 319-335-5647, Fax: 319-335-5660, E-mail: cee@engineering.uiowa.edu.
Website: https://cee.engineering.uiowa.edu

University of Maryland, College Park, Academic Affairs, College of Computer, Mathematical and Natural Sciences, Department of Biology, Program in Sustainable Development and Conservation Biology, College Park, MD 20742. Offers MS. *Program availability:* Part-time, evening/weekend. *Degree requirements:* For master's, internship, scholarly paper. *Entrance requirements:* For master's, GRE General Test, minimum GPA of 3.0, 3 letters of recommendation. Electronic applications accepted. *Faculty research:* Biodiversity, global change, conservation.

University of Massachusetts Amherst, Graduate School, College of Natural Sciences, Department of Environmental Conservation, Program in Sustainability Science, Amherst, MA 01003. Offers MS. *Program availability:* Part-time. *Degree requirements:* For master's, internship. *Entrance requirements:* Additional exam requirements/recommendations for international students: Required—TOEFL (minimum score 550 paper-based; 80 iBT), IELTS (minimum score 6.5). Electronic applications accepted.

University of Michigan, School for Environment and Sustainability, Program in Natural Resources and Environment, Ann Arbor, MI 48109. Offers behavior, education and communication (MS); conservation ecology (MS); environmental informatics (MS); environmental justice (MS); environmental policy and planning (MS); natural resources and environment (PhD); sustainable systems (MS); MS/JD; MS/MBA; MS/MPH; MS/MPP; MS/MSE; MS/MURP. Terminal master's awarded for partial completion of doctoral program. *Degree requirements:* For master's, practicum or group project; for doctorate, comprehensive exam, thesis/dissertation, oral defense of dissertation, preliminary exam. *Entrance requirements:* For master's, GRE General Test; for doctorate, GRE General Test, master's degree. Additional exam requirements/recommendations for international students: Required—TOEFL (minimum score 560 paper-based; 84 iBT), IELTS (minimum score 6.5). Electronic applications accepted. *Expenses:* Tuition, state resident: full-time $22,368; part-time $1201 per credit hour. Tuition, nonresident: full-time $45,156; part-time $2467 per credit hour. *Required fees:* $376 per term. Tuition and fees vary according to course load, degree level and program. *Faculty research:* Ecological science, social sciences, and sustainable systems.

University of New Brunswick Fredericton, School of Graduate Studies, Policy Studies Program, Fredericton, NB E3B 5A3, Canada. Offers citizen engagement/dispute resolution (M Phil); community development (M Phil); international development (M Phil); leadership (M Phil); sustainability/environmental issues (M Phil); worldviews (M Phil). *Program availability:* Part-time. *Degree requirements:* For master's, thesis, report. *Entrance requirements:* For master's, minimum GPA of 3.5. Additional exam requirements/recommendations for international students: Required—TWE (minimum score 5.5), TOEFL (minimum score 600 paper-based; 100 iBT) or IELTS (minimum score 7). Electronic applications accepted. *Faculty research:* International development, worldviews, citizenship/dispute resolution, sustainability/environmental issues, leadership, community development.

University of North Carolina at Asheville, Master of Liberal Arts and Sciences Program, Asheville, NC 28804-3299. Offers climate change and society (Graduate Certificate); environmental and cultural sustainability (Graduate Certificate). *Program availability:* Part-time, evening/weekend. *Faculty:* 7 full-time (1 woman), 3 part-time/adjunct (1 woman). *Students:* 1 full-time (0 women), 24 part-time (12 women); includes 3 minority (2 Black or African American, non-Hispanic/Latino; 1 Two or more races, non-Hispanic/Latino). Average age 44. 18 applicants, 83% accepted, 8 enrolled. In 2017, 19 master's awarded. *Degree requirements:* For master's, thesis or alternative. *Entrance requirements:* For master's and Graduate Certificate, essay, 3 letters of recommendation, transcript. Additional exam requirements/recommendations for international students: Required—TOEFL (minimum score 85 iBT), IELTS (minimum score 6.5). *Application deadline:* For fall admission, 4/15 priority date for domestic students; for spring admission, 11/15 priority date for domestic students. Applications are processed on a rolling basis. Application fee: $60. Electronic applications accepted. *Expenses:* $4,914. *Financial support:* Application deadline: 5/1; applicants required to submit FAFSA. *Unit head:* Gerard Voos, Director, Master of Liberal Arts and Sciences Program and the Asheville Graduate Center, 828-232-5040, E-mail: gvoos@unca.edu. *Application contact:* Jordan Dolfi, Program Coordinator, Master of Liberal Arts and Sciences Program and the Asheville Graduate Center, 828-251-6099, E-mail: jdolfi@unca.edu.
Website: https://mlas.unca.edu/

University of Notre Dame, Graduate School, Keough School of Global Affairs, Notre Dame, IN 46556. Offers global affairs (MGA); international peace studies (MGA); sustainable development (MGA).

University of Oklahoma, College of Atmospheric and Geographic Sciences, Department of Geography and Environmental Sustainability, Norman, OK 73019. Offers environmental sustainability (MS); geography (MA, MS, PhD), including geospatial technologies (MS), physical geography (MS). *Program availability:* Part-time. *Faculty:* 23 full-time (8 women). *Students:* 29 full-time (21 women), 10 part-time (5 women); includes 9 minority (2 Black or African American, non-Hispanic/Latino; 1 Asian, non-Hispanic/Latino; 4 Hispanic/Latino; 2 Two or more races, non-Hispanic/Latino), 9 international. Average age 29. 26 applicants, 69% accepted, 14 enrolled. In 2017, 8 master's, 4 doctorates awarded. *Degree requirements:* For master's, comprehensive exam (for some programs), thesis (for some programs); for doctorate, comprehensive exam (for some programs), thesis/dissertation (for some programs). *Entrance requirements:* For master's and doctorate, GRE, personal statement, transcripts, two letters of recommendation, writing sample. Additional exam requirements/recommendations for international students: Required—TOEFL (minimum score 79 iBT) or IELTS (minimum score 6.5). *Application deadline:* For fall admission, 1/15 for domestic and international students; for spring admission, 9/1 for domestic students, 11/1 for international students. Application fee: $50 ($100 for international students). Electronic applications accepted. *Expenses:* Tuition, state resident: full-time $5119; part-time $213.30 per credit hour. Tuition, nonresident: full-time $19,778; part-time $824.10 per credit hour. *Required fees:* $3458; $133.55 per credit hour. $126.50 per semester. *Financial support:* In 2017–18, 37 students received support, including 1 fellowship (averaging $5,000 per year), 14 research assistantships with full tuition reimbursements available (averaging $14,389 per year), 13 teaching assistantships with full tuition reimbursements available (averaging $14,024 per year); scholarships/grants and unspecified assistantships also available. Financial award application deadline: 6/1; financial award applicants required to submit FAFSA. *Faculty research:* Land cover land use change; economic geography; landscape ecology; environmental economics; renewable energy. *Total annual research expenditures:* $1.6 million. *Unit head:* Dr. Kirsten de Beurs, 405-325-5325, E-mail: kdebeurs@ou.edu. *Application contact:* Laurel Smith, Graduate Liaison, 405-325-5325, E-mail: laurel@ou.edu.
Website: http://geography.ou.edu

University of South Dakota, Graduate School, College of Arts and Sciences, Department of Sustainability and Environment, Vermillion, SD 57069. Offers sustainability (MS, PhD). Terminal master's awarded for partial completion of doctoral program. *Degree requirements:* For master's, thesis optional; for doctorate, thesis/dissertation. *Entrance requirements:* Additional exam requirements/recommendations for international students: Required—TOEFL (minimum score 550 paper-based; 79 iBT). Application fee: $35. *Financial support:* Applicants required to submit FAFSA. *Unit head:* Meghann Jarchow, Chair, 605-677-3115, E-mail: meghann.jarchow@usd.edu. *Application contact:* Graduate School, 605-657-6140, Fax: 605-677-6118, E-mail: grad@usd.edu.
Website: http://www.usd.edu/arts-and-sciences/sustainability

University of Southern California, Graduate School, Sol Price School of Public Policy, Master of Planning Program, Los Angeles, CA 90089. Offers sustainable cities (Graduate Certificate); transportation systems (Graduate Certificate); urban planning (M Pl); M Arch/M Pl; M Pl/MA; M Pl/MPP; M Pl/MRED; M Pl/MS; M Pl/MSW; MBA/M Pl; ML Arch/M Pl; MPA/M Pl. *Accreditation:* ACSP. *Program availability:* Part-time. *Degree requirements:* For master's, comprehensive exam, internship. *Entrance requirements:* For master's, GRE, GMAT. Additional exam requirements/recommendations for international students: Required—TOEFL (minimum score 600 paper-based; 100 iBT). Electronic applications accepted. *Faculty research:* Transportation and infrastructure, comparative international development, healthy communities, social economic development, sustainable community planning.

University of Southern California, Graduate School, Viterbi School of Engineering, Sonny Astani Department of Civil Engineering, Los Angeles, CA 90089. Offers applied mechanics (MS); civil engineering (MS, PhD); computer-aided engineering (ME, Graduate Certificate); construction management (MCM); engineering technology commercialization (Graduate Certificate); environmental engineering (MS, PhD); environmental quality management (ME); structural design (ME); sustainable cities (Graduate Certificate); transportation systems (MS, Graduate Certificate); water and waste management (MS). *Program availability:* Part-time, evening/weekend. Terminal master's awarded for partial completion of doctoral program. *Degree requirements:* For master's, thesis optional; for doctorate, thesis/dissertation. *Entrance requirements:* For master's and doctorate, GRE General Test. Additional exam requirements/recommendations for international students: Recommended—TOEFL. Electronic applications accepted. *Faculty research:* Geotechnical engineering, transportation engineering, structural engineering, construction management, environmental engineering, water resources.

University of South Florida, College of Global Sustainability, Tampa, FL 33620-9951. Offers energy, global, water and sustainable tourism (Graduate Certificate); global sustainability (MA), including building sustainable enterprise, climate change and sustainability, coastal sustainability, entrepreneurship, food sustainability and security, sustainability policy, sustainable energy, sustainable tourism, water. *Faculty:* 2 full-time (0 women). *Students:* 124 full-time (64 women), 77 part-time (45 women); includes 33 minority (12 Black or African American, non-Hispanic/Latino; 1 American Indian or Alaska Native, non-Hispanic/Latino; 1 Asian, non-Hispanic/Latino; 14 Hispanic/Latino; 5 Two or more races, non-Hispanic/Latino), 87 international. Average age 28. 220 applicants, 65% accepted, 101 enrolled. In 2017, 50 master's awarded. *Degree requirements:* For master's, comprehensive exam (for some programs), thesis or alternative, internship. *Entrance requirements:* For master's, minimum GPA of 3.0 in undergraduate coursework; at least two letters of recommendation (one must be academic); 200-250 word essay on student's background, professional goals, and reasons for seeking degree. Additional exam requirements/recommendations for international students: Required—TOEFL (minimum score 550 paper-based; 79 iBT). *Application deadline:* For fall admission, 6/1 for domestic students, 5/1 for international students; for spring admission, 10/15 for domestic students, 9/15 for international students. Electronic applications accepted. *Financial support:* In 2017–18, 22 students received support. *Faculty research:* Global sustainability, integrated resource management, systems thinking, green communities, entrepreneurship, ecotourism. *Total annual research expenditures:* $107,829. *Unit head:* Dr. Govindan Parayil, Dean, 813-974-9694, E-mail: gparayil@usf.edu.
Website: http://psgs.usf.edu/

University of South Florida, Innovative Education, Tampa, FL 33620-9951. Offers adult, career and higher education (Graduate Certificate), including college teaching, leadership in developing human resources, leadership in higher education; Africana studies (Graduate Certificate), including diasporas and health disparities, genocide and human rights; aging studies (Graduate Certificate), including gerontology; art research (Graduate Certificate), including museum studies; business foundations (Graduate Certificate); chemical and biomedical engineering (Graduate Certificate), including materials science and engineering, water, health and sustainability; child and family studies (Graduate Certificate), including positive behavior support; civil and industrial engineering (Graduate Certificate), including transportation systems analysis; community and family health (Graduate Certificate), including maternal and child health, social marketing and public health, violence and injury: prevention and intervention, women's health; criminology (Graduate Certificate), including criminal justice administration; data science for public administration (Graduate Certificate); digital humanities (Graduate Certificate); educational measurement and research (Graduate Certificate), including evaluation; English (Graduate Certificate), including comparative literary studies, creative writing, professional and technical communication; entrepreneurship (Graduate Certificate); environmental health (Graduate Certificate), including safety management; epidemiology and biostatistics (Graduate Certificate), including applied biostatistics, biostatistics, concepts and tools of epidemiology, epidemiology, epidemiology of infectious diseases; geography, environment and planning (Graduate Certificate), including community development, environmental policy and management, geographical information systems; geology (Graduate Certificate), including hydrogeology; global health (Graduate Certificate), including disaster management, global health and Latin American and Caribbean studies, global health practice, humanitarian assistance, infection control; government and international affairs (Graduate Certificate), including Cuban studies, globalization studies; health policy and management (Graduate Certificate), including health management and leadership, public health policy and programs; hearing specialist: early intervention (Graduate Certificate); industrial and management systems engineering (Graduate Certificate), including systems engineering, technology management; information studies (Graduate Certificate), including school library media specialist; information systems/decision sciences (Graduate Certificate), including analytics and business intelligence; instructional technology (Graduate Certificate), including distance education, Florida digital/virtual educator, instructional design, multimedia design, Web design; internal medicine, bioethics and medical humanities (Graduate Certificate), including biomedical ethics; Latin American and Caribbean studies (Graduate Certificate); leadership for coastal resiliency planning (Graduate Certificate); mass communications (Graduate Certificate), including multimedia journalism; mathematics and statistics (Graduate Certificate), including mathematics; medicine (Graduate Certificate), including aging and neuroscience, bioinformatics, biotechnology, brain fitness and memory management, clinical investigation, hand and upper limb rehabilitation, health informatics, health sciences, integrative weight management, intellectual property, medicine and gender, metabolic and nutritional medicine, metabolic cardiology, pharmacy sciences; national and competitive intelligence (Graduate Certificate); nursing (Graduate Certificate), including simulation based academic fellowship in advanced pain management; psychological and social foundations (Graduate Certificate), including career counseling, college teaching, diversity in education, mental health counseling, school counseling; public affairs (Graduate Certificate), including nonprofit management, public management, research administration; public health (Graduate Certificate), including assessing chemical toxicity and public health risks, health equity, pharmacoepidemiology, public health generalist, toxicology, translational research in adolescent behavioral health; public health practices (Graduate Certificate), including planning for healthy communities; rehabilitation and mental health counseling (Graduate Certificate), including integrative mental health care, marriage and family therapy, rehabilitation technology; secondary education (Graduate Certificate), including ESOL, foreign language education: culture and content, foreign language education: professional; social work (Graduate Certificate), including geriatric social work/clinical gerontology; special education (Graduate Certificate), including autism spectrum disorder, disabilities education: severe/profound; world languages (Graduate Certificate), including teaching English as a second language (TESL) or foreign language. *Unit head:* Dr. Cynthia DeLuca, Associate Vice President and Assistant Vice Provost, 813-974-3077, Fax: 813-974-7061, E-mail: deluca@usf.edu. *Application contact:* Owen Hooper, Director, Summer and Alternative Calendar Programs, 813-974-6917, E-mail: hooper@usf.edu.
Website: http://www.usf.edu/innovative-education/

The University of Texas at Austin, Graduate School, School of Architecture, Program in Sustainable Design, Austin, TX 78712-1111. Offers M Arch I, M Arch II, MSSD.

The University of Texas Rio Grande Valley, College of Sciences, School of Earth, Environmental, and Marine Sciences, Edinburg, TX 78539. Offers agricultural, environmental, and sustainability sciences (MS); ocean, coastal, and earth sciences (MS). *Expenses:* Tuition, state resident: full-time $5550; part-time $417 per credit hour. Tuition, nonresident: full-time $13,020; part-time $832 per credit hour. *Required fees:* $1169.

University of Vermont, Graduate College, The Rubenstein School of Environment and Natural Resources, Program in Leadership for Sustainability, Burlington, VT 05405. Offers MPS. *Program availability:* Part-time. *Students:* 36 (28 women). 22 applicants, 95% accepted, 16 enrolled. *Entrance requirements:* Additional exam requirements/recommendations for international students: Required—TOEFL (minimum iBT score of 90) or IELTS (6.5). *Application deadline:* For fall admission, 2/1 priority date for domestic and international students. Applications are processed on a rolling basis. Application fee: $65. Electronic applications accepted. *Expenses:* $646 per credit in-state, $1,100 per credit out-of-state. *Financial support:* Scholarships/grants available. Financial award application deadline: 4/30. *Unit head:* Matthew Kolan, Director, 802-656-4333, E-mail: matthew.kolan@uvm.edu. *Application contact:* Emil Tsao, Coordinator, 802-656-4333, E-mail: etsao@uvm.edu.
Website: https://www.uvm.edu/rsenr/leadership-sustainability/

University of Washington, Graduate School, College of the Environment, School of Environmental and Forest Sciences, Seattle, WA 98195. Offers bioresource science and engineering (MS, PhD); environmental horticulture (MEH); forest ecology (MS, PhD); forest management (MFR); forest soils (MS, PhD); restoration ecology (MS, PhD); restoration ecology and environmental horticulture (MS, PhD); social sciences (MS, PhD); sustainable resource management (MS, PhD); wildlife science (MS, PhD); MFR/MAIS; MPA/MS. *Accreditation:* SAF. *Program availability:* Part-time. *Degree requirements:* For master's, thesis; for doctorate, comprehensive exam, thesis/dissertation. *Entrance requirements:* For master's and doctorate, GRE, minimum GPA of 3.0. Additional exam requirements/recommendations for international students: Required—TOEFL. Electronic applications accepted. *Faculty research:* Ecosystem analysis, silviculture and forest protection, paper science and engineering, environmental horticulture and urban forestry, natural resource policy and economics, restoration ecology and environment horticulture, conservation, human dimensions, wildlife, bioresource science and engineering.

University of Washington, Graduate School, School of Law, Seattle, WA 98195-3020. Offers Asian law (LL M, PhD); intellectual property law and policy (LL M); law (JD); law of sustainable international development (LL M); taxation (LL M); JD/LL M; JD/MA; JD/MAIS; JD/MBA; JD/MPA; JD/MS; JD/PhD. *Accreditation:* ABA. *Degree requirements:* For master's, thesis; for doctorate, thesis/dissertation (for some programs). *Entrance requirements:* For master's, language proficiency (LL M in Asian law); for doctorate, LSAT (for JD). Additional exam requirements/recommendations for international students: Required—TOEFL. *Expenses:* Contact institution. *Faculty research:* Asian, international and comparative law, intellectual property law, health law, environmental law, taxation.

The University of Western Ontario, Faculty of Graduate Studies, Physical Sciences Division, Department of Earth Sciences, London, ON N6A 5B8, Canada. Offers environment and sustainability (MES); geology (M Sc, PhD); geology and environmental science (M Sc, PhD); geophysics (M Sc, PhD); geophysics and environmental science (M Sc, PhD). *Degree requirements:* For master's, thesis; for doctorate, thesis/dissertation, qualifying exam. *Entrance requirements:* For master's, honors in B Sc; for doctorate, M Sc. Additional exam requirements/recommendations for international students: Required—TOEFL. *Faculty research:* Geophysics, geochemistry, paleontology, sedimentology/stratigraphy, glaciology/quaternary.

University of Wisconsin–Madison, Graduate School, Gaylord Nelson Institute for Environmental Studies, Environmental Conservation Program, Madison, WI 53706-1380. Offers MS. *Degree requirements:* For master's, thesis or alternative, spring/summer leadership (internship) experience. *Entrance requirements:* For master's, GRE General Test (recommended for potential scholarship consideration). Additional exam requirements/recommendations for international students: Required—TOEFL (minimum score 550 paper-based, 80 iBT) or IELTS (6.5). Electronic applications accepted. *Expenses:* Contact institution. *Faculty research:* Geographic information systems, forestry, wildlife ecology, agroecology, landscape architecture, sociology, rural sociology, plant ecology, biodiversity, sustainability, sustainable development, conservation biology, conservation planning/management, land tenure.

University of Wisconsin–Stevens Point, College of Professional Studies, School of Education, Program in Educational Sustainability, Stevens Point, WI 54481-3897. Offers Ed D. *Program availability:* Online learning.

Walden University, Graduate Programs, School of Public Policy and Administration, Minneapolis, MN 55401. Offers criminal justice (MPA, MPP, MS, Graduate Certificate), including emergency management (MS, PhD), general program (MS), global leadership (MS, PhD), homeland security and policy coordination (MS, PhD), law and public policy (MS, PhD), policy analysis (MS, PhD), public management and leadership (MS, PhD), self-designed (MS), terrorism, mediation, and peace (MS, PhD); criminal justice and executive management (MS), including global leadership (MS, PhD); criminal justice leadership and executive management (MS), including emergency management (MS, PhD), general program, homeland security and policy coordination (MS, PhD), law and public policy (MS, PhD), policy analysis (MS, PhD), public management and leadership (MS, PhD), self-designed, terrorism, mediation, and peace (MS, PhD); emergency management (MPA, MPP, MS), including criminal justice (MS, PhD), general program (MS), homeland security (MS), public management and leadership (MS, PhD), terrorism and emergency management (MS); general program (MPA, MPP); global leadership (MPA, MPP); government management (Graduate Certificate); health policy (MPA, MPP); homeland security (Graduate Certificate); homeland security and policy coordination (MPA, MPP); international nongovernmental organizations (MPA, MPP); law and public policy (MPA, MPP); local government management for sustainable communities (MPA, MPP); nonprofit management (Graduate Certificate); nonprofit management and leadership (MPA, MPP, MS), including global leadership (MS, PhD), international nongovernmental organization (MS), local government for sustainable communities (MS), self designed (MS); online teaching in higher education (Post-Master's Certificate); policy analysis (MPA); public management and leadership (MPA, MPP, Graduate Certificate); public policy (Graduate Certificate); public policy and administration (PhD), including criminal justice (MS, PhD), emergency management (MS, PhD), global leadership (MS, PhD), health policy, homeland security and policy coordination (MS, PhD), international nongovernmental organizations, law and public policy (MS, PhD), local government management for sustainable communities, nonprofit management and leadership (MS, PhD), policy analysis (MS, PhD), public management and leadership (MS, PhD), terrorism, mediation, and peace (MS, PhD); strategic planning and public policy (Graduate Certificate); terrorism, mediation, and peace (MPA, MPP). *Program availability:* Part-time, evening/weekend, online only, 100% online. *Degree requirements:* For doctorate, thesis/dissertation, residency. *Entrance requirements:* For master's, bachelor's degree or higher; minimum GPA of 2.5; official transcripts; goal statement (for some programs); access to computer and Internet; for doctorate, master's degree or higher; three years of related professional or academic experience (preferred); minimum GPA of 3.0; goal statement and current resume (for select programs); official transcripts; access to computer and Internet; for other advanced degree, relevant work experience; access to computer and Internet. Additional exam requirements/recommendations for international students: Required—TOEFL (minimum score 550 paper-based, 79 iBT), IELTS (minimum score 6.5), Michigan English Language Assessment Battery (minimum score 82), or PTE (minimum score 53). Electronic applications accepted.

West Chester University of Pennsylvania, College of Education and Social Work, Department of Educational Foundations and Policy Studies, West Chester, PA 19383. Offers education for sustainability (Certificate); educational technology (Certificate); higher education policy and student affairs (MS); transformative education and social change (MS). *Program availability:* Part-time. *Students:* 35 full-time (21 women), 49 part-time (33 women); includes 15 minority (9 Black or African American, non-Hispanic/Latino; 1 Asian, non-Hispanic/Latino; 2 Hispanic/Latino; 3 Two or more races, non-Hispanic/Latino), 1 international. Average age 29. 77 applicants, 90% accepted, 51 enrolled. In 2017, 5 master's, 6 other advanced degrees awarded. *Degree requirements:* For master's, comprehensive exam (for some programs), thesis, 36 credits (42 credits for MS in higher education policy and student affairs). *Entrance requirements:* For master's, teaching certification (strongly recommended); for Certificate, minimum GPA of 3.0. Additional exam requirements/recommendations for international students: Required—TOEFL or IELTS. *Application deadline:* For fall admission, 5/15 for international students; for spring admission, 10/15 for international students. Applications are processed on a rolling basis. Application fee: $50. Electronic applications accepted. *Expenses:* Tuition, state resident: full-time $9000; part-time $500 per credit. Tuition, nonresident: full-time $13,500; part-time $750 per credit. *Required fees:* $2959; $149.79 per credit. *Financial support:* Scholarships/grants and unspecified assistantships available. Financial award application deadline: 2/15; financial award applicants required to submit FAFSA. *Faculty research:* Technology integration: preparing our teachers for the twenty-first century, critical pedagogy, education for sustainability. *Unit head:* Dr. John Elmore, Chair, 610-436-6934, Fax: 610-436-3102, E-mail: jelmore@wcupa.edu. *Application contact:* Office of Graduate Studies and Extended Education, 610-436-2943, Fax: 610-436-2763, E-mail: gradstudy@wcupa.edu.
Website: http://www.wcupa.edu/education-socialWork/profsecedu/

Xavier University, College of Arts and Sciences, Department of Interdisciplinary Studies, Cincinnati, OH 45207. Offers urban sustainability and resilience (MA). *Degree requirements:* For master's, thesis (for some programs), internship. *Entrance requirements:* For master's, MAT or GRE, official transcript, resume, 500-word statement of purpose, two letters of reference. Additional exam requirements/recommendations for international students: Required—TOEFL (minimum score 550 paper-based; 79 iBT). Electronic applications accepted. Application fee is waived when completed online. *Expenses:* Contact institution.

Urban and Regional Planning

Alabama Agricultural and Mechanical University, School of Graduate Studies, College of Agricultural, Life and Natural Sciences, Department of Community and Regional Planning, Huntsville, AL 35811. Offers urban and regional planning (MURP). *Accreditation:* ACSP. *Program availability:* Part-time, evening/weekend. *Degree requirements:* For master's, comprehensive exam. *Entrance requirements:* For master's, GRE General Test. Additional exam requirements/recommendations for international students: Required—TOEFL (minimum score 500 paper-based; 61 iBT). Electronic applications accepted. *Faculty research:* Urban and rural research, needs assessment and community trends through analysis of social indicators, fiscal impact studies, rural transportation, health care.

American University of Beirut, Graduate Programs, Faculty of Agricultural and Food Sciences, Beirut, Lebanon. Offers agricultural economics (MS); animal science (MS); ecosystem management (MSES); food safety (MS); food security (MS); food technology (MS); irrigation (MS); nutrition (MS); plant protection (MS); plant science (MS); poultry science (MS); public health nutrition (MS); rural community development (MS). *Program availability:* Part-time. *Faculty:* 16 full-time (4 women), 1 part-time/adjunct (0 women). *Students:* 76 full-time (58 women), 19 part-time (13 women); includes 6 minority (all Black or African American, non-Hispanic/Latino). Average age 25. 142 applicants, 72% accepted, 32 enrolled. In 2017, 20 master's awarded. *Degree requirements:* For master's, one foreign language, comprehensive exam, thesis (for some programs). *Entrance requirements:* Additional exam requirements/recommendations for international students: Required—TOEFL (minimum score 600 paper-based; 100 iBT), IELTS (minimum score 7.5). *Application deadline:* For fall admission, 2/10 for domestic and international students; for spring admission, 11/2 for domestic and international students. Application fee: $50. Electronic applications accepted. *Expenses: Tuition:* Full-time $17,244; part-time $958 per credit. *Required fees:* $740. Tuition and fees vary according to course load and program. *Financial support:* In 2017–18, 9 research assistantships with partial tuition reimbursements (averaging $1,800 per year), 47 teaching assistantships with full and partial tuition reimbursements (averaging $1,400 per year) were awarded; scholarships/grants, health care benefits, and unspecified assistantships also available. Financial award application deadline: 2/2. *Faculty research:* Refugee socio-economic vulnerability, nutrition in emergencies, forest and landscape restoration, broiler immunological response, vegetated infrastructure in deserts. *Total annual research expenditures:* $600,000. *Unit head:* Rabi Hassan Mohtar, Dean of Faculty of Agricultural and Food Sciences, 961-1-350000 Ext. 4400, Fax: 961-1-744460, E-mail: mohtar@aub.edu.lb. *Application contact:* Prof. Zaher Dawy, Graduate Council Chairperson, 961-1-374374 Ext. 4386, Fax: 961-1-374376, E-mail: graduate.council@aub.edu.lb.
Website: http://www.aub.edu.lb/fafs/Pages/default.aspx

American University of Beirut, Graduate Programs, Maroun Semaan Faculty of Engineering and Architecture, 1107 2020, Lebanon. Offers applied energy (ME); civil engineering (PhD); electrical and computer engineering (PhD); energy studies (MS); engineering management (MEM); environmental and water resources (ME); environmental technology (MSES); mechanical engineering (ME, PhD); urban design (MUD); urban planning and policy (MUPP). *Program availability:* Part-time, 100% online. *Faculty:* 98 full-time (21 women), 88 part-time/adjunct (27 women). *Students:* 337 full-time (176 women), 114 part-time (42 women). Average age 26. 502 applicants, 65% accepted, 118 enrolled. In 2017, 71 master's, 16 doctorates awarded. Terminal master's awarded for partial completion of doctoral program. *Degree requirements:* For master's, one foreign language, comprehensive exam, thesis optional; for doctorate, one foreign language, comprehensive exam, thesis/dissertation. *Entrance requirements:* For doctorate, GRE. Additional exam requirements/recommendations for international students: Required—TOEFL (minimum score 573 paper-based; 88 iBT); Recommended—IELTS (minimum score 7). *Application deadline:* For fall admission, 4/4 for domestic and international students; for spring admission, 11/3 for domestic and international students; for summer admission, 4/4 for domestic and international students. Applications are processed on a rolling basis. Application fee: $50. Electronic applications accepted. *Expenses:* $34,056 (for non-thesis ME/MS); $31,993 (for thesis ME/MS); $49,536 (for PhD). *Financial support:* In 2017–18, 26 students received support, including 92 fellowships with full tuition reimbursements available (averaging $14,400 per year), 65 research assistantships with full and partial tuition reimbursements available (averaging $5,000 per year), 129 teaching assistantships with full and partial tuition reimbursements available (averaging $1,326 per year); scholarships/grants, tuition waivers (full and partial), and unspecified assistantships also available. Financial award application deadline: 4/2. *Faculty research:* All areas in engineering, architecture and design. *Total annual research expenditures:* $1.7 million. *Unit head:* Prof. Alan Shihade, Dean, 961-1-374374 Ext. 3400, Fax: 961-1-744462, E-mail: as20@aub.edu.lb. *Application contact:* Dr. Salim Kanaan, Director, Admissions Office, 961-1-374374 Ext. 2590, Fax: 961-1-750775, E-mail: sk00@aub.edu.lb.
Website: http://www.aub.edu.lb/msfea/pages/default.aspx

American University of Sharjah, Graduate Programs, 26666, United Arab Emirates. Offers accounting (MS); biomedical engineering (MSBME); business administration (MBA); chemical engineering (MS Ch E); civil engineering (MSCE); computer engineering (MS); electrical engineering (MSEE); engineering systems management (MS, PhD); mathematics (MS); mechanical engineering (MSME); mechatronics engineering (MS); teaching English to speakers of other languages (MA); translation and interpreting (MA); urban planning (MUP). *Program availability:* Part-time, evening/weekend. *Students:* 108 full-time (73 women), 287 part-time (207 women). Average age 27. 203 applicants, 83% accepted, 121 enrolled. In 2017, 114 master's awarded. *Degree requirements:* For master's, thesis (for some programs). *Entrance requirements:* For master's, GMAT (for MBA). Additional exam requirements/recommendations for international students: Required—TOEFL (minimum score 550 paper-based; 80 iBT), TWE (minimum score 5); Recommended—IELTS (minimum score 6.5). *Application deadline:* For fall admission, 8/5 priority date for domestic students, 7/1 priority date for

international students; for spring admission, 12/30 priority date for domestic students, 12/9 for international students; for summer admission, 5/21 for domestic and international students. Applications are processed on a rolling basis. Application fee: $110. Electronic applications accepted. *Expenses: Tuition:* Full-time $20,000; part-time $1350 per credit. Tuition and fees vary according to degree level and program. *Financial support:* In 2017–18, 82 students received support, including 54 research assistantships, 54 teaching assistantships; scholarships/grants also available. Financial award application deadline: 6/3. *Faculty research:* Water pollution, management and waste water treatment, energy and sustainability, air pollution, Islamic finance, family business and small and medium enterprises. *Unit head:* Salwa Mohammed, Office of Graduate Studies, 971-6515-2934, E-mail: ogs@aus.edu. *Application contact:* Salwa H. Mohammed, Office of Graduate Studies, 971-65152934, E-mail: ogs@aus.edu.
Website: https://www.aus.edu/masters-degrees

Andrews University, School of Graduate Studies, College of Arts and Sciences, Department of Behavioral Science, Program in International Development, Berrien Springs, MI 49104. Offers community and international development (MSCID). *Program availability:* Online learning. *Faculty:* 10 full-time (2 women), 1 part-time/adjunct (0 women). *Students:* 18 full-time (13 women), 3 part-time (all women); includes 7 minority (3 Black or African American, non-Hispanic/Latino; 2 Asian, non-Hispanic/Latino; 2 Hispanic/Latino), 12 international. Average age 31. In 2017, 11 master's awarded. *Entrance requirements:* For master's, GRE General Test. Additional exam requirements/recommendations for international students: Required—TOEFL (minimum score 550 paper-based). Application fee: $40. *Unit head:* Dr. Duane C. McBride, Director, 269-471-3152. *Application contact:* Justina Clayburn, Supervisor of Graduate Admission, 800-253-2874, Fax: 269-471-6321, E-mail: graduate@andrews.edu.
Website: http://www.andrews.edu/grad/programs/community-and-international-development-off-campus.html

Arizona State University at the Tempe campus, College of Liberal Arts and Sciences, School of Geographical Sciences and Urban Planning, Tempe, AZ 85287-5302. Offers geographic information systems (MAS); geographical information science (Graduate Certificate); geography (MA, PhD); transportation systems (Graduate Certificate); urban and environmental planning (MUEP); urban planning (PhD). *Accreditation:* ACSP. Terminal master's awarded for partial completion of doctoral program. *Degree requirements:* For master's, thesis, interactive Program of Study (iPOS) submitted before completing 50 percent of required credit hours; for doctorate, comprehensive exam, thesis/dissertation, interactive Program of Study (iPOS) submitted before completing 50 percent of required credit hours. *Entrance requirements:* For master's and doctorate, GRE, minimum GPA of 3.0 or equivalent in last 2 years of work leading to bachelor's degree. Additional exam requirements/recommendations for international students: Required—TOEFL, IELTS, or PTE. Electronic applications accepted. *Expenses:* Contact institution.

Arizona State University at the Tempe campus, College of Public Programs, School of Community Resources and Development, Phoenix, AZ 85004-0685. Offers community resources and development (MS, PhD); nonprofit leadership and management (Graduate Certificate); nonprofit studies (MNpS); sustainable tourism (MAS). *Program availability:* Part-time, evening/weekend. Terminal master's awarded for partial completion of doctoral program. *Degree requirements:* For master's, thesis or alternative, interactive Program of Study (iPOS) submitted before completing 50 percent of required credit hours; for doctorate, comprehensive exam, thesis/dissertation, interactive Program of Study (iPOS) submitted before completing 50 percent of required credit hours. *Entrance requirements:* For master's and doctorate, GRE, minimum GPA of 3.0 or equivalent in last 2 years of work leading to bachelor's degree. Additional exam requirements/recommendations for international students: Required—TOEFL, IELTS, or PTE. Electronic applications accepted. *Expenses:* Contact institution.

Arizona State University at the Tempe campus, College of Public Programs, School of Public Affairs, Phoenix, AZ 85004-0687. Offers emergency management and homeland security (MA); program evaluation (MS); public administration (MPA, PhD), including nonprofit administration (MPA), urban management (MPA); public policy (MPP); MPA/MSW. *Accreditation:* NASPAA (one or more programs are accredited). *Program availability:* Part-time, evening/weekend. Terminal master's awarded for partial completion of doctoral program. *Degree requirements:* For master's, thesis or alternative, policy analysis or capstone project; interactive Program of Study (iPOS) submitted before completing 50 percent of required credit hours; for doctorate, comprehensive exam, thesis/dissertation, interactive Program of Study (iPOS) submitted before completing 50 percent of required credit hours. *Entrance requirements:* For master's, GRE, minimum GPA of 3.0 or equivalent in last 2 years of work leading to bachelor's degree; for doctorate, GRE, minimum GPA of 3.0 or equivalent in last 2 years of work leading to bachelor's degree, 3 letters of recommendation, resume, statement of goals, samples of research reports. Additional exam requirements/recommendations for international students: Required—TOEFL (minimum score 600 paper-based; 100 iBT), IELTS (minimum score 6.5). Electronic applications accepted. *Expenses:* Contact institution.

Auburn University, Graduate School, College of Architecture, Design, and Construction, Program in Community Planning, Auburn University, AL 36849. Offers MCP, MPA/MCP. *Program availability:* Part-time. *Faculty:* 23 full-time (8 women), 8 part-time/adjunct (0 women). *Students:* 1 (woman) full-time, all international. Average age 31. In 2017, 5 master's awarded. *Degree requirements:* For master's, oral exam, project. *Entrance requirements:* For master's, GRE General Test. *Application deadline:* Applications are processed on a rolling basis. Application fee: $50 ($60 for international students). Electronic applications accepted. *Expenses:* Tuition, state resident: full-time $10,974; part-time $519 per credit hour. Tuition, nonresident: full-time $29,658; part-time $1557 per credit hour. *Required fees:* $816 per semester. Tuition and fees vary according to degree level and program. *Financial support:* Federal Work-Study available. Support available to part-time students. Financial award application deadline: 3/15; financial award applicants required to submit FAFSA. *Unit head:* Dr. David Hill, Head, 334-844-5434. *Application contact:* Dr. George Flowers, Dean of the Graduate School, 334-844-2125.
Website: http://cadc.auburn.edu/studentservices/Pages/APLA/APLA_MCP_Degree.aspx

Ball State University, Graduate School, College of Architecture and Planning, Department of Urban Planning, Muncie, IN 47306. Offers urban and regional planning (MURP). *Accreditation:* ACSP. *Program availability:* Part-time. *Faculty:* 6. *Students:* 22 full-time (10 women), 14 part-time (7 women); includes 5 minority (3 Black or African American, non-Hispanic/Latino; 1 Asian, non-Hispanic/Latino; 1 Hispanic/Latino), 8 international. Average age 25. 23 applicants, 74% accepted, 9 enrolled. In 2017, 11 master's awarded. *Degree requirements:* For master's, thesis. *Entrance requirements:* For master's, minimum baccalaureate GPA of 2.75 or 3.0 in latter half of baccalaureate; at least three letters of recommendation (minimum of two from instructors); two-page personal statement (if GPA is below 3.0). Additional exam requirements/recommendations for international students: Required—TOEFL (minimum score 550 paper-based; 79 iBT), IELTS (minimum score 6.5). *Application deadline:* Applications are processed on a rolling basis. Application fee: $60. Electronic applications accepted. *Expenses:* Contact institution. *Financial support:* In 2017–18, 18 students received support. Research assistantships with partial tuition reimbursements available and unspecified assistantships available. Financial award application deadline: 3/1; financial award applicants required to submit FAFSA. *Faculty research:* Computer-assisted land-use analysis. *Unit head:* Dr. Nihal Perera, Interim Chairperson, 765-285-8606, E-mail: nperera@bsu.edu. *Application contact:* Dr. Nihal Perera, 765-285-8606, Fax: 765-285-2648, E-mail: nperera@bsu.edu.
Website: http://www.bsu.edu/planning

Ball State University, Graduate School, Miller College of Business, Interdepartmental Program in Business Administration, Muncie, IN 47306. Offers business administration (MBA); business essentials (Graduate Certificate); community and economic development (Certificate). *Accreditation:* AACSB. *Program availability:* Part-time, 100% online, blended/hybrid learning. *Students:* 33 full-time (15 women), 221 part-time (78 women); includes 20 minority (5 Black or African American, non-Hispanic/Latino; 8 Asian, non-Hispanic/Latino; 4 Hispanic/Latino; 1 Native Hawaiian or other Pacific Islander, non-Hispanic/Latino; 2 Two or more races, non-Hispanic/Latino), 8 international. Average age 31. 203 applicants, 41% accepted, 58 enrolled. In 2017, 70 master's awarded. *Entrance requirements:* For master's, GMAT or GRE, minimum baccalaureate GPA of 2.75 or 3.0 in latter half of baccalaureate, resume or curriculum vitae, four professional letters of recommendation. Additional exam requirements/recommendations for international students: Required—TOEFL (minimum score 550 paper-based; 79 iBT), IELTS (minimum score 6.5). *Application deadline:* For fall admission, 7/1 for domestic students; for spring admission, 12/1 for domestic students; for summer admission, 4/1 for domestic students. Applications are processed on a rolling basis. Application fee: $60. Electronic applications accepted. *Expenses:* Contact institution. *Financial support:* Research assistantships with partial tuition reimbursements, teaching assistantships with partial tuition reimbursements, and unspecified assistantships available. Financial award application deadline: 3/1; financial award applicants required to submit FAFSA. *Unit head:* Jason Webber, Director, 765-285-1931, Fax: 765-285-8818, E-mail: jjwebber@bsu.edu.
Website: http://www.bsu.edu/mba

Boston University, Metropolitan College, Program in City Planning, Boston, MA 02215. Offers MCP. *Program availability:* Part-time, evening/weekend. *Faculty:* 2 full-time (both women), 6 part-time/adjunct (2 women). *Students:* 14 full-time (4 women), 23 part-time (13 women); includes 4 minority (2 Black or African American, non-Hispanic/Latino; 2 Hispanic/Latino), 10 international. Average age 27. 59 applicants, 80% accepted, 15 enrolled. In 2017, 11 master's awarded. *Entrance requirements:* Additional exam requirements/recommendations for international students: Required—TOEFL (minimum score 84 iBT). *Application deadline:* For fall admission, 7/15 priority date for international students; for spring admission, 11/15 priority date for international students. Applications are processed on a rolling basis. Application fee: $85. Electronic applications accepted. *Expenses:* Contact institution. *Financial support:* In 2017–18, 5 research assistantships (averaging $4,200 per year) were awarded; career-related internships or fieldwork and unspecified assistantships also available. Support available to part-time students. Financial award applicants required to submit FAFSA. *Faculty research:* Housing, community development and land use planning, environmental management and planning, international comparative development planning. *Unit head:* Dr. Daniel P. LeClair, Chair, 617-353-3025, Fax: 617-358-3595, E-mail: dleclair@bu.edu. *Application contact:* Dr. Madhu Dutta-Koehler, Assistant Professor and Faculty Coordinator, 617-358-3264, Fax: 617-358-3595, E-mail: duttam@bu.edu.
Website: http://www.bu.edu/cityplanning/

★ **California Polytechnic State University, San Luis Obispo,** College of Architecture and Environmental Design, Department of City and Regional Planning, San Luis Obispo, CA 93407. Offers MCRP, MCRP/MS. *Accreditation:* ACSP. *Program availability:* Part-time. *Faculty:* 5 full-time (3 women), 2 part-time/adjunct (1 woman). *Students:* 32 full-time (13 women), 2 part-time (1 woman); includes 9 minority (4 Asian, non-Hispanic/Latino; 3 Hispanic/Latino; 2 Two or more races, non-Hispanic/Latino), 2 international. Average age 26. 50 applicants, 68% accepted, 16 enrolled. In 2017, 12 master's awarded. *Degree requirements:* For master's, comprehensive exam (for some programs), thesis. *Entrance requirements:* For master's, GRE. Additional exam requirements/recommendations for international students: Required—TOEFL (minimum score 80 iBT). *Application deadline:* For fall admission, 2/1 for domestic and international students; for winter admission, 11/1 for domestic students, 6/30 for international students. Applications are processed on a rolling basis. Application fee: $55. Electronic applications accepted. *Expenses:* Tuition, state resident: full-time $7176; part-time $4164 per year. *Required fees:* $3690; $3219 per year. $1073 per trimester. *Financial support:* Fellowships, research assistantships, career-related internships or fieldwork, institutionally sponsored loans, and unspecified assistantships available. Financial award application deadline: 3/2; financial award applicants required to submit FAFSA. *Faculty research:* Community sustainability, climate action planning, natural hazards, small town and rural planning, subdivision site design. *Unit head:* Cornelius Nuworsoo, Graduate Coordinator, E-mail: cnuworso@calpoly.edu.
Website: http://www.planning.calpoly.edu/

See Display on the next page and Close-Up on page 1305.

California State Polytechnic University, Pomona, Program in Urban and Regional Planning, Pomona, CA 91768-2557. Offers MURP. *Accreditation:* ACSP. *Program availability:* Part-time, evening/weekend. *Students:* 26 full-time (15 women), 17 part-time (5 women); includes 29 minority (1 Black or African American, non-Hispanic/Latino; 10 Asian, non-Hispanic/Latino; 18 Hispanic/Latino), 1 international. Average age 30. 76 applicants, 75% accepted, 43 enrolled. In 2017, 14 master's awarded. *Entrance requirements:* Additional exam requirements/recommendations for international students: Required—TOEFL (minimum score 580 paper-based). *Application deadline:* Applications are processed on a rolling basis. Application fee: $55. Electronic applications accepted. *Expenses:* Contact institution. *Financial support:* Application deadline: 3/2; applicants required to submit FAFSA. *Unit head:* Dr. Do-Hyung Kim, Graduate Coordinator, 909-869-4645, Fax: 909-869-4688, E-mail: dohyungkim@cpp.edu. *Application contact:* Deborah L. Brandon, Executive Director of Admissions and Enrollment Planning, 909-869-3427, Fax: 909-869-5315, E-mail: dlbrandon@cpp.edu.
Website: https://env.cpp.edu/urp/degree/master-urban-and-regional-planning

The Catholic University of America, School of Architecture and Planning, Washington, DC 20064. Offers architecture and planning (M Arch, MS Arch St); city and regional planning (M Arch); facilities management (MS Arch); regional development (Certificate); sustainable design (M Arch, Certificate). *Program availability:* Part-time. *Faculty:* 19 full-time (7 women), 9 part-time/adjunct (1 woman). *Students:* 61 full-time (24 women), 13 part-time (7 women); includes 31 minority (12 Black or African American, non-Hispanic/Latino; 1 American Indian or Alaska Native, non-Hispanic/Latino; 3 Asian, non-Hispanic/Latino; 8 Hispanic/Latino; 7 Two or more races, non-Hispanic/Latino), 11 international. Average age 28. 61 applicants, 90% accepted, 28 enrolled. In 2017, 46 master's awarded. *Degree requirements:* For master's, thesis. *Entrance requirements:* For master's, GRE (minimum score: 1000), minimum GPA of 2.8, portfolio, statement of purpose, official copies of academic transcripts, three letters of recommendation. Additional exam requirements/recommendations for international students: Required—TOEFL (minimum score 550 paper-based; 80 iBT). *Application deadline:* For fall admission, 1/15 priority date for domestic students, 7/1 for international students; for spring admission, 10/15 priority date for domestic students, 11/1 for international students. Applications are processed on a rolling basis. Application fee: $55. Electronic applications accepted. *Expenses:* Contact

institution. *Financial support:* Fellowships, research assistantships, teaching assistantships, Federal Work-Study, scholarships/grants, tuition waivers (full and partial), and unspecified assistantships available. Financial award application deadline: 2/1; financial award applicants required to submit FAFSA. *Faculty research:* Architectural history, cultural studies/sacred space, design technologies, digital media, real estate development, urban design. *Total annual research expenditures:* $106,977. *Unit head:* Randall Ott, Dean, 202-319-5784, Fax: 202-319-2023, E-mail: ott@cua.edu. *Application contact:* Dr. Steven Brown, Director of Graduate Admissions, 202-319-5057, Fax: 202-319-6533, E-mail: cua-admissions@cua.edu.
Website: https://architecture.catholic.edu/

Clark University, Graduate School, Department of International Development, Community, and Environment, Program in Community Development and Planning, Worcester, MA 01610-1477. Offers MA, MA/MBA. *Students:* 34 full-time (28 women); includes 2 minority (both Two or more races, non-Hispanic/Latino). Average age 23. 73 applicants, 60% accepted, 27 enrolled. In 2017, 21 master's awarded. *Degree requirements:* For master's, thesis. *Entrance requirements:* For master's, 2 references, resume or curriculum vitae, personal statement. Additional exam requirements/recommendations for international students: Required—TOEFL (minimum score 575 paper-based; 90 iBT), IELTS (minimum score 6.5). *Application deadline:* For fall admission, 4/15 for domestic and international students. Application fee: $75. Electronic applications accepted. *Expenses:* $5,685 tuition per unit, $490 fees. *Financial support:* Fellowships, research assistantships, teaching assistantships, institutionally sponsored loans, and scholarships/grants available. *Faculty research:* Urban revitalization, youth and gang violence, amenities, systemic education reform, housing for disabled residents, economic development in neighborhood planning. *Unit head:* Dr. Laurie Ross, Coordinator, 508-421-7642, E-mail: lross@clarku.edu. *Application contact:* Sawsan Berjawi, Manager of Academic and Student Affairs, 508-421-3846, Fax: 508-793-8820, E-mail: sberjawi@clarku.edu.
Website: http://www.clarku.edu/programs/masters-community-development-and-planning

Cleveland State University, College of Graduate Studies, Maxine Goodman Levin College of Urban Affairs, Program in Urban Planning and Development, Cleveland, OH 44115. Offers economic development (MUPD); environmental sustainability (MUPD); historic preservation (MUPD); housing and neighborhood development (MUPD); real estate development and finance (MUPD); urban economic development (Certificate); urban geographic information systems (MUPD); JD/MUPDD. *Accreditation:* ACSP. *Program availability:* Part-time, evening/weekend. *Faculty:* 16 full-time (8 women), 13 part-time/adjunct (5 women). *Students:* 20 full-time (7 women), 15 part-time (5 women); includes 1 minority (Black or African American, non-Hispanic/Latino), 2 international. Average age 28. 48 applicants, 56% accepted, 14 enrolled. In 2017, 24 master's awarded. *Degree requirements:* For master's, thesis or alternative, exit project. *Entrance requirements:* For master's, GRE General Test (minimum score: 50th percentile combined verbal and quantitative, 4.0 analytical writing), minimum GPA of 3.0. Additional exam requirements/recommendations for international students: Required—TOEFL (minimum score 550 paper-based; 78 iBT), IELTS (6.0), or International Test of English Proficiency (iTEP). *Application deadline:* For fall admission, 7/1 priority date for domestic students, 5/15 for international students; for spring admission, 11/15 for domestic students, 11/1 for international students; for summer admission, 4/1 for domestic students, 3/15 for international students. Applications are processed on a rolling basis. Application fee: $40. Electronic applications accepted. *Expenses:* Contact institution. *Financial support:* In 2017–18, 10 students received support, including 5 research assistantships with full tuition reimbursements available (averaging $7,200 per year), 3 teaching assistantships with partial tuition reimbursements available (averaging $2,400 per year); scholarships/grants, tuition waivers (full and partial), and unspecified assistantships also available. Support available to part-time students. Financial award application deadline: 3/1; financial award applicants required to submit FAFSA. *Faculty research:* Housing and neighborhood development, urban housing policy, environmental sustainability, economic development, GIS and planning decision support. *Unit head:* Dr. Stephanie Ryberg-Webster, Assistant Professor/Program Director, 216-802-3386, Fax: 216-687-2013, E-mail: s.ryberg@csuohio.edu. *Application contact:* David Arrighi, Graduate Academic Advisor, 216-523-7522, Fax: 216-687-5398, E-mail: d.arrighi@csuohio.edu.
Website: http://www.csuohio.edu/urban/mupd/mupd

College of Charleston, Graduate School, School of Humanities and Social Sciences, Program in Urban and Regional Planning, Charleston, SC 29424-0001. Offers Certificate. *Program availability:* Part-time, evening/weekend. *Entrance requirements:* Additional exam requirements/recommendations for international students: Required—TOEFL (minimum score 81 iBT). Electronic applications accepted.

Columbia University, Graduate School of Architecture, Planning, and Preservation, Program in Urban Planning, New York, NY 10027. Offers MS, PhD, JD/MS, M Arch/MS, MBA/MS, MIA/MS, MPH/MS, MS/MS. PhD offered through the Graduate School of Arts and Sciences. *Accreditation:* ACSP (one or more programs are accredited). *Degree requirements:* For master's, thesis. *Entrance requirements:* For master's, GRE General Test. *Expenses: Tuition:* Full-time $44,864; part-time $1704 per credit. *Required fees:* $2370 per semester. One-time fee: $105.

Concordia University, School of Graduate Studies, Faculty of Arts and Science, School of Community and Public Affairs, Montréal, QC H3G 1M8, Canada. Offers community economic development (Diploma).

Cornell University, Graduate School, Graduate Fields of Architecture, Art and Planning, Field of City and Regional Planning, Ithaca, NY 14853. Offers city and regional planning (MRP, PhD); environmental planning and design (MRP, PhD); historic preservation planning (MA); international development planning (MRP, PhD); planning theory and systems analysis (MRP, PhD); regional economics and development planning (MRP, PhD); regional science (MRP, PhD); social and health systems planning (MRP, PhD); urban and regional theory (MRP, PhD); urban planning history (MRP, PhD). *Accreditation:* ACSP (one or more programs are accredited). *Degree requirements:* For master's, thesis (MA); for doctorate, comprehensive exam, thesis/dissertation. *Entrance requirements:* For master's and doctorate, GRE General Test, 2 letters of recommendation. Additional exam requirements/recommendations for international students: Required—TOEFL (minimum score 600 paper-based; 77 iBT). Electronic applications accepted. *Faculty research:* Land use planning, economic development, international development, historic preservation, community development.

Cornell University, Graduate School, Graduate Fields of Architecture, Art and Planning, Field of Regional Science, Ithaca, NY 14853. Offers environmental studies (MA, MS, PhD); international spatial problems (MA, MS, PhD); location theory (MA, MS, PhD); multiregional economic analysis (MA, MS, PhD); peace science (MA, MS, PhD); planning methods (MA, MS, PhD); urban and regional economics (MA, MS, PhD). Terminal master's awarded for partial completion of doctoral program. *Degree requirements:* For master's, thesis; for doctorate, comprehensive exam, thesis/dissertation. *Entrance requirements:* For master's and doctorate, GRE General Test, 2 letters of recommendation. Additional exam requirements/recommendations for international students: Required—TOEFL (minimum score 600 paper-based; 77 iBT). Electronic applications accepted. *Faculty research:* Urban and regional growth, spatial economics, formation of spatial patterns by socioeconomic systems, non-linear dynamics and complex systems, environmental-economic systems.

Dalhousie University, Faculty of Architecture and Planning, School of Planning, Halifax, NS B3J 2X4, Canada. Offers M Eng, M Plan, MPS. *Degree requirements:* For master's, thesis. *Entrance requirements:* Additional exam requirements/recommendations for international students: Required—TOEFL, IELTS, CANTEST, CAEL, or Michigan English Language Assessment Battery. Electronic applications accepted.

Delta State University, Graduate Programs, College of Arts and Sciences, Division of Social Sciences and History, Program in Community Development, Cleveland, MS 38733-0001. Offers MS. *Program availability:* Part-time. *Degree requirements:* For master's, thesis or alternative.

East Carolina University, Graduate School, Thomas Harriot College of Arts and Sciences, Department of Geography, Planning, and Environment, Greenville, NC 27858-4353. Offers development and environmental planning (Certificate); economic development (Certificate); geographic information science and technology (Certificate); geography (MA), including geography, planning, rural development. *Program availability:* Part-time, evening/weekend, online learning. *Students:* 15 full-time (8 women), 6 part-time (2 women); includes 4 minority (3 Black or African American, non-Hispanic/Latino; 1 Hispanic/Latino). Average age 27. 14 applicants, 93% accepted, 8 enrolled. In 2017, 5 master's, 1 other advanced degree awarded. *Degree requirements:* For master's, comprehensive exam, thesis optional. *Entrance requirements:* For master's, GRE General Test. Additional exam requirements/recommendations for international students: Recommended—TOEFL (minimum score 78 iBT), IELTS (minimum score 6.5). *Application deadline:* For fall admission, 4/1 priority date for domestic and international students. Applications are processed on a rolling basis. Application fee: $75. Electronic applications accepted. *Expenses:* Tuition, state resident: full-time $4749; part-time $297 per credit hour. Tuition, nonresident: full-time $17,898; part-time $1119 per credit hour. *Required fees:* $2691; $224 per credit hour. Part-time tuition and fees vary according to course load and program. *Financial support:* Research assistantships with partial tuition reimbursements, teaching assistantships with partial tuition reimbursements, and Federal Work-Study available. Support available to part-time students. Financial award application deadline: 3/1. *Faculty research:* Coastal vulnerability and adaptation, emergency management, public understanding of risk, catastrophic events. *Unit head:* Dr. Thad Wasklewicz, Chair, 252-328-6230, E-mail: wasklewiczt@ecu.edu. *Application contact:* Dean of Graduate School, 252-328-6012, Fax: 252-328-6071, E-mail: gradschool@ecu.edu.
Website: http://www.ecu.edu/geog/

Eastern Kentucky University, The Graduate School, College of Arts and Sciences, Department of Government, Program in General Public Administration, Richmond, KY 40475-3102. Offers community development (MPA); community health administration (MPA); general public administration (MPA). *Accreditation:* NASPAA. *Program availability:* Part-time, evening/weekend. *Entrance requirements:* For master's, GRE General Test, minimum GPA of 2.5.

Eastern Michigan University, Graduate School, College of Arts and Sciences, Department of Geography and Geology, Programs in Urban and Regional Planning, Ypsilanti, MI 48197. Offers transportation planning and modeling (Graduate Certificate); urban and regional planning (MS). *Students:* 1 (woman) full-time, 13 part-time (6 women); includes 8 minority (4 Black or African American, non-Hispanic/Latino; 1 Asian, non-Hispanic/Latino; 1 Hispanic/Latino; 2 Two or more races, non-Hispanic/Latino), 1 international. Average age 28. 16 applicants, 56% accepted, 4 enrolled. In 2017, 6 master's awarded. Application fee: $45. *Application contact:* Dr. Heather Khan, Program Advisor, 734-487-8021, Fax: 734-487-6979, E-mail: hkhan3@emich.edu.

Eastern University, Department of Social Transformation, St. Davids, PA 19087-3696. Offers urban studies (MA), including community arts, community development, juvenile justice ministry, youth leadership. *Students:* 12 full-time (10 women), 17 part-time (14 women); includes 14 minority (10 Black or African American, non-Hispanic/Latino; 2 Hispanic/Latino; 2 Two or more races, non-Hispanic/Latino), 2 international. Average age 32. In 2017, 15 master's awarded. *Application deadline:* Applications are processed on a rolling basis. Application fee: $35. Electronic applications accepted. Application fee is waived when completed online. *Expenses:* Contact institution. *Unit head:* Michael Dziedziak, Executive Director of Enrollment, 800-452-0996, E-mail: gpsadmissions@eastern.edu.
Website: https://www.eastern.edu/academics/programs/urban-studies-department/master-of-arts-in-urban-studies

East Tennessee State University, School of Graduate Studies, College of Arts and Sciences, Department of Political Science, International Affairs and Public Administration, Johnson City, TN 37614. Offers economic development (Postbaccalaureate Certificate); economic development and planning (MPA); local government management (MPA); nonprofit and public financial management (MPA); urban planning (Postbaccalaureate Certificate). *Program availability:* Part-time. *Degree requirements:* For master's, internship, capstone. *Entrance requirements:* For master's, GRE General Test, three letters of recommendation. Additional exam requirements/recommendations for international students: Required—TOEFL (minimum score 550 paper-based; 79 iBT). *Application deadline:* For fall admission, 6/1 for domestic students, 4/29 for international students; for spring admission, 11/1 for domestic students, 9/29 for international students. Application fee: $55 ($65 for international students). Electronic applications accepted. *Financial support:* Research assistantships with full tuition reimbursements, teaching assistantships with full tuition reimbursements, career-related internships or fieldwork, institutionally sponsored loans, scholarships/grants, and unspecified assistantships available. Financial award application deadline: 7/1; financial award applicants required to submit FAFSA. *Faculty research:* Labor issues, presidency, public law in American politics, East Asian politics, European politics, Middle Eastern politics, development in comparative politics, international political economy, international relations, world politics in international affairs. *Unit head:* Dr. Andrew Battista, Chair, 423-439-6628, Fax: 423-439-4348, E-mail: battista@etsu.edu. *Application contact:* Dr. Andrew Battista, Chair, 423-439-6628, Fax: 423-439-4348, E-mail: battista@etsu.edu.
Website: http://www.etsu.edu/cas/polisci/

Florida Atlantic University, College for Design and Social Inquiry, School of Urban and Regional Planning, Boca Raton, FL 33431-0991. Offers MURP. *Accreditation:* ACSP. *Program availability:* Part-time, evening/weekend. *Faculty:* 3 full-time (1 woman). *Students:* 17 full-time (7 women), 12 part-time (5 women); includes 16 minority (10 Black or African American, non-Hispanic/Latino; 1 Asian, non-Hispanic/Latino; 4 Hispanic/Latino; 1 Two or more races, non-Hispanic/Latino), 1 international. Average age 30. 36 applicants, 33% accepted, 12 enrolled. In 2017, 24 master's awarded. *Entrance requirements:* For master's, GRE General Test, minimum GPA of 3.0. Additional exam requirements/recommendations for international students: Required—TOEFL (minimum score 500 paper-based; 61 iBT), IELTS (minimum score 6). *Application deadline:* For fall admission, 5/1 priority date for domestic students, 2/15 for international students; for spring admission, 11/1 priority date for domestic students, 7/15 for international students. Applications are processed on a rolling basis. Application fee: $30. *Expenses:* Tuition, state resident: full-time $7400; part-time $369.82 per credit. Tuition, nonresident: full-time $20,496; part-time $1042.81 per credit. *Financial support:* Fellowships with full tuition reimbursements, research assistantships, career-related internships or fieldwork, Federal Work-Study, institutionally sponsored loans, and tuition waivers (partial) available. Financial award application deadline: 4/1. *Faculty research:* Growth management, urban design, computer applications/geographical information systems, environmental planning. *Unit head:* 954-762-5652, E-mail: durp@fau.edu. *Application contact:* Alejandra Quintero, E-mail: mquinte5@fau.edu.
Website: http://www.fau.edu/durp/

Florida State University, The Graduate School, College of Social Sciences and Public Policy, Department of Urban and Regional Planning, Tallahassee, FL 32306-2280. Offers planning (MSP); urban and regional planning (PhD); JD/MSP; MA/MSP; MPH/MSP; MSP/MS. *Accreditation:* ACSP (one or more programs are accredited). *Program availability:* Part-time. *Faculty:* 10 full-time (4 women), 16 part-time/adjunct (4 women). *Students:* 74 full-time (40 women), 14 part-time (6 women); includes 33 minority (14 Black or African American, non-Hispanic/Latino; 6 Asian, non-Hispanic/Latino; 1 Hispanic/Latino; 12 Two or more races, non-Hispanic/Latino). Average age 28. 105 applicants, 59% accepted, 33 enrolled. In 2017, 31 master's, 1 doctorate awarded. *Degree requirements:* For master's, capstone project, internship; for doctorate, thesis/dissertation. *Entrance requirements:* For master's and doctorate, GRE General Test, minimum GPA of 3.0. Additional exam requirements/recommendations for international students: Required—TOEFL (minimum score 600 paper-based; 100 iBT); Recommended—IELTS (minimum score 7). *Application deadline:* For fall admission, 2/15 priority date for domestic students, 11/15 priority date for international students; for spring admission, 11/1 for domestic students, 9/1 for international students. Applications are processed on a rolling basis. Application fee: $30. Electronic applications accepted. *Financial support:* In 2017–18, 32 students received support, including 5 fellowships with full tuition reimbursements available (averaging $18,000 per year), 28 research assistantships with full tuition reimbursements available (averaging $9,600 per year), 6 teaching assistantships with full tuition reimbursements available (averaging $18,000 per year); career-related internships or fieldwork, Federal Work-Study, institutionally sponsored loans, and tuition waivers (partial) also available. Financial award application deadline: 2/15; financial award applicants required to submit FAFSA. *Faculty research:* Land use planning, environmental planning, developing countries, transportation, sustainable and healthy communities, neighborhood planning, climate change. *Total annual research expenditures:* $560,000. *Unit head:* Dr. Jeffrey R. Brown, Professor and Chairperson, 850-644-4510, Fax: 850-645-4841, E-mail: jrbrown3@fsu.edu. *Application contact:* Susan A. Taylor, Admissions Coordinator, 850-644-4510, Fax: 850-644-4841, E-mail: durp@coss.fsu.edu.
Website: http://www.coss.fsu.edu/durp/

Future Generations University, Program in Applied Community Change, Franklin, WV 26807. Offers conservation (MA). *Program availability:* Blended/hybrid learning. *Faculty:* 9 full-time (3 women), 12 part-time/adjunct (4 women). *Students:* 16 full-time (7 women); includes 13 minority (6 Black or African American, non-Hispanic/Latino; 4 Asian, non-Hispanic/Latino; 3 Hispanic/Latino). In 2017, 11 master's awarded. *Degree requirements:* For master's, portfolio. *Entrance requirements:* For master's, bachelor's degree, community involvement. Additional exam requirements/recommendations for international students: Recommended—TOEFL. *Application deadline:* Applications are processed on a rolling basis. Application fee: $0. Electronic applications accepted. *Financial support:* Scholarships/grants and tuition waivers (partial) available. Financial award applicants required to submit FAFSA. *Faculty research:* Sustainable communities, community engagement, peacebuilding, seed-scale community development. *Unit head:* Christie Hand, Chief Academic Officer, 304-358-2000. *Application contact:* Jodie Wimer, Registrar, 304-358-2000, E-mail: jwimer@future.edu.
Website: http://www.future.edu

Georgetown University, Graduate School of Arts and Sciences, School of Continuing Studies, Washington, DC 20057. Offers American studies (MALS); applied intelligence (MPS); Catholic studies (MALS); classical civilizations (MALS); emergency and disaster management (MPS); ethics and the professions (MALS); global strategic communications (MPS); hospitality management (MPS); human resources management (MPS); humanities (MALS); individualized study (MALS); integrated marketing communications (MPS); international affairs (MALS); Islam and Muslim-Christian relations (MALS); journalism (MPS); liberal studies (DLS); literature and society (MALS); medieval and early modern European studies (MALS); public relations and corporate communications (MPS); real estate (MPS); religious studies (MALS); social and public policy (MALS); sports industry management (MPS); systems engineering management (MPS); technology management (MPS); the theory and practice of American democracy (MALS); urban and regional planning (MPS); visual culture (MALS). MPS in systems engineering management offered jointly with Stevens Institute of Technology. *Entrance requirements:* Additional exam requirements/recommendations for international students: Required—TOEFL.

Georgia Institute of Technology, Graduate Studies, College of Design, School of City and Regional Planning, Atlanta, GA 30332-0001. Offers city and regional planning (PhD); economic development (MCRP); environmental planning and management (MCRP); geographic information systems (MCRP); land and community development (MCRP); land use planning (MCRP); transportation (MCRP); urban design (MCRP); MCP/MSCE. *Accreditation:* ACSP. *Degree requirements:* For master's, thesis, internship. *Entrance requirements:* For master's, GRE General Test, minimum GPA of 2.7. Additional exam requirements/recommendations for international students: Required—TOEFL. Electronic applications accepted.

Georgia State University, Andrew Young School of Policy Studies, Department of Public Management and Policy, Atlanta, GA 30303. Offers criminal justice (MPA); disaster management (Certificate); disaster policy (MPA); environmental policy (PhD); health policy (PhD); management and finance (MPA); nonprofit management (MPA, Certificate); nonprofit policy (MPA); planning and economic development (MPP, Certificate); policy analysis and evaluation (MPA), including planning and economic development; public and nonprofit management (PhD); public finance and budgeting (PhD), including science and technology policy, urban and regional economic development; public finance policy (MPA), including social policy; public health (MPA). *Accreditation:* NASPAA (one or more programs are accredited). *Program availability:* Part-time. *Faculty:* 17 full-time (9 women). *Students:* 125 full-time (75 women), 78 part-time (51 women); includes 90 minority (67 Black or African American, non-Hispanic/Latino; 5 Asian, non-Hispanic/Latino; 9 Hispanic/Latino; 9 Two or more races, non-Hispanic/Latino), 34 international. Average age 30. 275 applicants, 62% accepted, 88 enrolled. In 2017, 71 master's, 5 doctorates, 12 other advanced degrees awarded. Terminal master's awarded for partial completion of doctoral program. *Degree requirements:* For master's, thesis optional; for doctorate, comprehensive exam, thesis/dissertation. *Entrance requirements:* For master's and doctorate, GRE. Additional exam requirements/recommendations for international students: Required—TOEFL (minimum score 603 paper-based; 100 iBT) or IELTS (minimum score 7). *Application deadline:* For fall admission, 1/15 for domestic and international students. Application fee: $50. Electronic applications accepted. *Expenses:* Tuition, state resident: full-time $7020. Tuition, nonresident: full-time $22,518. *Required fees:* $2128. Tuition and fees vary according to degree level and program. *Financial support:* In 2017–18, fellowships (averaging $8,194 per year), research assistantships (averaging $8,068 per year), teaching assistantships (averaging $3,600 per year) were awarded; institutionally sponsored loans, scholarships/grants, health care benefits, and unspecified assistantships also available. Financial award application deadline: 2/1.

Faculty research: Public budgeting and finance, public management, nonprofit management, performance measurement and management, urban development. *Unit head:* Dr. Carolyn Bourdeaux, Chair and Professor, 404-413-0013, Fax: 404-413-0104, E-mail: cbourdeaux@gsu.edu.
Website: http://aysps.gsu.edu/pmap/

Harvard University, Graduate School of Arts and Sciences, Committee on Architecture, Landscape Architecture, and Urban Planning, Cambridge, MA 02138. Offers architecture (PhD); landscape architecture (PhD); urban planning (PhD). *Accreditation:* ACSP. *Degree requirements:* For doctorate, one foreign language, thesis/dissertation, oral exam. *Entrance requirements:* For doctorate, GRE General Test. Additional exam requirements/recommendations for international students: Required—TOEFL.

Harvard University, Graduate School of Design, Department of Urban Planning and Design, Cambridge, MA 02138. Offers urban planning (MUP); urban planning and design (MAUD, MLAUD). *Accreditation:* ACSP (one or more programs are accredited). *Entrance requirements:* For master's, GRE General Test. Additional exam requirements/recommendations for international students: Required—TOEFL (minimum score 600 paper-based; 104 iBT). Electronic applications accepted.

Hunter College of the City University of New York, Graduate School, School of Arts and Sciences, Department of Urban Policy and Planning, Program in Urban Planning, New York, NY 10065-5085. Offers MUP, JD/MUP. JD/MUP offered jointly with Brooklyn Law School. *Accreditation:* ACSP. *Program availability:* Part-time. *Degree requirements:* For master's, planning studio and internship. *Entrance requirements:* For master's, minimum 12 credits of course work in social sciences, 2 letters of recommendation. Additional exam requirements/recommendations for international students: Required—TOEFL. *Faculty research:* Community and economic development, transportation planning and policy, geographic information systems, housing, land use.

Indiana University of Pennsylvania, School of Graduate Studies and Research, College of Humanities and Social Sciences, Department of Geography and Regional Planning, Regional Planning Track, Indiana, PA 15705. Offers MS. *Program availability:* Part-time. *Faculty:* 10 full-time (2 women). *Students:* 2 full-time (1 woman). Average age 26. 3 applicants, 33% accepted, 1 enrolled. In 2017, 2 master's awarded. *Degree requirements:* For master's, thesis optional. *Entrance requirements:* Additional exam requirements/recommendations for international students: Required—TOEFL (minimum score 550 paper-based). *Application deadline:* Applications are processed on a rolling basis. Application fee: $50. Electronic applications accepted. *Expenses:* Tuition, state resident: full-time $12,000; part-time $500 per credit. Tuition, nonresident: full-time $18,000; part-time $750 per credit. *Required fees:* $4073; $165.55 per credit. $64 per term. *Financial support:* In 2017–18, 2 research assistantships with tuition reimbursements (averaging $2,970 per year) were awarded; fellowships with full tuition reimbursements, career-related internships or fieldwork, Federal Work-Study, scholarships/grants, and unspecified assistantships also available. Financial award application deadline: 4/15; financial award applicants required to submit FAFSA. *Unit head:* Dr. Richard Hoch, Graduate Coordinator, 724-357-5990, E-mail: richard.hoch@iup.edu.
Website: http://www.iup.edu/georegionalplan/grad/default.aspx

Iowa State University of Science and Technology, Department of Community and Regional Planning, Ames, IA 50011. Offers community and regional planning (MCRP); transportation (MS); M Arch/MCRP; MBA/MCRP; MCRP/MLA; MCRP/MPA. *Accreditation:* ACSP (one or more programs are accredited). *Degree requirements:* For master's, thesis or alternative. *Entrance requirements:* For master's, GRE General Test. Additional exam requirements/recommendations for international students: Required—TOEFL (minimum score 550 paper-based; 79 iBT), IELTS (minimum score 6.5). Electronic applications accepted. *Faculty research:* Economic development, housing, land use, geographic information systems planning in developing nations, regional and community revitalization, transportation planning in developing countries.

Jackson State University, Graduate School, College of Public Service, Department of Urban and Regional Planning, Jackson, MS 39217. Offers MA, PhD. *Accreditation:* ACSP. *Degree requirements:* For master's, comprehensive exam. *Entrance requirements:* For master's, GRE General Test. Additional exam requirements/recommendations for international students: Required—TOEFL (minimum score 520 paper-based; 67 iBT).

Kansas State University, Graduate School, College of Architecture, Planning and Design, Department of Interior Architecture and Product Design, Manhattan, KS 66506. Offers MIAPD. *Degree requirements:* For master's, thesis, oral exam, culminating project. *Entrance requirements:* For master's, minimum GPA of 3.0, portfolio. Additional exam requirements/recommendations for international students: Required—TOEFL (minimum score 600 paper-based; 95 iBT) or IELTS (minimum score 7). Electronic applications accepted. *Faculty research:* Planning interior spaces for exhibition; residential and commercial spaces; design of objects such as furniture, lighting, equipment, finishing treatments and accessories.

Kansas State University, Graduate School, College of Architecture, Planning and Design, Department of Landscape Architecture and Regional and Community Planning, Manhattan, KS 66506. Offers community development (MS); landscape architecture (MLA); regional and community planning (MRCP). MS offered online through the Great Plains Interactive Distance Education Alliance: Iowa State University, University of Nebraska, North Dakota State University, South Dakota State University. *Accreditation:* ACSP; ASLA. *Program availability:* Part-time, 100% online. Terminal master's awarded for partial completion of doctoral program. *Degree requirements:* For master's, thesis, oral exam. *Entrance requirements:* Additional exam requirements/recommendations for international students: Required—TOEFL (minimum score 600 paper-based), IELTS (minimum score 6.5). Electronic applications accepted. *Faculty research:* Community planning and design, design and implementation, geospatial modeling, fluvial and green systems, transportation systems.

Lesley University, Graduate School of Arts and Social Sciences, Cambridge, MA 02138-2790. Offers clinical mental health counseling (MA), including holistic counseling, school and community counseling, trauma studies; counseling psychology (MA, CAGS), including professional counseling (MA), school counseling (MA); creative writing (MFA); expressive therapies (MA, PhD, CAGS), including art (MA), clinical mental health counseling (MA), dance (MA), expressive therapies (MA), music (MA); independent studies (CAGS); independent study (MA); intercultural relations (MA, CAGS); interdisciplinary studies (MA), including individualized studies, integrative holistic health, mindfulness studies, peace and conflict transformation, trauma sensitive assessment, intervention, and consultation, women's studies; urban environmental leadership (MA). *Program availability:* Part-time, online learning. *Degree requirements:* For master's, internship, practicum, thesis (for expressive therapies); for doctorate, thesis/dissertation, arts apprenticeship, field placement; for CAGS, thesis, internship (for counseling psychology, expressive therapies). *Entrance requirements:* For master's, MAT (counseling psychology), interview, writing samples, art portfolio; for doctorate, GRE or MAT, interview, master's degree; for CAGS, interview, master's degree. Additional exam requirements/recommendations for international students: Required—TOEFL (minimum score 550 paper-based; 80 iBT). Electronic applications accepted. *Faculty research:* Psychotherapy and culture; psychotherapy and psychological trauma; women's issues in art, teaching and psychotherapy; community-based art, psycho-spiritual inquiry.

Massachusetts Institute of Technology, School of Architecture and Planning, Department of Urban Studies and Planning, Cambridge, MA 02139. Offers city planning (MCP); urban and regional planning (PhD); urban and regional studies (PhD); urban studies and planning (SM). *Accreditation:* ACSP (one or more programs are accredited). *Degree requirements:* For master's, thesis; for doctorate, comprehensive exam, thesis/dissertation. *Entrance requirements:* For master's and doctorate, GRE General Test. Additional exam requirements/recommendations for international students: Required—TOEFL, IELTS. Electronic applications accepted. *Faculty research:* City design and regional development; housing, community, and economic development; environmental policy; international development; infrastructure systems and climate change planning; spatial modeling and urban analytics.

McGill University, Faculty of Graduate and Postdoctoral Studies, Faculty of Engineering, School of Urban Planning, Montréal, QC H3A 2T5, Canada. Offers environmental planning (MUP); housing (MUP); transportation (MUP); urban design (MUP); urban planning, policy and design (PhD).

Michigan State University, The Graduate School, College of Agriculture and Natural Resources and College of Social Science, School of Planning, Design and Construction, East Lansing, MI 48824. Offers construction management (MS, PhD); environmental design (MA); interior design and facilities management (MA); international planning studies (MIPS); urban and regional planning (MURP). *Degree requirements:* For master's, thesis or alternative. *Entrance requirements:* Additional exam requirements/recommendations for international students: Required—TOEFL. Electronic applications accepted.

Minnesota State University Mankato, College of Graduate Studies and Research, College of Social and Behavioral Sciences, Urban and Regional Studies Institute, Mankato, MN 56001. Offers local government management (Certificate); non-profit leadership (Certificate); urban and regional studies (MA); urban planning (MA, Certificate). *Degree requirements:* For master's, one foreign language, comprehensive exam, thesis or alternative. *Entrance requirements:* For master's, minimum GPA of 3.0 during previous 2 years, 2 letters of recommendation. Additional exam requirements/recommendations for international students: Required—TOEFL. Electronic applications accepted.

Missouri State University, Graduate College, College of Natural and Applied Sciences, Department of Geography, Geology, and Planning, Springfield, MO 65897. Offers geography, geology, and planning (Certificate); natural and applied science (MNAS), including geography, geology and planning; secondary education (MS Ed), including earth science, physical geography. *Program availability:* Part-time, evening/weekend. *Faculty:* 18 full-time (4 women), 1 part-time/adjunct (0 women). *Students:* 27 full-time (10 women), 7 part-time (6 women); includes 2 minority (both Two or more races, non-Hispanic/Latino), 3 international. Average age 29. 27 applicants, 48% accepted, 13 enrolled. In 2017, 32 master's awarded. *Degree requirements:* For master's, comprehensive exam, thesis (for some programs). *Entrance requirements:* For master's, GRE General Test (MS, MNAS), minimum undergraduate GPA of 3.0 (MS, MNAS), 9-12 teacher certification (MS Ed). Additional exam requirements/recommendations for international students: Required—TOEFL (minimum score 550 paper-based; 79 iBT), IELTS (minimum score 6). *Application deadline:* For fall admission, 7/20 priority date for domestic students, 5/1 for international students; for spring admission, 12/20 priority date for domestic students, 9/1 for international students. Applications are processed on a rolling basis. Application fee: $35 ($50 for international students). Electronic applications accepted. *Expenses:* Tuition, state resident: full-time $2915; part-time $2021 per credit hour. Tuition, nonresident: full-time $5354; part-time $3647 per credit hour. *International tuition:* $11,992 full-time. *Required fees:* $173; $173 per credit hour. Tuition and fees vary according to class time, course level, course load, degree level, campus/location and program. *Financial support:* In 2017–18, 3 research assistantships with full tuition reimbursements (averaging $11,574 per year), 15 teaching assistantships with full tuition reimbursements (averaging $9,365 per year) were awarded; career-related internships or fieldwork, Federal Work-Study, institutionally sponsored loans, scholarships/grants, and unspecified assistantships also available. Financial award application deadline: 3/31; financial award applicants required to submit FAFSA. *Faculty research:* Stratigraphy and ancient meteorite impacts, environmental geochemistry of karst, hyperspectral image processing, water quality, small town planning. *Unit head:* Dr. Toby Dogwiler, Department Head, 417-836-5800, Fax: 417-836-6934, E-mail: tobydogwiler@missouristate.edu. *Application contact:* Stephanie Praschan, Director, Graduate Enrollment Management, 417-836-5330, Fax: 417-836-6200, E-mail: stephaniepraschan@missouristate.edu.
Website: http://geosciences.missouristate.edu/

Morgan State University, School of Graduate Studies, School of Architecture and Planning, Program in City and Regional Planning, Baltimore, MD 21251. Offers MCRP. *Accreditation:* ACSP. *Entrance requirements:* Additional exam requirements/recommendations for international students: Required—TOEFL (minimum score 550 paper-based). *Application deadline:* For fall admission, 2/1 priority date for domestic students; for spring admission, 10/1 priority date for domestic students. Applications are processed on a rolling basis. Application fee: $0. *Expenses:* Tuition, state resident: part-time $433 per credit. Tuition, nonresident: part-time $851 per credit. *Required fees:* $81.50 per credit. *Financial support:* Application deadline: 2/1. *Faculty research:* Nonprofit organizations, community development, urban design, transportation, international planning. *Unit head:* Daniel Campo, Program Director, 443-885-3514, E-mail: daniel.campo@morgan.edu. *Application contact:* Dr. Dean Campbell, Graduate Recruitment Specialist, 443-885-3185, Fax: 443-885-8226, E-mail: dean.campbell@morgan.edu.

New York University, Tandon School of Engineering, Department of Civil and Urban Engineering, Major in Urban Systems Engineering and Management, New York, NY 10012-1019. Offers MS. *Faculty:* 17 full-time (5 women), 38 part-time/adjunct (4 women). *Students:* 7 full-time (4 women), 11 part-time (5 women); includes 4 minority (3 Black or African American, non-Hispanic/Latino; 1 Hispanic/Latino), 9 international. Average age 28. 21 applicants, 76% accepted, 6 enrolled. In 2017, 4 master's awarded. *Entrance requirements:* Additional exam requirements/recommendations for international students: Required—TOEFL (minimum score 550 paper-based; 90 iBT); Recommended—IELTS (minimum score 7). *Application deadline:* For fall admission, 2/15 priority date for domestic and international students; for spring admission, 11/1 priority date for domestic and international students. Application fee: $75. *Expenses: Tuition:* Full-time $41,352; part-time $19,968 per year. *Required fees:* $2496; $1628 per unit. $814 per term. Tuition and fees vary according to course load and program. *Financial support:* Applicants required to submit FAFSA. *Total annual research expenditures:* $2.5 million. *Unit head:* Dr. Illan Juran, Program Director, 646-997-3717, E-mail: ijuran@nyu.edu. *Application contact:* Elizabeth Ensweiler, Senior Director of Graduate Enrollment and Graduate Admissions, 646-997-3182, E-mail: elizabeth.ensweiler@nyu.edu.

New York University, Wagner Graduate School of Public Service, Program in Urban Planning, New York, NY 10012-1019. Offers MUP, JD/MUP. *Accreditation:* ACSP (one or more programs are accredited). *Program availability:* Part-time. *Students:* Average age 27. 173 applicants, 71% accepted, 34 enrolled. In 2017, 53 master's awarded. *Degree requirements:* For master's, thesis or alternative, end event capstone program. *Entrance requirements:* Additional exam requirements/recommendations for international students: Required—TOEFL (minimum score 100 iBT), IELTS (minimum score 7.5), TWE. *Application deadline:* For fall admission, 1/5 for domestic and international students; for

spring admission, 10/1 for domestic and international students. Application fee: $85. Electronic applications accepted. *Expenses: Tuition:* Full-time $41,352; part-time $19,968 per year. *Required fees:* $2496; $1628 per unit. $814 per term. Tuition and fees vary according to course load and program. *Financial support:* In 2017–18, 26 students received support, including 10 fellowships with full and partial tuition reimbursements available (averaging $22,727 per year), 2 research assistantships with full tuition reimbursements available (averaging $56,524 per year); career-related internships or fieldwork, Federal Work-Study, scholarships/grants, health care benefits, and unspecified assistantships also available. Support available to part-time students. Financial award application deadline: 1/6; financial award applicants required to submit FAFSA. *Unit head:* Prof. Ingrid Gould Ellen, Director, 212-998-7533, Fax: 212-995-4164, E-mail: ingrid.ellen@nyu.edu. *Application contact:* Sandra Oliveira, Admissions Officer, 212-998-7414, Fax: 212-995-4611, E-mail: wagner.admissions@nyu.edu.
Website: http://wagner.nyu.edu/urbanplanning

North Dakota State University, College of Graduate and Interdisciplinary Studies, College of Arts, Humanities and Social Sciences, Department of Sociology and Anthropology, Program in Community Development, Fargo, ND 58102. Offers MA, MS. Electronic applications accepted.

Northern Arizona University, College of Social and Behavioral Sciences, Department of Geography, Planning, and Recreation, Flagstaff, AZ 86011. Offers applied geospatial sciences (MS); community planning (Certificate); geographic information systems (Certificate); parks and recreation management (MS). *Program availability:* Part-time, 100% online, blended/hybrid learning. *Faculty:* 18 full-time (9 women), 1 part-time/adjunct (0 women). *Students:* 22 full-time (16 women), 25 part-time (11 women); includes 7 minority (3 Black or African American, non-Hispanic/Latino; 2 Hispanic/Latino; 2 Two or more races, non-Hispanic/Latino), 2 international. Average age 33. 42 applicants, 86% accepted, 35 enrolled. In 2017, 14 master's, 7 other advanced degrees awarded. *Degree requirements:* For master's, variable foreign language requirement, comprehensive exam (for some programs), thesis (for some programs); for Certificate, comprehensive exam (for some programs). *Entrance requirements:* Additional exam requirements/recommendations for international students: Required—TOEFL (minimum score 80 iBT), IELTS (minimum score 6.5). *Application deadline:* For fall admission, 3/1 for domestic and international students; for spring admission, 10/1 for domestic and international students. Applications are processed on a rolling basis. Application fee: $65. Electronic applications accepted. *Expenses:* Tuition, state resident: full-time $9240; part-time $458 per credit hour. Tuition, nonresident: full-time $21,588; part-time $1199 per credit hour. *Required fees:* $1021; $14 per credit hour. $646 per semester. Tuition and fees vary according to course load, campus/location and program. *Financial support:* In 2017–18, 5 students received support, including 5 teaching assistantships with partial tuition reimbursements available (averaging $9,000 per year); institutionally sponsored loans, health care benefits, tuition waivers (partial), and unspecified assistantships also available. Financial award application deadline: 2/1; financial award applicants required to submit FAFSA. *Unit head:* Dr. Alan Lew, Chair, 928-523-6567, Fax: 928-523-2275. *Application contact:* Dana Mandino, Administrative Associate, 928-523-7988, Fax: 928-523-2275, E-mail: geog@nau.edu.
Website: https://nau.edu/SBS/GPR/

Northwest University, College of Social and Behavioral Sciences, Kirkland, WA 98033. Offers counseling psychology (MA, Psy D); international community development (MA). *Program availability:* Evening/weekend. *Entrance requirements:* For master's, 3 character references. Additional exam requirements/recommendations for international students: Required—TOEFL (minimum score 580 paper-based). *Expenses:* Contact institution.

The Ohio State University, Graduate School, College of Engineering, Austin E. Knowlton School of Architecture, Columbus, OH 43210. Offers architecture (M Arch); city and regional planning (MCRP, PhD); landscape architecture (M Land Arch). *Accreditation:* ACSP; ASLA. *Faculty:* 41. *Students:* 197 full-time (84 women), 6 part-time (2 women); includes 34 minority (9 Black or African American, non-Hispanic/Latino; 5 Asian, non-Hispanic/Latino; 15 Hispanic/Latino; 5 Two or more races, non-Hispanic/Latino), 35 international. Average age 26. In 2017, 66 master's, 8 doctorates awarded. *Entrance requirements:* For master's, GRE or GMAT (city and regional planning), portfolio (for architecture and landscape architecture); for doctorate, GRE or GMAT (city and regional planning), example of research or written work. Additional exam requirements/recommendations for international students: Required—TOEFL (minimum score 600 paper-based; 100 iBT), Michigan English Language Assessment Battery (minimum score 86); Recommended—IELTS (minimum score 8). *Application deadline:* For fall admission, 1/1 priority date for domestic students, 11/30 priority date for international students. Applications are processed on a rolling basis. Application fee: $60 ($70 for international students). Electronic applications accepted. *Financial support:* Fellowships, research assistantships, Federal Work-Study, institutionally sponsored loans, and unspecified assistantships available. Support available to part-time students. *Unit head:* Michael B. Cadwell, Professor/Director, 614-292-3174, E-mail: cadwell.1@osu.edu. *Application contact:* Graduate and Professional Admissions, 614-292-9444, Fax: 614-292-3895, E-mail: gpadmissions@osu.edu.
Website: http://knowlton.osu.edu/

Pratt Institute, School of Architecture, Program in City and Regional Planning, Brooklyn, NY 11205-3899. Offers MSCRP. *Accreditation:* ACSP. *Program availability:* Part-time. *Students:* 47 full-time (30 women), 26 part-time (15 women); includes 29 minority (13 Black or African American, non-Hispanic/Latino; 4 Asian, non-Hispanic/Latino; 10 Hispanic/Latino; 2 Two or more races, non-Hispanic/Latino), 16 international. Average age 29. 94 applicants, 89% accepted, 16 enrolled. In 2017, 24 master's awarded. *Degree requirements:* For master's, thesis. *Entrance requirements:* For master's, writing sample, bachelor's degree, transcripts, letters of recommendation, portfolio. Additional exam requirements/recommendations for international students: Required—TOEFL (minimum score 575 paper-based; 90 iBT). *Application deadline:* For fall admission, 1/5 for domestic and international students; for spring admission, 10/1 for domestic and international students. Application fee: $50 ($90 for international students). Electronic applications accepted. *Expenses: Tuition:* Full-time $30,834. *Required fees:* $1974. *Financial support:* Career-related internships or fieldwork, Federal Work-Study, institutionally sponsored loans, scholarships/grants, health care benefits, and unspecified assistantships available. Support available to part-time students. Financial award application deadline: 2/1; financial award applicants required to submit FAFSA. *Faculty research:* Advocacy planning, community development, comprehensive physical planning, transportation planning, real estate development. *Unit head:* Eve Baron, Chairperson, 718-687-5641, Fax: 718-636-3709, E-mail: ebaron@pratt.edu. *Application contact:* Natalie Capannelli, Director of Graduate Admissions, 718-636-3551, Fax: 718-399-4242, E-mail: ncapanne@pratt.edu.
Website: https://www.pratt.edu/academics/architecture/city-and-regional-planning/

See Display on page 105 and Close-Up on page 125.

Pratt Institute, School of Architecture, Program in Urban Placemaking and Management, Brooklyn, NY 11205-3899. Offers MS. *Students:* 24 full-time (15 women), 5 part-time (2 women); includes 7 minority (1 American Indian or Alaska Native, non-Hispanic/Latino; 4 Asian, non-Hispanic/Latino; 2 Hispanic/Latino), 17 international.

Average age 29. 37 applicants, 73% accepted, 13 enrolled. In 2017, 10 master's awarded. *Degree requirements:* For master's, thesis. *Entrance requirements:* For master's, resume, writing sample, work sample or portfolio. Additional exam requirements/recommendations for international students: Required—TOEFL (minimum score 575 paper-based; 90 iBT). *Application deadline:* For fall admission, 1/5 for domestic and international students; for spring admission, 10/1 for domestic and international students. Application fee: $50 ($90 for international students). Electronic applications accepted. *Expenses: Tuition:* Full-time $30,834. *Required fees:* $1974. *Financial support:* Career-related internships or fieldwork, Federal Work-Study, institutionally sponsored loans, scholarships/grants, health care benefits, and unspecified assistantships available. Support available to part-time students. Financial award application deadline: 2/1; financial award applicants required to submit FAFSA. *Unit head:* Eve Baron, Chairperson, 718-687-5641, Fax: 718-636-3709, E-mail: ebaron@pratt.edu. *Application contact:* Natalie Capannelli, Director of Graduate Admissions, 718-636-3551, Fax: 718-399-4242, E-mail: ncapanne@pratt.edu.
Website: https://www.pratt.edu/academics/architecture/urban-placemaking-and-management/

Queen's University at Kingston, School of Graduate Studies, School of Urban and Regional Planning, Kingston, ON K7L 3N6, Canada. Offers M Pl. *Program availability:* Part-time. *Degree requirements:* For master's, thesis optional. *Entrance requirements:* Additional exam requirements/recommendations for international students: Required—TOEFL (minimum score 580 paper-based). *Faculty research:* Housing, real estate development, human services, environmental services, land use planning.

Roger Williams University, School of Architecture, Art and Historic Preservation, Bristol, RI 02809. Offers architecture (M Arch); art and architectural history (MA); historical preservation (MS, Certificate); urban and regional planning (Certificate). *Faculty:* 18 full-time (5 women), 9 part-time/adjunct (1 woman). *Students:* 107 full-time (52 women), 9 part-time (5 women); includes 10 minority (1 Asian, non-Hispanic/Latino; 7 Hispanic/Latino; 2 Two or more races, non-Hispanic/Latino), 5 international. Average age 26. 92 applicants, 93% accepted, 58 enrolled. In 2017, 46 master's, 1 other advanced degree awarded. *Degree requirements:* For master's, thesis. *Entrance requirements:* For master's, portfolio, 2 letters of recommendation, college transcript, letter of intent. Additional exam requirements/recommendations for international students: Required—TOEFL (minimum score 85 iBT), IELTS (minimum score 6.5). *Application deadline:* For fall admission, 4/1 for domestic students; for spring admission, 11/15 for domestic students. Application fee: $50. Electronic applications accepted. *Expenses:* $1,463 per credit hour (for M Arch); $876 per credit hour (for MS and MA); $258 graduation fee. *Financial support:* In 2017–18, 116 students received support, including 116 research assistantships (averaging $2,776 per year); career-related internships or fieldwork, scholarships/grants, and unspecified assistantships also available. Financial award application deadline: 4/1; financial award applicants required to submit FAFSA. *Unit head:* Stephen White, Dean, 401-254-3607, E-mail: swhite@rwu.edu. *Application contact:* Marcus Hanscom, Director of Graduate Admissions, 401-254-3345, Fax: 401-254-3557, E-mail: gradadmit@rwu.edu.
Website: http://www.rwu.edu/graduate/programs/graduate-programs/architecture

Rutgers University–New Brunswick, Edward J. Bloustein School of Planning and Public Policy, Doctoral Program in Planning and Public Policy, New Brunswick, NJ 08901. Offers PhD. *Program availability:* Part-time. *Degree requirements:* For doctorate, comprehensive exam, thesis/dissertation. *Entrance requirements:* For doctorate, GRE, master's degree. Additional exam requirements/recommendations for international students: Required—TOEFL (minimum score 575 paper-based; 88 iBT). Electronic applications accepted. *Faculty research:* Housing and community development, land use and transportation, politics and policy analysis, urban and regional economics, international development.

Rutgers University–New Brunswick, Edward J. Bloustein School of Planning and Public Policy, Program in Urban Planning and Policy Development, New Brunswick, NJ 08901. Offers MCRP, MCRS, JD/MCRP, MBA/MCRP. *Accreditation:* ACSP (one or more programs are accredited). *Program availability:* Part-time, evening/weekend. *Entrance requirements:* For master's, GRE General Test. Additional exam requirements/recommendations for international students: Required—TOEFL (minimum score 575 paper-based; 88 iBT). Electronic applications accepted. *Faculty research:* Land use, transportation, housing, environmental planning, urban redevelopment, international development.

St. Francis Xavier University, Graduate Studies, Department of Adult Education, Antigonish, NS B2G 2W5, Canada. Offers adult education (M Ad Ed); community development (M Ad Ed). *Program availability:* Part-time, online learning. *Degree requirements:* For master's, thesis. *Entrance requirements:* For master's, minimum undergraduate B average, 2 years of work experience in field. Additional exam requirements/recommendations for international students: Required—TOEFL (minimum score 580 paper-based). *Faculty research:* Adult learning and development, religious education, women's issues, literacy, action research.

Saint Louis University, Graduate Programs, College for Public Health and Social Justice, Program in Urban Planning, St. Louis, MO 63103. Offers urban planning and development (MS). *Program availability:* Part-time. *Degree requirements:* For master's, comprehensive exam (for some programs), thesis (for some programs). *Entrance requirements:* For master's, GMAT, GRE General Test, or LSAT, three letters of recommendation, resume, professional goal statement, minimum GPA of 3.0. Additional exam requirements/recommendations for international students: Required—TOEFL (minimum score 525 paper-based). Electronic applications accepted. *Faculty research:* Urban politics, brown fields, e-government, and administration, evaluation research, community development, electronic government and governance.

San Diego State University, Graduate and Research Affairs, College of Professional Studies and Fine Arts, School of Public Affairs, Program in City Planning, San Diego, CA 92182. Offers MCP. *Program availability:* Part-time. *Entrance requirements:* For master's, GRE General Test. Additional exam requirements/recommendations for international students: Required—TOEFL. Electronic applications accepted. *Faculty research:* Community development, housing, sustainable development, visioning.

Savannah State University, Master of Public Administration Program, Savannah, GA 31404. Offers city management (MPA); human resources (MPA). *Accreditation:* NASPAA. *Program availability:* Part-time. *Degree requirements:* For master's, comprehensive exam, thesis, public service internship, capstone seminar. *Entrance requirements:* For master's, GRE General Test, GMAT, or MAT, minimum cumulative GPA of 2.5, 3 letters of recommendation, essay, official transcripts, resume, essay of 500-1000 words detailing reasons for pursuing degree. Additional exam requirements/recommendations for international students: Required—TOEFL. Electronic applications accepted. *Expenses:* Contact institution. *Faculty research:* Community development, human resources, leadership, conflict resolution, city management, non-profit management.

Southeastern University, College of Behavioral and Social Sciences, Lakeland, FL 33801-6099. Offers human services (MA); international community development (MA); marriage and family counseling (MS); professional counseling (MS); school counseling (MS); social work (MSW). *Program availability:* Evening/weekend. *Faculty:* 9 full-time (6 women), 7 part-time/adjunct (4 women). *Students:* 72 full-time (60 women), 9 part-time (all women); includes

28 minority (12 Black or African American, non-Hispanic/Latino; 2 Asian, non-Hispanic/Latino; 13 Hispanic/Latino; 1 Native Hawaiian or other Pacific Islander, non-Hispanic/Latino), 1 international. Average age 29. Application fee: $50. Electronic applications accepted. *Unit head:* Erica H. Sirrine, Dean, 863-667-5341, E-mail: ehsirrine@seu.edu.
Website: http://www.seu.edu/behavior/

State University of New York College of Environmental Science and Forestry, Department of Landscape Architecture, Syracuse, NY 13210-2779. Offers community design and planning (MLA, MS); cultural landscape studies and conservation (MLA, MS); landscape and urban ecology (MLA, MS). *Accreditation:* ASLA (one or more programs are accredited). *Program availability:* Part-time. *Faculty:* 10 full-time (4 women), 7 part-time/adjunct (5 women). *Students:* 27 full-time (16 women), 5 part-time (3 women); includes 5 minority (3 Black or African American, non-Hispanic/Latino; 1 Asian, non-Hispanic/Latino; 1 Hispanic/Latino), 5 international. Average age 25. 31 applicants, 65% accepted, 10 enrolled. In 2017, 9 master's awarded. *Degree requirements:* For master's, comprehensive exam (for some programs), thesis (for some programs). *Entrance requirements:* For master's, GRE General Test, minimum GPA of 3.0. Additional exam requirements/recommendations for international students: Required—TOEFL (minimum score 550 paper-based; 80 iBT), IELTS (minimum score 6), or STEP Eiken (grade 1). *Application deadline:* For fall admission, 2/1 priority date for domestic and international students; for spring admission, 11/1 priority date for domestic and international students. Applications are processed on a rolling basis. Application fee: $60. Electronic applications accepted. *Expenses:* Tuition, state resident: full-time $10,870; part-time $453 per credit. Tuition, nonresident: full-time $22,210; part-time $925 per credit. *Required fees:* $1435; $70.85 per credit. One-time fee: $25 full-time. Part-time tuition and fees vary according to course load. *Financial support:* In 2017–18, 9 students received support. Unspecified assistantships available. Financial award application deadline: 6/30; financial award applicants required to submit FAFSA. *Faculty research:* Site analysis and design, city and regional planning, community environments. *Total annual research expenditures:* $216,783. *Unit head:* Dr. Douglas Johnston, Chair, 315-470-6544, Fax: 315-470-6540, E-mail: dmjohnst@esf.edu. *Application contact:* Scott Shannon, Associate Provost for Instruction/Dean of the Graduate School, 315-470-6599, Fax: 315-470-6978, E-mail: esfgrad@esf.edu.
Website: http://www.esf.edu/la/

State University of New York College of Environmental Science and Forestry, Program in Environmental Science, Syracuse, NY 13210-2779. Offers biophysical and ecological economics (MPS); coupled natural and human systems (MPS); ecosystem restoration (MPS); environmental and community land planning (MPS, MS); environmental and natural resources policy (PhD); environmental communication and participatory processes (PhD); environmental monitoring and modeling (MPS); water and wetland resource studies (MPS, MS). *Program availability:* Part-time. *Faculty:* 1 full-time (0 women), 1 (woman) part-time/adjunct. *Students:* 57 full-time (36 women), 13 part-time (9 women); includes 5 minority (1 Black or African American, non-Hispanic/Latino; 2 Asian, non-Hispanic/Latino; 2 Hispanic/Latino), 26 international. Average age 30. 64 applicants, 63% accepted, 15 enrolled. In 2017, 15 master's, 4 doctorates awarded. Terminal master's awarded for partial completion of doctoral program. *Degree requirements:* For master's, thesis (for some programs); for doctorate, comprehensive exam, thesis/dissertation. *Entrance requirements:* For master's and doctorate, GRE General Test, minimum GPA of 3.0. Additional exam requirements/recommendations for international students: Required—TOEFL (minimum score 550 paper-based; 80 iBT), IELTS (minimum score 6). *Application deadline:* For fall admission, 2/1 priority date for domestic and international students; for spring admission, 11/1 priority date for domestic and international students. Applications are processed on a rolling basis. Application fee: $60. Electronic applications accepted. *Expenses:* Tuition, state resident: full-time $10,870; part-time $453 per credit. Tuition, nonresident: full-time $22,210; part-time $925 per credit. *Required fees:* $1435; $70.85 per credit. One-time fee: $25 full-time. Part-time tuition and fees vary according to course load. *Financial support:* In 2017–18, 20 students received support. Unspecified assistantships available. Financial award application deadline: 6/30; financial award applicants required to submit FAFSA. *Faculty research:* Environmental education/communications, water resources, land resources, waste management. *Total annual research expenditures:* $47,415. *Unit head:* Dr. Russell Briggs, Director of the Division of Environmental Science, 315-470-6989, Fax: 315-470-6700, E-mail: rdbriggs@esf.edu. *Application contact:* Scott Shannon, Associate Provost for Instruction/Dean of the Graduate School, 315-470-6599, Fax: 315-470-6978, E-mail: esfgrad@esf.edu.
Website: http://www.esf.edu/environmentalscience/graduate/

Syracuse University, Maxwell School of Citizenship and Public Affairs, CAS Program in Public Infrastructure Management and Leadership, Syracuse, NY 13244. Offers CAS. *Program availability:* Part-time. *Entrance requirements:* For degree, personal statement, resume, three letters of recommendation, official transcripts. Additional exam requirements/recommendations for international students: Required—TOEFL. *Application deadline:* For fall admission, 2/1 priority date for domestic students; for spring admission, 8/15 priority date for domestic and international students. Application fee: $75. *Financial support:* Application deadline: 1/1. *Faculty research:* Managerial leadership, public budgeting, financial management, engineering economics, infrastructure engineering and management. *Application contact:* Margaret Lane, Assistant Director, Executive Education Programs, 315-443-8708, E-mail: melane02@maxwell.syr.edu.
Website: http://www.maxwell.syr.edu/

Temple University, Tyler School of Art, Department of Planning and Community Development, Ambler, PA 19335. Offers city and regional planning (MS); sustainable community planning (Graduate Certificate); transportation planning (Graduate Certificate). *Accreditation:* ACSP. *Program availability:* Part-time, evening/weekend. *Faculty:* 3 full-time (1 woman), 8 part-time/adjunct (5 women). *Students:* 1 (woman) part-time. 23 applicants, 70% accepted, 1 enrolled. In 2017, 2 master's awarded. *Entrance requirements:* For master's, GRE or GMAT, 2 letters of recommendation, minimum undergraduate GPA of 3.0, statement of goals. Additional exam requirements/recommendations for international students: Required—TOEFL (minimum score 550 paper-based; 79 iBT). *Application deadline:* For fall admission, 3/1 for domestic students, 12/15 for international students; for spring admission, 11/1 for domestic students, 8/1 for international students. Applications are processed on a rolling basis. Application fee: $60. *Expenses:* Tuition, state resident: full-time $16,164; part-time $898 per credit hour. Tuition, nonresident: full-time $22,158; part-time $1231 per credit hour. *Required fees:* $890; $445 per semester. Full-time tuition and fees vary according to course load, degree level, campus/location and program. *Financial support:* Fellowships with full tuition reimbursements, research assistantships with full tuition reimbursements, Federal Work-Study, scholarships/grants, health care benefits, and unspecified assistantships available. Financial award application deadline: 1/15; financial award applicants required to submit FAFSA. *Faculty research:* Regional environmental planning, collaboration, management community development through sustainable food systems, storm water management and floodplain mapping, land use policy innovations, community planning for aging. *Unit head:* Lynn Mandarano, Chair, 267-468-8300, Fax: 267-468-8315, E-mail: lynn.mandarano@temple.edu.
Website: http://tyler.temple.edu/programs/planning-community-development

Texas A&M University, College of Architecture, Department of Landscape Architecture and Urban Planning, College Station, TX 77843. Offers land and property development (MLPD); landscape architecture (MLA); urban and regional planning (MUP); urban and regional science (PhD). *Accreditation:* ACSP (one or more programs are accredited); ASLA (one or more programs are accredited). *Faculty:* 30. *Students:* 163 full-time (84 women), 10 part-time (5 women); includes 22 minority (4 Black or African American, non-Hispanic/Latino; 4 Asian, non-Hispanic/Latino; 13 Hispanic/Latino; 1 Two or more races, non-Hispanic/Latino), 94 international. Average age 27. 186 applicants, 68% accepted, 62 enrolled. In 2017, 66 master's, 8 doctorates awarded. Terminal master's awarded for partial completion of doctoral program. *Degree requirements:* For master's, thesis optional, professional internship; for doctorate, comprehensive exam, thesis/dissertation, seminar. *Entrance requirements:* For master's, GMAT or GRE General Test, portfolio (MLA), minimum GPA of 3.0; for doctorate, GMAT or GRE General Test. Additional exam requirements/recommendations for international students: Required—TOEFL (minimum score 550 paper-based; 80 iBT), IELTS (minimum score 6), PTE (minimum score 53). *Application deadline:* For fall admission, 12/1 priority date for domestic and international students; for spring admission, 8/1 for domestic students. Applications are processed on a rolling basis. Application fee: $50 ($90 for international students). Electronic applications accepted. *Expenses:* Contact institution. *Financial support:* In 2017–18, 117 students received support, including 4 fellowships with tuition reimbursements available (averaging $25,450 per year), 45 research assistantships with tuition reimbursements available (averaging $6,952 per year), 18 teaching assistantships with tuition reimbursements available (averaging $8,427 per year); career-related internships or fieldwork, institutionally sponsored loans, scholarships/grants, traineeships, health care benefits, tuition waivers (full and partial), and unspecified assistantships also available. Support available to part-time students. Financial award application deadline: 3/15; financial award applicants required to submit FAFSA. *Faculty research:* Erosion control/water quality, geographic information systems/spatial information technology, transport hazards, international sustainable development. *Unit head:* Dr. Forster Ndubisi, Head, 979-845-1019, Fax: 979-862-1784. *Application contact:* Thena Morris, Administrative Assistant, 979-458-4306, E-mail: t-morris@tamu.edu.
Website: http://laup.arch.tamu.edu/

Texas Southern University, Barbara Jordan-Mickey Leland School of Public Affairs, Program in Urban Planning and Environmental Policy, Houston, TX 77004-4584. Offers MS, PhD. *Accreditation:* ACSP. *Program availability:* Part-time, evening/weekend. *Degree requirements:* For master's, comprehensive exam, thesis optional. *Entrance requirements:* For master's, GRE General Test, minimum GPA of 2.5. Additional exam requirements/recommendations for international students: Required—TOEFL. Electronic applications accepted.

Thomas Edison State University, John S. Watson School of Public Service and Continuing Studies, Trenton, NJ 08608. Offers community and economic development (MSM); environmental policy/environmental justice (MSM); homeland security (MSHS, MSM); information and technology for public service (MSM); nonprofit management (MSM); public and municipal finance (MSM); public health (MSM); public service administration and leadership (MSM); public service leadership (MPSL). *Program availability:* Part-time, online learning. *Entrance requirements:* Additional exam requirements/recommendations for international students: Required—TOEFL (minimum score 550 paper-based; 79 iBT). Electronic applications accepted.

Thomas Jefferson University, College of Architecture and the Built Environment, Program in Geospatial Technology for Geodesign, Philadelphia, PA 19107. Offers MS. *Program availability:* Part-time.

Tufts University, Graduate School of Arts and Sciences, Department of Urban and Environmental Policy and Planning, Medford, MA 02155. Offers community development (MA); environmental policy (MA); health and human welfare (MA); housing policy (MA); international environment/development policy (MA); public policy (MPP); MA/JD; MA/MBA; MA/MPH; MA/MS; MALD/MA. MALD/MA offered in connection with The Fletcher School of Law and Diplomacy; MA/MPH with School of Medicine; MA/MS with School of Nutrition Science and Policy or School of Engineering; MA/MBA with Boston College, Carroll School of Management; MA/JD with Boston College Law School. *Accreditation:* ACSP (one or more programs are accredited). *Program availability:* Part-time. *Students:* 95 full-time (68 women), 17 part-time (14 women); includes 34 minority (14 Black or African American, non-Hispanic/Latino; 10 Asian, non-Hispanic/Latino; 6 Hispanic/Latino; 4 Two or more races, non-Hispanic/Latino), 14 international. Average age 30. 153 applicants, 78% accepted, 51 enrolled. In 2017, 45 master's awarded. *Degree requirements:* For master's, thesis or alternative, internship. *Entrance requirements:* For master's, GRE General Test. Additional exam requirements/recommendations for international students: Required—TOEFL (minimum score 550 paper-based; 80 iBT), IELTS (minimum score 6.5). *Application deadline:* For fall admission, 1/15 for domestic and international students. Applications are processed on a rolling basis. Application fee: $85. Electronic applications accepted. *Expenses:* Contact institution. *Financial support:* Fellowships, research assistantships, teaching assistantships, career-related internships or fieldwork, Federal Work-Study, scholarships/grants, tuition waivers (full and partial), and unspecified assistantships available. Support available to part-time students. Financial award application deadline: 1/15. *Unit head:* Dr. Mary Davis, Graduate Program Director, 617-627-3394. *Application contact:* Office of Graduate Admissions, 617-627-3395, E-mail: gradadmissions@tufts.edu.
Website: http://ase.tufts.edu/uep/

Université de Montréal, Faculty of Environmental Design and Planning, Montréal, QC H3C 3J7, Canada. Offers environmental design and planning (M Sc A, PhD); environmental planning and design projects (DESS); game design (DESS); urban management for developing countries (DESS); urban planning (M Urb). DESS programs offered jointly with HEC Montreal and École Polytechnique de Montréal. *Accreditation:* ACSP. *Degree requirements:* For doctorate, thesis/dissertation, general exam. Electronic applications accepted. *Expenses:* Contact institution. *Faculty research:* Wayfinding, environmental evaluation, housing studies, urban design, urban and regional planning.

Université du Québec à Rimouski, Graduate Programs, Program in Regional Development, Rimouski, QC G5L 3A1, Canada. Offers MA, PhD, Diploma. PhD offered jointly with Université du Québec à Chicoutimi; Diploma with Université du Québec, École nationale d'administration publique. *Program availability:* Part-time. *Degree requirements:* For master's, thesis. *Entrance requirements:* For master's, appropriate bachelor's degree, proficiency in French.

Université du Québec en Outaouais, Graduate Programs, Program in Regional Development, Gatineau, QC J8X 3X7, Canada. Offers MA. *Program availability:* Part-time. *Degree requirements:* For master's, thesis (for some programs).

Université Laval, Faculty of Architecture, Planning and Visual Arts, Department of Regional Planning, Programs in Planning and Regional Development, Québec, QC G1K 7P4, Canada. Offers MATDR, PhD. Terminal master's awarded for partial completion of doctoral program. *Degree requirements:* For master's, thesis (for some programs); for doctorate, comprehensive exam, thesis/dissertation. *Entrance requirements:* For master's and doctorate, knowledge of French and English. Electronic applications accepted.

University at Albany, State University of New York, College of Arts and Sciences, Department of Geography and Planning, Albany, NY 12222-0001. Offers geographic information science (Certificate); geography (MA); regional planning (MRP); urban policy

(Certificate). *Program availability:* Part-time. *Faculty:* 13 full-time (3 women). *Students:* 32 full-time (13 women), 18 part-time (5 women); includes 9 minority (5 Black or African American, non-Hispanic/Latino; 2 Asian, non-Hispanic/Latino; 1 Hispanic/Latino; 1 Two or more races, non-Hispanic/Latino), 6 international. 46 applicants, 83% accepted, 21 enrolled. In 2017, 13 master's, 9 other advanced degrees awarded. *Entrance requirements:* Additional exam requirements/recommendations for international students: Required—TOEFL (minimum score 550 paper-based). *Application deadline:* For fall admission, 3/1 for domestic students, 5/1 for international students; for spring admission, 11/1 for international students. Applications are processed on a rolling basis. Application fee: $75. Electronic applications accepted. *Expenses:* Tuition, state resident: full-time $10,870; part-time $453 per credit hour. Tuition, nonresident: full-time $22,210; part-time $925 per credit hour. *Required fees:* $84.68 per credit hour. $508.06 per semester. Part-time tuition and fees vary according to course load and program. *Financial support:* Fellowships, teaching assistantships, career-related internships or fieldwork, Federal Work-Study, and institutionally sponsored loans available. Financial award application deadline: 3/1. *Faculty research:* Urban geography, social/cultural geography, urban planning, remote sensing, spatial analysis/geographic information systems. *Unit head:* Catherine Lawson, Chair, 518-442-4636, Fax: 518-442-4742, E-mail: lawsonc@albany.edu. *Application contact:* Michael DeRensis, Director, Graduate Admissions, 518-442-3980, Fax: 518-442-3922, E-mail: graduate@albany.edu.
Website: http://www.albany.edu/gp/

University at Buffalo, the State University of New York, Graduate School, School of Architecture and Planning, Department of Urban and Regional Planning, Buffalo, NY 12414. Offers community health and food systems (MUP); economic development (MUP); environment/land use (MUP); historic preservation (MUP, Certificate); neighborhood/community development (MUP); real estate development (MSRED); urban and regional planning (PhD); urban design (MUP); JD/MUP; M Arch/MUP. *Accreditation:* ACSP. *Program availability:* Part-time. *Faculty:* 13 full-time (6 women), 12 part-time/adjunct (3 women). *Students:* 76 full-time (27 women), 20 part-time (9 women); includes 17 minority (9 Black or African American, non-Hispanic/Latino; 5 Hispanic/Latino; 3 Two or more races, non-Hispanic/Latino), 20 international. Average age 27. 196 applicants, 20% accepted, 32 enrolled. In 2017, 35 master's, 1 doctorate, 5 other advanced degrees awarded. *Degree requirements:* For master's, thesis or alternative, project; for doctorate, comprehensive exam, thesis/dissertation. *Entrance requirements:* For master's, resume, three letters of recommendation, personal statement, transcripts; for doctorate, GRE, transcripts, three letters of recommendation, resume, research statement, writing sample. Additional exam requirements/recommendations for international students: Required—TOEFL (minimum score 79 iBT), IELTS (minimum score 6.5). *Application deadline:* For fall admission, 3/1 priority date for domestic and international students; for spring admission, 10/31 priority date for domestic students, 10/1 priority date for international students. Applications are processed on a rolling basis. Application fee: $75. Electronic applications accepted. *Expenses:* $13,382. *Financial support:* In 2017–18, 45 students received support, including 3 fellowships with full tuition reimbursements available (averaging $15,600 per year), 2 research assistantships with partial tuition reimbursements available (averaging $13,390 per year), 15 teaching assistantships with partial tuition reimbursements available (averaging $4,800 per year); career-related internships or fieldwork, Federal Work-Study, institutionally sponsored loans, scholarships/grants, health care benefits, and unspecified assistantships also available. Financial award application deadline: 3/1; financial award applicants required to submit FAFSA. *Faculty research:* Economic and international development, environmental and land use planning, GIS and spatial analysis, urban design and physical planning, neighborhood planning and community development, historic preservation. *Total annual research expenditures:* $1.3 million. *Unit head:* Dr. Daniel B. Hess, Professor and Chair, 716-829-3671 Ext. 109, Fax: 716-829-3256, E-mail: dbhess@buffalo.edu. *Application contact:* Donna Rogalski, Department Secretary, 716-829-3671, Fax: 716-829-3256, E-mail: dmr1@buffalo.edu.
Website: http://www.ap.buffalo.edu/planning/

The University of Arizona, College of Architecture, Planning, and Landscape Architecture, Planning Program, Tucson, AZ 85721. Offers MS. *Accreditation:* ACSP. *Entrance requirements:* For master's, GRE, 3 letters of recommendation, letter of intent. Additional exam requirements/recommendations for international students: Required—TOEFL (minimum score 573 paper-based; 80 iBT). Electronic applications accepted.

The University of British Columbia, Faculty of Applied Science, School of Community and Regional Planning, Vancouver, BC V6T 1Z2, Canada. Offers M Sc P, MAP, MCRP, PhD. *Accreditation:* ACSP. *Degree requirements:* For master's, thesis; for doctorate, thesis/dissertation, oral exam. *Entrance requirements:* For master's, GRE (recommended); for doctorate, MCRP or equivalent. Additional exam requirements/recommendations for international students: Required—TOEFL. Electronic applications accepted. *Expenses:* Contact institution. *Faculty research:* Natural resources management, international development, urban spatial, urban policy and community development planning.

University of California, Berkeley, Graduate Division, College of Environmental Design, Department of City and Regional Planning, Berkeley, CA 94720-1500. Offers MCP, PhD, JD/MCP, M Arch/MCP, MCP/MPH, MCP/MS, MLA/MCP. JD/MCP offered jointly with School of Law. *Accreditation:* ACSP. *Degree requirements:* For master's, comprehensive exam (for some programs), thesis (for some programs), professional project or thesis; for doctorate, thesis/dissertation, qualifying exam. *Entrance requirements:* For master's and doctorate, GRE General Test, minimum GPA of 3.0, 3 letters of recommendation. Additional exam requirements/recommendations for international students: Required—TOEFL (minimum score 570 paper-based; 90 iBT). Electronic applications accepted. *Faculty research:* Housing and project development, physical planning and design, community and economic development, geographic information systems, transportation.

University of California, Davis, Graduate Studies, Graduate Group in Community Development, Davis, CA 95616. Offers MS. *Degree requirements:* For master's, comprehensive exam (for some programs), thesis (for some programs). *Entrance requirements:* For master's, GRE General Test, minimum GPA of 3.0. Additional exam requirements/recommendations for international students: Required—TOEFL (minimum score 550 paper-based). Electronic applications accepted. *Faculty research:* Globalization; community economic change; urban and regional development; community planning design and sustainability; race, ethnic, and gender roles; community organization and political mobilization.

University of California, Irvine, School of Social Ecology, Department of Urban Planning and Public Policy, Irvine, CA 92697. Offers planning, policy and design (PhD); urban and regional planning (MURP). *Accreditation:* ACSP (one or more programs are accredited). *Students:* 116 full-time (62 women), 9 part-time (2 women); includes 55 minority (2 Black or African American, non-Hispanic/Latino; 17 Asian, non-Hispanic/Latino; 24 Hispanic/Latino; 1 Native Hawaiian or other Pacific Islander, non-Hispanic/Latino; 11 Two or more races, non-Hispanic/Latino), 38 international. Average age 28. 300 applicants, 66% accepted, 58 enrolled. In 2017, 49 master's, 6 doctorates awarded. *Degree requirements:* For doctorate, thesis/dissertation, research project. *Entrance requirements:* For master's and doctorate, GRE General Test, minimum GPA of 3.0. Additional exam requirements/recommendations for international students: Required—TOEFL (minimum score 550 paper-based). *Application deadline:* For fall admission, 1/15 priority date for domestic and international students. Application fee: $105 ($125 for international students). Electronic applications accepted. *Financial support:* Fellowships with tuition reimbursements, research assistantships with full tuition reimbursements, teaching assistantships with tuition reimbursements, institutionally sponsored loans, traineeships, health care benefits, and unspecified assistantships available. Financial award application deadline: 1/15; financial award applicants required to submit FAFSA. *Faculty research:* Community and social policy, economic development, land-use and growth management, transportation planning, environmental policy. *Unit head:* David L. Feldman, Chair, 949-824-4384, Fax: 949-824-3056, E-mail: feldmand@uci.edu. *Application contact:* Janet Gallagher, Graduate Coordinator, 949-824-9849, Fax: 949-824-8566, E-mail: janetg@uci.edu.
Website: http://uppp.soceco.uci.edu/

University of California, Los Angeles, Graduate Division, Luskin School of Public Affairs, Department of Urban Planning, Los Angeles, CA 90095. Offers MA, PhD, JD/MA, MA/MA, MBA/MA. *Accreditation:* ACSP (one or more programs are accredited). *Degree requirements:* For master's, comprehensive exam or thesis; for doctorate, thesis/dissertation, oral and written qualifying exams. *Entrance requirements:* For master's, GRE General Test (recommended); for doctorate, GRE General Test, master's degree in urban planning or related field. Additional exam requirements/recommendations for international students: Required—TOEFL. Electronic applications accepted. *Faculty research:* Industrial hazards, political economy of South and Southeast Asia, historic preservation, flexible production in U.S. and Western Europe, land-use controls.

University of Central Arkansas, Graduate School, College of Liberal Arts, Department of Geography, Conway, AR 72035-0001. Offers community and economic development (MS); geographic information systems (MGIS, Certificate). *Program availability:* Part-time, online learning. *Entrance requirements:* Additional exam requirements/recommendations for international students: Required—TOEFL (minimum score 550 paper-based). Electronic applications accepted.

University of Central Florida, College of Community Innovation and Education, School of Public Administration, Orlando, FL 32816. Offers emergency management and homeland security (Certificate); fundraising (Certificate); nonprofit management (MNM, Certificate); public administration (MPA); research administration (MRA); urban and regional planning (MS). *Accreditation:* NASPAA. *Program availability:* Part-time, evening/weekend. *Students:* 110 full-time (76 women), 290 part-time (215 women); includes 193 minority (96 Black or African American, non-Hispanic/Latino; 2 American Indian or Alaska Native, non-Hispanic/Latino; 13 Asian, non-Hispanic/Latino; 74 Hispanic/Latino; 8 Two or more races, non-Hispanic/Latino), 6 international. Average age 32. 255 applicants, 78% accepted, 152 enrolled. In 2017, 95 master's, 34 other advanced degrees awarded. *Degree requirements:* For master's, comprehensive exam, thesis or alternative, research report. *Entrance requirements:* For master's, letters of recommendation, goal statement, resume. Additional exam requirements/recommendations for international students: Required—TOEFL. *Application deadline:* For fall admission, 6/15 for domestic students; for spring admission, 11/1 for domestic students. Application fee: $30. Electronic applications accepted. *Expenses:* Tuition, state resident: part-time $288.16 per credit hour. Tuition, nonresident: part-time $1073.31 per credit hour. Tuition and fees vary according to program. *Financial support:* In 2017–18, 11 students received support, including 2 fellowships with partial tuition reimbursements available (averaging $5,300 per year), 6 research assistantships with partial tuition reimbursements available (averaging $9,637 per year), 3 teaching assistantships with partial tuition reimbursements available (averaging $9,390 per year); career-related internships or fieldwork, Federal Work-Study, institutionally sponsored loans, health care benefits, tuition waivers (partial), and unspecified assistantships also available. Financial award application deadline: 3/1; financial award applicants required to submit FAFSA. *Unit head:* Dr. Naim Kapucu, Director, 407-823-6096, Fax: 407-823-5651, E-mail: kapucu@ucf.edu. *Application contact:* Associate Director, Graduate Admissions, 407-823-2766, Fax: 407-823-6442, E-mail: gradadmissions@ucf.edu.
Website: https://www.cohpa.ucf.edu/publicadmin/

University of Central Oklahoma, The Jackson College of Graduate Studies, College of Liberal Arts, Department of Political Science, Edmond, OK 73034-5209. Offers political science (MA), including international affairs; public administration (MPA), including public and nonprofit management, urban management. *Program availability:* Part-time. *Faculty:* 11 full-time (4 women), 1 part-time/adjunct (0 women). *Students:* 42 full-time (21 women), 58 part-time (26 women); includes 33 minority (14 Black or African American, non-Hispanic/Latino; 3 American Indian or Alaska Native, non-Hispanic/Latino; 10 Hispanic/Latino; 6 Two or more races, non-Hispanic/Latino), 18 international. Average age 32. 127 applicants, 84% accepted, 29 enrolled. In 2017, 32 master's awarded. *Degree requirements:* For master's, comprehensive exam (for some programs), thesis (for some programs). *Entrance requirements:* For master's, 18 undergraduate hours in political science. Additional exam requirements/recommendations for international students: Required—TOEFL (minimum score 550 paper-based; 79 iBT), IELTS (minimum score 6.5). *Application deadline:* For fall admission, 7/15 for international students; for spring admission, 11/15 for international students. Applications are processed on a rolling basis. Application fee: $60. Electronic applications accepted. *Expenses:* Tuition, state resident: full-time $5375; part-time $268.75 per credit hour. Tuition, nonresident: full-time $13,295; part-time $664.75 per credit hour. *Required fees:* $626; $31.30 per credit hour. One-time fee: $50. Tuition and fees vary according to program. *Financial support:* In 2017–18, 20 students received support, including 3 research assistantships with partial tuition reimbursements available (averaging $3,943 per year), 4 teaching assistantships with partial tuition reimbursements available (averaging $7,394 per year); career-related internships or fieldwork, scholarships/grants, tuition waivers (partial), and unspecified assistantships also available. Financial award application deadline: 3/31; financial award applicants required to submit FAFSA. *Unit head:* Dr. Lou Furmanski, Department Chair, 405-974-5540, Fax: 405-974-3823. *Application contact:* Dr. Jan Hardt, Graduate Advisor, 405-974-5840, Fax: 405-974-3823, E-mail: gradcoll@uco.edu.
Website: http://sites.uco.edu/la/political-science/index.asp

University of Cincinnati, Graduate School, College of Design, Architecture, Art, and Planning, School of Planning, Program in Community Planning, Cincinnati, OH 45221. Offers MCP, JD/MCP. *Accreditation:* ACSP. *Degree requirements:* For master's, thesis. *Entrance requirements:* For master's, GRE General Test. Additional exam requirements/recommendations for international students: Required—TOEFL. *Expenses: Tuition, area resident:* Full-time $14,468. Tuition, state resident: full-time $14,968; part-time $754 per credit hour. Tuition, nonresident: full-time $24,210; part-time $1311 per credit hour. *International tuition:* $26,460 full-time. *Required fees:* $3958; $84 per credit hour. One-time fee: $85 full-time. Tuition and fees vary according to course load, degree level and program.

University of Colorado Denver, College of Architecture and Planning, Program in Design and Planning, Denver, CO 80217. Offers history of architecture, landscape and urbanism (PhD); sustainable and healthy environments (PhD). *Program availability:* Part-time. *Degree requirements:* For doctorate, comprehensive exam, thesis/dissertation. *Entrance requirements:* For doctorate, GRE (minimum score of 158 for both

verbal and quantitative; writing 4.0), minimum undergraduate GPA of 3.0, graduate 3.5; writing sample; three letters of recommendation; statement of personal and professional goals. Additional exam requirements/recommendations for international students: Required—TOEFL (minimum score 80 iBT); Recommended—IELTS (minimum score 6.8). Electronic applications accepted. *Expenses:* Contact institution. *Faculty research:* Land use and environmental planning and design; design and planning processes and practices; history, theory, and criticism of the built environment.

University of Colorado Denver, College of Architecture and Planning, Program in Urban and Regional Planning, Denver, CO 80217. Offers economic and community development planning (MURP); land use and environmental planning (MURP); urban place making (MURP). *Accreditation:* ACSP. *Program availability:* Part-time. *Degree requirements:* For master's, thesis, minimum of 51 semester hours. *Entrance requirements:* For master's, GRE (for students with an undergraduate GPA below 3.0), sample of writing or work project; statement of interest; resume; three letters of recommendation. Additional exam requirements/recommendations for international students: Required—TOEFL (minimum score 75 iBT). Electronic applications accepted. *Expenses:* Contact institution. *Faculty research:* Physical planning, environmental planning, economic development planning.

University of Detroit Mercy, School of Architecture, Detroit, MI 48221. Offers architecture (M Arch); community development (MA). *Entrance requirements:* For master's, BS in architecture, minimum GPA of 3.0, portfolio.

University of Florida, Graduate School, College of Design, Construction and Planning, Department of Urban and Regional Planning, Gainesville, FL 32611. Offers geographic information systems (MAURP); historic preservation (MAURP); sustainable design (MAURP); tropical conservation and development (MAURP); urban and regional planning (MAURP, MURP); wetland sciences (MAURP); JD/MAURP. *Accreditation:* ACSP (one or more programs are accredited). *Program availability:* Online learning. *Entrance requirements:* For master's, GRE General Test, minimum GPA of 3.0. Additional exam requirements/recommendations for international students: Required—TOEFL (minimum score 550 paper-based; 80 iBT), IELTS (minimum score 6). Electronic applications accepted. *Faculty research:* Planning and information systems, urban and environmental design, community and economic development, transportation and growth management.

University of Florida, Graduate School, College of Design, Construction and Planning, Doctoral Program in Design, Construction and Planning, Gainesville, FL 32611. Offers construction management (PhD); design, construction and planning (PhD); geographic information systems (PhD); historic preservation (PhD); interior design (PhD); landscape architecture (PhD); urban and regional planning (PhD). *Degree requirements:* For doctorate, thesis/dissertation. *Entrance requirements:* For doctorate, GRE General Test, minimum GPA of 3.0. Additional exam requirements/recommendations for international students: Required—TOEFL (minimum score 550 paper-based; 80 iBT), IELTS (minimum score 6). Electronic applications accepted. *Faculty research:* Architecture, building construction, urban and regional planning.

University of Hawaii at Manoa, Office of Graduate Education, College of Social Sciences, Department of Urban and Regional Planning, Honolulu, HI 96822. Offers community planning (MURP); disaster management and humanitarian assistance (Graduate Certificate); environmental planning and sustainability (MURP); international development planning (MURP); land use, transportation and infrastructure planning (MURP); planning studies (Graduate Certificate); urban and regional planning (PhD, Graduate Certificate). *Accreditation:* ACSP. *Program availability:* Part-time. *Entrance requirements:* For master's, GRE General Test, minimum GPA of 3.0; for doctorate, GRE General Test. Additional exam requirements/recommendations for international students: Required—TOEFL (minimum score 500 paper-based; 61 iBT), IELTS (minimum score 5).

University of Idaho, College of Graduate Studies, College of Art and Architecture, Program in Bioregional Planning and Community Design, Moscow, ID 83844. Offers MS. *Faculty:* 2. *Students:* 4. In 2017, 2 master's awarded. *Entrance requirements:* For master's, GRE or LSAT, minimum GPA of 3.0. Additional exam requirements/recommendations for international students: Required—TOEFL (minimum score 550 paper-based; 79 iBT), IELTS (minimum score 6.5), Michigan English Language Assessment Battery (minimum score of 77). *Application deadline:* Applications are processed on a rolling basis. Application fee: $60. Electronic applications accepted. *Expenses:* Tuition, state resident: full-time $6722; part-time $430 per credit hour. Tuition, nonresident: full-time $23,046; part-time $1337 per credit hour. *Required fees:* $2142; $63 per credit hour. *Financial support:* Applicants required to submit FAFSA. *Faculty research:* Environment and behavior interaction, geographic trade, design development, economic development, natural resource policy. *Unit head:* Dr. Shauna Corry, Interim Dean, 208-885-4409, E-mail: bioregionalplanning@uidaho.edu. *Application contact:* Sean Scoggin, Graduate Recruitment Coordinator, 208-885-4001, Fax: 208-805-4406, E-mail: graduateadmissions@uidaho.edu.
Website: http://www.uidaho.edu/caa/programs/biop

University of Illinois at Chicago, College of Urban Planning and Public Affairs, Department of Urban Planning and Policy, Chicago, IL 60607-7128. Offers MUPP, PhD. *Accreditation:* ACSP (one or more programs are accredited). *Program availability:* Part-time. *Degree requirements:* For master's, thesis or alternative, internship; for doctorate, thesis/dissertation. *Entrance requirements:* For master's and doctorate, GRE General Test, minimum GPA of 2.75, writing sample. Additional exam requirements/recommendations for international students: Required—TOEFL. Electronic applications accepted. *Expenses:* Contact institution. *Faculty research:* Urban and regional economic and workforce development issues, current policy issues and social trends, racial justice and related issues of poverty, quality of life of people living in Chicago and other great cities of the world.

University of Illinois at Urbana–Champaign, Graduate College, College of Fine and Applied Arts, Department of Urban and Regional Planning, Champaign, IL 61820. Offers regional planning (PhD); urban planning (MUP); JD/MUP; M Arch/MUP; MLA/MUP. *Accreditation:* ACSP (one or more programs are accredited).

The University of Iowa, Graduate College, Program in Urban and Regional Planning, Iowa City, IA 52242-1316. Offers MA, MS, JD/MA, MHA/MA, MHA/MS, MS/MA, MS/MS, MSW/MA, MSW/MS. *Accreditation:* ACSP. *Degree requirements:* For master's, thesis optional, portfolio. *Entrance requirements:* For master's, GRE General Test, minimum GPA of 3.0. Additional exam requirements/recommendations for international students: Required—TOEFL (minimum score 600 paper-based; 100 iBT). Electronic applications accepted.

The University of Kansas, Graduate Studies, College of Liberal Arts and Sciences, School of Public Affairs and Administration, Urban Planning Program, Lawrence, KS 66045. Offers MUP. *Accreditation:* ACSP. *Program availability:* Part-time. *Students:* 32 full-time (14 women), 2 part-time (both women); includes 7 minority (1 Black or African American, non-Hispanic/Latino; 5 Hispanic/Latino; 1 Two or more races, non-Hispanic/Latino), 5 international. Average age 28. 42 applicants, 74% accepted, 17 enrolled. In 2017, 15 master's awarded. *Entrance requirements:* For master's, GRE, three letters of reference, resume, statement of career goals and substantive interests in urban planning, official transcripts. Additional exam requirements/recommendations for international students: Required—TOEFL (minimum score 570 paper-based). *Application deadline:* For fall admission, 7/1 for domestic students, 6/1 for international students; for spring admission, 12/1 for domestic students, 11/1 for international students. Application fee: $65 ($85 for international students). Electronic applications accepted. *Financial support:* Fellowships, research assistantships, teaching assistantships, career-related internships or fieldwork, scholarships/grants, and unspecified assistantships available. Financial award application deadline: 2/15; financial award applicants required to submit FAFSA. *Faculty research:* Environmental land use, housing and economic development, community development and transportation, urban mass transportation, urban sprawl. *Unit head:* Stacey M. Swearingen White, Chair, 785-864-3530, E-mail: sswhite@ku.edu. *Application contact:* Pat Owens, Graduate Admission Contact, 785-864-4184, E-mail: ubpl@ku.edu.
Website: http://urbanplanning.ku.edu/

University of Louisville, Graduate School, College of Arts and Sciences, Department of Urban and Public Affairs, Louisville, KY 40208. Offers public administration (MPA), including human resources management, non-profit management, public policy and administration; urban and public affairs (PhD), including urban planning and development, urban policy and administration; urban planning (MUP), including administration of planning organizations, housing and community development, land use and environmental planning, spatial analysis. *Program availability:* Part-time, evening/weekend. *Faculty:* 12 full-time (5 women), 4 part-time/adjunct (1 woman). *Students:* 50 full-time (19 women), 20 part-time (17 women); includes 17 minority (6 Black or African American, non-Hispanic/Latino; 1 Asian, non-Hispanic/Latino; 4 Hispanic/Latino; 6 Two or more races, non-Hispanic/Latino), 4 international. Average age 31. 47 applicants, 70% accepted, 22 enrolled. In 2017, 20 master's, 2 doctorates awarded. Terminal master's awarded for partial completion of doctoral program. *Degree requirements:* For master's, internship; for doctorate, comprehensive exam, thesis/dissertation. *Entrance requirements:* For master's, GRE General Test, minimum GPA of 3.0; for doctorate, GRE General Test, master's degree in appropriate field. Additional exam requirements/recommendations for international students: Required—TOEFL (minimum score 550 paper-based; 79 iBT). *Application deadline:* Applications are processed on a rolling basis. Application fee: $65. *Expenses:* Contact institution. *Financial support:* Fellowships, research assistantships, tuition waivers (full and partial), and unspecified assistantships available. Financial award application deadline: 2/1. *Faculty research:* Urban theory, sustainability, public administration, urban planning, urban management. *Total annual research expenditures:* $240,308. *Unit head:* Dr. David Simpson, Chair, 502-852-8019, Fax: 502-852-4558, E-mail: dave.simpson@louisville.edu. *Application contact:* Latonia Craig, Director of Graduate Recruitment and Diversity Retention, 502-852-5207, Fax: 502-852-4558, E-mail: gradadm@louisville.edu.
Website: http://supa.louisville.edu

University of Manitoba, Faculty of Graduate Studies, Faculty of Architecture, Department of City Planning, Winnipeg, MB R3T 2N2, Canada. Offers MCP. *Degree requirements:* For master's, thesis.

University of Maryland, College Park, Academic Affairs, School of Architecture, Planning and Preservation, Program in Urban Studies and Planning, College Park, MD 20742. Offers urban and regional planning/design (PhD); urban studies and planning (MCP). *Accreditation:* ACSP. *Program availability:* Part-time, evening/weekend. *Entrance requirements:* For master's and doctorate, GRE General Test, minimum GPA of 3.0, 3 letters of recommendation. Additional exam requirements/recommendations for international students: Required—TOEFL. Electronic applications accepted. *Faculty research:* Policy analysis, urban planning, program planning and management, economic development planning.

University of Massachusetts Amherst, Graduate School, College of Social and Behavioral Sciences, Department of Landscape Architecture and Regional Planning, Dual Degree Program in Landscape Architecture and Regional Planning, Amherst, MA 01003. Offers MLA/MRP. *Accreditation:* ACSP; ASLA. *Program availability:* Part-time. *Entrance requirements:* Additional exam requirements/recommendations for international students: Required—TOEFL (minimum score 550 paper-based; 80 iBT), IELTS (minimum score 6.5). Electronic applications accepted.

University of Massachusetts Amherst, Graduate School, College of Social and Behavioral Sciences, Department of Landscape Architecture and Regional Planning, Program in Regional Planning, Amherst, MA 01003. Offers MRP, PhD, M Arch/MRP, MRP/MPPA. *Accreditation:* ACSP (one or more programs are accredited). *Program availability:* Part-time. Terminal master's awarded for partial completion of doctoral program. *Degree requirements:* For master's, thesis or alternative; for doctorate, comprehensive exam, thesis/dissertation. *Entrance requirements:* For master's and doctorate, GRE General Test. Additional exam requirements/recommendations for international students: Required—TOEFL (minimum score 550 paper-based; 80 iBT), IELTS (minimum score 6.5). Electronic applications accepted.

University of Massachusetts Amherst, Graduate School, Interdisciplinary Programs, Dual Degree Program in Regional Planning and Public Policy and Administration, Amherst, MA 01003. Offers MPPA/MRP. *Entrance requirements:* Additional exam requirements/recommendations for international students: Required—TOEFL (minimum score 550 paper-based; 80 iBT), IELTS (minimum score 6.5). Electronic applications accepted.

University of Massachusetts Boston, School for the Environment, Program in Urban Planning and Community Development, Boston, MA 02125-3393. Offers MS. *Students:* 13 full-time (6 women), 15 part-time (5 women); includes 9 minority (4 Black or African American, non-Hispanic/Latino; 3 Hispanic/Latino; 2 Two or more races, non-Hispanic/Latino), 4 international. Average age 30. 24 applicants, 67% accepted, 10 enrolled. *Expenses:* Tuition, state resident: full-time $17,375. Tuition, nonresident: full-time $33,915. *Required fees:* $355. *Unit head:* Dr. William Hagar, Interim Dean, 617-287-5777. *Application contact:* Graduate Admissions Coordinator, 617-287-6400, Fax: 617-287-6236, E-mail: bos.gadm@dpc.umassp.edu.

University of Massachusetts Lowell, College of Fine Arts, Humanities and Social Sciences, Program in Regional Economic and Social Development, Lowell, MA 01854. Offers MA, Graduate Certificate. *Program availability:* Part-time. *Entrance requirements:* For master's, GRE. Electronic applications accepted.

University of Memphis, Graduate School, College of Arts and Sciences, Department of City and Regional Planning, Memphis, TN 38152. Offers MCRP. *Accreditation:* ACSP. *Faculty:* 3 full-time (1 woman), 3 part-time/adjunct (0 women). *Students:* 22 full-time (12 women), 4 part-time (3 women); includes 3 minority (2 Black or African American, non-Hispanic/Latino; 1 Hispanic/Latino), 1 international. Average age 28. 16 applicants, 75% accepted, 10 enrolled. In 2017, 8 master's awarded. *Entrance requirements:* For master's, GRE General Test or MAT, personal statement, resume. Additional exam requirements/recommendations for international students: Required—TOEFL (minimum score 550 paper-based; 79 iBT). *Application deadline:* For fall admission, 4/15 priority date for domestic students; for spring admission, 12/1 for domestic students. Applications are processed on a rolling basis. Application fee: $35 ($60 for international students). Electronic applications accepted. *Expenses:* Contact institution. *Financial support:* In 2017–18, 14 students received support. Research assistantships, career-related internships or fieldwork, Federal Work-Study, scholarships/grants, and

unspecified assistantships available. Financial award application deadline: 2/1; financial award applicants required to submit FAFSA. *Faculty research:* Growth planning, site design, economic development, housing, smart growth. *Unit head:* Dr. Charles Santo, Chair/Director, 901-678-2161, Fax: 901-678-4162, E-mail: casanto@memphis.edu. Website: http://www.memphis.edu/planning/.

University of Michigan, Taubman College of Architecture and Urban Planning, Master of Urban and Regional Planning Program, Ann Arbor, MI 48109. Offers MURP. *Accreditation:* ACSP. *Degree requirements:* For master's, thesis or alternative. *Entrance requirements:* Additional exam requirements/recommendations for international students: Required—TOEFL (minimum score 83 iBT), GRE. Electronic applications accepted. *Expenses:* Contact institution. *Faculty research:* Housing community and economic development, transportation planning, physical planning and urban design, planning in developing countries, land use and environmental planning.

University of Michigan, Taubman College of Architecture and Urban Planning, Urban and Regional Planning PhD Program, Ann Arbor, MI 48109. Offers PhD. *Accreditation:* ACSP. *Degree requirements:* For doctorate, comprehensive exam, thesis/dissertation. *Entrance requirements:* Additional exam requirements/recommendations for international students: Required—TOEFL (minimum score 83 iBT), GRE. Electronic applications accepted. *Expenses:* Tuition, state resident: full-time $22,368; part-time $1201 per credit hour. Tuition, nonresident: full-time $45,156; part-time $2467 per credit hour. *Required fees:* $376 per term. Tuition and fees vary according to course load, degree level and program.

University of Minnesota, Twin Cities Campus, Graduate School, Humphrey School of Public Affairs, PhD Program in Public Affairs, Minneapolis, MN 55455. Offers management and governance (PhD); public policy (PhD); science, technology, and environmental policy (PhD); urban planning (PhD). *Program availability:* Part-time. *Degree requirements:* For doctorate, comprehensive exam, thesis/dissertation. *Entrance requirements:* For doctorate, GRE General Test. Additional exam requirements/recommendations for international students: Required—TOEFL (minimum score 650 paper-based; 100 iBT), IELTS (minimum score 7). Electronic applications accepted. *Expenses:* Contact institution. *Faculty research:* Public policy, urban/regional planning, public/nonprofit management and governance, science/technology/environmental policy.

University of Minnesota, Twin Cities Campus, Graduate School, Humphrey School of Public Affairs, Program in Urban and Regional Planning, Minneapolis, MN 55455. Offers MURP, JD/MURP, MURP/MPH, MURP/MS, MURP/MSW. *Accreditation:* ACSP (one or more programs are accredited). *Program availability:* Part-time. *Degree requirements:* For master's, thesis or alternative, internship or equivalent work experience. *Entrance requirements:* For master's, GRE General Test, minimum undergraduate GPA of 3.0. Additional exam requirements/recommendations for international students: Required—TOEFL (minimum score 600 paper-based; 100 iBT), IELTS (minimum score 7). Electronic applications accepted. *Expenses:* Contact institution. *Faculty research:* Policy planning, resource allocation planning, regulatory planning, program planning, project planning.

University of Nebraska–Lincoln, Graduate College, College of Agricultural Sciences and Natural Resources, Department of Agricultural Economics, Lincoln, NE 68588. Offers agribusiness (MBA); agricultural economics (MS, PhD); community development (M Ag). *Degree requirements:* For master's, thesis optional; for doctorate, comprehensive exam, thesis/dissertation. *Entrance requirements:* For master's and doctorate, GRE General Test. Additional exam requirements/recommendations for international students: Required—TOEFL (minimum score 550 paper-based). Electronic applications accepted. *Faculty research:* Marketing and agribusiness, production economics, resource law, international trade and development, rural policy and revitalization.

University of Nebraska–Lincoln, Graduate College, College of Architecture, Department of Community and Regional Planning, Lincoln, NE 68588. Offers MCRP, JD/MCRP, M Arch/MCRP, MCRP/MSCE. *Accreditation:* ACSP. *Degree requirements:* For master's, thesis optional. *Entrance requirements:* For master's, GRE General Test. Additional exam requirements/recommendations for international students: Required—TOEFL (minimum score 550 paper-based). Electronic applications accepted. *Faculty research:* Economic development, community development and improvement, social planning, land use planning, physical planning, environmental planning.

University of New Brunswick Fredericton, School of Graduate Studies, Policy Studies Program, Fredericton, NB E3B 5A3, Canada. Offers citizen engagement/dispute resolution (M Phil); community development (M Phil); international development (M Phil); leadership (M Phil); sustainability/environmental issues (M Phil); worldviews (M Phil). *Program availability:* Part-time. *Degree requirements:* For master's, thesis, report. *Entrance requirements:* For master's, minimum GPA of 3.5. Additional exam requirements/recommendations for international students: Required—TWE (minimum score 5.5), TOEFL (minimum score 600 paper-based; 100 iBT) or IELTS (minimum score 7). Electronic applications accepted. *Faculty research:* International development, worldviews, citizenship/dispute resolution, sustainability/environmental issues, leadership, community development.

University of New Mexico, Graduate Studies, School of Architecture and Planning, Program in Community and Regional Planning, Albuquerque, NM 87131-2039. Offers MCRP, MCRP/MA, MPA/MCRP. *Accreditation:* ACSP. *Program availability:* Part-time. *Faculty:* 13 full-time (8 women), 4 part-time/adjunct (2 women). *Students:* 31 full-time (18 women), 28 part-time (14 women); includes 36 minority (12 American Indian or Alaska Native, non-Hispanic/Latino; 21 Hispanic/Latino; 3 Two or more races, non-Hispanic/Latino), 5 international. Average age 34. 33 applicants, 85% accepted, 17 enrolled. In 2017, 21 master's awarded. *Entrance requirements:* For master's, minimum GPA of 3.0 in last two years of graduate study, 3 letters of recommendation, letter of intent, resume, copies of all official transcripts. Additional exam requirements/recommendations for international students: Required—TOEFL (minimum score 550 paper-based; 79 iBT). *Application deadline:* For fall admission, 1/30 priority date for domestic students, 1/30 for international students. Application fee: $50. Electronic applications accepted. *Financial support:* Fellowships, research assistantships with partial tuition reimbursements, teaching assistantships with partial tuition reimbursements, career-related internships or fieldwork, Federal Work-Study, institutionally sponsored loans, scholarships/grants, health care benefits, tuition waivers (full), and unspecified assistantships available. Support available to part-time students. Financial award application deadline: 3/1; financial award applicants required to submit FAFSA. *Faculty research:* Community development, urban and ecological design, land economics, community-based planning, environmental dispute resolution, environmental justice, indigenous planning, watershed management. *Unit head:* Dr. Teresa L. Cordova, Program Director, 505-277-3922, Fax: 505-277-0076, E-mail: tcordova@unm.edu. *Application contact:* Elizabeth M. Rowe, Senior Academic Advisor, 505-277-1303, Fax: 505-277-0076, E-mail: erowe@unm.edu. Website: http://www.unm.edu/~crp

University of New Orleans, Graduate School, College of Liberal Arts, Department of Planning and Urban Studies, Program in Urban and Regional Planning, New Orleans, LA 70148. Offers MURP. *Accreditation:* ACSP. *Degree requirements:* For master's, thesis. *Entrance requirements:* For master's, GRE General Test. Additional exam requirements/recommendations for international students: Required—TOEFL (minimum score 550 paper-based; 79 iBT), IELTS (minimum score 6.5). Electronic applications accepted. *Faculty research:* Urban economic development, environmental planning and analysis, social and cultural change.

The University of North Carolina at Chapel Hill, Graduate School, College of Arts and Sciences, Department of City and Regional Planning, Chapel Hill, NC 27599-3140. Offers city and regional planning (MCRP); planning (PhD); public policy analysis (PhD); JD/MCRP; MBA/MCRP; MPA/MCRP. *Accreditation:* ACSP (one or more programs are accredited). *Degree requirements:* For master's, project; for doctorate, comprehensive exam, thesis/dissertation. *Entrance requirements:* For master's and doctorate, GRE General Test. Additional exam requirements/recommendations for international students: Required—TOEFL (minimum score 550 paper-based). Electronic applications accepted. *Faculty research:* Developing areas, transportation, affordable housing, growth management, coastal zone management.

The University of North Carolina at Charlotte, College of Liberal Arts and Sciences, Department of Political Science and Public Administration, Charlotte, NC 28223-0001. Offers emergency management (Graduate Certificate); non-profit management (Graduate Certificate); public administration (MPA), including arts administration, emergency management, non-profit management, public budgeting and finance, urban management and policy; public budgeting and finance (Graduate Certificate); urban management and policy (Graduate Certificate). *Accreditation:* NASPAA. *Program availability:* Part-time, evening/weekend. *Faculty:* 19 full-time (9 women), 4 part-time/adjunct (1 woman). *Students:* 20 full-time (11 women), 61 part-time (41 women); includes 21 minority (12 Black or African American, non-Hispanic/Latino; 2 American Indian or Alaska Native, non-Hispanic/Latino; 1 Asian, non-Hispanic/Latino; 4 Hispanic/Latino; 2 Two or more races, non-Hispanic/Latino), 1 international. Average age 28. 48 applicants, 67% accepted, 22 enrolled. In 2017, 25 master's, 15 other advanced degrees awarded. *Degree requirements:* For master's, research project or thesis. *Entrance requirements:* For master's, GRE General Test, bachelor's degree, or its equivalent, from accredited college or university; minimum undergraduate GPA of 3.0; 3 letters of recommendation; statement of purpose; for Graduate Certificate, statement of purpose (1-2 pages in length) explaining applicant's career goals, how the Graduate Certificate fits into achieving those goals, and any relevant work experience; official transcripts; letters of recommendation. Additional exam requirements/recommendations for international students: Required—TOEFL (minimum score 523 paper-based, 70 iBT) or IELTS (6.5). *Application deadline:* For fall admission, 8/1 for domestic and international students; for spring admission, 12/1 for domestic and international students. Applications are processed on a rolling basis. Application fee: $75. Electronic applications accepted. *Expenses:* Tuition, state resident: full-time $4337. Tuition, nonresident: full-time $17,771. *Required fees:* $3211. Tuition and fees vary according to course load and program. *Financial support:* In 2017–18, 14 students received support, including 13 research assistantships (averaging $9,015 per year), 1 teaching assistantship (averaging $19,500 per year); career-related internships or fieldwork, Federal Work-Study, institutionally sponsored loans, scholarships/grants, and unspecified assistantships also available. Support available to part-time students. Financial award application deadline: 3/1; financial award applicants required to submit FAFSA. *Total annual research expenditures:* $419,411. *Unit head:* Dr. Greg Weeks, Chair, 704-687-7574, E-mail: gbweeks@uncc.edu. *Application contact:* Kathy B. Giddings, Director of Graduate Admissions, 704-687-5503, Fax: 704-687-1668, E-mail: gradadm@uncc.edu. Website: http://politicalscience.uncc.edu/

University of Oklahoma, Christopher C. Gibbs College of Architecture, Division of Architecture, Norman, OK 73019. Offers architecture (MS); data and digital representation (M Arch); design entrepreneurship and real estate (M Arch); planning, design and construction (PhD); resilient planning, design, and construction (M Arch). *Program availability:* Part-time. *Faculty:* 32 full-time (12 women), 2 part-time/adjunct (0 women). *Students:* 33 full-time (22 women), 9 part-time (2 women); includes 6 minority (2 Black or African American, non-Hispanic/Latino; 1 American Indian or Alaska Native, non-Hispanic/Latino; 1 Hispanic/Latino; 2 Two or more races, non-Hispanic/Latino), 13 international. Average age 29. 25 applicants, 72% accepted, 11 enrolled. In 2017, 7 master's awarded. Terminal master's awarded for partial completion of doctoral program. *Degree requirements:* For master's, variable foreign language requirement; for doctorate, variable foreign language requirement, comprehensive exam, thesis/dissertation. *Entrance requirements:* Additional exam requirements/recommendations for international students: Required—TOEFL (minimum score 79 iBT) or IELTS (minimum score 6.5). *Application deadline:* For spring admission, 5/1 for domestic students, 3/1 for international students. Applications are processed on a rolling basis. Application fee: $50 ($100 for international students). Electronic applications accepted. *Expenses:* Tuition, state resident: full-time $5119; part-time $213.30 per credit hour. Tuition, nonresident: full-time $19,778; part-time $824.10 per credit hour. *Required fees:* $3458; $133.55 per credit hour. $126.50 per semester. *Financial support:* In 2017–18, 34 students received support, including 17 research assistantships with partial tuition reimbursements available (averaging $12,585 per year), 1 teaching assistantship with partial tuition reimbursement available (averaging $10,372 per year); career-related internships or fieldwork, scholarships/grants, health care benefits, tuition waivers, and unspecified assistantships also available. Financial award application deadline: 6/1; financial award applicants required to submit FAFSA. *Faculty research:* Resiliency and sustainability; data and digital representation; design entrepreneurship and real estate. *Unit head:* Dr. Stephanie Pilat, Director, 405-325-9352, Fax: 405-325-7588, E-mail: architecture.director@ou.edu. *Application contact:* Marjorie Callahan, Graduate Liaison, Fax: 405-325-7588, E-mail: mcallahan@ou.edu. Website: http://arch.coa.ou.edu

University of Oklahoma, Christopher C. Gibbs College of Architecture, Division of Regional and City Planning, Norman, OK 73019. Offers community development (MRCP); physical planning (MRCP); MRCP/MLA. *Accreditation:* ACSP. *Program availability:* Part-time. *Students:* 24 full-time (12 women), 2 part-time (both women); includes 2 minority (1 American Indian or Alaska Native, non-Hispanic/Latino; 1 Hispanic/Latino), 6 international. Average age 27. 19 applicants, 89% accepted, 12 enrolled. In 2017, 15 master's awarded. Terminal master's awarded for partial completion of doctoral program. *Degree requirements:* For master's, comprehensive exam or thesis. *Entrance requirements:* Additional exam requirements/recommendations for international students: Required—TOEFL (minimum score 79 iBT) or IELTS (minimum score 6.5). *Application deadline:* For fall admission, 4/1 priority date for international students. Applications are processed on a rolling basis. Application fee: $50 ($100 for international students). Electronic applications accepted. *Expenses:* Tuition, state resident: full-time $5119; part-time $213.30 per credit hour. Tuition, nonresident: full-time $19,778; part-time $824.10 per credit hour. *Required fees:* $3458; $133.55 per credit hour. $126.50 per semester. *Financial support:* In 2017–18, 20 students received support, including 1 fellowship (averaging $5,000 per year), 7 research assistantships with full tuition reimbursements available (averaging $13,502 per year); teaching assistantships with full tuition reimbursements available, career-related internships or fieldwork, Federal Work-Study, scholarships/grants, health care benefits, tuition waivers, and unspecified assistantships also available. Financial award application deadline: 6/1; financial award applicants required to submit FAFSA. *Faculty research:* Food systems planning, the built environment and public health, community revitalization and minority communities, freight modeling. *Unit head:* Dr. Charles Warnken, Director, 405-325-2444, Fax: 405-325-7558, E-mail: cwarnken@ou.edu. Website: http://www.ou.edu/architecture/regional_city_planning.html

University of Oklahoma, Christopher C. Gibbs College of Architecture, Haskell and Irene Lemon Division of Construction Science, Norman, OK 73019. Offers construction management (MS); construction science (MCM); planning, design, and construction (PhD), including construction. *Program availability:* Part-time. *Students:* 19 full-time (5 women), 5 part-time (3 women); includes 7 minority (2 Black or African American, non-Hispanic/Latino; 3 Hispanic/Latino; 2 Two or more races, non-Hispanic/Latino), 9 international. Average age 32. 19 applicants, 74% accepted, 8 enrolled. In 2017, 10 master's awarded. Terminal master's awarded for partial completion of doctoral program. *Degree requirements:* For master's, thesis optional, special project; for doctorate, thesis/dissertation. *Entrance requirements:* For master's, minimum GPA of 3.5. Additional exam requirements/recommendations for international students: Required—TOEFL (minimum score 79 iBT) or IELTS (minimum score 6.5). Application fee: $50 ($100 for international students). Electronic applications accepted. *Expenses:* Tuition, state resident: full-time $5119; part-time $213.30 per credit hour. Tuition, nonresident: full-time $19,778; part-time $824.10 per credit hour. *Required fees:* $3458; $133.55 per credit hour. $126.50 per semester. *Financial support:* In 2017–18, 19 students received support, including 8 research assistantships with full and partial tuition reimbursements available (averaging $11,219 per year), 1 teaching assistantship with full and partial tuition reimbursement available (averaging $13,500 per year); fellowships with full and partial tuition reimbursements available, career-related internships or fieldwork, and scholarships/grants also available. Financial award application deadline: 6/1; financial award applicants required to submit FAFSA. *Faculty research:* Lean construction, construction safety, building information modeling, construction risk management, housing. *Unit head:* Ben Bigelow, Director, 405-325-6404, E-mail: bigelow@ou.edu. *Application contact:* Anthony Perrenoud, Graduate Liaison, 405-325-2674, E-mail: perrenoud@ou.edu.
Website: http://cns.ou.edu

University of Oregon, Graduate School, College of Design, School of Planning, Public Policy and Management, Program in Community and Regional Planning, Eugene, OR 97403. Offers MCRP. *Accreditation:* ACSP. *Program availability:* Part-time. *Degree requirements:* For master's, thesis or alternative. *Entrance requirements:* For master's, minimum GPA of 3.0. Additional exam requirements/recommendations for international students: Required—TOEFL. *Faculty research:* Community economic development, tourism, families in poverty.

University of Pennsylvania, School of Design, Department of City and Regional Planning, Philadelphia, PA 19104. Offers city and regional planning (PhD); city planning (MCP); GIS and spatial analysis (Certificate); land preservation (Certificate); urban design (Certificate); urban redevelopment (Certificate); urban spatial analytics (MUSA). *Accreditation:* ACSP (one or more programs are accredited). *Program availability:* Part-time. *Faculty:* 16 full-time (8 women), 3 part-time/adjunct (0 women). *Students:* 148 full-time (83 women), 5 part-time (2 women); includes 22 minority (5 Black or African American, non-Hispanic/Latino; 8 Asian, non-Hispanic/Latino; 6 Hispanic/Latino; 1 Native Hawaiian or other Pacific Islander, non-Hispanic/Latino; 2 Two or more races, non-Hispanic/Latino), 56 international. Average age 27. 395 applicants, 62% accepted, 101 enrolled. In 2017, 65 master's, 5 doctorates, 7 other advanced degrees awarded. *Degree requirements:* For doctorate, thesis/dissertation. *Entrance requirements:* Additional exam requirements/recommendations for international students: Required—TOEFL (minimum score 100 iBT); Recommended—IELTS (minimum score 7), TSE (minimum score 68). *Application deadline:* For spring admission, 1/12 for domestic students. Application fee: $80. Electronic applications accepted. *Financial support:* In 2017–18, 39 teaching assistantships (averaging $2,000 per year) were awarded; fellowships, research assistantships, and Federal Work-Study also available. Financial award application deadline: 2/15; financial award applicants required to submit FAFSA. *Faculty research:* Transportation planning, community and economic development, public private development, land use and environmental planning, urban design. *Unit head:* Dr. John Landis, Department Chair, 215-746-2340, E-mail: jlan@design.upenn.edu. *Application contact:* Roslynne Carter, Administrative Assistant, 215-898-8330, Fax: 215-898-5730, E-mail: admissions@design.upenn.edu.
Website: https://www.design.upenn.edu/city-regional-planning

University of Pittsburgh, Graduate School of Public and International Affairs, Master of International Development Program, Pittsburgh, PA 15260. Offers energy and environment (MID); governance and international public management (MID); human security (MID); nongovernmental organizations and civil society (MID); urban affairs and planning (MID); MID/JD; MID/MBA; MID/MPH; MID/MSIS; MID/MSW. *Program availability:* Part-time, evening/weekend. *Faculty:* 30 full-time (11 women), 14 part-time/adjunct (5 women). *Students:* 55 full-time (45 women), 6 part-time (4 women); includes 11 minority (4 Black or African American, non-Hispanic/Latino; 4 Asian, non-Hispanic/Latino; 3 Hispanic/Latino), 9 international. Average age 28. 71 applicants, 90% accepted, 10 enrolled. In 2017, 30 master's awarded. *Degree requirements:* For master's, thesis optional, capstone seminar. *Entrance requirements:* For master's, GRE General Test or GMAT, 2 letters of recommendation; undergraduate transcripts; resume; personal statement. Additional exam requirements/recommendations for international students: Required—TOEFL (minimum score 80 iBT); Recommended—IELTS (minimum score 7). *Application deadline:* For fall admission, 2/1 priority date for domestic students, 1/15 for international students; for spring admission, 11/1 priority date for domestic students, 8/1 for international students. Application fee: $50. Electronic applications accepted. *Expenses:* $23,140 per year in-state, $37,830 out-of-state. *Financial support:* In 2017–18, 38 students received support, including 2 fellowships with full tuition reimbursements available (averaging $37,000 per year), 3 research assistantships with full tuition reimbursements available (averaging $37,000 per year); career-related internships or fieldwork and scholarships/grants also available. Financial award application deadline: 2/1; financial award applicants required to submit FAFSA. *Faculty research:* Nongovernmental organizations and civil society, energy and environment, human security, urban affairs and planning, governance and international public management. *Total annual research expenditures:* $1.6 million. *Unit head:* Dr. John Keeler, Dean, 412-648-7605, Fax: 412-648-7601, E-mail: gspia@pitt.edu. *Application contact:* Dr. Michael Rizzi, Director of Student Services, 412-648-7640, Fax: 412-648-7641, E-mail: rizzim@pitt.edu.
Website: http://www.gspia.pitt.edu/

University of Pittsburgh, Graduate School of Public and International Affairs, Master of Public Administration Program, Pittsburgh, PA 15260. Offers energy and environment (MPA); governance and international public management (MPA); policy research and analysis (MPA); public and nonprofit management (MPA); urban affairs and planning (MPA); JD/MPA; MPH/MPA; MSIS/MPA; MSW/MPA. *Accreditation:* NASPAA. *Program availability:* Part-time, evening/weekend. *Faculty:* 30 full-time (11 women), 14 part-time/adjunct (5 women). *Students:* 100 full-time (75 women), 18 part-time (12 women); includes 13 minority (6 Black or African American, non-Hispanic/Latino; 3 Asian, non-Hispanic/Latino; 4 Hispanic/Latino), 54 international. Average age 26. 220 applicants, 87% accepted, 44 enrolled. In 2017, 54 master's awarded. *Degree requirements:* For master's, thesis optional, capstone seminar. *Entrance requirements:* For master's, GRE General Test or GMAT, 2 letters of recommendation, resume, undergraduate transcripts, personal statement. Additional exam requirements/recommendations for international students: Required—TOEFL (minimum score 80 iBT); Recommended—IELTS (minimum score 7). *Application deadline:* For fall admission, 2/1 priority date for domestic students, 1/15 priority date for international students; for spring admission, 11/1 priority date for domestic students, 8/1 priority date for international students. Application fee: $50. Electronic applications accepted. *Expenses:* $23,140 per year in-state, $37,830 out-of-state. *Financial support:* In 2017–18, 23 students received support, including 1 fellowship with full tuition reimbursement available (averaging $37,000 per year), 1 research assistantship with full tuition reimbursement available (averaging $37,000 per year); career-related internships or fieldwork and scholarships/grants also available. Financial award application deadline: 2/1; financial award applicants required to submit FAFSA. *Faculty research:* Urban affairs and planning, governance and international public management, public and nonprofit management, policy research and analysis, energy and environment. *Total annual research expenditures:* $1.6 million. *Unit head:* Dr. John Keeler, Dean, 412-648-7605, Fax: 412-648-7601, E-mail: gspia@pitt.edu. *Application contact:* Dr. Michael Rizzi, Director of Student Services, 412-648-7643, Fax: 412-648-7641, E-mail: rizzim@pitt.edu.
Website: http://www.gspia.pitt.edu

University of Puerto Rico–Río Piedras, Graduate School of Planning, San Juan, PR 00931-3300. Offers economic planning systems (MP); environmental planning (MP); social policy and planning (MP); urban and territorial planning (MP). *Accreditation:* ACSP. *Program availability:* Part-time. *Degree requirements:* For master's, comprehensive exam, thesis, planning project defense. *Entrance requirements:* For master's, PAEG, GRE, minimum GPA of 3.0, 2 letters of recommendation. *Faculty research:* Municipalities, historic Atlas, Puerto Rico, economic future.

University of Southern California, Graduate School, Sol Price School of Public Policy, Doctor of Philosophy in Urban Planning and Development Program, Los Angeles, CA 90089. Offers PhD. *Accreditation:* ACSP. *Degree requirements:* For doctorate, thesis/dissertation. *Entrance requirements:* For doctorate, GRE. Additional exam requirements/recommendations for international students: Required—TOEFL (minimum score 600 paper-based; 100 iBT). Electronic applications accepted. *Faculty research:* Transportation and infrastructure, healthy urban and place development, social economic development, sustainable community planning.

University of Southern California, Graduate School, Sol Price School of Public Policy, Doctor of Policy, Planning, and Development Program, Los Angeles, CA 90089. Offers DPPD. *Accreditation:* ACSP. *Program availability:* Part-time. *Degree requirements:* For doctorate, project. *Entrance requirements:* Additional exam requirements/recommendations for international students: Required—TOEFL (minimum score 600 paper-based; 100 iBT). Electronic applications accepted. *Faculty research:* Governance: effective institutions, leadership, management, healthy urban and place development, sustainability, community, public policy and planning, societal problem solving and analysis.

University of Southern California, Graduate School, Sol Price School of Public Policy, Master of Planning Program, Los Angeles, CA 90089. Offers sustainable cities (Graduate Certificate); transportation systems (Graduate Certificate); urban planning (M Pl); M Arch/M Pl; M Pl/MA; M Pl/MPP; M Pl/MRED; M Pl/MS; M Pl/MSW; MBA/M Pl; ML Arch/M Pl; MPA/M Pl. *Accreditation:* ACSP. *Program availability:* Part-time. *Degree requirements:* For master's, comprehensive exam, internship. *Entrance requirements:* For master's, GRE, GMAT. Additional exam requirements/recommendations for international students: Required—TOEFL (minimum score 600 paper-based; 100 iBT). Electronic applications accepted. *Faculty research:* Transportation and infrastructure, comparative international development, healthy communities, social economic development, sustainable community planning.

University of Southern Maine, College of Management and Human Service, Muskie School of Public Service, Program in Community Planning and Development, Portland, ME 04103. Offers MCPD, CGS, JD/MCPD. *Program availability:* Part-time, evening/weekend. *Degree requirements:* For master's, thesis, capstone project, field experience. *Entrance requirements:* For master's, GRE General Test or LSAT. Additional exam requirements/recommendations for international students: Required—TOEFL. Electronic applications accepted. *Faculty research:* Urban and regional growth and change, sustainability, responses to climate and environmental risks, food systems planning and policy, transportation, energy, landscape modeling and simulation.

University of South Florida, Innovative Education, Tampa, FL 33620-9951. Offers adult, career and higher education (Graduate Certificate), including college teaching, leadership in developing human resources, leadership in higher education; Africana studies (Graduate Certificate), including diasporas and health disparities, genocide and human rights; aging studies (Graduate Certificate), including gerontology; art research (Graduate Certificate), including museum studies; business foundations (Graduate Certificate); chemical and biomedical engineering (Graduate Certificate), including materials science and engineering, water, health and sustainability; child and family studies (Graduate Certificate), including positive behavior support; civil and industrial engineering (Graduate Certificate), including transportation systems analysis; community and family health (Graduate Certificate), including maternal and child health, social marketing and public health, violence and injury: prevention and intervention, women's health; criminology (Graduate Certificate), including criminal justice administration; data science for public administration (Graduate Certificate); digital humanities (Graduate Certificate); educational measurement and research (Graduate Certificate), including evaluation; English (Graduate Certificate), including comparative literary studies, creative writing, professional and technical communication; entrepreneurship (Graduate Certificate); environmental health (Graduate Certificate), including safety management; epidemiology and biostatistics (Graduate Certificate), including applied biostatistics, biostatistics, concepts and tools of epidemiology, epidemiology, epidemiology of infectious diseases; geography, environment and planning (Graduate Certificate), including community development, environmental policy and management, geographical information systems; geology (Graduate Certificate), including hydrogeology; global health (Graduate Certificate), including disaster management, global health and Latin American and Caribbean studies, global health practice, humanitarian assistance, infection control; government and international affairs (Graduate Certificate), including Cuban studies, globalization studies; health policy and management (Graduate Certificate), including health management and leadership, public health policy and programs; hearing specialist: early intervention (Graduate Certificate); industrial and management systems engineering (Graduate Certificate), including systems engineering, technology management; information studies (Graduate Certificate), including school library media specialist; information systems/decision sciences (Graduate Certificate), including analytics and business intelligence; instructional technology (Graduate Certificate), including distance education, Florida digital/virtual educator, instructional design, multimedia design, Web design; internal medicine, bioethics and medical humanities (Graduate Certificate), including biomedical ethics; Latin American and Caribbean studies (Graduate Certificate); leadership for coastal resiliency planning (Graduate Certificate); mass communications (Graduate Certificate), including multimedia journalism; mathematics and statistics (Graduate Certificate), including mathematics; medicine (Graduate Certificate), including aging and neuroscience, bioinformatics, biotechnology, brain fitness and memory management, clinical investigation, hand and upper limb rehabilitation, health informatics, health sciences, integrative weight management, intellectual property, medicine and gender, metabolic and nutritional medicine, metabolic cardiology, pharmacy sciences; national

and competitive intelligence (Graduate Certificate); nursing (Graduate Certificate), including simulation based academic fellowship in advanced pain management; psychological and social foundations (Graduate Certificate), including career counseling, college teaching, diversity in education, mental health counseling, school counseling; public affairs (Graduate Certificate), including nonprofit management, public management, research administration; public health (Graduate Certificate), including assessing chemical toxicity and public health risks, health equity, pharmacoepidemiology, public health generalist, toxicology, translational research in adolescent behavioral health; public health practices (Graduate Certificate), including planning for healthy communities; rehabilitation and mental health counseling (Graduate Certificate), including integrative mental health care, marriage and family therapy, rehabilitation technology; secondary education (Graduate Certificate), including ESOL, foreign language education: culture and content, foreign language education: professional; social work (Graduate Certificate), including geriatric social work/clinical gerontology; special education (Graduate Certificate), including autism spectrum disorder, disabilities education: severe/profound; world languages (Graduate Certificate), including teaching English as a second language (TESL) or foreign language. *Unit head:* Dr. Cynthia DeLuca, Associate Vice President and Assistant Vice Provost, 813-974-3077, Fax: 813-974-7061, E-mail: deluca@usf.edu. *Application contact:* Owen Hooper, Director, Summer and Alternative Calendar Programs, 813-974-6917, E-mail: hooper@usf.edu.
Website: http://www.usf.edu/innovative-education/

The University of Texas at Arlington, Graduate School, College of Architecture, Planning and Public Affairs, Program in Public and Urban Administration, Arlington, TX 76019. Offers PhD. *Program availability:* Part-time, evening/weekend. *Entrance requirements:* Additional exam requirements/recommendations for international students: Required—TOEFL (minimum score 550 paper-based). *Faculty research:* Personnel, non-profit organizational change, welfare policy, urban research.

The University of Texas at Arlington, Graduate School, College of Architecture, Planning and Public Affairs, Program in Urban Planning and Public Policy, Arlington, TX 76019. Offers PhD. *Accreditation:* ACSP. *Program availability:* Part-time, evening/weekend. *Entrance requirements:* Additional exam requirements/recommendations for international students: Required—TOEFL (minimum score 550 paper-based). Electronic applications accepted. *Faculty research:* Urban structure, GIS environmental resolutions, qualitative methods, planning history/theory.

The University of Texas at Austin, Graduate School, School of Architecture, Program in Community and Regional Planning, Austin, TX 78712-1111. Offers MSCRP, PhD, JD/MSCRP, MSCRP/MA. *Accreditation:* ACSP. *Degree requirements:* For master's, thesis; for doctorate, thesis/dissertation. *Entrance requirements:* For master's and doctorate, GRE General Test. Electronic applications accepted.

The University of Texas at San Antonio, College of Architecture, Construction and Planning, Program in Urban and Regional Planning, San Antonio, TX 78249-0617. Offers MS. *Program availability:* Part-time. *Faculty:* 1 full-time (0 women), 3 part-time/adjunct (1 woman). *Students:* 9 full-time (2 women), 9 part-time (2 women); includes 11 minority (2 Black or African American, non-Hispanic/Latino; 9 Hispanic/Latino), 2 international. Average age 33. 6 applicants, 83% accepted, 2 enrolled. In 2017, 7 master's awarded. *Entrance requirements:* For master's, GRE, transcripts, two letters of recommendation, letter of intent. Additional exam requirements/recommendations for international students: Required—TOEFL (minimum score 550 paper-based; 79 iBT), IELTS (minimum score 6.5). *Application deadline:* For fall admission, 6/15 for domestic students, 3/1 for international students. Application fee: $50 ($90 for international students). Electronic applications accepted. *Expenses:* Tuition, state resident: full-time $5495. Tuition, nonresident: full-time $21,938. *Required fees:* $1915. Tuition and fees vary according to program. *Total annual research expenditures:* $76,643. *Unit head:* Dr. Richard Tangum, Director, Center for Urban and Regional Planning Research, 210-458-2559, E-mail: richard.tangum@utsa.edu.
Website: http://cacp.utsa.edu/academic-programs/urban-and-regional-planning/explore-urban-and-regional-planning/

The University of Toledo, College of Graduate Studies, College of Languages, Literature and Social Sciences, Department of Geography and Planning, Toledo, OH 43606-3390. Offers geographic information science and applied geographics (Certificate); geography and planning (MA); spatially-integrated social science (PhD). *Program availability:* Part-time. *Degree requirements:* For master's, comprehensive exam, thesis; for doctorate, thesis/dissertation. *Entrance requirements:* For master's and doctorate, GRE General Test, minimum cumulative point-hour ratio of 2.7 for all previous academic work, three letters of recommendation; for Certificate, minimum cumulative point-hour ratio of 2.7 for all previous academic work, three letters of recommendation. Additional exam requirements/recommendations for international students: Required—TOEFL (minimum score 550 paper-based; 80 iBT). Electronic applications accepted.

University of Toronto, School of Graduate Studies, Faculty of Arts and Science, Department of Geography, Program in Planning, Toronto, ON M5S 1A1, Canada. Offers M Sc Pl, MUDS, PhD. *Program availability:* Part-time. *Degree requirements:* For master's, summer internship. *Entrance requirements:* For master's, bachelor's degree in planning, geography, social science or a closely related professional field, minimum B+ average in final year, 3 letters of reference; for doctorate, minimum A- or equivalent standing in previous master's program. Additional exam requirements/recommendations for international students: Required—TOEFL (minimum score 580 paper-based; 93 iBT), TWE (minimum score 5). Electronic applications accepted. *Expenses:* Contact institution.

University of Utah, Graduate School, College of Architecture and Planning, Department of City and Metropolitan Planning, Salt Lake City, UT 84112. Offers city and metropolitan planning (MCMP), including ecological planning, small town and resort planning, smart growth and transportation, urban design; metropolitan planning, policy and design (PhD). *Accreditation:* ACSP. *Program availability:* Part-time. *Faculty:* 4 full-time (2 women), 9 part-time/adjunct (2 women). *Students:* 41 full-time (17 women), 17 part-time (5 women); includes 10 minority (1 Black or African American, non-Hispanic/Latino; 1 Asian, non-Hispanic/Latino; 5 Hispanic/Latino; 3 Two or more races, non-Hispanic/Latino), 12 international. Average age 27. 33 applicants, 100% accepted, 16 enrolled. In 2017, 19 master's, 1 doctorate awarded. *Degree requirements:* For master's, thesis or alternative, comprehensive project; for doctorate, thesis/dissertation. *Entrance requirements:* For master's, GRE, minimum undergraduate GPA of 3.0; for doctorate, GRE, minimum GPA of 3.5. Additional exam requirements/recommendations for international students: Required—TOEFL (minimum score 500 paper-based; 61 iBT); Recommended—IELTS (minimum score 6). *Application deadline:* For fall admission, 1/15 priority date for domestic and international students; for spring admission, 11/1 for domestic and international students. Applications are processed on a rolling basis. Application fee: $55 ($65 for international students). Electronic applications accepted. *Expenses:* Contact institution. *Financial support:* In 2017–18, 25 students received support, including 1 fellowship with full tuition reimbursement available (averaging $25,000 per year), 3 research assistantships with tuition reimbursements available (averaging $16,000 per year), 21 teaching assistantships with tuition reimbursements available (averaging $10,000 per year); career-related internships or fieldwork, Federal Work-Study, scholarships/grants, health care benefits, and unspecified assistantships also available. Financial award application deadline: 1/15; financial award applicants required to submit FAFSA. *Faculty research:* Transportation, land-use, smart growth, public health, climate change, urban design, sustainable communities, community-based decision-making process, urban morphology, theory and practice in scenario-planning techniques, community-engaged teaching methodologies, interactions between federal environmental policies and state/local community development patterns, values in architecture and planning practices. *Total annual research expenditures:* $689,627. *Unit head:* Reid Ewing, Chair, 801-585-3745, Fax: 801-581-8217, E-mail: ewing@arch.utah.edu. *Application contact:* Saolo Utu, Recruitment and Admissions Advisor, 801-581-2361, Fax: 801-581-8217, E-mail: recruitment@arch.utah.edu.
Website: http://www.plan.utah.edu/

University of Virginia, School of Architecture, Department of Urban and Environmental Planning, Charlottesville, VA 22903. Offers MUEP, JD/MUEP, MPP/MUEP. *Accreditation:* ACSP (one or more programs are accredited). *Faculty:* 7 full-time (5 women). *Students:* 51 full-time (31 women); includes 7 minority (5 Black or African American, non-Hispanic/Latino; 2 Two or more races, non-Hispanic/Latino), 14 international. Average age 25. 86 applicants, 85% accepted, 24 enrolled. In 2017, 24 master's awarded. *Entrance requirements:* For master's, GRE General Test, previous course work in statistics, 3 letters of recommendation. Additional exam requirements/recommendations for international students: Required—TOEFL (minimum score 600 paper-based; 90 iBT). *Application deadline:* For fall admission, 1/15 for domestic students, 1/16 for international students. Applications are processed on a rolling basis. Application fee: $60. Electronic applications accepted. *Financial support:* Applicants required to submit FAFSA. *Faculty research:* Urban development, land use, environment, policy analysis, historic preservation. *Unit head:* Ellen Bassett, Chair, 434-924-6461, Fax: 434-982-2678, E-mail: bassette@virginia.edu. *Application contact:* 434-924-6442, Fax: 434-982-2678, E-mail: a-school-admissions@virginia.edu.
Website: http://www.arch.virginia.edu/academics/disciplines/planning

University of Washington, Graduate School, College of Built Environments, Department of Urban Design and Planning, Seattle, WA 98195. Offers urban design and planning (PhD); urban planning (MUP). *Accreditation:* ACSP (one or more programs are accredited). *Degree requirements:* For master's, thesis or alternative; for doctorate, thesis/dissertation. *Entrance requirements:* For master's and doctorate, GRE General Test, minimum GPA of 3.0. Additional exam requirements/recommendations for international students: Required—TOEFL. *Faculty research:* Land-use and growth management, urban form and travel behavior, geographic information systems/remote sensing, historic preservation, urban ecology and environmental planning.

University of Waterloo, Graduate Studies, Faculty of Environment, Program in Local Economic Development, Waterloo, ON N2L 3G1, Canada. Offers MAES. *Program availability:* Part-time. *Degree requirements:* For master's, internship, research paper. *Entrance requirements:* Additional exam requirements/recommendations for international students: Required—TOEFL, IELTS, PTE. Electronic applications accepted.

University of Waterloo, Graduate Studies, Faculty of Environment, School of Planning, Waterloo, ON N2L 3G1, Canada. Offers M Plan, MA, MAES, MES, PhD. *Program availability:* Part-time. *Degree requirements:* For master's, thesis (for some programs); for doctorate, comprehensive exam, thesis/dissertation. *Entrance requirements:* For master's, honors degree, minimum B+ average; for doctorate, master's degree, minimum A- average, resume. Additional exam requirements/recommendations for international students: Required—TOEFL, IELTS, PTE. Electronic applications accepted. *Faculty research:* Environmental planning, planning for resource development, urban planning and information systems, social planning, urban design.

University of West Georgia, College of Social Sciences, Carrollton, GA 30118. Offers criminology (MA); data analysis and evaluation methods (Postbaccalaureate Certificate); European Union studies (Postbaccalaureate Certificate); integrative health systems (Postbaccalaureate Certificate); nonprofit management and community development (Postbaccalaureate Certificate); psychology (MA, PhD), including consciousness and society (PhD); public administration (MPA); public management (Postbaccalaureate Certificate); sociology (MA). *Program availability:* Part-time, evening/weekend, 100% online, blended/hybrid learning. *Faculty:* 48 full-time (22 women). *Students:* 124 full-time (84 women), 73 part-time (46 women); includes 69 minority (56 Black or African American, non-Hispanic/Latino; 4 Asian, non-Hispanic/Latino; 6 Hispanic/Latino; 3 Two or more races, non-Hispanic/Latino), 10 international. Average age 32. 95 applicants, 89% accepted, 63 enrolled. In 2017, 44 master's, 2 doctorates, 4 other advanced degrees awarded. *Entrance requirements:* Additional exam requirements/recommendations for international students: Required—TOEFL (minimum score 523 paper-based; 69 iBT); Recommended—IELTS (minimum score 6.5). *Application deadline:* For fall admission, 7/15 for domestic students, 6/1 for international students; for spring admission, 11/30 for domestic students, 10/15 for international students; for summer admission, 5/15 for domestic students, 3/30 for international students. Applications are processed on a rolling basis. Application fee: $40. Electronic applications accepted. Tuition and fees vary according to degree level and program. *Financial support:* Fellowships, research assistantships, teaching assistantships, career-related internships or fieldwork, Federal Work-Study, institutionally sponsored loans, scholarships/grants, and unspecified assistantships available. Support available to part-time students. Financial award application deadline: 4/1; financial award applicants required to submit FAFSA. *Unit head:* Dr. N. Jane McCandless, Dean of Social Sciences, 678-839-5170, Fax: 678-839-5171, E-mail: jmccandl@westga.edu. *Application contact:* Dr. Toby Ziglar, Assistant Dean of the Graduate School, 678-839-1394, Fax: 678-839-1395, E-mail: graduate@westga.edu.
Website: https://www.westga.edu/coss

University of Wisconsin–Madison, Graduate School, College of Letters and Science, Department of Planning and Landscape Architecture, Madison, WI 53706-1380. Offers landscape architecture (MS); urban and regional planning (MS, PhD). *Accreditation:* ACSP (one or more programs are accredited). *Program availability:* Part-time. *Degree requirements:* For master's, thesis optional, internship; for doctorate, thesis/dissertation, 3 preliminary exams. *Entrance requirements:* For master's, GRE, minimum GPA of 3.0, previous course work in statistics; for doctorate, 1 year of experience, master's degree in related field. Electronic applications accepted. *Faculty research:* Land use, environmental planning, community development, economic development planning.

University of Wisconsin–Milwaukee, Graduate School, School of Architecture and Urban Planning, Department of Urban Planning, Milwaukee, WI 53201-0413. Offers MUP. *Accreditation:* ACSP. *Program availability:* Part-time. *Students:* 10 full-time (4 women), 1 part-time (0 women); includes 3 minority (1 Hispanic/Latino; 2 Two or more races, non-Hispanic/Latino), 1 international. Average age 31. 23 applicants, 65% accepted, 3 enrolled. In 2017, 23 master's awarded. *Degree requirements:* For master's, comprehensive exam, thesis or alternative. *Entrance requirements:* For master's, GRE General Test. Additional exam requirements/recommendations for international students: Required—TOEFL (minimum score 550 paper-based; 79 iBT), IELTS (minimum score 6.5). *Application deadline:* For fall admission, 1/1 priority date for domestic students; for spring admission, 9/1 for domestic students. Application fee: $56

($96 for international students). Electronic applications accepted. *Financial support:* Fellowships, research assistantships, teaching assistantships, career-related internships or fieldwork, health care benefits, and unspecified assistantships available. Support available to part-time students. Financial award application deadline: 4/15; financial award applicants required to submit FAFSA. *Unit head:* Robert Greenstreet, Dean, Architecture and Urban Planning, 414-229-4016. *Application contact:* Student Advising Office, 414-229-4015, E-mail: sarup-grad@uwm.edu.
Website: https://uwm.edu/sarup/urban-planning/

Utah State University, School of Graduate Studies, College of Agriculture and Applied Sciences, Department of Landscape Architecture and Environmental Planning, Logan, UT 84322. Offers bioregional planning (MS); landscape architecture (MLA). *Accreditation:* ASLA (one or more programs are accredited). *Degree requirements:* For master's, thesis. *Entrance requirements:* For master's, GRE General Test, minimum GPA of 3.0. Additional exam requirements/recommendations for international students: Required—TOEFL. *Faculty research:* Visual resource management, planning for wildlife, agricultural land preservation, watershed planning, community planning and design.

Utah State University, School of Graduate Studies, S.J. and Jessie E. Quinney College of Natural Resources, Department of Environment and Society, Logan, UT 84322. Offers bioregional planning (MS); geography (MA, MS); human dimensions of ecosystem science and management (MS, PhD); recreation resource management (MS, PhD). *Degree requirements:* For master's, comprehensive exam, thesis (for some programs). *Entrance requirements:* For master's and doctorate, GRE General Test, minimum GPA of 3.0. Additional exam requirements/recommendations for international students: Required—TOEFL. Electronic applications accepted. *Faculty research:* Geographic information systems/geographic and environmental education, bioregional planning, natural resource and environmental policy, outdoor recreation and tourism, natural resource and environmental management.

Vanderbilt University, Peabody College, Department of Human and Organizational Development, Nashville, TN 37240-1001. Offers community development and action (M Ed); human development counseling (M Ed). *Accreditation:* ACA; NCATE. *Program availability:* Blended/hybrid learning, on-campus immersion once every semester. *Faculty:* 31 full-time (20 women), 19 part-time/adjunct (9 women). *Students:* 104 full-time (87 women), 21 part-time (20 women); includes 18 minority (8 Black or African American, non-Hispanic/Latino; 2 Asian, non-Hispanic/Latino; 4 Hispanic/Latino; 4 Two or more races, non-Hispanic/Latino), 2 international. Average age 26. 186 applicants, 64% accepted, 55 enrolled. In 2017, 52 master's awarded. *Degree requirements:* For master's, comprehensive exam, thesis optional. *Entrance requirements:* For master's, GRE General Test. Additional exam requirements/recommendations for international students: Required—TOEFL (minimum score 550 paper-based; 80 iBT). *Application deadline:* For fall admission, 12/31 priority date for domestic and international students; for spring admission, 11/1 priority date for domestic and international students. Applications are processed on a rolling basis. Application fee: $0. Electronic applications accepted. *Financial support:* Fellowships with partial tuition reimbursements, research assistantships with partial tuition reimbursements, teaching assistantships with partial tuition reimbursements, Federal Work-Study, institutionally sponsored loans, scholarships/grants, tuition waivers (partial), and unspecified assistantships available. Support available to part-time students. Financial award application deadline: 1/15; financial award applicants required to submit FAFSA. *Faculty research:* Community psychology and community development; counseling and mental health services, prevention and positive youth development; organizational and community change; youth physical and behavioral health in schools and communities. *Unit head:* Dr. Paul Speer, Chair, 615-322-6881, Fax: 615-322-1141, E-mail: paul.w.speer@vanderbilt.edu. *Application contact:* Sherrie Lane, Educational Coordinator, 615-322-8484, Fax: 615-322-1141, E-mail: sherrie.a.lane@vanderbilt.edu.

Virginia Commonwealth University, Graduate School, L. Douglas Wilder School of Government and Public Affairs, Program in Urban and Regional Studies and Planning, Richmond, VA 23284-9005. Offers MURP. *Degree requirements:* For master's, thesis optional, internship. *Entrance requirements:* For master's, GRE General Test, GMAT, or LSAT, minimum GPA of 2.7. Additional exam requirements/recommendations for international students: Required—TOEFL (minimum score 600 paper-based; 100 iBT); Recommended—IELTS (minimum score 6.5). Electronic applications accepted.

Virginia Polytechnic Institute and State University, Graduate School, College of Architecture and Urban Studies, Blacksburg, VA 24061. Offers architecture (M Arch, MS); architecture and design research (PhD); building construction science management (MS); creative technologies (MFA); environmental design and planning (PhD); government and international affairs (MPIA); landscape architecture (MLA, PhD); planning, governance, and globalization (PhD); public administration and public affairs (MPA, PhD); urban and regional planning (MURPL). *Accreditation:* ASLA (one or more programs are accredited). *Faculty:* 139 full-time (58 women), 1 (woman) part-time/adjunct. *Students:* 339 full-time (165 women), 210 part-time (97 women); includes 115 minority (49 Black or African American, non-Hispanic/Latino; 1 American Indian or Alaska Native, non-Hispanic/Latino; 30 Asian, non-Hispanic/Latino; 29 Hispanic/Latino; 6 Two or more races, non-Hispanic/Latino), 136 international. Average age 32. 649 applicants, 49% accepted, 105 enrolled. In 2017, 142 master's, 18 doctorates awarded. *Degree requirements:* For master's, comprehensive exam (for some programs), thesis (for some programs); for doctorate, comprehensive exam (for some programs), thesis/dissertation (for some programs). *Entrance requirements:* For master's and doctorate, GRE/GMAT. Additional exam requirements/recommendations for international students: Required—TOEFL (minimum score 80 iBT). *Application deadline:* For fall admission, 8/1 for domestic students, 4/1 for international students; for spring admission, 1/1 for domestic students, 9/1 for international students. Applications are processed on a rolling basis. Application fee: $75. Electronic applications accepted. *Expenses:* Tuition, state resident: full-time $15,072; part-time $718.50 per credit hour. Tuition, nonresident: full-time $28,810; part-time $1448.25 per credit hour. *Required fees:* $2741; $502 per semester. Tuition and fees vary according to course load, campus/location and program. *Financial support:* In 2017–18, 17 research assistantships with full tuition reimbursements (averaging $18,561 per year), 41 teaching assistantships with full tuition reimbursements (averaging $17,340 per year) were awarded. Financial award application deadline: 3/1; financial award applicants required to submit FAFSA. *Total annual research expenditures:* $3.1 million. *Unit head:* Dr. Richard Blythe, Dean, 540-231-6416, Fax: 540-231-6332, E-mail: richbl1@vt.edu. *Application contact:* Christine Mattsson-Coon, Executive Assistant, 540-231-6416, Fax: 540-231-6332, E-mail: cmattsso@vt.edu.
Website: http://www.caus.vt.edu/

Wayne State University, College of Liberal Arts and Sciences, Department of Urban Studies and Planning, Detroit, MI 48202. Offers economic development (Graduate Certificate); urban studies and planning (MUP). *Accreditation:* ACSP. *Program availability:* Evening/weekend. *Students:* 12 full-time (9 women), 37 part-time (20 women); includes 21 minority (15 Black or African American, non-Hispanic/Latino; 1 American Indian or Alaska Native, non-Hispanic/Latino; 2 Hispanic/Latino; 3 Two or more races, non-Hispanic/Latino). Average age 30. 62 applicants, 47% accepted, 15 enrolled. In 2017, 16 master's awarded. *Degree requirements:* For master's, thesis or essay. *Entrance requirements:* For degree, graduate degree or actively pursuing a graduate degree at WSU; personal statement of interest. Additional exam requirements/recommendations for international students: Required—TOEFL (minimum score 550 paper-based; 79 iBT), TWE (minimum score 5.5), Michigan English Language Assessment Battery (minimum score 85); Recommended—IELTS (minimum score 6.5). *Application deadline:* For fall admission, 6/1 priority date for domestic students, 5/1 priority date for international students; for winter admission, 10/1 priority date for domestic students, 9/1 priority date for international students; for spring admission, 2/1 priority date for domestic students, 1/1 priority date for international students. Applications are processed on a rolling basis. Application fee: $50. Electronic applications accepted. *Expenses:* Tuition, state resident: full-time $10,224; part-time $638.98 per credit hour. Tuition, nonresident: full-time $22,145; part-time $1384.04 per credit hour. Tuition and fees vary according to course load and program. *Financial support:* In 2017–18, 14 students received support. Research assistantships, scholarships/grants, and unspecified assistantships available. Financial award applicants required to submit FAFSA. *Faculty research:* Community development, economic development, environmental planning, housing policy, land use planning and policy, local fiscal policy, local planning practices, neighborhood change, sustainable food systems. *Unit head:* Dr. Rayman Mohamed, Interim Chair, Associate Professor and Graduate Director, 313-577-3356, E-mail: rayman.mohamed@wayne.edu. *Application contact:* E-mail: dusp@wayne.edu.
Website: http://clas.wayne.edu/dusp/

West Chester University of Pennsylvania, College of Business and Public Management, Department of Geography and Planning, West Chester, PA 19383. Offers geographic information systems (Certificate); geography (MS); geography and planning (MURP); urban and regional planning (Certificate). *Program availability:* Part-time, evening/weekend. *Students:* 10 full-time (4 women), 10 part-time (5 women); includes 1 minority (Black or African American, non-Hispanic/Latino). Average age 29. 17 applicants, 94% accepted, 11 enrolled. In 2017, 10 master's, 11 other advanced degrees awarded. *Degree requirements:* For master's, 48 credits: 27 credits required, 21 credits electives (for MURP); 33 credits or 11 courses (for MS); thesis or independent research course; for Certificate, 12 credits or 4 courses (for geographic information systems); 18 credits or 6 courses (for urban and regional planning). *Entrance requirements:* For master's and Certificate, minimum GPA of 2.8, resume, two letters of recommendation. Additional exam requirements/recommendations for international students: Required—TOEFL or IELTS. *Application deadline:* For fall admission, 5/15 for international students; for spring admission, 10/15 for international students. Applications are processed on a rolling basis. Application fee: $50. Electronic applications accepted. *Expenses:* Tuition, state resident: full-time $9000; part-time $500 per credit. Tuition, nonresident: full-time $13,500; part-time $750 per credit. *Required fees:* $2959; $149.79 per credit. *Financial support:* Scholarships/grants and unspecified assistantships available. Financial award application deadline: 2/15; financial award applicants required to submit FAFSA. *Faculty research:* Sustainability and environmental conservation, land use/suburban planning, geographic information systems, transportation planning, housing, economic development. *Unit head:* Dr. Dottie Ives Dewey, Chair/Graduate Coordinator for Certificate Programs, 610-436-2746, Fax: 610-436-2889, E-mail: divesdewey@wcupa.edu. *Application contact:* Dr. Matin Katirai, Graduate Coordinator, 610-436-2392, Fax: 610-436-2889, E-mail: mkatirai@wcupa.edu.
Website: http://www.wcupa.edu/business-publicManagement/geographyPlanning/

Urban Studies

Arizona State University at the Tempe campus, College of Liberal Arts and Sciences, School of Human Evolution and Social Change, Tempe, AZ 85287-2402. Offers anthropology (MA, PhD), including anthropology (PhD), archaeology (PhD), bioarchaeology (PhD), evolutionary (PhD), museum studies (MA), sociocultural (PhD); applied mathematics for the life and social sciences (PhD); environmental social science (PhD), including environmental social science, urbanism; global health (MA, PhD), including complex adaptive systems science (PhD), evolutionary global health sciences (PhD), health and culture (PhD), urbanism (PhD); immigration studies (Graduate Certificate). Terminal master's awarded for partial completion of doctoral program. *Degree requirements:* For master's, thesis or alternative, interactive Program of Study (iPOS) submitted before completing 50 percent of required credit hours; for doctorate, comprehensive exam, thesis/dissertation, interactive Program of Study (iPOS) submitted before completing 50 percent of required credit hours. *Entrance requirements:* For master's and doctorate, GRE, minimum GPA of 3.0 or equivalent in last 2 years of work leading to bachelor's degree. Additional exam requirements/recommendations for international students: Required—TOEFL, IELTS, or PTE. Electronic applications accepted.

Azusa Pacific University, Azusa Pacific Seminary, Program in Pastoral Studies, Concentration in Urban Studies, Azusa, CA 91702-7000. Offers MAPS. *Degree requirements:* For master's, project.

Boston University, Metropolitan College, Program in Urban Affairs, Boston, MA 02215. Offers MUA. *Program availability:* Part-time, evening/weekend. *Faculty:* 2 full-time (both women), 6 part-time/adjunct (2 women). *Students:* 24 part-time (15 women); includes 14 minority (5 Black or African American, non-Hispanic/Latino; 2 Asian, non-Hispanic/Latino; 7 Hispanic/Latino). Average age 31. 21 applicants, 90% accepted, 10 enrolled. In 2017, 14 master's awarded. *Entrance requirements:* Additional exam requirements/recommendations for international students: Required—TOEFL. *Application deadline:* For fall admission, 7/15 priority date for domestic and international students; for spring admission, 12/15 for domestic students, 11/15 priority date for international students. Applications are processed on a rolling basis. Application fee: $85. Electronic

applications accepted. *Expenses:* Contact institution. *Financial support:* In 2017–18, 5 research assistantships (averaging $4,200 per year) were awarded; career-related internships or fieldwork, Federal Work-Study, and unspecified assistantships also available. Support available to part-time students. Financial award applicants required to submit FAFSA. *Faculty research:* Housing, community development and land use planning, environmental management and planning, international comparative development planning, sustainability. *Unit head:* Dr. Daniel P. LeClair, Chair, 617-353-3025, Fax: 617-358-3595, E-mail: dleclair@bu.edu. *Application contact:* Dr. Madhu Dutta-Koehler, Director, 617-358-2364, E-mail: duttam@bu.edu.

Brooklyn College of the City University of New York, School of Humanities and Social Sciences, Department of Political Science, Brooklyn, NY 11210-2889. Offers international affairs (MA); political science (MA); urban policy and administration (MA). *Program availability:* Part-time, evening/weekend. *Degree requirements:* For master's, comprehensive exam (for some programs), thesis or alternative, foreign language exam (for international affairs program). *Entrance requirements:* For master's, 2 letters of recommendation, personal statement. Additional exam requirements/recommendations for international students: Required—TOEFL (minimum score 500 paper-based; 61 iBT). *Faculty research:* Ethics and politics, politics of criminal justice, Western Europe, international law and politics, labor politics.

Cleveland State University, College of Graduate Studies, Maxine Goodman Levin College of Urban Affairs, Program in Urban Studies, Cleveland, OH 44115. Offers MS, Certificate. *Program availability:* Part-time, evening/weekend. *Faculty:* 23 full-time (11 women), 23 part-time/adjunct (6 women). *Students:* 2 full-time (1 woman), 15 part-time (7 women); includes 3 minority (2 Black or African American, non-Hispanic/Latino; 1 Two or more races, non-Hispanic/Latino), 2 international. Average age 35. 21 applicants, 29% accepted, 4 enrolled. In 2017, 4 master's awarded. *Degree requirements:* For master's, thesis or alternative, exit project. *Entrance requirements:* For master's, GRE General Test (minimum score: verbal and quantitative combined 40th percentile, analytical writing 4.0), minimum GPA of 3.0. Additional exam requirements/recommendations for international students: Required—TOEFL (minimum score 550 paper-based; 78 iBT), IELTS (6.0), or International Test of English Proficiency (iTEP). *Application deadline:* For fall admission, 7/1 priority date for domestic students, 5/15 for international students; for spring admission, 11/15 for domestic students, 11/1 for international students; for summer admission, 4/1 for domestic students, 3/15 for international students. Applications are processed on a rolling basis. Application fee: $40. Electronic applications accepted. *Expenses:* Contact institution. *Financial support:* In 2017–18, 4 students received support, including 1 research assistantship with full tuition reimbursement available (averaging $6,960 per year), 1 teaching assistantship with tuition reimbursement available (averaging $6,960 per year); scholarships/grants, tuition waivers (full and partial), and unspecified assistantships also available. Support available to part-time students. Financial award application deadline: 3/1; financial award applicants required to submit FAFSA. *Faculty research:* Environmental issues, economic development, urban and public policy, public management, community and neighborhood development. *Unit head:* Dr. Brian Mikelbank, Associate Professor/Program Director, 216-875-9980, Fax: 216-687-9342, E-mail: b.mikelbank@csuohio.edu. *Application contact:* David Arrighi, Graduate Academic Advisor, 216-523-7522, Fax: 216-687-5398, E-mail: d.arrighi@csuohio.edu.
Website: http://urban.csuohio.edu/academics/graduate/msus/

Cleveland State University, College of Graduate Studies, Maxine Goodman Levin College of Urban Affairs, Program in Urban Studies and Public Affairs, Cleveland, OH 44115. Offers communication (PhD); public administration (PhD); urban policy and development (PhD). *Program availability:* Part-time, evening/weekend. *Faculty:* 16 full-time (8 women), 13 part-time/adjunct (5 women). *Students:* 3 full-time (2 women), 24 part-time (14 women); includes 6 minority (4 Black or African American, non-Hispanic/Latino; 1 Hispanic/Latino; 1 Two or more races, non-Hispanic/Latino), 4 international. Average age 41. 32 applicants, 34% accepted, 2 enrolled. In 2017, 4 doctorates awarded. *Degree requirements:* For doctorate, comprehensive exam, thesis/dissertation. *Entrance requirements:* For doctorate, GRE General Test (minimum score: verbal and quantitative 50th percentile, analytical writing 4.0), minimum GPA of 3.5. Additional exam requirements/recommendations for international students: Required—TOEFL (minimum score 550 paper-based; 78 iBT), IELTS (6.0), or International Test of English Proficiency (iTEP). *Application deadline:* For fall admission, 1/31 for domestic and international students. Application fee: $40. Electronic applications accepted. *Expenses:* Contact institution. *Financial support:* In 2017–18, 15 students received support, including 1 research assistantship with full tuition reimbursement available (averaging $11,800 per year), 2 teaching assistantships with full tuition reimbursements available (averaging $11,800 per year); scholarships/grants, tuition waivers (full and partial), and unspecified assistantships also available. Support available to part-time students. Financial award application deadline: 3/1; financial award applicants required to submit FAFSA. *Faculty research:* Urban and public policy, public affairs. *Unit head:* Dr. Bill Bowen, Professor/PhD Program Director, 216-687-9226, E-mail: w.bowen@csuohio.edu. *Application contact:* David Arrighi, Graduate Academic Advisor, 216-523-7522, Fax: 216-687-5398, E-mail: d.arrighi@csuohio.edu.
Website: http://urban.csuohio.edu/academics/graduate/phd/

Columbus State University, Graduate Studies, College of Letters and Sciences, Department of Political Science and Public Administration, Columbus, GA 31907-5645. Offers public administration (MPA), including criminal justice, environmental policy, government administration, health services administration, political campaigning, urban policy. *Program availability:* Part-time, evening/weekend, 100% online, blended/hybrid learning. *Faculty:* 15 full-time (6 women), 14 part-time/adjunct (0 women). *Students:* 34 full-time (21 women), 44 part-time (24 women); includes 40 minority (32 Black or African American, non-Hispanic/Latino; 2 Asian, non-Hispanic/Latino; 3 Hispanic/Latino; 1 Native Hawaiian or other Pacific Islander, non-Hispanic/Latino; 2 Two or more races, non-Hispanic/Latino), 3 international. Average age 33. 68 applicants, 43% accepted, 21 enrolled. In 2017, 38 master's awarded. *Degree requirements:* For master's, comprehensive exam. *Entrance requirements:* For master's, GRE General Test, minimum GPA of 2.75, three letters of recommendation. Additional exam requirements/recommendations for international students: Required—TOEFL (minimum score 550 paper-based; 79 iBT). *Application deadline:* For fall admission, 6/30 for domestic students, 5/1 for international students; for spring admission, 11/1 for domestic and international students; for summer admission, 3/1 for domestic and international students. Applications are processed on a rolling basis. Application fee: $50. Electronic applications accepted. *Expenses:* Tuition, state resident: full-time $3708; part-time $2472 per year. Tuition, nonresident: full-time $14,418; part-time $9612 per year. *International tuition:* $19,218 full-time. *Required fees:* $1605. Tuition and fees vary according to program. *Financial support:* In 2017–18, 4 students received support, including 6 research assistantships with partial tuition reimbursements available (averaging $3,000 per year); career-related internships or fieldwork, Federal Work-Study, institutionally sponsored loans, scholarships/grants, tuition waivers (partial), and unspecified assistantships also available. Support available to part-time students. Financial award application deadline: 5/1; financial award applicants required to submit FAFSA. *Unit head:* Dr. Frederick Gordon, Director, 706-565-7875, E-mail: gordon_frederick@colstate.edu. *Application contact:* Catrina Smith-Edmond, Assistant Director for Graduate and Global Admission, 706-507-8824, Fax: 706-568-5091, E-mail: smithedmond_catrina@columbusstate.edu.
Website: http://politicalscience.columbusstate.edu/

Concordia University, School of Graduate Studies, Faculty of Arts and Science, Department of Geography, Planning and Environment, Montréal, QC H3G 1M8, Canada. Offers environmental assessment (M Env, Diploma); geography, urban and environmental studies (M Sc, PhD).

Fordham University, Graduate School of Arts and Sciences, Program in Urban Studies, New York, NY 10458. Offers MA. *Students:* 4 full-time (3 women), 8 part-time (3 women); includes 6 minority (5 Black or African American, non-Hispanic/Latino; 1 Asian, non-Hispanic/Latino). Average age 28. 20 applicants, 85% accepted, 2 enrolled. In 2017, 4 master's awarded. *Degree requirements:* For master's, internship or field work, research project. *Entrance requirements:* Additional exam requirements/recommendations for international students: Required—TOEFL. Application fee: $70. *Financial support:* Tuition waivers (partial) available. *Unit head:* Dr. Annika Hinze, Director, 718-817-3960, E-mail: rwakeman@fordham.edu. *Application contact:* Bernadette Valentino-Morrison, Director of Graduate Admissions, 718-817-4419, Fax: 718-817-3566, E-mail: valentinomor@fordham.edu.

Fresno Pacific University, Biblical Seminary, Program in Community Leadership and Transformation, Fresno, CA 93702-4709. Offers MA. Program offered in partnership with the Center for Community Transformation (CCT). *Entrance requirements:* For master's, bachelor's degree, minimum GPA of 2.5, personal profile statement, three letters of references, writing sample.

Hunter College of the City University of New York, Graduate School, School of Arts and Sciences, Department of Urban Policy and Planning, Program in Urban Affairs, New York, NY 10065-5085. Offers MS. *Program availability:* Part-time. *Degree requirements:* For master's, thesis or alternative, 2 formal reports, internship. *Entrance requirements:* For master's, minimum 12 credits of course work in social sciences. Additional exam requirements/recommendations for international students: Required—TOEFL. *Faculty research:* Women, tourism, youth, immigration, employment.

Indiana University Northwest, College of Arts and Sciences, Gary, IN 46408. Offers clinical counseling (MS), including drug and alcohol counseling; community development/urban studies (Graduate Certificate); computer information systems (Graduate Certificate); liberal studies (MLS); race-ethnic studies (Graduate Certificate); women's and gender studies (Graduate Certificate). *Program availability:* Part-time, evening/weekend. *Entrance requirements:* For master's, GRE (recommended for MS), minimum undergraduate GPA of 3.0, bachelor's degree from accredited university (for MS). Electronic applications accepted. *Expenses:* Contact institution.

Le Moyne College, Department of Education, Syracuse, NY 13214. Offers adolescent education (MS Ed, MST); adolescent education/special education (MS Ed, MST); adolescent English (MST), including grades 7-12; adolescent English/special education (MST), including grades 7-12; adolescent foreign language (MST), including grades 7-12; adolescent history (MST), including grades 7-12; childhood education (MS Ed); childhood education/special education (MS Ed); elementary education (MS Ed); general education (MS Ed); inclusive childhood education (MST); literacy education (MS Ed), including birth to grade 6, grades 5-12; school building leader (MS Ed); school building leadership (CAS); school district business leader (MS Ed, CAS); school district leader (MS Ed); school district leadership (CAS); secondary education (MS Ed); special education (MS Ed); teaching English to speakers of other languages (MS Ed); urban studies (MS Ed). *Accreditation:* TEAC. *Program availability:* Part-time, evening/weekend. *Faculty:* 7 full-time (5 women), 20 part-time/adjunct (12 women). *Students:* 30 full-time (19 women), 126 part-time (93 women); includes 15 minority (7 Black or African American, non-Hispanic/Latino; 1 American Indian or Alaska Native, non-Hispanic/Latino; 1 Asian, non-Hispanic/Latino; 6 Hispanic/Latino), 4 international. Average age 29. 139 applicants, 65% accepted, 76 enrolled. In 2017, 82 master's, 43 CASs awarded. *Degree requirements:* For master's, thesis. *Entrance requirements:* For master's, bachelor's degree with minimum undergraduate GPA of 3.0, 2 letters of recommendation, transcripts. Additional exam requirements/recommendations for international students: Required—TOEFL (minimum score 550 paper-based; 79 iBT); Recommended—IELTS (minimum score 6.5). *Application deadline:* For fall admission, 4/1 priority date for domestic and international students; for spring admission, 10/1 priority date for domestic and international students; for summer admission, 3/1 priority date for domestic and international students. Applications are processed on a rolling basis. Application fee: $50. Electronic applications accepted. *Expenses:* $700 per credit hour. *Financial support:* In 2017–18, 30 students received support. Career-related internships or fieldwork, scholarships/grants, and health care benefits available. Support available to part-time students. Financial award applicants required to submit FAFSA. *Faculty research:* Minority teachers, special education, multiculturalism, literacy, technology, media literacy learning, autism, school district organization, service-learning, higher level problem solving, teacher leadership. *Unit head:* Dr. Stephen C. Fleury, Chair, Department of Education, 315-445-4376, Fax: 315-445-4744, E-mail: fleurysc@lemoyne.edu. *Application contact:* Kristen P. Richards, Senior Director of Enrollment Management, 315-445-5444, Fax: 315-445-6092, E-mail: trapaskp@lemoyne.edu.
Website: http://www.lemoyne.edu/education

Long Island University–LIU Brooklyn, Richard L. Conolly College of Liberal Arts and Sciences, Brooklyn, NY 11201-8423. Offers biology (MS); chemistry (MS); clinical psychology (PhD); creative writing (MFA); English (MA); media arts (MA, MFA); political science (MA); psychology (MA); social science (MS); United Nations (Advanced Certificate); urban studies (MA); writing and production for television (MFA). *Program availability:* Part-time. *Faculty:* 32 full-time (13 women), 17 part-time/adjunct (6 women). *Students:* 178 full-time (123 women), 143 part-time (96 women); includes 128 minority (65 Black or African American, non-Hispanic/Latino; 22 Asian, non-Hispanic/Latino; 31 Hispanic/Latino; 10 Two or more races, non-Hispanic/Latino), 54 international. Average age 30. 629 applicants, 38% accepted, 74 enrolled. In 2017, 147 master's, 9 doctorates, 8 other advanced degrees awarded. Terminal master's awarded for partial completion of doctoral program. *Degree requirements:* For master's, comprehensive exam (for some programs), thesis (for some programs); for doctorate, thesis/dissertation. *Entrance requirements:* For doctorate, GRE. Additional exam requirements/recommendations for international students: Required—TOEFL (minimum score 550 paper-based, 79 iBT) or IELTS. *Application deadline:* Applications are processed on a rolling basis. Application fee: $50. Electronic applications accepted. *Expenses: Tuition:* Full-time $21,618; part-time $1201 per credit. *Required fees:* $1840; $920 per term. Tuition and fees vary according to course load. *Financial support:* In 2017–18, 214 students received support, including 120 fellowships with full and partial tuition reimbursements available (averaging $915 per year), 5 research assistantships with full and partial tuition reimbursements available (averaging $2,300 per year), 136 teaching assistantships with full and partial tuition reimbursements available (averaging $2,300 per year); career-related internships or fieldwork, Federal Work-Study, institutionally sponsored loans, scholarships/grants, and unspecified assistantships also available. Support available to part-time students. Financial award application deadline: 2/15; financial award applicants required to submit FAFSA. *Faculty research:* Quantum gravity and astrophysics; string theory; pharmaceutical biotechnology with a focus on molecular details of drug susceptibility/resistance mechanisms; entomology, population and

community ecology, agroecology, and biodiversity; psychotherapy process-outcome, particularly therapeutic alliance development, the role of common factors, and the study of treatment failures; personality pathology, borderline personality disorder and pathological narcissism. *Unit head:* Dr. Scott Krawczyk, Dean, 718-488-1003, E-mail: scott.krawczyk@liu.edu. *Application contact:* Bayu Sutrisno, Graduate Admissions Counselor, 718-488-1564, Fax: 718-780-6110, E-mail: bayu.sutrisno@liu.edu.

Loyola University Chicago, Graduate School, Program in Urban Affairs, Chicago, IL 60660. Offers MA. *Program availability:* Part-time, evening/weekend. *Faculty:* 2 full-time (both women), 3 part-time/adjunct (1 woman). *Students:* 1 (woman) full-time. Average age 21. 3 applicants, 100% accepted, 1 enrolled. *Entrance requirements:* For master's, GRE, three letters of recommendation, transcripts, statement of purpose. Additional exam requirements/recommendations for international students: Required—TOEFL. *Application deadline:* For fall admission, 6/30 for domestic students. Applications are processed on a rolling basis. Application fee: $0. Electronic applications accepted. *Expenses:* $1,033 per credit hour tuition, $432 pere semester mandatory fees. *Financial support:* Fellowships, research assistantships, unspecified assistantships, and Fulbright scholarships available. Financial award application deadline: 2/15; financial award applicants required to submit FAFSA. *Faculty research:* Urban public policy. *Unit head:* Dr. Annette Steinacker, Director, 773-508-3396. *Application contact:* Jill Schur, Director, Graduate Enrollment Management, 312-915-8902, E-mail: gradinfo@luc.edu.

Massachusetts Institute of Technology, School of Architecture and Planning, Department of Urban Studies and Planning, Cambridge, MA 02139. Offers city planning (MCP); urban and regional planning (PhD); urban and regional studies (PhD); urban studies and planning (SM). *Accreditation:* ACSP (one or more programs are accredited). *Degree requirements:* For master's, thesis; for doctorate, comprehensive exam, thesis/dissertation. *Entrance requirements:* For master's and doctorate, GRE General Test. Additional exam requirements/recommendations for international students: Required—TOEFL, IELTS. Electronic applications accepted. *Faculty research:* City design and regional development; housing, community, and economic development; environmental policy; international development; infrastructure systems and climate change planning; spatial modeling and urban analytics.

Minnesota State University Mankato, College of Graduate Studies and Research, College of Social and Behavioral Sciences, Urban and Regional Studies Institute, Mankato, MN 56001. Offers local government management (Certificate); non-profit leadership (Certificate); urban and regional studies (MA); urban planning (MA, Certificate). *Degree requirements:* For master's, one foreign language, comprehensive exam, thesis or alternative. *Entrance requirements:* For master's, minimum GPA of 3.0 during previous 2 years, 2 letters of recommendation. Additional exam requirements/recommendations for international students: Required—TOEFL. Electronic applications accepted.

Moody Bible Institute, Graduate School, Chicago, IL 60610-3284. Offers biblical studies (MABS, Graduate Certificate); intercultural studies (MAIS, Graduate Certificate); ministry (M Div, M Min); spiritual formation and discipleship (MASF, Graduate Certificate); urban studies (MA, Graduate Certificate). *Program availability:* Part-time. *Degree requirements:* For master's, 2 foreign languages, fieldwork (MABS); colloquium, field research project (MA Min). *Entrance requirements:* For master's, 30 hours in Bible/theology, 2 years of ministry experience (MA Min).

New Jersey City University, Debra Cannon Partridge Wolfe College of Education, Department of Educational Leadership and Counseling, Jersey City, NJ 07305-1597. Offers counselor education (MA); educational administration and supervision (MA); urban education (MA). *Accreditation:* TEAC. *Program availability:* Part-time, evening/weekend. *Entrance requirements:* Additional exam requirements/recommendations for international students: Required—TOEFL (minimum score 79 iBT).

New Jersey Institute of Technology, College of Architecture and Design, Newark, NJ 07102. Offers architecture (M Arch, MS Arch); infrastructure planning (MIP); urban systems (PhD). *Program availability:* Part-time, evening/weekend. *Faculty:* 31 full-time (8 women), 37 part-time/adjunct (14 women). *Students:* 40 full-time (23 women), 6 part-time (0 women); includes 10 minority (1 Black or African American, non-Hispanic/Latino; 3 Asian, non-Hispanic/Latino; 5 Hispanic/Latino; 1 Two or more races, non-Hispanic/Latino), 19 international. Average age 30. 129 applicants, 37% accepted, 10 enrolled. In 2017, 16 master's, 4 doctorates awarded. Terminal master's awarded for partial completion of doctoral program. *Degree requirements:* For master's, thesis (for some programs). *Entrance requirements:* For master's, GRE General Test, minimum GPA of 3.0. Additional exam requirements/recommendations for international students: Required—TOEFL (minimum score 550 paper-based; 79 iBT). *Application deadline:* For fall admission, 6/1 priority date for domestic students, 5/1 priority date for international students; for spring admission, 11/15 priority date for domestic and international students. Applications are processed on a rolling basis. Application fee: $75. Electronic applications accepted. *Expenses:* Contact institution. *Financial support:* In 2017–18, 31 students received support, including 6 fellowships (averaging $6,825 per year), 8 teaching assistantships (averaging $24,834 per year); career-related internships or fieldwork, Federal Work-Study, institutionally sponsored loans, scholarships/grants, traineeships, unspecified assistantships, and studio assistantships (1 averaging $10,000) also available. Financial award application deadline: 1/15. *Faculty research:* Building sciences, community and urban design history and theory, computer-aided architecture, material dynamics. *Unit head:* Anthony W. Schuman, Interim Dean, 973-596-6370, E-mail: anthony.w.schuman@njit.edu. *Application contact:* Stephen Eck, Director of Admissions, 973-596-3300, Fax: 973-596-3461, E-mail: admissions@njit.edu.
Website: http://architecture.njit.edu/

New York University, Tandon School of Engineering, Department of Civil and Urban Engineering, Major in Urban Systems Engineering and Management, New York, NY 10012-1019. Offers MS. *Faculty:* 17 full-time (5 women), 38 part-time/adjunct (4 women). *Students:* 7 full-time (4 women), 11 part-time (5 women); includes 4 minority (3 Black or African American, non-Hispanic/Latino; 1 Hispanic/Latino), 9 international. Average age 28. 21 applicants, 76% accepted, 6 enrolled. In 2017, 4 master's awarded. *Entrance requirements:* Additional exam requirements/recommendations for international students: Required—TOEFL (minimum score 550 paper-based; 90 iBT); Recommended—IELTS (minimum score 7). *Application deadline:* For fall admission, 2/15 priority date for domestic and international students; for spring admission, 11/1 priority date for domestic and international students. Application fee: $75. *Expenses:* Tuition: Full-time $41,352; part-time $19,968 per year. *Required fees:* $2496; $1628 per unit. $814 per term. Tuition and fees vary according to course load and program. *Financial support:* Applicants required to submit FAFSA. *Total annual research expenditures:* $2.5 million. *Unit head:* Dr. Illan Juran, Program Director, 646-997-3717, E-mail: ijuran@nyu.edu. *Application contact:* Elizabeth Ensweiler, Senior Director of Graduate Enrollment and Graduate Admissions, 646-997-3182, E-mail: elizabeth.ensweiler@nyu.edu.

Norfolk State University, School of Graduate Studies, School of Liberal Arts, Department of Sociology, Program in Urban Affairs, Norfolk, VA 23504. Offers MA. *Program availability:* Part-time. *Degree requirements:* For master's, thesis. *Entrance requirements:* For master's, minimum GPA of 2.5.

North Dakota State University, College of Graduate and Interdisciplinary Studies, Interdisciplinary Program in Transportation and Logistics, Fargo, ND 58102. Offers managerial logistics (MML); transportation and logistics (PhD); transportation and urban systems (MS). *Entrance requirements:* For doctorate, 1 year of calculus, statistics and probability, minimum GPA of 3.0. Additional exam requirements/recommendations for international students: Required—TOEFL (minimum score 550 paper-based; 79 iBT). *Faculty research:* Supply chain optimization, spatial analysis of transportation networks, advanced traffic analysis, transportation demand, railroad/intermodal freight.

Northeastern University, College of Social Sciences and Humanities, Boston, MA 02115. Offers criminology and criminal justice (MSCJ); criminology and justice policy (PhD); economics (MA, PhD); English (MA, PhD); international affairs (MA); law and public policy (PhD); political science (MA, PhD); public administration (MPA); public policy (MPP); security and resilience studies (MS); sociology (MA, PhD); urban and regional policy (MS); urban informatics (MS); world history (MA, PhD). *Program availability:* Online learning. *Faculty:* 242. *Students:* 491. In 2017, 143 master's, 38 doctorates awarded. *Degree requirements:* For doctorate, variable foreign language requirement, comprehensive exam, thesis/dissertation. *Entrance requirements:* For master's and doctorate, GRE. Additional exam requirements/recommendations for international students: Required—TOEFL, IELTS. Application fee: $75. Electronic applications accepted. *Expenses:* Contact institution. *Financial support:* Teaching assistantships, career-related internships or fieldwork, scholarships/grants, health care benefits, tuition waivers (full and partial), and unspecified assistantships available. Support available to part-time students. Financial award applicants required to submit FAFSA. *Unit head:* Dr. Uta Poiger, Dean, 617-373-5173, E-mail: college_of_social_sciences_and_humanities@neu.edu. *Application contact:* 617-373-5990, E-mail: gradcssh@northeastern.edu.
Website: http://www.northeastern.edu/cssh/

Queens College of the City University of New York, Division of Social Sciences, Department of Urban Studies, Queens, NY 11367-1597. Offers urban affairs (MA). *Program availability:* Part-time, evening/weekend. *Students:* 1 (woman) full-time, 79 part-time (56 women); includes 55 minority (26 Black or African American, non-Hispanic/Latino; 8 Asian, non-Hispanic/Latino; 18 Hispanic/Latino; 3 Two or more races, non-Hispanic/Latino), 4 international. Average age 38. *Degree requirements:* For master's, thesis. *Entrance requirements:* For master's, minimum GPA of 3.0. Additional exam requirements/recommendations for international students: Required—TOEFL (minimum score 61 iBT), IELTS (minimum score 5). *Application deadline:* For fall admission, 8/15 for domestic students; for spring admission, 1/15 for domestic students. Applications are processed on a rolling basis. Application fee: $125. Electronic applications accepted. *Financial support:* Career-related internships or fieldwork and unspecified assistantships available. Financial award application deadline: 4/1; financial award applicants required to submit FAFSA. *Unit head:* Tarry Hum, Chair, 718-997-5124, E-mail: tarry.hum@qc.cuny.edu. *Application contact:* Elizabeth D'Amico-Ramirez, Assistant Director of Graduate Admissions, 718-997-5203, E-mail: elizabeth.damicoramirez@qc.cuny.edu.
Website: http://qcurban.org/

Rutgers University–Newark, Graduate School, Program in Public Administration, Newark, NJ 07102. Offers health care administration (MPA); human resources administration (MPA); public administration (PhD); public management (MPA); public policy analysis (MPA); urban systems and issues (MPA). *Accreditation:* NASPAA (one or more programs are accredited). *Program availability:* Part-time, evening/weekend. *Degree requirements:* For master's, comprehensive exam, thesis or alternative; for doctorate, thesis/dissertation. *Entrance requirements:* For master's, GRE, minimum undergraduate B average; for doctorate, GRE, MPA, minimum B average. Electronic applications accepted. *Faculty research:* Government finance, municipal and state government, public productivity.

Rutgers University–Newark, Graduate School, Program in Urban Systems, Newark, NJ 07102. Offers PhD. Program offered jointly with New Jersey Institute of Technology.

Savannah State University, Master of Science in Urban Studies and Planning Program, Savannah, GA 31404. Offers MSUS. *Program availability:* Part-time. *Degree requirements:* For master's, thesis or capstone project. *Entrance requirements:* For master's, GRE or MAT, minimum cumulative GPA of 2.6, 3 letters of recommendation, statement of interest, official transcripts, curriculum vitae. Additional exam requirements/recommendations for international students: Required—TOEFL. Electronic applications accepted. *Expenses:* Contact institution.

Simon Fraser University, Office of Graduate Studies and Postdoctoral Fellows, Faculty of Arts and Social Sciences, Urban Studies Program, Vancouver, BC V6B 5K3, Canada. Offers M Urb, Graduate Diploma. *Program availability:* Part-time. *Degree requirements:* For master's, project. *Entrance requirements:* For master's, minimum GPA of 3.0 (on scale of 4.33) or 3.33 based on last 60 credits of undergraduate courses; for Graduate Diploma, minimum GPA of 2.5 (on scale of 4.33) or 2.67 based on last 60 credits of undergraduate courses. Additional exam requirements/recommendations for international students: Recommended—TOEFL (minimum score 580 paper-based; 93 iBT), IELTS (minimum score 7), TWE (minimum score 5). Electronic applications accepted. *Faculty research:* Urban history; public policy and culture; environmental, transportation, and energy policy; urban governance and administration; urban sustainability.

Temple University, College of Liberal Arts, Department of Geography and Urban Studies, Philadelphia, PA 19122-6096. Offers geographic information systems (PSM, Graduate Certificate); geography and urban studies (MA, PhD). *Faculty:* 22 full-time (7 women), 2 part-time/adjunct (1 woman). *Students:* 27 full-time (16 women), 22 part-time (10 women); includes 14 minority (9 Black or African American, non-Hispanic/Latino; 2 Asian, non-Hispanic/Latino; 3 Hispanic/Latino), 7 international. 53 applicants, 45% accepted, 15 enrolled. In 2017, 4 master's, 2 doctorates, 3 other advanced degrees awarded. *Degree requirements:* For master's, comprehensive exam, thesis or alternative. *Entrance requirements:* For master's, GRE General Test, minimum GPA of 3.0, 3 letters of recommendation; for doctorate, GRE, minimum GPA of 3.0, 3 letters of recommendation. Additional exam requirements/recommendations for international students: Required—TOEFL (minimum score 575 paper-based; 88 iBT). *Application deadline:* For fall admission, 1/15 for domestic students, 12/15 for international students; for spring admission, 10/15 for domestic students, 8/1 for international students. Applications are processed on a rolling basis. Application fee: $60. Electronic applications accepted. *Expenses:* Tuition, state resident: full-time $16,164; part-time $898 per credit hour. Tuition, nonresident: full-time $22,158; part-time $1231 per credit hour. *Required fees:* $890; $445 per semester. Full-time tuition and fees vary according to course load, degree level, campus/location and program. *Financial support:* Fellowships, teaching assistantships, career-related internships or fieldwork, Federal Work-Study, and tuition waivers (partial) available. Financial award application deadline: 1/15; financial award applicants required to submit FAFSA. *Faculty research:* Social justice, sustainability, globalization, geographic methods, urban processes. *Unit head:* Dr. C. Hamil Pearsall, Graduate Director, 215-204-3074, Fax: 215-204-7833, E-mail: hamil.pearsall@temple.edu. *Application contact:* Julia Falcon, Student Services Coordinator, 215-204-3386, E-mail: julia.falcon@temple.edu.
Website: http://www.cla.temple.edu/gus/

Tufts University, Graduate School of Arts and Sciences, Department of Urban and Environmental Policy and Planning, Medford, MA 02155. Offers community development (MA); environmental policy (MA); health and human welfare (MA); housing policy (MA); international environment/development policy (MA); public policy (MPP); MA/JD; MA/MBA; MA/MPH; MA/MS; MALD/MA. MALD/MA offered in connection with The Fletcher School of Law and Diplomacy; MA/MPH with School of Medicine; MA/MS with School of Nutrition Science and Policy or School of Engineering; MA/MBA with Boston College, Carroll School of Management; MA/JD with Boston College Law School. *Accreditation:* ACSP (one or more programs are accredited). *Program availability:* Part-time. *Students:* 95 full-time (68 women), 17 part-time (14 women); includes 34 minority (14 Black or African American, non-Hispanic/Latino; 10 Asian, non-Hispanic/Latino; 6 Hispanic/Latino; 4 Two or more races, non-Hispanic/Latino), 14 international. Average age 30. 153 applicants, 78% accepted, 51 enrolled. In 2017, 45 master's awarded. *Degree requirements:* For master's, thesis or alternative, internship. *Entrance requirements:* For master's, GRE General Test. Additional exam requirements/recommendations for international students: Required—TOEFL (minimum score 550 paper-based; 80 iBT), IELTS (minimum score 6.5). *Application deadline:* For fall admission, 1/15 for domestic and international students. Applications are processed on a rolling basis. Application fee: $85. Electronic applications accepted. *Expenses:* Contact institution. *Financial support:* Fellowships, research assistantships, teaching assistantships, career-related internships or fieldwork, Federal Work-Study, scholarships/grants, tuition waivers (full and partial), and unspecified assistantships available. Support available to part-time students. Financial award application deadline: 1/15. *Unit head:* Dr. Mary Davis, Graduate Program Director, 617-627-3394. *Application contact:* Office of Graduate Admissions, 617-627-3395, E-mail: gradadmissions@tufts.edu.
Website: http://ase.tufts.edu/uep/

Université du Québec à Montréal, Graduate Programs, Program in Urban Analysis and Management, Montréal, QC H3C 3P8, Canada. Offers MA. Program offered jointly with Université du Québec, École nationale d'administration publique and Université du Québec, Institut National de la Recherche Scientifique. *Program availability:* Part-time. *Entrance requirements:* For master's, appropriate bachelor's degree or equivalent and proficiency in French.

Université du Québec à Montréal, Graduate Programs, Program in Urban Studies, Montréal, QC H3C 3P8, Canada. Offers MA, PhD. *Program availability:* Part-time. *Degree requirements:* For doctorate, thesis/dissertation. *Entrance requirements:* For doctorate, appropriate master's degree or equivalent, proficiency in French.

Université du Québec, École nationale d'administration publique, Graduate Programs in Public Administration, Program in Urban Analysis and Management, Quebec, QC G1K 9E5, Canada. Offers MAGU. *Program availability:* Part-time. *Entrance requirements:* For master's, appropriate bachelor's degree, proficiency in French.

Université du Québec, Institut National de la Recherche Scientifique, Graduate Programs, Centre for Urbanisation Culture Societe, Montreal, QC G1K 9A9, Canada. Offers demography (M Sc, PhD); research practices and public action (MA, DESS); urban studies (M Sc, PhD). *Program availability:* Part-time. *Faculty:* 29 full-time. *Students:* 82 full-time (42 women), 12 part-time (10 women), 13 international. Average age 32. 35 applicants, 83% accepted, 23 enrolled. In 2017, 10 master's, 3 doctorates awarded. *Degree requirements:* For master's, thesis (for some programs); for doctorate, thesis/dissertation; for DESS, thesis or alternative. *Entrance requirements:* For master's, appropriate bachelor's degree, proficiency in French; for doctorate, appropriate master's degree, proficiency in French; for DESS, proficiency in French. *Application deadline:* For fall admission, 3/30 for domestic and international students; for winter admission, 11/1 for domestic and international students; for spring admission, 3/1 for domestic and international students. Application fee: $45. Electronic applications accepted. *Financial support:* In 2017–18, fellowships (averaging $16,500 per year) were awarded; research assistantships also available. *Faculty research:* Mobility and migration, cultural policies, knowledge mobilization, spatial analysis of data, social demography. *Unit head:* Hélène Belleau, Director, 514-499-4001, Fax: 514-499-4065, E-mail: helene.belleau@ucs.inrs.ca. *Application contact:* Sylvie Richard, Registrar, 418-654-2518, Fax: 418-654-3858, E-mail: sylvie.richard@adm.inrs.ca.
Website: http://www.ucs.inrs.ca

University at Albany, State University of New York, College of Arts and Sciences, Department of Sociology, Albany, NY 12222-0001. Offers demography (Certificate); sociology (MA, PhD); urban policy (Certificate). *Faculty:* 25 full-time (11 women). *Students:* 25 full-time (18 women), 53 part-time (39 women); includes 16 minority (4 Black or African American, non-Hispanic/Latino; 5 Asian, non-Hispanic/Latino; 5 Hispanic/Latino; 2 Two or more races, non-Hispanic/Latino), 22 international. 71 applicants, 37% accepted, 7 enrolled. In 2017, 5 doctorates awarded. Terminal master's awarded for partial completion of doctoral program. *Degree requirements:* For master's, thesis; for doctorate, thesis/dissertation, 2 specialization exams, research tool. *Entrance requirements:* For master's and doctorate, GRE General Test. Additional exam requirements/recommendations for international students: Required—TOEFL. *Application deadline:* For fall admission, 1/15 for domestic students, 5/1 for international students. Applications are processed on a rolling basis. Application fee: $75. Electronic applications accepted. *Expenses:* Tuition, state resident: full-time $10,870; part-time $453 per credit hour. Tuition, nonresident: full-time $22,210; part-time $925 per credit hour. *Required fees:* $84.68 per credit hour. $508.06 per semester. Part-time tuition and fees vary according to course load and program. *Financial support:* Fellowships, research assistantships, teaching assistantships, career-related internships or fieldwork, and Federal Work-Study available. Financial award application deadline: 3/15. *Faculty research:* Gender and equality, crime and deviance, aging, work and organizations, social demography. *Unit head:* Glenn Deane, Chair, 518-442-4666, Fax: 518-442-4936, E-mail: gdeane@albany.edu. *Application contact:* Michael DeRensis, Director, Graduate Admissions, 518-442-3980, Fax: 518-442-3922, E-mail: graduate@albany.edu.
Website: http://www.albany.edu/sociology/index.html

University of California, Irvine, School of Social Ecology, Department of Urban Planning and Public Policy, Irvine, CA 92697. Offers planning, policy and design (PhD); urban and regional planning (MURP). *Accreditation:* ACSP (one or more programs are accredited). *Students:* 116 full-time (62 women), 9 part-time (2 women); includes 55 minority (2 Black or African American, non-Hispanic/Latino; 17 Asian, non-Hispanic/Latino; 24 Hispanic/Latino; 1 Native Hawaiian or other Pacific Islander, non-Hispanic/Latino; 11 Two or more races, non-Hispanic/Latino), 38 international. Average age 28. 300 applicants, 66% accepted, 58 enrolled. In 2017, 49 master's, 6 doctorates awarded. *Degree requirements:* For doctorate, thesis/dissertation, research project. *Entrance requirements:* For master's and doctorate, GRE General Test, minimum GPA of 3.0. Additional exam requirements/recommendations for international students: Required—TOEFL (minimum score 550 paper-based). *Application deadline:* For fall admission, 1/15 priority date for domestic and international students. Application fee: $105 ($125 for international students). Electronic applications accepted. *Financial support:* Fellowships with tuition reimbursements, research assistantships with full tuition reimbursements, teaching assistantships with tuition reimbursements, institutionally sponsored loans, traineeships, health care benefits, and unspecified assistantships available. Financial award application deadline: 1/15; financial award applicants required to submit FAFSA. *Faculty research:* Community and social policy, economic development, land-use and growth management, transportation planning, environmental policy. *Unit head:* David L. Feldman, Chair, 949-824-4384, Fax: 949-824-3056, E-mail: feldmand@uci.edu. *Application contact:* Janet Gallagher, Graduate Coordinator, 949-824-9849, Fax: 949-824-8566, E-mail: janetg@uci.edu.
Website: http://uppp.soceco.uci.edu/

University of Delaware, Center for Energy and Environmental Policy, Newark, DE 19716. Offers energy and environmental policy (MA, MEEP, PhD); urban affairs and public policy (PhD), including technology, environment, and society. *Degree requirements:* For master's, analytical paper or thesis; for doctorate, comprehensive exam, thesis/dissertation. *Entrance requirements:* For master's, GRE General Test, minimum GPA of 3.0; for doctorate, GRE General Test, minimum GPA of 3.5. Additional exam requirements/recommendations for international students: Required—TOEFL. Electronic applications accepted. *Faculty research:* Sustainable development, renewable energy, climate change, environmental policy, environmental justice, disaster policy.

University of Delaware, College of Arts and Sciences, School of Public Policy and Administration, Program in Urban Affairs and Public Policy, Newark, DE 19716. Offers governance planning and management (PhD); historic preservation (MA); social and urban policy (PhD); technology, environment and society (PhD); urban affairs and public policy (MA). *Program availability:* Part-time. Terminal master's awarded for partial completion of doctoral program. *Degree requirements:* For master's, analytical paper or thesis; for doctorate, thesis/dissertation. *Entrance requirements:* For master's, GRE General Test, minimum GPA of 3.0; for doctorate, GRE General Test, minimum GPA of 3.5. Additional exam requirements/recommendations for international students: Required—TOEFL. Electronic applications accepted. *Faculty research:* Political economy; social policy analysis; technology and society; historic preservation; urban policy.

University of Lethbridge, School of Graduate Studies, Lethbridge, AB T1K 3M4, Canada. Offers addictions counseling (M Sc); agricultural biotechnology (M Sc); agricultural studies (M Sc, MA); anthropology (MA); archaeology (M Sc, MA); art (MA, MFA); biochemistry (M Sc); biological sciences (M Sc); biomolecular science (PhD); biosystems and biodiversity (PhD); Canadian studies (MA); chemistry (M Sc); computer science (M Sc); computer science and geographical information science (M Sc); counseling (MC); counseling psychology (M Ed); dramatic arts (MA); earth, space, and physical science (PhD); economics (MA); education (MA, PhD); educational leadership (M Ed); English (MA); environmental science (M Sc); evolution and behavior (PhD); exercise science (M Sc); French (MA); French/German (MA); French/Spanish (MA); general education (M Ed); geography (M Sc, MA); German (MA); health sciences (M Sc); individualized multidisciplinary (M Sc, MA); kinesiology (M Sc, MA); management (M Sc), including accounting, finance, human resource management and labor relations, information systems, international management, marketing, policy and strategy; mathematics (M Sc); music (M Mus, MA); Native American studies (MA); neuroscience (M Sc, PhD); new media (MA, MFA); nursing (M Sc, MN); philosophy (MA); physics (M Sc); political science (MA); psychology (M Sc, MA); religious studies (MA); sociology (MA); theatre and dramatic arts (MFA); theoretical and computational science (PhD); urban and regional studies (MA); women and gender studies (MA). *Program availability:* Part-time, evening/weekend. *Degree requirements:* For master's, thesis (for some programs); for doctorate, comprehensive exam, thesis/dissertation. *Entrance requirements:* For master's, GMAT (for M Sc in management), bachelor's degree in related field, minimum GPA of 3.0 during previous 20 graded semester courses, 2 years' teaching or related experience (M Ed); for doctorate, master's degree, minimum graduate GPA of 3.5. Additional exam requirements/recommendations for international students: Required—TOEFL (minimum score 580 paper-based; 93 iBT). Electronic applications accepted. *Faculty research:* Movement and brain plasticity, gibberellin physiology, photosynthesis, carbon cycling, molecular properties of main-group ring components.

University of Louisville, Graduate School, College of Arts and Sciences, Department of Urban and Public Affairs, Louisville, KY 40208. Offers public administration (MPA), including human resources management, non-profit management, public policy and administration; urban and public affairs (PhD), including urban planning and development, urban policy and administration; urban planning (MUP), including administration of planning organizations, housing and community development, land use and environmental planning, spatial analysis. *Program availability:* Part-time, evening/weekend. *Faculty:* 12 full-time (5 women), 4 part-time/adjunct (1 woman). *Students:* 50 full-time (19 women), 20 part-time (17 women); includes 17 minority (6 Black or African American, non-Hispanic/Latino; 1 Asian, non-Hispanic/Latino; 4 Hispanic/Latino; 6 Two or more races, non-Hispanic/Latino), 4 international. Average age 31. 47 applicants, 70% accepted, 22 enrolled. In 2017, 20 master's, 2 doctorates awarded. Terminal master's awarded for partial completion of doctoral program. *Degree requirements:* For master's, internship; for doctorate, comprehensive exam, thesis/dissertation. *Entrance requirements:* For master's, GRE General Test, minimum GPA of 3.0; for doctorate, GRE General Test, master's degree in appropriate field. Additional exam requirements/recommendations for international students: Required—TOEFL (minimum score 550 paper-based; 79 iBT). *Application deadline:* Applications are processed on a rolling basis. Application fee: $65. *Expenses:* Contact institution. *Financial support:* Fellowships, research assistantships, tuition waivers (full and partial), and unspecified assistantships available. Financial award application deadline: 2/1. *Faculty research:* Urban theory, sustainability, public administration, urban planning, urban management. *Total annual research expenditures:* $240,308. *Unit head:* Dr. David Simpson, Chair, 502-852-8019, Fax: 502-852-4558, E-mail: dave.simpson@louisville.edu. *Application contact:* Latonia Craig, Director of Graduate Recruitment and Diversity Retention, 502-852-5207, Fax: 502-852-4558, E-mail: gradadm@louisville.edu.
Website: http://supa.louisville.edu

University of Maryland, Baltimore County, The Graduate School, College of Arts, Humanities and Social Sciences, School of Public Policy, Baltimore, MD 21250. Offers public policy (MPP, PhD), including economics (PhD), educational policy, emergency services (PhD), environmental policy (MPP), evaluation and analytical methods, health policy, policy history (PhD), public management, urban policy. *Program availability:* Part-time, evening/weekend. *Faculty:* 10 full-time (5 women). *Students:* 50 full-time (24 women), 69 part-time (37 women); includes 35 minority (17 Black or African American, non-Hispanic/Latino; 1 American Indian or Alaska Native, non-Hispanic/Latino; 8 Asian, non-Hispanic/Latino; 5 Hispanic/Latino; 1 Native Hawaiian or other Pacific Islander, non-Hispanic/Latino; 3 Two or more races, non-Hispanic/Latino), 6 international. Average age 37. 60 applicants, 68% accepted, 25 enrolled. In 2017, 15 master's, 3 doctorates awarded. Terminal master's awarded for partial completion of doctoral program. *Degree requirements:* For master's, thesis, policy analysis paper, internship for pre-service; for doctorate, comprehensive exam, thesis/dissertation, comprehensive and field qualifying exams. *Entrance requirements:* For master's, GRE General Test, 3 academic letters of reference, resume, official transcripts; for doctorate, GRE General Test, 3 academic letters of reference, resume, research paper, official transcripts. Additional exam requirements/recommendations for international students: Required—TOEFL (minimum score 550 paper-based; 80 iBT), IELTS (minimum score 6.5). *Application deadline:* For

fall admission, 1/15 priority date for domestic students, 1/1 priority date for international students; for spring admission, 11/1 priority date for domestic students, 5/1 priority date for international students. Applications are processed on a rolling basis. Application fee: $50. Electronic applications accepted. *Expenses:* $28,061 in-state, $39,356 out-of-state to complete the degree (for MPP); $43,823 in-state, $61,508 out-of-state to complete the degree (for PhD). *Financial support:* In 2017–18, 26 students received support, including 26 research assistantships with full tuition reimbursements available (averaging $20,000 per year); Federal Work-Study, scholarships/grants, health care benefits, and unspecified assistantships also available. Financial award application deadline: 1/1; financial award applicants required to submit FAFSA. *Faculty research:* Education policy, health policy, urban and environmental policy, public management, evaluation and analytical method. *Unit head:* Dr. Susan Sterett, Director, 410-455-2140, Fax: 410-455-1172, E-mail: ssterett@umbc.edu. *Application contact:* Sally F. Helms, Administrator of Academic Affairs, 410-455-3202, Fax: 410-455-1172, E-mail: gradpubpol@umbc.edu.
Website: http://publicpolicy.umbc.edu/

University of New Orleans, Graduate School, College of Liberal Arts, Department of Planning and Urban Studies, Program in Urban Studies, New Orleans, LA 70148. Offers MS, PhD. *Degree requirements:* For master's, thesis; for doctorate, thesis/dissertation. *Entrance requirements:* For master's, GRE General Test. Additional exam requirements/recommendations for international students: Required—TOEFL (minimum score 550 paper-based; 79 iBT), IELTS (minimum score 6.5). Electronic applications accepted. *Faculty research:* Urban economic development, environmental planning and analysis, social and cultural change.

University of San Francisco, College of Arts and Sciences, Urban and Public Affairs Program, San Francisco, CA 94117. Offers MA. *Program availability:* Part-time. *Entrance requirements:* Additional exam requirements/recommendations for international students: Required—TOEFL, IELTS, PTE. Electronic applications accepted.

University of Wisconsin–Milwaukee, Graduate School, College of Letters and Science, Program in Urban Studies, Milwaukee, WI 53201-0413. Offers MS, PhD. *Unit head:* Joel Rast, Director, 414-229-4751, E-mail: jrast@uwm.edu. *Application contact:* General Letters and Science Support, 414-229-7711, E-mail: let-sci@uwm.edu.
Website: https://uwm.edu/urban-studies/

Virginia Polytechnic Institute and State University, Graduate School, College of Architecture and Urban Studies, Blacksburg, VA 24061. Offers architecture (M Arch, MS); architecture and design research (PhD); building construction science management (MS); creative technologies (MFA); environmental design and planning (PhD); government and international affairs (MPIA); landscape architecture (MLA, PhD); planning, governance, and globalization (PhD); public administration and public affairs (MPA, PhD); urban and regional planning (MURPL). *Accreditation:* ASLA (one or more programs are accredited). *Faculty:* 139 full-time (58 women), 1 (woman) part-time/adjunct. *Students:* 339 full-time (165 women), 210 part-time (97 women); includes 115 minority (49 Black or African American, non-Hispanic/Latino; 1 American Indian or Alaska Native, non-Hispanic/Latino; 30 Asian, non-Hispanic/Latino; 29 Hispanic/Latino; 6 Two or more races, non-Hispanic/Latino), 136 international. Average age 32. 649 applicants, 49% accepted, 105 enrolled. In 2017, 142 master's, 18 doctorates awarded. *Degree requirements:* For master's, comprehensive exam (for some programs), thesis (for some programs); for doctorate, comprehensive exam (for some programs), thesis/dissertation (for some programs). *Entrance requirements:* For master's and doctorate, GRE/GMAT. Additional exam requirements/recommendations for international students: Required—TOEFL (minimum score 80 iBT). *Application deadline:* For fall admission, 8/1 for domestic students, 4/1 for international students; for spring admission, 1/1 for domestic students, 9/1 for international students. Applications are processed on a rolling basis. Application fee: $75. Electronic applications accepted. *Expenses:* Tuition, state resident: full-time $15,072; part-time $718.50 per credit hour. Tuition, nonresident: full-time $28,810; part-time $1448.25 per credit hour. *Required fees:* $2741; $502 per semester. Tuition and fees vary according to course load, campus/location and program. *Financial support:* In 2017–18, 17 research assistantships with full tuition reimbursements (averaging $18,561 per year), 41 teaching assistantships with full tuition reimbursements (averaging $17,340 per year) were awarded. Financial award application deadline: 3/1; financial award applicants required to submit FAFSA. *Total annual research expenditures:* $3.1 million. *Unit head:* Dr. Richard Blythe, Dean, 540-231-6416, Fax: 540-231-6332, E-mail: richbl1@vt.edu. *Application contact:* Christine Mattsson-Coon, Executive Assistant, 540-231-6416, Fax: 540-231-6332, E-mail: cmattsso@vt.edu.
Website: http://www.caus.vt.edu/

Wayne State University, College of Fine, Performing and Communication Arts, Department of Communication, Detroit, MI 48202. Offers communication (PhD), including democratic participation and culture, identity and representation, media, society and culture, risk, crisis and conflict, wellness, work life and relationships;

communication and new media (Graduate Certificate); communication studies (MA); dispute resolution (MADR, Graduate Certificate), including community and urban studies (MADR), conflict area studies (MADR), health and family (MADR), international conflict and cooperation (MADR), professional practice (MADR), theory of conflict (MADR), workplace (MADR); health communication (Graduate Certificate); journalism (MA); media arts (MA); media studies (MA); public relations and organizational communication (MA); JD/MADR. Doctoral program admits for fall only. *Program availability:* Online learning. *Faculty:* 21. *Students:* 63 full-time (35 women), 87 part-time (55 women); includes 54 minority (39 Black or African American, non-Hispanic/Latino; 2 Asian, non-Hispanic/Latino; 7 Hispanic/Latino; 6 Two or more races, non-Hispanic/Latino), 10 international. Average age 34. 153 applicants, 39% accepted, 27 enrolled. In 2017, 26 master's, 7 doctorates, 8 other advanced degrees awarded. *Degree requirements:* For master's, thesis (for some programs). *Entrance requirements:* For master's, GRE (for MA if undergraduate GPA less than 3.2), personal statement; BA or BS in communication or related field with minimum upper-division GPA of 3.2 and minimum upper-division undergraduate GPA of 3.0, and sample of academic writing (for MA); undergraduate degree with minimum upper-division GPA of 3.0 and three letters of recommendation (for MADR); for doctorate, GRE, undergraduate degree in communication or related field; master's degree in communication or related field with minimum GPA of 3.5; letters of recommendation; personal statement; sample of written scholarship. Additional exam requirements/recommendations for international students: Required—TOEFL (minimum score 100 iBT), IELTS, TWE. Application fee: $50. Electronic applications accepted. *Expenses:* Contact institution. *Financial support:* In 2017–18, 57 students received support, including 5 fellowships with tuition reimbursements available (averaging $17,400 per year), 2 research assistantships with tuition reimbursements available (averaging $20,388 per year), 20 teaching assistantships with tuition reimbursements available (averaging $18,534 per year); scholarships/grants and unspecified assistantships also available. Financial award applicants required to submit FAFSA. *Faculty research:* Democratic participation and culture; identity and representation; media, society and culture; risk, crisis and conflict; wellness, work life, and relationships. *Unit head:* Dr. Lee Wilkins, Professor and Chair, 313-577-2943, E-mail: eh8899@wayne.edu. *Application contact:* E-mail: communication@wayne.edu.
Website: http://comm.wayne.edu/

Wayne State University, College of Liberal Arts and Sciences, Department of Political Science, Detroit, MI 48202. Offers political science (MA, PhD); public administration (MPA), including economic development policy and management, health and human services policy and management, human and fiscal resource management, nonprofit policy and management, organizational behavior and management, urban and metropolitan policy and management; JD/MA. *Accreditation:* NASPAA. *Faculty:* 18. *Students:* 48 full-time (20 women), 68 part-time (36 women); includes 37 minority (26 Black or African American, non-Hispanic/Latino; 3 Asian, non-Hispanic/Latino; 2 Hispanic/Latino; 6 Two or more races, non-Hispanic/Latino), 6 international. Average age 32. 105 applicants, 39% accepted, 20 enrolled. In 2017, 17 master's, 3 doctorates awarded. *Degree requirements:* For master's, comprehensive exam (for some programs), thesis (for some programs); for doctorate, thesis/dissertation. *Entrance requirements:* For master's, GRE General Test, substantial undergraduate preparation in the social sciences, minimum upper-division undergraduate GPA of 3.0, two letters of recommendation, personal statement; for doctorate, GRE General Test, 3 letters of recommendation; personal statement; interview. Additional exam requirements/recommendations for international students: Required—TOEFL (minimum score 550 paper-based; 79 iBT), TWE (minimum score 5.5), Michigan English Language Assessment Battery (minimum score 85); Recommended—IELTS (minimum score 6.5). *Application deadline:* For fall admission, 5/15 for domestic students, 5/1 priority date for international students; for winter admission, 10/15 for domestic students, 9/1 priority date for international students. Applications are processed on a rolling basis. Application fee: $50. Electronic applications accepted. *Expenses:* Contact institution. *Financial support:* In 2017–18, 44 students received support, including 6 fellowships with tuition reimbursements available (averaging $11,698 per year), 12 teaching assistantships with tuition reimbursements available (averaging $18,534 per year); research assistantships with tuition reimbursements available, scholarships/grants, health care benefits, and unspecified assistantships also available. Financial award applicants required to submit FAFSA. *Faculty research:* American government and politics, comparative politics, political methodology, political theory, public administration, public law, public policy, world politics/international relations, formal theory/modeling, gender and politics, international law, peace research, political economy, political psychology, politics of developing countries, race, religion, and ethnicity, urban politics. *Unit head:* Dr. Daniel Geller, Professor and Chair, 313-577-6328, E-mail: dgeller@wayne.edu. *Application contact:* Dr. Sharon Lean, Graduate Director, 313-577-2630, E-mail: gradpolisci@wayne.edu.
Website: http://clas.wayne.edu/politicalscience/

CALIFORNIA POLYTECHNIC STATE UNIVERSITY

Masters of City & Regional Planning

Program of Study

The Master of City & Regional Planning program at California Polytechnic State University cultivates talent, leadership, innovation and action-oriented research leading to the education of civic-minded and diverse students. The program provides an applied, comprehensive, professional planning education with, community, regional, and global awareness. The university prepares planners to develop communities and regions that are socially, ecologically, and economically sustainable.

The Master of City & Regional Planning degree (M.C.R.P.) is an applied, comprehensive, and professionally based program. It is open to students with high standards of academic achievement who wish to pursue careers in city and regional planning. It is structured to prepare graduates to function in a general context of city planning. The core courses cover planning theory, methods, law, and formulation and implementation of plans and policies. In addition, skill building in all aspects of planning communications (visual, verbal, written) is stressed.

The M.C.R.P. program is structured to meet the needs of those who have earned baccalaureate degrees in a variety of disciplines including, but not limited to, environmental studies, economics, business, geography, architecture, landscape architecture, civil engineering, political science, environmental or urban studies, natural resources management, and ecology. The program is six quarters (two years) in duration and consists of 72 approved units (not including courses necessary to compensate for deficiencies). The degree culminates in a thesis (CRP 599), professional project (CRP 596), or a community planning studio (CRP 556).

Research Opportunities

California Polytechnic State University has a thesis-based program that gives students strong research experience under the direct leadership of their faculty supervisor. As a result, they graduate with the skills to perform these tasks: 1) critically evaluate and apply scientific research, 2) gather, organize, analyze, and present planning information, and 3) transform information into knowledge for action.

The City & Regional Planning (CRP) Department is recognized locally and nationally for providing excellence in education. Since 2000, the American Planning Association has awarded the Outstanding Planning Award for Distinguished Leadership by a student to three CRP students. This achievement is unique among planning schools.

In addition, students regularly win awards for projects and studios from the American Planning Association. Students have won the annual Bank of America Low Cost Housing Challenge twice. According to the Planetizen Guide to Graduate Urban Planning Programs, California Polytechnic State University has consistently ranked near the top of programs for planning for the past 10 years. Its 2017 guide ranked the M.C.R.P. program 5th among small programs and 20th in the country.

Financial Aid

Graduate students may qualify for federal loans, emergency loans, state grants, scholarships, and veteran's benefits. Students may also pursue loans from private lenders, employer tuition remission programs, and scholarships from private sources.

Cost of Study

For the 2018–19 academic year, tuition and fees for the Master in City and Regional Planning program average $3,750 per term for California residents and $7,710 for nonresidents. The most current information on tuition and fees is available at https://afd.calpoly.edu/fees/.

Living and Housing

Graduate students can live in campus apartments complete with a full kitchen, private bathrooms, and the option of private or shared bedrooms. Costs for a University apartment per academic year range from $5,770 for an apartment with a double suite bedroom to $9,014 for an apartment with a private bedroom. There are also many opportunities for off-campus housing.

Location

California Polytechnic State University is located in San Luis Obispo, California. According to Colleges in California, its campus is one of the most beautiful in the state. The University is situated in an area known for its mild climate, natural beauty, and outdoor recreational options. Biking, hiking, and sailing are just some of the activities students can enjoy most of the year.

The University

California Polytechnic State University fosters scholarship, service, and teaching in a learn-by-doing environment. The application of theory to practice, active-learning methods, and field and laboratory work form the core of this academic approach. The University offers approximately 21,300 students nearly 190 bachelor's, master's, minor, and credential programs. This large offering enables students to create programs of study that reflect their academic and career interests.

California Polytechnic State University's commitment to providing high quality education earns it top honors. In its 2017 guidebook, U.S. News & World Report named it the best public, master's-level university in the west. This is the 24th consecutive year that the university has received this honor. The publisher also ranked it ninth among the best universities in the western region.

Faculty

Graduate faculty members in the City and Regional Planning Department are committed to helping their students succeed. They integrate theory, research, and practice to provide extensive knowledge and training. Students have an opportunity to form close working relationships with accomplished faculty like Hemalata C. Dandekar. Dr. Dandekar is a professor and the head of the City and Regional Planning Department, but also has practical experience as a licensed architect in state of California. Her research interests include architecture and planning methods, comparative issues of international development, housing, rural planning, urban form and design, vernacular, and women and development.

Applying

Most applicants with undergraduate degrees in political science, architecture or civil engineering are eligible to apply for the M.S. program.

California Polytechnic State University

Applicants with other undergraduate degrees are also eligible to apply but may require prerequisite course work.

All applicants must submit a statement of purpose; 3 letters of reference; and GRE scores. For applicants with degrees from outside the U.S., all of the above applies. In addition, the applicant's international credentials must be evaluated by AACRAO, ACEI, WES or IERF; proficiency in English must be demonstrated by taking TOEFL (Test of English as a Foreign Language) within the last 2 years with an Internet score of 80 or greater or ELTS (International English Language Testing System) must be taken within 2 years with a score of 6.5 or greater. TOFEL or ELTS is required to issue an I20 visa.

Candidates are strongly encouraged to submit their application materials by mid-January. As a relatively small, non-cohort program, it is important that candidates connect with the graduate coordinator, discuss potential areas of research, include these considerations in their statement of interest, and submit applications early. Applications are accepted through the online system Cal State Apply. The filing periods are listed at https://admissions.calpoly.edu/applicants/graduate/deadlines.html and all applicants are responsible for using the University's established applicant checklist for meeting admission deadlines. More information is available at grad.calpoly.edu.

Contact

California Polytechnic State University

City and Regional Planning

1 Grand Avenue

San Luis Obispo, California 93407

Phone: 805-756-1315

E-mail: crp@calpoly.edu

Website: www.planning.calpoly.edu

UNIVERSITY OF DELAWARE
School of Public Policy and Administration

Programs of Study

The School of Public Policy and Administration offers five graduate degree programs: a Master of Public Administration (M.P.A.), a Master of Arts (M.A.) in Urban Affairs and Public Policy, a Master of Public Policy (M.P.P.), a Master of Science (M.S.) in Disaster Science and Management, and a Master of Energy and Environmental Policy (M.E.E.P.). Graduate certificates are offered in Historic Preservation and Nonprofit and Voluntary Action. Ph.D. degrees are offered for Urban Affairs and Public Policy, Disaster Science and Management, and Energy and Environmental Policy.

The M.P.A. is a 36-credit, two-year professional degree program that prepares students for leadership positions in public affairs. It is the preferred professional degree for anyone whose ambition is a career in public or nonprofit management. The program boasts a strong, collaborative, faculty-student research environment and has been accredited by the Network of Schools of Public Policy, Affairs, and Administration (NASPAA) since 1982. Areas of specialization include nonprofit management, public policy analysis, emergency management, public management, or a student-designed area (with faculty approval).

The M.A. in Urban Affairs and Public Policy is a 36-credit program that typically involves four semesters of full-time study. It offers students a strong foundation in public policy theory and analysis with a strong focus on solving a variety of societal problems. The program is particularly strong in providing students with many opportunities to apply their new theoretical knowledge and analytical skills to real-world issues. This is done through the careful selection of elective courses, participation in a policy analysis studio, or writing a thesis. Most importantly, this application of skills occurs in the close collaboration with faculty and professional staff in conducting research and public service projects that have clear policy impact. These projects tend to be in the areas of disaster science and management, health policy, historic preservation, housing and community development, media and public policy, nonprofits and philanthropy, and urban and regional planning. The program also has a vibrant international component with study trips, organized and led by the faculty and professional staff, to various places in Europe, Asia, Latin America, and Africa.

The Master of Public Policy (M.P.P.) degree program offers 42 credits of coursework that are generally completed in 2 years of study. The program provides advanced analytic and substantive knowledge of public policy to educate professionals for work in the public, private, and non-profit sectors on issues of public concern at all levels, local to global. M.P.P. education trains students to rigorously analyze policy components so that policy that is crafted and later implemented will effectively address the complex issues that face our society. This interdisciplinary degree draws from multiple fields of study, including economics, political science, sociology, psychology, education, law, history, and public health. The SPPA M.P.P. degree focuses on professional skills in public policy analysis, evaluation, and communication.

The Ph.D. in Urban Affairs and Public Policy is an interdisciplinary, research-oriented degree that focuses on analysis of the critical policy challenges of our times. The program prepares scholars to create usable knowledge that can inform decision-making and improve the quality of life in communities at all scales, from cities to nations. The doctoral program prepares scholars to approach these multifaceted challenges from creative vantage points, reflecting diverse, international perspectives that transcend disciplinary views and embody the highest research standards. A concern for the global policy challenges and opportunities of an urbanizing world cuts across all research. Students work alongside faculty and researchers to create new knowledge and develop innovative approaches to expand the possibilities for community enhancement and policy improvement.

The School offers a nationally recognized internship program that places students in paid professional positions in international, national, state, and local government. All students in the School are eligible; the internship is a requirement for pre-service M.P.A. students.

The M.S. and Ph.D. program in Disaster Science and Management covers the theories, research methodologies, and policies informing efforts focused on emergency preparedness, mitigation, management and response. The M.S. degree requires 30 credits (non-thesis requires 24 credits). The Ph.D. degree requires 42 credits of graduate-level course work beyond the master's degree and 9 credits of dissertation.

The M.E.E.P. and Ph.D. in Energy and Environmental policy programs are the first of their kind in the United States. These programs have earned international recognition for being among the top three programs in this field. These programs combine rigorous academic studies, analysis and design of energy and environmental policies, and participation in public dialogues about the need for equitable futures. M.E.E.P. and Ph.D. faculty and students work critically and analytically on issues of climate change, energy transformation, renewable and nonrenewable energy options, environmental justice, smart cities, and sustainable development.

Research Facilities

The School is centrally located in its own building, with its own classrooms and student offices. One of the most distinguishing characteristics of the School of Public Policy and Administration is the integration of theory and practice through applied research projects with the affiliated research and public service centers, internationally known as the Delaware Model. Some full-time students are awarded research assistantships on projects in these centers.

The Biden Institute is a world-class intellectual center and destination for scholars, activists, policymakers, and national leaders. The mission at The Biden Institute is to influence, shape, and work to solve the most pressing domestic policy problems facing America. This research and policy center works to bring together the sharpest minds and the most powerful voices to address our nation's toughest problems. The Center for Applied Demography and Survey Research provides demographic and survey data and information on important public issues to researchers and policy makers at all levels (http://www.cadsr.udel.edu). The Center for Community Research and Service helps public, nonprofit, and private organizations in Delaware to design, implement, and evaluate policies and programs that address the needs of low- and moderate-income families and communities related to economic development, housing, and social services. The center also focuses on issues that are vital to the physical and emotional well-being of the world's population. These questions concern the delivery and financing of health care and the outcomes of health care provided (https://www.sppa.udel.edu/ccrs). The Center for Historic Architecture and Design focuses on shaping historic preservation planning and policy, reconstructing historic landscapes, documenting threatened historic properties, and advocating for the preservation of historic resources (https://www.sppa.udel.edu/chad/). The Institute for Public Administration links the resources of the University of Delaware (UD) with the management and policy information needs of public and nonprofit organizations (https://www.sppa.udel.edu/ipa).

Financial Aid

The School has competitive financial aid programs, including fellowships, research assistantships, and scholarships. Aid is awarded on merit and is limited by the various restrictions established by the sources of aid. Stipends for 2018–19 are $19,000 for Master's students ($20,000 for Ph.D.) for the full academic year. Additional special assistantships, fellowships, and internships are available to students through the University Graduate Scholar's Program, for both newly admitted and graduate students currently enrolled. All full-time doctoral students who are admitted are awarded four years of funding support through research and teaching assistantships, as well as fellowship opportunities. Master's-level awards are competitive and are based on many criteria, including challenging social, economic, educational, cultural, or other life circumstances; academic achievements; first generation graduate student status; and/or need as determined by federal income guidelines (FAFSA). Support is also available through the Delaware Legislative Fellows Program.

Cost of Study

All School of Public Policy and Administration graduate students receive some scholarship support, even if an assistantship is not available. These scholarships are residency-based. Graduate students will be billed by the credit. The 2018–19 rate is $1,827 per credit. Fully-matriculated students are automatically assessed nonrefundable charges/fees for health services, student-sponsored activities, and a recreational fee. For more information on tuition and funding support, see https://www.sppa.udel.edu/masters-programs/tuition-support-scholarships.

Living and Housing Costs

The University provides some graduate apartments, and there is plenty of off-campus housing in the surrounding community in many price ranges. For more information, students should contact the Housing Assignment Services Office (302-831-2491; http://www.udel.edu/has).

Student Group

In 2017–2018, the School had 54 students in the M.P.A. program, 25 in the M.A. and 40 in the Ph.D. Urban Affairs and Public Policy program, and 8 in the M.S. and 17 in the Ph.D. Disaster Science and Management program.

Student Outcomes

Graduates find career positions in government and nonprofit organizations and occasionally in the private sector with consulting firms. With UD's proximity to Washington, D.C.; Philadelphia; and New York, many graduates pursue positions in nearby metropolitan areas, as well as positions in state and local government in the region and in the nation. Several recent graduates have been successful in the highly competitive federal Presidential Management Fellowship Program.

Location

Located midway between Philadelphia and Baltimore, the main campus of the University of Delaware is in Newark, conveniently near New York City; Washington, D.C.; and the seashore. A community of 30,000, with a vibrant Main Street of coffeehouses, restaurants, and small shops, Newark is about 14 miles from Wilmington, Delaware's largest city.

The University

The University is a comprehensive land-, sea-, space-, and urban-grant institution of higher education with an enrollment of approximately 3,500 graduate students. The University offers 133 programs leading to a master's degree and 67 programs leading to a doctoral degree. In 2016, the University awarded 274 doctoral degrees and 889 master's degrees.

Applying

SPPA welcomes informal inquiries. Students seeking priority consideration for financial aid or admission to any of the graduate programs should apply by January 15. For current information on the criteria for admission, see https://www.sppa.udel.edu/masters-programs/masters-admissions/admission-criteria and https://www.sppa.udel.edu/doctoral-programs/ph-d-admissions/admission-criteria.

Correspondence and Information

School of Public Policy and Administration Admissions
University of Delaware
Newark, Delaware 19716-7310
Phone: 302-831-1687
Fax: 302-831-3296
E-mail: sppa@udel.edu
Website: http://www.sppa.udel.edu

THE FACULTY AND THEIR RESEARCH

At the core of the School of Public Policy and Administration are the dedicated faculty members, who are challenging teachers, seasoned researchers, and experienced practitioners. With interdisciplinary backgrounds as skilled executives, managers, and community leaders, they bring practical experience to the classroom and successfully blend a solid academic base with stimulating practical experience.

Maria P. Aristigueta, Charles P. Messick Professor in Public Administration; Director, School of Public Policy and Administration; and Senior Policy Fellow, Institute for Public Administration; D.P.A., USC, 1997. Administrative behavior, performance management, policy analysis, strategic management.

Philip J. Barnes, Assistant Professor, Ph.D., Delaware, 2015. Energy, environment.

Jane Case-Lilly, Assistant Professor of Instruction; Ph.D., Delaware, 2008. Organizational leadership, ethics, communication, decision making.

Nina P. David, Assistant Professor; Ph.D., Michigan, 2008. Land use planning and policy, regional planning and cooperation, growth management, architecture and urban design.

Eric D. Jacobson, Associate Professor and Policy Scientist, Institute for Public Administration; M.P.A., Delaware, 1981. Public economics, health policy, employee compensation and benefits, tourism development and research, analytical methods.

Jonathan Justice, Professor; Ph.D., Rutgers, 2003. Public financial management, nongovernmental public administration, urban policy and administration.

Gerald Kauffman, Assistant Professor and Project Director, Water Resources Agency; Ph.D., Delaware. Watershed policy, planning, and management; water resources government and finance; water resources engineering; hydrology and hydraulics.

James Kendra, Professor, Director, Disaster Research Center; Ph.D., Rutgers, 2000. Disasters, hurricanes, environment.

Erin Knight, Assistant Professor; Ph.D., Delaware, 2011. Equity, public health, evaluation.

Jerome R. Lewis, Associate Professor; Director, Institute for Public Administration; Ph.D., NYU, 1968. Public administration, personnel management, urban planning, political leadership.

John G. McNutt, Professor; Ph.D., Tennessee, 1991. Technology, nonprofit management, advocacy and government relations, community organization and planning.

Anthony E. Middlebrooks, Associate Professor; Ph.D., Wisconsin, 1999. Leadership formation and development, creativity and leadership, service and social justice, research methods.

James L. Morrison, Professor; Ed.D., Temple, 1971. Telecommunications and consumer policy, consumer environmental issues, consumer protection.

K. C. Morrison, Professor; Ph.D., Wisconsin, 1977. Comparative public administration, public administration, public policy and comparative politics.

Kathleen M. Murphy, Instructor and Coordinator, Conflict Resolution Program; M.P.A., Delaware. Conflict resolution, mediation, organizational and leadership development.

Steven W. Peuquet, Associate Professor and Director, Center for Community Research and Service; Ph.D., Pennsylvania, 1996. Strategic planning, housing, homelessness, electronic community networks, public policy analysis and evaluation.

Edward C. Ratledge, Associate Professor and Director, Center for Applied Demography and Survey Research; M.A., Delaware, 1972. Management information systems, econometrics, criminal justice systems.

Chandra Reedy, Professor and Interim Director, Center for Historic Architecture and Design; Ph.D., California, 2011. Preservation, conservation, archaeology.

Daniel Rich, University Professor of Public Policy; Director, Urban Affairs and Public Policy Ph.D. Program; Director, Community Engagement Initiative; Ph.D., MIT, 1972. Public policy and public management.

Breck Robinson, Associate Professor and Director, Public Policy Undergraduate Program; Ph.D., Tennessee, 1994. Financial institutions, public policy, development.

Andrea Sarzynski, Associate Professor; Ph.D., George Washington, 2006. Urbanization and environmental change; environmental policy and politics; urban and regional planning; science and policymaking.

Daniel Smith, Associate Professor and Director, Master of Public Administration Program; Ph.D., Georgia, 2008. Public budgeting and finance, public management, public policy.

Karen F. Stein, Associate Professor and Director, Organizational and Community Leadership Undergraduate Program; Ph.D., Delaware, 1984. Domestic elder abuse and neglect, leadership studies, consumer and family economic policy analysis.

Tibor Tóth, Assistant Professor; Ph.D., Delaware, 2005. Environment, health.

Joseph Trainor, Associate Professor; Ph.D., Delaware, 2008. Disasters, health, human behavior, organizations, evacuation.

Leland Ware, Louis L. Redding Chair for the Study of Law and Public Policy and Associate Director, School of Public Policy and Administration; J.D., Boston College, 1973. Employment discrimination law, civil rights law, civil procedure.

Harvey White, Professor of Practice; Ph.D., North Carolina at Chapel Hill, 1985. Human talent development and management, international development and management, social equity and environmental justice, health policy.

Danilo Yanich, Professor; Director, Urban Affairs and Public Policy Master's Program; and Associate Policy Scientist, Center for Community Research and Service; Ph.D., Delaware, 1980. Criminal justice policy, media and public policy, international comparative governance.

Section 26
Social Sciences

This section contains a directory of institutions offering graduate work in social sciences. Additional information about programs listed in the directory may be obtained by writing directly to the dean of a graduate school or chair of a department at the address given in the directory.

For programs offering related work, see also in this book *Area and Cultural Studies, Communication and Media, Criminology and Forensics, Economics, Geography, Family and Consumer Sciences, Political Science and International Affairs, Psychology and Counseling,* and *Sociology, Anthropology, and Archaeology.*

CONTENTS

Program Directory

Social Sciences

Assumption College, Resiliency in the Helping Professions Program, Worcester, MA 01609-1296. Offers CAGS, CGS. *Program availability:* Part-time, evening/weekend. *Faculty:* 1 (woman) full-time, 1 (woman) part-time/adjunct. *Students:* 6 part-time (all women); includes 1 minority (American Indian or Alaska Native, non-Hispanic/Latino). Average age 42. 4 applicants, 75% accepted, 2 enrolled. In 2017, 2 CAGSs awarded. *Entrance requirements:* For degree, bachelor's degree with minimum GPA of 3.0 (for CGS); master's degree (for CAGS); two letters of recommendation, official transcripts, personal statement, current resume. Additional exam requirements/recommendations for international students: Required—TOEFL (minimum score 540 paper-based; 76 iBT), IELTS (minimum score 6). *Application deadline:* Applications are processed on a rolling basis. Application fee: $30. *Expenses: Tuition:* Full-time $11,952; part-time $664 per credit. *Required fees:* $70 per term. *Financial support:* In 2017–18, 1 student received support. Tuition waivers (full and partial) and institutional discounts available. Financial award applicants required to submit FAFSA. *Unit head:* Lea Christo, Director, 508-767-7503, Fax: 508-798-2872, E-mail: l.christo@assumption.edu. *Application contact:* Karen Stoyanoff, Director of Recruitment for Graduate Enrollment, 508-767-7442, Fax: 508-799-4412, E-mail: graduate@assumption.edu.
Website: http://graduate.assumption.edu/resiliency-helping-professions/resiliency-helping-professions

Augusta University, College of Allied Health Sciences, Program in Public Health, Augusta, GA 30912. Offers environmental health (MPH); health informatics (MPH); health management (MPH); social and behavioral sciences (MPH). *Accreditation:* CEPH. *Program availability:* Part-time. *Degree requirements:* For master's, thesis (for some programs). *Entrance requirements:* For master's, GRE General Test, three letters of recommendation. Additional exam requirements/recommendations for international students: Required—TOEFL. Electronic applications accepted.

California Institute of Technology, Division of the Humanities and Social Sciences, Social Science Program, Pasadena, CA 91125-0001. Offers MS, PhD. Terminal master's awarded for partial completion of doctoral program. *Degree requirements:* For doctorate, thesis/dissertation. *Entrance requirements:* For doctorate, GRE General Test. Additional exam requirements/recommendations for international students: Required—TOEFL (minimum score 90 iBT); Recommended—TWE. Electronic applications accepted. *Faculty research:* Theoretical and applied microeconomics, experimental social science, political science, quantitative history, behavioral economics and neuroscience.

California State University, Chico, Office of Graduate Studies, College of Behavioral and Social Sciences, Social Science Program, Chico, CA 95929-0722. Offers MA. *Degree requirements:* For master's, thesis or project. *Entrance requirements:* For master's, GRE General Test or MAT, two letters of recommendation, statement of purpose. Additional exam requirements/recommendations for international students: Required—TOEFL (minimum score 550 paper-based; 80 iBT), IELTS (minimum score 6.5), PTE (minimum score 59). Electronic applications accepted.

California State University, San Bernardino, Graduate Studies, College of Social and Behavioral Sciences, Program in Social Sciences and Globalization, San Bernardino, CA 92407. Offers MA. *Faculty:* 3 full-time (1 woman), 3 part-time/adjunct (0 women). *Students:* 5 full-time (4 women), 17 part-time (7 women); includes 12 minority (all Hispanic/Latino), 1 international. Average age 33. 17 applicants, 88% accepted, 11 enrolled. In 2017, 11 master's awarded. *Entrance requirements:* Additional exam requirements/recommendations for international students: Required—TOEFL. *Application deadline:* For fall admission, 5/15 for domestic students. Application fee: $55. *Financial support:* Fellowships, research assistantships, teaching assistantships, and institutionally sponsored loans available. Financial award application deadline: 5/1. *Unit head:* Dr. Jose Munoz, Coordinator, 909-537-5524, E-mail: munoz@csusb.edu. *Application contact:* Dr. Dorota Huizinga, Dean of Graduate Studies, 909-537-3064, E-mail: dorota.huizinga@csusb.edu.

Campbellsville University, College of Arts and Sciences, Campbellsville, KY 42718-2799. Offers justice studies (MS); sport management (MA). *Program availability:* Part-time, evening/weekend, 100% online, blended/hybrid learning. *Faculty:* 12 full-time (4 women), 2 part-time/adjunct (1 woman). *Students:* 6 full-time (3 women), 28 part-time (12 women); includes 9 minority (all Black or African American, non-Hispanic/Latino), 1 international. Average age 29. 38 applicants, 66% accepted, 25 enrolled. In 2017, 5 master's awarded. *Degree requirements:* For master's, comprehensive exam, thesis optional. *Entrance requirements:* For master's, GRE General Test, minimum GPA of 2.9, letters of recommendation, college transcripts. Additional exam requirements/recommendations for international students: Recommended—TOEFL, IELTS. *Application deadline:* Applications are processed on a rolling basis. Application fee: $25. Electronic applications accepted. Application fee is waived when completed online. *Expenses:* $399 per credit hour. *Financial support:* In 2017–18, 2 students received support. Unspecified assistantships and employee tuition waivers available. Financial award application deadline: 6/1; financial award applicants required to submit FAFSA. *Unit head:* Dr. Mike Page, Dean, 270-789-5394. *Application contact:* Monica Bamwine, Assistant Director of Graduate Admissions, 270-789-5221, Fax: 270-789-5071, E-mail: mkbamwine@campbellsville.edu.
Website: http://www.campbellsville.edu/

Carnegie Mellon University, Dietrich College of Humanities and Social Sciences, Department of Social and Decision Sciences, Pittsburgh, PA 15213-3891. Offers behavioral decision research (PhD); social and decision science (PhD); strategy, entrepreneurship, and technological change (PhD). Terminal master's awarded for partial completion of doctoral program. *Degree requirements:* For doctorate, comprehensive exam, thesis/dissertation, research paper. *Entrance requirements:* For doctorate, GRE General Test. Additional exam requirements/recommendations for international students: Required—TOEFL. Electronic applications accepted. *Faculty research:* Organization theory, political science, sociology, technology studies.

The Citadel, The Military College of South Carolina, Citadel Graduate College, School of Humanities and Social Sciences, Department of Political Science, Charleston, SC 29409. Offers international politics and military affairs (MA); social science (MA). *Program availability:* Part-time, evening/weekend, 100% online, blended/hybrid learning. *Entrance requirements:* For master's, GRE (minimum combined score of 290 verbal and quantitative), MAT (minimum raw score of 396), written statement of purpose setting forth intentions, goals, and preparation for graduate study; at least 2 academic letters of recommendation addressing ability to undertake coursework at graduate level. Additional exam requirements/recommendations for international students: Required—TOEFL (minimum score 550 paper-based; 79 iBT). Electronic applications accepted. *Expenses:* Tuition, state resident: part-time $587 per credit hour. Tuition, nonresident: part-time $988 per credit hour. *Required fees:* $90 per term.

Colorado School of Mines, Office of Graduate Studies, Division of Humanities, Arts and Social Sciences, Golden, CO 80401. Offers international political economy (Graduate Certificate); science and technology policy (Graduate Certificate). *Program availability:* Part-time. *Students:* 2 full-time (1 woman); includes 1 minority (Hispanic/Latino), 1 international. Average age 37. 1 applicant, 100% accepted, 1 enrolled. *Entrance requirements:* Additional exam requirements/recommendations for international students: Required—TOEFL (minimum score 550 paper-based; 79 iBT). *Application deadline:* For fall admission, 12/15 priority date for domestic and international students; for spring admission, 9/1 priority date for domestic and international students. Application fee: $60 ($80 for international students). Electronic applications accepted. *Expenses:* Tuition, state resident: full-time $16,170. Tuition, nonresident: full-time $35,220. *Required fees:* $2216. *Financial support:* Fellowships, research assistantships, teaching assistantships, scholarships/grants, health care benefits, and unspecified assistantships available. Financial award application deadline: 12/15. *Unit head:* Dr. Hussain Amery, Department Head, 303-273-3339, E-mail: hamery@mines.edu. *Application contact:* Jody Lowther, Program Assistant, 303-384-2509, E-mail: jlowther@mines.edu.
Website: https://hass.mines.edu/

Columbia University, Graduate School of Arts and Sciences, New York, NY 10027. Offers African-American studies (MA); American studies (MA); anthropology (MA, PhD); art history and archaeology (MA, PhD); astronomy (PhD); biological sciences (PhD); biotechnology (MA); chemical physics (PhD); chemistry (PhD); classical studies (MA, PhD); classics (MA, PhD); climate and society (MA); conservation biology (MA); earth and environmental sciences (PhD); East Asia: regional studies (MA); East Asian languages and cultures (MA, PhD); ecology, evolution and environmental biology (MA), including conservation biology; ecology, evolution, and environmental biology (PhD), including ecology and evolutionary biology, evolutionary primatology; economics (MA, PhD); English and comparative literature (MA, PhD); French and Romance philology (MA, PhD); Germanic languages (MA, PhD); global French studies (MA); global thought (MA); Hispanic cultural studies (MA); history (PhD); history and literature (MA); human rights studies (MA); Islamic studies (MA); Italian (MA, PhD); Japanese pedagogy (MA); Jewish studies (MA); Latin America and the Caribbean: regional studies (MA); Latin American and Iberian cultures (PhD); mathematics (MA, PhD), including finance (MA); medieval and Renaissance studies (MA); Middle Eastern, South Asian, and African studies (MA, PhD); modern art: critical and curatorial studies (MA); modern European studies (MA); museum anthropology (MA); music (DMA, PhD); oral history (MA); philosophical foundations of physics (MA); philosophy (MA, PhD); physics (PhD); political science (MA, PhD); psychology (PhD); quantitative methods in the social sciences (MA); religion (MA, PhD); Russia, Eurasia and East Europe: regional studies (MA); Russian translation (MA); Slavic cultures (MA); Slavic languages (MA, PhD); sociology (MA, PhD); South Asian studies (MA); statistics (MA, PhD); theatre (PhD). Dual-degree programs require admission to both Graduate School of Arts and Sciences and another Columbia school. *Program availability:* Part-time. Terminal master's awarded for partial completion of doctoral program. *Degree requirements:* For master's, variable foreign language requirement, comprehensive exam (for some programs), thesis (for some programs); for doctorate, variable foreign language requirement, comprehensive exam (for some programs), thesis/dissertation. *Entrance requirements:* For master's and doctorate, GRE General Test, GRE Subject Test (for some programs). Additional exam requirements/recommendations for international students: Required—TOEFL, IELTS. Electronic applications accepted. *Expenses: Tuition:* Full-time $44,864; part-time $1704 per credit. *Required fees:* $2370 per semester. One-time fee: $105.

East Carolina University, Graduate School, Thomas Harriot College of Arts and Sciences, Department of Psychology, Greenville, NC 27858-4353. Offers health psychology (PhD), including clinical health psychology, occupational health psychology, pediatric school psychology; industrial and organizational psychology (MA); quantitative methods for the social and behavioral sciences (Certificate); MA/CAS. *Program availability:* Part-time, evening/weekend. *Students:* 77 full-time (52 women), 17 part-time (15 women); includes 12 minority (8 Black or African American, non-Hispanic/Latino; 3 Hispanic/Latino; 1 Two or more races, non-Hispanic/Latino). Average age 26. 221 applicants, 31% accepted, 22 enrolled. In 2017, 31 master's, 7 doctorates, 21 other advanced degrees awarded. *Degree requirements:* For doctorate, comprehensive exam, thesis/dissertation or alternative. *Entrance requirements:* For master's and doctorate, GRE General Test. Additional exam requirements/recommendations for international students: Recommended—TOEFL (minimum score 78 iBT), IELTS (minimum score 6.5). *Application deadline:* For fall admission, 12/1 priority date for domestic and international students. Applications are processed on a rolling basis. Application fee: $75. Electronic applications accepted. *Expenses:* Tuition, state resident: full-time $4749; part-time $297 per credit hour. Tuition, nonresident: full-time $17,898; part-time $1119 per credit hour. *Required fees:* $2691; $224 per credit hour. Part-time tuition and fees vary according to course load and program. *Financial support:* Research assistantships with partial tuition reimbursements, teaching assistantships with partial tuition reimbursements, Federal Work-Study, and traineeships available. Support available to part-time students. Financial award application deadline: 6/1. *Unit head:* Dr. Susan L. McCammon, Chair, 252-328-6357, E-mail: mccammons@ecu.edu. *Application contact:* Dean of Graduate School, 252-328-6012, Fax: 252-328-6071, E-mail: gradschool@ecu.edu.
Website: http://www.ecu.edu/psyc/

Eastern Michigan University, Graduate School, College of Arts and Sciences, Department of History and Philosophy, Program in Social Science, Ypsilanti, MI 48197. Offers MA. *Program availability:* Part-time, evening/weekend, online learning. *Students:* 2 full-time (1 woman), 6 part-time (4 women); includes 3 minority (all Black or African American, non-Hispanic/Latino). Average age 45. 1 applicant, 100% accepted, 1 enrolled. In 2017, 1 master's awarded. *Degree requirements:* For master's, thesis optional. *Entrance requirements:* Additional exam requirements/recommendations for international students: Required—TOEFL. *Application deadline:* Applications are processed on a rolling basis. Application fee: $45. *Financial support:* Fellowships, research assistantships with full tuition reimbursements, teaching assistantships with full tuition reimbursements, career-related internships or fieldwork, Federal Work-Study, institutionally sponsored loans, scholarships/grants, tuition waivers (partial), and unspecified assistantships available. Support available to part-time students. Financial award applicants required to submit FAFSA. *Application contact:* Dr. Ronald Delph, Director, 734-487-1018, Fax: 734-487-6835, E-mail: rdelph@emich.edu.

Elms College, Division of Social Sciences, Chicopee, MA 01013-2839. Offers applied behavior analysis (MS); autism spectrum disorders (MS, CAGS); communication sciences and disorders (CAGS). *Program availability:* Part-time. *Faculty:* 2 full-time (1 woman), 3 part-time/adjunct (1 woman). *Students:* 3 full-time (all women), 22 part-time (19 women); includes 1 minority (Black or African American, non-Hispanic/Latino).

Average age 31. 24 applicants, 75% accepted, 15 enrolled. In 2017, 6 master's, 3 other advanced degrees awarded. *Entrance requirements:* For degree, minimum GPA of 3.0. Additional exam requirements/recommendations for international students: Required—TOEFL. *Application deadline:* Applications are processed on a rolling basis. Application fee: $30. Electronic applications accepted. *Expenses: Tuition:* Full-time $13,860; part-time $770 per credit hour. *Required fees:* $200. Tuition and fees vary according to degree level and program. *Financial support:* Applicants required to submit FAFSA. *Unit head:* Dr. John Lambdin, Chair, Division of Social Sciences, 413-265-2442, E-mail: lambdinj@elms.edu. *Application contact:* School of Graduate and Professional Studies, 413-265-2445, E-mail: graduateeducation@elms.edu.

Evangel University, Department of Behavioral and Social Sciences, Springfield, MO 65802. Offers clinical mental health counseling (MS). *Program availability:* Part-time. *Faculty:* 6 full-time (4 women), 2 part-time/adjunct (1 woman). *Students:* 33 full-time (27 women), 6 part-time (5 women); includes 3 minority (all Hispanic/Latino). Average age 31. 30 applicants, 70% accepted, 16 enrolled. In 2017, 14 master's awarded. *Degree requirements:* For master's, comprehensive exam. *Entrance requirements:* For master's, GRE General Test, minimum undergraduate GPA of 3.0. Additional exam requirements/recommendations for international students: Required—TOEFL (minimum score 550 paper-based). *Application deadline:* For fall admission, 7/15 priority date for domestic students, 8/1 for international students; for spring admission, 11/15 priority date for domestic students, 12/1 for international students. Applications are processed on a rolling basis. Application fee: $25. Electronic applications accepted. Application fee is waived when completed online. *Expenses: Tuition:* Full-time $7200; part-time $4800 per credit hour. *Required fees:* $210; $155 per semester. *Financial support:* In 2017–18, 12 students received support. Unspecified assistantships available. Financial award application deadline: 4/1; financial award applicants required to submit FAFSA. *Unit head:* Dr. Christine Arnzen, Program Coordinator, 417-865-2815 Ext. 8618, E-mail: arnzenc@evangel.edu. *Application contact:* Michael Mann, Enrollment Coordinator, Graduate Studies, 417-865-2815 Ext. 8276, Fax: 417-575-5484, E-mail: mannm@evangel.edu.
Website: https://www.evangel.edu/departments/behavioral-social-sciences/about-the-department/

Florida Agricultural and Mechanical University, Division of Graduate Studies, Research, and Continuing Education, College of Social Sciences, Arts and Humanities, Department of History and Political Science, Program in Applied Social Science, Tallahassee, FL 32307-3200. Offers criminal justice (MASS); history (MASS); political science (MASS); public administration (MASS). *Program availability:* Part-time. *Degree requirements:* For master's, thesis optional. *Entrance requirements:* For master's, GRE General Test, minimum GPA of 3.0. *Faculty research:* Southern history, black history, election trends, Presidential history.

Graduate Theological Union, Graduate Programs, Berkeley, CA 94709-1212. Offers art and religion (MA, PhD, Th D); biblical languages (MA); biblical studies (MA); Biblical studies (PhD, Th D); Buddhist studies (MA); Christian spirituality (MA, PhD, Th D); cultural and historical studies of religions (MA, PhD, Th D); ethics and social theory (PhD, Th D); history (MA, PhD, Th D); homiletics (MA, PhD, Th D); interdisciplinary studies (PhD, Th D); Jewish studies (MA, PhD, Th D, Certificate); liturgical studies (MA, PhD, Th D); Near Eastern religions (PhD, Th D); Orthodox Christian studies (MA); religion and psychology (MA, PhD, Th D); religion and society/ethics and social theory (MA); systematic and philosophical theology (MA, PhD, Th D). PhD programs in Jewish studies and Near Eastern religions offered jointly with University of California, Berkeley. *Accreditation:* ATS. Terminal master's awarded for partial completion of doctoral program. *Degree requirements:* For master's, one foreign language, thesis; for doctorate, one foreign language, comprehensive exam, thesis/dissertation. *Entrance requirements:* For master's, GRE General Test; for doctorate, GRE General Test, MA or M Div. Additional exam requirements/recommendations for international students: Required—TOEFL. Electronic applications accepted.

Harrison Middleton University, Graduate Program, Tempe, AZ 85282. Offers education (MA, Ed D); humanities (MA); imaginative literature (MA); interdisciplinary studies (DA); jurisprudence (MA); natural science (MA); philosophy and religion (MA); social science (MA). *Program availability:* Part-time, evening/weekend, online learning. *Degree requirements:* For master's and doctorate, capstone project. *Entrance requirements:* For master's, interview; for doctorate, 2 academic letters of reference, interview, essay. Additional exam requirements/recommendations for international students: Required—TOEFL (minimum score 550 paper-based; 80 iBT). Electronic applications accepted. *Faculty research:* Japanese animation, educational leadership, war art, John Muir's wilderness.

Hollins University, Graduate Programs, Program in Liberal Studies, Roanoke, VA 24020. Offers humanities (MALS); interdisciplinary studies (MALS); leadership (MALS); social sciences (MALS); visual and performing arts (MALS). *Program availability:* Part-time, evening/weekend, 100% online, blended/hybrid learning. *Faculty:* 5 part-time/adjunct (2 women). *Students:* 5 full-time (4 women), 29 part-time (25 women); includes 9 minority (6 Black or African American, non-Hispanic/Latino; 1 Asian, non-Hispanic/Latino; 1 Hispanic/Latino; 1 Two or more races, non-Hispanic/Latino). Average age 40. 7 applicants, 86% accepted, 3 enrolled. In 2017, 11 master's awarded. *Degree requirements:* For master's, thesis. *Entrance requirements:* For master's, three letters of recommendation, interview, bachelor's degree, undergraduate transcripts, statement of educational objectives. Additional exam requirements/recommendations for international students: Required—TOEFL (minimum score 550 paper-based; 80 iBT), IELTS (minimum score 6.5). *Application deadline:* Applications are processed on a rolling basis. Application fee: $40. Electronic applications accepted. *Expenses:* Contact institution. *Financial support:* Scholarships/grants available. Financial award application deadline: 7/15; financial award applicants required to submit FAFSA. *Faculty research:* Diversity, gender and women's studies, political science, leadership. *Unit head:* Dr. Lorraine Lange, Director, 540-362-6576, Fax: 540-362-6288, E-mail: hugrad@hollins.edu. *Application contact:* Cathy S. Koon, Manager of Graduate Programs, 540-362-6326, Fax: 540-362-6288, E-mail: hugrad@hollins.edu.
Website: http://www.hollins.edu/academics/graduate-degrees/liberal-studies/

Humboldt State University, Academic Programs, College of Arts, Humanities, and Social Sciences, Program in Environment and Community, Arcata, CA 95521-8299. Offers MA. *Degree requirements:* For master's, thesis or alternative, qualifying exam. *Entrance requirements:* For master's, minimum GPA of 2.5, 3 letters of recommendation. Additional exam requirements/recommendations for international students: Required—TOEFL (minimum score 500 paper-based). *Faculty research:* Geography, political science, ethnic studies, anthropology, economics.

Indiana University Bloomington, Maurer School of Law, Bloomington, IN 47405-7000. Offers comparative law (MCL); juridical science (SJD); law (LL M, JD); law and social sciences (PhD); legal studies (Certificate); JD/MA; JD/MBA; JD/MLS; JD/MPA; JD/MS; JD/MSES. PhD offered through University Graduate School. *Accreditation:* ABA. *Degree requirements:* For master's, thesis or practicum; for doctorate, thesis/dissertation (for some programs), research seminar (for JD). *Entrance requirements:* For master's, LSAT, 3 letters of recommendation, law degree or license to practice; for doctorate, LSAT. Additional exam requirements/recommendations for international students: Required—TOEFL (minimum score 560 paper-based; 80 iBT). Electronic applications accepted. *Faculty research:* Environmental risk assessment and policy analysis, information privacy and security, judicial independence, accountability, ethics.

Indiana University–Purdue University Indianapolis, Richard M. Fairbanks School of Public Health, Indianapolis, IN 46202. Offers biostatistics (MS, PhD); environmental health (MPH); epidemiology (MPH, PhD); global health leadership (Dr PH); health administration (MHA); health policy (Graduate Certificate); health policy and management (MPH, PhD); health systems management (Graduate Certificate); product stewardship (MS); public health (Graduate Certificate); social and behavioral sciences (MPH). *Expenses:* Contact institution.

Massachusetts Institute of Technology, School of Humanities, Arts, and Social Sciences, Program in Science, Technology, and Society, Cambridge, MA 02139. Offers history, anthropology, and science, technology and society (PhD). *Degree requirements:* For doctorate, one foreign language, comprehensive exam, thesis/dissertation. *Entrance requirements:* For doctorate, GRE General Test. Additional exam requirements/recommendations for international students: Required—TOEFL, IELTS. Electronic applications accepted. *Faculty research:* History of science; history of technology; sociology of science and technology; anthropology of science and technology; science, technology, and society.

Mississippi College, Graduate School, College of Arts and Sciences, School of Humanities and Social Sciences, Department of History, Political Science, Administration of Justice, and Paralegal Studies, Clinton, MS 39058. Offers administration of justice (MSS); history (M Ed, MA, MSS); paralegal studies (Certificate); political science (MSS); social sciences (M Ed, MSS). *Program availability:* Part-time. *Degree requirements:* For master's, one foreign language, comprehensive exam, thesis (for some programs). *Entrance requirements:* For master's, GRE or NTE, minimum GPA of 2.5. Additional exam requirements/recommendations for international students: Recommended—TOEFL, IELTS. Electronic applications accepted.

Montclair State University, The Graduate School, College of Education and Human Services, MAT Program in Teaching, Montclair, NJ 07043-1624. Offers art (MAT); biology (MAT); chemistry (MAT); earth science (MAT); English (MAT); French (MAT); health and physical education (MAT); health education (MAT); mathematics (MAT); music (MAT); physical education (MAT); physical science (MAT); social studies (MAT); Spanish (MAT); teacher of English as a second language (MAT). *Degree requirements:* For master's, comprehensive exam, thesis or alternative. *Entrance requirements:* For master's, interview, 2 letters of recommendation. Additional exam requirements/recommendations for international students: Required—TOEFL (minimum score 83 iBT), IELTS (minimum score 6.5). Electronic applications accepted.

The New School, The New School for Social Research, New York, NY 10003. Offers M Phil, MA, MS, PhD. *Program availability:* Part-time. *Faculty:* 73 full-time (34 women), 14 part-time/adjunct (2 women). *Students:* 648 full-time (338 women), 155 part-time (92 women); includes 124 minority (21 Black or African American, non-Hispanic/Latino; 25 Asian, non-Hispanic/Latino; 55 Hispanic/Latino; 23 Two or more races, non-Hispanic/Latino), 279 international. Average age 31. 880 applicants, 76% accepted, 190 enrolled. In 2017, 152 master's, 60 doctorates awarded. Terminal master's awarded for partial completion of doctoral program. *Degree requirements:* For master's, comprehensive exam (for some programs), thesis (for some programs); for doctorate, variable foreign language requirement, comprehensive exam (for some programs), thesis/dissertation. *Entrance requirements:* For master's, letters of recommendation, writing sample, essays, official transcripts. Additional exam requirements/recommendations for international students: Required—TOEFL (minimum score 100 iBT), IELTS (minimum score 7), PTE (minimum score 68). *Application deadline:* For fall admission, 6/15 priority date for domestic and international students; for spring admission, 10/15 priority date for domestic and international students. Applications are processed on a rolling basis. Application fee: $50. Electronic applications accepted. *Expenses:* $2,100 per credit. *Financial support:* In 2017–18, 592 students received support, including 49 fellowships (averaging $38,451 per year), 28 research assistantships (averaging $13,911 per year), 146 teaching assistantships with full and partial tuition reimbursements available (averaging $8,625 per year); career-related internships or fieldwork, Federal Work-Study, scholarships/grants, and tuition waivers (full and partial) also available. Support available to part-time students. Financial award application deadline: 2/1; financial award applicants required to submit FAFSA. *Unit head:* Dr. William Milberg, Dean, The New School for Social Research, 212-229-5777, E-mail: milbergw@newschool.edu. *Application contact:* Dana Messinger, Director of Graduate Admission, 212-229-5150 Ext. 2300, E-mail: messingd@newschool.edu.
Website: http://www.newschool.edu/nssr

New York University, College of Global Public Health, New York, NY 10012. Offers biological basis of public health (PhD); community and international health (MPH); global health leadership (MPH); health systems and health services research (PhD); population and community health (PhD); public health nutrition (MPH); social and behavioral sciences (MPH); socio-behavioral health (PhD). *Accreditation:* CEPH. *Program availability:* Part-time, online learning. *Faculty:* 26 full-time (20 women), 104 part-time/adjunct (53 women). *Students:* 161 full-time (136 women), 70 part-time (54 women); includes 74 minority (24 Black or African American, non-Hispanic/Latino; 1 American Indian or Alaska Native, non-Hispanic/Latino; 27 Asian, non-Hispanic/Latino; 11 Hispanic/Latino; 4 Native Hawaiian or other Pacific Islander, non-Hispanic/Latino; 7 Two or more races, non-Hispanic/Latino), 39 international. Average age 29. 802 applicants, 70% accepted, 97 enrolled. In 2017, 1 master's awarded. *Degree requirements:* For master's, thesis (for some programs); for doctorate, thesis/dissertation. *Entrance requirements:* For master's and doctorate, GRE. Additional exam requirements/recommendations for international students: Required—TOEFL. *Application deadline:* For fall admission, 2/1 for domestic and international students. Applications are processed on a rolling basis. Electronic applications accepted. *Expenses:* Contact institution. *Financial support:* Federal Work-Study and scholarships/grants available. *Unit head:* Dr. Cheryl G. Healton, Director, 212-992-6741. *Application contact:* New York University Information, 212-998-1212.
Website: http://publichealth.nyu.edu/

North Dakota State University, College of Graduate and Interdisciplinary Studies, College of Arts, Humanities and Social Sciences, Department of Sociology and Anthropology, Fargo, ND 58102. Offers anthropology (MA, MS); community development (MA, MS); social science (MA, MS); sociology (MS). *Program availability:* Part-time. *Degree requirements:* For master's, thesis. *Entrance requirements:* For master's, GRE (for emergency management), course work in sociology, minimum GPA of 3.2. Additional exam requirements/recommendations for international students: Required—TOEFL. Electronic applications accepted. *Faculty research:* Medical sociology, demography, ethnology, archaeology.

Nova Southeastern University, College of Arts, Humanities, and Social Sciences, Fort Lauderdale, FL 33314-7796. Offers advanced conflict resolution practice (Graduate Certificate); child protection (MHS); college student affairs (MS); conflict analysis and resolution (MS, PhD); criminal justice (MS, PhD); cross-disciplinary studies (MA); developmental disabilities (MS); family studies (Graduate Certificate); family systems health care (Graduate Certificate); family therapy (MS, PhD); marriage and family therapy (DMFT); peace studies (Graduate Certificate); qualitative research (Graduate

Certificate); solution focused coaching (Graduate Certificate). *Accreditation:* AAMFT/ COAMFTE (one or more programs are accredited). *Program availability:* Part-time, evening/weekend, 100% online, blended/hybrid learning. *Faculty:* 29 full-time (18 women), 27 part-time/adjunct (21 women). *Students:* 303 full-time (238 women), 903 part-time (677 women); includes 689 minority (385 Black or African American, non-Hispanic/Latino; 4 American Indian or Alaska Native, non-Hispanic/Latino; 31 Asian, non-Hispanic/Latino; 234 Hispanic/Latino; 1 Native Hawaiian or other Pacific Islander, non-Hispanic/Latino; 34 Two or more races, non-Hispanic/Latino), 60 international. Average age 37. 624 applicants, 61% accepted, 285 enrolled. In 2017, 277 master's, 62 doctorates, 25 other advanced degrees awarded. *Degree requirements:* For master's, thesis optional, comprehensive exams, portfolios (for some programs), table-top exams (for some programs); for doctorate, comprehensive exam, thesis/dissertation, qualifying exams, portfolios (for some programs). *Entrance requirements:* For master's, interview, minimum GPA of 3.0, writing sample; for doctorate, interview, minimum GPA of 3.5, master's degree in related field, writing sample; for Graduate Certificate, minimum GPA of 3.0. Additional exam requirements/recommendations for international students: Required—TOEFL. *Application deadline:* For fall admission, 5/17 priority date for domestic and international students; for winter admission, 12/1 priority date for domestic and international students; for spring admission, 4/1 priority date for domestic and international students. Applications are processed on a rolling basis. Application fee: $50. Electronic applications accepted. *Expenses:* Contact institution. *Financial support:* In 2017–18, 170 students received support. Career-related internships or fieldwork, Federal Work-Study, scholarships/grants, and unspecified assistantships available. Financial award application deadline: 4/1; financial award applicants required to submit CSS PROFILE. *Faculty research:* Conflict resolution, family therapy, peace research, international conflict, multi-disciplinary studies, college student affairs, national security affairs, health care conflict resolution, family systems health care, advanced family systems, qualitative research, solution-focused coaching. *Unit head:* Dr. Honggang Yang, Dean, 954-262-3016, Fax: 954-262-3968, E-mail: yangh@nova.edu. *Application contact:* Marcia Arango, Student Recruitment Coordinator, 954-262-3006, Fax: 954-262-3968, E-mail: marango@nsu.nova.edu.
Website: http://cahss.nova.edu/

The Ohio State University, Graduate School, College of Food, Agricultural, and Environmental Sciences, School of Environment and Natural Resources, Columbus, OH 43210. Offers ecological restoration (MS, PhD); ecosystem science (MS, PhD); environment and natural resources (MENR); environmental social sciences (MS, PhD); fisheries and wildlife science (MS, PhD); forest science (MS, PhD); rural sociology (MS, PhD); soil science (MS, PhD). *Faculty:* 37. *Students:* 86 full-time (53 women), 8 part-time (4 women), 7 international. Average age 29. In 2017, 34 master's, 7 doctorates awarded. *Entrance requirements:* For master's and doctorate, GRE. Additional exam requirements/recommendations for international students: Required—TOEFL (minimum score 550 paper-based; 79 iBT), Michigan English Language Assessment Battery (minimum score 82); Recommended—IELTS (minimum score 7). *Application deadline:* For fall admission, 1/1 priority date for domestic students, 12/15 priority date for international students; for spring admission, 11/1 for domestic students, 9/15 for international students. Applications are processed on a rolling basis. Application fee: $60 ($70 for international students). Electronic applications accepted. *Financial support:* Fellowships, research assistantships, teaching assistantships, health care benefits, and unspecified assistantships available. *Unit head:* Dr. Jeff S. Sharp, Director, 614-292-9410, E-mail: sharp.123@osu.edu. *Application contact:* Graduate and Professional Admissions, 614-292-9444, Fax: 614-292-3895, E-mail: gpadmissions@osu.edu.
Website: http://senr.osu.edu/

Ohio University, Graduate College, College of Arts and Sciences, Program in Social Sciences, Athens, OH 45701-2979. Offers MSS. *Program availability:* Online learning. *Degree requirements:* For master's, oral exam. *Entrance requirements:* For master's, minimum GPA of 2.75. Additional exam requirements/recommendations for international students: Required—TOEFL (minimum score 600 paper-based). Electronic applications accepted.

Oregon State University, Interdisciplinary/Institutional Programs, Program in Environmental Sciences, Corvallis, OR 97331. Offers biogeochemistry (MA, MS, PSM, PhD); ecology (MA, MS, PSM, PhD); environmental education (MA, MS, PhD); quantitative analysis (PSM); social science (MA, MS, PSM, PhD); water resources (MA, MS, PhD). *Program availability:* Part-time. *Degree requirements:* For master's, variable foreign language requirement, thesis; for doctorate, thesis/dissertation. *Entrance requirements:* For master's and doctorate, GRE. Additional exam requirements/ recommendations for international students: Required—TOEFL (minimum score 80 iBT), IELTS (minimum score 6.5). *Application deadline:* For fall admission, 1/15 priority date for domestic and international students. Application fee: $75 ($85 for international students). *Unit head:* Dr. Carolyn Fonyo Boggess, Interim Director, 541-760-4196, E-mail: carolyn.fonyo@oregonstate.edu. *Application contact:* Dr. Carolyn Fonyo Boggess, Interim Director, 541-760-4196, E-mail: carolyn.fonyo@oregonstate.edu.
Website: http://gradschool.oregonstate.edu/environmental-sciences-graduate-program-esgp

Southern University and Agricultural and Mechanical College, Graduate School, College of Arts and Humanities, Department of History, Baton Rouge, LA 70813. Offers social sciences (MA). *Program availability:* Part-time. *Degree requirements:* For master's, thesis. *Entrance requirements:* For master's, GRE General Test. Additional exam requirements/recommendations for international students: Required—TOEFL (minimum score 525 paper-based).

Syracuse University, Maxwell School of Citizenship and Public Affairs, Programs in Social Sciences, Syracuse, NY 13244. Offers MA, PhD. *Program availability:* Part-time, evening/weekend, online learning. *Degree requirements:* For doctorate, comprehensive exam, thesis/dissertation. *Entrance requirements:* For master's, resume, personal statement, official transcripts, three letters of recommendation; for doctorate, GRE General Test, resume, personal statement, official transcripts, three letters of recommendation. Additional exam requirements/recommendations for international students: Required—TOEFL (minimum score 100 iBT). *Application deadline:* For fall admission, 3/15 priority date for domestic and international students. Application fee: $75. Electronic applications accepted. *Financial support:* Fellowships with full tuition reimbursements, research assistantships, and teaching assistantships available. Financial award application deadline: 1/1. *Faculty research:* Social and political theory and social policy, intergenerational relationships and social support systems, philanthropy. *Unit head:* Dr. Vernon Greene, Chair, 315-443-2275, Fax: 315-443-1463, E-mail: vgreene@maxwell.syr.edu. *Application contact:* Tammy Salisbury, Graduate Contact, 315-443-2275, E-mail: mtsalisb@maxwell.syr.edu.
Website: http://www.maxwell.syr.edu/

Texas A&M International University, Office of Graduate Studies and Research, College of Arts and Sciences, Department of Public Affairs and Social Research, Laredo, TX 78041. Offers criminal justice (MS); history and political thought (MA); political science (MA); public administration (MPA). *Degree requirements:* For master's, comprehensive exam (for some programs), thesis (for some programs). *Entrance requirements:* For master's, GRE General Test. Additional exam requirements/ recommendations for international students: Required—TOEFL (minimum score 550 paper-based; 79 iBT).

Towson University, College of Liberal Arts, Program in Social Science, Towson, MD 21252-0001. Offers MS. *Program availability:* Part-time, evening/weekend. *Students:* 7 full-time (4 women), 10 part-time (6 women); includes 7 minority (3 Black or African American, non-Hispanic/Latino; 1 Hispanic/Latino; 3 Two or more races, non-Hispanic/ Latino). *Entrance requirements:* For master's, minimum GPA of 3.0, 3 letters of recommendation, statement of intent. *Application deadline:* For fall admission, 1/17 for domestic students, 5/15 for international students; for spring admission, 10/15 for domestic students, 12/1 for international students. Applications are processed on a rolling basis. Application fee: $45. Electronic applications accepted. *Expenses:* Tuition, state resident: full-time $7960; part-time $398 per unit. Tuition, nonresident: full-time $16,480; part-time $824 per unit. *Required fees:* $2600; $130 per year. $390 per term. *Financial support:* Application deadline: 4/1. *Unit head:* Dr. Paul McCartney, Graduate Program Director, 410-704-5218, E-mail: pmccartney@towson.edu. *Application contact:* Coverley Beidleman, Assistant Director of Graduate Admissions, 410-704-5630, Fax: 410-704-3030, E-mail: cbeidleman@towson.edu.
Website: https://www.towson.edu/cla/departments/interdisciplinary/grad/socialscience/

Troy University, Graduate School, College of Arts and Sciences, Program in Social Science, Troy, AL 36082. Offers MS Sc. *Program availability:* Part-time, evening/ weekend. *Faculty:* 3 full-time (2 women), 2 part-time/adjunct (1 woman). *Students:* 15 full-time (11 women), 59 part-time (46 women); includes 11 minority (4 Black or African American, non-Hispanic/Latino; 2 Hispanic/Latino; 5 Two or more races, non-Hispanic/ Latino). Average age 37. 20 applicants, 85% accepted, 11 enrolled. *Degree requirements:* For master's, comprehensive exam, thesis optional. *Entrance requirements:* For master's, GRE (minimum score of 850 on old exam or 290 on new exam), MAT (minimum score of 385), or GMAT (minimum score of 380), bachelor's degree, minimum undergraduate GPA of 2.5 or 3.0 on last 30 semester hours, letter of recommendation. Additional exam requirements/recommendations for international students: Required—TOEFL (minimum score 523 paper-based; 70 iBT), IELTS (minimum score 6). *Application deadline:* For fall admission, 6/1 for international students; for spring admission, 10/15 for international students. Applications are processed on a rolling basis. Application fee: $50. Electronic applications accepted. *Expenses:* Tuition, state resident: part-time $417 per credit hour. Tuition, nonresident: part-time $834 per credit hour. *Required fees:* $42 per credit hour. $50 per semester. Tuition and fees vary according to campus/location. *Financial support:* Fellowships, career-related internships or fieldwork, and scholarships/grants available. Support available to part-time students. *Unit head:* Dr. Annette Allen, Chairman, Social Science, 334-808-6595, Fax: 334-670-3753, E-mail: aallen40379@troy.edu. *Application contact:* Jessica A. Kimbro, Director of Graduate Admissions, 334-670-3178, E-mail: jacord@troy.edu.

University at Buffalo, the State University of New York, Graduate School, College of Arts and Sciences, Program in Interdisciplinary Studies, Buffalo, NY 14260. Offers humanities (MA); natural sciences (MS); social sciences (MS). *Program availability:* Part-time. *Entrance requirements:* Additional exam requirements/recommendations for international students: Required—TOEFL (minimum score 550 paper-based; 79 iBT). *Application deadline:* For fall admission, 6/1 priority date for domestic students, 1/1 priority date for international students; for spring admission, 12/1 priority date for domestic students, 10/1 priority date for international students. Applications are processed on a rolling basis. Electronic applications accepted. *Financial support:* Fellowships, research assistantships, teaching assistantships, and unspecified assistantships available. *Unit head:* Danielle Lewis, Assistant Director, Strategic Programs, 716-645-1457, E-mail: dvegas@buffalo.edu.
Website: http://gradidp.buffalo.edu/

University of California, Merced, Graduate Division, School of Social Sciences, Humanities and Arts, Merced, CA 95343. Offers cognitive and information sciences (PhD); interdisciplinary humanities (MA, PhD); psychological sciences (MA, PhD); social sciences (MA, PhD); sociology (MA, PhD). *Faculty:* 101 full-time (49 women), 3 part-time/adjunct (1 woman). *Students:* 197 full-time (131 women), 2 part-time (1 woman); includes 86 minority (7 Black or African American, non-Hispanic/Latino; 17 Asian, non-Hispanic/Latino; 55 Hispanic/Latino; 1 Native Hawaiian or other Pacific Islander, non-Hispanic/Latino; 6 Two or more races, non-Hispanic/Latino), 33 international. Average age 31. 190 applicants, 41% accepted, 49 enrolled. In 2017, 7 master's, 10 doctorates awarded. Terminal master's awarded for partial completion of doctoral program. *Degree requirements:* For master's, variable foreign language requirement, comprehensive exam, thesis or alternative; for doctorate, variable foreign language requirement, comprehensive exam, thesis/dissertation. *Entrance requirements:* For master's and doctorate, GRE. Additional exam requirements/recommendations for international students: Required—TOEFL (minimum score 550 paper-based; 80 iBT); Recommended—IELTS (minimum score 7). *Application deadline:* For fall admission, 1/ 15 for domestic and international students. Application fee: $90 ($110 for international students). Electronic applications accepted. *Expenses:* Tuition, state resident: full-time $11,502; part-time $5751 per semester. Tuition, nonresident: full-time $26,604; part-time $13,302 per semester. *Required fees:* $564 per semester. *Financial support:* In 2017–18, 167 students received support, including 17 fellowships with full tuition reimbursements available (averaging $23,250 per year), 13 research assistantships with full tuition reimbursements available (averaging $15,387 per year), 162 teaching assistantships with full tuition reimbursements available (averaging $16,103 per year); scholarships/grants, traineeships, and health care benefits also available. Financial award application deadline: 1/15. *Faculty research:* Social inequality, critical race and ethnic studies, public health and health sciences, cognitive science and language acquisition, political institutions, literature, cultural studies, anthropology, art history, ethnomusicology, history. *Total annual research expenditures:* $1.2 million. *Unit head:* Dr. Jill Robbins, Dean, 209-228-7843, E-mail: jillrobbins@ucmerced.edu. *Application contact:* Tsu Ya, Director of Admissions and Academic Services, 209-228-4521, Fax: 209-228-6906, E-mail: tya@ucmerced.edu.

University of California, Santa Barbara, Graduate Division, College of Letters and Sciences, Division of Mathematics, Life, and Physical Sciences, Department of Psychological and Brain Sciences, Santa Barbara, CA 93106-9660. Offers cognitive science (PhD); psychology (PhD); quantitative methods in the social sciences (PhD); technology and society (PhD). Terminal master's awarded for partial completion of doctoral program. *Degree requirements:* For doctorate, comprehensive exam, thesis/ dissertation, teaching assistant training, progress report, papers, mini-convention presentation, 1 quarter of student teaching or teaching assistant class with section lab, continued participation in research and weekly area meetings. *Entrance requirements:* For doctorate, GRE General Test. Additional exam requirements/recommendations for international students: Required—TOEFL (minimum score 550 paper-based; 80 iBT) or IELTS (minimum score 7). Electronic applications accepted. *Faculty research:* Social psychology; developmental and evolutionary psychology; neuroscience and behavior; cognition, perception and cognitive neuroscience.

University of California, Santa Barbara, Graduate Division, College of Letters and Sciences, Division of Social Sciences, Department of Communication, Santa Barbara, CA 93106-4020. Offers cognitive science (PhD); communication (PhD); feminist studies

(PhD); language, interaction and social organization (PhD); quantitative methods in the social sciences (PhD); society and technology (PhD); MA/PhD. Terminal master's awarded for partial completion of doctoral program. *Degree requirements:* For doctorate, comprehensive exam, thesis/dissertation. *Entrance requirements:* For doctorate, GRE. Additional exam requirements/recommendations for international students: Required—TOEFL (minimum score 80 iBT), IELTS (minimum score 7). Electronic applications accepted. *Faculty research:* Interpersonal, intergroup, intercultural, organizational, health, media.

University of California, Santa Cruz, Division of Graduate Studies, Division of Humanities, Program in the History of Consciousness, Santa Cruz, CA 95064. Offers PhD. *Degree requirements:* For doctorate, one foreign language, thesis/dissertation, qualifying exam. *Entrance requirements:* For doctorate, GRE General Test. Additional exam requirements/recommendations for international students: Required—TOEFL (minimum score 550 paper-based; 83 iBT); Recommended—IELTS (minimum score 8). Electronic applications accepted. *Faculty research:* Interdisciplinary humanities and social sciences, political theory, cultural theory, feminist studies, literary theory.

University of Chicago, Division of the Social Sciences, The John U. Nef Committee on Social Thought, Chicago, IL 60637. Offers PhD. *Faculty:* 26. *Students:* 47 full-time (16 women); includes 8 minority (1 Black or African American, non-Hispanic/Latino; 2 Asian, non-Hispanic/Latino; 2 Hispanic/Latino; 3 Two or more races, non-Hispanic/Latino), 13 international. Average age 29. 95 applicants, 5% accepted, 3 enrolled. In 2017, 3 doctorates awarded. *Degree requirements:* For doctorate, one foreign language, thesis/dissertation. *Entrance requirements:* For doctorate, GRE General Test, 3 letters of recommendation, statement of purpose, transcripts, resume or curriculum vitae, writing sample (dependent on department). Additional exam requirements/recommendations for international students: Required—TOEFL (minimum score 104 iBT), IELTS (minimum score 7). *Application deadline:* For fall admission, 12/15 for domestic and international students. Application fee: $90. Electronic applications accepted. *Expenses:* $57,996 tuition. *Financial support:* In 2017–18, 6 students received support, including 5 fellowships with full tuition reimbursements available (averaging $27,000 per year); research assistantships, career-related internships or fieldwork, Federal Work-Study, institutionally sponsored loans, scholarships/grants, and health care benefits also available. Financial award application deadline: 12/15. *Unit head:* Prof. Robert Pippin, Chair, 773-702-5453, Fax: 773-834-1968, E-mail: r-pippin@uchicago.edu. *Application contact:* Office of the Dean of Students, 773-702-8415, E-mail: ssd-admissions@uchicago.edu.
Website: http://socialthought.uchicago.edu

University of Chicago, Division of the Social Sciences, Master of Arts Program in Computational Social Science, Chicago, IL 60637. Offers MA. *Faculty:* 7 full-time. *Students:* 58 full-time (31 women); includes 4 minority (2 Asian, non-Hispanic/Latino; 1 Hispanic/Latino; 1 Two or more races, non-Hispanic/Latino), 48 international. Average age 24. 113 applicants, 61% accepted, 35 enrolled. *Degree requirements:* For master's, thesis. *Entrance requirements:* For master's, GRE General Test, 3 letters of recommendation, statement of purpose, transcripts, resume or curriculum vitae, writing sample (dependent on department). Additional exam requirements/recommendations for international students: Required—TOEFL (minimum score 104 iBT), IELTS (minimum score 7). *Application deadline:* For fall admission, 1/4 priority date for domestic students, 1/4 for international students. Application fee: $90. Electronic applications accepted. *Expenses:* $57,996 tuition. *Financial support:* Federal Work-Study, institutionally sponsored loans, and scholarships/grants available. Financial award application deadline: 1/4. *Faculty research:* Social science data analytics, modeling social systems, cognitive neuroimaging, quantitative social science. *Unit head:* Dr. James Evans, Director, 773-702-9168, E-mail: jevans@uchicago.edu. *Application contact:* Office of the Dean of Students, 773-702-8415, E-mail: ssd-admissions@uchicago.edu.
Website: http://macss.uchicago.edu/

University of Chicago, Division of the Social Sciences, Master of Arts Program in the Social Sciences, Chicago, IL 60637. Offers MA. *Program availability:* Part-time. *Faculty:* 11 full-time. *Students:* 243 full-time (127 women), 2 part-time (both women); includes 41 minority (2 Black or African American, non-Hispanic/Latino; 18 Asian, non-Hispanic/Latino; 15 Hispanic/Latino; 6 Two or more races, non-Hispanic/Latino), 106 international. Average age 25. 1,068 applicants, 82% accepted, 245 enrolled. In 2017, 206 master's awarded. *Degree requirements:* For master's, thesis. *Entrance requirements:* For master's, GRE General Test, 3 letters of recommendation, statement of purpose, transcripts, resume or curriculum vitae, writing sample (dependent on department). Additional exam requirements/recommendations for international students: Required—TOEFL (minimum score 104 iBT), IELTS (minimum score 7). *Application deadline:* For fall admission, 1/4 priority date for domestic and international students. Application fee: $90. Electronic applications accepted. *Expenses:* $57,996 tuition. *Financial support:* In 2017–18, 172 students received support. Federal Work-Study, institutionally sponsored loans, and scholarships/grants available. Financial award application deadline: 1/4. *Unit head:* Prof. Dain Borges, Director, 773-702-8317, E-mail: mapssstaff@uchicago.edu. *Application contact:* Office of the Dean of Students, 773-702-8415, E-mail: ssd-admissions@uchicago.edu.
Website: http://mapss.uchicago.edu

University of Florida, Graduate School, College of Public Health and Health Professions, Programs in Public Health, Gainesville, FL 32611. Offers biostatistics (MPH); clinical and translational science (PhD); environmental health (MPH); epidemiology (MPH); health management and policy (MPH); public health (MPH, PhD, Certificate); public health practice (MPH); rehabilitation science (PhD); social and behavioral sciences (MPH); DPT/MPH; DVM/MPH; JD/MPH; MD/MPH; Pharm D/MPH. *Accreditation:* CEPH. *Program availability:* Online learning. *Degree requirements:* For master's, internship. *Entrance requirements:* For master's, GRE General Test, minimum GPA of 3.0. Additional exam requirements/recommendations for international students: Required—TOEFL (minimum score 550 paper-based; 80 iBT), IELTS (minimum score 6).

University of Illinois at Springfield, Graduate Programs, College of Education and Human Services, Program in Human Services, Springfield, IL 62703-5407. Offers alcohol and substance abuse (Graduate Certificate); alcoholism and substance abuse (MA); child and family services (MA); gerontology (MA); social services administration (MA). *Program availability:* Part-time, evening/weekend, 100% online, blended/hybrid learning. *Faculty:* 5 full-time (all women). *Students:* 8 full-time (7 women), 72 part-time (63 women); includes 38 minority (26 Black or African American, non-Hispanic/Latino; 9 Hispanic/Latino; 3 Two or more races, non-Hispanic/Latino). Average age 33. 49 applicants, 47% accepted, 20 enrolled. In 2017, 21 master's, 1 other advanced degree awarded. *Degree requirements:* For master's, internship; capstone project. *Entrance requirements:* For master's, minimum undergraduate GPA of 3.0, 2 letters of recommendation from professional or academic sources, statement of intent, interview. Additional exam requirements/recommendations for international students: Required—TOEFL (minimum score 500 paper-based; 61 iBT). *Application deadline:* Applications are processed on a rolling basis. Application fee: $60 ($75 for international students). Electronic applications accepted. *Expenses:* Tuition, state resident: full-time $7896; part-time $329 per credit hour. Tuition, nonresident: full-time $16,200; part-time $675 per credit hour. Tuition and fees vary according to program. *Financial support:* In 2017–18, research assistantships with full tuition reimbursements (averaging $10,249 per year), teaching assistantships with full tuition reimbursements (averaging $10,303 per year) were awarded; fellowships, career-related internships or fieldwork, Federal Work-Study, scholarships/grants, health care benefits, and unspecified assistantships also available. Support available to part-time students. Financial award application deadline: 11/15; financial award applicants required to submit FAFSA. *Unit head:* Dr. Carolyn Peck, Program Administrator, 217-206-7577, Fax: 217-206-6775, E-mail: peck.carolyn@uis.edu.
Website: http://www.uis.edu/humanservices

The University of Manchester, School of Social Sciences, Manchester, United Kingdom. Offers ethnographic documentary (M Phil); interdisciplinary study of culture (PhD); philosophy (PhD); politics (PhD); social anthropology (PhD); social anthropology with visual media (PhD); social change (PhD); social statistics (PhD); sociology (PhD); visual anthropology (M Phil).

University of Maryland, Baltimore County, The Graduate School, College of Arts, Humanities and Social Sciences, PhD Program in Gerontology at UMB/UMBC, Baltimore, MD 21201. Offers aging policy issues (PhD); epidemiology of aging (PhD); social, cultural, and behavioral sciences (PhD); MA/PhD; MS/PhD. Program offered with University of Maryland, Baltimore. *Program availability:* Part-time. *Faculty:* 15 part-time/adjunct (10 women). *Students:* 12 full-time (11 women), 8 part-time (7 women); includes 6 minority (3 Black or African American, non-Hispanic/Latino; 1 Asian, non-Hispanic/Latino; 2 Hispanic/Latino), 4 international. Average age 35. 10 applicants, 20% accepted, 2 enrolled. In 2017, 3 doctorates awarded. *Degree requirements:* For doctorate, comprehensive exam, thesis/dissertation. *Entrance requirements:* For doctorate, GRE General Test. Additional exam requirements/recommendations for international students: Required—TOEFL, TWE. *Application deadline:* For spring admission, 1/15 for domestic and international students. Application fee: $45. Electronic applications accepted. *Expenses: Required fees:* $132. *Financial support:* In 2017–18, 11 students received support, including 2 fellowships with full tuition reimbursements available (averaging $23,844 per year), 9 research assistantships with full tuition reimbursements available (averaging $20,000 per year); health care benefits and dissertation awards also available. Financial award application deadline: 2/1; financial award applicants required to submit FAFSA. *Faculty research:* Aging and health policy, behavioral aspects of aging, epidemiology of aging. *Total annual research expenditures:* $15.2 million. *Unit head:* Dr. John Schumacher, Co-Director, UMBC Campus, 410-455-3184, Fax: 410-455-2074, E-mail: jschuma@umbc.edu. *Application contact:* Justine Golden, Academic Coordinator, 410-706-4926, Fax: 410-706-4433, E-mail: jgold002@umaryland.edu.
Website: http://lifesciences.umaryland.edu/gerontologyphd/

University of Memphis, Graduate School, School of Public Health, Memphis, TN 38152. Offers biostatistics (MPH); environmental health (MPH); epidemiology (MPH, PhD); health systems and policy (PhD); health systems management (MPH); public health (MHA); social and behavioral sciences (MPH, PhD). *Program availability:* Part-time, evening/weekend. *Faculty:* 20 full-time (7 women), 4 part-time/adjunct (1 woman). *Students:* 111 full-time (76 women), 59 part-time (45 women); includes 77 minority (48 Black or African American, non-Hispanic/Latino; 18 Asian, non-Hispanic/Latino; 6 Hispanic/Latino; 5 Two or more races, non-Hispanic/Latino), 23 international. Average age 31. 100 applicants, 91% accepted, 60 enrolled. In 2017, 56 master's, 4 doctorates awarded. *Degree requirements:* For master's, comprehensive exam, thesis (for some programs), practicum/field experience; for doctorate, comprehensive exam, thesis/dissertation, residency. *Entrance requirements:* For master's, GRE or GMAT, letters of recommendation; letter of intent; for doctorate, GRE, letters of recommendation; personal statement. Additional exam requirements/recommendations for international students: Required—TOEFL (minimum score 550 paper-based; 79 iBT). *Application deadline:* For fall admission, 4/1 for domestic students; for spring admission, 11/1 for domestic students. Application fee: $35 ($60 for international students). Electronic applications accepted. *Expenses:* Contact institution. *Financial support:* In 2017–18, 46 students received support, including 8 research assistantships with full tuition reimbursements available (averaging $8,950 per year); Federal Work-Study, scholarships/grants, and unspecified assistantships also available. Financial award application deadline: 2/1; financial award applicants required to submit FAFSA. *Faculty research:* Health and medical savings accounts, adoption rates, health informatics, Telehealth technologies, biostatistics, environmental health, epidemiology, health systems management, social and behavioral sciences. *Unit head:* Dr. Lisa M. Klesges, Dean, 901-678-4501, E-mail: lmklsges@memphis.edu. *Application contact:* Dr. Marian Levy, Assistant Dean, 901-678-4514, Fax: 901-678-5023, E-mail: sph-admin@memphis.edu.
Website: http://www.memphis.edu/sph/

University of Michigan, School of Social Work, Interdisciplinary PhD Program in Social Work and Social Science, Ann Arbor, MI 48109. Offers social work and anthropology (PhD); social work and economics (PhD); social work and political science (PhD); social work and psychology (PhD); social work and sociology (PhD). Programs offered through the Rackham Graduate School. *Faculty:* 57 full-time (36 women). *Students:* 53 full-time (38 women); includes 27 minority (10 Black or African American, non-Hispanic/Latino; 2 American Indian or Alaska Native, non-Hispanic/Latino; 9 Asian, non-Hispanic/Latino; 6 Hispanic/Latino). Average age 32. 124 applicants, 6% accepted, 7 enrolled. In 2017, 10 doctorates awarded. *Degree requirements:* For doctorate, thesis/dissertation, oral defense of dissertation, preliminary exam. *Entrance requirements:* For doctorate, GRE General Test. Additional exam requirements/recommendations for international students: Required—TOEFL (minimum score 620 paper-based, 88 iBT) or IELTS. *Application deadline:* For fall admission, 12/1 for domestic and international students. Application fee: $75 ($90 for international students). Electronic applications accepted. *Expenses:* Contact institution. *Financial support:* In 2017–18, 59 students received support, including 24 fellowships with full tuition reimbursements available (averaging $17,600 per year), 7 research assistantships with full tuition reimbursements available (averaging $20,399 per year), 21 teaching assistantships with full tuition reimbursements available (averaging $20,399 per year); career-related internships or fieldwork, scholarships/grants, traineeships, health care benefits, tuition waivers (full and partial), and unspecified assistantships also available. Financial award application deadline: 12/1; financial award applicants required to submit FAFSA. *Faculty research:* Children and family, aging, community organization, health and mental health, police and evaluation. *Total annual research expenditures:* $4.1 million. *Unit head:* Dr. William Elliott, III, Director, 734-763-5768, E-mail: willelli@umich.edu. *Application contact:* Todd Huynh, Graduate Coordinator, 734-647-2554, Fax: 734-615-3192, E-mail: ssw.phd.info@umich.edu.
Website: https://ssw.umich.edu/offices/phd

University of Michigan–Flint, College of Arts and Sciences, Program in Social Sciences, Flint, MI 48502-1950. Offers gender studies (MA); global studies (MA); U.S. history and politics (MA). *Program availability:* Part-time. *Faculty:* 12 full-time (7 women), 6 part-time/adjunct (4 women). *Students:* 2 full-time (1 woman), 12 part-time (6 women); includes 4 minority (3 Black or African American, non-Hispanic/Latino; 1 Hispanic/Latino). Average age 43. 8 applicants, 88% accepted, 6 enrolled. In 2017, 11 master's

awarded. *Entrance requirements:* For master's, bachelor's degree from regionally-accredited institution, minimum overall undergraduate GPA of 3.0. Additional exam requirements/recommendations for international students: Required—TOEFL (minimum score 84 iBT), IELTS (minimum score 6.5). *Application deadline:* For fall admission, 8/1 for domestic students, 5/1 for international students; for winter admission, 11/15 for domestic students, 9/1 for international students; for spring admission, 3/15 for domestic students, 1/1 for international students; for summer admission, 5/15 for domestic students. Applications are processed on a rolling basis. Application fee: $55. Electronic applications accepted. *Expenses:* Contact institution. *Financial support:* Federal Work-Study, scholarships/grants, and unspecified assistantships available. Financial award application deadline: 3/1; financial award applicants required to submit FAFSA. *Unit head:* Dr. Adam Lutzker, Director, 810-762-3470, Fax: 810-762-3281, E-mail: alutzker@umflint.edu. *Application contact:* Bradley T. Maki, Director of Graduate Admissions, 810-762-3171, Fax: 810-766-6789, E-mail: bmaki@umflint.edu.
Website: http://www.umflint.edu/graduateprograms/social-sciences-ma

University of Northern Iowa, Graduate College, College of Social and Behavioral Sciences, MA Program in Social Science, Cedar Falls, IA 50614. Offers MA. *Entrance requirements:* For master's, minimum GPA of 3.0. Additional exam requirements/recommendations for international students: Required—TOEFL (minimum score 500 paper-based; 61 iBT).

University of Regina, Faculty of Graduate Studies and Research, Faculty of Arts, Department of Sociology and Social Studies, Regina, SK S4S 0A2, Canada. Offers social studies (MA); sociology (MA). *Program availability:* Part-time. *Faculty:* 9 full-time (4 women), 7 part-time/adjunct (all women). *Students:* 8 full-time (6 women), 5 part-time (3 women). 21 applicants, 29% accepted. In 2017, 3 master's awarded. *Degree requirements:* For master's, thesis. *Entrance requirements:* Additional exam requirements/recommendations for international students: Required—TOEFL (minimum score 580 paper-based; 80 iBT), IELTS (minimum score 6.5), PTE (minimum score 59). *Application deadline:* Applications are processed on a rolling basis. Application fee: $100. Electronic applications accepted. *Expenses:* $10,681. *Financial support:* In 2017–18, 1 fellowship (averaging $6,000 per year), 3 teaching assistantships (averaging $2,562 per year) were awarded; research assistantships and scholarships/grants also available. Financial award application deadline: 6/15. *Faculty research:* Social justice, international development, globalization, social policy, political economy. *Unit head:* Dr. John Conway, Department Head, 306-585-4052, Fax: 306-585-4815, E-mail: john.conway@uregina.ca. *Application contact:* Dr. Henry Chow, Graduate Coordinator, 306-585-5604, Fax: 306-585-4815, E-mail: henry.chow@uregina.ca.
Website: http://www.uregina.ca/arts/sociology-social-studies

University of South Florida Sarasota-Manatee, College of Liberal Arts and Social Sciences, Sarasota, FL 34243. Offers criminal justice (MA); education (MA); educational leadership (M Ed), including curriculum leadership, K-12 public school leadership, non-public/charter school leadership; elementary education (MAT); English education (MA); social work (MSW). *Program availability:* Part-time, 100% online, blended/hybrid learning. *Faculty:* 15 full-time (12 women), 8 part-time/adjunct (6 women). *Students:* 11 full-time (10 women), 43 part-time (37 women); includes 17 minority (7 Black or African American, non-Hispanic/Latino; 2 Asian, non-Hispanic/Latino; 8 Hispanic/Latino), 1 international. Average age 35. 62 applicants, 27% accepted, 14 enrolled. In 2017, 32 master's awarded. *Degree requirements:* For master's, comprehensive exam (for some programs). *Entrance requirements:* For master's, GRE. Additional exam requirements/recommendations for international students: Required—TOEFL (minimum score 550 paper-based; 79 iBT), IELTS (minimum score 6.5). *Application deadline:* For fall admission, 3/1 priority date for domestic students, 3/1 for international students; for spring admission, 10/1 priority date for domestic students, 10/1 for international students. Applications are processed on a rolling basis. Application fee: $30. Electronic applications accepted. *Expenses:* Tuition, state resident: full-time $8350; part-time $418 per credit hour. Tuition, nonresident: full-time $19,047; part-time $863 per credit hour. *Required fees:* $1689. Tuition and fees vary according to degree level and program. *Financial support:* In 2017–18, 1 student received support. Career-related internships or fieldwork, institutionally sponsored loans, scholarships/grants, health care benefits, and unspecified assistantships available. Support available to part-time students. Financial award application deadline: 3/1; financial award applicants required to submit FAFSA. *Faculty research:* Educational leadership, secondary education, elementary education, criminal justice, social work. *Total annual research expenditures:* $72,000. *Unit head:* Dr. Jane Rose, Dean, 941-359-4469, Fax: 941-359-4778, E-mail: jane.rose@sar.usf.edu. *Application contact:* Brandon Avery, Assistant Director, Admissions, 941-359-4331, E-mail: bavery@sar.usf.edu.

The University of Texas at Tyler, College of Arts and Sciences, Department of Social Sciences, Tyler, TX 75799-0001. Offers criminal justice (MS); public administration (MPA); sociology (MS). *Program availability:* Part-time, evening/weekend. *Degree requirements:* For master's, comprehensive exam, thesis optional. *Entrance requirements:* For master's, GRE General Test, minimum GPA of 3.0. Additional exam requirements/recommendations for international students: Required—TOEFL. *Faculty research:* Urban segregation, minority business, violent crime, gender discrimination.

University of the Virgin Islands, College of Liberal Arts and Social Sciences, St. Thomas, VI 00802. Offers M Psych, MPA. *Program availability:* Part-time, evening/weekend. *Degree requirements:* For master's, comprehensive exam, thesis or alternative. *Entrance requirements:* For master's, GRE, minimum GPA of 2.5. Additional exam requirements/recommendations for international students: Required—TOEFL (minimum score 550 paper-based). Electronic applications accepted. *Expenses:* Contact institution. *Faculty research:* Ethical issues of arbitration, spiritual leadership, accountability.

University of Toronto, School of Graduate Studies, Department of Public Health Sciences, Toronto, ON M5S 1A1, Canada. Offers biostatistics (M Sc, PhD); community health (M Sc); community nutrition (MPH), including nutrition and dietetics; epidemiology (MPH, PhD); family and community medicine (MPH); occupational and environmental health (MPH); social and behavioral health science (PhD); social and behavioral health sciences (MPH), including health promotion. *Accreditation:* CAHME (one or more programs are accredited). *Program availability:* Part-time. *Degree requirements:* For master's, thesis (for some programs), practicum; for doctorate, comprehensive exam, thesis/dissertation, oral thesis defense. *Entrance requirements:* For master's, 2 letters of reference, relevant professional/research experience, minimum B average in final year; for doctorate, 2 letters of reference, relevant professional/research experience, minimum B+ average. Additional exam requirements/recommendations for international students: Required—TOEFL (minimum score 580 paper-based; 93 iBT), TWE (minimum score 5). Electronic applications accepted. *Expenses:* Contact institution.

University of Washington, Graduate School, School of Public Health, Department of Health Services, Seattle, WA 98195. Offers community-oriented public health practice (MPH); health services (MPH, MS, PhD); health systems and policy (MPH); maternal and child health (MPH); social and behavioral sciences (MPH); MPH/JD; MPH/MD; MPH/MN; MPH/MPA; MPH/MS; MPH/MSD; MPH/MSW; MPH/PhD. *Program availability:* Online learning. *Faculty:* 51 full-time (24 women), 69 part-time/adjunct (36 women). *Students:* 156 full-time (133 women), 9 part-time (all women); includes 58 minority (12 Black or African American, non-Hispanic/Latino; 4 American Indian or Alaska Native, non-Hispanic/Latino; 25 Asian, non-Hispanic/Latino; 16 Hispanic/Latino; 1 Native Hawaiian or other Pacific Islander, non-Hispanic/Latino), 5 international. Average age 30. 288 applicants, 64% accepted, 82 enrolled. In 2017, 69 master's, 5 doctorates awarded. Terminal master's awarded for partial completion of doctoral program. Electronic applications accepted. *Expenses:* Contact institution. *Financial support:* Fellowships, research assistantships, teaching assistantships, institutionally sponsored loans, traineeships, and health care benefits available. Financial award applicants required to submit FAFSA. *Faculty research:* Public health practice, health promotion and disease prevention, maternal and child health, organizational behavior and culture, health policy. *Unit head:* Dr. Larry Kessler, Chair, 206-543-2703. *Application contact:* Programs Manager, 206-616-2926, Fax: 206-543-3964, E-mail: hservmph@u.washington.edu.
Website: http://depts.washington.edu/hserv/

Wilfrid Laurier University, Faculty of Graduate and Postdoctoral Studies, Faculty of Arts, Cultural Analysis and Social Theory Program, Waterloo, ON N2L 3C5, Canada. Offers body politics (MA); cultural representation and social theory (MA); gender, sexuality and embodiment (MA); globalization, identity and social movements (MA). *Program availability:* Part-time. *Entrance requirements:* For master's, honours BA in humanities, social science or interdisciplinary program with social theory, minimum B+ in final year of full-time study. Additional exam requirements/recommendations for international students: Required—TOEFL (minimum score 89 iBT). Electronic applications accepted. *Faculty research:* Globalization; identity and social movements; body politics: gender, sexuality and embodiment; cultural representation and social theory.

Worcester Polytechnic Institute, Graduate Admissions, Department of Social Science and Policy Studies, Worcester, MA 01609-2280. Offers interdisciplinary social science (PhD); system dynamics (MS, Graduate Certificate). *Program availability:* Part-time, evening/weekend, 100% online. *Faculty:* 4 full-time (2 women), 4 part-time/adjunct (1 woman). *Students:* 7 part-time (1 woman), 1 international. Average age 48. 5 applicants, 80% accepted, 2 enrolled. In 2017, 4 master's, 1 doctorate, 2 other advanced degrees awarded. *Entrance requirements:* For master's and doctorate, GRE General Test, 3 letters of recommendation, statement of purpose. Additional exam requirements/recommendations for international students: Required—TOEFL (minimum score 563 paper-based; 84 iBT), IELTS (minimum score 7). *Application deadline:* For fall admission, 1/1 priority date for domestic students, 1/1 for international students; for spring admission, 10/1 priority date for domestic students, 10/1 for international students. Applications are processed on a rolling basis. Application fee: $70. Electronic applications accepted. *Expenses: Tuition:* Full-time $26,226; part-time $1457 per credit. *Required fees:* $60; $30 per credit. One-time fee: $15. Tuition and fees vary according to course load. *Financial support:* Research assistantships, teaching assistantships, career-related internships or fieldwork, institutionally sponsored loans, scholarships/grants, and unspecified assistantships available. Financial award application deadline: 1/1. *Unit head:* Dr. Emily Douglas, Head, 508-831-5296, Fax: 508-831-5896, E-mail: emdouglas@wpi.edu. *Application contact:* Dr. Khalid Saeed, Graduate Coordinator, 508-831-5296, Fax: 508-831-5896, E-mail: saeed@wpi.edu.
Website: https://www.wpi.edu/academics/departments/social-science-policy-studies

Worcester Polytechnic Institute, Graduate Admissions, Programs in Interdisciplinary Studies, Worcester, MA 01609-2280. Offers bioscience administration (MS); nuclear science and engineering (Graduate Certificate); power systems management (MS); social science (PhD); system dynamics and innovation management (MS, Graduate Certificate); systems modeling (MS). *Program availability:* Part-time, evening/weekend, 100% online. *Students:* 5 full-time (3 women), 50 part-time (11 women); includes 16 minority (7 Black or African American, non-Hispanic/Latino; 5 Asian, non-Hispanic/Latino; 3 Hispanic/Latino; 1 Two or more races, non-Hispanic/Latino), 3 international. Average age 34. 25 applicants, 96% accepted, 13 enrolled. In 2017, 10 master's, 1 doctorate, 7 other advanced degrees awarded. Terminal master's awarded for partial completion of doctoral program. *Degree requirements:* For master's, thesis; for doctorate, comprehensive exam, thesis/dissertation. *Entrance requirements:* For master's and doctorate, 3 letters of recommendation. Additional exam requirements/recommendations for international students: Required—TOEFL (minimum score 563 paper-based; 84 iBT), IELTS (minimum score 7). *Application deadline:* For fall admission, 1/1 priority date for domestic students, 1/1 for international students; for spring admission, 10/1 priority date for domestic students, 10/1 for international students. Applications are processed on a rolling basis. Application fee: $70. Electronic applications accepted. *Expenses: Tuition:* Full-time $26,226; part-time $1457 per credit. *Required fees:* $60; $30 per credit. One-time fee: $15. Tuition and fees vary according to course load. *Financial support:* Institutionally sponsored loans, scholarships/grants, and unspecified assistantships available. Financial award application deadline: 1/1. *Unit head:* Michale McGrade, Dean, 508-831-5301, Fax: 508-831-5717, E-mail: grad@wpi.edu. *Application contact:* Lynne Dougherty, Administrative Assistant, 508-831-5301, Fax: 508-831-5717, E-mail: grad@wpi.edu.

Yale University, Yale School of Medicine, Yale School of Public Health, New Haven, CT 06520. Offers applied biostatistics and epidemiology (APMPH); biostatistics (MPH, MS, PhD), including global health (MPH); chronic disease epidemiology (MPH, PhD), including global health (MPH); environmental health sciences (MPH, PhD), including global health (MPH); epidemiology of microbial diseases (MPH, PhD), including global health (MPH); global health (APMPH); health management (MPH), including global health; health policy (MPH), including global health; health policy and administration (APMPH, PhD); occupational and environmental medicine (APMPH); preventive medicine (APMPH); social and behavioral sciences (APMPH, MPH), including global health (MPH); JD/MPH; M Div/MPH; MBA/MPH; MD/MPH; MEM/MPH; MFS/MPH; MM Sc/MPH; MPH/MA; MSN/MPH. MS and PhD offered through the Graduate School. *Accreditation:* CEPH. *Program availability:* Part-time. Terminal master's awarded for partial completion of doctoral program. *Degree requirements:* For master's, thesis, summer internship; for doctorate, comprehensive exam, thesis/dissertation, residency. *Entrance requirements:* For master's, GMAT, GRE, or MCAT, two years of undergraduate coursework in math and science; for doctorate, GRE General Test. Additional exam requirements/recommendations for international students: Required—TOEFL (minimum score 100 iBT). Electronic applications accepted. *Expenses:* Contact institution. *Faculty research:* Genetic and emerging infections epidemiology, virology, cost/quality, vector biology, quantitative methods, aging, asthma, cancer.

Section 27
Sociology, Anthropology, and Archaeology

This section contains a directory of institutions offering graduate work in sociology, anthropology, and archaeology. Additional information about programs listed in the directory may be obtained by writing directly to the dean of a graduate school or chair of a department at the address given in the directory.

For programs offering related work, see also in this book *Area and Cultural Studies, Art and Art History, History, Humanities, Language and Literature,* and *Psychology and Counseling.*

CONTENTS

Program Directories

Anthropology

American University, College of Arts and Sciences, Department of Anthropology, Washington, DC 20016-8003. Offers anthropology (PhD, Certificate); public anthropology (MA). *Program availability:* Part-time, evening/weekend. *Faculty:* 12 full-time (7 women), 2 part-time/adjunct (1 woman). *Students:* 44 full-time (31 women), 39 part-time (36 women); includes 19 minority (6 Black or African American, non-Hispanic/Latino; 2 Asian, non-Hispanic/Latino; 8 Hispanic/Latino; 3 Two or more races, non-Hispanic/Latino), 8 international. Average age 32. 58 applicants, 64% accepted, 18 enrolled. In 2017, 13 master's, 14 doctorates awarded. Terminal master's awarded for partial completion of doctoral program. *Degree requirements:* For master's, comprehensive exam, thesis or alternative; for doctorate, comprehensive exam, thesis/dissertation. *Entrance requirements:* For master's, GRE, sample of written work, personal statement, two letters of recommendation, transcripts, resume; for doctorate, GRE, sample of written work, personal statement, three letters of recommendation, resume, transcripts; for Certificate, statement of purpose, transcripts. Additional exam requirements/recommendations for international students: Required—TOEFL (minimum score 600 paper-based; 100 iBT). *Application deadline:* For fall admission, 2/1 priority date for domestic students; for spring admission, 11/1 for domestic students. Application fee: $55. *Expenses:* Contact institution. *Financial support:* Research assistantships, teaching assistantships, institutionally sponsored loans, and unspecified assistantships available. Financial award application deadline: 1/15; financial award applicants required to submit FAFSA. *Faculty research:* Poverty and race, lesbian and gay studies, class and culture, developing countries. *Unit head:* Dr. Daniel Sayers, Department Chair, 202-885-1833, Fax: 202-885-1837, E-mail: sayers@american.edu. *Application contact:* Jonathan Harper, Assistant Director, Graduate Recruitment, 202-855-3622, E-mail: jharper@american.edu.
Website: http://www.american.edu/cas/anthropology/

American University of Beirut, Graduate Programs, Faculty of Arts and Sciences, 1107 2020, Lebanon. Offers anthropology (MA); Arab and Middle Eastern history (PhD); Arabic language and literature (MA, PhD); archaeology (MA); art history and curating (MA); biology (MS); cell and molecular biology (PhD); chemistry (MS); clinical psychology (MA); computational sciences (MS); computer science (MS); economics (MA); education (MA), including administration and policy studies, elementary education, mathematics education, psychology school guidance, psychology test and measurements, science education, teaching English as a foreign language; English language (MA); English literature (MA); environmental policy planning (MS); financial economics (MAFE); general psychology (MA); geology (MS); history (MA); Islamic studies (MA); mathematics (MS); media studies (MA); Middle East studies (MA); philosophy (MA); physics (MS); political studies (MA); public administration (MA); public policy and international affairs (MA); sociology (MA); theoretical physics (PhD). *Program availability:* Part-time. *Faculty:* 108 full-time (36 women), 5 part-time/adjunct (4 women). *Students:* 251 full-time (180 women), 233 part-time (172 women). Average age 26. 425 applicants, 65% accepted, 121 enrolled. In 2017, 47 master's, 2 doctorates awarded. *Degree requirements:* For master's, one foreign language, comprehensive exam, thesis (for some programs), project; for doctorate, one foreign language, comprehensive exam, thesis/dissertation. *Entrance requirements:* For master's, GRE General Test (for some programs); for doctorate, GRE General Test (GRE Subject Test for theoretical physics). Additional exam requirements/recommendations for international students: Required—TOEFL (minimum score 583 paper-based; 97 iBT), IELTS (minimum score 7). *Application deadline:* For fall admission, 2/8 for domestic students; for spring admission, 11/3 for domestic students. Application fee: $50. Electronic applications accepted. *Expenses:* Contact institution. *Financial support:* In 2017–18, 29 fellowships, 40 research assistantships were awarded; teaching assistantships, scholarships/grants, tuition waivers (full and partial), and unspecified assistantships also available. Financial award application deadline: 4/4. *Unit head:* Dr. Nadia Maria El Cheikh, Dean, Faculty of Arts and Sciences, 961-1-374374 Ext. 3800, Fax: 961-1-744461, E-mail: nmcheikh@aub.edu.lb. *Application contact:* Rima Rassi, Graduate Studies Officer, 961-1-350000 Ext. 3833, Fax: 961-1-744461, E-mail: rr46@aub.edu.lb.
Website: http://www.aub.edu.lb/fas/pages/default.aspx

Arizona State University at the Tempe campus, College of Liberal Arts and Sciences, School of Human Evolution and Social Change, Tempe, AZ 85287-2402. Offers anthropology (MA, PhD), including anthropology (PhD), archaeology (PhD), bioarchaeology (PhD), evolutionary (PhD), museum studies (MA), sociocultural (PhD); applied mathematics for the life and social sciences (PhD); environmental social science (PhD), including environmental social science, urbanism; global health (MA, PhD), including complex adaptive systems science (PhD), evolutionary global health sciences (PhD), health and culture (PhD), urbanism (PhD); immigration studies (Graduate Certificate). Terminal master's awarded for partial completion of doctoral program. *Degree requirements:* For master's, thesis or alternative, interactive Program of Study (iPOS) submitted before completing 50 percent of required credit hours; for doctorate, comprehensive exam, thesis/dissertation, interactive Program of Study (iPOS) submitted before completing 50 percent of required credit hours. *Entrance requirements:* For master's and doctorate, GRE, minimum GPA of 3.0 or equivalent in last 2 years of work leading to bachelor's degree. Additional exam requirements/recommendations for international students: Required—TOEFL, IELTS, or PTE. Electronic applications accepted.

Ball State University, Graduate School, College of Sciences and Humanities, Department of Anthropology, Muncie, IN 47306. Offers anthropology (MA); interpretive ethnography (Certificate). *Program availability:* Part-time. *Faculty:* 8 full-time (5 women). *Students:* 10 full-time (8 women), 10 part-time (8 women); includes 1 minority (Hispanic/Latino). Average age 32. 15 applicants, 67% accepted, 9 enrolled. In 2017, 9 master's awarded. *Entrance requirements:* For master's, GRE General Test, minimum baccalaureate GPA of 2.75 or 3.0 in latter half of baccalaureate, official transcripts, goals statement, resume, three letters of recommendation. Additional exam requirements/recommendations for international students: Required—TOEFL (minimum score 550 paper-based; 79 iBT), IELTS (minimum score 6.5). *Application deadline:* For fall admission, 3/30 for domestic students. Applications are processed on a rolling basis. Application fee: $60. Electronic applications accepted. *Financial support:* In 2017–18, 10 students received support, including 6 research assistantships with partial tuition reimbursements available (averaging $10,809 per year). Financial award application deadline: 3/1; financial award applicants required to submit FAFSA. *Unit head:* Dr. S. Homes Hogue, Chairperson, 765-285-4845, Fax: 765-285-2163, E-mail: sshogue@bsu.edu. *Application contact:* Dr. Jennifer Erickson, Graduate Program Director, 765-285-1512, Fax: 765-285-2163, E-mail: jlerickson@bsu.edu.
Website: http://www.bsu.edu/anthropology

Binghamton University, State University of New York, Graduate School, Harpur College of Arts and Sciences, Department of Anthropology, Binghamton, NY 13902-6000. Offers anthropology (MA, PhD); biomedical anthropology (MS). *Program availability:* Part-time. *Faculty:* 23 full-time (10 women). *Students:* 71 full-time (48 women), 91 part-time (67 women); includes 27 minority (2 Black or African American, non-Hispanic/Latino; 1 American Indian or Alaska Native, non-Hispanic/Latino; 6 Asian, non-Hispanic/Latino; 12 Hispanic/Latino; 1 Native Hawaiian or other Pacific Islander, non-Hispanic/Latino; 5 Two or more races, non-Hispanic/Latino), 21 international. Average age 30. 102 applicants, 73% accepted, 31 enrolled. In 2017, 19 master's, 7 doctorates awarded. Terminal master's awarded for partial completion of doctoral program. *Degree requirements:* For master's, variable foreign language requirement, comprehensive exam (for some programs), thesis (for some programs); for doctorate, variable foreign language requirement, comprehensive exam, thesis/dissertation. *Entrance requirements:* For master's and doctorate, GRE General Test. Additional exam requirements/recommendations for international students: Required—TOEFL (minimum score 550 paper-based; 80 iBT). *Application deadline:* For fall admission, 4/15 priority date for domestic and international students; for spring admission, 10/15 priority date for domestic and international students. Application fee: $75. Electronic applications accepted. *Financial support:* In 2017–18, 49 students received support, including 1 fellowship with full tuition reimbursement available (averaging $5,000 per year), 1 research assistantship with full tuition reimbursement available (averaging $17,000 per year), 30 teaching assistantships with full tuition reimbursements available (averaging $15,000 per year); career-related internships or fieldwork, Federal Work-Study, institutionally sponsored loans, scholarships/grants, health care benefits, tuition waivers (full and partial), and unspecified assistantships also available. Financial award application deadline: 1/15; financial award applicants required to submit FAFSA. *Unit head:* Kathleen Sterling, Graduate Director, 607-777-2100, E-mail: sterling@binghamton.edu. *Application contact:* Ben Balkaya, Assistant Dean and Director, 607-777-2151, Fax: 607-777-2501, E-mail: balkaya@binghamton.edu.
Website: http://www.binghamton.edu/anthropology/

Biola University, Cook School of Intercultural Studies, La Mirada, CA 90639-0001. Offers anthropology (MA); applied linguistics (MA); intercultural education (PhD); intercultural studies (MA, PhD); linguistics (Certificate); linguistics and Biblical languages (MA); missiology (D Miss); missions (MA); teaching English to speakers of other languages (MA, Certificate). *Program availability:* Part-time, 100% online. *Faculty:* 19. *Students:* 127 full-time (64 women), 123 part-time (70 women); includes 72 minority (9 Black or African American, non-Hispanic/Latino; 2 American Indian or Alaska Native, non-Hispanic/Latino; 41 Asian, non-Hispanic/Latino; 17 Hispanic/Latino; 3 Two or more races, non-Hispanic/Latino), 26 international. In 2017, 28 master's, 16 doctorates awarded. *Entrance requirements:* For master's, minimum undergraduate GPA of 3.0; for doctorate, master's degree or equivalent, 3 years of cross-cultural experience, minimum graduate GPA of 3.3. Additional exam requirements/recommendations for international students: Required—TOEFL. *Application deadline:* For fall admission, 7/1 for domestic students, 6/1 for international students; for spring admission, 12/1 for domestic students; for summer admission, 5/1 for domestic students. Applications are processed on a rolling basis. Application fee: $65. Electronic applications accepted. *Financial support:* Scholarships/grants available. Support available to part-time students. Financial award applicants required to submit FAFSA. *Faculty research:* Linguistics, anthropology, intercultural studies, teaching English to speakers of other languages, missions, missiology. *Unit head:* Dr. Bulus Y. Galadima, Dean, 562-903-4844. *Application contact:* Graduate Admissions Office, 562-903-4752, E-mail: graduate.admissions@biola.edu.
Website: http://cook.biola.edu

Boise State University, College of Arts and Sciences, Department of Anthropology, Boise, ID 83725-0399. Offers anthropology (MA); applied anthropology (MAA). *Program availability:* Part-time. *Faculty:* 6. *Students:* 12 full-time (7 women), 3 part-time (2 women); includes 2 minority (both Hispanic/Latino), 1 international. Average age 31. *Degree requirements:* For master's, comprehensive exam, thesis (MA); project (MAA). *Entrance requirements:* For master's, GRE General Test. Additional exam requirements/recommendations for international students: Required—TOEFL (minimum score 550 paper-based; 80 iBT), IELTS (minimum score 6). *Application deadline:* For fall admission, 5/1 for domestic and international students. Application fee: $65 ($95 for international students). Electronic applications accepted. *Expenses:* Tuition, state resident: full-time $6471; part-time $390 per credit. Tuition, nonresident: full-time $21,787; part-time $685 per credit. *Required fees:* $2283; $100 per term. Part-time tuition and fees vary according to course load and program. *Financial support:* Scholarships/grants and unspecified assistantships available. Financial award application deadline: 2/15; financial award applicants required to submit FAFSA. *Unit head:* Dr. John Ziker, Department Chair, 208-426-2121, E-mail: jziker@boisestate.edu. *Application contact:* Dr. Mark Plew, Graduate Program Coordinator, 208-426-3444, E-mail: mplew@boisestate.edu.
Website: http://anthropology.boisestate.edu/

Boston University, Graduate School of Arts and Sciences, Department of Anthropology, Boston, MA 02215. Offers anthropology (PhD); applied anthropology (MA). *Students:* 42 full-time (30 women), 2 part-time (1 woman); includes 4 minority (1 Black or African American, non-Hispanic/Latino; 1 Asian, non-Hispanic/Latino; 2 Two or more races, non-Hispanic/Latino), 17 international. Average age 27. 100 applicants, 13% accepted, 8 enrolled. In 2017, 1 master's, 1 doctorate awarded. Terminal master's awarded for partial completion of doctoral program. *Degree requirements:* For master's, one foreign language, comprehensive exam, thesis or alternative; for doctorate, one foreign language, thesis/dissertation. *Entrance requirements:* For master's and doctorate, GRE General Test, 3 letters of recommendation, transcripts, personal statement. Additional exam requirements/recommendations for international students: Required—TOEFL (minimum score 550 paper-based; 84 iBT). *Application deadline:* For fall admission, 1/15 for domestic and international students. Application fee: $95. Electronic applications accepted. *Financial support:* In 2017–18, 41 students received support, including 10 fellowships with full tuition reimbursements available (averaging $22,000 per year), 17 teaching assistantships with full tuition reimbursements available (averaging $22,000 per year); Federal Work-Study, scholarships/grants, health care benefits, and unspecified assistantships also available. Support available to part-time students. Financial award application deadline: 1/15. *Unit head:* Thomas Barfield, Chair, 617-353-5028, Fax: 617-353-2610, E-mail: barfield@bu.edu. *Application contact:* Martin Wraga, Administrator, 617-353-2195, Fax: 617-353-2610, E-mail: mwraga@bu.edu.
Website: http://www.bu.edu/ANTHROP/

Boston University, School of Medicine, Division of Graduate Medical Sciences, Program in Forensic Anthropology, Boston, MA 02215. Offers MS. *Financial support:* Applicants required to submit FAFSA. *Unit head:* Dr. Tara L. Moore, Program Director, 617-638-4054, Fax: 617-638-4922, E-mail: tlmoore@bu.edu. *Application contact:* GMS Admissions Office, 617-638-5255, E-mail: askgms@bu.edu.
Website: http://www.bumc.bu.edu/gms/forensicanthropology/

Boston University, School of Medicine, Division of Graduate Medical Sciences, Program in Medical Anthropology and Cross Cultural Practice, Boston, MA 02215. Offers MS. *Unit head:* Dr. Linda Barnes, Director, 617-414-4534, Fax: 617-414-5511, E-mail: linda.barnes@bmc.org. *Application contact:* GMS Admissions Office, 617-638-5255, E-mail: askgms@bu.edu.
Website: http://www.bumc.bu.edu/gms/maccp/

Brandeis University, Graduate School of Arts and Sciences, Department of Anthropology, Waltham, MA 02454-9110. Offers anthropology/women's, gender, and sexuality studies (MA); Mesoamerican archaeology (MA, PhD); sociocultural anthropology (MA, PhD). *Program availability:* Part-time. *Faculty:* 9 full-time (5 women), 4 part-time/adjunct (1 woman). *Students:* 35 full-time (24 women), 1 part-time (0 women); includes 6 minority (3 Black or African American, non-Hispanic/Latino; 1 Hispanic/Latino; 2 Two or more races, non-Hispanic/Latino), 6 international. Average age 28. 50 applicants, 48% accepted, 8 enrolled. In 2017, 11 master's awarded. Terminal master's awarded for partial completion of doctoral program. *Degree requirements:* For master's, thesis; for doctorate, one foreign language, comprehensive exam, thesis/dissertation. *Entrance requirements:* For master's and doctorate, GRE General Test, sample of written work, resume, letters of recommendation, transcript. Additional exam requirements/recommendations for international students: Required—PTE (minimum score 68), TOEFL (minimum score 600 paper-based, 100 iBT) or IELTS (7). *Application deadline:* For fall admission, 1/15 priority date for domestic and international students. Applications are processed on a rolling basis. Application fee: $75. Electronic applications accepted. *Expenses: Tuition:* Full-time $48,720. *Required fees:* $88. Tuition and fees vary according to course load, degree level, program and student level. *Financial support:* In 2017–18, 34 students received support, including 11 fellowships with full tuition reimbursements available (averaging $24,480 per year), 15 teaching assistantships with partial tuition reimbursements available (averaging $3,200 per year); scholarships/grants, health care benefits, and tuition waivers (partial) also available. Support available to part-time students. Financial award application deadline: 4/15; financial award applicants required to submit FAFSA. *Faculty research:* Sociocultural anthropology, archaeology, gender and sexuality, linguistic anthropology, physical anthropology. *Unit head:* Dr. Sarah Lamb, Director of Graduate Studies, 781-736-2210, Fax: 781-736-2232, E-mail: lamb@brandeis.edu. *Application contact:* Laurel Carpenter, Academic Administrator, 781-736-2210, Fax: 781-736-2232, E-mail: lcarpent@brandeis.edu.
Website: http://www.brandeis.edu/gsas/programs/anthropology.html

Brigham Young University, Graduate Studies, College of Family, Home, and Social Sciences, Department of Anthropology, Provo, UT 84602. Offers MA. *Faculty:* 10 full-time (1 woman). *Students:* 15 full-time (11 women). Average age 25. 5 applicants, 80% accepted, 2 enrolled. In 2017, 2 master's awarded. *Degree requirements:* For master's, comprehensive exam, thesis. *Entrance requirements:* For master's, GRE General Test, minimum GPA of 3.0 in last 60 hours. Additional exam requirements/recommendations for international students: Required—TOEFL (minimum score 580 paper-based). *Application deadline:* For fall admission, 2/1 for domestic and international students. Application fee: $50. Electronic applications accepted. *Expenses: Tuition:* Full-time $6880; part-time $405 per credit hour. Tuition and fees vary according to course load, program and student's religious affiliation. *Financial support:* In 2017–18, 16 students received support, including 10 research assistantships (averaging $10,000 per year), 3 teaching assistantships (averaging $7,500 per year); fellowships, career-related internships or fieldwork, institutionally sponsored loans, and tuition waivers (partial) also available. Financial award application deadline: 3/1; financial award applicants required to submit FAFSA. *Faculty research:* Archaeology of the Southwest, near East, South America, and Mesoamerica; Mayan glyphs. *Total annual research expenditures:* $55,000. *Unit head:* Dr. James R. Allison, Chair/Graduate Coordinator, 801-422-3059, Fax: 801-422-7942, E-mail: jallison@byu.edu.
Website: http://anthropology.byu.edu/

Brown University, Graduate School, Department of Anthropology, Providence, RI 02912. Offers MA, PhD. *Degree requirements:* For doctorate, one foreign language, thesis/dissertation, preliminary exam.

California State University, Bakersfield, Division of Graduate Studies, School of Social Sciences and Education, Program in Anthropology, Bakersfield, CA 93311. Offers MA. *Faculty:* 1 full-time (0 women). *Students:* 4 full-time (1 woman), 10 part-time (7 women); includes 7 minority (6 Hispanic/Latino; 1 Two or more races, non-Hispanic/Latino). Average age 34. *Degree requirements:* For master's, thesis optional. *Entrance requirements:* For master's, GRE, minimum GPA of 2.5, 3 letters of recommendation. Additional exam requirements/recommendations for international students: Required—TOEFL (minimum score 550 paper-based). *Application deadline:* For fall admission, 5/1 for domestic students. Application fee: $55. *Expenses:* Tuition, state resident: full-time $7176; part-time $4164 per year. *Financial support:* In 2017–18, fellowships (averaging $1,850 per year) were awarded; Federal Work-Study, scholarships/grants, and tuition waivers (full and partial) also available. Financial award application deadline: 3/2; financial award applicants required to submit FAFSA. *Faculty research:* Human services, social science teaching. *Unit head:* Dr. Robert Yohe, Graduate Coordinator, 661-654-3457, Fax: 661-654-6909, E-mail: ryohe@csub.edu. *Application contact:* Debbie Blowers, Assistant Director of Admissions and Evaluations, 661-654-3381, E-mail: dblowers@csub.edu.
Website: https://www.csub.edu/anthropology/index.html

California State University, Chico, Office of Graduate Studies, College of Behavioral and Social Sciences, Department of Anthropology, Chico, CA 95929-0722. Offers anthropology (MA); museum studies (MA). *Degree requirements:* For master's, comprehensive exam, thesis, oral examination. *Entrance requirements:* For master's, GRE General Test, two letters of recommendation, statement of purpose, curriculum vitae, writing sample. Additional exam requirements/recommendations for international students: Required—TOEFL (minimum score 550 paper-based; 80 iBT), IELTS (minimum score 6.5), PTE (minimum score 59). Electronic applications accepted.

California State University, East Bay, Office of Graduate Studies, College of Letters, Arts, and Social Sciences, Department of Anthropology, Geography and Environmental Studies, Hayward, CA 94542-3000. Offers anthropology (MA); geography (MA). *Program availability:* Part-time. *Faculty:* 7 full-time (1 woman), 10 part-time/adjunct (8 women). *Students:* 2 part-time (both women); includes 1 minority (Hispanic/Latino). Average age 61. In 2017, 5 master's awarded. *Degree requirements:* For master's, variable foreign language requirement, project or thesis. *Entrance requirements:* For master's, minimum GPA of 3.0 in field. Additional exam requirements/recommendations for international students: Required—TOEFL (minimum score 550 paper-based). *Application deadline:* For fall admission, 6/1 for domestic and international students. Applications are processed on a rolling basis. Application fee: $55. Electronic applications accepted. *Financial support:* Fellowships, teaching assistantships, career-related internships or fieldwork, Federal Work-Study, institutionally sponsored loans, and scholarships/grants available. Support available to part-time students. Financial award application deadline: 3/2; financial award applicants required to submit FAFSA. *Faculty research:* Sustainability, water resources, geographic information systems (GIS), mapping. *Unit head:* Dr. David Larson, Chair, 510-885-3192, E-mail: david.larson@csueastbay.edu. *Application contact:* Prof. David Woo, Graduate Advisor

for Geography, 510-885-3160, Fax: 510-885-2353, E-mail: david.woo@csueastbay.edu.
Website: http://www20.csueastbay.edu/class/departments/ages/index.html

California State University, Fullerton, Graduate Studies, College of Humanities and Social Sciences, Department of Anthropology, Fullerton, CA 92831-3599. Offers MA. *Program availability:* Part-time. *Faculty:* 8 full-time (4 women). *Students:* 17 full-time (12 women), 8 part-time (6 women); includes 11 minority (1 Asian, non-Hispanic/Latino; 9 Hispanic/Latino; 1 Two or more races, non-Hispanic/Latino), 1 international. Average age 29. 30 applicants, 63% accepted, 15 enrolled. *Entrance requirements:* For master's, minimum GPA of 2.5 in last 60 hours of course work. Application fee: $55. *Financial support:* Career-related internships or fieldwork, Federal Work-Study, institutionally sponsored loans, and scholarships/grants available. Support available to part-time students. Financial award application deadline: 3/1; financial award applicants required to submit FAFSA. *Unit head:* Dr. Mitch Avila, Chair, 657-278-2272. *Application contact:* Admissions/Applications, 657-278-2371.

California State University, Long Beach, Graduate Studies, College of Liberal Arts, Department of Anthropology, Long Beach, CA 90840. Offers anthropology (MA); applied anthropology (MA). *Program availability:* Part-time. *Degree requirements:* For master's, one foreign language, comprehensive exam or thesis. Electronic applications accepted. *Faculty research:* Archeology of California, Fiji, and Ireland; cultures of American Indians and Mexico.

California State University, Los Angeles, Graduate Studies, College of Natural and Social Sciences, Department of Anthropology, Los Angeles, CA 90032-8530. Offers MA. *Program availability:* Part-time, evening/weekend. *Degree requirements:* For master's, one foreign language, comprehensive exam or thesis. *Entrance requirements:* Additional exam requirements/recommendations for international students: Required—TOEFL (minimum score 500 paper-based). *Faculty research:* Archaeology, folklore, petroglyphs, symbolism, medical anthropology.

California State University, Northridge, Graduate Studies, College of Social and Behavioral Sciences, Department of Anthropology, Northridge, CA 91330. Offers general anthropology (MA); public archaeology (MA). *Students:* 7 full-time (3 women), 11 part-time (7 women); includes 13 minority (12 Hispanic/Latino; 1 Two or more races, non-Hispanic/Latino). Average age 30. 22 applicants, 55% accepted, 8 enrolled. In 2017, 12 master's awarded. *Degree requirements:* For master's, thesis or alternative. *Entrance requirements:* For master's, GRE General Test or minimum GPA of 3.0. Additional exam requirements/recommendations for international students: Required—TOEFL. *Application deadline:* For fall admission, 11/30 for domestic students. Application fee: $55. *Financial support:* Career-related internships or fieldwork, Federal Work-Study, and institutionally sponsored loans available. Financial award application deadline: 3/1. *Unit head:* Dr. Suzanne Scheld, Chair, 818-677-3331.
Website: http://www.csun.edu/csbs/departments/anthropology/index.html

California State University, Sacramento, College of Social Sciences and Interdisciplinary Studies, Department of Anthropology, Sacramento, CA 95819. Offers MA. *Program availability:* Part-time. *Students:* 4 full-time (3 women), 14 part-time (9 women); includes 4 minority (1 American Indian or Alaska Native, non-Hispanic/Latino; 2 Asian, non-Hispanic/Latino; 1 Hispanic/Latino). Average age 37. 15 applicants, 53% accepted, 6 enrolled. In 2017, 1 master's awarded. *Degree requirements:* For master's, project or thesis; writing proficiency exam. *Entrance requirements:* For master's, minimum GPA of 3.0 during previous 2 years. Additional exam requirements/recommendations for international students: Required—TOEFL (minimum score 550 paper-based; 80 iBT); Recommended—IELTS, TSE. *Application deadline:* For fall admission, 3/1 for domestic and international students. Applications are processed on a rolling basis. Application fee: $55. Electronic applications accepted. *Expenses:* Contact institution. *Financial support:* Career-related internships or fieldwork, Federal Work-Study, and scholarships/grants available. Support available to part-time students. Financial award application deadline: 3/1; financial award applicants required to submit FAFSA. *Unit head:* Dr. Raghuraman Trichur, Chair, 916-278-4789, E-mail: rtrichur@csus.edu. *Application contact:* Jose Martinez, Graduate Admissions Supervisor, 916-278-7871, E-mail: martinj@skymail.csus.edu.
Website: http://www.csus.edu/anth

Canisius College, Graduate Division, College of Arts and Sciences, Department of Animal Behavior, Ecology and Conservation, Buffalo, NY 14208-1098. Offers anthrozoology (MS). Applicants accepted in fall only. *Program availability:* Part-time, evening/weekend, blended/hybrid learning. *Faculty:* 5 full-time (3 women), 3 part-time/adjunct (all women). *Students:* 23 full-time (all women), 32 part-time (26 women); includes 3 minority (1 Black or African American, non-Hispanic/Latino; 1 Hispanic/Latino; 1 Two or more races, non-Hispanic/Latino), 1 international. Average age 35. 78 applicants, 36% accepted, 20 enrolled. In 2017, 15 master's awarded. *Entrance requirements:* For master's, GRE (recommended), official transcript of all college work, bachelor's degree, minimum GPA of 3.0, three essays. Additional exam requirements/recommendations for international students: Required—TOEFL (minimum score 550 paper-based, 80 iBT), IELTS (minimum score 6.5), or CAEL (minimum score 70). *Application deadline:* For fall admission, 3/1 for domestic and international students. Applications are processed on a rolling basis. Application fee: $0. Electronic applications accepted. *Expenses: Tuition:* Full-time $22,860; part-time $820 per credit. *Required fees:* $720; $25 per credit. $65 per semester. One-time fee: $425. *Financial support:* Career-related internships or fieldwork, Federal Work-Study, scholarships/grants, tuition waivers (partial), and unspecified assistantships available. Support available to part-time students. Financial award application deadline: 4/30; financial award applicants required to submit FAFSA. *Faculty research:* Human animal relations; advocacy of animal welfare and conservation. *Unit head:* Dr. Sue Margulis, Program Director, 716-888-2773, E-mail: margulis@canisius.edu.
Website: http://www.canisius.edu/abec/

Carleton University, Faculty of Graduate Studies, Faculty of Arts and Social Sciences, Department of Sociology and Anthropology, Program in Anthropology, Ottawa, ON K1S 5B6, Canada. Offers MA. *Degree requirements:* For master's, comprehensive exam, thesis optional. *Entrance requirements:* For master's, honors degree. Additional exam requirements/recommendations for international students: Required—TOEFL. *Faculty research:* Culture, symbols and mind, anthropology of signs and symbols, Indigenous studies, anthropology of development and underdevelopment.

Case Western Reserve University, School of Graduate Studies, Department of Anthropology, Cleveland, OH 44106. Offers MA, PhD, MD/MA, MD/PhD, MPH/MA, MSN/MA, PhD/MPH. *Program availability:* Part-time. *Faculty:* 11 full-time (6 women), 7 part-time/adjunct (3 women). *Students:* 32 full-time (24 women), 1 (woman) part-time; includes 4 minority (1 Black or African American, non-Hispanic/Latino; 2 Asian, non-Hispanic/Latino; 1 Two or more races, non-Hispanic/Latino), 6 international. Average age 32. 22 applicants, 59% accepted, 6 enrolled. In 2017, 3 master's, 2 doctorates awarded. Terminal master's awarded for partial completion of doctoral program. *Degree requirements:* For master's, comprehensive exam, thesis optional; for doctorate, thesis/dissertation. *Entrance requirements:* For master's and doctorate, GRE General Test, statement of purpose; 3 letters of recommendation; official transcripts. Additional exam requirements/recommendations for international students: Required—TOEFL (minimum score 577 paper-based; 90 iBT), IELTS (minimum score 7). *Application deadline:* For fall

admission, 2/15 priority date for domestic students; for spring admission, 11/1 for domestic students. Applications are processed on a rolling basis. Application fee: $50. Electronic applications accepted. *Expenses: Tuition:* Full-time $43,854; part-time $1827 per credit hour. *Required fees:* $50; $50 per credit hour. Tuition and fees vary according to course load and program. *Financial support:* Research assistantships with tuition reimbursements, teaching assistantships with tuition reimbursements, career-related internships or fieldwork, and unspecified assistantships available. Support available to part-time students. Financial award application deadline: 2/15; financial award applicants required to submit CSS PROFILE or FAFSA. *Faculty research:* Medical anthropology, psychological anthropology, cross-cultural aging, physical anthropology, international health. *Unit head:* Lawrence P. Greksa, Professor and Chair, 216-368-6777, Fax: 216-368-5334, E-mail: lawrence.greksa@case.edu. *Application contact:* Linda Rinella, Department Administrator, 216-368-2264, Fax: 216-368-5334, E-mail: linda.rinella@case.edu.
Website: http://anthropology.case.edu/

The Catholic University of America, School of Arts and Sciences, Department of Anthropology, Washington, DC 20064. Offers MA. *Program availability:* Part-time. *Faculty:* 2 full-time (1 woman), 3 part-time/adjunct (1 woman). *Students:* 1 applicant. In 2017, 1 master's awarded. *Degree requirements:* For master's, one foreign language, comprehensive exam, thesis or alternative. *Entrance requirements:* For master's, GRE General Test, statement of purpose, official copies of academic transcripts, three letters of recommendation. Additional exam requirements/recommendations for international students: Required—TOEFL (minimum score 550 paper-based; 80 iBT). *Application deadline:* For fall admission, 2/1 priority date for domestic students, 7/1 for international students; for spring admission, 11/15 priority date for domestic students, 11/1 for international students. Applications are processed on a rolling basis. Application fee: $55. Electronic applications accepted. *Expenses:* Contact institution. *Financial support:* Fellowships, research assistantships, teaching assistantships, Federal Work-Study, scholarships/grants, tuition waivers (full and partial), and unspecified assistantships available. Financial award application deadline: 2/1; financial award applicants required to submit FAFSA. *Faculty research:* Medical anthropology, Latin American studies, ancient states and empires; political anthropology, cultural heritage studies, Middle East studies, Andean archaeology. *Unit head:* Dr. Anita Cook, Chair, 202-319-5080, Fax: 202-319-4782, E-mail: cook@cua.edu. *Application contact:* Dr. Steven Brown, Director of Graduate Admissions, 202-319-5057, Fax: 202-319-6533, E-mail: cua-admissions@cua.edu.
Website: http://anthropology.cua.edu/

Central European University, Department of Sociology and Social Anthropology, Budapest, Hungary. Offers MA, PhD. *Faculty:* 9 full-time (3 women), 4 part-time/adjunct (2 women). *Students:* 65 full-time (37 women). Average age 29. 288 applicants, 19% accepted, 33 enrolled. In 2017, 30 master's, 6 doctorates awarded. *Degree requirements:* For master's, one foreign language, thesis; for doctorate, one foreign language, comprehensive exam, thesis/dissertation. *Entrance requirements:* For master's and doctorate, interview. Additional exam requirements/recommendations for international students: Required—TOEFL (minimum score 570 paper-based); Recommended—IELTS (minimum score 6.5). *Application deadline:* For fall admission, 2/4 for domestic and international students. Application fee: $30. Electronic applications accepted. *Expenses: Tuition:* Full-time 12,000 euros. *Required fees:* 230 euros. One-time fee: 30 euros full-time. Tuition and fees vary according to course level, course load, degree level and program. *Financial support:* Fellowships, career-related internships or fieldwork, scholarships/grants, health care benefits, and tuition waivers (full and partial) available. *Faculty research:* Migration studies, post colonialism, studies of globalization, political and economic sociology, urban studies and sociologies of culture. *Unit head:* Dr. Dorit Geva, Head of Department, 36 1 327-3000 Ext. 2131, E-mail: sociology@ceu.edu. *Application contact:* Zsuzsanna Jaszberenyi, Admissions Officer, 361-324-3009, Fax: 367-327-3211, E-mail: admissions@ceu.edu.
Website: http://sociology.ceu.edu/

Central Washington University, School of Graduate Studies and Research, College of the Sciences, Program in Cultural and Environmental Resource Management, Ellensburg, WA 98926. Offers anthropology (MS); geography (MS). *Entrance requirements:* For master's, GRE, minimum GPA of 3.0. Additional exam requirements/recommendations for international students: Required—TOEFL (minimum score 550 paper-based; 79 iBT). *Application deadline:* For fall admission, 2/1 priority date for domestic students; for spring admission, 1/1 for domestic students. Applications are processed on a rolling basis. Application fee: $50. Electronic applications accepted. *Financial support:* Application deadline: 3/1; applicants required to submit FAFSA. *Unit head:* Dr. Karl Lillquist, Co-Director, 509-963-1188, Fax: 509-963-3224, E-mail: lillquis@cwu.edu. *Application contact:* Justine Eason, Admissions Program Coordinator, 509-963-3103, Fax: 509-963-1799, E-mail: masters@cwu.edu.

Clemson University, Graduate School, College of Behavioral, Social and Health Sciences, Department of Sociology, Anthropology and Criminal Justice, Clemson, SC 29634. Offers applied sociology (MS). *Program availability:* Part-time. *Faculty:* 17 full-time (12 women). *Students:* 14 full-time (8 women), 2 part-time (both women); includes 2 minority (both Black or African American, non-Hispanic/Latino), 6 international. Average age 28. 13 applicants, 77% accepted, 5 enrolled. In 2017, 8 master's awarded. *Degree requirements:* For master's, thesis optional. *Entrance requirements:* For master's, GRE General Test, unofficial transcripts, letters of recommendation. Additional exam requirements/recommendations for international students: Required—TOEFL (minimum score 80 iBT), IELTS (minimum score 6.5), PTE (minimum score 54). *Application deadline:* For fall admission, 2/1 priority date for domestic and international students. Applications are processed on a rolling basis. Application fee: $80 ($90 for international students). Electronic applications accepted. *Expenses:* $5,174 per semester full-time resident, $9,714 per semester full-time non-resident, $511 per credit hour part-time resident, $1,017 per credit hour part-time non-resident, $741 per credit hour online; other fees may apply per session. *Financial support:* In 2017–18, 5 students received support, including 5 teaching assistantships with partial tuition reimbursements available (averaging $11,000 per year); career-related internships or fieldwork also available. Financial award application deadline: 2/1. *Faculty research:* Environmental issues; social inequalities; health and medical development; sociology of food, nutrition, and food security. *Total annual research expenditures:* $36,371. *Unit head:* Dr. Catherine Weisensee, Interim Department Chair, 864-656-3238, E-mail: kweisen@clemson.edu. *Application contact:* Dr. William Haller, Graduate Program Coordinator, 864-656-3814, E-mail: whaller@clemson.edu.
Website: http://www.clemson.edu/cbshs/departments/sociology/

The College of William and Mary, Faculty of Arts and Sciences, Department of Anthropology, Williamsburg, VA 23187-8795. Offers MA, PhD. *Faculty:* 15 full-time (8 women). *Students:* 21 full-time (14 women), 1 part-time (0 women); includes 2 minority (1 Black or African American, non-Hispanic/Latino; 1 Hispanic/Latino), 3 international. Average age 30. 39 applicants, 23% accepted, 5 enrolled. In 2017, 5 master's, 5 doctorates awarded. Terminal master's awarded for partial completion of doctoral program. *Degree requirements:* For master's, thesis, fieldwork; for doctorate, one foreign language, comprehensive exam, thesis/dissertation, fieldwork. *Entrance requirements:* For master's and doctorate, GRE, course work in anthropology or history.

Additional exam requirements/recommendations for international students: Required—TOEFL. *Application deadline:* For fall admission, 1/15 for domestic and international students. Application fee: $50. Electronic applications accepted. *Financial support:* In 2017–18, 15 students received support. Fellowships, career-related internships or fieldwork, institutionally sponsored loans, scholarships/grants, and unspecified assistantships available. Financial award application deadline: 1/15; financial award applicants required to submit FAFSA. *Faculty research:* Historical archaeology, comparative colonialism, biocultural anthropology, African diaspora, historical archaeology of native America. *Total annual research expenditures:* $877,506. *Unit head:* Dr. Martin Gallivan, Chair, 757-221-3622, Fax: 757-221-1209, E-mail: mdgall@wm.edu. *Application contact:* Dr. Neil L. Norman, Director of Graduate Studies, 757-221-1960, Fax: 757-221-1066, E-mail: nlnorman@wm.edu.
Website: http://www.wm.edu/anthropology/

Colorado State University, College of Liberal Arts, Department of Anthropology and Geography, Fort Collins, CO 80523-1787. Offers anthropology (MA, PhD). *Program availability:* Part-time. *Faculty:* 10 full-time (4 women), 1 part-time/adjunct (0 women). *Students:* 18 full-time (13 women), 18 part-time (10 women); includes 2 minority (1 Asian, non-Hispanic/Latino; 1 Hispanic/Latino), 3 international. Average age 29. 27 applicants, 37% accepted, 5 enrolled. In 2017, 9 master's awarded. *Degree requirements:* For master's, thesis (for some programs); for doctorate, thesis/dissertation. *Entrance requirements:* For master's, GRE General Test, minimum GPA of 3.0, BA/BS, transcripts, statement of purpose, writing sample, 3 letters of recommendation; for doctorate, GRE General Test, master's degree in anthropology or geography, transcripts, statement of purpose, writing sample, 3 letters of recommendation. Additional exam requirements/recommendations for international students: Required—TOEFL (minimum score 550 paper-based; 80 iBT). *Application deadline:* For fall admission, 2/1 for domestic and international students. Application fee: $60 ($70 for international students). Electronic applications accepted. *Expenses:* Tuition, state resident: full-time $9917. Tuition, nonresident: full-time $24,312. *Required fees:* $2284. Tuition and fees vary according to course load and program. *Financial support:* In 2017–18, 15 teaching assistantships with full and partial tuition reimbursements (averaging $14,256 per year) were awarded; scholarships/grants and unspecified assistantships also available. *Faculty research:* Past and present human environments; how economic life, moral frameworks, and social identities intersect; international development processes in Vietnam and the Philippines; the relationship between expansive states and the societies conquered by them; human adaptation to disease and nutrition. *Total annual research expenditures:* $265,566. *Unit head:* Dr. Michelle M. Glantz, Professor and Chair, 970-491-4635, Fax: 970-491-7597, E-mail: mica.glantz@colostate.edu. *Application contact:* Dr. Mary Van Buren, Graduate Program Coordinator, 970-491-3781, Fax: 970-491-7597, E-mail: mary.vanburen@colostate.edu.
Website: http://anthropology.colostate.edu/

Columbia University, Graduate School of Arts and Sciences, New York, NY 10027. Offers African-American studies (MA); American studies (MA); anthropology (MA, PhD); art history and archaeology (MA, PhD); astronomy (PhD); biological sciences (PhD); biotechnology (MA); chemical physics (PhD); chemistry (PhD); classical studies (MA, PhD); classics (MA, PhD); climate and society (MA); conservation biology (MA); earth and environmental sciences (PhD); East Asia: regional studies (MA); East Asian languages and cultures (MA, PhD); ecology, evolution and environmental biology (MA), including conservation biology; ecology, evolution, and environmental biology (PhD), including ecology and evolutionary biology, evolutionary primatology; economics (MA, PhD); English and comparative literature (MA, PhD); French and Romance philology (MA, PhD); Germanic languages (MA, PhD); global French studies (MA); global thought (MA); Hispanic cultural studies (MA); history (PhD); history and literature (MA); human rights studies (MA); Islamic studies (MA); Italian (MA, PhD); Japanese pedagogy (MA); Jewish studies (MA); Latin America and the Caribbean: regional studies (MA); Latin American and Iberian cultures (PhD); mathematics (MA, PhD), including finance (MA); medieval and Renaissance studies (MA); Middle Eastern, South Asian, and African studies (MA, PhD); modern art: critical and curatorial studies (MA); modern European studies (MA); museum anthropology (MA); music (DMA, PhD); oral history (MA); philosophical foundations of physics (MA); philosophy (MA, PhD); physics (PhD); political science (MA, PhD); psychology (PhD); quantitative methods in the social sciences (MA); religion (MA, PhD); Russia, Eurasia and East Europe: regional studies (MA); Russian translation (MA); Slavic cultures (MA); Slavic languages (MA, PhD); sociology (MA, PhD); South Asian studies (MA); statistics (MA, PhD); theatre (PhD). Dual-degree programs require admission to both Graduate School of Arts and Sciences and another Columbia school. *Program availability:* Part-time. Terminal master's awarded for partial completion of doctoral program. *Degree requirements:* For master's, variable foreign language requirement, comprehensive exam (for some programs), thesis (for some programs); for doctorate, variable foreign language requirement, comprehensive exam (for some programs), thesis/dissertation. *Entrance requirements:* For master's and doctorate, GRE General Test, GRE Subject Test (for some programs). Additional exam requirements/recommendations for international students: Required—TOEFL, IELTS. Electronic applications accepted. *Expenses: Tuition:* Full-time $44,864; part-time $1704 per credit. *Required fees:* $2370 per semester. One-time fee: $105.

Concordia University, School of Graduate Studies, Faculty of Arts and Science, Department of Sociology and Anthropology, Montréal, QC H3G 1M8, Canada. Offers social and cultural analysis (PhD); social and cultural anthropology (MA); sociology (MA). *Degree requirements:* For master's, comprehensive exam or thesis. *Entrance requirements:* For master's, honors degree in sociology or equivalent. *Faculty research:* Community and ethnic relations, popular culture, regional development in Canada, industrial and social movements, social problems and policies.

Cornell University, Graduate School, Graduate Fields of Arts and Sciences, Field of Anthropology, Ithaca, NY 14853. Offers archaeological anthropology (PhD); biological anthropology (PhD); sociocultural anthropology (PhD). *Degree requirements:* For doctorate, one foreign language, comprehensive exam, thesis/dissertation, teaching experience. *Entrance requirements:* For doctorate, GRE General Test, 3 letters of recommendation, sample of written work. Additional exam requirements/recommendations for international students: Required—TOEFL (minimum score 550 paper-based; 77 iBT). Electronic applications accepted. *Faculty research:* Culture, engaged anthropology, political economy, area studies: Asia, Americas, Europe; interdisciplinary and ethnic studies: Asian-American studies.

Creighton University, Graduate School, College of Arts and Sciences, Program in Medical Anthropology, Omaha, NE 68178-0001. Offers MA. *Program availability:* Part-time, online only, blended/hybrid learning. *Faculty:* 13 full-time (8 women). *Students:* 3 full-time (all women), 13 part-time (9 women); includes 1 minority (Asian, non-Hispanic/Latino). Average age 34. In 2017, 7 master's awarded. *Degree requirements:* For master's, thesis optional. *Entrance requirements:* For master's, three recommendations; resume; statement of purpose; writing sample. Additional exam requirements/recommendations for international students: Required—TOEFL (minimum score 90 iBT). *Application deadline:* For summer admission, 1/15 for domestic and international students. Applications are processed on a rolling basis. Application fee: $50. Electronic applications accepted. Part-time tuition and fees vary according to course load, degree

level, campus/location and program. *Financial support:* Teaching assistantships and scholarships/grants available. Financial award application deadline: 3/15; financial award applicants required to submit FAFSA. *Unit head:* Dr. Alex Roedlach, Program Director, 402-280-2567, E-mail: alexanderroedlach@creighton.edu. *Application contact:* Lindsay Johnson, Director of Graduate and Adult Recruitment, 402-280-2703, Fax: 402-280-2423, E-mail: gradschool@creighton.edu.

Dalhousie University, Faculty of Arts and Social Science, Department of Sociology and Social Anthropology, Halifax, NS B3H 4R2, Canada. Offers social anthropology (MA, PhD); sociology (MA, PhD). *Entrance requirements:* Additional exam requirements/recommendations for international students: Required—TOEFL, IELTS, CANTEST, CAEL, or Michigan English Language Assessment Battery. Electronic applications accepted. *Faculty research:* Social inequality and social injustice; work, industry, and development (regional and international perspectives); health and illness.

East Carolina University, Graduate School, Thomas Harriot College of Arts and Sciences, Department of Anthropology, Greenville, NC 27858-4353. Offers MA. *Program availability:* Part-time. *Students:* 18 full-time (12 women), 5 part-time (all women); includes 3 minority (1 Black or African American, non-Hispanic/Latino; 2 Hispanic/Latino). Average age 27. 38 applicants, 50% accepted, 8 enrolled. In 2017, 9 master's awarded. *Degree requirements:* For master's, one foreign language, comprehensive exam, thesis or alternative. *Entrance requirements:* For master's, GRE General Test, minimum GPA of 3.0. Additional exam requirements/recommendations for international students: Recommended—TOEFL (minimum score 78 iBT), IELTS (minimum score 6.5). *Application deadline:* For fall admission, 3/1 priority date for domestic and international students. Applications are processed on a rolling basis. Application fee: $75. Electronic applications accepted. *Expenses:* Tuition, state resident: full-time $4749; part-time $297 per credit hour. Tuition, nonresident: full-time $17,898; part-time $1119 per credit hour. *Required fees:* $2691; $224 per credit hour. Part-time tuition and fees vary according to course load and program. *Financial support:* Research assistantships with partial tuition reimbursements available. Financial award application deadline: 3/1. *Faculty research:* Historic archaeology and bioarchaeology; human osteology, primatology, and forensic anthropology; applied anthropology, medical anthropology, and anthropology of religion. *Unit head:* Dr. Randolph Daniel, Jr., Interim Chair, 252-328-9455, E-mail: danieli@ecu.edu. *Application contact:* Dean of Graduate School, 252-328-6012, E-mail: gradschool@ecu.edu.
Website: http://www.ecu.edu/cs-cas/anth/

Eastern New Mexico University, Graduate School, College of Liberal Arts and Sciences, Department of Anthropology and Applied Archaeology, Portales, NM 88130. Offers anthropology (MA). *Program availability:* Part-time. *Degree requirements:* For master's, variable foreign language requirement, comprehensive exam, thesis. *Entrance requirements:* For master's, minimum GPA of 3.0, letters of recommendation, curriculum vitae, writing sample. Additional exam requirements/recommendations for international students: Required—TOEFL (minimum score 550 paper-based; 79 iBT), IELTS (minimum score 6). *Application deadline:* For fall admission, 7/20 priority date for domestic students, 6/20 priority date for international students; for spring admission, 12/15 priority date for domestic students, 11/15 priority date for international students. Applications are processed on a rolling basis. Application fee: $10. Electronic applications accepted. *Financial support:* Applicants required to submit FAFSA. *Faculty research:* Paleobotany, remote sensing, conservation archaeology, obsidian hydration. *Unit head:* Dr. Kathy Roler Durand, Graduate Coordinator, 575-562-2206, E-mail: kathy.durand@enmu.edu. *Application contact:* Barbara Senn, Anthropology Department Secretary, 575-562-2206, Fax: 575-562-2555, E-mail: barbara.senn@enmu.edu.
Website: http://liberal-arts.enmu.edu/anthro/graduate.shtml

Edinboro University of Pennsylvania, Department of History, Politics, Languages and Cultures, Edinboro, PA 16444. Offers social sciences (MA), including anthropology, history. *Program availability:* Part-time, evening/weekend. *Degree requirements:* For master's, thesis or alternative, competency exam. *Entrance requirements:* For master's, GRE or MAT, minimum QPA of 2.5. Electronic applications accepted.

Emory University, Laney Graduate School, Department of Anthropology, Atlanta, GA 30322-1100. Offers PhD. *Degree requirements:* For doctorate, thesis/dissertation, qualifying exams. *Entrance requirements:* For doctorate, GRE General Test. Additional exam requirements/recommendations for international students: Required—TOEFL. Electronic applications accepted. *Faculty research:* Primate behavioral ecology, comparative human biology, human growth and development, medical anthropology, globalization, gender and sexuality.

Florida Atlantic University, Dorothy F. Schmidt College of Arts and Letters, Department of Anthropology, Boca Raton, FL 33431-0991. Offers MA, MAT. *Program availability:* Part-time. *Faculty:* 7 full-time (4 women), 1 (woman) part-time/adjunct. *Students:* 26 full-time (16 women), 14 part-time (8 women); includes 12 minority (1 Black or African American, non-Hispanic/Latino; 1 Asian, non-Hispanic/Latino; 7 Hispanic/Latino; 3 Two or more races, non-Hispanic/Latino). Average age 29. 11 applicants, 73% accepted, 8 enrolled. In 2017, 8 master's awarded. *Degree requirements:* For master's, one foreign language, thesis. *Entrance requirements:* For master's, GRE General Test, minimum GPA of 3.0. Additional exam requirements/recommendations for international students: Required—TOEFL (minimum score 500 paper-based; 61 iBT), IELTS (minimum score 6). *Application deadline:* For fall admission, 7/1 priority date for domestic students, 2/15 for international students; for spring admission, 11/1 for domestic students, 7/15 for international students. Applications are processed on a rolling basis. Application fee: $30. Electronic applications accepted. *Expenses:* Tuition, state resident: full-time $7400; part-time $369.82 per credit. Tuition, nonresident: full-time $20,496; part-time $1042.81 per credit. *Financial support:* Fellowships, research assistantships with tuition reimbursements, teaching assistantships with tuition reimbursements, Federal Work-Study, and unspecified assistantships available. *Faculty research:* Archaeological, ethnological, ethnographical, osteological, paleoanthropological, and zoo-archaeological research. *Unit head:* Dr. Michael S. Harris, Chairman, 561-297-3233, Fax: 561-297-0084, E-mail: mharris@fau.edu.
Website: http://www.fau.edu/anthro/

George Mason University, College of Humanities and Social Sciences, Department of Sociology and Anthropology, Fairfax, VA 22030. Offers anthropology (MA); sociology (MA, PhD). *Faculty:* 24 full-time (13 women), 4 part-time/adjunct (2 women). *Students:* 35 full-time (27 women), 55 part-time (38 women); includes 21 minority (6 Black or African American, non-Hispanic/Latino; 1 American Indian or Alaska Native, non-Hispanic/Latino; 5 Asian, non-Hispanic/Latino; 7 Hispanic/Latino; 2 Two or more races, non-Hispanic/Latino), 6 international. Average age 32. 76 applicants, 68% accepted, 19 enrolled. In 2017, 19 master's, 7 doctorates awarded. *Degree requirements:* For master's, thesis; for doctorate, comprehensive exam, thesis/dissertation. *Entrance requirements:* For master's, official transcript; expanded goals statement; 3 letters of recommendation; writing sample; resume; 3 credits in undergraduate sociology theory, statistics and research methods (for sociology); 3 credits of sociocultural anthropology (for anthropology); for doctorate, GRE General Test, expanded goals statement; 3 letters of recommendation; writing sample; official transcript. Additional exam requirements/recommendations for international students: Required—TOEFL (minimum score 575 paper-based; 88 iBT), IELTS (minimum score 6.5), PTE (minimum score 59). *Application deadline:* For fall admission, 2/15 for domestic and international students; for

spring admission, 11/1 for domestic and international students. Application fee: $75 ($80 for international students). Electronic applications accepted. *Expenses:* Tuition, state resident: full-time $11,228; part-time $459.50 per credit. Tuition, nonresident: full-time $30,932; part-time $1280.50 per credit. *Required fees:* $3252; $135.50 per credit. Part-time tuition and fees vary according to course load and program. *Financial support:* In 2017–18, 24 students received support, including 6 fellowships (averaging $7,483 per year), 10 research assistantships with tuition reimbursements available (averaging $20,262 per year), 10 teaching assistantships with tuition reimbursements available (averaging $10,215 per year); career-related internships or fieldwork, Federal Work-Study, scholarships/grants, unspecified assistantships, and health care benefits (for full-time research or teaching assistantship recipients) also available. Support available to part-time students. Financial award application deadline: 3/1; financial award applicants required to submit FAFSA. *Faculty research:* Africa, American teenagers, black entrepreneurs, human rights, gambling. *Total annual research expenditures:* $80,740. *Unit head:* Amy Best, Department Chair, 703-993-1426, Fax: 703-993-1446, E-mail: abest@gmu.edu. *Application contact:* Nancy Hanrahan, Graduate Director, 703-993-1433, Fax: 703-993-1446, E-mail: nhanraha@gmu.edu.
Website: http://soan.gmu.edu

The George Washington University, Columbian College of Arts and Sciences, Department of Anthropology, Washington, DC 20052. Offers anthropology (MA, PhD); international development (MA); medical anthropology (MA); museum training (MA). *Program availability:* Part-time, evening/weekend. *Faculty:* 3 full-time (2 women), 18 part-time/adjunct (7 women). *Students:* 32 full-time (20 women), 16 part-time (13 women); includes 13 minority (1 Black or African American, non-Hispanic/Latino; 3 Asian, non-Hispanic/Latino; 5 Hispanic/Latino; 4 Two or more races, non-Hispanic/Latino), 9 international. Average age 28. 85 applicants, 42% accepted, 18 enrolled. In 2017, 14 master's awarded. *Degree requirements:* For master's, one foreign language, comprehensive exam, thesis or alternative. *Entrance requirements:* For master's, GRE General Test, minimum GPA of 3.0. Additional exam requirements/recommendations for international students: Required—TOEFL (minimum score 550 paper-based; 80 iBT). *Application deadline:* For fall admission, 1/15 priority date for international students; for spring admission, 9/15 priority date for domestic students, 9/1 priority date for international students. Applications are processed on a rolling basis. Application fee: $75. Electronic applications accepted. *Expenses: Tuition:* Full-time $28,800; part-time $1655 per credit hour. *Required fees:* $45; $2.75 per credit hour. *Financial support:* In 2017–18, 8 students received support. Fellowships, teaching assistantships, career-related internships or fieldwork, and Federal Work-Study available. Financial award application deadline: 1/15. *Unit head:* Richard Grinker, Chair, 202-994-6984, E-mail: rgrink@email.gwu.edu. *Application contact:* Information Contact, 202-994-6075, E-mail: anth@gwu.edu.
Website: http://anthropology.columbian.gwu.edu/

Georgia State University, College of Arts and Sciences, Department of Anthropology, Atlanta, GA 30302. Offers MA. *Program availability:* Part-time. *Faculty:* 10 full-time (7 women). *Students:* 29 full-time (26 women), 8 part-time (6 women); includes 9 minority (2 Black or African American, non-Hispanic/Latino; 2 Asian, non-Hispanic/Latino; 5 Hispanic/Latino), 6 international. Average age 29. 27 applicants, 85% accepted, 18 enrolled. In 2017, 22 master's awarded. *Degree requirements:* For master's, one foreign language, comprehensive exam, 33 to 36 credit hours, thesis/practicum defense. *Entrance requirements:* For master's, GRE, statement of purpose, writing sample, official transcripts, two letters of recommendation, curriculum vitae. Additional exam requirements/recommendations for international students: Required—TOEFL (minimum score 550 paper-based; 80 iBT), IELTS (minimum score 6.5). *Application deadline:* For fall admission, 3/15 for domestic and international students; for spring admission, 10/15 for domestic and international students. Applications are processed on a rolling basis. Application fee: $50. Electronic applications accepted. *Expenses:* Tuition, state resident: full-time $7020. Tuition, nonresident: full-time $22,518. *Required fees:* $2128. Tuition and fees vary according to degree level and program. *Financial support:* In 2017–18, research assistantships with full tuition reimbursements (averaging $4,000 per year) were awarded. Financial award applicants required to submit FAFSA. *Faculty research:* Archaeology, medical anthropology, linguistic anthropology, biological/physical anthropology, cultural anthropology. *Unit head:* Dr. Frank L. Williams, Chair, 404-413-5154, Fax: 404-413-5159, E-mail: frankwilliams@gsu.edu. *Application contact:* Dr. Emanuela Guano, Director of Graduate Studies, 404-413-5152, Fax: 404-413-5159, E-mail: eguano@gsu.edu.
Website: http://www.cas.gsu.edu/anthropology/

The Graduate Center, City University of New York, Graduate Studies, Program in Anthropology, New York, NY 10016-4039. Offers anthropological linguistics (PhD); archaeology (PhD); cultural anthropology (PhD); physical anthropology (PhD). *Faculty:* 39 full-time (14 women). *Students:* 166 full-time (103 women), 2 part-time (both women); includes 34 minority (5 Black or African American, non-Hispanic/Latino; 5 Asian, non-Hispanic/Latino; 21 Hispanic/Latino; 3 Two or more races, non-Hispanic/Latino), 39 international. Average age 33. 145 applicants, 14% accepted, 19 enrolled. In 2017, 14 doctorates awarded. *Degree requirements:* For doctorate, one foreign language, thesis/dissertation. *Entrance requirements:* For doctorate, GRE General Test. Additional exam requirements/recommendations for international students: Required—TOEFL. *Application deadline:* For fall admission, 1/8 priority date for domestic students. Application fee: $125. Electronic applications accepted. *Financial support:* In 2017–18, 111 students received support, including 88 fellowships, 16 research assistantships, 10 teaching assistantships; career-related internships or fieldwork, Federal Work-Study, institutionally sponsored loans, and tuition waivers (full and partial) also available. Financial award application deadline: 2/1; financial award applicants required to submit FAFSA. *Unit head:* Prof. Jeff Maskovsky, Acting Executive Officer, 212-817-8006, Fax: 212-817-1501, E-mail: jmaskovsky@gc.cuny.edu. *Application contact:* Information Contact, 212-817-8005, Fax: 212-817-1501, E-mail: anthro@gc.cuny.edu.

Harvard University, Graduate School of Arts and Sciences, Committee on Middle Eastern Studies, Cambridge, MA 02138. Offers anthropology and Middle Eastern studies (PhD); economics and Middle Eastern studies (PhD); fine arts and Middle Eastern studies (PhD); history and Middle Eastern studies (PhD); regional studies–Middle East (AM). Terminal master's awarded for partial completion of doctoral program. *Degree requirements:* For master's, one foreign language; for doctorate, 2 foreign languages, thesis/dissertation. *Entrance requirements:* For master's, GRE General Test; for doctorate, GRE General Test, 1 year of course work in Middle Eastern regional studies, proficiency in a related language. Additional exam requirements/recommendations for international students: Required—TOEFL.

Harvard University, Graduate School of Arts and Sciences, Department of Anthropology, Cambridge, MA 02138. Offers archaeology (PhD); biological anthropology (PhD); legal anthropology (AM); medical anthropology (AM); social anthropology (AM, PhD); social change and development (AM). Terminal master's awarded for partial completion of doctoral program. *Degree requirements:* For master's, 2 foreign languages, thesis (for some programs); for doctorate, 2 foreign languages, thesis/dissertation, laboratory and/or fieldwork; general, qualifying, or special exams. *Entrance requirements:* For master's and doctorate, GRE General Test. Additional exam requirements/recommendations for international students: Required—TOEFL.

Anthropology

Humboldt State University, Academic Programs, College of Arts, Humanities, and Social Sciences, Department of Anthropology, Arcata, CA 95521-8299. Offers applied anthropology (MA). *Program availability:* Part-time, online learning. *Degree requirements:* For master's, comprehensive exam, thesis, 180 hours of field placement/ internship. *Entrance requirements:* For master's, three letters of recommendation. Electronic applications accepted.

Hunter College of the City University of New York, Graduate School, School of Arts and Sciences, Department of Anthropology, New York, NY 10065-5085. Offers MA. *Program availability:* Part-time, evening/weekend. *Degree requirements:* For master's, comprehensive exam, thesis, language or statistics exam. *Entrance requirements:* For master's, GRE General Test, minimum 9 credits of course work in anthropology or a related field. Additional exam requirements/recommendations for international students: Required—TOEFL. *Faculty research:* Primatology, human ecology, archeology, political anthropology, primate and human evolution.

Idaho State University, Office of Graduate Studies, College of Arts and Letters, Department of Anthropology, Pocatello, ID 83209-8005. Offers MA, MS. *Program availability:* Part-time. *Degree requirements:* For master's, one foreign language, comprehensive exam, thesis, 4 semesters foreign language, oral defense. *Entrance requirements:* For master's, GRE General Test, GMAT or MAT, minimum GPA of 3.0 in all upper-division classes, 3 letters of recommendation. Additional exam requirements/ recommendations for international students: Required—TOEFL (minimum score 550 paper-based; 80 iBT). Electronic applications accepted. *Faculty research:* Native American studies: health care, language/ethnopoetics, prehistory, art, resource environmental management.

Indiana University Bloomington, University Graduate School, College of Arts and Sciences, Department of Anthropology, Bloomington, IN 47405. Offers anthropology (MA, PhD), including archaeology (PhD), bioanthropology (PhD), linguistic anthropology (PhD), social-cultural anthropology (PhD). *Degree requirements:* For master's, comprehensive exam (for some programs), thesis or alternative; for doctorate, 2 foreign languages, comprehensive exam, thesis/dissertation. *Entrance requirements:* For master's and doctorate, GRE General Test, minimum GPA of 3.0. Additional exam requirements/recommendations for international students: Required—TOEFL (minimum score 550 paper-based, 79 iBT) or IELTS. Electronic applications accepted. *Expenses:* Contact institution. *Faculty research:* Archaeology in social context; bioanthropology; anthropology of food and ecology; gender studies; communication, media and performance.

Iowa State University of Science and Technology, Department of Anthropology, Ames, IA 50011. Offers MA. *Degree requirements:* For master's, thesis. *Entrance requirements:* For master's, GRE General Test. Additional exam requirements/ recommendations for international students: Required—TOEFL (minimum score 550 paper-based; 79 iBT), IELTS (minimum score 6.5). Electronic applications accepted.

Johns Hopkins University, Zanvyl Krieger School of Arts and Sciences, Department of Anthropology, Baltimore, MD 21218. Offers PhD. *Degree requirements:* For doctorate, one foreign language, thesis/dissertation. *Entrance requirements:* For doctorate, GRE General Test. Additional exam requirements/recommendations for international students: Required—TOEFL, IELTS. Electronic applications accepted. *Faculty research:* Social and cultural anthropology of complex societies, gender politics, economic anthropology, religion.

Kent State University, College of Arts and Sciences, Department of Anthropology, Kent, OH 44242-0001. Offers MA. *Program availability:* Part-time. *Faculty:* 8 full-time (2 women), 1 (woman) part-time/adjunct. *Students:* 11 full-time (8 women), 9 part-time (5 women); includes 3 minority (1 Asian, non-Hispanic/Latino; 2 Two or more races, non-Hispanic/Latino). Average age 29. 12 applicants, 58% accepted, 6 enrolled. In 2017, 4 master's awarded. *Degree requirements:* For master's, thesis. *Entrance requirements:* For master's, GRE, statement of goals, three letters of recommendation, official transcript. Additional exam requirements/recommendations for international students: Required—TOEFL (minimum score 525 paper-based, 71 iBT), Michigan English Language Assessment Battery (minimum score 74), IELTS (minimum score 6.0) or PTE (minimum score 50). *Application deadline:* For fall admission, 2/1 for domestic and international students. Applications are processed on a rolling basis. Application fee: $45 ($70 for international students). Electronic applications accepted. *Expenses:* Tuition, state resident: full-time $11,310; part-time $515 per credit hour. Tuition, nonresident: full-time $20,396; part-time $928 per credit hour. *International tuition:* $18,544 full-time. *Financial support:* Research assistantships with full tuition reimbursements, teaching assistantships with full tuition reimbursements, career-related internships or fieldwork, Federal Work-Study, scholarships/grants, and unspecified assistantships available. Financial award application deadline: 2/1; financial award applicants required to submit FAFSA. *Unit head:* Dr. Mary Ann Raghanti, Chairperson, 330-672-9354, E-mail: mraghant@kent.edu. *Application contact:* Dr. Richard S. Meindl, Professor, 330-672-7998, E-mail: rmeindl@kent.edu.
Website: https://www.kent.edu/anthropology

Louisiana State University and Agricultural & Mechanical College, Graduate School, College of Humanities and Social Sciences, Department of Geography and Anthropology, Baton Rouge, LA 70803. Offers geography (MA, MS); geography and anthropology (PhD). *Faculty:* 27 full-time (13 women). *Students:* 59 full-time (36 women), 23 part-time (11 women); includes 14 minority (3 Black or African American, non-Hispanic/Latino; 1 American Indian or Alaska Native, non-Hispanic/Latino; 1 Asian, non-Hispanic/Latino; 8 Hispanic/Latino; 1 Two or more races, non-Hispanic/Latino), 22 international. Average age 30. 64 applicants, 55% accepted, 16 enrolled. In 2017, 16 master's, 6 doctorates awarded. *Financial support:* In 2017–18, 3 fellowships (averaging $22,799 per year), 26 research assistantships (averaging $19,473 per year), 28 teaching assistantships (averaging $17,412 per year) were awarded. *Total annual research expenditures:* $925,707.

McGill University, Faculty of Graduate and Postdoctoral Studies, Faculty of Arts, Department of Anthropology, Montréal, QC H3A 2T5, Canada. Offers anthropology (MA, PhD); medical anthropology (MA).

McGill University, Faculty of Graduate and Postdoctoral Studies, Faculty of Medicine, Department of Social Studies in Medicine, Montréal, QC H3A 2T5, Canada. Offers medical anthropology (MA, PhD); medical history (MA, PhD); medical sociology (MA, PhD).

McMaster University, School of Graduate Studies, Faculty of Social Sciences, Department of Anthropology, Hamilton, ON L8S 4M2, Canada. Offers MA, PhD. *Program availability:* Part-time. *Degree requirements:* For master's, thesis or alternative; for doctorate, one foreign language, comprehensive exam, thesis/dissertation, fieldwork. *Entrance requirements:* Additional exam requirements/recommendations for international students: Required—TOEFL (minimum score 580 paper-based). *Faculty research:* Medical anthropology, contemporary ethnography in an interdisciplinary perspective, archaeological and social theory, linguistics, folklore.

Memorial University of Newfoundland, School of Graduate Studies, Department of Anthropology, St. John's, NL A1C 5S7, Canada. Offers archaeology and physical anthropology (MA, PhD); social and cultural anthropology (MA, PhD). *Program availability:* Part-time. *Degree requirements:* For master's, comprehensive exam (for some programs), thesis (for some programs); for doctorate, comprehensive exam, thesis/dissertation, oral defense of thesis. *Entrance requirements:* For master's, 2nd class degree in related field. Electronic applications accepted. *Faculty research:* Early European settlements, ethnoarchaeology, economic/political anthropology, land claims and aboriginal rights, marine anthropology.

Mercyhurst University, Graduate Studies, Program in Anthropology, Erie, PA 16546. Offers archaeology and geological archaeology (MS); forensic and biological anthropology (MS). *Entrance requirements:* For master's, GRE or MAT, undergraduate degree in related field, interview, resume, essay, three professional references, transcripts. Additional exam requirements/recommendations for international students: Required—TOEFL.

Michigan State University, The Graduate School, College of Social Science, Department of Anthropology, East Lansing, MI 48824. Offers anthropology (MA, PhD); professional applications in anthropology (MA). Terminal master's awarded for partial completion of doctoral program. *Degree requirements:* For master's, comprehensive exam (for some programs); for doctorate, annual evaluation. *Entrance requirements:* Additional exam requirements/recommendations for international students: Required—TOEFL. Electronic applications accepted.

Minnesota State University Mankato, College of Graduate Studies and Research, College of Social and Behavioral Sciences, Department of Anthropology, Mankato, MN 56001. Offers applied anthropology (MS). *Program availability:* Part-time. *Degree requirements:* For master's, comprehensive exam, thesis. *Entrance requirements:* For master's, GRE. Additional exam requirements/recommendations for international students: Required—TOEFL. Electronic applications accepted.

Mississippi State University, College of Arts and Sciences, Department of Anthropology and Middle Eastern Cultures, Mississippi State, MS 39762. Offers MA. *Program availability:* Part-time. *Faculty:* 8 full-time (4 women). *Students:* 21 full-time (13 women), 20 part-time (12 women); includes 4 minority (1 Black or African American, non-Hispanic/Latino; 3 Hispanic/Latino), 4 international. Average age 29. 28 applicants, 68% accepted, 10 enrolled. In 2017, 13 master's awarded. *Degree requirements:* For master's, thesis. *Entrance requirements:* For master's, GRE, minimum GPA of 3.0 on last 60 hours of undergraduate courses. Additional exam requirements/ recommendations for international students: Required—TOEFL (minimum score 477 paper-based; 53 iBT); Recommended—IELTS (minimum score 4.5). *Application deadline:* For fall admission, 7/15 priority date for domestic students, 4/15 for international students; for spring admission, 11/1 priority date for domestic students, 9/1 for international students. Applications are processed on a rolling basis. Application fee: $60 ($80 for international students). Electronic applications accepted. *Expenses:* Tuition, state resident: full-time $8318; part-time $462.12 per credit hour. Tuition, nonresident: full-time $22,358; part-time $1242.12 per credit hour. *Required fees:* $110; $12.24 per credit hour. $6.12 per semester. *Financial support:* In 2017–18, 1 research assistantship (averaging $9,000 per year), 9 teaching assistantships with partial tuition reimbursements (averaging $9,400 per year) were awarded; Federal Work-Study, institutionally sponsored loans, scholarships/grants, and unspecified assistantships also available. Financial award application deadline: 3/15; financial award applicants required to submit FAFSA. *Faculty research:* Archaeology and bioarchaeology, environmental archaeology, cultural archaeology, research projects in Southeastern archaeology and bioarcheology. *Unit head:* Dr. William Cooke, Professor and Interim Head, 662-325-2795, Fax: 662-325-8690, E-mail: whc5@msstate.edu. *Application contact:* Nathan Drake, Admissions and Enrollment Assistant, 662-325-3804, E-mail: ndrake@grad.msstate.edu.
Website: http://www.amec.msstate.edu

Monmouth University, Graduate Studies, Program in Anthropology, West Long Branch, NJ 07764-1898. Offers MA. *Program availability:* Part-time, evening/weekend. *Faculty:* 5 full-time (3 women). *Students:* 6 full-time (all women), 29 part-time (20 women); includes 5 minority (1 Black or African American, non-Hispanic/Latino; 1 Asian, non-Hispanic/Latino; 3 Hispanic/Latino). Average age 32. In 2017, 6 master's awarded. *Degree requirements:* For master's, comprehensive exam (for some programs), thesis (for some programs). *Entrance requirements:* For master's, minimum undergraduate GPA of 3.0, 500-word essay highlighting personal and/or professional goals and objectives for graduate anthropology study, two professional letters of recommendation. Additional exam requirements/recommendations for international students: Required—TOEFL (minimum score 550 paper-based; 79 iBT), IELTS (minimum score 6), Michigan English Language Assessment Battery (minimum score 77) or Certificate of Advanced English (minimum score 160). *Application deadline:* For fall admission, 7/15 for domestic students, 6/1 for international students; for spring admission, 12/1 for domestic students, 11/1 for international students; for summer admission, 5/1 for domestic students. Applications are processed on a rolling basis. Application fee: $50. Electronic applications accepted. *Expenses: Tuition:* Full-time $21,366; part-time $7122 per credit. *Required fees:* $700; $175 per term. *Financial support:* In 2017–18, 12 students received support. Institutionally sponsored loans, scholarships/grants, and unspecified assistantships available. Support available to part-time students. Financial award applicants required to submit FAFSA. *Faculty research:* Historical archeology, early America, Native Americans, historic preservation, archeology of New Jersey and Northeast. *Unit head:* Dr. Veronica Davidov, Director, 732-571-7502, E-mail: vdavidov@monmouth.edu. *Application contact:* Andrea Thompson, Graduate Admission Counselor, 732-571-3452, Fax: 732-263-5123, E-mail: gradadm@monmouth.edu.
Website: https://www.monmouth.edu/graduate/ma-anthropology/

New Mexico Highlands University, Graduate Studies, College of Arts and Sciences, Department of Social and Behavioral Sciences, Las Vegas, NM 87701. Offers psychology (MS), including clinical psychology/counseling, general psychology; public affairs (MA), including applied sociology; Southwest studies (MA), including anthropology. *Program availability:* Part-time. *Degree requirements:* For master's, comprehensive exam, thesis or alternative. *Entrance requirements:* For master's, minimum undergraduate GPA of 3.0. Additional exam requirements/recommendations for international students: Required—TOEFL (minimum score 540 paper-based). *Faculty research:* Southwest Native American resettlement development, community-level interventions, neurochemistry of personality, comparative criminal justice, social theory and activism.

New Mexico State University, College of Arts and Sciences, Department of Anthropology, Las Cruces, NM 88003. Offers anthropology (MA); cultural resource management (Graduate Certificate); museum studies (Graduate Certificate). *Program availability:* Part-time. *Faculty:* 9 full-time (5 women), 1 part-time/adjunct (0 women). *Students:* 31 full-time (22 women), 19 part-time (12 women); includes 15 minority (2 Black or African American, non-Hispanic/Latino; 2 American Indian or Alaska Native, non-Hispanic/Latino; 9 Hispanic/Latino; 2 Two or more races, non-Hispanic/Latino), 3 international. Average age 34. 28 applicants, 64% accepted, 11 enrolled. In 2017, 12 master's, 17 other advanced degrees awarded. *Degree requirements:* For master's, thesis, internship, or special research project. *Entrance requirements:* For master's, minimum undergraduate GPA of 3.0. Additional exam requirements/recommendations for international students: Required—TOEFL (minimum score 550 paper-based; 79 iBT), IELTS (minimum score 6.5). *Application deadline:* For fall admission, 2/1 priority date for

domestic and international students; for spring admission, 10/1 priority date for domestic and international students. Applications are processed on a rolling basis. Application fee: $40 ($50 for international students). Electronic applications accepted. *Expenses:* Tuition, state resident: full-time $4390. Tuition, nonresident: full-time $15,309. *Required fees:* $853. *Financial support:* In 2017–18, 31 students received support, including 3 fellowships (averaging $4,390 per year), 11 teaching assistantships (averaging $9,486 per year); career-related internships or fieldwork, Federal Work-Study, scholarships/grants, traineeships, health care benefits, and unspecified assistantships also available. Support available to part-time students. Financial award application deadline: 3/1. *Unit head:* Dr. Rani Alexander, Department Head, 575-646-5809, E-mail: raalexan@nmsu.edu. *Application contact:* Dr. Lois Stanford, Graduate Advisor, 575-646-6092, E-mail: lstanfor@nmsu.edu.
Website: http://anthropology.nmsu.edu

The New School, The New School for Social Research, Department of Anthropology, New York, NY 10003. Offers MA, PhD. *Program availability:* Part-time. *Faculty:* 7 full-time (4 women), 1 (woman) part-time/adjunct. *Students:* 51 full-time (32 women), 6 part-time (5 women); includes 8 minority (1 Black or African American, non-Hispanic/Latino; 2 Asian, non-Hispanic/Latino; 4 Hispanic/Latino; 1 Two or more races, non-Hispanic/Latino), 29 international. Average age 31. 55 applicants, 87% accepted, 12 enrolled. In 2017, 8 master's, 7 doctorates awarded. Terminal master's awarded for partial completion of doctoral program. *Degree requirements:* For master's, variable foreign language requirement, comprehensive exam; for doctorate, one foreign language, comprehensive exam, thesis/dissertation. *Entrance requirements:* For master's, GRE, letters of recommendation, writing sample, essays, transcript; for doctorate, letters of recommendation, writing sample, essays, transcript. Additional exam requirements/recommendations for international students: Required—TOEFL (minimum score 100 iBT), IELTS (minimum score 7), PTE (minimum score 68). *Application deadline:* For fall admission, 1/5 priority date for domestic and international students; for spring admission, 10/15 priority date for domestic and international students. Applications are processed on a rolling basis. Application fee: $50. Electronic applications accepted. *Expenses:* $2,180 per credit. *Financial support:* In 2017–18, 49 students received support, including 8 fellowships (averaging $34,186 per year), 6 research assistantships (averaging $15,603 per year), 12 teaching assistantships with full and partial tuition reimbursements available (averaging $6,039 per year); Federal Work-Study, scholarships/grants, and tuition waivers (full and partial) also available. Support available to part-time students. Financial award application deadline: 2/1; financial award applicants required to submit FAFSA. *Unit head:* Dr. William Milberg, Dean, The New School for Social Research, 212-229-5777, E-mail: milbergw@newschool.edu. *Application contact:* Dana Messinger, Director of Graduate Admission, 212-229-5150 Ext. 2300, E-mail: messingd@newschool.edu.
Website: https://www.newschool.edu/nssr/anthropology/

New York University, Graduate School of Arts and Science, Department of Anthropology, New York, NY 10012-1019. Offers anthropology (MA, PhD), including archaeological anthropology, linguistic anthropology, physical anthropology, socio-cultural anthropology; anthropology and French studies (PhD); MA/Advanced Certificate; PhD/Advanced Certificate. *Program availability:* Part-time. *Students:* Average age 30. 357 applicants, 6% accepted, 15 enrolled. In 2017, 14 master's, 7 doctorates awarded. *Degree requirements:* For master's, thesis; for doctorate, one foreign language, comprehensive exam, thesis/dissertation. *Entrance requirements:* For master's and doctorate, GRE General Test. Additional exam requirements/recommendations for international students: Required—TOEFL. *Application deadline:* For fall admission, 12/18 priority date for domestic students, 12/18 for international students. Application fee: $100. *Expenses:* Tuition: Full-time $41,352; part-time $19,968 per year. *Required fees:* $2496; $1628 per unit. $814 per term. Tuition and fees vary according to course load and program. *Financial support:* Fellowships, research assistantships, teaching assistantships, career-related internships or fieldwork, Federal Work-Study, institutionally sponsored loans, scholarships/grants, health care benefits, and unspecified assistantships available. Financial award application deadline: 12/18; financial award applicants required to submit FAFSA. *Faculty research:* Sociocultural anthropology, archaeology, biological anthropology, linguistic anthropology. *Unit head:* Terry Harrison, Chair, 212-998-8550, Fax: 212-995-4014, E-mail: anthropology@nyu.edu. *Application contact:* Tejaswini Ganti, Director of Graduate Studies, 212-998-8550, Fax: 212-995-4014, E-mail: anthropology@nyu.edu.
Website: http://www.nyu.edu/gsas/dept/anthro/

North Carolina State University, Graduate School, College of Humanities and Social Sciences, Department of Sociology and Anthropology, Program in Anthropology, Raleigh, NC 27695. Offers bioarchaeology (MA); cultural anthropology (MA); environmental anthropology (MA).

North Dakota State University, College of Graduate and Interdisciplinary Studies, College of Arts, Humanities and Social Sciences, Department of Sociology and Anthropology, Fargo, ND 58102. Offers anthropology (MA, MS); community development (MA, MS); social science (MA, MS); sociology (MS). *Program availability:* Part-time. *Degree requirements:* For master's, thesis. *Entrance requirements:* For master's, GRE (for emergency management), course work in sociology, minimum GPA of 3.2. Additional exam requirements/recommendations for international students: Required—TOEFL. Electronic applications accepted. *Faculty research:* Medical sociology, demography, ethnology, archaeology.

Northern Arizona University, College of Social and Behavioral Sciences, Department of Anthropology, Flagstaff, AZ 86011. Offers anthropology (MA), including applied anthropology, research anthropology. *Faculty:* 28 full-time (18 women). *Students:* 33 full-time (21 women), 8 part-time (3 women); includes 15 minority (2 Black or African American, non-Hispanic/Latino; 1 American Indian or Alaska Native, non-Hispanic/Latino; 6 Hispanic/Latino; 6 Two or more races, non-Hispanic/Latino). Average age 28. 53 applicants, 58% accepted, 27 enrolled. In 2017, 26 master's awarded. *Degree requirements:* For master's, variable foreign language requirement, comprehensive exam (for some programs), thesis, fieldwork experience/internship, oral defense. *Entrance requirements:* For master's, minimum GPA of 3.0 overall and in all anthropology courses taken, with no grade below a C; 12 hours of required anthropology courses. Additional exam requirements/recommendations for international students: Required—TOEFL (minimum score 80 iBT), IELTS (minimum score 6.5). *Application deadline:* For fall admission, 1/15 for domestic and international students; for spring admission, 10/1 for domestic and international students. Applications are processed on a rolling basis. Application fee: $65. Electronic applications accepted. *Expenses:* Tuition, state resident: full-time $9240; part-time $458 per credit hour. Tuition, nonresident: full-time $21,588; part-time $1199 per credit hour. *Required fees:* $1021; $14 per credit hour. $646 per semester. Tuition and fees vary according to course load, campus/location and program. *Financial support:* In 2017–18, 17 students received support, including 16 teaching assistantships with partial tuition reimbursements available (averaging $9,000 per year); institutionally sponsored loans, health care benefits, tuition waivers (partial), and unspecified assistantships also available. Financial award application deadline: 2/1; financial award applicants required to submit FAFSA. *Faculty research:* Economic development, culture change, ethnohistory, archaeology of the Southwest, small town networks and HIV. *Unit head:* Dr. Kelley Hays-Gilpin, Chair/

Professor, 928-523-6564, Fax: 928-523-9135, E-mail: kelley.hays-gilpin@nau.edu. *Application contact:* Denise Stippick, Business Manager, 928-523-1339, Fax: 928-523-9135, E-mail: anthropology@nau.edu.
Website: https://nau.edu/SBS/Anthropology/

Northern Illinois University, Graduate School, College of Liberal Arts and Sciences, Department of Anthropology, De Kalb, IL 60115-2854. Offers MA. *Program availability:* Part-time. *Faculty:* 12 full-time (6 women). *Students:* 14 full-time (8 women), 13 part-time (8 women); includes 3 minority (2 Asian, non-Hispanic/Latino; 1 Hispanic/Latino), 3 international. Average age 30. 17 applicants, 82% accepted, 11 enrolled. In 2017, 16 master's awarded. *Degree requirements:* For master's, one foreign language, comprehensive exam, thesis optional. *Entrance requirements:* For master's, GRE General Test, minimum GPA of 2.75, 15 hours of course work in anthropology, course work in statistics. Additional exam requirements/recommendations for international students: Required—TOEFL (minimum score 550 paper-based). *Application deadline:* For fall admission, 6/1 for domestic students, 5/1 for international students; for spring admission, 11/1 for domestic students, 10/1 for international students. Applications are processed on a rolling basis. Application fee: $40. Electronic applications accepted. *Financial support:* In 2017–18, 7 research assistantships with full tuition reimbursements, 9 teaching assistantships with full tuition reimbursements were awarded; fellowships with full tuition reimbursements, career-related internships or fieldwork, Federal Work-Study, scholarships/grants, tuition waivers (full), and unspecified assistantships also available. Support available to part-time students. Financial award applicants required to submit FAFSA. *Faculty research:* Linguistic anthropology of Oceania, Mayan languages, human paleontology, primate evolution, dental anthropology. *Unit head:* Dr. Kendall Thu, Chair, 815-753-0479, Fax: 815-753-7027, E-mail: kthu@niu.edu. *Application contact:* Graduate School Office, 815-753-0395, E-mail: gradsch@niu.edu.
Website: http://www.niu.edu/anthro/

Northwestern University, The Graduate School, Judd A. and Marjorie Weinberg College of Arts and Sciences, Department of Anthropology, Evanston, IL 60208. Offers PhD, JD/PhD. Admissions and degrees offered through The Graduate School. *Degree requirements:* For doctorate, thesis/dissertation. *Entrance requirements:* For doctorate, GRE General Test. Additional exam requirements/recommendations for international students: Required—TOEFL. Electronic applications accepted. *Faculty research:* Archaeology of complex societies, gender, political/urban anthropology, linguistic anthropology, African studies.

The Ohio State University, Graduate School, College of Arts and Sciences, Division of Social and Behavioral Sciences, Department of Anthropology, Columbus, OH 43210. Offers MA, PhD. *Faculty:* 17. *Students:* 50 full-time (38 women), 3 part-time (all women). Average age 31. In 2017, 4 master's, 6 doctorates awarded. *Degree requirements:* For master's, thesis optional; for doctorate, one foreign language, thesis/dissertation. *Entrance requirements:* For master's and doctorate, GRE General Test, minimum GPA of 3.3 in undergraduate work, 3.5 in all previous graduate work (recommended). Additional exam requirements/recommendations for international students: Required—TOEFL (minimum score 550 paper-based; 79 iBT), Michigan English Language Assessment Battery (minimum score 82); Recommended—IELTS (minimum score 7). *Application deadline:* For fall admission, 11/19 priority date for domestic and international students. Applications are processed on a rolling basis. Application fee: $60 ($70 for international students). Electronic applications accepted. *Financial support:* Fellowships, research assistantships, teaching assistantships, Federal Work-Study, institutionally sponsored loans, and unspecified assistantships available. Support available to part-time students. *Unit head:* Dr. Kristen Gremillion, Chair and Professor, 614-292-4388, Fax: 614-292-4155, E-mail: gremillion.1@osu.edu. *Application contact:* Graduate and Professional Admissions, 614-292-9444, Fax: 614-292-3895, E-mail: gpadmissions@osu.edu.
Website: http://anthropology.osu.edu/

Oregon State University, College of Liberal Arts, Program in Applied Anthropology, Corvallis, OR 97331. Offers MA. *Degree requirements:* For master's, one foreign language, thesis. *Entrance requirements:* Additional exam requirements/recommendations for international students: Required—TOEFL (minimum score 80 iBT), IELTS (minimum score 6.5). *Application deadline:* For fall admission, 1/1 for domestic and international students. Application fee: $75 ($85 for international students). *Financial support:* Application deadline: 1/1. *Faculty research:* Historical anthropology, evolutionary anthropology, medical anthropology, anthropology of food, environmental anthropology. *Unit head:* Allen Thompson, Director of Graduate Studies, 541-737-5654, E-mail: thompsan@oregonstate.edu. *Application contact:* Dr. Kenneth Maes, Assistant Professor, 541-737-7870, E-mail: kenneth.maes@oregonstate.edu.
Website: http://liberalarts.oregonstate.edu/slcs/anthropology

Penn State University Park, Graduate School, College of the Liberal Arts, Department of Anthropology, University Park, PA 16802. Offers MA, PhD. *Unit head:* Dr. Susan Welch, Dean, 814-865-7691, Fax: 814-863-2085. *Application contact:* Lori Hawn, Director, Graduate Student Services, 814-865-1795, Fax: 814-863-4627, E-mail: l-gswww@lists.psu.edu.
Website: http://anth.la.psu.edu/

Portland State University, Graduate Studies, College of Liberal Arts and Sciences, Department of Anthropology, Portland, OR 97207-0751. Offers MA, MS. *Faculty:* 8 full-time (6 women), 6 part-time/adjunct (3 women). *Students:* 8 full-time (5 women), 14 part-time (11 women); includes 2 minority (1 Hispanic/Latino; 1 Two or more races, non-Hispanic/Latino). Average age 32. 22 applicants, 45% accepted, 3 enrolled. In 2017, 1 master's awarded. *Degree requirements:* For master's, one foreign language, thesis. *Entrance requirements:* For master's, GRE General Test, minimum GPA of 3.25 in upper-division anthropology course work, 3.0 overall; 3 letters of recommendation. Additional exam requirements/recommendations for international students: Required—TOEFL (minimum score 550 paper-based; 80 iBT), IELTS (minimum score 6.5). *Application deadline:* For fall admission, 2/1 for domestic and international students. Application fee: $65. *Expenses:* Tuition, state resident: full-time $14,436; part-time $401 per credit. Tuition, nonresident: full-time $21,780; part-time $605 per credit. *Required fees:* $1380; $22 per credit. $119 per quarter. One-time fee: $325. Tuition and fees vary according to program. *Financial support:* In 2017–18, 8 students received support, including 1 research assistantship with full tuition reimbursement available (averaging $11,526 per year), 4 teaching assistantships with full tuition reimbursements available (averaging $6,834 per year); career-related internships or fieldwork, Federal Work-Study, and unspecified assistantships also available. Support available to part-time students. Financial award application deadline: 3/1; financial award applicants required to submit FAFSA. *Faculty research:* Forensic anthropology, Northwest Coast prehistory, Native Americans, applied anthropology, urban anthropology. *Total annual research expenditures:* $691,496. *Unit head:* Dr. Virginia Butler, Chair, 503-725-3303, E-mail: virginia@pdx.edu. *Application contact:* Torrie Sisson, Office Coordinator, 503-725-3081, Fax: 503-725-3905, E-mail: anthdept@pdx.edu.
Website: http://www.pdx.edu/anthropology/

Portland State University, Graduate Studies, College of Liberal Arts and Sciences, Systems Science Program, Portland, OR 97207-0751. Offers computational intelligence (Certificate); computer modeling and simulation (Certificate); systems science (MS);

systems science/anthropology (PhD); systems science/business administration (PhD); systems science/civil engineering (PhD); systems science/economics (PhD); systems science/engineering management (PhD); systems science/general (PhD); systems science/mathematical sciences (PhD); systems science/mechanical engineering (PhD); systems science/psychology (PhD); systems science/sociology (PhD). *Faculty:* 2 full-time (0 women), 4 part-time/adjunct (0 women). *Students:* 12 full-time (4 women), 22 part-time (6 women); includes 6 minority (4 Hispanic/Latino; 2 Two or more races, non-Hispanic/Latino). Average age 37. 18 applicants, 94% accepted, 16 enrolled. In 2017, 6 master's awarded. *Degree requirements:* For master's, comprehensive exam (for some programs), thesis optional; for doctorate, variable foreign language requirement, comprehensive exam (for some programs), thesis/dissertation. *Entrance requirements:* For master's, GRE/GMAT (recommended), minimum GPA of 3.0 on undergraduate or graduate work, 2 letters of recommendation, statement of interest; for doctorate, GMAT, GRE General Test, minimum GPA of 3.0 undergraduate, 3.25 graduate; 3 letters of recommendation; statement of interest. Additional exam requirements/recommendations for international students: Required—TOEFL (minimum score 550 paper-based; 80 iBT). *Application deadline:* For fall admission, 1/15 for domestic and international students; for spring admission, 11/1 for domestic students. Application fee: $65. Electronic applications accepted. *Expenses:* Tuition, state resident: full-time $14,436; part-time $401 per credit. Tuition, nonresident: full-time $21,780; part-time $605 per credit. *Required fees:* $1380; $22 per credit. $119 per quarter. One-time fee: $325. Tuition and fees vary according to program. *Financial support:* In 2017–18, 1 teaching assistantship with full and partial tuition reimbursement (averaging $7,830 per year) was awarded; research assistantships, career-related internships or fieldwork, Federal Work-Study, scholarships/grants, and unspecified assistantships also available. Support available to part-time students. Financial award application deadline: 3/1; financial award applicants required to submit FAFSA. *Faculty research:* Systems theory and methodology, artificial intelligence neural networks, information theory, nonlinear dynamics/chaos, modeling and simulation. *Total annual research expenditures:* $169,034. *Unit head:* Dr. Wayne Wakeland, Chair, 503-725-4975, E-mail: wakeland@pdx.edu.
Website: http://www.pdx.edu/sysc/

Princeton University, Graduate School, Department of Anthropology, Princeton, NJ 08544-1019. Offers PhD. *Degree requirements:* For doctorate, variable foreign language requirement, thesis/dissertation. *Entrance requirements:* For doctorate, GRE General Test, sample of written work. Additional exam requirements/recommendations for international students: Required—TOEFL (minimum score 600 paper-based). Electronic applications accepted. *Faculty research:* Symbolic anthropology, social theory, gender studies, law and society, political and social anthropology.

Purdue University, Graduate School, College of Liberal Arts, Department of Anthropology, West Lafayette, IN 47907. Offers MS, PhD. *Faculty:* 16 full-time (11 women), 1 part-time/adjunct (0 women). *Students:* 21 full-time (17 women), 3 part-time (0 women); includes 5 minority (1 Asian, non-Hispanic/Latino; 3 Hispanic/Latino; 1 Two or more races, non-Hispanic/Latino), 3 international. Average age 28. 27 applicants, 30% accepted, 4 enrolled. In 2017, 5 master's, 3 doctorates awarded. Terminal master's awarded for partial completion of doctoral program. *Degree requirements:* For master's, thesis; for doctorate, comprehensive exam, thesis/dissertation. *Entrance requirements:* For master's, GRE General Test, minimum undergraduate GPA of 3.0 or equivalent; for doctorate, GRE General Test, minimum undergraduate GPA of 3.0 or equivalent; master's degree. Additional exam requirements/recommendations for international students: Required—TOEFL (minimum score 550 paper-based; 77 iBT), TWE. *Application deadline:* For fall admission, 12/1 for domestic and international students. Applications are processed on a rolling basis. Application fee: $60 ($75 for international students). Electronic applications accepted. *Financial support:* In 2017–18, 27 students received support. Fellowships, research assistantships, teaching assistantships, and tuition waivers (full) available. Support available to part-time students. Financial award application deadline: 2/15; financial award applicants required to submit FAFSA. *Faculty research:* Communiversity survey project, risk, fear, constrained behavior, archaeological services. *Unit head:* Ellen R. Gruenbaum, Head, 765-496-7422, E-mail: gruenbaum@purdue.edu. *Application contact:* Talin M. Lindsay, Graduate Contact, 765-496-7428, E-mail: tlindsay@purdue.edu.
Website: http://www.cla.purdue.edu/anthropology/

Rice University, Graduate Programs, School of Social Sciences, Department of Anthropology, Houston, TX 77251-1892. Offers archaeology (MA, PhD); social-cultural anthropology (MA, PhD). Terminal master's awarded for partial completion of doctoral program. *Degree requirements:* For master's, one foreign language, 3 major papers, dissertation proposal and language exam or thesis; for doctorate, one foreign language, thesis/dissertation. *Entrance requirements:* For master's and doctorate, research proposal. Additional exam requirements/recommendations for international students: Required—TOEFL (minimum score 90 iBT). Electronic applications accepted.

Rutgers University–New Brunswick, Graduate School-New Brunswick, Program in Anthropology, Piscataway, NJ 08854-8097. Offers MA, PhD. Terminal master's awarded for partial completion of doctoral program. *Degree requirements:* For master's, thesis or alternative; for doctorate, comprehensive exam, thesis/dissertation. *Entrance requirements:* For master's and doctorate, GRE General Test, writing sample. Additional exam requirements/recommendations for international students: Required—TOEFL. Electronic applications accepted. *Faculty research:* Human evolution, lithic technology, behavioral ecology, ethnicity, gender.

San Diego State University, Graduate and Research Affairs, College of Arts and Letters, Department of Anthropology, San Diego, CA 92182. Offers MA. *Degree requirements:* For master's, one foreign language, thesis. *Entrance requirements:* For master's, GRE General Test, 3 letters of recommendation, typed writing sample. Additional exam requirements/recommendations for international students: Required—TOEFL. Electronic applications accepted. *Faculty research:* Meso-American archaeology, cognitive anthropology, ethnomusicology, primate conservation, biomedical anthropology.

San Francisco State University, Division of Graduate Studies, College of Liberal and Creative Arts, Department of Anthropology, San Francisco, CA 94132-1722. Offers archaeology (MA); biological anthropology (MA); cultural anthropology (MA); visual anthropology (MA). *Faculty research:* Immigration, ethnicity, urban anthropology, Californian and Latin American archaeology. *Unit head:* Dr. Cynthia Wilczak, Chair, 415-338-2046, Fax: 415-338-6159, E-mail: anthro@sfsu.edu. *Application contact:* Dr. Douglass Bailey, Graduate Coordinator, 415-338-1427, Fax: 415-338-6159, E-mail: dwbailey@sfsu.edu.
Website: http://anthropology.sfsu.edu/

San Jose State University, Graduate Studies and Research, College of Social Sciences, San Jose, CA 95192-0107. Offers applied anthropology (MA); communication studies (MA); economics (MA), including applied economics, economics; environmental studies (MS); geography (MA); history (MA), including history, history education; Mexican American studies (MA); psychology (MA, MS), including clinical psychology (MS), industrial/organizational psychology (MS), research and experimental psychology (MA); public administration (MPA); social sciences (MS); sociology (MA). *Faculty:* 59 full-time (29 women), 18 part-time/adjunct (5 women). *Students:* 181 full-time (126 women), 221 part-time (127 women); includes 228 minority (15 Black or African American, non-Hispanic/Latino; 48 Asian, non-Hispanic/Latino; 112 Hispanic/Latino; 3 Native Hawaiian or other Pacific Islander, non-Hispanic/Latino; 50 Two or more races, non-Hispanic/Latino), 38 international. Average age 30. 532 applicants, 44% accepted, 156 enrolled. In 2017, 139 master's awarded. *Degree requirements:* For master's, one foreign language, comprehensive exam, thesis (for some programs), project, field work, professional work experience. *Entrance requirements:* Additional exam requirements/recommendations for international students: Required—TOEFL (minimum score 550 paper-based; 80 iBT), IELTS (minimum score 6.5), PTE (minimum score 53). *Application deadline:* For fall admission, 2/1 for domestic and international students. Applications are processed on a rolling basis. Application fee: $55. Electronic applications accepted. *Expenses:* Tuition, state resident: full-time $7176. Tuition, nonresident: full-time $16,680. Tuition and fees vary according to course load and program. *Financial support:* Fellowships, research assistantships, career-related internships or fieldwork, Federal Work-Study, scholarships/grants, tuition waivers (full and partial), and unspecified assistantships available. Support available to part-time students. Financial award application deadline: 4/28; financial award applicants required to submit FAFSA. *Unit head:* Dr. Walt Jacobs, Dean, 408-924-5300, Fax: 408-924-5303, E-mail: walter.jacobs@sjsu.edu.
Website: http://www.sjsu.edu/socialsciences/

Simon Fraser University, Office of Graduate Studies and Postdoctoral Fellows, Faculty of Arts and Social Sciences, Department of Sociology and Anthropology, Burnaby, BC V5A 1S6, Canada. Offers anthropology (MA, PhD); sociology (MA, PhD). *Degree requirements:* For master's, thesis; for doctorate, comprehensive exam, thesis/dissertation, cooperative education. *Entrance requirements:* For master's, minimum GPA of 3.0 (on scale of 4.33) or 3.33 based on last 60 credits of undergraduate courses; for doctorate, minimum GPA of 3.5 (on scale of 4.33). Additional exam requirements/recommendations for international students: Recommended—TOEFL (minimum score 580 paper-based; 93 iBT), IELTS (minimum score 7), TWE (minimum score 5). Electronic applications accepted. *Faculty research:* Globalization and development, health, environment and science, knowledge, culture and power, social justice, policy, law and society, women, gender and sexuality.

Sonoma State University, School of Social Sciences, Program in Cultural Resources Management, Rohnert Park, CA 94928. Offers MA. *Program availability:* Part-time. *Entrance requirements:* For master's, minimum GPA of 3.0. Additional exam requirements/recommendations for international students: Required—TOEFL (minimum score 500 paper-based). *Application deadline:* For fall admission, 1/31 for domestic students. Application fee: $55. *Financial support:* Career-related internships or fieldwork, scholarships/grants, traineeships, and unspecified assistantships available. Financial award application deadline: 3/2; financial award applicants required to submit FAFSA. *Unit head:* Alexis Boutin, Chair, Anthropology Department, 707-664-2312, Fax: 707-664-2505, E-mail: alexis.boutin@sonoma.edu.
Website: http://www.sonoma.edu/anthropology/graduate/master.html

Southern Illinois University Carbondale, Graduate School, College of Liberal Arts, Department of Anthropology, Carbondale, IL 62901-4701. Offers MA, PhD. *Degree requirements:* For master's, one foreign language, thesis; for doctorate, one foreign language, thesis/dissertation. *Entrance requirements:* For master's, GRE General Test, minimum GPA of 2.7; for doctorate, GRE General Test, minimum GPA of 3.25. Additional exam requirements/recommendations for international students: Required—TOEFL (minimum score 600 paper-based; 100 iBT). *Faculty research:* Archaeology, human variability, evolution, cultural ecology, social anthropology.

Southern Methodist University, Dedman College of Humanities and Sciences, Department of Anthropology, Dallas, TX 75205. Offers anthropology (PhD); medical anthropology (MA). Terminal master's awarded for partial completion of doctoral program. *Degree requirements:* For master's, one foreign language, comprehensive exam, thesis or alternative; for doctorate, one foreign language, comprehensive exam, thesis/dissertation, qualifying exam, defense of dissertation. *Entrance requirements:* For master's and doctorate, GRE General Test, minimum GPA of 3.0. Additional exam requirements/recommendations for international students: Required—TOEFL (minimum score 550 paper-based). *Faculty research:* Health and gender, Paleo-Indians, Mesoamerica, American southwest, migration and ethnicity.

Stanford University, School of Humanities and Sciences, Department of Anthropology, Stanford, CA 94305-2004. Offers anthropology (MA); archaeology (PhD); culture and society (PhD); ecology and environment (PhD). Terminal master's awarded for partial completion of doctoral program. *Degree requirements:* For master's, thesis; for doctorate, one foreign language, thesis/dissertation. *Entrance requirements:* For master's and doctorate, GRE General Test. Additional exam requirements/recommendations for international students: Required—TOEFL. Electronic applications accepted. *Expenses: Tuition:* Full-time $48,987; part-time $10,620 per quarter. One-time fee: $400. Tuition and fees vary according to program.

Stony Brook University, State University of New York, Graduate School, College of Arts and Sciences, Department of Anthropology, Stony Brook, NY 11794. Offers MA, PhD. *Program availability:* Part-time. *Faculty:* 13 full-time (6 women), 1 (woman) part-time/adjunct. *Students:* 27 full-time (19 women); includes 4 minority (1 Hispanic/Latino; 3 Two or more races, non-Hispanic/Latino), 6 international. Average age 29. 53 applicants, 15% accepted, 4 enrolled. In 2017, 4 master's, 2 doctorates awarded. *Degree requirements:* For master's, fieldwork; for doctorate, thesis/dissertation. *Entrance requirements:* For master's and doctorate, GRE General Test. Additional exam requirements/recommendations for international students: Required—TOEFL (minimum score 90 iBT). *Application deadline:* For fall admission, 1/15 for domestic students; for spring admission, 10/1 for domestic students. Application fee: $100. *Expenses:* Contact institution. *Financial support:* In 2017–18, 2 fellowships, 1 research assistantship, 16 teaching assistantships were awarded; career-related internships or fieldwork also available. *Faculty research:* Anthropology, archaeology, human evolution, paleontology, Africa. *Total annual research expenditures:* $189,190. *Unit head:* Dr. David Hicks, Chair, 631-632-7617, E-mail: david.hicks@stonybrook.edu. *Application contact:* Tara J. Powers, Coordinator, 631-632-7606, E-mail: tara.powers@stonybrook.edu.
Website: http://www.stonybrook.edu/commcms/anthropology/

Stony Brook University, State University of New York, Graduate School, College of Arts and Sciences, Interdepartmental Doctoral Program in Anthropological Sciences (IDPAS), Stony Brook, NY 11794. Offers PhD. *Students:* 27 full-time (19 women); includes 4 minority (1 Hispanic/Latino; 3 Two or more races, non-Hispanic/Latino), 6 international. 50 applicants, 14% accepted, 4 enrolled. In 2017, 2 doctorates awarded. *Degree requirements:* For doctorate, one foreign language, thesis/dissertation, fieldwork. *Entrance requirements:* For doctorate, GRE General Test. Additional exam requirements/recommendations for international students: Required—TOEFL (minimum score 90 iBT). *Application deadline:* For fall admission, 1/15 for domestic students; for spring admission, 10/1 for domestic students. Application fee: $100. Electronic applications accepted. *Expenses:* Tuition, state resident: full-time $10,870; part-time $453 per credit. Tuition, nonresident: full-time $22,210; part-time $925 per credit. *Financial support:* In 2017–18, 2 fellowships, 1 research assistantship, 16 teaching assistantships were awarded. *Unit head:* Prof. Andreas Koenig, Director, 631-632-1513, E-mail: andreas.koenig@stonybrook.edu. *Application contact:* Tara J. Powers,

Coordinator, 631-632-7606, Fax: 631-632-9165, E-mail: tara.powers@stonybrook.edu.
Website: https://www.stonybrook.edu/commcms/idpas/

Syracuse University, Maxwell School of Citizenship and Public Affairs, Programs in Anthropology, Syracuse, NY 13207. Offers MA, PhD. In 2017, 5 master's, 4 doctorates awarded. *Degree requirements:* For master's, thesis or alternative; for doctorate, one foreign language, comprehensive exam, thesis/dissertation. *Entrance requirements:* For master's and doctorate, GRE General Test, resume, three letters of recommendation, personal statement, official transcripts. Additional exam requirements/recommendations for international students: Required—TOEFL (minimum score 100 iBT). *Application deadline:* For fall admission, 12/15 priority date for domestic and international students. Application fee: $75. Electronic applications accepted. *Financial support:* Fellowships with full tuition reimbursements, research assistantships, and teaching assistantships available. Financial award application deadline: 1/1. *Faculty research:* Human diversity, globalization, ethnology, sociolinguistics, osteology. *Unit head:* Dr. John Burdick, Professor and Chair, Anthropology, 315-443-3822, E-mail: jsburdic@maxwell.syr.edu. *Application contact:* Prof. Robert Rubinstein, Director of Graduate Studies, 315-443-3837, E-mail: rar@syr.edu.
Website: https://www.maxwell.syr.edu/anthro/Graduate/Graduate_Admissions(2)/

Teachers College, Columbia University, Department of International and Transcultural Studies, New York, NY 10027-6696. Offers anthropology and education (MA, Ed D, PhD); applied anthropology (PhD); comparative and international education (MA, Ed D, PhD); international educational development (Ed M, MA, Ed D, PhD). *Program availability:* Part-time. *Students:* 150 full-time (120 women), 143 part-time (116 women); includes 95 minority (22 Black or African American, non-Hispanic/Latino; 33 Asian, non-Hispanic/Latino; 29 Hispanic/Latino; 11 Two or more races, non-Hispanic/Latino), 116 international. Average age 29. 433 applicants, 59% accepted, 120 enrolled. *Degree requirements:* For doctorate, thesis/dissertation. *Unit head:* Prof. Herve Varenne, Chair, 212-678-3190, E-mail: varenne@tc.columbia.edu. *Application contact:* David Estrella, Director of Admission, 212-678-3305, E-mail: estrella@tc.columbia.edu.

Temple University, College of Liberal Arts, Department of Anthropology, Philadelphia, PA 19122-6096. Offers PhD. *Program availability:* Part-time. *Faculty:* 16 full-time (7 women), 1 (woman) part-time/adjunct. *Students:* 29 full-time (21 women), 1 (woman) part-time; includes 8 minority (3 Black or African American, non-Hispanic/Latino; 4 Hispanic/Latino; 1 Two or more races, non-Hispanic/Latino), 1 international. 13 applicants. In 2017, 2 doctorates awarded. Terminal master's awarded for partial completion of doctoral program. *Degree requirements:* For doctorate, one foreign language, thesis/dissertation. *Entrance requirements:* For doctorate, GRE General Test, minimum GPA of 3.0; 3 letters of recommendation. Additional exam requirements/recommendations for international students: Required—TOEFL (minimum score 550 paper-based; 79 iBT). *Application deadline:* For fall admission, 1/15 for domestic students, 12/10 for international students. Application fee: $60. Electronic applications accepted. *Expenses:* Tuition, state resident: full-time $16,164; part-time $898 per credit hour. Tuition, nonresident: full-time $22,158; part-time $1231 per credit hour. *Required fees:* $890; $445 per semester. Full-time tuition and fees vary according to course load, degree level, campus/location and program. *Financial support:* Fellowships, research assistantships, teaching assistantships, career-related internships or fieldwork, Federal Work-Study, and institutionally sponsored loans available. Financial award application deadline: 1/15; financial award applicants required to submit FAFSA. *Faculty research:* Anthropology of visual communication, political economy of language, historical archaeology, bicultural adaptation. *Unit head:* Dr. Paul Garrett, Director of Graduate Studies, 215-204-7621, Fax: 215-204-1410, E-mail: paul.garrett@temple.edu. *Application contact:* Yvonne Davis, Department Coordinator, 215-204-7775, Fax: 215-204-1410, E-mail: yvonne.davis@temple.edu.
Website: https://www.cla.temple.edu/anthropology/

Texas A&M University, College of Liberal Arts, Department of Anthropology, College Station, TX 77843. Offers anthropology (MA, PhD); maritime archaeology and conservation (MS). *Faculty:* 24. *Students:* 54 full-time (33 women), 32 part-time (19 women); includes 14 minority (3 Black or African American, non-Hispanic/Latino; 1 American Indian or Alaska Native, non-Hispanic/Latino; 3 Asian, non-Hispanic/Latino; 5 Hispanic/Latino; 2 Two or more races, non-Hispanic/Latino), 9 international. Average age 32. 57 applicants, 39% accepted, 14 enrolled. In 2017, 10 master's, 6 doctorates awarded. *Degree requirements:* For doctorate, thesis/dissertation. *Entrance requirements:* For master's and doctorate, GRE General Test. Additional exam requirements/recommendations for international students: Required—TOEFL (minimum score 550 paper-based; 80 iBT), IELTS (minimum score 6), PTE (minimum score 53). *Application deadline:* For fall admission, 12/1 for domestic students. Application fee: $50 ($90 for international students). *Expenses:* Contact institution. *Financial support:* In 2017–18, 66 students received support, including 6 fellowships with tuition reimbursements available (averaging $25,970 per year), 15 research assistantships with tuition reimbursements available (averaging $10,871 per year), 25 teaching assistantships with tuition reimbursements available (averaging $11,130 per year); career-related internships or fieldwork, institutionally sponsored loans, scholarships/grants, traineeships, health care benefits, tuition waivers (full and partial), and unspecified assistantships also available. Support available to part-time students. Financial award application deadline: 3/15; financial award applicants required to submit FAFSA. *Faculty research:* Nautical archaeology, archaeological conservation, archaeological palynology, paleo ethnobotany, folklore. *Unit head:* Dr. Ted Goebel, Interim Department Head, 979-845-5242, E-mail: goebel@tamu.edu. *Application contact:* Marco Valadez, Academic Advisor, 979-845-9333, Fax: 979-845-4070, E-mail: mlvaladez@tamu.edu.
Website: http://anthropology.tamu.edu/html/home.html

Texas State University, The Graduate College, College of Liberal Arts, Program in Anthropology, San Marcos, TX 78666. Offers MA. *Program availability:* Part-time. *Faculty:* 23 full-time (11 women), 3 part-time/adjunct (all women). *Students:* 38 full-time (31 women), 13 part-time (11 women); includes 13 minority (2 Black or African American, non-Hispanic/Latino; 1 Asian, non-Hispanic/Latino; 7 Hispanic/Latino; 3 Two or more races, non-Hispanic/Latino), 1 international. Average age 26. 125 applicants, 30% accepted, 20 enrolled. In 2017, 13 master's awarded. *Degree requirements:* For master's, comprehensive exam, thesis. *Entrance requirements:* For master's, GRE (minimum score 300 verbal and quantitative preferred), baccalaureate degree from regionally-accredited university with minimum GPA of 3.0 on last 60 undergraduate semester hours, resume, statement of purpose detailing academic interest identifying possible areas of anthropological research, three letters of recommendation. Additional exam requirements/recommendations for international students: Required—TOEFL (minimum score 550 paper-based; 78 iBT), IELTS (minimum score 6.5). *Application deadline:* For fall admission, 1/15 for domestic and international students. Applications are processed on a rolling basis. Application fee: $40 ($90 for international students). Electronic applications accepted. *Expenses:* Tuition, state resident: full-time $7868; part-time $3934 per semester. Tuition, nonresident: full-time $17,828; part-time $8914 per semester. *Required fees:* $2092; $1435 per semester. Tuition and fees vary according to course load. *Financial support:* In 2017–18, 41 students received support, including 13 research assistantships (averaging $9,438 per year), 20 teaching assistantships (averaging $6,474 per year); Federal Work-Study, institutionally sponsored loans, scholarships/grants, and unspecified assistantships also available. Support available to part-time students. Financial award application deadline: 3/1; financial award applicants required to submit FAFSA. *Faculty research:* Identifying human remains of migrants in Texas, Archaeological Field School at the Cross Bar Ranch, body score to determine days to post-mortem interval, luminescence dating,. *Total annual research expenditures:* $168,601. *Unit head:* Dr. Emily Brunson, Graduate Advisor, 512-245-6753, E-mail: grad-anthropology@txstate.edu. *Application contact:* Dr. Andrea Golato, Dean of Graduate School, 512-245-2581, Fax: 512-245-8365, E-mail: gradcollege@txstate.edu.
Website: http://www.txstate.edu/anthropology/grad-program.html

Texas Tech University, Graduate School, College of Arts and Sciences, Department of Sociology, Anthropology and Social Work, Lubbock, TX 79409. Offers anthropology (MA); social work (MSW); sociology (MA). *Program availability:* Part-time. *Faculty:* 28 full-time (17 women), 5 part-time/adjunct (3 women). *Students:* 46 full-time (32 women), 7 part-time (all women); includes 19 minority (3 Black or African American, non-Hispanic/Latino; 14 Hispanic/Latino; 2 Two or more races, non-Hispanic/Latino), 2 international. Average age 28. 52 applicants, 44% accepted, 19 enrolled. In 2017, 22 master's awarded. *Degree requirements:* For master's, one foreign language, comprehensive exam (for some programs), thesis (for some programs). *Entrance requirements:* For master's, GRE (for MA in anthropology), two letters of recommendation, statement of purpose, writing sample, curriculum vitae; minimum GPA of 3.0 and coursework in sociology or closely-related fields (for MA in sociology); coursework in anthropology (for MA in anthropology). Additional exam requirements/recommendations for international students: Required—TOEFL (minimum score 550 paper-based; 79 iBT). *Application deadline:* For fall admission, 6/1 priority date for domestic students, 1/15 priority date for international students; for spring admission, 9/1 priority date for domestic students, 6/15 priority date for international students. Applications are processed on a rolling basis. Application fee: $60. Electronic applications accepted. *Expenses:* Contact institution. *Financial support:* In 2017–18, 43 students received support, including 35 fellowships (averaging $4,324 per year), 28 teaching assistantships (averaging $13,091 per year); research assistantships, Federal Work-Study, scholarships/grants, tuition waivers (partial), and unspecified assistantships also available. Financial award application deadline: 2/1; financial award applicants required to submit FAFSA. *Faculty research:* Sociology of criminology/deviance, population/migration, forensic anthropology, archaeology, social work (advanced generalist). *Total annual research expenditures:* $153,180. *Unit head:* Dr. Brett A. Houk, Chair and Associate Professor, 806-834-8107, Fax: 806-742-1088, E-mail: brett.houk@ttu.edu. *Application contact:* Dr. Martha Smithey, Associate Professor/Sociology Graduate Program Director, 806-834-1995, E-mail: martha.smithey@ttu.edu.
Website: http://www.depts.ttu.edu/sasw/

Trent University, Graduate Studies, Program in Anthropology, Peterborough, ON K9J 7B8, Canada. Offers MA. *Program availability:* Part-time. *Degree requirements:* For master's, thesis. *Entrance requirements:* For master's, honors degree. *Faculty research:* Paleoecology, trade and fortification networks, pre-Columbian art.

Tulane University, School of Liberal Arts, Department of Anthropology, New Orleans, LA 70118-5669. Offers PhD. Terminal master's awarded for partial completion of doctoral program. *Degree requirements:* For doctorate, 2 foreign languages, thesis/dissertation. *Entrance requirements:* For doctorate, GRE General Test. Additional exam requirements/recommendations for international students: Required—TOEFL. Electronic applications accepted. *Expenses: Tuition:* Full-time $50,920; part-time $2829 per credit hour. *Required fees:* $2040; $44.50 per credit hour. $580 per term. Tuition and fees vary according to course load, degree level and program. *Faculty research:* Linguistics, physical anthropology, sociocultural archaeology, Mesoamerica.

Universidad de las Américas Puebla, Division of Graduate Studies, School of Social Sciences, Program in Anthropology, Puebla, Mexico. Offers anthropology (MA); archaeology (MA). *Program availability:* Part-time, evening/weekend. *Degree requirements:* For master's, one foreign language, thesis. *Entrance requirements:* For master's, bachelor's degree in anthropology or equivalent. *Faculty research:* Archaeology, ethnography, and ethnohistory of Mesoamerica.

Université de Montréal, Faculty of Arts and Sciences, Department of Anthropology, Montréal, QC H3C 3J7, Canada. Offers M Sc, PhD. *Program availability:* Part-time. *Degree requirements:* For master's, thesis; for doctorate, thesis/dissertation, general exam. Electronic applications accepted. *Faculty research:* Archaeology, ethnolinguistics, ethnology.

Université Laval, Faculty of Social Sciences, Department of Anthropology, Programs in Anthropology, Québec, QC G1K 7P4, Canada. Offers MA, PhD. Terminal master's awarded for partial completion of doctoral program. *Degree requirements:* For master's, thesis; for doctorate, thesis/dissertation. *Entrance requirements:* For master's, knowledge of French, interview; for doctorate, knowledge of French, comprehensive of written English, knowledge of a third language. Electronic applications accepted.

University at Albany, State University of New York, College of Arts and Sciences, Department of Anthropology, Albany, NY 12222-0001. Offers MA, PhD. *Faculty:* 19 full-time (8 women). *Students:* 26 full-time (22 women), 13 part-time (11 women). Average age 29. 45 applicants, 67% accepted, 12 enrolled. In 2017, 8 master's, 6 doctorates awarded. Terminal master's awarded for partial completion of doctoral program. *Degree requirements:* For master's, comprehensive exam, thesis; for doctorate, 2 foreign languages, thesis/dissertation, field exams. *Entrance requirements:* For master's and doctorate, GRE. Additional exam requirements/recommendations for international students: Required—TOEFL (minimum score 550 paper-based). *Application deadline:* For fall admission, 3/15 priority date for domestic students, 4/1 for international students; for spring admission, 11/1 for international students. Applications are processed on a rolling basis. Application fee: $75. Electronic applications accepted. *Expenses:* Tuition, state resident: full-time $10,870; part-time $453 per credit hour. Tuition, nonresident: full-time $22,210; part-time $925 per credit hour. *Required fees:* $84.68 per credit hour. $508.06 per semester. Part-time tuition and fees vary according to course load and program. *Financial support:* Fellowships, research assistantships, teaching assistantships, and career-related internships or fieldwork available. Financial award application deadline: 3/15. *Faculty research:* Economic and ecological anthropology; language, culture, and cognition; symbolic and interpretive anthropology; human evolution, morphology, demography, and medical anthropology; spatial and settlement archaeology. *Unit head:* Lee Bickmore, Chair, 518-442-4700, Fax: 518-442-5710, E-mail: lbickmore@albany.edu. *Application contact:* Michael DeRensis, Director, Graduate Studies, 518-442-3980, Fax: 518-442-3922, E-mail: graduate@albany.edu.
Website: http://www.albany.edu/anthro/

University at Buffalo, the State University of New York, Graduate School, College of Arts and Sciences, Department of Anthropology, Buffalo, NY 14260. Offers MA, PhD. *Faculty:* 14 full-time (5 women), 3 part-time/adjunct (2 women). *Students:* 78 full-time (49 women), 2 part-time (both women); includes 6 minority (1 Black or African American, non-Hispanic/Latino; 1 American Indian or Alaska Native, non-Hispanic/Latino; 2 Asian, non-Hispanic/Latino; 2 Hispanic/Latino), 3 international. Average age 29. 48 applicants, 54% accepted, 14 enrolled. In 2017, 11 master's, 11 doctorates awarded. Terminal

master's awarded for partial completion of doctoral program. *Degree requirements:* For master's, project; for doctorate, one foreign language, comprehensive exam, thesis/dissertation, exam. *Entrance requirements:* For master's, GRE General Test, minimum GPA of 3.0; for doctorate, GRE General Test, minimum GPA of 3.2. Additional exam requirements/recommendations for international students: Required—TOEFL (minimum score 79 iBT). *Application deadline:* For fall admission, 12/15 priority date for domestic and international students; for winter admission, 5/1 for domestic students, 3/15 for international students. Applications are processed on a rolling basis. Application fee: $75. Electronic applications accepted. *Financial support:* In 2017–18, 8 fellowships with full tuition reimbursements (averaging $19,646 per year), 1 research assistantship with full tuition reimbursement (averaging $13,896 per year), 12 teaching assistantships with full tuition reimbursements (averaging $13,896 per year) were awarded; career-related internships or fieldwork, Federal Work-Study, and institutionally sponsored loans also available. Financial award application deadline: 12/15; financial award applicants required to submit FAFSA. *Faculty research:* Old and New World archaeology, medical anthropology, primatology, human evolution, anthropology of Europe, bioarchaeology. *Total annual research expenditures:* $800,000. *Unit head:* Dr. Donald Pollock, Chair, 716-645-0402, Fax: 716-645-3808. *Application contact:* Maria Portera, Graduate Coordinator, 716-645-2414, Fax: 716-645-3808, E-mail: mportera@buffalo.edu.
Website: http://www.buffalo.edu/cas/anthropology

The University of Alabama, Graduate School, College of Arts and Sciences, Department of Anthropology, Tuscaloosa, AL 35487. Offers MA, PhD. *Faculty:* 14 full-time (6 women), 2 part-time/adjunct (0 women). *Students:* 29 full-time (19 women), 4 part-time (3 women); includes 3 minority (2 Black or African American, non-Hispanic/Latino; 1 Hispanic/Latino), 2 international. Average age 30. 28 applicants, 54% accepted, 7 enrolled. In 2017, 8 master's, 2 doctorates awarded. *Degree requirements:* For master's, one foreign language, comprehensive exam, thesis optional; for doctorate, one foreign language, comprehensive exam, thesis/dissertation. *Entrance requirements:* For master's, GRE, bachelor's degree in anthropology or closely-related discipline, undergraduate coursework in at least three of four anthropology subdisciplines; for doctorate, master's degree in anthropology or closely-related discipline, undergraduate or graduate coursework in at least three of four anthropology subdisciplines. Additional exam requirements/recommendations for international students: Required—TOEFL. *Application deadline:* For fall admission, 1/31 for domestic and international students. Application fee: $50 ($60 for international students). Electronic applications accepted. *Financial support:* In 2017–18, 25 students received support, including 4 fellowships with full tuition reimbursements available (averaging $15,000 per year), 1 research assistantship with full tuition reimbursement available (averaging $13,500 per year), 21 teaching assistantships with full tuition reimbursements available (averaging $14,720 per year); Federal Work-Study and health care benefits also available. Financial award application deadline: 1/15. *Faculty research:* Medical anthropology, southeastern archaeology, Latin American archaeology, biological anthropology, cultural anthropology. *Total annual research expenditures:* $71,313. *Unit head:* Dr. Keith P. Jacobi, Chair and Professor, 205-348-1960, Fax: 205-348-7937, E-mail: kjacobi@ua.edu. *Application contact:* Dr. Christopher D. Lynn, Associate Professor and Director of Graduate Studies, 205-348-4162, Fax: 205-348-7937, E-mail: cdlynn@ua.edu.
Website: http://anthropology.ua.edu

The University of Alabama at Birmingham, College of Arts and Sciences, Program in Anthropology, Birmingham, AL 35294. Offers MA. Program offered jointly with The University of Alabama (Tuscaloosa). *Degree requirements:* For master's, one foreign language, thesis (for some programs). *Entrance requirements:* For master's, GRE General Test. Additional exam requirements/recommendations for international students: Required—TOEFL, TWE. Electronic applications accepted. *Faculty research:* Ethnicity, medical anthropology, primate conservation, pastoral systems, Southeastern archaeology.

University of Alaska Anchorage, College of Arts and Sciences, Department of Anthropology, Anchorage, AK 99508. Offers MA. *Degree requirements:* For master's, comprehensive exam, thesis (for some programs), practicum. *Entrance requirements:* For master's, GRE General Test. Additional exam requirements/recommendations for international students: Required—TOEFL (minimum score 550 paper-based).

University of Alaska Fairbanks, College of Liberal Arts, Department of Anthropology, Fairbanks, AK 99775-7720. Offers MA, PhD. *Program availability:* Part-time. *Degree requirements:* For master's, one foreign language, comprehensive exam, oral defense of project or thesis; for doctorate, one foreign language, comprehensive exam, thesis/dissertation, oral defense of dissertation. *Entrance requirements:* For master's, GRE General Test, bachelor's degree in anthropology with minimum cumulative undergraduate and major GPA of 3.0; for doctorate, GRE General Test, master's degree in anthropology. Additional exam requirements/recommendations for international students: Required—TOEFL (minimum score 550 paper-based; 79 iBT), IELTS (minimum score 6.5). Electronic applications accepted. *Faculty research:* Circumpolar archaeology and population biology; rural subsistence; arctic physical, biological and social anthropology; arctic ethno history; arctic linguistics.

University of Alberta, Faculty of Graduate Studies and Research, Department of Anthropology, Edmonton, AB T6G 2E1, Canada. Offers MA, PhD. *Degree requirements:* For master's, thesis; for doctorate, one foreign language, thesis/dissertation. *Entrance requirements:* For master's and doctorate, minimum GPA of 7.0 on a 9.0 scale in last 2 years. Additional exam requirements/recommendations for international students: Required—TOEFL. *Faculty research:* Cultural anthropology of North America, South East Asia; physical anthropology in osteology, forensic primatology; archaeology of North America, South America, Old World/Africa.

The University of Arizona, College of Social and Behavioral Sciences, School of Anthropology, Tucson, AZ 85721. Offers MA, MS, PhD, Graduate Certificate. *Program availability:* Part-time. Terminal master's awarded for partial completion of doctoral program. *Degree requirements:* For master's, thesis or alternative; for doctorate, one foreign language, thesis/dissertation. *Entrance requirements:* For master's and doctorate, GRE General Test, minimum GPA of 3.5, 2 letters of recommendation. Additional exam requirements/recommendations for international students: Required—TOEFL (minimum score 550 paper-based; 79 iBT). Electronic applications accepted. *Faculty research:* Archaeology of pre-Han China, cultural ecology, health and illness-related behavior, interaction of linguistic and social processes, human growth and development under stress.

University of Arkansas, Graduate School, J. William Fulbright College of Arts and Sciences, Department of Anthropology, Fayetteville, AR 72701. Offers MA, PhD. *Program availability:* Part-time, evening/weekend. In 2017, 8 master's awarded. *Degree requirements:* For master's, comprehensive exam. *Entrance requirements:* For master's, GRE General Test, minimum GPA of 3.0; for doctorate, GRE General Test. *Application deadline:* For fall admission, 8/1 for domestic students, 4/1 for international students; for spring admission, 12/1 for domestic students, 10/1 for international students; for summer admission, 4/15 for domestic students, 3/1 for international students. Applications are processed on a rolling basis. Application fee: $60. Electronic applications accepted. *Expenses:* Tuition, state resident: full-time $3782. Tuition, nonresident: full-time $10,238. *Financial support:* In 2017–18, 6 research

assistantships, 21 teaching assistantships were awarded; fellowships with tuition reimbursements, career-related internships or fieldwork, and Federal Work-Study also available. Support available to part-time students. Financial award application deadline: 4/1; financial award applicants required to submit FAFSA. *Unit head:* Dr. Justin Murphy Nolan, Department Chair, 479-575-2508, Fax: 479-575-6595, E-mail: jmnolan@uark.edu. *Application contact:* Dr. JoAnn D'Alisera, Graduate Coordinator, 479-575-4460, Fax: 479-575-6595, E-mail: daliser@uark.edu.
Website: https://fulbright.uark.edu/departments/anthropology/

The University of British Columbia, Faculty of Arts, Department of Anthropology, Vancouver, BC V6T 1Z1, Canada. Offers MA, PhD. *Program availability:* Part-time. *Degree requirements:* For master's, thesis; for doctorate, comprehensive exam, thesis/dissertation. *Entrance requirements:* For master's, BA in anthropology or equivalent with minimum B+ average in upper-level courses; for doctorate, MA in anthropology or equivalent. Additional exam requirements/recommendations for international students: Required—TOEFL. Electronic applications accepted. *Expenses:* Contact institution. *Faculty research:* Cultures of North America, East Asia, Oceania; museum studies; archaeology.

University of Calgary, Faculty of Graduate Studies, Faculty of Arts, Department of Anthropology, Calgary, AB T2N 1N4, Canada. Offers MA, PhD. *Degree requirements:* For master's, thesis; for doctorate, one foreign language, comprehensive exam, thesis/dissertation, candidacy exam. *Entrance requirements:* Additional exam requirements/recommendations for international students: Required—TOEFL. *Faculty research:* Primatology, culture and society, biosocial anthropology, political anthropology, evolutionary theory.

University of California, Berkeley, Graduate Division, College of Letters and Science, Department of Anthropology, Program in Anthropology, Berkeley, CA 94720-1500. Offers PhD. *Degree requirements:* For doctorate, thesis/dissertation. *Entrance requirements:* For doctorate, GRE General Test, minimum GPA of 3.0, 3 letters of recommendation. Additional exam requirements/recommendations for international students: Required—TOEFL (minimum score 570 paper-based; 90 iBT). Electronic applications accepted.

University of California, Berkeley, Graduate Division, College of Letters and Science, Department of Anthropology, Program in Medical Anthropology, Berkeley, CA 94720-1500. Offers PhD. Program held jointly with University of California, San Francisco. *Degree requirements:* For doctorate, thesis/dissertation. *Entrance requirements:* For doctorate, GRE General Test, minimum GPA of 3.0, 3 letters of recommendation. Additional exam requirements/recommendations for international students: Required—TOEFL (minimum score 570 paper-based; 90 iBT). Electronic applications accepted.

University of California, Davis, Graduate Studies, Program in Anthropology, Davis, CA 95616. Offers MA, PhD. Terminal master's awarded for partial completion of doctoral program. *Degree requirements:* For master's, one foreign language; for doctorate, one foreign language, thesis/dissertation. *Entrance requirements:* For master's and doctorate, GRE General Test, minimum GPA of 3.0. Additional exam requirements/recommendations for international students: Required—TOEFL (minimum score 550 paper-based). Electronic applications accepted. *Faculty research:* Archaeology, linguistics, biological and sociocultural anthropology.

University of California, Irvine, School of Social Sciences, Department of Anthropology, Irvine, CA 92697. Offers MA, PhD. *Students:* 56 full-time (39 women), 1 (woman) part-time; includes 19 minority (1 Black or African American, non-Hispanic/Latino; 2 American Indian or Alaska Native, non-Hispanic/Latino; 11 Hispanic/Latino; 5 Two or more races, non-Hispanic/Latino), 7 international. Average age 30. 84 applicants, 26% accepted, 10 enrolled. In 2017, 8 master's, 9 doctorates awarded. *Entrance requirements:* For master's, GRE, minimum GPA of 3.0; for doctorate, GRE General Test, minimum GPA of 3.0. Additional exam requirements/recommendations for international students: Required—TOEFL (minimum score 550 paper-based). *Application deadline:* For fall admission, 1/15 priority date for domestic and international students. Applications are processed on a rolling basis. Application fee: $105 ($125 for international students). Electronic applications accepted. *Financial support:* Fellowships, research assistantships with full tuition reimbursements, teaching assistantships, institutionally sponsored loans, traineeships, health care benefits, and unspecified assistantships available. Financial award application deadline: 3/1; financial award applicants required to submit FAFSA. *Faculty research:* Cognitive anthropology, sociology of culture, social structure, family and gender. *Unit head:* George Marcus, Chair, 949-824-5345, Fax: 949-824-6046, E-mail: gmarcus@uci.edu. *Application contact:* Tom Boellstorff, Graduate Program Director, 949-824-9944, Fax: 949-824-0646, E-mail: tboellst@uci.edu.
Website: http://www.anthropology.uci.edu/

University of California, Los Angeles, Graduate Division, College of Letters and Science, Department of Anthropology, Los Angeles, CA 90095. Offers MA, PhD. Terminal master's awarded for partial completion of doctoral program. *Degree requirements:* For master's, thesis; for doctorate, thesis/dissertation, oral and written qualifying exams. *Entrance requirements:* For master's and doctorate, GRE General Test, bachelor's degree; minimum undergraduate GPA of 3.0 (or its equivalent if letter grade system not used); writing sample. Additional exam requirements/recommendations for international students: Required—TOEFL. Electronic applications accepted.

University of California, Riverside, Graduate Division, Department of Anthropology, Riverside, CA 92521-0102. Offers MA, MS, PhD. *Program availability:* Part-time. Terminal master's awarded for partial completion of doctoral program. *Degree requirements:* For master's, comprehensive exams or thesis; for doctorate, one foreign language, comprehensive exam, thesis/dissertation, qualifying exams. *Entrance requirements:* For master's and doctorate, GRE General Test, sample of written work, minimum GPA of 3.2, 3 letters of recommendation. Additional exam requirements/recommendations for international students: Required—TOEFL (minimum score 550 paper-based; 80 iBT). Electronic applications accepted. *Expenses:* Tuition, state resident: full-time $5746. Tuition, nonresident: full-time $10,780. Tuition and fees vary according to campus/location and program. *Faculty research:* Transnational processes, border communities, political and cultural ecology, Mesoamerican and Western U.S. archaeology, applied anthropology.

University of California, San Diego, Graduate Division, Department of Anthropology, La Jolla, CA 92093. Offers PhD. *Students:* 56 full-time (38 women). 78 applicants, 24% accepted, 11 enrolled. In 2017, 5 doctorates awarded. *Degree requirements:* For doctorate, variable foreign language requirement, comprehensive exam, thesis/dissertation, 1-quarter teaching assistantship. *Entrance requirements:* For doctorate, GRE General Test, 3 letters of recommendation, statement of purpose. Additional exam requirements/recommendations for international students: Required—TOEFL (minimum score 550 paper-based; 80 iBT), IELTS (minimum score 7), PTE. *Application deadline:* For fall admission, 1/16 for domestic students. Application fee: $105 ($125 for international students). Electronic applications accepted. *Financial support:* Fellowships, research assistantships, teaching assistantships, and scholarships/grants available. Financial award applicants required to submit FAFSA. *Faculty research:* Anthropological archaeology, biological anthropology, sociocultural anthropology,

psychological anthropology, linguistic anthropology, anthropogony. *Unit head:* Steve Parish, Department Chair, 858-534-8880, E-mail: sparish@ucsd.edu. *Application contact:* Nikki Gee, Graduate Coordinator, 858-534-0107, E-mail: ngee@ucsd.edu. Website: http://anthropology.ucsd.edu/

University of California, San Francisco, Graduate Division, Program in Medical Anthropology, San Francisco, CA 94143. Offers PhD. Program offered jointly with University of California, Berkeley. *Degree requirements:* For doctorate, one foreign language, thesis/dissertation, 3 field statements. *Entrance requirements:* For doctorate, GRE General Test, master's degree in anthropology or a related social or health science. *Faculty research:* Ethnicity, gender, aging, international health, health policy.

University of California, Santa Barbara, Graduate Division, College of Letters and Sciences, Division of Social Sciences, Department of Anthropology, Santa Barbara, CA 93106-2014. Offers sociocultural anthropology (PhD); MA/PhD. Terminal master's awarded for partial completion of doctoral program. *Degree requirements:* For master's, comprehensive exam (for some programs), thesis (for some programs); for doctorate, comprehensive exam (for some programs), thesis/dissertation. *Entrance requirements:* For master's and doctorate, GRE General Test, statement of purpose, personal achievements statement, transcripts, writing sample, curriculum vitae, letters of recommendation. Additional exam requirements/recommendations for international students: Required—TOEFL (minimum score 550 paper-based; 80 iBT), IELTS (minimum score 7). Electronic applications accepted. *Faculty research:* Archaeology, bioarchaeology, biosocial anthropology, evolutionary ecology, evolutionary psychology, sociocultural anthropology.

University of California, Santa Cruz, Division of Graduate Studies, Division of Social Sciences, Department of Anthropology, Santa Cruz, CA 95064. Offers cultural anthropology (PhD). *Degree requirements:* For doctorate, thesis/dissertation, qualifying exam. *Entrance requirements:* For doctorate, GRE General Test. Additional exam requirements/recommendations for international students: Required—TOEFL (minimum score 550 paper-based; 83 iBT); Recommended—IELTS (minimum score 8). Electronic applications accepted. *Faculty research:* Culture and power, women's roles, AIDS, folklore.

University of Central Florida, College of Sciences, Department of Anthropology, Orlando, FL 32816. Offers anthropology (MA). *Students:* 32 full-time (24 women), 4 part-time (2 women); includes 6 minority (1 American Indian or Alaska Native, non-Hispanic/Latino; 4 Hispanic/Latino; 1 Two or more races, non-Hispanic/Latino). Average age 27. 29 applicants, 69% accepted, 12 enrolled. In 2017, 14 master's awarded. *Degree requirements:* For master's, thesis or alternative. *Entrance requirements:* For master's, GRE General Test, letters of recommendation, personal statement. Additional exam requirements/recommendations for international students: Required—TOEFL. *Application deadline:* For fall admission, 2/15 for domestic students; for spring admission, 11/1 for domestic students. Application fee: $30. Electronic applications accepted. *Expenses:* Tuition, state resident: part-time $288.16 per credit hour. Tuition, nonresident: part-time $1073.31 per credit hour. Tuition and fees vary according to program. *Financial support:* In 2017–18, 24 students received support, including 3 fellowships with partial tuition reimbursements available (averaging $5,333 per year), 1 research assistantship with partial tuition reimbursement available (averaging $11,256 per year), 21 teaching assistantships with partial tuition reimbursements available (averaging $9,088 per year); institutionally sponsored loans, scholarships/grants, and health care benefits also available. Financial award application deadline: 3/1; financial award applicants required to submit FAFSA. *Unit head:* Dr. Toshas Dupras, Chair, 407-823-6568, Fax: 407-823-3498, E-mail: tosha.dupras@ucf.edu. *Application contact:* Associate Director, Graduate Admissions, 407-823-2766, Fax: 407-823-6442, E-mail: gradadmissions@ucf.edu. Website: http://anthropology.cos.ucf.edu/

University of Chicago, Division of the Humanities, Department of Linguistics, Chicago, IL 60637. Offers anthropology and linguistics (PhD); linguistics (PhD). *Students:* 42 full-time (22 women); includes 10 minority (1 American Indian or Alaska Native, non-Hispanic/Latino; 2 Asian, non-Hispanic/Latino; 5 Hispanic/Latino; 2 Two or more races, non-Hispanic/Latino), 15 international. Average age 28. 100 applicants, 12% accepted, 6 enrolled. In 2017, 2 doctorates awarded. Terminal master's awarded for partial completion of doctoral program. *Degree requirements:* For doctorate, 2 foreign languages, thesis/dissertation. *Entrance requirements:* For doctorate, GRE General Test, 15-20 page writing sample, statement of purpose, 3 letters of recommendation, transcripts for all previous degrees and institutions attended. Additional exam requirements/recommendations for international students: Required—TOEFL (minimum score 104 iBT), IELTS (minimum score 7). *Application deadline:* For fall admission, 12/15 for domestic and international students. Application fee: $90. Electronic applications accepted. *Financial support:* In 2017–18, fellowships with full tuition reimbursements (averaging $27,000 per year) were awarded; teaching assistantships with full tuition reimbursements, Federal Work-Study, institutionally sponsored loans, scholarships/grants, and health care benefits also available. Financial award application deadline: 12/15. *Unit head:* Dr. Lenore Grenoble, Chair, 773-702-8522, E-mail: linguistics@uchicago.edu. *Application contact:* Michael Beetley, Assistant Dean of Students, Admissions and Fellowships, 773-702-1552, Fax: 773-834-9148, E-mail: humanitiesadmissions@uchicago.edu. Website: http://linguistics.uchicago.edu/

University of Chicago, Division of the Social Sciences, Department of Anthropology, Chicago, IL 60637. Offers archaeology (PhD); sociocultural and linguistic anthropology (PhD). *Faculty:* 23. *Students:* 129 full-time (74 women); includes 20 minority (6 Black or African American, non-Hispanic/Latino; 2 American Indian or Alaska Native, non-Hispanic/Latino; 2 Asian, non-Hispanic/Latino; 4 Hispanic/Latino; 6 Two or more races, non-Hispanic/Latino), 45 international. Average age 31. 260 applicants, 7% accepted, 11 enrolled. In 2017, 13 doctorates awarded. *Degree requirements:* For doctorate, one foreign language, thesis/dissertation. *Entrance requirements:* For doctorate, GRE General Test, 3 letters of recommendation, statement of purpose, transcripts, resume or curriculum vitae, writing sample (dependent on department). Additional exam requirements/recommendations for international students: Required—TOEFL (minimum score 104 iBT), IELTS (minimum score 7). *Application deadline:* For fall admission, 12/15 for domestic and international students. Application fee: $90. Electronic applications accepted. *Financial support:* In 2017–18, 16 students received support, including 12 fellowships with full tuition reimbursements available (averaging $27,000 per year); research assistantships, teaching assistantships, career-related internships or fieldwork, Federal Work-Study, institutionally sponsored loans, scholarships/grants, and health care benefits also available. Financial award application deadline: 12/15. *Unit head:* Dr. William Mazzarella, Chair, 773-834-4873, E-mail: mazzarel@uchicago.edu. *Application contact:* Office of the Dean of Students, 773-702-8415, E-mail: ssd-admissions@uchicago.edu. Website: http://anthropology.uchicago.edu

University of Cincinnati, Graduate School, McMicken College of Arts and Sciences, Department of Anthropology, Cincinnati, OH 45221. Offers MA. *Program availability:* Part-time. *Degree requirements:* For master's, thesis or alternative. *Entrance requirements:* For master's, GRE General Test. Additional exam requirements/recommendations for international students: Required—TOEFL; Recommended—TWE.

Electronic applications accepted. *Expenses: Tuition, area resident:* Full-time $14,468. Tuition, state resident: full-time $14,968; part-time $754 per credit hour. Tuition, nonresident: full-time $24,210; part-time $1311 per credit hour. *International tuition:* $26,460 full-time. *Required fees:* $3958; $84 per credit hour. One-time fee: $85 full-time. Tuition and fees vary according to course load, degree level and program. *Faculty research:* Medical anthropology, Mayan prehistory, southwestern U.S. prehistory, skeletal biology and paleoanthropology; immigrants; Mexico.

University of Colorado Boulder, Graduate School, College of Arts and Sciences, Department of Anthropology, Boulder, CO 80309. Offers MA, PhD. *Faculty:* 24 full-time (13 women). *Students:* 49 full-time (31 women), 1 part-time (0 women); includes 12 minority (1 American Indian or Alaska Native, non-Hispanic/Latino; 2 Asian, non-Hispanic/Latino; 7 Hispanic/Latino; 2 Two or more races, non-Hispanic/Latino), 2 international. Average age 32. 81 applicants, 21% accepted, 6 enrolled. In 2017, 12 master's, 6 doctorates awarded. Terminal master's awarded for partial completion of doctoral program. *Degree requirements:* For master's, comprehensive exam, thesis or alternative; for doctorate, one foreign language, thesis/dissertation. *Entrance requirements:* For master's, GRE General Test, minimum undergraduate GPA of 3.0; for doctorate, GRE General Test, minimum undergraduate GPA of 3.0, master's degree in anthropology. *Application deadline:* For fall admission, 1/10 for domestic students, 12/1 for international students. Applications are processed on a rolling basis. Application fee: $60 ($80 for international students). Electronic applications accepted. Application fee is waived when completed online. *Financial support:* In 2017–18, 131 students received support, including 39 fellowships (averaging $5,046 per year), 3 research assistantships with full and partial tuition reimbursements available (averaging $26,580 per year), 38 teaching assistantships with full and partial tuition reimbursements available (averaging $19,318 per year); institutionally sponsored loans, scholarships/grants, health care benefits, and unspecified assistantships also available. Financial award application deadline: 2/15; financial award applicants required to submit FAFSA. *Faculty research:* Anthropology; cultural/social anthropology; archaeology; ethnography; physical anthropology. *Total annual research expenditures:* $757,188. *Application contact:* E-mail: anthro@colorado.edu. Website: http://www.colorado.edu/anthropology

University of Colorado Denver, College of Liberal Arts and Sciences, Department of Anthropology, Denver, CO 80217. Offers archaeological studies (MA); biological anthropology (MA); medical anthropology (MA); sustainable development and political ecology (MA). *Program availability:* Part-time, evening/weekend. *Degree requirements:* For master's, comprehensive exam, thesis or alternative, 30-36 credit hours. *Entrance requirements:* For master's, GRE General Test, minimum GPA of 3.0 for all undergraduate studies, transcripts from all undergraduate/graduate institutions attended, prior training in anthropology, three letters of recommendation, statement of purpose. Additional exam requirements/recommendations for international students: Required—TOEFL (minimum score 537 paper-based; 75 iBT); Recommended—IELTS (minimum score 6.5). Electronic applications accepted. *Faculty research:* Applied medical anthropology, primate social behavior, environmental anthropology, Southwestern and Mexican archaeology, human ecology.

University of Connecticut, Graduate School, College of Liberal Arts and Sciences, Department of Anthropology, Storrs, CT 06269. Offers MA, PhD. Terminal master's awarded for partial completion of doctoral program. *Degree requirements:* For master's, comprehensive exam; for doctorate, thesis/dissertation. *Entrance requirements:* For master's and doctorate, GRE General Test. Additional exam requirements/recommendations for international students: Required—TOEFL (minimum score 550 paper-based). Electronic applications accepted.

University of Denver, Division of Arts, Humanities and Social Sciences, Department of Anthropology, Denver, CO 80208. Offers archaeology (MA); cultural anthropology (MA); museum and heritage studies (MA). *Program availability:* Part-time. *Faculty:* 8 full-time (2 women). *Students:* 3 full-time (all women), 23 part-time (20 women); includes 2 minority (1 Black or African American, non-Hispanic/Latino; 1 Hispanic/Latino), 1 international. Average age 25. 49 applicants, 59% accepted, 12 enrolled. In 2017, 9 master's awarded. *Degree requirements:* For master's, one foreign language, comprehensive exam, thesis (for some programs), tool, foreign language literacy, or course work. *Entrance requirements:* For master's, GRE General Test, bachelor's degree, transcripts, personal statement, two letters of recommendation. Additional exam requirements/recommendations for international students: Required—TOEFL (minimum score 550 paper-based; 80 iBT). *Application deadline:* For fall admission, 2/4 priority date for domestic and international students. Applications are processed on a rolling basis. Application fee: $65. Electronic applications accepted. *Expenses:* $31,935 per year full-time. *Financial support:* In 2017–18, 23 students received support. Teaching assistantships with tuition reimbursements available, career-related internships or fieldwork, Federal Work-Study, institutionally sponsored loans, scholarships/grants, and unspecified assistantships available. Support available to part-time students. Financial award application deadline: 2/15; financial award applicants required to submit FAFSA. *Faculty research:* Human diversity, human rights, historic archaeology, museums and heritage, high-tech field methods. *Unit head:* Dr. Larry Conyers, Professor and Chair, 303-871-2684, Fax: 303-871-2437, E-mail: lconyers@du.edu. Website: http://www.du.edu/ahss/anthropology

University of Florida, Graduate School, College of Liberal Arts and Sciences, Department of Anthropology, Gainesville, FL 32611. Offers anthropology (MA, MAT, PhD), including historic preservation (MA, PhD), tropical conservation and development, women's and gender studies (PhD). *Program availability:* Part-time. *Degree requirements:* For master's, thesis optional; for doctorate, comprehensive exam, thesis/dissertation. *Entrance requirements:* For master's and doctorate, GRE General Test, minimum GPA of 3.2. Additional exam requirements/recommendations for international students: Required—TOEFL (minimum score 550 paper-based; 80 iBT), IELTS (minimum score 6). Electronic applications accepted. *Faculty research:* Social and cultural anthropology, archaeology, biological anthropology, medical anthropology, linguistic anthropology.

University of Georgia, Franklin College of Arts and Sciences, Department of Anthropology, Athens, GA 30602. Offers anthropology (MA, PhD). *Degree requirements:* For master's, one foreign language, thesis; for doctorate, one foreign language, thesis/dissertation. *Entrance requirements:* For master's and doctorate, GRE General Test. Electronic applications accepted.

University of Guelph, Graduate Studies, College of Social and Applied Human Sciences, Department of Sociology and Anthropology, Guelph, ON N1G 2W1, Canada. Offers anthropology (MA); crime and criminal justice policy (MA); sociology (MA, PhD). *Degree requirements:* For master's, thesis or major paper; for doctorate, comprehensive exam, thesis/dissertation. *Entrance requirements:* For master's, minimum B+ average during previous 2 years of course work, honors BA or equivalent; for doctorate, must have an MA in Sociology, must have 80% or higher in graduate level studies. Additional exam requirements/recommendations for international students: Required—TOEFL (minimum score 550 paper-based; 89 iBT) or IELTS (minimum score 6.5). Electronic applications accepted. *Faculty research:* Rural and development sociology; education, employment, and the workplace; race, ethnicity, and native studies; criminology and deviance; social psychology.

Anthropology

University of Hawaii at Manoa, Office of Graduate Education, College of Social Sciences, Department of Anthropology, Honolulu, HI 96822. Offers MA, PhD. *Program availability:* Part-time. *Degree requirements:* For master's, thesis optional; for doctorate, comprehensive exam, thesis/dissertation. *Entrance requirements:* For master's and doctorate, GRE General Test. Additional exam requirements/recommendations for international students: Required—TOEFL (minimum score 560 paper-based; 83 iBT), IELTS (minimum score 5). *Faculty research:* Evolution of social complexity, ethnopharmacology, social interaction, faunal analysis, human ecology.

University of Houston, College of Liberal Arts and Social Sciences, Department of Comparative Cultural Studies, Houston, TX 77204. Offers anthropology (MA). *Program availability:* Part-time. *Degree requirements:* For master's, comprehensive exam, thesis. *Entrance requirements:* For master's, GRE General Test (minimum 500 verbal, 500 quantitative), minimum GPA of 3.0 in last 60 undergraduate hours. Additional exam requirements/recommendations for international students: Required—TOEFL (minimum score 550 paper-based; 79 iBT). Electronic applications accepted.

University of Idaho, College of Graduate Studies, College of Letters, Arts and Social Sciences, Department of Sociology and Anthropology, Moscow, ID 83844. Offers anthropology (MA). *Faculty:* 9. *Students:* 10 full-time, 7 part-time. Average age 32. In 2017, 10 master's awarded. *Degree requirements:* For master's, variable foreign language requirement. *Entrance requirements:* For master's, minimum GPA of 3.0. Additional exam requirements/recommendations for international students: Required—TOEFL (minimum score 79 iBT). *Application deadline:* For fall admission, 8/1 for domestic students; for spring admission, 12/15 for domestic students. Applications are processed on a rolling basis. Application fee: $60. Electronic applications accepted. *Expenses:* Tuition, state resident: full-time $6722; part-time $430 per credit hour. Tuition, nonresident: full-time $23,046; part-time $1337 per credit hour. *Required fees:* $2142; $63 per credit hour. *Financial support:* Research assistantships and teaching assistantships available. Financial award applicants required to submit FAFSA. *Unit head:* Dr. Mark Warner, Chair, 208-885-6751, E-mail: socanth@uidaho.edu. *Application contact:* Sean Scoggin, Graduate Recruitment Coordinator, 208-885-4723, Fax: 208-885-4406, E-mail: graduateadmissions@uidaho.edu.
Website: https://www.uidaho.edu/class/soc-anthro

University of Illinois at Chicago, College of Liberal Arts and Sciences, Department of Anthropology, Chicago, IL 60607-7128. Offers anthropology (MA, PhD); environmental and urban geography (MA), including environmental studies, urban geography. *Program availability:* Part-time. *Degree requirements:* For doctorate, comprehensive exam. *Entrance requirements:* For master's and doctorate, minimum GPA of 2.75. Additional exam requirements/recommendations for international students: Required—TOEFL. Electronic applications accepted. *Faculty research:* Archaeological, physical, and cultural anthropology; environmental and urban geography.

University of Illinois at Urbana–Champaign, Graduate College, College of Liberal Arts and Sciences, Department of Anthropology, Champaign, IL 61820. Offers MA, PhD. Terminal master's awarded for partial completion of doctoral program.

University of Indianapolis, Graduate Programs, College of Arts and Sciences, Department of Anthropology, Indianapolis, IN 46227-3697. Offers MS. *Entrance requirements:* For master's, GRE General Test (minimum score of 500 on both the verbal and quantitative sections), bachelor's degree with major or minor in anthropology or closely-related field; undergraduate or graduate coursework in anthropology and the natural sciences with minimum C grade (ideally, semester in cultural anthropology, biological anthropology, archeology, statistics, and geology); minimum cumulative undergraduate GPA of 3.2. Additional exam requirements/recommendations for international students: Required—TOEFL (minimum score 550 paper-based; 79 iBT).

The University of Iowa, Graduate College, College of Liberal Arts and Sciences, Department of Anthropology, Iowa City, IA 52242-1316. Offers MA, PhD. *Degree requirements:* For master's, thesis optional, exam; for doctorate, comprehensive exam, thesis/dissertation. *Entrance requirements:* For master's and doctorate, GRE General Test, minimum GPA of 3.0. Additional exam requirements/recommendations for international students: Required—TOEFL (minimum score 550 paper-based; 81 iBT). Electronic applications accepted.

The University of Kansas, Graduate Studies, College of Liberal Arts and Sciences, Department of Anthropology, Lawrence, KS 66045. Offers MA, PhD. *Students:* 27 full-time (18 women), 6 part-time (4 women); includes 1 minority (Black or African American, non-Hispanic/Latino), 5 international. Average age 31. 22 applicants, 50% accepted, 7 enrolled. In 2017, 4 master's, 5 doctorates awarded. *Entrance requirements:* For master's, GRE (for university fellowship), letter stating academic objectives and clearly indicating disciplinary track of interest; copy of curriculum vitae; transcripts of undergraduate and graduate study completed; three letters of recommendation; for doctorate, GRE (for university fellowship), letter stating academic objectives and clearly indicating disciplinary track of interest; copy of curriculum vitae; transcripts of undergraduate and graduate study completed; three letters of recommendation; professional writing sample. Additional exam requirements/recommendations for international students: Required—TOEFL. *Application deadline:* For fall admission, 1/5 for domestic and international students. Application fee: $65 ($85 for international students). Electronic applications accepted. *Financial support:* Fellowships, research assistantships, teaching assistantships, career-related internships or fieldwork, institutionally sponsored loans, and unspecified assistantships available. Financial award application deadline: 1/5; financial award applicants required to submit FAFSA. *Faculty research:* Archaeological, biological, cultural, linguistic, and applied anthropology. *Unit head:* Joane P. Nagel, Chair, 785-864-4114, E-mail: nagel@ku.edu. *Application contact:* Le-Thu Erazmus, Graduate Officer, 785-864-2630, E-mail: lerazmus@ku.edu.
Website: http://anthropology.ku.edu/

University of Kentucky, Graduate School, College of Arts and Sciences, Program in Anthropology, Lexington, KY 40506-0032. Offers MA, PhD. *Program availability:* Part-time. *Degree requirements:* For master's, comprehensive exam, thesis optional; for doctorate, one foreign language, comprehensive exam, thesis/dissertation. *Entrance requirements:* For master's, GRE General Test, minimum undergraduate GPA of 2.75; for doctorate, GRE General Test, minimum graduate GPA of 3.0. Additional exam requirements/recommendations for international students: Required—TOEFL (minimum score 550 paper-based). Electronic applications accepted. *Faculty research:* Applied social anthropology, developmental change, medical anthropology, culture history, ethnohistory.

University of Lethbridge, School of Graduate Studies, Lethbridge, AB T1K 3M4, Canada. Offers addictions counseling (M Sc); agricultural biotechnology (M Sc); agricultural studies (M Sc, MA); anthropology (MA); archaeology (M Sc, MA); art (MA, MFA); biochemistry (M Sc); biological sciences (M Sc); biomolecular science (PhD); biosystems and biodiversity (PhD); Canadian studies (MA); chemistry (M Sc); computer science (M Sc); computer science and geographical information science (M Sc); counseling (MC); counseling psychology (M Ed); dramatic arts (MA); earth, space, and physical science (PhD); economics (MA); education (MA, PhD); educational leadership (M Ed); English (MA); environmental science (M Sc); evolution and behavior (PhD); exercise science (M Sc); French (MA); French/German (MA); French/Spanish (MA); general education (M Ed); geography (M Sc, MA); German (MA); health sciences (M Sc); individualized multidisciplinary (M Sc, MA); kinesiology (M Sc, MA); management (M Sc), including accounting, finance, human resource management and labor relations, information systems, international management, marketing, policy and strategy; mathematics (M Sc); music (M Mus, MA); Native American studies (MA); neuroscience (M Sc, PhD); new media (MA, MFA); nursing (M Sc, MN); philosophy (MA); physics (M Sc); political science (MA); psychology (M Sc, MA); religious studies (MA); sociology (MA); theatre and dramatic arts (MFA); theoretical and computational science (PhD); urban and regional studies (MA); women and gender studies (MA). *Program availability:* Part-time, evening/weekend. *Degree requirements:* For master's, thesis (for some programs); for doctorate, comprehensive exam, thesis/dissertation. *Entrance requirements:* For master's, GMAT (for M Sc in management), bachelor's degree in related field, minimum GPA of 3.0 during previous 20 graded semester courses, 2 years' teaching or related experience (M Ed); for doctorate, master's degree, minimum graduate GPA of 3.5. Additional exam requirements/recommendations for international students: Required—TOEFL (minimum score 580 paper-based; 93 iBT). Electronic applications accepted. *Faculty research:* Movement and brain plasticity, gibberellin physiology, photosynthesis, carbon cycling, molecular properties of main-group ring components.

University of Louisville, Graduate School, College of Arts and Sciences, Department of Anthropology, Louisville, KY 40292-0001. Offers MA. *Program availability:* Part-time, evening/weekend. *Faculty:* 11 full-time (5 women), 5 part-time/adjunct (3 women). *Students:* 5 full-time (4 women), 11 part-time (8 women); includes 1 minority (Two or more races, non-Hispanic/Latino). Average age 32. 6 applicants, 33% accepted, 2 enrolled. In 2017, 3 master's awarded. *Degree requirements:* For master's, variable foreign language requirement, thesis optional. *Entrance requirements:* For master's, GRE, transcripts, statement of purpose, references. *Application deadline:* For fall admission, 11/1 priority date for domestic and international students; for spring admission, 4/1 priority date for domestic and international students. Applications are processed on a rolling basis. Application fee: $65. Electronic applications accepted. *Expenses:* Tuition, state resident: full-time $12,246; part-time $681 per credit hour. Tuition, nonresident: full-time $25,486; part-time $1417 per credit hour. *Required fees:* $196. Tuition and fees vary according to course load, program and reciprocity agreements. *Financial support:* In 2017–18, 1 teaching assistantship (averaging $12,000 per year) was awarded; scholarships/grants, health care benefits, and unspecified assistantships also available. *Faculty research:* Human-environment interaction, political economy, social justice, globalization, infectious diseases. *Total annual research expenditures:* $75,000. *Unit head:* Dr. Jonathan Haws, Chair and Professor, 502-852-2423, Fax: 502-852-4560, E-mail: johnathan.haws@louisville.edu. *Application contact:* Dr. Lisa Markowitz, Associate Professor, 502-852-2426, Fax: 502-852-6536, E-mail: lisa.markowitz@louisville.edu.
Website: http://louisville.edu/anthropology

University of Maine, Graduate School, College of Liberal Arts and Sciences, Department of Anthropology, Orono, ME 04469. Offers anthropology and environmental policy (PhD). *Faculty:* 10 full-time (5 women). *Students:* 7 full-time (5 women), 2 part-time (both women). Average age 31. 11 applicants, 36% accepted, 3 enrolled. *Degree requirements:* For doctorate, comprehensive exam, thesis/dissertation. *Entrance requirements:* For doctorate, GRE General Test. Additional exam requirements/recommendations for international students: Required—TOEFL (minimum score 80 iBT), IELTS (minimum score 6.5). *Application deadline:* For fall admission, 1/15 for domestic and international students. Application fee: $65. Electronic applications accepted. *Expenses:* Tuition, state resident: full-time $7722; part-time $429 per credit hour. Tuition, nonresident: full-time $25,146; part-time $1397 per credit hour. *Required fees:* $1162; $581 per credit hour. *Financial support:* In 2017–18, 11 students received support, including 1 fellowship (averaging $25,000 per year), 2 research assistantships (averaging $15,200 per year), 3 teaching assistantships (averaging $15,200 per year); scholarships/grants and unspecified assistantships also available. Financial award application deadline: 3/1. *Faculty research:* Historical ecology, human dimensions of climate change, conservation, indigenous studies. *Unit head:* Gregory Zaro, Chair, 207-581-1857, Fax: 207-581-1823, E-mail: gregory.zaro@umit.maine.edu. *Application contact:* Scott G. Delcourt, Assistant Vice President for Graduate Studies and Senior Associate Dean, 207-581-3291, Fax: 207-581-3232, E-mail: graduate@maine.edu.
Website: http://www.umaine.edu/anthropology/graduate-programs/

The University of Manchester, School of Arts, Histories and Cultures, Manchester, United Kingdom. Offers anthropology, media and performance (PhD); applied theatre professional (PhD); archaeology (PhD); art history and visual studies (PhD); arts management and cultural policy (PhD); classics and ancient history (PhD); composition (PhD); creative writing (PhD); drama (PhD); economic and social history (PhD); electroacoustic composition (PhD); English and American studies (PhD); history (PhD); humanitarianism and conflict response (PhD); museology (PhD); music (PhD); musicology (PhD); religions and theology (PhD).

The University of Manchester, School of Social Sciences, Manchester, United Kingdom. Offers ethnographic documentary (M Phil); interdisciplinary study of culture (PhD); philosophy (PhD); politics (PhD); social anthropology (PhD); social anthropology with visual media (PhD); social change (PhD); social statistics (PhD); sociology (PhD); visual anthropology (M Phil).

University of Manitoba, Faculty of Graduate Studies, Faculty of Arts, Department of Anthropology, Winnipeg, MB R3T 2N2, Canada. Offers MA, PhD. *Degree requirements:* For master's, thesis or alternative.

University of Maryland, College Park, Academic Affairs, College of Behavioral and Social Sciences, Department of Anthropology, College Park, MD 20742. Offers applied anthropology (MAA). *Program availability:* Part-time, evening/weekend. *Degree requirements:* For master's, internship. *Entrance requirements:* For master's, GRE General Test, minimum GPA of 3.0, 3 letters of recommendation. Additional exam requirements/recommendations for international students: Required—TOEFL. Electronic applications accepted. *Faculty research:* Archaeology, human biodiversity, cultural and resource management.

University of Massachusetts Amherst, Graduate School, College of Social and Behavioral Sciences, Department of Anthropology, Amherst, MA 01003. Offers MA, PhD. *Program availability:* Part-time. Terminal master's awarded for partial completion of doctoral program. *Degree requirements:* For master's, thesis or alternative; for doctorate, comprehensive exam, thesis/dissertation. *Entrance requirements:* Additional exam requirements/recommendations for international students: Required—TOEFL (minimum score 550 paper-based; 80 iBT), IELTS (minimum score 6.5). Electronic applications accepted.

University of Memphis, Graduate School, College of Arts and Sciences, Department of Anthropology, Memphis, TN 38152. Offers medical anthropology (MA). *Program availability:* Part-time. *Faculty:* 5 full-time (4 women), 2 part-time/adjunct (1 woman). *Students:* 15 full-time (13 women), 2 part-time (1 woman); includes 6 minority (4 Black or African American, non-Hispanic/Latino; 1 Asian, non-Hispanic/Latino; 1 Two or more races, non-Hispanic/Latino), 1 international. Average age 29. 9 applicants, 100% accepted, 7 enrolled. In 2017, 8 master's awarded. *Degree requirements:* For master's,

comprehensive exam, practicum. *Entrance requirements:* For master's, GRE General Test, minimum GPA of 3.0, letter of intent, 3 letters of recommendation. *Application deadline:* For fall admission, 1/31 priority date for domestic students; for spring admission, 9/1 priority date for domestic students. Applications are processed on a rolling basis. Application fee: $35 ($60 for international students). Electronic applications accepted. *Expenses:* Contact institution. *Financial support:* In 2017–18, 9 research assistantships with full tuition reimbursements (averaging $13,334 per year) were awarded; fellowships, teaching assistantships with full tuition reimbursements, career-related internships or fieldwork, Federal Work-Study, scholarships/grants, and unspecified assistantships also available. Financial award application deadline: 2/1; financial award applicants required to submit FAFSA. *Faculty research:* Community development, medical anthropology, environmental justice, health disparities, cultural identity and heritage. *Unit head:* Dr. Ruthbeth Finerman, Chair, 901-678-2080, Fax: 901-678-2069, E-mail: finerman@memphis.edu. *Application contact:* Dr. Katheryn Hicks, Coordinator of Graduate Studies, 901-678-3328, Fax: 901-678-2069, E-mail: kahicks2@memphis.edu.
Website: http://www.memphis.edu/anthropology

University of Michigan, Rackham Graduate School, College of Literature, Science, and the Arts, Department of Anthropology, Ann Arbor, MI 48109. Offers anthropological archaeology (PhD); biological anthropology (PhD); linguistic anthropology (PhD); sociocultural anthropology (PhD). *Faculty:* 42 full-time (18 women), 3 part-time/adjunct (1 woman). *Students:* 99 full-time (62 women); includes 23 minority (1 Black or African American, non-Hispanic/Latino; 2 American Indian or Alaska Native, non-Hispanic/Latino; 7 Asian, non-Hispanic/Latino; 10 Hispanic/Latino; 3 Two or more races, non-Hispanic/Latino), 17 international. Average age 30. 181 applicants, 12% accepted, 12 enrolled. In 2017, 9 doctorates awarded. *Degree requirements:* For doctorate, one foreign language, comprehensive exam, thesis/dissertation, preliminary examination, oral defense of dissertation. *Entrance requirements:* For doctorate, GRE General Test. Additional exam requirements/recommendations for international students: Required—TOEFL (minimum score 560 paper-based; 84 iBT). *Application deadline:* For fall admission, 12/15 for domestic and international students. Application fee: $75 ($90 for international students). Electronic applications accepted. *Expenses:* Tuition, state resident: full-time $22,368; part-time $1201 per credit hour. Tuition, nonresident: full-time $45,156; part-time $2467 per credit hour. *Required fees:* $376 per term. Tuition and fees vary according to course load, degree level and program. *Financial support:* In 2017–18, 72 students received support, including 36 fellowships with full tuition reimbursements available (averaging $19,000 per year), 7 research assistantships with full tuition reimbursements available (averaging $20,398 per year), 31 teaching assistantships with full tuition reimbursements available (averaging $20,398 per year); scholarships/grants, traineeships, health care benefits, tuition waivers (full), and unspecified assistantships also available. Financial award application deadline: 3/1; financial award applicants required to submit FAFSA. *Faculty research:* Sociocultural, linguistic, biological and archaeological anthropology. *Unit head:* Dr. Andrew Shryock, Chair, 734-764-7274, Fax: 734-763-6077. *Application contact:* Katia Kitchen, Graduate Program Assistant, 734-936-7933, Fax: 734-763-6077, E-mail: kitchenk@umich.edu.
Website: http://www.lsa.umich.edu/anthro/

University of Michigan, Rackham Graduate School, College of Literature, Science, and the Arts, Doctoral Program in Anthropology and History, Ann Arbor, MI 48109. Offers PhD. *Degree requirements:* For doctorate, 2 foreign languages, thesis/dissertation, oral defense of dissertation, preliminary exam. *Entrance requirements:* For doctorate, GRE General Test, writing sample. Additional exam requirements/recommendations for international students: Required—TOEFL. Electronic applications accepted. *Expenses:* Tuition, state resident: full-time $22,368; part-time $1201 per credit hour. Tuition, nonresident: full-time $45,156; part-time $2467 per credit hour. *Required fees:* $376 per term. Tuition and fees vary according to course load, degree level and program. *Faculty research:* Historical anthropology.

University of Michigan, School of Social Work, Interdisciplinary PhD Program in Social Work and Social Science, Ann Arbor, MI 48109. Offers social work and anthropology (PhD); social work and economics (PhD); social work and political science (PhD); social work and psychology (PhD); social work and sociology (PhD). Programs offered through the Rackham Graduate School. *Faculty:* 57 full-time (36 women). *Students:* 53 full-time (38 women); includes 27 minority (10 Black or African American, non-Hispanic/Latino; 2 American Indian or Alaska Native, non-Hispanic/Latino; 9 Asian, non-Hispanic/Latino; 6 Hispanic/Latino). Average age 32. 124 applicants, 6% accepted, 7 enrolled. In 2017, 10 doctorates awarded. *Degree requirements:* For doctorate, thesis/dissertation, oral defense of dissertation, preliminary exam. *Entrance requirements:* For doctorate, GRE General Test. Additional exam requirements/recommendations for international students: Required—TOEFL (minimum score 620 paper-based, 88 iBT) or IELTS. *Application deadline:* For fall admission, 12/1 for domestic and international students. Application fee: $75 ($90 for international students). Electronic applications accepted. *Expenses:* Contact institution. *Financial support:* In 2017–18, 59 students received support, including 24 fellowships with full tuition reimbursements available (averaging $17,600 per year), 7 research assistantships with full tuition reimbursements available (averaging $20,399 per year), 21 teaching assistantships with full tuition reimbursements available (averaging $20,399 per year); career-related internships or fieldwork, scholarships/grants, traineeships, health care benefits, tuition waivers (full and partial), and unspecified assistantships also available. Financial award application deadline: 12/1; financial award applicants required to submit FAFSA. *Faculty research:* Children and family, aging, community organization, health and mental health, police and evaluation. *Total annual research expenditures:* $4.1 million. *Unit head:* Dr. William Elliott, III, Director, 734-763-5768, E-mail: willelli@umich.edu. *Application contact:* Todd Huynh, Graduate Coordinator, 734-647-2554, Fax: 734-615-3192, E-mail: ssw.phd.info@umich.edu.
Website: https://ssw.umich.edu/offices/phd

University of Minnesota, Duluth, Graduate School, College of Liberal Arts, Department of Sociology/Anthropology, Duluth, MN 55812-2496. Offers criminology (MA); liberal studies (MLS). *Program availability:* Part-time. *Degree requirements:* For master's, thesis or alternative. *Entrance requirements:* For master's, interview, minimum GPA of 3.0, letters of recommendation. Additional exam requirements/recommendations for international students: Required—TOEFL. *Faculty research:* Nature of knowledge, philosophy of science, ecology, cultural studies, language.

University of Minnesota, Twin Cities Campus, Graduate School, College of Liberal Arts, Department of Anthropology, Minneapolis, MN 55455-0213. Offers MA, PhD. Terminal master's awarded for partial completion of doctoral program. *Degree requirements:* For master's, thesis optional; for doctorate, comprehensive exam, thesis/dissertation. *Entrance requirements:* For master's and doctorate, GRE. Additional exam requirements/recommendations for international students: Recommended—TOEFL. Electronic applications accepted. *Faculty research:* Psychological/psychoanalytic anthropology, gender and feminist anthropology, economic anthropology, medical anthropology, paleoanthropology.

University of Mississippi, Graduate School, College of Liberal Arts, University, MS 38677. Offers anthropology (MA); biology (MS, PhD); chemistry (MS, DA, PhD); creative writing (MFA); documentary expression (MFA); economics (MA, PhD); English (MA, PhD); experimental psychology (PhD); history (MA, PhD); mathematics (MS, PhD); modern languages (MA); music (MM); philosophy (MA); physics (MA, MS, PhD); political science (MA, PhD); Southern studies (MA); studio art (MFA). *Program availability:* Part-time. *Faculty:* 465 full-time (207 women), 82 part-time/adjunct (46 women). *Students:* 466 full-time (229 women), 72 part-time (34 women); includes 87 minority (38 Black or African American, non-Hispanic/Latino; 18 Asian, non-Hispanic/Latino; 24 Hispanic/Latino; 7 Two or more races, non-Hispanic/Latino), 121 international. Average age 29. *Degree requirements:* For doctorate, thesis/dissertation. *Entrance requirements:* For master's, GRE General Test, minimum GPA of 3.0; for doctorate, GRE General Test. Additional exam requirements/recommendations for international students: Required—TOEFL. *Application deadline:* For fall admission, 2/1 priority date for domestic students; for spring admission, 10/1 for domestic students. Applications are processed on a rolling basis. Application fee: $50. Electronic applications accepted. *Financial support:* Fellowships, research assistantships, teaching assistantships, career-related internships or fieldwork, Federal Work-Study, institutionally sponsored loans, scholarships/grants, and unspecified assistantships available. Financial award application deadline: 3/1; financial award applicants required to submit FAFSA. *Unit head:* Dr. Lee Michael Cohen, Dean, 662-915-7177, Fax: 662-915-5792, E-mail: libarts@olemiss.edu. *Application contact:* Dr. Christy M. Wyandt, Associate Dean of Graduate School, 662-915-7474, Fax: 662-915-7577, E-mail: cwyandt@olemiss.edu.

University of Missouri, Office of Research and Graduate Studies, College of Arts and Science, Department of Anthropology, Columbia, MO 65211. Offers MA, PhD. *Degree requirements:* For master's, thesis (for some programs); for doctorate, one foreign language, comprehensive exam, thesis/dissertation. *Entrance requirements:* For master's, GRE General Test (minimum score 1000 verbal and quantitative), minimum GPA of 3.25 in last 60 hours and in all anthropology courses; for doctorate, GRE General Test (minimum score 1000 verbal and quantitative), minimum GPA of 3.5 in previous graduate work. Additional exam requirements/recommendations for international students: Required—TOEFL (minimum score 500 paper-based; 61 iBT), IELTS (minimum score 5.5). Electronic applications accepted. *Faculty research:* Social/cultural anthropology, biological anthropology, archaeology.

University of Montana, Graduate School, College of Humanities and Sciences, Department of Anthropology, Missoula, MT 59812. Offers anthropology (MA, PhD); applied anthropology (PhD); applied medical anthropology (MA); cultural heritage (MA, PhD); forensic anthropology (MA); linguistic anthropology (MA). *Degree requirements:* For master's, thesis (for some programs). *Entrance requirements:* For master's, GRE General Test. Additional exam requirements/recommendations for international students: Required—TOEFL. *Faculty research:* Historical preservation, plateau-plains archaeology and ethnohistory.

University of Nebraska–Lincoln, Graduate College, College of Arts and Sciences, Department of Anthropology and Geography, Program in Anthropology, Lincoln, NE 68588. Offers MA. *Degree requirements:* For master's, thesis optional. *Entrance requirements:* For master's, GRE General Test. Additional exam requirements/recommendations for international students: Required—TOEFL (minimum score 500 paper-based). Electronic applications accepted. *Faculty research:* Cultural, archaeologic, linguistic, and physical anthropology.

University of Nevada, Las Vegas, Graduate College, College of Liberal Arts, Department of Anthropology, Las Vegas, NV 89154-5003. Offers MA, PhD. *Program availability:* Part-time. *Faculty:* 13 full-time (4 women), 1 part-time/adjunct (0 women). *Students:* 29 full-time (15 women), 13 part-time (8 women); includes 13 minority (1 American Indian or Alaska Native, non-Hispanic/Latino; 2 Asian, non-Hispanic/Latino; 7 Hispanic/Latino; 3 Two or more races, non-Hispanic/Latino), 1 international. Average age 33. 54 applicants, 26% accepted, 7 enrolled. In 2017, 2 master's, 3 doctorates awarded. *Degree requirements:* For master's, thesis, oral defense of thesis; for doctorate, comprehensive exam, thesis/dissertation, oral defense of dissertation. *Entrance requirements:* For master's, GRE General Test, 18 semester credit hours in anthropology with minimum GPA of 3.0; research paper; letter of intent; 3 letters of recommendation; for doctorate, GRE General Test, minimum GPA of 3.5 for previous graduate work; example of previous work; statement of intent; 3 letters of recommendation. Additional exam requirements/recommendations for international students: Required—TOEFL (minimum score 550 paper-based; 80 iBT), IELTS (minimum score 7). *Application deadline:* For fall admission, 2/1 for domestic students. Application fee: $60 ($95 for international students). Electronic applications accepted. *Expenses:* $275 per credit, $850 per course, $7,969 per year resident, $22,157 per year non-resident, $7,094 non-resident fee (7 credits or more), $1,307 annual health insurance fee. *Financial support:* In 2017–18, 25 students received support, including 1 fellowship with partial tuition reimbursement available (averaging $20,000 per year), 7 research assistantships with partial tuition reimbursements available (averaging $15,143 per year), 18 teaching assistantships with partial tuition reimbursements available (averaging $15,667 per year); institutionally sponsored loans, scholarships/grants, health care benefits, and unspecified assistantships also available. Financial award application deadline: 3/15; financial award applicants required to submit FAFSA. *Faculty research:* Food and nutrition, adaptive strategies, childhood and parenting, sexuality, gender and identity. *Total annual research expenditures:* $185,655. *Unit head:* Dr. Barbara Roth, Chair/Professor, 702-895-3646, Fax: 702-895-4823, E-mail: barbara.roth@unlv.edu. *Application contact:* Dr. Peter Gray, Graduate Coordinator, 702-895-3586, Fax: 702-895-4823, E-mail: peter.gray@unlv.edu.
Website: http://anthro.unlv.edu/

University of Nevada, Reno, Graduate School, College of Liberal Arts, Department of Anthropology, Reno, NV 89557. Offers MA, PhD. Terminal master's awarded for partial completion of doctoral program. *Degree requirements:* For master's, thesis; for doctorate, thesis/dissertation. *Entrance requirements:* For master's, GRE, minimum GPA of 2.75; for doctorate, GRE, minimum GPA of 3.0. Additional exam requirements/recommendations for international students: Required—TOEFL (minimum score 500 paper-based; 61 iBT), IELTS (minimum score 6). Electronic applications accepted. *Faculty research:* Ethnology, linguistics, cultural/medical/religious/ethnic relations, ecological anthropology, historical anthropology.

University of New Brunswick Fredericton, School of Graduate Studies, Faculty of Arts, Department of Anthropology, Fredericton, NB E3B 5A3, Canada. Offers MA. *Program availability:* Part-time. *Degree requirements:* For master's, thesis. *Entrance requirements:* For master's, minimum GPA of 3.0. Additional exam requirements/recommendations for international students: Required—TOEFL. Electronic applications accepted. *Faculty research:* Medical anthropology, anthropology of education, community-based fisheries, maritime archaeology, world prehistory, geoarchaeology, zooarchaeology socio-cultural anthropology, bioarchaeology, forensics, globalization, legal anthropology.

University of New Mexico, Graduate Studies, College of Arts and Sciences, Program in Anthropology, Albuquerque, NM 87131-2039. Offers archaeology (MA, MS, PhD); ethnology (MA, MS, PhD); evolutionary anthropology (PhD); public archaeology (MA, MS, PhD). *Faculty:* 28 full-time (10 women), 2 part-time/adjunct (0 women). *Students:* 47 full-time (34 women), 58 part-time (34 women); includes 25 minority (4 American Indian or Alaska Native, non-Hispanic/Latino; 1 Asian, non-Hispanic/Latino; 15 Hispanic/Latino; 5 Two or more races, non-Hispanic/Latino), 8 international. Average age 34. 58

applicants, 34% accepted, 20 enrolled. In 2017, 18 master's, 14 doctorates awarded. Terminal master's awarded for partial completion of doctoral program. *Degree requirements:* For master's, comprehensive exam (for some programs), thesis or alternative, 1-2 exams; for doctorate, one foreign language, comprehensive exam, thesis/dissertation, exam, proposal, oral defense, skill and/or second language. *Entrance requirements:* For master's and doctorate, GRE General Test, 3 letters of recommendation, letter of interest, transcripts. Additional exam requirements/recommendations for international students: Required—TOEFL (minimum score 550 paper-based), IELTS (minimum score 7). *Application deadline:* For fall admission, 1/4 for domestic and international students. Application fee: $50. Electronic applications accepted. *Financial support:* Fellowships, research assistantships with partial tuition reimbursements, teaching assistantships with partial tuition reimbursements, career-related internships or fieldwork, Federal Work-Study, institutionally sponsored loans, scholarships/grants, traineeships, health care benefits, tuition waivers (partial), and unspecified assistantships available. Support available to part-time students. Financial award application deadline: 3/1; financial award applicants required to submit FAFSA. *Faculty research:* Ethnology, archaeology, evolutionary anthropology, environment, water and land use, gender and social frameworks, Greater Southwest, Latin America, political economy, public anthropology. *Total annual research expenditures:* $875,790. *Unit head:* Michael W. Graves, Chair, 505-277-4524, Fax: 505-277-0874, E-mail: mwgraves@unm.edu. *Application contact:* Erika E. Gerety, Program Advisement Coordinator, 505-277-2732, Fax: 505-277-0874, E-mail: erika@unm.edu.
Website: http://www.unm.edu/~anthro/

The University of North Carolina at Chapel Hill, Graduate School, College of Arts and Sciences, Department of Anthropology, Chapel Hill, NC 27599-3115. Offers MA, PhD. Terminal master's awarded for partial completion of doctoral program. *Degree requirements:* For master's, variable foreign language requirement, thesis; for doctorate, variable foreign language requirement, comprehensive exam, thesis/dissertation. *Entrance requirements:* For master's and doctorate, GRE General Test, minimum GPA of 3.0. Additional exam requirements/recommendations for international students: Required—TOEFL. Electronic applications accepted. *Faculty research:* Archeology, ecology and evolution, medical anthropology, social systems, anthropology of meaning.

The University of North Carolina at Charlotte, College of Liberal Arts and Sciences, Department of Anthropology, Charlotte, NC 28223-0001. Offers MA. *Program availability:* Part-time. *Faculty:* 11 full-time (7 women), 1 part-time/adjunct (0 women). *Students:* 8 full-time (7 women), 10 part-time (8 women); includes 6 minority (2 Black or African American, non-Hispanic/Latino; 1 Asian, non-Hispanic/Latino; 1 Hispanic/Latino; 2 Two or more races, non-Hispanic/Latino). Average age 30. 28 applicants, 61% accepted, 7 enrolled. In 2017, 4 master's awarded. *Degree requirements:* For master's, research thesis or applied practicum and project report. *Entrance requirements:* For master's, GRE, three letters of recommendation from individuals who can comment on candidate's academic and professional promise, at least two from academic referees; statement of purpose that discusses applicant's specific interests in anthropology and professional goals; transcripts from all colleges or universities attended. Additional exam requirements/recommendations for international students: Required—TOEFL (minimum score 523 paper-based, 70 iBT) or IELTS (6.5). *Application deadline:* For fall admission, 3/1 priority date for domestic and international students. Applications are processed on a rolling basis. Application fee: $75. Electronic applications accepted. *Expenses:* Tuition, state resident: full-time $4337. Tuition, nonresident: full-time $17,771. *Required fees:* $3211. Tuition and fees vary according to course load and program. *Financial support:* In 2017–18, 7 students received support, including 3 research assistantships (averaging $8,659 per year), 4 teaching assistantships (averaging $9,125 per year); institutionally sponsored loans, scholarships/grants, and unspecified assistantships also available. Support available to part-time students. Financial award application deadline: 3/1. *Faculty research:* Impact of environment on the social strategies and reproductive careers of Sifaka; molecular anthropology: the application of genetic data; family abuse and women's health; aging cross-culturally; production and circulation of knowledge in material form; the relationship among knowledge, power, policy and practice as they pertain to health and health care; the development of ranked societies in prehistory. *Total annual research expenditures:* $92,416. *Unit head:* Dr. Steven Falconer, Chair, 704-687-7459, E-mail: sfalcon1@uncc.edu. *Application contact:* Kathy B. Giddings, Director of Graduate Admissions, 704-687-5503, Fax: 704-687-1668, E-mail: gradadm@uncc.edu.
Website: http://anthropology.uncc.edu/

University of North Georgia, Department of History, Anthropology and Philosophy, Dahlonega, GA 30597. Offers history (MA), including American history, military history, world history. *Program availability:* Part-time, evening/weekend. *Faculty:* 10 full-time (5 women), 1 part-time/adjunct (0 women). *Students:* 2 full-time (0 women), 13 part-time (4 women); includes 1 minority (Hispanic/Latino). Average age 34. 9 applicants, 78% accepted, 3 enrolled. In 2017, 2 master's awarded. *Degree requirements:* For master's, thesis optional. *Entrance requirements:* For master's, GRE, 3 recommendations, writing sample, letter of intent, minimum GPA of 3.0. Additional exam requirements/recommendations for international students: Required—TOEFL (minimum score 550 paper-based; 79 iBT), IELTS (minimum score 6.5). *Application deadline:* For fall admission, 4/1 priority date for domestic students. Applications are processed on a rolling basis. Application fee: $40. Electronic applications accepted. *Expenses:* Contact institution. *Financial support:* Unspecified assistantships available. Financial award application deadline: 3/17; financial award applicants required to submit FAFSA. *Unit head:* Dr. Jeff Pardue, Department Head, 678-717-3867. *Application contact:* Melinda Maxwell, Director of Graduate Admissions, 706-864-1543, E-mail: melinda.maxwell@ung.edu.
Website: http://ung.edu/history-anthropology-philosophy/

University of North Texas, Robert B. Toulouse School of Graduate Studies, Denton, TX 76203-5459. Offers accounting (MS); applied anthropology (MA, MS); applied behavior analysis (Certificate); applied geography (MA); applied technology and performance improvement (M Ed, MS); art education (MA); art history (MA); art museum education (Certificate); arts leadership (Certificate); audiology (Au D); behavior analysis (MS); behavioral science (PhD); biochemistry and molecular biology (MS); biology (MA, MS); biomedical engineering (MS); business analysis (MS); chemistry (MS); clinical health psychology (PhD); communication studies (MA, MS); computer engineering (MS); computer science (MS); counseling (M Ed, MS), including clinical mental health counseling (MS), college and university counseling, elementary school counseling, secondary school counseling; creative writing (MA); criminal justice (MS); curriculum and instruction (M Ed); decision sciences (MBA); design (MA, MFA), including fashion design (MFA), innovation studies, interior design (MFA); early childhood studies (MS); economics (MS); educational leadership (M Ed, Ed D); educational psychology (MS, PhD), including family studies (MS), gifted and talented (MS), human development (MS), learning and cognition (MS), research, measurement and evaluation (MS); electrical engineering (MS); emergency management (MPA); engineering technology (MS); English (MA); English as a second language (MA); environmental science (MS); finance (MBA, MS); financial management (MPA); French (MA); health services management (MBA); higher education (M Ed, Ed D); history (MA, MS); hospitality management (MS); human resources management (MPA); information science (MS); information systems (PhD); information technologies (MBA); interdisciplinary studies (MA, MS); international studies (MA); international sustainable tourism (MS); jazz studies (MM); journalism (MA, MJ, Graduate Certificate), including interactive and virtual digital communication (Graduate Certificate), narrative journalism (Graduate Certificate), public relations (Graduate Certificate); kinesiology (MS); linguistics (MA); local government management (MPA); logistics (PhD); logistics and supply chain management (MBA); long-term care, senior housing, and aging services (MA); management (PhD); marketing (MBA); mathematics (MA, MS); mechanical and energy engineering (MS, PhD); music (MA), including ethnomusicology, music theory, musicology, performance; music composition (PhD); music education (MM Ed, PhD); nonprofit management (MPA); operations and supply chain management (MBA); performance (MM, DMA); philosophy (MA); political science (MA); professional and technical communication (MA); radio, television and film (MA, MFA); rehabilitation counseling (Certificate); sociology (MA); Spanish (MA); special education (M Ed); speech-language pathology (MA); strategic management (MBA); studio art (MFA); teaching (M Ed); MBA/MS. *Program availability:* Part-time, evening/weekend, online learning. Terminal master's awarded for partial completion of doctoral program. *Degree requirements:* For master's, variable foreign language requirement, comprehensive exam (for some programs), thesis (for some programs); for doctorate, variable foreign language requirement, comprehensive exam (for some programs), thesis/dissertation; for other advanced degree, variable foreign language requirement, comprehensive exam (for some programs). *Entrance requirements:* For master's and doctorate, GRE, GMAT. Additional exam requirements/recommendations for international students: Required—TOEFL (minimum score 550 paper-based; 79 iBT). Electronic applications accepted.

University of Oklahoma, College of Arts and Sciences, Department of Anthropology, Norman, OK 73019. Offers anthropology (MA, PhD); applied linguistic anthropology (MA); archaeology (PhD); health and human biology (PhD); socio-cultural and linguistics (PhD); socio-cultural anthropology (MA). *Faculty:* 27 full-time (13 women). *Students:* 26 full-time (15 women), 23 part-time (17 women); includes 11 minority (5 American Indian or Alaska Native, non-Hispanic/Latino; 1 Hispanic/Latino; 5 Two or more races, non-Hispanic/Latino), 3 international. Average age 31. 29 applicants, 62% accepted, 15 enrolled. In 2017, 10 master's, 6 doctorates awarded. *Degree requirements:* For master's, thesis; for doctorate, comprehensive exam, thesis/dissertation. *Entrance requirements:* For master's and doctorate, GRE, minimum undergraduate GPA of 3.0; statement of purpose; 2 letters of recommendation. Additional exam requirements/recommendations for international students: Required—TOEFL (minimum score 79 iBT) or IELTS (minimum score 6.5). *Application deadline:* For spring admission, 2/1 for domestic and international students. Application fee: $50 ($100 for international students). Electronic applications accepted. *Expenses:* Tuition, state resident: full-time $5119; part-time $213.30 per credit hour. Tuition, nonresident: full-time $19,778; part-time $824.10 per credit hour. *Required fees:* $3458; $133.55 per credit hour. $126.50 per semester. *Financial support:* In 2017–18, 36 students received support, including 2 research assistantships with full tuition reimbursements available (averaging $14,670 per year), 10 teaching assistantships with full tuition reimbursements available (averaging $14,670 per year); career-related internships or fieldwork, Federal Work-Study, institutionally sponsored loans, health care benefits, and unspecified assistantships also available. Financial award application deadline: 6/1; financial award applicants required to submit FAFSA. *Faculty research:* North American archaeology; linguistics including applied; health and human biology; sociocultural anthropology; native North America. *Total annual research expenditures:* $1.3 million. *Unit head:* Dr. Diane Warren, Associate Professor and Department Chair, 405-325-7609, Fax: 405-325-7386, E-mail: dmwarren@ou.edu. *Application contact:* Dr. Patrick Livingood, Associate Professor and Graduate Liaison, 405-397-0215, Fax: 405-325-7386, E-mail: patrickl@ou.edu.
Website: http://cas.ou.edu/anthropology

University of Oregon, Graduate School, College of Arts and Sciences, Department of Anthropology, Eugene, OR 97403. Offers MA, MS, PhD. Terminal master's awarded for partial completion of doctoral program. *Degree requirements:* For master's, one foreign language; for doctorate, 2 foreign languages, thesis/dissertation. *Entrance requirements:* For master's and doctorate, GRE General Test. Additional exam requirements/recommendations for international students: Required—TOEFL. *Faculty research:* Prehistory, primatology, cultural anthropology of Native Americans, human evolution, Africa.

University of Ottawa, Faculty of Graduate and Postdoctoral Studies, Faculty of Social Sciences, Department of Sociology and Anthropology, Ottawa, ON K1N 6N5, Canada. Offers MA. *Degree requirements:* For master's, thesis or alternative. *Entrance requirements:* For master's, honors bachelor's degree or equivalent, minimum B average. Electronic applications accepted. *Faculty research:* Inter-ethnic relations, development, political policies.

University of Pennsylvania, School of Arts and Sciences, Graduate Group in Anthropology, Philadelphia, PA 19104. Offers AM, MS, PhD. *Faculty:* 17 full-time (8 women), 12 part-time/adjunct (7 women). *Students:* 62 full-time (43 women), 4 part-time (2 women); includes 11 minority (4 Black or African American, non-Hispanic/Latino; 1 Asian, non-Hispanic/Latino; 3 Hispanic/Latino; 3 Two or more races, non-Hispanic/Latino), 13 international. Average age 30. 157 applicants, 10% accepted, 11 enrolled. In 2017, 4 master's, 5 doctorates awarded. Terminal master's awarded for partial completion of doctoral program.
Website: http://www.sas.upenn.edu/graduate-division

University of Pittsburgh, Kenneth P. Dietrich School of Arts and Sciences, Department of Anthropology, Pittsburgh, PA 15260. Offers MA, PhD. *Program availability:* Part-time, online learning. *Faculty:* 20 full-time (8 women), 5 part-time/adjunct (2 women). *Students:* 62 full-time (41 women), 3 part-time (2 women); includes 4 minority (2 Black or African American, non-Hispanic/Latino; 2 Hispanic/Latino), 32 international. Average age 24. 105 applicants, 18% accepted, 11 enrolled. In 2017, 4 master's, 13 doctorates awarded. Terminal master's awarded for partial completion of doctoral program. *Degree requirements:* For master's, one foreign language, thesis or alternative; for doctorate, one foreign language, comprehensive exam, thesis/dissertation, preliminary exam. *Entrance requirements:* For master's and doctorate, GRE General Test. Additional exam requirements/recommendations for international students: Required—TOEFL (minimum score 550 paper-based; 90 iBT), IELTS (minimum score 6.5). *Application deadline:* For fall admission, 1/15 for domestic and international students. Applications are processed on a rolling basis. Application fee: $50. Electronic applications accepted. *Financial support:* In 2017–18, 24 fellowships with full tuition reimbursements (averaging $22,896 per year), 1 research assistantship with full tuition reimbursement (averaging $15,060 per year), 25 teaching assistantships with full tuition reimbursements (averaging $19,180 per year) were awarded; health care benefits, tuition waivers (full), and unspecified assistantships also available. Financial award application deadline: 1/15. *Faculty research:* Conflict studies; ethnicity, nationalism, and the state; Latin American archaeology; human evolutionary biology. *Total annual research expenditures:* $79,158. *Unit head:* Dr. Bryan Hanks, Chair, 412-648-7530, E-mail: bkh5@pitt.edu. *Application contact:* Phyllis J. Deasy, Graduate Administrator, 412-648-7504, E-mail: pdeasy@pitt.edu.
Website: http://www.anthropology.pitt.edu

University of Regina, Faculty of Graduate Studies and Research, Faculty of Arts, Department of Anthropology, Regina, SK S4S 0A2, Canada. Offers MA. Offered as a special case program. *Program availability:* Part-time. *Faculty:* 5 full-time (2 women), 1 part-time/adjunct (0 women). *Students:* 2 full-time (1 woman). 2 applicants, 50% accepted. *Degree requirements:* For master's, thesis. *Entrance requirements:* Additional exam requirements/recommendations for international students: Required—TOEFL (minimum score 580 paper-based; 80 iBT), IELTS (minimum score 6.5), PTE (minimum score 59). *Application deadline:* Applications are processed on a rolling basis. Application fee: $100. Electronic applications accepted. *Expenses:* $10,681. *Financial support:* Fellowships, research assistantships, teaching assistantships, and scholarships/grants available. Financial award application deadline: 6/15. *Unit head:* Dr. Tabias Sperlich, Department Head, 306-585-4773, E-mail: tobias.sperlich@uregina.ca.
Website: http://www.uregina.ca/arts/anthropology/

University of Rhode Island, Graduate School, College of Arts and Sciences, Department of History, Kingston, RI 02881. Offers archaeology and anthropology (MA); European history (MA), including European history, United States history; MLIS/MA. *Program availability:* Part-time. *Faculty:* 17 full-time (8 women). *Students:* 7 full-time (1 woman), 6 part-time (3 women). 12 applicants, 92% accepted, 5 enrolled. In 2017, 5 master's awarded. *Entrance requirements:* Additional exam requirements/recommendations for international students: Required—TOEFL. *Application deadline:* For fall admission, 7/15 for domestic students; for spring admission, 11/15 for domestic students. Application fee: $65. Electronic applications accepted. *Expenses:* Tuition, state resident: full-time $12,706; part-time $786 per credit. Tuition, nonresident: full-time $25,216; part-time $1401 per credit. *Required fees:* $1598; $45 per credit. One-time fee: $30 part-time. *Financial support:* In 2017–18, 3 teaching assistantships with tuition reimbursements (averaging $17,724 per year) were awarded. Financial award application deadline: 2/1; financial award applicants required to submit FAFSA. *Unit head:* Dr. Rod Mather, Chair, 401-874-4093, E-mail: rodmather@uri.edu. *Application contact:* Dr. Evelyn Sterne, Director of Graduate Studies, 401-874-4074, E-mail: sterne@uri.edu.
Website: http://www.uri.edu/artsci/his/

University of Saskatchewan, College of Graduate Studies and Research, College of Arts and Science, Department of Religion and Culture, Saskatoon, SK S7N 5A2, Canada. Offers MA. *Degree requirements:* For master's, thesis. *Entrance requirements:* Additional exam requirements/recommendations for international students: Required—TOEFL (minimum score 80 iBT); Recommended—IELTS (minimum score 6.5). Electronic applications accepted.

University of South Africa, College of Human Sciences, Pretoria, South Africa. Offers adult education (M Ed); African languages (MA, PhD); African politics (MA, PhD); Afrikaans (MA, PhD); ancient history (MA, PhD); ancient Near Eastern studies (MA, PhD); anthropology (MA, PhD); applied linguistics (MA); Arabic (MA, PhD); archaeology (MA); art history (MA); Biblical archaeology (MA); Biblical studies (M Th, D Th, PhD); Christian spirituality (M Th, D Th); church history (M Th, D Th); classical studies (MA, PhD); clinical psychology (MA); communication (MA, PhD); comparative education (M Ed, Ed D); consulting psychology (D Admin, D Com, PhD); curriculum studies (M Ed, Ed D); development studies (M Admin, MA, D Admin, PhD); didactics (M Ed, Ed D); education (M Tech); education management (M Ed, Ed D); educational psychology (M Ed); English (MA); environmental education (M Ed); French (MA, PhD); German (MA, PhD); Greek (MA); guidance and counseling (M Ed); health studies (MA, PhD), including health sciences education (MA), health services management (MA), medical and surgical nursing science (critical care general) (MA), midwifery and neonatal nursing science (MA), trauma and emergency care (MA); history (MA, PhD); history of education (Ed D); inclusive education (M Ed, Ed D); information and communications technology policy and regulation (MA); information science (MA, MIS, PhD); international politics (MA, PhD); Islamic studies (MA, PhD); Italian (MA, PhD); Judaica (MA, PhD); linguistics (MA, PhD); mathematical education (M Ed); mathematics education (MA); missiology (M Th, D Th); modern Hebrew (MA, PhD); musicology (MA, MMus, D Mus, PhD); natural science education (M Ed); New Testament (M Th, D Th); Old Testament (D Th); pastoral therapy (M Th, D Th); philosophy (MA); philosophy of education (M Ed, Ed D); politics (MA, PhD); Portuguese (MA, PhD); practical theology (M Th, D Th); psychology (MA, MS, PhD); psychology of education (M Ed, Ed D); public health (MA); religious studies (MA, D Th, PhD); Romance languages (MA); Russian (MA, PhD); Semitic languages (MA, PhD); social behavior studies in HIV/AIDS (MA); social science (mental health) (MA); social science in development studies (MA); social science in psychology (MA); social science in social work (MA); social science in sociology (MA); social work (MSW, DSW, PhD); socio-education (M Ed, Ed D); sociolinguistics (MA); sociology (MA, PhD); Spanish (MA, PhD); systematic theology (M Th, D Th); TESOL (teaching English to speakers of other languages) (MA); theological ethics (M Th, D Th); theory of literature (MA, PhD); urban ministries (D Th); urban ministry (M Th).

University of South Carolina, The Graduate School, College of Arts and Sciences, Department of Anthropology, Columbia, SC 29208. Offers MA, PhD. Terminal master's awarded for partial completion of doctoral program. *Degree requirements:* For master's, comprehensive exam, thesis; for doctorate, comprehensive exam, thesis/dissertation. *Entrance requirements:* For master's and doctorate, GRE General Test, letters of reference. Additional exam requirements/recommendations for international students: Required—TOEFL. Electronic applications accepted. *Faculty research:* Biocultural anthropology, archaeology, cultural anthropology.

University of Southern Mississippi, College of Arts and Letters, Department of Anthropology and Sociology, Hattiesburg, MS 39406-0001. Offers MA. *Program availability:* Part-time. *Students:* 5 full-time (4 women). In 2017, 23 master's awarded. *Degree requirements:* For master's, one foreign language, comprehensive exam, thesis (for some programs). *Entrance requirements:* For master's, GRE General Test, minimum GPA of 2.75 in last 2 years, 3.0 in field of study. Additional exam requirements/recommendations for international students: Required—TOEFL, IELTS. *Application deadline:* For fall admission, 3/15 priority date for domestic students, 3/1 for international students. Applications are processed on a rolling basis. Application fee: $60. Electronic applications accepted. *Expenses:* Tuition, state resident: full-time $3830. *Financial support:* Research assistantships with full tuition reimbursements, teaching assistantships with full tuition reimbursements, career-related internships or fieldwork, Federal Work-Study, institutionally sponsored loans, scholarships/grants, and unspecified assistantships available. Financial award application deadline: 3/15; financial award applicants required to submit FAFSA. *Faculty research:* Archaeology of North America, historic archaeology, bioarchaeology, ethnography of Europe, ethnography of Africa. *Unit head:* Ann Marie Kinnell, Chair, 601-266-4306, Fax: 601-266-6373, E-mail: ann.kinnell@usm.edu.
Website: https://www.usm.edu/anthropology-sociology

University of South Florida, College of Arts and Sciences, Department of Anthropology, Tampa, FL 33620-9951. Offers applied anthropology (MA, PhD), including archaeological and forensic sciences, biocultural medical anthropology, cultural resource management, heritage studies; medical anthropology (Graduate Certificate). *Program availability:* Part-time. *Faculty:* 22 full-time (15 women). *Students:* 73 full-time (50 women), 42 part-time (33 women); includes 30 minority (6 Black or African American, non-Hispanic/Latino; 2 Asian, non-Hispanic/Latino; 18 Hispanic/Latino; 1 Native Hawaiian or other Pacific Islander, non-Hispanic/Latino; 3 Two or more races, non-Hispanic/Latino), 6 international. Average age 32. 117 applicants, 36% accepted, 26 enrolled. In 2017, 16 master's, 7 doctorates awarded. *Degree requirements:* For master's, one foreign language, comprehensive exam, thesis; for doctorate, one foreign language, comprehensive exam, thesis/dissertation. *Entrance requirements:* For master's and doctorate, GRE, minimum GPA of 3.0, 3 letters of recommendation, statement of purpose, signed research ethics statement, resume or curriculum vitae; for Graduate Certificate, bachelor's degree with minimum GPA of 3.0. Additional exam requirements/recommendations for international students: Required—TOEFL (minimum score 550 paper-based; 79 iBT) or IELTS (minimum score 6.5). *Application deadline:* For fall admission, 12/15 priority date for domestic and international students. Application fee: $30. Electronic applications accepted. *Financial support:* In 2017–18, 19 students received support, including 14 research assistantships with tuition reimbursements available (averaging $14,475 per year), 52 teaching assistantships with partial tuition reimbursements available (averaging $12,540 per year); scholarships/grants and tuition waivers (partial) also available. Financial award application deadline: 1/15; financial award applicants required to submit FAFSA. *Faculty research:* Biocultural medical anthropology; archaeology and culture resource management in the Americas; community identity and heritage; urban community issues; verbal and nonverbal communications in media and education; global dynamics of sustainable resource management and economic development; social and cultural constructions of race, ethnicity, and gender. *Total annual research expenditures:* $1.1 million. *Unit head:* Dr. David Himmelgreen, Professor/Chair, 813-974-5455, E-mail: dhimmelg@usf.edu. *Application contact:* Dr. Rebecca Zarger, Associate Professor and Graduate Director, 813-974-0069, E-mail: rzarger@usf.edu.
Website: http://anthropology.usf.edu/graduate/

The University of Tennessee, Graduate School, College of Arts and Sciences, Department of Anthropology, Knoxville, TN 37996. Offers archaeology (MA, PhD); biological anthropology (MA, PhD); cultural anthropology (MA, PhD); zoo-archaeology (MA, PhD). *Degree requirements:* For master's, thesis; for doctorate, one foreign language, thesis/dissertation. *Entrance requirements:* For master's and doctorate, GRE General Test, minimum GPA of 2.7. Additional exam requirements/recommendations for international students: Required—TOEFL. Electronic applications accepted.

The University of Texas at Arlington, Graduate School, College of Liberal Arts, Department of Sociology and Anthropology, Program in Anthropology, Arlington, TX 79019. Offers MA. *Program availability:* Part-time, evening/weekend. *Degree requirements:* For master's, comprehensive exam, thesis or alternative. *Entrance requirements:* For master's, GRE General Test, minimum GPA of 3.0, 3 letters of recommendation. Additional exam requirements/recommendations for international students: Required—TOEFL (minimum score 550 paper-based). Electronic applications accepted.

The University of Texas at Austin, Graduate School, College of Liberal Arts, Department of Anthropology, Austin, TX 78712-1111. Offers archaeology (MA, PhD); cultural forms (MA, PhD); linguistic anthropology (MA, PhD); physical anthropology (MA, PhD); social anthropology (MA, PhD). *Program availability:* Part-time. Terminal master's awarded for partial completion of doctoral program. *Degree requirements:* For master's, thesis; for doctorate, one foreign language, thesis/dissertation. *Entrance requirements:* For master's and doctorate, GRE General Test. Additional exam requirements/recommendations for international students: Required—TOEFL. Electronic applications accepted.

The University of Texas at El Paso, Graduate School, College of Liberal Arts, Department of Sociology and Anthropology, El Paso, TX 79968-0001. Offers applied anthropology (Certificate); applied social sciences (Certificate); sociology (MA). *Program availability:* Part-time, evening/weekend. *Degree requirements:* For master's, thesis. *Entrance requirements:* For master's, GRE General Test, minimum GPA of 3.0. Additional exam requirements/recommendations for international students: Required—TOEFL. Electronic applications accepted. *Faculty research:* U.S.-Mexico border, social inequality, immigration, Chicano culture, Mexico.

The University of Texas at San Antonio, College of Liberal and Fine Arts, Department of Anthropology, San Antonio, TX 78249-0617. Offers MA, PhD. *Program availability:* Part-time. *Faculty:* 10 full-time (4 women), 1 part-time/adjunct (0 women). *Students:* 16 full-time (13 women), 47 part-time (33 women); includes 18 minority (1 Asian, non-Hispanic/Latino; 16 Hispanic/Latino; 1 Two or more races, non-Hispanic/Latino), 3 international. Average age 33. 35 applicants, 74% accepted, 14 enrolled. In 2017, 6 master's, 1 doctorate awarded. Terminal master's awarded for partial completion of doctoral program. *Degree requirements:* For master's, comprehensive exam, thesis; for doctorate, comprehensive exam, thesis/dissertation, proficiency in foreign language, statistics, or computer programming. *Entrance requirements:* For master's, GRE General Test, minimum GPA of 3.3 during last 60 hours (preferred), 18 hours in major field, three letters of recommendation, statement of purpose, writing sample; for doctorate, GRE General Test, minimum GPA of 3.3 (preferred), transcripts from all colleges and universities attended, 3 letters of recommendation, statement of purpose, writing sample. Additional exam requirements/recommendations for international students: Required—TOEFL (minimum score 550 paper-based; 79 iBT), IELTS (minimum score 6.5). *Application deadline:* For fall admission, 6/15 for domestic students, 3/1 for international students; for spring admission, 10/15 for domestic students, 9/15 for international students. Application fee: $50 ($90 for international students). Electronic applications accepted. *Expenses:* Contact institution. *Financial support:* Fellowships, research assistantships, teaching assistantships, scholarships/grants, and unspecified assistantships available. *Faculty research:* Political and cultural ecology, the archaeology of complexity, indigenous and environmental politics, primate and evolutionary ecology, medical anthropology. *Total annual research expenditures:* $418,448. *Unit head:* Dr. Jason Yaeger, Chair and Professor of Anthropology, 210-458-4075, Fax: 210-458-7811, E-mail: jason.yeager@utsa.edu.
Website: http://colfa.utsa.edu/ant/

University of Toronto, School of Graduate Studies, Faculty of Arts and Science, Department of Anthropology, Toronto, ON M5S 1A1, Canada. Offers M Sc, MA, PhD. *Program availability:* Part-time. *Degree requirements:* For master's, research paper; for doctorate, one foreign language, thesis/dissertation, language exam, thesis defense. *Entrance requirements:* For master's, minimum B+ average, 5 full-year anthropology courses, 2 letters of reference, statement of interest; for doctorate, minimum B+ average, master's degree in relevant area, resume, 2 letters of reference, statement of interest. Additional exam requirements/recommendations for international students: Required—TOEFL (minimum score 580 paper-based; 93 iBT), IELTS (minimum score 7), TWE (minimum score 5), Michigan English Language Assessment Battery (minimum score 85), or COPE (minimum score 4). Electronic applications accepted.

The University of Tulsa, Graduate School, Kendall College of Arts and Sciences, Department of Anthropology, Tulsa, OK 74104-3189. Offers MA, PhD, JD/MA. *Program availability:* Part-time. *Faculty:* 9 full-time (3 women). *Students:* 9 full-time (7 women), 6 part-time (all women); includes 2 minority (1 American Indian or Alaska Native, non-Hispanic/Latino; 1 Two or more races, non-Hispanic/Latino), 2 international. Average age 33. 16 applicants, 44% accepted, 3 enrolled. In 2017, 1 master's, 1 doctorate awarded. Terminal master's awarded for partial completion of doctoral program. *Degree*

requirements: For master's, thesis (for some programs); for doctorate, comprehensive exam, thesis/dissertation. *Entrance requirements:* For master's, GRE General Test. Additional exam requirements/recommendations for international students: Required—TOEFL (minimum score 577 paper-based; 91 iBT), IELTS (minimum score 6.5). *Application deadline:* Applications are processed on a rolling basis. Application fee: $55. Electronic applications accepted. *Expenses: Tuition:* Full-time $22,230. *Required fees:* $2000. Tuition and fees vary according to course load and program. *Financial support:* In 2017–18, 22 students received support, including 4 fellowships with full tuition reimbursements available (averaging $3,687 per year), 14 teaching assistantships with full tuition reimbursements available (averaging $12,500 per year); research assistantships with full tuition reimbursements available, career-related internships or fieldwork, Federal Work-Study, scholarships/grants, health care benefits, tuition waivers (full and partial), and unspecified assistantships also available. Support available to part-time students. Financial award application deadline: 2/1; financial award applicants required to submit FAFSA. *Faculty research:* Archaeology, paleoanthropology, zoo archaeology, Native American studies, ecological archaeology, lithic analysis, cultural anthropology. *Unit head:* Dr. Peter Stromberg, Chairperson, 918-631-2370, Fax: 918-631-2540, E-mail: peter-stromberg@utulsa.edu. *Application contact:* Dr. Thomas Foster, Advisor, 918-631-3082, Fax: 918-631-2540, E-mail: thomas-foster@utulsa.edu.
Website: http://artsandsciences.utulsa.edu/academics/departments-schools/anthropology/

University of Utah, Graduate School, College of Social and Behavioral Science, Department of Anthropology, Salt Lake City, UT 84112. Offers MA, MS, PhD. *Program availability:* Part-time. *Faculty:* 15 full-time (6 women), 6 part-time/adjunct (4 women). *Students:* 16 full-time (10 women), 14 part-time (6 women); includes 5 minority (2 Hispanic/Latino; 3 Two or more races, non-Hispanic/Latino), 1 international. Average age 26. 39 applicants, 28% accepted, 5 enrolled. In 2017, 2 master's, 2 doctorates awarded. *Degree requirements:* For master's, comprehensive exam, thesis optional, foreign language (for MA); for doctorate, variable foreign language requirement, comprehensive exam (for some programs), thesis/dissertation. *Entrance requirements:* For master's, GRE General Test, minimum undergraduate GPA of 3.0; for doctorate, GRE General Test, minimum GPA of 3.0. Additional exam requirements/recommendations for international students: Required—TOEFL (minimum score 500 paper-based). *Application deadline:* For fall admission, 12/29 for domestic and international students. Application fee: $55 ($65 for international students). Electronic applications accepted. *Expenses:* Contact institution. *Financial support:* In 2017–18, 18 students received support, including 1 fellowship with full tuition reimbursement available (averaging $7,500 per year), 2 research assistantships with full tuition reimbursements available (averaging $18,000 per year), 16 teaching assistantships with full tuition reimbursements available (averaging $15,000 per year); scholarships/grants, health care benefits, and unspecified assistantships also available. Financial award application deadline: 3/19. *Faculty research:* Hunter-gatherer ethnography, primate immuno-genetics, anthropogenic fire, human-female life history, archaic homonym and modern human genetics. *Total annual research expenditures:* $288,569. *Unit head:* Dr. Leslie Ann Knapp, Chair, 801-581-6251, Fax: 801-581-6252, E-mail: leslie.knapp@anthro.utah.edu. *Application contact:* Linda K. Morgan, Administrative Assistant, 801-581-6251, Fax: 801-581-6252, E-mail: linda.morgan@anthro.utah.edu.
Website: http://www.anthro.utah.edu/

University of Victoria, Faculty of Graduate Studies, Faculty of Social Sciences, Department of Anthropology, Victoria, BC V8W 2Y2, Canada. Offers MA. *Program availability:* Part-time. *Degree requirements:* For master's, comprehensive exam (for some programs), thesis (for some programs). *Entrance requirements:* For master's, minimum B+ average in last 2 years of undergraduate course work, writing sample. Additional exam requirements/recommendations for international students: Required—TOEFL (minimum score 575 paper-based), IELTS (minimum score 7).

University of Virginia, College and Graduate School of Arts and Sciences, Department of Anthropology, Charlottesville, VA 22903. Offers MA, PhD. *Faculty:* 17 full-time (5 women). *Students:* 39 full-time (25 women), 1 part-time (0 women); includes 5 minority (1 Black or African American, non-Hispanic/Latino; 1 Asian, non-Hispanic/Latino; 1 Hispanic/Latino; 2 Two or more races, non-Hispanic/Latino), 9 international. Average age 29. 47 applicants, 32% accepted, 6 enrolled. In 2017, 5 master's, 5 doctorates awarded. *Degree requirements:* For master's, one foreign language, thesis; for doctorate, 2 foreign languages, thesis/dissertation. *Entrance requirements:* For master's and doctorate, GRE General Test, GRE Subject Test, 3 letters of recommendation. Additional exam requirements/recommendations for international students: Required—TOEFL (minimum score 600 paper-based; 90 iBT), IELTS (minimum score 7). *Application deadline:* For fall admission, 12/15 for domestic and international students. Applications are processed on a rolling basis. Application fee: $60. Electronic applications accepted. *Financial support:* Application deadline: 3/15; applicants required to submit FAFSA. *Unit head:* Eve Danziger, Chair, 434-924-3002, Fax: 434-924-1350, E-mail: danziger@virginia.edu.
Website: http://anthropology.virginia.edu/

University of Washington, Graduate School, College of Arts and Sciences, Department of Anthropology, Seattle, WA 98195. Offers MA, PhD. *Faculty:* 32 full-time (16 women), 5 part-time/adjunct (3 women). *Students:* 55 full-time (33 women), 6 part-time (1 woman); includes 25 minority (3 Black or African American, non-Hispanic/Latino; 5 American Indian or Alaska Native, non-Hispanic/Latino; 5 Asian, non-Hispanic/Latino; 9 Hispanic/Latino; 1 Native Hawaiian or other Pacific Islander, non-Hispanic/Latino; 2 Two or more races, non-Hispanic/Latino), 12 international. Average age 32. 121 applicants, 12% accepted, 4 enrolled. In 2017, 8 master's, 6 doctorates awarded. Terminal master's awarded for partial completion of doctoral program. *Degree requirements:* For master's, comprehensive exam, thesis or alternative; for doctorate, variable foreign language requirement, comprehensive exam, thesis/dissertation. *Entrance requirements:* For doctorate, GRE General Test, minimum GPA of 3.6. Additional exam requirements/recommendations for international students: Recommended—TOEFL (minimum score 500 paper-based; 61 iBT). *Application deadline:* For fall admission, 12/15 for domestic and international students. Application fee: $85. Electronic applications accepted. *Financial support:* In 2017–18, 45 students received support, including 3 fellowships with full tuition reimbursements available (averaging $20,000 per year), 6 research assistantships with full tuition reimbursements available (averaging $21,000 per year), 23 teaching assistantships with full tuition reimbursements available (averaging $21,000 per year); institutionally sponsored loans, scholarships/grants, traineeships, health care benefits, tuition waivers (full and partial), and unspecified assistantships also available. Financial award application deadline: 1/15; financial award applicants required to submit FAFSA. *Faculty research:* Sociocultural anthropology, biological anthropology, archaeology, medical anthropology and global health. *Unit head:* Dr. Patricia Ann Kramer, Chair, 206-543-5240, Fax: 206-543-3285, E-mail: pakramer@uw.edu. *Application contact:* Catherine M. Zeigler, Graduate Program Advisor, 206-685-1562, Fax: 206-543-3285, E-mail: gradanth@uw.edu.
Website: https://anthropology.washington.edu

University of Waterloo, Graduate Studies, Faculty of Arts, Department of Anthropology, Waterloo, ON N2L 3G1, Canada. Offers anthropology (MA); public issues (MA). *Entrance requirements:* Additional exam requirements/recommendations for international students: Required—TOEFL, IELTS, PTE. Electronic applications accepted. *Faculty research:* Applied socio-cultural anthropology and archaeology.

The University of Western Ontario, Faculty of Graduate Studies, Social Sciences Division, Department of Anthropology, London, ON N6A 5B8, Canada. Offers MA, PhD. *Degree requirements:* For master's, thesis; for doctorate, thesis/dissertation. *Entrance requirements:* For master's, minimum B average, honors BA. Additional exam requirements/recommendations for international students: Required—TOEFL. Electronic applications accepted. *Faculty research:* Sociocultural anthropology, bioarchaeology, linguistics.

University of West Florida, College of Arts, Social Sciences, and Humanities, Division of Anthropology and Archaeology, Pensacola, FL 32514-5750. Offers anthropology (MA); historical archaeology (MA). *Degree requirements:* For master's, internship or thesis. *Entrance requirements:* For master's, GRE, transcripts; minimum GPA of 3.0; 3 letters of recommendation; writing sample; letter of intent describing background, study interests, and professional goals. Additional exam requirements/recommendations for international students: Required—TOEFL (minimum score 550 paper-based).

University of Wisconsin–Madison, Graduate School, College of Letters and Science, Department of Anthropology, Madison, WI 53706-1380. Offers archaeology (PhD); biological anthropology (PhD); cultural anthropology (PhD). Terminal master's awarded for partial completion of doctoral program. *Degree requirements:* For doctorate, thesis/dissertation. *Entrance requirements:* For doctorate, qualifying exam. Electronic applications accepted. *Faculty research:* Archaeology, biological, anthropology, cultural anthropology.

University of Wisconsin–Milwaukee, Graduate School, College of Letters and Science, Department of Anthropology, Milwaukee, WI 53201-0413. Offers anthropology (MS, PhD); museum studies (Graduate Certificate). *Students:* 62 full-time (47 women), 28 part-time (24 women); includes 9 minority (2 American Indian or Alaska Native, non-Hispanic/Latino; 1 Hispanic/Latino; 6 Two or more races, non-Hispanic/Latino). Average age 31. 29 applicants, 79% accepted, 18 enrolled. In 2017, 5 master's, 2 doctorates, 3 other advanced degrees awarded. *Degree requirements:* For master's, thesis or alternative; for doctorate, one foreign language, thesis/dissertation, departmental qualifying exam. *Entrance requirements:* For master's, GRE; for doctorate, GRE, minimum GPA of 3.0, master's degree. Additional exam requirements/recommendations for international students: Required—TOEFL (minimum score 550 paper-based; 79 iBT), IELTS (minimum score 6.5). *Application deadline:* For fall admission, 1/1 priority date for domestic students; for spring admission, 9/1 for domestic students. Application fee: $56 ($96 for international students). Electronic applications accepted. *Financial support:* Fellowships, research assistantships, teaching assistantships, career-related internships or fieldwork, unspecified assistantships, and project assistantships available. Support available to part-time students. Financial award application deadline: 4/15; financial award applicants required to submit FAFSA. *Unit head:* Thomas Malaby, Department Chair, 414-229-5247, E-mail: malaby@uwm.edu. *Application contact:* General Information Contact, 414-229-4982, Fax: 414-229-6967, E-mail: gradschool@uwm.edu.
Website: https://uwm.edu/letters-science/programs/?discipline-Anthropology

University of Wyoming, College of Arts and Sciences, Department of Anthropology, Laramie, WY 82071. Offers MA, PhD. *Program availability:* Part-time. Terminal master's awarded for partial completion of doctoral program. *Degree requirements:* For master's, one foreign language, comprehensive exam, thesis optional; for doctorate, one foreign language, comprehensive exam, thesis/dissertation. *Entrance requirements:* For master's and doctorate, GRE General Test, minimum GPA of 3.0. Electronic applications accepted. *Faculty research:* Paleo-Indian archaeology, osteology, faunal analysis, lithic analysis, hunter-gatherers.

Utah State University, School of Graduate Studies, College of Humanities and Social Sciences, Department of Sociology, Social Work, and Anthropology, Logan, UT 84322. Offers anthropology (MS); social work (MSW); sociology (MS, PhD). *Degree requirements:* For master's, thesis; for doctorate, comprehensive exam, thesis/dissertation. *Entrance requirements:* For master's, GRE General Test, minimum GPA of 3.0, recommendation letters; for doctorate, GRE General Test, minimum GPA of 3.0, recommendation letters, transcripts, personal statement, MS degree. Additional exam requirements/recommendations for international students: Required—TOEFL; Recommended—TWE. *Faculty research:* Demography, environmental/natural resource sociology, rural community change, international development, health studies.

Vanderbilt University, Department of Anthropology, Nashville, TN 37240-1001. Offers MA, PhD. *Faculty:* 14 full-time (4 women). *Students:* 30 full-time (22 women); includes 5 minority (all Hispanic/Latino), 10 international. Average age 33. 47 applicants, 9% accepted, 4 enrolled. In 2017, 5 doctorates awarded. *Degree requirements:* For master's, comprehensive exam, thesis or alternative; for doctorate, one foreign language, comprehensive exam, thesis/dissertation, general, qualifying, and final exams. *Entrance requirements:* For master's and doctorate, GRE General Test. Additional exam requirements/recommendations for international students: Required—TOEFL (minimum score 570 paper-based; 88 iBT). *Application deadline:* For fall admission, 1/15 for domestic and international students. Application fee: $0. Electronic applications accepted. *Financial support:* Fellowships with tuition reimbursements, research assistantships with full tuition reimbursements, teaching assistantships with full tuition reimbursements, career-related internships or fieldwork, Federal Work-Study, institutionally sponsored loans, scholarships/grants, and health care benefits available. Financial award application deadline: 1/15; financial award applicants required to submit CSS PROFILE or FAFSA. *Faculty research:* Archaeology, ethnohistory and ethnography, epigraphy, conflict theory, Latin America. *Unit head:* Dr. Beth Conklin, Chair, 615-343-6120, Fax: 615-343-0230, E-mail: beth.a.conklin@vanderbilt.edu. *Application contact:* John Janusek, Director of Graduate Studies, 615-343-6120, E-mail: john.w.janusek@vanderbilt.edu.
Website: http://as.vanderbilt.edu/anthropology/

Washington State University, College of Arts and Sciences, Department of Anthropology, Pullman, WA 99164. Offers archaeology (MA, PhD); cultural anthropology (PhD); evolutionary anthropology (MA, PhD). Program applications must be made through the Pullman campus. *Degree requirements:* For master's, one foreign language, comprehensive exam (for some programs), thesis; for doctorate, one foreign language, comprehensive exam, thesis/dissertation, written and oral preliminary exam. *Entrance requirements:* For master's and doctorate, GRE General Test, curriculum vitae, statement of intent, official transcripts, 3 letters of recommendation, one or two undergraduate papers (from BA/BS applicants), minimum GPA of 3.0. Additional exam requirements/recommendations for international students: Required—TOEFL (minimum score 550 paper-based), IELTS. Electronic applications accepted. *Faculty research:* Quantitative analysis of archaeological data, simulation of aspects of prehistoric behavior, subsistence strategies, language use, inequality and poverty, gender, pedagogy, Mexico/U.S. border region, childhood, infectious and parasitic diseases, the analysis of mitochondrial DNA (mtDNA) and Y-chromosomal DNA.

Washington University in St. Louis, The Graduate School, Department of Anthropology, St. Louis, MO 63130-4899. Offers PhD. Terminal master's awarded for

partial completion of doctoral program. *Degree requirements:* For doctorate, thesis/ dissertation. *Entrance requirements:* Additional exam requirements/recommendations for international students: Required—TOEFL. Electronic applications accepted. *Faculty research:* Sociocultural anthropology (including medical anthropology); archaeology; physical anthropology (including primate studies, paleontology and human biology).

Wayne State University, College of Liberal Arts and Sciences, Department of Anthropology, Detroit, MI 48202. Offers anthropology (MA, PhD); social work (PhD). Doctoral program admits for fall only. *Program availability:* Part-time. *Faculty:* 13. *Students:* 31 full-time (25 women), 25 part-time (16 women); includes 9 minority (4 Black or African American, non-Hispanic/Latino; 2 Hispanic/Latino; 3 Two or more races, non-Hispanic/ Latino), 3 international. Average age 33. 30 applicants, 33% accepted, 8 enrolled. In 2017, 9 master's, 3 doctorates awarded. *Degree requirements:* For master's, thesis (for some programs); for doctorate, one foreign language, thesis/dissertation. *Entrance requirements:* For master's, three letters of recommendation, completion of introduction to anthropology, letter of intent, writing sample, minimum undergraduate GPA of 3.2; for doctorate, GRE, bachelor's degree in anthropology or a related field, three letters of recommendation, completion of introduction to anthropology, letter of intent, writing sample, minimum undergraduate GPA of 3.2. Additional exam requirements/recommendations for international students: Required—TOEFL (minimum score 550 paper-based; 79 iBT), TWE (minimum score 5.5), Michigan English Language Assessment Battery (minimum score 85); Recommended—IELTS (minimum score 6.5). *Application deadline:* For fall admission, 1/10 for domestic and international students; for winter admission, 10/1 for domestic and international students. Application fee: $50. Electronic applications accepted. *Expenses:* Tuition, state resident: full-time $10,224; part-time $638.98 per credit hour. Tuition, nonresident: full-time $22,145; part-time $1384.04 per credit hour. Tuition and fees vary according to course load and program. *Financial support:* In 2017–18, 28 students received support, including 1 fellowship with tuition reimbursement available (averaging $16,000 per year), 1 research assistantship with tuition reimbursement available (averaging $18,885 per year), 6 teaching assistantships with tuition reimbursements available (averaging $18,534 per year); scholarships/grants and unspecified assistantships also available. Financial award applicants required to submit FAFSA. *Faculty research:* Anthropology of Detroit, archaeology, business and organizational anthropology, linguistic anthropology, cultural anthropology, medical anthropology, biological anthropology. *Unit head:* Dr. Andrea Sankar, Professor and Chair, 313-577-6961, E-mail: asankar@wayne.edu. *Application contact:* Dr. Stephen Chrisomalis, Director of Graduate Studies, 313-577-9922, E-mail: chrisomalis@wayne.edu.
Website: http://clas.wayne.edu/anthropology/

Western Kentucky University, Graduate Studies, Potter College of Arts and Letters, Department of Folk Studies and Anthropology, Bowling Green, KY 42101. Offers folk studies (MA). *Degree requirements:* For master's, comprehensive exam, thesis optional, written exam. *Entrance requirements:* For master's, GRE General Test, minimum GPA of 3.0. Additional exam requirements/recommendations for international students: Required—TOEFL (minimum score 555 paper-based; 79 iBT). *Faculty research:* Public folklore, folklore and education, vernacular belief, music and culture, historic presentation.

Western Michigan University, Graduate College, College of Arts and Sciences, Department of Anthropology, Kalamazoo, MI 49008. Offers MA. *Degree requirements:* For master's, comprehensive exam, thesis.

Western Washington University, Graduate School, College of Humanities and Social Sciences, Department of Anthropology, Bellingham, WA 98225-5996. Offers MA. *Program availability:* Part-time. *Degree requirements:* For master's, thesis. *Entrance requirements:* For master's, GRE General Test, minimum GPA of 3.0 in last 60 semester hours or last 90 quarter hours. Additional exam requirements/recommendations for international students: Required—TOEFL (minimum score 567 paper-based). Electronic applications accepted. *Faculty research:* Peoples and culture of the Pacific Rim; prehistory of North America; applied health; community-based action research; globalization and human rights.

Wichita State University, Graduate School, Fairmount College of Liberal Arts and Sciences, Department of Anthropology, Wichita, KS 67260. Offers MA. *Program availability:* Part-time. *Entrance requirements:* For master's, minimum GPA of 2.75 in last 60 hours, 3.0 in anthropology. *Unit head:* Dr. Peer H. Moore-Jansen, Chair, 316-978-3195, E-mail: pmojan@wichita.edu. *Application contact:* Jordan Oleson, Admission Coordinator, 316-978-3095, E-mail: jordan.oleson@wichita.edu.
Website: http://www.wichita.edu/anthropology

Yale University, Graduate School of Arts and Sciences, Department of Anthropology, New Haven, CT 06520. Offers M Phil, MA, PhD. *Degree requirements:* For doctorate, thesis/dissertation. *Entrance requirements:* For master's and doctorate, GRE General Test. *Faculty research:* Linguistics, national identity.

York University, Faculty of Graduate Studies, Faculty of Liberal Arts and Professional Studies, Program in Social Anthropology, Toronto, ON M3J 1P3, Canada. Offers MA, PhD. *Program availability:* Part-time. *Degree requirements:* For master's, thesis or alternative; for doctorate, comprehensive exam, thesis/dissertation. Electronic applications accepted.

Applied Social Research

American University, College of Arts and Sciences, Department of Sociology, Washington, DC 22016-8072. Offers public sociology (Certificate); social research (Certificate); sociology (MA). *Program availability:* Part-time, evening/weekend. *Faculty:* 13 full-time (9 women), 8 part-time/adjunct (5 women). *Students:* 6 full-time (4 women), 6 part-time (4 women); includes 5 minority (2 Black or African American, non-Hispanic/ Latino; 1 Hispanic/Latino; 2 Two or more races, non-Hispanic/Latino). Average age 28. 14 applicants, 93% accepted, 5 enrolled. In 2017, 1 master's awarded. *Degree requirements:* For master's, comprehensive exam, thesis or alternative. *Entrance requirements:* For master's, GRE, statement of purpose, transcripts, 2 letters of recommendation, resume; for Certificate, bachelor's degree, statement of purpose, transcripts, resume. Additional exam requirements/recommendations for international students: Required—TOEFL (minimum score 600 paper-based; 100 iBT). *Application deadline:* For fall admission, 2/1 priority date for domestic students; for spring admission, 11/1 priority date for domestic students. Application fee: $55. *Expenses:* Contact institution. *Financial support:* Research assistantships, teaching assistantships, institutionally sponsored loans, scholarships/ grants, and unspecified assistantships available. Financial award application deadline: 2/ 1; financial award applicants required to submit FAFSA. *Unit head:* Dr. Gloria Young, Department Chair, 202-885-2254, Fax: 202-885-2477, E-mail: gyoung@american.edu. *Application contact:* Jonathan Harper, Associate Director, Graduate Recruitment, 202-885-3622, E-mail: jharper@american.edu.
Website: http://www.american.edu/cas/sociology/

California State University, Dominguez Hills, College of Natural and Behavioral Sciences, Program in Sociology, Carson, CA 90747-0001. Offers social research (MA); sociology (MA). *Program availability:* Part-time, evening/weekend. *Degree requirements:* For master's, comprehensive exam, thesis. *Entrance requirements:* For master's, minimum GPA of 2.85. *Faculty research:* Community studies, social movements, criminology.

Concordia University Irvine, School of Theology, Irvine, CA 92612-3299. Offers Christian leadership (MA); research in theology (MA); theology and culture (MA). *Program availability:* Part-time, evening/weekend. *Degree requirements:* For master's, project/thesis or vicarage. *Entrance requirements:* For master's, official college transcript(s), statement of intent, 2 references, interview. Additional exam requirements/ recommendations for international students: Required—TOEFL. Electronic applications accepted. *Expenses:* Contact institution.

Florida State University, The Graduate School, College of Social Sciences and Public Policy, Department of Sociology, Tallahassee, FL 32306-2270. Offers applied social research (MS); sociology (MS, PhD); sociology of health and aging (MS). *Faculty:* 21 full-time (15 women). *Students:* 49 full-time (29 women), 6 part-time (5 women); includes 18 minority (5 Black or African American, non-Hispanic/Latino; 2 Asian, non-Hispanic/ Latino; 8 Hispanic/Latino; 3 Two or more races, non-Hispanic/Latino). Average age 28. 33 applicants, 33% accepted, 8 enrolled. In 2017, 13 master's, 12 doctorates awarded. *Degree requirements:* For doctorate, comprehensive exam, thesis/dissertation. *Entrance requirements:* For master's and doctorate, GRE General Test, minimum GPA of 3.0. Additional exam requirements/recommendations for international students: Required—TOEFL (minimum score 550 paper-based; 80 iBT). *Application deadline:* For fall admission, 12/15 priority date for domestic students, 12/15 for international students. Applications are processed on a rolling basis. Application fee: $30. Electronic applications accepted. *Expenses:* $479.32 per credit hour in-state; $1,110.72 per credit hour out-of-state. *Financial support:* In 2017–18, 55 students received support, including 3 fellowships with full tuition reimbursements available (averaging $25,115 per year), 4 research assistantships with full tuition reimbursements available (averaging $21,150 per year), 50 teaching assistantships with full tuition reimbursements available (averaging $21,150 per year); institutionally sponsored loans, scholarships/grants, health care benefits, and unspecified assistantships also available. Financial award application deadline: 12/15; financial award applicants required to submit FAFSA. *Faculty research:* Aging and health, demography, inequality (gender/race and social movements/politics). *Total annual research expenditures:* $371,977. *Unit head:* Dr. Kathryn Harker Tillman, Chair, 850-644-6416, E-mail: ktillman@fsu.edu. *Application contact:* Kimberly McClellan, Academic Specialist/Graduate Program Coordinator, 850-644-8329, E-mail: kmcclellan@fsu.edu.
Website: http://coss.fsu.edu/sociology/

Hunter College of the City University of New York, Graduate School, School of Arts and Sciences, Department of Sociology, Program in Applied Social Research, New York, NY 10065-5085. Offers MS. *Program availability:* Part-time, evening/weekend. *Degree requirements:* For master's, internship, research reports. *Entrance requirements:* For master's, GRE General Test or GMAT, 3 credits of course work in statistics, research methods, background in sociology or related social science. Additional exam requirements/recommendations for international students: Required—TOEFL. *Faculty research:* Consumer behavior, new electronic media, voting behavior, policy analysis, sociomedicine.

Laurentian University, School of Graduate Studies and Research, Programme in Sociology, Sudbury, ON P3E 2C6, Canada. Offers applied social research (MA). *Program availability:* Part-time. *Entrance requirements:* For master's, honors degree in sociology or equivalent. *Faculty research:* Work foundations, managing AIDS organization, tracking laid-off mine workers.

Loma Linda University, School of Behavioral Health, Department of Social Work and Social Ecology, Loma Linda, CA 92350. Offers criminal justice (MS); gerontology (MS); social policy and social research (PhD); social work (MSW). *Accreditation:* CSWE. *Degree requirements:* For master's, comprehensive exam, thesis optional; for doctorate, comprehensive exam, thesis/dissertation. *Entrance requirements:* For master's and doctorate, GRE General Test. Additional exam requirements/recommendations for international students: Required—TOEFL, Michigan English Language Assessment Battery. Electronic applications accepted.

The New School, The New School for Social Research, New York, NY 10003. Offers M Phil, MA, MS, PhD. *Program availability:* Part-time. *Faculty:* 73 full-time (34 women), 14 part-time/adjunct (2 women). *Students:* 648 full-time (338 women), 155 part-time (92 women); includes 124 minority (21 Black or African American, non-Hispanic/Latino; 25 Asian, non-Hispanic/Latino; 55 Hispanic/Latino; 23 Two or more races, non-Hispanic/ Latino), 279 international. Average age 31. 880 applicants, 76% accepted, 190 enrolled. In 2017, 152 master's, 60 doctorates awarded. Terminal master's awarded for partial completion of doctoral program. *Degree requirements:* For master's, comprehensive exam (for some programs), thesis (for some programs); for doctorate, variable foreign language requirement, comprehensive exam (for some programs), thesis/dissertation. *Entrance requirements:* For master's, letters of recommendation, writing sample, essays, official transcripts. Additional exam requirements/recommendations for international students: Required—TOEFL (minimum score 100 iBT), IELTS (minimum score 7), PTE (minimum score 68). *Application deadline:* For fall admission, 6/15 priority date for domestic and international students; for spring admission, 10/15 priority date for domestic and international students. Applications are processed on a rolling basis. Application fee: $50. Electronic applications accepted. *Expenses:* $2,100 per credit. *Financial support:* In 2017–18, 592 students received support, including 49 fellowships (averaging $38,451 per year), 28 research assistantships (averaging $13,911 per year), 146 teaching assistantships with full and partial tuition reimbursements available (averaging $8,625 per year); career-related internships or fieldwork, Federal Work-Study, scholarships/grants, and tuition waivers (full and partial) also available. Support available to part-time students. Financial award application deadline: 2/1; financial award applicants required to submit FAFSA. *Unit head:* Dr. William Milberg, Dean, The New School for Social Research, 212-229-5777, E-mail: milbergw@newschool.edu. *Application contact:* Dana Messinger, Director of Graduate Admission, 212-229-5150 Ext. 2300, E-mail: messingd@newschool.edu.
Website: http://www.newschool.edu/nssr

Applied Social Research

New York University, Steinhardt School of Culture, Education, and Human Development, Department of Humanities and Social Sciences in the Professions, Program in Applied Statistics for Social Science Research, New York, NY 10012-1019. Offers MS. *Students:* Average age 25. 72 applicants, 32% accepted, 2 enrolled. *Entrance requirements:* For master's, GRE, statement of purpose, resume/curriculum vitae, two letters of recommendation, transcripts. Additional exam requirements/recommendations for international students: Required—TOEFL. *Application deadline:* For fall admission, 12/1 priority date for domestic and international students. Electronic applications accepted. *Expenses: Tuition:* Full-time $41,352; part-time $19,968 per year. *Required fees:* $2496; $1628 per unit. $814 per term. Tuition and fees vary according to course load and program. *Faculty research:* Causal inference, multi-level models, multivariate analysis, psychometrics, survey research and design. *Unit head:* Dr. Jonathan L. Zimmerman, Chairperson, 212-998-5049, Fax: 212-995-4832. *Application contact:* 212-998-5030, Fax: 212-995-4328, E-mail: steinhardt.gradadmissions@nyu.edu.
Website: http://steinhardt.nyu.edu/humsocsci/applied_statistics/

Portland State University, Graduate Studies, School of Social Work, Portland, OR 97207-0751. Offers social work (MSW); social work and social research (PhD). *Accreditation:* CSWE (one or more programs are accredited). *Program availability:* Part-time. *Faculty:* 33 full-time (26 women), 46 part-time/adjunct (33 women). *Students:* 382 full-time (304 women), 232 part-time (197 women); includes 160 minority (29 Black or African American, non-Hispanic/Latino; 14 American Indian or Alaska Native, non-Hispanic/Latino; 23 Asian, non-Hispanic/Latino; 64 Hispanic/Latino; 1 Native Hawaiian or other Pacific Islander, non-Hispanic/Latino; 29 Two or more races, non-Hispanic/Latino), 4 international. Average age 34. 624 applicants, 42% accepted, 195 enrolled. In 2017, 205 master's, 4 doctorates awarded. *Degree requirements:* For master's, two 500-hour field placements; for doctorate, comprehensive exam, thesis/dissertation, residency. *Entrance requirements:* For master's, minimum GPA of 3.0 in upper-division course work or 2.75 overall, resume, 3 letters of reference, 3-4 page statement of purpose; for doctorate, GRE General Test, 4 references. Additional exam requirements/recommendations for international students: Required—TOEFL (minimum score 550 paper-based; 80 iBT). *Application deadline:* For fall admission, 2/1 for domestic and

international students. Application fee: $65. *Expenses:* Contact institution. *Financial support:* In 2017–18, 88 students received support, including 12 research assistantships with full and partial tuition reimbursements available (averaging $11,761 per year), 3 teaching assistantships with full and partial tuition reimbursements available (averaging $12,720 per year); career-related internships or fieldwork, Federal Work-Study, scholarships/grants, tuition waivers (full and partial), and unspecified assistantships also available. Support available to part-time students. Financial award application deadline: 3/1; financial award applicants required to submit FAFSA. *Faculty research:* Child welfare; child mental health; social welfare policies and services; work, family, and dependent care; adult mental health. *Total annual research expenditures:* $18 million. *Unit head:* Dr. Laura B. Nissen, Dean, 503-725-3997, Fax: 503-725-5545, E-mail: nissen@pdx.edu. *Application contact:* William Donlan, Director of MSW Program, 503-725-8977, E-mail: donlan@pdx.edu.
Website: https://www.pdx.edu/ssw/

Queens College of the City University of New York, Division of Social Sciences, Department of Sociology, Queens, NY 11367-1597. Offers data analytics and applied social research (MA). *Program availability:* Part-time, evening/weekend. *Students:* 4 full-time (3 women), 39 part-time (22 women); includes 29 minority (4 Black or African American, non-Hispanic/Latino; 9 Asian, non-Hispanic/Latino; 16 Hispanic/Latino), 7 international. Average age 29. *Degree requirements:* For master's, thesis optional. *Entrance requirements:* For master's, minimum GPA of 3.0. Additional exam requirements/recommendations for international students: Required—TOEFL (minimum score 100 iBT), IELTS (minimum score 7). *Application deadline:* For fall admission, 5/15 for domestic students; for spring admission, 12/1 for domestic students. Applications are processed on a rolling basis. Application fee: $125. Electronic applications accepted. *Financial support:* Career-related internships or fieldwork and unspecified assistantships available. Financial award application deadline: 4/1; financial award applicants required to submit FAFSA. *Unit head:* Dr. Andrew Beveridge, Chair, 718-997-2800, E-mail: andrew.beveridge@qc.cuny.edu. *Application contact:* Elizabeth D'Amico-Ramirez, Assistant Director of Graduate Admissions, 718-997-5203, E-mail: elizabeth.damicoramirez@qc.cuny.edu.
Website: http://qcsociology.org/

Archaeology

American University of Beirut, Graduate Programs, Faculty of Arts and Sciences, 1107 2020, Lebanon. Offers anthropology (MA); Arab and Middle Eastern history (PhD); Arabic language and literature (MA, PhD); archaeology (MA); art history and curating (MA); biology (MS); cell and molecular biology (PhD); chemistry (MS); clinical psychology (MA); computational sciences (MS); computer science (MS); economics (MA); education (MA), including administration and policy studies, elementary education, mathematics education, psychology school guidance, psychology test and measurements, science education, teaching English as a foreign language; English language (MA); English literature (MA); environmental policy planning (MS); financial economics (MAFE); general psychology (MA); geology (MS); history (MA); Islamic studies (MA); mathematics (MS); media studies (MA); Middle East studies (MA); philosophy (MA); physics (MS); political studies (MA); public administration (MA); public policy and international affairs (MA); sociology (MA); theoretical physics (PhD). *Program availability:* Part-time. *Faculty:* 108 full-time (36 women), 5 part-time/adjunct (4 women). *Students:* 251 full-time (180 women), 233 part-time (172 women). Average age 26. 425 applicants, 65% accepted, 121 enrolled. In 2017, 47 master's, 2 doctorates awarded. *Degree requirements:* For master's, one foreign language, comprehensive exam, thesis (for some programs), project; for doctorate, one foreign language, comprehensive exam, thesis/dissertation. *Entrance requirements:* For master's, GRE General Test (for some programs); for doctorate, GRE General Test (GRE Subject Test for theoretical physics). Additional exam requirements/recommendations for international students: Required—TOEFL (minimum score 583 paper-based; 97 iBT), IELTS (minimum score 7). *Application deadline:* For fall admission, 2/8 for domestic students; for spring admission, 11/3 for domestic students. Application fee: $50. Electronic applications accepted. *Expenses:* Contact institution. *Financial support:* In 2017–18, 29 fellowships, 40 research assistantships were awarded; teaching assistantships, scholarships/grants, tuition waivers (full and partial), and unspecified assistantships also available. Financial award application deadline: 4/4. *Unit head:* Dr. Nadia Maria El Cheikh, Dean, Faculty of Arts and Sciences, 961-1-374374 Ext. 3800, Fax: 961-1-744461, E-mail: nmcheikh@aub.edu.lb. *Application contact:* Rima Rassi, Graduate Studies Officer, 961-1-350000 Ext. 3833, Fax: 961-1-744461, E-mail: rr46@aub.edu.lb.
Website: http://www.aub.edu.lb/fas/pages/default.aspx

Arizona State University at the Tempe campus, College of Liberal Arts and Sciences, School of Human Evolution and Social Change, Tempe, AZ 85287-2402. Offers anthropology (MA, PhD), including anthropology (PhD), archaeology (PhD), bioarchaeology (PhD), evolutionary (PhD), museum studies (MA), sociocultural (PhD); applied mathematics for the life and social sciences (PhD); environmental social science (PhD), including environmental social science, urbanism; global health (MA, PhD), including complex adaptive systems science (PhD), evolutionary global health sciences (PhD), health and culture (PhD), urbanism (PhD); immigration studies (Graduate Certificate). Terminal master's awarded for partial completion of doctoral program. *Degree requirements:* For master's, thesis or alternative, interactive Program of Study (iPOS) submitted before completing 50 percent of required credit hours; for doctorate, comprehensive exam, thesis/dissertation, interactive Program of Study (iPOS) submitted before completing 50 percent of required credit hours. *Entrance requirements:* For master's and doctorate, GRE, minimum GPA of 3.0 or equivalent in last 2 years of work leading to bachelor's degree. Additional exam requirements/recommendations for international students: Required—TOEFL, IELTS, or PTE. Electronic applications accepted.

Boston University, Graduate School of Arts and Sciences, Department of Archaeology, Boston, MA 02215. Offers MA, PhD. *Students:* 19 full-time (16 women), 2 part-time (1 woman); includes 1 minority (Hispanic/Latino), 4 international. Average age 27. In 2017, 1 master's, 2 doctorates awarded. Terminal master's awarded for partial completion of doctoral program. *Degree requirements:* For master's, one foreign language, comprehensive exam, thesis or alternative; for doctorate, 2 foreign languages, comprehensive exam, thesis/dissertation. Application fee: $95. *Financial support:* In 2017–18, 17 students received support, including 2 fellowships with full tuition reimbursements available (averaging $22,000 per year), 2 research assistantships with full tuition reimbursements available (averaging $22,000 per year), 8 teaching assistantships with full tuition reimbursements available (averaging $22,000 per year); career-related internships or fieldwork, Federal Work-Study, scholarships/grants, and health care benefits also available. Support available to part-time students. *Unit head:*

Curtis Runnels, Chair, 617-358-1647, Fax: 617-353-6800, E-mail: runnels@bu.edu. *Application contact:* Maria Sousa, Senior Program Coordinator, 617-353-3415, Fax: 617-353-6800, E-mail: mhsousa@bu.edu.
Website: http://www.bu.edu/ARCHAEOLOGY/

Brown University, Graduate School, Department of Egyptology and Assyriology, Providence, RI 02912. Offers ancient western Asian studies (PhD); Egyptology (PhD); history of the exact sciences in antiquity (PhD). *Degree requirements:* For doctorate, 2 foreign languages, comprehensive exam, thesis/dissertation. *Entrance requirements:* For doctorate, GRE General Test.

Brown University, Graduate School, Joukowsky Institute for Archaeology and the Ancient World, Providence, RI 02912. Offers PhD. *Degree requirements:* For doctorate, thesis/dissertation.

Bryn Mawr College, Graduate School of Arts and Sciences, Department of Classical and Near Eastern Archaeology, Bryn Mawr, PA 19010-2899. Offers MA, PhD. *Program availability:* Part-time. *Faculty:* 4 full-time (3 women). *Students:* 11 full-time (8 women), 2 part-time (both women), 1 international. Average age 29. 12 applicants, 33% accepted, 2 enrolled. In 2017, 1 master's, 2 doctorates awarded. *Degree requirements:* For master's, 2 foreign languages, thesis; for doctorate, 3 foreign languages, comprehensive exam, thesis/dissertation. *Entrance requirements:* For master's and doctorate, GRE General Test, transcripts, three letters of recommendation, statement of interest, resume or curriculum vitae, writing sample. Additional exam requirements/recommendations for international students: Required—TOEFL (minimum score 600 paper-based; 100 iBT), IELTS (minimum score 7). *Application deadline:* For fall admission, 12/15 for domestic and international students. Application fee: $50. Electronic applications accepted. *Financial support:* In 2017–18, 13 students received support, including 10 fellowships with tuition reimbursements available (averaging $18,200 per year), 2 teaching assistantships with tuition reimbursements available (averaging $19,000 per year); Federal Work-Study, scholarships/grants, health care benefits, and tuition awards also available. Support available to part-time students. Financial award application deadline: 12/15. *Unit head:* Maria Dantis, Graduate Program Administrator, 610-526-5074, E-mail: gsas@brynmawr.edu.

California State University, Northridge, Graduate Studies, College of Social and Behavioral Sciences, Department of Anthropology, Northridge, CA 91330. Offers general anthropology (MA); public archaeology (MA). *Students:* 7 full-time (3 women), 11 part-time (7 women); includes 13 minority (12 Hispanic/Latino; 1 Two or more races, non-Hispanic/Latino). Average age 30. 22 applicants, 55% accepted, 8 enrolled. In 2017, 12 master's awarded. *Degree requirements:* For master's, thesis or alternative. *Entrance requirements:* For master's, GRE General Test or minimum GPA of 3.0. Additional exam requirements/recommendations for international students: Required—TOEFL. *Application deadline:* For fall admission, 11/30 for domestic students. Application fee: $55. *Financial support:* Career-related internships or fieldwork, Federal Work-Study, and institutionally sponsored loans available. Financial award application deadline: 3/1. *Unit head:* Dr. Suzanne Scheld, Chair, 818-677-3331.
Website: http://www.csun.edu/csbs/departments/anthropology/index.html

California State University, San Bernardino, Graduate Studies, College of Social and Behavioral Sciences, Program in Applied Archaeology, San Bernardino, CA 92407. Offers clinical psychology (MS). *Faculty:* 5 full-time (2 women). *Students:* 15 part-time (10 women); includes 3 minority (1 Black or African American, non-Hispanic/Latino; 1 American Indian or Alaska Native, non-Hispanic/Latino; 1 Hispanic/Latino). Average age 35. 19 applicants, 63% accepted, 10 enrolled. In 2017, 5 master's awarded. *Entrance requirements:* Additional exam requirements/recommendations for international students: Required—TOEFL. *Application deadline:* For fall admission, 5/20 for domestic students. Application fee: $55. *Financial support:* Application deadline: 3/1. *Unit head:* Dr. Wesley Niewoehner, Chair, 909-537-5567, Fax: 909-537-7645, E-mail: wniewoeh@csusb.edu.

Columbia University, Graduate School of Arts and Sciences, New York, NY 10027. Offers African-American studies (MA); American studies (MA); anthropology (MA, PhD); art history and archaeology (MA, PhD); astronomy (PhD); biological sciences (PhD); biotechnology (MA); chemical physics (PhD); chemistry (PhD); classical studies (MA, PhD); classics (MA, PhD); climate and society (MA); conservation biology (MA); earth

and environmental sciences (PhD); East Asia: regional studies (MA); East Asian languages and cultures (MA, PhD); ecology, evolution and environmental biology (MA), including conservation biology; ecology, evolution, and environmental biology (PhD), including ecology and evolutionary biology, evolutionary primatology; economics (MA, PhD); English and comparative literature (MA, PhD); French and Romance philology (MA, PhD); Germanic languages (MA, PhD); global French studies (MA); global thought (MA); Hispanic cultural studies (MA); history (PhD); history and literature (MA); human rights studies (MA); Islamic studies (MA); Italian (MA, PhD); Japanese pedagogy (MA); Jewish studies (MA); Latin America and the Caribbean: regional studies (MA); Latin American and Iberian cultures (PhD); mathematics (MA, PhD), including finance (MA); medieval and Renaissance studies (MA); Middle Eastern, South Asian, and African studies (MA, PhD); modern art: critical and curatorial studies (MA); modern European studies (MA); museum anthropology (MA); music (DMA, PhD); oral history (MA); philosophical foundations of physics (MA); philosophy (MA, PhD); physics (PhD); political science (MA, PhD); psychology (PhD); quantitative methods in the social sciences (MA); religion (MA, PhD); Russia, Eurasia and East Europe: regional studies (MA); Russian translation (MA); Slavic cultures (MA); Slavic languages (MA, PhD); sociology (MA, PhD); South Asian studies (MA); statistics (MA, PhD); theatre (PhD). Dual-degree programs require admission to both Graduate School of Arts and Sciences and another Columbia school. *Program availability:* Part-time. Terminal master's awarded for partial completion of doctoral program. *Degree requirements:* For master's, variable foreign language requirement, comprehensive exam (for some programs), thesis (for some programs); for doctorate, variable foreign language requirement, comprehensive exam (for some programs), thesis/dissertation. *Entrance requirements:* For master's and doctorate, GRE General Test, GRE Subject Test (for some programs). Additional exam requirements/recommendations for international students: Required—TOEFL, IELTS. Electronic applications accepted. *Expenses: Tuition:* Full-time $44,864; part-time $1704 per credit. *Required fees:* $2370 per semester. One-time fee: $105.

Cornell University, Graduate School, Graduate Fields of Arts and Sciences, Field of Archaeology, Ithaca, NY 14853. Offers environmental archaeology (MA); historical archaeology (MA); Latin American archaeology (MA); medieval archaeology (MA); Mediterranean and Near Eastern archaeology (MA); Stone Age archaeology (MA). *Degree requirements:* For master's, one foreign language, thesis. *Entrance requirements:* For master's, GRE General Test, 3 letters of recommendation, sample of written work. Additional exam requirements/recommendations for international students: Required—TOEFL (minimum score 550 paper-based; 77 iBT). Electronic applications accepted. *Faculty research:* Anatolia, Lydia, Sardis, classical and Hellenistic Greece, science in archaeology, North American Indians, Stone Age Africa, Mayan trade.

Cornell University, Graduate School, Graduate Fields of Arts and Sciences, Field of History of Art, Archaeology and Visual Studies, Ithaca, NY 14853. Offers 19th century art (PhD); African, African American and African diaspora (PhD); American art (PhD); ancient art and archaeology (PhD); Asian American art (PhD); Baroque art (PhD); comparative modernities (PhD); digital art (PhD); East Asian art (PhD); history of photography (PhD); Islamic art (PhD); Latin American art (PhD); medieval art (PhD); modern art (PhD); Renaissance art (PhD); Southeast Asian art (PhD); theory and criticism (PhD); visual studies (PhD). *Degree requirements:* For doctorate, one foreign language, comprehensive exam, thesis/dissertation, general exams in 3 areas. *Entrance requirements:* For doctorate, GRE General Test, sample of written work, 3 letters of recommendation. Additional exam requirements/recommendations for international students: Required—TOEFL (minimum score 550 paper-based; 77 iBT). Electronic applications accepted.

Florida State University, The Graduate School, College of Arts and Sciences, Department of Classics, Tallahassee, FL 32306-1510. Offers ancient history (MA); classical archaeology (MA); classical civilization (MA); classics (PhD), including classical archaeology, classics; Greek (MA); Greek and Latin (MA); Latin (MA). *Faculty:* 17 full-time (7 women), 2 part-time/adjunct (1 woman). *Students:* 41 full-time (30 women); includes 4 minority (2 Black or African American, non-Hispanic/Latino; 1 Asian, non-Hispanic/Latino; 1 Hispanic/Latino). Average age 25. 50 applicants, 40% accepted, 12 enrolled. In 2017, 8 master's, 6 doctorates awarded. Terminal master's awarded for partial completion of doctoral program. *Degree requirements:* For master's, 2 foreign languages, comprehensive exam, thesis or alternative; for doctorate, 4 foreign languages, comprehensive exam, thesis/dissertation. *Entrance requirements:* For master's, GRE General Test, minimum GPA of 3.0; for doctorate, GRE General Test, minimum GPA of 3.5. Additional exam requirements/recommendations for international students: Required—TOEFL (minimum score 550 paper-based; 80 iBT). *Application deadline:* For fall admission, 12/15 priority date for domestic students, 12/15 for international students. Applications are processed on a rolling basis. Application fee: $30. Electronic applications accepted. *Financial support:* In 2017–18, 39 students received support, including 1 fellowship with full tuition reimbursement available (averaging $18,000 per year), 2 research assistantships with full tuition reimbursements available (averaging $12,000 per year), 24 teaching assistantships with full tuition reimbursements available (averaging $12,400 per year); Federal Work-Study, scholarships/grants, tuition waivers (full), and unspecified assistantships also available. Financial award application deadline: 1/15; financial award applicants required to submit FAFSA. *Faculty research:* Greek and Latin literature, classical archaeology, mythology, ancient history, religion. *Total annual research expenditures:* $100,000. *Unit head:* Dr. Daniel J. Pullen, Chairman, 850-644-0304, Fax: 850-644-4073, E-mail: dpullen@fsu.edu. *Application contact:* Dr. Timothy Stover, Admissions Director, 850-644-4259, Fax: 850-644-4073, E-mail: tstover@fsu.edu.
Website: http://classics.fsu.edu/

Gordon-Conwell Theological Seminary, Graduate and Professional Programs, South Hamilton, MA 01982. Offers Biblical languages (MABL); church history (MACH); counseling (MACO); ministry (D Min); missions/evangelism (MAME); New Testament (MANT); Old Testament (MAOT); religion (MAR); theology (M Div, MATH, Th M, Th D). *Accreditation:* ACIPE; ATS (one or more programs are accredited). *Program availability:* Part-time, evening/weekend. *Degree requirements:* For master's, one foreign language, thesis optional; for doctorate, 2 foreign languages, thesis/dissertation. *Entrance requirements:* For master's, minimum GPA of 2.5; for doctorate, minimum GPA of 3.0.

The Graduate Center, City University of New York, Graduate Studies, Program in Anthropology, New York, NY 10016-4039. Offers anthropological linguistics (PhD); archaeology (PhD); cultural anthropology (PhD); physical anthropology (PhD). *Faculty:* 39 full-time (14 women). *Students:* 166 full-time (103 women), 2 part-time (both women); includes 34 minority (5 Black or African American, non-Hispanic/Latino; 5 Asian, non-Hispanic/Latino; 21 Hispanic/Latino; 3 Two or more races, non-Hispanic/Latino), 39 international. Average age 33. 145 applicants, 14% accepted, 19 enrolled. In 2017, 14 doctorates awarded. *Degree requirements:* For doctorate, one foreign language, thesis/dissertation. *Entrance requirements:* For doctorate, GRE General Test. Additional exam requirements/recommendations for international students: Required—TOEFL. *Application deadline:* For fall admission, 1/8 priority date for domestic students. Application fee: $125. Electronic applications accepted. *Financial support:* In 2017–18, 111 students received support, including 88 fellowships, 16 research assistantships, 10 teaching assistantships; career-related internships or fieldwork, Federal Work-Study, institutionally sponsored loans, and tuition waivers (full and partial) also available.

Financial award application deadline: 2/1; financial award applicants required to submit FAFSA. *Unit head:* Prof. Jeff Maskovsky, Acting Executive Officer, 212-817-8006, Fax: 212-817-1501, E-mail: jmaskovsky@gc.cuny.edu. *Application contact:* Information Contact, 212-817-8005, Fax: 212-817-1501, E-mail: anthro@gc.cuny.edu.

Harvard University, Graduate School of Arts and Sciences, Department of Anthropology, Cambridge, MA 02138. Offers archaeology (PhD); biological anthropology (PhD); legal anthropology (AM); medical anthropology (AM); social anthropology (AM, PhD); social change and development (AM). Terminal master's awarded for partial completion of doctoral program. *Degree requirements:* For master's, 2 foreign languages, thesis (for some programs); for doctorate, 2 foreign languages, thesis/dissertation, laboratory and/or fieldwork; general, qualifying, or special exams. *Entrance requirements:* For master's and doctorate, GRE General Test. Additional exam requirements/recommendations for international students: Required—TOEFL.

Harvard University, Graduate School of Arts and Sciences, Department of Near Eastern Languages and Civilizations, Cambridge, MA 02138. Offers Akkadian and Sumerian (AM, PhD); Arabic (AM, PhD); Armenian (AM, PhD); biblical history (AM, PhD); Hebrew (AM, PhD); Indo-Muslim culture (AM, PhD); Iranian (AM, PhD); Jewish history and literature (AM, PhD); Persian (AM, PhD); Semitic philology (AM, PhD); Syro-Palestinian archaeology (AM, PhD); Turkish (AM, PhD). *Degree requirements:* For doctorate, variable foreign language requirement, thesis/dissertation, general exams. *Entrance requirements:* For master's, GRE General Test; for doctorate, GRE General Test, proficiency in a Near Eastern language. Additional exam requirements/recommendations for international students: Required—TOEFL.

Harvard University, Graduate School of Arts and Sciences, Department of the Classics, Cambridge, MA 02138. Offers Byzantine Greek (PhD); classical archaeology (PhD); classical philology (PhD); classical philosophy (PhD); medieval Latin (PhD). *Degree requirements:* For doctorate, 4 foreign languages, thesis/dissertation, preliminary and special exams. *Entrance requirements:* For doctorate, GRE General Test. Additional exam requirements/recommendations for international students: Required—TOEFL.

Illinois State University, Graduate School, College of Arts and Sciences, Department of Sociology, Program in Historical Archaeology, Normal, IL 61790. Offers MA, MS.

Indiana University Bloomington, University Graduate School, College of Arts and Sciences, Department of Anthropology, Bloomington, IN 47405. Offers anthropology (MA, PhD), including archaeology (PhD); bioanthropology (PhD); linguistic anthropology (PhD); social-cultural anthropology (PhD). *Degree requirements:* For master's, comprehensive exam (for some programs), thesis or alternative; for doctorate, 2 foreign languages, comprehensive exam, thesis/dissertation. *Entrance requirements:* For master's and doctorate, GRE General Test, minimum GPA of 3.0. Additional exam requirements/recommendations for international students: Required—TOEFL (minimum score 550 paper-based, 79 iBT) or IELTS. Electronic applications accepted. *Expenses:* Contact institution. *Faculty research:* Archaeology in social context; bioanthropology; anthropology of food and ecology; gender studies; communication, media and performance.

Indiana University of Pennsylvania, School of Graduate Studies and Research, College of Humanities and Social Sciences, Department of Anthropology, Indiana, PA 15705. Offers applied archaeology (MA). *Program availability:* Part-time. *Faculty:* 5 full-time (3 women). *Students:* 19 full-time (7 women), 1 part-time (0 women); includes 2 minority (1 Asian, non-Hispanic/Latino; 1 Two or more races, non-Hispanic/Latino), 1 international. Average age 26. 18 applicants, 83% accepted, 9 enrolled. *Degree requirements:* For master's, thesis and/or internship. *Entrance requirements:* For master's, GRE, 2 letters of recommendation. Additional exam requirements/recommendations for international students: Required—TOEFL (minimum score 540 paper-based). *Application deadline:* Applications are processed on a rolling basis. Application fee: $50. Electronic applications accepted. *Expenses:* Tuition, state resident: full-time $12,000; part-time $500 per credit. Tuition, nonresident: full-time $18,000; part-time $750 per credit. *Required fees:* $4073; $165.55 per credit. $64 per term. *Financial support:* In 2017–18, 8 research assistantships with tuition reimbursements (averaging $3,095 per year) were awarded; fellowships with partial tuition reimbursements, Federal Work-Study, scholarships/grants, and unspecified assistantships also available. Financial award application deadline: 4/15; financial award applicants required to submit FAFSA. *Unit head:* Dr. Ben Ford, Chair, 724-357-2733, Fax: 724-357-7637, E-mail: ben.ford@iup.edu.
Website: http://www.iup.edu/anthropology/

Johns Hopkins University, Zanvyl Krieger School of Arts and Sciences, Department of Near Eastern Studies, Baltimore, MD 21218. Offers archaeology (PhD); Assyriology (PhD); Egyptology (PhD); Hebrew Bible/Northwest Semitics (PhD). *Faculty:* 8 full-time (2 women), 1 part-time/adjunct (0 women). *Students:* 22 full-time (13 women); includes 3 minority (1 Black or African American, non-Hispanic/Latino; 1 Asian, non-Hispanic/Latino; 1 Hispanic/Latino), 5 international. Average age 31. 54 applicants, 15% accepted, 4 enrolled. In 2017, 4 doctorates awarded. *Degree requirements:* For doctorate, 2 foreign languages, comprehensive exam, thesis/dissertation. *Entrance requirements:* For doctorate, GRE. Additional exam requirements/recommendations for international students: Required—TOEFL (minimum score 600 paper-based; 100 iBT); Recommended—IELTS. *Application deadline:* For fall admission, 12/15 for domestic and international students. Application fee: $75. Electronic applications accepted. *Expenses:* $10,434. *Financial support:* In 2017–18, 17 students received support, including 17 fellowships with full tuition reimbursements available (averaging $27,000 per year); teaching assistantships, career-related internships or fieldwork, Federal Work-Study, scholarships/grants, and health care benefits also available. Financial award application deadline: 4/15; financial award applicants required to submit FAFSA. *Faculty research:* Egyptology, Assyriology, Hebrew Bible/Northwest Semitic languages, Demotic Egyptian, archaeology. *Total annual research expenditures:* $64,479. *Unit head:* Dr. Glenn Schwartz, Chair, 410-516-8492, Fax: 410-516-5218, E-mail: schwartz@jhu.edu. *Application contact:* Glenda Hogan, Academic Program Coordinator, 410-516-7394, Fax: 410-516-5218, E-mail: ghogan@jhu.edu.
Website: http://neareast.jhu.edu/

Massachusetts Institute of Technology, School of Engineering, Department of Materials Science and Engineering, Cambridge, MA 02139. Offers archaeological materials (PhD, Sc D); materials engineering (Mat E); materials science and engineering (SM, PhD, Sc D). *Degree requirements:* For master's, thesis; for doctorate, comprehensive exam, thesis/dissertation; for Mat E, comprehensive exam, thesis. *Entrance requirements:* For master's and doctorate, GRE General Test. Additional exam requirements/recommendations for international students: Required—IELTS. Electronic applications accepted. *Faculty research:* Thermodynamics and kinetics of materials; structure, processing and properties of materials; electronic, structural and biological materials engineering; computational materials science; materials in energy, medicine, nanotechnology and the environment.

Memorial University of Newfoundland, School of Graduate Studies, Department of Anthropology, St. John's, NL A1C 5S7, Canada. Offers archaeology and physical anthropology (MA, PhD); social and cultural anthropology (MA, PhD). *Program availability:* Part-time. *Degree requirements:* For master's, comprehensive exam (for

some programs), thesis (for some programs); for doctorate, comprehensive exam, thesis/dissertation, oral defense of thesis. *Entrance requirements:* For master's, 2nd class degree in related field. Electronic applications accepted. *Faculty research:* Early European settlements, ethnoarchaeology, economic/political anthropology, land claims and aboriginal rights, marine anthropology.

Mercyhurst University, Graduate Studies, Program in Anthropology, Erie, PA 16546. Offers archaeology and geological archaeology (MS); forensic and biological anthropology (MS). *Entrance requirements:* For master's, GRE or MAT, undergraduate degree in related field, interview, resume, essay, three professional references, transcripts. Additional exam requirements/recommendations for international students: Required—TOEFL.

Michigan Technological University, Graduate School, College of Sciences and Arts, Department of Social Sciences, Houghton, MI 49931. Offers environmental and energy policy (MS, PhD); industrial archaeology (MS); industrial heritage and archaeology (PhD). *Faculty:* 29 full-time (14 women), 9 part-time/adjunct (2 women). *Students:* 21 full-time (10 women), 14 part-time; includes 3 minority (2 American Indian or Alaska Native, non-Hispanic/Latino; 1 Two or more races, non-Hispanic/Latino), 8 international. Average age 35. 62 applicants, 15% accepted, 7 enrolled. In 2017, 3 master's, 2 doctorates awarded. *Degree requirements:* For master's, thesis; for doctorate, comprehensive exam, thesis/dissertation. *Entrance requirements:* For master's and doctorate, GRE, statement of purpose, official transcripts, 3 letters of recommendation, writing sample, resume/curriculum vitae. Additional exam requirements/ recommendations for international students: Required—TOEFL (recommended minimum score 100 iBT) or IELTS (recommended minimum score of 7.0). *Application deadline:* For fall admission, 1/15 priority date for domestic and international students; for spring admission, 10/1 for domestic students. Applications are processed on a rolling basis. Application fee: $0. Electronic applications accepted. *Expenses:* Tuition, state resident: full-time $17,100; part-time $950 per credit. Tuition, nonresident: full-time $17,100; part-time $950 per credit. *Required fees:* $248; $124 per term. Tuition and fees vary according to course load and program. *Financial support:* In 2017–18, 23 students received support, including fellowships with tuition reimbursements available (averaging $15,790 per year), 5 research assistantships with tuition reimbursements available (averaging $15,790 per year), 13 teaching assistantships with tuition reimbursements available (averaging $15,790 per year); career-related internships or fieldwork, scholarships/grants, health care benefits, and unspecified assistantships also available. Financial award application deadline: 1/15. *Faculty research:* Industrial archaeology, Industrial heritage, environment policy, energy policy. *Total annual research expenditures:* $777,813. *Unit head:* Dr. Hugh S. Gorman, Chair, 906-487-2116, E-mail: hsgorman@mtu.edu. *Application contact:* Amy Spahn, Office Assistant, 906-487-2113, E-mail: aspahn@mtu.edu.
Website: http://www.mtu.edu/social-sciences/

New York University, Graduate School of Arts and Science, Institute of Fine Arts, Program in Art History and Archaeology, New York, NY 10012-1019. Offers architectural studies (PhD); art history and archaeology (MA, PhD); classical art and archaeology (PhD); curatorial studies (PhD); East and South Asian art (PhD); Near Eastern art and archaeology (PhD); MA/Diploma; PhD/Certificate. *Program availability:* Part-time. *Students:* Average age 31. 346 applicants, 43% accepted, 52 enrolled. In 2017, 47 master's, 24 doctorates awarded. Terminal master's awarded for partial completion of doctoral program. *Degree requirements:* For master's, 2 foreign languages, thesis or alternative, 2 qualifying papers; for doctorate, 2 foreign languages, thesis/dissertation. *Entrance requirements:* For master's, GRE General Test; for doctorate, GRE General Test, MA. Additional exam requirements/recommendations for international students: Required—TOEFL. *Application deadline:* For fall admission, 12/18 for domestic and international students. Application fee: $100. *Expenses: Tuition:* Full-time $41,352; part-time $19,968 per year. *Required fees:* $2496; $1628 per unit. $814 per term. Tuition and fees vary according to course load and program. *Financial support:* Fellowships, research assistantships, teaching assistantships, career-related internships or fieldwork, Federal Work-Study, and institutionally sponsored loans available. Financial award application deadline: 12/18; financial award applicants required to submit FAFSA. *Unit head:* Patricia Rubin, Chair, 212-992-5800, Fax: 212-992-5807, E-mail: ifa.program@nyu.edu. *Application contact:* Alexander Nagel, Director of Graduate Studies, 212-992-5800, Fax: 212-992-5807, E-mail: ifa.program@nyu.edu.
Website: http://www.nyu.edu/gsas/dept/fineart/

Princeton University, Graduate School, Department of Art and Archaeology, Princeton, NJ 08544-1019. Offers classical art and archaeology (PhD); East Asian art and archaeology (PhD). *Degree requirements:* For doctorate, 2 foreign languages, thesis/ dissertation. *Entrance requirements:* For doctorate, GRE General Test. Additional exam requirements/recommendations for international students: Required—TOEFL (minimum score 600 paper-based). Electronic applications accepted.

Rice University, Graduate Programs, School of Social Sciences, Department of Anthropology, Houston, TX 77251-1892. Offers archaeology (MA, PhD); social-cultural anthropology (MA, PhD). Terminal master's awarded for partial completion of doctoral program. *Degree requirements:* For master's, one foreign language, 3 major papers, dissertation proposal and language exam or thesis; for doctorate, one foreign language, thesis/dissertation. *Entrance requirements:* For master's and doctorate, research proposal. Additional exam requirements/recommendations for international students: Required—TOEFL (minimum score 90 iBT). Electronic applications accepted.

St. Cloud State University, School of Graduate Studies, College of Social Sciences, Program in Cultural Resource Management Archeology, St. Cloud, MN 56301-4498. Offers MS. *Entrance requirements:* For master's, GRE General Test, minimum GPA of 2.75. Additional exam requirements/recommendations for international students: Required—Michigan English Language Assessment Battery; Recommended—TOEFL (minimum score 550 paper-based).

San Francisco State University, Division of Graduate Studies, College of Liberal and Creative Arts, Department of Anthropology, San Francisco, CA 94132-1722. Offers archaeology (MA); biological anthropology (MA); cultural anthropology (MA); visual anthropology (MA). *Faculty research:* Immigration, ethnicity, urban anthropology, Californian and Latin American archaeology. *Unit head:* Dr. Cynthia Wilczak, Chair, 415-338-2046, Fax: 415-338-6159, E-mail: anthro@sfsu.edu. *Application contact:* Dr. Douglass Bailey, Graduate Coordinator, 415-338-1427, Fax: 415-338-6159, E-mail: dwbailey@sfsu.edu.
Website: http://anthropology.sfsu.edu/

Simon Fraser University, Office of Graduate Studies and Postdoctoral Fellows, Faculty of Environment, Department of Archaeology, Burnaby, BC V5A 1S6, Canada. Offers MA, PhD. *Degree requirements:* For master's, one foreign language, thesis; for doctorate, one foreign language, comprehensive exam, thesis/dissertation. *Entrance requirements:* For master's, minimum GPA of 3.0 (on scale of 4.33) or 3.33 based on last 60 credits of undergraduate courses; for doctorate, minimum GPA of 3.5 (on scale of 4.33). Additional exam requirements/recommendations for international students: Recommended—TOEFL (minimum score 580 paper-based; 93 iBT), IELTS (minimum score 7), TWE (minimum score 5). Electronic applications accepted. *Faculty research:* Archaeometry, cultural resource management, ethnoarchaeology, forensic anthropology, palaeoethnobotany, skeletal biology, zoo archaeology.

Stanford University, School of Humanities and Sciences, Department of Anthropology, Stanford, CA 94305-2004. Offers anthropology (MA); archaeology (PhD); culture and society (PhD); ecology and environment (PhD). Terminal master's awarded for partial completion of doctoral program. *Degree requirements:* For master's, thesis; for doctorate, one foreign language, thesis/dissertation. *Entrance requirements:* For master's and doctorate, GRE General Test. Additional exam requirements/ recommendations for international students: Required—TOEFL. Electronic applications accepted. *Expenses: Tuition:* Full-time $48,987; part-time $10,620 per quarter. One-time fee: $400. Tuition and fees vary according to program.

Trinity International University, Trinity Evangelical Divinity School, Deerfield, IL 60015-1284. Offers academic ministry (M Div); Biblical and Near Eastern archaeology and languages (MA); chaplaincy and ministry care (MA); Christian studies (Certificate); church and parachurch ministry (M Div); church history (MA, Th M); counseling (Th M); educational ministries (MA); educational ministry (Th M); educational studies (PhD); intercultural studies (MA, PhD); leadership and management (D Min); mental health counseling (MA); military chaplaincy (D Min); ministry (MA); missions (Th M); missions and evangelism (D Min); New Testament (MA, Th M); Old Testament (Th M); Old Testament and Semitic languages (MA); pastoral ministry and care (D Min); pastoral theology (Th M); preaching and teaching (D Min); spiritual formation and education (D Min); systematic theology (MA, Th M); theological studies (MA, PhD); urban ministry (MA). *Program availability:* Part-time, online learning. *Degree requirements:* For master's, comprehensive exam, thesis, fieldwork; for doctorate, comprehensive exam (for some programs), thesis/dissertation; for Certificate, comprehensive exam, integrative papers. *Entrance requirements:* For master's, GRE, MAT, minimum cumulative undergraduate GPA of 3.0; for doctorate, GRE, minimum cumulative graduate GPA of 3.2; for Certificate, GRE, MAT, minimum undergraduate GPA of 2.5. Additional exam requirements/recommendations for international students: Required—TOEFL (minimum score 580 paper-based), TWE (minimum score 4). Electronic applications accepted.

Universidad de las Américas Puebla, Division of Graduate Studies, School of Social Sciences, Program in Anthropology, Puebla, Mexico. Offers anthropology (MA); archaeology (MA). *Program availability:* Part-time, evening/weekend. *Degree requirements:* For master's, one foreign language, thesis. *Entrance requirements:* For master's, bachelor's degree in anthropology or equivalent. *Faculty research:* Archaeology, ethnography, and ethnohistory of Mesoamerica.

Université Laval, Faculty of Letters, Department of History, Programs in Archaeology, Québec, QC G1K 7P4, Canada. Offers MA, PhD. Terminal master's awarded for partial completion of doctoral program. *Degree requirements:* For master's, thesis; for doctorate, comprehensive exam, thesis/dissertation. *Entrance requirements:* For master's and doctorate, English test, knowledge of French. Electronic applications accepted.

University of Alberta, Faculty of Graduate Studies and Research, Department of History and Classics, Edmonton, AB T6G 2E1, Canada. Offers ancient history (PhD); classical archaeology (MA, PhD); classical literature (PhD); classics (MA); history (MA, PhD). *Program availability:* Part-time, evening/weekend. *Degree requirements:* For master's, one foreign language, thesis (for some programs); for doctorate, one foreign language, thesis/dissertation. *Entrance requirements:* For master's, minimum B+ average; for doctorate, minimum A- average. Additional exam requirements/ recommendations for international students: Required—TOEFL (minimum score 580 paper-based). Electronic applications accepted. *Faculty research:* Western Canada, classical archaeology, Britain, Eastern Europe, East Asia.

The University of British Columbia, Faculty of Arts, Department of Classical, Near Eastern and Religious Studies, Program in Classical and Near Eastern Archaeology, Vancouver, BC V6T 1Z1, Canada. Offers MA. *Degree requirements:* For master's, thesis.

University of Calgary, Faculty of Graduate Studies, Faculty of Arts, Department of Archaeology, Calgary, AB T2N 1N4, Canada. Offers MA. *Degree requirements:* For master's, thesis. *Entrance requirements:* For master's, BA or B Sc in anthropology or archaeology; statement of intent; sample of written work; curriculum vitae. Additional exam requirements/recommendations for international students: Required—TOEFL. Electronic applications accepted. *Faculty research:* Pre-history, ethnoarchaeology, Africa, Latin America, biological anthropology.

University of California, Berkeley, Graduate Division, College of Letters and Science, Department of Classics, Berkeley, CA 94720-1500. Offers classical archaeology (MA, PhD); classics (MA, PhD); Greek (MA); Latin (MA). Terminal master's awarded for partial completion of doctoral program. *Degree requirements:* For master's, one foreign language, exams; for doctorate, 2 foreign languages, thesis/dissertation, qualifying exam. *Entrance requirements:* For master's and doctorate, GRE General Test, minimum GPA of 3.0, 3 letters of recommendation. Additional exam requirements/ recommendations for international students: Required—TOEFL (minimum score 570 paper-based; 90 iBT), TWE. Electronic applications accepted. *Faculty research:* Greek and Latin literature, textual criticism, history, archaeology and philosophy.

University of California, Berkeley, Graduate Division, College of Letters and Science, Group in Ancient History and Mediterranean Archaeology, Berkeley, CA 94720-1500. Offers MA, PhD. Terminal master's awarded for partial completion of doctoral program. *Degree requirements:* For master's, one foreign language, exam or thesis; for doctorate, 2 foreign languages, thesis/dissertation, qualifying exam. *Entrance requirements:* For master's and doctorate, GRE General Test, minimum GPA of 3.0, 3 letters of recommendation. Additional exam requirements/recommendations for international students: Required—TOEFL (minimum score 570 paper-based; 90 iBT), TWE. Electronic applications accepted.

University of California, Los Angeles, Graduate Division, College of Letters and Science, Interdepartmental Program in Archaeology, Los Angeles, CA 90095. Offers MA, PhD. Terminal master's awarded for partial completion of doctoral program. *Degree requirements:* For master's, one foreign language, comprehensive exam, field experience; for doctorate, 2 foreign languages, thesis/dissertation, oral and written qualifying exams. *Entrance requirements:* For doctorate, GRE General Test, bachelor's degree; minimum undergraduate GPA of 3.0 (or its equivalent if letter grade system not used); writing sample. Additional exam requirements/recommendations for international students: Required—TOEFL. Electronic applications accepted.

University of California, Los Angeles, Graduate Division, College of Letters and Science, Interdepartmental Program in Conservation of Archaeological and Ethnographic Materials, Los Angeles, CA 90095. Offers MA. *Degree requirements:* For master's, one foreign language, thesis, eleven-month internship. *Entrance requirements:* For master's, GRE General Test, bachelor's degree; minimum undergraduate GPA of 3.0 (or its equivalent if letter grade system not used); proficiency in one foreign language; portfolio; writing sample; documented practical experience; interview. Additional exam requirements/recommendations for international students: Required—TOEFL.

University of Chicago, Division of the Social Sciences, Department of Anthropology, Chicago, IL 60637. Offers archaeology (PhD); sociocultural and linguistic anthropology (PhD). *Faculty:* 23. *Students:* 129 full-time (74 women); includes 20 minority (6 Black or African American, non-Hispanic/Latino; 2 American Indian or Alaska Native, non-Hispanic/Latino; 2 Asian, non-Hispanic/Latino; 4 Hispanic/Latino; 6 Two or more races, non-Hispanic/Latino), 45 international. Average age 31. 260 applicants, 7% accepted, 11 enrolled. In 2017, 13 doctorates awarded. *Degree requirements:* For doctorate, one foreign language, thesis/dissertation. *Entrance requirements:* For doctorate, GRE General Test, 3 letters of recommendation, statement of purpose, transcripts, resume or curriculum vitae, writing sample (dependent on department). Additional exam requirements/recommendations for international students: Required—TOEFL (minimum score 104 iBT), IELTS (minimum score 7). *Application deadline:* For fall admission, 12/15 for domestic and international students. Application fee: $90. Electronic applications accepted. *Financial support:* In 2017–18, 16 students received support, including 12 fellowships with full tuition reimbursements available (averaging $27,000 per year); research assistantships, teaching assistantships, career-related internships or fieldwork, Federal Work-Study, institutionally sponsored loans, scholarships/grants, and health care benefits also available. Financial award application deadline: 12/15. *Unit head:* Dr. William Mazzarella, Chair, 773-834-4873, E-mail: mazzarel@uchicago.edu. *Application contact:* Office of the Dean of Students, 773-702-8415, E-mail: ssd-admissions@uchicago.edu.
Website: http://anthropology.uchicago.edu

University of Colorado Denver, College of Liberal Arts and Sciences, Department of Anthropology, Denver, CO 80217. Offers archaeological studies (MA); biological anthropology (MA); medical anthropology (MA); sustainable development and political ecology (MA). *Program availability:* Part-time, evening/weekend. *Degree requirements:* For master's, comprehensive exam, thesis or alternative, 30-36 credit hours. *Entrance requirements:* For master's, GRE General Test, minimum GPA of 3.0 for all undergraduate studies, transcripts from all undergraduate/graduate institutions attended, prior training in anthropology, three letters of recommendation, statement of purpose. Additional exam requirements/recommendations for international students: Required—TOEFL (minimum score 537 paper-based; 75 iBT); Recommended—IELTS (minimum score 6.5). Electronic applications accepted. *Faculty research:* Applied medical anthropology, primate social behavior, environmental anthropology, Southwestern and Mexican archaeology, human ecology.

University of Denver, Division of Arts, Humanities and Social Sciences, Department of Anthropology, Denver, CO 80208. Offers archaeology (MA); cultural anthropology (MA); museum and heritage studies (MA). *Program availability:* Part-time. *Faculty:* 8 full-time (2 women). *Students:* 3 full-time (all women), 23 part-time (20 women); includes 2 minority (1 Black or African American, non-Hispanic/Latino; 1 Hispanic/Latino), 1 international. Average age 25. 49 applicants, 59% accepted, 12 enrolled. In 2017, 9 master's awarded. *Degree requirements:* For master's, one foreign language, comprehensive exam, thesis (for some programs), tool, foreign language literacy, or course work. *Entrance requirements:* For master's, GRE General Test, bachelor's degree, transcripts, personal statement, two letters of recommendation. Additional exam requirements/recommendations for international students: Required—TOEFL (minimum score 550 paper-based; 80 iBT). *Application deadline:* For fall admission, 2/4 priority date for domestic and international students. Applications are processed on a rolling basis. Application fee: $65. Electronic applications accepted. *Expenses:* $31,935 per year full-time. *Financial support:* In 2017–18, 23 students received support. Teaching assistantships with tuition reimbursements available, career-related internships or fieldwork, Federal Work-Study, institutionally sponsored loans, scholarships/grants, and unspecified assistantships available. Support available to part-time students. Financial award application deadline: 2/15; financial award applicants required to submit FAFSA. *Faculty research:* Human diversity, human rights, historic archaeology, museums and heritage, high-tech field methods. *Unit head:* Dr. Larry Conyers, Professor and Chair, 303-871-2684, Fax: 303-871-2437, E-mail: lconyers@du.edu.
Website: http://www.du.edu/ahss/anthropology

University of Lethbridge, School of Graduate Studies, Lethbridge, AB T1K 3M4, Canada. Offers addictions counseling (M Sc); agricultural biotechnology (M Sc); agricultural studies (M Sc, MA); anthropology (MA); archaeology (M Sc, MA); art (MA, MFA); biochemistry (M Sc); biological sciences (M Sc); biomolecular science (PhD); biosystems and biodiversity (PhD); Canadian studies (MA); chemistry (M Sc); computer science (M Sc); computer science and geographical information science (M Sc); counseling (MC); counseling psychology (M Ed); dramatic arts (MA); earth, space, and physical science (PhD); economics (MA); education (MA, PhD); educational leadership (M Ed); English (MA); environmental science (M Sc); evolution and behavior (PhD); exercise science (M Sc); French (MA); French/German (MA); French/Spanish (MA); general education (M Ed); geography (M Sc, MA); German (MA); health sciences (M Sc); individualized multidisciplinary (M Sc, MA); kinesiology (M Sc, MA); management (M Sc), including accounting, finance, human resource management and labor relations, information systems, international management, marketing, policy and strategy; mathematics (M Sc); music (M Mus, MA); Native American studies (MA); neuroscience (M Sc, PhD); new media (MA, MFA); nursing (M Sc, MN); philosophy (MA); physics (M Sc); political science (MA); psychology (M Sc, MA); religious studies (MA); sociology (MA); theatre and dramatic arts (MFA); theoretical and computational science (PhD); urban and regional studies (MA); women and gender studies (MA). *Program availability:* Part-time, evening/weekend. *Degree requirements:* For master's, thesis (for some programs); for doctorate, comprehensive exam, thesis/dissertation. *Entrance requirements:* For master's, GMAT (for M Sc in management), bachelor's degree in related field, minimum GPA of 3.0 during previous 20 graded semester courses, 2 years' teaching or related experience (M Ed); for doctorate, master's degree, minimum graduate GPA of 3.5. Additional exam requirements/recommendations for international students: Required—TOEFL (minimum score 580 paper-based; 93 iBT). Electronic applications accepted. *Faculty research:* Movement and brain plasticity, gibberellin physiology, photosynthesis, carbon cycling, molecular properties of main-group ring components.

The University of Manchester, Faculty of Life Sciences, Manchester, United Kingdom. Offers adaptive organismal biology (M Phil, PhD); animal biology (M Phil, PhD); biochemistry (M Phil, PhD); bioinformatics (M Phil, PhD); biomolecular sciences (M Phil, PhD); biotechnology (M Phil, PhD); cell biology (M Phil, PhD); cell matrix research (M Phil, PhD); channels and transporters (M Phil, PhD); developmental biology (M Phil, PhD); Egyptology (M Phil, PhD); environmental biology (M Phil, PhD); evolutionary biology (M Phil, PhD); gene expression (M Phil, PhD); genetics (M Phil, PhD); history of science, technology and medicine (M Phil, PhD); immunology (M Phil, PhD); integrative neurobiology and behavior (M Phil, PhD); membrane trafficking (M Phil, PhD); microbiology (M Phil, PhD); molecular and cellular neuroscience (M Phil, PhD); molecular biology (M Phil, PhD); molecular cancer studies (M Phil, PhD); neuroscience (M Phil, PhD); ophthalmology (M Phil, PhD); optometry (M Phil, PhD); organelle function (M Phil, PhD); pharmacology (M Phil, PhD); physiology (M Phil, PhD); plant sciences (M Phil, PhD); stem cell research (M Phil, PhD); structural biology (M Phil, PhD); systems neuroscience (M Phil, PhD); toxicology (M Phil, PhD).

The University of Manchester, School of Arts, Histories and Cultures, Manchester, United Kingdom. Offers anthropology, media and performance (PhD); applied theatre professional (PhD); archaeology (PhD); art history and visual studies (PhD); arts management and cultural policy (PhD); classics and ancient history (PhD); composition (PhD); creative writing (PhD); drama (PhD); economic and social history (PhD); electroacoustic composition (PhD); English and American studies (PhD); history (PhD); humanitarianism and conflict response (PhD); museology (PhD); music (PhD); musicology (PhD); religions and theology (PhD).

University of Massachusetts Boston, College of Liberal Arts, Program in Historical Archaeology, Boston, MA 02125-3393. Offers MA. *Program availability:* Part-time, evening/weekend. *Students:* 11 full-time (6 women), 42 part-time (27 women); includes 4 minority (1 Black or African American, non-Hispanic/Latino; 1 Hispanic/Latino; 2 Two or more races, non-Hispanic/Latino), 1 international. Average age 28. 22 applicants, 73% accepted, 10 enrolled. In 2017, 3 master's awarded. *Entrance requirements:* For master's, GRE General Test, minimum GPA of 2.75. *Application deadline:* For fall admission, 3/1 for domestic students; for spring admission, 11/1 for domestic students. *Expenses:* Tuition, state resident: full-time $17,375. Tuition, nonresident: full-time $33,915. *Required fees:* $355. *Financial support:* Research assistantships, teaching assistantships, career-related internships or fieldwork, Federal Work-Study, and unspecified assistantships available. Support available to part-time students. Financial award application deadline: 3/1; financial award applicants required to submit FAFSA. *Faculty research:* New World Colonialism, New England archeology, historical and urban archeology, archeological botany, ethnology. *Unit head:* Dr. Stephen Silliman, Associate Director, 617-287-6850, E-mail: stephen.silliman@umb.edu. *Application contact:* Graduate Admissions Coordinator, 617-287-6400, Fax: 617-287-6236, E-mail: bos.gadm@dpc.umassp.edu.

University of Memphis, Graduate School, College of Arts and Sciences, Department of Earth Sciences, Memphis, TN 38152. Offers earth sciences (MA, MS, PhD), including archaeology (MS), geography (MS), geology (MS), geophysics (MS), interdisciplinary studies (MS); geographic information systems (Graduate Certificate), including geographic information systems, GIS educator, GIS planning, GIS professional. *Program availability:* Part-time, evening/weekend. *Faculty:* 18 full-time (3 women), 4 part-time/adjunct (0 women). *Students:* 55 full-time (23 women), 24 part-time (4 women); includes 5 minority (1 Black or African American, non-Hispanic/Latino; 4 Asian, non-Hispanic/Latino), 19 international. Average age 31. 17 applicants, 82% accepted, 11 enrolled. In 2017, 7 master's, 5 doctorates, 3 other advanced degrees awarded. Terminal master's awarded for partial completion of doctoral program. *Degree requirements:* For master's, comprehensive exam, thesis, seminar presentation; for doctorate, comprehensive exam, thesis/dissertation, qualifying exam, submission of two manuscripts for publication in peer-reviewed journal or books. *Entrance requirements:* For master's, GRE General Test, 3 letters of recommendation, statement of research interests; for doctorate, GRE General Test, 2 letters of recommendation, resume, personal statement. Additional exam requirements/recommendations for international students: Required—TOEFL (minimum score 550 paper-based; 79 iBT). *Application deadline:* For fall admission, 1/15 for domestic students; for spring admission, 11/1 for domestic students. Applications are processed on a rolling basis. Application fee: $35 ($60 for international students). Electronic applications accepted. *Expenses:* Contact institution. *Financial support:* In 2017–18, 18 students received support, including 2 research assistantships with full tuition reimbursements available (averaging $17,000 per year), 13 teaching assistantships with full tuition reimbursements available (averaging $16,692 per year); fellowships with full tuition reimbursements available, Federal Work-Study, scholarships/grants, and unspecified assistantships also available. Financial award application deadline: 2/1; financial award applicants required to submit FAFSA. *Faculty research:* Hazards, active tectonics, geophysics, hydrology and water resources, spatial analysis. *Unit head:* Dr. Daniel Larsen, Chair, 901-678-4538, Fax: 901-678-2178, E-mail: dlarsen@memphis.edu. *Application contact:* Dr. Randel T. Cox, Graduate Coordinator, 901-678-4361, Fax: 901-678-2178, E-mail: randycox@memphis.edu.
Website: http://www.memphis.edu/earthsciences/

University of Michigan, Rackham Graduate School, College of Literature, Science, and the Arts, Department of Anthropology, Ann Arbor, MI 48109. Offers anthropological archaeology (PhD); biological anthropology (PhD); linguistic anthropology (PhD); sociocultural anthropology (PhD). *Faculty:* 42 full-time (18 women), 3 part-time/adjunct (1 woman). *Students:* 99 full-time (62 women); includes 23 minority (1 Black or African American, non-Hispanic/Latino; 2 American Indian or Alaska Native, non-Hispanic/Latino; 7 Asian, non-Hispanic/Latino; 10 Hispanic/Latino; 3 Two or more races, non-Hispanic/Latino), 17 international. Average age 30. 181 applicants, 12% accepted, 12 enrolled. In 2017, 9 doctorates awarded. *Degree requirements:* For doctorate, one foreign language, comprehensive exam, thesis/dissertation, preliminary examination, oral defense of dissertation. *Entrance requirements:* For doctorate, GRE General Test. Additional exam requirements/recommendations for international students: Required—TOEFL (minimum score 560 paper-based; 84 iBT). *Application deadline:* For fall admission, 12/15 for domestic and international students. Application fee: $75 ($90 for international students). Electronic applications accepted. *Expenses:* Tuition, state resident: full-time $22,368; part-time $1201 per credit hour. Tuition, nonresident: full-time $45,156; part-time $2467 per credit hour. *Required fees:* $376 per term. Tuition and fees vary according to course load, degree level and program. *Financial support:* In 2017–18, 72 students received support, including 36 fellowships with full tuition reimbursements available (averaging $19,000 per year), 7 research assistantships with full tuition reimbursements available (averaging $20,398 per year), 31 teaching assistantships with full tuition reimbursements available (averaging $20,398 per year); scholarships/grants, traineeships, health care benefits, tuition waivers (full), and unspecified assistantships also available. Financial award application deadline: 3/1; financial award applicants required to submit FAFSA. *Faculty research:* Sociocultural, linguistic, biological and archaeological anthropology. *Unit head:* Dr. Andrew Shryock, Chair, 734-764-7274, Fax: 734-763-6077. *Application contact:* Katia Kitchen, Graduate Program Assistant, 734-936-7933, Fax: 734-763-6077, E-mail: kitchenk@umich.edu.
Website: http://www.lsa.umich.edu/anthro/

University of Michigan, Rackham Graduate School, College of Literature, Science, and the Arts, Interdepartmental Program in Classical Art and Archaeology, Ann Arbor, MI 48109-1390. Offers MA, PhD. *Degree requirements:* For doctorate, 4 foreign languages, comprehensive exam, thesis/dissertation, ancient history exam, qualifying exam, preliminary exam. *Entrance requirements:* For doctorate, GRE General Test. Additional exam requirements/recommendations for international students: Required—TOEFL (minimum score 560 paper-based; 84 iBT). Electronic applications accepted. *Expenses:* Tuition, state resident: full-time $22,368; part-time $1201 per credit hour. Tuition, nonresident: full-time $45,156; part-time $2467 per credit hour. *Required fees:* $376 per term. Tuition and fees vary according to course load, degree level and program. *Faculty research:* Prehistoric art and archaeology, Greek art and archaeology, Roman art and archaeology, Near Eastern art and archaeology, archaeological theory and methodology.

University of Minnesota, Twin Cities Campus, Graduate School, College of Liberal Arts, Department of Classical and Near Eastern Studies, Minneapolis, MN 55455-0213.

Offers ancient and medieval art and archaeology (MA, PhD); classics (MA, PhD); Greek (MA, PhD); Latin (MA, PhD); religions in antiquity (MA). *Program availability:* Part-time. Terminal master's awarded for partial completion of doctoral program. *Degree requirements:* For master's, 2 foreign languages, comprehensive exam, thesis or alternative; for doctorate, variable foreign language requirement, comprehensive exam, thesis/dissertation. *Entrance requirements:* For master's and doctorate, GRE, 3 letters of recommendation, writing sample, copies of transcripts, personal statement. Additional exam requirements/recommendations for international students: Required—TOEFL. Electronic applications accepted. *Faculty research:* Greek and Latin literature, religions in antiquity, ancient Near East.

University of Missouri, Office of Research and Graduate Studies, College of Arts and Science, Department of Art History and Archaeology, Columbia, MO 65211. Offers MA, PhD. Terminal master's awarded for partial completion of doctoral program. *Degree requirements:* For master's, 2 foreign languages, thesis; for doctorate, 2 foreign languages, thesis/dissertation. *Entrance requirements:* For master's, GRE General Test (minimum score 1000 verbal and quantitative, 4.5 analytical), minimum GPA of 3.0, 3.3 in major field; at least 3 semesters in appropriate foreign language; for doctorate, GRE General Test, minimum GPA of 3.0; MA or equivalent in art history or classical archaeology; master's thesis. Additional exam requirements/recommendations for international students: Required—TOEFL (minimum score 500 paper-based; 61 iBT), IELTS (minimum score 5.5). Electronic applications accepted. *Faculty research:* Classical Mediterranean archaeology, medieval and Renaissance art, art and architecture of modern Europe and the Americas.

University of Nebraska–Lincoln, Graduate College, College of Arts and Sciences, Department of Anthropology and Geography, Lincoln, NE 68588. Offers anthropology (MA); geography (MA, PhD); professional archaeology (MA). *Degree requirements:* For master's, thesis optional. *Entrance requirements:* For master's, GRE General Test. Additional exam requirements/recommendations for international students: Required—TOEFL. Electronic applications accepted.

University of New Mexico, Graduate Studies, College of Arts and Sciences, Program in Anthropology, Albuquerque, NM 87131-2039. Offers archaeology (MA, MS, PhD); ethnology (MA, MS, PhD); evolutionary anthropology (PhD); public archaeology (MA, MS, PhD). *Faculty:* 28 full-time (10 women), 2 part-time/adjunct (0 women). *Students:* 47 full-time (34 women), 58 part-time (34 women); includes 25 minority (4 American Indian or Alaska Native, non-Hispanic/Latino; 1 Asian, non-Hispanic/Latino; 15 Hispanic/Latino; 5 Two or more races, non-Hispanic/Latino), 8 international. Average age 34. 58 applicants, 34% accepted, 20 enrolled. In 2017, 18 master's, 14 doctorates awarded. Terminal master's awarded for partial completion of doctoral program. *Degree requirements:* For master's, comprehensive exam (for some programs), thesis or alternative, 1-2 exams; for doctorate, one foreign language, comprehensive exam, thesis/dissertation, exam, proposal, oral defense, skill and/or second language. *Entrance requirements:* For master's and doctorate, GRE General Test, 3 letters of recommendation, letter of interest, transcripts. Additional exam requirements/recommendations for international students: Required—TOEFL (minimum score 550 paper-based), IELTS (minimum score 7). *Application deadline:* For fall admission, 1/4 for domestic and international students. Application fee: $50. Electronic applications accepted. *Financial support:* Fellowships, research assistantships with partial tuition reimbursements, teaching assistantships with partial tuition reimbursements, career-related internships or fieldwork, Federal Work-Study, institutionally sponsored loans, scholarships/grants, traineeships, health care benefits, tuition waivers (partial), and unspecified assistantships available. Support available to part-time students. Financial award application deadline: 3/1; financial award applicants required to submit FAFSA. *Faculty research:* Ethnology, archaeology, evolutionary anthropology, environment, water and land use, gender and social frameworks, Greater Southwest, Latin America, political economy, public anthropology. *Total annual research expenditures:* $875,790. *Unit head:* Michael W. Graves, Chair, 505-277-4524, Fax: 505-277-0874, E-mail: mwgraves@unm.edu. *Application contact:* Erika E. Gerety, Program Advisement Coordinator, 505-277-2732, Fax: 505-277-0874, E-mail: erika@unm.edu. Website: http://www.unm.edu/~anthro/

The University of North Carolina at Chapel Hill, Graduate School, College of Arts and Sciences, Department of Classics, Chapel Hill, NC 27599. Offers classical archaeology (MA, PhD); classics (MA, PhD). Terminal master's awarded for partial completion of doctoral program. *Degree requirements:* For master's, one foreign language, comprehensive exam, thesis; for doctorate, 2 foreign languages, comprehensive exam, thesis/dissertation. *Entrance requirements:* For master's and doctorate, GRE General Test, minimum GPA of 3.0. Electronic applications accepted.

University of Oklahoma, College of Arts and Sciences, Department of Anthropology, Norman, OK 73019. Offers anthropology (MA, PhD); applied linguistic anthropology (MA); archaeology (PhD); health and human biology (PhD); socio-cultural and linguistics (PhD); socio-cultural anthropology (MA). *Faculty:* 27 full-time (13 women). *Students:* 26 full-time (15 women), 23 part-time (17 women); includes 11 minority (5 American Indian or Alaska Native, non-Hispanic/Latino; 1 Hispanic/Latino; 5 Two or more races, non-Hispanic/Latino), 3 international. Average age 31. 29 applicants, 62% accepted, 15 enrolled. In 2017, 10 master's, 6 doctorates awarded. *Degree requirements:* For master's, thesis; for doctorate, comprehensive exam, thesis/dissertation. *Entrance requirements:* For master's and doctorate, GRE, minimum undergraduate GPA of 3.0; statement of purpose; 2 letters of recommendation. Additional exam requirements/recommendations for international students: Required—TOEFL (minimum score 79 iBT) or IELTS (minimum score 6.5). *Application deadline:* For spring admission, 2/1 for domestic and international students. Application fee: $50 ($100 for international students). Electronic applications accepted. *Expenses:* Tuition, state resident: full-time $5119; part-time $213.30 per credit hour. Tuition, nonresident: full-time $19,778; part-time $824.10 per credit hour. *Required fees:* $3458; $133.55 per credit hour. $126.50 per semester. *Financial support:* In 2017–18, 36 students received support, including 2 research assistantships with full tuition reimbursements available (averaging $14,670 per year), 10 teaching assistantships with full tuition reimbursements available (averaging $14,670 per year); career-related internships or fieldwork, Federal Work-Study, institutionally sponsored loans, health care benefits, and unspecified assistantships also available. Financial award application deadline: 6/1; financial award applicants required to submit FAFSA. *Faculty research:* North American archaeology; linguistics including applied; health and human biology; sociocultural anthropology; native North America. *Total annual research expenditures:* $1.3 million. *Unit head:* Dr. Diane Warren, Associate Professor and Department Chair, 405-325-7609, Fax: 405-325-7386, E-mail: dmwarren@ou.edu. *Application contact:* Dr. Patrick Livingood, Associate Professor and Graduate Liaison, 405-397-0215, Fax: 405-325-7386, E-mail: patrickl@ou.edu. Website: http://cas.ou.edu/anthropology

University of Pennsylvania, School of Arts and Sciences, Graduate Group in Art and Archaeology of the Mediterranean World, Philadelphia, PA 19104. Offers AM, PhD. *Program availability:* Part-time. *Faculty:* 14 full-time (8 women), 5 part-time/adjunct (4 women). *Students:* 19 full-time (12 women), 2 part-time (1 woman); includes 2 minority (both Two or more races, non-Hispanic/Latino), 2 international. Average age 30. 60 applicants, 13% accepted, 3 enrolled. In 2017, 3 doctorates awarded. Terminal master's awarded for partial completion of doctoral program. Website: http://www.sas.upenn.edu/graduate-division

University of Rhode Island, Graduate School, College of Arts and Sciences, Department of History, Kingston, RI 02881. Offers archaeology and anthropology (MA); European history (MA), including European history, United States history; MLIS/MA. *Program availability:* Part-time. *Faculty:* 17 full-time (8 women). *Students:* 7 full-time (1 woman), 6 part-time (3 women). 12 applicants, 92% accepted, 5 enrolled. In 2017, 5 master's awarded. *Entrance requirements:* Additional exam requirements/recommendations for international students: Required—TOEFL. *Application deadline:* For fall admission, 7/15 for domestic students; for spring admission, 11/15 for domestic students. Application fee: $65. Electronic applications accepted. *Expenses:* Tuition, state resident: full-time $12,706; part-time $786 per credit. Tuition, nonresident: full-time $25,216; part-time $1401 per credit. *Required fees:* $1598; $45 per credit. One-time fee: $30 part-time. *Financial support:* In 2017–18, 3 teaching assistantships with tuition reimbursements (averaging $17,724 per year) were awarded. Financial award application deadline: 2/1; financial award applicants required to submit FAFSA. *Unit head:* Dr. Rod Mather, Chair, 401-874-4093, E-mail: rodmather@uri.edu. *Application contact:* Dr. Evelyn Sterne, Director of Graduate Studies, 401-874-4074, E-mail: sterne@uri.edu. Website: http://www.uri.edu/artsci/his/

University of Saskatchewan, College of Graduate Studies and Research, College of Arts and Science, Department of Archaeology, Saskatoon, SK S7N 5A2, Canada. Offers MA, PhD. *Program availability:* Part-time. *Degree requirements:* For master's, thesis; for doctorate, comprehensive exam (for some programs), thesis/dissertation. *Entrance requirements:* Additional exam requirements/recommendations for international students: Required—TOEFL (minimum score 80 iBT); Recommended—IELTS (minimum score 6.5).

University of South Africa, College of Human Sciences, Pretoria, South Africa. Offers adult education (M Ed); African languages (MA, PhD); African politics (MA, PhD); Afrikaans (MA, PhD); ancient history (MA, PhD); ancient Near Eastern studies (MA, PhD); anthropology (MA, PhD); applied linguistics (MA); Arabic (MA, PhD); archaeology (MA); art history (MA); Biblical archaeology (MA); Biblical studies (M Th, D Th, PhD); Christian spirituality (M Th, D Th); church history (M Th, D Th); classical studies (MA, PhD); clinical psychology (MA); communication (MA, PhD); comparative education (M Ed, Ed D); consulting psychology (D Admin, D Com, PhD); curriculum studies (M Ed, Ed D); development studies (M Admin, MA, D Admin, PhD); didactics (M Ed, Ed D); education (M Tech); education management (M Ed, Ed D); educational psychology (M Ed); English (MA); environmental education (M Ed); French (MA, PhD); German (MA, PhD); Greek (MA); guidance and counseling (M Ed); health studies (MA, PhD), including health sciences education (MA), health services management (MA), medical and surgical nursing science (critical care general) (MA), midwifery and neonatal nursing science (MA), trauma and emergency care (MA); history (MA, PhD); history of education (Ed D); inclusive education (M Ed, Ed D); information and communications technology policy and regulation (MA); information science (MA, MIS, PhD); international politics (MA, PhD); Islamic studies (MA, PhD); Italian (MA, PhD); Judaica (MA, PhD); linguistics (MA, PhD); mathematical education (M Ed); mathematics education (MA); missiology (M Th, D Th); modern Hebrew (MA, PhD); musicology (MA, MMus, D Mus, PhD); natural science education (M Ed); New Testament (M Th, D Th); Old Testament (D Th); pastoral therapy (M Th, D Th); philosophy (MA); philosophy of education (M Ed, Ed D); politics (MA, PhD); Portuguese (MA, PhD); practical theology (M Th, D Th); psychology (MA, MS, PhD); psychology of education (M Ed, Ed D); public health (MA); religious studies (MA, D Th, PhD); Romance languages (MA); Russian (MA, PhD); Semitic languages (MA, PhD); social behavior studies in HIV/AIDS (MA); social science (mental health) (MA); social science in development studies (MA); social science in psychology (MA); social science in social work (MA); social science in sociology (MA); social work (MSW, DSW, PhD); socio-education (M Ed, Ed D); sociolinguistics (MA); sociology (MA, PhD); Spanish (MA, PhD); systematic theology (M Th, D Th); TESOL (teaching English to speakers of other languages) (MA); theological ethics (M Th, D Th); theory of literature (MA, PhD); urban ministries (D Th); urban ministry (M Th).

University of South Florida, College of Arts and Sciences, Department of Anthropology, Tampa, FL 33620-9951. Offers applied anthropology (MA, PhD), including archaeological and forensic sciences, biocultural medical anthropology, cultural resource management, heritage studies; medical anthropology (Graduate Certificate). *Program availability:* Part-time. *Faculty:* 22 full-time (15 women). *Students:* 73 full-time (50 women), 42 part-time (33 women); includes 30 minority (6 Black or African American, non-Hispanic/Latino; 2 Asian, non-Hispanic/Latino; 18 Hispanic/Latino; 1 Native Hawaiian or other Pacific Islander, non-Hispanic/Latino; 3 Two or more races, non-Hispanic/Latino), 6 international. Average age 32. 117 applicants, 36% accepted, 26 enrolled. In 2017, 16 master's, 7 doctorates awarded. *Degree requirements:* For master's, one foreign language, comprehensive exam, thesis; for doctorate, one foreign language, comprehensive exam, thesis/dissertation. *Entrance requirements:* For master's and doctorate, GRE, minimum GPA of 3.0, 3 letters of recommendation, statement of purpose, signed research ethics statement, resume or curriculum vitae; for Graduate Certificate, bachelor's degree with minimum GPA of 3.0. Additional exam requirements/recommendations for international students: Required—TOEFL (minimum score 550 paper-based; 79 iBT) or IELTS (minimum score 6.5). *Application deadline:* For fall admission, 12/15 priority date for domestic and international students. Application fee: $30. Electronic applications accepted. *Financial support:* In 2017–18, 19 students received support, including 14 research assistantships with tuition reimbursements available (averaging $14,475 per year), 52 teaching assistantships with partial tuition reimbursements available (averaging $12,540 per year); scholarships/grants and tuition waivers (partial) also available. Financial award application deadline: 1/15; financial award applicants required to submit FAFSA. *Faculty research:* Biocultural medical anthropology; archaeology and culture resource management in the Americas; community identity and heritage; urban community issues; verbal and nonverbal communications in media and education; global dynamics of sustainable resource management and economic development; social and cultural constructions of race, ethnicity, and gender. *Total annual research expenditures:* $1.1 million. *Unit head:* Dr. David Himmelgreen, Professor/Chair, 813-974-5455, E-mail: dhimmelg@usf.edu. *Application contact:* Dr. Rebecca Zarger, Associate Professor and Graduate Director, 813-974-0069, E-mail: rzarger@usf.edu. Website: http://anthropology.usf.edu/graduate

The University of Tennessee, Graduate School, College of Arts and Sciences, Department of Anthropology, Knoxville, TN 37996. Offers archaeology (MA, PhD); biological anthropology (MA, PhD); cultural anthropology (MA, PhD); zoo-archaeology (MA, PhD). *Degree requirements:* For master's, thesis; for doctorate, one foreign language, thesis/dissertation. *Entrance requirements:* For master's and doctorate, GRE General Test, minimum GPA of 2.7. Additional exam requirements/recommendations for international students: Required—TOEFL. Electronic applications accepted.

The University of Texas at Austin, Graduate School, College of Liberal Arts, Department of Anthropology, Austin, TX 78712-1111. Offers archaeology (MA, PhD); cultural forms (MA, PhD); linguistic anthropology (MA, PhD); physical anthropology (MA, PhD); social anthropology (MA, PhD). *Program availability:* Part-time. Terminal master's

awarded for partial completion of doctoral program. *Degree requirements:* For master's, thesis; for doctorate, one foreign language, thesis/dissertation. *Entrance requirements:* For master's and doctorate, GRE General Test. Additional exam requirements/recommendations for international students: Required—TOEFL. Electronic applications accepted.

University of West Florida, College of Arts, Social Sciences, and Humanities, Division of Anthropology and Archaeology, Pensacola, FL 32514-5750. Offers anthropology (MA); historical archaeology (MA). *Degree requirements:* For master's, internship or thesis. *Entrance requirements:* For master's, GRE, transcripts; minimum GPA of 3.0; 3 letters of recommendation; writing sample; letter of intent describing background, study interests, and professional goals. Additional exam requirements/recommendations for international students: Required—TOEFL (minimum score 550 paper-based).

University of Wisconsin–Madison, Graduate School, College of Letters and Science, Department of Anthropology, Madison, WI 53706-1380. Offers archaeology (PhD); biological anthropology (PhD); cultural anthropology (PhD). Terminal master's awarded for partial completion of doctoral program. *Degree requirements:* For doctorate, thesis/dissertation. *Entrance requirements:* For doctorate, qualifying exam. Electronic applications accepted. *Faculty research:* Archaeology, biological, anthropology, cultural anthropology.

Washington State University, College of Arts and Sciences, Department of Anthropology, Pullman, WA 99164. Offers archaeology (MA, PhD); cultural anthropology (PhD); evolutionary anthropology (MA, PhD). Program applications must be made through the Pullman campus. *Degree requirements:* For master's, one foreign language, comprehensive exam (for some programs), thesis; for doctorate, one foreign language, comprehensive exam, thesis/dissertation, written and oral preliminary exam. *Entrance requirements:* For master's and doctorate, GRE General Test, curriculum vitae, statement of intent, official transcripts, 3 letters of recommendation, one or two undergraduate papers (from BA/BS applicants), minimum GPA of 3.0. Additional exam requirements/recommendations for international students: Required—TOEFL (minimum score 550 paper-based), IELTS. Electronic applications accepted. *Faculty research:* Quantitative analysis of archaeological data, simulation of aspects of prehistoric behavior, subsistence strategies, language use, inequality and poverty, gender, pedagogy, Mexico/U.S. border region, childhood, infectious and parasitic diseases, the analysis of mitochondrial DNA (mtDNA) and Y-chromosomal DNA.

Washington University in St. Louis, The Graduate School, Department of Art History and Archaeology, St. Louis, MO 63130-4899. Offers AM, PhD. *Degree requirements:* For doctorate, 2 foreign languages, comprehensive exam, thesis/dissertation. *Entrance requirements:* For master's and doctorate, GRE General Test, sample of written work.

Electronic applications accepted. *Faculty research:* Ancient, medieval, Renaissance, early modern European, modern and contemporary European and American, and Asian art history; classical archaeology.

Wheaton College, Graduate School, Department of Biblical and Theological Studies, Wheaton, IL 60187-5593. Offers Biblical and theological studies (PhD); Biblical archaeology (MA); Biblical exegesis (MA); Biblical studies (MA); general theological studies (MA); historical and systematic theology (MA), including Biblical and theological studies; history of Christianity (MA), including Biblical and theological studies. *Program availability:* Part-time. *Faculty:* 7 full-time (1 woman), 2 part-time/adjunct (both women). *Students:* 50 full-time (14 women), 44 part-time (22 women); includes 16 minority (5 Black or African American, non-Hispanic/Latino; 7 Asian, non-Hispanic/Latino; 2 Hispanic/Latino; 2 Two or more races, non-Hispanic/Latino), 23 international. Average age 34. 103 applicants, 67% accepted, 34 enrolled. In 2017, 44 master's, 6 doctorates awarded. *Degree requirements:* For doctorate, thesis/dissertation. *Entrance requirements:* For master's, GRE General Test. Additional exam requirements/recommendations for international students: Required—TOEFL (minimum score 550 paper-based; 80 iBT), IELTS (minimum score 6.5). *Application deadline:* For fall admission, 1/1 priority date for domestic students, 1/1 for international students; for spring admission, 11/1 for domestic students. Applications are processed on a rolling basis. Application fee: $30. Electronic applications accepted. *Expenses: Tuition:* Full-time $19,800; part-time $825 per credit hour. Tuition and fees vary according to degree level and program. *Financial support:* Fellowships, scholarships/grants, and unspecified assistantships available. Financial award application deadline: 3/1; financial award applicants required to submit FAFSA. *Unit head:* Dr. David Capes, Associate Dean, 630-752-5054. *Application contact:* Director of Graduate Admissions, 630-752-5195, Fax: 630-752-7047, E-mail: graduate.admissions@wheaton.edu.
Website: https://www.wheaton.edu/academics/programs/theology/biblical-and-theological-graduate-studies/

Yale University, Graduate School of Arts and Sciences, Department of Near Eastern Languages and Civilizations, New Haven, CT 06520. Offers Arabic and Islamic studies (MA, PhD); archaeology of the ancient Near East (MA, PhD); Assyriology (MA, PhD); Egyptology (MA, PhD); Graeco-Arabic studies (MA, PhD); Northwest Semitic, Bible, comparative Semitics (MA, PhD). *Degree requirements:* For doctorate, 2 foreign languages, thesis/dissertation. *Entrance requirements:* For doctorate, GRE General Test.

Yale University, Graduate School of Arts and Sciences, Interdisciplinary Program in Archaeological Studies, New Haven, CT 06520. Offers MA. *Degree requirements:* For master's, thesis. *Entrance requirements:* For master's, GRE General Test.

Biological Anthropology

Duke University, Graduate School, Department of Evolutionary Anthropology, Durham, NC 27708. Offers cellular and molecular biology (PhD); gross anatomy and physical anthropology (PhD), including comparative morphology of human and non-human primates, primate social behavior, vertebrate paleontology; neuroanatomy (PhD). *Degree requirements:* For doctorate, one foreign language, thesis/dissertation. *Entrance requirements:* For doctorate, GRE General Test. Additional exam requirements/recommendations for international students: Required—TOEFL (minimum score 577 paper-based; 90 iBT) or IELTS (minimum score 7). Electronic applications accepted.

Kent State University, College of Arts and Sciences, School of Biomedical Sciences, Kent, OH 44242-0001. Offers biological anthropology (PhD); biomedical mathematics (MS, PhD); cellular and molecular biology (MS, PhD), including cellular biology and structures, molecular biology and genetics; neurosciences (MS, PhD); pharmacology (MS, PhD); physiology (MS, PhD). *Faculty:* 22 full-time (9 women), 3 part-time/adjunct (1 woman). *Students:* 75 full-time (46 women); includes 8 minority (1 Black or African American, non-Hispanic/Latino; 3 Asian, non-Hispanic/Latino; 2 Hispanic/Latino; 2 Two or more races, non-Hispanic/Latino), 25 international. Average age 28. 70 applicants, 23% accepted, 13 enrolled. In 2017, 23 master's, 5 doctorates awarded. Terminal master's awarded for partial completion of doctoral program. *Degree requirements:* For master's, thesis; for doctorate, comprehensive exam, thesis/dissertation. *Entrance requirements:* For master's, GRE, bachelor's degree, transcripts, minimum GPA of 3.0, goal statement, three letters of recommendation, academic preparation adequate to

perform graduate work in the desired field; for doctorate, GRE, master's degree, minimum GPA of 3.0, transcripts, goal statement, three letters of recommendation. Additional exam requirements/recommendations for international students: Required—TOEFL (minimum score 600 paper-based, 100 iBT), Michigan English Language Assessment Battery (minimum score 85), IELTS (minimum score 7.0) or PTE (minimum score 68). *Application deadline:* For fall admission, 1/1 for domestic and international students. Applications are processed on a rolling basis. Application fee: $45 ($70 for international students). Electronic applications accepted. *Expenses:* Tuition, state resident: full-time $11,310; part-time $515 per credit hour. Tuition, nonresident: full-time $20,396; part-time $928 per credit hour. *International tuition:* $18,544 full-time. *Financial support:* Research assistantships with full tuition reimbursements, teaching assistantships, and unspecified assistantships available. Financial award application deadline: 1/1. *Unit head:* Dr. Ernest J. Freeman, Director, School of Biomedical Sciences, 330-672-2363, E-mail: efreema2@kent.edu.
Website: http://www.kent.edu/biomedical/

Mercyhurst University, Graduate Studies, Program in Anthropology, Erie, PA 16546. Offers archaeology and geological archaeology (MS); forensic and biological anthropology (MS). *Entrance requirements:* For master's, GRE or MAT, undergraduate degree in related field, interview, resume, essay, three professional references, transcripts. Additional exam requirements/recommendations for international students: Required—TOEFL.

Cultural Anthropology

Brandeis University, Graduate School of Arts and Sciences, Department of Anthropology, Waltham, MA 02454-9110. Offers anthropology/women's, gender, and sexuality studies (MA); Mesoamerican archaeology (MA, PhD); sociocultural anthropology (MA, PhD). *Program availability:* Part-time. *Faculty:* 9 full-time (5 women), 4 part-time/adjunct (1 woman). *Students:* 35 full-time (24 women), 1 part-time (0 women); includes 6 minority (3 Black or African American, non-Hispanic/Latino; 1 Hispanic/Latino; 2 Two or more races, non-Hispanic/Latino), 6 international. Average age 28. 50 applicants, 48% accepted, 8 enrolled. In 2017, 11 master's awarded. Terminal master's awarded for partial completion of doctoral program. *Degree requirements:* For master's, thesis; for doctorate, one foreign language, comprehensive exam, thesis/dissertation. *Entrance requirements:* For master's and doctorate, GRE General Test, sample of written work, resume, letters of recommendation, transcript. Additional exam requirements/recommendations for international students: Required—PTE (minimum score 68), TOEFL (minimum score 600 paper-based, 100 iBT) or IELTS (7). *Application deadline:* For fall admission, 1/15 priority date for domestic and international students. Applications are processed on a rolling basis. Application fee: $75. Electronic applications accepted. *Expenses: Tuition:* Full-time $48,720. *Required fees:* $88. Tuition and fees vary according to course load, degree level, program and student level. *Financial support:* In 2017–18, 34 students received support, including 11 fellowships with full tuition reimbursements available (averaging $24,480 per year), 15 teaching assistantships with partial tuition reimbursements available (averaging $3,200 per year); scholarships/grants, health care benefits, and tuition waivers (partial) also available. Support available to part-time students. Financial award application deadline: 4/15; financial award applicants required to submit FAFSA. *Faculty research:*

Sociocultural anthropology, archaeology, gender and sexuality, linguistic anthropology, physical anthropology. *Unit head:* Dr. Sarah Lamb, Director of Graduate Studies, 781-736-2210, Fax: 781-736-2232, E-mail: lamb@brandeis.edu. *Application contact:* Laurel Carpenter, Academic Administrator, 781-736-2210, Fax: 781-736-2232, E-mail: lcarpent@brandeis.edu.
Website: http://www.brandeis.edu/gsas/programs/anthropology.html

California Institute of Integral Studies, School of Consciousness and Transformation, San Francisco, CA 94103. Offers anthropology and social change (MA, PhD); Asian philosophies and cultures (MA); creative inquiry/interdisciplinary arts (MFA); East-West psychology (MA, PhD); integral and transpersonal psychology (PhD); philosophy and religion (PhD), including ecology, spirituality, and religion, philosophy, cosmology, and consciousness, women's spirituality; philosophy, cosmology, and consciousness (Certificate); transformative leadership (MA); transformative studies (PhD); women, gender, spirituality and social justice (MA); writing and consciousness (MFA). *Program availability:* Part-time, evening/weekend, 100% online, blended/hybrid learning. *Students:* 392 full-time (265 women), 141 part-time (98 women); includes 145 minority (40 Black or African American, non-Hispanic/Latino; 1 American Indian or Alaska Native, non-Hispanic/Latino; 19 Asian, non-Hispanic/Latino; 54 Hispanic/Latino; 31 Two or more races, non-Hispanic/Latino), 61 international. Average age 43. 212 applicants, 96% accepted, 153 enrolled. In 2017, 49 master's, 36 doctorates awarded. Terminal master's awarded for partial completion of doctoral program. *Degree requirements:* For master's, thesis optional; for doctorate, comprehensive exam, thesis/dissertation, 1 foreign language (for Asian philosophies and cultures). *Entrance requirements:* For master's,

minimum GPA of 3.0, letters of recommendation, writing sample; for doctorate, master's degree, minimum GPA of 3.0, letters of recommendation, writing sample. Additional exam requirements/recommendations for international students: Required—TOEFL. *Application deadline:* For fall admission, 2/1 priority date for domestic and international students; for spring admission, 10/15 priority date for domestic and international students. Applications are processed on a rolling basis. Application fee: $65. Electronic applications accepted. *Expenses:* $21,400 tuition and fees (for MA); $28,390 (for MFA); $24,658 (for PhD). *Financial support:* Fellowships, research assistantships, teaching assistantships, career-related internships or fieldwork, Federal Work-Study, and scholarships/grants available. Support available to part-time students. Financial award application deadline: 4/15; financial award applicants required to submit FAFSA. *Faculty research:* Ecology and sustainability, philosophy and religion, East-West psychology, integrative health, social and cultural anthropology, transformative leadership. *Unit head:* Kathy Littles, Academic Dean, 415-575-6100, E-mail: klittles@ciis.edu. *Application contact:* Ellen Durst, Director of Admissions, 415-575-6100, Fax: 415-575-1268, E-mail: admissions@ciis.edu.
Website: http://www.ciis.edu/

Concordia University, School of Graduate Studies, Faculty of Arts and Science, Department of Sociology and Anthropology, Montréal, QC H3G 1M8, Canada. Offers social and cultural analysis (PhD); social and cultural anthropology (MA); sociology (MA). *Degree requirements:* For master's, comprehensive exam or thesis. *Entrance requirements:* For master's, honors degree in sociology or equivalent. *Faculty research:* Community and ethnic relations, popular culture, regional development in Canada, industrial and social movements, social problems and policies.

Cornell University, Graduate School, Graduate Fields of Arts and Sciences, Field of Anthropology, Ithaca, NY 14853. Offers archaeological anthropology (PhD); biological anthropology (PhD); sociocultural anthropology (PhD). *Degree requirements:* For doctorate, one foreign language, comprehensive exam, thesis/dissertation, teaching experience. *Entrance requirements:* For doctorate, GRE General Test, 3 letters of recommendation, sample of written work. Additional exam requirements/recommendations for international students: Required—TOEFL (minimum score 550 paper-based; 77 iBT). Electronic applications accepted. *Faculty research:* Culture, engaged anthropology, political economy, area studies: Asia, Americas, Europe; interdisciplinary and ethnic studies: Asian-American studies.

Duke University, Graduate School, Department of Cultural Anthropology, Durham, NC 27708. Offers physical anthropology (PhD), including comparative morphology of human and non-human primates, primate social behavior; social/cultural anthropology (PhD); JD/AM. *Degree requirements:* For doctorate, one foreign language, thesis/dissertation. *Entrance requirements:* For doctorate, GRE General Test. Additional exam requirements/recommendations for international students: Required—TOEFL (minimum score 577 paper-based; 90 iBT) or IELTS (minimum score 7).

The Graduate Center, City University of New York, Graduate Studies, Program in Anthropology, New York, NY 10016-4039. Offers anthropological linguistics (PhD); archaeology (PhD); cultural anthropology (PhD); physical anthropology (PhD). *Faculty:* 39 full-time (14 women). *Students:* 166 full-time (103 women), 2 part-time (both women); includes 34 minority (5 Black or African American, non-Hispanic/Latino; 5 Asian, non-Hispanic/Latino; 21 Hispanic/Latino; 3 Two or more races, non-Hispanic/Latino), 39 international. Average age 33. 145 applicants, 14% accepted, 19 enrolled. In 2017, 14 doctorates awarded. *Degree requirements:* For doctorate, one foreign language, thesis/dissertation. *Entrance requirements:* For doctorate, GRE General Test. Additional exam requirements/recommendations for international students: Required—TOEFL. *Application deadline:* For fall admission, 1/8 priority date for domestic students. Application fee: $125. Electronic applications accepted. *Financial support:* In 2017–18, 111 students received support, including 88 fellowships, 16 research assistantships, 10 teaching assistantships; career-related internships or fieldwork, Federal Work-Study, institutionally sponsored loans, and tuition waivers (full and partial) also available. Financial award application deadline: 2/1; financial award applicants required to submit FAFSA. *Unit head:* Prof. Jeff Maskovsky, Acting Executive Officer, 212-817-8006, Fax: 212-817-1501, E-mail: jmaskovsky@gc.cuny.edu. *Application contact:* Information Contact, 212-817-8005, Fax: 212-817-1501, E-mail: anthro@gc.cuny.edu.

Memorial University of Newfoundland, School of Graduate Studies, Department of Anthropology, St. John's, NL A1C 5S7, Canada. Offers archaeology and physical anthropology (MA, PhD); social and cultural anthropology (MA, PhD). *Program availability:* Part-time. *Degree requirements:* For master's, comprehensive exam (for some programs), thesis (for some programs); for doctorate, comprehensive exam, thesis/dissertation, oral defense of thesis. *Entrance requirements:* For master's, 2nd class degree in related field. Electronic applications accepted. *Faculty research:* Early European settlements, ethnoarchaeology, economic/political anthropology, land claims and aboriginal rights, marine anthropology.

North Carolina State University, Graduate School, College of Humanities and Social Sciences, Department of Sociology and Anthropology, Program in Anthropology, Raleigh, NC 27695. Offers bioarchaeology (MA); cultural anthropology (MA); environmental anthropology (MA).

Rice University, Graduate Programs, School of Social Sciences, Department of Anthropology, Houston, TX 77251-1892. Offers archaeology (MA, PhD); social-cultural anthropology (MA, PhD). Terminal master's awarded for partial completion of doctoral program. *Degree requirements:* For master's, one foreign language, 3 major papers, dissertation proposal and language exam or thesis; for doctorate, one foreign language, thesis/dissertation. *Entrance requirements:* For master's and doctorate, research proposal. Additional exam requirements/recommendations for international students: Required—TOEFL (minimum score 90 iBT). Electronic applications accepted.

San Francisco State University, Division of Graduate Studies, College of Liberal and Creative Arts, Department of Anthropology, San Francisco, CA 94132-1722. Offers archaeology (MA); biological anthropology (MA); cultural anthropology (MA); visual anthropology (MA). *Faculty research:* Immigration, ethnicity, urban anthropology, Californian and Latin American archaeology. *Unit head:* Dr. Cynthia Wilczak, Chair, 415-338-2046, Fax: 415-338-6159, E-mail: anthro@sfsu.edu. *Application contact:* Dr. Douglass Bailey, Graduate Coordinator, 415-338-1427, Fax: 415-338-6159, E-mail: dwbailey@sfsu.edu.
Website: http://anthropology.sfsu.edu/

Southern Illinois University Edwardsville, Graduate School, Program in Integrative Studies, Edwardsville, IL 62026. Offers cultural heritage and resources management (MA, MS); diversity training (MA, MS); organizational design thinking (MS); sustainability (MS). *Program availability:* Part-time, evening/weekend. *Degree requirements:* For master's, variable foreign language requirement, comprehensive exam (for some programs), thesis (for some programs). *Entrance requirements:* Additional exam requirements/recommendations for international students: Required—TOEFL (minimum score 550 paper-based; 79 iBT), IELTS (minimum score 6.5). Electronic applications accepted.

University of California, Santa Barbara, Graduate Division, College of Letters and Sciences, Division of Social Sciences, Department of Anthropology, Santa Barbara, CA 93106-2014. Offers sociocultural anthropology (PhD); MA/PhD. Terminal master's awarded for partial completion of doctoral program. *Degree requirements:* For master's, comprehensive exam (for some programs), thesis (for some programs); for doctorate, comprehensive exam (for some programs), thesis/dissertation. *Entrance requirements:* For master's and doctorate, GRE General Test, statement of purpose, personal achievements statement, transcripts, writing sample, curriculum vitae, letters of recommendation. Additional exam requirements/recommendations for international students: Required—TOEFL (minimum score 550 paper-based; 80 iBT), IELTS (minimum score 7). Electronic applications accepted. *Faculty research:* Archaeology, bioarchaeology, biosocial anthropology, evolutionary ecology, evolutionary psychology, sociocultural anthropology.

University of California, Santa Cruz, Division of Graduate Studies, Division of Social Sciences, Department of Anthropology, Santa Cruz, CA 95064. Offers cultural anthropology (PhD). *Degree requirements:* For doctorate, thesis/dissertation, qualifying exam. *Entrance requirements:* For doctorate, GRE General Test. Additional exam requirements/recommendations for international students: Required—TOEFL (minimum score 550 paper-based; 83 iBT); Recommended—IELTS (minimum score 8). Electronic applications accepted. *Faculty research:* Culture and power, women's roles, AIDS, folklore.

University of Denver, Division of Arts, Humanities and Social Sciences, Department of Anthropology, Denver, CO 80208. Offers archaeology (MA); cultural anthropology (MA); museum and heritage studies (MA). *Program availability:* Part-time. *Faculty:* 8 full-time (2 women). *Students:* 3 full-time (all women), 23 part-time (20 women); includes 2 minority (1 Black or African American, non-Hispanic/Latino; 1 Hispanic/Latino), 1 international. Average age 25. 49 applicants, 59% accepted, 12 enrolled. In 2017, 9 master's awarded. *Degree requirements:* For master's, one foreign language, comprehensive exam, thesis (for some programs), tool, foreign language literacy, or course work. *Entrance requirements:* For master's, GRE General Test, bachelor's degree, transcripts, personal statement, two letters of recommendation. Additional exam requirements/recommendations for international students: Required—TOEFL (minimum score 550 paper-based; 80 iBT). *Application deadline:* For fall admission, 2/4 priority date for domestic and international students. Applications are processed on a rolling basis. Application fee: $65. Electronic applications accepted. *Expenses:* $31,935 per year full-time. *Financial support:* In 2017–18, 23 students received support. Teaching assistantships with tuition reimbursements available, career-related internships or fieldwork, Federal Work-Study, institutionally sponsored loans, scholarships/grants, and unspecified assistantships available. Support available to part-time students. Financial award application deadline: 2/15; financial award applicants required to submit FAFSA. *Faculty research:* Human diversity, human rights, historic archaeology, museums and heritage, high-tech field methods. *Unit head:* Dr. Larry Conyers, Professor and Chair, 303-871-2684, Fax: 303-871-2437, E-mail: lconyers@du.edu.
Website: http://www.du.edu/ahss/anthropology

University of Michigan, Rackham Graduate School, College of Literature, Science, and the Arts, Department of Anthropology, Ann Arbor, MI 48109. Offers anthropological archaeology (PhD); biological anthropology (PhD); linguistic anthropology (PhD); sociocultural anthropology (PhD). *Faculty:* 42 full-time (18 women), 3 part-time/adjunct (1 woman). *Students:* 99 full-time (62 women); includes 23 minority (1 Black or African American, non-Hispanic/Latino; 2 American Indian or Alaska Native, non-Hispanic/Latino; 7 Asian, non-Hispanic/Latino; 10 Hispanic/Latino; 3 Two or more races, non-Hispanic/Latino), 17 international. Average age 30. 181 applicants, 12% accepted, 12 enrolled. In 2017, 9 doctorates awarded. *Degree requirements:* For doctorate, one foreign language, comprehensive exam, thesis/dissertation, preliminary examination, oral defense of dissertation. *Entrance requirements:* For doctorate, GRE General Test. Additional exam requirements/recommendations for international students: Required—TOEFL (minimum score 560 paper-based; 84 iBT). *Application deadline:* For fall admission, 12/15 for domestic and international students. Application fee: $75 ($90 for international students). Electronic applications accepted. *Expenses:* Tuition, state resident: full-time $22,368; part-time $1201 per credit hour. Tuition, nonresident: full-time $45,156; part-time $2467 per credit hour. *Required fees:* $376 per term. Tuition and fees vary according to course load, degree level and program. *Financial support:* In 2017–18, 72 students received support, including 36 fellowships with full tuition reimbursements available (averaging $19,000 per year), 7 research assistantships with full tuition reimbursements available (averaging $20,398 per year), 31 teaching assistantships with full tuition reimbursements available (averaging $20,398 per year); scholarships/grants, traineeships, health care benefits, tuition waivers (full), and unspecified assistantships also available. Financial award application deadline: 3/1; financial award applicants required to submit FAFSA. *Faculty research:* Sociocultural, linguistic, biological and archaeological anthropology. *Unit head:* Dr. Andrew Shryock, Chair, 734-764-7274, Fax: 734-763-6077. *Application contact:* Katia Kitchen, Graduate Program Assistant, 734-936-7933, Fax: 734-763-6077, E-mail: kitchenk@umich.edu.
Website: http://www.lsa.umich.edu/anthro/

The University of Tennessee, Graduate School, College of Arts and Sciences, Department of Anthropology, Knoxville, TN 37996. Offers archaeology (MA, PhD); biological anthropology (MA, PhD); cultural anthropology (MA, PhD); zoo-archaeology (MA, PhD). *Degree requirements:* For master's, thesis; for doctorate, one foreign language, thesis/dissertation. *Entrance requirements:* For master's and doctorate, GRE General Test, minimum GPA of 2.7. Additional exam requirements/recommendations for international students: Required—TOEFL. Electronic applications accepted.

University of Wisconsin–Madison, Graduate School, College of Letters and Science, Department of Anthropology, Madison, WI 53706-1380. Offers archaeology (PhD); biological anthropology (PhD); cultural anthropology (PhD). Terminal master's awarded for partial completion of doctoral program. *Degree requirements:* For doctorate, thesis/dissertation. *Entrance requirements:* For doctorate, qualifying exam. Electronic applications accepted. *Faculty research:* Archaeology, biological, anthropology, cultural anthropology.

Washington State University, College of Arts and Sciences, Department of Anthropology, Pullman, WA 99164. Offers archaeology (MA, PhD); cultural anthropology (PhD); evolutionary anthropology (MA, PhD). Program applications must be made through the Pullman campus. *Degree requirements:* For master's, one foreign language, comprehensive exam (for some programs), thesis; for doctorate, one foreign language, comprehensive exam, thesis/dissertation, written and oral preliminary exam. *Entrance requirements:* For master's and doctorate, GRE General Test, curriculum vitae, statement of intent, official transcripts, 3 letters of recommendation, one or two undergraduate papers (from BA/BS applicants), minimum GPA of 3.0. Additional exam requirements/recommendations for international students: Required—TOEFL (minimum score 550 paper-based), IELTS. Electronic applications accepted. *Faculty research:* Quantitative analysis of archaeological data, simulation of aspects of prehistoric behavior, subsistence strategies, language use, inequality and poverty, gender, pedagogy, Mexico/U.S. border region, childhood, infectious and parasitic diseases, the analysis of mitochondrial DNA (mtDNA) and Y-chromosomal DNA.

Demography and Population Studies

Bowling Green State University, Graduate College, College of Arts and Sciences, Department of Sociology, Bowling Green, OH 43403. Offers demography and population studies (MA); social psychology (MA); sociology (PhD). *Program availability:* Part-time. *Degree requirements:* For master's, thesis or alternative; for doctorate, comprehensive exam, thesis/dissertation. *Entrance requirements:* For master's and doctorate, GRE General Test. Additional exam requirements/recommendations for international students: Required—TOEFL. Electronic applications accepted. *Faculty research:* Applied demography, criminology and deviance, family studies, population studies, social psychology.

Cornell University, Graduate School, Graduate Fields of Agriculture and Life Sciences, Field of Development Sociology, Ithaca, NY 14853. Offers population and development (MS, PhD); rural and environmental sociology (MS, PhD); state, economy, and society (MS, PhD). *Degree requirements:* For doctorate, comprehensive exam, thesis/dissertation. *Entrance requirements:* For master's and doctorate, GRE General Test, 3 letters of recommendation. Additional exam requirements/recommendations for international students: Required—TOEFL (minimum score 550 paper-based; 77 iBT). Electronic applications accepted. *Faculty research:* Demography (population and development), environmental sociology, international and rural community development, political economy and ecology, sustainable agriculture.

Cornell University, Graduate School, Graduate Fields of Agriculture and Life Sciences, Field of Global Development, Ithaca, NY 14853. Offers development policy (MPS); international agriculture and development (MPS); international development (MPS); international nutrition (MPS); international planning (MPS); international population (MPS); science and technology policy (MPS). *Degree requirements:* For master's, project paper. *Entrance requirements:* For master's, GRE General Test (recommended), 2 years of development experience, 2 letters of recommendation. Additional exam requirements/recommendations for international students: Required—TOEFL (minimum score 550 paper-based; 77 iBT). Electronic applications accepted.

Florida State University, The Graduate School, College of Social Sciences and Public Policy, Center for Demography and Population Health, Tallahassee, FL 32306-2240. Offers demography (MS). *Program availability:* Part-time. *Faculty:* 10 full-time (6 women). *Students:* 10 full-time (4 women), 1 part-time (0 women); includes 2 minority (both Hispanic/Latino), 1 international. Average age 25. 11 applicants, 91% accepted, 9 enrolled. In 2017, 6 master's awarded. *Degree requirements:* For master's, thesis, minimum 27 hours' course work (including 18 hours of statistics and data analysis). *Entrance requirements:* For master's, GRE General Test, minimum upper-division GPA of 3.0. Additional exam requirements/recommendations for international students: Required—TOEFL (minimum score 550 paper-based; 80 iBT). *Application deadline:* For fall admission, 6/1 for domestic and international students; for spring admission, 11/1 for domestic and international students. Application fee: $30. Electronic applications accepted. *Expenses:* $15,818 in-state, $36,654 out-of-state. *Financial support:* In 2017–18, 10 students received support. Career-related internships or fieldwork, institutionally sponsored loans, scholarships/grants, and tuition waivers (full and partial) available. Financial award application deadline: 6/1. *Faculty research:* Aging and life course; families, children, youth; fertility and sexual behavior; mortality, morbidity, and health; mathematical demography. *Unit head:* Dr. Karin L. Brewster, Director, 850-644-7106, Fax: 850-644-8818, E-mail: karin.brewster@fsu.edu. *Application contact:* Julie Phillips von der Lieth, Program Assistant, 850-644-1762, Fax: 850-644-8818, E-mail: julie.phillips@fsu.edu.
Website: http://popcenter.fsu.edu

Harvard University, Harvard T.H. Chan School of Public Health, Department of Global Health and Population, Boston, MA 02115-6096. Offers global health and population (SM); population health sciences (PhD). *Program availability:* Part-time. *Faculty:* 47 full-time (18 women), 22 part-time/adjunct (7 women). *Students:* 121 full-time (87 women), 9 part-time (8 women); includes 9 minority (2 Black or African American, non-Hispanic/Latino; 6 Asian, non-Hispanic/Latino; 1 Hispanic/Latino), 27 international. Average age 29. 51 applicants, 55% accepted, 15 enrolled. In 2017, 28 master's, 10 doctorates awarded. *Degree requirements:* For master's, thesis; for doctorate, thesis/dissertation, qualifying exam. *Entrance requirements:* For master's, GRE, MCAT; for doctorate, GRE. Additional exam requirements/recommendations for international students: Recommended—TOEFL (minimum score 600 paper-based; 100 iBT), IELTS (minimum score 7). *Application deadline:* For fall admission, 12/1 for domestic and international students. Application fee: $120. Electronic applications accepted. *Financial support:* Fellowships, research assistantships, teaching assistantships, Federal Work-Study, scholarships/grants, traineeships, and unspecified assistantships available. Support available to part-time students. Financial award application deadline: 2/15; financial award applicants required to submit FAFSA. *Faculty research:* Health systems, international health policy, economics, population and reproductive health, ecology. *Unit head:* Dr. Wafaie W. Fawzi, Chair, 617-432-1232, Fax: 617-432-2435, E-mail: mina@hsph.harvard.edu. *Application contact:* Vincent W. James, Director of Admissions, 617-432-1031, Fax: 617-432-7080, E-mail: admissions@hsph.harvard.edu.
Website: http://www.hsph.harvard.edu/global-health-and-population/

Harvard University, Harvard T.H. Chan School of Public Health, PhD Program in Population Health Sciences, Boston, MA 02115. Offers environmental health (PhD); epidemiology (PhD); global health and population (PhD); nutrition (PhD); social and behavioral sciences (PhD). *Students:* 80 full-time (56 women); includes 23 minority (5 Black or African American, non-Hispanic/Latino; 7 Asian, non-Hispanic/Latino; 6 Hispanic/Latino; 5 Two or more races, non-Hispanic/Latino), 26 international. Average age 29. 469 applicants, 11% accepted, 42 enrolled. *Entrance requirements:* Additional exam requirements/recommendations for international students: Recommended—TOEFL, IELTS. *Application deadline:* For fall admission, 12/1 for domestic and international students. Electronic applications accepted. *Financial support:* Application deadline: 2/15; applicants required to submit FAFSA. *Unit head:* Bruce Villineau, Assistant Director, E-mail: phdphs@hsph.harvard.edu. *Application contact:* Vincent W. James, Director of Admissions, 617-432-1031, Fax: 617-432-7080, E-mail: admissions@hsph.harvard.edu.

Johns Hopkins University, Bloomberg School of Public Health, Department of Population, Family and Reproductive Health, Baltimore, MD 21205. Offers demography (MHS); population, family and reproductive health (MHS, MSPH, PhD). *Degree requirements:* For master's, essay, fieldwork; for doctorate, thesis/dissertation, 1-year full-time residency, oral and written exams. *Entrance requirements:* For master's and doctorate, GRE General Test, 3 letters of recommendation, curriculum vitae. Additional exam requirements/recommendations for international students: Required—TOEFL (minimum score 600 paper-based). Electronic applications accepted. *Faculty research:* Child and adolescent health and development, population and health and reproductive, perinatal and women's health.

Miami University, College of Arts and Science, Department of Sociology and Gerontology, Oxford, OH 45056. Offers gerontology (MGS); population and social gerontology (MPSG); social gerontology (PhD). *Students:* 30 full-time (26 women), 8 part-time (7 women); includes 5 minority (1 Black or African American, non-Hispanic/Latino; 3 Asian, non-Hispanic/Latino; 1 Hispanic/Latino), 12 international. Average age 32. In 2017, 7 master's, 2 doctorates awarded. *Expenses:* Tuition, state resident: full-time $13,812; part-time $575 per credit hour. Tuition, nonresident: full-time $30,860; part-time $1286 per credit hour. *Unit head:* Dr. Stephen Lippman, Chair and Associate Professor, 513-529-8515, E-mail: lippmas@miamioh.edu. *Application contact:* Dr. Jennifer Kinney, Director of Graduate Studies, 513-529-2915, E-mail: kinneyjm@miamioh.edu.
Website: http://www.MiamiOH.edu/sociology/

New York University, College of Global Public Health, New York, NY 10012. Offers biological basis of public health (PhD); community and international health (MPH); global health leadership (MPH); health systems and health services research (PhD); population and community health (PhD); public health nutrition (MPH); social and behavioral sciences (MPH); socio-behavioral health (PhD). *Accreditation:* CEPH. *Program availability:* Part-time, online learning. *Faculty:* 26 full-time (20 women), 104 part-time/adjunct (53 women). *Students:* 161 full-time (136 women), 70 part-time (54 women); includes 74 minority (24 Black or African American, non-Hispanic/Latino; 1 American Indian or Alaska Native, non-Hispanic/Latino; 27 Asian, non-Hispanic/Latino; 11 Hispanic/Latino; 4 Native Hawaiian or other Pacific Islander, non-Hispanic/Latino; 7 Two or more races, non-Hispanic/Latino), 39 international. Average age 29. 802 applicants, 70% accepted, 97 enrolled. In 2017, 1 master's awarded. *Degree requirements:* For master's, thesis (for some programs); for doctorate, thesis/dissertation. *Entrance requirements:* For master's and doctorate, GRE. Additional exam requirements/recommendations for international students: Required—TOEFL. *Application deadline:* For fall admission, 2/1 for domestic and international students. Applications are processed on a rolling basis. Electronic applications accepted. *Expenses:* Contact institution. *Financial support:* Federal Work-Study and scholarships/grants available. *Unit head:* Dr. Cheryl G. Healton, Director, 212-992-6741. *Application contact:* New York University Information, 212-998-1212.
Website: http://publichealth.nyu.edu/

Princeton University, Graduate School, Department of Sociology, Princeton, NJ 08544-1019. Offers sociology (PhD); sociology and demography (PhD). *Degree requirements:* For doctorate, variable foreign language requirement, thesis/dissertation. *Entrance requirements:* For doctorate, GRE General Test, GRE Subject Test (recommended), sample of written work. Additional exam requirements/recommendations for international students: Required—TOEFL (minimum score 600 paper-based). Electronic applications accepted.

Princeton University, Graduate School, Program in Population Studies, Princeton, NJ 08544-1019. Offers demography (PhD, Certificate); economics and demography (PhD); public affairs and demography (PhD); sociology and demography (PhD). *Degree requirements:* For doctorate, thesis/dissertation. *Entrance requirements:* For doctorate, GRE General Test. Additional exam requirements/recommendations for international students: Required—TOEFL (minimum score 600 paper-based). Electronic applications accepted. *Faculty research:* Models, fertility, infant and child mortality, migration.

Université de Montréal, Faculty of Arts and Sciences, Department of Demography, Montréal, QC H3C 3J7, Canada. Offers M Sc, PhD. Terminal master's awarded for partial completion of doctoral program. *Degree requirements:* For master's, one foreign language, thesis; for doctorate, one foreign language, thesis/dissertation, general exam. *Entrance requirements:* For master's, minimum GPA of 2.7. Electronic applications accepted. *Faculty research:* Historical demography, population and development, ethnic and linguistic groups, aging of population, family demography.

Université du Québec, Institut National de la Recherche Scientifique, Graduate Programs, Centre for Urbanisation Culture Societe, Montreal, QC G1K 9A9, Canada. Offers demography (M Sc, PhD); research practices and public action (MA, DESS); urban studies (M Sc, PhD). *Program availability:* Part-time. *Faculty:* 29 full-time. *Students:* 82 full-time (42 women), 12 part-time (10 women), 13 international. Average age 32. 35 applicants, 83% accepted, 23 enrolled. In 2017, 10 master's, 3 doctorates awarded. *Degree requirements:* For master's, thesis (for some programs); for doctorate, thesis/dissertation; for DESS, thesis or alternative. *Entrance requirements:* For master's, appropriate bachelor's degree, proficiency in French; for doctorate, appropriate master's degree, proficiency in French; for DESS, proficiency in French. *Application deadline:* For fall admission, 3/30 for domestic and international students; for winter admission, 11/1 for domestic and international students; for spring admission, 3/1 for domestic and international students. Application fee: $45. Electronic applications accepted. *Financial support:* In 2017–18, fellowships (averaging $16,500 per year) were awarded; research assistantships also available. *Faculty research:* Mobility and migration, cultural policies, knowledge mobilization, spatial analysis of data, social demography. *Unit head:* Hélène Belleau, Director, 514-499-4001, Fax: 514-499-4065, E-mail: helene.belleau@ucs.inrs.ca. *Application contact:* Sylvie Richard, Registrar, 418-654-2518, Fax: 418-654-3858, E-mail: sylvie.richard@adm.inrs.ca.
Website: http://www.ucs.inrs.ca

University at Albany, State University of New York, College of Arts and Sciences, Department of Sociology, Albany, NY 12222-0001. Offers demography (Certificate); sociology (MA, PhD); urban policy (Certificate). *Faculty:* 25 full-time (11 women). *Students:* 25 full-time (18 women), 53 part-time (39 women); includes 16 minority (4 Black or African American, non-Hispanic/Latino; 5 Asian, non-Hispanic/Latino; 5 Hispanic/Latino; 2 Two or more races, non-Hispanic/Latino), 22 international. 71 applicants, 37% accepted, 7 enrolled. In 2017, 5 doctorates awarded. Terminal master's awarded for partial completion of doctoral program. *Degree requirements:* For master's, thesis; for doctorate, thesis/dissertation, 2 specialization exams, research tool. *Entrance requirements:* For master's and doctorate, GRE General Test. Additional exam requirements/recommendations for international students: Required—TOEFL. *Application deadline:* For fall admission, 1/15 for domestic students, 5/1 for international students. Applications are processed on a rolling basis. Application fee: $75. Electronic applications accepted. *Expenses:* Tuition, state resident: full-time $10,870; part-time $453 per credit hour. Tuition, nonresident: full-time $22,210; part-time $925 per credit hour. *Required fees:* $84.68 per credit hour. $508.06 per semester. Part-time tuition and fees vary according to course load and program. *Financial support:* Fellowships, research assistantships, teaching assistantships, career-related internships or fieldwork, and Federal Work-Study available. Financial award application deadline: 3/15. *Faculty research:* Gender and equality, crime and deviance, aging, work and organizations, social demography. *Unit head:* Glenn Deane, Chair, 518-442-4666, Fax: 518-442-4936, E-mail: gdeane@albany.edu. *Application contact:* Michael DeRensis, Director, Graduate Admissions, 518-442-3980, Fax: 518-442-3922, E-mail: graduate@albany.edu.
Website: http://www.albany.edu/sociology/index.html

University of Alberta, Faculty of Graduate Studies and Research, Department of Sociology, Edmonton, AB T6G 2E1, Canada. Offers criminal justice (MA); demography (MA, PhD); sociology (MA, PhD). *Program availability:* Part-time. *Degree requirements:* For master's, thesis (for some programs); for doctorate, thesis/dissertation. *Faculty research:* Criminology, knowledge and culture, methods and theory, population studies, stratification.

University of California, Berkeley, Graduate Division, College of Letters and Science, Department of Demography, Berkeley, CA 94720-1500. Offers PhD. *Degree requirements:* For doctorate, thesis/dissertation, qualifying exam. *Entrance requirements:* For doctorate, GRE General Test, minimum GPA of 3.0, 3 letters of recommendation. Additional exam requirements/recommendations for international students: Required—TOEFL (minimum score 570 paper-based; 90 iBT). Electronic applications accepted.

University of California, Berkeley, Graduate Division, College of Letters and Science, Group in Sociology and Demography, Berkeley, CA 94720-1500. Offers MA, PhD. *Degree requirements:* For doctorate, thesis/dissertation, qualifying exam. *Entrance requirements:* For master's and doctorate, GRE General Test, minimum GPA of 3.0, 3 letters of recommendation. Electronic applications accepted.

University of California, Irvine, School of Social Sciences and School of Social Ecology, Program in Demographic and Social Analysis, Irvine, CA 92697. Offers MA. *Students:* 10 full-time (6 women); includes 3 minority (1 Asian, non-Hispanic/Latino; 2 Two or more races, non-Hispanic/Latino), 2 international. Average age 26. 22 applicants, 95% accepted, 10 enrolled. In 2017, 17 master's awarded. *Entrance requirements:* For master's, GRE, minimum GPA of 3.0. Additional exam requirements/recommendations for international students: Required—TOEFL (minimum score 550 paper-based). *Application deadline:* For fall admission, 1/15 priority date for domestic and international students. Application fee: $105 ($125 for international students). *Financial support:* Application deadline: 3/1. *Unit head:* Susan Brown, Graduate Director, 949-824-9382, Fax: 949-824-4717, E-mail: skbrown@uci.edu. *Application contact:* John Sommerhauser, Director of Graduate Affairs, 949-824-4074, E-mail: john.sommerhauser@uci.edu.
Website: http://www.demography.uci.edu/

University of Guelph, Ontario Veterinary College and Graduate Studies, Graduate Programs in Veterinary Sciences, Department of Population Medicine, Guelph, ON N1G 2W1, Canada. Offers epidemiology (M Sc, DV Sc, PhD); health management (DV Sc); population medicine and health management (M Sc); swine health management (M Sc); theriogenology (M Sc, DV Sc). *Degree requirements:* For master's, thesis; for doctorate, comprehensive exam, thesis/dissertation. *Entrance requirements:* Additional exam requirements/recommendations for international students: Required—TOEFL.

University of Hawaii at Manoa, John A. Burns School of Medicine, Department of Public Health Sciences and Epidemiology, Global Health and Population Studies Program, Honolulu, HI 96822. Offers Graduate Certificate. *Program availability:* Part-time. *Entrance requirements:* For degree, GRE General Test. Additional exam requirements/recommendations for international students: Required—TOEFL (minimum score 550 paper-based; 79 iBT), IELTS (minimum score 5).

University of Pennsylvania, School of Arts and Sciences, Graduate Group in Demography, Philadelphia, PA 19104. Offers AM, PhD. *Faculty:* 37 full-time (17 women), 12 part-time/adjunct (6 women). *Students:* 15 full-time (6 women); includes 3 minority (1 Black or African American, non-Hispanic/Latino; 1 Asian, non-Hispanic/Latino; 1 Hispanic/Latino), 8 international. Average age 29. 21 applicants, 14% accepted, 3 enrolled. In 2017, 1 master's, 6 doctorates awarded. Terminal master's awarded for partial completion of doctoral program. *Unit head:* Dr. Ralph M. Rosen, Associate Dean for Graduate Studies, 215-898-7156, Fax: 215-573-8068, E-mail: grad-dean@sas.upenn.edu. *Application contact:* Arts and Sciences Graduate Admissions, 215-573-5816, Fax: 215-573-8068, E-mail: gdasadmis@sas.upenn.edu.
Website: http://demog.pop.upenn.edu

University of Puerto Rico–Medical Sciences Campus, Graduate School of Public Health, Department of Social Sciences, Program in Demography, San Juan, PR 00936-5067. Offers MS. *Program availability:* Part-time. *Degree requirements:* For master's, thesis. *Entrance requirements:* For master's, GRE, previous course work in algebra and statistics.

The University of Texas at San Antonio, College of Public Policy, Department of Demography, San Antonio, TX 78207. Offers applied demography (PhD). *Program availability:* Part-time, evening/weekend. *Faculty:* 5 full-time (2 women). *Students:* 15 full-time (5 women), 21 part-time (9 women); includes 18 minority (5 Black or African American, non-Hispanic/Latino; 3 Asian, non-Hispanic/Latino; 10 Hispanic/Latino), 10 international. Average age 36. 11 applicants, 82% accepted, 9 enrolled. In 2017, 3 doctorates awarded. *Degree requirements:* For doctorate, comprehensive exam, thesis/dissertation, dissertation proposal defense. *Entrance requirements:* For doctorate, GRE, three letters of recommendation, statement of purpose, MA/MS. Additional exam requirements/recommendations for international students: Required—TOEFL (minimum score 550 paper-based; 79 iBT), IELTS (minimum score 6.5). *Application deadline:* For fall admission, 6/15 for domestic students, 3/1 for international students; for spring admission, 10/15 for domestic students, 9/15 for international students. Application fee: $50 ($90 for international students). Electronic applications accepted. *Expenses:* Tuition, state resident: full-time $5495. Tuition, nonresident: full-time $21,938. *Required fees:* $1915. Tuition and fees vary according to program. *Financial support:* Fellowships, research assistantships, and teaching assistantships available. *Faculty research:* International migration, health disparities and inequality, food security, poverty, demographic change in communities, demographics of energy use. *Unit head:* Dr. Johnelle Sparks, Department Chair, 210-458-3141, E-mail: johnelle.sparks@utsa.edu. *Application contact:* Dr. Corey Sparks, Graduate Advisor of Record, 210-458-3166, E-mail: corey.sparks@utsa.edu.
Website: http://copp.utsa.edu/demography/

The University of Texas Medical Branch, Graduate School of Biomedical Sciences, Program in Population Health Sciences, Galveston, TX 77555. Offers PhD.

University of Wisconsin–Madison, School of Medicine and Public Health, Population Health and Epidemiology Program, Madison, WI 53726. Offers epidemiology (MS, PhD); population health (MS, PhD), including epidemiology. *Program availability:* Part-time. *Faculty:* 21 full-time (10 women). *Students:* 36 full-time (31 women), 11 part-time (7 women); includes 8 minority (2 Black or African American, non-Hispanic/Latino; 3 Asian, non-Hispanic/Latino; 2 Hispanic/Latino; 1 Two or more races, non-Hispanic/Latino), 6 international. Average age 29. 45 applicants, 44% accepted, 10 enrolled. In 2017, 9 master's, 5 doctorates awarded. Terminal master's awarded for partial completion of doctoral program. *Degree requirements:* For master's, thesis, thesis defense; for doctorate, comprehensive exam, thesis/dissertation, qualifying exam, preliminary exam, dissertation defense. *Entrance requirements:* For master's and doctorate, GRE taken within the last 5 years (MCAT or LSAT acceptable for those with doctoral degrees), minimum GPA of 3.0, quantitative preparation (calculus, statistics, or other) with minimum B average. Additional exam requirements/recommendations for international students: Required—TOEFL (minimum score 580 paper-based; 92 iBT). *Application deadline:* For fall admission, 1/15 for domestic and international students. Application fee: $75. Electronic applications accepted. *Expenses:* $5,993 full-time resident per semster; $12,657 full-time nonresident per semester. *Financial support:* In 2017–18, 31 students received support, including 5 research assistantships with full tuition reimbursements available (averaging $25,000 per year), 2 teaching assistantships with full tuition reimbursements available (averaging $18,000 per year); fellowships, scholarships/grants, traineeships, health care benefits, and unspecified assistantships also available. Support available to part-time students. Financial award application deadline: 4/15; financial award applicants required to submit FAFSA. *Faculty research:* Epidemiology (cancer, environmental, aging, infectious and genetic disease), determinants of population health, health services research, social and behavioral health sciences, biostatistics. *Total annual research expenditures:* $16.6 million. *Unit head:* Mari Palta, Graduate Program Chair, 608-263-4029, Fax: 608-263-2820, E-mail: mpalta@wisc.edu. *Application contact:* Quinn H. Fullenkamp, Graduate Program Coordinator, 608-265-8108, Fax: 608-263-2820, E-mail: pophealth@mailplus.wisc.edu.
Website: https://pophealth.wisc.edu/grad

Rural Sociology

Cornell University, Graduate School, Graduate Fields of Agriculture and Life Sciences, Field of Development Sociology, Ithaca, NY 14853. Offers population and development (MS, PhD); rural and environmental sociology (MS, PhD); state, economy, and society (MS, PhD). *Degree requirements:* For doctorate, comprehensive exam, thesis/dissertation. *Entrance requirements:* For master's and doctorate, GRE General Test, 3 letters of recommendation. Additional exam requirements/recommendations for international students: Required—TOEFL (minimum score 550 paper-based; 77 iBT). Electronic applications accepted. *Faculty research:* Demography (population and development), environmental sociology, international and rural community development, political economy and ecology, sustainable agriculture.

Iowa State University of Science and Technology, Department of Sociology, Ames, IA 50011. Offers rural sociology (MS, PhD); sociology (MS, PhD). *Degree requirements:* For master's, thesis; for doctorate, thesis/dissertation. *Entrance requirements:* For master's and doctorate, GRE General Test. Additional exam requirements/recommendations for international students: Required—TOEFL (minimum score 550 paper-based; 79 iBT), IELTS (minimum score 6.5). Electronic applications accepted.

Iowa State University of Science and Technology, Program in Rural Sociology, Ames, IA 50011. Offers MS, PhD. *Degree requirements:* For master's, thesis; for doctorate, thesis/dissertation. *Entrance requirements:* For master's, GRE General Test; for doctorate, GRE General Test, master's degree. Additional exam requirements/recommendations for international students: Required—TOEFL (minimum score 550 paper-based; 79 iBT), IELTS (minimum score 6.5). Electronic applications accepted.

The Ohio State University, Graduate School, College of Food, Agricultural, and Environmental Sciences, School of Environment and Natural Resources, Columbus, OH 43210. Offers ecological restoration (MS, PhD); ecosystem science (MS, PhD); environment and natural resources (MENR); environmental social sciences (MS, PhD); fisheries and wildlife science (MS, PhD); forest science (MS, PhD); rural sociology (MS, PhD); soil science (MS, PhD). *Faculty:* 37. *Students:* 86 full-time (53 women), 8 part-time (4 women), 7 international. Average age 29. In 2017, 34 master's, 7 doctorates awarded. *Entrance requirements:* For master's and doctorate, GRE. Additional exam requirements/recommendations for international students: Required—TOEFL (minimum score 550 paper-based; 79 iBT), Michigan English Language Assessment Battery (minimum score 82); Recommended—IELTS (minimum score 7). *Application deadline:* For fall admission, 1/1 priority date for domestic students, 12/15 priority date for international students; for spring admission, 11/1 for domestic students, 9/15 for international students. Applications are processed on a rolling basis. Application fee: $60 ($70 for international students). Electronic applications accepted. *Financial support:* Fellowships, research assistantships, teaching assistantships, health care benefits, and unspecified assistantships available. *Unit head:* Dr. Jeff S. Sharp, Director, 614-292-9410, E-mail: sharp.123@osu.edu. *Application contact:* Graduate and Professional Admissions, 614-292-9444, Fax: 614-292-3895, E-mail: gpadmissions@osu.edu.
Website: http://senr.osu.edu/

Penn State University Park, Graduate School, College of Agricultural Sciences, Department of Agricultural Economics, Sociology, and Education, University Park, PA 16802. Offers agricultural and extension education (M Ed, MS, PhD, Certificate); applied youth, family and community education (M Ed); energy, environmental, and food economics (MS, PhD); rural sociology (MS, PhD). *Unit head:* Dr. Richard T. Roush, Dean, 814-865-2541, Fax: 814-865-3103. *Application contact:* Lori Hawn, Director, Graduate Student Services, 814-865-1795, Fax: 814-863-4627, E-mail: l-gswww@lists.psu.edu.
Website: http://aese.psu.edu/

University of Alberta, Faculty of Graduate Studies and Research, Department of Rural Economy, Edmonton, AB T6G 2E1, Canada. Offers agricultural economics (M Ag, M Sc, PhD); forest economics (M Ag, M Sc, PhD); rural sociology (M Ag, M Sc); MBA/M Ag. *Program availability:* Part-time. *Degree requirements:* For doctorate, thesis/dissertation. *Entrance requirements:* Additional exam requirements/recommendations for international students: Required—TOEFL. *Faculty research:* Agroforestry, development, extension education, marketing and trade, natural resources and environment, policy, production economics.

University of Missouri, Office of Research and Graduate Studies, College of Agriculture, Food and Natural Resources, Department of Rural Sociology, Columbia, MO 65211. Offers MS, PhD. *Program availability:* Part-time. *Degree requirements:* For doctorate, comprehensive exam, thesis/dissertation. *Entrance requirements:* For master's and doctorate, GRE General Test, minimum GPA of 3.0. Additional exam requirements/recommendations for international students: Required—TOEFL (minimum score 570 paper-based; 89 iBT). Electronic applications accepted. *Faculty research:*

Rural social organization; social change and development; sociology of agriculture; natural resource management; sociology of consumption, culture and organization; science, technology and society studies; social inequality; survey research; entrepreneurship; state and local public finance; community economics; rural development.

University of Montana, Graduate School, College of Humanities and Sciences, Department of Sociology, Missoula, MT 59812. Offers criminology (MA); inequality and social justice (MA); rural and environmental change (MA); sociology (MA). *Entrance requirements:* For master's, GRE General Test. Additional exam requirements/recommendations for international students: Required—TOEFL. *Faculty research:* Housing, homelessness, hunger, infant mortality, work safety.

University of Puerto Rico–Mayagüez, Graduate Studies, College of Agricultural Sciences, Department of Agricultural Economics and Rural Sociology, Mayagüez, PR

00681-9000. Offers MS. *Program availability:* Part-time. *Degree requirements:* For master's, comprehensive exam, thesis. *Entrance requirements:* For master's, bachelor's degree in agricultural economics or its equivalent. Electronic applications accepted. *Faculty research:* Farm management, agricultural development, agrimarketing, natural resource economics.

University of Wisconsin–Madison, Graduate School, College of Letters and Science, Department of Sociology, Madison, WI 53706-1380. Offers rural sociology (MS); sociology (MS, PhD). *Program availability:* Part-time. Terminal master's awarded for partial completion of doctoral program. *Degree requirements:* For master's, thesis, oral exam; for doctorate, thesis/dissertation, preliminary and final oral exams, 4 seminars. *Entrance requirements:* For master's and doctorate, GRE General Test. Additional exam requirements/recommendations for international students: Required—TOEFL. Electronic applications accepted.

Sociology

Acadia University, Faculty of Arts, Department of Sociology, Wolfville, NS B4P 2R6, Canada. Offers MA. *Entrance requirements:* For master's, honors degree, minimum GPA of 3.25. Additional exam requirements/recommendations for international students: Required—TOEFL (minimum score 630 paper-based; 93 iBT), IELTS (minimum score 6.5). *Application deadline:* For fall admission, 2/1 priority date for domestic and international students. Applications are processed on a rolling basis. Application fee: $50. *Financial support:* Application deadline: 2/1. *Faculty research:* Atlantic cultures, class analysis, gender and women's studies, religion, symbolism, development studies. *Unit head:* Dr. Saara Liinamaa, Graduate Studies Coordinator, 902-585-1494, E-mail: saara.liinamaa@acadiau.ca. *Application contact:* Karen Turner, Administrative Secretary, 902-585-1493, Fax: 902-585-1769, E-mail: karen.turner@acadiau.ca. Website: http://sociology.acadiau.ca/

American University, College of Arts and Sciences, Department of Sociology, Washington, DC 22016-8072. Offers public sociology (Certificate); social research (Certificate); sociology (MA). *Program availability:* Part-time, evening/weekend. *Faculty:* 13 full-time (9 women), 8 part-time/adjunct (5 women). *Students:* 6 full-time (4 women), 6 part-time (4 women); includes 5 minority (2 Black or African American, non-Hispanic/Latino; 1 Hispanic/Latino; 2 Two or more races, non-Hispanic/Latino). Average age 28. 14 applicants, 93% accepted, 5 enrolled. In 2017, 1 master's awarded. *Degree requirements:* For master's, comprehensive exam, thesis or alternative. *Entrance requirements:* For master's, GRE, statement of purpose, transcripts, 2 letters of recommendation, resume; for Certificate, bachelor's degree, statement of purpose, transcripts, resume. Additional exam requirements/recommendations for international students: Required—TOEFL (minimum score 600 paper-based; 100 iBT). *Application deadline:* For fall admission, 2/1 priority date for domestic students; for spring admission, 11/1 priority date for domestic students. Application fee: $55. *Expenses:* Contact institution. *Financial support:* Research assistantships, teaching assistantships, institutionally sponsored loans, scholarships/grants, and unspecified assistantships available. Financial award application deadline: 2/1; financial award applicants required to submit FAFSA. *Unit head:* Dr. Gloria Young, Department Chair, 202-885-2254, Fax: 202-885-2477, E-mail: gyoung@american.edu. *Application contact:* Jonathan Harper, Associate Director, Graduate Recruitment, 202-885-3622, E-mail: jharper@american.edu.
Website: http://www.american.edu/cas/sociology/

American University of Beirut, Graduate Programs, Faculty of Arts and Sciences, 1107 2020, Lebanon. Offers anthropology (MA); Arab and Middle Eastern history (PhD); Arabic language and literature (MA, PhD); archaeology (MA); art history and curating (MA); biology (MS); cell and molecular biology (PhD); chemistry (MS); clinical psychology (MA); computational sciences (MS); computer science (MS); economics (MA); education (MA), including administration and policy studies, elementary education, mathematics education, psychology school guidance, psychology test and measurements, science education, teaching English as a foreign language; English language (MA); English literature (MA); environmental policy planning (MS); financial economics (MAFE); general psychology (MA); geology (MS); history (MA); Islamic studies (MA); mathematics (MS); media studies (MA); Middle East studies (MA); philosophy (MA); physics (MS); political studies (MA); public administration (MA); public policy and international affairs (MA); sociology (MA); theoretical physics (PhD). *Program availability:* Part-time. *Faculty:* 108 full-time (36 women), 5 part-time/adjunct (4 women). *Students:* 251 full-time (180 women), 233 part-time (172 women). Average age 26. 425 applicants, 65% accepted, 121 enrolled. In 2017, 47 master's, 2 doctorates awarded. *Degree requirements:* For master's, one foreign language, comprehensive exam, thesis (for some programs), project; for doctorate, one foreign language, comprehensive exam, thesis/dissertation. *Entrance requirements:* For master's, GRE General Test (for some programs); for doctorate, GRE General Test (GRE Subject Test for theoretical physics). Additional exam requirements/recommendations for international students: Required—TOEFL (minimum score 583 paper-based; 97 iBT), IELTS (minimum score 7). *Application deadline:* For fall admission, 2/8 for domestic students; for spring admission, 11/3 for domestic students. Application fee: $50. Electronic applications accepted. *Expenses:* Contact institution. *Financial support:* In 2017–18, 29 fellowships, 40 research assistantships were awarded; teaching assistantships, scholarships/grants, tuition waivers (full and partial), and unspecified assistantships also available. Financial award application deadline: 4/4. *Unit head:* Dr. Nadia Maria El Cheikh, Dean, Faculty of Arts and Sciences, 961-1-374374 Ext. 3800, Fax: 961-1-744461, E-mail: nmcheikh@aub.edu.lb. *Application contact:* Rima Rassi, Graduate Studies Officer, 961-1-350000 Ext. 3833, Fax: 961-1-744461, E-mail: rr46@aub.edu.lb.
Website: http://www.aub.edu.lb/fas/pages/default.aspx

Angelo State University, College of Graduate Studies and Research, Archer College of Health and Human Services, Department of Psychology and Sociology, San Angelo, TX 76909. Offers industrial-organizational psychology (MS). *Program availability:* Part-time, evening/weekend. *Students:* 83 full-time (55 women), 41 part-time (28 women); includes 39 minority (8 Black or African American, non-Hispanic/Latino; 1 Asian, non-Hispanic/Latino; 28 Hispanic/Latino; 2 Two or more races, non-Hispanic/Latino), 6 international. Average age 32. *Degree requirements:* For master's, comprehensive exam, thesis optional. *Entrance requirements:* For master's, GRE General Test (for industrial and organizational psychology only), essay, letters of recommendation (for industrial and organizational psychology only). Additional exam requirements/recommendations for international students: Required—TOEFL or IELTS. *Application deadline:* For fall admission, 7/15 priority date for domestic students, 6/10 for international students; for spring admission, 12/1 priority date for domestic students, 11/1 for international students. Applications are processed on a rolling basis. Application fee: $40 ($50 for

international students). Electronic applications accepted. *Expenses:* Tuition, state resident: full-time $3856. Tuition, nonresident: full-time $11,324. *Required fees:* $2650. *Financial support:* Teaching assistantships, career-related internships or fieldwork, Federal Work-Study, scholarships/grants, and unspecified assistantships available. Support available to part-time students. Financial award application deadline: 3/1; financial award applicants required to submit FAFSA. *Unit head:* Dr. James N. Forbes, Chair, 325-486-6120, Fax: 325-942-2290, E-mail: james.forbes@angelo.edu. Website: http://www.angelo.edu/dept/psychology_sociology/

Arizona State University at the Tempe campus, College of Liberal Arts and Sciences, School of Social and Family Dynamics, Tempe, AZ 85287-3701. Offers family and human development (MS, PhD); infant-family practice (MAS); marriage and family therapy (MAS); sociology (MA, PhD). Terminal master's awarded for partial completion of doctoral program. *Degree requirements:* For master's, thesis or alternative, interactive Program of Study (iPOS) submitted before completing 50 percent of required credit hours; for doctorate, thesis/dissertation, interactive Program of Study (iPOS) submitted before completing 50 percent of required credit hours. *Entrance requirements:* For master's and doctorate, GRE, minimum GPA of 3.0 or equivalent in last 2 years of work leading to bachelor's degree. Additional exam requirements/recommendations for international students: Required—TOEFL, IELTS, or PTE. Electronic applications accepted. *Expenses:* Contact institution.

Arkansas State University, Graduate School, College of Humanities and Social Sciences, Department of Criminology, Sociology, and Geography, State University, AR 72467. Offers criminal justice (MA); sociology (MA); sociology education (SCCT). *Program availability:* Part-time. *Degree requirements:* For master's, one foreign language, comprehensive exam, thesis or alternative; for SCCT, comprehensive exam. *Entrance requirements:* For master's, GRE General Test or MAT, appropriate bachelor's degree, letters of recommendation, official transcripts, immunization records; for SCCT, GRE General Test or MAT, interview, master's degree, official transcript, immunization records. Additional exam requirements/recommendations for international students: Required—TOEFL (minimum score 550 paper-based; 79 iBT), IELTS (minimum score 6), PTE (minimum score 56). Electronic applications accepted.

Arkansas Tech University, College of Arts and Humanities, Russellville, AR 72801. Offers applied sociology (MS); English (M Ed, MA); history (MA); liberal arts (MLA); multi-media journalism (MA); psychology (MS); teaching English as a second language (MA). *Program availability:* Part-time, 100% online, blended/hybrid learning. *Students:* 35 full-time (22 women), 122 part-time (94 women); includes 34 minority (11 Black or African American, non-Hispanic/Latino; 2 Asian, non-Hispanic/Latino; 19 Hispanic/Latino; 2 Two or more races, non-Hispanic/Latino), 19 international. Average age 34. In 2017, 85 master's awarded. *Degree requirements:* For master's, comprehensive exam (for some programs), thesis (for some programs), project. *Entrance requirements:* Additional exam requirements/recommendations for international students: Required—TOEFL (minimum score 550 paper-based; 79 iBT), IELTS (minimum score 6.5), PTE (minimum score 58). *Application deadline:* For fall admission, 3/1 priority date for domestic students, 5/1 priority date for international students; for spring admission, 10/1 priority date for domestic and international students. Applications are processed on a rolling basis. Application fee: $40 ($90 for international students). Electronic applications accepted. *Expenses:* Tuition, state resident: full-time $6816; part-time $284 per credit hour. Tuition, nonresident: full-time $13,632; part-time $568 per credit hour. *Required fees:* $420 per semester. Tuition and fees vary according to course load. *Financial support:* In 2017–18, research assistantships with full and partial tuition reimbursements (averaging $4,800 per year), teaching assistantships with full and partial tuition reimbursements (averaging $4,800 per year) were awarded; career-related internships or fieldwork, Federal Work-Study, scholarships/grants, health care benefits, and unspecified assistantships also available. Support available to part-time students. Financial award application deadline: 4/15; financial award applicants required to submit FAFSA. *Unit head:* Dr. Jeffrey Woods, Dean, 479-968-0274, Fax: 479-964-0812, E-mail: jwoods@atu.edu. *Application contact:* Dr. Mary B. Gunter, Dean of Graduate College, 479-968-0398, Fax: 479-964-0542, E-mail: gradcollege@atu.edu.
Website: http://www.atu.edu/humanities/

Auburn University, Graduate School, Interdepartmental Programs, Graduate Programs in Sociology and Rural Sociology, Auburn University, AL 36849. Offers MA, MS. *Program availability:* Part-time. *Faculty:* 16 full-time (12 women), 6 part-time/adjunct (4 women). *Students:* 13 full-time (6 women), 5 part-time (3 women); includes 2 minority (1 Black or African American, non-Hispanic/Latino; 1 Hispanic/Latino), 1 international. Average age 29. 9 applicants, 100% accepted, 6 enrolled. In 2017, 4 master's awarded. *Degree requirements:* For master's, thesis, computer language (MS), foreign language (MA). *Entrance requirements:* For master's, GRE General Test. *Application deadline:* Applications are processed on a rolling basis. Application fee: $50 ($60 for international students). *Expenses:* Tuition, state resident: full-time $10,974; part-time $519 per credit hour. Tuition, nonresident: full-time $29,658; part-time $1557 per credit hour. *Required fees:* $816 per semester. Tuition and fees vary according to degree level and program. *Financial support:* Research assistantships and teaching assistantships available. Financial award application deadline: 3/15; financial award applicants required to submit FAFSA. *Unit head:* Deacue Fields, Chair, 334-844-5049. *Application contact:* Dr. George Flowers, Dean of the Graduate School, 334-844-4700.

Ball State University, Graduate School, College of Sciences and Humanities, Department of Sociology, Muncie, IN 47306. Offers MA. *Program availability:* Part-time. *Faculty:* 5 full-time (3 women). *Students:* 12 full-time (8 women), 3 part-time (2 women); includes 1 minority (Asian, non-Hispanic/Latino), 2 international. Average age 27. 12

applicants, 67% accepted, 4 enrolled. In 2017, 5 master's awarded. *Entrance requirements:* For master's, GRE General Test, minimum baccalaureate GPA of 2.75 or 3.0 in latter half of baccalaureate, three letters of recommendation. Additional exam requirements/recommendations for international students: Required—TOEFL (minimum score 550 paper-based; 79 iBT), IELTS (minimum score 6.5). *Application deadline:* Applications are processed on a rolling basis. Application fee: $60. Electronic applications accepted. *Financial support:* In 2017–18, 5 students received support, including 5 teaching assistantships with partial tuition reimbursements available (averaging $10,417 per year); research assistantships with partial tuition reimbursements available and unspecified assistantships also available. Financial award application deadline: 3/1; financial award applicants required to submit FAFSA. *Faculty research:* Retention policies for secondary education, community mental health. *Unit head:* Dr. Chad Menning, Chairperson/ Professor, 765-285-5977, Fax: 765-285-8980, E-mail: clmenning@bsu.edu.
Website: http://www.bsu.edu/sociology

Baylor University, Graduate School, College of Arts and Sciences, Department of Sociology, Waco, TX 76798-7326. Offers community analytics (PhD); health and society (PhD); sociology (MA); sociology of religion (PhD). *Faculty:* 13 full-time (3 women). *Students:* 20 full-time (7 women), 1 (woman) part-time; includes 4 minority (3 Hispanic/Latino; 1 Two or more races, non-Hispanic/Latino), 3 international. 20 applicants, 25% accepted, 4 enrolled. In 2017, 4 master's, 3 doctorates awarded. Terminal master's awarded for partial completion of doctoral program. *Degree requirements:* For master's, thesis; for doctorate, comprehensive exam, thesis/dissertation. *Entrance requirements:* For master's and doctorate, GRE General Test. Additional exam requirements/recommendations for international students: Required—TOEFL. *Application deadline:* For fall admission, 1/15 priority date for domestic and international students. Applications are processed on a rolling basis. Electronic applications accepted. *Financial support:* In 2017–18, 23 students received support, including 23 teaching assistantships with full tuition reimbursements available; research assistantships, career-related internships or fieldwork, Federal Work-Study, institutionally sponsored loans, scholarships/grants, health care benefits, and unspecified assistantships also available. Financial award application deadline: 1/15; financial award applicants required to submit FAFSA. *Faculty research:* Applied sociology, family, community, rural sociology, collective behavior/social movements, demography, racial and ethnic relations, criminology/delinquency, religion, health/medicine, aging. *Unit head:* Dr. Kevin D. Dougherty, Associate Professor and Graduate Program Director, 254-710-6232, Fax: 254-710-1175, E-mail: kevin_dougherty@baylor.edu. *Application contact:* Sharon Tate, Office Manager, 254-710-1165, Fax: 254-710-1175, E-mail: sharon_tate@baylor.edu.
Website: http://www.baylor.edu/sociology/

Binghamton University, State University of New York, Graduate School, Harpur College of Arts and Sciences, Department of Sociology, Binghamton, NY 13902-6000. Offers MA, PhD. *Program availability:* Part-time. *Faculty:* 16 full-time (7 women), 1 (woman) part-time/adjunct. *Students:* 10 full-time (7 women), 48 part-time (21 women); includes 4 minority (2 Black or African American, non-Hispanic/Latino; 1 Asian, non-Hispanic/Latino; 1 Hispanic/Latino), 33 international. Average age 36. 26 applicants, 46% accepted, 5 enrolled. In 2017, 7 master's, 6 doctorates awarded. Terminal master's awarded for partial completion of doctoral program. *Degree requirements:* For doctorate, comprehensive exam, thesis/dissertation. *Entrance requirements:* For master's and doctorate, GRE General Test, writing sample. Additional exam requirements/recommendations for international students: Required—TOEFL (minimum score 550 paper-based; 80 iBT). *Application deadline:* For fall admission, 1/15 priority date for domestic and international students. Application fee: $75. Electronic applications accepted. *Financial support:* In 2017–18, 26 students received support, including 1 research assistantship (averaging $13,500 per year), 20 teaching assistantships with full tuition reimbursements available (averaging $15,000 per year); career-related internships or fieldwork, Federal Work-Study, institutionally sponsored loans, scholarships/grants, health care benefits, tuition waivers (full and partial), and unspecified assistantships also available. Financial award applicants required to submit FAFSA. *Unit head:* Dr. Michael O. West, Chairperson, 607-777-2629, E-mail: mwest@binghamton.edu. *Application contact:* Ben Balkaya, Assistant Dean and Director, 607-777-2151, Fax: 607-777-2501, E-mail: balkaya@binghamton.edu.

Boston College, Graduate School of Arts and Sciences, Department of Sociology, Chestnut Hill, MA 02467-3800. Offers MA, PhD, MBA/MA, MBA/PhD. Terminal master's awarded for partial completion of doctoral program. *Degree requirements:* For master's, thesis optional; for doctorate, thesis/dissertation. *Entrance requirements:* For master's and doctorate, GRE General Test. Additional exam requirements/recommendations for international students: Required—TOEFL (minimum score 600 paper-based; 100 iBT), IELTS (minimum score 8). Electronic applications accepted. *Faculty research:* Social theory, race, gender studies, aging, global and transnational sociology, economic sociology, environmental sociology, political sociology, quantitative and statistical methodology.

Boston University, Graduate School of Arts and Sciences, Department of Sociology, Boston, MA 02215. Offers MA, PhD. *Students:* 43 full-time (30 women), 3 part-time (all women); includes 9 minority (3 Black or African American, non-Hispanic/Latino; 4 Hispanic/Latino; 2 Two or more races, non-Hispanic/Latino), 10 international. Average age 27. 141 applicants, 13% accepted, 7 enrolled. In 2017, 3 master's, 3 doctorates awarded. Terminal master's awarded for partial completion of doctoral program. *Degree requirements:* For master's, thesis; for doctorate, comprehensive exam, thesis/dissertation. *Entrance requirements:* For master's and doctorate, GRE General Test, 3 letters of recommendation, transcripts, personal statement, academic writing sample. Additional exam requirements/recommendations for international students: Required—TOEFL (minimum score 550 paper-based; 84 iBT). *Application deadline:* For fall admission, 1/15 for domestic and international students. Application fee: $95. Electronic applications accepted. *Financial support:* In 2017–18, 35 students received support, including 18 fellowships with full tuition reimbursements available (averaging $22,000 per year), research assistantships with full tuition reimbursements available (averaging $22,000 per year), 12 teaching assistantships with full tuition reimbursements available (averaging $22,000 per year); career-related internships or fieldwork, Federal Work-Study, scholarships/grants, and health care benefits also available. Financial award application deadline: 1/15. *Unit head:* Nazli Kibria, Chair, 617-358-0634, Fax: 617-353-4837, E-mail: nkibria@bu.edu. *Application contact:* Sarah Jordan, Department Administrator, 617-353-2591, Fax: 617-353-4837, E-mail: skjordan@bu.edu.
Website: http://www.bu.edu/sociology/

Bowling Green State University, Graduate College, College of Arts and Sciences, Department of Sociology, Bowling Green, OH 43403. Offers demography and population studies (MA); social psychology (MA); sociology (PhD). *Program availability:* Part-time. *Degree requirements:* For master's, thesis or alternative; for doctorate, comprehensive exam, thesis/dissertation. *Entrance requirements:* For master's and doctorate, GRE General Test. Additional exam requirements/recommendations for international students: Required—TOEFL. Electronic applications accepted. *Faculty research:* Applied demography, criminology and deviance, family studies, population studies, social psychology.

Brandeis University, Graduate School of Arts and Sciences, Department of Sociology, Waltham, MA 02454-9110. Offers social policy and sociology (PhD); sociology (PhD); sociology/women's, gender, and sexuality studies (MA). Offered jointly with The Heller School of Social Policy and Management. *Program availability:* Part-time. *Faculty:* 8 full-time (6 women), 7 part-time/adjunct (5 women). *Students:* 22 full-time (20 women); includes 5 minority (3 Asian, non-Hispanic/Latino; 2 Hispanic/Latino), 2 international. Average age 30. 81 applicants, 14% accepted, 5 enrolled. In 2017, 6 master's awarded. Terminal master's awarded for partial completion of doctoral program. *Degree requirements:* For master's, thesis, project or exam; for doctorate, comprehensive exam, thesis/dissertation, qualifying exam. *Entrance requirements:* For master's and doctorate, GRE General Test, resume, letters of recommendation, statement of purpose, critical writing sample, transcripts. Additional exam requirements/recommendations for international students: Required—PTE (minimum score 68), TOEFL (minimum score 600 paper-based, 100 iBT) or IELTS (7). *Application deadline:* For fall admission, 12/15 for domestic and international students. Applications are processed on a rolling basis. Application fee: $75. Electronic applications accepted. *Expenses: Tuition:* Full-time $48,720. *Required fees:* $88. Tuition and fees vary according to course load, degree level, program and student level. *Financial support:* In 2017–18, 14 students received support, including 10 fellowships with full tuition reimbursements available (averaging $24,480 per year), 6 teaching assistantships with partial tuition reimbursements available (averaging $3,200 per year); Federal Work-Study, scholarships/grants, health care benefits, and tuition waivers (partial) also available. Support available to part-time students. Financial award application deadline: 4/15; financial award applicants required to submit FAFSA. *Faculty research:* Gender and feminist studies; medical sociology; politics and social change; culture and religion. *Unit head:* Dr. Wendy Cadge, Director of Graduate Studies, 781-736-2641, E-mail: wcadge@brandeis.edu. *Application contact:* Lauren Jordahl, Department Administrator, 781-736-2644, E-mail: ljordahl@brandeis.edu.
Website: http://www.brandeis.edu/gsas/programs/sociology.html

Brigham Young University, Graduate Studies, College of Family, Home, and Social Sciences, Department of Sociology, Provo, UT 84602. Offers MS. *Faculty:* 16 full-time (3 women). *Students:* 9 full-time (7 women); includes 4 minority (1 American Indian or Alaska Native, non-Hispanic/Latino; 3 Hispanic/Latino). Average age 25. 7 applicants, 57% accepted, 2 enrolled. In 2017, 8 master's awarded. Terminal master's awarded for partial completion of doctoral program. *Degree requirements:* For master's, thesis. *Entrance requirements:* For master's, GRE General Test, minimum GPA of 3.0 in last 60 hours, writing sample, bachelor's degree in sociology or related field, 3 letters of recommendation, Honor Code commitment. Additional exam requirements/recommendations for international students: Required—TOEFL (minimum score 580 paper-based; 85 iBT), IELTS (minimum score 7). *Application deadline:* For fall admission, 1/15 for domestic and international students. Application fee: $50. Electronic applications accepted. *Expenses: Tuition:* Full-time $6880; part-time $405 per credit hour. Tuition and fees vary according to course load, program and student's religious affiliation. *Financial support:* In 2017–18, 8 students received support, including 8 research assistantships (averaging $18,400 per year); institutionally sponsored loans and unspecified assistantships also available. Financial award application deadline: 4/15. *Faculty research:* Demography, race and ethnicity, gender, rural and community, international development, comparative family. *Total annual research expenditures:* $33,500. *Unit head:* Dr. Richard B. Miller, Department Chair, 801-422-2860, Fax: 801-422-0625, E-mail: rick_miller@byu.edu. *Application contact:* Dr. Mikaela J. Dufur, Graduate Coordinator, 801-422-1720, Fax: 801-422-0625, E-mail: mikaela_dufur@byu.edu.
Website: http://sociology.byu.edu/

Brock University, Faculty of Graduate Studies, Faculty of Social Sciences, Program in Critical Sociology, St. Catharines, ON L2S 3A1, Canada. Offers MA.

Brooklyn College of the City University of New York, School of Humanities and Social Sciences, Department of Sociology, Brooklyn, NY 11210-2889. Offers MA, PhD. *Program availability:* Part-time, evening/weekend. *Degree requirements:* For master's, comprehensive exam or research essay. *Entrance requirements:* For master's, 12 upper-level credits in sociology, 2 letters of recommendation, essay. Additional exam requirements/recommendations for international students: Required—TOEFL (minimum score 500 paper-based; 61 iBT). Electronic applications accepted. *Faculty research:* Urbanization, religion, family, gender, research methods.

Brown University, Graduate School, Department of Sociology, Providence, RI 02912. Offers MA, PhD. *Degree requirements:* For master's, thesis; for doctorate, thesis/dissertation, oral exam. *Entrance requirements:* For master's and doctorate, GRE General Test.

California State University, Bakersfield, Division of Graduate Studies, School of Social Sciences and Education, Program in Sociology, Bakersfield, CA 93311. Offers MA. *Students:* 1 full-time (0 women), 5 part-time (3 women); includes 4 minority (2 Black or African American, non-Hispanic/Latino; 2 Hispanic/Latino). Average age 31. In 2017, 21 master's awarded. *Entrance requirements:* For master's, baccalaureate degree; minimum GPA of 2.5 overall, 3.0 in major. Additional exam requirements/recommendations for international students: Required—TOEFL (minimum score 500 paper-based). *Application deadline:* Applications are processed on a rolling basis. Application fee: $55. Electronic applications accepted. *Expenses:* Tuition, state resident: full-time $7176; part-time $4164 per year. *Financial support:* In 2017–18, fellowships (averaging $1,850 per year) were awarded; Federal Work-Study, scholarships/grants, and tuition waivers (full and partial) also available. Financial award application deadline: 3/2; financial award applicants required to submit FAFSA. *Unit head:* Dr. Doreen Anderson-Facile, Department Chair, 661-654-2368, Fax: 661-654-6909, E-mail: danderson_facile@csub.edu. *Application contact:* Debbie Blowers, Assistant Director of Admissions and Evaluations, 661-654-3381, E-mail: dblowers@csub.edu.
Website: https://www.csub.edu/sociology/index.html

California State University, Dominguez Hills, College of Natural and Behavioral Sciences, Program in Sociology, Carson, CA 90747-0001. Offers social research (MA); sociology (MA). *Program availability:* Part-time, evening/weekend. *Degree requirements:* For master's, comprehensive exam, thesis. *Entrance requirements:* For master's, minimum GPA of 2.85. *Faculty research:* Community studies, social movements, criminology.

California State University, Fullerton, Graduate Studies, College of Humanities and Social Sciences, Department of Sociology, Fullerton, CA 92831-3599. Offers MA. *Program availability:* Part-time. *Faculty:* 6 full-time (4 women), 1 part-time/adjunct (0 women). *Students:* 23 full-time (16 women), 14 part-time (8 women); includes 28 minority (2 Black or African American, non-Hispanic/Latino; 7 Asian, non-Hispanic/Latino; 17 Hispanic/Latino; 2 Two or more races, non-Hispanic/Latino), 1 international. Average age 29. 37 applicants, 59% accepted, 18 enrolled. *Entrance requirements:* For master's, minimum GPA of 3.0 in sociology, 2.5 in last 60 units. Application fee: $55. *Financial support:* Career-related internships or fieldwork, Federal Work-Study, institutionally sponsored loans, and scholarships/grants available. Support available to part-time students. Financial award application deadline: 3/1; financial award applicants required to submit FAFSA. *Faculty research:* Gerontology wellness clinic. *Unit head:*

Eileen Walsh, Chair, 657-278-3188, E-mail: ewalsh@fullerton.edu. *Application contact:* Admissions/Applications, 657-278-2371.

California State University, Los Angeles, Graduate Studies, College of Natural and Social Sciences, Department of Sociology, Los Angeles, CA 90032-8530. Offers MA. *Program availability:* Part-time, evening/weekend. *Degree requirements:* For master's, comprehensive exam or thesis. *Entrance requirements:* For master's, minimum GPA of 2.5 in last 90 units of course work. Additional exam requirements/recommendations for international students: Required—TOEFL (minimum score 500 paper-based). Electronic applications accepted. *Faculty research:* Criminal and delinquent careers, family and sex, ethnic minorities, demographic trends, human socialization and aging.

California State University, Northridge, Graduate Studies, College of Social and Behavioral Sciences, Department of Sociology, Northridge, CA 91330. Offers MA. *Accreditation:* CSWE. *Program availability:* Part-time, evening/weekend. *Students:* 16 full-time (14 women), 18 part-time (11 women); includes 21 minority (5 Black or African American, non-Hispanic/Latino; 3 Asian, non-Hispanic/Latino; 13 Hispanic/Latino). Average age 32. 39 applicants, 51% accepted, 14 enrolled. In 2017, 1 master's awarded. *Degree requirements:* For master's, thesis or alternative. *Entrance requirements:* For master's, GRE General Test. Additional exam requirements/ recommendations for international students: Required—TOEFL. *Application deadline:* For fall admission, 3/27 for domestic students; for spring admission, 10/17 for domestic students. Application fee: $55. *Financial support:* Career-related internships or fieldwork, Federal Work-Study, and institutionally sponsored loans available. Support available to part-time students. Financial award application deadline: 3/1. *Faculty research:* Crime and corrections, relationships between adult children and parents. *Unit head:* Karen Morgaine, Chair, 818-677-3591, E-mail: sociology@csun.edu.
Website: http://www.csun.edu/csbs/departments/sociology/index.html

California State University, Sacramento, College of Social Sciences and Interdisciplinary Studies, Department of Sociology, Sacramento, CA 95819. Offers MA. *Program availability:* Part-time. *Students:* 15 full-time (8 women), 27 part-time (14 women); includes 27 minority (5 Black or African American, non-Hispanic/Latino; 2 American Indian or Alaska Native, non-Hispanic/Latino; 5 Asian, non-Hispanic/Latino; 15 Hispanic/Latino), 1 international. Average age 29. 43 applicants, 49% accepted, 18 enrolled. In 2017, 5 master's awarded. *Degree requirements:* For master's, thesis or project; writing proficiency exam. *Entrance requirements:* For master's, minimum GPA of 3.0 during previous 2 years; completion of 18 undergraduate units in sociology. Additional exam requirements/recommendations for international students: Required—TOEFL (minimum score 550 paper-based; 80 iBT); Recommended—IELTS, TSE. *Application deadline:* For fall admission, 3/1 for domestic and international students. Applications are processed on a rolling basis. Application fee: $55. Electronic applications accepted. *Expenses:* Contact institution. *Financial support:* Teaching assistantships, career-related internships or fieldwork, Federal Work-Study, and scholarships/grants available. Support available to part-time students. Financial award application deadline: 3/1; financial award applicants required to submit FAFSA. *Unit head:* Dr. Bohsiu Wu, Chair, 916-278-6678, E-mail: bwu@csus.edu. *Application contact:* Jose Martinez, Graduate Admissions Supervisor, 916-278-7871, E-mail: martinj@skymail.csus.edu.
Website: http://www.csus.edu/soc

California State University, San Marcos, College of Humanities, Arts, Behavioral and Social Sciences, Program in Sociological Practice, San Marcos, CA 92096-0001. Offers MA. *Program availability:* Part-time, evening/weekend. *Entrance requirements:* For master's, minimum GPA of 3.0, statement of purpose, writing sample, official transcripts, three letters of recommendation. *Application deadline:* For fall admission, 2/15 for domestic students. Applications are processed on a rolling basis. Application fee: $55. Electronic applications accepted. *Expenses:* Tuition, state resident: full-time $7176. Tuition, nonresident: full-time $9504. *Faculty research:* Organized crime, juvenile detention, counseling services for minorities, mental-health facilities. *Unit head:* Dr. Richelle Swan, Graduate Coordinator, 760-750-4633, E-mail: rswan@csusm.edu.
Website: http://www.csusm.edu/sociology/graduatestudies/

Carleton University, Faculty of Graduate Studies, Faculty of Arts and Social Sciences, Department of Sociology and Anthropology, Program in Sociology, Ottawa, ON K1S 5B6, Canada. Offers MA, PhD. *Degree requirements:* For master's, thesis optional; for doctorate, one foreign language, comprehensive exam, thesis/dissertation. *Entrance requirements:* For master's, honors degree; for doctorate, master's degree. Additional exam requirements/recommendations for international students: Required—TOEFL. *Faculty research:* Canadian society and policy, inequality and mobility, race/ethnic relations, cultural studies, gender studies.

Case Western Reserve University, School of Graduate Studies, Department of Sociology, Cleveland, OH 44106. Offers MA, PhD. *Faculty:* 9 full-time (5 women), 5 part-time/adjunct (1 woman). *Students:* 34 full-time (28 women), 1 (woman) part-time; includes 9 minority (6 Black or African American, non-Hispanic/Latino; 1 Asian, non-Hispanic/Latino; 2 Two or more races, non-Hispanic/Latino), 6 international. Average age 33. 19 applicants, 42% accepted, 5 enrolled. In 2017, 6 master's, 5 doctorates awarded. Terminal master's awarded for partial completion of doctoral program. *Degree requirements:* For master's, comprehensive exam; for doctorate, comprehensive exam, thesis/dissertation. *Entrance requirements:* For master's and doctorate, GRE, curriculum vitae, writing sample, letter of intent, three letters of recommendation. Additional exam requirements/recommendations for international students: Required—TOEFL (minimum score 577 paper-based; 90 iBT); Recommended—IELTS (minimum score 7). *Application deadline:* For fall admission, 2/1 priority date for domestic students. Applications are processed on a rolling basis. Application fee: $50. Electronic applications accepted. *Expenses: Tuition:* Full-time $43,854; part-time $1827 per credit hour. *Required fees:* $50; $50 per credit hour. Tuition and fees vary according to course load and program. *Financial support:* Research assistantships, tuition waivers (full and partial), and student employment available. Financial award application deadline: 2/1; financial award applicants required to submit FAFSA. *Faculty research:* Sociology of aging and the life course, health and medical sociology, research design and methods. *Unit head:* Dr. Dale Dannefer, Professor and Chair, Department of Sociology, 216-368-2703, Fax: 216-368-2676, E-mail: dale.dannefer@case.edu. *Application contact:* Michelle Rizzuto, Department Administrator, 216-368-2214, Fax: 216-368-2676, E-mail: michelle.rizzuto@case.edu.
Website: http://sociology.case.edu/

The Catholic University of America, School of Arts and Sciences, Department of Sociology, Washington, DC 20064. Offers crime and justice studies (MA); global and comparative sociology (MA); public policy (MA). *Program availability:* Part-time. *Faculty:* 3 full-time (2 women), 3 part-time/adjunct (0 women). *Students:* 1 (woman) full-time, 1 (woman) part-time; includes 1 minority (Hispanic/Latino). Average age 24. 2 applicants. *Degree requirements:* For master's, comprehensive exam, thesis or alternative, two seminar papers. *Entrance requirements:* For master's, GRE General Test, statement of purpose, official copies of academic transcripts, three letters of recommendation. Additional exam requirements/recommendations for international students: Required—TOEFL (minimum score 550 paper-based; 80 iBT). *Application deadline:* For fall admission, 7/15 priority date for domestic students, 7/1 for international students; for spring admission, 11/15 priority date for domestic students, 11/1 for international students. Applications are processed on a rolling basis. Application fee: $55. Electronic applications accepted. *Expenses:* Contact institution. *Financial support:* Fellowships, research assistantships, teaching assistantships, Federal Work-Study, scholarships/grants, tuition waivers (full and partial), and unspecified assistantships available. Financial award application deadline: 2/1; financial award applicants required to submit FAFSA. *Faculty research:* Social movements, gender structure, political sociology, race and ethnic relations, evaluation methodologies. *Unit head:* Dr. David Walsh, Chair, 202-319-5445, Fax: 202-319-4980, E-mail: pumar@cua.edu. *Application contact:* Dr. Steven Brown, Director of Graduate Admissions, 202-319-5057, Fax: 202-319-6533, E-mail: cua-admissions@cua.edu.
Website: http://sociology.cua.edu/

Central European University, Department of Sociology and Social Anthropology, Budapest, Hungary. Offers MA, PhD. *Faculty:* 9 full-time (3 women), 4 part-time/adjunct (2 women). *Students:* 65 full-time (37 women). Average age 29. 288 applicants, 19% accepted, 33 enrolled. In 2017, 30 master's, 6 doctorates awarded. *Degree requirements:* For master's, one foreign language, thesis; for doctorate, one foreign language, comprehensive exam, thesis/dissertation. *Entrance requirements:* For master's and doctorate, interview. Additional exam requirements/recommendations for international students: Required—TOEFL (minimum score 570 paper-based); Recommended—IELTS (minimum score 6.5). *Application deadline:* For fall admission, 2/4 for domestic and international students. Application fee: $30. Electronic applications accepted. *Expenses: Tuition:* Full-time 12,000 euros. *Required fees:* 230 euros. One-time fee: 30 euros full-time. Tuition and fees vary according to course level, course load, degree level and program. *Financial support:* Fellowships, career-related internships or fieldwork, scholarships/grants, health care benefits, and tuition waivers (full and partial) available. *Faculty research:* Migration studies, post colonialism, studies of globalization, political and economic sociology, urban studies and sociologies of culture. *Unit head:* Dr. Dorit Geva, Head of Department, 36 1 327-3000 Ext. 2131, E-mail: sociology@ceu.edu. *Application contact:* Zsuzsanna Jaszberenyi, Admissions Officer, 361-324-3009, Fax: 367-327-3211, E-mail: admissions@ceu.edu.
Website: http://sociology.ceu.edu/

City College of the City University of New York, Graduate School, Colin Powell School for Civic and Global Leadership, Department of Sociology, New York, NY 10031-9198. Offers MA. *Degree requirements:* For master's, one foreign language, comprehensive exam, thesis. *Entrance requirements:* Additional exam requirements/ recommendations for international students: Required—TOEFL (minimum score 500 paper-based; 61 iBT). Electronic applications accepted. *Faculty research:* Urban sociology, criminology and deviance, race and ethnicity.

Clark Atlanta University, School of Arts and Sciences, Department of Sociology and Criminal Justice, Atlanta, GA 30314. Offers MA. *Program availability:* Part-time. *Faculty:* 5 full-time (4 women), 6 part-time/adjunct (1 woman). *Students:* 20 full-time (15 women), 3 part-time (1 woman); includes 14 minority (all Black or African American, non-Hispanic/Latino), 7 international. Average age 26. 8 applicants, 88% accepted, 5 enrolled. In 2017, 8 master's awarded. *Degree requirements:* For master's, one foreign language, comprehensive exam, thesis. *Entrance requirements:* For master's, GRE General Test, minimum GPA of 2.5. Additional exam requirements/recommendations for international students: Required—TOEFL (minimum score 500 paper-based; 61 iBT). *Application deadline:* For fall admission, 4/1 for domestic and international students; for spring admission, 11/1 for domestic and international students. Applications are processed on a rolling basis. Application fee: $40 ($55 for international students). Electronic applications accepted. *Financial support:* Scholarships/grants and unspecified assistantships available. Financial award application deadline: 4/30; financial award applicants required to submit FAFSA. *Faculty research:* Gerontology, geriatric education. *Unit head:* Dr. Obie Clayton, Chairperson, 404-880-8681, E-mail: oclayton@cau.edu.

Clemson University, Graduate School, College of Behavioral, Social and Health Sciences, Department of Sociology, Anthropology and Criminal Justice, Clemson, SC 29634. Offers applied sociology (MS). *Program availability:* Part-time. *Faculty:* 17 full-time (12 women). *Students:* 14 full-time (8 women), 2 part-time (both women); includes 2 minority (both Black or African American, non-Hispanic/Latino), 6 international. Average age 28. 13 applicants, 77% accepted, 5 enrolled. In 2017, 8 master's awarded. *Degree requirements:* For master's, thesis optional. *Entrance requirements:* For master's, GRE General Test, unofficial transcripts, letters of recommendation. Additional exam requirements/recommendations for international students: Required—TOEFL (minimum score 80 iBT), IELTS (minimum score 6.5), PTE (minimum score 54). *Application deadline:* For fall admission, 2/1 priority date for domestic and international students. Applications are processed on a rolling basis. Application fee: $80 ($90 for international students). Electronic applications accepted. *Expenses:* $5,174 per semester full-time resident, $9,714 per semester full-time non-resident, $511 per credit hour part-time resident, $1,017 per credit hour part-time non-resident; $741 per credit hour online; other fees may apply per session. *Financial support:* In 2017–18, 5 students received support, including 5 teaching assistantships with partial tuition reimbursements available (averaging $11,000 per year); career-related internships or fieldwork also available. Financial award application deadline: 2/1. *Faculty research:* Environmental issues; social inequalities; health and medical development; sociology of food, nutrition, and food security. *Total annual research expenditures:* $36,371. *Unit head:* Dr. Catherine Weisensee, Interim Department Chair, 864-656-3238, E-mail: kweisen@clemson.edu. *Application contact:* Dr. William Haller, Graduate Program Coordinator, 864-656-3814, E-mail: whaller@clemson.edu.
Website: http://www.clemson.edu/cbshs/departments/sociology/

Colorado State University, College of Liberal Arts, Department of Sociology, Fort Collins, CO 80523-1784. Offers MA, PhD. *Faculty:* 15 full-time (5 women). *Students:* 10 full-time (7 women), 30 part-time (20 women); includes 1 minority (Hispanic/Latino), 5 international. Average age 32. 45 applicants, 31% accepted, 7 enrolled. In 2017, 8 master's, 3 doctorates awarded. Terminal master's awarded for partial completion of doctoral program. *Degree requirements:* For master's, thesis (for some programs), practicum, professional paper; for doctorate, comprehensive exam, thesis/dissertation. *Entrance requirements:* For master's, GRE General Test, minimum GPA of 3.0, BA coursework in sociology, three letters of recommendation, official transcripts, statement of purpose; for doctorate, GRE General Test, minimum GPA of 3.0, BA and MA coursework in sociology, three letters of recommendation, official transcripts, statement of purpose. Additional exam requirements/recommendations for international students: Required—TOEFL (minimum score 550 paper-based; 80 iBT), IELTS (minimum score 6.5). *Application deadline:* For fall admission, 1/15 priority date for domestic and international students. Application fee: $60 ($70 for international students). Electronic applications accepted. *Expenses:* Tuition, state resident: full-time $9917. Tuition, nonresident: full-time $24,312. *Required fees:* $2284. Tuition and fees vary according to course load and program. *Financial support:* In 2017–18, 1 research assistantship (averaging $18,583 per year), 19 teaching assistantships (averaging $16,305 per year) were awarded; scholarships/grants and unspecified assistantships also available. Financial award applicants required to submit FAFSA. *Faculty research:* Public opinion on crime and justice issues; energy development; globalization; environmental flow cooperation on the Colorado River; criminology and criminal justice. *Total annual*

research expenditures: $234,357. *Unit head:* Pete Taylor, Chair, 970-491-6044, Fax: 970-491-2191, E-mail: pete.taylor@colostate.edu. *Application contact:* Dr. Michael Carolan, Associate Dean for Research and Graduate Affairs, 970-491-5797.
Website: http://sociology.colostate.edu/

Columbia University, Graduate School of Arts and Sciences, New York, NY 10027. Offers African-American studies (MA); American studies (MA); anthropology (MA, PhD); art history and archaeology (MA, PhD); astronomy (PhD); biological sciences (PhD); biotechnology (MA); chemical physics (PhD); chemistry (PhD); classical studies (MA, PhD); classics (MA, PhD); climate and society (MA); conservation biology (MA); earth and environmental sciences (PhD); East Asia: regional studies (MA); East Asian languages and cultures (MA, PhD); ecology, evolution and environmental biology (MA), including conservation biology; ecology, evolution, and environmental biology (PhD), including ecology and evolutionary biology, evolutionary primatology; economics (MA, PhD); English and comparative literature (MA, PhD); French and Romance philology (MA, PhD); Germanic languages (MA, PhD); global French studies (MA); global thought (MA); Hispanic cultural studies (MA); history (PhD); history and literature (MA); human rights studies (MA); Islamic studies (MA); Italian (MA, PhD); Japanese pedagogy (MA); Jewish studies (MA); Latin America and the Caribbean: regional studies (MA); Latin American and Iberian cultures (PhD); mathematics (MA, PhD), including finance (MA); medieval and Renaissance studies (MA); Middle Eastern, South Asian, and African studies (MA, PhD); modern art: critical and curatorial studies (MA); modern European studies (MA); museum anthropology (MA); music (DMA, PhD); oral history (MA); philosophical foundations of physics (MA); philosophy (MA, PhD); physics (PhD); political science (MA, PhD); psychology (PhD); quantitative methods in the social sciences (MA); religion (MA, PhD); Russia, Eurasia and East Europe: regional studies (MA); Russian translation (MA); Slavic cultures (MA); Slavic languages (MA, PhD); sociology (MA, PhD); South Asian studies (MA); statistics (MA, PhD); theatre (PhD). Dual-degree programs require admission to both Graduate School of Arts and Sciences and another Columbia school. *Program availability:* Part-time. Terminal master's awarded for partial completion of doctoral program. *Degree requirements:* For master's, variable foreign language requirement, comprehensive exam (for some programs), thesis (for some programs); for doctorate, variable foreign language requirement, comprehensive exam (for some programs), thesis/dissertation. *Entrance requirements:* For master's and doctorate, GRE General Test, GRE Subject Test (for some programs). Additional exam requirements/recommendations for international students: Required—TOEFL, IELTS. Electronic applications accepted. *Expenses: Tuition:* Full-time $44,864; part-time $1704 per credit. *Required fees:* $2370 per semester. One-time fee: $105.

Concordia University, School of Graduate Studies, Faculty of Arts and Science, Department of Sociology and Anthropology, Montréal, QC H3G 1M8, Canada. Offers social and cultural analysis (PhD); social and cultural anthropology (MA); sociology (MA). *Degree requirements:* For master's, comprehensive exam or thesis. *Entrance requirements:* For master's, honors degree in sociology or equivalent. *Faculty research:* Community and ethnic relations, popular culture, regional development in Canada, industrial and social movements, social problems and policies.

Cornell University, Graduate School, Graduate Fields of Agriculture and Life Sciences, Field of Development Sociology, Ithaca, NY 14853. Offers population and development (MS, PhD); rural and environmental sociology (MS, PhD); state, economy, and society (MS, PhD). *Degree requirements:* For doctorate, comprehensive exam, thesis/dissertation. *Entrance requirements:* For master's and doctorate, GRE General Test, 3 letters of recommendation. Additional exam requirements/recommendations for international students: Required—TOEFL (minimum score 550 paper-based; 77 iBT). Electronic applications accepted. *Faculty research:* Demography (population and development), environmental sociology, international and rural community development, political economy and ecology, sustainable agriculture.

Cornell University, Graduate School, Graduate Fields of Arts and Sciences, Field of Sociology, Ithaca, NY 14853. Offers economy and society (MA, PhD); gender and life course (MA, PhD); methodology (MA, PhD); organizations (MA, PhD); policy analysis (MA, PhD); political sociology/social movements (MA, PhD); racial and ethnic relations (MA, PhD); social networks (MA, PhD); social psychology (MA, PhD); social stratification (MA, PhD). Terminal master's awarded for partial completion of doctoral program. *Degree requirements:* For master's, thesis; for doctorate, thesis/dissertation, 1 year of teaching experience. *Entrance requirements:* For master's and doctorate, GRE General Test, 2 letters of recommendation, writing sample. Additional exam requirements/recommendations for international students: Required—TOEFL (minimum score 550 paper-based; 77 iBT). Electronic applications accepted. *Faculty research:* Comparative societal analysis, work and family, simulations, social class and mobility, racial segregation and inequality.

Dalhousie University, Faculty of Arts and Social Science, Department of Sociology and Social Anthropology, Halifax, NS B3H 4R2, Canada. Offers social anthropology (MA, PhD); sociology (MA, PhD). *Entrance requirements:* Additional exam requirements/recommendations for international students: Required—TOEFL, IELTS, CANTEST, CAEL, or Michigan English Language Assessment Battery. Electronic applications accepted. *Faculty research:* Social inequality and social injustice; work, industry, and development (regional and international perspectives); health and illness.

DePaul University, College of Liberal Arts and Social Sciences, Chicago, IL 60614. Offers Arabic (MA); Chinese (MA); critical ethnic studies (MA); English (MA); French (MA); German (MA); history (MA); interdisciplinary studies (MA, MS); international public service (MS); international studies (MA); Italian (MA); Japanese (MA); liberal studies (MA); nonprofit management (MNM); public administration (MPA); public health (MPH); public policy (MPP); public service management (MS); refugee and forced migration studies (MS); social work (MSW); sociology (MA); Spanish (MA); sustainable urban development (MA); women's and gender studies (MA); writing and publishing (MA); writing, rhetoric and discourse (MA); MA/PhD. *Program availability:* Part-time, evening/weekend, online learning. Terminal master's awarded for partial completion of doctoral program. *Degree requirements:* For master's, variable foreign language requirement, comprehensive exam (for some programs), thesis (for some programs). *Application deadline:* Applications are processed on a rolling basis. Application fee: $40. Electronic applications accepted. *Financial support:* Applicants required to submit FAFSA. *Unit head:* Dr. Guillermo Vasquez de Velasco, Dean, 773-325-7305. *Application contact:* Ann Spittle, Director of Graduate Admission, 773-325-8369, Fax: 312-476-3244, E-mail: graddepaul@depaul.edu.
Website: http://las.depaul.edu/

Duke University, Graduate School, Department of Sociology, Durham, NC 27708. Offers AM, PhD. Terminal master's awarded for partial completion of doctoral program. *Degree requirements:* For doctorate, thesis/dissertation. *Entrance requirements:* For master's and doctorate, GRE General Test. Additional exam requirements/recommendations for international students: Required—TOEFL (minimum score 577 paper-based; 90 iBT) or IELTS (minimum score 7). Electronic applications accepted.

East Carolina University, Graduate School, Thomas Harriot College of Arts and Sciences, Department of Sociology, Greenville, NC 27858-4353. Offers MA. *Program availability:* Part-time, evening/weekend. *Students:* 14 full-time (10 women), 4 part-time (3 women); includes 7 minority (all Black or African American, non-Hispanic/Latino), 1 international. Average age 29. 10 applicants, 100% accepted, 8 enrolled. In 2017, 6 master's awarded. *Degree requirements:* For master's, comprehensive exam, thesis or alternative. *Entrance requirements:* For master's, GRE General Test or MAT. Additional exam requirements/recommendations for international students: Recommended—TOEFL (minimum score 78 iBT), IELTS (minimum score 6.5). *Application deadline:* For fall admission, 6/15 priority date for domestic and international students; for spring admission, 11/15 priority date for domestic and international students. Applications are processed on a rolling basis. Application fee: $75. Electronic applications accepted. *Expenses:* Tuition, state resident: full-time $4749; part-time $297 per credit hour. Tuition, nonresident: full-time $17,898; part-time $1119 per credit hour. *Required fees:* $2691; $224 per credit hour. Part-time tuition and fees vary according to course load and program. *Financial support:* Fellowships with partial tuition reimbursements, research assistantships with partial tuition reimbursements, teaching assistantships with partial tuition reimbursements, and Federal Work-Study available. Support available to part-time students. Financial award application deadline: 3/1. *Unit head:* Dr. Bob Edwards, Chair, 252-328-4863, E-mail: edwardsr@ecu.edu. *Application contact:* Dean of Graduate School, 252-328-6012, Fax: 252-328-6071, E-mail: gradschool@ecu.edu.
Website: http://www.ecu.edu/soci/

Eastern Michigan University, Graduate School, College of Arts and Sciences, Department of Sociology, Anthropology and Criminology, Programs in Sociology, Ypsilanti, MI 48197. Offers sociology (MA); sociology - applied research specialty (MA). *Students:* 4 full-time (3 women), 11 part-time (9 women); includes 7 minority (4 Black or African American, non-Hispanic/Latino; 1 Asian, non-Hispanic/Latino; 2 Two or more races, non-Hispanic/Latino). Average age 31. 16 applicants, 75% accepted, 4 enrolled. In 2017, 2 master's awarded. Application fee: $45. *Application contact:* Dr. Solage Simoes, Graduate Coordinator, 734-487-0012, Fax: 734-487-9666, E-mail: ssimoes@emich.edu.
Website: http://www.emich.edu/sac/

East Tennessee State University, School of Graduate Studies, College of Arts and Sciences, Department of Sociology and Anthropology, Johnson City, TN 37614-1701. Offers applied sociology (MA); general sociology (MA). *Program availability:* Part-time, evening/weekend. *Degree requirements:* For master's, comprehensive exam, internship or thesis. *Entrance requirements:* For master's, GRE General Test, minimum GPA of 3.0 in sociology major, three letters of recommendation. Additional exam requirements/recommendations for international students: Required—TOEFL (minimum score 550 paper-based; 79 iBT). *Application deadline:* For fall admission, 6/1 for domestic students, 4/29 for international students; for spring admission, 11/1 for domestic students, 9/29 for international students. Application fee: $55 ($65 for international students). Electronic applications accepted. *Financial support:* Research assistantships with full tuition reimbursements, teaching assistantships with full tuition reimbursements, career-related internships or fieldwork, institutionally sponsored loans, scholarships/grants, tuition waivers (full), and unspecified assistantships available. Financial award application deadline: 7/1; financial award applicants required to submit FAFSA. *Faculty research:* Survey research methodologies, religion, sociology of sport, sociology of emotions, race and gender studies. *Unit head:* Dr. William N. Duncan, Chair, 423-439-6650, Fax: 423-439-5313, E-mail: duncanwn@etsu.edu. *Application contact:* Dr. William N. Duncan, Chair, 423-439-6650, Fax: 423-439-5313, E-mail: duncanwn@etsu.edu.
Website: http://www.etsu.edu/cas/sociology/

Emory University, Laney Graduate School, Department of Sociology, Atlanta, GA 30322-1100. Offers PhD. Terminal master's awarded for partial completion of doctoral program. *Degree requirements:* For doctorate, comprehensive exam, thesis/dissertation, 2 preliminary exams, research paper, paper presentation. *Entrance requirements:* For doctorate, GRE General Test, minimum GPA of 3.0. Additional exam requirements/recommendations for international students: Required—TOEFL. Electronic applications accepted. *Faculty research:* Political economy and global analysis, culture, social psychology, criminology, stratification.

Fayetteville State University, Graduate School, Program in Sociology, Fayetteville, NC 28301-4298. Offers MA. *Program availability:* Part-time, evening/weekend. *Faculty:* 3 full-time (1 woman). *Students:* 1 (woman) full-time, 11 part-time (9 women); includes 9 minority (6 Black or African American, non-Hispanic/Latino; 1 American Indian or Alaska Native, non-Hispanic/Latino; 2 Two or more races, non-Hispanic/Latino). Average age 35. 9 applicants, 100% accepted, 7 enrolled. In 2017, 3 master's awarded. *Degree requirements:* For master's, comprehensive exam, internship. *Entrance requirements:* For master's, GRE. Additional exam requirements/recommendations for international students: Required—TOEFL. *Application deadline:* For fall admission, 4/15 for domestic students; for spring admission, 10/15 for domestic students. Applications are processed on a rolling basis. Application fee: $40. Electronic applications accepted. *Expenses:* Tuition, state resident: full-time $8604. Tuition, nonresident: full-time $19,669. *Financial support:* Application deadline: 3/1; applicants required to submit FAFSA. *Faculty research:* Research methodology, African demography, urban sociology, aging and health, divided social problems, medical sociology, social change. *Unit head:* Dr. Nicole Lucas, Chairperson, 910-672-1122, Fax: 910-672-1378, E-mail: nlucas2@uncfsu.edu. *Application contact:* Latoya Parker, Academic Advisor, 910-672-2322, Fax: 910-672-1378, E-mail: lmparker01@uncfsu.edu.

Florida Atlantic University, Dorothy F. Schmidt College of Arts and Letters, Department of Sociology, Boca Raton, FL 33431-0991. Offers MA. *Program availability:* Part-time, evening/weekend. *Faculty:* 9 full-time (3 women). *Students:* 18 full-time (12 women), 7 part-time (3 women); includes 12 minority (5 Black or African American, non-Hispanic/Latino; 6 Hispanic/Latino; 1 Two or more races, non-Hispanic/Latino). Average age 30. 18 applicants, 72% accepted, 12 enrolled. In 2017, 8 master's awarded. *Degree requirements:* For master's, thesis (for some programs). *Entrance requirements:* For master's, GRE General Test, minimum GPA of 3.0. Additional exam requirements/recommendations for international students: Required—TOEFL, IELTS. *Application deadline:* For fall admission, 5/1 priority date for domestic and international students. Applications are processed on a rolling basis. Application fee: $30. Electronic applications accepted. *Expenses:* Tuition, state resident: full-time $7400; part-time $369.82 per credit. Tuition, nonresident: full-time $20,496; part-time $1042.81 per credit. *Financial support:* Teaching assistantships with tuition reimbursements and Federal Work-Study available. *Faculty research:* Gender/race/class, globalization, theory, social control, social movements. *Unit head:* Cathy King, Program Administrator, 561-297-3270, E-mail: cking11@fau.edu.
Website: http://www.fau.edu/sociology/

Florida International University, Steven J. Green School of International and Public Affairs, Department of Global and Sociocultural Studies, Miami, FL 33199. Offers MA, PhD. *Program availability:* Part-time, evening/weekend. *Faculty:* 30 full-time (10 women), 13 part-time/adjunct (8 women). *Students:* 38 full-time (19 women), 27 part-time (22 women); includes 36 minority (9 Black or African American, non-Hispanic/Latino; 1 Asian, non-Hispanic/Latino; 24 Hispanic/Latino; 2 Two or more races, non-Hispanic/Latino), 7 international. Average age 35. 45 applicants, 47% accepted, 16 enrolled. In 2017, 4 master's, 5 doctorates awarded. *Degree requirements:* For master's, thesis; for doctorate, comprehensive exam, thesis/dissertation. *Entrance requirements:* For master's, GRE General Test, 3 letters of recommendation; minimum undergraduate GPA of 3.25, 3.5 on any previous graduate work; written examples of academic or other

relevant professional work; for doctorate, GRE General Test, letter of intent; 3 letters of recommendation; minimum undergraduate GPA of 3.25, 3.5 on any previous graduate work; written examples of academic or other relevant professional work. Additional exam requirements/recommendations for international students: Required—TOEFL (minimum score 550 paper-based; 80 iBT). *Application deadline:* For fall admission, 6/1 for domestic students, 4/1 for international students; for spring admission, 10/1 for domestic students, 9/1 for international students. Applications are processed on a rolling basis. Application fee: $30. Electronic applications accepted. *Expenses:* Tuition, state resident: full-time $8912; part-time $446 per credit hour. Tuition, nonresident: full-time $21,393; part-time $992 per credit hour. *Required fees:* $390; $195 per semester. *Financial support:* Institutionally sponsored loans and scholarships/grants available. Financial award application deadline: 3/1; financial award applicants required to submit FAFSA. *Unit head:* Dr. Rod Neumann, Chair, 305-348-2936, Fax: 305-348-3605, E-mail: roderick.neumann@fiu.edu. *Application contact:* Nanett Rojas, Manager, Admissions Operations, 305-348-7464, Fax: 305-348-7441, E-mail: gradadm@fiu.edu.

Florida State University, The Graduate School, College of Social Sciences and Public Policy, Department of Sociology, Tallahassee, FL 32306-2270. Offers applied social research (MS); sociology (MS, PhD); sociology of health and aging (MS). *Faculty:* 21 full-time (15 women). *Students:* 49 full-time (29 women), 6 part-time (5 women); includes 18 minority (5 Black or African American, non-Hispanic/Latino; 2 Asian, non-Hispanic/Latino; 8 Hispanic/Latino; 3 Two or more races, non-Hispanic/Latino). Average age 28. 33 applicants, 33% accepted, 8 enrolled. In 2017, 13 master's, 12 doctorates awarded. *Degree requirements:* For doctorate, comprehensive exam, thesis/dissertation. *Entrance requirements:* For master's and doctorate, GRE General Test, minimum GPA of 3.0. Additional exam requirements/recommendations for international students: Required—TOEFL (minimum score 550 paper-based; 80 iBT). *Application deadline:* For fall admission, 12/15 priority date for domestic students, 12/15 for international students. Applications are processed on a rolling basis. Application fee: $30. Electronic applications accepted. *Expenses:* $479.32 per credit hour in-state; $1,110.72 per credit hour out-of-state. *Financial support:* In 2017–18, 55 students received support, including 3 fellowships with full tuition reimbursements available (averaging $25,115 per year), 4 research assistantships with full tuition reimbursements available (averaging $21,150 per year), 50 teaching assistantships with full tuition reimbursements available (averaging $21,150 per year); institutionally sponsored loans, scholarships/grants, health care benefits, and unspecified assistantships also available. Financial award application deadline: 12/15; financial award applicants required to submit FAFSA. *Faculty research:* Aging and health, demography, inequality (gender/race and social movements/politics). *Total annual research expenditures:* $371,977. *Unit head:* Dr. Kathryn Harker Tillman, Chair, 850-644-6416, E-mail: ktillman@fsu.edu. *Application contact:* Kimberly McClellan, Academic Specialist/Graduate Program Coordinator, 850-644-8329, E-mail: kmcclellan@fsu.edu.
Website: http://coss.fsu.edu/sociology/

George Mason University, College of Humanities and Social Sciences, Department of Sociology and Anthropology, Fairfax, VA 22030. Offers anthropology (MA); sociology (MA, PhD). *Faculty:* 24 full-time (13 women), 4 part-time/adjunct (2 women). *Students:* 35 full-time (27 women), 55 part-time (38 women); includes 21 minority (6 Black or African American, non-Hispanic/Latino; 1 American Indian or Alaska Native, non-Hispanic/Latino; 5 Asian, non-Hispanic/Latino; 7 Hispanic/Latino; 2 Two or more races, non-Hispanic/Latino), 6 international. Average age 32. 76 applicants, 68% accepted, 19 enrolled. In 2017, 19 master's, 7 doctorates awarded. *Degree requirements:* For master's, thesis; for doctorate, comprehensive exam, thesis/dissertation. *Entrance requirements:* For master's, official transcript; expanded goals statement; 3 letters of recommendation; writing sample; resume; 3 credits in undergraduate sociology theory, statistics and research methods (for sociology); 3 credits of sociocultural anthropology (for anthropology); for doctorate, GRE General Test, expanded goals statement; 3 letters of recommendation; writing sample; official transcript. Additional exam requirements/recommendations for international students: Required—TOEFL (minimum score 575 paper-based; 88 iBT), IELTS (minimum score 6.5), PTE (minimum score 59). *Application deadline:* For fall admission, 2/15 for domestic and international students; for spring admission, 11/1 for domestic and international students. Application fee: $75 ($80 for international students). Electronic applications accepted. *Expenses:* Tuition, state resident: full-time $11,228; part-time $459.50 per credit. Tuition, nonresident: full-time $30,932; part-time $1280.50 per credit. *Required fees:* $3252; $135.50 per credit. Part-time tuition and fees vary according to course load and program. *Financial support:* In 2017–18, 24 students received support, including 6 fellowships (averaging $7,483 per year), 10 research assistantships with tuition reimbursements available (averaging $20,262 per year), 10 teaching assistantships with tuition reimbursements available (averaging $10,215 per year); career-related internships or fieldwork, Federal Work-Study, scholarships/grants, unspecified assistantships, and health care benefits (for full-time research or teaching assistantship recipients) also available. Support available to part-time students. Financial award application deadline: 3/1; financial award applicants required to submit FAFSA. *Faculty research:* Africa, American teenagers, black entrepreneurs, human rights, gambling. *Total annual research expenditures:* $80,740. *Unit head:* Amy Best, Department Chair, 703-993-1426, Fax: 703-993-1446, E-mail: abest@gmu.edu. *Application contact:* Nancy Hanrahan, Graduate Director, 703-993-1433, Fax: 703-993-1446, E-mail: nhanraha@gmu.edu.
Website: http://soan.gmu.edu

The George Washington University, Columbian College of Arts and Sciences, Department of Sociology, Washington, DC 20052. Offers criminology (MA); sociology (MA). *Program availability:* Part-time, evening/weekend. *Students:* Average age 25. 43 applicants, 77% accepted, 14 enrolled. In 2017, 7 master's awarded. *Degree requirements:* For master's, comprehensive exam, thesis or alternative. *Entrance requirements:* For master's, GRE General Test, minimum GPA of 3.0. Additional exam requirements/recommendations for international students: Required—TOEFL (minimum score 550 paper-based; 80 iBT). *Application deadline:* For fall admission, 6/1 priority date for domestic students, 1/15 priority date for international students; for spring admission, 11/1 priority date for domestic students, 9/1 priority date for international students. Applications are processed on a rolling basis. Application fee: $75. Electronic applications accepted. *Expenses: Tuition:* Full-time $28,800; part-time $1655 per credit hour. *Required fees:* $45; $2.75 per credit hour. *Financial support:* In 2017–18, 7 students received support. Fellowships with full tuition reimbursements available, teaching assistantships, career-related internships or fieldwork, Federal Work-Study, and tuition waivers available. Financial award application deadline: 1/15. *Unit head:* Dr. Greg Squires, Chair, 202-994-7466, E-mail: squires@gwu.edu. *Application contact:* Information Contact, 202-994-6345, Fax: 202-994-3239, E-mail: soc@gwu.edu.
Website: http://sociology.columbian.gwu.edu/

Georgia Southern University, Jack N. Averitt College of Graduate Studies, College of Liberal Arts and Social Sciences, Program in Social Science, Statesboro, GA 30460. Offers MA. *Program availability:* Part-time, evening/weekend. *Faculty:* 17 full-time (9 women), 1 (woman) part-time/adjunct. *Students:* 29 full-time (23 women), 14 part-time (11 women); includes 14 minority (9 Black or African American, non-Hispanic/Latino; 2 Hispanic/Latino; 3 Two or more races, non-Hispanic/Latino), 1 international. Average age 27. 20 applicants, 85% accepted, 13 enrolled. In 2017, 17 master's awarded. *Degree requirements:* For master's, thesis optional. *Entrance requirements:* For

master's, GRE General Test. Additional exam requirements/recommendations for international students: Required—TOEFL (minimum score 550 paper-based; 80 iBT), IELTS (minimum score 6). *Application deadline:* For fall admission, 3/1 priority date for domestic and international students; for spring admission, 10/1 priority date for domestic students, 10/1 for international students. Applications are processed on a rolling basis. Application fee: $50. Electronic applications accepted. *Expenses:* Tuition, state resident: full-time $4986; part-time $3324 per year. Tuition, nonresident: full-time $21,982; part-time $15,352 per year. *Required fees:* $2092; $1802 per credit hour. $901 per semester. Tuition and fees vary according to course load, campus/location and program. *Financial support:* In 2017–18, 24 students received support, including 7 fellowships with full tuition reimbursements available (averaging $7,750 per year); career-related internships or fieldwork, Federal Work-Study, scholarships/grants, tuition waivers (full), and unspecified assistantships also available. Support available to part-time students. Financial award application deadline: 4/15; financial award applicants required to submit FAFSA. *Faculty research:* Anthropology, sociology, criminal justice, history, political science. *Total annual research expenditures:* $40,162. *Unit head:* Dr. Marieke VanWilligen, Department Chair, 912-478-5621, Fax: 912-478-0703, E-mail: mvanwilligen@georgiasouthern.edu.
Website: http://class.georgiasouthern.edu/socianth/

Georgia State University, College of Arts and Sciences, Department of Sociology, Atlanta, GA 30302-3083. Offers MA, PhD, MA/PhD. *Program availability:* Part-time, evening/weekend. *Faculty:* 23 full-time (15 women). *Students:* 66 full-time (47 women), 27 part-time (20 women); includes 55 minority (38 Black or African American, non-Hispanic/Latino; 1 American Indian or Alaska Native, non-Hispanic/Latino; 3 Asian, non-Hispanic/Latino; 6 Hispanic/Latino; 7 Two or more races, non-Hispanic/Latino), 4 international. Average age 32. 58 applicants, 74% accepted, 11 enrolled. In 2017, 6 master's, 10 doctorates awarded. Terminal master's awarded for partial completion of doctoral program. *Entrance requirements:* For master's and doctorate, GRE. Additional exam requirements/recommendations for international students: Required—TOEFL (minimum score 600 paper-based; 100 iBT). *Application deadline:* For fall admission, 4/15 for domestic students, 2/1 for international students; for spring admission, 4/15 for domestic and international students. Applications are processed on a rolling basis. Application fee: $50. Electronic applications accepted. *Expenses:* Tuition, state resident: full-time $7020. Tuition, nonresident: full-time $22,518. *Required fees:* $2128. Tuition and fees vary according to degree level and program. *Financial support:* In 2017–18, fellowships with tuition reimbursements (averaging $5,000 per year), research assistantships with tuition reimbursements (averaging $17,500 per year), teaching assistantships with tuition reimbursements (averaging $13,000 per year) were awarded; scholarships/grants and unspecified assistantships also available. Financial award application deadline: 2/1; financial award applicants required to submit FAFSA. *Faculty research:* Race and urban studies, gender and sexuality, family, health, life course. *Unit head:* Dr. Donald C. Reitzes, Department Chair, 404-413-6506, Fax: 404-413-6505, E-mail: dreitzes@gsu.edu. *Application contact:* Dr. Leslie Reid, Director of Graduate Studies, 404-413-6521, Fax: 404-413-6505, E-mail: lesleyreid@gsu.edu.
Website: http://cas.gsu.edu/graduate-studies/admissions/

The Graduate Center, City University of New York, Graduate Studies, Program in Sociology, New York, NY 10016-4039. Offers PhD. *Faculty:* 69 full-time (15 women). *Students:* 134 full-time (78 women), 2 part-time (both women); includes 34 minority (12 Black or African American, non-Hispanic/Latino; 7 Asian, non-Hispanic/Latino; 12 Hispanic/Latino; 1 Native Hawaiian or other Pacific Islander, non-Hispanic/Latino; 2 Two or more races, non-Hispanic/Latino), 33 international. Average age 34. 169 applicants, 28% accepted, 15 enrolled. In 2017, 13 doctorates awarded. *Degree requirements:* For doctorate, one foreign language, thesis/dissertation. *Entrance requirements:* For doctorate, GRE General Test, writing sample. Additional exam requirements/recommendations for international students: Required—TOEFL. *Application deadline:* For fall admission, 12/15 for domestic students. Application fee: $125. Electronic applications accepted. *Financial support:* In 2017–18, 129 students received support, including 98 fellowships, 13 research assistantships, 8 teaching assistantships; career-related internships or fieldwork, Federal Work-Study, institutionally sponsored loans, and tuition waivers (full and partial) also available. Financial award application deadline: 2/1; financial award applicants required to submit FAFSA. *Unit head:* Dr. Lynn Chancer, Executive Officer, 212-817-8783, Fax: 212-817-1536. *Application contact:* Les Gribben, Director of Admissions, 212-817-7470, Fax: 212-817-1624, E-mail: lgribben@gc.cuny.edu.

Harvard University, Graduate School of Arts and Sciences, Department of Sociology, Cambridge, MA 02138. Offers PhD. *Degree requirements:* For doctorate, thesis/dissertation, oral exams in 2 subfields. *Entrance requirements:* For doctorate, GRE General Test. Additional exam requirements/recommendations for international students: Required—TOEFL. *Faculty research:* Sociological theory, political theories, quantitative approaches to methodology.

Howard University, Graduate School, Department of Health, Human Performance and Leisure Studies, Washington, DC 20059-0002. Offers exercise physiology (MS); health education (MS); sports studies (MS), including sociology of sports, sports management; urban recreation (MS), including leisure studies. *Program availability:* Part-time, evening/weekend. *Degree requirements:* For master's, comprehensive exam, thesis. *Entrance requirements:* For master's, BS in human performance or related field. Additional exam requirements/recommendations for international students: Recommended—TOEFL. Electronic applications accepted. *Faculty research:* Health promotion, cardiovascular hypertension, physical activity, sport and human rights issues.

Howard University, Graduate School, Department of Sociology and Anthropology, Washington, DC 20059-0002. Offers sociology (MA, PhD). *Program availability:* Part-time, evening/weekend. *Degree requirements:* For master's, thesis; for doctorate, one foreign language, comprehensive exam, thesis/dissertation, RCR, writing exam. *Entrance requirements:* For master's, GRE General Test, minimum GPA of 3.0; for doctorate, GRE General Test, minimum GPA of 3.5. Additional exam requirements/recommendations for international students: Required—TOEFL. Electronic applications accepted. *Faculty research:* Medical sociology; criminology; race, class and gender; urban sociology.

Humboldt State University, Academic Programs, College of Arts, Humanities, and Social Sciences, Department of Sociology, Arcata, CA 95521-8299. Offers MA. *Degree requirements:* For master's, thesis or alternative, qualifying exam. *Entrance requirements:* For master's, minimum GPA of 2.5, 3 letters of recommendation. Additional exam requirements/recommendations for international students: Required—TOEFL (minimum score 500 paper-based). *Faculty research:* Sociology of women political activists, environmental dispute resolution, prosocial behavior.

Hunter College of the City University of New York, Graduate School, School of Arts and Sciences, Department of Sociology, New York, NY 10065-5085. Offers applied social research (MS). *Degree requirements:* For master's, internship. *Entrance requirements:* For master's, GRE General Test or GMAT, 3 credits of course work in statistics, 2 letters of recommendation. Additional exam requirements/recommendations for international students: Required—TOEFL.

Sociology

Idaho State University, Office of Graduate Studies, College of Arts and Letters, Department of Sociology, Social Work and Criminology, Pocatello, ID 83209-8114. Offers sociology (MA). *Program availability:* Part-time. *Degree requirements:* For master's, comprehensive exam, thesis, oral defense of thesis. *Entrance requirements:* For master's, GRE General Test (minimum 40th percentile in one of 3 sections), minimum undergraduate GPA of 3.0, 3 letters of recommendation. Additional exam requirements/recommendations for international students: Required—TOEFL (minimum score 550 paper-based; 80 iBT). Electronic applications accepted. *Faculty research:* Terrorism, social organization, family social work.

Illinois State University, Graduate School, College of Arts and Sciences, Department of Sociology, Normal, IL 61790. Offers historical archaeology (MA, MS); sociology (MA, MS). *Degree requirements:* For master's, thesis. *Entrance requirements:* For master's, GRE General Test, GRE Subject Test, minimum GPA of 2.4 in last 60 hours of course work. *Faculty research:* Japanese Saturday School (Kato).

Indiana University Bloomington, University Graduate School, College of Arts and Sciences, Department of Sociology, Bloomington, IN 47405-7000. Offers MA, PhD. Terminal master's awarded for partial completion of doctoral program. *Degree requirements:* For master's, thesis; for doctorate, comprehensive exam, thesis/dissertation. *Entrance requirements:* For master's and doctorate, GRE General Test. Additional exam requirements/recommendations for international students: Required—TOEFL. Electronic applications accepted. *Faculty research:* Social psychology, political sociology, sociological research methods, stratification/mobility, education.

Indiana University of Pennsylvania, School of Graduate Studies and Research, College of Humanities and Social Sciences, Department of Sociology, Program in Sociology, Indiana, PA 15705. Offers MA. *Program availability:* Part-time. *Faculty:* 14 full-time (11 women). *Students:* 8 full-time (6 women), 2 part-time (1 woman), 1 international. Average age 24. 14 applicants, 93% accepted, 4 enrolled. In 2017, 3 master's awarded. *Degree requirements:* For master's, thesis optional. *Entrance requirements:* For master's, GRE, 2 letters of recommendation. Additional exam requirements/recommendations for international students: Required—TOEFL (minimum score 550 paper-based). *Application deadline:* Applications are processed on a rolling basis. Application fee: $50. Electronic applications accepted. *Expenses:* Tuition, state resident: full-time $12,000; part-time $500 per credit. Tuition, nonresident: full-time $18,000; part-time $750 per credit. *Required fees:* $4073; $165.55 per credit. $64 per term. *Financial support:* In 2017–18, 8 research assistantships with tuition reimbursements (averaging $5,796 per year) were awarded; fellowships with full tuition reimbursements, career-related internships or fieldwork, Federal Work-Study, scholarships/grants, and unspecified assistantships also available. Financial award application deadline: 4/15; financial award applicants required to submit FAFSA. *Unit head:* Dr. Diane Shinberg, Coordinator, 724-357-4769, E-mail: shinberg@iup.edu.
Website: http://www.iup.edu/grad/sociology/default.aspx

Indiana University–Purdue University Indianapolis, School of Liberal Arts, Department of Sociology, Indianapolis, IN 46202. Offers general sociology (MA); medical sociology (MA).

Iowa State University of Science and Technology, Department of Sociology, Ames, IA 50011. Offers rural sociology (MS, PhD); sociology (MS, PhD). *Degree requirements:* For master's, thesis; for doctorate, thesis/dissertation. *Entrance requirements:* For master's and doctorate, GRE General Test. Additional exam requirements/recommendations for international students: Required—TOEFL (minimum score 550 paper-based; 79 iBT), IELTS (minimum score 6.5). Electronic applications accepted.

Jackson State University, Graduate School, College of Liberal Arts, Department of Criminal Justice and Sociology, Jackson, MS 39217. Offers criminology and justice services (MA); sociology (MA). *Program availability:* Part-time, evening/weekend. *Degree requirements:* For master's, comprehensive exam, thesis or alternative. *Entrance requirements:* For master's, GRE General Test. Additional exam requirements/recommendations for international students: Required—TOEFL (minimum score 520 paper-based; 67 iBT).

Johns Hopkins University, Zanvyl Krieger School of Arts and Sciences, Department of Sociology, Baltimore, MD 21218. Offers PhD. *Faculty:* 15 full-time (9 women), 2 part-time/adjunct (both women). *Students:* 3 full-time (1 woman). Average age 29. 138 applicants, 6% accepted, 3 enrolled. *Degree requirements:* For doctorate, thesis/dissertation. *Entrance requirements:* For doctorate, GRE General Test. Additional exam requirements/recommendations for international students: Required—TOEFL (minimum score 600 paper-based; 100 iBT), IELTS; Recommended—TWE. *Application deadline:* For fall admission, 12/31 for domestic and international students. Application fee: $75. Electronic applications accepted. *Financial support:* In 2017–18, 2 fellowships with full tuition reimbursements (averaging $23,000 per year), 5 research assistantships with full tuition reimbursements (averaging $23,000 per year), 11 teaching assistantships with full tuition reimbursements (averaging $23,000 per year) were awarded; institutionally sponsored loans, health care benefits, and tuition waivers (partial) also available. Financial award applicants required to submit CSS PROFILE or FAFSA. *Faculty research:* Education, immigration, race and gender, world systems, social policy. *Total annual research expenditures:* $599,554. *Unit head:* Dr. Andrew Cherlin, Chair, 410-516-2370, Fax: 410-516-7590, E-mail: cherlin@jhu.edu. *Application contact:* Linda Burkhardt, Academic Program Coordinator, 410-516-7627, Fax: 410-516-7590, E-mail: lindab@jhu.edu.
Website: http://www.soc.jhu.edu/

Kansas State University, Graduate School, College of Arts and Sciences, Department of Sociology, Anthropology and Social Work, Manhattan, KS 66506. Offers sociology (MA, PhD). *Program availability:* Part-time. *Degree requirements:* For master's, thesis or alternative; for doctorate, comprehensive exam, thesis/dissertation. *Entrance requirements:* For master's, GRE, minimum undergraduate GPA of 3.0; for doctorate, GRE, master's degree in sociology or related field. Additional exam requirements/recommendations for international students: Required—TOEFL (minimum score 550 paper-based; 79 iBT), IELTS (minimum score 6.5). Electronic applications accepted. *Faculty research:* Politics and development; criminology; community, agriculture, food, and environment; social inequalities.

Kent State University, College of Arts and Sciences, Department of Sociology, Kent, OH 44242-0001. Offers criminology and criminal justice (MA), including corrections, global security, policing, victimology; sociology (MA, PhD). PhD offered jointly with The University of Akron. *Program availability:* Part-time, 100% online. *Faculty:* 24 full-time (14 women), 4 part-time/adjunct (2 women). *Students:* 42 full-time (25 women), 51 part-time (36 women); includes 20 minority (15 Black or African American, non-Hispanic/Latino; 1 Asian, non-Hispanic/Latino; 3 Hispanic/Latino; 1 Two or more races, non-Hispanic/Latino). Average age 30. 39 applicants, 67% accepted, 19 enrolled. In 2017, 23 master's, 5 doctorates awarded. Terminal master's awarded for partial completion of doctoral program. *Degree requirements:* For master's, thesis, project, or internship; for doctorate, comprehensive exam, thesis/dissertation. *Entrance requirements:* For master's, minimum undergraduate GPA of 3.0, transcripts, goal statement, 3 letters of recommendation; for doctorate, GRE, minimum GPA of 3.0, transcripts, personal statement, 3 letters of recommendation. Additional exam requirements/recommendations for international students: Required—TOEFL (minimum score 587 paper-based, 94 iBT), Michigan English Language Assessment Battery (minimum score 82), IELTS (minimum score 7.0) or PTE (minimum score 65). *Application deadline:* For fall admission, 12/15 for domestic students, 12/1 for international students. Applications are processed on a rolling basis. Application fee: $45 ($70 for international students). Electronic applications accepted. *Expenses:* Tuition, state resident: full-time $11,310; part-time $515 per credit hour. Tuition, nonresident: full-time $20,396; part-time $928 per credit hour. *International tuition:* $18,544 full-time. *Financial support:* Research assistantships with full tuition reimbursements, teaching assistantships with full tuition reimbursements, scholarships/grants, and unspecified assistantships available. Financial award application deadline: 2/28. *Unit head:* Dr. Richard T. Serpe, Professor and Chair, 330-672-2562, E-mail: rserpe@kent.edu. *Application contact:* Dr. William Kalkhoff, Professor and Graduate Coordinator, 330-672-3712, E-mail: wkalkhof@kent.edu.
Website: http://www.kent.edu/sociology/

Lakehead University, Graduate Studies, Faculty of Social Sciences and Humanities, Department of Sociology, Thunder Bay, ON P7B 5E1, Canada. Offers gerontology (MA); health services and policy research (MA); sociology (MA); women's studies (MA). *Program availability:* Part-time, evening/weekend. *Degree requirements:* For master's, research project or thesis. *Entrance requirements:* For master's, minimum B average. Additional exam requirements/recommendations for international students: Required—TOEFL. *Faculty research:* Sociology of medicine, cultural and social change, health human resources, gerontology, women's studies.

Laurentian University, School of Graduate Studies and Research, Programme in Sociology, Sudbury, ON P3E 2C6, Canada. Offers applied social research (MA). *Program availability:* Part-time. *Entrance requirements:* For master's, honors degree in sociology or equivalent. *Faculty research:* Work foundations, managing AIDS organization, tracking laid-off mine workers.

Lehigh University, College of Arts and Sciences, Department of Sociology and Anthropology, Bethlehem, PA 18015. Offers sociology (MA). *Faculty:* 11 full-time (8 women). *Students:* 8 full-time (6 women), 1 (woman) part-time; includes 3 minority (1 Black or African American, non-Hispanic/Latino; 2 Hispanic/Latino), 2 international. Average age 27. 13 applicants, 69% accepted, 3 enrolled. In 2017, 3 master's awarded. *Degree requirements:* For master's, comprehensive exam, thesis optional. *Entrance requirements:* For master's, GRE General Test. Additional exam requirements/recommendations for international students: Required—TOEFL (minimum score 650 paper-based; 96 iBT). *Application deadline:* For fall admission, 1/15 for domestic and international students. Application fee: $75. Electronic applications accepted. *Expenses:* $1,460 per credit. *Financial support:* In 2017–18, 9 students received support, including 3 fellowships with full tuition reimbursements available, 6 teaching assistantships with full tuition reimbursements available; scholarships/grants also available. Financial award application deadline: 1/1. *Faculty research:* Urban sociology, medical sociology, policy studies, globalization. *Total annual research expenditures:* $11,525. *Unit head:* Dr. David Casagrande, Chair/Professor, 610-758-2672, Fax: 610-758-6552, E-mail: dac511@lehigh.edu. *Application contact:* Prof. Yuping Zhang, Graduate Program Director, 610-758-3820, Fax: 610-758-6552, E-mail: yuz307@lehigh.edu.
Website: http://cas.lehigh.edu/socanthro

Lincoln University, Graduate Studies, Jefferson City, MO 65101. Offers business administration (MBA), including accounting, management, management information systems, public administration/policy; elementary teaching (M Ed); environmental science (MS); guidance and counseling (M Ed), including community/agency counseling, elementary school, secondary school; higher education (MA); history (MA); integrated agricultural systems (MS); middle school (M Ed); natural sciences (MS); secondary teaching (M Ed); sociology (MA); sociology/criminal justice (MA). *Program availability:* Part-time, evening/weekend, 100% online, blended/hybrid learning. *Students:* 40 full-time (23 women), 64 part-time (32 women); includes 33 minority (30 Black or African American, non-Hispanic/Latino; 2 Hispanic/Latino; 1 Two or more races, non-Hispanic/Latino), 12 international. Average age 33. 48 applicants, 81% accepted, 22 enrolled. In 2017, 46 master's awarded. *Degree requirements:* For master's, comprehensive exam, thesis optional. *Entrance requirements:* For master's, GRE, MAT, or GMAT, minimum GPA of 2.75 overall, 3.0 in courses related to specialization; 3 letters of recommendation; minimum C average in English composition; personal statement of purpose. Additional exam requirements/recommendations for international students: Required—TOEFL (minimum score 500 paper-based; 61 iBT), IELTS (minimum score 5.5), Michigan English Language Assessment Battery (minimum score 80). *Application deadline:* For fall admission, 7/1 priority date for domestic students, 5/1 priority date for international students; for spring admission, 11/1 priority date for domestic students, 10/1 priority date for international students; for summer admission, 6/1 priority date for domestic students. Applications are processed on a rolling basis. Application fee: $30. Electronic applications accepted. *Expenses:* Tuition, state resident: part-time $291 per credit hour. Tuition, nonresident: part-time $541.50 per credit hour. *Financial support:* In 2017–18, 2 fellowships with tuition reimbursements, 3 research assistantships with tuition reimbursements were awarded; Federal Work-Study, scholarships/grants, and unspecified assistantships also available. Support available to part-time students. Financial award application deadline: 3/1; financial award applicants required to submit FAFSA. *Unit head:* Dr. Debra F. Greene, Interim Provost, 573-681-5247, Fax: 573-681-5106, E-mail: gradschool@lincolnu.edu. *Application contact:* Irasema Steck, Administrative Assistant, 573-681-5247, Fax: 573-681-5106, E-mail: gradschool@lincolnu.edu.
Website: http://www.lincolnu.edu/web/graduate-studies/graduate-studies

Louisiana State University and Agricultural & Mechanical College, Graduate School, College of Humanities and Social Sciences, Department of Sociology, Baton Rouge, LA 70803. Offers MA, PhD. *Faculty:* 19 full-time (7 women). *Students:* 44 full-time (19 women), 7 part-time (6 women); includes 20 minority (15 Black or African American, non-Hispanic/Latino; 1 Asian, non-Hispanic/Latino; 4 Hispanic/Latino), 10 international. Average age 32. 31 applicants, 45% accepted, 10 enrolled. In 2017, 7 master's, 5 doctorates awarded. *Financial support:* In 2017–18, 4 fellowships (averaging $31,861 per year), 8 research assistantships (averaging $23,695 per year), 30 teaching assistantships (averaging $20,020 per year) were awarded. *Total annual research expenditures:* $1.3 million.

Loyola University Chicago, Graduate School, Department of Sociology, Chicago, IL 60611. Offers sociology (MA, PhD). *Program availability:* Part-time, evening/weekend. *Faculty:* 17 full-time (10 women). *Students:* 35 full-time (19 women), 9 part-time (8 women); includes 15 minority (3 Black or African American, non-Hispanic/Latino; 5 Asian, non-Hispanic/Latino; 5 Hispanic/Latino; 2 Two or more races, non-Hispanic/Latino), 5 international. Average age 30. 41 applicants, 59% accepted, 12 enrolled. In 2017, 10 master's, 3 doctorates awarded. Terminal master's awarded for partial completion of doctoral program. *Degree requirements:* For master's, thesis or alternative; for doctorate, comprehensive exam, thesis/dissertation. *Entrance requirements:* For master's, GRE General Test (recommended); for doctorate, GRE General Test. Additional exam requirements/recommendations for international students: Required—TOEFL (minimum score 550 paper-based; 79 iBT), IELTS (minimum score 6.5). *Application deadline:* For fall admission, 1/5 for domestic and international students; for winter admission, 1/5 for domestic students, 1/4 for

international students. Electronic applications accepted. *Expenses:* $1,033 per credit hour tuition, $432 pere semester mandatory fees. *Financial support:* In 2017–18, 14 students received support, including 4 fellowships with full tuition reimbursements available (averaging $18,000 per year), 6 research assistantships with full tuition reimbursements available (averaging $18,000 per year), 4 teaching assistantships with full tuition reimbursements available (averaging $18,000 per year); Federal Work-Study, health care benefits, and tuition waivers (full and partial) also available. Financial award application deadline: 1/5; financial award applicants required to submit FAFSA. *Faculty research:* Medical, religion, urban, knowledge, culture. *Total annual research expenditures:* $160,000. *Unit head:* Dr. Marilyn Krogh, Chair, 773-508-3471, Fax: 773-508-7099, E-mail: mkrogh@luc.edu. *Application contact:* Dr. Marilyn Krogh, Graduate Program Director, 773-508-3445, Fax: 773-508-7099, E-mail: mkrogh@luc.edu.

Marshall University, Academic Affairs Division, College of Liberal Arts, Department of Sociology and Anthropology, Huntington, WV 25755. Offers sociology (MA). *Students:* 6 full-time (2 women), 5 part-time (3 women); includes 1 minority (Black or African American, non-Hispanic/Latino). Average age 30. In 2017, 2 master's awarded. *Degree requirements:* For master's, thesis optional. *Entrance requirements:* For master's, GRE. Application fee: $40. *Unit head:* Dr. Marty Loebach, Chair, 304-696-6700, E-mail: sociology@marshall.edu. *Application contact:* Information Contact, Graduate Admissions, 304-746-1900, Fax: 304-746-1902, E-mail: services@marshall.edu.

McGill University, Faculty of Graduate and Postdoctoral Studies, Faculty of Arts, Department of Sociology, Montréal, QC H3A 2T5, Canada. Offers medical sociology (MA); neo-tropical environment (MA); social statistics (MA); sociology (MA, PhD, Diploma).

McGill University, Faculty of Graduate and Postdoctoral Studies, Faculty of Medicine, Department of Social Studies in Medicine, Montréal, QC H3A 2T5, Canada. Offers medical anthropology (MA, PhD); medical history (MA, PhD); medical sociology (MA, PhD).

McMaster University, School of Graduate Studies, Faculty of Social Sciences, Department of Sociology, Hamilton, ON L8S 4M2, Canada. Offers MA, PhD. *Program availability:* Part-time. *Degree requirements:* For master's, thesis; for doctorate, comprehensive exam, thesis/dissertation. *Entrance requirements:* For master's and doctorate, minimum B+ average. Additional exam requirements/recommendations for international students: Required—TOEFL (minimum score 580 paper-based). *Faculty research:* Socialization and conversion, ethnic relations, international migration, racism, social implications of the Internet.

Memorial University of Newfoundland, School of Graduate Studies, Department of Sociology, St. John's, NL A1C 5S7, Canada. Offers gender (PhD); maritime sociology (PhD); sociology (M Phil, MA); work and development (PhD). *Program availability:* Part-time. *Degree requirements:* For master's, comprehensive exam, thesis optional, program journal (M Phil); for doctorate, one foreign language, comprehensive exam, thesis/dissertation, oral defense of thesis. *Entrance requirements:* For master's, 2nd class degree from university of recognized standing in area of study; for doctorate, MA, M Phil, or equivalent. Electronic applications accepted. *Faculty research:* Work and development, gender, maritime sociology.

Michigan State University, The Graduate School, College of Social Science, Department of Sociology, East Lansing, MI 48824. Offers MA, PhD. *Program availability:* Part-time. *Entrance requirements:* Additional exam requirements/recommendations for international students: Required—TOEFL (minimum score 550 paper-based), Michigan State University ELT (minimum score 85), Michigan English Language Assessment Battery (minimum score 83). Electronic applications accepted.

Middle Tennessee State University, College of Graduate Studies, College of Liberal Arts, Department of Sociology and Anthropology, Murfreesboro, TN 37132. Offers sociology (MA). *Program availability:* Part-time, evening/weekend, online learning. *Degree requirements:* For master's, comprehensive exam, thesis. *Entrance requirements:* For master's, GRE. Additional exam requirements/recommendations for international students: Required—TOEFL (minimum score 525 paper-based; 71 iBT) or IELTS (minimum score 6). Electronic applications accepted. *Faculty research:* Women's and gender studies, crime and deviance, aging studies, social organizations.

Minnesota State University Mankato, College of Graduate Studies and Research, College of Social and Behavioral Sciences, Department of Sociology and Corrections, Mankato, MN 56001. Offers sociology (MA); sociology: college teaching (MA); sociology: corrections (MS); sociology: human services planning and administration (MS). *Program availability:* Part-time. *Degree requirements:* For master's, comprehensive exam, thesis or alternative. *Entrance requirements:* For master's, minimum GPA of 3.0 during previous 2 years, 3 letters of reference, resume. Additional exam requirements/recommendations for international students: Required—TOEFL. Electronic applications accepted.

Mississippi State University, College of Arts and Sciences, Department of Sociology, Mississippi State, MS 39762. Offers MS, PhD. *Program availability:* Part-time. *Faculty:* 19 full-time (14 women). *Students:* 22 full-time (16 women), 12 part-time (9 women); includes 8 minority (5 Black or African American, non-Hispanic/Latino; 1 Asian, non-Hispanic/Latino; 1 Hispanic/Latino; 1 Two or more races, non-Hispanic/Latino), 2 international. Average age 29. 26 applicants, 50% accepted, 7 enrolled. In 2017, 2 master's, 2 doctorates awarded. *Degree requirements:* For master's, thesis optional, comprehensive oral or written exam; for doctorate, thesis/dissertation, comprehensive oral and written exam. *Entrance requirements:* For master's, minimum GPA of 3.0 on last two years of undergraduate courses or GRE; academic writing sample in English (student's choice); for doctorate, GRE, academic writing sample in English (student's choice). Additional exam requirements/recommendations for international students: Required—TOEFL (minimum score 477 paper-based; 53 iBT); Recommended—IELTS (minimum score 4.5). *Application deadline:* For fall admission, 4/15 priority date for domestic students, 5/1 for international students; for spring admission, 10/15 priority date for domestic students, 9/1 for international students. Applications are processed on a rolling basis. Application fee: $60 ($80 for international students). Electronic applications accepted. *Expenses:* Tuition, state resident: full-time $8318; part-time $462.12 per credit hour. Tuition, nonresident: full-time $22,358; part-time $1242.12 per credit hour. *Required fees:* $110; $12.24 per credit hour. $6.12 per semester. *Financial support:* In 2017–18, 2 research assistantships with full tuition reimbursements (averaging $16,272 per year), 11 teaching assistantships with partial tuition reimbursements (averaging $13,321 per year) were awarded; Federal Work-Study, institutionally sponsored loans, scholarships/grants, and unspecified assistantships also available. Financial award application deadline: 2/15; financial award applicants required to submit FAFSA. *Faculty research:* Community and regional development, criminology, natural resource development, family sociology, gender. *Total annual research expenditures:* $11.5 million. *Unit head:* Dr. Leslie Hossfeld, Professor and Head, 662-325-7880, Fax: 662-325-4564, E-mail: lh401@msstate.edu. *Application contact:* Lakan Drinker, Admissions and Enrollment Assistant, 662-325-8951, E-mail: ldrinker@grad.msstate.edu.
Website: http://www.sociology.msstate.edu/

Morehead State University, Graduate Programs, Caudill College of Arts, Humanities and Social Sciences, Department of Sociology, Social Work and Criminology, Morehead, KY 40351. Offers criminology (MA); general sociology (MA); gerontology

(MA); sociology regional analysis (MA); sociology/chemical dependency (MA). *Program availability:* Part-time, evening/weekend. *Degree requirements:* For master's, comprehensive exam, thesis (for some programs). *Entrance requirements:* For master's, GRE General Test, minimum GPA of 3.0 in sociology, 2.75 overall; 18 hours of course work in sociology, writing sample. Additional exam requirements/recommendations for international students: Required—TOEFL (minimum score 500 paper-based). Electronic applications accepted. *Faculty research:* Death and dying; aging, drinking, and drugs; economic development; adult children of alcoholics.

Morgan State University, School of Graduate Studies, College of Liberal Arts, Department of Sociology and Anthropology, Baltimore, MD 21251. Offers sociology (MA, MS). *Program availability:* Part-time, evening/weekend. *Entrance requirements:* Additional exam requirements/recommendations for international students: Required—TOEFL (minimum score 550 paper-based). *Application deadline:* For fall admission, 2/1 priority date for domestic students; for spring admission, 10/1 priority date for domestic students. Applications are processed on a rolling basis. Application fee: $0. *Expenses:* Tuition, state resident: part-time $433 per credit. Tuition, nonresident: part-time $851 per credit. *Required fees:* $81.50 per credit. *Financial support:* Application deadline: 2/1. *Faculty research:* Domestic violence, homelessness, social movements, marriage and family. *Unit head:* Dr. Stella Hargett, Interim Chairperson, 443-885-3518, Fax: 443-885-8242, E-mail: stella.hargett@morgan.edu. *Application contact:* Dr. Dean Campbell, Graduate Recruitment Specialist, 443-885-3185, Fax: 443-885-8226, E-mail: dean.campbell@morgan.edu.

Murray State University, College of Humanities and Fine Arts, Department of Political Science and Sociology, Murray, KY 42071. Offers MPA. *Program availability:* Part-time, evening/weekend. *Faculty:* 4 full-time (1 woman). *Students:* 28 full-time (18 women), 29 part-time (20 women); includes 18 minority (15 Black or African American, non-Hispanic/Latino; 1 Asian, non-Hispanic/Latino; 1 Hispanic/Latino; 1 Two or more races, non-Hispanic/Latino), 12 international. Average age 33. 102 applicants, 82% accepted, 25 enrolled. In 2017, 9 master's awarded. *Entrance requirements:* For master's, GRE or GMAT, minimum university GPA of 2.75. Additional exam requirements/recommendations for international students: Required—TOEFL (minimum score 527 paper-based; 71 iBT). *Application deadline:* Applications are processed on a rolling basis. Application fee: $40 ($50 for international students). Electronic applications accepted. *Expenses:* Tuition, state resident: full-time $9504. Tuition, nonresident: full-time $26,811. *International tuition:* $14,400 full-time. Tuition and fees vary according to course load, degree level and reciprocity agreements. *Financial support:* Federal Work-Study and unspecified assistantships available. Financial award applicants required to submit FAFSA. *Unit head:* Dr. Choong-Nam Kang, Chair, Department of Political Science and Sociology, 270-809-4213, Fax: 270-809-2688, E-mail: ckang1@murraystate.edu. *Application contact:* Kaitlyn Burzynski, Interim Assistant Director for Graduate Admission and Records, 270-809-5732, Fax: 270-809-3780, E-mail: msu.graduateadmissions@murraystate.edu.
Website: http://www.murraystate.edu/academics/CollegesDepartments/CollegeOfHumanitiesAndFineArts/politicalScienceandSociology/Programs/MastersPublicAdministrat

New Mexico Highlands University, Graduate Studies, College of Arts and Sciences, Department of Social and Behavioral Sciences, Las Vegas, NM 87701. Offers psychology (MS), including clinical psychology/counseling, general psychology; public affairs (MA), including applied sociology; Southwest studies (MA), including anthropology. *Program availability:* Part-time. *Degree requirements:* For master's, comprehensive exam, thesis or alternative. *Entrance requirements:* For master's, minimum undergraduate GPA of 3.0. Additional exam requirements/recommendations for international students: Required—TOEFL (minimum score 540 paper-based). *Faculty research:* Southwest Native American resettlement development, community-level interventions, neurochemistry of personality, comparative criminal justice, social theory and activism.

New Mexico State University, College of Arts and Sciences, Department of Sociology, Las Cruces, NM 88003. Offers MA. *Program availability:* Part-time, 100% online. *Faculty:* 9 full-time (6 women). *Students:* 10 full-time (6 women), 43 part-time (27 women); includes 14 minority (7 Black or African American, non-Hispanic/Latino; 2 Asian, non-Hispanic/Latino; 4 Hispanic/Latino; 1 Two or more races, non-Hispanic/Latino), 1 international. Average age 37. 44 applicants, 73% accepted, 21 enrolled. In 2017, 13 master's awarded. *Degree requirements:* For master's, comprehensive exam (for some programs), thesis (for some programs). *Entrance requirements:* Additional exam requirements/recommendations for international students: Required—TOEFL (minimum score 550 paper-based; 79 iBT), IELTS (minimum score 6.5). *Application deadline:* For fall admission, 3/15 for domestic and international students. Application fee: $40 ($50 for international students). Electronic applications accepted. *Expenses:* Tuition, state resident: full-time $4390. Tuition, nonresident: full-time $15,309. *Required fees:* $853. *Financial support:* In 2017–18, 12 students received support, including 5 teaching assistantships (averaging $8,482 per year); career-related internships or fieldwork, Federal Work-Study, scholarships/grants, traineeships, health care benefits, and unspecified assistantships also available. Support available to part-time students. Financial award application deadline: 3/1. *Faculty research:* Environmental sociology, borderland issues, gender; race and ethnicity; inequality; and popular culture. *Total annual research expenditures:* $426. *Unit head:* Dr. David G. LoConto, Department Head, 575-646-3448, Fax: 575-646-7601, E-mail: dloconto@nmsu.edu. *Application contact:* Dr. Sandra M. Way, Director of Graduate Studies, 575-646-3448, Fax: 575-646-7601, E-mail: sway@nmsu.edu.
Website: http://sociology.nmsu.edu/

The New School, The New School for Social Research, Department of Historical Studies, New York, NY 10011. Offers historical studies (MA); politics (PhD), including historical studies; sociology (PhD), including historical studies. *Program availability:* Part-time, evening/weekend. *Faculty:* 1 (woman) full-time. *Students:* 8 full-time (3 women), 3 part-time (2 women); includes 2 minority (1 Asian, non-Hispanic/Latino; 1 Hispanic/Latino), 1 international. Average age 28. 19 applicants, 95% accepted, 6 enrolled. In 2017, 3 master's awarded. *Degree requirements:* For master's, thesis. *Entrance requirements:* For master's, GRE, two letters of recommendation, writing sample, essays, transcripts. Additional exam requirements/recommendations for international students: Required—TOEFL (minimum score 100 iBT), IELTS (minimum score 7), PTE (minimum score 68). *Application deadline:* For fall admission, 1/15 priority date for domestic and international students; for spring admission, 10/15 priority date for domestic and international students. Applications are processed on a rolling basis. Application fee: $50. Electronic applications accepted. *Expenses:* $2,180 per credit. *Financial support:* In 2017–18, 8 students received support, including 5 teaching assistantships (averaging $5,520 per year); Federal Work-Study, scholarships/grants, health care benefits, and tuition waivers (full and partial) also available. Support available to part-time students. Financial award application deadline: 2/1; financial award applicants required to submit FAFSA. *Unit head:* Dr. William Milberg, Dean, The New School for Social Research, 212-229-5777, E-mail: milbergw@newschool.edu. *Application contact:* Dana Messinger, Director of Graduate Admission, 212-229-5150 Ext. 2300, E-mail: messingd@newschool.edu.
Website: http://www.newschool.edu/nssr/historical-studies/

Sociology

The New School, The New School for Social Research, Department of Sociology, New York, NY 10003. Offers historical studies (PhD); sociology (M Phil, MA). *Program availability:* Part-time. *Faculty:* 11 full-time (6 women), 2 part-time/adjunct (0 women). *Students:* 91 full-time (36 women), 5 part-time (4 women); includes 12 minority (7 Hispanic/Latino; 5 Two or more races, non-Hispanic/Latino), 55 international. Average age 33. 100 applicants, 76% accepted, 21 enrolled. In 2017, 23 master's, 8 doctorates awarded. Terminal master's awarded for partial completion of doctoral program. *Degree requirements:* For master's, comprehensive exam; for doctorate, one foreign language, thesis/dissertation. *Entrance requirements:* For master's and doctorate, GRE, letters of recommendation, writing sample, essays, transcripts. Additional exam requirements/recommendations for international students: Required—TOEFL (minimum score 92 iBT), IELTS (minimum score 7), PTE (minimum score 68). *Application deadline:* For fall admission, 5/5 priority date for domestic students, 6/15 priority date for international students; for spring admission, 10/15 priority date for domestic and international students. Applications are processed on a rolling basis. Application fee: $50. Electronic applications accepted. *Expenses:* $2,180 per credit. *Financial support:* In 2017–18, 62 students received support, including 15 fellowships (averaging $18,567 per year), 14 teaching assistantships (averaging $10,057 per year); Federal Work-Study, scholarships/grants, and tuition waivers (full and partial) also available. Support available to part-time students. Financial award application deadline: 2/1; financial award applicants required to submit FAFSA. *Unit head:* Eiko Ikegami, Program Chair, 212-229-5376 Ext. 4925, E-mail: ikegame1@newschool.edu. *Application contact:* Dana Messinger, Director of Graduate Admission, 212-229-5150 Ext. 2300, E-mail: socialresearchadmit@newschool.edu.
Website: https://www.newschool.edu/nssr/sociology/

New York University, Graduate School of Arts and Science, Department of Sociology, New York, NY 10012-1019. Offers French studies and sociology (PhD); sociology (MA, PhD); JD/MA. *Program availability:* Part-time. *Students:* Average age 31. 408 applicants, 15% accepted, 22 enrolled. In 2017, 26 master's, 9 doctorates awarded. Terminal master's awarded for partial completion of doctoral program. *Degree requirements:* For master's, thesis or alternative; for doctorate, comprehensive exam, thesis/dissertation. *Entrance requirements:* For master's and doctorate, GRE General Test. Additional exam requirements/recommendations for international students: Required—TOEFL. *Application deadline:* For fall admission, 1/4 priority date for domestic students, 1/4 for international students. Application fee: $100. *Expenses:* Tuition: Full-time $41,352; part-time $19,968 per year. *Required fees:* $2496; $1628 per unit. $814 per term. Tuition and fees vary according to course load and program. *Financial support:* Fellowships, research assistantships, teaching assistantships, Federal Work-Study, institutionally sponsored loans, scholarships/grants, health care benefits, and unspecified assistantships available. Financial award application deadline: 1/4; financial award applicants required to submit FAFSA. *Faculty research:* Political sociology and social movements; gender and inequality; deviance, law, and crime; education; stratification and theory. *Unit head:* Guillermina Jasso, Chair, 212-998-8340, Fax: 212-995-4140, E-mail: gsas.sociology.info@nyu.edu. *Application contact:* Paula England, Director of Graduate Studies, 212-998-8340, Fax: 212-995-4140, E-mail: gsas.sociology.info@nyu.edu.
Website: http://www.nyu.edu/gsas/dept/socio/

New York University, Steinhardt School of Culture, Education, and Human Development, Department of Humanities and Social Sciences in the Professions, Program in Sociology of Education, New York, NY 10012. Offers education policy (MA); social and cultural studies of education (MA); sociology of education (PhD). *Program availability:* Part-time. *Students:* Average age 26. 96 applicants, 45% accepted, 8 enrolled. In 2017, 24 master's, 2 doctorates awarded. *Entrance requirements:* For master's, letters of recommendation; for doctorate, GRE General Test, interview. Additional exam requirements/recommendations for international students: Required—TOEFL (minimum score 100 iBT). *Application deadline:* For fall admission, 12/1 priority date for domestic and international students; for spring admission, 10/1 for domestic and international students. Applications are processed on a rolling basis. Application fee: $75. Electronic applications accepted. *Expenses:* Tuition: Full-time $41,352; part-time $19,968 per year. *Required fees:* $2496; $1628 per unit. $814 per term. Tuition and fees vary according to course load and program. *Financial support:* Fellowships with full and partial tuition reimbursements, Federal Work-Study, institutionally sponsored loans, scholarships/grants, and tuition waivers (partial) available. Support available to part-time students. Financial award application deadline: 2/1; financial award applicants required to submit FAFSA. *Faculty research:* Legal and institutional environments of schools; social inequality; high school reform and achievement; urban schooling, economics and education, educational policy. *Unit head:* Prof. Lisa Stulberg, Program Director, 212-992-9373, Fax: 212-995-4832, E-mail: lisa.stulberg@nyu.edu. *Application contact:* 212-998-5030, Fax: 212-995-4328, E-mail: steinhardt.gradadmissions@nyu.edu.
Website: http://steinhardt.nyu.edu/humsocsci/sociology

North Carolina State University, Graduate School, College of Humanities and Social Sciences, Department of Sociology and Anthropology, Program in Sociology, Raleigh, NC 27695. Offers M Soc, MS, PhD. *Program availability:* Part-time. *Degree requirements:* For master's, practicum (M Soc), thesis (MS); for doctorate, comprehensive exam, thesis/dissertation. *Entrance requirements:* For master's and doctorate, GRE General Test, sample of written work. Electronic applications accepted. *Faculty research:* Inequity: gender, race and class; crime and social control; work and organizations; rural sociology; family and intimate relations.

North Dakota State University, College of Graduate and Interdisciplinary Studies, College of Arts, Humanities and Social Sciences, Department of Sociology and Anthropology, Fargo, ND 58102. Offers anthropology (MA, MS); community development (MA, MS); social science (MA, MS); sociology (MS). *Program availability:* Part-time. *Degree requirements:* For master's, thesis. *Entrance requirements:* For master's, GRE (for emergency management), course work in sociology, minimum GPA of 3.2. Additional exam requirements/recommendations for international students: Required—TOEFL. Electronic applications accepted. *Faculty research:* Medical sociology, demography, ethnology, archaeology.

Northeastern University, College of Social Sciences and Humanities, Boston, MA 02115. Offers criminology and criminal justice (MSCJ); criminology and justice policy (PhD); economics (MA, PhD); English (MA, PhD); international affairs (MA); law and public policy (PhD); political science (MA, PhD); public administration (MPA); public policy (MPP); security and resilience studies (MS); sociology (MA, PhD); urban and regional policy (MS); urban informatics (MS); world history (MA, PhD). *Program availability:* Online learning. *Faculty:* 242. *Students:* 491. In 2017, 143 master's, 38 doctorates awarded. *Degree requirements:* For doctorate, variable foreign language requirement, comprehensive exam, thesis/dissertation. *Entrance requirements:* For master's and doctorate, GRE. Additional exam requirements/recommendations for international students: Required—TOEFL, IELTS. Application fee: $75. Electronic applications accepted. *Expenses:* Contact institution. *Financial support:* Teaching assistantships, career-related internships or fieldwork, scholarships/grants, health care benefits, tuition waivers (full and partial), and unspecified assistantships available. Support available to part-time students. Financial award applicants required to submit FAFSA. *Unit head:* Dr. Uta Poiger, Dean, 617-373-5173, E-mail: college_of_social_sciences_and_humanities@neu.edu. *Application contact:* 617-373-5990, E-mail: gradcssh@northeastern.edu.
Website: http://www.northeastern.edu/cssh/

Northern Arizona University, College of Social and Behavioral Sciences, Department of Sociology and Social Work, Flagstaff, AZ 86011. Offers applied sociology (MA). *Program availability:* Part-time, 100% online, blended/hybrid learning. *Faculty:* 29 full-time (18 women), 1 (woman) part-time/adjunct. *Students:* 12 full-time (6 women), 2 part-time (1 woman); includes 3 minority (1 Black or African American, non-Hispanic/Latino; 2 Two or more races, non-Hispanic/Latino), 1 international. Average age 26. 18 applicants, 89% accepted, 14 enrolled. In 2017, 10 master's awarded. *Degree requirements:* For master's, variable foreign language requirement, comprehensive exam (for some programs), thesis (for some programs). *Entrance requirements:* For master's, minimum undergraduate GPA of 3.0, minimum of 250 volunteer and/or relevant paid human service work experience. Additional exam requirements/recommendations for international students: Required—TOEFL (minimum score 80 iBT), IELTS (minimum score 6.5). *Application deadline:* For fall admission, 2/1 for domestic and international students; for spring admission, 10/1 for domestic and international students. Applications are processed on a rolling basis. Application fee: $65. Electronic applications accepted. *Expenses:* Tuition, state resident: full-time $9240; part-time $458 per credit hour. Tuition, nonresident: full-time $21,588; part-time $1199 per credit hour. *Required fees:* $1021; $14 per credit hour. $646 per semester. Tuition and fees vary according to course load, campus/location and program. *Financial support:* In 2017–18, 11 students received support, including 11 teaching assistantships with partial tuition reimbursements available (averaging $9,000 per year); institutionally sponsored loans, health care benefits, tuition waivers (partial), and unspecified assistantships also available. Financial award application deadline: 2/1; financial award applicants required to submit FAFSA. *Faculty research:* Demography, death and dying, criminology, social policy, divorce. *Unit head:* Dr. Kathleen Ferraro, Chair, 928-523-9412, Fax: 928-523-6777, E-mail: kathleen.ferraro@nau.edu. *Application contact:* Caleb Buum, Administrative Assistant, 928-523-6562, Fax: 928-523-6777, E-mail: ssw@nau.edu.
Website: http://nau.edu/sbs/ssw/

Northern Illinois University, Graduate School, College of Liberal Arts and Sciences, Department of Sociology, De Kalb, IL 60115-2854. Offers MA. *Program availability:* Part-time. *Faculty:* 14 full-time (3 women). *Students:* 8 full-time (4 women), 7 part-time (4 women); includes 3 minority (all Hispanic/Latino). Average age 28. 10 applicants, 90% accepted, 4 enrolled. In 2017, 7 master's awarded. *Degree requirements:* For master's, comprehensive exam, thesis optional. *Entrance requirements:* For master's, GRE General Test, minimum GPA of 2.75; course work in social theory, social methods, and statistics. Additional exam requirements/recommendations for international students: Required—TOEFL (minimum score 550 paper-based). *Application deadline:* For fall admission, 6/1 for domestic students, 5/1 for international students; for spring admission, 11/1 for domestic students, 10/1 for international students. Applications are processed on a rolling basis. Application fee: $40. Electronic applications accepted. *Financial support:* In 2017–18, 18 teaching assistantships with full tuition reimbursements were awarded; fellowships with full tuition reimbursements, research assistantships with full tuition reimbursements, career-related internships or fieldwork, Federal Work-Study, scholarships/grants, tuition waivers (full), and unspecified assistantships also available. Support available to part-time students. Financial award applicants required to submit FAFSA. *Faculty research:* Welfare reform, interpersonal disputes, multicultural education, race and ethnicism, social control. *Unit head:* Dr. Mike Ezell, Acting Chair, 815-753-1194, Fax: 815-753-6302, E-mail: mezell@niu.edu. *Application contact:* Dr. Keri B. Burchfield, Director, Graduate Studies, 815-753-0302, E-mail: kburchfield@niu.edu.
Website: http://www.sociology.niu.edu/

Northwestern University, The Graduate School, Judd A. and Marjorie Weinberg College of Arts and Sciences, Department of Sociology, Evanston, IL 60208. Offers PhD, JD/PhD. Admissions and degrees offered through The Graduate School. *Degree requirements:* For doctorate, thesis/dissertation. *Entrance requirements:* For doctorate, GRE General Test. Additional exam requirements/recommendations for international students: Required—TOEFL. Electronic applications accepted. *Faculty research:* Sociology of culture, social organizations, social inequality, comparative/historical sociology, economic sociology.

Northwestern University, The Graduate School, Kellogg School of Management, Management Programs, Evanston, IL 60208. Offers accounting information and management (MBA, PhD); analytical finance (MBA); business administration (MBA); decision sciences (MBA); entrepreneurship and innovation (MBA); finance (MBA, PhD); health enterprise management (MBA); human resources management (MBA); international business (MBA); management and organizations (MBA, PhD); management and organizations and sociology (PhD); management and strategy (MBA); management studies (MS); managerial analytics (MBA); managerial economics (MBA); managerial economics and strategy (PhD); marketing (MBA, PhD); marketing management (MBA); media management (MBA); operations management (MBA, PhD); real estate (MBA); social enterprise at Kellogg (MBA); JD/MBA. *Program availability:* Part-time, evening/weekend. Terminal master's awarded for partial completion of doctoral program. *Degree requirements:* For doctorate, thesis/dissertation, 2 years of coursework, qualifying (field) exam and candidacy, summer research papers and presentations to faculty, proposal defense, final exam/defense. *Entrance requirements:* For master's, GMAT, GRE, interview, 2 letters of recommendation, college transcripts, resume, essays, Kellogg honor code; for doctorate, GMAT, GRE, statement of purpose, transcripts, 2 letters of recommendation, resume, interview. Additional exam requirements/recommendations for international students: Required—TOEFL, IELTS. Electronic applications accepted. *Expenses:* Contact institution. *Faculty research:* Business cycles and international finance, health policy, networks, non-market strategy, consumer psychology.

The Ohio State University, Graduate School, College of Arts and Sciences, Division of Social and Behavioral Sciences, Department of Sociology, Columbus, OH 43210. Offers PhD. *Faculty:* 29. *Students:* 61 full-time (36 women); includes 8 minority (all Hispanic/Latino), 10 international. Average age 28. In 2017, 7 doctorates awarded. *Entrance requirements:* For doctorate, GRE General Test. Additional exam requirements/recommendations for international students: Required—TOEFL (minimum score 600 paper-based; 100 iBT); Recommended—IELTS (minimum score 7). *Application deadline:* For fall admission, 12/1 for domestic students, 11/30 for international students. Applications are processed on a rolling basis. Application fee: $60 ($70 for international students). Electronic applications accepted. *Financial support:* Fellowships, research assistantships, teaching assistantships, Federal Work-Study, and institutionally sponsored loans available. Support available to part-time students. *Unit head:* Dr. Claudia Buchmann, Professor and Chair, 614-292-5452, E-mail: buchmann.4@osu.edu. *Application contact:* Graduate and Professional Admissions, 614-292-9444, Fax: 614-292-3895, E-mail: gpadmissions@osu.edu.
Website: http://sociology.osu.edu/

Ohio University, Graduate College, College of Arts and Sciences, Department of Sociology and Anthropology, Athens, OH 45701-2979. Offers sociology (MA). *Program*

availability: Part-time. *Degree requirements:* For master's, thesis or alternative. *Entrance requirements:* For master's, minimum GPA of 3.0; minimum of 20 hours in sociology including statistics, theory, and research methods. Additional exam requirements/recommendations for international students: Required—TOEFL (minimum score 550 paper-based; 80 iBT) or IELTS (minimum score 6.5). Electronic applications accepted. *Faculty research:* Criminology/deviance, gender studies, inequality, social psychology and rural poverty.

Oklahoma City University, Petree College of Arts and Sciences, Oklahoma City, OK 73106-1402. Offers applied behavioral studies (M Ed); applied sociology: nonprofit leadership (MA); creative writing (MFA); criminology (MS); early childhood education (M Ed); elementary education (M Ed); general studies (MLA); leadership/management (MLA); moving image arts (MFA); professional counseling (M Ed); teaching (MA); teaching English to speakers of other languages (MA). *Program availability:* Part-time, evening/weekend. *Faculty:* 6 full-time (2 women), 16 part-time/adjunct (10 women). *Students:* 84 full-time (61 women), 32 part-time (23 women); includes 31 minority (13 Black or African American, non-Hispanic/Latino; 3 American Indian or Alaska Native, non-Hispanic/Latino; 1 Asian, non-Hispanic/Latino; 9 Hispanic/Latino; 5 Two or more races, non-Hispanic/Latino), 30 international. Average age 34. 192 applicants, 67% accepted, 57 enrolled. In 2017, 65 master's awarded. *Degree requirements:* For master's, capstone/practicum. *Entrance requirements:* For master's, bachelor's degree from accredited institution with minimum GPA of 3.0, essay, recommendation letters. Additional exam requirements/recommendations for international students: Required—TOEFL (minimum score 550 paper-based; 80 iBT). *Application deadline:* Applications are processed on a rolling basis. Application fee: $50. Electronic applications accepted. *Expenses:* $8,580. *Financial support:* In 2017–18, 19 students received support. Federal Work-Study, institutionally sponsored loans, scholarships/grants, and tuition waivers (full and partial) available. Support available to part-time students. Financial award application deadline: 6/1; financial award applicants required to submit FAFSA. *Unit head:* Dr. Amy Cataldi, Dean, 405-208-5446, Fax: 405-208-5447, E-mail: acataldi@okcu.edu. *Application contact:* Michael Harrington, Director of Graduate Admissions, 800-633-7242, Fax: 405-208-5356, E-mail: gadmissions@okcu.edu.
Website: https://www.okcu.edu/artsci/home

Oklahoma State University, College of Arts and Sciences, Department of Sociology, Stillwater, OK 74078. Offers MS, PhD. *Faculty:* 15 full-time (6 women), 2 part-time/adjunct (both women). *Students:* 9 full-time (5 women), 14 part-time (8 women); includes 1 minority (Hispanic/Latino), 5 international. Average age 29. 19 applicants, 58% accepted, 7 enrolled. In 2017, 6 master's awarded. *Entrance requirements:* For master's and doctorate, GRE General Test. Additional exam requirements/recommendations for international students: Required—TOEFL (minimum score 550 paper-based; 79 iBT). *Application deadline:* For fall admission, 3/1 priority date for international students; for spring admission, 8/1 priority date for international students. Applications are processed on a rolling basis. Application fee: $40 ($75 for international students). Electronic applications accepted. *Expenses:* Tuition, state resident: full-time $4019; part-time $2679.60 per year. Tuition, nonresident: full-time $15,286; part-time $10,190.40 per year. *Required fees:* $2129; $1419 per unit. Tuition and fees vary according to program. *Financial support:* Research assistantships, teaching assistantships, career-related internships or fieldwork, Federal Work-Study, scholarships/grants, health care benefits, tuition waivers (partial), and unspecified assistantships available. Support available to part-time students. Financial award application deadline: 3/1; financial award applicants required to submit FAFSA. *Faculty research:* Criminology/correction/legal issues; race, ethnicity, and gender in American society; environmental conflict and population problems; international comparative research; social change and social movement in American culture. *Unit head:* Dr. Sharon Bird, Department Head, 405-744-6104, Fax: 405-744-5780, E-mail: sharon.bird@okstate.edu.
Website: http://sociology.okstate.edu

Old Dominion University, College of Arts and Letters, Program in Applied Sociology, Norfolk, VA 23529. Offers criminal justice (MA); general sociology (MA); women's studies (MA). *Program availability:* Part-time, evening/weekend. *Faculty:* 19 full-time (11 women). *Students:* 18 full-time (13 women), 2 part-time (1 woman); includes 10 minority (4 Black or African American, non-Hispanic/Latino; 1 Hispanic/Latino; 5 Two or more races, non-Hispanic/Latino). Average age 26. 26 applicants, 65% accepted, 12 enrolled. In 2017, 3 master's awarded. *Degree requirements:* For master's, thesis. *Entrance requirements:* For master's, GRE General Test, minimum GPA of 3.0; 12 credits in criminal justice, sociology, or women's studies. Additional exam requirements/recommendations for international students: Required—TOEFL. *Application deadline:* For fall admission, 3/1 for domestic and international students. Application fee: $50. Electronic applications accepted. *Expenses:* Contact institution. *Financial support:* In 2017–18, 8 students received support, including 2 research assistantships (averaging $10,000 per year), 6 teaching assistantships (averaging $10,000 per year); career-related internships or fieldwork, scholarships/grants, and unspecified assistantships also available. Financial award application deadline: 2/15. *Faculty research:* Quantitative methodology, theory, family, gender/class/race, crime. *Total annual research expenditures:* $350,000. *Unit head:* Dr. Ingrid Whitaker, Graduate Program Director, 757-683-3811, Fax: 757-683-5634, E-mail: iwhitake@odu.edu. *Application contact:* Dr. David C. Earnest, Associate Dean, 757-683-6077, Fax: 757-683-5746, E-mail: dearnest@odu.edu.
Website: http://al.odu.edu/sociology/gradprogram/graduatehome.shtml

Our Lady of the Lake University, College of Professional Studies, Program in Sociology, San Antonio, TX 78207-4689. Offers MA. *Program availability:* Part-time, evening/weekend, online learning. *Faculty:* 2 full-time (1 woman). *Students:* 9 full-time (all women), 2 part-time (both women); includes 6 minority (2 Black or African American, non-Hispanic/Latino; 4 Hispanic/Latino). Average age 33. 4 applicants, 100% accepted, 3 enrolled. In 2017, 4 master's awarded. *Entrance requirements:* For master's, official transcripts showing minimum B grade in undergraduate statistics course, personal statement, two letters of recommendation, interview. Additional exam requirements/recommendations for international students: Required—TOEFL. *Application deadline:* For fall admission, 6/15 for domestic and international students. Application fee: $40 ($50 for international students). Electronic applications accepted. *Expenses: Tuition:* Full-time $10,668; part-time $5334 per year. *Required fees:* $816; $816 per year. $408 per semester. *Financial support:* In 2017–18, 5 students received support. Federal Work-Study, scholarships/grants, unspecified assistantships, and tuition discounts available. Support available to part-time students. Financial award application deadline: 5/1; financial award applicants required to submit FAFSA. *Faculty research:* Community based population health. *Unit head:* Dr. Steve Blanchard, Professor of Sociology, 210-528-7119, E-mail: steveblanchard@ollusa.edu. *Application contact:* Office of Graduate Admissions, 210-431-3995 Ext. 2314, Fax: 210-431-3945, E-mail: gradadm@lake.ollusa.edu.
Website: http://www.ollusa.edu/s/1190/hybrid/default-hybrid-ollu.aspx?sid-1190&gid-1&pgid-7989

Oxford Graduate School, Graduate Programs, Dayton, TN 37321-6736. Offers family life education (M Litt); integration of religion and society (D Phil); organizational leadership (M Litt). *Entrance requirements:* For master's, official transcripts, three letters of recommendation, bachelor's degree or its equivalent, minimum undergraduate GPA of 3.0, minimum of 3 years of professional experience; for doctorate, official transcripts, three letters of recommendation, master's degree with minimum GPA of 3.0, minimum of 5 years of professional experience. *Expenses:* Contact institution.

Penn State University Park, Graduate School, College of the Liberal Arts, Department of Sociology and Criminology, University Park, PA 16802. Offers criminology (MA, PhD); sociology (MA, PhD). *Unit head:* Dr. Susan Welch, Dean, 814-865-7691, Fax: 814-863-2085. *Application contact:* Lori Hawn, Director, Graduate Student Services, 814-865-1795, Fax: 814-863-4627, E-mail: l-gswww@lists.psu.edu.
Website: http://sociology.la.psu.edu/

Portland State University, Graduate Studies, College of Liberal Arts and Sciences, Department of Sociology, Portland, OR 97207-0751. Offers MA, MS, PhD. *Program availability:* Part-time. *Faculty:* 17 full-time (11 women), 6 part-time/adjunct (2 women). *Students:* 20 full-time (11 women), 20 part-time (14 women); includes 8 minority (1 Black or African American, non-Hispanic/Latino; 1 Asian, non-Hispanic/Latino; 4 Hispanic/Latino; 2 Two or more races, non-Hispanic/Latino), 3 international. Average age 36. 49 applicants, 24% accepted, 10 enrolled. In 2017, 5 master's awarded. *Degree requirements:* For master's, variable foreign language requirement, thesis, oral defense of thesis; for doctorate, comprehensive exam, thesis/dissertation, proposal, research project. *Entrance requirements:* For master's, GRE General Test, GRE Subject Test, minimum GPA of 3.0 in upper-division course work or 2.75 overall, 3 letters of recommendation, personal statement, curriculum vitae/resume, writing sample. Additional exam requirements/recommendations for international students: Required—TOEFL (minimum score 550 paper-based; 80 iBT), IELTS (minimum score 6.5). *Application deadline:* For fall admission, 1/15 for domestic and international students. Applications are processed on a rolling basis. Application fee: $65. *Expenses:* Tuition, state resident: full-time $14,436; part-time $401 per credit. Tuition, nonresident: full-time $21,780; part-time $605 per credit. *Required fees:* $1380; $22 per credit. $119 per quarter. One-time fee: $325. Tuition and fees vary according to program. *Financial support:* In 2017–18, 20 students received support, including 1 research assistantship with full tuition reimbursement available (averaging $9,971 per year), 14 teaching assistantships with full and partial tuition reimbursements available (averaging $8,170 per year); fellowships, career-related internships or fieldwork, Federal Work-Study, and unspecified assistantships also available. Support available to part-time students. Financial award application deadline: 3/1; financial award applicants required to submit FAFSA. *Faculty research:* Urban sociology, gender and class, development, social change, race/ethnic/minority relations. *Total annual research expenditures:* $247,798. *Unit head:* Melissa Thompson, Chair, 503-725-3614, Fax: 503-725-3957, E-mail: mthomp@pdx.edu. *Application contact:* Ginny Garcia-Alexander, Professor/Graduate Director, 503-725-9572, E-mail: gin5@pdx.edu.
Website: https://www.pdx.edu/sociology/

Portland State University, Graduate Studies, College of Liberal Arts and Sciences, Systems Science Program, Portland, OR 97207-0751. Offers computational intelligence (Certificate); computer modeling and simulation (Certificate); systems science (MS); systems science/anthropology (PhD); systems science/business administration (PhD); systems science/civil engineering (PhD); systems science/economics (PhD); systems science/engineering management (PhD); systems science/general (PhD); systems science/mathematical sciences (PhD); systems science/mechanical engineering (PhD); systems science/psychology (PhD); systems science/sociology (PhD). *Faculty:* 2 full-time (0 women), 4 part-time/adjunct (0 women). *Students:* 12 full-time (4 women), 22 part-time (6 women); includes 6 minority (4 Hispanic/Latino; 2 Two or more races, non-Hispanic/Latino). Average age 37. 18 applicants, 94% accepted, 16 enrolled. In 2017, 6 master's awarded. *Degree requirements:* For master's, comprehensive exam (for some programs), thesis optional; for doctorate, variable foreign language requirement, comprehensive exam (for some programs), thesis/dissertation. *Entrance requirements:* For master's, GRE/GMAT (recommended), minimum GPA of 3.0 on undergraduate or graduate work, 2 letters of recommendation, statement of interest; for doctorate, GMAT, GRE General Test, minimum GPA of 3.0 undergraduate, 3.25 graduate; 3 letters of recommendation; statement of interest. Additional exam requirements/recommendations for international students: Required—TOEFL (minimum score 550 paper-based; 80 iBT). *Application deadline:* For fall admission, 1/15 for domestic and international students; for spring admission, 11/1 for domestic students. Application fee: $65. Electronic applications accepted. *Expenses:* Tuition, state resident: full-time $14,436; part-time $401 per credit. Tuition, nonresident: full-time $21,780; part-time $605 per credit. *Required fees:* $1380; $22 per credit. $119 per quarter. One-time fee: $325. Tuition and fees vary according to program. *Financial support:* In 2017–18, 1 teaching assistantship with full and partial tuition reimbursement (averaging $7,830 per year) was awarded; research assistantships, career-related internships or fieldwork, Federal Work-Study, scholarships/grants, and unspecified assistantships also available. Support available to part-time students. Financial award application deadline: 3/1; financial award applicants required to submit FAFSA. *Faculty research:* Systems theory and methodology, artificial intelligence neural networks, information theory, nonlinear dynamics/chaos, modeling and simulation. *Total annual research expenditures:* $169,034. *Unit head:* Dr. Wayne Wakeland, Chair, 503-725-4975, E-mail: wakeland@pdx.edu.
Website: http://www.pdx.edu/sysc/

Prairie View A&M University, College of Arts and Sciences, Division of Social Work, Behavioral and Political Sciences, Prairie View, TX 77446. Offers sociology (MA). *Program availability:* Part-time, evening/weekend. *Faculty:* 3 full-time (0 women), 1 (woman) part-time/adjunct. *Students:* 14 full-time (9 women), 6 part-time (4 women); all minorities (all Black or African American, non-Hispanic/Latino). Average age 29. 23 applicants, 96% accepted, 15 enrolled. In 2017, 1 master's awarded. *Degree requirements:* For master's, comprehensive exam, thesis (for some programs). *Entrance requirements:* For master's, GRE General Test. Additional exam requirements/recommendations for international students: Required—TOEFL (minimum score 550 paper-based; 79 iBT). *Application deadline:* For fall admission, 5/1 priority date for domestic and international students; for spring admission, 10/1 priority date for domestic students, 9/1 priority date for international students; for summer admission, 3/1 priority date for domestic students, 2/1 priority date for international students. Applications are processed on a rolling basis. Application fee: $50. Electronic applications accepted. *Expenses:* Tuition, state resident: part-time $242 per credit. Tuition, nonresident: part-time $695 per credit. *Required fees:* $149 per credit. *Financial support:* Career-related internships or fieldwork, Federal Work-Study, institutionally sponsored loans, and tuition waivers available. Financial award application deadline: 4/1; financial award applicants required to submit FAFSA. *Faculty research:* Social theory, political and military sociology, sociology of religion and education, media studies, African-American status attainment. *Unit head:* Dr. Walle Engedayehu, Division Head, 936-261-3202, Fax: 936-261-3229, E-mail: waengedayehu@pvamu.edu. *Application contact:* Pauline Walker, Administrative Assistant II, Research and Graduate Studies, 936-261-3521, Fax: 936-261-3529, E-mail: gradadmissions@pvamu.edu.
Website: http://www.pvamu.edu/swbps/

Princeton University, Graduate School, Department of Sociology, Princeton, NJ 08544-1019. Offers sociology (PhD); sociology and demography (PhD). *Degree requirements:* For doctorate, variable foreign language requirement, thesis/dissertation. *Entrance requirements:* For doctorate, GRE General Test, GRE Subject Test (recommended), sample of written work. Additional exam requirements/

recommendations for international students: Required—TOEFL (minimum score 600 paper-based). Electronic applications accepted.

Princeton University, Graduate School, Program in Population Studies, Princeton, NJ 08544-1019. Offers demography (PhD, Certificate); economics and demography (PhD); public affairs and demography (PhD); sociology and demography (PhD). *Degree requirements:* For doctorate, thesis/dissertation. *Entrance requirements:* For doctorate, GRE General Test. Additional exam requirements/recommendations for international students: Required—TOEFL (minimum score 600 paper-based). Electronic applications accepted. *Faculty research:* Models, fertility, infant and child mortality, migration.

Purdue University, Graduate School, College of Liberal Arts, Department of Sociology, West Lafayette, IN 47907. Offers MS, PhD. *Faculty:* 25 full-time (9 women), 1 part-time/adjunct (0 women). *Students:* 27 full-time (15 women), 5 part-time (1 woman); includes 3 minority (1 Black or African American, non-Hispanic/Latino; 1 Hispanic/Latino; 1 Two or more races, non-Hispanic/Latino), 8 international. Average age 29. 36 applicants, 39% accepted, 10 enrolled. In 2017, 2 master's, 6 doctorates awarded. *Degree requirements:* For master's, thesis; for doctorate, comprehensive exam, thesis/dissertation. *Entrance requirements:* For master's, GRE General Test, minimum undergraduate GPA of 3.0 or equivalent; for doctorate, GRE General Test, minimum undergraduate GPA of 3.0 or equivalent; master's degree in sociology with minimum GPA of 3.25 or equivalent. Additional exam requirements/recommendations for international students: Required—TOEFL (minimum score 78 iBT). *Application deadline:* For fall admission, 12/15 for domestic and international students. Application fee: $60 ($75 for international students). *Unit head:* Daniel V.A. Olson, Head, 765-494-4861, E-mail: dolson@purdue.edu. *Application contact:* Nicole A. Remley, Graduate Contact, 765-494-4673, E-mail: ncavanau@purdue.edu.
Website: http://www.cla.purdue.edu/sociology/

Queens College of the City University of New York, Division of Social Sciences, Department of Sociology, Queens, NY 11367-1597. Offers data analytics and applied social research (MA). *Program availability:* Part-time, evening/weekend. *Students:* 4 full-time (3 women), 39 part-time (22 women); includes 29 minority (4 Black or African American, non-Hispanic/Latino; 9 Asian, non-Hispanic/Latino; 16 Hispanic/Latino), 7 international. Average age 29. *Degree requirements:* For master's, thesis optional. *Entrance requirements:* For master's, minimum GPA of 3.0. Additional exam requirements/recommendations for international students: Required—TOEFL (minimum score 100 iBT), IELTS (minimum score 7). *Application deadline:* For fall admission, 5/15 for domestic students; for spring admission, 12/1 for domestic students. Applications are processed on a rolling basis. Application fee: $125. Electronic applications accepted. *Financial support:* Career-related internships or fieldwork and unspecified assistantships available. Financial award application deadline: 4/1; financial award applicants required to submit FAFSA. *Unit head:* Dr. Andrew Beveridge, Chair, 718-997-2800, E-mail: andrew.beveridge@qc.cuny.edu. *Application contact:* Elizabeth D'Amico-Ramirez, Assistant Director of Graduate Admissions, 718-997-5203, E-mail: elizabeth.damicoramirez@qc.cuny.edu.
Website: http://qcsociology.org/

Queen's University at Kingston, School of Graduate Studies, Faculty of Arts and Sciences, Department of Sociology, Kingston, ON K7L 3N6, Canada. Offers communication and Information technology (MA, PhD); feminist sociology (MA, PhD); socio-legal studies (MA, PhD); sociological theory (MA, PhD). *Program availability:* Part-time. *Degree requirements:* For master's, thesis; for doctorate, comprehensive exam, thesis/dissertation. *Entrance requirements:* For master's, honors bachelors degree in sociology; for doctorate, honors bachelors degree, masters degree in sociology. Additional exam requirements/recommendations for international students: Required—TOEFL. *Faculty research:* Social change and modernization, social control, deviance and criminology, surveillance.

Rice University, Graduate Programs, School of Social Sciences, Department of Sociology, Houston, TX 77251-1892. Offers PhD.

Roosevelt University, Graduate Division, College of Arts and Sciences, Department of Sociology and Sustainability Studies, Chicago, IL 60605. Offers community development and action (MA). *Program availability:* Part-time, evening/weekend. *Students:* 3 full-time (all women), 10 part-time (6 women); includes 9 minority (6 Black or African American, non-Hispanic/Latino; 2 Hispanic/Latino; 1 Two or more races, non-Hispanic/Latino). Average age 26. 12 applicants, 100% accepted, 7 enrolled. In 2017, 3 master's awarded. *Application deadline:* Applications are processed on a rolling basis. Application fee: $40. *Financial support:* Teaching assistantships and scholarships/grants available. Financial award applicants required to submit FAFSA. *Unit head:* Pamela Robert, Director of MA Community Development and Action Program, 312-341-3737, E-mail: probert@roosevelt.edu. *Application contact:* Sivling Lam, Graduate Admission Counselor, 312-341-3252, E-mail: slam02@roosevelt.edu.

Rutgers University–New Brunswick, Graduate School-New Brunswick, Program in Sociology, Piscataway, NJ 08854-8097. Offers MA, PhD. Terminal master's awarded for partial completion of doctoral program. *Degree requirements:* For master's, qualifying paper; for doctorate, thesis/dissertation, qualifying exam, qualifying papers. *Entrance requirements:* For master's, GRE General Test; for doctorate, GRE General Test, sample of written work. Additional exam requirements/recommendations for international students: Required—TOEFL. Electronic applications accepted. *Faculty research:* Comparative-historical, sex and gender, organizations and work, culture and cognition, economics, occupations/professions, religion.

St. John's University, St. John's College of Liberal Arts and Sciences, Department of Sociology and Anthropology, Queens, NY 11439. Offers criminology and justice (MA); sociology (MA). *Program availability:* Part-time, evening/weekend. *Faculty:* 14 full-time (8 women), 13 part-time/adjunct (4 women). *Students:* 35 full-time (23 women), 11 part-time (8 women); includes 18 minority (12 Black or African American, non-Hispanic/Latino; 2 Asian, non-Hispanic/Latino; 3 Hispanic/Latino; 1 Two or more races, non-Hispanic/Latino), 9 international. Average age 27. 70 applicants, 50% accepted, 15 enrolled. In 2017, 32 master's awarded. *Degree requirements:* For master's, comprehensive exam, thesis optional. *Entrance requirements:* For master's, letters of recommendation, transcripts, resume, personal statement. Additional exam requirements/recommendations for international students: Required—TOEFL (minimum score 80 iBT), IELTS (minimum score 6.5). *Application deadline:* For fall admission, 5/1 for domestic students; for spring admission, 11/1 for domestic students. Applications are processed on a rolling basis. Application fee: $70. Electronic applications accepted. *Expenses: Tuition:* Full-time $44,280; part-time $1230 per credit. *Required fees:* $340; $340 per credit. Tuition and fees vary according to course load, degree level and program. *Financial support:* Fellowships, research assistantships, teaching assistantships, scholarships/grants, tuition waivers, and unspecified assistantships available. Support available to part-time students. Financial award application deadline: 2/1; financial award applicants required to submit FAFSA. *Faculty research:* Community studies and gentrification, global financial crisis, insurance fraud, globalization, immigration and human rights. *Unit head:* Dr. Roberta Villalon, Chair, 718-990-5663, E-mail: villalonr@stjohns.edu. *Application contact:* Robert Medrano, Director of Graduate Admission, 718-990-1601, Fax: 718-990-5686, E-mail: gradhelp@stjohns.edu.
Website: https://www.stjohns.edu/academics/schools-and-colleges/st-johns-college-liberal-arts-and-sciences/sociology-and-anthropology

Sam Houston State University, College of Humanities and Social Sciences, Department of Sociology, Huntsville, TX 77341. Offers MA. *Program availability:* Part-time, evening/weekend, online learning. *Degree requirements:* For master's, comprehensive exam, thesis optional, professional paper. *Entrance requirements:* For master's, GRE General Test, minimum GPA of 3.0, letter of intent, letters of recommendation. Additional exam requirements/recommendations for international students: Required—TOEFL (minimum score 550 paper-based; 79 iBT), IELTS (minimum score 6.5). Electronic applications accepted.

San Diego State University, Graduate and Research Affairs, College of Arts and Letters, Department of Sociology, San Diego, CA 92182. Offers MA. *Degree requirements:* For master's, thesis. *Entrance requirements:* For master's, GRE General Test, 3 letters of recommendation, writing sample. Additional exam requirements/recommendations for international students: Required—TOEFL. Electronic applications accepted. *Faculty research:* The homeless and mentally ill, medical data relating to the homeless.

San Jose State University, Graduate Studies and Research, College of Social Sciences, San Jose, CA 95192-0107. Offers applied anthropology (MA); communication studies (MA); economics (MA), including applied economics, economics; environmental studies (MS); geography (MA); history (MA), including history, history education; Mexican American studies (MA); psychology (MA, MS), including clinical psychology (MS), industrial/organizational psychology (MS), research and experimental psychology (MA); public administration (MPA); social sciences (MS); sociology (MA). *Faculty:* 59 full-time (29 women), 18 part-time/adjunct (5 women). *Students:* 181 full-time (126 women), 221 part-time (127 women); includes 228 minority (15 Black or African American, non-Hispanic/Latino; 48 Asian, non-Hispanic/Latino; 112 Hispanic/Latino; 3 Native Hawaiian or other Pacific Islander, non-Hispanic/Latino; 50 Two or more races, non-Hispanic/Latino), 38 international. Average age 30. 532 applicants, 44% accepted, 156 enrolled. In 2017, 139 master's awarded. *Degree requirements:* For master's, one foreign language, comprehensive exam, thesis (for some programs), project, field work, professional work experience. *Entrance requirements:* Additional exam requirements/recommendations for international students: Required—TOEFL (minimum score 550 paper-based; 80 iBT), IELTS (minimum score 6.5), PTE (minimum score 53). *Application deadline:* For fall admission, 2/1 for domestic and international students. Applications are processed on a rolling basis. Application fee: $55. Electronic applications accepted. *Expenses:* Tuition, state resident: full-time $7176. Tuition, nonresident: full-time $16,680. Tuition and fees vary according to course load and program. *Financial support:* Fellowships, research assistantships, career-related internships or fieldwork, Federal Work-Study, scholarships/grants, tuition waivers (full and partial), and unspecified assistantships available. Support available to part-time students. Financial award application deadline: 4/28; financial award applicants required to submit FAFSA. *Unit head:* Dr. Walt Jacobs, Dean, 408-924-5300, Fax: 408-924-5303, E-mail: walter.jacobs@sjsu.edu.
Website: http://www.sjsu.edu/socialsciences/

Shippensburg University of Pennsylvania, School of Graduate Studies, College of Arts and Sciences, Department of Sociology and Anthropology, Shippensburg, PA 17257-2299. Offers organizational development and leadership (MS), including business, higher education structure and policy, historical administration, leadership in society, management information systems, public organizations. *Program availability:* Part-time, evening/weekend. *Faculty:* 4 full-time (2 women). *Students:* 14 full-time (6 women), 19 part-time (11 women); includes 7 minority (4 Black or African American, non-Hispanic/Latino; 2 Hispanic/Latino; 1 Two or more races, non-Hispanic/Latino), 1 international. Average age 26. 31 applicants, 81% accepted, 15 enrolled. In 2017, 22 master's awarded. *Degree requirements:* For master's, capstone experience including internship. *Entrance requirements:* For master's, interview (if GPA less than 2.75), current resume, personal goals statement. Additional exam requirements/recommendations for international students: Required—TOEFL (minimum score 550 paper-based, 68 iBT) or IELTS (minimum score 6). *Application deadline:* For fall admission, 4/30 for international students; for spring admission, 9/30 for international students. Applications are processed on a rolling basis. Application fee: $45. Electronic applications accepted. *Expenses:* Tuition, state resident: part-time $500 per credit. Tuition, nonresident: part-time $750 per credit. *Required fees:* $145 per credit. *Financial support:* In 2017–18, 12 students received support. Career-related internships or fieldwork, scholarships/grants, unspecified assistantships, and resident hall director and student payroll positions available. Support available to part-time students. Financial award application deadline: 3/1; financial award applicants required to submit FAFSA. *Unit head:* Dr. Barbara J. Denison, Departmental Chair and Program Coordinator, 717-477-1735, Fax: 717-477-4011, E-mail: bjdeni@ship.edu. *Application contact:* Maya T. Mapp, Director of Admissions, 717-477-1231, Fax: 717-477-4016, E-mail: mtmapp@ship.edu.
Website: http://www.ship.edu/odl/

Simon Fraser University, Office of Graduate Studies and Postdoctoral Fellows, Faculty of Arts and Social Sciences, Department of Sociology and Anthropology, Burnaby, BC V5A 1S6, Canada. Offers anthropology (MA, PhD); sociology (MA, PhD). *Degree requirements:* For master's, thesis; for doctorate, comprehensive exam, thesis/dissertation, cooperative education. *Entrance requirements:* For master's, minimum GPA of 3.0 (on scale of 4.33) or 3.33 based on last 60 credits of undergraduate courses; for doctorate, minimum GPA of 3.5 (on scale of 4.33). Additional exam requirements/recommendations for international students: Recommended—TOEFL (minimum score 580 paper-based; 93 iBT), IELTS (minimum score 7), TWE (minimum score 5). Electronic applications accepted. *Faculty research:* Globalization and development, health, environment and science, knowledge, culture and power, social justice, policy, law and society, women, gender and sexuality.

South Dakota State University, Graduate School, College of Agriculture and Biological Sciences, Department of Sociology and Rural Studies, Brookings, SD 57007. Offers sociology (MS, PhD). *Program availability:* Part-time, online learning. *Degree requirements:* For master's, comprehensive exam (for some programs), thesis, oral and written exams; for doctorate, comprehensive exam, thesis/dissertation, preliminary oral and written exams. *Entrance requirements:* Additional exam requirements/recommendations for international students: Required—TOEFL (minimum score 550 paper-based; 79 iBT). *Faculty research:* Demography, rural families, rural development, Native Americans, rural poverty, sociology of agriculture.

Southeastern Louisiana University, College of Arts, Humanities and Social Sciences, Department of Languages and Communication, Hammond, LA 70402. Offers health communications (MA); journalism (MA); marketing (MA); public relations (MA); sociology (MA). *Program availability:* Part-time, evening/weekend. *Faculty:* 5 full-time (3 women). *Students:* 7 full-time (6 women), 11 part-time (7 women); includes 10 minority (5 Black or African American, non-Hispanic/Latino; 3 Hispanic/Latino; 2 Two or more races, non-Hispanic/Latino). Average age 28. 133 applicants, 51% accepted, 10 enrolled. In 2017, 36 master's awarded. *Degree requirements:* For master's, comprehensive exam. *Entrance requirements:* For master's, GRE (minimum score 148 on Verbal section, 3.5 Written). Additional exam requirements/recommendations for international students: Required—TOEFL (minimum score 525 paper-based; 75 iBT). *Application deadline:* For

fall admission, 7/15 priority date for domestic students, 6/1 priority date for international students; for spring admission, 12/1 priority date for domestic students, 10/1 priority date for international students. Applications are processed on a rolling basis. Application fee: $20 ($30 for international students). Electronic applications accepted. *Expenses:* Tuition, state resident: full-time $6684. Tuition, nonresident: full-time $19,162. *Required fees:* $2088. *Financial support:* In 2017–18, 12 students received support, including 7 research assistantships (averaging $6,082 per year); career-related internships or fieldwork, Federal Work-Study, institutionally sponsored loans, scholarships/grants, traineeships, health care benefits, tuition waivers, and unspecified assistantships also available. Financial award application deadline: 5/1; financial award applicants required to submit FAFSA. *Faculty research:* Communicate with the millennial generation to enhance organizational effectiveness, conflict resolution and mediation among nations, journalism history, media law, media writing, media convergence, external compliances accreditation and strategic planning. *Unit head:* Dr. Lucia Harrison, Department Head, 985-549-2105, Fax: 985-549-5014, E-mail: lharrison@southeastern.edu. *Application contact:* Amanda Harper, Graduate Admissions Analyst, 985-549-5620, Fax: 985-549-5632, E-mail: admissions@southeastern.edu.
Website: http://www.southeastern.edu/acad_research/depts/lang_comm/index.html

Southeastern Louisiana University, College of Arts, Humanities and Social Sciences, Department of Sociology and Criminal Justice, Hammond, LA 70402. Offers criminal justice (MS); globalization and sustainability (MS). *Program availability:* Part-time, evening/weekend. *Faculty:* 5 full-time (0 women). *Students:* 14 full-time (9 women), 4 part-time (0 women); includes 5 minority (2 Black or African American, non-Hispanic/Latino; 1 Hispanic/Latino; 2 Two or more races, non-Hispanic/Latino), 1 international. Average age 26. 13 applicants, 46% accepted, 5 enrolled. In 2017, 12 master's awarded. *Degree requirements:* For master's, comprehensive exam, thesis (for some programs), internship research (for those who select an internship track). *Entrance requirements:* For master's, GRE General Test (verbal and quantitative). Additional exam requirements/recommendations for international students: Required—TOEFL (minimum score 500 paper-based; 61 iBT). *Application deadline:* For fall admission, 7/15 priority date for domestic students, 6/1 priority date for international students; for spring admission, 12/1 priority date for domestic students, 10/1 priority date for international students. Applications are processed on a rolling basis. Application fee: $20 ($30 for international students). Electronic applications accepted. *Expenses:* Tuition, state resident: full-time $6684. Tuition, nonresident: full-time $19,162. *Required fees:* $2088. *Financial support:* In 2017–18, 8 students received support, including 7 research assistantships (averaging $6,506 per year); teaching assistantships, career-related internships or fieldwork, Federal Work-Study, institutionally sponsored loans, scholarships/grants, and unspecified assistantships also available. Support available to part-time students. Financial award application deadline: 5/1; financial award applicants required to submit FAFSA. *Faculty research:* Criminology, environmental sociology, globalization, sociology of disasters, sociology of religion. *Unit head:* Dr. Kenneth Bolton, Department Head, 985-549-2110, Fax: 985-549-5961, E-mail: kbolton@southeastern.edu. *Application contact:* Amanda Harper, Graduate Admissions Analyst, 985-549-5620, Fax: 985-549-5632, E-mail: admissions@southeastern.edu.
Website: http://www.southeastern.edu/acad_research/depts/soc_cj/grad_degree/index.html

Southern Connecticut State University, School of Graduate Studies, School of Arts and Sciences, Department of Sociology, New Haven, CT 06515-1355. Offers MS. *Program availability:* Part-time, evening/weekend. *Degree requirements:* For master's, thesis or alternative. *Entrance requirements:* For master's, interview. Electronic applications accepted.

Southern Illinois University Carbondale, Graduate School, College of Liberal Arts, Department of Sociology, Carbondale, IL 62901-4701. Offers MA, PhD. *Program availability:* Part-time. *Degree requirements:* For master's, thesis; for doctorate, thesis/dissertation. *Entrance requirements:* For master's, GRE, minimum GPA of 2.7; for doctorate, GRE, minimum GPA of 3.25. Additional exam requirements/recommendations for international students: Required—TOEFL. *Faculty research:* Deviance, family, social stratification, social change, theory methodology, culture.

Southern Illinois University Edwardsville, Graduate School, College of Arts and Sciences, Department of Sociology and Criminal Justice Studies, Edwardsville, IL 62026. Offers sociology (MA). *Program availability:* Part-time. *Degree requirements:* For master's, thesis (for some programs), internship. *Entrance requirements:* Additional exam requirements/recommendations for international students: Required—TOEFL (minimum score 550 paper-based; 79 iBT), IELTS (minimum score 6.5). Electronic applications accepted.

Stanford University, School of Humanities and Sciences, Department of Sociology, Stanford, CA 94305-2004. Offers PhD. *Degree requirements:* For doctorate, thesis/dissertation, oral exam. *Entrance requirements:* For doctorate, GRE General Test. Additional exam requirements/recommendations for international students: Required—TOEFL. Electronic applications accepted. *Expenses:* Tuition: Full-time $48,987; part-time $10,620 per quarter. One-time fee: $400. Tuition and fees vary according to program.

Stony Brook University, State University of New York, Graduate School, College of Arts and Sciences, Department of Sociology, Stony Brook, NY 11794. Offers MA, PhD. *Faculty:* 19 full-time (9 women), 2 part-time/adjunct (both women). *Students:* 48 full-time (29 women), 2 part-time (both women); includes 13 minority (1 Black or African American, non-Hispanic/Latino; 5 Asian, non-Hispanic/Latino; 3 Hispanic/Latino; 4 Two or more races, non-Hispanic/Latino), 16 international. Average age 32. 51 applicants, 18% accepted, 5 enrolled. In 2017, 7 master's, 5 doctorates awarded. *Degree requirements:* For doctorate, thesis/dissertation, comprehensive exam or professional papers, field exam, teaching practicum. *Entrance requirements:* For doctorate, GRE General Test, minimum GPA of 3.0. Additional exam requirements/recommendations for international students: Required—TOEFL (minimum score 90 iBT). *Application deadline:* For fall admission, 1/15 for domestic students; for spring admission, 10/1 for domestic students. Application fee: $100. *Expenses:* Contact institution. *Financial support:* In 2017–18, 1 fellowship, 1 research assistantship, 23 teaching assistantships were awarded. *Faculty research:* Adolescents, disability studies, globalization, sociology, sociology of sex and gender. *Total annual research expenditures:* $77,818. *Unit head:* Dr. Daniel Levy, Chair, 631-632-7755, E-mail: daniel.levy@stonybrook.edu. *Application contact:* Wanda Vega, Coordinator, 631-632-7730, Fax: 631-632-8203, E-mail: wanda.olivera@stonybrook.edu.
Website: http://www.sunysb.edu/sociology/

Syracuse University, Maxwell School of Citizenship and Public Affairs, Programs in Sociology, Syracuse, NY 13244. Offers MA, PhD. *Degree requirements:* For master's, thesis; for doctorate, comprehensive exam, thesis/dissertation. *Entrance requirements:* For master's and doctorate, GRE General Test, three letters of recommendation, resume, personal statement, official transcripts. Additional exam requirements/recommendations for international students: Required—TOEFL (minimum score 100 iBT). *Application deadline:* For fall admission, 1/10 priority date for domestic and international students. Application fee: $75. Electronic applications accepted. *Financial support:* Fellowships with full tuition reimbursements, research assistantships, teaching assistantships, tuition waivers, and unspecified assistantships available. Financial award application deadline: 1/1. *Faculty research:* Qualitative methods and feminist methods, inequality studies, aging and the life course, sociological theory. *Unit head:* Dr. Madonna Harrington Meyer, Professor and Chair, Sociology, 315-443-6755, E-mail: mhm@maxwell.syr.edu. *Application contact:* Janet Coria, Recruiting Contact, 315-443-2347, E-mail: jmcoria@syr.edu.
Website: http://www.maxwell.syr.edu/soc/

Teachers College, Columbia University, Department of Education Policy and Social Analysis, New York, NY 10027-6696. Offers economics and education (Ed M, MA, PhD); education policy (Ed M, MA, Ed D, PhD); politics and education (Ed M, MA, Ed D, PhD); sociology and education (Ed M, MA, Ed D, PhD). *Students:* 144 full-time (109 women), 107 part-time (85 women); includes 100 minority (43 Black or African American, non-Hispanic/Latino; 17 Asian, non-Hispanic/Latino; 33 Hispanic/Latino; 7 Two or more races, non-Hispanic/Latino), 69 international. Average age 29. 524 applicants, 53% accepted, 104 enrolled. *Unit head:* Dr. Aaron Pallas, Chair, E-mail: amp155@tc.columbia.edu. *Application contact:* David Estrella, Director of Admissions, 212-678-3305, E-mail: estrella@tc.columbia.edu.
Website: http://www.tc.columbia.edu/education-policy-and-social-analysis/

Temple University, College of Liberal Arts, Department of Sociology, Philadelphia, PA 19122-6096. Offers MA, PhD. *Program availability:* Part-time, evening/weekend. *Faculty:* 16 full-time (7 women), 2 part-time/adjunct (both women). *Students:* 36 full-time (19 women), 2 part-time (both women); includes 10 minority (4 Black or African American, non-Hispanic/Latino; 1 Asian, non-Hispanic/Latino; 2 Hispanic/Latino; 3 Two or more races, non-Hispanic/Latino), 5 international. 51 applicants, 22% accepted, 9 enrolled. In 2017, 5 master's, 8 doctorates awarded. Terminal master's awarded for partial completion of doctoral program. *Degree requirements:* For doctorate, thesis/dissertation. *Entrance requirements:* For master's and doctorate, GRE General Test, minimum GPA of 3.0, 3 letters of recommendation. Additional exam requirements/recommendations for international students: Required—TOEFL (minimum score 600 paper-based; 100 iBT). *Application deadline:* For fall admission, 3/15 for domestic students, 12/15 for international students. Application fee: $60. Electronic applications accepted. *Expenses:* Tuition, state resident: full-time $16,164; part-time $898 per credit hour. Tuition, nonresident: full-time $22,158; part-time $1231 per credit hour. *Required fees:* $890; $445 per semester. Full-time tuition and fees vary according to course load, degree level, campus/location and program. *Financial support:* Fellowships with tuition reimbursements, research assistantships with tuition reimbursements, teaching assistantships with tuition reimbursements, career-related internships or fieldwork, Federal Work-Study, institutionally sponsored loans, and scholarships/grants available. Financial award application deadline: 1/15; financial award applicants required to submit FAFSA. *Faculty research:* Urban sociology, gender and sexuality, race and ethnicity, globalization, medical sociology. *Unit head:* Dr. Dustin Kidd, Graduate Director, 215-204-6850, E-mail: dustin.kidd@temple.edu. *Application contact:* Pamela Smallwood, Coordinator, 215-204-7750, Fax: 215-204-3352, E-mail: poppy@temple.edu.
Website: http://www.cla.temple.edu/sociology/

Texas A&M University, College of Liberal Arts, Department of Sociology, College Station, TX 77843. Offers sociology (MS, PhD). *Faculty:* 27. *Students:* 61 full-time (42 women), 13 part-time (9 women); includes 33 minority (11 Black or African American, non-Hispanic/Latino; 1 American Indian or Alaska Native, non-Hispanic/Latino; 3 Asian, non-Hispanic/Latino; 18 Hispanic/Latino), 11 international. Average age 32. 38 applicants, 87% accepted, 11 enrolled. In 2017, 13 doctorates awarded. *Degree requirements:* For master's, thesis or alternative; for doctorate, thesis/dissertation. *Entrance requirements:* For master's and doctorate, GRE General Test. Additional exam requirements/recommendations for international students: Required—TOEFL (minimum score 550 paper-based; 80 iBT), IELTS (minimum score 6), PTE. *Application deadline:* For fall admission, 12/15 for domestic students. Applications are processed on a rolling basis. Application fee: $50 ($90 for international students). Electronic applications accepted. *Expenses:* Contact institution. *Financial support:* In 2017–18, 65 students received support, including 6 fellowships with tuition reimbursements available (averaging $27,962 per year), 18 research assistantships with tuition reimbursements available (averaging $9,887 per year), 39 teaching assistantships with tuition reimbursements available (averaging $9,974 per year); career-related internships or fieldwork, institutionally sponsored loans, scholarships/grants, traineeships, health care benefits, tuition waivers (full and partial), and unspecified assistantships also available. Support available to part-time students. Financial award application deadline: 3/15; financial award applicants required to submit FAFSA. *Faculty research:* Crime, deviance, and law; culture; demography and human ecology; political and economic sociology; racial and ethnic relations; social psychology; Latino sociology; gender; Asian studies. *Unit head:* Dr. Jane Sell, Department Head, 979-845-6120, Fax: 979-862-4057, E-mail: j-sell@tamu.edu. *Application contact:* Dr. Wendy Leo Moore, Graduate Advisor, 979-845-5133, Fax: 979-862-4057, E-mail: wlmoore@tamu.edu.
Website: http://sociology.tamu.edu/

Texas A&M University–Commerce, College of Humanities, Social Sciences and Arts, Commerce, TX 75429. Offers applied criminology (MS); applied linguistics (MA, MS); art (MA, MFA); computational linguistics (Graduate Certificate); creative writing (Graduate Certificate); criminal justice management (Graduate Certificate); criminal justice studies (Graduate Certificate); English (MA, MS, PhD); film studies (Graduate Certificate); history (MA, MS); history of Christianity (Graduate Certificate); Holocaust studies (Graduate Certificate); homeland security (Graduate Certificate); music education (MM); music performance (MM); political science (MA, MS); public history (Graduate Certificate); sociology (MS); Spanish (MA); studies in children's and adolescent literature and culture (Graduate Certificate); teaching English to speakers of other languages (Graduate Certificate); theater (MA, MS); world history (Graduate Certificate). *Program availability:* Part-time. *Faculty:* 56 full-time (26 women), 10 part-time/adjunct (5 women). *Students:* 133 full-time (85 women), 439 part-time (311 women); includes 204 minority (79 Black or African American, non-Hispanic/Latino; 4 American Indian or Alaska Native, non-Hispanic/Latino; 9 Asian, non-Hispanic/Latino; 98 Hispanic/Latino; 14 Two or more races, non-Hispanic/Latino), 26 international. Average age 36. 261 applicants, 50% accepted, 113 enrolled. In 2017, 105 master's, 5 doctorates awarded. *Degree requirements:* For master's, one foreign language, comprehensive exam, thesis (for some programs); for doctorate, one foreign language, comprehensive exam, thesis/dissertation, departmental qualifying exam. *Entrance requirements:* For master's and doctorate, GRE General Test. Additional exam requirements/recommendations for international students: Required—TOEFL (minimum score 550 paper-based; 79 iBT), IELTS (minimum score 6). *Application deadline:* Applications are processed on a rolling basis. Application fee: $50. Electronic applications accepted. *Expenses:* Contact institution. *Financial support:* In 2017–18, 43 students received support, including 9 research assistantships with partial tuition reimbursements available (averaging $9,000 per year), 68 teaching assistantships with partial tuition reimbursements available (averaging $9,000 per year); Federal Work-Study, institutionally sponsored loans, scholarships/grants, health care benefits, and unspecified assistantships also available. Financial award application deadline: 5/1; financial award applicants required to submit FAFSA. *Unit head:* Dr. William F. Kuracina, Interim Dean, 903-886-5166, Fax: 903-886-5774, E-mail: william.kuracina@tamuc.edu. *Application contact:* Vicky Turner, Doctoral Degree and Special Programs Coordinator, 903-886-5167, E-mail: vicky.turner@tamuc.edu.
Website: http://www.tamuc.edu/academics/graduateSchool/programs/humanitiesSocialScienceArts/default.aspx

Sociology

Texas A&M University–Kingsville, College of Graduate Studies, College of Arts and Sciences, Department of Psychology and Sociology, Program in Sociology, Kingsville, TX 78363. Offers MA, MS. *Entrance requirements:* Additional exam requirements/recommendations for international students: Required—TOEFL (minimum score 550 paper-based; 79 iBT); Recommended—IELTS. Electronic applications accepted.

Texas Southern University, College of Liberal Arts and Behavioral Sciences, Department of Sociology, Houston, TX 77004-4584. Offers MA. *Program availability:* Part-time, evening/weekend. *Degree requirements:* For master's, comprehensive exam, thesis. *Entrance requirements:* For master's, GRE General Test, minimum GPA of 2.5. Additional exam requirements/recommendations for international students: Required—TOEFL. Electronic applications accepted. *Faculty research:* Sociocultural systems, ethnic and regional studies, community sociology.

Texas State University, The Graduate College, College of Liberal Arts, Program in Applied Sociology, San Marcos, TX 78666. Offers MS. *Program availability:* Part-time, evening/weekend. *Faculty:* 10 full-time (6 women), 2 part-time/adjunct (0 women). *Students:* 10 full-time (8 women), 9 part-time (6 women); includes 10 minority (3 Black or African American, non-Hispanic/Latino; 2 Asian, non-Hispanic/Latino; 5 Hispanic/Latino). Average age 31. 18 applicants, 72% accepted, 8 enrolled. In 2017, 1 master's awarded. *Degree requirements:* For master's, comprehensive exam. *Entrance requirements:* For master's, baccalaureate degree from regionally-accredited university with minimum GPA of 3.0 on last 60 undergraduate semester hours; background course work in sociological theory, statistics, and social research; statement of purpose describing personal goals and academic interest in relation to personal goals; three letters of recommendation. Additional exam requirements/recommendations for international students: Required—TOEFL (minimum score 550 paper-based; 78 iBT), IELTS (minimum score 6.5). *Application deadline:* For fall admission, 3/1 priority date for domestic and international students; for spring admission, 10/15 priority date for domestic students, 10/1 for international students; for summer admission, 4/15 for domestic students, 3/15 for international students. Applications are processed on a rolling basis. Application fee: $40 ($90 for international students). Electronic applications accepted. *Expenses:* Tuition, state resident: full-time $7868; part-time $3934 per semester. Tuition, nonresident: full-time $17,828; part-time $8914 per semester. *Required fees:* $2092; $1435 per semester. Tuition and fees vary according to course load. *Financial support:* In 2017–18, 15 students received support, including 1 research assistantship (averaging $11,855 per year), 6 teaching assistantships (averaging $12,627 per year); Federal Work-Study, institutionally sponsored loans, scholarships/grants, health care benefits, and unspecified assistantships also available. Support available to part-time students. Financial award application deadline: 3/1; financial award applicants required to submit FAFSA. *Faculty research:* Gender initiatives: women in culinary, evaluation of Harris County protective services, advancing peer support in integrated health care evaluation, evaluate people's community clinic's early childhood mental health program. *Total annual research expenditures:* $47,593. *Unit head:* Dr. Patti Giuffre, Graduate Advisor, 512-245-8983, E-mail: pg07@txstate.edu. *Application contact:* Dr. Andrea Golato, Dean of Graduate School, 512-245-2581, Fax: 512-245-8365, E-mail: gradcollege@txstate.edu.
Website: http://www.soci.txstate.edu

Texas State University, The Graduate College, College of Liberal Arts, Program in Sociology, San Marcos, TX 78666. Offers MA. *Program availability:* Part-time, evening/weekend. *Faculty:* 10 full-time (6 women), 2 part-time/adjunct (0 women). *Students:* 15 full-time (12 women), 8 part-time (7 women); includes 11 minority (4 Black or African American, non-Hispanic/Latino; 4 Hispanic/Latino; 3 Two or more races, non-Hispanic/Latino). Average age 26. 16 applicants, 75% accepted, 8 enrolled. In 2017, 15 master's awarded. *Degree requirements:* For master's, comprehensive exam, thesis optional. *Entrance requirements:* For master's, baccalaureate degree from regionally-accredited university with minimum GPA of 3.0 on last 60 undergraduate semester hours; background course work in sociological theory, statistics, and social research; statement of purpose describing personal goals, academic interest and career goals; 3 letters of recommendation. Additional exam requirements/recommendations for international students: Required—TOEFL (minimum score 550 paper-based; 78 iBT), IELTS (minimum score 6.5). *Application deadline:* For fall admission, 3/1 priority date for domestic and international students; for spring admission, 10/15 for domestic students, 10/1 for international students; for summer admission, 4/15 for domestic students, 3/15 for international students. Applications are processed on a rolling basis. Application fee: $40 ($90 for international students). Electronic applications accepted. *Expenses:* Tuition, state resident: full-time $7868; part-time $3934 per semester. Tuition, nonresident: full-time $17,828; part-time $8914 per semester. *Required fees:* $2092; $1435 per semester. Tuition and fees vary according to course load. *Financial support:* In 2017–18, 19 students received support, including 9 teaching assistantships (averaging $12,265 per year); research assistantships, Federal Work-Study, institutionally sponsored loans, scholarships/grants, health care benefits, and unspecified assistantships also available. Support available to part-time students. Financial award application deadline: 3/1; financial award applicants required to submit FAFSA. *Faculty research:* Evaluation of gender initiatives: women in culinary, Harris County protective services evaluation, advancing peer support in integrated health care evaluation. *Total annual research expenditures:* $47,593. *Unit head:* Dr. Patti Giuffre, Graduate Advisor, 512-245-8983, Fax: 512-245-2174, E-mail: pg07@txstate.edu. *Application contact:* Dr. Andrea Golato, Dean of Graduate School, 512-245-2581, Fax: 512-245-8365, E-mail: gradcollege@txstate.edu.
Website: http://www.soci.txstate.edu/Graduate-Degree/socigradprograms.html

Texas Tech University, Graduate School, College of Arts and Sciences, Department of Sociology, Anthropology and Social Work, Lubbock, TX 79409. Offers anthropology (MA); social work (MSW); sociology (MA). *Program availability:* Part-time. *Faculty:* 28 full-time (17 women), 5 part-time/adjunct (3 women). *Students:* 46 full-time (32 women), 7 part-time (all women); includes 19 minority (3 Black or African American, non-Hispanic/Latino; 14 Hispanic/Latino; 2 Two or more races, non-Hispanic/Latino), 2 international. Average age 28. 52 applicants, 44% accepted, 19 enrolled. In 2017, 22 master's awarded. *Degree requirements:* For master's, one foreign language, comprehensive exam (for some programs), thesis (for some programs). *Entrance requirements:* For master's, GRE (for MA in anthropology), two letters of recommendation, statement of purpose, writing sample, curriculum vitae; minimum GPA of 3.0 and coursework in sociology or closely-related fields (for MA in sociology); coursework in anthropology (for MA in anthropology). Additional exam requirements/recommendations for international students: Required—TOEFL (minimum score 550 paper-based; 79 iBT). *Application deadline:* For fall admission, 6/1 priority date for domestic students, 1/15 priority date for international students; for spring admission, 9/1 priority date for domestic students, 6/15 priority date for international students. Applications are processed on a rolling basis. Application fee: $60. Electronic applications accepted. *Expenses:* Contact institution. *Financial support:* In 2017–18, 43 students received support, including 35 fellowships (averaging $4,324 per year), 28 teaching assistantships (averaging $13,091 per year); research assistantships, Federal Work-Study, scholarships/grants, tuition waivers (partial), and unspecified assistantships also available. Financial award application deadline: 2/1; financial award applicants required to submit FAFSA. *Faculty research:* Sociology of criminology/deviance, population/migration, forensic anthropology, archaeology, social work

(advanced generalist). *Total annual research expenditures:* $153,180. *Unit head:* Dr. Brett A. Houk, Chair and Associate Professor, 806-834-8107, Fax: 806-742-1088, E-mail: brett.houk@ttu.edu. *Application contact:* Dr. Martha Smithey, Associate Professor/Sociology Graduate Program Director, 806-834-1995, E-mail: martha.smithey@ttu.edu.
Website: http://www.depts.ttu.edu/sasw/

Texas Woman's University, Graduate School, College of Arts and Sciences, Department of Sociology and Social Work, Denton, TX 76204. Offers social work (MS); sociology (MA, PhD). MSW offered jointly with The University of North Texas; PhD in sociology in partnership with the Federation of North Texas Universities. *Program availability:* Evening/weekend. *Faculty:* 6 full-time (2 women). *Students:* 2 full-time (both women), 54 part-time (39 women); includes 22 minority (15 Black or African American, non-Hispanic/Latino; 1 Asian, non-Hispanic/Latino; 5 Hispanic/Latino; 1 Two or more races, non-Hispanic/Latino), 2 international. Average age 39. 21 applicants, 81% accepted, 7 enrolled. In 2017, 6 master's, 6 doctorates awarded. Terminal master's awarded for partial completion of doctoral program. *Degree requirements:* For master's, comprehensive exam, thesis optional; for doctorate, comprehensive exam, thesis/dissertation. *Entrance requirements:* For master's, 2 letters of reference, 2-3 page statement of interest, minimum GPA of 3.0 in last 60 hours of undergraduate work and all graduate work; for doctorate, GRE General Test, minimum GPA of 3.5 on last 60 undergraduate hours and all graduate coursework, graduate statistics and social sciences research methods, 3 letters of reference, 2-3 page statement of interest. Additional exam requirements/recommendations for international students: Required—TOEFL (minimum score 550 paper-based; 79 iBT); Recommended—IELTS (minimum score 6.5), TSE (minimum score 53). *Application deadline:* For fall admission, 3/1 priority date for domestic and international students; for spring admission, 11/1 priority date for domestic students, 7/1 priority date for international students; for summer admission, 5/1 priority date for domestic students, 2/1 priority date for international students. Applications are processed on a rolling basis. Application fee: $50 ($75 for international students). Electronic applications accepted. *Expenses:* $8,520 per year full-time in-state, $17,720 per year full-time out-of-state. *Financial support:* In 2017–18, 27 students received support, including 16 teaching assistantships (averaging $26,125 per year); career-related internships or fieldwork, Federal Work-Study, institutionally sponsored loans, scholarships/grants, traineeships, health care benefits, and unspecified assistantships also available. Support available to part-time students. Financial award application deadline: 3/1; financial award applicants required to submit FAFSA. *Faculty research:* Victimology, ethnography, post-humanism health and the environment, domestic violence, social work and disabilities. *Unit head:* Dr. Celia Lo, Chair and Sociology Professor, 940-898-2052, Fax: 940-898-2067, E-mail: sociology@twu.edu. *Application contact:* Korie Hawkins, Associate Director of Admissions, Graduate Recruitment, 940-898-3188, Fax: 940-898-3081, E-mail: admissions@twu.edu.
Website: http://www.twu.edu/sociology/

Tulane University, School of Liberal Arts, Department of Sociology, New Orleans, LA 70118-5669. Offers MA. Terminal master's awarded for partial completion of doctoral program. *Degree requirements:* For master's, thesis. *Entrance requirements:* For master's, GRE General Test, minimum B average in undergraduate course work. Additional exam requirements/recommendations for international students: Required—TOEFL. Electronic applications accepted. *Expenses: Tuition:* Full-time $50,920; part-time $2829 per credit hour. *Required fees:* $2040; $44.50 per credit hour. $580 per term. Tuition and fees vary according to course load, degree level and program.

Université de Montréal, Faculty of Arts and Sciences, Department of Sociology, Montréal, QC H3C 3J7, Canada. Offers M Sc, PhD. *Degree requirements:* For master's, thesis; for doctorate, thesis/dissertation, general exam. *Entrance requirements:* For master's, minimum GPA of 3.0; for doctorate, minimum GPA of 3.5, proficiency in French. Electronic applications accepted. *Faculty research:* Sociological theory, economy, state and social movements, work, social politics and health.

Université du Québec à Montréal, Graduate Programs, Program in Social Intervention, Montréal, QC H3C 3P8, Canada. Offers MA. *Program availability:* Part-time. *Degree requirements:* For master's, thesis. *Entrance requirements:* For master's, appropriate bachelor's degree or equivalent, proficiency in French.

Université du Québec à Montréal, Graduate Programs, Program in Sociology, Montréal, QC H3C 3P8, Canada. Offers MA, PhD. *Program availability:* Part-time. *Degree requirements:* For master's, thesis optional; for doctorate, thesis/dissertation. *Entrance requirements:* For master's, appropriate bachelor's degree or equivalent, proficiency in French; for doctorate, appropriate master's degree or equivalent, proficiency in French.

Université Laval, Faculty of Social Sciences, Department of Sociology, Programs in Sociology, Québec, QC G1K 7P4, Canada. Offers MA, PhD. Terminal master's awarded for partial completion of doctoral program. *Degree requirements:* For master's, thesis; for doctorate, comprehensive exam, thesis/dissertation. *Entrance requirements:* For master's, English exam (comprehension of written English), French exam (for some), knowledge of French; for doctorate, English exam (comprehension of written English), French exam may be required, knowledge of French. Electronic applications accepted.

University at Albany, State University of New York, College of Arts and Sciences, Department of Communication, Albany, NY 12222-0001. Offers communication (MA); sociology and communication (PhD). *Program availability:* Part-time. *Faculty:* 11 full-time (6 women). *Students:* 31 full-time (26 women), 32 part-time (25 women); includes 13 minority (8 Black or African American, non-Hispanic/Latino; 2 Asian, non-Hispanic/Latino; 2 Hispanic/Latino; 1 Two or more races, non-Hispanic/Latino), 9 international. 71 applicants, 54% accepted, 19 enrolled. In 2017, 15 master's awarded. *Degree requirements:* For master's, comprehensive exam, thesis or alternative; for doctorate, comprehensive exam, thesis/dissertation. *Entrance requirements:* For master's, minimum GPA of 3.0; for doctorate, GRE, minimum GPA of 3.0. Additional exam requirements/recommendations for international students: Required—TOEFL (minimum score 550 paper-based). *Application deadline:* For fall admission, 2/20 priority date for domestic students, 5/1 for international students. Applications are processed on a rolling basis. Application fee: $75. Electronic applications accepted. *Expenses:* Tuition, state resident: full-time $10,870; part-time $453 per credit hour. Tuition, nonresident: full-time $22,210; part-time $925 per credit hour. *Required fees:* $84.68 per credit hour. $508.06 per semester. Part-time tuition and fees vary according to course load and program. *Financial support:* Fellowships, teaching assistantships, career-related internships or fieldwork, and institutionally sponsored loans available. Financial award application deadline: 3/1. *Faculty research:* Language and social interaction, campaign communication, media agenda-setting, high-speed management, organizational boundary-spanning. *Unit head:* Annis Golden, Chair, 518-442-4871, Fax: 518-442-3884, E-mail: agolden@albany.edu. *Application contact:* Michael DeRensis, Director, Graduate Admissions, 518-442-3980, Fax: 518-442-3922, E-mail: graduate@albany.edu.
Website: http://www.albany.edu/communication/

University at Albany, State University of New York, College of Arts and Sciences, Department of Sociology, Albany, NY 12222-0001. Offers demography (Certificate);

sociology (MA, PhD); urban policy (Certificate). *Faculty:* 25 full-time (11 women). *Students:* 25 full-time (18 women), 53 part-time (39 women); includes 16 minority (4 Black or African American, non-Hispanic/Latino; 5 Asian, non-Hispanic/Latino; 5 Hispanic/Latino; 2 Two or more races, non-Hispanic/Latino), 22 international. 71 applicants, 37% accepted, 7 enrolled. In 2017, 5 doctorates awarded. Terminal master's awarded for partial completion of doctoral program. *Degree requirements:* For master's, thesis; for doctorate, thesis/dissertation, 2 specialization exams, research tool. *Entrance requirements:* For master's and doctorate, GRE General Test. Additional exam requirements/recommendations for international students: Required—TOEFL. *Application deadline:* For fall admission, 1/15 for domestic students, 5/1 for international students. Applications are processed on a rolling basis. Application fee: $75. Electronic applications accepted. *Expenses:* Tuition, state resident: full-time $10,870; part-time $453 per credit hour. Tuition, nonresident: full-time $22,210; part-time $925 per credit hour. *Required fees:* $84.68 per credit hour. $508.06 per semester. Part-time tuition and fees vary according to course load and program. *Financial support:* Fellowships, research assistantships, teaching assistantships, career-related internships or fieldwork, and Federal Work-Study available. Financial award application deadline: 3/15. *Faculty research:* Gender and equality, crime and deviance, aging, work and organizations, social demography. *Unit head:* Glenn Deane, Chair, 518-442-4666, Fax: 518-442-4936, E-mail: gdeane@albany.edu. *Application contact:* Michael DeRensis, Director, Graduate Admissions, 518-442-3980, Fax: 518-442-3922, E-mail: graduate@albany.edu.
Website: http://www.albany.edu/sociology/index.html

University at Buffalo, the State University of New York, Graduate School, College of Arts and Sciences, Department of Sociology, Buffalo, NY 14260. Offers MA, PhD. *Program availability:* Part-time. *Faculty:* 17 full-time (8 women), 5 part-time/adjunct (4 women). *Students:* 53 full-time (28 women), 7 part-time (3 women); includes 23 minority (4 Black or African American, non-Hispanic/Latino; 1 American Indian or Alaska Native, non-Hispanic/Latino; 16 Asian, non-Hispanic/Latino; 1 Hispanic/Latino; 1 Two or more races, non-Hispanic/Latino). Average age 30. 49 applicants, 69% accepted, 18 enrolled. In 2017, 5 master's, 7 doctorates awarded. Terminal master's awarded for partial completion of doctoral program. *Degree requirements:* For master's, project or thesis; for doctorate, thesis/dissertation, qualifying paper. *Entrance requirements:* For master's and doctorate, GRE General Test. Additional exam requirements/recommendations for international students: Required—TOEFL (minimum score 550 paper-based; 79 iBT), IELTS (minimum score 6.5). *Application deadline:* For fall admission, 8/1 priority date for domestic students, 4/1 priority date for international students. Applications are processed on a rolling basis. Application fee: $75. Electronic applications accepted. *Financial support:* In 2017–18, 15 students received support, including 4 fellowships with full tuition reimbursements available (averaging $6,625 per year), 15 teaching assistantships with full tuition reimbursements available (averaging $14,100 per year); scholarships/grants, health care benefits, and tuition waivers (full) also available. Financial award application deadline: 1/15; financial award applicants required to submit FAFSA. *Faculty research:* Family and the life course, health, law and social policy, social inequalities, work and organizations. *Unit head:* Dr. Debra Street, Chair, 716-645-8475, Fax: 716-645-3934, E-mail: dastreet@buffalo.edu. *Application contact:* Dr. Mary Nell Trautner, Director of Graduate Studies, 716-645-8477, Fax: 716-645-3934, E-mail: trautner@buffalo.edu.

The University of Akron, Graduate School, Buchtel College of Arts and Sciences, Department of Sociology, Akron, OH 44325. Offers MA, PhD. PhD offered jointly with Kent State University. *Program availability:* Part-time. *Faculty:* 10 full-time (6 women), 2 part-time/adjunct (both women). *Students:* 21 full-time (13 women), 8 part-time (6 women); includes 9 minority (5 Black or African American, non-Hispanic/Latino; 3 Asian, non-Hispanic/Latino; 1 Hispanic/Latino), 3 international. Average age 31. 14 applicants, 64% accepted, 5 enrolled. In 2017, 4 master's, 2 doctorates awarded. Terminal master's awarded for partial completion of doctoral program. *Degree requirements:* For master's, thesis optional, oral defense of thesis, paper or oral exam; for doctorate, one foreign language, comprehensive exam, thesis/dissertation. *Entrance requirements:* For master's, GRE General Test, minimum GPA of 3.0, three letters of recommendation, writing sample, statement of purpose outlining educational and career objectives; for doctorate, GRE General Test, minimum GPA of 3.5, three letters of recommendation, writing sample, statement of purpose outlining educational and career objectives. Additional exam requirements/recommendations for international students: Required—TOEFL (minimum score 79 iBT), IELTS (minimum score 6.5). *Application deadline:* For fall admission, 1/15 priority date for domestic and international students. Application fee: $45 ($70 for international students). Electronic applications accepted. *Financial support:* In 2017–18, 19 teaching assistantships with full tuition reimbursements were awarded. *Faculty research:* Medical sociology, inequality, social psychology, criminology, mental health. *Total annual research expenditures:* $21,113. *Unit head:* Dr. Stacey Nofziger, Interim Department Chair, 330-972-5364, E-mail: sn18@uakron.edu. *Application contact:* Dr. John Zipp, Director of Graduate Studies, 330-972-6893, E-mail: jzipp@uakron.edu.
Website: http://www.uakron.edu/sociology/

The University of Alabama at Birmingham, College of Arts and Sciences, Program in Medical Sociology, Birmingham, AL 35294. Offers PhD. *Program availability:* Part-time. *Faculty:* 8 full-time (5 women), 4 part-time/adjunct (2 women). *Students:* 18 full-time (10 women), 4 part-time (all women); includes 7 minority (4 Black or African American, non-Hispanic/Latino; 1 American Indian or Alaska Native, non-Hispanic/Latino; 1 Asian, non-Hispanic/Latino; 1 Hispanic/Latino), 5 international. Average age 28. 14 applicants, 71% accepted, 8 enrolled. In 2017, 3 doctorates awarded. Terminal master's awarded for partial completion of doctoral program. *Degree requirements:* For doctorate, comprehensive exam, thesis/dissertation, student teaching, manuscript review. *Entrance requirements:* For doctorate, GRE, minimum GPA of 3.0 overall and in all previous graduate coursework, 3.2 on last 60 semester hours of baccalaureate work. Additional exam requirements/recommendations for international students: Required—TOEFL (minimum score 80 iBT), IELTS (minimum score 6.5). *Application deadline:* For fall admission, 3/1 for domestic students; for spring admission, 11/1 for domestic students; for summer admission, 4/1 for domestic students. Applications are processed on a rolling basis. Application fee: $60 for international students. Electronic applications accepted. *Financial support:* In 2017–18, 19 students received support, including fellowships with full tuition reimbursements available (averaging $34,000 per year), 1 research assistantship with full tuition reimbursement available (averaging $18,000 per year), 14 teaching assistantships with full tuition reimbursements available (averaging $18,000 per year); traineeships, health care benefits, and unspecified assistantships also available. *Faculty research:* Health disparities; aging and life course; gender, race, and mental health; family sociology; social psychology. *Total annual research expenditures:* $136,595. *Unit head:* Dr. Verna Keith, Department Chair, 205-934-3307, Fax: 205-975-5614, E-mail: vmkeith@uab.edu. *Application contact:* Holly Hebard, Director of Student and Academic Services, 205-934-8227, Fax: 205-934-8413, E-mail: gradschool@uab.edu.
Website: http://www.uab.edu/cas/sociology/graduate-programs

University of Alberta, Faculty of Graduate Studies and Research, Department of Sociology, Edmonton, AB T6G 2E1, Canada. Offers criminal justice (MA); demography (MA, PhD); sociology (MA, PhD). *Program availability:* Part-time. *Degree requirements:* For master's, thesis (for some programs); for doctorate, thesis/dissertation. *Faculty research:* Criminology, knowledge and culture, methods and theory, population studies, stratification.

The University of Arizona, College of Social and Behavioral Sciences, Department of Sociology, Tucson, AZ 85721. Offers MA, PhD. *Degree requirements:* For master's, publishable paper/oral; for doctorate, thesis/dissertation, 2 preliminary exams. *Entrance requirements:* For doctorate, GRE General Test, 3 letters of recommendation, writing samples. Additional exam requirements/recommendations for international students: Required—TOEFL (minimum score 630 paper-based). Electronic applications accepted. *Faculty research:* Organizations, social psychology, social movement, stratification, religion.

University of Arkansas, Graduate School, J. William Fulbright College of Arts and Sciences, Department of Sociology, Fayetteville, AR 72701. Offers MA. *Program availability:* Part-time. In 2017, 6 master's awarded. *Degree requirements:* For master's, thesis. *Application deadline:* For fall admission, 8/1 for domestic students, 4/1 for international students; for spring admission, 12/1 for domestic students, 10/1 for international students; for summer admission, 4/15 for domestic students, 3/1 for international students. Applications are processed on a rolling basis. Application fee: $60. Electronic applications accepted. *Expenses:* Tuition, state resident: full-time $3782. Tuition, nonresident: full-time $10,238. *Financial support:* In 2017–18, 5 research assistantships, 10 teaching assistantships were awarded; fellowships with tuition reimbursements, career-related internships or fieldwork, and Federal Work-Study also available. Support available to part-time students. Financial award application deadline: 4/1; financial award applicants required to submit FAFSA. *Unit head:* Dr. Anna Zajicek, Department Chair, 479-575-3205, Fax: 479-575-7981, E-mail: azajicek@uark.edu. *Application contact:* Shauna Morimoto, Vice-Chair/Director of Graduate Studies, 479-575-3205, Fax: 479-575-7981, E-mail: smorimot@uark.edu.
Website: https://fulbright.uark.edu/departments/sociology/

The University of British Columbia, Faculty of Arts, Department of Sociology, Vancouver, BC V6T 1Z1, Canada. Offers MA, PhD. *Degree requirements:* For master's, thesis; for doctorate, comprehensive exam, thesis/dissertation. *Entrance requirements:* For master's, BA in sociology or equivalent with minimum B+ average in upper-level courses; for doctorate, master's degree in sociology or equivalent. Additional exam requirements/recommendations for international students: Required—TOEFL. Electronic applications accepted. *Expenses:* Contact institution. *Faculty research:* Social and cultural theories and methods; gender, race, class and sexuality; environment economy and development politics; law and social movements.

University of Calgary, Faculty of Graduate Studies, Faculty of Arts, Department of Sociology, Calgary, AB T2N 1N4, Canada. Offers MA, PhD. Terminal master's awarded for partial completion of doctoral program. *Degree requirements:* For master's, thesis, prospectus; for doctorate, comprehensive exam, thesis/dissertation, oral and written candidacy exams, prospectus, qualifying paper. *Entrance requirements:* For master's, minimum GPA of 3.2; for doctorate, minimum GPA of 3.5. Additional exam requirements/recommendations for international students: Required—TOEFL or IELTS. Electronic applications accepted. *Faculty research:* Deviance, gender, medical, religion, ethnicity.

University of California, Berkeley, Graduate Division, College of Letters and Science, Department of Sociology, Berkeley, CA 94720-1500. Offers PhD. *Degree requirements:* For doctorate, thesis/dissertation, qualifying exam. *Entrance requirements:* For doctorate, GRE General Test, minimum GPA of 3.0, sample of academic written work, 3 letters of recommendation. Additional exam requirements/recommendations for international students: Required—TOEFL (minimum score 570 paper-based) or IELTS. Electronic applications accepted. *Faculty research:* Race, gender, political, stratification theory.

University of California, Davis, Graduate Studies, Program in Sociology, Davis, CA 95616. Offers MA, PhD. Terminal master's awarded for partial completion of doctoral program. *Degree requirements:* For master's, written exam; for doctorate, thesis/dissertation, professional paper, qualifying exam. *Entrance requirements:* For master's and doctorate, GRE General Test, minimum GPA of 3.0, writing sample. Additional exam requirements/recommendations for international students: Required—TOEFL (minimum score 550 paper-based). Electronic applications accepted. *Faculty research:* Collective behavior, social movements, comparative sociology, historical sociology, culture development, inequality.

University of California, Irvine, School of Social Sciences, Department of Sociology, Irvine, CA 92697. Offers social networks (PhD); social science (PhD); sociology and social relations (PhD). *Students:* 88 full-time (49 women), 3 part-time (all women); includes 42 minority (6 Black or African American, non-Hispanic/Latino; 10 Asian, non-Hispanic/Latino; 19 Hispanic/Latino; 7 Two or more races, non-Hispanic/Latino), 5 international. Average age 29. 127 applicants, 31% accepted, 22 enrolled. In 2017, 11 doctorates awarded. *Entrance requirements:* For doctorate, GRE General Test, minimum GPA of 3.0. *Application deadline:* For fall admission, 1/15 priority date for domestic students, 1/15 for international students. Applications are processed on a rolling basis. Application fee: $105 ($125 for international students). Electronic applications accepted. *Financial support:* Fellowships, research assistantships with full tuition reimbursements, teaching assistantships, institutionally sponsored loans, traineeships, health care benefits, and unspecified assistantships available. Financial award application deadline: 3/1; financial award applicants required to submit FAFSA. *Faculty research:* Cognitive anthropology, sociology of culture, social structure, family and gender. *Unit head:* Prof. Matt Huffman, Chair, 949-824-5341, E-mail: mhuffman@uci.edu. *Application contact:* Ann Hironaka, Graduate Program Director, 949-824-3504, E-mail: hironaka@uci.edu.
Website: http://www.sociology.uci.edu/

University of California, Los Angeles, Graduate Division, College of Letters and Science, Department of Sociology, Los Angeles, CA 90095. Offers MA, PhD. Terminal master's awarded for partial completion of doctoral program. *Degree requirements:* For master's, thesis or alternative, paper; for doctorate, thesis/dissertation, oral and written qualifying exams. *Entrance requirements:* For doctorate, GRE General Test, bachelor's degree; minimum undergraduate GPA of 3.0 (or its equivalent if letter grade system not used); writing sample. Additional exam requirements/recommendations for international students: Required—TOEFL. Electronic applications accepted.

University of California, Merced, Graduate Division, School of Social Sciences, Humanities and Arts, Merced, CA 95343. Offers cognitive and information sciences (PhD); interdisciplinary humanities (MA, PhD); psychological sciences (MA, PhD); social sciences (MA, PhD); sociology (MA, PhD). *Faculty:* 101 full-time (49 women), 3 part-time/adjunct (1 woman). *Students:* 197 full-time (131 women), 2 part-time (1 woman); includes 86 minority (7 Black or African American, non-Hispanic/Latino; 17 Asian, non-Hispanic/Latino; 55 Hispanic/Latino; 1 Native Hawaiian or other Pacific Islander, non-Hispanic/Latino; 6 Two or more races, non-Hispanic/Latino), 33 international. Average age 31. 190 applicants, 41% accepted, 49 enrolled. In 2017, 7 master's, 10 doctorates awarded. Terminal master's awarded for partial completion of doctoral program. *Degree requirements:* For master's, variable foreign language requirement, comprehensive exam, thesis or alternative; for doctorate, variable foreign language requirement, comprehensive exam, thesis/dissertation. *Entrance requirements:* For master's and

doctorate, GRE. Additional exam requirements/recommendations for international students: Required—TOEFL (minimum score 550 paper-based; 80 iBT); Recommended—IELTS (minimum score 7). *Application deadline:* For fall admission, 1/15 for domestic and international students. Application fee: $90 ($110 for international students). Electronic applications accepted. *Expenses:* Tuition, state resident: full-time $11,502; part-time $5751 per semester. Tuition, nonresident: full-time $26,604; part-time $13,302 per semester. *Required fees:* $564 per semester. *Financial support:* In 2017–18, 167 students received support, including 17 fellowships with full tuition reimbursements available (averaging $23,250 per year), 13 research assistantships with full tuition reimbursements available (averaging $15,387 per year), 162 teaching assistantships with full tuition reimbursements available (averaging $16,103 per year); scholarships/grants, traineeships, and health care benefits also available. Financial award application deadline: 1/15. *Faculty research:* Social inequality, critical race and ethnic studies, public health and health sciences, cognitive science and language acquisition, political institutions, literature, cultural studies, anthropology, art history, ethnomusicology, history. *Total annual research expenditures:* $1.2 million. *Unit head:* Dr. Jill Robbins, Dean, 209-228-7843, E-mail: jillrobbins@ucmerced.edu. *Application contact:* Tsu Ya, Director of Admissions and Academic Services, 209-228-4521, Fax: 209-228-6906, E-mail: tya@ucmerced.edu.

University of California, Riverside, Graduate Division, Department of Sociology, Riverside, CA 92521. Offers MA, PhD. *Faculty:* 19 full-time (10 women). *Students:* 45 full-time (24 women). 43 applicants, 33% accepted, 8 enrolled. *Degree requirements:* For doctorate, thesis/dissertation, 1 quarter of teaching experience, professional paper. *Entrance requirements:* For doctorate, GRE General Test, minimum GPA of 3.2. Additional exam requirements/recommendations for international students: Required—TOEFL (minimum score 550 paper-based; 80 iBT). *Application deadline:* For fall admission, 12/5 for domestic and international students. Application fee: $80 ($100 for international students). Electronic applications accepted. *Expenses:* Tuition, state resident: full-time $5746. Tuition, nonresident: full-time $10,780. Tuition and fees vary according to campus/location and program. *Financial support:* In 2017–18, 11 students received support. Fellowships with tuition reimbursements available, research assistantships, teaching assistantships with partial tuition reimbursements available, career-related internships or fieldwork, institutionally sponsored loans, health care benefits, and tuition waivers (full and partial) available. Financial award application deadline: 12/5; financial award applicants required to submit FAFSA. *Faculty research:* Crime/deviance, race/ethnic relations, family/gender, political economy/globalization, theory. *Unit head:* Dr. Jan E. Stets, Professor and Co-Chair, 951-827-3424, Fax: 951-827-3330, E-mail: jan.stets@ucr.edu. *Application contact:* Anna M. Wire, Graduate Affairs, 951-827-5145, Fax: 951-827-3330, E-mail: anna.wire@ucr.edu.
Website: http://www.sociology.ucr.edu/

University of California, San Diego, Graduate Division, Department of Sociology, La Jolla, CA 92093. Offers PhD. *Students:* 53 full-time (32 women). 146 applicants, 18% accepted, 11 enrolled. In 2017, 7 doctorates awarded. *Degree requirements:* For doctorate, comprehensive exam, thesis/dissertation. *Entrance requirements:* For doctorate, GRE General Test, minimum GPA of 3.0, writing sample, statement of purpose, 3 letters of recommendation. Additional exam requirements/recommendations for international students: Required—TOEFL (minimum score 550 paper-based; 80 iBT), IELTS (minimum score 7). *Application deadline:* For fall admission, 1/11 for domestic students. Application fee: $105 ($125 for international students). Electronic applications accepted. *Financial support:* Fellowships, teaching assistantships, scholarships/grants, and readerships, research and travel funds available. Financial award applicants required to submit FAFSA. *Faculty research:* Comparative and historical sociology; sociology of culture; sociology of science, technology, and medicine; social inequalities. *Unit head:* Isaac Martin, Chair, 858-534-5589, E-mail: iwmartin@ucsd.edu. *Application contact:* Teresa Eckert, Graduate Coordinator, 858-534-4627, E-mail: socphd@ucsd.edu.
Website: http://sociology.ucsd.edu/

University of California, San Francisco, Graduate Division, School of Nursing, Department of Social and Behavioral Sciences, San Francisco, CA 94143. Offers sociology (PhD). *Degree requirements:* For doctorate, one foreign language, thesis/dissertation. *Entrance requirements:* For doctorate, GRE General Test, statement of purpose, official transcripts, two letters of recommendation, scholarly writing example, curriculum vitae or resume. Additional exam requirements/recommendations for international students: Required—TOEFL (minimum score 84 iBT). *Faculty research:* Urban social relations; sociology of women's role in healing; sociology of work, occupations, and professions.

University of California, Santa Barbara, Graduate Division, College of Letters and Sciences, Division of Social Sciences, Department of Sociology, Santa Barbara, CA 93106-9430. Offers interdisciplinary emphasis: Black studies (PhD); interdisciplinary emphasis: environment and society (PhD); interdisciplinary emphasis: feminist studies (PhD); interdisciplinary emphasis: global studies (PhD); interdisciplinary emphasis: language, interaction and social organization (PhD); interdisciplinary emphasis: quantitative methods in the social sciences (PhD); interdisciplinary emphasis: technology and society (PhD); sociology (PhD); MA/PhD. Terminal master's awarded for partial completion of doctoral program. *Degree requirements:* For doctorate, comprehensive exam, thesis/dissertation. *Entrance requirements:* For doctorate, GRE General Test. Additional exam requirements/recommendations for international students: Required—TOEFL (minimum score 550 paper-based; 80 iBT), IELTS (minimum score 7). Electronic applications accepted. *Faculty research:* Gender and sexualities, race/ethnicity, social movements, conversation analysis, global sociology.

University of California, Santa Cruz, Division of Graduate Studies, Division of Social Sciences, Department of Sociology, Santa Cruz, CA 95064. Offers PhD. *Degree requirements:* For doctorate, thesis/dissertation, qualifying exam. *Entrance requirements:* For doctorate, GRE General Test. Additional exam requirements/recommendations for international students: Required—TOEFL (minimum score 550 paper-based; 83 iBT); Recommended—IELTS (minimum score 8). Electronic applications accepted. *Faculty research:* Globalization, political economy, and environment; inequality and identity; culture, knowledge, and power.

University of Central Florida, College of Sciences, Department of Sociology, Orlando, FL 32816. Offers applied sociology (MA); sociology (PhD). *Program availability:* Part-time, evening/weekend. *Students:* 48 full-time (36 women), 18 part-time (13 women); includes 26 minority (9 Black or African American, non-Hispanic/Latino; 2 Asian, non-Hispanic/Latino; 15 Hispanic/Latino), 1 international. Average age 31. 41 applicants, 71% accepted, 22 enrolled. In 2017, 15 master's, 8 doctorates awarded. *Degree requirements:* For master's, thesis or alternative; for doctorate, comprehensive exam, thesis/dissertation. *Entrance requirements:* For master's, GRE General Test, minimum GPA of 3.0 in last 60 hours of course work, letters of recommendation, personal statement; for doctorate, GRE General Test, master's degree in related field from accredited institution, letters of recommendation, personal statement, resume, writing sample. Additional exam requirements/recommendations for international students: Required—TOEFL. Application fee: $30. Electronic applications accepted. *Expenses:* Tuition, state resident: part-time $288.16 per credit hour. Tuition, nonresident: part-time $1073.31 per credit hour. Tuition and fees vary according to program. *Financial support:* In 2017–18, 34 students received support, including 13 fellowships with partial tuition reimbursements available (averaging $8,293 per year), 9 research assistantships with partial tuition reimbursements available (averaging $8,295 per year), 26 teaching assistantships with partial tuition reimbursements available (averaging $12,868 per year); career-related internships or fieldwork, Federal Work-Study, institutionally sponsored loans, health care benefits, tuition waivers (partial), and unspecified assistantships also available. Financial award application deadline: 3/1; financial award applicants required to submit FAFSA. *Faculty research:* Criminology/domestic violence, social inequalities, health, families and communities, social and behavioral sciences. *Unit head:* Dr. Elizabeth Mustaine, Chair, 407-823-6568, E-mail: elizabeth.mustaine@ucf.edu. *Application contact:* Associate Director, Graduate Admissions, 407-823-2766, Fax: 407-823-6442, E-mail: gradadmissions@ucf.edu.
Website: http://sociology.cos.ucf.edu/

University of Central Missouri, The Graduate School, Warrensburg, MO 64093. Offers accountancy (MA); accounting (MBA); applied mathematics (MS); aviation safety (MA); biology (MS); business administration (MBA); career and technical education leadership (MS); college student personnel administration (MS); communication (MA); computer science (MS); counseling (MS); criminal justice (MS); educational leadership (Ed D); educational technology (MS); elementary and early childhood education (MSE); English (MA); environmental studies (MA); finance (MBA); history (MA); human services/educational technology (Ed S); human services/learning resources (Ed S); human services/professional counseling (Ed S); industrial hygiene (MS); industrial management (MS); information systems (MBA); information technology (MS); kinesiology (MS); library science and information services (MS); literacy education (MSE); marketing (MBA); mathematics (MS); music (MA); occupational safety management (MS); psychology (MS); rural family nursing (MS); school administration (MSE); social gerontology (MS); sociology (MA); special education (MSE); speech language pathology (MS); superintendency (Ed S); teaching (MAT); teaching English as a second language (MA); technology (MS); technology management (PhD); theatre (MA). *Program availability:* Part-time, 100% online, blended/hybrid learning. *Faculty:* 337 full-time (145 women), 41 part-time/adjunct (28 women). *Students:* 785 full-time (398 women), 1,633 part-time (1,063 women); includes 231 minority (102 Black or African American, non-Hispanic/Latino; 4 American Indian or Alaska Native, non-Hispanic/Latino; 16 Asian, non-Hispanic/Latino; 52 Hispanic/Latino; 57 Two or more races, non-Hispanic/Latino), 692 international. Average age 30. In 2017, 2,605 master's, 122 other advanced degrees awarded. *Degree requirements:* For master's and Ed S, comprehensive exam (for some programs), thesis (for some programs). *Entrance requirements:* Additional exam requirements/recommendations for international students: Required—TOEFL (minimum score 550 paper-based; 79 iBT). *Application deadline:* For fall admission, 6/1 priority date for domestic and international students; for spring admission, 10/1 priority date for domestic and international students; for summer admission, 4/1 priority date for domestic and international students. Applications are processed on a rolling basis. Application fee: $30 ($75 for international students). Electronic applications accepted. *Expenses:* Tuition, state resident: full-time $8771; part-time $292.35 per credit hour. Tuition, nonresident: full-time $17,541; part-time $584.70 per credit hour. *Required fees:* $372; $24.78 per credit hour. *Financial support:* In 2017–18, 99 students received support. Research assistantships, teaching assistantships, career-related internships or fieldwork, Federal Work-Study, scholarships/grants, and administrative and laboratory assistantships available. Support available to part-time students. Financial award application deadline: 3/1; financial award applicants required to submit FAFSA. *Unit head:* Shellie Hewitt, Director of Graduate and International Student Services, 660-543-4621, Fax: 660-543-4778, E-mail: hewitt@ucmo.edu. *Application contact:* 660-543-4621, E-mail: admit_intl@ucmo.edu.
Website: http://www.ucmo.edu/graduate/

University of Central Oklahoma, The Jackson College of Graduate Studies, College of Liberal Arts, Department of Sociology, Gerontology, and Substance Abuse Studies, Edmond, OK 73034-5209. Offers gerontology (MA); substance abuse studies (MA), including substance abuse studies. *Program availability:* Part-time. *Faculty:* 8 full-time (6 women), 6 part-time/adjunct (3 women). *Students:* 31 full-time (25 women), 30 part-time (23 women); includes 25 minority (14 Black or African American, non-Hispanic/Latino; 1 American Indian or Alaska Native, non-Hispanic/Latino; 2 Asian, non-Hispanic/Latino; 3 Hispanic/Latino; 5 Two or more races, non-Hispanic/Latino), 3 international. Average age 39. 39 applicants, 92% accepted, 22 enrolled. In 2017, 21 master's awarded. *Degree requirements:* For master's, variable foreign language requirement, comprehensive exam (for some programs), thesis (for some programs). *Entrance requirements:* Additional exam requirements/recommendations for international students: Required—TOEFL (minimum score 550 paper-based; 79 iBT), IELTS (minimum score 6.5). *Application deadline:* For fall admission, 7/15 for international students; for spring admission, 11/15 for international students. Applications are processed on a rolling basis. Application fee: $60. Electronic applications accepted. *Expenses:* Tuition, state resident: full-time $5375; part-time $268.75 per credit hour. Tuition, nonresident: full-time $13,295; part-time $664.75 per credit hour. *Required fees:* $626; $31.30 per credit hour. One-time fee: $50. Tuition and fees vary according to program. *Financial support:* In 2017–18, 10 students received support, including 2 research assistantships with partial tuition reimbursements available (averaging $2,958 per year), 1 teaching assistantship with partial tuition reimbursement available (averaging $11,830 per year); career-related internships or fieldwork, scholarships/grants, tuition waivers (partial), and unspecified assistantships also available. Financial award application deadline: 3/31; financial award applicants required to submit FAFSA. *Unit head:* Dr. Douglas Reed, Chair, 405-974-5540, Fax: 405-974-3823, E-mail: gradcoll@uco.edu.
Website: http://www.uco.edu/la/soc-gero-sas/index.asp

University of Chicago, Division of the Social Sciences, Department of Sociology, Chicago, IL 60637. Offers PhD. *Faculty:* 27. *Students:* 95 full-time (44 women); includes 24 minority (6 Black or African American, non-Hispanic/Latino; 4 Asian, non-Hispanic/Latino; 10 Hispanic/Latino; 4 Two or more races, non-Hispanic/Latino), 37 international. Average age 30. 169 applicants, 19% accepted, 14 enrolled. In 2017, 14 doctorates awarded. *Degree requirements:* For doctorate, one foreign language, comprehensive exam, thesis/dissertation, 2 field exams. *Entrance requirements:* For doctorate, GRE General Test, 3 letters of recommendation, statement of purpose, transcripts, resume or curriculum vitae, writing sample (dependent on department). Additional exam requirements/recommendations for international students: Required—TOEFL (minimum score 104 iBT), IELTS (minimum score 7). *Application deadline:* For fall admission, 12/1 for domestic and international students. Application fee: $90. Electronic applications accepted. *Financial support:* In 2017–18, 14 students received support, including 14 fellowships with full tuition reimbursements available (averaging $27,000 per year); career-related internships or fieldwork, Federal Work-Study, institutionally sponsored loans, scholarships/grants, and health care benefits also available. Financial award application deadline: 12/1. *Unit head:* Karin Knorr Cetina, Chair, 773-834-3312, E-mail: knorr@uchicago.edu. *Application contact:* Office of the Dean of Students, 773-702-8415, E-mail: ssd-admissions@uchicago.edu.
Website: http://sociology.uchicago.edu

University of Cincinnati, Graduate School, McMicken College of Arts and Sciences, Department of Sociology, Cincinnati, OH 45221. Offers MA, PhD. *Program availability:*

Part-time. *Faculty:* 12 full-time (5 women). *Students:* 24 full-time (14 women), 16 part-time (8 women); includes 14 minority (8 Black or African American, non-Hispanic/Latino; 4 Asian, non-Hispanic/Latino; 2 Two or more races, non-Hispanic/Latino), 7 international. Average age 28. 43 applicants, 30% accepted, 7 enrolled. In 2017, 6 master's, 3 doctorates awarded. Terminal master's awarded for partial completion of doctoral program. *Degree requirements:* For master's, comprehensive exam (for some programs), thesis (for some programs); for doctorate, comprehensive exam, thesis/dissertation. *Entrance requirements:* For master's and doctorate, GRE General Test. Additional exam requirements/recommendations for international students: Required—TOEFL (minimum score 600 paper-based; 100 iBT), IELTS (minimum score 7). *Application deadline:* For fall admission, 4/1 for domestic and international students. Application fee: $65 ($70 for international students). Electronic applications accepted. *Expenses:* Contact institution. *Financial support:* In 2017–18, 21 students received support, including 1 fellowship with full tuition reimbursement available (averaging $20,600 per year), 10 research assistantships with full tuition reimbursements available (averaging $18,000 per year), 10 teaching assistantships with full tuition reimbursements available (averaging $18,000 per year); institutionally sponsored loans, scholarships/grants, tuition waivers (full), and unspecified assistantships also available. Financial award application deadline: 1/15. *Faculty research:* Urban, race, education, health, and methods. *Total annual research expenditures:* $72,600. *Unit head:* Dr. Steven Carlton-Ford, Department Head, 513-556-4716, Fax: 513-556-0057, E-mail: carltosl@ucmail.uc.edu. *Application contact:* Dr. Jeffrey M. Timberlake, Graduate Program Director, 513-556-4704, Fax: 513-556-0057, E-mail: timberjm@ucmail.uc.edu. Website: http://www.artsci.uc.edu/sociology

University of Colorado Boulder, Graduate School, College of Arts and Sciences, Department of Sociology, Boulder, CO 80309. Offers PhD. *Faculty:* 22 full-time (13 women). *Students:* 59 full-time (44 women), 1 (woman) part-time; includes 10 minority (1 Asian, non-Hispanic/Latino; 5 Hispanic/Latino; 4 Two or more races, non-Hispanic/Latino), 4 international. Average age 31. 77 applicants, 27% accepted, 10 enrolled. In 2017, 3 doctorates awarded. *Degree requirements:* For doctorate, comprehensive exam, thesis/dissertation. *Entrance requirements:* For doctorate, GRE General Test, GRE Subject Test, minimum undergraduate GPA of 2.75. *Application deadline:* For fall admission, 12/1 for domestic students; for spring admission, 12/1 for domestic students. Application fee: $60 ($80 for international students). Electronic applications accepted. Application fee is waived when completed online. *Financial support:* In 2017–18, 148 students received support, including 30 fellowships (averaging $10,960 per year), 16 research assistantships with full and partial tuition reimbursements available (averaging $23,834 per year), 38 teaching assistantships with full and partial tuition reimbursements available (averaging $20,486 per year); institutionally sponsored loans, scholarships/grants, health care benefits, and unspecified assistantships also available. Financial award application deadline: 2/15; financial award applicants required to submit FAFSA. *Faculty research:* Sociology; minorities and disadvantaged; demography; racism/race relations; sociology of sex and gender. *Total annual research expenditures:* $1.7 million. *Application contact:* E-mail: sociology@colorado.edu. Website: http://SOCSCI.colorado.edu/SOC/

University of Colorado Colorado Springs, College of Letters, Arts and Sciences, Department of Sociology, Colorado Springs, CO 80918. Offers MA. *Program availability:* Part-time, blended/hybrid learning. *Faculty:* 13 full-time (7 women), 9 part-time/adjunct (8 women). *Students:* 1 (woman) full-time, 22 part-time (16 women); includes 7 minority (1 Black or African American, non-Hispanic/Latino; 1 American Indian or Alaska Native, non-Hispanic/Latino; 4 Hispanic/Latino; 1 Two or more races, non-Hispanic/Latino). Average age 38. 24 applicants, 96% accepted, 6 enrolled. In 2017, 12 master's awarded. *Degree requirements:* For master's, thesis optional. *Entrance requirements:* For master's, minimum GPA of 3.0 or GRE. Additional exam requirements/recommendations for international students: Recommended—TOEFL (minimum score 550 paper-based; 100 iBT), IELTS (minimum score 7). *Application deadline:* For fall admission, 2/1 priority date for domestic and international students; for spring admission, 4/15 priority date for domestic and international students; for summer admission, 11/15 for domestic and international students. Applications are processed on a rolling basis. Application fee: $60 ($100 for international students). Electronic applications accepted. *Expenses:* $10,350 per year resident tuition, $20,935 nonresident, $11,961 nonresidential online; annual costs vary depending on program, course-load, and residency status. *Financial support:* In 2017–18, 5 students received support. Career-related internships or fieldwork, Federal Work-Study, scholarships/grants, and unspecified assistantships available. Support available to part-time students. Financial award application deadline: 3/1; financial award applicants required to submit FAFSA. *Faculty research:* Intersectionality, culture, justice studies and globalization and development. *Unit head:* Dr. Edwardo Portillos, Associate Professor/Director, Graduate Studies, 719-255-4143, Fax: 719-255-4450, E-mail: eportill@uccs.edu. *Application contact:* Rosemary Kelbel, Program Assistant, 719-255-4153, Fax: 719-255-4450, E-mail: rkelbel@uccs.edu. Website: http://www.uccs.edu/~soc/

University of Colorado Denver, College of Liberal Arts and Sciences, Department of Sociology, Denver, CO 80217. Offers MA. *Program availability:* Part-time, evening/weekend. *Degree requirements:* For master's, 36 credit hours, project or thesis. *Entrance requirements:* For master's, GRE (recommended), minimum combined GPA of 3.3 for all courses taken at undergraduate or graduate level, 3.5 for all sociology courses; writing sample; statement of intent; three letters of recommendation. Additional exam requirements/recommendations for international students: Required—TOEFL (minimum score 537 paper-based; 75 iBT); Recommended—IELTS (minimum score 6.5). Electronic applications accepted. *Faculty research:* Domestic violence, elderly and housing, family demography, immigrants and immigration, social determinants of health behaviors.

University of Colorado Denver, College of Liberal Arts and Sciences, Program in Humanities, Denver, CO 80217. Offers community health science (MSS); humanities (MH); international studies (MSS); philosophy and theory (MH); social justice (MSS); society and the environment (MSS); visual studies (MH); women's and gender studies (MSS). *Program availability:* Part-time, evening/weekend. *Degree requirements:* For master's, 36 credit hours, project or thesis. *Entrance requirements:* For master's, writing sample, statement of purpose/letter of intent, three letters of recommendation. Additional exam requirements/recommendations for international students: Required—TOEFL (minimum score 537 paper-based; 75 iBT); Recommended—IELTS (minimum score 6.5). Electronic applications accepted. *Faculty research:* Women and gender in the classical Mediterranean, communication theory and democracy, relationship between psychology and philosophy.

University of Connecticut, Graduate School, College of Liberal Arts and Sciences, Department of Sociology, Storrs, CT 06269. Offers MA, PhD. Terminal master's awarded for partial completion of doctoral program. *Degree requirements:* For master's, comprehensive exam; for doctorate, thesis/dissertation. *Entrance requirements:* For master's and doctorate, GRE General Test. Additional exam requirements/recommendations for international students: Required—TOEFL (minimum score 550 paper-based). Electronic applications accepted.

University of Delaware, College of Arts and Sciences, Department of Sociology and Criminal Justice, Newark, DE 19716. Offers criminology (MA, PhD); sociology (MA, PhD). *Degree requirements:* For master's, thesis; for doctorate, comprehensive exam, thesis/dissertation. *Entrance requirements:* For master's and doctorate, GRE, 3 letters of recommendation. Additional exam requirements/recommendations for international students: Required—TOEFL. Electronic applications accepted. *Faculty research:* Sex and gender, criminology/deviance, theory, methods, collective behavior.

University of Florida, Graduate School, College of Liberal Arts and Sciences, Department of Sociology and Criminology and Law, Gainesville, FL 32611. Offers criminology, law, and society (MA, PhD); sociology (MA, PhD), including sociology, tropical conservation and development, women's and gender studies (PhD); MA/JD. *Program availability:* Part-time. Terminal master's awarded for partial completion of doctoral program. *Degree requirements:* For master's, thesis optional; for doctorate, comprehensive exam, thesis/dissertation. *Entrance requirements:* For master's and doctorate, GRE, minimum GPA of 3.0. Additional exam requirements/recommendations for international students: Required—TOEFL (minimum score 550 paper-based; 80 iBT), IELTS (minimum score 6). Electronic applications accepted. *Faculty research:* Law and society, juvenile justice, criminal investigation procedures, deviance, biosocial criminology, environmental sociology, comparative race and ethnic studies, health and aging, families and gender.

University of Georgia, Franklin College of Arts and Sciences, Department of Sociology, Athens, GA 30602. Offers MA, PhD. *Degree requirements:* For master's, thesis; for doctorate, thesis/dissertation. *Entrance requirements:* For master's and doctorate, GRE General Test. Additional exam requirements/recommendations for international students: Required—TOEFL. Electronic applications accepted. *Faculty research:* Race, deviance, gender, culture.

University of Guelph, Graduate Studies, College of Social and Applied Human Sciences, Department of Sociology and Anthropology, Guelph, ON N1G 2W1, Canada. Offers anthropology (MA); crime and criminal justice policy (MA); sociology (MA, PhD). *Degree requirements:* For master's, thesis or major paper; for doctorate, comprehensive exam, thesis/dissertation. *Entrance requirements:* For master's, minimum B+ average during previous 2 years of course work, honors BA or equivalent; for doctorate, must have an MA in Sociology, must have 80% or higher in graduate level studies. Additional exam requirements/recommendations for international students: Required—TOEFL (minimum score 550 paper-based; 89 iBT) or IELTS (minimum score 6.5). Electronic applications accepted. *Faculty research:* Rural and development sociology; education, employment, and the workplace; race, ethnicity, and native studies; criminology and deviance; social psychology.

University of Hawaii at Manoa, Office of Graduate Education, College of Social Sciences, Department of Sociology, Honolulu, HI 96822. Offers MA, PhD. *Program availability:* Part-time. *Degree requirements:* For master's, thesis optional; for doctorate, comprehensive exam, thesis/dissertation. *Entrance requirements:* For master's and doctorate, GRE General Test. Additional exam requirements/recommendations for international students: Required—TOEFL (minimum score 500 paper-based; 61 iBT), IELTS (minimum score 5). *Faculty research:* Comparative sociology of Asia; population studies; crime, law, and deviance; health; aging and medical sociology.

University of Houston, College of Liberal Arts and Social Sciences, Department of Sociology, Houston, TX 77204. Offers MA. *Program availability:* Part-time. *Degree requirements:* For master's, thesis, 4 core courses, 36 hours. *Entrance requirements:* For master's, GRE (minimum score 1000), minimum GPA of 3.0; letters of recommendation, resume. Additional exam requirements/recommendations for international students: Required—TOEFL (minimum score 550 paper-based; 79 iBT). Electronic applications accepted. *Faculty research:* Immigration, public education, HIV/AIDS.

University of Houston–Clear Lake, School of Human Sciences and Humanities, Programs in Human Sciences, Houston, TX 77058-1002. Offers behavioral sciences (MA), including criminology, cross cultural studies, general psychology, sociology; clinical psychology (MA); criminology (MA); cross cultural studies (MA); family therapy (MA); fitness and human performance (MA); school psychology (MA). *Accreditation:* AAMFT/COAMFTE. *Program availability:* Part-time, evening/weekend, online learning. *Degree requirements:* For master's, thesis or alternative. *Entrance requirements:* For master's, GRE General Test. Additional exam requirements/recommendations for international students: Required—TOEFL (minimum score 550 paper-based). Electronic applications accepted. *Faculty research:* Smoking cessation, adolescent sexuality, white collar crime, serial murder, human factors/human computer interaction.

University of Illinois at Chicago, College of Liberal Arts and Sciences, Department of Sociology, Chicago, IL 60607-7128. Offers MA, PhD. Terminal master's awarded for partial completion of doctoral program. *Degree requirements:* For master's, comprehensive exam, thesis; for doctorate, thesis/dissertation, qualifying exam. *Entrance requirements:* For master's and doctorate, GRE General Test, minimum GPA of 3.0. Additional exam requirements/recommendations for international students: Required—TOEFL. Electronic applications accepted. *Faculty research:* Social psychology, social organization, applied sociology, demography and human ecology.

University of Illinois at Urbana–Champaign, Graduate College, College of Liberal Arts and Sciences, Department of Sociology, Champaign, IL 61820. Offers MA, PhD.

University of Indianapolis, Graduate Programs, College of Arts and Sciences, Department of Social Sciences, Indianapolis, IN 46227-3697. Offers applied sociology (MA). *Program availability:* Part-time, evening/weekend. *Degree requirements:* For master's, thesis optional. *Entrance requirements:* For master's, GRE Subject Test, minimum GPA of 3.0, letter of intent, 3 letters of recommendation. Additional exam requirements/recommendations for international students: Required—TOEFL (minimum score 550 paper-based). Electronic applications accepted.

The University of Iowa, Graduate College, College of Liberal Arts and Sciences, Department of Sociology, Iowa City, IA 52242-1316. Offers MA, PhD. *Degree requirements:* For master's, thesis optional, exam; for doctorate, comprehensive exam, thesis/dissertation. *Entrance requirements:* For master's and doctorate, GRE General Test, minimum GPA of 3.0. Additional exam requirements/recommendations for international students: Required—TOEFL (minimum score 600 paper-based; 100 iBT). Electronic applications accepted.

The University of Kansas, Graduate Studies, College of Liberal Arts and Sciences, Department of Sociology, Lawrence, KS 66045. Offers PhD. *Program availability:* Part-time. *Students:* 37 full-time (18 women), 1 (woman) part-time. Average age 32. 24 applicants, 58% accepted, 9 enrolled. In 2017, 5 doctorates awarded. *Entrance requirements:* For doctorate, GRE General Test, current resume, statement of academic interests and professional goals, writing sample of academic work, three recommendation letters, official transcripts. Additional exam requirements/recommendations for international students: Required—TOEFL or IELTS. *Application deadline:* For fall admission, 12/15 for domestic and international students. Application fee: $65 ($85 for international students). Electronic applications accepted. *Financial support:* Fellowships, research assistantships, teaching assistantships, scholarships/grants, and unspecified assistantships available. Financial award application deadline:

12/15. *Faculty research:* Culture, demography, environment, gender and sexuality, globalization, immigration and migration, life course, aging and family, medicine and health, political sociology, race and ethnicity, religion, social inequality and stratification, social theory. *Unit head:* Kelly H. Chong, Director, 785-864-4111, Fax: 785-864-5280, E-mail: socdept@ku.edu. *Application contact:* Corinne Butler, Graduate Secretary, 785-864-9419, Fax: 785-864-5280, E-mail: cleg@ku.edu.
Website: http://www.sociology.ku.edu/

University of Kentucky, Graduate School, College of Arts and Sciences, Program in Sociology, Lexington, KY 40506-0032. Offers MA, MS, PhD. *Program availability:* Part-time. *Degree requirements:* For master's, comprehensive exam, thesis optional; for doctorate, comprehensive exam, thesis/dissertation. *Entrance requirements:* For master's, GRE General Test, minimum undergraduate GPA of 2.75; for doctorate, GRE General Test, minimum graduate GPA of 3.0. Additional exam requirements/recommendations for international students: Required—TOEFL (minimum score 550 paper-based). Electronic applications accepted. *Faculty research:* Work organizations, social inequalities, rural sociology, criminology/deviance, medical sociology.

University of Lethbridge, School of Graduate Studies, Lethbridge, AB T1K 3M4, Canada. Offers addictions counseling (M Sc); agricultural biotechnology (M Sc); agricultural studies (M Sc, MA); anthropology (MA); archaeology (M Sc, MA); art (MA, MFA); biochemistry (M Sc); biological sciences (M Sc); biomolecular science (PhD); biosystems and biodiversity (PhD); Canadian studies (MA); chemistry (M Sc); computer science (M Sc); computer science and geographical information science (M Sc); counseling (MC); counseling psychology (M Ed); dramatic arts (MA); earth, space, and physical science (PhD); economics (MA); education (MA, PhD); educational leadership (M Ed); English (MA); environmental science (M Sc); evolution and behavior (PhD); exercise science (M Sc); French (MA); French/German (MA); French/Spanish (MA); general education (M Ed); geography (M Sc, MA); German (MA); health sciences (M Sc); individualized multidisciplinary (M Sc, MA); kinesiology (M Sc, MA); management (M Sc), including accounting, finance, human resource management and labor relations, information systems, international management, marketing, policy and strategy; mathematics (M Sc); music (M Mus, MA); Native American studies (MA); neuroscience (M Sc, PhD); new media (MA, MFA); nursing (M Sc, MN); philosophy (MA); physics (M Sc); political science (MA); psychology (M Sc, MA); religious studies (MA); sociology (MA); theatre and dramatic arts (MFA); theoretical and computational science (PhD); urban and regional studies (MA); women and gender studies (MA). *Program availability:* Part-time, evening/weekend. *Degree requirements:* For master's, thesis (for some programs); for doctorate, comprehensive exam, thesis/dissertation. *Entrance requirements:* For master's, GMAT (for M Sc in management), bachelor's degree in related field, minimum GPA of 3.0 during previous 20 graded semester courses, 2 years' teaching or related experience (M Ed); for doctorate, master's degree, minimum graduate GPA of 3.5. Additional exam requirements/recommendations for international students: Required—TOEFL (minimum score 580 paper-based; 93 iBT). Electronic applications accepted. *Faculty research:* Movement and brain plasticity, gibberellin physiology, photosynthesis, carbon cycling, molecular properties of main-group ring components.

University of Louisville, Graduate School, College of Arts and Sciences, Department of Sociology, Louisville, KY 40292. Offers applied sociology (PhD); sociology (MA). *Program availability:* Part-time, evening/weekend, 100% online. *Faculty:* 15 full-time (9 women), 4 part-time/adjunct (3 women). *Students:* 18 full-time (5 women), 7 part-time (6 women); includes 4 minority (3 Black or African American, non-Hispanic/Latino; 1 Hispanic/Latino), 1 international. Average age 35. 13 applicants, 69% accepted, 6 enrolled. In 2017, 3 master's, 2 doctorates awarded. Terminal master's awarded for partial completion of doctoral program. *Degree requirements:* For master's, thesis (for some programs); for doctorate, comprehensive exam, thesis/dissertation. *Entrance requirements:* For master's, official transcripts, three references. Additional exam requirements/recommendations for international students: Required—TOEFL (minimum score 550 paper-based; 79 iBT), IELTS (minimum score 6.5). *Application deadline:* For fall admission, 6/1 for domestic and international students; for spring admission, 11/1 for domestic and international students. Application fee: $65. Electronic applications accepted. *Expenses:* Contact institution. *Financial support:* In 2017–18, fellowships (averaging $18,000 per year), 2 research assistantships with full tuition reimbursements (averaging $18,000 per year), 9 teaching assistantships with full tuition reimbursements (averaging $18,000 per year) were awarded; tuition waivers (full) also available. Financial award application deadline: 1/5. *Faculty research:* Applied sociology/evaluation research; family; sex and gender; race, class, and gender; medical sociology. *Total annual research expenditures:* $6,821. *Unit head:* Dr. Ryan D. Schroeder, Associate Professor and Chair, 502-852-8010, Fax: 502-852-0099, E-mail: ryan.schroeder@louisville.edu. *Application contact:* Jonetta Weber, Director of Academic Services, 502-852-8028, Fax: 502-852-0099, E-mail: jonettaweber@louisville.edu.
Website: http://louisville.edu/sociology

The University of Manchester, School of Social Sciences, Manchester, United Kingdom. Offers ethnographic documentary (M Phil); interdisciplinary study of culture (PhD); philosophy (PhD); politics (PhD); social anthropology (PhD); social anthropology with visual media (PhD); social change (PhD); social statistics (PhD); sociology (PhD); visual anthropology (M Phil).

University of Manitoba, Faculty of Graduate Studies, Faculty of Arts, Department of Sociology, Winnipeg, MB R3T 2N2, Canada. Offers MA, PhD. *Degree requirements:* For master's, thesis.

University of Maryland, Baltimore County, The Graduate School, College of Arts, Humanities and Social Sciences, Department of Sociology, Anthropology, and Health Administration and Policy, Program in Applied Sociology, Baltimore, MD 21250. Offers MA. *Program availability:* Part-time, evening/weekend. *Faculty:* 18 full-time (13 women), 1 (woman) part-time/adjunct. *Students:* 13 full-time (10 women), 16 part-time (9 women); includes 10 minority (4 Black or African American, non-Hispanic/Latino; 3 Asian, non-Hispanic/Latino; 2 Hispanic/Latino; 1 Two or more races, non-Hispanic/Latino). Average age 27. 19 applicants, 63% accepted, 8 enrolled. In 2017, 9 master's awarded. *Degree requirements:* For master's, thesis or alternative. *Entrance requirements:* For master's, minimum GPA of 3.0. Additional exam requirements/recommendations for international students: Required—TOEFL. *Application deadline:* For fall admission, 3/15 for domestic students, 1/1 for international students; for spring admission, 11/15 for domestic students, 9/1 for international students. Application fee: $70. Electronic applications accepted. *Expenses: Required fees:* $132. *Financial support:* In 2017–18, 10 students received support, including 1 research assistantship with tuition reimbursement available, 9 teaching assistantships with tuition reimbursements available; health care benefits, unspecified assistantships, and tuition remission also available. *Faculty research:* Health, illness, and medicine; aging and the life course; diversity, gender, and culture; applied research methods. *Unit head:* Dr. Marina Adler, Graduate Program Director, 410-455-3155, Fax: 410-455-1154, E-mail: adler@umbc.edu. *Application contact:* Faith Dinh, Graduate Program Coordinator, 410-455-3365, Fax: 410-455-1154, E-mail: fdinh1@umbc.edu.
Website: http://sociology.umbc.edu/ma-in-applied-sociology/

University of Maryland, College Park, Academic Affairs, College of Behavioral and Social Sciences, Department of Sociology, College Park, MD 20742. Offers MA, PhD. *Degree requirements:* For master's, thesis; for doctorate, thesis/dissertation, 2 qualifying exams. *Entrance requirements:* For master's, GRE General Test, minimum GPA of 3.0, 3 letters of recommendation; for doctorate, GRE General Test, 3 letters of recommendation. Additional exam requirements/recommendations for international students: Required—TOEFL. Electronic applications accepted. *Faculty research:* Social psychology, sociology of work, sociology of the military, population studies, stratification.

University of Massachusetts Amherst, Graduate School, College of Social and Behavioral Sciences, Department of Sociology, Amherst, MA 01003. Offers MA, PhD. *Program availability:* Part-time. Terminal master's awarded for partial completion of doctoral program. *Degree requirements:* For master's, thesis or alternative; for doctorate, comprehensive exam, thesis/dissertation. *Entrance requirements:* For master's and doctorate, GRE General Test, writing sample, 3 letters of recommendation. Additional exam requirements/recommendations for international students: Required—TOEFL (minimum score 550 paper-based; 80 iBT), IELTS (minimum score 6.5). Electronic applications accepted.

University of Massachusetts Boston, College of Liberal Arts, Program in Applied Sociology, Boston, MA 02125-3393. Offers MA. *Program availability:* Part-time, evening/weekend. *Students:* 13 full-time (9 women), 2 part-time (1 woman); includes 6 minority (1 Black or African American, non-Hispanic/Latino; 4 Hispanic/Latino; 1 Two or more races, non-Hispanic/Latino). Average age 25. 21 applicants, 67% accepted, 9 enrolled. In 2017, 10 master's awarded. *Entrance requirements:* For master's, GRE or MAT, minimum GPA of 2.75. *Application deadline:* For fall admission, 3/1 for domestic students; for spring admission, 11/1 for domestic students. *Expenses:* Tuition, state resident: full-time $17,375. Tuition, nonresident: full-time $33,915. *Required fees:* $355. *Financial support:* Research assistantships, teaching assistantships, career-related internships or fieldwork, Federal Work-Study, and unspecified assistantships available. Support available to part-time students. Financial award application deadline: 3/1; financial award applicants required to submit FAFSA. *Faculty research:* Sociology of education, social deviance and control, women and development, race and ethnic group relations, criminology. *Unit head:* Dr. Russell Schutt, Director, 617-287-6250, E-mail: russell.schutt@umb.edu. *Application contact:* Graduate Admissions Coordinator, 617-287-6400, Fax: 617-287-6236, E-mail: bos.gadm@dpc.umassp.edu.

University of Massachusetts Boston, College of Liberal Arts, Program in Sociology, Boston, MA 02125-3393. Offers PhD. *Faculty:* 28 full-time (16 women), 17 part-time/adjunct (10 women). *Students:* 7 full-time (6 women), 20 part-time (17 women); includes 6 minority (2 Black or African American, non-Hispanic/Latino; 2 Asian, non-Hispanic/Latino; 1 Hispanic/Latino; 1 Two or more races, non-Hispanic/Latino). Average age 34. 24 applicants, 63% accepted, 6 enrolled. *Expenses:* Tuition, state resident: full-time $17,375. Tuition, nonresident: full-time $33,915. *Required fees:* $355. *Financial support:* Teaching assistantships and unspecified assistantships available. *Unit head:* Dr. Reef Youngreen, Director, 617-287-3909, E-mail: reef.youngreen@umb.edu. *Application contact:* Graduate Admissions Coordinator, 617-287-6400, Fax: 617-287-6236, E-mail: bos.gadm@dpc.umassp.edu.
Website: http://www.umb.edu/academics/cla/sociology/graduate_programs/phd_in_sociology

University of Massachusetts Lowell, College of Fine Arts, Humanities and Social Sciences, Program in Regional Economic and Social Development, Lowell, MA 01854. Offers MA, Graduate Certificate. *Program availability:* Part-time. *Entrance requirements:* For master's, GRE. Electronic applications accepted.

University of Memphis, Graduate School, College of Arts and Sciences, Department of Sociology, Memphis, TN 38152. Offers MA. *Program availability:* Part-time. *Faculty:* 5 full-time (3 women). *Students:* 16 full-time (11 women); includes 6 minority (3 Black or African American, non-Hispanic/Latino; 1 Hispanic/Latino; 2 Two or more races, non-Hispanic/Latino), 2 international. Average age 30. 8 applicants, 100% accepted, 6 enrolled. In 2017, 4 master's awarded. *Degree requirements:* For master's, comprehensive exam, thesis (for some programs). *Entrance requirements:* For master's, GRE General Test, 12 undergraduate hours in sociology, letters of reference, writing sample. Additional exam requirements/recommendations for international students: Required—TOEFL (minimum score 550 paper-based; 79 iBT). *Application deadline:* For fall admission, 7/1 for domestic students, 5/1 for international students; for spring admission, 12/1 for domestic students, 9/15 for international students. Applications are processed on a rolling basis. Application fee: $35 ($60 for international students). Electronic applications accepted. *Expenses:* Contact institution. *Financial support:* In 2017–18, 12 students received support, including 15 research assistantships with full tuition reimbursements available (averaging $14,990 per year); teaching assistantships with full tuition reimbursements available, Federal Work-Study, scholarships/grants, and unspecified assistantships also available. Financial award application deadline: 2/1; financial award applicants required to submit FAFSA. *Faculty research:* Globalization, medical, inequality, religion, urban. *Unit head:* Dr. Gretchen Peterson, Chair, 901-678-2241, Fax: 901-678-2525, E-mail: gpterson@memphis.edu. *Application contact:* Dr. Wesley James, Coordinator of Graduate Studies, 901-678-1631, Fax: 901-678-2525, E-mail: wes.james@memphis.edu.
Website: http://sociology.memphis.edu

University of Miami, Graduate School, College of Arts and Sciences, Department of Sociology, Coral Gables, FL 33124. Offers MA, PhD. *Program availability:* Part-time. Terminal master's awarded for partial completion of doctoral program. *Degree requirements:* For master's, thesis; for doctorate, comprehensive exam, thesis/dissertation. *Entrance requirements:* For master's and doctorate, GRE General Test. Additional exam requirements/recommendations for international students: Required—TOEFL (minimum score 515 paper-based). Electronic applications accepted. *Faculty research:* Crime, violence, mental health, ethnic relations, health.

University of Miami, Graduate School, School of Education and Human Development, Department of Educational and Psychological Studies, Program in Community and Social Change, Coral Gables, FL 33124. Offers MS Ed. *Program availability:* Part-time, evening/weekend. *Degree requirements:* For master's, thesis optional, capstone project or comprehensive exam. *Entrance requirements:* For master's, GRE General Test. Additional exam requirements/recommendations for international students: Required—TOEFL (minimum score 550 paper-based; 80 iBT); Recommended—IELTS (minimum score 6.5). Electronic applications accepted.

University of Miami, Graduate School, School of Education and Human Development, Department of Teaching and Learning, Program in Education and Social Change, Coral Gables, FL 33124. Offers MS Ed. *Program availability:* Part-time, evening/weekend. *Degree requirements:* For master's, electronic portfolio. *Entrance requirements:* For master's, GRE General Test. Additional exam requirements/recommendations for international students: Required—TOEFL (minimum score 550 paper-based; 80 iBT); Recommended—IELTS (minimum score 6.5). Electronic applications accepted.

University of Michigan, Rackham Graduate School, College of Literature, Science, and the Arts, Department of Sociology, Ann Arbor, MI 48109. Offers public policy and sociology (PhD); social work and sociology (PhD); sociology (PhD). *Faculty:* 41 full-time (21 women), 10 part-time/adjunct (4 women). *Students:* 72 full-time (50 women);

includes 27 minority (8 Black or African American, non-Hispanic/Latino; 4 Asian, non-Hispanic/Latino; 8 Hispanic/Latino; 7 Two or more races, non-Hispanic/Latino), 10 international. Average age 28. 253 applicants, 12% accepted, 17 enrolled. In 2017, 2 doctorates awarded. *Degree requirements:* For doctorate, comprehensive exam, thesis/dissertation, oral defense of dissertation, preliminary exam, dissertation prospectus. *Entrance requirements:* For doctorate, GRE General Test, letters of recommendation, writing sample, academic statement of purpose, personal statement, transcript. Additional exam requirements/recommendations for international students: Required—TOEFL (minimum score 560 paper-based; 84 iBT), IELTS (minimum score 6.5). *Application deadline:* For fall admission, 12/15 for domestic and international students. Application fee: $75 ($90 for international students). Electronic applications accepted. *Expenses:* Tuition, state resident: full-time $22,368; part-time $1201 per credit hour. Tuition, nonresident: full-time $45,156; part-time $2467 per credit hour. *Required fees:* $376 per term. Tuition and fees vary according to course load, degree level and program. *Financial support:* In 2017–18, 77 students received support, including 17 fellowships with full tuition reimbursements available (averaging $23,940 per year), 28 teaching assistantships with full tuition reimbursements available (averaging $23,782 per year); scholarships/grants, traineeships, health care benefits, and tuition waivers (full) also available. Financial award application deadline: 12/15. *Faculty research:* Power, history and social change; gender and sexuality; race and ethnicity; economic sociology; social demography. *Total annual research expenditures:* $269,377. *Unit head:* Karin A. Martin, Chair, 734-764-5554, Fax: 734-763-6887, E-mail: soc-chair@umich.edu. *Application contact:* Jessica Parks-Piatt, Graduate Program Coordinator, 734-647-4428, Fax: 734-763-6887, E-mail: lsa-soc-gradprogram@umich.edu.
Website: http://www.lsa.umich.edu/soc/

University of Michigan, School of Social Work, Interdisciplinary PhD Program in Social Work and Social Science, Ann Arbor, MI 48109. Offers social work and anthropology (PhD); social work and economics (PhD); social work and political science (PhD); social work and psychology (PhD); social work and sociology (PhD). Programs offered through the Rackham Graduate School. *Faculty:* 57 full-time (36 women). *Students:* 53 full-time (38 women); includes 27 minority (10 Black or African American, non-Hispanic/Latino; 2 American Indian or Alaska Native, non-Hispanic/Latino; 9 Asian, non-Hispanic/Latino; 6 Hispanic/Latino). Average age 32. 124 applicants, 6% accepted, 7 enrolled. In 2017, 10 doctorates awarded. *Degree requirements:* For doctorate, thesis/dissertation, oral defense of dissertation, preliminary exam. *Entrance requirements:* For doctorate, GRE General Test. Additional exam requirements/recommendations for international students: Required—TOEFL (minimum score 620 paper-based, 88 iBT) or IELTS. *Application deadline:* For fall admission, 12/1 for domestic and international students. Application fee: $75 ($90 for international students). Electronic applications accepted. *Expenses:* Contact institution. *Financial support:* In 2017–18, 59 students received support, including 24 fellowships with full tuition reimbursements available (averaging $17,600 per year), 7 research assistantships with full tuition reimbursements available (averaging $20,399 per year), 21 teaching assistantships with full tuition reimbursements available (averaging $20,399 per year); career-related internships or fieldwork, scholarships/grants, traineeships, health care benefits, tuition waivers (full and partial), and unspecified assistantships also available. Financial award application deadline: 12/1; financial award applicants required to submit FAFSA. *Faculty research:* Children and family, aging, community organization, health and mental health, police and evaluation. *Total annual research expenditures:* $4.1 million. *Unit head:* Dr. William Elliott, III, Director, 734-763-5768, E-mail: willelli@umich.edu. *Application contact:* Todd Huynh, Graduate Coordinator, 734-647-2554, Fax: 734-615-3192, E-mail: ssw.phd.info@umich.edu.
Website: https://ssw.umich.edu/offices/phd

University of Minnesota, Duluth, Graduate School, College of Liberal Arts, Department of Sociology/Anthropology, Duluth, MN 55812-2496. Offers criminology (MA); liberal studies (MLS). *Program availability:* Part-time. *Degree requirements:* For master's, thesis or alternative. *Entrance requirements:* For master's, interview, minimum GPA of 3.0, letters of recommendation. Additional exam requirements/recommendations for international students: Required—TOEFL. *Faculty research:* Nature of knowledge, philosophy of science, ecology, cultural studies, language.

University of Minnesota, Twin Cities Campus, Graduate School, College of Liberal Arts, Department of Sociology, Minneapolis, MN 55455. Offers MA, PhD. Terminal master's awarded for partial completion of doctoral program. *Degree requirements:* For master's, thesis optional; for doctorate, comprehensive exam, thesis/dissertation, preliminary written and oral exam, prospectus hearing, final oral defense and dissertation. *Entrance requirements:* For doctorate, GRE General Test, bachelor's degree, transcripts, minimum GPA of 3.0, personal statement, three letters of recommendation, writing sample. Additional exam requirements/recommendations for international students: Required—TOEFL (minimum score 587 paper-based; 95 iBT). Electronic applications accepted. *Faculty research:* Organizations, work, and markets; inequality: race, class, and gender; law, crime and deviance; family and life course; political sociology and social movements.

University of Missouri, Office of Research and Graduate Studies, College of Arts and Science, Department of Sociology, Columbia, MO 65211. Offers PhD. *Degree requirements:* For doctorate, one foreign language, comprehensive exam, thesis/dissertation. *Entrance requirements:* For doctorate, GRE General Test, minimum GPA of 3.0; 15 hours of undergraduate sociology with minimum B average, including one course each in sociological theory and basic statistics. Additional exam requirements/recommendations for international students: Required—TOEFL (minimum score 500 paper-based; 61 iBT). Electronic applications accepted.

University of Missouri–Kansas City, College of Arts and Sciences, Department of Sociology, Kansas City, MO 64110-2499. Offers MA. PhD (interdisciplinary) offered through the School of Graduate Studies. *Program availability:* Part-time, evening/weekend. *Degree requirements:* For master's, thesis optional. *Entrance requirements:* For master's, GRE, minimum GPA of 3.0 in major, 2.7 overall. Additional exam requirements/recommendations for international students: Required—TOEFL (minimum score 550 paper-based; 80 iBT). Electronic applications accepted. *Faculty research:* Gerontology, religious movements, urban community and neighborhoods.

University of Montana, Graduate School, College of Humanities and Sciences, Department of Sociology, Missoula, MT 59812. Offers criminology (MA); inequality and social justice (MA); rural and environmental change (MA); sociology (MA). *Entrance requirements:* For master's, GRE General Test. Additional exam requirements/recommendations for international students: Required—TOEFL. *Faculty research:* Housing, homelessness, hunger, infant mortality, work safety.

University of Nebraska at Omaha, Graduate Studies, College of Arts and Sciences, Department of Sociology and Anthropology, Omaha, NE 68182. Offers sociology (MA). *Program availability:* Part-time. *Degree requirements:* For master's, comprehensive exam (for some programs), thesis optional. *Entrance requirements:* For master's, 3 letters of recommendation, resume, statement of purpose, writing sample, minimum GPA of 3.0, official transcripts. Additional exam requirements/recommendations for international students: Required—TOEFL, IELTS, PTE. Electronic applications accepted.

University of Nebraska–Lincoln, Graduate College, College of Arts and Sciences, Department of Sociology, Lincoln, NE 68588. Offers MA, PhD. *Degree requirements:* For master's, thesis optional; for doctorate, comprehensive exam, thesis/dissertation. *Entrance requirements:* For master's and doctorate, GRE General Test, writing sample. Additional exam requirements/recommendations for international students: Required—TOEFL (minimum score 550 paper-based). Electronic applications accepted. *Faculty research:* Family, deviance and social control, ethnic studies, inequality (gender, race, and class).

University of Nevada, Las Vegas, Graduate College, College of Liberal Arts, Department of Sociology, Las Vegas, NV 89154-5003. Offers MA, PhD. *Program availability:* Part-time. *Faculty:* 12 full-time (4 women), 1 (woman) part-time/adjunct. *Students:* 29 full-time (17 women), 17 part-time (10 women); includes 13 minority (3 Black or African American, non-Hispanic/Latino; 1 Asian, non-Hispanic/Latino; 6 Hispanic/Latino; 3 Two or more races, non-Hispanic/Latino), 2 international. Average age 34. 23 applicants, 39% accepted, 5 enrolled. In 2017, 2 master's, 4 doctorates awarded. Terminal master's awarded for partial completion of doctoral program. *Degree requirements:* For doctorate, comprehensive exam, thesis/dissertation, oral defense. *Entrance requirements:* For doctorate, GRE General Test, 3 letters of recommendation; statement of purpose; writing samples. Additional exam requirements/recommendations for international students: Required—TOEFL (minimum score 550 paper-based; 80 iBT), IELTS (minimum score 7). *Application deadline:* For fall admission, 2/1 for domestic students. Application fee: $60 ($95 for international students). Electronic applications accepted. *Expenses:* Contact institution. *Financial support:* In 2017–18, 31 students received support, including 7 research assistantships with full and partial tuition reimbursements available (averaging $17,571 per year), 24 teaching assistantships with full and partial tuition reimbursements available (averaging $17,875 per year); institutionally sponsored loans, scholarships/grants, health care benefits, and unspecified assistantships also available. Financial award application deadline: 3/15; financial award applicants required to submit FAFSA. *Faculty research:* Urban and community studies, culture, sex and gender, health and environment, theory and social psychology. *Unit head:* Dr. Robert Futrell, Chair/Professor, 702-895-0270, Fax: 702-895-4800, E-mail: robert.futrell@unlv.edu. *Application contact:* Dr. Barbara Brents, Graduate Coordinator, 702-895-0261, Fax: 702-895-4800, E-mail: barb.brents@unlv.edu.
Website: http://www.unlv.edu/sociology

University of Nevada, Reno, Graduate School, College of Liberal Arts, School of Social Research and Justice Studies, Department of Sociology, Reno, NV 89557. Offers MA. *Degree requirements:* For master's, thesis optional. *Entrance requirements:* For master's, GRE General Test, minimum GPA of 2.75. Additional exam requirements/recommendations for international students: Required—TOEFL (minimum score 500 paper-based; 61 iBT), IELTS (minimum score 6). Electronic applications accepted. *Faculty research:* Statistics, politics and economics, religion and law, industry, theory stratification.

University of New Brunswick Fredericton, School of Graduate Studies, Faculty of Arts, Department of Sociology, Fredericton, NB E3B 5A3, Canada. Offers MA, PhD. *Program availability:* Part-time. *Degree requirements:* For master's, thesis; for doctorate, comprehensive exam, thesis/dissertation, 6 courses. *Entrance requirements:* For master's, minimum GPA of 3.5; for doctorate, MA in sociology with thesis or equivalent, curriculum vitae, statement of interest about intended research and why UNB was selected. Additional exam requirements/recommendations for international students: Required—TOEFL. Electronic applications accepted. *Faculty research:* Social policy, media, sociology and cooperative economy, charities and philanthropy, gender health and entrepreneurship, reproductive health and women, international development, criminology, environment, science and technology, family and domestic violence, sociology of health, health policy and social determinants of health, law and social policy.

University of New Hampshire, Graduate School, College of Liberal Arts, Department of Sociology, Durham, NH 03824. Offers MA, PhD. *Program availability:* Part-time. *Students:* 23 full-time (15 women), 6 part-time (4 women); includes 4 minority (1 Asian, non-Hispanic/Latino; 2 Hispanic/Latino; 1 Two or more races, non-Hispanic/Latino), 3 international. Average age 33. 26 applicants, 58% accepted, 5 enrolled. In 2017, 4 master's, 2 doctorates awarded. *Entrance requirements:* For master's, GRE General Test; for doctorate, GRE General Test, master's thesis or research. Additional exam requirements/recommendations for international students: Required—TOEFL (minimum score 550 paper-based; 80 iBT). *Application deadline:* For fall admission, 4/1 for domestic and international students. Application fee: $65. Electronic applications accepted. *Financial support:* In 2017–18, 15 students received support, including 1 research assistantship, 13 teaching assistantships; fellowships, career-related internships or fieldwork, Federal Work-Study, scholarships/grants, and tuition waivers (full and partial) also available. Support available to part-time students. Financial award application deadline: 2/15. *Unit head:* Cesar Rebellon, Chair, 603-862-2500. *Application contact:* Brenda Worden, Administrative Assistant, 603-862-2500, E-mail: sociology.dept@unh.edu.
Website: http://www.cola.unh.edu/sociology

University of New Mexico, Graduate Studies, College of Arts and Sciences, Program in Sociology, Albuquerque, NM 87131. Offers MA, PhD. *Program availability:* Part-time. *Faculty:* 15 full-time (9 women). *Students:* 14 full-time (9 women), 19 part-time (12 women); includes 12 minority (1 Black or African American, non-Hispanic/Latino; 1 American Indian or Alaska Native, non-Hispanic/Latino; 2 Asian, non-Hispanic/Latino; 7 Hispanic/Latino; 1 Two or more races, non-Hispanic/Latino), 2 international. Average age 33. 22 applicants, 45% accepted, 7 enrolled. In 2017, 4 master's awarded. Terminal master's awarded for partial completion of doctoral program. *Degree requirements:* For master's, thesis; for doctorate, comprehensive exam, thesis/dissertation. *Entrance requirements:* For master's and doctorate, GRE General Test, 2 writing samples, 3 letters of reference, letter of intent. Additional exam requirements/recommendations for international students: Required—TOEFL (minimum score 550 paper-based; 79 iBT), IELTS (minimum score 7). *Application deadline:* For fall admission, 1/15 priority date for domestic and international students; for spring admission, 9/30 for domestic students. Application fee: $50. Electronic applications accepted. *Financial support:* Fellowships, research assistantships, teaching assistantships with partial tuition reimbursements, institutionally sponsored loans, scholarships/grants, health care benefits, tuition waivers (partial), and unspecified assistantships available. Support available to part-time students. Financial award application deadline: 1/15; financial award applicants required to submit FAFSA. *Faculty research:* Criminology/crime/law/social control, sociology of health and medicine, social movements, race and ethnicity, comparative sociology, Latin American comparative sociology, political sociology, sociology of science and knowledge, sociology of education. *Unit head:* Dr. Richard Santos, Interim Departmental Chair, 505-277-2501, Fax: 505-277-8805, E-mail: santos@unm.edu. *Application contact:* Shannon Kindilien, Academic Advisor, 505-277-2501, Fax: 505-277-8805, E-mail: sadvisor@unm.edu.
Website: http://www.unm.edu/~socdept/

University of New Orleans, Graduate School, College of Liberal Arts, Department of Sociology, New Orleans, LA 70148. Offers MA. *Program availability:* Part-time, evening/

weekend. *Degree requirements:* For master's, thesis (for some programs). *Entrance requirements:* For master's, GRE General Test. Additional exam requirements/recommendations for international students: Required—TOEFL (minimum score 550 paper-based; 79 iBT), IELTS (minimum score 6.5). Electronic applications accepted. *Faculty research:* Environment and gender.

The University of North Carolina at Chapel Hill, Graduate School, College of Arts and Sciences, Department of Sociology, Chapel Hill, NC 27599. Offers MA, PhD. *Degree requirements:* For master's, comprehensive exam, thesis; for doctorate, comprehensive exam, thesis/dissertation. *Entrance requirements:* For master's and doctorate, GRE General Test, minimum GPA of 3.0. Additional exam requirements/recommendations for international students: Required—TOEFL (minimum score 550 paper-based). Electronic applications accepted. *Faculty research:* Comparative historical, work/organizations, religion, demography, stratification.

The University of North Carolina at Charlotte, College of Liberal Arts and Sciences, Department of Sociology, Charlotte, NC 28223-0001. Offers MA. *Program availability:* Part-time, evening/weekend. *Faculty:* 15 full-time (9 women). *Students:* 12 full-time (6 women), 3 part-time (1 woman); includes 4 minority (3 Black or African American, non-Hispanic/Latino; 1 Asian, non-Hispanic/Latino), 1 international. Average age 27. 18 applicants, 72% accepted, 9 enrolled. In 2017, 6 master's awarded. *Degree requirements:* For master's, thesis or practicum. *Entrance requirements:* For master's, GRE, minimum undergraduate GPA of 3.0; minimum of 18 hours of undergraduate course work in the social sciences, including social theory; demonstrated undergraduate competence in research methods and statistics. Additional exam requirements/recommendations for international students: Required—TOEFL (minimum score 523 paper-based, 70 iBT) or IELTS (6.5). *Application deadline:* For fall admission, 3/1 priority date for domestic and international students; for spring admission, 10/1 priority date for domestic and international students; for summer admission, 4/1 priority date for domestic and international students. Applications are processed on a rolling basis. Application fee: $75. Electronic applications accepted. *Expenses:* Tuition, state resident: full-time $4337. Tuition, nonresident: full-time $17,771. *Required fees:* $3211. Tuition and fees vary according to course load and program. *Financial support:* In 2017–18, 17 students received support, including 1 fellowship (averaging $47,476 per year), 9 research assistantships (averaging $11,063 per year), 7 teaching assistantships (averaging $11,229 per year); career-related internships or fieldwork, institutionally sponsored loans, scholarships/grants, and unspecified assistantships also available. Support available to part-time students. Financial award application deadline: 3/1; financial award applicants required to submit FAFSA. *Total annual research expenditures:* $535,405. *Unit head:* Dr. Stephanie Moller, Chair, 704-687-7824, Fax: 704-687-1397, E-mail: smoller@uncc.edu. *Application contact:* Kathy B. Giddings, Director of Graduate Admissions, 704-687-5503, Fax: 704-687-1668, E-mail: gradadm@uncc.edu.
Website: http://sociology.uncc.edu/

The University of North Carolina at Greensboro, Graduate School, College of Arts and Sciences, Department of Sociology, Greensboro, NC 27412-5001. Offers criminology (MA); sociology (MA). *Program availability:* Part-time. *Degree requirements:* For master's, comprehensive exam, thesis. *Entrance requirements:* For master's, GRE General Test. Additional exam requirements/recommendations for international students: Required—TOEFL. Electronic applications accepted.

The University of North Carolina Wilmington, College of Arts and Sciences, Department of Sociology and Criminology, Wilmington, NC 28403-3297. Offers MA. *Faculty:* 13 full-time (7 women). *Students:* 14 full-time (12 women), 5 part-time (0 women); includes 5 minority (1 Black or African American, non-Hispanic/Latino; 2 Hispanic/Latino; 2 Two or more races, non-Hispanic/Latino). Average age 24. 13 applicants, 54% accepted, 7 enrolled. In 2017, 6 master's awarded. *Degree requirements:* For master's, thesis or internship. *Entrance requirements:* For master's, GRE General Test, 3 letters of recommendation, statement of interest. Additional exam requirements/recommendations for international students: Required—TOEFL (minimum score 550 paper-based; 79 iBT), IELTS (minimum score 6.5). *Application deadline:* For fall admission, 2/15 priority date for domestic students. Applications are processed on a rolling basis. Application fee: $75. Electronic applications accepted. *Expenses:* Tuition, state resident: full-time $4626; part-time $226.76 per credit hour. Tuition, nonresident: full-time $17,834; part-time $874.22 per credit hour. *Required fees:* $2124. Tuition and fees vary according to program. *Financial support:* Research assistantships, teaching assistantships, scholarships/grants, and out-of-state tuition awards available. Financial award application deadline: 1/1; financial award applicants required to submit FAFSA. *Unit head:* Dr. Mike Maume, Chair, 910-962-7749, Fax: 910-962-7385, E-mail: maume@uncw.edu. *Application contact:* Dr. Daniel Buffington, Graduate Coordinator, 910-962-3434, Fax: 910-962-7385, E-mail: buffingtond@uncw.edu.
Website: http://www.uncw.edu/socgrad/index.html

University of North Dakota, Graduate School, College of Arts and Sciences, Department of Sociology, Grand Forks, ND 58202. Offers MA. *Degree requirements:* For master's, thesis, final examination. *Entrance requirements:* For master's, minimum GPA of 3.0. Additional exam requirements/recommendations for international students: Required—TOEFL (minimum score 550 paper-based; 79 iBT), IELTS (minimum score 6.5). Electronic applications accepted. *Faculty research:* Criminal justice studies, social psychology, research methods, corrections, social theory.

University of Northern Colorado, Graduate School, College of Humanities and Social Sciences, Department of Sociology, Greeley, CO 80639. Offers MA. *Program availability:* Part-time. *Degree requirements:* For master's, comprehensive exam. *Entrance requirements:* For master's, 2 letters of recommendation. Electronic applications accepted.

University of North Texas, Robert B. Toulouse School of Graduate Studies, Denton, TX 76203-5459. Offers accounting (MS); applied anthropology (MA, MS); applied behavior analysis (Certificate); applied geography (MA); applied technology and performance improvement (M Ed, MS); art education (MA); art history (MA); art museum education (Certificate); arts leadership (Certificate); audiology (Au D); behavior analysis (MS); behavioral science (PhD); biochemistry and molecular biology (MS); biology (MA, MS); biomedical engineering (MS); business analysis (MS); chemistry (MS); clinical health psychology (PhD); communication studies (MA, MS); computer engineering (MS); computer science (MS); counseling (M Ed, MS), including clinical mental health counseling (MS), college and university counseling, elementary school counseling, secondary school counseling; creative writing (MA); criminal justice (MS); curriculum and instruction (M Ed); decision sciences (MBA); design (MA, MFA), including fashion design (MFA), innovation studies, interior design (MFA); early childhood studies (MS); economics (MS); educational leadership (M Ed, Ed D); educational psychology (MS, PhD), including family studies (MS), gifted and talented (MS), human development (MS), learning and cognition (MS), research, measurement and evaluation (MS); electrical engineering (MS); emergency management (MPA); engineering technology (MS); English (MA); English as a second language (MA); environmental science (MS); finance (MBA, MS); financial management (MPA); French (MA); health services management (MBA); higher education (M Ed, Ed D); history (MA, MS); hospitality management (MS); human resources management (MPA); information science (MS); information systems (PhD); information technologies (MBA); interdisciplinary studies (MA, MS); international studies (MA); international sustainable tourism (MS); jazz studies (MM); journalism (MA, MJ, Graduate Certificate), including interactive and virtual digital communication (Graduate Certificate), narrative journalism (Graduate Certificate), public relations (Graduate Certificate); kinesiology (MS); linguistics (MA); local government management (MPA); logistics (PhD); logistics and supply chain management (MBA); long-term care, senior housing, and aging services (MA); management (PhD); marketing (MBA); mathematics (MA, MS); mechanical and energy engineering (MS, PhD); music (MA), including ethnomusicology, music theory, musicology, performance; music composition (PhD); music education (MM Ed, PhD); nonprofit management (MPA); operations and supply chain management (MBA); performance (MM, DMA); philosophy (MA); political science (MA); professional and technical communication (MA); radio, television and film (MA, MFA); rehabilitation counseling (Certificate); sociology (MA); Spanish (MA); special education (M Ed); speech-language pathology (MA); strategic management (MBA); studio art (MFA); teaching (M Ed); MBA/MS. *Program availability:* Part-time, evening/weekend, online learning. Terminal master's awarded for partial completion of doctoral program. *Degree requirements:* For master's, variable foreign language requirement, comprehensive exam (for some programs), thesis (for some programs); for doctorate, variable foreign language requirement, comprehensive exam (for some programs), thesis/dissertation; for other advanced degree, variable foreign language requirement, comprehensive exam (for some programs). *Entrance requirements:* For master's and doctorate, GRE, GMAT. Additional exam requirements/recommendations for international students: Required—TOEFL (minimum score 550 paper-based; 79 iBT). Electronic applications accepted.

University of Notre Dame, Graduate School, College of Arts and Letters, Division of Social Science, Department of Sociology, Notre Dame, IN 46556. Offers PhD. *Degree requirements:* For doctorate, thesis/dissertation, 2 area specialty exams. *Entrance requirements:* For doctorate, GRE General Test, GRE Subject Test (strongly recommended). Additional exam requirements/recommendations for international students: Required—TOEFL (minimum score 600 paper-based; 80 iBT). Electronic applications accepted. *Faculty research:* Cultural sociology, development, family, education, historical/comparative sociology.

University of Oklahoma, College of Arts and Sciences, Department of Sociology, Norman, OK 73019. Offers MA, PhD. *Program availability:* Part-time. *Faculty:* 14 full-time (7 women). *Students:* 19 full-time (8 women), 9 part-time (7 women); includes 5 minority (2 American Indian or Alaska Native, non-Hispanic/Latino; 1 Hispanic/Latino; 2 Two or more races, non-Hispanic/Latino), 3 international. Average age 32. 16 applicants, 81% accepted, 12 enrolled. In 2017, 4 master's, 5 doctorates awarded. Terminal master's awarded for partial completion of doctoral program. *Degree requirements:* For master's, thesis, 3 courses in statistics, 1 course in theory, 1 course in research methods, professionalization seminar; for doctorate, comprehensive exam, thesis/dissertation, 3 semesters of statistics, 2 semesters of theory, 1 semester of research methods, professionalization seminar, teaching seminar. *Entrance requirements:* For master's and doctorate, GRE. Additional exam requirements/recommendations for international students: Required—TOEFL (minimum score 79 iBT) or IELTS (minimum score 6.5). *Application deadline:* For fall admission, 1/1 for domestic and international students. Application fee: $50 ($100 for international students). Electronic applications accepted. *Expenses:* Tuition, state resident: full-time $5119; part-time $213.30 per credit hour. Tuition, nonresident: full-time $19,778; part-time $824.10 per credit hour. *Required fees:* $3458; $133.55 per credit hour. $126.50 per semester. *Financial support:* In 2017–18, 25 students received support, including 4 fellowships (averaging $4,125 per year), 18 teaching assistantships with full tuition reimbursements available (averaging $14,713 per year); health care benefits also available. Financial award application deadline: 6/1; financial award applicants required to submit FAFSA. *Faculty research:* Criminology; LGBTQ issues; race, class stratification, and gender; international/cross-national sociology; environmental sociology; sociology of religion. *Unit head:* Loretta E. Bass, Chair, 405-325-1751, Fax: 405-325-7825, E-mail: lbass@ou.edu. *Application contact:* Dr. Trina Hope, Graduate Liaison, 405-325-3647, Fax: 405-325-7825, E-mail: thope@ou.edu.
Website: http://www.ou.edu/cas/soc.html

University of Oregon, Graduate School, College of Arts and Sciences, Department of Sociology, Eugene, OR 97403. Offers MA, MS, PhD. *Program availability:* Part-time. Terminal master's awarded for partial completion of doctoral program. *Degree requirements:* For doctorate, thesis/dissertation. *Entrance requirements:* For master's and doctorate, GRE General Test, minimum GPA of 3.0. Additional exam requirements/recommendations for international students: Required—TOEFL. *Faculty research:* Criminology, environment, gender, labor, political economy.

University of Ottawa, Faculty of Graduate and Postdoctoral Studies, Faculty of Social Sciences, Department of Sociology and Anthropology, Ottawa, ON K1N 6N5, Canada. Offers MA. *Degree requirements:* For master's, thesis or alternative. *Entrance requirements:* For master's, honors bachelor's degree or equivalent, minimum B average. Electronic applications accepted. *Faculty research:* Inter-ethnic relations, development, political policies.

University of Pennsylvania, School of Arts and Sciences, Graduate Group in Sociology, Philadelphia, PA 19104. Offers AM, PhD. *Faculty:* 37 full-time (17 women), 12 part-time/adjunct (6 women). *Students:* 49 full-time (35 women), 2 part-time (both women); includes 22 minority (10 Black or African American, non-Hispanic/Latino; 5 Asian, non-Hispanic/Latino; 7 Hispanic/Latino), 14 international. Average age 29. 250 applicants, 9% accepted, 8 enrolled. In 2017, 7 master's, 9 doctorates awarded. Terminal master's awarded for partial completion of doctoral program.
Website: http://sociology.sas.upenn.edu/graduate_resources

University of Pittsburgh, Kenneth P. Dietrich School of Arts and Sciences, Department of Sociology, Pittsburgh, PA 15260. Offers MA, PhD. *Program availability:* Part-time, online learning. *Faculty:* 13 full-time (6 women). *Students:* 17 full-time (9 women); includes 10 minority (4 Black or African American, non-Hispanic/Latino; 3 Asian, non-Hispanic/Latino; 3 Hispanic/Latino), 5 international. Average age 33. 39 applicants, 5% accepted, 2 enrolled. In 2017, 4 master's, 8 doctorates awarded. *Degree requirements:* For master's, thesis; for doctorate, comprehensive exam, thesis/dissertation, preliminary exam. *Entrance requirements:* For master's and doctorate, GRE General Test, writing sample. Additional exam requirements/recommendations for international students: Required—TOEFL (minimum score 550 paper-based; 90 iBT), IELTS (minimum score 7). *Application deadline:* For fall admission, 1/15 for domestic and international students. Application fee: $50. Electronic applications accepted. *Financial support:* In 2017–18, 7 fellowships with full tuition reimbursements, 4 research assistantships with full tuition reimbursements, 16 teaching assistantships with full tuition reimbursements were awarded; career-related internships or fieldwork, Federal Work-Study, institutionally sponsored loans, scholarships/grants, traineeships, health care benefits, tuition waivers (full and partial), unspecified assistantships, and part-time instructor positions also available. Support available to part-time students. Financial award application deadline: 1/15. *Faculty research:* Collective behavior/social movements, comparative sociology/historical sociology, cultural sociology, political sociology, qualitative methodology, quantitative methodology, sex and gender, social change, theory. *Unit head:* Dr. Suzanne Staggenborg, Chair, 412-648-7582, Fax: 412-648-2799, E-mail: suzstagg@pitt.edu. *Application contact:* Graduate Coordinator, 412-648-7588, Fax: 412-648-2799.
Website: http://www.sociology.pitt.edu/graduate/

University of Puerto Rico–Río Piedras, College of Social Sciences, Department of Sociology, San Juan, PR 00931-3300. Offers MA. *Degree requirements:* For master's, comprehensive exam, thesis. *Entrance requirements:* For master's, GRE or PAEG, interview, minimum GPA of 3.0, letter of recommendation.

University of Regina, Faculty of Graduate Studies and Research, Faculty of Arts, Department of Sociology and Social Studies, Regina, SK S4S 0A2, Canada. Offers social studies (MA); sociology (MA). *Program availability:* Part-time. *Faculty:* 9 full-time (4 women), 7 part-time/adjunct (all women). *Students:* 8 full-time (6 women), 5 part-time (3 women). 21 applicants, 29% accepted. In 2017, 3 master's awarded. *Degree requirements:* For master's, thesis. *Entrance requirements:* Additional exam requirements/recommendations for international students: Required—TOEFL (minimum score 580 paper-based; 80 iBT), IELTS (minimum score 6.5), PTE (minimum score 59). *Application deadline:* Applications are processed on a rolling basis. Application fee: $100. Electronic applications accepted. *Expenses:* $10,681. *Financial support:* In 2017–18, 1 fellowship (averaging $6,000 per year), 3 teaching assistantships (averaging $2,562 per year) were awarded; research assistantships and scholarships/grants also available. Financial award application deadline: 6/15. *Faculty research:* Social justice, international development, globalization, social policy, political economy. *Unit head:* Dr. John Conway, Department Head, 306-585-4052, Fax: 306-585-4815, E-mail: john.conway@uregina.ca. *Application contact:* Dr. Henry Chow, Graduate Coordinator, 306-585-5604, Fax: 306-585-4815, E-mail: henry.chow@uregina.ca.
Website: http://www.uregina.ca/arts/sociology-social-studies

University of Saskatchewan, College of Graduate Studies and Research, College of Arts and Science, Department of Sociology, Saskatoon, SK S7N 5A2, Canada. Offers MA, PhD. *Degree requirements:* For master's, thesis; for doctorate, comprehensive exam (for some programs), thesis/dissertation. *Entrance requirements:* Additional exam requirements/recommendations for international students: Required—TOEFL (minimum score 80 iBT); Recommended—IELTS (minimum score 6.5). Electronic applications accepted.

University of South Africa, College of Human Sciences, Pretoria, South Africa. Offers adult education (M Ed); African languages (MA, PhD); African politics (MA, PhD); Afrikaans (MA, PhD); ancient history (MA, PhD); ancient Near Eastern studies (MA, PhD); anthropology (MA, PhD); applied linguistics (MA); Arabic (MA, PhD); archaeology (MA); art history (MA); Biblical archaeology (MA); Biblical studies (M Th, D Th, PhD); Christian spirituality (M Th, D Th); church history (M Th, D Th); classical studies (MA, PhD); clinical psychology (MA); communication (MA, PhD); comparative education (M Ed, Ed D); consulting psychology (D Admin, D Com, PhD); curriculum studies (M Ed, Ed D); development studies (M Admin, MA, D Admin, PhD); didactics (M Ed, Ed D); education (M Tech); education management (M Ed, Ed D); educational psychology (M Ed); English (MA); environmental education (M Ed); French (MA, PhD); German (MA, PhD); Greek (MA); guidance and counseling (M Ed); health studies (MA, PhD), including health sciences education (MA), health services management (MA), medical and surgical nursing science (critical care general) (MA), midwifery and neonatal nursing science (MA), trauma and emergency care (MA); history (MA, PhD); history of education (Ed D); inclusive education (M Ed, Ed D); information and communications technology policy and regulation (MA); information science (MA, MIS, PhD); international politics (MA, PhD); Islamic studies (MA, PhD); Italian (MA, PhD); Judaica (MA, PhD); linguistics (MA, PhD); mathematical education (M Ed); mathematics education (MA); missiology (M Th, D Th); modern Hebrew (MA, PhD); musicology (MA, MMus, D Mus, PhD); natural science education (M Ed); New Testament (M Th, D Th); Old Testament (D Th); pastoral therapy (M Th, D Th); philosophy (MA); philosophy of education (M Ed, Ed D); politics (MA, PhD); Portuguese (MA, PhD); practical theology (M Th, D Th); psychology (MA, MS, PhD); psychology of education (M Ed, Ed D); public health (MA); religious studies (MA, D Th, PhD); Romance languages (MA); Russian (MA, PhD); Semitic languages (MA, PhD); social behavior studies in HIV/AIDS (MA); social science (mental health) (MA); social science in development studies (MA); social science in psychology (MA); social science in social work (MA); social science in sociology (MA); social work (MSW, DSW, PhD); socio-education (M Ed, Ed D); sociolinguistics (MA); sociology (MA, PhD); Spanish (MA, PhD); systematic theology (M Th, D Th); TESOL (teaching English to speakers of other languages) (MA); theological ethics (M Th, D Th); theory of literature (MA, PhD); urban ministries (D Th); urban ministry (M Th).

University of South Alabama, College of Arts and Sciences, Department of Sociology, Anthropology and Social Work, Mobile, AL 36688. Offers sociology (MA). *Program availability:* Part-time, evening/weekend. *Faculty:* 4 full-time (1 woman). *Students:* 6 full-time (5 women); includes 3 minority (1 Black or African American, non-Hispanic/Latino; 2 Two or more races, non-Hispanic/Latino). Average age 33. 7 applicants, 14% accepted, 1 enrolled. In 2017, 3 master's awarded. *Degree requirements:* For master's, comprehensive exam, thesis optional. *Entrance requirements:* For master's, GRE General Test, minimum GPA of 3.0. Additional exam requirements/recommendations for international students: Required—TOEFL (minimum score 525 paper-based; 71 iBT), IELTS (minimum score 6). *Application deadline:* For fall admission, 7/15 priority date for domestic students, 6/15 priority date for international students; for spring admission, 12/1 priority date for domestic students, 5/1 priority date for international students; for summer admission, 5/1 for domestic students, 4/1 for international students. Applications are processed on a rolling basis. Application fee: $35. Electronic applications accepted. *Expenses:* Tuition, state resident: full-time $10,104; part-time $421 per semester hour. Tuition, nonresident: full-time $20,208; part-time $842 per semester hour. *Financial support:* In 2017–18, teaching assistantships with tuition reimbursements (averaging $9,000 per year) were awarded; fellowships, research assistantships, career-related internships or fieldwork, Federal Work-Study, institutionally sponsored loans, scholarships/grants, and unspecified assistantships also available. Support available to part-time students. Financial award application deadline: 3/15; financial award applicants required to submit FAFSA. *Faculty research:* Child welfare, social inequality, sociology of medicine, poverty, health disparities. *Unit head:* Dr. Roma S. Hanks, Chair, 251-460-6347, Fax: 251-460-7925, E-mail: rhanks@southalabama.edu. *Application contact:* Dr. Christopher Freed, Graduate Coordinator, Sociology, 251-460-6348, Fax: 251-460-7925, E-mail: cfreed@southalabama.edu.
Website: http://www.southalabama.edu/colleges/artsandsci/syansw

University of South Carolina, The Graduate School, College of Arts and Sciences, Department of Sociology, Columbia, SC 29208. Offers MA, PhD. *Program availability:* Part-time. Terminal master's awarded for partial completion of doctoral program. *Degree requirements:* For master's, thesis; for doctorate, comprehensive exam, thesis/dissertation. *Entrance requirements:* For master's and doctorate, GRE General Test. Additional exam requirements/recommendations for international students: Required—TOEFL (minimum score 570 paper-based; 75 iBT). Electronic applications accepted. *Faculty research:* Social psychology, social inequality.

University of Southern California, Graduate School, Dana and David Dornsife College of Letters, Arts and Sciences, Department of Sociology, Los Angeles, CA 90089. Offers PhD. *Degree requirements:* For doctorate, comprehensive exam, thesis/dissertation. *Entrance requirements:* For doctorate, GRE. Additional exam requirements/recommendations for international students: Required—TOEFL. Electronic applications accepted. *Faculty research:* Family, immigration, gender, culture, race.

University of South Florida, College of Arts and Sciences, Department of Sociology, Tampa, FL 33620-9951. Offers MA, PhD. *Program availability:* Part-time. *Faculty:* 10 full-time (7 women). *Students:* 34 full-time (20 women), 2 part-time (both women); includes 10 minority (2 Black or African American, non-Hispanic/Latino; 1 Asian, non-Hispanic/Latino; 5 Hispanic/Latino; 2 Two or more races, non-Hispanic/Latino), 6 international. Average age 30. 30 applicants, 57% accepted, 11 enrolled. In 2017, 4 master's, 3 doctorates awarded. *Degree requirements:* For master's, comprehensive exam, thesis; for doctorate, comprehensive exam, thesis/dissertation. *Entrance requirements:* For master's, GRE General Test, minimum GPA of 3.25 in undergraduate coursework, three letters of recommendation, personal statement (1-3 pages), academic writing sample; for doctorate, GRE General Test, minimum GPA of 3.5 in graduate work, three letters of recommendation, personal statement, writing sample. Additional exam requirements/recommendations for international students: Required—TOEFL minimum score 550 paper-based; 79 iBT or IELTS minimum score 6.5 (for PhD); TOEFL minimum score 600 paper-based (for MA). *Application deadline:* For fall admission, 1/15 priority date for domestic and international students. Application fee: $30. Electronic applications accepted. *Financial support:* In 2017–18, 18 students received support, including 21 teaching assistantships with tuition reimbursements available (averaging $12,581 per year); unspecified assistantships also available. Financial award application deadline: 3/1. *Faculty research:* Urban development and culture; social inequalities; identities and communities; social problems and social movements; globalization, power, and politics; immigration and migration; community, networks, and wellbeing. *Total annual research expenditures:* $203,661. *Unit head:* Dr. James Cavendish, Associate Professor and Chairperson, 813-974-2633, Fax: 813-974-6455, E-mail: jcavendi@usf.edu. *Application contact:* Dr. Sara Crawley, Associate Professor and Graduate Program Director, 813-974-0977, Fax: 813-974-6455, E-mail: scrawley@usf.edu.
Website: http://sociology.usf.edu

The University of Tennessee, Graduate School, College of Arts and Sciences, Department of Sociology, Knoxville, TN 37996. Offers criminology (MA, PhD); energy, environment, and resource policy (MA, PhD); political economy (MA, PhD). *Program availability:* Part-time. *Degree requirements:* For master's, thesis or alternative; for doctorate, thesis/dissertation. *Entrance requirements:* For master's, GRE General Test, minimum GPA of 3.0; for doctorate, GRE General Test, minimum GPA of 3.5. Additional exam requirements/recommendations for international students: Required—TOEFL. Electronic applications accepted.

The University of Texas at Arlington, Graduate School, College of Liberal Arts, Department of Sociology and Anthropology, Program in Sociology, Arlington, TX 76019. Offers MA. *Program availability:* Part-time, evening/weekend. *Degree requirements:* For master's, comprehensive exam, thesis or alternative. *Entrance requirements:* For master's, GRE General Test, 12 hours of undergraduate course work in sociology. Additional exam requirements/recommendations for international students: Required—TOEFL (minimum score 550 paper-based). Electronic applications accepted.

The University of Texas at Austin, Graduate School, College of Liberal Arts, Department of Sociology, Austin, TX 78712-1111. Offers MA, PhD. *Degree requirements:* For master's, thesis; for doctorate, thesis/dissertation. *Entrance requirements:* For master's and doctorate, GRE General Test. Additional exam requirements/recommendations for international students: Required—TOEFL. Electronic applications accepted. *Faculty research:* Criminology, demography, Latin America, health, political sociology.

The University of Texas at El Paso, Graduate School, College of Liberal Arts, Department of Sociology and Anthropology, El Paso, TX 79968-0001. Offers applied anthropology (Certificate); applied social sciences (Certificate); sociology (MA). *Program availability:* Part-time, evening/weekend. *Degree requirements:* For master's, thesis. *Entrance requirements:* For master's, GRE General Test, minimum GPA of 3.0. Additional exam requirements/recommendations for international students: Required—TOEFL. Electronic applications accepted. *Faculty research:* U.S.-Mexico border, social inequality, immigration, Chicano culture, Mexico.

The University of Texas at San Antonio, College of Liberal and Fine Arts, Department of Sociology, San Antonio, TX 78249-0617. Offers MS. *Program availability:* Part-time. *Faculty:* 9 full-time (2 women), 1 part-time/adjunct (0 women). *Students:* 10 full-time (5 women), 18 part-time (12 women); includes 12 minority (3 Black or African American, non-Hispanic/Latino; 9 Hispanic/Latino). Average age 29. 9 applicants, 100% accepted, 5 enrolled. In 2017, 13 master's awarded. *Degree requirements:* For master's, comprehensive exam, internship or thesis. *Entrance requirements:* For master's, GRE (waived if GPA 3.5 or above), BA/BS with 18 credit hours in field of study or other appropriate field of study; official transcripts; statement of purpose; academic writing sample; 3 letters of recommendation; minimum GPA of 3.0. Additional exam requirements/recommendations for international students: Required—TOEFL (minimum score 550 paper-based; 79 iBT), IELTS (minimum score 6.5). *Application deadline:* For fall admission, 6/15 for domestic students, 3/1 for international students; for spring admission, 10/15 for domestic students, 9/15 for international students. Application fee: $50 ($90 for international students). Electronic applications accepted. *Expenses:* Contact institution. *Financial support:* Fellowships, research assistantships, teaching assistantships, career-related internships or fieldwork, scholarships/grants, and unspecified assistantships available. Financial award applicants required to submit FAFSA. *Faculty research:* Border studies, Latino studies, race and ethnicity, cultural media, communications studies, family and child development, health and illness, religion. *Total annual research expenditures:* $1.1 million. *Unit head:* Dr. Xiaohe Xu, Chair, 210-458-4620, E-mail: xiaohe.xu@utsa.edu. *Application contact:* Dr. Terri Earnest, Graduate Advisor of Record, 210-458-6239, E-mail: terri.earnest@utsa.edu.
Website: http://colfa.utsa.edu/Sociology/

The University of Texas at Tyler, College of Arts and Sciences, Department of Social Sciences, Tyler, TX 75799-0001. Offers criminal justice (MS); public administration (MPA); sociology (MS). *Program availability:* Part-time, evening/weekend. *Degree requirements:* For master's, comprehensive exam, thesis optional. *Entrance requirements:* For master's, GRE General Test, minimum GPA of 3.0. Additional exam requirements/recommendations for international students: Required—TOEFL. *Faculty research:* Urban segregation, minority business, violent crime, gender discrimination.

The University of Texas Rio Grande Valley, College of Liberal Arts, Department of Sociology and Anthropology, Edinburg, TX 78539. Offers disaster studies (MA); sociology (MS). *Program availability:* Part-time, evening/weekend. *Faculty:* 14 full-time (4 women). *Students:* 16 full-time (12 women), 8 part-time (6 women); includes 21 minority (all Hispanic/Latino). Average age 30. 6 applicants, 83% accepted, 4 enrolled. In 2017, 4 master's awarded. *Entrance requirements:* For master's, GRE General Test, minimum undergraduate GPA of 3.0, bachelor's degree, official transcripts, personal statement, two letters of recommendation. Additional exam requirements/recommendations for international students: Required—TOEFL or IELTS. *Application deadline:* Applications are processed on a rolling basis. Application fee: $50 ($100 for international students). *Expenses:* Tuition, state resident: full-time $5550; part-time $417 per credit hour. Tuition, nonresident: full-time $13,020; part-time $832 per credit hour. *Required fees:* $1169. *Faculty research:* Sociology of education, sociology of health, sociology of religion, migration, race and ethnicity, gender, border studies, disaster studies. *Unit head:* Ramon Guerra, Chair, E-mail: ramon.guerra@utrgv.edu.

Sociology

The University of Toledo, College of Graduate Studies, College of Languages, Literature and Social Sciences, Department of Sociology and Anthropology, Toledo, OH 43606-3390. Offers sociology (MA). *Program availability:* Part-time. *Degree requirements:* For master's, thesis or alternative. *Entrance requirements:* For master's, GRE, minimum cumulative point-hour ratio of 2.7 for all previous academic work, three letters of recommendation, statement of purpose, transcripts from all prior institutions attended. Additional exam requirements/recommendations for international students: Required—TOEFL (minimum score 550 paper-based; 80 iBT). Electronic applications accepted. *Faculty research:* Medical and social gerontology, population, social movements, socioeconomic development, corporations and work, race and ethnicity.

University of Toronto, School of Graduate Studies, Faculty of Arts and Science, Department of Sociology, Toronto, ON M5S 1A1, Canada. Offers MA, PhD. *Program availability:* Part-time. *Degree requirements:* For doctorate, thesis/dissertation. *Entrance requirements:* For master's, GRE (for applicants from non-Canadian universities, recommended for those from Canadian universities), 5 full-year courses in sociology, basic research and statistical skills; 2 letters of reference; minimum B+ average in each of last two years of post-secondary education; for doctorate, GRE (for applicants from non-Canadian universities; recommended for those from Canadian universities), MA in sociology, minimum A- average, 2 letters of reference, statement of interest. Additional exam requirements/recommendations for international students: Required—TOEFL (minimum score 580 paper-based; 93 iBT), TWE (minimum score 5). Electronic applications accepted.

University of Utah, Graduate School, College of Social and Behavioral Science, Department of Sociology, Salt Lake City, UT 84112-1107. Offers M Stat, MA, MS, PhD. *Faculty:* 16 full-time (10 women), 5 part-time/adjunct (1 woman). *Students:* 15 full-time (14 women), 4 part-time (3 women); includes 3 minority (1 Black or African American, non-Hispanic/Latino; 1 Asian, non-Hispanic/Latino; 1 Hispanic/Latino), 3 international. Average age 25. 25 applicants, 40% accepted, 6 enrolled. In 2017, 2 master's, 6 doctorates awarded. Terminal master's awarded for partial completion of doctoral program. *Entrance requirements:* For master's and doctorate, GRE, minimum undergraduate GPA of 3.0. Additional exam requirements/recommendations for international students: Required—TOEFL (minimum score 550 paper-based). Application fee: $55 ($65 for international students). Electronic applications accepted. *Expenses:* Contact institution. *Financial support:* In 2017–18, 1 research assistantship with full tuition reimbursement (averaging $15,000 per year), 15 teaching assistantships with full tuition reimbursements (averaging $15,000 per year) were awarded; scholarships/grants, health care benefits, tuition waivers (full), and unspecified assistantships also available. Financial award application deadline: 12/1. *Faculty research:* Comparative international sociology, population studies, health disparities, environment, gender. *Total annual research expenditures:* $9,900. *Unit head:* Dr. Ming Wen, Chair, 801-581-6153, Fax: 801-585-3784, E-mail: ming.wen@soc.utah.edu. *Application contact:* Dr. Rebecca Utz, Director of Graduate Studies, 801-581-7922, Fax: 801-585-3784, E-mail: rebecca.utz@soc.utah.edu. Website: http://www.soc.utah.edu/

University of Victoria, Faculty of Graduate Studies, Faculty of Social Sciences, Department of Sociology, Victoria, BC V8W 2Y2, Canada. Offers MA, PhD. PhD by special arrangement. *Program availability:* Part-time. *Degree requirements:* For master's, thesis; for doctorate, thesis/dissertation, candidacy exam. *Entrance requirements:* For master's, minimum B+ average. Additional exam requirements/recommendations for international students: Required—TOEFL (minimum score 575 paper-based), IELTS (minimum score 7), TWE (minimum score 4). *Faculty research:* Social and political thought, social justice, health and aging, globalization and social psychology.

University of Virginia, College and Graduate School of Arts and Sciences, Department of Sociology, Charlottesville, VA 22903. Offers MA, PhD. *Faculty:* 19 full-time (10 women), 2 part-time/adjunct (0 women). *Students:* 31 full-time (24 women); includes 7 minority (3 Black or African American, non-Hispanic/Latino; 2 Asian, non-Hispanic/Latino; 1 Hispanic/Latino; 1 Two or more races, non-Hispanic/Latino), 11 international. Average age 29. 60 applicants, 22% accepted, 6 enrolled. In 2017, 4 master's, 6 doctorates awarded. *Degree requirements:* For master's, thesis; for doctorate, comprehensive exam, thesis/dissertation. *Entrance requirements:* For master's and doctorate, GRE General Test, GRE Subject Test, 2 letters of recommendation. Additional exam requirements/recommendations for international students: Required—TOEFL (minimum score 600 paper-based; 90 iBT), IELTS (minimum score 7). *Application deadline:* For fall admission, 1/1 for domestic and international students. Applications are processed on a rolling basis. Application fee: $60. Electronic applications accepted. *Financial support:* Applicants required to submit FAFSA. *Unit head:* Jeffrey Olick, Chair, 434-924-3526, Fax: 434-924-7028, E-mail: sociology@virginia.edu. *Application contact:* Isaac Reed, Director of Graduate Admissions, 434-982-7794, Fax: 434-924-7028, E-mail: iar2c@virginia.edu. Website: http://www.virginia.edu/sociology/

University of Washington, Graduate School, College of Arts and Sciences, Department of Sociology, Seattle, WA 98195. Offers MA, PhD. *Degree requirements:* For master's, thesis; for doctorate, thesis/dissertation. *Entrance requirements:* For master's and doctorate, GRE General Test, minimum GPA of 3.0. Additional exam requirements/recommendations for international students: Required—TOEFL. Electronic applications accepted. *Faculty research:* Demography, criminology, social psychology, race/ethnicity/inequality, family.

University of Waterloo, Graduate Studies, Faculty of Arts, Department of Sociology, Waterloo, ON N2L 3G1, Canada. Offers MA, PhD. *Program availability:* Part-time. *Degree requirements:* For master's, thesis (for some programs); for doctorate, one foreign language, thesis/dissertation. *Entrance requirements:* For master's, honors degree, minimum B+ average, resume, writing sample; for doctorate, master's degree, minimum A- average, resume, writing sample. Additional exam requirements/recommendations for international students: Required—TOEFL, IELTS, PTE. Electronic applications accepted. *Faculty research:* Theory, methods, stratification deviance, political sociology.

The University of Western Ontario, Faculty of Graduate Studies, Social Sciences Division, Department of Sociology, London, ON N6A 5B8, Canada. Offers MA, PhD. Terminal master's awarded for partial completion of doctoral program. *Degree requirements:* For master's, thesis (for some programs); for doctorate, one foreign language, comprehensive exam, thesis/dissertation. *Entrance requirements:* For master's, minimum B+ average, honors degree; for doctorate, minimum A- average. Additional exam requirements/recommendations for international students: Required—TOEFL. Electronic applications accepted. *Faculty research:* Social demography, class and change, health and aging, theory, methods.

University of West Georgia, College of Social Sciences, Carrollton, GA 30118. Offers criminology (MA); data analysis and evaluation methods (Postbaccalaureate Certificate); European Union studies (Postbaccalaureate Certificate); integrative health systems (Postbaccalaureate Certificate); nonprofit management and community development (Postbaccalaureate Certificate); psychology (MA, PhD), including consciousness and society (PhD); public administration (MPA); public management

(Postbaccalaureate Certificate); sociology (MA). *Program availability:* Part-time, evening/weekend, 100% online, blended/hybrid learning. *Faculty:* 48 full-time (22 women). *Students:* 124 full-time (84 women), 73 part-time (46 women); includes 69 minority (56 Black or African American, non-Hispanic/Latino; 4 Asian, non-Hispanic/Latino; 6 Hispanic/Latino; 3 Two or more races, non-Hispanic/Latino), 10 international. Average age 32. 95 applicants, 89% accepted, 63 enrolled. In 2017, 44 master's, 2 doctorates, 4 other advanced degrees awarded. *Entrance requirements:* Additional exam requirements/recommendations for international students: Required—TOEFL (minimum score 523 paper-based; 69 iBT); Recommended—IELTS (minimum score 6.5). *Application deadline:* For fall admission, 7/15 for domestic students, 6/1 for international students; for spring admission, 11/30 for domestic students, 10/15 for international students; for summer admission, 5/15 for domestic students, 3/30 for international students. Applications are processed on a rolling basis. Application fee: $40. Electronic applications accepted. Tuition and fees vary according to degree level and program. *Financial support:* Fellowships, research assistantships, teaching assistantships, career-related internships or fieldwork, Federal Work-Study, institutionally sponsored loans, scholarships/grants, and unspecified assistantships available. Support available to part-time students. Financial award application deadline: 4/1; financial award applicants required to submit FAFSA. *Unit head:* Dr. N. Jane McCandless, Dean of Social Sciences, 678-839-5170, Fax: 678-839-5171, E-mail: jmccandl@westga.edu. *Application contact:* Dr. Toby Ziglar, Assistant Dean of the Graduate School, 678-839-1394, Fax: 678-839-1395, E-mail: graduate@westga.edu. Website: https://www.westga.edu/coss

University of Windsor, Faculty of Graduate Studies, Faculty of Arts and Social Sciences, Department of Sociology and Anthropology, Windsor, ON N9B 3P4, Canada. Offers criminology (MA); sociology (MA); sociology-social justice (PhD). *Program availability:* Part-time. *Degree requirements:* For master's, thesis; for doctorate, comprehensive exam, thesis/dissertation. *Entrance requirements:* For master's, minimum B+ average; for doctorate, writing sample, minimum B+ average. Additional exam requirements/recommendations for international students: Required—TOEFL (minimum score 560 paper-based). Electronic applications accepted. *Faculty research:* Power and social change; criminology/deviance; social psychology; comparative development; race and ethnic relations; family, sex, and gender, social justice.

University of Wisconsin–Madison, Graduate School, College of Letters and Science, Department of Sociology, Madison, WI 53706-1380. Offers rural sociology (MS); sociology (MS, PhD). *Program availability:* Part-time. Terminal master's awarded for partial completion of doctoral program. *Degree requirements:* For master's, thesis, oral exam; for doctorate, thesis/dissertation, preliminary and final oral exams, 4 seminars. *Entrance requirements:* For master's and doctorate, GRE General Test. Additional exam requirements/recommendations for international students: Required—TOEFL. Electronic applications accepted.

University of Wisconsin–Milwaukee, Graduate School, College of Letters and Science, Department of Sociology, Milwaukee, WI 53201-0413. Offers MA, PhD. *Program availability:* Part-time. *Students:* 21 full-time (9 women), 3 part-time (1 woman); includes 6 minority (2 Black or African American, non-Hispanic/Latino; 1 Asian, non-Hispanic/Latino; 3 Two or more races, non-Hispanic/Latino), 3 international. Average age 32. 28 applicants, 29% accepted, 8 enrolled. In 2017, 4 master's, 4 doctorates awarded. *Entrance requirements:* For master's, GRE. *Application deadline:* For fall admission, 1/1 priority date for domestic students; for spring admission, 9/1 for domestic students. Application fee: $56 ($96 for international students). Electronic applications accepted. *Financial support:* Fellowships, teaching assistantships, career-related internships or fieldwork, unspecified assistantships, and project assistantships available. Support available to part-time students. Financial award application deadline: 4/15; financial award applicants required to submit FAFSA. *Unit head:* Donald Green, Department Chair, 414-229-4259, E-mail: dgreen@uwm.edu. *Application contact:* General Information Contact, 414-229-4982, Fax: 414-229-6967, E-mail: gradschool@uwm.edu. Website: http://www.uwm.edu/dept/sociology/

University of Wyoming, College of Arts and Sciences, Department of Sociology, Laramie, WY 82071. Offers MA. *Program availability:* Part-time. *Degree requirements:* For master's, thesis. *Entrance requirements:* For master's, GRE General Test, minimum GPA of 3.0. Additional exam requirements/recommendations for international students: Required—TOEFL (minimum score 525 paper-based). Electronic applications accepted. *Faculty research:* Gender, theory, international studies, law, social inequality.

Utah State University, School of Graduate Studies, College of Humanities and Social Sciences, Department of Sociology, Social Work, and Anthropology, Logan, UT 84322. Offers anthropology (MS); social work (MSW); sociology (MS, PhD). *Degree requirements:* For master's, thesis; for doctorate, comprehensive exam, thesis/dissertation. *Entrance requirements:* For master's, GRE General Test, minimum GPA of 3.0, recommendation letters; for doctorate, GRE General Test, minimum GPA of 3.0, recommendation letters, transcripts, personal statement, MS degree. Additional exam requirements/recommendations for international students: Required—TOEFL; Recommended—TWE. *Faculty research:* Demography, environmental/natural resource sociology, rural community change, international development, health studies.

Vanderbilt University, Department of Sociology, Nashville, TN 37240-1001. Offers MA, PhD. *Faculty:* 16 full-time (6 women). *Students:* 34 full-time (27 women); includes 15 minority (6 Black or African American, non-Hispanic/Latino; 5 Asian, non-Hispanic/Latino; 4 Hispanic/Latino), 3 international. Average age 28. 124 applicants, 6% accepted, 4 enrolled. In 2017, 5 master's, 2 doctorates awarded. *Degree requirements:* For master's, thesis; for doctorate, comprehensive exam, thesis/dissertation, area, qualifying, and final exams. *Entrance requirements:* For master's and doctorate, GRE General Test. Additional exam requirements/recommendations for international students: Required—TOEFL (minimum score 570 paper-based; 88 iBT). *Application deadline:* For fall admission, 1/15 for domestic and international students. Electronic applications accepted. *Financial support:* Fellowships with full tuition reimbursements, research assistantships, teaching assistantships with full tuition reimbursements, Federal Work-Study, institutionally sponsored loans, scholarships/grants, and health care benefits available. Financial award application deadline: 1/15; financial award applicants required to submit CSS PROFILE or FAFSA. *Faculty research:* Criminology; cultural sociology; gender, race, and ethics relations; deviant behavior and social control. *Unit head:* Dr. Larry Isaac, Chair, 615-322-7626, Fax: 615-322-7505, E-mail: larry.isaac@vanderbilt.edu. *Application contact:* Richard Pitt, Director of Graduate Studies, 615-322-7530, Fax: 615-322-7505, E-mail: r.pitt@vanderbilt.edu. Website: http://www.vanderbilt.edu/sociology/VDOS_Home.shtml

Virginia Commonwealth University, Graduate School, College of Humanities and Sciences, Department of Sociology, Richmond, VA 23284-9005. Offers digital sociology (MS). *Degree requirements:* For master's, thesis optional. *Entrance requirements:* For master's, GRE General Test. Additional exam requirements/recommendations for international students: Required—TOEFL (minimum score 600 paper-based; 100 iBT); Recommended—IELTS (minimum score 6.5). Electronic applications accepted.

Washington State University, College of Arts and Sciences, Department of Sociology, Pullman, WA 99164. Offers MA, PhD. Program applications must be made through the

Pullman campus. *Program availability:* Part-time. Terminal master's awarded for partial completion of doctoral program. *Degree requirements:* For master's, thesis; for doctorate, comprehensive exam, thesis/dissertation. *Entrance requirements:* For master's, bachelor's degree, minimum GPA of 3.0; for doctorate, MA in sociology, minimum GPA of 3.0. Additional exam requirements/recommendations for international students: Required—TOEFL (minimum score 550 paper-based). Electronic applications accepted. *Faculty research:* Criminology, environmental sociology, family, gender, social inequality.

Wayne State University, College of Liberal Arts and Sciences, Department of Sociology, Detroit, MI 48202. Offers applied sociological research methodology (MA); medical sociology/health (PhD); race/gender inequality (PhD); sociology (MA); urban/labor studies (PhD). *Faculty:* 11. *Students:* 26 full-time (19 women), 7 part-time (5 women); includes 8 minority (7 Black or African American, non-Hispanic/Latino; 1 Two or more races, non-Hispanic/Latino, 1 international. Average age 37. 29 applicants, 21% accepted, 3 enrolled. In 2017, 6 master's, 9 doctorates awarded. *Degree requirements:* For master's, comprehensive exam (for some programs), thesis (for some programs), oral exam, public defense of thesis/essay; for doctorate, comprehensive exam, thesis/dissertation. *Entrance requirements:* For master's, GRE General Test, minimum GPA of 3.3 in upper-division courses; substantial background in sociology, social science research methods, sociological theory, and basic statistics; three letters of reference (at least 2 from college/university faculty); writing sample; statement of interest; for doctorate, GRE General Test, minimum GPA of 3.5 in master's work; three letters of reference (at least 2 from college/university faculty); statement of interest; sample of written work. Additional exam requirements/recommendations for international students: Required—TOEFL (minimum score 600 paper-based; 100 iBT), TWE, Michigan English Language Assessment Battery (minimum score 85); Recommended—IELTS. *Application deadline:* For fall admission, 1/15 for domestic and international students. Application fee: $50. Electronic applications accepted. *Expenses:* Tuition, state resident: full-time $10,224; part-time $638.98 per credit hour. Tuition, nonresident: full-time $22,145; part-time $1384.04 per credit hour. Tuition and fees vary according to course load and program. *Financial support:* In 2017-18, 19 students received support, including 7 fellowships with tuition reimbursements available (averaging $14,429 per year), 8 teaching assistantships with tuition reimbursements available (averaging $18,534 per year); research assistantships with tuition reimbursements available, scholarships/grants, health care benefits, and unspecified assistantships also available. Financial award applicants required to submit FAFSA. *Faculty research:* Medical sociology, inequality, mental health and immigration, labor, women's menopause and midlife experiences. *Unit head:* Dr. Jeffrey Kentor, Chair and Professor, 313-577-8131, E-mail: jeffrey.kentor@wayne.edu. *Application contact:* Dr. Krista Brumley, Director of Graduate Studies, 313-577-1418, E-mail: kbrumley@wayne.edu.
Website: http://clas.wayne.edu/Sociology/

Western Illinois University, School of Graduate Studies, College of Arts and Sciences, Department of Sociology and Anthropology, Macomb, IL 61455-1390. Offers sociology (MA). *Program availability:* Part-time. *Students:* 10 full-time (3 women), 3 part-time (all women); includes 4 minority (1 Black or African American, non-Hispanic/Latino; 1 Hispanic/Latino; 2 Two or more races, non-Hispanic/Latino), 3 international. Average age 34. 11 applicants, 82% accepted, 5 enrolled. In 2017, 7 master's awarded. *Degree requirements:* For master's, thesis or alternative. *Entrance requirements:* Additional exam requirements/recommendations for international students: Required—TOEFL (minimum score 550 paper-based; 80 iBT). *Application deadline:* Applications are processed on a rolling basis. Application fee: $30. Electronic applications accepted. *Financial support:* Unspecified assistantships available. Financial award applicants required to submit FAFSA. *Unit head:* Dr. John Wozniak, Chairperson, 309-298-1056. *Application contact:* Dr. Nancy Parsons, Associate Provost and Director of Graduate Studies, 309-298-1806, Fax: 309-298-2345, E-mail: grad-office@wiu.edu.
Website: http://wiu.edu/sociology

Western Kentucky University, Graduate Studies, Potter College of Arts and Letters, Department of Sociology, Bowling Green, KY 42101. Offers criminology (MA); sociology (MA). *Program availability:* Online learning. *Degree requirements:* For master's, comprehensive exam, thesis optional, final exam. *Entrance requirements:* For master's, GRE General Test, minimum GPA of 3.0. Additional exam requirements/recommendations for international students: Required—TOEFL (minimum score 555 paper-based; 79 iBT). *Faculty research:* Criminology/delinquency, quantitative and survey research methodology, occupations/professions, sex and gender, demography.

Western Michigan University, Graduate College, College of Arts and Sciences, Department of Sociology, Kalamazoo, MI 49008. Offers MA, PhD. *Degree requirements:* For master's, thesis; for doctorate, one foreign language, thesis/dissertation.

West Virginia University, Eberly College of Arts and Sciences, Morgantown, WV 26506. Offers biology (MS, PhD); chemistry (MS, PhD); communication studies (MA, PhD); computational statistics (PhD); creative writing (MFA); English (MA, PhD); forensic and investigative science (MS); forensic science (PhD); geography (MA); geology (MA, PhD); history (MA, PhD); legal studies (MLS); math (MS); physics (MS, PhD); political science (MA, PhD); professional writing and editing (MA); psychology (MA); public administration (MPA); social work (MSW); sociology (MA, PhD); statistics (MS). *Program availability:* Part-time, evening/weekend, online learning. *Students:* 831 full-time (437 women), 236 part-time (142 women); includes 112 minority (35 Black or African American, non-Hispanic/Latino; 15 Asian, non-Hispanic/Latino; 29 Hispanic/Latino; 33 Two or more races, non-Hispanic/Latino), 235 international. Terminal master's awarded for partial completion of doctoral program. *Degree requirements:* For master's, thesis (for some programs); for doctorate, comprehensive exam, thesis/

dissertation. *Entrance requirements:* For master's and doctorate, GRE. Additional exam requirements/recommendations for international students: Required—TOEFL (minimum score 600 paper-based); Recommended—TWE. *Application deadline:* For spring admission, 2/15 priority date for domestic and international students. Applications are processed on a rolling basis. Application fee: $45. Electronic applications accepted. *Expenses:* Tuition, state resident: full-time $9450. Tuition, nonresident: full-time $24,390. *Financial support:* Fellowships with full tuition reimbursements, research assistantships with full tuition reimbursements, teaching assistantships with full tuition reimbursements, career-related internships or fieldwork, Federal Work-Study, institutionally sponsored loans, scholarships/grants, health care benefits, tuition waivers (full and partial), unspecified assistantships, and administrative assistantships available. Financial award application deadline: 2/1; financial award applicants required to submit FAFSA. *Faculty research:* Humanities, social sciences, life science, physical sciences, mathematics. *Unit head:* Dr. Mary Ellen Mazey, Dean, 304-293-4611, Fax: 304-293-6858, E-mail: mary.mazey@mail.wvu.edu. *Application contact:* Dr. Fred L. King, Associate Dean for Graduate Studies, 304-293-4611 Ext. 5205, Fax: 304-293-6858, E-mail: fred.king@mail.wvu.edu.
Website: http://www.as.wvu.edu/

Wichita State University, Graduate School, Fairmount College of Liberal Arts and Sciences, Department of Sociology, Wichita, KS 67260. Offers MA. *Program availability:* Part-time. *Unit head:* Dr. Jodie Hertzog, Chair, 316-978-3280, Fax: 316-978-3281, E-mail: jodie.hertzog@wichita.edu. *Application contact:* Jordan Oleson, Admissions Coordinator, 316-978-3095, Fax: 316-978-3253, E-mail: jordan.oleson@wichita.edu.
Website: http://www.wichita.edu/sociology

Wilfrid Laurier University, Faculty of Graduate and Postdoctoral Studies, Faculty of Arts, Department of Sociology, Waterloo, ON N2L 3C5, Canada. Offers health, family and well-being (MA); internationalization, migration and human rights (MA). *Entrance requirements:* For master's, honours BA with minimum B+ average and major in sociology. Additional exam requirements/recommendations for international students: Required—TOEFL (minimum score 89 iBT). Electronic applications accepted. *Faculty research:* Internationalization, migration and human rights, health, families, and well-being.

William Paterson University of New Jersey, College of Humanities and Social Sciences, Wayne, NJ 07470-8420. Offers applied sociology (MA); assessment and evaluation research (Certificate); bilingual education (Certificate); clinical and counseling psychology (MA); clinical psychology (Psy D); creative and professional writing (MFA); English (MA); history (MA); public policy and international affairs (MA); teaching English as a second language (Certificate). *Program availability:* Part-time. *Faculty:* 36 full-time (21 women), 10 part-time/adjunct (5 women). *Students:* 62 full-time (44 women), 102 part-time (71 women); includes 76 minority (12 Black or African American, non-Hispanic/Latino; 8 Asian, non-Hispanic/Latino; 50 Hispanic/Latino; 6 Two or more races, non-Hispanic/Latino), 6 international. Average age 33. 156 applicants, 51% accepted, 52 enrolled. In 2017, 39 master's awarded. *Degree requirements:* For master's, thesis (for some programs), internship (for some programs). *Entrance requirements:* For master's, GRE/MAT, minimum GPA of 3.0; 2 letters of recommendation; writing sample/personal statement. Additional exam requirements/recommendations for international students: Required—TOEFL (minimum score 550 paper-based; 79 iBT), IELTS (minimum score 6). *Application deadline:* For fall admission, 6/1 for domestic students, 3/1 for international students; for spring admission, 11/1 for domestic students, 10/1 for international students. Applications are processed on a rolling basis. Application fee: $50. Electronic applications accepted. *Expenses:* Tuition, state resident: full-time $13,920; part-time $6264 per year. Tuition, nonresident: full-time $21,700; part-time $9765 per year. *Required fees:* $80; $36 per year. Tuition and fees vary according to course load, degree level and program. *Financial support:* In 2017–18, 3,480 students received support. Career-related internships or fieldwork, Federal Work-Study, scholarships/grants, and unspecified assistantships available. Support available to part-time students. Financial award application deadline: 3/15; financial award applicants required to submit FAFSA. *Faculty research:* Relationship violence, work-family balance, social development of Japan, theories justifying war, reactions to trauma. *Total annual research expenditures:* $32,300. *Unit head:* Dr. Kara Rabbitt, Dean, 973-720-2180, Fax: 973-720-2955, E-mail: rabbittk@wpunj.edu. *Application contact:* Tinu Adeniran, Associate Director, Graduate Admissions, 973-720-2764, Fax: 973-720-2035, E-mail: adenirant@wpunj.edu.
Website: http://www.wpunj.edu/cohss

Yale University, Graduate School of Arts and Sciences, Department of Sociology, New Haven, CT 06520. Offers comparative and historical sociology (PhD); cultural sociology and social theory (PhD); social stratification and the life course (PhD). *Degree requirements:* For doctorate, thesis/dissertation. *Entrance requirements:* For doctorate, GRE General Test.

York University, Faculty of Graduate Studies, Faculty of Liberal Arts and Professional Studies, Program in Sociology, Toronto, ON M3J 1P3, Canada. Offers MA, PhD. *Program availability:* Part-time. *Degree requirements:* For master's, thesis or alternative; for doctorate, one foreign language, comprehensive exam, thesis/dissertation, analytical paper. Electronic applications accepted.

York University, Faculty of Graduate Studies, Program in Social and Political Thought, Toronto, ON M3J 1P3, Canada. Offers MA, PhD. *Program availability:* Part-time. *Degree requirements:* For master's, one foreign language, thesis or alternative, oral exams; for doctorate, one foreign language, comprehensive exam, thesis/dissertation. Electronic applications accepted.

Survey Methodology

University of Maryland, College Park, Academic Affairs, College of Behavioral and Social Sciences, Joint Program in Survey Methodology, College Park, MD 20742. Offers MS, PhD. Program offered with University of Michigan and Westat. *Degree requirements:* For master's, thesis (for some programs), scholarly paper; for doctorate, thesis/dissertation. *Entrance requirements:* For master's, GRE General Test (recommended), minimum GPA of 3.0, 3 letters of recommendation; for doctorate, GRE General Test, minimum GPA of 3.0, 3 letters of recommendation. Electronic applications accepted.

University of Michigan, Rackham Graduate School, Program in Survey Methodology, Ann Arbor, MI 48106. Offers data science (MS, PhD); social and psychological (MS, PhD); statistical (MS, PhD); survey methodology (Certificate). *Program availability:* Part-time. Terminal master's awarded for partial completion of doctoral program. *Degree requirements:* For master's, internships; for doctorate, comprehensive exam, thesis/dissertation. *Entrance requirements:* For master's and doctorate, GRE, 3 letters of

recommendation, academic statement of purpose, personal statement, resume or curriculum vitae, academic transcripts; for Certificate, 3 letters of recommendation, academic statement of purpose, personal statement, resume or curriculum vitae, academic transcripts. Additional exam requirements/recommendations for international students: Required—TOEFL (minimum score 560 paper-based; 84 iBT). Electronic applications accepted. *Expenses:* Contact institution. *Faculty research:* Survey methodology, web surveys, survey non-response, sample design methods, adaptive survey design.

University of Nebraska–Lincoln, Graduate College, Interdepartmental Area of Survey Research and Methodology, Lincoln, NE 68588. Offers MS, PhD. *Degree requirements:* For master's, comprehensive exam. *Entrance requirements:* For master's, GRE General Test or GMAT. Additional exam requirements/recommendations for international students: Required—TOEFL (minimum score 550 paper-based). Electronic applications accepted. *Faculty research:* Survey research and data analysis.

APPENDIXES

APPENDIXES

Institutional Changes
Since the 2018 Edition

Following is an alphabetical listing of institutions that have recently closed, merged with other institutions, or changed their names or status. In the case of a name change, the former name appears first, followed by the new name.

Argosy University, Dallas (Farmers Branch, TX): *closed.*

Argosy University, Denver (Denver, CO): *closed.*

Argosy University, Inland Empire (Ontario, CA): *closed.*

Argosy University, Nashville (Nashville, TN): *closed.*

Argosy University, Salt Lake City (Draper, UT): *closed.*

Argosy University, San Diego (San Diego, CA): *closed.*

Argosy University, San Francisco Bay Area (Alameda, CA): *closed.*

Argosy University, Sarasota (Sarasota, FL): *closed.*

Argosy University, Schaumburg (Schaumburg, IL): *closed.*

Arlington Baptist College (Arlington, TX): *name changed to Arlington Baptist University.*

Armstrong State University (Savannah, GA): *name changed to Georgia Southern University-Armstrong Campus.*

Art Center College of Design (Pasadena, CA): *name changed to ArtCenter College of Design.*

The Art Institute of California-San Francisco, a campus of Argosy University (San Francisco, CA): *closed.*

Augsburg College (Minneapolis, MN): *name changed to Augsburg University.*

Bristol University (Anaheim, CA): *closed.*

Claremont McKenna College (Claremont, CA): *no longer profiled by request from the institution. Graduate program is for students attending the Claremont Colleges.*

Coleman University (San Diego, CA): *closed.*

Digital Media Arts College (Boca Raton, FL): *merged into Lynn University (Boca Raton, FL).*

Episcopal Divinity School (Cambridge, MA): *merged into Union Theological Seminary in the City of New York (New York, NY).*

Everest University (Tampa, FL): *name changed to Altierus Career College and no longer offers graduate degrees.*

Fairleigh Dickinson University, College at Florham (Madison, NJ): *name changed to Fairleigh Dickinson University, Florham Campus.*

Faith Evangelical College & Seminary (Tacoma, WA): *name changed to Faith International University.*

Frank Lloyd Wright School of Architecture (Scottsdale, AZ): *name changed to School of Architecture at Taliesin.*

Future Generations Graduate School (Franklin, WV): *name changed to Future Generations University.*

Grace University (Omaha, NE): *closed.*

Greenville College (Greenville, IL): *name changed to Greenville University.*

Hazelden Graduate School of Addiction Studies (Center City, MN): *name changed to Hazelden Betty Ford Graduate School of Addiction Studies.*

Henley-Putnam University (San Jose, CA): *name changed to Henley-Putnam School of Strategic Security.*

Huntington College of Health Sciences (Knoxville, TN): *name changed to Huntington University of Health Sciences.*

The Institute for the Psychological Sciences (Arlington, VA): *name changed to Divine Mercy University.*

International College of the Cayman Islands (Newlands, Cayman Islands): *no longer accredited by agency recognized by USDE or CHEA.*

Johnson State College (Johnson, VT): *name changed to Northern Vermont University-Johnson.*

John Wesley University (High Point, NC): *closed.*

Kaplan University, Davenport Campus (Davenport, IA): *name changed to Purdue University Global.*

Knowledge Systems Institute (Skokie, IL): *no longer degree granting.*

Long Island University-Hudson at Westchester (Purchase, NY): *name changed to Long Island University-Hudson.*

Lutheran Theological Seminary at Gettysburg (Gettysburg, PA): *name changed to United Lutheran Seminary.*

The Lutheran Theological Seminary at Philadelphia (Philadelphia, PA): *name changed to United Lutheran Seminary.*

Lynchburg College (Lynchburg, VA): *name changed to University of Lynchburg.*

Lyndon State College (Lyndonville, VT): *name changed to Northern Vermont University-Lyndon.*

Marylhurst University (Marylhurst, OR): *closed.*

McNally Smith College of Music (Saint Paul, MN): *closed.*

Memphis College of Art (Memphis, TN): *closed.*

Mirrer Yeshiva (Brooklyn, NY): *name changed to Mirrer Yeshiva Central Institute.*

Mount Ida College (Newton, MA): *merged into University of Massachusetts Amherst (Amherst, MA).*

National American University (Rapid City, SD): *graduate programs now listed under National American University (Austin, TX).*

The Ohio State University-Mansfield Campus (Mansfield, OH): *name changed to The Ohio State University at Mansfield.*

The Ohio State University-Newark Campus (Newark, OH): *name changed to The Ohio State University at Newark.*

Our Lady of the Lake College (Baton Rouge, LA): *name changed to Franciscan Missionaries of Our Lady University.*

Philadelphia University (Philadelphia, PA): *merged into Thomas Jefferson University (Philadelphia, PA).*

Sacred Heart School of Theology (Hales Corners, WI): *name changed to Sacred Heart Seminary and School of Theology.*

Sewanee: The University of the South (Sewanee, TN): *name changed to The University of the South.*

Shepherd University (Los Angeles, CA): *closed.*

Silicon Valley University (San Jose, CA): *closed.*

South University (Novi, MI): *closed.*

South University (High Point, NC): *closed.*

South University (Cleveland, OH): *closed.*

University of Great Falls (Great Falls, MT): *name changed to University of Providence.*

University of Phoenix-Atlanta Campus (Sandy Springs, GA): *closed.*

University of Phoenix-Augusta Campus (Augusta, GA): *closed.*

University of Phoenix-Central Florida Campus (Orlando, FL): *closed.*

University of Phoenix-Charlotte Campus (Charlotte, NC): *closed.*

University of Phoenix-Colorado Campus (Lone Tree, CO): *closed.*

University of Phoenix-Colorado Springs Downtown Campus (Colorado Springs, CO): *closed.*

University of Phoenix-Columbus Georgia Campus (Columbus, GA): *closed.*

University of Phoenix-Jersey City Campus (Jersey City, NJ): *closed.*

University of Phoenix-New Mexico Campus (Albuquerque, NM): *closed.*

University of Phoenix-North Florida Campus (Jacksonville, FL): *closed.*

University of Phoenix-Southern Arizona Campus (Tucson, AZ): *closed.*

University of Phoenix-Southern California Campus (Costa Mesa, CA): *closed.*

University of Phoenix-South Florida Campus (Miramar, FL): *closed.*

University of Phoenix-Utah Campus (Salt Lake City, UT): *closed.*

University of Phoenix-Washington D.C. Campus (Washington, DC): *closed.*

University of Phoenix-Western Washington Campus (Tukwila, WA): *closed.*

University of Puerto Rico, Mayagüez Campus (Mayagüez, PR): *name changed to University of Puerto Rico-Mayagüez.*

University of Puerto Rico, Medical Sciences Campus (San Juan, PR): *name changed to University of Puerto Rico-Medical Sciences Campus.*

University of Puerto Rico, Río Piedras Campus (San Juan, PR): *name changed to University of Puerto Rico-Río Piedras.*

The University of South Dakota (Vermillion, SD): *name changed to University of South Dakota.*

Urbana University (Urbana, OH): *name changed to Urbana University-A Branch Campus of Franklin University.*

Virginia College in Birmingham (Birmingham, AL): *no longer offers graduate degrees.*

Warner Pacific College (Portland, OR): *name changed to Warner Pacific University.*

Wheelock College (Boston, MA): *merged with Boston University's School of Education.*

Wright Institute (Berkeley, CA): *name changed to The Wright Institute.*

Yeshiva Karlin Stolin Rabbinical Institute (Brooklyn, NY): *name changed to Yeshiva Karlin Stolin.*

Abbreviations Used in the Guides

The following list includes abbreviations of degree names used in the profiles in the 2019 edition of the guides. Because some degrees (e.g., Doctor of Education) can be abbreviated in more than one way (e.g., D.Ed. or Ed.D.), and because the abbreviations used in the guides reflect the preferences of the individual colleges and universities, the list may include two or more abbreviations for a single degree.

DEGREES

A Mus D	Doctor of Musical Arts
AC	Advanced Certificate
AD	Artist's Diploma
	Doctor of Arts
ADP	Artist's Diploma
Adv C	Advanced Certificate
AGC	Advanced Graduate Certificate
AGSC	Advanced Graduate Specialist Certificate
ALM	Master of Liberal Arts
AM	Master of Arts
AMBA	Accelerated Master of Business Administration
APC	Advanced Professional Certificate
APMPH	Advanced Professional Master of Public Health
App Sc	Applied Scientist
App Sc D	Doctor of Applied Science
AstE	Astronautical Engineer
ATC	Advanced Training Certificate
Au D	Doctor of Audiology
B Th	Bachelor of Theology
BN	Bachelor of Naturopathy
CAES	Certificate of Advanced Educational Specialization
CAGS	Certificate of Advanced Graduate Studies
CAL	Certificate in Applied Linguistics
CAPS	Certificate of Advanced Professional Studies
CAS	Certificate of Advanced Studies
CATS	Certificate of Achievement in Theological Studies
CE	Civil Engineer
CEM	Certificate of Environmental Management
CET	Certificate in Educational Technologies
CGS	Certificate of Graduate Studies
Ch E	Chemical Engineer
Clin Sc D	Doctor of Clinical Science
CM	Certificate in Management
CMH	Certificate in Medical Humanities
CMM	Master of Church Ministries
CMS	Certificate in Ministerial Studies
CNM	Certificate in Nonprofit Management
CPC	Certificate in Publication and Communication
CPH	Certificate in Public Health
CPS	Certificate of Professional Studies
CScD	Doctor of Clinical Science
CSD	Certificate in Spiritual Direction
CSS	Certificate of Special Studies
CTS	Certificate of Theological Studies
D Ac	Doctor of Acupuncture
D Admin	Doctor of Administration
D Arch	Doctor of Architecture
D Be	Doctor in Bioethics
D Com	Doctor of Commerce
D Couns	Doctor of Counseling
D Des	Doctorate of Design
D Div	Doctor of Divinity
D Ed	Doctor of Education
D Ed Min	Doctor of Educational Ministry
D Eng	Doctor of Engineering
D Engr	Doctor of Engineering
D Ent	Doctor of Enterprise
D Env	Doctor of Environment
D Law	Doctor of Law
D Litt	Doctor of Letters
D Med Sc	Doctor of Medical Science
D Mgt	Doctor of Management
D Min	Doctor of Ministry
D Miss	Doctor of Missiology
D Mus	Doctor of Music
D Mus A	Doctor of Musical Arts
D Phil	Doctor of Philosophy
D Prof	Doctor of Professional Studies
D Ps	Doctor of Psychology
D Sc	Doctor of Science
D Sc D	Doctor of Science in Dentistry
D Sc IS	Doctor of Science in Information Systems
D Sc PA	Doctor of Science in Physician Assistant Studies
D Th	Doctor of Theology
D Th P	Doctor of Practical Theology
DA	Doctor of Accounting
	Doctor of Arts
DACM	Doctor of Acupuncture and Chinese Medicine
DAIS	Doctor of Applied Intercultural Studies
DAOM	Doctorate in Acupuncture and Oriental Medicine
DAT	Doctorate of Athletic Training
	Professional Doctor of Art Therapy
DBA	Doctor of Business Administration
DBH	Doctor of Behavioral Health
DBL	Doctor of Business Leadership
DC	Doctor of Chiropractic
DCC	Doctor of Computer Science
DCD	Doctor of Communications Design
DCE	Doctor of Computer Engineering
DCL	Doctor of Civil Law
	Doctor of Comparative Law
DCM	Doctor of Church Music
DCN	Doctor of Clinical Nutrition
DCS	Doctor of Computer Science
DDN	Diplôme du Droit Notarial
DDS	Doctor of Dental Surgery
DE	Doctor of Education
	Doctor of Engineering
DED	Doctor of Economic Development
DEIT	Doctor of Educational Innovation and Technology
DEL	Doctor of Executive Leadership
DEM	Doctor of Educational Ministry
DEPD	Diplôme Études Spécialisées
DES	Doctor of Engineering Science
DESS	Diplôme Études Supérieures Spécialisées
DET	Doctor of Educational Technology
DFA	Doctor of Fine Arts
DGP	Diploma in Graduate and Professional Studies
DGS	Doctor of Global Security
DH Sc	Doctor of Health Sciences
DHA	Doctor of Health Administration
DHCE	Doctor of Health Care Ethics
DHL	Doctor of Hebrew Letters
DHPE	Doctorate of Health Professionals Education
DHS	Doctor of Health Science
DHSc	Doctor of Health Science
DIT	Doctor of Industrial Technology

	Doctor of Information Technology	EMHA	Executive Master of Health Administration
DJS	Doctor of Jewish Studies	EMHCL	Executive Master in Healthcare Leadership
DLS	Doctor of Liberal Studies	EMIB	Executive Master of International Business
DM	Doctor of Management	EMIR	Executive Master in International Relations
	Doctor of Music	EML	Executive Master of Leadership
DMA	Doctor of Musical Arts	EMPA	Executive Master of Public Administration
DMD	Doctor of Dental Medicine	EMPL	Executive Master in Policy Leadership
DME	Doctor of Manufacturing Management		Executive Master in Public Leadership
	Doctor of Music Education	EMS	Executive Master of Science
DMFT	Doctor of Marital and Family Therapy	EMTM	Executive Master of Technology Management
DMH	Doctor of Medical Humanities	Eng	Engineer
DML	Doctor of Modern Languages	Eng Sc D	Doctor of Engineering Science
DMP	Doctorate in Medical Physics	Engr	Engineer
DMPNA	Doctor of Management Practice in Nurse Anesthesia	Exec MHA	Executive Master of Health Administration
		Exec Ed D	Executive Doctor of Education
DN Sc	Doctor of Nursing Science	Exec MBA	Executive Master of Business Administration
DNAP	Doctor of Nurse Anesthesia Practice	Exec MPA	Executive Master of Public Administration
DNP	Doctor of Nursing Practice	Exec MPH	Executive Master of Public Health
DNP-A	Doctor of Nursing Practice - Anesthesia	Exec MS	Executive Master of Science
DNS	Doctor of Nursing Science	G Dip	Graduate Diploma
DO	Doctor of Osteopathy	GBC	Graduate Business Certificate
DOL	Doctorate of Organizational Leadership	GDM	Graduate Diploma in Management
DOM	Doctor of Oriental Medicine	GDPA	Graduate Diploma in Public Administration
DOT	Doctor of Occupational Therapy	GEMBA	Global Executive Master of Business Administration
DPA	Diploma in Public Administration		
	Doctor of Public Administration	GM Acc	Graduate Master of Accountancy
DPDS	Doctor of Planning and Development Studies	GMBA	Global Master of Business Administration
DPH	Doctor of Public Health	GP LL M	Global Professional Master of Laws
DPM	Doctor of Plant Medicine	GPD	Graduate Performance Diploma
	Doctor of Podiatric Medicine	GSS	Graduate Special Certificate for Students in Special Situations
DPPD	Doctor of Policy, Planning, and Development		
DPS	Doctor of Professional Studies	IEMBA	International Executive Master of Business Administration
DPT	Doctor of Physical Therapy		
DPTSc	Doctor of Physical Therapy Science	IMA	Interdisciplinary Master of Arts
Dr DES	Doctor of Design	IMBA	International Master of Business Administration
Dr NP	Doctor of Nursing Practice	IMES	International Master's in Environmental Studies
Dr OT	Doctor of Occupational Therapy		
Dr PH	Doctor of Public Health	Ingeniero	Engineer
Dr Sc PT	Doctor of Science in Physical Therapy	JCD	Doctor of Canon Law
DRSc	Doctor of Regulatory Science	JCL	Licentiate in Canon Law
DS	Doctor of Science	JD	Juris Doctor
DS Sc	Doctor of Social Science	JM	Juris Master
DScPT	Doctor of Science in Physical Therapy	JSD	Doctor of Juridical Science
DSI	Doctor of Strategic Intelligence		Doctor of Jurisprudence
DSJS	Doctor of Science in Jewish Studies		Doctor of the Science of Law
DSL	Doctor of Strategic Leadership	JSM	Master of the Science of Law
DSS	Doctor of Strategic Security	L Th	Licenciate in Theology
DSW	Doctor of Social Work	LL B	Bachelor of Laws
DTL	Doctor of Talmudic Law	LL CM	Master of Comparative Law
	Doctor of Transformational Leadership	LL D	Doctor of Laws
DV Sc	Doctor of Veterinary Science	LL M	Master of Laws
DVM	Doctor of Veterinary Medicine	LL M in Tax	Master of Laws in Taxation
DWS	Doctor of Worship Studies	LL M CL	Master of Laws in Common Law
EAA	Engineer in Aeronautics and Astronautics	M Ac	Master of Accountancy
EASPh D	Engineering and Applied Science Doctor of Philosophy		Master of Accounting
			Master of Acupuncture
ECS	Engineer in Computer Science	M Ac OM	Master of Acupuncture and Oriental Medicine
Ed D	Doctor of Education	M Acc	Master of Accountancy
Ed DCT	Doctor of Education in College Teaching		Master of Accounting
Ed L D	Doctor of Education Leadership	M Acct	Master of Accountancy
Ed M	Master of Education		Master of Accounting
Ed S	Specialist in Education	M Accy	Master of Accountancy
Ed Sp	Specialist in Education	M Actg	Master of Accounting
EDB	Executive Doctorate in Business	M Acy	Master of Accountancy
EDM	Executive Doctorate in Management	M Ad	Master of Administration
EE	Electrical Engineer	M Ad Ed	Master of Adult Education
EJD	Executive Juris Doctor	M Adm	Master of Administration
EMBA	Executive Master of Business Administration	M Adm Mgt	Master of Administrative Management
EMFA	Executive Master of Forensic Accounting	M Admin	Master of Administration

M ADU	Master of Architectural Design and Urbanism
M Adv	Master of Advertising
M AEST	Master of Applied Environmental Science and Technology
M Ag	Master of Agriculture
M Ag Ed	Master of Agricultural Education
M Agr	Master of Agriculture
M App Comp Sc	Master of Applied Computer Science
M App St	Master of Applied Statistics
M Appl Stat	Master of Applied Statistics
M Aq	Master of Aquaculture
M Ar	Master of Architecture
M Arc	Master of Architecture
M Arch	Master of Architecture
M Arch I	Master of Architecture I
M Arch II	Master of Architecture II
M Arch E	Master of Architectural Engineering
M Arch H	Master of Architectural History
M Bioethics	Master in Bioethics
M Biomath	Master of Biomathematics
M Cat	Master of Catechesis
M Ch E	Master of Chemical Engineering
M Cl D	Master of Clinical Dentistry
M Cl Sc	Master of Clinical Science
M Comm	Master of Communication
M Comp	Master of Computing
M Comp Sc	Master of Computer Science
M Coun	Master of Counseling
M Dent	Master of Dentistry
M Dent Sc	Master of Dental Sciences
M Des	Master of Design
M Des S	Master of Design Studies
M Div	Master of Divinity
M E Sci	Master of Earth Science
M Ec	Master of Economics
M Econ	Master of Economics
M Ed	Master of Education
M Ed T	Master of Education in Teaching
M En	Master of Engineering
M En S	Master of Environmental Sciences
M Eng	Master of Engineering
M Eng Mgt	Master of Engineering Management
M Engr	Master of Engineering
M Ent	Master of Enterprise
M Env	Master of Environment
M Env Des	Master of Environmental Design
M Env E	Master of Environmental Engineering
M Env Sc	Master of Environmental Science
M Ext Ed	Master of Extension Education
M Fin	Master of Finance
M Geo E	Master of Geological Engineering
M Geoenv E	Master of Geoenvironmental Engineering
M Geog	Master of Geography
M Hum	Master of Humanities
M IDST	Master's in Interdisciplinary Studies
M Jur	Master of Jurisprudence
M Kin	Master of Kinesiology
M Land Arch	Master of Landscape Architecture
M Litt	Master of Letters
M Mark	Master of Marketing
M Mat SE	Master of Material Science and Engineering
M Math	Master of Mathematics
M Mech E	Master of Mechanical Engineering
M Med Sc	Master of Medical Science
M Mgmt	Master of Management
M Mgt	Master of Management
M Min	Master of Ministries
M Mtl E	Master of Materials Engineering
M Mu	Master of Music
M Mus	Master of Music
M Mus Ed	Master of Music Education
M Music	Master of Music
M Pet E	Master of Petroleum Engineering
M Pharm	Master of Pharmacy
M Phil	Master of Philosophy
M Phil F	Master of Philosophical Foundations
M Pl	Master of Planning
M Plan	Master of Planning
M Pol	Master of Political Science
M Pr Met	Master of Professional Meteorology
M Prob S	Master of Probability and Statistics
M Psych	Master of Psychology
M Pub	Master of Publishing
M Rel	Master of Religion
M Sc	Master of Science
M Sc A	Master of Science (Applied)
M Sc AC	Master of Science in Applied Computing
M Sc AHN	Master of Science in Applied Human Nutrition
M Sc BMC	Master of Science in Biomedical Communications
M Sc CS	Master of Science in Computer Science
M Sc E	Master of Science in Engineering
M Sc Eng	Master of Science in Engineering
M Sc Engr	Master of Science in Engineering
M Sc F	Master of Science in Forestry
M Sc FE	Master of Science in Forest Engineering
M Sc Geogr	Master of Science in Geography
M Sc N	Master of Science in Nursing
M Sc OT	Master of Science in Occupational Therapy
M Sc P	Master of Science in Planning
M Sc Pl	Master of Science in Planning
M Sc PT	Master of Science in Physical Therapy
M Sc T	Master of Science in Teaching
M SEM	Master of Sustainable Environmental Management
M Serv Soc	Master of Social Service
M Soc	Master of Sociology
M Sp Ed	Master of Special Education
M Stat	Master of Statistics
M Sys E	Master of Systems Engineering
M Sys Sc	Master of Systems Science
M Tax	Master of Taxation
M Tech	Master of Technology
M Th	Master of Theology
M Tox	Master of Toxicology
M Trans E	Master of Transportation Engineering
M U Ed	Master of Urban Education
M Urb	Master of Urban Planning
M Vet Sc	Master of Veterinary Science
MA	Master of Accounting
	Master of Administration
	Master of Arts
MA Comm	Master of Arts in Communication
MA Ed	Master of Arts in Education
MA Ed/HD	Master of Arts in Education and Human Development
MA Ext	Master of Agricultural Extension
MA Islamic	Master of Arts in Islamic Studies
MA Min	Master of Arts in Ministry
MA Miss	Master of Arts in Missiology
MA Past St	Master of Arts in Pastoral Studies
MA Ph	Master of Arts in Philosophy
MA Psych	Master of Arts in Psychology
MA Sc	Master of Applied Science
MA Sp	Master of Arts (Spirituality)
MA Th	Master of Arts in Theology
MA-R	Master of Arts (Research)

MAA	Master of Applied Anthropology
	Master of Applied Arts
	Master of Arts in Administration
MAAA	Master of Arts in Arts Administration
MAAAP	Master of Arts Administration and Policy
MAAD	Master of Advanced Architectural Design
MAAE	Master of Arts in Art Education
MAAPPS	Master of Arts in Asia Pacific Policy Studies
MAAS	Master of Arts in Aging and Spirituality
MAASJ	Master of Arts in Applied Social Justice
MAAT	Master of Arts in Applied Theology
	Master of Arts in Art Therapy
MAB	Master of Agribusiness
	Master of Applied Bioengineering
MABA	Master's in Applied Behavior Analysis
MABC	Master of Arts in Biblical Counseling
MABE	Master of Arts in Bible Exposition
MABL	Master of Arts in Biblical Languages
MABM	Master of Agribusiness Management
MABS	Master of Arts in Biblical Studies
MABT	Master of Arts in Bible Teaching
MAC	Master of Accountancy
	Master of Accounting
	Master of Arts in Communication
	Master of Arts in Counseling
MACC	Master of Arts in Christian Counseling
MACCT	Master of Accounting
MACD	Master of Arts in Christian Doctrine
MACE	Master of Arts in Christian Education
MACH	Master of Arts in Church History
MACI	Master of Arts in Curriculum and Instruction
MACIS	Master of Accounting and Information Systems
MACJ	Master of Arts in Criminal Justice
MACL	Master of Arts in Christian Leadership
	Master of Arts in Community Leadership
MACM	Master of Arts in Christian Ministries
	Master of Arts in Christian Ministry
	Master of Arts in Church Music
	Master of Arts in Counseling Ministries
MACML	Master of Arts in Christian Ministry and Leadership
MACN	Master of Arts in Counseling
MACO	Master of Arts in Counseling
MAcOM	Master of Acupuncture and Oriental Medicine
MACP	Master of Arts in Christian Practice
	Master of Arts in Church Planting
	Master of Arts in Counseling Psychology
MACS	Master of Applied Computer Science
	Master of Arts in Catholic Studies
	Master of Arts in Christian Studies
MACSE	Master of Arts in Christian School Education
MACT	Master of Arts in Communications and Technology
MAD	Master in Educational Institution Administration
	Master of Applied Design
	Master of Art and Design
MADR	Master of Arts in Dispute Resolution
MADS	Master of Applied Disability Studies
MAE	Master of Aerospace Engineering
	Master of Agricultural Economics
	Master of Agricultural Education
	Master of Applied Economics
	Master of Architectural Engineering
	Master of Art Education
	Master of Arts in Education
	Master of Arts in English
MAEd	Master of Arts Education
MAEE	Master of Agricultural and Extension Education

MAEL	Master of Arts in Educational Leadership
MAEM	Master of Arts in Educational Ministries
MAEP	Master of Arts in Economic Policy
	Master of Arts in Educational Psychology
MAES	Master of Arts in Environmental Sciences
MAET	Master of Arts in English Teaching
MAF	Master of Arts in Finance
MAFE	Master of Arts in Financial Economics
MAFM	Master of Accounting and Financial Management
MAFS	Master of Arts in Family Studies
MAG	Master of Applied Geography
MAGU	Master of Urban Analysis and Management
MAH	Master of Arts in Humanities
MAHA	Master of Arts in Humanitarian Assistance
MAHCM	Master of Arts in Health Care Mission
MAHG	Master of American History and Government
MAHL	Master of Arts in Hebrew Letters
MAHN	Master of Applied Human Nutrition
MAHR	Master of Applied Historical Research
MAHS	Master of Arts in Human Services
MAHSR	Master in Applied Health Services Research
MAIA	Master of Arts in International Administration
	Master of Arts in International Affairs
MAICS	Master of Arts in Intercultural Studies
MAIDM	Master of Arts in Interior Design and Merchandising
MAIH	Master of Arts in Interdisciplinary Humanities
MAIOP	Master of Applied Industrial/Organizational Psychology
MAIS	Master of Arts in Intercultural Studies
	Master of Arts in Interdisciplinary Studies
	Master of Arts in International Studies
MAIT	Master of Administration in Information Technology
MAJ	Master of Arts in Journalism
MAJCS	Master of Arts in Jewish Communal Service
MAJPS	Master of Arts in Jewish Professional Studies
MAJS	Master of Arts in Jewish Studies
MAL	Master of Athletic Leadership
MALA	Master of Arts in Liberal Arts
MALCM	Master in Arts Leadership and Cultural Management
MALD	Master of Arts in Law and Diplomacy
MALER	Master of Arts in Labor and Employment Relations
MALL	Master of Arts in Language Learning
MALLT	Master of Arts in Language, Literature, and Translation
MALP	Master of Arts in Language Pedagogy
MALS	Master of Arts in Liberal Studies
MAM	Master of Acquisition Management
	Master of Agriculture and Management
	Master of Applied Mathematics
	Master of Arts in Management
	Master of Arts in Ministry
	Master of Arts Management
	Master of Aviation Management
MAMC	Master of Arts in Mass Communication
	Master of Arts in Ministry and Culture
	Master of Arts in Ministry for a Multicultural Church
MAME	Master of Arts in Missions/Evangelism
MAMFC	Master of Arts in Marriage and Family Counseling
MAMFT	Master of Arts in Marriage and Family Therapy
MAMHC	Master of Arts in Mental Health Counseling
MAMS	Master of Applied Mathematical Sciences
	Master of Arts in Ministerial Studies
	Master of Arts in Ministry and Spirituality

MAMT	Master of Arts in Mathematics Teaching
MAN	Master of Applied Nutrition
MANT	Master of Arts in New Testament
MAOL	Master of Arts in Organizational Leadership
MAOM	Master of Acupuncture and Oriental Medicine
	Master of Arts in Organizational Management
MAOT	Master of Arts in Old Testament
MAP	Master of Applied Politics
	Master of Applied Psychology
	Master of Arts in Planning
	Master of Psychology
	Master of Public Administration
MAP Min	Master of Arts in Pastoral Ministry
MAPA	Master of Arts in Public Administration
MAPC	Master of Arts in Pastoral Counseling
MAPE	Master of Arts in Physics Education
MAPM	Master of Arts in Pastoral Ministry
	Master of Arts in Pastoral Music
	Master of Arts in Practical Ministry
MAPP	Master of Arts in Public Policy
MAPS	Master of Applied Psychological Sciences
	Master of Arts in Pastoral Studies
	Master of Arts in Public Service
MAPW	Master of Arts in Professional Writing
MAQRM	Master's of Actuarial and Quantitative Risk Management
MAR	Master of Arts in Reading
	Master of Arts in Religion
Mar Eng	Marine Engineer
MARC	Master of Arts in Rehabilitation Counseling
MARE	Master of Arts in Religious Education
MARL	Master of Arts in Religious Leadership
MARS	Master of Arts in Religious Studies
MAS	Master of Accounting Science
	Master of Actuarial Science
	Master of Administrative Science
	Master of Advanced Study
	Master of American Studies
	Master of Animal Science
	Master of Applied Science
	Master of Applied Statistics
	Master of Archival Studies
MASA	Master of Advanced Studies in Architecture
MASC	Master of Arts in School Counseling
MASD	Master of Arts in Spiritual Direction
MASE	Master of Arts in Special Education
MASF	Master of Arts in Spiritual Formation
MASJ	Master of Arts in Systems of Justice
MASLA	Master of Advanced Studies in Landscape Architecture
MASM	Master of Aging Services Management
	Master of Arts in Specialized Ministries
MASP	Master of Arts in School Psychology
MASS	Master of Applied Social Science
MASW	Master of Aboriginal Social Work
MAT	Master of Arts in Teaching
	Master of Arts in Theology
	Master of Athletic Training
	Master's in Administration of Telecommunications
Mat E	Materials Engineer
MATCM	Master of Acupuncture and Traditional Chinese Medicine
MATDE	Master of Arts in Theology, Development, and Evangelism
MATDR	Master of Territorial Management and Regional Development
MATE	Master of Arts for the Teaching of English
MATESL	Master of Arts in Teaching English as a Second Language

MATESOL	Master of Arts in Teaching English to Speakers of Other Languages
MATF	Master of Arts in Teaching English as a Foreign Language/Intercultural Studies
MATFL	Master of Arts in Teaching Foreign Language
MATH	Master of Arts in Therapy
MATI	Master of Administration of Information Technology
MATL	Master of Arts in Teaching of Languages
	Master of Arts in Transformational Leadership
MATM	Master of Arts in Teaching of Mathematics
MATRN	Master of Athletic Training
MATS	Master of Arts in Theological Studies
	Master of Arts in Transforming Spirituality
MAUA	Master of Arts in Urban Affairs
MAUD	Master of Arts in Urban Design
MAURP	Master of Arts in Urban and Regional Planning
MAW	Master of Arts in Worship
MAWSHP	Master of Arts in Worship
MAYM	Master of Arts in Youth Ministry
MB	Master of Bioinformatics
MBA	Master of Business Administration
MBA-AM	Master of Business Administration in Aviation Management
MBA-EP	Master of Business Administration–Experienced Professionals
MBAA	Master of Business Administration in Aviation
MBAE	Master of Biological and Agricultural Engineering
	Master of Biosystems and Agricultural Engineering
MBAH	Master of Business Administration in Health
MBAi	Master of Business Administration–International
MBAICT	Master of Business Administration in Information and Communication Technology
MBC	Master of Building Construction
MBE	Master of Bilingual Education
	Master of Bioengineering
	Master of Bioethics
	Master of Biomedical Engineering
	Master of Business Economics
	Master of Business Education
MBEE	Master in Biotechnology Enterprise and Entrepreneurship
MBET	Master of Business, Entrepreneurship and Technology
MBI	Master in Business Informatics
MBIOT	Master of Biotechnology
MBiotech	Master of Biotechnology
MBL	Master of Business Leadership
MBLE	Master in Business Logistics Engineering
MBME	Master's in Biomedical Engineering
MBMSE	Master of Business Management and Software Engineering
MBOE	Master of Business Operational Excellence
MBS	Master of Biblical Studies
	Master of Biological Science
	Master of Biomedical Sciences
	Master of Bioscience
	Master of Building Science
	Master of Business and Science
	Master of Business Statistics
MBST	Master of Biostatistics
MBT	Master of Biomedical Technology
	Master of Biotechnology
	Master of Business Taxation
MBV	Master of Business for Veterans
MC	Master of Classics
	Master of Communication
	Master of Counseling

MC Ed	Master of Continuing Education
MC Sc	Master of Computer Science
MCA	Master of Commercial Aviation
	Master of Communication Arts
	Master of Criminology (Applied)
MCAM	Master of Computational and Applied Mathematics
MCC	Master of Computer Science
MCD	Master of Communications Disorders
	Master of Community Development
MCE	Master in Electronic Commerce
	Master of Chemistry Education
	Master of Christian Education
	Master of Civil Engineering
	Master of Control Engineering
MCEM	Master of Construction Engineering Management
MCEPA	Master of Chinese Economic and Political Affairs
MCHE	Master of Chemical Engineering
MCIS	Master of Communication and Information Studies
	Master of Computer and Information Science
	Master of Computer Information Systems
MCIT	Master of Computer and Information Technology
MCJ	Master of Criminal Justice
MCL	Master in Communication Leadership
	Master of Canon Law
	Master of Christian Leadership
	Master of Comparative Law
MCM	Master of Christian Ministry
	Master of Church Ministry
	Master of Church Music
	Master of Communication Management
	Master of Community Medicine
	Master of Construction Management
	Master of Contract Management
MCMin	Master of Christian Ministry
MCMM	Master in Communications and Media Management
MCMP	Master of City and Metropolitan Planning
MCMS	Master of Clinical Medical Science
MCN	Master of Clinical Nutrition
MCOL	Master of Arts in Community and Organizational Leadership
MCP	Master of City Planning
	Master of Community Planning
	Master of Counseling Psychology
	Master of Cytopathology Practice
	Master of Science in Quality Systems and Productivity
MCPD	Master of Community Planning and Development
MCR	Master in Clinical Research
MCRP	Master of City and Regional Planning
	Master of Community and Regional Planning
MCRS	Master of City and Regional Studies
MCS	Master of Chemical Sciences
	Master of Christian Studies
	Master of Clinical Science
	Master of Combined Sciences
	Master of Communication Studies
	Master of Computer Science
	Master of Consumer Science
MCSE	Master of Computer Science and Engineering
MCSL	Master of Catholic School Leadership
MCSM	Master of Construction Science and Management
MCT	Master of Commerce and Technology

MCTM	Master of Clinical Translation Management
MCTP	Master of Communication Technology and Policy
MCTS	Master of Clinical and Translational Science
MCVS	Master of Cardiovascular Science
MD	Doctor of Medicine
MDA	Master of Dietetic Administration
MDB	Master of Design-Build
MDE	Master in Design Engineering
	Master of Developmental Economics
	Master of Distance Education
	Master of the Education of the Deaf
MDH	Master of Dental Hygiene
MDI	Master of Disruptive Innovation
MDM	Master of Design Methods
	Master of Digital Media
MDP	Master in Sustainable Development Practice
	Master of Development Practice
MDR	Master of Dispute Resolution
MDS	Master in Data Science
	Master of Dental Surgery
	Master of Design Studies
	Master of Digital Sciences
MDSPP	Master in Data Science for Public Policy
ME	Master of Education
	Master of Engineering
	Master of Entrepreneurship
ME Sc	Master of Engineering Science
ME-PD	Master of Education–Professional Development
MEA	Master of Educational Administration
	Master of Engineering Administration
MEAE	Master of Entertainment Arts and Engineering
MEAP	Master of Environmental Administration and Planning
MEB	Master of Energy Business
MEBD	Master in Environmental Building Design
MEBT	Master in Electronic Business Technologies
MEC	Master of Electronic Commerce
Mech E	Mechanical Engineer
MEDS	Master of Environmental Design Studies
MEE	Master in Education
	Master of Electrical Engineering
	Master of Energy Engineering
	Master of Environmental Engineering
MEECON	Master of Energy Economics
MEEM	Master of Environmental Engineering and Management
MEENE	Master of Engineering in Environmental Engineering
MEEP	Master of Environmental and Energy Policy
MEERM	Master of Earth and Environmental Resource Management
MEH	Master in Humanistic Studies
	Master of Environmental Health
	Master of Environmental Horticulture
MEHS	Master of Environmental Health and Safety
MEIM	Master of Entertainment Industry Management
	Master of Equine Industry Management
MEL	Master of Educational Leadership
	Master of Engineering Leadership
	Master of English Literature
MELP	Master of Environmental Law and Policy
MEM	Master of Engineering Management
	Master of Environmental Management
	Master of Marketing
MEME	Master of Engineering in Manufacturing Engineering
	Master of Engineering in Mechanical Engineering
MENR	Master of Environment and Natural Resources

MENVEGR	Master of Environmental Engineering		MGM	Master of Global Management
MEP	Master of Engineering Physics		MGMA	Master of Greenhouse Gas Management and Accounting
MEPC	Master of Environmental Pollution Control		MGP	Master of Gestion de Projet
MEPD	Master of Environmental Planning and Design		MGPS	Master of Global Policy Studies
MER	Master of Employment Relations		MGREM	Master of Global Real Estate Management
MERE	Master of Entrepreneurial Real Estate		MGS	Master of Gender Studies
MERL	Master of Energy Regulation and Law			Master of Gerontological Studies
MES	Master of Education and Science			Master of Global Studies
	Master of Engineering Science		MH	Master of Humanities
	Master of Environment and Sustainability		MH Sc	Master of Health Sciences
	Master of Environmental Science		MHA	Master of Health Administration
	Master of Environmental Studies			Master of Healthcare Administration
	Master of Environmental Systems			Master of Hospital Administration
MESM	Master of Environmental Science and Management			Master of Hospitality Administration
MET	Master of Educational Technology		MHB	Master of Human Behavior
	Master of Engineering Technology		MHC	Master of Mental Health Counseling
	Master of Entertainment Technology		MHCA	Master of Health Care Administration
	Master of Environmental Toxicology		MHCD	Master of Health Care Design
METM	Master of Engineering and Technology Management		MHCI	Master of Human-Computer Interaction
			MHCL	Master of Health Care Leadership
MEVE	Master of Environmental Engineering		MHCM	Master of Health Care Management
MF	Master of Finance		MHE	Master of Health Education
	Master of Forestry			Master of Human Ecology
MFA	Master of Financial Administration		MHE Ed	Master of Home Economics Education
	Master of Fine Arts		MHEA	Master of Higher Education Administration
MFALP	Master of Food and Agriculture Law and Policy		MHHS	Master of Health and Human Services
MFAS	Master of Fisheries and Aquatic Science		MHI	Master of Health Informatics
MFC	Master of Forest Conservation			Master of Healthcare Innovation
MFCS	Master of Family and Consumer Sciences		MHID	Master of Healthcare Interior Design
MFE	Master of Financial Economics		MHIHIM	Master of Health Informatics and Health Information Management
	Master of Financial Engineering		MHIIM	Master of Health Informatics and Information Management
	Master of Forest Engineering			
MFES	Master of Fire and Emergency Services		MHK	Master of Human Kinetics
MFG	Master of Functional Genomics		MHM	Master of Healthcare Management
MFHD	Master of Family and Human Development		MHMS	Master of Health Management Systems
MFM	Master of Financial Management		MHP	Master of Health Physics
	Master of Financial Mathematics			Master of Heritage Preservation
MFPE	Master of Food Process Engineering			Master of Historic Preservation
MFR	Master of Forest Resources		MHPA	Master of Heath Policy and Administration
MFRC	Master of Forest Resources and Conservation		MHPCTL	Master of High Performance Coaching and Technical Leadership
MFRE	Master of Food and Resource Economics			
MFS	Master of Food Science		MHPE	Master of Health Professions Education
	Master of Forensic Sciences		MHR	Master of Human Resources
	Master of Forest Science		MHRD	Master in Human Resource Development
	Master of Forest Studies		MHRIR	Master of Human Resources and Industrial Relations
	Master of French Studies			
MFST	Master of Food Safety and Technology		MHRLR	Master of Human Resources and Labor Relations
MFT	Master of Family Therapy			
MFWCB	Master of Fish, Wildlife and Conservation Biology		MHRM	Master of Human Resources Management
			MHS	Master of Health Science
MFWS	Master of Fisheries and Wildlife Sciences			Master of Health Sciences
MFYCS	Master of Family, Youth and Community Sciences			Master of Health Studies
				Master of Hispanic Studies
MG	Master of Genetics			Master of Human Services
MGA	Master of Global Affairs			Master of Humanistic Studies
	Master of Government Administration		MHSA	Master of Health Services Administration
	Master of Governmental Administration		MHSM	Master of Health Systems Management
MGBA	Master of Global Business Administration		MI	Master of Information
MGC	Master of Genetic Counseling			Master of Instruction
MGCS	Master of Genetic Counselor Studies		MI Arch	Master of Interior Architecture
MGD	Master of Graphic Design		MIA	Master of Interior Architecture
MGE	Master of Geotechnical Engineering			Master of International Affairs
MGEM	Master of Geomatics for Environmental Management		MIAA	Master of International Affairs and Administration
	Master of Global Entrepreneurship and Management		MIAM	Master of International Agribusiness Management
MGIS	Master of Geographic Information Science		MIAPD	Master of Interior Architecture and Product Design
	Master of Geographic Information Systems			

MIB	Master of International Business
MIBS	Master of International Business Studies
MICLJ	Master of International Criminal Law and Justice
MICM	Master of International Construction Management
MID	Master of Industrial Design
	Master of Industrial Distribution
	Master of Innovation Design
	Master of Interior Design
	Master of International Development
MIDA	Master of International Development Administration
MIDP	Master of International Development Policy
MIDS	Master of Information and Data Science
MIE	Master of Industrial Engineering
MIF	Master of International Forestry
MIHTM	Master of International Hospitality and Tourism Management
MIJ	Master of International Journalism
MILR	Master of Industrial and Labor Relations
MIM	Master in Ministry
	Master of Information Management
	Master of International Management
	Master of International Marketing
MIMFA	Master of Investment Management and Financial Analysis
MIMLAE	Master of International Management for Latin American Executives
MIMS	Master of Information Management and Systems
	Master of Integrated Manufacturing Systems
MIP	Master of Infrastructure Planning
	Master of Intellectual Property
	Master of International Policy
MIPA	Master of International Public Affairs
MIPD	Master of Integrated Product Design
MIPER	Master of International Political Economy of Resources
MIPM	Master of International Policy Management
MIPP	Master of International Policy and Practice
	Master of International Public Policy
MIPS	Master of International Planning Studies
MIR	Master of Industrial Relations
	Master of International Relations
MIRD	Master of International Relations and Diplomacy
MIRHR	Master of Industrial Relations and Human Resources
MIS	Master of Imaging Science
	Master of Industrial Statistics
	Master of Information Science
	Master of Information Systems
	Master of Integrated Science
	Master of Interdisciplinary Studies
	Master of International Service
	Master of International Studies
MISE	Master of Industrial and Systems Engineering
MISKM	Master of Information Sciences and Knowledge Management
MISM	Master of Information Systems Management
MISW	Master of Indigenous Social Work
MIT	Master in Teaching
	Master of Industrial Technology
	Master of Information Technology
	Master of Initial Teaching
	Master of International Trade
MITA	Master of Information Technology Administration
MITM	Master of Information Technology and Management

MJ	Master of Journalism
	Master of Jurisprudence
MJ Ed	Master of Jewish Education
MJA	Master of Justice Administration
MJM	Master of Justice Management
MJS	Master of Judaic Studies
	Master of Judicial Studies
	Master of Juridical Studies
MK	Master of Kinesiology
MKM	Master of Knowledge Management
ML	Master of Latin
	Master's in Law
ML Arch	Master of Landscape Architecture
MLA	Master of Landscape Architecture
	Master of Liberal Arts
MLAS	Master of Laboratory Animal Science
	Master of Liberal Arts and Sciences
MLAUD	Master of Landscape Architecture in Urban Development
MLD	Master of Leadership Development
	Master of Leadership Studies
MLE	Master of Applied Linguistics and Exegesis
MLER	Master of Labor and Employment Relations
MLI Sc	Master of Library and Information Science
MLIS	Master of Library and Information Science
	Master of Library and Information Studies
MLM	Master of Leadership in Ministry
MLPD	Master of Land and Property Development
MLRHR	Master of Labor Relations and Human Resources
MLS	Master of Leadership Studies
	Master of Legal Studies
	Master of Liberal Studies
	Master of Library Science
	Master of Life Sciences
	Master of Medical Laboratory Sciences
MLSCM	Master of Logistics and Supply Chain Management
MLT	Master of Language Technologies
MLTCA	Master of Long Term Care Administration
MLW	Master of Studies in Law
MLWS	Master of Land and Water Systems
MM	Master of Management
	Master of Mediation
	Master of Ministry
	Master of Music
MM Ed	Master of Music Education
MM Sc	Master of Medical Science
MM St	Master of Museum Studies
MMA	Master of Marine Affairs
	Master of Media Arts
	Master of Ministry Administration
	Master of Musical Arts
MMAL	Master of Maritime Administration and Logistics
MMAS	Master of Military Art and Science
MMB	Master of Microbial Biotechnology
MMC	Master of Manufacturing Competitiveness
	Master of Mass Communications
MMCM	Master of Music in Church Music
MMCSS	Master of Mathematical Computational and Statistical Sciences
MME	Master of Management in Energy
	Master of Manufacturing Engineering
	Master of Mathematics for Educators
	Master of Mechanical Engineering
	Master of Mining Engineering
	Master of Music Education
MMEL	Master's in Medical Education Leadership

MMF	Master of Mathematical Finance		Master of Oriental Medicine
MMFC/T	Master of Marriage and Family Counseling/ Therapy	MOR	Master of Operations Research
MMFT	Master of Marriage and Family Therapy	MOT	Master of Occupational Therapy
MMG	Master of Management	MP	Master of Physiology
MMH	Master of Management in Hospitality		Master of Planning
	Master of Medical Humanities	MP Ac	Master of Professional Accountancy
MMI	Master of Management of Innovation	MP Acc	Master of Professional Accountancy
MMIS	Master of Management Information Systems		Master of Professional Accounting
MML	Master of Managerial Logistics		Master of Public Accounting
MMM	Master of Manufacturing Management	MP Aff	Master of Public Affairs
	Master of Marine Management	MP Th	Master of Pastoral Theology
	Master of Medical Management	MPA	Master of Performing Arts
MMP	Master of Marine Policy		Master of Physician Assistant
	Master of Medical Physics		Master of Professional Accountancy
	Master of Music Performance		Master of Professional Accounting
MMPA	Master of Management and Professional Accounting		Master of Public Administration
			Master of Public Affairs
MMQM	Master of Manufacturing Quality Management	MPAC	Master of Professional Accounting
MMR	Master of Marketing Research	MPAID	Master of Public Administration and International Development
MMRM	Master of Marine Resources Management	MPAP	Master of Physician Assistant Practice
MMS	Master in Migration Studies		Master of Public Administration and Policy
	Master of Management Science		Master of Public Affairs and Politics
	Master of Management Studies	MPAS	Master of Physician Assistant Science
	Master of Manufacturing Systems		Master of Physician Assistant Studies
	Master of Marine Studies	MPC	Master of Professional Communication
	Master of Materials Science	MPD	Master of Product Development
	Master of Mathematical Sciences		Master of Public Diplomacy
	Master of Medical Science	MPDS	Master of Planning and Development Studies
	Master of Medieval Studies	MPE	Master of Physical Education
MMSE	Master of Manufacturing Systems Engineering	MPEM	Master of Project Engineering and Management
MMSM	Master of Music in Sacred Music	MPFM	Master of Public Financial Management
MMT	Master in Marketing	MPH	Master of Public Health
	Master of Math for Teaching	MPHE	Master of Public Health Education
	Master of Music Therapy	MPHM	Master in Plant Health Management
	Master's in Marketing Technology	MPHS	Master of Population Health Sciences
MMus	Master of Music	MPHTM	Master of Public Health and Tropical Medicine
MN	Master of Nursing	MPIA	Master of Public and International Affairs
	Master of Nutrition	MPL	Master of Pastoral Leadership
MN NP	Master of Nursing in Nurse Practitioner	MPM	Master of Pastoral Ministry
MNA	Master of Nonprofit Administration		Master of Pest Management
	Master of Nurse Anesthesia		Master of Policy Management
MNAL	Master of Nonprofit Administration and Leadership		Master of Practical Ministries
MNAS	Master of Natural and Applied Science		Master of Professional Management
MNCL	Master of Nonprofit and Civic Leadership		Master of Project Management
MNCM	Master of Network and Communications Management		Master of Public Management
MNE	Master of Nuclear Engineering	MPNA	Master of Public and Nonprofit Administration
MNL	Master in International Business for Latin America	MPNL	Master of Philanthropy and Nonprofit Leadership
MNM	Master of Nonprofit Management	MPO	Master of Prosthetics and Orthotics
MNO	Master of Nonprofit Organization	MPOD	Master of Positive Organizational Development
MNPL	Master of Not-for-Profit Leadership	MPP	Master of Public Policy
MNpS	Master of Nonprofit Studies	MPPA	Master of Public Policy Administration
MNR	Master of Natural Resources		Master of Public Policy and Administration
MNRD	Master of Natural Resources Development	MPPAL	Master of Public Policy, Administration and Law
MNRES	Master of Natural Resources and Environmental Studies	MPPGA	Master of Public Policy and Global Affairs
MNRM	Master of Natural Resource Management	MPPM	Master of Public Policy and Management
MNRMG	Master of Natural Resource Management and Geography	MPRTM	Master of Parks, Recreation, and Tourism Management
MNRS	Master of Natural Resource Stewardship	MPS	Master of Pastoral Studies
MNS	Master of Natural Science		Master of Perfusion Science
MNSE	Master of Natural Sciences Education		Master of Planning Studies
MO	Master of Oceanography		Master of Political Science
MOD	Master of Organizational Development		Master of Preservation Studies
MOGS	Master of Oil and Gas Studies		Master of Prevention Science
MOL	Master of Organizational Leadership		Master of Professional Studies
MOM	Master of Organizational Management		Master of Public Service
		MPSA	Master of Public Service Administration

MPSG	Master of Population and Social Gerontology	MS Sc	Master of Social Science
MPSIA	Master of Political Science and International Affairs	MS Sp Ed	Master of Science in Special Education
		MS Stat	Master of Science in Statistics
MPSL	Master of Public Safety Leadership	MS Surg	Master of Science in Surgery
MPT	Master of Pastoral Theology	MS Tax	Master of Science in Taxation
	Master of Physical Therapy	MS Tc E	Master of Science in Telecommunications Engineering
	Master of Practical Theology		
MPVM	Master of Preventive Veterinary Medicine	MS-R	Master of Science (Research)
MPW	Master of Professional Writing	MSA	Master of School Administration
	Master of Public Works		Master of Science in Accountancy
MQF	Master of Quantitative Finance		Master of Science in Accounting
MQM	Master of Quality Management		Master of Science in Administration
	Master of Quantitative Management		Master of Science in Aeronautics
MQS	Master of Quality Systems		Master of Science in Agriculture
MR	Master of Recreation		Master of Science in Analytics
	Master of Retailing		Master of Science in Anesthesia
MRA	Master in Research Administration		Master of Science in Architecture
	Master of Regulatory Affairs		Master of Science in Aviation
MRC	Master of Rehabilitation Counseling		Master of Sports Administration
MRCP	Master of Regional and City Planning		Master of Surgical Assisting
	Master of Regional and Community Planning	MSAA	Master of Science in Astronautics and Aeronautics
MRD	Master of Rural Development		
MRE	Master of Real Estate	MSABE	Master of Science in Agricultural and Biological Engineering
	Master of Religious Education		
MRED	Master of Real Estate Development	MSAC	Master of Science in Acupuncture
MREM	Master of Resource and Environmental Management	MSACC	Master of Science in Accounting
		MSACS	Master of Science in Applied Computer Science
MRLS	Master of Resources Law Studies	MSAE	Master of Science in Aeronautical Engineering
MRM	Master of Resources Management		Master of Science in Aerospace Engineering
MRP	Master of Regional Planning		Master of Science in Applied Economics
MRRD	Master in Recreation Resource Development		Master of Science in Applied Engineering
MRS	Master of Religious Studies		Master of Science in Architectural Engineering
MRSc	Master of Rehabilitation Science	MSAEM	Master of Science in Aerospace Engineering and Mechanics
MRUD	Master of Resilient Design		
MS	Master of Science	MSAF	Master of Science in Aviation Finance
MS Cmp E	Master of Science in Computer Engineering	MSAG	Master of Science in Applied Geosciences
MS Kin	Master of Science in Kinesiology	MSAH	Master of Science in Allied Health
MS Acct	Master of Science in Accounting	MSAL	Master of Sport Administration and Leadership
MS Accy	Master of Science in Accountancy	MSAM	Master of Science in Applied Mathematics
MS Aero E	Master of Science in Aerospace Engineering	MSANR	Master of Science in Agriculture and Natural Resources
MS Ag	Master of Science in Agriculture		
MS Arch	Master of Science in Architecture	MSAS	Master of Science in Administrative Studies
MS Arch St	Master of Science in Architectural Studies		Master of Science in Applied Statistics
MS Bio E	Master of Science in Bioengineering		Master of Science in Architectural Studies
MS Bm E	Master of Science in Biomedical Engineering	MSAT	Master of Science in Accounting and Taxation
MS Ch E	Master of Science in Chemical Engineering		Master of Science in Advanced Technology
MS Cp E	Master of Science in Computer Engineering		Master of Science in Athletic Training
MS Eco	Master of Science in Economics	MSB	Master of Science in Biotechnology
MS Econ	Master of Science in Economics	MSBA	Master of Science in Business Administration
MS Ed	Master of Science in Education		Master of Science in Business Analysis
MS Ed Admin	Master of Science in Educational Administration	MSBAE	Master of Science in Biological and Agricultural Engineering
MS El	Master of Science in Educational Leadership and Administration		Master of Science in Biosystems and Agricultural Engineering
MS En E	Master of Science in Environmental Engineering	MSBCB	Master's in Bioinformatics and Computational Biology
MS Eng	Master of Science in Engineering	MSBE	Master of Science in Biological Engineering
MS Engr	Master of Science in Engineering		Master of Science in Biomedical Engineering
MS Env E	Master of Science in Environmental Engineering	MSBENG	Master of Science in Bioengineering
		MSBH	Master of Science in Behavioral Health
MS Exp Surg	Master of Science in Experimental Surgery	MSBM	Master of Sport Business Management
MS Mat SE	Master of Science in Material Science and Engineering	MSBME	Master of Science in Biomedical Engineering
		MSBMS	Master of Science in Basic Medical Science
MS Met E	Master of Science in Metallurgical Engineering	MSBS	Master of Science in Biomedical Sciences
MS Mgt	Master of Science in Management	MSBTM	Master of Science in Biotechnology and Management
MS Min	Master of Science in Mining		
MS Min E	Master of Science in Mining Engineering	MSC	Master of Science in Commerce
MS Mt E	Master of Science in Materials Engineering		Master of Science in Communication
MS Otol	Master of Science in Otolaryngology		Master of Science in Counseling
MS Pet E	Master of Science in Petroleum Engineering		Master of Science in Criminology

	Master of Strategic Communication
MSCC	Master of Science in Community Counseling
MSCD	Master of Science in Communication Disorders
	Master of Science in Community Development
MSCE	Master of Science in Chemistry Education
	Master of Science in Civil Engineering
	Master of Science in Clinical Epidemiology
	Master of Science in Computer Engineering
	Master of Science in Continuing Education
MSCEE	Master of Science in Civil and Environmental Engineering
MSCF	Master of Science in Computational Finance
MSCH	Master of Science in Chemical Engineering
MSChE	Master of Science in Chemical Engineering
MSCI	Master of Science in Clinical Investigation
MSCID	Master of Science in Community and International Development
MSCIS	Master of Science in Computer and Information Science
	Master of Science in Computer and Information Systems
	Master of Science in Computer Information Science
	Master of Science in Computer Information Systems
MSCIT	Master of Science in Computer Information Technology
MSCJ	Master of Science in Criminal Justice
MSCJA	Master of Science in Criminal Justice Administration
MSCJS	Master of Science in Crime and Justice Studies
MSCLS	Master of Science in Clinical Laboratory Studies
MSCM	Master of Science in Church Management
	Master of Science in Conflict Management
	Master of Science in Construction Management
	Master of Supply Chain Management
MSCMP	Master of Science in Cybersecurity Management and Policy
MSCNU	Master of Science in Clinical Nutrition
MSCP	Master of Science in Clinical Psychology
	Master of Science in Community Psychology
	Master of Science in Computer Engineering
	Master of Science in Counseling Psychology
MSCPE	Master of Science in Computer Engineering
MSCPharm	Master of Science in Pharmacy
MSCR	Master of Science in Clinical Research
MSCRP	Master of Science in City and Regional Planning
	Master of Science in Community and Regional Planning
MSCS	Master of Science in Clinical Science
	Master of Science in Computer Science
	Master of Science in Cyber Security
MSCSD	Master of Science in Communication Sciences and Disorders
MSCSE	Master of Science in Computer Science and Engineering
MSCTE	Master of Science in Career and Technical Education
MSD	Master of Science in Dentistry
	Master of Science in Design
	Master of Science in Dietetics
MSDM	Master of Security and Disaster Management
MSE	Master of Science Education
	Master of Science in Education
	Master of Science in Engineering
	Master of Science in Engineering Management
	Master of Software Engineering
	Master of Special Education
	Master of Structural Engineering

MSECE	Master of Science in Electrical and Computer Engineering
MSED	Master of Sustainable Economic Development
MSEE	Master of Science in Electrical Engineering
	Master of Science in Environmental Engineering
MSEH	Master of Science in Environmental Health
MSEL	Master of Science in Educational Leadership
MSEM	Master of Science in Engineering and Management
	Master of Science in Engineering Management
	Master of Science in Engineering Mechanics
	Master of Science in Environmental Management
MSENE	Master of Science in Environmental Engineering
MSEO	Master of Science in Electro-Optics
MSES	Master of Science in Embedded Software Engineering
	Master of Science in Engineering Science
	Master of Science in Environmental Science
	Master of Science in Environmental Studies
	Master of Science in Exercise Science
MSESE	Master of Science in Energy Systems Engineering
MSET	Master of Science in Educational Technology
	Master of Science in Engineering Technology
MSEV	Master of Science in Environmental Engineering
MSF	Master of Science in Finance
	Master of Science in Forestry
MSFA	Master of Science in Financial Analysis
MSFCS	Master of Science in Family and Consumer Science
MSFE	Master of Science in Financial Engineering
MSFM	Master of Sustainable Forest Management
MSFOR	Master of Science in Forestry
MSFP	Master of Science in Financial Planning
MSFS	Master of Science in Financial Sciences
	Master of Science in Forensic Science
MSFSB	Master of Science in Financial Services and Banking
MSFT	Master of Science in Family Therapy
MSGC	Master of Science in Genetic Counseling
MSH	Master of Science in Health
	Master of Science in Hospice
MSHA	Master of Science in Health Administration
MSHCA	Master of Science in Health Care Administration
MSHCPM	Master of Science in Health Care Policy and Management
MSHE	Master of Science in Health Education
MSHES	Master of Science in Human Environmental Sciences
MSHFID	Master of Science in Human Factors in Information Design
MSHFS	Master of Science in Human Factors and Systems
MSHI	Master of Science in Health Informatics
MSHP	Master of Science in Health Professions
	Master of Science in Health Promotion
MSHR	Master of Science in Human Resources
MSHRL	Master of Science in Human Resource Leadership
MSHRM	Master of Science in Human Resource Management
MSHROD	Master of Science in Human Resources and Organizational Development
MSHS	Master of Science in Health Science
	Master of Science in Health Services
	Master of Science in Homeland Security

MSHSR	Master of Science in Human Security and Resilience
MSI	Master of Science in Information
	Master of Science in Instruction
	Master of System Integration
MSIA	Master of Science in Industrial Administration
	Master of Science in Information Assurance
MSIB	Master of Science in International Business
MSIDM	Master of Science in Interior Design and Merchandising
MSIE	Master of Science in Industrial Engineering
MSIEM	Master of Science in Information Engineering and Management
MSIM	Master of Science in Industrial Management
	Master of Science in Information Management
	Master of Science in International Management
MSIMC	Master of Science in Integrated Marketing Communications
MSIMS	Master of Science in Identity Management and Security
MSIS	Master of Science in Information Science
	Master of Science in Information Studies
	Master of Science in Information Systems
	Master of Science in Interdisciplinary Studies
MSISE	Master of Science in Infrastructure Systems Engineering
MSISM	Master of Science in Information Systems Management
MSISPM	Master of Science in Information Security Policy and Management
MSIST	Master of Science in Information Systems Technology
MSIT	Master of Science in Industrial Technology
	Master of Science in Information Technology
	Master of Science in Instructional Technology
MSITM	Master of Science in Information Technology Management
MSJ	Master of Science in Journalism
	Master of Science in Jurisprudence
MSJC	Master of Social Justice and Criminology
MSJFP	Master of Science in Juvenile Forensic Psychology
MSJJ	Master of Science in Juvenile Justice
MSJPS	Master of Science in Justice and Public Safety
MSK	Master of Science in Kinesiology
MSL	Master in the Study of Law
	Master of School Leadership
	Master of Science in Leadership
	Master of Science in Limnology
	Master of Sports Leadership
	Master of Strategic Leadership
	Master of Studies in Law
MSLA	Master of Science in Legal Administration
MSLB	Master of Sports Law and Business
MSLFS	Master of Science in Life Sciences
MSLP	Master of Speech-Language Pathology
MSLS	Master of Science in Library Science
MSLSCM	Master of Science in Logistics and Supply Chain Management
MSLT	Master of Second Language Teaching
MSM	Master of Sacred Ministry
	Master of Sacred Music
	Master of School Mathematics
	Master of Science in Management
	Master of Science in Medicine
	Master of Science in Organization Management
	Master of Security Management
	Master of Strategic Ministry
	Master of Supply Management
MSMA	Master of Science in Marketing Analysis
MSMAE	Master of Science in Materials Engineering

MSMC	Master of Science in Management and Communications
	Master of Science in Mass Communications
MSME	Master of Science in Mathematics Education
	Master of Science in Mechanical Engineering
	Master of Science in Medical Ethics
MSMHC	Master of Science in Mental Health Counseling
MSMIT	Master of Science in Management and Information Technology
MSMLS	Master of Science in Medical Laboratory Science
MSMOT	Master of Science in Management of Technology
MSMP	Master of Science in Medical Physics
	Master of Science in Molecular Pathology
MSMS	Master of Science in Management Science
	Master of Science in Marine Science
	Master of Science in Medical Sciences
MSMSE	Master of Science in Manufacturing Systems Engineering
	Master of Science in Material Science and Engineering
	Master of Science in Material Science Engineering
	Master of Science in Mathematics and Science Education
MSMus	Master of Sacred Music
MSN	Master of Science in Nursing
MSNA	Master of Science in Nurse Anesthesia
MSNE	Master of Science in Nuclear Engineering
MSNS	Master of Science in Natural Science
	Master of Science in Nutritional Science
MSOD	Master of Science in Organization Development
	Master of Science in Organizational Development
MSOEE	Master of Science in Outdoor and Environmental Education
MSOES	Master of Science in Occupational Ergonomics and Safety
MSOH	Master of Science in Occupational Health
MSOL	Master of Science in Organizational Leadership
MSOM	Master of Science in Oriental Medicine
MSOR	Master of Science in Operations Research
MSOT	Master of Science in Occupational Technology
	Master of Science in Occupational Therapy
MSP	Master of Science in Pharmacy
	Master of Science in Planning
	Master of Speech Pathology
	Master of Sustainable Peacebuilding
MSPA	Master of Science in Physician Assistant
MSPAS	Master of Science in Physician Assistant Studies
MSPC	Master of Science in Professional Communications
MSPE	Master of Science in Petroleum Engineering
MSPH	Master of Science in Public Health
MSPHR	Master of Science in Pharmacy
MSPM	Master of Science in Professional Management
	Master of Science in Project Management
MSPNGE	Master of Science in Petroleum and Natural Gas Engineering
MSPPM	Master of Science in Public Policy and Management
MSPS	Master of Science in Pharmaceutical Science
	Master of Science in Political Science
	Master of Science in Psychological Services
MSPT	Master of Science in Physical Therapy
MSpVM	Master of Specialized Veterinary Medicine
MSRA	Master of Science in Recreation Administration
MSRE	Master of Science in Real Estate
	Master of Science in Religious Education

MSRED	Master of Science in Real Estate Development		Master of Teaching Arts
	Master of Sustainable Real Estate Development		Master of Tourism Administration
MSRLS	Master of Science in Recreation and Leisure Studies	MTC	Master of Technical Communications
		MTCM	Master of Traditional Chinese Medicine
MSRM	Master of Science in Risk Management	MTD	Master of Training and Development
MSRMP	Master of Science in Radiological Medical Physics	MTE	Master in Educational Technology
			Master of Technological Entrepreneurship
MSRS	Master of Science in Radiological Sciences	MTESOL	Master in Teaching English to Speakers of Other Languages
	Master of Science in Rehabilitation Science		
MSS	Master of Security Studies	MTHM	Master of Tourism and Hospitality Management
	Master of Social Science	MTI	Master of Information Technology
	Master of Social Services	MTID	Master of Tangible Interaction Design
	Master of Sports Science	MTL	Master of Talmudic Law
	Master of Strategic Studies	MTM	Master of Technology Management
	Master's in Statistical Science		Master of Telecommunications Management
MSSA	Master of Science in Social Administration		Master of the Teaching of Mathematics
MSSCM	Master of Science in Supply Chain Management		Master of Transformative Ministry
MSSD	Master of Arts in Software Driven Systems Design		Master of Translational Medicine
		MTMH	Master of Tropical Medicine and Hygiene
	Master of Science in Sustainable Design	MTMS	Master in Teaching Mathematics and Science
MSSE	Master of Science in Software Engineering	MTOM	Master of Traditional Oriental Medicine
	Master of Science in Special Education	MTPC	Master of Technical and Professional Communication
MSSEM	Master of Science in Systems and Engineering Management		
		MTR	Master of Translational Research
MSSI	Master of Science in Security Informatics	MTS	Master of Theatre Studies
	Master of Science in Strategic Intelligence		Master of Theological Studies
MSSIS	Master of Science in Security and Intelligence Studies	MTW	Master of Teaching Writing
		MTWM	Master of Trust and Wealth Management
MSSL	Master of Science in School Leadership	MUA	Master of Urban Affairs
MSSLP	Master of Science in Speech-Language Pathology	MUAP	Master's of Urban Affairs and Policy
		MUCD	Master of Urban and Community Design
MSSM	Master of Science in Sports Medicine	MUD	Master of Urban Design
	Master of Science in Systems Management	MUDS	Master of Urban Design Studies
MSSP	Master of Science in Social Policy	MUEP	Master of Urban and Environmental Planning
MSSS	Master of Science in Safety Science	MUP	Master of Urban Planning
	Master of Science in Systems Science	MUPD	Master of Urban Planning and Development
MSST	Master of Science in Security Technologies	MUPP	Master of Urban Planning and Policy
MSSW	Master of Science in Social Work	MUPRED	Master of Urban Planning and Real Estate Development
MSSWE	Master of Science in Software Engineering		
MST	Master of Science and Technology	MURP	Master of Urban and Regional Planning
	Master of Science in Taxation		Master of Urban and Rural Planning
	Master of Science in Teaching	MURPL	Master of Urban and Regional Planning
	Master of Science in Technology	MUS	Master of Urban Studies
	Master of Science in Telecommunications	Mus M	Master of Music
	Master of Science Teaching	MUSA	Master of Urban Spatial Analytics
MSTC	Master of Science in Technical Communication	MVP	Master of Voice Pedagogy
	Master of Science in Telecommunications	MVPH	Master of Veterinary Public Health
MSTCM	Master of Science in Traditional Chinese Medicine	MVS	Master of Visual Studies
		MWBS	Master of Won Buddhist Studies
MSTE	Master of Science in Telecommunications Engineering	MWC	Master of Wildlife Conservation
		MWPS	Master of Wood and Paper Science
	Master of Science in Transportation Engineering	MWR	Master of Water Resources
		MWS	Master of Women's Studies
MSTL	Master of Science in Teacher Leadership		Master of Worship Studies
MSTM	Master of Science in Technology Management	MWSc	Master of Wildlife Science
	Master of Science in Transfusion Medicine	MZS	Master of Zoological Science
MSTOM	Master of Science in Traditional Oriental Medicine	Nav Arch	Naval Architecture
		Naval E	Naval Engineer
MSUASE	Master of Science in Unmanned and Autonomous Systems Engineering	ND	Doctor of Naturopathic Medicine
			Doctor of Nursing
MSUD	Master of Science in Urban Design	NE	Nuclear Engineer
MSUS	Master of Science in Urban Studies	Nuc E	Nuclear Engineer
MSW	Master of Social Work	OD	Doctor of Optometry
MSWE	Master of Software Engineering	OTD	Doctor of Occupational Therapy
MSWREE	Master of Science in Water Resources and Environmental Engineering	PBME	Professional Master of Biomedical Engineering
		PC	Performer's Certificate
MT	Master of Taxation	PD	Professional Diploma
	Master of Teaching	PGC	Post-Graduate Certificate
	Master of Technology	PGD	Postgraduate Diploma
	Master of Textiles		
MTA	Master of Tax Accounting		

Ph L	Licentiate of Philosophy
Pharm D	Doctor of Pharmacy
PhD	Doctor of Philosophy
PhD Otol	Doctor of Philosophy in Otolaryngology
PhD Surg	Doctor of Philosophy in Surgery
PhDEE	Doctor of Philosophy in Electrical Engineering
PMBA	Professional Master of Business Administration
PMC	Post Master Certificate
PMD	Post-Master's Diploma
PMS	Professional Master of Science
	Professional Master's
Post-Doctoral MS	Post-Doctoral Master of Science
Post-MSN Certificate	Post-Master of Science in Nursing Certificate
PPDPT	Postprofessional Doctor of Physical Therapy
Pro-MS	Professional Science Master's
Professional MA	Professional Master of Arts
Professional MBA	Professional Master of Business Administration
Professional MS	Professional Master of Science
PSM	Professional Master of Science
	Professional Science Master's
Psy D	Doctor of Psychology
Psy M	Master of Psychology
Psy S	Specialist in Psychology
Psya D	Doctor of Psychoanalysis
S Psy S	Specialist in Psychological Services
Sc D	Doctor of Science
Sc M	Master of Science
SCCT	Specialist in Community College Teaching
ScDPT	Doctor of Physical Therapy Science

SD	Specialist Degree
SJD	Doctor of Juridical Sciences
SLPD	Doctor of Speech-Language Pathology
SM	Master of Science
SM Arch S	Master of Science in Architectural Studies
SMACT	Master of Science in Art, Culture and Technology
SMBT	Master of Science in Building Technology
SP	Specialist Degree
Sp Ed	Specialist in Education
Sp LIS	Specialist in Library and Information Science
SPA	Specialist in Arts
Spec	Specialist's Certificate
Spec M	Specialist in Music
Spt	Specialist Degree
SSP	Specialist in School Psychology
STB	Bachelor of Sacred Theology
STD	Doctor of Sacred Theology
STL	Licentiate of Sacred Theology
STM	Master of Sacred Theology
tDACM	Transitional Doctor of Acupuncture and Chinese Medicine
TDPT	Transitional Doctor of Physical Therapy
Th D	Doctor of Theology
Th M	Master of Theology
TOTD	Transitional Doctor of Occupational Therapy
VMD	Doctor of Veterinary Medicine
WEMBA	Weekend Executive Master of Business Administration
XMA	Executive Master of Arts

INDEXES

Displays and Close-Ups

Directories and Subject Areas

Following is an alphabetical listing of directories and subject areas. Also listed are cross-references for subject area names not used in the directory structure of the guides, for example, "City and Regional Planning (*see* Urban and Regional Planning)"

Graduate Programs in the Humanities, Arts & Social Sciences

Addictions/Substance Abuse Counseling
Administration (*see* Arts Administration; Public Administration)
African-American Studies
African Languages and Literatures (*see* African Studies)
African Studies
Agribusiness (*see* Agricultural Economics and Agribusiness)
Agricultural Economics and Agribusiness
Alcohol Abuse Counseling (*see* Addictions/Substance Abuse Counseling)
American Indian/Native American Studies
American Studies
Anthropology
Applied Arts and Design—General
Applied Behavior Analysis
Applied Economics
Applied History (*see* Public History)
Applied Psychology
Applied Social Research
Arabic (*see* Near and Middle Eastern Languages)
Arab Studies (*see* Near and Middle Eastern Studies)
Archaeology
Architectural History
Architecture
Archives Administration (*see* Public History)
Area and Cultural Studies (*see* African-American Studies; African Studies; American Indian/Native American Studies; American Studies; Asian-American Studies; Asian Studies; Canadian Studies; Cultural Studies; East European and Russian Studies; Ethnic Studies; Folklore; Gender Studies; Hispanic Studies; Holocaust Studies; Jewish Studies; Latin American Studies; Near and Middle Eastern Studies; Northern Studies; Pacific Area/Pacific Rim Studies; Western European Studies; Women's Studies)
Art/Fine Arts
Art History
Arts Administration
Arts Journalism
Art Therapy
Asian-American Studies
Asian Languages
Asian Studies
Behavioral Sciences (*see* Psychology)
Bible Studies (*see* Religion; Theology)
Biological Anthropology
Black Studies (*see* African-American Studies)
Broadcasting (*see* Communication; Film, Television, and Video Production)
Broadcast Journalism
Building Science
Canadian Studies
Celtic Languages
Ceramics (*see* Art/Fine Arts)
Child and Family Studies
Child Development
Chinese
Chinese Studies (*see* Asian Languages; Asian Studies)
Christian Studies (*see* Missions and Missiology; Religion; Theology)
Cinema (*see* Film, Television, and Video Production)
City and Regional Planning (*see* Urban and Regional Planning)
Classical Languages and Literatures (*see* Classics)
Classics
Clinical Psychology

Clothing and Textiles
Cognitive Psychology (*see* Psychology—General; Cognitive Sciences)
Cognitive Sciences
Communication—General
Community Affairs (*see* Urban and Regional Planning; Urban Studies)
Community Planning (*see* Architecture; Environmental Design; Urban and Regional Planning; Urban Design; Urban Studies)
Community Psychology (*see* Social Psychology)
Comparative and Interdisciplinary Arts
Comparative Literature
Composition (*see* Music)
Computer Art and Design
Conflict Resolution and Mediation/Peace Studies
Consumer Economics
Corporate and Organizational Communication
Corrections (*see* Criminal Justice and Criminology)
Counseling (*see* Counseling Psychology; Pastoral Ministry and Counseling)
Counseling Psychology
Crafts (*see* Art/Fine Arts)
Creative Arts Therapies (*see* Art Therapy; Therapies—Dance, Drama, and Music)
Criminal Justice and Criminology
Cultural Anthropology
Cultural Studies
Dance
Decorative Arts
Demography and Population Studies
Design (*see* Applied Arts and Design; Architecture; Art/Fine Arts; Environmental Design; Graphic Design; Industrial Design; Interior Design; Textile Design; Urban Design)
Developmental Psychology
Diplomacy (*see* International Affairs)
Disability Studies
Drama Therapy (*see* Therapies—Dance, Drama, and Music)
Dramatic Arts (*see* Theater)
Drawing (*see* Art/Fine Arts)
Drug Abuse Counseling (*see* Addictions/Substance Abuse Counseling)
Drug and Alcohol Abuse Counseling (*see* Addictions/Substance Abuse Counseling)
East Asian Studies (*see* Asian Studies)
East European and Russian Studies
Economic Development
Economics
Educational Theater (*see* Theater; Therapies—Dance, Drama, and Music)
Emergency Management
English
Environmental Design
Ethics
Ethnic Studies
Ethnomusicology (*see* Music)
Experimental Psychology
Family and Consumer Sciences—General
Family Studies (*see* Child and Family Studies)
Family Therapy (*see* Child and Family Studies; Clinical Psychology; Counseling Psychology; Marriage and Family Therapy)
Filmmaking (*see* Film, Television, and Video Production)
Film Studies (*see* Film, Television, and Video Production)
Film, Television, and Video Production
Film, Television, and Video Theory and Criticism
Fine Arts (*see* Art/Fine Arts)
Folklore
Foreign Languages (*see* specific language)
Foreign Service (*see* International Affairs; International Development)
Forensic Psychology
Forensic Sciences
Forensics (*see* Speech and Interpersonal Communication)
French
Gender Studies
General Studies (*see* Liberal Studies)

Genetic Counseling
Geographic Information Systems
Geography
German
Gerontology
Graphic Design
Greek (*see* Classics)
Health Communication
Health Psychology
Hebrew (*see* Near and Middle Eastern Languages)
Hebrew Studies (*see* Jewish Studies)
Hispanic and Latin American Languages
Hispanic Studies
Historic Preservation
History
History of Art (*see* Art History)
History of Medicine
History of Science and Technology
Holocaust and Genocide Studies
Home Economics (*see* Family and Consumer Sciences—General)
Homeland Security
Household Economics, Sciences, and Management (*see* Family and Consumer Sciences—General)
Human Development
Humanities
Illustration
Industrial and Labor Relations
Industrial and Organizational Psychology
Industrial Design
Interdisciplinary Studies
Interior Design
International Affairs
International Development
International Economics
International Service (*see* International Affairs; International Development)
International Trade Policy
Internet and Interactive Multimedia
Interpersonal Communication (*see* Speech and Interpersonal Communication)
Interpretation (*see* Translation and Interpretation)
Islamic Studies (*see* Near and Middle Eastern Studies; Religion)
Italian
Japanese
Japanese Studies (*see* Asian Languages; Asian Studies; Japanese)
Jewelry (*see* Art/Fine Arts)
Jewish Studies
Journalism
Judaic Studies (*see* Jewish Studies; Religion)
Labor Relations (*see* Industrial and Labor Relations)
Landscape Architecture
Latin American Studies
Latin (*see* Classics)
Law Enforcement (*see* Criminal Justice and Criminology)
Liberal Studies
Lighting Design
Linguistics
Literature (*see* Classics; Comparative Literature; specific language)
Marriage and Family Therapy
Mass Communication
Media Studies
Medical Illustration
Medieval and Renaissance Studies
Metalsmithing (*see* Art/Fine Arts)
Middle Eastern Studies (*see* Near and Middle Eastern Studies)
Military and Defense Studies
Mineral Economics
Ministry (*see* Pastoral Ministry and Counseling; Theology)
Missions and Missiology
Motion Pictures (*see* Film, Television, and Video Production)
Museum Studies
Music
Musicology (*see* Music)
Music Therapy (*see* Therapies—Dance, Drama, and Music)
National Security

Native American Studies (*see* American Indian/Native American Studies)
Near and Middle Eastern Languages
Near and Middle Eastern Studies
Northern Studies
Organizational Psychology (*see* Industrial and Organizational Psychology)
Oriental Languages (*see* Asian Languages)
Oriental Studies (*see* Asian Studies)
Pacific Area/Pacific Rim Studies
Painting (*see* Art/Fine Arts)
Pastoral Ministry and Counseling
Philanthropic Studies
Philosophy
Photography
Playwriting (*see* Theater; Writing)
Policy Studies (*see* Public Policy)
Political Science
Population Studies (*see* Demography and Population Studies)
Portuguese
Printmaking (*see* Art/Fine Arts)
Product Design (*see* Industrial Design)
Psychoanalysis and Psychotherapy
Psychology—General
Public Administration
Public Affairs
Public History
Public Policy
Public Speaking (*see* Mass Communication; Rhetoric; Speech and Interpersonal Communication)
Publishing
Regional Planning (*see* Architecture; Urban and Regional Planning; Urban Design; Urban Studies)
Rehabilitation Counseling
Religion
Renaissance Studies (*see* Medieval and Renaissance Studies)
Rhetoric
Romance Languages
Romance Literatures (*see* Romance Languages)
Rural Planning and Studies
Rural Sociology
Russian
Scandinavian Languages
School Psychology
Sculpture (*see* Art/Fine Arts)
Security Administration (*see* Criminal Justice and Criminology)
Slavic Languages
Slavic Studies (*see* East European and Russian Studies; Slavic Languages)
Social Psychology
Social Sciences
Sociology
Southeast Asian Studies (*see* Asian Studies)
Soviet Studies (*see* East European and Russian Studies; Russian)
Spanish
Speech and Interpersonal Communication
Sport Psychology
Studio Art (*see* Art/Fine Arts)
Substance Abuse Counseling (*see* Addictions/Substance Abuse Counseling)
Survey Methodology
Sustainable Development
Technical Communication
Technical Writing
Telecommunications (*see* Film, Television, and Video Production)
Television (*see* Film, Television, and Video Production)
Textile Design
Textiles (*see* Clothing and Textiles; Textile Design)
Thanatology
Theater
Theater Arts (*see* Theater)
Theology
Therapies—Dance, Drama, and Music
Translation and Interpretation
Transpersonal and Humanistic Psychology
Urban and Regional Planning

Urban Design
Urban Planning (*see* Architecture; Urban and Regional Planning; Urban Design; Urban Studies)
Urban Studies
Video (*see* Film, Television, and Video Production)
Visual Arts (*see* Applied Arts and Design; Art/Fine Arts; Film, Television, and Video Production; Graphic Design; Illustration; Photography)
Western European Studies
Women's Studies
World Wide Web (*see* Internet and Interactive Multimedia)
Writing

Graduate Programs in the Biological/ Biomedical Sciences & Health-Related Medical Professions

Acupuncture and Oriental Medicine
Acute Care/Critical Care Nursing Administration (*see* Health Services Management and Hospital Administration; Nursing and Healthcare Administration; Pharmaceutical Administration)
Adult Nursing
Advanced Practice Nursing (*see* Family Nurse Practitioner Studies)
Allied Health—General
Allied Health Professions (*see* Clinical Laboratory Sciences/Medical Technology; Clinical Research; Communication Disorders; Dental Hygiene; Emergency Medical Services; Occupational Therapy; Physical Therapy; Physician Assistant Studies; Rehabilitation Sciences)
Allopathic Medicine
Anatomy
Anesthesiologist Assistant Studies
Animal Behavior
Bacteriology
Behavioral Sciences (*see* Biopsychology; Neuroscience; Zoology)
Biochemistry
Bioethics
Biological and Biomedical Sciences—General Biological Chemistry (*see* Biochemistry)
Biological Oceanography (*see* Marine Biology)
Biophysics
Biopsychology
Botany
Breeding (*see* Botany; Plant Biology; Genetics)
Cancer Biology/Oncology
Cardiovascular Sciences
Cell Biology
Cellular Physiology (*see* Cell Biology; Physiology)
Child-Care Nursing (*see* Maternal and Child/Neonatal Nursing)
Chiropractic
Clinical Laboratory Sciences/Medical Technology
Clinical Research
Community Health
Community Health Nursing
Computational Biology
Conservation (*see* Conservation Biology; Environmental Biology)
Conservation Biology
Crop Sciences (*see* Botany; Plant Biology)
Cytology (*see* Cell Biology)
Dental and Oral Surgery (*see* Oral and Dental Sciences)
Dental Assistant Studies (*see* Dental Hygiene)
Dental Hygiene
Dental Services (*see* Dental Hygiene)
Dentistry
Developmental Biology Dietetics (*see* Nutrition)
Ecology
Embryology (*see* Developmental Biology)
Emergency Medical Services
Endocrinology (*see* Physiology)
Entomology
Environmental Biology

Environmental and Occupational Health
Epidemiology
Evolutionary Biology
Family Nurse Practitioner Studies
Foods (*see* Nutrition)
Forensic Nursing
Genetics
Genomic Sciences
Gerontological Nursing
Health Physics/Radiological Health
Health Promotion
Health-Related Professions (*see* individual allied health professions)
Health Services Management and Hospital Administration
Health Services Research
Histology (*see* Anatomy; Cell Biology)
HIV/AIDS Nursing
Hospice Nursing
Hospital Administration (*see* Health Services Management and Hospital Administration)
Human Genetics
Immunology
Industrial Hygiene
Infectious Diseases
International Health
Laboratory Medicine (*see* Clinical Laboratory Sciences/Medical Technology; Immunology; Microbiology; Pathology)
Life Sciences (*see* Biological and Biomedical Sciences)
Marine Biology
Maternal and Child Health
Maternal and Child/Neonatal Nursing
Medical Imaging
Medical Microbiology
Medical Nursing (*see* Medical/Surgical Nursing)
Medical Physics
Medical/Surgical Nursing
Medical Technology (*see* Clinical Laboratory Sciences/Medical Technology)
Medical Sciences (*see* Biological and Biomedical Sciences)
Medical Science Training Programs (*see* Biological and Biomedical Sciences)
Medicinal and Pharmaceutical Chemistry
Medicinal Chemistry (*see* Medicinal and Pharmaceutical Chemistry)
Medicine (*see* Allopathic Medicine; Naturopathic Medicine; Osteopathic Medicine; Podiatric Medicine)
Microbiology
Midwifery (*see* Nurse Midwifery)
Molecular Biology
Molecular Biophysics
Molecular Genetics
Molecular Medicine
Molecular Pathogenesis
Molecular Pathology
Molecular Pharmacology
Molecular Physiology
Molecular Toxicology
Naturopathic Medicine
Neural Sciences (*see* Biopsychology; Neurobiology; Neuroscience)
Neurobiology
Neuroendocrinology (*see* Biopsychology; Neurobiology; Neuroscience; Physiology)
Neuropharmacology (*see* Biopsychology; Neurobiology; Neuroscience; Pharmacology)
Neurophysiology (*see* Biopsychology; Neurobiology; Neuroscience; Physiology)
Neuroscience
Nuclear Medical Technology (*see* Clinical Laboratory Sciences/Medical Technology)
Nurse Anesthesia
Nurse Midwifery
Nurse Practitioner Studies (*see* Family Nurse Practitioner Studies)
Nursing Administration (*see* Nursing and Healthcare Administration)
Nursing and Healthcare Administration
Nursing Education
Nursing—General
Nursing Informatics

Nutrition
Occupational Health (*see* Environmental and Occupational Health; Occupational Health Nursing)
Occupational Health Nursing
Occupational Therapy
Oncology (*see* Cancer Biology/Oncology)
Oncology Nursing
Optometry
Oral and Dental Sciences
Oral Biology (*see* Oral and Dental Sciences)
Oral Pathology (*see* Oral and Dental Sciences)
Organismal Biology (*see* Biological and Biomedical Sciences; Zoology)
Oriental Medicine and Acupuncture (*see* Acupuncture and Oriental Medicine)
Orthodontics (*see* Oral and Dental Sciences)
Osteopathic Medicine
Parasitology
Pathobiology
Pathology
Pediatric Nursing
Pedontics (*see* Oral and Dental Sciences)
Perfusion
Pharmaceutical Administration
Pharmaceutical Chemistry (*see* Medicinal and Pharmaceutical Chemistry)
Pharmaceutical Sciences
Pharmacology
Pharmacy
Photobiology of Cells and Organelles (*see* Botany; Cell Biology; Plant Biology)
Physical Therapy
Physician Assistant Studies
Physiological Optics (*see* Vision Sciences)
Podiatric Medicine
Preventive Medicine (*see* Community Health and Public Health)
Physiological Optics (*see* Physiology)
Physiology
Plant Biology
Plant Molecular Biology
Plant Pathology
Plant Physiology
Pomology (*see* Botany; Plant Biology)
Psychiatric Nursing
Public Health—General
Public Health Nursing (*see* Community Health Nursing)
Psychiatric Nursing
Psychobiology (*see* Biopsychology)
Psychopharmacology (*see* Biopsychology; Neuroscience; Pharmacology)
Radiation Biology
Radiological Health (*see* Health Physics/Radiological Health)
Rehabilitation Nursing
Rehabilitation Sciences
Rehabilitation Therapy (*see* Physical Therapy)
Reproductive Biology
School Nursing
Sociobiology (*see* Evolutionary Biology)
Structural Biology
Surgical Nursing (*see* Medical/Surgical Nursing)
Systems Biology
Teratology
Therapeutics
Theoretical Biology (*see* Biological and Biomedical Sciences)
Therapeutics (*see* Pharmaceutical Sciences; Pharmacology; Pharmacy)
Toxicology
Transcultural Nursing
Translational Biology
Tropical Medicine (*see* Parasitology)
Veterinary Medicine
Veterinary Sciences
Virology
Vision Sciences
Wildlife Biology (*see* Zoology)
Women's Health Nursing
Zoology

Graduate Programs in the Physical Sciences, Mathematics, Agricultural Sciences, the Environment & Natural Resources

Acoustics
Agricultural Sciences
Agronomy and Soil Sciences
Analytical Chemistry
Animal Sciences
Applied Mathematics
Applied Physics
Applied Statistics
Aquaculture
Astronomy
Astrophysical Sciences (*see* Astrophysics; Atmospheric Sciences; Meteorology; Planetary and Space Sciences)
Astrophysics
Atmospheric Sciences
Biological Oceanography (*see* Marine Affairs; Marine Sciences; Oceanography)
Biomathematics
Biometry
Biostatistics
Chemical Physics
Chemistry
Computational Sciences
Condensed Matter Physics
Dairy Science (*see* Animal Sciences)
Earth Sciences (*see* Geosciences)
Environmental Management and Policy
Environmental Sciences
Environmental Studies (*see* Environmental Management and Policy)
Experimental Statistics (*see* Statistics)
Fish, Game, and Wildlife Management
Food Science and Technology
Forestry
General Science (*see* specific topics)
Geochemistry
Geodetic Sciences
Geological Engineering (*see* Geology)
Geological Sciences (*see* Geology)
Geology
Geophysical Fluid Dynamics (*see* Geophysics)
Geophysics
Geosciences
Horticulture
Hydrogeology
Hydrology
Inorganic Chemistry
Limnology
Marine Affairs
Marine Geology
Marine Sciences
Marine Studies (*see* Marine Affairs; Marine Geology; Marine Sciences; Oceanography)
Mathematical and Computational Finance
Mathematical Physics
Mathematical Statistics (*see* Applied Statistics; Statistics)
Mathematics
Meteorology
Mineralogy
Natural Resource Management (*see* Environmental Management and Policy; Natural Resources)
Natural Resources
Nuclear Physics (*see* Physics)
Ocean Engineering (*see* Marine Affairs; Marine Geology; Marine Sciences; Oceanography)
Oceanography
Optical Sciences
Optical Technologies (*see* Optical Sciences)
Optics (*see* Applied Physics; Optical Sciences; Physics)
Organic Chemistry

Paleontology
Paper Chemistry (*see* Chemistry)
Photonics
Physical Chemistry
Physics
Planetary and Space Sciences
Plant Sciences
Plasma Physics
Poultry Science (*see* Animal Sciences)
Radiological Physics (*see* Physics)
Range Management (*see* Range Science)
Range Science
Resource Management (*see* Environmental Management and Policy; Natural Resources)
Solid-Earth Sciences (*see* Geosciences)
Space Sciences (*see* Planetary and Space Sciences)
Statistics
Theoretical Chemistry
Theoretical Physics
Viticulture and Enology
Water Resources

Graduate Programs in Engineering & Applied Sciences

Aeronautical Engineering (*see* Aerospace/Aeronautical Engineering)
Aerospace/Aeronautical Engineering
Aerospace Studies (*see* Aerospace/Aeronautical Engineering)
Agricultural Engineering
Applied Mechanics (*see* Mechanics)
Applied Science and Technology
Architectural Engineering
Artificial Intelligence/Robotics
Astronautical Engineering (*see* Aerospace/Aeronautical Engineering)
Automotive Engineering
Aviation
Biochemical Engineering
Bioengineering
Bioinformatics
Biological Engineering (*see* Bioengineering)
Biomedical Engineering
Biosystems Engineering
Biotechnology
Ceramic Engineering (*see* Ceramic Sciences and Engineering)
Ceramic Sciences and Engineering
Ceramics (*see* Ceramic Sciences and Engineering)
Chemical Engineering
Civil Engineering
Computer and Information Systems Security
Computer Engineering
Computer Science
Computing Technology (*see* Computer Science)
Construction Engineering
Construction Management
Database Systems
Electrical Engineering
Electronic Materials
Electronics Engineering (*see* Electrical Engineering)
Energy and Power Engineering
Energy Management and Policy
Engineering and Applied Sciences
Engineering and Public Affairs (*see* Technology and Public Policy)
Engineering and Public Policy (*see* Energy Management and Policy; Technology and Public Policy)
Engineering Design
Engineering Management
Engineering Mechanics (*see* Mechanics)
Engineering Metallurgy (*see* Metallurgical Engineering and Metallurgy)

Engineering Physics
Environmental Design (*see* Environmental Engineering)
Environmental Engineering
Ergonomics and Human Factors
Financial Engineering
Fire Protection Engineering
Food Engineering (*see* Agricultural Engineering)
Game Design and Development
Gas Engineering (*see* Petroleum Engineering)
Geological Engineering
Geophysics Engineering (*see* Geological Engineering)
Geotechnical Engineering
Hazardous Materials Management
Health Informatics
Health Systems (*see* Safety Engineering; Systems Engineering)
Highway Engineering (*see* Transportation and Highway Engineering)
Human-Computer Interaction
Human Factors (*see* Ergonomics and Human Factors)
Hydraulics
Hydrology (*see* Water Resources Engineering)
Industrial Engineering (*see* Industrial/Management Engineering)
Industrial/Management Engineering
Information Science
Internet Engineering
Macromolecular Science (*see* Polymer Science and Engineering)
Management Engineering (*see* Engineering Management; Industrial/Management Engineering)
Management of Technology
Manufacturing Engineering
Marine Engineering (*see* Civil Engineering)
Materials Engineering
Materials Sciences
Mechanical Engineering
Mechanics
Medical Informatics
Metallurgical Engineering and Metallurgy
Metallurgy (*see* Metallurgical Engineering and Metallurgy)
Mineral/Mining Engineering
Modeling and Simulation
Nanotechnology
Nuclear Engineering
Ocean Engineering
Operations Research
Paper and Pulp Engineering
Petroleum Engineering
Pharmaceutical Engineering
Plastics Engineering (*see* Polymer Science and Engineering)
Polymer Science and Engineering
Public Policy (*see* Energy Management and Policy; Technology and Public Policy)
Reliability Engineering
Robotics (*see* Artificial Intelligence/Robotics)
Safety Engineering
Software Engineering
Solid-State Sciences (*see* Materials Sciences)
Structural Engineering
Surveying Science and Engineering
Systems Analysis (*see* Systems Engineering)
Systems Engineering
Systems Science
Technology and Public Policy
Telecommunications
Telecommunications Management
Textile Sciences and Engineering
Textiles (*see* Textile Sciences and Engineering)
Transportation and Highway Engineering
Urban Systems Engineering (*see* Systems Engineering)
Waste Management (*see* Hazardous Materials Management)
Water Resources Engineering

Graduate Programs in Business, Education, Information Studies, Law & Social Work

Accounting
Actuarial Science
Adult Education
Advertising and Public Relations
Agricultural Education
Alcohol Abuse Counseling (*see* Counselor Education)
Archival Management and Studies
Art Education
Athletics Administration (*see* Kinesiology and Movement Studies)
Athletic Training and Sports Medicine
Audiology (*see* Communication Disorders)
Aviation Management
Banking (*see* Finance and Banking)
Business Administration and Management—General
Business Education
Communication Disorders
Community College Education
Computer Education
Continuing Education (*see* Adult Education)
Counseling (*see* Counselor Education)
Counselor Education
Curriculum and Instruction
Developmental Education
Distance Education Development
Drug Abuse Counseling (*see* Counselor Education)
Early Childhood Education
Educational Leadership and Administration
Educational Measurement and Evaluation
Educational Media/Instructional Technology
Educational Policy
Educational Psychology
Education—General
Education of the Blind (*see* Special Education)
Education of the Deaf (*see* Special Education)
Education of the Gifted
Education of the Hearing Impaired (*see* Special Education)
Education of the Learning Disabled (*see* Special Education)
Education of the Mentally Retarded (*see* Special Education)
Education of the Physically Handicapped (*see* Special Education)
Education of Students with Severe/Multiple Disabilities
Education of the Visually Handicapped (*see* Special Education)
Electronic Commerce
Elementary Education
English as a Second Language
English Education
Entertainment Management
Entrepreneurship
Environmental Education
Environmental Law
Exercise and Sports Science
Exercise Physiology (*see* Kinesiology and Movement Studies)
Facilities and Entertainment Management
Finance and Banking
Food Services Management (*see* Hospitality Management)
Foreign Languages Education
Foundations and Philosophy of Education
Guidance and Counseling (*see* Counselor Education)
Health Education
Health Law
Hearing Sciences (*see* Communication Disorders)
Higher Education
Home Economics Education
Hospitality Management
Hotel Management (*see* Travel and Tourism)
Human Resources Development
Human Resources Management
Human Services
Industrial Administration (*see* Industrial and Manufacturing Management)
Industrial and Manufacturing Management

Industrial Education (*see* Vocational and Technical Education)
Information Studies
Instructional Technology (*see* Educational Media/Instructional Technology)
Insurance
Intellectual Property Law
International and Comparative Education
International Business
International Commerce (*see* International Business)
International Economics (*see* International Business)
International Trade (*see* International Business)
Investment and Securities (*see* Business Administration and Management; Finance and Banking; Investment Management)
Investment Management
Junior College Education (*see* Community College Education)
Kinesiology and Movement Studies
Law
Legal and Justice Studies
Leisure Services (*see* Recreation and Park Management)
Leisure Studies
Library Science
Logistics
Management (*see* Business Administration and Management)
Management Information Systems
Management Strategy and Policy
Marketing
Marketing Research
Mathematics Education
Middle School Education
Movement Studies (*see* Kinesiology and Movement Studies)
Multilingual and Multicultural Education
Museum Education
Music Education
Nonprofit Management
Nursery School Education (*see* Early Childhood Education)
Occupational Education (*see* Vocational and Technical Education)
Organizational Behavior
Organizational Management
Parks Administration (*see* Recreation and Park Management)
Personnel (*see* Human Resources Development; Human Resources Management; Organizational Behavior; Organizational Management; Student Affairs)
Philosophy of Education (*see* Foundations and Philosophy of Education)
Physical Education
Project Management
Public Relations (*see* Advertising and Public Relations)
Quality Management
Quantitative Analysis
Reading Education
Real Estate
Recreation and Park Management
Recreation Therapy (*see* Recreation and Park Management)
Religious Education
Remedial Education (*see* Special Education)
Restaurant Administration (*see* Hospitality Management)
Science Education
Secondary Education
Social Sciences Education
Social Studies Education (*see* Social Sciences Education)
Social Work
Special Education
Speech-Language Pathology and Audiology (*see* Communication Disorders)
Sports Management
Sports Medicine (*see* Athletic Training and Sports Medicine)
Sports Psychology and Sociology (*see* Kinesiology and Movement Studies)
Student Affairs
Substance Abuse Counseling (*see* Counselor Education)
Supply Chain Management
Sustainability Management
Systems Management (*see* Management Information Systems)
Taxation
Teacher Education (*see* specific subject areas)

Teaching English as a Second Language (*see* English as a Second Language)

Technical Education (*see* Vocational and Technical Education)

Transportation Management

Travel and Tourism

Urban Education

Vocational and Technical Education

Vocational Counseling (*see* Counselor Education)

Directories and Subject Areas in This Book

NOTES

NOTES

NOTES

NOTES

NOTES

NOTES

NOTES

NOTES

NOTES

NOTES

NOTES